REVELATION AND INSPIRATION

BY

BENJAMIN BRECKINRIDGE WARFIELD

Professor of Didactic and Polemic Theology
in the Theological Seminary of Princeton
New Jersey, 1887–1921

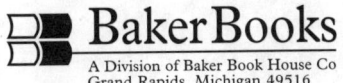
Baker Books

A Division of Baker Book House Co
Grand Rapids, Michigan 49516

PREFATORY NOTE

REV. BENJAMIN BRECKINRIDGE WARFIELD, D.D., LL.D., Professor of Didactic and Polemic Theology in the Theological Seminary of the Presbyterian Church at Princeton, New Jersey, provided in his will for the collection and publication of the numerous articles on theological subjects contained in encyclopaedias, reviews and other periodicals, and appointed a committee to edit and publish these papers. In pursuance of his instructions, this, the first volume containing his articles on Revelation and Inspiration, has been prepared under the editorial direction of this committee.

The contents of the succeeding volumes will be as follows: the articles on certain great Biblical doctrines, the critical articles on the Person of Christ, those on historical theology, on Perfectionism, articles on miscellaneous theological subjects, and the more important book reviews.

It is proposed to publish these volumes in as rapid succession as possible.

The generous permission to publish articles contained in this volume is gratefully acknowledged as follows: The Howard-Severance Co. for the articles taken from the International Standard Encyclopaedia, and D. Appleton & Co. for an article taken from the Universal Cyclopedia and Atlas.

The clerical preparation of this volume has been done by Miss Letitia N. Gosman, to whom the thanks of the committee are hereby expressed.

ETHELBERT D. WARFIELD
WILLIAM PARK ARMSTRONG
CASPAR WISTAR HODGE
Committee.

BIOGRAPHICAL SKETCH OF
BENJAMIN BRECKINRIDGE WARFIELD

BENJAMIN BRECKINRIDGE WARFIELD was born at "Grasmere" near Lexington, Kentucky, November 5, 1851.

His father, William Warfield, descended in the paternal line from a body of south of England puritans who were expelled from Virginia by Governor Berkeley when they refused to accept his proclamation of Charles II as king. They were given a refuge by the Roman Catholic colony of Maryland and settled at Annapolis and South River. On the maternal line he was descended from Scotch-Irish families who first settled in the Cumberland Valley in Pennsylvania.

His mother, Mary Cabell Breckinridge, was the daughter of Rev. Robert Jefferson Breckinridge, D.D., LL.D., distinguished as a preacher, Moderator of the General Assembly of the Presbyterian Church, president of Jefferson College, Pennsylvania, founder and president of the Theological Seminary at Danville, Kentucky, editor of the *Spirit of the Nineteenth Century* and the *Danville* (Kentucky) *Review,* ardent advocate of the emancipation of the slaves and of the maintenance of the Union, temporary chairman of the Republican Convention of 1864 which renominated Abraham Lincoln, and author of a system of theology entitled "The Knowledge of God Objectively and Subjectively Considered." Her mother, Sophonisba Preston, daughter of General Francis Preston of Virginia, belonged to one of the most vital stocks of the great Ulster immigration which settled the up-country of Virginia. To all of these people the political, educational and religious problems of the new country were of tremendous significance and the subject of fervid discussion and at times heated controversy.

Benjamin Warfield attended private schools in Lexington; and received his preparation chiefly from Lewis Barbour, afterwards professor of mathematics in Central University, and James K. Patterson, afterwards president of the State College of Kentucky. He entered the sophomore class of the College of New Jersey at Princeton in the autumn of 1868 and graduated with the highest honors of his class in 1871, when only nineteen years of age. He won the Thompson prize for the highest rank in the junior year, and prizes for essay and debate in the American Whig Society, and was one of the editors of the *Nassau Literary Magazine.*

His early tastes were strongly scientific. He collected birds' eggs, butterflies and moths, and geological specimens; studied the fauna and flora of his neighborhood; read Darwin's newly published books with enthusiasm; and counted Audubon's works on American birds and mammals his chief treasure. He was so certain that he was to follow a scientific career that he strenuously objected to studying Greek. But youthful objections had little effect in a household where the shorter catechism was ordinarily completed in the sixth year, followed at once by the proofs from the Scriptures, and then by the larger catechism, with an appropriate amount of Scripture memorized in regular course each Sabbath afternoon.

His special interests in college were mathematics and physics, in which he obtained perfect marks. He intended to seek the fellowship in experimental science, but was dissuaded by his father on the plea that he did not need the stipend in order to pursue graduate studies and it would be better for him to spend some time in Europe without being bound to any particular course of study.

His departure was delayed by family illness and he did not sail until February, 1872. After spending some time in Edinburgh he went to Heidelberg, and writing from there in midsummer he announced his decision to enter the Christian ministry. He had early made a profession of faith and united with the Second Presbyterian Church in Lexington, but no serious purpose of studying theology had ever been expressed by him. The atmosphere of his home was one of vital piety, and his mother constantly spoke of her hope that her sons might become preachers of the Gospel, but with the inheritance of the intellectual gifts of his mother's family he combined the reticence with regard to personal matters which was characteristic of his father. His decision was, therefore, a surprise to his family and most intimate friends.

In September, 1873, he entered the Theological Seminary of the Presbyterian Church at Princeton, and was graduated in May, 1876. He was licensed to preach by the Presbytery of Ebenezer (Kentucky) in 1875, was stated supply and received a call to the pastorate of the First Presbyterian Church of Dayton, Ohio, in the summer of 1876. But he decided to go abroad for further study. On August 3rd he was married to Miss Annie Pearce Kinkead, and soon after sailed for Europe, studying the following winter at Leipsic.

In the course of the year he was offered an appointment in the Old Testament Department at the Western Theological Seminary, but his mind, despite his early reluctance to the study of Greek, had already turned to the New Testament field. Returning in the late summer, he was for a time assistant pastor of the First Presbyterian Church of Baltimore. Accepting a call to become instructor in New Testament Language and Literature at the Western Theological Seminary, Allegheny, Pennsylvania, he entered upon his duties in September, 1878. The following year he was appointed professor and was ordained. He had already attracted attention by the first of his scholarly publications and in 1880 the degree of Doctor of Divinity was conferred upon him by the College of New Jersey.

The nine years he spent at the Western Theological Seminary were busy years of teaching and study and productive scholarship. In them he won a reputation as a teacher and exegete rarely attained by so young a man. When upon the death of Dr. Archibald Alexander Hodge in the autumn of 1886 he was called to succeed him in the historic Chair of Theology at Princeton many of his friends questioned the wisdom of a change. But recalling that Dr. Charles Hodge had been first a New Testament student and always a prince of exegetes, he determined to accept the call.

The years spent at Allegheny, useful and fruitful as they were, were years of training and preparation for the more than thirty-three years (1887–February, 1921) spent in the professorship at Princeton. Always deeply attached to the place, loving with an enthusiastic devotion the University and the Seminary, which he counted in very truth his *almae matres,* he venerated as only a pure and unselfish spirit can the great men and the hallowed memories which have made Princeton one of the notable seats of theological scholarship. His reverence for those who had taught him was equalled by his admiration of his colleagues, and the love which he delighted to express for those who had taught him was constantly reproduced in his affection for his younger colleagues and the successive classes of students who thronged his classrooms.

It may be that a certain intellectual austerity, a loftiness and aloofness from the common weaknesses of the human reason, are inseparable from the system of thought which is associated with the names of Calvin and Augustine and Paul, but it is never really incarnated in a great thinker without its inevitable counterpoise of the tenderest human sympathies. In Benjamin Warfield such sympathies found expression in a love for men, and especially of children, in a heart open to every appeal, and a strong, if undemonstrative, support of such causes as home and foreign missions and especially of the work for the freedmen. Always a diligent student, he also read widely over an unusual range of general literature, including poetry, fiction and drama, and often drew illustrations from the most unexpected sources.

He appreciated in a very high degree the value of an organ for the discussion of the theological questions of his time. In 1889 he became one of the editors of the *Presbyterian Review* in succession to Dr. Francis L. Patton. When that review was discontinued he planned and for twelve years conducted the *Presbyterian and Reformed Review,* which in 1902 was taken over by the Faculty of Princeton Theological Seminary and renamed the *Princeton Theological Review.*

In these reviews was published a large part of the material

gathered into this and succeeding volumes. Other portions are taken from various encyclopaedias and dictionaries, reviews, magazines and other publications to which he was a frequent contributor. He also published the following volumes: " Introduction to the Textual Criticism of the New Testament " (1886); " On the Revision of the Confession of Faith " (1890); " The Gospel of the Incarnation " (1893); " Two Studies in the History of Doctrine " (1893); " The Right of Systematic Theology " (1897); " The Significance of the Westminster Standards " (1898); " Acts and Pastoral Epistles " (1902); " The Power of God Unto Salvation " (1903); " The Lord of Glory " (1907); " Calvin as a Theologian and Calvinism Today " (1909); " Hymns and Religious Verses " (1910); " The Saviour of the World " (1914); " The Plan of Salvation " (1915); "Faith and Life " (1916); " Counterfeit Miracles " (1918).

He received from the College of New Jersey the degree of Doctor of Divinity in 1880; that of Doctor of Laws in 1892; and that of Doctor of Laws from Davidson College in 1892; that of Doctor of Letters from Lafayette College in 1911; and that of Sacrae Theologiae Doctor from the University of Utrecht in 1913.

He was stricken with angina pectoris on December 24, 1920, and died on February 16, 1921, at Princeton.

E. D. W.

CONTENTS

xi

OTHER ARTICLES ON INSPIRATION AND THE BIBLE

I

THE BIBLICAL IDEA OF REVELATION

THE BIBLICAL IDEA OF REVELATION [1]

I. The Nature of Revelation

THE religion of the Bible is a frankly supernatural religion. By this is not meant merely that, according to it, all men, as creatures, live, move and have their being in God. It is meant that, according to it, God has intervened extraordinarily, in the course of the sinful world's development, for the salvation of men otherwise lost. In Eden the Lord God had been present with sinless man in such a sense as to form a distinct element in his social environment (Gen. iii. 8). This intimate association was broken up by the Fall. But God did not therefore withdraw Himself from concernment with men. Rather, He began at once a series of interventions in human history by means of which man might be rescued from his sin and, despite it, brought to the end destined for him. These interventions involved the segregation of a people for Himself, by whom God should be known, and whose distinction should be that God should be "nigh unto them" as He was not to other nations (Deut. iv. 7; Ps. cxlv. 18). But this people was not permitted to imagine that it owed its segregation to anything in itself fitted to attract or determine the Divine preference; no consciousness was more poignant in Israel than that Jehovah had chosen it, not it Him, and that Jehovah's choice of it rested solely on His gracious will. Nor was this people permitted to imagine that it was for its own sake alone that it had been singled out to be the sole recipient of the knowledge of Jehovah; it was made clear from the beginning that God's mysteriously gracious dealing with it had as its ultimate end the blessing of the whole world (Gen. xii. 2.3; xvii. 4.5.6.16;

[1] Article " Revelation," from *The International Standard Bible Encyclopaedia*, James Orr, General Editor, v. 4, pp. 2573–2582. Pub. Chicago, 1915, by The Howard-Severance Co.

xviii. 18; xxii. 18; cf Rom. iv. 13), the bringing together again
of the divided families of the earth under the glorious reign
of Jehovah, and the reversal of the curse under which the
whole world lay for its sin (Gen. xii. 3). Meanwhile, however,
Jehovah was known only in Israel. To Israel God showed His
word and made known His statutes and judgments, and after
this fashion He dealt with no other nation; and therefore none
other knew His judgments (Ps. cxlvii. 19 f.). Accordingly,
when the hope of Israel (who was also the desire of all nations)
came, His own lips unhesitatingly declared that the salvation
He brought, though of universal application, was " from the
Jews " (Jn. iv. 22). And the nations to which this salvation
had not been made known are declared by the chief agent in
its proclamation to them to be, meanwhile, " far off," "having
no hope " and " without God in the world " (Eph. ii. 12), because they were aliens from the commonwealth of Israel and
strangers from the covenant of the promise.

The religion of the Bible thus announces itself, not as the
product of men's search after God, if haply they may feel after
Him and find Him, but as the creation in men of the gracious
God, forming a people for Himself, that they may show forth
His praise. In other words, the religion of the Bible presents
itself as distinctively a revealed religion. Or rather, to speak
more exactly, it announces itself as the revealed religion, as
the only revealed religion; and sets itself as such over against
all other religions, which are represented as all products, in a
sense in which it is not, of the art and device of man.

It is not, however, implied in this exclusive claim to revelation — which is made by the religion of the Bible in all the
stages of its history — that the living God, who made the
heaven and the earth and the sea and all that in them is, has
left Himself without witness among the peoples of the world
(Acts xiv. 17). It is asserted indeed, that in the process of His
redemptive work, God suffered for a season all the nations to
walk in their own ways; but it is added that to none of them
has He failed to do good, and to give from heaven rains and
fruitful seasons, filling their hearts with food and gladness.

And not only is He represented as thus constantly showing Himself in His providence not far from any one of them, thus wooing them to seek Him if haply they might feel after Him and find Him (Acts xvii. 27), but as from the foundation of the world openly manifesting Himself to them in the works of His hands, in which His everlasting power and Divinity are clearly seen (Rom. i. 20). That men at large have not retained Him in their knowledge, or served Him as they ought, is not due therefore to failure on His part to keep open the way to knowledge of Him, but to the darkening of their senseless hearts by sin and to the vanity of their sin-deflected reasonings (Rom. i. 21 ff.), by means of which they have supplanted the truth of God by a lie and have come to worship and serve the creature rather than the ever-blessed Creator. It is, indeed, precisely because in their sin they have thus held down the truth in unrighteousness and have refused to have God in their knowledge (so it is intimated); and because, moreover, in their sin, the revelation God gives of Himself in His works of creation and providence no longer suffices for men's needs, that God has intervened supernaturally in the course of history to form a people for Himself, through whom at length all the world should be blessed.

It is quite obvious that there are brought before us in these several representations two species or stages of revelation, which should be discriminated to avoid confusion. There is the revelation which God continuously makes to all men: by it His power and Divinity are made known. And there is the revelation which He makes exclusively to His chosen people: through it His saving grace is made known. Both species or stages of revelation are insisted upon throughout the Scriptures. They are, for example, brought significantly together in such a declaration as we find in Ps. xix: " The heavens declare the glory of God . . . their line is gone out through all the earth " (vers. 1.4); " The law of Jehovah is perfect, restoring the soul " (ver. 7). The Psalmist takes his beginning here from the praise of the glory of God, the Creator of all that is, which has been written upon the very heavens, that none may fail to see it.

From this he rises, however, quickly to the more full throated praise of the mercy of Jehovah, the covenant God, who has visited His people with saving instruction. Upon this higher revelation there is finally based a prayer for salvation from sin, which ends in a great threefold acclamation, instinct with adoring gratitude: " O Jehovah, my rock, and my redeemer " (ver. 14). " The heavens," comments Lord Bacon, " indeed tell of the glory of God, but not of His will according to which the poet prays to be pardoned and sanctified." In so commenting, Lord Bacon touches the exact point of distinction between the two species or stages of revelation. The one is adapted to man as man; the other to man as sinner; and since man, on becoming sinner, has not ceased to be man, but has only acquired new needs requiring additional provisions to bring him to the end of his existence, so the revelation directed to man as sinner does not supersede that given to man as man, but supplements it with these new provisions for his attainment, in his new condition of blindness, helplessness and guilt induced by sin, of the end of his being.

These two species or stages of revelation have been commonly distinguished from one another by the distinctive names of natural and supernatural revelation, or general and special revelation, or natural and soteriological revelation. Each of these modes of discriminating them has its particular fitness and describes a real difference between the two in nature, reach or purpose. The one is communicated through the media of natural phenomena, occurring in the course of Nature or of history; the other implies an intervention in the natural course of things and is not merely in source but in mode supernatural. The one is addressed generally to all intelligent creatures, and is therefore accessible to all men; the other is addressed to a special class of sinners, to whom God would make known His salvation. The one has in view to meet and supply the natural need of creatures for knowledge of their God; the other to rescue broken and deformed sinners from their sin and its consequences. But, though thus distinguished from one another, it is important that the two species or stages of revelation should not be set in opposition to one another, or the closeness of their mutual relations or the constancy of their interaction be obscured. They constitute together a unitary whole, and each is incomplete without the other. In its most general idea, revelation is rooted in creation and the relations with His intelligent creatures into which God has brought Himself by giving them being. Its object is to realize the end of man's creation, to be attained only through knowledge of God and perfect and unbroken communion with Him. On the entrance of sin into the world, destroying this communion with God and obscuring the knowledge of Him derived from Nature, another mode of revelation was necessitated, having also another content, adapted to the new relation to God and the new conditions of intellect, heart and will brought about by sin. It must not be supposed, however, that this new mode of revelation was an *ex post facto* expedient, introduced to meet an unforeseen contingency. The actual course of human development was in the nature of the case the expected and the intended course of human development, for which man was created; and revelation, therefore, in its double form was the Divine purpose for man from the beginning, and constitutes a unitary provision for the realization of the end of his creation in the actual circumstances in which he exists. We may distinguish in this unitary revelation the two elements by the coöperation of which the effect is produced; but we should bear in mind that only by their coöperation is the effect produced. Without special revelation, general revelation would be for sinful men incomplete and ineffective, and could issue, as in point of fact it has issued wherever it alone has been accessible, only in leaving them without excuse (Rom. i. 20). Without general revelation, special revelation would lack that basis in the fundamental knowledge of God as the mighty and wise, righteous and good, maker and ruler of all things, apart from which the further revelation of this great God's interventions in the world for the salvation of sinners could not be either intelligible, credible or operative.

Only in Eden has general revelation been adequate to the needs of man. Not being a sinner, man in Eden had no need of that grace of God itself by which sinners are restored to communion with Him, or of the special revelation of this grace of God to sinners to enable them to live with God. And not being a sinner, man in Eden, as he contemplated the works of God, saw God in the unclouded mirror of his mind with a clarity of vision, and lived with Him in the untroubled depths of his heart with a trustful intimacy of association, inconceivable to sinners. Nevertheless, the revelation of God in Eden was not merely " natural." Not only does the prohibition of the forbidden fruit involve a positive commandment (Gen. ii. 16), but the whole history implies an immediacy of intercourse with God which cannot easily be set to the credit of the picturesque art of the narrative, or be fully accounted for by the vividness of the perception of God in His works proper to sinless creatures. The impression is strong that what is meant to be conveyed to us is that man dwelt with God in Eden, and enjoyed with Him immediate and not merely mediate communion. In that case, we may understand that if man had not fallen, he would have continued to enjoy immediate intercourse with God, and that the cessation of this immediate intercourse is due to sin. It is not then the supernaturalness of special revelation which is rooted in sin, but, if we may be allowed the expression, the specialness of supernatural revelation. Had man not fallen, heaven would have continued to lie about him through all his history, as it lay about his infancy; every man would have enjoyed direct vision of God and immediate speech with Him. Man having fallen, the cherubim and the flame of a sword, turning every way, keep the path: and God breaks His way in a round-about fashion into man's darkened heart to reveal there His redemptive love. By slow steps and gradual stages He at once works out His saving purpose and molds the world for its reception, choosing a people for Himself and training it through long and weary ages, until at last when the fulness of time has come, He bares His arm and sends out the proclamation of His great salvation to all the earth.

Certainly, from the gate of Eden onward, God's general revelation ceased to be, in the strict sense, supernatural. It is, of course, not meant that God deserted His world and left it to fester in its iniquity. His providence still ruled over all, leading steadily onward to the goal for which man had been created, and of the attainment of which in God's own good time and way the very continuance of men's existence, under God's providential government, was a pledge. And His Spirit still everywhere wrought upon the hearts of men, stirring up all their powers (though created in the image of God, marred and impaired by sin) to their best activities, and to such splendid effect in every department of human achievement as to command the admiration of all ages, and in the highest region of all, that of conduct, to call out from an apostle the encomium that though they had no law they did by nature (observe the word "nature") the things of the law. All this, however, remains within the limits of Nature, that is to say, within the sphere of operation of Divinely directed and assisted second causes. It illustrates merely the heights to which the powers of man may attain under the guidance of providence and the influences of what we have learned to call God's "common grace." Nowhere, throughout the whole ethnic domain, are the conceptions of God and His ways put within the reach of man, through God's revelation of Himself in the works of creation and providence, transcended; nowhere is the slightest knowledge betrayed of anything concerning God and His purposes, which could be known only by its being supernaturally told to men. Of the entire body of "saving truth," for example, which is the burden of what we call "special revelation," the whole heathen world remained in total ignorance. And even its hold on the general truths of religion, not being vitalized by supernatural enforcements, grew weak, and its knowledge of the very nature of God decayed, until it ran out to the dreadful issue which Paul sketches for us in that inspired philosophy of religion which he incorporates in the latter part of the first chapter of the Epistle to the Romans.

Behind even the ethnic development, there lay, of course, the supernatural intercourse of man with God which had obtained before the entrance of sin into the world, and the supernatural revelations at the gate of Eden (Gen. iii. 8), and at the second origin of the human race, the Flood (Gen. viii. 21.22; ix. 1-17). How long the tradition of this primitive revelation lingered in nooks and corners of the heathen world, conditioning and vitalizing the natural revelation of God always accessible, we have no means of estimating. Neither is it easy to measure the effect of God's special revelation of Himself to His people upon men outside the bounds of, indeed, but coming into contact with, this chosen people, or sharing with them a common natural inheritance. Lot and Ishmael and Esau can scarcely have been wholly ignorant of the word of God which came to Abraham and Isaac and Jacob; nor could the Egyptians from whose hands God wrested His people with a mighty arm fail to learn something of Jehovah, any more than the mixed multitudes who witnessed the ministry of Christ could fail to infer something from His gracious walk and mighty works. It is natural to infer that no nation which was intimately associated with Israel's life could remain entirely unaffected by Israel's revelation. But whatever impressions were thus conveyed reached apparently individuals only: the heathen which surrounded Israel, even those most closely affiliated with Israel, remained heathen; they had no revelation. In the sporadic instances when God visited an alien with a supernatural communication — such as the dreams sent to Abimelech (Gen. xx.) and to Pharaoh (Gen. xl. xli.) and to Nebuchadnezzar (Dan. ii. 1 ff.) and to the soldier in the camp of Midian (Jgs. vii. 13) — it was in the interests, not of the heathen world, but of the chosen people that they were sent; and these instances derive their significance wholly from this fact. There remain, no doubt, the mysterious figure of Melchizedek, perhaps also of Jethro, and the strange apparition of Balaam, who also, however, appear in the sacred narrative only in connection with the history of God's dealings with His people and in their interest. Their unexplained appearance cannot in any event avail to modify the general fact that the life of the heathen peoples lay outside the supernatural revelation of God. The heathen were suffered to walk in their own ways (Acts xiv. 16).

II. The Process of Revelation

Meanwhile, however, God had not forgotten them, but was preparing salvation for them also through the supernatural revelation of His grace that He was making to His people. According to the Biblical representation, in the midst of and working confluently with the revelation which He has always been giving of Himself on the plane of Nature, God was making also from the very fall of man a further revelation of Himself on the plane of grace. In contrast with His general, natural revelation, in which all men by virtue of their very nature as men share, this special, supernatural revelation was granted at first only to individuals, then progressively to a family, a tribe, a nation, a race, until, when the fulness of time was come, it was made the possession of the whole world. It may be difficult to obtain from Scripture a clear account of why God chose thus to give this revelation of His grace only progressively; or, to be more explicit, through the process of a historical development. Such is, however, the ordinary mode of the Divine working: it is so that God made the worlds, it is so that He creates the human race itself, the recipient of this revelation, it is so that He builds up His kingdom in the world and in the individual soul, which only gradually comes whether to the knowledge of God or to the fruition of His salvation. As to the fact, the Scriptures are explicit, tracing for us, or rather embodying in their own growth, the record of the steady advance of this gracious revelation through definite stages from its first faint beginnings to its glorious completion in Jesus Christ.

So express is its relation to the development of the kingdom of God itself, or rather to that great series of Divine operations which are directed to the building up of the kingdom of God in the world, that it is sometimes confounded with them, or thought of as simply their reflection in the contemplating mind of man. Thus it is not infrequently said that revelation, meaning this special redemptive revelation, has been communicated in deeds, not in words; and it is occasionally elaborately argued that the sole manner in which God has revealed Himself as the Saviour of sinners is just by performing those mighty acts by which sinners are saved. This is not, however, the Biblical representation. Revelation is, of course, often made through the instrumentality of deeds; and the series of His great redemptive acts by which He saves the world constitutes the preëminent revelation of the grace of God — so far as these redemptive acts are open to observation and are perceived in their significance. But revelation, after all, is the correlate of understanding and has as its proximate end just the production of knowledge, though not, of course, knowledge for its own sake, but for the sake of salvation. The series of the redemptive acts of God, accordingly, can properly be designated "revelation" only when and so far as they are contemplated as adapted and designed to produce knowledge of God and His purpose and methods of grace. No bare series of unexplained acts can be thought, however, adapted to produce knowledge, especially if these acts be, as in this case, of a highly transcendental character. Nor can this particular series of acts be thought to have as its main design the production of knowledge; its main design is rather to save man. No doubt the production of knowledge of the Divine grace is one of the means by which this main design of the redemptive acts of God is attained. But this only renders it the more necessary that the proximate result of producing knowledge should not fail; and it is doubtless for this reason that the series of redemptive acts of God has not been left to explain itself, but the explanatory word has been added to it. Revelation thus appears, however, not as the mere reflection of the redeeming acts of God in the minds of men, but as a factor in the redeeming work of God, a component part of the series of His redeeming acts, without which that series would be incomplete and so far inoperative for its main end. Thus the Scriptures represent it, not confounding revelation with the series of the redemptive acts of God, but placing it among the redemptive acts of God and giving it a function as a substantive element in the operations by which the merciful God saves sinful men. It is therefore not made even a mere constant accompaniment of the redemptive acts of God, giving their explanation that they may be understood. It occupies a far more independent place among them than this, and as frequently precedes them to prepare their way as it accompanies or follows them to interpret their meaning. It is, in one word, itself a redemptive act of God and by no means the least important in the series of His redemptive acts.

This might, indeed, have been inferred from its very nature, and from the nature of the salvation which was being wrought out by these redemptive acts of God. One of the most grievous of the effects of sin is the deformation of the image of God reflected in the human mind, and there can be no recovery from sin which does not bring with it the correction of this deformation and the reflection in the soul of man of the whole glory of the Lord God Almighty. Man is an intelligent being; his superiority over the brute is found, among other things, precisely in the direction of all his life by his intelligence; and his blessedness is rooted in the true knowledge of his God — for this is life eternal, that we should know the only true God and Him whom He has sent. Dealing with man as an intelligent being, God the Lord has saved him by means of a revelation, by which he has been brought into an ever more and more adequate knowledge of God, and been led ever more and more to do his part in working out his own salvation with fear and trembling as he perceived with ever more and more clearness how God is working it out for him through mighty deeds of grace.

This is not the place to trace, even in outline, from the material point of view, the development of God's redemptive revelation from its first beginnings, in the promise given to Abraham — or rather in what has been called the Protevangelium at the gate of Eden — to its completion in the advent and work of Christ and the teaching of His apostles; a steadily advancing development, which, as it lies spread out to view in the pages of Scripture, takes to those who look at it from the consummation backward, the appearance of the shadow cast athwart preceding ages by the great figure of Christ. Even from the formal point of view, however, there has been pointed out a progressive advance in the method of revelation, conso-

nant with its advance in content, or rather with the advancing
stages of the building up of the kingdom of God, to subserve
which is the whole object of revelation. Three distinct steps in
revelation have been discriminated from this point of view.
They are distinguished precisely by the increasing independence of revelation of the deeds constituting the series of the redemptive acts of God, in which, nevertheless, all revelation is
a substantial element. Discriminations like this must not be
taken too absolutely; and in the present instance the chronological sequence cannot be pressed. But, with much interlacing,
three generally successive stages of revelation may be recognized, producing periods at least characteristically of what we
may somewhat conventionally call theophany, prophecy and
inspiration. What may be somewhat indefinitely marked off as
the Patriarchal age is characteristically " the period of Outward Manifestations, and Symbols, and Theophanies ": during it " God spoke to men through their senses, in physical
phenomena, as the burning bush, the cloudy pillar, or in sensuous forms, as men, angels, etc. . . . In the Prophetic age, on
the contrary, the prevailing mode of revelation was by means
of inward prophetic inspiration ": God spoke to men characteristically by the movements of the Holy Spirit in their
hearts. " Prevailingly, at any rate from Samuel downwards,
the supernatural revelation was a revelation in the hearts of
the foremost thinkers of the people, or, as we call it, prophetic
inspiration, without the aid of external sensuous symbols of
God " (A. B. Davidson, *OT Prophecy*, 1903, p. 148; cf. pp. 12-
14, 145 ff.). This internal method of revelation reaches its culmination in the New Testament period, which is preëminently
the age of the Spirit. What is especially characteristic of this
age is revelation through the medium of the written word,
what may be called apostolic as distinguished from prophetic
inspiration. The revealing Spirit speaks through chosen men
as His organs, but through these organs in such a fashion that
the most intimate processes of their souls become the instruments by means of which He speaks His mind. Thus at all
events there are brought clearly before us three well-marked

modes of revelation, which we may perhaps designate respectively, not with perfect discrimination, it is true, but not misleadingly, (1) external manifestations, (2) internal suggestion, and (3) concursive operation.

III. Modes of Revelation

Theophany may be taken as the typical form of " external manifestation "; but by its side may be ranged all of those mighty works by which God makes Himself known, including express miracles, no doubt, but along with them every supernatural intervention in the affairs of men, by means of which a better understanding is communicated of what God is or what are His purposes of grace to a sinful race. Under " internal suggestion " may be subsumed all the characteristic phenomena of what is most properly spoken of as " prophecy": visions and dreams, which, according to a fundamental passage (Num. xii. 6), constitute the typical forms of prophecy, and with them the whole " prophetic word," which shares its essential characteristic with visions and dreams, since it comes not by the will of man but from God. By " concursive operation " may be meant that form of revelation illustrated in an inspired psalm or epistle or history, in which no human activity — not even the control of the will — is superseded, but the Holy Spirit works in, with and through them all in such a manner as to communicate to the product qualities distinctly superhuman. There is no age in the history of the religion of the Bible, from that of Moses to that of Christ and His apostles, in which all these modes of revelation do not find place. One or another may seem particularly characteristic of this age or of that; but they all occur in every age. And they occur side by side, broadly speaking, on the same level. No discrimination is drawn between them in point of worthiness as modes of revelation, and much less in point of purity in the revelations communicated through them. The circumstance that God spoke to Moses, not by dream or vision but mouth to mouth, is, indeed, adverted to (Num. xii. 8) as a proof of the peculiar favor shown to Moses and even of the superior dignity of Moses above other organs of revelation: God admitted him to an intimacy of intercourse which He did not accord to others. But though Moses was thus distinguished above all others in the dealings of God with him, no distinction is drawn between the revelations given through him and those given through other organs of revelation in point either of Divinity or of authority. And beyond this we have no Scriptural warrant to go on in contrasting one mode of revelation with another. Dreams may seem to us little fitted to serve as vehicles of Divine communications. But there is no suggestion in Scripture that revelations through dreams stand on a lower plane than any others; and we should not fail to remember that the essential characteristics of revelations through dreams are shared by all forms of revelation in which (whether we should call them visions or not) the images or ideas which fill, or pass in procession through, the consciousness are determined by some other power than the recipient's own will. It may seem natural to suppose that revelations rise in rank in proportion to the fulness of the engagement of the mental activity of the recipient in their reception. But we should bear in mind that the intellectual or spiritual quality of a revelation is not derived from the recipient but from its Divine Giver. The fundamental fact in all revelation is that it is from God. This is what gives unity to the whole process of revelation, given though it may be· in divers portions and in divers manners and distributed though it may be through the ages in accordance with the mere will of God, or as it may have suited His developing purpose — this and its unitary end, which is ever the building up of the kingdom of God. In whatever diversity of forms, by means of whatever variety of modes, in whatever distinguishable stages it is given, it is ever the revelation of the One God, and it is ever the one consistently developing redemptive revelation of God.

On a *prima facie* view it may indeed seem likely that a difference in the quality of their supernaturalness would inevitably obtain between revelations given through such divergent modes. The completely supernatural character of revelations given in theophanies is obvious. He who will not allow that God speaks to man, to make known His gracious purposes toward him, has no other recourse here than to pronounce the stories legendary. The objectivity of the mode of communication which is adopted is intense, and it is thrown up to observation with the greatest emphasis. Into the natural life of man God intrudes in a purely supernatural manner, bearing a purely supernatural communication. In these communications we are given accordingly just a series of " naked messages of God." But not even in the Patriarchal age were all revelations given in theophanies or objective appearances. There were dreams, and visions, and revelations without explicit intimation in the narrative of how they were communicated. And when we pass on in the history, we do not, indeed, leave behind us theophanies and objective appearances. It is not only made the very characteristic of Moses, the greatest figure in the whole history of revelation except only that of Christ, that he knew God face to face (Deut. xxxiv. 10), and God spoke to him mouth to mouth, even manifestly, and not in dark speeches (Num. xii. 8); but throughout the whole history of revelation down to the appearance of Jesus to Paul on the road to Damascus, God has shown Himself visibly to His servants whenever it has seemed good to Him to do so and has spoken with them in objective speech. Nevertheless, it is expressly made the characteristic of the Prophetic age that God makes Himself known to His Servants " in a vision," " in a dream " (Num. xii. 6). And although, throughout its entire duration, God, in fulfilment of His promise (Deut. xviii. 18), put His words in the mouths of His prophets and gave them His commandments to speak, yet it would seem inherent in the very employment of men as instruments of revelation that the words of God given through them are spoken by human mouths; and the purity of their supernaturalness may seem so far obscured. And when it is not merely the mouths of men with which God thus serves Himself in the delivery of His messages, but their minds and hearts as well — the play of their religious feelings, or the processes of their logical reasoning, or the tenacity of their mem-

ories, as, say, in a psalm or in an epistle, or a history — the
supernatural element in the communication may easily seem
to retire still farther into the background. It can scarcely be a
matter of surprise, therefore, that question has been raised as
to the relation of the natural and the supernatural in such revelations, and, in many current manners of thinking and speaking of them, the completeness of their supernaturalness has
been limited and curtailed in the interests of the natural instrumentalities employed. The plausibility of such reasoning
renders it the more necessary that we should observe the
unvarying emphasis which the Scriptures place upon the absolute supernaturalness of revelation in all its modes alike.
In the view of the Scriptures, the completely supernatural
character of revelation is in no way lessened by the circumstance that it has been given through the instrumentality
of men. They affirm, indeed, with the greatest possible
emphasis that the Divine word delivered through men is
the pure word of God, diluted with no human admixture
whatever.

We have already been led to note that even on the occasion
when Moses is exalted above all other organs of revelation
(Num. xii. 6 ff.), in point of dignity and favor, no suggestion
whatever is made of any inferiority, in either the directness or
the purity of their supernaturalness, attaching to other organs
of revelation. There might never afterward arise a prophet in
Israel like unto Moses, whom the Lord knew face to face
(Deut. xxxiv. 10). But each of the whole series of prophets
raised up by Jehovah that the people might always know His
will was to be like Moses in speaking to the people only what
Jehovah commanded them (Deut. xviii. 15.18.20). In this great
promise, securing to Israel the succession of prophets, there is
also included a declaration of precisely how Jehovah would
communicate His messages not so much to them as through
them. " I will raise them up a prophet from among their brethren, like unto thee," we read (Deut. xviii. 18), " *and I will put
my words in his mouth,* and he shall speak unto them all that
I shall command him." The process of revelation through the

prophets was a process by which Jehovah put His words in the mouths of the prophets, and the prophets spoke precisely these words and no others. So the prophets themselves ever asserted. " Then Jehovah put forth his hand, and touched my mouth," explains Jeremiah in his account of how he received his prophecies, " and Jehovah said unto me, Behold, I have put my words in thy mouth " (Jer. i. 9; cf. v. 14; Isa. li. 16; lix. 21; Num. xxii. 35; xxiii. 5.12.16). Accordingly, the words " with which " they spoke were not their own but the Lord's: " And he said unto me," records Ezekiel, " Son of man, go, get thee unto the house of Israel, and speak with my words unto them " (Ezk. iii. 4). It is a process of nothing other than " dictation " which is thus described (2 S. xiv. 3.19), though, of course, the question may remain open of the exact processes by which this dictation is accomplished. The fundamental passage which brings the central fact before us in the most vivid manner is, no doubt, the account of the commissioning of Moses and Aaron given in Ex. iv. 10–17; vii. 1–7. Here, in the most express words, Jehovah declares that He who made the mouth can be with it to teach it what to speak, and announces the precise function of a prophet to be that he is " a mouth of God," who speaks not his own but God's words. Accordingly, the Hebrew name for " prophet " (nābhi'), whatever may be its etymology, means throughout the Scriptures just " spokesman," though not " spokesman " in general, but spokesman by way of eminence, that is, God's spokesman; and the characteristic formula by which a prophetic declaration is announced is: " The word of Jehovah came to me," or the brief " saith Jehovah " (יהוה־ נאם, neʾum Yahweh). In no case does a prophet put his words forward as his own words. That he is a prophet at all is due not to choice on his own part, but to a call of God, obeyed often with reluctance; and he prophesies or forbears to prophesy, not according to his own will but as the Lord opens and shuts his mouth (Ezk. iii. 26 f.) and creates for him the fruit of the lips (Isa. lvii. 19; cf. vi. 7; l. 4). In contrast with the false prophets, he strenuously asserts that he does not speak out of his own heart (" heart " in Biblical language includes the whole inner man), but all that he proclaims is the pure word of Jehovah.

The fundamental passage does not quite leave the matter, however, with this general declaration. It describes the characteristic manner in which Jehovah communicates His messages to His prophets as through the medium of visions and dreams. Neither visions in the technical sense of that word, nor dreams, appear, however, to have been the customary mode of revelation to the prophets, the record of whose revelations has come down to us. But, on the other hand, there are numerous indications in the record that the universal mode of revelation to them was one which was in some sense a vision, and can be classed only in the category distinctively so called.

The whole nomenclature of prophecy presupposes, indeed, its vision-form. Prophecy is distinctively a word, and what is delivered by the prophets is proclaimed as the "word of Jehovah." That it should be announced by the formula, "Thus saith the Lord," is, therefore, only what we expect; and we are prepared for such a description of its process as: "The Lord Jehovah . . . wakeneth mine ear to hear." He "hath opened mine ear" (Isa. l. 4.5). But this is not the way of speaking of their messages which is most usual in the prophets. Rather is the whole body of prophecy cursorily presented as a thing seen. Isaiah places at the head of his book: "The vision of Isaiah . . . which he saw" (cf. Isa. xxix. 10.11; Ob. ver. 1); and then proceeds to set at the head of subordinate sections the remarkable words, "The word that Isaiah . . . saw" (ii. 1); "the burden [margin "oracle"] . . . which Isaiah . . . did see" (xiii. 1). Similarly there stand at the head of other prophecies: "the words of Amos . . . which he saw" (Am. i. 1); "the word of Jehovah that came to Micah . . . which he saw" (Mic. i. 1); "the oracle which Habakkuk the prophet did see" (Hab. i. 1 margin); and elsewhere such language occurs as this: "the word that Jehovah hath showed me" (Jer. xxxviii. 21); "the prophets have seen . . . oracles" (Lam. ii. 14); "the word of Jehovah came . . . and I looked, and, behold" (Ezk. i. 3.4); "Woe unto the foolish prophets, that fol-

low their own spirit, and have seen nothing " (Ezk. xiii. 3);
" I . . . will look forth to see what he will speak with me, . . .
Jehovah . . . said, Write the vision " (Hab. ii. 1 f.). It is an
inadequate explanation of such language to suppose it merely
a relic of a time when vision was more predominantly the form
of revelation. There is no proof that vision in the technical
sense ever was more predominantly the form of revelation than
in the days of the great writing prophets; and such language
as we have quoted too obviously represents the living point of
view of the prophets to admit of the supposition that it was
merely conventional on their lips. The prophets, in a word,
represent the Divine communications which they received as
given to them in some sense in visions.

It is possible, no doubt, to exaggerate the significance of
this. It is an exaggeration, for example, to insist that therefore
all the Divine communications made to the prophets must
have come to them in external appearances and objective
speech, addressed to and received by means of the bodily eye
and ear. This would be to break down the distinction between
manifestation and revelation, and to assimilate the mode of
prophetic revelation to that granted to Moses, though these
are expressly distinguished (Num. xii. 6–8). It is also an exaggeration to insist that therefore the prophetic state must be
conceived as that of strict ecstasy, involving the complete
abeyance of all mental life on the part of the prophet (amen-
tia), and possibly also accompanying physical effects. It is
quite clear from the records which the prophets themselves
give us of their revelations that their intelligence was alert in
all stages of their reception of them. The purpose of both these
extreme views is the good one of doing full justice to the objectivity of the revelations vouchsafed to the prophets. If these
revelations took place entirely externally to the prophet, who
merely stood off and contemplated them, or if they were implanted in the prophets by a process so violent as not only to
supersede their mental activity but, for the time being, to annihilate it, it would be quite clear that they came from a source
other than the prophets' own minds. It is undoubtedly the fun-

damental contention of the prophets that the revelations given
through them are not their own but wholly God's. The significant language we have just quoted from Ezk. xiii. 3: "Woe
unto the foolish prophets, that follow their own spirit, and have
seen nothing," is a typical utterance of their sense of the complete objectivity of their messages. What distinguishes the
false prophets is precisely that they "prophesy out of their
own heart" (Ezk. xiii. 2–17), or, to draw the antithesis sharply,
that "they speak a vision of their own heart, and not out of
the mouth of Jehovah" (Jer. xxiii. 16.26; xiv. 14). But these
extreme views fail to do justice, the one to the equally important fact that the word of God, given through the prophets,
comes as the pure and unmixed word of God not merely to,
but from, the prophets; and the other to the equally obvious
fact that the intelligence of the prophets is alert throughout
the whole process of the reception and delivery of the revelation made through them.

That which gives to prophecy as a mode of revelation its
place in the category of visions, strictly so called, and dreams,
is that it shares with them the distinguishing characteristic
which determines the class. In them all alike the movements
of the mind are determined by something extraneous to the
subject's will, or rather, since we are speaking of supernaturally given dreams and visions, extraneous to the totality of
the subject's own psychoses. A power not himself takes possession of his consciousness and determines it according to its will.
That power, in the case of the prophets, was fully recognized
and energetically asserted to be Jehovah Himself or, to be
more specific, the Spirit of Jehovah (1S. x. 6.10; Neh. ix. 30;
Zec. vii. 12; Joel ii. 28.29). The prophets were therefore 'men
of the Spirit' (Hos. ix. 7). What constituted them prophets
was that the Spirit was put upon them (Isa. xlii. 1) or poured
out on them (Joel ii. 28.29), and they were consequently filled
with the Spirit (Mic. iii. 8), or, in another but equivalent locution, that "the hand" of the Lord, or "the power of the hand"
of the Lord, was upon them (2 K. iii. 15; Ezk. i. 3; iii. 14.22;
xxxiii. 22; xxxvii. 1; xl. 1), that is to say, they were under the

divine control. This control is represented as complete and compelling, so that, under it, the prophet becomes not the "mover," but the "moved" in the formation of his message. The apostle Peter very purely reflects the prophetic consciousness in his well-known declaration: ' No prophecy of scripture comes of private interpretation; for prophecy was never brought by the will of man; but it was as borne by the Holy Spirit that men spoke from God ' (2 Pet. i. 20.21).

What this language of Peter emphasizes — and what is emphasized in the whole account which the prophets give of their own consciousness — is, to speak plainly, the passivity of the prophets with respect to the revelation given through them. This is the significance of the phrase: ' it was as borne by the Holy Spirit that men spoke from God.' To be " borne " (φέρειν, *phérein*) is not the same as to be led (ἄγειν, *ágein*), much less to be guided or directed (ὀδηγεῖν, *hodēgeín*): he that is " borne " contributes nothing to the movement induced, but is the object to be moved. The term " passivity " is, perhaps, however, liable to some misapprehension, and should not be overstrained. It is not intended to deny that the intelligence of the prophets was active in the reception of their message; it was by means of their active intelligence that their message was received: their intelligence was the instrument of revelation. It is intended to deny only that their intelligence was active in the production of their message: that it was creatively as distinguished from receptively active. For reception itself is a kind of activity. What the prophets are solicitous that their readers shall understand is that they are in no sense co-authors with God of their messages. Their messages are given them, given them entire, and given them precisely as they are given out by them. God speaks through them: they are not merely His messengers, but " His mouth." But at the same time their intelligence is active in the reception, retention and announcing of their messages, contributing nothing to them but presenting fit instruments for the communication of them — instruments capable of understanding, responding profoundly to and zealously proclaiming them.

There is, no doubt, a not unnatural hesitancy abroad in thinking of the prophets as exhibiting only such merely receptive activities. In the interests of their personalities, we are asked not to represent God as dealing mechanically with them, pouring His revelations into their souls to be simply received as in so many buckets, or violently wresting their minds from their own proper action that He may do His own thinking with them. Must we not rather suppose, we are asked, that all revelations must be " psychologically mediated," must be given " after the mode of moral mediation," and must be made first of all their recipients' " own spiritual possession " ? And is not, in point of fact, the personality of each prophet clearly traceable in his message, and that to such an extent as to compel us to recognize him as in a true sense its real author? The plausibility of such questionings should not be permitted to obscure the fact that the mode of the communication of the prophetic messages which is suggested by them is directly contradicted by the prophets' own representations of their relations to the revealing Spirit. In the prophets' own view they were just instruments through whom God gave revelations which came from them, not as their own product, but as the pure word of Jehovah. Neither should the plausibility of such questionings blind us to their speciousness. They exploit subordinate considerations, which are not without their validity in their own place and under their own limiting conditions, as if they were the determining or even the sole considerations in the case, and in neglect of the really determining considerations. God is Himself the author of the instruments He employs for the communication of His messages to men and has framed them into precisely the instruments He desired for the exact communication of His message. There is just ground for the expectation that He will use all the instruments He employs according to their natures; intelligent beings therefore as intelligent beings, moral agents as moral agents. But there is no just ground for asserting that God is incapable of employing the intelligent beings He has Himself created and formed to His will, to proclaim His messages purely as He gives them to them; or of

making truly the possession of rational minds conceptions
which they have themselves had no part in creating. And there
is no ground for imagining that God is unable to frame His own
message in the language of the organs of His revelation without its thereby ceasing to be, because expressed in a fashion
natural to these organs, therefore purely His message. One
would suppose it to lie in the very nature of the case that if the
Lord makes any revelation to men, He would do it in the language of men; or, to individualize more explicitly, in the language of the man He employs as the organ of His revelation;
and that naturally means, not the language of his nation or
circle merely, but his own particular language, inclusive of all
that gives individuality to his self-expression. We may speak
of this, if we will, as " the accommodation of the revealing God
to the several prophetic individualities." But we should avoid
thinking of it externally and therefore mechanically, as if the
revealing Spirit artificially phrased the message which He
gives through each prophet in the particular forms of speech
proper to the individuality of each, so as to create the illusion
that the message comes out of the heart of the prophet himself.
Precisely what the prophets affirm is that their messages do
not come out of their own hearts and do not represent the workings of their own spirits. Nor is there any illusion in the phenomenon we are contemplating; and it is a much more intimate, and, we may add, a much more interesting phenomenon
than an external " accommodation " of speech to individual
habitudes. It includes, on the one hand, the " accommodation "
of the prophet, through his total preparation, to the speech in
which the revelation to be given through him is to be clothed;
and on the other involves little more than the consistent carrying into detail of the broad principle that God uses the instruments He employs in accordance with their natures.

No doubt, on adequate occasion, the very stones might cry
out by the power of God, and dumb beasts speak, and mysterious voices sound forth from the void; and there have not been
lacking instances in which men have been compelled by the
same power to speak what they would not, and in languages

whose very sounds were strange to their ears. But ordinarily when God the Lord would speak to men He avails Himself of the services of a human tongue with which to speak, and He employs this tongue according to its nature as a tongue and according to the particular nature of the tongue which He employs. It is vain to say that the message delivered through the instrumentality of this tongue is conditioned at least in its form by the tongue by which it is spoken, if not, indeed, limited, curtailed, in some degree determined even in its matter, by it. Not only was it God the Lord who made the tongue, and who made this particular tongue with all its peculiarities, not without regard to the message He would deliver through it; but His control of it is perfect and complete, and it is as absurd to say that He cannot speak His message by it purely without that message suffering change from the peculiarities of its tone and modes of enunciation, as it would be to say that no new truth can be announced in any language because the elements of speech by the combination of which the truth in question is announced are already in existence with their fixed range of connotation. The marks of the several individualities imprinted on the messages of the prophets, in other words, are only a part of the general fact that these messages are couched in human language, and in no way beyond that general fact affect their purity as direct communications from God.

A new set of problems is raised by the mode of revelation which we have called "concursive operation." This mode of revelation differs from prophecy, properly so called, precisely by the employment in it, as is not done in prophecy, of the total personality of the organ of revelation, as a factor. It has been common to speak of the mode of the Spirit's action in this form of revelation, therefore, as an assistance, a superintendence, a direction, a control, the meaning being that the effect aimed at — the discovery and enunciation of Divine truth — is attained through the action of the human powers — historical research, logical reasoning, ethical thought, religious aspiration — acting not by themselves, however, but under the prevailing assistance, superintendence, direction, control of the Divine Spirit. This manner of speaking has the advantage of setting this mode of revelation sharply in contrast with prophetic revelation, as involving merely a determining, and not, as in prophetic revelation, a supercessive action of the revealing Spirit. We are warned, however, against pressing this discrimination too far by the inclusion of the whole body of Scripture in such passages as 2 Pet. i. 20 f. in the category of prophecy, and the assignment of their origin not to a mere " leading " but to the " bearing " of the Holy Spirit. In any event such terms as assistance, superintendence, direction, control, inadequately express the nature of the Spirit's action in revelation by " concursive operation." The Spirit is not to be conceived as standing outside of the human powers employed for the effect in view, ready to supplement any inadequacies they may show and to supply any defects they may manifest, but as working confluently in, with and by them, elevating them, directing them, controlling them, energizing them, so that, as His instruments, they rise above themselves and under His inspiration do His work and reach His aim. The product, therefore, which is attained by their means is His product through them. It is this fact which gives to the process the right to be called actively, and to the product the right to be called passively, a revelation. Although the circumstance that what is done is done by and through the action of human powers keeps the product in form and quality in a true sense human, yet the confluent operation of the Holy Spirit throughout the whole process raises the result above what could by any possibility be achieved by mere human powers and constitutes it expressly a supernatural product. The human traits are traceable throughout its whole extent, but at bottom it is a Divine gift, and the language of Paul is the most proper mode of speech that could be applied to it: " Which things also we speak, not in words which man's wisdom teacheth, but which the Spirit teacheth " (1 Cor. ii. 13); " The things which I write unto you . . . are the commandment of the Lord " (1 Cor. xiv. 37).

It is supposed that all the forms of special or redemptive

revelation which underlie and give its content to the religion of
the Bible may without violence be subsumed under one or another of these three modes — external manifestation, internal
suggestion, and concursive operation. All, that is, except the
culminating revelation, not through, but in, Jesus Christ. As
in His person, in which dwells all the fulness of the Godhead
bodily, He rises above all classification and is *sui generis;* so
the revelation accumulated in Him stands outside all the divers
portions and divers manners in which otherwise revelation has
been given and sums up in itself all that has been or can be
made known of God and of His redemption. He does not so
much make a revelation of God as Himself is the revelation of
God; He does not merely disclose God's purpose of redemption, He is unto us wisdom from God, and righteousness and
sanctification and redemption. The theophanies are but faint
shadows in comparison with His manifestation of God in the
flesh. The prophets could prophesy only as the Spirit of Christ
which was in them testified, revealing to them as to servants
one or another of the secrets of the Lord Jehovah; from Him
as His Son, Jehovah has no secrets, but whatsoever the Father
knows that the Son knows also. Whatever truth men have
been made partakers of by the Spirit of truth is His (for all
things whatsoever the Father hath are His) and is taken by
the Spirit of truth and declared to men that He may be glorified. Nevertheless, though all revelation is thus summed up in
Him, we should not fail to note very carefully that it would
also be all sealed up in Him — so little is revelation conveyed
by fact alone, without the word — had it not been thus taken
by the Spirit of truth and declared unto men. The entirety of
the New Testament is but the explanatory word accompanying
and giving its effect to the fact of Christ. And when this fact
was in all its meaning made the possession of men, revelation
was completed and in that sense ceased. Jesus Christ is no less
the end of revelation than He is the end of the law.

IV. Biblical Terminology

There is not much additional to be learned concerning the nature and processes of revelation, from the terms currently employed in Scripture to express the idea. These terms are ordinarily the common words for disclosing, making known, making manifest, applied with more or less heightened significance to supernatural acts or effects in kind. In the English Bible (AV) the verb " reveal " occurs about fifty-one times, of which twenty-two are in the Old Testament and twenty-nine in the New Testament. In the Old Testament the word is always the rendering of a Hebrew term גָּלָה, gālāh, or its Aramaic equivalent גְּלָה, gᵉlāh, the root meaning of which appears to be " nakedness." When applied to revelation, it seems to hint at the removal of obstacles to perception or the uncovering of objects to perception. In the New Testament the word " reveal " is always (with the single exception of Lk. ii. 35) the rendering of a Greek term ἀποκαλύπτω, apokaluptō (but in 2 Thess. i. 7; 1 Pet. iv. 13 the corresponding noun ἀποκάλυψις, apokálupsis), which has a very similar basal significance with its Hebrew parallel. As this Hebrew word formed no substantive in this sense, the noun " revelation " does not occur in the English Old Testament, the idea being expressed, however, by other Hebrew terms variously rendered. It occurs in the English New Testament, on the other hand, about a dozen times, and always as the rendering of the substantive corresponding to the verb rendered " reveal " (apokálupsis). On the face of the English Bible, the terms " reveal," " revelation " bear therefore uniformly the general sense of " disclose," " disclosure." The idea is found in the Bible, however, much more frequently than the terms " reveal," " revelation " in English versions. Indeed, the Hebrew and Greek terms exclusively so rendered occur more frequently in this sense than in this rendering in the English Bible. And by their side there stand various other terms which express in one way or another the general conception.

In the New Testament the verb φανερόω, phaneróō, with the general sense of making manifest, manifesting, is the most common of these. It differs from *apokalúptō* as the more general and external term from the more special and inward. Other terms also are occasionally used: ἐπιφάνεια, *epipháneia,* "manifestation" (2 Thess. ii. 8; 1 Tim. vi. 14; 2 Tim. i. 10; iv. 1; Tit. ii. 13; cf. ἐπιφαίνω, *epiphaínō,* Tit. ii. 11; iii. 4); δεικνύω, *deiknúō* (Rev. i. 1; xvii. 1; xxii. 1.6.8; cf. Acts ix. 16; 1 Tim. iv. 15); ἐξηγέομαι, *exēgéomai* (Jn. i. 18), of which, however, only one perhaps — χρηματίζω, *chrēmatízō* (Mt. ii. 12.22; Lk. ii. 26; Acts x. 22; Heb. viii. 5; xi. 7; xii. 25); χρηματισμός, *chrēmatismós* (Rom. xi. 4) — calls for particular notice as in a special way, according to its usage, expressing the idea of a Divine communication.

In the Old Testament, the common Hebrew verb for "seeing" (רָאָה, *rā'āh*) is used in its appropriate stems, with God as the subject, for "appearing," "showing": "the Lord appeared unto . . ."; "the word which the Lord showed me." And from this verb not only is an active substantive formed which supplied the more ancient designation of the official organ or revelation: רֹאֶה, *rō'eh,* "seer"; but also objective substantives, מַרְאָה, *mar'āh,* and מַרְאֶה, *mar'eh* which were used to designate the thing seen in a revelation — the "vision." By the side of these terms there were others in use, derived from a root which supplies to the Aramaic its common word for "seeing," but in Hebrew has a somewhat more pregnant meaning, חָזָה, *hāzāh.* Its active derivative, חֹזֶה, *hōzeh,* was a designation of a prophet which remained in occasional use, alternating with the more customary נָבִיא, *nābhî,* long after רָאָה, *rō'eh,* had become practically obsolete; and its passive derivatives *hāzōn, hizzāyōn, hāzūth, mahăzeh* provided the ordinary terms for the substance of the revelation or "vision." The distinction between the two sets of terms, derived respectively from *rā'āh* and *hāzāh,* while not to be unduly pressed, seems to lie in the direction that the former suggests external manifestations and the latter internal revelations. The *rō'eh* is he to whom Divine manifestations, the *hōzeh* he to whom Divine communications, have been vouchsafed; the *mar'eh* is an appearance, the *hāzōn* and its companions a vision. It may be of interest to observe that *mar'āh* is the term employed in Num. xii. 6, while it is *ḥāzōn* which commonly occurs in the headings of the written prophecies to indicate their revelatory character. From this it may possibly be inferred that in the former passage it is the mode, in the latter the contents of the revelation that is emphasized. Perhaps a like distinction may be traced between the *ḥāzōn* of Dan. viii. 15 and the *mar'eh* of the next verse. The ordinary verb for " knowing," יָדַע, *yādhaʿ*, expressing in its causative stems the idea of making known, informing, is also very naturally employed, with God as its subject, in the sense of revealing, and that, in accordance with the natural sense of the word, with a tendency to pregnancy of implication, of revealing effectively, of not merely uncovering to observation, but making to know. Accordingly, it is paralleled not merely with גָּלָה, *gālāh* (Ps. xcviii. 2: ' The Lord hath *made known* his salvation; his righteousness hath he *displayed* in the sight of the nation '), but also with such terms as לָמַד, *lāmadh* (Ps. xxv. 4: ' *Make known* to me thy ways, O Lord: *teach* me thy paths '). This verb *yādhaʿ* forms no substantive in the sense of " revelation " (cf. דַּעַת, *daʿath*, Num. xxiv. 16; Ps. xix. 3).

The most common vehicles of the idea of " revelation " in the Old Testament are, however, two expressions which are yet to be mentioned. These are the phrase, " word of Jehovah," and the term commonly but inadequately rendered in the English versions by " law." The former (*dᵉbhar Yahweh*, varied to *dᵉbhar 'Ĕlōhīm* or *dᵉbhar hā-'Ĕlōhīm; cf. nᵉʾum Yahweh, massā, Yahweh*) occurs scores of times and is at once the simplest and the most colorless designation of a Divine communication. By the latter (*tōrāh*), the proper meaning of which is " instruction," a strong implication of authoritativeness is conveyed; and, in this sense, it becomes what may be called the technical designation of a specifically Divine communication. The two are not infrequently brought together, as in Isa. i. 10: " Hear the word of Jehovah, ye rulers of Sodom; give ear unto the law [margin " teaching "] of our God, ye people of Gomorrah "; or Isa. ii. 3; Mic. iv. 2; " For out of Zion shall go forth the law [margin " instruction "], and the word of Jehovah from Jerusalem." Both terms are used for any Divine communication of whatever extent; and both came to be employed to express the entire body of Divine revelation, conceived as a unitary whole. In this comprehensive usage, the emphasis of the one came to fall more on the graciousness, and of the other more on the authoritativeness of this body of Divine revelation; and both passed into the New Testament with these implications. " The word of God," or simply " the word," comes thus to mean in the New Testament just the gospel, " the word of the proclamation of redemption, that is, all that which God has to say to man, and causes to be said " looking to his salvation. It expresses, in a word, precisely what we technically speak of as God's redemptive revelation. " The law," on the other hand, means in this New Testament use, just the whole body of the authoritative instruction which God has given men. It expresses, in other words, what we commonly speak of as God's supernatural revelation. The two things, of course, are the same: God's authoritative revelation is His gracious revelation; God's redemptive revelation is His supernatural revelation. The two terms merely look at the one aggregate of revelation from two aspects, and each emphasizes its own aspect of this one aggregated revelation.

Now, this aggregated revelation lay before the men of the New Testament in a written form, and it was impossible to speak freely of it without consciousness of and at least occasional reference to its written form. Accordingly we hear of a Word of God that is written (Jn. xv. 25; 1 Cor. xv. 54), and the Divine Word is naturally contrasted with mere tradition, as if its written form were of its very idea (Mk. vii. 10); indeed, the written body of revelation — with an emphasis on its written form — is designated expressly ' the prophetic word ' (2 Pet. i. 19). More distinctly still, " the Law " comes to be thought of as a written, not exactly, code, but body of Divinely authoritative instructions. The phrase, " It is written in your law " (Jn. x. 34; xv. 25; Rom. iii. 19; 1 Cor. xiv. 21), acquires the precise sense of, " It is set forth in your authoritative Scriptures, all

the content of which is 'law,' that is, Divine instruction." Thus
" the Word of God," " the Law," came to mean just the written
body of revelation, what we call, and what the New Testament
writers called, in the same high sense which we give the term,
" the Scriptures." These " Scriptures " are thus identified with
the revelation of God, conceived as a well-defined *corpus,* and
two conceptions rise before us which have had a determining
part to play in the history of Christianity — the conception of
an authoritative Canon of Scripture, and the conception of this
Canon of Scripture as just the Word of God written. The
former conception was thrown into prominence in opposition
to the gnostic heresies in the earliest age of the church, and
gave rise to a richly varied mode of speech concerning the
Scriptures, emphasizing their authority in legal language,
which goes back to and rests on the Biblical usage of " Law."
The latter it was left to the Reformation to do justice to in its
struggle against, on the one side, the Romish depression of the
Scriptures in favor of the traditions of the church, and on the
other side the Enthusiasts' supercession of them in the interests of the " inner Word." When Tertullian, on the one hand,
speaks of the Scriptures as an " Instrument," a legal document, his terminology has an express warrant in the Scriptures'
own usage of *tōrāh,* " law," to designate their entire content.
And when John Gerhard argues that " between the Word of
God and Sacred Scripture, taken in a material sense, there is
no real difference," he is only declaring plainly what is definitely implied in the New Testament use of " the Word of
God " with the written revelation in mind. What is important
to recognize is that the Scriptures themselves represent the
Scriptures as not merely containing here and there the record
of revelations — " words of God," *tōrōth* — given by God, but
as themselves, in all their extent, a revelation, an authoritative
body of gracious instructions from God; or, since they alone,
of all the revelations which God may have given, are extant
— rather as the Revelation, the only " Word of God " accessible to men, in all their parts " law," that is, authoritative instruction from God.

LITERATURE. — Herman Witsius, " De Prophetis et Prophetia " in *Miscell. Sacr.*, I, Leiden, 1736, 1–318; G. F. Oehlor, *Theology of the OT*, ET, Edinburgh, 1874, I, part I (and the appropriate sections in other Bib. Theologies); H. Bavinck, *Gereformeerde Dogmatiek*[2], I, Kampen, 1906, 290–406 (and the appropriate sections in other dogmatic treatises); H. Voigt, *Fundamentaldogmatik*, Gotha, 1874, 173 ff; A. Kuyper, *Encyclopaedia of Sacred Theology*, ET, New York, 1898, div. III, ch. 11; A. E. Krauss, *Die Lehre von der Offenbarung*, Gotha, 1868; C. F. Fritzsche, *De revelationis notione biblica*, Leipzig, 1828; E. W. Hengstenberg, *The Christology of the OT*, ET[2], Edinburgh, 1868, IV, Appendix 6, pp. 396–444; E. König, *Der Offenbarungsbegriff des AT*, Leipzig, 1882; A. B. Davidson, *OT Prophecy*, 1903; W. J. Beecher, *The Prophets and the Promise*, New York, 1905; James Orr, *The Christian View of God and the World*, 1893, as per Index, " Revelation," and *Revelation and Inspiration*, London and New York, 1910. Also: T. Christlieb, *Modern Doubt and Christian Belief*, ET, New York, 1874; G. P. Fisher, *The Nature and Method of Revelation*, New York, 1890; C. M. Mead, *Supernatural Revelation*, 1889; J. Quirmbach, *Die Lehre des h. Paulus von der natürlichen Gotteserkenntnis*, etc., Freiburg, 1906.

II

THE IDEA OF REVELATION AND THEORIES OF REVELATION

THE IDEA OF REVELATION AND THEORIES OF REVELATION [1]

REVELATION [from Latin *revela'tio*, an unveiling, revealing, derivative of *revela're*, unveil; *re-*, back + *vela're*, to veil, derivative of *ve'lum*, a veil]: in its active meaning, the act of God by which he communicates to man the truth concerning himself — his nature, works, will, or purposes; in the passive meaning, the knowledge resultant upon such activity of God. The term is commonly employed in two senses: a wider — general revelation; and a narrower — special revelation. In its wider sense it includes all modes in which God makes himself known to men; or, passively, all knowledge concerning God however attained, inasmuch as it is conceived that all such knowledge is, in one way or another, wrought by him. In its narrower sense it is confined to the communication of knowledge in a supernatural as distinguished from a natural mode; or, passively, to the knowledge of God which has been supernaturally made known to men. The reality of general revelation is disputed by none but the anti-theist and agnostic, of whom one denies the existence of a God to make himself known, and the other doubts the capacity of the human intellect, if there be a God, to read the vestiges he has left of himself in his handiwork. Most types of modern theology explicitly allow that all knowledge of God rests on revelation; that God can be known only because and so far as he reveals himself. In this the extremest "liberals," such as Biedermann, Lipsius, and Pfleiderer, agree with the extremest "conservatives." Revelation is everywhere represented as the implication of theism, and as necessary to the very being of religion: "The man who does not believe that God can speak to him will not

[1] Article "Revelation," from *Universal Cyclopædia and Atlas*, R. Johnson ed. v. 10, pp. 79–81. Pub. N. Y., 1909, by D. Appleton and Co.

speak to God " (*A M. Fairbairn*). It is only with reference to
the reality of special revelation that debate concerning revelation continues; and it is this that Christian apologetics needs
to validate. Here, too, the controversy is ultimately with antitheistic presuppositions, with the postulates of an extreme deism or of an essential pantheism; but it is proximately with all
those types of thought which seek to mediate between deistic
or pantheizing conceptions and those of a truly Christian
theism.

In the eighteenth century the debate was chiefly with deism
in its one-sided emphasis upon the divine transcendence, and
with the several compromising schemes which grew up in the
course of the conflict, such as pure rationalism and dogmatistic
rationalism. The deist denied the reality of all special revelation, on the grounds that it was not necessary for man and was
either metaphysically impossible or morally unworthy of God.
Convinced of the reality of special revelation, the rationalist
still denied its necessity, while the dogmatist, admitting also
its necessity, denied that it constituted the authoritative
ground of the acceptance of truth. Kant's criticism struck a
twofold blow at rationalism. On the negative side his treatment of the theistic proofs discredited the basis of natural
(general) revelation, in which the rationalist placed his whole
confidence. Thus the way was prepared for philosophical agnosticism and for that Christian agnosticism which is exemplified in the school of Ritschl. On the positive side he prepared
the way for the idealistic philosophy, whose fundamentally
pantheistic presuppositions introduced a radical change in the
form of the controversy concerning the reality of a special revelation without in any way altering its essence. Instead of denying the supernatural with the deists, this new mode of thought
formally denied the natural. All thought was conceived as the
immanent work of God. This change of position antiquated the
forms of statement and argument which had been wrought out
against the deists; but the question at issue still remained the
same — whether there is any special revelation of God possible, actual, extant, whether man has received any other knowl-

edge of God than what is excogitable by the normal action of his own unaided faculties. Men's ontology of the human faculties and activities was changed; it was now affirmed that all that they excogitated was of God, and the natural was accordingly labeled supernatural. But a special supernatural interposition for a new gift of knowledge continued to be denied as strenuously as before. Thus it has come about that, in the nineteenth century, the controversy as to special revelation is no longer chiefly with the one-sided emphasis upon the transcendence of God of the deist, but with the equally one-sided emphasis upon the immanence of God of the pantheist, and with the various compromising schemes which have grown up in the course of the conflict, through efforts to mediate between pantheism and a truly Christian theism. It is no longer necessary to prove that God may and does speak in the souls of men; it is admitted on all hands that he reveals himself unceasingly through all the activities of creaturely minds. The task has come to be to distinguish between God's general and God's special revelations, to prove the possibility and actuality of the latter alongside of the former, and to vindicate for it a supernaturalness of a more immediate order than that which is freely attributed to all the thought of man concerning divine things.

In order to defend the idea of distinctively supernatural revelation against this insidious undermining, it has become necessary, in defining it in its highest and strictest sense, to emphasize the supernatural in the mode of knowledge and not merely in its source. When stress is laid upon the source only without taking into account the mode of knowledge, the way lies open to those who postulate immanent deity in all human thought to confound the categories of reason and revelation, and so practically to do away with the latter altogether. Even when the data on which our faculties work belong to a distinctively supernatural order, yet so long as the mode of acquisition of knowledge from them is conceived as purely human, the resultant knowledge remains natural knowledge; and, since intuition is a purely human mode of knowledge, so-called intuitions of divine truth would form no exception to this classification. Only such knowledge as is immediately communicated by God is, in the highest and strictest sense, supernaturally revealed. The differentia of revelation in its narrowest and strictest sense, therefore, is not merely that the knowledge so designated has God for its source, nor merely that it becomes the property of men by a supernatural agency, but further that it does not emerge into human consciousness as an acquisition of the human faculties, pure and simple.

Such a conception may give us a narrower category than that usually called special revelation. In contending for its reality it is by no means denied that there are other revelations of God which may deserve the name of special or supernatural in a distinctive sense. It is only affirmed that among the other modes in which God has revealed himself there exists also this mode of revelation, viz., a direct and immediate communication of truth, not only from God but by God, to minds which occupy relatively to the attainment of this truth a passive or receptive attitude, so that the mode of its acquisition is as supernatural as its source. In the knowledge of God which is acquired by man in the normal use of his own faculties — naturally, therefore, as to mode — some deserves the name of special and supernatural above the rest, because the data upon which the human faculties work in acquiring it belong to a supernatural order. Such knowledge forms an intermediate class between that obtained by the faculties working upon natural data and that obtained in a supernatural mode as well as from a supernatural source. Again, in the knowledge of God, communicated by the objective activities of his Spirit upon the minds of special organs of revelation — supernaturally, thus, as to immediate origin as well as to ultimate source — some may emerge into consciousness along the lines of the ordinary action of the human faculties. Such knowledge would form a still higher intermediate class — between that obtained by the natural faculties working according to their native powers on supernatural data and that obtained in a purely supernatural mode, as well as from a supernatural source and by a supernatural agency. These modes of revelation are not to be overlooked. But neither is it to be overlooked that among the ways in which God has revealed himself is also this way — that he has spoken to man as Spirit to spirit, mouth to mouth, and has made himself and his gracious purposes known to him in an immediate and direct word of God, which is simply received and not in any sense attained by man. In these revelations we reach the culminating category of special revelation, in which its peculiar character is most clearly seen. And it is these direct revelations which modern thought finds most difficult to allow to be real, and which Christian apologists must especially vindicate.

THEORIES OF REVELATION

In the state of the case which has just been pointed out, it is a matter of course that recent theories of revelation should very frequently leave no or but little place for the highest form of revelation, that by the direct word of God. The lowest class of theories represent revelation as taking place only through the purely natural activities of the human mind, and deny the reality of any special action of the Divine Spirit directly on the mind in the communication of revealed truth. Those who share this general position may differ very greatly in their presuppositions. They may, from a fundamentally deistic standpoint, jealously guard the processes of human thought from all intrusion on the part of God; or they may, from a fundamentally pantheistic standpoint, look upon all human thought as only the unfolding of the divine thought. They may differ also very greatly as to the nature and source of the objective data on which the mind is supposed to work in obtaining its knowledge of God. But they are at one in conceiving that which from the divine side is spoken of as revelation, as on the human side, simply the natural development of the moral and religious consciousness. The extreme deistic theory allows the possibility of no knowledge of God except what is obtained by the human mind working upon the data supplied by creation to the exclusion of providential government. Modern speculative theists correct the deistic conception by postulating an immanent divine activity, both in external providence and in mental action. The data on which the mind works are supplied, according to them, not only by creation, but also by God's moral government; and the theory grades upward in proportion as something like a special providence is admitted in the peculiar function ascribed to Israel in developing the idea of God, and the significance of Jesus Christ as the embodiment of the perfect relation between God and man is recognized. (Biedermann, " Christl. Dogmatik," i., 264; Lipsius, " Dogmatik," 41; Pfleiderer, " Religionsphilosophie," iv., 46.) The school of Ritschl, though they speak of a " positive revelation " in Jesus Christ, make no real advance upon this. Denying not only all mystical connection of the soul with God, but also all rational knowledge of divine things, they confine the data of revelation to the historical manifestation of Christ, which makes an impression on the minds of men such as justifies us in speaking of him as revealing God to us. (Herrmann, " Der Begriff der Offenbarung," and " Der Verkehr des Christen mit Gott "; Kaftan, " Das Wesen," etc.)

We are on higher ground, however, although still moving in essentially the same circle of conceptions as to the nature of revelation, when we rise to the theory which identifies revelation strictly with the series of redemptive acts (Koehler, " Stud. und Kritiken," 1852, p. 875). From this point of view, as truly as from that of the deist or speculative theist, revelation is confined to the purely external manifestation of God in a series of acts. It is differentiated from the conceptions of the deist and speculative theist only in the nature of the works of God, which are supposed to supply the data which are observed and worked into knowledge by the unaided activities of the human mind. In emphasizing here those acts of a special providence which constitute the redemptive activity of God, this theory for the first time lays the foundation for a distinction between general and special revelation; and it grades upward in proportion as the truly miraculous character of God's re-

THE IDEA AND THEORIES OF REVELATION

demptive work is recognized, and acts of a truly miraculous nature are included in it. And it rises above itself in proportion as, along with the supernatural character of the series of objective acts with which it formally identifies revelation, it recognizes an immediate action of God's Spirit on the mind of man, preparing, fitting, and enabling him to apprehend and interpret aright the revelation made objectively in the redemptive acts. J. Chr. K. Hofmann in his earlier work, " Prophecy and Fulfillment," announces this theory in a lower form, but corrects it in his later " Schriftbeweis." Richard Rothe (" Zur Dogmatik," p. 54) is an outstanding example of one of its higher forms. To him revelation consists fundamentally in the " manifestation " of God in the series of redemptive acts, by which God enters into natural history by means of an unambiguously supernatural and peculiarly divine history, and which man is enabled to understand and rightly to interpret by virtue of an inward work of the Divine Spirit that Rothe calls " inspiration." But this internal action of the Spirit does not communicate new truth; it only enables the subject to combine the elements of knowledge naturally received into a new combination, from which springs an essentially new thought which he is clearly conscious that he did not produce. The theory propounded by Prof. A. B. Bruce in his well-known lectures on " The Chief End of Revelation " stands possibly one stage higher than Rothe's, to which it bears a very express relation. Dr. Bruce speaks with great circumspection. He represents revelation as consisting in the " self-manifestation of God in human history as the God of a gracious purpose — the manifestation being made not merely or chiefly by words, but very specially by deeds " (p. 155); while he looks upon " inspiration " as " not enabling the prophets to originate a new idea of God," but " rather as assisting them to read aright the divine name and nature." Dr. Bruce transcends the position of the class of theorists here under consideration in proportion as he magnifies the office of inner " inspiration," and, above all, in proportion to the extent of meaning which he attaches to the saving clause that revelation is *not merely* by word, but *also* by deed. The theory commended by the great name of Bishop B. F. Westcott ("The Gospel of Life") is quite similar to Dr. Bruce's.

By these transitional theories we are already carried well into a second class of theories, which recognize that revelation is fundamentally the work of the Spirit of God in direct communication with the human mind. At its lowest level this conception need not rise above the pantheistic postulate of the unfolding of the life and thought of God within the world. The Divine Spirit stirs men's hearts, and feelings and ideas spring up, which are no less revelations of God than movements of the human soul. A higher level is attained when the action of God is conceived as working in the heart of man an inward certainty of divine life — as, for example, by Schultz ("Old Testament Theology"); revelation being confined as much as possible to the inner life of man apparently to avoid the recognition of objective miracle. A still higher level is reached where the action of the Spirit is thought of — after the fashion of Rothe, for example — as a necesary aid granted to certain men to enable them to apprehend and interpret aright the objective manifestation of God. The theory rises in character in proportion as the necessity of this action of the Spirit, its relative importance, and the nature of the effect produced by it are magnified. So long, however, as it conceives of this work of the Spirit as secondary, and ordinarily if not invariably successive to the series of redemptive acts of God, which are thought to constitute the real core of the revelation, it falls short of the biblical idea. According to the biblical representations, the fundamental element in revelation is not the objective process of redemptive acts, but the revealing operations of the Spirit of God, which run through the whole series of modes of communication proper to Spirit, culminating in communications by the objective word. The characteristic element in the Bible idea of revelation in its highest sense is that the organs of revelation are not creatively concerned in the revelations made through them, but occupy a receptive attitude. The contents of their messages are not something thought out, inferred, hoped, or feared by them, but something conveyed to them, often forced upon them by the irresistible might of the revealing Spirit. No conception can do justice to the Bible idea of revelation which neglects these facts. Nor is justice done even to the rational idea of revelation when they are neglected. Here, too, we must interpret by the highest category in our reach. " Can man commune with man," it has been eloquently asked, " through the high gift of language, and is the Infinite mind not to express itself, or is it to do so but faintly or uncertainly, through dumb material symbols, never by blessed speech? " (W. Morrison, " Footprints of the Revealer," p. 52.)

The Doctrine of Revelation

The doctrine of revelation which has been wrought out by Christian thinkers in their effort to do justice to all the biblical facts, includes the following features. God has never left himself without a witness. In the act of creation he has impressed himself on the work of his hands. In his work of providence he manifests himself as the righteous ruler of the world. Through this natural revelation men in the normal use of reason rise to a knowledge of God — a *notitia Dei acquisita,* based on the *notitia Dei insita* — which is trustworthy and valuable, but is insufficient for their necessities as sinners, and by its very insufficiency awakens a longing for a fuller knowledge of God and his purposes. To this purely natural revelation God has added a revelation of himself as the God of grace, in a connected series of redemptive acts, which constitute as a whole the mighty process of the new creation. To even the natural mind contemplating this series of supernatural acts which culminate in the coming of Christ, a higher knowledge of God should be conveyed than what is attainable from mere nature, though it would be limited to the capacity of the natural mind to apprehend divine things. In the process of the new creation God, however, works also inwardly by his regenerating grace, creating new hearts in men and illuminating their minds for apprehending divine things: thus, over against the new manifestation of himself in the series of redemptive acts, he creates a new subject to apprehend and profit by them. But neither by the presentation of supernatural facts to the mind nor by the breaking of the power of sin within, by which the eyes of the mind were holden that they should not see, is the human mind enabled to rise above itself, that it may know as God knows, unravel the manifestation of his gracious purposes from the incompleted pattern which he is weaving into the fabric of history, or even interpret aright an unexplained series of marvelous facts involving mysteries which " angels desire to look into." It may be doubted whether even the supreme revelation of God in Jesus Christ could have been known as such in the absence of preparatory, accompanying and succeeding explanatory revelations in words: " the kingdom of God cometh not with observation." God has therefore, in his infinite mercy, added a revelation of himself, strictly so called, communicating by his Spirit directly to men knowledge concerning himself, his works, will, and purposes. The modes of communication may be various — by dreams or visions, in ecstasy or theophany, by inward guidance, or by the simple objective word; but in all cases the object and result are the direct supernatural communication of special knowledge.

Of this special revelation it is to be said: (1) It was not given all at once, but *progressively,* " by divers portions and in divers manners," in the form of a regular historical development. (2) Its progressive unfolding stands in *a very express relation to the progress of God's redemptive work.* If it is not to be conceived, on the one hand, however, as an isolated act, wholly out of relation to God's redemptive work, neither is it to be simply identified with the series of his redemptive acts. The phrase, " revelation is for redemption and not for instruction," presents a false antithesis. Revelation as such is certainly just " to make wise," though it is to make wise only " unto salvation." It is not an alternative name for the redemptive process, but a specific part of the redemptive process. Nor does it merely grow out of the redemptive acts as their accompanying or following explanation; it is rather itself one of the redemptive acts, and takes its place along with the other redemptive acts, co-operative with them to the one great end. (3) *Its relation to miracles* has often been very unnecessarily confused by one-sided statements. Miracles are not merely credentials of revelation, but vehicles of revelation as well; but they are primarily credentials; and some of them are so barely " signs " as to serve no other purpose. As works of God, however, they are inevitably revelatory of God. Because the nature of the acts performed necessarily reveals the character of the actor is no proof, nevertheless, that their primary purpose was self-revelation; but this fact gives them a place in revelation itself; and as revelation as a whole is a substantial part of the redemptive work of God, also in the redemptive work of God. (4) *Its relation to predictive prophecy* is in some respects different. As a rule, at all events, predictive prophecy is primarily a part of revelation, and becomes a credential of it only secondarily, on account of the nature of the particular revelation which it conveys. When a revelation is, in its very contents, such as could come only from God, it obviously becomes a credential of itself as a revelation, and carries with it an evidence of the divine character of the whole body of revelation with which it stands in organic connection. (5) *Its relation to the Scriptures* is already apparent from what has been said. As revelation does not exist solely for the increase of knowledge, but by increasing knowledge to build up the kingdom of God, so neither did it come into being for no other purpose than the production of the Scriptures. The Scriptures also are a means to the one end, and exist only as a part of God's redemptive work. But if, thus, the Scriptures can not be exalted as the sole end of revelation, neither can they be degraded into the mere human record of revelation. They are themselves a substantial part of God's revelation; one form which his revealing activity chose for itself; and that its final and complete form, adopted as such for the very purpose of making God's revealed will the permanent and universal possession of man. Among the manifold methods of God's revelation, revelation through " inspiration " thus takes its natural place; and the Scriptures, as the product of this " inspiration," become thus a work of God; not only a substantial part of revelation, but, along with the rest of revelation, a substantial part of his redemptive work. Along with the other acts of God which make up the connected series of his redemptive acts, the giving of the Scriptures ranks as an element of the building up of the kingdom of God. That within the limits of Scripture there appears the record of revelations in a narrower and stricter sense of the term, in nowise voids its claim to be itself revelation. Scripture records the sequence of God's great redeeming acts. But it is much more than merely " the record, the interpretation, and the literary reflection of God's grace in history." Scripture records the direct revelations which God gave to men in days past, so far as those revelations were intended for permanent and universal use. But it is much more than a record of past revelations. It is itself the final revelation of God, completing the whole disclosure of his unfathomable love to lost sinners, the whole proclamation of his purposes of grace, and the whole exhibition of his gracious provisions for their salvation.

III

THE INSPIRATION OF THE BIBLE

THE INSPIRATION OF THE BIBLE [1]

THE subject of the Inspiration of the Bible is one which has been much confused in recent discussion. He who, seeking to learn the truth, should gather about him the latest treatises, bearing such titles as, " Inspiration, and other Lectures," " Inspiration and the Bible," " What is Inspiration? " " How did God inspire the Bible? " " The Oracles of God? " [2] — would find himself led by them in every conceivable direction at once. No wonder if he should stand stock-still in the midst of his would-be guides, confounded by the Babel of voices. The old formula, *quot homines tot sententiæ*, seems no longer adequate. Wherever five " advanced thinkers " assemble, at least six theories as to inspiration are likely to be ventilated. They differ in every conceivable point, or in every conceivable point save one. They agree that inspiration is less pervasive and less determinative than has heretofore been thought, or than is still thought in less enlightened circles. They agree that there is less of the truth of God and more of the error of man in the Bible than Christians have been wont to believe. They agree accordingly that the teaching of the Bible may be, in this, that, or the other, — here, there, or elsewhere, — safely neglected or openly repudiated. So soon as we turn to the constructive side, however, and ask wherein the inspiration of the Bible consists; how far it guarantees the trustworthiness of the Bible's teaching; in what of its elements is the Bible a divinely safeguarded guide to truth: the concurrence ends and hopeless dissension sets in. They agree only in their common destructive attitude towards some higher view of the inspiration of the Bible, of the presence of which each one seems supremely conscious.

[1] A lecture. From " Bibliotheca Sacra," v. 51, 1894, pp. 614–640. Pub. also in " King's Own," v. 6, Lond. 1895, pp. 791–794, 833–840, 926–933.

[2] Titles of recent treatises by Rooke, Horton, DeWitt, Smyth, and Sanday respectively.

It is upon this fact that we need first of all to fix our attention. It is not of the variegated hypotheses of his fellow-theorizers, but of some high doctrine of inspiration, the common object of attack of them all, that each new theorizer on the subject of inspiration is especially conscious, as standing over against him, with reference to which he is to orient himself, and against the claims of which he is to defend his new hypothesis. Thus they themselves introduce us to the fact that over against the numberless discordant theories of inspiration which vex our time, there stands a well-defined church-doctrine of inspiration. This church-doctrine of inspiration differs from the theories that would fain supplant it, in that it is not the invention nor the property of an individual, but the settled faith of the universal church of God; in that it is not the growth of yesterday, but the assured persuasion of the people of God from the first planting of the church until to-day; in that it is not a protean shape, varying its affirmations to fit every new change in the ever-shifting thought of men, but from the beginning has been the church's constant and abiding conviction as to the divinity of the Scriptures committed to her keeping. It is certainly a most impressive fact, — this well-defined, aboriginal, stable doctrine of the church as to the nature and trustworthiness of the Scriptures of God, which confronts with its gentle but steady persistence of affirmation all the theories of inspiration which the restless energy of unbelieving and half-believing speculation has been able to invent in this agitated nineteenth century of ours. Surely the seeker after the truth in the matter of the inspiration of the Bible may well take this church-doctrine as his starting-point.

What this church-doctrine is, it is scarcely necessary minutely to describe. It will suffice to remind ourselves that it looks upon the Bible as an oracular book, — as the Word of God in such a sense that whatever it says God says, — not a book, then, in which one may, by searching, find some word of God, but a book which may be frankly appealed to at any point with the assurance that whatever it may be found to say, that is the Word of God. We are all of us members in particular of the body of Christ which we call the church: and the life of the church, and the faith of the church, and the thought of the church are our natural heritage. We know how, as Christian men, we approach this Holy Book, — how unquestioningly we receive its statements of fact, bow before its enunciations of duty, tremble before its threatenings, and rest upon its promises. Or, if the subtle spirit of modern doubt has seeped somewhat into our hearts, our memory will easily recall those happier days when we stood a child at our Christian mother's knee, with lisping lips following the words which her slow finger traced upon this open page, — words which were her support in every trial and, as she fondly trusted, were to be our guide throughout life. Mother church was speaking to us in that maternal voice, commending to us her vital faith in the Word of God. How often since then has it been our own lot, in our turn, to speak to others all the words of this life! As we sit in the midst of our pupils in the Sabbath-school, or in the centre of our circle at home, or perchance at some bedside of sickness or of death; or as we meet our fellow-man amid the busy work of the world, hemmed in by temptation or weighed down with care, and would fain put beneath him some firm support and stay: in what spirit do we turn to this Bible then? with what confidence do we commend its every word to those whom we would make partakers of its comfort or of its strength? In such scenes as these is revealed the vital faith of the people of God in the surety and trustworthiness of the Word of God.

Nor do we need to do more than remind ourselves that this attitude of entire trust in every word of the Scriptures has been characteristic of the people of God from the very foundation of the church. Christendom has always reposed upon the belief that the utterances of this book are properly oracles of God. The whole body of Christian literature bears witness to this fact. We may trace its stream to its source, and everywhere it is vocal with a living faith in the divine trustworthiness of the Scriptures of God in every one of their affirmations. This is the murmur of the little rills of Christian speech which find their tenuous way through the parched heathen land of the early second century. And this is the mighty voice of the great river of Christian thought which sweeps through the ages, freighted with blessings for men. Dr. Sanday, in his recent Bampton Lectures on " Inspiration " — in which, unfortunately, he does not teach the church-doctrine — is driven to admit that not only may " testimonies to the general doctrine of inspiration " from the earliest Fathers, " be multiplied to almost any extent; but [that] there are some which go further and point to an inspiration which might be described as ' verbal ' "; " nor does this idea," he adds, " come in tentatively and by degrees, but almost from the very first." [3] He might have spared the adverb " almost." The earliest writers know no other doctrine. If Origen asserts that the Holy Spirit was co-worker with the Evangelists in the composition of the Gospel, and that, therefore, lapse of memory, error or falsehood was impossible to them,[4] and if Irenæus, the pupil of Polycarp, claims for Christians a clear knowledge that " the Scriptures are perfect, seeing that they are spoken by God's Word and his Spirit ";[5] no less does Polycarp, the pupil of John, consider the Scriptures the very voice of the Most High, and pronounce him the first-born of Satan, " whosoever perverts these oracles of the Lord." [6] Nor do the later Fathers know a different doctrine. Augustine, for example, affirms that he defers to the canonical Scriptures alone among books with such reverence and honor that he most " firmly believes that no one of their authors has erred in anything, in writing." [7] To precisely the same effect did the Reformers believe and teach. Luther adopts these words of Augustine's as his own, and declares that the whole of the Scriptures are to be ascribed to the Holy Ghost, and therefore cannot err.[8] Calvin demands that whatever is propounded in Scripture,

[3] Sanday, " Inspiration," p. 34.
[4] On Matt. xvi. 12 and Jno. vi. 18.
[5] Adv. Haer, ii. 28.
[6] Ep. ad Phil., cap. vii.
[7] Ep. ad Hier. lxxxii. 3.
[8] " Works " (St. Louis ed.), xix. 305; (Erlangen ed.), xxxvii. 11 and xxxviii. 33.

" without exception," shall be humbly received by us, — that the Scriptures as a whole shall be received by us with the same reverence which we give to God, " because they have emanated from him alone, and are mixed with nothing human." [9] The saintly Rutherford, who speaks of the Scriptures as a more sure word than a direct oracle from heaven,[10] and Baxter, who affirms that " all that the holy writers have recorded is true (and no falsehood in the Scriptures but what is from the errors of scribes and translators)," [11] hand down this supreme trust in the Scripture word to our own day — to our own Charles Hodge and Henry B. Smith, the one of whom asserts that the Bible " gives us truth without error," [12] and the other, that " all the books of the Scripture are equally inspired; . . . all alike are infallible in what they teach; . . . their assertions must be free from error." [13] Such testimonies are simply the formulation by the theologians of each age of the constant faith of Christians throughout all ages.

If we would estimate at its full meaning the depth of this trust in the Scripture word, we should observe Christian men at work upon the text of Scripture. There is but one view-point which will account for or justify the minute and loving pains which have been expended upon the text of Scripture, by the long line of commentators that has extended unbrokenly from the first Christian ages to our own. The allegorical interpretation which rioted in the early days of the church was the daughter of reverence for the biblical word; a spurious daughter you may think, but none the less undeniably a direct offspring of the awe with which the sacred text was regarded as the utterances of God, and, as such, pregnant with inexhaustible significance. The patient and anxious care with which the Bible text is scrutinized today by scholars, of a different spirit no doubt from those old allegorizers, but of equal reverence for

[9] "Institutes," i. 18; " Commentary on Romans," xv. 4, and on 2 Tim. iii. 16.

[10] " Free Disputation against Pretended Liberty of Conscience," p. 373.

[11] " Works," xv. 65.

[12] Henry B. Smith, " Sermon on Inspiration " (Cincinnati ed.), p. 19.

[13] Charles Hodge, " Syst. Theol.," i. 163.

the text of Scripture, betrays the same fundamental viewpoint, — to which the Bible is the Word of God, every detail of the meaning of which is of inestimable preciousness. No doubt there have been men who have busied themselves with the interpretation of Scripture, who have not approached it in such a spirit or with such expectations. But it is not the Jowetts, with their supercilious doubts whether Paul meant very much by what he said, who represent the spirit of Christian exposition. This is represented rather by the Bengels, who count no labor wasted, in their efforts to distill from the very words of Holy Writ the honey which the Spirit has hidden in them for the comfort and the delight of the saints. It is represented rather by the Westcotts, who bear witness to their own experience of the " sense of rest and confidence which grows firmer with increasing knowledge," as their patient investigation has dug deeper and deeper for the treasures hid in the words and clauses and sentences of the Epistles of John,[14] — to the sure conviction which forty years of study of the Epistle to the Hebrews has brought them that " we come nearer to the meaning of Scripture by the closest attention to the subtleties and minute variations of words and order." It was a just remark of one of the wisest men I ever knew, Dr. Wistar Hodge, that this is " a high testimony to verbal inspiration." [15]

Of course the church has not failed to bring this, her vital faith in the divine trustworthiness of the Scripture word, to formal expression in her solemn creeds. The simple faith of the Christian people is also the confessional doctrine of the Christian churches. The assumption of the divine authority of the scriptural teaching underlies all the credal statements of the church; all of which are formally based upon the Scriptures. And from the beginning, it finds more or less full expression in them. Already, in some of the formulas of faith which underlie the Apostles' Creed itself, we meet with the phrase " according to the Scriptures " as validating the items of belief; while in the Niceno-Constantinopolitan Creed, amid the meagre clauses

[14] B. F. Westcott, " The Epistles of St. John," p. vi.
[15] C. Wistar Hodge, " Presbyterian and Reformed Review," ii. 330.

outlining only what is essential to the doctrine of the Holy
Spirit, place is given to the declaration that He is to be found
speaking in the prophets — "who spake by the prophets." It
was in conscious dependence upon the immemorial teaching of
the church that the Council of Trent defined it as of faith in
the Church of Rome, that God is the author of Scripture, — a
declaration which has been repeated in our own day by the
Vatican Council, with such full explanations as are included in
these rich words: "The church holds" the books of the Old
and New Testaments, "to be sacred and canonical, not because, having been carefully composed by mere human industry, they were afterwards approved by her authority; nor
merely because they contain revelation with no admixture of
error; but because, having been written by the inspiration of
the Holy Ghost, they have God for their author." Needless to
say that a no less firm conviction of the absolute authority of
Scripture underlies all the Protestant creeds. Before all else,
Protestantism is, in its very essence, an appeal from all other
authority to the divine authority of Holy Scripture. The Augsburg Confession, the first Protestant creed, is, therefore, commended to consideration, only on the ground that it is "drawn
from the Holy Scriptures and the pure word of God." The
later Lutheran creeds, and especially the Reformed creeds,
grow progressively more explicit. It is our special felicity, that
as Reformed Christians, and heirs of the richest and fullest
formulation of Reformed thought, we possess in that precious
heritage, the Westminster Confession, the most complete, the
most admirable, the most perfect statement of the essential
Christian doctrine of Holy Scripture which has ever been
formed by man. Here the vital faith of the church is brought to
full expression; the Scriptures are declared to be the word of
God in such a sense that God is their author, and they, because
immediately inspired by God, are of infallible truth and divine
authority, and are to be believed to be true by the Christian
man, in whatsoever is revealed in them, for the authority of
God himself speaking therein.

Thus, in every way possible, the church has borne her testi-

mony from the beginning, and still in our day, to her faith in
the divine trustworthiness of her Scriptures, in all their affirmations of whatever kind. At no age has it been possible for
men to express without rebuke the faintest doubt as to the
absolute trustworthiness of their least declaration. Tertullian, writing at the opening of the third century, suggests, with
evident hesitation and timidity, that Paul's language in the
seventh chapter of First Corinthians may be intended to distinguish, in his remarks on marriage and divorce, between matters of divine commandment and of human arrangement. Dr.
Sanday is obliged to comment on his language: " Any seeming
depreciation of Scripture was as unpopular even then as it is
now." [16] The church has always believed her Scriptures to be
the book of God, of which God was in such a sense the author
that every one of its affirmations of whatever kind is to be
esteemed as the utterance of God, of infallible truth and
authority.

In the whole history of the church there have been but two
movements of thought, tending to a lower conception of the
inspiration and authority of Scripture, which have attained
sufficient proportions to bring them into view in an historical
sketch.

(1) The first of these may be called the Rationalistic view.
Its characteristic feature is an effort to distinguish between
inspired and uninspired elements within the Scriptures. With
forerunners among the Humanists, this mode of thought was
introduced by the Socinians, and taken up by the Syncretists
in Germany, the Remonstrants in Holland, and the Jesuits in
the Church of Rome. In the great life-and-death struggle of
the eighteenth century it obtained great vogue among the defenders of supernatural religion, in their desperate efforts to
save what was of even more importance, — just as a hard-
pressed army may yield to the foe many an outpost which
justly belongs to it, in the effort to save the citadel. In the nineteenth century it has retained a strong hold, especially upon
apologetical writers, chiefly in the three forms which affirm re-

[16] Sanday, " Inspiration," p. 42 (note).

spectively that only the *mysteries* of the faith are inspired, i. e.
things undiscoverable by unaided reason, — that the Bible is
inspired only in *matters of faith and practice,* — and that the
Bible is inspired only in its *thoughts or concepts,* not in its
words. But although this legacy from the rationalism of an evil
time still makes its appearance in the pages of many theological writers, and has no doubt affected the faith of a considerable number of Christians, it has failed to supplant in either
the creeds of the church or the hearts of the people the church-
doctrine of the plenary inspiration of the Bible, i. e. the doctrine that the Bible is inspired not *in part* but *fully,* in all its
elements alike, — things discoverable by reason as well as mysteries, matters of history and science as well as of faith and
practice, words as well as thoughts.

(2) The second of the lowered views of inspiration may be
called the Mystical view. Its characteristic conception is that
the Christian man has something within himself, — call it enlightened reason, spiritual insight, the Christian consciousness,
the witness of the Spirit, or call it what you will, — to the test
of which every " external revelation " is to be subjected, and
according to the decision of which are the contents of the Bible
to be valued. Very varied forms have been taken by this conception; and more or less expression has been given to it, in
one form or another, in every age. In its extremer manifestations, it has formerly tended to sever itself from the main
stream of Christian thought and even to form separated sects.
But in our own century, through the great genius of Schleiermacher it has broken in upon the church like a flood, and
washed into every corner of the Protestant world. As a consequence, we find men everywhere who desire to acknowledge as
from God only such Scripture as " finds them," — who cast the
clear objective enunciation of God's will to the mercy of the
currents of thought and feeling which sweep up and down in
their own souls, — who " persist " sometimes, to use a sharp
but sadly true phrase of Robert Alfred Vaughan's, " in their
conceited rejection of the light without until they have turned
into darkness their light within." We grieve over the inroads

which this essentially naturalistic mode of thought has made in the Christian thinking of the day. But great and deplorable as they have been, they have not been so extensive as to supplant the church-doctrine of the absolute authority of the objective revelation of God in his Word, in either the creeds of the church, or the hearts of the people. Despite these attempts to introduce lowered conceptions, the doctrine of the plenary inspiration of the Scriptures, which looks upon them as an oracular book, in all its parts and elements, alike, of God, trustworthy in all its affirmations of every kind, remains to-day, as it has always been, the vital faith of the people of God, and the formal teaching of the organized church.

The more we contemplate this church-doctrine, the more pressing becomes the question of what account we are to give of it, — its origin and persistence. How shall we account for the immediate adoption of so developed a doctrine of inspiration in the very infancy of the church, and for the tenacious hold which the church has kept upon it through so many ages? The account is simple enough, and capable of inclusion in a single sentence: this is the doctrine of inspiration which was held by the writers of the New Testament and by Jesus as reported in the Gospels. It is this simple fact that has commended it to the church of all ages as the true doctrine; and in it we may surely recognize an even more impressive fact than that of the existence of a stable, abiding church-doctrine standing over against the many theories of the day, — the fact, namely, that this church-doctrine of inspiration was the Bible doctrine before it was the church-doctrine, and is the church-doctrine only because it is the Bible doctrine. It is upon this fact that we should now fix our attention.

In the limited space at our disposal we need not attempt anything like a detailed proof that the church-doctrine of the plenary inspiration of the Bible is the Bible's own doctrine of inspiration. And this especially for three very obvious reasons:

First, because it cannot be necessary to prove this to our-

selves. We have the Bible in our hands, and we are accustomed
to read it. It is enough for us to ask ourselves how the apostles
and our Lord, as represented in its pages, conceived of what
they called " the Scriptures," for the answer to come at once to
our minds. As readers of the New Testament, we know that to
the men of the New Testament " the Scriptures " were the
Word of God which could not be broken, i. e. whose every word
was trustworthy; and that a simple " It is written " was therefore to them the end of all strife. The proof of this is pervasive
and level to the apprehension of every reader. It would be an
insult to our intelligence were we to presume that we had not
observed it, or could not apprehend its meaning.

Secondly, it is not necessary to prove that the New Testament regards " Scripture " as the mere Word of God, in the
highest and most rigid sense, to modern biblical scholarship.
Among untrammelled students of the Bible, it is practically
a matter of common consent that the writers of the New Testament books looked upon what they called " Scripture " as
divinely safeguarded in even its verbal expression, and as divinely trustworthy in all its parts, in all its elements, and in
all its affirmations of whatever kind. This is, of course, the
judgment of all those who have adopted this doctrine as their
own, because they apprehend it to be the biblical doctrine. It
is also the judgment of all those who can bring themselves to
refuse a doctrine which they yet perceive to be a biblical doctrine. Whether we appeal, among men of this class, to such
students of a more evangelical tendency, as Tholuck, Rothe,
Farrar, Sanday, or to such extremer writers as Riehm, Reuss,
Pfleiderer, Keunen, they will agree in telling us that the high
doctrine of inspiration which we have called the church-doctrine was held by the writers of the New Testament. This is
common ground between believing and unbelieving students
of the Bible, and needs, therefore, no new demonstration in the
forum of scholarship. Let us pause here, therefore, only long
enough to allow Hermann Schultz, surely a fair example of the
" advanced " school, to tell us what is the conclusion in this
matter of the strictest and coldest exegetical science. " The

Book of the Law," he tells us, "seemed already to the later poets of the Old Testament, the 'Word of God.' The post-canonical books of Israel regard the Law and the Prophets in this manner. And for the men of the New Testament, the Holy Scriptures of their people are already God's word in which God himself speaks." This view, which looked upon the scriptural books as verbally inspired, he adds, was the ruling one in the time of Christ, was shared by all the New Testament men, and by Christ himself, as a pious conception, and was expressly taught by the more scholastic writers among them.[17] It is hardly necessary to prove what is so frankly confessed.

The *third* reason why it is not necessary to occupy our time with a formal proof that the Bible does teach this doctrine, arises from the circumstance that even those who seek to rid themselves of the pressure of this fact upon them, are observed to be unable to prosecute their argument without an implied admission of it as a fact. This is true, for example, of Dr. Sanday's endeavors to meet the appeal of the church to our Lord's authority in defence of the doctrine of plenary inspiration.[18] He admits that the one support which has been sought by the church of all ages for its high doctrine has been the "extent to which it was recognized in the sayings of Christ himself." As over against this he begins by suggesting "that, whatever view our Lord himself entertained as to the Scriptures of the Old Testament, the record of his words has certainly come down to us through the medium of persons who shared the current view on the subject." This surely amounts to a full admission that the writers of the New Testament at least, held and taught the obnoxious doctrine. He ends with the remark that "when deductions have been made . . . there still remains evidence enough that our Lord, while on earth *did* use the common language of his contemporaries in regard to the Old Testament." This surely amounts to a full admission that Christ as well as his reporters taught the obnoxious doctrine.

This will be found to be a typical case. Every attempt to

---

[17] Hermann Schultz, "Grundriss d. Evang. Dogmatik," p. 7.

[18] "Inspiration," p. 393 *seq*.

escape from the authority of the New Testament enunciation of the doctrine of plenary inspiration, in the nature of the case begins by admitting that this is, in very fact, the New Testament doctrine. Shall we follow Dr. Sanday, and appeal from the apostles to Christ, and then call in the idea of *kenosis,* and affirm that in the days of his flesh, Christ did not speak out of the fulness and purity of his divine knowledge, but on becoming man had shrunk to man's capacity, and in such matters as this was limited in his conceptions by the knowledge and opinions current in his day and generation? In so saying, we admit, as has already been pointed out, not only that the apostles taught this high doctrine of inspiration, but also that Christ too, in whatever humiliation he did it, yet actually taught the same. Shall we then take refuge in the idea of *accommodation,* and explain that, in so speaking of the Scriptures, Christ and his apostles did not intend to teach the doctrine of inspiration implicated, but merely adopted, as a matter of convenience, the current language, as to Scripture, of the time? In so speaking, also, we admit that the actual language of Christ and his apostles expresses that high view of inspiration which was confessedly the current view of the day — whether as a matter of convenience or as a matter of truth, the Christian consciousness may be safely left to decide. Shall we then remind ourselves that Jesus himself committed nothing to writing, and appeal to the uncertainties which are accustomed to attend the record of teaching at second-hand? Thus, too, we allow that the words of Christ as transmitted to us do teach the obnoxious doctrine. Are we, then, to fall back upon the observation that the doctrine of plenary inspiration is not taught with equal plainness in every part of the Bible, but becomes clear only in the later Old Testament books, and is not explicitly enunciated except in the more scholastic of the New Testament books? In this, too, we admit that it is taught in the Scriptures; while the fact that it is taught not all at once, but with progressive clearness and fulness, is accordant with the nature of the Bible as a book written in the process of the ages and progressively developing the truth. Then, shall we affirm that our doctrine of inspiration is not to be derived solely from the teachings of the Bible, but from its teachings and phenomena in conjunction; and so call in what we deem the phenomena of the Bible to modify its teaching? Do we not see that the very suggestion of this process admits that the teaching of the Bible, when taken alone, i. e., in its purity and just as it is, gives us the unwelcome doctrine? Shall we, then, take counsel of desperation and assert that all appeal to the teaching of the Scriptures themselves in testimony to their own inspiration is an argument in a circle, appealing to their inspiration to validate their inspiration? Even this desperately illogical shift to be rid of the scriptural doctrine of inspiration, obviously involves the confession that this is the scriptural doctrine. No, the issue is not, What does the Bible teach? but, Is what the Bible teaches true? And it is amazing that any or all of such expedients can blind the eyes of any one to the stringency of this issue.

Even a detailed attempt to explain away the texts which teach the doctrine of the plenary inspiration and unvarying truth of Scripture, involves the admission that in their obvious meaning such texts teach the doctrine which it is sought to explain away. And think of explaining away the texts which inculcate the doctrine of the plenary inspiration of the Scriptures! The effort to do so is founded upon an inexplicably odd misapprehension — the misapprehension that the Bible witnesses to its plenary inspiration only in a text here and there: texts of exceptional clearness alone probably being in mind, — such as our Saviour's declaration that the Scriptures cannot be broken; or Paul's, that every scripture is inspired of God; or Peter's, that the men of God spake as they were moved by the Holy Ghost. Such texts, no doubt, do teach the doctrine of plenary inspiration, and are sadly in need of explaining away at the hands of those who will not believe this doctrine. As, indeed, we may learn from Dr. Sanday's treatment of one of them, that in which our Lord declares that the Scriptures cannot be broken. Dr. Sanday can only speak of this as " a passage of peculiar strangeness and difficulty "; " because," he tells us,

" it seems to mean that the *dicta* of Scripture, even where we should naturally take them as figurative, must be true." Needless to say that the only " strangeness and difficulty " in the text arises from the unwillingness of the commentator to approach the Scriptures with the simple trust in their detailed divine trustworthiness and authority which characterized all our Lord's dealings with them.

But no grosser misconception could be conceived than that the Scriptures bear witness to their own plenary inspiration in these outstanding texts alone. These are but the culminating passages of a pervasive testimony to the divine character of Scripture, which fills the whole New Testament; and which includes not only such direct assertions of divinity and infallibility for Scripture as these, but, along with them, an endless variety of expressions of confidence in, and phenomena of use of, Scripture which are irresistible in their teaching when it is once fairly apprehended. The induction must be broad enough to embrace, and give their full weight to, a great variety of such facts as these: the lofty titles which are given to Scripture, and by which it is cited, such as " Scripture," " the Scriptures," even that almost awful title, " the Oracles of God "; the significant *formulæ* by which it is quoted, " It is written," " It is spoken," " It says," " God says "; such modes of adducing it as betray that to the writer " Scripture says " is equivalent to " God says," and even its narrative parts are conceived as direct utterances of God; the attribution to Scripture, as such, of divine qualities and acts, as in such phrases as " the Scriptures foresaw "; the ascription of the Scriptures, in whole or in their several parts as occasionally adduced, to the Holy Spirit as their author, while the human writers are treated as merely his *media* of expression; the reverence and trust shown, and the significance and authority ascribed, to the very words of Scripture; and the general attitude of entire subjection to every declaration of Scripture of whatever kind, which characterizes every line of the New Testament. The effort to explain away the Bible's witness to its plenary inspiration reminds one of a man standing safely in his laboratory and elaborately expounding — possibly by the aid of diagrams and mathematical *formulæ* — how every stone in an avalanche has a defined pathway and may easily be dodged by one of some presence of mind. We may fancy such an elaborate trifler's triumph as he would analyze the avalanche into its constituent stones, and demonstrate of stone after stone that its pathway is definite, limited, and may easily be avoided. But avalanches, unfortunately, do not come upon us, stone by stone, one at a time, courteously leaving us opportunity to withdraw from the pathway of each in turn: but all at once, in a roaring mass of destruction. Just so we may explain away a text or two which teach plenary inspiration, to our own closet satisfaction, dealing with them each without reference to its relation to the others: but these texts of ours, again, unfortunately do not come upon us in this artificial isolation; neither are they few in number. There are scores, hundreds, of them: and they come bursting upon us in one solid mass. Explain them away? We should have to explain away the whole New Testament. What a pity it is that we cannot see and feel the avalanche of texts beneath which we may lie hopelessly buried, as clearly as we may see and feel an avalanche of stones! Let us, however, but open our eyes to the variety and pervasiveness of the New Testament witness to its high estimate of Scripture, and we shall no longer wonder that modern scholarship finds itself compelled to allow that the Christian church has read her records correctly, and that the church-doctrine of inspiration is simply a transcript of the biblical doctrine; nor shall we any longer wonder that the church, receiving these Scriptures as her authoritative teacher of doctrine, adopted in the very beginnings of her life, the doctrine of plenary inspiration, and has held it with a tenacity that knows no wavering, until the present hour.

But, we may be reminded, the church has not held with such tenacity to all doctrines taught in the Bible. How are we to account, then, for the singular constancy of its confession of the Bible's doctrine of inspiration? The account to be given is again simple, and capable of being expressed in a single sentence. It is due to an instinctive feeling in the church, that the trustworthiness of the Scriptures lies at the foundation of trust in the Christian system of doctrine, and is therefore fundamental to the Christian hope and life. It is due to the church's instinct that the validity of her teaching of doctrine as the truth of God, — to the Christian's instinct that the validity of his hope in the several promises of the gospel, — rests on the trustworthiness of the Bible as a record of God's dealings and purposes with men.

Individuals may call in question the soundness of these instinctive judgments. And, indeed, there is a sense in which it would not be true to say that the truth of Christian teaching and the foundations of faith are suspended upon the doctrine of plenary inspiration, or upon any doctrine of inspiration whatever. They rest rather upon the previous fact of revelation: and it is important to keep ourselves reminded that the supernatural origin and contents of Christianity, not only may be vindicated apart from any question of the inspiration of the record, but, in point of fact, always are vindicated prior to any question of the inspiration of the record. We cannot raise the question whether God has given us an absolutely trustworthy record of the supernatural facts and teachings of Christianity, before we are assured that there are supernatural facts and teachings to be recorded. The fact that Christianity is a supernatural religion and the nature of Christianity as a supernatural religion, are matters of history; and are independent of any, and of every, theory of inspiration.

But this line of remark is of more importance to the Christian apologist than to the Christian believer, as such; and the instinct of the church that the validity of her teaching, and the instinct of the Christian that the validity of his hope, are bound up with the trustworthiness of the Bible, is a perfectly sound one. This for three reasons:

First, because the average Christian man is not and cannot be a fully furnished historical scholar. If faith in Christ is to be always and only the product of a thorough historical investigation into the origins of Christianity, there would certainly be few who could venture to preach Christ and him crucified with entire confidence; there would certainly be few who would be able to trust their all to him with entire security. The Christian scholar desires, and, thank God, is able to supply, a thoroughly trustworthy historical vindication of supernatural Christianity. But the Christian teacher desires, and, thank God, is able to lay his hands upon, a thoroughly trustworthy record of supernatural Christianity; and the Christian man requires, and, thank God, has, a thoroughly trustworthy Bible to which he can go directly and at once in every time of need. Though, then, in the abstract, we may say that the condition of the validity of the Christian teaching and of the Christian hope, is no more than the fact of the supernaturalism of Christianity, historically vindicated; practically we must say that the condition of the persistence of Christianity as a religion for the people, is the entire trustworthiness of the Scriptures as the record of the supernatural revelation which Christianity is.

Secondly, the merely historical vindication of the supernatural origin and contents of Christianity, while thorough and complete for Christianity as a whole, and for all the main facts and doctrines which enter into it, does not by itself supply a firm basis of trust for all the details of teaching and all the items of promise upon which the Christian man would fain lean. Christianity would be given to us; but it would be given to us, not in the exact form or in all the fulness with which God gave it to his needy children through his servants, the prophets, and through his Son and his apostles; but with the marks of human misapprehension, exaggeration, and minimizing upon it, and of whatever attrition may have been wrought upon it by its passage to us through the ages. That the church may have unsullied assurance in the details of its teaching, — that the Christian man may have unshaken confidence in the details of the promises to which he trusts, — they need, and they know that they need, a thoroughly trustworthy Word of God in which God himself speaks directly to them all the words of this life.

Thirdly, in the circumstances of the present case, we cannot fall back from trust in the Bible upon trust in the historical vindication of Christianity as a revelation from God, inasmuch as, since Christ and his apostles are historically shown to have taught the plenary inspiration of the Bible, the credit of the previous fact of revelation — even of the supreme revelation in Christ Jesus — is implicated in the truth of the doctrine of plenary inspiration. The historical vindication of Christianity as a revelation from God, vindicates as the truth of God all the contents of that revelation; and, among these contents, vindicates, as divinely true, the teaching of Christ and his apostles, that the Scriptures are the very Word of God, to be trusted as such in all the details of their teaching and promises. The instinct of the church is perfectly sound, therefore, when she clings to the trustworthiness of the Bible, as lying at the foundation of her teaching and her faith.

Much less can she be shaken from this instinctive conviction by the representations of individual thinkers who go yet a step further, and, refusing to pin their faith either to the Bible or to history, affirm that " the essence of Christianity " is securely intrenched in the subjective feelings of man, either as such, or as Christian man taught by the Holy Ghost; and therefore that there is by no means needed an infallible objective rule of faith in order to propagate or preserve Christian truth in the world. It is unnecessary to say that " the essence of Christianity " as conceived by these individuals, includes little that is characteristic of Christian doctrine, life, or hope, as distinct from what is taught by other religions or philosophies. And it is perhaps equally unnecessary to remind ourselves that such individuals, having gone so far, tend to take a further step still, and to discard the records which they thus judge to be unnecessary. Thus, there may be found even men still professing historical Christianity, who reason themselves into the conclusion that " in the nature of the case, no external authority can possibly be absolute in regard to spiritual truth "; [19] just as men have been known to reason themselves into the conclusion that the external world has no objective reality and is naught but the projection of their own faculties.

[19] Professor W. F. Adeney, " Faith and Criticism," p. 90.

But as in the one case, so in the other, the common sense of men recoils from such subtleties; and it remains the profound persuasion of the Christian heart that without such an " external authority " as a thoroughly trustworthy Bible, the soul is left without sure ground for a proper knowledge of itself, its condition, and its need, or for a proper knowledge of God's provisions of mercy for it and his promises of grace to it, — without sure ground, in a word, for its faith and hope. Adolphe Monod gives voice to no more than the common Christian conviction, when he declares that, " If faith has not for its basis a testimony of God to which we must submit, as to an authority exterior to our personal judgment, and independent of it, then faith is no faith." [20] " The more I study the Scriptures, the example of Christ, and of the apostles, and the history of my own heart," he adds, " the more I am convinced, that a testimony of God, placed without us and above us, exempt from all intermixture of sin and error which belong to a fallen race, and received with submission on the sole authority of God, is the true basis of faith." [21]

It is doubtless the profound and ineradicable conviction, so expressed, of the need of an infallible Bible, if men are to seek and find salvation in God's announced purpose of grace, and peace and comfort in his past dealings with his people, that has operated to keep the formulas of the churches and the hearts of the people of God, through so many ages, true to the Bible doctrine of plenary inspiration. In that doctrine men have found what their hearts have told them was the indispensable safeguard of a sure word of God to them, — a word of God to which they could resort with confidence in every time of need, to which they could appeal for guidance in every difficulty, for comfort in every sorrow, for instruction in every perplexity; on whose " Thus saith the Lord " they could safely rest all their aspirations and all their hopes. Such a Word of God, each one of us knows he needs, — not a Word of God that speaks to us only through the medium of our fellow-men, men of like passions and weaknesses with ourselves, so that we have to feel

[20] " Life of Adolphe Monod," p. 224.   [21] Ibid., p. 357.

our way back to God's word through the church, through tradition, or through the apostles, standing between us and God; but a Word of God in which God speaks directly to each of our souls. Such a Word of God, Christ and his apostles offer us, when they give us the Scriptures, not as man's report to us of what God says, but as the very Word of God itself, spoken by God himself through human lips and pens. Of such a precious possession, given to her by such hands, the church will not lightly permit herself to be deprived. Thus the church's sense of her need of an absolutely infallible Bible, has co-operated with her reverence for the teaching of the Bible to keep her true, in all ages, to the Bible doctrine of plenary inspiration.

What, indeed, would the church be — what would we, as Christian men, be — without our inspired Bible? Many of us have, no doubt, read Jean Paul Richter's vision of a dead Christ, and have shuddered at his pictures of the woe of a world from which its Christ has been stolen away. It would be a theme worthy of some like genius to portray for us the vision of a dead Bible, — the vision of what this world of ours would be, had there been no living Word of God cast into its troubled waters with its voice of power, crying, " Peace! Be still! " What does this Christian world of ours not owe to this Bible! And to this Bible conceived, not as a part of the world's literature, — the literary product of the earliest years of the church; not as a book in which, by searching, we may find God and perchance somewhat of God's will: but as the very Word of God, instinct with divine life from the " In the beginning " of Genesis to the " Amen " of the Apocalypse, — breathed into by God, and breathing out God to every devout reader. It is because men have so thought of it that it has proved a leaven to leaven the whole lump of the world. We do not half realize what we owe to this book, thus trusted by men. We can never fully realize it. For we can never even in thought unravel from this complex web of modern civilization, all the threads from the Bible which have been woven into it, throughout the whole past, and now enter into its very fabric. And, thank God, much less can we ever untwine them in fact, and separate our mod-

orn life from all those Bible influences by which alone it is
blessed, and sweetened, and made a life which men may live.
Dr. Gardiner Spring published, years ago, a series of lectures in
which he sought to take some account of the world's obligations to the Bible, — tracing in turn the services it has rendered to religion, to morals, to social institutions, to civil and
religious liberty, to the freedom of slaves, to the emancipation
of woman and the sweetening of domestic life, to public and
private beneficence, to literary and scientific progress, and the
like.[22] And Adolphe Monod, in his own inimitable style, has
done something to awaken us as individuals to what we owe to
a fully trusted Bible, in the development of our character and
religious life.[23] In such matters, however, we can trust our imaginations better than our words, to remind us of the immensity of our debt.

Let it suffice to say that to a plenarily inspired Bible, humbly trusted as such, we actually, and as a matter of fact, owe all
that has blessed our lives with hopes of an immortality of bliss,
and with the present fruition of the love of God in Christ. This
is not an exaggeration. We may say that without a Bible we
might have had Christ and all that he stands for to our souls.
Let us not say that this might not have been possible. But
neither let us forget that, in point of fact, it is to the Bible that
we owe it that we know Christ and are found in him. And may
it not be fairly doubted whether you and I, — however it may
have been with others, — would have had Christ had there
been no Bible? We must not at any rate forget those nineteen
Christian centuries which stretch between us and Christ, whose
Christian light we would do much to blot out and sink in a
dreadful darkness if we could blot out the Bible. Even with the
Bible, and all that had come from the Bible to form Christian
lives and inform a Christian literature, after a millennium and
a half the darkness had grown so deep that a Reformation was
necessary if Christian truth was to persist, — a Luther was
necessary, raised up by God to rediscover the Bible and give it

---

[22] Gardiner Spring, " Obligations of the World to the Bible." (New York:
M. W. Dodd. 1855.)
[23]   Adolphe Monod, " L'Inspiration prouvée par ses Œuvres."

back to man. Suppose there had been no Bible for Luther to rediscover, and on the lines of which to refound the church, — and no Bible in the hearts of God's saints and in the pages of Christian literature, persisting through those darker ages to prepare a Luther to rediscover it? Though Christ had come into the world and had lived and died for us, might it not be to us, — you and me, I mean, who are not learned historians but simple men and women, — might it not be to us as though he had not been? Or, if some faint echo of a Son of God offering salvation to men could still be faintly heard even by such dull ears as ours, sounding down the ages, who would have ears to catch the fulness of the message of free grace which he brought into the world? who could assure our doubting souls that it was not all a pleasant dream? who could cleanse the message from the ever-gathering corruptions of the multiplying years? No: whatever might possibly have been had there been no Bible, it is actually to the Bible that you and I owe it that we have a Christ, — a Christ to love, to trust and to follow, a Christ without us the ground of our salvation, a Christ within us the hope of glory.

Our effort has been to bring clearly out what seem to be three very impressive facts regarding the plenary inspiration of the Scriptures, — the facts, namely, that this doctrine has always been, and is still, the church-doctrine of inspiration, as well the vital faith of the people of God as the formulated teaching of the official creeds; that it is undeniably the doctrine of inspiration held by Christ and his apostles, and commended to us as true by all the authority which we will allow to attach to their teaching; and that it is the foundation of our Christian thought and life, without which we could not, or could only with difficulty, maintain the confidence of our faith and the surety of our hope. On such grounds as these is not this doctrine commended to us as true?

But, it may be said, there are difficulties in the way. Of course there are. There are difficulties in the way of believing anything. There are difficulties in the way of believing that God is, or that Jesus Christ is God's Son who came into the world to save sinners. There are difficulties in the way of be-

lieving that we ourselves really exist, or that anything has real
existence besides ourselves. When men give their undivided
attention to these difficulties, they may become, and they have
become, so perplexed in mind, that they have felt unable to believe that God is, or that they themselves exist, or that there is
any external world without themselves. It would be a strange
thing if it might not so fare with plenary inspiration also. Difficulties? Of course there are difficulties. It is nothing to the
purpose to point out this fact. Dr. J. Oswald Dykes says with
admirable truth: " If men must have a reconciliation for all
conflicting truths before they will believe any; if they must
see how the promises of God are to be fulfilled before they will
obey his commands; if duty is to hang upon the satisfying of
the understanding, instead of the submission of the will, —
then the greater number of us will find the road of faith and
the road of duty blocked at the outset." [24] These wise words
have their application also to our present subject. The question is not, whether the doctrine of plenary inspiration has difficulties to face. The question is, whether these difficulties are
greater than the difficulty of believing that the whole church
of God from the beginning has been deceived in her estimate
of the Scriptures committed to her charge — are greater than
the difficulty of believing that the whole college of the apostles,
yes and Christ himself at their head, were themselves deceived
as to the nature of those Scriptures which they gave the church
as its precious possession, and have deceived with them twenty
Christian centuries, and are likely to deceive twenty more before our boasted advancing light has corrected their error, —
are greater than the difficulty of believing that we have no sure
foundation for our faith and no certain warrant for our trust
in Christ for salvation. We believe this doctrine of the plenary
inspiration of the Scriptures primarily because it is the doctrine which Christ and his apostles believed, and which they
have taught us. It may sometimes seem difficult to take our
stand frankly by the side of Christ and his apostles. It will
always be found safe.

[24] J. Oswald Dykes, " Abraham," etc. (1877), p. 257.

IV

THE BIBLICAL IDEA OF INSPIRATION

INSPIRATION [1]

THE word " inspire " and its derivatives seem to have come
into Middle English from the French, and have been employed
from the first (early in the fourteenth century) in a considerable number of significations, physical and metaphorical, secular and religious. The derivatives have been multiplied and
their applications extended during the procession of the years,
until they have acquired a very wide and varied use. Underlying all their use, however, is the constant implication of an
influence from without, producing in its object movements and
effects beyond its native, or at least its ordinary powers. The
noun " inspiration," although already in use in the fourteenth
century, seems not to occur in any but a theological sense until
late in the sixteenth century. The specifically theological sense
of all these terms is governed, of course, by their usage in Latin
theology; and this rests ultimately on their employment in the
Latin Bible. In the Vulgate Latin Bible the verb *inspiro* (Gen.
ii. 7; Wisd. xv. 11; Ecclus. iv. 12; 2 Tim. iii. 16; 2 Pet. i. 21)
and the noun *inspiratio* (2 Sam. xxii. 16; Job xxxii. 8; Ps. xvii.
16; Acts xvii. 25) both occur four or five times in somewhat
diverse applications. In the development of a theological nomenclature, however, they have acquired (along with other
less frequent applications) a technical sense with reference to
the Biblical writers or the Biblical books. The Biblical books
are called inspired as the Divinely determined products of inspired men; the Biblical writers are called inspired as breathed
into by the Holy Spirit, so that the product of their activities
transcends human powers and becomes Divinely authoritative.
Inspiration is, therefore, usually defined as a supernatural in-

[1] Article "Inspiration," from *The International Standard Bible Encyclopaedia*, James Orr General Editor, v. 3, pp. 1473–1483. Pub. Chicago, 1915, by
The Howard-Severance Co.

fluence exerted on the sacred writers by the Spirit of God, by
virtue of which their writings are given Divine trustworthiness.

Meanwhile, for English-speaking men, these terms have
virtually ceased to be Biblical terms. They naturally passed
from the Latin Vulgate into the English versions made from it
(most fully into the Rheims-Douay: Job xxxii. 8; Wisd. xv.
11; Ecclus. iv. 12; 2 Tim. iii. 16; 2 Pet. i. 21). But in the development of the English Bible they have found ever-decreasing place. In the English versions of the Apocrypha (both Authorized Version and Revised Version) " inspired " is retained
in Wisd. xv. 11; but in the canonical books the nominal form
alone occurs in the Authorized Version and that only twice:
Job xxxii. 8, " But there is a spirit in man: and the inspiration
of the Almighty giveth them understanding "; and 2 Tim. iii.
16, " All scripture is given by inspiration of God, and is profitable for doctrine, for reproof, for correction, for instruction in
righteousness." The Revised Version removes the former of
these instances, substituting " breath " for " inspiration "; and
alters the latter so as to read: " Every scripture inspired of God
is also profitable for teaching, for reproof, for correction, for instruction which is in righteousness," with a marginal alternative in the form of, " Every scripture is inspired of God and
profitable," etc. The word " inspiration " thus disappears from
the English Bible, and the word " inspired " is left in it only
once, and then, let it be added, by a distinct and even misleading mistranslation.

For the Greek word in this passage — θεόπνευστος, theó-
pneustos — very distinctly does not mean " inspired of God."
This phrase is rather the rendering of the Latin, divinitus inspirata, restored from the Wyclif (" Al Scripture of God yn-
spyrid is . . .") and Rhemish (" All Scripture inspired of God
is . . .") versions of the Vulgate. The Greek word does not
even mean, as the Authorized Version translates it, " given by
inspiration of God," although that rendering (inherited from
Tindale: " All Scripture given by inspiration of God is . . ."
and its successors; cf. Geneva: " The whole Scripture is given
by inspiration of God and is . . .") has at least to say for itself

that it is a somewhat clumsy, perhaps, but not misleading, paraphrase of the Greek term in the theological language of the day. The Greek term has, however, nothing to say of *in*spiring or of *in*spiration: it speaks only of a " spiring " or " spiration." What it says of Scripture is, not that it is " breathed into by God " or is the product of the Divine " inbreathing " into its human authors, but that it is breathed out by God, " God-breathed," the product of the creative breath of God. In a word, what is declared by this fundamental passage is simply that the Scriptures are a Divine product, without any indication of how God has operated in producing them. No term could have been chosen, however, which would have more emphatically asserted the Divine production of Scripture than that which is here employed. The " breath of God " is in Scripture just the symbol of His almighty power, the bearer of His creative word. " By the word of Jehovah," we read in the significant parallel of Ps. xxxiii. 6, " were the heavens made, and all the host of them by the breath of his mouth." And it is particularly where the operations of God are energetic that this term (whether רוּחַ, *rū*^{a}*h*, or נְשָׁמָה, *n*^{e}*shāmāh*) is employed to designate them — God's breath is the irresistible outflow of His power. When Paul declares, then, that " every scripture," or " all scripture " is the product of the Divine breath, " is God-breathed," he asserts with as much energy as he could employ that Scripture is the product of a specifically Divine operation.

(1) 2 Tim. iii. 16: In the passage in which Paul makes this energetic assertion of the Divine origin of Scripture he is engaged in explaining the greatness of the advantages which Timothy had enjoyed for learning the saving truth of God. He had had good teachers; and from his very infancy he had been, by his knowledge of the Scriptures, made wise unto salvation through faith in Jesus Christ. The expression, " sacred writings," here employed (ver. 15), is a technical one, not found elsewhere in the New Testament, it is true, but occurring currently in Philo and Josephus to designate that body of authoritative books which constituted the Jewish " Law." It appears

here anarthrously because it is set in contrast with the oral teaching which Timothy had enjoyed, as something still better: he had not only had good instructors, but also always " an open Bible," as we should say, in his hand. To enhance yet further the great advantage of the possession of these Sacred Scriptures the apostle adds now a sentence throwing their nature strongly up to view. They are of Divine origin and therefore of the highest value for all holy purposes.

There is room for some difference of opinion as to the exact construction of this declaration. Shall we render " Every Scripture " or " All Scripture " ? Shall we render " Every [or all] Scripture is God-breathed and [therefore] profitable," or " Every [or all] Scripture, being God-breathed, is as well profitable " ? No doubt both questions are interesting, but for the main matter now engaging our attention they are both indifferent. Whether Paul, looking back at the Sacred Scriptures he had just mentioned, makes the assertion he is about to add, of them distributively, of all their parts, or collectively, of their entire mass, is of no moment: to say that every part of these Sacred Scriptures is God-breathed and to say that the whole of these Sacred Scriptures is God-breathed, is, for the main matter, all one. Nor is the difference great between saying that they are in all their parts, or in their whole extent, God-breathed and therefore profitable, and saying that they are in all their parts, or in their whole extent, because God-breathed as well profitable. In both cases these Sacred Scriptures are declared to owe their value to their Divine origin; and in both cases this their Divine origin is energetically asserted of their entire fabric. On the whole, the preferable construction would seem to be, " Every Scripture, seeing that it is God-breathed, is as well profitable." In that case, what the apostle asserts is that the Sacred Scriptures, in their every several passage — for it is just " passage of Scripture " which " Scripture " in this distributive use of it signifies — is the product of the creative breath of God, and, because of this its Divine origination, is of supreme value for all holy purposes.

It is to be observed that the apostle does not stop here to

tell us either what particular books enter into the collection which he calls Sacred Scriptures, or by what precise operations God has produced them. Neither of these subjects entered into the matter he had at the moment in hand. It was the value of the Scriptures, and the source of that value in their Divine origin, which he required at the moment to assert; and these things he asserts, leaving to other occasions any further facts concerning them which it might be well to emphasize. It is also to be observed that the apostle does not tell us here everything for which the Scriptures are made valuable by their Divine origination. He speaks simply to the point immediately in hand, and reminds Timothy of the value which these Scriptures, by virtue of their Divine origin, have for the "man of God." Their spiritual power, as God-breathed, is all that he had occasion here to advert to. Whatever other qualities may accrue to them from their Divine origin, he leaves to other occasions to speak of.

(2) 2 Pet. i. 19–21: What Paul tells here about the Divine origin of the Scriptures is enforced and extended by a striking passage in 2 Pet. (i. 19–21). Peter is assuring his readers that what had been made known to them of " the power and coming of our Lord Jesus Christ " did not rest on " cunningly devised fables." He offers them the testimony of eyewitnesses of Christ's glory. And then he intimates that they have better testimony than even that of eyewitnesses. " We have," says he, " the prophetic word " (English versions, unhappily, " the word of prophecy "): and this, he says, is " more sure," and therefore should certainly be heeded. He refers, of course, to the Scriptures. Of what other " prophetic word " could he, over against the testimony of the eyewitnesses of Christ's " excellent glory " (Authorized Version) say that " we have " it, that is, it is in our hands? And he proceeds at once to speak of it plainly as " Scriptural prophecy." You do well, he says, to pay heed to the prophetic word, because we know this first, that " every prophecy of scripture . . ." It admits of more question, however, whether by this phrase he means the whole of Scripture, designated according to its character, as prophetic,

that is, of Divine origin; or only that portion of Scripture which we discriminate as particularly prophetic, the immediate revelations contained in Scripture. The former is the more likely view, inasmuch as the entirety of Scripture is elsewhere conceived and spoken of as prophetic. In that case, what Peter has to say of this " every prophecy of scripture " — the exact equivalent, it will be observed, in this case of Paul's " every scripture " (2 Tim. iii. 16) — applies to the whole of Scripture in all its parts. What he says of it is that it does not come " of private interpretation "; that is, it is not the result of human investigation into the nature of things, the product of its writers' own thinking. This is as much as to say it is of Divine gift. Accordingly, he proceeds at once to make this plain in a supporting clause which contains both the negative and the positive declaration: " For no prophecy ever came [margin " was brought "] by the will of man, but it was as borne by the Holy Spirit that men spoke from God." In this singularly precise and pregnant statement there are several things which require to be carefully observed. There is, first of all, the emphatic denial that prophecy — that is to say, on the hypothesis upon which we are working, Scripture — owes its origin to human initiative: " No prophecy ever was brought — ' came ' is the word used in the English version text, with ' was brought ' in Revised Version margin — by the will of man." Then, there is the equally emphatic assertion that its source lies in God: it was spoken by men, indeed, but the men who spoke it " spake from God." And a remarkable clause is here inserted, and thrown forward in the sentence that stress may fall on it, which tells us how it could be that men, in speaking, should speak not from themselves, but from God: it was " as borne " — it is the same word which was rendered " was brought " above, and might possibly be rendered " brought " here — " by the Holy Spirit " that they spoke. Speaking thus under the determining influence of the Holy Spirit, the things they spoke were not from themselves, but from God.

Here is as direct an assertion of the Divine origin of Scripture as that of 2 Tim. iii. 16. But there is more here than a simple assertion of the Divine origin of Scripture. We are advanced somewhat in our understanding of how God has produced the Scriptures. It was through the instrumentality of men who " spake from him." More specifically, it was through an operation of the Holy Ghost on these men which is described as " bearing " them. The term here used is a very specific one. It is not to be confounded with guiding, or directing, or controlling, or even leading in the full sense of that word. It goes beyond all such terms, in assigning the effect produced specifically to the active agent. What is " borne " is taken up by the " bearer," and conveyed by the " bearer's " power, not its own, to the " bearer's " goal, not its own. The men who spoke from God are here declared, therefore, to have been taken up by the Holy Spirit and brought by His power to the goal of His choosing. The things which they spoke under this operation of the Spirit were therefore His things, not theirs. And that is the reason which is assigned why " the prophetic word " is so sure. Though spoken through the instrumentality of men, it is, by virtue of the fact that these men spoke " as borne by the Holy Spirit," an immediately Divine word. It will be observed that the proximate stress is laid here, not on the spiritual value of Scripture (though that, too, is seen in the background), but on the Divine trustworthiness of Scripture. Because this is the way every prophecy of Scripture " has been brought," it affords a more sure basis of confidence than even the testimony of human eyewitnesses. Of course, if we do not understand by " the prophetic word " here the entirety of Scripture described, according to its character, as revelation, but only that element in Scripture which we call specifically prophecy, then it is directly only of that element in Scripture that these great declarations are made. In any event, however, they are made of the prophetic element in Scripture as written, which was the only form in which the readers of this Epistle possessed it, and which is the thing specifically intimated in the phrase " every prophecy *of scripture.*" These great declarations are made, therefore, at least of large tracts of Scripture; and if the entirety of Scripture is intended by the phrase "the prophetic word," they are made of the whole of Scripture.

(3) Jn. x. 34 f.: How far the supreme trustworthiness of Scripture, thus asserted, extends may be conveyed to us by a passage in one of Our Lord's discourses recorded by John (Jn. x. 34–35). The Jews, offended by Jesus' "making himself God," were in the act to stone Him, when He defended Himself thus: "Is it not written in your law, I said, Ye are gods? If he called them gods, unto whom the word of God came (and the scripture cannot be broken), say ye of him, whom the Father sanctified [margin "consecrated"] and sent unto the world, Thou blasphemest; because I said, I am the Son of God?" It may be thought that this defence is inadequate. It certainly is incomplete: Jesus made Himself God (Jn. x. 33) in a far higher sense than that in which "Ye are gods" was said of those "unto whom the word of God came": He had just declared in unmistakable terms, "I and the Father are one." But it was quite sufficient for the immediate end in view — to repel the technical charge of blasphemy based on His making Himself God: it is not blasphemy to call one God in any sense in which he may fitly receive that designation; and certainly if it is not blasphemy to call such men as those spoken of in the passage of Scripture adduced gods, because of their official functions, it cannot be blasphemy to call Him God whom the Father consecrated and sent into the world. The point for us to note, however, is merely that Jesus' defence takes the form of an appeal to Scripture; and it is important to observe how He makes this appeal. In the first place, He adduces the Scriptures as law: "Is it not written in your law?" He demands. The passage of Scripture which He adduces is not written in that portion of Scripture which was more specifically called "the Law," that is to say, the Pentateuch; nor in any portion of Scripture of formally legal contents. It is written in the Book of Psalms; and in a particular psalm which is as far as possible from presenting the external characteristics of legal enactment (Ps. lxxxii. 6). When Jesus adduces this passage, then, as written in the "law" of the Jews, He does it, not because it stands in this

psalm, but because it is a part of Scripture at large. In other words, He here ascribes legal authority to the entirety of Scripture, in accordance with a conception common enough among the Jews (cf. Jn. xii. 34), and finding expression in the New Testament occasionally, both on the lips of Jesus Himself, and in the writings of the apostles. Thus, on a later occasion (Jn. xv. 25), Jesus declares that it is written in the " law " of the Jews, " They hated me without a cause," a clause found in Ps. xxxv. 19. And Paul assigns passages both from the Psalms and from Isaiah to " the Law " (1 Cor. xiv. 21; Rom. iii. 19), and can write such a sentence as this (Gal. iv. 21 f.): " Tell me, ye that desire to be under the law, do ye not hear the law? For it is written . . ." quoting from the narrative of Genesis. We have seen that the entirety of Scripture was conceived as " prophecy "; we now see that the entirety of Scripture was also conceived as " law ": these three terms, the law, prophecy, Scripture, were indeed, materially, strict synonyms, as our present passage itself advises us, by varying the formula of adduction in contiguous verses from " law " to " scripture." And what is thus implied in the manner in which Scripture is adduced, is immediately afterward spoken out in the most explicit language, because it forms an essential element in Our Lord's defence. It might have been enough to say simply, " Is it not written in your law? " But Our Lord, determined to drive His appeal to Scripture home, sharpens the point to the utmost by adding with the highest emphasis: " and the scripture cannot be broken." This is the reason why it is worth while to appeal to what is " written in the law," because " the scripture cannot be broken." The word " broken " here is the common one for breaking the law, or the Sabbath, or the like (Jn. v. 18; vii. 23; Mt. v. 19), and the meaning of the declaration is that it is impossible for the Scripture to be annulled, its authority to be withstood, or denied. The movement of thought is to the effect that, because it is impossible for the Scripture — the term is perfectly general and witnesses to the unitary character of Scripture (it is all, for the purpose in hand, of a piece) — to be withstood, therefore this particular Scripture which is cited must be taken as of irrefragable authority. What we have here is, therefore, the strongest possible assertion of the indefectible authority of Scripture; precisely what is true of Scripture is that it " cannot be broken." Now, what is the particular thing in Scripture, for the confirmation of which the indefectible authority of Scripture is thus invoked? It is one of its most casual clauses — more than that, the very form of its expression in one of its most casual clauses. This means, of course, that in the Saviour's view the indefectible authority of Scripture attaches to the very form of expression of its most casual clauses. It belongs to Scripture through and through, down to its most minute particulars, that it is of indefectible authority.

It is sometimes suggested, it is true, that Our Lord's argument here is an *argumentum ad hominem,* and that his words, therefore, express not His own view of the authority of Scripture, but that of His Jewish opponents. It will scarcely be denied that there is a vein of satire running through Our Lord's defence: that the Jews so readily allowed that corrupt judges might properly be called " gods," but could not endure that He whom the Father had consecrated and sent into the world should call Himself Son of God, was a somewhat pungent fact to throw up into such a high light. But the argument from Scripture is not *ad hominem* but *e concessu;* Scripture was common ground with Jesus and His opponents. If proof were needed for so obvious a fact, it would be supplied by the circumstance that this is not an isolated but a representative passage. The conception of Scripture thrown up into such clear view here supplies the ground of all Jesus' appeals to Scripture, and of all the appeals of the New Testament writers as well. Everywhere, to Him and to them alike, an appeal to Scripture is an appeal to an indefectible authority whose determination is final; both He and they make their appeal indifferently to every part of Scripture, to every element in Scripture, to its most incidental clauses as well as to its most fundamental principles, and to the very form of its expression. This attitude toward Scripture as an authoritative document is, indeed, already intimated by their constant designation of it by the name of Scripture, the Scriptures, that is " the Document," by way of eminence; and by their customary citation of it with the simple formula, " It is written." What is written in this document admits so little of questioning that its authoritativeness required no asserting, but might safely be taken for granted. Both modes of expression belong to the constantly illustrated habitudes of Our Lord's speech. The first words He is recorded as uttering after His manifestation to Israel were an appeal to the unquestionable authority of Scripture; to Satan's temptations He opposed no other weapon than the final " It is written " ! (Mt. iv. 4.7.10; Lk. iv. 4.8). And among the last words which He spoke to His disciples before He was received up was a rebuke to them for not understanding that all things " which are written in the law of Moses, and the prophets, and psalms " concerning Him — that is (ver. 45) in the entire " Scriptures " — " must needs be " (very emphatic) " fulfilled " (Lk. xxiv. 44). " Thus it is written," says He (ver. 46), as rendering all doubt absurd. For, as He had explained earlier upon the same day (Lk. xxiv. 25 ff.), it argues only that one is " foolish and slow at heart " if he does not " believe in "(if his faith does not rest securely on, as on a firm foundation) " all " (without limit of subject-matter here) " that the prophets " (explained in ver. 27 as equivalent to " all the scriptures ") " have spoken."

The necessity of the fulfilment of all that is written in Scripture, which is so strongly asserted in these last instructions to His disciples, is frequently adverted to by Our Lord. He repeatedly explains of occurrences occasionally happening that they have come to pass " that the scripture might be fulfilled " (Mk. xiv. 49; Jn. xiii. 18; xvii. 12; cf. xii. 14; Mk. ix. 12.13). On the basis of Scriptural declarations, therefore, He announces with confidence that given events will certainly occur: " All ye shall be offended [literally " scandalized "] in me this night: *for* it is written . . ." (Mt. xxvi. 31; Mk. xiv. 27; cf. Lk. xx. 17). Although holding at His command ample means of escape, He bows before on-coming calamities, for, He asks, how otherwise "should the scriptures be fulfilled, that thus it must be?" (Mt. xxvi. 54). It is not merely the two disciples with whom He talked on the way to Emmaus (Lk. xxiv. 25) whom He rebukes for not trusting themselves more perfectly to the teaching of Scripture. "Ye search the scriptures," He says to the Jews, in the classical passage (Jn. v. 39), "because ye think that in them ye have eternal life; and these are they which bear witness of me; and ye will not come to me, that ye may have life!" These words surely were spoken more in sorrow than in scorn: there is no blame implied either for searching the Scriptures or for thinking that eternal life is to be found in Scripture; approval rather. What the Jews are blamed for is that they read with a veil lying upon their hearts which He would fain take away (2 Cor. iii. 15 f.). "Ye search the scriptures" — that is right: and "even you" (emphatic) "think to have eternal life in them" — that is right, too. But "it is these very Scriptures" (very emphatic) "which are bearing witness" (continuous process) "of me; and" (here is the marvel!) "ye will not come to me and have life!" — that you may, that is, reach the very end you have so properly in view in searching the Scriptures. Their failure is due, not to the Scriptures but to themselves, who read the Scriptures to such little purpose.

Quite similarly Our Lord often finds occasion to express wonder at the little effect to which Scripture had been read, not because it had been looked into too curiously, but because it had not been looked into earnestly enough, with sufficiently simple and robust trust in its every declaration. "Have ye not read even this scripture?" He demands, as He adduces Ps. cxviii. to show that the rejection of the Messiah was already intimated in Scripture (Mk. xii. 10; Mt. xxi. 42 varies the expression to the equivalent: "Did ye never read in the scriptures?"). And when the indignant Jews came to Him complaining of the Hosannas with which the children in the Temple were acclaiming Him, and demanding, "Hearest thou what these are saying?" He met them (Mt. xxi. 16) merely with, "Yea: did ye never read, Out of the mouths of babes and sucklings thou hast perfected praise? " The underlying thought of these passages is spoken out when He intimates that the source of all error in Divine things is just ignorance of the Scriptures: " Ye do err," He declares to His questioners, on an important occasion, " not knowing the scriptures " (Mt. xxii. 29); or, as it is put, perhaps more forcibly, in interrogative form, in its parallel in another Gospel: " Is it not for this cause that ye err, that ye know not the scriptures? " (Mk. xii. 24). Clearly, he who rightly knows the Scriptures does not err. The confidence with which Jesus rested on Scripture, in its every declaration, is further illustrated in a passage like Mt. xix. 4. Certain Pharisees had come to Him with a question on divorce and He met them thus: " Have ye not read, that he who made them from the beginning made them male and female, and said, For this cause shall a man leave his father and mother, and shall cleave to his wife; and the two shall become one flesh? . . . What therefore God hath joined together, let not man put asunder." The point to be noted is the explicit reference of Gen. ii. 24 to God as its author: " *He who made them* . . . said "; " what therefore *God* hath joined together." Yet this passage does not give us a saying of God's recorded in Scripture, but just the word of Scripture itself, and can be treated as a declaration of God's only on the hypothesis that all Scripture is a declaration of God's. The parallel in Mk. (x. 5 ff.) just as truly, though not as explicitly, assigns the passage to God as its author, citing it as authoritative law and speaking of its enactment as an act of God's. And it is interesting to observe in passing that Paul, having occasion to quote the same passage (1 Cor. vi. 16), also explicitly quotes it as a Divine word: " For, The twain, saith he, shall become one flesh " — the " he " here, in accordance with a usage to be noted later, meaning just " God."

Thus clear is it that Jesus' occasional adduction of Scripture as an authoritative document rests on an ascription of it to God as its author. His testimony is that whatever stands written in Scripture is a word of God. Nor can we evacuate this testimony of its force on the plea that it represents Jesus only in the days of His flesh, when He may be supposed to have reflected merely the opinions of His day and generation. The view of Scripture He announces was, no doubt, the view of His day and generation as well as His own view. But there is no reason to doubt that it was held by Him, not because it was the current view, but because, in His Divine-human knowledge, He knew it to be true; for, even in His humiliation, He is the faithful and true witness. And in any event we should bear in mind that this was the view of the resurrected as well as of the humiliated Christ. It was after He had suffered and had risen again in the power of His Divine life that He pronounced those foolish and slow of heart who do not believe all that stands written in all the Scriptures (Lk. xxiv. 25); and that He laid down the simple " Thus it is written " as the sufficient ground of confident belief (Lk. xxiv. 46). Nor can we explain away Jesus' testimony to the Divine trustworthiness of Scripture by interpreting it as not His own, but that of His followers, placed on His lips in their reports of His words. Not only is it too constant, minute, intimate and in part incidental, and therefore, as it were, hidden, to admit of this interpretation; but it so pervades all our channels of information concerning Jesus' teaching as to make it certain that it comes actually from Him. It belongs not only to the Jesus of our evangelical records but as well to the Jesus of the earlier sources which underlie our evangelical records, as anyone may assure himself by observing the instances in which Jesus adduces the Scriptures as Divinely authoritative that are recorded in more than one of the Gospels (e.g. " It is written," Mt. iv. 4.7.10 [Lk. iv. 4.8.10]; Mt. xi. 10; [Lk. vii. 27]; Mt. xxi. 13 [Lk. xix. 46; Mk. xi. 17]; Mt. xxvi. 31 [Mk. xiv. 21]; " the scripture " or " the scriptures," Mt. xix. 4 [Mk. x. 9]; Mt. xxi. 42 [Mk. xii. 10; Lk. xx. 17]; Mt. xxii. 29 [Mk. xii. 24; Lk. xx. 37]; Mt. xxvi. 56 [Mk. xiv. 49; Lk. xxiv. 44]). These passages alone would suffice to make clear to us the testimony of Jesus to Scripture as in all its parts and declarations Divinely authoritative.

The attempt to attribute the testimony of Jesus to His followers has in its favor only the undeniable fact that the testimony of the writers of the New Testament is to precisely the same effect as His. They, too, cursorily speak of Scripture by that pregnant name and adduce it with the simple " It is written," with the implication that whatever stands written in it is Divinely authoritative. As Jesus' official life begins with this " It is written " (Mt. iv. 4), so the evangelical proclamation begins with an " Even as it is written " (Mk. i. 2) ; and as Jesus sought the justification of His work in a solemn " Thus it is written, that the Christ should suffer, and rise again from the dead the third day " (Lk. xxiv. 46 ff.), so the apostles solemnly justified the Gospel which they preached, detail after detail, by appeal to the Scriptures, " That Christ died for our sins according to the scriptures " and " That he hath been raised on the third day according to the scriptures " (1 Cor. xv. 3.4; cf. Acts viii. 35; xvii. 3; xxvi. 22, and also Rom. i. 17; iii. 4.10; iv. 17; xi. 26; xiv. 11; 1 Cor. i. 19; ii. 9; iii. 19; xv. 45; Gal. iii. 10.13; iv. 22.27). Wherever they carried the gospel it was as a gospel resting on Scripture that they proclaimed it (Acts xvii. 2; xviii. 24.28); and they encouraged themselves to test its truth by the Scriptures (Acts xvii. 11). The holiness of life they inculcated, they based on Scriptural requirement (1 Pet. i. 16), and they commended the royal law of love which they taught by Scriptural sanction (Jas. ii. 8). Every detail of duty was supported by them by an appeal to Scripture (Acts xxiii. 5; Rom. xii. 19). The circumstances of their lives and the events occasionally occurring about them are referred to Scripture for their significance (Rom. ii. 26; viii. 36; ix. 33; xi. 8; xv. 9.21; 2 Cor. iv. 13). As Our Lord declared that whatever was written in Scripture must needs be fulfilled (Mt. xxvi. 54; Lk. xxii. 37; xxiv. 44), so His followers explained one of the most startling facts which had occurred in their experience by pointing out that " it was needful that the scripture should be fulfilled, which the Holy Spirit spake before by the mouth of David " (Acts i. 16). Here the ground of this constant appeal to Scripture, so that it is enough that a thing " is contained in scripture " (1 Pet. ii. 6) for it to be of indefectible authority, is plainly enough declared: Scripture must needs be fulfilled, for what is contained in it is the declaration of the Holy Ghost through the human author. What Scripture says, God says; and accordingly we read such remarkable declarations as these: " For the scripture saith unto Pharaoh, For this very purpose did I raise thee up " (Rom. ix. 17); " And the scripture, foreseeing that God would justify the Gentiles by faith, preached the gospel beforehand unto Abraham, . . . In thee shall all the nations be blessed " (Gal. iii. 8). These are not instances of simple personification of Scripture, which is itself a sufficiently remarkable usage (Mk. xv. 28; Jn. vii. 38.42; xix. 37; Rom. iv. 3; x. 11; xi. 2; Gal. iv. 30; 1 Tim. v. 18: Jas. ii. 23; iv. 5 f.), vocal with the conviction expressed by James (iv. 5) that Scripture cannot speak in vain. They indicate a certain confusion in current speech between " Scripture " and " God," the outgrowth of a deep-seated conviction that the word of Scripture is the word of God. It was not " Scripture " that spoke to Pharaoh, or gave his great promise to Abraham, but God. But " Scripture " and " God " lay so close together in the minds of the writers of the New Testament that they could naturally speak of " Scripture " doing what Scripture records God as doing. It was, however, even more natural to them to speak casually of God saying what the Scriptures say; and accordingly we meet with forms of speech such as these: " Wherefore, even as the Holy Spirit saith, To-day if ye shall hear His voice," etc. (Heb. iii. 7, quoting Ps. xcv. 7); " Thou art God . . . who by the mouth of thy servant David hast said, Why did the heathen rage," etc. (Acts iv. 25 Authorized Version, quoting Ps. ii. 1); " He that raised him from the dead . . . hath spoken on this wise, I will give you . . . because he saith also in another [place] . . ." (Acts xiii. 34, quoting Isa. lv. 3 and Ps. xvi. 10), and the like. The words put into God's mouth in each case are not words of God recorded in the Scriptures, but just Scripture words in themselves. When we take the two classes of passages together, in the one of which the Scriptures are spoken of as God, while in the other God is spoken of as if He were the Scriptures, we may perceive how close the identification of the two was in the minds of the writers of the New Testament.

This identification is strikingly observable in certain ca-
tenae of quotations, in which there are brought together a
number of passages of Scripture closely connected with one another. The first chapter of the Epistle to the Hebrews supplies
an example. We may begin with ver. 5: " For unto which of
the angels said he " — the subject being necessarily " God "
— " at any time, Thou art my Son, this day have I begotten
thee? " — the citation being from Ps. ii. 7 and very appropriate in the mouth of God — " and again, I will be to him a
Father, and he shall be to me a Son? " — from 2 S. vii. 14,
again a declaration of God's own — " And when he again bringeth in the firstborn into the world he saith, And let all the angels of God worship him " — from Deut. xxxii. 43, Septuagint,
or Ps. xcvii. 7, in neither of which is God the speaker — " And
of the angels he saith, Who maketh his angels winds, and his
ministers a flame of fire " — from Ps. civ. 4, where again God
is not the speaker but is spoken of in the third person — " but
of the Son he saith. Thy throne, O God, etc." — from Ps. xlv.
6.7 where again God is not the speaker, but is addressed —
" And, Thou, Lord, in the beginning," etc. — from Ps. cii. 25–
27, where again God is not the speaker but is addressed —
" But of which of the angels hath he said at any time, Sit thou
on my right hand? " etc. — from Ps. cx. 1, in which God is the
speaker. Here we have passages in which God is the speaker
and passages in which God is not the speaker, but is addressed
or spoken of, indiscriminately assigned to God, because they
all have it in common that they are words of Scripture, and as
words of Scripture are words of God. Similarly in Rom. xv.
9 ff. we have a series of citations the first of which is introduced
by " as it is written," and the next two by " again he saith,"
and " again," and the last by " and again, Isaiah saith," the
first being from Ps. xviii. 49; the second from Deut. xxxii. 43;
the third from Ps. cxvii. 1; and the last from Isa. xi. 10. Only
the last (the only one here assigned to the human author) is a
word of God in the text of the Old Testament.

This view of the Scriptures as a compact mass of words of
God occasioned the formation of a designation for them by

which this their character was explicitly expressed. This designation is " the sacred oracles," " the oracles of God." It occurs with extraordinary frequency in Philo, who very commonly refers to Scripture as " the sacred oracles " and cites its several passages as each an " oracle." Sharing, as they do, Philo's conception of the Scriptures as, in all their parts, a word of God, the New Testament writers naturally also speak of them under this designation. The classical passage is Rom. iii. 2 (cf. Heb. v. 12; Acts vii. 38). Here Paul begins an enumeration of the advantages which belonged to the chosen people above other nations; and, after declaring these advantages to have been great and numerous, he places first among them all their possession of the Scriptures: " What advantage then hath the Jew? or what is the profit of circumcision? Much every way: first of all, that they were intrusted with the oracles of God." That by " the oracles of God " here are meant just the Holy Scriptures in their entirety, conceived as a direct Divine revelation, and not any portions of them, or elements in them more especially thought of as revelatory, is perfectly clear from the wide contemporary use of this designation in this sense by Philo, and is put beyond question by the presence in the New Testament of habitudes of speech which rest on and grow out of the conception of Scripture embodied in this term. From the point of view of this designation, Scripture is thought of as the living voice of God speaking in all its parts directly to the reader; and, accordingly, it is cited by some such formula as " it is said," and this mode of citing Scripture duly occurs as an alternative to " it is written " (Lk. iv. 12, replacing " it is written " in Mt.; Heb. iii. 15; cf. Rom. iv. 18). It is due also to this point of view that Scripture is cited, not as what God or the Holy Spirit " said," but what He " says," the present tense emphasizing the living voice of God speaking in Scriptures to the individual soul (Heb. iii. 7; Acts xiii. 35; Heb. i. 7. 8. 10; Rom. xv. 10). And especially there is due to it the peculiar usage by which Scripture is cited by the simple " saith," without expressed subject, the subject being too well understood, when Scripture is adduced, to require stating; for who could

be the speaker of the words of Scripture but God only (Rom.
xv. 10; 1 Cor. vi. 16; 2 Cor. vi. 2; Gal. iii. 16; Eph. iv. 8; v.
14)? The analogies of this pregnant subjectless " saith " are
very widespread. It was with it that the ancient Pythagoreans
and Platonists and the mediaeval Aristotelians adduced each
their master's teaching; it was with it that, in certain circles,
the judgments of Hadrian's great jurist Salvius Julianus were
cited; African stylists were even accustomed to refer by it to
Sallust, their great model. There is a tendency, cropping out
occasionally, in the old Testament, to omit the name of God
as superfluous, when He, as the great logical subject always in
mind, would be easily understood (cf. Job xx. 23; xxi. 17; Ps.
cxiv. 2; Lam. iv. 22). So, too, when the New Testament writers
quoted Scripture there was no need to say whose word it was:
that lay beyond question in every mind. This usage, accordingly, is a specially striking intimation of the vivid sense which
the New Testament writers had of the Divine origin of the
Scriptures, and means that in citing them they were acutely
conscious that they were citing immediate words of God. How
completely the Scriptures were to them just the word of God
may be illustrated by a passage like Gal. iii. 16: " He saith not,
And to seeds, as of many; but as of one, And to thy seed, which
is Christ." We have seen Our Lord hanging an argument on
the very words of Scripture (Jn. x. 34); elsewhere His reasoning depends on the particular tense (Mt. xxii. 32) or word
(Mt. xxii. 43) used in Scripture. Here Paul's argument rests
similarly on a grammatical form. No doubt it is the grammatical form of the word which God is recorded as having spoken
to Abraham that is in question. But Paul knows what grammatical form God employed in speaking to Abraham only as
the Scriptures have transmitted it to him; and, as we have
seen, in citing the words of God and the words of Scripture he
was not accustomed to make any distinction between them. It
is probably the Scriptural word as a Scriptural word, therefore,
which he has here in mind: though, of course, it is possible
that what he here witnesses to is rather the detailed trustworthiness of the Scriptural record than its direct divinity —

if we can separate two things which apparently were not separated in Paul's mind. This much we can at least say without
straining, that the designation of Scripture as "scripture"
and its citation by the formula, "It is written," attest primarily its indefectible authority; the designation of it as
"oracles" and the adduction of it by the formula, "It says,"
attest primarily its immediate divinity. Its authority rests on
its divinity and its divinity expresses itself in its trustworthiness; and the New Testament writers in all their use of it
treat it as what they declare it to be — a God-breathed document, which, because God-breathed, as through and through
trustworthy in all its assertions, authoritative in all its declarations, and down to its last particular, the very word of God,
His "oracles."

That the Scriptures are throughout a Divine book, created
by the Divine energy and speaking in their every part with Divine authority directly to the heart of the readers, is the fundamental fact concerning them which is witnessed by Christ and
the sacred writers to whom we owe the New Testament. But
the strength and constancy with which they bear witness to
this primary fact do not prevent their recognizing by the side
of it that the Scriptures have come into being by the agency
of men. It would be inexact to say that they recognize a human
element in Scripture: they do not parcel Scripture out, assigning portions of it, or elements in it, respectively to God and
man. In their view the whole of Scripture in all its parts and in
all its elements, down to the least minutiae, in form of expression as well as in substance of teaching, is from God; but the
whole of it has been given by God through the instrumentality
of men. There is, therefore, in their view, not, indeed, a human
element or ingredient in Scripture, and much less human divisions or sections of Scripture, but a human side or aspect to
Scripture; and they do not fail to give full recognition to this
human side or aspect. In one of the primary passages which
has already been before us, their conception is given, if somewhat broad and very succinct, yet clear expression. No 'prophecy,' Peter tells us (2 Pet. i. 21), 'ever came by the will of

man; *but as borne by the Holy Ghost,* men spake from God.' Here the whole initiative is assigned to God, and such complete control of the human agents that the product is truly God's work. The men who speak in this "prophecy of scripture" speak not of themselves or out of themselves, but from "God": they speak only as they are "borne by the Holy Ghost." But it is they, after all, who speak. Scripture is the product of man, but only of man speaking from God and under such a control of the Holy Spirit as that in their speaking they are "borne" by Him. The conception obviously is that the Scriptures have been given by the instrumentality of men; and this conception finds repeated incidental expression throughout the New Testament.

It is this conception, for example, which is expressed when Our Lord, quoting Ps. cx., declares of its words that "David himself said in the Holy Spirit" (Mk. xii. 36). There is a certain emphasis here on the words being David's own words, which is due to the requirements of the argument Our Lord was conducting, but which none the less sincerely represents Our Lord's conception of their origin. They are David's own words which we find in Ps. cx., therefore; but they are David's own words, spoken not of his own motion merely, but "in the Holy Spirit," that is to say — we could not better paraphrase it — "as borne by the Holy Spirit." In other words, they are "God-breathed" words and therefore authoritative in a sense above what any words of David, not spoken in the Holy Spirit, could possibly be. Generalizing the matter, we may say that the words of Scripture are conceived by Our Lord and the New Testament writers as the words of their human authors when speaking "in the Holy Spirit," that is to say, by His initiative and under His controlling direction. The conception finds even more precise expression, perhaps, in such a statement as we find — it is Peter who is speaking and it is again a psalm which is cited — in Acts i. 16, "The Holy Spirit spake by the mouth of David." Here the Holy Spirit is adduced, of course, as the real author of what is said (and hence Peter's certainty that what is said will be fulfilled); but David's mouth is expressly designated as the instrument (it is the instrumental preposition that is used) by means of which the Holy Spirit speaks the Scripture in question. He does not speak save through David's mouth. Accordingly, in Acts iv. 25, ' the Lord that made the heaven and earth,' acting by His Holy Spirit, is declared to have spoken another psalm ' through the mouth of . . . David,' His " servant "; and in Mt. xiii. 35 still another psalm is adduced as " spoken through the prophet " (cf. Mt. ii. 5). In the very act of energetically asserting the Divine origin of Scripture the human instrumentality through which it is given is constantly recognized. The New Testament writers have, therefore, no difficulty in assigning Scripture to its human authors, or in discovering in Scripture traits due to its human authorship. They freely quote it by such simple formulae as these: " Moses saith " (Rom. x. 19); " Moses said " (Mt. xxii. 24; Mk. vii. 10; Acts iii. 22); " Moses writeth " (Rom. x. 5); " Moses wrote " (Mk. xii. 19; Lk. xx. 28); " Isaiah . . . saith " (Rom. x. 20); " Isaiah said " (Jn. xii. 39); " Isaiah crieth " (Rom. ix. 27); " Isaiah hath said before " (Rom. ix. 29); " said Isaiah the prophet " (Jn. i. 23); " did Isaiah prophesy " (Mk. vii. 6; Mt. xv. 7); " David saith " (Lk. xx. 42; Acts ii. 25; Rom. xi. 9); " David said " (Mk. xii. 36). It is to be noted that when thus Scripture is adduced by the names of its human authors, it is a matter of complete indifference whether the words adduced are comments of these authors or direct words of God recorded by them. As the plainest words of the human authors are assigned to God as their real author, so the most express words of God, repeated by the Scriptural writers, are cited by the names of these human writers (Mt. xv. 7; Mk. vii. 6; Rom. x. 5.19.20; cf. Mk. vii. 10 from the Decalogue). To say that " Moses " or " David says," is evidently thus only a way of saying that " Scripture says," which is the same as to say that " God says." Such modes of citing Scripture, accordingly, carry us little beyond merely connecting the name, or perhaps we may say the individuality, of the several writers with the portions of Scripture given through each. How it was given through them is left mean-

while, if not without suggestion, yet without specific explanation. We seem safe only in inferring this much: that the gift
of Scripture through its human authors took place by a process
much more intimate than can be expressed by the term " dictation," and that it took place in a process in which the control
of the Holy Spirit was too complete and pervasive to permit
the human qualities of the secondary authors in any way to
condition the purity of the product as the word of God. The
Scriptures, in other words, are conceived by the writers of the
New Testament as through and through God's book, in every
part expressive of His mind, given through men after a fashion
which does no violence to their nature as men, and constitutes
the book also men's book as well as God's, in every part expressive of the mind of its human authors.

If we attempt to get behind this broad statement and to
obtain a more detailed conception of the activities by which
God has given the Scriptures, we are thrown back upon somewhat general representations, supported by the analogy of the
modes of God's working in other spheres of His operation. It is
very desirable that we should free ourselves at the outset from
influences arising from the current employment of the term
" inspiration " to designate this process. This term is not a
Biblical term and its etymological implications are not perfectly accordant with the Biblical conception of the modes of
the Divine operation in giving the Scriptures. The Biblical
writers do not conceive of the Scriptures as a human product
breathed into by the Divine Spirit, and thus heightened in its
qualities or endowed with new qualities; but as a Divine product produced through the instrumentality of men. They do not
conceive of these men, by whose instrumentality Scripture is
produced, as working upon their own initiative, though ener-
gized by God to greater effort and higher achievement, but as
moved by the Divine initiative and borne by the irresistible
power of the Spirit of God along ways of His choosing to ends
of His appointment. The difference between the two conceptions may not appear great when the mind is fixed exclusively
upon the nature of the resulting product. But they are differ-

ing conceptions, and look at the production of Scripture from distinct points of view — the human and the Divine; and the involved mental attitudes toward the origin of Scripture are very diverse. The term "inspiration" is too firmly fixed, in both theological and popular usage, as the technical designation of the action of God in giving the Scriptures, to be replaced; and we may be thankful that its native implications lie as close as they do to the Biblical conceptions. Meanwhile, however, it may be justly insisted that it shall receive its definition from the representations of Scripture, and not be permitted to impose upon our thought ideas of the origin of Scripture derived from an analysis of its own implications, etymological or historical. The Scriptural conception of the relation of the Divine Spirit to the human authors in the production of Scripture is better expressed by the figure of "bearing" than by the figure of "inbreathing"; and when our Biblical writers speak of the action of the Spirit of God in this relation as a breathing, they represent it as a "breathing out" of the Scriptures by the Spirit, and not a "breathing into" the Scriptures by Him.

So soon, however, as we seriously endeavor to form for ourselves a clear conception of the precise nature of the Divine action in this "breathing out" of the Scriptures — this "bearing" of the writers of the Scriptures to their appointed goal of the production of a book of Divine trustworthiness and indefectible authority — we become acutely aware of a more deeply lying and much wider problem, apart from which this one of inspiration, technically so called, cannot be profitably considered. This is the general problem of the origin of the Scriptures and the part of God in all that complex of processes by the interaction of which these books, which we call the sacred Scriptures, with all their peculiarities, and all their qualities of whatever sort, have been brought into being. For, of course, these books were not produced suddenly, by some miraculous act — handed down complete out of heaven, as the phrase goes; but, like all other products of time, are the ultimate effect of many processes coöperating through long pe-

riods. There is to be considered, for instance, the preparation
of the material which forms the subject-matter of these books:
in a sacred history, say, for example, to be narrated; or in a
religious experience which may serve as a norm for record; or
in a logical elaboration of the contents of revelation which
may be placed at the service of God's people; or in the progressive revelation of Divine truth itself, supplying their culminating contents. And there is the preparation of the men to write
these books to be considered, a preparation physical, intellectual, spiritual, which must have attended them throughout
their whole lives, and, indeed, must have had its beginning in
their remote ancestors, and the effect of which was to bring the
right men to the right places at the right times, with the right
endowments, impulses, acquirements, to write just the books
which were designed for them. When " inspiration," technically so called, is superinduced on lines of preparation like
these, it takes on quite a different aspect from that which it
bears when it is thought of as an isolated action of the Divine
Spirit operating out of all relation to historical processes. Representations are sometimes made as if, when God wished to
produce sacred books which would incorporate His will — a
series of letters like those of Paul, for example — He was reduced to the necessity of going down to earth and painfully
scrutinizing the men He found there, seeking anxiously for the
one who, on the whole, promised best for His purpose; and
then violently forcing the material He wished expressed
through him, against his natural bent, and with as little loss
from his recalcitrant characteristics as possible. Of course,
nothing of the sort took place. If God wished to give His people a series of letters like Paul's, He prepared a Paul to write
them, and the Paul He brought to the task was a Paul who
spontaneously would write just such letters.

If we bear this in mind, we shall know what estimate to
place upon the common representation to the effect that the
human characteristics of the writers must, and in point of fact
do, condition and qualify the writings produced by them, the
implication being that, therefore, we cannot get from man a

pure word of God. As light that passes through the colored glass of a cathedral window, we are told, is light from heaven, but is stained by the tints of the glass through which it passes; so any word of God which is passed through the mind and soul of a man must come out discolored by the personality through which it is given, and just to that degree ceases to be the pure word of God. But what if this personality has itself been formed by God into precisely the personality it is, for the express purpose of communicating to the word given through it just the coloring which it gives it? What if the colors of the stained-glass window have been designed by the architect for the express purpose of giving to the light that floods the cathedral precisely the tone and quality it receives from them? What if the word of God that comes to His people is framed by God into the word of God it is, precisely by means of the qualities of the men formed by Him for the purpose, through which it is given? When we think of God the Lord giving by His Spirit a body of authoritative Scriptures to His people, we must remember that He is the God of providence and of grace as well as of revelation and inspiration, and that He holds all the lines of preparation as fully under His direction as He does the specific operation which we call technically, in the narrow sense, by the name of "inspiration." The production of the Scriptures is, in point of fact, a long process, in the course of which numerous and very varied Divine activities are involved, providential, gracious, miraculous, all of which must be taken into account in any attempt to explain the relation of God to the production of Scripture. When they are all taken into account we can no longer wonder that the resultant Scriptures are constantly spoken of as the pure word of God. We wonder, rather, that an additional operation of God — what we call specifically "inspiration," in its technical sense — was thought necessary. Consider, for example, how a piece of sacred history — say the Book of Chronicles, or the great historical work, Gospel and Acts, of Luke — is brought to the writing. There is first of all the preparation of the history to be written: God the Lord leads the sequence of occurrences through the development He has designed for them that they may convey their lessons to His people: a " teleological " or " aetiological " character is inherent in the very course of events. Then He prepares a man, by birth, training, experience, gifts of grace, and, if need be, of revelation, capable of appreciating this historical development and eager to search it out, thrilling in all his being with its lessons and bent upon making them clear and effective to others. When, then, by His providence, God sets this man to work on the writing of this history, will there not be spontaneously written by him the history which it was Divinely intended should be written? Or consider how a psalmist would be prepared to put into moving verse a piece of normative religious experience: how he would be born with just the right quality of religious sensibility, of parents through whom he should receive just the right hereditary bent, and from whom he should get precisely the right religious example and training, in circumstances of life in which his religious tendencies should be developed precisely on right lines; how he would be brought through just the right experiences to quicken in him the precise emotions he would be called upon to express, and finally would be placed in precisely the exigencies which would call out their expression. Or consider the providential preparation of a writer of a didactic epistle — by means of which he should be given the intellectual breadth and acuteness, and be trained in habitudes of reasoning, and placed in the situations which would call out precisely the argumentative presentation of Christian truth which was required of him. When we give due place in our thoughts to the universality of the providential government of God, to the minuteness and completeness of its sway, and to its invariable efficacy, we may be inclined to ask what is needed beyond this mere providential government to secure the production of sacred books which should be in every detail absolutely accordant with the Divine will.

The answer is, Nothing is needed beyond mere providence to secure such books — provided only that it does not lie in the Divine purpose that these books should possess qualities which rise above the powers of men to produce, even under the most complete Divine guidance. For providence is guidance; and guidance can bring one only so far as his own power can carry him. If heights are to be scaled above man's native power to achieve, then something more than guidance, however effective, is necessary. This is the reason for the superinduction, at the end of the long process of the production of Scripture, of the additional Divine operation which we call technically " inspiration." By it, the Spirit of God, flowing confluently in with the providentially and graciously determined work of men, spontaneously producing under the Divine directions the writings appointed to them, gives the product a Divine quality unattainable by human powers alone. Thus these books become not merely the word of godly men, but the immediate word of God Himself, speaking directly as such to the minds and hearts of every reader. The value of " inspiration " emerges, thus, as twofold. It gives to the books written under its " bearing " a quality which is truly superhuman; a trustworthiness, an authority, a searchingness, a profundity, a profitableness which is altogether Divine. And it speaks this Divine word immediately to each reader's heart and conscience; so that he does not require to make his way to God, painfully, perhaps even uncertainly, through the words of His servants, the human instruments in writing the Scriptures, but can listen directly to the Divine voice itself speaking immediately in the Scriptural word to him.

That the writers of the New Testament themselves conceive the Scriptures to have been produced thus by Divine operations extending through the increasing ages and involving a multitude of varied activities, can be made clear by simply attending to the occasional references they make to this or that step in the process. It lies, for example, on the face of their expositions, that they looked upon the Biblical history as teleological. Not only do they tell us that " whatsoever things were written aforetime were written for our learning, that through patience and through comfort of the scriptures we might have hope " (Rom. xv. 4; cf. Rom. iv. 23.24); they speak also of the course of the historical events themselves as guided for our benefit: " Now these things happened unto them by way of example " — in a typical fashion, in such a way that, as they occurred, a typical character, or predictive reference impressed itself upon them; that is to say, briefly, the history occurred as it did in order to bear a message to us — " and they were written for our admonition, upon whom the ends of the ages are come " (1 Cor. x. 11; cf. ver. 6). Accordingly, it has become a commonplace of Biblical exposition that " the history of redemption itself is a typically progressive one " (Küper), and is " in a manner impregnated with the prophetic element," so as to form a " part of a great plan which stretches from the fall of man to the first consummation of all things in glory; and, in so far as it reveals the mind of God toward man, carries a respect to the future not less than to the present " (P. Fairbairn). It lies equally on the face of the New Testament allusions to the subject that its writers understood that the preparation of men to become vehicles of God's message to man was not of yesterday, but had its beginnings in the very origin of their being. The call by which Paul, for example, was made an apostle of Jesus Christ was sudden and apparently without antecedents; but it is precisely this Paul who reckons this call as only one step in a long process, the beginnings of which antedated his own existence: " But when it was the good pleasure of God, who separated me, even from my mother's womb, and called me through his grace, to reveal his Son in me " (Gal. i. 15.16; cf. Jer. i. 5; Isa. xlix. 1.5). The recognition by the writers of the New Testament of the experiences of God's grace, which had been vouchsafed to them as an integral element in their fitting to be the bearers of His gospel to others, finds such pervasive expression that the only difficulty is to select from the mass the most illustrative passages. Such a statement as Paul gives in the opening verses of 2 Cor. is thoroughly typical. There he represents that he has been afflicted and comforted to the end that he might " be able to comfort them that are in any affliction, through the comfort wherewith " he had himself been " comforted of God." For, he explains, "Whether we are afflicted, it is for your comfort and salvation; or whether we are comforted, it is for your comfort, which worketh in the patient enduring of the same sufferings which we also suffer" (2 Cor. i. 4–6). It is beyond question, therefore, that the New Testament writers, when they declare the Scriptures to be the product of the Divine breath, and explain this as meaning that the writers of these Scriptures wrote them only as borne by the Holy Spirit in such a fashion that they spoke, not out of themselves, but "from God," are thinking of this operation of the Spirit only as the final act of God in the production of the Scriptures, superinduced upon a long series of processes, providential, gracious, miraculous, by which the matter of Scripture had been prepared for writing, and the men for writing it, and the writing of it had been actually brought to pass. It is this final act in the production of Scripture which is technically called "inspiration"; and inspiration is thus brought before us as, in the minds of the writers of the New Testament, that particular operation of God in the production of Scripture which takes effect at the very point of the writing of Scripture — understanding the term "writing" here as inclusive of all the processes of the actual composition of Scripture, the investigation of documents, the collection of facts, the excogitation of conclusions, the adaptation of exhortations as means to ends and the like — with the effect of giving to the resultant Scripture a specifically supernatural character, and constituting it a Divine, as well as human, book. Obviously the mode of operation of this Divine activity moving to this result is conceived, in full accord with the analogy of the Divine operations in other spheres of its activity, in providence and in grace alike, as confluent with the human activities operative in the case; as, in a word, of the nature of what has come to be known as "immanent action."

It will not escape observation that thus "inspiration" is made a mode of "revelation." We are often exhorted, to be sure, to distinguish sharply between "inspiration" and "revelation"; and the exhortation is just when "revelation" is taken in one of its narrower senses, of, say, an external mani-

festation of God, or of an immediate communication from God
in words. But " inspiration " does not differ from " revelation "
in these narrowed senses as genus from genus, but as a species
of one genus differs from another. That operation of God which
we call " inspiration," that is to say, that operation of the
Spirit of God by which He " bears " men in the process of composing Scripture, so that they write, not of themselves, but
" from God," is one of the modes in which God makes known
to men His being, His will, His operations, His purposes. It is
as distinctly a mode of revelation as any mode of revelation
can be, and therefore it performs the same office which all revelation performs, that is to say, in the express words of Paul,
it makes men wise, and makes them wise unto salvation. All
" special " or " supernatural " revelation (which is redemptive
in its very idea, and occupies a place as a substantial element
in God's redemptive processes) has precisely this for its end;
and Scripture, as a mode of the redemptive revelation of God,
finds its fundamental purpose just in this: if the " inspiration " by which Scripture is produced renders it trustworthy
and authoritative, it renders it trustworthy and authoritative
only that it may the better serve to make men wise unto salvation. Scripture is conceived, from the point of view of the writers of the New Testament, not merely as the record of revelations, but as itself a part of the redemptive revelation of God;
not merely as the record of the redemptive acts by which God
is saving the world, but as itself one of these redemptive acts,
having its own part to play in the great work of establishing
and building up the kingdom of God. What gives it a place
among the redemptive acts of God is its Divine origination,
taken in its widest sense, as inclusive of all the Divine operations, providential, gracious and expressly supernatural, by
which it has been made just what it is — a body of writings
able to make wise unto salvation, and profitable for making
the man of God perfect. What gives it its place among the
modes of revelation is, however, specifically the culminating
one of these Divine operations, which we call " Inspiration ";
that is to say, the action of the Spirit of God in so " bearing "

its human authors in their work of producing Scripture, as that in these Scriptures they speak, not out of themselves, but " from God." It is this act by virtue of which the Scriptures may properly be called " God-breathed."

It has been customary among a certain school of writers to speak of the Scriptures, because thus " inspired," as a Divine-human book, and to appeal to the analogy of Our Lord's Divine-human personality to explain their peculiar qualities as such. The expression calls attention to an important fact, and the analogy holds good a certain distance. There are human and Divine sides to Scripture, and, as we cursorily examine it, we may perceive in it, alternately, traits which suggest now the one, now the other factor in its origin. But the analogy with Our Lord's Divine-human personality may easily be pressed beyond reason. There is no hypostatic union between the Divine and the human in Scripture; we cannot parallel the " inscripturation " of the Holy Spirit and the incarnation of the Son of God. The Scriptures are merely the product of Divine and human forces working together to produce a product in the production of which the human forces work under the initiation and prevalent direction of the Divine: the person of Our Lord unites in itself Divine and human natures, each of which retains its distinctness while operating only in relation to the other. Between such diverse things there can exist only a remote analogy; and, in point of fact, the analogy in the present instance amounts to no more than that in both cases Divine and human factors are involved, though very differently. In the one they unite to constitute a Divine-human person, in the other they coöperate to perform a Divine-human work. Even so distant an analogy may enable us, however, to recognize that as, in the case of Our Lord's person, the human nature remains truly human while yet it can never fall into sin or error because it can never act out of relation with the Divine nature into conjunction with which it has been brought; so in the case of the production of Scripture by the conjoint action of human and Divine factors, the human factors have acted as human factors, and have left their mark on the product as such, and yet cannot have fallen into that error which we say it is human to fall into, because they have not acted apart from the Divine factors, by themselves, but only under their unerring guidance.

The New Testament testimony is to the Divine origin and qualities of " Scripture "; and " Scripture " to the writers of the New Testament was fundamentally, of course, the Old Testament. In the primary passage, in which we are told that " every " or " all Scripture " is " God-breathed," the direct reference is to the " sacred writings " which Timothy had had in knowledge since his infancy, and these were, of course, just the sacred books of the Jews (2 Tim. iii. 16). What is explicit here is implicit in all the allusions to inspired Scriptures in the New Testament. Accordingly, it is frequently said that our entire testimony to the inspiration of Scripture concerns the Old Testament alone. In many ways, however, this is overstated. Our present concern is not with the extent of " Scripture " but with the nature of " Scripture "; and we cannot present here the considerations which justify extending to the New Testament the inspiration which the New Testament writers attribute to the Old Testament. It will not be out of place, however, to point out simply that the New Testament writers obviously themselves made this extension. They do not for an instant imagine themselves, as ministers of a new covenant, less in possession of the Spirit of God than the ministers of the old covenant: they freely recognize, indeed, that they have no sufficiency of themselves, but they know that God has made them sufficient (2 Cor. iii. 5.6). They prosecute their work of proclaiming the gospel, therefore, in full confidence that they speak " by the Holy Spirit " (1 Pet. i. 12), to whom they attribute both the matter and form of their teaching (1 Cor. ii. 13). They, therefore, speak with the utmost assurance of their teaching (Gal. i. 7.8); and they issue commands with the completest authority (1 Thess. iv. 2.14; 2 Thess. iii. 6.12), making it, indeed, the test of whether one has the Spirit that he should recognize what they demand as commandments of God (1 Cor. xiv. 37). It would be strange, indeed, if these high claims were made for their oral teaching and commandments exclusively. In point of fact, they are made explicitly also for their written injunctions. It was " the things " which Paul was " writing," the recognition of which as commands of the Lord, he makes the test of a Spirit-led man (1 Cor. xiv. 37). It is his " word by this epistle," obedience to which he makes the condition of Christian communion (2 Thess. iii. 14). There seems involved in such an attitude toward their own teaching, oral and written, a claim on the part of the New Testament writers to something very much like the " inspiration " which they attribute to the writers of the Old Testament.

And all doubt is dispelled when we observe the New Testament writers placing the writings of one another in the same category of " Scripture " with the books of the Old Testament. The same Paul who, in 2 Tim. iii. 16, declared that ' every ' or ' all scripture is God-breathed ' had already written in 1 Tim. v. 18: " For the scripture saith, Thou shall not muzzle the ox when he treadeth out the corn. And, The laborer is worthy of his hire." The first clause here is derived from Deuteronomy and the second from the Gospel of Luke, though both are cited as together constituting, or better, forming part of the " Scripture " which Paul adduces as so authoritative as by its mere citation to end all strife. Who shall say that, in the declaration of the later epistle that " all " or " every " Scripture is God-breathed, Paul did not have Luke, and, along with Luke, whatever other new books he classed with the old under the name of Scripture, in the back of his mind, along with those old books which Timothy had had in his hands from infancy? And the same Peter who declared that every " prophecy of scripture " was the product of men who spoke " from God," being ' borne ' by the Holy Ghost (2 Pet. i. 21), in this same epistle (iii. 16), places Paul's Epistles in the category of Scripture along with whatever other books deserve that name. For Paul, says he, wrote these epistles, not out of his own wisdom, but " according to the wisdom given to him," and though there are some things in them hard to be understood, yet it is only " the ignorant and unstedfast " who wrest these difficult passages — as what else could be expected of men who wrest " also the other Scriptures " (obviously the Old Testament is meant) — " unto their own destruction " ? Is it possible to say that Peter could not have had these epistles of Paul also lurking somewhere in the back of his mind, along with " the other scriptures," when he told his readers that every " prophecy of scripture " owes its origin to the prevailing operation of the Holy Ghost? What must be understood in estimating the testimony of the New Testament writers to the inspiration of Scripture is that " Scripture " stood in their minds as the title of a unitary body of books, throughout the gift of God through His Spirit to His people; but that this body of writings was at the same time understood to be a growing aggregate, so that what is said of it applies to the new books which were being added to it as the Spirit gave them, as fully as to the old books which had come down to them from their hoary past. It is a mere matter of detail to determine precisely what new books were thus included by them in the category " Scripture." They tell us some of them themselves. Those who received them from their hands tell us of others. And when we put the two bodies of testimony together we find that they constitute just our New Testament. It is no pressure of the witness of the writers of the New Testament to the inspiration of the Scripture, therefore, to look upon it as covering the entire body of " Scriptures," the new books which they were themselves adding to this aggregate, as well as the old books which they had received as Scripture from the fathers. Whatever can lay claim by just right to the appellation of " Scripture," as employed in its eminent sense by those writers, can by the same just right lay claim to the " inspiration " which they ascribe to this Scripture."

LITERATURE. — J. Gerhard, " Loci Theolog.," Locus I; F. Turretin, " Instit.Theol.," Locus II; B. de Moor, " Comm. in J. Marckii Comp.," cap. ii; C. Hodge, " Syst. Theol.," New York, 1871, I, 151–86; Henry B. Smith, " The Inspiration of the Holy Scriptures," New York, 1855, new ed., Cincinnati, 1891; A. Kuyper, " Encyclopedie der heilige Godgeleerdheid," 1888–89, II, 347 ff., ET; " Enc of Sacred Theol.,"

New York, 1898, 341–563; also " De Schrift het woord Gods," Tiel, 1870; H. Bavinck, " Gereformeerde Dogmatiek," Kampen, 1006, I, 406–527; R. Haldane, " The Verbal Inspiration of the Scriptures Established," Edinburgh, 1830; J. T. Beck, " Einleitung in das System der christlichen Lehre," Stuttgart, 1838, 2d ed., 1870; A. G. Rudelbach, " Die Lehre von der Inspiration der heil. Schrift," *Zeitschrift für die gesammte Lutherische Theologie und Kirche*, 1840, 1, 1841, 1, 1842, 1; S. R. L. Gaussen, " Théopneustie ou inspiration plénière des saintes écritures[2]," Paris, 1842, ET by E. N. Kirk, New York, 1842; also " Theopneustia; the Plenary Inspiration of the Holy Scriptures," David Scott's tr., reëdited and revised by B. W. Carr, with a preface by C. H. Spurgeon, London, 1888; William Lee, " The Inspiration of the Holy Scriptures," Donellan Lecture, 1852, New York, 1857; James Bannerman, " Inspiration: the Infallible Truth and Divine Authority of the Holy Scriptures," Edinburgh, 1865; F. L. Patton, " The Inspiration of the Scriptures," Philadelphia, 1869 (reviewing Lee and Bannerman); Charles Elliott, " A Treatise on the Inspiration of the Holy Scriptures," Edinburgh, 1877; A. A. Hodge and B. B. Warfield, " Inspiration," *Presbyterian Review*, April, 1881, also tract, Philadelphia, 1881; R. Watts, " The Rule of Faith and the Doctrine of Inspiration," Edinburgh, 1885; A. Cave, " The Inspiration of the OT Inductively Considered," London, 1888; B. Manly, " The Bible Doctrine of Inspiration," New York, 1888; W. Rohnert, " Die Inspiration der heiligen Schrift und ihre Bestreiter," Leipzig, 1889; A. W. Dieckhoff, " Die Inspiration und Irrthumlosigkeit der heiligen Schrift," Leipzig, 1891; J. Wichelhaus, " Die Lehre der heiligen Schrift," Stuttgart, 1892; J. Macgregor, " The Revelation and the Record," Edinburgh, 1893; J. Urquhart, " The Inspiration and Accuracy of the Holy Scriptures," London, 1895; C. Pesch, " De Inspiratione Sacrae Scripturae," Freiburg, 1906; James Orr, " Revelation and Inspiration," London, 1910.

V

"SCRIPTURE," "THE SCRIPTURES," IN THE NEW TESTAMENT

"SCRIPTURE," "THE SCRIPTURES," IN THE NEW TESTAMENT [1]

THE scope of this article does not permit the full discussion in it of the employment of Scripture, or of the estimate put upon Scripture, by either our Lord or the writers of the New Testament. It is strictly limited to what is necessary to exhibit the use of the terms 'Scripture,' 'The Scriptures,' in the New Testament and the more immediate implications of this use.

This use was an inheritance, not an invention. The idea of a 'canon' of 'Sacred Scriptures,' and, with the idea, the 'canon' itself were derived by Christianity from Judaism. The Jews possessed a body of writings, consisting of 'Law, Prophets and (other) Scriptures (K'thubhim),' though they were often called for brevity's sake merely 'the Law and the Prophets' or even simply 'the Law.' These 'Sacred Scriptures'' (כִּתְבֵי הַקֹּדֶשׁ), — or, as they were very frequently pregnantly called, this 'Scripture' (הכתוב), or these 'Books' (הספרים) or, even sometimes, in the singular, this 'Book' (הספר) — were looked upon as all drawing their origin from divine inspiration and as possessed in all their extent of divine authority. Whatever stood written in them was a word of God, and was therefore referred to indifferently as something which 'the Scripture says' (אמר קרא or אמר הכתיב or כתיב קרא) or 'the All-merciful says' (אמר רחמנא), or even simply 'He says' (כן הוא אומר or merely ואומר) — that God is the speaker being too fully understood to require explicit expression. Every precept or dogma was supposed to be grounded in Scriptural teaching, and possessed authority only as buttressed by a Scriptural passage, introduced com-

---

[1] A condensation of this article was published in Dr. Hastings' "Dictionary of Christ and the Gospels," sub voc. *Scripture*. It has been thought desirable after this interval to print the entire article. (From *The Princeton Theological Review* v. VIII, 1910, pp. 561–612.)

115

monly by one of the formulas, 'for it is said' (שׁנאמר), or 'as it is written' (דכתיב or כדכתיב), though of course a great variety of less frequently occurring similar formulas of adduction are found.[2]

Greek-speaking Jews naturally tended merely to reproduce in their new language the designations and forms of adduction of the sacred books current among their compatriots. This process was no doubt facilitated by the existence among the Greeks themselves of a pregnant legislative use of γράφω, γραφή, γράμμα, in which they were already freighted with a certain implication of authority.[3] But it is very easy to make too much of this (as e. g., Deissmann does), and the simple fact should not be obscured that the Greek-speaking Jews follow the usage of the Jews in general. It may no doubt very possibly be due in part to his Graecizing tendencies that the Scriptures are spoken of by Josephus apparently with predilection as the "Sacred Books" (ἱεραὶ βίβλοι or ἱερὰ βιβλία) or "Sacred Scriptures" (ἱερὰ γράμματα) or more fully still as the "Books of the Sacred Scriptures" (αἱ ἱερῶν γραφῶν βίβλοι); and quoted with the formula γέγραπται or more frequently ἀναγέγραπται — all of which are forms which would be familiar to Greek ears, with a general implication of authority.[4] Perhaps, however, the influence of the Greek usage is more clearly traceable in certain passages of the LXX in which γραφή may seem to hover between the pregnant Greek

[2] Edersheim, "Life and Times of Jesus," etc., Ed. 1, I. p. 187, note 2; cf., in general, Surenhusius, ספר המשוה sive βίβλος καταλλαγῆς (1713), pp. 1–36; Döpke, "Hermeneutik der NT. Schriftsteller" (1829), I. pp. 60–69; Pinner, Translation of the Tract Berachoth, Introd. p. 21b; Zunz, "Gottesdienstliche Vorträge der Juden," p. 44; Weber, "Jüdische Theologie" (1897) § 20, p. 80 seq.; Schürer, "Jewish People" II. i. p. 311; Buhl, "Canon and Text," § 2; Ryle, "Canon of O. T.," Excursus E.

[3] Cf. the passages in the Lexicons, and especially in Deissmann, "Bible Studies," 112, 249, and Cremer, "Biblico-Theol. Lex." sub vocc. especially the later eds.

[4] Cf. Deissmann, "Bible Studies," p. 149, note 4. For Josephus' use of Scripture, in general, see Gerlach, "Die Weissagungen d. AT. in d. Schrift. d. F. Josephus (1863), and Dienstfertig, "Die Prophetologie in d. Religionsphilosophie d. ersten nachchristlichen Jahrhunderts" (1892), the latter of whom discusses Philo's ideas of Scripture also.

sense of authoritative 'ordinance,' and the pregnant Hebrew
sense of authoritative 'Scripture.' When, for example, we
read in I Chron. xv. 15, "And the sons of the Levites took
upon themselves with staves the Ark of God, ὡς ἐνετείλατο
Μωυσῆς ἐν λόγῳ θεοῦ κατὰ τὴν γραφήν," we scarcely know
whether we are to translate the κατὰ τὴν γραφήν (which has
no equivalent in the Hebrew) by "according to the precept,"
or by "according to the Scriptures." Something of the same
hesitancy is felt with reference to the similar passages:
II Chron. xxx. 5, "Because the multitude had not done it
lately κατὰ τὴν γραφήν" (= כַּכָּתוּב); II Chron. xxx. 18, "But
they ate the passover παρὰ τὴν γραφήν" (= בְּלֹא כַכָּתוּב);
II Esdr. vi. 18, "And they established the priests in their
courses and the Levites in their divisions for the service of
God in Jerusalem, κατὰ τὴν γραφὴν βίβλου Μωυσῆ" (= כִּכְתָב
סְפַר מֹשֶׁה); I Chron. xxviii. 19, "All these things David gave
to Solomon ἐν γραφῇ χειρὸς κυρίου" (= בִּכְתָב מִיַּד יְהֹוָה): II Chron.
xxxv. 4, "Prepare yourselves . . . κατὰ τὴν γραφὴν Δαυίδ . . .
καὶ διὰ χειρὸς Σαλωμὼν" (= בִּכְתָב דָּוִיד וּבְמִכְתַּב שְׁלֹמֹה); I Esdr. i. 4,
"κατὰ τὴν γραφὴν Δαυίδ" κτλ; and especially the very instruc-
tive passage II Esdr. vii. 22, "For which there is no γραφή."
Similarly in II Esdr. iii. 2, "κατὰ τὰ γεγραμμένα (= כַּכָּתוּב) in
the law of Moses," τὰ γεγραμμένα might very well appeal to
a Greek ear as simply "the prescriptions"; and there are a
series of passages in which γέγραπται might very readily be
taken in the Greek sense of "it is prescribed," such as Josh.
ix. 4, (viii. 31), II Kings xiv. 6, xxiii. 21, II Chron. xxiii. 18,
xxv. 4, Neh. x. 34, (35), 35, (37), Tob. i. 6. Should this interpretation be put on these passages, there would be left in the
LXX little unalloyed trace of the peculiar Jewish usage of
pregnantly referring to Scripture as such by that term, and
citing it with the authoritative 'It is written.' For clear instances of the former usage we should have to go to IV Macc.
xviii. 14, and of the latter to Dan. ix. 13, and to the Greek
additions to Job (xlii. 18).[5] Philo on the other hand is abso-

---

[5] IV Macc. xviii. 14, "And he reminded you of Ἡσαΐου γραφήν which says,
Though you pass through fire, &c."; Dan. ix. 13, "Καθὼς γέγραπται in the law

lutely determined in his usage by his inherited Jewish habits of thought. With him the Sacred books are by predilection a body of divine Oracles and are designated ordinarily either ὁ λόγος with various adjectival enhancements — 'prophetic,' 'divine,' 'sacred' — or, perhaps even more commonly, "the Oracles," or even "the Oracle," (οἱ χρησμοί, τὰ λόγια, ὁ χρησμός, τὸ λόγιον, or even possibly the anarthrous χρησμός, λόγιον); and are adduced (as is also most frequently the case in the Mishna, cf. Edersheim as cited) rather with the formula, "As it is said," than with the "As it is written" which would more naturally convey to Greek ears the sense of authoritative declarations. Of course Philo also speaks on occasion (for this too is a truly Jewish mode of speech) of these "Oracles" as "the Sacred Books" (ἰα ἱεραὶ βίβλοι. "De Vita Moysis," iii. 23, Mangey ii. 163; "Quod det. pot. insid." 44, Mangey i. 222), or as "the Sacred Scriptures" (αἱ ἱερώταται γραφαί, "De Abrah." i, Mangey ii. 2; ἱεραὶ γραφαί, "Quis rerum div. heres." 32, Mangey i. 495; τὰ ἱερὰ γράμματα, "Legat. ad Caium," 29, Mangey ii. 574); and adduces them with the pregnant γέγραπται. But the comparative infrequency of these designations in his pages is very noticeable.[6]

What it is of importance especially to note is that there was nothing left for Christianity to invent in the way of designating the Sacred Books taken over from the Jewish Church pregnantly as "Scripture," and currently adducing their authority with the pregnant 'It is written.' The Christian writers merely continued in their entirety the established usages of the Synagogue in this matter, already prepared to their hands in Hebrew and Greek alike. There is probably not a single mode of alluding to or citing Scripture in all the

---

of Moses, all this evil is come upon us"; Job xlii. 18, "And Job died an old man and full of days, γέγραπται δὲ that he shall rise again along with those whom the Lord will raise."

[6] Philo's designations of Scripture have been collected by Hornemann, "Observationes ad illustr. doctr. de V. T. ex Philone" (1775); more briefly by Eichhorn, "Einleitung in d. A. T.;" and less satisfactorily by Ryle, "Philo and Holy Scripture." Cf. The Presbyterian and Reformed Review, x. 504 (July, 1899) and xi. 235 (April, 1900).

New Testament which does not find its exact parallel among the Rabbis.[7] The New Testament so far evinces itself a thoroughly Jewish book. The several terms made use of in it, to be sure, as it was natural they should be, are employed with some sensitiveness to their inherent implications as Greek words; and the Greek legislative use of some of them gave them no doubt peculiar fitness for the service asked of them, and lent them a special significance to Gentile readers. But the application made of them by the New Testament writers nevertheless has its roots set in the soil of Jewish thought, from which they derive a fuller and deeper meaning than their most pregnant classical usage could accord them. Among these terms those which more particularly claim our attention at the moment are the two substantives γραφή and γράμμα, with their various qualifications, and the cognate verbal forms employed in citing writings pregnantly designated by these substantives. There is nothing in the New Testament usage of these terms peculiar to itself; and throughout the New Testament any differences that may be observed in their employment by the several writers are indicative merely of varying habits of speech within the limits of one well-settled general usage.

To the New Testament writers as to other Jews, the Sacred Books of what was in their circle now called the Old Covenant (II Cor. iii. 14), described according to their contents as "the Law, the Prophets and the Psalms" (Lk. xxiv. 44) — or more briefly as "the Law and the Prophets" (Matt. vii. 12, Lk. xvi. 16, cf. Acts xxviii. 23, Lk. xvi. 29–31) or merely as "the Law" (Jno. x. 34, I Cor. xiv. 21) or even "the Prophets," (Rom. xvi. 26),[8] — were, when thought of according to their nature, a body of "Sacred Scriptures" (Rom. i. 2, II Tim. iii. 16), or, with the omission of the unnecessary be-

---

[7] This has been shown in detail by, for example, Surenhusius and Döpke, as cited above.

[8] Sometimes the whole is spoken of, in accordance with its character as revelation, as "prophetical Scriptures" or "the Scriptures of the prophets" (cf. Matt. ii. 23, xi. 13, xxvi. 56; Lk. i. 70, xviii. 31, xxiv. 25, 27; Acts iii. 24, xiii. 27; Rom. i. 2, xvi. 26).

cause well-understood adjective, by way of eminence, "the Scriptures," "the Scripture," "Scripture," (Matt. xxii. 29, Jno. x. 35, I Pet. ii. 6). For employment in this designation, either of the substantives, γραφή or γράμμα, would apparently have been available; although of course with slightly differing suggestions arising from the differing implications of the forms and the respective general usages of the words. In Philo and Josephus the more usual of the two in this application is γράμμα, or, to speak more exactly, γράμματα, — for although γράμμα is sometimes in later Greek so employed in the singular [9] it is in the plural that this term most properly denotes that congeries of alphabetical signs which constitutes a book (cf. Latin, literae). In the New Testament on the contrary, this form is rare. The complete phrase, ἱερὰ γράμματα, which is found also both in Josephus (e. g. "Antt." proem. 3; iii. 7, 6; x. 10, 4; xiii. 5, 8) and in Philo (e. g., "DeVita Moys."i. 2, "Legat. ad Caium," 29) occurs in II Tim. iii. 15 as the current title of the Sacred Books, freighted with all its implications as such, or rather with those implications emphasized by its anarthrous employment, and particularly adverted to in the immediate context (verse 16).[10] Elsewhere in the New Testament, however, γράμματα scarcely occurs as a designation of Scripture. In Jno. v. 47, "But if ye believe not his (Moses') writings, how shall ye believe my (Jesus') words?" to be sure we must needs hesitate before we refuse to give to it this its most pregnant sense, especially since there appears to be an implication present that it would be more reprehensible to refuse trust to these "writings" of Moses than to the "words"

[9] Strabo, "Geog." i. 7, "Hecataeus left a γράμμα believed to be his from his other γραφή." Callimachus, "Epigr." xxiv. 4, "Plato's τὸ περὶ ψυχῆς γράμμα. In the Church Fathers τὸ θεῖον (or ἱερὸν) γράμμα occurs frequently for "Holy Scripture," e. g. Greg. Thaumat. in "Orig. orat. paneg. VI. ad fin.;" Epiphan. "Adv. Hær." III, ii. (lxxx. A.); Cyr. Al. "Epistula 50" (formerly 44): in Cyr. Al. "De Adver." p. 44, the N. T. is the νέον γράμμα; in Eus. h. e. x. 4fin, τῶν τεττάρων εὐαγγελίων τὸ γράμμα is the Gospels, etc.

[10] H. Holtzmann accordingly accurately comments on this passage: "The writer shares the Jewish view of the purely supernatural origin of Scripture in its strictest form, according to which 'theopneustie' is ascribed directly to the Scriptures." ("N. T. Theologie" ii. 261).

of Jesus Himself. But on the whole, the tendency of the most
recent exegesis to see in "his writings" here little more than
another way of saying "what he wrote," seems justified. The
only other passage which can come into consideration is
Jno. vii. 15, "How knoweth this man γράμματα, not having
learned?" in which some commentators still see a reference
to "the ἱερὰ γράμματα (II Tim. iii. 15) from which the Jewish
γραμματεῖς derived their title" (Th. Zahn,"Einleitung,"ii. 99).
Most readers, however, doubtless will agree that "letters"
in general are more naturally meant (cf. Acts xxvi. 24 and
Meyer's judicious note).[11] Practically, therefore, γράμμα is
eliminated; and γραφή, γραφαί, in their varied uses, remain
the sole terms employed in the New Testament in the sense
of "Scripture," "Scriptures."

This term, in singular or plural, occurs in the New Testament some fifty times (Gospels twenty-three, Acts seven,
Catholic Epistles six, Paul fourteen) and in every case bears
the technical sense in which it refers to the Scriptures by way
of eminence, the Scriptures of the Old Testament. This statement requires only such modification as is involved in noting
that from II Pet. iii. 16 (cf. I Tim. v. 18) it becomes apparent
that the New Testament writers were perfectly aware that
the term "Scripture" in its high sense was equally applicable
to their own writings as to the books included in the Old
Testament; or, to be more precise, that it included within
itself along with the writings which constituted the Old Testament those also which they were producing, as sharing with
the Old Testament books the high functions of the authoritative written word of God.[12] No modification needs to be

[11] For the currency of this sense, cf. G. Milligan, "Selections from the Greek
Papyri," p. 58, where commenting on the phrase μὴ ἰδότος γράμματα, he remarks:
"The phrase occurs in countless papyrus documents written either in whole or
in part by a scribe on behalf of the 'unlettered' author. Cf. the use of the corresponding adjective ἀγράμματος in Acts iv. 13 (cf. Jno. vii. 15, Ac. xxvi. 24) = 'unacquainted with literature or Rabbinical learning.'"

[12] On the significance of the plural αἱ γραφαί in 2 Pet. iii. 16, see below
p. 132. There is no justification for attempting to lower the high implication of
the term here (e. g. Huther, Spitta, Mayor in loc., Ladd "Doct. of Sacred Scripture," I. p. 211, note). The inclusion of New Testament books within the category

made for the benefit of the few passages in which words are
adduced as Scriptural which are not easily identified in the
Old Testament text.[13] The only passages which come strictly
under consideration here are Jno. vii. 38 and Jas. iv. 5, to
which may be added as essentially of the same kind (although
the term γραφή does not occur in connection with them),
I Cor. ii. 9, and Lk. ix. 49. It is enough to remark as to these
passages that, however difficult it may be to identify with
certainty the passages referred to, there is no reason to doubt
that Old Testament passages were in mind and were intended
to be referred to in every case (see Mayor on Jas. iv. 5, and
cf. Lightfoot on I Cor. ii. 9, Westcott on Jno. vii. 38, Godet
on Lk. xi. 49). In twenty out of the fifty instances in which
γραφή, γραφαί occur in the New Testament, it is the plural
form which is employed: and in all these cases except two the
article is present, — αἱ γραφαί the well-known Scriptures of
the Jewish people, or rather of the writer and his readers
alike. The two exceptions, moreover, are exceptions in appearance only, since in both cases adjectival definitions are
present, raising γραφαί to the same height to which the article
would have elevated it, and giving it the value of a proper
name (γραφαὶ ἅγιαι, Rom. i. 2, here first in extant literature;
γραφαὶ, προφητικαί, Rom. xvi. 26). The singular form occurs
some thirty times, and likewise with the article in every instance except these four: John xix. 37 'another Scripture';
II Tim. iii, 16 'every Scripture,' or 'all Scripture'; I Pet. ii. 6
'it is contained in Scripture'; II Pet. i. 20 'no prophecy of
Scripture.' Here too the exceptions, obviously, are only apparent, the noun being definite in every case whether by the
effect of its adjunct, or as the result of its use as a quasi-
proper-name. The distribution of the singular and plural forms
is perhaps worth noting. In Acts the singular (3) and plural
(4) occur with almost equal frequency: the plural prevails in
the Synoptic Gospels (Matt. plural only; Mk. plural 2 to 1;

of 'Scripture' is witnessed also in 1 Tim. v. 18, Ep. Barnabas iv. 14, 2 Clem.
Rom. ii. 4, and in the later Fathers *passim*. It is as early as literary Christianity.
    [13] See them in Hühn, "Die alttestamentlichen Citate," 270.

Lk. 3 to 1), while the singular prevails in the rest of the New Testament (Jno. 11 to 1; James 3 to 1; Peter 2 to 1, Paul 9 to 5). In the Gospels, the plural form occurs exclusively in Matthew, prevailingly in Mark and Luke, and rarely in John, of whom the singular is characteristic. The usage of the Gospels in detail is as follows: αἱ γραφαί, Matt. xxi. 42, xxii. 29, xxvi. 54, 56, Mk. xii. 24, xiv. 49, Lk. xxiv. 27, 32, 45, Jno. v. 39; ἡ γραφή, Mk. xii. 10, Lk. iv. 21, Jno. ii. 22, vii. 38, 42, x. 35, xiii. 18, xvii. 12, xix. 24, 28, 36, xx. 9; anarthrous γραφή, Jno. xix. 37 (but with ἑτέρα). No distinction is traceable between the usage of the Evangelists themselves and that of the Lord as reported by them. Matthew and Mark do not on their own account use the term at all, but only report it as used by our Lord: in Luke and John on the other hand it occurs not only in reports of our Lord's sayings (Lk. iv. 21, Jno. v. 39, vii. 38, 42, x. 35, xiii. 18, xvii. 12), and of the sayings of others (Lk. xxiv. 32), but also in the narrative of the Evangelists (Lk. xxiv. 27, 45, Jno. ii. 22, xix. 24, 28, 36, 37, xx. 9). To our Lord is ascribed the use indifferently of the plural (Matt. xxi. 42, xxii. 29, xxvi. 54, 56, Mk. xii. 24, xiv. 49, Jno. v. 39) and the singular (Mk. xii. 10, Lk. iv. 21, Jno. vii. 38, 42, x. 35, xiii. 18, xvii. 12), and that in all the forms of application in which the term occurs in the Gospels. So far as His usage of the term "Scripture" is concerned, our Lord is represented by the Evangelists, thus, as occupying precisely the same standpoint and employing precisely the same forms of designation, with precisely the same implications, which characterized the devout Jewish usage of His day. "Jesus," says B. Weiss, therefore, with substantial truth, "acknowledged the Scriptures of the Old Testament in their entire extent and their complete sacredness. 'The Scripture cannot be broken,' He says (Jno. x. 35) and forthwith grounds His argument upon its language." [14]

[14] "Das Leben Jesu," I. 441–442, E. T. II. 62–63. Cf. Haupt, "Die alttest. Citate in d. vier Evang." pp. 201–203: "We recognize first what no doubt scarcely requires proof, that Jesus treats the Old Testament in its entirety as the Word of God. Down to the smallest letter and most casual word (Matt. v. 18; Jno. x. 34) it is to Him truth, and that, religious truth." "An isolated expression of

That we may gather the precise significance of ἡ γραφή, αἱ γραφαί, as a designation of the Scriptures, it will be well to attend somewhat more closely to the origin of the term in Greek speech and to the implications it gathered to itself in its application to literary documents. Its history in its literary application does not seem to have been precisely the same as that of its congener, τὸ γράμμα, τὰ γράμματα. Γράμμα appears to have become current first in this reference as the appropriate appellation of an alphabetical sign, and to have grown gradually upward from this lowly employment to designate a document of less or greater extent, because such documents are ultimately made up of alphabetical signs. Although, therefore, the singular, τὸ γράμμα, came to be used of any written thing — from a simple alphabetical character up to complete works, or even unitary combinations of works, like the Scriptures, — it is apparently when applied to writings, most naturally employed of brief pieces like short inscriptions or proverbs, or to the shorter portions of documents such as the clauses of treaties, and the like; although it is also used of those longer formal sections of literary works which are more commonly designated technically "Books." It is rather the plural, τὰ γράμματα, which seems to suggest itself most readily not only for extended treatises, but indeed for complete documents of all kinds. When so employed, the plural form is accordingly not to be pressed. Such a phrase as "Moses' γράμματα" (Jno. v. 47) for example, need not imply that Moses wrote more than one "work"; it would rather mass whatever 'writings' of Moses are in mind into a single 'writing,' and would most naturally mean just, say, "the Pentateuch." Such a phrase as ἱερὰ γράμματα (II Tim. iii. 15),

precisely the book most subjective in its character in the whole canon is made use of and applied as meeting the case." Cf. also Franke, "Das Alt-Test. bei Johan." pp. 46, 48; H. Holtzmann, "N. T. Theologie," I. 45, 115; P. Gennrich, "Der Kampf um die Schrift," &c. 1898, p. 72: "In this late-Jewish, wholly unhistorical tradition, Jesus Himself and the oldest Christian authors were brought up; for them the whole Old Testament literature is already inspired (θεόπνευστος 2 Tim. iii. 16), every word, even those of the Psalms and of the Historical Books, an oracle."

again, need not bring the Old Testament books before our contemplation in their plurality, as a "Divine library"; but more probably conceives them together in the mass, as constituting a single sacred document, thought of as a unitary whole. On the other hand, γραφή, in its literary application, seems to have sprung somewhat lightly across the intervening steps, to designate which γράμμα is most appropriately used, and to have been carried at once over from the 'writing' in the sense of the script to the 'writing' in the sense of the scripture or document. Although therefore it of course exhibits more applications parallel with those of γράμμα than of any other term, its true synonymy in its higher literary use is rather with such terms as ἡ βίβλος (τὸ βιβλίον) and ὁ λόγος, in common with which it most naturally designates a complete literary piece, whether "Treatise" or "Book." Each of these terms, of course, preserves in all its applications something of the flavor of the primitive conception which was bound up with it. When thought of from the material point of view, as, so to say, so much paper, or, to speak more respectfully, from the point of sight of its extent, a literary work was apt therefore to be spoken of as a βίβλος (βιβλίον). When thought of as a rational product, thought presented in words, it was apt to be spoken of as a λόγος. Intermediate between the two stood γραφή (γράμμα) which was apt to come to the lips when the work was thought of as, so to speak, so much 'writing.' As between the two terms, γραφή and γράμμα, Dr. Westcott (on Jno. v. 47) suggests that the latter 'marks rather the specific form,' the former 'the scope of the record'; and this seems so far just that to γράμμα there clings a strong flavor of the 'letters' of which the document is made up, while γραφή looks rather to the completeness of the 'scripture.' To both alike so much of the implication of specific form clings as to lend them naturally to national and legislative employment with the implication of the "certa scriptio."[15]

<hr/>

[15] We meet the two words in a single context in Strabo, "Geog." i I. 7 (Ed. Didot, p. 5, line 50, seq.) where we are told that Hecataeus "left a γράμμα which is believed to be his ἐκ τῆς ἄλλης αὐτοῦ γραφῆς." Here γράμμα appears to be used where

To put the general matter in a nutshell, βίβλος (βιβλίον) may perhaps be said to be the more exact word for the 'book'; γραφή (γράμμα) for the 'document' inscribed in the 'book'; λόγος for the 'treatise' which the 'document' records; while as between γραφή and γράμμα, γράμμα, preserving the stronger material flavor, gravitates somewhat towards βίβλος (βιβλίον) while γραφή looks somewhat upwards towards λόγος. When in the development of the publishers' trade, the "great-book-system" of making books gave way for the purposes of convenience to the "small-book-system," and long works came to be broken up into "Books," each of which constituted a 'volume,'[16] these "Books" attached to themselves this whole series of designations and were called alike, — in each case with its own appropriate implications — βίβλοι, (βιβλία) γραφαί (γράμματα) and λόγοι: βίβλοι (βιβλία) because each book was written on a separate roll of papyrus and constituted one 'paper' or 'volume'; γραφαί (γράμματα) because each book was a separate document, a distinct 'scripture'; and λόγοι because each book was a distinct 'discourse' or rational work. Smaller sections than these "Books" were properly called περιοχάς, τόπους, χωρία, γράμματα (which last is the appropriate word for 'clauses') but very seldom if ever in the classics, γραφάς.[17]

The current senses of these several terms are, of course, more or less reflected as they occur in the pages of the New Testament. In the case of some of them, the New Testament usage simply continues that of profane Greek; in the case of others, new implications enter in which, while not superseding, profoundly modify their fundamental significance; in yet other cases, there is a development of usage beyond what is traceable in profane Greek. The passages in which two or

the mind is on the concrete object, and γραφή where it rests rather on the contents: that is, γράμμα seems to reach down towards βίβλος (βιβλίον), γραφή upwards towards λόγος. Does the singular γραφή bear here a plural or "collective" sense (Latin version: ex ceteris ejus scriptis)?

[16] Cf. Birt, "Das antike Buchwesen," 479.

[17] Cf., however, Eur. "Hipp." 1311, where Phaedra is said to have written ψευδεῖς γραφάς which may mean "false statements."

more of the terms in question are brought together are, naturally, especially instructive. When we read, for example, in
Lk. iii. 4 *seq.* ὡς γέγραπται ἐν βίβλῳ λόγων Ἡσαΐου τοῦ προφήτου, we perceive at once that what is quoted is a body of
λόγοι which are found in written form (γραφή: cf. I Cor. xv.
54, ὁ λόγος ὁ γεγραμμένος) in a βίβλος: the βίβλος is the volume
which contains the γραφή, which conveys or, perhaps better,
records the λόγοι. So again when we read in Lk. iv. 17 *seq.*
that there was delivered to our Lord the βιβλίον of Isaiah, on
opening which he found the τόπον, where a given thing ἦν
γεγραμμένον, and then closing the βιβλίον he remarked ἡ γραφή
αὕτη is fulfilled in your ears, we perceive that the βιβλίον is
the concrete volume — a thing to be handled, opened and
closed (cf. Rev. v. 3, 4, 5, x. 8, xx. 12), the manner of opening
and closing being, of course, unrolling and rolling (Rev. vi.
14, cf. Heb. x. 7, Birt, "Das antike Buchwesen," 116); and
that the γραφή is the document written in this βιβλίον; while
the various parts of this γραφή are formally τόποι, or when
attention is directed to their essential quality as sharers in
the authority of the whole, γραφαί (cf. Acts i. 16, "The γραφή
which the Holy Spirit spake through the mouth of" the
writer).

As might be inferred from these examples, βίβλος and
βιβλίον retain in the New Testament their current significations in profane Greek. Their application to sacred rather
than to secular books in no way modified their general sense.[18]
It brought, however, to them a richness of association which
prepared the way for that pregnant employment of them —
beginning not indeed in the New Testament but in even
earlier Hellenistic writings — to designate in its simple absoluteness the sacred volume, from which ultimately our
common term "The Bible" is supposed to have descended.[19]

---

[18] They may, of course, be applied even in profane Greek to "sacred" books.
Thus a magical formula among the Oxyrhynchus Papyri (Grenfell & Hunt,
"Oxyrhynchus Papyri," vi. p. 100, etc.) represents itself as an ἀντίγραφον ἱερᾶς
βίβλου.

[19] Αἱ βίβλοι (= הַסְּפָרִים) used absolutely, for the Old Testament as a whole,
occurs in Dan. ix. 2 (*cf.* Driver *in loc.*). Ἡ βίβλος absolutely for the Old Testa-

Throughout the New Testament the βίβλος or βιβλίον when applied to literary entities is just the "volume," that is to say, the concrete object, the "book" in the handleable sense. When we read of the βίβλος of the words of Isaiah (Lk. iii. 4), or of Moses (Mk. xii. 26) or of the Psalms (Lk. xx. 42, Acts i. 20) or of the Prophets, i. e., of the Twelve "Minor Prophets" (Acts vii. 42), the meaning is simply that each of these writings or collections of writings formed a single volume.[20] Similarly when we read of the βιβλίον of Isaiah (Lk. iv. 17) or of the Law (Gal. iii. 10), what is meant in each case is the volume formed by the document or documents named. The Gospel of John (Jno. xx. 30, xxi. 25) and the Book of Revelation (Rev. i. 11, xxii. 7, 9, 10, 18, 19) are spoken of as each a βιβλίον again because each existed in separation as a concrete unity. Accordingly βίβλοι are things which may be burned (Acts xix. 19); βιβλία, things which may be sprinkled (Heb. ix. 19) or carried about (II Tim. iv. 13), and may be made of parchment (II Tim. iv. 13). The Book of Life presented itself to the imagination as a volume in which names may be inscribed (βίβλος, Phil. iv. 3, Rev. iii. 5, xx. 15; βιβλίον, Rev. xiii. 8, xvii. 8, xx. 12, xxi. 27); the Book of Destiny as a volume in which is set down what is to come to pass (βιβλίον, Heb. x. 7, Rev. v. 1, 2, 3, 4, 5, 8, 9, x. 8). There is no essential difference in fundamental implication when in Matt. xix. 7, Mk. x. 4 βιβλίον is used for a "bill" of divorcement, or in Matt. i. 1, βίβλος, under the influence of the LXX, is employed of a genealogical register. In both instances it would

---

ment as a whole occurs first, apparently, in the "Letter of Aristeas" § 316 (cf. Thackeray, *Jewish Quarterly Review*, April, 1903, p. 391). Τὰ βιβλία absolutely of the Old Testament as a whole apparently occurs first in 2 Clem. xiv. 2 (cf. Lightfoot *in loco*). It has been customary to say that from the time of Chrysostom (*Hom.* 9 *in Coloss.*, *Hom.* 10 *in Genesim*) τὰ βιβλία occurs absolutely for the Scriptures as a whole (cf. Suicer, "Thesaur. Eccles." I. 687, 696; Reuss, "Hist. of the New Testament," § 320, E. T., p. 326). This usage is already found, however, in Clement Alex. and in Origen (ed. *Lommatsch*, i. 607). On the general subject see the detached note at the end of this article on the terms 'Bible,' 'Holy Bible' (page 149).

[20] Cf. Birt, "Das antike Buchwesen," 478–481, and especially Jerome, "Praef. Psal." and "Ep. ad Marcellam" as cited by Birt.

be understood that the document in question occupied a separate piece of papyrus or parchment and was therefore an entire "paper."

There is a much more marked enhancement of sense apparent in the New Testament use of λόγος. In Acts i. 1, to be sure, it occurs in the simple classical sense of "Book"; Luke merely points to his Gospel as "the first Book" of an extended historical treatise of which Acts is "the second Book"; and there is no implication of deeper meaning. The ordinary usage of λόγος, however, in the New Testament, is to express, in accordance with its employment in the Old Testament of the Prophetic word, the, or a, revelation from God, with no, or a very indistinct, reference to a written form. The Divine Word was, however, in the hands of the New Testament writers in a written form and allusion to this could not always fail. In passages like Jno. xv. 25, I Cor. xv. 54, the λόγος that is cited is distinctly declared to be written: "that the λόγος may be fulfilled that is written in their Law"; "then shall come to pass the λόγος that is written"; and with these there may be connected such passages as Jno. xii. 38, (cf. Lk. iv. 6): "that the word of Isaiah the prophet might be fulfilled," since, although it is not expressly stated, this λόγος too was in the hands of the New Testament writers in a written form. In this usage λόγος is a particular passage of Scripture viewed as a divine declaration. In Matt. xv. 6 (if this reading be accepted), Mk. vii. 13 (cf. Jno. v. 38, x. 35, Rom. xiii. 9, Gal. v. 14) in accordance with a familiar usage (cf. Ex. xxxiv. 28, οἱ δέκα λόγοι), the specific reference is to a divine commandment; but this commandment is thrown up in sharp contrast with "tradition" and is thought of distinctly as a written one. It is only in a passage like II Pet. i. 19 that λόγος comes to mean the entire Old Testament, after the fashion of Philo,[21] with the emphasis upon its divine character: that by "the prophetic word" here is meant not the prophetic portion of

---

[21] E. g. "De Plantat. Noe," 28, Mangey i. 347: "The prophetic word (ὁ προφητικὸς λόγος) seems to dignify the number four often throughout the νομοθεσίας, and especially in the catalogue of the creation of the universe."

Scripture but the Scriptures as a whole, conceived in accordance with their nature as "prophetic," that is to say as a
body of revelation, is made plain by the subsequent context,
where this prophecy is defined by the exegetical genitive as
just that prophecy which is Scripture πᾶσα προφητεία γραφῆς).
Thus λόγος, under the influence of the Old Testament usage
of the "Word of Jehovah," comes to mean in the New Testament specifically a divine revelation, and is applied to the
Old Testament to designate it, as written in the Books which
constitute it, the revealed Word of God.[22]

The λόγος, now, which was contained in the βίβλος (βιβλίον) (Lk. iii. 4), and of course contained in it only in written
form, was, naturally, conceived, as truly by the New Testament writers as by Greek writers in general, as a γραφή, (or
in the plural γραφαί). There seems to be no reason inherent
in the case, accordingly, why γραφή should not occur in the
New Testament in its simple classical sense of a "Treatise"
or (as λόγος does, Acts i. 1) of a "Book" or formal division of
a treatise. It may very properly be considered therefore merely
an accident that no instances are found in the New Testament of this general usage of the term without further implications.[23] It so occurs in Josephus ("Antt." III. viii. 10; IV.
viii. 44, of books of his own) and in Philo ("De Somniis," ad
init., Ἡ μὲν οὖν πρὸ ταύτης γραφὴ περιεῖχε — i. e., the preceding Book of the Treatise in hand); and it is repeatedly used
in the LXX to designate any piece of writing (cf. II Chron.
ii. 11, Neh. vii. 64, Dan. v. 5, I Macc. xiv. 27, 48). In point
of fact, however, γραφή (γραφαί) appears in the New Testament only in its application to the Sacred Scriptures, and
only in its high technical significance of "Scripture" by way
of eminence. It may be surmised that the long-established
employment of the term as a designation of the Scriptures
tended to withdraw it from common use on the lips of those

[22] This idea is still more emphatically expressed by the kindred term λόγια,
Rom. iii. 2, cf. Heb. v. 12, Acts vii. 38, the current use of which in this sense by
Philo is adverted to above (p. 118, note 6). See *The Presbyterian and Reformed
Review* for April 1900, pp. 217 *seq.*

[23] Cf. Zahn, "Einleitung," II. 99, 108, note 12.

to whom these Scriptures were a thing apart. It may even seem that a certain tendency is observable in the New Testament writers to distinguish between γραφή (γραφαί) and γράμμα (γράμματα) in favor of the former as the technical designation of the Scripture, while the latter is more freely employed for general uses. Certainly γράμματα occurs occasionally in the New Testament for non-sacred writings (Acts xxviii. 21, Lk. xvi. 6, 7) and for sacred writings indeed but without stress on their sacredness (Jno. v. 47, cf. vii. 15), while it is only rarely met with in the pregnant sense of Scripture (II Tim. iii. 15 only) and then only in an established phrase which may be supposed to have obtained a standing of its own. There seems also in γράμμα a naturally stronger implication of the material elements of the script, which may have formed the point of departure for a depreciatory employment of the term to designate the "mere letter" as distinguished from the "spirit" (cf. Rom. ii. 27, 29, vii. 6, II Cor. iii. 6, 7). On the other hand the free employment by later Christian writers of γραφή, γραφαί of secular compositions, and of both γράμμα and γράμματα in the high technical sense of "Scripture," so far militates against the supposition that already in New Testament Greek the former were hardening into the exclusive technical designations of "Scripture." Meanwhile the simple fact remains that in the New Testament while γράμματα is used freely, and with a single exception exclusively, without implication of sacredness, γραφή and γραφαί are employed solely as technical designations of Sacred Scripture and take their color in all their occurrences from this higher plane of usage. Throughout the New Testament the γραφή which alone is in question is conceived as rather the word of the Holy Spirit than of its human authors *through* whom merely it is spoken (Acts i. 16), and is therefore ever adduced as of indefectible, because of Divine, authority.

It is somewhat remarkable that even on this high plane of its technical application, in which it designates nothing but the Sacred Scriptures, γραφή never occurs in the New Testament, in accordance with its most natural and, in the classics, its most frequent sense of "Treatise," as a term to describe the several books of which the Old Testament is composed. It is tempting, no doubt, to seek to give it this sense in some of the passages where, occurring in the singular, it yet does not appear to designate the Scriptures as a whole; and even Dr. Hort seems for a moment almost inclined to yield to the temptation.[24] It is more tempting still to assume that behind the frequent use of the plural, αἱ γραφαί, to designate the Scriptures as a whole, there lies a previous current usage by which each Book which enters into the composition of these Scriptures was designated by the singular ἡ γραφή. In no single passage where the singular ἡ γραφή occurs, however, does it seem possible to give it a reference to the Book of Scripture to which the appeal is made. And the frequent employment in profane Greek of γραφαί in the plural for a single document [25] discourages the assumption that it, like τὰ βιβλία, has reference, when used as a designation of Scripture, to its composite character as a "Divine Library." It is true that in one unique passage, II Pet. iii. 16,[26] αἱ γραφαί bears a plural signification. But the items of which this plural is formed, as the grammatical construction implies, are not "treatises" (Huther, Kühl) but "passages" (De Wette). Peter says that the unlearned and unstable, of course, wrested the hard sayings of Paul's letters, as they were accustomed to wrest τὰς λοιπὰς γραφάς, i. e., "the other Scriptural statements," [27] due reverence for which should have protected

[24] On I Pet. ii. 6: note the "probably."

[25] E. g. of a letter, Euripides, "Iph. in Taur." 735, "Let him give an oath to me that he will bear τὰς γραφάς to Argos"; "Iph. in Aul." 363 (a line of doubtful genuineness), where Agamemnon is said to be secretly devising ἄλλας γραφάς; of a book, Georg. Sync., p. 168 τὴν ἐκ τῶν Κεφαλίωνος γραφῶν πρὸς τὸν Διόδωρον διαφωνίαν.

[26] On the meaning of this passage, see especially Bigg, in loc., and cf. Chase, Hastings', B. D., iii. 810.

[27] For γραφαί in the sense of "statements," cf. Eurip. "Hipp." 1311, where Phaedra is said, under the fear of disgrace, to have written ψευδεῖς γραφάς, probably not a "lying tablet" (γραφαί in its singular sense as in note 25 above) but "false statements." Cf. also Philo, "De Praem. et Poen." 11. near the end (Mangey, ii. 418), where he distributes the contents of the sacred volume into

them from such treatment, the implication being that no part of Scripture was safe in their hands. This is a sufficiently remarkable use of the plural, no other example of which occurs in the New Testament; it is, however, an entirely legitimate use of the plural [28] and in its context a perfectly natural one, which, nevertheless, just because it is a special usage determined by its context, stands somewhat apart from the general technical use of αἱ γραφαί to designate the body of Scriptures and cannot guide us to its interpretation. In no other passage where αἱ γραφαί occurs is there the slightest hint that its plural form is determined by the conception of the Scriptures as a congeries of authoritative passages; this interpretation of the current plural form may indeed be set aside at once as outside of the possibilities of the case.

If we may not speak quite so decisively of the possibility of the plural form resting on a conception of "the Scriptures" as made up of a collection of Books, it may at least be said that there is nothing in the New Testament use of the term to remove the general unlikelihood of that construction of it. There are indeed two or three passages in which γραφαί might appear at first sight to designate a body of documents. Such are, for example, Rom. xvi. 26, where we read of γραφαί προφητικαί, and especially Matt. xxvi. 56, where we read of αἱ γραφαὶ τῶν προφητῶν. In the case of Rom. xvi. 26, however,

---

αἱ ῥηταὶ γραφαί and αἱ καθ' ὑπόνοιαν ἀλληγορίαι, which may perhaps be taken as "literal statements" and "covert allegories." The use of γραφή in the sense of a "passage" of Scripture is found in Philo, the LXX and frequently in the New Testament (see below).

[28] Accordingly γραφαί is quite freely used by the Church Fathers of a plurality of passages of Scripture. The famous words in Polycarp "Ad Phil.," xii. 1 are probably not a case in point: *ut his Scripturis dictum est* here apparently refers back to the *in sacris libris* which just precedes them and not forward to the two passages adduced. From Justin on, however, numerous examples present themselves. Cf. e. g. Justin, "Contra Tryph." 65 (Otto. p. 230): "And Trypho said, Being importuned by so many Scriptures (τῶν τοσούτων γραφῶν) I do not know what to say about the Scripture (τῆς γραφῆς) which Isaiah said, according to which God says He will not give His glory to another." Again, "Cont. Tryph." 71 (Otto. p. 255, cf. note): They have taken away πολλὰς γραφάς from the LXX translation. Again, Clem. Alex. "Cohort. ad Gentes," 9 *ad init.* (Migne, i. 192D), "I could adduce μυρίας γραφάς not one of which shall pass away."

the very natural impression that here we have mention of the
several books which constitute the second of the sections of
the Jewish canon, known as "The Prophets," is almost certainly an error (cf. Vaughan *in loc.*). It is very unlikely that
the "prophetic writings" with this mention of which this
epistle closes are any other than the "Holy Scriptures" of
the prophets with mention of which it opens (Rom. i. 2); and
it is quite clear that these "Holy Scriptures" are much more
inclusive than the writings of the second section of the Jewish canon, — that they embrace in fact the entirety of Scripture, thought of here as of prophetic, that is, revelatory,
character (cf. Meyer, Weiss, Oltramare *in loc.;* Bleek on Heb.
i. 1). Nor need the "Scriptures of the prophets" of Matt. xxvi.
56 have any different meaning (cf. Swete on Mk. xiv. 49,
Morrison *in loc.*). It is quite true that the term "The Prophets"
is sometimes in Matthew (v. 17, vii. 12, xxii. 40) and in the
other Gospels (Lk. xvi. 16, 29, 31, xxiv. 44, Jno. i. 45) and in
the rest of the New Testament (Acts vii. 42, xiii. 15, xxiv. 14,
xxviii. 23, Rom. iii. 21) a technical term designating the second
section of the Jewish canon; but it is equally true that it is
sometimes used much more inclusively. For example in Matt.
ii. 23 the reference seems to be quite generally to the Old
Testament considered as a prophetic book (cf. Meyer *in loc.*);
and in Matt. xi. 13, "all the prophets and even the law prophesied," the Pentateuch is expressly included within the prophetic word (cf. II Pet. i. 19). Passages like Lk. i. 70, xi. 50
show that by these writers the whole Old Testament revelation was thought of as prophetic in character, while Lk.
xviii. 31 is certainly entirely general (cf. Acts iii. 24). The
most instructive passages, however, are doubtless those which
follow one another so closely in Lk. xxiv. 25, 27, 44. It can
hardly be doubted that the same body of books is intended
in all three of these references, which merely progressively
discriminate between the parts which make up the whole.
The simple "prophets" thus becomes first "Moses and indeed all the prophets" (cf. Hahn *in loc.*) — further defined as
the "whole Scripture" — and then "the Law of Moses, and

the Prophets and the Psalms." The term "the Prophets"
occurs thus in this brief context in three senses of varying
inclusiveness, and apparently lends itself as readily to the
widest as to the narrowest application. In these circumstances
there seems no reason why in Matt. xxvi. 56 "the Scriptures of
the Prophets" should be narrowed beyond the inclusiveness
of the suggestion of "the Scriptures" of the immediately preceding context (xxvi. 54) or of its own parallel in Mk. xiv. 49.
In other words there is every reason to believe that in this
passage the defining adjunct "of the Prophets" does not discriminate among the books which make up the Scriptures
and single out certain of these as prophetic, but rather describes the entire body of Scripture as prophetic in origin and
character, that is to say as a revelation from God.[29] Γραφαί
does not here, then, mean "books" "treatises," but αἱ
γραφαί, as in verse 54 and in the parallel passage, Mk. xiv.
49, means the one Divine book. That Lk. xxiv. 27, ἐν πάσαις
ταῖς γραφαῖς, lends itself readily to the same interpretation
requires no argument to show. If αἱ γραφαί is employed in a
singular sense, then πᾶσαι αἱ γραφαί means just the whole of
the document so designated, and is the exact equivalent of
πᾶσα ἡ γραφή or πᾶσα γραφή (II Tim. iii. 16 taken as a proper
noun). The truth seems to be, therefore, that as there is no
example in the New Testament of the use of ἡ γραφή in the
sense of one of the Books of Scripture, so there is no trace in
its use of αἱ γραφαί of an underlying consciousness of the composition of the Scriptures out of a body of such Books.[30]
Whether the plural αἱ γραφαί, or the singular ἡ γραφή, is employed, therefore, the meaning is the same; in either case the

[29] On this conception of the whole Old Testament as a prophetic book, cf.
Willis J. Beecher, "The Prophets and the Promise," 1905, pp. 168 seq.

[30] In Patristic usage, on the contrary, a very large variety of applications of
ἡ γραφή and αἱ γραφαί, in the sense of Biblical Books or more or less extensive
collections of Biblical Books, is found. Thus for example, in Athan. "Epist.
Encycl." 1 ad init. we meet with ἡ θεία τῶν Κριτῶνγ ραφή: in Eus. h. e. iii. 11 with
ἡ τοῦ εὐαγγελίου γραφή; in ibid. ii. i. 2. with ἡ ἱερὰ τῶν εὐαγγελίων γραφή; in Orig.
"Contr. Cels." i. 58, with ἡ εὐαγγελικὴ γραφή. In Origen, "Contr. Cels." vii. 24 and
in "Fragmenta in Prov." 2, we find ἡ παλαιὰ γραφή, and in another place (Migne,
i. 1365A) the corresponding νεώτεραι γραφαί where the plural is probably a real

application of the term to the Old Testament writings by the
writers of the New Testament is the outgrowth of their conception of these Old Testament writings as a unitary whole,
and designates this body of writings in its entirety as the one,
well-known, authoritative documentation of the Divine revelation. This is the fundamental fact with respect to the use
of these terms in the New Testament from which all the other
facts of their usage flow.

In saying this, we are brought at once, however, face to
face with what is probably the most remarkable fact about
the usage of ἡ γραφή in the New Testament. This is its occasional employment to refer, not merely, as was to be expected
from its form and previous history, to Scripture as a whole,
nor even as, had it so occurred in the New Testament, would
have been only a continuation of its profane usage, to the
several treatises which make up that whole, but to individual
passages of Scripture. This employment finds so little support in profane Greek, in which γράμμα rather than γραφή is
the current form for the adduction of clauses or fragmentary
portions of documents,[31] that it has often been represented as
a peculiarity of the New Testament and Patristic Greek.
Thus, for example, we read in Stephens' "Thesaurus" (*sub
voc.*): "In the New Testament and ecclesiastical books, ἡ
γραφή and αἱ γραφαί are used of the sacred writings which are
commonly called 'The Holy Scriptures.' But γραφή is sometimes in the New Testament employed peculiarly of a particular passage of Scripture." And Schaefer adds to this
merely a reference to a passage in one of the orations of

plural. This is also the case in, say, Eus. *h. e.* iii. 3 when he speaks of "the acknowledged γραφαί" of the New Testament, and (*ad init.*) mentions that II Peter had
been used by many μετὰ τῶν ἄλλων γραφῶν.

[31] E. g. Thucyd. v. 29: "They were angry with the Lacedemonians chiefly because among other things it was provided in the treaty with Athens that the
Lacedemonians and Athenians if agreed might add to or take away from them
whatever they pleased: this clause (τοῦτο τὸ γράμμα) aroused great uneasiness
among the Peloponnesians." Cf. Philo. "De Congr. erud. grat." 12 (Mangey
i. 527): "There is also in another place τὸ γράμμα τοῦτο inscribed" = Deut.
xxxii. 8; "Quod Deus Immut" 2 (Mangey i. 273): Κατὰ τὸ ἱερώτατον Μωϋσέως
γράμμα τοῦτο.

Valckenaer, where commenting on Acts xvii. 2–3, he remarks
that, in the New Testament, "passages of the Old Testament
such as are also designated περιοχάς, τόπους and χωρία are
sometimes also called γραφάς." [32] The usage does not seem,
however, to be peculiar to the New Testament and the Church
Fathers: it occurs also, though rarely, in the LXX and Philo,
and may claim therefore to be at least Hellenistic.[33] It is probably the outgrowth of the habit of looking upon the Scriptures as a unitary book of divine oracles, every part and passage of which is clothed with the authority which belongs to
the whole, and which is of course manifested in all its parts.
No doubt this extension of γραφή from a designation of Scripture as a whole to a designation of any given fragment of
Scripture, however small, was mediated by the circumstance
that in adducing the authority of 'Scripture' for any doctrine or practice, it was always inevitably not the whole of
'Scripture' but some special declaration of 'Scripture' which
was especially in mind as bearing upon the particular point
at the moment in hand. The transition was easy from saying "The Scripture says, namely in this or that passage,"
to saying of this and that passage specifically, "This Scripture says" and "Another Scripture says." When the entirety
of Scripture is "Scripture" to us, each passage may readily
be adduced as "Scripture" also, because "Scripture" is conceived as speaking in and through each passage. A step so
inviting was sure to be taken sooner or later. Whenever therefore γραφή occurs of a particular passage of Scripture, so far

[32] "Ti Hemsterhusii Orationes, . . . L. C. Valckenai Tres Orationes," etc.
Lugdunum Bat., 1784, p. 395.

[33] IV Macc. xviii. 14: "And he reminded you of τὴν Ἡσαΐου γραφήν which says,
Though you pass through fire." Philo, "Quis rerum div. her." 53 (Mangey, i. 511);
τὸ δὲ ἀκόλουθον προσυφαίνει τῇ γραφῇ φάσκων· ἐρρέθη πρὸς Ἀβραάμ; "De Praem. et
poen." 11 (Mangey ii. 418). Cf. The Presbyterian and Reformed Review, XI (April
1900) 245–6 notes. For the possibility of a classical use of γραφαί = "statements" see above p. 132 note 27. Of the ordinary Greek words for "passage"
of a writing, neither γράμμα nor χωρίον occurs in the New Testament; τόπος only
at Lk. iv. 17 and περιοχή only at Acts viii. 32 (cf. Dr. C. J. Vaughan on Rom.
iv. 3 and per contra, Meyer in loc. and cf. I Pet. ii. 6 and the commentators there.)
The place of all these terms is taken in the New Testament by γραφή.

from throwing in doubt its usage of Scripture as a whole, conceived as a unitary Divine authority, it rather presupposes this usage and is an outgrowth of it. It cannot surprise us therefore that ἡ γραφή occurs in the New Testament side by side in the two senses, and designates indifferently either Scripture as a whole, or a particular passage of Scripture, that is, is used indifferently "collectively" as it has not very exactly been called, and "particularly."

It has often, no doubt, been called in question whether both these senses do occur side by side in the New Testament. Possibly a desire to erect some well-marked and uniform distinction between the usage of the plural αἱ γραφαί and the singular ἡ γραφή, has not been wholly without its influence here. At all events the suggestion has every now and then been made that the singular ἡ γραφή bears in the New Testament the uniform sense of 'a passage of Scripture,' while it is the plural, αἱ γραφαί, alone which designates the Scriptures in their entirety. The famous Rationalist divine, Johannes Schulthess, for example, having occasion to comment briefly on the words πᾶσα γραφὴ Θεόπνευστος, II Tim. iii. 16, among other assertions of equal insecurity, makes this one: "γραφή in the singular never means in the New Testament βίβλος, much less the entirety of τῶν ἱερῶν γραμμάτων, but some particular passage." [34] Hitherto it has been thought enough to meet such assertions with a mere expression of dissent. Christiaan Sepp, for example, meets this one with equal brevity and point by the simple observation: "Passages like Jno. x. 35 prove the contrary." [35] But a new face has been put upon the matter by the powerful advocacy of the proposition "that the singular γραφή in the New Testament always means a *particular passage* of Scripture," by the late Bishop Lightfoot in a comment on Gal. iii. 22 which has on this account become famous. We must believe, however, that it is the weight of Dr. Lightfoot's justly great authority rather than the inherent reasonableness of the doctrine which

---

[34] "Lucubr. pro divin. discip. ac person. Jesu," etc. Turici 1828, p. 36 note.
[35] "De Leer des N. T. over de H. S. des O. V.," Amsterdam 1849, p. 70.

has given this opinion the great vogue which it appears to enjoy at present among English-speaking scholars. It was at once confuted, it is true, by Dr. C. J. Vaughan in a note on Rom. iv. 3; and in his own note on this passage Dr. Lightfoot seemed almost (not quite) persuaded to admit a doubt as to the usage of John, while reiterating, with respect to Paul at least, that in the matter of the use of γραφή in the singular of a single passage of Scripture "practice is absolute and uniform." Dr. Westcott took his stand by Dr. Lightfoot's side (see on Jno. ii. 22, x. 35) and labored to show that John's usage conforms to the canon asserted; and Dr. Hort, though with some apparent hesitation with respect to John and Paul — the only portions of the New Testament, it will be noticed, of which Drs. Westcott and Lightfoot express assurance — inclined on the whole to give his assent to their general judgment (on I Peter ii. 6). With more hesitancy, Dr. Swete remarks merely that "γραφή is a portion of Scripture," at least "almost always when the singular is used" (on Mk. xii. 10). General agreement in the view in question is expressed also, for example, by Page (Acts i. 16), Knowling (Acts viii. 32), Plummer (Lk. iv. 21), A. Stewart (Hastings' BD. I 286). It is difficult to believe, however, that the reasons assigned for this view are sufficient to bear the weight of the judgment founded on them. They suffice, certainly, to show — what is in itself sufficiently remarkable, — that ἡ γραφή is repeatedly employed in the New Testament of a particular passage of Scripture. But the attempt to carry this usage through all the instances in which the singular appears involves a violence of exegetical procedure which breaks down of itself. Out of the thirty instances in which the singular, ἡ γραφή occurs, about a score prove utterly intractable to the proposed interpretation, — these nineteen to wit: Jno. ii. 22, vii. 38, 42, x. 35, xvii. 12, xix. 28, xx. 9, Acts viii. 32, Rom. iv. 3, ix. 17, x. 11, xi. 2, Gal. iii. 8, 22, iv. 30, I Tim. v. 18, Jas. iv. 5, I Pet. ii. 6, II Pet. i. 20.[36] In point of fact, therefore, in

---

[36] Cf. Cremer, *sub. voc.*, who gives 17 passages, omitting of those above Jno. xvii. 12, xx. 9; T. Stephenson, "Expository Times" xiv. 475 *seq.* who in a well-

some two-thirds of the instances where γραφή is employed in the singular, its reference is to the Scripture as a whole, to that unitary written authority to which final appeal was made. In some of these passages it is no less than impossible to take it otherwise. In Jno. ii. 22, for example, there is absolutely no definite passage suggested, and Westcott seeks one to which to assign the reference only under the pressure of theory. The same is true of Jno. xx. 9, where the reference is quite as broad as in Lk. xxiv. 45. In Jno. x. 35 the argument depends upon the wide reference to Scripture as a whole, which forms its major premise. In Gal. iii. 22 there is absolutely nothing to suggest a reference to a special text rather than to the general tenor of Scripture, and Lightfoot supplies a special text only conjecturally and with hesitation. The personification of Scripture in such passages as Jas. iv. 5, Gal. iii. 8 carries with it the same implication. And the anarthrous use of γραφή in I Pet. ii. 6, II Pet. i. 20, cf. II Tim. iii. 16, is explicable only on the presupposition that ἡ γραφή had become so much the proper designation of Scripture that the term had acquired the value of a proper name, and was therefore treated as definite without, as with, the article. If anything were needed to render this supposition certain, it would be supplied by the straits to which expositors are brought who seek to get along without it.[37] Dr. Hort, for example, after declining to understand γραφή in I Pet. ii. 6 of Scripture in general, because he does not find "a distinct and recognized use of this sort," finally suggests that we should render "simply, 'in writing,'" so that "περιέχει ἐν γραφῇ shall be held equivalent to 'it stands written.'" But he is compelled to add: "That the quotation was authoritative, though not expressed, was doubtless implied, in accordance with the

classified list gives 18 passages, omitting Jno. xx. 9; E. Hühn, "Die alttestamentlichen Citate" etc., 1900, p. 276, who gives 23 passages, adding Jno. xiii. 18, xix. 24, 36, Jas. ii. 8. On the general question, cf. Vaughan, on Rom. iv. 3, Meyer on Jno. x. 35, Weiss on Jno. x. 35, Kübel on 2 Pet. i. 20, Abbott on Eph. iv. 8, Beet on Rom. ix. 17, "Encyc. Bibl." 4329, Francke, "Das A. T. bei Johan," p. 48, Haupt, "Die alttest. Citate in d. vier Evang.," p. 201.

[37] Cf. Zahn, "Einleitung," II, 108; Hort on I Pet. ii. 6.

familiar Jewish use of the words 'said,' 'written,'" — apparently not realizing that, if the quotation is authoritative then, "It stands written" is the equivalent of the authoritative employment of this phrase in the adduction of what is specifically Scripture, and therefore means here distinctly not, "It stands written — somewhere," but "It stands written in the (technically so-called) Scripture." This seems, therefore, to be only a roundabout way of saying that γραφή here means and definitely refers to the authoritative Scripture, and not any 'writing' indifferently. The same is inevitably true of II Pet. i. 20. It is impossible that by "every prophecy of Scripture" the writer can have meant "every prophecy which has been reduced to writing." [38] He undoubtedly intended the prophecies written in the Old Testament alone (cf., Bigg, Kübel, Keil *in loc.*); and this is but another way of saying that anarthrous γραφή is to him a technical designation of the Old Testament, or, in other words, that he uses it with precisely the implications with which we employ the term, "Scripture." [39] In the presence of such passages as these there seems to be no reason why we should fail to recognize that the employment of γραφή in the New Testament so far follows its profane usage, in which it is applied to entire documents and carries with it a general implication of completeness, that it in its most common reference designates the Old Testament to which it is applied in its completeness as a unitary whole. [40]

[38] Cf. Zahn, "Einleitung," II. p. 109.

[39] Presumably few will take refuge in the explanation suggested by Dr. E. H. Plumptre ("Smith's B. D." 2874), which understands the "prophecy" here of New Testament, not Old Testament prophets and renders, every prophetic utterance arising from, resting on, a γραφή — i. e. a passage of the Old Testament.

[40] Precisely the same is true of the usage of the term in at least the earlier Patristic literature, although a contrary impression might be taken from a remark at the close of Dr. Lightfoot's note on Gal. iii. 22. Ἡ γραφή of a passage of Scripture seems to be the rarer usage in, for example, the so-called Apostolical Fathers. It occurs with certainty, only at 1 Clem. xxiii. 3 (cf. xxv. 5), 2 Clem. xiv. 1, while ἡ γραφή = "Scripture" as a whole, seems to occur at least at 1 Clem. xxxiv. 6, xxxv. 7, xlii. 5; 2 Clem. vi. 8, xiv. 2; Barn. iv. 11, v. 4, vi. 12, xiii. 2, xvi. 5. (The plural αἱ γραφαί occurs in 1 Clem. xlv. 2, and in the formula αἱ ἱεραὶ γραφαί in 1 Clem. liii. 1 [Polyc. xii. 1].) In the later Fathers ἡ γραφή occurs in

It has seemed worth while to enter somewhat fully upon this matter, not only on account of its intrinsic interest and the importance given it in recent expositions, but also because the issue throws into a high light what is after all the fundamental fact about the New Testament use of ἡ γραφή, αἱ γραφαί. This is the implication which they bear not only of the uniqueness of the body of religious writings which they designate, entitling them to be spoken of as together, in a supereminent sense, "the Scriptures," or rather "the Scripture," or even "Scripture"; but also, along with this, of their irreducible unity, — as constituting in their entirety a single divinely authoritative "writing." Francke is quite within the limits of clear fact, when he remarks,[41] "The contemplation of the entire body of Scripture as a unitary word, in all its parts equally resting upon a single authority, and therefore possessing the same authority everywhere, forms the most essential presupposition of the designation of the collection of the written word as the γραφή." It only needs to be added that the same is true of its designation as αἱ γραφαί. What requires emphasis, in a word, is that the two designations ἡ γραφή and αἱ γραφαί are, so far as our evidence goes, strictly parallel; and neither is to be derived from the other. That the application of αἱ γραφαί to the Scriptures does not rest on a previous application of ἡ γραφή to each of the Books of Scripture, we have already had occasion to show. It is equally important to observe that the application to Scripture of ἡ γραφή is not a subsequent development resting on a previous usage by which Scripture was known as αἱ γραφαί. The contrary assumption is often tacitly made and it is sometimes quite plainly expressed, as, for example, in the concluding words of Dr. Lightfoot's note on Gal. iii. 22, where he tells us that "the transition from the 'Scriptures' to the 'Scripture' is analogous to the transition from τὰ βιβλία to the 'Bible.'" Precisely what is meant by the last clause of this

every conceivable variety of sense and application, but in none more distinctly than of Scripture as a whole.

[41] "Das A. T. bei Johan," p. 48.

statement is perhaps not perfectly clear. It is obvious, of course, that the designation of the Scripture as τὰ βιβλία antedates the misunderstanding of this term as a feminine singular, whence arose the Latin "Biblia" and our "Bible" treated as a singular — if this be really the history of the origin of these latter terms; but Dr. Lightfoot can hardly have meant that the use of ἡ γραφή as a designation of the Scripture arose similiarly through a misunderstanding of αἱ γραφαί as a singular. It would seem that he can only have meant that the progress was in both cases from a view of the sacred books which was fully conscious of their plurality to a conception of them which has swallowed up their plurality in a unitary whole. There is no proof, however, that such a movement of thought took place in either case. The fact seems to be that αἱ γραφαί was used from its earliest application to Scripture in a singular sense, in accordance with a current usage of the term in profane Greek. And we lack evidence that the Scriptures were known as τὰ βιβλία before they were known as ἡ βίβλος.[42] These two modes of speaking of Scripture appear to have been rather parallel than consecutive usages. And it is probable that the same is true of the designations αἱ γραφαί and ἡ γραφή as well. It is true enough that we meet with αἱ γραφαί, though somewhat rarely and perhaps ordinarily in the phrase [αἱ] ἱεραὶ γραφαί, in Philo[43] and Josephus, whereas ἡ γραφή of Scripture in general is said to occur first in the New Testament.[44] But it is not

---

[42] See above, p. 127, note 19.

[43] E. g. "De Abrahamo," 13 (Mangey ii, 10): αἱ γραφαί = "the Scriptures."

[44] Cf. Cremer, ed. 9, sub voc. γραφή II: "In Philo, and as it seems, also in Josephus, the singular does not occur of the Scriptures as a whole, although the plural does. Cf. αἱ ἀπογραφαί 2 Macc. ii. 1, ἀναγραφαί verse 14. The use of the singular in this sense seems accordingly to have first formed itself, or perhaps, more correctly to have manifested itself, in the New Testament community, and that in connection with its belief in the Messiah and its appeal to the Old Testament." The use of singular γραφή of the Scriptures is in any event not frequent in Philo and Josephus: and Cremer's inference is rash, even if the facts be as represented. It would be well, however, if the statement of fact were carefully verified. Cf. Josephus, "Antt." III. i. 7, fin. where he tells us that a γραφή was

probable that we are witnesses of the birth of a new usage in either case; and the evidence is too meagre to justify a pronouncement on the relative ages of the two forms. And in proportion as we recognize the singular sense of αἱ γραφαί and the rooting of both usages in a precedent Jewish mode of citing Scripture as the unitary Law of God, does all the probability of the proposed development pass away. In any event when the New Testament was in process of writing it was much too late in the day to speak of the formation of a sense of the unitary uniqueness of the Old Testament or of the rise of a usage in designating the Old Testament in which that sense would first come to its manifestation. Both that sense and modes of expressing it were an inheritance of the New Testament writers from a remote past, and find manifestation in the whole body of Jewish literature, not merely in the usage of the Rabbis, but in the pages of Philo as well. The truth seems to be that whether αἱ γραφαί is used or ἡ γραφή or anarthrous γραφή the implication is the same. In each case alike the Old Testament is thought of as a single document, set over against all other documents by reason of its unique authority based upon its Divine origin, on the ground of which it is constituted in every part and declaration the final arbiter of belief and practice. We need not, then, seek to discover subtle reasons for the distribution of these forms through the New Testament, asking why truly anarthrous γραφή is employed only by Peter (cf. II Tim. iii. 16); why John and Paul prevailingly use the singular, Matthew uniformly and Mark and Luke prevailingly the plural; and why our Lord is reported as employing the two numbers indifferently. These things are at most matters of literary habit; at least, matters of chance and occasion, like our own indifferent use of 'The Scriptures,' 'The Scripture,' 'Scripture.'

One of the outgrowths of the conception of the Old Testa-

---

deposited in the Temple which informs us that God foretold to Moses that water should be drawn thus from the rock. By this γραφή he means of course precisely what he elsewhere calls αἱ ἱεραί γραφαί: but he necessarily speaks of it indefinitely.

ment as a unitary Divine document, of indefectible authority in all its parts and declarations, was the habit of adducing
it for the ordinary purposes of instruction or debate by
such simple formulas as 'It is said,' 'It is written,' with the
pregnant implication that what is thus adduced as 'said' or
'written' is 'said' or 'written' by an authority recognized
as Divine and final. Both of these usages are richly illustrated in a variety of forms and with all high implications,
not only in the New Testament at large, but also in the Gospels,
and not only in the comments by the Evangelists but also in
reported sayings of our Lord. We are concerned here particularly only with the formula "It is written," in which the
consciousness of the written form, the documentary character, of the authority appealed to is most distinctly expressed.
In its most common form, this formula is the simple γέγραπται, used either absolutely, or, with none of its authoritative
implications thereby evacuated, with more or less precise definition of the place where the cited words can be found written.
By its side there occurs in John the resolved formula γεγραμμένον ἐστίν; and in the latter part of Luke there is a tendency
to adduce Scripture by means of a participial construction.[45]
These modes of citation have analogies in profane Greek,
especially in legislative usage.[46] But, as Cremer points out,
their use with reference to the Divine Scriptures, as it involves the adduction of an authority which rises immeasur-

---

[45] The various formulas may be commodiously reviewed in Hühn, "Die
alttestamentlichen Citate," pp. 272 seq.

[46] Cf. Cremer ed. 9 sub voc. γράφω, fin.; Deissmann, "Bible Studies," 112, 250.
A good example of the classical mode of expression may perhaps be found in the
third Philippic of Demosthenes (III. 41, 42, p. 122): "That our condition was
formerly quite different from this, I shall now convince you, not by any arguments of my own, but by a decree of your ancestors (γράμματα τῶν προγόνων) . . .
What then says the decree (τὰ γράμματα)? . . . In the laws importing capital cases
it is enacted (γέγραπται)" Deissmann calls attention to the fact that Josephus
uses γέγραπτα infrequently in his references to the Old Testament, preferring
ἀναγέγραπται; and refers to a passage in which he uses γέγραπται of a profane document. The passage is "Contr. Ap." IV. 18: "For if we may give credit to the
Phoenician records (ἀναγραφαῖς), it is recorded (γέγραπται) in them," etc. It should
be observed that this is not an instance of the absolute γέγραπται; but yet it is not
without an implication of (notarial) authority.

ably above all legislative authority, so is freighted with a significance to which the profane usage affords no key. In the Gospels, — if we may take the Gospels as an example of the whole — of the two forms, γέγραπται alone occurs in Matthew (ii. 5, iv. 6 in the narrative; iv. 4, iv. 7, 10, xi. 10, xxi. 13, xxvi. 24, 31 in the report of our Lord's words) and in Mark (i. 2 in the narrative; vii. 6, ix. 12, 13, xi. 17, xiv. 21, 27 in the report of our Lord's words), and predominantly in Luke (ii. 23, iii. 4, iv. 10 in the narrative; iv. 4, 8, vii. 27, x. 20, xix. 46, xxiv. 46 in the report of our Lord's words), but only once in John (viii. 17 in the report of our Lord's words). In the latter part of Luke the citation of Scripture is accomplished by the aid of the participle γεγραμμένον ([cf. iv. 17] xviii. 31, xx. 17, xxi. 22, xxii. 37, xxiv. 44), while in John the place of the formula γέγραπται (viii. 17 only) is taken by the resolved form γεγραμμένον ἐστίν (ii. 17, vi. 31, x. 34, xii. 14, cf. 16, in the narrative; vi. 45, [viii. 17], cf. xv. 25, in the report of our Lord's words). The significance of these formulas is perhaps most manifest when they are used absolutely, where they stand alone in bare authoritativeness, without indication of any kind whence the citation adduced is derived, the bald adduction being indication enough that it is the Divine authority of Scripture to which appeal is made. Instances of this usage are found in the Gospels for γέγραπται in Matt. iv. 4, 6, 7, 10, xi. 10, xxi. 13, xxvi. 24, 31, in Mk. vii. 6, ix. 12, 13, xi. 17, xiv. 21, 27, in Lk. iv. 4, 8, 10, vii. 27, xix. 46, xx. 17, xxii. 37; for γεγραμμένον ἐστίν in Jno. ii. 17, vi. 31, xii. 14, [16]. In only a single passage each in Matthew and Mark is there added an indication of the source of the citation (Matt. ii. 5, "it is written through the prophet"; Mk. i. 2, "it is written in Isaiah the prophet"). In Luke such defining adjuncts are more frequent (ii. 23, in the law of the Lord; iii. 4, in the book of the words of Isaiah the prophet; x. 26, in the law; xviii. 31, through the prophet; xxiv. 44, in the law of Moses and the prophets and the psalms, i. e., in Scripture, verse 45). In John also such definitions are not relatively rare (vi. 45, in the prophets; viii. 17, in your law;

x. 34, in your law; xv. 25, in the law). These fuller passages
while they identify the document from which the citation is
drawn, in no wise suggest that the necessity for such identification was felt; by their relative infrequency they rather
emphasize how unnecessary such specification was except as
an additional solemn invocation of the recognized source of
all religious authority. The bare "It is written" was the decisive adduction of the indefectible authority of the Scriptures of God, clothed as such, in all their parts and in all their
declarations, with His authority. We could scarcely imagine
a usage which would more illuminatingly exhibit the estimate
put upon Scripture as the expressed mind of God or the rooted
sense of its unity and its equal authoritativeness in all its
parts.[47]

We should not pass lightly over this high implication of
the employment of absolute γέγραπται to adduce the Scriptural word, and especially the suggestions of its relative frequency. No better index could be afforded of the sense of the
unitary authority of the document so cited which dominated
the minds of the writers of the New Testament and of our
Lord as reported by them. The consciousness of the human
authors, through whom the Scriptures were committed to
writing, retires into the background; thought is absorbed in
the contemplation of the divine authority which lies behind
them and expresses itself through them. Even when explanatory adjuncts are added indicating where the words to which
appeal is made are to be found written, they are so framed
as not to lessen this implication. Commonly there is given
only a bare reference to the written source of the words in
mind;[48] and when the human authors are named, it is not

[47] Cf. especially Cremer, *sub voc.* γράφω: and A. Kuyper, "Encyclopaedia of
Sacred Theology," pp. 433 *seq.*, 444 *seq.*

[48] "In the law and the prophets and the psalms," Lk. xxiv. 44; "in the law"
(of the whole Old Testament), Jno. x. 34, xv. 25, 1 Cor. xiv. 21; "in the (or your,
or their) law," Lk. x. 26; Jno. viii. 17; "in the law of Moses," 1 Cor. ix. 9; "in the
law of the Lord," Lk. ii. 23; "in the prophets," Jno. vi. 45, Acts xx. 14; "in
the book of the words of Isaiah the prophet," Luke iii. 4; "in the book of the
prophets," Acts vii. 42; "in the Book of Psalms," Acts i. 20 (cf. Luke xxi. 62,
Matt. xii. 36); "in the second Psalm," Acts xiii. 33. The closest definitions of

so much as the responsible authors of the words adduced as the intermediaries through whom the Divine authority expresses itself.[49] In the parallel usage by which the Scriptures are appealed to by "It is said" and similar formulas the implication in question is perhaps even more clear. In Matthew, for example, Scripture is often cited as "what was spoken through (διά)" the prophets (ii. 23) or the prophet (xiii. 35, xxi. 4), or more specifically through this or that prophet — Isaiah ([iii. 3], iv. 14, viii. 17, xii. 17, cf. Jno. xii. 38), or Jeremiah (ii. 17, xxvii. 9) or Daniel (xxiv. 15). In a few passages of this kind the implication is explicitly filled out, and we read that the Scripture is spoken "by the Lord" (ὑπὸ κυρίου) through (διά) the prophet (i. 22, ii. 15, cf., xxii. 31, "Have ye not *read* what was spoken by God *to you*," that is, in their Scriptures; Acts i. 16, "The Scriptures which the Holy Ghost spoke before through the words of David"; xxviii. 25, "The Holy Ghost spoke through Isaiah the prophet to your fathers"). A similar use of εἰρημένον or εἴρηται occurs in the writings of Luke, whether absolutely (Lk. iv. 12, [Rom. iv. 18]) or with indication of the place where it is said (Lk. ii. 24, Acts xiii. 40); and here too we find occasionally a suggestion that the human speaker is only the intermediary of the true speaker, God (Acts ii. 16, διά the prophet Joel). It is possibly, however, not in the Gospels that the general usage illustrated by these passages finds its fullest or most emphatic expression; but rather in the Epistle to the Hebrews, where the Scriptures are looked upon almost exclusively from the point of sight of this usage. Its height perhaps is attained in the designation of Scripture as τὰ λόγια (Rom. iii. 2, cf. Acts vii. 38, Heb. v. 12, I Pet. iv. 11) and the current citation of it by the subjectless φησίν (I Cor. vi. 16) or λέγει (Rom. xv. 10, II Cor. vi. 2, Gal. iii. 16, Eph. iv. 8, v. 14), the authoritative subject being taken for granted.[50] In the Gospels, however, we have place in the Gospels are probably "at the bush," Mk. xii. 26; and "at the place," Luke iv. 17.

[49] Matt. ii. 5, "*through* the prophet"; Luke xviii. 31, "*through* the prophet."
[50] Cf. *The Presbyterian and Reformed Review*, July 1899, p. 472, April 1900, p. 217.

sufficient illustration of the same general method of dealing
with Scripture, side by side with their treatment of it as
documentary authority, to evince that their writers and Jesus
as reported by them, shared the same fundamental view-
point.[51]

ON THE TERMS "BIBLE," "HOLY BIBLE."

The purpose of the following note is simply to bring together what seems to be currently known of the origin of the
terms "Bible," "Holy Bible." No attempt has been made to
go behind the universally accessible sources of information
upon which the general public depends, in order to gather
additional material. The object in view is merely to make
plain how incomplete the accessible knowledge of the history
of these terms is. It is remarkable that terms daily on the
lips of the entire Western world should have been left until
to-day without adequate historical explanation. The fact is,
however, beyond doubt. In a short letter printed in *The Expository Times* a few years ago [52] Eb. Nestle remarks that
"nobody as yet knows how the word 'Bible' found its way
into the European languages" and represents even Theodor
Zahn as declining the task of working out the story.[53] The

[51] The ἐρρέθη of Matt. v. 21, 27, 31, 33, 38, 43 (Cf. Rom. ix. 12, 26, Gal. iii. 16)
is not a formula of citation, — for which we should have the perfect, εἴρηκεν (Heb.
iv. 3, x. 9–15, xiii. 5) — but adduces the historical fact that such teaching as is
adduced was given to the ancients. J. A. Alexander (on Matt. v. 21) admirably
paraphrases: "You have (often) heard (it said by the scribes and leading Pharisees) that our fathers were commanded not to murder, and that consequently
he who murders (in the strict sense of the term) is liable to be condemned and
punished under the commandment." The subsequent instances, though in verses
27, 31, 38, 43 more or less abridged in the introductory formula, are governed by
the full formula of verse 21. In point of fact the commandments adduced, (with
additions to the first and last) are all found written in the Mosaic Law. But our
Lord does not say that they are found there; He merely says that His hearers had
often heard from their official teachers, that they were found there — "*Ye have
heard* that it was commanded . . ." So Spanheim, J. A. Alexander, etc.

[52] 1903–4, Vol. XV. pp. 565–566.

[53] What Zahn says, "Geschichte des N. T. Kanons" II. p. 944, is: "On the
origin and earliest spread of the modern use of 'Bible' among the Western peoples
I do not venture to say anything."

account which is ordinarily given is that βιβλία was current
in Greek in the sense of "the Bible"; that this was taken
over into Latin as a feminine singular, "Biblia"; and that
this form in turn passed thence into the several Western languages.[54] There is no step of this presumed process, however,
which is beyond dispute, and a great obscurity rests upon
the whole subject.

Th. Zahn [55] enters a strong denial with respect to the basis
of the development which is assumed. "For τὰ βιβλία as a
designation of the Old Testament," he says, "no usage can be
adduced." More broadly still: "The mediaeval and modern
employment of τὰ βιβλία in the sense of αἱ γραφαί, ἡ γραφή,
that is 'Bible,' is altogether alien to the ancient church."
The current representation on the faith of Suicer [56] that τὰ
βιβλία occurs first in the sense of 'Bible' in Chrysostom, he
continues, is "only a widely-spread error"; the passages Suicer
quotes do not support the representation.

To justify this last assertion Zahn examines the three passages which Suicer quotes from Chrysostom in support of his
statement that "Scriptura Sacra is called βιβλία simpliciter,"
and concludes that no one of them employs the term in that
sense. In one of them — Hom. 10 in Genes. (Montfaucon, iv.
81) not βιβλία simpliciter, but θεῖα βιβλία is used. In another
— Hom. 2 on certain passages of Genesis (Montfaucon, iv.
652) — Chrysostom declares that the Jews have no doubt
τὰ βιβλία, but we Christians alone τῶν βιβλίων θησαυρός, —
they τὰ γράμματα, we, however, both τὰ γράμματα and τὰ
νοήματα — not the Bible but the Pentateuch being in mind
and the very point of the statement requiring us to take the

[54] See e. g. A. Stewart, Hastings' DB, sub voc. 'Bible'; W. Sanday, Hastings'
ERE, sub voc. 'Bible'; Hilgenfeld, "Einleitung in das N. T." p. 30.
[55] "Geschichte des N. T. Kanons" II. pp. 943–4.
[56] Credner, "Geschichte des N. T. Kanons," 1860, p. 229: "Further it is well
known that for the collection of the sacred writings in general the name τὰ βιβλία
(Bible) occurs first in the usage of Chrysostom (cf. 'Suiceri Thesaurus,' sub voc.)."
Reuss, "History of the New Testament," E. T. p. 326 (§ 320): "From the time of
Chrysostom the canonical collection is called simply τὰ βιβλία." Ersch and
Gruber, art. "Bibel" ad init. Neither Credner's nor Reuss's statement is, how-
ever, quite justified by Suicer's words.

"Books" as merely so much paper, as the "letters" as only
so much ink. It is on the third passage, however, that Suicer
lays most stress, remarking of it, here "βιβλία is used absolutely and means Sacra Biblia." It is found in "Hom. ix. in
Epist. ad Coloss." (Montfaucon xi. 391) and runs as follows:
"Delay not, I beseech thee: thou hast the oracles (λόγια) of
God. . . . Hear, I beseech you, all ye who are careful for this
life, and procure βιβλία φάρμακα τῆς ψυχῆς. . . . If you will
have nothing else, get, then, the New [Testament: τὴν καινήν
used absolutely as frequently in Chrysostom], the Apostle,
the Acts, the Gospels, constant teachers, . . . This is the
cause of all our evils, — ignorance of τὰς γραφάς." Zahn remarks: "It is evident that the anarthrous βιβλία here is not
a name of the Bible, but designates the category 'Books,'
to which, among others, the New Testament belongs; books
too can be means of grace and constant teachers."

The average reader will no doubt feel that in his examination of these passages Zahn presses his thesis a little too
far.

The contrast in the second passage between the Books and
the Treasure hidden in them, between the Letter and the
Sense, of course, throws the emphasis on the *mere* Books and
the *mere* Letter. But this, so far from excluding, presupposes
rather, the technical usage of these terms, τὰ βιβλία, τὰ γράμματα, to mean "Bible," "Scripture." The terms are used here
certainly with primary reference to the Old Testament. But
this is not to the exclusion of the New. In the third passage —
in which the rich series of designations of Scripture brought
together should be observed: "the Oracles of God," "the
New [Testament]," "the Scriptures," — it is clear enough,
no doubt, that βιβλία is primarily a common noun. But it
does not seem clear that it does not contain in itself a suggestion of its use as a proper noun. Beyond question Chrysostom means by these βιβλία just the Bible; just the "Oracles
of God" of which he had spoken immediately before, inclusive of the New Testament of which he immediately afterwards speaks, and constituting "the Scriptures" of which he

speaks somewhat further on. He speaks of these Bible books
as remedial, and of course he speaks generally without an
article. The case is like the anarthrous ἱερὰ γράμματα of II Tim.
iii. 16, or the anarthrous 'Bible' when we congratulate ourselves that we live "in a land of an open Bible"; in both of
which instances the term is technical enough. When Chrysostom exhorted his hearers to get for themselves βιβλία which
will be medicaments for their souls, they caught under the
common noun βιβλία the implication of the technical τὰ βιβλία. These passages of Chrysostom, after all would seem then
to bear witness to the currency of the term τὰ βιβλία as the
synonym of αἱ γραφαί, ἡ γραφή.

But why should we confine ourselves to the passages cited
by Suicer? Sophocles defines τὰ βιβλία, if not, like Suicer, as
the sacred Books of the Christians, yet, similiarly, as "the
Sacred Books of the Hebrews," quoting for his definition the
Prologue to Ecclesiasticus, I Macc. xii. 9 (τὰ ἅγια), Josephus,
"Contr. Apion.," i. 8; and Clem. Alex. [Migne] i. 668 B,
Origen, [Migne] i. 1276, C. The three Jewish citations we
may leave for the moment to one side: in any case they do
not present us with an absolute τὰ βιβλία, meaning "the
Scriptures." Clement and Origen take us back two hundred
years before Chrysostom.

In the passage cited from Clement — it is "Paedagog."
iii. xii. *med.* — Clement is speaking of the goodness of the Instructor in setting forth his salutary commandments in the
great variety of the Scriptures. He had adduced our Lord's
great summary of the Law (Matt. xxii. 37–40) and His injunction to the rich young man "to keep the commandments";
and taking a new beginning from this injunction, he enlarges
on the Decalogue. "These things," he remarks, "are to be
observed," — and not these only, but along with them, "whatsoever else we see prescribed for us as we read τὰ βιβλία."
For example there is Isaiah i. 10, 17, 18, and the declaration
of Scripture that "good works are an acceptable prayer to
the Lord" — whatever the passage may be which Clement
may have had in mind when he wrote this. It is scarcely dis-

putable that by τὰ βιβλία here, used absolutely, there is meant
just "the *Sacred* Books," that is to say, "the Bible." The
immediately preceding reference is to the Decalogue, and the
immediately contiguous ones are to the Old Testament. But
it seems hardly possible to contend that τὰ βιβλία therefore
means here either the Decalogue, or the Pentateuch, or the
Old Testament, distinctively. It is altogether more probable
that it is equally comprehensive with the αἱ γραφαί of the
closely preceding context. We cannot accord with Sophocles'
opinion, then, that τὰ βιβλία here means "the Sacred Books
of the Hebrews": it seems to us to mean "the Sacred Books
of the Christians."

The passage cited by Sophocles from Origen is "Contra
Celsum" v. 60 (Ed. Koetschau, 1899, ii. p. 63: 22. 23). In it
the Hebrew Scriptures are clearly referred to by τὰ βιβλία. It
declares that Jews and Christians alike "confess that τὰ βιβλία were written by the Divine Spirit." But it does not follow
that τὰ βιβλία means with Origen the Old Testament as distinguished from the New, though Koetschau seems inclined
to hold this to be the fact. "The Books of the Holy Scriptures," he writes (*Prolegom.* i. p. xxxii.), "are with Origen
generally designated θεῖα βιβλία, γραφή (γραφαί) or γράμματα;
those of the Old Testament, βιβλία, παλαιὰ γραφή or παλαιὰ
γράμματα." This would seem to say that the absolute τὰ βιβλία with Origen is the synonym not of ἡ γραφή but of ἡ παλαιὰ γραφή, not of τὰ γράμματα but of τὰ παλαιὰ γράμματα.
There seems to be nothing in the Contra "Celsum," to be
sure, which will decisively refute this opinion. There we read
of "the sacred βιβλία of the Jews" or "of the Hebrews" (Koetschau, i. 304, 26; 305, 6): of "the βιβλία which the prophets
wrote in Hebrew" (ii. 208, 22; cf., i. 291, 12), or simply of
"the βιβλία of the Jews" (ii. 93, 18); but nowhere else than
in v. 60 (so far as Koetschau's confessedly incomplete index
indicates) do we meet with absolute τὰ βιβλία in the sense of
"The Scriptures." [57] But what shall we make of a passage like

[57] At ii. 120, 22, we read of "the book of Genesis," and at various passages of
secular "books" (ii. 63, 4; 58, 17; 109, 15; 152, 26; 293, 1.).

the following from the 'Fourteenth Homily on Jeremiah' (§ 12: Ed. Klostermann, 1901, p. 117, line 4)? "'For thy sins, then, will I give thy treasures for a spoil.' And he gave the treasures of the Jews to us, for they were the first to believe τὰ λόγια τοῦ θεοῦ, and only after them did we believe, God having taken the λόγια away from them and given them to us. And we say that 'the kingdom shall be taken away from them by God and given to a nation bringing forth the fruits thereof' has been said by the Saviour and shall be fulfilled. Not that ἡ γραφή has been taken away from them, but now, though they have the Law and the Prophets they do not understand the meaning that is in them. For they have τὰ βιβλία. But how was the kingdom of God taken from them? The meaning τῶν γραφῶν was taken from them," etc. It is worth while to pause and note the rich synonymy of "the Scriptures" here. And, noting it, we may well ask whether, if τὰ βιβλία, because it is used here with the eye on the Hebrew Scriptures, is to be taken as meaning distinctively the *Hebrew* Scriptures, this same is not true also of τὰ λόγια and ἡ γραφή and αἱ γραφαί. There is a subtle propriety in the adjustment of these three terms to the exact place in which each appears in the argument. Λόγια emphasizes the divine origin of the Scriptures; βιβλία looks upon them from the point of view of their external form; γραφή, of their significant contents. The terms could not be interchanged without some loss of exactness of speech: βιβλία accordingly stands where it does because it expresses the externalia of the Scriptures, sets them before us as "nothing but books" — so much paper. But in their general connotation the three terms are coextensive, and there is no reason for narrowing τὰ βιβλία to "the Old Testament" because it refers to the Old Testament here, which will not apply as well to τὰ λόγια and to ἡ γραφή, αἱ γραφαί. There is preserved for us in the "Philocalia" (Ch. v., ed. Robinson, 1893, pp. 43–48) a remarkable fragment of the Fifth Book of Origen's 'Commentary on John' (ed. Preuschen, 1903, pp. 100–105), in which Origen, speaking to the text, "Of the making of many books there is no end," rings the changes on βιβλίον and βιβλία and leaves a strong impression on the reader's mind that to him τὰ βιβλία would be exactly synonymous with τὰ θεῖα βιβλία. "But since," says he (Preuschen, p. 103, 12), "the proofs of this must be drawn from τῆς θείας γραφῆς, it will be most satisfactorily established if I am able to show that it is not in one Book only that it is written among us concerning Christ — taking τὰ βιβλία in its common sense. For we find it written in the Pentateuch," etc. Origen here, by telling us that τὰ βιβλία has a common sense, tells us also that it has a special sense, and that in this special sense it includes alike the New Testament in which we should expect to find Christ spoken of, and the Pentateuch where also He is spoken of; in a word it is the exact synonym of ἡ θεία γραφή.[58]

If we do not quite learn from Clement and Origen, therefore, — as Sophocles would have us learn — that, because it is used of the Sacred Books of the Hebrews, τὰ βιβλία means distinctively the "Sacred Books of the Hebrews," we do learn what Zahn would not have us learn, that it is used absolutely in the sense of "the Sacred Scriptures." We must now take note of the fact, however, that Zahn's primary object was to deny not that τὰ βιβλία, absolutely used, could mean "the Sacred Books," but precisely that it could mean the Sacred Books *of the Hebrews* — the Old Testament. His primary statement is that no usage can be adduced of τὰ βιβλία as a designation distinctively of the Old Testament. He is discussing the reading of a clause in II Clemens Rom. xiv. This clause couples together (in the Constantinople MS. followed by Lightfoot) τὰ βιβλία καὶ οἱ ἀπόστολοι, which, as Lightfoot remarks, is a rough designation of the Old and New Testaments. On the testimony of the Syriac version Zahn reads τὰ βιβλία τῶν προφητῶν καὶ οἱ ἀπόστολοι, and to strengthen his position argues that absolute τὰ βιβλία

[58] Preuschen indexes the following further occurrences of the plural τὰ βιβλία (apart from the passage, pp. 100–105) in the "Commentary on John:" p. 40, 21, τὰ τῆς καινῆς διαθήκης βιβλία; 117, 19, δι' ὅλων τῶν ἁγίων βιβλίων. At p. 9, 24 Origen opens an inquiry as to why ταῦτα τὰ βιβλία — that is the Gospels, — are called by the singular title of εὐαγγέλιον.

for "the Old Testament" is unexampled. We have already seen enough to prove to us that absolute τὰ βιβλία was quite readily used to designate the Old Testament — because the Old Testament was part of the Scriptures, that is of τὰ βιβλία in their pregnant sense. But whether τὰ βιβλία was used *distinctively* of the Old Testament — when the Old Testament was set over against the New — is another question.

This question need not wait long, however, for an answer. It cannot be doubted, and it is not doubted, that the Jews called their sacred writings, by way of eminence, "the Books." As Zahn very exactly declares [59] the Hebrew הספרים (Mishna Megilla i. 8) certainly underlies the usage of αἱ γραφαί, ἡ γραφή in the general sense of "the Bible." The antiquity of this phrase may be estimated from its occurrence in Daniel ix. 2: "I Daniel understood by 'the Books' . . .": "that is," says Driver, commenting on the passage, "the sacred books, the Scriptures" (cf. ספר in Ps. xl. 8, Is. xxix. 18). The Greek rendering of this passage gives us to be sure αἱ βίβλοι rather than τὰ βιβλία. But already in I Macc. xii. 9 we have the full phrase of which τὰ βιβλία is the natural abbreviation — τὰ βιβλία τὰ ἅγια, while Josephus gives us the parallel τὰ ἱερὰ βιβλία: and from these phrases τὰ βιβλία could not fail to be extracted, just as γραφαί, was extracted from αἱ ἅγιαι γραφαί, αἱ ἱεραὶ γραφαί, and the like. We meet with no surprise therefore the appearance of τὰ βιβλία in II Clems. xiv, as a distinctive designation of the Old Testament. It only advertises to us, what we knew beforehand, that the Old Testament was "the Books" before both Old and New Testaments were subsumed under that title, and that usage, in a community made up partly of Jews, for a time conserved, without prejudice to the equal authority of the New Testament Books, some lingering reminiscence of the older habit of speech. How easily the Old Testament might continue to be called τὰ βιβλία after the term had come to include New Books as well, may be illus-

[59] "Geschichte," etc. I. 87, note 1.

trated by a tendency which is observable in the earlier English usage of the word "Bible" (persisting even yet dialectically) to employ it of the Old Testament distinctively — as in the phrase "The Bible and the Testament," — not, of course, with any implication of inferiority for the New Testament books.[60] How long such a tendency to think of the Old Testament especially when the term τὰ βιβλία was heard continued to manifest itself in the early church, it would require a delicate investigation to determine. It is enough for the moment to note that II Clems. xiv witnesses to the presence of such a tendency in the first age, while such phrases as meet us in Melito of Sardis [61] — τὰ παλαιὰ βιβλία, τὰ τῆς παλαιᾶς διαθήκης βιβλία — warn us that the new conditions of the New Covenant with its New Books were already requiring a distinction, among the τὰ βιβλία by way of eminence, between the New and the Old Books which made up the whole. Τὰ βιβλία in a word to Jew and Christian alike meant just "the Holy Books," "the Books" by way of eminence, by the side of which could stand no others; and though ear and lip needed a space to adjust themselves to the increased content of the phrase when Christianity came bringing with it its contribution to the unitary collection, yet the adjustment was quickly made and if the memory of the earlier usage persisted for a while, τὰ βιβλία in Christian circles meant from the beginning in principle the whole body of Sacred Books and rapidly came to mean in practice nothing less.

We cannot agree with Zahn, then, that the usage of τὰ βιβλία in the early church provides no basis upon which the development of our term "Bible" could have taken place. But when we come to take the next step in the development of that term, we are constrained to assent to Nestle's declaration that nobody knows how the term "Bible" found its way into the European languages. The Latins did not take

---

[60] See the passages from the Oxford "Dictionary of the English Language," in note 82 below.
[61] Otto: ix. 414.

over the Greek word βιβλία, or its cognate βίβλοι, to designate the Biblical books. They had in their own *Liber* a term which· had already acquired a pregnant sense "in religion and public law" — as expressing "a religious book, Scripture, a statute book, codex" [62]; and which therefore readily lent itself to employment as the representative of the pregnant Greek terms which it translates, though it scarcely seems to have attained so absolute a use. Accordingly we find in use in the early church side by side with such Greek phrases as τὰ βιβλία τῆς παλαιᾶς, τῆς καινῆς διαθήκης, the Latin phrases, *Libri veteris, novi testamenti, (fœderis)*: [63] and over against the Greek βιβλία κανονικά, the Latin *libri regulares*, or as Rufinus puts it, *libri inter canonem conclusi*.[64] Jerome gave currency to the very appropriate term *Bibliotheca* as the designation of the corpus of the Sacred Books; and this term became later the technical term perhaps most frequently employed, so that Martianaeus in his "Prolegomena in divinam bibliothecam Hieron." i. §1,[65] speaking *de nomine Bibliothecae Divinae*, can very fairly say, "among the ancients, the sacred volume which we, at the present time, call Biblia, obtained the name of Bibliotheca Divina."[66] There is no trace of such a word as "Biblia" in Patristic Latin, and no such word is entered in the Latin Lexicons, — not even in

[62] Andrews' "Latin-English Lexicon," *sub voc.*

[63] Reuss, E. T. p. 308, § 303.

[64] Reuss, p. 321, § 316.

[65] Migne, "Patrol. Lat." xxviii. ("Hieron." vol. 14) pp. 33–34.

[66] M. Kähler, "Dogmatische Zeitfragen," [2] I. p. 362, writes: "It was very harmlessly intended and was not in contradiction of the usage followed by Christ Himself, when the Holy Scripture was called a Bibliotheca. . . . As, however, that designation 'Bibliotheca' never became the dominant one, and the Biblical one, 'the Scripture,' alone ultimately maintained itself, so the comprehensive name, 'the Bible,' attained general currency in the West before the ninth century." On this last point, he had already said, (p. 232 note 1): "As a popular designation 'Biblia' was in use long before its earliest provable occurrence in the ninth century," with appeal to: "Eb. Nestle, *Beil. zur Allg. Z.* 1904, No. 90, p. 117," — an article to which we have not access, though possibly we have its essential contents in the contemporarily printed note in the *Expository Times*, mentioned at the beginning of this discussion. It can be said that 'Bibliotheca' never became the dominant designation of the Scriptures only in contrast with such a designation as "the Scriptures."

the great Latin "Thesaurus" now publishing by the German Universities. We shall have to come to Du Cange's "Gloss. Med. et Inf. Latinitatis" to discover it. And when we discover it we are told very little about it except of its existence in the Latin of the early middle ages, and shortly afterwards in the vernaculars of the West.

There seems to be no serious inherent difficulty in conceiving the passage of a Greek neuter plural into Latin as a feminine singular. The thing appears not to be unexampled, and so might have happened to βιβλία. What we lack is clear evidence that βιβλία did pass into "Biblia," and exact information of the stages and processes by which the feat was accomplished. And the difficulty of the problem is vastly increased by the circumstances that the time when the transference is supposed to have taken place was not a time when there was rich intercourse between the East and the West, in which borrowing of terms would have been easy and natural; and that there was no obvious need upon the part of the West for such a term, which would render its borrowing of it natural. Yet the term is supposed to have been taken over with such completeness and heartiness as to have become the parent of the common nomenclature of the Scriptures in all the Western languages.[67] The difficulties raised by these considerations are so great that one finds himself questioning whether the origin of the term "Biblia" in Mediaeval Latin and of its descendants in the Western languages can be accounted for after the fashion suggested, and whether some other conjectural explanation of their origin might not wisely be sought for — as, for example, a contraction of the commonly current term "bibliotheca." [68] Some color might be lent to such a conjecture by the fact that "Biblia" and its descendants seem to have been from the first in use not

[67] Grimm, sub voc. "Bibel," enumerates as follows: Italian, bibbia, Spanish, biblia, French, bible, Middle High German, biblie, Dutch, bijbel, Islandic, biflja, Russian and Lithuanian, biblija, Polish, biblia, Bohemian, biblj, etc.

[68] The Latin "Thesaurus" tells us that " bibliotheca " occurs in titles variously contracted: "Compendia in titulis: by., byb., bybl., byblio., bibliot.," and in even completer forms.

merely in an ecclesiastical but also in a common sense — as
designations, that is, not merely of the Scriptures but of any
large book.[69] Appeal might be made also to the ease with
which the two terms 'Biblia' and 'Bibliotheca' took one the
other's place down at least to the fifteenth century.[70] What
we need, however, is not conjectures but a series of ascertained facts, and these are at the moment at our disposal in
very insufficient measure.

Du Cange can tell us only that the word "Biblia" occurs
in the "Imitatio Christi" I i. 3,[71] and in the "Diarium Belli
Hussitici," adding a quotation from a Chronicle, at the year
1228, to the·effect that "Stephen, archibishop of Canterbury . . . made postils super *totam Bibliam*." To this Diefenbach in the "Glossarium," which he published (1857) as a
supplement to Du Cange, merely adds an intimation that
certain fifteenth century glossaries contain "Biblia" in the
sense of a "large book," [72] as also "Biblie" and "Bibel"
(German). Becker in his "Catalogi Bibliothecarum Antiqui" is
able to cite earlier examples of "Biblia" from old catalogues
of libraries. The earliest — from the ninth century — comes
from the catalogue of an unknown French library; next in
age are two twelfth century examples — one from Monte
Cassiro and the other from Stederburg in Brunswick. The
English Latin catalogues in which he finds it begin with one
of the books at Durham, dating from 1266,[73] and by that

[69] See Diefenbach's addenda to Du Cange, *sub voc.* "Biblia." The Oxford Dictionary gives English examples from the fourteenth to the sixteenth centuries: e. g.
1377, Lang. " Piers Pl." B. xv. 87; "Of this matere I mygte mak a long bible";
1542, Udall, Erasm. "Apophth," 205a, "When he had read a long bible written
and sent to hym from Antipater." (The quotation from Z. Boyd 1629 does not
seem to us to belong here).

[70] This is adverted to in the Oxford Dictionary, *sub voc.* "Bible." The following citations are given: 1382, Wyclif, 2 *Macc.* ii. 13, "He makynge a litil bible
(Vulg. bibliothecam) gadride of cuntrees bokis"; c. 1425, in Wr.-Wülcker, *Voc.*
648, *Bibleoteca*, bybulle; 1483 *Cath. Angl.* 31, A Bybylle, *biblia*, *bibliotheca*.

[71] Si scires totam Bibliam.   [72] "Biblia, eyn gross buch."

[73] Cf. Eb. Nestle, *The Expository Times*, xv. pp. 565–566. The citation given
in the Oxford Dictionary from an Anglo-Latin occurrence of "biblia" in 1095 —
viz. from the Catalogue of the Lindisfarne books — Nestle shows to rest on an
error. This catalogue dates from the fourteenth or fifteenth century.

time the word was already in use in English,[74] and of course in French,[75] since the English usage rests on the French. How early it appears in the modern European languages we lack data to inform us. The German examples which Diefenbach quotes are from the fifteenth century and those which Heyne gives from the sixteenth,[76] while Grimm cites none earlier than the seventeenth. But if the Low-German "Fibel" is really a derivative of "Bibel," the common use of "Bibel" must have antedated the fifteenth century.[77] Littré gives no French example earlier than Joinville, who wrote at the beginning of the fourteenth century (1309). Its French usage must go well back of this, however, for as we have seen it had come from French into Middle English by that date. The name in ordinary use throughout the Middle Ages for what we call the "Bible" was "Bibliotheca," and we accordingly find that in Old English (Anglo-Saxon) "bibliothéce" alone occurs in this sense.[78] From the fourteenth

---

[74] The Oxford Dictionary cites from c. 1300, *Cursor M.* 1900: "As the bibul sais"; from 1330, R. Brunne, *Chron.* 290: "The bible may not lie."

[75] Littré ("Dictionaire de la Langue Française" I. *sub voc.*) cites only: "HIST. xiii^es. — Un cordelier vint à li au chastel de Yeres [Hières] et pour enseigner le roi, dit en son sermon, que il avoit leu la Bible et les livres qui parlent des princes mescreans, JOINV. 199." To this may be added Joinville, "Histoire de Saint Louis," Paris, Didot, 1874, p. 310 (cxi. 569): "L'endemain s'ala logier li roys devant la citei d'Arsur que l'on appelle Tyri en la Bible." On p. 320 (cxiii. 583) "Bible" occurs in the sense of "Balista," cf. Du Cange, *sub voc.* "Biblia I." The Century and the Standard Dictionaries both record this usage for English.

[76] Heyne, "Deutsches Wörterbuch" I. 1890, tells us *sub voc.* that Bibel is a borrowed word from the Greek neuter-plural Biblia, "Books," which since the late Middle-High-German, as in Middle Latin, has been looked on as a feminine singular, first in a form nearer to the Latin, and afterwards in that now current — with a reference to Diefenbach. His earliest citations are from Luther, who still has ("D. christliche Adel," 1520) "die biblien, das heilig gotis wort," but elsewhere ("Wider die himlischen Proph." 1525): "aus meine verdeutschten bibel."

[77] Cf. F. Kluge, "Etymologisches Wörterbuch d. deutschen Sprache," 6². ed. 1905 *sub voc.* "Fibel," where we are told that it was entered in Low-German Glossaries of the fifteenth century (first in 1419), was used by Luther, and duly registered since Henisch 1616. Kluge classifies "Bibel" as a Middle-High-German word."

[78] The Oxford Dictionary says: "In O. E. bibliotheca alone occurs." Nestle *l. c.* says: "The name commonly used throughout the Middle Ages was Bibliotheca"; and accordingly in O. E. and all mediaeval writers this term is used for

century on, however, "Bible" takes the place of "Biblio-théce." Chaucer uses it freely in both the ecclesiastical and common senses.[79] Purvey uses it as a word well-known in common currency, referring naturally to "the Bible late translated," and to that "simple creature" (as he called himself) "who hath translated the Bible out of the Latin into the English." The rapidity with which the term entered into general usage may be divined from the examples given by Richardson and Murray.

These lexicographers record no example, however, of the occurrence of the compound term, "The Holy Bible." It seems that this combination was somewhat late in establishing itself as the stated designation of the sacred book in English. It first finds a place on the title-page of an English Bible in the so-called "Bishops' Bible," the earliest issue of which dates from 1568: "The. holie. Bible. | conteynyng the olde | Testament and the newe." | [80] It, of course, continues on the title-pages of the numerous subsequent issues of this edition,[81] but it does not otherwise occur on the title-page of English Bibles until the appearance of the Douai Old Testament of 1610: "The | Holie Bible | ...." The Rheims trans-

complete Mss. of Old and New Testaments. The Anglo-Saxons also used "ge-writ" when speaking of the Bible.

[79] In the ecclesiastical sense: "Canterbury Tales:" Prolog. l. 438, "His studie was but litel on the Bible"; "Pardoner's Tale," l. 4652, "Looketh the Bible, and ther ye may it leere"; "The Wife's Preamble," l. 10729, "He knew of hem mo legendes and lyves | Than been of goode wyves in the Bible." In the general sense: "Canterbury Tales," Prol. to Canon's "Yeoman's Tale," l. 17257, "To tellen al wolde passen any Bible | That owher is"; "House of Fame," l. 1334 (Book iii. l. 244), If all the arms of the people he saw in his dream were described, "men myght make of hem a Bible twenty foote thykke."

[80] The *editio princeps* of the English Bible (Coverdale, 1535) bears the title: "Biblia | The Byble: that | is the holy Scrypture of the | Olde and New Testament." Matthew's Bible, of 1537, has: "The Byble, | which is all the holy Scrip- | ture: In whych are contayned the | Olde and Newe Testament —" Taverner's Bible, of 1539, has: "The most | sacred Bible, | whiche is the holy scripture, con- | teyning the old and new testament." The very popular and frequently reprinted "Genevan Bible" called itself, edition 1560: "The Bible | and | Holy Scriptures | conteyned in | the olde and Newe | Testament."

[81] E. g. 1573, 1574, 1575 bis, 1576, 1577 bis, 1578, 1584, 1585, 1588, 1591, 1595, 1602.

lators, in the preface of their New Testament, published in
1582, had indeed spoken of "the holy Bible" as "long since
translated by us into English, and the Old Testament lying
by us for lacke of goode meanes to publish the whole in such
sort as a worke of so great charge and importance requireth";
from which we may learn that, though the volume of 1610
contains only the Old Testament, the term "The Holie
Bible" upon its title is not to be confined to the Old Testament, as sometimes the phrase was confined in its Old English use.[82] The adoption of the term "The Holy Bible"
for the title-page of King James' version of 1611: "The |
Holy Bible, | conteyning the Old Testament, | and the
New | ," finally fixed it as the technical designation of the
book in English.

It is natural to assume that the current title of the Vulgate Latin Bible with which we are familiar — "Biblia Sacra"
— lay behind this English development; but it would be a
mistake to suppose that this was by any means the constant
designation of the Latin Bible in the earlier centuries of its
printing. A hasty glance over the lists of editions recorded
in Masch's Le Long (iii.) indeed leaves the impression that it
was only after the publication of the "authorized" Roman
edition of 1590, "Biblia Sacra Vulgatae Editionis," that this
designation finally established itself as regular; though it was,
of course, frequently employed before that. The original edition of John Fust and Peter Schoeffer indeed is described by
Le Long (p. 98) as "Biblia Sacra Latina juxta Vulgatam
editionem II vol. in folio." And the title of the great Complutensian Polyglot (1514–1517) is given as "Biblia Sacra." [83]
But these are not the actual titles of these books, and it is

[82] In the Oxford Dictionary are found the following examples of this odd usage
from the sixteenth century: Rastell, "Bk. Purgat." I. 1. "Neyther of the bokys of
the olde byble nor of the newe testament"; 1587, Golding, "De Mornay," xxiv.
357, "Certaine bookes which we call the Bible or Olde Testament." It may not be
out of place to note that Rastell wrote as a Romanist, Golding as a Protestant
controversialist.

[83] This is the actual title of the Antwerp Polyglot, 1569–1572, and of Walton's
Polyglot, 1657; but not of the Paris Polyglot.

not until near the opening of the second quarter of the sixteenth century that "Biblia Sacra" begins to appear on the title-pages of the Latin Bibles which were pouring from the press.[84] Osiander's edition (Norimbergae, 1522) has it: "Biblia sacra utriusque Testamenti," (p. 309), and of course transmitted it to its reprints (1523, 1527, 1529, 1530, 1543, 1559, 1564); Knoblauch's contemporary edition, on the other hand, (Argentorati, 1522) has rather: "Biblia sacrae scripturae Veteris omnia" (p. 314).[85] Among Catholic editions, one printed at Cologne in 1527: "Biblia sacra utriusque Testamenti" (p. 178), seems to be the earliest recorded by Le Long, which has this designation. It seems to have been, however, a Paris edition of the next year (1528): "Biblia sacra: integrum utriusque testamenti corpus completens," (repeated in 1534, 1543, 1548, 1549, 1550, 1551, 1552, 1560) which set the fashion of it. Somewhat equivalent forms appear by its side, such as: "Biblia Bibliorum opus sacrosanctum" (Lugduni, 1532), "Biblie sacre Textus" (Lugduni, 1531), and especially "Biblia Sacrosancta" (Lugduni, 1532, 1535, 1536, 1544, 1546, 1556, 1562: Basiliae 1547, 1551, 1557, 1562, 1569, 1578). But none of these became fixed as the technical designation of the volume, as Biblia Sacra tended to become from the opening of the second quarter of the sixteenth century, and ended by fairly becoming before that century closed.

The Romance languages seem to have followed this grow-

[84] The *editio princeps* has no title page; and the Complutensian Polyglot no general title-page. Cf. Fr. Kaulen, "Geschichte der Vulgata," 1868, pp. 305–6: — "The first editions contain only the naked text of the Vulgate, together with the Introductions of St. Jerome and the old *Argumenta*, as they appear already in the "Codex Amiatinus." A proper title is at first not present; and neither the sheets nor the pages show numeration. Instead of the title, the front page bears commonly a heading in large type: *Incipit prologus sancti iheronymi, incipit epistola scti iheronymi ad paulinum, prologus biblie*, and the like. The folio edition of Basle, 1487, bears as title merely the one word, 'Biblia.'. . . In a Nuremberg Bible of 1471 there stands for the first time as title, 'Biblia Vulgata' . . . By far the most common title is 'Biblia Latina,' accompanied in later editions by some addition giving the contents."

[85] Brylinger's edition, Basiliae, 1544 (1551, 1557, 1562, 1569, 1578) has: "Biblia Sacrosancta" —

ing Latin custom in the designation of their Bibles, although examples of the simple nomenclature persist (e. g., *La Bible qui est toute la sainte escriture*, Geneva, 1562, 1622, 1638, 1657, etc.). Among the Teutonic races, other than the English, however, it has been slower in taking root. German Bibles still call themselves "Biblia, das ist: die gantze Heilige Schrift," or in more modern form, "Die Bibel, oder die ganze Heilige Schrift," and Dutch Bibles similiarly, "Biblia, dat is de gantsche H. Schrifture," or more modernly, "Bijbel, dat is de gansche Heilige Schrift." Doubtless "die heilige Bibel" or "de heilige Bybel" — though not unexampled, — would seem somewhat harsh and unusual to Teutonic ears. Strange to say they would take more kindly apparently to such a phrase as "Das heilige Bibelbuch."

Our common phrase, "The Holy Bible," thus reveals itself as probably a sixteenth century usage, which has not yet been made the common property of the Christian world. In its substantive, it rests on an as yet insufficiently explained mediaeval usage, not yet traced further back than the ninth century. This usage in turn is commonly assigned for its origin to a borrowing from the Greek churches of their customary use of τὰ βιβλία to designate the Scriptures. Behind this lies a Jewish manner of speech. This appears to be all that can as yet be affirmed of the origin of our common term: "The Holy Bible."

VI

THE REAL PROBLEM OF INSPIRATION

THE REAL PROBLEM OF INSPIRATION [1]

A GREAT deal is being said of late of " the present problem
of inspiration," with a general implication that the Christian
doctrine of the plenary inspiration of the Scriptures has been
brought into straits by modern investigation, and needs now to
adapt itself to certain assured but damaging results of the scientific study of the Bible. Thus, because of an assumed " present distress," Canon Cheyne, in a paper read at the English
Church Congress of 1888, commended a most revolutionary
book of Mr. R. F. Horton's, called "Inspiration and the
Bible," [2] which explains away inspiration properly so called altogether, as the best book he could think of on the subject. And
Mr. Charles Gore defends the concessive method of treating
the subject of inspiration adopted in " Lux Mundi," by the
plea that the purpose of the writers of that volume " was ' to
succour a distressed faith,' by endeavoring to bring the Christian creed into its right relation to the modern growth of
knowledge, scientific, historical, critical." [3] On our side of the
water, Dr. Washington Gladden has published a volume which
begins by presenting certain " new " views of the structure of
the books of the Bible as established facts, and proceeds to the
conclusion that: " Evidently neither the theory of verbal inspiration nor the theory of plenary inspiration can be made to
fit the facts which a careful study of the writings themselves
brings before us. These writings are not inspired in the sense
which we have commonly given to that word." Accordingly he
recommends that under the pressure of these new views we admit not only that the Bible is not " infallible," but that its laws

---

[1] From *The Presbyterian and Reformed Review,* v. iv, 1893. pp. 177–221.

[2] " Inspiration and the Bible." An Inquiry. By Robert F. Horton, M.A.,
Late Fellow of New College, Oxford. Fourth Edition. London: T. Fisher Unwin,
1889.

[3] " Lux Mundi." Tenth Edition. London: John Murray, 1890. P. xi.

are "inadequate" and "morally defective," and its untrustworthiness as a religious teacher is so great that it gives us in places "blurred and distorted ideas about God and His truth."[4] And Prof. Joseph H. Thayer has published a lecture which represents as necessitated by the facts as now known, such a change of attitude towards the Bible as will reject the whole Reformed doctrine of the Scriptures in favor of a more "Catholic" view which will look upon some of the history recorded in the Bible as only "fairly trustworthy," and will expect no intelligent reader to consider the exegesis of the New Testament writers satisfactory.[5] A radical change in our conception of the Scriptures as the inspired Word of God is thus pressed upon us as now necessary by a considerable number of writers, representing quite a variety of schools of Christian thought.

Nevertheless the situation is not one which can be fairly described as putting the old doctrine of inspiration in jeopardy. The exact state of the case is rather this: that a special school of Old Testament criticism, which has, for some years, been gaining somewhat widespread acceptance of its results, has begun to proclaim that these results having been accepted, a "changed view of the Bible" follows which implies a reconstructed doctrine of inspiration, and, indeed, also a whole new theology. That this changed view of the Bible involves losses is frankly admitted. The nature of these losses is stated by Dr. Sanday in a very interesting little book [6] with an evident effort to avoid as far as possible "making sad the heart of the righteous whom the Lord hath not made sad," as consisting chiefly in making "the intellectual side of the connection between Christian belief and Christian practice a matter of greater difficulty than it has hitherto seemed to be," in rendering it "less

[4] "Who Wrote the Bible?" A Book for the People. By Washington Gladden. Boston: Houghton, Mifflin & Co., 1891. See pp. 61 (cf. pp. 57, 92 seq.), 21, 25, 154 (cf. pp. 105, 166, 37, etc.).

[5] "The Change of Attitude Towards the Bible." A lecture, etc. By Joseph Henry Thayer, Professor in Harvard University. Boston: Houghton, Mifflin & Co., 1891. See pp. 9, 10, 22, 52, 65.

[6] "The Oracles of God" (Longmans, 1891), pp. 5, 45, 76.

easy to find proof texts for this or that," and in making the use
of the Bible so much less simple and less definite in its details
that " less educated Christians will perhaps pay more deference to the opinion of the more educated, and to the advancing
consciousness of the Church at large." If this means all that it
seems to mean, its proclamation of an indefinite Gospel eked
out by an appeal to the Church and a scholastic hierarchy, involves a much greater loss than Dr. Sanday appears to think —
a loss not merely of the Protestant doctrine of the perspicuity
of the Scriptures, but with it of all that that doctrine is meant
to express and safeguard — the loss of the Bible itself to the
plain Christian man for all practical uses, and the delivery of
his conscience over to the tender mercies of his human instructors, whether ecclesiastical or scholastic. Dr. Briggs is more
blunt and more explicit in his description of the changes which
he thinks have been wrought. " I will tell you what criticism
has destroyed," he says in an article published a couple of
years ago. " It has destroyed many false theories about the
Bible; it has destroyed the doctrine of verbal inspiration; it
has destroyed the theory of inerrancy; it has destroyed the
false doctrine that makes the inspiration depend upon its attachment to a holy man." [7] And he goes on to remark further
" that Biblical criticism is at the bottom " of the " reconstruction that is going on throughout the Church " — " the demand
for revision of creeds and change in methods of worship and
Christian work." It is clear enough, then, that a problem has
been raised with reference to inspiration by this type of criticism. But this is not equivalent to saying that the established
doctrine of inspiration has been put in jeopardy. For there is
criticism and criticism. And though it may not be unnatural for
these scholars themselves to confound the claims of criticism
with the validity of their own critical methods and the soundness of their own critical conclusions, the Christian world can
scarcely be expected to acquiesce in the identification. It has
all along been pointing out that they were traveling on the

[7] The article appeared in *The Christian Union,* but we quote it from *Public
Opinion,* vol. x. No. 24 (March 25, 1891), p. 576.

wrong road; and now when their conclusions clash with well-established facts, we simply note that the wrong road has not unnaturally led them to the wrong goal. In a word, it is not the established doctrine of inspiration that is brought into distress by the conflict, but the school of Old Testament criticism which is at present fashionable. It is now admitted that the inevitable issue of this type of criticism comes into collision with the established fact of the plenary inspiration of the Bible and the well-grounded Reformed doctrine of Holy Scripture based on this fact.[8] The cry is therefore, and somewhat impatiently, raised that this fact and this doctrine must " get out of the way," and permit criticism to rush on to its bitter goal. But facts are somewhat stubborn things, and are sometimes found to prove rather the test of theories which seek to make them their sport.

Nevertheless, though the strain of the present problem should thus be thrown upon the shoulders to which it belongs, it is important to keep ourselves reminded that the doctrine of inspiration which has become established in the Church, is open to all legitimate criticism, and is to continue to be held only as, and so far as, it is ever anew critically tested and approved. And in view of the large bodies of real knowledge concerning the Bible which the labors of a generation of diligent critical study have accumulated, and of the difficulty which is always experienced in the assimilation of new knowledge and

[8] This remark, of course, does not imply that there are none who assert that the results of this type of criticism leave " inspiration " untouched. Dr. Driver does not stand alone when he says, in the Preface to his " Introduction to the Literature of the Old Testament ": " Criticism in the hands of Christian scholars does not banish or destroy the inspiration of the Old Testament; it *presupposes* it " (p. xix). But Prof. Driver would be the last to maintain that the " inspiration " which criticism leaves to the Old Testament is what the Church has understood by the plenary inspiration of the Bible. Accordingly, Prof. Robertson speaks directly to the point when he remarks in the Preface to his " Early Religion of Israel " (p. xi), that " such scholars would do an invaluable service to the Church, at the present time, if they would explain what they mean by inspiration in this connection." The efforts to do this, on our side of the water, are not reassuring. On the relation of the new views to inspiration see the lucid statement by Dr. E. C. Bissell in *The Hartford Seminary Record,* ii. 1.

its correlation with previously ascertained truth, it is becoming to take this occasion to remind ourselves of the foundations on which this doctrine rests, with a view to inquiring whether it is really endangered by any assured results of recent Biblical study. For such an investigation we must start, of course, from a clear conception of what the Church doctrine of inspiration is, and of the basis on which it is held to be the truth of God. Only thus can we be in a position to judge how it can be affected on critical grounds, and whether modern Biblical criticism has reached any assured results which must or may " destroy " it.

The Church, then, has held from the beginning that the Bible is the Word of God in such a sense that its words, though written by men and bearing indelibly impressed upon them the marks of their human origin, were written, nevertheless, under such an influence of the Holy Ghost as to be also the words of God, the adequate expression of His mind and will. It has always recognized that this conception of co-authorship implies that the Spirit's superintendence extends to the choice of the words by the human authors (verbal inspiration [9]), and preserves its product from everything inconsistent with a divine authorship — thus securing, among other things, that entire truthfulness which is everywhere presupposed in and asserted for Scripture by the Biblical writers (inerrancy). Whatever minor variations may now and again have entered into the mode of statement, this has always been the core of the Church doctrine of inspiration. And along with many other modes of commending and defending it, the primary ground on which it has been held by the Church as the true doctrine is that it is the doctrine of the Biblical writers themselves, and has therefore the whole mass of evidence for it which goes to show that the Biblical writers are trustworthy as doctrinal guides. It is the testimony of the Bible itself to its own origin

[9] It ought to be unnecessary to protest again against the habit of representing the advocates of " verbal inspiration " as teaching that the mode of inspiration was by dictation. The matter is fully explained in the paper: " Inspiration." By Profs. A. A. Hodge and B. B. Warfield. Philadelphia: Presbyterian Board of Publication, 1881, pp. 19 seq.

and character as the Oracles of the Most High, that has led the Church to her acceptance of it as such, and to her dependence on it not only for her doctrine of Scripture, but for the whole body of her doctrinal teaching, which is looked upon by her as divine because drawn from this divinely given fountain of truth.

Now if this doctrine is to be assailed on critical grounds, it is very clear that, first of all, criticism must be required to proceed against the evidence on which it is based. This evidence, it is obvious, is twofold. First, there is the exegetical evidence that the doctrine held and taught by the Church is the doctrine held and taught by the Biblical writers themselves. And secondly, there is the whole mass of evidence — internal and external, objective and subjective, historical and philosophical, human and divine — which goes to show that the Biblical writers are trustworthy as doctrinal guides. If they are trustworthy teachers of doctrine and if they held and taught this doctrine, then this doctrine is true, and is to be accepted and acted upon as true by us all. In that case, any objections brought against the doctrine from other spheres of inquiry are inoperative; it being a settled logical principle that so long as the proper evidence by which a proposition is established remains unrefuted, all so-called objections brought against it pass out of the category of objections to its truth into the category of difficulties to be adjusted to it. If criticism is to assail this doctrine, therefore, it must proceed against and fairly overcome one or the other element of its proper proof. It must either show that this doctrine is not the doctrine of the Biblical writers, or else it must show that the Biblical writers are not trustworthy as doctrinal guides. If a fair criticism evinces that this is not the doctrine of the Biblical writers, then of course it has " destroyed " the doctrine which is confessedly based on that supposition. Failing in this, however, it can " destroy " the doctrine, strictly speaking, only by undermining its foundation in our confidence in the trustworthiness of Scripture as a witness to doctrine. The possibility of this latter alternative must, no doubt, be firmly faced in our investigation of the phenomena of the Bible; but the weight of the evidence, be it small or great, for the general trustworthiness of the Bible as a source of doctrine, throws itself, in the form of a presumption, against the reality of any phenomena alleged to be discovered which make against its testimony. No doubt this presumption may be overcome by clear demonstration. But clear demonstration is requisite. For, certainly, if it is critically established that what is sometimes called, not without a touch of scorn, " the traditional doctrine," is just the Bible's own doctrine of inspiration, the real conflict is no longer with " the traditional theory of inspiration," but with the credibility of the Bible. The really decisive question among Christian scholars (among whom alone, it would seem, could a question of inspiration be profitably discussed), is thus seen to be, " What does an exact and scientific exegesis determine to be the Biblical doctrine of inspiration? "

The Biblical Doctrine of Inspiration Clear

The reply to this question is, however, scarcely open to doubt. The stricter and the more scientific the examination is made, the more certain does it become that the authors of the New Testament held a doctrine of inspiration quite as high as the Church doctrine. This may be said, indeed, to be generally admitted by untrammeled critics, whether of positive or of negative tendencies. Thus, for instance — to confine our examples to a few of those who are not able personally to accept the doctrine of the New Testament writers — Archdeacon Farrar is able to admit that Paul " shared, doubtless, in the views of the later Jewish schools — the Tanaim and Amoraim — on the nature of inspiration. These views . . . made the words of Scripture coextensive and identical with the words of God." [10] So also Otto Pfleiderer allows that Paul " fully shared the assumption of his opponents, the irrefragable authority of the letter as the immediately revealed Word of God." [11] Similarly, Tholuck recognizes that the application of the Old Tes-

[10] " Life of Paul," i. 49.   [11] " Paulinism," i. 88.

tament made by the author of the Epistle to the Hebrews, " rests on the strictest view of inspiration, since passages where God is not the speaker are cited as words of God or of the Holy Ghost (i. 6, 7, 8, iv. 4, 7, vii. 21, iii. 7, x. 15)." [12] This fact is worked out also with convincing clearness by the writer of an odd and sufficiently free Scotch book published a few years ago,[13] who formulates his conclusion in the words: " There is no doubt that the author of Hebrews, in common with the other New Testament writers, regards the whole Old Testament as having been dictated by the Holy Ghost, or, as we should say, plenarily, and, as it were, mechanically inspired." And more recently still Prof. Stapfer, of Paris,[14] though himself denying the reality not only of an infallibility for the Bible, but also of any inspiration for it at all, declaring that " the doctrine of an Inspiration distinct from Revelation and legitimating it, is an error " — yet cannot deny that Paul held a different doctrine — a doctrine which made the Old Testament to him the divine Word and the term, " It is written," equivalent to " God says." [15]

A detailed statement of the evidence is scarcely needed to support a position allowed by such general consent. But it will not be improper to adjoin a brief outline of the grounds on which the general consent rests. In the circumstances, however, we may venture to dispense with an argument drawn up from our own point of view,[16] and content ourselves with an extract from the brief statement of the grounds of his decision

[12] " Old Testament in the New," *Bibliotheca Sacra*, xi. 612.

[13] " Principles of Christianity," by James Stuart (1888), p. 346.

[14] " Séance de Rentrée des Cours de la Faculté de Théologie Protestante de Paris, le Mardi 3 Novembre," 1891. *Leçon d'Ouverture de M. le Prof. Edm. Stapfer.* Paris: Fischbacher, 1891. Pp. 26, 42.

[15] Compare also Kuenen, " Prophets," p. 449; Reuss, " History of Christian Theology in the Apostolic Age," i. p. 352 *seq.*; Riehm, " Der Lehrbegr. des Hebräerbriefes," i. pp. 173, 177, etc.

[16] Those who wish to see a very conclusive and thorough statement of Paul's doctrine of inspiration should consult Dr. Purves's paper on " St. Paul and Inspiration," published in *The Presbyterian and Reformed Rev.*, January, 1893. For our Lord's doctrine, see Dr. Caven's paper on " Our Lord's Testimony to the Old Testament," in the number of the *Review* for July, 1892.

given by another of those critical scholars who do not believe the doctrine of plenary inspiration, but yet find themselves constrained to allow that it is the doctrine of the New Testament writers. Richard Rothe [17] seeks, wrongly, to separate Christ's doctrine of the Old Testament from that of the apostles; our Lord obviously spoke of the Scriptures of His people out of the same fundamental conception of their nature and divinity as His apostles. But he more satisfactorily outlines the doctrine of the apostles as follows:

"We find in the New Testament authors the same theoretical view of the Old Testament and the same practice as to its use, as among the Jews of the time in general, although at the same time in the handling of the same conceptions and principles on both sides, the whole difference between the new Christian spirit and that of contemporary Judaism appears in sharp distinctness. Our authors look upon the words of the Old Testament as *immediate* words of God, and adduce them expressly as such, even those of them which are not at all related as direct sayings of God. They see nothing at all in the sacred volume which is simply the word of its human author and not at the same time the very Word of God Himself. In all that stands 'written' God Himself speaks to them, and so entirely are they habituated to think only of this that they receive the sacred Word written itself, as such, as God's Word, and hear God speaking in it *immediately*, without any thought of the human persons who appear in it as speaking and acting. The *historical* conception of their Bible is altogether foreign to them. Therefore they cite the abstract ἡ γραφή or αἱ γραφαί or γραφαὶ ἅγιαι (Rom. i. 2), or again τὰ ἱερὰ γράμματα (2 Tim. iii. 15), without naming any special author, as self-evidently God's Word, e.g., John vii. 38, x. 35, xix. 36, 37, xx. 9; Acts i. 16; James ii. 8; Rom. ix. 17; Gal. iii. 8, 22, iv. 30; 1 Pet. ii. 6; 2 Pet. i. 20, etc.; and introduce Old Testament citations with the formulas, now that God (Matt. i. 22, ii. 15; Acts iv. 25, xiii. 34; Rom. i. 2), now that the Holy Spirit (Acts i. 16, xxviii. 25; Heb. iii. 7, ix. 8, x. 15; cf. also Acts iv. 25; 1 Pet. i. 11; 2 Pet. i. 20) so speaks or has spoken. The Epistle to the Hebrews unhesitatingly adduces with a ὁ θεὸς λέγει and the like, even passages in which God is spoken of expressly in the third person (i. 6, 7, 8 *seq.*, iv. 4, 7, vii. 21, x. 30), and even (i. 10) cites a passage in which in the Old Testament text God

[17] " Zur Dogmatik," p. 177 *seq.*

Himself (according to the view of the author it is, however, the Son of God) is addressed, as a word spoken by God. In 2 Tim. iii. 16 the ἱερὰ γράμματα (verse 15) are expressly called θεόπνευστα, however the sentence may be construed or expounded; and however little a special theory of the inspiration of the Bible can be drawn from an expression of such breadth of meaning, nevertheless this *datum* avails to prove that the author shared in general the view of his Jewish contemporaries as to the peculiar character of the Old Testament books, and it is of especial importance inasmuch as it attributes the inspiration, without the least ambiguity, directly to the writings themselves, and not merely to their authors, the prophets. No doubt, in the teaching of the apostles the conception of prophetic inspiration to which it causally attributes the Old Testament, has not yet the sharp exactness of our ecclesiastical dogmatic conception; but it stands, nevertheless, in a very express analogy with it. . . . Moreover, it must be allowed that the apostolical writers, although they nowhere say it expressly, refer the prophetic inspiration also to the *actus scribendi* of the Biblical authors. The whole style and method of their treatment of the Old Testament text manifestly presupposes in them this view of this matter, which was at the time the usual one in the Jewish schools. With Paul particularly this is wholly incontrovertibly the case. For only on that view could he, in such passages as Rom. iv. 23, 24, xv. 4; 1 Cor. ix. 10, x. 11 — in which he distinguishes between the occurrence of the Old Testament facts and the recording of them — maintain of the latter that it was done with express teleological reference to the needs of the New Testament believers, at least so far as the selection of the matter to be described is concerned; and only on that view could he argue on the details of the letter of the Old Testament Scriptures, as he does in Gal. iii. 15, 16. We can, moreover, trace the continuance of this view in the oldest post-apostolical Church. . . . So far as the Old Testament is concerned, our ecclesiastical-dogmatic doctrine of inspiration can, therefore, in very fact, appeal to the authority, not indeed of the Redeemer Himself — for He stands in an entirely neutral attitude towards it — but no doubt of the apostles."

A keen controversialist like Rothe does not fail, of course — as the reader has no doubt observed — to accompany his exposition of the apostolic doctrine with many turns of expression designed to lessen its authority in the eyes of the reader, and to prepare the way for his own refusal to be bound by it; but neither does he fail to make it clear that this doctrine, although it is unacceptable to him, is the apostles' doctrine. The apostles' *doctrine,* let it be observed that we say. For even so bald a statement as Rothe's will suffice to uncover the fallacy of the assertion, which is so often made, that the doctrine of verbal inspiration is based on a few isolated statements of Scripture to the neglect, if not to the outrage, of its phenomena — a form of remark into which even so sober a writer as Dr. W. G. Blaikie has lately permitted himself to fall.[18] Nothing, obviously, could be more opposite to the fact. The doctrine of verbal inspiration is based on the broad foundation of the carefully ascertained *doctrine* of the Scripture writers on the subject. It is a product of Biblical Theology. And if men will really ask, not, " What do the creeds teach? What do the theologians say? What is the authority of the Church? but, What does the Bible itself teach us? " and " fencing off from the Scriptures all the speculations, all the dogmatic elaborations, all the doctrinal adaptations that have been made in the history of doctrine in the Church," " limit themselves strictly to the theology of the Bible itself " — according to the excellent programme outlined by Dr. Briggs [19] — it is to the doctrine of verbal inspiration, as we have seen, that they must come. It is not Biblical criticism that has " destroyed " verbal inspiration, but Dr. Briggs' scholastic theories that have drawn him away in this matter from the pure deliverances of Biblical Theology.[20]

Much more, of course, does such a statement as even Rothe's uncover the even deeper error of the assertion latterly becoming much too common, that, the doctrine of verbal inspiration, as a recent writer puts it,[21] " is based wholly upon an *a priori* assumption of what inspiration *must be,* and not upon

[18] " Letter to the Rev. Andrew A. Bonar, D.D.," etc. Edinburgh, 1890.

[19] " The Edward Robinson Chair of Biblical Theology in the Union Theological Seminary," New York (1891), pp. 5, 6.

[20] The substance of some of the preceding paragraphs was printed in *The Homiletical Review* for May, 1891, under the title of " The Present Problem of Inspiration."

[21] " Exegesis." An Address delivered at the Opening of the Autumn Term of Union Theological Seminary, September 24, 1891. By Marvin R. Vincent, D.D., Professor of Sacred Literature. New York: C. Scribner's Sons, 1891. P. 40.

the Bible as it actually exists." It is based wholly upon an exegetical fact. It is based on the exegetical fact that our Lord and His apostles held this doctrine of Scripture, and everywhere deal with the Scriptures of the Old Testament in accordance with it, as the very Word of God, even in their narrative parts. This is a commonplace of exegetical science, the common possession of the critical schools of the left and of the right, a prominent and unmistakable deliverance of Biblical Theology. And on the establishment of it as such, the real issue is brought out plainly and stringently. If criticism has made such discoveries as to necessitate the abandonment of the doctrine of plenary inspiration, it is not enough to say that we are compelled to abandon only a " particular theory of inspiration," though that is true enough. We must go on to say that that " particular theory of inspiration " is the theory of the apostles and of the Lord, and that in abandoning *it* we are abandoning *them* as our doctrinal teachers and guides, as our " exegetes," in the deep and rich sense of that word which Dr. Vincent vindicates for it.[22] This real issue is to be kept clearly before us, and faced courageously. Nothing is gained by closing our eyes to the seriousness of the problem which we are confronting. Stated plainly it is just this: Are the New Testament writers trustworthy guides in doctrine? Or are we at liberty to reject their authority, and frame contrary doctrines for ourselves? If the latter pathway be taken, certainly the doctrine of plenary inspiration is not the only doctrine that is " destroyed," and the labor of revising our creeds may as well be saved and the shorter process adopted of simply throwing them away. No wonder we are told that the same advance in knowledge which requires a changed view of the Bible necessitates also a whole new theology. If the New Testament writers are not trustworthy as teachers of doctrine and we have to go elsewhere for the source and norm of truth as to God and duty and immortality, it will not be strange if a very different system of doctrine from that delivered by the Scriptures and docilely received from them by the Church, results.

[22] *Op. cit.*, p. 5 *seq.*

And now, having uncovered the precise issue which is involved in the real problem of inspiration, let us look at it at various angles and thus emphasize in turn two or three of the more important results that spring from it.

I

Modifications of the Biblical Doctrine Undermine the Authority of the Scriptures

First, we emphasize the fact that, this being the real state of the case, we cannot modify the doctrine of plenary inspiration in any of its essential elements without undermining our confidence in the authority of the apostles as teachers of doctrine.

Logically, this is an immediate corollary of the proposition already made good. Historically, it is attested by the driftage of every school of thought which has sought to find a ground of faith in any lower than the Church's doctrine of a plenarily inspired Bible. The authority which cannot assure of a hard fact is soon not trusted for a hard doctrine. Sooner or later, in greater or less degree, the authority of the Bible in doctrine and life is replaced by or subordinated to that of reason, or of the feelings, or of the " Christian consciousness " — the " conscious experience by the individual of the Christian faith " — or of that corporate Christian consciousness which so easily hardens into simple ecclesiastical domination. What we are to accept as the truth of God is a comparatively easy question, if we can open our Bibles with the confident belief that what we read there is commended to us by a fully credible " Thus saith the Lord." But in proportion as we allow this or that element in it not to be safeguarded to us by this divine guarantee, do we begin to doubt the trustworthiness of more and more of the message delivered, and to seek other grounds of confidence than the simple " It is written " which sufficed for the needs of our Lord and His apostles. We have seen Dr. Sanday pointing to " the advancing consciousness of the Church at large," along with the consensus of scholars, as the ground of acceptance of doctrines as true, which will be more and more turned to when men can no longer approach the Bible so simply as heretofore. This is the natural direction in which to look, for men trained to lay that great stress on institutional Christianity which leads Mr. Gore to describe the present situation as one in which " it is becoming more and more difficult to believe in the Bible without believing in the Church." [23] Accordingly Dr. Sterrett also harmonizes his Hegelianism and Churchliness in finding the ground of Christian certitude in the " communal Christian consciousness," which is defined as the Church, as " objective, authoritative reason for every Christian," to which he must subordinate his individual reason.[24] Men of more individualistic training fall back rather on personal reason or the individual " Christian consciousness "; but all alike retire the Bible as a source of doctrine behind some other safeguard of truth.

It may not be without interest or value to subject the various pathways which men tread in seeking to justify a lower view of Scripture than that held and taught by the New Testament writers, to a somewhat close scrutiny, with a view to observing how necessarily they logically involve a gradual undermining of the trustworthiness of those writers as teachers of doctrine. From the purely formal point of view proper to our present purpose, four types of procedure may be recognized.

CHRIST VERSUS THE APOSTLES

1. There is first, that, of which Richard Rothe is an example, which proceeds by attempting to establish a distinction between the teaching of Christ and the teaching of His apostles, and refusing the latter in favor of the former.

As we have already remarked, this distinction cannot be made good. Rothe's attempt to establish it proceeds on the twofold ground, on the one hand, of an asserted absence from our Lord's dealings with the Scriptures of those extreme facts

[23] " Lux Mundi." American Ed. New York: John W. Lovell Co. P. 283.
[24] " Reason and Authority in Religion." By J. MacBride Sterrett, D.D., Professor in Seabury Divinity School. New York: T. Whittaker, 1891. P. 176.

of usage of it as the Word of God, and of those extreme statements concerning its divine character, on the ground of which in the apostles' dealing with it we must recognize their high doctrine of Scripture; and on the other hand, of an asserted presence in Christ's remarks concerning Scripture of hints that He did not share the conception of Scripture belonging to contemporary Judaism, which conception we know to have been the same high doctrine that was held by the apostles. He infers, therefore, that the apostles, in this matter, represent only the current Jewish thought in which they were bred, while Christ's divine originality breaks away from this and commends to us a new and more liberal way.

But in order to make out the first member of the twofold ground on which he bases this conclusion, Rothe has to proceed by explaining away, by means of artificial exegetical expedients, a number of facts of usage and deliverances as to Scripture, in which our Lord's dealings with Scripture culminate, and which are altogether similar in character and force to those on the basis of which he infers the apostles' high doctrine. These are such passages as the quotation in Matt. xix. 4, 5, of Adam's words as God's Word, which Lechler appeals to as decisive just as Rothe appeals to similar passages in the epistles — but which Rothe sets aside in a footnote simply with the remark that it is not decisive here; the assertion in John x. 35, that the " Scripture cannot be broken," which he sets aside as probably not a statement of Christ's own opinion but an *argumentum ad hominem,* and as in any case not available here, since it does not explicitly assert that the authority it ascribes to Scripture is due " to its origination by inspiration " — but which, as Dr. Robert Watts has shown anew,[25] is conclusive for

[25] " Faith and Inspiration." The Carey Lectures for 1884. By Robert Watts, D.D. London: Hodder & Stoughton, 1885. P. 139. "The sole question is: What, according to the language employed by Him, was His estimate of the Old Testament Scripture? It will be observed that He does not single out the passage on which He bases His argument, and testify of it that it is unbreakable, making its infallibility depend on His authority. Stated formally, His argument is as follows: Major — The Scripture cannot be broken. Minor — ' I said ye are God's,' is written in your law, which is Scripture. Conclusion — ' I said ye are

our Saviour's view of the entire infallibility of the whole Old Testament; the assertion in Matt. v. 18 (and in Luke xvi. 17) that not " one jot or one tittle (ἰῶτα ἓν ἢ μία κεραία) shall pass away from the law till all be fulfilled," which he sets aside with the remark that it is not the law-codex, but the law itself, that is here spoken of, forgetful of the fact that it is the law itself *as written* that the Lord has in mind, in which form alone, moreover, do " yodhs and horns " belong to it; the assertion in Matt. xxii. 43, that it was " in the Spirit " that David called the Messiah, " Lord," in the one hundredth and tenth Psalm, which he sets aside with the remark that this does prove that Jesus looked upon David as a prophet, but not necessarily that he considered the one hundred and tenth Psalm inspired, as indeed he does not say γράφει but καλεῖ — forgetful again that it is to the written David alone that Christ makes His appeal and on the very language written in the Psalm that He founds His argument.

No less, in order to make out the second member of the ground on which he bases his conclusion, does Rothe need to press passages which have as their whole intent and effect to rebuke the scribes for failure to understand and properly to use Scripture, into indications of rejection on Christ's part of the authority of the Scriptures to which both He and the scribes appealed. Lest it should be thought incredible that such a conclusion should be drawn from such premises, we transcribe Rothe's whole statement.

" On the other hand, we conclude with great probability that the Redeemer did *not* share the conception of His Israelitish contemporaries as to the inspiration of their Bible, as stated above, from the fact that He repeatedly expresses his dissatisfaction with the manner usual among them of looking upon and using the sacred books. He tells the scribes to their face that they do not understand the

---

God's' cannot be broken. . . . He argues the infallibility of the clause on which He founds His argument from the infallibility of the record in which it occurs. According to His infallible estimate, it was sufficient proof of the infallibility of any sentence or phrase of a clause, to show that it constituted a portion of what the Jews called ' the Scripture ' (ἡ γραφή)."

Scriptures (Matt. xxii. 29; Mark xii. 24), and that it is delusion for them to think to possess eternal life in *them,* therefore in a *book* (John v. 39), even as He also (in the same place) seems to speak disapprovingly of their searching of the Scriptures, because it proceeds from such a perverted point of view." [26]

Thus Jesus' *appeal* to the Scriptures as testifying to Him, and His rebuke to the Jews for not following them while professing to honor them, are made to do duty as a proof that He did not ascribe plenary authority to them.[27]

Furthermore, Rothe's whole treatment of the matter omits altogether to make account of the great decisive consideration of the general tone and manner of Christ's allusions and appeal to the Scriptures, which only culminate in such passages as he has attempted to explain away, and which not only are inconsistent with any other than the same high view of their authority, trustworthiness and inspiration, as that which Rothe infers from similar phenomena to have been the conception of the apostles, but also are necessarily founded on it as its natural expression. The distinction attempted to be drawn between Christ's doctrine of Holy Scripture and that of His apostles is certainly inconsistent with the facts.

But we are more concerned at present to point out that the attempt to draw this distinction must result in undermining utterly all confidence in the New Testament writers as teachers of doctrine. So far as the apostles are concerned, indeed, it would be more correct to say that it is the outgrowth and manifestation of an already present distrust of them as teachers of doctrine. Its very principle is appeal from apostolic teaching to that of Christ, on the ground that the former is not authoritative. How far this rejection of apostolic authority goes is evidenced by the mode of treatment vouchsafed to it. Immediately on drawing out the apostles' doctrine of inspiration, Rothe asks, " But now what dogmatic value has this fact? "

[26] " Zur Dogmatik," p. 177.

[27] Compare Meyer, *in loc.* (E. T., i. p. 262, note): " Even Rothe . . . takes δοκεῖτε in the sense of a *delusion,* namely, that they possessed eternal *life* in a *book.* Such explanations are opposed to the high veneration manifested by Jesus towards the Holy Scriptures, especially apparent in John. . . ."

And on the ground that "by their fruits ye shall know them," he proceeds to declare that the apostles' doctrine of Scripture led them into such a general use and mode of interpretation of Scripture as Rothe deems wholly unendurable.[28] It is not, then, merely the teaching of the apostles as to what the Scriptures are, but their teaching as to what those Scriptures teach, in which Rothe finds them untrustworthy. It would be impossible but that the canker should eat still more deeply.

Nor is it possible to prevent it from spreading to the undermining of the trustworthiness of even the Lord's teaching itself, for the magnifying of which the distinction purports to be drawn. The artificial manner in which the testimony of the Lord to the authority of the Scriptures is explained away in the attempt to establish the distinction, might be pleaded indeed as an indication that trust in it was not very deeply rooted. And there are other indications that had the Lord been explained to be of the apostles' mind as to Scripture, a way would have been found to free us from the duty of following His teaching.[29] For even *His* exegesis is declared not to be authoritative, seeing that " exegesis is essentially a scientific function, and conditioned on the existence of scientific means, which in relation to the Old Testament were completely at the command of Jesus as little as of His contemporaries "; and the principle of partial limitation at least to the outlook of His day which is involved in such a statement is fully accepted by Rothe.[30] All this may, however, be thought more or less per-

28 *Op. cit.*, pp. 181, 182.

29 *Op. cit.*, pp. 174, 175.

30 Even on an extreme Kenotic view, it is, however, not so certain that *error* should be attributed to the God-man. Prof. Gretillat, of Neuchatel, a Kenotist of the type of Gess and his own colleague Godet, is able to teach that " by reason of the relation which unites the intelligence with the will," our Lord must needs be free not only from sin, but also from all error (*Exposé de Theol. Syst.*, iv. 288). Tholuck occupied a position similar to Rothe's; yet he reminds us that: " Proofs might be brought to show that, even in questions pertaining to learned exegesis " — which are such as our Lord needed to *learn* as a man — " such as those concerning the historical connection of a passage, the author and age of a book, an original spiritual discernment without the culture of the schools may often divine the truth " (" Citations of the Old Testament in the New," tr. in *Bibliotheca Sacra,* xi. p. 615).

sonal to Rothe's own mental attitude, whereas the ultimate undermining of our Lord's authority as teacher of doctrine, as well as that of His apostles, is logically essential to the position assumed.

This may be made plain at once by the very obvious remark that we have no Christ except the one whom the apostles have given to us. Jesus Himself left no treatises on doctrine. He left no written dialogues. We are dependent on the apostles for our whole knowledge of Him, and of what He taught. The portraiture of Jesus which has glorified the world's literature as well as blessed all ages and races with the revelation of a God-man come down from heaven to save the world, is limned by his followers' pencils alone. The record of that teaching which fell from His lips as living water, which if a man drink of he shall never thirst again, is a record by his followers' pens alone. They have painted for us, of course, the Jesus that they knew, and as they knew Him. They have recorded for us the teachings that they heard, and as they heard them. Whatever untrustworthiness attaches to them as deliverers of doctrine, must in some measure shake also our confidence in their report of what their Master was and taught.

But the logic cuts even deeper. For not only have we no Christ but Him whom we receive at the apostles' hands, but this Christ is committed to the trustworthiness of the apostles as teachers. His credit is involved in their credit. He represents His words on earth as but the foundation of one great temple of doctrine, the edifice of which was to be built up by Him through their mouths, as they spoke moved by His Spirit; and thus He makes Himself an accomplice before the fact in all they taught. In proportion as they are discredited as doctrinal guides, in that proportion He is discredited with them. By the promise of the Spirit, He has forever bound His trustworthiness with indissoluble bands to the trustworthiness of His accredited agents in founding His Church, and especially by that great promise recorded for us in John xvi. 12–15: " I have yet many things to say unto you, but ye cannot bear them now. Howbeit when he, the Spirit of truth, is come, he will guide you into all truth; for he shall not speak of himself; but whatsoever he shall hear, that shall he speak: and he will show you things to come. He shall glorify me: for he shall receive of mine, and shall show it unto you. All things that the Father hath are mine: therefore said I, that he shall take of mine and shall show it unto you." Says Dr. C. W. Hodge: [31]

" It is impossible to conceive how the authority of the Master could be conveyed to the teaching of the disciples more emphatically than is here done by Christ. He identifies His teaching and the teaching of the Spirit as parts of one whole; His teaching is carrying out My teaching, it is calling to remembrance what I have told you; it is completing what I have begun. And to make the unity emphatic, He explains why He had reserved so much of His own teaching, and committed the work of revelation to the Spirit. He, in His incarnation and life, comprised all saving truth. He was the revealer of God and the truth and the life. But while some things He had taught while yet with them, He had many things to say which must be postponed because they could not yet bear them. . . . If Christ has referred us to the apostles as teachers of the truths which He would have us know, certainly this primary truth of the authority of the Scriptures themselves can be no exception. All questions as to the extent of this inspiration, as to its exclusive authority, as to whether it extends to words as well as doctrines, as to whether it is infallible or inerrant, or not, are simply questions to be referred to the Word itself."

In such circumstances the attempt to discriminate against the teaching of the apostles in favor of that of Christ, is to contradict the express teaching of Christ Himself, and thus to undermine our confidence in it. We cannot both believe Him and not believe Him. The cry, " Back to Christ! " away from all the imaginations of men's hearts and the cobweb theories which they have spun, must be ever the cry of every Christian heart. But the cry, " Back to Christ! " away from the teachings of His apostles, whose teachings He Himself represents as His

---

[31] Sermon on " The Promise of the Spirit," in the volume: " Princeton Sermons." By the Faculty of the Seminary. New York: Fleming H. Revell Co., 1893. P. 33. The whole of this noble sermon should be read.

own, only delivered by His Spirit through their mouths, is an invitation to desert Christ Himself. It is an invitation to draw back from the Christ of the Bible to some Christ of our own fancy, from the only real to some imaginary Christ. It is to undermine the credit of the whole historical revelation in and through the Christ of God, and to cast us for the ascertainment and authentication of truth on the native powers of our own minds.

ACCOMMODATION OR IGNORANCE?

2. Another method is that of those who seek to preserve themselves from the necessity of accepting the doctrine of inspiration held by the writers of the New Testament, by representing it as merely a matter of accommodation to the prejudices of the Jews, naturally if not necessarily adopted by the first preachers of the Gospel in their efforts to commend to their contemporaries their new teaching as to the way of life.

This position is quite baldly stated by a recent Scotch writer, to whose book, written with a frank boldness, a force and a logical acumen which are far above the common, too little heed has been paid as an indication of the drift of the times.[32] Says Mr. James Stuart:

" The apostles had not merely to reveal the Gospel scheme of salvation to their own and all subsequent ages, but they had to present it in such a form, and support it by such arguments, as should commend it to their more immediate hearers and readers. Notwithstanding its essentially universal character, the Gospel, as it appears in the New Testament, is couched in a particular form, suited to the special circumstances of a particular age and nation. Before the Gospel could reach the hearts of those to whom it was first addressed, prejudices had to be overcome, prepossessions had to be counted on and dealt with. The apostles, in fact, had just to take the men of their time as they found them, adapting their teaching accordingly. Not only so, but there is evidence that the apostles were themselves, to a very great extent, men of their own time, sharing many of the

[32] " The Principles of Christianity." Being an Essay towards a More Correct Apprehension of Christian Doctrine, Mainly Soteriological. By James Stuart, M.A. London: Williams & Norgate, 1888. P. 67 *seq.*

common opinions and even the common prejudices, so that, in arguing *ex concessis*, they were arguing upon grounds that would appear
to themselves just and tenable. Now one of the things universally
conceded in apostolic times was the inspiration and authority of the
Old Testament; another was the legitimacy of certain modes of interpreting and applying the Old Testament. The later Jews, as is
well known, cherished a superstitious reverence and attached an
overwhelming importance to the letter of the Old Testament, which
they regarded as the ' Word of God ' in the fullest and most absolute
sense that can possibly be put upon such an expression. The doctors
taught and the people believed that the sacred writings were not
only inspired, but inspired to the utmost possible or conceivable extent. In the composition of Scripture, the human author was nowhere,
and the inspiring Spirit everywhere; not the thoughts alone, but the
very words of Scripture were the Word of God, which He communicated by the mouth of the human author, who merely discharged the
duty of spokesman and amanuensis, so that what the Scripture contains is the Word of God in as complete and full a sense as if it had
been dictated by the lips of God to the human authors, and recorded
with something approaching to perfect accuracy. . . . Such being
the prevalent view of the inspiration and authority of the Old Testament writings, what could be more natural than that the apostles
should make use of these writings to enforce and commend their own
ideas? And if the Old Testament were to be used for such a purpose
at all, evidently it must be used according to the accepted methods;
for to have followed any other — assuming the possibility of such a
thing — would have defeated the object aimed at, which was to accommodate the Gospel to established prejudices."

Now, here too, the first remark which needs to be made is
that the assertion of " accommodation " on the part of the
New Testament writers cannot be made good. To prove " accommodation," two things need to be shown: first, that the
apostles did not share these views, and, secondly, that they
nevertheless accommodated their teaching to them. " Accommodation " properly so called cannot take place when the
views in question are the proper views of the persons themselves. But even in the above extract Mr. Stuart is led to allow
that the apostles shared the current Jewish view of the Scrip-

tures, and at a later point [33] he demonstrates this in an argument of singular lucidity, although in its course he exaggerates
the character of their views in his effort to fix a stigma of
mechanicalness on them. With what propriety, then, can he
speak of " accommodation " in the case? The fact is that the
theory of " accommodation " is presented by Mr. Stuart only
to enable him the more easily to refuse to be bound by the
apostolic teaching in this matter, and as such it has served
him as a stepping stone by which he has attained to an even
more drastic principle, on which he practically acts: that whenever the apostles can be shown to agree with their contemporaries, their teaching may be neglected. In such cases, he conceives of the New Testament writers " being inspired and
guided by current opinion," [34] and reasons thus: [35]

" Now it is unquestionable that the New Testament writers in so
regarding the Old Testament were not enunciating a new theory of
inspiration or interpretation, they were simply adopting and following out the current theory. . . . In matters of this kind . . . the
New Testament writers were completely dominated by the spirit of
the age, so that their testimony on the question of Scripture inspiration possesses no independent value." " If these popular notions were
infallibly correct before they were taken up and embodied in the
New Testament writings, they are infallibly correct still; if they
were incorrect before they were taken up and embodied in the New
Testament writings, they are incorrect still." [36]

This is certainly most remarkable argumentation, and the
principle asserted is probably one of the most singular to which
thinking men ever committed themselves, viz., that a body of
religious teachers, claiming authority for themselves as such,
are trustworthy *only* when they teach *novelties*. It is the
apotheosis of the old Athenian and new modern spirit, which
has leisure and heart " for nothing else but either to tell or

[33] P. 345 *seq.*
[34] P. 213.
[35] Pp. 348, 349.
[36] P. 70. The immediate reference of these last words is to matters of criticism and exegesis; but according to the contextual connection they would also
be used of matters of inspiration.

hear some new thing." Nevertheless, it is a principle far from uncommon among those who are seeking justification for them-selves in refusing the leadership of the New Testament writers in the matter of the authority and inspiration of the Scrip-tures. And, of late, it is, of course, taking upon itself in certain quarters a new form, the form imposed by the new view of the origin of Christian thought in Hellenic sources, which has been given such vogue by Dr. Harnack and rendered popular in English-speaking lands by the writings of the late Dr. Hatch. For example, we find it expressed in this form in the recent valuable studies on the First Epistle of Clement of Rome, by Lic. Wrede.[37] Clement's views of the Old Testament Scriptures are recognized as of the highest order; he looks upon them as a marvelous and infallible book whose very letters are sacred, as a veritable oracle, the most precious possession of the Church. These high views were shared by the whole Church of his day, and, indeed, of the previous age: " The view which Clement has of the Old Testament, and the use which he makes of it, show in themselves no essential peculiarities in compari-son with the most nearly related Christian writings, especially the Pauline epistles, the Epistle to the Hebrews and the Epis-tle of Barnabas." And yet, according to Wrede, this view rests on " the Hellenistic conception of inspiration, according to which the individual writers were passive instruments of God."[38] Whether, however, the contemporary influence is thought to be Jewish or Greek, it is obvious that the appeal to it in such matters has, as its only intention, to free us from the duty of following the apostles and can have as its only effect to undermine their authority. We may no doubt suppose at the beginning that we seek only to separate the kernel from the husk; but a principle which makes husk of all that can be shown to have anything in common with what was believed by any body of contemporaries, Hebrew or Greek, is so very

[37] "Untersuchungen zum ersten Klemensbriefe." Von Lic. Theol. W. Wrede, Privatdocent der Theologie in Göttingen. Göttingen: Vanderhoeck & Ruprecht's Verlag, 1891. Pp. 60, 75 seq.

[38] Compare the review of Wrede by Prof. H. M. Scott, in The Presbyterian and Reformed Review, January, 1893, p. 163.

drastic that it will leave nothing which we can surely trust. On this principle the Golden Rule itself is not authoritative, because something like it may be found in Jewish tradition and among the heathen sages. It certainly will not serve to make novelty the test of authority.

From the ethical point of view, however, this theory is preferable to that of " accommodation," and it is probable that part, at least, of the impulse which led Mr. Stuart to substitute it for the theory of " accommodation," with which he began, arose from a more or less clear perception of the moral implications of the theory of " accommodation." Under the impulse of that theory he had been led to speak of the procedure of the apostles in such language as this: " The sole principle that regulates all their appeals to the Old Testament, is that of obtaining, at whatever cost, support for their own favorite ideas." [39] Is it any wonder that the reaction took place and an attempt was made to shift the burden from the *veracity* to the *knowledge* of the New Testament writers? [40] In Mr. Stuart's case we see very clearly, then, the effect of a doctrine of " accommodation " on the credit of the New Testament writers. His whole book is written in order to assign reason why he will not yield authority to these writers in their doctrine of a sacrificial atonement. This was due to their Jewish type of thought. But when the doctrine of accommodation is tried as a ground for the rejection of their authority, it is found to cut too deeply even for Mr. Stuart. He wishes to be rid of the authority of the New Testament writers, not to impeach their veracity; and so he discards it in favor of the less plausible, indeed, but also less deeply cutting canon, that the apostles are not to be followed when they agree with contemporary thought, because in these elements they are obviously speaking out of their own consciousness, as the products of their day, and not as proclaimers of the *new* revelation in Christ. Their inspiration, in a word, " was not *plenary* or *universal* — extending, that is, to all matters whatever which they speak about — but *partial* or *special,* being limited to securing the accurate communication of that

[39] P. 66.   [40] P. 353.

plan of salvation which they had so profoundly experienced, and which they were commissioned to proclaim." [41] In all else " the New Testament writers are simply on a level with their contemporaries." It may not be uninstructive to note that under such a formula Mr. Stuart not only rejects the teachings of these writers as to the nature and extent of inspiration, but also their teaching as to the sacrificial nature of the very plan of salvation which they were specially commissioned to proclaim. But what it is our business at present to point out is that the doctrine of accommodation is so obviously a blow at not only the trustworthiness, but the very veracity of the New Testament authors, that Mr. Stuart, even after asserting it, is led to permit it to fall into neglect.

And must it not be so? It may be easy indeed to confuse it with that progressive method of teaching which every wise teacher uses, and which our Lord also employed (John xvi. 12 *seq.*); it may be easy to represent it as nothing more than that harmless wisdom which the apostle proclaimed as the principle of his life, as he went about the world becoming all things to all men. But how different it is from either! It is one thing to adapt the teaching of truth to the stage of receptivity of the learner; it is another thing to adopt the errors of the time as the very matter to be taught. It is one thing to refrain from unnecessarily arousing the prejudices of the learner, that more ready entrance may be found for the truth; it is another thing to adopt those prejudices as our own, and to inculcate them as the very truths of God. It was one thing for Paul to become " all things to all men " that he might gain them to the truth; it was another for Peter to dissemble at Antioch, and so confirm men in their error. The accommodation attributed to the New Testament writers is a method by which they did and do not undeceive but deceive; not a method by which they teach the truth more winningly and to more; but a method by which they may be held to have taught along with the truth also error. The very object of attributing it to them is to enable us to separate their teaching into two parts — the true

41 P. 258.

and the false; and to justify us in refusing a part while accepting a part at their hands. At the best it must so undermine the trustworthiness of the apostles as deliverers of doctrine as to subject their whole teaching to our judgment for the separation of the true from the false; at the worst, it must destroy their trustworthiness by destroying our confidence in their veracity. Mr. Stuart chose the better path; but he did so, as all who follow him must, by deserting the principle of accommodation, which leads itself along the worse road. With it as a starting point we must impeach the New Testament writers as lacking either knowledge or veracity.

Teaching versus Opinion

3. A third type of procedure, in defense of refusal to be bound by the doctrine of the New Testament writers as to inspiration, proceeds by drawing a distinction between the belief and the teaching of these writers; and affirming that, although it is true that they did believe and hold a high doctrine of inspiration, yet they do not explicitly teach it, and that we are bound, not by their opinions, but only by their explicit teaching.

This appears to be the conception which underlies the treatment of the matter by Archdeacon (then Canon) Farrar, in his " Life and Work of St. Paul." Speaking of Paul's attitude towards Scripture, Dr. Farrar says: [42]

" He shared, doubtless, in the views of the later Jewish schools — the Tanaim and Amoraim — on the nature of inspiration. These views, which we find also in Philo, made the words of Scripture co-extensive and identical with the words of God, and in the clumsy and feeble hands of the more fanatical Talmudists often attached to the dead letter an importance which stifled or destroyed the living sense. But as this extreme and mechanical literalism — this claim to absolute infallibility even in accidental details and passing allusions — this superstitious adoration of the letters and vocables of Scripture, as though they were the articulate vocables and immedi-

[42] *Op. cit.,* Vol. i. p. 49.

ato autograph of God — finds no encouragement in any part of
Scripture, and very distinct discouragement in more than one of the
utterances of Christ, so there is not a single passage in which any
approach to it is dogmatically stated in the writings of St. Paul."

This passage lacks somewhat more in point of clearness than it
does in point of rhetorical fire. But three things seem to be sufficiently plain: (1) That Dr. Farrar thinks that Paul shared
the views of the Tanaim, the Amoraim and Philo as to the
nature of inspiration. (2) That he admits that these views
claimed for Scripture " absolute infallibility even in accidental
details and passing allusions." (3) That nevertheless he does
not feel bound to accept this doctrine at Paul's hands, because,
though Paul held it, he is thought not to have " dogmatically
stated " it.

Now, the distinction which is here drawn seems, in general,
a reasonable one. No one is likely to assert infallibility for the
apostles in aught else than in their official teaching. And whatever they may be shown to have held apart from their official
teaching, may readily be looked upon with only that respect
which we certainly must accord to the opinions of men of such
exceptional intellectual and spiritual insight. But it is more
difficult to follow Dr. Farrar when it is asked whether this distinction can be established in the present matter. It does not
seem to be true that there are no didactic statements as to inspiration in Paul's letters, or in the rest of the New Testament,
such as implicate and carry into the sphere of matters taught,
the whole doctrine that underlies their treatment of Scripture.
The assertion in the term " theopneustic " in such a passage as
II Tim. iii. 16, for example, cannot be voided by any construction of the passage; and the doctrine taught in the assertion
must be understood to be the doctrine which that term connoted to Paul who uses it, not some other doctrine read into it
by us.

It is further necessary to inquire what sources we have in a
case like that of Paul, to inform us as to what his opinions
were, apart from and outside of his teachings. It might conceivably have happened that some of his contemporaries

should have recorded for us some account of opinions held by
him to which he has given no expression in his epistles; or
some account of actions performed by him involving the manifestation of judgment — somewhat similar, say, to Paul's own
account of Peter's conduct in Antioch (Gal. ii. 11 *seq.*). A presumption may be held to lie also that he shared the ordinary
opinions of his day in certain matters lying outside the scope
of his teachings, as, for example, with reference to the form of
the earth, or its relation to the sun; and it is not inconceivable
that the form of his language, when incidentally adverting to
such matters, might occasionally play into the hands of such a
presumption. But it is neither on the ground of such a presumption, nor on the ground of such external testimony, that
Dr. Farrar ascribes to him views as to inspiration similar to
those of his Jewish contemporaries. It is distinctly on the
ground of what he finds on a study of the body of official teaching which Paul has left to us. Dr. Farrar discovers that these
views as to the nature of Scripture so underlie, are so assumed
in, are so implied by, are so interwoven with Paul's official
teaching that he is unwillingly driven to perceive that they
were Paul's opinions. With what color of reason then can they
be separated from his teaching?

There is raised here, moreover, a very important and far-
reaching question, which few will be able to decide in Dr.
Farrar's sense. What is taught in the New Testament? And
what is the mode of its teaching? If we are to fall in with Dr.
Farrar and say that nothing is taught except what is " dogmatically stated " in formal didactic form, the occasional character of the New Testament epistles would become a source of
grave loss to us, instead of, as it otherwise is, a source of immense gain; the parabolic clothing of much of Christ's teaching would become a device to withhold from us all instruction
on the matters of which the parables treat; and all that is most
fundamental in religious truth, which, as a rule, is rather assumed everywhere in Scripture as a basis for particular applications than formally stated, would be removed out of the
sphere of Biblical doctrine. Such a rule, in a word, would op-

erate to turn the whole of Biblical teaching on its head, and to
reduce it from a body of principles inculcated by means of ex
amples into a mere congeries of instances hung in the air. The
whole advance in the attitude of Dogmatics towards the Scriptures which has been made by modern scholarship is, moreover,
endangered by this position. It was the fault of the older dogmatists to depend too much on isolated proof-texts for the
framing and defense of doctrine. Dr. Farrar would have us return to this method. The alternative, commended justly to us
by the whole body of modern scholarship, is, as Schleiermacher
puts it, to seek " a form of Scripture proof on a larger scale than
can be got from single texts," to build our systematic theology,
in a word, on the basis, not of the occasional dogmatic statements of Scripture alone, taken separately and, as it were, in
shreds, but on the basis of the theologies of the Scripture — to
reproduce first the theological thought of each writer or group
of writers and then to combine these several theologies (each
according to its due historical place) into the one consistent
system, consentaneous parts of which they are found to be.[43]
In rejecting this method, Dr. Farrar discredits the whole science of Biblical Theology. From its standpoint it is incredible
that one should attribute less importance and authoritativeness to the fundamental conceptions that underlie, color and
give form to all of Paul's teaching than to the chance didactic
statements he may have been led to make by this or that circumstance at the call of which his letters happened to be written. This certainly would be tithing mint and anise and cummin and omitting the weightier matters of the law.

That this mode of presenting the matter must lead, no less
than the others which have already come under review, to undermining the authority of the New Testament writers as deliverers of doctrine, must already be obvious. It begins by discrediting them as leaders in doctrinal thought and substituting
for this a sporadic authority in explicit dogmatic statements.

[43] The present writer has tried to state the true relations of Systematic and
Biblical theology in a discussion of " The Idea of Systematic Theology Considered as a Science " (Inaugural Address), pp. 22–28. A. D. F. Randolph & Co.,
1888. He ventures to refer the reader to it.

In Dr. Farrar's own hands it proceeds by quite undermining our confidence in the apostles as teachers, through an accusation lodged against them, not only of holding wrong views in doctrine, but even of cherishing as fundamental conceptions theological fancies which are in their very essence superstitious and idolatrous, and in their inevitable outcome ruinous to faith and honor. For Dr. Farrar does not mince matters when he expresses his opinion of that doctrine of inspiration — in its nature and its proper effects — which Philo held and the Jewish Rabbis and in which Paul, according to his expressed conviction, shared. " To say that every word and sentence and letter of Scripture is divine and supernatural, is a mechanical and useless shibboleth, nay, more, a human idol, and (constructively, at least) a dreadful blasphemy." It is a superstitious — he tells us that he had almost said fetish-worshiping — dogma, and " not only unintelligible, but profoundly dangerous." It " has in many ages filled the world with misery and ruin," and " has done more than any other dogma to corrupt the whole of exegesis with dishonest casuistry, and to shake to its centre the religious faith of thousands, alike of the most ignorant and of the most cultivated, in many centuries, and most of all in our own." [44] Yet these are the views which Dr. Farrar is forced to allow that Paul shared! For Philo " held the most rigid views of inspiration "; than him indeed " Aqiba himself used no stronger language on the subject " [45] — Aqiba, " the greatest of the Tanaites "; [46] and it was the views of the Tanaim, Amoraim and Philo, which Dr. Farrar tells us the apostle shared. How after this Dr. Farrar continues to look upon even the " dogmatic statements " of Paul as authoritative, it is hard to see. By construction he was a fetish worshiper and placed Scripture upon an idol's pedestal. The doctrines which he held and which underlie his teaching were unintelligible, useless, idolatrous, blasphemous and profoundly dangerous, and actu-

[44] " Inspiration." A Clerical Symposium. By the Rev. Archdeacon Farrar and others. London: James Nisbet and Co., 1888. 2d ed. Pp. 219, 241.

[45] " History of Interpretation." Bampton Lectures. By F. W. Farrar, D.D. London: Macmillan, 1880. P. 147.

[46] P. 71.

ally have shaken to its centre the religious faith of thousands.
On such a tree what other than evil fruits could grow?

No doubt something of this may be attributed to the exaggeration characteristic of Dr. Farrar's language and thought.
Obviously Paul's view of inspiration was not altogether identical with that of contemporary Judaism; it differed from it
somewhat in the same way that his use of Scripture differed
from that of the Rabbis of his day. But it is one with Philo's
and Aqiba's on the point which with Dr. Farrar is decisive:
alike with them he looked upon Scripture as " absolutely infallible, even in accidental details and passing allusions," as the
very Word of God, His " Oracles," to use his own high phrase,
and therefore Dr. Farrar treats the two views as essentially one.
But the situation is only modified, not relieved, by the recognition of this fact.

In any event the pathway on which we enter when we begin
to distinguish between the didactic statements and the fundamental conceptions of a body of incidental teaching, with a
view to accepting the former and rejecting the latter, cannot
but lead to a general undermining of the authority of the
whole. Only if we could believe in a quite mechanical and magical process of inspiration (from believing in which Dr. Farrar
is no doubt very far) by which the subject's " dogmatical statements " were kept entirely separate from and unaffected by
his fundamental conceptions, could such an attitude be logically possible. In that case we should have to view these " dogmatical statements " as not Paul's at all, standing, as they do
ex hypothesi, wholly disconnected with his own fundamental
thought, but as spoken through him by an overmastering spiritual influence; as a phenomenon, in a word, similar to the
oracles of heathen shrines, and without analogy in Scripture
except perhaps in such cases as that of Balaam. In proportion
as we draw back from so magical a conception of the mode of
inspiration, in that proportion our refusal of authority to the
fundamental conceptions of the New Testament writers must
invade also their " dogmatical statements." We must logically,
in a word, ascribe like authority to the whole body of their

teaching, in its foundation and superstructure alike, or we must withhold it in equal measure from all; or, if we withhold it from one and not the other, the discrimination would most naturally be made against the superstructure rather than against the foundation.

Facts versus Doctrine

4. Finally, an effort may be made to justify our holding a lower doctrine of inspiration than that held by the writers of the New Testament, by appealing to the so-called phenomena of the Scriptures and opposing these to the doctrine of the Scriptures, with the expectation, apparently, of justifying a modification of the doctrine taught by the Scriptures by the facts embedded in the Scriptures.

The essential principle of this method of procedure is shared by very many who could scarcely be said to belong to the class who are here more specifically in mind, inasmuch as they do not begin by explicitly recognizing the doctrine of inspiration held by the New Testament writers to be that high doctrine which the Church and the best scientific exegesis agree in understanding them to teach.[47] Every attempt to determine or

[47] On the contrary these writers usually minimize the Biblical definition of inspiration. Thus Dr. Marvin R. Vincent, who is immediately to be quoted (*op. c.* p. 15), tells us " Scripture does not define the nature and extent of its own inspiration. The oft-quoted passage of II Tim. iii. 16 really gives us no light on that point. . . . The passage does indeed point out certain *effects* which attend the use of inspired writings. . . . But after all, we are no nearer than ever to an answer to the question, What *is* inspiration? . . . So that we must fall back on the facts, on the phenomena of the Bible as we have it." But the deck is not cleared by such remarks; after all, Paul does assert *something* by calling the Scriptures Theopneustic, and what the thing is that he asserts in the use of this predicate, is not discoverable from an examination into what the Scriptures *are,* but only by an examination into what Paul *means;* but what *Paul understands* by theopneustic, Dr. Vincent makes no effort to investigate. This whole procedure is typical. Thus, for example, the Rev. J. Paterson Smyth, in his recent book, " How God Inspired the Bible " (p. 64), proceeds in an exactly similar manner. " Our theory of inspiration must be learned from the facts presented in the Bible, and in order to be correct it must be consistent with all these facts. . . . I want to find out what I can about inspiration. God has nowhere revealed to me exactly what it is. He has told me it is a divine

modify the Biblical doctrine of inspiration by an appeal to the actual characteristics of the Bible must indeed proceed on an identical principle. It finds, perhaps, as plausible a form of assertion possible to it in the declaration of Dr. Marvin R. Vincent [48] that " our only safe principle is that *inspiration is consistent with the phenomena of Scripture* " — to which one of skeptical turn might respond that whether *the inspiration claimed by Scripture* is consistent with the phenomena of Scripture after all requires some proof, while one of a more believing frame might respond that it is a safer principle that the phenomena of Scripture are consistent with its inspiration. Its crudest expression may be seen in such a book as Mr. Horton's " Inspiration and the Bible," which we have already had

---

influence, an in-breathing of the Holy Ghost on the spirit of the ancient writers. But I cannot tell how much that means or what effects I should expect from it. I have, therefore, no way of finding out except by examining the phenomena presented by the Bible itself." This method amounts simply to discarding the guidance of the doctrine of Scripture in favor of our own doctrine founded on our examination of the nature of Scripture. Mr. Smyth cannot close his eyes to certain outstanding facts on the surface of Scripture, indicatory of the doctrine as to Scripture held by the Biblical writers (pp. 36 and 106), though he makes no effort to collect and estimate all such phenomena. And when he realizes that some may be affected even by his meagre statement of them so far as to say that " the strong expressions just here quoted from some of the Bible writers, and even from our Lord Himself, convince me that the theory of verbal inspiration is most probably true," he has only such an answer as the following: " Well, reader, you will find a good many thoughtful people disagreeing with you. Why? Because, while fully receiving these arguments as a proof of God's inspiration of the Bible, they have looked a little further than the surface to judge how much God's inspiration implies, and they cannot believe from their examination of Scripture that it implies what is known as verbal inspiration " (p. 109). Mr. Smyth means by " verbal inspiration " the theory of mechanical dictation. But putting that aside as a man of straw, what it is difficult for us to understand is how " thoughtful people " can frame a theory of inspiration after only such shallow investigation of the Scriptural doctrine of inspiration, and how " thoughtful people " can assign their inability to believe a doctrine, an inability based on their own conception of what Scripture is, as any proof that that doctrine is not taught by the ." strong expressions " of the Bible writers and the Lord Himself. Is it any more rationalistic to correct the Scriptural doctrine of the origin of the universe from our investigations of the nature of things, than it is to correct the Scriptural doctrine of inspiration from our investigations of the nature of Scripture?

[48] *Mag. of Christian Lit.*, April, 1892.

occasion to mention. Mr. Horton chooses to retain the term, "inspiration," as representing "the *common sense* of Christians of all ages and in all places" as to the nature of their Scriptures,[49] but asserts that this term is to be understood to mean just what the Bible *is* — that is to say, whatever any given writer chooses to think the Bible to be. When Paul affirms in II Tim. iii. 16 that every Scripture is "inspired by God," therefore, we are not to enter into a philological and exegetical investigation to discover what Paul meant to affirm by the use of this word, but simply to say that Paul must have meant to affirm the Bible to be what we find it to be. Surely no way could be invented which would more easily enable us to substitute our thought for the apostles' thought, and to proclaim our crudities under the sanction of their great names. Operating by it, Mr. Horton is enabled to assert that the Bible is "inspired," and yet to teach that God's hand has entered it only in a providential way, by His dealings through long ages with a people who gradually wrought out a history, conceived hopes, and brought all through natural means to an expression in a faulty and often self-contradictory record, which we call inspired only "because by reading it and studying it we can find our way to God, we can find what is His will for us and how we can carry out that will."[50] The most naïve expression of the principle in question may be found in such a statement as the following, from the pen of Dr. W. G. Blaikie: "In our mode of dealing with this question the main difference between us is, that you lay your stress on certain general considerations, and on certain specific statements of Scripture. We, on the other hand, while accepting the specific statements, lay great stress also on the *structure* of Scripture as we find it, on certain phenomena which lie on the surface, and on the inextricable difficulties which are involved in carrying out your view in detail."[51] This statement justly called out the rebuke of Dr.

---

[49] *Op. cit.*, p. 5.
[50] *Op. cit.*, p. 240.
[51] "Letter to the Rev. Andrew A. Bonar, D.D." By William G. Blaikie, D.D., LL.D. 2d ed. Edinburgh: Macniven & Wallace, 1890. P. 5.

Robert Watts,[52] that " while the principle of your theory is a mere inference from apparent discrepancies not as yet explained, the principle of the theory you oppose is the formally expressed utterances of prophets and apostles, and of Christ Himself."

Under whatever safeguards, indeed, it may be attempted, and with whatever caution it may be prosecuted, the effort to modify the teaching of Scripture as to its own inspiration by an appeal to the observed characteristics of Scripture, is an attempt not to obtain a clearer knowledge of what the Scriptures teach, but to *correct* that teaching. And to *correct* the teaching of Scripture is to proclaim Scripture untrustworthy as a witness to doctrine. The procedure in question is precisely similar to saying that the Bible's doctrine of creation is to be derived not alone from the teachings of the Bible as to creation, but from the facts obtained through a scientific study of creation; that the Bible's doctrine as to man is to be found not in the Bible's deliverances on the subject, but " while accepting these, we lay great stress also on the *structure* of man as we find him, and on the inextricable difficulties which are involved in carrying out the Bible's teaching in detail "; that the Bible's doctrine of justification is to be obtained by retaining the term as commended by the common sense of the Christian world and understanding by it just what we find justification to be in actual life. It is precisely similar to saying that Mr. Darwin's doctrine of natural selection is to be determined not solely by what Mr. Darwin says concerning it, but equally by what we, in our own independent study of nature, find to be true as to natural selection. A historian of thought who proceeded on such a principle would scarcely receive the commendation of students of history, however much his writings might serve certain party ends. Who does not see that underlying this whole method of procedure — in its best and in its worst estate alike — there is apparent an unwillingness to commit ourselves without reserve to the *teaching* of the Bible, either because that

[52] " A Letter to the Rev. Prof. William G. Blaikie, D.D., LL.D." By Robert Watts, D.D., LL.D. Edinburgh: R. W. Hunter, 1890. P. 30.

teaching is distrusted or already disbelieved; and that it is a grave logical error to suppose that the teaching of the Bible as to inspiration can be corrected in this way any otherwise than by showing it not to be in accordance with the facts? The proposed method, therefore, does not conduct us to a somewhat modified doctrine of inspiration, but to a disproof of inspiration; by correcting the doctrine delivered by the Biblical writers, it discredits those writers as teachers of doctrine.

Let it not be said that in speaking thus we are refusing the inductive method of establishing doctrine. We follow the inductive method. When we approach the Scriptures to ascertain their doctrine of inspiration, we proceed by collecting the whole body of relevant facts. Every claim they make to inspiration is a relevant fact; every statement they make concerning inspiration is a relevant fact; every allusion they make to the subject is a relevant fact; every fact indicative of the attitude they hold towards Scripture is a relevant fact. But the characteristics of their own writings are not facts relevant to the determination of *their doctrine*. Nor let it be said that we are desirous of determining the true, as distinguished from the Scriptural, doctrine of inspiration otherwise than inductively. We are averse, however, to supposing that in such an inquiry the relevant " phenomena " of Scripture are not first of all and before all the claims of Scripture and second only to them its use of previous Scripture. And we are averse to excluding these primary " phenomena " and building our doctrine solely or mainly upon the characteristics and structure of Scripture, especially as determined by some special school of modern research by critical methods certainly not infallible and to the best of our own judgment not even reasonable. And we are certainly averse to supposing that this induction, if it reaches results not absolutely consentaneous with the teachings of Scripture itself, has done anything other than discredit those teachings, or that in discrediting them, it has escaped discrediting the doctrinal authority of Scripture.

Nor again is it to be thought that we refuse to use the actual characteristics of Scripture as an aid in, and a check upon, our exegesis of Scripture, as we seek to discover its doctrine of inspiration. We do not simply admit, on the contrary, we affirm that in every sphere the observed fact may throw a broad and most helpful light upon the written text. It is so in the narrative of creation in the first chapter of Genesis; which is only beginning to be adequately understood as science is making her first steps in reading the records of God's creative hand in the structure of the world itself. It is preëminently so in the written prophecies, the dark sayings of which are not seldom first illuminated by the light cast back upon them by their fulfillment. As Scripture interprets Scripture, and fulfillment interprets prediction, so may fact interpret assertion. And this is as true as regards the Scriptural assertion of the fact of inspiration as elsewhere. No careful student of the Bible doctrine of inspiration will neglect anxiously to try his conclusions as to the teachings of Scripture by the observed characteristics and " structure " of Scripture, and in trying he may and no doubt will find occasion to modify his conclusions as at first apprehended. But it is one thing to correct our exegetical processes and so modify our exegetical conclusions in the new light obtained by a study of the facts, and quite another to modify, by the facts of the structure of Scripture, the Scriptural teaching itself, as exegetically ascertained; and it is to this latter that we should be led by making the facts of structure and the facts embedded in Scripture co-factors of the same rank in the so-called inductive ascertainment of the doctrine of inspiration. Direct exegesis after all has its rights: we may seek aid from every quarter in our efforts to perform its processes with precision and obtain its results with purity; but we cannot allow its results to be " modified " by extraneous considerations. Let us by all means be careful in determining the doctrine of Scripture, but let us also be fully honest in determining it; and if we count it a crime to permit our ascertainment of the facts recorded in Scripture to be unduly swayed by our conception of the doctrine taught in Scripture, let us count it equally a crime to permit our ascertainment of its doctrine to be unduly swayed or colored by our conception of the nature of the facts of its structure or of the facts embedded in its record. We cannot, therefore, appeal from the doctrine of Scripture as exegetically established to the facts of the structure of Scripture or the facts embedded in Scripture, in the hope of modifying the doctrine. If the teaching and the facts of Scripture are in harmony the appeal is useless. If they are in disharmony, we cannot follow both — we must choose one and reject the other. And the attempt to make the facts of Scripture co-factors of equal rank with the teaching of Scripture in ascertaining the true doctrine of inspiration, is really an attempt to modify the doctrine taught by Scripture by an appeal to the facts, while concealing from ourselves the fact that we have modified it, and in modifying corrected it, and, of course, in correcting it, discredited Scripture as a teacher of doctrine.

Probably these four types of procedure will include most of the methods by which men are to-day seeking to free themselves from the necessity of following the Scriptural doctrine of inspiration, while yet looking to Scripture as the source of doctrine. Is it not plain that on every one of them the outcome must be to discredit Scripture as a doctrinal guide? The human mind is very subtle, but with all its subtlety it will hardly be able to find a way to refuse to follow Scripture in one of the doctrines it teaches without undermining its authority as a teacher of doctrine.

II

IMMENSE WEIGHT OF EVIDENCE FOR THE BIBLICAL DOCTRINE

It is only to turn another face of the proposition with which we are dealing towards us, to emphasize next the important fact, that, the state of the case being such as we have found it, the evidence for the truth of the doctrine of the plenary inspiration of Scripture is just the whole body of evidence which goes to show that the apostles are trustworthy teachers of doctrine.

Language is sometimes made use of which would seem to imply that the amount or weight of the evidence offered for the truth of the doctrine that the Scriptures are the Word of God in such a sense that their words deliver the truth of God without error, is small. It is on the contrary just the whole body of evidence which goes to prove the writers of the New Testament to be trustworthy as deliverers of doctrine. It is just the same evidence in amount and weight which is adduced in favor of any other Biblical doctrine. It is the same weight and amount of evidence precisely which is adducible for the truth of the doctrines of the Incarnation, of the Trinity, of the Divinity of Christ, of Justification by Faith, of Regeneration by the Holy Spirit, of the Resurrection of the Body, of Life Everlasting. It is, of course, not absurdly intended that every Biblical doctrine is taught in the Scriptures with equal clearness, with equal explicitness, with equal frequency. Some doctrines are stated with an explicit precision that leaves little to systematic theology in its efforts to define the truth on all sides, except to repeat the words which the Biblical writers have used to teach it — as for example the doctrine of Justification by Faith. Others are not formulated in Scripture at all, but are taught only in their elements, which the systematician must collect and combine and so arrive finally at the doctrine — as for example the doctrine of the Trinity. Some are adverted to so frequently as to form the whole warp and woof of Scripture — as for example the doctrine of redemption in the blood of Christ. Others are barely alluded to here and there, in connections where the stress is really on other matters — as for example the doctrine of the fall of the angels. But however explicitly or incidentally, however frequently or rarely, however emphatically or allusively, they may be taught, when exegesis has once done its work and shown that they are taught by the Biblical writers, all these doctrines stand as supported by the same weight and amount of evidence — the evidence of the trustworthiness of the Biblical writers as teachers of doctrine. We cannot say that

we will believe these writers when they assert a doctrine
a hundred times and we will not believe them if they assert
it only ten times or only once; that we will believe them in
the doctrines they make the main subjects of discourse,
but not in those which they advert to incidentally; that we
will believe them in those that they teach as conclusions
of formal arguments, but not in those which they use as
premises wherewith to reach those conclusions; that we will
believe them in those they explicitly formulate and dogmatically teach, but not in those which they teach only in
their separate parts and elements. The question is not *how*
they teach a doctrine, but *do* they teach it; and when that
question is once settled affirmatively, the weight of evidence
that commends this doctrine to us as true is the same in
every case; and that is the whole body of evidence which
goes to show that the Biblical writers are trustworthy as
teachers of doctrine. The Biblical doctrine of inspiration,
therefore, has in its favor just this whole weight and amount
of evidence. It follows on the one hand that it cannot rationally be rejected save on the ground of evidence which
will outweigh the whole body of evidence which goes to
authenticate the Biblical writers as trustworthy witnesses to
and teachers of doctrine. And it follows, on the other hand,
that if the Biblical doctrine of inspiration is rejected, our
freedom from its trammels is bought logically at the somewhat serious cost of discrediting the evidence which goes
to show that the Biblical writers are trustworthy as teachers
of doctrine. In this sense, the fortunes of distinctive Christianity are bound up with those of the Biblical doctrine of
inspiration.

Let it not be said that thus we found the whole Christian
system upon the doctrine of plenary inspiration. We found
the whole Christian system on the doctrine of plenary inspiration as little as we found it upon the doctrine of
angelic existences. Were there no such thing as inspiration,
Christianity would be true, and all its essential doctrines
would be credibly witnessed to us in the generally trust-

worthy reports of the teaching of our Lord and of His authoritative agents in founding the Church, preserved in the writings of the apostles and their first followers, and in the historical witness of the living Church. Inspiration is not the most fundamental of Christian doctrines, nor even the first thing we prove about the Scriptures. It is the last and crowning fact as to the Scriptures. These we first prove authentic, historically credible, generally trustworthy, before we prove them inspired. And the proof of their authenticity, credibility, general trustworthiness would give us a firm basis for Christianity prior to any knowledge on our part of their inspiration, and apart indeed from the existence of inspiration. The present writer, in order to prevent all misunderstanding, desires to repeat here what he has said on every proper occasion — that he is far from contending that without inspiration there could be no Christianity. "Without any inspiration," he added, when making this affirmation on his induction into the work of teaching the Bible [53] — "without any inspiration we could have had Christianity; yea, and men could still have heard the truth and through it been awakened, and justified, and sanctified, and glorified. The verities of our faith would remain historically proven to us — so bountiful has God been in His fostering care — even had we no Bible; and through those verities, salvation." We are in entire harmony in this matter with what we conceive to be the very true statement recently made by Dr. George P. Fisher, that "if the authors of the Bible were credible reporters of revelations of God, whether in the form of historical transactions of which they were witnesses, or of divine mysteries that were unveiled to their minds, their testimony would be entitled to belief,

[53] "Discourses Occasioned by the Inauguration of Benj. B. Warfield, D.D., to the Chair of New Testament Exegesis and Literature in the Western Theological Seminary, April 25, 1880." Pittsburgh, 1880. P. 46. Cf. "Inspiration." By Prof. A. A. Hodge and Prof. B. B. Warfield. Philadelphia: Presbyterian Board of Publication, 1881. Pp. 7, 8 (also in *The Presbyterian Review* for April, 1881). Also, "The Inspiration of the Scriptures." By Francis L. Patton, D.D. Philadelphia: Presbyterian Board of Publication, 1869. Pp. 22, 23, 54.

even if they were shut up to their unaided faculties in communicating what they had thus received." [54] We are in entire sympathy in this matter, therefore, with the protest
which Dr. Marcus Dods raised in his famous address at the
meeting of the Alliance of the Reformed Churches at London,
against representing that "the infallibility of the Bible is the
ground of the whole Christian faith." [55] We judge with him
that it is very important indeed that such a misapprehension, if it is anywhere current, should be corrected. What we
are at present arguing is something entirely different from
such an overstrained view of the importance of inspiration
to the very existence of Christian faith, and something
which has no connection with it. We do not think that the
doctrine of plenary inspiration is the ground of Christian
faith, but if it was held and taught by the New Testament
writers, we think it an element in the Christian faith; a very
important and valuable element; [56] an element that appeals
to our acceptance on precisely the same ground as every

[54] *The Congregationalist*, Nov. 3, 1892; *The Magazine of Christian Literature*,
Dec., 1892, p. 236, first column. This whole column should be read; its statement
and illustration are alike admirable.

[55] This address may be most conveniently consulted in *The Expositor* for
October, 1888, pp. 301, 302. In expressing our concurrence with portions of this
address and of Dr. Fisher's papers just quoted, we are not to be understood, of
course, as concurring with their whole contents.

[56] How important and valuable this element of the Christian faith is, it is not
the purpose of this paper to point out. Let it suffice here to say briefly that it is
(1) the element which gives detailed certitude to the delivery of doctrine in the
New Testament, and (2) the element by which the individual Christian is brought
into immediate relation to God in the revelation of truth through the prophets
and apostles. The importance of these factors in the Christian life could not be
overstated. The importance of the recognition of plenary inspiration to the preservation of sound doctrine is negatively illustrated by the progress of Rationalism, as
thus outlined briefly by Dr. Charles Hodge ("Syst. Theol.," iii. p. 195): "Those
who admitted the divine origin of the Scriptures got rid of its distinctive doctrines
by the adoption of a low theory of inspiration and by the application of arbitrary
principles of interpretation. Inspiration was in the first instance confined to the
religious teachings of the Bible, then to the ideas or truths, but not to the form
in which they were presented, nor to the arguments by which they were supported. . . . In this way a wet sponge was passed over all the doctrines of redemption and their outlines obliterated." It looks as if the Church were extremely
slow in reading the most obvious lessons of history.

other element of the faith, viz., on the ground of our recognition of the writers of the New Testament as trustworthy witnesses to doctrine; an element of the Christian faith, therefore, which cannot be rejected without logically undermining our trust in all the other elements of distinctive Christianity by undermining the evidence on which this trust rests. We must indeed prove the authenticity, credibility and general trustworthiness of the New Testament writings before we prove their inspiration; and even were they not inspired this proof would remain valid and we should give them accordant trust. But just because this proof is valid, we must trust these writings in their witness to their inspiration, if they give such witness; and if we refuse to trust them here, we have in principle refused them trust everywhere. In such circumstances their inspiration is bound up inseparably with their trustworthiness, and therefore with all else that we receive on trust from them.

On the other hand, we need to remind ourselves that to say that the amount and weight of the evidence of the truth of the Biblical doctrine of inspiration is measured by the amount and weight of the evidence for the general credibility and trustworthiness of the New Testament writers as witnesses to doctrine, is an understatement rather than an overstatement of the matter. For if we trust them at all we will trust them in the account they give of the person and in the report they give of the teaching of Christ; whereupon, as they report Him as teaching the same doctrine of Scripture that they teach, we are brought face to face with divine testimony to this doctrine of inspiration. The argument, then, takes the form given it by Bishop Wordsworth: "The New Testament canonizes the Old; the INCARNATE WORD sets His seal on the WRITTEN WORD. The Incarnate Word is God; therefore, the inspiration of the Old Testament is authenticated by God Himself." [57] And, again, the general trustworthiness of the writers of the New Testament gives us the right and imposes on us the duty of accepting their

[57] Wordsworth, "On the Canon," p. 51, Am. Ed.

witness to the relation the Holy Ghost bears to their teaching, as, for example, when Paul tells us that the things which they uttered they uttered "not in words taught by human wisdom, but in those taught by the Spirit; joining Spirit-given things with Spirit-given things" (1 Cor. ii. 13), and Peter asserts that the Gospel was preached by them "in the Holy Spirit" (I Peter i. 12); and this relation asserted to exist between the Holy Ghost and their teaching, whether oral or written (I Cor. xiv. 37; II Thess. ii. 15, iii. 6–14), gives the sanction of the Holy Ghost to their doctrine of Holy Scripture, whatever that is found to be. So that, even though we begin on the lowest ground, we may find ourselves compelled to say, as Bishop Wilberforce found himself compelled to say: "In brief, my belief is this: The whole Bible comes to us as 'the Word of God' under the sanction of God, the Holy Ghost." [58] The weight of the testimony to the Biblical doctrine of inspiration, in a word, is no less than the weight to be attached to the testimony of God—God the Son and God the Spirit.

But our present purpose is not to draw out the full value of the testimony, but simply to emphasize the fact that on the emergence of the exegetical fact that the Scriptures of the New Testament teach this doctrine, the amount and weight of evidence for its truth must be allowed to be the whole amount and weight of the evidence that the writers of the New Testament are trustworthy as teachers of doctrine. It is not on some shadowy and doubtful evidence that the doctrine is based — not on an *a priori* conception of what inspiration ought to be, not on a "tradition" of doctrine in the Church, though all the *a priori* considerations and the whole tradition of doctrine in the Church are also thrown in the scale for and not in that against this doctrine; but first on the confidence which we have in the writers of the New Testament as doctrinal guides, and ultimately on whatever evidence of whatever kind and force exists to justify that confidence. In this sense, we repeat, the cause of

[58] "Life of the Rt. Rev. S. Wilberforce, D.D.," Vol. III. p. 149.

distinctive Christianity is bound up with the cause of the Biblical doctrine of inspiration. We accept Christianity in all its distinctive doctrines on no other ground than the credibility and trustworthiness of the Bible as a guide to truth; and on this same ground we must equally accept its doctrine of inspiration. "If we may not accept its account of itself," asks Dr. Purves, pointedly, "why should we care to ascertain its account of other things?" [59]

III

IMMENSE PRESUMPTION AGAINST ALLEGED FACTS CONTRADICTORY OF THE BIBLICAL DOCTRINE

We are again making no new affirmation but only looking from a slightly different angle upon the same proposition with which we have been dealing from the first, when we emphasize next the fact, that the state of the case being as we have found it, we approach the study of the so-called "phenomena" of the Scriptures with a very strong presumption that these Scriptures contain no errors, and that any "phenomena" apparently inconsistent with their inerrancy are so in appearance only: a presumption the measure of which is just the whole amount and weight of evidence that the New Testament writers are trustworthy as teachers of doctrine.

It seems to be often tacitly assumed that the Biblical doctrine of inspiration cannot be confidently ascertained until all the facts concerning the contents and structure and characteristics of Scripture are fully determined and allowed for. This is obviously fallacious. What Paul, for example, believed as to the nature of Scripture is obviously an easily separable question from what the nature of Scripture really is. On the other hand, the assumption that we cannot confidently accept the Biblical doctrine of inspiration as true

[59] "St. Paul and Inspiration." Inaugural Address, etc. A. D. F. Randolph & Co., 1892. P. 52. *Presbyterian and Reformed Review*, January, 1893, p. 21.

until criticism and exegesis have said their last word upon
the structure, the text, and the characteristics of Scripture,
even to the most minute fact, is more plausible. But it is far
from obviously true. Something depends upon our estimate
of the force of the mass of evidence which goes to show the
trustworthiness of the apostles as teachers of truth, and of
the clearness with which they announce their teaching as
to inspiration. It is conceivable, for example, that the force
of the evidence of their trustworthiness may be so great
that we should be fully justified in yielding implicit confidence to their teaching, even though many and serious difficulties should stand in the way of accepting it. This, indeed,
is exactly what we do in our ordinary use of Scripture as a
source of doctrine. Who doubts that the doctrines of the
Trinity and of the Incarnation present difficulties to rational
construction? Who doubts that the doctrines of native demerit and total depravity, inability and eternal punishment
raise objections in the natural heart? We accept these doctrines and others which ought to be much harder to credit,
such as the Biblical teaching that God so loved sinful man
as to give His only-begotten Son to die for him, not because
their acceptance is not attended with difficulties, but because our confidence in the New Testament as a doctrinal
guide is so grounded in unassailable and compelling evidence,
that we believe its teachings despite the difficulties which
they raise. We do not and we cannot wait until all these
difficulties are fully explained before we yield to the teaching
of the New Testament the fullest confidence of our minds
and hearts. How then can it be true that we are to wait until
all difficulties are removed before we can accept with confidence the Biblical doctrine of inspiration? In relation to
this doctrine alone, are we to assume the position that we
will not yield faith in response to due and compelling evidence of the trustworthiness of the teacher, until all difficulties are explained to our satisfaction? — that we must
fully understand and comprehend before we will believe?
Or is the point this — that we can suppose ourselves possibly

mistaken in everything else except our determination of the characteristics and structure of Scripture and the facts stated therein? Surely if we do not need to wait until we understand how God can be both one and three, how Christ can be both human and divine, how man can be both unable and responsible, how an act can be both free and certain, how man can be both a sinner and righteous in God's sight, before we accept, on the authority of the teaching of Scripture, the doctrines of the Trinity, of the Incarnation, of man's state as a sinner, of God's eternal predestination of the acts of free agents, and of acceptance on the ground of Christ's righteousness, because of the weight of the evidence which goes to prove that Scripture trustworthy as a teacher of divine truth; we may on the same compelling evidence accept, in full confidence, the teaching of the same Scripture as to the nature of its own inspiration, prior to a full understanding of how all the phenomena of Scripture are to be adjusted to it.

No doubt it is perfectly true and is to be kept in mind that the claim of a writing to be infallible may be mistaken or false. Such a claim has been put forth in behalf of and by other writings besides the Bible, and has been found utterly inconsistent with the observed characteristics of those writings. An *a priori* possibility may be asserted to exist in the case of the Bible, that a comparison of its phenomena with its doctrine may bring out a glaring inconsistency. The test of the truth of the claims of the Bible to be inspired of God through comparison with its contents, characteristics and phenomena, the Bible cannot expect to escape; and the lovers of the Bible will be the last to deny the validity of it. By all means let the doctrine of the Bible be tested by the facts and let the test be made all the more, not the less, stringent and penetrating because of the great issues that hang upon it. If the facts are inconsistent with the doctrine, let us all know it, and know it so clearly that the matter is put beyond doubt. But let us not conceal from ourselves the greatness of the issues involved in the test, lest we approach the test in too light a spirit, and make shipwreck of faith in the trustworthiness of the apostles as teachers of doctrine, with the easy indifference of a man who corrects the incidental errors of a piece of gossip. Nor is this appeal to the seriousness of the issues involved in any sense an appeal to deal deceitfully with the facts concerning or stated in the Bible, through fear of disturbing our confidence in a comfortable doctrine of its infallibility. It is simply an appeal to common sense. If you are told that a malicious lie has been uttered by some unknown person you may easily yield the report a languid provisional assent; such things are not impossible, unfortunately in this sinful world not unexampled. But if it is told you of your loved and trusted friend, you will probably demand the most stringent proof at the point of your walking stick. So far as this, Robert Browning has missed neither nature nor right reason, when he makes his Ferishtah point out how much more evidence we require in proof of a fact which brings us loss than what is sufficient to command

> "The easy acquiescence of mankind
> In matters nowise worth dispute."

If it is right to test most carefully the claim of every settled and accepted faith by every fact asserted in rebuttal of it, it must be equally right, nay incumbent, to scrutinize most closely the evidence for an asserted fact, which, if genuine, wounds in its vitals some important interest. If it would be a crime to refuse to consider most carefully and candidly any phenomena of Scripture asserted to be inconsistent with its inerrancy, it would be equally a crime to accept the asserted reality of phenomena of Scripture, which, if real, strike at the trustworthiness of the apostolic witness to doctrine, on any evidence of less than demonstrative weight.

But we approach the consideration of these phenomena alleged to be inconsistent with the Biblical doctrine of inspiration not only thus with what may be called, though in a high sense, a sentimental presumption against their reality.

The presumption is an eminently rational one, and is capable of somewhat exact estimation. We do not adopt the doctrine of the plenary inspiration of Scripture on sentimental grounds, nor even, as we have already had occasion to remark, on *a priori* or general grounds of whatever kind. We adopt it specifically because it is taught us as truth by Christ and His apostles, in the Scriptural record of their teaching, and the evidence for its truth is, therefore, as we have also already pointed out, precisely that evidence, in weight and amount, which vindicates for us the trustworthiness of Christ and His apostles as teachers of doctrine. Of course, this evidence is not in the strict logical sense "demonstrative;" it is "probable" evidence. It therefore leaves open the metaphysical possibility of its being mistaken. But it may be contended that it is about as great in amount and weight as "probable" evidence can be made, and that the strength of conviction which it is adapted to produce may be and should be practically equal to that produced by demonstration itself. But whatever weight it has, and whatever strength of conviction it is adapted to produce, it is with this weight of evidence behind us and with this strength of conviction as to the unreality of any alleged phenomena contradictory of the Biblical doctrine of inspiration, that we approach the study of the characteristics, the structure, and the detailed statements of the Bible. Their study is not to be neglected; we have not attained through "probable" evidence apodeictic certainty of the Bible's infallibility. But neither is the reality of the alleged phenomena inconsistent with the Bible's doctrine, to be allowed without sufficient evidence. Their reality cannot be logically or rationally recognized unless the evidence for it be greater in amount and weight than the whole mass of evidence for the trustworthiness of the Biblical writers as teachers of doctrine.

It is not to be thought that this amounts to a recommendation of strained exegesis in order to rid the Bible of phenomena adverse to the truth of the Biblical doctrine of inspiration. It amounts to a recommendation of great care in the exegetical determination of these alleged phenomena; it amounts to a recommendation to allow that our exegesis determining these phenomena is not infallible. But it is far from recommending either strained or artificial exegesis of any kind. We are not bound to harmonize the alleged phenomena with the Bible doctrine; and if we cannot harmonize them save by strained or artificial exegesis they would be better left unharmonized. We are not bound, however, on the other hand, to believe that they are unharmonizable, because we cannot harmonize them save by strained exegesis. Our individual fertility in exegetical expedients, our individual insight into exegetical truth, our individual capacity of understanding are not the measure of truth. If we cannot harmonize without straining, let us leave unharmonized. It is not necessary for us to see the harmony that it should exist or even be recognized by us as existing. But it is necessary for us to believe the harmony to be possible and real, provided that we are not prepared to say that we clearly see that on any conceivable hypothesis (conceivable to us or conceivable to any other intelligent beings) the harmony is impossible — if the trustworthiness of the Biblical writers who teach us the doctrine of plenary inspiration is really safeguarded to us on evidence which we cannot disbelieve. In that case every unharmonized passage remains a case of difficult harmony and does not pass into the category of objections to plenary inspiration. It can pass into the category of objections only if we are prepared to affirm that we clearly see that it is, on any conceivable hypothesis of its meaning, clearly inconsistent with the Biblical doctrine of inspiration. In that case we would no doubt need to give up the Biblical doctrine of inspiration; but with it we must also give up our confidence in the Biblical writers as teachers of doctrine. And if we cannot reasonably give up this latter, neither can we reasonably allow that the phenomena apparently inconsistent with the former are real, or really inconsistent with it. And this is but to say that we approach

the study of these phenomena with a presumption against
their being such as will disprove the Biblical doctrine of
inspiration — or, we may add (for this is but the same thing
in different words), correct or modify the Biblical doctrine
of inspiration — which is measured precisely by the amount
and weight of the evidence which goes to show that the
Bible is a trustworthy guide to doctrine.

The importance of emphasizing these, as it would seem,
very obvious principles, does not arise out of need for a very
great presumption in order to overcome the difficulties
arising from the "phenomena" of Scripture, as over against
its doctrine of inspiration. Such difficulties are not specially
numerous or intractable. Dr. Charles Hodge justly characterizes those that have been adduced by disbelievers in the
plenary inspiration of the Scriptures, as "for the most part
trivial," "only apparent," and marvelously few "of any real
importance." They bear, he adds, about the same relation
to the whole that a speck of sandstone detected here and
there in the marble of the Parthenon would bear to that
building.[60] They do not for the most part require explaining
away, but only to be fairly understood in order to void them.
They constitute no real strain upon faith, but when approached in a candid spirit one is left continually marveling
at the excessive fewness of those which do not, like ghosts,
melt away from vision as soon as faced. Moreover, as every
student of the history of exegesis and criticism knows, they
are a progressively vanishing quantity. Those which seemed
most obvious and intractable a generation or two ago, remain to-day as only too readily forgotten warnings against

[60] "Systematic Theology," i. pp. 169, 170: We have purposely adduced this
passage here to enable us to protest against the misuse of it, which, in the exigencies of the present controversy, has been made, as if Dr. Hodge was in this passage admitting the reality of the alleged errors. The passage occurs in the reply
to objections to the doctrine, not in the development of the doctrine itself, and
is of the nature of an *argumentum ad hominem*. How far Dr. Hodge was from
admitting the reality of error in the original Biblical text may be estimated from
the frequency with which he asserts its freedom from error in the immediately
preceding context — pp. 152, 155, 163 (no less than three times on this page),
165, 166, 169 (no less than five times).

the ineradicable and inordinate dogmatism of the opponents of the inerrancy of the Bible, who over-ride continually every canon of historical and critical caution in their eager violence against the doctrine that they assail. What scorn they expressed of "apologists" who doubted whether Luke was certainly in error in assigning a "pro-consul" to Cyprus, whether he was in error in making Lysanias a contemporary tetrarch with the Herodian rulers, and the like. How easily that scorn is forgotten as the progress of discovery has one by one vindicated the assertions of the Biblical historians. The matter has come to such a pass, indeed, in the progress of discovery, that there is a sense in which it may be said that the doctrine of the inerrancy of the Bible can now be based, with considerable confidence, on its observed "phenomena." What marvelous accuracy is characteristic of its historians! Dr. Fisher, in a paper already referred to, invites his readers to read Archibald Forbes' article in the *Nineteenth Century* for March, 1892, on "Napoleon the Third at Sedan," that they may gain some idea of how the truth of history as to the salient facts may be preserved amid "hopeless and bewildering discrepancies in regard to details," in the reports of the most trustworthy eye-witnesses. The article is instructive in this regard. And it is instructive in another regard also. What a contrast exists between this mass of "hopeless and bewildering discrepancies in regard to details," among the accounts of a single important transaction, written by careful and watchful eye-witnesses, who were on the ground for the precise purpose of gathering the facts for report, and who were seeking to give an exact and honest account of the events which they witnessed, and the marvelous accuracy of the Biblical writers! If these "hopeless and bewildering discrepancies" are consistent with the honesty and truthfulness and general trustworthiness of the uninspired writers, may it not be argued that the so much greater accuracy attained by the Biblical writers when describing not one event but the history of ages — and a history filled with pitfalls for the unwary — has something moro than honesty and truthfulness behind it, and warrants the attribution to them of something more than general trustworthiness? And, if in the midst of this marvel of general accuracy there remain here and there a few difficulties as yet not fully explained in harmony with it, or if in the course of the historical vindication of it in general a rare difficulty (as in the case of some of the statements of Daniel) seems to increase in sharpness, are we to throw ourselves with desperate persistency into these "last ditches" and strive by our increased insistence upon the impregnability of *them* to conceal from men that the main army has been beaten from the field? Is it not more reasonable to suppose that these difficulties, too, will receive their explanation with advancing knowledge? And is it not the height of the unreasonable to treat them like the Sibylline books as of ever-increasing importance in proportion to their decreasing number? The importance of keeping in mind that there is a presumption against the reality of these "inconsistent phenomena," and that the presumption is of a weight measurable only by the weight of evidence which vindicates the general trustworthiness of the Bible as a teacher of doctrine, does not arise from the need of so great a presumption in order to overcome the weight of the alleged opposing facts. Those facts are not specially numerous, important or intractable, and they are, in the progress of research, a vanishing quantity.

The importance of keeping in mind the principle in question arises rather from the importance of preserving a correct logical method. There are two ways of approaching the study of the inspiration of the Bible. One proceeds by obtaining first the doctrine of inspiration taught by the Bible as applicable to itself, and then testing this doctrine by the facts as to the Bible as ascertained by Biblical criticism and exegesis. This is good logical procedure; and in the presence of a vast mass of evidence for the general trustworthiness of the Biblical writings as witnesses of doctrine, and for the appointment of their writers as teachers of divine truth to men, and for the presence of the Holy Spirit with and in them aiding them in their teaching (in whatever degree and with whatever effect) — it would seem to be the only logical and proper mode of approaching the question. The other method proceeds by seeking the doctrine of inspiration in the first instance through a comprehensive induction from the facts as to the structure and contents of the Bible, as ascertained by critical and exegetical processes, treating all these facts as co-factors of the same rank for the induction. If in this process the facts of structure and the facts embedded in the record of Scripture — which are called, one-sidedly indeed but commonly, by the class of writers who adopt this procedure, "the phenomena" of Scripture — alone are considered, it would be difficult to arrive at a precise doctrine of inspiration, at the best: though, as we have already pointed out, a degree and kind of accuracy might be vindicated for the Scriptures which might lead us to suspect and to formulate as the best account of it, some divine assistance to the writers' memory, mental processes and expression. If the Biblical facts and teaching are taken as co-factors in the induction, the procedure (as we have already pointed out) is liable to the danger of modifying the teaching by the facts without clear recognition of what is being done; the result of which would be the loss from observation of one main fact of errancy, viz., the inaccuracy of the teaching of the Scriptures as to their own inspiration. This would vitiate the whole result: and this vitiation of the result can be avoided only by ascertaining separately the teaching of Scripture as to its own inspiration, and by accounting the results of this ascertainment one of the facts of the induction. Then we are in a position to judge by the comparison of this fact with the other facts, whether this fact of teaching is in accord or in disaccord with those facts of performance. If it is in disaccord, then of course this disaccord is the main factor in the case: the writers are convicted of false teaching. If it is in accord, then, if the teaching is not proved by the accord, it is at least left credible, and may bo believed with whatever confidence may be justified by the evidence which goes to show that these writers are trustworthy as deliverers of doctrine. And if nice and difficult questions arise in the comparison of the fact of teaching with the facts of performance, it is inevitable that the relative weight of the evidence for the trustworthiness of the two sets of facts should be the deciding factor in determining the truth. This is as much as to say that the asserted facts as to performance must give way before the fact as to teaching, unless the evidence on which they are based as facts outweighs the evidence on which the teaching may be accredited as true. But this correction of the second method of procedure, by which alone it can be made logical in form or valid in result, amounts to nothing less than setting it aside altogether and reverting to the first method, according to which the teaching of Scripture is first to be determined, and then this teaching to be tested by the facts of performance.

The importance of proceeding according to the true logical method may be illustrated by the observation that the conclusions actually arrived at by students of the subject seem practically to depend on the logical method adopted. In fact, the difference here seems mainly a difference in point of view. If we start from the Scripture doctrine of inspiration, we approach the phenomena with the question whether they will negative this doctrine, and we find none able to stand against it, commended to us as true, as it is, by the vast mass of evidence available to prove the trustworthiness of the Scriptural writers as teachers of doctrine. But if we start simply with a collection of the phenomena, classifying and reasoning from them, whether alone or in conjunction with the Scriptural statements, it may easily happen with us, as it happened with certain of old, that meeting with some things hard to be understood, we may be ignorant and unstable enough to wrest them to our own intellectual destruction, and so approach the Biblical doctrine of inspiration set upon explaining it away. The value of having the Scripture doctrine as a clue in our hands, is thus fairly illustrated by the ineradicable inability of the whole negative school to distinguish between *difficulties* and *proved errors*. If then we ask what we are to do with the numerous phenomena of Scripture inconsistent with verbal inspiration, which, so it is alleged, "criticism" has brought to light, we must reply: Challenge them in the name of the New Testament doctrine, and ask for their credentials. They have no credentials that can stand before that challenge. No single error has as yet been demonstrated to occur in the Scriptures as given by God to His Church. And every critical student knows, as already pointed out, that the progress of investigation has been a continuous process of removing difficulties, until scarcely a shred of the old list of "Biblical Errors" remains to hide the nakedness of this moribund contention. To say that we do not wish to make claims "for which we have only this to urge, that they cannot be absolutely disproved," is not to the point; what is to the point is to say, that we cannot set aside the presumption arising from the general trustworthiness of Scripture, that its doctrine of inspiration is true, by any array of contradictory facts, each one of which is fairly disputable. We must have indisputable errors — which are not forthcoming.

The real problem brought before the Churches by the present debate ought now to be sufficiently plain. In its deepest essence it is whether we can still trust the Bible as a guide in doctrine, as a teacher of truth. It is not simply whether we can explain away the Biblical doctrine of inspiration so as to allow us to take a different view from what has been common of the structure and characteristics of the Bible. Nor, on the other hand, is it simply whether we may easily explain the facts, established as facts, embedded in Scripture, consistently with the teaching of Scripture as to the nature, extent and effects of inspiration. It is specifically whether the results proclaimed by a special school of Biblical criticism — which are of such a character, as is now admitted by all, as to necessitate, if adopted, a new view of the

Bible and of its inspiration — rest on a basis of evidence strong enough to meet and overcome the weight of evidence, whatever that may be in kind and amount, which goes to show that the Biblical writers are trustworthy as teachers of doctrine. If we answer this question in the affirmative, then no doubt we shall have not only a new view of the Bible and of its inspiration but also a whole new theology, because we must seek a new basis for doctrine. But if we answer it in the negative, we may possess our souls in patience and be assured that the Scriptures are as trustworthy witnesses to truth when they declare a doctrine of Inspiration as when they declare a doctrine of Incarnation or of Redemption, even though in the one case as in the other difficulties may remain, the full explanation of which is not yet clear to us. The real question, in a word, is not a new question but the perennial old question, whether the basis of our doctrine is to be what the Bible teaches, or what men teach. And this is a question which is to be settled on the old method, viz., on our estimate of the weight and value of the evidence which places the Bible in our hands as a teacher of doctrine.

VII

"GOD-INSPIRED SCRIPTURE"

"GOD-INSPIRED SCRIPTURE"

THE phrase, "Given by inspiration of God," or "Inspired of God," occurs, as is well-known, but once in the New Testament — in the classical passage, to wit, II Tim. iii. 16, which is rendered in the Authorized Version, "All Scripture *is* given by inspiration of God," and by the Revised Version, "Every Scripture inspired of God *is*, etc." The Greek word represented by it, and standing in this passage as an epithet or predicate of "Scripture" — θεόπνευστος — though occurring here only in the New Testament and found nowhere earlier in all Greek literature, has nevertheless not hitherto seemed of doubtful interpretation. Its form, its subsequent usage, the implications of parallel terms and of the analogy of faith, have combined with the suggestions of the context to assign to it a meaning which has been constantly attributed to it from the first records of Christian interpretation until yesterday.

This unvarying understanding of the word is thus reported by the leading lexicographers: Schleusner "New Test. Lexicon." Glasgow reprint of fourth Leipzig edition, 1824:

"Θεόπνευστος, ου, ὁ, ἡ, *afflatu divino actus, divino quodam spiritu afflatus*, et partim de *hominibus* usurpatur, *quorum sensus et sermones ad vim divinam referendi sunt*, v. c. *poëtis, faticidis, prophetis, auguribus*, qui etiam θεοδίδακτοι vocantur, partim de *ipsis rebus, notionibus, sermonibus, et scriptis, a Deo suggestis, et divino instructu natis*, ex θεὸς et πνέω *spiro*, quod, ut Latinum *afflo*, de diis speciatim usurpatur, quorum vi homines interdum ita agi existimabantur, ut notiones rerum, antea ignotarum, insolito quodam modo conciperent atque mente vehementius concitata in sermones sublimiores et elegantiores erumperent. Conf. *Cic.* pro Archia c. 14; *Virgil.* Aen. iii, 358, vi, 50. In N. T. semel legitur II Tim. iii. 16, πᾶσα γραφὴ θεόπνευστος omnis

¹ From *The Presbyterian and Reformed Review*, v. XI, pp. 89–130.

Scriptura divinitus inspirata, seu, quæ est originis divinæ. coll. II Pet i. 21. Syrus. . . . scriptura, quæ per spiritum scripta est. Conjunxit nempe actionem scribendi cum actione inspirandi. Apud *Plutarchum* T. ix. p. 583. ed. *Reiske*. θεόπνευστοι ὄνειροι sunt *somnia a diis immissa*."

Robinson "Greek and English Lexicon of the New Testament," new ed., New York, 1872:

"θεόπνευστος, ου, ὁ, ἡ, adj. (θεός, πνέω), *God-inspired, inbreathed of God*, II Tim. iii. 16 πᾶσα γραφὴ θεόπνευστος. — Plut. de Placit. Philosoph. 5. 2, τοὺς ὀνείρους τοὺς θεοπνεύστους. Phocylid. 121 τῆς δὲ θεοπνεύστου σοφίης λόγος ἐστὶν ἄριστος. Comp. Jos. c. Ap. 1. 7 [αἱ γραφαὶ] τῶν προφητῶν κατὰ τὴν ἐπίπνοιαν τὴν ἀπὸ τοῦ θεοῦ μαθόντων. Cic. pro Arch. 8, 'poetam . . . quasi divino quodam spiritu inflari.' "

Thayer-Grimm "Greek-English Lexicon of the New Testament," New York, 1887:

"θεόπνευστος, —ον, (θεός and πνέω), *inspired by God:* γραφή, i. e. the contents of Scripture, II Tim. iii. 16 [see πᾶς I. 1 c.]; σοφίη, [pseudo-] Phocyl. 121; ὄνειροι, Plut. de plac. phil. 5, 2, 3 p. 904f.; [Orac. Sibyll. 5, 406 (cf. 308); Nonn. paraphr. ev. Ioan. 1, 99]. (ἔμπνευστος also is used passively, but ἄπνευστος, εὔπνευστος, πυρίπνευστος, [δυσδιάπνευστος], actively [and δυσανάπνευστος appar. either act. or pass.; cf. W. 96 (92) note].)"

Cremer "Biblico-Theological Lexicon of New Testament Greek" ed. 2, E. T., Edinburgh, 1878:

"θεόπνευστος, *prompted by God, divinely inspired*. II Tim. iii. 16, πᾶσα γραφὴ θ. In profane Greek it occurs only in Plut. *de placit. philos.* v. 2, ὄνειροι θεόπνευστοι (κατ' ἀνάγκην γίνονται), opposed to φυσικοί. The formation of the word cannot be traced to the use of πνέω, but only of ἐμπνέω. Cf. Xen. *Hell.* vii. 4, 32, τὴν ἀρετὴν θεὸς μὲν ἐμπνεύσας; Plat. *Conv.* 179 B, μένος ἐμπνεῦσαι ἐνίοις τῶν ἡρώων τὸν θεόν; Hom. *Il.* xx. 110; *Od.* xix. 138. The simple verb is never used of divine action. How much the word corresponds with the Scriptural view is evident from II Pet. i. 21."

And the commentators generally will be found to speak no otherwise.

The completeness of this lexical consent has recently, however, been broken, and that by no less an authority than Prof.

Hermann Cremer himself, the second edition of whose great "Biblico-theological Lexicon" we have just adduced as in entire agreement with the current view. The date of issue of this edition, in its original German form, was 1872. The third edition was delayed until 1883. In the interval Dr. Cremer was called upon to write the article on "Inspiration" in the second edition of Herzog's "Realencyklopædie" (Vol. vi, *sub voc.*, pp. 746 *seq.*), which saw the light in 1880. In preparing this article he was led to take an entirely new view [2] of the meaning of θεόπνευστος, according to which it defines Scripture, in II Tim. iii. 16, not according to its origin, but according to its effect — not as "inspired of God," but as "inspiring its readers." The statement of his new view was transferred to the third edition of his "Lexicon" (1883; E. T. as "Supplement," 1886) very much in the form in which it appears in Herzog; and it has retained its place in the "Lexicon," with practically no alteration, ever since.[3] As its expression in Herzog was the earliest, and therefore is historically the most important, and as the article in the "Lexicon" is easily accessible in both German and English, and moreover does not

[2] The novelty of the view in question must not be pressed beyond measure. It was a new view in the sense of the text, but, as we shall subsequently see, it was no invention of Prof. Cremer's, but was derived by him from Ewald.

[3] That is at least to the eighth edition (1895), which is the last we have seen. The chief differences between the Herzog and "Lexicon" articles are found at the beginning and end — the latter being fuller at the beginning and the former at the end. The "Lexicon" article opens thus: "Θεόπνευστος, -ον, *gifted with God's Spirit, breathing the Divine Spirit* (but not, as Weiss still maintains = *inspired by God*). The term belongs only to Hellenistic and Ecclesiastical Greek, and as peculiar thereto is connected with expressions belonging to the sphere of heathen prophecy and mysteries, θεοφόρος, θεοφόρητος, θεοφορούμενος, θεήλατος, θεοκίνητος, θεοδέγμων, θεοδέκτωρ, θεοτρόπος, θεόμαντις, θεόφρων, θεοφράδμων, θεοφραδής, ἔνθεος, ἐνθουσιαστής, *et al.*, to which Hellenistic Greek adds two new words, θεόπνευστος and θεοδίδακτος, without, however, denoting what the others do — an ecstatic state." The central core of the article then runs parallel in both forms. Nothing is added in the "Lexicon," except (in the later editions) immediately after the quotations from Nonnus this single sentence: "This usage in Nonnus shows just that it is not to be taken as = *inspiratus*, inspired by God but as = filled with God's Spirit and therefore radiating it." Then follows immediately the next sentence, precisely as in Herzog, with which the "Lexicon" article then runs parallel to the quotation from Origen, immediately after which it breaks off.

essentially differ from what is said in Herzog, we shall quote here Dr. Cremer's statement of the case in preference from Herzog. He says:

"In theological usage, Inspiration denotes especially the influence of the Holy Spirit in the origination of the sacred Scriptures, by means of which they become the expression to us of the will of God, or the Word of God. The term comes from the Vulgate, which renders II Tim. iii. 16 πᾶσα γραφὴ θεόπνευστος, by *omnis Scriptura divinitus inspirata*. Whether the meaning of the Greek term is conveyed by this is at least questionable. It clearly belongs only to Hellenistic and Christian Greek. The notion that it was used also in classical Greek of poets and seers (Huther in his Commentary) and to express what Cicero says in his *pro Archia*, p. 8, *nemo vir magnus sine aliquo afflatu divino unquam fuit*, is certainly wrong. For θεόπνευστος does not occur at all in classical Greek or in profane Greek as a whole. In the unique passage, Plutarch, *de placit. phil.*, 5, 2 (Mor. 904, 2): τοὺς ὀνείρους τοὺς θεοπνεύστους κατ᾿ ἀνάγκην γίνεσθαι· τοὺς δὲ φυσικοὺς ἀνειδωλοποιουμένης ψυχῆς τὸ συμφέρον αὐτῇ κτλ., it is very probably to be ascribed to the copyist, and stands, as Wyttenbach conjectures, in the place of θεοπέμπτους. Besides this it occurs in Pseudo-Phocylides, v. 121: τῆς δὲ θεοπνεύστου σοφίης λόγος ἐστὶν ἄριστος — unless the whole line is, with Bernays, to be deleted as disturbing to the sense — as well as in the fifth book of the "Sibyllines," v. 308: Κύμη δ᾿ ἡ μωρὰ σὺν νάμασι τοῖς θεοπνεύστοις, and v. 406, Ἀλλὰ μέγαν γενετῆρα θεὸν πάντων θεοπνεύστων Ἐν θυσίαις ἐγέραιρον καὶ ἁγίας ἑκατόμβας. The Pseudo-Phocylides was, however, a Hellenist, and the author of the fifth book of the "Sibyllines" was, most probably, an Egyptian Jew living in the time of Hadrian. On Christian ground we find it in II Tim. iii. 16, which is possibly the earliest written employment of it to which we can point. Wetstein, on this passage, adduces the sentence from the *Vita Sabae* 16 (in Cotelerii *Monum.*): ἔφθασε τῇ τοῦ Χυ χάριτι ἡ πάντων θεοπνεύστων, πάντων χριστοφόρων αὐτοῦ συνοδία μέχρι ὁ ὀνομάτων, as well as the designation of Marcus Eremita as ὁ θεόπνευστος ἀνήρ. That the term has a passive meaning = 'gifted with God's Spirit,' 'divinely spirited,' (not 'inspired' as Ewald rightly distinguishes [4]) may be taken as indubitable from 'Sibyll.', v. 406 and the two passages last adduced. Never-

---

[4] The contrast is between "*göttlich begeistet*" and "*göttlich begeistert*." The reference to Ewald is given in the "Lexicon": *Jahrb. f. bibl. Wissenschaft*, vii. 68. *seq.*; ix. 91 *seq.*

theless γραφὴ θεόπνευστος does not seem easily capable of meaning
'inspired by God's Spirit' in the sense of the Vulgate; when connected
with such conceptions as γραφή here, νᾶμα, 'fountain,' 'Sibyll.' v. 308,
it would rather signify 'breathing a divine spirit,' in keeping with that
ready transition of the passive into the active sense which we see in
ἄπνευστος, εὔπνευστος, 'ill- or well-breathed' = 'breathing ill or well.'
Compare Nonnus, *paraphr. ev Jo.*, i, 102: οὗ ποδὸς ἄκρου ἀνδρομένην
παλάμην οὐκ ἄξιος εἰμὶ πελάσσας, λῦσαι μοῦνον ἱμάντα θεοπνεύστοιο πεδίλου,
with v. 129: βαπτίζειν ἀπύροισι καὶ ἀπνεύστοισι λοέτροις. In harmony
with this, it might be understood also in Phocyl. 121; the explanation,
'Wisdom gifted with the Divine Spirit,' at all events has in its favor
the fact that θεόπνευστος is given the same sense as when it is connected
with ἀνήρ, ἄνθρωπος. Certainly a transition to the sense, 'breathed by
God' = 'inspired by God' seems difficult to account for, and it would
fit, without forcing, only Phocyl. 121, while in II Tim. iii. 16, on the
assumption of this sense, there would be required a not altogether
easy metonyme. The sense 'breathing God's Spirit' is moreover in
keeping with the context, especially with the ὠφέλιμος πρὸς διδασκαλίαν
κτλ. and the τὰ δυνάμενά σε σοφίσαι, v. 15, as well as with the language
employed elsewhere, e. g., in the Epistle to the Hebrews, where what
the Scripture says is, as is well known, spoken of as the saying, the
word of the Holy Ghost. Cf. also Acts xxviii. 25. Origen also, *in Hom.
21 in Jerem.*, seems so to understand it: *sacra volumina Spiritus plenitudinem spirant.* Let it be added that the expression 'breathed by God,
inspired by God,' though an outgrowth of the Biblical idea, certainly,
so far as it is referred to the prophecy which does not arise out of the
human will (II Pet. i. 21), yet can scarcely be applied to the whole of
the rest of the sacred Scriptures — unless we are to find in II Tim.
iii. 16 the expression of a conception of sacred Scripture similar to the
Philonian. There is no doubt, however, that the Peshito understood
it simply = 'inspired by God' — yet not differently than as in Matt.
xxii. 43 we find: Δαυὶδ ἐν πνεύματι λαλεῖ. It translates כל כתב גיר בברוחא
אתכתב, 'for every Scripture which is written ἐν πνεύματι' — certainly
keeping prominently in the foreground the inspiration of the writer.
Similarly the Æthiopic renders: 'And every Scripture is in the (by
the) Spirit of the Lord and profits'; while the Arabic (deriving from
the original text) reads: 'And every Scripture which is divinely of
spiratio, divinam sapiens auram.' The rendering of the Peshito and
the explanations of the Greek exegetes would certainly lend great
weight to the *divinitus inspirata*, were not they explicable from the

dominant idea of the time — for which, it was thought, a suitable term was found in II Tim. iii. 16, nowhere else used indeed and coined for the purpose — but which was itself more or less taken over from the Alexandrian Judaism, that is to say, from heathenism."

Here, we will perceive, is a carefully reasoned attempt to reverse the previous lexical *consensus* as to the meaning of this important word. We have not observed many traces of the influence of this new determination of its import. The present writer, after going over the ground under Prof. Cremer's guidance, too hastily adopted his conclusion in a paper on "Paul's Doctrine of the Old Testament" published in *The Presbyterian Quarterly* for July, 1899; and an adverse criticism of Dr. Cremer's reasoning, from the pen of Prof. Dr. L. Schulze, of Rostock, appeared in the *Theologisches Literaturblatt* for May 22, 1896 (xvii, 21, pp. 253, 254), in the course of a review of the eighth edition of the "Lexicon." But there has not met our eye as yet any really thorough reëxamination of the whole matter, such as a restatement of it like Dr. Cremer's might have been expected to provoke. The case surely warrants and indeed demands it. Dr. Cremer's statement is more than a statement — it is an argument; and his conclusion is revolutionary, not indeed as to doctrine — for that rests on a broader basis than a single text or an isolated word — but as to the meaning borne by an outstanding New Testament term. It would seem that there is, then, no apology needed for undertaking a somewhat minute examination of the facts in the case under the guidance of Dr. Cremer's very full and well-reasoned statement.

It may conduce, in the end, to clearness of presentation if we begin somewhat *in medias res* by raising the question of the width of the usage of the word. Is it broadly a Greek word, or distinctively a Hellenistic word, or even a purely Christian word?

So far as appears from the usage as ascertained,[5] it would

[5] Of which the facts given by Cremer may for the present be taken as a fair conspectus, only adding that the word occurs not only in the editions of Plutarch,

seem to be post-Christian. Whether we should also call it Christian, coined possibly by Paul and used only in Christian circles, depends, in the present state of our knowledge, on the determination of two rather nice questions. One of these concerns the genuineness of the reading θεοπνεύστους in the tract on "The Opinions of Philosophers" (v, 2, 3), which has come down to us among the works of Plutarch, as well as in its dependent document, the "History of Philosophy" (106), transmitted among the works of Galen. The other concerns the character, whether Jewish or Jewish-Christian, of certain portions of the fifth book of the " Sibylline Oracles "and of the "Poem of Admonition," once attributed to Phocylides but now long recognized to be the work of a late Alexandrian Jew,[6] — in both of which the word occurs. Dr. Cremer considers the reading to be false in the Plutarchian tract, and thinks the fifth book of the "Sybillines" and the Pseudo-Phocylidian poem Jewish in origin. He therefore pronounces the word a Hellenistic one. These decisions, however, can scarcely be looked upon as certain; and they will bear scrutiny, especially as they are accompanied with some incidental errors of statement.

It would certainly require considerable boldness to decide with confidence upon the authorship of any given portion of the fifth book of the "Sibyllines." Friedlieb (whom Dr. Cremer follows) and Badt ascribe the whole book to a Jewish, but Alexandre, Reuss and Dechent to a Christian author; while others parcel it out variously between the two classes of sources — the most assigning the sections containing the word in question, however, to a Jewish author (Bleck, Lücke, Gfrörrer; Ewald, Hilgenfeld; Schürer). Schürer practically gives up in despair the problem of distributing the book to its several authors, and contents himself with saying that Jewish pieces preponderate and run in date from the first Christian century to Hadrian.[7] In these circumstances surely

"De plac. phil.," v. 2, 3, but also in the printed text of the dependent document printed among Galen's works under the title of "De hist. phil.," 106.

[6] Cf. Mahaffy, "History of Greek Literature" (American ed.), i. 188, note 1.

[7] "The Jewish People in the Time of Jesus Christ," E. T., II, iii. 286, whence the account given in the text is derived.

a certain amount of doubt may fairly be thought to rest on the Jewish or Christian origin of our word in the Sibylline text. On the other hand, there seems to be pretty good positive reason for supposing the Pseudo-Phocylidian poem to be in its entirety a Christian production. Its Jewish origin was still strenuously maintained by Bernays,[8] but its relation to the "Teaching of the Apostles" has caused the subject to be reopened, and we think has brought it to at least a probable settlement in favor of Scaliger's opinion that it is the work "ἀνωνύμου Christiani."[9] In the face of this probability the brilliant and attractive, but not always entirely convincing conjectures by which Bernays removed some of the Christian traits from the text may now be neglected: and among them that by which he discarded the line containing our word. So far then as its occurrence in the fifth book of the "Sibyllines" and in Pseudo-Phocylides is concerned, no compelling reason appears why the word may not be considered a distinctively Christian one: though it must at the same time be recognized that the sections in the fifth "Sibyl" in which it occurs are more probably Jewish than Christian.

With reference to the Plutarchian passage something more needs to be said. "In the unique passage, Plutarch *de plac. phil.* 5, 2 (904 F.): τῶν ὀνείρων τοὺς μὲν θεοπνεύστους κατ' ἀνάγκην γίνεσθαι· τοὺς δὲ φυσικούς ἀνειδωλοποιουμένης ψυχῆς τὸ συμφέρον αὐτῇ κτλ." says Dr. Cremer, "it is with the greatest probability to be ascribed to the transcriber, in whose mind θεόπνευστος lay in the sense of the Vulgate rendering, *divinitus inspirata*, and it stands, as Wyttenbach conjectures, for θεοπέμπτους." The remark concerning Wyttenbach is erroneous — only one of a series of odd misstatements which have dogged the textual notes on this passage. Wyttenbach prints θεοπνεύστους in his text and accompanies it with this textual

[8] See his "Gesammelte Abhandlungen," edited by Usener in 1885. Usener's Preface should be also consulted.

[9] So Harnack, "Theologische Literaturzeitung," 1885, No. 7, p. 160: also, J. R. Harris, "The Teaching of the Apostles and the Sibylline Books" (Cambridge, 1888): both give internal evidences of the Christian origin of the book. Cf. what we have said in *The Andover Review* for August, 1886, p. 219.

note: [10] "θεοπέμπτους *reposuit editor Lips. ut ex Gal. et Mosc. At in neutro haec reperio. Sane non est quare compilatori elegantias obtrudamus.*" Θεοπέμπτους is therefore not Wyttenbach's conjecture: Wyttenbach does not even accept it, and this has of late been made a reproach to him: [11] he ascribes it to "the Leipzig editor," that is to Christian Daniel Beck, whose edition of this tract was published at Leipzig, in 1787. But Wyttenbach even more gravely misquotes Beck than he has himself been misquoted by Dr. Cremer. For Beck, who prints in his text: τῶν ὀνείρων τοὺς μὲν θεοπνεύστους, annotates as follows: "Olim: τοὺς ὀνείρους τοὺς θεοπνεύστους — *Reddidi textis elegantiorem lectionem, quae in M. et G. est.* θεοπνεύστους *sapere Christianum librarium videtur pro* θεοπέμπτους." [12] That is to say, Wyttenbach has transferred Beck's note on τῶν ὀνείρων τοὺς μὲν to θεοπέμπτους. It is this clause and not θεοπέμπτους that Beck professes to have got out of the Moscow MS. and Galen: θεοπέμπτους he presents merely as a pure conjecture founded on the one consideration that θεοπνεύστους has a flavor of Christian scribe about it; and he does not venture to put θεοπέμπτους into the text. The odd thing is that Hutten follows Wyttenbach in his misrepresentation of Beck, writing in his note: "Beck. dedit θεοπέμπτους ut elegantiorem lectionem e Mosq. et Gal. sumptam. In neutro se hoc reperisse W. notat, addens, non esse quare compilatori elegantias obtrudamus. Cors. e Gal. notat τῶν ὀνείρων τοὺς μὲν θεοπνεύστους." [13] Corsini does indeed so report, his note running: "Paullo aliter" (i. e., from the ordinary text which he reprints from Stephens) "Galenus, τῶν ὀνείρων τοὺς μὲν θεοπνεύστους, somniorum ea quidem quae divinitus inspirata sint, etc." [14] But this is exactly what Beck says, and nothing other,

[10] Oxford 8vo edition, 1795–1830, Vol. IV, ii. 650.

[11] As by Diels in his "Doxographi Graci," p. 15: "*fuit scilicet* θεοπέμπτους, *quod sero intellectum est a Wyttenbachio in indice Plutarcheo. si Galenum inspexisset, ipsum illud* θεοπέμπτους *inventurus erat.*" But Diels' presentation of Galen was scarcely open to Wyttenbach's inspection: and the editions then extant read θεοπνεύστους as Corsini rightly tells us.

[12] "Plutarchi de Physicis Philosophorum Decretis," ed. Chr. Dan. Beckius, Leipzig, 1787.   [13] Tübingen, 1791–1804, Vol. XII (1800), p. 467.

[14] "Plutarchi de Placitis Philosophorum Libb. v." (Florentiæ, 1750).

except that he adds that this form is also found in the
Moscow MS. We must conclude that Hutten in looking at
Beck's note was preoccupied with Wyttenbach's misreport
of it. The upshot of the whole matter is that the reading
θεοπέμπτους was merely a conjecture of Beck's, founded solely
on his notion that θεοπνεύστους was a purely Christian term,
and possessing no diplomatic basis whatsoever. Accordingly
it has not found its way into the printed text of Plutarch: all
editions, with one exception, down to and including those of
Dübner-Döhner (Didot's "Bibliotheca") of 1856 and Bernardakis (Teubner's series) of 1893 read θεοπνεύστους.

A new face has been put on the matter, however, by the
publication in 1879 of Diels' "Doxographi Græci," in which the
whole class of ancient literature to which Plutarch's "De plac.
philos." belongs is subjected to a searching study, with a view
to tracing the mutual relations of the several pieces and the
sources from which they are constructed.[15] With this excursion into "higher criticism," into which there enters a highly
speculative element, that, despite the scientific thoroughness
and admirable acuteness which give the whole an unusually
attractive aspect, leaves some doubts in the mind of the sober
reader,[16] we have now happily little to do. Suffice it to say
that Diels looks upon the Plutarchian tract as an epitome of
a hypothetical Aëtios, made about 150 A.D. and already used
by Athenagoras (c. 177 A.D.):[17] and on the Galenic tract as
in its later portion an excerpt from the Plutarchian tract,
made about A.D. 500.[18] In the course of his work, he has

[15] A very clear account of Diels' main conclusions is given by Franz Susemihl
in his "Geschichte der Griechischen Literatur in der Alexandrinerzeit" (Leipzig,
1891–1892), ii. pp. 250, 251, as well as in Bursian's *Jahresbericht* for 1881 (VII,
i. 289 *seq.*). A somewhat less flattering notice by Max Heinze appears in Bursian
for 1880, p. 3 *seq.* Cf. Gerke, *sub voc.* "Aëtios," in the new edition of Pauly's
"Real-Encyclopædie" (Wissowa's ed., 1894), I, i. 705 *a*.

[16] Cf. the remarks of Max Heinze as above.

[17] It would be possible to hold, of course, that Athenagoras used not the
[Pseudo?-] Plutarch, but the hypothetical Aëtios, of which Diels considers the
former an excerpt: but Diels does not himself so judge: "anceps est quæstio utrum
excerpserit Athenagoras Plutarchi Placita an maius illud opus, cuius illa est
epitome. illud mihi probatur, hoc R. Volkmanno 'Leben Plut.,' i. 169. . . ." (p. 51).

[18] The relation of the Pseudo-Galen to the [Pseudo?-] Plutarch Diels ex-

framed and printed a careful recension of the text of both tracts,[19] and in both of them he reads at the place of interest to us, θεοπέμπτους.[20] Here for the first (and as yet only [21]) time θεοπέμπτους makes its appearance in the text of what we may, in deference to Diels' findings and after the example of Gerke,[22] call, at least, the "[Pseudo?-] Plutarch."[23] The key to the situation, with Diels, lies in the reading of the Pseudo-Galen: for as an excerpt from the [Pseudo?-] Plutarch the Pseudo-Galen becomes a valuable witness to its text, and is treated in this case indeed as a determinative witness, inasmuch as the whole MS. transmission of [Pseudo?-] Plutarch, so far as known, reads here θεοπνεύστους. Editing θεοπέμπτους in Pseudo-Galen, Diels edits it also, on that sole documentary ground, in [Pseudo?-] Plutarch. That we may form some estimate of the likelihood of the new reading, we must, therefore, form some estimate of its likelihood in the text of the Pseudo-Galen, as well as of the principles on which the text of the [Pseudo?-] Plutarch is to be framed.

The editions of Pseudo-Galen — including that of Kühn[24] —

presses thus: "Alter liber quo duce ex generali physicorum tanquam promulside ad largiorem dapam Galenus traducit est 'Plutarchus de Placidis philosophorum physicis.' Unde cum in prioribus pauca suspensa manu ut condimentum adspersa sint (c. 5, 20, 21), jam a c. 25 ad finem Plutarchus ita regnat, nihil aliud ut præterea adscitum esse appareat . . . ergo fœdioribus Byzantiorum soloecismis amputatis hanc partem ad codicum fidem descripsimus, non nullis Plutarcheæ emendationis auxilium, pluribus fortasse humanæ perversitatis insigne testimonium" (pp. 252, 253). [19] Plutarch's, pp. 267 *seq.*; Galen's, pp. 595 *seq.*

[20] Plutarch's "Ep.," v. 2, 3 (p. 416); Galen's "Hist. Phil.," 106 (p. 640).

[21] For Bernardakis reads θεοπνεύστους in his text (Teubner series, Plutarch's "Moralia," v. 351), recognizing at the same time in a note that the reading of Galen is θεοπέμπτους.

[22] In Pauly's "Real-Encyclopædie," new ed., s. v.

[23] It is not meant, of course, that Diels was the first to deny the tract to Plutarch. It has always been under suspicion. Wyttenbach, for example, rejects its Plutarchian claim with decision, and speaks of the tract in a tone of studied contempt, which is, indeed, reflected in the note already quoted from him, in the remark that we would not be justified in obtruding elegancies on a mere compiler. Cf. i. p. xli: "Porro, si quid hoc est, spurius liber utriusque nomine perperam fertur idem, Plutarchi qui dicitur *De Philosophorum Placitis*, Galeni *Historia philosophiæ*."

[24] Diels does not think highly of this portion of Kühn's edition: "Kuehnius, qui prioribus sui corporis voluminibus manum subinde admovit quamvis parum

have hitherto read θεοπνεύστους at our place, and from this we may possibly infer, that this is the reading of the common run of the MSS.[25] Diels constructs his text for this portion of the treatise from two kindred MSS. only, and records the readings of no others: as no variation is given upon our word, we may infer that these two MSS. at least agree in reading θεοπέμπτους. The former of them (Codex Laurentianus lxxiv, 3), of the twelfth or early thirteenth century, is described as transcribed "with incredible corruptness"; the latter (Codex Laurentianus lviii, 2), of the fifteenth century, as written more carefully: both represent a common very corrupt archetype.[26] This archetype is reconstructed from the consent of the two, and where they differ the preference is given to the former. The text thus framed is confessedly corrupt:[27] but though it must therefore be cautiously used, Diels considers it nevertheless a treasure house of the best readings for the [Pseudo?-] Plutarch.[28] Especially in the latter part of the [Pseudo?-] Plutarch, where the help of Eusebius and the other *eclogæ* fails, he thinks the case would often be desperate if we did not have the Pseudo-Galen. Three examples of the preservation of the right reading by it alone he gives us, one of them being our present passage, in which he follows, therefore, the reading of the Pseudo-Galen against the entire MS. transmission.

Diels considers the whole MS. transmission of the [Pseudo?-] Plutarch to take us back to an archetype of

felicem, postremo urgenti typothetæ ne inspectas quidem Charterianæ plagulas typis discribendas tradidisse fertur. neque aliter explicari potest, quod editio ambitiose suscepta tam misere absoluta est" (p. 241, 2).

[25] Though Diels informs us that the editors have made very little effort to ascertain the readings of the MSS.

[26] "Ex archetypo haud vetusto eodemque mendosissimo quattuor exempla transcripta esse, ac fidelius quidem Laur. A, peritius sed interpolate Laur. B." (p. 241).

[27] Diels' language is: "dolendum sane est libri condicionem tam esse desperatam ut etiam Plutarcheo archetypo comparato haud semel plane incertus hæreas, quid sibi velit compilator" (p. 12).

[28] "Verum quamvis sit summa opus cautione ne ventosi nebulonis commenta pro sincera memoria amplexemur, inest tamen in Galeno optimarum lectionum pæne intactus thesaurus" (p. 13).

about A.D. 1000, and selects from it three codices as nearest to the archetype,[29] viz., A = Codex Mosquensis 339 (nunc 352) of saec. xi. or xii. (the same as the Mosq. quoted by Beck), collated by Matthaei and in places reëxamined for Diels by Voelkelius; B = Codex Marcianus 521 [xcii, 7], of saec. xiv, very closely related to A, collated by Diels himself; and C = Codex Parisinus 1672 of saec. xiii. ex. vel. xiv. in which is a copy of a corpus of Plutarch put together by Planudes or a contemporary. Through these three codices he reaches the original apograph which stands at the root of all the extant MSS., and from it, by the aid of the excerpts from the tract — in our passage the Pseudo-Galen's only — he attains his text.

His note on our reading runs thus: "$\theta\epsilon o\pi\acute{\epsilon}\mu\pi\tau ovs$ G cf. Arist. de divinat. 2 p. 463b 13: $\theta\epsilon o\pi\nu\epsilon\acute{v}\sigma\tau ovs$ (A) B C, cf. Prol. p. 15." The parenthesis in which A is enclosed means that A is here cited from the silence of Matthaei's collation.[30] The reference to the Prolegomena is to the passage already alluded to, in which the Galenic reading $\theta\epsilon o\pi\acute{\epsilon}\mu\pi\tau ovs$ is cited as one of three chosen instances of excellent readings preserved by Galen alone. The note there runs thus: "alteri loco christiani librarii pius fraus nocuit. V. 2, 3, Ἡρόφιλος τῶν ὀνείρων τοὺς μὲν θ ε ο π ν ε ύ σ τ ο υ ς κατ' ἀνάγκην γίνεθαι. fuit scilicet $\theta\epsilon o\pi\acute{\epsilon}\mu\pi\tau ovs$, quod sero intellectum est a Wyttenbachio in indice Plutarcheo. si Galenum inspexisset, ipsum illud $\theta\epsilon o\pi\acute{\epsilon}\mu$-$\pi\tau ovs$ inventurus erat. simili fraude versus 121 Phocylideis a Byzantinis insertus est, ubi vox illa sacra [II Tim. iii. 16] I. Bernaysio interpolationis originem manifesto aperuit."

---

[29] "Codices manu scripti quotquot noti sunt ex archetypo circa millesimum annum scripto deducti sunt" (p. 33). "duo autem sunt recensendi Plutarchi instrumenta . . . unum recentius ex codicis petendum, inter quos A B C archetypo proximos ex ceterorum turba segregavi . . . alterum genus est excerptorum . . ." (p. 42).

[30] The readings of A are drawn from a collation of it with the Frankfort edition of 1620 published by C. F. Matthæi in his "Lectiones Mosquenses." In a number of important readings, the MS. has been reinspected for Diels by Voelkel with the result of throwing some doubt on the completeness of Matthæi's collation. Accordingly the MS. is cited in parenthesis whenever it is cited e silentio (see Diels, p. 33).

That is to say, the reading of the Pseudo-Galen is preferred to that of the MSS., because the reading θεοπνεύστους explains itself as a pious fraud of a Christian scribe, giving a place in the text of Plutarch to "this sacred word" — another example of which procedure is to be found in Pseudo-Phoc. 121, extruded by Bernays from the text on this very ground. On this remark, as on a hinge, turns, it would seem, the decision of the whole question. The problem of the reading, indeed, may be set forth at this point in the form of this alternative: — Which is most likely, — that θεοπνεύστους in the [Pseudo?-] Plutarch originated in the pious fraud of a Christian scribe? — or that θεοπέμπτους in the text of Pseudo-Galen edited by Diels originated in the error of a careless scribe?

When we posit the problem in this definite form we cannot feel at all certain that Diels' solution is the right one. There is an à priori unlikelihood in its way: deliberate corruption of texts is relatively rare and not to be assumed without good reason. The parallel from the Pseudo-Phocylides fails, now that it seems probable that the whole poem is of Christian origin. There seems no motive for such a pious fraud as is charged: what gain could be had from intruding θεοπνεύστους into the Plutarchian text? and what special sanctity attached to this word? And if a sacrosanct character be attributed to the word, could it not be equally plausibly argued that it was therefore offensive to the Christian consciousness in this heathen connection, and was accordingly replaced by the less sacred θεοπέμπτους, a word of heathen associations and indeed with a secondary sense not far from "extraordinary." [31] Or if it be now said that it is not intended to charge conscious fraud, it is pertinent to ask what special associations Christians had with the word θεόπνευστος in connection with dreams which would cause it to obtrude itself

---

[31] The general use of θεόπεμπτος is illustrated in the Lexicons, by the citation of Arist., "Ethic. Nic.," i. 9, 3, where happiness is spoken of as θεόπεμπτος in contrast to the attainment of virtue in effort; Longinus, c. 34, where we read of θεόπεμπτά τινα δωρήματα in contrast with ἀνθρώπινα; Themist, "Or." 13, p. 178 D, where ὁ Θ. νεανίος is found; Dion. Hal., T. 14. Liddell and Scott quote for the secondary sense of "extraordinary," Longus, 3, 18; Artem., i. 7.

unconsciously in such a connection. One is almost equally at a loss to account for the intrusion of the word in the place of the simpler θεόπεμπτος, whether the intrusion be looked upon as deliberate or unconscious. On the other hand, the substitution of θεόπεμπτος for θεόπνευστος in the text of Pseudo-Galen seems quite readily accountable, and that whether it be attributed to the original excerpter or to some later copyist of the tract. The term was associated with dreams in the minds of all acquainted with the literature of the subject. Diels himself refers us to a passage in Aristotle where the collocation occurs,[32] and familiar passages from Philo [33] and the "Clementina" [34] will suggest themselves to others. "God-sent dreams" must have almost had the rank of a "*terminus technicus.*" [35] Moreover the scribe had just written the word

[32] Arist., *de divinat*, 2 p. 463ᵇ 13: ὅλως δ'ἐπεὶ καὶ τῶν ἄλλων ζώων ὀνειρώττει τινὰ, θεόπεμπτα μὲν οὐκ ἄν εἴη τὰ ἐνύπνια, οὐδὲ γέγονε τούτου χάριν, δαιμόνια μέντοι· ἡ γὰρ φύσις δαιμονία, ἀλλ' οὐ θεία.

[33] Cf. Philo's tract περὶ τοῦ θεοπέμπτους εἶναι τοὺς ὀνείρους (Mangey., i. 620). Its opening words run (Yonge's translation, ii. 292): "The treatise before this one has contained our opinions as to those of τῶν ὀνείρων θεοπέμπτων classed in the first species . . . which are defined as dreams in which the Deity sends the appearances beheld in dreams according to his own suggestion (τὸ θεῖον κατὰ τὴν ἰδίαν ὑποβολὴς τὰς ἐν τοῖς ὕπνοις ἐπιπέμπειν φαντασίας)," whereas this later treatise is to discuss the second species of dreams, in which, "our mind being moved along with that of the universe, has seemed to be hurried away from itself and to be God-borne (θεοφορεῖσθαι) so as to be capable of preapprehension and fore-knowledge of the future." Cf. also § 22, τῆς θεοπέμπτου φαντασίας: § 33, θεοπέμπτους ὀνείρους: ii. § 1, τῶν θεοπέμπτων ὀνείρων. The superficial parallelism of Philo with what is cited from Herophilus is close enough fully to account for a scribe harking back to Philo's language — or even for the compiler of the Pseudo-Galen doing so.

[34] "Clementine Homilies," xvii. 15: "And Simon said: 'If you maintain that apparitions do not always reveal the truth, yet for all that visions and dreams, being God-sent (τὰ ὁράματα καὶ τὰ ἐνύπνια θεόπεμπτα ὄντα οὐ ψεύδεται) do not speak falsely in regard to those matters which they wish to tell.' And Peter said: 'You were right in saying that, being God-sent, they do not speak falsely (θεόπεμπτα ὄντα οὐ ψεύδεται. But it is uncertain if he who sees has seen a God-sent dream (εἰ ὁ ἰδὼν θεόπεμπτον ἑώρακεν ὄνειρον)." What has come to the "Clementine Homilies" is surely already a Christian commonplace.

[35] The immediately preceding paragraph in the Pseudo-Galen (§ 105), corresponding with [Pseudo?-] Plutarch, v. i. 1, 2.3 is edited by Diels thus: Πλάτων καὶ οἱ Στωικοὶ τὴν μαντικὴν εἰσάγουσι· καὶ γὰρ θεόπεμπτον εἶναι, ὅπερ ἐστὶν ἐνθεαστικὸν καὶ κατὰ τὸ θειότατον τῆς ψυχῆς, ὅπερ ἐστὶν ἐνθουσιαστικόν, καὶ τὸ ὀνειροπωλικὸν καὶ τὸ ἀστρονομικὸν καὶ τὸ ὀρνεοσκοπικόν. Ξενοφάνης καὶ Ἐπίκουρος ἀναιροῦσι τὴν μαντικήν.

in the immediate context, and that not without close contiguity with the word ὀνείρους,[36] and may be readily supposed
to have had it still lingering in his memory when he came to
write the succeeding section. In fine, the intrusion into the
text of θεοπνεύστους, a rare word and one suggested to a dull
or inattentive scribe by nothing, seems far less easy to account for than the intrusion of θεοπέμπτους, a common word,
an ordinary term in this connection, and a term suggested
to the scribe by the immediate context. On transcriptional
grounds certainly the former appears far more likely to be
original — "proclivi scriptioni praestat ardua."

The decisive consideration against θεοπνεύστους in the
mind of Diels — as it had been before him in the mind of
Beck — seems to have been, indeed, nothing but the assumption that θεόπνευστος, as a distinctively Christian word, must
argue a Christian hand, wherever it is found. That, however,
in our present study is precisely the matter under investigation; and we must specially guard against permitting to
intrude decisively into our premises what we propose to
arrive at only by way of conclusion. Whether the word be
genuine in the [Pseudo?-] Plutarch or not, is just one of the
most important factors in deciding whether it be a peculiarly
Christian word or not. An instructive parallel may be found
in the treatment accorded by some great authorities to the
cognate word θεόπνοος when it turned up in an inscription
which seems obviously heathen.[37] This inscription, inscribed
(about the third century) on the face of a man-headed sphinx
at Memphis, sings the praises of the sphinx's beauty—

Πυθαγόρας δὲ μόνον τὸ θυτικὸν οὐκ ἐγκρίνει. Ἀριστοτέλης καὶ Δικαίαρχος τοὺς ὀνείρους
εἰσάγουσιν, ἀθάνατον μὲν τὴν ψυχὴν οὐ νομίζοντες, θείου δέ τινος μετέχειν. Surely the scribe
or compiler who could transmute the section περὶ μαντικῆς in the [Pseudo?-]
Plutarch into this, with its intruded θεόπεμπτον before him and its allusion to
Aristotle on dreams, might be credited without much rashness with the intrusion
of θεοπέμπτους into the next section.

[36] Cf. in general E. Thrämer. Hastings *ERE*, VI, p. 542.

[37] It is duly recorded in Boeckh, "Corpus Inscript. Graec," 4700 b. (Add. iii).
It is also printed by Kaibel, "Epigrammata Græca" (Berlin, 1878), p. 428, but
not as a Christian inscription, but under the head of "Epigrammata dedicatoria:
V. proscynemata."

among the items mentioned being that ἐφύπερ[θ]ε πρόσωπον
ἔχει τὸ θ[ε]ό[πν]ουν, while, below, the body is that of the lion,
king of beasts. Boeckh comments on this: "Vs. 4, 5, recte legit
Letronnius, qui θεόπνοον monet Christianum quidam sonare."
But why should Letronnius infer Christianity from the word
θεόπνοον, or Boeckh think it worth while to record the fact?
Fortunately the heathen use of θεόπνοος is beyond question.[38]
It provides an excellent illustration, therefore, of the rashness of pronouncing words of this kind to be of Christian
origin; and suggests the hesitancy with which we should extrude such a word from the text of [Pseudo?-] Plutarch on
the sole ground that it "tastes of a Christian scribe." Surely
if a heathen could invent and use the one word, he might
equally well invent and use the other. And certainly it is a
great mistake to look upon compounds with θέος of this kind
as in any sense exclusively Christian. The long list of heathen
terms of this character given by Dr. Cremer, indeed, is itself
enough to indicate the heathen facility for their coinage.
Many such words, we may well believe, were found by
Christians ready made to their hand, and had only to be
adapted to their richer usage. What is more distinctively
Christian is the parallel list of words compounded with
πνεῦμα [39] or even χριστός [40] which were placed by their side,

[38] Porphyry: "Ant. Nymph.," 116: ἡγοῦντο γὰρ προσιζάνειν τῷ ὕδατι τὰς ψυχὰς
θεοπνόῳ ὄντι, ὥς φησιν ὁ Νουμήνιος· διὰ τοῦτο λέγων καὶ τὸν προφήτην εἰρηκέναι, ἐμφέρεσθαι
ἐπάνω τοῦ ὕδατος θεοῦ πνεῦμα — a passage remarkable for containing an appeal to
Moses (Gen. i. 5) by a heathen sage. "God-breathed water" is rendered by Hol-
stenius: "aquæ quæ divino spiritu foveretur"; by Gesnerus: "aquæ divinitus
afflatæ"; by Thomas Taylor: "water which is inspired by divinity." Pisid.
"Hexæm.," 1489: ἡ θεόπνους ἀκρότης (quoted unverified from Hase-Dindorf's
Stephens). The Christian usage is illustrated by the following citations, taken
from Sophocles: Hermes Tris., "Poem," 17. 14: τῆς ἀληθείας; Anastasius of Sinai,
Migne, 89. 1169 A: Those who do not have the love of God, "these, having a
diabolical will and doing the desires of their flesh, παραιτοῦνται ὡς πονηρὸν τὸ θεόμοιον, καὶ θεόκτιστον, καὶ θεόμοιον τῆς νοερᾶς καὶ θεοχαράκτου ἡμῶν ψυχῆς ὁμολογεῖν ἐν
Χριστῷ, καὶ τὴν ζωοποιὸν αὐτῆς καὶ συστατικὴν θεόπνουν ἐνέργειαν."

[39] πνευματοφόρος and πνευματοφορεῖσθαι are pre-Christian Jewish words, already
used in the LXX. (Hos. ix. 7, Zeph. iii. 4, Jer. ii. 24). Compounds of θεός found in
the LXX. are θεόκτιστος, II Macc. vi. 23; θεομαχεῖν, II Macc. vii. 19 [θεομάχος Sm.,
Job xxvi. 5, et al.]; θεοσέβεια, Gen. xx. 11 et al.; θεοσεβής Ex. xviii. 21 et al.

[40] No derivative of χριστός except χριστιανός is found in the New Testament.

such as [πνευματικός], πνευματοκίνητος, πνευματοφόρος, πνευματέμφορος; χριστόγραφος, χριστοδίδακτος, χριστοκίνητος, χριστόληπτος, χριστοφόρος.

As the reasons which have been determining with Diels in framing his text do not appear to us able to bear the weight laid on them, we naturally cannot adopt his text with any confidence. We doubt whether θεοπέμπτους was the original reading in the Pseudo-Galen; we doubt whether, if that were the case, we should on that ground edit it in the [Pseudo?-] Plutarch. Our feeling is decided that the intrusion of θεοπέμπτους into a text which originally read θεοπνεύστους would be far more easily accounted for than the reverse. One should be slow, of course, in rejecting a reading commended by such a scholarly tact as Diels'. But we may take courage from the fact that Bernardakis, with Diels' text before him, continues to read θεοπνεύστους even though recognizing θεοπέμπτους as the reading of Galen. We think we must be permitted to hold the matter still at least *sub judice* and to profess our inability in the circumstances to look upon the word as a purely Christian term.[41] It would be interesting to know what phraseology was used by Herophilus himself (born c. B.C. 300) in the passage which the [Pseudo?-] Plutarch excerpts. But this excerpt seems to be the only source of information we have in the matter,[42] and it would perhaps be overbold

The compounds are purely Patristic. See Lightfoot's note on Ignatius, Eph. ix; Phil. viii and the note in Migne's "Pat. Græc.," xi. 1861, at Adamantii "Dialogus de recta fide," § 5.

[41] In the Hase-Dindorf Stephens, *sub-voc.* θεόπνευστος, the passage, from the [Pseudo?-] Plutarch is given within square brackets in this form: ["Plut. Mor. p. 904F: τοὺς ὀνείρους τοὺς θεοπλούτους]." What is to be made of this new reading, we do not know. One wonders whether it is a new conjecture or a misprint. No earlier reference is given for θεόπλουτος in the "Thesaurus" than Chrysostom: "Ita Jobum appellat Jo. Chrystom, Vol. iv, p. 297, Suicer." Sophocles cites also Anast. Sinai. for the word: *Hexæmeron* XII *ad fin.* (Migne, 1076 D., Vol. 89): ὅπως τοῦτο καταβαλὼν ἐν ταῖς ψυχαῖς τραπεζισῶν σῶν ἄρρων σε δι' αὐτῶν τὴν θεόπλουτον καταπλουτήσω.

[42] So it may be confidently inferred from the summary of what we know of Herophilus given in Susemihl's "Geschichte der Griechisch. Literatur in d. Alexandrinerzeit," Vol. i, p. 792, or from Marx's "De Herophili . . . vita scriptis atque in medicina mentis" (Göttingen, 1840), p. 38. In both cases Herophilus' doctrine

to suppose that the compiler had preserved the very words of the great physician. Were such a presumption deemed plausible we should be forced to carry back the first known use of the word θεόπνευστος to the third century before Christ, but not to a *provenance* other than that Alexandria where its earliest use is otherwise traceable. Perhaps if we cannot call it a purely Christian term nor yet, with Dr. Cremer, an exclusively Hellenistic one, we may venture to think of it, provisionally at least, as belonging to Alexandrian Greek. Whether we should also say to late Alexandrian usage will possibly depend on the degree of likelihood we ascribe to its representing in the text of the [Pseudo?-] Plutarch an actual usage of Herophilus.

Our interest in determining the reading in the [Pseudo?-] Plutarch culminates, of course, in its bearing on the meaning of θεόπνευστος. Prof. Schulze's remark [43] that no copyist would have substituted θεόπνευστος here for θεόπεμπτος if linguistic usage had attached an active sense to the former, is no doubt quite just. This is admitted, indeed, by Dr. Cremer, who considers that the scribe to whom the substitution is thought to be due "had θεόπνευστος in his mind in the sense of the Vulgate rendering, *divinitus inspirata*"; and only seeks to break the force of this admission by urging that the constant exegetical tradition which assigned this meaning to θεόπνευστος, rests on a misunderstanding of the word and reads into it a sense derived from Alexandrian-Jewish conceptions of inspiration. This appeal from a fixed later to an assumed original sense of the word possesses force, no doubt, only in case that traces of such an assumed original sense can be adduced; and meanwhile the presence of θεόπνευστος as a synonym of θεόπεμπτος, even in the vocabulary of somewhat late scribes, must rank as one item in the evidence by which its meaning is to be ascertained. The whole face of the matter is changed, however, if θεόπνευστος be allowed to be probably

of dreams is gathered solely from our excerpts — in the case of Susemihl from "Aëtius" and in the case of Marx primarily from Galen with the support of Plutarch.   [43] *Loc. cit.*

or even possibly genuine in the [Pseudo?-] Plutarch. In that
case it could scarcely be thought to reflect the later Christian
conception of inspiration, imposed on Paul's term by thinkers
affected by Philo's doctrine of Scripture, but would stand as
an independent bit of evidence as to the original meaning of
the term. The clerical substitution of θεόπεμπτος for it under
the influence of literary associations would indeed, in this
case too, only witness to a synonymy in the mind of the
later scribes, who may well be supposed Christians and
sharers in the common conception that Christians read into
θεόπνευστος. But the implications of the passage itself would
be valid testimony to the original import of the term here
used. And it would seem quite clear that the implications of
the passage itself assign to it a passive sense, and that a
sense not very remote from θεόπεμπτος. "Herophilus says,"
we read, "that theopneustic dreams" ("dreams divinely inspired," Holland; "the dreams that are caused by divine
instinct," Goodwin), "come by necessity; but natural ones"
("natural dreams," Holland; "dreams which have their
origin from a natural cause," Goodwin), "from the soul's
imagery of what is fitting to it and its consequences," etc.[44]
The contrast here between dreams that are θεόπνευστοι and
those that are φυσικοί, the former of which are imposed on
the soul while the latter are its own production, would seem
certainly to imply that θεόπνευστος here imports something
nearly akin to "God-given," though naturally with implications of its own as to the mode of the giving. It might be

[44] In the common text the passage goes on to tell us of the dreams of mixed
nature, i. e., presumably partly divine and partly human in origin. But the idea
itself seems incongruous and the description does not very well fit the category.
Diels, therefore, conjectures πνευματικούς in its place in which case there are *three*
categories in the enumeration: Theopneustic, physical (i. e., the product of the
ψυχή or lower nature), and pneumatic, or the product of the higher nature. The
whole passage in Diels' recension runs as follows: Aët. 'Plac.,' p. 416 (Pseudo-
Plut., v. 2, 3): Ἡρόφιλος τῶν ὀνείρων τοὺς μὲν θεοπέμπτους κατ' ἀνάγκην γίνεσθαι,
τοὺς δὲ φυσικοὺς ἀνειδωλοποιουμένης ψυχῆς τὸ συμφέρον αὐτῇ καὶ τὸ πάντως ἐσόμενον, τοὺς
δὲ συγκραματικοὺς [πνευματικοὺς? Diels, but this is scarcely the right correction, cf.
Susemihl, "Gesch. d. Gr. Lit.," etc. i. 792] [ἐκ τοῦ αὐτομάτου] κατ' εἰδώλων πρόσπτωσιν,
ὅταν ἃ βουλόμεθα βλέπωμεν, ὡς ἐπὶ τῶν τὰς ἐρωμένας ὁρώντων ἐν ὕπνῳ γίνεται."

possible to read it as designating dreams that are breathed into by God, filled with His inspiration and thus made the vehicles of His message, if we otherwise knew that such is the implication of the term. But nothing so subtle as this is suggested by the language as it stands, which appears to convey merely the simple notion that theopneustic dreams differ from all natural ones, whether the latter belong to the higher or lower elements of our nature, in that they come from God and are therefore not necessarily agreeable to the soul's own image-making faculties or the product of its immanent desires, but take form and bear a meaning imposed on them from without.

There are few other instances of the occurrence of the word which have much chance of lying entirely outside the sphere of influence of its use in II Tim. iii. 16. In the first rank of these will certainly be placed the two instances in the fifth book of the "Sibyllines." The former of these occurs in a description of the city of Cyme, which is called the "foolish one," and described as cast down by wicked hands, "along with her theopneustic streams (νάμασι θεοπνεύστοις)" no longer to shout her boasts into the air but henceforth to remain "dead amid the Cymean streams." [45] The description skillfully brings together all that we know of Cyme — adverts to her former greatness ("the largest and noblest of all the Æolian cities," Strabo tells us,[46] and with Lesbos, "the metropolis" of all the rest), her reputation for folly (also adverted to and quaintly explained by Strabo), her present decadence, and her situation by running waters (a trait indicated also by her coins which show that there was a stream

---

[45] V. 308 seq. The full text, in Rzach's edition, runs:

Κύμη δ' ἡ μωρὴ σὺν νάμασιν οἷς θεοπνεύστοις
'Εν παλάμαις ἀθέων ἀνδρῶν ἀδίκων καὶ ἀθέσμων
'Ριφθεῖσ' οὐκ ἔτι τίσσον ἐς αἰθέρα ῥῆμα προδώσει·
'Αλλὰ μενεῖ νεκρὴ ἐνί νάμασι κυμαίοισιν.

[46] Strabo, "Rerum Geographicarum," liber xiii, iii. 6, pp. 622, 623 (Amsterdam ed., 1707, p. 924). A good summary may be read in Smith's "Dictionary of Greek and Roman Geography," i. 724, 725.

near by called Xanthus). It has been customary to understand by "the theopneustic streams" mentioned, some streams
or fountains in the neighborhood known for the presump-
tively oracular powers of their waters.[47] But there does not
seem to have been preserved any notice of the existence of
such oracular waters belonging to Cyme, and it makes against
this assumption that the Cymeans, like the rest of the Io-
nians and Æolians, were accustomed to resort for their oracles
to the somewhat distant Branchidæ, in the south.[48] It appears much more likely, then, that the streams adverted to
are natural streams and stand here only as part of the rather
full and very exact description of the town — the reference
being primarily to the Xanthus and to it as an element
merely in the excellence of the situation. In that case "theopneustic," here too, would seem to mean something akin
to "God-given," or perhaps more broadly still "divine," in
the sense of specially excellent and desirable.

The second Sibylline passage is a portion of a lament over
the destruction of the Temple at Jerusalem, wherein (we are
told) gold, "deceiver of the world and souls," was not worshiped, but men "adored in sacrifices, with pure and noble
hecatombs, the great Father-God of all theopneustic things."[49]
Here Alexandre translates, "Qui cælestis vitam pater omnibus afflat"; and Terry, "The God and mighty maker of
all breathing things."[50] And they seem supported in their
general conception by the fact that we appear to have before
us here only a slightly varied form of a formula met with
elsewhere in the Sibyllines. Thus, as Rzach points out, we

[47] Alexandre translates "plenis numine lymphis"; Dr. Terry, "inspired
streams."

[48] So Herodotus observes (i, 157).

[49] V. 408 *seq.* In Rzach's text the lines run:

> Οὐ γὰρ ἀκηδέστως αἰνεῖ θεὸν ἐξ ἀφανοῦς γῆς
> οὐδὲ πέτρην ποίησε σοφὸς τέκτων παρὰ τούτοις,
> οὐ χρυσὸν κόσμου ἀπάτην ψυχῶν τ' ἐσεβάσθη,
> ἀλλὰ μέγαν γενετῆρα θεὸν πάντων θεοπνεύστων
> ἐν θυσίαις ἐγέραιρ' ἁγίαις καλαῖς θ'ἑκατόμβαις.

[50] In this second edition, Dr. Terry has altered this to "The Mighty Father,
God of all things God-inspired": but this scarcely seems an improvement.

have at iii, 278 [51] a condemnation of those who "neither fear
nor desire to honor the deathless Father-God of all men," [52]
and at iii, 604, essentially the same phrase is repeated. We
seem, in a word, to meet here only with the Sibylline equivalent of the Homeric "πατὴρ ἀνδρῶν τε θεῶν τε." Accordingly
θεοπνεύστων would seem to stand here in the stead of ἀνθρώπων
in the parallel passages, and merely to designate men, doubtless with a reminiscence of Gen. ii. 7 — or perhaps, more
widely, creatures, with a reminiscence of such a passage as
Ps. civ. 30. In either event it is the creative power of God
that is prominently in the mind of the writer as he writes
down the word θεοπνεύστων, which is to him obviously the
proper term for "creatures" in correlation with the γενέτης
θεός.

By the side of these Sibylline passages it is perhaps
natural to place the line from the Pseudo-Phocylides, which
marks the culmination of his praise of "speech" as the
greatest gift of God — a weapon, he says, sharper than steel
and more to be desired than the swiftness of birds, or the
speed of horses, or the strength of lions, or the horns of bulls
or the stings of bees — "for best [of all] is the speech of
theopneustic wisdom," so that the wise man is better than
the strong one, and it is wisdom that rules alike in the field,
the city and the sea. It is certainly simplest to understand
"theopneustic wisdom" here shortly as "God-given wisdom." Undoubtedly it is itself the inspirer of the speech that
manifests it, and we might manage to interpret the θεοπνεύστου as so designating it — "God-inspiring, God-breathing wisdom." But this can scarcely be considered natural;
and it equally undoubtedly lies more closely at hand to
interpret it as designating the source of the wisdom itself
as lying in God. Wisdom is conceived as theopneustic, in a
word, because wisdom itself is thought of as coming from
God, as being the product of the divine activity — here

[51] οὐδὲ φοβηθεὶς ἀθάνατον γενετῆρα θεὸν πάντων ἀνθρώπων οὐκ ἔθελες τιμᾶν. Rzach
compares also Xenophon. "Fragm.," i. 1, M., εἷς θεὸς ἔν τε θεοῖσι καὶ ἀνθρώποισι
μέγιστος·

[52] Terry, Ed. 2: "the immortal Father, God of all mankind."

designated, as so frequently in the Old Testament, as operating as a breathing.

A passage that has come to light since Dr. Cremer's investigation for this word-study was made, is of not dissimilar implication. It is found in the recently published "Testament of Abraham,"[53] a piece which in its original form, its editor, Prof. James, assigns to a second-century Egyptian Jewish-Christian, though it has suffered much mediævalization in the ninth or tenth century. It runs as follows: "And Michael the archangel came immediately with a multitude of angels, and they took his precious soul ($\tau \grave{\eta} \nu$ $\tau \iota \mu \acute{\iota} \alpha \nu$ $\alpha \mathring{\upsilon} \tau o \hat{\upsilon}$ $\psi \upsilon \chi \acute{\eta} \nu$) in their hands in a God-woven cloth ($\sigma \iota \nu \delta \acute{o} \nu \iota$ $\theta \epsilon o \ddot{\upsilon} \phi \alpha \nu \tau \hat{\omega}$); and they prepared ($\mathring{\epsilon} \kappa \acute{\eta} \delta \epsilon \upsilon \sigma \alpha \nu$) the body of righteous Abraham unto the third day of his death with theopneustic ointments and herbs ($\mu \upsilon \rho \acute{\iota} \sigma \mu \alpha \sigma \iota$ $\theta \epsilon o \pi \nu \epsilon \acute{\upsilon} \sigma \tau o \iota \varsigma$ $\kappa \alpha \grave{\iota}$ $\mathring{\alpha} \rho \acute{\omega} \mu \alpha \sigma \iota \nu$), and they buried him in the land of promise." Here $\theta \epsilon \acute{o} \pi \nu \epsilon \upsilon \sigma \tau o \varsigma$ can hardly mean "God-breathing," and "God-imbued" is not much better; and though we might be tempted to make it mean "divinely sweet" (a kind of derivative sense of "God-redolent ointment"; for $\pi \nu \acute{\epsilon} \omega$ means also "to smell," "to breathe of a thing"), it is doubtless better to take it simply, as the parallel with $\theta \epsilon o \ddot{\upsilon} \phi \alpha \nu \tau \hat{\omega}$ suggests, as importing something not far from "God-given." The cloth in which the soul was carried up to God and the unguents with which the body was prepared for burial were alike from God — were "God-provided"; the words to designate this being chosen in each case with nice reference to their specific application, but covering to their writer little more specific meaning than the simple adjective "divine" would have done.

It is surely in this same category also that we are to place the verse of Nonnus which Dr. Cremer adduces as showing distinctly that the word $\theta \epsilon \acute{o} \pi \nu \epsilon \upsilon \sigma \tau o \varsigma$ "is not to be taken as equivalent to *inspiratus*, inspired by God, but as rather meaning filled with God's spirit and therefore radiating it." Nonnus is paraphrasing John i. 27 and makes the Baptist say: "And he that cometh after me stands to-day in your

[53] Recension A, chap. xx. p. 103, ed. James.

midst, the tip of whose foot I am not worthy to approach
with human hand though only to loose the thongs of the
theopneustic sandal." [54] Here surely the meaning is not directly that our Lord's sandal "radiated divinity," though
certainly that may be one of the implications of the epithet,
but more simply that it partook of the divinity of the divine
Person whose property it was and in contact with whom it
had been. All about Christ was divine. We should not go
far wrong, therefore, if we interpreted θεόπνευστος here simply
as "divine." What is "divine" is no doubt "redolent of
Divinity," but it is so called not because of what it does,
but because of what it is, and Nonnus' mind when he called
the sandal theopneustic was occupied rather with the divine
influence that made the sandal what it was, viz., something
more than a mere sandal, because it had touched those divine
feet, than with any influence which the sandal was now calculated to exert. The later line which Dr. Cremer asks us
to compare is not well calculated to modify this decision.
In it John i. 33 is being paraphrased and the Baptist is contrasting his mission with that of Christ who was to baptize
with fire and the Holy Spirit ἐν πυρὶ βαπτίζων καὶ πνεύματι).
He, John, was sent, on the contrary, he says, to baptize the
body of already regenerate men, and to do it in lavers that
are destitute of both fire and the spirit — fireless and spirit-
less (ἀπύροισι καὶ ἀπνεύστοισι λοετροῖς).[55] It may indeed be
possible to interpret, "unburning and unspiritualizing"; but
this does not seem the exact shade of thought the words are
meant to express; though in any case the bearing of the
phrase on the meaning of θεόπνευστος in the former line is of
the slightest.

Of the passages cited by Dr. Cremer there remain only
the two he derives from Wetstein, in which θεόπνευστος ap-

[54] Nonni Panopolitani "Paraphrasis in Joannem" (i. 27), in Migne, xliii. 753:

Καὶ ὀπίστερος ὅστις ἱκάνει
Σήμερον ὑμείων μέσος ἵσταται, οὗ ποδὸς ἄκρου,
'Ανδρομέην παλάμην οὐκ ἄξιός εἰμι πελάσσας,
Λῦσαι μοῦνον ἱμάντα θεοπνεύστοιο πεδίλου.

[55] *Op. cit.*, p. 756.

pears as an epithet of certain men. To these should be added
an inscription found at Bostra, in which a certain ecclesiastic
is designated an ἀρχιερεὺς θεόπνευστος.[56] Dr. Cremer himself
thinks it clear that in such passages we have a passive sense,
but interprets it as *divinely spirited*, "endued with the divine
spirit," rather than as "*divinely inspired*," — in accordance
with a distinction drawn by Ewald. Certainly it is difficult
to understand the word in this connection as expressing
simple origination by God; it was something more than the
mere fact that God made them that was intended to be
affirmed by calling Marcus and Antipater theopneustic men.
Nor does it seem very natural to suppose that the intention
was to designate them as precisely what we ordinarily mean
by God-inspired men. It lies very near to suppose, therefore,
that what it was intended to say about them, is that they
were God-pervaded men, men in whom God dwelt in an
especial manner; and this supposition may be thought to be
supported by the parallel, in the passage from the "Vita
Sabæ," with χριστοφόρος. Of whom this "caravan of all the-
opneustics, of all his christophers," was composed, we have
no means of determining, as Cotelerius' "Monumenta," from
which Wetstein quoted the passage, is not accessible to us
as we write. But the general sense of the word does not seem
to be doubtful. Ignatius, ("ad Ephes." ix.) tells us that all
Christians constitute such a caravan, of "God-bearers and
shrine-bearers, Christ-bearers, holy-thing-bearers, completely
clothed in the commandments of Christ"; and Zahn rightly
comments that thus the Christians appear as the real "ἔνθεοι
or ἐνθουσιάζοντες, since they carry Christ and God in them-

---

[56] It is given in Kaibel's "Epigrammata Græca," p. 477. Waddington supposes the person meant to be a certain Archbishop of Bostra, of date 457–474, an
opponent of Origenism, who is commemorated in the Greek Church on June 13.
The inscription runs as follows:

Δόξης] ὀρθοτό[ν]ου ταμίης καὶ ὑπέρμαχος ἐσθλός,
ἀρχιερεὺς θεόπνευστος ἐδείματο κάλλος ἄμετρον
'Αντίπατρ]ο[ς] κλυτόμητις ἀεθλοφόρους μετ' ἀγῶνας,
κυ[δ]αίνων μεγάλως θεομήτορα παρθένον ἀγνήν
Μαρίαν πολύυμνον, ἀκήρατον ἀγλαόδωρον·

selves." Particularly distinguished Christians might therefore very properly be conceived in a supereminent sense as
filled with God and bearers of Christ; and this might very
appropriately be expressed by the double attribution of θεόπνευστος and χριστοφόρος. Only it would seem to be necessary
to understand that thus a secondary and derived sense would
be attributed to θεόπνευστος, about which there should still
cling a flavor of the idea of origination. The θεόπνευστος ἀνήρ
is God-filled by the act of God Himself, that is to say, he is
a God-endowed man, one made what he is by God's own
efficiency. No doubt in usage the sense might suffer still
more attrition and come to suggest little more than "divine"
— which is the epithet given to Marcus of Scetis [57] by Nicephorus Callistus, ("H. E.,"xi, 35) — ὁ θεῖος Μάρκος — that is
to say "Saint Mark," of which ὁ θεόπνευστος Μάρκος is doubtless a very good synonym. The conception conveyed by θεόπνευστος in this usage is thus something very distinct from
that expressed by the Vulgate rendering, a Deo inspiratus,
when taken strictly; that would seem to require, as Ewald
suggests, some such form as θεέμπνευστος; the theopneustic
man is not the man "breathed into by God." But it is equally
distinct from that expressed by the phrase, "pervaded by
God," used as an expression of the character of the man so
described, without implication of the origin of this characteristic. What it would seem specifically to indicate is that
he has been framed by God into something other than what
he would have been without the divine action. The Christian
as such is as much God-made as the man as such; and the
distinguished Christian as such as much as the Christian at
large; and the use of θεόπνευστος to describe the one or the
other would appear to rest ultimately on this conception. He

[57] Wetstein cites the expression as applied (where, he does not say) to
"Marcus Ægyptus," by which he means, we suppose, Marcus of Scetis, mentioned
by Sozomen, H. E., vi. 29, and Nicephorus Callistus, H. E., xi. 35. Dr. Cremer
transmutes the designation into Marcus Eremita, who is mentioned by Nicephorus Callistus, H. E., xiv. 30, 54, and whose writings are collected in Migne,
lxv. 905 seq. The two are often identified, but are separately entered in Smith and
Wace.

is, in what he has become, the product of the divine energy —
of the divine breath.

We cannot think it speaking too strongly, therefore, to
say that there is discoverable in none of these passages the
slightest trace of an active sense of θεόπνευστος, by which it
should express the idea, for example, of "breathing the
divine spirit," or even such a quasi-active idea as that of
"redolent of God." Everywhere the word appears as purely
passive and expresses production by God. And if we proceed
from these passages to those much more numerous ones, in
which it is, as in II Tim. iii. 16, an epithet or predicate of
Scripture, and where therefore its signification may have
been affected by the way in which Christian antiquity understood that passage, the impression of the passive sense of the
word grows, of course, ever stronger. Though these passages
may not be placed in the first rank of material for the determination of the meaning of II Tim. iii. 16, by which they
may have themselves been affected; it is manifestly improper
to exclude them from consideration altogether. Even as part
bearers of the exegetical tradition they are worthy of adduction: and it is scarcely conceivable that the term should have
been entirely voided of its current sense, had it a different
current sense, by the influence of a single employment of it
by Paul — especially if we are to believe that its natural
meaning as used by him differed from that assigned it by
subsequent writers. The patristic use of the term in connection with Scripture has therefore its own weight, as evidence
to the natural employment of the term by Greek-speaking
Christian writers.

This use of it does not seem to occur in the very earliest
patristic literature: but from the time of Clement of Alexandria the term θεόπνευστος appears as one of the most common technical designations of Scripture. The following scattered instances, gathered at random, will serve to illustrate
this use of it sufficiently for our purpose. Clement of Alexandria: "Strom.," vii. 16, § 101 (Klotz, iii. 286; Potter,
894), "Accordingly those fall from their eminence who follow

not God whither He leads; and He leads us in the inspired Scriptures (κατὰ τὰς θεοπνεύστους γραφάς)"; "Strom.," vii. 16, § 103 (Klotz, iii. 287; Potter, 896), "But they crave glory, as many as willfully sophisticate the things wedded to inspired words (τοῖς θεοπνεύστοις λόγοις) handed down by the blessed apostles and teachers, by diverse arguments, opposing human teaching to the divine tradition for the sake of establishing the heresy"; "Protrept." 9, § 87 (Klotz., i. 73, 74; Potter 71), "This teaching the apostle knows as truly divine (θείαν): 'Thou, O Timothy,' he says, 'from a child hast known the holy letters which are able to make thee wise unto salvation, through faith that is in Jesus Christ'; for truly holy are those letters that sanctify and deify; and the writings or volumes that consist of these holy letters or syllables, the same apostle consequently calls 'inspired by God, seeing that they are profitable for doctrine,' etc." Origen: "De Principiis," iv, 8 (cf. also title to Book iv), "Having thus spoken briefly on the subject of the Divine inspiration of the Holy Scriptures (περὶ τοῦ θεοπνεύστου τῆς θείας γραφῆς)"; Migne, (11, 1276), "The Jews and Christians agree as to the inspiration of the Holy Scripture (θείῳ γεγράφθαι πνεύματι), but differ as to its interpretation"; (12, 1084), "Therefore the inspired books (θεόπνευστα βιβλία) are twenty-two"; (14, 1309), "The inspired Scripture"; (13, 664–5), "For we must seek the nourishment of the whole inspired Scripture (πάσης τῆς θεοπνεύστου γραφῆς); "Hom. xx. in Joshuam," 2 (Robinson's "Origen's Philocalia," p. 63), "Let us not then be stupefied by listening to Scriptures which we do not understand, but let it be to us according to our faith by which we believe that 'every Scripture, seeing that it is inspired (θεόπνευστος), is profitable': for you must needs admit one of two things regarding these Scriptures, either that they are not inspired (θεόπνευστοι) because they are not profitable, as the unbeliever takes it, or, as a believer, you must admit that since they are inspired (θεόπνευστοι) they are profitable"; "Selecta in Psalmos," Ps. i, 3 (Migne XII, ii. 1080; De la Rue, 527), "Being about to begin the interpretation of the Psalms, we prefix a very excellent tradition handed down by the Hebrew [58] to us generally concerning the whole divine Scripture (καθολικῶς περὶ πάσης θείας γραφῆς); for he affirmed that the whole inspired Scripture (τὴν ὅλην θεόπνευστον γραφήν). . . . But if 'the words of the Lord are pure words, fined silver, tried as the earth, purified seven times' (Ps. ii.

7) and the Holy Spirit has with all care dictated them accurately through the ministers of the word (μετὰ πάσης ἀκριβείας ἐξητασμένως τὸ ἅγιον πνεῦμα ὑποβέβληκεν αὐτὰ διὰ τῶν ὑπηρετῶν τοῦ λόγου), let the proportion never escape us, according to which the wisdom of God is first with respect to the whole theopneustic Scripture unto the last letter (καθ' ἢν ἐπὶ πᾶσαν ἔφθασε γραφὴν ἡ σοφία τοῦ θεοῦ θεόπνευστον μέχρι τοῦ τυχόντος γράμματος); and haply it was on this account that the Saviour said, 'One iota or one letter shall not pass from the law till all be fulfilled': and it is just so that the divine art in the creation of the world, not only appeared in the heaven and sun and moon and stars, interpenetrating their whole bodies, but also on earth did the same in paltry matter, so that not even the bodies of the least animals are disdained by the artificer. . . . So we understand concerning all the things written by the inspiration (ἐξ ἐπιπνοίας) of the Holy Spirit . . . ." Athanasius (Migne, 27, 214): πᾶσα γραφὴ ἡμῶν τῶν χριστιανῶν θεόπνευστός ἐστιν; (Migne, 25, 152): θεόπνευστος κάλεῖται; (Bened. Par., 1777, i. 767): "Saying also myself, 'Since many have taken in hand to set forth to themselves the so-called apocrypha and to sing them with τῇ θεοπνεύστῳ γραφῇ . . . .'" Cyrillus Hier., "Catechet.,"iv. 33: "This is taught us by αἱ θεόπνευστοι γραφαί of both the Old and New Covenant." Basil, "On the Spirit," xxi (ad fin.): "How can he who calls Scripture 'God-inspired' because it was written through the inspiration of the Spirit (ὁ θεόπνευστον τὴν γραφὴν ὀνομάζων, διὰ τῆς ἐπιπνοίας τοῦ ἁγίου πνεύματος συγγραφεῖσαν), use the language of one who insults and belittles Him?" "Letters," xvii. 3: "All bread is nutri-

---

[58] That is doubtless the Jewish teacher to whom he elsewhere refers, as, e. g., "De Principiis," iv. 20 (Ante-Nicene Library, N. Y. ed., iv. 375), where the same general subject is discussed.

tious, but it may be injurious to the sick; just so, all Scripture is God-inspired (πᾶσα γραφὴ θεόπνευστος) and profitable"; (Migne, xxx. 81): "The words of God-inspired Scripture (οἱ τῆς θεοπνεύστου γραφῆς λόγοι) shall stand on the tribune of Christ"; (Migne, 31, 744): "For every word or deed must be believed by the witness of the θεοπνεύστου γραφῆς, for the assurance of the good and the shame of the wicked"; (Migne, 31, 1080): "Apart from the witness of the θεοπνεύστων γραφῶν it is not possible, etc."; (Migne, 31, 1500): "From what sort of Scripture are we to dispute at this time? Πάντα ὁμότιμα, καὶ πάντα πνευματικά· πάντα θεόπνευστα, καὶ πάντα ὠφέλιμα"; (Migne, 31, 1536): "On the interpretation and remarking of the names and terms τῆς θεοπνεύστου γραφῆς"; (Migne, 32, 228): μεγίστη δὲ ὁδὸς πρὸς τὴν τοῦ καθήκοντος εὕρεσιν καὶ ἡ μελέτη τῶν θεοπνεύστων γραφῶν. Gregory Naz. (Migne, 35, 504): περὶ τοῦ θεοπνεύστου τῶν ἀγίων γραφῶν; (Migne, 36, 472, cf. 37, 589), περὶ τῶν γησίων βιβλίων τῆς θεοπνεύστου γραφῆς; (Migne, 36, 1589), τοῖς θεοπνεύστοις γραφαῖς. Gregory Nyssen, "Against Eunom.," vii. 1: "What we understand of the matter is as follows: Ἡ θεόπνευστος γραφή, as the divine apostle calls it, is the Scripture of the Holy Spirit and its intention is the profit of men"; (Migne, 44, 68), μόνης τῆς θεοπνεύστου διαθήκης. Cyrillus Alex. (Migne, 68, 225), πολυμερῶς καὶ πολυτρόπως ἡ θεόπνευστος γραφὴ τῆς διὰ χριστοῦ σωτηρίας προαναφωνεῖ τοὺς τύπους. Neilos Abbas (Migne, 79, 141, cf. 529): γραφὴ ἡ θεόπνευστος οὐδὲν λέγει ἀκαίρως κτλ. Theodoret of Cyrrhus ("H. E.", i. 6; Migne, iii. 920). John of Damascus (Migne, 85, 1041), etc.

If, then, we are to make an induction from the use of the word, we shall find it bearing a uniformly passive significance, rooted in the idea of the creative breath of God. All that is, is God-breathed ("Sibyll." v. 406); and accordingly the rivers that water the Cymean plain are God-breathed ("Sibyll." v. 308), the spices God provides for the dead body of His friend ("Testament of Abraham," A. xx), and above all the wisdom He implants in the heart of man (Ps.-Phocyl. 121), the dreams He sends with a message from Him (Ps.-Plut., v. 2, 3) and the Scriptures He gives His people (II Tim. iii. 16). By an extension of meaning by no means extreme, those whom He has greatly honored as His followers, whom He has created into His saints, are called God-breathed men (" Vita Sabæ " 16. Inscription in Kaibel); and even the sandals that have touched the feet of the Son of God are called God-breathed sandals (Nonnus), i. e., sandals that have been made by this divine contact something other than what they were: in both these cases, the word approaching more or less the broader meaning of "divine." Nowhere is there a trace of such an active significance as "God-breathing"; and though in the application of the word to individual men and to our Lord's sandals there may be an approach to the sense of "God-imbued," this sense is attained by a pathway of development from the simple idea of God-given, God-determined, and the like.

It is carefully to be observed, of course, that, although Dr. Cremer wishes to reach an active signification for the word in II Tim. iii. 16, he does not venture to assign an active sense to it immediately and directly, but approaches this goal through the medium of another signification. It is fully recognized by him that the word is originally passive in its meaning; it is merely contended that this original passive sense is not "God-inspired," but rather "God-filled" — a sense which, it is pleaded, will readily pass into the active sense of "God-breathing," after the analogy of such words as ἄπνευστος, εὔπνευστος, which from "ill- or well-breathed" came to mean "breathing ill or well." What is filled with God will certainly be redolent of God, and what is redolent of God will certainly breathe out God. His reasons for preferring the sense of "gifted or filled with God's Spirit, divinely spirited," to "God-inspired" for the original passive connotation of the word are drawn especially from what he thinks the unsuitableness of the latter idea to some of the connections in which the word is found. It is thought that, as an epithet of an individual man, as an epithet of Scripture or a fountain, and (in the later editions of the " Lexicon " at least) especially, as an epithet of a sandal, "God-inspired" is incongruous, and something like "filled with God's Spirit and therefore radiating it" is suggested. There is obviously some confusion here arising from the very natural contemplation of the Vulgate translation "*a Deo inspiratus*" as the alternative rendering to what is proposed. There is, we may well admit, nothing in the word θεόπνευστος to warrant the *in-* of the Vulgate rendering: this word speaks not of an "*in*spiration" by God, but of a "spiration" by God. The alternatives brought before us by Dr. Cremer's presentation are not to be confined, therefore, to the two, "Divinely spirited" and "Divinely *in*spired," but must be made to include the three, "Divinely spirited," "Divinely inspired," and "Divinely spired." The failure of Dr. Cremer to note this introduces, as we say, some confusion into his statement. We need only thus incidentally refer to it at this point, however. It is of more immediate importance to observe that what we are naturally led to by Dr. Cremer's remarks, is to an investigation of the natural meaning of the word θεόπνευστος under the laws of word-formation. In these remarks he is leaning rather heavily on the discussion of Ewald to which he refers us, and it will conduce to a better understanding of the matter if we will follow his directions and turn to our Ewald.

Ewald, like Dr. Cremer, is dissatisfied with the current explanation of θεόπνευστος and seeks to obtain for it an active sense, but is as little inclined as Dr. Cremer to assign an active sense directly to it. He rather criticises Winer,[59] for using language when speaking of θεόπνευστος which would seem to imply that such compounds could really be active — as if "it were to be taken as a passive, although such words as εὔπνευστος, ἄπνευστος are used actively." He cannot admit that any compound of a word like -πνευστος can be really active in primary meaning, and explains that εὔπνευστος means not so much "breathing good," i. e., propelling something good by the breath, as "endowed with good breath," and expresses, therefore, just like ἄπνευστος, "breathless,"

[59] "Jahrb. f. bibl. Wissenschaft," vii. 114.

i. e, "*dead*," a subjective condition, and is therefore to be compared with a half-passive verb, as indeed the word-form suggests. Just so, θεόπνευστος, he says, is not so much our "God-breathing" as our "full of God's Spirit," "permeated and animated by God's Spirit." Thus, he supposes θεόπνευστος to mean "blown through by God" (*Gottdurchwehet,* "God-pervaded"), rather than "blown into by God" (*Gotteinge-wehet,* "God-inspired") as the Vulgate (*inspiratus*) and Luther (*eingegeben*) render it — an idea which, as he rightly says, would have required something like θεέμπνευστος [60] (or we may say θεείσπνευστος) [61] to express it.

At first he seems to have thought that by this explanation he had removed all implication as to the origination of Scrip-

[60] In a note on p. 89, Ewald adds as to θεέμπνευστος that it is certainly true that such compounds are not common, and that this particular one does not occur: but that they are possible is shown by the occurrence of such examples as θεο-σύνακτος, θεοκατασκεύαστος, in which the preposition occurs: and *dem Laute nach,* the formation is like θεήλατος. There seems to be no reason, we may add, why, if it were needed, we should not have had a θεέμπνευστος by the side of θεόπνευστος, just as by the side of πνευματοφόρος we have πνευματέμφορος ("Etymologicum Magnum," 677, 28; John of Damascus, in Migne, 96, 837c.: Ἧσε προφητῶν πνευματέμφορον στόμα).

[61] For not even θεεμπνέω would properly signify "breathe into" but rather "breathe *in*," "inhale." It is by a somewhat illogical extension of meaning that the verb and its derivatives (ἔμπνευσις, ἔμπνοια) are used in the theological sense of "inspiration," in which sense they do not occur, however, either in the LXX. or the New Testament. In the LXX. ἔμπνευσις means a "blast," a "blowing" (Ps. xvii. (xviii.) 15; cf. the participle ἐμπνέων, Acts ix. 1); ἔμπνους, "living," "breathing" (II Macc. vii. 5, xiv. 45); and the participle πᾶν ἐμπνέον, "every living, breathing thing" (Deut. xx. 16; Josh. x. 28, 30, 35, 37, 39, 40; xi. 14; Wisd. xv. 11). Εἰσπνέω is properly used by the classics in the sense of "breathing into," "inspiring": it is not found in itself or derivatives in LXX. or the New Testament — though it occurs in Aq. at Ex. i. 5. How easily and in what a full sense, however, ἐμπνέω is used by ecclesiastical writers for "inspire" may be noted from such examples as Ign. " ad Mag.," 8: "For the divine (θειότατοι) prophets lived after Christ; for this cause also they were persecuted, being inspired by His grace (ἐμνεόμενοι ὑπὸ τῆς χάριτος αὐτοῦ) for the full persuasion of those that are disobedient." Theoph. of Antioch, " ad. Autol.," ii. 9: "Butt he men of God, πνευματοφόροι of the Holy Ghost, and becoming prophets ὑπ' αὐτοῦ τοῦ θεοῦ ἐμπνευσθέντες καὶ σοφισθέντες, be-came θεοδίδακτοι and holy and righteous." The most natural term for "inspired" in classic Greek one would be apt to think, would be ἔνθεος (ἔνθους), with τὸ ἔνθεον for "inspiration"; and after it, participial or other derivatives of ἐνθουσιάζω: but both εἰσπνέω and ἐμπνέω were used for the "inspiration" that consisted of "breathing *into*" even in profane Greek.

ture from the epithet: it expresses, he said,[62] what Scripture is — viz., pervaded by God, full of His Spirit — without the least hint as to how it got to be so. He afterwards came to see this was going too far, and contented himself with saying that though certainly implicating a doctrine of the origin of the Scriptures, the term throws the *emphasis* on its quality.[63] He now, therefore, expressed himself thus: "It is certainly undeniable that the new expression θεόπνευστος, II Tim. iii. 16, is intended to say very much what Philo meant, but did not yet know how to express sharply by means of such a compressed and strong term. For θεόπνευστος (like εὔπνευστος, accurately, 'well-breathed') must mean 'God-breathed' or 'God-animated' (*Gottbeathmet*, or *Gottbegeistert*), and, in accordance with the genius of the compressed, clear Greek compounds, this includes in itself the implication that the words are *spoken by the Spirit of God*, or by those who are inspired by God," — a thing which, he adds, is repeatedly asserted in Scripture to have been the case, as, for example, in II Pet. i. 21. On another occasion,[64] he substantially repeats this, objecting to the translations *inspiratus, eingegeben*, as introducing an idea not lying in the word and liable to mislead, affirming a general but not perfect accord of the idea involved in it with Philo's conception of Scripture, and insisting on the incomplete parallelism between the term and our dogmatic idea of "inspiration." "This term," he says, " no doubt expresses only what is everywhere presupposed by Philo as to Scripture and repeatedly said by him in other words; still his usage is not yet so far developed; and it is accordant with this that in the New Testament, also, it is only in one of the latest books that the word is thus used. This author was possibly the first who so applied it." Again, θεόπνευστος "means, purely passively, God-spirited (*Gottbegeistet*), or full of God's Spirit, not at all, when taken strictly, what we call discriminatingly God-inspired (*Gottbegeistert*) or filled with God's inspiration (*Begeisterung*), but in itself only,

---

[62] P. 88. [63] "Geschichte des Volkes Israel," vi. 245, note.
[64] "Jahrb. f. bibl. Wissenschaft," ix. 91.

In a quite general sense, God-breathed, God-inspired (*Gott-beathmet, Gottbegeistert*), or filled with the divine spirit. In itself, therefore, it permits the most divers applications and we must appeal purely to the context in each instance in order to obtain its exact meaning."

Here we have in full what Dr. Cremer says so much more briefly in his articles. In order to orient ourselves with reference to it, we shall need to consider in turn the two points that are emphasized. These are, first, the passive form and sense of the word; and, secondly, the particular passive sense attributed to it, to wit: *Gottbegeistet* rather than *Gottbegeistert*, "endowed with God's Spirit," rather than "inspired by God."

On the former point there would seem to be little room for difference of opinion. We still read in Schmiedel's Winer: "Verbals in -τος correspond sometimes to Latin participles in -*tus*, sometimes to adjectives in -*bilis*"; and then in a note (despite Ewald's long-ago protest), after the adduction of authorities, "θεόπνευστος, *inspiratus* (II Tim. iii. 16; passive like ἔμπνευστος, while εὔπνευστος, ἄπνευστος are active)."[65] To these Thayer-Grimm adds also πυρίπνευστος and δυσδιάπνευστος as used actively and δυσανάπνευστος as used apparently either actively or passively. Ewald, however, has already taught us to look beneath the "active" usage of εὔπνευστος and ἄπνευστος for the "half-passive" background, and it may equally be found in the other cases; in each instance it is a state or condition at least, that is described by the word, and it is often only a matter of point of view whether we catch the passive conception or not. For example, we shall look upon δυσδιάπνευστος as active or passive according as we think of the object it describes as a "slowly evaporating" or a "slowly evaporated" object — that is, as an object that only slowly evaporates, or as an object that can be only with difficulty evaporated. We may prefer the former expression; the Greeks preferred the latter: that is all. We fully accord

[65] Sec. 16, 2, p. 135. Cf. Thayer's Winer, p. 96; Moulton's, p. 120. Also Thayer's Buttmann, p. 190. The best literature of the subject will be found adduced by Winer.

with Prof. Schulze, therefore, when he says that all words
compounded with -πνευστος have the passive sense as their
original implication, and the active sense, when it occurs, is
always a derived one. On this showing it cannot be contended, of course, that θεόπνευστος may not have, like some
of its relatives, developed an active or quasi-active meaning,
but a passive sense is certainly implied as its original one,
and a certain presumption is thus raised for the originality
of the passive sense which is found to attach to it in its most
ordinary usage.[66]

This conclusion finds confirmation in a consideration
which has its bearing on the second point also — the consideration that compounds of verbals in -τος with θεός normally express an effect produced by God's activity. This is
briefly adverted to by Prof. Schulze, who urges that "the
closely related θεοδίδακτος, and many, or rather most, of the
compounds of θεο- in the Fathers, bear the passive sense,"
adducing in illustration: θεόβλαστος, θεοβούλητος, θεογένητος,
θεόγραπτος, θεόδμητος, θεόδοτος, θεοδώρητος, θεόθρεπτος, θεοκίνητος,
θεόκλητος, θεοποίητος, θεοφόρητος, θεόχρηστος, θεόχριστος. The
statement may be much broadened and made to cover the
whole body of such compounds occurring in Greek literature.
Let any one run his eye down the list of compounds of θεός
with verbals in -τος as they occur on the pages of any Greek
Lexicon, and he will be quickly convinced that the notion
normally expressed is that of a result produced by God. The
sixth edition of Liddell and Scott happens to be the one lying
at hand as we write; and in it we find entered (if we have

---

[66] Compounds of -πνευστος do not appear to be very common. Liddell and
Scott (ed. 6) do not record either ἀνά- or διά- or ἐπί- or even εὖ-; though the cognates
are recorded, and further compounds presupposing them. The rare word εὔπνευστος
might equally well express "breathing-well" quasi-actively, or "well-aired"
passively; just as ἄπνευστος is actually used in the two senses of "breathless" and
"unventilated": and a similar double sense belongs to δυσανάπνευστος. Ἔμπνευστος
does not seem to occur in a higher sense; its only recorded usage is illustrated by
Athenaeus, iv. 174, where it is connected with ὄργανα in the sense of wind-instru-
ments: its cognates are used of "inspiration." Only πυρίπνευστος = πυρίπνοος =
"fire-breathing" is distinctively active in usage: cf. ἀνάπνευστος, poetic for ἄπνευστος = "breathless."

counted aright), some eighty-six compounds of this type, of which, at least, seventy-five bear quite simply the sense of a result produced by God. We adjoin the list: θεήλατος, θεοβάστακτος, θεόβλυστος, θεοβούλητος, θεοβράβευτος, θεογένητος, θεόγνωστος, θεόγραπτος, θεοδέκτος, θεοδίδακτος, θεόδμητος, θεοδόμητος, θεόδοτος, θεοδώρητος, θεόθετος, θεοκατάρατος, θεοκατασκεύαστος, θεοκέλευστος, θεοκίνητος, θεόκλητος, θεόκμητος, θεόκραντος, θεόκριτος, θεόκτητος, θεόκτιστος, θεόκτιτος, θεοκυβέρνητος, θεοκύρωτος, θεόλεκτος, θεόληπτος, θεομακάριστος, θεομίσητος, θεόμυστος, θεόπαιστος, θεοπαράδοτος, θεοπάρακτος, θεόπεμπτος, θεοπέρατος, θεόπληκτος, θεόπλουτος, θεοποίητος, θεοπόνητος, θεοπρόσδεκτος, θεόπτυστος, θεόργητος, θεόρρητος, θέορτος, θεόσδοτος, θεόστρεπτος, θεοστήρικτος, θεοστύγητος, θεοσύλλεκτος, θεοσύμφυτος, θεοσύνακτος, θεόσυτος, θεοσφράγιστος, θεόσωστος, θεοτέρατος, θεότευκτος, θεοτίμητος, θεότρεπτος, θεοτύπωτος, θεοϋπόστατος, θεοΰφαντος, θεόφαντος, θεόφθεγκτος, θεοφίλητος, θεόφοιτος, θεοφόρητος, θεοφρούρητος, θεοφύλακτος, θεοχόλωτος, θεόχρηστος, θεόχριστος. The eleven instances that remain, as in some sort exceptions to the general rule, include cases of different kinds. In some of them the verbal is derived from a deponent verb and is therefore passive only in form, but naturally bears an active sense: such are θεοδήλητος (God-injuring), θεομίμητος (God-imitating), θεόσεπτος (feared as God). Others may possibly be really passives, although we prefer an active form in English to express the idea involved: such are, perhaps, θεόκλυτος ("God-heard," where we should rather say, "calling on the gods"), θεοκόλλητος ("God-joined," where we should rather say, "united with God"), θεόπρεπτος ("God-distinguished," where we should rather say, "meet for a god"). There remain only these five: θεαίτητος ("obtained from God"), θεόθυτος ("offered to the gods"), θεορράστος and the more usual θεόρροτος ("flowing from the gods"), and θεοχώρητος ("containing God"). In these the relation of θεός to the verbal idea is clearly not that of producing cause to the expressed result, but some other: perhaps what we need to recognize is that the verbal here involves a relation which we ordinarily express by a preposition, and that the sense would be suggested by some such phrases as "God-asked-of," "God-offered-to," "God-flowed-from," "God-made-room-for." In any event, these few ex-ceptional cases cannot avail to set aside the normal sense of this compound, as exhibited in the immense majority of the cases of its occurrence. If analogy is to count for anything, its whole weight is thrown thus in favor of the interpretation which sees in θεόπνευστος, quite simply, the sense of "God-breathed," i. e., produced by God's creative breath.

If we ask, then, what account is to be given of Ewald's and, after him, Prof. Cremer's wish, to take it in the specific sense of "God-spirited," that is, "imbued with the Spirit of God," we may easily feel ourselves somewhat puzzled to return a satisfactory answer. We should doubtless not go far wrong in saying, as already suggested, that their action is proximately due to their not having brought all the alternatives fairly before them. They seem to have worked, as we have said, on the hypothesis that the only choice lay between the Vulgate rendering, "God-inspired," and their own "God-imbued." Ewald, as we have seen, argues (and as we think rightly) that "God-*in*spired" is scarcely consonant with the word-form, but would have required something like θεέμ-πνευστος. Similarly we may observe Dr. Cremer in the second edition of his "Lexicon" (when he was arguing for the current conception) saying that "the formation of the word cannot be traced to the use of πνέω, but only of ἐμπνέω," and sup-porting this by the remark that "the simple verb is never used of divine action"; and throughout his later article, operating on the presumption that the rendering "*in*spired" solely will come into comparison with his own newly pro-posed one. All this seems to be due, not merely to the traditional rendering of the word itself, but also to the con-ception of the nature of the divine action commonly ex-pressed by the term, "inspiration," and indeed to the doc-trine of Holy Scripture, dominant in the minds of these scholars.[67] If we will shake ourselves loose from these obscur-

[67] Two fundamental ideas, lying at the root of all their thinking of Scripture, seem to have colored somewhat their dealing with this term: the old Lutheran

ing prepossessions and consider the term without preoccupation of mind, it would seem that the simple rendering
"God-breathed" would commend itself powerfully to us:
certainly not, with the Vulgate and Luther, "God-*in*breathed,"
since the preposition "in" is wholly lacking in the term and
is not demanded for the sense in any of its applications; but
equally certainly not "God-imbued" or "God-infused" in
the sense of imbued or infused *with* (rather than *by*) God,
since, according to all analogy, as well as according to the
simplest construction of the compound, the relation of
"God" to the act expressed is that of "agent." On any other
supposition than that this third and assuredly the most
natural alternative, "God-breathed," was not before their
minds, the whole treatment of Ewald and Dr. Cremer will
remain somewhat inexplicable.

Why otherwise, for example, should the latter have remarked, that the "word must be traced to the use of ἐμπνέω
and not to the simple verb πνέω?" Dr. Cremer, it is true,
adds, as we have said, that the simple verb is never used of
divine action. In any case, however, this statement is overdrawn. Not only is πνέω applied in a physical sense to God
in such passages of the LXX. as Ps. cxlvii. 7 (18) (πνεύσει τὸ
πνεῦμα αὐτοῦ) and Isa. xl. 24, and of Symmachus and Theodotion as Isa. xl. 7; and not only in the earliest Fathers is it
used of the greatest gifts of Christ the Divine Lord, in such
passages as Ign., "Eph." 17: — "For this cause the Lord received ointment on His head, that He might breathe incorruption upon His Church (ἵνα πνέῃ τῇ ἐκκλησίᾳ ἀφθαρσίαν)";
but in what may be rightly called the normative passage,

doctrine of the Word of God, and the modern rationalizing doctrine of the nature
of the Divine influence exerted in the production of Scripture. On account of the
latter point of view they seem determined not to find in Scripture itself any
declaration that will shut them up to "a Philonian conception of Scripture" as
the Oracles of God — the very utterances of the Most High. By the former they
seem predisposed to discover in it declarations of the wonder-working power of
the Word. The reader cannot avoid becoming aware of the influence of both these
dogmatic conceptions in both Ewald's and Cremer's dealing with θεόπνευστος. But
it is not necessary to lay stress on this.

Gen. ii. 7, it is practically justified, in its application to God, by the LXX. use of πνοή in the objective clause, and actually employed for the verb itself by both Symmachus and Theodotion. And if we will penetrate beneath the mere matter of the usage of a word to the conception itself, nothing could be more misleading than such a remark as Dr. Cremer's. For surely there was no conception more deeply rooted in the Hebrew mind, at least, than that of the creative "breath of God"; and this conception was assuredly not wholly unknown even in ethnic circles. To a Hebrew, at all events, the "breath of God" would seem self-evidently creative; and no locution would more readily suggest itself to him as expressive of the Divine act of "making" than just that by which it would be affirmed that He breathed things into existence. The "breath of the Almighty" — πνοὴ παντοκράτορος — was traditionally in his mouth as the fit designation of the creative act (Job xxxii. 8, xxxiii. 4); and not only was he accustomed to think of man owing his existence to the breathing of the breath of God into his nostrils (Gen. ii. 7, especially Symm. Theod.) and of his life as therefore the "breath of God" (πνεῦμα θεῖον, LXX., Job xxvii. 8), which God needs but to draw back to Himself that all flesh should perish (Job xxxiv. 14): but he conceived also that it was by the breath of God's mouth (πνεύματι τοῦ στώματος, Ps. xxxiii. 6), that all the hosts of the heavens were made, and by the sending forth of His breath, (πνεῦμα, Ps. civ. 30) that the multiplicity of animal life was created. By His breath even (πνοή, Job xxxvii. 10), he had been told, the ice is formed; and by His breath (πνεῦμα, Isa. xi. 5, cf. Job iv. 9) all the wicked are consumed. It is indeed the whole conception of the Spirit of God as the executive of the Godhead that is involved here: the conception that it is the Spirit of God that is the active agent in the production of all that is. To the Hebrew consciousness, creation itself would thus naturally appear as, not indeed an "*in*spiration," and much less an "infusion of the Divine essence," but certainly a "spiration"; and all that exists would appeal to it as, therefore, in the proper sense theopnoustic, i e., simply, "breathed by God," produced by the creative breath of the Almighty, the πνοὴ παντοκράτορος.

This would not, it needs to be remembered, necessarily imply an "immediate creation," as we call it. When Elihu declares that it is the breath of the Almighty that has given him life or understanding (Job xxxii. 8, xxxiii. 4), he need not be read as excluding the second causes by which he was brought into existence; nor need the Psalmist (civ. 30) be understood to teach an "immediate creation" of the whole existing animal mass. But each certainly means to say that it is God who has made all these things, and that by His breath: He breathed them into being — they are all θεόπ-νευστοι. So far from the word presenting a difficulty therefore from the point of view of its conception, it is just, after the nature of Greek compounds, the appropriate crystallization into one concise term of a conception that was a ruling idea in every Jewish mind. Particularly, then, if we are to suppose (with both Ewald and Cremer) that the word is a coinage of Paul's, or even of Hellenistic origin, nothing could be more natural than that it should have enshrined in it the Hebraic conviction that God produces all that He would bring into being by a mere breath. From this point of view, therefore, there seems no occasion to seek beyond the bare form of the word itself for a sense to attribute to it. If we cannot naturally give it the meaning of "God-*in*spired," we certainly do not need to go so far afield as to attribute to it the sense of "filled with God": the natural sense which belongs to it by virtue of its formation, and which is commended to us by the analogy of like compounds, is also most consonant with the thought-forms of the circles in which it perhaps arose and certainly was almost exclusively used. What the word naturally means from this point of view also, is "God-spirated," "God-breathed," "produced by the creative breath of the Almighty."

Thus it appears that such a conception as "God-breathed" lies well within the general circle of ideas of the Hellenistic writers, who certainly most prevailingly use the word. An application of this conception to Scripture, such as is made in II Tim. iii. 16, was no less consonant with the ideas concerning the origin and nature of Scripture which prevailed in the circles out of which that epistle proceeded. This may indeed be fairly held to be generally conceded.

The main object of Ewald's earlier treatment of this passage, to be sure, was to void the word θεόπνευστος of all implication as to the origination of Scripture. By assigning to it the sense of "God-pervaded," "full of God's Spirit," he supposed he had made it a description of what Scripture is, without the least suggestion of how it came to be such; and he did not hesitate accordingly, to affirm that it had nothing whatever to say as to the origin of Scripture.[68] But he afterwards, as we have already pointed out, saw the error of this position, and so far corrected it as to explain that, of course, the term θεόπνευστος includes in itself the implication that the words so designated are spoken by the Spirit of God or by men inspired by God — in accordance with what is repeatedly said elsewhere in Scripture, as, for example, in II Pet. i. 21 — yet still to insist that it throws its *chief emphasis* rather on the nature than the origin of these words.[69] And he never thought of denying that in the circles in which the word was used in application to Scripture, the idea of the origination of Scripture by the act of God was current and indeed dominant. Philo's complete identification of Scripture with the spoken word of God was indeed the subject under treatment by him, when he penned the note from which we have last quoted; and he did not fail explicitly to allow that the conceptions of the writer of the passage in II Timothy were very closely related to those of Philo. "It is certainly undeniable," he writes, "that the new term θεόπνευστος, II Tim. iii. 16, is intended to express very much what Philo meant, and did not yet know how to say sharply by means of so compressed and direct a term"; and again, in another place, "this term, no doubt, embodies only what is everywhere presupposed by

[68] "Jahrb. f. bibl. Wissenschaft," vii. 88, 114.
[69] "Geschichte des Volkes Israel," i. 245, note.

Philo as to the Scriptures, and is repeatedly expressed by him in other words; yet his usage is not yet so far developed; and it is in accordance with this that in the New Testament, too, it is only one of the latest writings which uses the term in this way." [70]

It would seem, to be sure, that it is precisely this affinity with Philo's conception of Scripture which Dr. Cremer wishes to exclude in his treatment of the term. "Let it be added," he writes, near the close of the extract from his *Herzog* article which we have given above, "that the expression 'breathed by God, inspired by God,' though an outgrowth of the Biblical idea, certainly, so far as it is referred to the prophecy which does not arise out of the human will (II Pet. i. 20), yet can scarcely be applied to the whole of the rest of Scripture — unless we are to find in II Tim. iii. 16 the expression of a conception of sacred Scripture similar to the Philonian." And a little later he urges against the testimony of the exegetical tradition to the meaning of the word, that it was affected by the conceptions of Alexandrian Judaism — that is, he suggests, practically of heathenism. There obviously lies beneath this mode of representation an attempt to represent the idea of the nature and origin of Scripture exhibited in the New Testament, as standing in some fundamental disaccord with that of the Philonian tracts; and the assimilation of the conception expressed in II Tim. iii. 16 to the latter as therefore its separation from the former. Something like this is affirmed also by Holtzmann when he writes: [71] "It is accordingly clear that the author shares the Jewish conception of the purely supernatural origin of the Scriptures in its straitest acceptation, according to which, therefore, the theopneusty is ascribed immediately to the Scriptures themselves, and not merely, as in II Pet. i. 21, to their writers; and so far as the thing itself is concerned there is nothing incorrect implied in the translation, *tota Scriptura*." The notion that the Biblical and the Philonian ideas of Scripture somewhat markedly

[70] "Jahrb.," etc., ix. 92.
[71] "Die Pastoralbriefe" u. s. w., p. 163.

differ is apparently common to the two writers: only Holtzmann identifies the idea expressed in II Tim. iii. 16 with the
Philonian, and therefore pronounces it to be a mark of late
origin for that epistle; while Cremer wishes to detach it from
the Philonian, that he may not be forced to recognize the
Philonian conception as possessing New Testament authorization.

No such fundamental difference between the Philonian
and New Testament conceptions as is here erected, however,
can possibly be made out; though whatever minor differences may be traceable between the general New Testament
conception and treatment of Scripture and that of Philo, it
remains a plain matter of fact that no other general view of
Scripture than the so-called Philonian is discernible in the
New Testament, all of whose writers — as is true of Jesus
Himself also, according to His reported words, — consistently look upon the written words of Scripture as the express
utterances of God, owing their origin to His direct spiration
and their character to this their divine origin. It is peculiarly
absurd to contrast II Pet. i. 21 with II Tim. iii. 16 (as Holtzmann does explicitly and the others implicitly), on the ground
of a difference of conception as to "inspiration," shown in the
ascription of inspiration in the former passage to the writers,
in the latter immediately to the words of Scripture. It is, on
the face of it, the "*word* of prophecy" to which Peter ascribes divine surety; it is *written* prophecy which he declares
to be of no "private interpretation"; and if he proceeds to
exhibit *how* God produced this sure written word of prophecy
— viz., through men of God carried onward, apart from
their own will, by the determining power of the Holy Ghost [72]
— surely this exposition of the mode of the divine action in
producing the Scriptures can only by the utmost confusion
of ideas be pleaded as a denial of the fact that the Scriptures
were produced by the Divine action. To Peter as truly as to
Paul, and to the Paul of the earlier epistles as truly as to the

[72] For the implications of the term φερόμενοι here (as distinguished from ἀγό-
μενοι) consult the fruitful discussion of the words in Schmidt's "Synonymik."

Paul of II Timothy, or as to Philo himself, the Scriptures are
the product of the Divine Spirit, and would be most appropriately described by the epithet of "God-breathed," i. e.,
produced by the breath, the inspiration, of God.

The entire distinction which it is sought to erect between
the New Testament and the Philonic conceptions of Scripture, as if to the New Testament writers the Scriptures were
less the oracles of God than to Philo, and owed their origin
less directly to God's action, and might therefore be treated
as less divine in character or operation, hangs in the mere
air. There may be fairly recognized certain differences between the New Testament and the Philonic conceptions of
Scripture; but they certainly do not move in this fundamental
region. The epithet "God-breathed," "produced by the creative breath of the Almighty," commends itself, therefore, as
one which would lie near at hand and would readily express
the fundamental view as to the origination of Scripture current among the whole body of New Testament writers, as
well as among the whole mass of their Jewish contemporaries,
amid whom they were bred. The distinction between the inspiration of the writers and that of the record, is a subtlety
of later times of which they were guiltless: as is also the
distinction between the origination of Scripture by the action
of the Holy Ghost and the infusing of the Holy Spirit into
Scriptures originating by human activity. To the writers of
this age of simpler faith, the Scriptures are penetrated by
God because they were given by God: and the question of
their effects, or even of their nature, was not consciously
separated from the question of their origin. The one sufficient
and decisive fact concerning them to these writers, inclusive
of all else and determinative of all else that was true of them
as the Word of God, was that they were "God-given," or,
more precisely, the product of God's creative "breath."

In these circumstances it can hardly be needful to pause
to point out in detail how completely this conception accords
with the whole New Testament doctrine of Scripture, and
with the entire body of phraseology currently used in it to

express its divine origination. We need only recall the declarations that the Holy Spirit is the author of Scripture (Heb. iii. 7, x. 15), "in whom" it is, therefore, that its human authors speak (Matt. xxii. 43; Mark xii. 36), because it is He that speaks what they speak "through them" (Acts i. 16, iv. 25), they being but the media of the prophetic word (Matt. i. 22, ii. 15, iii. 3, iv. 14, viii. 17, xii. 17, xiii. 35, xxi. 4, xxiv. 15, xxvii. 9, Luke xviii. 31, Acts ii. 16, xxvii. 25, Rom. i. 2, Luke i. 76, Acts i. 16, iii. 18, 21). The whole underlying conception of such modes of expression is in principle set forth in the command of Jesus to His disciples that, in their times of need, they should depend wholly on the Divine Spirit speaking in them (Matt. x. 20; Mark xiii. 11; cf. Luke i. 41, 67, xii. 12; Acts iv. 8): and perhaps even more decidedly still in Peter's description of the prophets of Scripture as "borne by the Holy Ghost," as πνευματόφοροι, whose words are, therefore, of no "private interpretation," and of the highest surety (II Pet. i. 21). In all such expressions the main affirmation is that Scripture, as the product of the activity of the Spirit, is just the "breath of God"; and the highest possible emphasis is laid on their origination by the divine agency of the Spirit. The primary characteristic of Scripture in the minds of the New Testament writers is thus revealed as, in a word, its Divine origin.

That this was the sole dominating conception attached from the beginning to the term θεόπνευστος as an epithet of Scripture, is further witnessed by the unbroken exegetical tradition of its meaning in the sole passage of the New Testament in which it occurs. Dr. Cremer admits that such is the exegetical tradition, though he seeks to break the weight of this fact by pleading that the unanimity of the patristic interpretation of the passage is due rather to preconceived opinions on the part of the Fathers as to the nature of Scripture, derived from Alexandrian Judaism, than to the natural effect on their minds of the passage itself. Here we are pointed to the universal consent of Jewish and Christian students of the Word as to the divine origin of the Scriptures they held

in common — a fact impressive enough of itself — as a reason
for discrediting the testimony of the latter as to the meaning
of a fundamental passage bearing on the doctrine of Holy
Scripture. One is tempted to ask whether it can be really
proved that the theology of Alexandrian Judaism exercised
so universal and absolute a dominion over the thinking of the
Church, that it is likely to be due to its influence alone that
the Christian doctrine of inspiration took shape, in despite
(as we are told) of the natural implications of the Christian
documents themselves. And one is very likely to insist that,
whatever may be its origin, this conception of the divine
origination of Scripture was certainly shared by the New
Testament writers themselves, and may very well therefore
have found expression in II Tim. iii. 16 — which would therefore need no adjustment to current ideas to make it teach
it. At all events, it is admitted that this view of the teaching
of II Tim. iii. 16 is supported by the unbroken exegetical
tradition; and this fact certainly requires to be taken into
consideration in determining the meaning of the word.

It is quite true that Dr. Cremer in one sentence does not
seem to keep in mind the unbrokenness of the exegetical tradition. We read: "Origen also, in ' Hom. 21 in Jerem.', seems
so [i. e., as Dr. Cremer does] to understand it [that is,
θεόπνευστος]: — sacra volumina spiritus plenitudinem spirant."
The unwary reader may infer from this that these words of
Origen are explanatory of II Tim. iii. 16, and that they therefore break the exegetical tradition and show that Origen assigned to that passage the meaning that "the Holy Scriptures
breathe out the plenitude of the Spirit." Such is, however,
not the case. Origen is not here commenting on II Tim. iii. 16,
but only freely expressing his own notion as to the nature of
Scripture. His words here do not, therefore, break the constancy of the exegetical tradition, but at the worst only the
universality of that Philonian conception of Scripture, to the
universality of which among the Fathers, Dr. Cremer attributes the unbrokenness of the exegetical tradition. What results from their adduction is, then, not a weakening of the

patristic testimony to the meaning of θεόπνευστος in II Tim. iii. 16, but (at the worst) a possible hint that Dr. Cremer's explanation of the unanimity of that testimony may not, after all, be applicable. When commenting on II Tim. iii. 16, Origen uniformly takes the word θεόπνευστος as indicatory of the origin of Scripture; though when himself speaking of what Scripture is, he may sometimes speak as Dr. Cremer would have him speak. It looks as if his interpretation of II Tim. iii. 16 were expository of its meaning to him rather than impository of his views on it. Let us, by way of illus-tration, place a fuller citation of Origen's words, in the pas-sage adduced by Dr. Cremer, side by side with a passage directly dealing with II Tim. iii. 16, and note the result.

Secundum istiusmodi expositiones decet sacras litteras credere nec unum quidem apicem habere vacuum sapientia Dei. Qui enim mihi homini præcipit dicens: *Non apparebis ante conspectum meum vacuus,* multo plus hoc ipse agit, ne aliquid vacuum loquatur. Ex plenitudine ejus accipientes prophetæ, ea, quæ erant de plenitudine sumpta, cecinerunt: et idcirco sacra volumina spiritus plenitudinem spirant, nihilque est sive in prophetia, sive in lege, sive in evangelio, sive in apostolo, quod non a plenitudine divinæ majestatis descendat. Quam-obrem spirant in scripturis sanctis hodieque plenitudinis verba. Spi-rant autem his, qui habent et oculos ad videnda cœlestia et aures ad audienda divina, et nares ad ea, quæ sunt plenitudinis, sentienda (Origen, "in Jeremiam Homilia," xxi, 2. Wirceburg ed., 1785, ix, 733).

Here Origen is writing quite freely: and his theme is the divine fullness of Scripture. There is nothing in Scripture which is vain or empty and all its fullness is derived from Him from whom it is dipped by the prophets. Contrast his manner, now, when he is expounding II Tim. iii. 16.

"Let us not be stupefied by hearing Scriptures which we do not understand; but let it be to us according to our faith, by which also we believe that every Scripture because it is theopneustic (πᾶσα γραφὴ θεόπνευστος οὖσα) is profitable. For you must needs admit one of two things regarding these Scriptures: either that they are not theopneus-tic since they are not profitable, as the unbeliever takes it; or, as a believer, you must admit that since they are theopneustic, they are profitable It is to be admitted, of course, that the profit is often received by us unconsciously, just as often we are assigned certain food for the benefit of the eyes, and only after two or three days does the digestion of the food that was to benefit the eyes give us assurance by trial that the eyes are benefited. . . . So, then, believe also concerning the divine Scriptures, that thy soul is profited, even if thy understanding does not perceive the fruit of the profit that comes from the letters, from the mere bare reading" [Origen, " Hom. XX in Josuam " 2, in J. A. Robinson's Origen's "Philocalia," p. 63).

It is obvious that here Origen does not understand II Tim. iii. 16, to teach that Scripture is inspired only because it is profitable, and that we are to determine its profitableness first and its inspiration therefrom; what he draws from the passage is that Scripture is profitable because it is inspired, and that though we may not see in any particular case how, or even that, it is profitable, we must still believe it to be profitable because it is inspired, i. e., obviously because it is given of God for that end.

It seemed to be necessary to adduce at some length these passages from Origen, inasmuch as the partial adduction of one of them, alone, by Dr. Cremer might prove misleading to the unwary reader. But there appears to be no need of multiplying passages from the other early expositors of II Tim. iii. 16, seeing that it is freely confessed that the exegetical tradition runs all in one groove. We may differ as to the weight we allow to this fact; but surely as a piece of testimony corroborative of the meaning of the word derived from other considerations, it is worth noting that it has from the beginning been understood only in one way — even by those, such as Origen and we may add Clement, who may not themselves be absolutely consistent in preserving the point of view taught them in this passage.[73]

[73] Cf. Prof. Schulze, loc. cit.: "Further, it should not be lost sight of (and Dr. Cremer does not do so) how the Church in its defenders has understood this word. There can be no doubt that in the conflict with Montanism, the traditional doctrine of theopneusty was grounded in the conception of θεόπνευστος, but never that of the Scriptures breathing out the Spirit of God. The passage which Cremer adduces from Origen gives no interpretation of this word, but only points to a quality of Scripture consequent on their divine origination by the Holy Spirit:

The final test of the sense assigned to any word is, of course, derived from its fitness to the context in which it is found. And Dr. Cremer does not fail to urge with reference to θεόπνευστος in II Tim. iii. 16, that the meaning he assigns to it corresponds well with the context, especially with the succeeding clauses; as well as, he adds, with the language elsewhere in the New Testament, as, for example, in the Epistle to the Hebrews, where what Scripture says is spoken of as the utterance, the saying of the Holy Ghost, with which he would further compare even Acts xxviii. 25.

That the words of Scripture are conceived, not only in Hebrews but throughout the New Testament, as the utterances of the Holy Ghost is obvious enough and not to be denied. But it is equally obvious that the ground of this conception is everywhere the ascription of these words to the Holy Ghost as their responsible author: *littera scripta manet* and remains what it was when written, viz., the words of the writer. The fact that all Scripture is conceived as a body of Oracles and approached with awe as the utterances of God certainly does not in the least suggest that these utterances may not be described as God-given words or throw a preference for an interpretation of θεόπνευστος which would transmute it into an assertion that they are rather God-giving words.

And the same may be said of the contextual argument. Naturally, if θεόπνευστος means "God-giving," it would as an epithet or predicate of Scripture serve very well to lay a foundation for declaring this "God-giving Scripture" also profitable, etc. But an equal foundation for this declaration is laid by the description of it as "God-given." The passage just quoted from Origen will alone teach us this. All that can be said on this score for the new interpretation, therefore,

and elsewhere when he adduces the rule of faith, the words run, *quod per spiritum dei sacræ scripturæ conscriptæ sint,* or *a verbo dei et spirita dei dictæ sunt:* just as Clem. Alex. also, when, in *Coh.* 71, he is commenting on the Pauline passage, takes the word in the usual way, and yet, like Origen, makes an inference from the God-likeness (as θεοποιεῖν) in Plato's manner, from the whole passage — though not deriving it from the word itself. For the use of the word in Origen, we need it note: *Sel. in Ps.,* ii. 527; *Hom. in Joh.,* vi. 134, Ed. de la R."

is that it also could be made accordant with the context; and as much, and much more, can be said for the old. We leave the matter in this form, since obviously a detailed interpretation of the whole passage cannot be entered into here, but must be reserved for a later occasion. It may well suffice to say now that obviously no advantage can be claimed for the new interpretation from this point of view. The question is, after all, not what can the word be made to mean, but what does it mean; and the witness of its usage elsewhere, its form and mode of composition, and the sense given it by its readers from the first, supply here the primary evidence. Only if the sense thus commended to us were unsuitable to the context would we be justified in seeking further for a new interpretation — thus demanded by the context. This can by no means be claimed in the present instance, and nothing can be demanded of us beyond showing that the more natural current sense of the word is accordant with the context.

The result of our investigation would seem thus, certainly, to discredit the new interpretation of θεόπνευστος offered by Ewald and Cremer. From all points of approach alike we appear to be conducted to the conclusion that it is primarily expressive of the origination of Scripture, not of its nature and much less of its effects. What is θεόπνευστος is "God-breathed," produced by the creative breath of the Almighty. And Scripture is called θεόπνευστος in order to designate it as "God-breathed," the product of Divine spiration, the creation of that Spirit who is in all spheres of the Divine activity the executive of the Godhead. The traditional translation of the word by the Latin *inspiratus a Deo* is no doubt also discredited, if we are to take it at the foot of the letter. It does not express a breathing *into* the Scriptures by God. But the ordinary conception attached to it, whether among the Fathers or the Dogmaticians, is in general vindicated. What it affirms is that the Scriptures owe their origin to an activity of God the Holy Ghost and are in the highest and truest sense His creation. It is on this foundation of Divine origin that all the high attributes of Scripture are built.

VIII

"IT SAYS:" "SCRIPTURE SAYS:" "GOD SAYS"

"IT SAYS:" "SCRIPTURE SAYS:" "GOD SAYS"[1]

IT would be difficult to invent methods of showing profound reverence for the text of Scripture as the very Word of God, which will not be found to be characteristic of the writers of the New Testament in dealing with the Old. Among the rich variety of the indications of their estimate of the written words of the Old Testament as direct utterances of Jehovah, there are in particular two classes of passages, each of which, when taken separately, throws into the clearest light their habitual appeal to the Old Testament text as to God Himself speaking, while, together, they make an irresistible impression of the absolute identification by their writers of the Scriptures in their hands with the living voice of God. In one of these classes of passages the Scriptures are spoken of as if they were God; in the other, God is spoken of as if He were the Scriptures: in the two together, God and the Scriptures are brought into such conjunction as to show that in point of directness of authority no distinction was made between them.

Examples of the first class of passages are such as these: Gal. iii. 8, "The Scripture, foreseeing that God would justify the heathen through faith, preached before the gospel unto Abraham, saying, In thee shall all the nations be blessed" (Gen. xii. 1-3); Rom. ix. 17, "The Scripture saith unto Pharaoh, Even for this same purpose have I raised thee up" (Ex. ix. 16). It was not, however, the Scripture (which did not exist at the time) that, foreseeing God's purposes of grace in the future, spoke these precious words to Abraham, but God Himself in His own person: it was not the not yet existent Scripture that made this announcement to Pharaoh, but God Himself through the mouth of His prophet Moses. These acts could be attributed to "Scripture" only as the

[1] From *The Presbyterian and Reformed Review*, Vol. x, 1899, pp. 472-510.

result of such a habitual identification, in the mind of the writer, of the text of Scripture with God as speaking, that it became natural to use the term "Scripture says," when what was really intended was "God, as recorded in Scripture, said."

Examples of the other class of passages are such as these: Matt. xix. 4, 5, "And he answered and said, Have ye not read that he which made them from the beginning made them male and female, and said, For this cause shall a man leave his father and mother, and shall cleave to his wife, and the twain shall become one flesh?" (Gen. ii. 24); Heb. iii. 7, "Wherefore, even as the Holy Ghost saith, To-day if ye shall hear his voice," etc. (Ps. xcv. 7); Acts iv. 24, 25, "Thou art God, who by the mouth of thy servant David hast said, Why do the heathen rage and the people imagine vain things" (Ps. ii. 1); Acts xiii. 34, 35, "He that raised him up from the dead, now no more to return to corruption, . . . hath spoken in this wise, I will give you the holy and sure blessings of David" (Isa. lv. 3); "because he saith also in another [Psalm], Thou wilt not give thy holy one to see corruption" (Ps. xvi. 10); Heb. i. 6, "And when he again bringeth in the first born into the world, he saith, And let all the angels of God worship him" (Deut. xxxii. 43); "and of the angels he saith, Who maketh his angels wings, and his ministers a flame of fire" (Ps. civ. 4); "but of the Son, *He saith*, Thy throne, O God, is for ever and ever," etc., (Ps. xlv. 7) and, "Thou, Lord, in the beginning," etc. (Ps. cii. 26). It is not God, however, in whose mouth these sayings are placed in the text of the Old Testament: they are the words of others, recorded in the text of Scripture as spoken to or of God. They could be attributed to God only through such habitual identification, in the minds of the writers, of the text of Scripture with the utterances of God that it had become natural to use the term "God says" when what was really intended was "Scripture, the Word of God, says."

The two sets of passages, together, thus show an absolute identification, in the minds of these writers, of "Scripture" with the speaking God.

In the same line with these passages are commonly ranged
certain others, in which Scripture seems to be adduced with
a subjectless λέγει or φησί, the authoritative subject — whether
the divinely given Word or God Himself — being taken for
granted. Among these have been counted such passages, for
example, as the following: Rom. ix. 15, "For he saith to
Moses, I will have mercy on whom I have mercy, and I will
have compassion on whom I have compassion" (Ex. xxxiii.
19); Rom. xv. 10, "And again he saith, Rejoice, ye Gentiles,
with his people" (Deut. xxxii. 43); and again, "Praise the
Lord, all ye Gentiles; and let all the people praise him"
(Ps. cvii. 1); Gal. iii. 16, "He saith not, And to seeds, as of
many; but as of one, And to thy seed (Gen. xiii. 15), which is
Christ"; Eph. iv. 8, "Wherefore he saith, When he ascended
on high, he led captivity captive, and gave gifts unto men"
(Ps. lxviii. 18); Eph. v. 14, "Wherefore he saith, Awake thou
that sleepest and arise from the dead and Christ shall shine
upon thee" (Isa. lx. 1); I Cor. vi. 16, "For the twain, saith
he, shall become one flesh" (Gen. ii. 24); I Cor. xv. 27, "But
when he saith, All things are put in subjection" (Ps. viii. 7);
II Cor. vi. 2, "For he saith, At an acceptable time, I hearkened unto thee, and in a day of salvation did I succor thee"
(Isa. xlix. 8); Heb. viii. 5, "For see, saith he, that thou make
all things according to the pattern that was showed thee in
the mount" (Ex. xxv. 40); James iv. 6, "Wherefore he saith,
God resisteth the proud but giveth grace to the humble"
(Prov. iii. 34).

There is room for difference of opinion, of course, whether
all these passages are cases in point. And there has certainly
always existed some difference of opinion among commentators as to the proper *subauditum* in such instances as are
allowed. The state of the case would seem to be fairly indicated by Alexander Buttmann, when he says:

"The predicates λέγει or φησίν are often found in the New Testament in quotations, ὁ θεός or even merely ἡ γραφή being always to be
supplied as subject; as I Cor. vi. 16, II Cor. vi. 2, Gal. iii. 16, Eph. iv.
8, v. 14, Heb. viii. 5, iv. 3 (εἴρηκεν). These subjects are also expressed,

as in Gal. iv. 30, I Tim v. 18, or to be supplied from the preceding context, as in Heb. i. 5 *seq.*" [2]

Of the alternatives thus offered, Jelf apparently prefers the one:

"In the New Testament we must supply προφήτης, ἡ γραφή, πνεῦμα, etc., before φησί, λέγει, μαρτυρεῖ." [3]

Winer and Blass take the other:

"The formulas of citation — λέγει, II Cor. vi. 2, Gal. iii. 16, Eph. iv. 8 al., φησί, I Cor. vi. 16, Heb. viii. 5; εἴρηκε, Heb. iv. 4 (cf. the Rabbinical ואומר); μαρτυρεῖ, Heb. vii. 17 (εἶπε, I Cor. xv. 27) — are probably in no instance impersonal in the minds of the New Testament writers. The subject (ὁ θεός) is usually contained in the context, either directly or indirectly; in I Cor. vi. 16 and Matt. xix. 5, φησί, there is an apostolic ellipsis (of ὁ θεός); in Heb. vii. 17, the best authorities have μαρτυρεῖται." [4]

"In the formulas of citation such as λέγει, II Cor. vi. 2, Gal. iii. 16, etc.; φησίν, I Cor. vi. 16, Heb. viii. 5; εἴρηκε, Heb. iv. 4 — ὁ θεός is to be understood ('*He* says'); in II Cor. x. 10, φησίν (א DE, etc. [?], 'one says'), appears to be a wrong reading for φασίν (B), unless perhaps a τις has dropped out (but cp. Clem. Hom., xi. 9 *ad init.*)." [5]

The commentators commonly range themselves with Winer and Blass. Thus, on Rom. ix. 15, Sanday and Headlam comment: "λέγει without a nominative for θεὸς λέγει is a common idiom in quotations," referring to Rom. xv. 10 as a parallel case. On Gal. iii. 16, Meyer says: "*sc.* θεός, which is derived from the historical reference of the previous ἐρρέθησαν, so well known to the reader"; and Alford: "viz., He who gave the promises — God"; and Sieffert: "οὐ λέγει *sc.* θεός which flows out of the historical relation (known to the reader) of the preceding ἐρρέθησαν (cf. Eph. iv. 8, v. 14)."

[2] "A Grammar of the New Testament Greek," Thayer's translation p. 134.
[3] Sec. 373, 3.
[4] Winer, Sec. 58, 9, γ; p. 656 of Moulton's translation.
[5] Blass' "Grammar of N. T. Greek"; English translation by H. St. J. Thackeray, M.A., p. 75.

On Eph. iv. 8, Meyer's comment runs: "*Who* says it (comp. v. 14) is obvious of itself, namely, *God*, whose word the Scripture is. See on I Cor. vi. 16; Gal. iii. 16; the supplying ἡ γραφή or τὸ πνεῦμα must have been suggested by the context (Rom. xv. 10). The manner of citation with the simple λέγει, obviously meant of God, has as its necessary presupposition, in the mind of the writer and readers, the Theopneustia of the Old Testament." Haupt, similarly: "The introduction of a citation with the simple λέγει, with which, of course, 'God' is to be supplied as subject, not 'the Scripture,' is found in Paul again v. 14, II Cor. vi. 2, Rom. xv. 10; similarly φησί, I Cor. vi. 16 (εἶπεν with the addition ὁ θεός, II Cor. vi. 16)." A similar comment is given by Ellicott, who adds at Eph. v. 14: "scil. ὁ θεός, according to the usual form of St. Paul's quotations; see notes on chap. iv. 8 and on Gal. iii. 16": though on I Cor. vi. 16 he speaks with less decision: "It may be doubted what nominative is to be supplied to this practically impersonal verb, whether ἡ γραφή (comp. John vii. 38, Rom. iv. 3, ix. 17, *al.*) or ὁ θεός (comp. Matt. xix. 5, II Cor. vi. 2, where this nominative is distinctly suggested by the context): the latter is perhaps the more natural: comp. Winer, *Gr.*, § 58, 9, and notes on Eph. iv. 8." On I Cor. vi. 16, Edwards comments: "sc. ὁ θεός, as in Rom. ix. 15. Cf. Matt. xix. 4, 5, where ὁ ποιήσας supplies a nom. to εἶπεν. Similarly in Philo and Barnabas φησί introduces citations from Scripture." On II Cor. vi. 2, Waite says: "A statement of God Himself is adduced"; and De Wette: "sc. θεός, who Himself speaks." On Heb. viii. 5, Bleek comments: "That there is to be understood as the subject of φησί, not, as Böhme thinks, ἡ γραφή, but ὁ θεός, can least of all be doubtful here, where actual words of God are adduced"; and Weiss: "This statement is now established (γάρ) by appeal to Ex. xxv. 40, which passage is characterized only by the interpolated φησίν (cf. Acts xxv. 22) as a divine oracle. . . . The subject of φησίν is, of course, God, neither ὁ χρηματισμός (Lün.) nor ἡ γραφή (Bhm.)." On James iv. 6, Mayor comments: "The subject understood is probably God, as above, i. 12, ἐπηγγείλαιυ, and Eph. iv. 8, v 14, where the same phrase occurs; others take it as ἡ γραφή. Cf. above, v. 5." [6]

Most of these passages have, on the other hand, been explained by some commentators on the supposition that it is ἡ γραφή that is to be supplied, as has sufficiently appeared indeed from the controversial remarks in the notes quoted above. This circumstance may be taken as precluding the necessity of adducing examples here.[7] Suffice it to say that those so filling in the *subauditum* are entirely at one with the commentators already quoted in looking upon the citations as treated by the New Testament writers as of divine authority, it being, in their apprehension, all one in this regard whether the *subauditum* is conceived as ἡ γραφή or as ὁ θεός.

In the meantime, however, there has occasionally showed itself a tendency to treat these subjectless verbs more or less as true impersonals. Thus we read in Delitzsch's note on Heb. viii. 5: "For 'see,' saith He, i. e., ὁ θεός, or taking φησί impersonally (that is, without a definite subject), 'it is said' (i. e., in Scripture), (Bernhardy, 'Synt.,' 419)." So Kern on James iv. 6 comments: "λέγει here *impersonaliter*, instead of the foregoing λέγει ἡ γραφή"; and accordingly Beyschlag, in his recent commentary says: "to λέγει, ἡ γραφή is to be supplied, or it is to be taken with Kern impersonally." Similarly Godet on I Cor. vi. 16 says: "The subject of the verb φησίν, *says he*, may be either Adam or Moses, or Scripture, or God Himself, or finally, as is shown by Heinrici, the verb may be a simple formula of quotation like our '*It is said.*' This form is frequently found in Philo." [8] Some such usage as is here

[6] So also Wandel: "James then cites the passage Prov. iii. 24, in which we must simply supply 'God' to λέγει."

[7] As a single example, take, e. g., Oltramare, on Eph. iv. 8: "Διὸ λέγει, scil. ἡ γραφή: In accord with the extreme frequency with which the New Testament is cited, Paul often cites by saying simply λέγει (v. 14, Rom. xv. 10, II Cor. vi. 2, Gal. iii. 16; cf. Rom. iv. 3, x. 17, I Tim. v. 18), or φησί (I Cor. vi. 16; cf. Heb. viii. 15), or εἶπε (I Cor. xv. 27). He understands the subject, which is understood of itself, γραφή or θεός (see Winer, *Gr.*, p. 486)."

[8] Earlier still De Wette explained the phrase in a somewhat similar way. His note on Eph. v. 8 runs: "Old Testament support. διὸ λέγει] *therefore* (because

supposed may seem actually to occur in the common text of Wisdom xv. 12 [9] and II Cor. x. 10.[10] But in both passages the true reading is probably φασίν; in neither instance is it clear that, if φησίν be read, it has no subject implied in the context; if φησίν be read and taken as equivalent to φασίν it still is not purely indefinite; and in any case the instances are not parallel, inasmuch as in neither of these passages is it Scripture, or indeed any document, that is adduced.

The fact that a few very able commentators have taken this unlikely line of exposition would call for nothing more than this incidental remark, were not our attention attracted somewhat violently to it by the dogmatic tone and extremity of contention of a recent commentator who has adopted this opinion. We refer to Dr. T. K. Abbott's comment on Eph. iv. 8, in his contribution to "The International Critical Commentary." It runs to a considerable length, but as on this very account it opens out somewhat more fully than usual this

Christ gives the gifts and according to the presupposition that all that concerns Christ is predicted in the Old Testament *it is said*, [heisst es] (cf. Gal. iii. 16, I Cor. vi. 16 — a formula of citation (also v. 14) like Jas. iv. 6, Acts xiii. 35, Heb. x. 5, not elsewhere found in the apostle (cf., however, II Cor. vi. 17) . . ." And again on Eph. v. 14 we read: "διὸ λέγει] *therefore it is said* [heisst es] (in the Scriptures). Cf. iv. 8." He supposes that, in the latter passage, Paul confuses a customary application of Scripture with the very words of Scripture.

[9] Grimm's note on the passage runs: "Instead of the rec. reading, φησίν, Alex. Ephr., 157, 248, 296, Compl. have φασίν. Nevertheless the author may here return to the singular, referring to the potter before depicted (see the following verses). Or φησί may stand impersonally, in the sense of 'heisst es,' 'sagt man,' Win., p. 462, 6th ed.; Müller, 'Philo's Buch von d. Weltschöpfung,' p. 44." Cf. further, below, p. 316.

[10] φησίν is placed by Tischendorf, Tregelles and Westcott and Hort in their texts: while φασίν is read by Lachmann and placed in their margins by Tregelles and Westcott and Hort. The former is read by אDEFGKLP, etc., by the cursives, and by the Vulgate and Coptic versions, while the latter is the reading of B, Old Latin and Syriac. Heinrici pertinently remarks (in his own "Commentary," 1887): "The reading φασίν, which Lachmann accepts, is just as strongly witnessed by B, the Itala and Peschitto as φησίν (אDFG Vulg. Copt.) and it almost looks as if φησίν were a correction occasioned by the succeeding ὁ τοιοῦτος (against Meyer)." Alford, who continues to read φησίν equally pertinently on that hypothesis, remarks: "φησίν, taken by Winer (Ed. 6, § 58, 96), De Wette and Meyer as impersonal, 'heisst es,' *'men say';* but why should not the τις of ver. 7, and ὁ τοιοῦτος of ver. 11, be the subject?" See further below, p. 316.

rather unwonted view of the construction, we shall venture to quote it *in extenso*. Dr. Abbott says:

"Διὸ λέγει. 'Wherefore it saith' = 'it is said.' If any substantive is to be supplied, it is ἡ γραφή; but the verb may well be taken impersonally, just as in colloquial English one may often hear: 'it says' or the like. Many expositors supply, however, ὁ Θεός. Meyer even says, 'Who says it is obvious of itself, namely, God, whose word the Scripture is.[11] Similarly Alford [12] and Ellicott.[13] If it were St. Paul's habit to introduce quotations from the Old Testament, by whomsoever spoken in the original text, with the formula ὁ Θεὸς λέγει, then this supplement here might be defended. But it is not. In quoting he sometimes says λέγει, frequently ἡ γραφὴ λέγει, at other times Δαβὶδ λέγει, 'Ησαΐας λέγει. There is not a single instance in which ὁ Θεός is either expressed or implied as the subject, except where in the original context God is the speaker, as in Rom. ix. 15. Even when that is the case

[11] [See above, p. 287.]

[12] ["*He* (viz., God, whose word the Scriptures are. See reff. [i. e., Rom. xii. 3, II Cor. x. 13, iv. 13, 16 = Paul only], and notes: not merely 'it,' *es heisst*, as, De Wette, *al.*: nor ἡ γραφή: had it been the subject it must have been expressed, as in Rom. iv. 3, ix. 17, *al.*) *says* (viz., Ps. lxviii. 18, see below: not in some Christian hymn, as Flatt and Storr — which would not agree with λέγει, nor with the treatment of the citation, which is plainly regarded as carrying the weight of Scripture.")]

[13] ["'*He saith*,' *sc.* ὁ θεός,, not ἡ γραφή. This latter nominative is several times inserted by St. Paul (Rom. iv. 3, ix. 17, x. 11, Gal. iv. 30, I Tim. v. 18), but is not therefore to be regularly supplied whenever there is an ellipsis (Bos, *Ellips.*, p. 54) without reference to the nature of the passages. The surest and in fact only guide is the context; when that affords no certain hint, we fall back upon the natural subject, ὁ θεός, whose words the Scriptures are; see notes on Gal. iii. 16." See further above, p. 287. At Gal. iii. 16, Ellicott had said: "'*He saith not*;' not ἡ γραφή (Bos, *Ellips.*, p. 54), as in Rom. xv. 10 — where the subst. is supplied from γέγραπται, ver. 9 — or τὸ πνεῦμα (Rück., Winer, *Gr.*, § 39, 1), which appears arbitrary, but the natural subject ὁ θεός, as in Eph. iv. 8, v. 14, and (φησί) I Cor. vi. 16, Heb. viii. 5. So apparently Syr., which here inserts *illi* after λέγει." The passage referred to in Bos (London ed. of 1825, pp. 57, 58) is as follows: "In the New Testament, where the Scripture of the Old Testament is cited, φησί or λέγει often occurs with ἡ γραφή understood — a word which actually stands in other passages: I Cor. vi. 16, Eph. v. 14, Gal. iii. 16. The same thing occurs in the Greek fathers. Marcus Eremita, in his earlier aphorisms, No. 106, οὐδεὶς, φησί, στρατευόμενος ἐμπλέκεται ταῖς τοῦ βίου πραγματείαις, 'No one, says (the Scripture, II Tim. ii. 4) going a-soldiering is entangled in the affairs of this life.' So, No. 134: φησί γὰρ, ὁ ὑψῶν ἑαυτὸν ταπεινωθήσεται, 'For, says (Scripture), he that exalteth himself shall be brought low.' There may be also understood *pro re nata* εὐαγγελιστής, προφητής, ἀπόστολος: but the other is more general and suits excellently. Schoettg."]

he does not hesitate to use a different subject, as in Rom. x. 19, 20:
'Moses saith,' 'Isaiah is very bold, and saith'; Rom. ix. 17, 'The
Scripture saith to Pharaoh.'

"This being the case, we are certainly not justified in forcing upon
the apostle here and in chap. v. 14 a form of expression consistent only
with the extreme view of verbal inspiration. When Meyer (followed
by Alford and Ellicott) says that ἡ γραφή must not be supplied unless
it is given by the context, the reply is obvious, namely, that, as above
stated, ἡ γραφὴ λέγει does, in fact, often occur, and therefore the
apostle might have used it here, whereas ὁ Θεὸς λέγει does not occur
(except in cases unlike this), and we have reason to believe could not
be used by St. Paul here. It is some additional confirmation of this
that both here and in chap. v. 14 (if that is a Biblical quotation) he
does not hesitate to make important alterations. This is the view taken
by Braune, Macpherson, Moule; the latter, however, adding that for
St. Paul 'the word of the Scripture and the word of its Author are
convertible terms.'

"It is objected that although φησί is used impersonally, λέγει is
not. The present passage and chap. v. 14 [14] are enough to prove the
usage for St. Paul, and there are other passages in his Epistles where
this sense is at least applicable; cf. Rom. xv. 10, where λέγει is parallel
to γέγραπται in ver. 9; Gal. iii. 16, where it corresponds to ἐρρήθησαν.
But, in fact, the impersonal use of φησί in Greek authors is quite different, namely = φασί, 'they say' (so II Cor. x. 10). Classical authors
had no opportunity of using λέγει as it is used here, as they did not
possess any collection of writings which could be referred to as ἡ
γραφή, or by any like word. They could say: ὁ νόμος λέγει and τὸ
λεγόμενον."

It is not, it will be observed, the fact that Dr. Abbott decides against the *subauditum*, ὁ Θεός, in these passages, which
calls for remark. As he himself points out, many others have
been before him in this. It is the extremity of his opinion that
first of all attracts attention. For it is to be noticed that,
though he sometimes speaks as if he understood an implied
ἡ γραφή, or some like term, as the subject of λέγει, that is not
his real contention. What he proposes is to take the verb
wholly indefinitely — as equivalent to "it is said," as if the

[14] [The text actually has "ver. 14," but we venture to correct the obvious
slip.]

source of the quotation were unimportant and its authority insignificant. This interpretation of his proposal is placed beyond doubt by his remarks on chap. v. 14. There we read:

"Διὸ λέγει. 'Wherefore it is said.' It is generally held that this formula introduces a quotation from canonical Scripture. . . . The difficulties disappear when we recognize that λέγει need not be taken to mean ὁ Θεὸς λέγει — an assertion which has been shown in iv. 8 to be untenable. It means, 'it says,' or 'it is said,' and the quotation may probably be from some liturgical formula or hymn — a supposition with which its rhythmical character agrees very well. . . . Theodoret mentions this opinion. . . . Stier adopts a similar view, but endeavors to save the supposed limitation of the use of λέγει by saying that in the Church the Spirit speaks. As there are in the Church prophets and prophetic speakers and poets, so there are liturgical expressions and hymns which are holy words. Comparing vv. 18, 19, Col. iii. 16, it may be said that the apostle is here giving us an example of this self-admonition by new spiritual songs."

So extreme an opinion, as we have already hinted, naturally finds, however, little support in the commentators, even in those quoted to buttress it, — of course, in its fundamental point. Braune says: "We must naturally supply ἡ γραφή, the Scripture, with λέγει, 'saith,' (James iv. 6, Rom. xv. 10, Gal. iii. 16, I Cor. vi. 16: φησίν), and not ὁ θεός (Meyer, Schenkel [15]), or ὁ λέγων (Bleek: the writer)": to which Dr. M. T. Riddle, his translator, however, adds: "The fact that Paul frequently supplies ἡ γραφή (Rom. iv. 3, ix. 17, x. 11, Gal. iv. 30, I Tim. v. 18) is against Braune's view; for in some of these passages there is a reason for its insertion (see "Romans," p. 314), and as the Scriptures are God's Word (Meyer), the natural aim and obvious subject is ὁ θεός. So Alford, Ellicott and most." Moule's comment runs: "Wherefore he saith] Or it, i. e., the Scripture, saith. St. Paul's usage

[15] ["With λέγει God is to be supplied as subject. From this way of adducing it, it is already clear that the cited words cannot be taken from a Christian hymn in use in the Church at Ephesus (Storr, Flatt), but must belong to the sacred, God-given Scripture." Accordingly at v. 14 he says: "In accordance with the formula (λέγει, chap. iv. 8) usual in adducing Scripture, it can scarcely be doubtful that the apostle intended to cite an Old Testament passage."]

in quotation leaves the subject of the verb undetermined here and in similar cases (see, e. g., chap. v. 14 [16]). For him the word of the Scripture and the word of its author are convertible terms." Macpherson alone, of those appealed to by Dr. Abbott, supports, in a somewhat carelessly written note, the indefinite interpretation put forward by Dr. Abbott, — being misled apparently by remarks of Lightfoot's and Westcott's. His comment runs:

"A very simple quotation formula is here employed, the single word λέγει. It is also similarly used (chap. v. 14; II Cor. vi. 2; Gal. iii. 16; Rom. xv. 10).[17] This word is frequently employed in the fuller formula, *The Scripture saith*, λέγει ἡ γραφή (Rom. iv. 3, x. 11, xi. 2; Jas. ii. 23, etc.); or the name of the writer of the particular scripture, Esaias, David, the Holy Spirit, the law (Rom. xv. 12; Acts xiii. 35; Heb. iii. 7; I Cor. xiii. 34, etc.).[18] Of λέγει, φησί, εἴρηκε, and similar words thus used, Winer ("Grammar," p. 656, 1882) says that probably in no instance are they impersonal in the minds of the New Testament writers, but that the subject, ὁ θεός, is somewhere in the context, and is to be supplied.[19] On the contrary, Lightfoot, in his note on Gal. iii. 16, remarks that λέγει, like the Attic φησί, seems to be used impersonally, the nominative being lost sight of. In our passage we have no nominative in the context which we can supply, and it seems better to render the phrase impersonally, *It is said*. The same word is used very frequently in the Epistle to the Hebrews, but always with God or Christ understood from the immediate context. Westcott very correctly remarks (p. 457) that the use of the formula in Eph. iv. 8, v. 14, seems to be of a different kind." [20]

[16] The comment there is simply: "he *saith*] or possibly *it* (the Scripture) *saith*." [17] [The parenthetical marks should doubtless be removed.]

[18] [This sentence seems formally incomplete; probably "is frequently employed" is to be supplied from the preceding clause.]

[19] [This scarcely gives a complete view of Winer's remark: he says that "the subject ὁ θεός) is *usually* contained in the context, either directly *or indirectly*," and proceeds to adduce cases of ellipsis.]

[20] [What Westcott apparently says is not that "the two passages in the Epistle to the Ephesians (iv. 8, v. 14, διὸ λέγει) appear to be different in kind" from the usage of Hebrews, but from the cases in the rest of the New Testament, where God is the subject of λέγει indeed, but "the reference is to words directly spoken by God." He possibly means, "different in kind" from the usage both of Hebrews and of the rest of the New Testament: but he does not seem to say this directly. See post, p. 305.]

Outside of these commentators quoted by himself, however, Prof. Abbott's extreme view has (as has, indeed, already incidentally appeared) the powerful support of Lightfoot and Heinrici. The former expresses his opinion not only in his note on Gal. iii. 16, to which Macpherson refers, but more fully and argumentatively in his note on I Cor. vi. 16 printed in his posthumous " Notes on the Epistles of St. Paul." In the former of these places he says:

"οὐ λέγει seems to be used impersonally, like the Attic φησί in quoting legal documents, the nominative being lost sight of. If so, we need not inquire whether ὁ θεός or ἡ γραφή is to be understood. Comp. λέγει, Rom. xv. 10, Eph. iv. 8, v. 14; and φησίν, I Cor. vi. 16, II Cor. x. 10 (v. l)."

In the latter, speaking more at large "as to the authority assigned to the passage" quoted by St. Paul, he says:

"What are we to understand by φησίν? Is ὁ θεός to be supplied or ἡ γραφή? To this question it is safest to reply that we cannot decide. The fact is that, like λέγει, φησίν when introducing a quotation seems to be used impersonally. This usage is common in Biblical Greek (λέγει, Rom. xv. 10, Gal. iii. 16, Eph. iv. 8, v. 14; φησίν, Heb. viii. 5, II Cor. x. 10 (v. l.), more common in classical Greek. Alford, after Meyer, objects to rendering φησίν impersonally here, as contrary to St. Paul's usage. But the only other occurrence of the phrase in St. Paul is II Cor. x. 10, where he is not introducing Scripture, but the objections of human critics and of more than one critic. If then φησίν be read there at all, it must be impersonal. The apostle's analogous use of λέγει points to the same conclusion. In Eph. v. 14 it introduces a quotation which is certainly not in Scripture, and apparently belonged to an early Christian hymn. We gather therefore that St. Paul's usage does not suggest any restriction here to ὁ θεός or ἡ γραφή. But we cannot doubt from the context that the quotation is meant to be authoritative."

In his own commentary on I Corinthians (1880), Heinrici writes as follows:

"To φησί, just as to λέγει (II Cor. vi. 2, Gal. iii. 16) nothing at all is to be supplied, but like *inquit* it stands, sometimes as the introduc-

tion to an objection (II Cor. x. 10, where Holsten refers to Bentley on
Horat., *Serm.*, i, 4, 78), sometimes as a general formula of citation.
It is especially often used in the latter sense by Philo, in the quotation
of Scripture passages, and by Arrian-Epictetus, who supplies many
most interesting parallels to the Pauline forms of speech. Schweig-
häuser, in his Index, under φησί, remarks of it: nec enim semper in
proferenda objectione locum habet illa formula, verum etiam in
citando exemplo ad id quod agitur pertinente. J. G. Müller (*Philo
the Jew's Book on the Creation*, Berlin, 1841, p. 44) says that φησί,
after the example of Plato (?), became gradually among the Hellenistic
Jews the standing formula of citation."

In his edition of Meyer's "Commentary on I Corinthians"
(eighth edition, 1896), this note reappears in this form:

"φησίν). Who? According to the usual view, God, whose words the
sayings of the Scripture are, even when they, like Gen. ii. 24 through
Adam, are spoken through another. Winer, 7 § 58, 9, 486: Buttmann,
117. But the impersonal sense '*es heisst*,' '*inquit*,' lies nearer the
Pauline usage; he coincides in this with Arrian-Epictetus and Philo,
with whom φησί sometimes introduces an objection, sometimes is the
customary formula of citation. Cf. II Cor. x. 10, vi. 2, I Cor. xv. 27,
Eph. iv. 8; Winer, as above; Müller, in Philo, *De op. mund.*, 44;
Heinrici, i. 181. In accordance with this, are the other supplements of
subject — ἡ γραφή or τὸ πνεῦμα (Rückert) — to be estimated."

Even in the extremity of his contention, therefore, Dr. Abbott, it seems, is not without support — on the philological
side, at least — in previous commentators of the highest rank.

He himself does not seem, however, quite clear in his own
mind: and his confusion of both considerations and commentators which make for the fundamentally diverse positions
that there is to be supplied with λέγει some such subject as
ἡ γραφή, and that there is nothing at all to be supplied but
the word is to be taken with entire indefiniteness, is indicatory of the main thing that calls for remark in Dr. Abbott's
note. For, why should this confusion take place? It is quite
evident that in interpreting the phrase the fundamental distinction lies between the view which supposes that a subject
to λέγει is so implied as to be suggested either by the con-

text or by the mind of the reader from the nature of the case, and that which takes λέγει as a case of true impersonal usage, of entirely indefinite subject. It is a minor difference among the advocates of the first of these views, which separates them into two parties — those which would supply as subject ὁ θεός, and those which would supply ἡ γραφή. That one of these subdivisions of the first class of views should be violently torn from its true comradeship and confused with the second view, betrays a preoccupation on Dr. Abbott's part, when dealing with this passage, with considerations not of purely exegetical origin. He is for the moment less concerned with ascertaining the meaning of the apostle than with refuting a special interpretation of his words: and therefore everything which stands opposed in any measure to the obnoxious interpretation appears to him to be "on his side." Put somewhat brusquely, this is as much as to say that Dr. Abbott is in this note dominated by dogmatic prejudice.

There do not lack other indications of this fact. The most obtrusive of them is naturally the language — scarcely to be called perfectly calm — with which the second paragraph of the note opens: "We are certainly not justified in forcing upon the apostle here and in chap. v. 14 a form of expression consistent only with the extreme view of verbal inspiration." Certainly not. But because we chance not to like "the extreme view of verbal inspiration," are we justified in forbidding the apostle to use a form of expression consistent only with it, and forcing upon him some other form of expression which we may consider consistent with a view of inspiration which we like better? Would it not be better to permit the apostle to choose his own form of expression and confine ourselves, as expositors, to ascertaining from his form of expression what view of inspiration lay in his mind, rather than seek to force his hand into consistency with our preconceived ideas? The whole structure of the note evinces, however, that it was not written in this purely expository spirit. Thus only can be explained a certain exaggerated dogmatism in its language, as if doubt were to be silenced by decision of manner if not by decisiveness of evidence. So also probably is to be explained a certain narrowness in the appeal to usage — that rock on which much factitious exegesis splits. Only, it is intimated, in case "it were St. Paul's habit to introduce quotations from the Old Testament, by whomso-ever spoken in the original text, with the formula ὁ θεὸs λέγει," "could this supplement here be defended." One asks in astonishment whether St. Paul really could make known his estimate of Scripture as the very voice of God which might naturally be quoted with the formula "God says," and so render the occurrence of that formula occasionally in his writings no matter of surprise, only by a habitual use of this exact formula in quoting Scripture. And one notes with-out surprise that the narrowness of Dr. Abbott's rule for the adduction of usage supplies no bar to his practice when he is arguing "on the other side." At the opening of the very next paragraph we read, "It is objected that although φησί is used impersonally, λέγει is not": and to this the answer is returned, "The present passage and chap. v. 14 are sufficient to prove the usage for St. Paul"; with the supplement, "And there are other passages in his epistles where this sense is at least applicable"; and further, "But in fact, the impersonal use of φησί in Greek authors is quite different." One fancies Dr. Abbott must have had a grim controversial smile upon his features when he wrote that last clause, which pleads that the meaning assigned to λέγει here is absolutely unexampled in Greek literature, not only for λέγει but even for φησί, as a reason for accepting it for λέγει here! But apart from this remarkable instance of skill in marshaling adverse facts — a skill not unexampled elsewhere in the course of this note, as any one who will take the trouble to examine the proof-texts adduced in it will quickly learn — might not the advo-cates of the supplement, ὁ θεός, say equally that "the present passage and chap. v. 14 are sufficient to prove the usage for St. Paul, and there are other passages in his epistles where this sense is at least applicable." And might they not support this statement with better proof-texts than those adduced by Dr. Abbott, or indeed with the same with better right; as well as with a more applicable supplementary remark than the one with which he really subverts his whole reasoning — such as this, for example, that elsewhere, in the New Testament, as for instance in the Epistle to the Hebrews, the usage contended for undoubtedly occurs, and a satisfactory basis is laid for it in the whole attitude of the entire body of New Testament writers, inclusive of Paul, toward the Old Testament? Certainly, reasoning so one-sided and dominated by preconceived opinions so blinding is thoroughly inconclusive. The note is, indeed, an eminent example of that form of argumentation which, to invert a phrase of Omar Khayyam's, "goes out at the same door at which it came in": and even though its contention should prove sound, can itself add nothing to the grounds on which we embrace it. At best it may serve as the starting-point of a fresh investigation into the proper interpretation of the phrase with which it deals.

For such a fresh investigation we should need to give our attention particularly to two questions. The first would inquire into the light thrown by Paul's method of introducing quotations from the Old Testament, upon his estimate of the text of the Old Testament, — with a view to determining whether it need cause surprise to find him adducing it with such a formula as "God says." Subsidiary to this it might be inquired whether it is accurate to say that "there is not a single instance in which ὁ θεός is either expressed or implied as the subject, except where in the original context God is the speaker," and further, if Paul's usage elsewhere can be accurately so described, whether that fact will warrant us in denying such an instance to exist in Eph. iv. 8. The second question would inquire into the general usage of the subjectless λέγει or φησί in and out of the New Testament, with a view to discovering what light may be thrown by it upon the interpretation of the passages in question. It might be incidentally asked in this connection whether it is a complete account to give of φησί in profane Greek to say that the "impersonal use of φησί in Greek authors is quite different from that of the New Testament, inasmuch as with them φησί = φασί, 'they say.'"

It is really somewhat discouraging at this late date to find it treated as still an open question, how Paul esteemed the written words of the Old Testament. And it brings us, as the French say, something akin to stupefaction, when Dr. Abbott goes further and uses language concerning Paul's attitude toward the Old Testament text which implies that Paul habitually distinguished, in point of authority, between those passages "where in the original context God is the speaker" and the rest of the volume, so that "we have reason to believe" that the formula ὁ θεὸς λέγει "could not be used by Paul" in introducing Scriptural language not recorded as spoken by God in the original context. He even suggests, indeed, that Paul shows an underlying doubt as to the Divine source of even the words attributed to God in the Old Testament text — "not hesitating to use a different subject" when quoting them, "as in Rom. x. 19, 20, 'Moses saith,' 'Isaiah is very bold and saith'; Rom. ix. 17, 'The Scripture saith to Pharaoh'" — and deals with the text of other portions with a freedom which exhibits his little respect for them — "not hesitating to make important alterations" in them. It would seem to require a dogmatic prejudice of the very first order to blind one to a fact so obvious as that with Paul "Scripture," as such, is conceived everywhere as the authoritative declaration of the truth and will of God — of which fact, indeed, no better evidence can be needed than the very texts quoted by Dr. Abbott in a contrary sense.

For, when Paul, in Rom. ix. 15, supports his abhorrent rejection of the supposition that there may be unrighteousness with God, with the divine declaration taken from Ex. xxxiii. 19, introduced with the formula, "For he" — that is, as Dr. Abbott recognizes, God — "saith to Moses," and then immediately, in Rom. ix. 17, supports the teaching of this declaration with the further word of God taken from Ex. ix. 16, introduced with the formula, "For the Scripture saith unto Pharaoh" — the one thing which is thrown into a relief above all others is that, with Paul, "God saith" and "Scripture saith" are synonymous terms, so synonymous in his habitual thought that he could not only range the two together in consecutive clauses, but use the second in a manner in which, taken literally, it is meaningless and can convey an appropriate sense only when translated back into its equivalent of "God saith." The present tense in both formulas, moreover, advises us that, despite the fact that in both instances they are words spoken by God which are cited, it is rather as part of that Scripture which to Paul's thinking is the ever-present and ever-speaking word of God that they are adduced. It is not as words which God once spoke (εἶπεν, LXX.) to Moses that the former passage is here adduced, but as living words still speaking to us — it is not as words Moses was once commanded to speak to Pharaoh that the second is here adduced, but as words recorded in the ever-living Scripture for our admonition upon whom the ends of the world have come. They are thus not assigned to Scripture in order to lower their authority: but rather as a mark of their abiding authority. And similarly when in that catena of quotations in Rom. x. 16–21, we read at ver. 19, "first Moses saith," and then at ver. 20, "and Isaiah is very bold and saith," both adducing words of God — the implication is not that Paul looks upon them as something less than the words of God and so cites them by the names of these human authors; but that it is all one to him to say, "God says," and "Moses says," or "Isaiah says": and therefore in this catena of quotations — in which are included four, not two, quotations — all the citations are treated as alike authoritative, though some are in the original context words of God and others (ver. 16) words of the prophet — and though some are adduced by the name of the prophet and some without assignment to any definitely named human source. The same implication, again, underlies the fact that

in the catena of quotations on Rom. xv. 9 *seq.*, the first is
introduced by καθὼς γέγραπται, the next two by καὶ πάλιν
λέγει and καὶ πάλιν, and the last by καὶ πάλιν 'Ησαΐας λέγει —
the first being from Ps. lxxviii. 50, the second from Deut.
xxxii. 43, the third from Ps. cxvii. 1, and only the last from
Isaiah — Isa. xi. 10: clearly it is all one to the mind of Paul
how Scripture is adduced — it is the fact that it is *Scripture*
that is important. So also it is no more true that in Gal. iii.
16, the λέγει "corresponds to ἐρρήθησαν" of the immediately
preceding context, than that it stands in line with the "and
the Scripture foreseeing that God would justify the Gentiles
by faith, preached the Gospel beforehand unto Abraham"
of iii. 8 — a thing which the Scripture as such certainly did
not do; and with the "for it is written" of iii. 10 and iii. 13,
and the unheralded quotations of the Scriptures as unquestioned authority of iii. 11 and iii. 12; and with the general
appeal in iii. 22 to the teaching of Scripture as a whole as
the sole testimony needed: the effect of the whole being to
evince in the clearest manner that to Paul the whole text
of Scripture, inclusive of Gen. xii. 3, Deut. xxvii. 26, Hab.
ii. 4, Lev. xviii. 5, and Gen. xxii. 18, was as such the living
word of the living God profitable to all ages alike for divine
instruction.

We need not go, indeed, beyond the first sentence of this
Epistle to the Romans from which all but one of Dr. Abbott's
citations are drawn, to learn Paul's conception of Scripture
as the crystallized voice of God. There he declares himself to
have been "separated unto the gospel of God which he promised afore by his prophets in the Holy Scriptures" (Rom. i.
2). Dr. George T. Purves, in a singularly well-considered and
impressive paper on "St. Paul and Inspiration," printed in
The Presbyterian and Reformed Review for January, 1893,[21]
justly draws out the meaning of this compressed statement
thus:

"Not only did Moses and the prophets speak from God, but the
sacred Scriptures themselves were in some way composed under divine

[21] Vol. iv, p. 13.

control. He not only affirms with Peter that 'moved by the Holy Ghost, *men* spake from God,' but that '*the Scriptures themselves are inspired by God.*' Paul plainly recognizes the human authorship of the books, and quotes Moses and David and Isaiah as speaking therein. But not only *through them,* but *in these books* of theirs did God also speak. Many readers notice the first part of Paul's statement, but not the second. God spake 'through the prophets *in the Holy Scriptures.*'"

This emphasis on the *written* Scriptures as themselves the product of a divine activity, making them as such the divine voice to us, is characteristic of the whole treatment of Scripture by Paul (I Cor. x. 11, Rom. xv. 4, iv. 23, I Cor. ix. 10, iv. 6): and it is thoroughly accordant with the point of view so exhibited, that he explicitly declares, not of the writers of Scripture, but of the sacred writings themselves, that they are theopneustic — breathed out, or breathed into by God (II Tim. iii. 16). For he applies this epithet not to "every prophet," but to "every *Scripture*" — that is, says Dr. Purves, to "the whole collection to which he had just referred as the 'sacred writings,' and all their parts": these *writings* are theopneustic. "By their inspiration, he evidently meant," continues Dr. Purves justly, "that, as writings, they were so composed under God's particular direction that both in substance and in form they were the special utterances of His mind and will.'

It could be nothing more than an accident if Paul, under the dominance of such a conception of Scripture, has nowhere happened to adduce from it a passage, taken out of a context in which God is not expressly made in the Old Testament narrative itself the speaker, with the formula, ὁ θεὸς λέγει, expressed or implied. If no instance of such an adduction occurs, it is worth while to note that fact, to be sure, as one of the curious accidents of literary usage; but as there is no reason to doubt that such a formula would be entirely natural on the lips of Paul, so there is no propriety in calling it impossible in Paul, or even in erecting a distinction between him and other New Testament writers on the ground that they do and he does not quote Scripture by such a

formula. As a matter of fact, the distinction suggested between passages in Scripture "where in the original context
God is the speaker" and passages where He is not the speaker
— as if the one could be cited with a "God says," and the
other not, — is foreign to Paul's conception and usage, as has
abundantly appeared already: so that whatever passages of
the former kind occur — "as in Rom. ix. 15," says Dr. Abbott — are really passages in which Scripture is quoted with
a "God says." It cannot be held to be certain, moreover, that
passages do not occur in which the "God says" introduces
words not ascribed to God in the original context — so long,
at least, as it is not obvious that "God" is not the *subauditum*
in passages like Acts xiii. 35, Rom. xv. 10, Gal. iii. 16. It is
no doubt, however, also worth observing that it is equally
matter of fact, that it is rather to the Epistle to the Hebrews
than to those that bear the name of Paul that we shall need
to go to find a body of explicit instances of the usage in
question. This is, as we have said, an interesting fact of
literary usage, but it is not to be pressed into an indication
of a divergent point of view toward "Scripture" between the
Epistle to the Hebrews and the epistles that bear Paul's
name.

Even Dr. Westcott seems, to be sure, so to press it. In
the interesting dissertation "On the Use of the Old Testament in the Epistle," which he has appended to his "Commentary on the Epistle to the Hebrews," he sets out in some
detail the facts that bear on the mode in which that epistle
cites the Old Testament:

"The quotations," he tells us, "are without exception made
anonymously. There is no mention anywhere of the name of the
writer (iv. 7 is no exception to the rule). God is presented as the
speaker through the person of the prophet, except in the one place
where He is directly addressed (ii. 6). . . . In two places the words are
attributed to Christ. . . . In two other places the Holy Spirit specially
is named as the speaker. . . . But it is worthy of notice that in each
of these two cases the words are also quoted as the words of God
(iv. 7, viii. 8). This assignment of the written word to God, as the

Inspirer of the message, is most remarkable when the words spoken by the prophet in his own person are treated as divine words — as words spoken by Moses: i. 6 (Deut. xxxii. 43); iv. 4, comp. vv. 5, 7, 8 (Gen. ii. 2); x. 30 (Deut. xxxii. 36); and by Isaiah: ii. 13 (Isa. viii. 17 f), comp. also xiii. 5 (Deut. xxxi. 6). Generally it must be observed that no difference is made between the word spoken and the word written. For us and for all ages the record is the voice of God. The record is the voice of God, and as a necessary consequence the record is itself living. . . . The constant use of the present tense in quotations emphasizes this truth: ii. 11, iii. 7, xii. 5. Comp. xii. 26." [22]

Every careful student will recognize this at once as a very clear and very true statement of the attitude of the author of the Epistle to the Hebrews toward the Old Testament. But we cannot help thinking that Dr. Westcott overshoots the mark when he throws it into strong contrast with the attitude of the rest of the New Testament writers to the Old Testament. When he says, for example: "There is nothing really parallel to this general mode of quotation in the other books of the New Testament" — meaning apparently to suggest, as the subsequent context indicates, that the author of this Epistle exhibits an identification in his mind of the written text of the Scriptures with the voice of God which is foreign to the other writers of the New Testament — he would seem to have attached far too great significance to what is, after all, so far as it is real, nothing more than one of those surface differences of individual usage which are always observable among writers who share the same fundamental view-point, or even in different treatises from the same hand. Entirely at one in looking upon the Scriptures as nothing less than τὰ λόγια τοῦ θεοῦ (Rom. iii. 2, Heb. v. 12 [23]) — in all their parts and phrases the utterance of God — the epistles that bear the name of Paul and this epistle yet chance to differ in the prevalent mode in which these "oracles" are adduced: the one in its formulas of citation emphasizing the sole fact that they are "oracles" it is quoting, the others,

---

[22] *Op. cit.*, pp. 285, 286, 287.

[23] Westcott, *in loc.*, "it seems more natural to refer it to the collected writings of the Old Testament."

that these "oracles" lie before them in *written* form. Let the
fact of this difference, of course, be noted: but let it not be
overstrained and, as if it were the sole relevant fact in the
field of view, made to bear the whole weight of a theory of
the relations of the two in their attitude toward Scripture.

Impossible as such a procedure should be in any case, it
becomes doubly so when we note the extremely narrow and
insecure basis for the conclusion drawn, which is offered by
the differences in usage adduced between Hebrews and the
rest of the New Testament — which means for us primarily
the epistles that bear the name of Paul. Says Dr. Westcott
in immediate sequence to what we have quoted from him:

"There is nothing really parallel to this general mode of quotation
in the other books of the New Testament. Where the word λέγει occurs
elsewhere, it is for the most part combined either with the name of the
prophet or with 'Scripture': e.g., Rom. x. 16, Ἡσαΐας λέγει; x. 19,
Μωυσῆς λέγει; xi. 9, Δαυεὶδ λέγει; iv. 3, ἡ γραφὴ λέγει; ix. 17, λέγει ἡ
γραφή, etc. Where God is the subject, as is rarely the case, the reference is to words directly spoken by God: II Cor. vi. 2, λέγει γὰρ (ὁ
θεός); Rom. ix. 15, τῷ Μωυσεῖ λέγει; ix. 25, ἐν τῷ Ὡσηὲ λέγει. Comp.
Rom. xv. 9–12 (γέγραπται . . . λέγει . . . . Ἡσαΐας λέγει). The two passages in the Epistle to the Ephesians (iv. 8, v. 14, διὸ λέγει) appear to
be different in kind."

The last remark is apparently intended to exclude Eph. iv.
8 and v. 14 from consideration.[24] The immediately preceding
one seems intended to suggest that the subject to be supplied
to λέγει in Rom. xv. 10, which carries with it also Rom. xv.
11, is ἡ γραφή; if we rather supply with Sanday-Headlam
θεός, this citation would afford an instance to the contrary.
Other cases similar to this, e. g., Acts xiii. 35 [25] and (with the

[24] What is meant may possibly be that these two passages in Ephesians are
analogous neither to the usage of Hebrews nor to that of the rest of the New
Testament, but stand out by themselves. In that case Dr. Westcott probably
means to take them as instances of the indefinite use of λέγει. Cf. above, p. 293.

[25] Cf. Meyer's note: "λέγει], the subject is necessarily that of εἴρηκεν, ver. 34,
and so, neither David (Bengel, Heinrichs and others), nor the Scriptures (Herrmann), but *God*, although Ps. xvi. 10 contains David's words addressed to God.
But David is considered as the interpreter of God, who has put the prayer into
his mouth. Comp. on Matt. xix. 5."

parallel φησί) I Cor. vi. 16,[26] are simply passed by in silence. If such cases were considered, perhaps the induction would be different.

It is possible, on the other hand, that the usage of the Epistle to the Hebrews also is conceived by Dr. Westcott a shade too narrowly. It scarcely seems sufficient to say of ii. 6, for example, that this passage is not an exception to the more general usage of the Epistle inasmuch as it is "the one place where God is directly addressed" — and is therefore not ascribed to Him, but to "some one somewhere." According to Dr. Westcott's own exposition,[27] we have in i. 10 also words addressed *to* God and yet cited as spoken *by* God, and in a number of passages words spoken *of* God nevertheless cited as spoken *by* Him; and, in a word, the fundamental principle of the mode of quotation used by this Epistle is that the words of Scripture as such are the living words of God and are cited as such indifferently — whether in the original context spoken by Him or by another of Him, to Him, or apart from Him. In any event, therefore, the citation in the present passage by the formula "someone hath somewhere borne witness" is an exception to the general usage of the Epistle, and evidences that the author of it, though conceiving Scripture as such as a body of divine oracles, did not really lose sight of the fact that these oracles were delivered through men, and might therefore be cited on occasion as the deliverances of these men. In other words, here is a mode of citation of the order affirmed to be charac-

---

[26] Cf. Meyer's note: "φησίν], who it is that says it, is self-evident, namely, *God*, the utterances of Scripture being His words, even when they may be spoken through another, as Gen. ii. 24 was through Adam. Comp. on Matt. xix. 5. Similarly Gal. iii. 16, Eph. iv. 8, Heb. viii. 5, I Cor. xv. 27. Ἡ γραφή, which is usually supplied here, would need to be suggested by the context, as in Rom. xv. 10. Rückert arbitrarily prefers τὸ πνεῦμα." "To take it *impersonally, 'it is said'* as in II Cor. x. 10, according to the well-known usage in the classics, would be without warrant from any other instance of Paul's quotations from Scripture. Comp. Winer, *Gr.*, p. 486 [English translation, 656]; Buttmann, *Neut. Gr.*, p. 117 [English translation, 134]."

[27] For he supposes the words quoted in i. 10 to be addressed not to Christ, but to God: "God through His Spirit so speaks in the Psalmist that words not directly addressed to Christ find their fulfillment in Him."

teristic of the letters bearing the name of Paul. It is at least
not beyond the limits of possibility that another such instance occurs in iv. 7: "saying in David." No doubt, "in
David," may be taken here, as Dr. Westcott takes it, as
meaning "in the person of David," i. e., through his prophetic utterances; but it seems, on the whole, much more
natural to take it as parallel to ἐν τῇ βίβλῳ Μωυσέως (Mark xii.
26), ἐν τῷ Ὡσηέ (Rom. ix. 25), and as meaning "in the book
of David "[28] — exhibiting the consciousness of the author
that he is quoting not merely "God," but God in the *written
Scripture* — written by the hand of men. This is the more
worth insisting on that it is really not absolutely certain that
the subject of the λέγων here is immediately "God" at all.
There is no subject expressed either for it or the ὁρίζει on
which it depends; and when we go back in the context for
an express subject it eludes us, and we shall not find it until
we arrive at the "even as the Holy Ghost saith" of iii. 7.
From that point on, we have a series of quotations, introduced, quite in the manner of Philo, with formulæ which
puzzle us as to their reference — whether to God, who is the
general subject of the whole context, or to Scripture, conceived as the voice of God (e. g., iii. 15, ἐν τῷ λέγεσθαι —
by whom? God? or "the Scripture" already quoted? iv. 4,
εἴρηκεν — who? God? or Scripture? iv. 5, καὶ ἐν τούτῳ πάλιν).
Something of the same kind meets us in the eighth chapter,
where quite in the manner of Philo, we begin at ver. 5:
"Even as Moses was oracularly warned when about to make
the tabernacle, for 'see,' φησίν, etc." and proceed at ver. 8,
with a subjectless λέγει, to close with ver. 13 with an equally
subjectless ἐν τῷ λέγειν. It certainly is not obvious that the
subject to be supplied to these three verbs is "God" rather
than "oracular Scripture."

One can but feel that with a due regard to these two
classes of neglected facts, a somewhat broader comparison of
the usage of the Epistle to the Hebrews and that of those

[28] So (according to Lünemann), Dindorf, Schulz, Böhme, Bleek, Ebrard
Alford, Woerner: add Lowrie, Riggenbach.

letters that bear the name of Paul would not leave an impression of such sharp and indubitable divergence in point of view as Dr. Westcott's statement is apt to suggest. In the Epistle to the Hebrews, the verb λέγω is used to introduce citations, (1) with *expressed* subject: ii. 6, "But someone somewhere hath borne witness, saying . . . ."; iii. 7, "Even as the Holy Ghost saith . . . ."; vi. 14, "God . . . . sware by himself, saying . . . .": (2) with subject to be *supplied from the preceding context*: i. 6, "And when he (God) again bringeth in the firstborn into the world, he saith . . . ."; i. 7, "And of the angels he (God) saith . . . ."; ii. 12, "He (Christ) is not ashamed to call them brethren, saying . . . ."; v. 6, "As he (God) saith also in another place . . . .": (3) with subject to be *supplied from the general knowledge of the reader:* x. 5, "Wherefore when he (Christ) cometh into the world, he saith . . . ."; x. 8, "Saying (Christ) above . . . ."; xii. 26, "But now hath he (God) promised, saying . . . .": (4) *without obvious subject:* iii. 15, "While it is said, To day, etc." (by whom? God? or the Scripture quoted, iii. 7 *seq.?*); iv. 7, "He [or it?] again defineth a certain time, saying in David . . . ."; viii. 8, "For finding fault with them, he [or it?] saith . . . ." (cf. viii. 13, "in that he [or it?] saith . . . ."). On the other hand, in the epistles that bear the name of Paul we may distinguish some four cases of the adduction of Scripture by the formula λέγει. (1) Sometimes, quoting Scripture *as a divine whole,* the formula runs ἡ γραφὴ λέγει or λέγει ἡ γραφή: Rom. iv. 3, ix. 17 (λέγει ἡ γραφὴ τῷ Φαραῷ), xi. 2 (ἡ γραφὴ ἐν Ἡλείᾳ), Gal. iv. 30, I Tim. v. 18. (2) Sometimes it is adduced *by the name of the author:* Δαυείδ λέγει, Rom. iv. 6, xi. 9; Ἡσαίας λέγει, Rom. x. 16, 20, xv. 12. (3) Sometimes it is quoted *by its contents:* ὁ νόμος λέγει, Rom. iii. 19, vii. 7, I Cor. ix. 8, 10, xiv. 34; the righteousness that is of faith λέγει, Rom. x. 6 (cf. ver. 10); ὁ χρηματισμός λέγει, Rom. xi. 4. (4) Sometimes it is adduced by the verb λέγει *without expressed subject.* (A) In some of these cases *the subject is plainly indicated* in the preceding context: Rom. ix. 25 = "God," from ver. 22; x. 10 = "the righteousness of faith," (?) from ver. 6; x. 21 =

"Isaiah," from ver. 20. (B) In others it is less clearly indicated and is *not altogether obvious:* [Acts xiii. 34 = "God," from εἴρηκεν?]; Rom. ix. 15 = "God," from ver. 14?; Rom. xv. 10 = "Scripture," from γέγραπται?; II Cor. vi. 2 = "God," from preceding context; Gal. iii. 16 = "God," from the promises?; Eph. iv. 8 and v. 12. It should be added that parallel to the use of the subjectless φησί in Heb. viii. 5 we have the similar use of it in I Cor. vi. 16.

When we glance over these two lists of phenomena we shall certainly recognize a difference between them: but the difference is not suggestive of such an extreme distinction as Dr. Westcott appears to indicate. The fact is that for its proper estimation we must rise to a higher viewpoint and look upon the two lists in the light of a much larger fact. For we cannot safely study this difference of usage as an isolated phenomenon: and we shall get the key to its interpretation into our hands only when we correlate it with a more general view of the estimate of Scripture and mode of adducing Scripture prevalent at the time and in the circles which are represented by these epistles. Dr. Westcott already points the way to this wider outlook, when at the end of his discussion he adds these words:

"The method of citation on which we have dwelt is peculiar to the Epistle [to the Hebrews] among the writings of the New Testament; but it is interesting to notice that there is in the Epistle of Clement a partial correspondence with it. Clement generally quotes the LXX. anonymously. He attributes the prophetic words to God (15, 21, 46), to Christ (16, 22), to the Holy Word (13, 56), to the Holy Spirit (13, 16). But he also, though rarely, refers to the writers (26, Job; 52, David), and to Books (57, Proverbs, 'the all virtuous Wisdom'), and not unfrequently uses the familiar form γέγραπται (14, 39, etc.). The quotations in the Epistle of Barnabas are also commonly anonymous, but Barnabas mentions several names of the sacred writers, and gives passages from the Law, the Prophets and the Psalms with the formula, 'the Prophet saith' (vi. 8; 2; 4, 6)."

And, he should have added, Barnabas also repeatedly adduces what he held to be the Word of God with the formulas γέγραπται (iv. 3, 14, v. 2, xi. 1, xiv. 6, xv. 1, xvi. 6) and λέγει ἡ γραφή (iv. 7, 11, v. 4, vi. 12, xiii. 2, xv. 5): and indeed passes from the one mode of citation to the other without the least jar, as, for example, in chap. v.: "For *it is written* concerning him, some things indeed with respect to Israel, and some with respect to us. For *it saith* this (Isa. liii. 5, 7). . . . . And the *Scripture saith* (Prov. i. 17). . . . And *still also this* (Jer. i. 25). . . . . For *God saith* (Zech. xiii. 6). . . . . For the *prophesier saith* (Ps. xxii. 21, etc.). . . . . And again *it saith* (Isa. l. 6)." Though adverting thus to these facts, however, Dr. Westcott quite misses their significance. What they mean is shortly this: that the two modes of citing Scripture thought to distinguish Hebrews and the letters that bear the name of Paul, do not imply well-marked distinctive modes of conceiving Scripture; but coëxist readily within the limits of one brief letter, like the letter of Clement or that of Barnabas. No wonder, when laid side by side, we found the usages of the two to present no sharply marked division line, but to crumble into one another along the edges. And when we look beyond Clement and Barnabas and take a general glance over the literature of the time, it is easily seen that we are looking in the two cases only at two fragments of one fact, and are seeing in each only one of the everywhere current methods of citing Scripture as the very Word of God. It seems inconceivable that one could rise from reading, say, twenty pages of Philo, for example, without being fully convinced of this.

Philo's fundamental conception of Scripture is that it is a book of oracles; each passage of it is a χρησμός or λόγιον, and the whole is therefore οἱ χρησμοί or τὰ λόγια: he currently quotes it, accordingly, as "the living voice" of God, and whole treatises of his may be read without meeting with a single citation introduced by γέγραπται or with the Scriptures once called ἡ γραφή. Nevertheless, when occasion serves, he adduces Scripture readily enough as ἡ γραφή, and cites it with γέγραπται, and calls it τὰ γράμματα. We have no more reason for assuming that such modes of citing Scripture would have been foreign to the author of the Epistle to the Hebrews (whose mode of citing Scripture is markedly Philonic) than we have for assuming that the author of the tract *de Mutatione Nominum*, in which they do not occur, but where Scripture is almost exclusively οἱ χρησμοί, or the author of the tracts *de Somniis*, where again they do not occur, but where Scripture is almost exclusively ὁ ἱερὸς (or ὁ θεῖος) λόγος (i. 14, 22, 33, 35, 37, 39, 42, ii. 4, 9, 37, etc.; i. 33, ii. 37) — which designations are rare again in *de Mutatione Nominum* (ὁ θ. λ., 20; ὁ ἱ. λ., 38) — held a different conception of Scripture from the author of the tract *de Legatione ad Caium* (§ 29) or the tract *de Abrahamo* (§ 1), in which the Scriptures are spoken of as τὰ γράμματα or αἱ γραφαί. There is no reason, in a word, why, if the Epistle to the Hebrews had contained even a single other verse, it might not have presented the "exotic," ἡ γραφή or γέγραπται. Because Philo or the author of this Epistle was especially accustomed to look on Scripture as a body of *oracles* and to cite it accordingly, is no reason why he should forget that it is a body of *written* oracles and be incapable on occasion of citing it from that point of view. Similarly because Paul ordinarily cites Scripture as *written* is no reason why he should not be firmly convinced that what is written in it is *oracles*, or should not occasionally cite it from that point of view. In a word, the two modes of citing Scripture brought into contrast by Bishop Westcott are not two mutually exclusive ways of citing Scripture, but two mutually complementary methods. The use of the one by any writer does not argue that the other is foreign to him; if we have enough written material from his hand, we are sure rather to find in him traces of the other usage also. This is the meaning of the presence in the Epistle to the Hebrews of suggestive instances of an approach to the citation of Scripture as a document: and of the presence in the epistles bearing the name of Paul of instances of modes of citation which hint of his conception of Scripture as an oracular book. Where and when the sense of the oracular character of the source of the quotation is predominatingly in mind it tends to be quoted with the simple φησί or λέγει, with the implication that it is God that says it: this is most richly exhibited in Philo, and, within the limits of the New Testament, most prevailingly in the Epistle to the Hebrews. Where and when, on the other hand, the consciousness that it is from a written source that the authoritative words are drawn is predominant in the mind, it tends to be quoted with the simple γέγραπται or the more formal ἡ γραφὴ λέγει: this is the mode in which it is most commonly cited in the epistles that bear the name of Paul. Both modes of citation rest on the common consciousness of the Divine authority of the matter cited, and have no tendency to exclude one another: they appear side by side in the same writer, and must be held to predominate variously in different writers only according to their prevailing habits of speaking of Scripture, and at different times in the same writer according as the circumstances under which he was writing threw the emphasis in his mind temporarily upon the Scriptures as written *oracles* or as *written* oracles.

From this point of view we may estimate Dr. Westcott's remark: "Nor can it be maintained that the difference of usage is to be explained by the difference of readers, as being [in Hebrews] Jews, for in the Gospels γέγραπται is the common formula (nine times in St. Matthew)." This remark, like his whole treatment of the subject, seems conceived in a spirit which is too hard and narrow, too drily statistical. No one, doubtless, would contend that the difference of readers directly produced the difference of usage, as if the Scriptures *must* be quoted to Jews as "oracles of God," and to Gentiles as "written documents." But it is far from obvious that the difference of readers may not, after all, have had very much to do with the prevalence of the one mode of citation in the Epistle to the Hebrews and of the other in the epistles that bear the name of Paul. The Jews were certainly accustomed to the current citation of the Scriptures as the living voice of God in oracular deliverances —

as the usage of Philo sufficiently indicates: and it may be that this was subtly felt the most impressive method of adducing the words of the Holy Book when addressing Jews. On the other hand, the heathen were accustomed to authoritative documents, cited currently, with an implication of their authority, by the formula γέγραπται: [29] and it may well be that this subtly suggested itself as the most telling way of adducing Scripture as authoritative law to the Gentiles. We need not ride such a notion too hard: but it at least seems far from inconceivable that the selfsame writer, addressing, on the one hand, a body of devout Jews, and, on the other, a body of law-loving Romans, might find himself using almost unconsciously modes of adducing Scripture suggestive, in the one case, of loving awe in its presence and, in the other, of its binding authority over the conscience. Be this as it may, however, it is quite clear that the fact that Paul ordinarily adduces Scripture with "the forms (καθώς) γέγραπται (sixteen times in the Epistle to the Romans), ἡ γραφὴ λέγει, and the like, which never occur in the Epistle to the Hebrews," implies no far-reaching difference of conception on his part from that exhibited by that Epistle, as to the fundamental character of the Scriptures as an oracular book — which, on the contrary, is just what he calls them (Rom. iii. 2) — and certainly raises no presumption against his occasionally quoting them as an oracular book with the formula so characteristic of the Epistle to the Hebrews, ὁ θεὸς λέγει, or its equivalents. And the fact that "Paul not unfrequently quotes the words of God as 'Scripture' simply (e. g., Rom. ix. 17)" so far from raising a presumption that he would not quote "Scripture" as "words of God," actually demonstrates the contrary, as it only in another way indicates the identification on his part of the written word with the voice of the speaking God.

If we approach the study of such texts as Eph. iv. 8, v.

---

[29] Cf. Deissmann, "Bibelstudien," 109; "Neue Bibelstudien," 77: and also for the implications, Kuyper, "Encyclopædia of Sacred Theology," pp. 433–435 and 444–445.

14, therefore, from the point of view of the Pauline conception of Scripture, there is no reason why they should not be understood as adducing Scripture with a high "God says." To say that "we have reason to believe" that such a formula "could not be used by Paul," is as wide of the mark as could well be. To say that it is a formula more in accordance with the point of view of the Epistle to the Hebrews, is to confound mere occasional differences in usage with fundamental differences in conception. To Paul, too, the Scriptures are a book of oracles, and though he cites them ordinarily as *written* oracles there is no reason why he should not occasionally cite them merely as *oracles*. And in any case, whether we take the *subauditum* in such passages as "God," or "Scripture," or prefer to render simply by "it," from Paul's point of view the meaning is all one: in any case, Scripture is to him the authoritative dictum of God and what it says is adduced as the authoritative word that ends all strife.

In seeking to estimate the likelihoods as to the meaning of such a locution as the διὸ λέγει of Eph. iv. 8, v. 14, we should not lose from sight, on the other hand, the fact that the Greek language was not partial to true "impersonals," that is, absolutely indefinite uses of its verbs. Says Jelf:

"Of impersonal verbs (in English, verbs with the indefinite *it*) the Greek language has but few." [30]

Says Kühner:

"Impersonal verbs, by which we understand a verb agreeing with the indefinite pronoun *it*, are not known to the Greek language: for expressions like δεῖ, χρή . . . λέγεται, etc. . . . the Greek always conceived as personal, in that the infinitive or subjoined sentence was considered the subject of these verbs." [31]

No doubt, the subject often suffers ellipsis — especially when it may be counted upon readily to suggest itself, either out

[30] § 373, 1. obs., 1.
[31] "Ausführ. Gram.," ii. 30 (§ 352).

of the predicate itself, or out of the context, or out of the
knowledge of the reader: and no doubt this implied subject
is sometimes the indefinite τις. But it remains true that as
yet there has turned up no single instance in all Greek literature of λέγει in the purely indefinite sense of "someone
says," equivalent to "it is said" in the meaning of general
rumor, or of a common proverb, or a current saying; and
though there have been pointed out instances of something
like this in the case of the kindred word φησί, it still remains
somewhat doubtful precisely how they are to be interpreted.
The forms commonly used to express this idea are either the
expressed τις, or the third person plural, as λέγουσι, φασί,
ὀνομάζουσιν, or the third person singular passive, as λέγεται,
or the second person singular optative or indicative of the
historical tenses, as φαίης ἄν, = dicas, or the like.[32]

We find it, indeed, occasionally asserted that φησί is used
sometimes or frequently as a pure impersonal, in the sense
of "it is said." The passage from Bernhardy, to be sure, to
which reference has been made in support of this assertion,
by more than one of the commentators adduced above, has
its primary interest not in this point, but in the different one
of the use of the singular φησί for the plural — like the Latin
inquit, and the English "says" in that vulgar colloquial locution in which it is made to do duty not only in the form
"he says," but also in such forms as "I says" and "you
says," and even "they says" and "we says." What Bernhardy remarks is:[33]

"*The rhetorical employment of the singular* for the plural rests on
the Greek peculiarity (K. 3, 5; 6, 13c.) of clearly conceiving and representing the multitude by means of the individual. A ready instance of
this is supplied by the formula φησί, like the Latin inquit an expression
for all persons and numbers for designating an indefinite speaker (den
beliebigen Redner) — 'heisst es'; and by the more classic εἰπέ μοι in
appeal to the multitude in Attic life, Arist. (as Pac., 385, εἰπέ μοι τί

---

[32] Jelf, § 373, 7: Kühner, l.c.: Jannaris ("A Historical Greek Grammar," 1161
seq.), treats the omitted subject no otherwise than Kühner.

[33] "Syntax.," 419.

ἢ ἀυχει' ἄνδρες; coll. *Eccl.*, 741), Plat. (clearly in a turn like εἰπέ μοι, ὦ Σώκρατές τε καὶ ὑμεῖς οἱ ἄλλοι), Demosth., *Phil.* i, p. 45; *Chers.*, p. 108; *Timocr.*, p. 718." [34]

The usage of φησί here more particularly adverted to — for all numbers and persons — seems a not uncommon one. Instances may possibly be found in the "Discourses" of Epictetus i. 29, 34 (Schenkl, p. 95). "Even athletes are dissatisfied with slight young men: 'He cannot lift me,' φησί," where φησί might perhaps be rendered by our vernacular, "says they," referring to "the athletes." Again, iv. 9, 15 (Schenkl, p. 383): "But learn from what the trainers of boys do. The boy has fallen: 'Rise,' φησί, 'wrestle again, till you become strong!'" where we may possibly have another 'says they,' viz., the trainers. Possibly again ii. 10, 20 (Schenkl, p. 133), "But consider, if you refer everything to a small coin, not even he who loses his nose is in your opinion damaged. 'Yes,' φησί, 'for he is mutilated in his body,'" where possibly φησί is "says you," referring to the collocutor, addressed in the preceding context in the second person — though, no doubt, another explanation is here possible. Indeed, in no one of the instances cited is it impossible to conceive a singular subject derived from the contextual plural as specially in mind. If φησί were genuine in Wisdom xv. 12,[35] II Cor. x. 10,[36] these might well supply other instances — the "says they" in each case continuing the contextual or implicated plural. But in none of these instances, it is to be observed, would the subject be conceived as in the strict sense "indefinite." It is a

[34] These references are added in a note: "Von φησί in späten manche nach Bentley, wie Dav. ad Cic. Tus. i. 39; Wytt. ad Plut., T. vi, p. 791. Von εἰπέ μοι, Heind. ad Euthyd., 29."

[35] Cf. Grimm's note, given above, p. 289.

[36] Meyer, *in loc.*, continues to read φησί. He says, "*It is said*, impersonal, as often with the Greeks. See Bernhardy, p. 419. The reading φασίν (Lachmann, following B. Vulg.), is a rash correction. Comp. Fritzsche, *ad Thesmoph.*, p. 189; Buttmann, *Neut. Gram.*, p. 119 [English translation, 136]." So in essence most commentators, including Flatt, Storr, Krause, De Wette, Kling, Waite. Rückert more warily comments: "φησίν is here properly recognized as a formula of adduction, without reference to the number of those speaking. See Winer (304)." Cf. above, p. 289.

perfectly definite subject that is present to the mind of the
writer, given either in the immediate context or in the
thorough understanding that exists between the writer and
reader. There is in them nothing whatever of the vagueness
that attaches to the French "on dit," or the German "man
sagt," or the English "it is said." The Greeks had other locutions for expressing this idea, and if it was ever expressed
by the simple φησί, only the slightest traces of it remain in
their extant literature.

In the seventh edition of the Greek Lexicon of Liddell &
Scott,[37] nevertheless, this usage is expressly assigned to φησί.
We read:

"φασί parenthetically, *they say, it is said*, Il. 5, 638, Od. 6, 42
and Att.; but in prose also φησί, like French *on dit*, Dem. 650, 13,
Plut. 2, 112 C., etc. (so Lat. *inquit, ait*, Gronov, Liv. 34, 3, Bent.
Hor. 1 Sat. 4, 79; — especially in urging an objection or counter-
argument, v. Interpp. Pers. Sat. 1, 40);—so also ἔφη, c. acc. et inf.,
Xen. An. i, 6, 6."

It is far from obvious, however, that the passages here adduced will justify precisely the usage which they are cited
to illustrate. In the passage from Demosthenes — ἔστω, φησὶν,
ὑπὲρ αὐτοῦ ἡ αὐτὴ τιμωρία, etc. — it seems to be quite clear,
as the previous sentence suggests and the editors recognize,[38]
that the subject of the φησί is ἕκαστος τῶν γεγραφότων, and is
far from a purely indefinite τις. The passage from Plutarch
("Consolatio ad Apollonium," xxi) is more specious. It runs:
ἀλλ' οὐ γὰρ ἤλπιζον, φησί, ταῦτα πείσεσθαι, οὐδὲ προσεδόκων;
and is translated in the Latin version, "At, inquiunt, præter
spem mihi hic casus et expectationem evenit"; and in Holland's old English version, "But haply you will say, I never
thought that this would have befallen unto me, neither did
I so much as doubt any such thing." A glance at the context,
however, is enough to show that there is no purely indefinite
φησί here, though it may be that we have here another instance of its usage without regard to number and person. In

[37] P. 1665a (Oxford, 1883).   [38] Whiston, Reiske, Weber.

any case, the subject is the quite definitely conceived inter-locutor of the passage. That the ἔφη adduced at the end of the note as in some degree of the same sort is not an indefinite ἔφη, but has the Clearchus of the immediately preceding context as its subject, is too obvious for remark. Clearchus was present by the request of Cyrus at the trial of Orontes, and when he came out he reported to his friends the manner in which the trial was conducted: "He said (ἔφη) that Cyrus began to speak as follows." It is not by such instances as these that the occurrence of a purely indefinite φησί can be established.[39]

The subjectless φησί, to be sure, does occur very thickly scattered over the face of Greek literature, introducing or emphasizing quotations, or adducing objections, or the like: but the "it" that is to be supplied to it is, ordinarily at least, a quite definite one with its own definite reference perfectly clear. A characteristic instance, often referred to, is that in Demosth., "Leptin," § 56:[40] καὶ γάρ τοι μόνῳ τῶν πάντων αὐτῷ τοῦτ᾽ ἐν τῇ στήλῃ γέγραπται, ἐπειδὴ Κόνων, φησίν, ἠλευθέρωσε τοὺς Ἀθηναίων συμμάχους. — Ἔστι δὲ τοῦτο τὸ γράμμα. . . . ." Here F. A. Wolf comments: "Absolute ibi interjectum est φησίν, aut, si mavis, subaudi ὁ γράψας"; and Schaefer adds: "Subaudi ἡ στήλη."[41] It does not appear why we should not render simply "it says": but this "it" is so far from an "'indefinite' it" that it has its clear reference to the inscription just mentioned. Perhaps even more instructive is a passage in the third Philippic [42] of Demosthenes, which runs as follows:

"That such is our present state, you yourselves are witnesses, and need not any testimony from me. That our state in former times was quite opposite to this, I shall now convince you, not by any arguments of mine, but by a decree of your ancestors (γράμματα τῶν

[39] We are indebted to Prof. S. S. Orris, of Princeton University, for suggestions in preparing this paragraph. He permits us to add that, in his opinion, "φησί is never equivalent to the general, indefinite *they say* or *it is said*."

[40] Reiske, p. 477; Dindorf, ii. 23.   [41] Reiske and Schaefer, vi. 162.

[42] iii. §§ 41, 42 (p. 122); "Oratores Attici," v. 214.

προγόνων), which they inscribed upon a brazen column (στήλην) erected in the citadel. . . . What, then, says the decree (τί οὖν λέγει τὰ γράμματα)? 'Let Arithmius,' it says (φησίν), 'of Zelia, the son of Pythonax, be accounted infamous and an enemy to the Athenians and their allies, both he and all his race.' . . . The sentence imported somewhat more, for, in the laws importing capital cases, it is enacted (γέγραπται) that 'when the legal punishment of a man's crime cannot be inflicted he may be put to death,' and it was accounted meritorious to kill him. 'Let not the infamous man,' saith the law, 'be permitted to live' (καὶ ἄτιμος, φησί, τεθνάτω), intimating that he is free from guilt who executes this sentence (τοῦτο δὴ λέγει, καθαρὸν τὸν τούτων τινὰ ἀποκτείναντα εἶναι)."

In both cases it is doubtless enough to render φησί, "it says," its function being in each case to call pointed attention to the words quoted: but the "it" is by no means "indefinite" in the sense that its reference was not very definitely conceived. On the second instance of its occurrence Wolf comments: "s. ὁ φονικὸς νόμος," [43] while Schaefer says: [44]

" Pleonastice positum cum γέγραπται praecesserit. Verumtamen h. l. sensum paulo magis juvat quam ubi post εἶπον, εἶπε, continuo sequitur ἔφην, ἔφη. Ad φησί subaudi ὁ νομοθέτης."

These instances will supply us with typical examples of the "absolute" φησί; and, in this sense, "subjectless φησί" is of very common occurrence indeed in Greek literature.

But really "subjectless φησί," i. e., φησί without any implied subject in context or common knowledge, which therefore we must take quite indefinitely, is very rare indeed, if not non-existent. Perhaps one of the most likely instances of such a usage is offered us by a passage in Plutarch's "Consolatio ad Apollonium," 34.[45] Holland's old version of it runs thus: [46]

"And verily in regard of him who is now in a blessed estate, it has not been naturall for him to remaine in this life longer than the terme prefixed and limited unto him; but after he had honestly performed

[43] Reiske-Schaefer, v. 579. [44] Op. cit., p. 581.
[45] P. 119 F (Wyttenbach, I. ii. 470). [46] P. 530 (20–30).

the course of his time, it was needfull and requisit for him to take the way for to returne unto his destinie that called for him to come unto her."

From this we may at least learn that φησίν here presented some difficulty, as Holland passes it by unrendered. The common Latin version restores it, reading the last clause thus: "Sed ita postulabit natura ut hoc expleto *fatale* quod aiunt *iter* conficeret, revocante eum jam ad se natura"; the Greek running thus: "ἀλλ' εὐτάκτως τοῦτον ἐκπλήσαντι πρὸς τὴν εἱμαρμένην ἐπανάγειν πορείαν, καλούσης αὐτῆς, φησίν, ἤδη πρὸς ἐαυτήν." The theory of the Latin version obviously is that φησίν here is to be taken indefinitely, that is as an index hand pointing to a current designation of death as an entering upon the "fated journey" — ἡ εἱμαρμένη πορεία. This is explained to us by Wyttenbach's note: [47]

"φησίν] non debebat offendere viros doctos. Est *ut ait poeta ille unde hoc sumptum est*. Videt hoc et Reiskius. Correxi versionem. De Tragici dicto in Animadversibus dicetur."

Accordingly, in the Animadversions,[48] he addresses himself first to showing that the expression here signalized was a current poetical saying — appealing to Plato,[49] Julian, Philo; and then adds:

"Cæterum φησίν ita elliptice usitatum est: v. c. Plutarcho, p. 135 B.,[50] 817 D., Dion. Chrys., p. 493 D., 532 A., 562 B. Notavit et Uptonus ad Epict. in Indice. In annotatoribus ad Lambertum Bosium de Ellipsibus unus Schoettgenius, idque ex uno Paulo Apostolo hunc usum annotavit, p. 74. Et. Latine ita dicitur *inquit*,

---

[47] I, ii. 470. [48] VI, ii. 791.

[49] Phaedo, 401 B. (115): "in these arrayed, [the soul] is ready to go on her journey to the world below, when her time comes. You, Simmias and Cebes, and all other men, will depart at some time or other. Me already, as the tragic poet would say, the voice of fate calls (ἐμὲ δὲ νῦν ἤδη καλεῖ, φαίη ἄν ἀνὴρ τραγικὸς, ἡ εἱμαρμένη)." The other passages adduced witness only to the currency of the phrase ἡ εἱμαρμένη πορεία. But the language of both Plutarch and Plato would seem to imply that the "calling" is certainly a part of the quotation.

[50] *Praecepta Sanit. Tuend.*, 135 B., οὐ κατά γε τὴν ἐμὴν, ἔφη, γνώμην. Wytt.: "ἔφη notat alterius dictum ut alibi φησί, de quo diximus, p. 119 F."

quod monuerunt J. F. Gronovius et A. Drakenborch. ad Livium
xxxiv. 3, J. A. Ernestus in Clav. Cic. voce *Inquit.*"

It does not seem, however, that Wyttenbach would have us
read the φησί here quite indefinitely, as adducing for example a current saying: judging from his own paraphrase
this might appear to him as a certain exaggeration of its
implication. Its office would seem rather to be to call attention to the words, to which it is adjoined, as quoted, and
thus, in the good understanding implied to exist between
the writer and his readers, to point definitely to its source:
so that it might be a proper note to it to say, "subaudi ὁ
τραγικός, vel ὁ ποιητής" — and this might be done with a
considerable emphasis on the ὁ; nay, the actual name of the
poet, well known to both writer and reader, though now lost
to us, might equally well be the *subauditum*, and such, indeed, may be the implication of the *subauditum* suggested
by Wyttenbach: *ut ait poeta ille unde hoc scriptum est.* Surely,
an instance like this is far from a clear case of the absolutely
indefinite or even generally undefining use of φησί.

Among the references with which Wyttenbach supports
his note, the most promising sends us to Epictetus, whose
"Discourses" abound in the most varied use of φησί, and
offer us at the same time one of our most valuable sources of
knowledge of the Greek in common use near the times of the
apostles.[51] We meet with many instances here which it has
been customary to explain as cases of φησί in a wholly indefinite reference. But the matter is somewhat complicated
by the facts that we are not reading here Epictetus' "Discourses" pure and simple, but Arrian's report of them; and
that Arrian may exercise his undoubted right to slip in a
φησί of his own whenever he specially wishes to keep his
readers' attention fixed upon the fact that they are his
master's words he is setting down, or perhaps even merely
out of the abiding sense, on his own part, that he is reporting Epictetus and not writing out of his own mind. When

[51] Cf. Heinrici as above, p. 481; and Blass, "Gram. of New Testament
Greek," English translation, p. 2.

such a φησί occurs at the beginning of a section it gives no trouble: every reader recognizes it at once as Arrian's. But when it occurs unexpectedly in the midst of a vivacious discussion, the reader who is not carrying with him the sense of Arrian's personality, standing behind the Epictetus he is attending to, is very apt to be stumbled by it, and to resort to some explanation of it on the theory that it is Epictetus' own and is to find its interpretation in the context. An attempt has been made by Schenkl in the index to his edition of Epictetus [52] to distinguish between the instances in which φησί occurs "inter Epicteti verba ab Arriano servata," and those in which it occurs "inter Arriani verba." It will be found that most of the instances where it has been thought markedly indefinite in its reference are classed by him in the second group and are thus made very definite indeed — the standing *subauditum* being "Epictetus." Opinions will, no doubt, differ as to the proper classification of a number of these: and in any case many instances remain which cannot naturally be so explained — occurring as they do in the midst of vividly conceived dramatic passages. In this very vividness of dramatic action, however, is doubtless to be found the explanation of these instances. So far are the verbs here from being impersonal, that the speakers in these little dialogues stood out before Epictetus' mind's eye as actual persons; and it is therefore that he so freely refers to them with his vivid φησί.

The following are some of the most striking examples of his usage of the word. "But now we admit that virtue produces one thing, and we declare that approaching near to it is another thing, namely progress or improvement. Such a person, φησίν, is already able to read Chrysippus by himself. Indeed, sir, you are making great progress" (i, 4, 9).[53] Here Schenkl suggests that the φησίν is Arrian's, and this would seem to be a good suggestion, as it illuminates the passage

[52] "Epicteti Dissertationes," etc. (Lipsiæ, 1894), Index, pp. 701, 702.

[53] We purposely use Long's translation, which, in all these instances, proceeds on the theory that the φησί is Epictetus' own.

in more ways than one. If not, the *subauditum* would seem
to be the collocutor of the paragraph: a "some one," no
doubt, but rather *the* "some one" most prominent in the
mind of writer and reader in this discussion. "But a man
may say, Whence shall I get bread to eat, when I have
nothing (καὶ πόθεν φάγω, φησί, μηδὲν ἔχων;) ?" (i. 9, 8). Here
again the φησί seems best explained as Arrian's (Schenkl):
if not, the *subauditum* is again the collocutor prominent
through the context, and only, in that sense, indefinite.
"Who made these things and devised them? 'No one,' you
say (φησίν). O amazing shamelessness and stupidity" (i. 16,
8). The reference is to the collocutor. "They are thieves and
robbers you may say (κλέπται, φησίν, εἰσι . . . .)" (i. 18, 3).
Either Arrian's (Schenkl), or with the collocutor as the *subauditum*. "How can you conquer the opinion of another
man? By applying terror to it, he replies (φησίν), I will
conquer it" (i, 29, 12). *Subaudi* the collocutor. "For why, a
man says (φησί), do I not know the beautiful and the ugly?"
(ii, 11, ?). Either Arrian's (Schenkl), or *subaudi* the collocutor. "How, he replies (φησίν), am I not good?" (ii, 13, 17).
Either Arrian's (Schenkl), or *subaudi* the collocutor. So also
similarly in ii, 22, 4; iii, 2, 5; iii, 5, 1, etc. Cf. also ii, 23, 16;
iii, 3, 12; 9, 15; 20, 12; 26, 19. Similarly, in the "Fragments"
we have this: "They are amusing fellows, said he (ἔφη =
Epictetus), who are proud of the things which are not in our
power. A man says, I (ἐγώ, φησί) am better than you, for I
possess much land and you are wasting with hunger. Another
says (ἄλλος λέγει). . . . ." ("Frag.," xviii. [Schw., 16]). Here the
φησί is brought in as the initial member of a series and in
contrast with ἄλλος λέγει: it would seem to be Epictetus' own,
therefore, and to mean "says one," as distinguished from
another; and thus it appears to be the most likely instance
of the "indefinite φησί" in the whole mass. But even it seems
an essentially different locution from the really indefinite
"it is said," "on dit," "man sagt."

A glance over the whole usage of φησί in Arrian-Epictetus
leaves on the mind a keen sense of the lively way in which the

word must have been interjected into Greek conversation, but does not greatly alter the impression of its essential implication which we derive from the general use of the word. Take a single instance of its current use in the "Discourses" in its relation to kindred words:

"So also Diogenes somewhere says (που λέγει) that there exists but one means of obtaining freedom — to die contentedly, and he writes (γράφει) to the king of the Persians, 'You cannot enslave the city of the Athenians, any more,' says he (φησίν), 'than fishes.' 'How? Can I not catch them?' 'If you catch them,' says he (φησίν), 'they will immediately leave you and be gone, just like fishes: for whatever one of them you catch dies, and if these men die when they are caught, what good will your preparations do you?'" (iv, 1, 30).

The lively effect given by such unexpected interpositions of φησίν is lost in our decorous translation of the New Testament examples: but it exists in them too. Thus: "But she, being urged on by her mother, 'Give me,' says she, 'here upon a charger, the head of John the Baptist'" (Matt. xiv. 8); "But he, 'Master, speak,' says he" (Luke vii. 40); "But Peter to them, 'Repent,' says he, 'and be baptized each one of you'" (Acts ii. 38); "'Let those among you,' says he, 'that are able, go down with me'" (Acts xxv. 5); "'To-morrow,' says he, 'thou shalt hear him'" (Acts xxv. 22); "But Paul, 'I am not mad,' says he, 'most noble Festus'" (Acts xxvi. 25).[54] The main function of φησί then would appear to be to keep the consciousness of the speaker reported clearly before the mind of the reader. It is therefore often used to mark the transition from indirect to direct quotation [55]: and it lent itself readily, therefore, to mark the adduction both

[54] The matter of this interposition is investigated for Plato by Stallbaum, p. 472 D., 580 D. — where he seems to have collected all the instances of interposed φαμέν in Plato. Cf. also Bornemann and Sauppe on Xenophon's *Memorab.*, iii. 5, 13, and the indices of Schenkl on Arrian-Epictetus and Thieme-Sturz on Xenophon (sub. voc. φάναι).

[55] On Acts xxv. 5, Blass has this note: "5 fit transitus ex or. obliqua in rectam, ut I. 4 al; hinc φησίν interpositum ut I. 4 β.," i. e., in the *Western* text of I, 4, which reads: "'Which ye heard,' says he, 'from my mouth.'" The interposition of a "he says," or some similar phrase, to keep the consciousness of the

of objections and of literary citations. But, one would imagine, it did not very readily lend itself to vague and indefinite references.

If we desire to find cases of "subjectless λέγει" in any way similar to those of φησί, we must apparently turn our back on profane Greek altogether.[56] We have fortunately in Philo, however, an author, the circumstances of whose writing made literary quotation as frequent with him as oral is in the lively pages of Epictetus' "Discourses." And in Philo's treatises λέγει takes its place by the side of its more common kinsman φησί, and is used in much the same way, though naturally somewhat less frequently. In harmony with his fundamental viewpoint — which looked on the Scriptures as a body of oracular sayings — Philo adduces Scripture commonly with verbs of "saying" — φησί, λέγεται, λέγει, εἶπεν (γέγραπται falling into the background). Passages so adduced are often woven into the fabric of his discussion of the contents of Scripture; and where the words adduced are words of a speaker in the Biblical narrative, the subject of the φησί or λέγει which introduces them naturally is often this speaker — whether God or some other person. Equally often, however, the subject given immediately or indirectly in the context is something outside of the narrative that is dealt with: in this case it is sometimes Moses, or "the prophet," or "the lawgiver" — at other times, "the Holy Word," or "the sacred Word," or "the Oracle," or "the Oracles" (ὁ θεῖος λόγος, ὁ ἱερὸς λόγος, ὁ χρησμός, τὸ λόγιον, οἱ χρησμοί, τὰ λόγια) — at other times still it is "God," under various designations. Often, however, the verb — φησί or λέγει — stands not only without expressed subject, but equally without indicated subject. The rendering of these cases has given students of Philo some trouble, arising out

hearer or reader bright on the fact that the words before him are *quoted* words is, of course, a general linguistic and not a specifically Greek usage. It is found in all languages. A Hebrew instance, for example, may be found in I Kgs. ii. 4.

[56] Schenkl catalogues in the "Discourses" of Epictetus two cases of interposited λέγει, quite in the style of φησί — iii. 19, 1 and "Fragment," xxi. 10 — but in both cases the subject is expressed.

of the apparent confusion, when the subject is expressed,
of the reference of the verb, — now to a speaker in the text
of Scripture and now to the author of the particular Scripture, to God as the author of all Scripture, or to Scripture
itself conceived as a living Word. This apparent confusion is
due solely to Philo's fundamental conception of Scripture as
an oracular book, which leads him to deal with its text as
itself the Word of God: he has himself fully explained the
matter,[57] and we should be able to steer clear of serious
difficulties with his explanation in our hands.

Nevertheless, a somewhat mechanical mode of dealing
with his citations has produced, on more than one occasion,
certain odd results. Prof. Ryle says: [58]

"The commonest forms of quotation employed by Philo are φησί,
εἶπεν, λέγει, λέγεται, γέγραπται γάρ. Whether the subject of φησί be
Moses or Scripture personified cannot in many cases be determined."

In no case is the subject strictly indeterminate, however, and
the failure to determine it aright may introduce confusion.
Thus, for example, in "De Confus. Ling.," § 26 (Mangey, i.
424), Philo mentions the Book of Judges, and cites it with
the subjectless φησί. Prof. Ryle comments thus: [59]

"He does not mention any opinion as to authorship, and introduces his quotation with his usual formula φησίν. We are hardly
justified in assuming that Philo intended Moses as the subject of
φησίν, and regarded him as the author of Judges (so Dr. Pick, *Journal
of Biblical Literature*, 1884). Moses is doubtless often spoken of by
Philo as if he were the personification of the Inspired Word; but we
cannot safely extend this idea beyond the range of the Pentateuch.
All that we can say is that φησίν, used in this quotation from Judges,
refers either to the unknown writer of this book or to the personification of Holy Scripture."

Or else, we may add, to God, the real author, in Philo's conception, of every word of Scripture. Prof. Ryle, however, has

---

[57] In "De Vita Mosis," iii. 23.   [58] "Philo and Holy Scripture," p. xlv.
[59] *Op. cit.*, p. xxv.

not caught precisely Dr. Pick's meaning: Dr. Pick does not commit himself to the extravagant view that wherever subjectless φησί occurs in Philo the *subauditum* "Moses" is implied: he only says, in direct words, that here — in this special passage — "Moses is introduced as speaking." It would seem obvious that he had a text before him which read "Moses says," and not simply "says," at this place. This text was doubtless nothing other than Yonge's English translation, which reads Moses here, as often elsewhere with as little warrant: "'For,' says Moses, 'Gideon swore, etc.'" [60] The incident illustrates the evil of mechanically supplying a supplement to these subjectless verbs — which cannot indeed be understood except on the basis of Philo's primary principle, that it is all one to say "Moses says," "the Scripture says," or "God says." The simple fact here is that Philo quotes Judges, as he does the rest of Scripture, with the subjectless "says," and with the same implication, viz., that Judges is to him a part of the Word of God.

As has been already hinted, by all means the commonest verb used by Philo thus, — without expressed or obviously indicated subject, — to introduce a Scripture passage, is φησί. Perhaps, however, the one instance to which we have incidentally adverted will suffice to illustrate the usage — other instances of which may be seen on nearly every page of Philo's treatises. It is of more interest for us to note that λέγει seems also to be used in the same subjectless way — examples of which may be seen, for instance, in the following places, "Legg. Allegor.," i, 15; ii, 4; iii, 8; "Quod Det. Pot. Insid.," 48; "De Posterit. Caini," 9; 22; 52; "De Gigant.," 11; 12; "De Confus. Ling.," 32; "De Migrat. Abrah.," 11; "Fragment. ex Joh. Monast." (ii, 668). In "Legg. Allegor.," i, 15, for instance, we have a string of quotations without obvious subject, introduced, the first by the subjectless φησίν, the next by the equally subjectless ἐπιφέρει πάλιν, and the third (from Exod. xx. 23) by λέγει δὲ καὶ ἐν ἑτέροις. In "Legg. Allegor.," ii, 4, we have Gen. ii. 19 intro-

[60] Vol. ii. p. 27.

duced by λέγει γὰρ without any obvious subject. Yonge translates this too by "For Moses says": but to obtain warrant
for this we should have to go back two pages and a half (of
Richter's text), quite to the beginning of the treatise, where
we find an apostrophe to the "prophet." In "De Posterit.
Caini," 22, λέγει ἐπὶ μὲν ᾿Αβραὰμ οὕτως (Gen. xi. 29), though
Yonge supplies "Moses" again, that would seem to be demonstrably absurd, as the passage proceeds to place "Moses,"
in parallelism with Abraham, in the *object*. Similarly the passages adduced from "De Gigant.," 11 and 12 (Num. xiv. 44
and Deut. xxxiv. 6) are *about* Moses, and it would scarcely
do to fill out the ellipsis of subject with his name. Examples
need not, however, be multiplied.

It would seem quite clear that both the subjectless φησί
frequently, and the subjectless λέγει less often, occur in Philo
after a fashion quite similar to the instances adduced from
the New Testament. And it would seem to be equally clear
that the lack of a subject in their case is not indicative of
indefiniteness, but rather of definiteness in their reference.
Philo does not adduce passages of Scripture with the bare
φησί or λέγει because he knows or cares very little whence
they come or with what authority; but because he and his
readers alike both know so well the source whence they are
derived, and yield so unquestionably to its authority, that it
is unnecessary to pause to indicate either. The use of the bare
φησί or λέγει in citations from Scripture is in his case, obviously, the outgrowth and the culminating sign of his absolute confidence in Scripture as the living voice of God,
fully recognized as such both by himself and his readers. In
the same sense in which to the dying Sir Walter Scott there
was but one "Book," to him and his readers there was but
one authoritative divine Word, and all that was necessary in
adducing it was to indicate the fact of adduction. The φησί
or λέγει serves thus primarily the function of "quotation
marks" in modern usage: but under such circumstances and
with such implications that bare quotation marks carry with
them the assurance that the words adduced are divine words.

It would seem to be very easy, in these circumstances, to give ourselves more uneasiness than is at all necessary as to the precise *subauditum* which we are to assume with these verbs. It may serve very well to render them simply, "It says," with the implication that Philo is using the *codex* of Scripture as the living voice of God speaking to him and his readers. The case, in a word, would seem to be very similar to that of the common New Testament formula of quotation γέγραπται — meaning not that what is adduced is somewhere written, but that it is the authoritative law that is being adduced. Just so, "It says," in such a case would mean not that somebody or something says what is adduced, but that the Word of God says it. As the one usage is the natural outgrowth of the conception of the Scriptures as a written authoritative law, the other is the equally natural outgrowth of the conception of Scripture as the living voice of God. How very natural a development this usage is, may be illustrated by the fact that something very similar to it may be met with in colloquial English. In the same circles where we may hear God spoken of as simply "He," as if it were dangerous to name His name too freely, we may also occasionally hear the Bible quoted with a simple "It says," or even with an elision of the "it," as "'Tsays": and yet the "it," though treated thus cavalierly, is in reality a very emphatic "It" indeed — the phrase being the product of awe in the presence of "the Book," and importing that there is but one "It" that could be thought of in the case. Somewhat similarly, in the case of Philo, the Scriptures are cited with the bare φησί, λέγει, because, in his mind and in the circles which he addressed, there stood out so far above all other voices this one Voice of God embodied in His Scriptures, that none other would be thought of in the case. The phrase is the outgrowth of reverence for the Word and of unquestioning submission to it: and the fundamental fact is that no special subject is expressed simply because none was needed and it would be all one whether we understood as subject, Moses, the prophet and lawgiver — the holy or sacred Word or the oracle — or

finally, God Himself. In any case, and with any *subauditum*,
the real subject conceived as speaking is GOD.[61]

If now, in the light of the facts we have thus brought to
our recollection, we turn back to the New Testament passages in which the Old Testament is cited with a simple φησί
or λέγει, it may not be impossible for us to perceive their real
character and meaning. There would seem to be absolutely
no warrant in Greek usage for taking λέγει, and but very
little, if any, for taking φησί really indefinitely: and even if
there were, it would be inconceivable that the New Testament writers, from their high conception of "Scripture,"
should have adduced Scripture with a simple "it is said" —
somewhere, by some one — without implication of reverence
toward the quoted words or recognition of the authority inherent in them. It is rather in the usage of Philo that we find
the true analogue of these examples. Like Philo, the author
of the Epistle to the Hebrews looks upon Scripture as an
oracular book, and all that it says, God says to him: and
accordingly, like Philo, he adduces its words with a simple
"it says," with the full implication that this "it says" is a
"God says" also. Whenever the same locution occurs elsewhere in the New Testament, it bears naturally the same
implication. There is no reason why we should recognize the
Philonic φησί in Heb. viii. 5, and deny it in I Cor. vi. 16: or
why we should recognize the Philonic λέγει in Heb. viii. 8
and deny it in Acts xiii. 35, Rom. ix. 15, xv. 10, II Cor. vi. 2,
Gal. iii. 16, or in Eph. iv. 8, v. 14. Only in case it were very
clear that Paul did not share the high conception of Scripture as the living voice of God which underlies this usage in

[61] The reverent use of an indefinite may be illustrated from the mode of
citation adopted in Heb. ii. 6 — "one hath somewhere testified" — a mode of citation not uncommon in Philo [as, for example, *de Temul.* (ed. Mang., i. 365), εἶπε
γάρ πού τις (i. e., Abraham, Gen. xx. 12), and other examples in Bleek, II, i. 239].
Delitzsch correctly explains: "The citation is thus introduced with a special
solemnity, the author naming neither the place whence he takes it nor the original
speaker, but making use (as Philo frequently) of the vague term πού τις, so that
the important testimony itself becomes only the more conspicuous, like a grand
pictured figure in the plainest, narrowest frame."

Philo and the Epistle to the Hebrews, could we hesitate to
understand this phrase in him as we understand it in them.
But we have seen that such is not the case: and his use in
adducing Scripture of the subjectless φησί and λέγει quite in
their manner is, rightly viewed, only another indication,
among many, that his conception of Scripture was fundamentally the same with theirs, and it cannot be explained
away on the assumption that it was fundamentally different.

It does not indeed follow that on every occasion when a
Scripture passage is introduced by a φησί or a λέγει it is to
be explained as an instance of this subjectless usage — even
though a subject for it is given or plainly implied in the immediate context. That is not possible even in Philo, where
the introductory formula often finds its appropriate subject
expressed in the preceding context. But it does follow that
we need not and ought not resort to unnatural expedients
to find a subject for such a φησί or λέγει in the context, or
that acquiescing, whenever that seems more natural, in its
subjectlessness, we should seek to explain away its high
implications.[62] Men may differ as to the number of clear

[62] The matter is approached in a sensible and helpful way by Viteau, in his
"Étude sur le Grec du N. T.: sujet, complement et attribute" (1896), p. 61. He
is treating of the subject to be mentally supplied, i. e., of the case where the
reader may be fairly counted upon to supply the subject, and he remarks (inter
alia): "76 (9). There is a kind of mental subject peculiar to the New Testament.
When events of the Old Testament are spoken of, these events are supposed to
be known to the reader or the hearer, who is invited to supply the subject of the
verb mentally. . . . 77 (10). There is still another kind of mental subject peculiar
to the New Testament and kindred to the preceding. In the citations made by
the New Testament the subject is often lacking, as well for the verb which announces the citation as for the verb in the citation itself. The reader is supposed
to recognize the passage and is invited to supply the subject. (a) For the verbs
which announce the citation there occur as subjects: ὁ θεός, Acts ii. 17; ὁ προφήτης,
Acts vii. 48; Δαυείδ, Rom. iv. 6; Μωϋσῆς, Rom. x. 19; Ἡσαίας, Rom. xv. 12; ἡ γραφή,
Gal. iv. 30. When the verb has no subject, the reader is to supply it mentally:
Acts xiii. 34, 35, εἴρηκεν and λέγει, the subject is ὁ θεός, according to the LXX.,
Es. lv. 3, and Ps. xv. 10; Rom. xv. 10, πάλιν λέγει (ὁ Μωϋσῆς), according to Deut.
xxxii. 43; Eph. iv. 8, λέγει (ὁ θεός or Δαυείδ), according to Ps. lxvii. 19; Eph. v. 14,
διὸ λέγει, those who regard the passage as imitated or partially cited from the Old
Testament give Ἡσαίας as the subject of λέγει, according to Isa. lx. 1, 2, but if we
regard this passage as containing some κῶλα of an early hymn (in imitation of

instances of such a usage, that may be counted in the New Testament. But most will doubtless agree that some may be counted: and will doubtless place among them Eph. iv. 8 and v. 14. Some will contend, no doubt, that in the latter of these texts, the passage adduced is not derived from the Old Testament at all. That, however, is "another story," on which we cannot enter now, but on which we must be content to differ. We pause only to say that we reckon among the reasons why we should think the citation here is derived from the Old Testament, just its adduction by διὸ λέγει — which would seem to advise us that Paul intended to quote the oracular Word.

There may be room for difference of opinion again as to the precise *subauditum* which it will be most natural to assume with these subjectless verbs: whether ὁ θεός or ἡ γραφή. In our view it makes no real difference in their implication: for, in our view, the very essence of the case is, that, under the force of their conception of the Scriptures as an oracular book, it was all one to the New Testament writers whether they said "God says" or "Scripture says." This is made very clear, as their real standpoint, by their double identification of Scripture with God and God with Scripture, to which we adverted at the beginning of this paper, and by which Paul, for example, could say alike "the *Scripture* saith to Pharaoh" (Rom. ix. 17) and "*God* . . . . saith, Thou wilt not give thy Holy One to see corruption" (Acts xiii. 34). We may well be content in the New Testament as in Philo to translate the phrase wherever it occurs, "It says" — with the implication that *this* "It says" is the same as "Scripture says," and that this "Scripture says" is the same as "God says." It is this implication that is really the fundamental fact in the case.

Isaiah) we must supply as the subject τις, 'it is said,' 'it is sung' (96a); Heb. viii. 5, φησίν (ὁ θεός), according to Ex. xxv. 40." We do not accord, of course, with the remark on Eph. v. 14; and we miss in Viteau's remarks the expected reference to the deeper fact in the case.

IX

"THE ORACLES OF GOD"

"THE ORACLES OF GOD"[1]

THE purpose of this paper is to bring together somewhat more fully than can be easily found in one place elsewhere, the material for forming a judgment as to the sense borne by the term [τὰ] λόγια, as it appears in the pages of the New Testament. This term occurs only four times in the New Testament. The passages, as translated by the English revisers of 1881, are as follows: "Moses . . . who received living *oracles* to give unto us" (Acts vii. 38); "They [the Jews] were intrusted with *the oracles* of God" (Rom. iii. 2); "When by reason of the time ye ought to be teachers, ye have need again that some one teach you the rudiments of the first principles of *the oracles* of God" (Heb. v. 12); "If any man speaketh let him speak as it were *oracles* of God" (I Peter iv. 11). The general sense of the term is obvious on the face of things: and the commentators certainly do not go wholly wrong in explaining it. But the minor differences that emerge in their explanations are numerous, and seem frequently to evince an insufficient examination of the usage of the word: and the references by which they support their several views are not always accessible to readers who would fain test them, so that the varying explanations stand, in the eyes of many, as only so many *obiter dicta* between which choice must be made, if choice is made at all, purely arbitrarily. It has seemed, therefore, as if it would not be without its value if the usage of the word were exhibited in sufficient fullness to serve as some sort of a touchstone of the explanations that have been offered of it. We are sure, at any rate, that students of the New Testament remote from libraries will not be sorry to have at hand a tolerably full account of the usage of the word: and we are not without hope that

[1] From *The Presbyterian and Reformed Review*, Vol. XI. 1900, pp. 217–260.

a comprehensive view of it may help to correct some long-standing errors concerning its exact meaning, and may, indeed, point not obscurely to its true connotation — which is not without interesting implications. Upheld by this hope we shall essay to pass in rapid review the usage of the term in Classic, Hellenistic and Patristic Greek, and then to ask what, in the light of this usage, the word is likely to have meant to the writers of the New Testament.

I. It may be just as well at the outset to disabuse our minds of any presumption that a diminutive sense is inherent in the term λόγιον, as a result of its very form.[2] Whether we explain it with Meyer-Weiss [3] as the neuter of λόγιος and point to λογίδιον [4] as the proper diminutive of this stem; or look upon it with Sanday-Headlam [5] as originally the diminutive of λόγος, whose place as such was subsequently, viz., when it acquired the special sense of "oracle," taken by the strengthened diminutive λογίδιον — it remains true that no trace of a diminutive sense attaches to it as we meet it on the pages of Greek literature.[6]

We are pointed, to be sure, to a scholium on the "Frogs" of Aristophanes (line 942) as indicating the contrary. The passage is the well-known one in which Euripides is made to

[2] So very commonly: as, e. g., by Grimm ("Lexicon in N. T.," s. v.), Bleek ("Der Brief an die Hebräer," ii. 2, 114, on Heb. v. 12), Philippi ("Com. on Romans," E. T., i. 105, on Rom. iii. 2), Morrison ("Expos. of 3d Chap. of Rom.," p. 14).   [3] "Com. on Romans," on Rom. iii. 2 (E. T., i. 140, note 1).

[4] Plato, "Eryx.," 401, E.: ἐτάραττέ γε αὐτὸν . . . τὸ λογίδιον; Isocrates, "Contra Sophistas," 295 B. (Didot, 191): τοσούτῳ δὲ χείρους ἐγένοντο τῶν περὶ τὰς ἔριδας καλινδουμένων, ὅσον οὗτοι μὲν τοιαῦτα λογίδια διεξιόντες . . .; Aristophanes, "Vesp.," 64: ἀλλ' ἔστιν ἡμῖν λογίδιον γνώμην ἔχον | ὑμῶν μὲν αὐτῶν οὐχὶ δεξιώτερον. Cf. Blaydes on the passage in Aristophanes.

[5] "Com. on Rom.," on Rom. iii. 2: "The old account of λόγιον as a diminutive of λόγος is probably correct, though Mey.-W. make it neuter of λόγιος on the ground that λογίδιον is the proper diminutive. The form λογίδιον is rather a strengthened diminutive which, by a process common in language, took the place of λόγιον when it acquired the sense of 'oracle.'" When they add that it was as "a brief condensed saying" that the oracle was called λόγιον, they have no support in the literature.

[6] Jelf, who looks upon it as a diminutive, cites it as an extreme example of the fact that many simple diminutives in -ιον have lost their diminutive force — such as θηρίον, βιβλίον: λόγιον, he says, "has assumed a peculiar meaning." In any event, thus, no diminutive meaning clings to λόγιον.

respond to Æschylus' inquiry as to what things he manufactured. "Not winged horses," is the reply (as Wheelwright
translates it), "By Jupiter, nor goat-stags, such as thou, Like
paintings on the Median tapestry, But as from thee I first
received the art, Swelling with boastful pomp and heavy
words, I paréd it straight and took away its substance, *With
little words*, and walking dialogues,[7] And white beet mingled,
straining from the books A juice of pleasant sayings, — then
I fed him With monodies, mixing Ctesiphon." It is upon the
word here translated "with little words," but really meaning "verselets" (Blaydes: *versiculis*) — ἐπυλλίοις — that the
scholium occurs. It runs: Ἀντὶ τοῦ λογίοις μικροῖς· ὡς δὲ βρέφος
βρεφύλλιον, καὶ εἶδος εἰδύλλιον· οὕτω καὶ ἔπος ἐπύλλιον.[8] That is
to say, ἐπύλλιον is a diminutive of the same class as βρεφύλλιον
and εἰδύλλιον,[9] and means λόγιον μικρόν. Since the idea of
smallness is explicit in the adjective attached to λόγιον here,
surely it is not necessary to discover it also in the noun,[10]
especially when what the scholiast is obviously striving to
say is not that ἐπυλλίοις means "little wordlets," but "little
verses." The presence of μικροῖς here, rather is conclusive evidence that λογίοις by itself did not convey a diminutive
meaning to the scholiast. If we are to give λόγιον an unexampled sense here, we might be tempted to take it, therefore, as intended to express the idea "verses" rather than
the tautological one of "little words" or even "little maxims"
or "little sayings." And it might fairly be pleaded in favor of
so doing that λόγιον in its current sense of "oracle" not only
lies close to one of the ordinary meanings of ἔπος ("Od.," 12,
266; Herod., 1, 13, and often in the Tragedians), but also,
because oracles were commonly couched in verse, might
easily come to suggest in popular speech the idea of "verse,"

---

[7] ἐπυλλίοις καὶ περιπάτοις καὶ τευτλίοισι λευκοῖς.

[8] Dindorf, iv. ii. p. 113, on line 973.

[9] Blaydes adds some other instances: "Ejusdem formæ diminutiva sunt
εἰδύλλιον, βρεφύλλιον, μειρακύλλιον, ζωύλλιον, κρεύλλιον, ξενύλλιον."

[10] With this λόγιον μικρόν compare the βραχέα λόγια of Justin Martyr, "Contra
Tryph.," c. 18. When the idea of *brevity* needed to be conveyed, it would seem
that an adjective expressive of this idea was required to be added.

so that a λόγιον μ ι κ ρ ό ν would easily obtrude itself as the exact synonym of ἐπύλλιον, in Euripides' sense, i. e., in the sense of short broken verses. There is no reason apparent on the other hand why we should find a diminutive implication in the word as here used, and in any case, if this is intended, it is a sense unillustrated by a single instance of usage.

And the unquestionable learning of Eustathius seems to assure us that to Greek ears λόγιον did not suggest a diminutive sense at all. He is commenting on line 339 of the Second Book of the "Iliad," which runs,

πῆ δὴ συνθεσίαι τε καὶ ὅρκια βήσεται ἡμῖν,

and he tells us that ὅρκιον in Homer is not a diminutive, but is a formation similar to λόγιον, which means "an oracle": Οὐχ ὑποκοριστικὸν δὲ παρ' Ὁμήρῳ οὐδὲ . . . τὸ ἴχνιον. Ὥσπερ δὲ τὰ ὅρκια παρωνόμασται ἐκ τοῦ ὅρκου, οὕτω καὶ ἐκ τοῦ λόγου τὰ λόγια ἤγουν οἱ χρησμοί.[11] There is no direct statement here, to be sure, that λόγιον is not a diminutive; that statement is made — with entire accuracy — only of ὅρκιον and ἴχνιον:[12] nor is the derivation suggested for λόγιον, as if it came directly from λόγος, perhaps scientifically accurate. But there is every indication of clearness of perception in the statement: and it could scarcely be given the form it has, had λόγιον stood in Eustathius' mind as the diminutive of λόγος. It obviously represented to him not a diminutive synonym of λόγος, but an equal synonym of χρησμός. What λόγιον stood for, in his mind, is very clearly exhibited, further, in a comment which he makes on the 416th line of the First Book of the "Odyssey," where Telemachus declares that he does not "care for divinations such as my mother seeks, summoning a diviner to the hall":

οὔτε θεοπροπίης ἐμπάζομαι, ἥν τινα μήτηρ
ἐς μέγαρον καλέσασα θεοπρόπον ἐξερέηται.

[11] Ed. Bas., i. 177; Rom. i. 233: Weigel's Leipzig ed. (here used), i. 189.

[12] Liddell and Scott say, s. v.: "ὅρκιον is not with Buttm., "Lexil.," s. v., to be regarded as a dim. of ὅρκος, but rather as neuter of ὅρκιος, with which ἱερόν or ἱερά may be supplied"; "Dim. of ἴχνος only in form (v. Chandler, "Accent.," § 340)." Cf. in general Jelf, "Grammar," §§ 56, 2, and 335, c (Vol. i. pp. 53, 337).

Eustathius wishes us to note that θεοπρόπος means the μάντις, θεοπροπία his art, and θεοπρόπιον the message he delivers, which Eustathius calls the χρησμῴδημα, and informs us is denominated by the Attics also λόγιον. He says: 'Ιστέον δὲ ὅτι θεοπρόπος μὲν ἄλλως, ὁ μάντις. θεοπροπία δὲ, ἡ τέχνη αὐτοῦ. θεοπρόπιον δὲ, τὸ χρησμῴδημα, ὃ καὶ λόγιον ἔλεγον οἱ 'Αττικοί.[13] To Eustathius, thus λόγιον was simply the exact synonym of the highest words in use to express a divine communication to men — θεοπρόπιον,[14] χρησμῴδημα, χρησμός. Similarly Hesychius' definition runs: Λόγια: θέσφατα, μαντεύματα, (προ)φητεύματα, φῆμαι, χρησμοί. In a word, λόγιον differs from λόγος not as expressing something smaller than it, but as expressing something more sacred.

The Greek synonymy of the notion "oracle" is at once extraordinarily full and very obscure. It is easy to draw up a long list of terms — μαντεῖα, μαντεύματα, πρόφαντα, θεοπρόπια, ἐπιθεσπισμοί θέσφατα, θεσπίσματα, λόγια, and the like; but exceedingly difficult, we do not say to lay down hard and fast lines between them, but even to establish any shades of difference among them which are consistently reflected in usage. M. Bouché-Leclercq, after commenting on the poverty of the Latin nomenclature, continues as to the Greek:[15]

" The Greek terminology is richer and allows analysis of the different senses, but it is even more confused than abundant. The Greeks, possessors of a flexible tongue, capable of rendering all the shades of thought, often squandered their treasures, broadening the meaning of

[13] Ed. Bas., pp. 1426, 1427; ed. Rom., p. 69; ed. Leipzig, i. p. 72.
[14] A scholium on the passage in the "Odyssey" brings out the meaning of θεοπρόπιον, to wit: τὸ ἐκ θεοῦ λεγόμενον, ἐξ οὗ καὶ θεοπρόπος ὁ τὰ τοῦ θεοῦ λέγων. Cf. also the Homeric Lexicons on the word: e. g., Ebeling, s. v. θεοπροπίη et θεοπρόπιον: "Sententia deorum, judicium quod dii (Juppiter potissimum et Appollo) cum vate (vel cum deo) communicant, vates cum aliis hominibus, oraculum. Cf. Nægelsb., H[omerische] Th[eologie], 187. Ap. 87, 4 μάντευμα τὸ ἐκ θεοῦ προλεγόμενον. Cf. Suid., i. 2, 1144 Hes."; and Capelle under same heading: "Alles was von den Göttern (bes[onders] Apollon und Zeus) angezeigt und durch den θεοπρόπος gedeutet wird, 'die von den Göttern eingegebenen Offenbarungen' (Nægelsb. zu A. 385. Cf. 'Hom. Th.,' S. 187), also Weissagung, Göttergebot, Götterbescheid, Orakel."
[15] "Histoire de la Divination dans l'Antiquité" (Paris, Leroux, 1879), Vol. ii. pp. 229, 230.

words at pleasure, multiplying synonyms without distinguishing between them, and thus disdaining the precision to which they could attain without effort. We shall seek in vain for terms especially appropriated to divination by oracles. From the verb χρῆσθαι, which signifies in Homer 'to reveal' in a general way, come the derivatives χρησμός and χρηστήριον. The latter, which dates from Hesiod and the Homerides, designates the place where prophecies are dispensed and, later, the responses themselves, or the instrument by which they are obtained. Χρησμός, which comes into current usage from the time of Solon, is applied without ambiguity to inspired and versified prophecies, but belongs equally to the responses of the oracles and those of free prophets. The word μαντεῖον in the singular designates ordinarily the place of consultation; but in the plural it is applied to the prophecies themselves of whatever origin. In the last sense it has a crowd of synonyms of indeterminate and changeable shades of meaning. The grammarians themselves have been obliged to renounce imposing rules on the capricious usage and seeking recognition for their artificial distinctions. We learn once more the impossibility of erecting precise definitions for terms which lack precision."

Among the distinctions which have been proposed but which usage will not sustain is the discrimination erected by the scholiast on Euripides, "Phœniss.," 907,[16] which would reserve θέσφατα, θεσπίσματα, χρησμοί for oracles directly from the gods, and assign μαντεῖαι and μαντεύματα to the responses of the diviners. The grain of truth in this is that in μάντις, μαντεύεσθαι, μαντεία, etymologically, what is most prominent is the idea of a special unwonted capacity, attention being directed by these words to the strong spiritual elevation which begets new powers in us. While, on the other hand, in θεσπίζειν the reference is directly to the divine inspiration, which, because it is normally delivered in song, is referred to by such forms as θεσπιῳδός, θεσπιῳδεῖν. Χρησμός, on the other hand, seems an expression which in itself has little direct reference either to the source whence or the form in which the oracle comes, but describes the oracle from the point of view of what it is in itself — viz., a "communication" —

---

[16] The scholium runs: θέσφατα, θεσπίσματα, χρησμοὶ τὸ αὐτὸ, ἐλέγοντο δὲ ἐπὶ θεῶν· μαντεῖαι δὲ καὶ μαντεύματα ἐπὶ μάντεων ἀνθρώπων.

going back, as it does, to χρῆν, the original sense of which
seems to be "to bestow," "to communicate." [17] Λόγιον doubtless may be classed with χρησμός in this respect — it is *par
excellence* the "utterance," the "saying." It would seem to be
distinguished from χρησμός by having even less reference than
it to the source whence — something as "a declaration" is
distinguished from "a message." If we suppose a herald coming with the cry, "A communication from the Lord," and
then, after delivering the message, adding: "This is His
utterance," it might fairly be contended that in strict precision the former should be χρησμός and the latter λόγιον, in
so far as the former term may keep faintly before the mind
the *source* of the message as a thing given, while the latter
may direct the attention to its *content* as *the very thing* received, doubtless with a further connotation of its fitness to
its high origin. Such subtlety of distinction, however, is not
sure to stamp itself on current use, so that by such etymological considerations we are not much advanced in determining the ordinary connotation of the words in usage.

A much more famous discrimination, and one which much
more nearly concerns us at present, has been erected on what
seems to be a misapprehension of a construction in Thucydides. In a passage which has received the compliment of
imitation by a number of his successors,[18] the historian is
describing the agitation caused by the outbreak of the Pe-

[17] The above is abstracted from J. H. Heinr. Schmidt in his "Handbuch der
Lateinischen und Griechischen Synonymik" (1889), §21, pp. 77–82. The original
meaning assigned to χρῆν (*darreichen, ertheilen*) is supported by a reference to
Vaniček, p. 250. Surely it is a much more reasonable determination than that
of Bouché-Leclercq ("Hist. de la Divination," i. 192), who would derive it from a
cleromantic idea, as if χράω signified first of all "entailler." So he conceives
ἀναιρεῖν to refer to the lot, as we say to "draw lots," as if the Pythoness "drew
her revelations as we draw lots." Schmidt refers the use of this word to the early
idea that the words came up out of the depths of the earth.

[18] E. g., Polybius, 3, 112, 8: "All the oracles preserved in Rome were in everybody's mouth (πάντα δ' ἦν τὰ παρ' αὐτοῖς λόγια πᾶσι τότε διὰ στόματος) and every
temple and house was full of prodigies and miracles: in consequence of which the
city was one scene of vows, sacrifices, supplicatory processions and prayers"
(Schuchburgh's translation). Appian, 2, 115, δείματα τὰ γὰρ ἄλογα πολλοῖς ἐνέπιπτε
περὶ ὅλην 'Ιταλίαν. Καὶ μαντευμάτων παλαιῶν ἐπιφοβωτέρων ἐμνημόνευον. Dionys. Hal.,

loponnesian war, one symptom of which was the passion for oracles which was developed. "All Hellas," he says,[19] "was excited by the coming conflict between the two cities. Many were the prophecies circulated, and many the oracles chanted by diviners (καὶ πολλὰ μὲν λόγια ἐλέγοντο, πολλὰ δὲ χρησμολόγοι ᾖδον), not only in the cities about to engage in the struggle, but throughout Hellas." And again, as the Lacedæmonians approached the city, one of the marks he, at a later point, notes of the increasing excitement is that "soothsayers (χρησμολόγοι) were repeating oracles (ᾖδον χρησμούς) of the most different kinds, which all found in some one or other enthusiastic listeners." [20] On a casual glance the distinction appears to lie on the surface of the former passage that λόγια are oracles in prose and χρησμοί oracles in verse: and so the scholiast [21] on the passage, followed by Suidas [22] defines. But it is immediately obvious on the most cursory glance into Greek literature that the distinction thus suggested will not hold. The χρησμοί are, to be sure, commonly spoken of as sung; and the group of words χρησμῳδός, χρησμῳδέω, χρησμῳδία, χρησμῴδημα, χρησμῴδης, χρησμῳδικός, witnesses to the intimate connection of the two ideas. But this arises out of the nature of the case, rather than out of any special sense attached to the word χρησμός: and accordingly, by the side of this group of words, we have others which, on the one hand, compound χρησμός with terms not implicative of singing (χρησμηγορέω, χρησμαγόρης — χρησμοδοτέω, χρησμοδότης, χρησμοδότημα — χρησμολογέω, χρησμολόγος, χρησμολογία, χρησμολόγιον, χρησμολογική, χρησμολέσχης — χρησμοποιός), and, on the other hand, compound other words for oracles with words denoting singing (θεσπιῳδέω, θεσπιῴδημα, θεσπιῳδός). The fact

---

"Ant.," vii. 68: χρησμοί τ' ᾔδοντο ἐν πολλοῖς χωρίοις κτλ. Dio Cassius, 431, 66 and 273, 64, where we read of λόγια παντοῖα ᾔδετο.

[19] ii. 8, Jowett's translation (i. p. 99).

[20] ii. 21, Jowett's translation (i. 109).

[21] In Didot's appendix, p. 416: Λόγιά ἐστι τὰ παρὰ τοῦ θεοῦ λεγόμενα καταλογάδην· χρησμοὶ δὲ οἵτινες ἐμμέτρως λέγονται, θεοφορουμένων τῶν λεγόντων.

[22] Ed. Bekker, p. 666: λόγια τὰ παρὰ θεοῦ λεγόμενα καταλογάδην, χρησμοὶ δὲ οἵτινες ἐμμέτρως λέγοντα' θεοφορουμένων τῶν λεγόντων.

is that, as J. H. Heinr. Schmidt [23] points out in an interesting discussion, the natural expression of elevated feeling was originally in song: so that the singer comes before the poet and the poet before the speaker. It was thus as natural for the ancients to say vati-*cinium* as it is for moderns to say Weis-*sagung* or sooth-*saying:* but as the custom of written literature gradually transformed the consciousness of men, their thought became more logical and less pictorial until even the Pythia ceased at last to speak in verse. Meanwhile, old custom dominated the oracles. They were chanted: they were couched in verse: and the terms which had been framed to describe them continued to bear this implication. Even when called λόγια, they prove to be ordinarily [24] in verse; and these also are said to be sung, as we read, for example, in Dio Cassius (431, 66 and 273, 64): λόγια παντοῖα ᾔδετο. What appears to be a somewhat constant equivalence in usage of the two terms χρησμός and λόγιον, spread broadly over the face of Greek literature, seems in any event to negative the proposed distinction. Nor does the passage in Thucydides when more closely examined afford any real ground for it. After all, λόγια and χρησμοί are not contrasted in this passage: the word χρησμοί does not even occur in it. The stress of the distinction falls, indeed, not on the nouns, but on the verbs, the point of the remark being that oracles were scattered among the people by every possible method.[25] If we add that

[23] In his "Handbuch der Lateinischen und Griechischen Synonymik" (Leipzig, 1889), § 21 (pp. 77–82).

[24] So for example in Aristophanes' "Knights" *passim* (see below) and in Porphyry's collection of Oracles.

[25] This is the explanation of Croiset in the very sensible brief note he gives on the passage in his attractive edition of Thucydides (Paris, Hachette & Cie., 1886): He says: "λόγια, oracles: according to the scholiast, oracles in prose in contrast with χρησμοί or oracles in verse; but it may be seen in Aristophanes ("Knights," 999–1002), that the two expressions were synonyms: the distinction bears here only on the manner in which these oracles were spread among the people; ἐλέγοντο signifies: they were hawked about from mouth to mouth, without the intervention of the diviners (ἐλέγοντο in the plural, despite the neuter subject, because it is the idea of *diversity* that dominates, rather than an idea of *collectivity;* cf. Curtius "Gr. gr.," § 363, Rem. 1); ᾖδον is the appropriate word in speaking of χρησμολόγοι or oracle-deliverers whose business was to *recite* the prophecies in verse."

the second πολλά is probably not to be resolved into πολλούς
χρησμούς,[26] the χρησμούς being derived from the χρησμῳλόγοι,
but is to have λόγια supplied with it from the preceding
clause, the assumed distinction between λόγια and χρησμοί
goes up at once in smoke. Λόγια alone are spoken of: and
these λόγια are said to be both spoken and sung.[27]

So easy and frequent is the interchange between the two
terms that it seems difficult to allow even the more wary
attempts of modern commentators to discriminate between
them. These ordinarily turn on the idea that λόγια is the
more general and χρησμός the more specific word, and go
back to the careful study of the Baron de Locella,[28] in his
comment on a passage in (the later) Xenophon's "Ephesiaca."
Locella's note does indeed practically cover the ground. He
begins by noting the interchange of the two words in the
text before him. Then he offers the definition that *oraculorum
responsa* are generically λόγια, whether in prose or verse, adducing the λόγια παλαιά of Eurip., "Heracl.," 406, and the
λόγιον πυθόχρηστον of Plutarch, "Thes.," i. 55, as instances of
λόγια undoubtedly couched in verse; while versified oracles,

[26] So still Franz Müller in his handy edition of this second book (Paderborn,
1886).

[27] So Steup-Classen in the fourth edition of Classen's "Second Book of Thucydides," brought out by Steup (Berlin, 1889). They say: "ἐλέγοντο : the unusual
plural doubtless on account of the variety and diffusion of the λόγια : cf. 5, 26, 2;
6, 62, 4. Λόγια, according to the usage of the anaphora, is to be understood with
πολλά in both instances (B. supposes the anaphora would require the prepositing
of the noun, as I. 3; but there νεότης is emphasized by καί, which is not the case
here with λόγια). Ἐλέγοντο : circulated by the mouth of the people, without
fixed or metrical form, which would be given them or preserved for them by
the χρησμολόγοι who were occupied professionally in the collection (hence —
λόγοι) and interpretation of transmitted prophecies (cf. Herod. 7, 6, 142;
Schömann, *Gr. Alt.*, 2³, 304). The distinction is between ἐλέγοντο and ᾖδον, not the
object of the λόγια."

[28] Pp. 152, 153 of his edition of the piece (Vienna, 1796). It is reprinted entire
in Peerlkamp's edition (Haarlem, 1818) with this addition by the later editor:
"λόγια Latinis interdum *dictiones*, *dicta*, *sermones*, et *logia;* cf. Heins. *ad Ovid.*,
Her. v. 33 et Observ. Misc. V. I. T. I., p. 276. *Apollodorus* in Biblioth. saepe
permutat λόγια et χρησμούς, qui quum scribit I, vi. § 1, τοῖς δὲ θεοῖς λόγιον ἦν
mireris interpretem reddentem *rumor erat inter deos.* De discrimine λόγια inter et
χρησμούς eadem jam ex *Aristophane* ejusque Schol. notarat *Tresling.* Adv. pag.
46, 47, addens *L. Bos* ad Rom. iii. 2 et *Alberti* Obs. Phil. pag. 298 *seq.*"

originally in hexameters and later in iambic trimeters are, specifically, χρησμοί — whence χρησμῳδέω is *vaticinor*, χρησ-μῳδία, *vaticinium*, and χρησμῳδός, *vates*. As thus the difference between the two words is that of genus and species, they may be used promiscuously for the same oracle. It is worth the trouble, he then remarks, to inspect how often λόγιον and χρησμός are interchanged in the "Knights" of Aristophanes between verses 109 and 1224, from which the error of the scholiast on Thucydides, ii. 8, is clear and of Suidas following him, in making λόγιον specifically an oracle in prose, and χρησ-μός one in verse. He then quotes Eustathius on the "Iliad," ii. ver. 233, and on the "Odyssey," i. ver. 1426; adduces the gloss, λόγιον, ὁ χρησμός; and asks his readers to note what Stephens adduces from Camerarius against this distinction.[29] The continued designation by Greek writers of the prose Pythian oracles as χρησμοί is adverted to, Plutarch's testi-mony being dwelt on: and relevant scholia on Aristophanes' "Av"., 960, and "Nub.," 144, are referred to. It is not strange that Locella's finding, based on so exhaustive a survey of the relevant facts, should have dominated later commentators, who differ from it ordinarily more by way of slight modifi-cation than of any real revision — suggesting that λόγια, being the more general word, is somewhat less sacred;[30] or somewhat less precise;[31] or somewhat less ancient.[32] The common difficulty with all these efforts to distinguish the two words is that there is no usage to sustain them. When the two words occur together it is not in contrast but in

---

[29] Stephens (ed. Dindorf-Hase) merely adduces Camerarius' testimony: "So Cam., adding that the discrimination of the grammarians is a false one, although the passage in Thucydides, i (*sic.*) [8] seems to agree with it."

[30] This seems to be what Haack (on Thucyd., ii. 8) means when he defines λόγια as *auguria, præsagia vatum*, and χρησμοί as *oracula deorum*.

[31] This seems the gist of Bredow's view (on Thucyd., ii. 8): "χρησμός cum verbis χρᾶν et χρεῖσθαι oraculorum propriis cohaerens definite oraculum divinum vocatur; λόγιον autem aperte generalius vocabulorum est, sermo ominosus, verbum faticidium quod non interrogatus vel deus, vel vates elocutus est." Poppo and Gœller *ad loc.* quote these views but add nothing of value to them.

[32] Bouché-Leclercq seems almost inclined to revert to Eustathius' statement and look upon λόγιον as "an expression peculiar to the Attic dialect, as πρόφαντα (Herod., v. 63; ix. 93) is an Ionic expression" (*op. cit.*, ii. 130, note 4).

apparently complete equivalence, and when λόγιον appears
apart from χρησμός it is in a sense which seems in no way to
be distinguishable from it. The only qualification to which
this statement seems liable, arises from a faintly-felt suspicion that, in accordance with their etymological implications already suggested, χρησμός has a tendency to appear
when the mind of the speaker is more upon the source of
the "oracle" and λόγιον when his mind is more upon its
substance.

Even in such a rare passage as Eurip., "Heracl.," 406,
where the two words occur in quasi-contrast, we find no
further ground for an intelligible distinction between them:

"Yet all my preparations well are laid:
Athens is all in arms, the victims ready
Stand for the gods for whom they must be slain.
By seers the city is filled with sacrifice
For the foes' rout and saving of the state.
All prophecy-chanters have I caused to meet,
Into old public oracles have searched,
And secret, for salvation of this land.[33]
And mid their manifest diversities,
In one thing glares the sense of all the same —
They bid me to Demeter's daughter slay,
A maiden of a high-born father sprung." [34]

And ordinarily they display an interchangeability which
seems almost studied, it is so complete and, as it were,
iterant. Certainly, at all events, it is good advice to follow, to
go to Aristophanes' "Knights" to learn their usage. In that
biting play Demos — the Athenian people — is pictured as
"a Sibyllianizing old man" with whom Cleon curries favor
by plying him with oracles,

ᾄδει δὲ χρησμούς· ὁ δὲ γέρων σιβυλλιᾷ.[35]

---

[33] χρησμῶν δ' ἀοιδοὺς πάντας εἰς ἓν ἁλίσας | ἤλεγξα καὶ βέβηλα καὶ κεκρυμμένα | λόγια παλαιὰ τῇ δὲ γῇ σωτήρια.
[34] Way's translation, 398 seq.
[35] Line 61. Blaydes says: "sensus est, senes enim oracula amat."

Nicias steals τοὺς χρησμούς from Cleon, and brings τὸν ἱερὸν χρησμόν to Demosthenes, who immediately on reading it exclaims, ὦ λόγια! [36] "DEM.: Ὦ λόγια. Give me quick the cup! NIC.: Behold, what says the χρησμός? DEM.: Pour on! NIC.: Is it so stated in the λογίοις? DEM.: O Bacis!" To cap the climax, the scholiast remarks on ὦ λόγια: "(μαντεύματα): he wonders when he reads τὸν χρησμόν." Only a little later,[37] Demosthenes is counseling the Sausage Vender not to "slight what the gods by τοῖς λογίοισι have given" him and receives the answer: "What then says ὁ χρησμός?" and after the contents of it are explained the declaration, "I am flattered by τὰ λόγια." As the dénouement approaches, Cleon and the Sausage Vender plead that their oracles may at least be heard (lines 960–961: οἱ χρησμοί). They are brought, and this absurd scene is the result: "CLEON: Behold, look here — and yet I've not got all. S. V.: Ah, me! I burst — 'and yet I've not got all!' DEM.: What are these? CLEON: Oracles (λόγια). DEM.: All! CLEON: Do you wonder? By Jupiter, I've still a chestful left. S. V.: And I an upper with two dwelling rooms. DEM.: Come, let us see whose oracles (οἱ χρησμοί) are these? CLEON: Mine are of Bacis. DEM.: Whose are thine? S. V.: Of Glamis, his elder brother." And when they are read they are all alike in heroic measure.

It is not in Aristophanes alone, however, that this equivalence meets us: the easy interchange of the two words is, we may say, constant throughout Greek literature. Thus, for example, in the "Corinthiaca" of Pausanias (ii. 20, 10) an oracle is introduced as τὸ λόγιον, and commented on as ὁ χρησμός.[38] In Diodorus Siculus, ii. 14,[39] Semiramis is said to have gone

---

[36] Line 120. Wheelwright's translation is used throughout.   [37] Line 194.

[38] πρότερον δὲ ἔτι τὸν ἀγῶνα τοῦτον προεσήμηνεν ἡ Πυθία, καὶ τὸ λόγιον εἴτε ἄλλως εἴτε καὶ ὡς συνεὶς ἐδήλωσεν Ἡρόδοτος·

'Αλλ' ὅταν ἡ θήλεια τὸν ἄρρενα νικήσασα
ἐξελάσῃ καὶ κῦδος ἐν 'Αργείοισιν ἄρηται
πολλὰς 'Αργείων ἀμφιδρυφέας τότε θήσει.

Τὰ μὲν ἐς τὸ ἔργον τῶν γυναικῶν ἔχοντα τοῦ χρησμοῦ ταῦτα ἦν. In. v. 3, 1; iv. 9, 4; ix. 37, 4 in like manner χρησμός is identified with μάντευμα.

[39] Bekker, i. 150.

τὸ Ἄμμον χρηυυμένη τῷ θεῷ πcρὶ τῆς ἰδίας τελευτῆς, and, the narrative continues, λέγεται αὐτῇ γενέσθαι λόγιον. Similarly in Plutarch's "De Defectu Orac.," v.[40] we have the three terms τὸ χρηστηρίον, τὸ λόγιον and τὰ μαντεῖα ταῦτα equated: in "De Mul. Virt.," viii.[41] the λόγια are explained by what was ἐχρήσ-θη: in "Quæstiones Romanæ," xxi.[42] λόγια came by way of a χρησμῳδεῖν. In the "Ephesiaca" of the later Xenophon metrical μαντεύματα are received, the recipients of which are in doubt what τὰ τοῦ θεοῦ λόγια can mean, until, on consideration, they discover a likely interpretation for the χρησμόν that seems to meet the wish of the God who ἐμαντεύσατο.[43]

How little anything can be derived from the separate use of λόγιον to throw doubt on its equivalence with χρησμός as thus exhibited, may be observed from the following instances of its usage, gathered together somewhat at random: [44]

Herodotus, i. 64: "He purified the island of Delos, according to the injunctions of an oracle (ἐκ τῶν λογίων)"; i. 120: "We have found even oracles sometimes fulfilled in unimportant ways (τῶν λογίων ἔνια)"; iv. 178: "Here in this lake is an island called Phla, which it is said the Lacedæmonians were to have colonized according to an oracle (τὴν νῆσον Λακεδαιμονίοισί φασι λόγιον εἶναι κτίσαι)"; viii. 60: "Where an oracle has said that we are to overcome our enemies (καὶ λόγιόν ἐστι τῶν ἐχθρῶν κατύπερθε)"; viii. 62: "which the prophecies declare we are to colonize (τὰ λόγια λέγει)." Aristophanes," Vesp.," 799: ὅρα τὸ χρῆμα, τὰ λόγι' ὡς περαίνεται; "Knights," 1050, ταυτὶ τελεῖσθαι τὰ λόγι' ἤδη μοι δοκεῖ. Polybius, viii. 30, 6: "For the eastern quarter of Tarentum is full of monuments, because those who die there are to this day all buried within the walls, in obedience to an ancient oracle (κατά τι λόγιον ἀρχαῖον)." Diodorus Siculus ap. Geog. Sync., p. 194 D ("Corpus Scriptorum Historiæ Byzantinæ," i. 366), "Fabius says an oracle came to Æneas (Αἰνείᾳ γενέσθαι λόγιον), that a quadruped should direct him

[40] ii. 412 D.
[41] ii. 247 D. ἀποπειρώμενοι τῶν λογίων. Ἐχρήσθη γὰρ αὐτοῖς· . . .
[42] ii. 268 E. ἀποφθέγγεσθαι λόγια, καὶ χρησμῳδεῖν τοῖς ἐρωτῶσιν· . . .
[43] i. 6.
[44] The word, as will be seen, is as old as Herodotus: on the other hand — if we may trust the indices — it does not seem to occur in Homer (Dunbar's "Concordance" [to Odyssey], Gehring's "Index"), Hesiod (Paulsen's "Index"), Plato (Ast's "Lexicon") or Aristotle, Xenophon or Sophocles.

to the founding of a city." Ælian,"Var. Hist.," ii.41: "Moreover My-
cerinus the Egyptian, when there was brought to him the prophecy
from Budo (τὸ ἐκ Βούτης μαντεῖον), predicting a short life, and he wished to
escape the oracle (τὸ λόγιον) . . ." Arrian, "Expedit. Alex.," ii. 3, 14
(Ellendt., i. 151): ὡς τοῦ λογίου τοῦ ἐπὶ τῇ λύσει τοῦ δεσμοῦ ξυμβεβηκότος;
vii. 16, 7 (Ellendt., ii. 419), "But when Alexander had crossed the
river Tigris with his army, pushing on to Babylon, the wise men of
the Chaldeans (Χαλδαίων οἱ λόγιοι) met him and separating him from
his companions asked him to check the march to Babylon. For they
had an oracle from their God Belus (λόγιον ἐκ τοῦ θεοῦ τοῦ Βήλου) that
entrance into Babylon at that time would not be for his good. But he
answered them with a verse (ἔπος) of the poet Euripides, which runs
thus: 'The best μάντις is he whose conclusion is good.'" Plutarch,
"Non posse suaviter vivi," etc., 24 (1103 F.): "What of that? (quoth
Zeuxippus). Shall the present discourse be left imperfect and unfinished because of it? and feare we to alledge the oracle of the gods (τὸ
λόγιον πρὸς 'Επίκουρον λέγοντες) when we dispute against the Epicureans? No (quoth I againe) in any wise, for according to the sentence
of Empedocles, 'A good tale twice a man may tell, and heare it told as
oft full well';" "Life of Theseus," § 26 (p. 12 C, Didot, p. 14), "He
applied to himself a certain oracle of Apollo's (λόγιόν τι πυθόχρηστον)"
§ 27 (p. 12 E, Didot, p. 14): "At length Theseus, having sacrificed to
Fear, according to the oracle (κατά τι λόγιον)"; "Life of Fabius," § 4
(Didot, p. 210), 'Εκινήθησαν δὲ τότε πολλαὶ καὶ τῶν ἀπορρήτων καὶ χρησί-
μων αὐτοῖς βίβλων, ἃς Σιβυλλείους καλοῦσι· καὶ λέγεται συνδραμεῖν ἔνια τῶν
ἀποκειμένων ἐν αὐταῖς λογίων πρὸς τὰς τύχας καὶ τὰς πράξεις ἐκείνας. Pausanias, "Attica" [I. 44, 9] (taken unverified from Wetstein): θύσαντος
Αἰακοῦ κατὰ δή τι λόγιον τῷ Πανελληνίῳ Διΐ. Polyænus, p. 37 (Wetstein)
[I, 18]: ὁ θεὸς ἔχρησε — οἱ πολέμιοι τὸ λόγιον εἰδότες — τοῦ λογίου πε-
πληρωμένου; p. 347 [IV, 3, 27], ἣν δὲ λόγιον 'Απόλλωνος. Aristeas, p. 119
(Wetstein): εὐχαριστῶ μὲν, ἄνδρες, ὑμῖν, τῷ δὲ ἀποστείλαντι μᾶλλον· μέγιστον δὲ τῷ θεῷ, οὗτινός ἐστι τὰ λόγια ταῦτα.

A survey of this somewhat miscellaneous collection of
passages will certainly only strengthen the impression we derived from those in which λόγιον and χρησμός occur together
— that in λόγιον we have a term expressive, in common usage
at least, of the simple notion of a divine revelation, an oracle,
and that independently of any accompanying implication of
length or brevity, poetical or prose form, directness or in-

directness of delivery. This is the meaning of λόγιον in the mass of profane Greek literature. As we have already suggested, the matter of the derivation of the word is of no great importance to our inquiry: [45] but we may be permitted to add that the usage seems distinctly favorable to the view that it is to be regarded rather as, in origin, the neuter of λόγιος used substantively, than the diminutive of λόγος. No implication of brevity seems to attach to the word in usage; and its exclusive application to "oracles" may perhaps be most easily explained on the supposition that it connotes fundamentally "a wise saying," and implies at all times something above the ordinary run of "words." [46]

II. It was with this fixed significance, therefore, that the word presented itself to the Jews of the later centuries before Christ, when the changed conditions were forcing them to give a clothing in Greek speech to their conceptions, derived from the revelation of the old covenant; and thus to prepare the way for the language of the new covenant. The oldest monument of Hellenistic Greek — the Septuagint Version of the Sacred Books, made probably in the century that stretched between 250 and 150 B.C. — is, however, peculiarly ill-adapted to witness to the Hellenistic usage of this word. As lay in the nature of the case, and, as we shall see later, was the actual fact, to these Jewish writers there were no "oracles" except what stood written in these sacred books themselves, and all that stood written in them were "oracles of God." In a translation of the books themselves, naturally this, the most significant Hellenistic application of the word

---

[45] See above, p. 336.

[46] Dr. Addison Alexander, with his usual clearness, posits the alternative admirably (on Acts vii. 38): "The Greek word (λόγια) has been variously explained as a diminutive of (λόγος) *word*, meaning a brief, condensed and frequent utterance; or as the neuter of an adjective (λόγιος) meaning rational, profound, wise, and as a substantive, a wise saying." It would seem difficult to rise from a survey of the classical usage without an impression that it justifies the latter derivation. This usage is stated with perfect accuracy by DeMoor ("Com. in Marckii Compend.," i. 13): τὸ λόγιον "when used substantively may be considered as more emphatic than τὸ ῥῆμα or even ὁ λόγος: for this term means with the Greeks not any kind of word, but specifically an *oracle*, a *divine response*."

"oracles," could find little place. And though the term might be employed within the sacred books to translate such a phrase as, say, "the word of God," in one form or another not infrequently met with in their pages, the way even here was clogged by the fact that the Hebrew words used in these phrases only imperfectly corresponded to the Greek word λόγιον, and were not very naturally represented by it. Though the ordinary Hebrew verb for *"saying"* — אָמַר [47] — to which etymologically certain high implications might be thought to be natural, had substantival derivatives, yet these were fairly effectually set aside by a term of lower origin — דָּבָר [48] — which absorbed very much the whole field of the conception "word." [49] The derivatives of מַאֲמַר, אֵמֶר, אִמְרָה, אֶמְרָה, אֹמֶר–אָמַר — in accordance with their etymological impress of loftiness or authority, are relegated to poetic speech (except מַאֲמַר, which occurs only in Esther i. 15, ii. 20, ix. 32, and has the sense of *commandment*) and are used comparatively seldom.[50] Nevertheless, it was to one of these that the Septuagint translators fitted the word λόγιον. To דָּבָר they naturally consecrated the general terms λόγος, ῥῆμα, πρᾶγμα: while

---

[47] It occurs, according to the Brown-Gesenius "Lexicon," no less than 5287 times; according to Girdlestone ("Synonyms of the O. T.," ed. 2, p. 205), it "is generally rendered in the LXX. ἔπω and λέγω." There seems to be inherent in the word an undertone of loftiness or authoritativeness due possibly to its etymological implication of "prominence." Its derivations are accordingly mostly poetical words designating a lofty speech or authoritative speech.

[48] The verb, of doubtful origin, occurs according to Brown-Gesenius, 1142 times, and is generally rendered in the LXX. (Girdlestone, *loc. cit.*) λαλέω. The noun occurs 1439 times and is rendered "generally λόγος, sometimes ῥῆμα, and in 35 passages, πρᾶγμα."

[49] There is also the poetic word מָלַל and its derivative noun מִלָּה — a word "used in 30 passages, 19 of which are in Job and 7 in Daniel," and rendered in the LXX. λόγος and ῥῆμα (Girdlestone).

[50] אֹמֶר, "except in Josh. xxiv. 27 (E) used exclusively in poetry, 48 times, of which 22 are in Proverbs and 11 in Job" (Driver on Deut. xxxii. 1). אִמְרָה "only found in poetry (36 times, of which 19 are in Ps. cxix.)" (Driver on Deut. xxxii. 2). אֶמְרָה, Lam. ii. 17 only. מַאֲמַר, Esth. i. 15, ii. 20, ix. 32 only. On the general subject of their poetic usage see Green, "General Introduction to the O. T.: The Text," p. 19; Bleek, "Introduction to the O. T.," E. T., i. 98; Hävernick, "Einleitung," i. 172; Gesenius, "Geschichte der hebräischen Sprache," p. 22, and "Lehrgebäude," Register, p. 892; Vogel, "De Dialecto Poetica."

they adjusted λόγιων as well as might be to אִמְרָה, and left
to one side meanwhile its classical synonyms [51] — except
μαντεία and its cognates, which they assigned, chiefly, of
course, in a bad sense, to the Hebrew קסם in the sense of
"divination."

אִמְרָה is, to be sure, in no sense an exact synonym of
λόγιον. It is simply a poetical word of high implications, prevailingly, though not exclusively, used of the "utterances"
of God, and apparently felt by the Septuagint translators to
bear in its bosom a special hint of the authoritativeness or
awesomeness of the "word" it designates. It is used only
some thirty-six times in the entire Old Testament (of which
no less than nineteen are in Ps. cxix.), and designates the
solemn words of men (Gen. iv. 23, cf. Isa. xxix. 4 bis., xxviii.
23, xxxii. 9; Ps. xvii. 6; Deut. xxxii. 2) as well as, more prevailingly, those of God. In adjusting λόγιον to it the instances
of its application to human words are, of course, passed by
and translated either by λόγος (Gen. iv. 23; Isa. xxix. 4 bis.;
Isa. xxviii. 23, xxxii. 9), or ῥῆμα (Deut. xxxii. 2; Ps. xvii. 6).
In a few other instances, although the term is applied to
"words of God," it is translated by Greek words other than
λόγιον (II Sam. xxii. 31, LXX. ῥῆμα, and its close parallel,
Prov. xxx. 5, LXX. λόγοι, though in the other parallels,
Ps. xii. 7, xviii. 31, the LXX. has λόγια; Ps. cxix. [41][52], 154,
where the LXX. has λόγος; in Ps. cxxxviii. 2, the LXX. reads
τὸ ἅγιόν σου, on which Bæthgen remarks, in loc., that "ἅγιον
seems to be a corruption for λόγιον," which is read here by
Aquila and the Quinta). In the remaining instances of its
occurrences, however — and that is in the large majority of
its occurrences — the word is uniformly rendered by λόγιον

---

[51] χρησμός, for example, which we have found the constant accompaniment of
λόγιον in the classics and shall find always by its side in Philo, does not occur in
the LXX. at all. The cognates χρηματίζω (Jer. xxxii. (25) 30, xxxiii. (26) 2, xxxvi.
(29) 23, xxxvii. (30) 2, χρηματισμός (Prov. xxiv. 69 (xxxi. 1), II Macc. ii. 4), χρημα-
τιστηρί (I Kgs. viii. 6), are, however, found, and in their high sense. It is somewhat
overstrained for Delitzsch (on Heb. viii. 5, E. T., Vol. ii. 32) to say: "The Septuagint word for the deliverance of a divine oracle or injunction is χρηματίζειν
(τοὺς λόγους) τινί or πρός τινα:" χρηματίζειν is found in this sense only in the LXX.

(Deut. xxxiii. 9; Ps. xii. 7 *bis.*, xviii. 31, cv. 19, cxix. 11, 38 [41],[52] 50, 58, 67, 76, 82, 103, 116, 123, 133, 140, 148, 158, 162, 170, 172, cxlvii. 15; Isa. v. 24). If there is a fringe of usage of אִמְרָה thus standing outside of the use made of λόγιον, there is, on the other side, a corresponding stretching of the use made of λόγιον beyond the range of אִמְרָה — to cover a few passages judged by the translators of similar import. Thus it translates אֹמֶר in Num. xxiv. 4, 16; Ps. xviii. 15 [xix. 15], cvi. [cvii.] 11, and דָּבָר in Ps. cxviii. [cxix.] 25, 65, 107, 169, [cxlvii. 8]; Isa. xxviii. 13; and it represents in a few passages λόγον, a variation from the Hebrew, viz., Ps. cxviii. [cxix.]; Isa. xxx. 11, 27 *bis.* In twenty-five instances of its thirty-nine occurrences, however, it is the rendering of אִמְרָה.[53] It is also used twice in the Greek apocrypha (Wis. xvi. 11; Sir. xxxvi. 19 [16]), in quite the same sense. In all the forty-one instances of its usage, it is needless to say, it is employed in its native and only current sense, of "oracle," a sacred utterance of the Divine Being, the only apparent exception to this uniformity of usage (Ps. xviii. 15 [xix. 15]) being really no exception, but, in truth, significant of the attitude of the translators to the text they were translating — as we shall see presently.

What led the LXX. translators to fix upon אִמְרָה as the nearest Hebrew equivalent to λόγιον,[54] we have scanty material for judging. Certainly, in Psalm cxix, where the word most frequently occurs, it is difficult to erect a distinction between its implications and those of דָּבָר with which it seems to be freely interchanged, but which the LXX. trans-

---

Jeremiah. A very rich body of illustrations for the New Testament usages (Luke ii. 26, Acts x. 22, Heb. viii. 5) might, however, be culled from Philo.

[52] In some codd. but in the edd. we read, κατὰ τὸ ἔλεός σου.

[53] The passages are already enumerated just above.

[54] The other versions add nothing of importance. At Ps. cxix. 41 the אִמְרָה rendered ἔλεος by LXX. is rendered λόγιον by Aq. and Th. In Ps. cxxxvii. (cxxxviii). 2 the אִמְרָה rendered by LXX. ἅγιον (though Bæthgen remarks that this seems merely a corruption of λόγιον) is rendered λόγιον by Aq. and Quinta. In Isa. xxxii. 9, the אִמְרָה rendered in LXX. by λόγοι is given as λόγιον by Aq., a case quite parallel with Ps. xviii. 15 (xix. 15) in LXX. In Jer. viii. 9 the phrase בִּדְבַר־יהוָה is rendered in Aq. by λόγιον.

lators keep reasonably distinct from it by rendering it prevailingly by λόγος,[55] while equally prevailingly reserving
λόγιον for אִמְרָה.[56] Perhaps the reader may faintly feel even
in this Psalm, that אִמְרָה was to the writer the more sacred
and solemn word, and was used, in his rhetorical variation of
his terms, especially whenever the sense of the awesomeness
of God's words or the unity of the whole revelation of God [57]
more prominently occupied his mind; and this impression is
slightly increased, perhaps, in the case of the interchange of
λόγιον and λόγος in the Greek translation. When we look beyond this Psalm we certainly feel that something more requires to be said of אִמְרָה than merely that it is poetic.[58] It is
very seldom applied to human words and then only to the
most solemn forms of human speech — Gen. xxiv. 23 (LXX.,
λόγοι); Deut. xxxii. 2 (LXX., ῥῆμα); Ps. xxvii. (LXX., ῥῆμα);
cf. Isa. xxix. 4 bis (LXX., λόγοι) where the speaker is Jerusalem whose speech is compared to the murmuring of familiar
spirits or of the dead,[59] and Isa. xxviii. 23, xxxii. 9, where the
prophet's word is in question. It appears to suggest itself
naturally when God's word is to receive its highest praises

[55] The statistics of this Psalm are: אִמְרָה is used 19 times: being translated by
λόγιον 17 times, viz., at verses 11, 38, 50, 58, 67, 76, 82, 103, 115, 123, 133, 140,
148, 158, 162, 170, 172; at v. 41 it is translated τὸ ἔλεος, though some codices read
τὸν λόγον and some τὸ λόγιον; at v. 154 it is translated by λόγον. דָּבָר is used 23 times:
being translated by λόγος 15 times, viz., at verses 9, 16, 17, 28, 42, 43, 49, 74, 81,
89, 101, 130, 147, 160, 161; by λόγιον 4 times, viz., at verses 25, 65, 107, 109; by
ἐντολή twice, viz., at verses 57, 139; by νόμος at v. 105, and by λαός at v. 114 (though
some cod. read λόγοι or λόγος). Λόγιον is used 23 times: being the translation of אִמְרָה
17 times, viz., at verses 11, 38, 50, 58, 67, 76, 82, 103, 115, 123, 133, 140, 148, 158,
162, 170, 172; of דָּבָר 4 times (25, 65, 107, 169); of הֶסֶד once (124) and of מִשְׁפָּט
once (149). Λόγος is used 17 times: being the translation of דָּבָר 15 times, viz.,
at verses 9, 16, 17, 28, 42, 43, 49, 74, 81, 89, 101, 130, 147, 160, 161 and of אִמְרָה
once (154, cf. 41), while once (42a) it is inserted without warrant from the Hebrew.

[56] Delitzsch on v. 9 seq.: "The old classic (e. g., xviii. 31), אִמְרָתֶךָ alternates
throughout with דְּבָרֶךָ; both are intended collectively." Perowne on v. 11: "WORD,
or rather 'saying,' 'speech,' distinct from the word employed, for instance, in v. 9.
Both words are constantly interchanged throughout the Psalm."

[57] Delitzsch on v. 145–152: "אִמְרָה is here as in verses 140, 158, the whole
Word of God, whether in its requirements or its promises."

[58] Driver on Deut. xxxii. 2: "Only found in poetry (36 times, of which 19 are
in Ps. 119); cf. Isa. xxviii. 23, xxxii. 9."

[59] On this passage cf. König, "Offenbarungsbegriff," ii. 149, 150.

(II Sam. xxii. 31; Ps. xii. 7, xviii. 31; Prov. xxx. 5; Ps. cxxxviii. 2), or when the word of Jehovah is conceived as power or adduced in a peculiarly solemn way (Ps. cxlvii. 18 [60]; Isa. v. 24). Perhaps the most significant passage is that in Psalm cv. 19, where the writer would appear to contrast man's word with God's word, using for the former דָּבָר (LXX., λόγος) and for the latter אִמְרָה (LXX., λόγιον): Joseph was tried by the word of the Lord until his own words came to pass.[61] Whatever implications of superior solemnity attached to the Hebrew word אִמְרָה, however, were not only preserved, but emphasized by the employment of the Greek term λόγιον to translate it — a term which was inapplicable, in the nature of the case, to human words, and designated whatever it was applied to as the utterance of God. We may see its lofty implications in the application given to it outside the usage of אִמְרָה — in Num. xxiv. 4, for example, where the very solemn description of Balaam's deliverances — "oracle of the hearer of the words of God" (אִמְרֵי־אֵל) — is rendered most naturally φησὶν ἀκούων λόγια ἰσχυροῦ. Here, one would say, we have the very essence of the word, as developed in its classical usage, applied to Biblical conceptions: and it is essentially this conception of the "unspeakable oracles of God" (Sir., xxxvi. 19, [16]) that is conveyed by the word in every instance of its occurrence.

An exception has been sometimes found, to be sure, in Ps. xviii. 15 (xix. 14), inasmuch as in this passage we have the words of the Psalmist designated as τὰ λόγια: "And the words (τὰ λόγια) of my mouth and the meditation of my heart shall be continually before thee for approval, O Lord, my help and my redeemer." In this passage, however — and

[60] "The God of Israel is the Almighty Governor of nature. It is He who sends His fiat (אִמְרָתוֹ) after the manner of the וַיֹּאמֶר of the history of creation, cf. xxxiii. 9), earthward. . . . The word is His messenger (cf. in cvii. 20), etc." Delitzsch, in loc.

[61] It seems certainly inadequate to render אִמְרָה by "saying," as is very frequently done, e. g., by Dr. John DeWitt in his "Praise Songs of Israel" (we have only the first edition at hand), by Dr. Maclaren in the cxix. Psalm ("Expositor's Bible") and by Dr. Driver at Ps. cv. 19; cf. cxlvii. 15 seq. This English word suggests nothing of the lofty implications which seem to have attached to the Hebrew term.

in Isa. xxxii. 9 as rendered by Aquila, which is similar — we
would seem to have not so much an exception to the usage
of τὰ λόγια as otherwise known, as an extension of it. The
translators have by no means used it here of the words of a
human speaker, but of words deemed by them to be the
words of God, and called τὰ λόγια just because considered
the "tried words of God." This has always been perceived
by the more careful expositors. Thus Philippi [62] writes:

"Psalm xix. 14 supplies only an apparent exception, since τὰ
λόγια τοῦ στόματός μου there, as spoken through the Holy Spirit, may
be regarded as at the same time, λόγια θεοῦ."

And Morrison: [63]

"In Psalm xix. 15 (14) the term thus occurs: 'let the words of my
mouth (τὰ λόγια τοῦ στόματός μου = אִמְרֵי־פִי, from אָמַר), and the meditation of my heart, be acceptable in thy sight, O Lord, my strength
and my Redeemer.' But even here the term may be fitly regarded as
having its otherwise invariable reference. The Septuagint translator
looked upon the sacred writer as giving utterance in his Psalm — *the
words of his mouth* — to diviner thoughts than his own, to the thoughts
of God Himself. He regarded him as 'moved' in what he said, 'by
the Holy Ghost.'" [64]

In a word, we have here an early instance of what proves to
be the standing application of τὰ λόγια on Hellenistic lips —
its application to the Scripture word as such, as the special
word of God that had come to them. The only ground of
surprise that can emerge with reference to its use here, therefore, is that in this instance it occurs within the limits of the
Scriptures themselves: and this is only significant of the
customary employment of the term in this application —
for, we may well argue, it was only in sequence to such a
customary employment of it that this usage could intrude
itself thus, unobserved as it were, into the Biblical text itself.

[62] On Rom. iii. 2.
[63] On Rom. iii. 2 (pp. 14, 15).
[64] Possibly Bleek *in loc.* Heb. v. 12 means the same thing when he says the
word stands here of "the inspired religious song of the poet."

It is scarcely necessary to do more than incidentally advert to the occasional occurrence of λόγιον = λογεῖον in the Septuagint narrative, as the rendering of the Hebrew חשׁן, that is, to designate the breastplate of the high priest, which he wore when he consulted Jehovah.[65] Bleek writes, to be sure, as follows: [66]

"How fully the notion of an utterance of God attended the word according to the usage of the Alexandrians too is shown by the circumstance that the LXX. employed it for the oracular breastplate of the High Priest (חשׁן), Ex. xxviii. 15, 22 seq., xxix. 5, xxxix. 8 seq.; Lev. viii. 8; Sir. xlv. 12, for which λογεῖον, although found in Codd. Vat. and Alex., is apparently a later reading; λόγιον, to which the Latin translation rationale goes back, has also Josephus, "Ant.," iii. 7, 5, for it: ἐσσήνης (חשׁן) μὲν καλεῖται, σημαίνει δὲ τοῦτο κατὰ τὴν Ἑλλήνων γλῶτταν λόγιον; c. 8, 9: ὅθεν Ἕλληνες . . . τὸν ἐσσήνην λόγιον καλοῦσιν; viii. 3, 8. And similarly apparently Philo, as may be inferred from his expositions, in that he brings it into connection with λόγος, reason, although with him too the reading varies between the two forms: see "Legg. Allegor.," iii. 40, p. 83, A. B.; § 43, p. 84, C. "Vit. Mos.," iii. 11, p. 670 C.; § 12, p. 672 B.; § 13, p. 673 A. "De Monarch.," ii. 5, p. 824 A."

It is much more probable, however, that we have here an itacistic confusion by the copyists, than an application by the Septuagint translators of λόγιον to a new meaning. This confusion may have had its influence on the readers of the LXX., and may have affected in some degree their usage of the word: but it can have no significance for the study of the use of the word by the LXX. itself.

III. Among the readers of the Septuagint it is naturally to Philo that we will turn with the highest expectations of light on the Hellenistic usage of the word: and we have already seen Bleek pointing out the influence upon him of the

---

[65] Ex. xxviii. 15, 22, 23, 24, 24, 26, xxix. 5, 5 A. R., xxxv. 27, xxxvi. 15, 16, 22, 24, 25, 27, 29, 29; Lev. viii. 8, 8; Sir. xlv. 10. Also in Aq.: Ex. xxv. 6 (7), xxviii. 4, xxxv. 9. In Sm.: Ex. xxviii. 4, 28. In Th.: Ex. xxv. 6 (7), xxviii. 4, 23, 23, xxviii. 24, 26, 28, xxxv. 9.

[66] Hebrews, pp. 115, 116, note.

LXX. use of λόγιον — λογείον. Whatever minor influence of this kind the usage of the Septuagint may have had on him, however, Philo's own general employment of the word carries on distinctly that of the profane authors. In him, too, the two words χρησμός and λόγιον appear as exact synonyms, interchanging repeatedly with each other, to express what is in the highest sense the word of God, an oracle from heaven. The only real distinction between his usage of these words and that of profane authors arises from the fact that to Philo nothing is an oracle from heaven, a direct word of God, except what he found within the sacred books of Israel.[67] And the only confusing element in his usage springs

[67] It is not intended to deny that Philo recognized a certain divine influence working beyond the limits of Scripture: but he does this without prejudice to his supreme regard for the Scriptures as the only proper oracles of God. At the opening of the tractate "Quod Omn. Prob. Lib." (§ 1, M. 444, 445), he gives expression in the most exalted terms to his appreciation of the value of Greek thought: the Pythagoreans are a most sacred brotherhood (ἱερώτατος θίασος) whose teachings are κάλα, and all men who have genuinely embraced philosophy (φιλοσοφίαν γνησίως ἠσπάσαντο) have found one of their λόγοι a θεσμὸν ἰσούμενον χρησμῷ. Elsewhere he speaks of Parmenides, Empedocles, Zeno and Cleanthes and their like as "divi homines" constituting a "sacer coetus" ("De Prov.," § 48), who did not cast their teachings in verse only because it was fitting that they should not be quite gods ("De Prov.," § 42). But even here the χρησμός is the standard to which their teaching is only likened: with all their wisdom they fall short of deity; and it is the utterance of deity alone which is "oracular" — and this utterance is discernible only in the Scriptures of the Jews. We venture to quote here the statements of Prof. James Drummond ("Philo Judæus," i. pp. 13 seq.): The Scriptures "were the 'oracles,' the 'sacred' or 'divine word,' whose inspiration extended to the most minute particulars. Philo distinguishes indeed different kinds of inspiration, but the distinction did not affect its divine authority. . . . Communion between God and man is among the permanent possibilities of our race; and Philo goes so far as to say that every good and wise man has the gift of prophecy, while it is impossible for the wicked man to become an interpreter of God ("Quis rer. div. heres." 52 [i. 510]). It is true that he is referring here primarily to the good men in the Scriptures, but he seems to regard them as representatives of a general law. He did not look upon himself as a stranger to this blessed influence, but sometimes 'a more solemn word' spoke from his own soul, and he ventured to write down what it said to him ("Cherubim," 9 [i. 143]). In one passage he fully records his experience ("Migrat. Abrah.," 7 [i. 441]). . . . Elsewhere he refers to the suggestions of the Spirit which was accustomed to commune with him unseen ("De Somniis," ii. 38 [i. 692]). . . . But he ascribed to the Biblical writers a fullness of this divine enthusiasm, and consequent infallibility of utterance, which he claimed for no others."

from the fact that the whole contents of the Jewish sacred books are to him "oracles," the word of God; so that he has no nomenclature by which the oracles recorded in the Scriptures may be distinguished from the oracles which the Scriptures as such are. He has no higher words than λόγιον and χρησμός by which to designate the words of God which are recorded in the course of the Biblical narrative: he can use no lower words than these to designate the several passages of Scripture he adduces, each one of which is to him a direct word of God. Both of these uses of the words may be illustrated from his writings almost without limit. A few instances will suffice.

In the following, the "oracle" is a "word of God" recorded in the Scriptures [68]:

"For he inquires whether the man is still coming hither, and the sacred oracle answers (ἀποκρίνεται τὸ λόγιον), 'He is hidden among the stuff' (I Sam. x. 22)" ("De Migrat. Abrah.," § 36, pp. 418 E). "For after the wise man heard the oracle which being divinely given said (θεσπισθέντος λογίου τοιούτου) 'Thy reward is exceeding great' (Gen. xv. 1), he inquired, saying. . . . And yet who would not have been amazed at the dignity and greatness of him who delivered this oracle (τοῦ χρησμῷ δούντος)?" ("Quis rer. div. her.," § 1, pp. 481 D). "And he (God) mentions the ministrations and services by which Abraham displayed his love to his master in the last sentence of the divine oracle given to his son (ἀκροτελεύτιον λογίου τοῦ χρησθέντος αὐτοῦ τῷ υἱεῖ) ("Quis rer. div. her.," § 2, pp. 482 E). "To him (Abraham), then, being conscious of such a disposition, an oracular command suddenly comes (θεσπίζεται λόγιον), which was never expected (Gen. xxii. 1) . . . and without mentioning the oracular command (τὸ λόγιον) to anyone . . ." ("De Abrah.," § 32, P., p. 373 E). "[Moses] had appointed his brother high-priest in accordance with the will of God that had been declared unto him (κατὰ τὰ χρησθέντα λόγια")) ("De Vita Moysis," iii.

[68] Yonge's translation (in Bohn's Ecclesiastical Library) is made use of in these citations. The paging of Mangey is often given and sometimes that of the Paris edition: but the edition of Richter is the one that has been actually used. The shortcomings of Yonge's translation (cf. Edersheim's article, "Philo," in Smith and Wace's "Dictionary of Christian Biography," iv. 367 A, note o), will be evident to the reader; but when important for our purpose will be correctable from the Greek clauses inserted.

21, P., p. 569 D). "Moses . . . being perplexed . . . besought God to decide the question and to announce his decision to him by an oracular command (χρησμῷ). And God listened to his entreaty· and gave him an oracle (λόγιον θεσπίζει). . . . We must proceed to relate the oracular commands (λόγια χρησθέντα). He says . . . (Num. ix. 10)" ("De Vita Moysis," iii. 30, P., p. 687 D). "And Balaam replied, All that I have hitherto uttered have been oracles and words of God (λόγια καὶ χρησμοί), but what I am going to say are merely the suggestions of my own mind. . . . Why do you give counsel suggesting things contrary to the oracles of God (τοῖς χρησμοῖς) unless indeed that your counsels are more powerful than his decrees (λογίων)?" ("De Vita Moysis," i. 53, P., p. 647 D). "Was it not on this account that when Cain fancied he had offered up a blameless sacrifice an oracle (λόγιον) came to him ? . . . And the oracle is as follows (τὸ δὲ λόγιόν ἐστι τοιόνδε) (Gen. iv. 7)" ("De Agricult.," § 29, M. i. 319). "And a proof of this may be found in the oracular answer given by God (τὸ θεσπισθὲν λόγιον) to the person who asked what name he had: 'I am that I am'" ("De Somniis," i. § 40, M. 1, 655). "But when he became improved and was about to have his name changed, he then became a man born of God (ἄνθρωπος θεοῦ) according to the oracle that was delivered to him (κατὰ τὸ χρησθὲν αὐτῷ λόγιον), 'I am thy God'" ("De Gigant.," § 14, M. 1, 271). "For which reason, a sacred injunction to the following purport (διὸ καὶ λόγιον ἐχρήσθη τῷ σοφῷ τοιόνδε) 'Go thou up to the Lord, thou and Aaron,' etc. (Gen. xxiv. i.). And the meaning of this injunction is as follows: 'Go thou up, O soul'" ("De Migrat. Abrah.," § 31, M. 1, 462). "For which account an oracle of the all-merciful God has been given (λόγιον τοῦ ἵλεω θεοῦ μεστὸν ἡμερότητος) full of gentleness, which shadows forth good hopes to those who love instruction in these times, 'I will never leave thee nor forsake thee' (Jos. i. 5)" ("De Confus. Ling.," § 32, M. i. 430). "Do you not recollect the case of the soothsayer Balaam ? He is represented as hearing the oracles of God (λόγια θεοῦ) and as having received knowledge from the Most High, but what advantage did he reap from such hearing, and what good accrued to him from such knowledge ?" ("De Mutat. Nominum," § 37). "There are then a countless number of things well worthy of being displayed and demonstrated; and among them one which was mentioned a little while ago; for the oracle (τὸ λόγιον) calls the person who was really his grandfather, the father of the practiser of virtue, and to him who was really his father it has not given any such title; for it says, 'I am the Lord God of Abraham, thy Father' (Gen. xxviii. 13), and in reality he was his grandfather, and, again, 'the God of Isaac,' not adding this time, 'thy Father' ('De Somniis,' i. § 27)." "And there is something closely resembling this in the passage of Scripture (*lit.* the oracle: τὸ χρησθὲν λόγιον) concerning the High Priest (Lev. xvi. 17)" ("De Somniis," ii. § 34).

On the other hand, in the following instances, the reference is distinctly to Scripture as such:

"And the following oracle given with respect to Enoch (τὸ χρησθὲν ἐπὶ Ἐνὼχ λόγιον) proves this: 'Enoch pleased God and he was not found' (Gen. v. 24)" ("De Mutat. Nom.," § 4).

It is a portion of the narrative Scriptures which is thus adduced.

"But let us stick to the subject before us and follow the Scripture (ἀκολουθήσαντες τῷ λογίῳ) and say that there is such a thing as wisdom existing, and that he who loves wisdom is wise" (*do*).

Here τὸ λόγιον is either Scripture in general, or, perhaps more probably, the passage previously under discussion and still in mind (Gen. v. 24).

"Μαρτυρεῖ δέ μοι λόγιον τὸ χρησθὲν ἐπὶ τοῦ Ἀβραάμ τόδε, 'He came into the place of which the Lord God had told him; and having looked up with his eyes, he saw the place afar off (Gen. xxii. 9)'" ("De Somniis," i. 11).

This narrative passage of Scripture is here cited as λόγιον τὸ χρησθέν.

"This is a boast of a great and magnanimous soul, to rise above all creation, and to overleap its boundaries and to cling to the great uncreated God above, according to his sacred commands (κατὰ τὰς ἱερὰς ὑφηγήσεις) in which we are expressly enjoined 'to cleave unto him' (Deut. xxx. 20). Therefore he in requital bestows himself as their inheritance upon those who do cleave unto him and who serve him without intermission; and the sacred Scripture (λόγιον) bears its testimony in behalf of these, when it says, 'The Lord himself is his inheritance' (Deut. x. 9)" ("De Congressu erud. grat.," § 24, p. 443).

Here the anarthrous λόγιον is probably to be understood of "a passage of Scripture" — viz., that about to be cited.

"Moreover she (Consideration) confirmed this opinion of hers by the sacred scriptures (χρησμοῖς), one of which ran in this form (ἑνὶ μὲν τοιῷδε — without verb) (Deut. iv. 4). . . . She also confirmed her statement by another passage in Scripture of the following purport (ἑτέρῳ τοιῷδε χρησμῷ) (Deut. xxx. 15) . . . and in another passage we read (καὶ ἐν ἑτέροις) (Deut. xxx. 20). And again this is what the Lord himself hath said . . . (Lev. x. 3) . . . as it is also said in the Psalms (Ps. cxiii. 25) . . . but Cain, that shameless man, that parricide, is nowhere spoken of in the Law (οὐδαμοῦ τῆς νομοθεσίας) as dying: but there is an oracle delivered respecting him in such words as these (ἀλλὰ καὶ λόγιον ἔστιν ἐπ᾽ αὐτῷ χρησθὲν τοιοῦτον): 'The Lord God put a mark upon Cain' (Gen. iv. 15)" ("De Profug.," § 11, M. i. 555).

Here it is questionable whether "the Law" (ἡ νομοθεσία) is not broad enough to include all the passages mentioned — from Genesis, Leviticus and the Psalms — as it is elsewhere made to include Joshua ("De Migrat. Abrah.," § 32, M. i, 464. See Ryle: p. xix). At all events, whatever is in this νομοθεσία is a χρησθὲν λόγιον: the passage more particularly adduced being a narrative one.

"After the person who loves virtue seeks a goat by reason of his sins, but does not find one; for already as the sacred Scripture tells us (ὡς δηλοῖ τὸ λόγιον), 'It hath been burnt' (Lev. x. 16) . . . Accordingly the Scripture says (φησὶν οὖν ὁ χρησμός) that Moses 'sought and sought again,' a reason for repentance for his sins in mortal life . . . on which account it is said in the Scripture (διὸ λέγεται) (Lev. xvi. 20)" ("De Profug.," § 28, M. i. 569).

Here τὸ λόγιον seems to mean not so much a passage in Scripture as "Scripture" in the abstract: Lev. x. 16 not being previously quoted in this context. The same may be said of the reference of ὁ χρησμός in the next clause and of the simple λέγεται lower down — the interest of the passage turning on the entire equivalence of the three modes of adducing Scripture.

"This then is the beginning and preface of the prophecies of Moses under the influence of inspiration (τῆς κατ᾽ ἐνθουσιασμὸν προφητείας Μωϋσέως). After this he prophesied (θεσπίζει) . . . about food . . . being full of inspiration (ἐπιθειάσας). . . . Some thinking, perhaps, that what was said to them was not an oracle (οὐ χρησμούς). . . . But the father established the oracle by his prophet (τὸ λόγιον τοῦ προφήτου). . . . He gave a second instance of his prophetical inspiration in the oracle (λόγιον, anarthrous) which he delivered about the seventh day" ("De Vit. Moysis," iii. 35 and 36).

"And the holy oracle that has been given (τὸ χρησθὲν λόγιον = 'the delivered oracle'; Ryle, 'the utterance of the oracle') will bear witness, which expressly says that he cried out loudly and betrayed clearly by his cries what he had suffered from the concrete evil, that is from the body" ("Quod det. pot. insid.," § 14, M. I., 200).

Here the narrative in Gen. iv, somewhat broadly taken, including vers. 8 and 10, is called τὸ χρησθὲν λόγιον.

"There is also something like this in the sacred scriptures where the account of the creation of the universe is given and it is expressed more distinctly (τὸ παραπλήσιον καὶ ἐν τοῖς περὶ τῆς τοῦ παντὸς γενέσεως χρησθεῖσι λογίοις περιέχεται σημειωδέστερον). For it is said to the wicked man, 'O thou man, that hast sinned; cease to sin' (Gen. iv. 7)" ("De Sobriet.," § 10, M. 1, 400).

Here there is a formal citation of a portion of Scripture, viz., the portion "concerning the creation of the universe," which means, probably, the Book of Genesis (see Ryle's "Philo and Holy Scripture," p. xx); and this is cited as made up of "declared oracles," ἐν τοῖς χρησθεῖσι λογίοις. The Book of Genesis is thus to Philo a body of χρησθέντα λόγια.

"And this is the meaning of the oracle recorded in Deuteronomy (παρ' ὃ καὶ λόγιον ἔστι τοιοῦτον ἀναγεγραμμένον ἐν Δευτερονομίῳ), 'Behold I have put before thy face life and death, good and evil'" ("Quod Deus Immut.," § 10, M. i. 280).

Here the "oracle" is a "written" thing; and it is written in a well-known book of oracles, viz., in "Deuteronomy," the second book of the Law. This book, and of course the others like it, consists of written oracles.

"And the words of scripture show this, in which (δηλοῖ δὲ τὸ λόγιον ἐν ᾧ) it is distinctly stated that 'they both of them went together, and came to the plain which God had mentioned to them (Gen. xxii. 3)" ("De Migrat. Abrah." § 30, M. i. 462).

"And for this reason the following scripture has been given to men (διὸ λόγιον ἐχρήσθη τοιόνδε), 'Return to the land of thy father and to thy family, and I will be with thee' (Gen. xxxi. 3)" ("De Migrat. Abrah.," § 6, M. i. 440).

Here, though the words are spoken in the person of God, the generalized use of them seems to point to their Scriptural expression as the main point.

"Moses chose to deliver each of the ten commandments (ἕκαστον θεσπίζειν τῶν δέκα λογίων) in such a form as if they were addressed not to many persons but to one" ("De Decem Oracul.," περὶ τῶν Δέκα Λογίων, § 10).

"And the sacred scripture (λόγιον, anarthrous) bears its testimony in behalf of this assertion, when it says: 'The Lord himself is his inheritance' (Deut. x. 9)" ("De Congr. Erud. Grat.," § 24, M. i. 538).

"For there is a passage in the word of God (λόγιον γὰρ ἔστιν) that . . . (Lev. xxvi. 3)" ("De praem. et poen.," § 17, M. ii. 424).

Both classes of passages thus exist in Philo's text in the greatest abundance — no more those which speak of words of God recorded in Scripture as λόγια than those which speak of the words of Scripture as such as equally λόγια. Nor are we left to accord the two classes of passages for ourselves. Philo himself, in what we may call an even overstrained attempt at systematization, elaborately explains how he distinguishes the several kinds of matter which confront him in Scripture. The fullest statement is probably that in the "De Vita Moysis," iii, 23 (Mangey, ii, 163). Here he somewhat artificially separates three classes of "oracles," all having equal right to the name. It is worth while to transcribe enough of the passage to set its essential contents clearly before us. He is naturally in this place speaking directly of Moses — as indeed commonly in his tracts, which are confined, generally speaking, to an exposition of the Pentateuch: but his words will apply also to the rest of the "sacred books," which he uniformly treats as the oracles of God alike with the Pentateuch.[69] He writes:

[69] Cf. on this matter Edersheim in Smith and Wace's "Dictionary of Christian Biography," art. "Philo" (Vol. iv. pp. 386, 387): The only books "of which

"Having shown that Moses was a most excellent king and law-giver and high priest, I come in the last place to show that he was also the most illustrious of the prophets (προφητῶν). I am not unaware, then, that all the things that are written in the sacred books are oracles delivered by him (ὡς πάντα εἰσὶ χρησμοὶ ὅσα ἐν ταῖς ἱεραῖς βίβλοις ἀναγέγραπται χρησθέντες δι' αὐτοῦ): and I will set forth what more particularly concerns him, when I have first mentioned this one point, namely, that of the sacred oracles (τῶν λογίων) some are represented as delivered in the person of God by His interpreter, the divine prophet (ἐκ προσώπου τοῦ θεοῦ δι' ἑρμηνέως τοῦ θείου προφήτου), while others are put in the form of question and answer (ἐκ πεύσεως καὶ ἀποκρίσεως ἐθεσπίσθη), and others are delivered by Moses in his own character, as a divinely prompted lawgiver possessed by divine inspiration (ἐκ προσώπου Μωϋσέως ἐπιθειάσαντος καὶ ἐξ αὐτοῦ κατασχεθέντος).

"Therefore all the earliest [Gr. πρῶτα = the first of the three classes enumerated] oracles are manifestations of the whole of the divine virtues and especially of that merciful and boundless character by means of which He trains all men to virtue, and especially the race which is devoted to His service, to which He lays open the road leading to happiness. The second class have a sort of mixture and communication (μίξιν καὶ κοινωνίαν) in them, the prophet asking information on the subjects as to which he is in difficulty and God answering him and instructing him. The third sort are attributed to the lawgiver, God having given him a share in His prescient power by means of which he is enabled to foretell the future.

"Therefore we must for the present pass by the first; for they are too great to be adequately praised by any man, as indeed they could

it may with certainty be said that they are not referred to by Philo, are Esther and the Song of Solomon. The reference to Ecclesiastes is very doubtful, much more so than that to Daniel (p. 387 a)." Cf. also Ryle, "Philo and Holy Scripture," pp. 16–35: "It is abundantly clear that to Philo the Pentateuch was a Bible within a Bible, and that he only occasionally referred to other books, whose sanctity he acknowledged, as opportunity chanced to present itself" (p. 27). Cf. also Ewald, "History of Israel," E. T., vii. 204, 205: "Although he uses, and generally in the order in which they are now found in the Hebrew Canon, the other books much less *gradatim* than the Pentateuch, their authors are, nevertheless, considered by him as of equal holiness and divinity with Moses, and inasmuch as from his whole view and treatment of the Scriptures, he can attribute but little importance to their authors as authors, or to their names and temporal circumstances, he likes to call them all simply friends, or associates, or disciples of Moses, or prefers still more to quote the passage to which he refers simply as a sacred song, sacred word, etc." "It is only the books which we now find collected in the

scarcely be panegyrized worthily by the heaven itself and the nature of the universe; and they are also uttered by the mouth, as it were, of an interpreter (καὶ ἄλλως λέγεται ὡσανεὶ δι' ἑρμηνέως). But (δὲ) interpretation and prophecy differ from one another. And concerning the second kind I will at once endeavor to explain the truth, connecting with them the third species also, in which the inspired character (ἐνθουσιῶδες) of the speaker is shown, according to which he is most especially and appropriately looked upon as a prophet." [70]

A somewhat different distribution of material — now from the point of view, not of mode of oracular delivery, but of nature of contents — is given at the opening of the tract "De præm. et poen." (§ 1, init.):

"We find then that in the sacred oracles delivered by the prophet Moses (τῶν διὰ τοῦ προφήτου Μωϋσέως λογίων) there are three separate characters: for a portion of them relates to the creation of the world, a portion is historical, and the third portion is legislative."

Hebrew Canon which he regarded as holy, and he was both sufficiently learned and careful not to rank all the others which were at that time gradually appended to the Greek Bible upon an equality with them." Cf. also Lee, "The Inspiration of Holy Scripture," pp. 69, 70.

[70] Compare Ewald, "The History of Israel," E. T., vii. 203, 204: "The sacred Scriptures are to Philo so immediately divine and holy, that he consistently finds in them simply the divine word rather than Scripture, and therefore really everywhere speaks less of the *Sacred Scriptures* than of divine oracles [χρησμοί, λόγια] of which they were wholly composed, or, when he desires to designate them briefly as a whole, of *the sacred* and *divine Word*, as if the same Logos, of whom he speaks so much elsewhere, were symbolized and incorporated in them for all time, as far as that is possible in a book [ὁ ἱερὸς, more rarely ὁ θεῖος λόγος, likewise ὁ ὀρθὸς λόγος (e. g., i. 308, 27; 681, 17; cf. esp., ii. 163, 44) is the expression which he constantly uses in this case; cf. esp. i. 676, 37 *seq.;* 677, 12]. It is true that in the case of the general subject matter, of the Pentateuch for instance, he makes a certain distinction, inasmuch as some of the oracles come to the prophet, as a mere interpreter directly as from the presence and voice of God alone, while others are revealed to him by God in answer to his interrogations, and again others have their origin in himself when in an inspired state of mind. But he makes this threefold distinction simply because he found it in reading particular passages of the Bible, and not with a view of further reflecting upon it and drawing references from it. On the contrary, he regards and treats all the sentences and words of the Scripture as on a perfect equality and teaches expressly that sacred Scripture must be interpreted and applied, as forming even to its smallest particles, one inseparable whole [cf. esp. "Auch.," ii. 170, 212 *seq.;* in other respects, cf. i. 554, 14, and many other passages of a similar character]."

Accordingly in the tract "De Legat. ad Caium," § 31 (Mangey, ii. 577), we are told of the high esteem the Jews put on their laws:

"For looking upon their laws as oracles directly given to them by God Himself (θεόχρηστα γὰρ λόγια τοὺς νόμους εἶναι ὑπολαμβάνοντες) and having been instructed in this doctrine from their earliest infancy, they bear in their souls the images of the commandments contained in these laws as sacred."

By the side of this passage should be placed doubtless another from the "De Vita Contemplativa," §3, since it appears that we may still look on this tract as Philo's:

"And in every house there is a sacred shrine . . . Studying in that place the laws and sacred oracles of God enunciated by the holy prophets (νόμους καὶ λόγια δεσπισθέντα διὰ προφητῶν) and hymns and psalms and all kinds of other things by reason of which knowledge and piety are increased and brought to perfection."

It is not strange that out of such a view of Scripture Philo should adduce every part of it alike as a λόγιον. Sometimes, to be sure, his discrimination of its contents into classes shows itself in the formulæ of citation; and we should guard ourselves from being misled by this. Thus, for example, he occasionally quotes a λόγιον "from the mouth (or 'person') of God" — which does not mean that Scriptures other than these portions thus directly ascribed to God as speaking, are less oracular than these, but only that these are oracles of his first class — those that "are represented as delivered from the person of God (ἐκ προσώπου τοῦ θεοῦ) by his interpreter, the divine prophet." A single instance or two will suffice for examples:

"And the sacred oracle which is delivered as" [dele "as"] "from the mouth" [or "person"] "of the ruler of the universe (λόγιον ἐκ προσώπου θεσπισθὲν τοῦ τῶν ὅλων ἡγεμόνος) speaks of the proper name of God as never having been revealed to anyone [71] when God is repre-

---

[71] The translation here is unusually expanded: the Greek runs Δηλοῖ δὲ καὶ λ. ε. π. θ. τ. τ. ὅ. ἡ. περὶ τοῦ μεδενὶ δεδηλῶσθαι ὄνομά τι αὐτοῦ κύριον, κτλ.

sented as saying, 'For I have not shown them my name' (Gen. vi. 3)" ("De Mutat. Nom.," § 2). "And the oracles" (οἱ χρησμοί which is a standing term for 'the Scriptures' in Philo) "bear testimony, in which it is said to Abraham ἐκ προσώπου τοῦ θεοῦ (Gen. xvii. 1)" (ditto, § 5). "And he (Jeremiah the prophet) like a man very much under the influence of inspiration (ἅτε τὰ πολλὰ ἐνθουσιῶν) uttered an oracle in the character of God (χρησμόν τινα ἐξεῖπεν ἐκ προσώπου τοῦ θεοῦ) speaking in this manner to most peaceful virtue: 'Hast thou not called me as thy house' etc. (Jer. iii. 4)" ("De Cherub.," § 14, M. i. 148).

The other oracles, delivered not ἐκ προσώπου τοῦ θεοῦ but in dialogue or in the person of the prophet, are, however, no less oracular or authoritative. To Philo all that is in Scripture is oracular, every passage is a λόγιον, of whatever character or length; and the whole, as constituted of these oracles, is τὰ λόγια, or perhaps even τὸ λόγιον — the mass of logia or one continuous logion.

It is not said, be it observed, that Philo's sole mode of designating Scripture, or even his most customary mode, is as τὰ λόγια. As has already been stated, he used χρησμός equally freely with λόγιον for passages of Scripture, and οἱ χρησμοί apparently even more frequently than τὰ λόγια for the body of Scripture. Instances of the use of the two terms interchangeably in the same passage have already been incidentally given.[72] A very few passages will suffice to illustrate his constant use of χρησμός and οἱ χρησμοί separately.

In the following instances he adduces passages of Scripture, each as a χρησμός:

"On this account also the oracle (ὁ χρησμός) which bears testimony against the pretended simplicity of Cain says, 'You do not think as you say' (Gen. iv. 15)" ("Quod det. potiori insid.," § 45, M. i. 223). "And of the supreme authority of the living God, the sacred scripture is a true witness (ὁ χρησμὸς ἀληθὴς μάρτυς) which speaks thus (Lev. xxv. 23)" ("De Cherub.," § 31, M. i. 158). "For a man will come forth, says the word of God (φησὶν ὁ χρησμός) leading a host and warring furiously, etc. (Num. xxiv. 7)" ("De Praem. et Poen.," § 16, M. ii. 423). "And the sacred scripture bears witness to this fact

[72] "De Profug.," §§ 11 and 28; "De Vita Moysis," i. 53; iii. 23, 30, 35, 36.

(μαρτυρεῖ δὲ ὁ περὶ τούτων χρησμός): for it says (Num. xxiii. 19)" ("De Migrat. Abrah.," § 20, M. i. 454). "For though there was a sacred scripture (χρησμοῦ γὰρ ὄντος) that 'There should be no harlot among the daughters of the seer, Israel' (Deut. xxiii. 17)" ("De Migrat. Abrah.," § 39, M. i. 472). "And witness is borne to this assertion by the scripture (μάρτυς δὲ καὶ χρησμός) in which it is said: 'I will cause to live,' etc. (Deut. xxxii. 39)" ("De Somniis," ii. 44, M. i. 698). "The oracle (ὁ χρησμός) given to the all-wise Moses, in which these words are contained" ("Quod det. pot. insid.," § 34, M. i. 215). "Which also the oracle (ὁ χρησμός) said to Cain" (do., § 21). "And I know that this illustrious oracle was formerly delivered from the mouth of the prophet (στόματι δ' οἶδά ποτε προφητικῷ θεσπισθέντα διάπυρον τοιόνδε χρησμόν), 'Thy fruit,' etc., (Hos. xiv. 9)" ("De Mutat. Nom.," § 24, M. ii. 599). In this last case it is to be noticed that the "oracle" is taken from Hosea: the corresponding passage in "De Plant. Noe.," § 33, M. 1, 350, should be compared: "And with this assertion, this oracle delivered by one of the prophets is consistent, etc. (Hos. xiv. 9) (τούτῳ καὶ παρά τινι τῶν προφητῶν χρησθὲν συνᾴδει τόδε)."

Two other passages may be adduced for their inherent interest. The first from " De Profug.," §32 (M. i. 573), where we read:

"There are passages written in the sacred scriptures (οἱ ἀναγρα-φέντες χρησμοί) which give proof of these things. What they are we must now consider. Now in the very beginning of the history of the law there is a passage to the following effect (Gen. ii. 6) (ᾄδεταί τις ἐν ἀρχῇ τῆς νομοθεσίας μετὰ τὴν κοσμοποιίαν εὐθὺς τοιόσδε)."

Here there is a precise designation where, among " the written χρησμοί," a certain one (τις) of them may be found, viz., in the beginning of "The Legislation" immediately after "The Creation" (cf. Ryle, p. xxi, note 1). The other is from the first book of the " De Somniis," § 27 (M. i. 646):

"These things are not my myth, but an oracle (χρησμός) written on the sacred tables (ἐν ταῖς ἱεραῖς ἀναγεγραμμένος στήλαις), For it says (Gen. xlvi. 1)."

This passage in Genesis is thus an oracle "written in the sacred tablets" — and thus this phrase emerges as one of

Philo's names for the Scriptures. Elsewhere we read somewhat more precisely:

"Now these are those men who have lived irreproachably and admirably, whose virtues are durably and permanently recorded as on pillars in the sacred scriptures (ὧν τὰς ἀρετὰς ἐν ταῖς ἱερωτάταις ἐστηλιτεῦσθαι γραφαῖς συμβέβηκεν)" ("De Abrah.," § 1, M. ii. 2). "There is also in another place the following sentence (γράμμα) deeply engraven (ἐστηλιτευμένον), (Deut. xxxii. 8)" ("De Congr. Erud. Grat.," § 12, M. i. 527).

The "Scriptures" thus bear to Philo a monumental character: they are a body of oracles written, and more — a body of oracles permanently engraved to be a lasting testimony forever.

The designations for Scripture in Philo are, indeed, somewhat various — such as ἱεραὶ γραφαί ("Quis rerum div. heres," § 32 M. i. 495); ἱεραὶ βίβλοι ("Quod det. pot. insid.," § 44, M. i. 222); τοῖς ἱεροῖς γράμμασιν ("Legat. ad Caium.," §29, M. ii. 574). But probably none are used so frequently as, on the one hand, λόγος, with various adjectival enhancements — such as ὁ προφητικὸς λόγος ("De Plantat. Noe," § 28, M. i. 437), ὁ θεῖος λόγος ("Legg. Alleg.," iii, § 3, M. i. 89; "De Mutat. Nom.," § 20; "De Somniis," i. 33, ii. 37), and ὁ ἱερὸς λόγος ("De Ebriet.," § 36, M. i. 379; "De Mut. Nominum," § 38; "De Somniis," i. 14, 22, 33, 35, 37, 39, 42; ii. 4, 9, 37, etc.); and especially, on the other hand, οἱ χρησμοί, occurring at times with extraordinary frequency.[73] Some passages illustrative of this last usage are the following:

"For the sacred Scriptures (οἱ χρησμοί) say that he entered into the darkness" ("De Mutat. Nom.," § 2). "But the sacred oracles (οἱ χρησμοί) are witnesses of that in which Abraham is addressed (the words being put in the mouth of God), (ἐν οἷς λέγεται τῷ 'Αβραὰμ ἐκ προσώπου τοῦ θεοῦ) (Gen. xvii. 1)" (do. § 5). "And these are not my

[73] Philo's designations of Scripture have been collected by Cl. Frees Hornemann, in his "Observationes ad illustr. doctr. de Can. V. T. ex. Philone" (1775); more briefly by Eichhorn in his "Einl. in d. A. Test."; and in a not altogether complete or exact list by Ryle, "Philo and Holy Scripture."

words only but those of the most holy scriptures (χρησμῶν τῶν ἱερω-
τάτων, — anarthrous to bring out the quality in contrast to ἐμὸς μῦθος),
in which certain persons are introduced as saying . . ." (do. § 28). Of
Isaiah xlviii. 22 it is said in do. § 31: λόγος γὰρ ὄντως καὶ χρησμός ἐστι
θεῖος. "Accordingly the holy scriptures (οἱ χρησμοί) tell us that . . ."
(do. § 36). "Therefore the sacred scriptures (οἱ χρησμοί) represent Leah
as hated" (do. § 44) "For she is represented by the sacred oracles (διὰ
τῶν χρησμῶν) as having left off all womanly ways (Gen. xviii. 12)"
("De Ebrietat.," § 14, M. i. 365). "On which account the holy scripture (οἱ χρησμοί) very beautifully represent it as 'a little city and yet
not a little one'" ("De Abrah.," § 31, M. ii. 25). "Therefore the
sacred scriptures (οἱ χρησμοί) say (Gen. xxiv. 1)" ("De Sobriet.," § 4,
M. i. 395). "According as the sacred scriptures (οἱ χρησμοί) testify, in
which it is said (Ex. viii. 1)" ("De Confus. Ling.," § 20, M. i. 419).
"On which account it is said in the sacred scriptures (ἐν χρησμοῖς)
(Deut. vii. 7)" ("De Migrat. Abrah.," § 11, M. i. 445). "God having
drawn up and confirmed the proposition, as the Scriptures (οἱ χρησμοί)
show, in which it is expressly stated that (Deut. xxx. 4)" ("De Confus.
Ling.," § 38, M. i. 435).

When we combine these passages with those in which
λόγιον occurs it will probably not seem too much to say that
the dominant method of conceiving the Bible in Philo's mind
was as a book of oracles. Whether he uses the word λόγιον or
χρησμός, it is, of course, all one to him. Indeed, that nothing
should be lacking he occasionally uses also other synonyms.
For example, here is an instance of the Homeric word θεοπρόπιον cropping out: "For there is extant an oracle delivered to
the wise man in which it is said (Lev. xxvi. 12), (καὶ γὰρ ἐστι
χρησθὲν τῷ σοφῷ θεοπρόπιον ἐν ᾧ λέγεται)" ("De Somniis," i,
§ 23). And this oracular conception of Scripture is doubtless
the reason why it is so frequently quoted in Philo by the subjectless φησί, λέγει, λέγεται (instead of, say, γέγραπται). There
are in general, speaking broadly, three ways in which one
fully accepting the divine origin and direct divine authority
of Scripture may habitually look upon it. He may think of
it as a library of volumes and then each volume is likely to
be spoken of by him as a γραφή and the whole, because the
collection of volumes, as αἱ γραφαί, or, when the idea of its

unity is prominently in mind, as itself ἡ γραφή. On the other hand, the sense of its composite character may be somewhat lost out of habitual thought, swallowed up in the idea of its divine unity, and then its several sentences or passages are apt to be thought and spoken of as each a γράμμα, and the whole, because made up of these sentences or passages, as τὰ γράμματα. Or, finally, the sense of the direct divine utterance of the whole to the soul, and of its immediate divine authority, may overshadow all else and the several sentences or passages of the book be each conceived as an unmediated divine word coming directly to the soul — and then each passage is likely to be called a λόγιον or χρησμός, and the whole volume, because the sum of these passages, τὰ λόγια or οἱ χρησμοί — or occasionally, when its unity is prominently in mind, one great τὸ λόγιον or ὁ χρησμός. Each of these three ways of looking at the Scriptures of the Old Testament finds expression in Philo,[74] in Josephus and in the New Testament. But it is the last that is most characteristic of the thought of Philo, and the first possibly of the writers of the New Testament: [75] while perhaps we may suspect that the intermediate

---

[74] As to γραφαί, see "Quis rerum div. heres," § 32 (Mangey, i. 495), παρ' ὃ καὶ ἐν ἱεραῖς γραφαῖς λέγεται; "De Abrah.," § 1 (M. ii. 2), "Now these are those men who have lived irreproachably . . . whose virtues are durably and permanently recorded as on pillars, ἐν ταῖς ἱερωτάταις γραφαῖς." As to γράμμα, γράμματα, see "De Congr. Erud. Grat.," § 12 (M. i. 527), Ἔστι δὲ καὶ ἑτέρωθι τὸ γράμμα τοῦτο ἐστηλιτευμένον (Deut. xxxii. 8)"; "Quod Deus Immut.," § 2 (M. i. 273), "For in the first book of Kings (= I Sam. i. 20), she (Hannah) speaks in this manner: 'I give him (Samuel) unto thee freely,' the expression here used being equivalent to 'I give him unto thee whom thou hast given unto me,' κατὰ τὸ ἱερώτατον Μωϋσέως γράμμα τοῦτο, 'My gifts and my offerings, and my firstfruits, ye shall observe to offer unto me'"; "Legat. ad Caium," § 29 (M. ii. 574), "You have never been trained in the knowledge of the sacred Scriptures (τοῖς ἱεροῖς γράμμασιν"; "De Vita M.," iii. 39; etc.

[75] In the New Testament γράμμα does not occur in the sense of a passage of Scripture — as indeed τὰ γράμματα occurs of Scripture only in II Tim. iii. 15, cf. John v. 47. The place of γράμμα in this sense is taken in the New Testament by γραφή, though it is extreme to say with Lightfoot on Gal. iii. 22 (cf. Westcott on John ii. 22) that γραφή, always in the New Testament refers to a particular passage. On the other hand this use of γραφή is far from being peculiar to the New Testament as seems to be implied by Stephens ("Thes." sub. voc.). Not only does it occur familiarly in the Fathers, as e. g. (from Sophocles): Clems. Rom., ii. 2; Justin

one was most congenial to the thought of Josephus, who, as a man of affairs and letters rather than of religion, would naturally envisage the writings of the Old Testament rather as documents than as oracles.

From this survey we may be able to apprehend with some accuracy Philo's place in the development of the usage of the word λόγιον. He has received it directly from profane Greek as one of a series of synonyms — λόγιον, χρησμός, θεοπρόπιον, etc. — denoting a direct word from God, an "oracle." He has in no way modified its meaning except in so far as a heightening of its connotation was inseparable from the transference of it from the frivolous and ambiguous oracles of heathendom to the revelations of the God of Israel, a heightening which was, no doubt, aided by the constant use of the word in the Septuagint — Philo's Bible — to translate the Hebrew אִמְרָה with all its high suggestions. But in this transference he has nevertheless given it a wholly new significance, in so far as he has applied it to a fixed written revelation and thus impressed on it entirely new implications. In his hands, λόγιον becomes, by this means, a synonym of γράμμα, and imports "a passage of Scripture" — conceived, of course, as a direct oracle from God. And the plural becomes a synonym of τὰ γράμματα, αἱ γραφαί, οἱ βίβλοι, ὁ λόγος — or whatever other terms are used to express the idea of "the Holy Scriptures" — and imports what we call "the Bible," of course with the implication that this Bible is but a congeries of "oracles," or

Mart., "Advs. Tryph.," cc. 56, 65 (a very instructive case), 69, 71 (cf. Otto's note here) and elsewhere; Clems. Alex., "Cohort ad Gentes.," ix. ad init.: but also in Philo, as e. g., "De Praem. et Poen.," § 11 near the end (M. ii. 418): "Being continually devoted to the study of the Holy Scriptures both in their literal sense and also in the allegories figuratively contained in them (ἐν ταῖς ῥηταῖς γραφαῖς καὶ ἐν ταῖς ὑπόνοιαν ἀλληγορίαις)," and "Quis rerum div. her.," § 53 (M. i. 511): "And the historian connects with his preceding account what follows in consistency with it, saying . . . (τὸ δὲ ἀκόλουθον προσυφαίνει τῇ γραφῇ φάσκων)." Of course Philo sometimes uses ἡ γραφή in the non-technical sense also, of a human treatise: thus at the opening of "De Somniis" he refers to what was contained in the preceding treatise (ἡ μὲν οὖν πρὸ ταύτης γραφὴ περιεῖχε). What is said in the text is not intended to traverse such facts as these, indicating other usages; but is meant only to suggest in a broad way what seems to be the primary distinction between the three usages; the subsequent development undergone by them is another story.

direct utterances of God, or even in its whole extent one great "oracle" or utterance of God — that it is, in a word, the pure and absolute "Word of God." But when we say that λόγιον is in Philo's hands the equivalent of "a passage of Scripture," we must guard against supposing that there is any implication of brevity attaching to it: its implication is that of direct divine utterance, not of brevity; and "the passage" in mind and designated by λόγιον may be of any length, conceived for the time and the purpose in hand as a unitary deliverance from God, up to the whole body of Scripture itself.[76] Similarly τὰ λόγια in Philo has not yet hardened into a simple synonym of "Scripture," but designates any body of the "oracles" of which the whole Scripture is composed — now the "ten commandments," now the Book of Genesis, now the Pentateuch, now the Jewish Law in general.[77]

There is little trace in Philo of the application made in the LXX. of λόγιον to the high priestly breastplate, by which it came to mean, not only the oracular deliverance, but the place or instrument of divination — though, quoting the LXX. as freely as he does, Philo could not help occasionally incorporating such a passage in his writings. We read, for example, in the "Legg. Allegor.," iii, § 40 (M. i. 111):

"At all events the Holy Scripture (ὁ ἱερὸς λόγος), being well aware how great is the power of the impetuosity of each passion, anger and appetite, puts a bridle in the mouth of each, having appointed reason (τὸν λόγον) as their charioteer and pilot. And first of all it speaks thus of anger, in the hope of pacifying and curing it, 'And you shall put manifestation and truth' [the Urim and Thummim] 'in the oracle of judgment (ἐπὶ τὸ λόγιον τῶν κρίσεων) and it shall be on the breast of Aaron, when he comes into the Holy Place before the Lord' (Ex.

---

[76] Thus of the passage cited above: in "Quod det pot. insid.," § 14, the reference is to the narrative of Gen. iv; in "De Vita Moysis," iii. 35, to the whole legislation concerning food; in "De Profug.," § 28, and "De Mutat. Nom.," § 4, apparently to the whole Bible.

[77] "De Decem Oraculis," title and § 10; "De Sobrietate," § 10; "De Praem. et Poen.," § 1; "De Vita Moysis," iii. § 23; "De Legat. ad Caium," § 31; "De Vita Contemplativa," § 3.

xxviii. 30). Nor by the oracle (λόγιον) is here meant the organs of speech which exist in us. . . . For Moses here speaks not of a random, spurious oracle (λόγιον) but of the oracle of judgment, which is equivalent to saying a well-judged and carefully examined oracle."

Thus Philo gradually transmutes the λόγιον = λογεῖον of his text into the λόγιον = χρησμός of his exposition: and it is a little remarkable how little influence this LXX. usage has on his own use of the word. With him λόγιον is distinctively a passage of Scripture, and the congeries of these passages make τὰ λόγια.

That this usage is not, however, a *peculium* of Philo's merely, is evidenced by a striking passage from Josephus, in which it appears in full development. For example, we read:

"The Jews, by demolishing the tower of Antonia, had made their temple square, though they had it written in their sacred oracles (ἀναγεγραμμένον ἐν τοῖς λογίοις) that their city and sanctuary should be taken when their temple should become square. But what most stirred them up was an ambiguous oracle (χρησμός) that was found also in their sacred writings (ἐν τοῖς ἱεροῖς εὑρημένος γράμμασιν) that about that time one from their country should become ruler of the world. The Jews took this prediction to belong to themselves, and many wise men were thereby deceived in their judgment. Now this oracle (τὸ λόγιον) certainly denoted the rule of Vespasian" ("De Bello Jud.," vi. 5, 4).

In this short passage we have most of the characteristics of the Philonean usage repeated: here is the interchangeable usage of λόγιον and χρησμός, on the one hand, and of τὰ λόγια and τὰ γράμματα, on the other: the sacred writings of the Jews are made up of "oracles," so that each portion of them is a λόγιον and the whole τὰ λόγια. [78]

IV. That this employment of τὰ λόγια as a synonym of αἱ γραφαί was carried over from the Jewish writers to the early Fathers, Dr. Lightfoot has sufficiently shown in a brief but effective passage in his brilliant papers in reply to the

[78] Cf. the echo of Josephus' language in Tacitus, "Hist.," v. 13: "Pluribus persuasio inerat, *antiquis sacerdotum litteris* (= ἐν τοῖς ἱεροῖς γράμμασι) contineri, eo ipso tempore fore ut valesceret Oriens profectique Judæa rerum potirentur. Quae *ambages* (= χρησμὸς ἀμφίβολος = τὸ λόγιον) Vespasianum et Titum praedixerant."

author of "Supernatural Religion."[79] It is not necessary to go over the ground afresh which Dr. Lightfoot has covered. But, for the sake of a general completeness in the presentation of the history of the word, it may be proper to set down here some of the instances of its usage in this sense among the earlier Fathers. Clement of Rome, after having quoted examples from the Scriptures at length, sums up the lesson thus: "The humility, therefore, and the submissiveness of so many great men, who have thus obtained a good report, hath through obedience made better not only us, but also the generations which were before us, even them that received his oracles in fear and truth" (c. 19); again (c. 53), "For ye know, and know well the sacred Scriptures (τὰς ἱερὰς γραφάς), dearly beloved, and ye have searched into the oracles of God (τὰ λόγια τοῦ θεοῦ)"; and still again (c. 62), "And we have put you in mind of these things the more gladly, since we knew well that we were writing to men who are faithful and highly accounted and have diligently searched into the oracles of the teaching of God (τὰ λόγια τῆς παιδείας τοῦ θεοῦ)." The same phenomenon obviously meets us here as in Philo: and Harnack [80] and Lightfoot [81] both naturally comment to this effect on the middle instance — the former calling especially attention to the equation drawn between the two phrases for Scripture, and the latter to the fact, as shown by the Scriptures immediately adduced, that the mind of the writer in so designating Scripture was not on "any divine precept or prediction, but *the example of Moses.*" Equally strikingly, we read in II Clem., xiii, "For the Gentiles when they hear from our mouth the oracles of God, marvel at them for their beauty and greatness. . . . . For when they hear from us that God saith, 'It is no thank unto you, if ye love them that love you, but this is thank unto you, if you love your enemies and them that hate you [Luke vi. 32]' — when they hear these things, I say, they marvel at their exceeding goodness."

[79] *The Contemporary Review*, August, 1875, p. 400; "Essays on the Work entitled Supernatural Religion" (1889), p. 173.
[80] *In loc.*   [81] *Loc. cit.*

"The point to be observed," says Lightfoot,[82] "is that the expression here refers to an *evangelical* record." Similarly Polycarp, c. vii, writes: "For every one 'who will not confess that Jesus Christ is come in the flesh is antichrist' (I John iv. 2, 3); and whosoever shall not confess the testimony of the cross is of the devil; and whosoever shall pervert the oracles of the Lord (τὰ λόγια τοῦ κυρίου) to his own lusts and say there is neither resurrection nor judgment, that man is the firstborn of Satan." On this passage Zahn, followed by Lightfoot, very appropriately adduces the parallel in the Preface to Irenæus' great work, "Against Heresies," where he complains of the Gnostics "falsifying the oracles of the Lord (τὰ λόγια Κυρίου), becoming bad exegetes of what is well said": while later ("Hær.," i. 8, 1) the same writer speaks of the Gnostics' art in adapting the dominical oracles (τὰ κυριακὰ λόγια) to their opinions, a phrase he equates with "the oracles of God," and uses in a context which shows that he has the whole complex of Scripture in mind. In precisely similar wise, Clement of Alexandria is found calling the Scriptures the "oracles of truth" ("Coh. ad Gent.," p. 84 ed. Potter), the "oracles of God" ("Quis Div. Sal.," 3) and the "inspired oracles" ("Strom.," i. 392); and Origen, "the oracles," "the oracles of God" "De Prin.," iv. 11; in Matt., x. § 6): and Basil, the "sacred oracles," "the oracles of the Spirit" ("Hom.," xi. 5; xii. 1). The Pseudo-Ignatius ("ad Smyr.," iii) writes: "For the oracles (τὰ λόγια) say: 'This Jesus who was taken up from you into heaven,' etc. [Acts i. 11]" — where the term certainly is just the equivalent of ἡ γραφή.[83] And Photius tells us ("Bibl.," 228) that the Scriptures recognized by Ephraem, Patriarch of Antioch (*circa* 525–545 A.D.), consisted of the Old Testament, the Dominical Oracles (τὰ κυριακὰ λόγια) and the Preaching of the Apostles" — where the adjective κυριακά is obviously intended to limit the broad τὰ λόγια, so that the phrase means just "the Gospels."

[82] *In loc.*
[83] Cf. what Prof. Ropes says of this passage in *The American Journal of Theology*, October, 1899 (iii. 698) and his strictures on Resch's use of it.

Dr. Lightfoot's object in bringing together such passages, it will be remembered, was to fix the sense of λόγια in the description which Eusebius gives of the work of Papias and in his quotations from Papias' remarks about the Gospels of Matthew and Mark. Papias' book, we are told by Eusebius ("H. E.," iii, 39), was entitled Λογίων κυριακῶν ἐξηγήσεις — that is, obviously, from the usage of the words, it was a commentary on the Gospels, or less likely, on the New Testament: and he is quoted as explaining that Matthew wrote τὰ λόγια in the Hebrew language and that Mark made no attempt to frame a σύνταξιν τῶν κυριακῶν λογίων,[84] or, as is explained in the previous clause, of τὰ ὑπὸ τοῦ Χριστοῦ ἢ λεχθέντα ἢ πραχθέντα — that is, as would seem again to be obvious, each wrote his section of the "Scriptures" in the manner described. The temptation to adjust these Papian phrases to current theories of the origin of the Gospels has proved too strong, however, to be withstood even by the demonstration of the more natural meaning of the words provided by Dr. Lightfoot's trenchant treatment: and we still hear of Papias' treatise on the "Discourses of the Lord," and of the "Book of Discourses" which Papias ascribes to Matthew and which may well be identified (we are told) with the "Collection of Sayings of Jesus," which criticism has unearthed as lying behind our present Gospels.[85] Indeed, as time has run on,

---

[84] Or λόγων, as is read by both Schwegler and Heinichen: contra Routh, Lightfoot and Gebhardt-Harnack.

[85] If there ever was such a "Collection of Sayings of Jesus," the natural title of it would certainly not be τὰ κυριακὰ λόγια, but something like the ἡ σύνταξις τῶν κυριακῶν λόγων which Papias says (if we adopt the reading λόγων) Mark did not write. We observe with astonishment, the venerable Prof. Godet saying, in his recent volume on the Gospels, that the existence of such collections of λόγια is now put beyond doubt by the discovery of the Oxyrhynchus fragment. The last word has doubtless not been said as to the nature and origin of this fragment: but that it was a collection of ΛΟΓΙΑ rests solely on the ascription of that title to it by its editors — a proceeding which in turn rests solely on their traditional misunderstanding of the Papian phrase. And that Matthew's "Logia" were "Logia" like these is scarcely a supposable case to a critic of Prof. Godet's views. Meanwhile we cannot but account it unfortunate that Messrs. Grenfell and Hunt should have attached so misleading a title to their valuable discovery: to which it is suitable only in one aspect, viz., as describing these "sayings" of Jesus as (in

there seems in some quarters even a growing disposition to
neglect altogether the hard facts of usage marshaled by Dr.
Lightfoot, and to give such rein to speculation as to the
meaning of the term λόγια as employed by Papias, that the
last end of the matter would appear to threaten to be worse
than the first. We are led to use this language by a recent construction of Alfred Resch's, published in the "Theologische
Studien" dedicated to Bernhard Weiss on his seventieth birthday. Let us, however, permit Resch to speak for himself. He
is remarking on the identification of the assumed fundamental gospel (*Urevangelium*) with the work of Matthew
mentioned by Papias. He says:

"Thus the name — λόγια — and the author — Matthew —
seemed to be found for this *Quellenschrift*. In the way of this
assumption there stood only the circumstance that the name 'λόγια'
did not seem to fit the *Quellenschrift* as it had been drawn out by
study of the Gospels, made wholly independently of the notice of
Papias — since it yielded a treatise of mixed narrative and discourses.
This circumstance led some to characterize the *Quellenschrift*, in
correspondence with the name λόγια, as a mere collection of discourses; while others found in it a reason for sharply opposing the
identification of the Logia of Matthew and the fundamental gospel
(*Urevangelium*), or even for discrediting the whole notice of Papias
as worthless and of no use to scholars. No one, however, thought of
looking behind the λόγια for the hidden Hebrew name, although it was
certainly obvious that a treatise written in Hebrew could not fail to
have a Hebrew title. And I must myself confess that only in 1895,
while the third volume of my 'Aussercanonischen Paralleltexte' was
passing through the press, did it occur to me to ask after the Hebrew
name of the λόγια. But with the question the answer was self-evidently at once given: הְדְּבָרִים,[86] therefore דִּבְרֵי יֵשׁוּעַ. To this answer attached itself at once, however, the reminiscence of titles ascribed in
the Old Testament to a whole series of *Quellenschriften*: דִּבְרֵי שְׁמוּאֵל,
דִּבְרֵי גָד הַחֹזֶה (הָרֹאֶה), דִּבְרֵי נָתָן הַנָּבִיא, דִּבְרֵי דָוִיד הַמֶּלֶךְ. (cf. I Chron. xxix.
29); דִּבְרֵי מַלְכֵי יִשְׂרָאֵל, דִּבְרֵי מְנַשֶּׁה, סֵפֶר דִּבְרֵי שְׁלֹמֹה (I Kings xi. 41); (II

the conception of the compiler, as the constant λέγει shows) "oracular utterances"
of present and continuous authority.

[86] Why should Resch, we may ask, think of דבר instead of אמרה as the
Hebrew original of λόγιον? Cf. above p. 353.

Chron. xxxiii. 18). As, then, there in the Old Testament, it is just historical *Quellenschriften* of biographical contents that bear the name of דְּבָרִים, so this New Testament *Quellenschrift*, the title דִּבְרֵי יֵשׁוּעַ. It contained therefore the history of Him of whom the prophets had prophesied, Who was greater than Solomon, David's Son and David's Lord and the King of Israel. And as the LXX. had translated the title דִּבְרֵי, certainly unskillfully enough by λόγοι, so Papias or his sponsor (*Gewährsmann*) by λόγια. The sense, however, of the Hebrew דְּבָרִים is, as Luther very correctly renders it — 'Histories.' Cf. Heft iii. 812. By this discovery of the original title, the New Testament *Quellenschrift* which from an unknown had already become a known thing, has now become from an unnamed a named thing. The desiderated x has been completely found." [87]

Criticism like this certainly scorns all facts. The Hebrew word דבר, meaning a "word," passed by a very readily understood process into the sense of "thing." In defining the term as used in the titles which Resch adduces, Dr. Driver says: [88] "*words*: hence *affairs*, *things* — in so far as they are done, 'acts'; in so far as they are narrated, 'history.'" The word דבר thus readily lent itself, in combinations like those adduced by Resch, to a double meaning: and it is apparently found in both these senses. In instances like דִּבְרֵי קֹהֶלֶת (Eccl. i. 1, cf. Prov. xxx. 1, xxxi. 5; Jer. i. 1; Am. i. 1; Neh. i. 1) it doubtless means "words of Koheleth," and the like. In the instances adduced by Resch, it is doubtless used in the secondary sense of "history." The Greek word λόγος, by which דבר was ordinarily translated in the LXX., while naturally not running through a development of meaning exactly parallel to that of דבר, yet oddly enough presented a fair Greek equivalent for both of these senses of דִּבְרֵי, used in titles: and why Resch should speak of λόγοι as unskillfully used in the titles he adduces, does not appear on the surface of things. Certainly, from Herodotus down, οἱ λόγοι bore the specific meaning of just "Histories," as afterwards it bore the sense of "prose writings": and the early Greek historians

---

[87] *Op. cit.*, p. 121 *seq.*
[88] "Introduction," last ed., 527, note 1.

were called accordingly οἱ λογογράφοι.[89] The LXX. translators, in a word, could scarcely have found a happier Greek rendering for the titles of the *Quellenschriften* enumerated in I Chron. xxix. 29, 30, etc. Who, however, could estimate the unskillfulness of translating דברי in such titles by λόγια — a word which had no such usage and indeed did not readily lend itself to an application to human "words?" Papias (or his sponsor) must have been (as Eusebius calls him) a man of mean capacity indeed, so to have garbled Matthew's Hebrew. It should be noted, further, that Papias does not declare, as Resch seems to think, that Matthew wrote τὰ λόγια τοῦ 'Ιησοῦ, or even τὰ κυριακὰ λόγια — it is Papias' own book whose title contains this phrase; and it will be hard to suppose that Papias (or his sponsor) was a man of such mean capacity as to fancy the simple τὰ λόγια a fair equivalent for the Hebrew דברי ישוע in the sense of " The History of Jesus." If he did so, one does not wonder that he has had to wait two thousand years for a reader to catch his meaning. Such speculations, in truth, serve no other good purpose than to exhibit how far a-sea one must drift who, leaving the moorings of actual usage, seeks an unnatural meaning for these phrases. Their obvious meaning is that Papias wrote an " Exposition of the Gospels," and that he speaks of Matthew's and Mark's books as themselves sections of those "Scriptures" which he was expounding. Under the guidance of the usage of the word, this would seem the only tenable opinion.[90]

It is not intended, of course, to imply that there is no trace among the Fathers of any other sense attaching to the

[89] See Liddell and Scott, *sub. voc.*, iv. and v.

[90] We must account it, then, as only another instance of that excess of caution which characterizes his application of the "apologetical" results of investigation, when Dr. Sanday still holds back from this conclusion and writes thus: "The word λόγια, indeed, means 'oracles' and not 'discourses.' But while the term 'the oracles' might well from the first have been applied to our Lord's words it is hardly likely that it should so early have been applied to a writing of the New Testament as such. Moreover, even when the inspiration of the New Testament had come to be as clearly recognized as that of the Old Testament, the term 'the oracles' would not have been a fitting one for a single work, simply on the ground that it formed part of the collection" (Hastings' "Bible Dictionary," ii. p. 235 a).

words τὸ λόγιον, τὰ λόγια, than "the Scriptures" as a whole.
Other applications of the words were found standing side
by side with this in Philo, and they are found also among
the Fathers. Τὸ λόγιον, used of a specific text of Scripture, for
example, is not uncommon in the Fathers. It is found, for instance, in Justin Martyr, "Apol.," i. 32: "And Jesse was his
forefather κατὰ τὸ λόγιον " — to wit, Isa. xi. 1, just quoted.
It is found in Clement of Alexandria ("Strom.," ii. Migne, i.
949a), where Isa. vii. 9 is quoted and it is added: "It was
this λόγιον that Heraclitus of Ephesus paraphrased when he
said . . . ." It is found repeatedly in Eusebius' "Ecclesiastical History," in which the Papian passages are preserved, as,
e. g., ix. 7, ad fin., "So that, according to that divine (θεῖον)
λόγιον," viz., Matt. xxiv. 24; x. 1, 4, "the λόγιον thus enjoin-
ing us," viz., Ps. xcvii. (xcviii.) 1; x. 4, 7, "concerning which a
certain other divine λόγιον thus proclaims," viz., Ps. lxxxvi.
(lxxxvii.) 3. Τὰ λόγια is also used in the Fathers, as in Philo,
for any body of these Scriptural λόγια, however small or large
(i. e., for any given section of Scripture) — as, e. g., for the Ten
Commandments. It is so used, for instance, in the "Apostolical
Constitutions," ii. 26: "Keep the fear of God before your eyes,
always remembering τῶν δέκα τοῦ θεοῦ λογίων "; and also in
Eusebius (H. E., ii. 18, 5). So, again, we have seen it, modified
by qualifying adjectives, used for the Gospels — and indeed
it seems to be employed without qualifications in this sense
in Pseudo-Justin's "Epistola ad Zeram et Serenum" (Otto, i.

Apart altogether from the fact that these caveats are founded on a demonstrably
mistaken conception of the origin of the New Testament Canon, they are in themselves invalid. The term λόγια was contemporaneously applied to writings of the
New Testament as such — as a glance at II Clem. xiii. and Polycarp vii. will
show — and as Lightfoot's note on the former passage, correcting his less careful
earlier note on the latter passage, points out. And that τὰ λόγια could easily refer
to any definite portion of the congeries of "oracles" known also as "Scripture,"
Philo's usage as indicated above (p. 374) sufficiently exhibits. For the rest, it cannot be doubted that Papias was understood by all his early readers to mean by
his τὰ λόγια of Matthew, just Matthew's Gospel. This has been sufficiently shown
("Einleitung," ii. 265) by Zahn, who in his rich and fundamentally right remarks
on the subject both here and elsewhere (e. g., pp. 254 seq. and "Geschichte d.
Kanons," i. 857 seq., ii. 790 seq.) supplies another instance of how near a great
scholar can come to the truth of a matter without precisely adopting it.

70*b*). It is further sometimes used apparently not of the Scripture text as such, but of certain oracular utterances recorded in it — as, for example, when Justin says to Trypho (c. 18): "For since you have read, O Trypho, as you yourself admitted, the doctrines taught by our Saviour, I do not think that I have done foolishly in adding some short utterances of his (βραχέα τοῦ ἐκείνου λόγια) to the prophetic statements" — to wit, words of Jesus recorded in Matt. xxi, xxiii and Luke xi, here put on a level with the oracles of the prophets, but apparently envisaged as spoken. All these are usages that have met us before.

But there are lower usages also discoverable in the later Patristic writers at least. There is an appearance now and then indeed as if the word was, in popular speech, losing something of its high implication of "solemn oracular utterances of God," and coming to be applied as well to the words of mere men [91] — possibly in sequence to its application to the words of prophets and apostles as such and the gradual wearing down, in the careless popular consciousness, of the distinction between their words as prophets and apostles and their words as men; possibly, on the other hand, in sequence to the freer use of the word in profane speech and the wearing away of its high import with the loss of reverence for the

[91] In the thirty-fifth chapter of the fourth book of Origen's "Against Celsus," there is a passage which is given this appearance in Dr. Crombie's excellent English translation, printed in the "Ante-Nicene Library" (Am. Ed., iv. 512): "And yet if Celsus had wished honestly to overturn the genealogy which he deemed the Jews to have so shamelessly arrogated, in boasting of Abraham and his descendants (as their progenitors), he ought to have quoted all the passages bearing on the subject; and, in the first place, to have advocated his cause with such arguments as he thought likely to be convincing, and in the next to have bravely refuted, by means of what appeared to him to be the true meaning, and by arguments in its favor, the errors existing on the subject (καὶ τοῖς ὑπὲρ αὐτῆς λογίοις τὰ κατὰ τὸν τόπον)." The rendering of λογίοις here by "arguments," however, is certainly wrong. The whole context is speaking of Celsus' misrepresentation of the teaching of the Hebrew Scriptures; and what Origen would have him do is to point out the *passages in them* which will bear out his allegations. According to Koetschau's index the word occurs but twice elsewhere in the treatise "Against Celsus," viz., V. xxix. *ad fin.*, and VI. lxxvii. near the end (inserted by Koetschau from Philoc. 85, 16): and in both of these cases the high meaning of the word is unmistakable.

thing designated. Thus we read as early as in the "Acts of
Xanthippe and Polyxena," edited by Prof. James for the
"Cambridge Texts and Studies," and assigned by him to the
middle of the third century (c. 28, p. 78), the following dialogue, in the course of a conversation between Polyxena and
Andrew, "the apostle of the Lord": "Andrew saith: 'Draw
not near me, child, but tell me who thou art and whence.'
Then saith Polyxena: 'I am a great friend of these here (ξένη
τῶν ἐνταῦθα), but I see thy gracious countenance and thy logia
are as the logia of Paul and I presume thee, too, to belong to
his God.'" If we may assume this to mark a transition stage
in the usage, we may look upon a curious passage in John of
Damascus as marking almost the completion of the sinking
of the word to an equivalence to ῥήματα. It occurs in his
"Disput. Christiani et Saraceni" (Migne, i. 1588, iii. 1344).
The Saracenic disputant is represented as eager to obtain an
acknowledgment that the Word of God, that is Christ, is a
mere creature, and as plying the Christian with a juggle on
the word λόγια. He asks whether the λόγια of God are create
or increate. If the reply is "create," the rejoinder is to be:
"Then they are not gods, and you have confessed that
Christ, who is the Word (λόγος) of God is not God." If, on
the other hand, the reply is "increate," the rejoinder apparently is to be that the λόγια of God nevertheless are not
properly gods, and so again Christ the λόγος is not God. Accordingly John instructs the Christian disputant to refuse
to say either that they are create or that they are increate,
but declining the dilemma, to reply merely: "I confess one
only Λόγος of God that is increate, but my whole Scripture
(γραφή) I do not call λόγια, but ῥήματα θεοῦ." On the Saracen
retorting that David certainly says τὰ λόγια (not ῥήματα) of
the Lord are pure λόγια, the Christian is to reply that the
prophet speaks here τροπολογικῶς, and not κυριολογικῶς, that
is to say, not by way of a direct declaration, but by way of
an indirect characterization. It is a remarkable logomachy
that we are thus treated to: and it seems to imply that in
John's day λόγια had sunk to a mere synonym of ῥήματα.

That men had then ceased to speak of the whole γραφή as τὰ θεῖα λόγια we know not to have been the case: but apparently this language was now made use of with no more pregnancy of meaning than if they had said τὰ θεῖα ῥήματα.[92] This process seems to have continued, and in the following passage from a work of the opening of the eleventh century — the "Life of Nilus the Younger," published in the 120th volume of Migne's "Pat. Græc." (p. 97 D), — we have an instance of the extreme extension of the application of the word: "Then saith the Father to him: 'It is not fitting that thou, a man of wisdom and high-learning, should think or speak τὰ τῶν κοινῶν ἀνθρώπων λόγια.'"[93] And accordingly we cannot be surprised to find that in modern Greek the word is employed quite freely of human speech. Jannaris tells us that it is used in the sense of "maxim," and that in colloquial usage τὰ λόγια may mean "promise" — in both of which employments there may remain a trace of its original higher import.[94] While Kontopoulos gives as the English equivalents of λόγιον, the follow-

[92] Dr. F. W. Farrar, with his fatal facility for quoting phrases in senses far other than those attached to them by their authors (other instances meet us in his dealing with the formula "Scriptura complectitur Verbum Dei" and with the word "Inspiration" in the same context, — see pp. 369, 370 of work cited) makes a thoroughly wrong use of this passage ("Hist. of Interpretation," p. 374, note 2). He says: "But as far back as the eighth century the eminently orthodox Father, St. John of Damascus, had said, 'We apply not to the written word of Scripture the title due to the Incarnate Word of God.' He says that when the Scriptures are called λόγια θεοῦ the phrase is only figurative, 'Disput. Christiani et Saraceni' (see Lupton, St. John of Damascus, p. 95)." But John says the Scriptures are called without figure ῥήματα τοῦ θεοῦ: he only means to say they are not God's Word in the same sense that the Logos is: in comparison with Him who is the only incarnate Word of God, they are only figuratively words of God, but they are real words of God, nevertheless, His ῥήματα, by which designation, rather than λόγια, John would have them called, not to avoid confessing them to be God's utterances, but to escape a Moslem jibe.

[93] An instance of the secular use of the word in this lowered meaning, is found doubtless in the Scholium on the "Frogs" of Aristophanes adduced above, p. 336. The date of this Scholium is uncertain, but it seems to belong to the later strata of the Scholia. It is not found in the "Ravenna MS.," which Rutherford is publishing; nor in the "Venetus" (Marc. 474), cf. Blaydes, "Ranae," p. 391; nor indeed in four out of the six MSS. used by Dindorf (iv. 2, p. 113).

[94] In his "Concise Dictionary of English and Modern Greek," sub. vocc. "word" and "saying."

ing list. "A saying, a word; a maxim; a motto, an oracle; τὰ θεῖα λόγια, the divine oracles, the sacred Scriptures." [95]

Thus not only all the usages of the word found, say, in Philo, are continued in the Fathers, but there is an obvious development to be traced. But this development itself is founded on and is a witness to the characteristic usage of the word among the Fathers — that, to wit, in which it is applied to the inspired words of prophets and apostles. And by far the most frequent use of the word in the Patristic writings seems to be that in which it designates just the Holy Scriptures. Their prevailing usage is very well illustrated by that of Eusebius. We have already quoted a number of passages from his "Ecclesiastical History" in which he seems to adduce special passages of Scripture, each as a λόγιον. More common is it for him to refer to the whole Scriptures as τὰ λόγια, or rather (for this is his favorite formula) τὰ θεῖα λόγια — and that whether he means the Old Testament (which in the "Præp. Evang.," ii. 6 [Migne, iii. 140 A], he calls τὰ Ἑβραίων λόγια), or the New Testament, or refers to the prophetic or the narrative portions. Instances may be found in "H. E.," v., 17, 5, where we are told that Miltiades left monuments of his study of the θεῖα λόγια; vi. 23, 2, where the zeal of Origen's friend Ambrose for the study of the θεῖα λόγια is mentioned as enabling Origen to write his commentaries on the θεῖαι γραφαί; ix. 9, 8, where a sentence from Ex. xv. 1 is quoted as from the θεῖα λόγια; x. 4, 28, where Ps. lvii. (lviii.), 7 is quoted from the θεῖα λόγια; "Palestinian Martyrs," xi. 2, where the devotion of the Palestinian martyrs to the θεῖα λόγια is adverted to. Even the singular — τὸ λόγιον — seems occasionally used by Eusebius (as by Philo) as a designation of the whole Scripture fabric. We may suspect this to be the case in "H. E.," x. 4, 43, when we read of "the costly cedar of Lebanon of which τὸ θεῖον λόγιον has not been unmindful, saying, 'The forests of the Lord shall rejoice and the cedars of Lebanon which he planted' (Ps. cv. [civ.] 16)." And we cannot doubt it at "H. E.," ii. 10, 1, where we read concerning Herod Agrippa,

[95] In his "New Lexicon of Modern Greek and English," *sub voc.*

that "as ἡ τῶν πράξεων γραφή relates, he proceeded to Cæsarea and . . . . τὸ λόγιον relates 'that the angel of the Lord smote him'" — in which account it is worth while to observe the coincidence of Josephus' narrative with τὴν θείαν γραφήν. Here, of course, τὸ λόγιον is primarily the Book of Acts — but as the subsequent context shows, it represents that book only as part of the sacred Scriptures, so that τὸ λόγιον emerges as a complete synonym of ἡ θεία γραφή. Whatever other usage may from time to time emerge in the pages of the Fathers, the Patristic usage of the term, κατ' ἐξοχήν, is as a designation of the "Scriptures" conceived as the Word of God.[96]

In the light of these broad facts of usage, certain lines may very reasonably be laid down within which our interpretation of [τὰ] λόγια in the New Testament instances of its occurrence should move. It would seem quite certain, for example, that no lower sense can be attached to it in these instances, than that which it bears uniformly in its classical and Hellenistic usage: it means, not "words" barely, simple "utterances," but distinctively "oracular utterances," divinely authoritative communications, before which men stand in awe and to which they bow in humility: and this high meaning is not merely implicit, but is explicit in the term. It would seem clear again that there are no implications of brevity in the term: it means not short, pithy, pregnant sayings, but high, authoritative, sacred utterances; and it may be applied equally well to long as to short utterances — even though they extend to pages and books and treatises. It would seem to be clear once more that there are no implications in the term of what may be called the literary nature of the utterances to which it is applied: it characterizes the utterances to which it is applied as emanations from God, but whether they be prophetic or narrative or legal, parenetic or promissory in character, is entirely indifferent: its whole

---

[96] Sophocles, in his "Lexicon," gives also the following references for this sense: Titus of Bostra (Migne, xviii. 1253 B); Serapion of Egypt (Migne, xl. 908 C, 909 B). References might be added, apparently, indefinitely.

function is exhausted in declaring them to be God's own utterances.[97] And still further, it would seem to be clear that it is equally indifferent to the term whether the utterances so designated be oral or written communications: whether oral or written it declares them to be God's own Word, and it had become customary to designate the written Word of God by this term as one that was felt fitly to describe the Scriptures as an oracular book — either a body of oracles, or one continuous oracular deliverance from God's own lips.

This last usage is so strikingly characteristic of the Hellenistic adaptation of the term that a certain presumption lies in favor of so understanding it in Hellenistic writings, when the Scriptural revelation is in question: though this presumption is, of course, liable to correction by the obvious implications of the passages as wholes. In such a passage as Rom. iii. 2 this presumption rises very high indeed, and it would seem as if the word here must be read as a designation of the "Scriptures" as such, unless very compelling reasons to the contrary may be adduced from the context. That the mind of the writer may seem to some to be particularly dwelling upon this or that element in the contents of the Scriptures cannot be taken as such a compelling reason to the contrary: for nothing is more common than for a writer to be thinking more particularly of one portion of what he is formally adducing as a whole. The paraphrase of Wetstein appears in this aspect, therefore, very judicious: "They have the Sacred Books, in which are contained the oracles and especially the prophecies of the advent of the Messiah and the calling of the Gentiles; and by these their minds should be prepared": though, so far as this paraphrase may seem to separate between the Sacred Books and the Oracles they contain, it is unfortunate. The very point of this use of the word is that it *identifies* the Sacred Books with the Oracles;

[97] It is therefore a perfectly blind comment that we meet with in Gerhard Heine's recent "Synonymik des N. T. Griechisch" (1898), p. 157 — when in contrast to λόγος as the "reasonable expression" of the νοῦς, τὸ λόγιον is said to be "more the separate utterance, with the (occasional?) accessory notion of promise (Rom. iii. 2)."

and in this aspect of it Dr. David Brown's comment is more
satisfactory: "That remarkable expression, denoting 'Divine
Communications' in general, is transferred to the sacred
Scriptures to express their oracular, divinely authoritative
character." The case is not quite so simple in Heb. v. 12: but
here, too, the well-balanced comment of Dr. Westcott appears to us to carry conviction with it: "The phrase might
refer to the new revelation given by Christ to His apostles
(comp. c. i. 2); but it seems more natural to refer it to the
collective writings of the Old Testament which the Hebrew
Christians failed to understand." In Acts vii. 38 the absence
of the article introduces no real complication: it merely emphasizes the qualitative aspect of the matter; what Moses
received was emphatically *oracles* — which is further enhanced by calling them "lively," i. e., they were not merely
dead, but living, effective, operative oracles. The speaker's
eye is obviously on Moses as the recipient of these oracles,
and on the oracles as given by God to Moses, as is recorded
in the Pentateuch: but the oracles his eye is on are those
recorded in the Pentateuch, and that came to Moses, not for
himself, but for the Church of all ages — "to give *to us*."
Here we may hesitate to say, indeed, that λόγια means just
the "Scriptures"; but what it means stands in a very express
relation to the Scriptures, and possibly was not very sharply
distinguished from the Scriptures by the speaker. With the
analogies in Philo clearly in our mind, we should scarcely go
far wrong if we conceived of λόγια here as meaning to the
speaker those portions of Scripture in which Moses recorded
the revelations vouchsafed to him by God — conceived as
themselves these revelations recorded. In I Peter iv. 11 the
interpretation is complicated by the question that arises concerning the charisma that is intended, as well as by the casting of the phrase into the form of a comparison: "let him
speak *as it were* oracles of God." It is not clear that the
Divine Scriptures as such are meant here; but the term, in
any case, retains all its force as a designation of sacred,
solemn divine utterances: the speaker is to speak as becomes

one whose words are not his own, but the very words of
God — oracles proclaimed through his mouth. Whether it is
the exercise of the prophetic gift in the strict sense that is
adverted to, so that Peter's exhortation is that the prophet
should comport himself in his prophesying as becomes one
made the vehicle of the awful words of revelation; or only
the gift of teaching that is in question, so that Peter's exhortation is that he who proclaims the word of God, even
in this lower sense, shall bear himself as befits one to whom
are committed the Divine oracles for explanation and enforcement — must be left here without investigation. In
either case the term is obviously used in its highest sense and
implies that the λόγια of God are His own words, His awe-
some utterances.

What has thus been said in reference to these New Testament passages is intended to go no further in their explanation than to throw the light of the usage of the word upon
their interpretation. Into their detailed exegesis we cannot
now enter. We cannot pass by the general subject, however,
without emphasizing the bearing these passages have on the
New Testament doctrine of Holy Scripture. It will probably
seem reasonable to most to interpret Rom. iii. 2 as certainly,
Heb. v. 12 as probably, and Acts vii. 38 as very likely making reference to the written Scriptures; and as bearing witness to the conception of them on the part of the New
Testament writers as "the oracles of God." That is to say,
we have unobtrusive and convincing evidence here that the
Old Testament Scriptures, as such, were esteemed by the
writers of the New Testament as an oracular book, which in
itself not merely contains, but is the "utterance," the very
Word of God; and is to be appealed to as such and as such
deferred to, because nothing other than the crystallized
speech of God. We merely advert to this fact here without
stopping to develop its implications or to show how consonant this designation of the Scriptures as the "Oracles of
God" is with the conception of the Holy Scriptures entertained by the New Testament writers as otherwise made

known to us. We have lately had occasion to point out in
this *Review* some of the other ways in which this conception
expresses itself in the New Testament writings.[98] He who
cares to look for it will find it in many ways written largely
and clearly and indelibly on the pages of the New Testament.
We content ourselves at this time, however, with merely
pointing out that the designation of the Scriptures as τὰ λόγια
τοῦ θεοῦ fairly shouts to us out of the pages of the New Testament, that to its writers the Scriptures of the Old Testament
were the very Word of God in the highest and strictest sense
that term can bear — the express utterance, in all their parts
and each and every of their words, of the Most High — the
"oracles of God." Let him that thinks them something other
and less than this, reckon, then, with the apostles and prophets of the New Covenant — to whose trustworthiness as witnesses to doctrinal truth he owes all he knows about the New
Covenant itself, and therefore all he hopes for through this
New Covenant.

[98] See article entitled, "It Says; Scripture Says; God Says," in the number of
this *Review* for July, 1899, and also article entitled, "God-Inspired Scripture,"
in the number for January, 1900.

X

INSPIRATION AND CRITICISM

INSPIRATION AND CRITICISM [1]

Fathers and Brothers:

It is without doubt a very wise provision by which, in institutions such as this, an inaugural address is made a part of the ceremony of induction into the professorship. Only by the adoption of some such method could it be possible for you, as the guardians of this institution, responsible for the principles here inculcated, to give to each newly-called teacher an opportunity to publicly declare the sense in which he accepts your faith and signs your standards. Eminently desirable at all times, this seems particularly so now, when a certain looseness of belief (inevitable parent of looseness of practice) seems to have invaded portions of the Church of Christ, — not leaving even its ministry unaffected; — when there may be some reason to fear that "enlightened clerical gentlemen may sometimes fail to look upon subscription to creeds as our covenanting forefathers looked upon the act of putting their names to theological documents, and as mercantile gentlemen still look upon endorsement of bills." [2] And how much more forcibly can all this be pled when he who appears before you at your call, is young, untried and unknown. I wish, therefore, to declare that I sign these standards not as a necessary form which must be submitted to, but gladly and willingly as the expression of a personal and cherished conviction; and, further, that the system taught in these symbols is the system which will be drawn out of the Scriptures in the prosecution of the

---

[1] The same points may be found discussed in "The Bible Doctrine of Inspiration," read at the Summer School of the Amer. Inst. of Christian Philosophy, July 7, 1893. Inaugural Address delivered upon the occasion of Dr. Warfield's induction into the Chair of New Testament Literature and Exegesis in the Western Theological Seminary.

[2] Peter Bayne in "The Puritan Revolution."

teaching to which you have called me, — not, indeed, because commencing with that system the Scriptures can be made to teach it, but because commencing with the Scriptures I cannot make them teach anything else.

This much of personal statement I have felt it due both to you and myself to make at the outset; but having done with it, I feel free to turn from all personal concerns.

In casting about for a subject on which I might address you, I have thought I could not do better than to take up one of our precious old doctrines, much attacked of late, and ask the simple question: What seems the result of the attack? The doctrine I have chosen, is that of "Verbal Inspiration." But for obvious reasons I have been forced to narrow the discussion to a consideration of the inspiration of the New Testament only; and that solely as assaulted in the name of criticism. I wish to ask your attention, then, to a brief attempt to supply an answer to the question:

Is the Church Doctrine of the Plenary Inspiration of the New Testament Endangered by the Assured Results of Modern Biblical Criticism?

At the very outset, that our inquiry may not be a mere beating of the air, we must briefly, indeed, but clearly, state what we mean by the Church Doctrine. For, unhappily, there are almost as many theories of inspiration held by individuals as there are possible stages imaginable between the slightest and the greatest influence God could exercise on man. It is with the traditional doctrine of the Reformed Churches, however, that we are concerned; and that we understand to be simply this: — *Inspiration is that extraordinary, supernatural influence (or, passively, the result of it,) exerted by the Holy Ghost on the writers of our Sacred Books, by which their words were rendered also the words of God, and, therefore, perfectly infallible.* In this definition, it is to be noted: 1st. That this influence is a supernatural one — something different from the inspiration of the poet or man of genius. Luke's accuracy is not left by it with only the safeguards which "the diligent and accurate Suetonius" had. 2d. That it is an extraordinary influence — something different from the ordinary action of the Spirit in the conversion and sanctifying guidance of believers. Paul had some more prevalent safeguard against false-teaching than Luther or even the saintly Rutherford. 3d. That it is such an influence as makes the words written under its guidance, the words of God; by which is meant to be affirmed an absolute infallibility (as alone fitted to divine words), admitting no degrees whatever — extending to the very word, and to all the words. So that every part of Holy Writ is thus held alike infallibly true in all its statements, of whatever kind.

Fencing around and explaining this definition, it is to be remarked further:

1st. That it purposely declares nothing as to the mode of inspiration. The Reformed Churches admit, that this is inscrutable. They content themselves with defining carefully and holding fast the effects of the divine influence, leaving the mode of divine action by which it is brought about draped in mystery.

2d. It is purposely so framed as to distinguish it from revelation; — seeing that it has to do with the communication of truth not its acquirement.

3d. It is by no means to be imagined that it is meant to proclaim a mechanical theory of inspiration. The Reformed Churches have never held such a theory:[3] though dishonest, careless, ignorant or over-eager controverters of its doctrine have often brought the charge. Even those special theologians in whose teeth such an accusation has been oftenest thrown (e. g., Gaussen) are explicit in teaching that the human element is never absent.[4] The Reformed Churches

[3] See Dr. C. Hodge's "Systematic Theology," page 157, Vol. I.

[4] Cf. Gaussen's "Theopneusty," New York, 1842; pp. 34, 36, 44 *seq. et passim*. In these passages he explicitly declares that the human element is never absent. Yet he has been constantly misunderstood: thus, Van Oosterzee ("Dog.," i. p. 202), Dorner ("Protestant Theo.," ii. 477) and even late English and American writers who, if no others, should have found it impossible to ascribe a me-

hold, indeed, that every word of the Scriptures, without exception, is the word of God; but, alongside of that, they hold equally explicitly that every word is the word of man. And, therefore, though strong and uncompromising in resisting the attribution to the Scriptures of any failure in absolute truth and infallibility, they are before all others in seeking, and finding, and gazing on in loving rapture, the marks of the fervid impetuosity of a Paul — the tender saintliness of a John — the practical genius of a James, in the writings which through them the Holy Ghost has given for our guidance. Though strong and uncompromising in resisting all effort to separate the human and divine, they distance all competitors in giving honor alike to both by proclaiming in one breath that all is divine and all is human. As Gaussen so well expresses it, "We all hold that every verse, without exception, is from men, and every verse, without exception, is from God"; "every word of the Bible is as really from man as it is from God."

4th. Nor is this a mysterious doctrine — except, indeed, in the sense in which everything supernatural is mysterious. We are not dealing in puzzles, but in the plainest facts of spiritual experience. How close, indeed, is the analogy here with all that we know of the Spirit's action in other spheres! Just as the first act of loving faith by which the regenerated

---

chanical theory to a man who had abhorrently repudiated it in an English journal and in a note prefixed to the subsequent English editions of his work. (See: "It is Written," London: Bagster & Sons, 3d edition, pp. i–iv.) In that notice he declares that he wishes "loudly to disavow" this theory, "that he feels the greatest repugnance to it," "that it is gratuitously attributed to him," "that he has never, for a single moment, entertained the idea of keeping it," etc. Yet so late a writer as President Bartlett, of Dartmouth (*Princeton Review*, January, 1880, p. 34), can still use Gaussen as an example of the mechanical theory. Gaussen's book ought never to have been misunderstood; it is plain and simple. The cause of the constant misunderstanding, however, is doubtless to be found in the fact that his one object is to give a proof of the existence of an everywhere present divine element in the Scriptures, — not to give a rounded statement of the doctrine of inspiration. He has, therefore, dwelt on the divinity, and only incidentally adverted to the humanity exhibited in its pages. Gaussen may serve us here as sufficient example of the statement in the text. The doctrine stated in the text is the doctrine taught by all the representative theologians in our own church.

soul flows out of itself to its Saviour, is at once the consciously-chosen act of that soul and the direct work of the Holy Ghost; so, every word indited under the analogous influence of inspiration was at one and the same time the consciously self-chosen word of the writer and the divinely-inspired word of the Spirit. I cannot help thinking that it is through failure to note and assimilate this fact, that the doctrine of verbal inspiration is so summarily set aside and so unthinkingly inveighed against by divines otherwise cautious and reverent. Once grasp this idea, and how impossible is it to separate in any measure the human and divine. It is all human — every word, and all divine. The human characteristics are to be noted and exhibited; the divine perfection and infallibility, no less.

This, then, is what we understand by the church doctrine: — a doctrine which claims that by a special, supernatural, extraordinary influence of the Holy Ghost, the sacred writers have been guided in their writing in such a way, as while their humanity was not superseded, it was yet so dominated that their words became at the same time the words of God, and thus, in every case and all alike, absolutely infallible.

I do not purpose now to undertake the proof of this doctrine. I purpose rather to ask whether, assuming it to have been accepted by the Church as apparently the true one, modern biblical criticism has in any of its results reached conclusions which should shake our previously won confidence in it. It is plain, however, that biblical criticism could endanger such a doctrine only by undermining it — by shaking the foundation on which it rests — in other words by attacking the proof which is relied on to establish it. We have, then, so far to deal with the proofs of the doctrine. It is evident, now, that such a doctrine must rest primarily on the claims of the sacred writers. In the very nature of the case, the writers themselves are the prime witnesses of the fact and nature of their inspiration. Nor does this argument run in a vicious circle. We do not assume inspiration

in order to prove inspiration. We assume only honesty and
sobriety. If a sober and honest writer claims to be inspired
by God, then here, at least, is a phenomenon to be accounted for. It follows, however, that besides their claims,
there are also secondary bases on which the doctrine of the
plenary inspiration of the Scriptures rests, and by the shaking of which it can be shaken. These are: — first, the allowance of their claims by the contemporaries of the writers,
— by those of their contemporaries, that is, who were in a
position to judge of the truth of such claims. In the case of
the New Testament writers this means the contemporary
church, who had the test of truth in its hands: "Was God
visibly with the Apostles, and did He seal their claims with
His blessing on their work?" And, secondly, the absence of
all contradictory phenomena in or about the writings themselves. If the New Testament writers, being sober and
honest men, claim verbal inspiration, and this claim was
allowed by the contemporary church, and their writings in
no respect in their character or details negative it, then it
seems idle to object to the doctrine of verbal inspiration on
any critical grounds.

In order, therefore, to shake this doctrine, biblical criticism must show: either, that the New Testament writers do
not claim inspiration; or, that this claim was rejected by the
contemporary church; or, that it is palpably negatived by
the fact that the books containing it are forgeries; or, equally
clearly negatived by the fact that they contain along with
the claim errors of fact or contradictions of statement. The
important question before us to-day, then, is: Has biblical
criticism proved any one of these positions?

I. Note, then, in the first place, that modern biblical
criticism does not in any way weaken the evidence that the
New Testament writers claim full, even verbal, inspiration.
Quite the contrary. The careful revision of the text of the
New Testament and the application to it of scientific principles of historico-grammatical exegesis, place this claim
beyond the possibility of a doubt. This is so clearly the case,

that even those writers who cannot bring themselves to admit the truth of the doctrines, yet not infrequently begin by admitting that the New Testament writers claim such an inspiration as is in it presupposed. Take, for instance, the twin statements of Richard Rothe: "To wish to maintain the inspiration of the subject-matter, without that of the words, is a folly; for everywhere are thoughts and words inseparable," and "It is clear that the orthodox theory of inspiration [by which he means the very strictest] is countenanced by the authors of the New Testament." If we approach the study of the New Testament under the guidance of and in the use of the methods of modern biblical science, more clearly than ever before is it seen that its authors make such a claim. Not only does our Lord promise a supernatural guidance to his Apostles, both at the beginning of their ministry (Matthew x. 19, 20) and at the close of his life (Mark xii. 11; Luke xxi. 12, cf. John xiv and xvi) but the New Testament writers distinctly claim divine authority. With what assurance do they speak — exhibiting the height of delirium, if not the height of authority. The historians betray no shadow of a doubt as to the exact truth of their every word, — a phenomenon hard to parallel elsewhere among accurate and truth-loving historians who commonly betray less and less assurance in proportion as they exhibit more and more painstaking care. The didactic writers claim an absolute authority in their teaching, and betray as little shadow of doubt as to the perfectly binding character of their words (II Cor. x. 7, 8). If opposed by an angel from heaven, the angel is indubitably wrong and accursed (Gal. i. 7, 8). Therefore, how freely they deal in commands (I Thes. iv. 2, 11; II Thes. iii. 6–14); commands, too, which they hold to be absolutely binding on all; so binding that it is the test of a Spirit-led man to recognize them as the commandments of God (I Cor. xiv. 37), and no Christian ought to company with those who reject them (II Thes. iii. 6–14). Nor is it doubtful that this authority is claimed specifically for the written word. In I Cor. xiv. 37, it is specifically "the things which I am writing" that must be recognized as the commands of the Lord; and so in II Thes. ii. 15; iii. 6–14, it is the teaching transmitted by letter as well as by word of mouth that is to be immediately and unquestionably received.

Now, on what is this immense claim of authority grounded? If a mere human claim, it is most astounding impudence. But that it is not a mere human claim, is specifically witnessed to. Paul claims to be but the transmitter of this teaching (II Thes. iii. 6; παρά); it is, indeed, his own (II Thes. iii. 14, ἡμῶν), but still, the transmitted word is God's word (I Thes. ii. 13). He speaks, indeed, and issues commands, but they are not his commands, but Christ's, in virtue of the fact that they are given through him by Christ (I Thes. iv. 2). The other writers exhibit the same phenomena. Peter distinctly claims that the Gospel was preached in (ἐν) the Holy Spirit (I Peter, i. 12); and John calls down a curse on those who would in any way alter his writing (Rev. xxii. 18, 19; cf. I John, v. 10). These, we submit, are strange phenomena if we are to judge that these writers professed no inspiration.

"But," we are asked, "is this all?" We answer, that we have but just begun. All that we have said is but a cushion for the specific proof to rest easily on. For here we wish to make two remarks:

1. *The inspiration which is implied in these passages, is directly claimed elsewhere.* We will now appeal, however, to but two passages. Look at I Cor. vii. 40, where the best and most scientific modern exegesis proves that Paul claimed for his "opinion" expressed in this letter direct divine inspiration, saying, "this is my opinion," and adding, not in modesty, or doubt, but in meiotic irony, "and it seems to me that I have the Spirit of God." If this interpretation be correct, and with the "it seems to me" and the very emphatic "I" staring us in the face, drawing the contrast so sharply between Paul and the impugners of his authority, it seems indubitably so; then it is clear that Paul claims here

a direct divine inspiration in the expression of even his "opinion" in his letters. Again look for an instant at I Cor. ii. 13. "Which things, also we utter not in words taught by human wisdom, but in those taught by the Spirit; joining spiritual things with spiritual things;" where modern science, more clearly even than ancient faith, sees it stated that both the matter and the manner of this teaching are from the Holy Ghost — both the thoughts and the words — yes, the words themselves. "It is not meet," says the Apostle, "that the things taught by the Holy Ghost should be expressed in merely human words; there must be Spirit-given words to clothe the Spirit-given doctrines. Therefore, I utter these things not in the words taught by human wisdom — not even in the most wisely-chosen human words — but in those taught by the Spirit, joining thus with Spirit-given things (as was fit) only Spirit-given words." It is impossible to deny that here there is clearly taught a *suggestio verborum*. Nor will it do to say that this does not bear on the point at issue, seeing that λόγος and not ῥῆμα is the term used. Not only is even this subterfuge useless in the face of what we will have still to urge, but it is even meaningless here. No one supposes that the mere grammatical forms separately considered are inspired: the claim concerns words in their ordered sequence — in their living flow in the sentences — and this is just what is expressed by λόγοι. This passage thus stands before us distinctly claiming verbal inspiration. The two together seem reconcilable with nothing less far reaching than the church doctrine.

2. But we must turn to our second remark. It is this: *The New Testament writers distinctly place each other's writings in the same lofty category in which they place the writings of the Old Testament; and as they indubitably hold to the full — even verbal — inspiration of the Old Testament, it follows that they claim the same verbal inspiration for the New.* Is it doubted that the New Testament writers ascribe full inspiration to the Old Testament? Modern science does not doubt it; nor can anyone doubt it who will but listen to the words of

the New Testament writers in the matter. The whole New
Testament is based on the divinity of the Old, and its inspiration is assumed on every page. The full strength of the
case, then, cannot be exhibited. It may be called to our
remembrance, however, that not only do the New Testament writers deal with the Old as divine, but that they
directly quote it as divine. Those very lofty titles, "Scripture," "The Scriptures," "The Oracles of God," which they
give it, and the common formula of quotation, "It is written," by which they cite its words, alone imply their full
belief in its inspiration. And this is the more apparent that
it is evident that for them to say, "Scripture says," is
equivalent to their saying, "God says," (Romans ix. 17; x.
19; Galatians iii. 8.) Consequently, they distinctly declare
that its writers wrote in the Spirit (Matthew xxii. 43; cf.
Luke xx. 42; and Acts ii. 24); the meaning of which is made
clear by their further statement that God speaks their
words (Matthew i. 22; ii. 15, etc.), even those not ascribed
to God in the Old Testament itself (Acts xiii. 35; Hebrews
viii. 8; i. 6, 7, 8; v. 5; Eph. iv. 8), thereby evincing the fact
that what the human authors speak God speaks through
their mouths (Acts iv. 25). Still more narrowly defining the
doctrine, it is specifically stated that it is the Holy Ghost
who speaks the written words of Scripture (Hebrews iii. 7)
— yea, even in the narrative parts (Hebrews iv. 4). In direct
accordance with these statements, the New Testament
writers use the very words of the Old Testament as authoritative and "not to be broken." Christ, himself, so deals with
a tense in Matthew xxii. 32, and twice elsewhere founds an
argument on the words (John x. 34; Matthew xxii. 43);
and it is in connection with one of these word arguments
that his divine lips declare "the Scriptures cannot be
broken." His Apostles follow his example (Galatians iii: 16).
Still, further, we have, at least, two didactic statements in
the New Testament, directly affirming the inspiration of the
Old (II Timothy iii. 16, and II Peter i. 21). In one of these it
is declared that every Scripture is God-inspired; in the other,

that no prophecy ever came by the will of man, but borne along by the Holy Ghost it was that holy men of God spoke. It is, following the best results of modern critical exegesis, therefore, quite certain that the New Testament writers held the full verbal inspiration of the Old Testament. Now, they plainly place the New Testament books in the same category. The same Paul, who wrote in II Timothy, "Every Scripture is God-inspired," quotes in its twin letter, 1 Timothy, a passage from Luke's Gospel calling it "Scripture" (I Timothy, v. 18), — nay, more, — parallelizing it as equally Scripture with a passage from the Old Testament. And the same Peter, who gave us our other didactic statements, and in the same letter, does the same for Paul that Paul did for Luke, and that even more broadly, declaring (II Peter iii. 16) that all Paul's Epistles are to be considered as occupying the same level as the rest of the Scriptures. It is quite indisputable, then, that the New Testament writers claim full inspiration for the New Testament books.

Now none of these points are weakened in either meaning or reference by the application of the principles of critical exegesis. In every regard they are strengthened. We can be quite bold, therefore, in declaring that modern criticism does not set aside the fact that the New Testament writers claim the very fullest inspiration.

II. We must ask, then, secondly, if modern critical investigation has shown that this claim of inspiration was disallowed by the contemporaries of the New Testament writers. Here again our answer must be in the negative. The New Testament writings themselves bristle with the evidences that they expected and received a docile hearing; parties may have opposed them, but only parties. And again, all the evidence that exists coming down to us from the sub-apostolic church — be it more or less voluminous, yet such as it is admitted to be by the various schools of criticism — points to a very complete reception of the New Testament claims. No church writer of the time can be pointed out who made a distinction derogatory to the New Testament, between it and the Old Testament, the Divine authority of which latter, it is admitted, was fully recognized in the church. On the contrary, all of them treat the New Testament with the greatest respect, hold its teachings in the highest honor, and run the statement of their theology into its forms of words as if they held even the forms of its statements authoritative. They all know the difference between the authority exercised by the New Testament writers and that which they can lawfully claim. They even call the New Testament books, and that, as is now pretty well admitted, with the fullest meaning, "Scripture." Take a few examples: No result of modern criticism is more sure than that Clement of Rome, himself a pupil of Apostles, wrote a letter to the Corinthians in the latter years of the first century; and that we now possess that letter, its text witnessed to by three independent authorities and therefore to be depended on. That epistle exhibits all the above-mentioned characteristics, except that it does not happen to quote any New Testament text specifically as Scripture. It treats the New Testament with the greatest respect, it teaches for doctrines only what it teaches, it runs its statements into New Testament forms, it imitates the New Testament style, it draws a broad distinction between the authority with which Paul wrote and that which it can claim, it declares distinctly that Paul wrote "most certainly in a spirit-led way" ($\dot{\epsilon}\pi$' $\dot{\alpha}\lambda\eta\theta\epsilon\dot{\iota}\alpha\varsigma$ $\pi\nu\epsilon\nu\mu\alpha\tau\iota\kappa\hat{\omega}\varsigma$. c. 47.) Again, even the most sceptical of schools place the Epistle of Barnabas in the first or at the very beginning of the second century, and it again exhibits these same phenomena, — moreover quoting Matthew definitely as Scripture. One of the latest triumphs of a most acute criticism has been the vindication of the genuineness of the seven short Greek letters of Ignatius, which are thus proved to belong to the very first years of the second century and to be the production again of one who knew Apostles. In them again we meet with the same phenomena. Ignatius even knows of a collected New Testament equal in authority to the Divinely inspired Old Testament. But we need not multiply detailed evidence; every piece of Christian writing which is even probably to be assigned to one who knew or might have known the Apostles, bears like testimony. This is absolutely without exception. They all treat the New Testament books as differentiated from all other writings, and no single voice can be adduced as raised against them. The very heretics bear witness to the same effect; anxious as they are to be rid of the teaching of these writings they yet hold them authoritative and so endeavor to twist their words into conformity with their errors. And if we follow the stream further down its course, the evidence becomes more and more abundant in direct proportion to the increasing abundance of the literary remains and their change from purely practical epistles or addresses to Jews and heathen to controversial treatises between Christian parties. It is exceedingly clear, then, that modern criticism has not proved that the contemporary church resisted the assumption of the New Testament writers or withstood their claim to inspiration: directly the contrary. Every particle of evidence in the case exhibits the apostolic church, not as disallowing, but as distinctly recognizing the absolute authority of the New Testament writings. In the brief compass of the extant fragments of the Christian literature of the first two decades of the second century we have Matthew and Ephesians distinctly quoted as Scripture, the Acts and Pauline Epistles specifically named as part of the Holy Bible, and the New Testament consisting of evangelic records and apostolic writings clearly made part of one sacred collection of books with the Old Testament.[5] Let us bear in mind that the belief of the early church in the inspiration of the Old Testament is beyond dispute, and we will see that the meaning of all this is simply this: The apostolic church certainly accepted the New Testament books as inspired by God. Such are the results of critical enquiry into the opinions

---

[5] See Barn, 4, Poly. 12. Test. xii., Patt. Benj. 10. Ign. Phil. 5, 8, etc.

on this subject of the church writers standing next to the Apostles.

III. If then, the New Testament writers clearly claim verbal inspiration and the apostolic church plainly allowed that claim, any objection to this doctrine must proceed by attempting to undermine the claim itself. From a critical standpoint this can be done only in two ways: It may be shown that the books making it are not genuine and therefore not authentic, in which case they are certainly not trustworthy and their lofty claims must be set aside as part of the impudence of forgery. Or it may be shown that the books, as a matter of fact, fall into the same errors and contain examples of the same mistakes which uninspired writings are guilty of, — exhibit the same phenomena of inaccuracy and contradiction as they, — and therefore, of course, as being palpably fallible by their very character disprove their claims to infallibility. It is in these two points that the main strength of the opposition to the doctrine of verbal inspiration lies, — the first being urged by unbelievers, who object to any doctrine of inspiration, the second by believers, who object to the doctrine of plenary and universal inspiration. The question is: Has either point been made good?

1. In opposition to the first, then, we risk nothing in declaring that *modern biblical criticism has not disproved the authenticity of a single book of our New Testament.* It is a most assured result of biblical criticism that every one of the twenty-seven books which now constitute our New Testament is assuredly genuine and authentic. There is, indeed, much that arrogates to itself the name of criticism and has that honorable title carelessly accorded to it, which does claim to arrive at such results as set aside the authenticity of even the major part of the New Testament. One school would save five books only from the universal ruin. To this, however, true criticism opposes itself directly, and boldly proclaims every New Testament book authentic. But thus two claimants to the name of criticism appear, and the

question arises, before what court can the rival claims be adjudicated? Before the court of simple common sense, it may be quickly answered. Nor is it impossible to settle once for all the whole dispute. By criticism is meant an investigation with three essential characteristics: (1) a fearless, honest mental abandonment, apart from presuppositions, to the facts of the case, (2) a most careful, complete and unprejudiced collection and examination of the facts, and (3) the most cautious care in founding inferences upon them. The absence of any one of these characteristics throws grave doubts on the results; while the acme of the uncritical is reached when in the place of these critical graces we find guiding the investigation that other trio, — bondage to preconceived opinion, — careless, incomplete or prejudiced collection and examination of the facts, — and rashness of inference. Now, it may well be asked, is that true criticism which starts with the presupposition that the supernatural is impossible, proceeds by a sustained effort to do violence to the facts, and ends by erecting a gigantic historical chimera — overturning all established history — on the appropriate basis of airy nothing? And, is not this a fair picture of the negative criticism of the day? Look at its history, — see its series of wild dreams, — note how each new school has to begin by executing justice on its predecessor. So Paulus goes down before Strauss, Strauss falls before Baur, and Baur before the resistless logic of his own negative successors. Take the grandest of them all, — the acutest critic that ever turned his learning against the Christian Scriptures, and it will require but little searching to discover that Baur has ruthlessly violated every canon of genuine criticism. And if this is true of him, what is to be said of the school of Kuenen which now seems to be in the ascendant? We cannot now follow theories like this into details. But on a basis of a study of those details we can remark without fear of successful contradiction that the history of modern negative criticism is blotted all over and every page stained black with the proofs of work undertaken with its conclusion already foregone and prosecuted in a spirit that was blind to all adverse evidence.[6] Who does not know, for example, of the sustained attempts made to pack the witness box against the Christian Scriptures? — the wild denials of evidence the most undeniable, — the wilder dragging into court of evidence the most palpably manufactured? Who does not remember the remarkable attempt to set aside the evidence arising from Barnabas' quotation of Matthew as Scripture, on the ground that the part of the epistle which contained it was extant only in an otherwise confessedly accurate Latin version; and when Tischendorf dragged an ancient Greek copy out of an Eastern monastery and vindicated the reading, who does not remember the astounding efforts then made to deny that the quotation was from Matthew, or to throw doubt on the early date of the epistle itself? Who does not know the disgraceful attempt made to manufacture, — yes simply to manufacture, — evidence against John's gospel, persevered in in the face of all manner of refutation until it seems at last to have received its death blow through one stroke of Dr. Lightfoot's trenchant pen on "the silence of Eusebius?" [7] In every way, then, this criticism evinces itself as false.

But false as it is, its attacks must be tested and the opposition of true criticism to its results exhibited. The attack, then, proceeds on the double ground of internal and external evidence. It is claimed that the books exhibit such contradictions among themselves and errors in historical fact, as evince that they cannot be authentic. It is claimed,

---

[6] We hear much of "apologists" undertaking critical study with such preconceived theories as render the conclusion foregone. Perhaps this is sometimes true, but it is not so necessarily. A Theist, believing that there is a personal God, is open to the proof as to whether any particular message claiming to be a revelation is really from him or not, and according to the proof, he decides. A Pantheist or Materialist begins by denying the existence of a personal God, and hence the possibility of the supernatural. If he begins the study of an asserted revelation, his conclusion is *necessarily* foregone. An honest Theist, thus, is open to evidence either way; an honest Pantheist or Materialist is not open to any evidence for the supernatural. See some fine remarks on this subject by Dr. Westcott, *Contemporary Review*, xxx. p. 1070.

[7] *Contemporary Review*, xxv. p. 169.

moreover, that external evidence such as would prove them to have existed in the Apostolic times is lacking. How does true criticism meet these attacks?

Joining issue first with the latter statement, sober criticism meets it with a categorical denial. It exhibits the fact that every New Testament book, except only the mites Jude, II and III John, Philemon and possibly II Peter, are quoted by the generation of writers immediately succeeding the Apostles, and are thereby proved to have existed in the apostolic times; and that even these four brief books which are not quoted by those earliest authors in the few and brief writings which have come down from them to us, are so authenticated afterwards as to leave no rational ground of doubt as to their authenticity.

It is admitted on all hands that there is less evidence for II Peter than for any other of our books. If the early date of II Peter then can be made good, the early date of all the rest follows *a fortiori;* and there can be no doubt but that sober criticism fails to find adequate grounds for rejecting II Peter from the circle of apostolic writings. It is an outstanding fact that at the beginning of the third century this epistle was well known; it is during the early years of that century that we meet with the first explicit mention of it, and then it is quoted in such a way as to exhibit the facts that it was believed to be Peter's and was at that time most certainly in the canon. What has to be accounted for, then, is how came it in the canon of the early third century? It was certainly not put there by those third century writers; their notices utterly forbid this. Then, it must have been already in it in the second century. But when in that century did it acquire this position? Can we believe that critics like Irenaeus, or Melito, or Dionysius would have allowed it to be foisted before their eyes into a collection they held all-holy? It could not, then, have first attained that entrance during the latter years of the second century; and that it must have been already in the New Testament, received and used by the great writers of the fourth quarter of the second century, seems scarcely open to doubt. Apart from this reasoning, indeed, this seems established; Clement of Alexandria certainly had the book, Irenaeus also in all probability possessed it. If, now, the book formed a part of the canon current in the fourth quarter of the second century, there can be little doubt but that it came from the bosom of the Apostolic circle. One has but to catch from Irenaeus, for instance, the grounds on which he received any book as scripture, to be convinced of this. The one and all-important *sine-qua-non* was that it should have been handed down from the fathers, the pupils of the Apostles, as the work of the Apostolic circle. And Irenaeus was an adequate judge as to whether this was the case; his immediate predecessor in the Episcopal office at Lyons was Pothinus, whose long life spanned the whole intervening time from the Apostles, and his teacher was Polycarp, who was the pupil of John. That a book formed a part of the New Testament of this period, therefore authenticates it as coming down from those elders who could bear personal witness to its authorship. This is one of the facts of criticism apart from noting which it cannot proceed. The question, then, is not: do we possess independently of this, sufficient evidence of the Petrine authorship of the book to place it in the canon? but: do we possess sufficient evidence against its Petrine authorship, to reject it from the canon of the fourth quarter of the second century authenticated as that canon as a whole is? The answer to the question cannot be doubtful when we remember that we have absolutely no evidence against the book; but, on the contrary, that all the evidence of whatever kind which is in existence goes to establish it. There is some slight reason to believe, for instance, that Clement of Rome had the letter, more that Hermas had it and much that Justin had it. There is also a good probability that the early author of the Testaments of the XII. Patriarchs had and used it. Any one of these references, independently of all the rest, would, if made good, throw the writing of the book back into the first century. Each supports the others, and the sum of the probabilities raised by all, is all in direct support of the inference drawn from the reception of the book by later generations, so that there seems to be really no room for reasonable doubt but that the book rightly retains its position in our New Testament. This conclusion gains greatly in strength when we compare the data on which it rests, with what is deemed sufficient to authenticate any other ancient writing. We find at least two most probable allusions to II Peter within a hundred years after its composition, and before the next century passes away we find it possessed by the whole church and that as a book with a secured position in a collection super-authenticated as a whole. Now, Herodotus, for instance, is but once quoted in the century which followed its composition, but once in the next, not at all in the next, only twice in the next, and not until the fifth century after its composition is it as fully quoted as II Peter during its second century. Yet who doubts the genuineness of the histories of Herodotus? Again the first distinct quotation from Thucydides does not occur until quite two centuries after its composition; while Tacitus is first cited nearly a century after his death, by Tertullian. Yet no one can reasonably doubt the genuineness of the histories of either Thucydides or Tacitus.[8] We hazard nothing then, in declaring that no one can reasonably doubt the authenticity of the better authenticated II Peter.

If now such a conclusion is critically tenable in the case of II Peter, what is to be said of the rest of the canon? There are some six writings which have come down to us, which were written within twenty years after the death of John; these six brief pieces alone, as we have said, prove the prior existence of the whole New Testament, with the exception of Jude, II and III John, Philemon and (possibly) II Peter, and the writers of the succeeding years vouch for and multiply their evidence. In the face of such contemporary testimony as this, negative criticism cannot possibly deny the authen-

[8] See Rawlinson's "Hist. Evid.," p. 370 f.

ticity of our books. A strenuous effort has consequently been
made to break the force of this testimony. The genuineness
of these witnessing documents themselves has been attacked
or else an attempt has been made to deny that their quotations are from the New Testament books. Neither the one
effort nor the other, however, has been or can be successful.
And yet with what energy have they been prosecuted! We
have already seen what wild strivings were wasted in an
attempt to get rid of Barnabas' quotation of Matthew.
That whole question is now given up; it is admitted that the
quotation is from Matthew; and it is admitted that Barnabas was written in the immediately sub-apostolic times.
But Barnabas quotes not only Matthew, but I Corinthians
and Ephesians, and in Keim's opinion witnesses also to the
prior existence of John. This may be taken as a type of the
whole controversy. The references to the New Testament
books in the Apostolic fathers are too plain to be disputed
and it is simply the despair of criticism that is exhibited by
the invention of elaborate theories of accidental coincidences
or of endless series of hypothetical books to which to assign
them. The quotations are too numerous, too close, and glide
too imperceptibly and regularly from mere adoption of
phrases into accurate citations of authorities, to be explained away. They therefore stand, and prove that the
authors of these writings already knew the New Testament
books and esteemed them authoritative.

Nor has the attempt to deny the early date of these
witnessing writers fared any better. The mere necessity of the
attempt is indeed fatal to the theory it is meant to support;
if to exhibit the unauthenticity of the New Testament books,
we must hold all subsequent writings unauthentic too, it
seems plain that we are on a false path. And what violence
is done in the attempt! For instance, the Epistle of Polycarp
witnesses to the prior existence of Matthew, Luke, Acts,
eleven Epistles of Paul, I Peter and I John; and as Polycarp
was a pupil of John, his testimony is very strong. It must
then be got rid of at all hazards. But Irenaeus was Poly-

carp's pupil, and Irenaeus explicitly cites this letter and
declares it to be Polycarp's genuine production; and no one
from his time to ours has found cause to dispute his statement
until it has become necessary to be rid of the testimony of the
letter to our canon. But if Polycarp's letter be genuine, it sets
its own date and witnesses in turn to the letters of Ignatius,
which themselves bear internal testimony to their own early
date; and these letters of Ignatius testify not only to the prior
individual existence of Matthew, John, Romans, I Corinthians, Ephesians, Philippians, I Thessalonians and I John;
but also to the prior existence of an authoritative Divinely-
inspired New Testament. This is but a specimen of the linked
character of our testimony. Not only is it fairly abundant,
but it is so connected by evidently undesigned, indeed, but
yet indetachable articulations, that to set aside any one important piece of it usually necessitates such a wholesale attack on the literature of the second century as to amount
to a *reductio ad absurdum*. We may, then, boldly formulate as
our conclusion that external evidence imperiously forbids the
dethronement of any New Testament book from its place in
our canon.

What, then, are we to do with the internal evidence that
is relied upon by the negative school? What, but set it
summarily aside also? It amounts to a twofold claim:
(1.) The sacred writers are hopelessly inconsistent with one
another, and (2.) they are at variance with contemporary
history. Of course, disharmony between the four gospels,
and between Acts and the Epistles is what is mainly relied
on under the first point, and it must be admitted that much
learning and acuteness has been expended on the effort to
make out this disharmony. But it is to be noted: (1.) That
even were it admitted up to the full extent claimed, it would
be no proof of unauthenticity; it would be no more than
that found between secular historians admitted to be
authentic, when narrating the same actions from different
points of view. And (2.) in no case has it been shown that
disharmony must be admitted. No case can be adduced

where a natural mode of harmonizing cannot be supplied, and it is a reasonable principle, recognized among critics of secular historians, that two writers must not be held to be contradictory where any natural mode of harmonizing can be imagined. Otherwise it amounts to holding that we know fully and thoroughly all the facts of the case, — better even than eye-witnesses seem ever to know them. In order to gain any force at all, therefore, for this objection, both the extent and degree of the disharmony has been grossly exaggerated. Take an example: It is asserted that the two accounts (in Matthew and Luke) of the events accompanying our Lord's birth are mutually exclusive. But even a cursory examination will show that there is not a single contradiction between them. How then is the charge of disharmony supported? In two ways: First, by erecting silence into contradiction. Since Matthew does not mention the visit of the shepherds, he is said to contradict Luke who does. Since Luke does not mention the flight into Egypt he is said to contradict Matthew who does. And secondly, by a still more astounding method which proceeds by first confounding two distinct transactions and then finding irreconcilable contradictions between them. Thus Strauss calmly enumerates no less than five discrepancies between Matthew's account of the visit of the angel to Joseph and Luke's account of the visit of the angel to Mary. On the same principle we might prove both Motley's "Dutch Republic" and Kingslake's "Crimean War" to be unbelievable histories by gravely setting ourselves to find "discrepancies" between the account in the one of the brilliant charges of Egmont at St. Quentin and the account in the other of the great charge of the six hundred at Balaclava. This is not an unfair example of the way in which the New Testament is dealt with in order to exhibit its internal disharmony. We are content, however, that it should pass for an extreme case. For it will suffice for our present purpose to be able to say that if the New Testament books are to be proved unauthentic by their internal contradictions, by parity of reasoning the world has never yet seen an authentic writing. In fact so marvelously are our books at one that, leaving the defensive, the harmonist may take the offensive and claim this unwonted harmony as one of the chief evidences of Christianity. Paley has done this for the Acts and Epistles; and it can be done also for the Gospels.

Perhaps we ought to content ourselves with merely repeating this same remark in reference to the charge that the New Testament writers are at variance with contemporary history. So far is this from being true that one of the strongest evidences for Christianity is the utter accord with the minute details of contemporary history which is exhibited in its records. There has been no lack indeed of "instances" of disaccord confidently put forth; but in every case the charge has recoiled on the head of its maker. Thus, the mention of Lysanias in Luke iii. 1 was long held the test case of such inaccuracy and sceptics were never weary of dwelling upon it; until it was pointed out that the whole "error" was not Luke's but — the sceptic's. Josephus mentions this Lysanias and in such a way that he should not have been confounded with his older namesake; and inscriptions have been brought to light which explicitly assign him to just Luke's date. And so this stock example vanishes into the air from which it was made. The others have met a like fate. The detailed accuracy of the New Testament writers in historical matters is indeed wonderful, and is more and more evinced by every fresh investigation. Every now and then a monument is dug up, touching on some point adverted to in the New Testament; and in every case only to corroborate the New Testament. Thus not only has Luke long ago been proved accurate in calling the ruler of Cyprus a "proconsul," but Mr. Cesnola has lately brought to light a Cyprian inscription which mentions that same Proconsul Paulus whom Luke represents Paul as finding on the island. — ("Cyprus," p. 425.) Let us but consider the unspeakable complication of the political history of those times; — the frequent changes of provinces from senatorial to imperial and *vice versa*, — the many alterations of boundaries and vacillations of relation to the central power at Rome, — which made it the most complicated period the world has ever seen, and renders it the most dangerous ground possible for a forger to enter upon; — and how impossible is it to suppose that a book whose every most incidental notice of historical circumstances is found after most searching criticism to be minutely correct, — which has threaded all this labyrinth with firm and unfaltering step, — was the work of unlearned forgers, writing some hundred years after the facts they record. Confessedly accurate Roman historians have not escaped error here; even Tacitus himself has slipped.[9] To think that a second century forger could have walked scathless among all the pitfalls that gaped around him, is like believing a blind man could thread a row of a hundred cambric needles at a thrust. If we merely apply the doctrine of probabilities to the accuracy of these New Testament writers they are proved to be the work of eyewitnesses and wholly authentic.[10]

We can, then, at the end, but repeat the statement with which we began: Modern negative criticism neither on internal nor on external grounds has been able to throw any doubt on the authenticity of a single book of our New Testament. Their authenticity, accuracy and honesty are super-vindicated by every new investigation. They are thus proved to be the productions of sober, honest, accurate men; they claim verbal inspiration; their claim was allowed by the contemporary church. So far modern criticism has gone step by step with traditional faith. There remains but one critical ground on which the doctrine we are considering can be disputed. Do these books in their internal character negative their claim? Are the phenomena of the writings in conflict with the claim they put forth? We must, then, in conclusion consider this last refuge of objection.

2. Much has been already said incidentally which bears

[9] Cf. "Annal," xi. p. 23.
[10] See this slightly touched on by Dr. Peabody, *Princeton Rev.*, March, 1880.

on this point; but something more is needed. An amount of accuracy which will triumphantly prove a book to be genuine and surely authentic, careful and honest, may fall short of proving it to be the very word of God. The question now before us is: Granting the books to be in the main accurate, are they found on the application of a searching criticism to bear such a character as will throw destructive objection in the way of the dogma that they are verbally from God? This inquiry opens a broad — almost illimitable — field, utterly impossible to treat fully here. It may be narrowed somewhat, however, by a few natural observations. (1). It is to be remembered that we are not defending a mechanical theory of inspiration. Every word of the Bible is the word of God according to the doctrine we are discussing; but also and just as truly, every word is the word of a man. This at once sets aside as irrelevant a large number of the objections usually brought from the phenomena of the New Testament against its verbal inspiration. No finding of traces of human influence in the style, wording or forms of statement or argumentation touches the question. The book is throughout the work of human writers and is filled with the signs of their handiwork. This we admit on the threshold; we ask what is found inconsistent with its absolute accuracy and truth. (2). It is to be remembered, again, that no objection touches the question, that is obtained by pressing the primary sense of phrases or idioms. These are often false; but they are a necessary part of human speech. And the Holy Ghost in using human speech, used it as He found it. It cannot be argued then that the Holy Spirit could not speak of the sun setting, or call the Roman world "the whole world." The current sense of a phrase is alone to be considered; and if men so spoke and were understood correctly in so speaking, the Holy Ghost, speaking their speech would also so speak. No objection then is in point which turns on a pressure of language. Inspiration is a means to an end and not an end in itself; if the truth is conveyed accurately to the ear that listens to it, its full end is obtained. (3). And we must remember again that no objection is valid which is gained by overlooking the prime question of the intentions and professions of the writer. Inspiration, securing absolute truth, secures that the writer shall do what he professes to do; not what he does not profess. If the author does not profess to be quoting the Old Testament *verbatim*, — unless it can be proved that he professes to give the *ipsissima verba*, — then no objection arises against his verbal inspiration from the fact that he does not give the exact words. If an author does not profess to report the exact words of a discourse or a document — if he professes to give, or it is enough for his purposes to give, an abstract or general account of the sense or the wording, as the case may be, — then it is not opposed to his claim to inspiration that he does not give the exact words. This remark sets aside a vast number of objections brought against verbal inspiration by men who seem to fancy that the doctrine supposes men to be false instead of true to their professed or implied intention. It sets aside, for instance, all objection against the verbal inspiration of the Gospels, drawn from the diversity of their accounts of words spoken by Christ or others, written over the cross, etc. It sets aside also all objection raised from the freedom with which the Old Testament is quoted, so long as it cannot be proved that the New Testament writers quote the Old Testament in a different sense from that in which it was written, in cases where the use of the quotation turns on this change of sense. This cannot be proved in a single case.

The great majority of the usual objections brought against the verbal inspiration of the Sacred Scriptures from their phenomena, being thus set aside, the way is open to remarking further, that no single argument can be brought from this source against the church doctrine which does not begin by *proving* an error in statement or contradiction in doctrine or fact to exist in these sacred pages. I say, that does not begin by *proving* this. For if the inaccuracies are apparent only, — if they are not indubitably inaccuracies,

— they do not raise the slightest presumption against the full, verbal inspiration of the book. Have such errors been pointed out? That seems the sole question before us now. And any sober criticism must answer categorically to it, No! It is not enough to point to passages *difficult* to harmonize; they cannot militate against verbal inspiration unless it is not only *impossible* for us to harmonize them, but also unless they are of such a character that they are clearly contradictory, so that if one be true the other cannot by any possibility be true. No such case has as yet been pointed out. Why should the New Testament harmonics be dealt with on other principles than those which govern men in dealing with like cases among profane writers? There, it is a first principle of historical science that any solution which affords a possible method of harmonizing any two statements is preferable to the assumption of inaccuracy or error — whether those statements are found in the same or different writers. To act on any other basis, it is clearly acknowledged, is to assume, not prove, error. We ask only that this recognized principle be applied to the New Testament. Who believes that the historians who record the date of Alexander's death — some giving the 28th, some the 30th of the month — are in contradiction? [11] And if means can be found to harmonize them, why should not like cases in the New Testament be dealt with on like principles? If the New Testament writers are held to be independent and accurate writers, — as they are by both parties in this part of our argument, — this is the only rational rule to apply to their writings; and the application of it removes every argument against verbal inspiration drawn from assumed disharmony. Not a single case of disharmony can be proved.

The same principle, and with the same results, may be applied to the cases wherein it is claimed that the New Testament is in disharmony with the profane writers of the times, or other contemporary historical sources. But it is hardly necessary to do so. At the most, only three cases of

[11] For methods by which these are harmonized, see Lee "Inspiration," p. 350.

cvon possible errors in this sphere can be now even plausibly claimed: the statements regarding the taxing under Quirinius, the revolt under Theudas, and the lordship of Aretas over Damascus. But Zumpt's proof that Quirinius was twice governor of Syria, the first time just after our Lord's birth, sets the first of these aside; whereas the other two, while not corroborated by distinct statements from other sources, yet are not excluded either. Room is found for the insignificant revolt of this Theudas — who is not to be confounded with his later and more important namesake — in Josephus' statement that at this time there were "ten thousand" revolts not mentioned by him. And the lordship of Aretas over Damascus is rendered very probable by what we know from other sources of the posture of affairs in that region, as well as by the significant absence of Roman-Damascene coinage for just this period. Even were the New Testament writers in direct conflict in these or in other statements, with profane sources, it would still not be proven that the New Testament was in error. There would still be an equal chance, to say the least (much too little as it is), that the other sources were in error. But it is never in such conflict; and, therefore, cannot be charged with having fallen into historical error, unless we are prepared to hold that the New Testament writers are not to be believed in any statement which cannot be independently of it proved true; in other words, unless it be assumed beforehand to be untrustworthy. This, again, is to assume, not prove error. Not a single case of error can be proved.

We cannot stop to mention even the fact that no doctrinal contradictions, or scientific errors can be proved. The case stands or falls confessedly on the one question: Are the New Testament writers contradictory to each other or to other sources of information in their record of historical or geographical facts? This settled, indubitably all is settled. We repeat, then, that all the fierce light of criticism which has so long been beating upon their open pages has not yet been able to settle one indubitable error on the New

Testament writers. This being so, no argument against their claim to write under a verbal inspiration from God can be drawn from the phenomena of their writings. No phenomena can be pled against verbal inspiration except errors, — no error can be proved to exist within the sacred pages; that is the argument in a nut-shell. Such being the result of the strife which has raged all along the line for decades of years, it cannot be presumptuous to formulate our conclusion here as boldly as after the former heads of discourse: — Modern criticism has absolutely no valid argument to bring against the church doctrine of verbal inspiration, drawn from the phenomena of Scripture. This seems indubitably true.

It is, indeed, well for Christianity that it is. For, if the phenomena of the writings were such as to negative their distinct claim to full inspiration, we cannot conceal from ourselves that much more than their verbal inspiration would have to be given up. If the sacred writers were not trustworthy in such a witness-bearing, where would they be trustworthy? If they, by their performance, disproved their own assertions, it is plain that not only would these assertions be thus proven false, but, also, by the same stroke the makers of the assertions convicted of either fanaticism or dishonesty. It seems very evident, then, that there is no standing ground between the two theories of full verbal inspiration and no inspiration at all. Gaussen is consistent; Strauss is consistent: but those who try to stand between! It is by a divinely permitted inconsistency that they can stand at all. Let us know our position. If the New Testament, claiming full inspiration, did exhibit such internal characteristics as should set aside this claim, it would not be a trustworthy guide to salvation. But on the contrary, since all the efforts of the enemies of Christianity — eager to discover error by which they might convict the precious word of life of falsehood — have proved utterly vain, the Scriptures stand before us authenticated as from God. They are, then, just what they profess to be; and criticism only secures to them the more firmly the position they claim. Claiming to be verbally inspired, that claim was allowed by the church which received them, — their writers approve themselves sober and honest men, and evince the truth of their claim, by the wonder of their performance. So, then, gathering all that we have attempted to say into one point, we may say that modern biblical criticism has nothing valid to urge against the church doctrine of verbal inspiration, but that on the contrary it puts that doctrine on a new and firmer basis and secures to the church Scriptures which are truly divine. Thus, although nothing has been urged formally as a proof of the doctrine, we have arrived at such results as amount to a proof of it. If the sacred writers clearly claim verbal inspiration and every phenomenon supports that claim, and all critical objections break down by their own weight, how can we escape admitting its truth? What further proof do we need?

With this conclusion I may fitly close. But how can I close without expression of thanks to Him who has so loved us as to give us so pure a record of His will, — God-given in all its parts, even though cast in the forms of human speech, — infallible in all its statements, — divine even to its smallest particle! I am far from contending that without such an inspiration there could be no Christianity. Without any inspiration we could have had Christianity; yea, and men could still have heard the truth, and through it been awakened, and justified, and sanctified and glorified. The verities of our faith would remain historically proven true to us — so bountiful has God been in his fostering care — even had we no Bible; and through those verities, salvation. But to what uncertainties and doubts would we be the prey! — to what errors, constantly begetting worse errors, exposed! — to what refuges, all of them refuges of lies, driven! Look but at those who have lost the knowledge of this infallible guide: see them evincing man's most pressing need by inventing for themselves an infallible church, or even an infallible Pope. Revelation is but half revelation unless it be infallibly communicated; it is but half communicated unless it be infallibly recorded. The heathen in their blindness are our witnesses of what becomes of an unrecorded revelation. Let us bless God, then, for His inspired word! And may He grant that we may always cherish, love and venerate it, and conform all our life and thinking to it! So may we find safety for our feet, and peaceful security for our souls.

APPENDIX I

THE DIVINE ORIGIN OF THE BIBLE
THE GENERAL ARGUMENT

THE DIVINE ORIGIN OF THE BIBLE [1]

WHEN the Christian asserts his faith in the divine origin of his Bible, he does not mean to deny that it was composed and written by men or that it was given by men to the world. He believes that the marks of its human origin are ineradicably stamped on every page of the whole volume. He means to state only that it is not merely human in its origin. If asked where and how the divine has entered this divine-human book, he must reply: "Everywhere, and in almost every way conceivable." Throughout the whole preparation of the material to be written and of the men to write it; throughout the whole process of the gathering and classification and use of the material by the writers; throughout the whole process of the actual writing, — he sees at work divine influences of the most varied kinds, extending all the way from simply providential superintendence and spiritual illumination to direct revelation and inspiration.

It is of great importance to distinguish between these various ways in which the divine has been active in originating the Scriptures, but it is of vastly greater importance to fix the previous fact that it is in the Scriptures at all and has entered them in any way. The present essay aims, therefore, without raising any of the many questions which concern the distinguishing of the various activities of God in originating his Scriptures, to busy itself with the one previous question: *Is there reason to believe that God has been concerned at all in the origin of the Bible?*

The question thus proposed is a very general one. And it is a very immense one — almost limitless. It is, of course, utterly impossible to do more than touch upon it in any reasonable space, and all that could be urged in a single paper or in any reasonably circumscribed series of papers would bear a very small proportion to all that might be urged — to the mighty case that could be made out. No attempt can be made, therefore, toward fullness of treatment. A series of propositions most baldly stated will only be laid down one after the other, and it will be left to the reader to develop and illustrate them and bring out their combined force, which will, however, it is hoped, be immediately partly evident from their simple statement. An effort will also be made, in the choice of the propositions and their ordering,

[1] Pub. 1882, by the Presbyterian Board of Publication, Philadelphia, Pa.

to frame an argument of a kind which will demand, as of right, entrance into every mind; one, therefore, which will depend for its force on no original assumptions, but will begin rather with simple and patent facts — will simply put these facts together and then inquire what kind of facts they are and what they imply. Thus the reasoning will take the form of an inquiry rather than an argument — of an induction rather than a demonstration. The conclusions reached may not be so sharply and accurately defined as if reached by other methods, but they have the advantage of being obtained by a process to every step of which every man's mind ought to be open.

Our purpose is to look upon the Bible simply as one of the facts of the universe, of which every theory of the universe must take account, and for which, just as surely as for gravitation, it must make account or itself die, and then ask (and press the question): What kind of a cause must be assumed to account for it just as it is and just as it arose in the world? Thus we may inductively come to an answer to the query: "Must we assume superhuman activities at work in the genesis of this book?"

Without further introduction, we begin the inquiry at once.

I. The History of the Bible

1. The basal fact from which our inquiry takes its start is the very indisputable and patent one that in the world there is such a book as THE BIBLE. There is a definite volume, well known and always the same in contents, about which there need be no mistake, which goes under this name, and under this name is accessible to all. This very patent fact is the first that we need to notice.

2. It is another fact, hardly less patent than the last, that this book occupies a unique position in the world of civilized man. No other book stands to-day among men for what the Bible stands for. We are not asserting here that it has a right to the position it occupies or the power it exerts: we simply assert that it is undeniable that it holds that position and exercises that power.

The legislation of civilized nations is profoundly affected by its teaching; the social habits of cultured people are largely determined by its scheme of life; the governmental forms of powerful countries are built on its principles, and their functions are carried on under its sanctions. Rulers are entrusted with the exercise of their powers, witnesses are credited in the deposition of their testimony, only after oaths sworn upon or according to it. Everywhere it has percolated through the fabric of civilization, and modern society is built up upon the lines drawn by it.

Still further, where it most dominates, there is most life. It is the great Protestant nations — those who most rest upon this book — which are the most prominent nations, the most full of abounding life and enterprising energy, the most impressive on the destinies of man. It is even the pioneer of civilization; instead of following, it breaks the way for material advancement. Go where you will, if you find life, you will find also the Bible; and you will find it in the very midst of the organism. You will find it in the hall of legislation, and in the laws that are there framed; in the courts of justice, and in the justice that is there administered; in the colleges of learning, and in the learning that is there imparted; at the home-firesides, and in the moral training and homely virtues which are there inculcated. In a word, it is, as no other book has ever been to a single nation, bound up with all civilization and progress and culture.

3. It is worth our notice, still further, that this position of power and influence has been attained and held by the Bible through a most remarkable history. Confined for ages to a rough, isolated corner of the globe, in the keeping of a small and peculiar tribe of men, it almost without a moment's warning, like a great lake receiving a new accession of waters, immediately on completion, burst all boundaries and deluged the world. It came commended by no external pomp of appearance, attended with no force of arms. Alone and single-handed, in the face of stinging contempt and bloodthirsty cruelty, it opposed ancient prejudices, long-settled habits, customs and religions, every consideration of self-interest or indulgence or safety, and swept them away like so many straws. By its simple, despised presence among men it conquered. It mattered not where it went; human society in every stage of development, under every form of administration, and composed of every race of men, everywhere alike yielded itself to it.

We cannot overstate the case; it is even impossible for us to mentally realize the profundity of the change induced. Look only at the straws of external action which, veering suddenly around, advertise to us the change of wind beneath and behind. See the revolution in the sentiment which the sight of a *cross* kindled.

Who can estimate, again, the profound revolution which was necessary in men's very habits of thought, in their inmost consciousness, before *sacrificial ordinances* could fall into neglect. Just think of it. From the beginning of the world sacrifices had been universal. Men knew, and had from the beginning known, no other way to express the deepest facts of their consciences. The habit had been ground in upon the race not only for a lifetime, but for a worldtime. Everybody everywhere spontaneously fled to this rite as the fit expression of the sense of sin and the hope of deliverance. And yet, in little more than fifty years after the introduction of Christianity into his province, Pliny complains that it had almost put a stop to sacrifices there. A world-habit, dominant from the beginning, thus rolled back upon itself in a single generation! We cannot possibly appreciate the greatness of this conquest. Sacrifices had been almost the whole life of the people: from childhood sacrifices had met each man in every form, in every quarter, in every act, in every duty of every day's business. Not only could he not engage in any of the graver duties of the citizen without being confronted with them everywhere; he could not rise from his bed in the morning, retire to it at night, partake of his necessary sustenance, without a recognition of a god or the performance of a rite at every step. And yet Christianity came, not undermining the principle which underlay sacrifices, but emphasizing it, and still they fled away from its presence.

Beneath such external changes, conceive, if you can, the immense revolution that was wrought. Not only was the whole practice of religion altered, but also the whole theory of religion; not only the whole practice of morals, but the whole theory of morals. Vices in former repute were suddenly raised to the highest pinnacle of virtues; virtues in former repute were thrust down to the lowest hell of vices. Everything was overturned.

Is it asked whether the human means employed in gaining this grand victory were not sufficient to account for it? Look at them. A dozen ignorant peasants proclaiming a crucified Jew as the founder of a new faith; bearing as the symbol of their worship an instrument which was the sign of ignominy, slavery and crime; preaching what must have seemed an absurd doctrine of humility, patient suffering and love to enemies — graces undreamed of before; demanding what must have seemed an absurd worship for one who had died like a malefactor and a slave, and making what must have seemed an absurd promise of everlasting life through one who had himself died, and that between two thieves.

Did their voices fall on willing or docile ears? This was the age of those princes of scoffers, Celsus and Lucian.

Did they prosecute their work in peace and quietude? They were thrown to the lions until the very beasts were satiated with their prey. Their blood seemed only to water the field of the Lord.

Thus, in the face of all discouragement and cruel persecution, the Bible found itself established with incredible rapidity in the hearts of an immense Christendom. In less than seventy years it was known over all the then known world; within little more than a single century it had won to itself "almost the greater part of the whole state."

Do you say that this, despite all appearances, must have been an exceptional age and an exceptional experience? We reply that it is the experience of the ages. When corruption had brought back an age of darkness and the Bible was once more lost from real life, it required but a Luther to tear off the veil for it to re-enact the same history and sow Europe with the blood of its votaries till a harvest could be reaped of equal victory. It cannot be necessary to repeat the story of the noble conflict. You know it well, and know that it was a Bible war and a Bible victory. The same history is even now working itself out about us. Madagascar, under our eyes, has repeated it. Every corner of the globe has felt the tingling of the mighty impulse. Even here, in America, we are living amid historical wonders, our eyes unopened to the sight. Rapidly as the population of the United States has grown since 1800, the proportionate increase of the votaries of the Bible has outstripped it. Yet so quietly has it all been done that we live utterly oblivious of it until, through painfully gathered statistics, the fact is made to look us squarely in the face.

How certain a fact, then, it is that the Bible has reached its present wonderful position and influence through a most remarkable history, and a history which it is still continuing on exactly the same lines!

4. It is important to note, next, that throughout all this history, and still to-day, this great influence which the Bible has exerted has been, and is still, purely and only *beneficent*. All its power has been exerted in the direction of the elevation of man and loving ministry to his needs. Of course we are in no danger of forgetting that the truth of this statement has been of late challenged in some quarters. But neither can we forget three other facts: 1. That it is not challenged by the well-informed and unprejudiced even among those who deny the divine origin of the Bible. 2. That the methods by which it is attempted to make the Bible appear in any other *rôle* than that of a cornucopia of good for man will (as Dr. Fisher has lately very clearly shown) avail equally to prove that love is a curse and the household fireside, with all its blessings, a very nest of corruption. Of course, it is not denied, either of love or of the Bible, that it sometimes has been the cause of pain; each has often ennobled man through the pain and self-sacrifice called out by it. Nor is it denied of either that it has been made at times the excuse of crime, but both have cried out upon the wickedness which would hide behind their sacred skirts. 3. That those who put forth the challenge have been led to do it only because the teaching of the Bible has so leavened society and the usages of modern life that it is almost impossible for men to believe that the world could ever have existed without the restraining and ennobling influences which now seem naturally to dominate us, and yet which really have their root in the Bible. A true picture of the boon which this book has really been to the world can be obtained only by an examination of two classes of facts — those belonging to the condition of society before it entered into its beneficent reign on the one hand, and on the other those belonging to the condition into which society lapses when-

ever the Bible in any degree loses its hold upon men. The shameless-ness of Roman society under the early emperors will give us the norm of the one; the horrors of the Italian renascence and of the French Revolution will give us the norm of the other. It is not necessary to stop now to pollute these pages with the recital of the depths of deg-radation from which the Bible rescued man, and from which its potent influence (witness the Italian renascence and the Reign of Terror) alone keeps him rescued: they may be read in any accredited history of the times, and it is certainly justifiable to assume as fact what is recognized as fact by all competent historians.

Thus, then, the Bible is seen to tread the ages like the fabled goddess under whose beneficent footfall sprang beautiful flowers wher-ever she went. Hospitals and asylums and refuges for the sick, the miserable and the afflicted grow like heaven-bedewed blossoms in its path. Woman, whose equality with man Plato considered a sure mark of social disorganization, has been elevated; slavery has been driven from civilized ground; letters have been given by Christian missiona-ries, under the influence of the Bible and in order to its publication, to whole peoples and races. Who can estimate that boon? Thus Cyril and Methodius gave alphabet and written language to the vast hordes of the Sclaves; thus Ulphilas, to the whole race of Teutons; thus even Egypt, mother of letters, first received a manageable alphabet. Thus still to-day tribes and peoples sunk in barbarism are being lifted by the Bible to the ranks of literary nations. So the work goes on, and still to-day, as ever before, the Bible stands in all the world exercising everywhere its immense power in the restraining of all evil passions, in the advancement of all that is good and tender and elevating, in pouring out benefits unspeakable to the individual and the state.

5. All this immense influence for good which the Bible is exercis-ing over the minds and hearts of men is due to a most deep-seated and steadfast conviction in their minds that it is from God and con-stitutes a law given from heaven for amending the lives and amelio-rating the condition of men.

If this be a fanaticism, it is a most beneficent and a most remark-able fanaticism, far from easy to account for on the hypothesis that it is a fanaticism. Did men rush to embrace a delusion which had nothing to commend it to them amid the scoffs of Celsus and the ridicule of Lucian, against their every interest and against their every inclination, and that when the majesty of Rome was unsheathed to fright them back and the jaws of the lions yawned to engulf them? Men do not usually spring so to die for a delusion which offers so little and threatens so much. Then, too, how has the fanaticism so grown? How is it that it still holds captive so many millions of those whose intellect is of the clearest and whose culture is of the highest? How is it that it still embraces the civilized world? But, however it be attempted to account for it, here is the fact. The great influence which the Bible has ever exercised has been always, and still is accounted for by those who yield to it on their sincere conviction that this book, which differs so in power from all other volumes, differs from them equally in origin, being alone of books *God's book*, while all others are men's.

6. This conviction is traced by them not solely to the visible power and influence of the book, nor solely, conjoined with that, to the manifest grandeur and divinity of its contents and character, but also (continuing to dwell now on external particulars) to marvelous circumstances which attended the giving of this marvelous book to the world. Those who wrote its latter portion and sent the whole abroad asserted that they acted under commission from God and authenticated their mission by a series of astounding miracles. Thus the miracle of the book is appropriately believed to have sprung from the center of a God-endowed company.

We cannot pause now to prove that these miracles really occurred. All that can be said is that the testimony they rest on is irrefragable, and that they must be admitted to have occurred or the foundations of all history are swept away at a stroke. It is enough here to note how appropriately the wonderful history which has been wrought out by the Bible is made to spring from open miracles. All is here consistent and appropriate; and if those miracles which are asserted to have happened really happened, all is explained and constitutes a harmonious whole. Otherwise, we are landed in great difficulties and inconsistencies.

If we will ponder the facts which we have so baldly stated, it seems that we must conclude that the external history of this book is such as will so harmonize with a supernatural origin for it as to take away all strangeness from the assertion of such an origin. And what is that but saying that the history of the book suggests a supernatural origin for it — even raises a presumption in favor of such an origin for it? This book is certainly unique in the power it possesses: is it not unique in its source of power? It is certainly furnished with an influence possessed by no other book. Whence came it?

II. THE STRUCTURE OF THE BIBLE

And now let us open the volume and see what kind of a book this is which has exerted such remarkable power through so long and so wonderful a history. We have all, doubtless, a notion of the kind of book a volume is likely to be which will exercise vast influence over men — a masterly argument, say, well ordered and set foursquare

against all possible opposition, each part fitted with consummate skill
to each other part, and the whole driven with relentless force and unswerving purpose straight to the intended goal; or a fervid appeal,
say, based on the primal emotions of the heart, with burning and well-
chosen words touching each string of that mystic harp, beating out
from them all one burst of answering music. A consummate master of
thought and speech may be thus conceived of as so catching the
human heart as to hold it almost permanently. Yet his influence would
be limited — notably, by this: the radius of the circle of his sympathies. Certainly no man has yet arisen able to frame a writing of
universal and age-long influence, simply because no one has arisen
yet wholly above the environment of the social customs and age-
influence in which he was bred. And certainly it is inconceivable that
a book should exert great influence over a wide expanse of territory
and through long stretches of time which was not consciously framed
for influence by an intelligent and competent mind. All this being
true, it is assuredly worth our most serious attention that the Bible
is the only book in existence which has any pretensions to being universal and lasting in its influence; *and yet, if it be not of superhuman
origin, it could not have been framed consciously for influence.* Let us
look into this fact somewhat more closely.

7. On first throwing open this wonderful volume we are struck
immediately with the fact that it is not a book, but rather a congeries
of books. No less than sixty-six separate books, one of which consists
itself of one hundred and fifty separate compositions, immediately
stare us in the face. These treatises come from the hands of at least
thirty distinct writers, scattered over a period of some fifteen hundred
years, and embrace specimens of nearly every kind of writing known
among men. Histories, codes of law, ethical maxims, philosophical
treatises, discourses, dramas, songs, hymns, epics, biographies, letters
both official and personal, vaticinations, — every kind of composition
known beneath heaven seems gathered here in one volume.

Their writers, too, were of like diverse kinds. The time of their
labors stretches from the hoary past of Egypt to and beyond the
bright splendor of Rome under Augustus. They appear to have been
of every sort of temperament, of every degree of endowment, of every
time of life, of every grade of attainment, of every condition in the
social scale. Looked at from a purely external point of view, the
volume is a rough bale of drift from the sea of Time, a conglomerate
of *débris* brought down by the waters and cast in a heap together.
Nay, not only are there heterogeneous, but seemingly positively conflicting, elements in it. One half is a mass of Hebrew writings held
sacred by a race which cannot look with patience on the other half,
which is a mass of Greek writings claiming to set aside the legislation

of a large part of its fellow. Yet it is this congeries of volumes which has had, and still has, this immense influence. The Hebrew half never conquered the world until the Greek half was added to it; the Greek half did not conquer save by the aid of the Hebrew half. The whole mass, in all its divinity, has attained the kingship.

The question which will not down is, Can the miraculous power of this book be explained by the measure of power to which other books are able to attain? Where does this book, seemingly thus cast together by some whirlpool of time, get its influence? If influence is not *natural* to such a volume, must it not point to something *supernatural* in it? Whence came it?

8. We may look, however, on a still greater wonder. Let us once penetrate beneath all this primal diversity and observe the internal character of the volume, and a most striking unity is found to pervade the whole; so that, in spite of having been thus made up of such diverse parts, it forms but one organic whole. The parts are so linked together that the absence of any one book would introduce confusion and disorder. The same doctrine is taught from beginning to end, running like a golden thread through the whole and stringing book after book upon itself like so many pearls. Each book, indeed, adds something in clearness, definition, or even increment, to what the others proclaim; but the development is orderly and constantly progressive. One step leads naturally to the next; the pearls are certainly chosen in the order of stringing.

An unbroken historical continuity pervades the whole book. It is even astonishing how accurately the parts historically dovetail together, jag to jag, into one connected and consistent whole. Malachi ends with a finger-post pointing through the silent ages to a path clearly seen in the Gospels. The New Testament fits on to the Old silently and noiselessly, but exactly, just as one stone of the Jewish temple fitted its fellow prepared for it by exact measurement in the quarries; so that, on any careful consideration of the two coexisting phenomena — utter diversity in origin of these books, and yet utter nicety of combination of one with all — it is as impossible to doubt that they were meant each for the other, were consciously framed each for its place, as it is to doubt that the various parts of a complicated machine, when brought from the factory and set up in its place of future usefulness, were all carefully framed for one another.

But just see where this lands us. Unless we are prepared to allow to a man some fifteen hundred years of conscious existence and intellectual supervision of the work, we are shut up here to the admission of a superhuman origin for this book. It is difficult to see how this argument can be really escaped. It will be perceived that it is analogous to what is often urged from the phenomena of the natural universe to prove for it a divine origin. Indeed, all the arguments urged in the one sphere are also capable of being urged in the other. The gradual framing of the Bible through a period of fifteen hundred years excludes human supervision. Now, the Bible, as a whole, is a result or an effect in the universe, and it must have had, as such, an adequate cause, which, since the result is an intelligent one, must have been an intelligent cause: there is the ontological argument, and it proves a superhuman intelligent cause for the Bible. It consists of orderly arranged parts, of an orderly developed scheme: there is the cosmological argument, and again it proves the activity of an intelligent cause (and much else not now to be brought out) of at least fifteen hundred years' duration. It is itself a cause of marvelous effects in the world for the production of which it is most admirably designed, and its whole inner harmony and all its inner relations are most deeply graven with the marks of a design kept constantly before some intelligent mind for at least fifteen hundred years: there is the argument from design, attaining equally far-reaching and cogent conclusions as in the realm of nature. The analogy need not, however, be drawn out further. An atheist of the present day spoke only sober truth when he declared that the divine origin of the Bible and the divine origin of the world must stand or fall together. The arguments which will prove the one prove also the other. Butler proved this proposition long ago. It stands indubitable; so that absolute atheism or Christianity must be our only choice.

9. Another point in which the unity of the Bible is strikingly apparent needs our attention next: amid all the diversity of its subject-matter, it may yet be said that almost the whole book is taken up with the *portraiture of one person*. On its first page he comes for a moment before our astonished eyes; on the last he lingers still before their adoring gaze. And from that first word in Genesis which describes him as the "seed of the woman" and at the same time her deliverer — with occasional moments of absence, just as the principal character of a play is not always on the stage, and yet with constant development of character — to the end, where he is discovered sitting on the great white throne and judging the nations, the one consistent but gradually developed portraiture grows before our eyes. Not a false stroke is made. Every touch of the pencil is placed just where it ought to stand as part of the whole. There is nowhere the slightest trace of wavering or hesitancy of hand. The draughtsman is certainly a consummate artist. And, as the result of it all, the world is possessed of the strongest, most consistent, most noble literary portraiture to be found in all her literature.

Yet we are asked to believe that this grand result has been attained, not by the skilled limning of a Michelangelo, but by the disconnected dabblings of a score and a half of untrained forgers, who, moreover, were ever at cross-purposes with each other. Why, if the creation and successful dramatization, through a few short years, of such a character as Hamlet required the genius of a Shakespeare, what genius was required for this astoundingly successful creation and dramatization of such a character as that of the GOD-MAN through the ages of ages and æons of æons — from the time when at his Father's side he sat, coequal with him, before all worlds, to the time when these same worlds shall be swallowed up in the final fire! One should certainly rather risk his sanity in the assertion that the play of "Hamlet" had formed itself by the fortuitous concourse of the alphabetical signs and made its own portraiture of the subtle Dane, than on the assertion that this portraiture of the GOD-MAN had been attained apart from the constant supervision and active labor of a consummate mind. If we should thus consider this portraiture only as a fiction, it would demand for its author something more than has yet been seen in man. As it is undeniable now that it occupies the chiefest portion of the Bible from Genesis to Revelation, and binds the portions it occupies together as a consistent dramatization of it-self, it is equally undeniable that these portions of the Bible, at any rate, owe their origin to a mind able to superintend their composition for at least fifteen hundred years with a genius hitherto unexampled among men.

10. One other bond of connection between the parts of the volume must needs be adverted to briefly — that formed by numer-ous predictions of coming events given in the earlier portions and accounts of the fulfillment of them in later portions, by which these later portions are proved to be but the intended outgrowth and con-clusion of the former. These predictions run through an immense range both of time and of circumstance, and are made too precise and detailed in form, and too precise and detailed in the account of their fulfillment, for it to be possible to doubt, on the one hand, that they were real predictions, or, on the other, that they were really fulfilled. Thus the various books are drawn close together; and if the Bible, externally considered, may be likened to a bale of drift, these proph-ecies, given in one part and reaching their fulfillment in another, are the strong cords which bind the bale securely together and make it one whole. The unity induced by this means is, indeed, complete and most conclusive to its own divine origin.

11. Thus we are led to appeal to *prophecy*, and that not only to prove the unity of the plan of Scripture, but, independent of and far above that — by its very nature as prediction of things yet hidden in the future — as an irrefragable proof of the divine origin of the whole of the closely-knit volume in which it finds place. It is not a

function of human intellect to read the secrets of unborn ages; and the existence in this book of accurate, detailed predictions of even unimportant and certainly incalculable events of the far future demonstrates its divine origin.

It is, of course, impossible in this brief essay to illustrate the character and convincingness of Scripture prophecy, or even to indicate instances of its unquestionable fulfillment in detail. Were there space, we might point to the immense number of independent predictions, seemingly opposite, or even contradictory, to one another, before their fulfillment, found on the coming of Christ to be harmoniously gathered up and fulfilled in his unique personality and work — predictions covering not only the great outlines of his work and the marked traits of his person, but publishing ages beforehand the very village in which he should first see the light, the homage on the one hand, and the abuse on the other, which he should receive, the life he should live and the death he should die, even to the most minute description of the pains he should suffer and the scoffs he should endure as he hung upon the tree — yea, even the exact price of his blood and fate of his betrayer. Or, again, we might point to that ever-living witness to the truth of prophecy in the Jewish race upon whom everything that has been prophesied has been and is being duly fulfilled; or, again, to an infinite multitude of minute details of predictions touching many races and nations which have with infinite might fulfilled themselves everywhere. Space would fail, however, for such an enumeration. And it is the less necessary, now that the feverish efforts, on the part of those who wish to escape from the power of the Bible, to assign later dates to the prophetical books than most cogent proof from many quarters will allow, amount to an admission that the prophetical element in them cannot be denied. In prophecy, therefore, we have a continual miracle set in the midst of the Bible, to stand in all ages as a sure proof that it comes from God. As each prediction is in turn fulfilled before the eyes of each age which witnesses it, a miracle performs itself (and attests itself in the act) which is as cogent and sufficient evidence of the divine origin of the Bible as if all the miracles of the apostolical age were rewrought in our presence to reaffirm its teaching. Thus we see, in perhaps a new light, the meaning of our Lord's pregnant saying: "If they hear not Moses and the prophets, neither will they be persuaded, though one rise from the dead."

As, then, when we considered the external history of the Bible, we were driven back, step by step, through marvelous circumstances to open miracles of power proclaiming and demonstrating the divine origin of the book, so here, as soon as we look within it in even the most cursory way, we repeat the same process and move back from marvel to marvel, until we reach the open miracle of prophecy, again independently proving the divine origin of the book after a fashion which cannot be escaped or legitimately questioned.

III. The Teaching of the Bible

The same process is only again repeated, and cumulative evidence for the divine origin of the Bible obtained, when we look somewhat deeper into its contents and ask after the character and witness of its teaching — a subject broad as the earth itself and full of self-evidence, but upon which we have as yet not even cast a glance. The character and the nature of the contents of the Bible alone are enough to prove its divine origin. If men cannot have made the miracles of power by which its publication to the world was accompanied, nor the miracles of prophecy by which its progress through the world has been accompanied, no more can they have manufactured the miracles of teaching of which its contents consist. Independently of all other evidence, the *miracle of the contents* demands a divine origin. This, again, may be made plainer by some specifications, which again, however, must be presented in a very naked and fragmentary way.

12. Let us note, then, first of all, the unspeakable elevation and grandeur both of the teaching itself which this book presents and of the assumptions on which it bases that teaching.

The conception of God which is here presented — how unutterably divine is it! Apart from the Bible, man has never reached to such a conception. This element of it, and that element of it, has, indeed, through the voice of nature, separately dawned upon his soul; but the complete ideal is conveyed to him only by this book. Infinite and eternal spirit — pure and ineffable — unlimited by matter, or space or time, infinite, eternal and unchangeable in essence and attributes! And what a circle of attributes! Infinite power, infinite wisdom, infinite justice, infinite holiness, infinite goodness, infinite mercy, infinite pity, infinite love! Verily, if this conception be not a true image of a really existent God, the human heart must say it ought to be. And this is the conception of God which the Bible holds up before us — more than that, which it dramatizes through an infinite series of infinitely varied actions through a period of millenniums of years in perfect consistency of character. Everywhere in its pages God appears as the all-powerful, all-wise, necessarily just and holy One; everywhere as the all-good, all-merciful, necessarily pitiful and loving One. Never is a single one of these ineffable perfections lost or hidden or veiled.

The Bible's conception of the nature of man is of like nobility. Framed in the image of God, he was made like him not only in the passive qualities, but also in his endowment of active capacities. Even freedom of action — unbound ability to choose his own future — were placed in his grasp. So, also, the Bible's teaching as to the duties that man, even after he has made his fatal choice, owes to God and his neighbor, all founded on the principle of love; its teaching as to the possibilities before man and the destiny in store for him, culminating in the possibility of his enthronement as co-ruler of the universe with his divine Redeemer; its teaching as to the relation of man to the physical and irrational universe as responsible head over it; its teaching as to the origin of this universe itself and its purpose and destiny, — all reach the acme of grandeur. These instances must serve us as specimens of the grandeur of its teaching.

13. We must note, still further, that both the general tenor of the Bible and its special assertions are all in precise accord "with what the profoundest learning shows to be the actual state of the universe, as well as what the deepest and largest experience establishes as the actual course of nature." And it is a very pertinent question how it happens that the Bible was able, alone of ancient books, to forestall the conclusions of the latest science of the nineteenth century. It has taken scientific thought up to to-day to bring its conceptions of the origin of the world to the point at which Moses stood some three millenniums ago. This, again, must serve us now as a specimen fact (among a multitude) proving that "whoever wrote this book knew more than we know, and knew it distinctly when we knew nothing."

Yet, although possessed of a knowledge thus unspeakably advanced beyond all of their time, the writers of this book do not seem to have been proud of their possession or anxious to display it; they do not even formally transmit their knowledge, but simply act and speak on its presupposition; so that when we reach an equal stage of advancement to theirs, without having been hitherto conscious of its presence, we suddenly find it there continually implied and constantly underlying every part. It is thus always most deeply felt by those most conversant with the progress of knowledge, and yet does not in any degree clog the understanding of the book for the purpose for which it was given by those who are as yet ignorant of the basis of physical or philosophical fact assumed.

14. Thus we are led to take note of another general characteristic of biblical teaching — the fact that all its great truths are universal truths; i.e., truths capable of reaching and making entrance into and taking a strong hold upon the heart of man as man, and of all men equally, independently of their race-affinities, intellectual advancement or social standing. That this should be so is undoubtedly a great wonder, and it is redoubled when we remember that it is correlated with great and remarkable knowledge. Usually, when the profound philosopher speaks, he needs philosophers for his audience; and yet here is a book which naturally and without effort betrays acquaint-

ance with the deepest reaches of modern discovery, and yet in its every accent speaks home to the child as readily as to the sage.

In still another respect this same fact — namely, that the truths of the Bible "find us" — has probative force, since, herefrom, it is equally evident that the Bible is suited to man and that its asserted truths are instinctively recognized by man as actual truths. The Bible thus certainly comes with a message to man — one that is recognized by each man who needs its words as specially for him, and that is witnessed to instinctively by each as true. How does it happen that this book, alone among books, reaches the heart alike of the Bushman and of a Newton? of a savage lost in the horrors of savagery and of a Faraday sitting aloft on the calm and clear if somewhat chill heights of science? This universality of effect seems to prove a corresponding universality of intention. But who of men has ever been able to hold before him as recipients of his book all men of all ages? Who has been able to calculate upon the hearts and characters of men removed from him by such stretches of both time and circumstance? Who could have been able to adapt a message penned in a corner, ages agone, to the mental position of the nineteenth century and the hearts of a Newton and a Faraday? Yet we must assume for the Bible an author who was capable of this. Was Moses capable of it? Was an anonymous forger of his name?

15. We must, however, turn to note another general characteristic of Scripture — the remarkable simplicity of its manner and the transparent honesty of its tone; so that its words, even when describing the most utter marvels, possess that calm, quiet ring which stamps them with indubitable truthfulness. If we are asked why we trust a friend in whom we have every confidence, and credit his every statement, we may be somewhat at a loss for a definite answer. "We know him," we say. This same evidence is good also for a book. We may judge of the truthfulness of men's writings by all those little intangible characteristics which when united go toward making a very strong impression of actual proof, but which one by one are almost too small to adduce or even notice, just as we may judge of the trustiness of men's characters by all the innumerable looks, gestures, chance expressions, little circumstances which make their due impression on us. Combined, they are convincing, though each by itself might seem ambiguous or valueless. The conclusion in each case is, however, valid and rational, and the evidence is unmistakably good evidence. Now, for the Bible, this evidence is unusually strong; and thus it happens that men who do not know how to reason, and who are incapable of following a closely-reasoned argument, are accepting the Bible on all sides of us on truly rational and valid evidence, and accepting it on like evidence as divine. They are continually reading accounts of

miracles so numerous and so striking that the witnesses of them could not be mistaken; so embedded in a narrative of such artlessness, gravity, honesty, intelligence, straightforwardness as palpably to be neither fraud nor fancy that they form part and parcel of it and are absolutely inseparable from it; so embedded in a narrative which approves itself by a thousand simple and inimitable hints and traits to be transparently truthful and trustworthy that they must stand or fall with it. Now, this is most rational evidence, and evidence so strong that it is as difficult for the honest mind to resist it as it is for us to express it.

16. It becomes surely, then, of sufficient importance to justify special notice that in the midst of this narrative, and scattered all through it, we find calm and simple, but frequent, constant, and steadfast, assertions of a divine origin for itself. So honest and transparently truthful a narrative, filled with marks everywhere of superhuman knowledge, naturally enough does not, in the pride of human nature, claim all this superhuman knowledge for its human authors, but ascribes it all to God; naturally enough empties its human authors of any credit for knowledge before the time of knowledge and plans beyond the reach of man and ascribes it all to God. And its very honesty and simplicity of statement, the transparent honesty of this statement, proves the assertion truthful and trustworthy. Here, then, once more, we reach through orderly steps, exhibiting at each stage marks of God's hand, the assertion of a divine origin; here, once more, after walking through the aisles and nave and choir of a grand cathedral filled all along with the marks of genius in its planning and execution, we reach again the wall, and, lo! on it the marks of the chisel and the superscription of the Architect that prove it was made by a competent mind and did not *grow*.

It is very difficult to see but that the argument, if fully drawn out and illustrated, is conclusive.

IV. Special Characteristics of the Bible

Another, and an even more cogent, argument might be presented from a consideration of some special characteristics either of the whole Bible or of some of its parts — an argument hitherto untouched. This argument would soon, however, grow much too vast to be included in this essay. We must content ourselves with only pointing at a distance to only one particular which might, were there space, be urged most convincingly.

17. We refer to the *progressive character of the teaching* included in this book, with the special cases which might be adduced under that head. It begins with first principles expressed in outward symbol, and advances gradually to the full system, working out its approaches

in history before delivering it in dogma. We do not urge simply that this progressive scheme is consistent with a divine origin for it; we urge that this supremely wise method of delivering truth and training a people, taken in connection with the unity of the system throughout the whole, is consistent with nothing else. No *doctrinaire* made this Bible — see what kind of work they do in the history of Middle-Age Florence and Revolutionary France — but a most consummate statesman who knew what was in man and how to mould him to his purposes.

We would appeal, in this connection — progressiveness — specially to the practical and practicable character of Old-Testament legislation. And thus we are led to assert that those very passages concerning polygamy and kindred themes (which have been made an occasion of gibe against the Scriptures) are themselves a most cogent argument for their divine origin. We Americans ought to know by this time that the best way to secure polygamy unharmed and enshrine it unconquerably under the protection of a nation is to write on the statute-books inoperative laws against it. The Bible was framed by too wise a statesman to fall into that error, and we who enjoy Christian homes to-day have to thank God for it. The unspeakable wisdom of dealing at that age, and under those circumstances, with polygamy, divorce, slavery by regulative laws, which in regulating discouraged, and in discouraging destroyed them, makes strongly for a superhuman origin of the legislation.

So, again, growing out of this same progressive system, we could appeal most strongly to the ritualistic system of symbolical worship given to the Jews and by law secured from failure, by which object lessons — all schoolmasters to lead to something better and higher — were ineffaceably taught to a whole nation, which was thus prepared to receive the spiritual lesson meant for it.

Still again we should appeal to the wise method of New-Testament legislation through great principles rather than specific ordinances, thus securing absolute universality in connection with perfect definiteness; or again to the remarkable tenderness and beauty of this legislation, especially apparent in the cases of slaves, wives and children and temporal rulers — a phenomenon in the age when it was given enough of itself to suggest a divine origin for the one book which contains it; or still again to the wise silence of the same legislation on many subjects on which it must have been very tempting then to legislate, but legislation on which we can see now would have imperiled the success of the main purpose for which the book was given and obtained no corresponding gain.

On all these and like points, however, it is not now possible to touch. We pass on, therefore, to our last remark.

V. Impossibility of Accounting for the Bible

18. That the Bible, thus standing in the world, being of such sort, and having had such a history, has yet to be accounted for on the hypothesis that it had only a human origin. Here it stands, just such a fact in the universe, a substantive thing, tangible and that can be examined. The ingenuity of men has been feverishly busy with it these hundreds of years. Yet the world still awaits a theory which will render an adequate account of it on any other hypothesis than that it came from God. Theories have been attempted, but one after another they have broken down of their own weight or have had justice executed upon them by fellow-unbelieving hands amid the plaudits of all men of all parties. Thus it happens that up to to-day no hypothesis except that of superhuman interference has been able to stand a half century as an account of the origin of this book. What is this but the confession that without the assumption of superhuman interference this book cannot be accounted for? that these miraculous claims and these miraculous assertions cannot be rationally or satisfactorily explained away? Look for one moment at the efforts made to account on natural grounds for the miraculous element in the New Testament. First, a school arose which tried to work on the assumption that whenever a miracle is recorded the event described did really happen, indeed, but that it has been exaggeratedly and mistakenly described as miraculous, and not merely natural, by the New-Testament writers. The sick were healed, but by medicinal means; the dead were raised, but only from seeming, not real, death. That attempt to explain away the miraculous failed, as requiring as great a series of miracles of wonderful coincidences as it explained away. Another then arose which wished to account for it all as a series of myths, holding that there was a kernel of truth in each event described, but that this kernel had gathered much falsehood around it as it rolled through time, from mouth to mouth, before it got recorded in our Bible, just as a snowball grows almost unrecognizably greater as it rolls down a long slope. But this attempt was wrecked hopelessly on the lack of a soil for the myths to grow in (that is, of snow to frame the balls of) and of time for them to increase in (that is, of any hill for them to roll down). Then another rose on its ruins — an elaborate theory of party strifes and forgeries and reforgeries of books in every conceivable interest; so that the same material was worked over and over again by false and designing men, to serve each new notion, until the final outcome was our New Testament. Again this theory was wrecked on the lack of time for all this elaborate process before the date at which adequate proof is in hand for the existence of the books. The whole elaborate scheme falls with the failure of the

attempted rape of the second century. It cannot be true unless all history is false.

Time is lacking for the New Testament to have grown in, if considered a product of time; whence, then, came it? Soil is lacking for it to have developed in, if considered a human development; then, whence came it? All schemes which have hitherto been invented to account for its origin without God have pitiably failed, and there is no particular reason to look for anything more cogent to be advanced in the future. If, however, this book cannot be accounted for apart from God, we seem shut up to account for it as from him. Certainly, the only rational course is to accept it as from him until it is able to be rationally accounted for without his interference.

With this we may fitly close our inquiry. The query with which we started seems abundantly answered. A supernatural origin for the Bible appears cumulatively proven.

In closing, it would be well for us to take note of one or two facts in regard to the argument which has been offered. Let it be observed, then:

1. That no attempt has been made to distinguish between a superhuman and a divine origin for the Bible. This is not because the two are not separable, but only because they are, in our present argument, practically the same.

2. That no attempt has been made to distinguish between the divine origin of the system and that of the books recording that system. This, again, is not because the two are not separable, but only because, so far as the argument has been pressed — though not much farther — the two need not be practically separated.

3. That no question has been raised as to the extent of the divine in the Bible. This is due to three facts: Because this question need not be raised primarily for the establishment of the faith, but is necessarily a consequent one to be raised after the general divine origin of the book is admitted; because, again, the humble Christian often looks upon and draws life from the Bible without raising this question, simply accepting what he reads as divinely given to strengthen his faith; and because, again, it was impossible in one essay to treat both questions.

4. That, nevertheless, the facts and arguments which have been adduced in a general way to prove the general divine origin of the Bible not only prepare the way, but even, narrowly questioned, will raise a strong presumption, for the further conclusions that this book has been not only in a general way given by God, but also specifically inspired in the giving, that thus its every word is from him, and that it is worthy of our reverent and loving credence in its every particular.

APPENDIX II

THE CANON OF THE NEW TESTAMENT:
HOW AND WHEN FORMED

THE FORMATION OF THE CANON OF
THE NEW TESTAMENT[1]

In order to obtain a correct understanding of what is called the formation of the Canon of the New Testament, it is necessary to begin by fixing very firmly in our minds one fact which is obvious enough when attention is once called to it. That is, that the Christian church did not require to form for itself the idea of a "canon," — or, as we should more commonly call it, of a "Bible," — that is, of a collection of books given of God to be the authoritative rule of faith and practice. It inherited this idea from the Jewish church, along with the thing itself, the Jewish Scriptures, or the "Canon of the Old Testament." The church did not grow up by natural law: it was founded. And the authoritative teachers sent forth by Christ to found His church, carried with them, as their most precious possession, a body of divine Scriptures, which they imposed on the church that they founded as its code of law. No reader of the New Testament can need proof of this; on every page of that book is spread the evidence that from the very beginning the Old Testament was as cordially recognized as law by the Christian as by the Jew. The Christian church thus was never without a "Bible" or a "canon."

But the Old Testament books were not the only ones which the apostles (by Christ's own appointment the authoritative founders of the church) imposed upon the infant churches, as their authoritative rule of faith and practice. No more authority dwelt in the prophets of the old covenant than in themselves, the apostles, who had been "made sufficient as ministers of a new covenant"; for (as one of themselves argued) "if that which passeth away was with glory, much more that which remaineth is in glory." Accordingly not only was the gospel they delivered, in their own estimation, itself a divine revelation, but it was also preached "in the Holy Ghost" (I Pet. i. 12); not merely the matter of it, but the very words in which it was clothed were "of the Holy Spirit" (I Cor. ii. 13). Their own commands were, therefore, of divine authority (I Thess. iv. 2), and their writings were the depository of these commands (II Thess. ii. 15). "If any man obeyeth not our word by this epistle," says Paul to one church (II Thess. iii. 14), "note that man, that ye have no company with

---

[1] Pub. 1892, by the American Sunday School Union, Philadelphia, Pa.

him." To another he makes it the test of a Spirit-led man to recognize that what he was writing to them was "the commandments of the Lord" (I Cor. xiv. 37). Inevitably, such writings, making so awful a claim on their acceptance, were received by the infant churches as of a quality equal to that of the old "Bible"; placed alongside of its older books as an additional part of the one law of God; and read as such in their meetings for worship — a practice which moreover was required by the apostles (I Thess. v. 27; Col. iv. 16; Rev. i. 3). In the apprehension, therefore, of the earliest churches, the "Scriptures" were not a *closed* but an *increasing* "canon." Such they had been from the beginning, as they gradually grew in number from Moses to Malachi; and such they were to continue as long as there should remain among the churches "men of God who spake as they were moved by the Holy Ghost."

We say that this immediate placing of the new books — given the church under the seal of apostolic authority — among the Scriptures already established as such, was inevitable. It is also historically evinced from the very beginning. Thus the apostle Peter, writing in A.D. 68, speaks of Paul's numerous letters not in contrast with the Scriptures, but as among the Scriptures and in contrast with "the *other* Scriptures" (II Pet. iii. 16) — that is, of course, those of the Old Testament. In like manner the apostle Paul combines, as if it were the most natural thing in the world, the book of Deuteronomy and the Gospel of Luke under the common head of "Scripture" (I Tim. v. 18): "For the Scripture saith, 'Thou shalt not muzzle the ox when he treadeth out the corn' [Deut. xxv. 4]; and, 'The laborer is worthy of his hire'" (Luke x. 7). The line of such quotations is never broken in Christian literature. Polycarp (c. 12) in A.D. 115 unites the Psalms and Ephesians in exactly similar manner: "In the sacred books, . . . as it is said in these Scriptures, 'Be ye angry and sin not,' and 'Let not the sun go down upon your wrath.'" So, a few years later, the so-called second letter of Clement, after quoting Isaiah, adds (ii. 4): "And another Scripture, however, says, 'I came not to call the righteous, but sinners'" — quoting from Matthew, a book which Barnabas (*circa* 97–106 A.D.) had already adduced as Scripture. After this such quotations are common.

What needs emphasis at present about these facts is that they obviously are not evidences of a gradually-heightening estimate of the New Testament books, originally received on a lower level and just beginning to be tentatively accounted Scripture; they are conclusive evidences rather of the estimation of the New Testament books from the very beginning as Scripture, and of their attachment as Scripture to the other Scriptures already in hand. The early Christians did not, then, first form a rival "canon" of "new books" which came only

gradually to be accounted as of equal divinity and authority with the
"old books"; they received new book after new book from the apostolical circle, as equally "Scripture" with the old books, and added
them one by one to the collection of old books as additional Scriptures, until at length the new books thus added were numerous enough
to be looked upon as another *section* of the Scriptures.

The earliest name given to this new section of Scripture was
framed on the model of the name by which what we know as the
Old Testament was then known. Just as it was called "The Law and
the Prophets and the Psalms" (or "the Hagiographa"), or more
briefly "The Law and the Prophets," or even more briefly still "The
Law"; so the enlarged Bible was called "The Law and the Prophets,
with the Gospels and the Apostles" (so Clement of Alexandria,
"Strom." vi. 11, 88; Tertullian, "De Præs. Hær." 36), or most briefly
"The Law and the Gospel" (so Claudius Apolinaris, Irenæus); while
the new books apart were called "The Gospel and the Apostles," or
most briefly of all "The Gospel." This earliest name for the new
Bible, with all that it involves as to its relation to the old and briefer
Bible, is traceable as far back as Ignatius (A.D. 115), who makes use
of it repeatedly (e. g., "ad Philad." 5; "ad Smyrn." 7). In one passage
he gives us a hint of the controversies which the enlarged Bible of the
Christians aroused among the Judaizers ("ad Philad." 6). "When I
heard some saying," he writes, "'Unless I find it in the *Old [Books]*
I will not believe the *Gospel*,' on my saying, 'It is written,' they
answered, 'That is the question.' To me, however, Jesus Christ *is*
the Old [Books]; his cross and death and resurrection, and the faith
which is by him, the undefiled Old [Books] — by which I wish, by
your prayers, to be justified. The priests indeed are good, but the
High Priest better," etc. Here Ignatius appeals to the "Gospel" as
Scripture, and the Judaizers object, receiving from him the answer
in effect which Augustine afterward formulated in the well-known
saying that the New Testament lies hidden in the Old and the Old
Testament is first made clear in the New. What we need now to observe, however, is that to Ignatius the New Testament was not a
different book from the Old Testament, but part of the one body of
Scripture with it; an *accretion*, so to speak, which had grown upon it.

This is the testimony of all the early witnesses — even those
which speak for the distinctively Jewish-Christian church. For example, that curious Jewish-Christian writing, "The Testaments of the
XII. Patriarchs" (Benj. 11), tells us, under the cover of an *ex post
facto* prophecy, that the "work and word" of Paul, i.e., confessedly
the book of Acts and Paul's Epistles, "shall be written in the Holy
Books," i. e., as is understood by all, made a part of the existent Bible.
So even in the Talmud, in a scene intended to ridicule a "bishop" of

the first century, he is represented as finding Galatians by "sinking himself deeper" into the same "Book" which contained the Law of Moses ("Babl. Shabbath," 116 a and b). The details cannot be entered into here. Let it suffice to say that, from the evidence of the fragments which alone have been preserved to us of the Christian writings of that very early time, it appears that from the beginning of the second century (and that is from the end of the apostolic age) a collection (Ignatius, II Clement) of "New Books" (Ignatius), called the "Gospel and Apostles" (Ignatius, Marcion), was already a part of the "Oracles" of God (Polycarp, Papias, II Clement), or "Scriptures" (I Tim., II Pet., Barn., Polycarp, II Clement), or the "Holy Books" or "Bible" (Testt. XII. Patt.).

The number of books included in this added body of New Books, at the opening of the second century, cannot be satisfactorily determined by the evidence of these fragments alone. The section of it called the "Gospel" included Gospels written by "the apostles and their companions" (Justin), which beyond legitimate question were our four Gospels now received. The section called "the Apostles" contained the book of Acts (The Testt. XII. Patt.) and epistles of Paul, John, Peter and James. The evidence from various quarters is indeed enough to show that the collection in general use contained all the books which we at present receive, with the possible exceptions of Jude, II and III John and Philemon. And it is more natural to suppose that failure of very early evidence for these brief booklets is due to their insignificant size rather than to their non-acceptance.

It is to be borne in mind, however, that the extent of the collection may have — and indeed is historically shown actually to have — varied in different localities. The Bible was circulated only in hand-copies, slowly and painfully made; and an incomplete copy, obtained say at Ephesus in A.D. 68, would be likely to remain for many years the Bible of the church to which it was conveyed; and might indeed become the parent of other copies, incomplete like itself, and thus the means of providing a whole district with incomplete Bibles. Thus, when we inquire after the history of the New Testament Canon we need to distinguish such questions as these: (1) When was the New Testament Canon completed? (2) When did any one church acquire a completed canon? (3) When did the completed canon — the complete Bible — obtain universal circulation and acceptance? (4) On what ground and evidence did the churches with incomplete Bibles accept the remaining books when they were made known to them?

The Canon of the New Testament was completed when the last authoritative book was given to any church by the apostles, and that was when John wrote the Apocalypse, about A.D. 98. Whether the church of Ephesus, however, had a completed Canon when it received the Apocalypse, or not, would depend on whether there was any epistle, say that of Jude, which had not yet reached it with authenticating proof of its apostolicity. There is room for historical investigation here. Certainly the whole Canon was not universally received by the churches till somewhat later. The Latin church of the second and third centuries did not quite know what to do with the Epistle to the Hebrews. The Syrian churches for some centuries may have lacked the lesser of the Catholic Epistles and Revelation. But from the time of Irenæus down, the church at large had the whole Canon as we now possess it. And though a section of the church may not yet have been satisfied of the apostolicity of a certain book or of certain books; and though afterwards doubts may have arisen in sections of the church as to the apostolicity of certain books (as e. g. of Revelation): yet in no case was it more than a respectable minority of the church which was slow in receiving, or which came afterward to doubt, the credentials of any of the books that then as now constituted the Canon of the New Testament accepted by the church at large. And in every case the principle on which a book was accepted, or doubts against it laid aside, was the historical tradition of apostolicity.

Let it, however, be clearly understood that it was not exactly apostolic *authorship* which in the estimation of the earliest churches, constituted a book a portion of the "canon." Apostolic authorship was, indeed, early confounded with canonicity. It was doubt as to the apostolic authorship of Hebrews, in the West, and of James and Jude, apparently, which underlay the slowness of the inclusion of these books in the "canon" of certain churches. But from the beginning it was not so. The principle of canonicity was not apostolic authorship, but *imposition by the apostles as "law."* Hence Tertullian's name for the "canon" is "*instrumentum*"; and he speaks of the Old and New *Instrument* as we would of the Old and New Testament. That the apostles so imposed the Old Testament on the churches which they founded — as their "Instrument," or "Law," or "Canon" — can be denied by none. And in imposing new books on the same churches, by the same apostolical authority, they did not confine themselves to books of their own composition. It is the Gospel according to Luke, a man who was not an apostle, which Paul parallels in I Tim. v. 18 with Deuteronomy as equally "Scripture" with it, in the first extant quotation of a New Testament book as Scripture. The Gospels which constituted the first division of the New Books, — of "The Gospel and the Apostles," — Justin tells us, were "written by the apostles and their companions." The authority of the apostles, as by divine appointment founders of the church, was embodied in whatever books they imposed on the church as law, not merely in those they themselves had written.

The early churches, in short, received, as we receive, into their New Testament all the books historically evinced to them as given by the apostles to the churches as their code of law; and we must not mistake the historical evidences of the slow circulation and authentication of these books over the widely-extended church, for evidence of slowness of "canonization" of books by the authority or the taste of the church itself.

BIBLICAL DOCTRINES

BY

BENJAMIN BRECKINRIDGE WARFIELD

Professor of Didactic and Polemic Theology
in the Theological Seminary of Princeton
New Jersey, 1887-1921

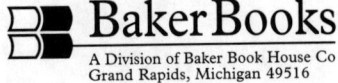

Baker Books

A Division of Baker Book House Co
Grand Rapids, Michigan 49516

I
PREDESTINATION

PREFATORY NOTE

Rev. Benjamin Breckinridge Warfield, D.D., LL.D., Professor of Didactic and Polemic Theology in the Theological Seminary of the Presbyterian Church in the United States of America, at Princeton, New Jersey, provided in his will for the collection and publication of the numerous articles on theological subjects contained in encyclopaedias, reviews and other periodicals, and appointed a committee to edit and publish these papers. In pursuance of his instructions the first volume, entitled "Revelation and Inspiration," was published in 1927 by the Oxford University Press; this, the second volume, containing Dr. Warfield's articles on Biblical Doctrines, has been prepared under the editorial direction of this committee. In it the biblical references have been retained in the forms which were used in the several articles; but, while lacking in uniformity, it is believed that the abbreviations will readily be understood.

The generous permission to publish articles contained in this volume is gratefully acknowledged as follows: The Howard-Severance Co. for the articles taken from the "International Standard Encyclopaedia," Charles Scribner's Sons for the articles taken from "A Dictionary of the Bible," edited by James Hastings, and from "A Dictionary of Christ and the Gospels," edited by James Hastings.

The clerical preparation of this volume has been done by Miss Letitia N. Gosman, to whom the thanks of the committee are hereby expressed.

Ethelbert D. Warfield
William Park Armstrong
Caspar Wistar Hodge
Committee.

I
PREDESTINATION

CONTENTS

v

PREDESTINATION [1]

I. The Terms

The words 'predestine,' 'predestinate,' 'predestination' seem not to have been domiciled in English literary use until the later period of Middle English (they are all three found in Chaucer: "Troylous and Cryseyde," 966; "Orisoune to the Holy Virgin," 69; translation of "Boëthius," b. 1, pr. 6, l. 3844; the Old English equivalent seems to have been 'fore-stihtian,' as in Ælfric's "Homilies," ii. 364, 366, in renderings of Rom. i. 4, viii. 30). 'Predestine,' 'predestination' were doubtless taken over from the French, while 'predestinate' probably owes its form directly to the Latin original of them all. The noun has never had a place in the English Bible, but the verb in the form 'predestinate' occurs in every one of its issues from Tindale to the Authorized Version. Its history in the English versions is a somewhat curious one. It goes back, of course, ultimately to the Latin *'prædestino'* (a good classical but not pre-Augustan word; while the noun *'prædestinatio'* seems to be of Patristic origin), which was adopted by the Vulgate as its regular rendering of the Greek προορίζω, and occurs, with the sole exception of Acts iv. 28 (Vulgate *decerno*), wherever the Latin translators found that verb in their text (Rom. i. 4, viii. 29, 30, I Cor. ii. 7, Eph. i. 5, 11). But the Wyclifite versions did not carry 'predestinate' over into English in a single instance, but rendered in every case by 'before ordain' (Acts iv. 28 'deemed'). It was thus left to Tindale to give the word a place in the English Bible. This he did, however, in only one passage, Eph. i. 11, doubtless under the influence of the Vulgate. His ordinary rendering of προορίζω is 'ordain before' (Rom. viii. 29, Eph. i. 5; cf. I Cor. ii. 7, where

[1] Article "Predestination," from *A Dictionary of the Bible*, ed. by James Hastings, v. 4, pp. 47–63. Pub. N. Y. 1909, by Charles Scribner's Sons.

3

the 'before' is omitted apparently only on account of the succeeding preposition into which it may be thought, therefore,
to coalesce), varied in Rom. viii. 30 to 'appoint before'; while,
reverting to the Greek, he has 'determined before' at Acts iv.
28 and, following the better reading, has 'declared' at Rom.
i. 4. The succeeding English versions follow Tindale very
closely, though the Genevan omits 'before' in Acts iv. 28 and,
doubtless in order to assimilate it to the neighbouring Eph.
i. 11, reads 'did predestinate' in Eph. i. 5. The larger use of
the word was due to the Rhemish version, which naturally
reverts to the Vulgate and reproduces its *prædestino* regularly
in 'predestinate' (Rom. i. 4, viii. 29, 30, I Cor. ii. 7, Eph. i. 5,
11; but Acts iv. 28 'decreed'). Under this influence the Authorized Version adopted 'predestinate' as its ordinary rendering
of $\pi\rho oo\rho i\zeta\omega$ (Rom. viii. 29, 30, Eph. i. 5, 11), while continuing
to follow Tindale at Acts iv. 28 'determined before,' I Cor.
ii. 7 'ordained,' as well as at Rom. i. 4 'declared,' in margin
'Greek determined.' Thus the word, tentatively introduced
into a single passage by Tindale, seemed to have intrenched
itself as the stated English representative of an important
Greek term. The Revised Version has, however, dismissed it
altogether from the English Bible and adopted in its stead the
hybrid compound 'foreordained' as its invariable representa-
tive of $\pi\rho oo\rho i\zeta\omega$ (Acts iv. 28, Rom. viii. 29, 30, I Cor. ii. 7,
Eph. i. 5, 11), — in this recurring substantially to the language
of Wyclif and the preferred rendering of Tindale. None other
than a literary interest, however, can attach to the change
thus introduced: 'foreordain' and 'predestinate' are exact
synonyms, the choice between which can be determined only
by taste. The somewhat widespread notion that the seventeenth century theology distinguished between them, rests on
a misapprehension of the evidently carefully-adjusted usage
of them in the Westminster Confession, iii. 3 ff. This is not,
however, the result of the attribution to the one word of a
'stronger' or to the other of a 'harsher' sense than that borne
by its fellow, but a simple sequence of a current employment
of 'predestination' as the precise synonym of 'election,' and

a resultant hesitation to apply a term of such precious associations to the foreordination to death. Since then the tables have been quite turned, and it is questionable whether in popular speech the word 'predestinate' does not now bear an unpleasant suggestion.

That neither word occurs in the English Old Testament is due to the genius of the Hebrew language, which does not admit of such compound terms. Their place is taken in the Old Testament, therefore, by simple words expressive of purposing, determining, ordaining, with more or less contextual indication of previousness of action. These represent a variety of Hebrew words, the most explicit of which is perhaps יָצַר (Ps. cxxxix. 16, Isa. xxii. 11, xxxvii. 26, xlvi. 11), by the side of which must be placed, however, יָעַץ (Isa. xiv. 24, 26, 27, xix. 12, xix. 17, xxiii. 9, Jer. xlix. 20, l. 45), whose substantival derivative עֵצָה (Job xxxviii. 2, xlii. 3, Jer. xxiii. 19, Prov. xix. 21, Ps. xxxiii. 11, cvii. 11, Isa. xiv. 26, xlvi. 10, 11, Ps. cvi. 13, Isa. v. 19, xix. 17, Jer. xlix. 20, l. 45, Mic. iv. 12) is doubtless the most precise Hebrew term for the Divine plan or purpose, although there occurs along with it in much the same sense the term מַחֲשָׁבָה (Jer. xviii. 11, xxix. 11, xlix. 30, l. 45, Isa. lv. 8, Jer. li. 29, Mic. iv. 12, Ps. xcii. 6, a derivative of חָשַׁב (Gen. l. 20, Mic. ii. 3, Jer. xviii. 11, xxvi. 3, xxix. 11, xxxvi. 3, xlix. 50, l. 45, Lam. ii. 8). In the Aramaic portion of Daniel (iv. 14 (17), 21 (24) the common later Hebrew designation of the Divine decree (used especially in an evil sense) גְּזֵרָה occurs: and חק is occasionally used with much the same meaning (Ps. ii. 7, Zeph. ii. 2, Ps. cv. 10 = I Chron. xvi. 17, Job xxiii. 14). Other words of similar import are זָמַם (Jer. iv. 28, li. 12, Lam. ii. 19, Zec. i. 6, viii. 14, 15) with its substantive מְזִמָּה (Job xlii. 2, Jer. xxiii. 20, xxx. 24, li. 11); חָפֵץ (Ps. cxv. 3, cxxxv. 6, Prov. xxi. 1, Isa. lv. 11, Jon. i. 14, Judg. xiii. 23, Isa. ii. 25, Isa. liii. 10) with its substantive חֵפֶץ (Isa. xlvi. 10, xliv. 28, xlviii. 14, liii. 10); חָרַץ (Job xiv. 5, Isa. x. 22, 23, xxviii. 22, Dan. ix. 26, 27, xi. 36); חָתַךְ (Dan. ix. 24); הוֹאִיל (I Sam. xii. 22, I Chron. xvii. 27, II Sam. vii. 29). To express that special act of predestination which we know as 'election,' the Hebrews commonly utilized

the word בָּחַר (of Israel, Deut. iv. 37, vii. 6, 7, x. 15, xiv. 2, Isa.
xli. 8, 9, xliii. 10, 30, xliv. 1, 2, Jer. xxxiii. 24; and of the future,
Isa. xiv. 1, lxv. 9, 15, 22; of Jehovah's servant, xlii. 1, xlix. 7;
of Jerusalem, Deut. xii. 14, 18, 26, xiv. 25, xv. 20, xvi. 7, 15, 16,
xvii. 8, 10, xviii. 6, xxxi. 11, Jos. ix. 27, I Kings viii. 44, 48, xi.
13, 32, 36, xiv. 21, II Kings xxi. 7, xxiii. 27) with its substantive
בָּחִיר (exclusively used of Jehovah's 'elect,' II Sam. xxi. 6, I
Chron. xvi. 13, Ps. lxxxix. 4, cv. 6, 43, cvi. 5, 23, Isa. xlii. 1, xliii.
20, xlv. 4, lxv. 9, 15, 22), and occasionally the word יָדַע in a pregnant sense (Gen. xviii. 19, Amos. iii. 2, Hos. xiii. 5, cf. Ps. i. 6,
xxxi. 8(7), xxxvii. 18, Isa. lviii. 3); while it is rather the execution of this previous choice in an act of separation that is
expressed by הִבְדִּיל (Lev. xx. 24, xx. 26, I Kings viii. 53).

In the Greek of the New Testament the precise term
προορίζω (Acts iv. 28, I Cor. ii. 7, Rom. viii. 29, 30, Eph. i. 5,
11) is supplemented by a number of similar compounds, such
as προτάσσω (Acts xvii. 26); προτίθημι (Eph. i. 9) with its
more frequently occurring substantive, πρόθεσις (Rom. viii.
28, ix. 11, Eph. i. 11, iii. 11, II Tim. i. 9); προετοιμάζω (Rom.
ix. 23, Eph. ii. 10) and perhaps προβλέπω in a similar sense of
providential pre-arrangement (Heb. xi. 40), with which may
be compared also προεῖδον (Acts ii. 31, Gal. iii. 8); προγιγ-
νώσκω (Rom. viii. 29, xi. 2, I Pet. i. 20) and its substantive
πρόγνωσις (I Pet. i. 2, Acts ii. 23); προχειρίζω (Acts xxii. 14,
iii. 20) and προχειροτονέω (Acts iv. 41). Something of the same
idea is, moreover, also occasionally expressed by the simple
ὁρίζω (Luke xxii. 22, Acts xvii. 26, 31, ii. 23, Heb. iv. 7, Acts
x. 42), or through the medium of terms designating the will,
wish, or good-pleasure of God, such as βουλή (Luke vii. 30,
Acts ii. 23, iv. 28, xiii. 36, xx. 27, Eph. i. 11, Heb. vi. 17, cf.
βούλημα Rom. ix. 19 and βούλομαι Heb. vi. 17, Jas. i. 18, II
Pet. iii. 9), θέλημα (e. g., Eph. i. 5, 9, 11, Heb. x. 7, cf. θέλησις
Heb. ii. 4, θέλω, e. g., Rom. ix. 18, 22), εὐδοκία (Luke ii. 14,
Eph. i. 5, 9, Phil. ii. 13, cf. εὐδοκέω Luke. xii. 32, Col. i. 19, Gal.
i. 15, I Cor. i. 21). The standing terms in the New Testament
for God's sovereign choice of His people are ἐκλέγεσθαι, in
which both the composition and voice are significant (Eph. i. 4,

Mark xiii. 20, John xv. 16 twice, 19, I Cor. i. 27 twice, Jas. ii. 5; of Israel, Acts xiii. 17; of Christ, Luke ix. 35; of the disciples, Luke vi. 13, John vi. 70, xiii. 18, Acts i. 2; of others, Acts i. 24, xv. 7), ἐκλεκτός (Matt. [xx. 16] xxii. 14, xxvi. 22, 24, 31, Mark xiii. 20, 22, 27, Luke xviii. 7, Rom. viii. 33, Col. iii. 12, II Tim. ii. 10, Tit. i. 1, I Pet. i. 1, [ii. 9], Rev. xvii. 14; of individuals, Rom. xvi. 13, II John i. 13; of Christ, Luke xxiii. 35, John xiii. 18; of angels, I Tim. v. 21), ἐκλογή (Acts ix. 15, Rom. ix. 11. xi. 5, 7, 28, I Thes. i. 4, II Pet. i. 10), — words which had been prepared for this New Testament use by their employment in the Septuagint — the two former to translate בָּחַר and בָּחִיר. In II Thes. ii. 13 αἱρέομαι is used similarly.

II. PREDESTINATION IN THE OLD TESTAMENT

No survey of the terms used to express it, however, can convey an adequate sense of the place occupied by the idea of predestination in the religious system of the Bible. It is not too much to say that it is fundamental to the whole religious consciousness of the Biblical writers, and is so involved in all their religious conceptions that to eradicate it would transform the entire scriptural representation. This is as true of the Old Testament as of the New Testament, as will become sufficiently manifest by attending briefly to the nature and implications of such formative elements in the Old Testament system as its doctrines of God, Providence, Faith, and the Kingdom of God.

Whencesoever Israel obtained it, it is quite certain that Israel entered upon its national existence with the most vivid consciousness of an almighty personal Creator and Governor of heaven and earth. Israel's own account of the clearness and the firmness of its apprehension of this mighty Author and Ruler of all that is, refers it to His own initiative: God chose to make Himself known to the fathers. At all events, throughout the whole of Old Testament literature, and for every period of history recorded in it, the fundamental conception of God remains the same, and the two most persistently emphasized elements in it are just those of might and personality: before everything else, the God of Israel is the Omnipotent Person. Possibly the keen sense of the exaltation and illimitable power of God which forms the very core of the Old Testament idea of God belongs rather to the general Semitic than to the specifically Israelitish element in its religion; certainly it was already prominent in the patriarchal God-consciousness, as is sufficiently evinced by the names of God current from the beginning of the Old Testament revelation, — *El, Eloah, Elohim, El Shaddai,* — and as is illustrated endlessly in the Biblical narrative. But it is equally clear that God was never conceived by the Old Testament saints as abstract power, but was ever thought of concretely as the all-powerful Person, and that, moreover, as clothed with all the attributes of moral personality, — pre-eminently with holiness, as the very summit of His exaltation, but along with holiness, also with all the characteristics that belong to spiritual personality as it exhibits itself familiarly in man. In a word, God is pictured in the Old Testament, and that from the beginning, purely after the pattern of human personality, — as an intelligent, feeling, willing Being, like the man who is created in His image in all in which the life of a free spirit consists. The anthropomorphisms to which this mode of conceiving God led were sometimes startling enough, and might have become grossly misleading had not the corrective lain ever at hand in the accompanying sense of the immeasurable exaltation of God, by which He was removed above all the weaknesses of humanity. The result accordingly was nothing other than a peculiarly pure form of Theism. The grosser anthropomorphisms were fully understood to be figurative, and the residuary conception was that of an infinite Spirit, not indeed expressed in abstract terms nor from the first fully brought out in all its implications, but certainly in all ages of the Old Testament development grasped in all its essential elements. (Cf. the art. GOD).

Such a God could not be thought of otherwise than as the free determiner of all that comes to pass in the world which is the product of His creative act; and the doctrine of Providence (פְּקֻדָּה) which is spread over the pages of the Old Testament

fully bears out this expectation. The almighty Maker of all
that is is represented equally as the irresistible Ruler of all
that He has made: Jehovah sits as King for ever (Ps. xxix. 10).
Even the common language of life was affected by this pervasive point of view, so that, for example, it is rare to meet
with such a phrase as 'it rains' (Amos iv. 7), and men by preference spoke of God sending rain (Ps. lxv. 9 f., Job xxxvi. 27,
xxxviii. 26). The vivid sense of dependence on God thus witnessed extended throughout every relation of life. Accident or
chance was excluded. If we read here and there of a מִקְרֶה it
is not thought of as happening apart from God's direction
(Ruth ii. 3, I Sam. vi. 9, xx. 26, Eccl. ii. 14, cf. I Kings
xxii. 34, II Chron. xviii. 33), and accordingly the lot was an
accepted means of obtaining the decision of God (Jos. vii. 16,
xiv. 2, xviii. 6, I Sam. x. 19, Jon. i. 7), and is didactically recognized as under His control (Prov. xvi. 33). All things without
exception, indeed, are disposed by Him, and His will is the
ultimate account of all that occurs. Heaven and earth and all
that is in them are the instruments through which He works
His ends. Nature, nations, and the fortunes of the individual
alike present in all their changes the transcript of His purpose.
The winds are His messengers, the flaming fire His servant:
every natural occurrence is His act: prosperity is His gift, and
if calamity falls upon man it is the Lord that has done it (Amos
iii. 5, 6, Lam. iii. 33–38, Isa. xlvii. 7, Eccl. vii. 14, Isa. liv. 16).
It is He that leads the feet of men, wit they whither or not;
He that raises up and casts down; opens and hardens the heart;
and creates the very thoughts and intents of the soul. So poignant is the sense of His activity in all that occurs, that an appearance is sometimes created as if everything that comes to
pass were so ascribed to His immediate production as to exclude the real activity of second causes. It is a grave mistake,
nevertheless, to suppose that He is conceived as an unseen
power, throwing up, in a quasi-Pantheistic sense, all changes
on the face of the world and history. The virile sense of the
free personality of God which dominates all the thought of the
Old Testament would alone have precluded such a conception.

Nor is there really any lack of recognition of 'second causes,'
as we call them. They are certainly not conceived as independent of God: they are rather the mere expression of His stated
will. But they are from the beginning fully recognized, both in
nature — with respect to which Jehovah has made covenant
(Gen. viii. 21, 22, Jer. xxxi. 35, 36, xxxiii. 20, 25, Ps. cxlviii. 6,
cf. Jer. v. 22, Ps. civ. 9, Job xxxviii. 10, 33, xiv. 5), establishing
its laws (חֻקּוֹת Job xxviii. 25, 28, Isa. xl. 12, Job xxxviii. 8–11,
Prov. viii. 29, Jer. v. 22, Ps. civ. 9, xxxiii. 7, Isa. xl. 26) — and
equally in the higher sphere of free spirits, who are ever conceived as the true authors of all their acts (hence God's proving of man, Gen. xxii. 1, Ex. xvi. 4, xx. 20, Deut. viii. 2, 16,
xiii. 3, Judg. iii. 1, 4, II Chron. xxxii. 31). There is no question
here of the substitution of Jehovah's operation for that of the
proximate causes of events. There is only the liveliest perception of the governing hand of God behind the proximate causes,
acting through them for the working out of His will in every
detail. Such a conception obviously looks upon the universe
teleologically: an almighty moral Person cannot be supposed
to govern His universe, thus in every detail, either unconsciously or capriciously. In His government there is necessarily
implied a plan; in the all-pervasiveness and perfection of His
government is inevitably implied an all-inclusive and perfect
plan: and this conception is not seldom explicitly developed.

It is abundantly clear on the face of it, of course, that this
whole mode of thought is the natural expression of the deep
religious consciousness of the Old Testament writers, though
surely it is not therefore to be set aside as 'merely' the religious
view of things, or as having no other rooting save in the imagination of religiously-minded men. In any event, however, it is
altogether natural that in the more distinctive sphere of the
religious life its informing principle of absolute dependence on
God should be found to repeat itself. This appears particularly
in the Old Testament doctrine of faith, in which there sounds
the keynote of Old Testament piety, — for the religion of the
Old Testament, so far from being, as Hegel, for example, would
affirm, the religion of fear, is rather by way of eminence the

religion of trust. Standing over against God, not merely as creatures, but as sinners, the Old Testament saints found no ground of hope save in the free initiative of the Divine love. At no period of the development of Old Testament religion was it permitted to be imagined that blessings might be wrung from the hands of an unwilling God, or gained in the strength of man's own arm. Rather it was ever inculcated that in this sphere, too, it is God alone that lifts up and makes rich, He alone that keeps the feet of His holy ones; while by strength, it is affirmed, no man shall prevail (I Sam. ii. 9). 'I am not worthy of the least of all thy mercies' is the constant refrain of the Old Testament saints (Gen. xxxii. 10); and from the very beginning, in narrative, precept and prophetic declaration alike, it is in trust in the unmerited love of Jehovah alone that the hearts of men are represented as finding peace. Self-sufficiency is the characteristic mark of the wicked, whose doom treads on his heels; while the mark of the righteous is that he lives by his faith (Hab. ii. 4). In the entire self-commitment to God, humble dependence on Him for all blessings, which is the very core of Old Testament religion, no element is more central than the profound conviction embodied in it of the free sovereignty of God, the God of the spirits of all flesh, in the distribution of His mercies. The whole training of Israel was directed to impressing upon it the great lesson enunciated to Zerubbabel, 'Not by might, nor by power, but by my Spirit, saith the Lord of hosts' (Zech. iv. 6) — that all that comes to man in the spiritual sphere, too, is the free gift of Jehovah.

Nowhere is this lesson more persistently emphasized than in the history of the establishment and development of the kingdom of God, which may well be called the cardinal theme of the Old Testament. For the kingdom of God is consistently represented, not as the product of man's efforts in seeking after God, but as the gracious creation of God Himself. Its inception and development are the crowning manifestation of the free grace of the Living God working in history in pursuance of His loving purpose to recover fallen man to Himself. To this end He preserves the race in existence after its sin, saves a seed from the destruction of the Flood, separates to Himself a family in Abraham, sifts it in Isaac and Jacob, nurses and trains it through the weakness of its infancy, and gradually moulds it to be the vehicle of His revelation of redemption, and the channel of Messianic blessings to the world. At every step it is God, and God alone, to whom is ascribed the initiative; and the most extreme care is taken to preserve the recipients of the blessings consequent on His choice from fancying that these blessings come as their due, or as reward for aught done by themselves, or to be found in themselves. They were rather in every respect emphatically not a people of their own making, but a people that God had formed that they might set forth His praise (Isa. xliii. 21). The strongest language, the most astonishing figures, were employed to emphasize the pure sovereignty of the Divine action at every stage. It was not because Israel was numerous, or strong, or righteous, that He chose it, but only because it pleased Him to make of it a people for Himself. He was as the potter, it as the clay which the potter moulds as he will; it was but as the helpless babe in its blood cast out to die, abhorred of man, which Jehovah strangely gathers to His bosom in unmerited love (Gen. xii. 1, 3, Deut. vii. 6–8, ix. 4–6, x. 15, 16, I Sam. xii. 22, Isa. xli. 8, 9, xliii. 20, xlviii. 9–11, Jer. xviii. 1 f., xxxi. 3, Hos. ii. 20, Mal. i. 2, 3). There was no element in the religious consciousness of Israel more poignantly realized, as there was no element in the instruction they had received more insisted on, than that they owed their separation from the peoples of the earth to be the Lord's inheritance, and all the blessings they had as such received from Jehovah, not to any claim upon Him which they could urge, but to His own gracious love faithfully persisted in in spite of every conceivable obstacle.

In one word, the sovereignty of the Divine will as the principle of all that comes to pass, is a primary postulate of the whole religious life, as well as of the entire world-view of the Old Testament. It is implicated in its very idea of God, its whole conception of the relation of God to the world and to the changes which take place, whether in nature or history, among the nations or in the life-fortunes of the individual; and also in its entire scheme of religion, whether national or personal. It lies at the basis of all the religious emotions, and lays the foundation of the specific type of religious character built up in Israel.

The specific teaching of the Old Testament as to predestination naturally revolves around the two foci of that idea which may be designated general and special, or, more properly, cosmical and soteriological predestination; or, in other words, around the doctrines of the Divine Decree and the Divine Election. The former, as was to be expected, is comparatively seldom adverted to — for the Old Testament is fundamentally a soteriological book, a revelation of the grace of God to sinners; and it is only at a somewhat late period that it is made the subject of speculative discussion. But as it is implied in the primordial idea of God as an Almighty Person, it is postulated from the beginning and continually finds more or less clear expression. Throughout the Old Testament, behind the processes of nature, the march of history and the fortunes of each individual life alike, there is steadily kept in view the governing hand of God working out His preconceived plan — a plan broad enough to embrace the whole universe of things, minute enough to concern itself with the smallest details, and actualizing itself with inevitable certainty in every event that comes to pass.

Naturally, there is in the narrative portions but little formal enunciation of this pervasive and all-controlling Divine teleology. But despite occasional anthropomorphisms of rather startling character (as, e.g., that which ascribes 'repentance' to God, Gen. vi. 6, Joel ii. 13, Jon. iv. 2, Jer. xviii. 8, 10, xxvi. 3, 13), or rather, let us say, just because of the strictly anthropomorphic mould in which the Old Testament conception of God is run, according to which He is ever thought of as a personal spirit, acting with purpose like other personal spirits, but with a wisdom and in a sovereignty unlike that of others because infinitely perfect, these narrative portions of the Old Testament also bear continual witness to the universal Old

Testament teleology. There is no explicit statement in the narrative of the creation, for example, that the mighty Maker of the world was in this process operating on a preconceived plan; but the teleology of creation lies latent in the orderly sequence of its parts, culminating in man for whose advent all that precedes is obviously a preparation, and is all but expressed in the Divine satisfaction at each of its stages, as a manifestation of His perfections (cf. Ps. civ. 31). Similarly, the whole narrative of the Book of Genesis is so ordered — in the succession of creation, fall, promise, and the several steps in the inauguration of the kingdom of God — as to throw into a very clear light the teleology of the whole world-history, here written from the Divine standpoint and made to centre around the developing Kingdom. In the detailed accounts of the lives of the patriarchs, in like manner, behind the external occurrences recorded there always lies a Divine ordering which provides the real plot of the story in its advance to the predetermined issue. It was not accident, for example, that brought Rebecca to the well to welcome Abraham's servant (Gen. xxiv), or that sent Joseph into Egypt (Gen. xlv. 8, l. 20; 'God meant [חשׁב] it for good'), or guided Pharaoh's daughter to the ark among the flags (Ex. ii), or that, later, directed the millstone that crushed Abimelech's head (Judg. ix. 53), or winged the arrow shot at a venture to smite the king in the joints of the harness (I Kings xxii. 34). Every historical event is rather treated as an item in the orderly carrying out of an underlying Divine purpose; and the historian is continually aware of the presence in history of Him who gives even to the lightning a charge to strike the mark (Job xxxvi. 32).

In the Psalmists and Prophets there emerges into view a more abstract statement of the government of all things according to the good-pleasure of God (Ps. xxxiii. 11, Jer. x. 12, li. 15). All that He wills He does (Ps. cxv. 3, cxxxv. 6), and all that comes to pass has pre-existed in His purpose from the indefinite past of eternity ('long ago' Isa. xxii. 11, 'of ancient times' Isa. xxxvii. 26 = II Kings xix. 25), and it is only because it so pre-existed in purpose that it now comes to pass (Isa. xiv.

24, 27, xlvi. 11, Zech. i. 6, Job xlii. 2, Jer. xxiii. 20, Jon. i. 14,
Isa. xl. 10). Every day has its ordained events (Job xiv. 5,
Ps. cxxxix. 16). The plan of God is universal in its reach, and
orders all that takes place in the interests of Israel — the Old
Testament counterpart to the New Testament declaration that
all things work together for good to those that love God. Nor
is it merely for the national good of Israel that God's plan has
made provision; He exercises a special care over every one of
His people (Job v. 15 f., Ps. xci, cxxi, lxv. 3, xxxvii, xxvii. 10,
11, cxxxix. 16, Jon. iii. 5, Isa. iv. 3, Dan. xii. 1). Isaiah especially is never weary of emphasizing the universal teleology
of the Divine operations and the surety of the realization of
His eternal purpose, despite the opposition of every foe (xiv.
24–27, xxxi. 2, xl. 13, lviii. 8–11) — whence he has justly earned
the name of the prophet of the Divine sovereignty, and has
been spoken of as the Paul, the Augustine, the Calvin of the
Old Testament.

It is, however, especially in connexion with the Old Testament doctrine of the Wisdom (חׇכְמׇה) of God, the chief depository
of which is the so-called *Hokhmah* literature, that the idea
of the all-inclusive Divine purpose (עֵצׇה and מַחְשׇׁבוֹת) in which
lies predetermined the whole course of events — including
every particular in the life of the world (Amos iii. 7) and in
the life of every individual as well (Ps. cxxxix. 14–16, Judg.
i. 2) — is speculatively wrought out. According to this developed conception, God, acting under the guidance of all His
ethical perfections, has, by virtue of His eternal wisdom, which
He 'possessed in the beginning of his way' (Prov. viii. 22),
framed 'from everlasting, from the beginning,' an all-inclusive
plan embracing all that is to come to pass; in accordance with
which plan He now governs His universe, down to the least
particular, so as to subserve His perfect and unchanging purpose. Everything that God has brought into being, therefore,
He has made for its specific end (Prov. xvi. 4, cf. iii. 19, 20,
Job xxviii. 23, xxxviii, xli, Isa. xl. 12 f., Jer. x. 12, 13); and
He so governs it that it shall attain its end, — no chance can
escape (Prov. xvi. 33), no might or subtlety defeat His direc-

tion (Prov. xxi. 30, 31, xix. 21, xvi. 9, cf. Isa. xiv. 24, 27, Jer. x. 23), which leads straight to the goal appointed by God from the beginning and kept steadily in view by Him, but often hidden from the actors themselves (Prov. xx. 24, cf. iii. 6, xvi. 1–9, xix. 21, Job xxxviii. 2, xlii. 3, Jer. x. 23), who naturally in their weakness cannot comprehend the sweep of the Divine plan or understand the place within it of the details brought to their observation — a fact in which the Old Testament sages constantly find their theodicy. No different doctrine is enunciated here from that which meets us in the Prophets and Psalmists, — only it is approached from a philosophical-religious rather than from a national-religious view-point. To prophet and sage alike the entire world — inanimate, animate, moral — is embraced in a unitary teleological world-order (Ps. xxxiii. 6, civ. 24, cxlviii. 8, Job ix. 4, xii. 13, xxxvii); and to both alike the central place in this comprehensive world-order is taken by God's redemptive purpose, of which Israel is at once the object and the instrument, while the savour of its saltness is the piety of the individual saint. The classical term for this all-inclusive Divine purpose (עֵצָה) is accordingly found in the usage alike of prophet, psalmist, and sage, — now used absolutely of the universal plan on which the whole world is ordered (Job xxxviii. 2, xlii. 3, cf. Delitzsch and Budde, in loc.), now, with the addition of 'of Jehovah,' of the all-comprehending purpose, embracing all human actions (Prov. xix. 21 and parallels; cf. Toy, in loc.), now with explicit mention of Israel as the centre around which its provisions revolve (Ps. xxxiii. 11, cvii. 11, cf. Delitzsch, in loc.; Isa. xiv. 26, xxv. 1, xlvi. 10, 11), and anon with more immediate concern with some of the details (Ps. cvi. 13, Isa. v. 19, xix. 17, Jer. xlix. 20, l. 45, Mic. iv. 12).

There seems no reason why a Platonizing colouring should be given to this simple attributing to the eternal God of an eternal plan in which is predetermined every event that comes to pass. This used to be done, e. g., by Delitzsch (see, e. g., on Job xxviii. 25–28, Isa. xxii. 11; "Biblical Psychology," I. ii.), who was wont to attribute to the Biblical writers, especially of

the "Hokhmah" and the latter portion of Isaiah, a doctrine of
the pre-existence of all things in an ideal world, conceived as
standing eternally before God at least as a pattern if not even
as a quasi-objective mould imposing their forms on all His
creatures, which smacked more of the Greek Academics than
of the Hebrew sages. As a matter of course, the Divine mind was
conceived by the Hebrew sages as eternally contemplating all
possibilities, and we should not do them injustice in supposing
them to think of its 'ideas' as the *causa exemplaris* of all that
occurs, and of the Divine intellect as the *principium dirigens*
of every Divine operation. But it is more to the point to note
that the conceptions of the Old Testament writers in regard
to the Divine decree run rather into the moulds of 'purpose'
than of 'ideas,' and that the roots of their teaching are planted
not in an abstract idea of the Godhead, but in the purity of
their concrete theism. It is because they think of God as a person, like other persons purposeful in His acts, but unlike other
persons all-wise in His planning and all-powerful in His performing, that they think of Him as predetermining all that
shall come to pass in the universe, which is in all its elements
the product of His free activity, and which must in its form and
all its history, down to the least detail, correspond with His
purpose in making it. It is easy, on the other hand, to attribute
too little 'philosophy' to the Biblical writers. The conception
of God in His relation to the world which they develop is beyond question anthropomorphic; but it is no unreflecting anthropomorphism that they give us. Apart from all question of
revelation, they were not children prattling on subjects on
which they had expended no thought; and the world-view they
commend to us certainly does not lack in profundity. The subtleties of language of a developed scholasticism were foreign to
their purposes and modes of composition, but they tell us as
clearly as, say, Spanheim himself ("Decad. Theol." vi. § 5), that
they are dealing with a purposing mind exalted so far above
ours that we can follow its movements only with halting steps,
— whose thoughts are not as our thoughts, and whose ways
are not as our ways (Isa. lv. 8; cf. xl. 13, 28, xxviii. 29, Job xi.

7 f., Ps. xcii 5, cxxxix. 14 f., cxlvii. 5, Eccl. iii. 11). Least of all in such a theme as this were they liable to forget that infinite exaltation of God which constituted the basis on which their whole conception of God rested.

Nor may they be thought to have been indifferent to the relations of the high doctrine of the Divine purpose they were teaching. There is no scholastic determination here either; but certainly they write without embarrassment as men who have attained a firm grasp upon their fundamental thought and have pursued it with clearness of thinking, no less in its relations than in itself; nor need we go astray in apprehending the outlines of their construction. It is quite plain, for example, that they felt no confusion with respect to the relation of the Divine purpose to the Divine foreknowledge. The notion that the almighty and all-wise God, by whom all things were created, and through whose irresistible control all that occurs fulfils the appointment of His primal plan, could govern Himself according to a foreknowledge of things which — perhaps apart from His original purpose of present guidance — *might haply* come to pass, would have been quite contradictory to their most fundamental conception of God as the almighty and all-sovereign Ruler of the universe, and, indeed, also of the whole Old Testament idea of the Divine foreknowledge itself, which is ever thought of in its due relation of dependence on the Divine purpose. According to the Old Testament conception, God foreknows only because He has pre-determined, and it is therefore also that He brings it to pass; His foreknowledge, in other words, is at bottom a knowledge of His own will, and His works of providence are merely the execution of His all-embracing plan. This is the truth that underlies the somewhat incongruous form of statement of late becoming rather frequent, to the effect that God's foreknowledge is conceived in the Old Testament as 'productive.' Dillmann, for example, says ("Handbuch der alttestamentlichen Theologie," p. 251): 'His foreknowledge of the future is a productive one; of an otiose foreknowledge or of a *præscientia media* . . . there is no suggestion.' In the thought of the Old Testament writers, however, it is not God's foreknowledge that produces the events of the future; it is His irresistible providential government of the world He has created for Himself: and His foreknowledge of what is yet to be rests on His pre-arranged plan of government. His 'productive foreknowledge' is but a transcript of His will, which has already determined not only the general plan of the world, but every particular that enters into the whole course of its development (Amos iii. 7, Job xxviii. 26, 27), and every detail in the life of every individual that comes into being (Jer. i. 5, Ps. cxxxix. 14–16, Job xxiii. 13, 14).

That the acts of free agents are included in this 'productive foreknowledge,' or rather in this all-inclusive plan of the life of the universe, created for the Old Testament writers apparently not the least embarrassment. This is not because they did not believe man to be free, — throughout the whole Old Testament there is never the least doubt expressed of the freedom or moral responsibility of man, — but because they did believe God to be free, whether in His works of creation or of providence, and could not believe He was hampered or limited in the attainment of His ends by the creatures of His own hands. How God governs the acts of free agents in the pursuance of His plan there is little in the Old Testament to inform us; but that He governs them in even their most intimate thoughts and feelings and impulses is its unvarying assumption: He is not only the creator of the hearts of men in the first instance, and knows them altogether, but He fashions the hearts of all in all the changing circumstances of life (Ps. xxxiii. 15); forms the spirit of man within him in all its motions (Zech. xii. 1); keeps the hearts of men in His hands, turning them whithersoever He will (Prov. xxi. 1); so that it is even said that man knows what is in his own mind only as the Lord reveals it to him (Amos iv. 13). The discussion of any antinomy that may be thought to arise from such a joint assertion of the absolute rule of God in the sphere of the spirit and the freedom of the creaturely will, falls obviously under the topic of Providential Government rather than under that of the Decree: it requires to be adverted to here only that we may clearly note the fact that the Old Testament teachers, as they did not hesitate to affirm the absolute sway of God over the thoughts and intents of the human heart, could feel no embarrassment in the inclusion of the acts of free agents within the all-embracing plan of God, the outworking of which His providential government supplies.

Nor does the moral quality of these acts present any apparent difficulty to the Old Testament construction. We are never permitted to imagine, to be sure, that God is the author of sin, either in the world at large or in any individual soul — that He is in any way implicated in the sinfulness of the acts performed by the perverse misuse of creaturely freedom. In all God's working He shows Himself pre-eminently the Holy One, and prosecutes His holy will, His righteous way, His all-wise plan: the blame for all sinful deeds rests exclusively on the creaturely actors (Ex. ix. 27, x. 16), who recognize their own guilt (II Sam. xxiv. 10, 17) and receive its punishment (Eccl. xi. 9 compared with xi. 5). But neither is God's relation to the sinful acts of His creatures ever represented as purely passive: the details of the doctrine of *concursus* were left, no doubt, to later ages speculatively to work out, but its assumption underlies the entire Old Testament representation of the Divine modes of working. That anything — good or evil — occurs in God's universe finds its account, according to the Old Testament conception, in His positive ordering and active concurrence; while the moral quality of the deed, considered in itself, is rooted in the moral character of the subordinate agent, acting in the circumstances and under the motives operative in each instance. It is certainly going beyond the Old Testament warrant to speak of the 'all-productivity of God,' as if He were the only efficient cause in nature and the sphere of the free spirit alike; it is the very delirium of misconception to say that in the Old Testament God and Satan are insufficiently discriminated, and deeds appropriate to the latter are assigned to the former. Nevertheless, it remains true that even the evil acts of the creature are so far carried back to God that they too are affirmed to be included in His all-embracing decree, and to be brought about, bounded and utilized in His providential government. It is He that hardens the heart of the sinner that persists in his sin (Ex. iv. 21, vii. 3, x. 1, 27, xiv. 4, 8, Deut. ii. 30, Jos. xi. 20, Isa. lxiii. 17); it is from Him that the evil spirits proceed that trouble sinners (I Sam. xvi. 14, Judg. ix. 23, I Kings xxii, Job i.); it is of Him that the evil impulses that rise in sinners' hearts take this or that specific form (II Sam. xxiv. 1). The philosophy that lies behind such representations, however, is not the pantheism which looks upon God as the immediate cause of all that comes to pass; much less the pandaimonism which admits no distinction between good and evil; there is not even involved a conception of God entangled in an undeveloped ethical discrimination. It is the philosophy that is expressed in Isa. xlv. 5 f., 'I am the Lord, and there is none else; beside me there is no God. . . . I am the Lord, and there is none else. I form the light and create darkness; I make peace and create evil; I am the Lord that doeth all these things'; it is the philosophy that is expressed in Prov. xvi. 4, 'The Lord hath made everything for its own end, yea, even the wicked for the day of evil.' Because, over against all dualistic conceptions, there is but one God, and He is indeed God; and because, over against all cosmotheistic conceptions, this God is a Person who acts purposefully; there is nothing that is, and nothing that comes to pass, that He has not first decreed and then brought to pass by His creation or providence. Thus all things find their unity in His eternal plan; and not their unity merely, but their justification as well; even the evil, though retaining its quality as evil and hateful to the holy God, and certain to be dealt with as hateful, yet does not occur apart from His provision or against His will, but appears in the world which He has made only as the instrument by means of which He works the higher good.

This sublime philosophy of the decree is immanent in every page of the Old Testament. Its metaphysics never come to explicit discussion, to be sure; but its elements are in a practical way postulated consistently throughout. The ultimate end in view in the Divine plan is ever represented as found in God alone: all that He has made He has made for Himself, to set forth His praise; the heavens themselves with all their splendid furniture exist but to illustrate His glory; the earth and all that is in it, and all that happens in it, to declare His majesty; the whole course of history is but the theatre of His self-manifestation, and the events of every individual life indicate His nature and perfections. Men may be unable to understand the place which the incidents, as they unroll themselves before their eyes, take in the developing plot of the great drama: they may, nay, must, therefore stand astonished and confounded before this or that which befalls them or befalls the world. Hence arise to them problems — the problem of the petty, the problem of the inexplicable, the problem of suffering, the problem of sin (e. g., Eccl. xi. 5). But, in the infinite wisdom of the Lord of all the earth, each event falls with exact precision into its proper place in the unfolding of His eternal plan; nothing, however small, however strange, occurs without His ordering, or without its peculiar fitness for its place in the working out of His purpose; and the end of all shall be the manifestation of His glory, and the accumulation of His praise. This is the Old Testament philosophy of the universe — a world-view which attains concrete unity in an absolute Divine teleology, in the compactness of an eternal decree, or purpose, or plan, of which all that comes to pass is the development in time.

Special or Soteriological Predestination finds a natural place in the Old Testament system as but a particular instance of the more general fact, and may be looked upon as only the general Old Testament doctrine of predestination applied to the specific case of the salvation of sinners. But as the Old Testament is a distinctively religious book, or, more precisely, a distinctively soteriological book, that is to say, a record of the gracious dealings and purposes of God with sinners, soteriological predestination naturally takes a more prominent place in it than the general doctrine itself, of which it is a particular application. Indeed, God's saving work is thrown out into such prominence, the Old Testament is so specially a record of the establishment of the kingdom of God in the world, that we easily get the impression in reading it that the core of God's general decree is His decree of salvation, and that His whole plan for the government of the universe is subordinated to His purpose to recover sinful man to Himself. Of course there is some slight illusion of perspective here, the materials for correcting which the Old Testament itself provides, not only in more or less specific declarations of the relative unimportance of what befalls man, whether the individual, or Israel, or the race at large, in comparison with the attainment of the Divine end; and of the wonder of the Divine grace concerning itself with the fortunes of man at all (Job xxii. 3 f., xxxv. 6 f., xxxviii, Ps. viii. 4): but also in the general disposition of the entire record, which places the complete history of sinful man, including alike his fall into sin and all the provisions for his recovery, within the larger history of the creative work of God, as but one incident in the greater whole, governed, of course, like all its other parts, by its general teleology. Relatively to the Old Testament record, nevertheless, as indeed to the Biblical record as a whole, which is concerned directly only with God's dealings with humanity, and that, especially, a sinful humanity (Gen. iii. 9, vi. 5, viii. 21, Lev. xviii. 24, Deut. ix. 4, I Kings viii. 46, Ps. xiv. 1, li. 5, cxxx. 3, cxliii. 2, Prov. xx. 9, Eccl. vii. 20, Isa. i. 4, Hos. iv. 1, Job xv. 14, xxv. 4, xiv. 4), soteriological predestination is the prime matter of importance; and the doctrine of election is accordingly thrown into relief, and the general doctrine of the decree more incidentally adverted to. It would be impossible, however, that the doctrine of election taught in the Old Testament should follow other lines than those laid down in the general doctrine of the decree, — or, in other words, that God should be conceived as working in the sphere of grace in a manner that would be out of accord with the fundamental conception entertained by these writers of the nature of God and His relations to the universe.

Accordingly, there is nothing concerning the Divine election more sharply or more steadily emphasized than its graciousness, in the highest sense of that word, or, in other terms, its absolute sovereignty. This is plainly enough exhibited even in the course of the patriarchal history, and that from the beginning. In tho very hour of man's first sin, God intervenes *sua sponte* with a gratuitous promise of deliverance; and at every stage afterwards the sovereign initiation of the grace of God — the Lord of the whole earth (Ex. xix. 5) — is strongly marked, as God's universal counsel of salvation is more and more unfolded through the separation and training of a people for Himself, in whom the whole world should be blessed (Gen. xii. 3, xviii. 18, xxii. 18, xxvi. 4, xxviii. 14): for from the beginning it is plainly indicated that the whole history of the world is ordered with reference to the establishment of the kingdom of God (Deut. xxxii. 8, where the reference seems to be to Gen. xi). Already in the opposing lines of Seth and Cain (Gen. iv. 25, 26) a discrimination is made; Noah is selected as the head of a new race, and among his sons the preference is given to Shem (Gen. ix. 25), from whose line Abraham is taken. Every fancy that Abraham owed his calling to his own desert is carefully excluded, — he was 'known' of God only that in him God might establish His kingdom (Gen. xviii. 19); and the very acme of sovereignty is exhibited (as St. Paul points out) in the subsequent choice of Isaac and Jacob, and exclusion of Ishmael and Esau; while the whole Divine dealing with the patriarchs — their separation from their kindred, removal into a strange land, and the like — is evidently understood as intended to cast them back on the grace of God alone. Similarly, the covenant made with Israel (Ex. xix–xxiv) is constantly assigned to the sole initiative of Divine grace, and the fact of election is therefore appropriately set at the head of the Decalogue (Ex. xx. 2; cf. xxxiv. 6, 7); and Israel is repeatedly warned that there was nothing in it which moved or could move God to favour it (e. g., Deut. iv. 37, vii. 7, viii. 17, ix. 4, x. 11, Ezk. xvi. 1 f., Amos ix. 7). It has already been pointed out by what energetic figures this fundamental lesson was impressed on the Israelitish consciousness, and it is only true to say that no means are left unused to drive home the fact that God's gracious election of Israel is an absolutely sovereign one, founded solely in His unmerited love, and looking to nothing

ultimately but the gratification of His own holy and loving
impulses, and the manifestation of His grace through the formation of a heritage for Himself out of the mass of sinful men,
by means of whom His saving mercy should advance to the
whole world (Isa. xl, xlii, lx, Mic. iv. 1, Amos iv. 13, v. 8,
Jer. xxxi. 37, Ezk. xvii. 22, xxxvi. 21, Joel ii. 28). The simple
terms that are employed to express this Divine selection —
'know' (יָדַע), 'choose' (בָּחַר) — are either used in a pregnant
sense, or acquire a pregnant sense by their use in this connexion.
The deeper meaning of the former term is apparently not
specifically Hebrew, but more widely Semitic (it occurs also
in Assyrian; see the *Dictionaries* of Delitzsch and Muss-
Arnolt *sub. voc.*, and especially Haupt in "Beiträge zur Assyrio-
logie," i. 14, 15), and it can create no surprise, therefore, when
it meets us in such passages as Gen. xviii. 19 (cf. Ps. xxxvii. 18
and also i. 6, xxxi. 8; cf. Baethgen and Delitzsch *in loc.*), Hos.
xiii. 5 (cf. Wünsche *in loc.*) in something of the sense expressed
by the scholastic phrase, *nosse cum affectu et effectu;* while in
the great declaration of Amos iii. 2 (cf. Baur and Gunning *in
loc.*), 'You only have I known away from all the peoples of the
earth,' what is thrown prominently forward is clearly the elective love which has singled Israel out for special care. More
commonly, however, it is בָּחַר that is employed to express
God's sovereign election of Israel: the classical passage is, of
course, Deut. vii. 6, 7 (see Driver *in loc.*, as also, of the love
underlying the 'choice,' at iv. 37, vii. 8), where it is carefully
explained that it is in contrast with the treatment accorded to
all the other peoples of the earth that Israel has been honoured
with the Divine choice, and that the choice rests solely on the
unmerited love of God, and finds no foundation in Israel itself.
These declarations are elsewhere constantly enforced (e. g., iv.
37, x. 15, xiv. 2), with the effect of throwing the strongest
possible emphasis on the complete sovereignty of God's choice
of His people, who owe their 'separation' unto Jehovah (Lev.
xx. 24, 26, I Kings viii. 33) wholly to the wonderful love of
God, in which He has from the beginning taken knowledge of
and chosen them.

It is useless to seek to escape the profound meaning of this fundamental Old Testament teaching by recalling the undeveloped state of the doctrine of a future life in Israel, and the national scope of its election, — as if the sovereign choice which is so insisted on could thus be confined to the choice of a people as a whole to certain purely earthly blessings, without any reference whatever to the eternal destiny of the individuals concerned. We are here treading very close to the abyss of confusing progress in the delivery of doctrine with the reality of God's saving activities. The cardinal question, after all, does not concern the extent of the knowledge possessed by the Old Testament saints of the nature of the blessedness that belongs to the people of God; nor yet the relation borne by the election within the election, by the real Israel forming the heart of the Israel after the flesh, to the external Israel: it concerns the existence of a real kingdom of God in the Old Testament dispensation, and the methods by which God introduced man into it. It is true enough that the theocracy was an earthly kingdom, and that a prominent place was given to the promises of the life that now is in the blessings assured to Israel; and it is in this engrossment with earthly happiness and the close connexion of the friendship of God with the enjoyment of worldly goods that the undeveloped state of the Old Testament doctrine of salvation is especially apparent. But it should not be forgotten that the promise of earthly gain to the people of God is not entirely alien to the New Testament idea of salvation (Matt. vi. 37, I Tim. iv. 8), and that it is in no sense true that in the Old Testament teaching, in any of its stages, the blessings of the kingdom were summed up in worldly happiness. The covenant blessing is rather declared to be *life*, inclusive of all that that comprehensive word is fitted to convey (Deut. xxx. 15; cf. iv. 1, viii. 1, Prov. xii. 28, viii. 35); and it found its best expression in the high conception of 'the favour of God' (Lev. xxvi. 11, Ps. iv. 8, xvi. 2, 5, lxiii. 4); while it concerned itself with earthly prosperity only as and so far as that is a pledge of the Divine favour. It is no false testimony to the Old Testament saints when they are described as looking for the city that has the foundations and as enduring as seeing the Invisible One: if their hearts were not absorbed in the contemplation of the eternal future, they were absorbed in the contemplation of the Eternal Lord, which certainly is something even better; and the representation that they found their supreme blessedness in outward things runs so grossly athwart their own testimony that it fairly deserves Calvin's terrible invective, that thus the Israelitish people are thought of not otherwise than as a 'sort of herd of swine which (so, forsooth, it is pretended) the Lord was fattening in the pen of this world' ("Inst." II. x. 1). And, on the other hand, though Israel as a nation constituted the chosen people of God (I Chron. xvi. 13, Ps. lxxxix. 4, cv. 6, 13, cvi. 5), yet we must not lose from sight the fact that the nation as such was rather the symbolical than the real people of God, and was His people at all, indeed, only so far as it was, ideally or actually, identified with the inner body of the really 'chosen' — that people whom Jehovah formed for Himself that they might set forth His praise (Isa. xliii. 20, lxv. 9, 15, 22), and who constituted the real people of His choice, the 'remnant of Jacob' (Isa. vi. 13, Amos ix. 8–10, Mal. iii. 10; cf. I Kings xix. 18, Isa. viii. 18). Nor are we left in doubt as to how this inner core of actual people of God was constituted; we see the process in the call of Abraham, and the discrimination between Isaac and Ishmael, between Jacob and Esau, and it is no false testimony that it was ever a 'remnant according to the election of grace' that God preserved to Himself as the salt of His people Israel. In every aspect of it alike, it is the sovereignty of the Divine choice that is emphasized, — whether the reference be to the segregation of Israel as a nation to enjoy the earthly favour of God as a symbol of the true entrance into rest, or the choice of a remnant out of Israel to enter into that real communion with Him which was the joy of His saints, — of Enoch who walked with God (Gen. v. 22), of Abraham who found in Him his exceeding great reward (Gen. xv. 1), or of David who saw no good beyond Him, and sought in Him alone his inheritance and his cup. Later times may have enjoyed fuller knowledge of what the grace of God had in store for His saints — whether in this world or that which is to come; later times may have possessed a clearer apprehension of the distinction between the children of the flesh and the children of the promise: but no later teaching has a stronger emphasis for the central fact that it is of the free grace of God alone that any enter in any degree into the participation of His favour. The kingdom of God, according to the Old Testament, in every circle of its meaning, is above and before all else a stone cut out of the mountain 'without hands' (Dan. ii. 34, 44, 45).

III. Predestination among the Jews

The profound religious conception of the relation of God to the works of His hands that pervades the whole Old Testament was too deeply engraved on the Jewish consciousness to be easily erased, even after growing legalism had measurably corroded the religion of the people. As, however, the idea of law more and more absorbed the whole sphere of religious thought, and piety came to be conceived more and more as right conduct before God instead of living communion with God, men grew naturally to think of God more and more as abstract unapproachableness, and to think of themselves more and more as their own saviours. The post-canonical Jewish writings, while retaining fervent expressions of dependence on God as the Lord of all, by whose wise counsel all things exist and work out their ends, and over against whom the whole world, with every creature in it, is but the instrument of His will of good to Israel, nevertheless threw an entirely new emphasis on the autocracy of the human will. This emphasis increases until in the later Judaism the extremity of heathen self-sufficiency is reproduced, and the whole sphere of the moral life is expressly reserved from Divine determination. Meanwhile also heathen terminology was intruding into Jewish speech. The Platonic πρόνοια, προνοεῖν, for example, coming in doubtless through the medium of the Stoa, is found not only in Philo (περὶ προνοίας), but also in the Apocryphal books (Wis. vi. 7, xiv. 3, xvii. 2, III Mac. iv. 21, v. 30, IV Mac. ix. 24, xiii.

18, xvii. 22; cf. also Dan. vi. 18, Septuagint 19); the perhaps even
more precise as well as earlier ἐφορᾶν occurs in Josephus (*BJ* ii.
viii. 14), and indeed also in the Septuagint, though here doubtless in a weakened sense (II Mac. xii. 22, xv. 2, cf. III Mac.
ii. 21, as also Job xxxiv. 24, xxviii. 24, xxii. 12, cf. xxi. 16; also
Zech. ix. 1); while even the fatalistic term εἱμαρμένη is employed by Josephus (*BJ* ii. viii. 14; *Ant.* xiii. v. 9, xviii. i. 3)
to describe Jewish views of predestination. With the terms there
came in, doubtless, more or less of the conceptions connoted
by them.

Whatever may have been the influences under which it was
wrought, however, the tendency of post-canonical Judaism was
towards setting aside the Biblical doctrine of predestination to
a greater or less extent, or in a larger or smaller sphere, in order
to make room for the autocracy of the human will, the רשות, as
it was significantly called by the Rabbis (*Bereshith Rabba*, c.
22). This disintegrating process is little apparent perhaps in the
Book of Wisdom, in which the sense of the almightiness of God
comes to very strong expression (xi. 22, xii. 8–12). Or even in
Philo, whose predestinarianism (*de Legg. Allegor.* i. 15, iii. 24,
27, 28) closely follows, while his assertion of human freedom
(*Quod Deus sit immut.* 10) does not pass beyond that of the
Bible: man is separated from the animals and assimilated to
God by the gift of 'the power of voluntary motion' and suitable emancipation from necessity, and is accordingly properly
praised or blamed for his intentional acts; but it is of the grace
of God only that anything exists, and the creature is not giver
but receiver in all things; especially does it belong to God alone
to plant and build up virtues, and it is impious for the mind,
therefore, to say 'I plant'; the call of Abraham, Isaac, Jacob
was of pure grace without any merit, and God exercises the
right to 'dispose excellently,' prior to all actual deeds. But
the process is already apparent in so early a book as Sirach.
The book at large is indeed distinctly predestinarian, and such
passages as xvi. 26–30, xxiii. 20, xxxiii. 11–13, xxxix. 20, 21
echo the teachings of the canonical books on this subject. But,
while this is its general character, another element is also pres-

ent: an assertion of human autocracy, for example, which is without parallel in the canonical books, is introduced at xv. 11–20, which culminates in the precise declaration that 'man has been committed to the hand of his own counsel' to choose for himself life or death. The same phenomena meet us in the Pharisaic Psalms of Solomon (B.C. 70–40). Here there is a general recognition of God as the great and mighty King (ii. 34, 36) who has appointed the course of nature (xviii. 12) and directs the development of history (ii. 34, ix. 4, xvii. 4), ruling over the whole and determining the lot of each (v. 6, 18), on whom alone, therefore, can the hope of Israel be stayed (vii. 3, xvii. 3), and to whom alone can the individual look for good. But, alongside of this expression of general dependence on God, there occurs the strongest assertion of the moral autocracy of the human will: 'O God, our works are in our own souls' election and control, to do righteousness or iniquity in the works of our hand' (ix. 7).

It is quite credible, therefore, when Josephus tells us that the Jewish parties of his day were divided, as on other matters, so on the question of the Divine predestination — the Essenes affirming that fate (εἱμαρμένῃ, Josephus' affected Græcizing expression for predestination) is the mistress of all, and nothing occurs to men which is not in accordance with its destination; the Sadducees taking away 'fate' altogether, and considering that there is no such thing, and that human affairs are not directed according to it, but all actions are in our own power, so that we are ourselves the causes of what is good, and receive what is evil from our own folly; while the Pharisees, seeking a middle ground, said that some actions, but not all, are the work of 'fate,' and some are in our own power as to whether they are done or not (*Ant.* xiii. v. 9). The distribution of the several views among the parties follows the general lines of what might have been anticipated — the Essenic system being pre-eminently supranaturalistic, and the Sadducean rationalistic, while there was retained among the Pharisees a deep leaven of religious earnestness tempered, but not altogether destroyed (except in the extremest circles), by their ingrained legalism. The middle ground, moreover, which Josephus ascribes to the Pharisees in their attempt to distribute the control of human action between 'fate' and 'free will,' reflects not badly the state of opinion presupposed in the documents we have already quoted. In his remarks elsewhere (*BJ* ii. viii. 14; *Ant.* xviii. i. 3) he appears to ascribe to the Pharisees some kind of a doctrine of *concursus* also — a κρᾶσις between 'fate' and the human will by which both co-operate in the effect: but his language is obscure, and is coloured doubtless by reminiscences of Stoic teaching, with which philosophical sect he compares the Pharisees as he compares the Essenes with the Epicureans.

But whatever may have been the traditional belief of the Pharisees, in proportion as the legalistic spirit which constituted the nerve of the movement became prominent, the sense of dependence on God, which is the vital breath of the doctrine of predestination, gave way. The Jews possessed the Old Testament Scriptures in which the Divine lordship is a cardinal doctrine, and the trials of persecution cast them continually back upon God; they could not, therefore, wholly forget the Biblical doctrine of the Divine decree, and throughout their whole history we meet with its echoes on their lips. The laws of nature, the course of history, the varying fortunes of individuals, are ever attributed to the Divine predestination. Nevertheless, it was ever more and more sharply disallowed that man's moral actions fell under the same predetermination. Sometimes it was said that while the decrees of God were sure, they applied only so long as man remained in the condition in which he was contemplated when they were formed; he could escape all predetermined evil by a change in his moral character. Hence such sayings as, 'The righteous destroy what God decrees' (*Tanchuma* on דברים); 'Repentance, prayer, and charity ward off every evil decree' (*Rosh-hashana*). In any event, the entire domain of the moral life was more and more withdrawn from the intrusion of the decree; and Cicero's famous declaration, which Harnack says might be inscribed as a motto over Pelagianism, might with equal right be accepted as the working hypothesis

of the later Judaism: 'For gold, land, and all the blessings of
life we have to return thanks to God; but no one ever returned
thanks to God for virtue' (*de Nat. Deorum*, iii. 36). We read
that the Holy One determines prior to birth all that every one
is to be — whether male or female, weak or strong, poor or
rich, wise or silly; but one thing He does not determine —
whether he is to be righteous or unrighteous; according to
Deut. xxx. 15 this is committed to one's own hands. Accordingly, it is said that 'neither evil nor good comes from God;
both are the results of our deeds' (*Midrash rab*, on ראה, and
Jalkut there); and again, 'All is in the hands of God except
the fear of God' (*Megilla* 25a); so that it is even somewhat
cynically said, 'Man is led in the way in which he wishes to go'
(*Maccoth* 10); 'If you teach him right, his God will make him
know' (Isa. xxviii. 26; Jerusalem *Challah* i. 1). Thus the deep
sense of dependence on God for all goods, and especially the
goods of the soul, which forms the very core of the religious
consciousness of the writers of the Old Testament, gradually
vanished from the later Judaism, and was superseded by a
self-assertiveness which hung all good on the self-determination
of the human spirit, on which the purposes of God waited, or
to which they were subservient.

IV. PREDESTINATION IN THE NEW TESTAMENT

The New Testament teaching starts from the plane of the
Old Testament revelation, and in its doctrines of God, Providence, Faith, and the Kingdom of God repeats or develops in
a right line the fundamental deliverances of the Old Testament,
while in its doctrines of the Decree and of Election only such
advance in statement is made as the progressive execution of
the plan of salvation required.

In the teaching of our Lord, as recorded in the Synoptic
Gospels, for example, though there is certainly a new emphasis
thrown on the Fatherhood of God, this is by no means at the
expense of His infinite majesty and might, but provides only
a more profound revelation of the character of 'the great King'

(Matt. v. 35), the 'Lord of heaven and earth' (Matt. xi. 25, Luke x. 21), according to whose good pleasure all that is comes to pass. He is spoken of, therefore, specifically as the 'heavenly Father' (Matt. v. 48, vi. 14, 26, 32, xv. 13, xviii. 35, xxiii. 9, cf. v. 16, 45, vi. 1, 9, vii. 11, 21, x. 32, 33, xii. 50, xvi. 17, xviii. 14, 19, Mark xi. 25, 26, Luke xi. 13) whose throne is in the heavens (Matt. v. 34, xxiii. 22), while the earth is but the footstool under His feet. There is no limitation admitted to the reach of His power, whether on the score of difficulty in the task, or insignificance in the object: the category of the impossible has no existence to Him 'with whom all things are possible' (Matt. xix. 26, Mark x. 27, Luke xviii. 27, Matt. xxii. 29, Mark xii. 24, xiv. 36), and the minutest occurrences are as directly controlled by Him as the greatest (Matt. x. 29, 30, Luke xii. 7). It is from Him that the sunshine and rain come (Matt. v. 45); it is He that clothes with beauty the flowers of the field (Matt. vi. 28), and who feeds the birds of the air (Matt. vi. 26); not a sparrow falls to the ground without Him, and the very hairs of our heads are numbered, and not one of them is forgotten by God (Matt. x. 29, Luke xii. 6). There is, of course, no denial, nor neglect, of the mechanism of nature implied here; there is only clear perception of the providence of God guiding nature in all its operations, and not nature only, but the life of the free spirit as well (Matt. vi. 6, viii. 13, xxiv. 22, vii. 7, Mark xi. 23). Much less, however, is the care of God thought of as mechanical and purposeless. It was not simply of sparrows that out Lord was thinking when He adverted to the care of the heavenly Father for them, as it was not simply for oxen that God was caring when He forbade them to be muzzled as they trod out the corn (I Cor. ix. 9); it was that they who are of more value than sparrows might learn with what confidence they might depend on the Father's hand. Thus a hierarchy of providence is uncovered for us, circle rising above circle, — first the wide order of nature, next the moral order of the world, lastly the order of salvation or of the kingdom of God, — a preformation of the dogmatic, *schema* of *providentia generalis*, *specialis*, and *specialissima*. All these work together for the one end of advancing the whole world-fabric to its goal; for the care of the heavenly Father over the works of His hand is not merely to prevent the world that He has made from falling into pieces, and not merely to preserve His servants from oppression by the evil of this world, but to lead the whole world and all that is in it onwards to the end which He has appointed for it, — to that παλιγγενεσία of heaven and earth to which, under His guiding hand, the whole creation tends (Matt. xix. 28, Luke xx. 34).

In this divinely-led movement of 'this world' towards 'the world that is to come,' in which every element of the world's life has part, the central place is naturally taken by the spiritual preparation, or, in other words, by the development of the Kingdom of God which reaches its consummation in the 're-generation.' This Kingdom, our Lord explains, is the heritage of those blessed ones for whom it has been prepared from the foundations of the world (Matt. xxv. 34, cf. xx. 23). It is built up on earth through a 'call' (Matt. ix. 13, Mark ii. 17, Luke v. 32), which, however, as mere invitation is inoperative (Matt. xxii. 2–14, Luke xiv. 16–23), and is made effective only by the exertion of a certain 'constraint' on God's part (Luke xiv. 23), — so that a distinction emerges between the merely 'called' and the really 'chosen' (Matt. xxii. 14). The author of this 'choice' is God (Mark xiii. 20), who has chosen His elect (Luke xviii. 7, Matt. xxiv. 22, 24, 31, Mark xiii. 20–22) before the world, in accordance with His own pleasure, distributing as He will of what is His own (Matt. x. 14, 15); so that the effect of the call is already predetermined (Matt. xiii), all providence is ordered for the benefit of the elect (Matt. xxiv. 22), and they are guarded from falling away (Matt. xxiv. 24), and, at the last day, are separated to their inheritance prepared for them from all eternity (Matt. xxv. 34). That, in all this process, the initiative is at every point taken by God, and no question can be entertained of precedent merit on the part of the recipients of the blessings, results not less from the whole underlying conception of God in His relation to the course of providence than from the details of the teaching itself. Every means is utilized, however, to enhance the sense of the free sovereignty of God in the bestowment of His Kingdom; it is 'the lost' whom Jesus comes to seek (Luke xix. 10), and 'sinners' whom He came to call (Mark ii. 17); His truth is revealed only to 'babes' (Matt. xi. 25, Luke x. 21), and He gives His teaching a special form just that it may be veiled from them to whom it is not directed (Mark iv. 11), distributing His benefits, independently of merit (Matt. xx. 1–16), to those who had been chosen by God therefor (Mark xiii. 20).

In the discourses recorded by St. John the same essential spirit rules. Although, in accordance with the deeper theological apprehension of their reporter, the more metaphysical elements of Jesus' doctrine of God come here to fuller expression, it is nevertheless fundamentally the same doctrine of God that is displayed. Despite the even stronger emphasis thrown here on His Fatherhood, there is not the slightest obscuration of His infinite exaltation: Jesus lifts His eyes up when He would seek Him (xi. 41, xvii. 1); it is in heaven that His house is to be found (xiv. 2); and thence proceeds all that comes from Him (i. 51, iii. 13, vi. 31, 32, 33, 38, 41, 49, 50, 58); so that God and heaven come to be almost equivalent terms. Nor is there any obscuration of His ceaseless activity in governing the world (v. 17), although the stress is naturally thrown, in accordance with the whole character of this Gospel, on the moral and spiritual side of this government. But the very essence of the message of the Johannine Jesus is that the will ($\theta\epsilon\lambda\eta\mu\alpha$) of the Father (iv. 34, v. 30, vi. 38, 39, 40, vii. 17, ix. 31, cf. iii. 8, v. 21, xvii. 24, xxi. 22, 23) is the principle of all things; and more especially, of course, of the introduction of eternal life into this world of darkness and death. The conception of the world as lying in the evil one and therefore judged already (iii. 18), so that upon those who are not removed from the evil of the world the wrath of God is not so much to be poured out as simply abides (iii. 36, cf. I John iii. 14), is fundamental to this whole presentation. It is therefore, on the one hand, that Jesus represents Himself as having come not to condemn the world, but to save the world (iii. 17, viii. 12, ix. 5, xii. 47, cf. iv. 42), and all that He does as having for its end the introduction of life

into the world (vi. 33, 51); the already condemned world
needed no further condemnation, it needed saving. And it is
for the same reason, on the other hand, that He represents the
wicked world as incapable of coming to Him that it might have
life (viii. 43, 21, xiv. 17, x. 33), and as requiring first of all a
'drawing' from the Father to enable it to come (vi. 44, 65);
so that only those hear or believe on Him who are 'of God'
(viii. 47, cf. xv. 19, xvii. 14), who are 'of his sheep' (x. 26).

There is undoubtedly a strong emphasis thrown on the
universality of Christ's mission of salvation; He has been sent
into the world not merely to save some out of the world, but
to save the world itself (iii. 16, vi. 51, xii. 47, xvii. 21, cf. i. 29,
I John iv. 14, ii. 2). But this universality of destination and
effect by which it is 'the world' that is saved, does not imply
the salvation of each and every individual in the world, even
in the earlier stages of the developing salvation. On the contrary, the saving work is a process (xvii. 20); and, meanwhile,
the coming of the Son into the world introduces a crisis, a sifting by which those who, because they are 'of God,' 'of his
sheep,' are in the world, but not of it (xv. 19, xvii. 14), are
separated from those who are of the world, that is, of their
father the devil (viii. 44), who is the Prince of this world (xii.
31, xiv. 30, xvi. 11). Obviously, the difference between men
that is thus manifested is not thought of as inhering, after a
dualistic or semi-Gnostic fashion, in their very natures as such,
or as instituted by their own self-framed or accidentally received dispositions, much less by their own conduct in the
world, which is rather the result of it, — but, as already pointed
out, as the effect of an act of God. All goes back to the will of
God, to accomplish which, the Son, as the Sent One, has come;
and therefore also to the consentient will of the Son, who gives
life, accordingly, to whom He will (v. 21). As no one can come
to Him out of the evil world, except it be given him of the
Father (vi. 65, cf. vi. 44), so all that the Father gives Him
(vi. 37, 39) and only such (vi. 65), come to Him, being drawn
thereunto by the Father (vi. 44). Thus the Son has 'his own in
the world' (xiii. 1), His 'chosen ones' (xiii. 18, xv. 16, 19),

whom by His choice He has taken out of the world (xv. 19, xvii. 6, 14, 16); and for these only is His high-priestly intercession offered (xvii. 9), as to them only is eternal life communicated (x. 28, xvii. 2, also iii. 15, 36, v. 24, vi. 40, 54, viii. 12). Thus, what the dogmatists call *gratia præveniens* is very strikingly taught; and especial point is given to this teaching in the great declarations as to the new birth recorded in John iii, from which we learn that the recreating Spirit comes, like the wind, without observation, and as He lists (iii. 8), the mode of action by which the Father 'draws' men being thus uncovered for us. Of course this drawing is not to be thought of as proceeding in a manner out of accord with man's nature as a psychic being; it naturally comes to its manifestation in an act of voluntary choice on man's own part, and in this sense it is 'psychological' and not 'physical'; accordingly, though it be God that 'draws,' it is man that 'comes' (iii. 21, vi. 35, 41, xiv. 6). There is no occasion for stumbling therefore in the ascription of 'will' and 'responsibility' to man, or for puzzling over the designation of 'faith,' in which the 'coming' takes effect, as a 'work' of man's (vi. 29). Man is, of course, conceived as acting humanly, after the fashion of an intelligent and voluntary agent; but behind all his action there is ever postulated the all-determining hand of God, to whose sovereign operation even the blindness of the unbelieving is attributed by the evangelist (xii. 39 f.), while the receptivity to the light of those who believe is repeatedly in the most emphatic way ascribed by Jesus Himself to God alone. Although with little use of the terminology in which we have been accustomed to expect to see the doctrines of the decree and of election expressed, the substance of these doctrines is here set out in the most impressive way.

From the two sets of data provided by the Synoptists and St. John, it is possible to attain quite a clear insight into the conception of predestination as it lay in our Lord's teaching. It is quite certain, for example, that there is no place in this teaching for a 'predestination' that is carefully adjusted to the foreseen performances of the creature; and as little for a 'decree' which may be frustrated by creaturely action, or an 'election' which is given effect only by the creaturely choice: to our Lord the Father is the omnipotent Lord of heaven and earth, according to whose pleasure all things are ordered, and who gives the Kingdom to whom He will (Luke xii. 32, Mark xi. 26, Luke x. 21). Certainly it is the very heart of our Lord's teaching that the Father's good-pleasure is a *good* pleasure, ethically right, and the issue of infinite love; the very name of Father as the name of God by preference on His lips is full of this conception; but the very nerve of this teaching is, that the Father's will is all-embracing and omnipotent. It is only therefore that His children need be careful for nothing, that the little flock need not fear, that His elect may be assured that none of them shall be lost, but all that the Father has given Him shall be raised up at the last day. And if thus the elective purpose of the Father cannot fail of its end, neither is it possible to find this end in anything less than 'salvation' in the highest sense, than entrance into that eternal life to communicate which to dying men our Lord came into the world. There are elections to other ends, to be sure, spoken of: notably there is the election of the apostles to their office (Luke vi. 13, John vi. 70); and Christ Himself is conceived as especially God's elect one, because no one has the service to render which He has (Luke ix. 35, xxiii. 35). But the elect, by way of eminence; 'the elect whom God elected,' for whose sake He governs all history (Mark xiii. 20); the elect of whom it was the will of Him who sent the Son, that of all that He gave Him He should lose nothing, but should raise it up at the last day (John vi. 39); the elect whom the Son of Man shall at the last day gather from the four winds, from the uttermost parts of the earth to the uttermost part of heaven (Mark xiii. 27): it would be inadequate to suppose that these are elected merely to opportunities or the means of grace, on their free cultivation of which shall depend their undecided destiny; or merely to the service of their fellow-men, as agents in God's beneficent plan for the salvation of the race. Of course this election is to privileges and means of grace; and without these the great end of the election would not be attained: for the 'election' is given effect only by the 'call,' and manifests itself only in faith and the holy life. Equally of course the elect are 'the salt of the earth' and 'the light of the world,' the few through whom the many are blessed; the eternal life to which they are elected does not consist in or with the silence and coldness of death, but only in and with the intensest activities of the conquering people of God. But the prime end of their election does not lie in these things, and to place exclusive stress upon them is certainly to gather in the mint and anise and cummin of the doctrine. That to which God's elect are elected is, according to the teaching of Jesus, all that is included in the idea of the Kingdom of God, in the idea of eternal life, in the idea of fellowship with Christ, in the idea of participation in the glory which the Father has given His Son. Their choice, and the whole development of their history, according to our Lord's teaching, is the loving work of the Father: and in His keeping also is the consummation of their bliss. Their segregation, of course, leaves others not elected, to whom none of their privileges are granted; from whom none of their services are expected; with whom their glorious destiny is not shared. This, too, is of God. But this side of the matter, in accordance with Jesus' mission in the world as Saviour rather than as Judge, is less dwelt upon. In the case of neither class, that of the elect as little as that of those that are without, are the purposes of God wrought out without the co-operation of the activities of the subjects; but in neither case is the decisive factor supplied by these, but is discoverable solely in the will of God and the consonant will of the Son. The 'even so, Father; for so it seemed good in thy sight' (Matt. xi. 26, Luke x. 21), is to our Lord, at least, an all-sufficient theodicy in the face of all God's diverse dealings with men.

The disciples of Jesus continue His teaching in all its elements. We are conscious, for example, of entering no new atmosphere when we pass to the *Epistle of James*. St. James, too, finds his starting-point in a profound apprehension of the exaltation and perfection of God, — defining God's nature, indeed, with a phrase that merely repeats in other words the pene-

trating declaration that 'God is light' (I John i. 5), which,
reflecting our Lord's teaching, sound the keynote of the beloved disciple's thought of God (Jas. i. 17), — and particularly in a keen sense of dependence on God (iv. 15, v. 7), to
which it was an axiom that every good thing is a gift from Him
(i. 17). Accordingly, salvation, the pre-eminent good, comes
purely as His gift, and can be ascribed only to His will (i. 18);
and its exclusively Divine origin is indicated by the choice that
is made of those who receive it — not the rich and prosperous,
who have somewhat perhaps which might command consideration, but the poor and miserable (ii. 5). So little does this Divine
choice rest on even faith, that it is rather in order to faith (ii. 5),
and introduces its recipients into the Kingdom as firstfruits of
a great harvest to be reaped by God in the world (i. 18).

Similarly, in the *Book of Acts*, the whole stress in the matter
of salvation is laid on the grace of God (xi. 23, xiii. 43, xiv. 3,
26, xv. 40, xviii. 27); and to it, in the most pointed way, the
inception of faith itself is assigned (xviii. 27). It is only slightly
varied language when the increase in the Church is ascribed to
the hand of the Lord (xi. 21), or the direct act of God (xiv. 27,
xviii. 10). The explicit declaration of ii. 47 presents, therefore,
nothing peculiar, and we are fully prepared for the philosophy
of the redemptive history expressed in xiii. 48, that only those
'ordained to eternal life' believed — the believing that comes
by the grace of God (xviii. 27), to whom it belongs to open the
heart to give heed to the gospel (xvi. 14), being thus referred
to the counsel of eternity, of which the events of time are only
the outworking.

The general philosophy of history thus suggested is implicit
in the very idea of a promissory system, and in the recognition
of a predictive element in prophecy, and is written large on
the pages of the *historical books* of the New Testament. It is
given expression in every declaration that this or that event
came to pass 'that it might be fulfilled which was spoken by
the prophets,' — a form of statement in which our Lord had
Himself betrayed His teleological view of history, not only as
respects details (John xv. 25, xvii. 12), but with the widest refer-

ence (Luke xxi. 22), and which was taken up cordially by His followers, particularly by Matthew (i. 22, ii. 15, 23, iv. 14, viii. 17, xii. 17, xiii. 35, xxi. 4, xxvi. 56, John xii. 38, xviii. 9, xix. 24, 28, 36). Alongside of this phrase occurs the equally significant 'δεῖ of the Divine decree,' as it has been appropriately called, by which is suggested the necessity which rules over historical sequences. It is used with a view now to Jesus' own plan of redemption (by Jesus Himself, Luke ii. 49, iv. 43, ix. 22, xiii. 33, xvii. 25, xxiv. 7, John iii. 14, x. 16, xii, 34; by the evangelist, Matt. xvi. 21), now to the underlying plan of God (by Jesus, Matt. xxiv. 6, Mark xiii. 7, 10, Luke xxi. 9; by the writer, Matt. xvii. 10, Mark ix. 11, Acts iii. 21, ix. 16), anon to the prophetic declaration as an indication of the underlying plan (by Jesus, Matt. xxvi. 56, Luke xxii. 37, xxiv. 26, 44; by the writer, John xx. 9, Acts i. 16, xvii. 3). This appeal, in either form, served an important apologetic purpose in the first proclamation of the gospel; but its fundamental significance is rooted, of course, in the conception of a Divine ordering of the whole course of history to the veriest detail.

Such a teleological conception of the history of the Kingdom is manifested strikingly in the speech of St. Stephen (Acts vii.), in which the developing plan of God is rapidly sketched. But it is in such declarations as those of St. Peter recorded in Acts ii. 23, iv. 28 that the wider philosophy of history comes to its clearest expression. In them everything that had befallen Jesus is represented as merely the emerging into fact of what had stood beforehand prepared for in 'the determinate counsel and foreknowledge of God,' so that nothing had been accomplished, by whatever agents, except what 'his hand and his counsel has foreordained to come to pass.' It would not be easy to frame language which should more explicitly proclaim the conception of an all-determining decree of God governing the entire sequence of events in time. Elsewhere in *the Petrine discourses* of Acts the speech is coloured by the same ideas: we note in the immediate context of these culminating passages the high terms in which the exaltation of God is expressed (iv. 24 f.), the sharpness with which His sovereignty in the 'call'

($\pi\rho\sigma\kappa\alpha\lambda\acute{\epsilon}o\mu\alpha\iota$) is declared (ii. 39), and elsewhere the repeated emergence of the idea of the necessary correspondence of the events of time with the predictions of Scripture (i. 16, ii. 24, iii. 21). The same doctrine of predestination meets us in the pages of *St. Peter's Epistles*. He does, indeed, speak of the members of the Christian community as God's elect (I i. 1, ii. 9, v. 13, II i. 10), in accordance with the apostolic habit of assuming the reality implied in the manifestation; but this is so far from importing that election hangs on the act of man that St. Peter refers it directly to the elective foreknowledge of God (I i. 2), and seeks its confirmation in sanctification (II i. 10), — even as the stumbling of the disobedient, on the other hand, is presented as a confirmation of their appointment to disbelief (I ii. 8). The pregnant use of the terms 'foreknow' ($\pi\rho\sigma\gamma\iota\nu\acute{\omega}\sigma\kappa\omega$) and 'foreknowledge' ($\pi\rho\acute{\sigma}\gamma\nu\omega\sigma\iota\varsigma$) by St. Peter brought to our attention in these passages (Acts ii. 23, I Pet. i. 2, 20), where they certainly convey the sense of a loving, distinguishing regard which assimilates them to the idea of election, is worthy of note as another of the traits common to him and St. Paul (Rom. viii. 29, xi. 2, only in the New Testament). The usage might be explained, indeed, as the development of a purely Greek sense of the words, but it is much more probably rooted in a Semitic usage, which, as we have seen, is not without example in the Old Testament. A simple comparison of the passages will exhibit the impossibility of reading the terms of mere prevision (cf. Cremer *sub voc.*, and especially the full discussion in K. Müller's "Die Göttliche Zuvorersehung und Erwählung," etc. pp. 38 f., 81 f.; also Gennrich, "Theol. Studien und Kritiken," 1898, 382–395; Pfleiderer, "Urchristenthum," 289, "Paulinismus," 268; and Lorenz, "Lehrsystem," etc. 94).

The *teaching of St. John* in Gospel and Epistle is not distinguishable from that which he reports from his Master's lips, and need not here be reverted to afresh. The same fundamental view-points meet us also in the Apocalypse. The emphasis there placed on the omnipotence of God rises indeed to a climax. There only in the New Testament (except II Cor. vi. 18), for example, is the epithet παντοκράτωρ ascribed to Him (i. 8, iv. 8, xi. 17, xv. 3, xvi. 7, 14, xix. 6, 15, xxi. 22, cf. xv. 3, vi. 10); and the whole purport of the book is the portrayal of the Divine guidance of history, and the very essence of its message that, despite all surface appearances, it is the hand of God that really directs all occurrences, and all things are hastening to the end of His determining. Salvation is ascribed unvaryingly to the grace of God, and declared to be His work (xii. 10, xix. 1). The elect people of God are His by the Divine choice alone: their names are from the foundation of the world written in the Lamb's Book of Life (xiii. 8, xvii. 8, xx. 12–15, xxi. 27), which is certainly a symbol of Divine appointment to eternal life revealed in and realized through Christ; nor shall they ever be blotted out of it (iii. 5). It is difficult to doubt that the destination here asserted is to a complete salvation (xix. 9), that it is individual, and that it is but a single instance of the completeness of the Divine government to which the world is subject by the Lord of lords and King of kings, the Ruler of the earth and King of the nations, whose control of all the occurrences of time in accordance with His holy purposes it is the supreme object of this book to portray.

Perhaps less is directly said about the purpose of God in the *Epistle to the Hebrews* than in any other portion of the New Testament of equal length. The technical phraseology of the subject is conspicuously absent. Nevertheless, the conception of the Divine counsel and will underlying all that comes to pass (ii. 10), and especially the entire course of the purchase (vi. 17, cf. x. 5–10, ii. 9) and application (xi. 39, 31, ix. 15) of salvation, is fundamental to the whole thought of the Epistle; and echoes of the modes in which this conception is elsewhere expressed meet us on every hand. Thus we read of God's eternal counsel (βουλή, vi. 17) and of His precedent will (θέλημα, x. 10) as underlying His redemptive acts; of the enrolment of the names of His children in heaven (xii. 23); of the origin in the energy of God of all that is good in us (xiii. 21); and, above all, of a 'heavenly call' as the source of the whole renewed life of the Christian (iii. 1, cf. ix. 15).

When our Lord spoke of 'calling' (καλέω, Matt. ix. 13, Mark ii. 17, Luke v. 32, and, parabolically, Matt. xxii. 3, 4, 8, 9, Luke xiv. 8, 9, 10, 12, 13, 16, 17, 24; κλητός, Matt. xxii. 14 [xx. 16]) the term was used in the ordinary sense of 'invitation,' and refers therefore to a much broader circle than the 'elect' (Matt. xxii. 14); and this fundamental sense of 'bidding' may continue to cling to the term in the hands of the evangelists (Matt. iv. 21, Mark i. 20, cf. Luke xiv. 7, John ii. 2), while the depth of meaning which might be attached to it, even in such a connotation, may be revealed by such a passage as Rev. xix. 9 'Blessed are they which are bidden to the marriage supper of the Lamb.' On the lips of the apostolic writers, however, the term in its application to the call of God to salvation took on deeper meanings, doubtless out of consideration of the author of the call, who has but to speak and it is done (cf. Rom. iv. 17). It occurs in these writers, when it occurs at all, as the synonym no longer of 'invitation,' but rather of 'election' itself; or, more precisely, as expressive of the temporal act of the Divine efficiency by which effect is given to the electing decree. In this profounder sense it is practically confined to the writings of St. Paul and St. Peter and the *Epistle to the Hebrews*, occurring elsewhere only in Jude 1, Rev. xvii. 14, where the children of God are designated the 'called,' just as they are (in various collocations of the term with the idea of election) in Rom. i. 6, 7, I Cor. i. 2, Rom. viii. 28, I Cor. i. 24 (cf. Rom. i. 1, I Cor. i. 1). Κλητός, as used in these passages, does not occur in the *Epistle to the Hebrews*, but in iii. 1 κλῆσις occurs in a sense indistinguishable from that which it bears in St. Paul (Rom. xi. 29, I Cor. i. 26, Eph. i. 18, iv. 1, 4, Phil. iii. 14, II Thes. i. 11, II Tim. i. 9) and St. Peter (II Pet. i. 10); and in ix. 15 (cf. special applications of the same general idea, v. 4, xi. 8), καλέω bears the same deep sense expressed by it in St. Paul (Rom. viii. 30 twice, ix. 11, 24, I Cor. i. 9, vii. 15, 17, 18 twice, 20, 21, 22 twice, 24, Gal. i. 6, 15, v. 8, 13, Eph. iv. 1, 4, Col. iii. 15, I Thes. ii. 12, iv. 7, v. 24, II Thes. ii. 14, II Tim. i. 9) and in St. Peter (I i. 15, ii. 9, 21, iii. 9, v. 10, II i. 3, cf. προσκαλέω, Acts ii. 39, and in the language of St. Luke, Acts xiii. 2, xvi. 10). The contrast into which the 'called' (iii. 1) are brought in this Epistle with the 'evangelized' (iv. 2, 6), repeating in other terms the contrast which our Saviour institutes between the 'elect' and 'called' (Matt. xxii. 14), exhibits the height of the meaning to which the idea of the 'call' has climbed. It no longer denotes the mere invitation, — that notion is now given in 'evangelize,' — but the actual ushering into salvation of the heirs of the promise, who are made partakers of the heavenly calling, and are called to the everlasting inheritance just because they have been destined thereunto by God (i. 14), and are enrolled in heaven as the children given to the Son of God (ii. 13).

It was reserved, however, to the Apostle Paul to give to the fact of predestination its fullest New Testament presentation. This was not because St. Paul exceeded his fellows in the strength or clearness of his convictions, but because, in the prosecution of the special task which was committed to him in the general work of establishing Christianity in the world, the complete expression of the common doctrine of predestination fell in his way, and became a necessity of his argument. With him, too, the roots of his doctrine of predestination were set in his general doctrine of God, and it was fundamentally because St. Paul was a theist of a clear and consistent type, living and thinking under the influence of the profound consciousness of a personal God who is the author of all that is and, as well, the upholder and powerful governor of all that He has made, according to whose will, therefore, all that comes to pass must be ordered, that he was a predestinarian; and more particularly he too was a predestinarian because of his general doctrine of salvation, in every step of which the initiative must be taken by God's unmerited grace, just because man is a sinner, and, as a sinner, rests under the Divine condemnation, with no right of so much as access to God, and without means to seek, much less to secure, His favour. But although possessing no other sense of the infinite majesty of the almighty Person in whose hands all things lie, or of the issue of all saving acts from His free grace, than his companion apostles, the course of the special work in which St. Paul was engaged, and the exigencies of the special controversies in which he was involved, forced him to a fuller expression of all that is implied in these convictions. As he cleared the whole field of Christian faith from the presence of any remaining confidence in human works; as he laid beneath the hope of Christians a righteousness not self-wrought but provided by God alone; as he consistently offered this God-provided righteousness to sinners of all classes without regard to anything in them by which they might fancy God could be moved to accept their persons, — he was inevitably driven to an especially pervasive reference of salvation in each of its elements to the free grace of God, and to an especially full exposition on the one hand of the course of Divine grace in the several acts which enter into the saving work, and on the other to the firm rooting of the whole process in the pure will of the God of grace. From the beginning to the end of his ministry, accordingly, St. Paul conceived himself, above everything else, as the bearer of a message of undeserved grace to lost sinners, not even directing his own footsteps to carry the glad tidings to whom he would (Rom. i. 10, I Cor. iv. 19, II Cor. ii. 12), but rather led by God in triumphal procession through the world, that through him might be made manifest the savour of the knowledge of Christ in every place — a savour from life unto life in them that are saved, and from death unto death in them that are lost (II Cor. ii. 15, 16). By the 'word of the cross' proclaimed by him the essential character of his hearers was thus brought into manifestation, — to the lost it was foolishness, to the saved the power of God (I Cor. i. 18): not as if this essential character belonged to them by nature or was the product of their own activities, least of all of their choice at the moment of the proclamation, by which rather it was only revealed; but as finding an explanation only in an act of God, in accordance with the working of Him to whom all differences among men are to be ascribed (I Cor. iv. 7) — for God alone is the Lord of the harvest, and all the increase, however diligently man may plant and water, is to be accredited to Him alone (I Cor. iii. 5 f.).

It is naturally the soteriological interest that determines in

the main St. Paul's allusions to the all-determining
God, — the letters that we have from him come from
evangelist, — but it is not merely a soteriological c
that he is expressing in them, but the most fundamental postulate of his religious consciousness; and he is accordingly constantly correlating his doctrine of election with his general
doctrine of the decree or counsel of God. No man ever had an
intenser or more vital sense of God, — the eternal (Rom. xvi.
26) and incorruptible (i. 23) One, the only wise One (xvi. 27),
who does all things according to His good-pleasure (I Cor. xv.
38, xii. 18, Col. i. 19), and whose ways are past tracing out
(Rom. xi. 33); before whom men should therefore bow in the
humility of absolute dependence, recognizing in Him the one
moulding power as well in history as in the life of the individual (Rom. ix.). Of Him and through Him and unto Him, he
fervently exclaims, are all things (Rom. xi. 36, cf. I Cor. viii.
6); He is over all and through all and in all (Eph. iv. 6, cf. Col.
i. 16); He worketh all things according to the counsel of His
will (Eph. i. 11): all that is, in a word, owes its existence and
persistence and its action and issue to Him. The whole course
of history is, therefore, of His ordering (Acts xiv. 16, xvii. 26,
Rom. i. 18 f., iii. 25, ix–xi, Gal. iii. iv.), and every event that
befalls is under His control, and must be estimated from the
view-point of His purposes of good to His people (Rom. viii.
28, I Thes. v. 17, 18), for whose benefit the whole world is
governed (Eph. i. 22, I Cor. ii. 7, Col. i. 18). The figure that is
employed in Rom. ix. 22 with a somewhat narrower reference,
would fairly express St. Paul's world-view in its relation to the
Divine activity: God is the potter, and the whole world with
all its contents but as the plastic clay which He moulds to His
own ends; so that whatsoever comes into being, and whatsoever uses are served by the things that exist, are all alike of
Him. In accordance with this world-view St. Paul's doctrine of
salvation must necessarily be interpreted; and, in very fact,
he gives it its accordant expression in every instance in which
he speaks of it.

There are especially *three chief passages* in which the apostle so fully expounds his fundamental teaching as to the relation of salvation to the purpose of God, that they may fairly claim our primary attention.

(a) The first of these — Rom. viii. 29, 30 — emerges as part of the encouragement which the apostle offers to his readers in the sad state in which they find themselves in this world, afflicted with fears within and fightings without. He reminds them that they are not left to their weakness, but the Spirit comes to their aid: 'and we know,' adds the apostle, — it is no matter of conjecture, but of assured knowledge, — 'that with them that love God, God co-operates with respect to all things for good, since they are indeed the called according to [His] purpose.' The appeal is obviously primarily to the universal government of God: nothing takes place save by His direction, and even what seems to be grievous comes from the Father's hand. Secondarily, the appeal is to the assured position of his readers within the fatherly care of God: they have not come into this blessed relation with God accidentally or by the force of their own choice; they have been 'called' into it by Himself, and that by no thoughtless, inadvertent, meaningless, or changeable call; it was a call 'according to purpose,' — where the anarthrousness of the noun throws stress on the purposiveness of the call. What has been denominated 'the golden chain of salvation' that is attached to this declaration by the particle 'because' can therefore have no other end than more fully to develop and more firmly to ground the assurance thus quickened in the hearts of the readers: it accordingly enumerates the steps of the saving process in the purpose of God, and carries it thus successively through the stages of appropriating foreknowledge, — for 'foreknow' is undoubtedly used here in that pregnant sense we have already seen it to bear in similar connexions in the New Testament, — predestination to conformity with the image of God's Son, calling, justifying, glorifying; all of which are cast in the past tense of a purpose in principle executed when formed, and are bound together as mutually implicative, so that, where one is present, all are in principle present with it. It accordingly follows that, in St.

Paul's conception, glorification rests on justification, which in turn rests on vocation, while vocation comes only to those who had previously been predestinated to conformity with God's Son, and this predestination to character and destiny only to those afore chosen by God's loving regard. It is obviously a strict doctrine of predestination that is taught. This conclusion can be avoided only by assigning a sense to the 'foreknowing' that lies at the root of the whole process, which is certainly out of accord not merely with its ordinary import in similar connexions in the New Testament, nor merely with the context, but with the very purpose for which the declaration is made, namely, to enhearten the struggling saint by assuring him that he is not committed to his own power, or rather weakness, but is in the sure hands of the Almighty Father. It would seem little short of absurd to hang on the merely contemplative foresight of God a declaration adduced to support the assertion that the lovers of God are something deeper and finer than even lovers of God, namely, 'the called according to *purpose*,' and itself educing the joyful cry, 'If God is for us, who is against us?' and grounding a confident claim upon the gift of all things from His hands.

(*b*) The even more famous section, Rom. ix, x, xi, following closely upon this strong affirmation of the suspension of the whole saving process on the predetermination of God, offers, on the face of it, a yet sharper assertion of predestination, raising it, moreover, out of the circle of the merely individual salvation into the broader region of the historical development of the kingdom of God. The problem which St. Paul here faces grew so directly out of his fundamental doctrine of justification by faith alone, with complete disregard of all question of merit or vested privilege, that it must have often forced itself upon his attention, — himself a Jew with a high estimate of a Jew's privileges and a passionate love for his people. He could not but have pondered it frequently and deeply, and least of all could he have failed to give it treatment in an Epistle like this, which undertakes to provide a somewhat formal exposition of his whole doctrine of justification.

Having shown the necessity of such a method of salvation as he proclaimed, if sinful men were to be saved at all (i. 18–iii. 20), and then expounded its nature and evidence (iii. 21–v. 21), and afterwards discussed its intensive effects (vi. 1–viii. 39), he could not fail further to explain its extensive effects — especially ,when they appeared to be of so portentous a character as to imply a reversal of what was widely believed to have been God's mode of working heretofore, the rejection of His people whom He foreknew, and the substitution of the alien in their place. St. Paul's solution of the problem is, briefly, that the situation has been gravely misconceived by those who so represent it; that nothing of the sort thus described has happened or will happen; that what has happened is merely that in the constitution of that people whom He has chosen to Himself and is fashioning to His will, God has again exercised that sovereignty which He had previously often exercised, and which He had always expressly reserved to Himself and frequently proclaimed as the principle of His dealings with the people emphatically of His choice. In his exposition of this solution St. Paul first defends the propriety of God's action (ix. 6–24), then turns to stop the mouth of the objecting Jew by exposing the manifested unfitness of the Jewish people for the kingdom (ix. 30–x. 21), and finally expounds with great richness the ameliorating circumstances in the whole transaction (xi. 1–36). In the course of his defence of God's rejection of the mass of contemporary Israel, he sets forth the sovereignty of God in the whole matter of salvation — 'that the purpose of God according to election might stand, not of works, but of Him that calleth' — with a sharpness of assertion and a clearness of illustration which leave nothing to be added in order to throw it out in the full strength of its conception. We are pointed illustratively to the sovereign acceptance of Isaac and rejection of Ishmael, and to the choice of Jacob and not of Esau before their birth and therefore before either had done good or bad; we are explicitly told that in the matter of salvation it is not of him that wills, or of him that runs, but of God that shows mercy, and that has mercy on whom He wills, and whom He wills He hardens; we are pointedly directed to behold in God the potter who makes the vessels which proceed from His hand each for an end of His appointment, that He may work out His will upon them. It is safe to say that language cannot be chosen better adapted to teach predestination at its height.

We are exhorted, indeed, not to read this language in isolation, but to remember that the ninth chapter must be interpreted in the light of the eleventh. Not to dwell on the equally important consideration that the eleventh chapter must likewise be interpreted only in the light of the ninth, there seems here to exhibit itself some forgetfulness of the inherent continuity of St. Paul's thought, and, indeed, some misconception of the progress of the argument through the section, which is a compact whole and must express a much pondered line of thought, constantly present to the apostle's mind. We must not permit to fall out of sight the fact that the whole extremity of assertion of the ninth chapter is repeated in the eleventh (xi. 4–10); so that there is no change of conception or lapse of consecution observable as the argument develops, and we do not escape from the doctrine of predestination of the ninth chapter in fleeing to the eleventh. This is true even if we go at once to the great closing declaration of xi. 32, to which we are often directed as to the key of the whole section — which, indeed, it very much is: 'For God hath shut up all unto disobedience, that he might have mercy upon all.' On the face of it there could not readily be framed a more explicit assertion of the Divine control and the Divine initiative than this; it is only another declaration that He has mercy on whom He will have mercy, and after the manner and in the order that He will. And it certainly is not possible to read it as a declaration of universal salvation, and thus reduce the whole preceding exposition to a mere tracing of the varying pathways along which the common Father leads each individual of the race severally to the common goal. Needless to point out that thus the whole argument would be stultified, and the apostle convicted of gross exaggeration in tone and language where otherwise we find only impressive solemnity, rising at times into natural anguish. It is enough to observe that the verse cannot bear this sense in its context. Nothing is clearer than that its purpose is not to minimise but to magnify the sense of absolute dependence on the Divine mercy, and to quicken apprehension of the mystery of God's righteously loving ways; and nothing is clearer than that the reference of the double 'all' is exhausted by the two classes discussed in the immediate context, — so that they are not to be taken individualistically but, so to speak, racially. The intrusion of the individualistic-universalistic sentiment, so dominant in the modern consciousness, into the interpretation of this section, indeed, is to throw the whole into inextricable confusion. Nothing could be further from the nationalistic-universalistic point of view from which it was written, and from which alone St. Paul can be understood when he represents that in rejecting the mass of contemporary Jews God has not cast off His people, but, acting only as He had frequently done in former ages, is fulfilling His promise to the kernel while shelling off the husk. Throughout the whole process of pruning and ingrafting which he traces in the dealings of God with the olive-tree which He has once for all planted, St. Paul sees God, in accordance with His promise, saving His people. The continuity of its stream of life he perceives preserved throughout all its present experience of rejection (xi. 1–10); the gracious purpose of the present confinement of its channel, he traces with eager hand (xi. 11–15); he predicts with confidence the attainment in the end of the full breadth of the promise (xi. 15–32), — all to the praise of the glory of God's grace (xi. 33–36). There is undoubtedly a universalism of salvation proclaimed here; but it is an eschatological, not an individualistic universalism. The day is certainly to come when the whole world — inclusive of all the Jews and Gentiles alike, then dwelling on the globe — shall know and serve the Lord; and God in all His strange work of distributing salvation is leading the course of events to that great goal; but meanwhile the principle of His action is free, sovereign grace, to which alone it is to be attributed that any who are saved in the meantime enter into their inheritance, and through which alone shall the final goal of the race itself be attained. The central thought of the whole discussion, in a word, is that Israel does not owe the promise to the fact that it is Israel, but conversely owes the fact that it is Israel to the promise, — that 'it is not the children of the flesh that are the children of God, but the children of the promise that are reckoned for a seed' (ix. 8). In these words we hold the real key to the whole section; and if we approach it with this key in hand we shall have little difficulty in apprehending that, from its beginning to its end, St. Paul has no higher object than to make clear that the inclusion of any individual within the kingdom of God finds its sole cause in the sovereign grace of the choosing God, and cannot in any way or degree depend upon his own merit, privilege, or act.

Neither, with this key in our hand, will it be possible to raise a question whether the election here expounded is to eternal life or not rather merely to prior privilege or higher service. These too, no doubt, are included. But by what right is this long section intruded here as a substantive part of this Epistle, busied as a whole with the exposition of 'the power of God unto salvation to every one that believeth, to the Jew first and also to the Greek,' if it has no direct concern with this salvation? By what chance has it attached itself to that noble grounding of a Christian's hope and assurance with which the eighth chapter closes? By what course of thought does it reach its own culmination in that burst of praise to God, on whom all things depend, with which it concludes? By what accident is it itself filled with the most unequivocal references to the saving grace of God 'which hath been poured out on the vessels of his mercy which he afore prepared for glory, even on us whom he also called, not from the Jews only, but also from the Gentiles'? If such language has no reference to salvation, there is no language in the New Testament that need be interpreted of final destiny. Beyond question this section does explain to us some of the grounds of the mode of God's action in gathering a people to Himself out of the world; and in doing this, it does reveal to us some of the ways in which the distri-

bution of His electing grace serves the purposes of His kingdom on earth; reading it, we certainly do learn that God has
many ends to serve in His gracious dealings with the children
of men, and that we, in our ignorance of His multifarious purposes, are not fitted to be His counsellors. But by all this, the
fact is in no wise obscured that it is primarily to salvation that
He calls His elect, and that whatever other ends their election
may subserve, this fundamental end will never fail; that in
this, too, the gifts and calling of God are not repented of, and
will surely lead on to their goal. The difficulty which is felt by
some in following the apostle's argument here, we may suspect,
has its roots in part in a shrinking from what appears to them
an arbitrary assignment of men to diverse destinies without
consideration of their desert. Certainly St. Paul as explicitly
affirms the sovereignty of reprobation as of election, — if these
twin ideas are, indeed, separable even in thought: if he represents God as sovereignly loving Jacob, he represents Him
equally as sovereignly hating Esau; if he declares that He has
mercy on whom He will, he equally declares that He hardens
whom He will. Doubtless the difficulty often felt here is, in
part, an outgrowth of an insufficient realization of St. Paul's
basal conception of the state of men at large as condemned
sinners before an angry God. It is with a world of lost sinners
that he is representing God as dealing; and out of that world
building up a Kingdom of Grace. Were not all men sinners,
there might still be an election, as sovereign as now; and there
being an election, there would still be as sovereign a rejection:
but the rejection would not be a rejection to punishment, to
destruction, to eternal death, but to some other destiny consonant to the state in which those passed by should be left.
It is not indeed, then, because men are sinners that men are
left unelected; election is free, and its obverse of rejection must
be equally free: but it is solely because men are sinners that
what they are left to is destruction. And it is in this universalism of ruin rather than in a universalism of salvation that St.
Paul really roots his theodicy. When all deserve death it is a
marvel of pure grace that any receive life; and who shall gain-

say the right of Him who shows this miraculous mercy, to have mercy on whom He will, and whom He will to harden?

(c) In Eph. i. 1–12 there is, if possible, an even higher note struck. Here, too, St. Paul is dealing primarily with the blessings bestowed on his readers, in Christ, all of which he ascribes to the free grace of God; but he so speaks of these blessings as to correlate the gracious purpose of God in salvation, not merely with the plan of operation which He prosecutes in establishing and perfecting His kingdom on earth, but also with the all-embracing decree that underlies His total cosmical activity. In opening this circular letter, addressed to no particular community whose special circumstances might suggest the theme of the thanksgiving with which he customarily begins his letters, St. Paul is thrown back on what is common to Christians; and it is probably to this circumstance that we owe the magnificent description of the salvation in Christ with which the Epistle opens, and in which this salvation is traced consecutively in its preparation (vv. 4, 5), its execution (6, 7), its publication (8–10), and its application (11–14), both to Jews (11, 12) and to Gentiles (13, 14). Thus, at all events, we have brought before us the whole ideal history of salvation in Christ from eternity to eternity — from the eternal purpose as it lay in the loving heart of the Father, to the eternal consummation, when all things in heaven and earth shall be summed up in Christ. Even the incredible profusion of the blessings which we receive in Christ, described with an accumulation of phrases that almost defies exposition, is less noticeable here than the emphasis and reiteration with which the apostle carries back their bestowment on us to that primal purpose of God in which all things are afore prepared ere they are set in the way of accomplishment. All this accumulation of blessings, he tells his readers, has come to them and him only in fulfilment of an eternal purpose — only because they had been chosen by God out of the mass of sinful men, in Christ, before the foundation of the world, to be holy and blameless before Him, and had been lovingly predestinated unto adoption through Jesus Christ to Him, in accordance with the good-pleasure of His

will, to the praise of the glory of His grace. It is therefore, he
further explains, that to them in the abundance of God's
grace there has been brought the knowledge of the salvation
in Christ, described here as the knowledge of the mystery of
the Divine will, according to His good-pleasure, which He purposed in Himself with reference to the dispensation of the fulness of the times, to sum up all things in the universe in Christ,
— by which phrases the plan of salvation is clearly exhibited
as but one element in the cosmical purpose of God. And thus
it is, the apostle proceeds to explain, only in pursuance of this
all-embracing cosmical purpose that Christians, whether Jews
or Gentiles, have been called into participation of these blessings, to the praise of the glory of God's grace, — and of the
former class, he pauses to assert anew that their call rests on
a predestination according to the purpose of Him that works
all things according to the counsel of His will. Throughout
this elevated passage, the resources of language are strained to
the utmost to give utterance to the depth and fervour of St.
Paul's conviction of the absoluteness of the dominion which
the God, whom he describes as Him that works all things according to the counsel of His will, exercises over the entire universe, and of his sense of the all-inclusive perfection of the
plan on which He is exercising His world-wide government —
into which world-wide government His administration of His
grace, in the salvation of Christ, works as one element. Thus
there is kept steadily before our eyes the wheel within wheel of
the all-comprehending decree of God: first of all, the inclusive
cosmical purpose in accordance with which the universe is
governed as it is led to its destined end; within this, the purpose relative to the kingdom of God, a substantive part, and,
in some sort, the hinge of the world-purpose itself; and still
within this, the purpose of grace relative to the individual, by
virtue of which he is called into the Kingdom and made sharer
in its blessings: the common element with them all being that
they are and come to pass only in accordance with the good-
pleasure of His will, according to His purposed good-pleasure,
according to the purpose of Him who works all things in ac-

cordance with the counsel of His will; and therefore all alike redound solely to His praise.

In these outstanding passages, however, there are only expounded, though with special richness, ideas which govern the Pauline literature, and which come now and again to clear expression in each group of St. Paul's letters. The whole doctrine of election, for instance, lies as truly in the declaration of II Thes. ii. 13 or that of II Tim. i. 9 (cf. II Tim. ii. 19, Tit. iii. 5) as in the passages we have considered from Romans (cf. I Cor. i. 26–31) and Ephesians (cf. Eph. ii. 10, Col. i. 27, iii. 12, 15, Phil. iv. 3). It may be possible to trace minor distinctions through the several groups of letters in forms of statement or modes of relating the doctrine to other conceptions; but from the beginning to the end of St. Paul's activity as a Christian teacher his fundamental teaching as to the Christian calling and life is fairly summed up in the declaration that those that are saved are God's 'workmanship created in Christ Jesus unto good works, which God afore prepared that they should walk in them' (Eph. ii. 10).

The most striking impression made upon us by a survey of the whole material is probably the intensity of St. Paul's practical interest in the doctrine — a matter fairly illustrated by the passage just quoted (Eph. ii. 10). Nothing is more noticeable than his zeal in enforcing its two chief practical contents — the assurance it should bring to believers of their eternal safety in the faithful hands of God, and the ethical energy it should arouse within them to live worthily of their vocation. It is one of St. Paul's most persistent exhortations, that believers should remember that their salvation is not committed to their own weak hands, but rests securely on the faithfulness of the God who has called them according to His purpose (e. g., I Thes. v. 24, I Cor. i. 8 f., x. 13, Phil. i. 6). Though the appropriation of their salvation begins in an act of faith on their own part, which is consequent on the hearing of the gospel, their appointment to salvation itself does not depend on this act of faith, nor on any fitness discoverable in them on the foresight of which God's choice of them might be supposed to be

based, but (as I Thes. ii. 13 already indicates) both the preaching of the gospel and the exercise of faith consistently appear
as steps in the carrying out of an election not conditioned on
their occurrence, but embracing them as means to the end set
by the free purpose of God. The case is precisely the same with
all subsequent acts of the Christian life. So far is St. Paul from
supposing that election to life should operate to enervate moral
endeavour, that it is precisely from the fact that the willing and
doing of man rest on an energizing willing and doing of God,
which in turn rest on His eternal purpose, that the apostle derives his most powerful and most frequently urged motive for
ethical action. That tremendous 'therefore,' with which at the
opening of the twelfth chapter of Romans he passes from the
doctrinal to the ethical part of the Epistle, — from a doctrinal
exposition the very heart of which is salvation by pure grace
apart from all works, and which has just closed with the fullest
discussion of the effects of election to be found in all his writings, to the rich exhortations to high moral effort with which
the closing chapters of this Epistle are filled, — may justly be
taken as the normal illation of his whole ethical teaching. His
Epistles, in fact, are sown (as indeed is the whole New Testament) with particular instances of the same appeal (e. g., I
Thes. ii. 12, II Thes. ii. 13–15, Rom. vi, II Cor. v. 14, Col. i. 10,
Phil. i. 21, ii. 12, 13, II Tim. ii. 19). In Phil. ii. 12, 13 it attains,
perhaps, its sharpest expression: here the saint is exhorted to
work out his own salvation with fear and trembling, just because it is God who is working in him both the willing and the
doing because of His 'good-pleasure' — obviously but another
way of saying, 'If God is for us, who can be against us?'

There is certainly presented in this a problem for those who
wish to operate in this matter with an irreconcilable 'either,
or,' and who can conceive of no freedom of man which is under
the control of God. St. Paul's theism was, however, of too pure
a quality to tolerate in the realm of creation any force beyond
the sway of Him who, as he says, is over all, and through all,
and in all (Eph. iv. 6), working all things according to the counsel of His will (Eph. i. 11). And it must be confessed that it is

more facile than satisfactory to set his theistic world-view summarily aside as a 'merely religious view,' which stands in conflict with a truly ethical conception of the world — perhaps even with a repetition of Fritzsche's jibe that St. Paul would have reasoned better on the high themes of 'fate, free-will, and providence' had he sat at the feet of Aristotle rather than at those of Gamaliel. Antiquity produced, however, no ethical genius equal to St. Paul, and even as a teacher of the foundations of ethics Aristotle himself might well be content to sit rather at his feet; and it does not at once appear why a so-called 'religious' conception may not have as valid a ground in human nature, and as valid a right to determine human conviction, as a so-called 'ethical' one. It can serve no good purpose even to proclaim an insoluble antinomy here: such an antinomy St. Paul assuredly did not feel, as he urged the predestination of God not more as a ground of assurance of salvation than as the highest motive of moral effort; and it does not seem impossible for even us weaker thinkers to follow him some little way at least in looking upon those twin bases of religion and morality — the ineradicable feelings of dependence and responsibility — not as antagonistic sentiments of a hopelessly divided heart, but as fundamentally the same profound conviction operating in a double sphere. At all events, St. Paul's pure theistic view-point, which conceived God as in His providential *concursus* working all things according to the counsel of His will (Eph. i. 11) in entire consistency with the action of second causes, necessary and free, the proximate producers of events, supplied him with a very real point of departure for his conception of the same God, in the operations of His grace, working the willing and the doing of Christian men, without the least infringement of the integrity of the free determination by which each grace is proximately attained. It does not belong to our present task to expound the nature of that Divine act by which St. Paul represents God as 'calling' sinners 'into communion with his Son,' itself the first step in the realization in their lives of that conformity to His image to which they are predestinated in the counsels of eternity, and of which the first manifestation is that faith in the Redeemer of God's elect out of which the whole Christian life unfolds. Let it only be observed in passing that he obviously conceives it as an act of God's almighty power, removing old inabilities and creating new abilities of living, loving action. It is enough for our present purpose to perceive that even in this act St. Paul did not conceive God as dehumanizing man, but rather as energizing man in a new direction of his powers; while in all his subsequent activities the analogy of the *concursus* of Providence is express. In his own view, his strenuous assertion of the predetermination in God's purpose of all the acts of saint and sinner alike in the matter of salvation, by which the discrimination of men into saved and lost is carried back to the free counsel of God's will, as little involves violence to the ethical spontaneity of their activities on the one side, as on the other it involves unrighteousness in God's dealings with His creatures. He does not speculatively discuss the methods of the Divine providence; but the fact of its universality — over all beings and actions alike — forms one of his most primary presuppositions; and naturally he finds no difficulty in postulating the inclusion in the prior intention of God of what is subsequently evolved in the course of His providential government.

V. The Bible Doctrine of Predestination

A survey of the whole material thus cursorily brought before us exhibits the existence of a consistent Bible doctrine of predestination, which, because rooted in, and indeed only a logical outcome of, the fundamental Biblical theism, is taught in all its essential elements from the beginning of the Biblical revelation, and is only more fully unfolded in detail as the more developed religious consciousness and the course of the history of redemption required.

The *subject* of the DECREE is uniformly conceived as God in the fulness of His moral personality. It is not to chance, nor to necessity, nor yet to an abstract or arbitrary will, — to God acting inadvertently, inconsiderately, or by any necessity of nature, — but specifically to the almighty, all-wise, all-holy, all-righteous, faithful, loving God, to the Father of our Lord and Saviour Jesus Christ, that is ascribed the predetermination of the course of events. Naturally, the contemplation of the plan in accordance with which all events come to pass calls out primarily a sense of the unsearchable wisdom of Him who framed it, and of the illimitable power of Him who executes it; and these attributes are accordingly much dwelt upon when the Divine predestination is adverted to. But the moral attributes are no less emphasized, and the Biblical writers find their comfort continually in the assurance that it is the righteous, holy, faithful, loving God in whose hands rests the determination of the sequence of events and all their issues. Just because it is the determination of God, and represents Him in all His fulness, the decree is ever set forth further as in its *nature* eternal, absolute, and immutable. And it is only an explication of these qualities when it is further insisted upon, as it is throughout the Bible, that it is essentially one single composite purpose, into which are worked all the details included in it, each in its appropriate place; that it is the pure determination of the Divine will — that is, not to be confounded on the one hand with an act of the Divine intellect on which it rests, nor on the other with its execution by His power in the works of creation and providence; that it is free and unconditional — that is, not the product of compulsion from without nor of necessity of nature from within, nor based or conditioned on any occurrence outside itself, foreseen or unforeseen; and that it is certainly efficacious, or rather constitutes the unchanging norm according to which He who is the King over all administers His government over the universe. Nor is it to pass beyond the necessary implications of the fundamental idea when it is further taught, as it is always taught throughout the Scriptures, that the *object* of the decree is the whole universe of things and all their activities, so that nothing comes to pass, whether in the sphere of necessary or free causation, whether good or bad, save in accordance with the provisions of the primal plan, or more precisely save as the outworking in fact of what had

lain in the Divine mind as purpose from all eternity, and is now
only unfolded into actuality as the fulfilment of His all-determining will. Finally, it is equally unvaryingly represented that
the *end* which the decreeing God had in view in framing His
purpose is to be sought not without but within Himself, and
may be shortly declared as His own praise, or, as we now commonly say, the glory of God. Since it antedates the existence
of all things outside of God and provides for their coming into
being, they all without exception must be ranked as means to
its end, which can be discovered only in the glory of the Divine
purposer Himself. The whole Bible doctrine of the decree revolves, in a word, around the simple idea of purpose. Since
God is a Person, the very mark of His being is purpose. Since
He is an infinite Person, His purpose is eternal and independent, all-inclusive and effective. Since He is a moral Person,
His purpose is the perfect exposition of all His infinite moral
perfections. Since He is the personal creator of all that exists,
His purpose can find its final cause only in Himself.

Against this general doctrine of the decree, the Bible doctrine of ELECTION is thrown out into special prominence, being, as it is, only a particular application of the general doctrine
of the decree to the matter of the dealings of God with a sinful
race. In its fundamental characteristics it therefore partakes
of all the elements of the general doctrine of the decree. It, too,
is necessarily an act of God in His completeness as an infinite
moral Person, and is therefore eternal, absolute, immutable —
the independent, free, unconditional, effective determination
by the Divine will of the objects of His saving operations. In
the development of the idea, however, there are certain elements which receive a special stress. There is nothing that is
more constantly emphasized than the absolute *sovereignty* of
the elective choice. The very essence of the doctrine is made,
indeed, to consist in the fact that, in the whole administration
of His grace, God is moved by no consideration derived from
the special recipients of His saving mercy, but the entire account of its distribution is to be found hidden in the free counsels of His own will. That it is not of him that runs, nor of him

that wills, but of God that shows mercy, that the sinner obtains salvation, is the steadfast witness of the whole body of Scripture, urged with such reiteration and in such varied connexions as to exclude the possibility that there may lurk behind the act of election considerations of foreseen characters or acts or circumstances — all of which appear rather as results of election as wrought out in fact by the *providentia specialissima* of the electing God. It is with no less constancy of emphasis that the roots of the Divine election are planted in His unsearchable love, by which it appears as *the supreme act of grace.* Contemplation of the general plan of God, including in its provisions every event which comes to pass in the whole universe of being during all the ages, must redound in the first instance to the praise of the infinite wisdom which has devised it all; or as our appreciation of its provisions is deepened, of the glorious righteousness by which it is informed. Contemplation of the particular element in His purpose which provides for the rescue of lost sinners from the destruction due to their guilt, and their restoration to right and to God, on the other hand draws our thoughts at once to His inconceivable love, and must redound, as the Scriptures delight to phrase it, to the praise of His glorious grace. It is ever, therefore, specifically to the love of God that the Scriptures ascribe His elective decree, and they are never weary of raising our eyes from the act itself to its source in the Divine compassion. A similar emphasis is also everywhere cast on the *particularity* of the Divine election. So little is it the designation of a mere class to be filled up by undetermined individuals in the exercise of their own determination; or of mere conditions, or characters, or qualities, to be fulfilled or attained by the undetermined activities of individuals, foreseen or unforeseen; that the Biblical writers take special pains to carry home to the heart of each individual believer the assurance that he himself has been from all eternity the particular object of the Divine choice, and that he owes it to this Divine choice alone that he is a member of the class of the chosen ones, that he is able to fulfil the conditions of salvation, that he can hope to attain the character on which alone God can look with complacency, that he can look forward to an eternity of bliss as his own possession. It is the very nerve of the Biblical doctrine that each individual of that enormous multitude that constitutes the great host of the people of God, and that is illustrating the character of Christ in the new life now lived in the strength of the Son of God, has from all eternity been the particular object of the Divine regard, and is only now fulfilling the high destiny designed for him from the foundation of the world.

The Biblical writers are as far as possible from obscuring the doctrine of election because of any seemingly unpleasant corollaries that flow from it. On the contrary, they expressly draw the corollaries which have often been so designated, and make them a part of their explicit teaching. Their doctrine of election, they are free to tell us, for example, does certainly involve a corresponding *doctrine of preterition*. The very term adopted in the New Testament to express it — ἐκλέγομαι, which, as Meyer justly says (Eph. i. 4), '*always* has, and must *of logical necessity* have, a reference to *others* to whom the chosen would, without the ἐκλογή, still belong' — embodies a declaration of the fact that in their election others are passed by and left without the gift of salvation; the whole presentation of the doctrine is such as either to imply or openly to assert, on its every emergence, the removal of the elect by the pure grace of God, not merely from a state of condemnation, but out of the company of the condemned — a company on whom the grace of God has no saving effect, and who are therefore left without hope in their sins; and the positive just reprobation of the impenitent for their sins is repeatedly explicitly taught in sharp contrast with the gratuitous salvation of the elect despite their sins. But, on the other hand, it is ever taught that, as the body out of which believers are chosen by God's unsearchable grace is the mass of justly condemned sinners, so the destruction to which those that are passed by are left is the righteous recompense of their guilt. Thus the discrimination between men in the matter of eternal destiny is distinctly set forth as taking place in the interests of mercy and for the sake of salvation:

from the fate which justly hangs over all, God is represented as in His infinite compassion rescuing those chosen to this end in His inscrutable counsels of mercy to the praise of the glory of His grace; while those that are left in their sins perish most deservedly, as the justice of God demands. And as the broader lines of God's gracious dealings with the world lying in its iniquity are more and more fully drawn for us, we are enabled ultimately to perceive that the Father of spirits has not distributed His elective grace with niggard hand, but from the beginning has had in view the restoration to Himself of the whole world; and through whatever slow approaches (as men count slowness) He has made thereto — first in the segregation of the Jews for the keeping of the service of God alive in the midst of an evil world, and then in their rejection in order that the fulness of the Gentiles migh tbe gathered in, and finally through them Israel in turn may all be saved — has ever been conducting the world in His loving wisdom and His wise love to its destined goal of salvation, — now and again, indeed, shutting up this or that element of it unto disobedience, but never merely in order that it might fall, but that in the end He might have mercy upon all. Thus the Biblical writers bid us raise our eyes, not only from the justly condemned lost, that we may with deeper feeling contemplate the marvels of the Divine love in the saving of sinners not better than they and with no greater claims on the Divine mercy; but from the relatively insignificant body of the lost, as but the prunings gathered beneath the branches of the olive-tree planted by the Lord's own hand, to fix them on the thrifty stock itself and the crown of luxuriant leafage and ever more richly ripening fruit, as under the loving pruning and grafting of the great Husbandman it grows and flourishes and puts forth its boughs until it shall shade the whole earth. This, according to the Biblical writers, is the end of election; and this is nothing other than the salvation of the world. Though in the process of the ages the goal is not attained without prunings and fires of burning, — though all the wild-olive twigs are not throughout the centuries grafted in, — yet the goal of a saved world shall at the end be gloriously realized. Meanwhile, the hope of the world, the hope of the Church, and the hope of the individual alike, is cast solely on the mercy of a freely electing God, in whose hands are all things, and not least the care of the advance of His saving grace in the world. And it is undeniable that whenever, as the years have passed by, the currents of religious feeling have run deep, and the higher ascents of religious thinking have been scaled, it has ever been on the free might of Divine grace that Christians have been found to cast their hopes for the salvation alike of the world, the Church, and the individual; and whenever they have thus turned in trust to the pure grace of God, they have spontaneously given expression to their faith in terms of the Divine election.

LITERATURE. — The Biblical material can best be surveyed with the help of the Lexicons on the terms employed (especially Cremer), the commentaries on the passages, and the sections in the several treatises on Biblical Theology dealing with this and cognate themes; among these last, the works of Dillmann on the Old Testament, and Holtzmann on the New Testament, may be especially profitably consulted. The Pauline doctrine has, in particular, been made the subject of almost endless discussion, chiefly, it must be confessed, with the object of softening its outlines or of explaining it more or less away. Perhaps the following are the more important recent treatises: — Poelman, "de Jesu Apostolorumque, Pauli præsertim, doctrina de prædestinatione divina et morali hominis libertate," Gron. 1851; Weiss, "Predestinationslehre des Ap. Paul.," in "Jahrbb. f. D. Theol." 1857, p. 54 f.; Lamping, "Pauli de prædestinatione decretorum enarratio," Leov. 1858; Goens, "Le rôle de la liberté humaine dans la prédestination Paulinienne," Lausanne, 1884; Ménégoz, "La prédestination dans la théologie Paulinienne," Paris, 1885; Dalmer, "Zur Paulinischen Erwählungslehre," in "Greifswälder Studien," Gütersloh, 1895. The publication of Karl Müller's valuable treatise on "Die Göttliche Zuvorersehung und Erwählung," etc. (Halle, 1892), has called out a new literature on the section Rom. ix–xi, the most important items in which are probably the reprint of Beyschlag's "Die Paulinische Theodicee" (1896, first published in 1868), and Dalmer, "Die Erwählung Israels nach der Heilsverkündigung des Ap. Paul." (Gütersloh, 1894), and Kühl, "Zur Paulinischen Theodicee," in the "Theologische Studien," presented to B. Weiss (Göttingen, 1897). But of these only Goens recognizes the double predestination; even Müller, whose treatise is otherwise of the first value, argues against it, and so does Dalmer in his very interesting discussions; the others are still less in accordance with their text (cf. the valuable critical note on the recent literature in Holtzmann's "N. T. Theologie," ii. 171–174).

Discussions of the doctrine of post-Canonical Judaism may be found in Hamburger, "Real-Encyc." ii. 102 f., article "Bestimmung"; F. Weber, "Jüd. Theol." 148 ff., 205 ff.; Schürer, *HJP* ii. ii. 14 f. (cf. p. 2 f., where the passages from Josephus are collected); Edersheim, "Life and Times of Jesus," i. 316 ff., article "Philo" in Smith and Wace, 383 [a], and "Speak. Com." on Ecclesiasticus, pp. 14, 16; Ryle and James, "Psalms of Solomon" on ix. 7 and Introd.; Montet, "Origines des partissaducéen et pharisien," 258 f.; Holtzmann, "N. T. Theologie," i. 32, 55; P. J. Muller, "De Godsleer der middeleeuwische Joden," Groningen, 1898; further literature is given in Schürer. — For post-Canonical Christian discussion, see the literature at the end of article ELECTION in the present work, v. i. p. 681.

II

THE FORESIGHT OF JESUS

THE FORESIGHT OF JESUS[1]

The interest of the student of the Gospels, and of the life of Jesus which forms their substance, in the topic of this article, is two-fold. Jesus is represented in the Gospels as at once the object and the subject of the most detailed foresight. The work which He came to do was a work ordained in the counsels of eternity, and in all its items prepared for beforehand with the most perfect prevision. In addressing Himself to the accomplishment of this work Jesus proceeded from the beginning in the fullest knowledge of the end, and with the most absolute adjustment of every step to its attainment. It is from this double view-point that each of the Evangelists depicts the course of our Lord's life on earth. They consentiently represent Him as having come to perform a specific task, all the elements of which were not only determined beforehand in the plan of God, but adumbrated, if somewhat sporadically, yet with sufficient fulness for the end in view, in the prophecies of the Old Testament. And they represent Him as coming to perform this task with a clear consciousness of its nature and a competent control of all the means for its discharge, so that His whole life was a conscientious fulfilment of a programme, and moved straight to its mark. The conception of foresight thus dominates the whole Evangelical narrative.

It is not necessary to dwell at length upon the Evangelists' conception of our Lord's life and work as *the fulfilment of a plan Divinely predetermined for Him.* It lies on the face of their narratives that the authors of the Gospels had no reservation with respect to the all-embracing predestination of God (cf. Hastings' *DB* iv. 54–56); and least of all could they exclude

[1] Article "Foresight" from *A Dictionary of Christ and the Gospels*, ed. by James Hastings, D.D., v. i, pp. 608–615. Pub. N. Y. 1908, by Charles Scribner's Sons.

71

from it this life and work which was to them the hinge upon which all history turns. To them accordingly our Lord is by way of eminence 'the man of destiny,' and His whole life (Lk. ii. 49, iv. 43) was governed by 'the δεῖ of the Divine counsel.' Every step of His pathway was a 'necessity' to Him, in the fulfilment of the mission for which He had 'come forth' (Mk. i. 38, cf. Swete), or as St. Luke (iv. 43) in quite Johannine wise (v. 23, 24, 30, 36, 38, vi. 29, 38, 39, 40 *et passim*) expresses it, 'was sent' (cf. Mt. x. 40, Mk. ix. 37, Lk. ix. 48, x. 16; Mt. xv. 24, xxi. 37, Mk. xii. 6, Lk. xx. 13, cf. Swete on Mk. ix. 37). Especially was all that concerned His departure, the accomplishment of which (Lk. ix. 31, cf. v. 51) was His particular task, under the government of this 'Divine necessity' (Mt. xvi. 21, xxvi. 54, Mk. viii. 31, Lk. ix. 22, xvii. 25, xxii. 22, 37, xxiv. 7, 44, Jn. iii. 14, xx. 9, cf. Acts ii. 23, iii. 18, iv. 28, and Westcott on Jn. xx. 9). His final journey to Jerusalem (Mt. xvi. 21), His rejection by the rulers (Mk. viii. 31, Lk. ix. 22, xvii. 25), His betrayal (Lk. xxiv. 7), arrest (Mt. xxvi. 54), sufferings (Mt. xxvi. 54, Mk. viii. 31, Lk. ix. 22, xvii. 25), and death (Mt. xvi. 21, Mk. viii. 31, Lk. ix. 22) by crucifixion (Lk. xxiv. 7, Jn. iii. 14), His rising again (Jn. xx. 9) on the third day (Mt. xvi. 21, Mk. viii. 31, Lk. ix. 22, xxiv. 7, 46) — each item alike is declared to have been 'a matter of necessity in pursuance of the Divine purpose' (Meyer, Mt. xxiv. 6), 'a necessary part of the destiny assigned our Lord' (Meyer, Mt. xxvi. 54). 'The death of our Lord' thus appears 'not as the accidental work of hostile caprice, but (cf. Acts ii. 23, iii. 18) the necessary result of the Divine predestination (Lk. xxii. 22), to which Divine δεῖ (Lk. xxiv. 26) the personal free action of man had to serve as an instrument' (Meyer, Acts iv. 28).

How far the several events which entered into this life had been prophetically announced is obviously, in this view of it, a mere matter of detail. All of them lay open before the eyes of God; and the only limit to pre-announcement was the extent to which God had chosen to reveal what was to come to pass, through His servants the prophets. In some instances, however, the prophetic announcement is particularly adduced as the ground on which recognition of the necessity of occurrence rests. The fulfilment of Scripture thus becomes regulative of the life of Jesus. Whatever stood written of Him in the Law or the Prophets or the Psalms (Lk. xxiv. 44) must needs (δεῖ) be accomplished (Mt. xxvi. 54, Lk. xxii. 37, xxiv. 26, Jn. xx. 9). Or, in another form of statement, particularly frequent in Mt. (i. 22, ii. 15, 23, iv. 14, viii. 17, xii. 17, xiii. 35, xxi. 4, xxvi. 56) and Jn. (xii. 38, xiii. 18, xv. 25, xvii. 12, xix. 24, 36), but found also in the other Evangelists (Mk. xiv. 49, Lk. iv. 21), the several occurrences of His life fell out as they did, 'in order that what was spoken by the Lord' through the prophets or in Scripture, 'might be fulfilled' (cf. Mt. ii. 17, xxvi. 54, xxvii. 9, Lk. xxiv. 44; in Jn. xviii. 9, 32, Lk. xxiv. 44 declarations of Jesus are treated precisely similarly). That is to say, 'what was done stood . . . in the connexion of the Divine necessity, as an actual fact, by which prophecy was destined to be fulfilled. The Divine decree expressed in the latter *must* be accomplished, and *to that end this . . . came to pass*, and that, *according to the whole of its contents*' (Meyer, Mt. i. 22). The meaning is, not that there lies in the Old Testament Scriptures a complete predictive account of all the details of the life of Jesus, which those skilled in the interpretation of Scripture might read off from its pages at will. This programme in its detailed completeness lies only in the Divine purpose; and in Scripture only so far forth as God has chosen to place it there for the guidance or the assurance of His people. The meaning is rather that all that stands written of Jesus in the Old Testament Scriptures has its certain fulfilment in Him; and that enough stands written of Him there to assure His followers that in the course of His life, and in its, to them, strange and unexpected ending, He was not the prey of chance or the victim of the hatred of men, to the marring of His work or perhaps even the defeat of His mission, but was following step by step, straight to its goal, the predestined pathway marked out for Him in the counsels of eternity, and sufficiently revealed from of old in the Scriptures to enable all who were not 'foolish and slow of heart to believe in all that the prophets have spoken,' to perceive that the Christ must needs have lived just this life and fulfilled just this destiny.

That the whole course of the life of Jesus, and especially its culmination in the death which He died, was foreseen and afore-prepared by God, enters, thus, into the very substance of the Evangelical narrative. It enters equally into its very substance that *this life was from the beginning lived out by Jesus Himself in full view of its drift and its issue.* The Evangelists are as far from representing Jesus as driven blindly onwards by a Divine destiny unknown to Himself, along courses not of His own choosing, to an unanticipated end, as they are from representing Him as thwarted in His purposes, or limited in His achievement, or determined or modified in His aims or methods, by the conditions which from time to time emerged in His way. The very essence of their representation is that Jesus came into the world with a definite mission to execute, of the nature of which He was perfectly aware, and according to which He ordered the whole course of His life as it advanced under His competent control unswervingly to its preconceived mark. In their view His life was lived out, not in ignorance of its issues, or in the form of a series of trials and corrections, least of all in a more or less unavailing effort to wring success out of failure; but in complete knowledge of the counsels of God for Him, in perfect acquiescence in them, and in careful and voluntary fulfilment of them. The 'Divine δεῖ' which governed His life is represented as fully recognized by Himself (Mt. xvi. 21, Mk. viii. 31, Lk. iv. 43, ix. 22, xvii. 25, xxiv. 7, Jn. iii. 14, xii. 34), and the fulfilment of the intimations of prophecy in His life as accepted by Him as a rule for His voluntary action (Mt. xxvi. 54, Lk. xxii. 37, xxiv. 26, 44, Jn. xx. 9, Mk. xiv. 49, Lk. iv. 21, Jn. xiii. 18, xv. 25, xvii. 12; cf. Mt. xiii. 14, xv. 7, xxiv. 15, xxvi. 56, Mk. vii. 6). Determining all things, determined by none, the life He actually lived, leading up to the death He actually died, is in their view precisely the life which from the beginning He intended to live, ending in precisely the death in which, from the beginning, He intended this life to issue, undeflected by so much as a hair's-breadth from the straight path He had from the start marked out for Himself in the fullest prevision and provision of all the so-called chances and changes which might befall Him. Not only were there no surprises in life for Jesus and no compulsions; there were not even 'influences,' as we speak of 'influences' in a merely human career. The mark of this life, as the Evangelists depict it, is its calm and quiet superiority to all circumstance and condition, and to all the varied forces which sway other lives; its prime characteristics are voluntariness and independence. Neither His mother, nor His brethren, nor His disciples, nor the people He came to serve, nor His enemies bent upon His destruction, nor Satan himself with his temptations, could move Him one step from His chosen path. When men seemed to prevail over Him they were but working His will; the great 'No one has taken my life away from me; I have power to lay it down, and I have power to take it again' (Jn. x. 18), is but the enunciation for the supreme act, of the principle that governs all His movements. His own chosen pathway ever lay fully displayed before His feet; on it His feet fell quietly, but they found the way always unblocked. What He did, He came to do; and He carried out His programme with unwavering purpose and indefectible certitude. So at least the Evangelists represent Him. (Cf. the first half of a striking article on "Die Selbständigkeit Jesu," by Trott, in Luthardt's "Zeitschrift für kirchl. Wissenschaft u. kirchl. Leben," 1883, iv. 233–241; in its latter half the article falls away from its idea, and ends by making Jesus absolutely dependent on Scripture for His knowledge of God and Divine things: 'We have no right whatever to maintain that Jesus received revelations from the Father otherwise than through the medium of the sacred Scriptures; that is a part of His complete humanity' (p. 238).)

The signature of this supernatural life which the Evangelists depict Jesus as living, lies thus in the perfection of the foresight by which it was governed. Of the reality of this foresight they leave their readers in no doubt, nor yet of its completeness. They suggest it by the general picture they draw of the self-directed life which Jesus lived in view of His mission. They record repeated instances in which He mentions beforehand events yet to occur, or foreshadows the end from the beginning. They connect these manifestations of foresight with the possession by Him of knowledge in general, in comprehension and penetration alike far beyond what is native to man. It may perhaps be natural to surmise in the first instance that they intend to convey merely the conviction that in Jesus was manifested a prophet of supreme greatness, in whom, as the culminating example of prophecy (cf. Acts iii. 22, 23), resided beyond precedent the gifts proper to prophets. There can be no question that to the writers of the Gospels Jesus was 'the incarnate ideal of the prophet, who, as such, forms a class by Himself, and is more than a prophet' (this is what Schwartz-kopff thinks Him, "The Prophecies of Jesus Christ," p. 7). They record with evident sympathy the impression made by Him at the outset of His ministry, that God had at last in Him visited His people (Mk. vi. 15, Lk. vii. 16, Jn. iv. 19, ix. 17); they trace the ripening of this impression into a well-settled belief in His prophetic character (Mt. xxi. 11, Lk. xxiv. 19, Mt. xxi. 46, Lk. vii. 39, Jn. vii. 40); and they remark upon the widespread suspicion which accompanied this belief, that He was something more than *a* prophet — possibly one of the old prophets returned, certainly a very special prophet charged with a very special mission for the introduction of the Messianic times (Mt. xvi. 14, Mk. vi. 15, viii. 28, Lk. ix. 8, 19, Jn. vi. 14, vii. 40). They represent Jesus as not only calling out and accepting this estimate of Him, but frankly assuming a prophet's place and title (Mt. xiii. 57, Mk. vi. 4, Lk. iv. 24, Jn. iv. 44, Lk. xiii. 33), exercising a prophet's functions, and delivering prophetic discourses, in which He unveils the future (Mt. xxiv. 21, Mk. xiii. 23, Jn. xiv. 29; cf. Mt. xxviii. 6, Lk. xxiv. 44, and such passages as Mt. xxvi. 32, 34, Mk. xvi. 7). Nevertheless it is very clear that in their allusions to the supernatural knowledge of Jesus, the Evangelists suppose themselves to be illustrating something very much greater than merely prophetic inspiration. The specific difference between Jesus and a prophet, in their view, was that while a prophet's human knowledge is increased by many things revealed to him by God (Amos. iii. 7), Jesus participated in all the fulness of the Divine knowledge (Mt. xi. 27, Lk. x. 22, Jn. xvi. 15, xviii. 4, xvi. 30, xxi. 17), so that all that is knowable lay open before Him (Jn. xvii. 10). The Evangelists, in a word, obviously intend to attribute Divine omniscience to Jesus, and in their adduction of instances of His supernatural knowledge, whether with respect to hidden things or to those yet buried in the future, are illustrating His possession of this Divine omniscience (cf. Muirhead, "The Eschatology of Jesus," p. 119, where, in partial correction of the more inadequate statement of p. 48, there is recognized in the Evangelists at least a 'tendency' to attribute to our Lord 'Divine dignity' and 'literal omniscience').

That this is the case with St. John's Gospel is very commonly recognized (for a plain statement of the evidence see Karl Müller, "Göttliches Wissen und göttliche Macht des johann. Christus," 1882, § 4, pp. 29–47: "Zeugnisse des vierten Evangeliums für Jesu göttliches Wissen"). It is not too much to say, indeed, that one of the chief objects which the author of that Gospel set before himself was to make clear to its readers the superhuman knowledge of Jesus, with especial reference, of course, to His own career. It therefore records direct ascriptions of omniscience to Jesus, and represents them as favourably received by Him (Jn. xvi. 30, xxi. 17; cf. Liddon, "The Divinity of our Lord," ed. 4, 1869, p. 466). It makes it almost the business of its opening chapters to exhibit this omniscience at work in the especially Divine form (Lk. xvi. 15, Acts i. 24, Heb. iv. 12, Ps. cxxxviii (cxxxix). 2, Jer. xvii. 10. xx. 12; cf. Swete on Mk. ii. 8) of immediate, universal, and complete knowledge of the thoughts and intents of the human heart (cf. Westcott on Jn. ii. 25), laying down the general thesis in ii. 24, 25 (cf. vi. 64, 70, xxi. 17), and illustrating it in detail in the cases of all with whom Jesus came into contact in the opening days of His ministry (cf. Westcott on Jn. i. 47), Peter (i. 42), Philip (i. 43), Nathanael (i. 47), Mary (ii. 4), Nicodemus (iii.), the woman of Samaria (iv.). In the especially striking case of the choice of Judas Iscariot as one of the Apostles, it expressly explains that this was due to no ignorance of Judas' character or of his future action (vi. 64, 70, xiii. 11), but was done as part of our Lord's voluntary execution of His own well-laid plans. It pictures Jesus with great explicitness as prosecuting His whole work in full knowledge of all the things that were coming upon Him (Jn. xviii. 4, cf. Westcott), and with a view to subjecting them all to His governing hand, so that His life from the beginning should run steadily onward on the lines of a thoroughly wrought-out plan (Jn. i. 47, ii. 19, 24, iii. 14, vi. 51, 64, 70, vii. 6, viii. 28, x. 15, 18, xii. 7, 23, xiii. 1, 11, 21, 38, xiv. 29, xvi. 5, 32, xviii. 4, 9).

It is difficult to see, however, why St. John's Gospel should be separated from its companions in this matter (Schenkel says frankly that it is only because there is no such passage in St. John's Gospel as Mk. xiii. 32, on which see below. Whatever else must be said of W. Wrede's "Das Messiasgeheimnis," etc., 1901, it must be admitted that it has broke down this artificial distinction between the Gospel of John and the Synoptics). If they do not, like St. John (xvi. 30, xxi. 17), record direct ascriptions of precise omniscience to Jesus by His followers, they do, like St. John, represent Him as Himself claiming to be the depository and distributer of the Father's knowledge (Mt. xi. 21–30, Lk. x. 22–24). Nor do they lag behind St. John in attributing to Jesus the Divine prerogative of reading the heart (Mt. ix. 4, Meyer; Mk. ii. 5, 8, viii. 17, xii. 15, 44, Swete, p. lxxxviii; Lk. v. 22, vii. 39) or the manifestation, in other forms, of God-like omniscience (Mt. xvii. 27, xxi. 2, Mk. xi. 2, xiv. 13, Lk. v. 4, xix. 30, xxii. 10; cf. O. Holtzmann, "War Jesus Ekstatiker?" p. 14 and p. 15, note). Least of all do they fall behind St. John in insisting upon the perfection of the foresight of Jesus in all matters connected with His own life and death (Mt. ix. 15, xii. 40, xvi. 21, xx. 18, 22, 28, xxvi. 2, 21, 34, 50, Mk. ii. 19, viii. 31, ix. 31, x. 33, 39, 45, xi. 2, xiv. 8, 13, 18, 30, Lk. v. 34, ix. 22, 44, 51, xii. 50, xiii. 35, xvii. 25, xviii. 31, xix. 30, xxii. 10, 21, 34, 37, xxiv. 44). Nothing could exceed the detailed precision of these announcements, — a characteristic which has been turned, of course, to their discredit as genuine utterances of Jesus by writers who find difficulty with detailed prediction. 'The form and contents of these texts,' remarks Wrede ('Messiasgeheimnis," etc. p. 88), 'speak a language which cannot be misunderstood. They are nothing but a short summary of the Passion history — "cast, of course, in the future tense."' '"The Passion-history,"' he proceeds, quoting Eichhorn, '"could certainly not be more exactly related in few words."' In very fact, it is perfectly clear — whether they did it by placing upon His lips predictions He never uttered and never could have uttered, is another question — that the Evangelists designed to represent Jesus as endowed with the absolute and unlimited foresight consonant with His Divine nature (see Liddon, "The Divinity of our Lord," ed. 4, p. 464 ff.; and cf. A. J. Mason, "The conditions of our Lord's Life on Earth," pp. 155–194).

The force of this representation cannot be broken, of course, by raising the question afresh whether the supernatural knowledge attributed by the Evangelists to our Lord may not, in many of its items at least, if not in its whole extent, find its analogues, after all, in human powers, or be explained as not different in kind from that of the prophets (cf. e. g., Westcott, "Additional Note on Jn. ii. 24"; A. J. Mason, "Conditions," etc. pp. 162–163). The question more immediately before us does not concern our own view of the nature and origin of this knowledge, but that of the Evangelists. If we will keep these two questions separate we shall scarcely be able to doubt that the Evangelists mean to present this knowledge as one of the marks of our Lord's Divine dignity. In interpreting them we are not entitled to parcel out the mass of the illustrations of His supernormal knowledge which they record to differing sources, as may fall in with our own conceptions of the inherent possibilities of each case; finding indications in some instances merely of His fine human instinct, in others of His prophetic inspiration, while reserving others — if such others are left to us in our analysis — as products of His Divine intuition. The Evangelists suggest no such lines of cleavage in the mass; and

they must be interpreted from their own standpoint. This finds
its centre in their expressed conviction that in Jesus Christ
dwelt the fulness of the knowledge of God (Mt. xi. 27, Lk. x.
22, Jn. viii. 38, xvi. 15, xvii. 10). To them His knowledge of
God and of Divine things, of Himself in His Person and mission, of the course of His life and the events which would befall Him in the prosecution of the work whereunto He had been
sent, of the men around Him, — His followers and friends,
the people and their rulers, — down to the most hidden depths
of their natures and the most intimate processes of their secret
thoughts, and of all the things forming the environment in
which the drama He was enacting was cast, however widely
that environment be conceived, or however minutely it be contemplated, — was but the manifestation, in the ever-widening
circles of our human modes of conception, of the perfect apprehension and understanding that dwelt changelessly in His
Divine intelligence. He who knew God perfectly, — it were
little that He should know man and the world perfectly too;
all that affected His own work and career, of course, and with
it, equally of course, all that lay outside of this (cf. Mason,
"Conditions," etc. p. 168): in a word, unlimitedly, all things.
Even if nothing but the Law of Parsimony stood in the way,
it might well be understood that the Evangelists would be deterred from seeking, in the case of such a Being, other sources
of information besides His Divine intelligence to account for
all His far-reaching and varied knowledge. At all events, it is
clearly their conviction that all He knew — the scope of which
was unbounded and its depth unfathomed, though their record
suggests rather than fully illustrates it — found its explanation
in the dignity of His person as God manifest in the flesh.

Nor can the effect of their representation of Jesus as the
subject of this all-embracing Divine knowledge be destroyed
by the discovery in their narratives of another line of representation in which our Lord is set forth as living His life out
under the conditions which belong naturally to the humanity
He had assumed. These representations are certainly to be
neglected as little as those others in which His Divine omnis-

cience is suggested. They bring to our observation another side
of the complex personality that is depicted, which, if it cannot
be said to be as emphatically insisted upon by the Evangelists,
is nevertheless, perhaps, equally pervasively illustrated. This
is the true humanity of our Lord, within the scope of which He
willed to live out His life upon earth, that He might accomplish
the mission for which He had been sent. The suggestion that
He might break over the bounds of His mission, in order that
He might escape from the ruggedness of His chosen path, by
the exercise whether of His almighty power (Mt. iv. 3 f., Lk.
iv. 3 f.) or of His unerring foresight (Mt. xvi. 22 ‖), He treated
first and last as a temptation of the Evil One — for 'how then
should the Scriptures be fulfilled that thus it must be' (Mt.
xxvi. 54 ‖)? It is very easy, to be sure, to exaggerate the indications in the Evangelists of the confinement of our Lord's
activities within the limits of human powers. It is an exaggeration, for example, to speak as if the Evangelists represent
Him as frequently surprised by the events which befell Him:
they never predicate surprise of Him, and it is only by a very
precarious inference from the events recorded that they can
ever be supposed even to suggest or allow place for such an
emotion in our Lord. It is an exaggeration again to adduce our
Lord's questions as attempts to elicit information for His own
guidance: His questions are often plainly dialectical or rhetorical, or, like some of His actions, solely for the benefit of
those 'that stood around.' It is once more an exaggeration to
adduce the employment in many cases of the term γινώσκω,
when the Evangelists speak of our Lord's knowledge, as if it
were thereby implied that this knowledge was freshly born in
His mind: the assumed distinction, but faintly marked in
Greek literature, cannot be traced in the usage of the terms
γνῶναι and εἰδέναι in their application to our Lord's knowledge;
these terms even replace one another in parallel accounts of
the same instance (Mt. xxii. 18‖Mk. xii. 15; [Mt. ix. 4]‖Mk.
ii. 8, Lk. v. 22; cf. Mt. xii. 25, Lk. vi. 8, ix. 47, xi. 17, Jn. vi. 61);
γνῶναι is used of the undoubted Divine knowledge of our Lord
([Mt. xi. 25] Lk. x. 22, Jn. x. 15, xvii. 25, Mt. vii. 23; cf. Jn.

ii. 24, 25, v. 42, x. 14, 27); and indeed of the knowledge of God Himself (Lk. x. 22, xvi. 15, Jn. x. 15 [Mt. xi. 27]): and, in any event, there is a distinction which in such nice inquiries should not be neglected, between saying that the occurrence of an event, being perceived, was the occasion of an action, and saying that knowledge of the event, perceived as occurring, waited on its occurrence. Gravely vitiated by such exaggerations as most discussions of the subject are, enough remains, however, after all exaggeration is pruned away, to assure us, not indeed that our Lord's life on earth was, in the view of the Evangelists, an exclusively human one; or that, apart from the constant exercise of His will to make it such, it was controlled by the limitations of humanity; but certainly that it was, in their view, lived out, so far as was consistent with the fulfilment of the mission for which He came — and as an indispensable condition of the fulfilment of that mission — under the limitations belonging to a purely human life. The classical passages in this reference are those striking statements in the second chapter of Luke (ii. 40, 52) in which is summed up our Lord's growth from infancy to manhood, including, of course, His intellectual development and His own remarkable declaration recorded in Mt. xxiv. 36, Mk. xiii. 32, in which He affirms His ignorance of the day and hour of His return to earth. Supplemented by their general dramatization of His life within the range of the purely human, these passages are enough to assure us that in the view of the Evangelists there was in our Lord a purely human soul, which bore its own proper part in His life, and which, as human souls do, grew in knowledge as it grew in wisdom and grace, and remained to the end, as human souls must, ignorant of many things, — nay, which, because human souls are finite, must ever be ignorant of much embraced in the universal vision of the Divine Spirit. We may wonder why the 'day and hour' of His own return should remain among the things of which our Lord's human soul continued ignorant throughout His earthly life. But this is a matter about which surely we need not much concern ourselves. We can never do more than vaguely guess at the law which governs the inclusions and exclusions which characterize the knowledge-contents of any human mind, limited as human minds are not only qualitatively but quantitatively; and least of all could we hope to penetrate the principle of selection in the case of the perfect human intelligence of our Lord; nor have the Evangelists hinted their view of the matter. We must just be content to recognize that we are face to face here with the mystery of the Two Natures, which, although they do not, of course, formally enunciate the doctrine in so many words, the Evangelists yet effectively teach, since by it alone can consistency be induced between the two classes of facts which they present unhesitatingly in their narratives. Only, if we would do justice to their presentation, we must take clear note of two of its characteristics. They do not simply, in separated portions of their narratives, adduce the facts which manifest our Lord's Divine powers and His human characteristics, but interlace them inextricably in the same sections of the narratives. And they do not subject the Divine that is in Christ to the limitations of the human, but quite decisively present the Divine as dominating all, and as giving play to the human only by a constant, voluntary withholding of its full manifestation in the interests of the task undertaken. Observe the story, for example, in Jn. xi, which Dr. Mason ("Conditions," etc. p. 143) justly speaks of as 'indeed a marvellous weaving together of that which is natural and that which is above nature.' 'Jesus learns from others that Lazarus is sick, but knows without any further message that Lazarus is dead; He weeps and groans at the sight of the sorrow which surrounds Him, yet calmly gives thanks for the accomplishment of the miracle before it has been accomplished.' This conjunction of the two elements is typical of the whole Evangelical narrative. As portrayed in it our Lord's life is distinctly duplex; and can be consistently construed only by the help of the conception of the Two Natures. And just as distinctly is this life portrayed in these narratives as receiving its determination not from the human, but from the Divine side. If what John undertakes to depict is what was said and done by the incarnated Word, no less what the Synoptics essay is to present the Gospel (as Mark puts it) of Jesus Christ the Son of God. It is distinctly a supernatural life that He is represented by them all as living; and the human aspect of it is treated by each alike as an incident in something more exalted, by which it is permitted, rather than on which it imposes itself. Though passed as far as was befitting within the limits of humanity, this life remains at all times the life of God manifest in the flesh, and, as depicted by the Evangelists, never escapes beyond the boundaries set by what was suitable to it as such.

The actual instances of our Lord's foresight which are recorded by the Evangelists are not very numerous outside of those which concern the establishment of the Kingdom of God, with which alone, of course, their narratives are particularly engaged. Even the few instances of specific exhibitions of foreknowledge of what we may call trivial events owe their record to some connexion with this great work. Examples are afforded by the foresight that the casting of the nets at the exact time and place indicated by our Lord would secure a draught of fishes (Lk. v. 4, cf. Jn. xxi. 6); that the first fish that Peter would take when he threw his hook into the sea would be one which had swallowed a stater (Mt. xvii. 27); that on entering a given village the disciples should find an ass tied, and a colt with it, whose owners would be obedient to our Lord's request (Mt. xxi. 2 ||); and that on entering Jerusalem to make ready for the final passover-feast they should meet a man bearing a pitcher, prepared to serve the Master's needs (Mk. xiv. 13). In instances like these the interlacing of prevision and provision is very intimate, and doubt arises whether they illustrate most distinctly our Lord's Divine foresight or His control of events. In other instances the element of foresight comes, perhaps, more purely forward: such are possibly the predictions of the offence of the disciples (Mt. xxvi. 31||), the denial of Peter (xxvi. 34||), and the treachery of Judas (xxvi. 21||). There may be added the whole series of utterances in which our Lord shows a comprehensive foresight of the career of those whom He called to His service (Mt. iv. 19, x. 17, 21, xx. 22,

xxiv. 9 f., Jn. xvi. 1 f.); and also that other series in which He
exhibits a like full foreknowledge of the entire history of the
Kingdom of God in the world (cf. especially the parables of the
Kingdom, and such passages as Mt. xvi. 18, xxiv. 5, 24, xxi. 43,
xxiv. 14, xxvi. 13, Lk. xix. 11, Jn. xiv. 18, 19). It is, however,
particularly with reference to His own work in establishing the
Kingdom, and in regard to the nature of that work, that stress
is particularly laid upon the completeness of His foreknowledge. His entire career, as we have seen, is represented by all
the Evangelists as lying plainly before Him from the beginning,
with every detail clearly marked and provided for. It is especially, however, with reference to the three great events in which
His work in establishing His Kingdom is summed up — His
death, His resurrection, His return — that the predictions become numerous, if we may not even say constant. Each of the
Evangelists represents Him, for example, as foreseeing His
death from the start (Jn. ii. 19, iii. 14, Mt. xii. 40, ix. 15, Mk.
ii. 19, Lk. xii. 49, v. 34; cf. Meyer on Mt. ix. 15, xvi. 21; Weiss
on Mk. viii. 31; Denney, "Death of Christ," p. 18; Wrede,
"Messiasgeheimnis," p. 19, etc.), and as so ordering His life as
to march steadfastly forward to it as its chosen climax (cf. e. g.,
Wrede, p. 84: 'It is accordingly the meaning of Mark that
Jesus journeys to Jerusalem because it is His will to die there').
He is represented, therefore, as avoiding all that could lead up
to it for a time, and then, when He was ready for it, as setting
Himself steadfastly to bring it about as He would; as speaking
of it only guardedly at first, and afterwards, when the time was
ripe for it, as setting about assiduously to prepare His disciples
for it. Similarly with respect to His resurrection, He is reported
as having it in mind, indeed, from the earliest days of His
ministry (Jn. ii. 19, Mt. xii. 40, xvi. 21, Mk. viii. 31, Lk. ix.
22), but adverting to it with pædagogical care, so as to prepare
rather than confuse the minds of His disciples. The same in
substance may be said with reference to His return (Mt. x.
23, xvi. 27, Mk. viii. 38, ix. 1, Lk. ix. 26, 27).

A survey in chronological order of the passages in which
He is reported as speaking of these three great events of the

future, cannot fail to leave a distinct impression on the mind not only of the large space they occupy in the Evangelical narrative, but of the great place they take as foreseen, according to that narrative, in the life and work of our Lord. In the following list the passages in which He adverts to His death stand in the order given them in Robinson's "Harmony of the Gospels": Jn. ii. 19, iii. 14, Mt. xii. 40 (cf. xvi. 4, Lk. xi. 32), Lk. xii. 49, 50, Mt. ix. 15 (Mk. ii. 19, Lk. v. 34), Jn. vi. 51, vii. 6–8, Mt. xvi. 21 (Mk. viii. 31, Lk. ix. 22), Lk. ix. 31, Mt. xvii. 17 (Mk. ix. 12), Mt. xvii. 22, 23 (Mk. ix. 31, Lk. ix. 44), Lk. ix. 51, Jn. vii. 34, viii. 21, 25, ix. 5, x. 11, 15, Lk. xiii. 32, xvii. 25, Mt. xx. 18, 19 (Mk. x. 33, Lk. xviii. 31), Jn. xii. 28, Mt. xx. 22 (Mk. x. 38), Mt. xx. 28 (Mk. x. 45), Mt. xxi. 39 (Mk. xii. 8, Lk. xx. 14), Jn. xii. 23, Mt. xxvi. 2, Jn. xiii. 1, 33, Mt. xxvi. 28 (Mk. xiv. 24, Lk. xxii. 20), Mt. xxvi. 31 (Mk. xiv. 27, Jn. xiv. 28), Jn. xv. 13, xvi. 5, xvi. 16, xviii. 11, Mt. xxvi. 54 (Jn. xviii. 11), Lk. xxiv. 26, 46.

The following allusions to His resurrection are in the same order: Jn. ii. 19, Mt. xii. 40 (Lk. xi. 30), Mt. xvi. 21 (Mk. viii. 31, Lk. ix. 22), Mt. xvii. 9 (Mk. ix. 9), Mt. xvii. 23 (Mk. ix. 31), Jn. x. 18 [xvi. 16], Mt. xx. 19 (Mk. x. 34, Lk. xviii. 33), Mt. xxvi. 32 (Mk. xiv. 28) [Mt. xxviii. 6||Lk. xxiv. 8], Lk. xxiv. 46.

The following are, in like order, the allusions to His return: Mt. x. 23, xvi. 27 (Mk. viii. 38, ix. 1, Lk. ix. 26, 27), Mk. x. 40, Lk. xvii. 22, Mt. xix. 28, xxiii. 39, xxiv. 3 (Mk. xiii. 4, Lk. xxi. 7), Mt. xxiv. 34–37 (Mk. xiii. 30, Lk. xxi. 32), Mt. xxiv. 44, xxv. 31, xxvi. 64 (Mk. xiv. 62, Lk. xxii. 69).

The most cursory examination of these series of passages in their setting, and especially in their distribution through the Evangelical narrative, will evince the cardinal place which the eschatological element takes in the life of the Lord as depicted in the Gospels. In particular, it will be impossible to escape the conviction that it is distinctly the teaching of the Evangelists that Jesus came into the world specifically to die, and ordered His whole life wittingly to that end. As Dr. Denney puts it (expounding Jn. x. 17, on which see also Westcott's note), 'Christ's death is not an incident of His life, it is the aim of it.'

The laying down of His life is not an accident in His career, it is His vocation; it is that in which the Divine purpose of His life is revealed.' 'If there was a period in His life during which He had other thoughts, it is antecedent to that at which we have any knowledge of Him' ("Death of Christ," pp. 259 and 18). Nothing could therefore be more at odds with the consentient and constant representations of the Evangelists than to speak of the 'shadow of the cross' as only somewhat late in His history beginning to fall athwart our Lord's pathway; of the idea that His earthly career should close in gloom as 'distinctly emerging in the teaching of Jesus only at a comparatively late period,' and as therefore presumably not earlier 'clear in His mind': unless, indeed, it be the accompanying more general judgment that 'there was nothing extraordinary or supernatural in Jesus' foreknowledge of His death,' and that 'His prophecy was but the expression of a mind which knew that it could not cease to be obedient while His enemies would not cease to be hostile' (A. M. Fairbairn, "The Expositor," 1897, i.; vol. iv. [1896] 283, 285). It is not less unwarranted to speak of Him as bowing to His fate only 'as the will of God, to which He yielded Himself up to the very end only with difficulty, and at best against His will' (Wernle, "Synopt. Frage," 200).

Such expressions as these, however, advise us that a very different conception from that presented by the Evangelists has found widespread acceptance among a class of modern scholars, whose efforts have been devoted to giving to our Lord's life on earth a character more normally human than it seems to possess as it lies on the pages of the Evangelists. The negative principle of the new constructions offered of the course and springs of our Lord's career being rejection of the account given by the Evangelists, these scholars are thrown back for guidance very much upon their own subjective estimate of probabilities. The Gospels are, however, the sole sources of information for the events of our Lord's life, and it is impossible to decline their aid altogether. Few, accordingly, have been able to discard entirely the general framework of the life of

Christ they present (for those who are inclined to represent Jesus as making no claim even to be the Messiah, see H. J. Holtzmann, "Lehrbuch der neutestamentlichen Theologie" i. 280, note; Meinhold as there referred to; and Wrede, "Das Messiasgeheimnis," especially Appendix vii.). Most have derived enough from the Gospels to assume that a crisis of some sort occurred at Cæsarea Philippi, where the Evangelists represent our Lord as beginning formally and frankly to prepare His disciples for His death (Mt. xvi. 21||).

Great differences arise at once, however, over what this crisis was. Schenkel supposes that it was only at this point in His ministry that Jesus began to think Himself the Messiah; Strauss is willing to believe He suspected Himself to be the Messiah earlier, and supposes that He now first began to proclaim Himself such; P. W. Schmidt and Lobstein imagine that on this day He both put the Messianic crown upon His head and faced death looming in His path; Weizsäcker and Keim allow that He thought and proclaimed Himself the Messiah from the beginning, and suppose that what is new here is that only now did He come to see with clearness that His ministry would end in His death, — and as death for the Messiah means return, they add that here He begins His proclamation of His return in glory. To this Schenkel and Hase find difficulty in assenting, feeling it impossible that the Founder of a spiritual kingdom should look forward to its consummation in a physical one, and insisting, therefore, that though Jesus may well have predicted the destruction of His enemies, He can scarcely have foretold His own coming in glory. On the other hand, Strauss and Baur judge that a prediction of the destruction of Jerusalem too closely resembles what actually occurred not to be *post eventum*, but see no reason why Jesus should not have dreamed of coming back on the clouds of heaven. As to His death, Strauss thinks He began to anticipate it only shortly before His last journey to Jerusalem; while Holsten cannot believe that He realized what was before Him until He actually arrived at Jerusalem, and even then did not acquiesce in it (so Spitta). That He went to Jerusalem for the purpose of dying,

neither Weizsäcker, nor Brandt, nor H. Holtzmann, nor Schult-
zen will admit, though the two last named allow that He foresaw that the journey would end in His death; or at least that
it possibly would, adds Pünjer, since, of course, a possibility
of success lay open to Him (cf. H. J. Holtzmann, "Lehrb. der
neutestamentlichen Theologie," i, 285–286, note). As many
men, so many opinions. As the positive principle of construction in all these schemes of life for Jesus is desupernaturaliza-
tion, they differ, so far as the prophetic element in His teaching
as reported by the Evangelists is concerned, chiefly in the
measure in which they explain it as due more or less entirely
to the Evangelists carrying their own ideas, or the ideas of the
community in which they lived, back into Jesus' mouth; or
allow it more or less fully to Jesus, indeed, but only in a form
which can be thought of as not rising above the natural prog-
nostications of a man in His position. A few deny to Jesus the
entire series of predictions reported in the Gospels, and assign
them in mass to the thought of the later community (e. g., Eichhorn, Wrede). A few, on the other hand, allow the whole, or
nearly the whole, series to Jesus, and explain them all naturalistically. Most take an intermediate position, determined by the
principle that all which seems to each critic incapable of naturalistic explanation as utterances of Jesus shall be assigned to
later origin. Accordingly, the concrete details in the alleged
predictions are quite generally denied to Jesus, and represented
as easily explicable modifications, in accordance with the actual
course of events, of what Jesus really said. The prediction of
resurrection on the third day, for example, is held by many
(e. g., Schwartzkopff) to be too precise a determination, and is
therefore excluded from the prophecy, or explained as only a
periphrasis for an indefinite short time, after the analogy of
Hos. vi. 2 (so even B. Weiss). To others a prediction of a resurrection at all seems incredible (Strauss, Schenkel, Weizsäcker,
Keim, Brandt), and it is transmuted into, at most, a premonition of future victory. By yet others (as Holsten) even the anticipation of death is doubted, and nothing of forecast is left
to Jesus except, possibly, a vague anticipation of difficulty and

suffering; while with others even this gives way, and Jesus is
represented as passing either the greater part of His life (Fairbairn), or the whole of it, in joyful expectation of more or less
unbroken success, or at least, however thickly the clouds gathered over His head, in inextinguishable hope in God and His
interposition in His behalf (cf. the brief general sketch of
opinions in Wrede, "Messiasgeheimnis," p. 85).

Thus, over-against the 'dogmatic' view of the life of
Christ, set forth in the Evangelists, according to which Jesus
came into the world to die, and which is dominated, therefore,
by foresight, is set, in polar opposition to it, a new view, calling
itself 'historical,' the principle of which is the denial to Jesus
of any foresight whatever beyond the most limited human forecast. No pretence is ordinarily made that this new view is given
support by the Evangelical records; it is put forward on *a
priori* or general grounds — as, for example, the only psychologically possible view (e. g., Schwartzkopff, "Prophecies of
Christ," p. 28; cf. Denney, "Death of Christ," p. 11, and especially the just strictures of Wrede, "Messiasgeheimnis," pp.
2, 3). It professes to find it incredible that Jesus entered upon
His ministry with any other expectation than success. Contact
with men, however, it allows, brought gradually the discovery
of the hopelessness of drawing them to His spiritual ideals; the
growing enmity of the rulers opened before Him the prospect
of disaster; and thus there came to Him the slow recognition,
first of the possibility, and then of the certainty, of failure; or,
at least, since failure was impossible for the mission He had
come to perform, of the necessity of passing through suffering
to the ultimate success. So slowly was the readjustment to this
new point of view made, that even at the end — as the prayer
at Gethsemane shows — there remained a lingering hope that
the extremity of death might be avoided. So far as a general
sketch can be made of a view presented by its several adherents
with great variety of detail, this is the essential fabric of the
new view (cf. the general statements of Kähler, "Zur Lehre
von der Versöhnung," 159; Denney, "Death of Christ," 11;
Wrede, "Messiasgeheimnis," 86). Only such parts of the pre-

dictive element of the teaching attributed to Jesus in the Gospels as are thought capable of naturalistic interpretation are incorporated into this new construction. By those who wish to bring in as much as possible, it is said, for example, that our Lord was too firmly persuaded of His Messianic appointment and function, and was too clear that this function centred in the establishment of the Kingdom, to accept death itself as failure. When He perceived death impending, that meant to Him, therefore, return; and return to bring in the Messianic glory meant resurrection. When He thought and spoke of death, therefore, He necessarily thought and spoke also of resurrection and return; the three went inevitably together; and if He anticipated the one, He must have anticipated the others also. Under this general scheme all sorts of opinions are held as to when, how, and under what impulses Jesus formed and taught this eschatological programme. As notable a construction as any holds that He first became certain of His Messiahship in an ecstatic vision which accompanied His baptism; that the Messiah must suffer was already borne in upon His conviction in the course of His temptation; but it was not until the scene at Cæsarea Philippi that He attained the happy assurance that the Messianic glory lay behind the dreadful death impending over Him. This great conviction, attained in principle in the ecstasy of that moment, was, nevertheless, only gradually assimilated. When Jesus was labouring with His disciples, He was labouring also with Himself. In this particular construction (it is O. Holtzmann's) an element of 'ecstasy' is introduced; more commonly the advances Jesus is supposed to make in His anticipations are thought to rest on processes of formal reasoning. In either case, He is pictured as only slowly, under the stress of compelling circumstances, reaching convictions of what awaited Him in the future; and thus He is conceived distinctly as the victim rather than as the Lord of His destiny. So far from entering the world to die, and by His death to save the world, and in His own good time and way accomplishing this great mission, He enters life set upon living, and only yields step by step reluctantly to the hard

fate which inexorably closes upon Him. That He clings through
all to His conviction of His Messiahship, and adjusts His hope
of accomplishing His Messianic mission to the overmastering
pressure of circumstances, — is that not a pathetic trait of
human nature? Do not all enthusiasts the like? Is it not precisely the mark of their fanaticism? The plain fact is, if we may
express it in the brutal frankness of common speech, in this
view of Jesus' career He miscalculated and failed; and then
naturally sought (or His followers sought for Him) to save the
failure (or the appearance of failure) by inventing a new *dénouement* for the career He had hoped for in vain, a new dénouement which — has it failed too? Most of our modern
theorizers are impelled to recognize that it too has failed. When
Jesus so painfully adjusted Himself to the hard destiny which
more and more obtruded itself upon His recognition, He taught
that death was but an incident in His career, and after death
would come the victory. Can we believe that He foresaw that
thousands of years would intervene between what He represented as but an apparent catastrophe and the glorious reversal
to which He directed His own and His followers' eyes? On the
contrary, He expected and He taught that He would come
back soon — certainly before the generation which had witnessed His apparent defeat had passed away; and that He
would then establish that Messianic Kingdom which from the
beginning of His ministry He had unvaryingly taught was at
hand. He did not do so. Is there any reason to believe that
He ever will return? Can the 'foresight' which has repeatedly
failed so miserably be trusted still, — for what we choose to
separate out from the mass of His expectations as the core of
the matter? On what grounds shall we adjust the discredited
'foresight' to the course of events, obviously unforeseen by
Him, since His death? Where is the end of these 'adjustments'? Have we not already with 'adjustment' after 'adjustment' transformed beyond recognition the expectations
of Jesus, even the latest and fullest to which He attained, and
transmuted them into something fundamentally different, —
passed, in a word, so far beyond Him, that we retain only an

artificial connexion with Him and His real teaching, a connexion mediated by little more than a word?

That in this modern construction we have the precise contradictory of the conception of Jesus and of the course of His
life on earth given us by the Evangelists, it needs no argument
to establish. In the Gospel presentation, foresight is made the
principle of our Lord's career. In the modern view He is credited
with no foresight whatever. At best, He was possessed by a
fixed conviction of His Messianic mission, whether gained in
ecstatic vision (as, e. g., O. Holtzmann) or acquired in deep
religious experiences (as, e. g., Schwartzkopff); and He felt an
assurance, based on this ineradicable conviction, that in His
own good time and way God would work that mission out for
Him; and in this assurance He went faithfully onward fulfilling
His daily task, bungling meanwhile egregiously in His reading
of the scroll of destiny which was unrolling for Him. It is an
intensely, even an exaggeratedly, human Christ which is here
offered us: and He stands, therefore, in the strongest contrast
with the frankly Divine Christ which the Gospels present to
us. On what grounds can we be expected to substitute this for
that? Certainly not on grounds of historical record. We have
no historical record of the self-consciousness of Jesus except
that embodied in the Gospel dramatization of His life and the
Gospel report of His teaching; and that record expressly contradicts at every step this modern reconstruction of its contents
and development. The very principle of the modern construction is reversal of the Gospel delineation. Its peculiarity is that,
though it calls itself the 'historical' view, it has behind it no
single scrap of historical testimony; the entirety of historical
evidence contradicts it flatly. Are we to accept it, then, on the
general grounds of inherent probability and rational construction? It is historically impossible that the great religious movement which we call Christianity could have taken its origin and
derived its inspiration — an inspiration far from spent after
two thousand years — from such a figure as this Jesus. The
plain fact is that in these modern reconstructions we have
nothing but a sustained attempt to construct a naturalistic

Jesus; and their chief interest is that they bring before us with unwonted clearness the kind of being the man must have been who at that time and in those circumstances could have come forward making the claims which Jesus made without supernatural nature, endowment, or aid to sustain Him. The value of the speculation is that it makes superabundantly clear that no such being could have occupied the place which the historical Jesus occupied; could have made the impression on His followers which the historical Jesus made; could have become the source of the stream of religious influence which we call Christianity, as the historical Jesus became. The clear formulation of the naturalistic hypothesis, in the construction of a naturalistic Jesus, in other words, throws us violently back upon the Divine Jesus of the Evangelists as the only Jesus that is historically possible. From this point of view, the labours of the scholars who have with infinite pains built up this construction of Jesus' life and development have not been in vain.

What, then, is to be said of the predictions of Jesus, and especially of the three great series of prophecies of His death, resurrection, and return, with respect to their contents and fulfilment? This is not the place to discuss the eschatology of Jesus. But a few general remarks seem not uncalled for. The topic has received of late much renewed attention with very varied results, the number and variety of constructions proposed having been greatly increased above what the inherent difficulty of the subject will account for, by the freedom with which the Scripture data have been modified or set aside on socalled critical grounds by the several investigators. Nevertheless, most of the new interpretations also may be classified under the old categories of futuristic, preteristic, and spiritualistic.

The spiritualistic interpretation — whose method of dealing with our Lord's predictions readily falls in with a widespread theory that it is 'contrary to the spirit and manner of genuine prophecy to predict actual circumstances like a soothsayer' (Muirhead, "Eschatology of Jesus," p. 10; Schwartzkopff, "Prophecies of Jesus Christ," 78, 250, 258, 275, 312, etc.) — has received a new impulse through its attractive presentation by Erich Haupt ("Eschatolog. Aussagen Jesu," etc., 1895). Christ's eschatology, says Haupt, is infinitely simple, and all that He predicts is to be accomplished in a heavenly way which passes our comprehension; there is no soothsaying in His utterances — 'nowhere any predictions of external occurrences, everywhere only great moral religious laws which must operate everywhere and always, while nothing is said of the form in which they must act' (p. 157). A considerable stir has been created also by the revival (Schleiermacher, Weisse) by Weiffenbach ("Der Wiederkunftsgedanke Jesu," 1873, "Die Frage der Wiederkunft Jesu," 1901) of the identification of the return of Christ with His resurrection, although this view has retained few adherents since its refutation by Schwartzkopff ("The Prophecies of Jesus Christ," 1895), whose own view is its exact contradictory, viz., that by His resurrection Jesus meant just His return. The general conception, however, that 'for Jesus the hope of resurrection and the thought of return fell together,' so that 'when Jesus spoke of His resurrection He was thinking of His return, and *vice versa*' (O. Holtzmann, "War Jesus Ekstatiker?" 67, note), is very widely held. The subsidiary hypothesis (first suggested by Colani) of the inclusion in the great eschatological discourse attributed by the Evangelists to our Lord of a 'little Apocalypse' of Jewish or Jewish Christian origin, by which Weiffenbach eased his task, has in more or less modified form received the widest acceptance (cf. H. J. Holtzmann, "Lehrbuch der neutestamentlichen Theologie," i. 327, note), but rests on no solid grounds (cf. Weiss, Beyschlag, Haupt, Clemen). Most adherents of the modern school are clear that Jesus expected and asserted that He would return in Messianic glory for the consummation of the Kingdom; and most of them are equally clear that in this expectation and assertion, Jesus was mistaken (cf. H. J. Holtzmann, "Lehrbuch der neutestamentlichen Theologie," i. 312 f.). 'In the expectation that the kingdom was soon to come,' says Oscar Holtzmann in a passage typical enough of this whole school of exposition ("War Jesus Ekstatiker?" p. 133), 'Jesus

erred in a human way'; and in such passages as Mk. ix. 1'
xiii. 30, Mt. x. 23 he considers that the error is obvious. He
adds, 'That such an error on the part of Jesus concerning not
a side-issue but a fundamental point of His faith, — His first
proclamation began, according to Mk. i. 15, with the πεπλή-
ρωται ὁ καιρὸς καὶ ἤγγικεν ἡ βασιλεία τοῦ θεοῦ, — does not facilitate faith in Jesus is self-evident; but this error of Jesus is for
His Church a highly instructive and therefore highly valuable
warning to distinguish between the temporary and the permanent in the work of Jesus.' Not every one even of this school
can go, however, quite this length. Even Schwartzkopff, while
allowing that Jesus erred in this matter, wishes on that very
account to think of the mere definition of times and seasons
as belonging to the form rather than to the essence of His
teaching ("The Prophecies of Jesus Christ," 1895, Eng. tr.
1897, p. 319; "Konnte Jesus irren?" 1896, p. 3); and in that
Baldensperger is in substantial agreement with him ("Selbst-
bewusstsein Jesu[1], p. 148, ed.[2], p. 205). From the other side, E.
Haupt ("Eschatolog. Aussagen Jesu," 1895, p. 138 f.) urges
that Jesus must be supposed to have been able to avoid all
errors, at least in the religious sphere, even if they concern
nothing but the form; while Weiffenbach ("Die Frage," etc.
p. 9) thinks we should hesitate to suppose Jesus could have
erred in too close a definition of the time of His advent, when
He expressly confesses that He was ignorant of its time (cf.
Muirhead, "Eschat. of Jesus," 48–50, and especially 117).
Probably Fritz Barth ("Die Hauptprobleme des Lebens Jesu,"
1899, pp. 167–170) stands alone in cutting the knot by appealing to the conditionality of all prophecy. According to him,
Jesus did, indeed, predict His return as coincident with the
destruction of Jerusalem; but all genuine prophecy is conditioned upon the conduct of the human agents involved —
'between prediction and fulfilment the conduct of man intrudes as a codetermining factor on which the fulfilment depends.' Thus this prediction has not failed, but its fulfilment
has only been postponed — in accordance, it must be confessed,
not with the will of God, but with that of man. It is difficult

to see how Jesus is thus shielded from the imputation of defective foresight; but at least Barth is able on this view still to look for a return of the Lord.

The difficulty which the passages in our Saviour's teaching under discussion present to the reverent expositor is, of course, not to be denied or minimized. But surely this difficulty would need to be much more hopeless than it is before it could compel or justify the assumption of error 'in One who has never been convicted of error in anything else' (Sanday in Hastings' *DB* ii. 635 — the whole passage should be read). The problem that faces us in this matter, it is apparent, in the meantime, is not one which can find its solution as a corollary to a speculative general view of our Lord's self-consciousness, its contents, and development. It is distinctly a problem of exegesis. We should be very sure that we know fully and precisely all that our Lord has declared about His return — its what and how and when — before we venture to suggest, even to our most intimate thought, that He has committed so gross an error as to its what and how and when as is so often assumed; especially as He has in the most solemn manner declared concerning precisely the words under consideration that heaven and earth shall pass away, but not His words. It would be sad if the passage of time has shown this declaration also to be mistaken. Meanwhile, the perfect foresight of our Lord, asserted and illustrated by all the Evangelists, certainly cannot be set aside by the facile assumption of an error on His part in a matter in which it is so difficult to demonstrate an error, and in which assumptions of all sorts are so little justified. For the detailed discussion of our Lord's eschatology, including the determination of His meaning in these utterances, reference must, however, be made to works treating expressly of this subject.

III

THE SPIRIT OF GOD IN THE OLD TESTAMENT

THE SPIRIT OF GOD IN THE OLD TESTAMENT [1]

THE doctrine of the Spirit of God is an exclusively Biblical doctrine. Rückert tells us that the idea connoted by the term is entirely foreign to Hellenism, and first came into the world through Christianity.[2] And Kleinert, in quoting this remark, adds that what is peculiarly anti-heathenish in the conception is already present in the Old Testament.[3] It would seem, then, that what is most fundamental in the Biblical doctrine of the Spirit of God is common to both Testaments.

The name meets us in the very opening verses of the Old Testament, and it appears there as unannounced and unexplained as in the opening verses of the New Testament. It is plain that it was no more a novelty in the mouth of the author of Genesis than in the mouth of the author of Matthew. But though it is common to both Testaments, it is not equally common in all parts of the Bible. It does not occur as frequently in the Old Testament as in the New. It is found as often in the Epistles of Paul as in the whole Old Testament. It is not as pervasive in the Old Testament as in the New. It fails in no New Testament book, except the three brief personal letters Philemon and II and III John. On the other hand, in only some half of the thirty-nine Old Testament books is it clearly mentioned,[4] while in as many as sixteen all definite allusion to it seems to be lacking.[5] The principle which governs the use

[1] From *The Presbyterian and Reformed Review*, v. vi, 1895, pp. 665–687.

[2] " Korinthierbriefe " i, p. 80.

[3] Article, " Zur altest. Lehre vom Geiste Gottes," in the " Jahrbb. für deutsch. Theologie " for 1867, i, p. 9.

[4] These are Genesis, Exodus, Numbers, Judges, I and II Samuel, I and II Kings, II Chronicles, Nehemiah, Job, Psalms, Isaiah, Ezekiel, Joel, Micah, Haggai, Zechariah. Deuteronomy and I Chronicles may be added, although they do not contain the explicit phrase, "the Spirit of God" or "the Spirit of Jehovah."

[5] These are Leviticus, Joshua, Ruth, Ezra, Esther, Ecclesiastes, Song of Songs, Jeremiah, Lamentations, Hosea, Amos, Obadiah, Jonah, Nahum, Habakkuk and Zephaniah. Proverbs, Daniel and Malachi may, for one reason or another, remain unclassified.

or disuse of it does not lie on the surface. Sometimes it may, perhaps, be partly due to the nature of the subject treated. But if mention of the Spirit of God fails in Leviticus, it is made in Numbers; if it fails in Joshua and Ruth, it is made in Judges and Samuel; if it fails in Ezra, it is made in Nehemiah; if it fails in Jeremiah, it is made in Isaiah and Ezekiel; if it fails in seven or eight of the minor prophets, it is made in the remaining four or five. Whether it occurs in an Old Testament book seems to depend on a number of circumstances which have little or no bearing on the history of the doctrine. We need only note that the name "Spirit of God" meets us at the very opening of revelation, and it, or its equivalents, accompanies us sporadically throughout the volume. The Pentateuch and historical books provide us with the outline of the doctrine; its richest depositories among the prophets are Isaiah and Ezekiel, from each of which alone probably the whole doctrine could be derived.[6]

In passing from the Old Testament to the New, the reader is conscious of no violent discontinuity in the conception of the Spirit which he finds in the two volumes. He may note the increased frequency with which the name appears on the printed page. But he would note this much the same in passing from the earlier to the later chapters of the *Epistle to the Romans*. He may note an increased definiteness and fulness in the conception itself. But something similar to this he would note in passing from the Pentateuch to Isaiah, or from Matthew to John or Paul. The late Professor Smeaton may have overstated the matter in his interesting Cunningham Lectures on "The Doctrine of the Holy Spirit." "We find," he says, "that the doctrine of the Spirit taught by the Baptist, by Christ and by

---

[6] "There is one writer of the Old Testament, in whom all lines and rays of this development come together, and who so stood in the matter of time and of inner manner that they had to come together in this point of unity, if the Old Testament had otherwise found such. This is Ezekiel" (Kleinert, *op. cit.* p. 45). "Isaiah has scattered throughout his prophecies allusions to the Spirit so manifold and various in express descriptions and in brief turns of phrase, that it might not be difficult to put together from his words, the complete doctrine of the Spirit" (Smeaton, "Doctrine of the Holy Spirit," p. 35).

the Apostles, was in every respect the same as that with which the Old Testament church was familiar. We nowhere find that their Jewish hearers on any occasion took exception to it. The teaching of our Lord and His Apostles never called forth a question or an opposition from any quarter — a plain proof that on this question nothing was taught by them which came into collision with the sentiments and opinions which up to that time had been accepted, and still continued to be current among the Jews." Some such change in the conception of God doubtless needs to be recognized as that which Dr. Denney describes in the following words: "The Apostles were all Jews, — men, as it has been said, with monotheism as a passion in their blood.[7] They did not cease to be monotheists when they became preachers of Christ, but they instinctively conceived God in a way in which the old revelation had not taught them to conceive him. . . . Distinctions were recognized in what had once been the bare simplicity of the Divine nature. The distinction of Father and Son was the most obvious, and it was enriched, on the basis of Christ's own teaching, and of the actual experience of the Church, by the further distinction of the Holy Spirit."[8] But if there be any fundamental difference between the Old and the New Testament conceptions of the Spirit of God, it escapes us in our ordinary reading of the Bible, and we naturally and without conscious straining read our New Testament conceptions into the Old Testament passages.

We are, indeed, bidden to do this by the New Testament itself. The New Testament writers identify their "Holy Spirit" with the "Spirit of God" of the older books. All that is attributed to the Spirit of God in the Old Testament, is attributed by them to their personal Holy Ghost. It was their own Holy Ghost who was Israel's guide and director and whom Israel rejected when they resisted the leading of God (Acts vii. 51). It was in Him that Christ (doubtless in the person of Noah) preached to the antediluvians (I Pet. iii. 18). It was He who was the author of faith of old as well as now (II Cor. iv. 13).

[7] Fairbairn, "Christ in Modern Theology," p. 377.
[8] James Denney, "Studies in Theology," p. 70.

It was He who gave Israel its ritual service (Heb. ix. 8). It was He who spoke in and through David and Isaiah and all the prophets (Matt. xxii. 43, Mark xii. 36, Acts i. 16, xxviii. 25, Heb. iii. 7, x. 15). If Zechariah (vii. 12) or Nehemiah (ix. 20) tells us that Jehovah of Hosts sent His word by His Spirit by the hands of the prophets, Peter tells us that these men from God were moved by the Holy Ghost to speak these words (II Pet. i. 21), and even that it was specifically the Spirit of Christ that was in the prophets (I Pet. i. 11). We are assured that it was in Jesus upon whom the Holy Ghost had visibly descended, that Isaiah's predictions were fulfilled that Jehovah would put His Spirit upon his righteous servant (Isa. xlii. 1) and that (Isa. lxi. 1) the Spirit of the Lord Jehovah should be upon Him (Matt. xii. 18, Luke iv. 18, 19). And Peter bids us look upon the descent of the Holy Spirit at Pentecost as the accomplished promise of Joel that God would pour out His Spirit upon all flesh (Joel ii. 27, 28, Acts ii. 16).[9] There can be no doubt that the New Testament writers identify the Holy Ghost of the New Testament with the Spirit of God of the Old.

This fact, of course, abundantly justifies the instinctive Christian identification. We are sure, with the surety of a divine revelation, that the Spirit of God of the Old Testament is the personal Holy Spirit of the New. But this assurance does not forestall the inquiry whether this personal Spirit was so fully revealed in the Old Testament that those who were dependent on that revelation alone, without the inspired commentary of the New, were able to know Him as He is known to us who enjoy the fuller light. The principle of the progressive delivery of doctrine in the age-long process of God's self-revelation, is not only a reasonable one in itself and one which is justified by the results of investigation, but it is one which is assumed in the Scriptures themselves as God's method of revealing Himself, and which received the practical endorsement of our Saviour in His manner of communicating His saving truth to men. The question is still an open one, therefore, how much of the doc-

---

[9] Cf. also the promise of Ezek. xxxvi. 27 and I Thes. iv. 8 (see Toy, "Quotations in the New Testament," p. 202). Cf. also Luke i. 17.

trine of the Holy Spirit as it lies in its completeness in the pages of the New Testament had already been made the property of the men of the old dispensation; in other words, what the Old Testament doctrine of the Spirit of God is. We may not find this inconsistent with the fuller New Testament teaching, but we may find it fall short of the whole truth revealed in the latter days in God's Son.

The deep unity between the New and Old Testament conceptions lies, in one broad circumstance, so upon the surface of the two Testaments that our attention is attracted to it at the outset of any investigation of the material. In both Testaments the Spirit of God appears distinctly as *the executive of the Godhead*. If in the New Testament God works all that He does by the Spirit, so in the Old Testament the Spirit is the name of God working. The Spirit of God is in the Old Testament the executive name of God — "the divine principle of activity everywhere at work in the world." [10] In this common conception lies doubtless the primary reason why we pass from one Testament to the other without sense of discontinuity in the doctrine of the Spirit. The further extent in which this unity may be traced will depend on the nature of the activities which are ascribed to the Spirit in both Testaments.

The Old Testament does not give us, of course, an exhaustive record of all God's activities. It is primarily an account of God's redemptive work prior to the coming of the Messiah — of the progress, in a word, so far, of the new creation of grace built upon the ruins of the first creation, a short account of which is prefixed as background and basis. In the nature of the case, we learn from the Old Testament of those activities of God only which naturally emerge in these accounts; and accordingly the doctrine of the Spirit of God as the divine principle of activity, as taught in the Old Testament, is necessarily confined to the course of divine activities in the first and the initial

[10] These words are C. F. Schmid's ("Biblical Theology of the New Testament,' Div. ii. § 24, p. 145, E. T.). Cf. Smeaton, *op. cit.* p. 36: "Events occurring in the moral government of God, are (in the Old Testament) also ascribed to the Spirit as the Executive of all the divine purposes."

stages of the second creation. In other words, it is subsumable under the two broad captions of God in the world, and God in His people. It is from this that the circumstance arises which has been frequently noted, that, after the entrance of sin into the world, the work of the Spirit of God on men's spirits is always set forth in the Old Testament in the interests and in the spirit of the kingdom of God.[11] The Old Testament is concerned after the sin of man only with the recovery of man; it traces the preparatory stages of the kingdom of God, as God laid its foundations in a chosen nation in whom all the nations of the earth were to be blessed. The segregation of Israel and the establishment of the theocracy thus mark the first steps in the new creation; and following this course of divine working, the doctrine of the Spirit in the new creation as taught in the Old Testament naturally concerns especially the activities of God in the establishment and development of the theocracy and in the preparation of a people to enjoy its blessings. In other words, it falls under the two captions of His national, or rather churchly, and of His individual work. Thus the Old Testament teaching concerning the Spirit, brings before us three spheres of His activity, which will correspond broadly to the conceptions of God in the world, God in the theocracy, and God in the soul.

Broadly speaking, these three spheres of the Spirit's activity appear successively in the pages of the Old Testament. In these pages the Spirit of God is introduced to us primarily in His cosmical, next in His theocratic, and lastly in His individual relations.[12] This is, of course, due chiefly to the natural

---

[11] Kleinert, op. cit., p. 30: "The Old Testament everywhere knows only of an influence of the Divine Spirit upon the human Spirit in the interest and sphere of the Kingdom of God, which is in Israel and is to come through Israel." Hävernick, "Theologie des alten Testaments" p. 77: "Of a communication of the Spirit in the narrower sense, after the entrance of sin, there can be question only in the Theocracy." Oehler, "Biblical Theology of the Old Testament," § 65: "But the Spirit as רוּחַ יְהוָֹה, or to express it more definitely רוּחַ קֹדֶשׁ יְהוָה only acts within the sphere of revelation. It rules within the Theocracy."

[12] For example, in the Pentateuch His working is perhaps exclusively cosmical and theocratic-official, (Oehler, op. cit. § 65); while His ethical work in individuals, is throughout the Old Testament, more a matter of prophecy than of present enjoyment (Dale, "Christian Doctrine," p. 317).

correspondence of the aspects of His activity which are presented with the course of history, and is not to be taken so strictly as to imply that the revelations relative to each sphere of His working occur exclusively in a single portion of the Old Testament. It supplies us, however, not only with the broad outlines of the historical development of the doctrine of the Spirit in the Old Testament, but also with a logical order of presentation for the material. Perhaps we may also say, in passing, that it suggests a course of development of the doctrine of the Spirit which is at once most natural and, indeed, rationally inevitable, and, as Dr. Dale points out,[13] closely correspondent with what have come to be spoken of as the "traditional" dates attributed to the books of the Old Testament. These books, standing as they stand in this dating, are in the most natural order for the development of this doctrine.

THE COSMICAL SPIRIT

I. The Spirit of God is first brought before us in the Old Testament, then, in His relations to the first creation, or in what may be called his cosmical relations. In this connection He is represented as the source of all order, life and light in the universe. He is the divine principle of all movement, of all life and of all thought in the world. The basis of this conception is already firmly laid in the first passage in which the Spirit of God is mentioned (Gen. i. 2). In the beginning, we are told, God created the heavens and the earth. And then the process is detailed by which the created earth, at first waste and void, with darkness resting upon the face of the deep, was transformed by successive fiats into the ordered and populous world in which we live. As the ground of the whole process, we are informed that "the Spirit of God was brooding upon the face of the waters," as much as to say that the obedience, and the precedent power of obedience, of the waste of waters to the successive creative words — as God said, Let there be light; Let

---

[13] Dale, "Christian Doctrine," p. 318. A striking passage both for its presentation of this fact and for its unwillingness to accept its implications.

there be a firmament; Let the waters bo gathered together; Let the waters and the earth bring forth — depended upon the fact that the Spirit of God was already brooding upon the formless void. To the voice of God in heaven saying, Let there be light! the energy of the Spirit of God brooding upon the face of the waters responded, and lo! there was light. Over against the transcendent God, above creation, there seems to be postulated here God brooding upon creation, and the suggestion seems to be that it is only by virtue of God brooding upon creation that the created thing moves and acts and works out the will of God. The Spirit of God, in a word, appears at the very opening of the Bible as God immanent; and, as such, is set over against God transcendent. And it is certainly very instructive to observe that God is conceived as immanent already in what may be called the formless world-stuff which by His immanence in it alone it constituted a stuff from which on the divine command an ordered world may emerge.[14] The Spirit of God thus appears from the outset of the Old Testament as the principle of the very existence and persistence of all things, and as the source and originating cause of all movement and order and life. God's thought and will and word take effect in the world, because God is not only over the world, thinking and willing and commanding, but also in the world, as the principle of all activity, *executing:* this seems the thought of the author of the Biblical cosmogony.[15]

[14] Cf. Schultz, "Old Testament Theology," E. T. ii, 184: "Over the lifeless and formless mass of the world-matter this Spirit broods like a bird on its nest, and thus transmits to it the seeds of life, so that afterwards by the word of God it can produce whatever God wills."

[15] Compare some very instructive words as to this account of creation, by the Rev. John Robson, D.D. of Aberdeen (*The Expository Times*, July, 1894, vol. v. No. 10, pp. 467, *sq.*): "The divine agents in creation are brought before us in the opening of the Book of Genesis, and in the opening of the Gospel of John. The object of John in his Gospel is to speak of Jesus Christ, the Word of God; and so he refers only to His agency in the work of creation. The object of Moses in Genesis is to tell the whole divine agency in that work; so in his narrative we have the work of the Spirit recognized. But he does not ignore the Word of God; he begins his account of each epoch or each day of creation with the words, 'And God said.' We do not find in Genesis the theological fulness that we do in subsequent writers in the Bible; but we do find in it the elements of all that we subse-

A series of Old Testament passages range themselves under this conception and carry it forward. It is by the Spirit of God, says Job, that the heavens are garnished (xxvi. 13). Isaiah compares the coming of the God of vengeance, repaying fury to His adversaries and recompense to His enemies, to the bursting forth "of a pent-in stream which the Spirit of Jehovah driveth" (lix. 19); and represents the perishing of flesh as like the withering of the grass and the fading of the flower when "the Spirit of Jehovah bloweth upon it" (xl. 7). In such passages the Spirit appears as the principle of cosmical processes. He is also the source of all life, and, as such, the executor of Him with whom, as the Psalmist says, is the fountain of life (Ps. xxxvi. 10 [9]). The Psalmist accordingly ascribes the being of all creatures to Him: "Thou sendest forth thy Spirit, they are created" (Ps. civ. 30). "The Spirit of God hath made me," declares Job, "and the breath of the Almighty giveth me life" (xxxiii. 4). Accordingly he represents life to be due to the persistence of the Spirit of God in his nostrils (xxvii. 3), and therefore its continuance to be dependent upon the continuance of the Spirit with man: "If He set His heart upon man, if He gather unto Himself His Spirit and His breath all flesh shall perish together, and man shall turn again unto dust" (xxxiv. 14, 15, cf. xii. 10). He is also the source of all intellectual life. Elihu tells us that it is not greatness, nor years, but the Spirit of God that gives understanding: "There is a Spirit in man, and the breath of the Almighty giveth them understanding" (Job xxxii. 8) — a thought which is probably only expressed in another way in Prov. xx. 27, which declares that the spirit of man is "the lamp of the Lord, searching all the innermost parts of the belly." That the Spirit is the source also of all ethical life seems to follow from the obscure passage, Genesis vi. 3: "And the Lord said, My Spirit shall not strive with man for ever, for that he

quently learn or deduce regarding the divine agency in creation. . . . Two agents are mentioned: 'The Spirit of God brooding on the surface of the waters,' and at each new stage of creative development, the Word of God expressed in the words 'God said.' . . . There is thus the Spirit of God present as a constant energy, and there is the Word of God giving form to that energy, and at each new epoch calling new forms into being."

also is flesh." Apparently there is here either a direct threat
from Jehovah to withdraw that Spirit by virtue of which alone
morality could exist in the world, or else a threat that He will,
on account of their sin, withdraw the Spirit whose presence
gives life so that men may no longer be upheld in their wicked
existence, but may sink back into nothingness. In either case
ethical considerations come forward prominently, — the occasion of the destruction of mankind is an ethical one, and the
gift of life appears as for ethical ends. This, however, is an element in the conception of the Spirit's work which comes to
clear enunciation only in another connection.

It would not be easy to overestimate the importance of the
early emergence of this doctrine of the immanent Spirit of God,
side by side with the high doctrine of the transcendence of God
which pervades the Old Testament. Whatever tendency the
emphasis on the transcendence of God might engender towards
Deistic conceptions would be corrected at once by such teaching as to the immanent Spirit; while in turn any tendencies to
Pantheistic or Cosmotheistic conceptions which it might itself
arouse would be corrected not only by the prevailing stress
upon the divine transcendence, but also by the manner in
which the immanence of God is itself presented. For we cannot
sufficiently admire the perfection with which, in delivering the
doctrine of the immanent Spirit, all possibility is excluded of
conceiving of God as entangled in creation — as if the Spirit
of God were merely the physical world-spirit, the proper
ground rather than effecting cause of cosmical activities. In
the very phraseology of Genesis i. 2, for example, the moving
Spirit is kept separate from the matter to which He gives movement; He *broods over* rather than is merged in the waste of
waters; He acts upon them and cannot be confounded with
them as but another name for their own blind surging. So in the
104th Psalm (verses 29, 30) the creative Spirit is *sent forth* by
God, and is not merely an alternative name for the unconscious
life-ground of nature. It is a thing which is *given* by God and
so produces life (Isa. xlii. 5). Though penetrating all things (Ps.
cxxxix. 7) and the immanent source of all life-activities (Ps.

civ. 30), it is nevertheless always the *personal* cause of physical, psychical and ethical activities. It exercises choice. It is not merely the *general* ground of all such activities; it is the determiner as well of all the *differences* that exist among men. So, for example, Elihu appeals to the Spirit of understanding that is in him (Job xxxii. 8). It is not merely the ground of the *presence* of these powers; it is also to it that their *withdrawal* is to be ascribed (Isa. xl. 7, Gen. vi. 3). Nor are its manifestations confined altogether to what may be called *natural* modes of action; room is left among them for what we may call truly *supernatural* activity (I Kgs. xviii. 12, II Kgs. ii. 16, cf. II Kgs. xix. 7, Isa. xxxvii. 7). All nature worship is further excluded by the clearness of the identification of the Spirit of God with the God over all. Thus the unity of God was not only preserved but emphasized, and men were taught to look upon the emergence of divine powers and effects in nature as the work of His hands. "Whither shall I go," asks the Psalmist, "from thy Spirit? or whither shall I flee from thy presence" (Ps. cxxxix. 7)? Here the spiritual presence of God is obviously the presence of the God over all in His Spirit. "Who hath . . . meted out heaven with a span? . . . Who hath meted out the Spirit of Jehovah, or being his counsellor hath taught him?" asks Isaiah (xl. 12, 13) in the same spirit. Obviously the Spirit of God was not conceived as the impersonal ground of life and understanding, but as the personal source of all that was of being, life and light in the world, not as apart from but as one with the great God Almighty in the heavens. And yet, as immanent in the world, He is set over against God transcendent in a manner which prepares the way for His hypostatizing and so for the Christian doctrine of the Trinity.

It requires little consideration to realize how greatly the Old Testament conception of God is enriched by this teaching. In particular, it behooves us to note how, side by side with the emphasis that is laid upon God as the maker of all things, this doctrine lays an equal emphasis on God as the upholder and governor of all things. Side by side with the emphasis which is laid on the unapproachable majesty of God as the transcendent

Person, it lays an equal emphasis on God as the immanent agent in all world changes and all world movements. It thus lays firmly the foundation of the Christian doctrine of Providence — God in the world and in history, leading all things to their destined goal. If without God there was not anything made that has been made, so without God's Spirit there has not anything occurred that has occurred.

The Theocratic Spirit

II. All this is still further emphasized in the second and predominant aspect in which the Spirit of God is brought before us in the Old Testament, viz., in His relations to the second creation.

1. Here, primarily, He is presented as the source of all the supernatural powers and activities which are directed to the foundation and preservation and development of the kingdom of God in the midst of the wicked world. He is thus represented as the theocratic Spirit as pointedly as He is represented as the world-spirit. We are moving here in a distinctly supernatural atmosphere and the activities which come under review belong to an entirely supernatural order. There are a great variety of these activities, but they have this in common: they are all endowments of the theocratic organs with the gifts requisite for the fulfilment of their functions.[16]

There are, for example, the supernatural gifts of strength, resolution, energy, courage in battle which were awakened in chosen leaders for the service of God's people. Thus we are told that the Spirit of Jehovah came upon Othniel to fit him for his work as judge of Israel (Judg. iii. 10), and clothed itself

[16] Oehler, "Old Testament Theology," § 65: "But the Spirit as רוּחַ יְהוָֹה, or to express it more definitely רוּחַ קֹדֶשׁ יְהוָֹה, only acts within *the sphere of revelation*. It rules within the theocracy (Isa. lxiii. 11, Hag. ii. 5, Neh. ix. 20) but not as if all citizens of the Old Testament Theocracy as such participated in this Spirit, which Moses expresses as a wish (Num. xi. 29), but which is reserved for the future community of salvation (John iii. 1). In the Old Testament the Spirit's work in the divine kingdom is rather that of *endowing the organs of the theocracy with the gifts required for their calling*, and those gifts of office in the Old Testament are similar to the gifts of grace in the New Testament, I Cor. xii. ff."

with Gideon (vi. 34), and came upon Jephthah (xi. 29), and, most remarkably of all, came mightily upon and moved Samson, endowing him with superhuman strength (xiii. 25, xiv. 6, 19, xv. 14). Similarly the Spirit of God came mightily upon Saul (I Sam. xi. 6) and upon David (I Sam. xvi. 13), and clothed Amasai (I Chron. xii. 18). Then, there are the supernatural gifts of skill by which artificers were fitted to serve the kingdom of God in preparing a worthy sanctuary for the worship of the King. There were, for instance, those whom Jehovah had filled with the spirit of wisdom and who were, therefore, wise-hearted to make Aaron's sacred garments (Ex. xxviii. 3). And especially we are told that Jehovah had filled Bezalel "with the Spirit of God, in wisdom and in understanding, and in knowledge, and in all manner of workmanship, to devise cunning works, to work in gold, and in silver, and in brass, and in cutting of stones for setting, and in carving of wood, to work in all manner of workmanship" (Ex. xxxi. 3 f. cf. xxxv. 31): — and that he should therefore preside over the work of the wise-hearted, in whom the Lord had put wisdom, for the making of the tabernacle and its furniture. Similarly when the temple came to be built, the pattern of it, we are told, was given of Jehovah "by his Spirit" to David (I Chron. xxviii. 12). Quite near to these gifts, but on a higher plane, lies the supernatural gift of wisdom for the administration of judgment and government. Moses was so endowed. And, therefore, the seventy elders were also endowed with it, to fit them to share his cares: "And I will take of the Spirit which is upon thee," said Jehovah, "and will put it upon them; and they shall bear the burden of the people with thee" (Num. xi. 17, 25).[17] It is in this sense also, doubtless, that Joshua is said to have been full of the Spirit of wisdom (Num. xxvii. 18, Deut. xxxiv. 9).[18] In these aspects, the gift of the Spirit, appearing as it does as an endowment for office, is sometimes sacramentally con-

[17] The idea of communicating to others the Spirit already resting on one occurs again in II Kings ii. 9, 15, of the communication of Elijah's Spirit (of Prophecy) to Elisha. Cf. Oehler, "Biblical Theology of the Old Testament," § 65.
[18] Cf. the prayer and endowment of Solomon, in I Kgs. iii.

nected with symbols of conference: in the case of Joshua with the laying on of hands (Deut. xxxiv. 9), in the cases of Saul and David with anointing (I Sam. x. 1, xvi. 13). Possibly its symbolical connection in Samson's case with Nazaritic length of hair may be classed in the same general category.

Prominent above all other theocratic gifts of the Spirit, however, are the gifts of supernatural knowledge and insight, culminating in the great gift of Prophecy. This greatest of gifts in the service of the Kingdom of God is sometimes very closely connected with the other gifts which have been mentioned. Thus the presence of the Spirit in the seventy elders in the wilderness, endowing them to share the burden of judgment with Moses, was manifested by prophetic utterance (Num. xi. 25). The descent of the Spirit upon Saul was likewise manifested by his prophesying (I Sam. x. 6, 10). Sometimes the Spirit's presence in the prophet even manifests itself in the production in others of what may be called sympathetic prophecy accompanied with ecstasy. Instances occur in the cases of the messengers sent by Saul and of Saul himself, when they went to apprehend David (I Sam. xix. 20, 23); and in these cases the phenomenon served the ulterior purpose of a protection for the prophets.[19] In the visions of Ezekiel the presence of the inspiring Spirit is manifested in physical as well as in mental effects (Ezek. iii. 12, 14, 24, viii. 3, xi. 1, 5, 24, xxxvii. 1). Thus clear it is that all these work one and the same Spirit.

In all cases, however, Prophecy is the free gift of the Spirit of God to special organs chosen for the purpose of the revelation of His will. It is so represented in the cases of Balaam (Num. xxiv. 2), of Saul (I Sam. x. 6), of David (I Sam. xvi. 13), of Azariah the son of Oded (II Chron. xv. 1), of Jahaziel the son of Zechariah (II Chron. xx. 14), of Zechariah the son of Jehoiada (II Chron. xxiv. 20). To Hosea, "the man that hath the Spirit" was a synonym for "prophet" (ix. 7). Isaiah (xlviii. 16) in a somewhat puzzling sentence declares, "The Lord God hath sent me and His Spirit," which seems to con-

---

[19] Compare the cases of the communication of the Spirit, in a different way, in Num. xi. 17, 25, 26 and II Kgs. ii. 9, 15 — already mentioned.

join the Spirit either with Jehovah as the source of the mission, or else with the prophet as the bearer of the message; and, in either case, refers the prophetic inspiration to the Spirit. A very full insight into the nature of the Spirit's work in prophetic inspiration is provided by the details which Ezekiel gives of the Spirit's mode of dealing with him in communicating his visions. While the richness of the prophetic endowment is indicated to us by Micah (iii. 8): "But I truly am full of power by the Spirit of the Lord, and of judgment, and of might, to declare unto Jacob his transgression, and to Israel his sin." There are, however, two passages that speak quite generally of the whole body of prophets as Spirit-led men, which, in their brief explicitness, deserve to be called the classical passages as to prophetic inspiration. In one of these, — the great psalm-prayer of the Levites recorded in the ninth chapter of Nehemiah, — God is first lauded for "giving His good Spirit to instruct" His people, by the mouth of Moses; and then further praised for enduring this people through so many years and "testifying against them by His Spirit through His prophets" (Neh. ix. 20, 30). Here the prophets are conceived as a body of official messengers, through whom the Spirit of God made known His will to His people through all the ages. In exactly similar wise, Zechariah testifies that the Lord of Hosts had sent His words "by His Spirit by the hand of the former prophets" (Zech. vii. 12). These are quite comprehensive statements. They include the whole series of the prophets, and they represent them as the official mouthpieces of the Spirit of God, serving the people of God as His organs.[20]

It is sufficiently clear that an official character attaches to all the manifestations of what we have called the theocratic Spirit. The theocratic Spirit appears to be represented as the executive of the Godhead within the sacred nation, the divine power working in the nation for the protection, governing, instruction and leading of the people to its destined goal. The

---

[20] In such passages as Gen. xli. 38, Dan. iv. 8, ix. 18 and v. 11, 14, we have "the Spirit of the Gods" as the equivalent of "the Spirit of God" on the lips of heathen.

Levitic prayer in the ninth chapter of Nehemiah traces the history of God's people with great fulness; and all through this history represents God as not only looking down from heaven upon His people, leading them, but, as it were, working within them, inspiring organs for their government and instruction. — "clothing Himself with these" organs as the media of His working, as the expressive Hebrew sometimes suggests (Judges vi. 34, I Chron. xii. 18, II Chron. xxiv. 20). The aspect in which the theocratic Spirit seems to be conceived is as God in His people, manifesting Himself through inspired instruments in supernatural leading and teaching. Very illuminating as to the mode of His working are the instructions given to Zerubbabel through the prophets Zechariah and Haggai. He — and, with him, all the people of the land — is counseled to be strong and of good courage, "for I am with you, saith the Lord of Hosts, according to the word that I covenanted with you when you came out of Egypt, and my Spirit abideth among you: fear ye not" (Hag. ii. 5). "This is the word of the Lord unto Zerubbabel, saying, Not by might, nor by power, but by my Spirit, saith the Lord of Hosts" (Zech. iv. 6). The mountains of opposition are to be reduced to a plain; but not by armed force. The symbol of the source of strength is the seven lamps burning brightly by virtue of perennial supplies from the living olives growing by their side; thus, by a hidden, divine supply of deathless life, the Church of God lives and prospers in the world. Not indeed as if God so inhabited Israel, that all that the house of Israel does is of the Lord. "Shall it be said, O house of Israel, Is the Spirit of the Lord straitened? — are these his doings? Do not my words do good to him that walketh uprightly?" (Micah ii. 7). The gift of the Spirit is only for good. But there is very clearly brought before us here the fact and the mode of God's official inspiration. The theocratic Spirit represents, in a word, the presence of God with His people. And in the Old Testament teaching concerning it, is firmly laid the foundation of the Christian doctrine of God in the Church, leading and guiding it, and supplying it with all needed instruction, powers and graces for its preservation in the world.

We must not omit to observe that in this higher sphere of the theocratic Spirit, the freedom and, so to speak, detachment of the informing Spirit is even more thoroughly guarded than in the case of His cosmical relations. If in the lower sphere the Spirit hovered over rather than was submerged in matter, so here He acts upon His chosen organs in the same sense from without, so that it is impossible to confound His official gifts with their native powers, however exalted. The Spirit here, too, is given by God (Num. xi. 29, Isa. xlii. 1). God puts it on men or fills men with it (Num. xi. 25, Ex. xxviii. 3, xxxi. 3); or the Spirit comes (Jud. iii. 10, xi. 29), comes mightily (xiv. 6, 19, etc., I Sam. xi. 6) upon men, falls on them (Ezek. xi. 5), breaks in upon them, seizes them violently, as it were, and puts them on as a garment (Judg. vi. 34). And this is no less true of the prophets than of the other organs of the Spirit's theocratic work: they are all the instruments of a mighty power, which, though in one sense it is conceived as the endowment of the theocratic people, in another sense is conceived as seizing upon its organs from without and above. And "because it is thus fundamentally a power seizing man powerfully, often violently," it is often replaced by the locution, "the hand of Jehovah," [21] which is, in this usage, the equivalent of the Spirit of Jehovah (II Kgs. iii. 15, Ezek. i. 3, iii. 14, 22, xxxiii. 22, xxxvii. 1, xl. 1). The intermittent character of the theocratic gifts still further emphasized their gift by a personal Spirit working purposively. They were not permanent possessions of the theocratic organs, to be used according to their own will, but came and went according to the divine gift.[22] The theocratic gifts of the Spirit are, in a word, everywhere emphatically gifts *from* God as well as *of* God; and every tendency to conceive of them as formally the

[21] Cf. Orelli, "The Old Testament Prophecy," etc., E. T. p. 11, and also Oehler, "Biblical Theology of Old Testament," § 65 *ad fin.*

[22] Cf. A. B. Davidson, (*The Expositor*, July, 1895, p. 1): "The view that prevailed among the people — and it seems the view of the Old Testament writers themselves — appears to have been this: the prophet did not speak out of a general inspiration of Jehovah, bestowed upon him once for all, as, say, at his call; each particular word that he spoke, whether a prediction or a practical counsel, was due to a special inspiration, exerted on him for the occasion." The statement might well have been stronger.

result of a general inspiration of the nation instead of a special inspiration of the chosen organs is rebuked by every allusion to them. God working in and through man, by whatever variety of inspiration, works divinely and from above. He is no more merged in His church than in the creation, but is, in all His operations alike, the free, transcendent Spirit, dividing to each man severally as He will.

The representations concerning the official theocratic Spirit culminate in Isaiah's prophetic descriptions of the Spirit-endowed Messiah:

"And there shall come forth a shoot out of the stock of Jesse, and a branch out of his roots shall bear fruit: and the Spirit of the Lord shall rest upon him, the Spirit of wisdom and understanding, the Spirit of counsel and might, the Spirit of knowledge and of the fear of the Lord; and his delight shall be in the fear of the Lord: and he shall not judge after the sight of his eyes, neither reprove after the hearing of his ears: but with righteousness shall he judge the poor, and reprove with equity for the meek of the earth: and he shall smite the earth with the rod of his mouth, and with the breath of his lips shall he slay the wicked. And righteousness shall be the girdle of his loins, and faithfulness the girdle of his reins" (Isa. xi. 1 sq.).

"Behold my servant whom I uphold; my chosen in whom my soul delighteth: I have put my Spirit upon him; he shall bring forth judgment to the Gentiles. . . . He shall bring forth judgment in truth. He shall not fail nor be discouraged, till he have set judgment in the earth; and the isles shall wait for his law. Thus saith God the Lord, he that created the heavens, and stretched them forth; he that spread abroad the earth and that which cometh out of it; he that giveth breath unto the people upon it and Spirit to them that walk therein; I the LORD have called thee in righteousness, and will hold thine hand and will keep thee, and give thee for a covenant of the people, for a light of the Gentiles; to open the blind eyes, to bring out the prisoners from the dungeon, and them that sit in darkness out of the prison-house. I am the Lord: that is my name: and my glory will I not give to another, neither my praise unto graven images" (Isa. xlii. 1 sq.).

"The Spirit of the Lord God is upon me" — this is the response of the Messiah to such gracious promises — "because the Lord hath anointed me to preach good-tidings unto the meek; he hath sent me to bind up the broken hearted, to proclaim liberty to the captives, and the opening of the prison to them that are bound; to proclaim the acceptable year of the Lord, and the day of vengeance of our God; to comfort all that mourn; to appoint unto them that mourn in Zion, to give unto them a garland for ashes, the oil of gladness for mourning, the garment of praise for the spirit of heaviness; that they might be called trees of righteousness, the planting of the Lord, that he might be glorified" (Isa. lxi. 1 *sq.*).

No one will fail to observe in these beautiful descriptions of the endowments of the Messiah, how all the theocratic endowments which had been given separately to others unite upon Him; so that all previous organs of the Spirit appear but as partial types of Him to whom as we are told in the New Testament, God "giveth not the Spirit by measure" (John iii. 34). Here we perceive the difference between the Messiah and other recipients of the Spirit. To them the Spirit had been "meted out" (Isa. xl. 13), according to their place and function in the development of the kingdom of God; upon Him it was poured out without measure. By Him, accordingly, the kingdom of God is consummated. The descriptions of the spiritual endowments of the Messiah are descriptions also, as will no doubt have been noted, of the consummated kingdom of God. His endowment also was not for himself but for the kingdom; it, too, was official. Nevertheless, it was the source in Him of all personal graces also, the opulence and perfection of which are fully described. And thus He becomes the type not only of the theocratic work of the Spirit, but also of His work upon the individual soul, perfecting it after the image of God.

THE INDIVIDUAL SPIRIT

2. And this brings us naturally to the second aspect in which the Spirit is presented to us in relation to the new creation — His relation to the individual soul, working inwardly in the spirits of men, fitting the children of God for the kingdom of God, even as, working in the nation as such, He, as theocratic Spirit, was preparing God's kingdom for His people. In this

aspect He appears specifically as the Spirit of grace. As He is
the source of all cosmical life, and of all theocratic life, so is
He also the source of all spiritual life. He upholds the soul in
being and governs it as part of the great world He has created;
He makes it sharer in the theocratic blessings which He brings
to His people; but He deals with it, too, within, conforming it
to its ideal. In a word, the Spirit of God, in the Old Testament,
is not merely the immanent Spirit, the source of all the world's
life and all the world's movement; and not merely the inspiring
Spirit, the source of His church's strength and safety and of its
development in accordance with its special mission; He is as
well the indwelling Spirit of holiness in the hearts of God's
children. As Hermann Schultz puts it: "The mysterious impulses which enable a man to lead a life well-pleasing to God,
are not regarded as a development of human environment, but
are nothing else than 'the Spirit of God.' which is also called
as being the Spirit peculiarly God's — His Holy Spirit." [23]

We have already had occasion to note that these personal
effects of the Spirit's work are sometimes very closely connected
with others of His operations. Already as the immanent Spirit
of life, indeed, as we saw, there did not lack a connection of
His activity with ethical considerations (Gen. vi. 3). We will
remember, too, that Nehemiah recalls the goodness — i.e., possibly the graciousness — of the Spirit, when He came to instruct Israel in the person of Moses in the wilderness: "Thou
gavest also thy good Spirit to instruct them" (Neh. ix. 20).[24]
When the Spirit came upon Saul, endowing him for his theocratic work, it is represented as having also a very far-reaching
personal effect upon him. "The Spirit of the Lord will come
mightily upon thee," says Samuel, "and thou shalt prophesy
with them, and shalt be turned into another man" (I Sam. x. 6).
"And it was so" adds the narrative, "that when he had turned
his back to go from Samuel, God gave him a new heart," or,

[23] *Op. cit.* ii, p. 203. The passage is cited for its main idea: we demur, of course,
to some of its implications.

[24] In Num. xiv. 24 we are told that Caleb followed the LORD fully, "because
he had another spirit in him," from that which animated his rebellious fellows.
Possibly the Spirit of the Lord may be intended.

as the Hebrew has it, "turned him a new heart." Possibly such revolutionary ethical consequences ordinarily attended the official gift of the Spirit, so that the gloss may be a true one which makes II Peter i. 21 declare that they were "holy men of God" who spake as they were moved by the Holy Ghost.[25]

At all events this conception of a thorough ethical change characterises the Old Testament idea of the inner work of the Spirit of Holiness, as He first comes to be called in the Psalms and Isaiah (Ps. li. 11; Isa. lxiii. 10, 11 only).[26] The classical passage in this connection is the Fifty-first Psalm — David's cry of penitence and prayer for mercy after Nathan's probing of his sin with Bathsheba. He prays for the creation within him of a new heart and the renewal of a right spirit within him; and he represents that all his hopes of continued power of new life rest on the continuance of God's holy Spirit, or of the Spirit of God's holiness, with him. Possibly the Spirit is here called holy, primarily, because He is one who cannot dwell in a wicked heart; but it seems also to be implicated that David looks upon Him as the author within him of that holiness without which he cannot hope to see the Lord. A like conception meets us in another Psalm ascribed to David, the One Hundred and Forty-third "Teach me to do thy will; for thou art my God: thy Spirit is good; lead me in the land of uprightness." The two conceptions of the divine grace and holiness are also combined by Isaiah in an account of how Israel had been, since the days of Moses, dealing ungratefully with God, and, by their rebellion, grieving "the Holy Spirit whom He had graciously put in

---

[25] Exceptions are found, of course; such as the cases of Balaam, Samson, etc. Cf. H. G. Mitchell, "Inspiration in the Old Testament," in *Christian Thought* for December 1893, p. 190.

[26] Cf. F. H. Woods, in *The Expository Times*, July, 1895, p. 462–463: "It may be extremely difficult to say what was the precise meaning which prophet or psalmist attached to the phrases, 'the Spirit of God' and 'the Spirit of Holiness.' But such language, at any rate, shows that they realised the divine character of that inward power which makes for holiness and truth. 'Cast me not away from Thy presence, and take not the Spirit of Thy holiness from me' (Ps. li. 11). 'And now the Lord God hath sent me, and His Spirit' (Isa. xlviii. 16). 'Not by might, nor by power, but by My Spirit, saith Jehovah of Hosts' (Zech. iv. 6). In such passages as these we can see the germ of the fuller Christian thought."

the midst of them" (Isa. lxiii. 10, 11).[27] The conception may primarily be that the Spirit given to guide Israel was a Spirit of holiness in the sense that He could not brook sin in those with whom He dealt, but the conception that He would guide them in ways of holiness underlies that.

This aspect of the work of the Spirit of God is most richly developed, however, in prophecies of the future. In the Messianic times, Isaiah tells us, the Spirit shall be poured out from on high with the effect that judgment shall dwell in the wilderness and righteousness shall abide in the peaceful field (Isa. xxxii. 15). It is in such descriptions of the Messianic era as a time of the reign of the Spirit in the hearts of the people, that the opulence of His saving influences is developed. It is He who shall gather the children of God into the kingdom, so that no one shall be missing (Isa. xxxiv. 16). It is He who, as the source of all blessings, shall be poured out on the seed with the result that it shall spring up in the luxuriant growth and bear such rich fruitage that one shall cry 'I am the Lord's,' and another shall call himself by the name of Jacob, and another shall write on his hand, 'Unto the Lord,' and shall surname himself by the name of Israel (Isa. xliv. 3 *sq.*). It is His abiding presence which constitutes the preëminent blessing of the new covenant which Jehovah makes with His people in the day of redemption: "And as for me, this is my covenant with them, saith the Lord: my Spirit that is upon thee, and my words which I have put in thy mouth, shall not depart out of thy mouth, nor out of the mouth of thy seed, nor out of the mouth of thy seed's seed, saith the Lord, from henceforth and for ever" (Isa. lix. 21). The gift of the Spirit as an abiding presence in the heart of the individual is the crowning Messianic blessing. To precisely the same effect is the teaching of Ezekiel. The new heart and new spirit is one of the burdens of his message (xi. 19, xviii. 31, xxxvi. 26): and these are the Messianic gifts of God to His people through the Spirit. God's people are dead; but He will open their graves and cause them to come up out of their graves: "And I will put my Spirit in you, and ye

[27] Cf. Psalm cvi. 13.

shall live" (xxxvii. 14). They are in captivity; he will bring them out of captivity: "Neither will I hide my face any more from them: for I have poured out my Spirit upon the house of Israel, saith the Lord God" (xxxix. 29). Like promises appear in Zechariah: "And I will pour upon the house of David, and upon the inhabitants of Jerusalem, the Spirit of grace and supplication; and they shall look upon me whom they have pierced" (xii. 10). It is the converting Spirit of God that is spoken of. One thing only is left to complete the picture, — the clear declaration that, in these coming days of blessing, the Spirit hitherto given only to Israel shall be poured out upon the whole world. This Joel gives us in that wonderful passage which is applied by Peter to the out-pouring begun at Pentecost: "And it shall come to pass afterward," says the Lord God through His prophet, "that I will pour out my Spirit upon all flesh; . . . and also upon the servants and upon the handmaids in those days will I pour out my Spirit. . . . And it shall come to pass, that whosoever shall call on the name of the Lord shall be delivered" (ii. 28–32).

In this series of passages, the indwelling Spirit of the New Testament is obviously brought before us — the indwelling God, author of all holiness and of all salvation. Thus there are firmly laid by them the foundations of the Christian doctrine of Regeneration and Sanctification, — of God in the soul quickening its powers of spiritual life and developing it in holiness. Nor can it be a ground of wonder that this aspect of His work is less frequently dwelt upon than His theocratic activities; nor that it is chiefly in prophecies of the future that the richer references to it occur.[28] This was the time of theocratic development; the old dispensation was a time of preparation for the fulness of spiritual graces. It is rather a ground of wonder that even in few and scattered hints and in prophecies of the times of the Spirit yet to come, such a deep and thorough grasp upon His individual work should be exhibited.

By its presentation of this work of the Spirit in the heart,

[28] See such wonder, nevertheless, expressed by Dr. Dale, in a striking passage in his "Christian Doctrine," p. 317.

the Old Testament completes its conception of the Spirit of God — the great conception of the immanent, inspiring, indwelling God. In it the three great ideas are thrown prominently forward, of God in the world, God in the Church, God in the soul: the God of Providence, the immanent source of all that comes to pass, the director and governor of the world of matter and spirit alike; the God of the Church, the inspiring source of all Church life and of all Church gifts, through which the Church is instructed, governed, preserved and extended; and the God of grace, the indwelling source of all holiness and of all religious aspirations, emotions and activities. Attention has already been called to the great enrichment which was brought to the general conception of God by this doctrine of the Spirit of God in its first aspect. The additional aspects in which He is presented in the pages of the Old Testament of course still further enrich and elevate the conception. By throwing a still stronger emphasis on the personality of the Spirit they made even wider the great gulf that already yawned between all Pantheising notions and the Biblical doctrine of the Personal God, the immanent source of all that comes to pass. And they bring out with great force and clearness the conceptions of grace and holiness as inherent in the idea of God working, and thus operate to deepen the ethical conception of the Divine Being. It is only as a personal, choosing, gracious and holy God, who bears His people on His heart for good, and who seeks to conform them in life and character to His own holiness — that we can conceive the God of the Old Testament, if we will attend to its doctrine of the Spirit. Thus the fundamental unity of the conception with that of the Holy Ghost of the New Testament grows ever more obvious, the more attentively it is considered. The Spirit of God of the Old Testament performs all the functions which are ascribed to the Holy Ghost of the New Testament, and bears all the same characteristics. They are conceived alike both in their nature and in their operations. We cannot help identifying them.

Such an identification need not involve, however, the assertion that the Spirit of God was conceived in the Old Testament as the Holy Ghost is in the New, as a distinct hypostasis in the divine nature. Whether this be so, or, if so in some measure, how far it may be true, is a matter for separate investigation. The Spirit of God certainly acts as a person and is presented to us as a person, throughout the Old Testament. In no passage is He conceived otherwise than personally — as a free, willing, intelligent being. This is, however, in itself only the pervasive testimony of the Scriptures to the personality of God. For it is equally true that the Spirit of God is everywhere in the Old Testament identified with God. This is only its pervasive testimony to the divine unity. The question for examination is, how far the one personal God was conceived of as embracing in His unity hypostatical distinctions. This question is a very complicated one and needs very delicate treatment. There are, indeed, three questions included in the general one, which for the sake of clearness we ought to keep apart. We may ask, May the Christian properly see in the Spirit of God of the Old Testament the personal Holy Spirit of the New? This we may answer at once in the affirmative. We may ask again, Are there any hints in the Old Testament anticipating and adumbrating the revelation of the hypostatic Spirit of the New? This also, it seems, we ought to answer in the affirmative. We may ask again, Are these hints of such clearness as actually to reveal this doctrine, apart from the revelation of the New Testament? This should be doubtless answered in the negative. There are hints, and they serve for points of attachment for the fuller New Testament teaching. But they are only hints, and, apart from the New Testament teaching, would be readily explained as personifications or ideal objectivations of the power of God. Undoubtedly, side by side with the stress put upon the unity of God and the identity of the Spirit with the God who gives it, there is a distinction recognized between God and His Spirit — in the sense at least of a discrimination between God over all and God in all, between the Giver and the Given, between the Source and the Executor of the moral law. This distinction already emerges in Genesis i. 2; and it does not grow less observable as we advance through the Old

Testament. It is prominent in the standing phrases by which, on the one hand, God is spoken of as sending, putting, placing, pouring, emptying His Spirit upon man, and on the other the Spirit is spoken of as coming, resting, falling, springing upon man. There is a sort of objectifying of the Spirit over against God in both cases; in the former case, by sending Him from Himself God, as it were, separates Him from Himself; in the latter, He appears almost as a distinct person, acting *sua sponte*. Schultz does not hesitate to speak of the Spirit even in Genesis i. 2 as appearing "as very independent, just like a hypostasis or person."[29] Kleinert finds in this passage at least a tendency towards hypostatizing — though he thinks this tendency was not subsequently worked out.[30] Perhaps we are warranted in saying as much as this — that there is observable in the Old Testament, not, indeed, an hypostatizing of the Spirit of God, but a tendency towards it — that, in Hofmann's cautious language, the Spirit appears in the Old Testament "as somewhat distinct from the 'I' of God which God makes the principle of life in the world."[31] A preparation, at least, for the full revelation of the Trinity in the New Testament is observable;[32] points of connection with it are discoverable; and so Christians are able to read the Old Testament without offence, and to find without confusion their own Holy Spirit in its Spirit of God.[33]

[29] *Op. cit.* ii. p. 184.

[30] *Op. cit.* pp. 55–56.

[31] "Schriftbeweis," i. p. 187.

[32] Cf. Oehler, *op. cit.* § 65, note 5. He looks on Isa. xliii. 16 as implying personality and reminds us that the Old Testament prepared the way for the œconomic Trinity of the new. Cf. also Dale, "Christian Doctrine," p. 317.

[33] Cf. Dr. Hodge's admirable summary statement: "Even in the first chapter of Genesis, the Spirit of God is represented as the source of all intelligence, order and life in the created universe; and in the following books of the Old Testament He is represented as inspiring the prophets, giving wisdom, strength and goodness to statesmen and warriors, and to the people of God. This Spirit is not an agency but an agent, who teaches and selects; who can be sinned against and grieved; and who in the New Testament is unmistakably revealed as a distinct person. When John the Baptist appeared, we find him speaking of the Holy Spirit as of a person with whom his countrymen were familiar, as an object of Divine worship and the giver of saving blessings. Our divine Lord also takes this truth for granted,

More than this could scarcely be looked for. The elements in the doctrine of God which above all others needed emphasis in Old Testament times were naturally His unity and His personality. The great thing to be taught the ancient people of God was that the God of all the earth is one person. Over against the varying idolatries about them, this was the truth of truths for which Israel was primarily to stand; and not until this great truth was ineffaceably stamped upon their souls could the personal distinctions in the Triune-God be safely made known to them. A premature revelation of the Spirit as a distinct hypostasis could have wrought nothing but harm to the people of God. We shall all no doubt agree with Kleinert [34] that it is pragmatic in Isidore of Pelusium to say that Moses knew the doctrine of the Trinity well enough, but concealed it through fear that Polytheism would profit by it. But we may safely affirm this of God the Revealer, in the gradual delivery of the truth concerning Himself to men. He reveals the whole truth, but in divers portions and in divers manners: and it was incident to the progressive delivery of doctrine that the unity of the Godhead should first be made the firm possession of men, and the Trinity in that unity should be unveiled to them only afterwards, when the times were ripe for it. What we need wonder over is not that the hypostatical distinctness of the Spirit is not more clearly revealed in the Old Testament but that the approaches to it are laid so skillfully that the doctrine of the hypostatical Holy Spirit of the New Testament finds so many and such striking points of attachment in the Old Testament, and yet no Israelite had ever been disturbed in repeating with hearty faith his great Sch'ma, "Hear O Israel, the Lord our God is one Lord" (Deut. vi. 4). Not until the whole doctrine of the Trinity was ready to be manifested in

and promised to send the Spirit as a Paraclete, to take his place, to instruct, comfort and strengthen them; whom they were to receive and obey. Thus, without any violent transition, the earliest revelations of this mystery were gradually unfolded, until the triune God, Father, Son and Spirit, appears in the New Testament as the universally recognized God of all believers" (Charles Hodge, "Systematic Theology," i. p. 447).

[34] *Op. cit.* p. 56.

such visible form as at the baptism of Christ — God in heaven, God on earth and God descending from heaven to earth — could any part of the mystery be safely uncovered.

There yet remains an important query which we cannot pass wholly by. We have seen the rich development of the doctrine of the Spirit in the Old Testament. We have seen the testimony the Old Testament bears to the activity of the Spirit of God throughout the old dispensation. What then is meant by calling the new dispensation the dispensation of the Spirit? What does John (vii. 39) mean by saying that the Spirit was not yet given because Jesus was not yet glorified? What our Lord Himself, when he promised the Comforter, by saying that the Comforter would not come until He went away and sent Him (John xvi. 7); and by breathing on His disciples, saying, "Receive ye the Holy Spirit" (John xx. 22)? What did the descent of the Spirit at Pentecost mean, when He came to inaugurate the dispensation of the Spirit? It cannot be meant that the Spirit was not active in the old dispensation. We have already seen that the New Testament writers themselves represent Him to have been active in the old dispensation in all the varieties of activity with which He is active in the new. Such passages seem to have diverse references. Some of them may refer to the specifically miraculous endowments which characterized the apostles and the churches which they founded.[35] Others refer to the world-wide mission of the Spirit, promised, indeed, in the Old Testament, but only now to be realized. But there is a more fundamental idea to be reckoned with still. This is the idea of the preparatory nature of the Old Testament dispensation. The old dispensation was a preparatory one and must be strictly conceived as such. What spiritual blessings came to it were by way of prelibation.[36] They were

[35] Cf. Redford, "Vox. Dei.," p. 236.

[36] Smeaton (*Op. cit.* p. 49) comments on John vii. 37 *sq.* thus: "But the apostle adds that 'the Spirit was not yet' because Christ's glorification had not yet arrived. He does not mean that the Spirit did not yet exist — for all Scripture attests His eternal preëxistence — nor that His regenerative efficacy was still unknown — for countless millions had been regenerated by His power since the first promise in Eden — but that these operations of the Spirit had been but an

many and various. The Spirit worked in Providence no less universally then than now. He abode in the Church not less really then than now. He wrought in the hearts of God's people not less prevalently then than now. All the good that was in the world was then as now due to Him. All the hope of God's Church then as now depended on Him. Every grace of the godly life then as now was a fruit of His working. But the object of the whole dispensation was only to prepare for the outpouring of the Spirit upon all flesh. He kept the remnant safe and pure; but it was primarily only in order that the seed might be preserved. This was the fundamental end of His activity, then. The dispensation of the Spirit, properly so-called, did not dawn until the period of preparation was over and the day of outpouring had come. The mustard seed had been preserved through all the ages only by the Spirit's brooding care. Now it is planted, and it is by His operation that it is growing up into a great tree which shades the whole earth, and to the branches of which all the fowls of heaven come for shelter. It is not that His work is more real in the new dispensation than in the old. It is not merely that it is more universal. It is that it is directed to a different end — that it is no longer for the mere preserving of the seed unto the day of planting, but for the perfecting of the fruitage and the gathering of the harvest. The Church, to use a figure of Isaiah's, was then like a pent-in stream; it is now like that pent-in stream with the barriers broken down and the Spirit of the Lord driving it. It was He who preserved it in being when it was pent in. It is He who is now driving on its gathered floods till it shall cover the earth as the waters cover the sea. In one word, that was a day in which the Spirit restrained His power. Now the great day of the Spirit is come.

anticipation of the atoning gift of Christ rather than a GIVING. The apostle speaks comparatively, not absolutely." Compare further the eloquent words on page 53 with the quotation there from Goodwin.

IV

THE BIBLICAL DOCTRINE OF
THE TRINITY

THE BIBLICAL DOCTRINE OF THE TRINITY [1]

THE term "Trinity" is not a Biblical term, and we are not using Biblical language when we define what is expressed by it as the doctrine that there is one only and true God, but in the unity of the Godhead there are three coeternal and coequal Persons, the same in substance but distinct in subsistence. A doctrine so defined can be spoken of as a Biblical doctrine only on the principle that the sense of Scripture is Scripture. And the definition of a Biblical doctrine in such un-Biblical language can be justified only on the principle that it is better to preserve the truth of Scripture than the words of Scripture. The doctrine of the Trinity lies in Scripture in solution; when it is crystallized from its solvent it does not cease to be Scriptural, but only comes into clearer view. Or, to speak without figure, the doctrine of the Trinity is given to us in Scripture, not in formulated definition, but in fragmentary allusions; when we assembled the *disjecta membra* into their organic unity, we are not passing from Scripture, but entering more thoroughly into the meaning of Scripture. We may state the doctrine in technical terms, supplied by philosophical reflection; but the doctrine stated is a genuinely Scriptural doctrine.

In point of fact, the doctrine of the Trinity is purely a revealed doctrine. That is to say, it embodies a truth which has never been discovered, and is indiscoverable, by natural reason. With all his searching, man has not been able to find out for himself the deepest things of God. Accordingly, ethnic thought has never attained a Trinitarian conception of God, nor does any ethnic religion present in its representations of the Divine Being any analogy to the doctrine of the Trinity.

[1] Article "Trinity" from *The International Standard Bible Encyclopaedia*, James Orr, General editor, v. v, pp. 3012–3022. Pub. Chicago, The Howard-Severance Co. 1915.

Triads of divinities, no doubt, occur in nearly all polytheistic religions, formed under very various influences. Sometimes, as in the Egyptian triad of Osiris, Isis and Horus, it is
the analogy of the human family with its father, mother and
son which lies at their basis. Sometimes they are the effect of
mere syncretism, three deities worshipped in different localities
being brought together in the common worship of all. Sometimes, as in the Hindu triad of Brahma, Vishnu and Shiva, they
represent the cyclic movement of a pantheistic evolution, and
symbolize the three stages of Being, Becoming and Dissolution.
Sometimes they are the result apparently of nothing more than
an odd human tendency to think in threes, which has given the
number three widespread standing as a sacred number (so H.
Usener). It is no more than was to be anticipated, that one or
another of these triads should now and again be pointed to as
the replica (or even the original) of the Christian doctrine of
the Trinity. Gladstone found the Trinity in the Homeric mythology, the trident of Poseidon being its symbol. Hegel very
naturally found it in the Hindu Trimurti, which indeed is very
like his pantheizing notion of what the Trinity is. Others have
perceived it in the Buddhist Triratna (Söderblom); or (despite
their crass dualism) in some speculations of Parseeism; or,
more frequently, in the notional triad of Platonism (e. g.,
Knapp); while Jules Martin is quite sure that it is present in
Philo's neo-Stoical doctrine of the "powers," especially when
applied to the explanation of Abraham's three visitors. Of late
years, eyes have been turned rather to Babylonia; and H. Zimmern finds a possible forerunner of the Trinity in a Father, Son,
and Intercessor, which he discovers in its mythology. It should
be needless to say that none of these triads has the slightest
resemblance to the Christian doctrine of the Trinity. The Christian doctrine of the Trinity embodies much more than the
notion of "threeness," and beyond their "threeness" these
triads have nothing in common with it.

As the doctrine of the Trinity is indiscoverable by reason,
so it is incapable of proof from reason. There are no analogies
to it in Nature, not even in the spiritual nature of man, who is

made in the image of God. In His trinitarian mode of being, God is unique; and, as there is nothing in the universe like Him in this respect, so there is nothing which can help us to comprehend Him. Many attempts have, nevertheless, been made to construct a rational proof of the Trinity of the Godhead. Among these there are two which are particularly attractive, and have therefore been put forward again and again by speculative thinkers through all the Christian ages. These are derived from the implications, in the one case, of self-consciousness; in the other, of love. Both self-consciousness and love, it is said, demand for their very existence an object over against which the self stands as subject. If we conceive of God as self-conscious and loving, therefore, we cannot help conceiving of Him as embracing in His unity some form of plurality. From this general position both arguments have been elaborated, however, by various thinkers in very varied forms.

The former of them, for example, is developed by a great seventeenth century theologian — Bartholomew Keckermann (1614) — as follows: God is self-conscious thought: and God's thought must have a perfect object, existing eternally before it; this object to be perfect must be itself God; and as God is one, this object which is God must be the God that is one. It is essentially the same argument which is popularized in a famous paragraph (§ 73) of Lessing's "The Education of the Human Race." Must not God have an absolutely perfect representation of Himself — that is, a representation in which everything that is in Him is found? And would everything that is in God be found in this representation if His necessary reality were not found in it? If everything, everything without exception, that is in God is to be found in this representation, it cannot, therefore, remain a mere empty image, but must be an actual duplication of God. It is obvious that arguments like this prove too much. If God's representation of Himself, to be perfect, must possess the same kind of reality that He Himself possesses, it does not seem easy to deny that His representations of everything else must possess objective reality. And this would be as much as to say that the eternal objective coexistence of all that God can conceive is given in the very idea of God, and that is open pantheism. The logical flaw lies in including in the perfection of a representation qualities which are not proper to representations, however perfect. A perfect representation must, of course, have all the reality proper to a representation; but objective reality is so little proper to a representation that a representation acquiring it would cease to be a representation. This fatal flaw is not transcended, but only covered up, when the argument is compressed, as it is in most of its modern presentations, in effect to the mere assertion that the condition of self-consciousness is a real distinction between the thinking subject and the thought object, which, in God's case, would be between the subject ego and the object ego. Why, however, we should deny to God the power of self-contemplation enjoyed by every finite spirit, save at the cost of the distinct hypostatizing of the contemplant and the contemplated self, it is hard to understand. Nor is it always clear that what we get is a distinct hypostatization rather than a distinct substantializing of the contemplant and contemplated ego: not two persons in the Godhead so much as two Gods. The discovery of the third hypostasis — the Holy Spirit — remains meanwhile, to all these attempts rationally to construct a Trinity in the Divine Being, a standing puzzle which finds only a very artificial solution.

The case is much the same with the argument derived from the nature of love. Our sympathies go out to that old Valentinian writer — possibly it was Valentinus himself — who reasoned — perhaps he was the first so to reason — that "God is all love," "but love is not love unless there be an object of love." And they go out more richly still to Augustine, when, seeking a basis, not for a theory of emanations, but for the doctrine of the Trinity, he analyzes this love which God is into the triple implication of "the lover," "the loved" and "the love itself," and sees in this trinary of love an analogue of the Triune God. It requires, however, only that the argument thus broadly suggested should be developed into its details for its artificiality to become apparent. Richard of St. Victor works it out as follows: It belongs to the nature of *amor* that it should turn to another as *caritas*. This other, in God's case, cannot be the world; since such love of the world would be inordinate. It can only be a person; and a person who is God's equal in eternity, power and wisdom. Since, however, there cannot be two Divine substances, these two Divine persons must form one and the same substance. The best love cannot, however, confine itself to these two persons; it must become *condilectio* by the desire that a third should be equally loved as they love one another. Thus love, when perfectly conceived, leads necessarily to the Trinity, and since God is all He can be, this Trinity must be real. Modern writers (Sartorius, Schöberlein, J. Müller, Liebner, most lately R. H. Grützmacher) do not seem to have essentially improved upon such a statement as this. And after all is said, it does not appear clear that God's own all-perfect Being could not supply a satisfying object of His all-perfect love. To say that in its very nature love is self-communicative, and therefore implies an object other than self, seems an abuse of figurative language.

Perhaps the ontological proof of the Trinity is nowhere more attractively put than by Jonathan Edwards. The peculiarity of his presentation of it lies in an attempt to add plausibility to it by a doctrine of the nature of spiritual ideas or ideas of spiritual things, such as thought, love, fear, in general. Ideas of such things, he urges, are just repetitions of them, so that he who has an idea of any act of love, fear, anger or any other act or motion of the mind, simply so far repeats the motion in question; and if the idea be perfect and complete, the original motion of the mind is absolutely reduplicated. Edwards presses this so far that he is ready to contend that if a man could have an absolutely perfect idea of all that was in his mind at any past moment, he would really, to all intents and purposes, be over again what he was at that moment. And if he could perfectly contemplate all that is in his mind at any given moment, as it is and at the same time that it is there in its first and direct existence, he would really be two at that time, he would be twice at once: "The idea he has of himself would be himself again." This now is the case with the Divine Being. "God's idea of Himself is absolutely perfect, and therefore is an express and perfect image of Him, exactly like Him in every respect. . . . But that which is the express, perfect image of God and in every respect like Him is God, to all intents and purposes, because there is nothing wanting: there is nothing in the Deity that renders it the Deity but what has something exactly answering to it in this image, which will therefore also render that the Deity." The Second Person of the Trinity being thus attained, the argument advances. "The Godhead being thus begotten of God's loving [having?] an idea of Himself and showing forth in a distinct Subsistence or Person in that idea, there proceeds a most pure act, and an infinitely holy and sacred energy arises between the Father and the Son in mutually loving and delighting in each other. . . . The Deity becomes all act, the Divine essence itself flows out and is as it were breathed forth in love and joy. So that the Godhead therein stands forth in yet another manner of Subsistence, and there proceeds the Third Person in the Trinity, the Holy Spirit, viz., the Deity in act, for there is no other act but the act of the will." The inconclusiveness of the reasoning lies on the surface. The mind does not consist in its states, and the repetition of its states would not, therefore, duplicate or triplicate it. If it did, we should have a plurality of Beings, not of Persons in one Being. Neither God's perfect idea of Himself nor His perfect love of Himself reproduces Himself. He differs from His idea and His love of Himself precisely by that which distinguishes His Being from His acts. When it is said, then, that there is nothing in the Deity which renders it the Deity but what has something answering to it in its image of itself, it is enough to respond — except the Deity itself. What is wanting to the image to make it a second Deity is just objective reality.

Inconclusive as all such reasoning is, however, considered as rational demonstration of the reality of the Trinity, it is very far from possessing no value. It carries home to us in a very suggestive way the superiority of the Trinitarian conception of God to the conception of Him as an abstract monad, and thus brings important rational support to the doctrine of the Trinity, when once that doctrine has been given us by revelation. If it is not quite possible to say that we cannot conceive of God as eternal self-consciousness and eternal love, without conceiving Him as a Trinity, it does seem quite necessary to say that when we conceive Him as a Trinity, new fulness, richness, force are given to our conception of Him as a self-conscious, loving Being, and therefore we conceive Him more adequately than as a monad, and no one who has ever once conceived Him as a Trinity can ever again satisfy himself with a monadistic conception of God. Reason thus not only performs the important negative service to faith in the Trinity, of showing the self-consistency of the doctrine and its consistency with other known truth, but brings this positive rational support to it of discovering in it the only adequate conception of God as self-conscious spirit and living love. Difficult, therefore, as the idea of the Trinity in itself is, it does not come to us as an added burden upon our intelligence; it brings us rather the solution of the deepest and most persistent difficulties in our conception of God as infinite moral Being, and illuminates, enriches and elevates all our thought of God. It has accordingly become a commonplace to say that Christian theism is the only stable theism. That is as much as to say that theism requires the enriching conception of the Trinity to give it a permanent hold upon the human mind — the mind finds it difficult to rest in the idea of an abstract unity for its God; and that the human heart cries out for the living God in whose Being there is that fulness of life for which the conception of the Trinity alone provides.

So strongly is it felt in wide circles that a Trinitarian conception is essential to a worthy idea of God, that there is abroad a deep-seated unwillingness to allow that God could ever have made Himself known otherwise than as a Trinity. From this point of view it is inconceivable that the Old Testament revelation should know nothing of the Trinity. Accordingly, I. A. Dorner, for example, reasons thus: "If, however — and this is the faith of universal Christendom — a living idea of God must be thought in some way after a Trinitarian fashion, it must be antecedently probable that traces of the Trinity cannot be lacking in the Old Testament, since its idea of God is a living or historical one." Whether there really exist traces of the idea of the Trinity in the Old Testament, however, is a nice question. Certainly we cannot speak broadly of the revelation of the doctrine of the Trinity in the Old Testament. It is a plain matter of fact that none who have depended on the revelation embodied in the Old Testament alone have ever attained to the doctrine of the Trinity. It is another question, however, whether there may not exist in the pages of the Old Testament turns of expression or records of occurrences in which one already acquainted with the doctrine of the Trinity may fairly see indications of an underlying implication of it. The older writers discovered intimations of the Trinity in such phenomena as the plural form of the Divine name *Ĕlōhīm*, the occasional employment with reference to God of plural pronouns ("Let us make man in our image," Gen. i. 26; iii. 22; xi. 7; Isa. vi. 8), or of plural verbs (Gen. xx. 13; xxxv. 7), certain repetitions of the name of God which seem to distinguish between God and God (Ps. xlv. 6, 7; cx. 1; Hos. i. 7), threefold liturgical formulas Num. vi. 24, 26; Isa. vi. 3), a certain tendency to hypostatize the conception of Wisdom (Prov. viii.), and especially the remarkable phenomena connected with the appearances of the Angel of Jehovah (Gen. xvi. 2–13, xxii. 11. 16; xxxi. 11, 13; xlviii. 15, 16; Ex. iii. 2, 4, 5; Jgs. xiii. 20–22). The tendency of more recent authors is to appeal, not so much to specific texts of the Old Testament, as to the very "organism of revelation" in the Old Testament in which there is perceived an underlying suggestion "that all things owe their existence and persistence to a threefold cause," both with reference to the first creation, and, more plainly, with reference to the second creation. Passages like Ps. xxxiii. 6; Isa. lxi. 1; lxiii. 9–12; Hag. ii. 5, 6, in which God and His Word and His Spirit are brought together, co-causes of effects, are adduced. A tendency is pointed out to hypostatize the Word of God on the one hand (e. g., Gen. i. 3; Ps. xxxiii. 6; cvii. 20; cxlvii. 15–18; Isa.

lv. 11); and, especially in Ezek. and the later Prophets, the Spirit of God, on the other (e. g., Gen. i. 2; Isa. xlviii. 16; lxiii. 10; Ezek. ii. 2; viii. 3; Zec. vii. 12). Suggestions — in Isa. for instance (vii. 14; ix. 6) — of the Deity of the Messiah are appealed to. And if the occasional occurrence of plural verbs and pronouns referring to God, and the plural form of the name *Ĕlōhīm*, are not insisted upon as in themselves evidence of a multiplicity in the Godhead, yet a certain weight is lent them as witnesses that "the God of revelation is no abstract unity, but the living, true God, who in the fulness of His life embraces the highest variety" (Bavinck). The upshot of it all is that it is very generally felt that, somehow, in the Old Testament development of the idea of God there is a suggestion that the Deity is not a simple monad, and that thus a preparation is made for the revelation of the Trinity yet to come. It would seem clear that we must recognize in the Old Testament doctrine of the relation of God to His revelation by the creative Word and the Spirit, at least the germ of the distinctions in the Godhead afterward fully made known in the Christian revelation. And we can scarcely stop there. After all is said, in the light of the later revelation, the Trinitarian interpretation remains the most natural one of the phenomena which the older writers frankly interpreted as intimations of the Trinity; especially of those connected with the descriptions of the Angel of Jehovah no doubt, but also even of such a form of expression as meets us in the "Let us make man in our image" of Gen. i. 26 — for surely verse 27: "And God created man in his own image," does not encourage us to take the preceding verse as announcing that man was to be created in the image of the angels. This is not an illegitimate reading of New Testament ideas back into the text of the Old Testament; it is only reading the text of the Old Testament under the illumination of the New Testament revelation. The Old Testament may be likened to a chamber richly furnished but dimly lighted; the introduction of light brings into it nothing which was not in it before; but it brings out into clearer view much of what is in it but was only dimly or even not at all perceived before. The mystery of the Trinity is not revealed in the Old Testament; but the mystery of the Trinity underlies the Old Testament revelation, and here and there almost comes into view. Thus the Old Testament revelation of God is not corrected by the fuller revelation which follows it, but only perfected, extended and enlarged.

It is an old saying that what becomes patent in the New Testament was latent in the Old Testament. And it is important that the continuity of the revelation of God contained in the two Testaments should not be overlooked or obscured. If we find some difficulty in perceiving for ourselves, in the Old Testament, definite points of attachment for the revelation of the Trinity, we cannot help perceiving with great clearness in the New Testament abundant evidence that its writers felt no incongruity whatever between their doctrine of the Trinity and the Old Testament conception of God. The New Testament writers certainly were not conscious of being "setters forth of strange gods." To their own apprehension they worshipped and proclaimed just the God of Israel; and they laid no less stress than the Old Testament itself upon His unity (Jn. xvii. 3; I Cor. viii. 4; I Tim. ii. 5). They do not, then, place two new gods by the side of Jehovah as alike with Him to be served and worshipped; they conceive Jehovah as Himself at once Father, Son and Spirit. In presenting this one Jehovah as Father, Son and Spirit, they do not even betray any lurking feeling that they are making innovations. Without apparent misgiving they take over Old Testament passages and apply them to Father, Son and Spirit indifferently. Obviously they understand themselves, and wish to be understood, as setting forth in the Father, Son and Spirit just the one God that the God of the Old Testament revelation is; and they are as far as possible from recognizing any breach between themselves and the Fathers in presenting their enlarged conception of the Divine Being. This may not amount to saying that they saw the doctrine of the Trinity everywhere taught in the Old Testament. It certainly amounts to saying that they saw the Triune God whom they worshipped in the God of the Old

Testament revelation, and felt no incongruity in speaking of their Triune God in the terms of the Old Testament revelation. The God of the Old Testament was their God, and their God was a Trinity, and their sense of the identity of the two was so complete that no question as to it was raised in their minds.

The simplicity and assurance with which the New Testament writers speak of God as a Trinity have, however, a further implication. If they betray no sense of novelty in so speaking of Him, this is undoubtedly in part because it was no longer a novelty so to speak of Him. It is clear, in other words, that, as we read the New Testament, we are not witnessing the birth of a new conception of God. What we meet with in its pages is a firmly established conception of God underlying and giving its tone to the whole fabric. It is not in a text here and there that the New Testament bears its testimony to the doctrine of the Trinity. The whole book is Trinitarian to the core; all its teaching is built on the assumption of the Trinity; and its allusions to the Trinity are frequent, cursory, easy and confident. It is with a view to the cursoriness of the allusions to it in the New Testament that it has been remarked that "the doctrine of the Trinity is not so much heard as overheard in the statements of Scripture." It would be more exact to say that it is not so much inculcated as presupposed. The doctrine of the Trinity does not appear in the New Testament in the making, but as already made. It takes its place in its pages, as Gunkel phrases it, with an air almost of complaint, already "in full completeness" (*völlig fertig*), leaving no trace of its growth. "There is nothing more wonderful in the history of human thought," says Sanday, with his eye on the appearance of the doctrine of the Trinity in the New Testament, "than the silent and imperceptible way in which this doctrine, to us so difficult, took its place without struggle — and without controversy — among accepted Christian truths." The explanation of this remarkable phenomenon is, however, simple. Our New Testament is not a record of the development of the doctrine or of its assimilation. It everywhere presupposes the doctrine as the fixed possession of the Christian community; and the process by which it became the possession of the Christian community lies behind the New Testament.

We cannot speak of the doctrine of the Trinity, therefore, if we study exactness of speech, as revealed in the New Testament, any more than we can speak of it as revealed in the Old Testament. The Old Testament was written before its revelation; the New Testament after it. The revelation itself was made not in word but in deed. It was made in the incarnation of God the Son, and the outpouring of God the Holy Spirit. The relation of the two Testaments to this revelation is in the one case that of preparation for it, and in the other that of product of it. The revelation itself is embodied just in Christ and the Holy Spirit. This is as much as to say that the revelation of the Trinity was incidental to, and the inevitable effect of, the accomplishment of redemption. It was in the coming of the Son of God in the likeness of sinful flesh to offer Himself a sacrifice for sin; and in the coming of the Holy Spirit to convict the world of sin, of righteousness and of judgment, that the Trinity of Persons in the Unity of the Godhead was once for all revealed to men. Those who knew God the Father, who loved them and gave His own Son to die for them; and the Lord Jesus Christ, who loved them and delivered Himself up an offering and sacrifice for them; and the Spirit of Grace, who loved them and dwelt within them a power not themselves, making for righteousness, knew the Triune God and could not think or speak of God otherwise than as triune. The doctrine of the Trinity, in other words, is simply the modification wrought in the conception of the one only God by His complete revelation of Himself in the redemptive process. It necessarily waited, therefore, upon the completion of the redemptive process for its revelation, and its revelation, as necessarily, lay complete in the redemptive process.

From this central fact we may understand more fully several circumstances connected with the revelation of the Trinity to which allusion has been made. We may from it understand, for example, why the Trinity was not revealed in the Old Testament. It may carry us a little way to remark, as it has been customary to remark since the time of Gregory of Nazianzus, that it was the task of the Old Testament revelation to fix firmly in the minds and hearts of the people of God the great fundamental truth of the unity of the Godhead; and it would have been dangerous to speak to them of the plurality within this unity until this task had been fully accomplished. The real reason for the delay in the revelation of the Trinity, however, is grounded in the secular development of the redemptive purpose of God: the times were not ripe for the revelation of the Trinity in the unity of the Godhead until the fulness of the time had come for God to send forth His Son unto redemption, and His Spirit unto sanctification. The revelation in word must needs wait upon the revelation in fact, to which it brings its necessary explanation, no doubt, but from which also it derives its own entire significance and value. The revelation of a Trinity in the Divine unity as a mere abstract truth without relation to manifested fact, and without significance to the development of the kingdom of God, would have been foreign to the whole method of the Divine procedure as it lies exposed to us in the pages of Scripture. Here the working-out of the Divine purpose supplies the fundamental principle to which all else, even the progressive stages of revelation itself, is subsidiary; and advances in revelation are ever closely connected with the advancing accomplishment of the redemptive purpose. We may understand also, however, from the same central fact, why it is that the doctrine of the Trinity lies in the New Testament rather in the form of allusions than in express teaching, why it is rather everywhere presupposed, coming only here and there into incidental expression, than formally inculcated. It is because the revelation, having been made in the actual occurrences of redemption, was already the common property of all Christian hearts. In speaking and writing to one another, Christians, therefore, rather spoke out of their common Trinitarian consciousness, and reminded one another of their common fund of belief, than instructed one another in what was already the common property of all. We are to look for, and we shall find, in the New Testament allusions to the Trinity, rather evidence of how the Trinity, believed in by all, was conceived by the authoritative teachers of the church, than formal attempts, on their part, by authoritative declarations, to bring the church into the understanding that God is a Trinity.

The fundamental proof that God is a Trinity is supplied thus by the fundamental revelation of the Trinity in fact: that is to say, in the incarnation of God the Son and the outpouring of God the Holy Spirit. In a word, Jesus Christ and the Holy Spirit are the fundamental proof of the doctrine of the Trinity. This is as much as to say that all the evidence of whatever kind, and from whatever source derived, that Jesus Christ is God manifested in the flesh, and that the Holy Spirit is a Divine Person, is just so much evidence for the doctrine of the Trinity; and that when we go to the New Testament for evidence of the Trinity we are to seek it, not merely in the scattered allusions to the Trinity as such, numerous and instructive as they are, but primarily in the whole mass of evidence which the New Testament provides of the Deity of Christ and the Divine personality of the Holy Spirit. When we have said this, we have said in effect that the whole mass of the New Testament is evidence for the Trinity. For the New Testament is saturated with evidence of the Deity of Christ and the Divine personality of the Holy Spirit. Precisely what the New Testament is, is the documentation of the religion of the incarnate Son and of the outpoured Spirit, that is to say, of the religion of the Trinity, and what we mean by the doctrine of the Trinity is nothing but the formulation in exact language of the conception of God presupposed in the religion of the incarnate Son and outpoured Spirit. We may analyze this conception and adduce proof for every constituent element of it from the New Testament declarations. We may show that the New Testament everywhere insists on the unity of the Godhead; that it constantly recognizes the Father as God, the Son as God and the Spirit as God; and that it cursorily presents these three to us as distinct Persons. It is not necessary, however, to enlarge here on facts so obvious. We may content ourselves with simply observing that to the New Testament there is but one only living and true God; but that to it Jesus Christ and the Holy Spirit are each God in the fullest sense of the term; and yet Father, Son and Spirit stand over against each other as I, and Thou, and He. In this composite fact the New Testament gives us the doctrine of the Trinity. For the doctrine of the Trinity is but the statement in well-guarded language of this composite fact. Throughout the whole course of the many efforts to formulate the doctrine exactly, which have followed one another during the entire history of the church, indeed, the principle which has ever determined the result has always been determination to do justice in conceiving the relations of God the Father, God the Son and God the Spirit, on the one hand to the unity of God, and, on the other, to the true Deity of the Son and Spirit and their distinct personalities. When we have said these three things, then — that there is but one God, that the Father and the Son and the Spirit is each God, that the Father and the Son and the Spirit is each a distinct person — we have enunciated the doctrine of the Trinity in its completeness.

That this doctrine underlies the whole New Testament as its constant presupposition and determines everywhere its forms of expression is the primary fact to be noted. We must not omit explicitly to note, however, that it now and again also, as occasion arises for its incidental enunciation, comes itself to expression in more or less completeness of statement. The passages in which the three Persons of the Trinity are brought together are much more numerous than, perhaps, is generally supposed; but it should be recognized that the formal collocation of the elements of the doctrine naturally is relatively rare in writings which are occasional in their origin and practical rather than doctrinal in their immediate purpose. The three Persons already come into view as Divine Persons in the annunciation of the birth of Our Lord: 'The Holy Ghost shall come upon thee,' said the angel to Mary, 'and the power of the Most High shall overshadow thee: wherefore also the holy thing which is to be born shall be called the Son

of God; (Lk. i. 35 m; cf. Mt. i. 18 ff.). Here the Holy Ghost is
the active agent in the production of an effect which is also
ascribed to the power of the Most High, and the child thus
brought into the world is given the great designation of "Son
of God." The three Persons are just as clearly brought before
us in the account of Mt. (i. 18 ff.), though the allusions to them
are dispersed through a longer stretch of narrative, in the course
of which the Deity of the child is twice intimated (ver. 21:
'It is He that shall save *His* people from their sins'; ver. 23:
'They shall call His name Immanuel; which is, being interpreted, *God-with-us*'). In the baptismal scene which finds record by all the evangelists at the opening of Jesus' ministry
(Mt. iii. 16, 17; Mk. i. 10, 11; Lk. iii. 21, 22; Jn. i. 32–34), the
three Persons are thrown up to sight in a dramatic picture in
which the Deity of each is strongly emphasized. From the
open heavens the Spirit descends in visible form, and 'a voice
came out of the heavens, Thou art my Son, the Beloved, in
whom I am well pleased.' Thus care seems to have been taken
to make the advent of the Son of God into the world the revelation also of the Triune God, that the minds of men might as
smoothly as possible adjust themselves to the preconditions of
the Divine redemption which was in process of being wrought
out.

With this as a starting-point, the teaching of Jesus is Trini-
tarianly conditioned throughout. He has much to say of God
His Father, from whom as His Son He is in some true sense
distinct, and with whom He is in some equally true sense one.
And He has much to say of the Spirit, who represents Him as
He represents the Father, and by whom He works as the Father
works by Him. It is not merely in the Gospel of John that
such representations occur in the teaching of Jesus. In the Synoptics, too, Jesus claims a Sonship to God which is unique (Mt.
xi. 27; xxiv. 36; Mk. xiii. 32; Lk. x. 22; in the following passages the title of "Son of God" is attributed to Him and accepted by Him: Mt. iv. 6; viii. 29; xiv. 33; xxvii. 40, 43, 54;
Mk. iii. 11; xv. 39; Lk. iv. 41; xxii. 70; cf. Jn. i. 34, 49; ix. 35;
xi. 27), and which involves an absolute community between

the two in knowledge, say, and power: both Mt. (xi. 27) and Lk. (x. 22) record His great declaration that He knows the Father and the Father knows Him with perfect mutual knowledge: "No one knoweth the Son, save the Father; neither doth any know the Father, save the Son." In the Synoptics, too, Jesus speaks of employing the Spirit of God Himself for the performance of His works, as if the activities of God were at His disposal: "I by the Spirit of God" — or as Luke has it, "by the finger of God" — "cast out demons" (Mt. xii. 28; Lk. xi. 20; cf. the promise of the Spirit in Mk. xiii. 11; Lk. xii. 12).

It is in the discourses recorded in John, however, that Jesus most copiously refers to the unity of Himself, as the Son, with the Father, and to the mission of the Spirit from Himself as the dispenser of the Divine activities. Here He not only with great directness declares that He and the Father are one (x. 30; cf. xvii. 11, 21, 22, 25) with a unity of interpenetration ("The Father is in me, and I in the Father," x. 38; cf. xvi. 10, 11), so that to have seen Him was to have seen the Father (xiv. 9; cf. xv. 21); but He removes all doubt as to the essential nature of His oneness with the Father by explicitly asserting His eternity ("Before Abraham was born, I am," Jn. viii. 58), His co-eternity with God ("had with thee before the world was," xvii. 5; cf. xvii. 18; vi. 62), His eternal participation in the Divine glory itself ("the glory which I had with thee," in fellowship, community with Thee "before the world was," xvii. 5). So clear is it that in speaking currently of Himself as God's Son (v. 25; ix. 35; xi. 4; cf. x. 36), He meant, in accordance with the underlying significance of the idea of sonship in Semitic speech (founded on the natural implication that whatever the father is that the son is also; cf. xvi. 15; xvii. 10), to make Himself, as the Jews with exact appreciation of His meaning perceived, "equal with God" (v. 18), or, to put it brusquely, just "God" (x. 33). How He, being thus equal or rather identical with God, was in the world, He explains as involving a coming forth (ἐξῆλθον, exélthon) on His part, not merely from the presence of God (ἀπό, apó, xvi. 30; cf. xiii. 3) or from fellowship with God (παρά, *pará*, xvi. 27; xvii. 8), but from out of God Himself (ἐκ, *ek*, viii. 42; xvi. 28). And in the very act of thus asserting that His eternal home is in the depths of the Divine Being, He throws up, into as strong an emphasis as stressed pronouns can convey, His personal distinctness from the Father. 'If God were your Father,' says He (viii. 42), 'ye would love *me:* for *I* came forth and am come out of God; for neither have I come of *myself*, but it was *He* that sent *me.*' Again, He says (xvi. 26, 27): 'In that day ye shall ask in my name: and I say not unto you that *I* will make request of the Father for you; for *the Father Himself* loveth you, because ye have loved *me*, and have believed that it was *from fellowship with the Father* that *I* came forth; I came from out of the Father, and have come into the world.' Less pointedly, but still distinctly, He says again (xvii. 8): 'They know of a truth that it was *from fellowship with Thee* that I came forth, and they believed that it was Thou that didst send me.' It is not necessary to illustrate more at large a form of expression so characteristic of the discourses of Our Lord recorded by John that it meets us on every page: a form of expression which combines a clear implication of a unity of Father and Son which is identity of Being, and an equally clear implication of a distinction of Person between them such as allows not merely for the play of emotions between them, as, for instance, of love (xvii. 24; cf. xv. 9 [iii. 35]; xiv. 31), but also of an action and reaction upon one another which argues a high measure, if not of exteriority, yet certainly of exteriorization. Thus, to instance only one of the most outstanding facts of Our Lord's discourses (not indeed confined to those in John's Gospel, but found also in His sayings recorded in the Synoptists, as e. g., Lk. iv. 43 [cf. || Mk. i. 38]; ix. 48; x. 16; iv. 34; v. 32; vii. 19; xix. 10), He continually represents Himself as on the one hand sent by God, and as, on the other, having come forth from the Father (e. g., Jn. viii. 42; x. 36; xvii. 3; v. 23, *et saepe*).

It is more important to point out that these phenomena of interrelationship are not confined to the Father and Son, but are extended also to the Spirit. Thus, for example, in a context

in which Our Lord had emphasized in the strongest manner
His own essential unity and continued interpenetration with
the Father ("If ye had known me, ye would have known my
Father also"; "He that hath seen me hath seen the Father";
"I am in the Father, and the Father in me"; "The Father
abiding in me doeth his works," Jn. xiv. 7, 9, 10), we read as
follows (Jn. xiv. 16–26): 'And *I* will make request of the
Father, and He shall give you *another* [thus sharply distinguished from Our Lord as a distinct Person] Advocate, that
He may be with you forever, the Spirit of Truth . . . He
abideth with you and shall be in you. I will not leave you orphans; I come unto you. . . . In that day ye shall know
that I am in the Father. . . . If a man love me, he will
keep my word; and my Father will love him and we [that is,
both Father and Son] will come unto him and make our abode
with him. . . . These things have I spoken unto you while
abiding with you. But the Advocate, the Holy Spirit, whom
the Father will send in my name, *He* shall teach you all things,
and bring to your remembrance all that *I* said unto you.' It
would be impossible to speak more distinctly of three who were
yet one. The Father, Son and Spirit are constantly distinguished from one another — the Son makes request of the
Father, and the Father in response to this request gives an
Advocate, "another" than the Son, who is sent in the Son's
name. And yet the oneness of these three is so kept in sight
that the coming of this "another Advocate" is spoken of without embarrassment as the coming of the Son Himself (vs. 18,
19, 20, 21), and indeed as the coming of the Father and the
Son (ver. 23). There is a sense, then, in which, when Christ
goes away, the Spirit comes in His stead; there is also a sense
in which, when the Spirit comes, Christ comes in Him; and
with Christ's coming the Father comes too. There is a distinction between the Persons brought into view; and with it an
identity among them; for both of which allowance must be
made. The same phenomena meet us in other passages. Thus,
we read again (xv. 26): 'But when there is come the Advocate
whom *I* will send unto you from [fellowship with] the Father,

the Spirit of Truth, which goeth forth from [fellowship with] the Father, *He* shall bear witness of *me*.' In the compass of this single verse, it is intimated that the Spirit is personally distinct from the Son, and yet, like Him, has His eternal home (in fellowship) with the Father, from whom He, like the Son, comes forth for His saving work, being sent thereunto, however, not in this instance by the Father, but by the Son.

This last feature is even more strongly emphasized in yet another passage in which the work of the Spirit in relation to the Son is presented as closely parallel with the work of the Son in relation to the Father (xvi. 5 ff.). 'But now I go unto Him that sent me. . . . Nevertheless *I* tell you the truth: it is expedient for you that *I* go away; for, if I go not away the Advocate will not come unto you; but if I go I will send Him unto you. And *He*, after He is come, will convict the world . . . of righteousness because I go to the Father and ye behold me no more. . . . I have yet many things to say unto you, but ye cannot bear them now. Howbeit when *He*, the Spirit of truth is come, He shall guide you into all the truth; for He shall not speak from Himself; but what things soever He shall hear, He shall speak, and He shall declare unto you the things that are to come. *He* shall glorify *me:* for He shall take of mine and shall show it unto you. All things whatsoever *the Father* hath are *mine:* therefore said I that He taketh of mine, and shall declare it unto you.' Here the Spirit is sent by the Son, and comes in order to complete and apply the Son's work, receiving His whole commission from the Son — not, however, in derogation of the Father, because when we speak of the things of the Son, that is to speak of the things of the Father.

It is not to be said, of course, that the doctrine of the Trinity is formulated in passages like these, with which the whole mass of Our Lord's discourses in John are strewn; but it certainly is presupposed in them, and that is, considered from the point of view of their probative force, even better. As we read we are kept in continual contact with three Persons who act, each as a distinct person, and yet who are in a deep, underlying sense, one. There is but one God — there is never any question of that — and yet this Son who has been sent into the world by God not only represents God but is God, and this Spirit whom the Son has in turn sent unto the world is also Himself God. Nothing could be clearer than that the Son and Spirit are distinct Persons, unless indeed it be that the Son of God is just God the Son and the Spirit of God just God the Spirit.

Meanwhile, the nearest approach to a formal announcement of the doctrine of the Trinity which is recorded from Our Lord's lips, or, perhaps we may say, which is to be found in the whole compass of the New Testament, has been preserved for us, not by John, but by one of the synoptists. It too, however, is only incidentally introduced, and has for its main object something very different from formulating the doctrine of the Trinity. It is embodied in the great commission which the resurrected Lord gave His disciples to be their "marching orders" "even unto the end of the world": "Go ye therefore, and make disciples of all the nations, baptizing them into the name of the Father and of the Son and of the Holy Spirit" (Mt. xxviii. 19). In seeking to estimate the significance of this great declaration, we must bear in mind the high solemnity of the utterance, by which we are required to give its full value to every word of it. Its phrasing is in any event, however, remarkable. It does not say, "In the names [plural] of the Father and of the Son and of the Holy Ghost"; nor yet (what might be taken to be equivalent to that), "In the name of the Father, and in the name of the Son, and in the name of the Holy Ghost," as if we had to deal with three separate Beings. Nor, on the other hand, does it say, "In the name of the Father, Son and Holy Ghost," as if "the Father, Son and Holy Ghost" might be taken as merely three designations of a single person. With stately impressiveness it asserts the unity of the three by combining them all within the bounds of the single Name; and then throws up into emphasis the distinctness of each by introducing them in turn with the repeated article: "In the name of the Father, and of the Son, and of the Holy Ghost" (Au-

thorized Version). These three, the Father, and the Son, and
the Holy Ghost, each stand in some clear sense over against the
others in distinct personality: these three, the Father, and
the Son, and the Holy Ghost, all unite in some profound sense
in the common participation of the one Name. Fully to comprehend the implication of this mode of statement, we must
bear in mind, further, the significance of the term, "the name,"
and the associations laden with which it came to the recipients
of this commission. For the Hebrew did not think of the name,
as we are accustomed to do, as a mere external symbol; but
rather as the adequate expression of the innermost being of its
bearer. In His name the Being of God finds expression; and
the Name of God — "this glorious and fearful name, Jehovah
thy God" (Deut. xxviii. 58) — was accordingly a most sacred
thing, being indeed virtually equivalent to God Himself. It is
no solecism, therefore, when we read (Isa. xxx. 27), "Behold,
the name of Jehovah cometh"; and the parallelisms are most
instructive when we read (Isa. lix. 19): 'So shall they fear the
Name of Jehovah from the west, and His glory from the rising
of the sun; for He shall come as a stream pent in which the
Spirit of Jehovah driveth.' So pregnant was the implication
of the Name, that it was possible for the term to stand absolutely, without adjunction of the name itself, as the sufficient
representative of the majesty of Jehovah: it was a terrible
thing to 'blaspheme the Name' (Lev. xxiv. 11). All those
over whom Jehovah's Name was called were His, His possession
to whom He owed protection. It is for His Name's sake, therefore, that afflicted Judah cries to the Hope of Israel, the Saviour thereof in time of trouble: 'O Jehovah, Thou art in the
midst of us, and Thy Name is called upon us; leave us not'
(Jer. xiv. 9); and His people find the appropriate expression of
their deepest shame in the lament, 'We have become as they
over whom Thou never barest rule; as they upon whom Thy
Name was not called' (Isa. lxiii. 19); while the height of joy
is attained in the cry, 'Thy Name, Jehovah, God of Hosts,
is called upon me' (Jer. xv. 16; cf. II Chron. vii. 14; Dan. ix.
18, 19). When, therefore, Our Lord commanded His disciples

to baptize those whom they brought to His obedience "into
the name of . . . ," He was using language charged to them
with high meaning. He could not have been understood otherwise than as substituting for the Name of Jehovah this other
Name "of the Father, and of the Son, and of the Holy Ghost";
and this could not possibly have meant to His disciples anything else than that Jehovah was now to be known to them by
the new Name, of the Father, and the Son, and the Holy
Ghost. The only alternative would have been that, for the
community which He was founding, Jesus was supplanting
Jehovah by a new God; and this alternative is no less than
monstrous. There is no alternative, therefore, to understanding Jesus here to be giving for His community a new Name to
Jehovah and that new Name to be the threefold Name of
"the Father, and the Son, and the Holy Ghost." Nor is there
room for doubt that by "the Son" in this threefold Name, He
meant just Himself with all the implications of distinct personality which this carries with it; and, of course, that further
carries with it the equally distinct personality of "the Father"
and "the Holy Ghost," with whom "the Son" is here associated, and from whom alike "the Son" is here distinguished.
This is a direct ascription to Jehovah the God of Israel, of a
threefold personality, and is therewith the direct enunciation
of the doctrine of the Trinity. We are not witnessing here the
birth of the doctrine of the Trinity; that is presupposed. What
we are witnessing is the authoritative announcement of the
Trinity as the God of Christianity by its Founder, in one of
the most solemn of His recorded declarations. Israel had worshipped the one only true God under the Name of Jehovah;
Christians are to worship the same one only and true God
under the Name of "the Father, and the Son, and the Holy
Ghost." This is the distinguishing characteristic of Christians;
and that is as much as to say that the doctrine of the Trinity
is, according to Our Lord's own apprehension of it, the distinctive mark of the religion which He founded.

A passage of such range of implication has, of course, not
escaped criticism and challenge. An attempt which cannot be

characterized as other than frivolous has even been made to dismiss it from the text of Matthew's Gospel. Against this, the whole body of external evidence cries out; and the internal evidence is of itself not less decisive to the same effect. When the "universalism," "ecclesiasticism," and "high theology" of the passage are pleaded against its genuineness, it is forgotten that to the Jesus of Matthew there are attributed not only such parables as those of the Leaven and the Mustard Seed, but such declarations as those contained in viii. 11, 12; xxi. 43; xxiv. 14; that in this Gospel alone is Jesus recorded as speaking familiarly about His church (xvi. 18; xviii. 17); and that, after the great declaration of xi. 27 ff., nothing remained in lofty attribution to be assigned to Him. When these same objections are urged against recognizing the passage as an authentic saying of Jesus' own, it is quite obvious that the Jesus of the evangelists cannot be in mind. The declaration here recorded is quite in character with the Jesus of Matthew's Gospel, as has just been intimated; and no less with the Jesus of the whole New Testament transmission. It will scarcely do, first to construct a priori a Jesus to our own liking, and then to discard as "unhistorical" all in the New Testament transmission which would be unnatural to such a Jesus. It is not these discarded passages but our a priori Jesus which is unhistorical. In the present instance, moreover, the historicity of the assailed saying is protected by an important historical relation in which it stands. It is not merely Jesus who speaks out of a Trinitarian consciousness, but all the New Testament writers as well. The universal possession by His followers of so firm a hold on such a doctrine requires the assumption that some such teaching as is here attributed to Him was actually contained in Jesus' instructions to His followers. Even had it not been attributed to Him in so many words by the record, we should have had to assume that some such declaration had been made by Him. In these circumstances, there can be no good reason to doubt that it was made by Him, when it is expressly attributed to Him by the record.

When we turn from the discourses of Jesus to the writings

of His followers with a view to observing how the assumption of the doctrine of the Trinity underlies their whole fabric also, we naturally go first of all to the letters of Paul. Their very mass is impressive; and the definiteness with which their composition within a generation of the death of Jesus may be fixed adds importance to them as historical witnesses. Certainly they leave nothing to be desired in the richness of their testimony to the Trinitarian conception of God which underlies them. Throughout the whole series, from I Thess., which comes from about 52 A.D., to II Tim., which was written about 68 A.D., the redemption, which it is their one business to proclaim and commend, and all the blessings which enter into it or accompany it are referred consistently to a threefold Divine causation. Everywhere, throughout their pages, God the Father, the Lord Jesus Christ, and the Holy Spirit appear as the joint objects of all religious adoration, and the conjunct source of all Divine operations. In the freedom of the allusions which are made to them, now and again one alone of the three is thrown up into prominent view; but more often two of them are conjoined in thanksgiving or prayer; and not infrequently all three are brought together as the apostle strives to give some adequate expression to his sense of indebtedness to the Divine source of all good for blessings received, or to his longing on behalf of himself or of his readers for further communion with the God of grace. It is regular for him to begin his Epistles with a prayer for "grace and peace" for his readers, "from God our Father, and the Lord Jesus Christ," as the joint source of these Divine blessings by way of eminence (Rom. i. 7; I Cor. i. 3; II Cor. i. 2; Gal. i. 3; Eph. i. 2; Phil. i. 2; II Thess. i. 2; I Tim. i. 2; II Tim. i. 2; Philem. ver. 3; cf. I Thess. i. 1). It is obviously no departure from this habit in the essence of the matter, but only in relative fulness of expression, when in the opening words of the Epistle to the Colossians the clause "and the Lord Jesus Christ" is omitted, and we read merely: "Grace to you and peace from God our Father." So also it would have been no departure from it in the essence of the matter, but only in relative fulness of expression, if in any instance the name of the Holy Spirit had chanced to be adjoined to the other two, as in the single instance of II Cor. xiii. 14 it is adjoined to them in the closing prayer for grace with which Paul ends his letters, and which ordinarily takes the simple form of, "the grace of our Lord Jesus Christ be with you" (Rom. xvi. 20; I Cor. xvi. 23; Gal. vi. 18; Phil. iv, 23; I Thess. v. 28; II Thess. iii. 18; Philem. ver. 25; more expanded form, Eph. vi. 23, 24; more compressed, Col. iv. 18; I Tim. vi. 21; II Tim. iv. 22; Tit. iii. 15). Between these opening and closing passages the allusions to God the Father, the Lord Jesus Christ, and the Holy Spirit are constant and most intricately interlaced. Paul's monotheism is intense: the first premise of all his thought on Divine things is the unity of God (Rom. iii. 30; I Cor. viii. 4; Gal iii. 20; Eph. iv. 6; I Tim. ii. 5; cf. Rom. xvi. 22; I Tim. i. 17). Yet to him God the Father is no more God than the Lord Jesus Christ is God, or the Holy Spirit is God. The Spirit of God is to him related to God as the spirit of man is to man (I Cor. ii. 11), and therefore if the Spirit of God dwells in us, that is God dwelling in us (Rom. viii. 10 ff.), and we are by that fact constituted temples of God (I Cor. iii. 16). And no expression is too strong for him to use in order to assert the Godhead of Christ: He is "our great God" (Tit. ii. 13); He is "God over all" (Rom. ix. 5); and indeed it is expressly declared of Him that the "fulness of the Godhead," that is, everything that enters into Godhead and constitutes it Godhead, dwells in Him. In the very act of asserting his monotheism Paul takes Our Lord up into this unique Godhead. "There is no God but one," he roundly asserts, and then illustrates and proves this assertion by remarking that the heathen may have "gods many, and lords many," but "to us there is one God, the Father, of whom are all things, and we unto him; and one Lord, Jesus Christ, through whom are all things, and we through him" (I Cor. viii. 6). Obviously, this "one God, the Father," and "one Lord, Jesus Christ," are embraced together in the one God who alone is. Paul's conception of the one God, whom alone he worships, includes, in other words, a recognition that within the unity of His Being, there exists such a distinction of Persons as is given us in the "one God, the Father" and the "one Lord, Jesus Christ."

In numerous passages scattered through Paul's Epistles, from the earliest of them (I Thess. i. 2–5; II Thess. ii. 13, 14) to the latest (Tit. iii. 4–6; II Tim. i. 3, 13, 14), all three Persons, God the Father, the Lord Jesus Christ and the Holy Spirit, are brought together, in the most incidental manner, as co-sources of all the saving blessings which come to believers in Christ. A typical series of such passages may be found in Eph. ii. 18; iii. 2–5, 14, 17; iv. 4–6; v. 18–20. But the most interesting instances are offered to us perhaps by the Epistles to the Corinthians. In I Cor. xii. 4–6 Paul presents the abounding spiritual gifts with which the church was blessed in a threefold aspect, and connects these aspects with the three Divine Persons. "Now there are diversities of gifts, but the same Spirit. And there are diversities of ministrations, and the same Lord. And there are diversities of workings, but the same God, who worketh all things in all." It may be thought that there is a measure of what might almost be called artificiality in assigning the endowments of the church, as they are graces to the Spirit, as they are services to Christ, and as they are energizings to God. But thus there is only the more strikingly revealed the underlying Trinitarian conception as dominating the structure of the clauses: Paul clearly so writes, not because "gifts," "workings," "operations" stand out in his thought as greatly diverse things, but because God, the Lord, and the Spirit lie in the back of his mind constantly suggesting a threefold causality behind every manifestation of grace. The Trinity is alluded to rather than asserted; but it is so alluded to as to show that it constitutes the determining basis of all Paul's thought of the God of redemption. Even more instructive is II Cor. xiii. 14, which has passed into general liturgical use in the churches as a benediction: "The grace of the Lord Jesus Christ, and the love of God, and the communion of the Holy Spirit, be with you all." Here the three highest redemptive blessings are brought together, and attached distributively to the three Persons of the Triune God. There is again no formal teaching

of the doctrine of the Trinity; there is only another instance of
natural speaking out of a Trinitarian consciousness. Paul is
simply thinking of the Divine source of these great blessings;
but he habitually thinks of this Divine source of redemptive
blessings after a trinal fashion. He therefore does not say, as
he might just as well have said, "The grace and love and communion of God be with you all," but "The grace of the Lord
Jesus Christ, and the love of God, and the communion of the
Holy Spirit, be with you all." Thus he bears, almost unconsciously but most richly, witness to the trinal composition of
the Godhead as conceived by Him.

The phenomena of Paul's Epistles are repeated in the other
writings of the New Testament. In these other writings also it
is everywhere assumed that the redemptive activities of God
rest on a threefold source in God the Father, the Lord Jesus
Christ, and the Holy Spirit; and these three Persons repeatedly
come forward together in the expressions of Christian hope or
the aspirations of Christian devotion (e. g., Heb. ii. 3, 4; vi.
4–6; x. 29–31; I Pet. i. 2; ii. 3–12; iv. 13–19; I Jn. v. 4–8; Jude
vs. 20, 21; Rev. i. 4–6). Perhaps as typical instances as any are
supplied by the two following: "According to the foreknowledge of God the Father, in sanctification of the Spirit, unto
obedience and sprinkling of the blood of Jesus Christ" (I Pet.
i. 2); "Praying in the Holy Spirit, keep yourselves in the love
of God, looking for the mercy of our Lord Jesus Christ unto
eternal life" (Jude vs. 20, 21). To these may be added the
highly symbolical instance from the Apocalypse: 'Grace to
you and peace from Him which is and was and which is to come;
and from the Seven Spirits which are before His throne; and
from Jesus Christ, who is the faithful witness, the firstborn of
the dead, and the ruler of the kings of the earth' (Rev. i. 4, 5).
Clearly these writers, too, write out of a fixed Trinitarian consciousness and bear their testimony to the universal understanding current in apostolical circles. Everywhere and by all
it was fully understood that the one God whom Christians
worshipped and from whom alone they expected redemption
and all that redemption brought with it, included within His

undiminished unity the three: God the Father, the Lord Jesus Christ, and the Holy Spirit, whose activities relatively to one another are conceived as distinctly personal. This is the uniform and pervasive testimony of the New Testament, and it is the more impressive that it is given with such unstudied naturalness and simplicity, with no effort to distinguish between what have come to be called the ontological and the economical aspects of the Trinitarian distinctions, and indeed without apparent consciousness of the existence of such a distinction of aspects. Whether God is thought of in Himself or in His operations, the underlying conception runs unaffectedly into trinal forms.

It will not have escaped observation that the Trinitarian terminology of Paul and the other writers of the New Testament is not precisely identical with that of Our Lord as recorded for us in His discourses. Paul, for example — and the same is true of the other New Testament writers (except John) — does not speak, as Our Lord is recorded as speaking, of the Father, the Son, and the Holy Spirit, so much as of God, the Lord Jesus Christ, and the Holy Spirit. This difference of terminology finds its account in large measure in the different relations in which the speakers stand to the Trinity. Our Lord could not naturally speak of Himself, as one of the Trinitarian Persons, by the designation of "the Lord," while the designation of "the Son," expressing as it does His consciousness of close relation, and indeed of exact similarity, to God, came naturally to His lips. But He was Paul's Lord; and Paul naturally thought and spoke of Him as such. In point of fact, "Lord" is one of Paul's favorite designations of Christ, and indeed has become with him practically a proper name for Christ, and in point of fact, his Divine Name for Christ. It is naturally, therefore, his Trinitarian name for Christ. Because when he thinks of Christ as Divine he calls Him "Lord," he naturally, when he thinks of the three Persons together as the Triune God, sets Him as "Lord" by the side of God — Paul's constant name for "the Father" — and the Holy Spirit. Question may no doubt be raised whether it would have been possible for Paul to have

done this, especially with the constancy with which he has
done it, if, in his conception of it, the very essence of the Trinity
were enshrined in the terms "Father" and "Son." Paul is
thinking of the Trinity, to be sure, from the point of view of a
worshipper, rather than from that of a systematizer. He designates the Persons of the Trinity therefore rather from his relations to them than from their relations to one another. He sees
in the Trinity his God, his Lord, and the Holy Spirit who
dwells in him; and naturally he so speaks currently of the three
Persons. It remains remarkable, nevertheless, if the very essence of the Trinity were thought of by him as resident in the
terms "Father," "Son," that in his numerous allusions to the
Trinity in the Godhead, he never betrays any sense of this. It
is noticeable also that in their allusions to the Trinity, there is
preserved, neither in Paul nor in the other writers of the New
Testament, the order of the names as they stand in Our Lord's
great declaration (Mt. xxviii. 19). The reverse order occurs,
indeed, occasionally, as, for example, in I Cor. xii. 4–6 (cf.
Eph. iv. 4–6); and this may be understood as a climactic arrangement and so far a testimony to the order of Mt. xxviii.
19. But the order is very variable; and in the most formal enumeration of the three Persons, that of II Cor. xiii. 14, it stands
thus: Lord, God, Spirit. The question naturally suggests itself
whether the order Father, Son, Spirit was especially significant
to Paul and his fellow-writers of the New Testament. If in their
conviction the very essence of the doctrine of the Trinity was
embodied in this order, should we not anticipate that there
should appear in their numerous allusions to the Trinity some
suggestion of this conviction?

　　Such facts as these have a bearing upon the testimony of
the New Testament to the interrelations of the Persons of the
Trinity. To the fact of the Trinity — to the fact, that is, that
in the unity of the Godhead there subsist three Persons, each
of whom has his particular part in the working out of salvation — the New Testament testimony is clear, consistent, pervasive and conclusive. There is included in this testimony
constant and decisive witness to the complete and undiminished

Deity of each of these Persons; no language is too exalted to apply to each of them in turn in the effort to give expression to the writer's sense of His Deity: the name that is given to each is fully understood to be "the name that is above every name." When we attempt to press the inquiry behind the broad fact, however, with a view to ascertaining exactly how the New Testament writers conceive the three Persons to be related, the one to the other, we meet with great difficulties. Nothing could seem more natural, for example, than to assume that the mutual relations of the Persons of the Trinity are revealed in the designations, "the Father, the Son, and the Holy Spirit," which are given them by Our Lord in the solemn formula of Mt. xxviii. 19. Our confidence in this assumption is somewhat shaken, however, when we observe, as we have just observed, that these designations are not carefully preserved in their allusions to the Trinity by the writers of the New Testament at large, but are characteristic only of Our Lord's allusions and those of John, whose modes of speech in general very closely resemble those of Our Lord. Our confidence is still further shaken when we observe that the implications with respect to the mutual relations of the Trinitarian Persons, which are ordinarily derived from these designations, do not so certainly lie in them as is commonly supposed.

It may be very natural to see in the designation "Son" an intimation of subordination and derivation of Being, and it may not be difficult to ascribe a similar connotation to the term "Spirit." But it is quite certain that this was not the denotation of either term in the Semitic consciousness, which underlies the phraseology of Scripture; and it may even be thought doubtful whether it was included even in their remoter suggestions. What underlies the conception of sonship in Scriptural speech is just "likeness"; whatever the father is that the son is also. The emphatic application of the term "Son" to one of the Trinitarian Persons, accordingly, asserts rather His equality with the Father than His subordination to the Father; and if there is any implication of derivation in it, it would appear to be very distant. The adjunction of the adjective "only begotten" (Jn. i. 14; iii. 16–18; I Jn. iv. 9) need add only the idea of uniqueness, not of derivation (Ps. xxii. 20; xxv. 16; xxxv. 17; Wisd. vii. 22 m.); and even such a phrase as "God only begotten" (Jn. i. 18 m.) may contain no implication of derivation, but only of absolutely unique consubstantiality; as also such a phrase as "the first-begotten of all creation" (Col. i. 15) may convey no intimation of coming into being, but merely assert priority of existence. In like manner, the designation "Spirit of God" or "Spirit of Jehovah," which meets us frequently in the Old Testament, certainly does not convey the idea there either of derivation or of subordination, but is just the executive name of God — the designation of God from the point of view of His activity — and imports accordingly identity with God; and there is no reason to suppose that, in passing from the Old Testament to the New Testament, the term has taken on an essentially different meaning. It happens, oddly enough, moreover, that we have in the New Testament itself what amounts almost to formal definitions of the two terms "Son" and "Spirit," and in both cases the stress is laid on the notion of equality or sameness. In Jn. v. 18 we read: 'On this account, therefore, the Jews sought the more to kill him, because, not only did he break the Sabbath, but also called God his own Father, making himself equal to God.' The point lies, of course, in the adjective "own." Jesus was, rightly, understood to call God "his *own* Father," that is, to use the terms "Father" and "Son" not in a merely figurative sense, as when Israel was called God's son, but in the real sense. And this was understood to be claiming to be all that God is. To be the Son of God in any sense was to be like God in that sense; to be God's *own* Son was to be exactly like God, to be "equal with God." Similarly, we read in I Cor. ii. 10, 11: 'For the Spirit searcheth all things, yea, the deep things of God. For who of men knoweth the things of a man, save the spirit of man which is in him? Even so the things of God none knoweth, save the Spirit of God.' Here the Spirit appears as the substrate of the Divine self-consciousness, the principle of God's knowledge of Himself: He is, in a word, just God Himself in the innermost essence of His Being. As the spirit of man is the seat of human life, the very life of man itself, so the Spirit of God is His very life-element. How can He be supposed, then, to be subordinate to God, or to derive His Being from God? If, however, the subordination of the Son and Spirit to the Father in modes of subsistence and their derivation from the Father are not implicates of their designation as Son and Spirit, it will be hard to find in the New Testament compelling evidence of their subordination and derivation.

There is, of course, no question that in "modes of operation," as it is technically called — that is to say, in the functions ascribed to the several Persons of the Trinity in the redemptive process, and, more broadly, in the entire dealing of God with the world — the principle of subordination is clearly expressed. The Father is first, the Son is second, and the Spirit is third, in the operations of God as revealed to us in general, and very especially in those operations by which redemption is accomplished. Whatever the Father does, He does through the Son (Rom. ii. 16; iii. 22; v. 1, 11, 17, 21; Eph. i. 5; I Thess. v. 9; Tit. iii. v) by the Spirit. The Son is sent by the Father and does His Father's will (Jn. vi. 38); the Spirit is sent by the Son and does not speak from Himself, but only takes of Christ's and shows it unto His people (Jn. xvii. 7 ff.); and we have Our Lord's own word for it that 'one that is sent is not greater than he that sent him' (Jn. xiii. 16). In crisp decisiveness, Our Lord even declares, indeed: 'My Father is greater than I' (Jn. xiv. 28); and Paul tells us that Christ is God's, even as we are Christ's (I Cor. iii. 23), and that as Christ is "the head of every man," so God is "the head of Christ" (I Cor. xi. 3). But it is not so clear that the principle of subordination rules also in "modes of subsistence," as it is technically phrased; that is to say, in the necessary relation of the Persons of the Trinity to one another. The very richness and variety of the expression of their subordination, the one to the other, in modes of operation, create a difficulty in attaining certainty whether they are represented as also subordinate the one to the other in modes of subsistence. Question is raised in each

case of apparent intimation of subordination in modes of subsistence, whether it may not, after all, be explicable as only
another expression of subordination in modes of operation. It
may be natural to assume that a subordination in modes of
operation rests on a subordination in modes of subsistence;
that the reason why it is the Father that sends the Son and
the Son that sends the Spirit is that the Son is subordinate to
the Father, and the Spirit to the Son. But we are bound to bear
in mind that these relations of subordination in modes of operation may just as well be due to a convention, an agreement,
between the Persons of the Trinity — a "Covenant" as it is
technically called — by virtue of which a distinct function in
the work of redemption is voluntarily assumed by each. It is
eminently desirable, therefore, at the least, that some definite
evidence of subordination in modes of subsistence should be
discoverable before it is assumed. In the case of the relation of
the Son to the Father, there is the added difficulty of the incarnation, in which the Son, by the assumption of a creaturely
nature into union with Himself, enters into new relations with
the Father of a definitely subordinate character. Question has
even been raised whether the very designations of Father and
Son may not be expressive of these new relations, and therefore without significance with respect to the eternal relations
of the Persons so designated. This question must certainly be
answered in the negative. Although, no doubt, in many of the
instances in which the terms "Father" and "Son" occur, it
would be possible to take them of merely economical relations,
there ever remain some which are intractable to this treatment, and we may be sure that "Father" and "Son" are applied to their eternal and necessary relations. But these terms,
as we have seen, do not appear to imply relations of first and
second, superiority and subordination, in modes of subsistence;
and the fact of the humiliation of the Son of God for His earthly
work does introduce a factor into the interpretation of the
passages which import His subordination to the Father, which
throws doubt upon the inference from them of an eternal relation of subordination in the Trinity itself. It must at least be

said that in the presence of the great New Testament doctrines of the Covenant of Redemption on the one hand, and of the Humiliation of the Son of God for His work's sake and of the Two Natures in the constitution of His Person as incarnated, on the other, the difficulty of interpreting subordinationist passages of eternal relations between the Father and Son becomes extreme. The question continually obtrudes itself, whether they do not rather find their full explanation in the facts embodied in the doctrines of the Covenant, the Humiliation of Christ, and the Two Natures of His incarnated Person. Certainly in such circumstances it were thoroughly illegitimate to press such passages to suggest any subordination for the Son or the Spirit which would in any manner impair that complete identity with the Father in Being and that complete equality with the Father in powers which are constantly presupposed, and frequently emphatically, though only incidentally, asserted for them throughout the whole fabric of the New Testament.

The Trinity of the Persons of the Godhead, shown in the incarnation and the redemptive work of God the Son, and the descent and saving work of God the Spirit, is thus everywhere assumed in the New Testament, and comes to repeated fragmentary but none the less emphatic and illuminating expression in its pages. As the roots of its revelation are set in the threefold Divine causality of the saving process, it naturally finds an echo also in the consciousness of everyone who has experienced this salvation. Every redeemed soul, knowing himself reconciled with God through His Son, and quickened into newness of life by His Spirit, turns alike to Father, Son and Spirit with the exclamation of reverent gratitude upon his lips, "My Lord and my God!" If he could not construct the doctrine of the Trinity out of his consciousness of salvation, yet the elements of his consciousness of salvation are interpreted to him and reduced to order only by the doctrine of the Trinity which he finds underlying and giving their significance and consistency to the teaching of the Scriptures as to the processes of salvation. By means of this doctrine he is able to think

clearly and consequently of his threefold relation to the saving
God, experienced by Him as Fatherly love sending a Redeemer,
as redeeming love executing redemption, as saving love applying redemption: all manifestations in distinct methods and by
distinct agencies of the one seeking and saving love of God.
Without the doctrine of the Trinity, his conscious Christian
life would be thrown into confusion and left in disorganization
if not, indeed, given an air of unreality; with the doctrine of
the Trinity, order, significance and reality are brought to every
element of it. Accordingly, the doctrine of the Trinity and the
doctrine of redemption, historically, stand or fall together. A
Unitarian theology is commonly associated with a Pelagian
anthropology and a Socinian soteriology. It is a striking testimony which is borne by F. E. Koenig ("Offenbarungsbegriff
des AT," 1882, I, 125): "I have learned that many cast off
the whole history of redemption for no other reason than because they have not attained to a conception of the Triune
God." It is in this intimacy of relation between the doctrines
of the Trinity and redemption that the ultimate reason lies
why the Christian church could not rest until it had attained
a definite and well-compacted doctrine of the Trinity. Nothing
else could be accepted as an adequate foundation for the experience of the Christian salvation. Neither the Sabellian nor
the Arian construction could meet and satisfy the data of the
consciousness of salvation, any more than either could meet
and satisfy the data of the Scriptural revelation. The data of
the Scriptural revelation might, to be sure, have been left unsatisfied: men might have found a *modus vivendi* with neglected,
or even with perverted Scriptural teaching. But perverted or
neglected elements of Christian experience are more clamant
in their demands for attention and correction. The dissatisfied
Christian consciousness necessarily searched the Scriptures, on
the emergence of every new attempt to state the doctrine of
the nature and relations of God, to see whether these things
were true, and never reached contentment until the Scriptural
data were given their consistent formulation in a valid doctrine
of the Trinity. Here too the heart of man was restless until it

found its rest in the Triune God, the author, procurer and applier of salvation.

The determining impulse to the formulation of the doctrine of the Trinity in the church was the church's profound conviction of the absolute Deity of Christ, on which as on a pivot the whole Christian conception of God from the first origins of Christianity turned. The guiding principle in the formulation of the doctrine was supplied by the Baptismal Formula announced by Jesus (Mt. xxviii. 19), from which was derived the ground-plan of the baptismal confessions and "rules of faith" which very soon began to be framed all over the church. It was by these two fundamental *principia* — the true Deity of Christ and the Baptismal Formula — that all attempts to formulate the Christian doctrine of God were tested, and by their molding power that the church at length found itself in possession of a form of statement which did full justice to the data of the redemptive revelation as reflected in the New Testament and the demands of the Christian heart under the experience of salvation.

In the nature of the case the formulated doctrine was of slow attainment. The influence of inherited conceptions and of current philosophies inevitably showed itself in the efforts to construe to the intellect the immanent faith of Christians. In the second century the dominant neo-Stoic and neo-Platonic ideas deflected Christian thought into subordinationist channels, and produced what is known as the Logos-Christology, which looks upon the Son as a prolation of Deity reduced to such dimensions as comported with relations with a world of time and space; meanwhile, to a great extent, the Spirit was neglected altogether. A reaction which, under the name of Monarchianism, identified the Father, Son, and Spirit so completely that they were thought of only as different aspects or different moments in the life of the one Divine Person, called now Father, now Son, now Spirit, as His several activities came successively into view, almost succeeded in establishing itself in the third century as the doctrine of the church at large. In the conflict between these two opposite tendencies the church

gradually found its way, under the guidance of the Baptismal
Formula elaborated into a "Rule of Faith," to a better and
more well-balanced conception, until a real doctrine of the
Trinity at length came to expression, particularly in the West,
through the brilliant dialectic of Tertullian. It was thus ready
at hand, when, in the early years of the fourth century, the
Logos-Christology, in opposition to dominant Sabellian tendencies, ran to seed in what is known as Arianism, to which the
Son was a creature, though exalted above all other creatures
as their Creator and Lord; and the church was thus prepared
to assert its settled faith in a Triune God, one in being, but in
whose unity there subsisted three consubstantial Persons. Under the leadership of Athanasius this doctrine was proclaimed
as the faith of the church at the Council of Nice in 325 A.D.,
and by his strenuous labors and those of "the three great Cap-
padocians," the two Gregories and Basil, it gradually won its
way to the actual acceptance of the entire church. It was at
the hands of Augustine, however, a century later, that the doctrine thus become the church doctrine in fact as well as in
theory, received its most complete elaboration and most carefully grounded statement. In the form which he gave it, and
which is embodied in that "battle-hymn of the early church,"
the so-called Athanasian Creed, it has retained its place as the
fit expression of the faith of the church as to the nature of its
God until today. The language in which it is couched, even in
this final declaration, still retains elements of speech which owe
their origin to the modes of thought characteristic of the Logos-
Christology of the second century, fixed in the nomenclature
of the church by the Nicene Creed of 325 A.D., though carefully guarded there against the subordinationism inherent in
the Logos-Christology, and made the vehicle rather of the Nicene doctrines of the eternal generation of the Son and procession of the Spirit, with the consequent subordination of the
Son and Spirit to the Father in modes of subsistence as well as
of operation. In the Athanasian Creed, however, the principle
of the equalization of the three Persons, which was already the
dominant motive of the Nicene Creed — the *homooúsia* — is so

strongly emphasized as practically to push out of sight, if not quite out of existence, these remanent suggestions of derivation and subordination. It has been found necessary, nevertheless, from time to time, vigorously to reassert the principle of equalization, over against a tendency unduly to emphasize the elements of subordinationism which still hold a place thus in the traditional language in which the church states its doctrine of the Trinity. In particular, it fell to Calvin, in the interests of the true Deity of Christ — the constant motive of the whole body of Trinitarian thought — to reassert and make good the attribute of self-existence (*autotheotōs*) for the Son. Thus Calvin takes his place, alongside of Tertullian, Athanasius and Augustine, as one of the chief contributors to the exact and vital statement of the Christian doctrine of the Triune God.

LITERATURE. — F. C. Baur, "Die christliche Lehre von der Dreieinigkeit Gottes," 3 vols., Tübingen, 1841–1843; Dionysius Petavius, "De Trinitate (vol. ii, of "De Theologicis Dogmaticis," Paris, 1647); G. Bull, "A Defence of the Nicene Creed" (1685), 2 vols., Oxford, 1851; G. S. Faber, "The Apostolicity of Trinitarianism," 2 vols., 1832; Augustine, "On the Holy Trinity" (vol. iii of "Nicene and Post-Nicene Fathers of the Christian Church," 1–228), New York, 1887; Calvin, "Institutes of the Christian Religion," I, ch. xiii; C. Hodge, "Systematic Theology and Index," I, New York, 1873, 442–482; H. Bavinck, "Gereformeerde Dogmatiek²," II, Kampen, 1908, 260–347 (gives excellent references to literature); S. Harris, "God, the Creator, and Lord of All," New York, 1896; R. Rocholl, "Der christliche Gottesbegriff," Göttingen, 1900; W. F. Adeney, "The Christian Conception of God," London, 1909, 215–246; J. Lebreton, "Les origines du dogme de la Trinité," Paris, 1910; J. C. K. Hofmann, "Der Schriftbeweis²," Nördlingen, 1857–1860, I, 85–111; J. L. S. Lutz, "Biblische Dogmatik," Pforzheim, 1847, 319–394; R. W. Landis, "A Plea for the Catholic Doctrine of the Trinity," Philadelphia, 1832; E. H. Bickersteth, "The Rock of Ages," etc., London, 1860, New York, 1861; E. Riggenbach, "Der trinitarische Taufbefehl,

Mt. xxviii. 19" (in Schlatter and Cremer, "Beiträge zur Förderung christlicher Theologie," 1903, VII; also 1904, VIII); F. J. Hall, "The Trinity," London and New York, 1910, 100–141; J. Pearson, "An Exposition of the Creed," ed. Chevallier and Sinker, Cambridge, 1899; J. Howe, "Calm Discourse on the Trinity," in "Works," ed. Hunt, London, 1810–1822; J. Owen, "Vindication of the Doctrine of the Holy Trinity," and "Saint's Fellowship with the Trinity," in "Works," Gould's ed., London, 1850–1855; J. Edwards, "Observations concerning the Scripture Economy of the Trinity," etc., New York, 1880, also "An Unpublished Essay on the Trinity," New York, 1903; J. R. Illingworth, "The Doctrine of the Trinity Apologetically Considered," London and New York, 1907; A. F. W. Ingram, "The Love of the Trinity," New York, 1908.

[NOTE. — In this article the author has usually given his own renderings of original passages, and not those of any particular VS. — EDITORS.]

V

THE PERSON OF CHRIST

THE PERSON OF CHRIST [1]

It is the purpose of this article to make as clear as possible the conception of the Person of Christ, in the technical sense of that term, which lies on — or, if we prefer to say so, beneath — the pages of the New Testament. Were it its purpose to trace out the process by which this great mystery has been revealed to men, a beginning would need to be taken from the intimations as to the nature of the person of the Messiah in Old Testament prophecy, and an attempt would require to be made to discriminate the exact contribution of each organ of revelation to our knowledge. And were there added to this a desire to ascertain the progress of the apprehension of this mystery by men, there would be demanded a further inquiry into the exact degree of understanding which was brought to the truth revealed at each stage of its revelation. The magnitudes with which such investigations deal, however, are very minute; and the profit to be derived from them is not, in a case like the present, very great. It is, of course, of importance to know how the person of the Messiah was represented in the predictions of the Old Testament; and it is a matter at least of interest to note, for example, the difficulty experienced by Our Lord's immediate disciples in comprehending all that was involved in His manifestation. But, after all, the constitution of Our Lord's person is a matter of revelation, not of human thought; and it is pre-eminently a revelation of the New Testament, not of the Old Testament. And the New Testament is all the product of a single movement, at a single stage of its development, and therefore presents in its fundamental teaching a common character. The whole of the New Testament was written within the limits of about half a century; or,

[1] Article "Person of Christ" from *The International Standard Bible Encyclopaedia*, James Orr, General editor, v. 4, pp. 2338–2348. Pub. Chicago, 1915, by Howard-Severance Co.

if we except the writings of John, within the narrow bounds of a couple of decades; and the entire body of writings which enter into it are so much of a piece that it may be plausibly represented that they all bear the stamp of a single mind. In its fundamental teaching, the New Testament lends itself, therefore, more readily to what is called dogmatic than to what is called genetic treatment; and we shall penetrate most surely into its essential meaning if we take our start from its clearest and fullest statements, and permit their light to be thrown upon its more incidental allusions. This is peculiarly the case with such a matter as the person of Christ, which is dealt with chiefly incidentally, as a thing already understood by all, and needing only to be alluded to rather than formally expounded. That we may interpret these allusions aright, it is requisite that we should recover from the first the common conception which underlies them all.

I. THE TEACHING OF PAUL

We begin, then, with the most didactic of the New Testament writers, the apostle Paul, and with one of the passages in which he most fully intimates his conception of the person of his Lord, Phil. ii. 5–9. Even here, however, Paul is not formally expounding the doctrine of the Person of Christ; he is only alluding to certain facts concerning His person and action perfectly well known to his readers, in order that he may give point to an adduction of Christ's example. He is exhorting his readers to unselfishness, such unselfishness as esteems others better than ourselves, and looks not only on our own things but also on those of others. Precisely this unselfishness, he declares, was exemplified by Our Lord. He did not look upon His own things but the things of others; that is to say, He did not stand upon His rights, but was willing to forego all that He might justly have claimed for Himself for the good of others. For, says Paul, though, as we all know, in His intrinsic nature He was nothing other than God, yet He did not, as we all know right well, look greedily on His condition of equality with God, but made no account of Himself, taking the form of a servant, being made in the likeness of men; and, being found in fashion as a man, humbled Himself, becoming obedient up to death itself, and that, the death of the cross. The statement is thrown into historical form; it tells the story of Christ's life on earth. But it presents His life on earth as a life in all its elements alien to His intrinsic nature, and assumed only in the performance of an unselfish purpose. On earth He lived as a man, and subjected Himself to the common lot of men. But He was not by nature a man, nor was He in His own nature subject to the fortunes of human life. By nature He was God; and He would have naturally lived as became God — 'on an equality with God.' He became man by a voluntary act, 'taking no account of Himself,' and, having become man, He voluntarily lived out His human life under the conditions which the fulfilment of His unselfish purpose imposed on Him.

The terms in which these great affirmations are made deserve the most careful attention. The language in which Our Lord's intrinsic Deity is expressed, for example, is probably as strong as any that could be devised. Paul does not say simply, "He was God." He says, "He was in the form of God," employing a turn of speech which throws emphasis upon Our Lord's possession of the specific quality of God. "Form" is a term which expresses the sum of those characterizing qualities which make a thing the precise thing that it is. Thus, the "form" of a sword (in this case mostly matters of external configuration) is all that makes a given piece of metal specifically a sword, rather than, say, a spade. And "the form of God" is the sum of the characteristics which make the being we call "God," specifically God, rather than some other being — an angel, say, or a man. When Our Lord is said to be in "the form of God," therefore, He is declared, in the most express manner possible, to be all that God is, to possess the whole fulness of attributes which make God God. Paul chooses this manner of expressing himself here instinctively, because, in adducing Our Lord as our example of self-abnegation, his mind is naturally resting, not on the bare fact that He is God, but on the richness and fulness of His being as God. He was all this, yet He did not look on His own things but on those of others.

It should be carefully observed also that in making this great affirmation concerning Our Lord, Paul does not throw it distinctively into the past, as if he were describing a mode of being formerly Our Lord's, indeed, but no longer His because of the action by which He became our example of unselfishness. Our Lord, he says, "being," "existing," "subsisting" "in the form of God" — as it is variously rendered. The rendering proposed by the Revised Version margin, "being originally," while right in substance, is somewhat misleading. The verb employed means "strictly 'to be beforehand,' 'to be already' so and so" (Blass, "Grammar of NT Greek," English translation, 244), "to be there and ready," and intimates the existing circumstances, disposition of mind, or, as here, mode of subsistence in which the action to be described takes place. It contains no intimation, however, of the cessation of these circumstances or disposition, or mode of subsistence; and that, the less in a case like the present, where it is cast in a tense (the imperfect) which in no way suggests that the mode of subsistence intimated came to an end in the action described by the succeeding verb (cf. the parallels, Lk. xvi. 14, 23; xxiii. 50; Acts ii. 30; iii. 2; II Cor. viii. 17; xii. 16; Gal. i. 14). Paul is not telling us here, then, what Our Lord was once, but rather what He already was, or, better, what in His intrinsic nature He is; he is not describing a past mode of existence of Our Lord, before the action he is adducing as an example took place — although the mode of existence he describes was Our Lord's mode of existence before this action — so much as painting in the background upon which the action adduced may be thrown up into prominence. He is telling us who and what He is who did these things for us, that we may appreciate how great the things He did for us are.

And here it is important to observe that the whole of the action adduced is thrown up thus against this background — not only its negative description to the effect that Our Lord (although all that God is) did not look greedily on His (consequent) being on an equality with God; but its positive description as well, introduced by the "but . . . ." and that in both of its elements, not merely that to the effect (ver. 7) that 'he took no account of himself' (rendered not badly by the Authorized Version, He "made himself of no reputation"; but quite misleading by the Revised Version, He "emptied himself"), but equally that to the effect (ver. 8) that "he humbled himself." It is the whole of what Our Lord is described as doing in vs. 6–8, that He is described as doing despite His "subsistence in the form of God." So far is Paul from intimating, therefore, that Our Lord laid aside His Deity in entering upon His life on earth, that he rather asserts that He retained His Deity throughout His life on earth, and in the whole course of His humiliation, up to death itself, was consciously ever exercising self-abnegation, living a life which did not by nature belong to Him, which stood in fact in direct contradiction to the life which was naturally His. It is this underlying implication which determines the whole choice of the language in which Our Lord's earthly life is described. It is because it is kept in mind that He still was "in the form of God," that is, that He still had in possession all that body of characterizing qualities by which God is made God, for example, that He is said to have been made, not man, but "in the likeness of man," to have been found, not man, but "in fashion as a man"; and that the wonder of His servanthood and obedience, the mark of servanthood, is thought of as so great. Though He was truly man, He was much more than man; and Paul would not have his readers imagine that He had become merely man. In other words, Paul does not teach that Our Lord was once God but had become instead man; he teaches that though He was God, He had become also man.

An impression that Paul means to imply, that in entering upon His earthly life Our Lord had laid aside His Deity, may be created by a very prevalent misinterpretation of the central clause of his statement — a misinterpretation unfortunately given currency by the rendering of the English Revised Version:

"counted it not a prize to be on an equality with God, but emptied himself," varied without improvement in the American
Revised Version to: "counted not the being on an equality
with God a thing to be grasped, but emptied himself." The
former (negative) member of this clause means just: He did
not look greedily upon His being on an equality with God; did
not "set supreme store" by it (see Lightfoot on the clause). The
latter (positive) member of it, however, cannot mean in antithesis to this, that He therefore "emptied himself," divested Himself of this, His being on an equality with God, much less that
He "emptied himself," divested Himself of His Deity ("form
of God") itself, of which His being on an equality with God is
the manifested consequence. The verb here rendered "emptied" is in constant use in a metaphorical sense (so only in the
New Testament: Rom. iv. 14; I Cor. i. 17; ix. 15; II Cor. ix. 3)
and cannot here be taken literally. This is already apparent
from the definition of the manner in which the "emptying"
is said to have been accomplished, supplied by the modal clause
which is at once attached: by "taking the form of a servant."
You cannot "empty" by "taking" — *adding*. It is equally apparent, however, from the strength of the emphasis which, by
its position, is thrown upon the "himself." We may speak of
Our Lord as "*emptying* Himself" of something else, but
scarcely, with this strength of emphasis, of His "emptying
Himself" of something else. This emphatic "Himself," interposed between the preceding clause and the verb rendered
"emptied," builds a barrier over which we cannot climb backward in search of that of which Our Lord emptied Himself.
The whole thought is necessarily contained in the two words,
"emptied *Himself*," in which the word "emptied" must therefore be taken in a sense analogous to that which it bears in the
other passages in the New Testament where it occurs. Paul,
in a word, says here nothing more than that Our Lord, who did
not look with greedy eyes upon His estate of equality with
God, emptied Himself, if the language may be pardoned, of
Himself; that is to say, in precise accordance with the exhortation for the enhancement of which His example is adduced,

that He did not look on His own things. 'He made no account of Himself,' we may fairly paraphrase the clause; and thus all question of what He emptied Himself of falls away. What Our Lord actually did, according to Paul, is expressed in the following clauses; those now before us express more the moral character of His act. He took "the form of a servant," and so was "made in the likeness of men." But His doing this showed that He did not set overweening store by His state of equality with God, and did not account Himself the sufficient object of all the efforts. He was not self-regarding: He had regard for others. Thus He becomes our supreme example of self-abnegating conduct.

The language in which the act by which Our Lord showed that He was self-abnegating is described, requires to be taken in its complete meaning. He took "the form of a servant, being made in the likeness of men," says Paul. The term "form" here, of course, bears the same full meaning as in the preceding instance of its occurrence in the phrase "the form of God." It imparts the specific quality, the whole body of characteristics, by which a servant is made what we know as a servant. Our Lord assumed, then, according to Paul, not the mere state or condition or outward appearance of a servant, but the reality; He became an actual "servant" in the world. The act by which He did this is described as a "taking," or, as it has become customary from this description of it to phrase it, as an "assumption." What is meant is that Our Lord took up into His personality a human nature; and therefore it is immediately explained that He took the form of a servant by "being made in the likeness of men." That the apostle does not say, shortly, that He assumed a human nature, is due to the engagement of his mind with the contrast which he wishes to bring out forcibly for the enhancement of his appeal to Our Lord's example, between what Our Lord is by nature and what He was willing to become, not looking on His own things but also on the things of others. This contrast is, no doubt, embodied in the simple opposition of 'God and man; it is much more pungently expressed in the qualificative terms, "form of God" and "form

of a servant." The Lord of the world became a servant in the
world; He whose right it was to rule took obedience as His
life-characteristic. Naturally therefore Paul employs here a
word of quality rather than a word of mere nature; and then
defines his meaning in this word of quality by a further epexegetical clause. This further clause — "being made in the likeness of men" — does not throw doubt on the reality of the
human nature that was assumed, in contradiction to the emphasis on its reality in the phrase "the form of a servant." It,
along with the succeeding clause — "and being found in fashion as a man" — owes its peculiar form, as has already been
pointed out, to the vividness of the apostle's consciousness,
that he is speaking of one who, though really man, possessing
all that makes a man a man, is yet, at the same time, infinitely
more than a man, no less than God Himself, in possession of
all that makes God God. Christ Jesus is in his view, therefore
(as in the view of his readers, for he is not instructing his readers
here as to the nature of Christ's person, but reminding them of
certain elements in it for the purposes of his exhortation), both
God and man, God who has "assumed" man into personal
union with Himself, and has in this His assumed manhood
lived out a human life on earth.

The elements of Paul's conception of the person of Christ
are brought before us in this suggestive passage with unwonted
fulness. But they all receive endless illustration from his occasional allusions to them, one or another, throughout his
Epistles. The leading motive of this passage, for example, reappears quite perfectly in II Cor. viii. 9, where we are exhorted
to imitate the graciousness of Our Lord Jesus Christ, who became for our sakes (emphatic) poor — He who was (again an
imperfect participle, and therefore without suggestion of the
cessation of the condition described) rich — that we might by
His (very emphatic) poverty be made rich. Here the change
in Our Lord's condition at a point of time perfectly understood
between the writer and his readers is adverted to and assigned
to its motive, but no further definition is given of the nature
of either condition referred to. We are brought closer to the

precise nature of the act by which the change was wrought by such a passage as Gal. iv. 4. We read that "When the fulness of the time came, God sent forth his Son, born of a woman, born under the law, that he might redeem them that were under the law." The whole transaction is referred to the Father in fulfilment of His eternal plan of redemption, and it is described specifically as an incarnation: the Son of God is born of a woman — He who is in His own nature the Son of God, abiding with God, is sent forth from God in such a manner as to be born a human being, subject to law. The primary implications are that this was not the beginning of His being; but that before this He was neither a man nor subject to law. But there is no suggestion that on becoming man and subject to law, He ceased to be the Son of God or lost anything intimated by that high designation. The uniqueness of His relation to God as His Son is emphasized in a kindred passage (Rom. viii. 3) by the heightening of the designation to that of God's "own Son," and His distinction from other men is intimated in the same passage by the declaration that God sent Him, not in sinful flesh, but only "in the likeness of sinful flesh." The reality of Our Lord's flesh is not thrown into doubt by this turn of speech, but His freedom from the sin which is associated with flesh as it exists in lost humanity is asserted (cf. II Cor. v. 21). Though true man, therefore (I Cor. xv. 21; Rom. v. 21; Acts xvii. 31), He is not without differences from other men; and these differences do not concern merely the condition (as sinful) in which men presently find themselves; but also their very origin: they are from below, He from above — 'the first man is from the earth, earthy; the second man is from heaven' (I Cor. xv. 47). This is His peculiarity: He was born of a woman like other men; yet He descended from Heaven (cf. Eph. iv. 9; Jn. iii. 13). It is not meant, of course, that already in heaven He was a man; what is meant is that even though man He derives His origin in an exceptional sense from heaven. Paul describes what He was in heaven (but not alone in heaven) — that is to say before He was sent in the likeness of sinful flesh (though not alone before this) — in the great terms of "God's Son," "God's own Son," "the form of God," or yet again in words whose import cannot be mistaken, 'God over all' (Rom. ix. 5). In the last cited passage, together with its parallel earlier in the same epistle (Rom. i. 3), the two sides or elements of Our Lord's person are brought into collocation after a fashion that can leave no doubt of Paul's conception of His twofold nature. In the earlier of these passages he tells us that Jesus Christ was born, indeed, of the seed of David according to the flesh, that is, so far as the human side of His being is concerned, but was powerfully marked out as the Son of God according to the Spirit of Holiness, that is, with respect to His higher nature, by the resurrection of the dead, which in a true sense began in His own rising from the dead. In the later of them, he tells us that Christ sprang indeed, as concerns the flesh, that is on the human side of His being, from Israel, but that, despite this earthly origin of His human nature, He yet is and abides (present participle) nothing less than the Supreme God, "God over all [emphatic], blessed forever." Thus Paul teaches us that by His coming forth from God to be born of woman, Our Lord, assuming a human nature to Himself, has, while remaining the Supreme God, become also true and perfect man. Accordingly, in a context in which the resources of language are strained to the utmost to make the exaltation of Our Lord's being clear — in which He is described as the image of the invisible God, whose being antedates all that is created, in whom, through whom and to whom all things have been created, and in whom they all subsist — we are told not only that (naturally) in Him all the fulness dwells (Col. i. 19), but, with complete explication, that 'all the fulness of the Godhead dwells in him bodily' (Col. ii. 9); that is to say, the very Deity of God, that which makes God God, in all its completeness, has its permanent home in Our Lord, and that in a "bodily fashion," that is, it is in Him clothed with a body. He who looks upon Jesus Christ sees, no doubt, a body and a man; but as he sees the man clothed with the body, so he sees God Himself, in all the fulness of His Deity, clothed with the humanity. Jesus Christ is therefore God "manifested in the flesh" (I Tim. iii. 16), and His appearance on earth is an "epiphany" (II Tim. i. 10), which is the technical term for manifestations on earth of a God. Though truly man, He is nevertheless also our "great God" (Tit. ii. 13).

II. Teaching of the Epistle to the Hebrews

The conception of the person of Christ which underlies and finds expression in the Epistle to the Hebrews is indistinguishable from that which governs all the allusions to Our Lord in the Epistles of Paul. To the author of this epistle Our Lord is above all else the Son of God in the most eminent sense of that word; and it is the Divine dignity and majesty belonging to Him from His very nature which forms the fundamental feature of the image of Christ which stands before his mind. And yet it is this author who, perhaps above all others of the New Testament writers, emphasizes the truth of the humanity of Christ, and dwells with most particularity upon the elements of His human nature and experience.

The great Christological passage which fills chap. ii of the Epistle to the Hebrews rivals in its richness and fulness of detail, and its breadth of implication, that of Phil. ii. It is thrown up against the background of the remarkable exposition of the Divine dignity of the Son which occupies chap. i (notice the "therefore" of ii. 1). There the Son had been declared to be "the effulgence of his (God's) glory, and the very image of his substance, through whom the universe has been created and by the word of whose power all things are held in being; and His exaltation above the angels, by means of whom the Old Covenant had been inaugurated, is measured by the difference between the designations "ministering spirits" proper to the one, and the Son of God, nay, God itself (i. 8, 9), proper to the other. The purpose of the succeeding statement is to enhance in the thought of the Jewish readers of the epistle the value of the salvation wrought by this Divine Saviour, by removing from their minds the offence they were in danger of taking at His lowly life and shameful death on earth. This earthly humiliation finds its abundant justification, we are told, in the greatness of the end which it sought and attained. By it Our Lord has, with His strong feet, broken out a pathway along which, in Him, sinful man may at length climb up to the high destiny which was promised him when it was declared he should have dominion over all creation. Jesus Christ stooped only to conquer, and He stooped to conquer not for Himself (for He was in His own person no less than God), but for us.

The language in which the humiliation of the Son of God is in the first instance described is derived from the context. The establishment of His Divine majesty in chap. i had taken the form of an exposition of His infinite exaltation above the angels, the highest of all creatures. His humiliation is described here therefore as being "made a little lower than the angels" (ii. 9). What is meant is simply that He became man; the phraseology is derived from Ps. viii., Authorized Version, from which had just been cited the declaration that God has made man (despite his insignificance) "but a little lower than the angels," thus crowning him with glory and honor. The adoption of the language of the psalm to describe Our Lord's humiliation has the secondary effect, accordingly, of greatly enlarging the reader's sense of the immensity of the humiliation of the Son of God in becoming man: He descended an infinite distance to reach man's highest conceivable exaltation. As, however, the primary purpose of the adoption of the language is merely to declare that the Son of God became man, so it is shortly afterward explained (ii. 14) as an entering into participation in the blood and flesh which are common to men: "Since then the children are sharers in flesh and blood, he also himself in like manner partook of the same." The voluntariness, the reality, the completeness of the assumption of humanity by the Son of God, are all here emphasized.

The proximate end of Our Lord's assumption of humanity is declared to be that He might die; He was "made a little lower than the angels . . . because of the suffering of death" (ii. 9); He took part in blood and flesh in order "that through death . . ." (ii. 14). The Son of God as such could not die; to Him belongs by nature an "indissoluble life" (vii. 16 m.).

If he was to die, therefore, He must take to Himself another nature to which the experience of death were not impossible (ii. 17). Of course it is not meant that death was desired by Him for its own sake. The purpose of our passage is to save its Jewish readers from the offence of the death of Christ. What they are bidden to observe is, therefore, Jesus, who was made a little lower than the angels because of the suffering of death, 'crowned with glory and honor, that by the grace of God the bitterness of death which he tasted might redound to the benefit of every man' (ii. 9), and the argument is immediately pressed home that it was eminently suitable for God Almighty, in bringing many sons into glory, to make the Captain of their salvation perfect (as a Saviour) by means of suffering. The meaning is that it was only through suffering that these men, being sinners, could be brought into glory. And therefore in the plainer statement of verse 14 we read that Our Lord took part in flesh and blood in order "that through death he might bring to nought him that has the power of death, that is, the devil; and might deliver all them who through fear of death were all their lifetime subject to bondage"; and in the still plainer statement of verse 17 that the ultimate object of His assimilation to men was that He might "make propitiation for the sins of the people." It is for the salvation of sinners that Our Lord has come into the world; but, as that salvation can be wrought only by suffering and death, the proximate end of His assumption of humanity remains that He might die; whatever is more than this gathers around this.

The completeness of Our Lord's assumption of humanity and of His identification of Himself with it receives strong emphasis in this passage. He took part in the flesh and blood which is the common heritage of men, after the same fashion that other men participate in it (ii. 14); and, having thus become a man among men, He shared with other men the ordinary circumstances and fortunes of life, "in all things" (ii. 17). The stress is laid on trials, sufferings, death; but this is due to the actual course in which His life ran — and that it might run in which He became man — and is not exclusive of other human experiences. What is intended is that He became truly a man, and lived a truly human life, subject to all the experiences natural to a man in the particular circumstances in which He lived.

It is not implied, however, that during this human life — "the days of his flesh" (v. 7) — He had ceased to be God, or to have at His disposal the attributes which belonged to Him as God. That is already excluded by the representations of chap. i. The glory of this dispensation consists precisely in the bringing of its revelations directly by the Divine Son rather than by mere prophets (i. 1), and it was as the effulgence of God's glory and the express image of His substance, upholding the universe by the word of His power, that this Son made purification of sins (i. 3). Indeed, we are expressly told that even in the days of the flesh, He continued still a Son (v. 8), and that it was precisely in this that the wonder lay: that though He was and remained (imperfect participle) a Son, He yet learned the obedience He had set Himself to (cf. Phil. ii. 8) by the things which He suffered. Similarly, we are told not only that, though an Israelite of the tribe of Judah, He possessed "the power of an indissoluble life" (vii. 16 m.), but, describing that higher nature which gave Him this power as an "eternal Spirit" (cf. "spirit of holiness," Rom. i. 4), that it was through this eternal Spirit that He could offer Himself without blemish unto God, a real and sufficing sacrifice, in contrast with the shadows of the Old Covenant (ix. 14). Though a man, therefore, and truly man, sprung out of Judah (vii. 14), touched with the feeling of human infirmities (iv. 15), and tempted like as we are, He was not altogether like other men. For one thing, He was "without sin" (iv. 15; vii. 26), and, by this characteristic, He was, in every sense of the words, separated from sinners. Despite the completeness of His identification with men, He remained, therefore, even in the days of His flesh different from them and above them.

III. Teaching of Other Epistles

It is only as we carry this conception of the person of Our Lord with us — the conception of Him as at once our Supreme Lord, to whom our adoration is due, and our fellow in the experiences of a human life — that unity is induced in the multiform allusions to Him throughout, whether the Epistles of Paul or the Epistle to the Hebrews, or, indeed, the other epistolary literature of the New Testament. For in this matter there is no difference between those and these. There are no doubt a few passages in these other letters in which a plurality of the elements of the person of Christ are brought together and given detailed mention. In I Pet. iii. 18, for instance, the two constitutive elements of His person are spoken of in the contrast, familiar from Paul, of the "flesh" and the "spirit." But ordinarily we meet only with references to this or that element separately. Everywhere Our Lord is spoken of as having lived out His life as a man; but everywhere also He is spoken of with the supreme reverence which is due to God alone, and the very name of God is not withheld from Him. In I Pet. i. 11 His preëxistence is taken for granted; in Jas. ii. 1 He is identified with the Shekinah, the manifested Jehovah — 'our Lord Jesus Christ, the Glory'; in Jude verse 4 He is "our only Master [Despot] and Lord"; over and over again He is the Divine Lord who is Jehovah (e. g., I Pet. ii. 3, 13; II Pet. iii. 2, 18); in II Pet. i. 1, He is roundly called "our God and Saviour." There is nowhere formal inculcation of the entire doctrine of the person of Christ. But everywhere its elements, now one and now another, are presupposed as the common property of writer and readers. It is only in the Epistles of John that this easy and unstudied presupposition of them gives way to pointed insistence upon them.

IV. Teaching of John

In the circumstances in which he wrote, John found it necessary to insist upon the elements of the person of Our

Lord — His true Deity, His true humanity and the unity of His person — in a manner which is more didactic in form than anything we find in the other writings of the New Testament. The great depository of his teaching on the subject is, of course, the prologue to his Gospel. But it is not merely in this prologue, nor in the Gospel to which it forms a fitting introduction, that these didactic statements are found. The full emphasis of John's witness to the twofold nature of the Lord is brought out, indeed, only by combining what he says in the Gospel and in the Epistles. "In the Gospel," remarks Westcott (on Jn. xx. 31), "the evangelist shows step by step that the historic Jesus was the Christ, the Son of God (opposed to mere 'flesh'); in the Epistle he re-affirms that the Christ, the Son of God, was true man (opposed to mere 'spirit'; I Jn. iv. 2)." What John is concerned to show throughout is that it was "the true God" (I Jn. v. 20) who was "made flesh" (Jn. i. 14); and that this 'only God' (Jn. i. 18, Revised Version, margin "God only begotten") has truly come "in . . . flesh" (I Jn. iv. 2). In all the universe there is no other being of whom it can be said that He is God come in flesh (cf. II Jn. ver. 7, He that "cometh in the flesh," whose characteristic this is). And of all the marvels which have ever occurred in the marvelous history of the universe, this is the greatest — that 'what was from the beginning' (I Jn. ii. 13, 14) has been heard and gazed upon, seen and handled by men (I Jn. i. 1).

From the point of view from which we now approach it, the prologue to the Gospel of John may be said to fall into three parts. In the first of these, the nature of the Being who became incarnate in the person we know as Jesus Christ is described; in the second, the general nature of the act we call the incarnation; and in the third, the nature of the incarnated person.

John here calls the person who became incarnate by a name peculiar to himself in the New Testament — the "Logos" or "Word." According to the predicates which he here applies to Him, he can mean by the "Word" nothing else but God Himself, "considered in His creative, operative, self-revealing, and communicating character," the sum total of what is Divine

(C. F. Schmid). In three crisp sentences he declares at the outset His eternal subsistence, His eternal intercommunion with God, His eternal identity with God: 'In the beginning the Word was; and the Word was with God; and the Word was God' (Jn. i. 1). "In the beginning," at that point of time when things first began to be (Gen. i. 1), the Word already "was." He antedates the beginning of all things. And He not merely antedates them, but it is immediately added that He is Himself the creator of all that is: 'All things were made by him, and apart from him was not made one thing that hath been made' (i. 3). Thus He is taken out of the category of creatures altogether. Accordingly, what is said of Him is not that He was the first of existences to come into being — that 'in the beginning He already had come into being' — but that 'in the beginning, when things began to come into being, He already *was*.' It is express eternity of being that is asserted: "the imperfect tense of the original suggests in this relation, as far as human language can do so, the notion of absolute, supra-temporal existence" (Westcott). This, His eternal subsistence, was not, however, in isolation: "And the Word was with God." The language is pregnant. It is not merely coexistence with God that is asserted, as of two beings standing side by side, united in a local relation, or even in a common conception. What is suggested is an active relation of intercourse. The distinct personality of the Word is therefore not obscurely intimated. From all eternity the Word has been with God as a fellow: He who in the very beginning already "was," "was" also in communion with God. Though He was thus in some sense a second along with God, He was nevertheless not a separate being from God: "And the Word was" — still the eternal "was" — "God." In some sense distinguishable from God, He was in an equally true sense identical with God. There is but one eternal God; this eternal God, the Word is; in whatever sense we may distinguish Him from the God whom He is "with," He is yet not another than this God, but Himself is this God. The predicate "God" occupies the position of emphasis in this great declaration, and is so placed in the sentence as to be thrown up in sharp contrast with the phrase "with God," as if to prevent inadequate inferences as to the nature of the Word being drawn even momentarily from that phrase. John would have us realize that what the Word was in eternity was not merely God's coeternal fellow, but the eternal God's self.

Now, John tells us that it was this Word, eternal in His subsistence, God's eternal fellow, the eternal God's self, that, as "come in the flesh," was Jesus Christ (I Jn. iv. 2). "And the Word became flesh" (Jn. i. 14), he says. The terms he employs here are not terms of substance, but of personality. The meaning is not that the substance of God was transmuted into that substance which we call "flesh." "The Word" is a personal name of the eternal God; "flesh" is an appropriate designation of humanity in its entirety, with the implications of dependence and weakness. The meaning, then, is simply that He who had just been described as the eternal God became, by a voluntary act in time, a man. The exact nature of the act by which He "became" man lies outside the statement; it was matter of common knowledge between the writer and the reader. The language employed intimates merely that it was a definite act, and that it involved a change in the life-history of the eternal God, here designated "the Word." The whole emphasis falls on the nature of this change in His life-history. He became *flesh*. That is to say, He entered upon a mode of existence in which the experiences that belong to human beings would also be His. The dependence, the weakness, which constitute the very idea of flesh, in contrast with God, would now enter into His personal experience. And it is precisely because these are the connotations of the term "flesh" that John chooses that term here, instead of the more simply denotative term "man." What he means is merely that the eternal God became man. But he elects to say this in the language which throws best up to view what it is to become man. The contrast between the Word as the eternal God and the human nature which He assumed as flesh, is the hinge of the statement. Had the evangelist said (as he does in I Jn. iv. 2) that the Word 'came in flesh,' it would have been the continuity throug the change which would have been most emphasized. When he says rather that the Word became flesh, while the continuity of the personal subject is, of course, intimated, it is the reality and the completeness of the humanity assumed which is made most prominent.

That in becoming flesh the Word did not cease to be what He was before entering upon this new sphere of experiences, the evangelist does not leave, however, to mere suggestion. The glory of the Word was so far from quenched, in his view, by His becoming flesh, that he gives us at once to understand that it was rather as "trailing clouds of glory" that He came. "And the Word became flesh," he says, and immediately adds: "and dwelt among us (and we beheld his glory, glory as of the only begotten from the Father), full of grace and truth" (i. 14). The language is colored by reminiscences from the Tabernacle, in which the Glory of God, the Shekinah, dwelt. The flesh of Our Lord became, on its assumption by the Word, the Temple of God on earth (cf. Jn. ii. 19), and the glory of the Lord filled the house of the Lord. John tells us expressly that this glory was visible, that it was precisely what was appropriate to the Son of God as such. "And we beheld his glory," he says; not divined it, or inferred it, but perceived it. It was open to sight, and the actual object of observation. Jesus Christ was obviously more than man; He was obviously God. His actually observed glory, John tells us further, was a "glory as of the only begotten from the Father." It was unique; nothing like it was ever seen in another. And its uniqueness consisted precisely in its consonance with what the unique Son of God, sent forth from the Father, would naturally have; men recognized and could not but recognize in Jesus Christ the unique Son of God. When this unique Son of God is further described as "full of grace and truth," the elements of His manifested glory are not to be supposed to be exhausted by this description (cf. ii. 11). Certain items of it only are singled out for particular mention. The visible glory of the incarnated Word was such a glory as the unique Son of God, sent forth from the Father, who was full of grace and truth, would naturally manifest.

That nothing should be lacking to the declaration of the continuity of all that belongs to the Word as such into this new sphere of existence, and its full manifestation through the veil of His flesh, John adds at the close of his exposition the remarkable sentence: 'As for God, no one has even yet seen him; God only begotten, who is in the bosom of the Father — He hath declared him' (i. 18 m.). It is the incarnate Word which is here called 'only begotten God.' The absence of the article with this designation is doubtless due to its parallelism with the word "God" which stands at the head of the corresponding clause. The effect of its absence is to throw up into emphasis the quality rather than the mere individuality of the person so designated. The adjective "only begotten" conveys the idea, not of derivation and subordination, but of uniqueness and consubstantiality: Jesus is all that God is, and He alone is this. Of this 'only begotten God' it is now declared that He "is" — not "was," the state is not one which has been left behind at the incarnation, but one which continues uninterrupted and unmodified — "into" — not merely "in" — "the bosom of the Father" — that is to say, He continues in the most intimate and complete communion with the Father. Though now incarnate, He is still "with God" in the full sense of the external relation intimated in i. 1. This being true, He has much more than seen God, and is fully able to "interpret" God to men. Though no one has ever yet seen God, yet he who has seen Jesus Christ, "God only begotten," has seen the Father (cf. xiv. 9; xii. 45). In this remarkable sentence there is asserted in the most direct manner the full Deity of the incarnate Word, and the continuity of His life as such in His incarnate life; thus He is fitted to be the absolute revelation of God to man.

This condensed statement of the whole doctrine of the incarnation is only the prologue to a historical treatise. The historical treatise which it introduces, naturally, is written from the point of view of its prologue. Its object is to present Jesus Christ in His historical manifestation, as obviously the Son of God in flesh. "These are written," the Gospel testifies, "that ye may believe that Jesus is the Christ, the Son of God" (xx. 31); that Jesus who came as a man (i. 30) was thoroughly known in His human origin (vii. 27), confessed Himself man (viii. 40), and died as a man dies (xix. 5), was, nevertheless, not only the Messiah, the Sent of God, the fulfiller of all the Divine promises of redemption, but also the very Son of God, that God only begotten, who, abiding in the bosom of the Father, is His sole adequate interpreter. From the beginning of the Gospel onward, this purpose is pursued: Jesus is pictured as ever, while truly man, yet manifesting Himself as equally truly God, until the veil which covered the eyes of His followers was wholly lifted, and He is greeted as both Lord and God (xx. 28). But though it is the prime purpose of this Gospel to exhibit the Divinity of the man Jesus, no obscuration of His manhood is involved. It is the Deity of the man Jesus which is insisted on, but the true manhood of Jesus is as prominent in the representation as in any other portion of the New Testament. Nor is any effacement of the humiliation of His earthly life involved. For the Son of man to come from heaven was a descent (iii. 13), and the mission which He came to fulfil was a mission of contest and conflict, of suffering and death. He brought His glory with Him (i. 14), but the glory that was His on earth (xvii. 22) was not all the glory which He had had with the Father before the world was, and to which, after His work was done, He should return (xvii. 5). Here too the glory of the celestial is one and the glory of the terrestrial is another. In any event, John has no difficulty in presenting the life of Our Lord on earth as the life of God in flesh, and in insisting at once on the glory that belongs to Him as God and on the humiliation which is brought to Him by the flesh. It is distinctly a duplex life which he ascribes to Christ, and he attributes to Him without embarrassment all the powers and modes of activity appropriate on the one hand to Deity and on the other to sinless (Jn. viii. 46; cf. xiv. 30; I Jn. iii. 5) human nature. In a true sense his portrait of Our Lord is a dramatization of the God-man which he presents to our contemplation in his prologue.

V. Teaching of the Synoptic Gospels

The same may be said of the other Gospels. They are all dramatizations of the God-man set forth in thetical exposition in the prologue to John's Gospel. The Gospel of Luke, written by a known companion of Paul, gives us in a living narrative the same Jesus who is presupposed in all Paul's allusions to Him. That of Mark, who was also a companion of Paul, as also of Peter, is, as truly as the Gospel of John itself, a presentation of facts in the life of Jesus with a view to making it plain that this was the life of no mere man, human as it was, but of the Son of God Himself. Matthew's Gospel differs from its fellows mainly in the greater richness of Jesus' own testimony to His Deity which it records. What is characteristic of all three is the inextricable interlacing in their narratives of the human and Divine traits which alike marked the life they are depicting. It is possible, by neglecting one series of their representations and attending only to the other, to sift out from them at will the portrait of either a purely Divine or a purely human Jesus. It is impossible to derive from them the portrait of any other than a Divine-human Jesus if we surrender ourselves to their guidance and take off of their pages the portrait they have endeavored to draw. As in their narratives they cursorily suggest now the fulness of His Deity and now the completeness of His humanity and everywhere the unity of His person, they present as real and as forcible a testimony to the constitution of Our Lord's person as uniting in one personal life a truly Divine and a truly human nature, as if they announced this fact in analytical statement. Only on the assumption of this conception of Our Lord's person as underlying and determining their presentation, can unity be given to their representations; while, on this supposition, all their representations fall into their places as elements in one consistent whole. Within the limits of their common presupposition, each Gospel has no doubt its own peculiarities in the distribution of its emphasis. Mark lays particular stress on the Divine power of the man Jesus, as evidence of His supernatural being; and on the irresistible impres-

sion of a veritable Son of God, a Divine being walking the earth
as a man, which He made upon all with whom He came into
contact. Luke places his Gospel by the side of the Epistle to
the Hebrews in the prominence it gives to the human development of the Divine being whose life on earth it is depicting and
to the range of temptation to which He was subjected. Matthew's Gospel is notable chiefly for the heights of the Divine
self-consciousness which it uncovers in its report of the words
of Him whom it represents as nevertheless the Son of David,
the Son of Abraham; heights of Divine self-consciousness which
fall in nothing short of those attained in the great utterances
preserved for us by John. But amid whatever variety there
may exist in the aspects on which each lays his particular emphasis, it is the same Jesus Christ which all three bring before
us, a Jesus Christ who is at once God and man and one individual person. If that be not recognized, the whole narrative of
the Synoptic Gospels is thrown into confusion; their portrait of
Christ becomes an insoluble puzzle; and the mass of details
which they present of His life-experiences is transmuted into
a mere set of crass contradictions.

VI. Teaching of Jesus

1. The Johannine Jesus. — The Gospel narratives not only
present us, however, with dramatizations of the God-man, according to their authors' conception of His composite person.
They preserve for us also a considerable body of the utterances
of Jesus Himself, and this enables us to observe the conception
of His person which underlay and found expression in Our
Lord's own teaching. The discourses of Our Lord which have
been selected for record by John have been chosen (among
other reasons) expressly for the reason that they bear witness
to His essential Deity. They are accordingly peculiarly rich in
material for forming a judgment of Our Lord's conception of
His higher nature. This conception, it is needless to say, is precisely that which John, taught by it, has announced in the prologue to his Gospel, and has illustrated by his Gospel itself,

compacted as it is of these discourses. It will not be necessary to present the evidence for this in its fulness. It will be enough to point to a few characteristic passages, in which Our Lord's conception of His higher nature finds especially clear expression.

That He was of higher than earthly origin and nature, He repeatedly asserts. "Ye are from beneath," he says to the Jews (viii. 23), "I am from above: ye are of this world; I am not of this world" (cf. xvii. 16). Therefore, He taught that He, the Son of Man, had "descended out of heaven" (iii. 13), where was His true abode. This carried with it, of course, an assertion of preëxistence; and this preëxistence is explicitly affirmed: "What then," He asks, "if ye should behold the Son of man ascending where he was before?" (vi. 62). It is not merely preexistence, however, but eternal preëxistence which He claims for Himself: "And now, Father," He prays (xvii. 5), "glorify thou me with thine own self with the glory which I had with thee before the world was" (cf. ver. 24); and again, as the most impressive language possible, He declares (viii. 58 A.V.): "Verily, verily, I say unto you, Before Abraham was, I am," where He claims for Himself the timeless present of eternity as His mode of existence. In the former of these two last-cited passages, the character of His preëxistent life is intimated; in it He shared the Father's glory from all eternity ("before the world was"); He stood by the Father's side as a companion in His glory. He came forth, when He descended to earth, therefore, not from heaven only, but from the very side of God (viii. 42; xvii. 8). Even this, however, does not express the whole truth; He came forth not only from the Father's side where He had shared in the Father's glory; He came forth out of the Father's very being — "I came out from the Father, and am come into the world" (xvi. 28; cf. viii. 42). "The connection described is internal and essential, and not that of presence or external fellowship" (Westcott). This prepares us for the great assertion: "I and the Father are one" (x. 30), from which it is a mere corollary that "He that hath seen me hath seen the Father" (xiv. 9; cf. viii. 19; xii. 45).

In all these declarations the subject of the affirmation is the actual person speaking: it is of Himself who stood before men and spoke to them that Our Lord makes these immense assertions. Accordingly, when He majestically declared, "I and the Father are" (plurality of persons) "one" (neuter singular, and accordingly singleness of being), the Jews naturally understood Him to be making Himself, the person then speaking to them, God (x. 33; cf. v. 18; xix. 7). The continued sameness of the person who has been, from all eternity down to this hour, one with God, is therefore fully safeguarded. His earthly life is, however, distinctly represented as a humiliation. Though even on earth He is one with the Father, yet He "descended" to earth; He had come out from the Father and out of God; a glory had been left behind which was yet to be returned to, and His sojourn on earth was therefore to that extent an obscuration of His proper glory. There was a sense, then, in which, because He had "descended," He was no longer equal with the Father. It was in order to justify an assertion of equality with the Father in power (x. 25, 29) that He was led to declare: "I and my Father are one" (x. 30). But He can also declare "The Father is greater than I" (xiv. 28). Obviously this means that there was a sense in which He had ceased to be equal with the Father, because of the humiliation of His present condition, and in so far as this humiliation involved entrance into a status lower than that which belonged to Him by nature. Precisely in what this humiliation consisted can be gathered only from the general implication of many statements. In it He was a "man": 'a man who hath told you the truth, which I have heard from God' (viii. 40), where the contrast with "God" throws the assertion of humanity into emphasis (cf. x. 33). The truth of His human nature is, however, everywhere assumed and endlessly illustrated, rather than explicitly asserted. He possessed a human soul (xii. 27) and bodily parts (flesh and blood, vi. 53 ff.; hands and side, xx. 27); and was subject alike to physical affections (weariness, iv. 6, and thirst, xix. 28, suffering and death), and to all the common human emotions — not merely the love of compassion (xiii. 34; xiv. 21; xv. 8–13), but the love of simple affection which we pour out on "friends" (xi. 11; cf.

xv. 14, 15), indignation (xi. 33, 38) and joy (xv. 11; xvii. 13).
He felt the perturbation produced by strong excitement (xi. 33;
xii. 27; xiii. 21), the sympathy with suffering which shows itself
in tears (xi. 35), the thankfulness which fills the grateful heart
(vi. 11, 23; xi. 41. Only one human characteristic was alien
to Him: He was without sin: "the prince of the world," He
declared, "hath nothing in me" (xiv. 30; cf. viii. 46). Clearly
Our Lord, as reported by John, knew Himself to be true God
and true man in one indivisible person, the common subject of
the qualities which belong to each.

2. The Synoptic Jesus. — (a) Mk. xiii. 32: The same is
true of His self-consciousness as revealed in His sayings recorded by the synoptists. Perhaps no more striking illustration
of this could be adduced than the remarkable declaration recorded in Mk. xiii. 32 (cf. Mt. xxiv. 36): 'But of that day or
that hour knoweth no one, not even the angels in heaven, nor
yet the Son, but the Father.' Here Jesus places Himself, in an
ascending scale of being, above "the angels in heaven," that is
to say, the highest of all creatures, significantly marked here
as supramundane. Accordingly, He presents Himself elsewhere
as the Lord of the angels, whose behests they obey: "The Son
of man shall send forth his angels, and they shall gather out of
his kingdom all things that cause stumbling, and them that do
iniquity" (Mt. xiii. 41), "And he shall send forth his angels
with a great sound of a trumpet, and they shall gather together his elect from the four winds, from one end of heaven
to the other" (Mt. xxiv. 31; cf. xiii. 49; xxv. 31; Mk. viii. 38).
Thus the "angels of God" (Lk. xii. 8, 9; xv. 10) Christ designates as His angels, the "kingdom of God" (Mt. xii. 28; xix.
24; xxi. 31, 43; Mk. and Lk. often) as His Kingdom, the "elect
of God" (Mk. xiii. 20; Lk. xviii. 7; cf. Rom. viii. 33; Col. iii. 12;
Tit. i. 1) as His elect. He is obviously speaking in Mk. xiii. 22
out of a Divine self-consciousness: "Only a Divine being can
be exalted above angels" (B. Weiss). He therefore designates
Himself by His Divine name, "the Son," that is to say, the
unique Son of God (ix. 7; i. 11), to claim to be whom would for
a man be blasphemy (Mk. xiv. 61, 64). But though He desig-

nates Himself by this Divine name, He is not speaking of what He once was, but of what at the moment of speaking He is: the action of the verb is present, "knoweth." He is claiming, in other words, the supreme designation of "the Son," with all that is involved in it, for His present self, as He moved among men: He is, not merely was, "the Son." Nevertheless, what He affirms of Himself cannot be affirmed of Himself distinctively as "the Son." For what He affirms of Himself is ignorance — "not even the Son" knows it; and ignorance does not belong to the Divine nature which the term "the Son" connotes. An extreme appearance of contradiction accordingly arises from the use of this terminology, just as it arises when Paul says that the Jews "crucified the Lord of glory" (I Cor. ii. 8), or exhorts the Ephesian elders to "feed the church of God which he purchased with his own blood" (Acts xx. 28 m.); or John Keble praises Our Lord for "the blood of souls by Thee redeemed." It was not the Lord of Glory as such who was nailed to the tree, nor have either "God" or "souls" blood to shed.

We know how this apparently contradictory mode of speech has arisen in Keble's case. He is speaking of men who are composite beings, consisting of souls and bodies, and these men come to be designated from one element of their composite personalities, though what is affirmed by them belongs rather to the other; we may speak, therefore, of the "blood of souls" meaning that these "souls," while not having blood as such, yet designate persons who have bodies and therefore blood. We know equally how to account for Paul's apparent contradictions. We know that he conceived of Our Lord as a composite person, uniting in Himself a Divine and a human nature. In Paul's view, therefore, though God as such has no blood, yet Jesus Christ who is God has blood because He is also man. He can justly speak, therefore, when speaking of Jesus Christ, of His blood as the blood of God. When precisely the same phenomenon meets us in Our Lord's speech of Himself, we must presume that it is the outgrowth of precisely the same state of things. When He speaks of "the Son" (who is God) as ignorant, we must understand that He is designating Himself as "the

Son" because of His higher nature, and yet has in mind the ignorance of His lower nature; what He means is that the person properly designated "the Son" is ignorant, that is to say with respect to the human nature which is as intimate an element of His personality as is His Deity.

When Our Lord says, then, that "the Son knows not," He becomes as express a witness to the two natures which constitute His person as Paul is when he speaks of the blood of God, or as Keble is a witness to the twofold constitution of a human being when he speaks of souls shedding blood. In this short sentence, thus, Our Lord bears witness to His Divine nature with its supremacy above all creatures, to His human nature with its creaturely limitations, and to the unity of the subject possessed of these two natures.

(b) Other passages: Son of Man and Son of God: All these elements of His personality find severally repeated assertions in other utterances of Our Lord recorded in the Synoptics. There is no need to insist here on the elevation of Himself above the kings and prophets of the Old Covenant (Mt. xii. 41 ff.), above the temple itself (Mt. xii. 6), and the ordinances of the Divine Law (Mt. xii. 8); or on His accent of authority in both His teaching and action, His great "I say unto you" (Mt. v. 21, 22), 'I will; be cleansed' (Mk. i. 41; ii. 5; Lk. vii. 14); or on His separation of Himself from men in His relation to God, never including them with Himself in an "Our Father," but consistently speaking distinctively of "my Father" (e. g., Lk. xxiv. 49) and "your Father" (e. g., Mt. v. 16); or on His intimation that He is not merely David's Son but David's Lord, and that a Lord sitting on the right hand of God (Mt. xxii. 44); or on His parabolic discrimination of Himself a Son and Heir from all "servants" (Mt. xxi. 33 ff.); or even on His ascription to Himself of the purely Divine functions of the forgiveness of sins (Mk. ii. 8) and judgment of the world (Mt. xxv. 31), or of the purely Divine powers of reading the heart (Mk. ii. 8; Lk. ix. 47), omnipotence (Mt. xxiv. 30; Mk. xiv. 62) and omnipresence (Mt. xviii. 20; xxviii. 10). These things illustrate His constant assumption of the possession of Divine dignity and attributes; the claim itself is more directly made in the two great designations which He currently gave Himself, the Son of Man and the Son of God. The former of these is His favorite self-designation. Derived from Dan. vii. 13, 14, it intimates on every occasion of its employment Our Lord's consciousness of being a supramundane being, who has entered into a sphere of earthly life on a high mission, on the accomplishment of which He is to return to His heavenly sphere, whence He shall in due season come back to earth, now, however, in His proper majesty, to gather up the fruits of His work and consummate all things. It is a designation, thus, which implies at once a heavenly preëxistence, a present humiliation, and a future glory; and He proclaims Himself in this future glory no less than the universal King seated on the throne of judgment for quick and dead (Mk. viii. 31; Mt. xxv. 31). The implication of Deity imbedded in the designation, Son of Man, is perhaps more plainly spoken out in the companion designation, Son of God, which Our Lord not only accepts at the hands of others, accepting with it the implication of blasphemy in permitting its application to Himself (Mt. xxvi. 63, 65; Mk. xiv. 61, 64; Lk. xxii. 29, 30), but persistently claims for Himself both, in His constant designation of God as His Father in a distinctive sense, and in His less frequent but more pregnant designation of Himself as, by way of eminence, "the Son." That His consciousness of the peculiar relation to God expressed by this designation was not an attainment of His mature spiritual development, but was part of His most intimate consciousness from the beginning, is suggested by the sole glimpse which is given us into His mind as a child (Lk. ii. 49). The high significance which the designation bore to Him is revealed to us in two remarkable utterances preserved, the one by both Matthew (xi. 27 ff.) and Luke (x. 22 ff.), and the other by Matthew (xxviii. 19).

(c) Mt. xi. 27; xxviii. 19: In the former of these utterances, Our Lord, speaking in the most solemn manner, not only presents Himself, as the Son, as the sole source of knowledge of God and of blessedness for men, but places Himself in a position, not of equality merely, but of absolute reciprocity and interpenetration of knowledge with the Father. "No one," He says, "knoweth the Son, save the Father; neither doth any know the Father, save the Son . . ." varied in Luke so as to read: "No one knoweth who the Son is, save the Father; and who the Father is, save the Son . . ." as if the being of the Son were so immense that only God could know it thoroughly; and the knowledge of the Son was so unlimited that He could know God to perfection. The peculiarly pregnant employment here of the terms "Son" and "Father" over against one another is explained to us in the other utterance (Mt. xxviii. 19). It is the resurrected Lord's commission to His disciples. Claiming for Himself all authority in heaven and on earth — which implies the possession of omnipotence — and promising to be with His followers 'alway, even to the end of the world '— which adds the implications of omnipresence and omniscience — He commands them to baptize their converts 'in the name of the Father and of the Son and of the Holy Ghost.' The precise form of the formula must be carefully observed. It does not read: 'In the names' (plural) — as if there were three beings enumerated, each with its distinguishing name. Nor yet: 'In the name of the Father, Son and Holy Ghost,' as if there were one person, going by a threefold name. It reads: 'In the name [singular] of the Father, and of the [article repeated] Son, and of the [article repeated] Holy Ghost,' carefully distinguishing three persons, though uniting them all under one name. The name of God was to the Jews Jehovah, and to name the name of Jehovah upon them was to make them His. What Jesus did in this great injunction was to command His followers to name the name of God upon their converts, and to announce the name of God which is to be named on their converts in the threefold enumeration of "the Father" and "the Son" and "the Holy Ghost." As it is unquestionable that He intended Himself by "the Son," He here places Himself by the side of the Father and the Spirit, as together with them constituting the one God. It is, of course, the Trinity which He is describing; and that is as much as to say that He announces Himself as one of the persons of the Trinity. This is what Jesus, as reported by the Synoptics, understood Himself to be.

In announcing Himself to be God, however, Jesus does not deny that He is man also. If all His speech of Himself rests on His consciousness of a Divine nature, no less does all His speech manifest His consciousness of a human nature. He easily identifies Himself with men (Mt. iv. 4; Lk. iv. 4), and receives without protest the imputation of humanity (Mt. xi. 19; Lk. vii. 34). He speaks familiarly of His body (Mt. xxvi. 12, 26; Mk. xiv. 8; xiv. 22; Lk. xxii. 19), and of His bodily parts — His feet and hands (Lk. xxiv. 39), His head and feet (Lk. vii. 44–46), His flesh and bones (Lk. xxiv. 39), His blood (Mt. xxvi. 28, Mk. xiv. 24; Lk. xxii. 20). We chance to be given indeed a very express affirmation on His part of the reality of His bodily nature; when His disciples were terrified at His appearing before them after His resurrection, supposing Him to be a spirit, He reassures them with the direct declaration: "See my hands and my feet, that it is I myself: handle me, and see; for a spirit hath not flesh and bones, as ye behold me having" (Lk. xxiv. 39). His testimony to His human soul is just as express: "My soul," says He, "is exceeding sorrowful, even unto death" (Mt. xxvi. 38; Mk. xiv. 34). He speaks of the human dread with which He looked forward to His approaching death (Lk. xii. 50), and expresses in a poignant cry His sense of desolation on the cross (Mt. xxvii. 46; Mk. xv. 34). He speaks also of His pity for the weary and hungering people (Mt. xv. 32; Mk. viii. 2), and of a strong human desire which He felt (Lk. xxii. 15). Nothing that is human is alien to Him except sin. He never ascribes imperfection to Himself and never betrays consciousness of sin. He recognizes the evil of those about Him (Lk. xi. 13; Mt. vii. 11; xii. 34, 39; Lk. xi. 29), but never identifies Himself with it. It is those who do the will of God with whom He feels kinship (Mt. xii. 50), and He offers Himself to the morally sick as a physician (Mt. ix. 12). He proposes Himself as an example of the highest virtues (Mt. xi. 28 ff.) and pronounces him blessed who shall find no occasion of stumbling in Him (Mt. xi. 6).

These manifestations of a human and Divine consciousness

simply stand side by side in the records of Our Lord's self-expression. Neither is suppressed or even qualified by the other. If we attend only to the one class we might suppose Him to proclaim Himself wholly Divine; if only to the other we might equally easily imagine Him to be representing Himself as wholly human. With both together before us we perceive Him alternately speaking out of a Divine and out of a human consciousness; manifesting Himself as all that God is and as all that man is; yet with the most marked unity of consciousness. He, the one Jesus Christ, was to His own apprehension true God and complete man in a unitary personal life.

VII. The Two Natures Everywhere Presupposed

There underlies, thus, the entire literature of the New Testament a single, unvarying conception of the constitution of Our Lord's person. From Matthew where He is presented as one of the persons of the Holy Trinity (xxviii. 19) — or if we prefer the chronological order of books, from the Epistle of James where He is spoken of as the Glory of God, the Shekinah (ii. 1) — to the Apocalypse where He is represented as declaring that He is the Alpha and the Omega, the First and the Last, the Beginning and the End (i. 8, 17; xxii. 13), He is consistently thought of as in His fundamental being just God. At the same time from the Synoptic Gospels, in which He is dramatized as a man walking among men, His human descent carefully recorded, and His sense of dependence on God so emphasized that prayer becomes almost His most characteristic action, to the Epistles of John in which it is made the note of a Christian that He confesses that Jesus Christ has come in flesh (I Jn. iv. 2) and the Apocalypse in which His birth in the tribe of Judah and the house of David (v. 5; xxii. 16), His exemplary life of conflict and victory (iii. 21), His death on the cross (xi. 8) are noted, He is equally consistently thought of as true man. Nevertheless, from the beginning to the end of the whole series of books, while first one and then the other of His two natures comes into repeated prominence, there is never a question of conflict between the two, never any confusion in their relations, never any schism in His unitary personal action; but He is obviously considered and presented as one, composite indeed, but undivided personality. In this state of the case not only may evidence of the constitution of Our Lord's person properly be drawn indifferently from every part of the New Testament, and passage justly be cited to support and explain passage without reference to the portion of the New Testament in which it is found, but we should be without justification if we did not employ this common presupposition of the whole body of this literature to illustrate and explain the varied representations which meet us cursorily in its pages, representations which might easily be made to appear mutually contradictory were they not brought into harmony by their relation as natural component parts of this one unitary conception which underlies and gives consistency to them all. There can scarcely be imagined a better proof of the truth of a doctrine than its power completely to harmonize a multitude of statements which without it would present to our view only a mass of confused inconsistencies. A key which perfectly fits a lock of very complicated wards can scarcely fail to be the true key.

VIII. Formulation of the Doctrine

Meanwhile the wards remain complicated. Even in the case of our own composite structure, of soul and body, familiar as we are with it from our daily experience, the mutual relations of elements so disparate in a single personality remain an unplumbed mystery, and give rise to paradoxical modes of speech, which would be misleading, were not their source in our duplex nature well understood. We may read, in careful writers, of souls being left dead on battlefields, and of everybody's immortality. The mysteries of the relations in which the constituent elements in the more complex personality of Our Lord stand to one another are immeasurably greater than in our simpler case. We can never hope to comprehend how the infinite God and a finite humanity can be united in a single person; and it is very easy to go fatally astray in attempting to explain the interactions in the unitary person of natures so diverse from one another. It is not surprising, therefore, that so soon as serious efforts began to be made to give systematic explanations of the Biblical facts as to Our Lord's person, many one-sided and incomplete statements were formulated which required correction and complementing before at length a mode of statement was devised which did full justice to the Biblical data. It was accordingly only after more than a century of controversy, during which nearly every conceivable method of construing and misconstruing the Biblical facts had been proposed and tested, that a formula was framed which successfully guarded the essential data supplied by the Scriptures from destructive misconception. This formula, put together by the Council of Chalcedon, 451 A.D., declares it to have always been the doctrine of the church, derived from the Scriptures and Our Lord Himself, that Our Lord Jesus Christ is "truly God and truly man, of a reasonable soul and body; consubstantial with the Father according to the Godhead, and consubstantial with us according to the manhood; in all things like unto us, without sin; begotten before all ages of the Father according to the Godhead, and in these latter days, for us and for our salvation, born of the Virgin Mary, the Mother of God, according to the manhood; one and the same Christ, Son, Lord, Only-begotten, to be acknowledged in two natures inconfusedly, unchangeably, indivisibly, inseparably; the distinction of natures being by no means taken away by the union, but rather the property of each nature being preserved, and concurring in one Person and one subsistence, not parted or divided into two persons, but one and the same Son, and Only-begotten, God, the Word, the Lord Jesus Christ." There is nothing here but a careful statement in systematic form of the pure teaching of the Scriptures; and therefore this statement has stood ever since as the norm of thought and teaching as to the person of the Lord. As such, it has been incorporated, in one form or another, into the creeds of all the great branches of the church; it underlies and gives their form to all the allusions to Christ in the great mass of preaching and song which has accumulated during the centuries; and it has supplied the background of the devotions of the untold multitudes who through the Christian ages have been worshippers of Christ.

LITERATURE. — The appropriate sections in the treatises on the Biblical theology of the New Testament; also A. B. Bruce, "The Humiliation of Christ," 2d ed., Edinburgh, 1881; R. L. Ottley, "The Doctrine of the Incarnation," London, 1896; H. C. Powell, "The Principle of the Incarnation," London, 1896; Francis J. Hall, "The Kenotic Theory," New York, 1898; C. A. Briggs, "The Incarnation of the Lord," New York, 1902; G. S. Streatfeild, "The Self-Interpretation of Jesus Christ," London, 1906; B. B. Warfield, "The Lord of Glory," New York, 1907; James Denney, "Jesus and the Gospel," London, 1908; M. Lepin, "Christ and the Gospel: or, Jesus the Messiah and Son of God," Philadelphia, 1910; James Stalker, "The Christology of Jesus," New York, 1899; D. Somerville, "St. Paul's Conception of Christ," Edinburgh, 1897; E. H. Gifford, "The Incarnation: a Study of Phil. ii. 5–11," London, 1897; S. N. Rostron, "The Christology of St. Paul," London, 1912; E. Digges La Touche, "The Person of Christ in Modern Thought," London, 1912.

[NOTE. — In this article the author has usually given his own translation of quotations from Scripture, and not that of any particular VS.]

VI

"GOD OUR FATHER AND THE LORD JESUS CHRIST"

"GOD OUR FATHER AND THE LORD JESUS CHRIST"[1]

IN the opening sentence of the very first of Paul's letters which have come down to us — and that is as much as to say, in the very first sentence which, so far as we know, he ever wrote, — he makes use of a phrase in speaking of the Christians' God, which at once attracts our interested attention. According to the generous way he had of thinking and speaking of his readers at the height of their professions, he describes the church at Thessalonica as living and moving and having its being in God. But, as it was a Christian church which he was addressing, he does not content himself, in this description, with the simple term "God." He uses the compound phrase, "God the Father and the Lord Jesus Christ." The Thessalonians, he says, because they were Christians, lived and moved and had their being "in God the Father and the Lord Jesus Christ."

It is quite clear that this compound phrase was not new on Paul's lips, coined for this occasion. It bears on its face the evidence of a long and familiar use, by which it had been worn down to its bare bones. All the articles have been rubbed off, and with them all other accessories; and it stands out in its baldest elements as just "God Father and Lord Jesus Christ." Plainly we have here a mode of speaking of the Christians' God which was customary with Paul.

We are not surprised, therefore, to find this phrase repeated in precisely the same connection in the opening verses of the next letter which Paul wrote — II Thessalonians — with only the slight variation that an "our" is inserted with "God the Father," — "in God our Father and the Lord Jesus Christ." The significance of this variation is, probably, that, although it is a customary formula which is being employed, it has not hardened into a mechanically repeated series of mere words.

[1] From *The Princeton Theological Review*, v. xv, 1917, pp. 1–20.

It is used with lively consciousness of its full meaning, and with such slight variations of wording from time to time as the circumstances of each case, or perhaps the mere emotional movement of the moment, suggested.

This free handling of what is, nevertheless, clearly in essence a fixed formula, is sharply illustrated by a third instance of its occurrence. Paul uses it again in the opening sentence of the third letter which he wrote, — that to the Galatians. Here it is turned, however, end to end, while yet preserving all its essential elements; and is set in such a context as to throw its fundamental meaning into very strong emphasis. Paul was called upon to defend to the Galatians the validity of his apostleship, and he characteristically takes occasion to assert, in the very first words which he wrote to them, that he received it from no human source, — no, nor even through any human intermediation, — but directly from God. The way he does this is to announce himself as "an apostle not from men, neither through man, but through Jesus Christ and God the Father" — "who," he adds, "raised Him from the dead." The effect of the addition of these last words is to throw the whole emphasis of the clause on "Jesus Christ"; even "God the Father" is defined in relation to Him. Yet the whole purpose of the sentence is to assert the divine origin of Paul's apostleship in strong contrast with any possible human derivation of it. Clearly, the phrase "Jesus Christ and God the Father" denotes something purely Divine. It is in effect a Christian periphrasis for "God." And in this Christian periphrasis for "God" the name of Jesus Christ takes no subordinate place.

It will conduce to our better apprehension of the nature and implications of this Christian periphrasis for "God" which Paul employs in the opening words of each of the first three of his epistles, if we will set side by side the actual words in which it is phrased in these three instances.

I Thess. i. 1: ἐν θεῷ πατρὶ καὶ κυρίῳ Ἰησοῦ Χριστῷ.

II Thess. i. 1: ἐν θεῷ πατρὶ ἡμῶν καὶ κυρίῳ Ἰησοῦ Χριστῷ.

Gal. i. 1: διὰ Ἰησοῦ Χριστοῦ καὶ θεοῦ πατρὸς τοῦ ἐγείραντος αὐτὸν ἐκ νεκρῶν.

It is not, however, merely or chiefly in these three instances that Paul uses this Christian periphrasis for God. It is the apostle's custom to bring the address which he prefixes to each of his letters to a close in a formal prayer that the fundamental Christian blessings of grace and peace (or, in the letters to Timothy, grace, mercy and peace) may be granted to his readers. In this prayer he regularly employs this periphrasis to designate the Divine Being to whom the prayer is offered. It fails to appear in this opening prayer in two only of his thirteen letters; and its failure to appear in these two is useful in fixing its meaning in the other eleven. It is quite clear that Paul intends to say the same thing in all thirteen instances: they differ only in the fulness with which he expresses his identical meaning. When he says in I Thess. i. 1 only "Grace to you and peace," he is not expressing a mere wish; he is invoking the Divine Being in prayer; and his mind is as fully on Him as if he had formally named Him. And when he names this Divine Being whom he is invoking in this prayer, in Col. i. 2, "God our Father," — "Grace to you and peace from God our Father" — his meaning is precisely the same as when he names Him in the companion letter, Eph. i. 2, "God our Father and the Lord Jesus Christ" — "Grace to you and peace from God our Father and the Lord Jesus Christ" — or in a similar prayer at the end of the same letter, Eph. vi. 23, "God the Father and the Lord Jesus Christ" — "Peace to the brethren and love along with faith from God the Father and the Lord Jesus Christ." In every instance Paul is invoking the Divine Being and only the Divine Being. Once he leaves that to be understood from the nature of the case. Once he names this Being simply "God the Father." In the other eleven instances he gives Him the conjunct name, which ordinarily takes the form of "God our Father and the Lord Jesus Christ," — obviously employing a formula which had become habitual with him in such formal prayers.

That we may see at a glance how clear it is that Paul is making use here of a fixed formula in his designation of the Christians' God, and may observe at the same time the amount of freedom which he allows himself in repeating it in these very formal prayers, we bring together the series of these opening prayers, in the chronological order of the epistles in which they occur.

I Thess. i. 1: χάρις ὑμῖν καὶ εἰρήνη.

II Thess. i. 2: χάρις ὑμῖν καὶ εἰρήνη ἀπὸ θεοῦ πατρὸς καὶ κυρίου Ἰησοῦ Χριστοῦ.

Gal. i. 3: χάρις ὑμῖν καὶ εἰρήνη ἀπὸ θεοῦ πατρὸς ἡμῶν καὶ κυρίου Ἰησοῦ Χριστοῦ.

I Cor. i. 3: χάρις ὑμῖν καὶ εἰρήνη ἀπὸ θεοῦ πατρὸς ἡμῶν καὶ κυρίου Ἰησοῦ Χριστοῦ.

II Cor. i. 2: χάρις ὑμῖν καὶ εἰρήνη ἀπὸ Θεοῦ πατρὸς ἡμῶν καὶ κυρίου Ἰησοῦ Χριστοῦ.

Rom. i. 7: χάρις ὑμῖν καὶ εἰρήνη ἀπὸ θεοῦ πατρὸς ἡμῶν καὶ κυρίου Ἰησοῦ Χριστοῦ.

Eph. i. 2: χάρις ὑμῖν καὶ εἰρήνη ἀπὸ θεοῦ πατρὸς ἡμῶν καὶ κυρίου Ἰησοῦ Χριστοῦ.

[Eph. vi. 23: εἰρήνη τοῖς ἀδελφοῖς καὶ ἀγάπη μετὰ πίστεως ἀπὸ θεοῦ πατρὸς καὶ κυρίου Ἰησοῦ Χριστοῦ.]

Col. i. 2: χάρις ὑμῖν καὶ εἰρήνη ἀπὸ θεοῦ πατρὸς ἡμῶν.

Phile. 3: χάρις ὑμῖν καὶ εἰρήνη ἀπὸ θεοῦ πατρὸς ἡμῶν καὶ κυρίου Ἰησοῦ Χριστοῦ.

Phil. i. 2: χάρις ὑμῖν καὶ εἰρήνη ἀπὸ θεοῦ πατρὸς ἡμῶν καὶ κυρίου Ἰησοῦ Χριστοῦ.

I Tim. i. 2: χάρις ἔλεος εἰρήνη ἀπὸ θεοῦ πατρὸς καὶ Χριστοῦ Ἰησοῦ τοῦ κυρίου ἡμῶν.

Tit. i. 4: χάρις καὶ εἰρήνη ἀπὸ θεοῦ πατρὸς καὶ Χριστοῦ Ἰησοῦ τοῦ σωτῆρος ἡμῶν.

II Tim. i. 2: χάρις ἔλεος εἰρήνη ἀπὸ θεοῦ πατρὸς καὶ Χριστοῦ Ἰησοῦ τοῦ κυρίου ἡμῶν.

Alfred Seeberg, seeking evidence of the survival of old Christian formulas in the literature of the New Testament, very naturally fixes on these passages, and argues that we have here a combination of the names of God the Father and the Lord Jesus Christ in prayer which Paul found already in use in the Christian community when he attached himself to it, and which

he took over from it. It is a hard saying when Ernst von Dobschütz professes himself ready to concede that Paul received
this combination of names from his predecessors, but sharply
denies that he received it as a "fixed formula." One would
have supposed it to lie on the face of Paul's use of it that he
was repeating a formula; while it might be disputed whether
it was a formula of his own making or he had adopted it from
others. It goes to show that it was not invented by Paul, that it
is found not only in other connections in Paul's writings, as we
have seen, but also in other New Testament books besides his.

Jas. i. 1: θεοῦ καὶ κυρίου 'Ιησοῦ Χριστοῦ δοῦλος.

II Pet. i. 2: ἐν ἐπιγνώσει τοῦ θεοῦ καὶ 'Ιησοῦ τοῦ κυρίου ἡμῶν.

II Jno. 3: ἔσται μεθ' ἡμῶν χάρις ἔλεος εἰρήνη παρὰ θεοῦ πατρὸς καὶ παρὰ 'Ιησοῦ Χριστοῦ τοῦ υἱοῦ τοῦ πατρός.

In the presence of these passages it is difficult to deny that we
have in the closely knit conjunction of these two Divine names
part of the established phraseology of primitive Christian religious speech.

It would not be easy to exaggerate the closeness with which
the two names are knit together in this formula. The two persons brought together are not, to be sure, absolutely identified.
They remain two persons, to each of whom severally there
may be ascribed activities in which the other does not share.
In Gal i. 1 we read of "Jesus Christ and God the Father who
raised Him from the dead." In Gal. i. 3, we read of "God the
Father and our Lord Jesus Christ who gave Himself for our
sins." The epithets by which they are described, moreover, are
distinctive, — the Father, our Father, the Lord, our Lord, our
Saviour. There is no obscuration, then, of the peculiarities of
the personalities brought together. But their equalization is
absolute. And short of thoroughgoing identification of persons
the unity expressed by their conjunction seems to be complete.

How complete this unity is may be illustrated by another
series of passages. J. B. Lightfoot has called attention to the
symmetrical structure of the two Epistles to the Thessalonians.
Each is divided into two parts ("the first part being chiefly

narrative and explanatory, and the second hortatory"), and
each of these parts closes with a prayer introduced by αὐτὸς δέ
followed by the Divine name, — a construction not found elsewhere in these epistles. Clearly there is formal art at work here;
and it will repay us to bring together the opening words of the
four prayers, including the designations by which God is invoked in each.

I Thess. iii. 11: αὐτὸς δὲ ὁ θεὸς καὶ πατὴρ ἡμῶν καὶ ὁ κύριος
ἡμῶν Ἰησοῦς.

I Thess. v. 23: αὐτὸς δὲ ὁ θεὸς τῆς εἰρήνης.

II Thess. ii. 16: αὐτὸς δὲ ὁ κύριος ἡμῶν Ἰησοῦς Χριστὸς καὶ
ὁ θεὸς ὁ πατὴρ ἡμῶν ὁ ἀγαπήσας ἡμᾶς καὶ δοὺς παρά-
κλησιν αἰωνίαν καὶ ἐλπίδα ἀγαθὴν ἐν χάριτι.

II Thess. iii. 16: αὐτὸς δὲ ὁ κύριος τῆς εἰρήνης.

It is remarkable how illuminating the mere conjunction of
these passages is. Taking I Thess. iii. 11 in isolation, we might
wonder whether we ought to read it, "God Himself, even our
Father and our Lord Jesus," or "Our God and Father Himself,
and our Lord Jesus," or "Our God and Father and our Lord
Jesus, Himself." So, taking it in isolation, we might hesitate
whether we should construe II Thess. ii. 16, "Our Lord Jesus
Christ Himself, and God our Father," or "Our Lord Jesus
Christ and God our Father, Himself." The commentators accordingly divide themselves among these views, each urging
reasons which scarcely seem convincing for his choice. But so
soon as we bring the passages together it becomes clear that the
αὐτός is to be construed with the whole subject following it in
every case, and thus a solid foundation is put beneath the opinion arrived at on other grounds by Martin Dibelius, Ernst von
Dobschütz and J. E. Frame, that in I Thess. iii. 11 and II
Thess. ii. 16, the αὐτός binds together the two subjects, God
and the Lord, as the conjunct object of Paul's prayer.

The four prayers are in every sense of the word parallel.
The petition is substantially the same in all. It cannot be
imagined that the Being to whom the several prayers are addressed was consciously envisaged as different. Paul is in every

case simply bringing his heart's desire for his converts before his God. Yet, in describing the God before whom he lays his petition, he fairly exhausts the possibilities of variety of designation which the case affords. As a result, God the Father and the Lord Jesus Christ could not be more indissolubly knit together as essentially one. Both are mentioned in two of the addresses, but the order in which they are mentioned is reversed from one to the other, and all the predicates in both instances are cast in the singular number. In the other two addresses only one is named, but it is a different one in each case, although an identical epithet is attributed to them both. We learn thus not only that Paul prays indifferently to God and to the Lord — in precisely the same way, for precisely the same things, and with precisely the same attitude of mind and heart, expressed in identical epithets, — but also that he prays thus indifferently to God or the Lord separately and to God and the Lord together. And when he prays to the two together, he does all that it is humanly possible to do to make it clear that he is thinking of them not as two but as one. Interchanging the names, so that they stand indifferently in the order "God and the Lord," or "the Lord and God," he binds them together in a single "self"; and then, proceeding with his prayer, he construes this double subject, thus bound together in a single "self," in both cases alike with a singular verb, — "Now our Lord Jesus Christ and God our Father who loved us . . . Himself," he prays, "may He comfort your hearts and establish them in every good work and word." "Now our God and Father and our Lord Jesus, Himself," he prays again, "may He direct our way unto you": and then he proceeds immediately, continuing the prayer, but now with only one name, though obviously with no change in the Being addressed, — "and may the Lord make you to increase and abound in love toward one another and toward all men." If it was with any difference of consciousness that Paul addressed God or the Lord, or God and the Lord together, in his prayers, he certainly has taken great pains to obscure that fact. If he had intended to show plainly that to him God and the Lord were so one that

God and the Lord conjoined were still one to his consciousness, he could scarcely have found more effective means of doing so. There is probably no instance in all Paul's epistles where God and the Lord are mentioned together, that they are construed with a plural adjective or verb.

We should not pass without notice that it is in the passages from II Thessalonians that ὁ κύριος is given relative prominence. In the two passages from I Thessalonians ὁ θεός comes forward, while in those from II Thessalonians it is ὁ κύριος. That is in accordance with the general character of II Thessalonians, which is distinctively a κύριος epistle. Proportionately to the lengths of the two epistles, while θεός occurs about equally often in each, κύριος occurs about twice as often in the second as in the first. We do not pause to inquire into the causes of this superior prominence of κύριος in II Thessalonians, although it may be worth remarking in passing that in both epistles it is relatively prominent in the hortatory portions. Whatever, however, may have been the particular causes which brought about the result in this case, the result is in itself one which could not have been brought about if θεός and κύριος had not stood in the consciousness of Paul in virtual equality as designations of Deity. For the phenomenon amounts at its apex, — as we see in the four passages more particularly before us — to the simple replacement of θεός by κύριος as the designation of Deity. And that means at bottom that Paul knows no difference between θεός and κύριος in point of rank; they are both to him designations of Deity and the discrimination by which the one is applied to the Father and the other to Christ is (so far) merely a convention by which two that are God are supplied with differentiating appellations by means of which they may be intelligibly spoken of severally. With respect to the substance of the matter there seems no reason why the Father might not just as well be called κύριος and Christ θεός.

Whether the convention by which the two appellations are assigned respectively to the Father as θεός and to Christ as κύριος is ever broken by Paul, is a question of little intrinsic importance, but nevertheless of some natural interest. It is probable that Paul never, — not only in these epistles to the Thessalonians, but throughout his epistles, — employs κύριος of the Father. The term seems to appear uniformly in his writings, except in a few (not all) quotations from the Old Testament, as a designation of Christ. Thus the Old Testament divine name κύριος (Jehovah) is appropriated exclusively to Christ; and that in repeated instances even when the language of the Old Testament is adduced, — which Paul carries over to and applies to Christ as the Lord there spoken of. The question whether Paul ever applies the term θεός to Christ is brought sharply before us by the form in which the formula, the use of which we are particularly investigating, occurs in II Thess. i. 12. There we read of Paul's constant prayer that "our God" should count his readers worthy of their calling and fulfil with reference to them every good pleasure of goodness and work of faith with power, to the end that "the name of our Lord Jesus" might be glorified in them, and they in Him, κατὰ τήν χάριν τοῦ θεοῦ ἡμῶν καὶ κυρίου 'Ιησοῦ Χριστοῦ.

It will probably be allowed that in strictness of grammatical rule, rigidly applied, this should mean, "according to the grace of our God and Lord Jesus Christ," or, if we choose so to phrase it, "according to the grace of our God, even the Lord Jesus Christ." All sorts of reasons are advanced, however, why the strict grammatical rule should not be rigidly applied here. Most of them are ineffective enough and testify only to the reluctance of expositors to acknowledge that Paul can speak of Christ as "God." This reluctance is ordinarily given expression either in the simple empirical remark that it is not in accordance with the usage of Paul to call Christ God, or in the more far-reaching assertion that it is contrary to Paul's doctrinal system to represent Christ as God. Thus, for example, W. Bornemann comments briefly: "In themselves, these words might be so taken as to call Jesus here both God and Lord. That is, however, improbable, according to the Pauline usage elsewhere." This mild statement is particularly interesting as a recession from the strong ground taken by G. Lünemann, whose commentary on the Thessalonian epistles in the Meyer series

Bornemann's superseded. Lünemann argues the question at
some length and one might almost say with some heat. "According to Hofmann and Riggenbach," he writes, "Christ is
here named both our God and our Lord, — an interpretation
which, indeed, grammatically is no less allowable than the interpretation of the doxology ὁ ὢν ἐπὶ πάντων θεὸς εὐλογητὸς εἰς
τοὺς αἰῶνας, Rom. ix. 5, as an apposition to Χριστός; but is
equally inadmissible as it would contain an un-Pauline thought:
on account of which also Hilgenfeld, "Zeitschr.f.d. wiss. Theol.,"
Halle, 1862, p. 264, in the interest of the supposed spuriousness
of the Epistle, has forthwith appropriated to himself this discovery of Hofmann." Ernst von Dobschütz, who has superseded Bornemann as Bornemann superseded Lünemann, is as
sure as Lünemann that it is un-Pauline to call Christ God; but
as he is equally sure that this passage does call Christ God, he
has no alternative but to deny the passage to Paul, — though
he prefers to deny to him only this passage and not, like Hilgenfeld, the whole Epistle. "But an entirely un-Pauline trait meets
us here," he writes, "that to τοῦ θεοῦ ἡμῶν there is added
καὶ κυρίου Ἰησοῦ Χριστοῦ· Not that the combination, God our
Father and the Lord Jesus Christ, is not original-Pauline (see
on I Thess. i. 1), but that what stands here must be translated,
'Of our God and Lord Jesus Christ' as Hofmann and Wohlenberg rightly maintain. This, however, is in very fact in the
highest degree un-Pauline (Lünemann) in spite of Rom. ix. 5,
and has its parallel only in Tit. ii. 13, 'Of our Great God and
Saviour, Christ Jesus,' or II Pet. i. 1, 11, 'Of our God (Lord)
and Saviour, Jesus Christ.'" H. J. Holtzmann, as is his wont,
sums up the whole contention crisply: "In the entire compass
of the Pauline literature, only II Thess. i. 12 and Tit. ii. 13
supply two equally exegetically uncertain parallels" to Rom.
ix. 5 "while, in Eph. iv. 6, God the Father is ὁ ἐπὶ πάντων."

It is manifest that reasoning of this sort runs great risk of
merely begging the question. The precise point under discussion is whether Paul does ever, or could ever, speak of Christ
as God. This passage is offered in evidence that he both can
and does. It is admitted that there are other passages which

may be adduced in the same sense. There is Rom. ix. 5 which everybody allows to be Paul's own. There is Tit. ii. 13 which occurs in confessedly distinctively "Pauline literature." There is Acts xx. 28, credibly attributed to Paul by one of his pupils. There is II Pet. i. 1 to show that the usage was not unknown to other of the New Testament letter-writers. It is scarcely satisfactory to say that all these passages are as "exegetically uncertain" as II Thess. i. 12 itself. This "exegetical uncertainty" is in each case imposed upon the passage by reluctance to take it in the sense which it most naturally bears, and which is exegetically immediately given. It is as exegetically certain, for example, as any thing can be purely exegetically certain, that in Rom. ix. 5 Paul calls Christ roundly "God over all." It is scarcely to be doubted that this would be universally recognized if Romans could with any plausibility be denied to Paul, or even could be assigned to a date subsequent to that of, say, Colossians. The equivalent may be said of each of the other passages *mutatis mutandis*. The reasoning is distinctly circular which denies to each of these passages in turn its natural meaning on the ground of lack of supporting usage, when this lack of supporting usage is created by a similar denial on the same ground of its natural meaning to each of the other passages. The ground of the denial in each case is merely the denial in the other cases. Meanwhile the usage is there, and is not thus to be denied away. If it may be, any usage whatever may be destroyed in the same manner.

In these circumstances there seems no reason why the ordinary laws of grammar should not determine our understanding of II Thess. i. 12. We may set it down here, therefore, with its parallels in Tit. ii. 13 and II Pet. i. 1 in which the same general phrasing even more clearly carries this sense.

II Thess. i. 12: τὴν χάριν τοῦ θεοῦ ἡμῶν καὶ κυρίου Ἰησοῦ Χριστοῦ.

Tit. ii. 13: καὶ ἐπιφάνειαν τῆς δόξης τοῦ μεγάλου θεοῦ καὶ σωτῆρος ἡμῶν Χριστοῦ Ἰησοῦ.

II Pet. i. 1: πίστιν ἐν δικαιοσύνῃ τοῦ θεοῦ ἡμῶν καὶ σωτῆρος Ἰησοῦ Χριστοῦ.

In these passages the conjunction, in which God and Christ are brought together in the general formula which we are investigating, reaches its culmination in an express identification of them. We have seen that the two are not only united in this formula on terms of complete equality, but are treated as in some sense one. Grammatically at least, they constitute one "self" (αὐτός); and they are presented in nearly every phraseology possible as the common source of Christian blessing and the unitary object of Christian prayer. Their formal identification would seem after this to be a matter of course, and we may be a little surprised that the recognition of it should be so strenuously resisted. The explanation is no doubt to be sought in the consideration that so long as this formal identification is not acknowledged to be expressly made, those who find difficulty in believing that Christ is included by Paul in the actual Godhead may feel the way more or less open to explain away by one expedient or another the identity of the two, manifoldly implied in the general representation indeed, but not formally announced.

Expositor after expositor, at any rate, may be observed introducing into his reproduction of Paul's simple equalization, or rather, unification, of God and the Lord, qualifying phrases of his own which tend to adjust them to his personal way of thinking of the relations subsisting between the two. C. J. Ellicott already found occasion to rebuke this practice in G. Lünemann and A. Koch. The former explains that Paul conjoins Christ with God in his prayers, because, according to Paul's conception — "see Usteri, "Lehrb." ii. 2. 4, p. 315" — Christ, as sitting at the right hand of God, has a part in the government of the world. The latter, going further, asserts that Paul brings the two together only because he regards Christ "as the wisdom and power of God." Few expositors entirely escape the temptation to go thus beyond what is written. It is most common, perhaps, to follow the path in which Lünemann walks, and to declare that Paul unites the two persons because Christ by His exaltation has been made for the time co-regnant with God over the universe, or perhaps only over the Church. Quite frequently, however, it is asserted, more like Koch, that the unity instituted between them amounts merely to a unity of will, or even only to a harmony of operation. At the best it is explained that our Lord is placed by the side of God only because it is through Him as intermediary that the blessings which have their source in God are received or are to be sought. An especially flagrant example of the substitution of quite alien phraseology for Paul's, in a professed restatement of his conception, is afforded by David Somerville in his Cunningham Lectures on "St. Paul's Conception of Christ." He tells us that Paul's "conjunction of God and Christ in his stated greetings to the churches indicated his belief that a co-partnership of Divine power and honor was included in the exaltation of Christ to be Lord." It obviously smacks, however, less of Paul than of Socinus to speak of the relation of Christ to God as a "co-partnership of Divine power and honor," and of this co-partnership of Divine power and honor between them as resulting from Christ becoming Lord by His exaltation.

Benjamin Jowett, with that fine condescension frequently exhibited by the "emancipated," remarks on Chrysostom's comment on Gal. i. 3: "This is the mind not of the Apostolic but of the Nicene age." He does not stay to consider that the mind of his own age and coterie may in such a matter be as much further removed than that of the Nicene age from the mind of the Apostolic age in substance as it is in time. Nevertheless it may be admitted that even the Nicene commentators were prone to read their own conceptions of the relations of Christ to God explanatorily into Paul's simple equalization of them. Athanasius appeals, — as he was thoroughly entitled to do, — to Paul's conjunction of God the Father and the Lord Jesus Christ as the common source of grace and the common object of prayer, against the Arian contention that the Father and the Son are concordant, indeed, in will but not one in being. In the eleventh section of the third of his Orations against the Arians he gives expression to this appeal thus: "Therefore also, as we said just now, when the Father gives grace and peace, the Son also gives it, as Paul signifies in every epistle, writing,

'Grace to you and peace, from God our Father and the Lord
Jesus Christ.' For one and the same grace is from the Father
in the Son, as the light of the sun and of the radiance is one,
and as the sun's illumination is effective through the radiance;
and so, when he prays for the Thessalonians, in saying, 'Now
God even the Father and the Lord Jesus Christ Himself, may
He direct our way unto you,' he has guarded the unity of the
Father and of the Son. For he has not said, 'May they direct,'
as of a double grace given from two, from This and That, but,
'May he direct,' to show that the Father gives it through the
Son." This is not to emphasize the unity of the Father and the
Son more strongly than Paul does: it is only to repeat Paul's
testimony to their unity. But Athanasius cannot repeat Paul's
testimony to their unity without interpolating his own conception of the manner in which this unity is to be conceived. One
and the same grace comes to us from the Father and the Son,
he gives us to understand, because the grace of the Father
comes to us in the Son; one and the same prayer is addressed
to the Father and the Son, because whatever the Father gives
He gives through the Son. This explanation is interpolated into
Paul's language. Paul places God and the Lord absolutely side
by side, as joint source of the blessings he seeks for his readers;
addresses his prayers for benefits he desires for his readers to
them in common; treats them, in a word, as one. Athanasius'
explanations are, of course, not as gross interpolations into the
text as Arius'; but they are no less real interpolations. The outstanding fact governing Paul's collocation of God and the Lord,
is that he makes no discrimination between them whatever,
but treats them as a unity.

This is well brought out in the remarks of Chrysostom on
which Jowett had his eye when he accused him of intruding a
Nicene meaning on the text. These remarks are on the prepositions in Gal. i. 1 and Rom. i. 7. Had Paul written in the former
of these passages, says Chrysostom, either "through Jesus
Christ," or "through God the Father," alone, the Arians
would have had their explanation of his having done so, in the
interests of some essential distinction between the Father and

the Son. But Paul "leaves no opening for such a cavil, by mentioning at once both the Son and the Father, and making the
language apply to both." "This he does," he adds, "not as
referring the acts of the Son to the Father, but to show that the
expression implies no distinction of essence." On Rom. i. 7 he
remarks similarly on the use of "from" with both the Father
and the Son. "For he did not say, 'Grace be unto you and
peace, from God the Father, through the Lord Jesus Christ,'
but 'from God the Father and the Lord Jesus Christ.'" There
is no imposing of a Nicene sense on Paul's language here. There
is a simple reflection, as in a clear mirror, of the exact sense of
the texts in hand, with an emphasis on their underlying implication of oneness between God and our Lord.

We are constantly pointed to I Cor. viii. 6, to be sure, as
in some way supplying a warrant for supposing an unexpressed
subordinationism to be hidden beneath the surface of all of
Paul's equalizations of God the Father and the Lord Jesus
Christ. It is exceedingly difficult, however, to see how this
passage can be made to supply such a warrant. It lies open to
the sight of all, of course, that in it the one God the Father
and the one Lord Jesus Christ, — who are included in the one
only God that, it is understood by all, alone exists, — are differentiated by the particular relations in which the first and
the second creations alike are said to stand to them severally.
All things are said to be "of" God the Father and "through"
the Lord Jesus Christ; Christians are said to be "unto" the
one and "by means of" the other. These characterizations are
of course, not made at random; and it is right to seek diligently
for their significance. It would doubtless be easy, however, to
press such prepositional distinctions too far, as such passages
as Rom. xi. 36 and Col. i. 16 may advise us. Perhaps it would
not be wrong to say that they are to be taken rather eminently
than exclusively. What it is at the moment especially important
that we observe, however, is that they concern the relations of
God the Father and the Lord Jesus Christ *ad extra* and say
nothing whatever of their relations to one another. With respect to their relations to one another, what the passage tells

us is that they are both embraced in that one God which, it is declared with great emphasis, alone exists. We must not permit to fall out of sight that the whole passage is dominated by the clear-cut assertion that "there is no God but one" (verse 4, at the end). Of this assertion the words now particularly before us (verse 6b) are the positive side of an explication and proof (verse 5, γάρ). And the thing for us distinctly to note is that Paul explicates the assertion that there is no God but one by declaring, as if that was quite *ad rem*, that Christians know but one God the Father and one Lord Jesus Christ. There meets us here again, we perceive, — as underlying and giving its force to this assertion, — the precise formula we have been having under consideration. And it meets us after a fashion which brings very strikingly to our attention once more that, when Paul says "God the Father and the Lord Jesus Christ," he has in mind not two Gods, much less two beings of unequal dignity, a God and a Demi-god, or a God and a mere creature, — but just one God. Though Christians have one God the Father and one Lord Jesus Christ, they know but one only God.

The essential meaning of the passage is wholly unaffected by the question whether in the words, "There is no God but one" at the end of verse 4, we have Paul's own language or that of his Corinthian correspondents repeated by him. We may read the verse, if we choose, — perhaps we ought to, — "Concerning the meats offered to idols, then, we are perfectly well aware that, as you say, there is no idol in the world, and there is no God but one." Still, the assertion that there is no God but one rules the succeeding verses, which, introduced as its justification, become in effect a reiteration of it. "There is no God but one, *for* — for, although there are indeed so-called Gods, whether in heaven or on earth, — as there are Gods a-plenty and Lords a-plenty! — yet for us there is one God the Father . . . and one Lord Jesus Christ. . . ." Obviously this can mean nothing else than that the "one God the Father and one Lord Jesus Christ" of the Christians is just the one only God which exists. To attempt to make it mean anything else is to stultify the whole argument. You cannot prove that only one God exists by pointing out that you yourself have two.

We are referred, it is true, to the declaration that the heathen have not only many Gods, but also many Lords, and we are bidden to see in their one God the Father and one Lord Jesus Christ a parallel among the Christians to this state of affairs among the heathen. And then we are further instructed that it is only fair to suppose that Paul felt some difference in grade between the Gods and the Lords of the heathen and, in paralleling the two objects of Christian worship with them respectively, intended to intimate a discrimination in rank between God the Father and the Lord Jesus Christ. On this ground, we are then asked to conclude that Paul does not range the Lord Jesus Christ here along with God the Father within the Godhead, but adjoins Him to God the Father as an additional and inferior object of reverence, placed distinctly as "Lord" outside the category of "God." This whole construction, however, is purely artificial and has no standing ground in the world of realities. There is no evidence that the heathen discriminated between the designations "God" and "Lord" in point of dignity to the disadvantage of the latter; this, at the end of the day, has to be admitted by both Johannes Weiss and W. Bousset, who yet urge that Paul must be supposed to presuppose such a distinction here. Paul, however, intimates in no way at all that he felt any such distinction on his part; on the contrary he includes the "Gods many" and "Lords many" of the heathen without question in their "so-called Gods" on equal terms. Least of all is it possible to separate off "one God the Father" from its fellow "one Lord Jesus Christ," linked to it immediately by the simple "and," and make the former alone refer back to the "There is no God but one." Paul obviously includes both "God the Father" and "the Lord Jesus Christ" within this one only God whom alone he and his readers alike recognize as existing. It would void his whole argument if Jesus Christ were conceived of as a second and inferior object of worship outside the limits of the one only

God. The thing which above all others the passage says plainly, is that the acknowledgment by Christians of "one God the Father and one Lord Jesus Christ" accords with the fundamental postulate that "there is no God but one." And that can mean nothing else than that God the Father and the Lord Jesus Christ together make but one God. So far from this passage throwing itself athwart the implications of the repeated employment by Paul, as by others of the writers of the New Testament, of the formula in which God the Father and the Lord Jesus Christ are conjoined as the one object of Christian prayer and source of Christian blessings, it brings a notable support to them. It supplies what is in effect an explicit assertion of the fact on which this formula implicitly proceeds. It declares that the one God of the Christians includes in His Being both "God the Father" and "the Lord Jesus Christ." Christians acknowledge but one God; and these are the one God which Christians acknowledge.

Something of the same thing that Paul expresses by this conjunction of God the Father and the Lord Jesus Christ, John expresses in his own phraseology by the conjunction of the Father and the Son, — as in I Jno. ii. 24: "If what you heard from the beginning abide in you, you also shall abide in the Son and the Father"; or II Jno. 9, in the reverse order: "He that abideth in the teaching, the same hath the Father and the Son"; as well as in II Jno. 3, already quoted: "Grace, mercy, peace shall be with us, from God the Father, and from Jesus Christ, the Son of the Father." It is true, but not adequate, to say that John never thinks of Christ apart from God and never thinks of God apart from Christ. With him, to have the Son is to have the Father also, and to have the Father is to have the Son also. The two are as inseparable in fact as in thought. The terminology is different, but the idea is the same as that which underlies Paul's unification of God the Father and the Lord Jesus Christ.

Clearly the suggestions of this formula carry us into the midst not only of Paul's Christology but of his conception of God — which obviously is not simple. Short of this, they bring

us face to face with two matters of great preliminary importance to the correct apprehension of Paul's doctrines of Christ
and of God, which have been much discussed of late, not always very illuminatingly. We mean the matters of the significance of the title "Lord" which is so richly applied to Christ
in the New Testament writings, and of the meaning of the
adoration of Christ which is everywhere reflected in these writings. We must deny ourselves the pleasure of following out these
suggestions here. It must content us for the moment to have
pointed out a line of approach to the correct understanding of
these great matters which, surely, cannot be neglected in any
earnest attempt to reach the truth concerning them, and which,
if not neglected, will certainly conduct us to very high conclusions in regard to them.

THE CHRIST THAT PAUL PREACHED

THE CHRIST THAT PAUL PREACHED [1]

"THE monumental Introduction of the Epistle to the Romans" — it is thus that W. Bousset speaks of the seven opening verses of the Epistle — is, from the formal point of view, merely the Address of the Epistle. In primary purpose and fundamental structure it does not differ from the Addresses of Paul's other Epistles. But even in the Addresses of his Epistles Paul does not confine himself to the simple repetition of a formula. Here too he writes at his ease and shows himself very much the master of his form.

It is Paul's custom to expand one or another of the essential elements of the Address of his Epistles as circumstances suggested, and thus to impart to it in each several instance a specific character. The Address of the Epistle to the Romans is the extreme example of this expansion. Paul is approaching in it a church which he had not visited, and to which he apparently felt himself somewhat of a stranger. He naturally begins with some words adapted to justify his writing to it, especially as an authoritative teacher of Christian truth. In doing this he is led to describe briefly the Gospel which had been committed to him, and that particularly with regard to its contents.

There is very strikingly illustrated here a peculiarity of Paul's style, which has been called "going off at a word." His particular purpose is to represent himself as one authoritatively appointed to teach the Gospel of God. But he is more interested in the Gospel than he is in himself; and he no sooner mentions the Gospel than off he goes on a tangent to describe it. In describing it, he naturally tells us particularly what its contents are. Its contents, however, were for him summed up in Christ. No sooner does he mention Christ than off he goes

[1] From *The Expositor*, 8th ser., v. xv, 1918, pp. 90–110.

again on a tangent to describe Christ. Thus it comes about that this passage, formally only the Address of the Epistle, becomes actually a great Christological deliverance, one of the chief sources of our knowledge of Paul's conception of Christ. It presents itself to our view like one of those nests of Chinese boxes; the outer encasement is the Address of the Epistle; within that fits neatly Paul's justification of his addressing the Romans as an authoritative teacher of the Gospel; within that a description of the Gospel committed to him; and within that a great declaration of who and what Jesus Christ is, as the contents of this Gospel.

The manner in which Paul approaches this great declaration concerning Christ lends it a very special interest. What we are given is not merely how Paul thought of Christ, but how Paul preached Christ. It is the content of "the Gospel of God," the Gospel to which he as "a called apostle" had been "separated," which he outlines in these pregnant words. This is how Paul preached Christ to the faith of men as he went up and down the world "serving God in his spirit in the Gospel of His Son." We have no abstract theologoumena here, categories of speculative thought appropriate only to the closet. We have the great facts about Jesus which made the Gospel that Paul preached the power of God unto salvation to every one that believed. Nowhere else do we get a more direct description of specifically the Christ that Paul preached.

The direct description of the Christ that Paul preached is given us, of course, in the third and fourth verses. But the wider setting in which these verses are embedded cannot be neglected in seeking to get at their significance. In this wider setting the particular aspect in which Christ is presented is that of "Lord." It is as "Lord" that Paul is thinking of Jesus when he describes himself in the opening words of the Address — in the very first item of his commendation of himself to the Romans — as "the slave of Christ Jesus." "Slave" is the correlate of "Lord," and the relation must be taken at its height. When Paul calls himself the slave of Christ Jesus, he is calling Christ Jesus his Lord in the most complete sense which can be ascribed to that word (cf. Rom. i. 1, Col. iii. 4). He is declaring that he recognises in Christ Jesus one over against whom he has no rights, whose property he is, body and soul, to be disposed of as He will. This is not because he abases himself. It is because he exalts Christ. It is because Christ is thought of by him as one whose right it is to rule, and to rule with no limit to His right.

How Paul thought of Christ as Lord comes out, however, with most startling clearness in the closing words of the Address. There he couples "the Lord Jesus Christ" with "God our Father" as the common source from which he seeks in prayer the divine gifts of grace and peace for the Romans. We must renounce enervating glossing here too. Paul is not thinking of the Lord Jesus Christ as only the channel through which grace and peace come from God our Father to men; nor is he thinking of the Lord Jesus Christ as only the channel through which his prayer finds its way to God our Father. His prayer for these blessings for the Romans is offered up to God our Father and the Lord Jesus Christ together, as the conjoint object addressed in his petition. So far as this Bousset's remark is just: "Prayer to God in Christ is for Pauline Christianity, too, a false formula; adoration of the Kyrios stands in the Pauline communities side by side with adoration of God in unreconciled reality."

Only, we must go further. Paul couples God our Father and the Lord Jesus Christ in his prayer on a complete equality. They are, for the purposes of the prayer, for the purposes of the bestowment of grace and peace, one to him. Christ is so highly exalted in his sight that, looking up to Him through the immense stretches which separate Him from the plane of human life, "the forms of God and Christ," as Bousset puts it, "are brought to the eye of faith into close conjunction." He should have said that they completely coalesce. It is only half the truth — though it is half the truth — to say that, with Paul, "the object of religious faith, as of religious worship, presents itself in a singular, thoroughgoing dualism." The other half of the truth is that this dualism resolves itself into a complete unity. The two, God our Father and the Lord Jesus Christ, are steadily recognized as two, and are statedly spoken of by the distinguishing designations of "God" and "Lord." But they are equally steadily envisaged as one, and are statedly combined as the common object of every religious aspiration and the common source of every spiritual blessing. It is no accident that they are united in our present passage under the government of the single preposition, "from," — "Grace to you and peace from God our Father and the Lord Jesus Christ." This is normal with Paul. God our Father and the Lord Jesus Christ are not to him two objects of worship, two sources of blessing, but one object of worship, one source of blessing. Does he not tell us plainly that we who have one God the Father and one Lord Jesus Christ yet know perfectly well that there is no God but one (I Cor. viii. 4, 6)?

Paul is writing the Address of his Epistle to the Romans, then, with his mind fixed on the divine dignity of Christ. It is this divine Christ who, he must be understood to be telling his readers, constitutes the substance of his Gospel-proclamation. He does not leave us, however, merely to infer this. He openly declares it. The Gospel he preaches, he says, concerns precisely "the Son of God . . . Jesus Christ our Lord." He expressly says, then, that he presents Christ in his preaching as "our Lord." It was the divine Christ that he preached, the Christ that the eye of faith could not distinguish from God, who was addressed in common with God in prayer, and was looked to in common with God as the source of all spiritual blessings. Paul does not speak of Christ here, however, merely as "our Lord." He gives Him the two designations: "the Son of God . . . Jesus Christ our Lord." The second designation obviously is explanatory of the first. Not as if it were the more current or the more intelligible designation. It may, or it may not, have been both the one and the other; but that is not the point here. The point here is that it is the more intimate, the more appealing designation. It is the designation which tells what Christ is to us. He is our Lord, He to whom we go in prayer, He to whom we look for blessings, He to whom all our religious emotions turn, on whom all our hopes are set — for this life and for that to come. Paul tells the Romans that this is the Christ that he preaches, their and his Lord whom both they and he reverence and worship and love and trust in. This is, of course, what he mainly wishes to say to them; and it is up to this that all else that he says of the Christ that he preaches leads.

The other designation — "the Son of God" — which Paul prefixes to this in his fundamental declaration concerning the Christ that he preached, supplies the basis for this. It does not tell us what Christ is to us, but what Christ is in Himself. In Himself He is the Son of God; and it is only because He is the Son of God in Himself, that He can be and is our Lord. The Lordship of Christ is rooted by Paul, in other words, not in any adventitious circumstances connected with His historical manifestation; not in any powers or dignities conferred on Him or acquired by Him; but fundamentally in His metaphysical nature. The designation "Son of God" is a metaphysical designation and tells us what He is in His being of being. And what it tells us that Christ is in His being of being is that He is just what God is. It is undeniable — and Bousset, for example, does not deny it, — that, from the earliest days of Christianity on, (in Bousset's words) "Son of God was equivalent simply to equal with God" (Mark xiv. 61–63; John x. 31–39).

That Paul meant scarcely so much as this, Bousset to be sure would fain have us believe. He does not dream, of course, of supposing Paul to mean nothing more than that Jesus had been elevated into the relation of Sonship to God because of His moral uniqueness, or of His community of will with God. He is compelled to allow that "the Son of God appears in Paul as a supramundane Being standing in close metaphysical relation with God." But he would have us understand that, however close He stands to God, He is not, in Paul's view, quite equal with God. Paul, he suggests, has seized on this term to help him through the frightful problem of conceiving of this second Divine Being consistently with his monotheism. Christ is not quite God to him, but only the Son of God. Of such refinements, however, Paul knows nothing. With him too the maxim rules that whatever the father is, that the son is also: every father begets his son in his own likeness. The Son of God is necessarily to him just God, and he does not scruple to declare this Son of God all that God is (Phil. ii. 6; Col. ii. 9) and even to give him the supreme name of "God over all" (Rom. ix. 5).

This is fundamentally, then, how Paul preached Christ — as the Son of God in this supereminent sense, and therefore our divine Lord on whom we absolutely depend and to whom we owe absolute obedience. But this was not all that he was accustomed to preach concerning Christ. Paul preached the historical Jesus as well as the eternal Son of God. And between these two designations — Son of God, our Lord Jesus Christ — he inserts two clauses which tell us how he preached the historical Jesus. All that he taught about Christ was thrown up against the background of His deity: He is the Son of God, our Lord. But who is this that is thus so fervently declared to be the Son of God and our Lord? It is in the two clauses which are now to occupy our attention that Paul tells us.

If we reduce what he tells us to its lowest terms it amounts just to this: Paul preached the historical Christ as the promised Messiah and as the very Son of God. But he declares Christ to be the promised Messiah and the very Son of God in language so pregnant, so packed with implications, as to carry us into the heart of the great problem of the two-natured person of Christ. The exact terms in which he describes Christ as the promised Messiah and the very Son of God are these: "Who became of the seed of David according to the flesh, who was marked out as the Son of God in power according to the Spirit of holiness by the resurrection of the dead." This in brief is the account which Paul gives of the historical Christ whom he preached.

Of course there is a temporal succession suggested in the declarations of the two clauses. They so far give us not only a description of the historical Christ, but the life-history of the Christ that Paul preached. Jesus Christ became of the seed of David at His birth and by His birth. He was marked out as the Son of God in power only at His resurrection and by His resurrection. But it was not to indicate this temporal succession that Paul sets the two declarations side by side. It emerges merely as the incidental, or we may say even the accidental, result of their collocation. The relation in which Paul sets the two declarations to one another is a logical rather than a temporal one: it is the relation of climax. His purpose is to exalt Jesus Christ. He wishes to say the great things about Him. And the two greatest things he has to say about Him in His historical manifestation are these — that He became of the seed of David according to the flesh, that He was marked out as the Son of God in power according to the Spirit of holiness by the resurrection of the dead.

Both of these declarations, we say, are made for the purpose of extolling Christ: the former just as truly as the latter. That Christ came as the Messiah belongs to His glory: and the particular terms in which His Messiahship is intimated are chosen in order to enhance His glory. The word "came," "became" is correlated with the "promised afore" of the preceding verse. This is He, Paul says, whom all the prophets did before signify, and who at length came — even as they signified — of the seed of David. There is doubtless an intimation of the preëxistence of Christ here also, as J. B. Lightfoot properly instructs us: He who was always the Son of God now "became" of the seed of David. But this lies somewhat apart from the main current of thought. The heart of the declaration resides in the great words, "Of the seed of David." For these are great words. In declaring the Messiahship of Jesus Paul adduces His royal dignity. And he adduces it because he is thinking of the majesty of the Messiahship. We must beware, then, of reading this clause depreciatingly, as if Paul were making a concession in it: "He came, no doubt, . . . He came, indeed, . . . of the seed of David, but . . ." Paul never for an instant thought of the Messiahship of Jesus as a thing to be apologised for. The relation of the second clause to the first is not that of opposition, but of climax; and it contains only so much of contrast as is intrinsic in a climax. The connection would be better expressed by an "and" than by a "but"; or, if by a "but," not by an "indeed . . . but," but by a "not only . . . but." Even the Messiahship, inexpressibly glorious as it is, does not exhaust the glory of Christ. He had a glory greater than even this. This was but the beginning of His glory. But it was the beginning of His glory. He came into the world as the promised Messiah, and He went out of the world as the demonstrated Son of God. In these two things is summed up the majesty of His historical manifestation.

It is not intended to say that when He went out of the world, He left His Messiahship behind Him. The relation of the second clause to the first is not that of supersession but that of superposition. Paul passes from one glory to another, but he is as far as possible from suggesting that the one glory extinguished the other. The resurrection of Christ had no tendency to abolish His Messiahship, and the exalted Christ remains "of the seed of David." There is no reason to doubt that Paul would have exhorted his readers when he wrote these words with all the fervour with which he did later to "remember Jesus Christ, risen from the dead, of the seed of David" (II Tim. ii. 8). "According to my Gospel," he adds there, as an intimation that it was as "of the seed of David" that he was accustomed to preach Jesus Christ, whether as on earth as here, or as in heaven as there. It is the exalted Jesus that proclaims Himself in the Apocalypse "the root and the offspring of David" (Rev. xxii. 16, v. 5), and in whose hands "the key of David" is found (iii. 7).

And as it is not intimated that Christ ceased to be "of the seed of David" when He rose from the dead, neither is it intimated that He then first became the Son of God. He was already the Son of God when and before He became of the seed of David: and He did not cease to be the Son of God on and by becoming of the seed of David. It was rather just because He was the Son of God that He became of the seed of David, to become which, in the great sense of the prophetic announcements and of His own accomplishment, He was qualified only by being the Son of God. Therefore Paul does not say He was made the Son of God by the resurrection of the dead. He says he was defined, marked out, as the Son of God by the resurrection of the dead. His resurrection from the dead was well adapted to mark Him out as the Son of God: scarcely to make Him the Son of God. Consider but what the Son of God in Paul's usage means; and precisely what the resurrection was and did. It was a thing which was quite appropriate to happen to the Son of God; and, happening, could bear strong witness to Him as such: but how could it make one the Son of God?

We might possibly say, no doubt, with a tolerable meaning, that Christ was installed, even constituted, "Son of God in power" by the resurrection of the dead — if we could see our way to construe the words "in power" thus directly with "the Son of God." That too would imply that He was already the Son of God before He rose from the dead, — only then in weakness; what He had been all along in weakness He now was constituted in power. This construction, however, though not impossible, is hardly natural. And it imposes a sense on the preceding clause of which it itself gives no suggestion, and which it is reluctant to receive. To say, "of the seed of David" is not to say weakness; it is to say majesty. It is quite certain, indeed, that the assertion "who was made of the seed of David" cannot be read concessively, preparing the way for the celebration of Christ's glory in the succeeding clause. It stands rather in parallelism with the clause that follows it, asserting with it the supreme glory of Christ.

In any case the two clauses do not express two essentially different modes of being through which Christ successively passed. We could think at most only of two successive stages of manifestation of the Son of God. At most we could see in it a declaration that He who always was and continues always to be the Son of God was manifested to men first as the Son of David, and then, after His resurrection, as also the exalted Lord. He always was in the essence of His being the Son of God; this Son of God became of the seed of David and was installed as — what He always was — the Son of God, though now in His proper power, by the resurrection of the dead. It is assuredly wrong, however, to press even so far the idea of temporal succession. Temporal succession was not what it was in Paul's mind to emphasize, and is not the ruling idea of his assertion. The ruling idea of his assertion is the celebration of the glory of Christ. We think of temporal succession only because of the mention of the resurrection, which, in point of fact, cuts our Lord's life-manifestation into two sections. But Paul is not adducing the resurrection because it cuts our Lord's life-manifestation into two sections; but because of the demonstration it brought of the dignity of His person. It is quite indifferent to his declaration when the resurrection took place. He is not adducing it as the producing cause of a change in our Lord's mode of being. In point of fact it did not produce a change in our Lord's mode of being, although it stood at the opening of a new stage of His life-history. What it did, and what Paul adduces it here as doing, was that it brought out into plain view who and what Christ really was. This, says Paul, is the Christ I preach — He who came of the seed of David, He who was marked out in power as the Son of God, by the resurrection of the dead. His thought of Christ runs in the two molds — His Messiahship, His resurrection. But he is not particularly concerned here with the temporal relations of these two facts.

Paul does not, however, say of Christ merely that He became of the seed of David and was marked out as the Son of God in power by the resurrection of the dead. He introduces a qualifying phrase into each clause. He says that He became of the seed of David "according to the flesh," and that He was marked out as the Son of God in power "according to the Spirit of holiness" by the resurrection of the dead. What is the nature of the qualifications made by these phrases?

It is obvious at once that they are not temporal qualifications. Paul does not mean to say, in effect, that our Lord was Messiah only during His earthly manifestation, and became the Son of God only on and by means of His resurrection. It has already appeared that Paul did not think of the Messiahship of our Lord only in connection with His earthly manifestation, or of His Sonship to God only in connection with His

post-resurrection existence. And the qualifying phrases themselves are ill-adapted to express this temporal distinction. Even
if we could twist the phrase "according to the flesh" into meaning "according to His human manifestation" and violently
make that do duty as a temporal definition, the parallel phrase
"according to the Spirit of holiness" utterly refuses to yield to
any treatment which could make it mean, "according to His
heavenly manifestation." And nothing could be more monstrous than to represent precisely the resurrection as in the
case of Christ the producing cause of — the source out of which
proceeds — a condition of existence which could be properly
characterised as distinctively "spiritual." Exactly what the
resurrection did was to bring it about that His subsequent
mode of existence should continue to be, like the precedent,
"fleshly"; to assimilate His post-resurrection to His pre-resurrection mode of existence in the matter of the constitution of
His person. And if we fall back on the ethical contrast of the
terms, that could only mean that Christ should be supposed to
be represented as imperfectly holy in His earthly stage of existence, and as only on His resurrection attaining to complete
holiness (cf. I Cor. xv. 44, 46). It is very certain that Paul did
not mean that (II Cor. v. 21).

It is clear enough, then, that Paul cannot by any possibility
have intended to represent Christ as in His pre-resurrection
and His post-resurrection modes of being differing in any way
which can be naturally expressed by the contrasting terms
"flesh" and "spirit." Least of all can he be supposed to have
intended this distinction in the sense of the ethical contrast
between these terms. But a further word may be pardoned as
to this. That it is precisely this ethical contrast that Paul intends has been insisted on under cover of the adjunct "of
holiness" attached here to "spirit." The contrast, it is said, is
not between "flesh" and "spirit," but between "flesh" and
"spirit of holiness"; and what is intended is to represent Christ,
who on earth was merely "Christ according to the flesh" —
the "flesh of sin" of course, it is added, that is "the flesh which
was in the grasp of sin" — to have been, "after and in conse-

quence of the resurrection," "set free from 'the likeness of
(weak and sinful) flesh.'" Through the resurrection, in other
words, Christ has for the first time become the holy Son of
God, free from entanglement with sin-cursed flesh; and, having
thus saved Himself, is qualified, we suppose, now to save others,
by bringing them through the same experience of resurrection
to the same holiness. We have obviously wandered here sufficiently far from the declarations of the Apostle; and we have
landed in a *reductio ad absurdum* of this whole system of interpretation. Paul is not here distinguishing times and contrasting
two successive modes of our Lord's being. He is distinguishing
elements in the constitution of our Lord's person, by virtue of
which He is at one and the same time both the Messiah and
the Son of God. He became of the seed of David with respect
to the flesh, and by the resurrection of the dead was mightily
proven to be also the Son of God with respect to the Spirit of
holiness.

It ought to go without saying that by these two elements
in the constitution of our Lord's person, the flesh and the spirit
of holiness, by virtue of which He is at once of the seed of David
and the Son of God, are not intended the two constituent elements, flesh and spirit, which go to make up common humanity.
It is impossible that Paul should have represented our Lord as
the Messiah only by virtue of His bodily nature; and it is absurd to suppose him to suggest that His Sonship to God was
proved by His resurrection to reside in His mental nature or
even in His ethical purity — to say nothing now of supposing
him to assert that He was made by the resurrection into the
Son of God, or into "the Son of God in power" with respect
to His mental nature here described as holy. How the resurrection — which was in itself just the resumption of the body
— of all things, could be thought of as constituting our Lord's
mental nature the Son of God passes imagination; and if it be
conceivable that it might at least prove that He was the Son
of God, it remains hidden how it could be so emphatically
asserted that it was only with reference to His mental nature,
in sharp contrast with His bodily, thus recovered to Him, that

this was proved concerning Him precisely by His resurrection. Is Paul's real purpose here to guard men from supposing that our Lord's bodily nature, though recovered to Him in this great act, the resurrection, entered into His Sonship to God? There is no reason discoverable in the context why this distinction between our Lord's bodily and mental natures should be so strongly stressed here. It is clearly an artificial distinction imposed on the passage.

When Paul tells us of the Christ which he preached that He was made of the seed of David "according to the flesh," he quite certainly has the whole of His humanity in mind. And in introducing this limitation, "according to the flesh," into his declaration that Christ was "made of the seed of David," he intimates not obscurely that there was another side — not aspect but element — of His being besides His humanity, in which He was not made of the seed of David, but was something other and higher. If he had said nothing more than just these words: "He was made of the seed of David according to the flesh," this intimation would still have been express; though we might have been left to speculation to determine what other element could have entered into His being, and what He must have been according to that element. He has not left us, however, to this speculation, but has plainly told us that the Christ he preached was not merely made of the seed of David according to the flesh, but was also marked out as the Son of God, in power, according to the Spirit of holiness by the resurrection of the dead. Since the "according to the flesh" includes all His humanity, the "according to the Spirit of holiness" which is set in contrast with it, and according to which He is declared to be the Son of God, must be sought outside of His humanity. What the nature of this element of His being in which He is superior to humanity is, is already clear from the fact that according to it He is the Son of God. "Son of God" is, as we have already seen, a metaphysical designation asserting equality with God. It is a divine name. To say that Christ is, according to the Spirit of holiness, the Son of God, is to say that the Spirit of holiness is a designation of His divine nature.

Paul's whole assertion therefore amounts to saying that, in one element of His being, the Christ that he preached was man, in another God. Looked at from the point of view of His human nature He was the Messiah — "of the seed of David." Looked at from the point of view of His divine nature, He was the Son of God. Looked at in His composite personality, He was both the Messiah and the Son of God, because in Him were united both He that came of the seed of David according to the flesh and He who was marked out as the Son of God in power according to the Spirit of holiness by the resurrection of the dead.

We may be somewhat puzzled by the designation of the divine nature of Christ as "the Spirit of holiness." But not only is it plain from its relation to its contrast, "the flesh," and to its correlate, "the Son of God," that it is His divine nature which is so designated, but this is made superabundantly clear from the closely parallel passage, Rom. ix. 5. There, in enumerating the glories of Israel, the Apostle comes to his climax in this great declaration, — that from Israel Christ came. But there, no more than here, will he allow that it was the whole Christ who came — as said there from the stock of Israel, as said here from the seed of David. He adds there too at once the limitation, "as concerns the flesh," — just as he adds it here. Thus he intimates with emphasis that something more is to be said, if we are to give a complete account of Christ's being; there was something about Him in which He did not come from Israel, and in which He is more than "flesh." What this something is, Paul adds in the great words, "God over all." He who was from Israel according to the flesh is, on the other side of His being, in which He is not from Israel and not "flesh," nothing other than "God over all." In our present passage, the phrase, "Spirit of holiness" takes the place of "God over all" in the other. Clearly Paul means the same thing by them both.

This being very clear, what interests us most is the emphasis which Paul throws on holiness in his designation of the divine nature of Christ. The simple word "Spirit" might have been ambiguous: when "the Spirit of holiness" is spoken of, the divine nature is expressly named. No doubt, Paul might have used the adjective, "holy," instead of the genitive of the substantive, "of holiness"; and have said "the Holy Spirit." Had he done so, he would have as expressly intimated deity as in his actual phrase. But he would have left open the possibility of being misunderstood as speaking of that distinct Holy Spirit to which this designation is commonly applied. The relation in which the divine nature which he attributes to Christ stands to the Holy Spirit was in Paul's mind no doubt very close; as close as the relation between "God" and "Lord" whom he constantly treats as, though two, yet also one. Not only does he identify the activities of the two (e. g., Rom. viii. 9 ff.); but also, in some high sense, he identifies them themselves. He can make use, for example, of such a startling expression as "the Lord is the Spirit" (II Cor. iii. 17). Nevertheless it is perfectly clear that "the Lord" and "the Spirit" are not one person to Paul, and the distinguishing employment of the designations "the Spirit," "the Holy Spirit" is spread broadcast over his pages. Even in immediate connection with his declaration that "the Lord is the Spirit," he can speak with the utmost naturalness not only of "the Spirit of the Lord," but also of "the Lord of the Spirit" (II Cor. iii. 17 f.). What is of especial importance to note in our present connection is that he is not speaking of an endowment of Christ either from or with the Holy Spirit; although he would be the last to doubt that He who was made of the seed of David according to the flesh was plenarily endowed both from and with the Spirit. He is speaking of that divine Spirit which is the complement in the constitution of Christ's person of the human nature according to which He was the Messiah, and by virtue of which He was not merely the Messiah, but also the very Son of God. This Spirit he calls distinguishingly the Spirit of holiness, the Spirit the very characteristic of which is holiness. He is speaking not of an acquired holiness but of an intrinsic holiness; not, then, of a holiness which had been conferred at the time of or attained by means of the resurrection from the dead; but of a holiness which had always been the very quality of Christ's being. He is not

representing Christ as having first been after a fleshly fashion
the son of David and afterwards becoming by or at the resurrection from the dead, after a spiritual fashion, the holy Son of
God. He is representing Him as being in his very nature essentially and therefore always and in every mode of His manifestation holy. Bousset is quite right when he declares that there is
no reference in the phrase "Spirit of holiness" to the preservation of His holiness by Christ in His earthly manifestation, but
that it is a metaphysical designation describing according to
its intrinsic quality an element in the constitution of Christ's
person from the beginning. This is the characteristic of the
Christ Paul preached; as truly His characteristic as that He
was the Messiah. Evidently in Paul's thought of deity holiness
held a prominent place. When he wishes to distinguish Spirit
from spirit, it is enough for him that he may designate Spirit
as divine, to define it as that Spirit the fundamental characteristic of which is that it is holy.

It belongs to the very essence of the conception of Christ
as Paul preached Him, therefore, that He was of two natures,
human and divine. He could not preach Him at once as of the
seed of David and as the Son of God without so preaching
Him. It never entered Paul's mind that the Son of God could
become a mere man, or that a mere man could become the Son
of God. We may say that the conception of the two natures is
unthinkable to us. That is our own concern. That a single
nature could be at once or successively God and man, man and
God, was what was unthinkable to Paul. In his view, when we
say God and man we say two natures; when we put a hyphen
between them and say God-man, we do not merge them one
in the other but join the two together. That this was Paul's
mode of thinking of Jesus, Bousset, for example, does not
dream of denying. What Bousset is unwilling to admit is that
the divine element in his two-natured Christ was conceived by
Paul as completely divine. Two metaphysical entities, he says,
combined themselves for Paul in the person of Christ: one of
these was a human, the other a divine nature: and Paul, along
with the whole Christian community of his day, worshipped

this two-natured Christ, though he (not they) ranked Him in his thought of His higher nature below the God over all.

The trouble with this construction is that Paul himself gives a different account of the matter. The point of Paul's designation of Christ as the Son of God is, not to subordinate Him to God, as Bousset affirms, but to equalize Him with God. He knows no difference in dignity between his God and his Lord; to both alike, or rather to both in common, he offers his prayers; from both alike and both together he expects all spiritual blessings (Rom. i. 7). He roundly calls Christ, by virtue of His higher nature, by the supreme name of "God over all" (Rom. ix. 5). These things cannot be obscured by pointing to expressions in which he ascribes to the Divine-human Christ a relation of subordination to God in His saving work. Paul does not fail to distinguish between what Christ is in the higher element of His being, and what He became when, becoming poor that we might be made rich, He assumed for His work's sake the position of a servant in the world. Nor does he permit the one set of facts to crowd the other out of his mind. It is no accident that all that he says about the historical two-natured Christ in our present passage is inserted between His two divine designations of the Son of God and Lord; that the Christ that he preached he describes precisely as "the Son of God — who was made of the seed of David according to the flesh, who was marked out as the Son of God in power according to the Spirit of holiness by the resurrection of the dead — Jesus Christ our Lord." He who is defined as on the human side of David, on the divine side the Son of God, this two-natured person, is declared to be from the point of view of God, His own Son, and — as all sons are — like Him in essential nature; from the point of view of man, our supreme Lord, whose we are and whom we obey. Ascription of proper deity could not be made more complete; whether we look at Him from the point of view of God or from the point of view of man, He is God. But what Paul preached concerning this divine Being belonged to His earthly manifestation; He was made of the seed of David, He was marked out as God's Son. The conception of the two natures is not with Paul a negligible speculation attached to his Gospel. He preached Jesus. And he preached of Jesus that He was the Messiah. But the Messiah that he preached was no merely human Messiah. He was the Son of God who was made of the seed of David. And He was demonstrated to be what He really was by His resurrection from the dead.

This was the Jesus that Paul preached: this and none other.

VIII

JESUS' MISSION, ACCORDING TO HIS OWN TESTIMONY

JESUS' MISSION, ACCORDING TO HIS OWN TESTIMONY [1]

(SYNOPTICS)

Under the title of "*'I came': the express self-testimony of Jesus to the purpose of His sending and His coming,*" Adolf Harnack has published a study of the sayings of Jesus reported in the Synoptic Gospels, which are introduced by the words "I came" or, exceptionally, "I was sent," or their equivalents.[2] These, says he, are "programmatic" sayings, and deserve as such a separate and comprehensive study, such as has not heretofore been given to them. In his examination of them, he pursues the method of, first, gathering the relevant sayings together and subjecting them severally to a critical and exegetical scrutiny; and, then, drawing out from the whole body of them in combination Jesus' own testimony to His mission.

It goes without saying that, in his critical scrutiny of the passages, Harnack proceeds on the same presuppositions which govern his dealing with the Synoptic tradition in general; that is to say, on the presuppositions of the "Liberal" criticism, which he applies, however, here as elsewhere, with a certain independence. It goes without saying also, therefore, that the passages emerge from his hands in a very mauled condition; brought as far as it is possible to bring them, even with violence, into line with the "Liberal" view of what the mission of Jesus ought to have been. It is reassuring, however, to observe that, even so, they cannot be despoiled of their central testimony. That Jesus proclaimed Himself to have come — to have been sent — on a mission of salvation, of salvation of the lost, Harnack is constrained to present as their primary content. By the side of this, it is true, he places a second purpose — to ful-

[1] From *The Princeton Theological Review*, v. xiii, 1915, pp. 513–586.

[2] *Zeitschrift für Theologie und Kirche*, 1912, xxii, pp. 1–30.

fil the law, that is, to fill it out, to complete it. Accordingly, he says, Jesus' self-testimony is to the effect that "the purpose of His coming, and therewith His significance, are given in this — that He is at once Saviour and Lawgiver." Behind both lies, no doubt, love, as the propulsive cause — "I came to minister" — and yet Jesus is perfectly aware that His purpose is not to be attained without turmoil and strife — "I came to cast fire upon the land and to bring a sword." These sayings, he remarks in conclusion, contain very few words; and yet is not really everything said in them? Shall we call it an accident that "under the superscription 'I came,' the purpose, the task, the manner of Jesus' work, all seem to be really exhaustively stated, and even the note of a bitter and plaintive longing is not lacking"?

It seems to be well worth while to follow Harnack's example and to make this series of sayings in which our Lord's testimony to the nature of His mission has been preserved for us in the Synoptic record, the object of a somewhat careful examination. Approaching them free from the "Liberal" presuppositions which condition Harnack's dealing with them, we may hope to obtain from them a more objective understanding than he has been able to attain of how Jesus really thought of His mission.

I

Our differences with Harnack begin with even so simple a matter as the collection of the passages. He discovers eight, as follows: Mt. x. 34 ff. = Lk. xii. 51, 53; Mk. ii. 17 = Mt. ix. 13 = Lk. v. 32; Mk. x. 45 = Mt. xx. 28; Lk. xii. 49; Lk. xix. 10; Lk. ix. 56; Mt. v. 17, Mt. xv. 24. This list, however, seems to us to require a certain amount of correction.

(1) We are compelled to omit from it Lk. ix. 56, as, despite the vigorous defence of its genuineness by Theodor Zahn,[3] certainly spurious.

---

[3] "Das Evangelium des Lucas" ausgelegt von Theodor Zahn, 1913, pp. 400 ff., 765 ff. The grounds on which the omission of the passage is justified are sufficiently stated by F. J. A. Hort, "The New Testament in the Original Greek," [ii], Appendix, 1881, pp. 59 ff.

Harnack's argument in its favor suffers somewhat from a confusion of it with some neighboring interpolations. Because he supposes himself to discover certain Lucan characteristics in these, he concludes that this too is Lucan in origin. Because some of them appear to have stood in Marcion's Gospel he assumes that this also stood in that Gospel. It is a matter of complete indifference, meanwhile, whether it stood in Marcion's Gospel or not. It may be urged, to be sure, that it is easier to suppose that it was stricken out of Luke because of Marcion's misuse of it, than that it was taken over into Luke from the Gospel of that "first-born of Satan." Meanwhile, there is no decisive evidence that it stood in Marcion's Gospel; [4] and, if it had a place there, there is no reason to suppose that it was taken over thence into Luke. It was, on the contrary, already current in certain Lucan texts before Marcion. [5]

The method of criticism which is employed by Harnack here, — a method with which Hilgenfeld used to vex us and of which Harnack and Bousset and Conybeare seem to have served themselves especially heirs [6] — is, let us say it frankly, thoroughly vicious. Its one effort is at all costs to get behind the total formal transmission, and in the attempt to do this it is tempted to prefer to the direct evidence, however great in mass and conclusive in effect, any small item of indirect evidence which may be unearthed, however weak in its probative force or ambiguous in its bearing. The fundamental principle of this method of criticism naturally does not commend itself to those who have made the criticism of texts their business. Even an Eduard Norden sounds a salutary warning against

[4] Cf. Zahn, as cited, p. 767: "On the other hand we do not as yet know whether Marcion had this third questionable passage also (verse 56ᵃ: ὁ γὰρ υἱὸς . . . σῶσαι in his Gospel. Tertullian, however, had precisely this passage in his text. . . ."

[5] The character of its attestation implies as much. Accordingly Tischendorf remarks ad loc.: "It is unquestionable from the witnesses, especially the Latin and Syriac, that the whole of this interpolation was current in MSS. already in the second century."

[6] This vicious critical method is thetically asserted by H. J. Holtzmann, "Einleitung," § 49, ed. 2, p. 49. It has been recently defended in principle by G. Kittel, TSK, 1912, 85, pp. 367–373.

it,[7] and the professional critics of the New Testament text reject it with instructive unanimity.[8] Nobody doubts that wrong readings were current in the second century and it goes but a little way towards showing that a reading is right to show that it was current in the second century. Many of the most serious corruptions which the text of the New Testament has suffered had already entered it in the first half of that century. The matter of importance is not to discover which of the various readings at any given passage chances to appear earliest, by a few years, in the citations of that passage which have happened to be preserved to us in extant writings. It is to determine which of them is a genuine part of the text as it came from its author's hands. For the determination of this question Harnack's method of criticism advances us directly not a single step, and indirectly (through, that is, the better ascertainment of the history of the transmission of the text) but a little way.

When, now Harnack deserts the textual question and suggests that it is of little importance whether the passage be a genuine portion of the Gospel of Luke or not, since in any event it comes from an ancient source, he completely misses the state of the case. This professed saying of Jesus has no independent existence. It exists only as transmitted in Luke's Gospel. If it is spurious there, we have no evidence whatever that it was spoken by Jesus. It comes to us as a saying of Jesus' only on the faith of its genuineness in Luke. Falling out of Luke it falls out of existence. There is no reason to suppose that it owes its origin to anything else than the brooding mind of some devout scribe — or, if we take the whole series of interpolations in verses 54–56 together, we may say to the brooding minds of a series of scribes, supplementing the work one of another —

---

[7] "Agnostos Theos," 1913, p. 301: "The philologist knows from experience that the manuscript transmission must be given a higher value than the indirect."

[8] Cf. C. R. Gregory, "Prolegomena" to the eighth edition of Tischendorf's New Testament, "Pars Ultima," 1894, p. 1138; "Textkritik des Neuen Testaments," ii, 1902, p. 754; "Canon and Text of the New Testament," 1907, p. 422; E. Miller in Scriverner's "Introduction," etc., ed. 4, ii, pp. 188–189; Hammond, "Outlines," etc., ed. 2, p. 66. On the general subject, see Ll. J. M. Bebb, in the Oxford "Studia Biblica," ii, 1890, p. 221.

whose pen — or pens — filled out more or less unconsciously
the suggestions of the text which was in process of copying.
The manuscripts are crowded with such complementary interpolations, — E. S. Buchanan, for example, has culled many
instructive examples from Latin manuscripts[9] — and none
could bear more clearly on its face the characteristic marks of
the class than those now before us. "And when His disciples
James and John saw, they said, Lord, wilt Thou that we bid
fire to come down from heaven and consume them [as [also]
Elias did]? But He turned and rebuked them and said, ye
know not what manner of spirit ye are of. [[For] the Son of
Man came not to destroy [men's] lives, but to save them]."

(2) As an offset to the omission of Lk. ix. 56 we should insert
into the list Mk. i. 38 = Lk. iv. 43.

This passage Harnack rejects on the ground that no reference is made to the mission of Jesus in Mark's "for to this end
came I out," His coming forth from Capernaum alone being
meant; while Luke's specific, "for therefore was I sent" is due
merely to a misunderstanding on Luke's part of Mark's statement. The major premiss of the conclusion thus reached is obviously a particular hypothesis of the composition of the Synoptic
Gospels and especially of the relation of Luke to Mark. On
this hypothesis, Mark is the original "Narrative-Source," and
the matter common to Luke and Mark is derived directly by
Luke from Mark. We cannot share this hypothesis: the matter
presented by both Luke and Mark seems to us rather to be
derived by both alike from a common source (call it the "Primi-

---

[9] In his "Sacred Latin Texts" (i, 1912; ii, 1914, iii, 1914) Buchanan is
accustomed to give lists of striking readings occurring in the manuscript he is
editing. Here are a few from the Irish codex, Harl., 1023: Lk. i. 57, And she brought
forth *according to the word of God* a son; viii. 12, Take heed how ye hear *the word
of God;* xi. 3, Give us today for bread, *the word of God from heaven;* xv. 29, But as
soon as this *son of the devil came;* Jno. vi. 44, No man can come unto me except
the Father which sent me *and the Holy Spirit* draw him; viii. 12, He that followeth
me shall not walk in darkness, but shall have the *eternal* light of the life *of God.*
See also "The Records Unrolled," 1911. The parallel is made more striking by
Buchanan's tendency to think such readings more original than those of the critical texts. The lengths he would go in this contention may be observed in his pamphlet: "The Search for the Original Words of the Gospel," 1914.

tive Mark" — *Urmarkus* — if you like) underlying both. But assuredly no hypothesis could be more infelicitous as an explanation of the relation of Luke to Mark in our present passage. If Luke is here drawing directly on Mark, he certainly uses a very free hand. The same general sense could scarcely be conveyed by two independent writers more diversely. This is apparent even to the reader of the English version, for the difference extends to the whole literary manner, the very conception and presentation of the incident. It is much more striking in the Greek, for the difference permeates so thoroughly the language employed by the two writers as to approach the limit of the possible. In the verse which particularly concerns us, for example, it is literally true that except at most the two words, translated diversely in the English version, in Mark "to this end," in Luke "therefore," [10] no single word is the same in the two accounts. If there is anything clear from the literary standpoint, it is clear that Luke is not here drawing upon Mark but is giving an independent account. In that case, Luke's report of what our Lord said cannot be summarily set aside as a mere misunderstanding of Mark.

It may still be said, of course, that what Luke gives us is a deliberate alteration of Mark. Something like this appears to be the meaning of C. G. Montefiore, who writes: "Luke's 'I was sent' (i. e. by God) is a grandiose and inaccurate interpretation of Mark's 'I came forth' (from the city)." Alfred Loisy traces at length what he conceives to be the transformation of the simple record of facts given by Mark into the announcement of a principle by Luke. "The difference between the historical tradition and the theological point of view," he remarks, "appears very clearly in the words of Christ; '*Let us go elsewhere* . . . it is for this *that I came out*'; and '*It must needs be that I proclaim* to other towns *the kingdom of God* — I was sent for that.'" It is the same general conception that underlies H. A. W. Meyer's explanation that Mark's "expression is original, but had already acquired in the tradition that Luke

---

[10] We give to εἰς τοῦτο the benefit of the doubt in Lk. iv. 43. Probably the right reading is ἐπὶ τοῦτο.

here follows a doctrinal development with a higher meaning." And the step from this is not a long one to H. J. Holtzmann's representation of Luke's "I was sent" as a transition-step to the doctrinal language of John. Luke's language, however, bears no appearance of being a correction, conscious or unconscious, either of Mark's or anybody else's statement: it looks rather very much like an independent account of a well-transmitted saying of Jesus'. And we are moving ever further from the actual state of the case, in proportion as we introduce into our explanation the principle of a developing tradition with its implication of lapse of time. There is no decisive reason for supposing that Luke wrote later than Mark. And it is no less unjustified to describe his point of view than his Gospel as later than Mark's. The two Gospels were written near the same time, — Mark's being probably, indeed, a few years the younger.[11] They came out of the same circle, the missionary circle of Paul. And they reflect the same tradition in the same stage of development, if we may speak of stages of development regarding a tradition in which we can trace no growth whatever. If the element of time be eliminated, and we speak merely of differing temperaments, there might be more propriety in attributing a more theological tendency to the one than to the other. When a matter of historical accuracy is involved, however, Luke surely is not a historian who can be lightly set aside in his statements of fact. His representation that Jesus spoke here of His divine mission and not merely of His purpose in leaving the city that morning, makes on purely historical grounds as strong a claim upon our credence as any contradictory representation which may be supposed to be found in Mark, especially as it was confessedly no unwonted thing for Jesus to speak of His divine mission.

In point of fact, however, there is no difference of repre-

---

[11] A. Plummer's dating of Mark ("The Gospel According to St. Mark," 1914), between 65 and 70 A. D., probably nearer the latter than the former date (we should say about A. D. 68), seems to us the only reasonable one: cf. Johannes Weiss, "Die Schriften des Neuen Testaments," I¹, 1906, p. 32 (cf. also p. 35): "about the year 70, probably somewhat earlier." On the other hand Harnack's later view of the date of Luke as prior to A. D. 63 seems to be not improbable.

sentation between Luke and Mark. Mark too reports Jesus as speaking of His divine mission. The possibility that he does so is allowed by Harnack himself, when he writes: "The probability is altogether preponderant that in the words of Jesus (Mark i. 38), 'Let us go elsewhere into the next towns that I may preach there also; for to this end came I forth,' the 'came I forth' (ἐξῆλθον) has no deeper sense, but takes up again the 'went out' (ἐξῆλθεν) of verse 35: 'And in the morning, a great while before day, He rose up and went out [from Capernaum] and departed.'" Others, making the same general contention, open the door to this possibility still wider. C. G. Montefiore comments: "'I came out' — i. e., from the city. But the phrase is odd. Does it mean 'from heaven'? In that case it would be a late 'theological' reading." In similar doubt Johannes Weiss writes: "It is not altogether clear whether He means 'For this purpose I left the house so early,' or 'For this purpose I have come out from God — come into the world' (it is thus that Luke understood the text)." Mark's meaning is, then, not so clearly that Jesus referred merely to His coming out from Capernaum, nor indeed is it quite so simple, as it is sometimes assumed to be.

Harnack is scarcely right in any event in making the "I came out" of verse 38 both refer to Jesus' leaving Capernaum and resume the "He went out" of verse 35. It is not at all likely that the "He went out" of verse 35 refers to His leaving Capernaum. The statements as to Jesus' movements in verse 35 are remarkably circumstantial: they tell us that Jesus, having got up [12] before dawn, went out and went forth to a desert place. It is not the "went out" (ἐξῆλθεν) but the "went forth" (ἀπῆλθεν) which refers to His departure from Capernaum: the "went out" means that He "went out of doors," "out of the house." This is very generally recognized. It is recognized, for example by both Loisy and Montefiore, as well as by Holtzmann before them, all of whom understand the "going out" of verse 38 of "leaving the town." It is recognized also by

---

[12] Cf. Holtzmann's note: "ἀναστάς is to be taken here literally, therefore not merely as = קַיָּם." Cf. also G. Wohlenberg's note.

Johannes Weiss, who saves the back reference to it of verse 38 by making the "I came out" of that verse too mean "from the house." Surely, however, it would be too trivial to make Jesus say: "It was for this reason that I left the house so early this morning — that I might preach also in the neighboring towns." Was He to visit all those towns that day, and therefore needed to make an early start? Mark apparently means us to understand, on the contrary, that the reason of His leaving the house so early was that He might find retirement for prayer. The "coming out" of verse 38 is then, in any case, not a resumption of that of verse 35, but a new "coming out" not previously mentioned. What reason is there for referring it back to the "going forth" ($\dot{a}\pi\hat{\eta}\lambda\theta\epsilon\nu$, "departed") from Capernaum of verse 35? Would it be much less trivial to make Jesus say that He came out from Capernaum so early that morning to preach throughout Galilee than that He came out of the house for that purpose? The solemn declaration, "For to this end came I out" must have a deeper meaning than this. In point of fact He did "come" in this deeper meaning to preach; and He did fulfil this purpose and preached throughout Galilee as Mark had just duly recorded (i. 14). Is it not much more natural that He should have said this here, and that His biographer should have recorded that He said it, than that He should have said and been recorded as saying that He came out of Capernaum that morning early with this purpose in view? We cannot but think G. Wohlenberg right in pronouncing such an understanding of the declaration "superficial." Jesus seems clearly to be making here a solemn reference to His divine mission.[13]

(3) There is another passage with Harnack's dealing with which we cannot agree. This is Luke xii. 49–53.

Harnack rends this closely knit paragraph into fragments; discards two of its five constituent sentences altogether; and, separating the other three into two independent sayings, identifies one of these (verses 51, 53) with Mt. x. 34 ff. and leaves

[13] So J. A. Alexander, J. J. Van Oosterzee, E. Klostermann, H. B. Swete, A. Plummer, *et al.* Mayer *ad loc.* gives older names.

the other (verses 49, 50) off to itself. This drastic treatment of
the passage seems to have been suggested to him by the comment on it of Julius Wellhausen.[14] This comment runs as
follows:

The three first verses do not square with one another. The fire
which Jesus longs for is an abiding, universal effect, the baptism of
death a passing personal experience, the prospect of which he dreads.
What stands here is not: My death is the necessary precondition of
my great historical effect. Rather, the declarations of verse 49 and
verse 50 are presented as parallel, although they are not so. Just as
little is verse 50 homogeneous with verse 51. But neither do verses
49 and 51 agree together; the wished-for fire can have nothing to do
with the terrible division of families. The whole of verse 50 and the
second half of verse 49 are lacking in Marcion. In their absence, a
connection would no doubt be instituted; the fire would be the inward
war, and Luke would be reduced to Matthew (x. 34, 35). I have,
however, no confidence whatever in this reading of Marcion's, but
rather believe that Luke has brought together wholly disparate things
according to some sort of association of ideas.

This slashing criticism Harnack reproduces in its main features,
as follows:

Luke would undoubtedly have these two verses [49 and 50] considered as fellows: they are bound together by δέ, are framed similarly, and close even with a rhyme. But their contents are so diverse
as to interpose a veto on their conjunction. It has been in vain, moreover, that the expositors have tried to build a bridge between the two
verses. Every bridge is wrecked on the consideration that the first
verse refers to the action of Jesus, the second to something which
threatens Him; for it is impossible to think in the second verse of
baptism in general (Jesus' own baptism of suffering is meant, see Mk.
x. 39), since the words, "How am I straitened, etc.," would then be
wholly unintelligible or would have to be explained in a very artificial
manner. The contention also that the eschatological idea connects
the two verses is wrong; for the futures which the two verses contem-

---

[14] A. Loisy appears not unwilling also to make a discreet use of Wellhausen's
disintegrating criticism in his attempt to show how Luke concocted his narrative.
Montefiore after reporting Wellhausen's criticism, expresses doubt regarding it,
and then slips off into the lines of his favorite mentor, Loisy.

plate are different. Add that the "fire" of the first verse has nothing to do with the "baptism with fire"; for Jesus could not say of that fire that He came "to cast" it upon the earth. It is therefore to be held that Luke who often follows external associations of ideas, has been led to put the two verses transmitted to him together by the similarity of their structure, and because some connection between fire and baptism hovered before his mind. He has similarly again made an arbitrary connection in the case of the next verse, when he adjoins the saying about peace and sword of which we have already spoken. This saying too can scarcely have been spoken in the same breath with ours, precisely because it exhibits a certain relationship with it but is differently oriented.

The superficiality of this criticism is flagrant. It owes whatever plausibility it may possess to the care which is taken not to go below the surface. So soon as we abstract ourselves from the mere vocables and attend to the thought the logical unity of the paragraph becomes even striking. Even in form of statement, however, the passage is clearly a unity. Harnack himself calls attention to the structure of verses 49 and 50 as a plain intimation that they form a pair in their author's intention, and the bridge which he desiderates to connect them he himself indicates in the "but" by which the author, before the expositors busied themselves with the matter, expressly joins them. When Jesus had given expression to the pleasure that it would give Him to see the fire He had come to cast into the world already kindled, it was altogether natural that He should add an intimation of what it was that held this back — He must die first. And nothing could be more natural than that He should proceed then to speak further of the disturbance which His coming should create. It would be difficult to find a series of five verses more inseparately knit together. That such rents should exist between them as are asserted, and they be invisible to H. J. Holtzmann, say, or Johannes Weiss, neither of whom is commonly either unable or unwilling to see flaws in the evangelical reports of Jesus' sayings is, to say the least, very remarkable; and a unitary understanding of the passage which commends itself in its general features alike to these expositors and, say, Theodor Zahn, can scarcely be summarily cast aside as impossible. It is quite instructive to observe that the lack of harmony between verses 49 and 50, which is the hinge of the disintegrating criticism of the passage, is so little obvious to, say, Johannes Weiss, that it is precisely to the combination of these two verses that he directs us to attend if we wish really to understand Jesus' state of mind with reference to His death. "The parallelism of the fire and baptism, preserved only by Luke," he urges, "is one of Jesus' most important sayings, because we can perceive from it how Jesus thought of His end." "How Jesus really thought of His future," he says in another place, "a declaration like Luke xii. 49 f., perhaps shows." [15]

Looking, thus, upon Lk. xii. 49–53 as a closely knit unit, it would be difficult for us to accept Harnack's identification of Lk. xii. 51, 53, torn from its context, with Mt. x. 34–36, also removed from its context; and the assignment of the "saying," thus preserved by both Matthew and Luke, to the hypothetical "Discourse-Source," which it is now fashionable to cite by the symbol "Q." Even apart from this difficulty, however, the equation of the two passages would not commend itself to us. The phraseology in which they are severally cast is distinctly different. The decisive matter, however, is the difference in the settings into which they are severally put by the two evangelists. Both of the sections in which they severally occur, confessedly present difficulties to the harmonist, and the dispositions which harmonists have made of them in their arrangement of the evangelical material vary greatly. [16] It seems to be reasonably clear, however, that in the tenth chapter of Mat-

[15] "Die Schriften," etc.[1], i, pp. 438 and 138. Weiss even speaks of Mk. x. 38 as "no doubt an echo of Lk. xii. 50" (p. 160), but it is not perfectly clear what he means by this (it is retained in the second edition).

[16] For example, Edward Robinson, having placed Mt. x. 34 ff. in its natural position in his § 62, preposits Lk. xii. 49 ff. to his § 52. John H. Kerr, on the contrary, retaining the same natural position for Mt. x. 34 ff. (at his § 50), more correctly places Lk. xii. 49 ff. at his § 90. C. W. Hodge, Sr., "Syllabus of Lectures on the Gospel History," 1888, p. 73, very properly speaks of Robinson's "dislocation" of the material of Luke as "the principal blot on his harmony": "he breaks up the connection just where commentators find a striking unity."

thew and the twelfth chapter of Luke we are dealing with two
quite distinct masses of material, spoken by our Lord on separate occasions. We may be sorry to forego any advantage which
may be thought to accrue from the assignment of one of the
sayings of Jesus in which He speaks of His mission to the hypothetical "Discourse-Source." [17] But we cannot admit that there
is involved any loss of authenticity for the two sayings in question. We see no reason to suppose that the source or sources,
from which the two evangelists drew severally the sayings they
have reported to us, compared unfavorably, in point of trustworthiness as vehicles of the tradition of Jesus' sayings, with
the hypothetical "Discourse-Source," from which they both
sometimes draw in common. On the whole the certainty that
Jesus said what is here attributed to Him is increased by His
being credibly reported to have said it twice in very similar language and to entirely the same effect.

We therefore amend Harnack's list at this point also, and instead of listing the two sayings as Mt. x. 34–36 = Lk. xii. 51, 53,
and Lk. xii. 49, 50, give them as Mt. x. 34–36 and Lk. xii. 49–53.

As the result of this survey of the material, we find ourselves, like Harnack, with eight "sayings" at our disposal, although these eight are not precisely the same as those which
he lists. Arranged, as nearly as the chronological order can be
made out, in the order in which they were spoken, they are as
follows: Mk. i. 38 = Lk. iv. 43; Mt. v. 17; Mk. ii. 17 = Mt.
ix. 13 = Lk. v. 32; Mt. x. 34 f.; Mt. xv. 24; Lk. xii. 49 ff.; Mk.
x. 45 = Mt. xx. 28; Lk. xix. 10.[18] Five of these sayings are

[17] Willoughby C. Allen and A. Plummer deny that Mt. x. 34 ff. and Lk. xii.
51 ff. come from Q. "Phraseology and context alike differ," says Allen. "The
two evangelists draw from different sources."

[18] Along with these there are certain other sayings which come illustratively
into consideration. Primary among them is Mt. xi. 3 ff. = Lk. vii. 20 ff. which
Harnack (p. 23) is tempted to include in the list itself as a ninth saying. Others
are: Mk. xi. 9, 10 = Mt. xxi. 9 = Lk. xix. 38 = Jno. xii. 13; Mt. xxiii. 39;
Mt. xi. 18, 19 = Lk. vii. 33, 34. Cf. also Mt. x. 40; Mk. ix. 37 = Lk. ix. 48;
Lk. x. 16. There may be added [Mk. ix. 11 = Mt. xvii. 13; Mt. iii. 11 = Lk. iii.
16]. We have made some remarks on the general subject in "The Lord of Glory,"
pp. 39 f., 76 f., 126 f., 190 f.

found in Matthew; four in Luke; and three in Mark. As no one of them is found only in Matthew and Luke we need not insist that any of them is derived from the hypothetical "Discourse-Source" (Q), to which are commonly assigned the portions of the Synoptics found in Matthew and Luke but lacking in Mark. As all of these sayings are found in either Matthew or in Luke (and one in both) there seems to be no good reason, however, why some (or all) of them may not possibly have had a place in a document from which both Matthew and Luke are supposed to draw.[19] One is found in all three Gospels, one in Mark and Matthew, and one in Mark and Luke. These three at least, two of them very confidently in the form in which we have them, and the third (Mk. i. 38 = Lk. iv. 43) very possibly in one of the forms in which it has come to us, may be thought to have stood in the hypothetical "Narrative-Source" (*Urmarkus*). And it is possible that all the others may have stood in it too, since all the Gospels draw from it. Three are found in Matthew alone and two in Luke alone. These are at no disadvantage in point of trustworthiness in comparison with their companions which occur in more than one Gospel. Apart from the fact that they may have stood in any source from which their companions were drawn but did not chance to be taken from it by more than one evangelist, the determination that some of the sources used by the evangelists were drawn upon by more than one of them has no tendency to depreciate the value of those which were drawn upon by only one. No doubt the hypothetical "Narration-Source" which lies behind all three of the Synoptics is a very old document and is very highly commended to us by the confident dependence of them all upon it. There is no sound reason for assigning any of these Gospels to a date later than the sixties, and Luke and Matthew may easily have come from a considerably earlier date. A document underlying them all must have existed in

[19] We may quote here, say, Johannes Weiss, who says ("Die Schriften[1]," i, p. 33): "Possibly there belongs to it yet many another [passage] which is found only in Matthew, or only in Luke." As we ourselves believe that Mark also knew the "Discourse-Source," we might add also "or only in Mark."

the fifties and may be carried back almost to any date subsequent to the facts it records. But much the same may be said of a document underlying any one of the Synoptics: a document drawn on by one of them only may be just as old and just as authoritative as one drawn on by all of them. The matter of primary importance does not concern the particular hypothetical document — they are all hypothetical — from which it may be supposed that our Gospels have derived this saying or that. The disentangling of the hypothetical sources from which they may be supposed to have derived the several items of their narratives is a mere literary matter. We know nothing of these sources after we have disentangled them except that they all are earlier than the Gospels which used them; and that when the contents of each are gathered together and scrutinized, the contents of them all prove to be, from the historical point of view, all of a piece. This is the fundamental fact concerning them which requires recognition. The tradition of Jesus' sayings and doings, gathered out of earlier sources (written or oral) and preserved by the Synoptic Gospels, is a homogeneous tradition, and the original tradition. Behind it there lies nothing but the facts. Whether written down in the fifties or the forties or the thirties: whether some short interval separates its writing from the facts it records — say ten or twenty years — or no interval at all; no trace whatever exists of any earlier tradition of any kind behind it. It is for us at least the absolute beginning. In these circumstances we are justified in holding with confidence to all the sayings of Jesus transmitted to us in these Gospels. It is not that we cannot get behind these Gospels: it is that we can get behind them and find behind them nothing but what is in them.[20]

The term used by our Lord in these passages to express the fact of His mission is normally the simple "I came" (ἦλθον, Mk. ii. 17, Mt. v. 17, ix. 13, Mt. x. 34, Lk. xii. 49; cf. ἦλθεν, Mk. x. 45, Mt. xx. 28). But variations from this "technical term" occur. Once, after it has been once employed, it is varied on

[20] See the state of the case as presented in the *Princeton Theological Review*, 1913, xi, 2, pp. 195–269.

repetition to "the more elegant" (as Harnack calls it) term for public manifestation, "I came forth" ($\pi\alpha\rho\epsilon\gamma\epsilon\nu\delta\mu\eta\nu$, Lk. xii. 49, 51). Once, in a parallel, the tense is changed to "I have come" ($\epsilon\lambda\eta\lambda\upsilon\theta\alpha$, Lk. v. 32). Once the compound "I came out" ($\epsilon\xi\eta\lambda\theta o\nu$, Mk. i. 38) is used. And in two passages, "I was sent" (Lk. iv. 43, Mt. xv. 24; cf. Mk. ix. 37 = Lk. ix. 48, Mt. x. 40, Lk. x. 16) takes the place of "I came." In the majority of cases our Lord speaks directly of Himself as the one whose mission He is describing, in the first person: "I came," "I was sent," "I came out." In a few instances, however, He speaks of Himself in the third person under the designation of "the Son of Man" — "the Son of Man came" (Mk. x. 45 = Mt. xx. 28, Lk. xix. 10). There is a difference also in the nature and, so to say, the profundity of the reference to His mission. Sometimes He is speaking only of His personal ministry in "the days of His flesh," and the manner of its performance (Mk. i. 38 = Lk. iv. 43, Mt. xv. 24, cf. Lk. xix. 10). Sometimes His mind is on the circumstantial effects of the execution of His mission (Mt. x. 34 ff., Lk. xii. 49 ff.). Sometimes the horizon widens and the ultimate ethical result of His work is indicated (Mt. v. 17). Sometimes the declaration cuts to the bottom and the fundamental purpose of His mission is announced with respect both to the object sought and the means of its accomplishment (Mk. ii. 17 = Mt. ix. 13 = Lk. v. 32; Lk. xix. 10; Mk. x. 45 = Mt. xx. 28): "I came not to call the righteous but sinners"; "The Son of Man came to seek and to save that which was lost"; "The Son of Man came not to be ministered unto but to minister, and to give His life a ransom for many." It should not pass without notice that it is in these last instances only that our Lord deserts the simple form of statement with the personal pronoun, "I came," and substitutes for it the solemn declaration, "the Son of Man came."

II

In investigating the meaning of these sayings severally it is not necessary to follow carefully the chronological order of

their utterance. In a broad sense they increase in richness of
contents as our Lord's ministry develops itself. It was not until late in His ministry, for example, that our Lord spoke insistently of His death and His allusions to His mission in His
later ministry reflect this change. Nevertheless these sayings
do not grow uniformly in richness as time goes on, and it will
be more convenient to arrange them arbitrarily in order of
relative richness of content than strictly to follow the chronological sequence. The order to be pursued has been suggested
at the close of the immediately preceding paragraph.

1

Mk. i. 38: And He saith unto them, Let us go elsewhere into the next towns, that I may preach there also; for to this end came I out.	Lk. iv. 43: But He said unto them, I must preach the good tidings of the kingdom of God to the other cities also; for to this end was I sent.

As reported by Mark, in this saying Jesus declares His
mission in the briefest and simplest terms possible. It was just
to preach. "For to this end came I out," He says; namely "to
preach." [21] The context intimates, it is true, that this preaching was to be done in the first instance in the immediately
neighboring towns: "Let us go elsewhere into the next towns
that I may preach there also." It lay in the nature of the case
that any preaching intended to extend over the land should
begin with the nearest towns, and that these therefore should
be particularly in mind in the announcement. But that the
preaching was not intended to be limited to these "next"
towns [22] is clear enough in itself, and is made quite plain (so
far as the understanding of the reporter, at least, is concerned)
by the next verse, which tells us what Jesus did by way of fulfilling the mission which He here announces: "And He went

[21] Cf. G. Wohlenberg *in loc.*: "The εἰς τοῦτο, verse 38, means just the κηρύσσειν
in general, not especially the κἀκεῖ κηρύσσειν."

[22] In the parallel, Luke says simply, "to the other cities," which suggests
no other limitation than what Th. Zahn (p. 247) calls "the self-evident one" of
"the other Jewish cities of Palestine."

into their synagogues throughout all Galilee,[23] preaching and casting out devils." Luke in the parallel, extends the boundaries even further. "And He was preaching in the synagogues of Judaea," he says, — but without prefixing the emphatic "all." By "Judaea" he means "Palestine as a whole,"[24] but, as the omission of the "all" already advises us, he does not intend to assert that there was no part of Palestine to which Jesus did not carry His Gospel, so much as that His mission was distinctively to Palestine.[25] In a word, Jesus announces His mission here as a mission to the Jewish people: He came out, was sent, to preach to the Jews.

The emphasis thus laid on preaching as the substance of Jesus' mission does not, however, so set preaching in contrast, say, to the working of miracles as to exclude the latter from any place in His mission. It has become fashionable in one school of expositors to see in the accounts which the evangelists give here a more or less complete misunderstanding of Jesus' motives in leaving Capernaum, although these are supposed nevertheless to shimmer through the narrative sufficiently to guide "the seeing eye." [26] When Jesus is represented as moved by a desire to preach in other places, less than half the truth, it is said, is told. What really determined His action was a desire to get away from Capernaum. And the reason for His desire to get away from Capernaum was that a thaumaturgical function had been thrust upon Him there. He fled from this in the night (Mk. i. 35). What He really announced in the words here misleadingly reported, was that His mission

[23] Cf. Mt. iv. 23: "And He went about in all Galilee, teaching in their synagogues, and preaching the good tidings of the Kingdom, and healing all manner of disease, and all manner of sickness among the people." The emphasis in both Mark and Matthew is on the completeness with which Galilee was covered by this itinerant preaching.

[24] See especially Th. Zahn, p. 248, and pp. 61 f. Cf. A. Loisy, i, p. 462: "Luke has chosen a general term in order to signify that the mission of Jesus was for the whole country, conformably to what was said in verse 43 (B. Weiss, "Einleitung," pp. 307–308)." Also, B. Weiss, C. F. Keil, Johannes Weiss in loc. Wellhausen: "Judaea (verse 44) includes Galilee in it: cf. i. 5; vi. 17; vii. 17, and D. xxiii. 5." Godet rejects the reading "Judaea" as "absurd."

[25] We are following Th. Zahn here (p. 248).

[26] So, e. g., H. J. Holtzmann, A. Loisy, J. Weiss. C. G. Montefiore draws back.

was to preach, not to work miracles. So far from permitting this to shimmer through them however, the narratives of the evangelists flatly contradict it. Mark, for example, tells us that in leaving Capernaum Jesus did not leave His miracles behind Him: "And He went into their synagogues throughout all Galilee, preaching, and casting out devils." The parallel in Matthew (iv. 23) enlarges on this: "And He went about in all Galilee, teaching in their synagogues and preaching the Gospel of the kingdom, and healing all manner of disease and all manner of sickness among the people." It may be easy to say, as Johannes Weiss for example does say, that such statements do not correspond with what really happened, and that Luke in his parallel account (iv. 44) has done well to omit them. But it is not so easy thus lightly to erase, not a couple of remarks merely, but the entire presentation of Jesus' work by the evangelists. According to their account, not merely at Capernaum in the beginning, but throughout His whole ministry, "mighty works" were as characteristic a feature of Jesus' ministry as His mighty word itself.[27] There is not the least justification in the narratives themselves, moreover, for the attempted re-reading of their implications. There is no suggestion in them that Jesus was "betrayed into thaumaturgical works" at Capernaum. There is no hint that He was shocked or troubled by His abounding miracles there, or that He looked upon them as a scattering of His energies, or a diversion of Him from His proper task or as making a draft upon His strength. They are represented rather as His crown of glory. He is not represented as fleeing from them and as endeavoring to confine Himself to activities of a different nature. He is represented rather as looking upon them as the seal of His mission and His incitement to its full accomplishment. "I must needs preach in *the other* towns": "that I may preach there *also*." Not a contrast with His work at Capernaum, but a repetition of it, is what He hopes for elsewhere. The whole contrast lies between Capernaum and the rest of the land: between a local and an itinerant

[27] Cf. the conjunction of the two in Jesus' instructions to the Twelve, Mt. x. 5–8, and His reply to the Baptist's question, Mt. xi. 4–5.

ministry. What He had done in Capernaum, He felt the divine necessity of His mission driving Him to do also in the other cities. And therefore "He went into their synagogues throughout all Galilee preaching, and casting out devils." The ground of Jesus' leaving Capernaum lay, shortly, as Holtzmann recognizes it to be Luke's purpose to intimate, solely in "the universality of His mission." [28]

What Jesus came out to preach in fulfilment of His mission Mark's statement does not tell us. It says simply, "I came out to preach." But this is not to leave it in doubt. It was too well understood to require statement. Mark had just told his readers summarily that "after John was delivered up, Jesus came into Galilee, preaching the glad-tidings of God, and saying, The time is fulfilled and the kingdom of God is at hand: repent ye and believe in the glad-tidings" (cf. Mt. iv. 17). When he tells them now that Jesus announced His mission to be to preach, it is perfectly evident that it is just this preaching which he has in mind. The parallel in Luke declares this in so many words. "I must needs," Jesus is there reported as saying, "proclaim the glad-tidings of the kingdom of God, for to this end was I sent." The accent of necessity is here sounded. It were impossible that Jesus should do anything other than preach just this Gospel of the kingdom of God. His mission to this end lays a compulsion upon Him: He was sent to do precisely this, and needs must do it.[29] Jesus' mission is to preach a Gospel, the Gospel of the kingdom of God.

For Jesus so to describe His mission, clearly was to lay claim to the Messianic function. Preaching the glad-tidings of the kingdom of God is the Messianic proclamation. The accompanying miracles are the signs of the Messiah. Accordingly when the Baptist sent to Jesus inquiring, "Art thou He that Cometh or look we for another?" Jesus replied by pointing to these things: "the blind receive their sight, and the lame walk, the lepers are cleansed, and the deaf hear, and the dead are

[28] P. 333: "The ground of His flight, verse 43 finds in the universality of His mission."

[29] On the accent of "necessity" in Jesus' life, see Hastings' "Dictionary of Christ and the Gospels," article "Foresight," at the beginning.

raised up, and the poor have the glad-tidings preached to them." [30] "He that Cometh" is a Messianic title, and therefore, as Harnack reminds us, those who heard Jesus say, "For I say unto you, ye shall not see me henceforth, till ye shall say, Blessed is He that cometh in the name of the Lord," understood Him to be speaking of the Messiah, and would have understood that just the same if the words "in the name of the Lord" had been wanting.[31] The question lies near at hand, accordingly, whether Jesus merely by speaking of "coming," "being sent," does not lay claim to Messianic dignity. In that case those terms would be used pregnantly. The Baptist "came," neither eating nor drinking, as truly as Jesus "came" eating and drinking (Mt. xi. 18; cf. xxi. 32). The prophet is "sent" as truly as the Messiah (Lk. iv. 26; Mt. xiii. 37 = Lk. xiii. 34; Jno. i. 6, 8, iii. 28). What the words openly declare is a consciousness of divine mission; and the two modes of expression differ according as the emphasis falls on the divine source of the mission ("I was sent") or on its voluntary performance ("I came").[32] Something more needs to be added, therefore, to mark the mission which they assume, plainly as Messianic. That something more is added in the present passage by the purpose which is declared to be subserved by the mission. That purpose is the Messianic proclamation. He who came to preach the glad-tidings of the kingdom of God and who could point to the signs of the Messiah accompanying His preaching, has come as the Messiah.

Jesus, however, does not here say merely "I came." He says, "I came *out*," and the preposition should not be neglected. At the least it must refer to Jesus' coming publicly forward

[30] Mt. xi. 3 ff. = Lk. vii. 20 ff. Harnack (p. 23) says: "The question whether the miracles which are enumerated are to be understood spiritually is to be answered in the negative for Matthew and Luke, and probably also for Jesus Himself." But that places Harnack in a quandary: "But that Jesus should have spoken here literally of raising the dead is nevertheless not easy to acknowledge."

[31] P. 1: Mt. xxiii. 39 = Lk. xiii. 35.

[32] Cf. Th. Zahn's words "Das Evangelium des Matthäus³," p. 610, distinguishing between "the execution of a commission laid on Him by God (Mt. x. 40, ὁ ἀποστείλας με, xv. 24; xxi. 37)" and "the purpose and meaning of His life comprehended by Himself (ἦλθεν)."

and entering upon the task of public teacher. J. J. van Ooster-
zoo insists upon this sense: "The Saviour speaks simply of the
purpose for which He now appeared publicly as a teacher."[33]
That, however, in this Messianic context, appears scarcely adequate. We seem to be compelled to see in this term a reference
to Jesus' manifestation as Messiah with whatever that may
carry with it. This is apparently what C. F. Keil and G. Wohlenberg have in mind. According to the former, the phrase "I
came out" is used here absolutely in the sense of coming into
publicity, coming into the world; and if, he adds, we wish to
supply anything we may add in thought $\pi\alpha\rho\dot{\alpha}$ or $\dot{\alpha}\pi\dot{o}$ $\tau o\hat{v}$ $\theta\epsilon o\hat{v}$ —
as we may find in Jno. xiii. 3; xvi. 27, 30. Similarly the latter
considers the reference to be to Jesus' entrance upon His Messianic calling, and adds that it is not surprising if the expression
tempts us to find in it an allusion to the coming forth from the
Father such as John speaks of at xiii. 3; xvi. 27, 30; xvii. 8.
Even if we follow this path to its end and say simply, with J.
A. Alexander, F. Godet, A. Plummer, H. B. Swete and others,
that when He says, "I came out" Jesus means, "I came out
from God" or "from heaven" we are not going beyond the
implications of the Messianic reference. If Jesus thought Himself the Messiah there is no reason why He may not be supposed
to have thought of Himself as that transcendent Messiah
which was "in the air" in "the days of His flesh." That He
did think of Himself as the transcendent Messiah is indeed
already evident from His favorite self-designation of the Son
of Man, — as reported by Mark as by the other evangelists.
The Son of Man carries with it the idea of preëxistence. When
then Mark records that He spoke of His mission as a "coming
out," the phrase may very well come before us as the vehicle
of Jesus' consciousness of His preëxistence; and F. Godet is
speaking no less critically than theologically when he remarks
that "Mark's term appears to allude to the incarnation, Luke's
only refers to the mission of Jesus." [34]

[33] On Lk. iv. 43.

[34] It is less obvious that the simple "I came" presupposes preëxistence as
many commentators insist (e. g., A. Plummer, "Matthew," p. 156, note 2, cf.
A. M. McNeille on Mt. x. 40). But on this see below pp. 568, 581 ff.

When we say Messiah we say Israel. We naturally revert here, then, to Jesus' testimony that His mission was to preach the Gospel of the Kingdom of God to the cities of Judaea. He is obviously speaking not of the utmost reach of His mission, but of the limits of His personal ministry. His personal ministry, however, He describes as distinctively to the Jews. He "came out," He "was sent," to proclaim the glad-tidings of the imminence of that Kingdom to the people of God to whom the Kingdom had been promised. This was, in its external aspects, His mission.

2

Mt. xv. 24: And He answered and said, I was not sent but unto the lost sheep of the house of Israel.

What in the former saying is given a perhaps somewhat unarresting positive expression is in this saying asserted in a strong, almost startling, negative form. Jesus declares that His mission was not only to the Jews, but to them only. Denying a request from His disciples that He should exercise His miraculous powers for the healing of a heathen girl who was suffering from possession, He justifies the denial by explaining that His mission was not to the heathen but solely to the Jews: "I was not sent but to the lost sheep of the house of Israel." The language in which He clothes this explanation had been employed by Him on a previous occasion. When He was sending His disciples on their first mission He laid, first of all, this charge upon them: "Go not into any way of the Gentiles, and enter not into any city of the Samaritans; but go rather to the lost sheep of the house of Israel" (Mt. x. 5–6). The circumstantial negative clauses act as definitions of the language of the positive clause. This language is just as sharply definite in our present saying. Jesus declares that He has no mission to the heathen. His mission is distinctively to the Jews.

It may be possible to exaggerate, however, the exclusiveness of this declaration. After all, it has a context. And it should not be overlooked that despite the emphasis of His assertion that He had no mission to the heathen, Jesus healed this heathen girl. Nor can it quite be said that He healed her by way of exception; overpersuaded, perhaps, by the touching plea of her mother, or even, perhaps, instructed by her shrewd common-sense to a wider apprehension of the scope of His mission than He had before attained. When He threw Himself back on His mission, He invoked in His justification the authority of God.[35] And therefore, in adducing His mission, He employs the phrase "I was sent" rather than "I came." By that phrase He appeals to Him with whose commission He was charged, and transfers the responsibility for the terms of His mission to Him.[36] After this it can scarcely be supposed that He overstepped the terms of His mission, as He understood them, in healing the heathen child. In other words, when He declares, "I was not sent but unto the lost sheep of the house of Israel," He is not to be understood as declaring that His mission was so exclusively to the Jews that the heathen had no part in it whatever.

The whole drift of the incident as recorded whether by Mark or by Matthew bears out this conclusion. The precise point which is stressed in both accounts alike is, not that the Jews have the exclusive right to the benefits of Jesus' mission, but that the preference belongs to them. This is given open expression in Jesus' words as reported by Mark, "Let the children *first* be fed; it is not meet to take the children's bread and cast it to the dogs." But it is equally the implication of Mat-

---

[35] Montefiore is quite right in saying: "The explanation is that God had ordered this limitation."

[36] In only two of the sayings in which Jesus expounds His mission (Lk. iv. 43, Mt. xv. 24) is the form "I was sent" employed. It is perhaps not without significance that in the only one of these which has a parallel (Lk. iv. 43), it is not the simple "I came" which stands in this parallel (Mk. i. 38), but a form which more pointedly refers to the source of the mission in God ("I came out"). The "I was sent" is reflected in its active equivalent in the "Johannine" (Jno. xiii. 20) phrase of Mt. x. 40; Mk. ix. 37 = Lk. ix. 48; Lk. x. 16, in which the unity of the sent and sender is suggested. Note the emphasis placed on Jesus' employment of "I was sent" in our present passage by F. L. Steinmeyer, "The Miracles of Our Lord," pp. 140 ff., and J. Laidlaw, "The Miracles of Our Lord," p. 252. Th. Zahn remarks that here for the first time in Matthew is Jesus presented as the ἀπόστολος of God, and adds: "cf. xv. 24; xxi. 37 as correlate of the ἦλθον of v. 17; ix. 13; x. 34. Apart from John cf. Heb. iii. 1, Clem., I Cor. xl, 1."

thew's account.[37] Jesus does not suggest that the dogs [38] shall
have nothing; but that they shall have only the dogs' portion.
What the portion of the dogs is, is not here indicated. It is only
intimated that they have a portion. The children have the
preference, of course: but there is something also for the dogs.
Jesus' whole conversation in this incident is certainly peda-
gogically determined. He employed the application of this
heathen woman to Him in order to teach His disciples the real
scope of His mission. There is no contradiction between His
declaration to them that He was sent distinctively to Israel
and His subsequent healing of the heathen child. He heals the
child not in defiance of the terms of His mission, but because
it fell within its terms; and He commends the mother because
she had found the right way: "And He said unto her, *For this
saying*, go thy way: the devil is gone out of thy daughter."
A comment of Alfred Edersheim's sums up not badly the teaching of the incident: "when He breaks the bread to the children,
in the breaking of it the crumbs must fall all around." [39]

Obviously what Jesus tells us here is very much what Paul
tells us, when, summing up his Gospel ringingly as the power
of God unto salvation to every one that believes, he adds, "To
the Jew first and also to the Greek" (Rom. i. 16, cf. ii. 10).
Many "Liberal" expositors therefore represent Mark as corrupting the record of Jesus' conversation when he puts on
Jesus' lips a sharp assertion of this principle: "Let the children
first be filled." [40] "If the Jews have only the *first* right," comments Johannes Weiss, for example, "it follows that the hea-

[37] This is solidly shown by Th. Zahn.

[38] It has been often pointed out that the use of the diminutive here softens
the apparent harshness of the language. Shall we say "doglings"?

[39] "Life and Times of Jesus the Messiah[1]," ii, 1883, p. 41.

[40] H. J. Holtzmann (p. 184): "*Let first* ($\pi\rho\tilde{\omega}\tau\sigma\nu$ = prius, maxim from Rom.
i. 16; ii. 9, 10) *the children* (Israelites) *be filled*"; this explanation, which still
leaves room for the satisfaction of the mother, is simply lacking in Mt. xv. 26,
and therefore the conclusion is commonly drawn that in the narrative of Mark
we have a deliberate mitigation, a dependence upon the later, Pauline mission,
and therefore secondary work (so Hilgenfeld, last in *ZWTh*, 1889, p. 497; B. and J.
Weiss, Jülicher, "Gleichnisreden," ii, p. 256 f., even Wittichen p. 188, and with
more reserve, Wernle, p. 133)."

then too have a right. This is an echo from the Epistle to the Romans, i. 10, — the Jew first, then the Greek!" [41] It is not, however, merely in this sharp assertion of it that this principle is given expression in the narrative of the incident. It is present as truly in the account of Matthew as in that of Mark. The whole drift of both accounts alike — the climax of which is found not in any word of Jesus' but in a marvellous word of His petitioner's — is that there is something left for the dogs after the children are filled: "Even the dogs under the table eat of the crumbs of the children"; "even the dogs eat of the crumbs that fall from the table of their masters." Had there been no provision for the Gentiles, indeed, Jesus could scarcely have expected His disciples to recognize Him as that "One to Come" with whose mission there had from the beginning been connected blessings for the Gentiles also. The evangelists are not drawing from Paul when they represent Jesus as teaching that His mission was to Israel and yet extends in its beneficial effects to the world (cf. especially Mt. viii. 11; xxviii. 19).[42] Paul on the contrary is reflecting the teaching of Jesus as reported by the evangelists when, as Jesus proclaimed Himself to have been sent only to Israel, he declares Him to have been made a minister of the circumcision; [43] and when, as Jesus suggests that nevertheless there is in His mission a blessing for Gentiles also, he declares that by His ministry to the circumcision not only is the truth of God exalted and the promises unto the fathers confirmed, but mercy is brought to the Gentiles also (Rom. xv. 8 ff.).

How His mission could be distinctively for Israel and yet contain in it a blessing for the Gentiles also Jesus does not here explain to His disciples. He is content to fix the fact in their

[41] "Schriften," etc.[1], i, 1906, p. 128.

[42] Wellhausen represents Mark as free from such universalizing utterances. Nowhere does it put such a statement as Mt. viii. 11 f. on Jesus' lips; and only in the eschatological discourse, Mk. xiii. 10, do we find a prediction of the extension of the preaching of the Gospel to the heathen attributed to Jesus. Montefiore adds xiv. 9. The implication is, of course, that neither of these passages is authentic.

[43] "Christ has become minister of the circumcised," comments H. A. W. Meyer; "for to devote His activity to the welfare of the Jewish nation was, according to promise, the duty of His Messianic office, cf. Mt. xx. 28, xv. 24."

minds by the awakening object-lesson of this memorable miracle in which His saving power goes out of Himself and effects its beneficent result across the borders of a strange land.[44] We can scarcely go astray, however, if we distinguish here, as in the case of Mark i. 38 = Lk. iv. 43, between His personal ministry and the wider working of His mission. When He says, "I was not sent but to the lost sheep of the house of Israel," He has His personal ministry in mind. It will hardly be doubted that this was the understanding of the evangelist. C. G. Montefiore, for example, paraphrases thus: "His disciples shall convert the world; He Himself is sent only to Israel." "Jesus says that He has been sent to the lost sheep of Israel only. This looks like a 'narrow' tradition. But it is not. It is intended to explain the undoubted but perplexing fact that Jesus the universal Saviour and Mediator, did actually confine Himself to the Jews. The explanation is that God had ordered this limitation. After His resurrection, He will send His disciples to all the world." [45] Did Jesus Himself have no anticipation of this course of events, or purpose with reference to it? It should go without saying that, just because He conceived His mission as Messianic, He necessarily conceived it both as immediately directed to Israel, and as in its effects extending also to the Gentiles. That was how the mission of the Messiah had been set forth in those prophecies on which He fed. We cannot be surprised, then, that it is customary to recognize that it is to His personal ministry alone that Jesus refers when He declares that He "was not sent but to the lost sheep of the house of Israel."[46]

The Messianic character of His mission is already implied

[44] "It has been remarked," says Wellhausen ("Das Ev. Marci," 1903, p. 60), "that this is up to now the only example in Mark in which Jesus heals from a distance, by His mere word." "This is the second example of a miracle wrought from a distance," says Loisy (i, p. 977). "The first was wrought on the centurion's son." Then he cites Augustine's remarks in "Quaest. Ev.," i, 18.

[45] Vol. ii, pp. 657, 658.

[46] So from Augustine and Jerome down. H. A. W. Meyer expresses the general opinion when he says: "It was not intended that Christ should come to the *Gentiles* in the days of His flesh, but that He should do so at the subsequent period (xxviii. 19) in the person of the Spirit acting through the medium of the Apostolic preaching (Jno. x. 16, Eph. ii. 17)." Cf. Th. Zahn: "His personal and

in the terms in which He here describes it. When He speaks of "the lost sheep of the house of Israel," His mind is on the great messianic passage, Ezek. xxxiii., xxxiv., in which Jehovah promises that He Himself will feed His sheep, "and seek that which was lost"; and that He will "set up one shepherd over them, and he shall feed them, even my servant David; he shall feed them and he shall be their shepherd." [47] When, with His mind on this prophecy, Jesus spoke of His mission as to "the lost sheep of the house of Israel" it may admit of question whether the genitive is epexegetical or partitive, — whether He conceives His mission to be directed to Israel as a whole, conceived as having wandered from God, or to that portion of Israel which had strayed [48] — but it can admit of no question that He conceived of those to whom His mission was directed as "lost." He thought of His mission, therefore, as distinctively a saving mission, and He might just as well have said, "I was sent to save the lost sheep of the house of Israel." Harnack is quite right, therefore, when, after calling attention to the adoption of the language of Ezek. xxxiv. 15, 16, he adds: "And the mission to the lost sheep contains implicitly the 'to seek and to save.'" How He is to accomplish the saving of the lost sheep of the house of Israel, Jesus does not in this utterance tell us. He tells us only that He has come, as the promised Messiah, with this mission entrusted to Him, — to save these lost sheep.

immediate vocation." Also, R. C. Trench, "Notes on the Miracles of Our Lord," second American ed., 1852, p. 274; J. Laidlaw, "The Miracles of Our Lord," 1890, p. 252; A. Edersheim, "Life and Times," etc.[1], 1883, ii, p. 40.

[47] Observe the address of the petitioner in our passage (Mt. xv. 22), "O Lord, Son of David," which is not repelled by Jesus. "Spoken by a heathen," remarks Edersheim (ii, p. 39), "these words were an appeal, not to the Messiah of Israel, but to an Israelitish Messiah." They supply the starting point for a conversation, however, in which the Messiah of Israel brings relief to the heathen.

[48] That in Mt. x. 6, "the lost sheep of the house of Israel," the genitive is not partitive seems to be shown by the contrast of verse 5: the disciples are to go, not to Gentiles or the Samaritans, but to Israel, described here as "lost sheep." Cf. H. A. W. Meyer in loc.: "Such sheep (ix. 36) were all, seeing that they were without faith in Him, the heaven-sent Shepherd." The same phrase in Mt. xv. 24, in a similar contrast (with the Canaanitish woman), might naturally be held to be used in the same broad sense. Israel as a whole in that case would be the "lost sheep."

3

Mt. x. 34 ff.: Think not that I came to cast peace on the earth; I came not to cast peace but a sword. For I came to set a man at variance against his father, and the daughter against her mother, and the daughter-in-law against her mother-in-law: and a man's foes shall be they of his own household.

In this context Jesus is preparing His disciples for the persecutions which awaited them. They must not think their case singular: their Teacher and Lord had Himself suffered‚ before them. Nor must they imagine that they are deserted: the Father has not forgotten them. And after all, such things belong in their day's work. They have not been called to ease but to struggle. Strife then is their immediate portion; but after the strife comes the reward.

When Jesus introduces what He has to say with the words, "Think not," He intimates that He is correcting a false impression, prevalent among His hearers (cf. v. 17).[49] His reference can only be to expectations of a kingdom of peace founded on Old Testament prophecy.[50] Since these expectations are focussed upon His own person He is obviously speaking out of a Messianic consciousness; and is assuming for Himself the rôle of the Messiah, come to introduce the promised kingdom.[51] Of course He does not mean to deny that the Messianic kingdom which He has come to introduce is the eternal kingdom of peace promised in the prophets. He is only warning His followers that the Messianic peace must be conquered before it is

[49] Cf. B. Weiss (Meyer, 9, 1898) and A. Plummer *in loc.*, and A. Loisy, i, p. 891.

[50] G. S. Goodspeed, "Israel's Messianic Hope," 1900, p. 123: "All the seers of Israel look forward out of their present, whether gloomy or bright, to a golden age of peace." W. A. Brown, Hastings' "Dictionary of the Bible," iii, p. 733ᵃ: "Among the blessings to which Israel looks forward in the Messianic times, none is more emphasized than peace." Cf. A. Loisy, i, p. 891.

[51] Neglecting this, Harnack speaks inadequately when he writes: "This discourse is not Messianic in the literal sense — even John the Baptist could, it would appear, have said it — but in the burden of the discourse and in the saying, 'I came for this purpose,' there lies a claim which soars above the prophets and the Baptist. For Jesus implicitly demands here that the severest sacrifices be made and the enmity of the nearest kindred be incurred, *for the sake of His person* "

enjoyed. As His mind at the moment is on the individual, He describes the strife which awaits His followers in terms of the individual's experience. The language in which He does this is derived from an Old Testament passage (Micah vii. 6) in which the terrible disintegration of natural relationships incident to a time of deep moral corruption is described. The dissolution of social ties which His followers shall have to face will be like this. Let them gird themselves to meet the strain upon them loyally. For, as the succeeding verses show, it is distinctly a question of personal loyalty that is at issue.[52]

It should be observed that Jesus does not say merely, "Think not that I came to *send* (or *bring*) peace upon the earth," as our English versions have it. He says, "Think not that I came to *cast* peace upon the earth." The energy of the expression should not be evaporated (cf. vii. 6). What Jesus denies is that He has come to fling peace suddenly and immediately upon the earth,[53] so that all the evils of life should at once and perfectly give way to the unsullied blessedness of the consummated kingdom. Such seems to have been the expectation of His followers. He undeceives them by telling them plainly that He came on the contrary to cast a sword. Strife and struggle lie immediately before them, and the peace to which they look forward is postponed. The pathway upon which they have adventured in attaching themselves to Him leads indeed to peace, but it leads through strife.

When Jesus says that He came to cast a sword upon the earth and to set men at variance with one another, the declaration of purpose must not be weakened into a mere prediction of result.[54] He is speaking out of the fundamental presupposi-

---

[52] Cf. the excellent remarks of Th. Zahn, p. 415.

[53] So B. Weiss, "Das Matthaeusevangelium und seine Lucas-Parallelen," 1876, p. 281, also in Meyer, 9th ed., 1898, and in "Die Vier Evangelien," etc., 1900, *in loc.* So also H. J. Holtzmann, "Die Synoptiker³," 1901, p. 235, who remarks: "Thus Jesus strikes out of the picture of the Messianic age, at least for the immediately following transitional period, the joy and peace predicted in Micah. iv. 3, v. iv, Zech. ix. 9, 10, and brings war into prospect in its stead, in reminiscence of Ex. xxxii. 27, Ezek. vi. 3, xiv. 17, xxi. 12."

[54] It is often so weakened. Thus e. g., A. Loisy: "The appearance of the Christ has therefore, for consequence — not for end, but the Biblical language does not

tion of the universal government of God, which had just found expression in the assertion that not even a sparrow, or indeed a hair of our heads, falls to the ground "apart from our Father" (verses 29–31). The essence of the declaration lies in the assurance that nothing is to befall His followers by chance or the hard necessity of things, but all that comes to them comes from Him.[55] Not merely the ultimate end, but all the means which lead up to this end — in a linked chain of means and ends — are of His appointment and belong to the arrangements which He has made for His people. They are to face the strife which lies before them, therefore, as a part of the service they owe to Him (verses 37 ff.), their Master and Lord (verses 24 f.). This strife is not indeed all that Jesus came to bring, but this too He came to bring; and when He casts it upon the earth, He is fulfilling so far His mission. He "came," "was sent" (verse 40) to "cast a sword."

In this saying, too, we perceive, Jesus is dealing with what we may without impropriety speak of as a subordinate element of His mission. He does not mean that the sole or the chief purpose of His coming was to stir up strife. He means that the strife which His coming causes has its part to play in securing the end for which He came. When He said in Mk. i. 38 = Lk. iv. 43, "I came to preach," He was looking through the preaching, as means, to the end which it was to subserve. When He said in Mt. xv. 24 that He was not sent but to the lost sheep of the house of Israel, He did not forget the wider end of which His ministry to Israel should be the means. So, when He says, "I came to cast a sword upon the earth," He is thinking of the strife which He thus takes up unto His plan not for itself but as an instrument by which His ultimate purpose should be reached. He tells us nothing of how long this strife is to last,

make a sharp distinction between the two — the division signified by the sword." Also, B. Weiss (Meyer, 9th ed., 1898): "What is the immediate, inevitable consequence of His coming, Jesus announces as its purpose." Cf. A. H. McNeille on Mt. x. 34.

[55] Cf. B. Weiss, "Das Matthaeusevangelium," etc., 1876, p. 281: "It does not come like an unavoidable evil which is connected with the sought-for good, but it is foreseen and intended by Him."

or through what steps and stages it is to pass into the peace which waits behind it. Is He speaking only of the turmoil which must accompany the acceptance of Him as Messiah by His own people, involving as it does adjustment to the revised Messianic ideal which He brought? [56] Is He speaking in a "springing sense" of the ineradicable conflict of His Gospel with worldly ideals, through age after age, until at last "the end shall come"? [57] Or is He speaking of the "growing pains" which must accompany the steady upward evolution through all the ages of the religion which He founded? [58] The passage itself tells us nothing more than that Jesus came to cast a sword upon the earth; that there were to result from His coming strife and strain; and that only through this strife and strain is the full purpose for which He came attainable. For what is more than this we must go elsewhere. Only let us bear well in mind that the note of the saying is not discouragement but confidence. There rings through it the "Fear not!" of verse 31.

[56] This appears to be A. Loisy's idea: "Because the proclamation of the kingdom has as its immediate effect (had not the Saviour found this Himself in His own home?) to cause discord in families — one accepting the faith, another rejecting it, and this discord placing believers and unbelievers at odds." See also C. G. Montefiore: "The sword does not mean war between nations, but dissension between families, of which one member remains a Jew, while another becomes a Christian."

[57] This appears to be A. Plummer's meaning: "So long as men's wills are opposed to the Gospel there can be no peace. . . . Once more Christ guards His disciples against being under any illusions. They have entered the narrow way, and it leads to tribulation, before leading to eternal life."

[58] Something like this seems to be Johannes Weiss' meaning: "This saying belongs to the most characteristic and the most authentic sayings of Jesus concerning Himself: 'I came not to bring peace on the earth but a sword.' Jesus must have felt deeply how utterly His proclamation stood in contradiction with what men were accustomed to hear and wished to hear. And what He Himself in His parental home seems to have experienced, that he foresees as a universal phenomenon which He portrays by means of words derived from Micah: a cleft is to go through families; and indeed it is to be the young generation which shall oppose the old ('three against two and two against three' says Luke: the wife of the son lives in the house of her parents-in-law). Jesus does not reprehend this, and offers no exhortation against loss of piety. He simply posits it as an inevitable fact. Thus it has always been a thousand times over; and it may be to the elders a warning and to the children a consolation, that even the Gospel of Jesus must create so painful a division."

There underlies it the "I too will confess him before my Father in heaven" of verse 32. And it passes unobserved into the "He who loses His life for my sake shall find it" of verse 39, and the "whosoever shall give to drink to one of these little ones a cup of cold water only in the name of a disciple, verily I say unto you, he shall not lose his reward" of verse 42. Jesus warns His followers of the stress and strain before them. But He does this as one who buckles their armor on them and sends them forth to victory. The word on which the discussion closes is "Reward."

4

Lk. xii. 49–53: I came to cast fire upon the earth; and how I wish that it was already kindled! But I have a baptism to be baptized with; and how am I straitened until it be accomplished! Think ye that I am come to give peace in the earth? I tell you, Nay; but rather division: for there shall be from henceforth five in one house divided, three against two and two against three. They shall be divided, father against son, and son against father; mother against daughter, and daughter against her mother; mother-in-law against her daughter-in-law, and daughter-in-law against her mother-in-law.

To some of the questions started by Mt. x. 34 ff., answers are suggested by the present saying. Here too Jesus is protecting His followers against the false expectation which they had been misled into forming, that He, the Messiah, would at once introduce the promised reign of peace.[59] In repelling this expectation, His own claim to the Messianic dignity and function is given express intimation. He corrects, not their estimate of His person or vocation, but their conception of the nature of the Messianic work. The language in which He makes this correction is very strong: "Ye think that it is peace that I am come to give in the earth. Not at all, I tell you; nothing but division."[60] The emphasis which, by its position, falls on the word "fire" in the first clause, corresponds with this strength

[59] Cf. Hahn's note *in loc.*
[60] A. Plummer: "I came not to send *any other thing than* division." Th. Zahn: "Think ye that I am come to give peace on earth? No, I say to you, nothing else than division." Cf. II Cor. i. 13.

of language and prepares the way for it: "It is fire that I came
to cast upon the earth." [61] It is clear that the two sentences
belong together and constitute together but a single statement.
The "fire" of the one is, then, taken up and explained by the
"division" of the other, just as the "came" ($\tilde{\eta}\lambda\theta\text{o}\nu$) of the one
is repeated in the "am come" ($\pi\alpha\rho\epsilon\gamma\epsilon\nu\acute{o}\mu\eta\nu$) of the other, and
the "cast" ($\beta\alpha\lambda\epsilon\hat{\iota}\nu$) of the one by the "give" ($\delta\text{o}\hat{\upsilon}\nu\alpha\iota$) of the
other. The greater energy of the language in the former decla-
ration is due to its being the immediate expression of Jesus'
own thought and feeling: "It is fire that I came to cast upon
the earth"; whereas in its repetition it is the thought of His
followers to which He gives expression: "Ye think that it is
peace that I am here [62] to give." What it is of chief importance
for us to observe is that by the "fire" which He has come to
cast upon the earth, Jesus means just the "division" [63] which
He describes in the subsequent clauses in much the same language in which He had spoken of it in Mt. x. 34 ff. That is to
say, He has in mind, here as there, a great disarrangement of
social relationships which He speaks of as the proximate result
of the introduction of the Kingdom of God into the world.

No more here than there does Jesus mean to represent this
discord which He declares He came to give in the earth, as the
proper purpose or the ultimate result of His coming.[64] The

[61] Cf. Plummer's note.

[62] $\pi\alpha\rho\alpha\gamma\acute{\iota}\nu\text{o}\mu\alpha\iota$ "to come to the side of," is, says Harnack, a "more elegant"
word than $\check{\epsilon}\rho\chi\text{o}\mu\alpha\iota$, and Luke has varied the $\tilde{\eta}\lambda\theta\text{o}\nu$ of verse 49 to the $\pi\alpha\rho\epsilon\gamma\epsilon\nu\acute{o}\mu\eta\nu$
of verse 51 for the sake of better literary form. If Luke was really the author
of all the nice touches with which he is credited, he would need to be recognized
as one of the most "exquisite" writers of literary history. The variations of language between the parallel statements of verses 49 and 51 are grounded in the
nature of the case and reflect the truth of life. It is better to explain $\pi\alpha\rho\epsilon\gamma\epsilon\nu\acute{o}\mu\eta\nu$
as the natural phrase to express the disciples' thought of Jesus' "coming" rela-
tively to themselves, than to give it with Thayer-Grimm the sense of "coming
forth," "making one's public appearance" (Mt. iii. 1, Heb. ix. 11).

[63] Cf. Loisy, p. 892: "In view of the expressions chosen and of the progress
of the discourse, the fire is nothing else than the discord introduced into the world
by the preaching of the Gospel, or, better still perhaps the movement excited for
or against the religion of Jesus by the Apostolic preaching, from which the discord
arose."

[64] Cf. Zahn, p. 516: "That the ultimate purpose of His life and work is to
bring peace upon the earth, Jesus of course does not here deny" [cf. to the con-

strength of the language in which He declares it to be His purpose in coming to produce this dissension, shuts off, indeed, all
view beyond. When He says, "Ye think it is peace that I am
here to give on the earth. Not at all, I tell you: nothing but
division," He is thinking, of course, only of the immediate results, and, absorbed in them, leaving what lies beyond for the
time out of sight. The absoluteness of the language is like the
absoluteness of the, "I was not sent but to the lost sheep of
the house of Israel." But something does lie beyond. This not
only belongs to the nature of the case, but is already intimated
in the last clause of the first sentence (verse 49): "It is fire that
I came to cast on the earth, and how I wish that it was already
kindled." Clearly Jesus did not long for the kindling of the fire
for the fire's own sake; but for the sake of what would come out
of the fire.

What this clause particularly teaches us, however, is that
the fire which Jesus came to cast on the earth was not yet
kindled. The clause is of recognized difficulty and has been
variously rendered. Most of these renderings yield, however,
the same general sense; and it is reasonably clear that the meaning is represented with sufficient accuracy by, "And how I
wish that it was already kindled." [65] For even the fire which
He came to cast upon the world, Jesus thus points to the future.
Not even it has yet been kindled. The peace which His followers
were expecting lies yet beyond it. He was not to give peace in
the world but nothing but division: yet even the division was
not yet come — for even that His followers were to look forward. He is, then, not accounting to His followers for the trials
they were enduring: He is warning them of trials yet to come.
He is saying to them in effect, "In the world ye shall have

trary, Acts x. 36, Lk. i. 79, Isa. ix. 6, Eph. ii. 14–17], "but only that the intended
and immediate consequence of His coming and manifestation is a universal condition of peace upon earth, — a thing which even the angels on the night of His
birth did not proclaim. . . ."

[65] So Kuinoel, Olshausen, De Wette, Bleek, Meyer, B. Weiss, Holtzmann,
Zahn. On this use of the τί see A. T. Robertson, "A Grammar of the Greek of the
New Testament," 1914, on Lk. xii. 49 as per Index, and Zahn *in loc.* p. 514, note
54. On the εἰ ἤδη ἀνήφθη see Zahn *in loc.* and note 53.

tribulation"; but the subaudition also is present, "But be of good cheer; I have overcome the world." These things He was speaking to them, therefore, that despite the impending tribulation, they might have the peace which they were expecting — at least in sure prospect.

From the strong wish which Jesus expresses that the fire which He came to cast upon the earth had already been kindled, Harnack takes occasion to represent Him as a disappointed man. Harnack explains the fire which Jesus says He came to cast upon the earth as "an inflammation and refining agitation of spirits," and discovers an immense pathos in Jesus' inability to see that it had as yet been kindled.

Jesus moved with pain, acknowledges that the fire does not yet burn . . . What Jesus wishes, yes, what He speaks of as the purpose of His coming, He does not yet see fulfilled — the great trying and refining agitation of spirits in which the old is consumed and the new is kindled. That "men of violence" (βασταί) are necessary that the kingdom of God may be taken, He says at Mt. xi. 12. To become such a man of violence (βαστής) one must be kindled from the fire. This fire He fain would bring, He has brought; but it will not yet burn; hence His pained exclamation. Elsewhere, only in the saying about Jerusalem (Mt. xxiii. 37) does this pained complaint of the failure of results come to such sharp expression.

It is needless to point out that this whole representation is in direct contradiction with the context. Harnack has prepared the way for it by cutting off the context and taking the single sentence of verse 49 in complete isolation. In so doing, he has rendered it impossible, however, confidently to assign any particular meaning to that, in that case, perfectly insulated saying. It is in this state equally patient to a dozen hypothetical meanings. The sense which Harnack puts upon it is simply imposed upon it from his own subjectivity: he merely ascribes to Jesus the feelings which, from his general conception of His person and work, he supposes He would naturally express in such an exclamation. Fortunately, the context interposes a decisive negative to the ascription. We have here not the weak wail of disappointment, but a strong assertion of conscious control.

That, indeed, is sufficiently clear from the declaration itself. When Jesus asserts, "It is to cast fire upon the earth that I came" it is anything but the consciousness of impotence that is suggested to us. And the note of power vibrating in the assertion is not abolished by the adjoined expression of a wish that this fire was already kindled. No doubt there is an acknowledgment that the end for which He came was not yet fully accomplished: He had not finished His work which He came to do. But this does not involve confession either of disappointment at the slowness of its accomplishment, or fear that it may never be accomplished. The very form of the acknowledgment suggests confidence in the accomplishment. When Jesus says, "Would that it was already kindled"! He expresses no uncertainty that it will in due time be kindled. And even the time, He does not put outside of His power. He even tells us why it has not already been kindled. And the reason proves to lie in the orderly prosecution of His task. "How I wish," He exclaims, "that it was already kindled! But . . ." He himself is postponing the kindling: "But I have a baptism to be baptized with." The fire cannot be kindled until He has undergone His baptism.[66] Its kindling is contingent upon that. No doubt He looks forward to this baptism with apprehension: "And how am I straitened till it be accomplished"! But with no starting back. It is to be accomplished: and His face is set to its accomplishment. The entire course of events lies clearly in His view, and fully within His power. He has come to cast fire on the earth; but one of the means through which this fire is to be cast on the earth is a baptism with which He is to be baptized. This baptism is a dreadful experience which oppresses His soul as He looks forward to it. He could wish it were all well over. But He has no thought of doubting its accomplishment or of shrinking from His part in it. It is a veritable pre-Gethsemane which is revealed to us here.[67] But as in the actual Gethsemane, with the "Let this cup pass from me," there is conjoined the, "Nevertheless not my will but thine be done."

[66] So Holtzmann (p. 374), and Zahn (p. 515).
[67] Cf. "Princeton Biblical and Theological Studies," 1912, pp. 71 f.

That the baptism with which Jesus declares that He is to be baptized (cf. Mk. x. 38) is His death is unquestionable and is unquestioned. What we learn, then, is that the kindling of the fire which He came to cast upon the earth is in some way consequent upon His death.[68] Of the manner of His death He tells us nothing, save what we may infer from the oppression of spirit which its prospect causes Him. Of the nature of its connection with the kindling of the fire which He came to cast upon the earth He tells us as little. We may be sure, indeed, that the relation of the two events is not a merely chronological one of precedence and subsequence. The relation between such events cannot be merely chronological; the order of time which is imperative in the development of Jesus' mission can never be a purely arbitrary temporal order. We must assume that the death of Jesus stands in some causal relation to the kindling of the fire He came to cast on the earth. What this causal relation is He does not, however, tell us here. Can we think of His death as needed to prepare Him to execute His task of casting fire upon the earth? Shall we think of His death giving impressiveness to His teaching and example and so creating in all hearts that crisis which issues in the decision by which there is produced the division with which the fire is identified? Or are we to think of His death entering in some yet more intimate manner into the production of this crisis, lying in some yet more fundamental manner at the basis of His efficient activity in the world? Jesus is silent. He tells us only that His death has a part to play in the kindling of the fire which He came to cast upon the earth; and that before it — and that means with-

[68] The "from henceforth" of verse 52 introduces no difficulty; cf. H. A. W. Meyer's comment: "Jesus already realizes His approaching death." "The lighting up of this fire," he remarks at an earlier point, "which by means of His teaching and work He had already prepared, was to be effected by His death (see ἀπὸ τοῦ νῦν verse 52) which became the subject of offense, as, on the other hand, of His divine courage of faith and life (cf. ii. 35)." A. Loisy is altogether unreasonable when he writes (p. 893): "In making Jesus say that the divisions will exist henceforth, 'from now,' the evangelist appears to forget that, according to him, the fire of discord should be kindled only later, when the Saviour had been baptized in death; but with him the time when Jesus spoke and that of His death were almost confounded together."

out it — that fire cannot be kindled. He tells us that His death
is indispensable to His work; but He does not explain how it is
indispensable.

Meanwhile we are advanced greatly in our understanding
of what Jesus means by the "fire," the "sword," the "division"
which, according to His statement in Mt. x. 34 ff., Lk. xii. 49 ff.,
He came to cast on the earth. And our sense of His control
over the events by which His mission is accomplished is greatly
deepened. What He came to do, He will do; even though in
order to do it, He must die: even though He die — nay, just
because He dies — He will do it. He came to set the world on
fire. He came to die that He might set the world on fire. He
wishes that the conflagration was already kindled: He is oppressed by the prospect before Him as He walks the path to
death. But let no man mistake Him or His progress in the performance of His mission. His death, He will accomplish: the
fire He will kindle. Men may fancy that He is come to give
peace: not at all: nothing but division. That primarily. We
shall see the whole world turned up-side-down (Acts xvii. 6).
After that, no doubt, we shall see what we shall see. But the
implication is express that, in whatever we shall see, will be
included at least that peace which, after all said, lies at the
end of the sequence.

5

Mt. v. 17, 18: Think not that I came to destroy the law or the
prophets: I came not to destroy, but to fulfil. For, verily I say unto
you, Till heaven and earth pass away, one jot or one tittle shall in
no wise pass away from the law, till all things be accomplished.

"Think not," says Jesus to His disciples, "that I came to
destroy the law or the prophets." That is as much as to say
that they were thinking it, or at least were in danger of thinking it.[69] And that is as much as to say that He was recognized

[69] It is unreasonable for Johannes Weiss (p. 246) to say: "The error that
Jesus came to destroy the law and the prophets was no doubt current in the time
of the evangelist in certain circles, but cannot be proved for the life-time of Jesus,
at least in the case of His disciples." Harnack refutes Weiss on his own ground
(pp. 19 f.): but no refutation is needed beyond the words themselves.

by them as the Messiah, and that He was speaking to them on
the presupposition of His Messiahship, and of His Messianic
mission. On the basis of such a prophecy as that on the New
Covenant in Jer. xxxi. 31 ff.[70] it was not unnatural to think
of the Messiah as a new law-giver under whom "the old law
should be annulled and a new spiritual law given in its stead."[71]
This point of view, we know, existed among the later Jews,[72]
and could hardly fail to have its part to play in the Messianic
conceptions of Jesus' time. That Jesus needed to guard His
disciples against it was, thus, a matter of course,[73] and it was
most natural that He should take opportunity to do so after
the great words in which He greeted them as the salt of the
earth and the light of the world, and exhorted them to let their
light so shine before men that their good works should be seen
and their Father in heaven be glorified. In guarding them
against it He declares, almost expressly following out the
thought of Jeremiah's prediction with respect to the writing
of the law on the heart (Jer. xxxi. 33), that He came not to
abrogate but to perfect. Thus, in the most striking way possible, Jesus lays claim to the Messianic dignity.

Richness and force is given to Jesus' declaration, "I came
not to destroy but to fulfil," by the absence of an expressed
object. The object naturally taken over from the preceding

[70] Cf. F. Giesebrecht, "Com. on Jer.," 1894, *in loc.:* "For Jeremiah, to whom
it was a matter of course that the old covenant would not last forever, there can
therefore lie in the future only a new covenant, as with Isa. lv. 3; lix. 21, lx. 20,
lxi. 8, and Ezek. xxxiv. 25, xxxvii, 26. The old covenant had proved its insufficiency by the people's not keeping it and not being able to keep it. And since
every good and perfect gift comes from above, God must for the future give the
strength which the people lack for keeping the law, or else no stable, abiding
relation between God and the people is ever possible. The requirement envisag-
ing the people now in external letters must become one with the mind and will
of man. . . . He has not yet attained to the conception of a 'new heart,' Ezek. xi.
19, xxx. 2 ff.; Ps. li. 12, although he thinks of an inward influencing of the heart
by divine power, so that it acquires a new attitude towards the content of the
law."

[71] These words are quoted from A. F. Gfrörer, "Das Jahrhundert des Heils,"
1838, ii, p. 341.

[72] See Gfrörer as cited, and especially the citation (p. 342) from the book
Siphra on Levit. xxvi. 9.

[73] H. A. W. Meyer states the matter excellently with respect to our passage.

clause is a double one, "the law or the prophets." The development in the subsequent verses deals only with the law. The statement itself stands in majestic generality. Jesus declares that His mission was not a destroying but a fulfilling one. In making this declaration, His mind was particularly engaged with the law, as the course of the subsequent discussion suggests; or rather with the Scriptures of the Old Covenant as a whole, thought of at the moment from the point of view of the righteousness which they inculcate, as the collocation of the "law" and the "prophets" in the preceding clause suggests. But His mind is engaged with the law as an application [74] of the general principle asserted, rather than as exhausting its whole content. He presents Himself quite generally as not an abrogator but a perfecter.

The commentators are at odds with one another as to the exact meaning which should be assigned to the word "fulfil." Some insist that, in its application to the law, it means nothing but to do what the law commands: Theodor Zahn, for example, employing a lucid figure, describes the law — or more broadly the written Word — as an empty vessel which is fulfilled when it receives the content appropriate to it, — law in obedience, prophecy in occurrence.[75] Others urge that "to fulfil the law" means to fill the law out, to bring it to its full and perfect formulation: [76] Theophylact beautifully illustrates this idea by likening Jesus' action to that of a painter who does not abrogate the sketch which he completes into a picture. The generality of the expression surely requires us to assign to it its most inclusive meaning, and we do not see that Th. Keim can be far wrong when he expounds "to fulfil" as "to teach the law, to do it, and to impose it." It is clear enough from the subsequent context that when Jesus applied to the law His broad declaration that He had come not as an abrogator but as a fulfiller, He had in mind both the perfecting and the keeping of the law. In point of fact, He presents Himself both as the legislator developing the law into its fullest implications (verses 21 ff.),

---

[74] See Zahn's discussion here. [75] P. 213 f.

[76] So H. A. W. Meyer, and A. H. McNeille.

and as the administrator, securing full obedience to the law (verses 18–20). The two functions are fairly included in the one act spoken of by Jeremiah — whose prophecy we have seen reason to suppose underlay Jesus' remark — as writing the law on the heart. To write the law on the heart is at once to perfect it — to give it its most inclusive and most searching meaning — and to secure for it spontaneous and therefore perfect obedience. It is to obtain these two ends that Jesus declares that He came, when He represents His mission to be that of "fulfiller" with reference to the law.

Harnack, nevertheless, lays all the stress on the single element of legislation.[77] Jesus, he supposes, presents Himself here as lawgiver; and what He declares, he paraphrases thus: "I came not to break, that is, to dissolve the law together with the prophets: I came not in general to dissolve but to consummate, that is, to make complete." He explains:

The exact opposite to καταλύσαι is to "establish," to "ratify." But Jesus intends to say something more than this. He is not satisfied, as Wellhausen finely remarks, with the positive but chooses the superlative. Not to ratify, that is to say, to establish (see Rom. iii. 31), is His intention, but to consummate. That could be done, with reference to the law, in a twofold manner, either by strengthening its authority, or by completing its contents. Since, however, the former cannot be thought of — because the law possesses divine authority — only the latter can be meant; and it is precisely this to which expression is given in verses 21–48. In this discourse the law is completed thus — that what "was said to them of old time" remains indeed in existence (οὐ καταλύω) but is completed by deeper and stricter commands which go to the bottom and direct themselves to the disposition, through which moreover it comes about that many definitions are supplanted by others. Those that are replaced do not appear, however, to be abrogated because the legislative intention of Jesus does not look upon the previous legislation as false but as incomplete, and completes it.

What is said here is not without its importance. Jesus does present Himself as a lawgiver come to perfect the law, by un-

[77] So also Wellhausen.

covering the depths of its meaning, and thus extending its manifest reach. How He, thus, as legislator brings the law to its perfection He shows in the specimen instances brought together in verses 21–48. But, saying this, we have said only half of what must be said. What Jesus is primarily concerned for here, is not the completer formulation of the law but its better keeping. And what He proclaims His mission fundamentally to be is less the perfecting of the law as a "doctrine" as Harnack puts it — "our verses [17–19] too are spoken by Him as *legislator*, that is, they contain a doctrine" — (although this too enters into His mission) than the perfecting of His disciples as righteous men (a thing which could not be done without the perfecting of the law as a "doctrine"). The immediately succeeding context of His proclamation of His mission as not one of destruction but of fulfilment, deals not with the formulation of the law but with its observance (verses 18–20).

"I came not," says Jesus, "to destroy but to fulfil, — *for* . . ." And, then, with this "for," He immediately grounds His assertion in the further one that the whole law in all its details, down to its smallest minutiae, remains permanently in force and shall be obeyed. "For, verily I say unto you, until heaven and earth pass away, not one jot or one tittle shall pass away from the law until all [of them] be accomplished." This assertion is made with the utmost solemnity: "Verily, I say unto you"; and there are two elements in it neither of which should be allowed to obscure the other. On the one hand it is asserted with an emphasis which could not easily be made stronger, that the law in its smallest details remains in undiminished authority so long as the world lasts. Jesus has not come to abrogate the law — on the contrary the law will never be abrogated, not even in the slightest of its particulars — the dotting of an "i" or the crossing of a "t" — so long as the world endured. But Jesus does not content Himself with this "canonizing of the letter" as H. J. Holtzmann calls it, certainly without exaggeration. The law, remaining in all its details in undiminished authority, is, on the other hand, to be perfectly observed. Jesus declares that while the world lasts no jot or tittle

of the law shall pass away — until they all, all the law's merest
jots and tittles, shall be accomplished. He means to say not
merely that they should be accomplished, but that they shall
be accomplished. The words are very emphatic. The "all,"
standing in correlation with the "one" of the "one jot" and
"one tittle," declares that all the jots and all the tittles of the
law shall be accomplished. Not one shall fail. The expression
itself is equivalent to a declaration that a time shall come when
in this detailed perfection, the law shall be observed. This
amounts to a promise that the day shall surely come for which
we pray when, in accordance with Jesus' instruction we ask,
"Thy Kingdom come, Thy will be done as in heaven so on
earth." So far from coming to abrogate the law, He comes then
to get the law kept; not merely to republish it, in all its reach,
whether of the jots and tittles of its former publication, or of
its most deeply cutting and widely reaching interpretation, but
to reproduce it in actual lives, to write it on the hearts of men
and in their actual living. "Therefore," He proceeds to tell
His disciples (verses 19–20), the "breaking" [78] of one of the
least of these — these jots and tittles of — commandments, and
the teaching of men so, is no small matter for them. Their place
in the kingdom of heaven depends on their faithfulness to the
least of them; and unless their righteousness far surpasses that
of the Scribes and Pharisees with all their, no doubt misplaced,
strictness, they shall have no place in that kingdom at all.

In a word, we do not understand the nature of the mission
which Jesus here ascribes to Himself until we clearly see that
it finds its end in the perfecting of men. His purpose in coming
is not accomplished in merely completing the law: it finds its
fulfilment in bringing men completely to keep the completed
law. If we speak of Him as legislator, then, we mean that He
claims plenary authority with respect to the law. The law is
His, and He uses it as an instrument in the accomplishment of
His great end, the making of men righteous. He knows what is
in the law, and He brings all its content out, with the most

[78] That $\lambda\acute{v}\sigma\eta$, verse 19, is "break," not "abrogate," the parallel $\pi o\iota\acute{\eta}\sigma\eta$
sufficiently shows.

searching analysis. But this is but the beginning. He came to make this law, thus nobly expounded, the actual law of human lives. Abrogate it? Nothing could be further from His purpose. He came rather to fulfil it, to work it out into its most wide-reaching applications, and to work it, thus worked-out, into men's lives. Those who are His disciples will not be behind the Scribes and Pharisees themselves in the perfection of their obedience to its very jots and tittles. But their righteousness will not be the righteousness of the Scribes and Pharisees. The difference will be that their obedience will not be confined to these jots and tittles. In their lives there will be "accomplished" the whole law of God in its highest and profoundest meaning. Their lives will be a perfect transcript in act of the law of God, a perfect reflection of the will of God in life. It is for this that Jesus says that He "came." When this complete moralization of His disciples shall be accomplished; how, by what means, in what stages this perfect righteousness is to be made theirs; He does not tell us here. He tells us merely that He "came" to do this thing: so that His disciples shall be truly the salt of the earth which has not lost its savor, the light of the world which cannot be hid.

6

| Mk. ii. 17: And when Jesus heard it, He saith unto them, They that are whole have no need of a physician, but they that are sick: I came not to call the righteous but sinners. | Mat. ix. 12–13: But when He heard it, He said, They that are whole have no need of a physician, but they that are sick. But go ye and learn what this meaneth, I desire mercy and not sacrifice: for I came not to call the righteous, but sinners. | Lk. v. 31: And Jesus answering said unto them, They that are whole have no need of a physician but they that are sick. I am not come to call the righteous but sinners to repentance. |

In the immediately preceding saying (Mt. v. 17), Jesus tells us that He came to make men righteous. In this He tells us

what manner of men they are whom He came to make righteous. They are sinners. "I came not to call righteous but
sinners." The anarthrous terms throw the qualities of the opposing classes into strong relief. Of course Jesus means by these
terms the really righteous and really sinful. This Harnack perceives. "The righteous," he rightly remarks, "are really, apart
from all irony, the righteous; and the sinners are really the
sinners; and Jesus says that His life-calling is not to call the
one but the other." Here, says Harnack, is an immense paradox. "It is one of the greatest milestones in the history of religion," he declares; "for Jesus puts His call in contrast with
all that had hitherto been considered the presupposition of
religion." So Celsus, he adds, already saw; and that is the reason
of his passion when he writes: [79]

Those who invite to the solemnization of other mysteries make
proclamation as follows: "He who has clean hands and an understanding tongue, come hither," or "He who is pure from all fault,
and who is conscious in his soul of no sin, and who has led a noble
and righteous life, come hither." This is what is proclaimed by those
who promise expiation of sins! Let us hear, on the other hand, what
kind of people the Christians invite: "Him who is a sinner, a fool, a
simpleton, in a word an unfortunate — him will the Kingdom of God
receive. By the sinner they mean the unjust, the thief, the burglar,
the poisoner, the sacrilegious, the grave-robber. If one wished to re-
cruit a robber band, it would be such people that he would collect.

The contrast here is very arresting and very instructive.
But we can scarcely call it paradoxical to invite sinners to
salvation — as Origen did not fail to remind Celsus. Paradox
is already expressly excluded when Luke, in his record, adds
the words, "to repentance." There is no paradox in calling not
righteous but sinners — to repentance. Harnack, no doubt,
asserts that this addition is "inappropriate." So little inappropriate is it, however, that it would necessarily be understood
even if it were not expressed, and it is understood in the records
of Matthew and Mark where it is not expressed. There can be
no doubt that Jesus came preaching precisely repentance (Mk.

[79] Origen, "Contra Celsum," iii. 59.

i. 15, Mt. iv. 17): and when He says that He came to call not righteous but sinners, it is clear that this was just because He was calling to repentance. All paradox, moreover, is already excluded by the preceding "parable" of which this declaration is the plain explanation: "They that are strong," says Jesus, "have no need of a physician, but they that are sick: I came not to call righteous but sinners." If Jesus' mission is like that of a physician and its end is healing, how could it be directed to the strong? Just because He came to save, He came to call only sinners. "But," says Harnack, "we have no certainty that this saying stood originally in this context (see Wellhausen on the passage), nor that the saying of Jesus originally combined both clauses." And if it did (he contends), — it would not yield the idea of calling to repentance. For in that case, sin would be likened to sickness, and sickness requires healing, not repentance. It is best, then, to take the simple words, "I came not to call righteous but sinners" by themselves. They need no presupposition to be supplied by the preceding "parable": "they stand on their own feet with equal surety." This is obviously special pleading. Harnack does not desire the qualifications provided by the context, and therefore will have no context. Meanwhile, it is clear that Jesus who came preaching the Gospel of God, and crying Repent! (Mk. i. 15, Mt. iv. 17) — to preach which Gospel He declares that He "was sent," (Lk. iv. 43) — very naturally represents that His mission is not to righteous but sinners; and equally naturally likens His work to that of a physician who deals not with well people but with the sick. He does not mean by this to say that sin is merely a sickness and that sinners must therefore be dealt with in the unmixed tenderness of a healer of diseases; but that the terms of His mission like those of a physician cast His lot with the derelicts of the world. He has come to call sinners, and where would men expect to find Him except with sinners?

When Jesus declares, "I came not to call righteous but sinners," then, He uses the words "righteous" and "sinners" in all seriousness, in their literal senses. By "righteous," He does not mean the Pharisees; nor by "sinners" the publicans.

Nevertheless it is clear that He so far takes His start from the Pharisaic point of view that He accepts its estimate of His table-companions as sinners. He does not deny that those with whom He ate were sinners.[80] His defence is not that they were miscalled sinners, but that His place was with sinners, whom He came to call.[81] Similarly His employment of the term "righteous" may not be free from a slight infusion of ironic reference to the Pharisees, who, by their question, contrasted themselves with the others and thus certainly ranked themselves with those "which trusted in themselves that they were righteous and set the rest at nought" (Lk. xviii. 9). His saying would at least raise in their own minds the question where they came in; and thus would act as a probe to enable them to "come to themselves" and to form a juster estimate of themselves. That such a probing of their consciences was within the intention of Jesus, is made clear by a clause in His declaration, preserved only by Matthew, interposed between the "parable" of the physician and the plain statement of the nature of His mission: "But go and learn what this meaneth, I desire mercy and not sacrifice" (Mt. ix. 13).[82] He is as far as possible from implying, therefore, that the Pharisees were well and had no need of His curative ministrations. He rather subtly suggests to them (and perhaps with Hos. vi. 6 in mind we would better not say so subtly either) that they deceived themselves if they fancied that to be the case. In thus intimating that the Pharisees were themselves sinners, He intimates that there were none righteous. A. Jülicher, it is true, vigorously asserts the contrary,[83] and in-

[80] Cf. H. A. W. Meyer on Mt. ix. 10: "Observe that Jesus Himself by no means denies the πονηρὸν εἶναι in regard to those associated with Him at table, ver. 12 f. They were truly diseased ones," sinners.

[81] Cf. Johannes Weiss (p. 167): "The answer which He gives to the criticism of the Scribes neither provides a complete analysis of His motives nor wholly reveals what He holds as to the publicans and sinners. He justifies His conduct only by an immediately obvious reason against which there is nothing to adduce: 'The strong have no need of a physician, but the sick' . . . He goes to those who need help and where He can help."

[82] Cf. H. A. W. Meyer in loc.: "Through that quotation from the Scriptures . . . it is intended to make the Pharisees understand how much they too were sinners."

[83] "Die Gleichnisreden Jesu," ii, pp. 175, 322.

sists that the "righteous" must be as actually existing a class
of men as "sinners": and A. Loisy follows him in this. Jesus,
looking out upon mankind, saw that some were righteous and
some sinners. With the righteous, He had nothing to do; they
needed no saving. It was to the sinners only that He had a
mission; and His mission to them was, as Luke is perfectly
right in adding, to call them to repentance. There were many
who needed no repentance (Lk. xv. 2), but no sinner can be
saved without repentance, and Luke's motive in adding "to
repentance" is to make this clear and thus to guard against
Jesus' call of sinners being taken in too broad, not to say too
loose, a sense. This, however, is quite inconsistent with the whole
drift of the narrative. Jesus is not separating mankind into two
classes and declaring that His mission is confined to one of
these classes. He is contemplating men from two points of view
and declaring that His mission presupposes the one point of
view rather than the other. Reprobation of Him had been expressed, because He associated with publicans and sinners. He
does not pursue the question of the justice of the concrete
contrast — though, as we have seen, not failing to drop hints
even of it. He responds simply, "That is natural, I came on a
mission not to righteous men but to sinners." The question
whether any righteous men actually existed is not raised.[84]
The point is that His mission is to sinners, and that it ought
to occasion no surprise, therefore, that He is found with sinners.[85]

What Jesus does in this saying, therefore, is to present Himself as the Saviour of sinners.[86] He came to call sinners; He is

[84] So far rightly, H. H. Wendt, "The Teaching of Jesus," E. T., vol. ii,
p. 51: "In these words He left quite untouched the question whether any were
truly righteous in His sense."
[85] Cf. J. A. Alexander: "The distinction which He draws is not between two
classes of men, but between two characters or conditions of the whole race."
[86] J. Weiss will not allow that Jesus spoke more than the "parable" of the
physician; but he recognizes that the Evangelist, by the main saying he puts into
Jesus' mouth reflects the belief of the community that Jesus is the Saviour of
sinners: "All those called into the community, felt themselves saved sinners, and
in the retrospect of the whole work of Jesus, He appears as the savior of sinners.
Cf. Lk. xix. 10."

the physician who brings healing to sick souls. He does not tell
us how He saves sinners. He speaks only of "calling them," of
calling them "to repentance." From this we may learn that an
awakened sense of wrong-doing, and a "change of heart,"
issuing in a changed life, enter into the effects of their "calling," — that, in a word, it issues in a transformed mind and
life. But nothing is told us of the forces brought to bear on
sinners to bring about these results. Meanwhile Jesus declares
explicitly that His mission in the world was to "call sinners."
That was no doubt implicit in all the definitions of this mission
which have heretofore come before us. It is here openly proclaimed. Harnack says this saying is not Messianic, "because,"
he explains, "it has nothing to do with the Judgment or the
Kingdom." When He who came to announce the Kingdom of
God, calling on men to repent, called sinners to repentance, —
had that nothing to do with the Kingdom? A "call to repentance" — has that not the Judgment in view? Who in any case
is the Saviour of Sinners if not the Messiah? And who but the
Messiah could proclaim with majestic brevity, "I came not to
call righteous but sinners"?

7

Lk. xix. 10: — For the Son of Man came to seek and to save that
which was lost.

This saying is very much a repetition of the immediately
preceding one in more searching language. Harnack himself
points out the closeness of their relation. "This saying," says
he, "in the best way completes that one, with which it is intimately connected; the 'sinners' are the 'lost,' but in being
'called' they are 'saved.'" The expressive language of the present saying is derived from the great Messianic prophecy of
Ezek. xxxiv. 11 ff., which Jesus has taken up and applies to
Himself and His mission. Harnack is thoroughly justified,
therefore, in saying: "What is most important about this saying, along with its contents, is that Jesus claims for Himself
the work which God proclaimed through the prophets as His
own future work." The whole figurative background of the

saying, and its peculiarities of language as well, are taken from
Ezekiel. "Thus saith the Lord Jehovah," we read there: "Behold I myself, even I, will search for my sheep, and will seek
them out. As a shepherd seeketh out his flock in the day that
he is among his sheep that are scattered abroad, so will I seek
out my sheep and I will deliver them . . . I will seek that
which was lost, and will bring again that which was driven
away, and will bind up all that which was broken, and will
strengthen that which was sick. . . ." Jesus obviously means
to say that He came like this shepherd, with the particular
task laid upon Him to seek and to save what was lost. Because
the statement is introduced as the reason, we might almost
say the justification, of His saving that "sinful man," Zacchaeus, the word "came" is put prominently forward,[87] with the
effect of declaring with great emphasis that it was the very
purpose of Jesus' "coming" "to seek and to save that which
is lost." Here too Harnack's observations are just:

'Ηλθεν is given the first place here with emphasis. Thus it is
made very clear that the salvation of what is lost (see Mt. x. 6, xv.
24; Lk. xv. 6, 9, 32) is the main purpose of Jesus' coming. What appears often in the parables and in separate sayings, is here collected
into a general declaration, which elevates the saving activity of Jesus
above all that is accidental. He Himself testifies that it is His proper
work.

The term "lost" here is a neuter singular, used collectively.[88]
It is simply taken over in this form from Ezek. xxxiv. 16, where
Jehovah declares: "I will seek that which was lost." [89] In explaining His saving of Zacchaeus, Jesus assigns him to the class
to seek and save which He declares to be His particular mission.
Precisely what He meant by speaking of the objects of His
saving actively as "lost" has been made the subject of some

[87] Cf. H. A. W. Meyer: "ἦλθε: emphatically placed first."
[88] Cf. the similar use of the collective neuter in Jno. vi. 37, xvii. 2, 24.
[89] Harnack therefore remarks that Wellhausen rightly supplies "sheep,"
translating: "For the Son of man came to seek and save das verlorene Schaf."
Is the employment of the singular, "Schaf," here accurate? Wellhausen can
scarcely intend it to apply to Zacchaeus as the example of a class.

discussion. Hermann Cremer, for example, wishes us to bear in mind that "lost sheep" may always be found again; that they exist, so to speak for the purpose of being found. And A. B. Bruce, taking up this notion, even reduces the idea of "the lost" to that of "the neglected," and invites us to think of Jesus' mission as directed to "the neglected classes." [90] Such minimizing interpretations are not only wholly without support in the usage of the terms, and in the demands of the passages in which they occur. They are derogatory to the mission which Jesus declares that He came to execute. He speaks of His mission in tones of great impressiveness, as involving supremely great accomplishments. Obviously "the lost" which He declares that He came to seek and to save were not merely neglected people but veritably lost people, lost beyond retrieval save only as He not merely sought them but in some great sense saved them. The solemnity with which Jesus speaks of having come as the Saviour of "the lost" will not permit us to think lightly of their condition, which necessarily carries with it thinking lightly also of His mission and achievement.

The solemnity of this declaration is much enhanced by Jesus' designation of Himself in it by the great title of "the Son of Man." He does not say here simply, as in the sayings we have heretofore had before us, "I came," or "I was sent," but, speaking of Himself in the third person, "The Son of Man came." By thus designating Himself He does far more than explicitly declare Himself the Messiah and His mission the Messianic mission, thus justifying His adoption of Ezekiel's language to describe it. He declares Himself the transcendent Messiah, and in so doing declares His mission, to put it shortly, a divine work, not merely in the sense that it was prosecuted under the divine appointment, but in the further sense that it

[90] "The Kingdom of God," p. 136. Bruce allows that the middle voice of the verb ἀπόλλυμι sometimes imports "irretrievable perdition," but he will allow no such connotation to "the neuter participle τὸ ἀπολωλός." The neuter participle τὸ ἀπολωλός is found in the absolute sense of the "the lost," however, only in Lk. xix. 10. The participle occurs, however, as a qualifier of substantives in Lk. xv. 4, 6, 24, 32, Mt. x. 6, xv. 24. These are all the passages which Bruce has to go on: they obviously do not sustain his contention.

was executed by a divine agent. Great pregnancy is at once imparted to the simple verb "came" by giving it the transcendent Son of Man for its subject. To say "I came" may mean nothing more than a claim to divine appointment. But to say, "the Son of Man came" transports the mind back into the pretemporal, heavenly existence of the Son of Man and conveys the idea of His voluntary descent to earth. We recall here the language of Mk. i. 38, and see that intimation that Jesus thought of His work on earth as a mission of a visitant from a higher sphere, raised into the position of an explicit assertion. We perceive that Jesus is employing a high solemnity of utterance which necessarily imparts to every word of His declaration its deepest significance. The terms "lost," "saved" must be read in their most pregnant sense. Jesus represents those whom He came to seek and save as "lost"; but He declares that the Son of Man who came from heaven for the purpose has power to "save" them. The stress lies on the greatness of the agent, which carries with it the greatness of the achievement, and that in turn carries with it the hopelessness, apart from this achievement by this agent, of the condition of the "lost." It is with the fullest meaning that Jesus represents Himself here as the Saviour of the lost.

If Jesus represents Himself here as the Saviour of the lost, however, does He not represent Himself as the Saviour of the lost of Israel only? We have heard Him in a previous saying, with the same passage from Ezekiel lying in the background, declaring, "I was not sent but to the lost sheep of the house of Israel" (Mt. xv. 24). Is not salvation here similarly declared to have been brought by Him to Zacchaeus' house only because Zacchaeus too was a son of Abraham? [91] Jesus is speaking, primarily, of course, of His own personal ministry, which was strictly confined to Israel.[92] It was in the prosecution of His

[91] Cf. the language of Lk. xiii. 16. We cannot take the words in a spiritual sense, even with the modification suggested by Holtzmann and Plummer who combine the two senses.

[92] Cf. Zahn p. 623, note 73: "According to the whole evangelical tradition, Jesus repeatedly indeed visited localities with a preponderant heathen population, and even worked some healings there (cf. Lk. viii. 27–39, Mt. xv. 26–28, xv.

personal ministry to Israel that He came to Zacchaeus' house, bringing salvation. When He justifies doing this by appealing to the terms of His mission as the Saviour of the lost, He naturally has primary reference to the salvation of Zacchaeus, that Son of Abraham, and may be said by the "lost" to mean, in the first instance, such as he. Must we understand Him as having the lost specifically of Israel therefore exclusively in view? The evangelist who has recorded these words for us certainly did not so understand them. They are in themselves quite general. The Gentiles too are sinners, and are comprehended too under the word "lost." However they may have lain outside the scope of Jesus' personal ministry, they did not lie beyond the horizon of His saving purpose.[93] If we cannot quite say that He tells us here that His mission of salvation extends to them also, we need not contend that He tells us that it does not. The declaration has, in point of fact, nothing to say of the extension of His mission. It absorbs itself in the definition of its intensive nature. It is a mission of salvation. It is a mission to the "lost." Jesus in it declares that the explicit purpose of His coming was to save the lost. This is the great message which this saying brings us.

8

Mk. x. 45: For verily the Son of Man came not to be ministered unto, but to minister, and to give His life a ransom for many.	Mt. xx. 28: Even as the Son of Man came not to be ministered unto, but to minister, and to give His life a ransom for many.

Although Harnack too includes this saying among Jesus' testimonies to the purpose of His "coming," he nevertheless, expresses grave doubt of its authenticity; and this doubt passes,

29–39, and see "Commentary on Matthew[3]," pp. 531 ff.), but He never preached to the heathen or even once entered a heathen's house (cf. Lk. vii. 2–10, Jno. vii. 35, xix, 20–32, and see "Commentary on John[3]," pp. 391 f. 511, 518)."

[93] Cf. in Luke, iii. 5, 6; iv. 24 ff.; xiii. 18–21, 29; xiv. 22 f.; xx. 16; xxiv. 47. See above in Mt. xv. 24. On the universalism of Luke, cf. Hastings' "Dictionary of the Bible," vol. iii, pp. 172 f. On the universalism of Jesus, cf. F. Spitta, "Jesus und die Heidenmission," 1909, and the article "Missions" in Hastings' "Dictionary of Christ and the Gospels."

with respect to the latter member of it, into decisive rejection. The grounds on which he bases this doubt and rejection are three.[94] The saying is not recorded in Lk. xxii. 24–34, a passage which Harnack chooses to consider another and older form of the tradition reproduced in Mt. xx. 20–28 = Mk. x. 35–45. The transition from "ministering" to "giving the life as a ransom," Harnack represents as, although not unendurable, yet unexpected and hard: "ministry" is the act of a servant and no servant is in a position to ransom others. Nowhere else, except in the words spoken at the Last Supper, is there preserved in the oldest tradition an announcement by Jesus that He was to give His life instead of others.[95] As these reasons bear chiefly upon the latter portion of the saying, Harnack contents himself with rejecting it, and allows to Jesus the former half, which commends itself to him, moreover, by its paradoxical form and the pithiness of its contents. The statement of these grounds of doubt is their sufficient refutation. There is no reason to suppose that the incident recorded in Lk. xxii. 24–36 is the same as that recorded in Mt. xx. 20–28 = Mk. x. 35–45. The differences are decisive.[96] Jesus does not represent the giving of one's life as a ransom for others as a servant's function, or

[94] In these criticisms Harnack pretty closely follows Wellhausen, "Das Evangelium Marci," 1903, p. 91: "The ἀπολύτρωσις through the death of Jesus intrudes into the Gospel only here: immediately before, He did not die *for* others and in their stead, but He died *before* them that they might die afterwards. The words καὶ δοῦναι κτλ. are lacking in Lk. xxii. 27. They do not in fact fit in with διακονῆσαι, for that means 'wait at table' as the third and fourth evangelists rightly understand. The passage from serving to giving life as a ransom is a μετάβασις εἰς ἀλλὸ γένος. It is explained by the service at the Lord's Supper, where Jesus administers His flesh and blood with bread and wine." Wellhausen is an adept at this sort of carping, surface verbal criticism.

[95] Johannes Weiss, "Die Schriften," etc.[1],i. p. 161, tells us that the grounds on which recent criticism denies the saying to Jesus are these three — which may be compared with Harnack's: "First, the entire life-activity of the Lord is here reviewed ('He came'); secondly, the term 'ransom' and the whole series of conceptions opened up by it, do not occur elsewhere in Jesus' preaching; and thirdly, the parallel declaration from the Discourse-Source, Lk. xxii. 27, contains nothing of the redemptive death." That is to say, in brief, Jesus cannot have said what He is here reported to have said, because He is not reported to have said it often.

[96] Cf. G. Hollmann, "Die Bedeutung des Todes Jesu" and Runze as there quoted.

even ascribe the act to a servant. He represents the giving of one's life as a ransom for others as a supreme act of service for one, not Himself a servant, to render when He gave Himself to service to the uttermost. Harnack himself allows that in one other saying, at least, Jesus does represent His death as offered for others, and, indeed, in a subsequent passage, himself extracts all the probative force from this objection, by pointing out that no presumption can lie against Jesus' expressing Himself concerning His death as He is here reported as doing (p. 26):

Whether Jesus Himself expressly included in the service which He performed, the giving of His life as a ransom for many, we must leave an open question; but the matter is not of so much importance as is commonly supposed. If His eye was always fixed upon His death (and the zealous effort to throw this into doubt is, considering the situation in which He ordinarily stood, simply whimsical) and knew Himself as the good shepherd, John has only said the most natural thing in the world when he puts on Jesus' lips the declaration that the good shepherd gives his life for the sheep. Whether Jesus really said it, whether He, in another turn of phrase, represented His life as a thing of value for the ransoming of others, is not to be certainly determined; but if He designated His life in general as "service" then His death is properly included in it, for the highest service is — so it has been and so it will remain — the giving of the life.[97]

The case being so; it is surely unreasonable to deny to Jesus words credibly reported from His lips in which He declares that His ministry culminated in the giving of His life for others,

[97] Somewhat similarly, Johannes Weiss, who denies Mk. x. 45, Mk. xx. 28, to Jesus but allows to Him Lk. xxii. 27, writes ("Die Schriften[1]," vol. i, pp. 161–162): "It is, however, of course not inconceivable that Jesus should have included also His approaching death in this work of service and love. It is even probable that He was of the conviction that His death would somehow accrue to the advantage of the men for whom He had labored in word and deed. But whether He thought directly of a sacrificial death, or of a vicarious punishment, such as is described by Isaiah in the Fifty-third chapter, — that must remain doubtful, cf. xiv. 24." Why — when He certainly knew Isaiah liii, certainly applied it to Himself, and is credibly reported to have spoken of His death as a sacrificial offering (Mk. xiv. 24) and as a vicarious punishment (Mk. x. 45)? The discussion by H. J. Holtzmann, "Synopt[3].," p. 160 is notable from the same point of view.

merely because He is not reported as having frequently made this great declaration.[98]

There is the less reason for doubting that we have before us here an authentic saying of Jesus', because it was eminently natural and to be expected that Jesus, at this stage of His ministry, when describing the nature of His mission, should not pause until He had intimated the place of His death in it. According to the representation of all the evangelists, it was characteristic of this period of His ministry that He spoke much and very insistently of the death which He should accomplish at Jerusalem, and of the indispensableness of this death for the fulfilment of His task. "From that time," says Matthew, marking the beginning of a period, "began Jesus to show unto His disciples, how that He must go unto Jerusalem . . . and be killed." [99] His insistence upon this teaching during this period is marked by all the evangelists again and again,[100] and it was immediately after the third of these insistences which have been recorded for us that the incident is introduced by Matthew and Mark which occasioned the declaration before us. Jesus' preoccupation with His death is strikingly betrayed by His allusion to it even in His response to the ambitious request of James and John, and that in such a manner as to show that it held, in His view, an indispensable place in His work.[101] It would have been unnatural, if when, in the sequel to this incident, He came to reveal to His disciples the innermost nature of His mission as one of self-sacrificing devotion, He had made no allusion whatever to the death in which it culminated, and the indispensableness of which to its accomplishment He was at the time earnestly engaged in impressing upon them.

[98] It is purely arbitrary for Harnack to add in a note: "If the declaration," as to giving His life as a ransom, "comes from Jesus, we have at least no guaranty that it was spoken in connection with the διακονεῖν and was introduced by ἦλθον." There is no justification in any legitimate method of criticism for thus rending unitary sayings into fragments and dealing with each clause as a separate entity. [99] Mt. xvi. 21; cf. Mk. viii. 31; Lk. ix. 22.

[100] Mt. xvii. 22 f., Mk. ix. 30 f., Lk. ix. 43 ff.: Mt. xx. 17 ff., Mk. x. 32 ff., Lk. xviii., 31 ff. [101] Mt. xx. 22, Mk. x. 38.

The naturalness, not to say inevitableness, of an allusion to
His death in this saying has not prevented some expositors, it
is true, from attempting violently to explain away the open
allusion which is made to it.[102] Thus, for example, Ernest D.
Burton [103] wishes us to believe that "to give His life" means
not "to die" but "to live," — "to devote His life-energies"
— and that Jesus here without direct reference to His death
is only exhorting His followers to devote their lives without
reserve to the service of their fellows. In support of this desperate contention, he urges that he has not been able to find
elsewhere the exact phrase, "to give life," used as a synonym
of "to die." [104] It does not seem very difficult to find; [105] but
in any event Burton might have remembered that this phrase
is not so much used here as the synonym of "to die," as the
wider phrase "to give His life a ransom for" is used as a synonym for "to die instead of." [106] In other words, the employment of the term "to give" is determined here by the idea of
a ransom — which is a thing given, whether it be money or

[102] Not Harnack, whose phrase: "The announcement that Jesus gave His
life as a λύτρον for others, that is to say, was to die for all" . . . indicates his
conception of the meaning of the words.

[103] "Biblical Ideas of Atonement," 1909, pp. 114 ff.

[104] He finds the phrase "give your lives" in the exhortations of Mattathias
to his sons, I Macc. ii. 50 f.; but he supposes it to mean there, "to devote your life
energies," an interpretation which did not suggest itself to Josephus, "Antt." xii.
6. 3, Niese iii. pp. 120f. (cf. Sirach xxix. 15, and, with παραδίδωμι, Acts xv. 26,
Hermas, "Sim.," ix. 28.2; Just. "Apol." i, 50 from Isa. 53, 12).

[105] See preceding note, and also cf. Ex. xxi. 23: δώσει ψυχὴν ἀντὶ ψυχῆς. A.
Seeberg, "Der Tod Christi," etc., 1895, p. 350, says: "The words δοῦναι τὴν ψυχήν
refer in any case to death, for this formula which corresponds to the Hebrew
נֶפֶשׁ נָתַן occurs frequently in the sense of the surrender of the life in death." In
a note he cites Ex. xxi. 23, I Macc. ii. 55, Sr. xxix. 15, with other less close
parallels. There can be no doubt that "to give His life" means to Clement of
Alexandria, for instance, "Paed." I, ix, somewhat past the middle, simply to die.

[106] Cf. Th. Zahn, "Das Ev. d. Matthaeus[1]," 1903, p. 604, ed. 3, 1910, p. 611:
"The greatest service, however, will be done by Him only in the gift of His life.
No doubt this is not said clearly by δοῦναι τὴν ψυχὴν αὐτοῦ by itself; δοῦναι rather
finds its necessary supplement only in the object-predicate λύτρον ἀντὶ πολλῶν.
But just this action described so figuratively, can take place only in a voluntary
endurance of death; for no one can give a purchase-price for another without in
doing so depriving himself of it."

blood — and not by the idea of 'dying. [107] Its employment carries with it, indeed, the implication that Jesus' death was a voluntary act — He gave it; but the thought is not completed until the purpose for which He gave it is declared — He gave it as a ransom.

In this context, the saying occurs as an enforcement of Jesus' exhortation to His disciples to seek their greatness in service. He adduces His own example. "For even the Son of Man," He says, "came not to be ministered unto but to minister, and to give His life a ransom for many." To enhance His example He designates Himself by the transcendent title, "The Son of Man." [108] If any, the Son of Man might expect "to be ministered unto" in His sojourn on earth. In His sojourn on earth — for, when we say "Son of Man" we intimate that His earthly life is a sojourn. The eye fixes itself at once on a heavenly origin and a heavenly issue; and we necessarily think of pomp and glory. If even the Son of Man "came" not to be ministered unto but to minister, what shall we say of the proper life-ideal for others? Jesus is not speaking of the manner of His daily life on earth when He speaks here of "coming" to serve. The manner of His daily life on earth was not that of a servant. He lived among His followers as their Master and Lord, claiming their obedience and receiving their reverence. [109] He did not scruple to accept from others or to apply to Himself titles of the highest, even of superhuman, dignity. In this very saying He speaks of Himself by a title which assigns to Him a transcendent being. It was not the manner of His earthly life but

[107] Cf. H. A. W. Meyer, on Mt. xx. 28 (E. T., ii, p. 51): " δοῦναι is made choice of, because the ψυχή (the soul, as the principle of the life of the body) is conceived of as a λύτρον (a ransom)." Note Josephus, "Antt." xiv. 7.1: λύτρον ἀντὶ πάντων ἔδοκεν, and cf. LXX Ex. xxi. 30, xxx. 12.

[108] Cf. Harnack (p. 10): "That Jesus says here, not 'I' but 'the Son of Man' is explained from the contents of the saying, which acquires force from Jesus' laying claim at the same time to the (future) Messianic dignity." This is saying too little and its says it with a wrong implication, but it allows the main matter. Jesus' use of "the Son of Man" here plays the same part that Paul's phrase "being in the form of God" plays in Phil. ii. 6.

[109] Cf. the striking presentation of the facts here by Zahn, "Matthew¹," p. 603.

the mere fact of this earthly life for Him, which He speaks of as a servile mission. That He was on earth at all; that He, the heavenly one, demeaned Himself to a life in the world; this was what required explanation. And the explanation was, service.

This was not news to His followers. He is not informing them of something hitherto unimagined by them. He is reminding them of a great fact concerning Himself which, He intimates, it were well for them to bear in mind. He "came," not to exercise the lordship which belongs naturally to a great one like Himself, but to perform a service. What the service which He came to perform was, and how He performs it He tells us by mentioning a single item, but that single item one lying so much at the center that it is in effect the whole story. "To minister *and* to give His life a ransom" are not presented as two separate things. They are one thing presented in general and in particular. The "and" is not merely copulative; it is intensive,[110] and may almost be read epexegetically: "The Son of Man came to minister, *namely* to give His life a ransom.[111] It is in "to give His life a ransom" that the declaration culminates; on it that it rests; through it that it conveys its real meaning. For this is the wonderful thing of which Jesus reminds His followers, to compose their ambitious rivalries — that He, the Son of Man, came unto the world to die. Dying was the service by way of eminence which He came to perform. Dying in the stead of others who themselves deserved to die [112] — that they need not die. We do not catch the drift of this great saying until we perceive that all its emphasis gathers itself up upon the declaration that Jesus came into the world just to die as a ransom.

The mode in which the service which Jesus came to render

[110] Cf. H. A. W. Meyer: "intensive: adding on the *highest act*, the culminating point in the διακονῆσαι."

[111] Cf. Seeberg, p. 348: "Jesus became man, in order as Messiah, to give His life in death, for of course the words δοῦναι τὴν ψυχήν give the content of διακονῆσαι."

[112] Whoever the "many" are, they certainly include the "sinners" whom He "came to call" (Mk. ii. 17, Mt. ix. 13, Lk. v. 32) and "the lost" whom "He came to seek and save" (Lk. xix. 10). For these "sinners" and "lost" He came to give His life a ransom. This is the way He saves them.

to others is performed is described here, then, in the phrase, "to give His life a ransom for many." It would be difficult to make the language more precise. Jesus declares that He came to die; to die voluntarily; to die voluntarily in order that His death may serve a particular purpose. This particular purpose He describes as a "ransom"; and the idea of a "ransom" is explicated by adding that, in thus giving His life as a ransom, His given life, His death, is set over against others in a relation of equivalence, takes their place and serves their need and so releases them.[113]

It is always possible to assign to each word in turn in a statement like this the least definite or the most attenuated meaning which is ever attached to it in its varied literary applications, and thus to reduce the statement as a whole literally to insignificance. Thus Jesus' strong and precise assertion that He came into the world in order to give His life as a ransom-price for the deliverance of many has been transmuted into the expression of a dawning recognition by Him that His death had became inevitable and of a more or less strong hope, or expectation, that it might not be quite a fatal blow to His wish to be of use, but might in some way or to some extent prove of advantage to His followers.[114] According to H. H.

[113] Cf. H. A. W. Meyer on Mt. xx. 28: "ἀντί denotes *substitution*. That which is given as a *ransom* takes the *place* (is given *instead*) of those who are to be set free in consideration thereof." The "meaning is strictly and specifically defined by λύτρον (כֹּפֶר) according to which ἀντί can only be understood in the sense of *substitution*, the act of which the ransom is presented as an equivalent to secure the deliverance of those on whose behalf it is paid." In the κοινή, ἀντί seems to be going out of use. Instead of it ὑπέρ is employed (L. Rademacher, "N. T. Grammatik," 1911, pp. 115–116). It must therefore be held to be fully intended when used.

[114] Cf. C. G. Montefiore, vol. i, p. 260: "Moreover Jesus may just conceivably have realized that His death would be to the advantage of many; that many would enter the Kingdom as the effect of His death. Menzies takes this view. He thinks 'Jesus became reconciled to the prospect of death when He saw that He was to die for the benefit of others.' This is a possible view, though I think it an unlikely one. It is rebutted by Pfleiderer, "Urchristentum," i, p. 372. Holtzmann thinks that λύτρον here is a translation of an Aramaic word which may merely mean 'deliverance.' Jesus 'delivered' people by causing them to repent . . ." "Holtzmann" at the end of this extract is a misprint for "Hollmann": see G. Hollmann, "Die Bedeutung des Todes Jesu," 1901, pp. 124 f.: "The following is

Wendt,[115] for example, Jesus makes no reference whatever here to the "ransoming" of individual souls from the guilt and punishment of sin: "it is more correct to say that Jesus meant the bringing about of the salvation of the Messianic end-time in a wholly general sense."

Because He now, as death threatened Him for His works' sake, was determined rather to give His life up than be untrue to the vocation imposed on Him by God (Jno. x. 11–18); and because in strong trust in God, He was assured that His death would work out not for the destruction but for the furthering of His work; He could designate His yielding up of His life a "ransom," that is a means for bringing about the Messianic "liberation" for all those who would permit themselves to be led by Him to the Messianic salvation.

According to Friedrich Niebergall,[116] on the other hand, there is no objective reference in the allusion to a ransom: "the figure is doubtless here only an expression for the religious impression that by Christ's death we are liberated from evil Powers." In a similar vein Johannes Weiss says: [117]

When Mark wrote this declaration it was immediately intelligible to all his readers. For their religious life was governed by the fundamental feeling that they were liberated from the dominion of the devil and the demons (cf. I Cor. xii. 2, Gal. iv. 8) and therewith delivered from the terrible destruction which impended over the kingdom of sin at the end of the ages.

Questions, such as have been raised by the dogmaticians, as to the meaning of the saying "will no longer occupy us," says Weiss, "if we keep the main idea in mind, that the immediate

then to be summarily derived from our passage: (1) that Jesus' death stands on the same plane with Jesus' life-work; (2) (negatively) that it prevents many souls from falling into destruction; (3) (positively) that it brings many hitherto unbelieving to salvation. There can be added as most probable that (4) their salvation lies in the operation of μετανοια."

[115] "System der Christl. Lehre," pp. 308 ff., 323.

[116] Lietzmann's "Handbuch zum N. T.," v, 1909, pp. 102 f.

[117] "Die Schriften," etc¹. v. i, p. 161. He speaks of the statement as Mark's, not Jesus'.

liberation from the dominion of demonic tyrants which was felt directly by the ancient Christians was a mark of the ministering love of the Christ who gave His life for them."

Comments like these merely lead away from the simple, penetrating declaration of Jesus, the meaning of which is perfectly clear in itself,[118] and is further fixed by the testimony of His followers. For Jesus' declaration did not fall fruitless to the ground: it finds an echo in the teaching of His followers, and in this echo we can hear His own tones sounding.[119] It marks the very extremity of perverseness, when an attempt is made to reverse the relation of this key-declaration and its echoes in the apostolical writings, explaining it as rather an echo of them. How this is managed may be read briefly in, say, H. J. Holtzmann's comment on Mk. x. 45.

The thought of the Discourse-Source, Lk. xxii. 27, is so expressed here in Paulinizing form (cf. Rom. xv. 3) that Jesus also is represented as having found His vocation only in service (Phil. ii. 7, I Cor. ix. 19), and as having yielded up His life in that service (Phil. ii. 8). . . . While, however, the disciple can only "lose" his life in the service of his Lord (Mk. viii. 35 = Mt. x. 39, xvi. 25 = Lk. ix. 24, xvii. 33), it is the part of the Lord to give it voluntarily, according to Gal. i. 4, ii. 20. Especially, however, the "give His life a ransom for many" corresponds to the "who gave Himself a ransom for all" of I Tim. ii. 6 and the "He gave Himself for us that He might ransom us" of Titus ii. 14, that is, the idea of Jesus is glossed by a reminiscence of the Pauline doctrine of redemption.

Perverse as this is, it at least fixes the sense of Jesus' declaration. The attempt to represent it as a reminiscence of the Pauline doctrine of redemption shows at any rate that it is identical with the Pauline doctrine of redemption.

It lies in the nature of the case that a brief saying, consisting of only two short clauses, made, moreover, not for itself but in

[118] We content ourselves with referring here to the excellent remarks of James Denney, "The Death of Christ[3]," 1903, pp. 36 ff., cap. pp. 42 ff.

[119] Cf. Zahn, p. 605, note 90: "The conception of the redemption (redemptio) wrought by Jesus and especially by His death, would not recur everywhere in the New Testament, if it did not go back to Jesus Himself." Zahn then cites the details.

order to enforce an exhortation to conduct becoming in followers of Jesus, should not tell us all we should like to know of the great matter which it thus allusively brings before us. Many questions arise for guidance on which we must look elsewhere. Fortunately answers to some of them are supplied by the sayings which have already engaged our attention. We can scarcely refuse to correlate Jesus' testimony in them, for example, that He came "to call sinners," that He came "to save the lost" with His testimony here that He came to do many a service, — above all, this service, by His death to ransom them. Undoubtedly the giving of His life as a ransom is the manner in which He saves the lost. And undoubtedly by the "lost" are meant just "sinners," and by "sinners" in turn are meant those who are not "righteous," that is to say the guilt-laden.[120] What we have here, then, is a declaration by Jesus that He came to save lost sinners by giving His life a ransom for them. The effect, called in a former saying "salvation," is clearly in the first instance relief from the penalties due to their sin: He purchases lost sinners out of the obligations which they have incurred by their sin, by giving His life a ransom for them. That is as far perhaps as our particular saying will carry us. Others of the sayings which have come before us, however, carry us further. They tell us that Jesus secures for lost sinners also perfected righteousness of life — and perhaps something like that is after all suggested in this saying also, for it too has to do with conduct. His disciples are exhorted to follow Jesus' example, and it is implied that His example is a perfect one. The ransom-paying certainly lies at the bottom of all and of that alone is there explicit mention. But there is a call to perfection of life too: and not a call to it merely, but a provision for it. In a word there is a complete "salvation" hinted at here: relief from sin both in its curse and its power. Say that it is in this its completeness only hinted at. That is to say that it *is* hinted at.

---

[120] Cf. Harnack (p. 24): "The 'lost' and the 'sinners' are, however, still more closely characterized by the contrast 'not the righteous,' — they are really the dying and guilt-laden, who must perish without Him."

III

We shall only in the briefest possible manner sum up the results of this survey of the eight sayings in which, according to the report of the Synoptics, Jesus declared the purpose of His mission. In doing so we may take our start from the remarks with which Harnack opens the summary of the results of his survey of practically the same series of sayings. "The eight sayings from the Synoptics which we have collected and studied," says he, "contain very few words, but how much is said in them! On investigation they compose a unity which is equally important for the characterization of Jesus, and for the compass and range of His work." We shall wish to say a word each on both of these matters.

First of all, we note, then, that these sayings are not without their teaching as to Jesus' person. The simple phrases, "I came," "I was sent," naturally, do not of themselves testify to more than Jesus' consciousness of a divine mission. It is quite clear, however, that this divine mission of which He thus expresses consciousness, stands in His mind as that of the Messiah. He speaks in all these sayings out of the Messianic consciousness and assumes in them all Messianic functions. Even that, however, does not exhaust their implications.[121] There is a certain pregnancy of speech in them, a certain majesty of tone, a certain presupposition of voluntariness in the action expressed by the "I came," — of active acquiescence lying behind the "I was sent" — which have constantly led expositors to feel in them a claim greater than that to the Messianic dignity itself. Harnack will not admit that even the specifically Messianic consciousness speaks through them, and yet is constrained to exclaim (p. 28):

Who, then is this "I" that here "came". . . Undoubtedly there lies in that "I came," no matter who is meant, something

[121] A. Seeberg, "Der Tod Christi," etc., 1895, p. 348, is quite right when he says: "All the passages in which a coming of Jesus into the world is spoken of (Mk. ii. 17, Mt. v. 17, ix. 13, Lk. v. 32, xii. 49, xix. 10) fix their eyes upon a nearer or more distant purpose of His Messianic vocation."

authoritative and final. There lies in it the consciousness of a divine mission, as indeed it is interchanged with the expression "I was sent." The finality, however, is given by the definitions of purpose. He who came to perfect the law, He who was sent to recover the lost sheep, that is, to fulfil the prediction of the coming of God Himself, He who came with fire and sword — He comes as the final and ultimate one.

To others, even this seems inadequate; and they are right. Justice may be done by it to the impression which the reader receives from these sayings of the majesty of the speaker; scarcely to the impression which they equally make on him of the speaker's sense of complete control over all the circumstances of His mission, including the mission itself. It is this strong impression which expresses itself in the constant tendency of expositors to see in the "I came," "I was sent" a testimony by Jesus not merely to His divine mission but to His heavenly origin. "In the coming of Jesus," expounds A. Seeberg, for example,[122] "it is not some kind of an appearance (*Auftreten*) of Jesus in the world that is spoken of, but His entrance (*Eintritt*) into the world, such as is unmistakably spoken of in Jno. xvi. 28, where the coming into the world corresponds to the going away to the Father."

Unquestionably in some of these sayings Jesus speaks out of a consciousness of preëxistence. That is not merely suggested by the appearance in one of them, instead of the simple "I came" of a more significant "I came out" (Mk. i. 38), which is scarcely completely satisfied by any other supplement than "from heaven" or "from the Father." It is clearly presupposed in two of them by the employment, instead of the personal pronoun, of the descriptive periphrasis, "the Son of Man," the particular Messianic designation which especially emphasizes preëxistence (Lk. xix. 10, Mk. x. 45 = Mt. xx. 28). The declaration of Mk. x. 45 = Mt. xx. 28 runs most strikingly on the same lines with Phil. ii. 5 ff., and bears similar testimony to the preëxistent glory of the great exemplar of humility, whom both passages hold up to view. The whole force of the example presented turns on the immense incongruity of the Son of Man

[122] As cited.

appearing in the rôle of a servant; this force would be much decreased, if not destroyed, if the Son of Man had never been anything but a servant, was in His own nature a servant, and was fitted only for a servant's rôle. That three out of eight of these sayings thus imply the preëxistence of Jesus, and take their coloring from this implication, perhaps sufficiently accounts for the tendency of commentators to read the whole of them from this point of sight. We know at least that He who says in them, "I came," "I was sent," was conscious of having come from heaven to perform the mission which He ascribes to Himself.

In this implication of a preëxistence in glory, distinct in some of these sayings, possibly to be assumed in them all, they range themselves by the side of the more numerous similar sayings of Jesus recorded in the Gospel of John.[123] "The not infrequent addition, 'into the world,'" remarks Harnack, in commenting on these, "shows a new horizon, alien to Jesus Himself." Not so. The difference in this as in other things, between the Synoptic and the Johannine record, is rather quantitative than qualitative. This Johannine feature too is found in the Synoptic record; but in fewer instances.

It is not, however, of the person of Jesus, but, as was to be expected — for do they not speak of His mission? — of His work, that we learn most from these sayings. According to their teaching Jesus' work may be fairly summed up in the one word, "salvation." He came to call "sinners"; He came to seek and save "the lost"; He came to give His life a "ransom" for many. Everything else which Jesus testifies that He came to do takes a place subordinate and subsidiary to "salvation." Even the "fulfilling" of the law. Harnack is wrong in attempting to coördinate the two functions of Saviour and Lawgiver in Jesus' testimony to His mission. "According to His self testimony, the purpose of His coming and thus His significance is given in this — that He is at once Saviour and Lawgiver.

---

[123] The Johannine passages are adverted to by Harnack twice, pp. 2 and 22. For a synoptical view of them see B. F. Westcott in the "additional note" on Jno. xx. 21.

. . . Redeemer and Lawgiver: all that constitutes the significance of His coming is exhausted in that collocation . . . Programmatic in the strict sense are only these two sayings: 'I
came to save' and 'I came to fulfil the law.'" [124] Jesus does
declare that He came to fulfil the law, and by this He means
also "to fill it out," to complete and perfect it, so that it shall
be a faultless transcript of the will of God, the Righteous One.
But not this only, or even mainly. He means more fundamentally that He came to get the law observed, so that it shall be
perfectly expressed in righteous lives. His mind is more on the
transforming of law-breakers into law-keepers, than on the
perfecting of the codex itself. That is to say, He is thinking of
salvation; of salvation in its ultimate effects. And what could
be more poignant than to declare side by side, "I came not to
call righteous but sinners," "I came to make human lives the
perfect reflection of the law of God"?

Those whom Jesus came to call, He describes as sinners
and as lost, that is to say as lost sinners; as those who can lay
claim to no righteousness of their own and who have no power
to obtain any, that is to say as helpless dependents on Him
the Saviour. To them He comes to preach the Gospel of the
Kingdom; He calls them to repentance; He seeks them out and
saves them; He gives His life a ransom for them; He writes
the law of God upon their hearts. This is the process of His
"salvation." Their own energies are enlisted: He preaches the
Gospel of the Kingdom to them and calls them to repentance.
Their hearts are changed: He writes the law of God upon their
hearts and sets them spontaneously to fulfil it. But beneath all
this, there lies something deeper still which attracts to itself
especially His greatest word: "I came to save." He gives His
life a ransom for them. And it is only as He thus ransoms them
by the gift of Himself that they cease to be "lost"; and having
thus ceased to lie under the curse, can cease also to lie under
the power of sin.

Harnack pushes this greatest declaration, "I came to give
my life a ransom for many" into the background. It makes

[124] Pp. 25–26.

little difference, he hints, whether Jesus ever said it or not. Jesus certainly died. And if all His work in the world was comprehended — as He witnesses that it was — in the category of ministry, then of course His death was included in this ministry. We may even say it was the culmination of His ministry, since the gift of one's life is the highest ministry which he can render. But the main matter is that Jesus declares that He came into the world to minister — whether by living or dying. "What it has meant in history that Jesus expressly said that He did not come to be ministered unto but to 'minister' — that cannot be expressed in words! All the advance in ethics, in these nineteen centuries which have flowed by, has had its most powerful lever in this." [125]

Imitatio Christi! It certainly is the most powerful lever to move men to endeavor which has ever entered the world; it has revolutionized all conceptions of values; it has transformed the whole spirit of conduct and changed the entire aspect of life. But it has one indispensable precondition. Only living things can imitate anything. Dead things must be brought to life. Lost things must be found. Sinners must be saved. Even the heathen knew that he may see the good and yet pursue the bad. The awakened soul cries out, O wretched man that I am who shall deliver me out of this body of death? Jesus has done for us something far greater than set us a good example, and summon us to its imitation: something without which there could have been no imitation of His example; no transformed ethics; no transfigured lives. He has undoubtedly set before our eyes in living example the perfect law of love. But He has done more than that. He has written it on our hearts. He has given us new ideals. And He has given us something even above that. He has given us the power to realize these ideals. In one word, He has brought to us newness of life. And He has obtained for us this newness of life by His own blood.

It is this that Jesus declares when He says, "I came to give my life a ransom for many." And therefore this is the greatest declaration of all. In it He shows us not how He has become our

[125] P. 26.

supreme example merely, but how He has become our Saviour.
He has set us a perfect example. He has given us a new ideal.
But He has also given us His life. And in giving us His life,
He has given us life. For "He gave His life a ransom instead of
many."

IX

THE NEW TESTAMENT TERMINOLOGY OF "REDEMPTION"

THE NEW TESTAMENT TERMINOLOGY
OF "REDEMPTION"[1]

The most direct, but not the exclusive,[2] vehicle in the Greek of the New Testament of the idea which we commonly express in our current speech by the term "redeem" and its derivatives, is provided by a group of words built up upon the Greek term λύτρον, "ransom."[3] The exact implications of this group of words as employed by the writers of the New Testament have been brought into dispute.[4] It seems desirable therefore to look afresh into their origin and usage sufficiently to become clear as to the matter, and the inquiry may perhaps be thought to possess enough intrinsic interest to justify going a little farther afield in it, and entering somewhat more into details, than would be necessary for the immediate purpose in hand.

[1] From *The Princeton Theological Review*, v. xv, 1917, pp. 201–249.

[2] Compare for example, the use of ἀγοράζω I Cor. vi. 20, vii. 23, II Pet. ii. 1, Rev. v. 9, xiv. 3, 4; ἐξαγοράζω Gal. iii. 13, iv. 5; περιποιέομαι Acts xx. 28.

[3] λύτρον Mt. xx. 28, Mk x. 45; ἀντίλυτρον I Tim. ii. 6; λυτροῦσθαι Lk. xxiv. 21, Tit. ii. 14, I Pet. i. 18; λύτρωσις Lk. i. 68, ii. 38, Heb. ix. 12; ἀπολύτρωσις Lk. xxi. 28, Rom. iii. 24, viii. 23, I Cor. i. 30, Eph. 1, 7, 14, iv. 30, Col. i. 14, Heb. ix. 15, xi. 35; [λυτρωτής] Acts vii. 35.

[4] Cf. what Johannes Weiss says in his comment on I Cor. i. 30b (Meyer series): "Whereas heretofore the notion of ἀπολύτρωσις has been carefully investigated with reference to its shade of meaning (whether it is to be taken simply generally as = 'Deliverance,' or — because of the λυτρ — as = 'Ransoming') and also with reference to the particular relations of the notion (Who was the former owner? What is the ransom price? Who pays it? Why is it of so great value?), the tendency of the day is to push all these questions aside as wrongly put: Paul uses here a common *terminus technicus*, as a piece of current coin, with regard to which he reckons on a ready understanding; it is approximately = σωτηρία; accordingly it is translated simply 'Deliverance,' and no questions are asked with respect to a more exact explanation. This is generally right. . . ." Weiss himself conceives the term to be used primarily of the eschatological salvation, but to have received (like others of the kind) a certain predating and not to have lost entirely the idea of ransoming, though laying the stress on the effects rather than the means.

I

To begin at the beginning, at any rate, the ultimate base
to which this group of words goes back seems to be represented
by the Sanscrit Lû, which bears the meaning of "to cut," or
"to clip"; hence it is inferred that the earliest implication of
the general Indo-European root LU was to set free by cutting
a bond. The Greek primitive of this base, λύειν, has the general
meaning of "to loose," which is applied and extended in a great
variety of ways. When applied to men, its common meaning is
"'to loose, release, set free,' especially from bonds or prison,
and so, generally, from difficulty, or danger." It developed a
particular usage with reference to prisoners,[5] which is of interest
to us. In this usage, it means, in the active voice, "to release
on receipt of ransom," "to hold to ransom"; and in the middle
voice, "to secure release by payment of ransom," "to ransom"
in the common sense of that word,[6] passing on to a broader

---

[5] See Liddell and Scott, *Sub voc.* I. 2. c.

[6] This distinctive usage of the active and middle may be excellently observed
in the First and Twenty Fourth Books of the "Iliad." In the opening lines of
Book I we are told that Chryses came to the ships of the Achæans to ransom
(λυσόμενος, line 13) his daughter, bearing a boundless ransom (ἄποινα); and that
accordingly he supplicated the Achæans to ransom (λῦσαι [λύσατε], line 20) her
to him and accept the ransom (ἄποινα). Agamemnon, however, declared roundly
that he would not ransom (λύσω, line 29) her, and this was brought home to him
in the subsequent council by Chalcas who charged him with not having ransomed
(ἀπέλυσε) her and accepted the ransom (ἄποινα), and required him now (lines
95 ff.) no longer to look for ransom but to give (δόμεναι) the maiden to her father
unbought (ἀπριάτην) and unransomed (ἀνάποινον). Similarly, early in Book xxiv
we read that Here despatched Thetis to Achilles (lines 115–116) to chide him for
holding Hector's body and not ransoming (ἀπέλυσεν) it, and to see to it, that, respecting her, he now ransomed (λύσῃ) it; and added that she will send Iris to Priam
bidding him go and ransom (λύσασθαι) his son bearing gifts to Achilles. Accordingly
Thetis goes and chides Achilles (line 135) for holding Hector's body and not
ransoming (ἀπέλυσας) it, and bids him ransom (λῦσαι) it, accepting the ransom
(ἄποινα) offered for the corpse: while Iris goes to Troy and urges Priam to go
(line 144) to the ships and ransom (λύσασθαι) his son, carrying gifts to Achilles.
Stephanus, "Thesaurus," *sub voc.* observes that the French word *Delivrer* has the
same two senses; "for *Delivrer un prisonnier* is said both concerning him who redeems him and concerning him who releases him to a redeemer." The same is
true of the English word, "to deliver" and also, indeed, of the English word "to
ransom."

usage of simply "to redeem" (in which it is applied not merely to prisoners but to animals and landed property [7]) and even "to buy." [8] It also acquired the sense of paying debts, and, when used with reference to wrong-doings, a sense of "undoing" or "making up for," which is not far removed from that of making atonement for, them.[9]

Naturally, the usual derivatives and compounds are formed from λύειν. Among the former the abstract active substantive, λύσις, is especially interesting to us because among its various senses it reflects both of the usages of its primitive to which we have just called attention. It is used of a release, deliverance, effected by the payment of a ransom — a "ransoming." [10] And it is used of a cleansing from guilt by means of an expiation — an "atonement." [11] Little less interesting, however, are the nouns of agent, of which several are formed, bearing the general sense of "deliverer" — λύσιος (λύσειος), λυτήρ (λύτειρα), λύτωρ. Λύσιος was used in the Dionysiac myth as an epithet of Dionysus,[12] and in the Orphics a great part was played by the θεοὶ λύσιοι.[13] In the Second Book of the "Republic," [14] Plato makes Adeimantos, performing the office of advocatus diaboli, urge in favor of being wicked and reaping its gains, that the penalties

---

[7] Liddell and Scott adduce ἵππον Xen. "An." 7. 8. 6; τὸ χωρίον Dem. 1215.20.

[8] Liddell and Scott adduce "to buy from a pimp," Ar. "Vesp." 1353.

[9] Cf. the usages classified by Liddell and Scott under IV, V = e.g. "to atone for, make up for, like Latin luere, rependere," as "to atone for sins," "to pay wages in full, to quit oneself of them," in the sense of "loosing" an obligation. According to the Greek conception wrong-doing was inevitably followed by punishment. "On the other hand, the punishment itself was sometimes regarded as an expiation of the guilt. So the death of Laius' murderer was to 'loose' i.e., undo, the effect of the original deed (Sophocles, "Oed. Tyr." 100 f.); so the chorus pray that Orestes' deed, a just manslaughter, may 'loose' the blood of long past murders (Æsch. "Choeph." 803 f.; cf. Eurip. "Her. Fur." 40)" — Arthur Fairbanks, Hastings' ERE, v, p. 653a.

[10] E. g., Homer, "Il." xxiv. 655: "And there might be delay in the ransoming of the corpse (ἀνάβλησις λύσιος νεκροῖο)."

[11] E. g., Plato, "Rep." 364 E. where it is said that λύσεις καὶ καθαρμοὶ τῶν ἀδικημάτων — "expiations and atonements for sin" (Jowett) — are made by the Orphics both for the living and the dead. Cf. E. Rohde, "Psyche²," 1898, ii, p. 127 f.

[12] See E. Rohde, as cited, p. 50, note 2; and Roscher, "Ausführlices Lexikon der Griechischen und Römischen Mythologie," vol. ii, col. 2212.

[13] Cf. Rohde, as cited, p. 124.   [14] P. 366. AB: Jowett, ii, p. 187.

of wickedness may very easily be escaped: the gods can be propitiated, and so we can sin and pray, and then sin and pray some more, — and if you talk of a dread hereafter, why, are there not mysteries and λύσιοι θεοί to whom we can look for deliverance? The form λυτήρ obtained sufficient currency to render it possible for the Christian poet Nonnus, the paraphrast of John, to employ it as a designation of our Lord, whom he calls "the Deliverer of the whole human race (ὅλης Λυτῆρα γενέθλης)." [15] But Nonnus was somewhat precious in his choice of words.

The prepositional compounds are numerous and appear to have been in wide use to express the many modifications which the general notion of "loosing" was capable of receiving from them.[16] We are naturally most interested in those of them which are employed of releasing men from chains or bondage, or broadly from other evils. Among these the special implication of ἀναλύειν is that the release effected is a restoration. In ἐκλύειν — the exact etymological equivalent of the German *Auslösung* (or its doublet *Erlösung*, which has become the standing German designation of the Christian Redemption) — the emphasis falls on the deliverance which is wrought by the release in question, and this form tends to be employed when the idea of relief is prominent. It is, however, with ἀπολύειν — in itself a close synonym of ἐκλύειν — that we are most nearly concerned. It is employed alternatively with the simple λύειν, and like that term developed a discriminating use of the active and middle voices to express respectively releasing on the receipt or releasing by the payment of a ransom. Thus, like λύειν, it came to mean not merely releasing but distinctively ransoming, and is used in that sense of the action of both of the parties involved.[17]

[15] On Jno. xvii. 21: Migne, xliii, col. 888. Nonnus is ordinarily assigned to the end of the fourth or the beginning of the fifth century.

[16] Ἀναλύειν, ἀνάλυσις, ἀναλυτήρ, ἀναλύτης; ἀπολύειν, ἀπόλυσις; διαλύειν, διάλυσις, διαλυτής, διάλυτος, διαλυτικός; ἐκλύειν, ἔκλυσις, ἐκλυτήριος, τὸ ἐκλυτήριον, ἔκλυτος; ἐπιλύειν, ἐπίλυσις, ἐπιλυτέον, ἐπιλυτικός; καταλύειν, κατάλυσις, κατάλυμα, καταλυτήριον, καταλύτης, καταλυτής, καταλύσιμος, καταλυτέος, καταλυτικός; παραλύειν, παράλυσις, παραλυτέον, παραλυτικός; προλύειν, προλύται; ὑπολύειν, ὑπόλυσις.

[17] See Liddell and Scott, *sub voc.*, II. "In 'Iliad' always = ἀπολυτρόω [*to set at liberty*], to let go free *on receipt of ransom*, . . . 24, 115, al.: Med. *to set free*

The particular derivative of λύειν with which we are at the moment directly concerned — λύτρον — belongs to that class of derivatives usually spoken of as "instrumental," which denote the instrument or means by which the action of the verb is accomplished.[18] The particular actions expressed by the verb λύειν for the performance of which λύτρον denotes the instrument are those to which we have called especial attention above, — ransoming and atoning — the former regularly and the latter by way of exception. It commonly means just a ransom; infrequently, however, it means an expiation; [19] and very rarely it passes over into the general sense of a recompense.[20] "Λύτρον 'means of deliverance' (Lösemittel)," says Franz Steinleitner [21] quite accurately, "is employed by the old writers almost universally (mostly in the plural) in the sense of the ransom (Lösegeld) paid or to be paid for prisoners, in accordance with the use of λύειν for the liberation (Auslösung) of prisoners, especially by ransoming (Loskauf)." It is only a special application of this general sense when the word is found in use in inscriptions and papyri as the technical term for the manu-

by payment of ransom, to ransom, redeem, χαλκοῦ τε χρυσοῦ τ' ἀπολυσόμεθ' at a price of . . ., 'Il.' 22.50; so too in 'Att.,' ἀπολύεσθαι πολλῶν χρημάτων Xen. 'Hell.' 4.8, 21." Th. Zahn ("Römerbrief," p. 179, note 50) has a note illustrating this double usage of ἀπολύειν active and middle. Cf. above note 5.

[18] Cf. W. E. Jelf, "A Grammar of the Greek Language⁴," 1866, vol. i, p. 338 (§ 335, e): "Instrumental: (signifying the instrument or means by which a certain end is obtained) in τρον and τρα (contracted from τήριον, τήρια), as σεῖστρον, a rattle, δίδακτρον, schooling-money, λοῦτρον, bathing-water, bath." Cf. G. Hollmann, "Die Bedeutung des Todes Jesu," 1901, p. 104, note 2: "That λύτρον is derived from λύω is certain. From λύτρον is λυτρόω then formed like μετρέω from μέτρον. Compare further χύω, χύτρα, ἰάομαι, ἰατρός etc., Brugmann, "Griech. Gramm." 1900, p. 192 f. Numerous examples are given in Kühner-Blass, "Ausführl. Gramm. der griech. Sprache," 1892, iv. p. 271."

[19] Cf. H. Cremer, "Biblisch-theologisches Wörterbuch³," 1883 (cf. E. T., p. 408), sub voc.: "Meanwhile it should be taken into consideration that λύτρον in profane Greek denotes also the means of expiation with reference to the intended result as in Æsch. "Choeph." 48, λύτρον αἵματος, following λύειν, in the sense of expiatory acts."

[20] Liddell and Scott, sub voc.: "3. generally, a recompense, λύτρον καμάτων Pind. I. 8 (7). 1."

[21] "Die Beicht in Zusammenhange mit der sakralen Rechtspflege, in der Antike," 1913, p. 37.

mission-price of slaves.[22] Its occurrence on two late inscriptions of a piacular character found near Könes in Lydia, on the other hand, illustrates its less common use of a means, an instrument, of expiation.[23] Both of these are, however, only special applications serving rather to illustrate than to qualify the essential meaning of the term as just the price paid as a ransom in order to secure release.[24]

The formation of λύτρον was not due to any serious need of a term of its significance. It has synonyms enough.[25] Its forma-

[22] "The same word," continues Steinleitner, "in the plural, is employed in three documents of the first century after Christ, from Oxyrhynchus, in which slaves are emancipated; and stands in the same sense in the singular as well as in the plural in the Thessalian stone-records of slave-manumissions." He refers for the papyri to the "Oxyrhynchus Papyri," Part I, ed. by Grenfell-Hunt (London 1898) p. 105, no. XLVIII, . . . no. XLIX; Part IV (London 1904) p. 199, no. 722, line 24 f., line 29/30 . . . line 39/40; and also to L. Mitteis, "Papyri aus Oxyrhynchos," in "Hermes," vol. xxxiv (1899) p. 103 f. For the inscriptions he refers to Gualterus Rensch, "De Manumissionum titulis apud Thessalos," Dissert.-"Inaugural. Philologica," Halis Sax., 1908. Cf. also A. Deissmann, "Light from the Ancient East," (1910) pp. 324 ff., especially 331 ff.: he gives the literature.

[23] They are described and expounded by Steinleitner, as cited. The longer of the two inscriptions reads: "Έτους σκζ. Artemidorus, the son of Diodotus and Amia, together with his six kinsmen, witting and unwitting, λύτρον according to the command of Mem Tyrannos and Zeus Ogmenos and the Gods with him." Steinleitner explains: "They liberate Artemidorus and his kindred from the God to whom they have become indebted through a transgression, which had occurred partly wittingly and partly unwittingly, by means of a λύτρον to which the God had himself given the injunction through a dream-image or the mouth of the priest. This λύτρον consists in this case certainly not of money, but of the confession of guilt (Schuld) and the erection of the public expiatory monument." It is quite unnecessary, however, to labor to derive this expiatory usage of λύτρον from its use as the price of the manumission of slaves. The expiatory use was current from the days of Pindar and Aeschylus. What these inscriptions show is that λύτρον was in use not only of the emancipation price of slaves but also of the expiatory offering for guilt, until after the Christian era. Cf. also Deissmann, op.cit., p. 332, note 2.

[24] Stephanus' definition very fairly describes its fundamental significance: "Redemptorium, Redemptionis Pretium, Pretium redempti, sine adjectione, quod Bud. ex Livio affert; Quod pro redemptione dependitur, Pretium quo captivi redimuntur; ab ea sc. verbi λύεσθαι signif. qua ponitur pro Redimo."

[25] ἄλλαγμα, ἀντάλλαγμα, τιμή, ποινή, ἄποινα, ζωάγρια, ἀντίψυχον. Ἄποινα is regularly used in the "Iliad" in the sense of λύτρον, λύτρα; perhaps also in that of ζωάγρια; the verb ἀποινάω formed from it and used in the active of demanding the fine from the murderer, is in the middle the synonym of λυτροῦν to hold to ransom.

tion must be traced to the natural influence of its primitive, λύειν, dominating the mind when the idea of ransoming occupied it, and leading to the framing from it of derived vocables expressive of that idea. It "came natural" to a Greek, in other words, when he wished to say ransom, to say λύτρον, because when he thought of ransoming he thought in terms of λύειν. This is an indication of the strength of the association of the idea of ransoming with λύειν; but, after all, the idea of ransoming was connected with λύειν only by association. It was not the intrinsic sense of that verb but only a signification which had — however firmly — been attached to it by usage. Accordingly the process of word-formation which began with λύτρον did not stop with it. It went on and built upon it a new verb with the distinctive meaning of just ransoming, — λυτροῦν, λυτροῦσθαι, — which meant and could mean nothing but to release for or by a ransom.[26] If λύειν, by a convention of speech, had come to express the idea of ransoming, this remained a mere convention of speech: the word intrinsically meant nothing more than to loose, to release, and was used in this wider sense side by side with its employment in the sense of ransoming. But λυτροῦν meant intrinsically just to ransom and nothing else, and could lose, not the suggestion merely, but the open assertion of specifically ransoming as the mode of deliverance of which it spoke, only by suffering such a decay of its native sense as to lose its very heart. He who said λυτροῦν, λυτροῦσθαι said λύτρον, and he who said λύτρον not merely intimated but asserted ransom. The only reason for the existence of this verb was to set by the side of the ambiguous λύειν (ἀπολύειν) an unambiguous term which would convey with surety, and without aid from the context or from the general understanding ruling its use, the express sense of ransoming. We are not surprised to observe therefore that throughout the whole history of profane Greek literature λυτροῦν, λυτροῦσθαι

---

[26] Jelf, "Grammar," as cited, vol. i, p. 332 (§ 330, c): "Verbs in όω mostly from substantives and adjectives of the II. decl.; . . . have all a factitive meaning, *making to be* that which the primitive expresses, as πυρόω, *I set on fire* from πῦρ; χρυσόω, *I gild*, from χρυσός; δηλόω, *I make known* from δῆλος."

maintained this sense unbrokenly. Its one meaning is just "to ransom"; in the active voice in the sense of to release on receipt of a ransom, and in the middle voice in the sense of to release by the payment of a ransom. We could ask no better proof of this than that neither H. Oltramare [27] nor Th. Zahn,[28] both of whom have sought diligently, has been able to discover an instance to the contrary.

Of course the derivatives and compounds of λυτροῦν, λυτροῦσθαι continue to convey the idea of ransoming. Impulse for forming them could arise only from a feeling out for unambiguous terms to express this idea. For the wider notion of deliverance the derivatives and compounds of the primitive, λύειν, λύεσθαι lay at hand. Not many derivatives and compounds of λυτροῦν, λυτροῦσθαι seem, it is true, to have been formed, and those that were formed appear to occur only sparsely in profane Greek literature. Of the derivatives [29] we

[27] "Commentaire sur l'Épitre aux Romains," 1881, i, p. 308.

[28] "Römerbrief¹," p. 179. Zahn remarks that the regular meaning of the active λυτροῦν, ἀπολυτροῦν is *dimittere*, and of the middle λυτροῦσθαι, ἀπολυτροῦσθαι is *redimere*, the λύτρον being supposed in both cases. It is his view, however, that in the middle sense, "to ransom," the λύτρον may be neglected and the verb come to mean merely "to deliver." When he comes to give vouchers, however, (p. 181, note 52), he fails to find any in profane Greek for this loose sense. He cites indeed only three passages from profane Greek: Plato, "Theat.," 165. E; Polyb. 18 (al. 17), 16, 1; Plutarch, "Cimon," 9; all of which expressly intimate a ransom-price as paid. Plato, "Theat." 165. E (Jowett iii, p. 368): "He will have got you into his net, out of which you will not escape, until you have come to an understanding about the sum which is to be paid for your release." Polybius, 18 (al. 17), 16, 1 (Shuckburgh ii. 216): "King Attalus had for some time past been held in extraordinary honor by the Sicyonians, ever since the time that he ransomed the sacred land of Apollo for them at the cost of a large sum of money." Plutarch, "Cimon," 9 (Perrin ii. 432–433): "But a little time after the friends and kinsmen of the captives came home from Phrygia and Lydia and ransomed every one of them at a great price, so that Cimon had four months' pay and rations for his fleet, and besides that, much gold from the ransom (λύτρον) left over for the city."

[29] The Lexicons record no other uncompounded derivative as occurring in profane Greek except λυτρωτέον, Aristot. "Eth. Nic.," 9.2.4 (see next note). Other derivatives, for which no vouchers from profane Greek are given, include: λύτρωμα, from a Christian hymn — "the precious redemption of our Jesus"; λυτρώσιμος, Photius and Suidas, "redeemmable"; λυτρωτήριος, "Chron. Pasch.," "redeeming"; λυτρωτής, LXX. and Acts, "redeemer"; λυτρωτικός, Theodorus Prodromus, "of or for ransoming."

need concern ourselves only with λύτρωσις; of the compounds [30] only with ἀπολυτροῦν, ἀπολυτροῦσθαι and its derivative, ἀπολύτρωσις.

Λύτρωσις is so rare in profane Greek that it appears to have turned up heretofore only in a single passage, Plutarch, "Aratus" XI. There we read of Aratus that "having a present of five and twenty talents sent him from the king, he took them, it is true, but gave them all to his fellow-citizens who wanted money, among other purposes for the ransoming of those who had been taken prisoners (εἴς τε τἆλλα καὶ λύτρωσιν αἰχμαλώτων)."

'Ἀπολυτροῦν (active voice) occurs somewhat more frequently, but ἀπολυτροῦσθαι (middle voice) and ἀπολύτρωσις are again very rare. How the active, ἀπολυτροῦν is employed, may

---

[30] The Lexicons record such compound derivatives as the following: 'Ἀντιλυτρωτέον Aristot. "Eth. Nic.," 9.2.4: "But perhaps this is not always the case: for instance, must a person who has been ransomed (λυτρωθέντι) from robbers, ransom in return (ἀντιλυτρωτέον) him who ransomed (λυσάμενον) him, whoever he may be? Or should he repay him who has not been taken prisoner, but demands payment as a debt? Or should he ransom (λυτρωτέον) his father rather than the other? For it would seem that he ought to ransom his father even in preference to himself." Διαλύτρωσις, Polyb. 6.58.11: "But they frustrated the calculations of Hannibal and the hopes he had formed of the ransoming of the men" (there is no suggestion of mutual ransoming — "exchange of prisoners" we should say: on the contrary, it is a distinctly one-sided transaction, — the Romans were to pay three minae for each man); 27.11.2 (al. 14): "Just about the time when Perseus retired for the winter from the Roman war, Antenor arrived at Rhodes from him to negotiate for the ransom of Diophanes and those who were on board with him. Thereupon there arose a great dispute among the statesmen as to what course they ought to take. Philophenax, Theatetus and their party were against entering into such an arrangement upon any terms, Deinon and Polyaratus were for doing so. Finally they did enter upon an arrangement for their redemption." 'Ἐκλυτροῦσθαι, Scholium on Homer. "Odyss.," IV. 33: When princely Telemachus and the proud son of Nestor arrived at Menelaus' palace, Eteoneus asks whether they are to be received or sent about their business. Menelaus replies that of course they are to be received: they had themselves often had to depend on the courtesy of strangers, "and we must look to Zeus henceforth to keep us safe from harm." The Scholium explains this as meaning that they would have to hope, "that after these things he (Zeus) may deliver (ἐκλυτρώσηται) us from the impending distress." There is no obvious implication of ransoming here, but Liddell and Scott quite naturally define the word, with this sole voucher, "to redeem by payment of ransom." 'Ἐπίλυτρος, set at liberty for ransom, Strabo, ii, p. 496: "Ἃ δ'ἂν λάβωσιν ἐπίλυτρα ποιοῦνται ῥᾳδίως. Παραλυτρούμενος is given by Athenaeus Grammaticus, p. 368, as the name of a comedy by Sotades.

be seen from the following examples, which are all that the lexicographers adduce. Plato, "Laws," XI, § 919 A (Jowett, iv, p. 430): He "treats them as enemies and captives who are at his mercy, and will not release (ἀπολυτρώσῃ) them until they have paid the highest, most exorbitant and base price." The Epistle of Philip to the Athenians in Demosthenes 159, 15: "He put Amphilochus to ransom (ἀπολύτρωσε) for nine talents." Polybius 2.6.6: "They made a truce with the inhabitants to deliver up all freemen and the city of Phoenice for a fixed ransom (ἀπολυτρώσαντες)." Polybius 22.21.8: "On a large sum of gold being agreed to be paid for the woman, he led her off to put her to ransom (ἀπολυτρώσαν)." Stephanus adds that Lucian somewhere says of Achilles that "he ransomed (ἀπολύτρωσας) the body of Hector for a small sum."

For the middle, ἀπολυτροῦσθαι, only late passages are cited. Th. Zahn, however, remarks very properly,[31] that while "the middle ἀπολυτροῦσθαι is very rare, and is not to be found in the Bible," it nevertheless "lies in essentially the same sense as the middle λυτροῦσθαι at the basis of the use of the passive in Zeph. iii. 1 (iii. 3),[32] and in Plutarch, 'Pompey,' 24." In this passage of Plutarch [33] we read that Helo who had been taken captive by pirates "was ransomed (ἀπελυτρώθη) with a great sum." In these passages ἀπολυτροῦσθαι is the passive of the middle, not of the active, sense. The lexicographers cite only two passages in which the middle is actually found. Polyaenus, a Macedonian rhetorician of the time of Marcus Aurelius and Lucius Verus, relates how Aristocrates the Athenian, entering a Spartan port in a ship disguised as peaceful, was able by this ruse to slay some and to abduct others as prisoners, which last, he adds, "Aristocles ransomed with a great sum (οὓς πολλῶν χρημάτων Ἀριστοκλῆς ἀπολυτρώσατο)."[34] That is the manuscript

---

[31] "Römerbrief¹⁻²," p. 181, note 52.

[32] The LXX here reads, ὢ ἡ ἐπιφανὴς καὶ ἀπολελυτρωμένη πόλις — "Alas, the glorious and ransomed city." Oltramare (on Rom. 3.24) wishes to render, "relaxed, licentious." Morison supports Zahn quite properly in insisting on the sense of ransomed. [33] Reiske, p. 775.

[34] "Strategemata," v. 40: Ed. Mursinna, Berlin, 1756, p. 326. In a note it is said: "Read, Ἀριστοκράτης. For ἀπολυτρώσατο is not redemit, but pro redemptione

reading. Nevertheless the modern editors, adopting an emendation of Casaubon's, print 'Αριστοκράτης for 'Αριστοκλῆς. By this
correction the meaning of ἀπολυτρώσατο is transformed, and we
are made to read it, "Extorted a great sum for their ransom":
that is to say, the middle is given the active sense. This result
is unacceptable in view of the regular middle sense preserved
in λύεσθαι, ἀπολύεσθαι, λυτροῦσθαι implied for ἀπολυτροῦσθαι
in the passive use noted above, and actually appearing in the
middle ἀπολυτροῦσθαι elsewhere. It must be held questionable,
therefore, whether the text of the passage has been rightly
settled by the editors: we need a different subject or else a different voice for the verb. There can be no question that in the
only remaining passage in which it is cited, the Emperor Julian
uses ἀπολυτροῦσθαι in its expected middle sense, and as the
general equivalent of λυτροῦσθαι. "Whom, then," he says,[35]
"are we to regard as a slave? Shall it be him whom we buy for
so many silver drachmas, for two minae, or for ten staters
of gold? Probably you will say that such a man is truly a slave.
And why? Is it because we have paid down money for him to
the seller? But in that case the prisoners of war whom we ransom (λυτρούμεθα) would be slaves. And yet the law on the one
hand grants these their freedom when they have come safe
home, and we on the other hand ransom (ἀπολυτρούμεθα) them
not that they may become slaves, but that they may be
free. Do you see then that in order to make a ransomed man
(λυτρωθέντα) a slave it is not enough to pay down a sum of
money . . .?"[36]

exegit. Casaubon." Accordingly the Teubner Ed. 1877, edited by Melber, p. 270,
prints 'Αριστοκράτης in the text with the note, "'Αριστοκράτης Casaubon; 'Αριστοκλῆς
F." "F" is the archetype from which all extant MSS. are descended. It reads
'Αριστοκλῆς which Casaubon in the editio princeps (Lugdunum Batavorum 1589)
already suggested should be changed to 'Αριστοκράτης on the ground reported
above. Whatever may be the true reading, the reason assigned for the proposed
emendation is a bad one. For not only does the middle ἀπολυτροῦσθαι but the middle of the simple λυτροῦσθαι and the middles λύεσθαι and ἀπολύεσθαι before them,
all mean distinctly not put to ransom but ransom.

[35] "Sixth Oration, to the Uneducated Cynics": "Works," ed. by W. C.
Wright, 1913, vol. ii. p. 44; ed. Teubner, 1875. vol. i. p. 253.

[36] Stephanus cites also the late Christian writer Nicetas, "Paraphrasis [carm.
arcan.] S. Gregorii Naz," ed. Dronk, pp. 26. 221; i.e., Migne, "Patr. Graec." 38.

The noun ἀπολύτρωσις might express the action of either the
active or the middle of the verb from which it is formed.[37]
Zahn remarks:[38] "For the corresponding use of ἀπολύτρωσις"
— that is to say for the use of it in a sense corresponding to the
middle sense of the verb, "to secure release by paying ransom" — "it seems that undoubted examples are lacking. Polybius, 6.58.11; 27.11.3, uses διαλύτρωσις in its stead, and most
writers content themselves with λύτρωσις." This is already to
say that the use of ἀπολύτρωσις in this sense has the support of
its cognates; and certainly there is nothing in its own very rare
usage to object. The lexicons give, it is true, only a single instance of the word's occurrence — Plutarch, "Pompey," 24 [39]
— and in this instance it expresses the action of the active voice
of the verb.[40] "Music," we read, "and dancing and banquets
all along the shore, and seizings of officers and ransomings of
captured cities (καὶ πόλεων αἰχμαλώτων ἀπολυτρώσεις) were a reproach to the Roman supremacy."[41] Another instance, however, has turned up in an inscription from Kos of the first or
second Christian century, in which the word expresses the action

705. Nicetas simply speaks of what Christ did that he might redeem (ἀπολυτρώ-
σηται) men.

[37] Zahn, "Römerbrief ¹," pp. 179–181 says: "We must bear in mind that according as we take our start from the regular sense of the active λυτροῦν, ἀπολυτροῦν
(dimittere) or from that of the middle, λυτροῦσθαι, ἀπολυτροῦσθαι (redimere), the
derived substantive will designate either the action of him who discharges or releases from duress" (there should be added: "on receipt of a ransom") "him
that is in duress to him, or the action of him who by means of the payment of
a ransom, or else without such a payment" (there is no justification in profane
Greek for this last clause) "secures the release of one in duress to another, be it
person or thing."   [38] P. 181. Note 52.   [39] Reiske, p. 754.

[40] So it is rightly taken both by Zahn (p. 181, note 52) and Oltramare (i.
310).

[41] Liddell and Scott refer also to Philo, 2. 463 [Mangey], that is to say to
"Quod Omn. Prob. Liber," § 17. med.: "He judged a violent death preferable to
the life that was before him, and despairing of ransoming (ἀπολύτρωσιν), he cheerfully slew himself." Here ἀπολύτρωσις expresses distinctly the action of the middle
voice of the verb. In the account given by Aristeas in the earlier portion of his
letter to Philocrates (cf., also Josephus, "Antt." XII. ii. 2 ff.) of the liberation of the
Jews by Ptolemy Philadelphus, the changes are rung on ἀπολύειν, ἀπόλυσις,
ἀπολυτροῦν (20), ἀπολύτρωσις (12, 33) in the sense of securing release by payment
of a ransom. The transaction was not a mere liberation, but involved the payment
of a ransom — twenty drachmas for each (20 and 22), — the whole sum amount-

of the middle voice. The inscription is speaking of that form of manumission of slaves, very widely current after the period of the Diadochi and illustrated by a great number of inscriptions at Delphi, in which the slave really purchased his own liberty, but did so through the intermediation of priests so as ostensibly to be purchased by a god. The purchase money deposited in the temple for the purpose is called the λύτρον or λύτρα. In the inscription in question, those who perform the ἀπελευθέρωσις are instructed "not to make formal record of the ἀπολύτρωσις until the priests have reported that the necessary sacrifice has been made." [42] Both Deissmann and Zahn apparently suppose that the paralleling of ἀπολύτρωσις here with ἀπελευθέρωσις empties it of its specific meaning. This is obviously unjustified: the transaction was a manumission (ἀπελευθέρωσις) which took place by means of a payment (λύτρον, λύτρα) and was therefore, more exactly described, a ransoming (ἀπολύτρωσις). We are clearly to interpret: those who make the manumission are not to record the sale until the whole transaction is actually completed; and the two terms are respectively in their right places.[43]

ing to more than 400 talents (20): "More than 400 talents τῆς ἀπολυτρώσεως" that is to say "of redemption money," says Josephus (Niese III. 77, line 11). Cf. § 27 with Josephus XII. ii. 2 ad fin.

[42] A. Deissmann, "Light from the Ancient East," p. 331, note 4; cf., Th. Zahn, "Römerbrief[1]," p. 180, note 51. Both Deissmann and Zahn give the fundamental references.

[43] Naturally the details of the transactions in which slaves purchased their freedom varied endlessly. There are instances on record in which the money is paid down, but the manumission is to take effect only at some future time, say at the master's death. There are others in which the manumission is so far only partial that the slave remains bound to certain specified services. On the other hand there are instances in which the manumission is accomplished on credit, that is to say, it is enjoyed on sufferance until the price is paid in. This class of freedmen appears to have been known as πάλαι ἐλεύθεροι. "To such a suspended freedom," writes L. Mitteis ("Reichsrecht und Volksrecht," etc., 1891, p. 388), "must be reckoned the remission of the purchase money (Lösegeld) in the will of the master, as in the testament of Lyko ("Diog. Laert.," v. 61–64), where we read: Δημητρίῳ μὲν ἐλευθέρῳ πάλαι ὄντι ἀφίημι τὰ λύτρα [to Demetrius who is a πάλαι ἐλεύθερος I remit the purchase-money]; E. Curtius has already correctly recognized that a πάλαι ἐλεύθερος who is still in debt for his purchase money, is certainly no real freeman, but only a statu liber ("Anecdot.," p. 11)."

Throughout the whole history of the profane usage of the derivatives of λύτρον, we perceive, the intrinsic significance of λύτρον continuously determines their meaning.[44] This was to be expected. The case is not similar to that of such a word as, say, "dilapidated" in English which readily loses in figurative usages all suggestion of its underlying reference to stones; or even to that of such a word as "redeem" itself in English, which easily rubs off its edges and comes to mean merely to buy out and even simply to release. The bases of these words are foreign to English speech and do not inevitably obtrude themselves on the consciousness of every one who employs them. Λύτρον was a distinctively Greek word, formed from a Greek primitive in everyday use, according to instinctively working Greek methods of word-formation, carrying with them regular modifications of sense. No Greek lips could frame it, no Greek ear could hear it, in any of its derivatives, without consciousness of its intrinsic meaning. This is, of course, not to say that the word could not conceivably lose its distinctive sense. But in words of this kind the processes of such decay are difficult, and illustrations of it are comparatively rare; especially when as in this instance, the terms in question stand out on a background of a far more widely current use of their primitive in the broader sense. A Greek might well be tempted to use λύειν and its derivatives in the sense of λυτροῦν and its derivatives; and in point of fact he did so use them copiously. But it would not be natural for him to reverse the process and use λυτροῦν and its derivatives in the sense of λύειν. It may be natural for us, standing at a sales-counter, to say "I will take that," meaning to "buy"; but it would never be natural for us to say, "I will buy that," meaning merely to "take." In the group of words built up around λύτρον the Greek language offered to the New Testament a series of terms which distinctly said "ransom"; and just in proportion as we think of the writers of the New Testament as using Greek naturally we must think of them as feeling the intrinsic significance of these words as they used

[44] The only apparent exception which we have noted is the use of ἐκλυτροῦσθαι in a scholium on Homer, "Odyss.," IV. 35; see above, note 30.

them, and as using them only when they intended to give expression to this their intrinsic significance. It is safe to say that no Greek, to the manner born, could write down any word, the center of which was λύτρον, without consciousness of ransoming as the mode of deliverance of which he was speaking.

The fact is not to be obscured, of course, that the writers of the New Testament were not in the strict sense Greeks. At the most Luke enjoys that unique distinction; and even he may have been in the wide sense a Hellenist rather than in the strict sense a Hellene. The rest were Jews: even Paul, coming out of the Diaspora, yet was able to speak in Aramaic; and apart from him and the author of the Epistle to the Hebrews, they were all of immediate Palestinian origin and traditions. Moreover they all had in their hands the Septuagint version of the Old Testament and may be thought to have derived their Greek religious terminology from it. We must, therefore, ascertain, we are told, how the group of words built up on λύτρον are employed in the Septuagint before we can venture to pass upon the sense in which they are used in the New Testament. And in turning to the Septuagint, it must be confessed, a surprising thing confronts us. Words of this group are certainly employed in the Septuagint without clear intimation of ransoming. This remarkable phenomenon is worthy of our careful and discriminating attention.

II

A considerable number of words of this group occur in the Septuagint — λύτρον, [ἀντίλυτρον], λυτροῦσθαι, λύτρωσις, λυτρωτής, λυτρωτός, ἀπολυτροῦν, ἀπολύτρωσις, ἐκλύτρωσις. Some of these, however, occur very seldom, and only one, λυτροῦσθαι, is copiously employed.

'Αντίλυτρον was printed in some of the early editions at Ps. xlviii. (xlix.) 9, but has been eliminated in the modern critical texts.

Λύτρον occurs nineteen times and always, of course, in the quite simple sense of a ransom-price. H. Oltramare gives a very

good account of its usage.[45] "Λύτρον, usually in the plural
λύτρα, (= כֹּפֶר, פִּדְיוֹן, גְּאֻלָּה) [46] designates an indemnification, a
pecuniary compensation, given in exchange for a cessation of
rights over a person or even a thing, *ransom*. It is used for the
money given to redeem a field, Lev. xxv. 24 — the life of an
ox about to be killed, Ex. xxi. 30 — one's own life in arrest of
judicial proceedings, Num. xxxv. 31, 32, or of vengeance, Prov.
vi. 35, — the first-born over whom God had claims, Num. iii.
46, 48, 51, Lev. xviii. 15, etc. It is ordinarily used of the ransom
given for redemption from captivity or slavery, Lev. xix. 20,
Isa. xlv. 13, etc."

The adjective λυτρωτός occurs only twice, in a single connection (Lev. xxv. 31, 32), in which we are told that the houses
in unwalled villages and in the Levitical cities were alike at all
times redeemable (λυτρωταὶ διαπαντὸς ἔσονται: representing
גְּאֻלָּה).

The compound active noun, ἐκλύτρωσις, occurs only a single
time (Num. iii. 49): "And for τὰ λύτρα . . . thou shalt take
five shekels apiece . . . and thou shalt give the money to
Aaron and to his sons as λύτρα of the supernumerary among
them; . . . and Moses took the money, τὰ λύτρα of the supernumerary, for the ἐκλύτρωσις of the Levites . . . and Moses
gave τὰ λύτρα of the supernumeraries to Aaron and his sons."

The compound verb, ἀπολυτροῦν occurs twice, once in the
active voice (Ex. xxi. 8 [47] for the Hiphil of פדה) and once in

---

[45] "Comm. sur L'Épitre aux Romains," 1881, i. p. 308.

[46] כֹּפֶר six times: Ex. xxi. 30, xxx. 12, Num. xxxv. 31, 32, Prov. vi. 35, xiii. 8;
פִּדְיוֹן seven times: Num. iii. 46, 48, 51; Ex. xxi. 30; Num. iii. 49, Lev. xix. 20,
Num. xviii. 15; גְּאֻלָּה five times, Lev. xxv. 24, 26, 51, 52; xxvii. 31; also מְהִיר once,
Isa. xlv. 13. Cf. G. Hollmann, "Die Bedeutung des Todes Jesu," 1901, p. 102.
Hollmann notes that λύτρα occurs in the same sentence as the rendering both of
כֹּפֶר and פִּדְיוֹן in Ex. xxi. 30, "If there be laid on him a כֹּפֶר he shall give for the
פִּדְיוֹן of his life whatever is laid on him."

[47] A. Seeberg, "Der Tod Christi," p. 218 says that in this passage "the
master to whom the Israelitish maiden bought by him does not prove to be pleasing, is required הפדה, which the LXX translate ἀπολυτρώσει αὐτήν, and that of
course cannot mean, 'he shall buy her free' but only 'he shall free her.'" But
verse 11 opposes her going out for nothing, "without money," to the disposal of
her required in verse 8, — which therefore must be for money. Undoubtedly the
E. V. renders rightly: "Then shall he let her be redeemed," in accordance with

the passive voice (Zeph. iii. 1 (3) for the Niphal of נאל). In both instances the idea of ransoming is express; and, as Th. Zahn points out, the sense in which the passive is used in Zeph. iii. 1 (3) presupposes the middle, ἀπολυτροῦσθαι, in the sense of "to deliver by the payment of a ransom." Thus this verb bears the distinctive active and middle senses in the Septuagint which it and its congeners bear in profane Greek.

So far the Septuagint usage shows no modification of that of profane Greek. No modification can be assumed even with reference to ἀπολύτρωσις, the active substantive derived from ἀπολυτροῦν, ἀπολυτροῦσθαι. This term occurs only in Dan. iv. 32 (29 or 30) LXX in a context which at first sight might mislead us into giving it the undifferentiated signification of just "deliverance." "And at the end of the seven years," we read, "the time of my ἀπολυτρώσεως came, and my sins and my ignorance were fulfilled in the sight of the God of heaven." The "deliverance" here spoken of, however, must be held to be defined by the preceding context as resting on a "ransoming." There is a manifest reference back from this verse to iv. 24 where the king is exhorted to pray God concerning his sins and "to redeem (λύτρωσαι) all his iniquities with almsgiving." [48] No doubt the emphasis is thrown on the result of the ransoming, on the deliverance in which it has at last issued. This is doubtless the reason why the compound term is used here — ἀπολύτρωσις, — the ἀπό in which, signifying "away from," shifting the emphasis from the process to the effects. The two terms, λυτροῦσθαι, verse 24, and ἀπολύτρωσις, verse 32, are respectively in their right places.

When we turn to the verb λυτροῦσθαι itself and its two sub-

the proper sense of the active voice of the verb — "to release for a ransom." Joseph Wirtz, "Die Lehre von der Apolytrosis," 1906, p. 2 and p. 3, note 2 has the right interpretation.

[48] Cf. Dan. iv. 24, Theod.: "Therefore, O King, let my counsel be acceptable to thee and λύτρωσαι thy sins with almsgivings and thine iniquities with mercies to the poor." The Aramaic word rendered by λύτρωσαι here is p'rak — to take away: λύτρωσαι accordingly represents a term which does not specifically express a ransoming (cf. S. R. Driver in loc.); cf. note 56. Nevertheless the purchase price is expressed and therefore λύτρωσαι is appropriate.

stantival derivatives, λύτρωσις and λυτρωτής, we find ourselves in deeper water.

Λύτρωσις occurs eight times,[49] representing the Hebrew bases נאל and פדה, each four times. In four of its occurrences, it is employed in the simple literal sense of ransoming or redeeming (Lev. xxv. 29, 29, 48; Num. xviii. 16); and in yet another (Ps. xlviii. (xlix.) 8), — "the price of the redemption of his soul" — it is used equally of ransoming by a price, although now in the higher, spiritual sphere. In the remaining three instances an implication of a ransom-price is less clear: Ps. cx. (cxi), 9, "He sent redemption to His people; He commanded His covenant forever"; Ps. cxxix (cxxx), 7, "For with the Lord is mercy, and with Him is plenteous redemption"; Isa. lxiii. 4, "For the day of recompense (ἀνταποδόσεως) is upon them, and the year of redemption is at hand." Passages like these will naturally receive their precise interpretation from the implication of the usage of their more copiously employed primitive, λυτροῦσθαι.

Similarly the noun of agent, λυτρωτής, which occurs only twice (Ps. xviii (xix), 14; lxxvii (lxxviii), 35, representing נאל) — in both instances as an epithet of God, "our Redeemer" — will necessarily receive its exact shade of meaning from the general usage of its primitive, λυτροῦσθαι.

This verb, λυτροῦσθαι, occurs some hundred and five times. It usually has at its base either נאל (about forty-two times) or פדה (about forty times),[50] and rarely פרק (five times). Sometimes, of course, there is no Hebrew base (Sir. xlviii. 20, xlix. 10, l. 24, li. 2, 3; Zech. iii. 15; I Macc. iv. 11). It is employed in more than one shade of meaning.

First, it is used quite literally to express the redeeming of a thing by the payment for it of a ransom price. Thus, for example: Ex. xiii. 13, "Every one of an ass that openeth the womb, thou shalt exchange for a sheep; but if thou wilt not exchange, thou shalt *redeem* it; every firstborn of a man of thy sons, thou shalt *redeem*"; Levit. xix. 20, "If any one lie carnally

---

[49] We do not concern ourselves with Judges i. 15.

[50] For the Hebrew synonyms פדה and נאל, see R. D. Wilson, *PTR* July 1919, p. 431.

with a woman, and she is a house-slave, kept for a man, and she has not been *redeemed* with a ransom (λύτροις) and freedom has not been given to her, . . . they shall not be put to death, because she was not set free"; Num. xviii. 15–17, "And everything which openeth the womb of all flesh, whatsoever they offer unto the Lord, from man unto beast, shall be thine; nevertheless the firstborn of men *shall be redeemed* with a ransom (λύτροις), and the firstborn of unclean beasts thou shalt *redeem*. And its redemption (λύτρωσις) is from a month old; the valuation (συντίμησις) is five sheckels, according to the sacred sheckel — there are twenty obols." In this simple literal usage the word occurs about twenty-seven times; but it seems to be confined to Exodus (six times), Leviticus (eighteen times) and Numbers (three times).[51]

Sharply differentiated from this literal usage is a parallel one in which λυτροῦσθαι is applied to the deliverance from Egypt. Here there is at least no emphasis placed on the deliverance being in mode a ransoming. The stress is thrown rather on the power exerted in it and the mind is focussed on the mightiness of the transaction. This is so marked that B. F. Westcott is led by it to declare,[52] too broadly, of the use of λυτροῦσθαι and its derivatives in the Septuagint, that "the idea of the exertion of a mighty force, the idea that the 'redemption' costs much, is everywhere present." It is at least clear that the idea that the redemption from Egypt was the effect of a great expenditure of the divine power and in that sense cost much, is prominent in the allusions to it, and seems to constitute the central idea sought to be conveyed. The earliest passage in which this usage occurs is typical of the whole series: Ex. vi. 6, "Go, speak to the sons of Israel, saying, I am the Lord, and I will lead you forth from the tyranny of the Egyptians, and deliver (ῥύσομαι) you from your bondage and *redeem* (λυτρώσομαι) you with a high hand and a great judgment; and I will take you to myself for my people, and I will be to you a God and ye shall

[51] Ex. xiii. 13 bis, 15, xxxiv. 20 bis; Lev. xix. 20, xxv. 25, 30, 33, 48, 49 bis, 54, xxvii. 13, 15, 19, 20 bis, 27, 28, 29, 31, 33; Num. xviii. 15 bis, 17. Cf. Dan. iv. 24.
[52] "Hebrews³," p. 298, med.

know that I am the Lord your God which bringeth you out from the oppression of the Egyptians." Other examples are: Deut. ix. 26, "And I prayed to God and said, O Lord, king of the Gods, destroy not thy people and thy portion which thou didst *redeem*, and didst lead forth out of Egypt by thy great might and by thy strong hand and by thy high hand"; Neh. i. 10, "And these are thy children and thy people, whom thou didst *redeem* by thy great power and by thy strong hand"; Ps. lxxvi (lxxvii) 15, 16, "Thou art the God that doest wonders, thou didst make known among the peoples thy power, thou didst *redeem* with thine arm thy people, the sons of Jacob and Joseph." This usage of the deliverance out of Egypt in might lies in the Pentateuch side by side with the former, occurring in Exodus (three times), and Deuteronomy (six times), and occurs on occasion in the later books.[53]

Similarly to its employment to express the fundamental national deliverance from Egypt in the divine might, λυτροῦσθαι is used of other great national deliverances in which the power of Jehovah was manifested. In "the praise of famous men and of our fathers which begat us," that fills the later chapters of Sirach, the word is employed repeatedly in this sense: (xlviii. 20), "But they called upon the Lord which is merciful and stretched out their hands towards him; and immediately the Holy One heard them out of heaven, and *delivered* them by the ministry of Esay"; (xlix. 10), "And of the twelve prophets let the memorial be blessed, and let their bones flourish again out of their place; for they comforted Jacob, and *delivered* them by assured hope"; (l. 22, 24), "Now, then bless ye the God of all, which only doeth wondrous things everywhere. . . . That he would confirm his mercy with us and *deliver* us at his time." The general point of view finds clear expression in I Macc. iv. 10, 11, "Now, therefore, let us cry unto heaven, if peradventure the Lord will have mercy upon us, and remember the covenant

[53] Ex. vi. 6, xv. 13, 16; Deut. vii. 8, ix. 26, xiii. 5 (6), xv. 15, xxi. 8, xxiv. 18; II Sam. vii. 23 bis; I Chron. xvii. 21 bis, Neh. i. 10, Esther iv. 16, (9); Ps. lxxvi. (lxxvii.) 15, cv. (cvi.) 10, cvi. (cvii.) 2 bis; cxxxv. (cxxxvi.) 24; Mic. vi. 4 (Isa. lxiii. 9?).

of our fathers, and destroy this host before our face this day: that so all the heathen may know that there is one that *delivereth* and saveth (σώζειν) Israel."

Among these great deliverances wrought for Israel, the chief place is taken, of course, by its second great cardinal emancipation — that from the Babylonian captivity. The employment of λυτροῦσθαι to express this deliverance is naturally comparatively frequent, and as naturally it shades insensibly into the expression of the Messianic deliverance of which this liberation (along with that from Egypt) is treated as the standing type. We may find the key-note struck, perhaps, in Jer. xxvii. (l.) 33, 34: "Thus saith the Lord, Oppressed have been the children of Israel and the children of Judah: all they that have taken them captive, together oppress them because they refuse to let them go. And *their redeemer* is strong, the Lord Almighty is his name; he shall judge judgment with his adversary, that he may destroy the land and disquiet the inhabitants of Babylon. A sword is upon the Chaldeans and upon the inhabitants of Babylon! . . ." How close the eschatological application lies may be illustrated by Isa. li. 11–13 (9–11): "Awake, awake Jerusalem and put on the strength of thine arm; awake as in the beginning of day, as the generation of eternity. Art thou not she that dried the sea, the deep waters of the abyss? that madest the depths of the sea a way for the delivered (ῥυομένοις) and the *redeemed* to pass through? For by the Lord shall they return, and shall come into Zion with joy and eternal exultation." And we seem fairly on eschatological ground in Isa. xxxv. 9–10: "And there shall be no lion there, neither shall any of the evil beasts go up upon it, nor be found there, but the *redeemed* and the gathered on account of the Lord shall walk in it, and they shall return and come into Zion with joy and everlasting joy shall be over their heads." [54]

Not essentially different is the employment of the word to

[54] In this general class there may be counted such passages as Isa. xli. 14, xliii.14, xliv. 22, 23, 24, lxii. 12, lxiii. 9, Jer. xv. 21, xxxviii. (xxxi.) 11, Hos. vii. 13, xiii. 14, Mic. iv. 10, Zeph. (iii. 1) iii. 15, Zech. x. 8 and perhaps Ps. xxiv. (xxv.) 22, xliii. (xliv.) 26, lxxiii. (lxiv.) 2, cxxix. (cxxx.) 8.

express the intervention of God for the deliverance of an individual either from some great specific evil or from evil in general — the term rising in the latter case fully into the spiritual region. A couple of very instructive instances occur in the Septuagint: Daniel iii. 88, "Bless ye the Lord, Ananias, Adzarias and Misael, hymn and exalt him forever; because he liberated (ἐξείλατο) us from hades, and saved (ἔσωσεν) us from the bonds of death, and delivered (ἐρρύσατο) us from the midst of the burning flame, and *redeemed* (ἐλυτρώσατο) us from the fire"; vi. 27, "I, Darius, will worship and serve him all my days, for the idols made with hands cannot save (σῶσαι) as the God of Daniel *redeemed* Daniel." Quite similarly we read in II Sam. iv. 9 (and I Kings i. 29): "And David answered Rechab and Baanah his brother, . . . and said unto them, As the Lord liveth, who hath *redeemed* my soul out of all adversity"; and in Ps. cxliii. (cxliv.) 9–10: "O God, I will sing a new song to thee, . . . who giveth salvation unto kings, who *redeemeth* David his servant from the hurtful sword" (cf. vii. 2–3). "I will thank thee, O Lord King," says the son of Sirach in his concluding prayer (li. 1 ff.), "and I will praise thee, O God my Savior (σωτῆρα), I give thanks to thy name, because thou hast become my defender and helper, and hast *redeemed* my body from destruction, and from the snare of the slanderous tongue, from the lips that forge a falsehood, and hast become my helper against my adversaries and hast *redeemed* me, according to the multitude of thy mercies and name, from the teeth of them that were ready to devour me, from the hand of those that seek my life, from the manifold afflictions which I had. . . ." [55] The Psalms afford a number of examples in which this individual redemption in the region of the spirit is spoken of. The note that sounds through them is struck in Ps. xxxiii. (xxxiv.), 23: "The Lord will *redeem* the souls of his servants, and none of them that hope in him shall go wrong." [56]

---

[55] Cf. Ps. lviii. (lix.) 1, lxviii. (lxix.) 18, cxviii. (cxix.) 134.

[56] Cf. Ps. xxv. (xxvi.) 11, xxx. (xxxi.) 5, xxxi. (xxxii.) 7, xlviii. (xlix.) 15, liv. (lv.) 18, lxx. (lxxi.) 23, lxxi. (lxxii.) 14, cii. (ciii.) 4, cxviii. (cxix.) 154; cf. Lam. iii. 58.

The redeeming power in all this range of applications of λυτροῦσθαι is uniformly conceived as divine. It is to God, the Lord God Almighty, alone that redemption is ascribed, whether it be the redemption of Israel or of the individual, or whether it be physical or spiritual. God and God alone is the Redeemer alike of Israel and of the individual, in every case of deliverance of whatever order. We hear in Sirach, it is true, of the Holy One redeeming Israel by the hand of Isaiah (xlviii. 20); and indeed, in a somewhat confused sentence, of the twelve prophets, or of their bones, redeeming Jacob (xlix. 10) — or are we to assume that God is understood as the nominative of the verbs and read: "But God comforted Israel and redeemed them by the faith of hope"? There are besides two negative statements which may seem to imply the possibility of a human redeemer. The one is found in Ps. vii. 2–3, and the other, — a very instructive passage — in Lam. v. 8.[57] In Ps. vii. 2–3 David prays: "O Lord, my God, in thee do I put my hope, save (σῶσον) me from all that persecute me, and deliver (ῥῦσαι) me; let him not seize my soul, like a lion, while there is none to redeem (λυτρουμένου) or to save (σώζοντος)." In Lam. v. 8 we read: "Slaves, have ruled over us: there is none to redeem (λυτρούμενος) out of their hand." In neither instance is it intimated, however, that a human redeemer could be found: despair is rather expressed, and the cry is for the only Redeemer that can suffice. It is only in Dan. iv. 24 that we find a clear reference to a human redeemer. "Entreat him concerning thy sins and redeem thine iniquities with alms" (LXX); "redeem thy sins with alms" (Theod.). Here the king is exhorted to ransom his own soul by his good works. This conception, however, cuts athwart the whole current of the usage of λυτροῦσθαι in the Septuagint elsewhere when it is a matter of spiritual redemption. How little such a point of view accords with that elsewhere connected with λυτροῦσθαι may be learned from Ps. xlviii. (xlix.) 8–10:

[57] In both cases the Hebrew word rendered by λυτροῦσθαι is פרק, as it is also in Ps. cxxxv (cxxxvi), 24; cf. the corresponding Aramaic in Dan. iv. 24 (and Driver's note on it). On this word see Giesebrecht, ZATW, 1881, p. 285 and the note of Baethgen on Ps. vii. 3. It is literally "to snatch away," "to rescue"; cf. Brown-Driver in loc. Cf. note 48.

"A brother redeemeth (λυτροῦται) not: shall a man redeem
(λυτρώσεται)? He shall not give to God an expiation (ἐξίλασμα)
for himself or the price of the redemption (τὴν τιμὴν τῆς λυτρώσεως) of his soul though he labor forever and live to the end,
so that he should not see corruption." The sense of ὁ λυτρούμενος
in Prov. xxiii. 10–11: "Remove not the ancient landmarks and
enter not into the possession of orphans, for he that redeemeth
them is a powerful Lord, and judgeth thy judgment with thee,"
may be open to some question. It is probably the intention of
the Septuagint translators to intimate that the poor are under
the especial protection of the God who is the "redeemer" by
way of eminence of the needy.

The emphasis put upon the power of God manifested in
redemption which accompanies the entire usage of λυτροῦσθαι
except in its literal sense, may tempt us to suppose that the
notion of ransoming has been altogether lost in this usage.
This is in point of fact widely taken for granted. B. F. Westcott, for example, writes:[58] "It will be obvious from the usage
of the LXX. that the idea of a ransom received by the power
from which the captive is delivered is practically lost in
λυτροῦσθαι &c." Such a statement is in any case fatally defective. It takes no account of the large use of λυτροῦσθαι in the
Pentateuch in the purely literal sense (cf. Dan. iv. 24). It is
doubtful, however, whether it can be fully sustained even with
respect to the use of λυτροῦσθαι of the divine deliverance. No
doubt, as has already been pointed out, the sense of the power
of God exerted in the deliverances wrought by Him comes so
forcibly forward as to obscure the implication of ransoming.
This is pushed so far into the background as to pass out of
sight; and not infrequently it seems to be pushed not only out
of sight but out of existence. In a passage like Dan. iii. 88 LXX,
for example, there seems no place left for ransom-paying; and
the same may appear to be true of such passages as Dan. vi.
27 LXX, Lam. v. 8, Ps. vii. 2. Nor does the synonymy in which
the word sometimes stands encourage seeking for it such an
underlying idea: Ex. vi. 6, ῥύσομαι, λυτρώσομαι; Ps. vii. 2–3,

[58] "Hebrews[3]," p. 298.

σῶσον, ῥῦσαι, λυτρουμένου, σώζοντος; Ps. lviii. (lix.) 2–3, ἐξελοῦ, λύτρωσαι, ῥῦσαι; Ps. cv. (cvi.) 10, ἔσωσεν, ἐλυτρώσατο; Hos. xiii. 14, ῥύσομαι, λυτρώσομαι; Dan. iii. 88 LXX, ἐξείλετο, ἔσωσεν, ἐρρύσατο, ἐλυτρώσατο; Dan. vi. 27 LXX, σῶσαι, ἐλυτρώσατο; I Macc. iv. 10, 11, λυτρούμενος, σώζων.

Nevertheless, as Westcott himself perceives, there is an abiding implication that the redemption has cost something: "the idea that the redemption costs much," says he, "is everywhere present." Perhaps we may say that, in this underlying suggestion, the conception of price-paying intrinsic in λυτροῦσθαι is preserved, and in this the reason may be found why it appears to be employed only when the mind is filled with the feeling that the redemption wrought has entailed the expenditure of almighty power.

It is going too far, in any case, however, to say that the idea of ransoming "is practically lost in λυτροῦσθαι, &c." in their Septuagint usage — as, to be sure the insertion of the word "practically" may show that Westcott himself felt. Whatever may be the implications of λυτροῦσθαι when used to designate the intervention of God in His almighty power for the deliverance of His people, there is evidence enough to show that the feeling of ransoming as the underlying sense of the word remained ever alive in the minds of the writers. That could not in any event fail to be the fact, because of the parallel use of λυτροῦσθαι in its literal sense; we must not permit to fall out of memory that λυτροῦσθαι is employed in its literal sense in more than a fourth of all its occurrences in the Septuagint. Every now and then moreover the consciousness of the underlying sense of ransoming is thrown up to observation. This may be the case in a passage like Ps. lxxiii. (lxxiv.) 2: "Remember thy synagogue which thou didst acquire (ἐκτήσω = purchase) of old; thou didst redeem (ἐλυτρώσω) the rod of thine inheritance." It is more clearly the case in a passage like Isa. lii. 3: "Ye were sold for nought (δωρεάν) and ye shall not be redeemed (λυτρωθήσεσθε) with money." There is an intimation here that no ransom price (in the sense intended) is to be paid for Israel; its redemption is to be wrought by the might of

Jehovah. But it is equally intimated that a redemption without a price paid is as anomalous a transaction as a sale without money passing. That is to say, here is an unexceptionable testimony that the term λυτροῦσθαι in itself was felt to imply a ransom price. Another passage in point is provided by Ps. xlviii. (xlix.) 8: "A brother redeemeth (λυτροῦται) not: shall a man redeem (λυτρῶσεται)? He shall not give to God an expiation (ἐξίλασμα) for himself, and the price of the redemption (τὴν τιμὴν τῆς λυτρώσεως) of his soul, though he labor forever." To redeem is distinctly set forth here as the giving of a price which operates as an expiation: and the inability of a man to redeem a man out of the hand of God turns precisely on his inability to pay the price. Perhaps the most instructive passage, however, will be found in Isa. xliii. 1 ff.: "Fear not," Jehovah here says to His people, "because I have redeemed (ἐλυτρωσάμην) thee. . . . I have made Egypt thy price (ἄλλαγμα) and Ethiopia and Soene in thy stead (ὑπὲρ σοῦ) . . . . And I will give men for thee (ὑπὲρ σοῦ) and rulers for thy head." Such passages as these, it surely does not require to be said, could not have been written by and to men in whose minds the underlying implication of ransoming had faded out of the terms employed. They bear witness to a living consciousness of this implication, and testify that, though λυτροῦσθαι and its derivatives may be employed to describe a redemption wrought in the almighty power of God, that was not in forgetfulness that redemption was properly a transaction which implies paying a price.

III

The broader use of λυτροῦσθαι (λύτρωσις, λυτρωτής) by the Septuagint of God's deliverance of His people, may not unfairly be said to throw the emphasis so strongly on the almightiness of the power manifested as to obscure, if not to obliterate, intimation of its mode as a ransoming. The assumption is frequently made that this usage is simply projected into the New Testament and determines the sense of all the terms of this group which are found in the New Testament.

This assumption is met, however, by the initial difficulty that the usage of the New Testament is not even formally a continuation of that of the Septuagint. The usage of the Septuagint in question is distinctly a usage of λυτροῦσθαι, and affects only it and, to a limited extent, its two immediate derivatives, λύτρωσις (Ps. cx. (cxi.) 9, cxxix. (cxxx.) 7, Isa. lxiii. 4) and λυτρωτής (Ps. xviii. (xix.) 15, lxxvii. (lxxviii.) 35), which could not fail to be drawn somewhat into the current of any extended usage of λυτροῦσθαι. The more proper usage of other members of the group, and indeed even of these members of it in a large section of their employment, remains untouched. On the other hand, the usage of the New Testament is characteristically a usage of ἀπολύτρωσις, an otherwise rare form, which appears never to occur — itself or its primitive, ἀπολυτροῦν, ἀπολυτροῦσθαι, — whether in profane Greek,[59] or in the Septuagint,[60] or in writers directly dependent on the Septuagint,[61] in any other than its intrinsic sense of ransoming. It would be plausible to suggest that the Septuagint usage in question is continued in the λύτρωσις of Luke i. 68, ii. 38 and λυτροῦσθαι of Luke xxiv. 21 where redemption is spoken of on the plane of Old Testament expectation. But the suggestion loses all plausibility when extended beyond this. It would be more plausible to argue that the form ἀπολύτρωσις was selected by the New Testament writers in part purposely to avoid the ambiguities which might arise from the Septuagint associations clinging to λυτροῦσθαι. The simple fact, however, is that the characteristic terminology in the two sets of writings is different.

This formal difference in the usages of the two sets of writers is immensely reinforced by a material difference in the presuppositions underlying what they severally wrote. Whatever may have been the nature of the expectations which the Old Testament saints cherished as to the mode of the divine deliverance

[59] Plato, "Laws," 919. A; Demosthenes 159, 15; Polybius 2.6.6, 22.21.8; Lucian; Plutarch, "Pompey," 24; Polyaenus, "Strat.," V. 40; Julian Imp., "Orat., vi," Teubner I. 253; Inscription from Kos. The passages are given above.

[60] Ex. xxi. 8, Zeph. iii. 1 (3), Dan. LXX. iv. 24.

[61] Philo, Mangey, ii. 463; Josephus, Niese, III. 77. 11; Aristeas, Wendland, 4.12; 7.19; 12.8.

to which they looked forward, the New Testament writers wrote of it, as a fact lying in the past, under the impression of a revolutionary experience of it as the expiatory death of the Son of God. It would have been unnatural to the verge of impossibility for them to speak of it colorlessly as to this central circumstance, especially when using phraseology with respect to it which in its intrinsic connotation emphasized precisely this circumstance. We must not obscure the fact that something had happened between the writing of the Old Testament and the New, something which radically affected the whole conception of the mode of the divine deliverance, and which set the development of Jewish and Christian ideas and expressions concerning it moving thenceforward on widely divergent pathways. It may sound specious when the Jewish eschatological conceptions are represented as supplying an analogy, according to which the New Testament phraseology may be understood. We may be momentarily impressed when it is explained that, as the Jews have set the Messiah as the great Deliverer (גואל) by the side of Moses, the first Deliverer (גואל.הראשון), and expect him, as Moses led Israel out of Egypt, to achieve the final Deliverance (גאלה) and bring Israel home, without any interruption by an expiatory suffering and death, and merely by the power of his own personal righteousness,[62] — so we must understand the New Testament writers, borrowing their language from the Jewish eschatology, to ascribe to Christ merely the Messianic deliverance, without any implication that it is wrought by an act of ransoming. But we can be only momentarily impressed by such representations. Between the Jewish and the New Testament conceptions of the Messianic deliverance there is less an analogy than a fundamental contradiction. There had taken place, first of all, on the part of the Christians what it is fashionable to speak of as a "predating" of the Messianic expectations: the redemption of God's people does not wait, with them, for the end-time, but has already been in principle wrought and awaits only its full realization in all its

[62] Cf. F. Weber, "Jüdische Theologie auf Grund des Talmud und verwandter Schriften²," 1897, p. 359 f. (§ 79.2); also p. 361.

effects, in the end-time. And precisely what has already been
wrought, contributing the very hinge on which the whole conception of the Messianic deliverance turns, is just that act of
expiation which is wholly absent from the Jewish representation.
If, in other words, the Jews looked only for a Deliverance,
wrought by sheer power, the Christians put their trust precisely
in a Redemption wrought in the blood of Christ. Of course so
fundamental a difference could not fail to reflect itself in the
language employed to give expression to the divergent conceptions. And that, again, may be, in part, the account to give of
the adoption by the New Testament writers of the rare form
ἀπολύτρωσις instead of the more current λυτροῦσθαι colored by
Septuagint conceptions, to describe the redemption in Christ.
That they conceived this redemption in terms of ransoming is
made clear in any event by repeated contextual intimations to
that effect.[63]

[63] Even Johannes Weiss is constrained to allow that it is probable that the
idea of ransoming was felt in the New Testament usage, as appears from his very
instructive comment on I Cor. i. 30: "The σωτηρία, the ζωή, is the benefit which is
obtained for us by the ἀπολύτρωσις. How far the conception of *ransom* is still felt
in this is not to be debated here. Paul thinks in our passage more of the *effect* than
of the *means* of the deliverance. But it is very probable (from passages like Gal.
iii. 13, I Pet. 1. 18) that this shade is still felt." How impossible it is to eliminate
the idea of purchase from the conceptions of the New Testament writers is illustrated by the admission by writers who argue for the wider notion of ἀπολύτρωσις
that it lies expressed in other language by the side of the general notion of deliverance expressed by ἀπολύτρωσις. This is done, for example, by A. Ritschl. It is
done also by H. Oltramare (on Rom. iii. 24): "That the idea of *ransom* is Scriptural," he says, "is incontestable; but who proves to us that ἀπολύτρωσις is the
equivalent of these expressions?" — that is to say, such as are found in Mt. xx.
28, I Tim. ii. 6, I Pet. i. 18, I Cor. vi. 20, Gal. iii. 13. Similarly B. F. Westcott
("Hebrews[3]," pp. 298–299), after arguing that the idea of ransom has faded from
"λυτροῦσθαι etc." in the LXX and its place has been taken by that of power, is disinclined to confine the expenditure which God makes in the New Testament conception to that of might alone. Love or self-sacrifice, he suggests, may be the
thing expended. He therefore remarks that in "the spiritual order" the idea of
deliverance must be supplemented by that of purchase; and he adduces the passages in which that is expressed. He concludes with the dictum: "The Christian,
it appears, is bought at the price of Christ's Blood for God." Like Ritschl he is
only concerned to show that the idea is not intrinsic in the term λυτροῦσθαι
(ἀπολύτρωσις): it is a fact that we are bought to God by the blood of Christ, but
this fact is not expressed by this term. The ingenuity required to validate this
position (see especially Ritschl here) is its sufficient refutation.

The attempts which have been made to construe the terms derived from λυτροῦσθαι, employed by the writers of the New Testament [64] of the deliverance wrought by Christ, as inexpressive of their intrinsic implication that the deliverance intimated was in the mode of a ransoming, were foreordained to failure in the presence of general considerations like this. H. Oltramare's extended discussion in his comments on Rom. iii. 24 is often referred to as a typical instance of these attempts.[65] This, however, is rather unfair to them. Oltramare's argument is vitiated from the beginning by failure to discriminate between the differing usages of the active and middle voices of the whole series of verbs, λύειν, ἀπολύειν, λυτροῦν, ἀπολυτροῦν by which the active means "to put to ransom" and the middle "to ransom." It loses itself speedily accordingly in mere paradoxes. Of course he cites no passages from the Greek authors in which any of these terms is employed without intimation of a ransom-paying: to all appearance such passages do not exist. He is compelled to rely entirely therefore on the Septuagint usage of λυτροῦσθαι mechanically treated. He allows, of course, that λυτροῦσθαι (with which he confounds also λυτροῦν) "signifies properly and etymologically to release, to liberate an object by giving to its holder or to one who has rights in it, a sum in return for which he desists from his possession, or from his rights, to *ransom*, to *redeem*." He very strangely, because it thus signifies "to secure a release by paying a ransom," sets it in contrast with ἀπολυτροῦν which he represents as meaning "to put to ransom," without observing that he has thus set the purely middle use of the one over against the purely active use of the other. Thus he parcels out between the two verbs the

[64] We remind ourselves that these include a somewhat rare use of λυτροῦσθαι itself (Luke xxiv. 21; Tit. ii. 14, I Pet. i. 18) and its derivative λύτρωσις (Luke i. 68, ii. 38, Heb. ix. 12), with a relatively large use of ἀπολύτρωσις (Luke xxi. 28; Rom. iii. 24, viii. 23, I Cor. i. 30; Eph. i. 7, 14; Col. i. 14, Heb. ix. 15, xi. 35). Λυτρωτής occurs Acts vii. 35, but of Moses, not of Christ. Λύτρον occurs at Mt. xx. 28, Mark x. 45, and ἀντίλυτρον at I Tim. ii. 6.

[65] E.g. by Sanday-Headlam, on Rom. iii. 24, whose own conclusion is that "the idea of the λύτρον retains its full force, that it is identical with the τιμή, and that both are ways of describing the Death of Christ. The emphasis is on the *cost* of man's redemption."

distinctive usages which obtain between the active and middle of each of them. "'Ἀπολυτρόω," he says, "does not have the sense of the simple verb, 'to ransom' = redimere: we do not know a single example of it. The prefix ἀπό (as in ἀπολύω, ἀφίημι) so emphasizes the idea of liberating, delivering, that in profane authors, ἀπολυτροῦν signifies properly to *release* for a ransom, to hold to ransom." Even this is not all. For he now proceeds to conclude that "ἀπολύτρωσις designates therefore the action of releasing for a demanded ransom." "Its meaning is such," he continues gravely, "that if we absolutely insist on giving to ἀπολύτρωσις the sense of 'deliverance for ransom,' the expression διὰ τῆς ἀπολυτρώσεως τῆς ἐν Χριστῷ 'Ιησοῦ signifies 'by the *release*, the *ransom-taking* which is found in Jesus Christ' — that is to say that Jesus delivers us by demanding a ransom of us, far from by paying it for us." He sees but one way of escape from this conclusion. "Very happily," he concludes, "ἀπολύτρωσις is also used in the sense of *deliverance*, liberation, without any accessory idea of ransoming. All that it seems to have preserved of the radical is that it speaks principally of releasing from that which binds, confines, impedes, or shuts up." He has no evidence to present for this cardinal assertion, however, except the fact that Schleusner cites from the Old Testament the passage "χρόνος τῆς ἀπολυτρώσεως ἦλθε." As we know, this passage comes from Dan. iv. 32 LXX, where the context suggests that the deliverance had been purchased by almsgiving. To it Oltramare can add only certain New Testament passages in which he finds no accessory idea of ransoming notified. This is all quite incompetent.

Th. Zahn's discussion, distributed through his notes on the same passage, is free, of course, from such eccentricities, and constitutes in its several parts a careful presentation of all the evidence which can possibly be brought together for taking ἀπολύτρωσις in Rom. iii. 24 in the undifferentiated sense of deliverance. No evidence, of course, for this sense of the term is adduced from the usage of any derivative of λύτρον by a profane author: and no decisive instance is adduced from any quarter of the use of the term itself in this undifferentiated sense.[66] The force of the argument is dependent wholly on the cumulative effect of the discussion of the several terms λυτ ροῦσθαι, λύτρωσις, ἀπολυτροῦν, ἀπολύτρωσις successively. In these discussions the more utilizable passages from the Septuagint are skilfully marshalled; certain New Testament passages in which there is no express intimation in the context that the deliverance in question is a ransoming (as if the form of the word itself and its appropriate usage elsewhere counted for nothing!) are added; and a few Patristic passages are subjoined. Despite the thoroughness of the research and the exhaustive adduction of the material, the whole discussion remains unconvincing. The reader rises from it with the conviction that an unnatural meaning is being thrust upon the term on insufficient grounds, and that, after all is said, "redemption" continues to mean redemption.

  Much more formidable than either Oltramare's or Zahn's argument is that which is developed with his usual comprehensiveness and vigor by Albrecht Ritschl in the second volume of his great work on "Justification and Reconciliation." [67] Ritschl begins by speaking of the use of λυτροῦν and its derivatives by the Septuagint to render the Hebrew stems גאל and פדה. These stems, he remarks, had originally, like the Greek terms, the sense of delivering specifically by means of purchase. This im-

---

[66] The only vouchers cited (pp. 179–180, note 51) are Rom. viii. 23, Eph. i. 14, iv. 30, and Clem. Alex. "Strom." VII. 56, to which Dan. iv. 30 Theod: ὁ χρόνος τῆς ἀπολυτρώσεως is added p. 179, note 49. Clement, "Strom." VII. 10 (56) looks forward to a time when we shall live "with gods according to the will of God," "after we shall have been redeemed (ἀπολυθέντων) from all chastisement and punishment which we shall have had to endure as salutary· chastening in consequence of our sins." "After which redemption (ἀπολύτρωσιν)," he continues, "the rewards and honors are assigned to those who have become perfect, when they have got done with purification, and ceased from all service, though it be holy service, and among saints." They enter into eternal contemplation and receive the name of Gods and live with other Gods who have before been elevated to this condition by the Savior. Here the ἀπολύτρωσις is conceived as a release from punishment and the moment of thought is fixed on the final removal of the soul to its rest. It is an instance of the so-called "eschatological sense" of the term, and "deliverance" would convey the main thought. But it does not follow that the idea of ransoming is eliminated, or that the term ἀπολύτρωσις is not employed because this "deliverance" is felt to rest at bottom on a ransoming.

[67] Edition 3, 1899, pp. 222 ff.

plication of purchase had been lost, however, in usage. Their etymological implication was similarly lost, of course, by the Greek terms which were employed to render them, through an assimilation to the Hebrew terms which they rendered. These Greek terms came to the New Testament writers, therefore, with this broadened sense; and the New Testament writers naturally continued to employ them in it. If they are sometimes used by the New Testament writers in connections in which the original sense of purchasing might seem to be intimated, it is nevertheless not to be assumed that their original sense has reasserted itself. It is more natural to read them in these passages too in the broadened sense in which they have been inherited from the Septuagint. Paul, for example, must be supposed to have had the Hebrew in mind when he cited from the Septuagint, and to have taken from it his religious phraseology. This would hold him, when he used the Greek words, to the sense which they have as renderings of the broadened Hebrew terms. Of course, it may be argued that the Apostolic use of these words is rather controlled by our Lord's declaration that He came into the world to give His life as a ransom for many (Mark x. 45). But there is really no proof that this saying was known to Paul, to say nothing of its having determined the sense in which he employed terms only remotely related to the word used. The impression is left on the mind, rather, that Paul has chosen the compound term ἀπολύτρωσις instead of the simple λύτρωσις of the Septuagint, because by it the idea of separation from, or liberation, is thrown into great emphasis: he wishes, in a word, to say not ransoming but deliverance.

The steps in this argument are the successive assertions that: (1) The Hebrew words נאל and פדה had lost their original connotation of purchase; (2) The Greek words used to translate them must as a consequence have lost theirs; (3) The Septuagint usage of these Greek words must have extended itself into the New Testament; (4) The ordinary usage of these terms in the New Testament is in point of fact of this undifferentiated sort; (5) The instances of their use which do not seem of this sort must be nevertheless interpreted in harmony with this usage.

No one of these propositions is, however, unqualifiedly true. (1) Though the original senses of גאל and פדה — to redeem and to ransom [68] — are sometimes submerged in their figurative use, they are so far from being wholly obliterated that the words are copiously employed quite literally, and it is repeatedly made clear that even in the most extreme extension of their figurative use their etymological significance does not wholly cease to be felt. (2) The Greek terms fitted to these Hebrew terms seem to have been selected to render them because they were their closest Greek representatives in their literal sense. The use of these Greek terms to render the Hebrew is evidence therefore that they retained their fundamental meaning of redemption, ransoming; and though they naturally acquired from the Hebrew terms their figurative meanings when they were used to express them, there is no evidence that they ever really lost their native implications. It is misleading to speak of "the Septuagint usage" of these Greek terms, as if this "extended" usage were the only usage they have in the Septuagint. Λυτροῦσθαι, the most important of the Septuagint terms, is used in twenty-seven out of the one hundred and five instances in which it occurs in its literal sense of ransoming, redeeming; λύτρωσις is used in five out of its eight occurrences in the sense of redemption, ransoming; all the compounds derived from λυτροῦν are used solely in this sense. (3) In point of fact, the New Testament usage is not a "projection" of the Septuagint usage. The terminology of the New Testament is different from that of the Septuagint, and therefore the terminology of the New Testament was very certainly not derived from that of the Septuagint. Are we to suppose that the New Testament writers carried over the senses of the Septuagint terms without carrying over the terms which were the vehicles of those senses? The fundamental assumption, moreover, that the New Testament writers derived their whole phraseology from the Septuagint — Ritschl even speaks of Paul's "Greek

[68] Cf. Driver, on Deut. vii. 8.

speech, formed from the Septuagint" — cannot be justified. The Greek speech of the New Testament writers is the common speech of their day and generation and their terminology more naturally reflects a popular usage of the time. (4) It is not the fact that the ordinary usage of the derivatives of λύτρον in the New Testament is without modal implications. The contextual implications rather show ordinarily that the modal implications are present. (5) There is not only no reason why a broadened sense should be made normative for these derivatives and imposed upon them in defiance of their natural implication to the contrary, but in several instances they are so recalcitrant to it that it cannot be imposed upon them without intolerable violence.

A brief survey of the New Testament passages seems to be desirable in order to justify the last two of these remarks.[69]

Despite Ritschl's protest we must take our starting-point from our Lord's own description of His mission on earth as to give His life a ransom for many (Mt. xx. 28, Mark x. 45). This could not fail to determine for His followers their whole conception of the nature of His redemptive work.[70] We cannot be surprised, therefore, to find one of them, echoing His very words, describing His work as a giving of Himself as a ransom (ἀντί-λυτρον) for all (I Tim. ii. 6). Nor can we profess to be doubtful of his meaning when the same writer, writing at nearly the same time, but using now the verbal form, tells us that "our great God and Savior gave Himself for us that He might redeem (λυτροῦσθαι) us from all iniquity and purify unto Himself a people for His own possession, zealous of good works" (Tit. i. 14); or when another of the New Testament writers, closely affiliated with this one, and writing at about the same time, reminds the Christians that they "were redeemed (λυτροῦσθαι), not with corruptible things, with silver or gold, from their vain manner of life handed down from their fathers, but with precious blood, as of a lamb without blemish and without spot,

[69] For a fuller discussion of the implications of the New Testament usage, see the Article, "Redemption" in Hastings' "Dictionary of the Apostolic Church."

[70] Cf. A. Deissmann, "Light from the Ancient East," p. 331 and note 6.

even the blood of Christ" (I Pet. i. 18). There is in these passages an express intimation that the deliverance described by the verb λυτροῦσθαι as wrought by our Lord, was wrought in the mode of a ransoming. He gave Himself in working it. He gave His blood, as a lamb's blood is given at the altar. We cannot fail to hear here the echoes of His own declaration, that He came to give His life a ransom for many, or to perceive that the verb λυτροῦσθαι is employed in its native etymological sense of a deliverance by means of a price paid. It is not less clear that the noun λύτρωσις is used in the same natural sense in Heb. ix. 12, where, as in I Pet. i. 18, the blood of Jesus is compared with less precious things — here with the blood of goats and calves — and He is asserted, by means of this His own blood, to have "procured eternal redemption." No subtlety of interpretation can rid such passages of their implication of ransoming.

The specialty of the New Testament usage lies, however, not in these simple forms, but in the large use made of the rare compound substantive, ἀπολύτρωσις. This unusual form occurs seven times in the Epistles of Paul, twice in the Epistle to the Hebrews and once in the Gospel of Luke.[71] The preposition ἀπό ("away from") with which it is compounded, no doubt, calls especial attention to the deliverance wrought by the ransoming intimated; and we are prepared, therefore, to see this form used when the mind is directed rather to the effects than to the process of the ransoming.[72] That does not justify us, however, in supposing the term to declare the effects alone, with a total neglect of the process, namely ransoming, by which they are

[71] "This rare word," exclaims Deissmann (p. 331, note 2) "occurs seven times in St. Paul!"

[72] This is what Chrysostom means, in his comment on Rom. iii. 24, when he says: "And he said not simply, λύτρωσις (ransoming) but ἀπολύτρωσις (ransoming away), so that we come not again into the same bondage." Our ransoming *removed* us from the bondage under which we had suffered so that we were in no danger of falling back into it. Cf., R. C. Trench, "Synonyms of the N. T.," 1871, p. 273; A. Deissmann, "Light from the Ancient East," p. 331, note 3. This is probably also all that Theophylact means when he defines ἀπολύτρωσις as "recall (ἐπανάκλητις) from captivity," not intending to deny that a ransoming is intimated (as Trench and Deissmann suppose) but emphasizing the reference to the effects of the transaction.

attained. In point of fact, in a number of instances the deliverance declared is in one way or another distinctly defined by the context as having been obtained by the payment of a price. Thus, in Heb. ix. 15, we are told that this deliverance was wrought by a death; in Eph. i. 7 by the blood of Christ; in Rom. iii. 24 by His being offered as a propitiatory sacrifice.

The implications of the term being fixed by its usage in such passages, it is necessarily interpreted in accordance with them on the other occasions where it occurs. Some of these are so closely connected with these normative passages, indeed, as to be inevitably carried on with them in the same sense. Thus Eph. i. 14 must be read in connection with Eph. i. 7; and Col. i. 14 but repeats Eph. i. 14 and cannot bear a different meaning. From these passages, however, we learn that the effects of the ransoming intimated by ἀπολύτρωσις stretch into the far future and are not all reaped until the end itself. Thus the key is given us for the understanding of it in its "eschatological" application, as it occurs in Luke xxi. 28, Rom. viii. 33, Eph. iv. 30.[73] In such passages the ultimate effects of the ransoming wrought by Jesus in His death are spoken of, not some new and different deliverance, unconnected with that ransoming or with any ransoming, and most certainly not some ransoming distinct from that. The mind of the writer is on the death of Christ as the procuring cause of the deliverance which he is representing by his employment of this term as obtained only at such a cost.

No doubt there are a couple of passages in which there is

---

[73] Cf. J. B. Lightfoot's comment on Eph. 1. 7: — "The ἀπολύτρωσις may be two-fold: (1) it may be *initial* and *immediate*, the liberation from the consequences of past sin and the inauguration of a new and independent life, as here: so Rom. iii. 24, I Cor. i. 30, Col. i. 14, Heb. ix. 15; or (2) *future* and *final*, the ultimate emancipation from the power of evil in all its forms, as in Luke xxi. 28. . . . Rom. viii. 23; comp. Heb. xi. 35. In the latter sense it is used below, ver. 14, and iv. 30. . . ." The point to be emphasized is that the only difference between these two classes of passages concerns the particular effects of the one "ransoming" by the blood of Christ which are for the moment engaging the mind of the writer as he thinks of what Christ has ransomed us *away from*. There is no specifically "eschatological sense" of ἀπολύτρωσις; there is only an eschatological application of the ransoming which has been wrought by Christ's gift of Himself.

less to go upon. There is nothing in I Cor. i. 30, for example,[74] which would independently fix the sense of the term as there used. But it is unnecessary that there should be, in the presence of so firmly established a significance for it. We must, of course, read it here in accordance with its etymological implications supported by its usage elsewhere: particularly in a writer like Paul whose whole thought of "redemption" is coloured through and through with the blood of Christ.[75] And there is certainly no reason why we should not conceive the deliverance spoken of in Heb. xi. 35 as one to be purchased by some price which the victims were unwilling to pay. That is indeed implied in the declaration that they would not accept deliverance, because they were looking for a better resurrection. Does it not mean that they would not accept deliverance, on the terms, say, apostasy, on which alone it could be had? It is quite clear in sum that ἀπολύτρωσις in the New Testament is conceived, in accordance with its native connotation, and its usage elsewhere, distinctly as a ransoming; and that that implication must be read in it on every occasion of its occurrence.

There remain, to be sure, three or four instances of the occurrence of the simple forms — λυτροῦσθαι Luke xxiv. 21, λύτρωσις Luke i. 68, ii. 38, λυτρωτής Acts vii. 35 — all in writings of Luke — which have the peculiarity of standing on the plane of the Old Testament dispensation, and of being consequently unaffected in their suggestions by the new revelation which had come in the ransoming death of Christ. When Zacharias blessed the Lord, the God of Israel, because in the promise to him of a son, He had "visited and brought redemption for His people" (Luke i. 68); when Anna spoke of God "to all those that were looking for the redemption of Jerusalem" (Luke ii. 38); when the two disciples, on their journey to Emmaus, bewailed to one another the death of Jesus, because they had

---

[74] Cf. Johannes Weiss' comment on this passage.

[75] G. P. Wetter, "Charis," 1913, p. 21, says strikingly: "Something great, something not to be understood, has happened to all men. And this great thing is an act of God, an ἀπολύτρωσις, a ransoming, of course out of the earlier condition of wrath and condemnation, and that means with Paul that it happened on the cross."

hoped that "it was He that should redeem Israel" — it is clear
enough that we are still on Old Testament ground. The redemptive "death which Jesus was to accomplish at Jerusalem" is
not in sight to illuminate and give precision to the ideas which
inform the language. In these passages, belonging to the dawn
of the new dispensation, the usage of the Septuagint may not
unnaturally be thought to prolong itself. And this point of
view may, no doubt, not unnaturally be extended to such a passage as Acts vii. 35, where Moses, thought of as a type of Christ,
is called a "redeemer." Even this is not to say, however, that
λυτροῦσθαι, λύτρωσις, λυτρωτής stand in these passages wholly
without implication of ransoming. As they were written down
by Luke, they doubtless were written down with Calvary read
into their heart. As they were originally spoken they were doubtless informed with longings which though surer of the deliverance promised than instructed in the precise manner in which it
should be wrought, were not without some premonitions, vague
and unformed, perhaps, that it would be costly. Those who
spoke these words were not mere Jews (as we might say); they
were the "quiet in the land" whose hearts were instructed
above their fellows. After all, the main fact is that in the Old
Testament, and in these few echoes of the Old Testament usage
"in the beginnings of the Gospel," before the light of the cross
had shined upon the world, the great deliverance which was
longed for from God, was spoken of, not in the use of terms
which expressed merely deliverance — of which plenty to
choose from lay at hand — but in the use of terms which
enshrined in their heart the conception of ransoming.

Whatever we may think, however, of these few phrases
preserved by Luke from the speech of men still only looking
forward to the Gospel, they obviously stand apart from the
general New Testament usage. That usage, whether of λυτροῦσθαι (Tit. ii. 14, I Pet. i. 18), λύτρωσις (Heb. ix. 12), or of
ἀπολύτρωσις (Luke xxi. Rom. iii. 24, viii. 23, I Cor. i. 30, Eph.
i. 7, 14, iv. 30, Col. i. 14, Heb. ix. 15, xi. 35), is very distinctly
a usage in which the native sense of this group of words — the
express sense of ransoming — is clearly preserved. We shall

not do justice to the New Testament use of these terms unless we read them in every instance of their occurrence as intimating that the deliverance which they assert has been accomplished, in accordance with the native sense of the words in which it is expressed, by means of a ransom-paying.

IV

It is not of large importance, but it is not without an interest of its own to observe how this group of terms is used in the earliest Patristic literature. Three currents of inheritance unite here, and the effect is naturally to impart to the resultant usage a certain lack of consistency and sureness. There was the general Greek tradition, which gave to all the members of the group the uniform connotation of ransoming. There was the Septuagint modification of the simple terms, which wrought the more powerfully because the Septuagint supplied a rich body of quotable passages that were everywhere employed as vehicles of Christian faith and hope. And there was the New Testament usage in which the deliverance wrought by Christ is distinctly presented as a ransoming, but in which also a certain tendency is manifested to throw the emphasis on the effects of this ransoming and especially on its ultimate effect in delivering us from the wrath of God at the end-time. We can observe the influence of all these currents at work.

In the first age, to be sure, there is no very copious use made of this group of terms. Only λύτρον, λυτροῦσθαι and λύτρωσις occur, for example, in the Apostolic Fathers; and they only sparingly.

Λύτρον occurs twice and in both instances, of course, in its natural sense of "ransom." "Thou shalt work with thy hands," says Barnabas (xix. 10), commanding diligence in business, "for a ransom for thy sins." And in the Epistle to Diognetus, the greatness and power of God in our salvation is beautifully praised because "in pity He took upon Himself our sins and Himself parted with His own Son as a ransom for us, the holy for the lawless, the guiltless for the evil, the just for the unjust, the incorruptible for the corruptible, the immortal for the mortal."

Λυτροῦσθαι occurs nine times. In some of these occurrences, it has reference to human rather than divine acts. One of these is I Clem. lv. "Many among ourselves have delivered themselves to bondage that they might ransom others." The native notion of ransoming intrinsic to the verb is here expressed very purely. This note is less clearly struck in Hermas, "Mand.," viii. 10. Hermas is giving a catalogue of Christian duties. "Hear now what follow upon these," he says: "To minister to widows, to visit the orphans and the needy, to ransom the servants of God from their afflictions, to be hospitable." And the note of ransoming appears to have sunk into silence in another passage of Hermas ("Vis.," iv. 1, 7). Pursued by a dreadful beast, he says, "And I began to cry and to beseech the Lord that He would deliver me from him." Dependence appears to be put on the might of God.

In none of these instances is there reference to the great normal deliverance which the redemption of God is. This is spoken of, however, in Ignatius' Christ-like prayer for the persecutors of his friends (Phil. ii. 1): "May those who treated them with dishonor be redeemed through the grace of Jesus Christ." And it is spoken of also in Barnabas' exhortation (xix. 2): "Thou shalt glorify Him that redeemed thee from death." Neither passage gives clear intimation of how the redemption spoken of is supposed to be wrought. Nor indeed does the earlier passage in Barnabas (xiv. 4–8) in which, within the space of a few lines, he uses λυτροῦσθαι of the saving work of our Lord no less than four times. We quote Lightfoot's version with its odd variations in the rendering of the term: "Even the Lord Jesus, who was prepared beforehand hereunto, that, appearing in person, He might *redeem* out of darkness our hearts which had already been paid over unto death. . . . For it is written how the Father chargeth Him to *deliver* us from darkness. . . . We perceive, then, whence we are *ransomed*. Again the prophet saith, . . . 'Thus saith the Lord that *ransomed* thee, even God.'" The citation at the end is from Isa.

xlix. 6 ff. where the Septuagint has ὁ ῥυσάμενος. Why Barnabas substitutes ὁ λυτρωσάμενος is a matter of conjecture. Possibly it was inadvertent. Possibly it was due to his having already written λυτροῦσθαι three times, and he adjusts his text to the language of the passage into which he brings it. Possibly he substitutes a term which more exactly describes what Christ actually did — Christianizes Isaiah's language, in a word. In the only remaining passage in which λυτροῦσθαι occurs in the Apostolic Fathers, II Clem. xvii. 4, it is used in the so-called "eschatological sense," illustrated in the New Testament by Luke xxi. 28, Rom. viii. 23, Eph. i. 14, iv. 30, Col. i. 14: "The Lord said, 'I will come to gather together all the peoples, tribes and tongues.' And He means by this the day of His epiphany, when, coming, He shall redeem us, each according to his works."

The only other form which occurs in the Apostolic Fathers is λύτρωσις and it occurs only twice (I Clem. xii. 7, Did. iv. 6, cf. Barn. xix. 10 as v.r. for λύτρον). In Did. iv. 6, the Christians are being exhorted to almsgiving, and quite after the Jewish fashion (cf. Dan. iv. 24 Theod.) the exhortation takes the form: "If thou hast aught passing through thy hands, thou shalt give a ransom for thy sins." Almsgiving is a means of securing deliverance: it is the purchase-price paid for immunity from deserved punishment. In I Clem. xii. 7, the scarlet thread which Rahab hung out of the window is declared to have showed beforehand that "through the blood of the Lord there shall be redemption unto all them that believe and hope in God." Here also the sense is distinctly that of ransoming, and the price paid for redemption is noted as Christ's blood.

This is rather a meagre showing for the currency of the language of redemption in the first age of the Church. The Apostolic Fathers are notable, however, for poverty of doctrinal content: perhaps it is only natural that this doctrine too finds only occasional allusion in them. We receive no impression that λυτροῦσθαι and its derivatives are employed as technical terms, as established vehicles of a definite doctrine. They appear to be cursorily used in the several senses and applications in which they would naturally suggest themselves to writers of the varied inheritance of these first Christians. The term which comes nearest to a technical term in the New Testament — Paul's ἀπολύτρωσις — does not occur here at all. And the terms that do occur are dealt with freely and librate in their suggestion between the two extremes of a strict ransoming and an undifferentiated deliverance — with the balance falling, as was natural, in the direction of the stricter signification.

When we advance to the next age — the age of the Apologists — we meet with similar phenomena, though for a different reason. Apologies are no more natural receptacles of doctrinal terms than practical letters. No single term of our group of words occurs in a single Apology of this epoch. The whole period would be barren of these terms were it not that the Dialogue between Justin and Trypho happens to have been written in it. It this Dialogue, λυτροῦσθαι appears seven times, and λύτρωσις, λυτρωτής and ἀπολύτρωσις each once. Here it will be observed, first in Christian literature, is our Lord called "Redeemer" (λυτρωτής). And here first in uninspired Christian literature does Paul's ἀπολύτρωσις reappear — and it does not appear here of Christ's redemption of His people to which usage Paul had consecrated it, but only of the redemption of Israel through Moses.

It is clear that the mind of this writer is not on these terms as technical terms for the Christian salvation, described in its mode. Of the ten passages in which they occur six are citations from the Old Testament: xix. 6 (Ez. xx. 12, 20), "That ye may know that I am God who redeemed you" (LXX: "who sanctifieth you"); xxvi. 3 (Isa. lxii. 12), "And he shall call it a holy nation, redeemed by the Lord"; xxxiv. 5 (Ps. lxxii. 14); "He shall redeem their souls from usury and injustice"; cxix. 3 (Isa. lxii. 12), "And they shall call them the holy people, redeemed of the Lord"; xxvi. 4 (Isa. lxiii. 4), "For the day of retribution has come upon them, and the year of redemption (λύτρωσις) is present"; xxx. 3 (Ps. xviii. (xix.) 15), "For we call him Helper and Redeemer (λυτρωτής)." In two more of them the allusion is not to the Christian redemption but to the Deliverance of Israel from Egypt: cxxxi. 3, "Ye who were redeemed from

Egypt with a high hand and a visitation of great glory, when the sea was parted for you"; lxxxvi. 1, "Moses was sent with a rod to effect the redemption ($ἀπολύτρωσις$) of the people; and with this in his hands at the head of the people he divided the sea."

Only two passages remain in which Justin uses $λυτροῦσθαι$ at his own instance of the Christian redemption.

The first of these is lxxxiii. 3. Here Justin is commenting on the Jewish attempt to interpret Ps. cx. 1 ff. of Hezekiah: "The Lord saith to my Lord, Sit at my right hand, till I make thine enemies my footstool. He shall send forth a rod of power over Jerusalem, and it shall rule in the midst of thine enemies. In the splendor of the saints before the morning star have I begotten thee. The Lord hath sworn and will not repent, Thou art a priest forever after the order of Melchizedek." He asks scornfully, "Who does not admit then, that Hezekiah is no priest after the order of Melchizedek? And who does not know that he is not the redeemer ($λυτρούμενος$) of Jerusalem? And who does not know that he neither sent a rod of power over Jerusalem, nor ruled in the midst of her enemies; but that it was God who averted from him the enemies after he mourned and was afflicted? But our Jesus. . . ." The reference to Jesus here is only indirect and the exact nature of the redemption spoken of is not clear.

The other passage, lxxxvi. 6, is clearer. It runs: "Our Christ by being crucified on the tree, and by purifying us with water, has redeemed us, though plunged in the direst offences which we have committed, and has made us a house of prayer and adoration." Here it is from sin that we are said to have been redeemed, both from its guilt and from its pollution. The redeeming act is seen in the crucifixion; while the cleansing by baptism is associated with that as co-cause of the effect. The whole process of salvation is thus included in what is called redemption; the impetration and application of salvation alike. There is a price paid; and there is a work wrought. So broadly does Justin conceive of the scope of $λυτροῦσθαι$.

We need not pursue the matter further. With Justin we are

already a hundred years later than the New Testament usage. We perceive that, under the varied influences moulding its usage, the idea of redemption in the early fathers is at once very deep and very broad. It has not lost the implication of ransoming with which it began, but it embraces the whole process of salvation, which, beginning with our ransoming by the precious blood of Jesus, proceeds with our purification from sin, to end only with our deliverance from the final destruction and our ushering into the eternal glory. The breadth of the reference is interestingly illustrated in the opening words of the beautiful letter of the Churches of Lyons and Vienne in Gaul. It is the New Testament word ἀπολύτρωσις which is used here. "The servants of Christ residing at Vienne and Lyons in Gaul," the letter begins, "to the brethren throughout Asia and Phrygia who hold with us the same faith and hope of redemption, peace and grace and glory from God the Father and Christ Jesus our Lord." [76] "Who have the same faith and hope in the redemption that we have" — οἱ αὐτὴν τῆς ἀπολυτρώσεως ἡμῖν πίστιν καὶ ἐλπίδα ἔχοντες.

Adolf Harnack [77] warns us against supposing that the terms σωτηρία, ἀπολύτρωσις and the like refer always — or regularly — to deliverance from sin. "In the superscription of the Epistle from Lyons, for example," he says, "it is manifestly the future redemption that is to be understood by ἀπολύτρωσις." Harnack's fault lies in introducing an illicit alternative. It is not a matter of *either* the redemption from sin *or* the future deliverance from wrath. Both are embraced. The writers of the letter speak not only of the common hope of redemption, but before that of the common faith in redemption: "to all that have the same *faith and hope* in redemption that we have." It is a redemption that has taken place in the past and that extends in its effects into the farthest future, of which they speak.

It was just this comprehensiveness of redemption, meeting all our needs here and hereafter, that filled the hearts of the fathers with adoring gratitude. They did not think of eliminat-

[76] Eusebius, H. E., V. 1. 3.
[77] "History of Dogma," E. T., i. p. 202 note (German ed., i. p. 145 note).

ing the fundamental ransoming in which it consisted on the
one side, because their outlook on its effects extended on the
other to the final deliverance from the wrath of God. There is
therefore a marked tendency among the fathers to speak of
Christ's work as double, past and future. Christ came, says Origen,[78] "in order that λυτρωθῶμεν καὶ ῥυσθῶμεν from the enemy"
— not for the one or the other, but for both. "Christ endured
death for our sakes," says Eusebius,[79] "giving Himself as a
λύτρον καὶ ἀντίψυχον for those who are to be saved by Him." He
died as a ransom certainly: but the salvation purchased by
this ransom-price works itself out steadily in its successive
stages unto the very end. This is the key to the "broad" use
of λυτροῦσθαι and its derivatives of the redemption that is in
Christ Jesus.[80]

[78] "Hom. XIV on Jer.," Ed. Klostermann, III. 116.1.

[79] Fragment on "The Theophany," Migne, xxiv. 633 B.

[80] We have no concern here with the Patristic doctrine of the ransoming
from Satan; see J. Wirtz, "Die Lehre von der Apolytrosis," 1906, on the early
history of that.

X

"REDEEMER" AND "REDEMPTION"

"REDEEMER" AND "REDEMPTION" [1]

There is no one of the titles of Christ which is more precious to Christian hearts than "Redeemer." There are others, it is true, which are more often on the lips of Christians. The acknowledgment of our submission to Christ as our Lord, the recognition of what we owe to Him as our Saviour, — these things, naturally, are most frequently expressed in the names we call Him by. "Redeemer," however, is a title of more intimate revelation than either "Lord" or "Saviour." It gives expression not merely to our sense that we have received salvation from Him, but also to our appreciation of what it cost Him to procure this salvation for us. It is the name specifically of the Christ of the cross. Whenever we pronounce it, the cross is placarded before our eyes and our hearts are filled with loving remembrance not only that Christ has given us salvation, but that He paid a mighty price for it.

It is a name, therefore, which is charged with deep emotion, and is to be found particularly in the language of devotion. Christian song is vocal with it. How it appears in Christian song, we may see at once from old William Dunbar's invocation, "My King, my Lord, and my Redeemer sweit." Or even from Shakespeare's description of a lost loved-one as "The precious image of our dear Redeemer." Or from Christina Rossetti's,

> "Up Thy Hill of Sorrows
> Thou all alone,
> Jesus, man's Redeemer,
> Climbing to a Throne."

Best of all perhaps from Henry Vaughan's ode which he inscribes "To my most merciful, my most loving, and dearly-

[1] From *The Princeton Theological Review*, vol. xiv, 1916, pp. 177–201. Opening Address, delivered in Miller Chapel, Princeton Theological Seminary, September 17, 1915. Some references and explanatory notes have been added.

loved Redeemer; the ever blessed, the only Holy and Just One, Jesus Christ, *The Son of the living God, and the Sacred Virgin Mary*," and in which he sings to

> "My dear Redeemer, the world's light,
> And life too, and my heart's delight."

Terms of affection gather to it. Look into your hymns. Fully eight and twenty of those in our own "Hymnal" celebrate our Lord under the name of "Redeemer." [2]

> Let our whole soul an offering be
> To our Redeemer's Name;
> While we pray for pardoning grace,
> Through our Redeemer's Name;
> Almighty Son, Incarnate Word,
> Our Prophet, Priest, Redeemer, Lord;
> To that dear Redeemer's praise
> Who the covenant sealed with blood;
> O for a thousand tongues to sing
> My dear Redeemer's praise;
> To our Redeemer's glorious Name
> Awake the sacred song;
> Intercessor, Friend of sinners,
> Earth's Redeemer, plead for me;
> All hail, Redeemer, hail,
> For Thou hast died for me;
> Let us learn the wondrous story
> Of our great Redeemer's birth;
> Guide where our infant Redeemer is laid;
> My dear Redeemer and my Lord;
> All glory, laud and honor
> To Thee Redeemer, King;
> Your Redeemer's conflict see;

[2] The references are (by Hymns and Verses): 52. 3; 54. 2; 59. 2; 73. 3; 147.1; 148. 1; 150. 3; 162. 4; 172. 6; 190. 1,5; 197.1; 216. 1; 218. 1; 239. 3; 276. 1; 293. 3; 300. 1; 311.2; 331. 3; 401. 4; 445. 3; 454. 3; 476. 5; 555. 1; 569. 3; 593. 2; 649. 2; 651. 1.

Maker and Redeemer,
  Life and Health of all;
Our blest Redeemer, ere He breathed
  His tender, last farewell;
Here the Redeemer's welcome voice
  Spreads heavenly peace around;
The church our blest Redeemer saved
  With His own precious blood;
The slain, the risen Son,
  Redeemer, Lord alone;
The path our dear Redeemer trod
  May we, rejoicing, tread;
Till o'er our ransomed nature
  The Lamb for sinners slain,
Redeemer, King, Creator,
  In bliss returns to reign;
O the sweet wonders of that cross
  Where my Redeemer loved and died;
Once, the world's Redeemer, dying,
  Bore our sins upon the Tree;
Redeemer, come: I open wide
  My heart to thee;
I know that my Redeemer lives;
For, every good
  In the Redeemer came;
A heart resigned, submissive, meek,
  My great Redeemer's throne;
Jesus, merciful Redeemer;
Father, and Redeemer, hear.

From our earliest childhood the preciousness of this title
has been impressed upon us. In "The Shorter Catechism," as
the most precise and significant designation of Christ, from the
point of view of what He has done for us, it takes the place of the
more usual "Saviour," which never occurs in that document.
Thus there is permanently imprinted on the hearts of us all,
the great fact that "the only Redeemer of God's elect is the

Lord Jesus Christ"; through whom, in the execution of His offices of a Prophet, of a Priest, and of a King, God delivers us out of the estate of sin and misery and brings us into an estate of salvation.[3] The same service is performed for our sister, Episcopalian, communion by its "Book of Common Prayer." The title "Redeemer" is applied in it to Christ about a dozen times:[4]

> O God the Son, Redeemer of the world;
> Our blessed Saviour and Redeemer;
> Joyfully receive Him for our Redeemer;
> Jesus Christ, our Mediator and Redeemer;
> The merits of our Saviour and Redeemer;
> O Lord, our Saviour and Redeemer;
> Jesus Christ, our only Saviour and Redeemer;
> Our Redeemer and the author of everlasting life;
> Our Redeemer and the author of everlasting life;
> O Lord our strength and our Redeemer;
> Only Mediator and Redeemer.

This constant pregnant use of the title "Redeemer" to express our sense of what we owe to Christ, has prevailed in the Church for, say, a millennium and a half. It comes with a little shock of surprise to learn that it has not always prevailed. In the first age of the Church, however, the usage had not become so characteristic of Christians as to stamp itself upon their literary remains. So far as appears, the first occurrence of the epithet "Redeemer" as applied to Christ in extant Christian literature is in Justin Martyr's "Dialogue with Trypho the Jew," which was written about the middle of the second century.[5] And it does not seem to occur frequently for a couple of centuries more. This is not to say that it was not in use among

[3] Questions, 20 and 21.

[4] According to the concordance of the (American) "Book of Common Prayer," published by the Rev. J. Courtney Jones, 1898. The actual number, as will be seen, is eleven.

[5] "Dial.," 30. 3: "For we call Him Helper (Βοηθόν) and Redeemer (Λυτρωτήν), the power of whose name even the Demons do fear"; cf. 83.3 Justin is applying to Christ the language of Ps. xviii. 14 (LXX: E. V. xix. 14). Λυτρωτής occurs in the LXX only at Ps. xviii. 14 and Ps. lxxvii. (lxxviii) 35.

Christians during this early period. When Eusebius opens the tenth Book of his "Church History" with the words, "Thanks for all things be given unto God the omnipotent Ruler and King of the universe, and the greatest thanks to Jesus Christ, the Saviour and Redeemer of our souls," it is quite clear that he is not describing Christ by an unwonted name. Even more clear is it that Justin is not inventing a new name for Christ when he tells Trypho that Christians depend upon Jesus Christ to preserve them from the demons which they had served in the time of their heathenism, "for we call Him Helper and Redeemer, the power of whose name even the demons do fear." Indeed, he explicitly tells us that the Christians were accustomed to employ this name of Christ: "*we call Him Redeemer*" he says. Nevertheless it seems hardly likely that so little trace of the use of this designation would have been left in the extant literature of the day, if it had occupied then quite the place it has occupied in later ages. This applies also to the New Testament. For, despite the prominence in the New Testament of the idea of redemption wrought by Christ, the designation "Redeemer" is not once applied to Christ in the New Testament. The word "Redeemer" occurs, indeed, only a single time in the New Testament, and then as a title of Moses, not of Christ, — although it is applied to Moses only as a type of Christ and presupposes its employment of Christ.[6]

The comparative rarity of the use of this title of Christ in the first age of the Church is probably due, in part at least, to the intense concreteness of the Greek term ($\Lambda \upsilon \tau \rho \omega \tau \acute{\eta} s$) which our "Redeemer" represents, and the definiteness with which it imputes a particular function to our Lord, as Saviour. This gave it a sharply analytical character, which, perhaps, militated against its adoption into wide devotional use until the analytical edges had been softened a little by habit. A parallel may perhaps be found in the prevalence in the New Testament of the locution, "He died in our behalf" over the more analyti-

[6] Acts vii. 35; cf. H. A. W. Meyer and J. A. Alexander *in loc.* Christ is called "Deliverer" only once in the New Testament (Rom. xi. 26) and then by an adaptation of an Old Testament passage.

cally exact, "He died in our stead." The latter occurs; occurs frequently enough to show that it expresses the fact as it lay in the minds of the New Testament writers. But these writers expressed themselves instinctively rather in the former mode because it was a more direct expression of the sense of benefit received, which was the overpowering sentiment which filled their hearts. That Christ died instead of them was the exact truth, analytically stated; that He died for their sake was the broad fact which suffused their hearts with loving emotion.

The word "Redeemer" is of course of Latin origin, and we owe it, together with its cognates "redemption," "redeem," "redeemed," to the nomenclature of Latin theology, and ultimately to the Latin Bible. These Latin words, however, do not, at their best, exactly reproduce the group of Greek words which they represent in the New Testament, although they are underlaid by the same fundamental idea of purchase. Etymologically, *redimo*, 'redeem,' means to buy *back*, while the Greek term which it renders in the New Testament (λυτροῦσθαι) means rather to buy *out*, or, to employ its exact equivalent, to *ransom*. Our English word "ransom" is, of course, philologically speaking, only a doublet of "redemption." But, in losing the significant form of that word, it has more completely than that word lost also the suggestion that the purchase which it intimates is a re-purchase. It might have been better, therefore, if, instead of "redemption," "to redeem," "redeemed," "redeemer," we had employed as the representatives of the Greek terms (λυτροῦσθαι, λύτρωσις, ἀπολύτρωσις, λυτρωτής) "ransom," "to ransom," "ransomed," "ransomer."

Of these, only the noun, "ransom" has actually a place in the English New Testament, — in the great passage in which our Lord Himself declares that He "came, not to be ministered unto but to minister, and to give His life a ransom for many" (Mt. xx. 28 = Mk. x. 45), and in its echo in the scarcely less great declaration of Paul that the one mediator between God and men, Himself man, Christ Jesus, "gave Himself a ransom for all" (I Tim. ii. 6). Nevertheless these terms, emphatically defining, like the Greek terms which they represent, the work

of Christ in terms of ransoming, have made a place for themselves in the language of Christian devotion only a little inferior to that of those which somewhat less exactly define it in
terms of redeeming. The noun of agent, "Ransomer," is used,
it is true, comparatively rarely; although its use, as a designation of Christ, seems actually to have preceded in English
literature that of "Redeemer," or even of its forerunner, the
now obsolete "Redemptor." The earliest citation for "Redeemer" given by the "Oxford Dictionary," at all events,
comes from the middle of the fifteenth century [7] — of "Redemptor" from the late fourteenth [8] — while "Ransomer" is
cited from the "Cursor Mundi," some half a century earlier:
"Christ and king and ranscouer . . ." "Ransomer" is found
side by side with "Redeemer" in William Dunbar's verses at
the opening of the sixteenth century: "Thy Ransonner with
woundis fyve"; and is placed literally by its side by John Foxe
in the "Book of Martyrs" in the middle of that century, apparently as more closely defining the nature of the saving act
of Him whom Foxe calls "the onlie sauior, redeemer and raun-
somer of them which were lost in Adam our forefather."

The other forms have, however, been more widely used in
all ages of English literature. The character of their earlier use
may be illustrated again from William Dunbar who tells us
that "the heaven's king is clad in our nature, Us from the death
with ransom to redress"; or from a couple of very similar instances from even earlier verses. In one, Christ is described as
Him "that deyid up on the rood, To raunsoun synfull creature." [9] In the other He is made Himself to say

> "Vpon a crosse nayled I was for the,
> Soffred deth to pay the rawnison." [10]

Milton, our theological poet by way of eminence, not only
speaks of Christ as, in rising, raising with Himself, "His breth-

[7] "1432–1450, tr. *Higden* (Rolls) viii, 201: 'A man . . . havynge woundes
in his body lyke to the woundes of Criste, seyenge that he was redemer of man.'"

[8] "1377, Langland: 'And after his resurrecioun Redemptor was his name.'"

[9] "Oxford Dictionary," *sub voc.*: "1414, Brampton, *Penit. Ps.* (Percy
Society), 28." [10] "Political Poems," etc. (ed. Furnivale), p. 111.

ren, ransom'd with His own dear life," but discriminatingly describes Him as "man's friend, his mediator, his design'd both ransom and redeemer voluntarie." "We learn with wonder," says Cowper, almost in Milton's manner, "how this world began, who made, who marr'd, and who has ransom'd man." Or, coming at once to our own days Tennyson can put upon the lips of a penitent sinner, the desire to minister (as he expresses it) "to poor sick people, richer in His eyes who ransom'd us, and haler too, than I." Let us appeal, however, again to our hymns.

Surprisingly few instances appear, in the hymns gathered in our own "Hymnal" at least, of the use of the noun "ransom," for which direct warrant is given in the text of our English New Testament. Only, it appears, these three: [11]

> Father of heaven, whose love profound
> A ransom for our souls hath found;
> I'd sing the precious blood He spilt
> My ransom from the dreadful guilt
> Of sin and wrath divine;
> Jesus, all our ransom paid,
> All Thy Father's will obeyed,
> Hear us, Holy Jesus.

But as over against the dozen times that the word "redeemed" occurs [12] in this "Hymnal" we have counted no fewer than twenty-two times in which the word "ransomed" occurs. In a couple of these instances, the two words stand together: [13]

> He crowns thy life with love,
> When ransomed from the grave;
> He that redeemed my soul from hell,
> Hath sovereign power to save.

[11] 59. 1; 159. 2; 227. vi, 1. The verb "ransom," of course, also occurs (e. g. 141. 6); see below, note 14, for the form "ransomed."

[12] Redeemed, 55. 5; 88. 2; 130. 4; 150. 4; 172. 3; 236. 4; 336. 1; 383. 5; 396. 2; 453. 5; 546. 1; 642. 1. Consult, however, the following also: Redeeming, 81.1; 179. 3; 223. 5; 332. 2; 402. 2; 441. 4; 470. 2; 609. 1; Redemption, 141. 4; 152. 2; 258. 4; 259. 1; 264. 1; 265. 4; 394. 1; 395. 1; 406. 2; 435. 4.

[13] 130. 4; 453. 5.

And when, redeemed from sin and hell,
With all the ransomed throng I dwell.

The others run as follows:[14]

Then be His love in Christ proclaimed
  With all our ransomed powers;
Ransomed, healed, restored, forgiven,
  Who like me His praise should sing;
Sing on your heavenly way,
  Ye ransomed sinners, sing;
Ye ransomed from the fall,
  Hail Him who saves you by His grace;
Bring our ransomed souls at last
  Where they need no star to guide;
One, the light of God's own presence
  O'er His ransomed people shed;
A wretched sinner, lost to God,
  But ransomed by Emanuel's blood;
Thy ransomed host in glory;
My ransomed soul shall be
  Through all eternity
    Offered to thee;
Our ransomed spirits rise to Thee;
Let none whom He hath ransomed fail to greet Him;
When we, a ransomed nation,
  Thy scepter shall obey;
Till o'er our ransomed nature
  The Lamb for sinners slain,
Redeemer, King, Creator,
  In bliss returns to reign;
Till all the ransomed number
  Fall down before the throne;
Blessed are the sons of God,
They are bought with Christ's own blood,
They are ransomed from the grave;

[14] 132. 4; 134. 1; 154. 4; 157. 4; 189. 4; 303. 2; 325. 2; 354. 4; 375. 4; 390. 4;
395. 5; 399. 2; 401. 4; 420. 3; 421. 1; 441. 3; 444. 1; 512. 2; 636. 4.

> Till all the ransomed church of God
>   Be saved to sin no more;
> Thy blood, O Lord, was shed
>   That I might ransomed be;
> Where streams of living water flow
>   My ransomed soul He leadeth;
> His laud and benediction
> Thy ransomed people raise.

It does not appear, then, that Christian emotion would have found any more difficulty in gathering about the term "ransom" and its derivatives, and consecrating them as the channel of its expression, than it has found in gathering around and consecrating "redeem" and its derivatives. Had these terms taken their proper place in our English New Testament as the exact renderings of the Greek terms now less precisely rendered by "redeem" and its derivatives, and had they from the English New Testament entered into our familiar Christian speech, there is no reason to doubt that "Christ our Ransomer" would now be as precious to the Christian heart as "Christ our Redeemer" is. There is certainly no one who will not judge with old John Brown that "a Ransomer," especially one who has ransomed us "at such a rate," "will be most tender" of His ransomed ones;[15] and His ransomed ones, realizing what His ransoming of them involved, may be trusted — if we may take the language of our hymns as indications — to speak of Him with the deepest gratitude and love. Nor should we consider it a small gain that then the sense of the New Testament representations would have been conveyed to us more precisely and with their shades of meaning and stresses of emphasis more clearly and sharply presented. After all is said, the New Testament does not set forth the saving work of Christ as a redemption, but as a ransoming; and does not present Him to us therefore so much as our Redeemer as our Ransomer; and

---

[15] John Brown, "Life of Faith in Time of Trial and Affliction," etc., 1678 (ed. 1726, p. 161; ed. 1824, p. 129): "And sure a Ransomer who hath purchased many persons to himself, at such a Rate, will be most tender of them, and will not take it well, that any wrong them."

it is a pity that we have been diverted by the channels through which we have historically received our religious phraseology from the adoption and use in our familiar speech of the more exact terminology.

One of the gains which would have accrued to us had this more exact terminology become our current mode of speech concerning our Lord's saving action, is that we should then have been measurably preserved from a danger which has accompanied the use of "redeem" and its derivatives to describe it — a danger which has nowadays become very acute — of dissipating in our thought of it all that is distinctive in our Lord's saving action. We are not saying, of course, that "ransom," any more than other terms, is immune from that disease of language by which, in the widening application of terms, they suffer a progressive loss of their distinctive meaning. But "ransom" has, in point of fact, retained with very great constancy its intrinsic connotation of purchase. It may possibly be that, in an extreme extension of its application, it is occasionally employed in the loose sense of merely "to rescue." The "Standard Dictionary" gives that as one of its definitions, marking it as "archaic"; though the "Oxford Dictionary" supplies no citations supporting it. At all events, the word does not readily lend itself to evacuating extensions of application; and when we say "to ransom" our minds naturally fix themselves on a price paid as the means of the deliverance intimated. The word is essentially a modal word; it emphasizes the means by which the effect it intimates is accomplished, and does not exhaust itself merely in declaring the effect. The same, of course, may be said in principle of "redeem." But this word has suffered far more from attrition of meaning than "ransom," and indeed had already lost the power inevitably to suggest purchase before it was adopted into specifically Christian use. We shall not forget, of course, what we have just noted, that "ransom" and "redeem" are at bottom one word; that they are merely two English forms of the Latin *redimo*. It is, no doubt, inexact, therefore, to speak of the usage of the Latin *redimo* and its derivatives as if it belonged to the early history

of "redeem" more than to that of "ransom." Nevertheless it
is convenient and not really misleading to do so, when we have
particularly in mind the use of the two words in Christian devotional speech. "To redeem" has come into our English New
Testament and our English religious usage in direct and continuous descent from its previous usage in Latin religious
speech and the Latin Bible; while "to ransom" has come in
from without, bringing with it its own set of implications, fixed
through a separate history. And what needs to be said is that
"to ransom" has quite firmly retained its fixed sense of securing a release by the payment of a price, while "to redeem"
had already largely lost this sense when it was first applied in
the Latin New Testament to render Greek terms, the very
soul of which was this intimation of the payment of a price,
and needed to reacquire this emphasis through the influence
of these terms shining through it; and that it moreover continues to be employed in general usage today in very wide and
undistinctive senses which naturally react more or less injuriously upon the particular meaning which it is employed in
Christian usage to convey.[16]

The Latin verb *redimo* already in its classical usage was
employed not only, in accordance with its composition, in the
sense of "to buy back," and not merely more broadly in the
sense of "to buy," — whether to "buy off" or "to buy up";
but, also in more extended applications still, in the senses
simply of "to release" or "rescue," "to acquire" or "obtain,"
or even "to obviate" or "avert." It had acquired, indeed, a
special sense of "to undertake," "to contract," "to hire" or
"to farm." In accordance with this special sense, its derivative,
redemptor, in all periods of the language, was used, as the synonym of the less common *conductor*, of a contractor, undertaker,
purveyor, farmer, — as when Cicero speaks of the *redemptor*
who had contracted to build a certain column, or Pliny of the
redemptor who farmed the tolls of a bridge. When Christ was

---

[16] When R. C. Trench, "The Study of Words," ed. 15, 1874, p. 312, counsels
the school-teacher to insist both on the idea of *purchase*, and on that of purchasing
back, in all usages of Redemption, he is indulging in an etymological purism which
the general use of the word will not sustain.

called the *Redemptor*, then, there was some danger that the
notion conveyed to Latin ears might be nearer that which is
conveyed to us by a Sponsor or a Surety (the seventeenth
century divines spoke freely of Christ as our "Undertaker")
than that of a Ransomer; and this danger was obviated only
by the implication of the Greek terms which this and its companion Latin terms represented and by which, and the contexts
natural to them, they were held to their more native significance, not, indeed, of buying back, but of buying off. The persistence of the secular use of these terms, parallel with the
religious, but with a more or less complete neglect of their original implication of purchase — through the whole period of their
use in Latin, and later of the use of their descendants in English — has constituted a perpetual danger that they would, by
assimilation, lose their specific implication of purchase in their
religious usage also. Obviously in these circumstances they cannot throw up an effective barrier against the elimination from
them of the idea of purchase even in their religious applications,
on the setting in of any strong current of thought and feeling in
that direction. Men who have ceased to think of the work of
Christ in terms of purchasing, and to whom the whole conception of His giving His life for us as a ransom, or of His pouring
out His blood as a price paid for our sins, has become abhorrent,
feel little difficulty, therefore, in still speaking of Him as our
Redeemer, and of His work as a Redemption, and of the Christianity which He founded as a Redemptive Religion. The ideas
connected with purchase are not so inseparably attached to
these terms in their instinctive thought that the linguistic feeling is intolerably shocked by the employment of them with no
implication of this set of ideas. Such an evacuation of these
great words, the vehicles thus far of the fundamental Christian
confession, of their whole content as such, is now actually going
on about us. And the time may be looked forward to in the
near future when the words "Redeemer" "redemption" "redeem" shall have ceased altogether to convey the ideas which
it has been thus far their whole function in our religious terminology to convey.

What has thus been going on among us has been going on at a much more rapid pace in Germany, and the process has reached a much more advanced stage there than here. German speech was much less strongly fortified against it than ours. It has been the misfortune of the religious terminology of Germany, that the words employed by it to represent the great ransoming language of the New Testament are wholly without native implication of purchase. Redeem, redemption, Redeemer, at least in their fundamental etymological suggestion, say purchase as emphatically as the Greek terms, built up around the notion of ransom, which they represent; and they preserve this implication in a large section of their usage. The German *erlösen, Erlösung, Erlöser*, on the contrary, contain no native suggestion of purchase whatever; and are without any large secular usage in which such an implication is distinctly conveyed.[17] They mean in themselves just deliver, deliverance, Deliverer, and they are employed nowhere, apart from their religious application, with any constant involvement of the mode in which the deliverance is effected. One of their characteristic usages, we are told by Jacob Grimm, is as the standing expression in the *Märchen* for the act of disenchanting (equivalent to *entzaubern*); in such phrases, for example, as "the princess is now *erlöst*," "the serpent can be *erlöst* by a kiss," "at twelve o'clock they were all *erlöst*."[18] If you will turn over the pages of the brother Grimm's "Kinder-

---

[17] Kluge, in his etymological dictionary of the German language, under "er-," tells us it is the new-high-German equivalent of the old-high-German "ir-," "ar-," "ur-," and refers us to the emphasized "ur-" for information. Under that form, he tells us that "er-" is the unemphasized form of the prefix, and adds: "The prefix means *aus, ursprünglich, anfänglich*." Thus it appears that *erlösen* is a weaker way of saying *auslösen;* and the usage bears that out, *auslösen* tending to suggest "extirpation," *erlösen*, "deliverance." By this feeling, apparently, G. Hollmann, "Die Bedeutung des Todes Jesu," 1901, pp. 108–109, is led to parallel *Auslösung* with *Loskaufung* as strong terms in contrast with *Erlösung* paralleled with *Befreiung*. The Greek equivalents of *erlösen* and *auslösen* are ἀπολύειν and ἐκλύειν, both of which are found in the New Testament, but elsewhere in senses more significant for our purposes. In the Iliad ἀπολύειν (like the simple λύειν) bears even the acquired sense of "to ransom." It is interesting to note that in Job xix. 25, for "my Redeemer" (גֹּאֲלִי), the LXX reads ὁ ἐκλύειν με.

[18] "Deutsches Wörterbuch," iii, 1862, *sub voc.*

und Haus-Märchen," you will come about the middle of the book upon the tale of "The King of the Golden Mountain," and may read in it of how a young merchant's son comes one day to a magnificent castle and finds in it nothing but a serpent. "The serpent, however," we read on, "was a bewitched maiden, who rejoiced when she saw him and said to him, 'Art thou come, my *Erlöser?* I have already waited twelve years for thee, this kingdom is bewitched and thou must *erlösen* it.'" A still more instructive passage may be met with a few pages earlier, in the tale of "The Lark." There, when the traveller found himself in the clutches of a lion, he begged to be permitted to ransom *(loskaufen)* himself with a great sum, and so to save *(retten)* himself; but the lion himself, who was, of course, an enchanted prince, was — at the proper time and by the proper means — neither ransomed nor saved, but simply *erlöst. Erlösen, Erlösung, Erlöser* of themselves awaken in the consciousness of the hearer no other idea than that of deliverance; and although, in religious language, they may have acquired suggestions of purchase by association — through their employment as the representatives of the Greek terms of ransoming and the contexts of thought into which they have thus been brought, — these do not belong to them intrinsically and fall away at once when external supports are removed.

We cannot feel surprise accordingly, when we meet in recent German theological discussion — as we repeatedly do — an express distinction drawn between *Loskaufung,* "ransoming," as a narrow term intimating the manner in which a given deliverance is effected, and *Erlösung,* "deliverance," as a broad term, declaring merely the fact of deliverance, with no intimation whatever of the mode by which it is effected. Thus, for example, Paul Ewald commenting on Eph. i. 7, remarks [19] that there is no reason why ἀπολύτρωσις should be taken there as meaning, "ransoming" *(Loskaufung)*, rather than "in the more general sense of *Erlösung*," that is to say, of "deliver-

[19] "Kommentar zum N. T. herausgegeben von T. Zahn," x, 1905, p. 7 note. So also Zahn himself in vol. vi¹⁻², p. 181, note 52 (cf. also p. 179, note 50): "Accordingly, λύτρωσις, *Loskaufung,* Lev. xxv. 48, Plut. "Aratus," 11; in the wider sense, 'deliverance,' *Erlösung,* Ps. cx. (cxi.) 9, Lk. i. 68, ii. 38, Heb. ix. 12; I Clem. xii. 7."

ance." Similarly A. Seeberg speaks [20] of ἀπυλύτρωσις as having lost in the New Testament its etymological significance, and come to mean, as he says, "nothing more than *Erlösung*," that is, "deliverance." And again G. Hollmann declares [21] that the Hebrew verb פָּדָה while meaning literally "to ransom" (*loskaufen*), yet, in the majority of the passages in which it occurs, means simply "to liberate," "to deliver" (*befreien, erlösen*); that is to say, "to free," "to liberate," and not "to ransom," are in his mind synonymous with *erlösen*. We are not concerned for the moment with the rightness, or the wrongness, of the opinions expressed by these writers with respect to the meaning of the Biblical terms which they are discussing. What concerns us now is only that, in endeavoring to fix their meaning, these writers expressly discriminate the term *erlösen* from *loskaufen*, and expressly assign to it the wide meaning "to deliver," and thus bring it into exact synonymy with such other non-modal words as "to free," "to liberate." We may speculate as to what might have been the effect on the course of German religious thought if, from the beginning, some exact reproductions of the Greek words built up around the idea of ransom — such as say *loskaufen, Loskaufung, Loskaufer,* — had been adopted as their representatives in the pages of the German New Testament, and, consequent upon that, in the natural expression of the religious thought and feeling of German Christians. But we can scarcely doubt that it has been gravely injurious to it, that, in point of fact, a loose terminology, importing merely deliverance, has taken the place of the more exact Greek terms, in the expression of religious thought and feeling; and thus German Christians have been habituated to express their conceptions of Christ's saving act in language which left wholly unnoted the central fact that it was an act of purchase.

The way to the reversion which has thus taken place of late in German religious speech, from the narrower significance which had long been attached in Christian usage to the word *Erlösung*, "ransoming," to its wider, native sense, "deliver-

---

[20] "Der Tod Christi," etc., 1905, p. 218.

[21] "Die Bedeutung des Todes Jesu," etc., 1901, pp. 102, 108–109.

ance," was led — like the way to so many other things which
have acted disintegratingly upon Christian conceptions — by
Schleiermacher. So, at least, Julius Kaftan tells us. "Schleiermacher," says he,[22] "explained the peculiar nature of Christianity by means of the notion of *Erlösung*. Christianity is the
religion in which every thing is related to the *Erlösung* accomplished by Jesus of Nazareth. It dates from this that the word
is employed by us in a comprehensive sense. We say of the Lord
that He is our *Erlöser*. We sum up what He has brought us in
this word, *Erlösung*." Kaftan himself is of the opinion that
justice is scarcely done to the definition of Christianity when
it is thus identified with *Erlösung*, deliverance, taken in the
wide, undifferentiated sense given it by Schleiermacher, and
after him by the so-called "Liberal theology." A closer definition, he thinks, is needed. But it is very significant that he
seeks this closer definition by emphasizing not the mode in
which the deliverance is wrought, but rather the thing from
which the deliverance is effected. "The word *Erlösung*," he
says, "is of a *formal* nature. That it may have its full sense,
there must be added *that from which* we are *erlöst*." This he
declares is, in the Christian, the New Testament conception,
the world. And so, he goes on to assert with great emphasis,
"The fundamental idea of Christianity is *Erlösung* from the
world."

We are not concerned here with the justice of the opinion
thus expressed. We are not even concerned for the moment
with the assimilation which results from this opinion of Christianity with certain other religions, the fundamental idea of
which is deliverance from the world. We pause only in passing
to note that Kaftan explicitly admits that it was "the history
of religion which opened his eyes to the fact that in Christianity as in other religions of deliverance (*Erlösungsreligionen*)
Erlösung from the world is the chief and fundamental conception." What we are for the moment interested in is the clearness with which Kaftan ascribes to the word *Erlösung* the wide
sense of "deliverance," with no implication whatever of "ran-

[22] *Zeitschrift für Theologie und Kirche*, 1908, 18, p. 238.

soming." Christianity, it is said, like other religions of high grade, is an *Erlösungsreligion*, a religion of deliverance. "We have today," we read,[23] "attained a wider survey of the religious life of humanity, a wider one, I mean, than that of the older teachers. We have learned that even outside of Christianity, whether really or supposedly, there is something like *Erlösung* (deliverance.) From this the arrangement has resulted, in the classification of religions, that we designate the highest stage of the religious life, that of the spiritual religions, also that of the *Erlösungsreligionen* (religions of deliverance)." That is to say, there is a class of religions, — no doubt, it embraces only the highest, the spiritual, religions, — which may justly be called *Erlösungsreligionen*, religions of deliverance, and Christianity belongs to this class. When we speak of *Erlösung* with reference to Christianity, we mean the same kind of a thing which we mean when we speak of it with reference to these other religions. As one of the *Erlösungsreligionen* (religions of deliverance) Christianity like the rest offers man deliverance. In point of fact, the deliverance which Christianity offers, according to Kaftan, is just a subjective change of mind and heart; he can write currently such a phrase as "*Erlösung oder Wiedergeburt*" (deliverance or regeneration.[24]) *Erlösung* (deliverance) in other words, as applied to describe the benefits conferred by Christianity, has come to mean for him just the better ethical life of Christians.

The classification of religions of which Kaftan avails himself in this discussion is derived ultimately from Hermann Siebeck, whose "Hand-book of the Philosophy of Religion" enjoys great vogue among Germans of Ritschlian tendency. This classification has not, however, commended itself universally. Many, like C. P. Tiele for example, strongly object to the distinguishing of a class of *Erlösungsreligionen* (religions of deliverance), which is placed at the apex of the series of religions. In reality, they say, all religions are *Erlösungsreligionen* (religions of deliverance). Precisely what religion is, always and everywhere, is a means of deliverance from some evil or other,

[23] P. 239. [24] "Dogmatik³⁻⁴," p. 459.

felt as such. Does not the proverb say, *not lehrt beten* — a sense of need is the mother of all religion? [25] The designation *Erlösungsreligionen* (religions of deliverance) has, however, evidently come to stay, whether it be taken discriminatingly as the designation of a particular class of religions, or merely descriptively as a declaration of the essential nature of all religions. And it is rapidly becoming the accepted way of speaking of Christianity to call it an *Erlösungsreligion* — a religion of deliverance, — whether it is meant thereby to assign it to a class or merely to indicate its nature. The point to be noted is that *Erlösung* is employed in these phrases in its looser native sense of deliverance, not in its narrower, acquired sense of ransoming. When Christianity is declared to be an *Erlösungsreligion* all that is meant is that it offers like all other religions, or very eminently like some other religions, a deliverance of some kind or other to men.

What gives this importance for us, is that these phrases have passed over from German into English, partly through the translation into English of the German books which employ them, partly by the adoption of the phrases themselves by native English writers for use in their own discussions. And in passing over into English, these phrases have not been exactly rendered with a care to reproducing their precise sense

[25] According to Rudolf Eucken, "Christianity and the New Idealism," E. T., 1909, p. 115, "That which drives men to religion is the break with the world of their experience, the failure to find satisfaction in what this world offers or is able to offer." It is probably something like this that Henry Osborn Taylor, "Deliverance," 1915, p. 5, means, when he says: "Evidently every 'religion' is a means of adjustment or deliverance." According to this all religions represent efforts of men to adjust themselves "to the fears and hopes of their natures," thus attaining peace or even "freedom of action in which they accomplish their lives." This "adjustment," Taylor speaks of as a "deliverance," that is to say, no doubt, deliverance from the discomfort of non-adjustment with its clogging effects on life. In this view religion is deliverance from conscious maladjustment of life. The implication is, apparently, that all men are to this extent conscious of being out of joint, in one way or another, with themselves or the universe in which they live, and struggle after adjustment. Thus religion arises, or rather the various religions, since they differ much both in the maladjustments they feel and their methods of correcting them. And there are even modes of adjustment which have been tried that cannot be called "religions."

in unambiguous English, but have been mechanically transferred into what are supposed to be the corresponding conventional English equivalents for the terms used.[26] Thus we have learned in these last days to speak very freely of "redemptive religions" or "religions of redemption," and it has become the fashion to describe Christianity as a "redemptive religion" or a "religion of redemption," — while yet the conception which lies in the mind is not that of redemption in the precise sense, but that of deliverance in its broadest connotation. This loose German usage has thus infected our own, and is coöperating with the native influences at work in the same direction, to break down the proper implications of our English redemptive terminology.[27]

You see, that what we are doing today as we look out upon our current religious modes of speech, is assisting at the death bed of a word. It is sad to witness the death of any worthy thing, — even of a worthy word. And worthy words do die, like any other worthy thing — if we do not take good care of them. How many worthy words have already died under our

[26] Thus, for example, Paul Wernle writes, "Die Anfänge unserer Religion[1]," p. 106, of Paul's view of Christianity: "Es war ihm ganz Erlösungsreligion"; "Jesus Erlöser, nicht Gesetzgeber, das war seine Parole." W. M. Macgregor, "Christian Freedom," 1914, p. 85, knowing what he is about, rightly translates: "To Paul Christianity was altogether a religion of deliverance." But the English translation of Wernle's book ("The Beginnings of Christianity," 1903, i, p. 176) renders: "Christianity was entirely a religion of redemption for him": " Jesus the Redeemer, not the lawgiver, was his watchword." This is, of course, a truer description of Paul's actual point of view; but it is not what Wernle means to say of him. Similarly Rudolf Eucken constantly speaks of Christianity as an "ethical" or "moral" "Erlösungsreligion" and of the particular "Erlösungstat" to which, as such, it points us (e. g. "Hauptprobleme der Religionsphilosophie der Gegenwart[4-5]," 1912, pp. 124, 126, 129). His translators ("Christianity and the New Idealism," 1909, pp. 114, 117, 119, 120) render as constantly "the religion of moral redemption," "act of redemption," although Eucken has no proper "redemption" whatever in mind, — as indeed the adjective "ethical," "moral" shows sufficiently clearly. An ethical revolution may be a deliverance but it is not properly a "redemption."

[27] For example, on the basis of this note: "Beyschlag ('N. T. Theol.' II. 157) frankly takes ἀπολυτροῦν, ἐλευθεροῦν, ἐξαιρεῖν (Gal. i. 4), ἀγοράζειν as synonymous," W. M. Macgregor, "Christian Freedom," 1914, p. 276. He retires into the background of all of them, all other notion than that of "Emancipation," that is, the notion of the weakest and least modal of them all.

very eyes, because we did not take care of them! Tennyson calls our attention to one of them. "The grand old name of gentleman," he sings, "defamed by every charlatan, and soil'd with all ignoble use." If you persist in calling people who are not gentlemen by the name of gentleman, you do not make them gentlemen by so calling them, but you end by making the word gentleman mean that kind of people. The religious terrain is full of the graves of good words which have died from lack of care — they stand as close in it as do the graves today in the flats of Flanders or among the hills of northern France. And these good words are still dying all around us. There is that good word "Evangelical." It is certainly moribund, if not already dead. Nobody any longer seems to know what it means. Even our Dictionaries no longer know. Certainly there never was a more blundering, floundering attempt ever made to define a word than "The Standard Dictionary's" attempt to define this word; and the "Century Dictionary" does little better. Adolf Harnack begins one of his essays with some paragraphs animadverting on the varied and confused senses in which the word "Evangelical" is used in Germany.[28] But he betrays no understanding whatever of the real source of a great part of this confusion. It is that the official name of the Protestant Church in a large part of Germany is "The Evangelical Church." When this name was first acquired by that church it had a perfectly defined meaning, and described the church as that kind of a church. But having been once identified with that church, it has drifted with it into the bog. The habit of calling "Evangelical" everything which was from time to time characteristic of that church or which any strong party in that church wished to make characteristic of it — has ended in robbing the term of all meaning. Along a somewhat different pathway we have arrived at the same state of affairs in America. Does anybody in the world know what "Evangelical" means, in our current religious speech? The other day, a professedly evangelical pastor, serving a church which is certainly committed by its formularies to an evangelical confession, having

[28] "Aus Wissenschaft und Leben," 1911, ii, pp. 213 ff.

occasion to report in one of our newspapers on a religious meeting composed practically entirely of Unitarians and Jews, remarked with enthusiasm upon the deeply evangelical character of its spirit and utterances.

But we need not stop with "Evangelical." Take an even greater word. Does the word "Christianity" any longer bear a definite meaning? Men are debating on all sides of us what Christianity really is. Auguste Sabatier makes it out to be just altruism; Josiah Royce identifies it with the sentiment of loyalty; D. C. Macintosh explains it as nothing but morality. We hear of Christianity without dogma, Christianity without miracle, Christianity without Christ. Since, however, Christianity is a historical religion, an undogmatic Christianity would be an absurdity; since it is through and through a supernatural religion, a non-miraculous Christianity would be a contradiction; since it is Christianity, a Christless Christianity would be — well, let us say lamely (but with a lameness which has perhaps its own emphasis), a misnomer. People set upon calling unchristian things Christian are simply washing all meaning out of the name. If everything that is called Christianity in these days is Christianity, then there is no such thing as Christianity. A name applied indiscriminately to everything, designates nothing.

The words "Redeem," "Redemption," "Redeemer" are going the same way. When we use these terms in so comprehensive a sense — we are following Kaftan's phraseology — that we understand by "Redemption" whatever benefit we suppose ourselves to receive through Christ, — no matter what we happen to think that benefit is — and call Him "Redeemer" merely in order to express the fact that we somehow or other relate this benefit to Him — no matter how loosely or unessentially — we have simply evacuated the terms of all meaning, and would do better to wipe them out of our vocabulary. Yet this is precisely how modern Liberalism uses these terms. Sabatier, who reduces Christianity to mere altruism, Royce who explains it in terms of loyalty, Macintosh who sees in it only morality — all still speak of it as a "Redemptive

Religion," and all are perfectly willing to call Jesus still by the title of "Redeemer,"— although some of them at least are quite free to allow that He seems to them quite unessential to Christianity, and Christianity would remain all that it is, and just as truly a "Redemptive Religion," even though He had never existed.

I think you will agree with me that it is a sad thing to see words like these die like this. And I hope you will determine that, God helping you, you will not let them die thus, if any care on your part can preserve them in life and vigor. But the dying of the words is not the saddest thing which we see here. The saddest thing is the dying out of the hearts of men of the things for which the words stand. As ministers of Christ it will be your function to keep the things alive. If you can do that, the words which express the things will take care of themselves. Either they will abide in vigor; or other good words and true will press in to take the place left vacant by them. The real thing for you to settle in your minds, therefore, is whether Christ is truly a Redeemer to you, and whether you find an actual Redemption in Him, — or are you ready to deny the Master that bought you, and to count His blood an unholy thing? Do you realize that Christ is your Ransomer and has actually shed His blood for you as your ransom? Do you realize that your salvation has been bought, bought at a tremendous price, at the price of nothing less precious than blood, and that the blood of Christ, the Holy One of God? Or, go a step further: do you realize that this Christ who has thus shed His blood for you is Himself your God? So the Scriptures teach: [29]

> The blood of God outpoured upon the tree!
> So reads the Book.   O mind, receive the thought,

[29] Acts xx. 28, "Feed the church of God which He hath purchased with His own blood." The reading "God" is, as F. J. A. Hort says, "assuredly genuine," and the emphasis upon the blood being His own is very strong. There is no justification for correcting the text conjecturally, as Hort does, to avoid this. If the reading "Lord" were genuine, the meaning would be precisely the same: "Lord" is not a lower title than "God." in such connections. I Cor. ii. 8, "They would not have crucified the Lord of Glory," is an exact parallel.

Nor helpless murmur thou hast vainly sought
Thought-room within thee for such mystery.
Thou foolish mindling! Do'st thou hope to see
   Undazed, untottering, all that God hath wrought?
   Before His mighty "shall," thy little "ought"
Be shamed to silence and humility!
Come mindling, I will show thee what 'twere meet
   That thou shouldst shrink from marvelling, and flee
   As unbelievable, — nay, wonderingly,
With dazed, but still with faithful praises, greet:
Draw near and listen to this sweetest sweet, —
   Thy God, O mindling, shed His blood for *thee!*

XI
CHRIST OUR SACRIFICE

CHRIST OUR SACRIFICE [1]

"ACCORDING to the New Testament, primitive Christianity, when it used the words 'Jesus redeems us by His blood,' was thinking of the ritual sacrifice, and this conception is diffused throughout the whole New Testament; it is a fundamental idea, universal in primitive Christianity, with respect to the significance of Jesus' death." So remarks Paul Fiebig;[2] and W. P. Paterson, summarizing Albrecht Ritschl,[3] emphasizes the assertion. "The interpretation of Christ's death as a sacrifice," says he,[4] "is imbedded in every important type of New Testament teaching." By the limitation implied in the words, "every important type," he means only to allow for the failure of allusions to this interpretation in the two brief letters, James and Jude, the silence of which, he rightly explains, "raises no presumption against the idea being part of the common stock of Apostolic doctrine." It was already given expression by Jesus Himself (Mt. xxvi. 28, Mk. xiv. 24, I Cor. xi. 25, Mt. xx. 28, Mk. x. 45),[5] and it is elaborated by the Apostles in a great variety of obviously spontaneous allusions. They not only expressly state that Christ was offered as a sacrifice.[6] They work out the correspondence between His death and the different forms of Old Testament sacrifice.[7] They show that the differ-

---

[1] From *The Princeton Theological Review*, v. xv, 1917, pp. 385–422.

[2] "Jesu Blut ein Geheimnis?" 1906, p. 27.

[3] "Die Christliche Lehre der Rechtfertigung und Versöhnung[3]," 1889, v. ii, pp. 161 ff.

[4] Hastings' "Dictionary of the Bible," v. iv, 1902, p. 343 b.

[5] Fiebig, as cited, p. 19, remarks on the connection in the Jewish mind of the idea of purchasing, ransoming, with sacrifice, — referring to F. Weber, "Jüdische Theologie," etc[2]., 1897, pp. 313, 324.

[6] E. g., προσφορά, Eph. v. 2, Heb. x. 10, 14 (for the meaning of προσφορά see Heb. x. 18), θυσία, Eph. v. 2, Heb. ix. 26; cf. Rom. iii. 25, ἱλαστήριον; viii. 3, περὶ ἁμαρτίας.

[7] Paterson (from whom we are taking this summary), as cited, notes: "esp. the Sin-offering (Rom. viii. 3, Heb. xiii. 11, I Pet. iii. 18), the Covenant-sacrifice

ent acts of the Old Testament sacrificial ritual were repeated in Christ's experience.[8] They ascribe the specific effects of sacrifice to his death.[9] They dwell particularly, in truly sacrificial wise, on the saving efficacy of His out-poured blood.[10] William Warburton did not speak a bit too strongly when he wrote, more than a hundred and fifty years ago: "One could hardly have thought it possible that any man who had read the Gospels with their best interpreters, the authors of the Epistles, should ever have entertained a doubt whether the death of Christ was a real sacrifice."[11]

(Heb. ix. 15–22), the sacrifices of the Day of Atonement (Heb. ii. 17, ix. 12 ff.), and of the Passover (I Cor. v. 7)." Cf. Sanday-Headlam, "Romans[1]," p. 92.

[8] Paterson enumerates: "the slaying of the immaculate victim (Rev. v. 6, xiii. 8), the sprinkling of the blood both in the sanctuary as in the Sin-offering (Heb. ix. 13 ff.), and on the people as in the Covenant-sacrifice (I Pet. i. 2), and the destruction of the victim, as in the Sin-offering, without the gate (Heb. xiii. 13)" — referring to Ritschl ii. 157 ff.; and Sanday-Headlam, "Romans," p. 91.

[9] E. g.: "Expiation, or pardon of sin," says Paterson. Sanday-Headlam mention as examples of passages in which the death of Christ is directly connected with forgiveness of sin: Mt. xxvi. 28; Acts v. 30 f., apparently; I Cor. xv. 3; II Cor. v. 21; Eph. i. 7; Col. i. 14 and 20; Tit. ii. 14; Heb. i. 3, ix. 28, x. 12, al.; I Pet. ii. 24, iii. 18; I John ii. 2, iv. 10; Rev. i. 5.

[10] Paterson: "A saving efficacy is ascribed to the blood of the cross of Christ, and in these cases the thought clearly points to the forms of the altar (Rom. iii. 25, v. 9, I Cor. x. 16, Eph. i. 7, ii. 13, Col. i. 20, Heb. ix. 12, 14; I Pet. i. 2, 19; I John i. 7, v. 6, 8; Rev. i. 5)." Cf. Sanday-Headlam, "Romans," p. 91 f. The matter is very interestingly presented by Fiebig, as cited, pp. 11–27 under the title: "What, according to the New Testament, did primitive Christianity think in connection with the words, 'Jesus has redeemed us by His blood'?" He takes his start, for the survey of a conception which he says is diffused throughout the whole New Testament, from I Pet. i. 17–19, the only key to which he declares to be "sacrifice, and indeed sacrifice as it was known to every Jew (and in a corresponding way to every heathen) from his daily life and from the festivals and duties of his religion, that is ritual sacrifice." From this passage he then proceeds through the New Testament and shows that the blood of Christ is used throughout the volume in a sacrificial sense, so that whenever we meet with an allusion to the blood of Jesus we meet with a reference to His death as a sacrifice.

[11] "The Divine Legation of Moses," Book ix, chapter ii, quoted in a note at the end of his excellent chapter on "The New Testament Description of the Atoning Work of Christ as Sacrificial," by Alfred Cave, "The Scriptural Doctrine of Sacrifice and Atonement[2]," 1890, pp. 274–289. Cave himself says (p. 289): "Not only portions but the whole New Testament — not only the New Testament teaching but any type of that teaching — must be cast aside unless the work of Christ be in some sense or other regarded as a sacrifice."

It would be strange in these circumstances if, in attempting
to determine the Biblical conception of the nature of the work
of Christ, appeal were not made to the sacrificial system; and
it were not argued that the nature of Christ's work is exhibited
in the nature of the sacrificial act. Whatever a sacrifice is, that
Christ's work is. It will be obvious, however, that we are liable
to fall into a certain confusion here. Jesus Himself and the
Apostles speak of Christ's work as sacrificial, and it is clear (as
Paterson duly points out [12]) that this is on their lips no figure
of speech or mere illustration, but is intended to declare the
simple fact. It is quite plain, then, that His work was conceived
by them to be of precisely that nature which a sacrifice was
understood by them to be. But it is by no means so plain that
they conceived His work to be of the nature which we may understand a sacrifice to be. Failure to regard this very simple
distinction has brought untold confusion into the discussion.
If we would comprehend the teaching of the writers of the New
Testament when they call Christ a sacrifice, we must, of course,
not assume out of hand that their idea of a sacrifice and ours

[12] As cited: "Nor for the apostolic age was the description of Christ's death
as a sacrifice of the nature of a mere illustration. The apostles held it to be a
sacrifice in the most literal sense of the word." Paterson goes on to assign reasons.
George F. Moore, "Encyclopaedia Biblica," v. iv. 1903, col. 4232 f. interposes a
caveat: "To begin with, it is necessary to say that in describing the death of
Christ as a sacrifice the New Testament writers are using figurative language.
Some modern theologians, indeed, still affirm that 'the apostles held it to be a
sacrifice in the most literal sense of the word'; but such writers do not expect us
to take their 'literal' literally. The author of the Epistle to the Hebrews, for example, regarded the death of Christ as the true sacrifice, because by it was really
effected what the Old Testament sacrifices only prefigured; but he was too good
an Alexandrian to identify 'true' with 'literal.'" What Moore maintains is that
the death of Christ was not believed to be expiatory because it was known to be
a sacrifice, but that it was spoken of as a sacrifice because it was recognized to be
expiatory. He does not doubt that the death of Christ was believed actually to
have wrought the expiation which the sacrifices were understood to figure. "The
association of expiation with sacrifice in the law and in the common ideas of the
time leads to the employment of sacrificial figures and terms in speaking of the
work of Christ; and even in Hebrews, where the idea of the death of Christ as a
sacrifice is most elaborately developed, it is plain that the premise of the whole
is that Christ by His death made a real expiation for the sins of men, by which
they are redeemed." We take it that it is just this that Paterson means by speaking
of Christ's death as a "literal" sacrifice.

are identical. The investigation of the previous question of the
notion they attached to a sacrifice must form our starting-point.
So little is this mode of procedure always adopted, however,
that it is even customary for writers on the subject to go so
far afield at this point as to introduce a discussion not of the
idea of sacrifice held by the founders of the Christian religion,
or even current in the Judaism of their day, or even embodied
in the Levitical system; but of the idea of sacrifice in general,
conceived as a world-wide mode of worship. The several theories
of the fundamental conception which underlies sacrificial worship in the general sense are set forth; a choice is made among
them; and this theory is announced as ruling the usage of the
term when applied to Christ. Christ is undoubtedly our sacrifice, it is said: but a sacrifice is a rite by which communion
with God is established and maintained, or by which a complete
surrender to God is symbolized, or by which recognition is
made of the homage we owe to Him as our God, or by which
God's suffering love is manifested. As if the question of importance were what we mean by a sacrifice, and not what the New
Testament writers mean by it.

It is manifestly of the highest importance, therefore, that
we should keep separate three very distinct questions, to each
of which a great deal of interest attaches, although they have
very different bearings on the determination of the nature of
Christ's work. These three questions are: (1) What is the fundamental idea which underlies sacrificial worship as a world-
phenomenon? (2) What is the essential implication of sacrifice
in the Levitical system? (3) What is the conception of sacrifice
which lay in the minds of the writers of the New Testament,
when they represented Jesus as a sacrifice and ascribed to His
work a sacrificial character, in its mode, its nature and its
effects? The distinctness of these questions is strikingly illustrated by the circumstance that not infrequently a different
response is given to each of them by the same investigator. It
may be said in general that few doubt that the conception of
sacrifice at least dominant among the Jews of Christ's time
was distinctly piacular: and, although it is more frequently

questioned whether all the writers of the New Testament were
in agreement with this conception, it is practically undoubted
that some of them were, and generally admitted that all were.
The majority of scholars agree also that the piacular conception
informs sacrificial worship in the Levitical system. On the other
hand speculation has as yet found no common ground with
respect to the fundamental conception which is supposed to
underlie sacrificial worship in general, and in this field hypothesis still jostles with hypothesis in what seems an endless controversy.

Question may even very legitimately be raised whether the
assumption can be justified which is commonly (but of course
not universally) made that a single fundamental idea underlies
all sacrificial worship the world over. There seems no reason in
the nature of things why a similar mode of worship may not
have grown up in various races of men, living in very different
circumstances, to express differing conceptions; and it certainly
cannot be doubted that very diverse conceptions, in the long
practice of the rite by these various races in their constantly
changing circumstances, attached themselves, from time to
time and from place to place, to the sacrificial mode of worship
common to all. The Biblical narrative may lead us to suppose,
to be sure, that sacrificial worship began very early in the history of the human race: it may seem to be carried back, indeed,
to the very dawn of history, and to be definitely assigned in its
origin to no later period than the second generation of men.
But at the same time we seem to be advertized that at the very
inception of sacrificial worship different conceptions were embodied in it by its several practitioners. It is difficult to believe
at least that we are expected to understand that the whole
difference in the acceptability to Jehovah of the two offerings
of Cain and Abel hung on the different characters of the two
offerers: [13] we are told that Jehovah had respect not merely

---

[13] This nevertheless is the common view. Driver supposes that the different
treatment of the sacrifices can hardly have had its ground in "anything except
the different spirit and temper actuating the two brothers": but he recognizes
(without comment) that there is "another view," namely, "that there underlies

unto Abel and not unto Cain, but also to Abel's offering and not to Cain's. The different characters of the two men seem rather to be represented as expressing themselves in differing conceptions of man's actual relation to God and of the conditions of approval by Him and the proper means of seeking His favor.

It can scarcely be reading too much between the lines to suppose that the narrative in the fourth chapter of Genesis is intended on the one hand to describe the origin of sacrificial worship, and on the other to distinguish between two conceptions of sacrifice and to indicate the preference of Jehovah for the one rather than the other. These two conceptions are briefly those which have come to be known respectively as the piacular theory and the symbolical, or perhaps we should rather call it the gift, theory. In this view we are not to suppose that Cain and Abel simply brought each a gift to the Lord from the increase which had been granted him, to acknowledge thereby the overlordship of Jehovah and to express subjection and obedience to Him: and that it is merely an accident that Cain's offering, as that of a husbandman, was of the fruit of the ground, while Abel's, as that of a shepherd, was of the firstlings of the flock. There is no reason apparent why Jehovah should prefer a lamb to a sheaf of wheat.[14] The difference surely goes deeper, for it was "by faith" that Abel offered under God a more excellent sacrifice than Cain — which seems to suggest that the supreme excellence of his sacrifice is to be sought not in the mere nature of the thing offered, but in the attitude of

the story some early struggle between two theories of sacrifice, which ended by the triumph of the theory that the right offering to be made consisted in the life of an animal." Dillmann says: "The reason must therefore lie in the dispositions presupposed in the offerings"; but quotes Hofmann, "Schriftbeweis²," i, p. 585 for the view that "Abel had in mind the expiation of sin, while Cain had not" — "of which," says Dillmann, "there is no indication whatever." Similar ground is taken, for example, by Kalisch, Keil, Delitzsch ("New Commentary"), Lange, W. P. Paterson (Articles "Abel" and "Cain" in Hastings' *B.D.*).

[14] Gunkel thinks there is: Jehovah is the God of nomads. The old narrator, he says, would be surprised that anyone should wonder why Jahve had respect to Abel's offering and not to Cain's: he means just that Jahve loved the shepherd and flesh-offerings but would have nothing to do with the cultivator and fruit-offerings. Similarly Tuch: the story comes from nomads.

the offerer.[15] What seems to be implied is that Cain's offering was an act of mere homage; Abel's embodied a sense of sin, an act of contrition, a cry for succor, a plea for pardon. In a word, Cain came to the Lord with an offering in his hand and the Homage theory of sacrifice in his mind: Abel with an offering in his hand and the Piacular theory of sacrifice in his heart. And it was therefore, that Jehovah had respect to Abel's offering and not to Cain's. If so, while we may say that sacrifice was invented by man, we must also say that by this act piacular sacrifice was instituted by God.[16] In other modes of conceiving it, sacrifice may represent the reaching out of man towards God: in its piacular conception it represents the stooping down of God to man. The fundamental difference is that in the one case sacrifice rests upon consciousness of sin and has its refer-

[15] The allusion in Heb. xii. 24 is taken by some commentators as a reference to Abel's offering rather than to his death. Bleek (p. 954) says: "It may be mentioned merely in a historical interest that with the Erasmian reading (τὸ Ἀβελ), by Hammond, Akersloot, and Snabel (*Amoenitatt theologiae emblematicae et typicae*, p. 109 ff.), the blood of Abel is understood of the blood of the sacrificial animal offered by him; and that the first, with the received reading (τὸν Ἀβελ), wishes to refer the τόν to the ῥαντισμόν in order to obtain the same sense." This interpretation has had great vogue in America, owing to its advocacy by the popular commentaries of Albert Barnes, 1843, F. S. Sampson, 1856, George Junkin 1873. Its significance for the matter of the nature of Abel's sacrifice may be perceived from the comment of Joseph B. McCaul, 1871, p. 317 f., who combines the two views: "Abel, being dead, can speak only figuratively. He does so by his faith, manifested by his bringing a vicarious sacrifice according to the Divine will. He therefore speaks, not only by the blood of his martyrdom, but also by the blood of his sacrifice, which latter obtained testimony from God that it was acceptable and accepted. It was *then* that God openly expressed his Divine selection of blood, to the exclusion of all other means of ransom, for the redemption of the soul. In the term 'the blood of Abel,' therefore, may be included the blood of all vicarious victims afterwards offered, in accordance with God's appointment, until the sacrifice of the death of Christ superseded them."

[16] Here perhaps is to be found the reply to the representation made for example by J. K. Mozley, "The Doctrine of the Atonement," 1916, p. 13, note 2, to the effect that writers of the school "which ignores or rejects modern criticism of the Old Testament" — represented by P. Fairbairn, "Typology of the Scriptures," W. L. Alexander, "Biblical Theology," A. Cave, "Scriptural Doctrine of Sacrifice"— had to explain how it is that the first sacrifices mentioned (those of Cain and Abel) "are not said to have been in any way ordered by God." The question of the origin of sacrifice, human or divine, Mozley says is no longer discussed. For a hint as to its literature see Cave, p. 41, note 2.

ence to the restoration of a guilty human being to the favor of a condemning God: in the other it stands outside of all relation to sin and has its reference only to the expression of the proper attitude of deference which a creature should preserve towards his Maker and Ruler.[17]

[17] This explanation of the narrative of "the first sacrifices" is not popular with the critical commentators. Skinner (in accordance with the alternative view of the passage mentioned by Driver) thinks that "the whole manner of the narrative" suggests that we here have "the initiation of sacrifice," and that, if this be accepted, it follows "that the narrative proceeds on a *theory* of sacrifice; the idea, viz. that animal sacrifice alone is acceptable to Yahwe." Why this should be so, he does not say. Franz Delitzsch, who in his "New Commentary on Genesis," will not look further for the reason of the difference in the treatment of the offerings than the different dispositions of the offerers, in his earlier "Commentary on Genesis," amid much inconsistent matter, has this to say: "The unbloody offering of Cain, as such, was only the expression of a grateful present, or, taken in its deepest significance, a consecrated offering of self: but man needs, before all things, the expiation of his death-deserving sins, and for this, the blood obtained through the slaying of the victim serves as a symbol." J. C. K. Hofmann, "Schriftbeweis[2]," i, pp. 584–585 remarks that the cultivation of the soil and the keeping of beasts were employments alike open to men: but he who adopted the one, dealing with a soil which was *cursed*, had to thank God for the yield it made despite sin, while he who adopted the other, in view of the provision God had made for hiding man's nakedness, had before him God's grace in hiding sin. If, now, Cain was satisfied to bring of the fruit of the earth to God, he was thanking God only for a prolongation of this present life, which he had gained by his own labor: while Abel, bringing the best beasts of his flock, gave Him thanks for the forgiveness of sin, the abiding symbol of which was the clothing given by God. "A grateful attitude such as Abel's had as its presupposition, however, the penitent faith in the word of God which saw in this divine clothing of human nakedness an approach to the forgiveness of sins which rests on the gracious will of God to man." Because Abel's sacrifice embodied this idea, it was acceptable to God and he received the witness that he was righteous. J. J. Murphy comments: "The fruit of the soil offered to God is an acknowledgment that the means of this earthly life are due to Him. This expresses the barren faith of Cain, not the living faith of Abel. The latter had entered deeply into the thought that life itself is forfeited to God by transgression, and that only by an act of mercy can the Author of life restore it to the penitent, trusting, submissive, loving heart." The remarks of "C. H. M." on the passage are very clear and pointed to the same effect. See them cited by A. H. Strong, "Syst. Theol.," ed. 1907, p. 727. J. C. Jones, "Primeval Revelation," 1897, p. 313 ff. gives a glowing popular expression to the same view. J. S. Candlish, "The Christian Salvation," 1899, p. 15, thinks that Abel's sacrifice plainly involves the confession of sin and compares his worship with that of the Publican in the parable, and Cain's to that of the Pharisee. T. J. Crawford, "Doctrine of Holy Scripture Respecting the Atonement[2]," 1875, p. 280, says that Abel's faith may have had respect not to a revelation with regard to

The appearance of two such sharply differentiated conceptions side by side in the earliest Hebrew tradition does not encourage us to embark on ambitious speculations which would seek the origin of all sacrificial doctrines in a single primitive idea out of which they have gradually unfolded in the progress of time and through many stages of increasing culture. We have been made familiar with such genetic constructions by the writings especially of E. B. Tylor, W. Robertson Smith, and Smith's follower and improver, J. G. Frazer.[18] In Tylor's view the beginning of sacrifice is to be found in a gift made by a savage to some superior being from which he hoped to receive a benefit. The gods grew gradually greater and more distant; and the gift was correspondingly spiritualized, until it ended by becoming the gift of the worshipper's self. Thus out of the offer of a bribe there gradually evolved its opposite — an act of self-abnegation and renunciation. The start is taken, according to W. Robertson Smith, rather from a common meal in which the totem animal, which is also the god, is consumed with a view to the assimilation of it by the worshippers and their assimilation to it. When the animal eaten came to be thought of as provided by the worshipper, the idea of gift came in; as all totemistic meals had for their object the maintenance or renewal of the bond between the worshipper and the god, the conception of expiation lay near — for what is expiation but the restitution of a broken bond? [19] H. Hubert and M.

sacrificial worship, but with regard to a promised Redeemer; this sacrifice may have expressed that faith. If so, God's acceptance of it gave a divine warrant to future sacrifice.

[18] We are abstracting in this account the illuminating survey by MM. Hubert and Mauss in the "L'Année Sociologique," II, 1897–1898, pp. 29 ff. They tell us, that Robertson Smith has been followed by E. Sidney Hartland, "The Legend of Perseus," 1894–1896, and "with theological exaggeration" by F. B. Jevons, "Introduction to the History of Religion," 1896.

[19] After threatening to become the dominant theory, this theory has recently lost ground, chiefly on account of the totemistic elements connected with it. See the criticisms by B. Stade, "Biblische Theologie des Alten Testaments," v. i, pp. 156–159; and M. J. Lagrange, "Études sur les religions Sémitiques," pp. 246 ff. The "gift" theory accordingly holds the field. W. R. Inge, "Christian Mysticism," 1899, p. 355, appears to prefer to suppose that neither conception is the source of the other: "There have always been two ideas of sacrifice, alike

Mauss are certainly wise in eschewing this spurious geneticism, and contenting themselves with seeking merely to isolate the common element discoverable in all sacrificial acts. It must be confessed, however, that we are not much advanced even by their less ambitious labors. Sacrifices, they tell us, are, broadly, rites designed by the consecration of a victim, to modify the moral state, or, as they elsewhere express it, to affect the religious state, of the offerers.[20] This is assuredly the most formal of formal definitions. All that differentiates sacrifices from other religious acts, so far as appears from it, is that they, as the others do not, seek their common end "by the consecration of a victim." Nor are we carried much further, when, at the end of their essay, we are told [21] that what binds together all the divers forms of sacrifice into a unity, is that it is always one process which is employed for their varied ends. "This process," it is then said, "consists in establishing a connection between the sacred world and the profane world by the intervention of a victim, that is to say, by something destroyed in the course of the ceremony." Sacrifice, we thus learn, is just — sacrifice. But what this sacrifice is, in its fundamental meaning, we seem not to be very clearly told. An impression is left on the mind that the word "sacrifice" embraces so great a variety of differing transactions that only a very formal definition can include them all.

Our guides having left us thus in the lurch, perhaps we cannot do better than simply survey the chief theories which have been suggested as to the fundamental idea embodied in sacrificial worship, quite in the flat. In doing so, we may take a hint from the two forms of conception brought before us in the narrative of the sacrifices of Cain and Abel and derive from them our principle of division. The theories part into two broad classes, which look upon sacrifices respectively as designed and adapted to express the religious feelings of man con-

in savage and civilized cults, — the mystical in which it is a *communion*, the victim who is slain and eaten being himself the god, or a symbol of the god; and the *commercial*, in which something valuable is offered to the god in the hope of receiving some benefit in exchange." This is very likely true as a general proposition.

[20] As cited, pp. 41 and 89.   [21] P. 133.

ceived merely as creature, or as intended to meet the needs of man as sinner. The theories of the first class are by far the more numerous, and, nowadays at least, by far the more popular. Perhaps, thinking of sacrifices as a world-wide usage as at this point we are, we may say also that these theories are very likely to embody the true account of the meaning of much of the sacrificial worship, at least, which has overspread the globe. For man, even in the formation of his religious rites is doubtless no more ready to remember that he is a sinner craving pardon than that he is a creature claiming protection. Deep-rooted as the sense of sin is in every normal human conscience, and sure as it is sporadically to express itself and to color all serious religious observances, the pride of man is no less ready to find manifestation even in his religious practices. Let us look at the chief varieties of these two great classes of theories in a rapid enumeration.

The chief theories of sacrifice which allow no place to sin in its essential implications, may perhaps be collected into three groups to which may be assigned the names of theories of Recognition, of Gift and of Communion.

The theories to which we have given the name of theories of Recognition are also known as Homage or Symbolical theories. Their common characteristic is that they conceive sacrifices to be at bottom symbolical rites by means of which the worshipper gives expression to his religious feelings or aspirations or needs: "acts go before words." At their highest level these theories represent the worshipper as expressing thus his recognition of the deity, his own relation of dependence upon Him and subjection to Him, and his readiness to act in accordance with this relation and to render the homage and obedience due from him. The name of William Warburton is connected with these theories in this general form.[22] A slightly different turn is given to the general conception by Albrecht Ritschl.[23] According to him, even in the case of the later sacrificial system of Israel, the sacrifices express (with no reference

---

[22] Cf. "The Divine Legation of Moses," etc. iv. 4.
[23] Cf. "Rechtfertigung und Versöhnung³," ii. 201–203.

whatever to sin in the symbolism) only the awe and religious fear which the creature in his inadequacy feels in the presence of deity: man seeks "to cover" his weakness in the face of the destroying glory of God (Gen. xxxii. 31, Judges vi. 23, xiii. 22). There are others, to be sure, who are not so careful to exclude a reference to sin and, in speaking of the sacrifices of Israel at least, suppose that what is symbolized includes a hatred of sin, as well as self-surrender to God: in their hands the theory passes therefore upward into the other main class. On the other hand, in their lowest forms, theories of this group tend to pass downward into conceptions which look upon sacrifices as merely magical rites. The thing symbolized may be supposed to be not a spiritual attitude at all but a physical need. Primitive worshippers only exhibited before the deity the object they required, and this was supposed to operate upon the deity (something after the fashion of sympathetic magic) as a specimen, securing from Him the thing desired. Theorists of this order do not scruple to point to the "shew-bread" displayed in the temple of Israel and the offering of first-fruits as instances in point.

The theories which look upon sacrifices as essentially gifts, presents, intended to please the deity,[24] and thus to gain favor with Him, part into two divisions according as the gifts are conceived more as bribes or more as fines, that is according as they are conceived as designed more to curry favor with the deity, or more to make amends for faults — or, from the point of view of the deity, as a sort of police regulation, to punish or check wrong doing. In either case the idea of sin may come into play and the theory pass upward into the other main class. The chief representative of this type of theory among the old writers is J. Spencer, who looks upon it as self-evident that this was the primitive view of sacrifice.[25] The anthropologists (E. B. Tylor, Herbert Spencer) have given it great vogue in

[24] J. Jeremias, "Encyclopaedia Biblica," v. iv. col. 4119 says, in a representative assertion: "Sacrifice rests ultimately on the idea that it gives pleasure to the deity (cf. Dillmann, "Leviticus," 376)." So A. Dillmann, "Exodus und Leviticus[3]," p. 416: "The characteristic of sacrifice is a gift; that which differentiates it from other gifts is that it is enjoyed by the divinity."

[25] J. Spencer, "De Legibus Hebraeorum Ritualibus," 1727, v. ii. p. 762.

our day; and it is doubtless the most commonly held theory of
the fundamental nature of sacrifice at present (e. g., H. Schultz,
B. Stade, A. B. Davidson, G. F. Moore).[26] In one of the lower
forms of this general theory the gifts are conceived as food
supplied to the deity — who is supposed to share in the human
need of being fed.[27] It is an advance on the crudest form of this
conception when it is the savour or odor of the sacrifice which
is supposed to be pleasing to the deity, and the food is thought
to be conveyed to Him through the medium of burning. When
the food is supposed to be shared between the offerer and the
deity, an advance is made to the next group of theories.

This group of theories looks upon sacrifices as essentially
formal acts of communion with the deity — a common meal,
say, partaken of by worshipper and worshipped, the fundamental motive being to gratify the deity by giving or sharing
with Him a meal.[28] This general view is often improved upon
by a reference to the custom of establishing covenants by common meals, and becomes thereby a "meal-covenant" or "table-
bond" theory. In this form it was already suggested by A. A.
Sykes who speaks of sacrifices as joint meals, which are, he
says, "acts of engaging in covenants and leagues."[29] It is a
further addition to this theory to say that it was conceived that
a physical union was induced between the deity and the worshipper, by the medium of the common meal.[30] And the notion

[26] Hubert and Mauss, as cited, p. 30, remark that "it is certain that sacrifices
were generally in some degree gifts, conferring on the believer rights upon his
God." They add in a note: "See a somewhat superficial brochure by Nitzsch,
'Idee und Stufen des Opferkultus,' Kiel, 1889"; and then, that "at bottom"
this theory is held by Wilken, "Over eene Nieuwe Theorie des Offers" in "De
Gids," 1891, pp. 535 ff. and by L. Marillier in the *Revue d'Histoire des Religions*, 1897–1898. Marillier connects sacrifices, however, with magical rites by
which the deity is bent to the worshipper's will by the liberation of a magical
force through the effusion of the victim's blood. The idea of "gift" grew out of
this, through the medium of the cult of the dead.
[27] E. G. Piepenbring, "Théologie de l'ancien Testament," p. 56.
[28] W. P. Paterson, Hastings' "Dictionary of the Bible," iv. p. 331 b.
[29] A. A. Sykes, "Essay on the Nature etc. of Sacrifices," 1748, p. 75.
[30] J. Wellhausen, "Skizzen und Vorarbeiten," 1897; W. R. Smith, "Religion of the Semites²," 1894; as applied to Israel, H. Schultz, *American Journal
of Theology*, 1900, p. 269.

has reached its height when the meal is thought of as essentially a feeding on the God Himself whether by symbol, or through the medium of a totem animal, or by magical influence.[31] H. C. Trumbull actually utilizes this conception to explain the mode of action of the Lord's Supper.[32]

One of the things which strikes us very sharply as we review these three groups of theories is the little place given in them to the slaughter, or more broadly the destruction, of the victim, or, more broadly, the offering. This comes forward in them all as incidental to the rite, rather than as its essence. In the third group the sacrificial feast — which follows on the sacrifice itself — assumes the main place; in the second it is the oblation which is emphasized as of chief importance; even in the first the slaughter is not cardinal, — at the best it is a prerequisite that the blood may be obtained, which is represented as the valuable thing, to present to the deity. This cirsumstance alone is probably fatal to the validity of these theories as accounts whether of sacrifice in general or sacrifice in Israel; and very certainly as providing an explanation of the meaning of the New Testament writers when they speak of our Lord as a sacrifice. There is reason to believe that the slaughter of the victim or destruction of the offering constitutes the essential act of sacrifice; and certainly in the New Testament it is precisely in the blood of Christ or in His cross, symbols of His death, that the essence of His sacrificial character is found.[33]

When we turn to the theories of sacrifice in which a reference to sin is made fundamental, we meet first with that form of the Symbolical theory in which the sacrifice is supposed to be the vehicle for the expression of the worshipper's "confession, his regret, his petition for forgiveness," [34] — that is to say, in one word, his repentance and his engagement to give back

[31] J. G. Frazer, "The Golden Bough[2]," 1900.

[32] "The Blood Covenant," 1888, at the end; see also his "The Covenant of Salt," 1899.

[33] Hubert and Mauss, as cited, p. 74. On the usage of the Hebrew word Zebach as a generic term for sacrifice, see Cave, as cited, pp. 511 ff.

[34] H. Schultz, *American Journal of Theology*, 1900, p. 310.

his life to God. Influential advocates of this view are K. C. W. F. Bähr, G. F. Oehler and F. D. Maurice.[35] By its side we meet also that form of the Gift theory in which the sinning worshipper is supposed to approach his judge with (on the lower level) a bribe, or (on the higher level) the fine for his fault in his hand. The former view is appropriate only to lower stages of culture, in which justice is supposed to go by favor. Even in the higher heathen opinion, so to think of the gods was held to be degrading to them: "Even a good man," says Cicero, "will refuse to accept presents from the wicked." [36] When the gift is thought of as amends for a fault, however, we have entered upon more distinctly ethical ground. It is, nevertheless, only in the Piacular or Expiatory view that theories of sacrifice reach their ethical culmination. In this view the offerer is supposed to come before God burdened with a sense of sin and seeking to expiate its guilt. The victim which he offers is looked upon as his substitute, to which is transferred the punishment which is his due; and the penalty having been thus vicariously borne, the offerer may receive forgiveness for his sin. Among the older writers W. Outram is usually looked upon as the type of this view: he explains the death of the victim as "some evil inflicted on one party in order to expiate the guilt of another in the sense of delivering the guilty from punishment and procuring the forgiveness of sin." [37] The general view has been held not only by such writers as P. Fairbairn, J. H. Kurtz, E. W. Hengstenberg, but also by such others as W. Gesenius, W. M. L. de Wette and even Bruno Bauer. E. Westermarck himself defines "the original idea in sacrifice a piaculum, a substitute for the offerer." [38]

A matter of importance which it may be well to observe in passing is that in no one of these theories are sacrifices sup-

[35] See Paterson (as cited, p. 341 a), who gives this form of the Symbolical Theory the not very satisfactory name of The Prayer Theory.

[36] "De Leg.," ii. 16.

[37] "De Sacrificiis libri duo," 1677 (E. T., "Two Dissertations on Sacrifices" . . . 1828) p. 248.

[38] J. J. Reeve, in the "International Standard Bible Encyclopaedia," p. 2640 quoting from "The Origin and Development of Moral Ideas," 1906. For Westermarck's notions as to expiating sacrifice at large, see v. i. pp. 61–72.

posed to terminate immediately upon the offerer and to have their direct effect upon him. The offerer offers them; but it is to the deity that he offers them; and their direct effect, whatever it may be, is naturally upon the deity. Of course the offerer seeks a benefit for himself by his offerings, and in this sense ultimately they terminate on him; and in some instances their operation upon him is conceived quite mechanically.[39] Nevertheless it is always through their effect on the deity that they are supposed to affect men, and their immediate effect is upon the deity himself. The nearest to an exception to this is provided by those theories in which the stress is laid on the sacrificial feast, or rather, among these, by those theories in which the worshipper is supposed to "eat the God" and thereby to become sharer in his divine qualities. Even this notion, however, is an outgrowth of the general conception which rules all sacrificial worship, that the purpose of the sacrifice is so to affect the deity as to secure its favorable regard for the worshipper or its favorable action in his behalf or upon him. This conception is no doubt extended in this special case to a great extreme, in representing the benefit hoped for, sought and obtained, to be the actual transfusion of the deity's powers into the

[39] Hubert and Mauss, as cited, p. 41, seeking a comprehensive definition, fix on this: "Sacrifice is a religious act which, by the consecrating of a victim, modifies the state of the moral person who offers it or of certain objects in which that person is interested." The meaning of this is amplified in an earlier passage (p. 37): "In sacrifice on the contrary" — as distinguished, that is, from such acts, as, say, anointing — "the consecration extends beyond the thing consecrated; it extends among others, to the moral person who defrays the cost of the ceremony. The believer who has supplied the victim, the object consecrated, is not at the end of the operation what he was at its beginning. He has acquired a religious character which he did not have, or he is relieved from an unfavorable character by which he was afflicted: he is elevated to a state of grace, or he has issued from a state of sin. In either case he is religiously transformed." In a note on the same page, on the basis of certain Hindu texts, they add: "These *benefits* from the sacrifice are, in our view, necessary reactions (*contrecoups*) of the rite. They are not due to a free divine will which theology interpolates little by little between the religious act and its sequences." On this view sacrifices are assimilated to magical acts, and their effects are conceived somewhat on the analogy of what is known as the reflex action of prayer. But if the deity is thought of merely as the object from which the sacrifices rebound to the offerer, it is on it nevertheless that they must first strike that they may rebound.

worshipper's person. Even so, however, the fundamental idea of sacrifices is retained — the securing of something from the deity for the worshipper; and this is something very different from a transaction intended directly to call out action on the part of the worshipper himself. It is in effect subversive of the whole principle of sacrificial worship to imagine that sacrifices are offered directly to affect the worshippers and to secure action from them: their purpose is to affect the deity and to secure beneficial action on its part. "The purpose of sacrifice," says J. Jeremias justly,[40] "is invariably to influence the deity in favour of the sacrificer." Every time the writers of the New Testament speak of the work of Christ under the rubric of a sacrifice, therefore, they bear witness — under any theory of sacrifice current among scholars — that they conceive of His work as directed Godward and as intended directly to affect God, not man.

It must be borne steadily in mind that the theories of sacrificial worship which we have been enumerating do not necessarily represent the judgment of their adherents on the nature and implications of sacrificial worship in the developed ritual of Israel, and much less in the decadence of Israelitish religion which is thought to have been in progress when the New Testament books were written. These theories are general theories and are put forward as attempts to determine the ideas which gave birth to and in this sense underlie all sacrificial worship. The adherents of these theories for the most part recognize that in the course of the history of sacrificial worship many changes of conception took place, here, there, and elsewhere; many new ideas were incorporated and many old ones lost. They are quite prepared to look for and to trace out in the history of sacrificial worship, therefore, at least a "development," and this "development" is not thought of as necessarily running on the same lines — certainly not *pari passu* — in every nation. Though these theorists are inclined, therefore, to conceive all sacrificial worship as rooting in one notion, they are ordinarily willing to recognize that the "development" of sacrificial worship may have taken, or actually did take, its own

[40] "Encyclopaedia Biblica," col. 4120.

direction in each region of the earth and among each people, as the conditions of its existence and modifying influences may have varied from time to time or from place to place. The history of sacrificial worship in Israel becomes thus a special subject of investigation; and scholars engaged upon it have wrought out their schemes of "development," beginning, each, with his own theory of the origin and essential presuppositions of sacrificial worship, and leading up through the stages recognized by him to the culmination of Israelitish sacrificial worship in the Levitical system. When we say that the sacrificial worship of Israel culminated in the Levitical system, this has a special significance for the investigations in question, seeing that they ordinarily proceed more or less completely on the assumption of the schematization of the development of religion in Israel which has been worked out by the Graf-Wellhausen school. This places the Levitical system at the end of the long development, and looks upon it as the final outcome of the actual religious effort of Israel. From this point of view we are apt to have, therefore, successively, discussions of sacrificial worship in the primitive Semitic ages, in the early Israelitish times, in the prophetic period, and in the prescriptions of the Levitical law. Thus a long course of development is interposed between the origin of sacrifices and the enactments of the Levitical legislation; and the theorists are free from all embarrassment when they find sacrifices bearing a very different meaning and charged with very different implications in the Levitical system from what they had conceived their fundamental, that is, speaking historically, their primitive meaning and implication to be. It is not surprising, therefore, that in point of fact, the theorizers do ordinarily find the conceptions expressed in the Levitical system different from the fundamental ideas which they suppose to have been originally embodied in sacrificial worship.

It is quite common for them to find this difference precisely in this, — that the Levitical system is the elaborate embodiment of the piacular idea, while in earlier times some one of the other conceptions of sacrifice prevailed. On this view it is customary to say that the idea of expiation is first elaborated in the post-exilic period, in which the sin-offering takes the first place among types of sacrifices, and that special expiatory sacrifices are mentioned first in Ezekiel (xl. 39, xlii. 13, xliii. 19). The assumptions in this construction, to be sure, are challenged on both sides.

It is pointed out, on the one side, that the rise of special expiatory sacrifices is not the same thing as the rise of the conception of expiation in connection with sacrifices. A. Kuenen notes,[41] for example, that the burnt-offering, which is thought the oldest of all sacrifices, was offered in earlier times in those cases for which, in the completed legislation, the expiatory sacrifices proper were required; and indeed it is clear that the whole burnt-offering can still be expiatory in the late document which is isolated as P (Lev. i. 4, xiv. 20, xvi. 24). And Robertson Smith does not hesitate to declare [42] that "the atoning function of sacrifice is not confined to a particular class of oblation, but belongs to all sacrifices." Of course this declaration is made from his own point of view; but it is not valid merely from his point of view. For him all sacrifices go back to a primitive form in which the object is to maintain or to reinstate communion with the God. Expiation is in his view only the re-establishment of the broken bond: the original totemistic sacrifice had all the effects of an expiatory rite; and in all the developments which have followed, this element in their significance has never been lost. All trace of totemism is effaced; but the sense of expiation always abides and thus becomes the constant feature of sacrifices. Hubert and Mauss arrive at the same result along another pathway.[43] In all sacrifices there is a thing offered — the victim, we may call it for brevity's sake. This victim is an intermediary. When we say intermediary, however, we say representative. And when we say representative, we say broadly, substitute. "This is why the offerer inserts between the religious forces and himself intermediaries, the chief of which is the victim. If he went through this rite to the

[41] "The Religion of Israel," ii. p. 263.
[42] "Religion of the Semites²," p. 237.   [43] As cited, p. 134.

end himself, he would find in it death and not life. The victim takes his place. It alone enters into the dangerous region of the sacrifice, it succumbs there, and it is there in order to succumb. The offerer remains under cover; the gods take the victim instead of taking him. *It ransoms him.*" "There is no sacrifice," they add emphatically, "in which there does not intervene some idea of ransom." We may take it to be sufficiently clear, then, that, whatever conceptions may have from time to time and from place to place dominated the minds of sacrificial worship, the one constant idea which has always been present in it is precisely that of piacular mediation. And it is very plain indeed that we cannot look upon the Levitical legislation as the introduction of the piacular conception into the sacrificial system of Israel.

The criticism directed from the other side against the assumptions of the theory in question cannot be held to be so successful. The general contention of this criticism is that, while it is to be admitted that the drift in Israel was towards the piacular conception, yet that drift had not reached its goal in the Levitical system, which thus at best marks only a stage in the progress towards it. There are some indeed who will not grant even so much as this. They see very definitely expressed in the Levitical system too some quite different conception of sacrificial worship, the Homage conception, say, or the Communion conception, according to which respectively the sacrifices are thought of as analogous to prayers or to sacraments. Others find it more convenient simply to deny that any definite conception whatever informs the Levitical system. The framers of this legislation were not clear in their own minds what was the real nature of sacrificial worship, but were content to practice it as an ordinance of God and to leave the mode of its operation in that mystery which probably enhanced rather than curtailed its influence upon the awe-stricken consciousness of the worshipper.[44] This extreme view has obtained a very considerable vogue, but need scarcely be taken seriously. It is plain

[44] R. Smend, "Lehrb. d. A. T. Religionsgeschichte," p. 324, cf. G. F. Moore, "Encyclopaedia Biblica," col. 4226. Compare also A. B. Davidson, "Theology

enough that the Levitical system is something more than a series of blind rites, the whole value of the performance of which lies in the manifestation of implicit obedience to God. And it is generally allowed that the sacrificial conception of Israel, one stage in the development of which is marked by the Levitical system, was moving towards the idea of expiation to which it ultimately attained. Rudolf Smend, for instance, who supposes that the earliest sacrificial ideas of Israel saw in the sacrifices only acts of homage, yet considers that these ideas were steadily modified in later ages until they had run through all the stages up to that of reparation of sin — although he thinks it doubtful if the Israelites ever attained to a truly substitutionary theory.[45] H. J. Holtzmann, while insisting that the penal interpretation is not that of the law, feels compelled to admit that it was nevertheless the popular doctrine of the Jews and that traces of it found their way into the code itself.[46] A. B. Davidson, who believes that the earliest idea connected with sacrifice in Israel was that of "a gift to placate God," considers that this idea still underlies the law, and yet "in later times the other side was more prominent, that the death of the creature was of the nature of penalty, by the exaction of which the righteousness of Jehovah was satisfied." [47] "This idea," he adds, "seems certainly expressed in Isa. liii; at least these two points appear to be stated there, that the sins of the people, i.e., the penalties for them, were laid on the servant and borne by him; and secondly, that thus the people were relieved from the penalty, and their sins being borne were forgiven." That there was a substitution in the law itself is recognized, on the other

of the Old Testament," pp. 352–354, where he says that the author of Leviticus has contented himself with stating the fact that the offering of a life atones, suggesting no explanation of why or how it atones. But he proceeds to remark that we can scarcely agree with Riehm that the blood atones merely because it is ordained that it shall, but should no doubt assume that there was a reason for the ordination, understood or not by the worshipper but no doubt at least dimly felt.

[45] As cited, p. 128.

[46] "Lehrbuch der Neutestamentlichen Theologie¹," 1897, v. i, pp. 67-68.

[47] "Theology of the Old Testament," p. 355, cf. 353. The use made of Davidson by W. L. Walker, "The Gospel of Reconciliation," 1909, p. 21, seems scarcely justified.

hand, by A. Dillmann, although he insists that this was not a substitution in kind, but of something not itself sin-bearing.[48]

W. Robertson Smith is well known as the powerful advocate of one of the lowest possible theories of the meaning of the primitive sacrifices of the Semites — that which sees the origin of sacrifice in a meal in which the worshipper was supposed to become physically imbued with the God on whom he fed in symbol. But he did not imagine that the Semitic peoples continued permanently to be sunk in this crass notion. Following Robertson Smith's guidance, W. P. Paterson adopts the common-meal conception of primitive sacrifice — "the fundamental motive was to gratify God by giving or sharing with Him a meal" — but fully recognizes that such changes had taken place in the progress of time that the Levitical system was just an elaborate embodiment of the piacular idea. In his view the whole system — in all its elements, and that not merely of animal but even of vegetable offerings — "contemplated the community as being in a state of guilt, and requiring to be reconciled to God." In it, in short, sacrifices "have in fact become — not excepting the Peace-offering in its later interpretation — piacular sacrifices which dispose God to mercy, procure the forgiveness of sin and avert punishment."[49] Accordingly he expounds the matter thus:[50] "The expiation of guilt is the leading purpose of the Levitical sacrifices. Their office is to cover or make atonement for sin. The word employed to describe this specific effect is כִּפֶּר. This efficacy is connected with all four kinds of principal offerings; the objects of the covering are persons and sins; the covering takes place before God, and it stands in a specially close relation to the sprinkling of the blood and the burning of the sacrificial flesh (Lev. i. 4,

---

[48] "A. T. Theologie," pp. 488–489.

[49] Hastings' "Dictionary of the Bible," v. iv, p. 338 b: "The Meat-offering also covered from sin and delivered from its consequences."

[50] As cited, p. 339 a. Cf. p. 342 a, where he sums up: "More likely is it that the step deemed by Holtzmann inevitable at a later stage was already taken, and that the chaos of confused ideas resulting from the discredit of old views was averted by the assertion of the substitutionary idea — 'the most external indeed, but also the simplest, the most generally intelligible, and the readiest answer to the question as to the nature of expiation.'"

etc.)." It is not to be doubted, of course, that elements of adoration and of sacramental communion also enter into the sacrificial rites of the Levitical system: nothing could be clearer than that in the several sacrificial ordinances, a variety of religious motives find appropriate expression, and a variety of religious impressions are aimed at and produced. But it would seem quite impossible to erect these motives and impressions into the main, and certainly not into the sole, notion expressed or object sought in these ordinances. It may be confidently contended that, present as they undoubtedly are, they are present as subsidiary and ancillary to the fundamental function of the sacrifice, which is to propitiate the offended deity in behalf of sinful man. Any unbiased study of the Levitical system must issue, as it seems to us, in the conviction that this system is through and through, in its intention and effect, piacular.

It is, naturally, quite possible to contend that it is not of the first importance for the interpretation of the New Testament writers, when they represent our Lord as a sacrifice, to determine what the conception of sacrifice was which underlay the Levitical legislation. It may be urged that the ideas of the writers of the New Testament were not influenced so much by the Levitical system, as by the notion of sacrifice current in the Jewish thought of their time. As we have seen, however, there are very few who doubt that the Jews in the time when the New Testament was in writing held the doctrine of substitutive expiation in connection with the sacrificial system. George F. Moore is one of these few.[51] He is quite sure that the idea of *poena vicaria* is a pure importation into the Old Testament, the prevailing conception of sacrifice in which he conceives to be that of "gift." And he seems to imply that the later Jewish doctors were of a quite indefinite mind as to how the sacrifice operated in expiating sin. "The theory that the victim's life is put in place of the owner's," he remarks, "is nowhere hinted at"; and he adds that this is "perhaps because the Jewish doctors understood better than our theologians what sin-offerings and trespass offerings were, and what they were for." We

[51] "Encyclopaedia Biblica," v. iv, coll. 4223–4226.

must leave it to him to make clear to himself — he has not made it clear to us — how such offerings could have been understood to "atone" — to make expiation for sin and to propitiate the offended deity — by the interposition of a slain victim, without any idea of vicarious penalty creeping in.

Even G. B. Stevens will not go the lengths of this. He apparently agrees with Moore, indeed, that the idea of the *poena vicaria* is absent from Old Testament sacrifices. But he seems to allow it even a determining place in the later Judaism. His prime contention at this point is, indeed, that it was from this later Judaism that Paul, for example, derived this conception. For he admits that in Paul, at least, "we have here the idea of satisfaction by substitution"; [52] and the precise thing on which he insists is that "this legalistic scheme which Paul wrought out of the materials of current Jewish thought." [53] He never tires in fact of scoring this teaching of Paul's as a mere remnant of Phariseeism,[54] in which, therefore, Christians are not bound to follow him. He is clearly so far right in this that this conception was part of Pharisaic belief. There are two conceptions indeed which beyond question — and probably no one questions it — lay together in the minds of the men of the New Testament times, forming the presuppositions of their thought concerning sin and its forgiveness. The one is that atonement for sin was wrought by the sacrifices; the other that vicarious sufferings availed for atonement. The former conception is crisply expressed by Heinrich Weinel thus: "At that time almost the only thought connected with sacrifice was that of a propitiatory rite, accompanied by the shedding of blood." [55] With respect to the latter H. H. Wendt points out the currency in the time of Jesus of "the idea of the expiatory significance of sufferings for guilt, and of the substitutionary significance of the excessive sufferings of the righteous for the sins of others." [56]

[52] "The Christian Doctrine of Salvation," p. 62, cf. p. 65.
[53] As cited, p. 66.
[54] As cited, pp. 73–75.　　　　　　　　[55] "Saint Paul," E. T., p. 302.
[56] "Teaching of Jesus," E. T., v. ii, p. 243. He refers in support to F. Weber, "Jüdische Theologie²," 1897, § 70, p. 326 ff. and to E. Schürer, "Geschichte des jüdischen Volkes," v. ii, p. 466 (E. T. Div. II. v. ii, p. 186).

Needless to say both facts thus expressed are fully recognized even by, say, G. F. Moore. He tells us that in the Palestinian schools of the first and second Christian centuries, "the effect of sacrifice is expressed as in the Pentateuch, by the verb *kipper*, 'make propitiation,' 'expiation,'" and that "the general principle is that all private sacrifices atone, except peace offerings (including thank offerings), with which no confession of sin is made." [57] And he tells us as explicitly not only that an expiatory character was attributed to suffering, but that "the suffering and death of righteous men" were held "to atone for the sins of others." [58] It would seem inconceivable that such relatable ideas could be kept apart in the mind which gave harborage to both: it is inhuman for us to imagine that men, merely because they lived a few hundred years ago, were incapable of putting even one and one together. And as we read over, say, the ceremonial for the Day of Atonement in the Mishnah tractate *Yoma* we can scarcely fail to see that this one and one were put together. Paul Fiebig occupies a general position very similar to that of G. F. Moore: he is eager to make it clear that the men of old time in their religious rites troubled themselves very little about ideas, and lived much more in usages and ceremonies carried out with painful exactness. Yet he cannot refuse to add: [59] "This is not to say that the ritual of the Day of Atonement did not suggest a variety of ideas, — this idea for example: 'You, a sinner, have really deserved death, but this sacrificial animal now bears the punishment of your sin.' Or this: 'The sacrificial animal now bears the sin away into the wilderness; so soon as the goat which is sent to Azazel (cf. Lev. xvi.) into the wilderness is gone, the sins have also disappeared.' Ideas of substitution and reparation, of bearing the curse of sin, — and also of a gift by means of which the deity is to be propitiated — are suggested here. The sacrificial animal might also be thought of as a purchase price, as ransom-money, and the whole sacrifice be placed under the point of view of ransoming. All these ideas were suggested

[57] As cited, col. 4223. [58] As cited, col. 4226, cf. col. 4232.
[59] "Jesu Blut ein Geheimnis?" 1906, p. 33.

and were simply and easily to be read out of the ritual." We think it necessary to say, not merely that such ideas as these might be suggested by the ceremonial of the Day of Atonement, and — each in its own measure — by the several varieties of sacrifice which were in use; but that they were inevitably suggested by them and, in point of fact, formed the circle of ideas which make up in their entirety what we may justly think of as the sacrificial conception of the time.[60]

Whether, then, we look to the Levitical system or to the conceptions current at the time when the New Testament was written as determining the sense of the writers of the New Testament when they spoke of Christ as a sacrifice, the most natural meaning that can be attached to the term on their lips is that of an expiatory offering propitiating God's favor and reconciling Him to guilty man. An attempt may be made, to be sure, to break the force of this finding by representing sacrificial worship to have fallen so much into the background in the time of our Lord that it no longer possessed importance for the religious thought of the day. Martin Brückner tells us

[60] It is by a misapprehension that J. K. Mozley, "The Doctrine of Atonement," 1916, p. 20, supporting himself on G. B. Stevens, seems to deny the sacrificial character of the scape-goat: "As to the ritual of the Day of Atonement, here also the old opinion is not as firmly established as might appear at first sight. The culminating point is the sending away of the goat 'for Azazel,' but we must remember that 'the flesh of this goat was not burned; atonement was not made by its blood; it was not a sacrifice at all.'" The quotation is from Stevens, as cited, p. 11. On the other hand Hugo Gressmann, "Der Ursprung der israelitisch-jüdischen Eschatologie," 1905, pp. 328–329 sees the sacrificial idea at its height represented in the scape-goat. He is speaking of the Ebed and adverting to the ascription of "a substitutive expiatory character" to his sufferings and death, and remarks: "The sacrificial idea stands in the background. We have materially an exact parallel in the goat of Azazel which was offered as an expiatory sacrifice on the great Day of Atonement. . . . The goat is burdened with the sin of the congregation and offered substitutionally for it. For the expulsion of the goat is only a specific form of sacrifice (Hubert et Mauss, "Essai sur la nature et la fonction du sacrifice" in L'Année Sociologique Second quar., Paris, 1898, p. 75). The expiatory significance which is attached to the death of the Ebed fully corresponds with the expiatory character which is ascribed here to the goat." At the place cited, supplemented at pp. 78f. and 92, Hubert and Mauss assign the scape-goat to its right category and expound convincingly its character as an expiatory sacrifice, thus supplying a corrective to the exposition of W. R. Smith on which Stevens supports himself.

that there is no exposition of the Jewish theory of sacrifice
given in W. Bousset's book on the "Religion of Judaism" because "there wasn't any." [61] Supposing, however, the fact to
be as stated — that the doctrine of sacrifice played so small a
part in the religion of the later Judaism that it may be treated
as negligible in a summary of the religious conceptions of the
time, — that would only add significance to the employment
of it by the New Testament writers as a paradigm into which
to run their conception of the work of Christ. The further they
must be supposed to have gone afield to find this rubric, the
more importance they must be supposed to have attached to
it as a vehicle of their doctrine. We are not inquiring into the
abstract likelihood of the New Testament writers making use
of a rare rubric: their use of it is not in dispute.[62] We are estimating the measure of significance which must be attributed
to their use of a rubric which they actually employ. The less a
mere matter-of-course their employment of it can be shown to
be, the more it must be recognized that they had a distinct purpose in using it and the more weight must be assigned to its
implications in their hands. Brückner's remark, therefore, that
sacrificial worship had become in the time of Christ "without
importance" for Jewish theology reacts injuriously upon his
main contention in the passage where it occurs — namely that
it was without importance for Paul.

It has become almost a fashion to speak minimizingly of
Paul's employment of the category of sacrifice in his explanation of Christ's work, and it is interesting to observe how hard
Nemesis treads on the heels of the attempt to do so. Brückner's
instance affords a very good example. What he wishes to do is
to lower the importance of the conception of sacrifice in Paul's
system of thought concerning the work of Christ. He seeks to
do this by suggesting that the sacrificial language served with
Paul little further purpose than to express the notion of sub-

[61] "Die Entstehung des paulinischen Christologie," 1903, p. 231.

[62] Of course nothing is ever absolutely undisputed. Paterson, as cited, p. 343,
b, very properly remarks: "It has been denied that Paul adopts the category
(Schmidt, "Die paul. Christologie," p. 84) but the denial rests on dogmatic rather
than on exegetical grounds (Ritschl, ii. p. 161)."

stitution. "The idea of a sacrifice," he remarks, "came into consideration for Paul only as an illustration of a conception: the thing which he intended lies in the theory of substitution" — a substitution which, he proceeds to show, includes in it the idea of "a substitutive punishment." Paul, in other words, calls Christ a sacrifice only with a view to showing that Christ too offered Himself as a substitutive expiation of our sins. What more could he be supposed to have intended? The contrast between the minimizing tone adopted and the effect of the facts adduced to support it, is perhaps even more striking in the remarks of A. E. J. Rawlinson, writing in the collection of Oxford essays published under the title of "Foundations."[63] With Paul, he tells us, Christ is spoken of as a sacrifice only by way of "an occasional illustration or a momentary point of comparison." He refers to Christ as "our Passover, sacrificed for us," as "making peace by his blood," as in some sense a "propitiation." "Apart from the three phrases quoted in the text," he adds in a note, "and the statement in Ephesians v. 2, 'Even as Christ also loved you and gave Himself up for us, an offering and a sacrifice to God, for an odour of a sweet smell' — where the self-oblation of Christ is compared not to a sin-offering, but to a burnt-offering, — there do not appear to be any passages in St. Paul which interpret the work of Christ in sacrificial terms." Not Gal. iii. 13 (Deut. xxi. 23), since "sacrificial victims were never regarded as 'accursed.'" Not in the idea of vicarious suffering — which is not a sacrificial idea — only the scape-goat being a sin-bearer (Lev. xvi.) and the scape-goat not being sacrificed. The reader will scarcely escape the impression that a great deal of unavailing trouble is being expended here in an effort to remove unwelcome facts out of the way. And it will not be strange if he wonders what advantage is supposed to be gained from insisting that Paul has made little use of the category of sacrifice for expounding his view of the nature of Christ's work, so long as it is recognized that he does employ it, and that therefore it must be understood to be a suitable expression of his view. "St. Paul does not appear to have made

[63] "Foundations," 1912, p. 194.

great use of Old Testament ideas of sacrifice," remarks J. K. Mozley:[64] "Ritschl indeed in the second volume of his great work, lays stress on the importance of the sacrificial system for Paul's doctrine, but we can hardly go beyond the balanced statement of Dr. Stevens ("Christian Doctrine of Salvation," p. 63): 'While Paul has made a less frequent and explicit use of sacrificial ideas than we should have expected, it is clear that the system supplied one of the forms of thought by which he interpreted Christ's death.'" That allowed, however, and all is allowed: agree that the rubric of sacrifice lent itself naturally to the expression of what Paul would convey concerning the death of Christ,[65] and we might as well say frankly with Paterson that to Paul, "the sacrifice of Christ had the significance of the death of an innocent victim in the room of the guilty," and add with him, with equal frankness: "It is vain to deny that St. Paul freely employs the category of substitution, involving the conception of the imputation or transference of moral qualities" — although it might perhaps be well to use some more exact phraseology in saying it than Paterson has managed to employ.

There is one book of the New Testament of which it has proved impossible for even the hardiest to deny that Christ's death is presented in it as a sacrifice. We refer, of course, to the Epistle to the Hebrews. In it not only is Christ's death directly described as a sacrifice, but all the sacrificial language is gathered about it in the repeated allusions which are made

[64] "The Doctrine of the Atonement," 1916, p. 79, note.

[65] Is perhaps part of the difficulty which so many writers feel on this matter due to approaching it from a wrong angle, and thinking not so much of Paul's expressing his convictions concerning Christ's death in terms of sacrifice as of his imposing on the death of Christ mechanically ideas derived from the sacrifices? Paul's conviction that Christ had died for our sins, bearing them in His own body on the tree, is the primary thing: the sacrificial language he applies to it is one of his modes of stating this fundamental fact. He begins always with the great fact of the expiatory death of Christ. "Ménégoz has admirably remarked," says Orello Cone justly in a parallel matter, "that Paul's faith in the expiatory sacrifice of Christ was not the conclusion of a process of reasoning on the relation between the mercy and justice of God, but, on the contrary, the apostle's ideas on the justice and mercy of God were founded on his faith in the expiatory death of Christ."

to it as such.[66] Nor is it doubtful that it is distinctly of expiatory sacrifices that the author is thinking when he presents Christ as dying a sacrificial death. He even uses of it "that characteristic term inseparably associated in the Old Testament with these sacrifices" (ἱλάσκομαι, ii. 17) the absence of which from the allusion to Christ's sacrifice in other parts of the New Testament has been made a matter of remark — although it is not really absent from them, but is present in its derivatives (ἱλαστήριον, Rom. iii. 25; ἱλασμός, I John ii. 2, iv. 10) justifying fully Paterson's remark [67] that "the idea of cancelling guilt, of which a vital moment is liability to punishment, is associated with Christ's sacrifice in Heb. ii. 17, I John ii. 2 (ἱλάσκεσθαι with ἁμαρτίας as object, and so 'to expiate')." The Epistle to the Hebrews does not, however, really stand apart from the rest of the New Testament in these things, as, indeed, we have just incidentally pointed out with reference to the Levitical term for sacrificial expiation, employed as it is by Paul and John as well as by this author. It only has its own points to make and distributes the emphasis to suit them. Even in such a peculiar matter as the ascription to Christ at once of the functions of priest and sacrifice, it may possibly have a parallel in Eph. v. 2.[68] The fact is, as Paterson broadly asserts in words

[66] B. F. Westcott, "Epistle to the Hebrews," p. 299, speaks of Christ's sacrifice as being presented in the Epistle to the Hebrews "in three distinct aspects," "(1) as a Sacrifice of Atonement (ix. 14, 15); (2) as a Covenant Sacrifice (ix. 15–17); and (3) as a Sacrifice which is the ground-work of a Feast (xiii. 10, 11)." This is true; but it is possible to press analysis over-far. The "Sacrifice which is the ground-work of a Feast" is the sacrifice of which we hear in the institution of the Lord's Supper, and this is distinctly a "Covenant Sacrifice." The "Covenant Sacrifice" (ix. 15, 17) is a sacrifice for sin (ix. 12, 26), and is therefore fundamentally piacular and atoning, as indeed its relation to the passover-lamb sufficiently intimates. In His sacrifice Christ fulfilled all the functions of sacrifice, and thus there are varied aspects in which His sacrifice may be looked upon. But above all else, He made expiation for the sins of His people by immolating Himself on the altar — thus putting away sin by the sacrifice of Himself.

[67] As cited, p. 344 a.

[68] Cf. J. K. Mozley, "The Doctrine of the Atonement," 1916, p. 82, note 1: "Eph. 1, 7 also refutes Pfleiderer's statement (ii. 175) that in this Epistle Christ is not the expiatory sacrifice, but the sacrificing priest. The latter idea is certainly that of v. 2, but St. Paul may as easily have united the two conceptions as did the writer to the Hebrews."

which were quoted from him at the opening of this discussion,
that every important type of New Testament teaching, including the teaching of Christ Himself, concurs in representing
Christ as a sacrifice, and in conceiving of the sacrifice which it
represents Christ as being, as a substitutive expiation. We say,
including Christ Himself; and we may say that with our eye
exclusively on the Synoptic Gospels. The language of Mt. xx.
28, Mk. x. 45 is sacrificial language; and it is very distinctly
substitutive language, — "In the place of many." That of Mt.
xxvi. 28, Mk. xiv. 24, Lk. xxii. 20 (the critical questions which
have been raised about these passages are negligible) is sacrificial language; and it is equally distinctly expiatory language
— "Blood shed for many," "For the remission of sins." [69]

The possibility of underrating the wealth and importance
of the allusions of the writers of the New Testament to the
death of Christ as sacrificial, in the sense of expiatory, appears
to depend upon a tendency to recognize such allusions only
when express references to sacrifices are made in connection
with it, if we should not even say only when didactic expositions
of it as a sacrifice are developed. Nothing can be more certain,
for example, than that the references to the "blood" of Jesus
are one and all ascriptions of a sacrificial character and effect
to His death. [70] Nevertheless, we meet with attempts to explain
these ascriptions away. Thus, for example, G. F. Moore writes
as follows, having more particularly in mind Paul's usage: [71]
"Evidence of a more pervasive association of Christ's death
with sacrifice has been sought in the references to his blood
as the ground of the benefits conferred by his death (Rom. iii.
25, v. 9): the thought of sacrifice is so constantly associated
with his death, it is said, that the one word suffices to suggest

[69] Cf. the discussion of these passages by Mozley, as cited, chapter ii.

[70] In general these references comprise: (1) certain general passages, Heb. ix.
14, 20, x. 29, xii. 24, I Pet. i. 19, I John i. 7; (2) certain eucharistic passages, Mt.
xxvi. 28, Mk. xiv. 24, Luke xxii. 20, I Cor. xi. 25; John vi. 53, 54, 55, 56, I Cor.
x. 16; (3) the formula, διὰ τῆς αἵματος (or its equivalent), Acts xx. 28, Eph. i. 7,
Col. i. 20, Heb. ix. 12, xiii. 12 (I John v. 6), Rev. xii. 11; and (4) the formula
ἐν τῷ αἵματι (or its equivalent) Rom. iii. 25, v. 9, I Cor. xi. 25 (27) Eph. ii. 13,
Heb. x. 19 (xiii. 25), I John v. 6, Rev. i. 5, v. 9, vii. 14.

[71] "Encyclopaedia Biblica," coll. 4229–4230.

it. But in view of the infrequency, to say the least, of sacrificial metaphors in the greater epistles, it is doubtful whether αἷμα is not used merely in allusion to Jesus' violent death. Nor is the case clearer in Col. i. 20, Eph. i. 7, ii. 13; the really noteworthy thing is that the context contains no suggestion of sacrifice either in thought or phrase." Such argumentation seems to us merely perverse. The discovery of allusions to the sacrificial character of Christ's death in the reiterated mention of His blood is not a mere assumption deriving color only from the frequency of other references to His sacrificial death; it has its independent ground in the nature of these allusions themselves. In every instance mentioned, so far from the context containing no suggestion of sacrifice, it is steeped in sacrificial suggestions. Is there no sacrificial suggestion in such language as this: "Whom God set forth as a propitiation, through faith, in His blood"? Or in such language as this: "While we were yet sinners Christ died for us: much more then having been now justified by His blood, we shall be saved by Him from the wrath"? Or as this: "And by Him to reconcile all things unto Him, having made peace through the blood of His cross"? Or as this: "In whom we have redemption through His blood, the forgiveness of sins"? Or as this: "But now in Christ Jesus you who once were far off have been made nigh in the blood of Christ"? This is the very language of the altar: "propitiation," "reconciliation," "redemption," "forgiveness." It passes all comprehension how it could be suggested that the word "blood" could be employed in such connections "merely in allusion to Jesus' violent death." And that particularly when Jesus' death was not actually an especially bloody death. "Another remarkable thing," says Paul Fiebig.[72] "is this: why is precisely the 'blood' of Jesus so often spoken of? Why is the redemption and the forgiveness of sins so often connected with the 'blood' of Jesus? This is remarkable; for the death on the cross was not so very bloody that it should be precisely the blood of Jesus which so impressed the eye-witnesses and the first Christians. The Evangelists moreover (except John xix.

[72] As cited, p. 11.

35 f.) say nothing about it. This special emphasis on the blood
cannot be explained therefore from the kind of death Jesus
died." If we really wish to know what the New Testament
writers had in mind when they spoke of the blood of Jesus we
have only to permit them to tell us themselves. They always
adduce it in the sacrificial sense. In his survey of the passages
Fiebig begins [73] not unnaturally with I Pet. i. 17–19. "Knowing that ye were redeemed, not with corruptible things, with
silver or gold, from your vain manner of life handed down from
your fathers: but with precious blood as of a lamb without
blemish and without spot, Christ." His comment runs thus:
"Here the clause 'as of a pure and unspotted lamb' makes
quite clear what the popular and at that time wholly clear
conception is which provides the key to the problem of the
redemptive significance of the blood of Jesus. This conception
is the sacrifice; and of course the sacrifice such as every Jew
(and in corresponding fashion, every heathen) knew it from his
daily life and from the festivals and duties of his religion."
This is of course only one passage; but in this case the adage
is true, *ab uno disce omnes,* — we may spare ourselves the survey of the whole series.

The theology of the writers of the New Testament is very
distinctly a "blood theology." But their reiterated reference
of the salvation of men to the blood of Christ is not the only
way in which they represent the work of Christ as in its essential character sacrificial. In numerous other forms of allusion
they show that they conceived the idea of sacrifice to supply
a suitable explanation of its nature and effect. We may avail
ourselves of words of James Denney to sum up the matter
briefly, — words which are in certain respects over-cautious,
but which contain the essence of the matter. "We have every
reason to believe," says he,[74] "that sacrificial blood universally,
and not only in special cases, was associated with propitiatory
power. 'The atoning function of sacrifice,' as Robertson Smith
put it, speaking of primitive times, 'is not confined to a par-

[73] P. 13.
[74] "The Death of Christ," ed. 1903, pp. 53–54.

ticular class of oblation, but belongs to all sacrifices.' [75] Dr. Driver has expressed the same opinion with regard to the Levitical legislation. . . . Criticizing Ritschl's explanation of sacrifice and its effect, he says,[76] it seems better to suppose that though the burnt-, peace- and meat-offerings were not offered *expressly*, like the sin- and guilt-offerings, for the forgiveness of sin, they nevertheless (in so far as *kipper* is predicated of them) were regarded as 'covering' or neutralizing, the offerer's unworthiness to appear before God and so, though in a much less degree than the sin- or guilt-offering, as effectively *Kappārā* in the sense ordinarily attached to the word, viz. 'propitiation.' Instead of saying 'in a much less degree' I should prefer to say 'with a less specific reference or application,' but the point is not material. What it concerns us to note is that the New Testament, while it abstains from interpreting Christ's death by any special prescriptions of the Levitical law, constantly uses sacrificial language to describe that death, and in doing so unequivocally recognizes in it a propitiatory character — in other words, a reference to sin and its forgiveness." What this fundamentally means is that the New Testament writers, in employing this language to describe the death of Christ, intended to represent that death as performing the functions of an expiatory sacrifice; wished to be understood as so representing it; and could not but be so understood by their first readers who were wonted to sacrificial worship.

An interesting proof that they were so understood is supplied by a remarkable fact emphasized in a striking passage by Adolf Harnack.[77] Wherever the Christian religion went, there blood-sacrifice ceased to be offered — just as the tapers go out when the sun rises. Christ's death was recognized everywhere where it became known as the reality of which they were the shadows. Having offered His own body once for all and by this one offering perfected forever them that are sanctified, it

---

[75] "Religion of the Semites," p. 219.

[76] Hastings' "Dictionary of the Bible," s.v. "Propitiation," p. 132.

[77] "Das Wesen des Christentums," ed. 1900, pp. 98–99: E. T., "What is Christianity?" 1901, pp. 157 ff.

was well understood that there remained no more offering for sin. "The death of Christ," says Harnack — "of this there can be no doubt — made an end to blood-sacrifices in the history of religion." "The instinct which led to them found its satisfaction and therefore its end in the death of Christ." "His death had the value of a sacrificial death; for otherwise it would not have had the power to penetrate into that inner world out of which the blood-sacrifices proceeded," — and, penetrating into it, to meet, and to satisfy all the needs which blood-sacrifices had been invented to meet and satisfy.

The whole world thus adds its testimony to the sacrificial character of Christ's death as it has received it, and as it rests upon it. As to the world's need of it, and as to the place it takes in the world, we shall let a sentence of C. Bigg's teach us. "The study of the great Greek and Roman moralists of the Empire," he tells us,[78] "leaves upon my own mind a strong conviction that the fundamental difference between heathenism of all shades and Christianity is to be discovered in the doctrine of Vicarious Sacrifice, that is to say, in the Passion of our Lord." This is as much as to say that not only is the doctrine of the sacrificial death of Christ embodied in Christianity as an essential element of the system, but in a very real sense it constitutes Christianity. It is this which differentiates Christianity from other religions. Christianity did not come into the world to proclaim a new morality and, sweeping away all the supernatural props by which men were wont to support their trembling, guilt-stricken souls, to throw them back on their own strong right arms to conquer a standing before God for themselves. It came to proclaim the real sacrifice for sin which God had provided in order to supersede all the poor fumbling efforts which men had made and were making to provide a sacrifice for sin for themselves; and, planting men's feet on this, to bid them go forward. It was in this sign that Christianity conquered, and it is in this sign alone that it continues to conquer. We may think what we will of such a religion. What cannot be denied is that Christianity is such a religion.

[78] "The Church's Task under the Roman Empire," pp. x.–xi.

XII

ON THE BIBLICAL NOTION OF "RENEWAL"

ON THE BIBLICAL NOTION OF "RENEWAL"[1]

The terms "renew," "renewing," are not of frequent occurrence in our English Bible. In the New Testament they do not occur at all in the Gospels, but only in the Epistles (Paul and Hebrews), where they stand, respectively, for the Greek terms ἀνακαινόω (II Cor. iv. 16, Col. iii. 10) with its cognates, ἀνακαινίζω (Heb. vi. 6) and ἀνανεόομαι (Eph. iv. 23), and ἀνακαίνωσις (Rom. xii. 2, Tit. iii. 5). If we leave to one side II Cor. iv. 16 and Heb. vi. 6, which are of somewhat doubtful interpretation, it becomes at once evident that a definite theological conception is embodied in these terms. This conception is that salvation in Christ involves a radical and complete transformation wrought in the soul (Rom. xii. 2, Eph. iv. 23) by God the Holy Spirit (Tit. iii. 5, Eph. iv. 24), by virtue of which we become "new men" (Eph. iv. 24, Col. iii. 10), no longer conformed to this world (Rom. xii. 2, Eph. iv. 22, Col. iii. 9), but in knowledge and holiness of the truth created after the image of God (Eph. iv. 24, Col. iii. 10, Rom. xii. 2). The conception, it will be seen, is a wide one, inclusive of all that is comprehended in what we now technically speak of as regeneration, renovation and sanctification. It embraces, in fact, the entire subjective side of salvation, which it represents as a work of God, issuing in a wholly new creation (II Cor. v. 17, Gal. vi. 15, Eph. ii. 10). What is indicated is, therefore, the need of such a subjective salvation by sinful man, and the provision for this need made in Christ (Eph. iv. 20, Col. iii. 11, Tit. iii. 6).

The absence of the terms in question from the Gospels does not in the least argue the absence from the teaching of the Gospels of the thing expressed by them. This thing is so of the essence of the religion of revelation that it could not be absent from any stage of its proclamation. That it should be

[1] From *The Princeton Theological Review*, v. ix, 1911, pp. 242–267.

absent would require that sin should be conceived to have wrought no subjective injury to man, so that he would need for his recovery from sin only an objective cancelling of his guilt and reinstatement in the favor of God. This is certainly not the conception of the Scriptures in any of their parts. It is uniformly taught in Scripture that by his sin man has not merely incurred the divine condemnation but also corrupted his own heart; that sin, in other words, is not merely guilt but depravity: and that there is needed for man's recovery from sin, therefore, not merely atonement but renewal; that salvation, that is to say, consists not merely in pardon but in purification. Great as is the stress laid in the Scriptures on the forgiveness of sins as the root of salvation, no less stress is laid throughout the Scriptures on the cleansing of the heart as the fruit of salvation. Nowhere is the sinner permitted to rest satisfied with pardon as the end of salvation; everywhere he is made poignantly to feel that salvation is realized only in a clean heart and a right spirit.

In the Old Testament, for example, sin is not set forth in its origin as a purely objective act with no subjective effects, or in its manifestation as a series of purely objective acts out of all relation to the subjective condition. On the contrary, the sin of our first parents is represented as no less corrupting than inculpating; shame is as immediate a fruit of it as fear (Gen. iii. 7). And, on the principle that no clean thing can come out of what is unclean (Job xiv. 4), all that are born of woman are declared "abominable and corrupt," to whose nature iniquity alone is attractive (Job xv. 14–16). Accordingly, to become sinful, men do not wait until the age of accountable action arrives. Rather, they are apostate from the womb, and as soon as they are born go astray, speaking lies (Ps. lviii. 3): they are even shapen in iniquity and conceived in sin (Ps. li. 5). The propensity (יֵצֶר) of their heart is evil from their youth (Gen. viii. 21), and it is out of the heart that all the issues of life proceed (Prov. iv. 23, xx. 11). Acts of sin are therefore but the expression of the natural heart, which is deceitful above all things and desperately sick (Jer. xvii. 9). The only hope of an amendment of the life, lies accordingly in a change of heart; and this change of heart is the desire of God for His people (Deut. v. 29) and the passionate longing of the saints for themselves (Ps. li. 10). It is, indeed, wholly beyond man's own power to achieve it. As well might the Ethiopian hope to change his skin and the leopard his spots as he who is wonted to evil to correct his ways (Jer. xiii. 23); and when it is a matter of cleansing not of hands but of heart — who can declare that he has made his heart clean and is pure from sin (Prov. xx. 9)? Men may be exhorted to circumcise their hearts (Deut. x. 16, Jer. iv. 4), and to make themselves new hearts and new spirits (Ezek. xviii. 31); but the background of such appeals is rather the promise of God than the ability of man (Deut. v. 29, Ezek. xi. 19, cf. Keil *in loc.*). It is God alone who can "turn" a man "a new heart" (I Sam. x. 9), and the cry of the saint who has come to understand what his sin means, and therefore what cleansing from it involves, is ever, "Create (בְּרָא) in me a new heart, O God, and renew (חָדֵשׁ) a steadfast spirit within me" (Ps. li. 10[12]). The express warrant for so great a prayer is afforded by the promise of God who, knowing the incapacity of the flesh, has Himself engaged to perfect His people. He will circumcise their hearts, that they may love the Lord their God with all their heart and with all their soul; and so may live (Deut. xxx. 6). He will give them a heart to know Him that He is the Lord; that so they may really be His people and He their God (Jer. xxiv. 7). He will put His law in their inward parts and write it in their heart so that all shall know Him (Jer. xxxi. 33, cf. xxxii. 39). He will take the stony heart out of their flesh and give them a heart of flesh, that they may walk in His statutes and keep his ordinances and do them, and so be His people and He their God (Ezek. xi. 19). He will give them a new heart and take away the stony heart out of their flesh; and put His Spirit within them and cause them to walk in His statutes and keep His judgments and do them: that so they may be His people and He their God (Ezek. xxxvi. 26, cf. xxxvii. 14). Thus the expectation of a new heart was made a substantial part of the Messianic promise, in which was embodied the whole hope of Israel.

It does not seem open to doubt that in these great declarations we have the proclamation of man's need of "renewal" and of the divine provision for it as an essential element in salvation.[2] We must not be misled by the emphasis placed in the Old Testament on the forgiveness of sins as the constitutive fact of salvation, into explaining away all allusions to the cleansing of the heart as but figurative expressions for pardon. Pardon is no doubt frequently set forth under the figure or symbol of washing or cleansing: but expressions such as those which have been adduced go beyond this. When, then, it is suggested [3] that Psalm li, for example, "contains only a single prayer, namely, that for forgiveness"; and that "the cry, 'Create in me a clean heart' is not a prayer for what we call renewal" but only for "forgiving grace," we cannot help thinking the contention an extravagance, — an extravagance, moreover, out of keeping with its author's language elsewhere, and indeed in this very context where he speaks quite simply of the pollution as well as the guilt of sin as included in the scope of the confession made in this psalm.[4] The word "create" is a strong one and appears to invoke from God the exertion of His almighty power for the production of a new subjective state of things: and it does not seem easy to confine the word "heart" to the signification "conscience" as if the prayer were merely that the conscience might be relieved from its sense of guilt. Moreover, the parallel clause, "Renew a steadfast spirit within me," does not readily lend itself to the purely objective inter-

---

[2] "The necessity of a change of disposition for the reception of salvation is indicated (Jer. xxxi. 33, Ezek. xxxvi. 35)"— König, "Offenbarungsbegriff d.A.T.," II, p. 398, note. "Indications are not wholly lacking that some of the prophets, at least, believed man unable to make himself acceptable before God . . . It is God who cleanses the heart and life by purging away the dross (Isa. i. 25, vi. 7, Jer. xxxi. 31–34, xxxiii. 8)"— J. M. P. Smith, "Biblical Ideas of Atonement," 1909, p. 28. "Ezekiel is even so bold as to declare that we amend our lives because God gives us a new heart and a new spirit (xi. 19)"— *Expository Times*, Feb. 1908, p. 240).

[3] Cf. A. B. Davidson, "Theology of the O. T.," p. 232.

[4] P. 234; cf. in general p. 244: There is, therefore, both guilt and pollution to be removed in the realization in Israel of the life of God. Similarly Delitzsch *in loc.*: "the prayer for justification is followed by the prayer for renewing."

pretation.[5] That the transformation of the heart promised in the great prophetic passages must also mean more than the production of a clear conscience, is equally undeniable and indeed is not denied. When Jeremiah (xxxi. 31–33), for example, represents God as declaring that what shall characterize the New Covenant which He will make with the House of Israel, is that He will put His law in the inward parts of His people and write it in their hearts, he surely means to say that God promises to work a subjective effect in the hearts of Israel, by virtue of which their very instincts and most intimate impulses shall be on the side of the law, obedience to which shall therefore be but the spontaneous expression of their own natures.[6]

It is equally important to guard against lowering the conception of the Divine holiness in the Old Testament until the demand of God that His people shall be holy as He is holy,[7] and the provisions of His Grace to make them holy by an inner creative act, are robbed of more or less of their deeper ethical meaning. Here, too, some recent writers are at fault, speaking at times almost as if holiness in God were merely a sort of fastidiousness, over against which is set not so much all sin as uncleanness, as all uncleanness, as in this sense sin.[8] The idea is that what

[5] Baethgen's comment on the verse runs: "The singer knows that for the steadfastness of heart sought in verse 8, there is needed a new creation, a rebirth. בָּרָא in the Kal is always used only of the divine production. The heart is the central organ of the whole religious moral life; the parallel רוּחַ is its synonym. Steadfast (נכוֹן) the spirit is called so far as it does not hesitate between good and evil."

[6] Cf. e. g., A. B. Davidson, "Hastings' BD," i, pp. 514 sq.: "Jehovah will make a new covenant with Israel, that is, forgive their sins and write His law on their hearts — the one in His free grace, the other by His creative act"; also iv, p. 119 a, and the fine exposition of Ezek. xxxvi. 17–38 in the "Theology of the O. T.," p. 343. On the other hand Giesebrecht, "Handkom. Jer.," p. 171 thinks "Jeremiah has not yet advanced to the 'new heart' (Ezek. xi. 19, xxxvi. 26 sq., Ps. li. 12); what he is thinking of is an inner influence on the heart by divine power, so that it attains a new attitude to the contents of the law." But this divine power is certainly conceived as creative. "The prophets," says Gunkel, "Die Wirkungen des heiligen Geistes," 1909, p. 77, "were convinced that God Himself must interfere in order to produce the ideal condition which He demands. The ideal kingdom in which dwell piety and righteousness cannot, therefore, be a result of the natural development of the people, but it can come into existence only by an act of God, by a miracle, by the outpouring of the divine Spirit."

[7] Cf. Dillmann, "Alttest. Theologie," pp. 421–422.

[8] E. g., A. B. Davidson, "Theology of O. T.," pp. 348 sq.

this somewhat squeamish God did not find agreeable those who served Him would discover it well to avoid; rather than that all sin is necessarily abominable to the holy God and He will not abide it in His servants. This lowered view is sometimes even pushed to the extreme of suggesting [9] that "it is nowhere intimated that there is any danger to the sinner because of his uncleanness;" if he is "cut off" that is solely on account of his disobedience in not cleansing himself, not on account of the uncleanness itself. The extremity of this contention is its sufficient refutation. When the sage declares that no one can say "I have made my heart clean, I am pure from sin" (Prov. xx. 9), he clearly means to intimate that an unclean heart is itself sinful. The Psalmist in bewailing his inborn sinfulness and expressing his longing for truth in the inward parts and wisdom in the hidden parts, certainly conceived his unclean heart as properly sinful in the sight of God (Ps. li). The prophet abject before the holy God (Isa. vi) beyond question looked upon his uncleanness as itself iniquity requiring to be taken away by expiatory purging. It would seem unquestionable that throughout the Old Testament the uncleanness which is offensive to Jehovah is sin considered as pollution, and that salvation from sin involves therefore a process of purification as well as expiation.

The agent by whom the cleansing of the heart is effected is in the Old Testament uniformly represented as God Himself, or, rarely, more specifically as the Spirit of God, which is the Old Testament name for God in His effective activity. It has, indeed, been denied that the Spirit of God is ever regarded in the Old Testament as the worker of holiness.[10] But this extreme position cannot be maintained.[11] It is true enough that the

---

[9] *Ibid.*, pp. 352–353, against Riehm.

[10] Cf. e. g., Beversluis, "De heilige Geest en zijne Werkingen," 1896, p. 38: "Although the spirit of God may, no doubt, be brought into connection with a moral renewing (in Ezek. xxxvi. 27) nevertheless an ethical operation of the Spirit of God is nowhere taught in the Old Testament."

[11] Cf. e. g., Swete, "Hastings' BD.," ii, pp. 403–404; and Davidson, *ibid.*, iv, p. 119 a: "Later prophets perceive that man's spirit must be determined by an operation of God who will write His law on it (Jer. xxxi. 33), or who will put His own Spirit within him as the impulsive principle of his life (Isa. xxxii. 15, Ezek. xxxvi. 26 ff.)."

Spirit of God comes before us in the Old Testament chiefly as the Theocratic Spirit endowing men as servants of the Kingdom, and after that as the Cosmical Spirit, the principle of all world-processes; and only occasionally as the creator of new ethical life in the individual soul.[12] But it can scarcely be doubted that in Ps. li. 11 [13] God's Holy Spirit, or the Spirit of God's holiness, is conceived in that precise manner, and the same is true of Psalm cxliii. 10 (cf. Isa. lxiii. 10, 11 and see Gen. vi. 3, Neh. ix. 20, I Sam. x. 6, 9).[13] It is chiefly, however, in promises of the future that this aspect of the Spirit's work is dwelt upon.[14] The recreative activity of the Spirit of God is even made the crowning Messianic blessing (Isa. xxxii. 15, xxxiv. 16, xliv. 3, on the latter of which see Giesebrecht, "Die Berufsbegabung," etc., p. 144, lix. 21, Ezek. xi. 19, xviii. 31, xxxvi. 27, xxxvii. 14, xxxix. 29, Zech. xii. 10); and this is as much as to say that the promised Messianic salvation included in it provision for the renewal of men's hearts as well as for the expiation of their guilt.[15]

It would be distinctly a retrogression from the Old Testament standpoint, therefore, if our Lord — Himself, in accordance with Old Testament prophecy (e. g., Isa. xi. 1, xlii. 1, lxi. 1), endowed with the Spirit (Mt. iii. 16, iv. 1, xii. 18, 28, Mk. i. 10, 12, Lk. iii. 22, iv. 1, 14, 18, x. 21, Jno. i. 32, 33) above

[12] Cf. *The Presbyterian and Reformed Review*, Oct. 1895, pp. 669 *sq.*

[13] As even Gunkel allows, "Die Wirkungen, &c².," p. 77: "On the other hand the Spirit appears as the principle of religion and morality in Ezek. xxxvi. 27; Isa. xxviii. 6; xxxii. 15 *sq.*, with which Zech. xii. 10 may be compared. To these may be added the passages, not cited by Wendt, Isa. xi. 2 and Ps. li. 13; cxliii. 10, the two last of which have far the most significance for our problem, because they present the doctrine of the Spirit in its relation to the life of pious individuals" (cf. pp. 78 and 79). Delitzsch, on Ps. li. 12, 13, thinks it nevertheless a mistake to take "the Holy Spirit" here as "the Spirit of grace" as distinct from the "Spirit of office." David, he says, is thinking of himself as king, as Israelite, and as man, without distinguishing between them: the Spirit in his mind is that with which he was anointed (I Sam. xvi. 13); and he speaks of His total effects without differentiation.

[14] Cf. Gunkel, as cited, p. 78, and Delitzsch on Ps. li. 12, 13; also Dalman, "Words of Jesus," p. 296: "Jeremiah and Ezekiel recognized a miraculous transformation in the heart of the people of the future."

[15] Cf. in general, *The Presbyterian and Reformed Review*, Oct. 1895, art. "The Spirit of God in the O. T.," pp. 679 ff.

measure (Jno. iii. 34) [16] — had neglected the Messianic promise
of spiritual renewal. In point of fact, He began His ministry as
the dispenser of the Spirit (Mt. iii. 11, Mk. i. 8, Lk. iii. 16, Jno.
i. 33). And the purpose for which He dispensed the Spirit is
unmistakably represented as the cleansing of the heart. The
distinction of Jesus is, indeed, made to lie precisely in this, —
that whereas John could baptise only with water, Jesus baptised with the Holy Spirit: the repentance which was symbolized by the one was wrought by the other. And this repentance
($\mu\epsilon\tau\acute{a}\nu o\iota a$) was no mere vain regret for an ill-spent past ($\mu\epsilon\tau a$-
$\mu\acute{\epsilon}\lambda\epsilon\iota a$), or surface modification of conduct, but a radical transformation of the mind which issues indeed in "fruits worthy
of repentance" (Lk. iii. 8) but itself consists in an inward reversal of mental attitude.

There is little subsequent reference in the Synoptic Gospels,
to be sure, to the Holy Spirit as the renovator of hearts. It is
made clear, indeed, that He is the best of gifts and that the
Father will not withhold Him from those that ask Him (Lk.
xi. 13), and that He abides in the followers of Jesus and works
in and through them (Mt. x. 20, Mk. xiii. 11, Lk. xii. 12); and
it is made equally clear that He is the very principle of holiness,
so that to confuse His activity with that of unclean spirits
argues absolute perversion (Mt. xii. 31, Mk. iii. 29, Lk. xii. 10).
But these two things do not happen to be brought together in
these Gospels.[17]

In the Gospel of John, on the other hand, the testimony of
the Baptist is followed up by the record of the searching conversation of our Lord with Nicodemus, in which Nicodemus is
rebuked for not knowing — though "the teacher of Israel" —
that the Kingdom of God is not for the children of the flesh
but only for the children of the Spirit (cf. Mt. iii. 9). Nicodemus
had come to our Lord as to a teacher, widely recognized as
having a mission from God. Jesus repels this approach as falling
far below recognizing Him for what He really was and for
what he had really come to do. As a divinely sent teacher He

---

[16] For on the whole it seems best so to understand this verse.
[17] See in general, however, Bruce, "The Kingdom of God," p. 259.

solemnly assures Nicodemus that something much more effective than teaching is needed: "Verily, verily, I say unto thee,
except a man be born anew he cannot see the Kingdom of God"
(iii. 3). And then, when Nicodemus, oppressed by the sense of
the profundity of the change which must indeed be wrought in
man if he is to be fitted for the Kingdom of God, despairingly
inquires "How can this be?" our Lord explains equally solemnly that it is only by a sovereign, recreating work of the
Holy Spirit, that so great an effect can be wrought: "Verily,
verily, I say unto thee, except a man be born of water and
the Spirit he cannot enter into the Kingdom of God"(iii. 5).
Nor, he adds, ought such a declaration to cause surprise:
what is born of the flesh can be nothing but flesh; only what is
born of the Spirit is spirit. He closes the discussion with a
reference to the sovereignty of the action of the Spirit in regenerating men: as with the wind which blows where it lists,
we know nothing of the Spirit's coming except Lo, it is here!
(iii. 8). About the phrase, "Born of water and the Spirit"
much debate has been had; and various explanations of it
have been offered. The one thing which seems certain is that
there can be no reference to an external act, performed by men,
of their own will: for in that case the product would not be
spirit but flesh, neither would it come without observation. Is
it fanciful to see here a reference back to the Baptist's, "I indeed baptise with water; He baptises with the Holy Spirit"?
The meaning then would be that entrance into the Kingdom
of God requires, if we cannot quite say not only repentance
but also regeneration, yet at least we may say both repentance
and regeneration. In any event it is very pungently taught
here that the precondition of entrance into the Kingdom of
God is a radical transformation wrought by the Spirit of God
Himself.[18]

[18] Cf. Wendt, "The Teaching of Jesus," E. T., ii, 91: "Jesus here at the
outset declares, in the only passage in the Fourth Gospel where the conception
of the Kingdom of God is directly mentioned, that a complete new birth, taking
place from the commencement, and, indeed, a birth from the Spirit of God, is
indispensably necessary in order both to seeing (that is, experiencing) and to
entering the Kingdom of God (vss. 3 and 5)."

Beyond this fundamental passage there is little said in John's Gospel of the renovating activities of the Spirit. The communication of the Spirit of xx. 22 seems to be an official endowment; and although in vii. 39 the allusion appears to be to the gift of the Spirit to believers at large, the stress seems to fall rather on the blessing they bring to others by virtue of this endowment, than on that they receive themselves. There remains only the great promise of the Paraclete. It would probably be impossible to attribute more depth or breadth of meaning than rightfully belongs to them, to the passages which embody this promise (xiv. 16, 26, xv. 26, xvi. 7, 13). But the emphasis appears to be laid in them upon the illuminating (cf. also Lk. i. 15, 41, 67, ii. 25, 26; Mt. xxii. 43) more than upon the sanctifying influences of the Spirit, although assuredly the latter are not wholly absent (xvi. 7–11).

Elsewhere in John, although apart from any specific reference to the Spirit as the agent, repeated expression is given to the fundamental conception of renewal. Men lie dead in their sins and require to be raised from the dead if they are to live (xi. 25, 26); it is the prerogative of the Son to quicken whom He will (v. 21); it is impossible for men to come to the Son, unless they be drawn by the Father (vi. 44); being in the Son it is only of the Father that they can bear fruit (xv. 1). Similarly in the Synoptics there is lacking nothing to this teaching, except the specific reference of the effects to the Holy Spirit. What is required of men is nothing less than perfection even as the heavenly Father is perfect (Mt. v. 48 — the New Testament form of the Old Testament "Ye shall be holy for I am holy, Jehovah your God," Lev. xix. 2). And this perfection is not a matter of external conduct but of internal disposition. One of the objects of the "Sermon on the Mount" is to deepen the conception of righteousness and to carry back both sin and righteousness into the heart itself (Mt. v. 20). Accordingly, the external righteousness of the Scribes and Pharisees is pronounced just no righteousness at all; it is the cleansing merely of the outside of the cup and of the platter (Mt. xxiii. 25), and they are therefore but as whited sepulchres, which outwardly

appear beautiful but inwardly are full of dead men's bones
(Mt. xxiii. 27, 28). True cleansing must begin from within; and
this inward cleansing will cleanse the outside also (Mt. xxiii.
26, xv. 11). The fundamental principle is that every tree brings
forth fruit according to its nature, whether good or bad; and
therefore the tree must be made good and its fruit good, or
else the tree corrupt and its fruit corrupt (Mt. vii. 17, xii. 33,
xv. 11, Mk. vii. 15, Lk. vi. 43, xi. 34). So invariable and all-
inclusive is this principle in its working, that it applies even
to the idle words which men speak, by which they may therefore be justly judged: none that are evil can speak good things,
"for it is out of the abundance of the heart that the mouth
speaketh" (Mt. xii. 34). Half-measures are therefore unavailing
(Mt. vi. 21); a radical change alone will suffice — no mere
patching of the new on the old, no pouring of new wine into
old bottles (Mt. ix. 16, 17, Mk. ii. 21, 22, Lk. v. 36, 39). He
who has not a wedding-garment — the gift of the host — even
though he be called shall not be chosen (Mt. xxii. 11, 12).

Accordingly when — in the Synoptic parallel to the conversation with Nicodemus — the rich young ruler came to Jesus
with his heart set on purchase (as a rich man's heart is apt to
be set), pleading his morality, Jesus repelled him and took occasion to pronounce upon not the difficulty only but the impossibility of entrance into the Kingdom of heaven on such
terms (Mt. xix. 23, Mk. x. 23, Lk. xviii. 24). The possibility
of salvation, He explains, just because it involves something
far deeper than this, rests in the hands of God alone (Mt. xix.
26, Mk. x. 27, Lk. xviii. 27). Man himself brings nothing to it;
the Kingdom is received in naked helplessness (Mt. xix. 21 ||).
It is not without significance that, in all the Synoptics, the
conversation with the rich young ruler is made to follow immediately upon the incident of the blessing of the little children
(Mt. xix. 13 ||). When our Lord says, with reference to these
children (they were mere babies, Lk. xviii. 15),[19] that, "Of
such is the kingdom of heaven," he means just to say that the
kingdom of heaven is never purchased by any quality whatever,

[19] Cf. "Hastings' DCG.," art. "Children."

to say nothing now of deed: whosoever enters it enters it as a child enters the world, — he is born into it by the power of God. In these two incidents, of the child set in the midst and of the rich young ruler, we have, in effect, acted parables of the new birth; they exhibit to us how men enter the kingdom and set the declaration made to Nicodemus (Jno. iii. 1 *sq.*) before us in vivid object-lesson. And if the kingdom can be entered thus only in nakedness as a child comes into the world, all stand before it in like case and it can come only to those selected therefor by God Himself: where none have a claim upon it the law of its bestowment can only be the Divine will (Mt. xi. 27, xx. 15).[20]

The broad treatment characteristic of the Gospels only partly gives way as we pass to the Epistles. Discriminations of aspects and stages, however, begin to become evident; and with the increased material before us we easily perceive lines of demarcation which perhaps we should not have noted with the Gospels only in view. In particular we observe two groups of terms standing over against one another, describing, respectively, from the manward and from the Godward side, the great change experienced by him who is translated from the power of darkness into the kingdom of the Son of God's love (Col. i. 13). And within the limits of each of these groups, we observe also certain distinctions in the usage of the several terms which make it up. In the one group are such terms as μετανοεῖν with its substantive μετάνοια, and its cognate μεταμέλεσθαι, and ἐπιστρέφειν and its substantive ἐπιστροφή. These tell us what part man takes in the change. The other group includes such terms as γεννηθῆναι ἄνωθεν or ἐκ τοῦ θεοῦ or ἐκ τοῦ πνεύματος, παλινγενεσία, ἀναγεννᾶν, ἀποκυεῖσθαι, ανανεοῦσθαι, ἀνακαινοῦσθαι, ἀνακαίνωσις. These tell what part God takes in the change. Man repents, makes amendment, and turns to God. But it is by God that men are renewed, brought forth, born again into newness of life. The transformation which to human vision manifests itself as a change of life (ἐπιστροφή) resting upon a radical change of mind (μετάνοια), to Him who searches

[20] Cf. Wendt, as cited, p. 54–55 note.

the heart and understands all the movements of the human soul is known to be a creation (κτίζειν) of God, beginning in a new birth from the Spirit (γεννηθῆναι ἄνωθεν ἐκ τοῦ πνεύματος) and issuing in a new divine product (ποίημα), created in Christ Jesus, into good works prepared by God beforehand that they may be walked in (Eph. ii. 10).

There is certainly synergism here; but it is a synergism of such character that not only is the initiative taken by God (for "all things are of God," II Cor. v. 18, cf. Heb. vi. 6), but the Divine action is in the exceeding greatness of God's power, according to the working of the strength of His might which He wrought in Christ when He raised Him from the dead (Eph. i. 19). The "new man" which is the result of this change is therefore one who can be described no otherwise than as "created" (κτισθέντα) in righteousness and holiness of truth (Eph. iv. 24), after the image of God significantly described as "He who created him" (τοῦ κτίσαντος αὐτόν, Col. iii. 10), — that is not He who made him a man, but He who has made him by an equally creative efflux of power this new man which he has become.[21] The exhortation that we shall "put on" this new man (Eph. iv. 24, cf. iii. 9, 10), therefore does not imply that either the initiation or the completion of the process by which the "new creation" (καινὴ κτίσις; II Cor. v. 17, Gal. vi. 15) is wrought lies in our own power; but only urges us to that diligent coöperation with God in the work of our salvation, to which He calls us in all departments of life (I Cor. iii. 9), and the classical expression of which in this particular department is found in the great exhortation of Phil. ii. 12, 13 where we are encouraged to work out our own salvation thoroughly to the end, with fear and trembling, on the express ground that it is God who works in us both the willing and doing for His good pleasure. The express inclusion of "renewal" in the exhortation (Eph. iv. 23 ἀνανεοῦσθαι; Rom. xii. μεταμορφοῦσθε τῇ ἀνακαινώσει) is indication enough that this "renewal" is a process wide enough to include in itself the whole synergistic "working out" of salvation (κατεργάζεσθε, Phil. ii. 12). But it has no tendency

[21] Cf. Lightfoot in loc.

to throw doubt upon the underlying fact that this "working out" is both set in motion (τὸ θέλειν) and given effect (τὸ ἐνεργεῖν), only by the energizing of God (ὁ ἐνεργῶν ἐν ὑμῖν), so that all (τὰ πάντα) is from God (ἐκ τοῦ θεοῦ, II Cor. v. 18). Its effect is merely to bring "renewal" (ἀνακαίνωσις) into close parallelism with "repentance" (μετάνοια) — which itself is a gift of God (II Tim. ii. 25, cf. Acts v. 31, xi. 18) as well as a work of man — as two names for the same great transaction, viewed now from the Divine, and now from the human point of sight.

It will not be without interest to observe the development of μετανοεῖν, μετάνοια into the technical term to denote the great change by which man passes from death in sin into life in Christ.[22] Among the heathen writers, the two terms μεταμέλεσθαι, μεταμέλεια and μετανοεῖν, μετάνοια, although no doubt affected in their coloring by their differing etymological suggestions, and although μετανοεῖν, μετάνοια seems always to have been the nobler term, were practically synonymous. Both were used of the dissatisfaction which is felt in reviewing an unworthy deed; both of the amendment which may grow out of this dissatisfaction. Something of this undiscriminating usage extends into the New Testament. In the only three instances in which μεταμέλεσθαι occurs in the Gospels (Mt. xxi. 29, 32, xxvii. 3, cf. Heb. vii. 21 from Old Testament), it is used of a repentance which issued in the amended act; while in Lk. xvii. 3, 4 (but there only) μετανοεῖν may very well be understood of a repentance which expended itself in regret. Elsewhere in the New Testament μεταμέλεσθαι is used in a single instance only (except Heb. vii. 21 from Old Testament) and then it is brought into contrast with μετάνοια as the emotion of regret is contrasted with a revolution of mind (II Cor. vii. 8 sq.). The Apostle had grieved the Corinthians with a letter and had regretted it (μετεμελόμην); he had, however, ceased to regret it (μεταμέλομαι), because he had come to perceive that their grief had led the

[22] Cf. Trench, "Synonyms of the N. T.," § lxix. Also Effie Freeman Thompson, Ph.D., "ΜΕΤΑΝΟΕΩ and ΜΕΤΑΜΕΛΕΙ in Greek Literature until 100 A.D.," 1908, p. 29 especially the summary of New Testament usage pp. 28–29: μετανοεῖν is not used in the New Testament of the intellect or sensibilities but always of voluntative action; and prevailingly not of specific but of generic choice.

Corinthians to repent of their sin (μετάνοια), and certainly the salvation to which such a repentance tends is not to be regretted (ἀμεταμέλητον). Here μεταμέλεσθαι is the painful review of the past; but so little is μετάνοια this, that it is presented as a result of sorrow, — a total revolution of mind traced by the Apostle through the several stages of its formation in a delicate analysis remarkable for its insight into the working of a human soul under the influence of a strong revulsion (verse 11). Its roots were planted in godly sorrow, its issue was amendment of life, its essence consisted in a radical change of mind and heart towards sin. In this particular instance it was a particular sin which was in view; and in heathen writers the word is commonly employed of a specific repentance of a specific fault. In the New Testament this, however, is the rarer usage.[23] Here it prevailingly stands for that fundamental change of mind by which the back is turned not upon one sin or some sins, but upon all sin, and the face definitely turned to God and to His service, — of which therefore a transformed life (ἐπιστροφή) is the outworking.[24] It is not itself this transformed life, into which it issues, any more than it is the painful regret out of which it issues. No doubt, it may spread its skirts so widely as to include on this side the sorrow for sin and on that the amendment of life; but what it precisely is, and what in all cases it emphasises, is the inner change of mind which regret induces and which itself induces a reformed life. Godly sorrow works repentance (II Cor. vii. 10): when we "turn" to God we are doing works worthy of repentance (Acts iii. 19, xxvi. 20, cf. Lk. iii. 8).

It is in this, its deepest and broadest sense, that μετάνοια corresponds from the human side to what from the divine point of sight is called ἀνακαίνωσις; or, rather, to be more precise, that μετάνοια is the psychological manifestation of ἀνακαί-

[23] Lk. xvii. 3, 4, Acts viii. 22, II Cor. vii. 9, 10, xii. 21, Heb. xii. 17; cf. also Rev. ii. 5, 5, 16, 21, 22, iii. 3, 19.

[24] Mt. iii. 2, iv. 17, xi, 20, 21, xii. 41, Mk. i. 15, vi. 12, Lk. x. 13, xi. 32, xiii. 3, 5, xv. 7. 10, xvi. 30, Acts ii. 38, iii. 19, xvii. 30, xxvi. 20, Mt. iii. 8, 11, Mk. i. 4, Lk. iii. 3, 8, v. 32, xv. 7, xxiv. 47, Acts v. 31, xi. 18, xiii. 24, xix. 4, xxvi. 20, Rom. ii. 4, II Tim. ii. 25, Heb. vi. 1, 6, II Pet. iii. 9, Rev. ix. 20, 21, xvi. 9, 11, cf. ii. 5, 5, 16, 21, 22, iii. 3, 19.

νωσις. This "renewal" (ἀνακαινοῦσθαι, ἀνακαίνωσις, ἀνανεοῦσθαι) is the broad term of its own group. It may be, to be sure, that παλινγενεσία should take its place by its side in this respect. In one of the only two passages in which it occurs in the New Testament (Mt. xix. 28) it refers to the repristination not of the individual, but of the universe, which is to take place at "the end": and this usage tends to stamp upon the word the broad sense of a complete and thoroughgoing restoration. If in Tit. iii. 5 it is applied to the individual in such a broad sense, it would be closely coextensive in meaning with the ἀνακαίνωσις by the side of which it stands in that passage, and would differ from it only as a highly figurative differs from a more literal expression of the same idea.[25] Our salvation, the Apostle would in that case say, is not an attainment of our own, but is wrought by God in His great mercy, by means of a regenerating washing, to wit, a renewal by the Holy Spirit.

The difficulty we experience in confidently determining the scope of παλινγενεσία, arising from lack of a sufficiently copious usage to form the basis of our induction, attends us also with the other terms of its class. Nevertheless it seems tolerably clear that over against the broader "renewal" expressed by ἀνακαινοῦσθαι and its cognates and perhaps also by παλινγενεσία, ἀναγεννᾶν (I Pet. i. 23) and with it, its synonym ἀποκυεῖσθαι (James i. 18) are of narrower connotation. We have, says Peter, in God's great mercy been rebegotten, not of corruptible seed, but of incorruptible, by means of the Word of the living and abiding God. It is in accordance with His own determination, says James, that we have been brought forth by the Father of Lights, from whom every good gift and every perfect boon comes, by means of the Word of truth. We have here an effect, the efficient agent in working which is God in His unbounded mercy, while the instrument by means of which it is wrought is "the word of good-tidings which has been preached" to us, that is to say, briefly, the Gospel of Jesus Christ. The issue is, equally briefly, just salvation. This salvation is characteristically described by Peter as awaiting its consummation in the

---

[25] So e. g., Weiss *in loc.*

future, while yet it is entered upon here and now not only (verse 4 *sq.*) as a "living hope" which shall not be put to shame (because it is reserved in heaven for us, and we meanwhile are guarded through faith for it by the power of God), but also in an accordant life of purity as children of obedience who would fain be like their Father and as He is holy be also ourselves holy in all manner of living. James intimates that those who have been thus brought forth by the will of God may justly be called "first fruits of His creatures," where the reference assuredly is not to the first but to the second creation, that is to say, they who have already been brought forth by the word of truth are themselves the product of God's creative energy and are the promise of the completed new creation when all that is shall be delivered from the bondage of corruption into the liberty of the glory of the children of God (Rom. viii. 19 *sq.*, Mt. xix. 28).

The new birth thus brought before us is related to the broader idea of "renewal" (ἀνακαίνωσις) as the initial stage to the whole process. The conception is not far from that embodied by our old Divines in the term "effectual calling" which they explained to be "by the Word and Spirit"; it is nowadays perhaps more commonly but certainly both less Scripturally and less descriptively spoken of as "conversion." It finds its further explanation in the Scriptures accordingly not under the terms ἐπιστρέφειν, ἐπιστροφή, which describe to us that in which it issues, but under the terms καλέω, κλῆσις [26] which describe to us precisely what it is. By these terms, which are practically confined to Paul and Peter, the follower of Christ is said to owe his introduction into the new life to a "call" from God — a call distinguished from the call of mere invitation (Mt. xxii. 14), as "the call according to purpose" (Rom. viii. 28), a call which cannot fail of its appropriate effect, because there works in it the very power of God. The notion of the new birth is confined even more closely still to its initial step in our Lord's discourse to Nicodemus, recorded in the opening verses of the third chapter of John's Gospel. Here the whole emphasis is thrown upon

[26] Cf. "Hastings' B. D.," ιν, 57 b.

the necessity of the new birth and its provision by the Holy Spirit. No one can see the Kingdom of God unless he be born again; and this new birth is wrought by the Spirit. Its advent into the soul is unobserved; its process is inscrutable; its reality is altogether an inference from its effects. There is no question here of means. That the ἐξ ὕδατος of verse 5 is to be taken as presenting the external act of baptism as the proper means by which the effect is brought about, is, as we have already pointed out, very unlikely. The axiom announced in verse 6 that all that is born of flesh is flesh and only what is born of the Spirit is spirit seems directly to negative such an interpretation by telling us flatly that we cannot obtain a spiritual effect from a physical action. The explanation of verse 8 that like the wind, the Spirit visits whom He will and we can only observe the effect and say Lo, it is here! seems inconsistent with supposing that it always attends the act of baptism and therefore can always be controlled by the human will. The new birth appears to be brought before us in this discussion in the purity of its conception; and we are made to perceive that at the root of the whole process of "renewal" there lies an immediate act of God the Holy Spirit upon the soul by virtue of which it is that the renewed man bears the great name of Son of God. Begotten not of blood, nor of the will of the flesh, nor of the will of man, but of God (Jno. i. 13), his new life will necessarily bear the lineaments of his new parentage (I Jno. iii. 9, 10; v. 4, 18): kept by Him who was in an even higher sense still begotten of God, he overcomes the world by faith, defies the evil one (who cannot touch him), and manifests in his righteousness and love the heritage which is his (I Jno. ii. 29, iv. 7, v. 1). Undoubtedly the Spirit is active throughout the whole process of "renewal"; but it is doubtless the peculiarly immediate and radical nature of his operation at this initial point which gives to the product of His renewing activities its best right to be called a new creation (II Cor. v. 17, Gal. vi. 15), a quickening (Jno. v. 21, Eph. ii. 5), a making alive from the dead (Gal. iii. 21).

We perceive, then, that the Scriptural phraseology lays be-

fore us, as its account of the great change which the man experiences who is translated from what the Scriptures call
darkness to what they call God's marvellous light (Eph. v. 8,
Col. i. 13, I Pet. ii. 9, I Jno. ii. 8) a process; and a process which
has two sides. It is on the one side a change of the mind and
heart, issuing in a new life. It is on the other side a renewing
from on high issuing in a new creation. But the initiative is
taken by God: man is renewed unto repentance: he does not
repent that he may be renewed (cf. Heb. vi. 6). He can work
out his salvation with fear and trembling only because God
works in him both the willing and the doing. At the basis of
all there lies an enabling act from God, by virtue of which alone
the spiritual activities of man are liberated for their work
(Rom. vi. 22, viii. 2). From that moment of the first divine
contact the work of the Spirit never ceases: while man is
changing his mind and reforming his life, it is ever God who is
renewing him in true righteousness. Considered from man's
side the new dispositions of mind and heart manifest themselves
in a new course of life. Considered from God's side the renewal
of the Holy Spirit results in the production of a new creature,
God's workmanship, with new activities newly directed. We
obtain thus a regular series. At the root of all lies an act seen
by God alone, and mediated by nothing, a direct creative act
of the Spirit, the new birth. This new birth pushes itself into
man's own consciousness through the call of the Word, responded
to under the persuasive movements of the Spirit; his conscious
possession of it is thus mediated by the Word. It becomes
visible to his fellow-men only in a turning to God in external
obedience, under the constant leading of the indwelling Spirit
(Rom. viii. 14). A man must be born again by the Spirit to become God's son. He must be born again by the Spirit and Word
to become consciously God's son. He must manifest his new
spiritual life in Spirit-led activities accordant with the new
heart which he has received and which is ever renewed
afresh by the Spirit, to be recognized by his fellow-men as
God's son. It is the entirety of this process, viewed as the work
of God on the soul, which the Scriptures designate "renewal."

It must not be supposed that it is only in these semi-technical terms, however, that the process of "renewal" is spoken of in the Epistles of the New Testament any more than in the Gospels. There is, on the contrary, the richest and most varied employment of language, literal and figurative, to describe it in its source, or its nature, or its effects. It is sometimes suggested, for example, under the image of a change of vesture (Eph. iv. 24, Col. iii. 9, 10, cf. Gal iii. 27, Rom. xiii. 14): the old man is laid aside like soiled clothing, and the new man put on like clean raiment. Sometimes it is represented, in accordance with its nature, less figuratively, as a metamorphosis (Rom. xii. 2): by the renewing of our minds we become transformed beings, able to free ourselves from the fashion of this world and prove what is the will of God, good and acceptable and perfect. Sometimes it is more searchingly set forth as to its nature as a reanimation (Jno. v. 21, Eph. ii. 4–6, Col. ii. 12, 13, Rom. vi. 3, 4): we are dead through our trespasses and the uncircumcision of our flesh; God raises us from this death and makes us sit in the heavenly places with Christ. Sometimes with less of figure and with more distinct reference to the method of the divine working, it is spoken of as a recreation (Eph. ii. 10, iv. 24, Col. iii. 10), and its product, therefore, as a new creature (II Cor. v. 17, Gal. vi. 15): we emerge from it as the workmanship of God, created in Christ Jesus unto good works. Sometimes with more particular reference to the nature and effects of the transaction, it is defined rather as a sanctification, a making holy (ἁγιάζω, I Thess. v. 23, Rom. xv. 16, Rev. xxii. 11; ἁγνίζω, I Pet. i. 22; ἁγιασμός, I Thess. iv. 3, 7, Rom. vi. 19, 22, Heb. xii. 14, II Thess. ii. 13, I Pet. i. 2; cf. Ellicott, on I Thess. iv. 3, iii. 13): and those who are the subjects of the change are, therefore, called "saints" (ἅγιοι, e. g., Rom. viii. 27, I Cor. vi. 1, 2, Col. i. 12). Sometimes again, with more distinct reference to its sources, it is spoken of as the "living" (Gal. ii. 20, Rom. vi. 9, 10, Eph. iii. 17) or "forming" (Gal. iv. 19, cf. Eph. iii. 17, I Cor. ii. 16, II Cor. iii. 8) of Christ in us, or more significantly (Rom. viii. 9, 10, Gal. iv. 6) as the indwelling of Christ or the Spirit in us, or with greater precision

as the leading of the Spirit (Rom. viii. 14, Gal. v. 18): and its
subjects are accordingly signalized as Spiritual men, that is,
Spirit-determined, Spirit-led men (πνευματικοί, I Cor. ii. 15, iii.
1, Gal. vi. 1, cf. I Pet. ii. 5), as distinguished from carnal men,
that is, men under the dominance of their own weak, vicious
selves (ψυχικοί, I Cor. ii. 14, Jude 19, σαρκικοί, I Cor. iii. 3).
None of these modes of representation more clearly define the
action than the last mentioned. For the essence of the New
Testament representation certainly is that the renewal which
is wrought upon him who is by faith in Christ, is the work of
the Spirit of Christ, who dwells within His children as a power
not themselves making for righteousness, and gradually but
surely transforms after the image of God, not the stream of
their activities merely, but themselves in the very centre of
their being.

The process by which this great metamorphosis is accomplished is laid bare to our observation with wonderful clearness
in Paul's poignant description of it, in the seventh chapter of
Romans. We are there permitted to look in upon a heart into
which the Spirit of God has intruded with His transforming
power. Whatever peace it may have enjoyed is broken up. All
its ingrained tendencies to evil are up in arms against the intruded power for good. The force of evil habit is so great that
the Apostle, in its revelation to him, is almost tempted to
despair. "O wretched man that I am," he cries, "who shall
deliver me out of the body of this death?" Certainly not himself. None knows better than he that with man this is impossible. But he bethinks himself that the Spirit of the most high
God is more powerful than even ingrained sin; and with a
great revulsion of heart he turns at once to cry his thanks to
God through Jesus Christ our Lord. This conflict he sees within
him, he sees now to bear in it the promise and potency of victory; because it is the result of the Spirit's working within him,
and where the Spirit works, there is emancipation from the
law of sin and death. The process may be hard — a labor, a
struggle, a fight; but the end is assured. No matter how far
from perfect we yet may be, we are not in the flesh but in the

Spirit if the Spirit of God dwells in us; and we may take heart of faith from that circumstance to mortify the deeds of the body and to enter upon our heritage as children of God. Here in brief compass is the Apostle's whole doctrine of renewal. Without holiness we certainly shall not see the Lord: but he in whom the Holy Spirit dwells, is already potentially holy; and though we see not yet what we shall be, we know that the work that is begun within us shall be completed to the end. The very presence of strife within us is the sign of life and the promise of victory.

The church has retained, on the whole, with very considerable constancy the essential elements of this Biblical doctrine of "renewal." In the main stream of Christian thought, at all events, there has been little tendency to neglect, much less to deny it, at least theoretically. In all accredited types of Christian teaching it is largely insisted upon that salvation consists in its substance of a radical subjective change wrought by the Holy Spirit, by virtue of which the native tendencies to evil are progressively eradicated and holy dispositions are implanted, nourished and perfected.

The most direct contradiction which this teaching has received in the history of Christian thought was that given it by Pelagius at the opening of the fifth century. Under the stress of a one-sided doctrine of human freedom, in pursuance of which he passionately asserted the inalienable ability of the will to do all righteousness, Pelagius was led to deny the need and therefore the reality of subjective operations of God on the soul ("grace" in the inner sense) to secure its perfection; and this carried with it as its necessary presupposition the denial also of all subjective injury wrought on man by sin. The vigorous reassertion of the necessity of subjective grace by Augustine put pure Pelagianism once for all outside the pale of recognized Christian teaching; although in more or less modified or attentuated forms, it has remained as a widely spread tendency in the churches, conditioning the purity of the supernaturalism of salvation which is confessed.

The strong emphasis laid by the Reformers upon the objec-

tive side of salvation, in the enthusiasm of their rediscovery of
the fundamental doctrine of justification, left its subjective
side, which was not in dispute between them and their nearest
opponents, in danger of falling temporarily somewhat out of
sight. From the comparative infrequency with which it was in
the first stress of conflict insisted on, occasion, if not given, was
at least taken, to represent that it was neglected if not denied.
Already in the first generation of the Reformation movement,
men of mystical tendencies like Osiander arraigned the Protestant teaching as providing only for a purely external salvation.
The reproach was eminently unjust, and although it continues
to be repeated up to to-day, it remains eminently unjust. Only
among a few Moravian enthusiasts, and still fewer Antinomians, and, in recent times, in the case of certain of the Neo-
Kohlbrüggian party, can a genuine tendency to neglect the
subjective side of salvation be detected. With all the emphasis
which Protestant theology lays on justification by faith as the
root of salvation, it has never failed to lay equal emphasis on
sanctification by the Spirit as its substance. Least of all can
the Reformed theology with its distinctive insistence upon "irresistible grace" — which is the very heart of the doctrine of
"renewal" — be justly charged with failure to accord its rights
to the great truth of supernatural sanctification. The debate
at this point does not turn on the reality or necessity of sanctification, but on the relation of sanctification to justification.
In clear accord with the teaching of Scripture, Protestant theology insists that justification underlies sanctification, and not
vice versa. But it has never imagined that the sinner could get
along with justification alone. It has rather ever insisted that
sanctification is so involved in justification that the justification cannot be real unless it be followed by santification. There
has never been a time when it could not recognize the truth in
and (when taken out of its somewhat compromising context)
make heartily its own such an admirable statement of the
state of the case as the following: [27] — "However far off it
may be from us or we from it, we cannot and ought not to think

[27] W. P. Du Bose, "The Gospel in the Gospels," p. 175.

of our salvation as anything less than our own perfected and completed sinlessness and holiness. We may be, to the depths of our souls, grateful and happy to be sinners pardoned and forgiven by divine grace. But surely God would not have us satisfied with that as the end and substance of the salvation He gives us in His Son. Jesus Christ is the power of God in us unto salvation. It does not require an exercise of divine power to extend pardon; it does require it to endow and enable us with all the qualities, energies, and activities that make for, and that make holiness and life. See how St. Paul speaks of it when he prays, That we may know the exceeding greatness of God's power to usward who believe, according to that working of the strength of His might which he wrought in Christ when He raised Him from the dead."

LITERATURE: — The literature of the subject is copious but also rather fragmentary. The best aid is afforded by the discussions of the terms employed in the Lexicons and of the passages which fall in review in the Commentaries: after that the appropriate sections in the larger treatises in Biblical Theology, and in the fuller Dogmatic treatises are most valuable. The articles of J. V. Bartlet in Hastings' B. D. on "Regeneration" and "Sanctification" should be consulted, — they also offer a suggestion of literature; as do also the articles, "Bekehrung," "Gnade," "Wiedergeburt" in the several editions of Herzog. There are three of the prize publications of the Hague Society which have a general bearing on the subject: G. W. Semler's and S. K. Theoden van Velzen's "Over de voortdurende Werking des H. G.," (1842) and E. I. Issel's "Der Begriff der Heiligkeit im N. T.," (1887). Augustine's Anti-Pelagian treatises are fundamental for the dogmatic treatment of the subject; and the Puritan literature is rich in searching discussions, — the most outstanding of which are possibly: Owen, "Discourse concerning the Holy Spirit" ("Works": Edinburgh, 1852, v. iii.); T. Goodwin, "The Work of the Holy Ghost in our Salvation" ("Works": Edinburgh, 1863, v. vi.); Charnock, "The Doctrine of Regeneration," Phil. 1840; Marshall, "The Gospel Mystery of Sanctification," London [1692], Edinburgh, 1815; Edwards, "The Religious Affections." Cf. also Köberle, "Sünde und Gnade im relig. Leben des Volkes Israel bis auf Christum," 1905; Vömel, "Der Begriff der Gnade im N. T.," 1903; J. Kuhn: "Die christl. Lehre der göttlichen Gnade" (Part I) 1868; A. Dieckmann, "Die christl. Lehre von der Gnade," 1901; Storr, "De Spiritus Sancti in mentibus nostris efficientia," 1779; J. P. Stricker, "Diss. Theol. de Mutatione homini secundum Jesu et App. doct. subeunda," 1845. — P. Gennrich, "Die Lehre von der Wiedergeburt: die christl. Zentrallehre in dogmengeschichtlicher und religionsgeschichtlicher Beleuchtung," 1907; and "Wiedergeburt und Heiligung mit Bezug auf die gegenwärtigen Strömungen des religiösen Lebens," 1908; H. Bavinck, "Roeping en Wedergeboorte," 1903; J. T. Marshall, art. "Regeneration" in Hastings' *ERE* v. x.

XIII

THE BIBLICAL DOCTRINE OF FAITH

FAITH[1]

I. THE PHILOLOGICAL EXPRESSION OF FAITH

THE verb 'to believe' in the Authorized Version of the Old Testament uniformly represents the Hebrew הֶאֱמִין, Hiphil of אָמַן, except, of course, in Dan. vi. 23 where it represents the corresponding Aramaic form. The root, which is widely spread among the Semitic tongues, and which in the word 'Amen' has been adopted into every language spoken by Christian, Jew, or Mohammedan, seems everywhere to convey the fundamental ideas of 'fixedness, stability, steadfastness, reliability.' What the ultimate conception is which underlies these ideas remains somewhat doubtful, but it would appear to be rather that of 'holding' than that of 'supporting' (although this last is the sense adopted in "Oxf. Heb. Lex."). In the simple species the verb receives both transitive and intransitive vocalization. With intransitive vocalization it means 'to be firm,' 'to be secure,' 'to be faithful,' and occurs in biblical Hebrew only in the past participle, designating those who are 'faithful' (II Sam. xx. 19, Ps. xii. 1, xxxi. 23). With transitive vocalization it occurs in biblical Hebrew only in a very specialized application, conveying the idea, whether as participle or verbal noun, of 'caretaking' or 'nursing' (II Kings x. 1, 5, Est. ii. 7, Ru. iv. 16, II Sam. iv. 4, Num. xi. 12, Isa. xlix. 23, Lam. iv. 5; cf. II Kings xviii. 16 'pillars' and [the Niphal] Isa. lx. 4), the implication in which seems to be that of 'holding,' 'bearing,' 'carrying.' The Niphal occurs once as the passive of transitive Qal (Isa. lx. 4): elsewhere it is formed from intransitive Qal, and is used very much in the same sense. Whatever holds, is steady, or can be depended upon, whether a wall which securely

---

[1] Article "Faith," from "A Dictionary of the Bible," ed. by James Hastings, v. i, pp. 827–838. Pub. N. Y. 1905, by Charles Scribner's Sons.

holds a nail (Isa. xxii. 23, 25), or a brook which does not fail
(Jer. xv. 18), or a kingdom which is firmly established (II Sam.
vii. 16), or an assertion which has been verified (Gen. xlii. 20),
or a covenant which endures for ever (Ps. lxxxix. 28), or a heart
found faithful (Neh. ix. 8), or a man who can be trusted (Neh.
xiii. 13), or God Himself who keeps covenant (Deut. vii. 9),
is נֶאֱמָן. The Hiphil occurs in one passage in the primary
physical sense of the root (Job xxxix. 24). Elsewhere it bears
constantly the sense of 'to trust,' weakening down to the simple
'to believe' (Ex. iv. 31, Ps. cxvi. 10, Isa. vii. 9, xxviii. 16,
Hab. i. 5). Obviously it is a subjective causative, and expresses
the acquisition or exhibition of the firmness, security, reliability, faithfulness which lies in the root-meaning of the verb,
in or with respect to its object. The מַאֲמִין is therefore one whose
state of mind is free from faintheartedness (Isa. vii. 9) and
anxious haste (Isa. xxviii. 16), and who stays himself upon the
object of his contemplation with confidence and trust. The implication seems to be, not so much that of a passive dependence
as of a vigorous active commitment. He who, in the Hebrew
sense, exercises faith, is secure, assured, confident (Deut.
xxviii. 66, Job xxiv. 22, Ps. xxvii. 13), and lays hold of the object of his confidence with firm trust.

The most common construction of הֶאֱמִין is with the preposition בְ, and in this construction its fundamental meaning seems
to be most fully expressed. It is probably never safe to represent
this phrase by the simple 'believe'; the preposition rather introduces the person or thing in which one believes, or on which one
believingly rests as on firm ground. This is true even when the
object of the affection is a thing, whether divine words, commandments, or works (Ps. cvi. 12, cxix. 66, lxxviii. 32), or
some earthly force or good (Job xxxix. 12, xv. 31, xxiv. 22,
Deut. xxviii. 66). It is no less true when the object is a person,
human (I Sam. xxvii. 12, Prov. xxvi. 25, Jer. xii. 6, Mic. vii. 5)
or superhuman (Job iv. 18, xv. 15), or the representative of
God, in whom therefore men should place their confidence
(Ex. xix. 9, II Chron. xx. 20). It is above all true, however,
when the object of the affection is God Himself, and that in-

differently whether or not the special exercise of faith adverted
to is rooted in a specific occasion (Gen. xv. 6, Ex. xiv. 31,
Num. xiv. 11, xx. 12, Deut. i. 32, II Kings xvii. 14, II Chron.
xx. 20, Ps. lxxviii. 22, Jon. iii. 5). The weaker conception of 'believing' seems, on the other hand, to lie in the construction
with the preposition ל, which appears to introduce the person
or thing, not on which one confidingly rests, but to the testimony of which one assentingly turns. This credence may be
given by the simple to every untested word (Prov. xiv. 15); it
may be withheld until seeing takes the place of believing (I
Kings x. 7, II Chron. ix. 6); it is due to words of the Lord and
of His messengers, as well as to the signs wrought by them
(Ps. cvi. 24, Isa. liii. 1, Ex. iv. 8, 9). It may also be withheld
from any human speaker (Gen. xlv. 26, Ex. iv. 1, 8, Jer. xl. 14,
II Chron. xxxii. 15), but is the right of God when He bears
witness to His majesty or makes promises to His people (Isa.
xliii. 10, Deut. ix. 23). In this weakened sense of the word the
proposition believed is sometimes attached to it by the conjunction כִּי (Ex. iv. 5, Job ix. 16, Lam. iv. 12). In its construction with the infinitive, however, its deeper meaning comes
out more strongly (Judg. xi. 20, Job xv. 22, Ps. xxvii. 13), and
the same is true when the verb is used absolutely (Ex. iv. 31,
Isa. vii. 9, xxviii. 16, Ps. cxvi. 10, Job xxix. 24, Hab. i. 5). In
these constructions faith is evidently the assurance of things
hoped for, the conviction of things not seen.

No hiphilate noun from this root occurs in the Old Testament. This circumstance need not in itself possess significance;
the notions of 'faith' and 'faithfulness' lie close to one another, and are not uncommonly expressed by a single term (so
πίστις, fides, faith). As a matter of fact, however, 'faith,' in its
active sense, can barely be accounted an Old Testament term.
It occurs in the Authorized Version of the Old Testament only
twice: Deut. xxxii. 20 where it represents the Hebrew אֵמֻן and
Hab. ii. 4 where it stands for the Hebrew אֱמוּנָה; and it would
seem to be really demanded in no passage but Hab. ii. 4. The
very point of this passage, however, is the sharp contrast
which is drawn between arrogant self-sufficiency and faithful

dependence on God. The purpose of the verse is to give a reply to the prophet's inquiry as to God's righteous dealings with the Chaldæans. Since it is by faith that the righteous man lives, the arrogant Chaldæan, whose soul is puffed up and not straight within him, cannot but be destined to destruction. The whole drift of the broader context bears out this meaning; for throughout this prophecy the Chaldæan is ever exhibited as the type of insolent self-assertion (i. 7, 11, 16), in contrast with which the righteous appear, certainly not as men of integrity and steadfast faithfulness, but as men who look in faith to God and trustingly depend upon His arm. The obvious reminiscence of Gen. xv. 6 throws its weight into the same scale, to which may be added the consent of the Jewish expositors of the passage. Here we have, therefore, thrown into a clear light the contrasting characteristics of the wicked, typified by the Chaldæan, and of the righteous: of the one the fundamental trait is self-sufficiency; of the other, faith. This faith, which forms the distinctive feature of the righteous man, and by which he obtains life, is obviously no mere assent. It is a profound and abiding disposition, an ingrained attitude of mind and heart towards God which affects and gives character to all the activities. Here only the term occurs in the Old Testament; but on this its sole occurrence it rises to the full height of its most pregnant meaning.

The extreme rarity of the noun 'faith' in the Old Testament may prepare us to note that even the verb 'to believe' is far from common in it. In a religious application it occurs in only some thirteen Old Testament books, and less than a score and a half times. The thing believed is sometimes a specific word or work of God (Lam. iv. 12, Hab. i. 5), the fact of a divine revelation (Ex. iv. 5, Job ix. 16), or the words or commandments of God in general (with ‎ב Ps. cvi. 12, cxix. 66). In Ex. xix. 9 and II Chron. xx. 20 God's prophets are the object of His people's confidence. God Himself is the object to which they believingly turn, or on whom they rest in assured trust, in some eleven cases. In two of these it is to Him as a faithful witness that faith believingly turns (Deut. ix. 23, Isa. xliii. 10).

In the remainder of them it is upon His very person that faith
rests in assured confidence (Gen. xv. 6, Ex. xiv. 31, Num. xiv.
11, xx. 12, Deut. i. 32, II Kings xvii. 14, II Chron. xx. 20, Ps.
lxxviii. 22, Jon. iii. 5). It is in these instances, in which the construction is with ב, together with those in which the word is
used absolutely (Ex. iv. 31, Isa. vii. 9, xxviii. 16, Ps. cxvi. 10),
to which may be added Ps. xxvii. 13 where it is construed with
the infinitive, that the conception of religious believing comes
to its rights. The typical instance is, of course, the great word
of Gen. xv. 6, 'And Abram believed in the LORD, and he counted
it to him for righteousness'; in which all subsequent believers,
Jewish and Christian alike, have found the primary example
of faith. The object of Abram's faith, as here set forth, was not
the promise which appears as the occasion of its exercise;
what it rested on was God Himself, and that not merely as
the giver of the promise here recorded, but as His servant's
shield and exceeding great reward (xv. 1). It is therefore not
the assentive but the fiducial element of faith which is here
emphasized; in a word, the faith which Abram gave Jehovah
when he 'put his trust in God' (ἐπίστευσεν τῷ θεῷ LXX), was
the same faith which later He sought in vain at the hands of
His people (Num. xiv. 11, cf. Deut. i. 32, II Kings xvii. 14),
and the notion of which the Psalmist explains in the parallel,
'They believed not in God, and trusted not in his salvation'
(Ps. lxxviii. 22). To believe in God, in the Old Testament sense,
is thus not merely to assent to His word, but with firm and unwavering confidence to rest in security and trustfulness upon
Him.

In the Greek of the Septuagint πιστεύειν takes its place as
the regular rendering of הֶאֱמִין and is very rarely set aside in
favour of another word expressing trust (Prov. xxvi. 25 πείθεσ-
θαι). In a few cases, however, it is strengthened by composition
with a preposition (Deut. i. 32, Judg. xi. 20, II Chron. xx. 20,
cf. Sir. i. 15, ii. 10 etc., I Macc. i. 30, vii. 16 etc., ἐμπιστεύειν;
Mic. vii. 5, καταπιστεύειν); and in a few others it is construed
with prepositions (ἔν τινι, Jer. xii. 6, Ps. lxxviii. 22, Dan. vi. 23,
I Sam. xxvii. 12, II Chron. xx. 20, Mic. vii. 5, Sir. xxxv. 21;

ἐπί τινα, Isa. xxviii. 16 (?), III Macc. ii. 7; ἐπί τινι, Wis. xii. 2; εἰς τινα, Sir. xxxviii. 31; κατά τινα, Job iv. 18, xv. 15, xxiv. 22).

It was by being thus made the vehicle for expressing the high religious faith of the Old Testament that the word was prepared for its New Testament use. For it had the slightest possible connection with religious faith in classical speech. Resting ultimately on a root with the fundamental sense of 'binding,' and standing in classical Greek as the common term for 'trusting,' 'putting faith in,' 'relying upon,' shading down into 'believing,' it was rather too strong a term for ordinary use of that ungenial relation to the gods which was characteristic of Greek thought, and which was substantively expressed by πίστις — the proper acknowledgment in thought and act of their existence and rights. For this νομίζειν was the usual term, and the relative strength of the two terms may be observed in their use in the opening sections of Xenophon's "Memorabilia" (I. i. 1 and 5), where Socrates is charged with not believing in the gods whom the city owned (νομίζειν τοὺς θεούς), but is affirmed to have stood in a much more intimate relation to them, to have trusted in them (πιστεύειν τοῖς θεοῖς). Something of the same depth of meaning may lurk in the exhortation of the Epinomis (980 C), Πιστεύσας τοῖς θεοῖς εὔχου. But ordinarily πιστεύειν τοῖς θεοῖς appears as the synonym of νομίζειν τοὺς θεούς, and imports merely the denial of atheism (Plut. "de Superst.," ii.; Arist. "Rhet.," ii. 17). It was only by its adoption by the writers of the Septuagint to express the faith of the Old Testament that it was fitted to take its place in the New Testament as the standing designation of the attitude of the man of faith towards God.

This service the Septuagint could not perform for πίστις also, owing to the almost complete absence of the noun 'faith' in the active sense from the Old Testament; but it was due to a Hellenistic development on the basis of the Old Testament religion, and certainly not without influence from Gen. xv. 6 and Hab. ii. 4 that this term, too, was prepared for New Testament use. In classical Greek πίστις is applied to belief in

the gods chiefly as implying that such belief rests rather on
trust than on sight (Plut. "Mor.," 756 B). Though there is no
suggestion in this of weakness of conviction (for πίστις expresses a strong conviction, and is therefore used in contrast
with 'impressions'), yet the word, when referring to the gods,
very rarely rises above intellectual conviction into its naturally
more congenial region of moral trust (Soph. "Oed. Rex," 1445).
That this, its fuller and more characteristic meaning, should
come to its rights in the religious sphere, it was necessary that
it should be transferred into a new religious atmosphere. The
usage of Philo bears witness that it thus came to its rights on
the lips of the Greek-speaking Jews. It is going too far, to be
sure, to say that Philo's usage of 'faith' is scarcely distinguishable from that of New Testament writers. The gulf that separates the two is very wide, and has not been inaptly described
by saying that with Philo, faith, as the queen of the virtues,
is the righteousness of the righteous man, while with St. Paul,
as the abnegation of all claim to virtue, it is the righteousness
of the unrighteous. But it is of the utmost significance that, in
the pages of Philo, the conception is filled with a content which
far transcends any usage of the word in heathen Greek, and
which is a refraction of the religious conceptions of the Old
Testament. Fundamental to his idea of it as the crowning virtue of the godly man, to be attained only with the supremest
difficulty, especially by creatures akin to mortal things, is his
conception of it as essentially a changeless, unwavering 'standing by God' (Deut. v. 31), — binding us to God, to the exclusion of every other object of desire, and making us one with
Him. It has lost that soteriological content which is the very
heart of faith in the Old Testament; though there does not absolutely fail an occasional reference to God as Saviour, it is,
with Philo, rather the Divinity, τὸ ὄν, upon which faith rests,
than the God of grace and salvation; and it therefore stands
with him, not at the beginning but at the end of the religious
life. But we can perceive in the usage of Philo a development
on Jewish ground of a use of the word πίστις to describe that
complete detachment from earthly things, and that firm con-

viction of the reality and supreme significance of the things not seen, which underlies its whole New Testament use.

The disparity in the use of the terms 'faith' and 'believe' in the two Testaments is certainly in a formal aspect very great. In contrast with their extreme rarity in the Old Testament, they are both, though somewhat unevenly distributed and varying in relative frequency, distinctly characteristic of the whole New Testament language, and oddly enough occur about equally often (about 240 times each). The verb is lacking only in Col., Philem., II Pet., II and III Jn., and the Apocalypse; the noun only in the Gospel of John and II and III Jn.: both fail only in II and III Jn. The noun predominates not only in the epistles of St. Paul, where the proportion is about three to one, and in St. James (about five to one), but very markedly in the Epistle to the Hebrews (about sixteen to one). In St. John, on the other hand, the verb is very frequent, while the noun occurs only once in I Jn. and four times in the Apocalypse. In the other books the proportion between the two is less noteworthy, and may fairly be accounted accidental. In the Old Testament, again, 'faith' occurs in the active sense in but a single passage; in the New Testament it is the passive sense which is rare. In the Old Testament in only about half the instances of its occurrence is the verb 'to believe' used in a religious sense; in the New Testament it has become so clearly a technical religious term, that it occurs very rarely in any other sense. The transitive usage, in which it expresses entrusting something to someone, occurs a few times both in the active (Lk. xvi. 11, Jn. ii. 24) and the passive (I Cor. ix. 17, Gal. ii. 7, I Thess. ii. 4, I Tim. i. 11, Tit. i. 3); but besides this special case there are very few instances in which the word does not express religious believing, possibly only the following: Jn. ix. 18, Acts ix. 26, I Cor. xi. 18, Mt. xxiv. 23, 26, Mk. xiii. 21, II Thess. ii. 11, cf. Acts xiii. 41, xv. 11, Jn. iv. 21, I Jn. iv. 1. The classical construction with the simple dative which prevails in the Septuagint retires in the New Testament in favour of constructions with prepositions and the absolute use of the verb; the construction with the dative occurs about forty-five times, while that with prepositions occurs some sixty-three times, and the verb is used absolutely some ninety-three times.

When construed with the dative, πιστεύειν in the New Testament prevailingly expresses believing assent, though ordinarily in a somewhat pregnant sense. When its object is a thing, it is usually the spoken (Lk. i. 20, Jn. iv. 50, v. 47, xii. 38, Rom. x. 16, cf. II Thess. ii. 11) or written (Jn. ii. 22, v. 47, Acts xxiv. 14, xxvi. 27) word of God; once it is divine works which should convince the onlooker of the divine mission of the worker (Jn. x. 38). When its object is a person it is rarely another than God or Jesus (Mt. xxi. 25, 32, Mk. xi. 31, Lk. xx. 5, Jn. v. 46, Acts viii. 12, I Jn. iv. 1), and more rarely God (Jn. v. 24, Acts xvi. 34, xxvii. 25, Rom. iv. 3 (17), Gal. iii. 6, Tit. iii. 8, Jas. ii. 23, I Jn. v. 10) than Jesus (Jn. iv. 21, v. 38, 46, vi. 30, viii. 31, 45, 46, x. 37, 38, xiv. 11, Acts xviii. 8, II Tim. i. 12). Among these passages there are not lacking some, both when the object is a person and when it is a thing, in which the higher sense of devoted, believing trust is conveyed. In I Jn. iii. 23, for example, we are obviously to translate, not 'believe the name,' but 'believe in the name of his Son, Jesus Christ,' for in this is summed up the whole Godward side of Christian duty. So there is no reason to question that the words of Gen. xv. 6 are adduced in Rom. iv. 3, Gal. iii. 6, Jas. ii. 23 in the deep sense which they bear in the Old Testament text; and this deeper religious faith can scarcely be excluded from the belief in God adverted to in Acts xvi. 34, Tit. iii. 8 (cf. Jn. v. 24), or from the belief in Jesus adverted to in II Tim. i. 12 (cf. Jn. v. 38, vi. 30), and is obviously the prominent conception in the faith of Crispus declared in Acts xviii. 8. The passive form of this construction occurs only twice — once of believing assent (II Thess. i. 10), and once with the highest implications of confiding trust (I Tim. iii. 16). The few passages in which the construction is with the accusative (Jn. xi. 26, Acts xiii. 41, I Cor. xi. 18, xiii. 7, I Jn. iv. 16) take their natural place along with the commoner usage with the dative, and need not express more than crediting, although over one or two of them there floats a shadow of a deeper implication. The same may be said of the cases of attraction in Rom.

iv. 17 and x. 14. And with these weaker constructions must be
ranged also the passages, twenty in all (fourteen of which occur
in the writings of St. John), in which what is believed is joined
to the verb by the conjunction ὅτι. In a couple of these the matter believed scarcely rises into the religious sphere (Jn. ix. 18,
Acts ix. 26); in a couple more there is specific reference to
prayer (Mk. xi. 23, 24); in yet a couple more it is general faith
in God which is in mind (Heb. xi. 6, Jas. ii. 19). In the rest,
what is believed is of immediately soteriological import — now
the possession by Jesus of a special power (Mt. ix. 28), now
the central fact of His saving work (Rom. x. 9, I Thess. iv. 14),
now the very hinge of the Christian hope (Rom. vi. 8), but
prevailingly the divine mission and personality of Jesus Himself (Jn. vi. 69, viii. 24, xi. 27, 42, xiii. 19, xiv. 10, xvi. 27,
30, xvii. 8, 21, xx. 31, I Jn. v. 1, 5). By their side we may
recall also the rare construction with the infinitive (Acts xv. 11,
Rom. xiv. 2).

When we advance to the constructions with prepositions, we
enter a region in which the deeper sense of the word — that of
firm, trustful reliance — comes to its full rights. The construction with ἐν, which is the most frequent of the constructions
with prepositions in the Septuagint, retires almost out of use in
the New Testament; it occurs with certainty only in Mk. i. 15,
where the object of faith is 'the gospel,' though Jn. iii. 15, Eph.
i. 13 may also be instances of it, where the object would be
Christ. The implication of this construction would seem to be
firm fixedness of confidence in its object. Scarcely more common
is the parallel construction of ἐπί with the dative, expressive of
steady, resting repose, reliance upon the object. Besides the
quotation from Isa. xxviii. 16, which appears alike in Rom. ix.
33, x. 11, I Pet. ii. 6, this construction occurs only twice: Lk.
xxiv. 25, where Jesus rebukes His followers for not 'believing
on,' relying implicitly upon, all that the prophets have spoken;
and I Tim. i. 16, where we are declared to 'believe on' Jesus
Christ unto salvation, i.e., to obtain salvation by relying upon
Him for it. The constructions with prepositions governing the
accusative, which involve an implication of 'moral motion,

mental direction towards,' are more frequently used. That with
ἐπί, indeed, occurs only seven times (four of which are in Acts).
In two instances in Rom. iv. where the reminiscence of the
faith of Abraham gives colour to the language, the object on
which faith is thus said relyingly to lay hold is God, described,
however, as savingly working through Christ — as He that
justifies the ungodly, He that raised Jesus our Lord from the
dead. Elsewhere its object is Christ Himself. In Mt. xxvii. 42
the Jewish leaders declare the terms on which they will become
'believers on' Jesus; in Acts xvi. 31 this is the form that is
given to the proclamation of salvation by faith in Christ —
'turn with confident trust to Jesus Christ,' and appropriately,
therefore, it is in this form of expression that those are designated who have savingly believed on Christ (Acts ix. 42, xi.
17, xxii. 19). The special New Testament construction, however,
is that with εἰς, which occurs some forty-nine times, about four-
fifths of which are Johannine and the remainder more or less
Pauline. The object towards which faith is thus said to be
reliantly directed is in one unique instance 'the witness which
God hath witnessed concerning his Son' (I Jn. v. 10), where we
may well believe that 'belief in the truth of the witness is carried on to personal belief in the object of the witness, that is,
the Incarnate Son Himself.' Elsewhere the object believed on,
in this construction, is always a person, and that very rarely
God (Jn. xiv. 1, cf. I Jn. v. 10, and also I Pet. i. 21, where, however, the true reading is probably πιστοὺς εἰς θεόν), and most
commonly Christ (Mt. xviii. 6, Jn. ii. 11, iii. 16, 18, 36, iv. 39,
vi. 29, 35, 40, vii. 5, 31, 38, 39, 48, viii. 30, ix. 35, 36, x. 42, xi.
25, 26, 45, 48, xii. 11, 37, 42, 44, 44, 46, xiv. 1, 12, xvi. 9, xvii.
20, Acts x. 43, xiv. 23, xix. 4, Rom. x. 14, 14, Gal. ii. 16, Phil.
i. 29, I Pet. i. 8, I Jn. v. 10, cf. Jn. xii. 36, i. 12, ii. 23, iii. 18, I Jn.
v. 13). A glance over these passages will bring clearly out the
pregnancy of the meaning conveyed. It may be more of a question wherein the pregnancy resides. It is probably sufficient to
find it in the sense conveyed by the verb itself, while the preposition adjoins only the person towards whom the strong feeling
expressed by the verb is directed. In any event, what these pas-

sages express is 'an absolute transference of trust from ourselves to another,' a complete self-surrender to Christ.

Some confirmation of this explanation of the strong meaning of the phrase πιστεύειν εἰς may be derived from the very rich use of the verb absolutely, in a sense in no way inferior. Its absolute use is pretty evenly distributed through the New Testament occurring 29 times in John, 23 times in Paul, 22 times in Acts, 15 times in the Synoptics, and once each in Hebrews, James, I Peter, and Jude; it is placed on the lips of Jesus some 18 times. In surprisingly few of these instances is it used of a non-religious act of crediting, — apparently only in our Lord's warning to His followers not to believe when men say '"Lo, here is the Christ," or "here"' (Mt. xxiv. 23, 26, Mk. xiii. 21). In equally surprisingly few instances is it used of specific acts of faith in the religious sphere. Once it is used of assent given to a specific doctrine — that of the unity of God (Jas. ii. 19). Once it is used of believing prayer (Mt. xxi. 22). Four times in a single chapter of John it is used of belief in a specific fact — the great fact central to Christianity of the resurrection of Christ (Jn. xx. 8, 25, 29, 29). It is used occasionally of belief in God's announced word (Lk. i. 45, Acts xxvi. 27), and occasionally also of the credit given to specific testimonies of Jesus, whether with reference to earthly or heavenly things (Jn. iii. 12, 12, i. 50, Lk. xxii. 67), passing thence to general faith in the word of salvation (Lk. viii. 12, 13). Twice it is used of general soteriological faith in God (Jude 5, Rom. iv. 18), and a few times, with the same pregnancy of implication, where the reference, whether to God or Christ, is more or less uncertain (Jn. i. 7, Rom. iv. 11, II Cor. iv. 13, 13). Ordinarily, however, it expresses soteriological faith directed to the person of Christ. In a few instances, to be sure, the immediate trust expressed is in the extraordinary power of Jesus for the performance of earthly effects (the so-called 'miracle faith'), as in Mt. viii. 13, Mk. v. 36, ix. 23, 24, Lk. viii. 50, Jn. iv. 48, xi. 40; but the essential relation in which this faith stands to 'saving faith' is clearly exhibited in Jn. iv. 48 compared with v. 53 and ix. 38, and Jn. xi. 40 compared with v. 15 and xii. 39; and, in any case, these passages are insignificant in number when compared with the great array in which the reference is distinctly to saving faith in Christ (Mk. ix. 42, xv. 32 [Jn. iii. 15], Jn. iii. 18. iv. 41, 42, 53, v. 44, vi. 36, 47, 64, 64, ix. 38, x. 25, 26, xi. 15, xii. 39, xiv. 29, xvi. 31, xix. 35, xx. 31, Acts ii. 44, iv. 4, 32, v. 14, viii. 13, xi. 21, xiii. 12, 39, 48, xiv. 1, xv. 5, 7, xvii. 12, 34, xviii. 8, 27, xix. 2, 18, xxi. 20, 25, Rom. i. 16, iii. 22, x. 4, 10, xiii. 11, xv. 13, I Cor. i. 21, iii. 5, xiv. 22, xv. 2, 11, Gal. iii. 22, Eph. i. 13, 19, I Thess. i. 7, ii. 10, 13, II Thess. i. 10, Heb. iv. 3, I Pet. ii. 7). A survey of these passages will show very clearly that in the New Testament 'to believe' is a technical term to express reliance on Christ for salvation. In a number of them, to be sure, the object of the believing spoken of is sufficiently defined by the context, but, without contextual indication of the object, enough remain to bear out this suggestion. Accordingly, a tendency is betrayed to use the simple participle very much as a verbal noun, with the meaning of 'Christian': in Mk. ix. 42, Acts xi. 21, I Cor. i. 21, Eph. i. 13, 19, I Thess. i. 7, ii. 10, 13 the participial construction is evident; it may be doubted, however, whether οἱ πιστεύσαντες is not used as a noun in such passages as Acts ii. 44, iv. 32, II Thess. i. 10, Heb. iv. 3; and in Acts v. 14 πιστεύοντες is perhaps generally recognized as used substantively. Before the disciples were called 'Christians' (Acts xi. 26, cf. xxvi. 28, I Pet. iv. 16) it would seem, then, that they were called 'believers,' — those who had turned to Christ in trusting reliance (οἱ πιστεύσαντες), or those who were resting on Christ in trusting reliance (οἱ πιστεύοντες); and that the undefined 'to believe' had come to mean to become or to be a Christian, that is, to turn to or rest on Christ in reliant trust. The occasional use of οἱ πιστοί in an equivalent sense (Acts x. 45, Eph. i. 1, I Tim. iv. 3, 12, I Pet. i. 21, Rev. xvii. 14), for which the way was prepared by the comparatively frequent use of this adjective in the classically rare active sense (Jn. xx. 27, Acts xvi. 1, I Cor. vii. 14, II Cor. vi. 15, Gal. iii. 9, I Tim. iv. 10, v. 16, vi. 2, Tit. i. 6), adds weight to this conclusion; as do also the use of ἄπιστοι of 'unbelievers,' whether in the simple (I Cor. vi. 6, vii. 12–15, x. 27, xiv. 22–24, I Tim. v. 8) or deepened sense (II Cor.

iv. 4, vi. 14 f., Tit. i. 15, cf. Jn. xx. 27, Mt. xvii. 17, Mk. ix. 19, Lk. ix. 41), and the related usage of the words ἀπιστία (Mk. ix. 24 (xvi. 14), Mt. xiii. 58, Mk. vi. 6, Rom. iv. 20, xi. 20, 23, I Tim. i. 13, Heb. iii. 12, 19), ἀπιστέω (Mk. xvi. 11 (16), Lk. xxiv. 11, 41, Acts xxviii. 24, I Pet. ii. 7), and ὀλιγόπιστος (Mt. vi. 30, viii. 26, xiv. 31, xvi. 8, Lk. xii. 28), ὀλιγοπιστία (Mt. xvii. 20).

The impression which is thus derived from the usage of πιστεύειν is only deepened by attending to that of πίστις. As already intimated, πίστις occurs in the New Testament very rarely in its passive sense of 'faithfulness,' 'integrity' (Rom. iii. 3 of God; Mt. xxiii. 23, Gal. v. 22, Tit. ii. 10, of men; cf. I Tim. v. 12 'a pledge'; Acts xvii. 31 'assurance'; others add I Tim. vi. 11, II Tim. ii. 22, iii. 10, Philem. 5). And nowhere in the multitude of its occurrences in its active sense is it applied to man's faith in man, but always to the religious trust that reposes on God, or Christ, or divine things. The specific object on which the trust rests is but seldom explicitly expressed. In some six of these instances it is a thing, but always something of the fullest soteriological significance — the gospel of Christ (Phil. i. 27), the saving truth of God (II Thess. ii. 13), the working of God who raised Jesus from the dead (Col. ii. 12, cf. Acts xiv. 9, iii. 16), the name of Jesus (Acts iii. 16), the blood of Jesus (Rom. iii. 25), the righteousness of Jesus (II Pet. i. 1). In as many more the object is God, and the conception is prevailingly that of general trust in God (Mk. xi. 22, Rom. xiv. 22, I Thess. i. 8, Heb. vi. 1, I Pet. i. 21, cf. Col. ii. 12). In most instances, however, the object is specified as Christ, and the faith is very pointedly soteriological (Acts xx. 21, xxiv. 24, xxvi. 18, Gal. ii. 16, 16, 20. Rom. iii. 22, 26, Gal. iii. 22, 26, Eph. i. 15, iii. 12, iv. 13, Phil. iii. 9, Col. i. 4, ii. 5, I Tim. i. 14, iii. 13, 15, II Tim. i. 13, iii. 15, Philem. 5, Jas. ii. 1, Rev. ii. 13, xiv. 12). Its object is most frequently joined to πίστις as an objective genitive, a construction occurring some seventeen times, twelve of which fall in the writings of Paul. In four of them the genitive is that of the thing, namely in Phil. i. 27 the gospel, in II Thess. ii. 13 the saving truth, in Col. ii. 12 the almighty working of God, and in Acts iii. 16 the name of Jesus. In one of them it is God (Mk. xi.

22). The certainty that the genitive is that of object in these cases is decisive with reference to its nature in the remaining cases, in which Jesus Christ is set forth as the object on which faith rests (Rom. iii. 22, 26, Gal. ii. 16, 16, 20, iii. 22, Eph. iii. 12, iv. 13, Phil. iii. 9, Jas. ii. 1, Rev. ii. 13, xiv. 12). Next most frequently its object is joined to faith by means of the preposition ἐν (9 times), by which it is set forth as the basis on which faith rests, or the sphere of its operation. In two of these instances the object is a thing — the blood or righteousness of Jesus (Rom. iii. 25, II Pet. i. 1); in the rest it is Christ Himself who is presented as the ground of faith (Gal. iii. 26, Eph. i. 15, Col. i. 4, I Tim. i. 14, iii. 13, II Tim. i. 13, iii. 15). Somewhat less frequently (5 times) its object is joined to πίστις by means of the preposition εἰς, designating, apparently, merely the object with reference to which faith is exercised (cf. especially Acts xx. 21); the object thus specified for faith is in one instance God (I Pet. i. 21), and in the others Christ (Acts xx. 21, xxiv. 24, xxvi. 18, Col. ii. 5). By the side of this construction should doubtless be placed the two instances in which the preposition πρός is used, by which faith is said to look and adhere to God (I Thess. i. 8) or to Christ (Philem. 5). And it is practically in the same sense that in a single instance God is joined to πίστις by means of the preposition ἐπί as the object to which it restingly turns. It would seem that the pregnant sense of πίστις as self-abandoning trust was so fixed in Christian speech that little was left to be expressed by the mode of its adjunction to its object.

Accordingly, the use of the word without specified object is vastly preponderant. In a few of such instances we may see a specific reference to the general confidence which informs believing prayer (Lk. xviii. 8, Jas. i. 6, v. 15). In a somewhat greater number there is special reference to faith in Jesus as a worker of wonders — the so-called 'miracle faith' (Mt. viii. 10, ix. 2, 22, 29, xv. 28 [xvii. 20] [xxi. 21], Mk. ii. 5, iv. 40, v. 34, x. 52, Lk. v. 20, vii. 9, viii. 25, 48, xvii. 19, xviii. 42, Acts iii. 16, xiv. 9) — although how little this faith can be regarded as non-soteriological the language of Mt. ix. 2, Mk. ii. 5, Lk. v. 20 shows, as well as the parallelism between·Lk. vii. 50 (cf. viii.

48, xvii. 19) and Mt. ix. 22, Mk. v. 34. The immense mass of
the passages in which the undefined πίστις occurs, however, are
distinctly soteriological, and that indifferently whether its implied object be God or Christ. Its implied reference is indeed
often extremely difficult to fix; though the passages in which it
may, with some confidence, be referred to Christ are in number about double those in which it may, with like confidence, be
referred to God. The degree of clearness with which an implied
object is pointed to in the context varies, naturally, very greatly;
but in a number of cases there is no direct hint of object in the
context, but this is left to be supplied by the general knowledge
of the reader. And this is as much as to say that πίστις is so used
as to imply that it had already become a Christian technical
term, which needed no further definition that it might convey
its full sense of saving faith in Jesus Christ to the mind of every
reader. This tendency to use it as practically a synonym for
'Christianity' comes out sharply in such a phrase as οἱ ἐκ πίστεως
(Gal. iii. 7, 9), which is obviously a paraphrase for 'believers.'
A transitional form of the phrase meets us in Rom. iii. 26,
τὸν ἐκ πίστεως 'Ιησοῦ; that the 'Ιησοῦ could fall away and leave
the simple οἱ ἐκ πίστεως standing for the whole idea, is full of
implications as to the sense which the simple undefined πίστις
had acquired in the circles which looked to Jesus for salvation.
The same implications underlie the so-called objective use of
πίστις in the New Testament. That in such passages as Acts vi.
7, Gal. i. 23, iii. 23, vi. 10, Phil. i. 25, Jude 3, 20 it conveys the
idea of 'the Christian religion' appears plain on the face of the
passages; and by their side can be placed such others as the
following, which seem transitional to them, namely: Acts xvi.
5, I Cor. xvi. 13, Col. i. 23, I Tim. i. 19, iv. 1, 6, v. 8, Tit. i. 13,
and, at a slightly further remove, such others as Acts xiii. 8,
Rom. i. 5, xvi. 26, Phil. i. 25, I Tim. iii. 9, vi. 10, 12, II Tim. iii.
8, iv. 7, Tit. i. 4, iii. 15, I Pet. v. 9. It is not necessary to suppose that πίστις is used in any of these passages as *doctrina fidei;*
it seems possible to carry through them all the conception of
'*subjective* faith conceived of *objectively* as a power,' — even
through those in Jude and I Timothy, which are more com-

monly than any others interpreted as meaning *doctrina fidei*. But this generally admitted objectivizing of subjective faith makes πίστις, as truly as if it were understood as *doctrina fidei*, on the verge of which it in any case trembles, a synonym for 'the Christian religion.' It is only a question whether 'the Christian religion' is designated in it from the side of doctrine or life; though it be from the point of view of life, still 'the faith' has become a synonym for 'Christianity,' 'believers' for 'Christians,' 'to believe' for 'to become a Christian,' and we may trace a development by means of which πίστις has come to mean the religion which is marked by and consists essentially in 'believing.' That this development so rapidly took place is significant of much, and supplies a ready explanation of such passages as Gal. iii. 23, 25, in which the phrases 'before the faith came' and 'now that faith is come' probably mean little more than before and after the advent of 'Christianity' into the world. On the ground of such a usage, we may at least re-affirm with increased confidence that the idea of 'faith' is conceived of in the New Testament as the characteristic idea of Christianity, and that it does not import mere 'belief' in an intellectual sense, but all that enters into an entire self-commitment of the soul to Jesus as the Son of God, the Saviour of the world.

II. The Historical Presentation of Faith

It lies on the very surface of the New Testament that its writers were not conscious of a chasm between the fundamental principle of the religious life of the saints of the old covenant and the faith by which they themselves lived. To them, too, Abraham is the typical example of a true believer (Rom. iv., Gal. iii., Heb. xi., Jas. ii.); and in their apprehension 'those who are of faith,' that is, 'Christians,' are by that very fact constituted Abraham's sons (Gal. iii. 7, Rom. iv. 16), and receive their blessing only along with that 'believer' (Gal. iii. 9) in the steps of whose faith it is that they are walking (Rom. iv. 12) when they believe on Him who raised Jesus our Lord from the dead (Rom. iv. 24). And not only Abraham, but the whole series of Old Testament heroes are conceived by them to be examples of the same faith which was required of them 'unto the gaining of the soul' (Heb. xi.). Wrought in them by the same Spirit (II Cor. iv. 13), it produced in them the same fruits, and constituted them a 'cloud of witnesses' by whose testimony we should be stimulated to run our own race with like patience in dependence on Jesus, 'the author and finisher of our faith' (Heb. xii. 2). Nowhere is the demand of faith treated as a novelty of the new covenant, or is there a distinction drawn between the faith of the two covenants; everywhere the sense of continuity is prominent (Jn. v. 24, 46, xii. 38, 39, 44, I Pet. ii. 6), and the 'proclamation of faith' (Gal. iii. 2, 5, Rom. x. 16) is conceived as essentially one in both dispensations, under both of which the law reigns that 'the just shall live by his faith' (Hab. ii. 4, Rom. i. 17, Gal. iii. 11, Heb. x. 38). Nor do we need to penetrate beneath the surface of the Old Testament to perceive the justice of this New Testament view. Despite the infrequency of the occurrence on its pages of the terms 'faith,' 'to believe,' the religion of the Old Testament is obviously as fundamentally a religion of faith as is that of the New Testament. There is a sense, to be sure, in which all religion presupposes faith (Heb. xi. 6), and in this broad sense the religion of Israel, too, necessarily rested on faith. But the religion of Israel was a religion of faith in a far more specific sense than this; and that not merely because faith was more consciously its foundation, but because its very essence consisted in faith, and this faith was the same radical self-commitment to God, not merely as the highest good of the holy soul, but as the gracious Saviour of the sinner, which meets us as the characteristic feature of the religion of the New Testament. Between the faith of the two Testaments there exists, indeed, no further difference than that which the progress of the historical working out of redemption brought with it.

The hinge of Old Testament religion from the very beginning turns on the facts of man's sin (Gen. iii.) and consequent unworthiness (Gen. iii. 2–10), and of God's grace (Gen. iii. 15) and consequent saving activity (Gen. iii. 4, iv. 5, vi. 8, 13 f.).

This saving activity presents itself from the very beginning also under the form of promise or covenant, the radical idea of which is naturally faithfulness on the part of the promising God with the answering attitude of faith on the part of the receptive people. Face to face with a holy God, the sinner has no hope except in the free mercy of God, and can be authorized to trust in that mercy only by express assurance. Accordingly, the only cause of salvation is from the first the pitying love of God (Gen. iii. 15, viii. 21), which freely grants benefits to man; while on man's part there is never question of merit or of a strength by which he may prevail (I Sam. ii. 9), but rather a constant sense of unworthiness (Gen. xxxii. 10), by virtue of which humility appears from the first as the keynote of Old Testament piety. In the earlier portions of the Old Testament, to be sure, there is little abstract statement of the ideas which ruled the hearts and lives of the servants of God. The essence of patriarchal religion is rather exhibited to us in action. But from the very beginning the distinctive feature of the life of the pious is that it is a life of faith, that its regulative principle is drawn, not from the earth but from above. Thus the first recorded human acts after the Fall — the naming of Eve, and the birth and naming of Cain — are expressive of trust in God's promise that, though men should die for their sins, yet man should not perish from the earth, but should triumph over the tempter; in a word, in the great promise of the Seed (Gen. iii. 15). Similarly, the whole story of the Flood is so ordered as to throw into relief, on the one hand, the free grace of God in His dealings with Noah (Gen. vi. 8, 18, viii. 1, 21, ix. 8), and, on the other, the determination of Noah's whole life by trust in God and His promises (Gen. vi. 22, vii. 5, ix. 20). The open declaration of the faith-principle of Abraham's life (Gen. xv. 6) only puts into words, in the case of him who stands at the root of Israel's whole national and religious existence, what not only might also be said of all the patriarchs, but what actually is most distinctly said both of Abraham and of them through the medium of their recorded history. The entire patriarchal narrative is set forth with the design and effect of exhibiting the life of the servants of God as a life of faith, and it is just by the fact of their implicit self-commitment to God that throughout the narrative the servants of God are differentiated from others. This does not mean, of course, that with them faith took the place of obedience: an entire self-commitment to God which did not show itself in obedience to Him would be self-contradictory, and the testing of faith by obedience is therefore a marked feature of the patriarchal narrative. But it does mean that faith was with them the precondition of all obedience. The patriarchal religion is essentially a religion, not of law but of promise, and therefore not primarily of obedience but of trust; the holy walk is characteristic of God's servants (Gen. v. 22, 24, vi. 9, xvii. 1, xxiv. 40, xlviii. 15), but it is characteristically described as a walk 'with God'; its peculiarity consisted precisely in the ordering of life by entire trust in God, and it expressed itself in conduct growing out of this trust (Gen. iii. 20, iv. 1, vi. 22, vii. 5, viii. 18, xii. 4, xvii. 23, xxi. 12, 16, xxii.). The righteousness of the patriarchal age was thus but the manifestation in life of an entire self-commitment to God, in unwavering trust in His promises.

The piety of the Old Testament thus began with faith. And though, when the stage of the law was reached, the emphasis might seem to be thrown rather on the obedience of faith, what has been called 'faith in action,' yet the giving of the law does not mark a fundamental change in the religion of Israel, but only a new stage in its orderly development. The law-giving was not a setting aside of the religion of promise, but an incident in its history; and the law given was not a code of jurisprudence for the world's government, but a body of household ordinances for the regulation of God's family. It is therefore itself grounded upon the promise, and it grounds the whole religious life of Israel in the grace of the covenant God (Ex. xx. 2). It is only because Israel are the children of God, and God has sanctified them unto Himself and chosen them to be a peculiar people unto Him (Deut. xiv. 1), that He proceeds to frame them by His law for His especial treasure (Ex. xix. 5; cf. Tit. ii. 14). Faith, therefore, does not appear as one of the precepts of the law, nor as a virtue superior to its precepts, nor yet as a substitute for keeping them; it rather lies behind the law as its presupposition. Accordingly, in the history of the giving of the law, faith is expressly emphasized as the presupposition of the whole relation existing between Israel and Jehovah. The signs by which Moses was accredited, and all Jehovah's deeds of power, had as their design (Ex. iii. 12, iv. 1, 5, 8, 9, xix. 4, 9) and their effect (Ex. iv. 31, xii. 28, 34, xiv. 31, xxiv. 3, 7, Ps. cvi. 12) the working of faith in the people; and their subsequent unbelief is treated as the deepest crime they could commit (Num. xiv. 11, Deut. i. 32, ix. 23, Ps. lxxviii. 22, 32, cvi. 24), as is even momentary failure of faith on the part of their leaders (Num. xx. 12). It is only as a consequent of the relation of the people to Him, instituted by grace on His part and by faith on theirs, that Jehovah proceeds to carry out His gracious purposes for them, delivering them from bondage, giving them a law for the regulation of their lives, and framing them in the promised land into a kingdom of priests and a holy nation. In other words, it is a precondition of the law that Israel's life is not of the earth, but is hid with God, and is therefore to be ordered by His precepts. Its design was, therefore, not to provide a means by which man might come into relation with Jehovah, but to publish the mode of life incumbent on those who stand in the relation of children to Jehovah; and it is therefore that the book of the law was commanded to be put by the side of the ark of the covenant of the LORD, that it might be a witness against the transgressions of Israel (Deut. xxxi. 26).

The effect of the law was consonant with its design. Many, no doubt, looked upon it in a purely legalistic spirit, and sought, by scrupulous fulfilment of it as a body of external precepts, to lay the foundation of a claim on God in behalf of the nation or the individual, or to realize through it, as a present possession, that salvation which was ever represented as something future. But, just in proportion as its spirituality and inwardness were felt, it operated to deepen in Israel the sense of shortcoming and sin, and to sharpen the conviction that from the grace of God alone could salvation be expected. This humble frame of conscious dependence on God was met by a twofold proclamation.

On the one hand, the eyes of God's people were directed more longingly towards the future, and, in contrast with the present failure of Israel to realize the ordinances of life which had been given it, a new dispensation of grace was promised in which the law of God's kingdom should be written upon the heart, and should become therefore the instinctive law of life of His people (Jer. xxiv. 7, xxxi. 11 f., Ezek. xxxvi 25 f.; cf. Ezek. xvi. 60, Joel iii., Jos. ii. 9 f.). It lay in the very nature of the Old Testament dispensation, in which the revelation of God was always incomplete, the still unsolved enigmas of life numerous, the work of redemption unfinished, and the consummation of the kingdom ever yet to come, that the eyes of the saints should be set upon the future; and these deficiencies were felt very early. But it also lay, in the nature of the case, that the sense of them should increase as time passed and the perfecting of Israel was delayed, and especially as the whole national and religious existence of Israel was more and more put in jeopardy by assaults from without and corruption from within. The essence of piety came thus to be ever more plainly proclaimed as consisting in such a confident trust in the God of salvation as could not be confounded either by the unrighteousness which reigned in Israel or by Jehovah's judgments on Israel's sins, — such a confidence as even in the face of the destruction of the theocracy itself, could preserve, in enduring hope, the assurance of the ultimate realization of God's purposes of good to Israel and the establishment of the everlasting kingdom. Thus hopeful waiting upon Jehovah became more and more the centre of Israelitish piety, and Jehovah became before all 'the Hope of Israel' (Jer. xiv. 8, xvii. 13, l. 7, cf. Ps. lxxi. 5). On the other hand, while thus waiting for the salvation of Israel, the saint must needs stay himself on God (Isa. xxvi. 3, l. 10), fixing his heart on Jehovah as the Rock of the heart (Ps. lxxiii. 26), His people's strength (Ps. xlvi. 1) and trust (Ps. xl. 4, lxv. 5, lxxi. 5, Jer. xvii. 7). Freed from all illusion of earthly help, and most of all from all self-confidence, he is meanwhile to live by faith (Hab. ii. 4). Thus, along with an ever more richly expressed corporate hope, there is found also an ever more richly expressed individual

trust, which finds natural utterance through an ample body of
synonyms bringing out severally the various sides of that perfect commitment to God that constitutes the essence of faith.
Thus we read much of trusting in, on, to God, or in His word,
His name, His mercy, His salvation (בָּטַח), of seeking and finding refuge in God or in the shadow of His wings (חָסָה), of committing ourselves to God (גָּלַל), setting confidence (כְּסֶל) in Him,
looking to Him (הִבִּיט), relying upon Him (נִשְׁעַן), staying upon
Him (נִסְמַךְ), setting or fixing the heart upon Him (הֵכִין לֵב),
binding our love on Him (חָשַׁק), cleaving to Him (דָּבַק). So, on
the hopeful side of faith, we read much of hoping in God (קִוָּה),
waiting on God (יִחֵל), of longing for Him (חִכָּה), patiently waiting for Him (הִתְחוֹלֵל), and the like.

By the aid of such expressions, it becomes possible to form
a somewhat clear notion of the attitude towards Him which was
required by Jehovah of His believing people, and which is
summed up in the term "faith." It is a reverential (Ex. xiv. 31,
Num. xiv. 11, xx. 12) and loving faith, which rests on the strong
basis of firm and unshaken conviction of the might and grace
of the covenant God and of the trustworthiness of all His words,
and exhibits itself in confident trust in Jehovah and unwavering
expectation of the fulfilment of, no doubt, all His promises, but
more especially of His promise of salvation, and in consequent
faithful and exclusive adherence to Him. In one word, it consists in an utter commitment of oneself to Jehovah, with confident trust in Him as guide and saviour, and assured expectation of His promised salvation. It therefore stands in contrast,
on the one hand, with trust in self or other human help, and on
the other with doubt and unbelief, despondency and unfaithfulness. From Jehovah alone is salvation to be looked for, and it
comes from His free grace alone (Deut. vii. 7, viii. 18, ix. 5,
Amos iii. 2, Hos. xiii. 5, Ezek. xx. 6, Jer. xxxix. 18, Mal. i. 2), and
to those only who look solely to Him for it (Isa. xxxi. 1, lvii. 13,
xxviii. 16, xxx. 15, Jer. xvii. 5, xxxix. 18, Ps. cxviii. 8, cxlvi. 3,
xx. 7, I Sam. xvii. 45, Job xxxi. 24, Ps. lii. 9). The reference of
faith is accordingly in the Old Testament always distinctly
soteriological; its end the Messianic salvation; and its essence

a trusting, or rather an entrusting of oneself to the God of salvation, with full assurance of the fulfilment of His gracious purposes and the ultimate realization of His promise of salvation for the people and the individual. Such an attitude towards the God of salvation is identical with the faith of the New Testament, and is not essentially changed by the fuller revelation of God the Redeemer in the person of the promised Messiah. That it is comparatively seldom designated in the Old Testament by the names of 'faith,' 'believing,' seems to be due, as has been often pointed out, to the special place of the Old Testament in the history of revelation, and the adaptation of its whole contents and language to the particular task in the establishment of the kingdom of God which fell to its writers. This task turned on the special temptations and difficulties of the Old Testament stage of development, and required emphasis to be laid on the majesty and jealousy of Jehovah and on the duties of reverence, sincerity, and patience. Meanwhile, the faith in Him which underlies these duties is continually implied in their enforcement, and comes to open expression in frequent paraphrase and synonym, and as often in its own proper terms as is natural in the circumstances. Especially in the great crises of the history of redemption (Gen. xv., Ex. iv. 5, xix. 9, Isa. vii.) is the fundamental requirement of faith rendered explicit and prominent.

On the coming of God to His people in the person of His Son, the promised Messianic King, bringing the salvation, the hope of which had for so many ages been their support and stay, it naturally became the primary task of the vehicles of revelation to attract and attach God's people to the person of their Redeemer. And this task was the more pressing in proportion as the form of the fulfilment did not obviously correspond with the promise, and especially with the expectations which had grown up on the faith of the promise. This fundamental function dominates the whole New Testament, and accounts at once for the great prominence in its pages of the demand for faith, by which a gulf seems to be opened between it and the Old Testament. The demand for faith in Jesus as the Redeemer so long hoped for, did indeed create so wide a cleft in the consciousness of the times that the term faith came rapidly to be appropriated to Christianity and 'to believe' to mean to become a Christian; so that the old covenant and the new were discriminated from each other as the ages before and after the 'coming of faith' (Gal. iii. 23, 25). But all this does not imply that faith now for the first time became the foundation of the religion of Jehovah, but only suggests how fully, in the new circumstances induced by the coming of the promised Redeemer, the demand for faith absorbed the whole proclamation of the gospel. In this primary concern for faith the New Testament books all necessarily share; but, for the rest, they differ among themselves in the prominence given to it and in the aspects in which it is presented, in accordance with the place of each in the historical development of the new life; and that is as much as to say in accordance with the historical occasion out of which each arose and the special object to subserve which each was written.

Indeed, the word 'to believe' first appears on the pages of the New Testament in quite Old Testament conditions. We are conscious of no distinction even in atmosphere between the commendation of faith and rebuke of unbelief in Exodus or the Psalms and the same commendation and rebuke in the days just before the 'coming of faith' (Lk. i. 20, 45); these are but specific applications of the thesis of prophetism, expressed positively in II Chron. xx. 20 and negatively in Isa. vii. 9. Already, however, the dawn of the new day has coloured the proclamation of the Baptist, the essence of which Paul sums up for us as a demand for faith in the Coming One (Acts xix. 4), and which John reports to us (Jn. iii. 36). In the synoptic report of the teaching of Jesus, the same purpose is the dominant note. All that Jesus did and taught was directed to drawing faith to Himself. Up to the end, indeed, He repelled the unbelieving demand that He should 'declare plainly' the authority by which He acted and who He really was (Mt. xxi. 23, Lk. xxii. 67): but this was only that He might, in His own way, the more decidedly confound unbelief and assert His divine majesty. Even when He spoke of general faith in God (Mk. xi. 22), and that confident trust which becomes men approaching the Almighty in prayer (Mt. xxi.

22‖Mk. ix. 24, Lk. xviii. 8), He did it in a way which inevitably directed attention to His own person as the representative of God on earth. And this accounts for the prevalence, in the synoptic report of His allusions to faith, of a reference to that exercise of faith which has sometimes been somewhat sharply divided from saving faith under the name of 'miracle faith' (Mt. viii. 10, 13 ‖ Lk. vii. 9; Mt. ix. 2; Mt. ix. 22 ‖ Mk. v. 34, Lk. viii. 48; Mt. ix. 28, 29; Mt. xv. 28; Mt. xvii. 20 ‖ Mk. ix. 20; Mt. xxi. 21, 22, cf. Lk. xvii. 6; Mk. iv. 40; Mk. v. 36 ‖ Lk. viii. 50; Mk. x. 52 ‖ Lk. xviii. 42; Lk. vii. 9). That in these instances we have not a generically distinct order of faith, directed to its own peculiar end, but only a specific movement of that entire trust in Himself which Jesus would arouse in all, seems clear from the manner in which He dealt with it, — now praising its exercise as a specially great exhibition of faith quite generally spoken of (Lk. vii. 9), now pointing to it as a manifestation of that believing to which 'all things are possible' (Mk. ix. 23), now connecting with it not merely the healing of the body but the forgiveness of sins (Mt. ix. 2), and everywhere using it as a means of attaching the confidence of men to His person as the source of all good. Having come to His own, in other words, Jesus took men upon the plane on which He found them, and sought to lead them through the needs which they felt, and the relief of which they sought in Him, up to a recognition of their greater needs and of His ability to give relief to them also. That word of power, 'Thy faith hath saved thee,' spoken indifferently of bodily wants and of the deeper needs of the soul (Lk. vii. 50), not only resulted, but was intended to result, in focusing all eyes on Himself as the one physician of both body and soul (Mt. viii. 17). Explicit references to these higher results of faith are, to be sure, not very frequent in the synoptic discourses, but there are quite enough of them to exhibit Jesus' specific claim to be the proper object of faith for these effects also (Lk. viii. 12, 13, xxii. 32, Mt. xviii. 6 ‖ Mk. ix. 42, Lk. vii. 50), and to prepare the way for His rebuke, after His resurrection, of the lagging minds of His followers, that they did not understand all these things (Lk. xxiv. 25, 45), and for His great commission to Paul to go and open men's eyes that they might receive 'remission of sins and an inheritance among the sanctified by faith in Him' (Acts xxvi. 18).

It is very natural that a much fuller account of Jesus' teaching as to faith should be given in the more intimate discourses which are preserved by John. But in these discourses, too, His primary task is to bind men to Him by faith. The chief difference is that here, consonantly with the nature of the discourses recorded, much more prevailing stress is laid upon the higher aspects of faith, and we see Jesus striving specially to attract to Himself a faith consciously set upon eternal good. In a number of instances we find ourselves in much the same atmosphere as in the Synoptics (iv. 21 *sq.*, 48 *sq.*, ix. 35); and the method of Jesus is the same throughout. Everywhere He offers Himself as the object of faith, and claims faith in Himself for the highest concerns of the soul. But everywhere He begins at the level at which He finds His hearers, and leads them upward to these higher things. It is so that He deals with Nathanael (i. 51) and Nicodemus (iii. 12); and it is so that He deals constantly with the Jews, everywhere requiring faith in Himself for eternal life (v. 24, 25, 38, vi. 35, 40, 47, vii. 38, viii. 24, x. 25, 36, xii. 44, 46), declaring that faith in Him is the certain outcome of faith in their own Scriptures (v. 46, 47), is demanded by the witness borne Him by God in His mighty works (x. 25, 36, 37), is involved in and is indeed identical with faith in God (v. 25, 38, vi. 40, 45, viii. 47, xii. 44), and is the one thing which God requires of them (vi. 29), and the failure of which will bring them eternal ruin (iii. 18, v. 38, vi. 64, viii. 24). When dealing with His followers, His primary care was to build up their faith in Him. Witness especially His solicitude for their faith in the last hours of His intercourse with them. For the faith they had reposed in Him He returns thanks to God (xvii. 8), but He is still nursing their faith (xvi. 31), preparing for its increase through the events to come (xiii. 19, xvi. 29), and with almost passionate eagerness claiming it at their hands (xiv. 1, 10, 11, 12). Even after His resurrection we find Him restoring the faith of the waverer (xx. 29) with words which pronounce a special blessing on those who should hereafter believe on less compelling evidence — words whose point is not fully caught until we realize that they contain an intimation of the work of the apostles as, like His own, summed up in bringing men to faith in Him (xvii. 20, 21).

The record in Acts of the apostolic proclamation testifies to the faithfulness with which this office was prosecuted by Jesus' delegates (Acts iii. 22, 23). The task undertaken by them was, by persuading men (Acts xvii. 4, xxviii. 24), to bring them unto obedience to the faith that is in Jesus (Acts vi. 7, Rom. i. 5, xvi. 26, cf. II Thess. i. 8, II Cor. x. 5). And by such 'testifying faith towards our Lord Jesus Christ' (Acts xx. 21, cf. x. 43) there was quickly gathered together a community of 'believers' (Acts ii. 44, iv. 4, 32), that is, of believers in the Lord Jesus Christ (Acts v. 14, ix. 42, xi. 17, xiv. 23), and that not only in Jerusalem but beyond (viii. 12, ix. 42, x. 45, xi. 21, xiii. 48, xiv. 1), and not only of Jews (x. 45, xv. 1, xxi. 20) but of Gentiles (xi. 21, xiii. 48, xiv. 1, xv. 7, xvii. 12, 34, xviii. 27, xix. 18, xxi. 25). The enucleation of this community of believers brought to the apostolic teachers the new task of preserving the idea of faith, which was the formative principle of the new community, and to propagate which in the world, pure and living and sound, was its chief office. It was inevitable that those who were called into the faith of Christ should bring into the infant Church with them many old tendencies of thinking, and that within the new community the fermentation of ideas should be very great. The task of instructing and disciplining the new community soon became unavoidably one of the heaviest of apostolic duties; and its progress is naturally reflected in their letters. Thus certain differences in their modes of dealing with faith emerge among New Testament writers, according as one lays stress on the deadness and profitlessness of a faith which produces no fruit in the life, and another on the valuelessness of a faith which does not emancipate from the bondage of the law; or as one lays stress on the perfection of the object of faith and the necessity of keeping the heart set upon it, and another on the necessity of preserving in its purity that subjective attitude

towards the unseen and future which constitutes the very essence of faith; or as one lays stress on the reaching out of faith
to the future in confident hope, and another on the present enjoyment by faith of all the blessings of salvation.

It was to James that it fell to rebuke the Jewish tendency to
conceive of the faith which was pleasing to Jehovah as a mere
intellectual acquiescence in His being and claims, when imported into the Church and made to do duty as 'the faith of our
Lord Jesus Christ, the Glory' (ii. 1). He has sometimes been
misread as if he were depreciating faith, or at least the place
of faith in salvation. But it is perfectly clear that with James,
as truly as with any other New Testament writer, a sound faith
in the Lord Jesus Christ as the manifested God (ii. 1) lies at the
very basis of the Christian life (i. 3), and is the condition of all
acceptable approach to God (i. 6, v. 15). It is not faith as he
conceives it which he depreciates, but that professed faith
(λέγῃ, ii. 14) which cannot be shown to be real by appropriate
works (ii. 18), and so differs by a whole diameter alike from the
faith of Abraham that was reckoned unto him for righteousness
(ii. 23), and from the faith of Christians as James understood
it (ii. 1, i. 3, cf. i. 22). The impression which is easily taken from
the last half of the second chapter of James, that his teaching
and that of Paul stand in some polemic relation, is, nevertheless,
a delusion, and arises from an insufficient realization of the
place occupied by faith in the discussions of the Jewish schools,
reflections of which have naturally found their way into the
language of both Paul and James. And so far are we from needing to suppose some reference, direct or indirect, to Pauline
teaching to account for James' entrance upon the question
which he discusses, that this was a matter upon which an earnest teacher could not fail to touch in the presence of a tendency
common among the Jews at the advent of Christianity (cf. Mt.
iii. 9, vii. 21, xxiii. 3, Rom. ii. 17), and certain to pass over into
Jewish-Christian circles: and James' treatment of it finds, indeed, its entire presupposition in the state of things underlying
the exhortation of i. 22. When read from his own historical
standpoint, James' teachings are free from any disaccord with

those of Paul, who as strongly as James denies all value to a faith which does not work by love (Gal. v. 6, I Cor. xiii. 2, I Thess. i. 3). In short, James is not depreciating faith: with him, too, it is faith that is reckoned unto righteousness (ii. 23), though only such a faith as shows itself in works can be so reckoned, because a faith which does not come to fruitage in works is dead, non-existent. He is rather deepening the idea of faith, and insisting that it includes in its very conception something more than an otiose intellectual assent.

It was a far more serious task which was laid upon Paul. As apostle to the Gentiles he was called upon to make good in all its depth of meaning the fundamental principle of the religion of grace, that the righteous shall live by faith, as over-against what had come to be the ingrained legalism of Jewish thought now intruded into the Christian Church. It was not, indeed, doubted that faith was requisite for obtaining salvation. But he that had been born a Jew and was conscious of the privileges of the children of the promise, found it hard to think that faith was all that was requisite. What, then, was the advantage of the Jew? In defence of the rights of the Gentiles, Paul was forced in the most uncompromising way to validate the great proposition that, in the matter of salvation, there is no distinction between Jew and Gentile, — that the Jew has no other righteousness than that which comes through faith in Jesus Christ (Gal. ii. 15 *sq.*), and that the Gentile fully possesses this righteousness from faith alone (Gal. iii. 7 *sq.*); in a word, that the one God, who is God of the Gentiles also, 'shall justify the circumcision by faith, and the uncircumcision through faith' (Rom. iii. 30). Thus was it made clear not only that 'no man is justified by the law' (Gal. ii. 16, iii. 11, Rom. iii. 20), but also that a man is justified by faith apart from law-works (Rom. iii. 28). The splendid vigour and thoroughness of Paul's dialectic development of the absolute contrast between the ideas of faith and works, by virtue of which one peremptorily excludes the other, left no hiding-place for a work-righteousness of any kind or degree, but cast all men solely upon the righteousness of God, which is apart from the law and comes through faith unto all that believe (Rom. iii. 21, 22). Thus, in vindicating the place of faith as the only instrument of salvation, Paul necessarily dwelt much upon the object of faith, not as if he were formally teaching what the object is on which faith savingly lays hold, but as a natural result of his effort to show from its object the all-sufficiency of faith. It is because faith lays hold of Jesus Christ, who was delivered up for our trespasses and was raised for our justification (Rom. iv. 25), and makes us possessors of the righteousness provided by God through Him, that there is no room for any righteousness of our own in the ground of our salvation (Rom. x. 3, Eph. ii. 8). This is the reason of that full development of the object of faith in Paul's writings, and especially of the specific connexion between faith and the righteousness of God proclaimed in Christ, by which the doctrine of Paul is sometimes said to be distinguished from the more general conception of faith which is characteristic of the Epistle to the Hebrews. This more general conception of faith is not, however, the peculiar property of that epistle, but is the fundamental conception of the whole body of biblical writers in the Old Testament and in the New Testament (cf. Mt. vi. 25, xvi. 23, Jn. xx. 29, 31, I Pet. i. 8), including Paul himself (II Cor. iv. 18, v. 7, Rom. iv. 16–22, viii. 24); while, on the other hand, the Epistle to the Hebrews, no less than Paul, teaches that there is no righteousness except through faith (x. 38, xi. 7, cf. xi. 4).

That in the Epistle to the Hebrews it is the general idea of faith, or, to be more exact, the subjective nature of faith, that is dwelt upon, rather than its specific object, is not due to a peculiar conception of what faith lays hold upon, but to the particular task which fell to its writer in the work of planting Christianity in the world. With him, too, the person and work of Christ are the specific object of faith (xiii. 7, 8, iii. 14, x. 22). But the danger against which, in the providence of God, he was called upon to guard the infant flock, was not that it should fall away from faith to works, but that it should fall away from faith into despair. His readers were threatened not with legalism but with 'shrinking back' (x. 39), and he needed, therefore, to emphasize not so much the object of faith as the duty of

faith. Accordingly, it is not so much on the righteousness of
faith as on its perfecting that he insists; it is not so much its
contrast with works as its contrast with impatience that he impresses on his readers' consciences; it is not so much to faith
specifically in Christ and in Him alone that he exhorts them as
to an attitude of faith — an attitude which could rise above the
seen to the unseen, the present to the future, the temporal to
the eternal, and which in the midst of sufferings could retain
patience, in the midst of disappointments could preserve hope.
This is the key to the whole treatment of faith in the Epistle to
the Hebrews — its definition as the assurance of things hoped
for, the conviction of things not seen (xi. 1); its illustration and
enforcement by the example of the heroes of faith in the past,
a list chosen and treated with the utmost skill for the end in
view (xi.); its constant attachment to the promises (iv. 1, 2,
vi. 12, x. 36, 38, xi. 9); its connexion with the faithfulness (xi.
11, cf. x. 23), almightiness (xi. 19), and the rewards of God (xi.
6, 26); and its association with such virtues as boldness (iii. 6,
iv. 16, x. 19, 35), confidence (iii. 14, xi. 1), patience (x. 36, xii. 1),
hope (iii. 6, vi. 11, 18, x. 23).

With much that is similar to the situation implied in Hebrews, that which underlies the Epistles of Peter differs from it
in the essential particular that their prevailingly Gentile readers
were not in imminent danger of falling back into Judaism. There
is, accordingly, much in the aspect in which faith is presented in
these epistles which reminds us of what we find in Hebrews, as,
for example, the close connexion into which it is brought with
obedience (I Pet. i. 2, 22, ii. 7, iii. 1, iv. 17), its prevailing reference to what is unseen and future (I Pet. i. 5, 7–10, 21), and its
consequent demand for steadfastness (v. 9, cf. i. 7), and especially for hope (i. 21, cf. i. 3, 13, iii. 5, 15). Yet there is a noteworthy difference in the whole tone of the commendation of
faith, which was rooted, no doubt, in the character of Peter, as
the tone of his speeches recorded in Acts shows, but which also
grew out of the nature of the task set before him in these letters.
There is no hint of despair lying in the near background, but
the buoyancy of assured hope rings throughout these epistles.

Having hearkened to the prophet like unto Moses (Deut. xviii. 15, 19, Acts iii. 22, 23), Christians are the children of obedience (I Pet. i. 14), and through their precious faith (I Pet. i. 7, II Pet. i. 1) possessors of the preciousness of the promises (I Pet. ii. 7). As they have obeyed the voice of God and kept His covenant, they have become His peculiar treasure, a kingdom of priests and a holy nation (Ex. xix. 5, I Pet. ii. 9). Naturally, the duty rests upon them of living, while here below, in accordance with their high hopes (I Pet. i. 13, II Pet. i. 5). But in any event they are but sojourners and pilgrims here (I Pet. ii. 11, i. 1, 17), and have a sure inheritance reserved for them in heaven (i. 4), unto which they are guarded through faith by the power of God (i. 5). The reference of faith in Peter is therefore characteristically to the completion rather than to the inception of salvation (i. 5, 9, ii. 6, cf. Acts xv. 11). Of course this does not imply that he does not share the common biblical conception of faith: he is conscious of no difference of view from that of the Old Testament (I Pet. ii. 6); and, no less than with James, with him faith is the fountain of all good works (I Pet. i. 7, 21, v. 9, II Pet. i. 5); and, no less than with Paul, with him faith lays hold of the righteousness of Christ (II Pet. i. 1). It only means that in the circumstances of his writing he is led to lay special emphasis on the reference of faith to the consummated salvation, in order to quicken in his readers that hope which would sustain them in their persecutions, and to keep their eyes set, not on their present trials, but, in accordance with faith's very nature, on the unseen and eternal glory.

In the entirely different circumstances in which he wrote, John wished to lay stress on the very opposite aspect of faith. For what is characteristic of John's treatment of faith is insistence not so much on the certainty and glory of the future inheritance which it secures, as on the fulness of the present enjoyment of salvation which it brings. There was pressing into the Church a false emphasis on knowledge, which affected to despise simple faith. This John met, on the one hand, by deepening the idea of knowledge to the knowledge of experience, and, on the other, by insisting upon the immediate entrance of every believer into the possession of salvation. It is not to be supposed, of course, that he was ready to neglect or deny that out-reaching of faith to the future on which Peter lays such stress: he is zealous that Christians shall know that they are children of God from the moment of believing, and from that instant possessors of the new life of the Spirit; but he does not forget the greater glory of the future, and he knows how to use this Christian hope also as an incitement to holy living (I Jn. iii. 2). Nor are we to suppose that, in his anti-Gnostic insistence on the element of conviction in faith, he would lose sight of that central element of surrendering trust which is the heart of faith in other portions of the Scriptures: he would indeed have believers know what they believe, and who He is in whom they put their trust, and what He has done for them, and is doing, and will do, in and through them; but this is not that they may know these things simply as intellectual propositions, but that they may rest on them in faith and know them in personal experience. Least of all the New Testament writers could John confine faith to a merely intellectual act: his whole doctrine of faith is rather a protest against the intellectualism of Gnosticism. His fundamental conception of faith differs in nothing from that of the other New Testament writers; with him, too, it is a trustful appropriation of Christ and surrender of self to His salvation. Eternal life has been manifested by Christ (Jn. i. 4, I Jn. i. 1, 2, v. 11), and he, and he only, who has the Son has the life (I Jn. v. 12). But in the conflict in which he was engaged he required to throw the strongest emphasis possible upon the immediate entrance of believers into this life. This insistence had manifold applications to the circumstances of his readers. It had, for example, a negative application to the antinomian tendency of Gnostic teaching, which John does not fail to press (I Jn. i. 5, ii. 4, 15, iii. 6): 'whosoever believeth that Jesus is the Christ is begotten of God' (I Jn. v. 1), and 'whosoever is begotten of God doeth no sin' (I Jn. iii. 9). It had also a positive application to their own encouragement: the simple believer was placed on a plane of life to which no knowledge could attain; the new life received by faith gave the victory over the world; and John boldly challenges experience to point to any who have overcome the world but he that believes that Jesus is the Son of God (I Jn. v. 4, 5). Accordingly, it is characteristic of John to announce that 'he that believeth hath eternal life' (Jn. iii. 36, v. 24, vi. 47, 54, I Jn. iii. 14, 15, v. 11, 12, 13). He even declares the purpose of his writing to be, in the Gospel, that his readers 'may believe that Jesus is the Christ, the Son of God, and that, believing, they may have life in his name' (xx. 31); and in the First Epistle, that they that believe in the name of the Son of God 'may know that they *have* eternal life' (I Jn. v. 13).

III. The Biblical Conception of Faith

By means of the providentially mediated diversity of emphasis of the New Testament writers on the several aspects of faith, the outlines of the biblical conception of faith are thrown into very high relief.

Of its *subjective nature* we have what is almost a formal definition in the description of it as an 'assurance of things hoped for, a conviction of things not seen' (Heb. xi. 1). It obviously contains in it, therefore, an element of knowledge (Heb. xi. 6), and it as obviously issues in conduct (Heb. xi. 8, cf. v. 9, I Pet. i. 22). But it consists neither in assent nor in obedience, but in a reliant trust in the invisible Author of all good (Heb. xi. 27), in which the mind is set upon the things that are above and not on the things that are upon the earth (Col. iii. 2, cf. II Cor. iv. 16–18, Mt. vi. 25. The examples cited in Heb. xi are themselves enough to show that the faith there commended is not a mere belief in God's existence and justice and goodness, or crediting of His word and promises, but a practical counting of Him faithful (xi. 11), with a trust so profound that no trial can shake it (xi. 35), and so absolute that it survives the loss of even its own pledge (xi. 17). So little is faith in its biblical conception merely a conviction of the understanding, that, when that is called faith, the true idea of faith needs to be built up above this word (Jas. ii. 14 ff.). It is a movement of the whole inner man (Rom. x. 9, 10), and is set in contrast with an unbelief that is akin, not to ignorance but to disobedience (Heb. iii. 18, 19, Jn. iii. 36, Rom. xi. 20, 30, xv. 31, I Thess. i. 8, Heb. iv. 2, 6, I Pet. i. 7, 8, iii. 1, 20, iv. 18, Acts xiv. 2, xix. 9), and that grows out of, not lack of information, but that aversion of the heart from God (Heb. iii. 12) which takes pleasure in unrighteousness (II Thess. ii. 12), and is so unsparingly exposed by our Lord (Jn. iii. 19, v. 44, viii. 47, x. 26). In the breadth of its idea, it is thus the going out of the heart from itself and its resting on God in confident trust for all good. But the scriptural revelation has to do with, and is directed to the needs of, not man in the abstract, but sinful man; and for sinful man this hearty reliance on God necessarily becomes humble trust in Him for the fundamental need of the sinner — forgiveness of sins and reception into favour. In response to the revelations of His grace and the provisions of His mercy, it commits itself without reserve and with abnegation of all self-dependence, to Him as its sole and sufficient Saviour, and thus, in one act, empties itself of all claim on God and casts itself upon His grace alone for salvation.

It is, accordingly, solely from its *object* that faith derives its value. This object is uniformly the God of grace, whether conceived of broadly as the source of all life, light, and blessing, on whom man in his creaturely weakness is entirely dependent, or, whenever sin and the eternal welfare of the soul are in view, as the Author of salvation in whom alone the hope of unworthy man can be placed. This one object of saving faith never varies from the beginning to the end of the scriptural revelation; though, naturally, there is an immense difference between its earlier and later stages in fulness of knowledge as to the nature of the redemptive work by which the salvation intrusted to God shall be accomplished; and as naturally there occurs a very great variety of forms of statement in which trust in the God of salvation receives expression. Already, however, at the gate of Eden, the God in whom the trust of our first parents is reposed is the God of the gracious promise of the retrieval of the injury inflicted by the serpent; and from that beginning of knowledge the progress is steady, until, what is implied in the

primal promise having become express in the accomplished
work of redemption, the trust of sinners is explicitly placed in
the God who was in Christ reconciling the world unto Himself
(II Cor. v. 19). Such a faith, again, could not fail to embrace
with humble confidence all the gracious promises of the God of
salvation, from which indeed it draws its life and strength; nor
could it fail to lay hold with strong conviction on all those revealed truths concerning Him which constitute, indeed, in the
varied circumstances in which it has been called upon to persist
throughout the ages, the very grounds in view of which it has
been able to rest upon Him with steadfast trust. These truths,
in which the 'Gospel' or glad-tidings to God's people has been
from time to time embodied, run all the way from such simple
facts as that it was the very God of their fathers that had appeared unto Moses for their deliverance (Ex. iv. 5), to such
stupendous facts, lying at the root of the very work of salvation
itself, as that Jesus is the Christ, the Son of God sent of God to
save the world (Jn. vi. 69, viii. 24, xi. 42, xiii. 19, xvi. 27, 30,
xvii. 8, 21, xx. 31, I Jn. v. 15), that God has raised Him from
the dead (Rom. x. 9, I Thess. iv. 14), and that as His children
we shall live with Him (Rom. vi. 8). But in believing this variously presented Gospel, faith has ever terminated with trustful
reliance, not on the promise but on the Promiser, — not on the
propositions which declare God's grace and willingness to save,
or Christ's divine nature and power, or the reality and perfection of His saving work, but on the Saviour upon whom, because of these great facts, it could securely rest as on One able
to save to the uttermost. Jesus Christ, God the Redeemer, is
accordingly the one object of saving faith, presented to its embrace at first implicitly and in promise, and ever more and more
openly until at last it is entirely explicit and we read that 'a
man is not justified save through faith in Jesus Christ' (Gal. ii.
16). If, with even greater explicitness still, faith is sometimes
said to rest upon some element in the saving work of Christ, as,
for example, upon His blood or His righteousness (Rom. iii. 25,
II Pet. i. 1), obviously such a singling out of the very thing in
His work on which faith takes hold, in no way derogates from

its repose upon Him, and Him only, as the sole and sufficient Saviour.

The *saving power* of faith resides thus not in itself, but in the Almighty Saviour on whom it rests. It is never on account of its formal nature as a psychic act that faith is conceived in Scripture to be saving, — as if this frame of mind or attitude of heart were itself a virtue with claims on God for reward, or at least especially pleasing to Him (either in its nature or as an act of obedience) and thus predisposing Him to favour, or as if it brought the soul into an attitude of receptivity or of sympathy with God, or opened a channel of communication from Him. It is not faith that saves, but faith in Jesus Christ: faith in any other saviour, or in this or that philosophy or human conceit (Col. ii. 16, 18, I Tim. iv. 1), or in any other gospel than that of Jesus Christ and Him as crucified (Gal. i. 8, 9), brings not salvation but a curse. It is not, strictly speaking, even faith in Christ that saves, but Christ that saves through faith. The saving power resides exclusively, not in the act of faith or the attitude of faith or the nature of faith, but in the object of faith; and in this the whole biblical representation centres, so that we could not more radically misconceive it than by transferring to faith even the smallest fraction of that saving energy which is attributed in the Scriptures solely to Christ Himself. This purely mediatory function of faith is very clearly indicated in the regimens in which it stands, which ordinarily express simple instrumentality. It is most frequently joined to its verb as the dative of means or instrument (Acts xv. 9, xxvi. 18, Rom. iii. 28, iv. 20, v. 2, xi. 20, II Cor. i. 24, Heb. xi. 3, 4, 5, 7, 8, 9, 11, 17, 20, 21, 23, 24 ‖ 27, 28, 29, 30, 31); and the relationship intended is further explained by the use to express it of the prepositions ἐκ (Rom. i. 17, 17, iii. 26, 30, iv. 16, 16, v. 1, ix. 30, 32, x. 6, xiv. 23, 23, Gal. ii. 16, iii. 7, 8, 9, 11, 12, 27, 28, v. 5, I Tim. i. 5, Heb. x. 38, Jas. ii. 24) and διά (with the genitive, never with the accusative, Rom. iii. 22, 25, 30, II Cor. v. 7, Gal. ii. 16, iii. 14, 26, II Tim. iii. 15, Heb. vi. 12, xi. 33, 39, I Pet. i. 5), — the fundamental idea of the former construction being that of source or origin, and of the latter that of mediation or instrumentality, though they are used together in the same context, apparently with no distinction of meaning (Rom. iii. 25, 26, 30, Gal. ii. 16). It is not necessary to discover an essentially different implication in the exceptional usage of the prepositions ἐπί (Acts iii. 16, Phil. iii. 9) and κατά (Heb. xi. 7, 13, cf. Mt. ix. 29) in this connexion: ἐπί is apparently to be taken in a quasi-temporal sense, 'on faith,' giving the occasion of the divine act, and κατά very similarly in the sense of conformability, 'in conformity with faith.' Not infrequently we meet also with a construction with the preposition ἐν which properly designates the sphere, but which in passages like Gal. ii. 20, Col. ii. 7, II Thess. ii. 13 appears to pass over into the conception of instrumentality.

So little indeed is faith conceived as containing in itself the energy or ground of salvation, that it is consistently represented as, in its *origin*, itself a gratuity from God in the prosecution of His saving work. It comes, not of one's own strength or virtue, but only to those who are chosen of God for its reception (II Thess. ii. 13), and hence is His gift (Eph. vi. 23, cf. ii. 8, 9, Phil. i. 29), through Christ (Acts iii. 16, Phil. i. 29, I Pet. i. 21, cf. Heb. xii. 2), by the Spirit (II Cor. iv. 13, Gal. v. 5), by means of the preached word (Rom. x. 17, Gal. iii. 2, 5); and as it is thus obtained from God (II Pet. i. 1, Jude 3, I Pet. i. 21), thanks are to be returned to God for it (Col. i. 4, II Thess. i. 3). Thus, even here all boasting is excluded, and salvation is conceived in all its elements as the pure product of unalloyed grace, issuing not from, but in, good works (Eph. ii. 8–12). The place of faith in the process of salvation, as biblically conceived, could scarcely, therefore, be better described than by the use of the scholastic term 'instrumental cause.' Not in one portion of the Scriptures alone, but throughout their whole extent, it is conceived as a boon from above which comes to men, no doubt through the channels of their own activities, but not as if it were an effect of their energies, but rather, as it has been finely phrased, as a gift which God lays in the lap of the soul. 'With the heart,' indeed, 'man believeth unto righteousness'; but this believing does not arise of itself out of any heart indifferently, nor is it grounded in the heart's own potencies; it is grounded rather in the freely-giving goodness of God, and comes to man as a benefaction out of heaven.

The *effects* of faith, not being the immediate product of faith itself but of that energy of God which was exhibited in raising Jesus from the dead and on which dependence is now placed for raising us with Him into newness of life (Col. ii. 12), would seem to depend directly only on the fact of faith, leaving questions of its strength, quality, and the like more or less to one side. We find a proportion, indeed, suggested between faith and its effects (Mt. ix. 29, viii. 13, cf. viii. 10, xv. 28, xvii. 20, Lk. vii. 9, xvii. 6). Certainly there is a fatal doubt, which vitiates with its double-mindedness every approach to God (Jas. i. 6–8, cf. iv. 8, Mt. xxi. 21, Mk. xi. 23, Rom. iv. 20, xiv. 23, Jude 22). But Jesus deals with notable tenderness with those of 'little faith,' and His apostles imitated Him in this (Mt. vi. 30 f., 20, xiv. 31, xvi. 8, xvii. 20, Lk. xii. 28, Mk. ix. 24, Lk. xvii. 5, cf. Rom. xiv. 1, 2, I Cor. viii. 7, and see DOUBT). The effects of faith may possibly vary also with the end for which the trust is exercised (cf. Mk. x. 51 ἵνα ἀναβλέψω with Gal. ii. 16 ἐπιστεύσαμεν ἵνα δικαιωθῶμεν). But he who humbly but confidently casts himself on the God of salvation has the assurance that he shall not be put to shame (Rom. xi. 11, ix. 33), but shall receive the end of his faith, even the salvation of his soul (I Pet. i. 9). This salvation is no doubt, in its idea, received all at once (Jn. iii. 36, I Jn. v. 12); but it is in its very nature a process, and its stages come, each in its order. First of all, the believer, renouncing by the very act of faith his own righteousness which is out of the law, receives that 'righteousness which is through faith in Christ, the righteousness which is from God on faith' (Phil. iii. 9, cf. Rom. iii. 22, iv. 11, ix. 30, x. 3, 10, II Cor. v. 21, Gal. v. 5, Heb. xi. 7, II Pet. i. 1). On the ground of this righteousness, which in its origin is the 'righteous act' of Christ, constituted by His 'obedience' (Rom. v. 18, 19), and comes to the believer as a 'gift' (Rom. v. 17), being reckoned to him apart from works (Rom. iv. 6), he that believes in Christ is justified in God's sight, received into His favour, and made the recipient of the

Holy Spirit (Jn. vii. 39, cf. Acts v. 32), by whose indwelling men are constituted the sons of God (Rom. viii. 13). And if children, then are they heirs (Rom. viii. 17), assured of an incorruptible, undefiled, and unfading inheritance, reserved in heaven for them; and meanwhile they are guarded by the power of God through faith unto this gloriously complete salvation (I Pet. i. 4, 5). Thus, though the immediate effect of faith is only to make the believer possessor before the judgment-seat of God of the alien righteousness wrought out by Christ, through this one effect it draws in its train the whole series of saving acts of God, and of saving effects on the soul. Being justified by faith, the enmity which has existed between the sinner and God has been abolished, and he has been introduced into the very family of God, and made sharer in all the blessings of His house (Eph. ii. 13 f.). Being justified by faith, he has peace with God, and rejoices in the hope of the glory of God, and is enabled to meet the trials of life, not merely with patience but with joy (Rom. v. 1 f.). Being justified by faith, he has already working within him the life which the Son has brought into the world, and by which, through the operations of the Spirit which those who believe in Him receive (Jn. vii. 39), he is enabled to overcome the world lying in the evil one, and, kept by God from the evil one, to sin not (I Jn. v. 19). In a word, because we are justified by faith, we are, through faith, endowed with all the privileges and supplied with all the graces of the children of God.

LITERATURE. — Schlatter, "Der Glaube im NT" (includes a section on "Der Glaube vor Jesus") is the most comprehensive work on the biblical idea of faith. The general subject is also treated by Lutz, "Biblische Dogmatik," p. 312; H. Schultz, "Gerechtigkeit aus dem Glauben im A. u. NT" (in *JDTh*, 1862, p. 510); Hofmann, "Schriftbeweis," i, p. 381; Riehm, "Lehrbr. d. Hebräerbr.," p. 700; Cremer, "Bib. Theol. Lex." s. πίστις, πιστεύω; Hatch, "Essays in Biblical Greek," p. 83. For OT, cf. the relevant sections in the treatises on "OT Theology," especially those of Oehler, H. Schultz, Riehm, Dillmann; and the commentaries on the passages, especially Delitzsch on Genesis and Hab-

akkuk. For NT, cf. Huther, "ζωή und πιστεύειν im NT" (in
JBDTh, 1872, p. 182), and the relevant sections in the general
treatises on "NT Theology," especially those of Neander
("Pflanzung," etc.), Schmid, Reuss, Weiss, Beyschlag, Holtzmann, and in the treatises on the theology of the several NT
writers, such as Wendt, "The Teaching of Jesus"; Usteri, "Paul-
inischer Lehrbegr."; Pfleiderer, "Paulinism"; Stevens, "The
Pauline Theology"; Lipsins, "Paulinische Rechtfertigungslehre"; Schnedermann, "De fidei ratione ethica Paulina"; Haus-
leiter, "Was versteht Paulus unter christlichem Glauben?" (in
"Greifswalder Studien," p. 159); Riehm, "Lehrbegr. d. Hebräerbr."; Reuss, "Die Johan. Theologie" (in "Beiträge zur d.
Theol. Wissenschaft," i, 56); Köstlin, "Lehrbegr. Johann.";
Weiss, "Der Johann. Lehrbegr."; Stevens, "The Johannine The-
ology"; Weiss, "Der Petrin. Lehrbegr.": also such commentaries
as Rückert on "Romans"; Sanday-Headlam on "Romans";
Lightfoot on "Galatians"; Haupt on "I John"; Mayor on
"James"; Spitta on "James." The whole body of doctrinal dis-
cussion may be reviewed in De Moor, "Commentarius in J.
Marckii Compendium," iv, p. 287 f.; cf. also John Ball, "A
Treatise of Faith" (3rd ed. London, 1637), Julius Köstlin, "Der
Glaube, sein Wesen, Grund und Gegenstand" (1889), and "Der
Glaube und seine Bedeutung für Erkentniss, Leben und Kirche"
(1891). For some interesting historical notes, see Harnack, "Die
Lehre von der Seligkeit allein durch den Glauben in der alten
Kirche" (in Zeitschrift. f. Theol. u. Kirche, 1895, p. 88); E.
König, "Der Glaubensact des Christen" (1891); and for a gen-
eral survey, Cunningham, "Historical Theology," ii, pp. 56 ff.

XIV

THE TERMINOLOGY OF LOVE IN THE NEW TESTAMENT

THE TERMINOLOGY OF LOVE IN THE NEW TESTAMENT [1]

I

CONSIDERED as a monument of the Greek language at a particular stage of its development, the New Testament is a very interesting document; and not least so in the terminology which it employs to express the emotion of love. The end-terms of this development, so far as it is open to our observation, are found — we are speaking in broad categories — in the literature which we know as "classical" on the one side, and in the speech of the modern Greek world on the other. In passing from one of these end-terms to the other, a complete revolution has been wrought in the terminology of love; a revolution so radical that the ordinary verb for "to love" in classical Greek has lost that sense altogether in modern Greek, its place being taken by a verb in comparatively infrequent use in the classics; while the ordinary substantive for "love" in modern Greek, formed from this latter verb, does not occur even once in the whole range of classical Greek literature. Coming in somewhere between these two end-terms, the New Testament, flanked on the one side by the Septuagint version of the Old Testament and its accompanying Apocrypha, and on the other by the Apostolic Fathers, forms a compact body of literature in which alone we can observe the revolution in progress; or, we should better say, in which this revolution suddenly appears to sight already nearly completed. Without any heralding in the secular literature, all at once in this religious literature the change presents itself to our view as in principle already an accomplished fact.

All the terms expressing the idea of love current either in classical or in modern Greek are found in this body of religious literature. But they are found in it in such distribution as to

[1] From *The Princeton Theological Review*, v. xvi, 1918, pp. 1–45, 153–203.

make it evident that we are witnessing the dying of one usage while the other has already reached its vigorous youth. This phenomenon is the more impressive because this body of literature stands out in this respect in a certain isolation. Neither in the secular literature of the early Christian centuries, nor even in the immediately succeeding religious literature — in the Greek of the Apologists and the early Church Fathers — is the change in usage anything like so manifest. We have an odd feeling that, with respect to the expression of the idea of love at least, the Greek of the New Testament (along with that of the Septuagint and the Apostolic Fathers) has run ahead of its time, and reflects a stage in the development of the language not yet by some centuries generally attained. This is due doubtless in part to the extremely popular character of these writings. They tap for us the Greek language of their day as it was actuaally spoken; and enable us to see how far the spoken Greek was outstripping in its development the language of "the prigs who write books." In the Apologists at any rate we have a partial return to the more literary usage, with the effect that the language of the New Testament (with the Septuagint and Apostolic Fathers) seems more modern than that of even the Christian writers that came after them.

There are four verbs which, with their accompanying nouns (of course there are also various derivatives), are employed by the classical writers to express the idea of love. Of these $\phi\iota\lambda\epsilon\hat{\iota}\nu$ ($\phi\iota\lambda\dot{\iota}\alpha$) is in universal use as the general term for love, though naturally it has its specific implication which on occasion comes sharply into sight. By its side stand its synonyms, $\dot{\epsilon}\rho\hat{\alpha}\nu$, $\dot{\epsilon}\rho\hat{\alpha}\sigma\theta\alpha\iota$ ($\ddot{\epsilon}\rho\omega\varsigma$), $\sigma\tau\dot{\epsilon}\rho\gamma\epsilon\iota\nu$ ($\sigma\tauο\rho\gamma\dot{\eta}$), $\dot{\alpha}\gamma\alpha\pi\hat{\alpha}\nu$ ($\dot{\alpha}\gamma\dot{\alpha}\pi\eta\sigma\iota\varsigma$), each of which also is no doubt employed (with decreasing frequency in the order in which they are here set down) to express every kind of love, but each with a specific implication which comes clearly into evidence whenever there is occasion for it to do so. What we mean to say is that, as synonyms, these terms do not so much cover a common ground over the edge of which each extends at a particular place to occupy an additional field all its own; as that they are so used that, within the common ground which they all alike cover, each has a particular quality or aspect which it alone emphasizes, and which it alone is fitted to bring into sight. If we should endeavor to hit off the special implication of each with a single word, we might perhaps say that with στέργειν it is nature, with ἐρᾶν passion, with φιλεῖν pleasurableness, with ἀγαπᾶν preciousness. The idea of love includes all these things, and these terms come severally to mind, therefore, in speaking of love, whenever love is contemplated from the angle of the special implication of each. If it is a question of the constitutional efflux of natural affection στέργειν is the most expressive word to use. If, of the blind impulse of absorbing passion, ἐρᾶν. If, of the glow of heart kindled by the perception of that in the object which affords us pleasure, φιλεῖν. If, of an awakened sense of value in the object which causes us to prize it, ἀγαπᾶν. It is probable that no one of the terms is ever used wholly without some sense in the speaker's mind of its specific implication. Nevertheless each of them is actually employed of every kind and degree of love — because there is no object which is fitted to call out the emotion of love at all which cannot be approached from numerous angles and envisaged from distinct points of view. Not merely differences in the objects on which the affection terminates, but also differences in the mental attitude of its subjects, determine the appropriateness of one or another of the terms, when love is spoken of.

We may take στέργειν as an illustration.[2] We have no doubt that the characterization of it by J. H. Heinrich Schmidt is substantially right. "Στέργειν," he writes,[3] "does not denote a passionate love or disposition, not a longing after something that takes our heart captive and gives to our efforts a distinc-

---

[2] Στέργειν, στοργή are not found in Homer, but are in good Attic use, and, though not of such common occurrence as, say φιλεῖν, φιλία, yet remain in constant employment throughout the whole history of the language, and apparently survive in modern Greek. N. Contopoulos in his "Modern Greek and English Dictionary," at least, lists both, with the definitions, for στέργω, of "to consent, to agree, to comply, to answer; to embrace with natural affection; to love"; and for στοργή, "tenderness, affection." Its etymology seems to be obscure. W. Prellwitz, "Etym. Wörterb².," 1905, records only Keltic analogies, with a reference to Stokes, *BB*. 23. 58.

[3] "Synonymik der griechischen Sprache," iii, 1879, p. 480 (136. § 4).

tive goal; it designates rather the quiet and abiding feeling within us, which resting on an object as near to us, recognizes that we are closely bound up with it and takes satisfaction in this recognition." "Of this sort," he adds, "is love to parents, to wife and children, to our close relations particularly, and then to our country and our king. There is revealed in στέργειν, accordingly, the inner life of the heart which belongs to man by nature; while φιλεῖν shows the inclination which springs out of commerce with a person or thing, or is called out by qualities in a thing which are agreeable to us; and ἐρᾶν expresses a passion pressing outward and seeking satisfaction." Nevertheless we can understand that one who, rising from reading this characterization, should light upon a passage like Plutarch's description of Pericles' love for Aspasia, might feel some doubts of its adequacy. "The affection (ἀγάπησις) which Pericles had for Aspasia," he explains,[4] "seems to have been rather of a passionate (ἐρωτική) kind." Discarding his wife, "he took Aspasia and loved her exceedingly (ἔστερξε διαφερόντως). Twice a day, as they say, on going out and on coming in from the market place, he would salute her with a loving kiss (καταφιλεῖν)." Στέργειν is used here of a distinctly erotic love, such as we might expect to be expressed rather by ἐρᾶν, and seems to be described, as distinguished from ἀγάπησις, precisely by its quality as passion. And certainly it is not of "natural affection" in the ordinary sense of that phrase that Meleager expects us to think when he asks concerning Eros, "Is not Ares his mother's lover (στέργει)?"[5] So little is it always conceived as independent of attractive qualities in its object, moreover, that Xenophon, in a discussion of the transitoriness of love (he is speaking of sexual love), uses it, when raising the question whether under the best circumstance — when namely the love is not only warm but mutual (ἢν δὲ καὶ ἀμφότερα στέρξωσι) — it can survive the fading

---

[4] Plutarch, "Pericles," 24 (ed. B. Perrin, pp. 70–71).

[5] "The Greek Anthology," v, 180 (ed. W. R. Paton, I, p. 216). Other instances of the use of στέργειν, στοργή of illicit love are found in v, 8 (p. 132); v, 166 (p. 206); v, 191 (p. 222); vii, 476 (v. ii, p. 258). In v, 180 (p. 216) we have also an instance of the use of στέργει with object of thing in the sense of yearning: "And yearns for anger like the waves."

of the charms of one or the other party.[6] Passages like these show how widely the application of στέργειν, στοργή is extended; and how nearly out of sight its specific implication of love as a natural movement of the soul — as something almost like gravitation or some other force of blind nature — may retire. Yet it probably never retires quite out of sight: the use of the word doubtless always suggests that in some way or other the love in question is natural, even if we must add that it has become natural only by the acquisition of a second nature. Even the love of sense may be conceived of, from this point of view, as a constitutional action of mere nature.[7]

Other and more numerous passages present themselves in which the native meaning of the word is thrown up strongly to observation. When Euripides wishes to reproach a father who has contracted a second marriage with neglect of the children of his dead wife, he naturally uses στέργειν of the love for them that he has lost. The passage contains a contrast between φιλεῖ and στέργει which puts a sharper point upon the specific meaning of the latter. "Hast learned this only now, That no man loves (φιλεῖ) his neighbor as himself? Good cause have some; with most 'tis greed of gain — As here: their sire for a bride's sake loves (στέργει) not these," [8] The guilt and tragedy of the situation are greatly increased by the fact that it is a natural and constitutional movement of the human heart which is outraged. Accordingly ἄστοργος — it is worth while to note it in passing, for ἄστοργος is a New Testament word — is a word of terrible significance. "Especially, however," writes Schmidt,[9] "is the meaning of στέργειν and στοργή illustrated by ἄστοργος, 'loveless.' It designates the unfeeling and hard, whose heart is warmed by no noble sentiment; it is applied particularly to inhuman parents, but also to animals who do not love their young. . . . How sharply the meaning of the word is differentiated is shown by the fact that it is used of women who have

---

[6] Xenophon, "Symposium," viii, 14: cf. 21.

[7] Στέργειν, στοργή are comparatively rarely used of the love of mere sense.

[8] Euripides, "Medea," 80–88 (A. S. Way's translation).

[9] As cited, pp. 489–490.

many love-affairs and who therefore are very certainly not ἀνέραστοι, but on the other hand lack the nobler love to their husbands."

It is this that is the natural use of στέργειν, and it occurs in it very frequently. An instructive instance is found in a passage in Plato's "Laws." [10] "I maintain," he writes, "that this colony of ours has a father and mother, which is no other than the colonizing state. Well, I know that many colonies have been, and will be, at enmity with their parents. But in early days the child, as in a family, loves and is beloved; even if there come a time later, when the tie is broken, still, while he is in want of education, he naturally loves his parents and is beloved by them, and flies to them for protection, and finds in them his natural defense in time of need; and this parental feeling already exists in the Cnosians." Some other term for love could no doubt have been employed in this passage. But the employment of the phrase στέργει τε καὶ στέργεται, which, in an effort to convey its implication, Jowett renders, "*naturally* loves his parents . . .," gives particular force to the remark; this is precisely what children and parents feel to one another.

Another instructive passage is found in the Ninth Book of Aristotle's "Nicomachaeon Ethics." It will repay us to run rapidly through it. Aristotle is remarking on the odd fact of experience that benefactors love (φιλεῖν) the benefited, rather than the other way round. The explanation is, he suggests, that the benefited stand to the benefactors in a relation somewhat like that of their product. It is to be noted, he says, that those who have conferred favors love and prize (φιλοῦσι καὶ ἀγαπῶσι, 'feel affection for and value') those who receive them quite irrespective of any hope they may cherish of a return. This is a feeling common to all artificers: each loves (ἀγαπᾷ) his own especial product much more than he could possibly be loved (ἀγαπηθείη, 'prized') by it, could life be conferred upon it. The poets supply the supreme illustration; their love for their poems is inordinate (ὑπεραγαπῶσι, 'the value that they place upon them'), and has a

[10] Page 754 B. (Jowett's translation of the Dialogues, 1874 v. iv, p. 276): καθάπερ παῖς . . . στέργει τε καὶ στέργεται ὑπὸ τῶν γεννησάντων.

truly parental quality (στέργοντες ὥσπερ τέκνα). It is a just simile: every workman lives in the product of his energy, for what is
living but the expenditure of energy? We love (στέργειν) what
we make, because what we make is the extension of ourselves,
and to love it is to love our own being. It will be noted that in
this passage στέργειν is raised so much above φιλεῖν and ἀγαπᾶν
that it is called in to give the specific quality of a ὑπεραγαπᾶν.
When our love becomes strong and tender like a parents' love
for his children it is most naturally described by στέργειν.

It is not, however, precisely the strength or the tenderness
of a love which qualifies it to be described by στέργειν. It is its
obligatoriness — if we may use that term in a quasi-natural
rather than an openly moral sense; its "necessity" under the
circumstances; a necessity by virtue of which its absence becomes not merely distressing but also reprehensible.[11] This is
the proper term for the love which constitutes the cement by
which any natural or social unit is bound together, and which is
due from one member of every such unit to another. Of course
such a unit may be mentally created out of any relation, natural
or artificial, permanent or temporary; and the use of στέργειν
of the sentiment existing between individuals is evidence that
they are, for the moment at least, thought of as constituting
such a unit, — as "bound together in some bundle of life." Accordingly it is used of the love which binds friends together,
and which a friend has the right to expect from his friend. "I
do not love a friend who loves with words (λόγοις δ' ἐγὼ φιλοῦσαν
οὐ στέργω φίλην)," says Antigone:[12] and what she means is that
she does not look upon one whose professed affection expresses
itself only in words as bound up in one bundle of life with her
and so worthy of the name of friend. Similarly when Lichas

[11] For the note of necessity in στέργειν see Schmidt, as cited, p. 482. Schmidt
even says that with στέργειν it is often not a matter of pleasure at all, and never
a matter of sensuous pleasure: it often conveys the meaning of yielding quickly
and with constant mind to the inevitable. He cites such passages as Sophocles,
"Phil.," 538: I think that no other man would endure to look on such a sight, "but
I have learned by hard necessity to στέργειν ills" — that is, to acquiesce in them,
accept them, take them as belonging to me; so "Lys.," 33. 4: it was necessary to
στέργειν this fortune. This sense of toleration — "to put up with" — is shared by
it with αἰνεῖν and ἀγαπᾶν.

advises Deianeira to receive Iole, in the words στέργε τὴν γυ-
ναῖκα,[13] he means something more than is expressed in the several
current renderings: "bear this woman with patience," "suffer
this maiden gladly," "treat the girl kindly": he means, take
her into a recognized relation to yourself, involving a duty of
affectionate treatment. The isolation of Menon the Thracian
could not be more strongly expressed than by Xenophon's description: "He evidently had no affection (στέργεν) for anyone";[14] it is implied that he was lacking in all that goes to bind
a man to his fellows and them to him. When the sausage-vender
cries out to Demos in Aristophanes' play:[15] May I be minced up
into very small meat indeed, εἰ μὴ σε φιλῶ, καὶ μὴ στέργω, — he
quickly corrects the protestation of mere personal sentiment
for Demos to an assertion of such a love for him as implied
identification of himself with him. Demos here represents a
whole people whom the sausage-vender describes as his friends,
to whom he asserts himself to be bound by a — not merely class
but organic — affection. It is just as easy to think of the whole
world as such an organic unity, compacted together by mutual
φιλανθρωπία. The Christian Apologists, rising to this conception, naturally give expression to it in the forms of speech long
consecrated to such things. We are φιλανθρωπότατοι to such
an extent, says Athenagoras,[16] that we do not love (στέργειν)
merely our friends (φίλους), for 'if ye love (ἀγαπῶνται) those
that love you,' says He, 'what reward will ye have?'" And
Justin:[17] "But concerning our loving all (περὶ δὲ τοῦ στέργειν
ἅπαντας), He taught us, 'If ye love those that love you (ἀγα-
πᾶτε τοὺς ἀγαπῶντας ὑμᾶς), what new thing do ye do?'" It is
exceedingly instructive to observe these writers, in the act of
citing our Lord's great commandment of universal love, replacing His ἀγαπᾶν with στέργειν in the interests of their own
feeling for the solidarity of the human race. Στέργειν, we see,
is the love of solidarity.[18]

[12] Line 543.
[13] "Trach.," line 486.
[14] "Anabasis," ii, 6. 23.
[15] "Eq.," line 769 (al. 715 or 748).
[16] 12. D (Otto, p. 56).
[17] "Apol.," i, 15.
[18] Aristotle, "Nic. Ethics," viii. 4, discusses what happens to the lover and
his mistress (ἐραστῇ καὶ ἐρωμένῳ) when the grounds on which their love (φιλία) is

And if the Deity be solidary with men — as Plato and the Stoics taught? Why, then, of course, στέργειν could be used of the love that binds the Deity and men together. Even the gods many and lords many could be said so to love, each its votaries. "This is right, Mr. Busybody, right," we read in Aristophanes: [19] "for the Muses of the lyre love us well (ἐμὲ γὰρ ἔστερξαν εὔλυροί τε Μοῦσαι)." And on a higher plane Athene is made to declare that she loves (στέργειν), even as one that tends plants, the race that has taken graft from the righteous.[20] But gods many and lords many are divisive things. We must come at least to the recognition of τὸ θεῖον before we can effectively conceive the divine and the human as bound up in one bundle of life, the cement of which is love. It is not without its deep significance, therefore, that the Emperor Constantine begins the oration which he delivered to "the Assembly of the Saints" with an allusion to the love (στοργή) to the Deity implanted in men,[21] and closes it with an assertion of the love (στοργή) of God to man, which is manifested in His providence.[22]

What has been said of στέργειν may in substance be repeated of ἐρᾶν, mutatis mutandis. What ἐρᾶν conveys [23] is the idea of passion; and since all love is a passion ἐρᾶν is applicable to all

built fall away. Sometimes the love (φιλία) passes away too. Sometimes — if the two are alike in their natures — custom has inspired them with an abiding affection and it holds (ἐὰν ἐκ τῆς συνηθείας τὰ ἤθη στέρξωσιν ὁμοήθεις ὄντες). Their love is thought of as στοργή only when they are conceived as constituting together a unity by reason of their similar natures.

[19] "Frogs," line 229.

[20] Æschylus, "Eumenides," line 912. The passage is a difficult one. We have followed Verrall. E. H. Plumptre renders thus: "For I, like gardener shepherding his plants, This race of just men, freed from sorrow, love."

[21] C. 2: "Eusebius Werke," ed. I. A. Heikel, v. i, 1902, p. 155 (τὴν πρὸς τὸ θεῖον στοργὴν ἔμφυτον).

[22] C. 25: as above, p. 192 (τὴν τοῦ θεοῦ πρόνοιαν καὶ τὴν πρὸς τοὺς ἀνθρώπους στοργήν).

[23] The derivation of the word is uncertain. It is ordinarily referred to the primitive Aryan root RA (see for example Skeat, "Etymolog. Dict. of the English Language," no. 289; cf. LAS, no. 324 which is an expansion of RA), which is given the senses of "to rest, to be delighted, to love." W. Prellwitz connects with the Old-Indian aris, with the meaning of trustworthy; but notes that Uhlenbeck, "Kurzgef. etym. Wörterb. d. altind. Sprache" connects aris with Gothic aljam, Old High German ellen, with the sense of "ardor."

love; but since ἐρᾶν emphasizes the passion of love it is above all applicable to especially passionate forms of love. It is naturally used, therefore, frequently to express the sexual appetite. This is not because it is a base word: it is no more intrinsically base than any other word for love. It is because its very heart is passion, and it therefore lends itself especially to express a love which is nothing but passion. But it just as readily lends itself to express a passion which is all love, and it accordingly is also used in the very strongest sense in which a term for love can be employed. Its characteristic uses thus lie at the two extremes of low and high, although of course it may be applied to any kind or degree of love lying between, if only it be for the moment thought of as passion. Schmidt [24] has persuaded himself that the fundamental idea of the word is absorbing preöccupation with its object, complete engrossment with it, the setting of the whole mind upon it — in accordance with a passage in Aristotle's "Rhetoric" [25] which tells us that people in love (ἐρῶντες), no matter what they are doing — talking or writing or acting — are always brooding with delight on the beloved one τοῦ ἐρωμένου). Aristotle, however, seems to be only noting here a familiar effect of the passion which ἐρᾶν really expresses.

    It is one of the most characteristic applications of ἐρᾶν which is illustrated by a frequently quoted passage from Xenophon's "Cyropaedeia." [26] This passage is a part of a disquisition designed to prove the voluntariness of love, and runs as follows. "'Do you observe,' said he, 'how fire burns all alike? That is its nature. But of beautiful things, we love (ἐρῶσι) some and some we do not: and one [loves] one [person], another another; for it is a matter of free-will, and each loves (ἐρᾷ) what he

[24] Page 475 (136. 2).
[25] I. 11. ii, ed. E. M. Cope, 1877, v. i, p. 209; Cope, however, explains the passage as saying that lovers take pleasure in busying themselves with the beloved object in his absence, talking about him and sketching his features, and doing everything they can think of to recall him to their memories.
[26] 5. 1. 10.–12. We use a version that lies at hand, but have enclosed in square brackets some of the words which have been inserted by the translator to give greater lucidity to the passage, in order that the reader may not be misled with respect to the frequency of the occurrence of ἐρᾶν, or with respect to apparent variations in the term used.

pleases. For example, a brother does not [fall in] love [with] (ἐρᾷ) his sister, but somebody else [falls in love with] her; neither does a father [fall in love with] his daughter, but someone else does; for fear of God and the law of the land are sufficient to prevent [such] love (ἔρωτα). But,' he went on, 'if a law should be passed forbidding those who did not eat to be hungry, those who did not drink to be thirsty, forbidding people to be cold in the winter or hot in summer, no such law could ever bring men to obey its provisions, for they are so constituted by nature as to be subject to the control of such circumstances. But love (ἐρᾶν) is a matter of free-will; at any rate every one loves (ἐρᾷ) what suits his taste as he does his clothes and shoes.'" And then the discussion proceeds to raise the question of slavery to the passion of this love, and deals with it lamely enough — on the theory that love is purely a matter of will. Here certainly it is said distinctly that "a brother οὐκ ἐρᾷ a sister — nor a father a daughter," and that assuredly means that ἐρᾶν designates distinctively sexual passion. So it does — in this passage: and this is one of the most characteristic applications of the term. It is not, however, its only application. In point of fact it may just as well be said of a given brother or father that he does ἐρᾷ his sister or daughter as that he does not. We read for example in a fragment of Euripides: [27] "There is nothing dearer (ἥδιον) to children than their mother: love (ἐρᾶτε) your mother, children. There is no other love (ἔρως) so sweet as this loving (ἐρᾶν)."

When ἐρᾶν is employed in this latter fashion, something much more, not less lofty than φιλεῖν is meant. Phrases in which it is brought into immediate contrast with φιλεῖν to express something better than it, occur not infrequently. Plutarch, for example, tells us [28] that Brutus was said to have been liked (φιλεῖσθαι) by the masses for his virtue, but loved (ἐρᾶσθαι) by his friends; and Xenophon transmits [29] an exhortation in identical terms — that we should seek not only to be liked (φιλεῖν)

[27] Eur., Frag. "Erecth.," 19 (Dind.) ap. Stob. 79, p. 454. (Teubner's ed. of Euripides' Works, ed. by A. Nauck, 1892, v. iii, p. 90, fragment 360).

[28] "Brutus," c. 29.   [29] "Hi.," xi. 11.

but loved (ἐρᾶν) by men. Dio Chrysostom draws the same contrast in a passage [30] which we may quote more at length for the sake of its discriminating use of the several terms for love. Cattle, says he, love (φιλεῖν, 'are fond of') their herdsmen, and horses their drivers — they love and exalt them; dogs love (ἀγαπᾶν, 'prize') the huntsmen — love and guard them; all irrational things recognize and love (φιλεῖν, 'are fond of') those that take care of them: how shall a king, then who is gentle and benevolent (ἥμερον καὶ φιλάνθρωπον) fail to be not only liked (φιλεῖν) but also loved (ἐρᾶν) by men? In passages like these ἐρᾶν is exalted above φιλεῖν not φιλεῖν depressed below ἐρᾶν. The contrasted renderings "like" and "love" do not do justice to either. Both words mean "love" and what is intended to be expressed by ἐρᾶν is that high love of exalted devotion which, from this point of view, soars above all other love.

The same essential contrast between the two notions — the contrast between a love of liking and a love of passion — may occur, no doubt, with the balance of approbation tipped the other way. Thus Plato can tell us of some lovers really loving (φιλεῖν) the objects of their passion (ἐρᾶν).[31] And Aristotle can speak similarly of lovers who really have affection for one another (φιλοῦσιν οἱ ἐρώμενοι).[32] It is possible also to draw quite a different contrast between the two words, a contrast turning on the fact that passion is blind while true affection can see.[33] Meanwhile we are effectually warned off from conceiving ἔρως as essentially a base word and confounding it with ἐπιθυμία [34]

[30] i. p. 4M.

[31] "Phaedr.," 231 C: τούτους μάλιστά φασι φιλεῖν ὡς ἂν ἐρῶσι: "regard with affection those for whom they have a passion" (Liddell and Scott, 8th ed. 1901); "feel the highest (moral) affections for those who have inspired them with the sensual passion" (E. M. Cope, "The Rhetoric of Aristotle," 1877, i, p. 293).

[32] "Anal. Pr.," 2.29.1.

[33] Apollon., "De Constr.," p. 292.1 cited by Stephanus, "Thesaurus," 1829–1863, v. 3, col. 1966.

[34] Cope, op. cit., i, 293 describes ἔρως shortly as "the sexual form of ἐπιθυμία or natural appetite," supporting himself on Plato, "Phaedrus," 237D: "It is evident to all that ἔρως is an ἐπιθυμία," and "Timaeus," 42A: "Love is a mixture of pleasure and pain," which, he adds, is "the characteristic of ἐπιθυμία." This applies to ἔρως, however, only in one of its uses.

in order that we may escape confounding it with φιλία. We may
observe the close affinity and real distinction of the three notions in a passage of Plato's which is, perhaps, the more instructive because in it ἐρᾶν is used in its lower application and still is
separated from ἐπιθυμεῖν as sharply as from φιλεῖν. "No one who
desires (ἐπιθυμεῖ) or loves (ἐρᾷ) another," we read,[35] "could ever
have desired (ἐπιθύμει) or loved (ἦρα) him or become his friend
(ἐφίλει) had he not in some way been congenial to his beloved
(τῷ ἐρωμένῳ)." In every stage of its progress, attraction implies
inherent congeniality: but the stages of attraction — desire,
love, abiding affection — are distinct. When this is true of ἐρᾶν at
its lowest, what are we to say of it at its highest, when it passes
above φιλεῖν itself and the series runs lust, affection, ardent love?

"Like our 'love' of which it is almost an exact equivalent,"
writes Charles Bigg,[36] "ἔρως may be applied to base uses, but it
is not, like ἐπιθυμία, a base word. From the time of Parmenides,
it had been capable of the most exalted signification." . . . We
need not stay, however, to refer to the elevated doctrine of the
Platonic Eros in detail. Through it, if no otherwise, an association of high things with ἔρως was formed, which penetrated
wherever the influence of Platonic thought extended. It is not
merely in Plotinus' great conception of the νοῦς ἐρῶν that this
lofty usage is continued. That the world ἔρως was not felt to be
a term of evil suggestion is abundantly certified by the readiness with which Jew and Christian alike, touched by the same
influences, employed it of their divine love. With Philo, it is
precisely the ἔρως οὐράνιος which leads to God, and brings all
the virtues to their perfection.[37] He often cites with deep feeling
the great declaration of Deut. xxx. 20: "This is thy life, and
thy length of days, — to love (ἀγαπᾶν) the Lord thy God";
and he does not scruple to define its ἀγαπᾶν in terms of ἔρως.
"This is the most admirable definition of immortal life," he
comments on one occasion:[38] "to be occupied by a love and

[35] "Lysis," 221D, 222A (Jowett, i, p. 63).
[36] "The Christian Platonists of Alexandria²," 1913, p. 7.
[37] "De Praem. et Poen.," (Mangey, ii, 421).
[38] "De Profugis," § 11 (Mangey, i. 554–555). Cf. the remarks of W. Lütgert,
"Die Liebe im Neuen Testament," 1905, p. 48.

affection (ἔρωτι καὶ φιλίᾳ) to God which has nothing to do with flesh and body." To Philo, thus, ἔρως (along with φιλία) is a constituent element of ἀγάπη (for Philo has ἀγάπη), when conceived in its highest stretches, as the very substance of immortal life. There is a famous passage in Ignatius' letter to the Romans [39] in which he gives, or has been misunderstood to give, Christ Himself the name of Ἔρως: "My Love has been crucified," he says. We need not go into the vexed question of the real meaning which Ignatius intends to convey by this phrase.[40] It affords as striking evidence that ἔρως was not felt to be an intrinsically base term, that such a phrase should have been facilely misunderstood by Christian writers as referring to Christ, as that it should have been actually applied to Him by Ignatius. It does not appear that Origen was aware of the currency of any other interpretation of the words than his own, when he cites them in the prologue to his commentary on the Song of Songs in support of his contention that ἔρως and ἀγάπη may be used indifferently of love in its highest sense. "It makes then no difference in the Sacred Scriptures," Rufinus renders him as writing,[41] "whether caritas is spoken of or amor or dilectio; except that the name of caritas is exalted so that God Himself is called Caritas. . . . Take accordingly whatever is written of caritas as said of amor, caring nothing for the names. For the same virtue is shared by each. . . . It makes no difference whether God is said amari or diligi. Neither do I think that, if any one should give God the name of Amor, as John does that of Caritas, he would be blameworthy. I remember, in fine, that one of the saints, Ignatius by name, said of Christ, 'My Amor is crucified,' and I do not think him reprehensible for this." Later writers, especially those of mystical tendencies, naturally

[39] Ch. vii.

[40] The two sides of the question have been well stated and argued respectively by J. B. Lightfoot in his comment on the passage ("My (earthly) passion has been crucified": he actually renders it in his version of the letter, "My lust has been crucified"), and by Charles Bigg in the preface to his Bampton Lectures on "The Christian Platonists of Alexandria" ("My (divine) Love has been crucified"). There is a third possible view: "My preference (for death) has been crucified."

[41] "Prologue to the Song of Songs," Lommatzsch, xiv, pp. 299, 301, 302.

follow Origen's reading of Ignatius. The Pseudo-Dionysius is even prepared to say that the name of "Ερως was thought by some to be more divine than that of 'Αγάπη.[42] But instances of the employment of words of this stem in a high sense are of course not lacking in earlier Christian writers: Justin,[43] Clement,[44] and Origen himself [45] use ἔρως of divine love, and Clement calls our Lord ὁ ἐραστός.[46]

Clearly it is ardor not lasciviousness which gives its "form" to ἐρᾶν (ἔρως) as a designation of love. Our senses may be inflamed by passion, but the love of the seraphs "who of all love Godhead most" also burns with pure flame. 'Ερᾶν (ἔρως) is not the exclusive possession either of the one or of the other; by virtue of its fundamental implication of passion it is the appropriate designation of both. The prominent employment of it of these two end-terms of the series of varieties of love may leave the impression that the middle region is left uninvaded by it. Schmidt, endeavoring to explain its general usage in a word,[47] even says formally that, when the object is a person, then either sensuous love is to be understood by ἐρᾶν or the highest and more or less passionate love. The vacation of the middle space is, however, an illusion. Since ἐρᾶν imports passion, the most passionate love is prevailingly designated by it; but since all love is passion all love may be spoken of in its terms. Whether it is employed will be determined by whether the love spoken of is at the moment thought of as passion. 'Ερᾶν, says Aristotle,[48] is a kind of φιλία; when φιλία goes to excess, that is ἐρᾶν.

As it is over against φιλεῖν (φιλία) that ἐρᾶν (ἔρως) stands out as designating the love of passion, we are sometimes tempted to render φιλεῖν in contrast with it by "like"; and, indeed, because all love is passion, in doing so to define it below the concept of love altogether. But, although the words, because each has a

---

[42] Cited with other mystical writers by Lightfoot, as above.
[43] "Dial.," viii. 1.   [44] "Cohort.," 71.
[45] "In Joann.," I. 14. (11): ed. Preuschen, p. 14, line 29.
[46] "Strom.," vi. 9. (72).   [47] As cited, p. 475.
[48] "Eth. Nic.," ix. 10; 1171A. 12: ἐρᾶν . . . ὑπερβολὴ γὰρ τις εἶναι βούλεται φιλίας. But as he is thinking of ἐρᾶν in its sensual application, he adds: τοῦτο δὲ πρὸς ἕνα.

specific implication, may be set in contrast with one another, they do not receive their specific implications as contrasts of one another, and they are not to be defined as contradictories. Because ἐρᾶν means passionate love, we are not to imagine that φιλεῖν expresses a love which is devoid of passion, — whatever kind of love that may be. It is true enough that φιλεῖν may be employed when no implication of passion is felt; and is the proper word to employ when relatively unimpassioned manifestations of love are described, as for example for what we may call "friendly love." But this is not because it excludes passion but because it describes love from a different angle and the presence or absence of passion is indifferent to it. It is just as appropriate for the strongest and most impassioned as it is for the quietest and least ardent love: no love lies outside its field. "Φιλεῖν," says T. D. Woolsey justly,[49] "we need not say, is as early as the earliest Greek literature itself, and as wide in its meaning as our verb to *love*, running through all kinds and degrees of the feeling, from the love of family and friend down to mere liking, and to *being wont* to do a thing; and passing over from the sphere of innocent to that of licentious love, whether passionate or merely sensual."

The approach of φιλεῖν to the idea of love is made through the sense of the agreeable.[50] It is the eudaimonistic term for love. Whatever in an object is adapted to give pleasure when perceived, tends to call out affection; and this affection is what φιλεῖν expresses. It may be quiet or it may be passionate; it may be strong or it may be weak; it may be noble or it may be base: all this depends on the quality in the object which calls out the response and the nature of the subject which responds to the appeal. "Of φιλεῖν," says Schmidt,[51] "it is first of all to be said that it is the general designation for our 'love,' and has for its peculiarity that it designates an inner predilection (*Neigung*) for persons, and has for its contradictories μισεῖν and ἐχθαίρειν;

---

[49] *The Andover Review*, August, 1885, p. 167.

[50] The etymology of φιλεῖν is not very clear. G. Heine, "Synonymik des Neutestamentlichen Griechisch," 1898, p. 154, suggests for φίλος (after Vaniček): "one's own, that to which one is accustomed, and on which he depends, dear, worthy."   [51] Pp. 476–477.

but, even when the presentation leaves no ambiguity, it can designate the love of sense. The notion of φιλεῖν can be traced back to the disposition which grows out of an inner community (*Gemeinschaft*). We find therefore in Homer the meaning of 'to be in a friendly way at one's side,' 'to interest oneself in him in a friendly manner.' This happens, for example, on the part of the gods when they assist men in battle, or qualify them for manifold things: on the part of men, when they offer hospitality. For these transactions Homer has exact expressions, and φιλεῖν is expressly distinguished from ξεινίζειν or δέξασθαι. The word designates, therefore, only generally the treatment of another as one that is dear (φίλος) to me, or my friend (again φίλος), and the context must show what kind of action is meant."

When Liddell and Scott say that "the ancients carefully distinguished between φιλεῖν and ἐρᾶν," that is formally right, though we should prefer to say "instinctively" rather than "carefully." When, however, they add: "But φιλεῖν sometimes comes very near in sense to ἐρᾶν," citing passages in which φιλεῖν is used for the love of sense, a certain misunderstanding seems involved. Φιλεῖν is used from the earliest dawn of Greek literature as clearly of the love of sense as of any other kind of love. But this is not to "come very near the sense of ἐρᾶν": it is only to describe the same love which ἐρᾶν describes as passion, from its own point of view as delight. Nor is it easy to understand what Schmidt means when he appears to suggest that φιλεῖν is applied to the love of sense only by a euphemism — "by way of insinuation": nor how the passage from Plato to which he appeals for the purpose can be thought to lend support to this opinion. What we read in this passage [52] is merely that it is said of lovers (τοὺς ἐρῶντας) that they show a very special affection (φιλεῖν) for those they are in love with (ἐρῶσι), because they are prepared to do hateful things for the pleasuring of their beloved ones (τοῖς ἐρωμένοις). Φιλεῖν here is certainly not used euphemistically for ἐρᾶν; it is simply the broad word for love used here in contrast with ἐρᾶν which is employed of a special variety of love. The employment of φιλεῖν for the love of sense is from the

[52] "Phaedr.," 231C.

beginning perfectly frank and outspoken. Take, for example, these frequentative imperfects from Homer: "a concubine whom he φιλέεσκεν";[53] "Melantho μισγέσκετο καὶ φιλέεσκεν Eurymachus."[54] They do not in any way differ from the frequentative imperfect in "Il.," vi, 15: "and he was loved (φίλος ἦν) by men, for, dwelling by the road, φιλέεσκεν all to his house," — except in the nature of the acts to which they are applied. The son of Teuthras showed himself a φίλος to men by keeping open-house and welcoming all comers. The concubines of Amyntor and Melantho showed themselves φίλαι to their lovers by fulfilling the function of mistresses to them. The usage is as simple and direct in the one case as in the other. The constant use in Homer of φιλότης with μίγνυμι should dispel all doubt on this point. And what could be franker than the use of φιλεῖν in Herodotus iv, 176?

The Greeks were very much preoccupied with the topic of Friendship: Plato, Xenophon, Aristotle discuss it endlessly: "in the circles of the philosophical schools interest in it far surpassed that of the family life."[55] Φιλεῖν was an ideal word for the expression of this form of affection, and this became one of its chief applications. Not, however, to the exclusion of other applications in which it gave expression to every variety of love which sentient beings could experience. Even, *pace* Hermann Cremer,[56] the love of God to men and of men to God. Cremer has permitted himself the sweeping statement: "To attribute love at all to the Deity was utterly impossible to the Greek." He supports himself on two passages from Aristotle, neither of which supports him. In both passages Aristotle is (of course) discussing Friendship, — not the term φιλία but the "friendship" which φιλία is in these discussions employed to express. What he is suggesting is not that God can neither love nor be loved in any sense, but that there is a certain incongruity

[53] "Il.," ix, 450.   [54] "Odyss.," xviii, 325.

[55] W. Lütgert, "Die Liebe im N.T.," 1905, p. 37: he sends us to E. Curtius, "Altertum und Gegenwart," i, p. 183 ff. for the matter. Consult also the remarks of Paul Kleinert, "Th. S. K.," 86 (1913) i, pp. 16 f.

[56] "Supplement to Biblico-Theological Lexicon of New Testament" Greek 1886, p. 593 (*sub voc.* Ἀγάπη).

in speaking of God and man as united in the specific bond which
we call "friendship." "Friendship" is a form of love which
more properly obtains between equals: between superiors and
inferiors the assertion of some other tie would be more appropriate. The matter is not of large intrinsic importance; but it is
worth while to transcribe the passages somewhat at length for
their illustrative value.

In them, as elsewhere,[57] Aristotle divides friendship (φιλία)
into three kinds, based respectively on virtue (ἀρετή), utility
(χρήσιμον) and pleasure (ἡδύ); and then he divides the whole
again into the cases between equals and those between unequals.
True friendship is mutual and is found among equals only; love
between unequals is only in a modified sense "friendship."
"First, then," he writes in the former of the two passages now
before us,[58] "we must determine what kind of friendship (φιλία)
we are in search of. For there is, people think, a friendship
(φιλία) towards God (πρὸς θεόν) and towards things without
life; but here they are wrong. For friendship (φιλία), we maintain, exists only where there can be a return of affection (ἀντιφιλεῖσθαι: why not say, "return of the friendship"?), but friendship (φιλία) toward God (πρὸς θεόν) does not admit of love being
returned (ἀντιφιλεῖσθαι: why not say, "of the friendship being
returned"?), nor at all of loving (τὸ φιλεῖν: why not say "of
friendly feeling"?). For it would be strange if one were to say
that he loved Zeus (φιλεῖν τὸν Δία: why not say "felt friendly
to"?). Neither is it possible to have affection returned (ἀντιφιλεῖσθαι: why not say, "to have friendship returned"?) by lifeless objects, though there is a love (φιλία) for such things, for
instance wine, or something else of that sort. Therefore, it is
not love (φιλία) towards God of which we are in search, nor love
towards things without life, but love towards things with life,
that is, where there can be a return of affection (ἀντιφιλεῖν)."
Aristotle is not arguing here that there can be no such thing as

[57] E. g., "Eth. Nic.," viii, 2. 1: "For it appears that not everything is loved
(φιλεῖσθαι) but [only] τὸ φιλητόν: this is good (ἀγαθόν) or pleasant (ἡδύ) or useful
(χρήσιμον)."

[58] "Magna Moralia," II. 11: p. 1208 B. The translation of St. George Stock
is used.

love on the part of God, or to God; or that this love may not be properly expressed in either case by φιλεῖν, φιλία. He is busying himself only with that mutual affection which we know as friendship; and it is this that he says is impossible between man and God because of the inequality between them. It is incongruous to say that Zeus and I are a pair of friends, — we might almost as well say we are a brace of good fellows or *par nobile fratrum*. He is speaking here, in a word, only of love based on mutual agreeability (ἡδύ) in which what is necessary is to be agreeable (τὸ ἡδέσιν εἶναι).[59] If the love in question is based on utility or virtue, on the other hand, the case is different.[60]

The other passage [61] takes up the case when love is based on virtue. "These, then," writes Aristotle here, "are three kinds of friendship (φιλία); and in all of them the word friendship (φιλία) implies a kind of equality. For even those who are friends (φίλοι) through virtue are mutually friends by a sort of equality of virtue. But another variety is the friendship [say rather 'love'] of superiority to inferiority, e. g. as the virtue of a god is superior to that of a man (for this is another kind of friendship [φιλία; say 'love']), and in general that of ruler to subject; just as justice in this case is different, for here it is a proportional equality — not numerical equality (κατ᾽ ἀναλογίαν; κατ᾽ ἀριθμόν). Into this class falls the relation of father to son, and of benefactor to beneficiary; and there are varieties of these again, e. g. there is a difference between the relation of father to son, and of husband to wife, the latter being that of ruler to subject, the former that of benefactor to beneficiary. In these varieties there is not at all, or at least not in equal degree, the return of love for love (ἀντιφιλεῖσθαι: say 'mutual loving'). For it would be ridiculous to accuse God because the love one receives in return from Him is not equal to the love given Him, (τὸ ἀντιφιλεῖσθαι ὡς φιλεῖτε), or for the subject to make the same complaint against his ruler. For the part of a ruler is to receive,

---

59 "Magna Moralia," p. 1210 A.

60 "Magna Moralia," p. 1210 A: "It is evident then that friendship (φιλία) based on utility occurs among things the most opposite."

61 "Ethica Eudemia," vii, 3 (p. 1238b). J. Solomon's version is used.

not to give, love (φιλεῖσθαι οὐ φιλεῖν) or at least to give love (φιλεῖν) in a different way. And the pleasure (ἡδονή) is different, and that of the man who needs nothing over his own possessions or child, and that of him who lacks over what comes to him, are not the same. Similarly also with those who are friends [say rather 'who love one another'] through use or pleasure, some are on an equal footing with each other, in others there is the relation of superiority and inferiority. Therefore those who think themselves to be on the former footing find fault if the other is not equally useful to and a benefactor of them; and similarly with regard to pleasure. This is obvious in the case of lover and beloved (ἐν τοῖς ἐρωτικοῖς); for this is frequently a cause of strife between them. The lover (ὁ ἐρῶν) does not perceive that the passion (προθυμίαν) in each has not the same reason; therefore Ænicus has said, 'a beloved (ὁ ἐρώμενος) not a lover (ἐρῶν), would say such things.' But they think that there is the same reason for the passion of each." We are here told that although friendship, properly so called — that is, mutual affection based on congeniality or reciprocal agreeability — can scarcely exist between beings so unequal as God and man, yet love can; as readily as it can exist between ruler and subject, or father and son. The term "love" (φιλία) is wide enough to describe all such cases, as it is wide enough also, as we learn at the end of the passage, to describe the mutual affection which binds "lovers" together: ἐρᾶν is a species of φιλεῖν, because, no matter with what passion, it also rests on something agreeable perceived in its object.

We have seen that from the beginning there was a natural tendency to carry φιλεῖν over from the sentiment of love itself to its expression in outward act. Thus in a passage from the Iliad already quoted,[62] Teuthramides is represented as habitually showing himself friendly by keeping open-house — πάντας γὰρ φιλέεσκεν, "he made all welcome." Similarly Penelope is described in the Odyssey as receiving all visitors well and giving them welcome (φιλέει):[63] a phrase matched by a similar one in the Iliad: "I entertained (φίλησα) them." [64] Along this line of

---

[62] "Il.," vi, 15.   [63] "Odyss.," xiv, 128.   [64] "Il.," iii, 207.

development φιλεῖν early began to acquire the specialized sense of "to kiss." "Φιλεῖν," writes Schmidt,[65] "means directly, with or without the addition of τῷ στόματι, to kiss, therefore that act which sensibly and externally brings to expression the fellow-ship of lovers or friends and, in general of those connected by a close bond (also of parents and children)." This usage does not yet occur in Homer: he employs κυνέω, κύσαι for kissing. But it made its appearance soon afterwards,[66] and ultimately com-pletely superseded the richer and higher uses of the word. In Modern Greek φιλῶ means nothing else but "to kiss." [67] In odd contrast with this development, ἀγαπᾶν, the great rival of φιλεῖν in the expression of the general idea of love — a rival which finally drove it entirely from the field, — appears from the first in an analogous usage and is thought by many to have begun as a term to express the external manifestations of affection and only afterward to have come to be applied to the emotion itself. At least the external sense is predominant in Homer, both for ἀγαπᾶν and for its more frequently occurring doublet ἀγαπάζειν;[68] and it remained in occasional use through-out the whole history of Greek letters. The range of suggestion of the word in this external sense is rather wide. The instances in Homer may ordinarily be brought under the broad category of "welcoming," with suggestions of "embracing," or other signs of hearty welcome. Thus Penelope asks forgiveness for not "welcoming" her husband properly on his first appearing,[69] "or," explains T. D. Woolsey,[70] "treating him with affection," remarking that Eustathius glosses with ἐφιλοφρονησάμην. Again we read:[71] "As a father, feeling kindly, welcomes his son (φίλα φρονέων ἀγαπάζει)." And yet again,[72] bringing φιλεῖν and ἀγαπᾶν together in this external sense: "Our people do not

[65] As cited, p. 477.

[66] Herodotus, Xenophon and Attic writers generally.

[67] E. A. Sophocles says ("Bibliotheca Sacra," July 1889, p. 525): "As to the modern φιλῶ, it retains only the meaning, to kiss."

[68] It is the sense of all the instances in which ἀγαπᾶν or ἀγαπάζειν occurs in Homer, except one — "Odyss.," xxi, 289, where it means "to acquiesce in," "be content with." Cf. Cope, as cited, p. 295.

[69] "Odyss.," xxiii, 214. [70] Andover Review, August 1885, p. 167.

[71] "Odyss.," xvi, 17. [72] "Odyss.," vii, 33.

φιλοῦσι a stranger ἀγαπαζόμενοι — "do not receive him with signs of regard," as Liddell and Scott gloss it. In a very similar passage,[73] we read of the swineherd kissing (κύνεον) Odysseus' head and shoulders ἀγαπαζόμενος, that is to say with a display of affection. And we find in Pindar [74] a passage like this: "And with mild words they welcomed him," where the action through which the affection is shown is defined as kind speech. In Euripides, in whom ἀγαπᾶν, ἀγαπάζειν occur only three times (they do not occur at all in Æschylus or Sophocles), they "are only used in the sense of tender offices to the dead":[75] as, for example, "Suppliants," 764: "You would have said so had you seen when he *treated lovingly* (Woolsey glosses: "made much of") the dead." In the light of such passages it is probable that when Xenophon, speaking of the transports of delight with which the Greeks at first welcomed the Hyrcanians as friends, says [76] that they almost carried them about in their bosoms ἀγαπῶντες, the ἀγαπῶντες means something more definite than "affectionately" — say "fondlingly." In an interesting passage in Plutarch [77] the sense is certainly "fondle." "On seeing certain wealthy foreigners in Rome carrying puppies and young monkeys about in their bosoms and fondling them (ἀγαπώντων), Caesar asked," we are told, "if the women in their country did not bear children. Thus in right princely fashion he rebuked those who squander on animals that proneness to love (φιλητικόν) and loving affection (φιλόστοργον) which is ours by nature and which is due only to our fellow men." In this passage the native sentiment of "fondness" and the stirrings of "natural affection" are given expression through other forms of speech; ἀγαπᾶν is employed of the external acts in which these movements of soul are manifested.

The persistence of this external use of ἀγαπᾶν is illustrated by its appearance in the letters of Ignatius. A probable instance occurs in "Smyrn.," 9: "In my absence and in my presence ye

---

[73] "Odyss.," xxi, 224.   [74] "Pyth.," iv, 241.

[75] John U. Powell in his edition of the "Phoenissae," 1911, p. 206. The passages are "Phoeniss.," 1327; "Suppl.," 764; Helen.," 937. Cf. also Woolsey, as cited, p. 167.

[76] "Cyrop.," vii, v. 50: ed. Holden, 1890, p. 74.   [77] "Pericles," 1.

ἠγαπήσατε me," where Lightfoot renders "cherished." The instance in "Magn.," 6 can scarcely be doubted. E. A. Abbott fills out the passage thus:[78] "Since then I beheld in faith and *embraced* (in the spirit) the whole multitude (of the Magnesian church) in the above-mentioned persons (of their deputation)."[79] But the most interesting passage is "Polyc.," 2: "In all things I am devoted to thee — I, and my bonds which you ἠγάπησας." "Kissing the chains" of the prisoners of Christ, it seems, was a current figure by which the early Christians expressed their ardent sympathy for their martyrs.[80] Bunsen, followed by Th. Zahn, therefore, translates here, "which thou didst kiss."[81] Lightfoot demurs to this as too specific, and points out that the precise sense of "kissing" is not elsewhere verifiable for ἀγαπᾶν, — although he is very willing to allow that the actual thing referred to by the broader term may well have been in this instance kissing the chains. He proposes the synonyms, "didst welcome, caress, fondle," and somewhat infelicitously translates in his version, "cherished." Interest in this discussion is increased by the suggestion that, when we read in Mk. x. 21 of the rich young ruler that "Jesus looked on him and ἠγάπησεν αὐτόν," we are to understand the ἠγάπησεν not of the sentiment of loving but of the act of caressing: Jesus, in a word, kissed the young man in greeting him. This suggestion was made by Frederick Field a third of a century ago,[82] and has often since been repeated.[83] It does not commend itself particularly from an exegetical point of view:[84] but the fact that, as

[78] "Johannine Vocabulary," 1905, p. 261, note (1744, iv, b).

[79] Lightfoot *in loc.* comments: "'*welcomed, embraced.*' The word here refers to external tokens of affection, according to its original meaning."

[80] "Acta Pauli et Thec.," 18: καταφιλούσης his chains: Tertullian, "Ad. Uxor.," ii, 4, *osculanda* the martyr's chains.

[81] See Zahn, "Ignatius von Antiochien," 1873, p. 415, and also his comment on the passage itself.

[82] "Otium Novicense," Pars Tertia, 1881., *ad loc.*

[83] See [J. Hastings], *Expository Times*, xviii, 99 (Hastings generalizes: "In any case the word is that word for loving which means manifesting love in action"); Edwin A. Abbott, "Johannine Vocabulary," 1905, pp. 257 ff.; J. H. Moulton and G. Milligan, "The Vocabulary of the New Testament," i, 1914, p. 12, *sub voc.* ἀγαπᾶν.

[84] Swete, for example, rejects it decisively.

Abbott points out, the phrase is rendered in one Latin MS. "osculatus est eum" supports the supposition that ἀγαπᾶν was in use in the sense of kissing during the early Christian centuries. The collocation of the words in the comment of Clement of Alexandria, likewise adduced by Abbott, suggests that he also may have understood ἠγάπησεν here in the sense of an external manifestation. "Accordingly Jesus," he writes, "does not convict him as one that had failed to fulfil all the words of the Law; on the contrary He" — so Abbott paraphrases — "loves and greets him with unusual courtesy." The Greek words are ἀγαπᾷ καὶ ὑπερασπάζεται; and it would not be unnatural to give them both an external meaning.[85]

This usage of ἀγαπᾶν of the manifestation of love in act, although possibly (we can scarcely say very probably) original,[86] and certainly real, is yet, in any case too infrequent to be of large importance for the explanation of the word. Unlike the corresponding usage of φιλεῖν it was a waning instead of a waxing usage; and therefore it exercised less and less influence on the general usage of the word. After all said, the word stands in Greek literature as a term for loving itself, not for external manifestations of love, more or fewer. And like other terms for love, it is applied to all kinds and degrees of love. This includes also the love of sense. It is true it seems to have acquired this application only slowly, and, one would think, with some difficulty. There is nothing in the native implication of the word to

[85] It would be easy to reply, it is true, that both might be given an internal meaning, and perhaps the usage of ὑπερασπάζεται encourages this view.

[86] J. B. Lightfoot argues for the originality of the external sense in an article published in the *Cambridge Journal of Classical Philology*, v. iii (1857), no. 7, p.9 2; and again in his note on Ignatius "ad Polyc.," 2, where he states the case with his accustomed compressed force. "The word," he says, "seems originally to have referred to the *outward demonstration of affection*. . . . This original sense appears still more strongly in ἀγαπάζω. The application of the term to the *inward feeling* of love is a later development, and the earlier meaning still appears occasionally." But after all it is difficult to believe that the word began with this external sense, and Homer does not record an absolutely primitive usage. E. M. Cope, *op. cit.*, pp. 295-296 properly therefore rejects this reading of the history of the word. Liddell and Scott's article on ἀγαπάω exaggerates the externality of the term and might even give the impression that the internal affection of love scarcely falls within its range at all.

suggest such an application; and the conjecture lies close that it was not until it had become the general term for love in common use for the whole notion that it was applied to this variety of love also, — at first doubtless by way of pure euphemism. Such euphemistic applications to the sexual impulse of all words denoting love are inevitable;[87] and unhappily many good words, euphemistically applied to lower uses, end by losing their native senses and sinking permanently to the level to which they have thus stooped, — as, for example, our English words "libertine," "harlot."[88] Fortunately this did not happen to ἀγαπᾶν, although its extention to cover the love of sense also became a fixed part of its ordinary usage. Liddell and Scott remark that it is "used of sexual love like ἐρᾶν, only in late writers, as Lucian "Jup. Trag.," 2;[89] for in Xenophon, "Mem.," I. 5. 4. πόρνας ἀγαπᾶν is not = ἐρᾶν, but *to be content*, or *satisfied* with such gratifications."[90] This explanation of the passage in Xenophon is certainly right. But it is not quite exact to speak of the appearance of this usage in Lucian, say, as marking its beginning. It already occurs in Plato.[91] And in any event the Septuagint is three or four hundred years older than Lucian, and not only is ἀγαπᾶν — and also its substantive (not found in the classical writers)

---

[87] Cf. "The Oxford Dictionary of the English Language," *sub voc.* "Love, subst.," no. 6 (p. 464 med.): "the animal instinct between the sexes and its gratification." Maurice Hewlett, "The Fool Errant," 1905, p. 247: "We ate frugally, drank a little wine and water, loved temperately, and slept profoundly."

[88] Cf. on this subject the excellent remarks of R. C. Trench, "On the Study of Words," ed. N. Y. 1855, pp. 50 ff.

[89] Lucian, "Jup. Trag.," 2: Hera accused Zeus of having a love-affair (ἐρωτικόν) on hand and, plagued by love (ἔρωτος), of thinking of falling through some roof into the lap of his ἀγαπωμένης. So, "Vera Hist.," ii, 25: Cinyres had fallen in love (ἤρα) with Helen, and she was plainly also enamoured (ἀγαπῶσα) with him; so, driven by love and despair (ὑπ' ἔρωτος καὶ ἀμηχανίας), they ran off. A hundred years before Lucian, Plutarch has the usage: cf. the passages cited by Thayer under φιλέω.

[90] J. S. Watson translates: "Who could find pleasure in the company of such a man, who, he would be aware, felt more delight in eating and drinking than in intercourse with his friends, and preferred the company of harlots to that of his fellows?" This sense of "to be satisfied with," is a not infrequent one for ἀγαπᾶν.

[91] Cope, as cited, p. 296: "In Plato's "Symposium," 180 B, it takes the place of ἐρᾶν in the representation of the lowest and most sensual form of the passion or appetite of love, ὅταν ὁ ἐρώμενος τὸν ἐραστὴν ἀγαπᾷ, ἢ ὅταν ὁ ἐραστὴς τὰ παιδικά."

ἀγάπη — used in it of the love of sense, but so used of it as to make it plain that they had long been used of it, and had become the current terms for the expression of this form of love also. To be convinced of this we have only to read the thirteenth chapter of II Samuel, — the story of Amnon and Thamar — the whole shocking narrative of which is carried on with ἀγαπᾶν and ἀγάπη, culminating in verse 15: "And Amnon hated her with exceeding great hatred, because the hatred with which he hated her was greater than the love (ἀγάπην) wherewith he loved (ἠγάπησεν) her." This love was mere lust: and it is very apparent that ἀγαπᾶν and ἀγάπη are used of it with perfect simplicity, undisturbed by any intruding consciousness of incongruity. This phenomenon means, of course, that in the Greek of the Septuagint we tap a stratum of the language of more popular character than that which meets us in the literary monuments of the times; and we see changes not only preparing but already accomplished in it which the recognized literary mode of the times had not yet accepted. Meanwhile, for literary Greek, it remains generally true that ἀγαπᾶν had not yet acquired the breadth of usage which led to its frequent application to the love of sense also; and so far as appears it did not acquire it for two or three centuries to come.

In the monuments of classical literature, ἀγαπᾶν, although in use from the beginning and occupying a distinctive place of its own, is never a very common word. It, and its doublet ἀγαπάζειν, occur in Homer but ten times, in Euripides but three times, and not at all in Æschylus or Sophocles.[92] The substantive ἀγάπησις is rare before, say, Plutarch;[93] while ἀγάπη appears first in the Septuagint, and has not as yet turned up with certainty in any secular writing.[94] Ἀγαπᾶν owes its peculiarity

---

[92] According to T. D. Woolsey, as cited, the indices record ἀγαπάω, ἀγαπητός, ἀγαπητῶς for Demosthenes twenty-two times; for Plato eighteen; for Lysias and Isocrates, each three times. These figures are, however, misleading: in Isocrates, for example, the words are of much more frequent occurrence.

[93] Cf. Lobeck on Phrynicus, p. 352, and Stephanus sub voc. Thayer sub voc. ἀγάπη, seems to intimate that the word appears first in Aristotle: Liddell and Scott, in Plato.

[94] The facts are carefully stated by Moulton and Milligan, as cited, sub voc.

to its etymological associations, which could not fail to suggest themselves to every Greek ear. Connected with ἄγαμαι, it conveyed the ideas of astonishment, wonder, admiration, approbation.[95] It expresses thus, distinctively, the love of approbation, or, we might say, the love of esteem, as over against the love of pure delight which lies rather in the sphere of φιλεῖν. It is from the apprehension of the preciousness rather than of the pleasantness of its object that it derives its impulse, and its content thus lies closer to the notion of prizing than to that of liking.[96] It is beside the mark to speak of it as a "weaker,"[97] or as a "colder"[98] word than φιλεῖν: the distinction between the two lies in a different plane from these things. A love rooted in the perception in its object of something pleasing (that is, of the order of φιλεῖν), or of something valuable (that is, of the order of ἀγαπᾶν), may alike be very weak or very strong, very cold or very warm: these things are quite indifferent to the distinction and will be determined by other circumstances, which may be present or absent in either case.

It is even more wide of the mark to speak of ἀγαπᾶν as distinctively voluntary love, or reasonable love. The former is the position taken with great emphasis by Cremer (it is also the

[95] On this etymology see Cope, as cited, p. 294, also p. 296. Other etymological suggestions are made. Cremer, in his third edition, finds the fundamental notion to be, "to find one's satisfaction in something"; but in his tenth edition reverts to the simple suggestion of a connection with ἄγαμαι in the sense of admiring. W. Prellwitz traces the word back to an Old-Aryan root Pō (Old-Indian Pā) bearing the sense of "protecting"; hence ἀγα-πός, "protecting," and the denominative ἀγαπάω, "entertain," or, as in Homer, "welcome." This view of the etymology favors the external sense of the word as original.

[96] Cope, as cited, p. 294, remarks that, whatever be the true derivation of the word, "this notion of selection or affection, conceived, on the ground of admiration, respect, and esteem, certainly enters into its meaning. Xen. "Mem.," ii. 7.9 is decisive on this point." On p. 295 he surveys the copious material in Aristotle's "Nicomachaean Ethics" and concludes that in every instance the word may, and in many instances it must, carry the implication of esteem. It is the *worth* of the object of preference which underlies the affection expressed by it.

[97] So e. g., Schmidt.

[98] So e. g., Gildersleeve. Woolsey, as cited, p. 182, with Trench in his mind, says very appositely: "We naturally avoid or distrust attaching this quality of coldness to ἀγαπάω or ἀγάπη; and while we ascribe to these words the consent of the will and benevolent regard, we do not strip them of feeling."

view of Cope); the latter is strongly argued for by Schmidt. "We shall make no mistake," says Cremer,[99] "if we define the distinction thus — that φιλεῖν designates the love of the natural inclination, of the emotion (*Affects*), the so-to-say originally involuntary love — *amare*, — while ἀγαπᾶν designates love as an effect (*Richtung*) of the will, *diligere*." It may be suspected that those who speak thus have in part misled themselves by the Latin analogy. The parallel is, it is true, very close with respect to the usage of the two pairs of words; but it does not extend to the etymological implications on which in each case the usage rests.[100] The conception underlying *diligere* is that of selection; the word bears an implication of choice in it. There is no such underlying suggestion in ἀγαπᾶν, its place being taken by the emotion of admiration.[101] In point of fact, the rise in the heart of love for an object perceived to be precious, is just as "originally involuntary," just as much a matter of pure feeling, as the rise in it of love for an object perceived to be delightful. The distinction between these two varieties of love rests on the differing qualities of the object to which they are the reactions, not on the presence or absence of volition in their production. "There can but two things create love," says Jeremy Taylor: [102] "perfection and usefulness; to which answer on our part, first,

[99] These sentences stand in all the editions from the third (1883) to the tenth (1915). Under ἀγάπη he says (ed. 10, p. 14): "It designates *the love which chooses its object with decisive will*."

[100] It may be worth noting that Liddell and Scott, in explaining the distinction between ἐρᾶν and φιλεῖν, say it is that between *amare* and *diligere;* and in explaining the distinction between φιλεῖν and ἀγαπᾶν, say that *this* is that between *amare* and *diligere*. That is to say, φιλεῖν appears now as *diligere* and now as *amare* to meet the needs of the case.

[101] There is no philological reason for supposing that the peculiarity of ἀγαπᾶν among the terms for loving was that it suggested that love is a voluntary emotion. There is also no trace of such a distinction having been made in usage by the Greeks. In arguing for it we are arguing without regard to the Greek consciousness. We have had occasion to observe Xenophon insisting that ἐρᾶν expresses a voluntary act. But it was not ἐρᾶν distinctively that he had in mind: what he was really arguing was that love as such, under any designation, is a voluntary act. It was a psychological, not a philological, question in which he was interested.

[102] "The Rule and Exercises of Holy Living," ch. IV, sec. 3 (p. 21 of v. ii, of the Temple Classics edition).

admiration, and secondly desire; and both these are centered in love." This is a piece of good psychology.

The form of statement which Schmidt prefers is that ἀγαπᾶν designates the love which arises by "rational reflection."[103] Citing a passage from Aristotle's "Rhetoric"[104] where he speaks of φιλεῖσθαι as being "ἀγαπᾶσθαι for one's own sake," Schmidt argues that "it follows from this passage that ἀγαπᾶν is not, like φιλεῖν, an inclination attached to the person himself, as called into being by close companionship and fellowship in many things, but a love for which we can give ourselves an account with our understanding; less sentiment than reflection."[105] As a result, he concludes that "the ἀγαπῶν holds the qualities of a person in view, the φιλῶν the person himself; the former gives itself a justification of its inclination, while to the latter it arises immediately out of an intercourse which is agreeable to oneself." This reasoning rests on a confusion between the production of an emotion by rational considerations, and the justification of it on rational grounds. Of course the love of ἀγαπᾶν is more capable of justification on rational grounds than the love of φιλεῖν. It is the product of the apprehension of valuable qualities in the object, and may be defended by the exhibition of the value of these qualities. The love of φιλεῖν, on the other hand, as the product of the apprehension of agreeable qualities in the object, may be able to give no better defence of itself than the traditional dislike of Dr. Fell: "I do not like you, Dr. Fell; the reason why I cannot tell." But this subsequent justification to reason of the love of ἀγαπᾶν affords no warrant for declaring it the product of will acting on rational considerations. The perception of those qualities constituting the object admirable is an act the same in kind as the perception of those qualities constituting it agreeable; and the reaction of the subject in the emotion of love is an act of the same nature in both cases. The reaction of the subject in the love of the order which is expressed by ἀγαπᾶν is just as instinctive and just as immediate an affectional movement of the soul, as in the order of love

103 As cited, p. 482.   104 I. 11. 17.
105 Trench and Cope hold much the same view.

expressed by φιλεῖν. The two differ not in their psychological
nature but in the character of the apprehended qualities to
which they are emotional responses. It is meaningless to say
that the one terminates on the person himself and the other
only on certain of his qualities: both terminate, of course, on
the person whose quality as precious or agreeable as apprehended has called them into being.

It is only by an artificial explanation of it, furthermore, that
Aristotle's phrase, — that "φιλεῖσθαι is ἀγαπᾶσθαι for our own
sake" — can be made to suggest that ἀγαπᾶν expresses a love
based on rational considerations. It only suggests that Aristotle
saw in φιλεῖν a love which found its account in the agreeableness
of the object. What Aristotle is saying in this passage is that it
is pleasant alike to love and to be loved; for one loves only because he enjoys it; and if he is loved — that makes him happy
because he fancies there must be something fine in him to call
out the passion. He explains this by adding that φιλεῖσθαι is
ἀγαπᾶσθαι for one's own sake. Here is a quasi-definition of
φιλεῖν: φιλεῖν is a love founded on nothing outside the object.
But the most that can be inferred about ἀγαπᾶν is that it is a
love which has cognizable ground. To conclude that that ground
is or may be outside the object, or must be of the nature of a
rational consideration operating through acts of reflection, and
judgment, and will, is sufficiently illegitimate to be absurd. The
actual ground of the particular act of ἀγαπᾶν here spoken of is
the total personality of the object conceived as good, and as
therefore justifying his becoming the object of φιλεῖν. Φιλεῖν is
subsumed under ἀγαπᾶν taken for the moment as a wider category; and the ἀγαπᾶν which includes the φιλεῖν in itself cannot
have as such a ground of essentially different nature.[106]

[106] Cope, as cited, v. i, p. 214, paraphrases Aristotle's phrase thus: "And being liked or loved is to be valued, esteemed, for one's own sake and for nothing
else." He remarks: "It is probable that little or no distinction is here intended to
be made between φιλεῖν and ἀγαπᾶν, since it is the end and not the process that
is here in question, and they seem to be used pretty nearly as synonyms. They
represent two different aspects of love, as a natural affection or emotion, and as
an acquired value, which we express by esteem." We probably get Aristotle's whole
meaning when we say that when we are loved, there is implied in that that we
are valued for our own sake.

We are not left by the ancients, however, without very clear intimation of how they conceived φιλεῖν and ἀγαπᾶν in relation to one another. There is, for example, what amounts to a direct definition of the two words in their distinctive meanings in an interesting passage in the "Memorabilia" of Xenophon, with which the commentators have rather fumbled.[107] B. L. Gildersleeve, in that unfortunate edition of Justin Martyr (1877) which brought only grief to his admirers, goes the length of saying,[108] with his eye on this passage, that "Xenophon uses ἀγαπᾶν and φιλεῖν as absolute synonyms"; and, what is even stranger, Moulton and Milligan repeat this judgment — for this special passage at least with the added emphasis of pronouncing it "undeniable." [109] These, however, are eccentric opinions. That a distinction is made between the two words lies on the face of the passage and is, of course, universally recognized.[110] The only question that is open is what precisely that distinction is. What has often been overlooked is that Xenophon actually defines the two terms in the clauses, which, because their relations to one another have not been accurately caught, have given the commentators all their trouble. Socrates,

---

[107] "Memorabilia," II, vii. 9 and 12. We give the text of the passage in the translation of J. A. Watson. Fourteen free women — his relatives — had been introduced into Aristarchus' house as dependents. Socrates' comment and advice was this: "Under present circumstances, as I should suppose, you neither feel attached (φιλεῖν) to your relatives nor they to you, for you find them burdensome to you, and they see that you are annoyed with their company. For such feelings there is danger that dislike may grow stronger and stronger, and that previous friendly inclination may be diminished. But if you take them under your direction so that they may be employed, you will love (φιλήσεις) them, when you see that they are serviceable to you, and they will grow attached to you (ἀγαπήσουσιν) when they find that you feel satisfaction in their society; and remembering past services with greater pleasure, you will increase the friendly feeling resulting from them, and consequently grow more attached and better disposed toward each other." Aristarchus took this advice and the result was: "they loved (ἐφίλον) Aristarchus as their protector, and he loved (ἠγάπα) them as being of use to him."

[108] P. 135.

[109] As cited, p. 2, sub voc. ἀγαπᾶν.

[110] J. H. H. Schmidt, as cited, p. 483, has a full and excellent discussion of the passage, which leaves no doubt of the general distinction that is drawn. Edward M. Cope, as cited, p. 294, pronounces it "decisive" in the matter. Cf. also T. D. Woolsey, as cited, p. 168; and E. A. Abbott, as cited, p. 240.

we are told, found Aristarchus peevish, because, owing to the
civil disturbances of the time, he had had fourteen female relatives — sisters, nieces, cousins — dumped on him, and he did
not see why he should be held responsible for their support. He
did not like it; and the women, on their part, did not like the
condition of affairs either. "Neither do you φιλεῖς them," says
Socrates in diagnosing the situation, "nor they you": a settled
mutual dislike threatened to be the outcome. The remedy which
Socrates proposed was that Aristarchus should put the women
to work at useful employment; and he promised that, on that
being done, their indifference to each other would pass away:
Aristarchus would acquire an affection for them arising out of a
sense of their value to him; and they would come to prize him
on perceiving his pleasure in them. "You will φιλήσεις them,"
says Socrates, "when you see that they are profitable to you;
and they will ἀγαπήσουσιν you, when they perceive that you
take pleasure in them." What is to be observed is that the
clauses here are so balanced that the participial adjunct in each
defines the verb in the other; so that what is said is equivalent
to saying: "You will φιλήσεις them when you see that they
ἀγάπουσιν you; and they will ἀγαπήσουσιν you when they perceive that you φιλεῖς them." Instead of mutual dislike, a mutual
liking and esteem will supervene. To the φιλεῖν, then, in the
first clause the "take pleasure in" of the other corresponds:
and to the ἀγαπᾶν of the second clause the "being profitable to
you" of the first corresponds: and thus we have in effect definitions of the two verbs — φιλεῖν is taking pleasure in, ἀγαπᾶν is
ascribing value to. Now, Xenophon continues, Aristarchus tried
it and it worked. He put the women to work and at once there
was a change: "They ἐφίλουν him as a protector, and he ἠγάπα
them as profitable." They came to take pleasure in his protection, and he came to value them for their profitable labor. The
relation of protector of useless women, as barely tolerated dependents, with their natural resentment of a grudging bounty,
passed, by the simple expedient of the introduction of productive employment, into a relation of mutual affection and esteem.
They came to like the man who gave them back their self-

respect; he came to prize the women whose labor brought him profit. The words in this last clause, so far from reversing their positions as compared with the former (this is the chief source of the difficulty the commentators find in the passage) are in their right places according to their definitions there. Φιλεῖν, defined there as delighting in, is properly used here to describe the attitude of the women towards their protector: ἀγαπᾶν, defined there as attaching value to, is properly employed here of the attitude of an employer to profitable workers.

The definition of ἀγαπᾶν which Xenophon here gives us — by which it expresses the love of prizing as over against the love of simple liking — verifies itself in a survey of the general usage of the word. This may be illustrated by attending to the other passages in which φιλεῖν and ἀγαπᾶν are brought together, that are cited by Abbott in connection with his discussion of this one. We see at once that it is Xenophon's distinction which is in the mind of Dio Cassius,[111] when he tells us that it was said to the Roman people at the death of Julius Caesar: Ye ἐφιλήσατε him as a father, and ἠγαπήσατε him as a benefactor — that is to say, they both felt true affection for him and greatly valued him. The case is equally simple with the passage from Plato's "Lysis"[112] with which Abbott deals with somewhat clumsy fingers, ascribing to ἀγαπᾶν the sense of "being drawn towards," and to φιλεῖν that of "drawing towards oneself." The passage is taken from a long discussion on friendship which is conducted throughout with φιλεῖν, φιλία, φιλοί, until, it having been concluded that only the good can be friends, the question is raised, How can those be valued (ἀγαπηθείη) by each other who can be of no use to one another, and how can one who is not valued (ἀγαπῷτο) be a friend? The good man being sufficient to himself — so far as he is good — stands in need of nothing; and therefore would not attach value (ἀγαπῷη) to anything; and because he cannot attach value (ἀγαπῷη) to anything, he cannot be fond (φιλοί) of anything. And yet they who do not make much of one another (μὴ περὶ πολλοῦ ποιούμενοι ἑαυτούς) cannot be friends. These last words, "make much of" define for us the

111 xliv, 48, p. 175.　　　　　112 P. 215B (cf. Jowett, p. 54).

sense in which ἀγαπᾶν has been used throughout; and we perhaps can hardly do better than render the crucial sentences: "He who lacks nothing will attach value to nothing (οὐδὲ τὶ ἀγαπῷη ἄν)": "what he does not attach value to, he cannot be fond of (ὃ δὲ μὴ ἀγαπῷη, οὐδ' ἄν φιλοί)." A little later in the discussion [113] the two words are coupled in the reverse order from that in which they occur in Dio Cassius. We read: "For if there is nothing to hurt us any longer we should have no need of anything that would do us good. Thus would it be clearly seen that we did but ἠγαπῶμεν καὶ ἐφιλοῦμεν the good on account of the evil, and as the remedy of the evil which was the disease; but if there had been no disease there would have been no need of a remedy." Jowett renders the pair of verbs by "love and desire" which certainly is wrong. Woolsey renders much better by "highly judge and love"; adding the comment: "The latter word contains something more of feeling, while the former contains more of regard, and a higher degree of respect." We can scarcely do better than render: "And thus it would be clear that we attached value to the good and looked with affection on it, only on account of the evil." Abbott's last example is drawn from Ælian's description of Hiero's love for his brothers.[114] He lived on terms of great intimacy with them, we are told, "holding them in very high regard (πάνυ σφόδρα ἀγάπησις), and being loved (φιληθεῖς) by them in return." The meaning seems to be what we might express by saying that he valued his brothers and they repaid him by true affection.

It is not intended to suggest that the content of ἀγαπᾶν is exhausted by the concepts esteem, value, prize. The word expresses the notion of love. What is contended for is that the particular manner love which the word is adapted to express, is the love which is the product of the apprehension of value in its object, and which is therefore informed by a feeling of its preciousness, so that it moves in a region closely akin to that of esteeming, valuing, prizing. The region in which it moves is, indeed, so closely akin to that of these conceptions, that there

---

[113] P. 220D (cf. Jowett, p. 61).
[114] "Var. Hist.," ix, 1 (Tauchnitz ed. p. 124).

are occasions when the idea it expresses is scarcely distinguishable from them. Take for example these two instances from Isocrates.[115] "The same opinion is also held concerning the Lacedemonians; for in their case their defeat at Thermopylae is more admired (ἄγωνται) than their other victories, and the trophy erected over them by the barbarians is an object of esteem (ἀγαπῶσι) and frequent visits (θεωροῦσι), while those set up by the Lacedemonians over others, far from being commended (ἐπαινοῦσι), are regarded with displeasure; for the former is considered to be a sign of valor, the latter of a desire for self-aggrandizement" (V. 148). "Now, I am surprised that those who consider it impossible that any such policy should be effected do not know from their own experience, or have not heard from others, that there have been indeed many terrible wars the parties to which have been reconciled and done each other great service. What could exceed the enmity between Xerxes and the Hellenes? Yet every one knows that both we and the Lacedemonians were more pleased (ἀγαπήσοντες) with the friendship (φιλία) of Xerxes than with that of those who helped us to found our respective empires" (V. 42). In the former passage ἀγαπῶσι καὶ θεωροῦσι are put in a sort of parallel with οὐκ ἐπαινοῦσιν ἀλλ᾽ ἀηδῶς ὁρῶσιν, and may perhaps be not inadequately represented by "prized and gazed at," as over against "not praised but looked askance at." The idea conveyed by ἀγαπήσαντες in the latter passage lies very close to that of "prized more," "valued more" "set more store by." Nevertheless Isocrates preferred to employ a word which said these things with a slight difference; a slight difference which enhanced the effect. He preferred to say that the trophy at Thermopylae was loved, and that the Greeks loved the friendship of Xerxes more than that of their allies — employing, however, for "loved" a term through which sounded the notions of esteeming, valuing, prizing, rather than that of enjoying.

We see the same implications shining through the word

---

[115] V. 148; V. 42. We draw these passages from Schmidt (p. 485), who presents them as involving no question of real love, but only of an esteeming or valuing.

when we read in Demosthenes such phrases as these: "Neither did I love (ἠγάπησα) Philip's gifts," for which Woolsey suggests, "neither did I value":[116] "These he loves (ἀγαπᾷ) and keeps around him," which Woolsey renders "these he makes much of."[117] Examples, however, need not be multiplied. The word designates love — "without reference to sensuousness, close-intercourse, or heart-inwardness" — from the distinct point of view of the recognition of worthiness in its object. It is, therefore, intrinsically a noble word for love; or, let us give to it its rights and say definitely it is the noble word for love. It is in its right company when Plutarch [118] joins it with τιμᾶν and σέβεσθαι in the declaration that "the people ought to love and honor and revere the gods according to righteousness." But like other noble words it was possible for it to lose the sharpness and force of its higher suggestions. It became ultimately, in the development of the language, the general word for love. And in proportion as it became the general word for love and was applied without thought to all kinds of love, it naturally lost more or less of the power to suggest its own specific implications. The time came when it could be applied to the basest forms of love without consciousness of incongruity. Its lofty implications remained, however, embedded in its very form, and could always be recalled to consciousness and observation by a simple emphasis. And as long as any other term for love was current, sharing the field with it, it was always possible to throw the high implications intrinsic to it up to sight by merely setting the two in contrast.

This, then, is the equipment of the Greek language for the expression of the idea of love, which is revealed to us in the monuments of classical Greek. There were, we see, four terms which served as vehicles of it. Φιλεῖν held the general field, though not without its distinctive implications which were on occasion thrown into clear emphasis, and which were always more or less felt coloring the conception of love as it expressed itself by its means in current speech. These implications repre-

---

[116] "De Corona," p. 263, 7 Reiske. [117] "De Olynth.," ii, p. 23, 23.
[118] "Aristides," 6.3.

sented love as the response of the human spirit to what appealed to it as pleasurable; therefore at bottom as a delight. Φιλεῖν was supported on both sides, however, by other terms of other implications. There was στέργειν in which love was presented as a natural outflow of the heart to objects conceived as in one way or another bound up very closely with it and making, therefore, a claim upon it for affection. There was ἐρᾶν which conceived love as an overmastering passion, seizing upon and absorbing into itself the whole mind. And there was, on the other side, ἀγαπᾶν which presented love as the soul's sense of the value and preciousness of its object and its response to its recognized worth in admiring affection.[119]

During the classical period these terms did not so much encroach on the dominance of φιλεῖν in the literary expression of love as rather come to its aid, bringing into fuller expression the several sides and aspects of love. A change, however, was preparing beneath the surface, in the broad region of popular speech. How this change was inaugurated, through what stages it passed, what were the forces which drove it forward, we are left to conjecture to suggest. There is no direct evidence available. We only know that in that body of literature constituted by the New Testament, along with the Septuagint version of the Old Testament and the Apostolic Fathers, a body of literature the peculiarity of which is that it dips into the popular speech,

[119] How fully these synonyms covered the idea of love in its complete range is illustrated by the opening words of Deutsch's article on "Love (Jewish)" in Hastings' *ERE.* viii, p. 173b. In transcribing what he says we insert the Greek terms at appropriate places. "The dictionaries define love as 'a feeling of strong personal attachment, induced by that which delights (φιλεῖν) or commands admiration (ἀγαπᾶν).' The subdivisions of this sentiment comprise the impulses of attachment, due to sexual instinct, or the mutual affections of man and woman (ἐρᾶν); the impulses which direct the mutual affections of members of one family, parents and children, brothers and other relatives (στέργειν); the attachment that springs from sympathetic sentiments of people with harmonious character, friendship (φιλία); and finally, the various metaphorical usages of the word, as the love for moral and intellectual ideals." He adds: "To the last class belongs the religious concept of love for God, while the particular Biblical conception of God's love for Israel is closely related to the idea of paternal affection." As we shall see when we come to speak of the usage of the Septuagint, these higher religious conceptions were brought under ἀγαπᾶν.

we suddenly see the change well on its way. The most outstanding feature of it is the retirement of φιλεῖν into the background and the substitution for it of ἀγαπᾶν as the general term for love. We must not permit to fall out of sight that this means the general adoption of the noblest word for love the language possessed as its common designation in every-day speech. One may well suppose that an ethical force was working in such a change.[120] Such a supposition would find support in the general deepening of the ethical life which, as we know, was taking place during the closing centuries of the old era. We may readily suppose that in the increasing seriousness of the times the current conception of love too may have grown more grave; and that it may have, therefore, seemed less and less appropriate to speak of it in any lighter than the highest available terms. Whatever may have been the cause, however, it is plain matter of fact that ἀγαπᾶν, a word of essential nobility in its native implications, did gradually through the years become the ordinary term for the expression of love in the most general sense. And this necessarily wrought a distinct ennoblement of the common speech with respect to love.

The effect of the change on ἀγαπᾶν itself naturally was not so happy. The application of it indiscriminately to every form and quality of love unavoidably reduced its current acceptation to the level of every form and quality of love. The native implications of the word could not, to be sure, be entirely eradicated. But they could be covered up and hidden so as not to be noted in the ordinary use of it, and only now and again brought back into view, when in one way or another they were thrown into emphasis. How thoroughly they were thus obscured we should not have been able to guess had we the witness of the New Testament alone in our hands. The Septuagint, however, reveals it to us. There ἀγαπᾶν appears as in such a sense the general term for love that it is readily applied to every form and quality of love, apparently in the case of the lower forms with-

[120] Woolsey's remark (as cited, p. 169): "Such a change . . . must have come from a higher condition of moral feeling," is sound in itself although made in a connexion not easily justified.

out any consciousness whatever of its higher connotations. This phenomenon occurs, it is true, occasionally also in classical Greek. It is incidental to the free use of any word that it should get its edges worn off in the process, and become more or less a mere symbol for the general idea connected with it, without regard to any specific modifications of that general idea which it may embody. But it becomes much more marked in the Septuagint. Because ἀγαπᾶν has become the general word for love, what was exceptional in the classics has here become the rule. In the Septuagint the word has lost the precision of its specific notion and become merely a general term to express a general idea. A much nobler term for love has come into general use for the expression of the broad idea of love; and this ennobles the whole speech concerning love. But the word itself has suffered loss in thus permitting itself to be applied indifferently to all kinds and conditions of love.

On another side, however, the employment of ἀγαπᾶν as the general term for love brought it a great elevation in its Septuagint usage. If there was no love too low to be spoken of in its terms, there was equally no love too high for its use of it. And the application of it to describe the higher aspects of love as presented in the Old Testament revelation added great stretches to its range upwards. We are in the presence here of a double movement through which ἀγαπᾶν was prepared for its use in the New Testament. By the obscure linguistic revolution wrought among the peoples of Greek speech, as a result of which ἀγαπᾶν superseded φιλεῖν as the general Greek term for the expression of the idea of love, intrinsically the noblest word for love the Greek language afforded, came naturally to the hands of the Septuagint translators for rendering the idea of love as it appeared in the pages of the Old Testament. By the rendering of the idea of love throughout the Old Testament by ἀγαπᾶν, the whole content of the Old Testament idea of love was poured into that term, expanding it in its suggestions upwards, and training it to speak in tones indefinitely exalted. The total effect of this double change was immensely to extend the range of the word. As it was the noblest word for love in Greek speech,

its range could be extended, on its becoming the general word
for love, only downward. It was extended also upwards only
by becoming the vehicle for the deepened conception of love
which has been given to the world by the self-revelation of God
in the Scriptures. When we open the Septuagint, therefore, and
see ἀγαπᾶν lying on its pages as the general term for love, we
are in the presence of some very notable phenomena in the
preparation of the terminology of love in the New Testament.

The story of the Septuagint usage of the terms for love is
almost told by the simple statistics. The verb ἀγαπᾶν occurs in
the Septuagint about two hundred and sixty-six times, φιλεῖν
about thirty-six times, ἐρᾶσθαι only three times, and στέργειν
just once. Even this does not give the whole state of the case,
for in the majority of its occurrences φιλεῖν is used in the sense
of "to kiss." It occurs only sixteen or seventeen times with the
meaning of "love." That is to say, this word, the common word
for love in the classics, is used in the Septuagint in only a little
more than five per cent of the instances where love falls to be
mentioned: in nearly ninety-five per cent ἀγαπᾶν is used. Here
is a complete reversal of the relative positions of the two words.

In more than a third of the instances in which φιλεῖν is used
of loving, moreover, it is used of things — food or drink, or the
like (Gen. xxvii. 4, 9, 14, Prov. xxi. 17, Hos. iii. 1, Isa. lvi. 10),
leaving only a half a score of instances in which it is employed of
love of persons. In all these instances (except Tob. vi. 14,
where it is a demon that is in question) it is a human being to
whom the loving is ascribed. The love ascribed to him ranges
from mere carnal love (Jer. xxii. 22 [paralleled with ἐρασταί],
Lam. i. 2, Tob. vi. 14, cf. Tob. vi. 17), through the love of a
father for his son (Gen. xxxvii. 4), to love for Wisdom (Prov.
viii. 17, xxix. 3, Wisd. viii. 2). Cremer drops the remark: "In
two passages only does φιλεῖν occur as perfectly synonymous
with ἀγαπάω, Prov. viii. 17, xxix. 3." [121] This cannot mean
that ἀγαπᾶν does not occur in the senses in which φιλεῖν is used

---

[121] "Biblisch-Theologisches Wörterbuch der Neutestamentlichen Gräci-
tät³," 1883, p. 11, near bottom: E. T., p. 592, bottom. The remark seems to have
been omitted from 10th ed., 1915.

in the other passages: ἀγαπᾶν is used in all these senses. What is really meant is that in these two passages alone φιλεῖν bears a sense which Cremer is endeavoring to fix on ἀγαπᾶν as its distinctive meaning — the sense of high ethical love. In both passages it is love to Wisdom that is spoken of: "I (Wisdom) ἀγαπῶ them that φιλοῦντας me" (viii. 17); "When a man loves (φιλοῦντος) wisdom, his father rejoices" (xxix. 3); and they bear witness that this high love could readily be expressed by φιλεῖν, as well as by ἀγαπᾶν. It is not obvious, however, that φιλεῖν is used in these passages as perfectly synonymous with ἀγαπᾶν. On the face of Prov. viii. 17, there is a difference between the love (ἀγαπᾶν) ascribed to Wisdom and that (φιλεῖν) ascribed to her votaries, if the distribution of the words be allowed any significance. Perhaps it may be conjectured that some flavor clings to φιλεῖν which renders it less suitable for the graver affection proper to Wisdom herself.

Despite the fewness of the occurrences of φιλεῖν, there are quite a number of instances in which it is brought into more or less close conjunction with ἀγαπᾶν, and a glance over these may help us to some notion of the relation which the two words bear to one another. Gen. xxxvii. 3, 4: "And Jacob ἠγάπα Joseph more than all his sons. . . . And his brothers, seeing that his father φιλεῖ him above all his sons, hated him." Prov. viii. 17: "I (Wisdom) ἀγαπῶ them that φιλοῦντας me." Prov. xxi. 17: "A poor man ἀγαπᾷ mirth, φιλῶν wine and oil in abundance." Isa. lvi. 6, 10: "The strangers that attach themselves unto the Lord . . . to ἀγαπᾶν the name of the Lord. . . . Dumb dogs, . . . φιλοῦντες to slumber." Lam. i. 2: "Weeping, she weeps in the night and her tears are upon her cheeks; and there is none of all that ἀγαπώντων her to comfort her; all those that φιλοῦντες her have dealt treacherously with her." Hos. iii. 1: "And the Lord said to me, Go yet and ἀγάπησον a woman that ἀγαπῶσαν evil things and an adulteress, even as the Lord ἀγαπᾷ the children of Israel, and they have respect to strange gods, and φιλοῦσι cakes and raisins." Wisdom viii. 2, 3: "Her (Wisdom) I ἐφίλησα, and sought out from my youth, and I desired to make her my wife and was an ἐραστής of her beauty. . . . Yea, the

Lord of all things Himself ἠγάπησεν her" (and then immediately below, at verse 7: "If a man ἀγαπᾷ righteousness"). Perhaps we should add Prov. xix. 7, 8, in which the noun φιλία and the verb ἀγαπᾶν occur, in distinct clauses no doubt, which yet stand rather close together: "Every one who hates a poor brother is also far from φιλία. . . . He that procures wisdom ἀγαπᾷ himself."

To fill out the general picture we may adjoin a few passages in which other combinations of terms for love are made. In his praise of woman in I Esd. iv. 14 ff., Zorobabel brings together these two statements — that a man can look a lion in the face, and can plunder and rob in the darkness — all to bring his spoil to τῇ ἐρωμένῃ; "yea a man ἀγαπᾷ his own wife more than father or mother." In Jer. xxii. 22, we read: "The wind shall tend all thy shepherds and thy ἐρασταί shall go into captivity; for then shalt thou be ashamed and disgraced by all τῶν φιλούντων σε." In Prov. vii. 18: "Come, and let us enjoy φιλίας until the morning; come, and let us embrace ἔρωτι." And again, in Sir. xxvii. 17, 18: "Στέρξον a friend (φίλον) and be faithful unto him; but if thou betrayest his secrets . . . thou hast lost the φιλίαν of thy neighbor."

It cannot be pretended that it is an easy task to find one's way through these passages, assigning a distinctive sense to each term. By one thing we are struck, however, at the first glance. In all the combinations of ἀγαπᾶν and φιλεῖν, the higher rôle is assigned to ἀγαπᾶν. The historian tells us in Gen. xxxvii. 3 that Jacob ἠγάπα Joseph; but when he repeats what the envious brothers said, φιλεῖν is used, as if they would suggest that their father's special love for him was an ungrounded preference. It is Wisdom who ἀγαπᾷ her votaries (Prov. viii. 17); they, on their part, φιλοῦνται her; and the Lord ἠγάπησεν Wisdom, while her servant ἐφίλησε her (Wisd. viii. 2, 3). There is some appearance here that ἀγαπᾶν was felt to be in some way the more appropriate word with which to express love of a superhuman order. Only in the case of Lam. i. 2 does the variation from ἀγαπᾶν to φιλεῖν seem to be purely rhetorical; and there the variation imitates a variation in the underlying Hebrew, and gives ἀγαπᾶν the place of honor.[122] Similarly, in the passages in which ἀγαπᾶν does not occur there appears to be in mind always some valid distinction between the terms that are used, although it is not always easy clearly to grasp it. It must be confessed, for example, that it is difficult to discover the precise reason for the variation from ἐρασταί to φιλοῦντες in Jer. xxii. 22, or from φιλία to ἔρως in Prov. vii. 18. In the former of these passages it is obvious enough, of course, that the φιλοῦντες are intended to embrace both the shepherds and the lovers, and doubtless that is the reason that a broader word is chosen. In the latter the variation in terms reflects a variation in the underlying Hebrew, but it is not clear that it reflects it accurately, or what is the exact distinction intended. The general impression left by the series of passages is that the several terms for love were used quite freely and with various natural interchanges, as substantial synonyms; but that ἀγαπᾶν was felt to be in some sense of the highest suggestion, and when they were brought into contrast, the higher place was instinctively given to it.

Certainly ἀγαπᾶν is used with the utmost freedom for every conceivable variety of love, from the love of mere lust on the one hand (e. g., II Sam. xiii. 1, 4, 15, Isa. lvii. 8, Ezek. xvi. 37) up to the purest earthly love on the other (Lev. xix. 18, 34, Deut. x. 19, I Sam. xviii. 1, xx. 17, II Sam. i. 23), and beyond that to the highest love which man can feel, love to God (Ex. xx. 6, Deut. v. 10, vi. 5, vii. 9, x. 12, xi. 1, 13, 22, xiii. 3, xix. 9, xxx. 6, 16, 20, Judges viii. 3, Jos. xxii. 5, xxiii. 11, I Kings iii. 3, Ps. xvii. 1, xxx. 23, lxviii. 37, xcvi. 10, cxvi. 7), and even above that, to the inexplicable love of God Himself to His people (Deut. iv. 37, vii. 8, 13, x. 15, xxiii. 5, II Sam. xii. 24, II Chron. ii. 11, ix. 8, Isa. xliii. 4, xlviii. 14, lxiii. 9, Jer. xxxviii. 3, Mal. i. 2, Prov. iii. 12). It is quite true that it is used for the higher reaches of love far more frequently than for the lower-lying varieties. This was the inevitable effect of the proportionate place occupied by the higher and lower forms of love in the pages of the Old Testa-

---

[122] According to Gesenius, אֹהֵב means "a friend, loving and beloved, intimate, different from רֵעַ, a companion": רֵעַ, he says, implies less than אֹהֵב. In the text, ἀγαπᾶν represents אֹהֵב and φιλεῖν רֵעַ.

ment, and argues little as to the relative adaptability of the
term for expressing them severally. The plain fact is that $\dot{\alpha}\gamma\alpha\pi\hat{\alpha}\nu$
is the general term for love in the Greek Old Testament, em-
ployed in some ninety-five per cent of the instances in which
love is mentioned; and therefore it is employed of the several
varieties of love, not in accordance with its fitness to express
one or another of them, but in accordance with the relative
frequency of their occurrence in the Old Testament. The five
per cent or so of occurrences which are left to be expressed by
other terms seem not to be divided off from the rest on the
ground of the intrinsic unfitness of $\dot{\alpha}\gamma\alpha\pi\hat{\alpha}\nu$ to express them.
They include next to no kinds of love which $\dot{\alpha}\gamma\alpha\pi\hat{\alpha}\nu$ is not employed to express in other passages.[123] It is not to be supposed,
of course, that pure caprice has determined the employment of
these terms in these few instances. There is doubtless always a
reason for the selection which is made; and ordinarily the appropriateness of the term actually employed can be more or
less clearly felt. But it does not appear that the reason for
passing over $\dot{\alpha}\gamma\alpha\pi\hat{\alpha}\nu$ in these cases was ordinarily its intrinsic
incapacity for the expression of the specific love that is spoken
of. As the general word for love it no doubt could have been
used without impropriety throughout.

It is possible, moreover, to overpress the intrinsic signifi-
cance of the predominant use of $\dot{\alpha}\gamma\alpha\pi\hat{\alpha}\nu$ for the higher varieties
of love. Both $\phi\iota\lambda\epsilon\hat{\iota}\nu$ (Prov. viii. 17, xxix. 3) and $\dot{\epsilon}\rho\hat{\alpha}\sigma\theta\alpha\iota$ (Prov. iv.
6, Wisd. viii. 2), along with it (Prov. viii. 21), are used for love
to Wisdom. But no other term except $\dot{\alpha}\gamma\alpha\pi\hat{\alpha}\nu$ happens to be
employed of God's love to man, or of man's love to God, or even
of that love to our neighbor which with them constitutes the
three conceptions in which is summed up the peculiarity of the
teaching on love of the religion of revelation. This is a notable
fact; and it had notable consequences. It did not, however, so
much result from, as result in, that elevation of $\dot{\alpha}\gamma\alpha\pi\hat{\alpha}\nu$ above
other terms for love, which fits it alone to express these high
forms. It is probable that had the Septuagint translators found
$\phi\iota\lambda\epsilon\hat{\iota}\nu$ still in use as the general term for love, they would have

[123] But see below page 373.

employed it as their own general word, and it would have fallen
to it therefore to be used to express these higher forms of love.
Instead, they found ἀγαπᾶν, an intrinsically higher word than
φιλεῖν and more suitable for the purpose; and they trained it to
convey these still higher conceptions also. Thus they stamped
ἀγαπᾶν with a new quality, and prepared it for its use in the
New Testament. What is of importance to bear in mind, however, is that the elevation of ἀγαπᾶν to this new dignity was not
due to its greater intrinsic fitness to express these new conceptions (though it was intrinsically more fit to do so), but to the
circumstance that it happened to be the general term for love
in current use when the Septuagint was written. This is proved
by the fact that it was not employed by the Septuagint writers
as a special word for the expression of the loftier aspects of love
alone, but as a general word to express all kinds and conditions
of love. It is simply the common term for love in the Greek Old
Testament, and the new dignity which clothes it as it leaves the
Old Testament has been contributed to it by the Old Testament
itself.

The account given of ἀγαπᾶν by Hermann Cremer, while
in its central statement perfectly just, is deformed by some remarkable inaccuracies, arising from a fruitless attempt to establish certain stated exceptions to this central statement.
"The New Testament usage with reference to the words
ἀγαπᾶν, ἀγάπη, ἀγαπητός," he writes,[124] "is in a very special
manner a consistent and complete one. It was prepared for by
the use, presented by the Septuagint, of ἀγαπάω for the Hebrew
אהב in the whole range of its applications, with one or two characteristic exceptions. The Hebrew word includes in itself the
significance of all three Greek synonyms" [i. e., φιλεῖν, ἐρᾶν, and
ἀγαπᾶν]; "it is especially frequently used in an application in
which the Greeks do not speak of love, that is to say, of the
love enjoined for God and His will, as well as of the love ascribed to God Himself (Deut. vii. 13, x. 15, 18, xxiii. 6, II Sam.
xii. 24, Ps. lxxviii. 68, lxxxvii. 2, cxlvi. 8, Isa. xliii. 4, xlviii. 14,

[124] As cited. We are quoting from 10th ed., 1915, but the passage has remained substantially unaltered since the 3d ed., 1883.

lxiii. 9), particularly the last, which is a conception beyond the imagination of the Greeks.[125] Apart, now, from a few passages in which the rendering is only according to the sense (Mic. iii. 2 = ζητεῖν, Prov. xviii. 21 = κρατεῖν, xvii. 19 = χαίρειν), אהב is regularly translated by ἀγαπᾶν, *with the exception of* when it stands for sensual love (sixteen times in all), in which case ἐρᾶν, ἐραστής are constantly used (see above), and when it denotes a sensuous inclination or a natural affection (ten times), and then it is rendered by φιλεῖν and its compounds — Gen. xxvii. 4, 9, 14, Isa. lvi. 10, Ecc. iii. 8; cf. II Chron. xxvi. 10, φιλογεωργός, A, אהב אדמה, as also two passages where there is mention of an objectionable disposition, I Kings xi. 1 φιλογύναιος (φιλογύνης, B), and Prov. xvii. 19, φιλομαρτήμων." W. G. Ballantine, commenting on the latter half of this passage, remarks trenchantly, but we are afraid not unjustly:[126] " Cremer's assertions regarding the translation of אהב in the Septuagint are sheer misstatements, as anyone who has Trommius' Concordance in his hands can see. We have already referred to half a score of passages where ἀγαπάω, as the translation of אהב, expresses lustful love. Φιλέω, as we saw above, but once expresses a natural affection, and but four times a sensual inclination. Ἀγαπάω expresses a natural affection in Gen. xxii. 2, xxv. 28, xxxvii. 3, xliv. 20, Ruth iv. 15, Prov. iv. 3, xiii. 24. Ἐράω translates אהב but twice. Cremer says that ἀγαπάω 'never means *to do anything willingly, to be wont to do'; yet we have it in Jer. xiv. 10, 'They have loved to move their feet,' and in Jer. v. 31, 'And my people loved to have it so.'*"

Cremer's statement certainly conveys the impression that ἀγαπᾶν is never used in the canonical Septuagint (as a rendering of אהב) for sensual love, or for a sensuous inclination or natural affection, its place being taken in the former case (there being sixteen instances in all) by ἐρᾶν, ἐραστής, and in the latter (ten instances) by φιλεῖν and its compounds. For the sixteen cases of ἐρᾶν rendering אהב, used of sensual love, he refers us to a

[125] On these assertions see *The Princeton Theological Review*, January 1918, pp. 20ff.

[126] "Bibliotheca Sacra," July, 1889, p. 534.

list previously given — "see above," he says — and that list
proves to run as follows: " Ἐρᾶν is found only in a few passages
in the Old Testament (Esth. ii. 17, Prov. iv. 6, = אהב; Wisd.
viii. 2; ἐραστής, Ez. xvi. 33, 36, 37, xxiii. 5, 9, 22, Jer. xxii. 20,
22, Lam. i. 19, Hos. ii. 7, 9, 12, 14, 15, the stated rendering of
the Hebrew מְאָהֵב in the sensual sense)." There are seventeen
passages enumerated here; but they are not seventeen passages
in which אהב and מאהב are used in a sensual sense and are rendered by ἐρᾶν and ἐραστής; they profess to be passages rather
in which ἐρᾶν and ἐραστής are found in the Old Testament —
Wisd. viii. 2, of course, having no Hebrew base. They do not,
to be sure, exhaust the list of occurrences of words of this
group in the Old Testament: ἐρᾶσθαι occurs three times, not
two as here (add I Esdr. iv. 24); ἔρως, not mentioned here,
occurs twice (Prov. vii. 18, xxiv. 51 [xxx. 16]); and ἐραστής
appears nineteen times, as against the fifteen here enumerated.
But much less do the sixteen of them which are renderings of אהב
justify the description of them given in the main passage. One
of the two passages cited for ἐρᾶν, indeed — "Love (Wisdom),
and she shall keep thee" (Prov. iv. 6) — refers to high ethical
love; as does also indeed Wisd. viii. 2 (ἐραστής), "I was a lover
of her (Wisdom's) beauty." The other passage cited for ἐρᾶν,
"And the king loved Esther and she found favor beyond all the
virgins; and he put on her the queen's crown" (Esth. ii. 17),
while certainly referring to sexual love, can scarcely be spoken
of as referring to dishonorable love, as neither, indeed, can
I Esd. iv. 24, the third passage in which ἐρᾶν occurs (not mentioned by Cremer): "And when he hath stolen, spoiled, and
robbed, he bringeth it to his beloved (ἐρωμένη); wherefore a
man loveth (ἀγαπᾷ) his wife better than father and mother."

As it is thus clear that the words of the ἐρᾶν group do not
always express lustful, and not even always sexual, love, it is even
more clear that sensual or even lustful love is not expressed exclusively by words of this group. We have seen the carnal love
of a demon for a mortal maid expressed by φιλεῖν (Tob. vi. 15),
and the wicked lovers of Zion, in parallelism with ἐρασταί, expressed by φιλοῦντες (Jer. xxii. 22). The Hebrew piel participle

מאהב, rendered in the fifteen passages enumerated by Cremer by ἐρασταί, occurs also in Jer. xxx. 14, Zech. xiii. 6, the former of which is certainly of the same class with its fellows, and the latter not certainly of a different class (so Hengstenberg). In Jer. xxx. 14, however, it is rendered by οἱ φιλοί, "All thy lovers have forgotten thee," and in Zech. xiii. 6, taken as a singular, by ὁ ἀγαπητός, "With these I was wounded in my beloved house," or, as in the Alexandrian MS., "in the house of my beloved." It has already been intimated that numerous passages exist in which sensual love is expressed by ἀγαπᾶν. If we are to take sensual love in a sense broad enough to include Cremer's examples, we may adduce such passages as Gen. xxiv. 67, xxix. 30, 32, xxxiv. 3, Ex. xxi. 5, Deut. xxi. 15, 16, Judges xiv. 16, xvi. 15, I Sam. i. 5, xviii. 28, II Chron. xi. 21, Ecc. ix. 9, and perhaps even I Kings xi. 2. If dishonorable love is to be insisted upon, we may refer to II Sam. xiii. 1, 4, 15, Ezek. xvi. 37, Hos. iii. 1, or we may content ourselves with the single passage Isa. lvii. 8: "Thou hast loved (ἠγάπησας) those that lay with thee, and now hast multiplied thy whoredom (πορνείαν) with them." It is beyond question that not ἐρᾶν but ἀγαπᾶν is the regular word to express sexual love in the Septuagint, and this fact is not to be obscured by pointing to ἐραστής as the standing word for "lover" — which is a different matter.

No assertion could be more unfortunate, then, than that ἐρᾶν is the constant vehicle in the Septuagint for the expression of sensual love; and it is no mitigation to confine the assertion to the instances of renderings of אהב by ἐρᾶν. Unless, indeed, it be held even more unfortunate to assert that φιλεῖν and its compounds supply the stated means of the expression of the love of sensuous inclination or natural affection — connected with the further implication that there are only ten instances in which love of this kind comes to expression in the Old Testament. A full list of the ten instances he has in mind is not given by Cremer, and it would be difficult to fill out such a list with instances exactly like the half-dozen which he adduces. These half-dozen instances do represent one side of the usage of φιλεῖν and its compounds — a usage in which it perhaps holds a

unique position in Old Testament Greek. We are not sure that
ἀγαπᾶν is found in any precisely similar applications. There is
even an appearance that such applications are avoided for
ἀγαπᾶν. Look, for example, at Prov. xxi. 17: "A poor man
loveth (ἀγαπᾶν) mirth, loving (φιλῶν) wine and oil in abundance." There seems to be reflected here a distinction in the
usage of the two terms, according to which φιλεῖν and not
ἀγαπᾶν is preferred for loving food and drink, just as in English
we say we "like" but only abusively that we "love" articles
of diet. But this is only a pocket in the usage of φιλεῖν, and does
not justify the broad characterization formulated by Cremer.
The love expressed by φιλεῖν includes also the elevated love of
Wisdom by her votaries (Prov. viii. 17, xxix. 3); and if Ecc. iii.
8, "There is a time to love (φιλῆσαι) and a time to hate" shows
that natural affections are expressed by φιλεῖν, what does Sir.
xiii. 15, "Every beast loves (ἀγαπᾷ) his like, and every man his
neighbor" [127] show? The fundamental fault of Cremer's statement lies in a zeal to mark off a special region within which each
term — ἐρᾶν, φιλεῖν, and above all, ἀγαπᾶν — shall be confined.
Accordingly, he arbitrarily narrows the range of the usage of
each, and very especially of ἀγαπᾶν. In point of fact, the usage
of ἀγαπᾶν covers the whole field which אהב itself covers, and
there is no real variety of love for which it is not employed somewhere or other in the Septuagint. Even such a conspectus of the
kinds of love for which it is used as that drawn up by Ballantine
in the following summary is only generally complete, although
it will doubtless serve to bring home to us the very wide field
covered by the word. "It is the word," he says, [128] "in constant
use to express (1) God's love to man, (2) God's love for truth
and other virtues and worthy objects, (3) man's love for God,
(4) man's love for salvation and worthy objects, (5) man's conscientious love for man, (6) ordinary human friendship, (7)
parental and filial affection, (8) the love of husband and wife,

[127] Lütgert, "Die Liebe im Neuen Testament," 1905, p. 35, remarks: "Here
the commandment of love comes forward as a law of nature, and that because it
ought to be presented as a rational thing." He is presenting it as an instance of
the rationalization of Jewish thought under the influence of Hellenism.

[128] As cited, p. 527.

(9) impure sexual love, (10) man's love for cursing and other vices and sinful objects."

One of the most striking accompaniments of the appearance of ἀγαπᾶν in the Septuagint as the general term for love, is the appearance by its side of two abstract substantives formed from this stem — ἀγάπησις and ἀγάπη. The classical writers got along without these substantives. Ἀγάπησις has, it is true, been turned up in Aristotle. But it does not come into wide use in profane literature until Plutarch — after the opening of the Christian era. Ἀγάπη has not hitherto been discovered in any profane author at all, unless a somewhat conjectural reading in Philodemus, an Epicurean writer of the first century before Christ, be an exception.[129] In a true sense, then, both of these words make their first appearance in the Septuagint. Ἀγαπᾶν itself was in comparatively limited use among the classical writers; and, with στοργή, ἔρως and φιλία in their hand, they apparently felt no need of a substantive representing the peculiar quality of ἀγαπᾶν, in order to give expression to all their conceptions of love. When, however, ἀγαπᾶν became the general word for love, a need for corresponding substantives seems to have come to be felt, and they were supplied. Of course the Septuagint did not invent these substantives: not even ἀγάπη, which is not found in any earlier writing. It took them over with ἀγαπᾶν from the common usage of the people. This appears very clearly from the nature of their use in the Septuagint. They are used as general terms for love, covering the whole range of the conception, and with the utmost simplicity and directness. A very careless manner of speaking of ἀγάπη is current, as if it were in some way a gift of revealed religion to the world, not to say a direct product of divine inspiration. When Trench says that "It should never be forgotten that the substantive ἀγάπη is a

---

[129] The treatise is known from Herculaneum papyri alone, and the reading in question is restored thus: δι' ἀ[γ]άπης ἐ[ναρ]γοῦς. It is recorded in Crönert's revision of Passow's Lexicon, *sub voc.*, who accompanies it with a note, "sicher (?)"; and it is reported from his record by Moulton and Milligan, *sub voc.* G. A. Deissmann, "Bible Studies," 1901, p. 200, points out a scholium to Thucydides II. 51, which reads "φιλανθρωπίας καὶ ἀγάπης." But there is no telling how late this scholium may be, or whether the glossator was a Christian or not.

purely Christian word, no example of its use occurring in any
heathen writer whatever," he has no doubt by a mere slip of the
pen said "Christian" when the historical revelation of God in
its entirety was what was in his mind. That correction, however,
will not save his remark from being misleading. It is not true
that "the word was born within the bosom of revealed religion"; it is true only that it has hitherto been found in the use
only of adherents of revealed religion. What Zezschwitz means
by saying that it "first makes its appearance as a current term
in the Song of Solomon" is not clear, unless it be that it occurs
more frequently in the Song of Solomon than in any other Old
Testament book (eleven times as over against eight in the whole
Old Testament besides). The plain fact about the word is that,
as it appears in the pages of the Septuagint, it bears all the marks
of being already an old word with a settled general usage.

Additional evidence of its general currency is supplied by
its appearance in Aristeas (second or first century B.C.) and
Philo (early first century A.D.). Each uses it a single time, and
both in a noble sense — as the content of true piety. Aristeas,
positing the question, What is equal to beauty? answers: [130]
"Piety (εὐσέβεια); for that is an excellent beauty. But its power
consists in ἀγάπη; for this is a gift of God. And," he adds, to
the king whose inquiry he is answering, "you possess this, embracing in it all that is good." [131] Philo writes more elaborately
to much the same effect. "And therefore it is," says he,[132] "that
it appears to me that with these two principal assertions above

[130] § 229; ed. Wendland, p. 63. Aristeas uses ἀγαπᾶν (§ 123), ἀγάπησις (§§ 44,
265, 270) and ἀγάπη (§ 229); apparently not ἐρᾶν, ἔρως, or στέργειν, στοργή, at
all; nor even φιλεῖν, but φιλία, §§ 40, 44, 225, 228, 231, φίλος a half-dozen times
and compounds of φιλ- including φιλανθρωπεῖν, φιλανθρωπία, φιλανθρωπότερον.

[131] Ἀγάπησις is used in a less exalted sense. In § 44 (p. 15), Eleazar writes to
Ptolemy that he would endeavor to do all that the king had asked, "for this is a
mark of φιλίας and ἀγαπήσεως." Here ἀγάπησις is used of national amity (Done:
"confederation and amity"). In § 270 (p. 73) it is said that a king ought to trust
men whose loyalty (εὔνοια) towards him is indisputable, "for this is a mark of
ἀγαπήσεως rather than of ill-will and timeserving." For § 265 see note 22. The
verb ἀγαπᾶν is used very distinctly in its native sense of valuing in § 123.

[132] "Quod Deus sit Immutabilis," § 14, near the end; ed. Mangey, p. 283;
ed. Cohn, v. ii, p. 72: Yonge's translation is used.

mentioned, namely that God is as a man and that God is not as
a man, are connected two other principles consequent upon and
connected with them, namely that of fear and that of love
(φόβον τε καὶ ἀγάπην); for I see that all the exhortations of the
laws to piety (εὐσέβειαν) are referred either to the love (τὸ
ἀγαπᾶν) or the fear of the living God. To those, therefore, who
do not attribute either the parts or the passions of man to the
living God, but who, as becomes the majesty of God, honor
(τιμῶσι) Him in Himself, and by Himself alone, to love (τὸ
ἀγαπᾶν) Him is most natural; but to the others it is most appropriate to fear Him." It would, of course, be possible to say
that both Aristeas and Philo got the word from the Septuagint;
but it would be very difficult to prove that, and it seems vastly
unlikely. Their use of it is highly individual,[133] and their independence in employing it is supported by its appearance in
other Greek versions of the Old Testament in passages in which
it is not found in the Septuagint.

There is a superficial appearance that ἀγάπη and ἀγάπησις
are used by the Septuagint far less freely than ἀγαπᾶν. The verb
certainly occurs much more frequently than the substantives —
it, about two hundred and sixty-six times; they, together, only
thirty times — ἀγάπη twenty times and ἀγάπησις ten. The relatively small number of the occurrences of the substantives is
accounted for in part, however, by the comparative infrequency
of the noun אַהֲבָה in the Hebrew Old Testament, which the
Septuagint translates. That substantive occurs only forty times,
in sixteen of which it is rendered by ἀγάπη (which include all
the occurrences of ἀγάπη in which it has a Hebrew base), six
by ἀγάπησις (all its occurrences with a Hebrew base), and thirteen by some form of the verb ἀγαπᾶν,[134] while it is rendered in
only five instances by φιλία (a little more than half of its occurrences with a Hebrew base). That is to say, it is rendered in
nearly ninety per cent of its occurrences by some form of the

[133] On Philo's independence of the Septuagint in his use of the word, see
Deissmann, as cited, p. 199; and Moulton and Milligan, as cited, sub voc.
[134] In Gen. xxix. 20, I Sam. xviii. 3, the clause containing אהבה is omitted in
the Septuagint as printed whether by Tischendorf or by Swete; but it is supplied
in some MSS.

ἀγαπᾶν group, and in nearly half of these by ἀγάπη itself. The
question remains an open one naturally why the translators resorted so frequently to a paraphrase of the verb to render the
Hebrew substantive, and did not in all instances employ the
substantive ἀγάπη; they paraphrase by the verb (thirteen times)
almost as often as they render by ἀγάπη (sixteen times). The
distribution of the several manners of rendering אהבה through
the Septuagint is also rather odd. The paraphrase by the verb
is fairly evenly distributed through the volume from the Pentateuch to the Prophets and Psalms (none in the Wisdom books).
No substantive for love occurs in the Greek Bible, on the other
hand, until II Samuel; practically none until the Poetical and
Prophetic books.[135] The use of these substantives belongs thus
almost entirely to the latter portion of the Septuagint. And even
there their distribution is somewhat notable. The use of ἀγάπη
centers in the Song of Solomon: it occurs in it no less than eleven
times, more than half of all its occurrences in the Septuagint;
it and its verb (ἀγαπᾶν) are the sole vehicles in this book of the
notion of love. Outside the Song of Solomon, it occurs only
eight times, widely scattered through the volume. Ἀγάπησις is
found in five of its ten occurrences in the Prophets, and in four
of the others in the Poetical books. Φιλία occurs only in two well-
marked groups: in the great Wisdom books, Proverbs, Wisdom,
and Sirach, and in I and II Maccabees. It is well to note this
last fact, because it contributes to the understanding of what
seems, at first sight, a preponderance in the use of φιλία over
ἀγάπη and ἀγάπησις. Φιλία occurs thirty-five times, and ἀγάπη
and ἀγάπησις together but thirty times. More than half of the
occurrences of φιλία, however, fall in I and II Maccabees, where
it is employed exclusively in the highly differentiated sense —
one might even say the technical sense — of political amity.[136]
Only sixteen instances remain (all in the Wisdom literature) for
the expression of love in the ordinary applications of the word.

[135] The exceptions to the last statement are ἀγάπη, II Sam. i. 26, xiii. 15, and
ἀγάπησις, II Sam. i. 26.
[136] I Macc. viii. 1, 12, 17; x. 54; xii. 1, 3, 8, 16; xiv. 18, 22; xv. 17; II Macc.
iv. 11; I Macc. xii. 10, with ἀδελφότητα; x. 20, 23, 26 paralleled with συνθήκη.

After all, therefore, the chief vehicle for the idea of love in the Septuagint, even in its substantival expression, is furnished by the terms of the ἀγαπᾶν group. 'Αγάπη, ἀγάπησις together occur thirty times, φιλία sixteen, ἔρως twice (Prov. vii. 18, xxiv. 51 [xxx. 16], and στοργή not at all in the Septuagint proper, but four times in III and IV Maccabees (III Macc. v. 32, IV Macc. xiv. 13, 14, 17).

In range of meaning, ἀγάπη is spread thinly over the whole field; necessarily thinly, because of the infrequency of its occurrence. Its preponderant sense is sexual love. That is secured for it by its eleven occurrences in the Song of Solomon. But outside the Song of Solomon it is used in II Sam. xiii. 15 of the merely lustful love of Amnon for Thamar, as well as in the figurative passage Jer. ii. 2. In II Sam. i. 26, it is used of "the love of women" to which Jonathan's love there spoken of as ἀγάπησις) is compared: "Thy ἀγάπησις to me was wonderful, beyond the ἀγάπη of women" — as if ἀγάπη had some special fitness for the expression of the "love of women." At the opposite extreme are the four passages in the Wisdom books which carry us up to the highest reaches to which human love can ascend. The transition is made by two passages in Ecclesiastes (ix. 1, 6) in which it is used quite generally of love, as a universal human emotion, in contrast with hate: "My heart hath seen how the righteous and the wise and their works are in the hands of God, and there is no man that knoweth whether (it is) love or hate": "But the dead know nothing . . . and their love and their hate and their envy have perished." In Wisdom vi. 18 we have a passage built up in a kind of sorites, which reminds us of the passage in Aristeas: "For the most unerring beginning of wisdom is desire of discipline, and heed to discipline is love, and love is the keeping of her laws, and attention to the laws is the assurance of incorruption, and incorruption bringeth near to God." Here the love of wisdom is the secret of law-keeping and a step on the stairs that lead up to God. The climax is reached, however, in Wisd. iii. 9 and Sir. xlviii. 11, where love to God is spoken of, and its exceeding great reward. In the former passage we read: "They that put their trust in

Him shall understand the truth, and they that are faithful in
love" — that is, in love to Him — "shall abide with Him, because there is grace and mercy for His elect." In the latter, the
"famous men, even our fathers that begat us," are praised in
these great words: "Blessed are they that saw Thee, and they
that have fallen asleep in love; for we too shall surely live." [137]
The employment of the word in the other Greek versions of the
Old Testament is remarkable chiefly for a tendency to invade
with it the book of Proverbs, which in the Septuagint is the
especial field of $\phi\iota\lambda\iota\alpha$. Aquila and Theodotion both use it in
vii. 18 of sexual love; Aquila and Symmachus in x. 12, where it
stands in contrast with hate; and all three, Aquila, Symmachus,
and Theodotion in xv. 17, where it is praised as the condition
of all happiness in life. Besides, it is used by Symmachus, in addition to some passages in the Song of Solomon (Aquila also
uses it in one of these), in Psalm xxxii. 5, and Ezekiel xvi. 8.
Commenting on this usage, Moulton and Milligan remark that
it shows that the word "retained in independent writers the
connotations we find in Canticles and Ecclesiastes." [138] The
evidence as a whole goes to show that it was in full popular use
during the later pre-Christian centuries as a general word for
love of all kinds and degrees; and that it was taken over by the
Septuagint writers in this general sense, and employed by them
indiscriminately to express the idea of love as it fell to their
task to speak of it. The effect was, as in the case of $\dot{\alpha}\gamma\alpha\pi\hat{\alpha}\nu$, to
add depth to the word, because it was employed to express,
among other kinds of love, also that love to God which is characteristic of the Biblical revelation.

It remains somewhat of a puzzle why the Septuagint
writers, in no less than thirteen instances of the occurrence of
אהבה, preferred to translate it by forms of $\dot{\alpha}\gamma\alpha\pi\hat{\alpha}\nu$; and the oc-
currence of $\dot{\alpha}\gamma\dot{\alpha}\pi\eta\sigma\iota\varsigma$ by the side of $\dot{\alpha}\gamma\dot{\alpha}\pi\eta$ in their pages is susceptible of the interpretation that $\dot{\alpha}\gamma\dot{\alpha}\pi\eta$ did not hold the whole
field in the popular Greek of the time, but shared it with the

---

[137] In this passage $\dot{\alpha}\gamma\dot{\alpha}\pi\eta\sigma\iota\varsigma$ is printed by both Tischendorf and Swete;
$\dot{\alpha}\gamma\dot{\alpha}\pi\eta$ is read by א. ﹔ ﻡ

[138] As cited, *sub voc.* $\dot{\alpha}\gamma\dot{\alpha}\pi\eta$, near end.

sister word. The instances in which אהבה is paraphrased by
forms of the verb the more call for remark, because they move
in the high places. There is no instance of sexual love among
them except [Gen. xxix. 20] where this form of love is at its
height; and but three [four] in which love from man to man is
spoken of (Ps. cviii. 4, I Sam. xx. 17 *bis*, [xviii. 3]), and in two
[three] of these it is the supreme type of human love which is
celebrated, the love of David and Jonathan: "And Jonathan
swore yet again unto David because he loved (ἠγάπησε) the
life of him that loved (ἀγαπῶντος) him." After that, we have an
instance in which the love of mercy is expressed by it (Micah
vi. 8), and all the others speak of the supernal love of God to
man (Deut. vii. 8, I Kings x. 9, II Chron. ii. 11, ix. 8, Isa. lxiii.
9, Hos. iii. 1, ix. 15). Why should the Septuagint writers refuse
just these passages to ἀγάπη and paraphrase them? One of the
results is that they render אהבה, in no instance in which it expresses either love to God or God's love, by ἀγάπη; the instances
in which ἀγάπη is used to express love to God (Wisd. iii. 9, Sir.
xlviii. 11) come from that portion of the Septuagint which has
no Hebrew base, as does also the instance in which ἀγάπη is
used of love to Wisdóm. The general concept of love as distinguished from hate (Ecc. ix. 1, 6) is the highest to which ἀγάπη
attains when rendering אהבה. The impression made by these
facts is increased when we observe that the usage of ἀγάπησις
in general also moves on a higher plane than that of ἀγάπη. In
only one instance does it allude to sexual love (Jer. ii. 33). In
three others it is the love of man to man that is in question —
II Sam. i. 26, Ps. cviii. 5, and we add Prov. xxx. 15 (xxiv. 50),
where the noun is used adverbially to strengthen the verb:
"the horse-leech had three daughters ἀγαπώμεναι ἀγαπήσει,
loved with love," i. e., dearly loved. In one instance (Sir. xl. 20)
it expresses man's love to Wisdom, and in two (Hab. iii. 4, Sir.
xlviii. 11) man's love to God. In three instances (Jer. xxxviii.
3, Hos. xi. 4, Zeph. iii. 17) it expresses the love of God to man.
Certainly an appearance is created that ἀγάπη lent itself with
less readiness to the expression of the higher than of the lower
forms of love. Perhaps just because it was the most popular

word for love in circulation, though it was a perfectly general term and was used for all forms of love alike, its chief associations were with those forms of love which fell to be most frequently mentioned in everyday speech. It was accordingly predominantly used for those forms of love in the Septuagint, and owes the exaltation of meaning with which it comes out of its hands less to its own usage in the Septuagint than to its association with ἀγαπᾶν. There is a sense, then, in which we may speak — as Moulton and Milligan do — of "its redemption from use as a mere successor to the archaic ἔρως," although we should not ourselves make use of just this language. It was the successor of the classical φιλία, not of ἔρως; ἔρως was scarcely "archaic," as its continued use in much later Greek shows; and we think it a mistake to speak of ἔρως as if it were exclusively a designation of sexual love. Nor can we ascribe quite the rôle which Moulton and Milligan do to "Alexandrian Jews of the first century B.C." in the "redemption" of the word. We see this redemption taking place in Aristeas and Philo, it is true; but we do not see it in the Jewish translators of the Old Testament (Aquila, Symmachus, Theodotion). After it leaves the Septuagint we get no full evidence of the usage of the word until we reach the New Testament. We are chary of concluding from the single instance of its use, each, in Aristeas and Philo, that it was they and such as they who wrought the work. All that we can be sure of is that the redemption of the word was the work of those who had learned what love is from the Divine revelation. If the word was not "born in the bosom of revealed religion," it was apparently redeemed to its nobler uses under the influences of that religion.[139]

[139] Naturally the daily use of the word in its lower senses was not inhibited by its acquisition of its higher senses. It has continued up to the present day. Witness the lines of Christopoulos: Εἰς βουνὸν ἐγὼ κι' ὁ Ἔρως Κ' ἡ ἀγάπη μου μαζή . . . ; or those of Zalokostas: Ἀπὸ τὴ μέση μὲ ἅρπαξε, μὲ φίλησε στὸ στόμα Καὶ μοῦπε· γιὰ ἀναστεναγμοὺς, Γιὰ τῆς ἀγάπης τοὺς καϋμοὺς Εἶσαι μικρὸς ἀκόμα. When Clement of Alexandria ("Paed.," III. xi. 257) tells us that love is not to be estimated by kissing, but by kind deeds (ἀγάπη δὲ οὐκ ἐν φιλήματι, ἀλλ' ἐν εὐνοίᾳ κρίνεται), that involves the understanding that there was an ἀγάπη which expressed itself in kissing; and a similar implication lies in Chrysostom's declaration (Hom. vii. on Romans) that ἀγάπη does not consist in empty words or mere

Of the other substantives used for love in the Septuagint, φιλία is, of course, the most important. We have already pointed out the odd division of its usage into two well-marked groups. We are concerned now only with the sixteen instances in which it occurs in the great Wisdom books — nine in Proverbs, two in Wisdom, and five in Sirach. Its usage here is a broad one; but, although it starts at the same low level with ἀγάπη, it does not scale the same heights. It is used occasionally of purely sexual love, even when this appears as mere lust (Prov. v. 19; vii. 18, where it is parallel with ἔρως in the same sense; Sir. ix. 8). It is used once of love, or perhaps we may even say here, of friendship, to God: "For she (Wisdom) is an eternal treasure to men, those who possess which have prepared φιλίαν to God" (Wisd. vii. 14). And it is used once of love to Wisdom herself: "And great good is in φιλία of her" (Wisd. viii. 18). But in the majority of cases it expresses merely that love which binds men together in the friendly intercourse of life: Prov. x. 12, xv. 17, parallel with χάρις, xvii. 9, xix. 7, xxv. 10, parallel with χάρις, xxvii. 5, Sir. vi. 17, xxii. 20, xxv. 1, "harmony of brothers, and φιλία of neighbors, and a wife and husband who agree together," xxvii. 18, "στέρξον a friend and be faithful with him; but if thou betray his secrets . . . thou hast destroyed the φιλίαν of thy neighbor." These are all natural uses of φιλίαν, quite in accordance with its previous history. The impression is conveyed that it has suffered less from the revolution which had been wrought in the common terms for love than its verb.

Φίλος has apparently suffered not at all. It occurs with extraordinary frequency (about a hundred and eighty-two times), and is used quite along classical lines, chiefly as a noun to designate those who are bound to one another by an affection which does not root in ties of kinship (consult such conjunctions as "friends and neighbors," Ps. xxxvii. 12, lxxxvii. 18, Prov. xiv.

substantives, but in care and works. Even in the horrible story told by Epiphanius ("Adv. Haer.," 1. ii. xxvi, 4; Migne 1. 337c) of the Gnostic orgies, where the man bade the woman, "arise, do τὴν ἀγάπην with your brother," using ἀγάπη, as Sophocles says, κακεμφάτως, — ποιεῖν τὴν ἀγάπην was the standing phrase for celebrating the 'Αγάπη — the current use of ἀγάπη of the sexual act is doubtless implied.

20, xviii. 25; "friends and kindred," Prov. xvii. 9). Ἀγαπητός (twenty-two times) occupies a different field, and can scarcely be said to encroach upon that appropriated to φίλος. It is used chiefly in the singular — often of an only child (Gen. xxii. 2, 12, 16 [Judg. xi. 34], Amos viii. 10, Zech. xii. 10) [140] — to designate one especially loved; and there is already a class which is called God's ἀγαπητοί, beloved ones, so that this phrase is here seen in the making (Ps. lix. 5, cvii. 6, cxxvi. 2). Of course, compounds in φιλ- abound; the Greek language has never lost them, and has never formed corresponding compounds in ἀγαπ- which might supersede them.[141] Of these we are particularly interested in such as φιλάδελφος (II Macc. xv. 14, IV Macc. xiii. 21, xv. 10); φιλαδελφία (IV Macc. xiii. 23, 26, xiv. 1); φιλανθρωπεῖν (II Macc. xiii. 23); φιλάνθρωπος (I Esd. viii. 10, Wisd. i. 6, vii. 23, xii. 19, II Macc. iv. 11, IV Macc. v. 12); φιλανθρώπως (II Macc. ix. 27, III Macc. iii. 20); φιλανθρωπία (II Macc. vi. 22, xiv. 9, III Macc. iii. 15, 18); φιλόστοργος (IV Macc. xv. 13); φιλοστόργως (II Macc. ix. 21); φιλοστοργία (II Macc. vi. 20, IV Macc. xv. 6, 9). By φιλαδελφία and its companions, love to one's people — in this case the Jews — or, in other words, patriotism is expressed. Φιλανθρωπία with its group is used as a general term for kindness, graciousness, such as that shown by superiors to inferiors, especially by monarchs to those having official dealings with them (consult the paralleling of the adverb with ἐπιεικῶς, "fairly," "moderately," in II Macc. ix. 27).[142] The fundamental sense

---

[140] Cf. Swete on Mk. i. 11: "'Αγαπητός in the LXX answers to יָחִיד (μονογενής) unicus, cf. Hort, "Two Dissertations," pp. 49f.) in seven instances out of fifteen." Also Zahn on Mat. iii. 17 (ed. 3, 1910, p. 149, note 68). The usage is classical from Homer down: cf. e. g., W. W. Goodwin, "Demosthenes against Midias," 1906, p. 95; or more fully R. Whiston, "Demosthenes," 1868, 11, p. 324; and Holden, "Xenophon's Cyropaedia, iv. vi. 5; Fritzsche "Aristotle's Eth. Eud.," iii. 6, 1233 and in criticism E. M. Cope, "Aristotle's Rhetoric," 1897, p. 150, esp. note.

[141] An exception like the Homeric ἀγαπήνωρ only proves the rule.

[142] Similarly Aristeas, § 290, ed. Wendland, p. 77, says that Ptolemy's greatness consisted not in the glory of his power and wealth, but in his ἐπιεικία καὶ φιλανθρωπία, "moderation and graciousness." Similarly in § 208, φιλάνθρωπος is "humane," and in § 36, φιλανθρωπότερον is "very graciously." In § 265, p. 71, on the other hand it is said apparently that the most necessary thing for a king to have is the φιλανθρωπία καὶ ἀγάπησις, "good feeling and affection" of his subjects, "for with these will come an indissoluble bond of loyalty (εὐνοίας)."

of φιλοστοργία and its group comes out clearly in IV Macc. xv. 6, 9, 13, where it is used of mother-love; in other passages its application is extended to any strong affection: "I would with *fitting affection* have remembered your kindness" (II Macc. ix. 21); "there are things which it is not lawful to do even *for natural love* of life" (II Macc. vi. 20). A great elevation of sense awaited these words in the future as a new religious spirit was breathed into them. "Be φιλόστοργοι to one another in φιλαδελφία," says Paul (Rom. xii. 10), plumbing the depths of the feeling of brotherhood. "But when the φιλανθρωπία of our Savior, God, appeared," he writes again (Tit. iii. 4), soaring to the heights of the divine "humanity." Or we may find our examples of the heightened sense of the terms, if we prefer, in the φιλαδελφία which Clement of Rome (xlviii. 1) demands that the Corinthian Christians should more fully manifest; or in the φιλοστοργία which the writer of the Epistle to Diognetus (i. 1) asserts to be the cement which binds the Christian brotherhood together; or in the "great φιλανθρωπία καὶ ἀγάπη" for which this latter writer celebrates his God (ix. 5).

It is worth while, perhaps, to turn directly from the Septuagint to the Apostolic Fathers, that we may observe how the great revolution in the usage of the Greek terms for love, of which we get our first glimpse in the Septuagint, looks, after its complete adjustment to the high conceptions of divine revelation. The Greek of the Apostolic Fathers is, like the Greek of the Septuagint, fundamentally the popular Greek of its day; but, no doubt, it can scarcely be looked upon as simply the same popular Greek upon which the writers of the Septuagint draw, at a later stage of its development. The religious language of the Apostolic Fathers has been profoundly influenced directly by the usage of the Septuagint itself. From the Septuagint they derive a large part of their religious inspiration, and upon it they draw in great part for the vocabulary in which they express their religious conceptions. Still more profoundly the religious language of the Apostolic Fathers has been influenced by the usage of the New Testament, itself deeply affected by that of the Septuagint. The fundamental basis of the language of the Apostolic Fathers nevertheless is the common Greek of the day; and that, needless to say, is just the common Greek which the Septuagint uses, at a stage of its development some three centuries later. To say this, obviously, is to question the propriety of describing the Greek of the Septuagint as in any very distinctive sense Judaic or Alexandrian. In the matter of the linguistic phenomena which are for the moment occupying our attention — the supersession of φιλεῖν by ἀγαπᾶν as the general term for loving, the coming of the substantive ἀγάπη into employment — it happens, no doubt, that they meet us first in the writings of Alexandrian Jews; and we may be tempted to conjecture on that ground that they are peculiarities of the speech of Alexandrian Jews. This conjecture loses its plausibility, however, when the usages in question are observed in an even more extreme form in the Apostolic Fathers. The Apostolic Fathers were not Jews of Alexandria; they fairly ring the Mediterranean basin in their provenience; and it is incredible that, great as is the influence of the Septuagint upon their religious terminology, it has given them their fundamental language. Whenever a usage is common to the Septuagint, Philo, and the Apostolic Fathers, it is safe to say not only that it was familiar to the Greek-speaking Jews of Alexandria, but also that it was not alien to the Greek-speaking world at the opening of the Christian era.[143]

The compositions of the Apostolic Fathers differ very greatly in general character and subject-matter from the series of writings which the Septuagint translators rendered into Greek. If we think of the Apostolic Fathers in their narrowest compass, as including only the Epistles of Clement, Barnabas, Ignatius, and Polycarp, they are merely a collection of hortatory letters, devoted to the enforcement of religious and ethical duty. In such writings we may anticipate relatively more frequent mention of love as a religious and ethical conception on the one hand, and much less mention of it as a mere fact of daily

[143] See some apposite remarks on the general matter in A. Thumb, "Die griechische Sprache im Zeitalter des Hellenismus," 1901, pp. 182 f. and 185. On the affinity of the Greek of Philo and Biblical Greek, cf. H. A. A. Kennedy, "Sources of New Testament Greek," 1895, p. 67.

occurrence on the other, than was natural in a varied assemblage of historical, poetical, and prophetic writings such as we have in the Septuagint. The addition to these simple letters of the other compositions which it is the custom to class with them under the caption of Apostolic Fathers — the homily commonly called II Clement, the book of Church-order known as the Teaching of the Apostles, the lengthy Apocalypse which goes under the name of the Shepherd of Hermas, the anonymous apology called the Epistle to Diognetus — brings no great change into the linguistic character of the whole. So far as the usage of the terms denoting love is concerned, these books are all of a piece, a fact which gives us confidence in viewing them as mirroring the established usage in the Christian churches of the time.

The chief fact which attracts our attention is a negative one: that φιλεῖν, φιλία have practically no place in these writings. Each occurs but a single time; and both in sufficiently weak senses. Ignatius exhorts Polycarp (ii. 1) thus: "If to good scholars only thou dost feel kindly (φιλῆς), this is not thankworthy in thee; rather bring the pestilent to submission by gentleness." The content of φιλεῖν here lies close to πραΰτης: to love is not much more than being mild and gentle in behavior. Hermas ("Mand.," 10, 1, 4) reprobates being "mixed up in business affairs, and riches, and heathen entanglements (φιλίαις), and the many other concerns of this world." Even φίλος occurs only eight times; and the list of compounds of φιλ- is comparatively small. [144] It looks almost as if φιλεῖν was ready to vanish away. Even ἐρᾶν (Ign. "Pol.," iv. 3, "Rom.," ii. 1, vii. 2), ἔρως ("Rom.," vii. 2), and στέργειν (I Clem. i. 3; Polyc. "Philip.," iv. 2) occur more frequently. Στέργειν is used in its fundamental sense of natural affection — here of the love of wives for their husbands — and in one of the instances of its occurrence is brought into contrast with ἀγαπᾶν as a word of deeper intensity of significance: I Clem. i. 3: "Loving their own husbands as is meet";

[144] φιλαδελφία, φιλανθρωπία, φιλάνθρωπος, φιλαργυρέω, φιλαργυρία, φιλάργυρος, φιλοδέσποτος, φιλόζωος, φιλονεικία, φιλόνεικος, φιλοξενία, φιλόξενος, φιλοπονεῖν, φιλόσοφος, φιλοστοργία, φιλότεκνος, φιλοτιμία, φιλόϋλος: eighteen.

Polyc. "ad Philip.," iv. 2: "And, then, let us teach our wives also to walk in the faith that hath been given unto them, and in ἀγάπῃ and ἀγνείᾳ, στεργούσας their own husbands in all truth, and ἀγαπώσας all men equally in all chastity." Ἐρᾶν is in every instance used of "desiring" something or "desiring" to do something — in one case preparing the way for the famous exclamation, which has already been spoken of, "My Ἔρως has been crucified!"

Quite a different state of affairs meets the eye when we look at ἀγαπᾶν and its accompanying noun and verbal adjective. Ἀγαπᾶν occurs about seventy-nine times; ἀγάπη about ninety-four times; and ἀγαπητός about twenty-five times, of which seventeen are in the plural ἀγαπητοί. Ignatius (20, 40, 6) and I Clement (8, 27, 18) are the largest depositories of these terms; but ἀγαπᾶν and ἀγάπη at least are fairly well distributed through the whole series of writers.[145] Too much stress must not be laid upon the fact that no instances of the lower senses of ἀγαπᾶν, ἀγάπη occur; that, for example, in no single case is either term used of sexual love. There was little occasion to speak of sexual love in these writings. But it may be worth noting that it almost seems as if ἀγαπᾶν was felt as a contrast to sexual love. When the twelve virgins require Hermas to pass the night with them, at all events, they emphasize that it is to be as a brother and not as a husband; and they add, "Hereafter we will dwell with thee, for we ἀγαπῶμεν thee exceedingly" (*Sim.* ix. 11, 3; cf. *Vis.* i. 1, "I began to ἀγαπᾶν her as a sister"). This could scarcely have been said precisely thus, unless ἀγαπᾶν had been felt in the circles for which Hermas wrote as a word of higher than sexual suggestion. A somewhat similar impression may be made when we read in Polycarp ("Philip.," iv. 2) an exhortation to wives to walk in the faith that has been given them, στεργούσας their own husbands in all truth, and ἀγαποῦσας all men equally in all chastity." The words could not easily change places, and ἀγαπᾶν appears to be contrasted with even the purest sexual

[145] Ἀγαπητός is found only in I Clement (18 times), Ignatius (6), and the Martyrium of Polycarp, Hermas, and the Didache (each once). Ἀγαπητοί is almost a *peculium* of I Clement (15 times to Ignatius' 2).

love. Saying this, however, is in any event saying too little for these special writings. The usage of ἀγαπᾶν and ἀγάπη alike in them is at the top of their applications. They are here very distinctly words of ethical and spiritual import. This too, no doubt, finds its account less in the implications of the words themselves than in the subjects dealt with in these writings. But it has this not unimportant significance with respect to the words themselves, that, when these high ethical and spiritual aspects of love were dealt with, it was, among the words for love, ἀγαπᾶν and ἀγάπη which suggested themselves to express them; and that with such inevitableness that only these terms were employed for the purpose. No doubt we must keep in consideration that ἀγαπᾶν and ἀγάπη were very distinctly the common words for love and may have been the first terms to suggest themselves for the expression of any kind of love. There were, however, other terms still in use, and they would have been employed had there been any unnaturalness in using ἀγαπᾶν, ἀγάπη in these high senses.

There is an occasional use of ἀγαπᾶν with the infinitive, to express what one "loves" or would "love" to do (e. g., Ign. "Trall.," iv. 2: "I *desire* to suffer"). But what is almost uniformly expressed by it is the love of the Christian proclamation in its three great exemplifications of the love of God or of Christ to man, the love of God's people to Him or to Christ, and the love of the Christian brethren to one another. Polycarp accordingly tells (iii. 3) the Philippians that Paul's letter to them had the power to build them up into the faith given to them, "which is the mother of us all, while hope followeth after, and love goeth before — love," he proceeds to explain, "towards God and Christ and towards our neighbor." Christians are "the children of love," as Barnabas phrases it; or as Polycarp calls Ignatius and his companions ("Philip.," i. *init.*) "the followers of the True Love," that is to say, of Christ, here called by the great title of 'Η Ἀληθῆς Ἀγάπη; and if they are to be imitators of Him who so loved us ("Diog.," x. 3), they must love," love in Christ," "love according to Jesus Christ." "Faith is the beginning, and love the end of life" (Ign. "Eph.," xiv. 1); "faith and love are all in all and nothing is preferred before them" (Ign. "Smyr.," vi. 1). As a typical passage, exhibiting the lofty sense which these terms had acquired in the familiar speech of these Christians, we may take perhaps the encomium on love which Clement pens to the Corinthians, inciting them to practice it in their own lives. It is full, it is true, of echoes of Paul's great hymn to love in the thirteenth chapter of his own First Letter to the Corinthians; but it is not less representative of the speech of the Apostolic Fathers on that account. "Let him that hath love in Christ," we read (c. 49), "fulfil the commandments of Christ. Who can declare the bond of the love of God? Who is sufficient to tell the majesty of its beauty? The height whereunto love exalteth is unspeakable. Love joineth us with God; love endureth all things, is longsuffering in all things. There is nothing vulgar, nothing arrogant in love. Love hath no divisions, love maketh no seditions, love doeth all things in concord. In love were all God's elect made perfect; without love nothing is well-pleasing to God; in love the Master took us unto Himself; for the love which He had towards us, Jesus Christ our Lord hath given His blood for us by the will of God, and His flesh for our flesh, and His life for our lives. Ye see, dearly beloved, how great and marvelous a thing is love, and there is no declaring its perfection. Who is sufficient to be found therein save those to whom God shall vouchsafe it?" It is this kind of love which, in the Apostolic Fathers, ἀγαπᾶν and ἀγάπη are practically exclusively used to express. "Oh the exceeding great φιλανθρωπία καὶ ἀγάπη of God" ("Diog.," ix. 2): "How wilt thou ἀγαπήσας Him that so προαγαπήσαντα thee!" (x. 2–3): "Now He that raised Him from the dead will raise us also if ἀγαπῶμεν the things that He ἠγά-πησεν" (Polyc. "Philip.," ii. 2). This is the circle through which the idea of love runs in them.

It ought perhaps to be mentioned before we leave the subject that in Ign. "Smyrn.," viii. 2 we have an instance of a usage of ἀγάπη created by Christianity and vocal with the significance which love had for Christianity. "It is not lawful," we read, "apart from the bishop either to baptize or ἀγάπην ποιεῖν" — that is to say, as the parallel with baptizing suggests, "celebrate the Lord's Supper." [146] The Lord's Supper was the feast of love. "I wish the bread of God," says Ignatius in another place ("Rom.," vii. 3), "which is the flesh of Christ, who was the seed of David; and I wish for a draught of His blood, which is love (ἀγάπη) incorruptible." And in yet another place ("Trall.," viii. 1): "Do ye, then, arm yourselves with gentleness and recover yourselves in faith, which is the flesh of the Lord, and in love (ἀγάπη) which is the blood of Jesus Christ." An extension of the usage of ἀγάπη like this is vocal with the place which the conception and the word had taken in the Christian community.

The New Testament stands between the Septuagint and the Apostolic Fathers, receiving from the one, giving to the other, sharing the particular type of Greek common to both. In this type of Greek, ἀγαπᾶν, ἀγάπη had become the general terms for the expression of love; and the Greek of the New Testament participates fully in this usage. Ἀγαπᾶν occurs about a hundred and forty-one times in the New Testament, ἀγάπη about a hundred and eighteen times, and ἀγαπητός about sixty-one times, while φιλεῖν (excluding three instances in which it means "to kiss": Mat. xxvi. 48, Mk. xiv. 44, Lk. xxii. 47) occurs only about twenty-two times, φιλία but once, and even φίλος only about twenty-nine times. Ἐρᾶν, ἔρως, and στέργειν, στοργή do not occur at all. It is perhaps worth while also to observe the distribution of the several terms through the New Testament. The book of Acts contains no one of them except φίλος (x. 24, xix. 31, xxvii. 3) and ἀγαπητός (xv. 25).[147] Hebrews has ἀγαπᾶν and ἀγάπη each twice; James ἀγαπᾶν three times and φιλία once — the only occurrence of φιλία in the New Testament; I Peter ἀγαπᾶν four times and ἀγάπη three times; II Peter ἀγαπᾶν twice and ἀγάπη twice; Jude ἀγαπᾶν once and ἀγάπη three times. Φιλεῖν does not occur in Hebrews or any of the Catholic Epistles; φιλία only in James. In the Synoptic Gospels ἀγαπᾶν occurs twenty-three times (8, 6, 9), φιλεῖν five times (4, 0, 1); ἀγάπη only twice (once each in Matthew

[146] See Jude 12 and II Peter ii. 13, and compare Lightfoot's note on the passage.

[147] It contains besides only φιλανθρώπως, xxvii. 3.

and Luke). The great depository of ἀγαπᾶν is John: it occurs thirty-seven times in the Gospel, twenty-eight times in the First Epistle, and twice and once in II and III John respectively — making sixty-eight times in all, to which may be added four times in Revelation. Next to John comes Paul, with thirty-three occurrences, distributed through all the epistles except Philippians, Philemon, II Timothy, and Titus. Ephesians is the most copiously supplied of the Epistles (ten times), and Romans next (seven times). With ἀγάπη the tables are turned. It is predominately a Pauline term, being found in every epistle without exception (I Cor. fourteen, II Cor. ten, Eph. ten, showing the highest figures), and totaling seventy-eight occurrences. Over against this copious use by Paul, it is found in John only twenty-eight times (Gospel seven times, I John eighteen, II John two, III John one, to which Rev. adds two). Ἀγαπητός also is a Pauline term, its sixty-one occurrences being distributed thus: Synoptic Gospels nine times, Acts once, Paul twenty times, Hebrews once, James three times, Peter eight times, Jude three times, John's Epistles ten times. It is particularly in the Gospels that φιλεῖν is used: in John thirteen times, and in the Synoptics five (4, 0, 1). In all of Paul's epistles it occurs but twice, twice also in Revelation, and nowhere else in the New Testament. We may perhaps generalize by saying that ἀγαπᾶν is distributed fairly evenly through the New Testament with some accumulation in the Gospel and First Epistle of John; that ἀγάπη is predominantly a Pauline word with a secondary depository in I John; and that φιλεῖν belongs particularly to the Gospel of John and after that to the Synoptics.

The highly preponderating use of ἀγαπᾶν, ἀγάπη in the New Testament is not due primarily to the deliberate selection of these terms by the writers of the New Testament as the fittest to express the high idea of love to which they had to give expression, though they were the fittest of Greek words to express this high idea and had moreover been prepared to express it by their usage in the Septuagint.[148] It is due primarily to the cur-

---

[148] E. F. Gelpke, "Theolog. Studien und Kritiken," 1849, pp. 646 f., gives the following account of these words as they came to the hands of the writers of

rency of these terms in the Greek native to the New Testament writers as the general terms for love — for love at its highest, no doubt, but also for love at its lowest. There can be little doubt that, had the New Testament writers had occasion to speak at large of sexual love — to write, for example, a series of narratives like those of Genesis xxiv. and Judges xvi. and I Samuel xiii. — they would have employed ἀγαπᾶν and ἀγάπη in them just as the writers of the Septuagint have done. Ballantine is so far quite right, when, criticizing Trench's suggestion that the explanation of the absence of ἔρως, ἐρᾶν, ἐραστής from the New Testament is, no doubt, in part "that these words" by the corrupt use of the world "had become so steeped in earthly sensuous passion," carried such an atmosphere of this about with them, "that the truth of God abstained from the defiling contact with them," he declares [149] that "This family of words was not used for Christian love for the very same reason that ἐπιθυμέω and its family were not used, namely, because they were not the general words in Hellenistic Greek for *love*." When he proceeds to say that "they were not used in their own

the New Testament. "The older profane writers know only the verb and adjective, not, however, the noun, precisely in which it was that the Christian writers found the abstract expression, recurring on every page, of the sentiment which bound all believers together. The verb, moreover, is found already with profane writers in the purer sense of reverential love, although it was later interchanged also, when conceived sensuously, with φιλεῖν, amare, the expression for personal affection. This usage is not only recognized in the LXX, where the word, it must be confessed, is used even more sensuously, and nevertheless also of the more sacred affection (Gen. xxii. 2); and again in the New Testament; but also it receives, first in this connection, its full content, as this follows of itself from the most Christian of all Christian declarations, I John iv. 8, ὁ θεὸς ἀγάπη ἐστίν (the abstract term is used, with the sense that God is the personal Love, presenting Himself personally), and from the religion of the spirit freed from all particularism and all sensuous elements. The word acquired, however, an entirely new, peculiarly Christian, sense, still further in the new demonstration of love conditioned by the deepened sentiment of love. Accordingly the word is used (1) of the love of God for Jesus and of Jesus for God, and of the love of both for men, and then again of the love of men for God and Christ, derived from the love of God and Christ, and of the love of men for one another inseparable from this as its vital basis; and then (2) of the actual, powerfully arising manifestation of love, the loving conduct in word and deed, I John iii. 1, cf. James iv, 8."

[149] "Bibliotheca Sacra," July 1889, p. 533.

proper senses simply because there was no occasion to refer to
those ideas by *any* words," he is right in the main affirmation,
but wrong, as we have seen, in seeming to assign sexual love to
ἐρᾶν, ἔρως as their "proper sense." The simple truth is that the
New Testament writers use ἀγαπᾶν, ἀγάπη to express the idea
of love because it was the word for love current in their circle
and lying thus directly in their way. They do not use ἐρᾶν, ἔρως,
στέργειν, στοργή because they had no such occasion, in speaking
of love, to throw up into emphasis the peculiar implications of
these words — of passion or of nature — as to demand their
employment. So far as such occasion arose, they had no difficulty with the words (Rev. xii. 10, φιλόστοργος; Rom. i. 31,
II Tim. iii. 3, ἄστοργος). They do not push φιλεῖν into the background; they found it in the background, — from which they
do not draw it, not because they looked upon it as a base word,
but because it had become too inexpressive a word to meet their
needs, especially since the Septuagint had communicated to the
ordinarily current word for love additional shades of suggestion
which enlarged its range of application precisely on the side on
which the New Testament writers desired to speak of love.
When φιλεῖν served their purpose better than ἀγαπᾶν, they used
φιλεῖν; but this use could not escape being exceptional just because ἀγαπᾶν had become the general word for love, and the
Septuagint had prepared it for New Testament use by filling
it with the content which the New Testament writers most
needed to express.

In the actual use which the New Testament writers make of
φιλεῖν it is made evident that its distinctive suggestions have
not faded out of sight; it is because of these distinctive suggestions that the New Testament writers occasionally make use of
it — as it was doubtless because of them that it maintained its
shrunken, if we cannot yet say its precarious, existence in the
current speech of the day. It is meaningless for Gildersleeve to
say that "The larger use of ἀγαπᾶν in Christian writers is perhaps due to the avoidance of φιλεῖν in the sense of 'kissing,'"
although Moulton and Milligan think it worth while to quote
the remark. And we can hardly account for Woolsey's sugges-

tion that "The increased use of ἀγάπη and its family in the Septuagint and in the Christian Scriptures is probably to be accounted for by the frequent use of φιλεῖν and its derivatives in denoting sensual love, and in covering up foul acts under the veil of words so common and important." 'Αγαπᾶν had itself been current from its earliest recorded usage in senses as external as "kissing"; and in the Septuagint itself it is employed in senses quite as foul as any for which φιλεῖν was ever used. Ballantine's remark is again quite apposite: "If husbands are commanded to ἀγαπᾶν their wives because the other verb would have suggested sensual passion, it is unaccountable that wives should be commanded to be φίλανδροι (Tit. ii. 4). If men are not commanded to φιλεῖν God, as being inappropriate, it is strange that they are condemned for not being φιλόθεοι (II Tim. iii. 4)." The plain fact is that φιλεῖν had come to be comparatively little used because, ἀγαπᾶν having superseded it as the general term for love in common use, there was very little need for it. It had shrunken from the general term for love to the designation of a particular aspect of love, and was called for only when this particular aspect of love required emphasizing.

It is only right, then, that we should look, in each instance of its employment, for the reason why φιλεῖν is preferred instead of the prevailing ἀγαπᾶν. That such a reason exists it is natural to assume. It is not easy to believe that a body of writers have deserted their habitual usage in a few instances without some reason for it. This reason may, no doubt, be found in merely grammatical or purely rhetorical considerations, or in personal habits of speech belonging to individual writers; but it may also be rooted in the underlying implications of the words themselves by which a rarer form is given the advantage in special circumstances. It may not be easy to trace it; but pure caprice is not to be lightly assumed; and ordinarily some special fitness in the language actually employed may at least be suggested, if not actually shown. We may take the usage of Paul as an example. It is sheerly incredible that he should desert his copious use of ἀγαπᾶν (ἀγάπη) in just two instances in favor of φιλεῖν without some reason for it. We may perhaps see that reason in the more pointed suggestion of personal predilection which φιλεῖν conveys. This appears fairly clear in the case of I Cor. xvi. 22, when we observe that οὐ φιλεῖ there, in accordance with a frequent usage of οὐ in conditional clauses, coalesce in a sharply positive notion, so that we are to read, not "If anyone falls short of really loving the Lord," but, "If anyone not-loves the Lord" — that is to say, "hates Him." Φιλεῖν rather than ἀγαπᾶν is the proper word to use, remarks T. C. Edwards, because it expresses a natural affection, in this negative statement a personal antipathy. Paul "is thinking of a deep-seated antipathy, a malignant hatred of Jesus Christ": "If anyone turns away from Jesus Christ with antipathy." It is not of failure to love Jesus Christ supremely of which Paul is speaking; it is of failure to love Him at all. It is more difficult to see our way in Tit. iii. 15, "Salute them that love us in faith"; but the same general influences may not improperly be assumed to have determined the language here too. As Huther remarks, φιλεῖν may here mark "the inner personal relation." In other words, Paul is sending greetings to certain personal friends in the Christian body. The addition of ἐν πίστει is not fatal to this assumption. It may mean no more than that these friends of Paul's were also fellow-Christians (cf. for the order of the words, Eph. vi. 1).

When we turn to the larger body of instances which confront us in the Synoptic Gospels, we find ourselves in the same atmosphere. Only in a single passage has φιλεῖν a personal object, Mat. x. 37: "He that loveth father or mother more than me is not worthy of me; and he that loveth son or daughter more than me is not worthy of me." Th. Zahn's comment seems to meet the case: "Jesus declares him unworthy of Him, who, in the case of the decision under consideration, permits love to parents and children to obtain the upper hand of love to Jesus (cf. viii. 21 ff.). Through the contrast with kindred, to whom we are bound by natural love, already prepared for in verse 25 (οἰκιακοί, as verse 36), it is brought about that Jesus here represents the right relation to His person by φιλεῖν, not by ἀγαπᾶν (v. 43–46, vi. 24), because only φιλεῖν clearly expresses the hearty affection (*Zuneigung*) which roots in affinity — whether bodily or elective." That is to say the love of Jesus' people for Him is expressed here by φιλεῖν because thus it is brought expressly into comparison with the love of affinity: this spiritual affinity is to take precedence of all other. What He is saying is, not that His people must give their supreme love to Him rather than others, but that they must manifest in their conduct that their fundamental inclination, "drawing," is to Him above others; He must be supremely attractive to them.

In the other Synoptic instances φιλεῖν is followed by the accusative of the thing (Mt. xxiii. 6, Lk. xx. 46), or in one case (Mt. vi. 5) construed in the same sense with the infinitive — the only passage in the New Testament in which either φιλεῖν or ἀγαπᾶν is construed with the infinitive. From the point of view of the classical usage, φιλεῖν is properly used in these passages; and it bears its ordinary classical sense in them [150] — which is not quite the sense that ἀγαπᾶν bears in similar constructions. In its best classical usage, ἀγαπᾶν with the accusative of the thing means not so much to like a thing, to be pleased with it, as to content oneself with it; with the infinitive not so much to be wont to do a thing, as to put up with it. Meyer is perfectly right, then, when he finds φιλεῖν the proper word at Mt. vi. 5, and comments: "*They have pleasure in it*, they *love* to do it — a usage frequently met with in the classical writers." We must note, however, that ἀγαπᾶν with the infinitive had already acquired this sense in the Septuagint (e. g., Ps. xxxiii. 13, Prov. xx. 16, Jer. v. 31, xiv. 10), and is repeatedly used in the New Testament with the accusative of the thing in the sense of liking, taking pleasure in,[151] not of contenting ourselves with, putting up with; and indeed we have merely to turn to Lk. xi.

---

[150] Schmidt remarks (p. 479): "Even when applied to things, φιλεῖν retains its ordinary meaning and designates therefore the satisfaction in things which are pleasing (φιλία) to us, the possession of which, or contact with which, is pleasant to us. Even evil or contemptible things are included, Aristotle, "Eth. Nic.," 8.2.1: 'For it appears that not everything is loved, but τὸ φιλητόν, and this is the good, or the pleasant, or the useful.'"

[151] Lk. xi. 43, Jno. iii. 19, xii. 43, II Thess. ii. 16, I Pet. iii. 10, II Pet. ii. 15, I Jno. ii. 15, Rev. xii. 11, 15.

43 to find ἀγαπᾶν instead of φιλεῖν in a passage which seems the exact parallel of Mt. xxiii. 6, although φιλεῖν is used at Lk. xx. 46. We are in the presence, here, apparently of an unsettled usage. It seems still to be more natural to use φιλεῖν in the sense of liking things, or of liking to do things; but ἀγαπᾶν is fast encroaching upon it in this usage also.

So long as φιλεῖν remained in use at all in this sense, one would think it would be inevitable in such a passage as Rev. xxii. 15: "Without are the dogs, and the sorcerers, and the fornicators, and the murderers, and the idolaters, and everyone that loveth and doeth a lie." It is a personal affinity with the false, inward kinship with it, leading to its outward practice, which is intimated; [152] and this is even more emphatically asserted if the other order of the words be adopted, and the progress of thought be from the mere doing of a lie to personal identification with it. The use of φιλεῖν in Rev. iii. 19 is probably determined by the contrast between the treatment described and the sentiment asserted. What our Lord is saying is that reproof and chastening from Him are proof, not of hatred but of love; and it was natural to employ in this assertion the most personal and therefore in such a connexion the most emotional term for love. The emphasis on the pronoun should not be neglected: "As for me, whomsoever *I* love, I reprove and chasten." The most intimate relations are suggested, and the most intimate feelings are naturally put forward: it is the love of a parent disciplining his child for its good which is pictured. And the use of φιλεῖν is all the more striking, that in the underlying passage, Prov. iii. 12, "For whom the Lord loves, He rebukes," ἀγαπᾶν is the word employed. There is an advance made even on this affecting passage of Proverbs in tenderness of expression.[153]

It is especially in the Gospel of John that φιλεῖν occurs

---

[152] Cf. Swete *in loc.*: "ὁ φιλῶν goes deeper than ὁ ποιῶν; he who loves falsehood is in his nature akin to it, and has through his love of it proved his affinity to Satan, who is ὁ πατὴρ αὐτοῦ (Jno. viii. 44)."

[153] Cf. Swete *in loc.*: φιλῶ (Bengel: Philadelphiensem ἠγάπησεν, Laodicensem φιλεῖ) is perhaps deliberately preferred to the less emotional and less human ἀγαπῶ (i. 5, iii. 9) notwithstanding the use of the latter in Prov. iii. 12 (LXX. ὃν γὰρ ἀγαπᾷ Κύριος ἐλέγχει), which supplies the groundwork of the thought."

(thirteen times), as indeed does ἀγαπᾶν also (thirty-seven times).[154] In about one out of every four instances of the occurrence of a verb for love in this Gospel, φιλεῖν is employed; the proportion is even greater for Revelation, no doubt (one out of three), and not very much less in the Synoptic Gospels, but the absolute number of occurrences in these cases is not large enough to be impressive. In all of its occurrences in John's Gospel, moreover, except one (xii. 25), φιλεῖν has a personal object. The single instance in which it is construed with the accusative of a thing (xii. 25) is altogether similar to the instances of like construction in the Synoptic Gospels and Revelation. Loving is brought in it into sharp contrast with hating: "He who loves his life shall lose it, and he who hates his life in this world shall preserve it unto eternal life." It is a proverbial saying of universal application, adduced here in support of the solemn declaration of the preceding verse that fruit-bearing comes through sacrifice. The loving of life spoken of, then, is such pleasure in it, such a fixing of the heart upon it and doting on it, that nothing else comes into consideration in comparison with it. Pure joy in living, says our Lord in effect, is a short-sighted policy, because there lies something beyond this living which is absorbing our attention. Undoubtedly φιλεῖν is the appropriate word to express this idea, and has a pungency when employed to express it which the more customary ἀγαπᾶν would lack.

In one of the instances in John in which the object is personal, the subject is "the world"; and those whom the world is said to love are described as "its own" (xv. 19): "If the world

---

[154] A fresh study of ἀγαπᾶν and φιλεῖν, especially in John, by Sally Neil Roach taking its point of departure from G. B. Stevens, "Johannine Theology," Ch. xi.; is printed in *The Review and Expositor*, 1913, x. pp. 531 ff. Her discrimination of terms is as follows (p. 533): "'Αγαπᾶν (and the same is true of the noun, ἀγάπη) carries with it *invariably* the idea of the rights or the good of the object, sought at the cost of the subject, while φιλεῖν as uniformly suggests the pleasure of the subject as associated with and derived from the object." She speaks of this as looking upon ἀγαπᾶν as the altruistic, and φιλεῖν as the egoistic term for love. Perhaps the same general idea might be better expressed by distinguishing the two as the love of benevolence and the love of complacency; and perhaps better still as the love of regard and the love of delight. All the Johannine passages in which φιλεῖν occurs are examined with a view to validating the suggested distinction.

hateth you, ye know that it hath hated me first: if ye were of
the world, the world would love its own; but because ye are not
of the world, but I have chosen you out of the world, therefore
the world hateth you." The appropriateness of φιλεῖν here is
striking: it is very especially adapted to express the love of
inner affinity — the love that grows out of the perception of
something in the object especially attractive to the subject;
and inner affinity is precisely what is emphasized here. Had
ἀγαπᾶν been used, the simple fact of the love would be stated,
and the fitness, inevitableness, of the love and hatred spoken
of would have remained unexpressed.[155]

In two other instances what is spoken of is the love of the
man Jesus for a friend (xi. 3, 36, cf. xi. 11): "Behold, he whom
Thou lovest is sick"; "Behold, how He loved him!" Here, too,
the use of φιλεῖν is so obviously appropriate as to seem inevitable; the love of friendship might almost seem to be the special
field of φιλεῖν. Ἀγαπᾶν of course, could have been employed
in its stead. It is actually used in xi. 5, where the Evangelist
states the simple objective fact, for the purpose of his narrative: "Now Jesus ἠγάπα Martha, and her sister, and Lazarus";
that is to say, Jesus felt sincere regard for them. Φιλεῖν is used
when the words are taken off of the lips of the anxious sisters
in their petition for aid, and of the Jews when they observed
Jesus' tears. It emphasizes the personal intimacy of the affection, such personal intimacy as justified the appeal to Him for
prompt aid, and His tears at the grave.[156] It is Jesus' human
heart which is here unveiled to us.

Quite close to these instances lies the employment of φιλεῖν
in xx. 2 to express the affection of Jesus for John and Peter.
Mary Magdalene, we are told, when she saw the stone removed
from the grave on the Resurrection morn, "runneth and cometh
to Simon Peter and the other disciple whom Jesus loved

[155] Cf. Karl Horn, "Abfassung, Geschichtlichkeit und Zweck vom Evang.
des Johannes, Kap. 21," 1904, p. 170: "In xv. 19, it is said very significantly:
'If ye were of the world, ὁ κόσμος would love its own'; therefore natural inclination
(Zuneigung) to that which is of kindred nature and has sprung from the same root
is what is expressed."

[156] This is excellently shown by Horn, as above.

(ἐφίλει)" — where it seems most natural to understand both disciples to be described as loved by Jesus.[157] "The disciple whom Jesus ἠγάπα" is the standing description of John in the latter part of the Gospel (xiii. 23, xix. 26, xxi. 7, 20); and obviously ἠγάπα is used in this description of intimate personal affection, and not of what we may speak of as the official love of Jesus for His disciples or of the saving love of the Redeemer for His children. Woolsey does not go too far, when, having regard to the imperfect tense, he remarks: [158] "It was an intimacy between the Master and the disciple of no short acquaintance. . . . He loved him with a continuous love." It has disturbed the commentators, therefore, that in the one instance of xx. 2, ἐφίλει has displaced the ἠγάπα. One has been tempted to say it is because Peter is included with John in this one instance, to which it has been added that Peter was now under a cloud. Another has gone a step further and suggested that it is because "the beloved disciple himself had temporarily fallen into unbelief and was for the moment not worthy of the higher love" expressed by ἀγαπᾶν.[159] These suggestions take for granted that ἀγαπᾶν, even in such a connexion, conveys a "higher" sense than φιλεῖν. Such an assumption underlies Woolsey's description of Jesus' love for John, as expressed in the ἠγάπα, not only in such terms as this: "He discerned in His disciple lovely traits. . . . His love for John was a tried, strong, personal love, such as the man Jesus could feel for some souls with especial endowments which few possessed"; but also in such as these: "And it was a religious love which no one could so correctly feel as He who had an intuitive knowledge of hearts. . . . It was an earthly love of a heavenly soul." [160] Φιλεῖν, it is suggested, might be used to denote such love as this, but it could not express it; ἀγαπᾶν alone could express it, and would be the only natural word to employ in order to express it. This seems to leave the question, Why, then, is ἠγάπα replaced by ἐφίλει in

[157] So Westcott in loc.: cf. what Woolsey says, Andover Review, August 1885, p. 166.
[158] As cited, p. 167.
[159] E. A. Abbott, "Johannine Vocabulary," p. 241, bottom (1728 p.).
[160] As cited, p. 167.

John xx. 2, more clamorous than ever. Woolsey's own explanation [161] is not very clear, and indeed does not profess to be. "It
is in this place," he says, "not altogether plain why ἐφίλει is
used instead of ἠγάπα. Meyer, in his remark on the passage, says
that ἐφίλει expresses the remembrance of Christ with a more
tender sensibility,[162] to which B. Weiss seems to assent. Westcott [163] in like manner thinks that a personal affection is more
strikingly shown than it would be by ἠγάπα. The Vulgate translates as elsewhere by *amabat*. All these explanations concur in
something like this: That Jesus was conceived of under the
power of a new affection." The meaning of this appears to be
that in the interval between the death of our Lord and their assurance that He had entered upon His heavenly dominion, the
disciples dropped into both thinking and speaking of Him from
the point of view of His humanity. This involves the assumptions that ἐφίλει is here employed from Mary Magdalene's
standpoint, or at least from the standpoint of the incident described, not from that of the Evangelist, writing after the
recovery of faith; and that ἠγάπα was a word of such high significance that it would be inappropriate to use it of a simple man's
affection for his friends. We transcribe, however, Woolsey's own
exposition of his not very clear meaning: "It was natural that,
when the Lord showed Himself again to His disciples, they
could not but feel a want of nearness and familiarity which
helped them in their earthly intercourse with Him. Until their
faith grew, and they believed more joyfully in their divine
Master, the human sight and presence were supports which
sustained them while away from Him. But ἀγαπῶ returns in
xxi. 15 and 20, as to the divine Saviour, as soon as the presence
of Jesus began to be apprehended again by the help of sight.

---

[161] P. 177.

[162] Meyer, E. T., ii, p. 367, says: "With ἐφίλει the recollection speaks with
more feeling." What he means is apparently that John, recording the events in
his Gospel, was at this point suffused with deeper feeling than he ordinarily felt
as the recollection rushed over him of the personal affection which Jesus showed
toward him "in the days of His flesh"; and this expressed itself in ἐφίλει.

[163] Westcott's actual phraseology is that ἐφίλει here "marks a personal affection."

Faith grew stronger, and the loss of Jesus' presence was an enlargement of the sway of the nobler principle, and was no more felt to be an absence."

Perhaps the difficulty we feel in accounting for ἐφίλει at John xx. 2 arises in large part from approaching the question from only one side. We begin with the ἠγάπα of xiii. 23, xix. 26, xxi. 7, 20, and ask why the alteration to ἐφίλει in xx. 2. Let us reverse the question, and ask why ἠγάπα is used in xiii. 23 and its companions. In itself considered, ἐφίλει is altogether in place in xx. 2; this is the proper word to express the love of friendship, however warm. What really needs accounting for is why in the parallel passages ἠγάπα is used instead. It is customary to think at once of the high connotations of ἀγαπᾶν, and to develop, as Woolsey does, the aspects of nobility which may be discovered in Jesus' love for John. It may be easier to say simply that, in the type of Greek employed in the New Testament, ἀγαπᾶν was the current word for love, and was consequently in place whenever love of any kind was spoken of; and that the only thing that is illustrated by the appearance of ἐφίλει in xx. 2 is the emergence on one occasion of the more exact term for the particular variety of love that is here in question. 'Εφίλει might have stood in xiii. 23 and its companions, and ἠγάπα might have stood in xx. 2; in the former case the more specific word would have been used in all the instances, in the latter the more general. We learn from the actual distribution of the usage nothing of the specific meaning of ἀγαπᾶν; but we do learn something of the specific meaning of φιλεῖν. If we demand that a reason shall be rendered for the replacing of the general by the specific term just at xx. 2 and nowhere else, we do not know that a satisfactory answer can be given. We can only say that such an explanation as Meyer's is not without plausibility — that the circumstances he was in the act of narrating flooded John's mind as he wrote with an especially tender reminiscence of his Master's human love for His disciples.

From a passage like John xxi. 15–17 we learn something of the specific meaning of both words. The two words appear here side by side in contrast with one another, with the inevitable result that what is distinctive of each is thrown into relief. That anyone should doubt that the words are used here in distinctive senses would seem incredible prior to experience. The list of those who have expressed such doubt, however, is neither short nor undistinguished, running as it does from Grotius to Gildersleeve.[164] It is, however, as Moulton and Milligan remark,[165] "in so severely simple a writer as John it is extremely hard to reconcile ourselves to a meaningless use of synonyms, where the point would seem to lie in the identity of the word employed." In point of fact, our Lord does not put to Peter three times over the same question. Altering the question progressively, He drives the probe into Peter's conscience deeper and deeper. On the first occasion Jesus asks him: "Simon, son of John, dost thou ἀγαπᾷς me more than these?" — have you a deeper devotion [166] to me than the rest of my disciples? In his answer, spoken in deep humility, the repentant Peter avoids all comparison with his fellows, and merely asseverates his personal love for his master: "Assuredly, Lord; thou knowest that I φιλῶ Thee." In His second question, Jesus accordingly omits the comparison, and asks of Peter only whether he himself has the requisite devotion to His person: "He saith to him again, a second time, Simon, son of John, ἀγαπᾷς me?" Again Peter responds in the same humble spirit as before, waiving the question of proper devotion, and asseverating only his personal affection: "Assuredly Lord; Thou knowest that I φιλῶ Thee." Then, the third time, Jesus pushes the probe to the bottom and demands of Peter with sharp directness and brevity whether he has any real affection for Him: "He saith to him the

[164] "Justin Martyr," 1877, p. 135. Among later writers of the same mind, cf. W. G. Ballantine, "Bibliotheca Sacra," July 1889, pp. 524 ff.; John A. Cross, *The Expositor*, 1893, iv, vii, pp. 312 ff.; Max Eberhardt, "Ev. Joh. c. 21: ein exegetischer Versuch," 1897, p. 52; cf. also G. B. Stevens, "The Johannine Theology," ch. xi.

[165] As cited, p. 2.

[166] Roach, as cited, p. 544, on her principle, paraphrases ἀγαπᾶν here, not inaptly: "Do you love Me so that you can surrender your life to My interests?"; and φιλεῖν, in Peter's response: "Yes, Lord, Thou knowest that my heart goes out to Thee and my pleasure is found in Thee." This is, clearly, what was really meant by the terms — however we arrive at it.

third time, Simon, son of John, dost thou φιλεῖς me?" "And Peter was grieved because He said to him this third time, Dost thou φιλεῖς me? and he saith to Him" (omitting this time the asseveration, "Assuredly," because the precise assertion he had to make had been called in question), "Lord, Thou knowest all things; Thou dost see" (surely, surely the Lord must see it!) "that I φιλῶ Thee."

Of course there is no question here of our Lord's question, "Dost thou ἀγαπᾷς me?" "sounding too cold to Peter," because all the pulses of his heart were beating with earnest affection toward his Lord.[167] It is "humility and a feeling of unworthiness which leads Peter to choose another expression."[168] He could not in his heart-broken penitence assert of himself the ἀγαπᾶν which he had not illustrated in his acts; but he could not be false to his deep sense of real affection. Ἀγαπᾶν and φιλεῖν emerge, therefore, as respectively the love of complete devotion and the love (as Meyer phrases it) "of personal heart emotion"; the love of surrendering obedience and the love (as Westcott phrases it) of "personal attachment," "the feeling of natural love." Th. Zahn supposes [169] that the question of our Lord to Peter had as one of its ends, "bringing him to the consciousness that the love of the Lord which is a mark of a right disciple and the spring of his duty-doing, is not a matter of natural temperament, but a fruit of victory over inborn nature."[170] Therefore he supposes Him, avoiding the term which expresses the product of the natural temperament, to ask Peter

[167] So Trench: so also Henry Burton, *The Expositor*, v, i. p. 462 (1895), who paraphrases ἀγαπᾶν here, as the broader and weaker word of the two, by, "Do you care for me?" and represents it as "too cold, too distant for Peter's passionate soul," who asserts that he does not merely "care for" but loves His Lord.

[168] So rightly Woolsey, as cited, p. 182.   [169] P. 684.

[170] Cf. A. Klöpper. *Zeitschrift für wiss. Theologie*, 1899, 42, p. 363, who supposes the contrast to be between the expression of a natural human inclination (φιλεῖν) and the efflux of such a love as might be expressed in Pauline phrase as ἀγάπη ἐν πνεύματι (Col. i. 8). In general he finds the distinction drawn by Schmidt from the classical writers valid for John also. Ἀγαπᾶν is, however, he says, almost always used in the higher, spiritual sense, iii. 35, x. 17, xiv. 21 (of God); xiii. 1, 23, xix. 26, xi. 5 (of Christ); viii. 42, xiii. 34, xiv. 15, 21 (of the disciples).

whether he loved Him in this way; whereas Peter clings to the simple asseveration of his natural personal love to Jesus — until our Lord is driven, in order to prove his heart fully, to challenge that also, and so to compel Peter to face the possibility that even this personal love for his master had failed. Whatever may be said of the details of this exposition, it is certainly sound so far as this: that in this conversation ἀγαπᾶν and φιλεῖν are brought into contrast as in a sense the higher and the lower love — although these terms are somewhat infelicitous and may be misleading; perhaps we would better say, as the love of reverent devotion and the love of emotional attachment. And what is of most importance to observe is that the term which bore in its bosom the implication of reverent devotion had become for the men of the New Testament age the general word for love, while the term which expressed in its native suggestion the love of emotional attachment was in process of passing out of use. It is difficult to overstate the importance of this fact for the ready expression of the new revelation of love which the New Testament brought, in terms of current speech. The term which it was most natural to use of love, and which was in most familiar use among the people for love, was a term of such native connotation that it readily received and intelligibly expressed the new revelation of love.

Three instances alone remain, in which φιλεῖν is used by John, and in these three instances it is used of love in its highest relations. In one of them it expresses the love of Christ's people for Him their divine Saviour (xvi. 27); in another, the love of the Father for His people (xvi. 27); in the last, the love of the Father for His Son (v. 20). Here we are scaling the heights, and are discovering that φιλεῖν is not too low a word to be applied to the love which God Himself feels, or the love to God's only Son, whether on the part of His people, or even on the part of His Father. It is quite clear that the intrinsic implication of φιλεῖν is not low, not to say evil. It is differentiated from ἀγαπᾶν fundamentally by the side from which it approaches love and the aspect in which it describes it. It is applicable to all love which can be approached from that side or viewed in that aspect. If it is prevailingly employed in the New Testament of the lower grades of love, that is only because these lower grades of love are more naturally approached from the point of view from which φιλεῖν approaches love, and the comparative rarity of its occurrences afforded few opportunities for its application to exercises of love of the higher order. We must bear in mind that ἀγαπᾶν is the general term for love in the New Testament, and the use of φιλεῖν is in any event exceptional. We could expect it to be employed for manifestations of love such as in their nature ἀγαπᾶν would naturally express, only in the few instances in which, for one reason or another, it was desirable to throw up into view the aspect which φιλεῖν naturally expresses.

An example is supplied by v. 20: "For the Father φιλεῖ the Son and showeth Him all that He doeth" — the only passage in the New Testament in which the love of the Father to the Son is described otherwise than by ἀγαπᾶν. As compared with iii. 35: "The Father ἀγαπᾷ the Son and hath given all things into His hand," this passage might, on a surface view, be taken as a mere repetition of that, with a meaningless change in the verb. Such is, however, not the case; the difference in the verbs corresponds with an important difference in the sense conveyed. The thought of iii. 35 is fixed on the greatness of the Son whom the Father honors by His love; in v. 20 it is fixed on the fatherly tenderness with which the Father loves the Son. Zahn very properly comments, therefore: "Φιλεῖν was more suitable here than the ἀγαπᾶν of the otherwise parallel sentence in iii. 35, because φιλεῖν recalls the natural affection of the human father to his son, or of a friend to a friend, in contrast, say, with the relation of the master to the servant (xv. 13–15)." [171]

A similar account may be given of the two instances in xvi. 27: "For the Father Himself loveth you, because ye have loved Me, and have believed that I have come forth from with the Father." This is the only place in the New Testament where

[171] Cf. Horn, as cited, p. 170: Φιλεῖν stands very suitably at v. 20: 'The Father loves the Son and shows Him all that He Himself does.' For here the more intimate relation of the filial relation of the Son to the Father is suggested, and at the same time, it is thought of as one wholly natural, resting on elective affinity. The Son 'can' nothing of Himself."

God is said to φιλεῖν man — though it would be better to say,
His children, for that enters into the case (but see Rev. iii. 19).
And this is also the only place where φιλεῖν is used "of the affection of the disciples for their Lord" (yet consult xxi. 17 and I
Cor. xvi. 22). Horn comments:[172] "The ὁ πατὴρ φιλεῖ ὑμᾶς of
xvi. 27 has a different meaning from iii. 16: οὕτως γὰρ ἠγάπησεν
ὁ θεὸς τὸν κόσμον. The latter is pitying love to the as yet unre-
deemed world, alien to God; the former is the natural pleasure
of the Father in His believers, approved as faithful."[173] He
adds in a note: "ἀγαπᾶν could, of course, stand here, as in the
similar passage, xvii. 23 'in order that the world may know
that Thou didst send me and didst love them even as Thou
didst love me'; but the sense would not be precisely the same."
What the difference in the sense of the two passages is, Horn
does not tell us — although that is the particular point under
discussion. Commenting on xvii. 23, he says, indeed: "In xvii.
23 the love of *the Father to the disciples* is spoken of as ἀγαπᾶν,
since it belongs to them (cf. 20) because of their faith in Jesus."
If that, however, would require ἀγαπᾶν to be used, it surely
would have been used in both passages. And it looks as if φιλεῖν
as the expression of the love of affinities would be equally appropriate in both passages. Perhaps it is enough to say that
ἀγαπᾶν is used as a matter of course in xvii. 23, as the general
word for love in common use — it needs no accounting for;
while φιλεῖν in xvi. 27 is used to emphasize the affinity between
God and His believers.

The abstract substantive connected with φιλεῖν — φιλία —
occurs only a single time in the New Testament, Jas. iv. 4,
where we read the arraignment: "Adulteresses! know ye not
that the φιλία of the world is enmity with God?" It is customary
to render φιλία here by "friendship," a course which the φίλος
of the next clause makes especially convenient. But it may be
well to guard against attributing to it too specific a notion. The
implication is that of finding one's pleasure, satisfaction, in

[172] As cited, p. 170.
[173] This is in effect the love of benevolence in distinction from the love of
complacency. Compare note 154.

the world, with a suggestion that by this one's affinity with the world is betrayed. The notion is similar to that expressed in John xv. 19: "If ye were of the world, the world would love its own" — for φιλία intimates mutual affection. To be at friends with the world is to love and to be loved by the world, to be bound by mutual ties to it. 'Αγαπᾶν would scarcely have expressed so much.

It may fairly be claimed that a survey of the passages in which φιλεῖν, φιλία occur leaves an impression of the naturalness of their use in these cases. But what should be kept ever fresh in mind is that the employment of them is highly exceptional, and rests on a background of a very copious use of ἀγαπᾶν, ἀγάπη — chiefly to express the great conceptions of love which permeate the Christian revelation. The equipment of the New Testament to express the idea of love consists, thus, in the possession in ἀγαπᾶν, ἀγάπη, of a high general term the native suggestion of which was a worthy one, and which had already been trained by the writers of the Septuagint to receive the great conceptions of revealed religion; and the possession by its side, of a subsidiary term by which, when occasion offered, a special aspect of love could be thrown into view — that aspect, to wit, in which love appears as the response of the soul to the perception of something which pleases it, is congenial to it, in the object. This is, to be sure, not as rich an equipment as was possessed by the Greek of the classical writers. It possessed four terms φιλεῖν, φιλία; ἐρᾶν, ἔρως; στέργειν, στοργή; ἀγαπᾶν, ἀγάπησις. But the comparative poverty of its terminology is offset in the case of the New Testament by the intrinsic superiority of its general term for love, ἀγαπᾶν, and by the higher content which it had acquired by its employment to express the conceptions of love embodied in the divine revelation. We must guard also against supposing that the resources for its expression of loving activities were absolutely exhausted by these, its direct vehicles. There were other terms which it might call to its aid when it wished to speak of love in one or another of its active exercises. There were such terms, for example, as οἰκτείρω, ἐλεέω, σπλαγχνίζομαι, with their accompany-

ing substantives, and above all there was χάρις. As it was this
aspect of love — love in gracious action — that the New Testament writers had most occasion to celebrate, their vocabulary
was not quite so restricted as it sounds, when we say that only
ἀγαπᾶν, ἀγάπη, with an exceptional use of φιλεῖν, φιλία, lay at
their disposal.

It does not fall within our present purpose, however, to
discuss the number and variety, or the nature and use, of such a
subsidiary vocabulary. Let it only be further noted that compounds in φιλ- are in the New Testament, as in the Greek
literature of all ages, numerous,[174] and that some of these compounds were significant, on one side or another, for the expression of love. We may mention, for example, such as φιλαδελφία
(five times), φιλάδελφος (once), φίλανδρος (once), φιλανθρωπία
(twice), φιλάνθρωπος (once), φιλόθεος (once), φιλοξενία (twice),
φιλόξενος (three times), φιλόστοργος[175] (once), φιλότεκνος (once).
By the aid of such forms a number of modifications of the idea
of love are given expression. After all said, however, it is not
the variety of the vehicles for the expression of love for which
the New Testament is notable, but the depth and height of the
conception of love which it is able to express through its fundamental terms, ἀγαπᾶν and ἀγάπη. The great fact which comes to
view is that, in the providence of God, the noblest word which
the Greek language afforded for the expression of love came into
its hands as the natural term for it to use to express its conception of love, and that, as already trained to express love at the
height of its conception by its use for that purpose in the Septuagint version of the Old Testament.

LITERATURE. — J. H. Heinrich Schmidt, "Synonymik der
griechischen Sprache," III, 1879, pp. 474–491 (= § 136: on
ἐρᾶν, φιλεῖν, στέργειν, ἀγαπᾶν). Edward Meredith Cope, on
στοργή, ἔρως, φιλεῖν, ἀγαπᾶν, in "The Rhetoric of Aristotle,

[174] Add to those mentioned in the text: φιλάγαθος, φιλαργυρία, φιλάργυρος,
φιλήδονος, φιλονεικία, φιλόνεικος, φιλοπρωτεύω, φιλοσοφία, φιλόσοφος, φιλοτιμέομαι, φι-
λοφρόνως, φιλόφρων.
[175] Consult on φιλόστοργος in the New Testament, E. Hoehne, Zeitschrift f.
k. Wissenschaft und k. Leben, 1882 (III.) p. 6.

with a Commentary," 1877, v. i, pp. 292–296 (printed also in the *Journal of Philology*, v. i, No. 1 (1868), pp. 88–93). J. B. Lightfoot, in *The Cambridge Journal of Classical and Sacred Philology*, v. iii, (1857), No. 7, pp. 92 ff. (see also Lightfoot's comment on Ignatius, "Rom.," vii, p. 222). R. C. Trench, "Synonyms of the New Testament," 9th ed., 1880, xii, on ἀγαπάω, φιλέω. J. A. H. Tittmann, "Remarks on the Synonyms of the N. T.," E. T. in "The Biblical Cabinet," v. iii, 1833, pp. 90–97. Hermann Cremer, "Biblisch-theologisches Wörterbuch der Neutestamentlichen Gräcität," 10th ed., 1915, *sub voc.* E. Buonaiuti, "I vocaboli d'amore nel Nuovo Testamento," in the "Rivista Storico-critica di Scienze Teologiche," v. v, 1909, pp. 257–264. E. Höhne, "Zum Neutestamentlichen Sprachgebrauch: 1. Ἀγαπᾶν, φιλεῖν, σπλαγχνίζεσθαι," in Luthardt's *Zeitschrift für k. Wissenschaft und k. Leben*, III, 1882, pp. 6–19. K. A. G. von Zezschwitz, "Profangräcität und biblischer Sprachgeist," 1859, p. 62. W. G. Ballantine, "Lovest Thou Me?" in "Bibliotheca Sacra," July 1889, v. xlvi, pp. 524–542. Sally Neil Roach, "Love in Its Relation to Service," in *The Review and Expositor*, 1913, v. x, pp. 531–553. T. D. Woolsey, "The Disciple Whom Jesus Loved," in *The Andover Review*, iv. 1885, August, pp. 163–185. G. A. Deissmann, "Bible Studies," E. T., 1901, pp. 198 ff. W. M. Ramsay, *The Expository Times*, ix. p. 568. Fr. Vermeil, "Étude sur le 21, Chap. de l'Évang. selon S. Jean," 1861. John A. Cross, "On St. John xxi. 15–17," in *The Expositor*, iv. vii., 1893, pp. 312–320. Henry Burton, "The Breakfast on the Shore," in *The Expositor* v. i, 1895, pp. 450–472. A. Klöpper, "Das 21. Kap. des 4. Evang. erläutert," in *Zeitschrift für wiss. Theologie*, 1899, pp. 337–381. Max Eberhardt, "Evang. Joh. c. 21; ein exeget. Versuch," 1897. K. Horn, "Abfassung, Geschichtlichkeit und Zweck vom Evang. des Johannes, Kap. 21.," 1904, pp. 167–171. R. H. Strachan, "The Appendix to the Fourth Gospel," in *The Expositor*, viii, vii, 1914, pp. 263 ff. H. W. Magoun, "The Bible Champion," Oct. and Nov. 1919, pp. 404 ff., 446 ff.

XV

THE PROPHECIES OF ST. PAUL

THE PROPHECIES OF ST. PAUL [1]

I. — I AND II THESSALONIANS

THE whole teaching, whether oral or written, of the Apostles of the New Testament, was essentially prophetic. St. Paul, in entire harmony with the Old Testament conception, defines a prophet to be one who "knows mysteries and knowledge" (I Cor. xiii. 2) and "speaks to men edification and exhortation and consolation" (I Cor. xiv. 3). This is a fair description of his own work; his Epistles are full of mysteries and knowledge, and speak to men edification, strengthening, and comfort. Among the mysteries which they declare — the word, we must remember, does not denote something inherently inscrutable, but only something as yet unknown and needing to be revealed — there are not lacking some that have to do with the future. We may properly speak, therefore, of Paul's prophecies, even in that narrow sense in which the word is popularly used, and which makes it synonymous with predictions. It is in this sense, indeed, although under a mild protest, that we use it in these papers. Our purpose is to study the predictions of Paul.

We begin with his earliest writings, the Epistles to the Thessalonians, which were written at Corinth in A.D. 52 and 53. As is well known to every careful reader of the New Testament, these Epistles are also the richest in predictions of all Paul's writings. It is not too much to say that their main burden is the Coming of the Lord. To explanations concerning this, their only didactic portions are given; and, in the first Epistle at least, a constant allusion to it is woven like a golden thread throughout its whole texture, and each section, whatever its subject, is sure to reach its climax in a reference to it (i. 10; ii. 19; iii. 13; v. 23). This seems strange to some. And it has been suggested, either that the Apostle in his early ministry made

[1] From *The Expositor*, 3d ser. v. iv, 1886, pp. 30–44, 131–148, 439–452.

more of the Second Advent in his teaching than growing wisdom
permitted him to do later; or else, that at this particular period,
amid the special trials of his work — the persecutions in Macedonia, the chill indifference at Athens, the discouragements
that met him at Corinth — he had his heart turned more than
was usual with him to the blessed consolation of a Christian's
expectation of the coming glory. Both of these explanations are
entirely gratuitous. A sufficient reason for this marked peculiarity lies at the hand of all in that other fact that distinguishes
these letters from all their fellows — they are the only letters
that have come down to us, which were addressed to an infant
community just emerged from heathenism.

For it is undeniable that the staple of Paul's preaching to
the Gentiles was God and the Judgment. When addressing
Jews he could appeal to prophecy, and he preached Jesus to
them as Him whom all the prophets pointed unto, the Messiah
whom God had graciously promised. But with Gentiles he could
appeal only to conscience; and he preached Jesus to them as
Him through whom God would judge the world in righteousness, whereof He hath given assurance to all men in that He
hath raised Him from the dead. The address on the Areopagus,
which was delivered only a few months before I Thessalonians
was written, admirably illustrates how the Apostle tried to
reach the consciences of his heathen hearers; and the totality
of the message delivered in it was God (Acts xvii. 24–29) and
the Judgment (Acts xvii. 30, 31). But if Christ coming for
judgment was thus the very centre and substance of Paul's
proclamation to the Gentiles, it would not be strange if he had
dwelt upon it to the Thessalonians also. And that he had
preached just in this strain to them, when, so shortly before
writing this letter, he was with them, he tells us himself (I
Thess. i. 9, 10). For, what he chiefly thanks God for in their
case is that they "turned unto God from idols" in order to do
two things: — "serve the living and true God," and "await
patiently His Son from the heavens, whom He raised from the
dead, Jesus, our deliverer from the coming wrath." The parallel
with the speech on Mars' Hill is precise; it almost looks as if

the Apostle had repeated at Athens the sermon that had been so effective at Thessalonica.

But we not only learn thus how it happens that Paul dwells so much on the Second Advent when writing to the Thessalonians, but we learn also what is much more important, — how he himself thought of the Advent and in what aspect he proclaimed it. Plainly to him it was above all things else the Judgment. It was the Judgment Day that he announced in its proclamation; and this was the lever with which he prized at Gentile consciences. "The day in which God will judge the world in righteousness" was what he proclaimed to the Athenians, and that it was just this that was in mind in I Thess. i. 10 is evident from the office assigned to the expected Jesus, — "the Deliverer from the coming wrath." In harmony with this, every passage in which the Second Advent is adverted to in these Epistles conceives of it pointedly as the Judgment Day. The Apostle's eager desire for the purity and sanctification of his readers is always referred to the Advent: he wishes to have them to boast of before the Lord Jesus at His coming (I Thess. ii. 19), — he prays that their hearts may be established unblameworthy in holiness before God at the coming of our Lord Jesus (I Thess. iii. 13), — he beseeches the God of peace to preserve them in their whole being and all their faculties blameless, at the coming of our Lord Jesus Christ (I Thess. v. 23), — he declares that the Day of the Lord will bring sudden destruction upon the wicked (I Thess. v. 3), and will draw a sharp line in justice between the good and bad (II Thess. i. 9). He speaks of the Advent freely as the "Day of the Lord" (I Thess. v. 2, 4; II Thess. i. 10), a term which from Joel down had stood in all prophecy as the synonym of the final judgment.

The most important passage in this point of view is II Thess. i. 6–10, where the matter is not only treated at large, but the statements are explicit. Here the declaration is distinctly made that "at the revelation of the Lord Jesus from heaven (ἐν τῇ ἀποκαλύψει) together with the angels of His power, in a fire of flame," God will justly recompense affliction to those who persecuted the Thessalonians, and rest or relief to them.

Both the statement of what is to occur and the definition of the time when it is to occur are to be here observed; and as the one can refer to nothing else than the distribution of rewards and punishments for the deeds done in the body, so the other can have no other reference than to the act of the coming of Christ. Both matters are made even plainer by what follows. The Apostle proceeds to declare broadly that this revelation of Jesus of which he is speaking is as one giving vengeance to those ignorant of God and those disobedient to the gospel — a vengeance that comes in the way of justice, and consists in eternal destruction away from the face of the Lord and from the glory of His might. And so closely and even carefully is the time defined, that to the exact statement that all this occurs at the revelation of Christ from heaven, it is added at the end, that this "eternal destruction" takes place whenever (ὅταν) the Lord gloriously comes, — "at that day." Unless the Apostle is here representing the persecutors of the Thessalonians as partakers in the horrors of the punitive side of the Second Advent because he expected and here asserts that the Advent was to come before that generation passed away — and this will not satisfy the general representation of verses 8 *seq.* — it is certain that he here thinks of the Advent, considered as an act and not as a state, as the last judgment itself, when

"Nil inultum remanebit."

In this case it would presuppose a general resurrection.

That Paul had a resurrection in mind as accompanying the Second Advent is certain from another important passage (I Thess. iv. 13–18). The Thessalonians did not doubt that Jesus had risen from the dead (v. 14); but they had not realized even in thought all the consequents of this great fact. Like certain at a somewhat later date at Corinth, they did not understand that all men that die rise again by virtue of Christ's conquest of death. And thus, as they saw one and another of their own number "fall on sleep," they sorrowed inordinately over them, like the rest that have no hope. It is not exactly clear what they thought of the state of the dead, — whether they conceived of them as with Christ indeed, in Paradise, but condemned to an eternity of shade existence, separated from the body for ever, which seems to have been the case with their Corinthian fellow-errorists, — or whether they fancied that with the cessation of bodily activity, the whole life went out, as may be hinted in the sad words that they sorrowed as the rest who have no hope (v. 13). In either case the Apostle brings them quick consolation in the glad announcement that the resurrection of Christ implies that of those who have fallen asleep; and that, raised through Jesus, God will bring them with Him at His coming (v. 14). With this assurance he makes Christ's coming doubly precious to them. Then proceeding to more minute details, he declares that those who are alive and are left unto the coming of the Lord shall in no wise be beforehand with those who have fallen asleep; for the Lord will come with a shout, and with an archangel's voice, and with a blast of the trumpet of God, which will pierce even into the grave. Thus the rising of Christ's dead is secured before He reaches the earth; and only after they have joined the throng, are the living along with them to be caught up in (or on) clouds unto His meeting, — into the air, to "swell the triumph of His train." "So," adds the Apostle, "we shall be always with the Lord" (v. 17). Dire, then, as the coming will be to those who know not God and who obey not the gospel, it will be bliss unspeakable to those in Christ; and as the results, on the one side, are "eternal destruction away from the face of the Lord and from the glory of His might" (II Thess. i. 9); so on the other they will be eternal dwelling with the Lord (I Thess. iv. 17). It goes without saying that the Apostle has the believing dead only in his mind in our present passage (iv. 16). How could he in such a passage speak of any other? But is not the parallel too close for us not to suspect that, as in the one case both the living and dead in Christ shall partake in the bliss and the living shall not precede the dead, so in the other the living who are left unto the Coming shall not precede those who have passed away, in receiving the terrible doom, and that the blare of the trumpet of God veritably

"Coget omnes ante thronum"?

Or is it more probable that Paul believed and taught that the Lord would certainly come before that generation passed away? There is no room to doubt that the Thessalonians expected the Advent in their own time. Their feelings towards death (I Thess. iv. 13 *seq.*) would be otherwise inexplicable. And it is worthy of note that the Apostle does not correct them in this belief. He points out to them that to fall asleep was not to miss the glory of the Advent, but that whether they waked or slept they should live together with their Lord (I Thess. v. 10). But he says no word that would declare them mistaken in expecting to live until "that day." On the contrary, he expresses himself in terms that left the possibility open that the Lord might come while they were still alive and left on the earth (I Thess. iv. 15, 17). This was far from asserting that the Lord would come in that generation; but, in the connexion in which the words stand, they would have been impossible had the Apostle felt justified in asserting that He would not come. And this appears to be the exact difference between the attitude of the Thessalonians and that of Paul; they confidently expected the Lord in their own day — he was in complete uncertainty when He would come. That He would assuredly come, to bring sudden destruction (I Thess. v. 3) upon all appointed unto wrath (v. 9) and rest and salvation to those in Christ, he was sure; but the times and seasons he knew perfectly were hidden in the Father's power (I Thess. v. 1). He might come soon — when He did come, it would be, he knew, with the unexpectedness of a thief in the night (I Thess. v. 2). But meanwhile, whether it found him waking or sleeping was of no moment; and though it became him to watch (I Thess. v. 6), yet the watch was to be not a nervous expectancy, but a quiet and patient waiting (I Thess. i. 10, ἀναμένειν, cf. Judith viii. 17). But if, just because the "when" was unknown, the Apostle could not confidently expect the Lord in his own time, the categorical assertion that the Advent would bring "eternal destruction away from the face of the Lord" (II Thess. i. 9) to the special persecutors of the Thessalonians, rests on his view of the Advent as synchronous with the final judgment and presupposes a general resurrection.

The very moderation of the Apostle's attitude made it difficult for the excited Thessalonians to yield themselves to his leading. Certainly his first letter did not allay their fanaticism. Things went rather from bad to worse, and so certain were they that the Lord was coming at once, that they fell an easy prey to every one who should cry "Lo, here!" or "Lo, there!" and even, apparently from this cause, began to neglect their daily business and became mere busybodies, refusing to work, and eating the bread of others. The Apostle sternly rebukes their disorder, and commands that they work with quietness; and with a view to preserving them from sudden agitation whenever any one chose to declare "The day of the Lord is upon us!" he points out certain events that must come before the Lord. That this practical, ethical purpose was the occasion of the important revelation in II Thess. ii. 1–12, the Apostle tells us himself (ii. 2). And a simple glance at his words is enough to expose the almost ludicrous inappropriateness of the contention of some that the error of the Thessalonians was not feverish expectancy of the Lord's coming, but the belief that the day of the Lord had already come and had brought none of the blessings they had expected from it, — not the Lord Himself, nor their resurrected friends, — nothing of all that the Apostle had taught and they had hoped.[2] What the Apostle says is that he wishes to save them from being suddenly shaken from their senses or troubled by any statement from any quarter, as that the day of the Lord was upon them. The passage is parallel to and probably founded upon the words of our Lord in His

[2] This curious misinterpretation is founded on a pressure of the verb ἐνέστηκεν, ii. 2, in forgetfulness of three things. (1) That this verb is a compound of ἴστημι, not of εἰμί, and means, not "is in progress," but "is upon us," in the two senses of "to threaten," and "to be actual" (especially in the participle). While it *may* mean "to be present," therefore, it *need not* mean it, and is not likely to in such a case. (2) That the clause "either by spirit or by word, or by letter as if from us," is an essential part of the context, the omission of which falsifies the text. What the Apostle says is *not* "be not troubled — as that the day of the Lord," etc. *but* "be not troubled *by any statement* as that the day of the Lord is upon us!" — something essentially different, which excludes the above interpretation. (3) That the broad context renders this explanation impossible and meaningless.

warning to His disciples not to be led astray or deceived by any "who should say, 'Lo, here is the Christ!' or 'Here!'" (Mt. xxiv. 23), and is already a valuable indication that throughout this whole section Paul has the great apocalyptic discourse of Jesus in mind and is to be interpreted from it.

The impression has become very widespread that, owing to the lack on our part of the previous information to which Paul alludes as given by him on a former occasion to the Thessalonians (verses 5 and 6), the interpretation of this prophecy must remain for all time a sealed riddle to us. That two important events, called by Paul "the apostasy," and "the revelation of the man of sin," the latter of which was at the time deterred by something else mysteriously designated "the restraint," or "the restrainer," were to take place before the coming of the Lord — this, we are told, is all that we can know, and any effort to obtain any defined outlines for the misty shapes thus barely named to us only succeeds in bringing the dense darkness in which they are steeped into tangibility and visibility. We find it difficult to believe the matter so hopeless. On the contrary, the broad outlines, at least, of the prophecy appear to us sufficiently clear; and we believe that a sound method of study will give the humble student who is willing to put a stern check on his imagination and follow the leading of the exegetical hints alone, an adequately exact understanding of its chief details.

First of all, we must try to keep fresh in our minds the great principle that all prophecy is ethical in its purpose, and that this ethical end controls not only what shall be revealed in general, but also the details of it and the very form which it takes. Next, we must not fail to observe that our present prophecy is not independent of previous ones, — that its roots are in Daniel, and from beginning to end it is full of allusions to our Lord's great apocalyptic discourse. Still again, we must bear in mind that it comes from a hand which throughout these Epistles preserves an attitude of uncertainty of the "times and seasons," and so expresses himself as to imply that he believed that the Lord might come, in despite of all these preliminary events, in his own day.

If, holding fast to these principles, we approach the prophecy itself, we observe first of all, that although the three things — the Apostasy, the Revelation of the Man of Sin, and the Coming of the Lord — are brought together, they are not declared to be closely connected, or immediately consecutive to one another. The mere "and" of verse 3 reveals nothing beyond the simple fact that both of those events must come to pass before the Lord comes. So too for all that the prophecy tells us, both of these evil developments might come and pass away, and be succeeded by ages on ages which in turn might pass away, and yet men be able to say, "Where is the promise of His coming?" To point to the declaration in verse 8, that "the Lord Jesus shall destroy" the lawless one — almost, "blow him away" — "with the breath of His mouth and abolish him with the manifestation of His presence," as proving that he will still be lording it on earth when the Lord comes to his destruction, is to neglect the apparent indications of the context. For this assertion does not go, in either vividness or literality of expression, beyond what is stated just before of the generation then living (II Thess. i. 7, 9); and it is inserted here not as a chronological detail — and is out of place (cf. verses 9, seq.) if considered a chronological detail — but as part of the description of the lawless one, and for the ethical purpose of keeping in the mind of the reader his judgment by God and his final fate. In a word, this statement only declares of the Man of Sin what was just before declared of the lesser enemies of the Gospel, and what was in I Thess. v. 3 seq. declared of all to whom wrath is appointed — that he shall meet with destruction at the Second Coming of the Lord. The revelation of the Man of Sin is not, then, necessarily to be sought at the end of time: we know of it, only that it will succeed the removal of the "restraint," and precede, by how much we are not told, the coming of the Lord.

We cannot fail to observe, however, next, that in his description of the Man of Sin, the Apostle has a contemporary, or nearly contemporary phenomenon in mind. The withholding power is already present. Although the Man of Sin is not yet revealed, as a mystery his essential "lawlessness" is already working — "only until the present restrainer be removed from the midst." He expects him to sit in "the temple of God," which perhaps most naturally refers to the literal temple in Jerusalem, although the Apostle knew that the out-pouring of God's wrath on the Jews was close at hand (I Thess. ii. 16). And if we compare the description which the Apostle gives of him with our Lord's address on the Mount of Olives (Mt. xxiv.), to which, as we have already hinted, Paul makes obvious allusion, it becomes at once in the highest degree probable that in the words, "he that exalteth himself against all that is called God, or is worshipped, so that he sitteth in the sanctuary of God showing himself that he is God," Paul can have nothing else in view than what our Lord described as "the abomination of desolation which was spoken of by Daniel the prophet, standing in the holy place" (Mt. xxiv. 15); and this our Lord connects immediately with the beleaguering of Jerusalem (cf. Luke xxi. 20). This obvious parallel, however, not only places the revelation of the Man of Sin in the near future, but goes far towards leading us to his exact identification. Our Lord's words not only connect him with the siege of Jerusalem, but place him distinctly among the besiegers; and, led by the implication of the original setting of the phrase (in Dan. xi. 36) which Paul uses, we cannot go far wrong in identifying him with the Roman emperor.

Whether a single emperor was thought of or the line of emperors, is a more difficult question. The latter hypothesis will best satisfy the conditions of the problem; and we believe that the line of emperors, considered as the embodiment of persecuting power, is the revelation of iniquity hidden under the name of the Man of Sin. With this is connected in the description certain other traits of Roman imperialism — more especially the rage for deification, which, in the person of Caligula, had already given a foretaste of what was to come. It was Nero, then, the first persecutor of the Church, — and Vespasian the miracle-worker,[3] — and Titus, who introduced his divine-

[3] Tac., "Hist.," iv. 82; Suet., "Vesp.," 7; Dio Cass., lxvi. 8.

self and his idolatrous insignia into the Holy of Holies, perhaps with a directly anti-Christian intent,[4] — and Domitian, — and the whole line of human monsters whom the world was worshipping as gods, on which, as a nerve-cord of evil, these hideous ganglia gathered, — these and such as these it was that Paul had in mind when he penned this hideous description of the son of perdition, every item of which was fulfilled in the terrible story of the emperors of Rome.

The restraining power, on this hypothesis, appears to be the Jewish state. For the continued existence of the Jewish state was both graciously and naturally a protection to Christianity, and hence a restraint on the revelation of the persecuting power. Graciously, it was God's plan to develop Christianity under the protection of Judaism for a short set time, with the double purpose of keeping the door of salvation open to the Jews until all of their elect of that generation should be gathered in and the apostasy of the nation should be rendered doubly and trebly without excuse, and of hiding the tender infancy of the Church within the canopy of a protecting sheath until it should grow strong enough to withstand all storms. Naturally, the effect of the continuance of Judaism was to conceal Christianity from notice through a confusion of it with Judaism — to save it thus from being declared an illicit religion — and to enable it to grow strong under the protection accorded to Jewish worship. So soon as the Jewish apostasy was complete and Jerusalem given over to the Gentiles — God deserting the temple which was no longer His temple to the fury of the enemies, of those who were now His enemies — the separation of Christianity from Judaism, which had already begun, became evident to every eye; the conflict between the new faith and heathenism culminating in and now alive almost only in the Emperor-worship, became intense; and the persecuting power of the empire was inevitably let loose. Thus the continued existence of Judaism was in the truest sense a restraint on the persecution of Christians, and its destruction gave the signal for the lawless one to be revealed in his time.

[4] Sulp. Sev., "Sacr. Hist.," ii. 30, §§ 6. 7.

If the masculine form of "the restrainer" in verse 7 demands interpretation as a person — which we more than doubt — it might possibly be referred without too great pressure to James of Jerusalem, God's chosen instrument in keeping the door of Christianity open for the Jews and by so doing continuing and completing their probation. Thus he may be said to have been the upholder of the restraining power, the savour of the salt that preserved the Christians from persecution, and so in a high sense the restrainer.

Finally, in this interpretation, the apostasy is obviously the great apostasy of the Jews, gradually filling up all these years and hastening to its completion in their destruction. That the Apostle certainly had this rapidly completing apostasy in his mind in the severe arraignment that he makes of the Jews in I Thess. ii. 14–16, which reached its climax in the declaration that they were continually filling up more and more full the measure of their sins, until already the measure of God's wrath was prematurely (ἔφθασεν) filled up against them and was hanging over them like some laden thunder-cloud ready to burst and overwhelm them, — adds an additional reason for supposing his reference to be to this apostasy — above all others, "the" apostasy — in this passage.

We venture to think that the core of this interpretation may be accounted very probable, — so much of it as this: that the Apostle had in view in this prophecy a development in the immediate future closely connected with the Jewish war and the destruction of Jerusalem, although not as if that were the coming of Christ for which he was patiently waiting, but rather in full recognition of its being only the culmination of the Jewish apostasy and the falling of God's wrath upon them to the uttermost. When he declares that these events must precede the coming of Christ, this no doubt was clear evidence that the Advent was not to be looked for immediately; but was in no wise inconsistent with uncertainty whether it would come during that generation or not. As a matter of mere fact the growing apostasy of the Jews was completed — the abomination of desolation had been set up in the sanctuary — Jerusalem and the temple, and the Jewish state were in ruins — Christianity stood naked before her enemies — and the persecuting sword of Divus Cæsar was unsheathed and Paul had himself felt its keenness: all the prophecy had been fulfilled before two decades had passed away.

Let us gather up for the close, in brief recapitulation, the events which Paul predicts in these two Epistles. First of all, and most persistently of all, he predicts the coming of the Lord from heaven unto judgment, with its glorious accompaniments of hosts of angels, the shout, the voice of the archangel and the blast of the trumpet of God that awake the dead. Thus, he predicts the resurrection of Christ's dead to partake in the glory of His coming. Then, he foretells the results of the judgment — eternal destruction from the face of God for the wicked, and everlasting presence with the Lord for His own. Of the time of the Advent the Apostle professes ignorance; he only knows that it will come unexpectedly. But he does know that before it the apostasy of the Jews must be completed, and the persecuting power of the Roman state be revealed. This apostasy and its punishment he sees is immediately ready for completion (I Thess. ii. 16). Finally, he mentions having previously foretold the persecutions under which the Thessalonians were already suffering (I Thess. iii. 4).

II. — The Epistles to the Galatians, Corinthians, and Romans

When we pass from the Epistles to the Thessalonians to the next group of letters — those to the Galatians, Corinthians and Romans, all four of which were written in the course of a single year, some five years later (A.D. 57–58) — we are at once aware of a great diminution in the allusions to the future. Galatians contains rather more matter than both letters to the Thessalonians, but does not contain a single prediction; and the much longer letter to the Romans, while alluding now and then to what the future was to bring forth, contains no explicit mention of the Second Advent. The first letter to the Corinthians is three times as long as both letters to the Thessalonians, but contains rather less predictive matter. We should not be far wrong if we estimated that these four letters, in about nine times the space, give us about as much eschatological matter as the two letters to the Thessalonians.

The contrast exists in nothing else, however, except the mere matter of amount. The two groups of letters are thoroughly at one in their teaching as to the future — at one, but not mere repetitions of one another. This group is continually supplying what almost seems to be explanations and extensions of the revelations in Thessalonians, so that it exhibits as great an advance in what is revealed as decrease in the relative amount of space given to revelations. So clear is it that the Apostle's preaching to all heathen communities was in essence the same, and that all grew up to the stature of manhood in Christ through practically the same stages, that we may look upon the Thessalonian letters as if they had been addressed to the infancy of every Church, and treat those at present before us as if they were intended to supplement them. This is probably the true account of the very strong appearance of being supplementary and explanatory to those in the letters to Thessalonica, which the predictions in this group of letters are continually presenting.

In these as in those, the Second Advent is represented primarily and most prominently in the aspect of judgment — as the last judgment. Here, too, the desire for moral perfection is referred constantly to it, as for example in I Cor. i. 8 cf. 7, where the actual moment in mind is that of the revelation of the Lord Jesus Christ. The mutual glorying of the Apostle and his readers in each other is to be "in the day of our Lord Jesus" (I Cor. i. 8). This is the day of punishment also: the incestuous man is delivered now unto Satan to be punished in the flesh in order that his spirit may be saved in the day of the Lord (I Cor. v. 5); and in exactly similar wise, those who are visited with bodily ills for unworthy partaking of the Lord's Supper, receive this chastening that they may not be condemned with the world (I Cor. xi. 32). The sanction of the anathema pronounced against all who do not love the Lord is Maranatha — "the Lord cometh!" (I Cor. xvi. 22). His coming is indeed so sharply defined as the time of judging, in the mind of Paul, that he advises his readers to "judge nothing before the time, until the Lord come" (I Cor. iv. 5). The connotation of "the day of the Lord" was to him so entirely judgment, that the word "day" had come to mean judgment to him, and he actually uses it as its synonym, speaking of a "human day," for "human judgment" (I Cor. iv. 3). Of like import is the representation of the second coming as the great day of revelation of character. Of the builders on the edifice of God's Church it is declared that "each man's work shall be made manifest by 'the day.'" "For the day is revealed in fire, and each man's work, of what sort it is, — the fire itself shall test." "If any man's work abideth, he shall receive reward; if any man's work is burned up, he shall be mulcted, but himself shall be saved, but so as through fire" (I Cor. iii. 13–15). It is scarcely an extension of this teaching to declare openly that when the Lord comes, He "will both bring to light the hidden things of darkness, and make manifest the counsels of the hearts; and then shall his praise come to each from God" (I Cor. iv. 5).

In the light of this it is evident what time the Apostle has in mind when he declares that "all of us must needs be made manifest [5] before the judgment-seat of Christ, that each may receive the things [done] through the body according to what he practised, whether good or bad" (II Cor. v. 10); and which day to him was "the day when God shall judge the secrets of men according to my gospel, by Jesus Christ" — "the day of wrath and revelation of the righteous judgment of God" (Rom. ii. 16, 5). Yet, in this last passage it is beyond all question that the Apostle has in mind the final judgment, when God "will render to every man according to his works," and the two verses which have been adduced are respectively the opening and closing verse of the splendid passage in which Paul gives us his fullest description of the nature and standards of the awful trial to which all men, whether Jews or Gentiles, whether those

[5] φανερωθῆναι, cf. φανερόν, I Cor. iii. 13; φανερώσει, I Cor. iv. 5.

who have law or those who have no law, are summoned "in the day when God shall judge the secrets of men according to my gospel through Christ Jesus." Elsewhere in Romans, where judgment necessarily holds an important place in the general argument, the wrath of God is kept hanging over ungodliness and unrighteousness (i. 18; iii. 5; v. 9) and the coming judgment is held before the eyes of the reader (iii. 6; xiv. 10).

For the realization of such a judgment scene (Rom. ii. 5–16; II Cor. v. 10; Rom. xiv. 10), a resurrection is presupposed, and the reference of the Apostle is obvious when he expresses his confidence that "He who raised up Jesus shall raise up us also with Jesus, and shall present us with you" (II Cor. iv. 14; cf. v. 10; also I Cor. vi. 14). In this compressed sentence, there is pointed out the relation of our resurrection both to the judgment ($\pi\alpha\rho\alpha\sigma\tau\hat{\eta}\sigma\epsilon\iota$, cf. Col. i. 22) as preceding and in order to it, and to the resurrection of Christ ($\sigma\grave{\upsilon}\nu$ $\text{'}I\eta\sigma\hat{\upsilon}$, cf. the use of $\sigma\upsilon\nu\epsilon\gamma\epsilon\acute{\iota}\rho\omega$ in Col. ii. 12; iii. 1) as included in it as a necessary result and part of it. The latter matter is made very plain by the remarkably simple way in which Jesus is declared in Rom. i. 4 to have been marked out as the Son of God "by the resurrection of the dead" — a phrase which has no meaning except on the presupposition that the raising of Jesus was the beginning of the resurrection of the dead and part and parcel of it (cf. also Rom. vi. 4; viii. 11, etc.).

At this point our attention is claimed by that magnificent combined argument and revelation contained in the 15th chapter of I Corinthians, which has been the instruction and consolation of the saints through all Christian ages. The occasion which called it forth was singularly like and singularly unlike that which gave rise to the parallel revelation in I Thessalonians. As in the one Church so in the other, there were those who failed to grasp the great truth of the Resurrection, and laid their dead away without hope of their rising again. But in Thessalonica this was due to sorrowing ignorance; in Corinth, to philosophizing pride of intellect. And in the one case, the Apostle meets it with loving instruction; in the other, with a brilliant refutation which confounds opposition, and which, although carrying a tender purpose buried in its bosom, as all the world has felt, yet flashes with argument and even here and there burns with sarcasm. The Corinthian errorists appear to have been spiritualistic philosophizers, perhaps of the Platonic school, who, convinced of the immortality of the soul, thought of the future life as a spiritual one in which men attained perfection apart from, perhaps largely because separate from, the body. They looked for and desired no resurrection; and their formula, perhaps somewhat scoffingly and certainly somewhat magisterially pronounced, was: "There is no rising again of dead men." It is instructive to observe how the Apostle meets their assertion. They did not deny the resurrection of Christ (I Cor. xv. 2, 11) — probably explaining it as a miracle like the reänimation of Lazarus. Yet the Apostle begins by laying firm the proofs of Christ's resurrection (xv. 1–11), and doing this in such a way as to suggest that they needed primary instruction. He "makes known to them," rather than reminds them of the Gospel which he and all the Apostles preached and all Christians believed. With this opening sarcasm, he closes the way of retreat through a denial of the resurrection of Christ, and then presses as his sole argument the admitted fact that Christ had risen. How could they deny that dead men rise, when Christ, who was a dead man, had risen? If there is no resurrection of dead men, then not even is Christ risen. It is plain that their whole position rested on the assertion of the impossibility of resurrection; to which it was a conclusive reply that they confessed it in one case. Having uncovered their logical inconsistency, Paul leaves at once the question of fact and presses at length the hideous corollaries that flow from their denial of the possibility of dead men rising, through its involved denial that Jesus, the dead man, had risen — aiming, no doubt, at arousing a revulsion against a doctrine fruitful of such consequences (xv. 14–34).

Having thus moved his readers to shame, he proceeds to meet squarely their real objection to the resurrection, by a full explanation of the nature of the resurrection-body (xv. 35–50), to which he adjoins a revelation concerning the occurrences of the last day (xv. 51–58). To each of these we should give a moment's attention.

The intimate connexion of our resurrection with that of Christ, which we have seen Paul everywhere insisting upon, would justify the inference that the nature of our resurrection-bodies was revealed to men in His resurrection-body, that was seen and handled of men for forty days. This is necessarily implied in the assumption that underlies the argument at I Cor. xv. 12 *sq.*, and is almost openly declared at verse 49; II Cor. iv. 14; Rom. viii. 11. In our present passage, however, the Apostle reserves this for the last, and begins by setting forth from natural analogies the possibility of a body being truly one's own body and yet differing largely from that which has hitherto been borne. This is an assertion of sameness and difference. At verse 42 he proceeds to explain the differences in detail. As the change in the form of expression advises us, the enumeration divides itself into two parts at the end of verse 43 — the former portion describing in threefold contrast, the physical, and the latter in a single pregnant phrase the moral difference. On the one hand the new bodies that God will give us will no longer be liable to corruption, dishonour or weakness. On the other, they will no longer be under the power of the only partially sanctified human nature, but rather will be wholly informed, determined and led by the Holy Ghost (verse 44). That this is the meaning of the much disputed phrase: "It is sown a natural (psychic) body, it is raised a spiritual (pneumatic) body," is demonstrable from the usage of the words employed. It is plain matter of fact that "psychic" in the New Testament naturally means and is uniformly used to express "self-led" in contrast to "God-led," and therefore, unconverted or unsanctified; while "pneumatic" never sinks in the New Testament so low in its connotation as the human spirit, but always (with the single exception of Eph. vi. 12, where superhuman evil spirits are in mind) refers to "Spirit" in its highest sense, — the Holy Ghost.[6] In this compressed phrase, thus, the Apostle declares

[6] This is gradually becoming recognized by the best expositors. Compare the satisfactory article on πνευματικός in the *third* edition of Cremer's "Biblico-

that in this life believers do not attain to complete sanctification (Rom. vii. 14–viii. 11), but groan in spirit awaiting the redemption of the body (Rom. viii. 23, vii. 24); while in the heavenly life even their bodies will no longer retain remainders of sin, but will be framed by (Rom. viii. 11), filled with, and led by the Holy Ghost. The incomparable importance of this moral distinction over the merely physical ones is illustrated by the Apostle's leaving them to devote the next five verses to the justification of this, closing (verse 50) with a chiasmic recapitulation in which he pointedly puts the moral difference first: "Now this I say, brethren, that flesh and blood cannot inherit the kingdom of God, neither doth corruption inherit incorruption." For, that "flesh and blood" must here be understood ethically and not physically is already evident from the preceding context and is put beyond question by the settled ethical sense of the phrase — which is, of course, used in the New Testament also only in its established ethical sense, and could not be used otherwise without misleading the reader. All crass inferences that have been drawn from it, therefore, in a physical sense are illegitimate to start with, and are negatived to end with by the analogy of Christ's resurrection-body, which we have seen Paul to understand to be a case under the rule, and which certainly had flesh and bones (Luke xxiv. 39). Paul does not deny to our resurrection-body, therefore, materiality, which would be a *contradictio in adjecto*; he does not deny "flesh" to it, — which he hints, rather, will be its material, though of "another" kind than we are used to (verse 39); he denies to it

Theological Lexicon of N. T. Greek," with the very unsatisfactory one in the second edition. He now tells us that the word is used "in profane Greek only in a physical or physiological sense, commonly the former; — in biblical Greek only in a religious, that is religio- or soteriologico-psychological sense = belonging to the Holy Ghost or determined by the Holy Ghost," p. 675, cf. p. 676. (The reader needs to be warned that he will find no hint of Cremer's entire rewriting of this article, in the *Supplement* to their edition of Cremer's Lexicon issued by T. & T. Clark this year.) So Meyer's latest view (to which he did not correct the Commentary throughout) is given in his Com. on I Cor., E. T., p. 298, *note:* "Πνευματικός" is nowhere "in the New Testament the opposite of *material*, but of *natural* (I Pet. ii. 5 not excluded); and the πνεῦμα to which πνευματικός refers is always (except Eph. vi. 12, where it is the *diabolic* spirit-world that is spoken of) the *Divine* πνεῦμα." The italics are his own.

"fleshliness" in any, even the smallest degree, and weakness of any and every sort. In a word, he leaves it human but makes it perfect.

After so full an explanation of the nature of the resurrection-body, it was inevitable that deeper questions should arise concerning the fate of those found by the advent still clothed in their bodies of humiliation. Hence a further revelation was necessary beyond what had been given to the Thessalonians, and the Apostle adds to that, that those found living shall be the subjects of an instantaneous change which will make them fit companions for the perfected saints that have slept. For when the trumpet sounds and the dead are raised incorruptible, they too in the twinkling of an eye shall be "changed." And the change is for them as for the dead a putting on of incorruption and of immortality. The spectacle of these multitudes, untouched by death, receiving their perfect and immortal bodies is the great pageant of the conquest of death, and the Apostle on witnessing it in spirit cannot restrain his shout of victory over that whilom enemy of the race, whose victory is now reversed and the sinews of whose fatal sting wherewith it had been wont to slay men are now cut. So complete is Christ's conquest that it looses its hold over its former victims and the men still living cannot die. The rapidity of action on "the great day" is also worth notice. The last trump sounds — the dead spring forth from the grave — the living in the twinkling of an eye are changed — and all together are caught up into the air to His meeting, — or ever the rushing train of angels that surround their Lord and ours can reach the confines of the earth. Truly events stay not, when the Lord comes.

Important as these revelations are, they become almost secondary when compared with the contents of that wonderful passage I Cor. xv. 20–28, the exceeding richness of which is partially accounted for by the occasion of its utterance. It comes in the midst of Paul's effort to move his readers by painting the terrible consequences of denial of the possibility of resurrection, involving denial of the fact that Christ has risen. He feels the revulsion he would beget in them, and relieves his overburdened heart by suddenly turning to rest a moment on the certainty of Christ's rising, and to sweep his eye over all the future, noting the effects of that precious fact up to the end. He begins by reasserting the inclusion of our resurrection in that of Christ, who was but the first-fruits of those asleep, and then justifies it by an appeal to the parallel of Adam's work of destruction, declaring, apparently, that as physical death came upon all men through Adam's sin, so all men shall be rescued from its bondage by Christ's work of redemption. The context apparently confines the word "death" in these verses to its simple physical sense, while on the contrary the "all" of both clauses seems unlimited, and the context appears to furnish nothing to narrow its meaning to a class. They thus assert the resurrection of all men without distinction as dependent on and the result of Christ's work, just as all men, even the redeemed, taste of death as the result of Adam's sin. "But" the Apostle adds, returning to the Christian dead, "this resurrection though certain, is not immediate; each rises in his own place in the ranks — Christ is the first-fruits, then His own rise at His coming; then is the end" (verses 23, 24). The interminable debates that have played around the meaning of this statement are the outgrowth of strange misconceptions. Because the resurrection of the wicked is not mentioned it does not at all follow that it is excluded; the whole section has nothing to do with the resurrection of the wicked (which is only incidentally included and not openly stated in the semi-parenthetic explanations of verses 21 and 22), but, like the parallel passage in I Thessalonians, confines itself to the Christian dead. Nor is it exegetically possible to read the resurrection of the wicked into the passage as a third event to take place at a different time from that of the good, as if the Apostle had said: "Each shall rise in his own order; Christ the first-fruits, — then Christ's dead at His coming, — then, the end of the resurrection, namely of the wicked." The term "the end," is a perfectly definite one with a set and distinct meaning, and from Matthew (e.g. xxiv. 6, cf. 14) throughout the New Testament, and in these very epistles (I Cor. i. 8; II Cor. i. 13, 14), is the standing designation of the

"end of the ages," or the "end of the world." It is illegitimate
to press it into any other groove here. Relief is not however got
by varying the third term, so as to make it say that "then
comes the end, accompanied by the resurrection of the wicked,"
for this is importing into the passage what there is absolutely
nothing in it to suggest. The word τάγμα does not in the least
imply succession; but means "order" only in the sense of that
word in such phrases as "orders of society." Neither does the
"they that are Christ's" prepare the mind to expect a statement as to "those who are not Christ's," any more than in
Rom. ix. 6, when we hear of "Israel," and "those of Israel,"
we expect immediately to hear of "those not of Israel." The
contrast is entirely absorbed by the "Christ" of the preceding
clause, and only the clumsiness of our English gives a different
impression. Not only, however, is there no exegetical basis for
this exposition in this passage; the whole theory of a resurrection of the wicked at a later time than the resurrection of
the just is excluded by this passage. Briefly, this follows from
the statement that after the coming of Christ, "then comes the
end" (verse 24). No doubt the mere word "then" (εἶτα) does
not assert immediateness, and for ought necessarily said in it,
"the end" might be only the next event mentioned by the
Apostle, although the intervening interval should be vast and
crowded with important events. But the context here necessarily limits *this* "then" to immediate subsequence.

Exegetically this follows, indeed, from the relation of verse
28 to 23 *b*, for the long delay asserted in which it assigns the
reason: Christ's children rise not with Him, because death is
the last enemy to be conquered by Him, and their release from
death cannot, therefore, come until all His conquests are completed. The matter can be reduced, however, to the stringency
of a syllogism. "The end" is declared to take place "whenever
Christ giveth over (the immediateness is asserted by the present) the kingdom to God"; and this occurs "whenever He shall
have conquered" all His enemies, the last of which to be conquered is death (verse 26). Shortly, then, the end comes so soon
as death is conquered. But death is already conquered when it

is forced to loose its hold on Christ's children; and that is at the Parousia (ver. 23). If any should think to escape this, as if it were an inference, it would be worth while to glance at verse 54, where it is, as we have seen, asserted that the victory over death is complete and his sting destroyed at the Second Advent, and that the rising of Christ's dead is a result of this completed conquest. The end then is synchronous with the victory over death, which itself is synchronous with the second coming, and if the wicked rise at all (which verses 21, 22 assert), it is all one whether we say they rise at the Advent or at the end, since these two are but two names for the same event. Of this, indeed, Paul's language elsewhere should have convinced us: "who shall also confirm you unto the end, unaccusable in the day of our Lord Jesus Christ" (I Cor. i. 8), "I hope ye will acknowledge unto the end, . . . that we are your glorying even as ye are also ours, in the day of our Lord Jesus" (II Cor. i. 14). So then, the Second Advent is represented to be itself "THE END."

With the emergence of this fact, the importance of our present passage is revealed. It is immediately seen to open to us the nature of the whole dispensation in which we are living, and which stretches from the First to the Second Advent, as a period of advancing conquest on the part of Christ. During its course He is to conquer "every rulership and every authority and power" (verse 24), and "to place all His enemies under His feet" (verse 25), and it ends when His conquests complete themselves by the subjugation of the "last enemy," death. We purposely say, period of "conquest," rather than of "conflict," for the essence of Paul's representation is not that Christ is striving against evil, but progressively (ἔσχατος, verse 26) over-coming evil, throughout this period. A precious passage in the Epistle to the Romans (xi. 25 sq., cf. verse 15) draws the veil aside to gladden our eyes with a nearer view of some of these victories; telling us that "the fulness of the Gentiles shall be brought into" the Church, and after that "all Israel shall be saved," and by their salvation great blessings, — such a spirit-ual awakening as can only be compared to "life from the dead" — shall be brought to all God's people. There may be some doubt as to the exact meaning of these phrases. The "fulness of the Gentiles," however, in accordance with the usual sense of the genitive with "pleroma," and the almost compulsion of the context, should mean, not the Gentile contingent to the elect, but the whole body of the Gentiles.[7] And "Israel" almost certainly means not the true but the fleshly "Israel." In this case, the prophecy promises the universal Christianization of the world, — at least the nominal conversion of all the Gentiles and the real salvation of all the Jews. In any understanding of it, it promises the widest practicable extension of Christianity, and reveals to us Christ going forth to victory. But in this, which seems to us the true understanding, it gives us a glimpse of the completion of His conquest over spiritual wickedness, and allows us to see in the spirit the fulfilment of the prayer, "Thy kingdom come, Thy will be done in earth even as it is in heaven." It is natural to think that such a victory cannot be wrought until the end is hastening — that with its completion nothing will remain to be conquered but death itself. But the Apostle does not tell us this,[8] and we know not from him how long the converted earth is to await its coming Lord.

[7] The exegetical question really turns on the sense to be given to Ἰσραήλ in xi. 26. If τὸ πλήρωμα τῶν ἐθνῶν in verse 25, means "those of the Gentiles who go towards filling up the kingdom," then πᾶς Ἰσραήλ of verse 26, must of necessity be the spiritual Israel, distinguished from Ἰσραήλ of verse 25, by the inclusive πᾶς. Then the sense would be that "hardening has befallen Israel" temporarily — viz. until the Gentile contingent comes in, — and thus ("in this way," the most natural sense of οὕτως), ALL Israel shall be saved; — not part only, but all. So that the passage continues to justify the temporary rejection of Israel by its gracious purpose, viz. that thus the Gentiles receive their calling, and all God's children, out of every nation, are saved. On the other hand if, as is most natural and usual, τῶν ἐθνῶν is genitive of what is filled up, so that the phrase means, the whole body of the Gentiles, then there is no thought to carry over from it to condition πᾶς Ἰσραήλ in verse 26, and it naturally follows in sense the Ἰσραήλ of verse 25. The sense then is that which is suggested in the text. That Ἰσραήλ of verse 26 is the fleshly Israel seems to follow from the succeeding context, as well as from the difficulty of taking the words in two different senses in so narrow a context. But if so, this carries the meaning of the "fulness of the Gentiles" with it, and the interpretation given in the text is the only admissible one.

[8] I shall not deny that the ζωὴ ἐκ νεκρῶν of ver. 15 may mean the general resurrection, but it is an unexampled phrase for this conception and cannot be asserted to mean it. Nor in this context is it natural to so understand it.

An even more important fact faces us in the wonderful revelation we have been considering (I Cor. xv. 20–28): the period between the two advents is the period of Christ's kingdom, and when He comes again it is not to institute His kingdom, but to lay it down (verses 24, 28). The completion of His conquest, which is marked by conquering "the last enemy," death (verse 28), which in turn is manifest when the just arise and Christ comes (verses 54, 23), marks also the end of His reign (verse 25) and the delivery of the kingdom to God, even the Father (verse 24). This is indubitably Paul's assertion here, and it is in perfect harmony with the uniform representation of the New Testament, which everywhere places Christ's kingdom before and God's after the Second Advent. The contrast in Mt. xiii. 41 and 43 is not accidental. We cannot enter into the many deep questions that press for discussion when this ineffable prediction is even approached. Suffice it to say that when we are told that Jesus holds the kingship for a purpose (verse 25), namely the completion of His mediatorial work, and that when it is accomplished He will restore it to Him who gave it to Him (verse 28), and thus the Father will again become "all relations among all creations," — nothing is in the remotest way suggested inconsistent with the co-equal Deity of the Son with the Father and His eternal co-regnancy with Him over the universe. Manifestly we must distinguish between the mediatorial kingship which Jesus exercises by appointment of His Father, and the eternal kingship which is His by virtue of His nature, and which is one with God's own.

As to the duration of Christ's kingdom — or in other words the length of time that was to elapse before the Lord came — Paul says nothing in this passage. Nor does he anywhere in these Epistles speak more certainly about it than in those to the Thessalonians (I Cor. i. 7; xi. 26). He so expresses himself as to leave the possibility open that the Lord might come in his own time (I Cor. xv. 51); but he makes it a matter for experience to decide whether He will or not (II Cor. v. 1, ἐάν with the subjunctive, cf. verse 3 *sq.*). It is only through misunderstanding that passages have been adduced as asserting a brief life for the world. When (I Cor. x. 11) the "ends of the ages" are said to have already come, a technical term is used which declares that after this present inter-adventual period there remains no further earthly dispensation, but nothing is implied as to the duration of these "last times" (*acharith hayyamim*). So, when (I Cor. vii. 25–29) the Corinthians are advised to refrain from earthly entanglements because of "the impending distress," which should shortly tear asunder every human tie, there is nothing to show that the Apostle had the Second Advent in mind, and everthing in the Neronian persecution and the wars of succession and the succeeding trials to Christians to fully satisfy the prediction.[9] The very difficult passage at Rom. xiii. 11–14 appears also to have been misapplied to the advent by the modern exegesis. Its obvious parallels are Eph. v. 1–14 and I Thess. v. 1–11. The whole gist of the passage turns on moral awaking; and the word "salvation" appears to refer to the consummation of salvation in a subjective rather than objective sense (Rom. x. 10; II Thess. ii. 13); while the aorist, "When we believed," seems not easily to lend itself to furnishing a *terminus a quo* for the calculation of time, but rather to express the act by which their salvation was brought closer. So that the meaning of the passage would seem to be: "Fulfil the law of love, I say. I appeal to you for renewed efforts by your knowledge of the time: that it is high time for you at length to awake out of sleep. Long ago when you believed, you professed to have come out of darkness into light, and to have shaken yourselves free from the inertia as well as deeds of the night. Now salvation is closer to us than it was when we made that step. Having begun, we have advanced somewhat towards the goal. The night of sin in which the call for repentance found us is passing away. Let us take off at length our night-clothes, and buckle on the armour for the good fight — yea, let us rid our-

---

[9] The reference of the phrase, "for the fashion of this world passeth away" (verse 31) is not to the broad but the narrow context, justifying the immediately preceding statement, that those who use the world should be as those not using it. It is but equivalent to the line, "This world is all a fleeting show," and is parallel to I John ii. 17. Although it may have some reference to the Second Advent, as the day of renovation, it does not affect verses 20 and 29.

selves of all that belongs to the night, and put on the Lord Jesus Himself." If this understanding is correct, the Apostle does not count the days and assert that the time that had elapsed since his conversion had nearly run the sands of all time out, but rather appeals to his readers to renew their strenuous and hearty working out of their salvation by the encouragement that they had already progressed somewhat on the road, and could more easily and hopefully take a second step.

There remain two very interesting passages (II Cor. v. 1–10; Rom. viii. 18–25) which give us an insight as no others do into the Apostle's personal feelings towards this life, death, and the Advent. Nowhere else are the trials under which he suffered life so clearly revealed to us as in the opening chapters of II Corinthians. Amid them all, the very allusions to which, lightly touched as they are, appal us, the Apostle is upheld by the greatness of his ministry and the greatness of his hope. Though his outward man is worn away — what then? He need not faint, for his inward man is renewed day by day, and this affliction is light compared with the eternal weight of glory in store for him. He longs for the rest of the future life (cf. also Rom. vii. 25); but he shrinks from death. He could desire rather to be alive when the Lord comes, and that he might put on "the house from God, the dwelling not made with hands, eternal in the heavens," over this "earthly tent-dwelling" which he now inhabits. He only desires — does not expect this; he does not at all know whether he shall be found not naked when the putting-on time comes. But he longs for relief from the burdens of life, that somehow this mortality may be swallowed up of life. And when he bethinks him that to be at home in the body is to be abroad from the Lord, the other world is so glorious to him that he is not only willing but even desires ("rather," verse 8) to enter it even "naked" — he is well pleased to go abroad from the body and go home to the Lord. Like Bunyan and the sweet singer, Paul, looking beyond the confines of earth, can only say, "Would God that I were there!" This longing for relief from earthly life is repeated in Romans (vii. 25), and the groaning expectation of the consummation as the swallowing up of corruption in incorruption is attributed in the wonderful words of Romans viii. 18 *sq.* to the whole of the lower creation. All nature, says Paul, travails in the same longing. And the consummation brings not only relief to Christ's children, who have received the firstfruits of the Spirit, in the redemption of the body, but also deliverance and renovation to all nature as well. This noble conception was implied already in the teaching of the Old Testament, not only in its declaration that the world was cursed for man's sake (Rom. viii. 20), but in the prediction of a new heavens and a new earth (verse 21). Paul here simply takes his position in the company of the prophets.

The glories of the future world find comparative expression again in I Cor. xiii. 10–13 as not only spiritual but eternal and perfect. There are besides two rapid allusions to future glories which are so slightly touched on in contexts of stinging satire as not fully to explain themselves. The one reminds the saints that they shall judge the world and angels (I Cor. vi. 2, 3), and the other assumes that at some time or other, they are to come to a kingship (I Cor. iv. 8). Out of our present epistles alone the time and circumstances when these promises shall be fulfilled can scarcely be confidently asserted. We can only say that if the reigning of the saints refers to a co-reigning with Christ (cf. II Tim. ii. 12), it must be fulfilled before Christ lays down His kingdom. And in like manner the judging must come before the Advent, unless it refers only to the part the saints take in the last judgment scene (cf. Mt. xix. 28; xxv. 31). The Apostle expects his readers to understand his allusions out of knowledge obtained elsewhere than in these epistles. Perhaps he has in mind such "words of the Lord" as are recorded in Luke xxii. 29, 30. For us, the whole matter may rest for the present *sub judice*.

III. — The Later Epistles

The distribution of predictive passages through the letters written by St. Paul during his first imprisonment, — Ephesians,

Colossians, Philemon and Philippians (A.D. 62 and 63), — is analogous to what we have observed in the preceding group. In the more theological and polemical letters, as there, so here, such passages are few, while in the more practical and personal letters they are comparatively numerous. The Second Advent is not directly mentioned at all in Ephesians, and only once, and then very incidentally, in Colossians; while, although the brief and purely occasional letter to Philemon naturally enough contains no allusions to the future, the Epistle to the Philippians, which resembles in general manner and contents the letters to the Corinthians and Thessalonians, like them too is full of them. The nature of the eschatological matter which is found in each epistle is in striking harmony with its purpose and general character: in Ephesians and Colossians it is confined to allusions, sometimes somewhat obscure, to eschatological facts which are introduced usually with a theological or polemic object; in Philippians, where Paul pours out his heart, it is free and rich, and usually has a direct personal design of encouragement or consolation. In all these epistles alike, however, it is introduced only incidentally — no section has it as its chief end to record the future; but in Philippians it is more fully and lovingly dwelt upon, in Ephesians and Colossians more allusively touched. It is not surprising, under such circumstances, that very little is revealed to us concerning the future in these epistles beyond what was already contained in the earlier letters, the teaching of which most commonly furnishes the full statement of the facts here briefly referred to. Now and then, however, they cast a ray of light on points or sides of the truth which were not before fully illuminated, and thus enable us to count distinct gains from their possession. Nowhere are they out of harmony with what the earlier epistles have revealed.

The eschatological contents of the twin letters, Ephesians and Colossians, will illustrate all this very sharply. Much is made in them of an inheritance of hope laid up in heaven for the saints in light (Eph. i. 14, cf. ii. 7; Col. i. 12, i. 5: cf. iii. 24). The time of its realization is when Christ our life shall be manifested, at which time we also shall be manifested with Him in glory (Col. iii. 4). It is clearly presupposed that the reception of the inheritance is conditioned on a previous judgment. We must be made meet for it by the Father, by a deliverance from the power of darkness and translation into the kingdom of Him by whom we have redemption, the forgiveness of our sins (Col. i. 12). Whatsoever good thing each one does, the same he shall certainly receive from the Lord (Eph. vi. 8). The inheritance itself is thus a recompense for our service here (Col. iii. 24). Judgment again is implied in the constant undertone of allusion to a presentation of us by God or Christ, pure and blameless and unaccusable at once before Christ and in Christ (Eph. i. 22; Col. i. 22, 28). But if Christ is thus the judge, we naturally enough are to live our life here in His fear (Eph. v. 21). The resurrection of the saints is implied now and then (Col. ii. 12, 13; cf. Eph. v. 23), and once asserted in the declaration that Christ has become "the first-born from the dead, that in all things He might have the pre-eminence" (Col. i. 18). The nature of this inter-adventual period is explained with apparent reference to some such teaching as is given in I Cor. xv. 25, to be a period of conflict (Eph. vi. 12), and its opening days are hence said to be evil (Eph. v. 16), though, no doubt, the evil will decrease as conflict passes into victory. The enemies of the Lord are named as principalities and powers, and their subjugation was potentially completed at His death and resurrection (Col. ii. 15). The actual completion of the victory and subjection of all things to the Son is briefly re-stated in each epistle. In the one it is declared that God has purposed with reference to the dispensation of the fulness of the times (i.e. this present dispensation of the ends of the ages, I Cor. x. 11) to gather again all things as under one head in Christ, the things in the heavens and the things upon earth (Eph. i. 10). In the other it is said that it was the Father's good pleasure that all the fulness should dwell in the Son, and that through Him all things should be reconciled to Him, whether things upon the earth or things in the heavens, and that this reconciliation should be wrought by His blood outpoured on the cross (Col. i. 19). The only difference between such statements and such a one as II Cor. v. 19 is that these deal with the universe, while that treats only of man, and hence these presuppose the full teaching implied in I Cor. xv. 10–28 and Rom. viii. 18–25, and sum up in a single pregnant sentence the full effects of the Saviour's work. The method of Christ's attack on the principalities and powers and world-rulers of this darkness and spiritual hosts of wickedness, and the means by which He will work His victory, are declared at Eph. vi. 12; from which we learn — as we might have guessed from Rom. xi. 25, *sq.* — that Christians are His soldiers in this holy war, and it is through our victory that His victory is known. It is easy to see that there is nothing new in all this, and yet there is much that has the appearance of being new. We see everything from a different angle; the light drops upon it from a new point, and the effect is to bring out new relations in the old truths and give us a feeling of its substantialness. We become more conscious that we are looking at solid facts, with fronts and backs and sides, standing each in due and fixed relations to all.

The Epistle to the Philippians differs from the others of its group only in dwelling more lingeringly on the matters it mentions, and thus transporting us back into the full atmosphere of Corinthians and Thessalonians. Here, too, Paul thinks of the advent chiefly in the aspect of the judgment at which we are to receive our eternal approval and reward or disapproval and rejection. He is sure that He who began a good work in His readers will perfect it, until the day of Jesus Christ (i. 6); he prays that they may be pure and void of offence against the day of Christ (i. 10); he desires them to complete their Christian life that he may have whereof to glory in the day of Christ that he did not run in vain, neither labour in vain (ii. 16). These sentences might have come from any of the earlier epistles. The events of the day of the Lord are detailed quite in the spirit of the earlier epistles in iii. 20, 21. Our real home, the commonwealth in which is our citizenship, is heaven, from whence we patiently await a Saviour, the Lord Jesus Christ, who shall fashion anew the body of our humiliation so that it shall be

conformed to the body of His glory, according to the working
whereby He is able to subdue all things unto Himself. These
two verses compress within their narrow compass most of the
essential features of Paul's eschatology: Christ's present enthronement as King of the state in which our citizenship is, in
heaven, from whence we are to expect Him to return in due time;
our resurrection and the nature of our new bodies on the one side
as no longer bodies of humiliation, on the other as like Christ's
resurrection body, and hence glorious; Christ's conquest of all
things to Himself, and last of all of death, in our resurrection,
of which, therefore, all His other conquests are a guerdon.

The description of our resurrection bodies as conformed to
Christ's glorified body is important in itself, and all the more
so as it helps us to catch the meaning of the almost immediately
preceding statement (iii. 10 *sq.*) of Paul's deep desire "to know
Christ and the power of His resurrection and the fellowship of
His suffering, becoming conformed unto His death, if by any
means he may attain to the resurrection of the dead." It has
become somewhat common to see in this passage a hint that
Paul knew only of a resurrection of the redeemed, and himself
expected to rise only in case he was savingly united to Christ.
This exposition receives, no doubt, some colour from the phraseology used; but when we observe the intensely moral nature
of the longing, as expressed in the immediately subsequent context, we cannot help limiting the term "resurrection from the
dead" here, by the added idea of resurrection to glory, and the
full statement of verse 21 inevitably throws back its light upon
it. It is not mere resurrection that Paul longs for; he gladly
becomes conformed to Christ in His death that he may be conformed to Him in His resurrection also, and the gist of the whole
passage is bound up in this idea of conformity to Christ, with
which it opens (verse 10) and with which it closes (verse 21).
To think of two separate resurrections here — of the just and
the unjust — in the former of which Paul desires to rise, is to
cut the knot, not untie it. Nothing in the language suggests
it — the "resurrection from the dead" is as unlimited [10] as the

[10] On ἐξανάστασις, see Meyer *in loc.*

"death" that precedes it. Nothing in the context demands or even allows it. Nothing anywhere in Paul's writings justifies it. It is inconsistent with what we have found Paul saying about the Second Advent and its relation to the end, at I Cor. xv. 20–28. And finally it is contradicted by his explicit statements concerning the general resurrection, in the discourses in Acts which are closest in time to the date of these letters, and which ought to be considered along with them, especially Acts xxiv. 15, where in so many words the resurrection is made to include both the just and unjust (cf. xxiii. 6; xxvi. 8, 23; xxviii. 20). The limitation which the context supplies in our present passage is not that of class, much less that of time, but that of result; Paul longs to be conformed to Christ in resurrection as in death — he is glad to suffer with Him that he may be also glorified together with Him. Yea, he counts his sufferings but refuse, if he may gain Christ and *be found in Him,* clothed in the righteousness which is by faith. This is the ruling thought which conditions the statements of verse 11, and is openly returned to at verse 21.

The mention of the subjection of all things to Christ in verse 21, which recalls the teaching of I Cor. xv. 20–28 again, was already prepared for by the account of the glory which God gave the Son as a reward for His work of suffering, in ii. 9–11. There His supreme exaltation is stated to have been given Him of God for a purpose — that all creation should be subjected to Him, should bow the knee to His Name and confess Him to be Lord to the glory of God the Father. The completion of this purpose Paul here (iii. 21) asserts Christ to have the power to bring about, but nothing is implied in either passage as to the rapidity of its actual realization.

Some have thought, however, that in this epistle also Paul expresses his confidence that all should be fulfilled in his own time. Plainly, however, the reference of the completion of our moral probation, or of our victory over the present humiliation, to the Second Advent goes no further than to leave the possibility of its coming in our generation open (i. 6; iii. 21), and the latter at least is conditioned by the desire for a good resurrection, which is earnestly expressed immediately before. "The Lord is at hand" (iv. 5) would be more to the point, if its reference to time and the Second Advent were plainer. But although it was early so understood (e. g., by Barnabas), it can hardly be properly so taken. It is, indeed, scarcely congruous to speak of a person as near in time; we speak of events or actions, times or seasons as near, meaning it temporally; but when we say a person is near, we mean it inevitably of a space-relation. And the connexion of the present verse points even more strongly in the same direction. Whether we construe it with what goes before, or with what comes after — whether we read "Let your gentleness be known to all men, [for] the Lord is near," or "The Lord is near, [therefore] be anxious for nothing, but in everything . . . let your requests be made known unto God," — the reference to God's continual nearness to the soul for help is preferable to that to the Second Advent. And if, as seems likely, the latter connexion be the intended one, the contextual argument is pressing. The fact that the same phrase occurs in the Psalter in the space-sense, and must have been therefore in familiar use in this sense by Paul and his readers alike, while the asyndetic, proverbial way in which it is introduced here gives it the appearance of a quotation, adds all that was needed to render this interpretation of it here certain.

The Apostle's real feelings towards the future life are clearly exposed to us in the touching words of i. 21 *sq.*, the close resemblance of which to II Cor. v. 1–10 is patent. Here he does not refer in the remotest way to a hope of living to see the advent, but begins where he ended in II Corinthians, with the assertion of his personal preference for death rather than life, because death brought the gain of being with Christ, "which is far better." Even the "naked" intermediate state of the soul, between death and resurrection, is thus in Paul's view to be chosen rather than a life at home in the body but abroad from the Lord. Yet he does not therefore choose to die: "but what if to live in the flesh — this means fruit of my work?" he pauses to ask himself, and can but answer that he is in a strait betwixt the two, and finally that since to die is advantageous to himself

PROPHECIES OF ST. PAUL

alone, while to live is more needful for his converts, he knows
he shall abide still a while in this world. To him, too, man here
is but

> "a hasty traveller
> Posting between the present and the future,
> That baits awhile in this dull fleshly tavern";

and yet, though this tent-dwelling is seen by him in all its
insufficiency and inefficiency, like the good Samaritan he is
willing to prolong his stay in even so humble a caravanserai
(iii. 21) for the succouring of his fellows — nay, like the Lord
Himself, he counts the glory of the heavenly life not a thing to
be graspingly seized, so long as by humbling himself to the form
of a tenant here he may save the more. The spirit that was in
Christ dwelt within him.

The eschatology of the Pastoral Epistles — I Timothy,
Titus, and II Timothy (A.D. 67, 68) — the richest depository
of which is the Second Epistle to Timothy, is indistinguishable
from that of the other Pauline letters. In these letters again the
Second Advent is primarily and most prominently conceived as
the closing act of the world, the final judgment of men, and
therefore the goal of all their moral endeavours. Timothy is
strenuously exhorted "to keep the commandment," that is, the
evangelical rule of life, "spotless and irreproachable until the
appearing of our Lord Jesus Christ" (I Tim. vi. 14). All of
Paul's confidence is based on his persuasion that Jesus Christ,
the abolisher of death and bringer of life and incorruption to
light through the Gospel, is able to guard his deposit [11] "against
that day" (II Tim. i. 12), and that there is laid up for him the
crown of righteousness which the Lord, the righteous Judge,
shall give him at that day (II Tim. iv. 8). "And not to me only,"
he adds, as if to guard against his confidence seeming one personal to himself, "but also to all them that have loved His
appearing." Though at that day the Lord will render to Alexander according to his works (II Tim. iv. 14), he will grant
mercy to Onesiphorus (II Tim. i. 16); and in general he will at-

[11] τὴν παραθήκην μου = "what I have entrusted to him."

tach to godliness the promise both of the life that now is and that which is to come (I Tim. iv. 8).

It follows, therefore, that for all those in Christ the Second Advent is a blessed hope to be waited for with patience, but also with loving desire and longing. Christians are described as those that love Christ's appearing (II Tim. iv. 8), and the hope of it is blessed (Titus ii. 13) because it is the epiphany of the glory of our great God and Saviour Jesus Christ, even as the former coming was the epiphany of His grace (Titus ii. 13, cf. 11). It is implied that as the grace so the glory is for Christ's children. What this glory consists in is not, however, very sharply defined. It is the deposit of life and incorruption that the Saviour holds in trust for His children (II Tim. i. 12). It is the crown of righteousness which the righteous Judge will bestow upon them (II Tim. iv. 8). It is freedom from all iniquity (Titus ii. 14). It is the actual inheritance of the eternal life now hoped for (Titus iii. 7). But all this is description rather than definition. Nothing is said of resurrection except that they gravely err who think it already past (II Tim. ii. 18), nothing of the new bodies to be given to the saints, or of any of the glories that accompany the final triumph. What is said describes only the full realization of what is already enjoyed in its first fruits here or what comes in some abundance in the imperfect intermediate state.

For the glories of the advent do not blind Paul to the bliss of a Christian's hope in "this world," whether in the body or out of the body. In the fervid music of a Christian hymn the Apostle assures his son Timothy of his own steadfast faith in the faithful saying (II Tim. ii. 11–13):—

> "If we died with Him, we shall also live with Him;
> If we endure we shall also reign with Him;
> If we shall deny Him, He will also deny us;
> If we are faithless — He abideth faithful,
> For He cannot deny Himself."

And death itself, he says, can but "save him into Christ's heavenly kingdom" (II Tim. iv. 18). The partaking in Christ's death and life in this passage seems to be meant ethically; and the co-regnancy with the Lord that is promised to the suffering believer apparently concerns the being with Christ in the heavenly kingdom, — whether in the body or abroad from the body. Thus the Apostle is not here contemplating the glories of the advent, but comforting and strengthening himself with the profitableness of godliness in its promise of the life that now is, under the epiphany of God's grace, when we can be but looking for the epiphany of His glory. That he expects death (for now he was sure of death, II Tim. iv. 6) to introduce him into Christ's heavenly kingdom advertises to us that that kingdom is now in progress, and II Tim. iv. 1 is in harmony with this just because it tells us nothing at all of the time of the kingdom.[12]

About Christ's reign and work as king — in other words, concerning the nature of this period in which we live — these epistles are somewhat rich in teaching. These "latter times" or "last days"[13] — for these are, according to the fixed usage of the times, the designations under which the Apostle speaks of the dispensation of the Spirit, — are not to be an age of idleness or of sloth among Christians; but, in harmony with the statements of the earlier letters, which represented it as a time of conflict with and conquest of evil, it is here pictured as a time in which apostasies shall occur (I Tim. iv. 1), and false doctrines flourish along with evil practices (II Tim. iii. 1, sq.), when the just shall suffer persecution, and evil men and impostors wax worse and worse (II Tim. iii. 13), and, even in the Church, men shall not endure sound doctrine, but shall introduce teachers after their own lusts (II Tim. iv. 3 sq.). It would be manifestly illegitimate to understand these descriptions as necessarily covering the life of the whole dispensation on the earliest verge of which the prophet was standing. Some of these evils had al-

---

[12] Notice that the correct translation is: "I charge thee before God and Christ Jesus who shall judge the quick and the dead, and by His appearing and by His kingdom." Each item is adduced entirely separately; the Apostle is accumulating the incitements to action, not giving a chronological list, which, in any case, the passage does not furnish.

[13] ἐν ὑστέροις καιροῖς, I Tim. iv. 1; ἐν ἐσχάταις ἡμέραις, II Tim. iii. 1.

ready broken out in his own times, others were pushing up the ground preparatory to appearing above it themselves. It is historically plain to us, no doubt, that they suitably describe the state of affairs up to at least our own day. But we must remember that all the indications are that Paul had the first stages of "the latter times" in mind, and actually says nothing to imply either that the evil should long predominate over the good, or that the whole period should be marked by such disorders.

When the Lord should come, he indeed keeps as uncertain in these epistles as in all his former ones. In II Timothy he expects his own death immediately, and he contemplates it with patience and even joy, no longer with the shrinking expressed in II Corinthians. It is all the more gratuitous to insist here that the natural reference of Timothy's keeping the faith to the advent as the judgment (I Tim. vi. 14), implies that he confidently expected that great closing event at once or very soon. On the contrary it is reiterated in the same context that God alone knows the times and seasons, in the assertion that God would show the epiphany of our Lord Jesus Christ "in His own times." Beyond this the Apostle never goes; and it is appropriate that in his earliest and latest epistles especially he should categorically assert the absolute uncertainty of the time of the consummation (I Thess. v. 1; I Tim. vi. 15). Surely an intense personal conviction that the times and seasons were entirely out of his knowledge can alone account for so consistent an attitude of complete uncertainty.

It appears to be legitimate to affirm in the light of the preceding pages that it is clear that there is such a thing as a Pauline eschatology; a consistent teaching on the last things which runs through the whole mass of his writings, not filling them, indeed, as some would have us believe, but appearing on their surface like daisies in a meadow — here in tolerable profusion, there in quite a mass, there scattered one by one at intervals of some distance — everywhere woven into it as constituent parts of the turf carpeting. The main outlines of this eschatology are repeated over and over again, and exhibited from many separate points of view, until we know them from every side and are confident of their contour and exact nature. Details are added to the general picture by nearly every letter; and each detail falls so readily into its place in the outline as to prove both that the Apostle held a developed scheme of truth on this subject, and that we are correctly understanding it. A general recapitulation of the broadest features of his doctrine will alone be necessary in closing.

Paul, then, teaches that as Jesus has once come in humiliation, bringing grace into the world, and God has raised Him to high exaltation and universal dominion in reward for His sufferings and in order to the completion of His work of redemption; so when He shall have put all His enemies under His feet, He shall come again to judgment in an epiphany of glory, to close the dispensation of grace and usher in the heavenly blessedness. The enemies to be conquered are principalities and powers and world-rulers of this darkness and spiritual hosts of wickedness; this whole period is the period of advancing conquest and will end with the victory over the last enemy, death, and the consequent resurrection of the dead. In this advancing conquest Christ's elect are His soldiers, and the conversion of the world — first of the Gentiles, then of the Jews — marks the culminating victory over the powers of evil. How long this conflict continues before it is crowned with complete victory, how long the supreme and sole kingship of Christ endures before He restores the restored realm to His father, the Apostle leaves in complete uncertainty. He predicts the evil days of the opening battle, the glad days of the victory; and leaves all questions of times and seasons to Him whose own times they are. At the end, however, are the general resurrection and the general judgment, when the eternal rewards and punishments are awarded by Christ as judge, and then, all things having been duly gathered together thus again under one head by Him, he subjects them all to God that He may once more become "all relations among all creations." That the blessed dead may be fitted to remain for ever with the Lord, He gives them each his own body, glorified and purified and rendered the willing organ of the Holy Ghost. Christ's living, though they die not, are "changed" to a like glory. Not only man, but all creation feels the renovation and shares in the revelation of the sons of God, and there is a new heaven and a new earth. And thus the work of the Redeemer is completed, the end has come, and it is visible to men and angels that through Him in whom it was His pleasure that all the fulness should dwell, God has at length reconciled all things unto Himself, having made peace through the blood of His cross — through Him, whether things upon the earth or things in the heavens — yea, even us, who were in times past alienated and enemies, hath He reconciled in the body of His flesh through death, to present us holy and without blemish and unreproachable before Him.

THE MILLENNIUM AND THE APOCALYPSE

THE MILLENNIUM AND THE APOCALYPSE [1]

OF the section of the Apocalypse which extends (according to his division of the book) from xx. 1 to xxi. 8, Kliefoth remarks, as he approaches its study, that "because the so-called millennium is included in its compass, it has been more than any other part of the book tortured by tendency-exposition into a variety of divergent senses." [2] This is undoubtedly true: but in reprobating it, we must not permit ourselves to forget that there is a sense in which it is proper to permit our understanding of so obscure a portion of Scripture to be affected by the clearer teaching of its more didactic parts. We must guard, no doubt, against carrying this too far and doing violence to the text before us in the interests of Bible-harmony. But within due limits, surely, the order of investigation should be from the clearer to the more obscure. And it is to be feared that there has been much less tendency-interpretation of Rev. xx in the interest of preconceived theory, than there has been tendency-interpretation of the rest of Scripture in the interest of conceptions derived from misunderstandings of this obscure passage.

Nothing, indeed, seems to have been more common in all ages of the Church than to frame an eschatological scheme from this passage, imperfectly understood, and then to impose this scheme on the rest of Scripture *vi et armis*. To realize this, we have but to recall the manifold influences which have wrought not only on eschatological dreaming, but on theological thought and on Christian life itself, out of the conception summed up in the term "the millennium." Yet not only the word, but, as Kliefoth has himself solidly shown,[3] the thing, is unknown to Scripture outside of this passage.[4] And not only so, but there

---

[1] From *The Princeton Theological Review*, v. 2, 1904, pp. 599–617.

[2] "Die Offenbarung des Johannes," 1874, III, 254.

[3] "Christliche Eschatologie," 1886, pp. 183 *sq.*

[4] "Once, and only once," says the "Encyc. Bibl.," 3095, "in the New Testament we hear of a millennium." W. A. Brown, in Hastings' "Bible Dict.," III,

are not a few passages of Scripture — as Kliefoth also has shown [5] — which seem definitely to exclude the whole conception, and which must be subjected to most unnatural exegetical manipulation to bring them into harmony with it at all. We need not raise the question whether Scripture can contradict Scripture: in our day, certainly, there is no lack of expositors who would feel little difficulty in expounding the eschatology of Revelation as definitely the *antipodes* of that, say, of Paul, not to say the eschatology of one section of Revelation as the precise contradictory of that of another. But surely, for those who look upon the Bible as something other than the chance driftage of the earliest age of Christianity, it is at least undesirable to assume such an antagonism beforehand; and on the emergence of apparent inconsistencies it certainly becomes in the first instance incumbent upon us to review our expositions under the impulse of at least the possibility that they may prove to be in error. We shall not proceed far in such an undertaking, as it seems to us, before we discover that the traditional interpretation of Revelation which yields the notion of a "millennium" is at fault; and that this book, when taken in its natural and self-indicated sense, needs no harmonizing with the eschatology of the rest of the New Testament, for the simple reason that its eschatology is precisely the same with that of its companion books.

In order to make this good, it will not be necessary to do more than pass in rapid review the series of visions which constitute the particular section of the Apocalypse of which the millennium-passage forms a part. The structure of the book,

---

371. The period of 1000 years seems to be applied to such a conception first in the Slavonic "Book of the Secrets of Enoch," 33: 1, 2 (see "Encyc. Bibl.," 1368; Hastings, I, 711*a*, III, 371*a*) which is dated by Charles in the first half of the first century. It is there based on the idea of a Sabbatical week: as the world was created in six days followed by a day of rest, so the world will last 6000 years followed by 1000 years of rest. The same idea seems to underlie Barnabas, c. 15, though Dr. Salmond, "Christian Doct. of Immort.," 1895, p. 438, does not think so. Cf. Gebhardt, "The Doctrine of the Apocalypse," E. T., pp. 277–278.

[5] *Ibid.*, pp. 187–188. Cf. Milligan, "Baird Lectures on the Revelation of St. John," 1886, pp. 205 *sq.*; and "Expositor's Bible: The Book of Revelation," 1889, pp. 345 *sq.*

made up as it is of seven parallel sections,[6] repeating with progressive clearness, fullness and richness the whole history of the inter-adventual period, and thus advancing in a spiral fashion to its climax, renders it possible to do this without drawing too much on a knowledge of the whole book. We have only to bear clearly in mind a few primary principles, apart from which no portion of the book can be understood, and we need not despair of unlocking the secrets of this section also.

These primary principles are, with the greatest possible brevity, the following: 1. The principle of *recapitulation*.[7] That is to say, the structure of the book is such that it returns at the opening of each of its seven sections to the first advent, and gives in the course of each section a picture of the whole inter-adventual period — each successive portraiture, however, rising above the previous one in the stress laid on the issue of the history being wrought out during its course. The present section, being the last, reaches, therefore, the climax, and all its emphasis is thrown upon the triumph of Christ's kingdom. 2. The principle of *successive visions*. That is to say, the several visions following one another within the limits of each section, though bound to each other by innumerable links, yet are presented as separate visions, and are to be interpreted, each, as a complete picture in itself. 3. The principle of *symbolism*. That is to say — as is implied, indeed, in the simple fact that we are brought face to face here with a series of visions significant of events — we are to bear continually in mind that the whole fabric of the book is compact of symbols. The descriptions are descriptions not of the real occurrences themselves, but of symbols of the real occurrences; and are to be read strictly as such. Even more than in the case of parables, we are to avoid pressing

---

[6] The plan of the book is, then, something like the following: Prologue, I: 1–8; seven parallel sections divided at III: 22, VIII: 1, XI: 19, XIV: 20, XVI: 21 and XIX: 20; Epilogue, XXII: 6–21. The subdivisions of the several sections follow, each, its own course.

[7] This principle of *recapitulatio* was announced by Augustine, and perfected by Nicolas Colladon (1584) and David Pareus (1618), and especially by Cocceius and Vitringa. A very large number of expositors have employed its fundamental principle, as, among later ones, for instance, Hofmann, Hengstenberg, Ebrard, Kienlen; but with varying degrees of judiciousness.

details in our interpretation of symbols: most of the details are
details of the symbol, designed purely to bring the symbol
sharply and strongly before the mind's eye, and are not to be
transferred by any method of interpretation whatever directly
to the thing symbolized. The symbol as a whole symbolizes the
real event: and the details of the picture belong primarily only
to the symbol. Of course, now and then a hint is thrown out
which may seem more or less to traverse this general rule: but,
as a general rule, it is not only sound but absolutely necessary for
any sane interpretation of the book. 4. The principle of *ethical purpose*. That is to say, here as in all prophecy it is the spiritual and
ethical impression that rules the presentation and not an annal-
istic or chronological intent. The purpose of the seer is to make
known indeed — to make wise — but not for knowledge's own
sake, but for a further end: to make known unto action, to make
wise unto salvation. He contents himself, therefore, with what
is efficacious for his spiritual end and never loses himself in
details which can have no other object than the satisfaction of
the curiosity of the mind for historical or other knowledge.

One of the effects of the recognition of these primary principles — an effect the perception of which is no more interesting
in itself than fruitful for the interpretation of the book — is the
transference of the task of the interpreter from the region of
minute philology to that of broad literary appreciation. The
ascertainment of the meaning of the Apocalypse is a task, that
is to say, not directly of verbal criticism but of sympathetic
imagination: the teaching of the book lies not immediately in
its words, but in the wide vistas its visions open to the fancy.
It is the seeing eye, here, therefore, rather than the nice scales
of linguistic science, that is needful more obviously than in
most sections of Scripture.

If, now, we approach the study of the section at present before us under the guidance of these principles, it is probable that
we shall not find it impossible to follow at least its main drift.

The section opens with a vision of the victory of the Word
of God, the King of Kings and Lord of Lords over all His ene-

mies. We see Him come forth from heaven girt for war, followed by the armies of heaven; the birds of the air are summoned to the feast of corpses that shall be prepared for them: the armies of the enemy — the beasts and the kings of the earth — are gathered against Him and are totally destroyed; and "all the birds are filled with their flesh" (xix. 11–21). It is a vivid picture of a complete victory, an entire conquest, that we have here; and all the imagery of war and battle is employed to give it life. This is the symbol. The thing symbolized is obviously the complete victory of the Son of God over all the hosts of wickedness. Only a single hint of this signification is afforded by the language of the description, but that is enough. On two occasions we are carefully told that the sword by which the victory is won proceeds *out of the mouth* of the conqueror (verses 15 and 21). We are not to think, as we read, of any literal war or manual fighting, therefore; the conquest is wrought by the spoken word — in short, by the preaching of the Gospel. In fine, we have before us here a picture of the victorious career of the Gospel of Christ in the world. All the imagery of the dread battle and its hideous details are but to give us the impression of the completeness of the victory. Christ's Gospel is to conquer the earth: He is to overcome all His enemies.

There is, of course, nothing new in this. The victory of the Gospel was predicted over and over again even in Old Testament times under the figure of a spiritual conquest. It is thus also that Paul pictures it. It is thus that John himself elsewhere portrays it: it is indeed the staple representation of this whole book. In particular we perceive that this splendid vision is, after all, only the expansion of the parallel vision given in the second verse of the sixth chapter. When the first seal was opened, "And I saw," says the seer, "and, behold, a white horse, and he that sat thereon had a bow; and there was given unto him a crown: and he came forth conquering, and to conquer." It is the same scene that is now before us, only strengthened and made more emphatic as befits its place near the end of the book. We recall now the principle of "recapitulation" which governs the structure of the book, and see that this first vision of the last section, in accordance with the general method of the book, returns to the beginning and portrays for us, as vi. 2 and xii. 1 do, the first coming of the Lord and the purpose and now, with more detail and stress, the issue of this coming. What we have here, in effect, is a picture of the whole period between the first and second advents, seen from the point of view of heaven. It is the period of the advancing victory of the Son of God over the world, emphasizing, in harmony with its place at the end of the book, the completeness of the victory. It is the eleventh chapter of Romans and the fifteenth of I Corinthians in symbolical form: and there is nothing in it that was not already in them — except that, perhaps, the completeness of the triumph of the Gospel is possibly somewhat more emphasized here.

With the opening of the twentieth chapter the scene changes (xx. 1–10). Here we are not smitten in the face with the flame and flare of war: it is a spectacle of utter peace rather that is presented to us. The peace is, however, it must be observed, thrown up against a background of war. The vision opens with a picture of the descent of an angel out of heaven who binds "the dragon, the old serpent, which is the Devil and Satan," for a thousand years. Then we see the saints of God reigning with their Lord, and we are invited to contemplate the blessedness of their estate. But when Satan is bound we are significantly told that after the thousand years "he must be loosed for a little time." The saints themselves, moreover, we are informed, have not attained their exaltation and blessedness save through tribulation. They have all passed through the stress of this beast-beset life — have all been "beheaded" for the testimony of Jesus. And at the end we learn of the renewed activity of Satan and his final destruction by fire out of heaven.

This thousand-year peace that is set before us is therefore a peace hedged around with war. It was won by war; the participants in it have come to it through war; it ends in war. What now is this thousand-year peace? It is certainly not what we have come traditionally to understand by the "millennium," as is made evident by many considerations, and sufficiently so by this one: that those who participate in it are spoken of as mere "souls" (ver. 4) — "the souls of them that had been beheaded for the testimony of Jesus and for the Word of God." It is not disembodied souls who are to constitute the Church during its state of highest development on earth, when the knowledge of the glory of God covers the earth as the waters cover the sea. Neither is it disembodied souls who are thought of as constituting the kingdom which Christ is intending to set up in the earth after His advent, that they may rule with Him over the nations. And when we have said this, we are surely following hard on the pathway that leads to the true understanding of the vision. The vision, in one word, is a vision of the peace of those who have died in the Lord; and its message to us is embodied in the words of xiv. 13: "Blessed are the dead which die in the Lord, from henceforth" — of which passage the present is indeed only an expansion.

The picture that is brought before us here is, in fine, the picture of the "intermediate state" — of the saints of God gathered in heaven away from the confused noise and garments bathed in blood that characterize the war upon earth, in order that they may securely await the end.[8] The thousand years, thus, is the whole of this present dispensation, which again is placed before us in its entirety, but looked at now relatively not to what is passing on earth but to what is enjoyed "in Paradise." This, in fact, is the meaning of the symbol of a thousand years. For, this period between the advents is, on earth, a broken time — three and a half years, a "little time" (ver. 3)[9]

[8] So far L. Kraussold ("Das tausendjährige Reich," u. s. w., 1863) is right: "The souls of the righteous live before God and with God — that is their first resurrection." But though he thus correctly interprets the "first resurrection" of the intermediate state, he does not see that the "millennium" is the intermediate period.

[9] Cf. Milligan, "Baird Lectures," pp. 213–214; "Expositor's Bible," pp. 340–341. The *term* 'three and a half years' does not occur in the Apocalypse, but its equivalents, forty-two months (xi. 2, xiii. 5) and 1260 days (xi. 3, xii. 6) do, as well as the corresponding phrase "a time and times and half a time" (xii. 14), which is derived of course from Daniel vii. 25, xii. 7. All these designations alike "express the whole time of the Church's militant and suffering condition in the

— which, amid turmoil and trouble, the saints are encouraged to look upon as of short duration, soon to be over. To the saints in bliss it is, on the contrary, a long and blessed period passing slowly and peacefully by, while they reign with Christ and enjoy the blessedness of holy communion with Him — "a thousand years." [10]

Of course the passage (xx. 1–10) does not give us a direct description of "the intermediate state." We must bear in mind that the book we are reading is written in symbols and gives us a direct description of nothing that it sets before us, but always a direct description only of the symbol by which it is represented. In the preceding vision (xix. 11–21) we had no direct description of the triumph and progress of the Gospel, but only of a fierce and gruesome war: the single phrase that spoke of the slaying sword as "proceeding out of the mouth" of the conqueror alone indicated that it was a conquest by means of persuading words. So here we are not to expect a direct description of the "intermediate state": were such a description given, that would be evidence enough that the intermediate state was not intended, but was rather the symbol of something else. The single hint that it is of the condition of the "souls" of those who have died in Christ and for Christ that the seer is speaking, is enough here to direct our thoughts in the right direction. What is described, or rather, to speak more exactly — for it is a course of events that is brought before us — what is narrated to us is the chaining of Satan "that he should deceive the nations no more"; the consequent security and glory of Christ's hitherto persecuted people; and the subsequent destruction of Satan. It is a description in the form of a narrative:

world, the whole time between the First and Second Coming of the Lord" (Milligan: Com. in Schaff's "Pop. Com. on N. T." on xi. 2, pp. 93, 94, where there is a clear and full statement). For the equivalent phrase "a little time" the references at the head of this note will suffice.

[10] Cf. Lee ("Speaker's Com." on xx. 2, p. 792): "That the period of a *'thousand years'* is to be taken figuratively is in accordance with such texts as Ps. xc. 4, . . . or II Peter iii. 8 . . . A space of time absolutely *long* is denoted. . . . A very great although not a countless number is signified. . . . . We are to understand a long though finite duration, beginning from the First Advent of Christ (I Cor. xv. 24, 25)."

the element of time and chronological succession belongs to the symbol, not to the thing symbolized. The "binding of Satan" is, therefore, in reality, not for a season, but with reference to a sphere; and his "loosing" again is not after a period but in another sphere: it is not subsequence but exteriority that is suggested. There is, indeed, no literal "binding of Satan" to be thought of at all: what happens, happens not to Satan but to the saints, and is only represented as happening to Satan for the purposes of the symbolical picture. What actually happens is that the saints described are removed from the sphere of Satan's assaults. The saints described are free from all access of Satan — he is bound with respect to them: outside of their charmed circle his horrid work goes on. This is indicated, indeed, in the very employment of the two symbols "a thousand years" and "a little time." A "thousand years" is the symbol of heavenly completeness and blessedness; the "little time" of earthly turmoil and evil. Those in the "thousand years" are safe from Satan's assaults: those outside the thousand years are still enduring his attacks. And therefore he, though with respect to those in the thousand years bound, is not destroyed; and the vision accordingly requires to close with an account of his complete destruction, and of course this also must needs be presented in the narrative form of a release of Satan, the gathering of his hosts and their destruction from above.

We may perhaps profitably advert to some of the traits that go to show that it is the children of God gathered in Paradise that are in view in the description of the rest and security that occupies the central section of the vision (vers. 4–6). We are told that the seer saw "thrones, and those that sat upon them, and judgment was given to them." Our Lord, we will remember, is uniformly represented as having been given a Messianic kingship in reward for His redemptive death, in order that He might carry out His mediatorial work to the end.[11] Those who, being His, go away from the body and home to the Lord, are accordingly conceived by the seer as ascending the throne with Him to share His kingship — not forever, however, but for a

[11] E. g., Phil. ii. 10.

thousand years, *i.e.*, for the Messianic period. Then, when the last enemy has been conquered and He restores the kingdom to the Father,[12] their co-reign with Him ceases, because His Messianic kingdom itself ceases. These reigning saints, now, are described as "souls" — a term which carries us back irresistibly to vi. 9, where we read of "the souls of them that had been slain for the Word of God resting underneath the altar," a passage of which the present is an expanded version. Similarly here, too, we are told that these souls are "of them that had been beheaded for the testimony of Jesus and for the Word of God, and such as worshipped not the beast, neither his image and received not the mark upon their forehead and upon their hand." The description in the symbol is drawn from the fate of martyrs; but it is not literal martyrs that are meant in the thing symbolized. To the seer all of Christ's saints are martyrs of the world. "For in the eyes of John," as has been well said, "all the disciples of a martyred Lord are martyrs": "Christ's Church is a martyr Church, she dies in her Master's service and for the world's good."[13] These all, dying in Christ, die not but live — for Christ is not Lord, any more than God is God, of the dead but the living. We must catch here the idea that pervades the whole of Jewish thought — inculcated as it is with the most constant iteration by the whole Old Testament revelation — that death is the penalty of sin and that restoration from death, that is resurrection, is involved, therefore, in reception into the favor of God. It is this that underlies and gives its explanation to our Lord's famous argument for the resurrection to which we have just alluded. And it is this, doubtless, that underlies also the seer's designation in our passage of the state of the souls in Paradise with their Lord, saved in principle if not in complete fruition, as "the first resurrection." "This," he says, "is the first resurrection"; and he pronounces those blessed who have part in it, and declares that over them "the

---

[12] I Cor. xv. 54.

[13] Milligan, "The Expositor's Bible: the Book of Revelation," pp. 182, 344. Cf. his beautiful words in Schaff's "Popular Commentary, The Revelation," *in loc.* IV.

second death" has no power. Subsequently he identifies "the
second death" with eternal destruction (ver. 14) in the lake of
fire — the symbol throughout these visions of the final state
of the wicked. To say that "the second death" has no power
over the saints of whom he is here speaking is to say at once
that they have already been subjected to the "first death,"
which can mean only that they have suffered bodily death, and
that they are "saved souls" with their life hidden with Christ
in God. That is to say, they are the blessed dead — the dwellers
in the "intermediate state." The "first resurrection" is here,
therefore, the symbolical description of what has befallen those
who while dead yet live in the Lord; and it is set in contrast with
the "second resurrection," which must mean the restoration of
the bodily life. As partakers of this "first resurrection" they
are set in contrast with "the rest of the dead" — who were to
"live not" until "the thousand years should be finished." This
phrase advertises us once more that those of whom the seer
speaks are themselves in a sense "dead," and as they are declared repeatedly to be *living* — living and reigning with Christ
— this cannot refer to spiritual death, but must find its reference to bodily death. Though dead, therefore, in this bodily
sense, they were yet alive — alive in the paradise of God with
Christ. The rest of the dead, on the other hand — those not
alive with Christ — wait for the end to live again: they are in
every sense dead — already suffering the penalty of sin and to
be restored to even bodily life only to be plunged into the terrible "second death."

It seems scarcely possible to read over these three verses,
however cursorily, without meeting thus with constant reminders that the peace and security pictured is the peace and
security of the blessed dead, seated in the heavenly places, in
their Lord, on the throne of the universe in company with Him.
Any hesitancy we may feel to adopt this view appears to arise
chiefly from the difficulty we naturally experience in reading
this apparently historical narrative as a descriptive picture of
a state — in translating, so to speak, the dynamic language of
narrative into the static language of description. Does not the

very term "a thousand years" suggest the lapse of time? And must we not, therefore, interpret what is represented as occurring before and after this thousand years as historical precedents and subsequents to it? Natural as this feeling is, we are persuaded it is grounded only on a certain not unnatural incapacity to enter fully into the seer's method and to give ourselves entirely to his guidance. If he elected to represent a state of completeness and perfection by a symbol which suggested lapse of time when taken in its literal meaning, he had no choice but to represent what was outside this state as *before* or *after*: that belonged to the very vehicle of representation. Now it is quite certain that the number 1000 represents in Bible symbolism absolute perfection and completeness; and that the symbolism of the Bible includes also the use of a period of time in order to express the idea of greatness, in connection with thoroughness and completeness.[14] It can scarcely be necessary to insist here afresh on the symbolical use of numbers in the Apocalypse and the necessity consequently laid upon the interpreter to treat them consistently not merely as symbols but as symbols embodying definite ideas. They constitute a language, and like any other language they are misleading unless intended and read as expressions of definite ideas. When the seer says seven or four or three or ten, he does not name these numbers at random but expresses by each a specific notion. The sacred number seven in combination with the equally sacred number three forms the number of holy perfection ten, and when this ten is cubed into a thousand the seer has said all he could say to convey to our minds the idea of absolute completeness. It is of more importance doubtless, however, to illustrate the use of time-periods to convey the idea of completeness. Ezek. xxxix. 9 provides an instance. There the completeness of the conquest of Israel over its enemies is expressed by saying that seven years shall be consumed in the burning up of the débris of battle: they "shall go forth," we read, "and shall make fires of the weapons and burn them, both the shields and the bucklers, the bows and the arrows, and the hand-staves and

---

[14] Dr. Milligan has shown this very convincingly.

the spears, and they shall *make fires of them seven years.*" It were absurd to suppose that it is intended that the fires shall actually endure seven years. We have here only a hyperbole to indicate the greatness of the mass to be consumed and the completeness of the consumption. A somewhat similar employment of the time-phrase to express the idea of greatness is found in the twelfth verse of the same chapter, where, after the defeat of Gog "and all his multitude," it is said, "And seven months shall the children of Israel be burying of them that they may cleanse the land." That is to say, the multitude of the dead is so great that by way of hyperbole their burial is said to consume seven months. The number seven employed by Ezekiel in these passages is replaced by the number a thousand in our present passage, with the effect of greatly enhancing the idea of greatness and of completeness conveyed. When the saints are said to live and reign with Christ a thousand years the idea intended is that of inconceivable exaltation, security and blessedness — a completeness of exaltation, security and blessedness beyond expression by ordinary language.

We can scarcely go the length of Dr. Milligan, nevertheless, and say that the time-element is wholly excluded from our passage. After all it is the intermediate state that is portrayed and the intermediate state has duration. But it is within the limits of sobriety to say that the time-element retires into the background and the stress is laid on the greatness and completeness of the security portrayed. This is, however, portrayed under a time-symbol: and the point now is that, this being so, the very necessity of the symbolism imposed on the writer the representation of the other elements of the symbol also by time-expressions. Accordingly in the picture which he draws for us the vision of the security of the saints is preceded and followed by scenes represented as occurring before and after it, but to be read as occurring merely outside it. The chaining of Satan is not in the event a preliminary transaction, on which the security of the saints follows: nor is the loosing of Satan a subsequent transaction, on which the security of the saints ceases. The saints rather escape entirely beyond the reach of Satan when they ascend to their Lord and take their seats on His throne by His side, and there they abide nevermore subject to his assaults. This is indeed suggested in the issue (verse 9*b*), where the destruction of Satan is compassed by a fire from heaven and not through the medium of a battle with the saints. But while the saints abide in their security Satan, though thus "bound" relatively to them, is loosed relatively to the world — and that is what is meant by the statement in verse 3*c* that "he must be loosed for a little time" — which is the symbol of the inter-adventual period, in the world; and not less in verses 7–10. We must here look on the time-element, we repeat, as belonging wholly to the symbol and read in the interpretation space-elements in its place. The intermediate state is in one word conceived of not out of relation to the "world," but as, so to speak, a safe haven of retreat in the midst of the world: the world is around it, and there Satan still works and deceives, but he who escapes through the one door of "beheading" for Christ's sake, rises not only to security but to a kingdom.

As we scrutinize the text closely with this scheme of interpretation in mind, the apparent difficulties that stand in its path give way one after another. One clause alone seems so recalcitrant as not to lend itself readily to the proposed interpretation. This occurs in the middle of verse 3. There it is affirmed that Satan is chained "that he should deceive the nations no more." Under Dr. Milligan's interpretation of the thousand years' security, which he applies not to the saints in glory with their Lord — the intermediate state — but to the saints in conflict on earth — the militant state — this clause seems no doubt hopeless. But if we are to understand that it is the intermediate state that is portrayed, the difficulty which it presents does not seem to be insuperable. In its general meaning the clause indeed is only the extreme point of the temporal-machinery in which the vision is cast. If what is *spacially* distinct, so to speak, in the reality, is to be represented in the figure as *temporally* distinct, there seems no way in which it can be done except by saying that Satan is first bound so as not to act, in order that he may be afterward loosed so as to act. The only real difficulty lies in the word "nations." Should we not expect "saints" instead — for is it not merely with reference to the saints that Satan is supposed to be bound? And is not the word "nations" the standing denomination in the Apocalypse of precisely the anti-Christian hosts? The only solution that readily suggests itself turns on the supposition that the word "nations" may be used here in its wider inclusive sense, and not of "those without" in contrast with God's people. The term "world" occurs in this double sense, and there seems no reason why "nations" should not also, especially since it is continually understood that the "nations" include God's people in the making (xxii. 2). Possibly little more is intended to be conveyed by the phrase in verse 3 than "to bring out and express that aspect of Satan by which he is specially distinguished in the Apocalypse" — that is to say, to declare simply that "Satan the deceiver" was bound,[15] and what is more than this belongs to the drapery of the symbolism. In verse 8 it appears to have a slightly different turn given it. There is a special propriety in its suggesting in this context "those without" indeed, but those without not so much the circle of Christ's people in general as Christ's people as gathered into the secure haven of the intermediate state. In a word, it seems that we may understand the "nations" here, not of the anti-Christian world in contrast with the Christian, but of the world on earth in contrast with the saints gathered in Paradise. As such the "nations" may include Christians also, but Christians not yet departed to their security — nay their monarchy — with their Lord. If these suggestions be allowed, something will certainly be gained towards a suitable interpretation of the clause. But it cannot be pretended that a real solution of its difficulties has been offered in any case; it remains a dark spot in an otherwise lucid paragraph and must be left for subsequent study to explain.

If the interpretation we have urged be adopted, this vision, therefore, as a whole (xx. 1–20), in sharp contrast with the pre-

---

[15] We are quoting here from Dr. Milligan's "Baird Lectures," first ed., pp. 223–225 note, which seems to us more suggestive than the note in "The Expositor's Bible" volume, pp. 350–351.

ceding one (xix. 11–21), which pictured the strife of God's people in the world, brings before us the spectacle of the peace of God's saints gathered in heaven. It, too, embraces the whole inter-adventual period, but that period as passed in the security and glory of the intermediate state. This is set forth, however, not out of relation to the militant Church on earth, but as, so to speak, its other side. It is as if the seer had said, Look on this picture and on that: neither alone, but the two in combination supply the true picture of the course of events between the first and second advents. The Church toiling and struggling here below is but half the story: the Church gathering above is the other half. And both speed them to the end. For the one it is a period of conflict, though of a conflict advancing to victory. For the other it is a period of restful security, nay of royal ruling. It is the conjunction of the two that constitutes this inter-adventual period; and, together, they pass onward to the end:

> Blessèd that flock safe penned in Paradise;
> Blessèd this flock which tramps in weary ways;
> All form one flock, God's flock; all yield Him praise
> By joy or pain, still tending towards the prize."

Accordingly this vision is followed by a third, in which is depicted the last judgment, in which all — both in earth and heaven — partake. That this is the *general* judgment seems to be obvious on the face of it. Those whom it concerns are described as "the dead, both great and small," which seems to be an inclusive designation. That it is not merely the wicked who are summoned to it appears from the fact that not only the "book of deeds," but also the "book of life" is employed in it, and it is only those whose names are not found written in the book of life that are cast into the lake of fire — whence it seems to follow that some are present whose names are written in the "book of life." The destruction of "death and Hades" does not imply that the judgment is over the enemies of God only, but merely that hereafter, as Paul, too, says, death shall be no more. There is, no doubt, the "second death," but this is the lake of fire, that is to say, the eternal torment. It is, thus, the great final assize that is here presented to our contemplation: implying the general resurrection and preparing the entrance into eternal destiny. The former fulfills the proleptic declaration in verse 5 that "the rest of the dead lived not until the thousand years should be finished": now they are finished and "the second resurrection," in which all — not Christ's people only — share, takes place: and accordingly they, too, are, in this reference, classed among "the dead" (ver. 12). The latter is adverted to, so far as the wicked are concerned, with the brevity consonant with this culminating part of the Apocalypse, in the concluding verse of the chapter: "And if any was not found written in the book of life, he was cast into the lake of fire." With respect to the destiny of God's saints, the things the seer has to say of them require new visions.

The scene, therefore, shifts at once and a new vision is presented to us (xxi. 1–8). It is the vision of the consummated kingdom of God. There is a new heaven and a new earth: and the new Jerusalem, the city of God, descends from heaven: and God makes His dwelling in its midst: and the happy inheritance of the saints is exhibited to us in all its richness and blessedness. To enhance the value and desirableness of this picture of holy bliss destined for God's people it is set between two declarations of the fate of the wicked (xx. 15, xxi. 8).

Nor is this all. For this vision is followed immediately by a symbolical description of the glorified people of God under the similitude of a city (xxi. 9–xxii. 5). It is the bride, the wife of the Lamb (verse 9) that is depicted: and she is described as a perfect and glorious city in which the Lord makes His abode, and which He Himself supplies with all that it can need. This is not a picture of heaven, be it observed: it is a picture of the heavenly estate of the Church — not merely of the ideal of the Church, but of the ideal of the Church as *realized*, after the turmoil of earth and the secluded waiting in Paradise alike are over. We quite agree with Dr. Milligan then when, in his latest exposition, he expounds the vision as a "detailed account of the true Church under the figure of a city," and remarks that this "city is really a figure, not of a place but of a people: it is not the final home of the redeemed: it is the redeemed themselves." But we cannot go with him when he adds that it is "essentially a picture, not of the future, but of the present; of the ideal condition of Christ's true people, of His 'little flock' on earth, in every age." [16] True, it may be that "every blessing limned in upon this canvas is *in principle* the believer's now," but the realization of these blessings for the Church, as a whole, is surely reserved until the time when that Church shall at length be presented to its Lord "a glorious Church, not having spot or wrinkle or any such thing, but holy and without blemish." "And I saw," said the seer, when he was contemplating the consummating glory (xxi. 2), "the holy city, new Jerusalem, coming down out of heaven from God, made ready as a bride adorned for her husband." But now, gazing in vision on the consummated glory, he has even more to show us. "Come hither," the angel said to him (xxi. 9), and "I will show thee the bride, *the Lamb's wife*." The marriage has now taken place, it is no longer the bride preparing for her husband, or even the bride adorned for her husband: it is the bride, "*the Lamb's wife*." "The Church," says Dr. Milligan himself in an earlier and in this point, we belive, a better exposition, "is not only espoused *but married to her Lord*." Gazing on the beautiful traits limned for us, we see not indeed what we are, but what we shall be, and who can wonder if we cry with the sweet singer, Would God we were there!

It is not our purpose to go into a detailed exegesis of these visions. We content ourselves with this mere suggestion of their essential contents, satisfied to draw out from them merely the great features of the eschatology of the Apocalypse, culminating as it does in this section in which is summed up its entire teaching. So far as serves this purpose, we venture to hope that the exposition will commend itself as reasonable: and it will

---

[16] "Expositor's Bible" volume on "The Book of Revelation" (1889), pp. 364, 368, 373. In his earlier "Commentary" in Dr. Schaff's "Popular Com. on the N. T.," Dr. Milligan had interpreted this vision of the consummated Church — though not of the Church so much as of its "eternal home," *i.e.*, heaven.

be wise not to lose ourselves in doubtful details of exegesis which might cloud the light that shines on the more general outline. Our main hesitation turns upon the distribution of the several visions. As we have read the section, we have separated it into only five visions. The whole structure of the Apocalypse is, however, dominated by the number seven. With a prologue and an epilogue the book is compounded of seven parallel and yet climactically wrought-out main sections. Four of these are formally subdivided into seven subsections each. It seems probable that this sevenfold structure runs through the remaining sections also, although it is not formally announced in them, and is left, therefore, for the reader to trace. On this ground we should expect the section now engaging our attention — xix. 11–xxii. 5 — to offer us a series of seven visions. But only five have been signalized by us. The suspicion lies close that we have in subdividing the section into its constituent visions missed two of its division lines. We think it very likely we have done so, but we have not been able to put our finger on obvious lines of cleavage, and have preferred to let the material fall apart where it naturally falls apart and to attempt no artificial dissecting. Possibly the points of separation may present themselves more clearly to others. In any event, it seems probable that if two separate visions have been confused by us into one, it is because they are very closely related visions, from one of which to the other there is rather progress than transition. In that very probable case the main lines of exposition would not be affected: and the purpose of our present enterprise would be secured as fully as if we had succeeded in separating between them.

What, then, is the eschatological outline we have gained from a study of this section? Briefly stated it is as follows. Our Lord Jesus Christ came to conquer the world to Himself, and this He does with a thoroughness and completeness which seems to go beyond even the intimations of Romans xi and I Cor. xv. Meanwhile, as the conquest of the world is going on below, the saints who die in the Lord are gathered in Paradise to reign with their Lord, who is also Lord of all, and who is from His throne directing the conquest of the world. When the victory is completely won there supervenes the last judgment and the final destruction of the wicked. At once there is a new heaven and a new earth and the consummation of the glory of the Church. And this Church abides forever (xxii. 5), in perfection of holiness and blessedness. In bare outline that is what our section teaches. It will be noted at once that it is precisely the teaching of the didactic epistles of Paul and of the whole New Testament with him. No attempts to harmonize as the several types of teaching are necessary, therefore, for their entire harmony lie on the surface. John knows no more of two resurrections — of the saints and of the wicked — than does Paul: and the whole theory of an intervening millennium — and indeed of a millennium of any kind on earth — goes up in smoke. We are forced, indeed, to add our assent to Kliefoth's conclusion, that "the doctrine of a thousand-year kingdom has no foundation in the prophecies of the New Testament, and is therefore not a dogma but merely a hypothesis lacking all Biblical ground." [17] The millennium of the Apocalypse is the blessedness of the saints who have gone away from the body to be at home with the Lord.

But this conclusion obviously does not carry with it the denial that a "golden age" yet lies before the Church, if we may use this designation in a purely spiritual sense. As emphatically as Paul, John teaches that the earthly history of the Church is not a history merely of conflict with evil, but of conquest over evil: and even more richly than Paul, John teaches that this conquest will be decisive and complete. The whole meaning of the vision of xix. 11–21 is that Christ Jesus comes forth not to war merely but to victory; and every detail of the picture is laid in with a view precisely to emphasizing the thoroughness of this victory. The Gospel of Christ is, John being witness, completely to conquer the world. He says nothing, any more than Paul does, of the period of the endurance of this conquered world. Whether the last judgment and the consummated kingdom are to follow immediately upon its conquest — his visions

[17] "Christl. Eschatol.," 1886, p. 188.

are as silent as Paul's teaching. But just on that account the possibility of an extended duration for the conquered earth lies open: and in any event a progressively advancing conquest of the earth by Christ's Gospel implies a coming age deserving at least the relative name of "golden." Perhaps a distinction may be made between a converted earth and a sanctified earth: such a distinction seems certainly more accordant with the tone of these visions than that more commonly suggested between a witnessed-to earth and a converted earth. The Gospel assuredly must be preached to the whole world as a witness, before the Lord comes. These visions seem to go farther and to teach that the earth — the whole world — must be won to Christ before He comes: and that it is precisely this conquest of it that He is accomplishing during the progress of this inter-adventual period.

Whether they go so far as to say that this winning of the world implies the complete elimination of evil from it may be more doubtful. In favor of the one view is the tremendous emphasis laid on the overthrow of all Christ's enemies, which must mean precisely his spiritual opponents — all that militates against the perfection of His rule over the hearts of men. In favor of the other is the analogy of the individual life, in which complete sanctification lags behind after the life has been in principle won to God. Perhaps it may even be said that a perfect life is not to be thought possible for sin-born men in the conditions of this sin-cursed world. Perhaps it may be affirmed that what is thus true of each individual must be true of the congeries of these individuals which we call the world. Perhaps it may be maintained on such grounds as these that as the perfecting of the individual waits for the next life, so the perfecting of the world must wait until the conquest is over — the last assize is held — and the New Jerusalem descends from heaven. In a word, that the perfected world — with all that means — is not to be discovered at xix. 21, but at xxi. 1, and that the description of it is to be read therefore in xxi. 9–xxii. 5, and at no previous point. No doubt there is an element of speculation in such suppositions, and we may well be content to leave the text to teach its own lessons, without additions from us. These lessons, however, at least include as much as this: that there is a "golden age" before the Church — at least an age relatively golden gradually ripening to higher and higher glories as the Church more and more fully conquers the world and all the evil of the world; and ultimately an age absolutely golden when the perfected Church is filled with the glory of the Lord in the new earth and under the new heavens. All the aspirations of the prophets, all the dreams of the seers, can surely find satisfaction in this great vision.

Meanwhile, the saints of God do not need to await the consummation of the ages before they enter into the joy of their Lord. Even "in this world" they receive their reward. The seer, in his vision, sees their accumulated hosts. But through all the years they are gathering, —

> "They are flocking from the East
>   And the West,
> They are flocking from the North
>   And the South,
> Every moment setting forth,
>
>   *   *   *   *   *   *
>
> Palm in hand, and praise in mouth,
> They are flocking up the path
>   To their rest."

This their "rest" is the "Millennium" of the Apocalypse.

LIST OF OTHER ARTICLES ON BIBLICAL DOCTRINES

CHRISTOLOGY AND CRITICISM

BY

BENJAMIN BRECKINRIDGE WARFIELD

Professor of Didactic and Polemic Theology
in the Theological Seminary of Princeton
New Jersey, 1887–1921

Baker Books
A Division of Baker Book House Co
Grand Rapids, Michigan 49516

PREFATORY NOTE

REV. BENJAMIN BRECKINRIDGE WARFIELD, D.D., LL.D., Professor of Didactic and Polemic Theology in the Theological Seminary of the Presbyterian Church at Princeton, New Jersey, provided in his will for the collection and publication of the numerous articles on theological subjects which he contributed to encyclopaedias, reviews and other periodicals, and appointed a committee to edit and publish these papers. In pursuance of his instructions, this, the third volume, containing his historico-critical articles on the Person and work of Christ, has been prepared under the editorial direction of this committee.

The generous permission to publish articles contained in this volume is gratefully acknowledged as follows: Funk and Wagnalls, for the article taken from "The New Schaff-Herzog Encyclopaedia of Religious Knowledge," The University of Chicago Press for the articles taken from *The American Journal of Theology*, Harvard Divinity School, for the articles taken from *The Harvard Theological Review*, and Mr. Leroy Phillips for the article taken from *The Hibbert Journal*.

The clerical preparation of this volume has been done by Miss Letitia N. Gosman and Mr. Johannes G. Vos, to whom the thanks of the committee are hereby expressed.

ETHELBERT D. WARFIELD
WILLIAM PARK ARMSTRONG
CASPAR WISTAR HODGE
Committee.

CONTENTS

I

THE DIVINE MESSIAH IN THE
OLD TESTAMENT

THE DIVINE MESSIAH IN THE OLD TESTAMENT [1]

THE question whether the Old Testament has any testimony to give as to the Deity of our Lord, when strictly taken, resolves itself into the question whether the Old Testament holds out the promise of a Divine Messiah. To gather the intimations of a multiplicity in the Divine unity which may be thought to be discoverable in the Old Testament,[2] has an important indeed, but, in the first instance at least,[3] only an indirect bearing on this precise question. It may render, it is true, the primary service of removing any antecedent presumption against the witness of the Old Testament to the Deity of the Messiah, which may be supposed to arise from the strict monadism of Old Testament monotheism. It is quite conceivable, however, that the Messiah might be thought to be Divine, and yet God not be conceived pluralistically. And certainly there is no reason why, in the delivery of doctrine, the Deity of the Messiah might not be taught before the multiplicity in the unity of the Godhead had been revealed. In the history of Christian doctrine the conviction of the Deity of Christ was

[1] From *The Princeton Theological Review,* xiv. 1916, pp. 379–416.

[2] As H. P. Liddon does in the former portion of the lecture in which he deals with the "Anticipations of Christ's Divinity in the Old Testament" ("The Divinity of our Lord and Saviour, Jesus Christ." Bampton Lectures for 1866. Ed. 4, 1869, pp. 44 ff.). Similarly E. W. Hengstenberg gives by far the greater part of his essay on "The Divinity of the Messiah in the Old Testament" ("Christology of the Old Testament," 1829, E. T. of ed. 2, 1865, pp. 282–331), — namely from p. 284 on — to a discussion of the Angel of Jehovah.

[3] For such questions remain as, for example, whether the Angel of Jehovah be not identified in the Old Testament itself with the Messiah (Daniel, Malachi). So G. F. Oehler (art. "Messias" in Herzog's "Realencyc.," p. 417; "Teol. des A. T.," ii. pp. 144, 265; "The Theology of the Old Testament," E. T. American ed., pp. 446, 528), A. Hilgenfeld, "Die jüdische Apokolyptik," pp. 47 ff. Cf. E. Riehm, "Messianic Prophecy," E. T.[2] pp. 195, 282, who cites these references in order to oppose them.

the condition, not the result, of the formulation of the doctrine of the Trinity.

It cannot be said in any case, therefore, that the discovery of a Divine Messiah in the Old Testament is dependent on the discovery also in the Old Testament of intimations of multiplicity in the unity of the Godhead. The two things go together in the sense that the discovery of either would be a natural preparation for the discovery of the other; that it would supply a matrix into which the other would nicely fit; and would set over against it a correlative doctrine with which it would readily unite to form a rational system. The two doctrines, though interdependent and mutually supporting one another in the system of which they form parts, are nevertheless not so dependent on one another that one of them might not conceivably be true without the other, and certainly not so that one could not conceivably be taught before the other. It seems in every way best, therefore, when inquiring after Old Testament intimations of the Deity of Christ, to keep this inquiry distinct from the parallel inquiry into possible Old Testament intimations of the multiplex constitution of the Godhead.

It is quite clear, at the outset, that the writers of the New Testament and Christ Himself understood the Old Testament to recognize and to teach that the Messiah was to be of divine nature. For example, they without hesitation support their own assertions of the Deity of Christ by appeals to Old Testament passages in which they find the Deity of the Messiah afore-proclaimed. This habit may be observed, as well as anywhere else perhaps, in the first chapter of the Epistle to the Hebrews. There, the author, after having announced the exalted nature of the Son, as the effulgence of the glory and the very image of the substance of God, illustrates His superiority to the angels, the highest of creatures, by appealing to a series of Old Testament passages, in which a " more excellent name " than is given to angels is shown to belong of right to Him. The exaltation of the Son to the right hand of the majesty on high, he says, is in accordance with the intrinsic dignity of His person as manifested in this " more excellent name." The " more excellent name" which he cites from the Old Testament is in the first instance none other than that of Son itself, whence we learn that when the Old Testament gives to the Messiah the designation of Son of God — or we would better say, when it ascribes Sonship to God to Him (for it is after this broader fashion that the author develops his theme) — it ascribes to Him, in the view of the author of this Epistle, a super-angelic dignity of person.[4] Of this Son, now, he goes on to say that, in contrast with the names of mere ministry given to the angels, there are ascribed to Him the supreme names of "God" and "Lord"; and with the names all the dignities and functions which they naturally connote. These great names of "God" and "Lord" are apparently not adduced as new names, additional to that of "Son," but as explications of the contents of that one "more excellent name"; and thus we are advised of the loftiness of the name of "Son" in the mind of this writer.[5] From this catena of passages we perceive, then, that in the view of this writer the Old Testament presents to our contemplation a Messiah who is not merely transcendent but sheerly Divine; to whom the great names of "Son of God," "God," "Lord" belong of right, and to whom are ascribed all the dignities, powers and functions which these great names suggest.

The passages of Scripture relied upon by the author of the Epistle to the Hebrews to make his point are, broadly speaking, derived from what we know as the Messianic Psalms. More particularly, his argument depends especially on citations from the Second, Forty-fifth, and Hundred-and-tenth Psalms. Ex-

---

[4] This representation of the author, embodied in the sharp demand: "Unto which of the angels said he at any time, Thou art my son?" has given the commentators some trouble in view of the designation of the angels in the Old Testament as "Sons of God." The notes of A. B. Davidson and Franz Delitzsch may be profitably consulted. When G. Hollmann, *in loc.*, pp. 204–205, remarks: "There is meant not the mere name of son, which is used in the Old Testament, as of the people, the king, and others, so also of angels but *the* name of Son, which is described in verses 2 and 3, according to its contents and its peculiarity," he is right in the substance of the matter but hardly in form.

[5] Cf. Lünemann (in Meyer, E. T. p. 83) on the passage.

cept for an allusion in Rev. xix. 8 the Forty-fifth Psalm is not elsewhere cited in the New Testament. But the Second and Hundred-and-tenth seem to have been much in the minds, and passages from them much on the lips, of its writers. To the Second, the very term Messiah, Christ, as applied to our Lord, goes back, as well as His loftier designation of Son of God; and it is adduced with great reverence as the Old Testament basis of these titles not only by the author of the Epistle to the Hebrews (i. 5; v. 5), but by the original apostles (Acts iv. 24–26) and by Paul (Acts xiii. 33) as reported in the Acts, while its language has supplied to the Book of Revelation its standing phrases for describing the completeness of our Lord's conquest of the world (Rev. ii. 27; xii. 5; xix. 15). It was the Hundred-and-tenth Psalm which first gave expression to the Session of the Messiah at the right-hand of God, and not only is it repeatedly referred to with reference to this great fact by the Epistle to the Hebrews (i. 13; v. 6; vii. 17–21; x. 13), but Paul adopts its language when speaking of the exaltation of Christ (I Cor. xv. 25) and Peter, in his initial proclamation of the Gospel at Pentecost, employs it in proof that Jesus has been raised to the right-hand of God and made Lord of Salvation (Acts ii. 32–36). Even more to the point, Jesus Himself adduces it to confound His opponents, who, harping on the title " Son of David," had forgotten that David himself recognized this, his greater Son as also his Lord. " And Jesus answered and said, we read in Mark's narrative (xii. 35–37; cf. Mt. xxii. 45–46; Lk. xx. 41–44), How say the Scribes that the Christ is the Son of David? David himself said in the Holy Spirit, The Lord said unto my Lord, Sit thou on my right hand, till I make thine enemies the footstool of thy feet. David himself calleth Him Lord; and whence then is He his Son? " We shall let Johannes Weiss tell us what this means. The Scribes, says he,[6] had built up a whole system of doctrine about the Messiah, and an important caption in it ran that He (according to the prophesy, for example, of Is. xi. 1) is (the present is timeless: He must be it: that is required by the doctrine) a descendant

[6] " Die Schriften des Neuen Testaments,[1] 1906, i. p. 175.

of David. " This declaration Jesus proves untenable, since David in his Psalm cx inspired by the Holy Spirit, calls the Messiah his ' Lord,' and, therefore, to put it bluntly, looks up to Him with religious veneration. . . . It follows from this that He must be a higher being than David himself. . . . Jesus accordingly shows here that his conception of the Messiah was different from the current political one. According to the Book of Daniel, and according to the convictions of the pious circle out of which the so-called Apocalypses came the Messiah comes down from heaven, ' the man on the clouds.' That Jesus also thought thus we have already seen." Johannes Weiss writes, of course, from his own point of view, which we do not share in many of its implications — as, for example, in the assumption that Jesus repudiates descent from David. He makes, however, the main matter perfectly clear. Jesus saw in the Hundred-and-tenth Psalm a reference to the transcendent Messiah in which He Himself believed.[7] In Jesus' view, therefore, the transcendent Messiah is already an object of Old Testament revelation.

What Jesus and the writers of the New Testament saw in the Messianic references of the Psalms, it is natural that those who share their view-point should also see in them. How the matter looks to one of the most searching expounders of the Scriptures that God has as yet given His church — we mean E. W. Hengstenberg — he sums up himself for us in a passage brief enough to quote in its entirety.[8] He has no difficulty in speaking directly of passages in the Psalms " which contain a reference to the superhuman nature of the Messiah ; — passages," he adds,

on which we must the less think of forcing another meaning as in the prophets (for example, in Is. ix. where even Hitzig is obliged to recognize it) there is found something unquestionably similar.

---

[7] Cf. the discussion of the meaning of Jesus' question and comment, F. Godet in loc. Luke (E. T. ii. pp. 251–254) : and also J. A. Alexander on Mk. xii. p. 37.

[8] " Commentary on the Psalms," E. T. iii. appendix, p. lvi. in the essay " On the Doctrinal Matter of the Psalms," near the beginning.

Such indications [he continues] pervade all the Messianic Psalms; and quite naturally. For the more deeply the knowledge of human sinfulness, impotence and nothingness sunk into Israel (compare, for example, Ps. ciii. 14–16), the less could men remain satisfied with the thought of a merely human redeemer, who, according to the Israelitish manner of contemplation, could do extremely little. A human king (and all the strictly Messianic Psalms have to do with Messiah as king), even of the most glorious description, could never accomplish what the idea of the kingdom of God imperiously required, and what had been promised even in the first announcement respecting the Messiah, namely, the bringing the nations into obedience, blessing all the families of the earth, and acquiring the sovereignty of the world. In Psalm ii. 12, the Messiah is presented *simpliciter* as the Son of God, as He, confidence in whom brings salvation, whose wrath is perdition. In Psalm xlv. 6–7 He is named God, Elohim. In Psalm lxxii. 5, 7, 17, eternity of dominion is ascribed to Him. In Psalm cx. 1, He at last appears as the Lord of the community of saints and of David himself, sitting at the right hand of the Almighty, and installed in the full enjoyment of Divine authority over heaven and earth.

That the state of the case may be fully before us, it will be useful to place by the side of this brief statement a somewhat more lengthy one, the tone of which very fairly represents the spirit of devout students of Scripture of the middle of last century. For a reason which will appear later, it seems to us to be an unusually instructive statement, to the entire compass of which it will repay us to give attention. We draw it from William Binnie's work on the Psalms: [9]

Respecting the Person of Christ, the testimony of the Psalms is copious and sufficiently distinct. For one thing, it is everywhere assumed that He is the Kinsman of His people. The Christ of the Old Testament is one who is to be born of the seed of *Abraham* and *family of David*. The modern Rationalists, in common with the unbelieving Jews of all ages, refuse to go further. They will not recognize in Him more than man, maintaining with great confidence that superhuman dignity is never attributed to the Messiah, either in the

[9] "The Psalms: Their History, Teachings and Use," 1870, pp. 200 ff.

law, or the prophets, or the psalms. It would be strange indeed if
the fact were so. The disciples were slow of heart to receive any
truth that happened to lie out of the line of their prior expectations,
— any truth of which the faithful who lived before the incarnation
had had no presentiment; yet we know that they readily accepted
the truth that Jesus was more than man. The Cross of Christ was
long an offence to them. It was not without a long struggle that they
were constrained to acknowledge the abrogation of the Mosaic law
and the opening of the door of faith to the Gentiles. But there is no
trace of any similar struggle in regard to Christ's *superhuman dignity*. The moment Nathaniel recognized in Jesus of Nazareth the expected Redeemer, he cried out, " Rabbi, thou art the Son of God ";
and, long before the close of the public ministry, Peter, in the name
of all the rest, made the articulate profession of faith, " Thou art
the Christ, the Son of the living God." They believed Him to be the
Son of God, in a sense in which it would have been blasphemy to
affirm the same of any mere man. Instead, therefore, of deeming it
a thing incredible, or highly improbable, that intimations of Christ's
superhuman dignity should be found in the psalms, we think it in
every way likely that they will be discoverable on a diligent search.
In truth they are neither few nor recondite. Take these three verses:

" Thy throne, O God, is for ever and ever:
   A scepter of equity is the scepter of Thy kingdom " (xlv. 6).
" Jehovah hath said unto me, Thou art my Son;
   This day have I begotten Thee " (ii. 7).
" Thus saith Jehovah to my Lord,
   Sit Thou at my right hand,
   Until I lay Thy foes as a footstool at Thy feet " (cx. 1).

I do not forget the attempts that have been made to put a lower
sense on each of these passages. I do not think they are successful.
But suppose it were admitted to be just possible to put on each of
them separately, a meaning that should come short of the ascription
of superhuman dignity to the Son of David, we should still be entitled to deduce an argument in favor of our interpretation from the
fact that in so many separate places, He is spoken of in terms which
most naturally suggest the thought of a superhuman person. From
the exclamation of Nathaniel it is evident that the thought did suggest itself to the Jews, before the veil of unbelief settled down upon

their hearts in the reading of the Old Testament. The truth is that, if a man reject the eternal Godhead of Christ, he must either lay the Psalms aside or sing them with bated breath. The Messiah whom they celebrate is fairer than the sons of men, one whom the peoples shall praise for ever and ever (Ps. xlv. 2, 17). The ancient Jews understood the particular psalms now quoted to refer to the Messiah; and no one who heartily believes in the inspiration of the Psalter will be at a loss to discern in it more testimonies to the proper Divinity of the Hope of Israel than could well have been discovered before His incarnation and death lighted up so many dark places of the ancient Scriptures. It will be sufficient for our purpose to indicate a single example. The coming of Jehovah to establish a reign of righteousness in all the earth is exultingly announced in several lofty psalms. It may be doubted, indeed, whether the ancient Jews were able to link these to the person of the Messiah; but we are enabled to do it, and have good ground to know that it was of Him that the Spirit spoke in them from the first. The announcement is thus made in the Ninety-sixth Psalm:

11. " Let the heavens rejoice and let the earth be glad;
        Let the sea roar, and the fulness thereof;
12. Let the field be joyful, and all that is therein:
        Then shall all the trees of the wood shout for joy
13. Before Jehovah: for He cometh, for He cometh to judge the earth:
        He shall judge the world with righteousness,
        And the peoples with His faithfulness."

We know whose advent this is. No Christian can doubt that the proper response to the announcement is that furnished by the Book of Revelation, " Amen. Even so, come Lord Jesus."

The circumstance which lends peculiar instructiveness to this statement is that, although conceived in a popular vein, and addressed rather to instruct the popular mind than to meet the difficulties raised by sceptical criticism; although written with absolutely no fear of sceptical criticism before the eye, — witness the unhesitating employment of John's Gospel as testimony to historical fact — and of course without knowledge of the phases of criticism which belong particularly to the twentieth century: it yet in all its main assertions fits so nicely into the present state of critical opinion that it might well have been written yesterday instead of fifty years ago. For example, it was rather bold fifty years ago to declare that it was the cross purely and simply, and not the assertion of a superhuman dignity for Christ, which was an offence to our Lord's Jewish contemporaries. Such a declaration is a commonplace today. There are few things which are more vigorously asserted by the latest phase of sceptical criticism than that the doctrine of a superhuman Messiah was native to pre-Christian Judaism. "The house was already prepared," declares W. Bousset; [10] " the faith in Jesus only needed to enter it." The whole secret of the Christology of the New Testament, explains Hermann Gunkel,[11] lies in the fact that it was the Christology of pre-Christian Judaism before it was the Christology of Christianity. It came from afar — this picture of the heavenly King, he intimates; but it had taken such hold of men that they could not free themselves from it.

Nothing could lie further from the purpose of writers of this tendency, of course, than to justify faith in the superhuman nature of Jesus. Of nothing are they more firmly convinced than that Jesus was merely a man. The whole object of their particular reading of the history of the Jewish Messianic ideal is, indeed, to smooth the way for a credible account of the immediate acceptance of Jesus by His followers as a superhuman being, although He was really only human. The pre-Christian conception of the Messiah, they say, involved the ascription to Him of a superhuman nature, and the acceptance of Jesus as Messiah, therefore, necessarily carried with it the ascription to Him of a superhuman nature.[12] But one of the results of this point of view is, naturally, that the mind is released from the prepossessions which formerly hindered recognition of traces of belief in a superhuman Messiah in the earlier Jewish literature. Hermann Gunkel, for example, having con-

[10] " Die jüdische Apokalyptik," p. 59.

[11] " Zum religionsgeschichtlichen Verständnis des Neuen Testaments," 1903, p. 93.

[12] Cf. W. Wrede, " Paul," E. T. 1907, pp. 151 ff.; H. Weinel, " Saint Paul," E. T. 1906, p. 313.

cluded that the conception of the heavenly Christ must have arisen somewhere before the New Testament, and having found traces of it in the Jewish Apocalypses, is able to see something like it also, centuries earlier, in the prophets.[13] Traits of a mythical God-King shine through the picture which the Prophets draw of the Messiah. " He receives already in Isaiah names which belong literally to no man — God-Hero, Father of Eternity (Is. ix. 5); He is the King of the Golden Age, in which sheep and wolf lie down together (Is. xi.); especially striking is it that His birth is celebrated with various mysterious statements (Is. ix. 5, Mic. v. 2) — for a just-born human child cannot aid His people, though perhaps a Divine child can. It is observable that other prophets and many Psalmists speak of a God, who is to be King of the whole world; that is, Jahveh, whose coronation and ascension (Ps. xlvii. 6, 9; lvii. 12) in the End-time are sung especially by many Psalmists." And so, he adds, we can feel no sort of wonder " when we meet in the later Apocalypses with a heavenly figure who is sometime to descend from heaven and establish a blessed kingdom on earth. This figure of the divine king is no new creation of Apocalyptic Judaism. It is the same figure which already lies at the basis of the prophetic hope." [14] The appeal to such passages as Ps. xlv. 6; ii. 7; cx. 1; xcvi. 11–13, as indications that the Messiah was thought of by the Psalmists as a superhuman being may now, then, hope for a more sympathetic hearing, in critical circles, than could be expected for it fifty years ago.

It undoubtedly does not make for edification to observe the expedients which have been resorted to by expositors to escape recognizing that these Psalms do ascribe a superhuman nature and superhuman powers to the Messiah. What they have done with Ps. xlv. 6 — to take it as an example [15] — " in order to avoid the addressing of the king with the word *Elohim*," as Franz Delitzsch puts it,[16] may be conveniently glanced

---

[13] *Op. cit.*, p. 93.

[14] *Op. cit.*, pp. 24–25.

[15] The helplessness with which they face the passage is illustrated by the note of G. S. Goodspeed, " Israel's Messianic Hope," 1900, p. 69.

[16] " Psalms," E. T. ii. p. 82. The spirit in which expositors approach the

at in the summary statement given by J. A. Selbie.[17] Rather than take it as it stands, they would prefer, it seems, to translate vilely, " Thy throne is God," " Thy throne of God," " Thy throne is of God," or to rewrite the text and make it say something else, — " Thy throne [its foundation is firmly fixed], God [has established it]," or " Thy throne [shall be] for ever." [18] Even Franz Delitzsch who turns away from such violent avoidances,[19] can permit the Psalmist his own word, only if he may be allowed an equally violent reduction of its meaning. Because, immediately after addressing the King by the great name of " God," — a name which in this class of Psalms confessedly means just God and nothing else [20] — the Psalmist refers the King to " God, thy God," Delitzsch supposes that the Psalmist must use " God " when applied to the King in some lowered sense. " Since elsewhere earthly authorities," he reasons,

are also called *Elohim* (Ex. xxi. 6; xxii. 7 ff.; Ps. lxxxii, cf. cxxxviii, 1) because they are God's representatives and the bearers of His image upon earth, so the king who is celebrated in this Psalm may be all the more readily styled *Elohim*, when in his heavenly beauty, his irresistible doxa or glory, and his divine holiness, he seems to the Psalmist to be the perfected realization of the close relationship in

---

matter is illustrated by the remark of J. H. Kurtz, " Zur Theologie der Psalmen," 1865, pp. 52 f.: if " God " *can* be taken in a lower sense here, it *must*. Kurtz wishes to translate, " Thy throne of God."

[17] Hastings' *B.D.* iv. pp. 756–757.

[18] T. K. Cheyne, " The Origin and Religious Contents of the Psalter," 1891, pp. 181–182, while adopting the penultimate of these expedients, makes himself somewhat merry over the rest. In his " The Book of Psalms," 1904, i. p. 198, he has eliminated the verse and no longer considers the (mutilated) Psalm to be addressed to an earthly king. " It has now," he says, " become superfluous to look for a contemporary king as the hero of the poem. . . ." It is " really a Messianic poem; the King, as the Targum says, is ' King Messiah.' " It is a " description of the ideal King."

[19] That is to say in his " Commentary on the Psalms." In his later " Messianic Prophecy," 1891, E. T. p. 115, he appears to accept the rendering, " Thy throne of God " as probable.

[20] Delitzsch himself says: " It is certainly true that the custom with the Elohim Psalms of using *Elohim* as of equal dignity with Jahve is not favorable to this supposition."

which God has set David and his seed to Himself. He calls Him
Elohim just as Isaiah calls the exalted royal child, whom he exultingly salutes in Ch. ix. 1–6, *'El Gibbōr*. He gives Him this
name, because in the transparent exterior of His fair humanity,
he sees the glory and holiness of God as having attained a salutary
or merciful conspicuousness among men. At the same time, however, he guards this calling of the king by the name of *Elohim* against
being misapprehended, by immediately distinguishing the God, who
stands above him, from the divine king, by the words " *Elohim*, Thy
God," which, in the Korahitic Psalms, and in the Elohimic Psalms in
general, is equivalent to " Jahve, thy God " (xliii. 4; xlviii. 15; l. 7),
and the two words are accordingly united by *Munach*.

Delitzsch does not believe, indeed, that when this is said,
all has been said. According to his view, this was all that the
writer of the Psalm meant; he was as far as possible from assigning Deity in any sense to the King he was addressing; he
applies the term "God" to Him only in a lower sense of the
word. But " the Church," in adopting this Psalm into its sacred
use, attached another meaning to it, referring a song " which
took its origin from some passing occasion, as a song for all
ages, to the great King of the future, the goal of its hope."
Its prophetically Messianic sense was " therefore not the original sense of the Psalm," though it was very ancient,[21] and
was, indeed, conferred upon it by its admission into the
Psalter.[22]

It is a refreshing return to common sense when the new
critical school renounces these artificialities of interpretation,
and begins by recognizing that the Psalmist in calling the King
"God," means precisely what he says, namely to ascribe the
Divine name to the King he is addressing. The sense is quite
clear, says Hermann Gunkel,[23] and we must not follow the

[21] How ancient we may learn from the remark: " Just as Ezek. xxi. 32
refers back to שׁלה, Gen. xlix. 10, *'El Gibbōr*, among the names of the Messiah
in Is. ix. 6 (cf. Zech. xii. 8) refers back in a similar manner to Ps. xlv. 5."
[22] "Psalms," E. T. ii. pp. 73–74; cf. i. p. 67 and especially p. 70; also
"Hebrews," E. T. i. p. 77, " Messianic Prophecy," E. T. p. 114.
[23] Ausgewählte Psalmen," [2] 1911, pp. 106 f. Similarly H. Gressmann,
" Der Ursprung der israelitisch-jüdischen Eschatologie," 1905, pp. 255–256.

multitude in explaining it away, and much less in altering the text. But, having recognized so much, Gunkel stops right there. The Messianic understanding of the Psalm (although that not only of the New Testament but of Judaism as well, from at least the time of the LXX), cannot come into consideration "for our scientific interpretation." Just an Israelitish king is meant, very likely Jeroboam II. That he is called " God " by the Psalmist is merely a solitary survival of a habit of speech common in the nations surrounding Israel, and, as we see here, not without its examples in Israel. "Veneration of kings as Gods was not rare in the ancient East; we are not surprized, therefore, that such a declaration meets us just once on the lips of an Israelitish singer. There was, no doubt, in ancient Israel a strong opposing current against such deification of the ruler; the genuine Jahve-religion, as it was advocated by the prophets, wishes that Jahve alone shall be God, and speaks with horror of everything human that would place itself by His side." We may learn from a passage like this, however,

that the distinction between the Divine and the human was not always and everywhere in Israel perfectly strictly conceived. There are many other passages also in which God and king are spoken of in the same breath; in which the king is compared with God or His angel; or in which he is called God's Son; and when Solomon built himself a throne, which stood on six steps flanked by lions, he imitated in it the throne of the highest God of heaven who sits high aloft above the seven heavenly stages, guarded by demons. Such a declaration as the singer's shows us, then, that there were tendencies approaching heathenism in ancient Israel, especially in the palace. In Israel, as elsewhere, it belonged to the court-style to promise an eternal dominion to the king, or eternal life to his house.

Hugo Gressmann [24] so far agrees with this, that he supposes that, in Ps. xlv. 6, we have a solitary " survival from a period when it was more customary in Israel to call the king God "; "although," he adds, "the usage had perhaps never been very common." But he improves upon it by thinking of

[24] *Op. cit.*, pp. ff.

this custom as really little more than an instance of an inflated court-style, which had become acclimated in Israel, too,
on the basis of general oriental models. The language which is
employed of the king in such Psalms as the Second, Forty-
fifth, Seventy-second and Hundred-and-tenth, cannot be
taken literally, of course, of any earthly monarch. But, says
Gressmann, it was never intended to be taken literally. It is
merely the language of couŕt-flattery and was fully understood to mean nothing. This was the language in which kings
had been spoken of and to, say in Babylon, from of old. It had
found its way, no doubt indirectly, possibly through Phoenicia,
into Israel; and had been popularized there merely as a matter
of court-form. Of course, it was gradually modified, in its
Israelitish use, in the direction of an ever closer assimilation of
it to the Israelitish point of view. The deification of the king,
for example, regular in the case of the Babylonian-Assyrian
kings and a dogma in Egypt, was more and more eliminated
from the court-style as it was employed in Israel. " In the
whole Old Testament, the (reigning) King is addressed only
a single time by the title of God: 'Thy throne, O God,
stands for ever and ever'" (Ps. xlv. 6). Other remnants of
similarly inflated flattery have, however, better maintained
their place. World-wide dominion is promised to the king;
eternal life and power are ascribed to him; he is presented
as the (adopted) Son of God. All such modes of speech are
merely relics of a court-style which originated elsewhere, and
which, as used in Israel, was without meaning. "From the
technical designation of the king as Son of God (II Sam. vii. 14,
Ps. ii. 7) no inferences can be drawn as to the deification of the
king. For it was merely the style to speak thus of the king,
and, when it is the style to speak thus, nobody asks whether
it has any meaning or not." [25] " The style permits the court-
poet to praise any and every king as a world-ruler, even though
the world which he really rules be no bigger than Israel." [26]
What we learn from such language is not how Israel thought of
its king, and much less how Israel thought of its Messiah.

[25] P. 256.   [26] P. 262.

There is no reference to the Messiah in this language; and Israel did not think thus of its king. What we learn is only where Israel got its court-style, and how that court-style was slowly modified in its use in Israel, to suit Israelitish modes of conception, until it was at last almost cleansed of its assimilation of the monarch to God.

The parallel between Delitzsch's and Gressmann's treatments of Ps. xlv. 6 should not be missed. Both start with the recognition that the Psalmist addresses the king as "God." Both set themselves at once to empty that fact of its significance. Delitzsch pursues a philological method, and concludes that, in such a connection, "God" does not mean God, but rather something which is not God. Gressmann follows the religio-historical method, and concludes that, in such instances, "God" means just nothing at all; it is mere bombast. That the view taken of the Psalm by either was not the view taken of it by those who gave it a place in the Psalter, at least, each is compelled to allow. It owes its place in the Psalter in fact, as neither would deny, precisely to its not having been understood to speak meaninglessly, or even moderately, of any earthly king, but, in the loftiest of ascriptions, of King Messiah. The question which presses for answer is whether it is possible thus to evacuate the language of the Psalm of its meaning. That Gressmann's method of evacuating it has some tactical advantage over that of the "psychological school" may be admitted. He is at least relieved from the necessity of accounting for the language employed from the Psalmist's own experience. He avoids so far, therefore, the impact of the pointed questions of Ernst Sellin: [27] "When did an Anointed of Juda ever have dominion over the peoples of the earth, against which they could rebel? When were the ends of the earth really promised by God to such an one, for his possession (Ps. ii.)? When and how could a king of Israel be called 'God,' and his sons be constituted princes over the whole world, as is done in Ps. xlv. 7, 17; when did such an one rule from the Euphrates to the end of the earth, like the king of lxxii. 8; and finally

[27] "Der alttestamentliche Prophetismus," 1912, p. 169.

when did such an one lead a host out of the dew of the morning and hold judgment among the peoples like him of cx. 6? "
But what advantage is it to escape these questions, only to fall into the way of the still more pointed one, When was it possible in Israel to ascribe to its kings *simpliciter* such Divine qualities and functions? Or, as Sellin sharply puts it, How could a king in Israel be directly addressed as God, as in Ps. xlv. 6? [28]

Is it adequate to say that it was natural for Israel to imitate the court-style of its neighbors, and that this court-style in its Israelitish employment had worn itself down, through long years of use, into a mere set of meaningless words? Kings had not existed in Israel for ever and ever; and Israel differed from the surrounding nations precisely in this — that there was but one God in Israel, and the king was not this God. "The deification of princes is everywhere else directly perhorrescent in Israel," remarks Sellin, and declares that there is but one solution possible: " a hymn which celebrated the Divine World-Savior is taken as the basis of a wedding-song addressed to an earthly king, and he is lauded as the introducer of the new age, which this world-savior is expected sometime to introduce." [29] That is to say, on the foundation of the new religio-historical point of view, Sellin returns in effect (although not altogether without defect, it must be allowed) to the old typical-messianic method of interpreting these Psalms. [30]

[28] Cf. T. K. Cheyne, "The Origin and Religious Contents of the Psalter," 1891, p. 181: "But from the severely monotheistic Jewish point of view, to represent this king as God, was impossible (Zech. xii. 8 is no proof to the contrary)." Also Gunkel, when speaking of Ps. xx. writes ("Ansgewählte Psalmen," [3] p. 41 f.) : "The piety is accordingly clear, which guards the singer from glorifying the king too much. This tone dominates also the other Royal Songs (xx. xxi. lxxii. cx. ii.) contained in the Psalter; they do not, or at least not in the first rank, glorify the king, but the God who protects and blesses him; a somewhat different ' more heathenish ' note sounds, on the other hand, in the very ancient song, Ps. xlv. The deification of the King which was at home in the ancient orient from primitive times, was certainly an abomination to these pious people."

[29] " Die israelitisch-jüdische Heilandserwartung," 1909, p. 16 (the second and third parts of the fifth volume of the " Biblische Zeit- und Streitfragen ").

[30] " Prophetismus," p. 129: " The right way to solve the riddle has been pointed out by Gunkel, though only by a modernization of what used to be

They speak of the contemporary kings, but through them they speak of the Great King yet to come. And their language can receive its full meaning only when it is read with reference to Him.

In order that we may apprehend Sellin's point of view, we shall need to have it before us in a somewhat broadened statement.[31] What we are particularly indebted to him for is the clearness with which he throws up to observation the main fact, that the center of Israel's eschatology lay in the settled expectation of the universal establishment of the reign of Jehovah. The way he puts it is, " Jahve is to come and simply be manifested as Lord — that is the kernel of the whole eschatology." [32] But alongside of this expectation there runs, he tells us, throughout the literature, the hope of the coming of a world-savior, the coming of whom is described in much the same language as the coming of Jehovah Himself. We may be tempted to identify the two after a fashion which will eliminate Jehovah's coming in favor of that of this savior: Jehovah comes only in His representative. The difficulty is that, in the documents, the identification goes beyond the coming to the figures themselves. Nor will it quite meet the case to say that Jehovah's representative is clothed with the attributes of Jehovah. The epithets given to Him pass beyond official identification and imply personal identity. And yet not such personal identity as excludes all distinction, or even all subordination.

---

contended for by Franz Delitzsch and others, when they said that David was here always the type of the Messiah. Hymns were written by court-poets to actual Israelitish or Jewish kings, on the occasion of their coronation or marriage, which transferred to them the long existent hope of the divine world-savior, and these songs became also prophecies."

[31] An admirable account of Sellin's views in their historical setting has been given to the readers of *The Princeton Theological Review* (October, 1913, xi. pp. 630–649) by J. Oscar Boyd under the title of " The Source of Israel's Eschatology." W. Nowack's criticisms of the " Heilandserwartung " in the *Theologische Rundschau* for 1912, xv. pp. 91–96, and of the " Prophetismus " in the same Journal for 1914, xvii. pp. 65–68, are also worth consulting.

[32] " Prophetismus," p. 174. Cf. p. 172: " The coming of God as Lord and King, we have already presented as the kernel of the Old-Israelitish Eschatology of woe and weal."

We are confronted in this figure with a problem very similar
to that which meets us in the mysterious figure of the Angel
of Jehovah and similar methods of solving it will naturally occur to us. Now, as Sellin makes clear, this figure of a world-
savior is both original and aboriginal in Israel. It was not, as
Gunkel and Gressmann imagine, derived at a comparatively
late date from the myths of Israel's oriental neighbors. The
myths of Israel's oriental neighbors, in point of fact, knew nothing of such a figure. " The old-oriental literature," writes Sellin,[33] " has been searched with the greatest zeal, especially during the last decade for traces of a hope of a Divine Savior, of a
new era of salvation to be brought in by him, and a return of
Paradise. . . . But I hold it to be my duty to say at once
without reserve, that not the slightest trace of proof has been
adduced, that this era is to be introduced by a great and
miraculous Divine-human ruler of the End-time. Absolutely
all that has been said, up to today, of an old-oriental ' expectation of a redeemer-king ' is merely construction, — or, where is
there a Babylonian or Egyptian text which speaks of such a future redeemer as Jacob's blessing speaks of Shiloh, — and the
like? . . . *The eschatological king is not known by the ancient
orient.*" [34] It is quite possible that in expounding and adorning its expectation, Israel may have employed figures and conceptions derived from without. But the expectation itself is
certainly its own. " The specifically Israelitish character and
the original parentage of its kernel are firmly established; and
its roots are not set in mythology but in the religion of Israel,
in Israel's belief in the God of Sinai, to whom in the end the
world must belong." [35]

Throughout the whole course of the history of Israel, we
may trace this expectation of a Savior running parallel with
the fundamental expectation of the coming of God as Ruler
and King. The parallel is very complete.

[33] P. 175 f.

[34] We observe that even Meinhold thanks Sellin for saying this: " I am
glad that Sellin declares strongly and clearly that ' the eschatological king is
not known to the ancient orient' — naturally Israel excepted " (" Theolog.
Literaturzeitung," 1913, 19, 580).   [35] P. 183.

" He too is the ruler over the peoples (Gen. xlix. 10; Ps. lxxii. 11),
to the ends of the earth (Deut. xxxiii. 17; Mic. v. 3; Zech. ix. 10 f.),
the scepter-bearer over the nations (Num. xxiv. 17–19; Ps. xlv. 17)
to whose dominion there are no limits (Is. ix. 6), etc.; he too bears
sometimes but not often the title of " King " (Ps. xlv. 2; lxxii. 1;
Zech. ix. 9; Jer. xxiii. 5), elsewhere those of " Judge " (Mic. v. 1),
" Father " (Is. ix. 5), " Anointed " or " Son of Jehovah " (Ps. ii. 2, 7).
Precisely as the activity of the one, so that of the other is three-fold:
it is his to destroy the enemies (Num. xxiv. 17 b; Deut. xxxiii. 17;
Ps. ii. 9; xlv. 6; cx. 1, 2, 5); he has to judge (Is. ix. 6 b; xi. 3; Jer.
xxiii. 5 b; Ps. lxxii. 6); and finally he has to " save " (Zech. ix. 9;
Jer. xxiii. 6; Ps. lxxii. 4, 12), above all by bringing social betterment,
Paradise, and universal peace (Gen. xlix. 11, 12; Is. vii. 15; xi. 4, 6–9;
Mic. iv. 4 a, 5 b; Zech. iii. 9 b, 10; ix. 10; Ps. lxxii. 12, 16).[36] . . .
Moreover he is given a name, " Immanuel," by which his appearance
is notified as the fulfilment of Balaam's prophecy of the end of the
days, " Jahve, his God, is with him "; and he is further designated as
" Star " (Num. xxiv. 17), as " God-Hero " (Is. ix. 5), as " God's
Son " (Ps. ii. 7); . . . [and] exegesis is continually bringing us back
to the idea that Is. vii. 14, Mic. v. 2 assume thoroughly a miraculous
birth for him without the aid of a man; . . . [and] there is promised to him when scarcely born, the dominion of the world (Gen.
xlix. 10; Is. ix. 5; Mic. v. 3).[37]

The kernel of the whole matter is this:[38] " Israel's savior is,
throughout the whole course of the Old Testament history the
counterpart of the World-God who is sometime to bring woe
and weal; precisely as of the one, so of the other there sounds
out — from the oldest to the latest sources — although, no
doubt with external differences, the mighty ' He comes ' (cf.
Gen. xlix. 10), ' He appears ' (Num. xxiv. 17), ' He cometh '
(Zech. ix. 9), ' He is born ' (Is. vii. 14, ix. 4), ' He comes forth '
(xi. 1), ' He comes forth ' (Mic. v. 1), ' He is raised up ' (Jer.
xxiii. 5), ' until He comes ' (Ez. xxi. 32), ' I will raise up ' (xxxiv.
23), ' I bring ' (Zech. iii. 8), ' I saw, there come ' (Dan. vii.
13)." This continually recurring assurance that the Paradise-
prince will come to destroy all enemies and judge even to the
ends of the earth, forms the deepest core of the mystery — it is

[36] Pp. 172–173.   [37] P. 173.   [38] P. 181.

expressed by a single word in Hebrew, יָבֹא, in English, " He comes." [39] It stamps the religion of the Old Testament as specifically a religion of hope. " Yes, for us the Old Testament religion, from the very beginning is a religion of hope, prepared from the very beginning sometime to become the world-religion; the Old Testament God from the beginning the God of heaven and earth; who, it is true, first of all chose only that one people, but looked forward to the day when He should destroy all other Gods and bring all other peoples to His feet." [40] It is from Sinai, and from the revelation-act at Sinai alone that this religion of hope can have derived. " Here, and only here, can a foundation be laid for viewing the whole history from the point of sight of waiting for the appearance of the world-God, who is to fill the universe with His glory." [41] But as no man could look upon this His glory and live, an organ for its manifestation was necessary, and a type of this organ was given in the Paradisiacal man, who, though a creature of God, was made in the image of the Divine glory and destined for communion with Him and the enjoyment of dominion over the world. Back to this figure, the old-oriental directed his eyes. " But in the old-Israelitish eschatology, this backwards directed longing became suddenly something wholly different — a clear, distinct, religiously oriented, historical expectation directed to the future: Jahve, the God of Sinai, will Himself, in this man, who, no doubt, is a creature, but who was with Him before the mountains were, — in this, His Chosen-One, His Servant, His Son — Himself come to establish the world-dominion, to judge Israel, and the peoples, to bring Paradise and the world-peace. There is no parallel to this assured confidence in the ancient orient." [42]

There are elements in this brilliant piece of constructive work which will require correction. The use made of the Paradisiacal man in the account given of the origin of Israel's expectation of a Savior, and the apparently defective Christology in part founded upon this, attract dissenting attention. But this ought not to blind us to the value of the broad pres-

[39] P. 193.   [40] P. 192.   [41] P. 182.   [42] P. 182.

entation given us here of the eschatological hope of Israel, including, as it does, the correlation of the hope of the coming Savior with the hope of what we have been accustomed to speak of as "the advent of Jehovah." It has been usual to separate these two things mechanically and to set them over against one another as quite independent, and indeed never even osculating, items of Israel's belief.[43] Gunkel even represents them as mutually exclusive. " In the whole eschatology," he says,[44] " we can distinguish two tendencies, both of which speak of a coming King; whereas the one calls the king David or David's Son, in the other Jahve Himself in the Ruler of the future; everywhere where God's kingdom is spoken of, the human king is lacking, for a ' Messiah ' has no place in ' God's kingdom.' " Charles A. Briggs, while he does not go so far as to represent these two elements of Old Testament eschatology as mutually contradictory, yet thinks, equally extremely, of the whole body of Old Testament Messianic hopes as a congeries of unharmonized items standing off in isolation from one another. " There are in the Old Testament," he says,[45] " two distinct lines of Messianic idea — the one predicting the advent of God for redemption and judgment, the other predicting the advent of a redemptive man. The redemptive man is conceived sometimes as the Seed of the Woman or Seed of Abraham, as the Lion of Judah, as the Second Moses, as the Son of David, the Son of God, the Messiah, as the Martyr Servant, as the Priest King, as the Martyr Shepherd, as the Son of Man. It is impossible to combine these in any unity, so far as the Old Testament is concerned. And there is not the slightest indication that there is any coincidence of the line of the divine advent with the line of the advent of any of these human Messiahs." The effect of a comprehensive presentation of the material like Sellin's is thoroughly to do away with such

---

[43] E.g. E. Riehm, " Messianic Prophecy," E. T.[2] 1891, p. 282, supporting himself on Oehler, " Prolegomena zur Theologie des A. T.," pp. 67 f. and art. " Messias," in Herzog's " Realencyklopädie," pp. 408 f. So also Ottley, Hastings' *B.D.* ii. p. 459a, repeating Riehm.

[44] " Ausgewählte-Psalmen," [3] pp. 191 f.

[45] " The Incarnation of the Word," 1902, p. 173.

impressions. The complete synthesis of the various representations waits, of course, for the fulfilment of them all in one Person. But it becomes clear at least that the hope of the coming of the world-savior, which includes in it the more specifically defined " Messianic " hope, is but another aspect of the hope of the coming of Jehovah to judge the world and to introduce the eternal kingdom of peace. One of the results of this is that the testimony of the Old Testament to " the transcendent Messiah " becomes pervasive. We no longer look for it in a text here and there which we are tempted to explain away as unexpected, perhaps intolerable, exaggerations, but rather see it involved in the entire drift of the eschatological expectations of the Old Testament, and view the special texts in which it finds particularly poignant expression as only the natural high lights thrown up upon the surface of the general picture.

This underlying coalescence of the advent of Messiah and the advent of Jehovah is perhaps more commonly vaguely felt than is generally recognized. It seems to be thus felt — in his own way and from his own point of view, of course, — by Gressmann.[46]

In the Israelitish eschatology [he writes] the Messiah and Jahve alternate. That is already intelligible, because the Messiah is ultimately a Divine figure, a God-king, and is thus elevated into the sphere of Deity. It becomes more intelligible when we observe a second parallel fact. Almost everywhere where Jahve meets us in the eschatology of weal, He is presented in a quite distinctive way. We can refer the descriptions which are given of Him and the functions which are ascribed to Him to the conception of the eschatological king. With respect to the thing, not to the person, the Jahve here described and the Messiah were originally as it seems counterparts: the functions of the two are still almost identical. The Messiah is described more as a King exalted into God, Jahve more as God exalted into the King. It is no doubt possible that in the eschatology which influenced the Israelitish religion, a single figure which united in itself the traits of both, occupied a middle ground. In its passage to Israel this figure was divided, and the one, the more divine, side

46 " Der Ursprung," etc., p. 294.

of its being was assigned to Jahve, the other, the more human side of its being to the Messiah. The eschatological hero, which originally bore rich mythical traits, that are still perceptible in the older prophecy, up to Isaiah and Micah, is in the course of time ever more degraded into an earthly king, and acquired a purely national character. Jahve, however, was inhibited from this development, since He could not lose the Divine type. Accordingly we may perhaps again ascribe to the *original* eschatological figure the things which in the *present* tradition are no longer said of the Messiah, but only now of Jahve.[47]

Such a speculation cannot commend itself to sober thought; but the fact that it suggests itself to Gressmann hints of what he finds in the Old Testament descriptions of the Messiah, and of the relation which the hope of His coming bore to the hope of the advent of Jehovah, and indeed which His person bore to the person of Jehovah. He who reads the Old Testament, however cursorily, will not escape a sense, however dim, that he is brought into contact in it with a Messiah who is more than human in the fundamental basis of His being, and in whose coming Jehovah visits His people in some more than representative sense.

It is naturally the customary representation of Franz Delitzsch that the two lines of prediction never meet in the pages of the Old Testament, but wait for their conjunction until He to whom they both point had come. Says he: [48]

For the announcement of salvation in the Old Testament runs on two parallel lines: the one has for its termination the Anointed of Jahve, who rules all nations out of Zion; the other the Lord Himself, sitting above the Cherubim, to whom all the earth does homage. These two lines do not meet in the Old Testament; it is only the fulfilment that makes it plain, that the advent of the Anointed One and the advent of Jahve is one and the same. . . . An allegory may serve to illustrate the way in which the Old Testament proclamation of salvation unfolds itself. The Old Testament in relation to the Day of the New Testament is Night. In this Night there rise in opposite directions, two stars of Promise. The one describes its path from

[47] P. 301.   [48] "Psalms," E. T. i. p. 67 f., cf. p. 70.

above downwards; it is the promise of Jahve who is about to come. The other describes its path from below upwards: it is the hope which rests on the seed of David, the prophecy of the Son of David, which at the outset assumes a thoroughly human and merely earthly character. These two stars meet at last, they blend together into one star: the Night vanishes and it is Day. This one Star is Jesus Christ, Jahve and the Son of David in one person, the King of Israel and at the same time the Redeemer of the world — in a word, the God-man! [49]

Elsewhere however he speaks with a juster divination: [50]

We find indeed undeniable traces in the Old Testament of a prophetic *presentiment* that the great Messias of the future, who was destined to accomplish what had been vainly looked for in David and Solomon, etc., should also present in His own person an unexampled union of human and divine. The mystery of the incarnation is still veiled under the Old Testament, and yet the two great lines of prophecy running through it — one leading on to a final manifestation of Jehovah, the other to the advent of a Son of David — do so meet and coalesce at certain points, as by the light thus generated, to burst through the veil. This is as clear as day in the one passage, Is. ix. 5, where the Messias is plainly called אל גבור (the Mighty God), an ancient traditional appellation for the Most High (Deut. x. 17; cf. Jer. xxxii. 8; Neh. ix. 32; Ps. xxiv. 8). And so (Jer. xxiii. 6) He is entitled " Jehovah our righteousness," following which, as Biesenthal has shown (p. 7), the ancient synagogue recognized Jehovah (יהוה) as one of the names of the Messiah.[51]

That the New Testament writers throughout proceed on the assumption that all those Old Testament passages in which the Advent of Jehovah is spoken of refer to the coming of the Messiah, Delitzsch himself is led to tell us when commenting

---

[49] " Psalms," E. T. ii. p. 300 (on Ps. lxxii). Cf. the similar statement of W. T. Davidson, in Hastings' *B.D.* iv. p. 151. Delitzsch seems to imply that it is only to Jehovah and not to the Messiah that the function of Savior is ascribed (cf. G. Dalman, " Words of Jesus," p. 295) ; this can be sustained only if we take the term " the Messiah " in too narrow a sense.

[50] " Hebrews," E. T. i. p. 79.

[51] Cf. on this Messianic title, A. Edersheim, " The Life and Times of Jesus the Messiah," [1] 1883, i. p. 178, who gives the references.

on the catena of passages adduced in the first chapter of Hebrews in support of the Deity of Christ, among which are some
of this kind.[52] Their consciousness of the identity of the two
comings "finds an utterance," as Delitzsch reminds us, "at
the very threshold of the evangelical history." (Lk. i. 17, 26)
when Malachi's prediction of the coming of Elijah "before the
day of Jehovah" to prepare His way, is adduced as fulfilled in
John the Baptist the forerunner of Jesus.[53] We shall at once
recall also the similar appeal of all three of the Synoptic Gospels to Is. xliii. 3, as fulfilled in John the Baptist. In Jesus they
saw all the lines of Messianic prediction converge; and they
declare Him no less the Jehovah who was expected to come to
save His people, than the Son of David or the Suffering Servant
of God. "When St. Mark tells us," remarks Charles A. Briggs
justly, "that St. John the Baptist was the herald of the advent
of Yahweh, at the beginning of the Gospel, what else can he
mean than that Jesus Christ whose redemptive life is the theme
of his Gospel was the very Yahweh?" And, we add, what can
he mean except that, in predicting this advent of Jehovah,
Isaiah was proclaming the Deity of the Messiah in whose
coming it was to be fulfilled? The same is true also, of course,
of Matthew and Luke in their parallel passages, so that Briggs
is thoroughly justified [54] in summing up "with confidence" in
the remark that "the three Synoptic Evangelists agree in
thinking of Jesus Christ as the Yahweh of the Old Testament,
and that His advent, as heralded by St. John the Baptist, was
the Divine advent of the Second Isaiah, as well as the human
advent of the Servant of Yahweh; in other words that they
saw in Jesus Christ the Messiah of history, the coincidence of
the line of the divine redeemer with the line of the human
Messiah; that they saw all the Messianic ideals combine in
Him." The only difference between John and the other Evangelists here is that the identification of the Baptist with the
voice crying in the wilderness, "Prepare ye the way of Jeho-

---

[52] "Hebrews," E. T. i. pp. 71–72.
[53] Cf. A. B. Davidson, "Old Testament Prophecy," 1913, p. 412. Cf. also
pp. 311 and 147.   [54] P. 182.

vah," which the others make on their own account, John quotes
from the lips of the Baptist. Briggs thinks the identification
can scarcely have been made by the Baptist.[55] Such a judgment is certainly rash in view of the exalted conception which
the Baptist in any event expresses of Him whose mere forerunner he undoubtedly recognizes himself as being. His shoe-
latchets he declares himself unworthy to unloose; he calls Him
the Lamb of God which taketh away the sin of the world; he
even gives Him the great name of the Son of God — a name
which in this context must surely bear its metaphysical sense
(cf. verses 7 and 25). Beginning on this note, the New Testament proceeds throughout its whole extent on the unchanging
supposition that in the coming of Jesus Christ there is fulfilled the repeated Old Testament promise, made in Psalm
and Prophet alike, that God is to visit His people, in His own
good time, to save them. It is therefore, indeed, so we are told,
that He is called Jesus, — precisely because " it is He that shall
save His people from their sins " — He, that is, Jesus, shall
save His people, that is, Jesus' people, — in fulfilment of the
promise of the Saving Jehovah.

Among the high lights thrown up on the surface of the general picture of the Divine Messiah, as it lies on the pages of the
Old Testament, such a passage as Is. ix. 6 challenges attention
with the same insistency as Ps. xlv. 6, and has met with much
the same treatment at the hands of the expositors. There have
always been some, of course, who have not shrunk from reading
the passage as it stands, and giving it its obvious meaning.
Outstanding instances are supplied by E. W. Hengstenberg
and J. A. Alexander. Alexander, speaking of the hypothesis
that by the child mentioned by the prophet, Hezekiah is
meant — an hypothesis once much in vogue, but now out of
date — and the unnatural explanations of particular terms
which it compelled, writes: [56]

The necessity of such explanations is sufficient to condemn the
exegetical hypothesis involving it, and shows that this hypothesis

[55] P. 171.
[56] " Commentary on the Prophecies of Isaiah," 1874, i. p. 204.

has only been adopted to avoid the natural and striking application of the words to Jesus Christ, as the promised *child*, emphatically *born for us* and *given to us*, as the *Son* of God, and the *Son* of man, as being *wonderful* in his person, works, and *sufferings* — a *counsellor*, prophet, and authoritative teacher of the truth, a wise administrator of the Church, and confidential adviser of the individual believer — a real man and yet the *mighty God* — eternal in his own existence, and the *giver of eternal life* to others — the great *peacemaker* between God and man, between Jew and Gentile, the umpire between nations, the abolisher of war, and the giver of internal peace to all who *being justified by faith have peace with God through our Lord Jesus Christ* (Rom. v. 1). The doctrine that this prophecy relates to the Messiah was not disputed even by the Jews, until the virulence of the anti-Christian controversy drove them from the ground which their own progenitors had steadfastly maintained. In this departure from the truth they have been followed by some learned writers who are Christians only in the name, and to whom may be applied with little alteration, what one of them (Gesenius) has said with respect to the ancient versions of this very text, viz., that the general meaning put upon it may be viewed as the criterion of a Christian and an anti-Christian writer.

Hengstenberg's remarks we prefer to give through the medium of T. K. Cheyne, who, in one of the stages of his ever-shifting opinion, adopts the core of them as his own. In an essay on " The Christian Element in the Book of Isaiah," Cheyne remarks: [57]

Both parts of Isaiah give us to understand clearly (and not as a mere ὑπόνοια) that the agent of Jehovah in the work of government and redemption is himself divine. Not indeed the much vexed passage in iv. 2, where, even if the date of this prophecy allowed us to suppose an allusion to the Messiah, " sprout of Jehovah " is much too vague a phrase to be a synonym of " God's Only-begotten Son." But the not less famous *'El Gibbōr* in ix. 6 may and must still be quoted. As Hengstenberg remarks it " can only signify God-Hero, a Hero who is infinitely exalted above all human heroes by the circumstance that he is *God*. To the attempts at weakening the import of the name, the passage x. 21, [where *'El Gibbōr* is used of

[57] " The Prophecies of Isaiah," [3] 1884, ii. p. 209.

Jehovah] appears a very inconvenient obstacle." [58] And who can doubt that, granting the subject of chap. liii. to be an individual, he must be the incarnation of the Divine?

Cheyne's direct comment on the passage itself in this work needs to be read in the light of these remarks to preserve it from ambiguity; but he doubtless means it to be taken in much the same sense which he unambiguously expresses here. "The meaning of the phrase," he declares,[59] "is defined by x. 21, where it occurs again of Jehovah"; that is to say, the Messiah is declared to be God in the same sense in which Jehovah is God. When he proceeds to say, "It would be uncritical to infer that Isaiah held the metaphysical oneness of the Messiah and Jehovah," he does not require to mean more than that Isaiah is not to be inferred to have as yet clearly formulated in his mind the doctrine of the Trinity, — and need not be supposed to have adjusted in his thinking the Deity of the Messiah to the fundamental doctrine of the unity of the Godhead. But when he goes on to say, "But he evidently does conceive the Messiah, somewhat as the Egyptians, Assyrians and Babylonians regarded their kings, as an earthly representation of Divinity (see on xiv. 13–14)," the comparison, although probably inevitable, yet tends to lower the conception of *'El Gibbōr* beyond its power to stretch. Accordingly Cheyne continues: "No doubt this development of the Messianic doctrine was accelerated by contact with foreign nations; still it is in harmony with fundamental Biblical ideas and expressions. This particular title of the Messiah is, no doubt, unique. But if even a Davidic king may be described as 'sitting upon the throne of Jehovah' (I Chr. xxix. 23), and the Davidic family be said, in a predictive passage it is true, to be 'as God (*ēlohīm*), as the (or, an) angel of Jehovah' (Zech. xii. 8), much more may similar titles be applied to the Messiah. The last comparison would, indeed, be especially suitable to the Messiah, and it is a little strange that we do not find it." So far the

[58] "Christology of the Old Testament," Edinburgh ed., ii. p. 88.
[59] *Op cit.,* i. p. 61 f.

tendency seems to be to lower the implication of the title,[60] but
the lost ground is now recovered: " But we do find the Messiah,
in a well-known Psalm, invited to sit at the right hand of Jehovah (Ps. cx. 1), and it is only a step further to give him the express title, ' God the Mighty One.' It is no doubt a very great
title. The word selected for ' God ' is not ēlohīm, which is applied to the judicial authority (Ex. xxi. 6, xxii. 8), to Moses
(Ex. vii. 1), and to the apparition of Samuel (I Sam. xxviii.
13); but el which, whenever it denotes (as it generally does;
and in Isaiah always) Divinity, does so in an absolute sense;
— it is never used hyperbolically or metaphorically." [61]

The thing most insisted upon by Cheyne in these remarks
is that 'El Gibbōr can mean nothing but " Mighty God"; as
Is. x. 21 shows. It illustrates the uncertainty of touch which
characterizes the " Liberal" criticism of this type, that, in his
later book on Isaiah, he simply deserts this ground and explains 'El Gibbōr as describing the ideal king as indued from
on high with might, and comments somewhat blindly: " x. 21,
which shows that we are not to render divine hero; the king
seems to Isaiah in his lofty enthusiasm, like one of those angels
(as we moderns call them), who, in old time were said to mix
with men, and even contend with them, and who, as superhuman beings, were called by the name of 'el (Gen. xxxii. 22–
32)." If Is. x. 21, where Cheyne himself renders 'El Gibbōr,
" the Mighty God " (p. 23), shows that this term cannot be
rendered " divine hero," but at least, as he himself renders
it, " Mighty Divinity," — which seems synonymous with
" Mighty God " — it is difficult to see how Isaiah by its use designates the ideal king (not now the Messiah) an angel and not
a God. By reducing the person spoken of from the Messiah
to the king, and the dignity ascribed to him from the Divine

[60] In his later work: " The Book of the Prophet Isaiah: A New English
Translation," 1898, p. 145, Cheyne actually lowers his view of the meaning
of 'El Gibbōr.
[61] Cf. Hengstenberg, " Christology," ii. p. 85 on the meaning of 'El
and the impossibility of rendering it (as Gesenius does) by " hero "; cf. also
the citations given by J. D. Davis, in the " Princeton Biblical and Theological
Studies," 1912, p. 99.

to the angelic rank, Cheyne has, no doubt, effectually removed
the passage from the category of Old Testament testimonies
to the Deity of the Messiah. But he appears to have done so
only at the cost not only of some violence, but also of some
confusion.

It is to attain this end that the exegesis of the " Old Liberal school " is particularly directed, and the exegesis seems
patient of nearly any conclusion which falls short of ascribing
Deity to the Messiah.[62] E. Kautzsch can lay it down dogmatically as a principle of exegesis, which must govern the
rendering of 'El Gibbōr, that " an absolute predication of Godhead, even in the case of the Messiah, would be inconceivable
in the Old Testament." [63] He therefore denies that it is possible to take the term as "hero God," and insists on translating it " God of a hero," that is " Godlike hero." And George
Adam Smith can actually permit himself to write such sentences as these: [64]

In any case the application of these prophecies to Jesus Christ must
be made with discrimination. They have been too hastily used as
predictions of the Godhead of the Messiah. But not even do the
names in Chapter ix. 6, f. imply Deity; while all the functions attributed to the promised King are human. Isaiah's Messiah is an
earthly monarch of the stock of David, and with offices that are
political, both military and judicial. He is not the mediator of
spiritual gifts to his people: forgiveness, a new knowledge of God
and the like. It is only in this, that he saves the people of God from
destruction and reigns over them with justice in the fear of God,
that he can be regarded as a type of Jesus Christ.

We have only to place by the side of this an equally brief statement emanating from a newer school, for its marvellousness
to strike the eye. Martin Brückner writes: [65]

[62] The various senses which have been put upon the words 'El Gibbōr
have been collected and discussed by J. D. Davis, as cited, pp. 93–105.

[63] Hastings' B.D., extra volume, 1904, p. 695b.

[64] " Modern Criticism and the Preaching of the Old Testament," 1901,
p. 161; cf. Hastings' B.D., ii. p. 491.

[65] " Die Entstehung der paulinischen Christologie," 1903, p. 97, note.

In any case " the old-prophetic Messiah-consciousness," for example, of Isaiah, would not be, on the assumption of the genuineness of his Christology, that of a " purely human King of David's
line " but that of the Apocalyptic introducer of the blessed end-
time. For a Messiah who reigns " without end " (ix. 6), who is called
the God-Hero and the Eternal One, who is the personal concentration of the spirit (xi. 2 ff.), and destroys the wicked with the
breath of his mouth (xi. 4), is not " purely human " but superhuman, wholly apart from this — that the kingdom over which he
reigns is the miraculous kingdom of peace and blessedness, the
splendor of which is the light of the benighted peoples (ix. 1 ff.;
xi. 7 ff.).

The several representatives of the " Old Liberal school "
differ very much among themselves, of course, in details of
interpretation. The thing which they are agreed upon is that
the Messiah is called *'El Gibbōr* — whatever that may be made
to mean — not because he is himself Divine, but because he is
the representative of Jehovah on earth. It is allowed that the
description given of him scales all the heights permissible to
such a representative. " In the brilliant picture of chapter ix.,"
writes G. S. Goodspeed,[66] " the child who occupies the throne
of David is to overthrow the enemy and to rule for ever and
ever. The names which are given to him describe a personage
more glorious than any prophet has hitherto mentioned, except perhaps the writer of Psalm xlv." But, however glorious,
they fall short of declaring him divine. " These divine titles,"
writes James Crichton,[67] " do not necessarily " — what is the
function of this " necessarily " here? — " imply that in the
mind of the prophet the Messianic king is God in the metaphysical sense — the essense of the divine nature is not a dogmatic conception in the Old Testament " — surely a blind
remark! — " but only that Jehovah is present in Him in perfect wisdom and power, so that He exercises over His people
for ever a fatherly and peaceful rule." Perhaps, however, Eduard Riehm may still stand as the typical representative of

[66] " Israel's Messianic Hope," 1900, p. 120.
[67] Orr's, " International Standard Bible Encyclopaedia," 1915, p. 2040.

this system of interpretation. The Messiah, says he,[68] is represented in Old Testament prophecy

as a human king, an offspring from the stem of David, whose eminence is far above the position of all other men, and whose personality has about it something wonderful and mysterious. Although it is nowhere indicated that he is to enter the world in an extraordinary and wonderful manner,[69] he yet, as the earthly representative of the Divine King, and his instrument in establishing His kingdom, and exercising His government, stands in an absolutely unique and intimate relationship to God, Whose Spirit rests upon him as upon no other, and Whose almighty power, wisdom, righteousness and helpful grace work through him in such full measure that in and through his government God's great name, that is, His revealed glory is made known. In other words, God makes him the organ of His self-revelation, just as elsewhere He uses the " angel of Jehovah." Hence, even the divine designation *'El Gibbōr* (God-hero) is one of the names ascribed to him; and hence also, even in a more general announcement applied to the house of David, there occurs the expression: " it shall be as *God* and the *angel of Jehovah* before " the inhabitants of Jerusalem. Both in the kingdom of God and in humanity, the Messiah assumes thus a central position, not only as their " head " but also as the mediating organ whence proceed the judicial and saving operations and the self-revelation of the Divine King.

It is no more than this that A. F. Kirkpatrick says when he expounds the Isaian declaration as follows: [70]

The fourfold name of this prince declares his marvellous nature and proclaims him to be, in an extraordinary and mysterious way, the representative of Jehovah. The title, *Wonderful Counsellor* conveys the idea of his endowment with supernatural wisdom in that counsel which was peculiarly the function of a king. *Mighty God* expresses his divine greatness and power, as the unique representative of Jehovah, who is Himself the *Mighty God* (x. 21). *Eternal Father* describes his paternal tenderness and unending care for his people.

---

[68] " Messianic Prophecy," 2 1884, E. T. 1891, p. 280; cf. p. 182.

[69] This means, of course that Riehm does not regard Is. vii. 14, Mic. v. 1 as involving this for the Messiah.

[70] " The Doctrine of the Prophets," 2 1897, p. 193.

Prince of Peace denotes the character and end of his government. His advent is still future but it is assured. *The zeal of Jehovah of hosts will perform this.*

To the exposition of the term "the Mighty God" Kirkpatrick attaches a footnote, which without comment adduces the following words from C. Orelli: "In such passages the Old Testament revelation falls into a self-contradiction, from which only a miracle has been able to deliver us, the Incarnation of the Son of God." Thus, and thus only, does he intimate that he is aware that the treatment of the epithet "Mighty God" as a suitable one for a merely human representative of Jehovah, however unique, does violence to all linguistic propriety.

Orelli, from whom the quotation is taken, it is needless to say, did not write the words taken over from him on any such hypothesis. In his opinion the prophet has in view a truly superhuman figure and one gets the impression, as he reads Orelli's exposition of the passage, that, so far as he fails to give its full meaning, the failure is due to a defect in his Christological thought, rather than to unwillingness to take the prophet at the height of his meaning. He writes: [71]

When in the first name a miraculous, divine character is ascribed to the ruler in his capacity of counsellor, planning for his people's good, this is saying more than that his wisdom far exceeds that usual among rulers; it is affirmed that his wisdom is related to the human as divine. Just so, the second predicate attributes to him energy in action. He is called *strong God*, not merely a divine hero: *a God of a hero*, for גִּבּוֹר is an adjective, and the phrase cannot be understood differently than in x. 21, where it is used of the Lord Himself. In this second name, also, doubtless, a definite expression of his dignity, one side of his working, is taken into view, namely, his divine energy in action, as in the first the superhuman grandeur of his counsel; but his person itself is thereby raised to divine greatness. He is called *strong God* in a way that would be inapplicable to a man, unless the one God who rightly bears the name *strong God* were perfectly set forth in this His Anointed One. In such passages, the Old Testament revelation falls into a self-contradiction, from which only

71 "Old Testament Prophecy," E. T. 1885, p. 274 f.

a miracle has been able to deliver us, the Incarnation of the Son of God. Elsewhere it draws the sharpest limit between the holy God and the sinful child of man, and its superiority to heathen religions depends in great part on this limit. Prophecy gradually lets this limit drop, in proof that the aim of God's action is to transcend it and to unite Himself most closely with humanity. In such oracles we Christians find no deification of the human, such as is the order of the day on heathen soil. Otherwise prophecy would be a retrogression from the teaching of the law into naturalism and heathen idealism. But in such oracles we find a clear proof that even in the time of the old covenant the Spirit of God was consciously striving after the goal that we see reached in the new.

" Divine wisdom," he continues after a page or two,[72] " divine strength, paternal love faithful as God's, divine righteousness and peace are ascribed to him, in such a way, indeed, that his person also appears divine: he perfectly exhibits God to the world; consequently his dominion is really God's dominion on earth. Every Judaizing and rationalizing attempt to adapt the insignia conferred on the Messiah here to a man of our nature, degrades them, and with them the Spirit who framed them." After this there is nothing left to say except what V. H. Stanton says with the simplicity of truth: [73] " Language is used " in this passage " to which only the person of a truly Divine Messiah could adequately correspond." This appears to be recognized, after his own fashion, even by G. B. Gray, when he comments: [74]

Some of the names singly and even more in combination, are, as applied to men, unparalleled in the Old Testament, and on this account are regarded by Gressmann (p. 280 ff.) as mythological and traditional; cf. also Rosenmüller, *Scholia*. . . . The Child is to be more than mighty . . . more than a mighty man . . . more than a mighty king; he is to be a mighty אל, God. This attribution of divinity, implying that the Messiah is to be a kind of demi-God, is without clear analogy in the Old Testament, for Ps. xlv. 7 (6) is ambiguous.

The language in which this comment is couched, as well as the direct reference to him, recalls us to the effect on the

---

[72] P. 277.   [73] " Jewish and Christian Messiah," p. 104.
[74] " Isaiah " (International Critical Commentary), 1912, i. p. 173.

interpretation of the passage of the new point of view introduced by Gressmann and his fellow-workers in the field of the
history of religion.[75] The essence of this new point of view lies
in the contention that the religious development and the religious language of Israel are to be explained after the analogy
of the religious development and the religious language of
the neighboring peoples; and on the assumption of a common body of old-oriental mythical ideas underlying them all
alike. How this applies to the Messianic conceptions of Israel
Gunkel briefly explains to us. He says: [76]

The figure of the Messiah, too, belongs to this originally mythological material. It is true that the new David or sprout of David
whom the prophets expect, is only a man, though endowed with
divine powers, and the hope that such a king should arise and bless
Israel is primarily a purely natural one. But there are traits in this
figure of a king, nevertheless, which intimate to us that this expected
king was originally a God-king. Already in Isaiah he receives names
which literally belong to no man: God-hero, Father óf Eternity;
he is the king of the Golden Age when sheep and wolf lie down together; particularly striking is it that his birth is celebrated repeatedly with mysterious statements, and that the salvation of Israel
is hoped for from it: for a fresh-born human child cannot help his
people, though no doubt a divine child could. We notice also that
other prophets and many psalmists speak of a God who is to be
King of the whole world; that is, Jahveh whose enthronement and
ascension in the last times the Psalmists particularly sing. The whole
material falls most beautifully into order if we assume that the
Israelitish hope of a king was preceded by an alien mythical one,
according to which a new God ascends as King the throne of the
world. And it therefore does not surprise us when we meet in the
later Apocalypses with a heavenly figure who is to come from heaven
and establish a blessed kingdom on earth. This figure of a divine
king is, therefore, no new creation of Apocalyptic Judaism: but it
is the same figure which already lies at the foundation of the prophetic hopes."

[75] Cf. for example Julius Boehmer, " Reichgottesspuren in der Völker-
welt " in Schlatter and Lütgert's " Beiträge zur Fördering christlicher Theologie," 1906, x.–i. p. 87.
[76] " Zum religionsgeschichtlichen Verständnis," p. 24 f.

This ingenious construction has been worked out into greater detail by Gressmann and set forth by him in perhaps as attractive a form as it is capable of receiving.[77] The difficulty with it is that it requires too many assumptions, and that these assumptions receive no support from the facts. As we have already seen, the ancient orient knows nothing of an eschatological king.[78] Israel knows as little of a deified King.[79] The whole mythological framework of the edifice thus breaks down. E. Sellin has solidly shown, moreover, that the entire development which it is here sought to explain on the basis of an alien mythology taken over by Israel from its neighbors, is purely native to Israel and has its roots set in the revelation-act at Sinai.[80]

The promulgation of this new view, however, has focussed attention on the prophetic language to which it seeks to assign a mythological significance, — with the effect of rendering the current attempts to explain that language away absurd. It has become quite clear in the course of the discussion that the prophets do attribute a divine nature and do ascribe divine functions to the Messiah. Indeed, the entire body of "results" of the "Old Liberal" criticism concerning the development of the Messianic hope — which it tended to relegate more and more completely to post-exilic times — has been hopelessly broken up.[81] It has again been made plain that the Messianic

[77] "Der Ursprung," pp. 250–301. Arthur Drews, of course, makes the most of it, in his fashion: "Christusmythe,"[1] pp. 8–9.

[78] See above, pp. 10–11.

[79] Gressmann writes, *op. cit.*, p. 285: "The general religious presupposition under which alone a figure like that of the God-King could be formed, is the king-deification, which, to be sure cannot be proved for Israel, but certainly may be for its neighboring nations."

[80] "Der alttestament. Prophetismus," p. 183: "The specifically Israelitish character and the original grounding of its kernel is certain. And its roots are set not in mythology but in the religion of Israel, in Israel's belief in the God of Sinai, to whom in the end the world must belong." So, p. 182: "The real root of the expectation of a Savior lies also here in the revelation act of Sinai. Here and here only could a foundation be laid for viewing the whole history under the point of sight of waiting for the appearance of the world-God, who is to fill the universe with His glory."

[81] Cf. what Sellin says, "Der alttestament. Prophetismus," pp. 167–168.

hope was aboriginal in Israel, and formed, indeed, in all ages
the heart of Israelitish religion. In sequence to this, much of
the disintegrating criticism of the documents which had been
indulged in for the purpose of giving a semblance of versimili-
tude to the hypothesis of the late origin of the Messianic development, has become antiquated; the integrity and early
date of sections and passages hitherto removed to a late period
have been restored; and the unity of the Messianic hope in
Israel, throughout all ages, has been vindicated, — so that,
from the beginning down through the Apocalypses of the later
Judaism and the songs of the earlier chapters of the Gospel
of Luke, we see exhibited essentially a single unitary hope.
In a passage written with great restraint, Herman Bavinck
describes the effect produced by the introduction of the new
view, thus.[82]

In place of the feverish efforts which were more and more ruling
in the dominant school of literary criticism to remove all Messianic
prediction to post-exilic times, it is now acknowledged that the pre-
exilic prophets, not only themselves cherished such Messianic expectations, but also presuppose them among the people; nor have
they themselves excogitated them and proclaimed them as novelties
to the people; but they have received them from the past and are
building on expectations which have existed from ancient times and
have been current in Israel. Accordingly this new tendency among
Old Testament scholars, as good as altogether discards the earlier
interpolation hypothesis and recognizes a high antiquity for all
eschatological ideas concerning the day of the Lord, the destruction
of enemies, the deliverance of the people, the appearance of the
Messiah, the consummation of the kingdom of God, and the like,
and in the figure of the Messiah, as presented in the Old Testament,
permits to come again fully to their rights even the supernatural
traits, such as the miraculous birth (Is. vii. 14; Mic. v. 1), the divine
names (Is. ix. 5) and so forth. Numerous texts and pericopes, which
were considered post-exilic by the earlier critics, now again rank as
genuine, and the so-called Christology of the Old Testament finds
itself thus once more restored more or less fully to its rights and its
value.

[82] "Gereformeerde Dogmatiek," [3] 1910, p. 249.

Perhaps there is no passage which more immediately suggests itself, when we ask after Old Testament testimonies to the transcendence of the Messiah than Daniel's account of his great vision of one like unto a Son of Man coming with the clouds of heaven (vii. 13, 14). So far as appears no doubt was felt as to the Messianic reference of this vision until modern times.[83] Even the Rationalists, as Hengstenberg points out,[84] though with strong temptations to reject it, yet for the most part recognized its Messianic character. And even up to the present day, when it has become the " Liberal " tradition [85] that, by the " one like unto a son of man," not the Messiah but the Israelitish people is intended, not only does the original Messianic interpretation still hold its own, but can be spoken of still by S. R. Driver, for example, as " the current interpretation." [86] Perhaps Hermann Schultz and Eduard Riehm may be taken as fair examples of how those " Liberals " who still cling to the interpretation of the vision of an individual, wish it to be understood. Schultz, who decides for this personal application only as probable, supposes [87] that Daniel conceived of the Messiah as a being dwelling with God in the heavens, like one of the angel-princes of whom he also speaks as like sons of men.[88] Riehm [89] will not allow even so much. He will not agree that there is in the vision any hint that the " one like

[83] The solitary exceptions of Ephraem Syrus among the Church Fathers and of Abenezra among the Jews may be left out of account.

[84] " Christology," iii. p. 88. He mentions De Wette, Bertholdt, Gesenius van Lengerke, Maurer.

[85] It is this that Sellin means when he says that the figure is " according to the dominant exposition simply a representation of the people of God " (" Der israelitisch-jüdische Heilandserwartung," p. 70).

[86] " The Book of Daniel " (" The Cambridge Bible for Schools and Colleges ") 1900, p. 102; cf. list of supporters of the two views on p. 108, note 4.

[87] " Alttestamentliche Theologie," 5 1896, pp. 635 f.

[88] This is probably the ruling view among those " Liberals " who allow the personal interpretation. For example, A. Schweitzer, writes (*The Expositor,* Nov. 1913, p. 444) : " In the Book of Daniel the view is taken that there is no longer a ruling Davidic family from which a ruler could be raised up to be Messiah. The author, therefore, expects that God will confer the supreme power in the coming world-age on an angelic Being who possesses human form and has the appearance of a ' son of man ' (Dan. vii. 13–14)."

[89] " Messianic Prophecy," p. 196.

unto a son of man " is of Divine or of angelic, or even in any sense of heavenly (as in Beyschlag's " heavenly man ") nature. The prophet, he insists, gives no intimation of the origin of this Being, beyond the constant presupposition that he belongs with " the saints of the Most High." He is represented as being in heaven and coming thence " *only because* he is the representative and organ of the God of heaven," and a " superhuman character and a divine position and dignity " are thus " lent, as it were, to Him." That is to say we can learn from this passage only that this Being comes from God, in the sense that he is sent by God to do God's work in the world.

The element of truth in this reasoning lies in its refusal to separate the " one like unto a son of man " completely from humanity, as if he were presented as a purely heavenly Being, and thus dissevered wholly from the entire course of Messianic expectation heretofore, in which the Messiah uniformly appears in close connection with Israel from whom He springs. It is the more important to point out the inconsequence of the total transcendentalizing of the Messiah on the basis of this vision, that the novelty of the vision in the history of the Messianic expectation lies precisely in its throwing up the transcendental element of the Messianic figure into such a strong light as apparently to neglect, if not quite to obscure, its human side. " Now," writes Sellin,[90] " the expectation here presented to us is new in so far as this Future Ruler appears in Daniel absolutely as a heavenly Being, borne on clouds, standing before the heavenly throne of God; that there is complete silence as to His human derivation; that He, although He also has human traits, is a heavenly Being; that, on the other hand, all actual earthly traits such as are always attributed by the prophets to the Savior, because He is born into this world, are stripped off. In this expectation of Daniel's all and every earthly human being is transcended; the Savior comes no longer from this world, no matter how miraculously given by God, but wholly and exclusively from the transcendental world." This side of the matter may be capable thus of exag-

[90] " Der israelitisch-jüdische Heilandserwartung," p. 72 f.

geration, but it is clearly hopeless to represent a figure in any measure so presented to us, as wholly human, as Riehm would fain do. If it must be held that room is left for human traits not here insisted upon, the traits which are insisted upon are obviously distinctly superhuman, or, we should rather say, distinctly divine. This is already apparent from his representation as coming with (or on) the clouds. It is always the Lord, as Hengstenberg already pointed out,[91] who appears with, or on, the clouds of heaven; none but the Lord of nature can ride on the clouds of heaven; and the clouds, as Michaelis says, "are characteristic of divine majesty." Julius Grill is quite right when he throws into emphasis[92] that "majesty" is the one characteristic which is insisted upon in the "one like unto a son of man." He is not represented as coming from heaven to earth (Holsten, Appel), or as going from earth to heaven, or as coming out of obscurity into manifestation (H. Holtz-mann). What he is represented as doing is simply drawing nigh to the throne. "What is emphasized in Daniel vii. 13 is the immediate vicinity of God into which the ' one like unto a son of man ' is brought," says Grill, and compares Ps. cx. 1, and Jer. xxx. 21. "It is," he says again,[93] "a veritable coronation act which the author has seen and wishes to describe."

The investigation of the passage by Grill has apparently become the starting-point for a new movement of "Liberal" authors towards recognizing its reference to an individual figure. This does not appear to be due to any peculiar strength or special novelty in Grill's manner of prosecuting the discussion; the reasons which he presents for understanding the passage thus, are very much the same that have been repeatedly urged before. But he approaches the question from a new angle and his readers have been prepared to follow his suggestion by their participation in his general presuppositions.

[91] "Christology," iii. 83: so also Pusey, "Daniel the Prophet,"[2] 1868, p. 85 f. Cf. Driver, *in loc.*: "*with the clouds of heaven:* in superhuman majesty and state."

[92] "Untersuchungen über die Entstehung des vierten Evangeliums," i. 1902, p. 52.

[93] P. 54.

Grill himself thinks of a purely heavenly being as presented to us here, an angel, perhaps Michael, perhaps a higher Being still, "a most exalted personal intermediary between God and the world; and," he somewhat unexpectedly adds, "a transcendent prototype of the God-pleasing humanity ultimately to be realized in the people of the Most High." Nathaniel Schmidt had already [94] expressed a similar view, interpreting the man-like Being as an angel and more particularly as Michael, the guardian angel of Israel; and his view had attracted to itself Frank C. Porter.[95] In a later article [96] Schmidt restates his view, citing Grill in support of it in general, but declining to accept the somewhat incongruous addition by which Grill attempts to combine the two main interpretations of the passage — that the man-like Being is an exalted heavenly personage and that he is the type of the saints of God. "Whether Michael or any other angel was ever thought of as the ideal Israelite," he declares to be doubtful. T. K. Cheyne [97] follows in Schmidt's steps, and, as was his wont, seeks to improve on him. Schmidt strongly repels the idea that Daniel's figure is the Messiah; to him this figure is distinctively a heavenly being, — angelic or more probably super-angelic, Michael or one higher still than Michael. To Cheyne,[98] he is both the Messiah, and "an angel, presumably Michael, the great prince-angel who defends the interests of the people of Israel," — or rather Michael, the somewhat obscured representative of Marduk who was no angel but a God; in a word "a degraded (but an honorably degraded) deity," a "great superhuman (and originally divine) personage," "the heavenly Messiah" who, having played a great rôle in the creation of the world and the deliverance from Egypt (as the Angel of Jehovah) is in the last days to "redeem the world and mankind." In sharp contrast with Cheyne, Paul Volz,[99] while following

---

[94] *Journal of Biblical Literature,* xix, 1900.
[95] "Hastings' *B.D.,*" iv. p. 260.
[96] "Encyclopaedia Biblica," iv. 1903, p. 4710 f.
[97] "Bible Problems," 1904, pp. 213 ff.
[98] Pp. 73, 214, ff.
[99] "Jüdische Eschatologie," 1903, pp. 101 f., 214 ff.

Grill in rejecting the symbolical interpretation and seeing in the one " like unto a son of man " an individual being, is clear that Michael is not meant, nor any angelic being, but a simple man, the Lord-Messiah, the Lord of the new world, to whom is to be given the dominion of the world, and all the peoples and all the times. " He is certainly not the symbolical representative of the Kingdom of God, but the prince of his Kingdom. He is the representative (*Stellvertreter*) of God, to whom the power and honor and dominion belong; he stands, however, also in direct relation to the people of the seer, to the people Israel, his dominion is their dominion " — in short, he is the Messiah. Though he thus belongs to the category of man, he is not, however, forthwith to be assigned to the earthly sphere. He comes from heaven. The old myth of a primitive man comes into view here: a primitive man created as the opponent of the primitive beasts, the demonic monsters, who is to deliver the cosmos from them and secure the heavenly beings from their assaults. " This primitive Savior was brought forward, now, by the Apocalyptists for their eschatological purposes: Daniel recalls that man of whom the myth speaks and sees him in the vision; the Savior of the primitive age becomes the Savior of the last age, and the one as the other has to do with the beasts; the Apocalypse of Daniel, nevertheless, pays no further attention to the primitive existence of this man." According to Volz, then, Daniel's " one like unto a son of man " is, indeed, a transcendent being, but yet only a man, though a heavenly man: conceived on the lines of the primitive man and so far a reproduction of him; but not precisely that primitive man and therefore not necessarily preëxistent.

All this, now, Gressmann turns right as its head.[100] All investigators are agreed, says he with fine neglect of his colleagues, that in the text as it lies before us, the Man stands as a symbol of Israel, as the beasts do of the heathen kingdoms. But this is only a use to which Daniel has put a borrowed figure: " the originality of the reworker consists only in this — that he has reinterpreted the Man of Israel." Whatever else

[100] " Der Ursprung," usw. p. 340.

there is in the passage, we may safely employ for the reconstruction of the old myth, and adventuring on this path we find
in the Man a parallel figure to the Messiah, who, according to
the old Israelitish conception, was to stand at the beginning of
the new age and all the peoples be subject to Him. He is, no
doubt, an angel, but no common angel, the highest angel
rather, the Being who is the greatest of all, next after only the
Ancient of Days; hence He is not Gabriel or Michael — they
are not high enough. We cannot give Him a name; we must
be modest and say merely that this angel means that eschatological figure, whom everybody knows as the eschatological
man which in the end of the days is to be made the Lord of the
world. In the heathen form of this myth, which lies behind the
Jewish one, He was, of course, a God; and this God has only
been degraded into an angel in consequence of Jewish monotheism. It was as an angel therefore that He came to Daniel;
and Daniel turned Him into a symbol of Israel. The development thus proceeded in directly the opposite direction from
what is commonly thought. Israel is not here represented as
one like unto a son of man; but the man is represented as Israel.

Sellin [101] makes it his primary task to draw the teeth of
Gressmann's mythology. He takes his start frankly from Gressmann's findings. It is true enough, he says, that the Messianic
conception is wider than that of the Son of David; wider and
older. We may see proofs of this all through the prophets.
Witness what we are told in them of the birth of Immanuel
from the Almah who was with child, of the travail of the
Yoledhah, of the seven shepherds and eight princes of the fifth
chapter of Micah, of the " Mighty God " and other great names
of the ninth chapter of Isaiah, above all of the eating of milk

[101] In Sellin's view, Dan. vii. 13, in the original Biography of Daniel,
" referred to the proclamation of the Saviour as the Second Adam, as a heavenly
man, free from all that is earthly, and to His kingdom "; but the later author
of the Apocalypse of Daniel — that is, our Daniel — has transferred this to
the whole people of God. So he explains in " Prophetismus," p. 97, note 1.
In the discussion in " Heilandserwartung," pp. 70 ff., he deals with Daniel's
presentation of " one like unto a son of man " as an individual figure without
raising question of the composition of the passage.

and honey, the picture of the King of Paradise riding on the ass, and the like.[102] But why represent these things as borrowed goods? Why, above all, think of Daniel's Man, who certainly was not invented by Daniel, but was already known to his readers, as a recent importation from heathendom? Rather, Daniel throws himself back on the prophets before him where we may find these things fragmentarily alluded to; as, for example, in Isaiah, and everywhere in the Old Israelitish expectations of a Being coming out of the Divine sphere. What we have in Daniel is not something new to Israel, but the primaeval Jewish expectation of a Savior newborn, stripped of this-world traits, and transformed into the sphere of the transcendental world.[103]

So, the discussion goes on. But it does not remain without results. And the main result of it is, that assurance is rendered doubly sure that in the " one like unto a son of man " of Dan. vii. 13, we have a superhuman figure, a figure to whose superhuman character justice is not done until it is recognized as expressly divine. It was understood to be a superhuman figure by everyone who appealed to it and built his Messianic hopes upon its basis throughout the whole subsequent development of the Jewish Church.[104] Wherever, in the Apocalyptic literature we meet with the figure of the Son of Man, it is transcendentally conceived.[105] When our Lord Himself derived from it His favorite self-designation of Son of Man,[106] He too took it

[102] " Die alttestamentliche Religion im Rahmen der andern altorientalischen," 1908, p. 45.

[103] " Der israelitisch-jüdische Heilandserwartung," pp. 70 ff.

[104] Cf. A. Dillmann, " Handb. der alttest. Theologie," p. 538 : " Finally the whole exegetical tradition from the Book of Enoch (which is directly dependent on Daniel) on, has even understood by this title the king of the kingdom. I cannot help holding that this interpretation is right. In this case we have not only the beginning of the development of the earthly kingdom of God into a βασιλεία τῶν οὐρανῶν here, but also its head is designated as like an angelic being (for these are elsewhere in Daniel also designated כְּבַר אֱנָשׁ), a preëxistent Being present already in heaven who in the fulness of the times will come and establish the eternal kingdom of heaven."

[105] Cf. W. Bousset, " Religion des Jüdentums,"[1] p. 24 ff. (In ed. 2, pp. 301 f. the more relevant part of this statement is eliminated).

[106] Cf. H. J. Holtzmann, " Lehrbuch der Neutestament. Theologie,"[1] i.

over in a transcendental sense; and meant by applying it to
Himself to present Himself as a heavenly Being who had come
forth from heaven and descended to earth on a mission of
mercy to lost men. On every occasion on which our Lord called
Himself the Son of Man thus, He bears His witness to the
transcendental character of the figure presented to Daniel.
There is no reason apparent today why His judgment of the
seer's meaning should be revised. If by his "one like to a son
of man" Daniel meant to bring before us the figure of an
individual being, and that seems to us to be beyond question,
— it is very certain that the individual the figure of whom he
brings before us is superhuman, or rather Divine.

In attempting to illustrate the testimony of the Old Testament to the deity of the Messiah we have laid particular stress
on the great declarations in Ps. xlv. 6, Is. ix. 6 and Dan. vii. 13.
These are, as we have said, high lights shining out brightly
on the surface of a pervasive implication. They are not the
only points which shine out on its surface with special brilliancy. We might just as well have chosen to dwell, instead,
on Ps. ii. or Ps. cx. or Mic. v. 2, or Jer. xxiii. 6 or Zech. xiii. 7
or Mal. iii. 1, and the like.[107] A selection, however, had to be
made and we have endeavored to select those particular points
on which the light seemed to shine with the purest illumination. We should be sorry to leave the impression, however, that
the testimony of the Old Testament to the Deity of the Messiah
is dependent upon these particular passages, and their fellows.
The salient fact regarding it is that it is an essential element
in the eschatological system of the Old Testament and is in-

---

p. 247: "The reference of the term back to Dan. vii. 13 (already essayed by
expositors of the Reformation period like Chemnitz and recommended by
Ewald and Hitzig) is to-day the, at all events, most recognized and most
assured result of the discussions of the 'Son of Man,' vexed in so many points."

[107] F. E. König, "Offenbarungsbegriff," ii. p. 398, illustrating how the light
of salvation breaks now and again through the veil of Old Testament conceptions, by which it is covered in the Old Testament announcements, observes
(among other things) that "the superhumanness of the mediator grows ever
clearer (Is. ix. 6 ff., xi. 1 ff.; Mat. v. 1)." Cf. Ottley, Hastings' *B.D.*, ii. p. 459 f.

separably imbedded in the hope of the coming of God to His kingdom which formed the heart of Israelitish religion from its origin. We have only to free ourselves from the notion that the Messianic hope was the product of the monarchy and to realize that, however closely it becomes attached to the Davidic dynasty in one of its modes of expression, it was an aboriginal element in the religion of Israel, to understand how little it can be summed up in the expectation of the coming of an earthly king. It is one of the chief merits of the new school of research that it is making this ever more and more clear.

Meanwhile, it is an unhappy fact that we may search in vain through many of the current treatises on the Messianic hope for intimations that it included the promise of a Divine Redeemer. It is much, indeed, if we find a hearty recognition that a Messianic figure occupied an essential place in it; at least during the larger space of the history of Israelitish religion. Even devout-minded students have been sometimes tempted to represent Messianic prophecy as fulfilled " not so much in the personality and work of Christ as in the religion of Christ." [108] When the person of the Messiah is given its rights, however, as the center of Messianic prophecy, it is still often insisted that He was conceived purely as a human being, — as Trypho, Justin Martyr's collocutor in the famous dialogue, contended in the second century. At the best, we get such a concession as A. Dillmann's. " We have then," says he,[109] " in this whole series of Messianic prophesies certainly the portrait of a sovereign of the kingdom, endowed with Divine attributes and powers, but nowhere a God or God-man; on the other hand, however, the Book of Daniel advances to a still higher, metaphysical or mystical view of His nature . . . an already existing being preëxisting in the heavens, who in the fulness of the times comes and establishes the kingdom of the saints." [110] On this A. B. Davidson makes less than no advance,

[108] Cf. F. H. Woods, " The Hope of Israel," 1896, p. 184.

[109] " Handbuch der Alttestament. Theologie," pp. 538–539.

[110] The schematization of the Messianic hope worked out from this point of view is very clearly presented by C. F. Kent, " The Sermons, etc., of Israel's Prophets," 1910, pp. 45–47.

when he declares [111] — shall we not say, evidently not without some misgivings? — " In Is. ix. xi. it is not taught that Messiah is God, but that Jehovah is fully present in Him. The general eschatological idea was that the presence of Jehovah in person among men would be their salvation. The prophet gives a particular turn to this general idea, representing that Jehovah shall be present in the Davidic king. The two are not identified but Jehovah is fully manifested in the Messiah." The sufficient answer to such comments is that they are obviously minifying in intention; they are endeavors not to concede too much where concession is seen to be nevertheless necessary. We do not wonder that Davidson feels constrained to add: " The passage goes very far." Pity it is that he could not see his way to go the whole length that it goes.

Happily, however, there have always been some who, standing less under the blight of the current critical theories, have been able to see more clearly. Thus, for example, F. Godet has seen his way to declare [112] that " the idea of the Divinity of the Messiah " is "the soul of the entire Old Testament"; and, after adducing Isaiah's designation of Him as "Wonderful," " Mighty God," and Micah's discrimination of His historical birth at Bethlehem from His prehistoric birth " from everlasting," and Malachi's calling Him " Adonai coming to His temple," to sum up in these sentences: "There was in the whole of the Old Testament from the patriarchal theophanies down to the latest prophetic visions, a constant current towards the incarnation as the goal of all these revelations. The appearance of the Messiah presents itself more and more clearly to the view of the prophets as the perfect theophany, the final coming of Jehovah." It is upon this thread of Old Testament teaching, he goes on to remark — broken off in the Rabbinical development — that Jesus laid hold in His assertion of the dignity of His person as Messiah. These words might well have been written today; they express admirably the new insight which we have obtained unto the nature and development of Old Testament eschatology.

[111] Hastings' *B.D.*, iv. p. 124 f.; similarly, " Old Testament Prophecy," 1903, pp. 367–368. [112] " Commentary on Luke," E. T. ii. p. 251.

II

MISCONCEPTION OF JESUS, AND BLAS-
PHEMY OF THE SON OF MAN

MISCONCEPTION OF JESUS, AND BLAS-
PHEMY OF THE SON OF MAN [1]

IT IS, perhaps, not always appreciated how great a popular excitement was roused when, as Mark puts it, "after that John was delivered up, Jesus came into Galilee, preaching the Gospel of God, and saying, The time is fulfilled, and the Kingdom of God is at hand" (Mk. i. 14, 15). It is not the fault of the Evangelists if it is not fully understood. Mark, for example, adverts no less than eight times before he reaches the middle of his third chapter to the enthusiasm which attended Jesus wherever He appeared. We shall perceive how nearly this constitutes the main subject of these opening chapters of his Gospel, if we will but read consecutively the passages in which it is spoken of. "And the report of Him went out straightway everywhere into all the region of Galilee round about" (i. 28). "And at even when the sun did set they brought unto Him all that were sick, and them that were possessed with devils. And all the city were gathered together at the door" (i. 32, 33). "And they found Him and say unto Him, All are seeking Thee" (i. 37). "Insomuch that Jesus could no more openly enter into a city, and was without in desert places; and they came to Him from every quarter" (i. 45). "And when He entered again into Capernaum after some days it was noised that He was in the house. And many were gathered together so that there was no longer room for them, no, not even about the door . . . and when they could not come nigh Him for the crowd, they uncovered the roof where He was" (ii. 1, 2, 4). "And He went forth again by the seaside, and all the multitude resorted unto Him" (ii. 13). "And Jesus with His disciples withdrew to the sea; and a great multitude from Galilee followed: and from Judea, and from Jerusalem, and from Idumea,

[1] From *The Princeton Theological Review*, xii. 1914, pp. 367–410.

and beyond Jordan, a great multitude hearing what great things He did, came unto Him. And He spoke to His disciples that a little boat should wait on Him because of the crowd, lest they should throng Him " (iii. 7–9). " And He cometh into a house, and the multitude cometh together again, so that they could not so much as eat bread " (iii. 20).[2] We may almost fancy that we can observe the crowds which thronged Jesus ever increasing in number and persistency under our eyes: they gather at the door (i. 32–34); there is no longer room even at the door (ii. 2); they are so continually with Him that He has no opportunity even to eat (iii. 20). But we note that, already at i. 45 (cf. i. 37), they had not only made the city inaccessible to Him, but had populated the very desert to which He withdrew; and at iii. 9 (cf. iv. 1) they so thronged Him even on the open sea-shore as to compel Him to take refuge in a boat and speak to them thence. The agency by which this great public agitation was created was not merely the proclamation that the Kingdom of God was at hand, but the manifestation of its actual presence in the abounding miracles of healing which were performed (Mat. xii. 28, Lk. xi. 20).[3] Disease and death must have been almost eliminated for a brief season from Capernaum and the region which lay immediately around Capernaum as a center. No wonder the public mind was thrown into a state of profound perturbation, and, the enthusiasm spreading, men flocked from every quarter to see this great thing, questioning with one another what it all meant.

Meanwhile, there were necessarily many who were not drawn into the movement but remained rather, whether momentarily or permanently, merely spectators of it. Of these there were in particular two classes who nevertheless could not look with indifference upon the wave of popular excitement

[2] So, consecutively, iv. 1, v. 21, 24, 27, 31, vi. 34, vii. 24, 33, viii. 1, ix. 14, 25, x. 1, 46.

[3] Cf. E. von Dobschütz, *The Expositor*, VII. ix. (1910), p. 334: " This ' is come ' (ἔφθασε) must mean something more than the usual ' is at hand ' (ἤγγικεν); it is the solemn declaration that the Kingdom is present in Jesus' acting; His casting out of devils proves that the powers of the Kingdom are at work." Cf. also H. J. Holtzmann, " Synoptiker," [3] p. 243.

sweeping through the land as it rose to its crest. These were those who felt responsible for Jesus Himself on the one hand, and on the other those who felt responsible for the religion of the community,— for we must bear in mind that the movement was from first to last a distinctly and intensely religious one. The circle of Jesus' relations (perhaps we may take the word for the moment in a rather broader sense than that of its current usage) and the body of the constituted religious guides of the people must each have been compelled to form at once a preliminary judgment upon the movement, and to act upon it. Nor was it likely that in either case this judgment would be favorable. Inevitably, in each case alike, it would be the expression of anxiety not to say of irritation. It is this natural judgment of what we may call the two interested classes that Mark records for us when, as he tells of the concourse of the crowd again to Jesus on His return to Capernaum after His second circuit in Galilee (Mk. iii. 20), he adds: " And when His relations heard it, they came forth to take charge of Him, for they said, He is out of His mind. And the scribes who came down from Jerusalem said, He hath Beelzebul, and it is by the prince of the demons that He casteth out the demons" (Mk. iii. 21, 22). The two judgments are as opposed as are the springs of emotion out of which they rise. It is pity that we hear the echoes of in the one; anger in the other. Jesus' relations, who, it must be observed, had a mere hearsay knowledge of the movement which was sweeping over Galilee in His train — He had not yet been to Nazareth (Mk. vi. 1),[4] — judged from the reports of His conduct which had reached them that He was not altogether Himself, and were prepared to take the responsibility of restraining Him. The scribes, who had heard His words and witnessed His works, could not deny that a supernatural power was operative among them; but, being unwilling to accredit this to a divine, ascribed it rather to a demoniac source, and thus sought to break the influence of Jesus with

[4] Lk. iv. 16 ff. seems to be a different visit (implied also in Mt. iv. 12, 13) which took place before His Galilean ministry had fairly begun (cf. Meyer, on Mt. xiii. 53).

the people. The two have in common only that they pass an
unfavorable judgment upon the movement as a whole.

The naturalness of this unfavorable judgment in each case,[5]
in the circumstances in which it was formed, has not prevented
its being appealed to, in each instance, in disproof of the supernaturalness of Jesus' person and ministry. It is urged that, if
Jesus was really a divine person and His ministry was accompanied by obviously supernatural effects, such as are narrated
in the Gospels, it would be inconceivable that those who stood
nearest to Him and knew Him best, should have pronounced
Him out of His mind. And it is urged again that, in His defence
of Himself from the charge of the scribes that He was possessed of a demon and wrought His wonders by the power of the
evil one, Jesus so far from asserting that He was a divine
person actually contrasts Himself with the divine Spirit as
one to speak against whom were a venial sin while to speak
against the Spirit is unpardonable blasphemy,—obviously
because the Spirit is divine. That we may form a right estimate
of these representations, we should look a little closely at the
relevant passages.

I

It is Mark alone who tells us of the judgment passed upon
Jesus by His relations. The words in which he does it are these:
"And He cometh home, and the crowd cometh together again,
so that they were not able even to eat bread. And when His
relations heard it they came forth to take charge of Him; for
they said, He is out of His mind."

The opening words, which we have rendered: "And He
cometh home," are translated by many rather: "And He
cometh into a house." [6] This statement is then explained as the

---

[5] Cf. A. Schweitzer, *The Expositor*, November 1913, p. 449, who remarks
of them: "This only means, however, that the former [the scribes] wished at
all costs to discredit Him with the people, and that His relatives noticed a
change in Him and could not understand how He could come forward as a
teacher and prophet."

[6] James Moffat, who in 1901 ("The Historical New Testament" p. 280),
had correctly rendered: "Then He comes home," has substituted for this in

fundamental statement of the passage, preparing the way, and setting the scene, for the whole remainder of the chapter. Thus a certain emphasis is made to fall on Jesus' actual entrance into a house. We certainly should not in this case, however, expect the ambiguous simple ἔρχομαι to be used, — the εἰς following which might indeed be ordinarily best rendered " to " (compare "unto," Mt. ii. 11, viii. 14, ix. 23, 28, Mk. 1. 29, etc.). His actual entrance into the house may thus even be left in some doubt (compare Mk. v. 38, 39: "and they come to the house . . . and entering it . . ."). The more precise εἰσέρχομαι we may feel sure would have been employed had this been the meaning which was intended to be conveyed, especially if the emphasis which is assumed in the interpretation in question falls upon it (compare Mt. x. 12, xii. 4, 29, Mk. ii. 26, iii. 27, vi. 10, vii. 17, 24, ix. 28, Lk. ix. 4). Moreover it is not easy to find an adequate reason in the immediate context for so formal a statement that Jesus did so simple a thing as to "come into a house." We may say [7] that Jesus went into a house obviously to seek rest and to take food (verse 20): but his need of these things seems to supply no sufficient reason for so formal a record of so slender a circumstance as His going into a house. It is customary, therefore, to go further afield and to seek the real reason of the record in the preparation it gives for the subsequent narrative, the eye being particularly fixed on the statement of verse 31, that His mother and brothers " stood without." [8] Thus, however, an extraordinary method of composition is ascribed to the evangelist. We are to suppose that, having begun an account of Jesus' relations to His family with

---

1913 (" The New Testament: A New Translation "): " They went indoors." This would exactly render the words in a different context: and the implication of " home " is in it. But it misses the point here.

[7] With B. Weiss (1878).

[8] B. Weiss *in loc.*: " He goes into a house, because it was in a house that the incident took place which the narrative has in mind (cf. verse 31) " (Meyer on Mark, ed. 6, 1878) ; " Emphasized in contrast to His sojourn at the sea-side or on the mountain-top (verses 7, 13), because the scene, iii. 31 ff. takes place in a house and Mark wishes to prepare for this," (Meyer on Mark, ed. 8, 1892; ed. 9, 1901) ; " Prepares for the narrative of iii. 31 ff., which what immediately follows, therefore, only introduces," (" Die vier Evangelien," 1900, p. 186).

iii. 20, 21, Mark suddenly breaks off and thrusts in a long
account of His relations with the scribes, only to return without
warning again to His family at iii. 31, leaving all the sutures
unclosed. We are to treat the whole narrative enclosed in
verses 22–30, in other words, as a parenthesis, and to expound
verses 20, 21 immediately in connection with verses 31 ff., as if
the intermediate section were not there — although it grows
naturally out of, and forms a natural whole with, verses 20, 21.[9]

Such results as these would seem to be a sufficient indication that a false. start has been taken when we render the
opening clause: "And He cometh into a house." In point
of fact the phrase may in itself just as well mean: "And
He cometh home " (compare viii. 3, 26 with defining pronouns
and ii. 1, v. r. pregnantly with verb of rest: vii. 17, ix. 28 where
εἰς οἶκον is connected with εἰσέρχομαι, are different — render
"indoors "); and this sense is strongly recommended by the
context. Jesus had been at the seaside (verse 7) and on the
mountain (verse 13): He now returns "home," that is to say,
to Capernaum (compare i. 21, ii. 1). The narrative is composed
of circuits out from Capernaum and returns to Capernaum, as
the center of Jesus' active work: this is one of the points at
which His return to His base of operations is intimated, and, as

---

[9] The difficulties arising from this construction become flagrantly apparent in the course of A. Loisy's skilful efforts to overcome them (" Les
Synoptiques," i. pp. 696 ff.) : " To consider only the present order of the texts,
it might be said that Mark, having deliberately neglected (not been ignorant
of) a fact which did not have in itself any particular prominence, substituted
for it, in preparation for an incident which he intended to recount after the
discourse of the Saviour [to the scribes], the mention of a judgment passed
upon Jesus by His own family, which, though less unfavorable than that of the
Pharisees, does not fail to exhibit in a sufficiently startling light, the relations
of the new preacher with His own people. The *mise en scène* is the sufficiently
natural preamble of the incident concerning the family of Jesus: what is
secondary is the connection of the disputation with this incident and the
artifice which has permitted Mark to neglect the teaching of the possessed
man which in the common source of the Synoptics served as the introduction
to the disputation. . . . What is said of the family does not attach itself
without some embarassment to the context: but this is a piece of unskilfulness
which belongs to the redaction, arising possibly from the fact that the preamble, though conceived with a view to the anecdote, does not belong to the
traditional basis of the narrative."

on the former occasions (i. 32, ii. 3; compare i. 45 where R.V.mg.
questions whether εἰσπόλιν may not be " *the city*," as indeed
A.V. had boldly translated it [10]), the crowd immediately gathers. In this case, the close connection which has been assumed
between iii. 20 and iii. 31 falls away; the misleading prominence into which the simple opening statement of verse 20
has been thrown is removed; and that statement resumes its
natural place as only one of the numerous intimations in this
narrative of Jesus' alternating excursions from Capernaum
and returns to it (i. 21–35; ii. 1–13; iii. 1–7; iii. 20; iv. 1).

The chief interest of this determination lies in its bearing
on the interpretation of the phrase in verse 21 which we have
translated " His relations." If verses 20, 21 were not written
specifically in preparation for verses 31ff.; verses 22–30 are not
a parenthesis; and verses 31–35 record a new incident: then
the phrase " His relations " in verse 21 does not find its explanation in " His mother and His brothers " of verse 31 —
as is very commonly represented — but must be independently
interpreted. This phrase,[11] in Greek writers generally, bears
ordinarily the meaning of " legates," " representatives," and
it still commonly occurs in the papyri in the sense of " agents,"
" representatives." By the side of this usage, however, there
is found another, less common but nevertheless constant, in
which it bears the sense, either broadly of " adherents," " followers," or more narrowly of " household," " family," or " kindred." It is obvious that it is in this latter general sense that
it is employed in our passage, but it is not easy to fix the exact
limits of its connotation. That Jesus' disciples — His ad-

[10] Render " into town."
[11] For discussions of the meaning of the phrase, see especially Fritzsche
in loc. and F. Field, " Notes on the Translation of the N. T.," p. 25 (he argues
for the meaning "household"). For the usage of the phrase in the papyri,
see J. H. Moulton, *The Expositor,* VI. vii. p. 118, viii. p. 436; " Prolegomena,"
etc., pp. 106–107;*The Expository Times,* xx, p. 476. At " Prolegomena," pp.
106–107, he says: "Οἱ παρ' αὐτοῦ is exceedingly common [in the papyri] to
denote 'his agents' or 'representatives.' It has hitherto been less easy to find
parallels for Mk. iii. 21, where it must mean 'his family'; see Swete and
Field *in loc.* We can now cite GH 36 (ii./B.C.) οἱ παρ' ἡμῶν πάντες BU 998
(ii./B.C.) and Par. P. 36 (ii./B.C.)."

herents, followers — are not intended, is clear, since a contrast is drawn with them (verse 20, αὐτούς). Our English versions — Authorized and Revised, — render the term " friends," not badly if it be taken, as it obviously is intended to be, in a personal, rather than an official sense.[12] The margin of the Authorized Version proposes instead the narrower " kinsmen," following in this the Wycliffite " kynnesmen " and the Genevan " kynesfolkes." The modern versions continue the same line: George R. Noyes, " relations "; James Moffat, 1901, " relatives "; *Twentieth Century New Testament,* " relations "; Samuel Lloyd, " kinsmen "; James Moffat, 1913, " family."[13] It can scarcely be doubted that this is practically what is meant, though too restricted a sense should not be insisted upon.[14] Obviously those are intended who bore such a relation to Jesus that they felt themselves responsible for Him, and that they would naturally be looked to by others to take charge of Him in the contingency of His needing to be kept under some restraint. We might think, in the varying circumstances which would render each natural, of His clansmen, of His fellow-townsmen, of His responsible friends, of His blood-kinsmen, of His household, of His family, of His parents, of His brothers.[15] In the absence of closer contextual definition, only the known circumstances of Jesus' case could supply us with confident guidance in fixing upon the precise persons intended. All that is intimated here is that His natural guardians were inclined to judge Him to be out of His mind, and were prepared to take measures to put Him under the restraint required by His sad condition. Who these natural guardians were we can

[12] F. C. Conybeare, " Myth, Magic and Morals," 1909, p. 72, insists *suo more* that the rendering " friends " is a " falsification of the text " with the intention of " deceiving English readers who cannot read Greek." The rebuke administered to him by J. H. Moulton, *The Expository Times,* xx. p. 476, is richly deserved.

[13] But Weymouth, "The Modern Speech New Testament," retains the A. V., " friends." Weizsäcker renders " die Seinigen "; Th. Zahn, " Forschungen," etc., iv. p. 332, " die Angehörigen," as also P. W. Schmiedel, cf. note 41 below.

[14] Cf. Swete's note.

[15] Theophylact defines: οἱ οἰκεῖοι αὐτοῦ, with οἱ ἀπὸ τῆς αὐτῆς πατρίδος and οἱ ἀδελφοὶ αὐτοῦ as alternatives.

only conjecturally supply from our further knowledge. There are some who feel quite sure that His mother could not be included among them, because they find it difficult or impossible to believe that she should have so cruelly misjudged Him.[16] There are others, on the contrary,[17] who are prepared to assert confidently, if not even violently, that His mother was included among them; sometimes, apparently, for no other reason than that thus the passage may be exploited as inconsistent, say, with the representations of the Infancy-chapters of Matthew and Luke or in general with the doctrine of the supernatural origin of Jesus. Too great confidence on either part seems misplaced. The passage itself gives us no guidance; and general considerations appear indecisive.

It is important to observe, however, that the judgment informed as to His condition by Jesus' friends or kinsfolk — according to our broader or narrower understanding of the phrase — was founded on hearsay evidence only. " When His relations *heard* . . .," we read. The meaning can hardly be, merely, that as soon as they heard that He had come home, they went forth to lay hands on Him. Nor does it seem likely that the meaning is merely that they went forth to lay hands on Him when they heard that, on His coming home, a multitude had gathered about Him. The article before " multitude " is probably genuine; and, if genuine, should not be neglected. And, in any event, the " again " has its rights. What appears to be meant is that His relations were moved to their action by the reports which reached them of the great excitement that had been raised by His ministry throughout Galilee, a culminating manifestation of which was seen in this renewed gathering of the crowd at His house.[18] The reports which had

---

[16] Th. Zahn, " Forschungen," etc., vi. p. 332: " We are scarcely to think of Mary among them . . . the word, ἐξέστη is not suitable in the mouth of the mother, and the intention to use physical force against the madman is attributable only to the men not to the women."

[17] Conybeare, as above.

[18] Cf. A. B. Bruce, *in loc.*: " not to be restricted to what is mentioned in verse 20; refers to the whole Galilean ministry with its cures, and crowds, and constant strain."

reached them of the thronging multitudes that attended His
whole work in Galilee and of the popular enthusiasm which
followed His movements, led them to suppose Him to be laboring under over-excitement and to undertake the duty of putting
Him under restraint.

If His friends, however, had not themselves witnessed His
work and knew of its effects only from hearsay, it is not likely
that they were living in Capernaum which was the center of
His activity and the seat of the most constant popular enthusiasm. On the other hand, in His circuits out from Capernaum
He had not yet visited Nazareth (Mk. vi. 1, Mt. xiii. 54).[19]
If Nazareth was the home of His friends here mentioned, therefore, their dependence on rumor for knowledge of His work and
its effects, is in harmony with what we read in Lk. iv. 23 ff.,[20]
Mk. vi. 5, Mt. xiii. 58. It is, indeed, frequently supposed that
not Jesus alone, but His family also, had removed from Nazareth to Capernaum at the very beginning of His ministry
(Jno. ii. 12).[21] This, however, is little likely in itself;[22] and it
would compel us to suppose either that their settlement at
Capernaum was quickly abandoned ("and they remained
there not many days"[23]), or that by Jesus' friends in our present passage, not "His mother and His brethren and His disciples" are intended, but some broader circle of those responsible for Him. If Jesus' "friends" in the responsible sense of
our passage were dwelling in Capernaum — especially if these
"friends" be understood as precisely His mother and brothers,

---

[19] We have already noted (note 4) that Luke iv. 16 ff. seems to record
an earlier visit to Nazareth before His systematic Galilean ministry had
begun. Besides Meyer's note at Mt. xiii. 53–58 (E. T. p. 372) cf. Godet's notes
on Lk. iv. 23 (E. T. i. p. 238), and John ii. 12 (E. T. ii. p. 19). Luke iv. 23 of
course offers a difficulty for this view.

[20] Cf. Godet, i. p. 237: "This speech betrays an ironical doubt respecting
those marvellous things which were attributed to Him."

[21] So Wieseler, De Wette, Tholuck, Ewald: cf. esp. Th. Zahn, in loc.
(p. 163 and note 3) and "Forschungen," vi. p. 331.

[22] Cf. Meyer's note on Jno. ii. 12 (E. T. i. p. 149).

[23] Cf. Westcott's note on Jno. ii. 12: "This is perhaps mentioned to show
that at present Capernaum was not made the permanent residence of the Lord,
as it became afterwards."

constituting His "household" — it would be inexplicable that His returning "home" should not have been to their house; and not only would their personal lack of acquaintance with His work or movements ("when they heard") be inexplicable, but the action ascribed to them ("they went forth") would be inappropriate. It would seem that we must think of the "friends" in question as living somewhere out of the path of His work hitherto, and away from the "home" to which He returned from the sea-side and mountain-top. The elimination of His disciples — who belonged to the party which returned from Cana — from the "friends" of our present passage is not only required by the situation in our passage itself, but is in harmony with the statement of Jno. ii. 11, that they already believed in Him. For, a certain measure of unbelief is, of course, implied in the judgment passed on Him by His "friends" here. If His brothers are meant, as seems intrinsically probable, this is in harmony with Jno. vii. 5, from which we learn that they remained unbelieving until the end.[24] The phrases of Jno. vii. 3–5 form, indeed, a very pungent commentary on our passage.

The measure of the unbelief — we designedly use the milder term, instead of the stronger, "disbelief" — which is implied in the judgment and action of Jesus' "friends" recorded in our passage is deserving of some consideration. That we may form an estimate of it it would be well to ascertain with some exactness what is really meant by the term, "He is beside Himself." Many insist that there is no real difference between this judgment upon Jesus and that expressed by the scribes in the words, "He hath Beelzebul" (verse 22).[25] Madness, it is urged, was explained as demoniacal possession, and to say that one was mad was all one with saying that he was possessed.[26] On the

[24] Cf. Swete's note: "The family of Jesus was doubtless inspired by a desire for His safety, but their interpretation of His enthusiasm implied want of faith in Him, cf. Jno. vii. 5; the Mother perhaps was overpersuaded by the brethren."

[25] E.g. H. J. Holtzmann (p. 127), who remarks that Theophylact already explains correctly: δαίμονα ἔχει.

[26] Cf. E. Renan, "Vie de Jesus"[2] 1863, p. 263, note 4 (E. T. of the twenty-third and final ed. 1913, p. 273, note 3): "This phrase 'Thou hast a demon' (Mt. xi. 18, Lk. vii. 33, Jno. vii. 20, viii. 48 ff., x. 20 ff.) should be rendered by

face of it, however, this view is untenable. Possession and insanity are not clearly identified in the Evangelical narratives. It is not even intimated that they were constantly associated.[27] In our present passage they even seem to be expressly distinguished. Mark clearly desires to contrast the judgments passed on Jesus by His friends and His enemies, as, though both uncomprehending, yet the pitying and the condemnatory judgment. Even, however, should we identify all mental alienation with possession, the degree of alienation implied in any given instance would still remain undetermined; the effects of the possession would naturally be very varied, and might on occasion involve only the slightest, perhaps the most temporary unbalancing. In any case, therefore, we are thrown back upon what is actually said.

The term employed [28] in the present passage is not a strong

---

'Thou art insane,' as it is said in Arabic *medjnoun enté*. This verb, δαιμονᾶν has also in the whole of classical antiquity the sense of ' to be insane.' " In the text, however, it is said: " But here again the difficulties must not be exaggerated. The disorders explained by possessions were often very slight. In our day, in Syria, people are regarded as insane or possessed by a demon (the two notions are the same, *medjnoun*) who have only some little eccentricity (*bizarrerie*)."

[27] The physical accompaniment of possession mentioned in Mt. ix. 32, Lk. xi. 14 is only dumbness, in Mt. xii. 22, blindness and dumbness, in Lk. xiii. 10–17, curvature of the spine; Cf. also Mt. xv. 22, Mk. vii. 26, xvi. 9, Lk. iv. 33, viii. 2 in none of which cases is insanity indicated. Only in a single instance is mania expressly intimated, and that only by its contrasting state (Mk. v. 15, Lk. viii. 35; cf. 2 Cor. v. 13). W. M. Alexander, " Demonic Possession in the New Testament," 1902, upholding the thesis that " all cases designated ' demoniac' belong to the category ' Lunacy or Idiocy ' " (p. 147), establishes his diagnosis in only three cases (Mk. i. 21–26 = Lk. iv. 31–37; Mt. viii. 28–34 = Mk. v. 1–17, Lk. viii. 26–37; Mt. xvii. 14–20 = Mk. ix. 14–29, Lk. ix. 37–43); and in two of these only with difficulty and at the cost of the enlargement of the category of "lunacy" by the addition of "and idiocy." He then applies this diagnosis, without express warrant from the text, to all other cases of possession. John x. 20 need not be read as identifying all possession with lunacy, but may only identify this particular case of lunacy with possession as its cause: cf. Jno. vii. 20, viii. 48.

[28] J. H. Heinrich Schmidt in § 174 of his *Synonymik der Griechischen Sprache* deals with the terms which designate a perverted state of mind (he had dealt in § 147 with these which express a mental deficiency, especially ἄφρων and ἄνους). He divides them into three groups: (1) Words which in

one and need not imply a serious state of mental disturbance. The fundamental implication of the word is no more than that the subject is thrown out of his normal state into a condition of strong, perhaps ungovernable, emotion. The emotion in question may be of the most varied kind, but commonly in the New Testament usage of the word (uniformly except for our present passage and II Cor. v. 13) it is that of amazement, perhaps with a suggestion of bewilderment.[29] In the special usage illustrated by our present passage (cf. II Cor. v. 13), in which it expresses that state of mental aberration which we also describe as " not one's self," it need not import more than an overwrought condition in which it might be thought that the prudent conduct of life would be unlikely and could become impossible. In this general sense, it occurs nowhere else in the New Testament except in II Cor. v. 13, where (to say nothing of demoniacal possession) it certainly does not suggest either raving madness or irrational insanity, but describes on the contrary an ecstatic state in which the Apostle saw a ground for much glorying (xii. 1).[30] We need not imagine, then, that

---

the first instance designate the violent utterances of a disturbed mind; (2) words which express more the inward disorder by which the soul is carried away by senseless passions; (3) words which rather describe the soul which thinks and feels in a disturbed manner. Ἐξίστημι (ἔκστασις) is not included in his lists; but this may be in part because he leaves to one side such terms as require the addition of a φρενός or φρενῶν, or some contextual indication, to define the meaning; and confines himself to such as bear in themselves their significance.

[29] Mt. xii. 23; Mk. ii. 12, v. 42, vi. 51; Lk. ii. 47, viii. 56, xxiv. 22; Acts ii. 7–12, viii. 9, 11, 13, ix. 21, x. 45, xii. 16 = " amazed "; Mk. iii. 21, II Cor. v. 13 = " demented." Cf. ἔκστασις: Mk. v. 42, xvi. 8; Lk. v. 26; Acts iii. 10 = " amazement "; Acts x. 10, xi. 5, xxii. 17 = " trance." Cf. Art. " Amazement " in Hastings' DCG.

[30] Cf. C. F. G. Heinrici, " Das zweite Sendschreiben des Apostel Paulus an die Korinthier," 1887, pp. 277 f.: " The fundamental sense of ἐξίστημι to be out of oneself, as this is brought about through the experience of an over-mastering impression, makes the word equally suitable for describing conditions of very high emotions, like amazement, joy, terror; and emotions which lie beyond the limits of sound mental life (ἐν ἑαυτῷ εἶναι ... ἐντὸς ἑαυτοῦ γίνεσθαι), whether of the nature of insanity or of rapture. In the latter sense σωφρονεῖν is the technical contrast to ἐκστῆναι, and it is accordingly introduced here for the purpose of indicating experiences which had for the Apostle a signif-

Jesus' friends saw in Him a maniac; we need only understand, — what surely would not be unnatural in men who had as yet at least no sense of the nature of His mission — that they were led by the reports which had come to them to believe that He was in a state of exaltation which endangered His health and safety and needed some soothing hand to guard Him from Himself.[31]

That they felt His condition to be serious, may be inferred from the fact that they were prepared " to lay hold upon Him." Yet exaggeration must be shunned here too. The term, no doubt emphasizes in its ground-idea the thought of force, even of violence; but, beginning thus with the notion of taking forcible possession of, it came to be employed also of simply taking possession of, with the idea of force quite out of sight, and ended by meaning merely to obtain, to get (Acts xxvii. 13), and, indeed, merely to cling to (Mt. xxviii. 9, Acts iii. 11), to retain, to hold (Mt. vii. 3, 4, 8, 9, 10). There is no need in our present passage to emphasize the idea of violence, as if His kinsmen wished " to seize " Jesus.[32] Even " to lay hold upon

icance similar to that of the rapture which is described later. In this connection the expression then suggests that ecstatic conditions which remain, in their content and source, obscure for the estimate of all others, cannot be the subject of boasting before others. . . . The key to the full understanding of the contrast of ἐκστῆναι and σωφρονεῖν is supplied, however, only by the detailed description of the ecstacy in the polemic concluding sections, which has been mentioned. (xii. 1 f.) . . .' "

[31] Cf. A. Loisy, " Evang. Synopt," i. p. 698: " They do not say that Jesus had lost His mind, the word which the Evangelist employs not having this precise meaning in the usage of the New Testament, but being used to designate every transport of astonishment, of admiration, of stupor, of enthusiasm; but they believed Him to be in a state of mystical exaltation, which made Him lose the real sense of life and of His own condition." A. B. Bruce, in loc., goes to an extreme when he says: " In the opinion of His friends, He was in a state of excitement bordering on insanity." Perhaps the English word " transport " presents as fair a rendering of the term here as can be found.

[32] H. J. Holtzmann: " Their purpose is to apprehend Him; to possess themselves of Him, κρατ . αὐτ., like vi. 17, xii. 12, xiv. 1; they would seek out the morbidly overstrained member of the family who had become strange and incomprehensible to them, and, no doubt for His own advantage, but still forcibly, withdraw Him from public life." Wohlenberg: " In order to seize Jesus (κρατῆσαι), to possess themselves of Him, if not to take Him into custody, yet in some sense forcibly to apprehend Him; cf. xii. 12, xiv. 1, 46."

Him " is too strong a rendering. " To get Him " is nearer to what it intended; and the idea is not so much to put Him in ward as to take Him in charge. Of course the idea of compulsion underlies everything: His relations were acting under the impression that He was in need of kindly control and were prepared to protect Him from Himself. But it is the idea of protection which dominates the statement, rather than that of compulsion.

Such a judgment upon Jesus' activities, and such an attitude towards His person, were inevitable for those of His kindred who, feeling responsible for Him, were yet ill-informed concerning His person and work. There were some of His kindred, no doubt, to whom such a judgment and attitude would have been at this stage impossible. James and John were of His kindred,[33] and there may have been others of those closest to Him who, with them, already, in the full sense of Jno. ii. 11, " believed on Him." But it is not necessary to pronounce this judgment of His work and attitude toward His person incompatible with any measure of faith in Him; or even with a high degree of faith in Him if imperfectly informed whether of what was to be expected of Him or of what He was actually doing. There is no compelling reason for insisting that His mother was of the number of those of whom it is said here that they were led to believe that He was " beside Himself " and in need of some protective care. But neither does there seem to be any compelling reason for assuming that she could not possibly be of their number.[34] Mary too (like John the Baptist, Mt. xi. 2 ff.), may have had searchings of heart before she adjusted herself to the Great Reality; and, in the meantime,

---

B. Weiss: " In order to apprehend Him, possess themselves of Him. . . . In spite of the strongly colored expression of Mk. we are by no means to think of a hostile act (Klostermann), but at the most of a kindly compulsion, which they thought to exercise in His own interest to protect Him in the keeping of the family from further crowding."

[33] As Wohlenberg reminds us.

[34] So, e.g. Wohlenberg: " From all that we otherwise know of Mary, His Mother, it must be taken as absolutely excluded that she should come forward in any way antagonistically to Jesus."

as she had exercised control over her son in His infancy (Lk.
ii. 51), so in the first days of His ministry she may have fancied
that she saw indications that He still required her motherly
care. There would be implied in this, not " a total unbelief in
His pretentions, but only an imperfect view of them." [35] Where
no belief in His pretentions existed such an attitude towards
Him as is here intimated, was, as we have said, not only natural
but inevitable. His unbelieving brothers, however kindly, must
have thought Him in some sense out of His mind, and must
have faced the duty of casting around Him some protection.[36]

Natural, however, as the judgment of Jesus and the attitude towards His person which are here recorded, are in the
circumstances and to the persons to which they are ascribed,
the critics have laid hold upon them as representing a point of
view regarding Jesus, or at least regarding Mary, which is
inconsistent with the supernaturalistic tradition of Jesus. On
this ground they seek to account for the fact that this section
appears in Mark's Gospel only. It was omitted by Matthew
and Luke, they tell us, because not consonant with their point
of view. In what respect Mark's point of view as to the person
of Jesus, or his reverence for Jesus, differs from that of Matthew and Luke, it is meanwhile difficult to perceive. The mere
presence of this passage in one of the Evangelists is proof

[35] The words we have quoted are from the excellent comment of J. A.
Alexander on Mk. iii. 21, where, however, he is speaking not of Mary but of
Jesus' friends in general, to whom is to be attributed also absence or deficiency
of faith. " This," says Alexander, was " a very natural and intelligible state of
mind at this stage of the history, and on the part of those whose spiritual
or religious feelings were less strong and well-defined than their natural
affections or humanity." With Mary also in mind, he repeats in his comment
on verse 31, that " nothing could be more natural and pardonable than precisely such solicitude, which is perfectly compatible with true faith and
affection, but imperfect views both of His person and mission."

[36] Cf. G. Salmon, " The Human Element in the Gospels," 1907, p. 203:
" To the Christian reader it is shocking that any one should be able to suppose that our Lord was out of His mind; yet, if we consider the circumstances,
we perceive that the idea was one most likely to occur as it often has done
since, when followers of His who were afterwards venerated as saints, had judgments passed on them by sensible men of the world. It is in itself perfectly
credible that our Lord should have made the impression commonly produced
by one who steps completely out of the beaten track."

enough that it contains nothing contradictory to the reverence
for Jesus' person which is common to them all.[37] Nevertheless
P. W. Schmiedel gives this passage a place among his nine
" pillar-passages " which he pronounces absolutely credible,
as preserving traditions of the real Jesus, precisely on the
ground that they make assertions about Jesus which could
not have been invented by His worshipping followers, and
must therefore have thrust themselves upon this or that
Evangelist merely by the force of their undeniable authenticity.
This is evidenced, he declares, by the fact that they have been
omitted by others of the Evangelists as offensive to their
reverence for Jesus.[38] On this view, Matthew and Luke are supposed to have had this statement before them and to have
omitted it, because it seemed to them derogatory to Jesus'
dignity that those nearest to Him should, even at the outset
of His ministry, have been led to fear that He might be beside
Himself; and Schmiedel labors [39] to show that Matthew's narrative, for example, retains signs of having been consciously
adapted from Mark's. It is more usual, however, to suppose
that Mark's statement has been omitted by the other Gospels
(presumed to be later than Mark and to be in large part based
on it) in the interests of growing reverence for Mary as the
mother of our Lord, rather than directly of reverence for
Jesus.[40] And, indeed, Schmiedel himself when dealing with the
passage at large lapses into this point of view.[41] In a passage

[37] Cf. *The Princeton Theological Review,* xi. 2 (April, 1913), pp. 252 ff.

[38] " Encyclopaedia Biblica," col. 1881; cf. *The Princeton Theological
Review,* xi. 2 (April, 1913), pp. 204 ff.

[39] Coll. 1847–1848.

[40] H. J. Holtzmann may serve as a typical instance (" Synoptiker "[3] p.
68): " Mark in the most significant way stands alone with the notice in verse
21, since Matthew and Luke already are unable to reconcile themselves to this
conception of Mary, and therefore the reparation to be spoken of at Lk. ii.
48." Accordingly at p. 323, he follows Pfleiderer in supposing that the " Behold
thy father and I have sought thee " of Lk. ii. 48 is a reminiscence of Mk. iii.
32, " Behold thy Mother and thy brothers seek thee," and serves the further
purpose of counteracting what is said in Mk. iii. 21 (not in Luke) together
with its consequences in iii. 31–35 (Lk. xviii. 19–21) and to soften the shadow
thrown by it on Mary.

[41] " Das vierte Evangelium gegenüber den drei ersten," 1906, p. 18:

like this, it is suggested, Mark accordingly preserves an earlier and truer tradition of the attitude of Jesus' kinsfolk to His person and work than can be found in the later Gospels, whether John or Matthew and Luke. It must be borne in mind, however, that, according to John also, the brothers of Jesus did not believe in Him (Jno. vii. 5), and must therefore have held much the view of Him which is placed on the lips of Jesus' kinsmen in our present passage. The attitude of Mary towards Him alone, can come into question; and it is upon it, accordingly, that the contrast between Matthew and Luke, with their " Infancy chapters " in which Mary's supernatural information as to her son is exploited, and Mark, which has nothing of this kind, is insisted upon.

The whole case hangs on the suppositions that Mary was included among the kinsmen of Jesus mentioned in Mk. iii. 21, and that the judgment upon Jesus there ascribed to His kinsmen would be impossible to the Mary of the opening chapters of Matthew and Luke. We have seen that neither supposition is necessary, or, indeed, in the presence of any good reasons to the contrary, even reasonable. We may accept the statement of Mk. iii. 20, 21 as intrinsically self-evidencing and therefore " absolutely credible " as a genuine historical fact, without any fear of discrediting thereby either the Infancy chapters of Matthew and Luke or the historical tradition of the supernatural Jesus which constitutes the substance of all the Evangelical records. The attempts to account for the absence of this statement from Matthew and Luke as deliberate omission on dogmatic grounds are accordingly altogether ineffective

---

" We must observe moreover the rôle which *Jesus' Mother* plays in the miracle at Cana. Although Jesus had never before worked a miracle (Jno. ii. 11) she knows beforehand that He is going to work one and says to the servants, although she is rebuffed by Him, ' Whatever He bids you, do.' How entirely different it is in Mark! Here (iii. 21) Jesus' kinsmen (*Angehörigen*) go out to lay hold of Him because they said, ' He is beside Himself.' Who these kinsmen were we very soon learn (iii. 31-35): His mother and His brothers come to Him and call Him out of the house. And it is only from their purpose to put a stop to His work and to confine Him to His home that His rude answer finds its explanation: ' Who is my mother and my brothers? He who does the will of God, the same is my brother and sister and mother.' "

and the endeavor to discover in the narratives of Matthew and Luke hidden signs of acquaintance with [42] and conscious alteration of Mark's text are too flimsy to justify notice. The entire fact is that we are indebted to Mark for a piece of information altogether natural in itself and consonant with the entire body of facts recorded in the other Evangelists, which nevertheless they do not also preserve for us. This might be inexplicable if we were compelled to suppose that each Evangelist has told us all he knew, or all he knew which he thought "fit to print." But it is just what we should expect on the supposition — which is the only tenable one — that each Evangelist, though serving himself, to a very great extent, with common sources of information, has yet set down in his Gospel from the general store, only what commended itself to him as suitable for his purpose and adapted to advance his particular object in writing.

The naturalness and, indeed, inevitableness of the judgment that Jesus was out of His mind on the part of men not ill-disposed towards Him but yet unable to accept His claims for Himself at their face value, is illustrated by the return to this judgment by a type of modern unbelief. A large literature has in recent years grown up around the suggestion that Jesus was more or less of unsound mind. Whether He is explained as a paranoiac lunatic or merely as a visionary ecstatic, it is inevitable that those who cannot see in Him the Divine Being He proclaimed Himself to be, should think His lofty estimate of Himself too lofty and should seek the account of His too lofty estimate of Himself in some — greater or less — mental derangement. We can scarcely look upon a like judgment among His contemporaries as strange when we are so familiar with it to-day; or urge its existence among His contemporaries as evidence of anything more than it witnesses to to-day. In simple fact, Jesus' career was not that of an ordinary man: and the dilemma is inevitable that He was

---

[42] We do not doubt that the incident recorded in Mark iii. 20–21 was known to the authors of both Matthew and Luke, as was much else which they (as writing freely, each for his own particular end) do not record.

either something more than a normal man or something less. We, like His contemporaries, — and His contemporaries like us — have only the alternatives: either supernatural or subnormal, either Divine or else " out of His mind." [43]

II

It is again Mark alone who records the extreme expression of the hatred of the scribes towards Jesus in their ascription to Him of demoniacal possession.[44] All three of the Synoptics, however, report the charge made by His enemies that it was by the aid of Beelzebul, the prince of the demons, that He cast out demons.[45] The solemn warning against blasphemy against the Holy Spirit which Jesus founded upon this charge, occurs — in one form or another — in all three Gospels, though in this connection only in Matthew and Mark,[46] while in Luke it appears in another context.[47] As it is solely with this warning that we are now concerned, we transcribe it in its three forms. " Verily, I say unto you, All things shall be forgiven unto the sons of men, their sins, and their blasphemies wherewithsoever they shall blaspheme; but whosoever shall blaspheme against the Holy Spirit hath never forgiveness, but is guilty of an eternal sin. Because they said, He hath an unclean Spirit " (Mk. iii. 28–30). " And everyone who shall speak a word against the Son of Man, it shall be forgiven unto him; but unto him that blasphemeth against the Holy Spirit, it shall not be forgiven " (Lk. xii. 10). " Therefore I say unto you, every sin and blasphemy shall be forgiven unto men, but the blasphemy against the Spirit shall not be forgiven. And whosoever shall speak a word against the Son of Man, it shall be forgiven unto him; but whosoever shall speak against the Holy Spirit, it shall not be forgiven unto him, neither in this world nor in that which is to come " (Mat. xii. 31, 32).

[43] Cf. what is said with respect to W. Heitmüller's hesitations and difficulties in *The Princeton Theological Review,* xii. 2 (April, 1914), pp. 315 ff.

[44] Mk. iii. 22–30; cf. Jno. x. 20, vii. 20, viii. 48.

[45] Mt. xii. 22–27; Mk. iii. 22–30; Lk. xi. 14–23; the parallel, Mt. ix. 34 is not genuine.   [46] Mt. xii. 31, 32; Mk. iii. 28–30.   [47] Lk. xii. 10.

Let us begin by looking at Mark's account.

Mark alone, as we have said, records the opprobrious judgment of the scribes upon Jesus and His work, that He was possessed by Beelzebul. This is formally due, probably, to the circumstance that Mark alone introduces his account of this incident in contrast with the judgment passed upon Jesus by His friends: here is the judgment passed upon Him by His enemies. It is intimated, however, that there is a closer connection between this opprobrious judgment of His enemies and Jesus' warning concerning blasphemy against the Spirit than merely that it formed the formal occasion of the discourse of which the warning is a part. Mark expressly tells us that it was precisely because the scribes attributed demoniacal possession to Him that Jesus was led to give His solemn warning (verse 30). That is to say, it was precisely in this ascription that their blasphemous words against the Holy Spirit culminated, or, at least, that their words approached most dangerously the unpardonable sin of blasphemy against the Spirit. It might infer a dangerous approach to blasphemy against the Spirit by whom He wrought His mighty works to say that He wrought them by means of Beelzebul. But He was able to argue that question. The assertion that He in whom the Holy Spirit dwelt beyond measure was possessed (instead) by an unclean Spirit, advanced so far beyond this, however, that not argument but quick warning was demanded.

The solemnity with which Mark represents Jesus as introducing the declaration regarding blasphemy is marked by its opening formula: "Verily, I say unto you . . ." And the weight given to it by this solemn opening formula is sustained throughout in the stately march of its words. The declaration begins with an impressive proclamation of the forgivableness, in the wide mercy of God, of all human sin. The words are so arranged as to throw the emphasis upon the universality of this forgivableness: [48] "Verily, I say unto you, that *all things* shall be forgiven to the sons of men " — a solemn periphrasis for

---

[48] Meyer: "The order of the words places them so far apart as to place a great emphasis on πάντα." So also Weiss, Holtzmann and others.

the mere " to men." Then this universal " all things " is more closely defined according to its nature, all " acts of sin "; and then the specific sins now more particularly in mind are brought to sight, — all " the blasphemies wherewithsoever they may blaspheme." The effect is to create a most moving sense of the amplitude of the divine forgiveness. All the acts of sin which the sons of men may commit; all the blasphemies where-with they may blaspheme: all these may be forgiven. It is with the force of a great contrast that the single exception is then brought in: all, all is forgivable except this one thing: " But whosoever shall blaspheme against the Holy Ghost " — the particular form of the designation is chosen which throws the emphasis on His quality of *holiness* [49] — " hath not for-giveness." This was startling enough: but it is rendered even more so by the addition emphatically at the end, of the awful words — " for ever ": " hath not forgiveness — for ever." And then the already strained emphasis is still further enhanced by a repetition of the declaration of the hopelessness of this sin, in the negative form: " But is guilty of an eternal sin," — a sin, that is, which can never in all eternity be expiated or remitted. At the end, the Evangelist adds under the influence of the dread solemnity of the whole, the justification of this terrible warning. " Because," he says, " they said, He hath an unclean spirit." Because they accused Him of being possessed by an unclean spirit, He thus in awe-inspiring words warns them that blasphemy against that Spirit which is holiness itself, by whom He was really informed, is an eternally unfor-givable sin.

The terms " blaspheme," " blasphemy," are obviously em-ployed in this passage in their highest sense of irreverent and impious speech with respect to the Divine Being. The words, no doubt, are capable of employment in a more general sense, to express any reviling or calumniating speech against men. They are actually used in this general sense in the New Testa-ment, including (though with Jesus only as their object) the

---

[49] Τὸ πνεῦμα τὸ ἅγιον; cf. Swete *in loc.*: " The repeated article brings the holiness of the Spirit into prominence."

Synoptic Gospels (Mt. xxvii. 39, Mk. xv. 29, Lk. xxii. 65, xxiii. 39). As the discourse of which it forms the climax has its start in a defamatory speech concerning Jesus, it might be colorably contended that they bear this more general sense in our passage.[50] But the extreme elevation of the language scarcely admits of this lower interpretation of the terms on which the whole turns as on its hinge. Why should such solemn assurance be given that among all the sins which will be forgiven the sons of men shall be included even (the " and " has a slight ascensive force) " the railings wherewith they may rail " — unless those " railings " possessed some special heinousness, as, for example, sins against the majesty of God? Otherwise, this sentence, in other respects so impressive in diction, would end on a sad anti-climax. It would be equivalent to saying: All their robberies and adulteries and murders shall be forgiven to men, yea even whatever bad language they may use. A similar incongruity would be created with the succeeding context, were the general sense of the terms insisted upon here. The heightening of the sin of blasphemy against the Holy Spirit would lose its force if the contrast against which it is thrown up were nothing more than detraction of our neighbors. The full effect of the passage becomes apparent only when we recognize that blasphemy against the Holy Spirit is set as unforgivable over against other — not merely slanders but — veritable blasphemies, described as capable of being pardoned. Moreover the terms " to blaspheme," " blasphemy," when used absolutely, had acquired a technical meaning practically equivalent to these terms in our current English,[51] and they cannot be taken in a lower sense here without violence. No simple reader could possibly understand them in any other sense than that of insults to the Divine Being.

It is, no doubt, a startling result of distinguishing blasphemy against the Holy Spirit from blasphemies against God

[50] They are so explained, for example, by Wellhausen *in loc.* A parallel to the passage so understood is found in I Sam. ii. 25.

[51] The verb: Mt. ix. 3, xxvi. 65; Mk. ii. 7; Jno. x. 36, but cf. Lk. xxii. 65; and the noun: Mt. xii. 31, xxvi. 65; Lk. v. 21; Jno. x. 33, but cf. Mt. xv. 19; Mk. xii. 22.

in general, that thus the Holy Spirit is set over against God in general and blasphemy against the Holy Spirit is declared more unpardonable than general blasphemy against God. Startling as this result is, however, it must just be accepted; it is impossible to believe that the contrast in our passage lies only between blasphemy against God and slander against fellow-men — as if what were said were, You can calumniate your fellow-men and it may be forgiven, but if you blaspheme God there is no forgiveness — for ever. We must not be stumbled by the indications of a Trinitarian background in Jesus' speech. Such indications pervade His speech in much greater measure than is commonly recognized. They are present, indeed, in all the expressions of His divine self-consciousness, and we should not forget that it is in His words that the Trinitarian formula finds its most precise enunciation in the New Testament (Mt. xxviii. 19). Meanwhile, what is necessary to recognize at the moment is only that Jesus here declares that blasphemy against the Holy Spirit specifically, not blasphemy in general, is unforgivable; and that He declares this with an emphasis which can only be understood as singling this sin out among all sins as a sin of very singular heinousness. The reason of this seems to reside in the fact that the holiness of God is especially manifested in the Holy Spirit. His designation here is accordingly so phrased as to throw His holiness particularly into prominence: " But whosoever shall blaspheme against the Spirit, that Holy One." [52] Because the holiness of God is peculiarly manifested in the Spirit, whose very name is Holy,[53] insulting words spoken against this Holy Spirit are a peculiarly heinous sin.

Mark reports only the contrast which Jesus drew between blasphemy of specifically the Holy Spirit and blasphemy in general. He communicates no specific declaration with respect to the pardonableness of blasphemy against Jesus' own person. The inference to be drawn from this omission may be variously

[52] Τὸ πνεῦμα τὸ ἅγιον not τὸ ἅγιον πνεῦμα as in Lk. xii. 10 or the simple τὸ πνεῦμα of Mt. xii. 31 (but in the more emphatic repetition of verse 32 τὸ πνεῦμα τὸ ἅγιον as in Mk. iii. 29).

[53] Cf. Is. lvii. 15.

conceived. It may be said that Jesus (according to Mark's conception) never thought of injurious words spoken against His person as "blasphemy." Conscious of His (mere, perhaps sinful) humanity, and setting Himself in all His thought in contrast with God, as a humble creature of His hands, He cannot speak of "blasphemy" with reference to Himself, but only with reference to God, inclusive of course of the Holy Spirit. He can contrast blasphemy against the Holy Ghost and blasphemy against God in general, but not "blasphemy" against Himself and blasphemy against God, the Holy Spirit. Or, more subtly seeking the same end — the presentation of Jesus as in His own estimate of Himself, merely a human being — it may be said that Jesus identifies here opprobrious words against Himself with blasphemy against the Holy Spirit and means to declare that they are the unpardonable sin.[54] The occasion of His remarks was the ascription to Him of demoniacal possession, and the attribution of His miracles to Satanic agency. This He declares to be unpardonable blasphemy, because He really has within Him the Divine Spirit and works His miracles by the Spirit, that is to say, by "the finger" of God. To vilify Him is unpardonably to blaspheme the Holy Spirit within Him by whom all His works are wrought. That the injurious words spoken against Him when it was declared that He was possessed of a demon are represented by Him as blasphemy (or as coming very near to blasphemy) of the Holy Spirit is indeed clear: that is precisely what Mark affirms in verse 30. But this does not identify all opprobrious words against His person with blasphemy against the Holy Spirit: it rather distinguishes between His person and

[54] Cf. H. J. Holtzmann, "Synoptiker"[3] 1901, p. 128: "Here, therefore in contrast with Mt. xii. 32; Lk. xii. 10 the unforgivable sin consists precisely in blasphemy of Jesus, who, no doubt, possesses His power of exorcism through the Spirit, Mt. xii. 28." Similarly cf. P. W. Schmiedel, "Protestantische Monatshefte," ii. (1898) p. 304: "With Mark, blasphemy of the Messiah is thought to be by no means forgivable, since he expressly indicates (verse 30) as the occasion of the declaration, the contention of the opponents from verse 22 that Jesus was in collusion with Beelzebul or even possessed by him, and therefore wishes to say that there lies in this a blasphemy of the Holy Spirit working in Jesus."

that of the Spirit, the point of the warning being that such words against Him as these particular words approached to the unpardonable sin because they expressly assailed not Him but the Spirit working in Him. In Mark's report, therefore, there is no express reference to blasphemy against the Son of Man and if it is included at all it must be included in the general reference to " the blasphemies wherewithsoever the sons of men blaspheme "; and these all, with the sole exception of blasphemy against the Holy Spirit, are expressly declared to be forgivable. Since only blasphemy against the Holy Spirit is unpardonable, then, of course blasphemy against His own person is already declared to be pardonable and there is no clamant need of explicating further so obvious a fact. With this understanding of the implications of the passage it stands in harmony with the conception of Jesus' person which underlies the whole of Mark's Gospel (cf. e.g., xiii. 32) and with the more explicated assertion of his companion Evangelists in this place, both of whom speak of a blasphemy of the Son of Man which — like these undefined blasphemies spoken of by Mark — is pardonable. Unless there is some decisive reason why this should not be included in these, it is only reasonable to see it in them.[55] Mark in that case does not explicitly adduce blasphemy against the Son of Man as pardonable only because its pardonableness is already sufficiently asserted in the emphasized declaration that all blasphemies, with the sole exception of that against the Holy Spirit, are pardonable.

Let us now look somewhat closely at the reports of the other Evangelists.

Luke gives the declaration its most compressed form, and places it in a wholly different connection from that in which it appears in Mark and Matthew. It may well be, indeed, that he is recording a different utterance of Jesus' of the same general purport. There is no intrinsic reason why Jesus may

[55] Cf. Meyer (E. T. i. p. 59): " The less is it to be said that Mark places on a par the blasphemy against the Person of Jesus (Mt. xii. 31 f.) and that against the Holy Spirit (Köstlin, p. 318), or that he has ' already given up ' the former blasphemy (Hilgenfeld). It is included in fact, in verse 28." This note is retained by Weiss.

not have made such a declaration more than once. In any event, however, the declaration given by Luke is of the same general contents as that given by Mark and Matthew.

It is not a little difficult to be quite sure of the exact reference of the blasphemy against the Holy Ghost which is spoken of in Luke's report. On the face of it the declaration is quite general, that blasphemy against the Holy Spirit shall not be forgiven; and no closer definition is supplied by the context. We may conjecture that the reference is to blasphemy of the Holy Spirit speaking in the disciples when put upon their trial (verses 11, 12),[56] or that the denial of the Son (verse 9) is here declared to be, when the act not of His enemies, but of His disciples, not merely " speaking a word against the Son of Man," but actually the unpardonable sin of blasphemy against the Holy Spirit, operative in them.[57] But such conjectures have little to support them.

There is a certain parallelism between the two clauses of verse 10 and those of verses 8, 9, which may warrant us in taking the two pairs of antitheses together as alike under the influence of the solemn opening phrase: " But I say unto you " (verse 8). In that case, we have here two combined encouragements and warnings:

(1a) " Every one who shall confess Me before men, him shall the Son of Man also confess before the angels of God:
    (1b) But he that denieth Me in the presence of men, shall be denied in the presence of the angels of God.

(2a) And every one who shall speak a word against the Son of Man, it shall be forgiven him:
    (2b) But unto him that blasphemeth against the Holy Spirit, it shall not be forgiven."

[56] So J. Weiss. Cf. Th. Zahn who broadens it to include the whole witnessing work of the disciples.

[57] So Hofmann, " Schriftbeweis " ii. 2, p. 342. Cf. especially G. L. Hahn's note.

Thus a gnomic character attaches to these twin declarations which lends them great impressiveness and gives to each member of each of them almost equal force. We must, it seems, assume, then, that our Lord advancing, in verse 10, to the climax of His combined encouragement and warning, makes two declarations of generally equal importance, — that to wit, blasphemy against His own person will be forgiven, and blasphemy against the Holy Spirit will not be forgiven. Closer definition wherein either blasphemy against His person or blasphemy against the Spirit consists is lacking, and would perhaps be out of place in such crisp, proverbial utterances.

We have spoken of " blasphemy " in both clauses, because it seems quite clear that the variation in their language, from " every one who *shall speak a word* against the Son of Man " in the former, to " to him who *blasphemeth* the Holy Ghost " in the latter, is without significance (cf. Mt. xii. 32, where " speak against " is common to both clauses).[58] Obviously the contrast between the two cases consists not in any difference in the nature of the offence committed, but in some difference in the persons against whom the offence is committed. What is in effect declared is that an offence will be forgiven when committed against the Son of Man which will not be forgiven when committed against the Holy Spirit. There is undoubtedly suggested here a certain subordination of the Son of Man to the Holy Spirit, — if we cannot say exactly in dignity of person, yet in the heinousness of the sin of blasphemy when committed against the two respectively. The ground of this distinction is in no way intimated unless it be hinted by the designations by which the two persons are described — " the Son of Man " and " the Holy Spirit." It is difficult to discover, however, in these designations, the desired implications of lowliness on the one hand and of exaltation on the other. " The Son of Man " is an exalted title and is employed to suggest the humiliation rather than the humility of Jesus' life on earth;

[58] Godet (E. T. ii. p. 93) on the contrary emphasizes the difference, as if the forgivableness of the " speaking a word against " the Son of Man depended on the precise point that this was not a " blasphemous " word.

the form of the title " the Holy Spirit " here is not (as in Mk. iii. 29) that which most strongly emphasizes His holiness and consequently His exaltation. Perhaps it would be wise to read the two designations, therefore, so far as simply denotative and not to seek in them for subtle contrasting connotations.

It is meanwhile easy also to misinterpret the contrast in dignity between the two persons involved in the differing treatment of blasphemy against them. It is of immense significance that Jesus should have thought it important to assure his followers that blasphemy against His person could be forgiven.[59] It would be bathos to say that every one who spoke a word against a man could be forgiven but not he who blasphemed the Holy Ghost. A high sense of the dignity of His person underlies the mere adduction of the case of blasphemy against Himself as a sin that might be forgiven. Otherwise that might go without saying. No doubt the immediately preceding declaration that those who denied Him would be denied before the angels of God (verse 9) somewhat prepares the way for such a further declaration. But that cannot empty of its significance the setting side by side of the Son of Man and Holy Spirit as if they had something in common which required that any difference in dealing with sins against them should be expressly notified. The title " Son of Man " moreover is taken up from verse 8 where it is a title of dignity. The effect of its repetition in verse 10 is clearly to aggravate the sin of speaking against Him: the reason why this sin is forgivable cannot be, therefore, that it is a little sin. It is the greatness of the grace of Jesus which is celebrated in this promise of forgiveness as truly as it is the heinousness of the sin of blasphemy against the Holy Spirit which is emphasized in the refusal of forgiveness for it in the succeeding clause. We cannot say, then, that the difference in the treatment of blasphemy against the Son of Man and against the Holy Spirit is rooted in an intrinsic difference between the two persons. It must rest on some other ground, and those seem to be led by a right

[59] And if we consider to " speak a word against " something less than to " blaspheme " the implication is even more striking.

instinct who seek it in the humiliation of the Son of Man in
His servant-form on earth,[60] and the culminating manifestation of the holiness of God in the Holy Spirit, — though these
things rather underlie the compressed statement before us
than find expression in it. It is abundantly clear at all events
that there is no depreciation of the dignity of the person of
Jesus in the contrast that is drawn between blasphemy against
Him as forgivable and blasphemy against the Holy Ghost as
unforgivable. That it is possible to blaspheme the Son of Man,
itself means that the Son of Man is divine.[61]

All the more clear is it that it is not intended to declare
that it is only blasphemy against the Son of Man among blasphemies which is capable of forgiveness. The gist of the declaration is not that only blasphemy against the Son of Man is
forgivable, but that only blasphemy against the Holy Spirit is
unforgivable. It is the latter, not the former, which is singled
out as unique in its treatment. Blasphemy against the Son of
Man takes its place, therefore, as one of a class, — the class of
forgivable blasphemies. Wherever it may rank within this
class, it has its place in this class. In substance of meaning,
accordingly, the declaration of Jesus reported by Luke is identical with that reported by Mark. When Mark makes Jesus
declare that " all the blasphemies wherewithsoever the sons of
men blaspheme," except that against the Holy Spirit, are forgivable, blasphemy against Jesus' own person is naturally included among forgivable blasphemies. When Luke reports
Jesus as declaring that blasphemy against the Holy Spirit alone
is unforgivable and even blasphemy against the Son of Man
may be forgiven, it is necessarily implied that all other blasphemies are forgivable. The essence of both statements is that
there is no blasphemy that is unforgivable except that against
the Holy Spirit. One explicitly contrasts with this as forgivable,
all other blasphemies; the other, even blasphemy against the
Son of Man. The ultimate content of both contrasts is the same.

The most notable characteristic of Matthew's report of our
Lord's declaration is its comprehensiveness, by which it is

[60] Mt. xx. 28; Mk. x. 45.   [61] Cf. A. B. Bruce *in loc.*

markedly distinguished from the compressed report of Luke. In substance, it combines the reports of Mark and Luke; but it does this in language so different from theirs that it is impossible to suppose that one Evangelist is directly dependent upon another. Matthew is obviously giving us an independent report of the substance of what was said by Jesus.

Matthew alone introduces the declaration by an illative particle, connecting it with the preceding discourse. The connection appears to be with the entire preceding discourse. It was because the Pharisees accused Him of casting out demons by Beelzebul, and because this was obviously absurd, and it was clear to every single eye that it was by the Spirit of God that He was casting out the demons (and therefore in Him the Kingdom of God had come upon them), that He solemnly (" I say unto you ") warns them against blasphemy of the Spirit. This warning is couched in language of intense impressiveness, and is so ordered as to throw the heinousness of blasphemy against the Spirit into the most poignant emphasis. It contains a double declaration of the unforgivableness of this sin. The former of these is more general in character and contrasts this blasphemy with other blasphemies in general (verse 31). The latter advances to a more pungent assertion and contrasts it specifically with blasphemy against the Son of Man, as more heinous than even it. The effect of the whole is to isolate the sin of blasphemy against the Holy Spirit with even startling distinctness and energy as the only sin which is entirely and forever incapable of pardon.

The former member of this striking declaration is clothed in language of extreme and impressive simplicity. " Every sin and blasphemy," we read — the addition " and blasphemy " descending from the genus to the particular species under discussion, and the combination of the terms focussing attention on the sinfulness of blasphemy: " Every sin and blasphemy shall be forgiven to man, but the blasphemy " — " *the* blasphemy," isolating the particular blasphemy under discussion — " the blasphemy of the Spirit shall not be forgiven." " Blasphemy " in the first clause is evidently used in its technical

84 CHRISTOLOGY AND CRITICISM

sense and imports insult to the Divine majesty: and "the blasphemy of the Spirit" is separated from this only as a particular from the general. Every term employed is the simplest and most direct attainable, and the construction is wholly free from rhetorical heightening. The simple abstract "sin" is used, instead of the more unusual derivative "acts of sin" of Mark; the simple "blasphemy" instead of Mark's emphasized "the blasphemies wherewithsoever the sons of men blaspheme." The universal "every" is attached simply to its substantives instead of separated from them for increased emphasis. We have the simple "to men" instead of the solemn "to the sons of men" of Mark. Even the simplest designation of the Holy Spirit possible is employed — the mere "the Spirit." The statement takes on, indeed, something of the baldness of a legislative enactment: there is not a superfluous particle in it, and not a single rhetorical flourish. It just simply states a fact of tremendous significance, and leaves it at that: "Every sin (including blasphemy) shall be forgiven to men; but blasphemy of the Spirit shall not be forgiven."

To this naked statement of fact, there is adjoined, now, a repetition which is something more than a repetition. It adds nothing in substance to what was said in the preceding statement. But it adds a great deal to it in tone and effect. It has the nature of a startling specific application of a general doctrine, with the effect of carrying the general doctrine home with tremendous force. All is said when it is said, "Every blasphemy shall be forgiven except blasphemy of the Spirit." But this all is said with quite new energy when it is added: "Even if any one blasphemes the Son of Man, he shall be forgiven, but not if he blasphemes the very Spirit of holiness — no, not for ever." The "and" by which this second member of the declaration is connected with the first, is not merely copulative, nor merely consecutive ("and so"). What follows is not merely an illustration of the general principle or a consequence drawn from it. The "and" has an ascensive force and introduces what is in effect a climax. Perhaps its force may be brought out by rendering it by some such term as "yea": "Every blasphemy

shall be forgiven; yea if one blaspheme the Son of Man. . . ."
It is not merely *an* instance which is adduced; but *the* instance,
which will illustrate above every other instance the incredible
reach of the forgiveness that is extended, and which will therefore supply the best background up against which may be
thrown the heinousness of blasphemy of the Spirit which cannot be forgiven. The blasphemy which cannot be forgiven
when even blasphemy of the Son of Man is forgiven, must be
heinous indeed.

That " whosoever shall speak a word against the Son of
Man " is just a periphrasis for " whosoever shall blaspheme
against the Son of Man " is obvious. There would be an anti-
climax if it were made to mean anything less than blasphemy.
To declare that every blasphemy shall be forgiven and then
add in climacteric illustration of this declaration that even the
speaking a word against the Son of Man — which is something
less than blasphemy — shall be forgiven would yield only
bathos. The progress of the argument requires us, therefore,
to take this " speaking a word against the Son of Man " as itself blasphemy in the sense of the preceding declaration. We
rise here, not sink, in the definition of the sin. The progress
consists in a change, not in the matter of the sin, but in the
adduction of an object by which its heinousness is heightened.
And, we must add, the heightening is, in the nature of the case,
to the extreme limit. Blasphemy against the Son of Man is the
extremity of blasphemy which can be forgiven. Beyond that
limit, it becomes unforgivable. It is not a little sin, then, which
is adduced; it is the greatest of forgivable sins. And therefore
the title of dignity, " Son of Man," is employed to designate
the object on which it terminates. To blaspheme the Son of
Man is a sin so dreadful that it might be thought unforgivable;
and the heinousness of the unforgivable sin may be estimated
when it is perceived that it is more heinous than this. Clearly
the Son of Man is not mere man: it is only because He is not
mere man, indeed, that " speaking a word against Him " is
blasphemy.

That by " speaking a word against Him " just blasphemy is

meant is clear also from the employment of this same phrase in the next clause of blasphemy of the Spirit. For, that this clause must repeat the last clause of the first member of the declaration is beyond dispute: and we do not rise to our climaxes by weakening our expressions. And in this second member all the other expressions are heightened: Jesus designates Himself " the Son of Man " here for the first time in this context; the simple " Spirit " of the former member of the declaration gives place here to the solemnly emphatic " the Spirit, the Holy One"; the simple negative, " shall not be forgiven " of the former member is expanded here to the awe-inspiring, " shall not be forgiven, neither in this world, nor in that which is to come." It would seem, then, that the periphrasis, " to speak a word against," is treated as a more, rather than a less, impressive way of saying " to blaspheme " than the word itself: it is the thing, not the term, that is condemned, and apparently it is felt that the thing is more precisely, and therefore more forcibly, expressed by the periphrasis than by the simple word, which, after all, is very fairly defined by the periphrasis.

By the employment of this periphrasis in this passage with respect to blasphemy against the Holy Spirit we are aided in determining the precise nature of the sin which our Lord pronounced unforgivable. It would seem that it is just speaking injurious or insulting words against the Holy Spirit; such words as are illustrated, — or at least approached — by the opprobrious attribution of acts of the Holy Spirit to Beelzebul. Matthew does not say, as Mark says, that our Lord has particular reference to the ascription to Him of demoniacal possession. What he says is that our Lord was led to give this tremendous warning to the Pharisees, because they declared that it was by Beelzebul, the prince of the demons, that He was casting out demons, this being in effect an identification of the Holy Spirit by whom He wrought His cures with the foul spirit. He bids them, therefore, to beware. The mercy of God is very wide; every sin and blasphemy may be forgiven to men — except only blasphemy of the Spirit; yea, though one speak a word against the Son of Man it may be forgiven; but if one speak against the Spirit, that Holy One, it shall not be forgiven — to all eternity.

The comprehensiveness of Matthew's report of Jesus' declaration, embracing as it does the substance of both what Mark and what Luke reports, affords a temptation to look upon Matthew's report as artificially made up from a combination of what is reported by the other evangelists. We have already pointed out, however, that the divergence of the language in Matthew's report from that of Mark's and Luke's respectively, renders this hypothesis untenable. If there ever were three reports purporting to give the substance of a single utterance — and actually giving it in complete harmony — which bore decisive marks of literary independence of one another, these three reports do. Nevertheless the temptation to explain the three as two divergent reports in Mark and Luke, and a conflation of them in Matthew, has proved too strong for the Synoptical critics to resist.

Which of the two brief divergent reports is to be held the more original, the critics are less agreed. Wellhausen is sure that Mark, along with Mt. xii. 31, has preserved in substance the original form, and that what was meant by it is that railing against men may be forgiven but not blasphemy against God. According to this view Jesus did not declare blasphemy against His own person to be pardonable, the version of Luke and Mt. xii. 32 resting upon a misunderstanding of the underlying Aramaic phrase for " man " which transmuted it into a title of the Messiah, " the Son of Man," used as a personal self-designation by Jesus.[62] The fundamental assumption here is, of course, that the reason why Jesus did not declare blasphemy against His person to be pardonable is that He never could have connected the idea of blasphemy with that of " speaking a word against " Himself, conceiving of Himself, as He did, as merely a human being.[63] P. W. Schmiedel, on the other hand,

[62] Cf. Arnold Meyer and Lietzmann as cited by P. W. Schmiedel, "Protestantische Monatshefte," ii. 1898, p. 304; also " Encyclopaedia Biblica," col. 1848, note 1.

[63] N. Schmidt, " The Prophet of Nazareth," p. 112, has a similar view,

is equally sure that the original form has been preserved by Luke, or rather by the fuller Mt. xii. 31, 32, while Mark represents a dogmatic alteration of this in the interests of the dignity of Jesus' person, men having come to entertain so high an opinion of Jesus' person that it offended them to have it said that blasphemy of even the Holy Spirit would be more unpardonable than blasphemy of Him.[64] According to this view Jesus declares speaking a word against Him to be pardonable because He conceives Himself to be only human, while the Holy Spirit is a periphrasis for God: the upshot of His teaching being just that we may speak against men and be forgiven but we cannot blaspheme God and expect pardon. The pathways over which the two interpretations would travel are different; the goal which they reach is the same; Jesus was only human and spoke out of a purely human consciousness.[65]

---

although he takes Mt. xii. 32 as preserving the original saying, in which, he supposes, *bar nasha,* in the sense of " man," stood in the place now occupied by " the Son of Man," in the sense of Jesus, the Messiah: " He was careful to distinguish between an attack upon a fellow-man and a denunciation of the Spirit that operated in Him, saying: ' If any one speaks against *bar nasha,* — i.e. man — that may be pardoned him, but he that speaks against the Holy Spirit can have no pardon.' No one in the audience could have understood him to say, ' you may blaspheme the Messiah with impunity, but not the Holy Ghost.' The distinction is clearly between the divine spirit and the human instrumentality." C. G. Montefiore, " Synopt. Gospels " ii. p. 624, says quite impartially that this interpretation seems " very strained."

[64] " Encyclopaedia Biblica," col. 1848: " In their worship of Jesus it must have appeared to them in itself the greatest possible blasphemy to say that blasphemy against Jesus could be forgiven."

[65] Cf. the discussion of the opposing views in Schmiedel's article in the " Protestantische Monatshefte," ii. 1908, pp. 303–307: an excellent brief account of them is given by S. R. Driver in Hastings' *BD* iv. p. 588, at the close of his article on the " Son of Man." E. von Dobschütz, " Theologische Studien und Kritiken " 85 (1912) p. 340, is sure that we have two reports here, but will not decide which is the more original, contenting himself with remarking that the double attestation gives us peculiar surety that something of the sort was said by Jesus: " When we read in the Mark-tradition (Mk. iii. 28 f.; Mt. xii. 31), ' All sins are forgiven to the sons of men and the blasphemies wherewithsoever they blaspheme, but he who blasphemes the Holy Ghost has no forgiveness forever '; but on the other hand in the Q-tradition (Lk. xii. 10; Mt. xii. 32), ' He who speaketh anything against the Son of Man, that will be forgiven him, but he who speaketh against the Holy Spirit, to him it will

So sure is Schmiedel that Mt. xii. 31, 32 presents to our view a purely human Jesus, that he includes this passage among those "pillar passages" which he announces as the foundation stones of a truly scientific knowledge of Jesus, — on the precise ground that they could never have been invented by worshippers of Jesus (as all the Evangelists were) but must have come to them as part of an authentic tradition of a human Jesus. This true tradition, he contends, was altered by one or another of the Evangelists in accordance with their later worship of Jesus.[66] Jesus here, he tells us, is represented as frankly ranging Himself with men, speaking against whom is pardonable; and as separating Himself from the Spirit of God to speak against whom is unpardonable.[67] That the passage in Matthew will not bear the meaning which Schmiedel puts upon it, we have already seen. Jesus does not place Himself there among men, and subordinate Himself to God in His essential nature. He does not say there that calumniation of men may be forgiven but never blasphemy against God. What He says may be forgiven is precisely blasphemy, in its strict

---

not be forgiven (neither in this nor in the future world) '; it is clear that we have before us two conceptions and also two translations: *bar nasa* is in one taken collectively, "sons of men," in the other as the well-known personal self-designation of Jesus. The one is a modification of the other, although it is not altogether easy to say in what direction the theology of the community has worked here; it is clear, however that through this double attestation a declaration of Jesus to His Pharisaic opponents as to unpardonable sin is assured."

[66] "Encyclopaedia Biblica," col. 1881; cf. col. 1848 (d and note 1). See *The Princeton Theological Review*, April, 1913, pp. 204, 252.

[67] The following is Schmiedel's most lucid statement of his view of the bearing of the passage ("Das vierte Evangelium," etc., p. 33): "In John Jesus knows, then, nothing higher than Himself, the bliss or misery of men for time and eternity is determined by whether they believe or do not believe in His divine origin. In the Synoptics, He knows something higher than Himself. He says in Mt. xii. 31, 32: 'Every sin and blasphemy will be forgiven to men, but blasphemy against the Spirit will not be forgiven. And whosoever speaks a word against the Son of Man, it will be forgiven him; but whosoever speaks a word against the Holy Ghost, it will not be forgiven him, either in this world or in the next.' Therefore He places His person below the Holy Spirit, i.e. below the holy work which He advocates." Cf. Karl Thieme, "Die christliche Demut," i. 1906, p. 139.

sense. He declares that speaking a word against His person is blasphemy in the strict sense; and that this may be forgiven only because blasphemy may be forgiven.[68] And though He subordinates Himself to the Holy Spirit, at least in manifestation, to this extent, that blasphemy against Him may be forgiven but blasphemy against the Holy Spirit not, it is illegitimate to interpret this as implying a subordination of Himself to the Spirit in intrinsic dignity of person: blasphemy against God may also be forgiven but blasphemy against the Holy Spirit not. It may be difficult to determine precisely why blasphemy against the Spirit is made unpardonable and blasphemy against the Son of Man not: no doubt the reason lies in some discrimination in the modes of divine manifestation in the two persons. But this difficulty affords no reason for cutting the knot by representing Jesus as definitely subordinating Himself — and God also — in dignity of person to the Holy Spirit.

It has been frequently remarked that it is only in the two passages, Mt. xii. 32 and Lk. xii. 10, that (as, for example,

[68] W. Beyschlag, " Die Christologie des Neuen Testaments," 1866, p. 24, had written — no doubt with wrong suggestions, but for the final matter very justly, as we think — as follows (we use Bruce's rendering): " Let us consider the relation here indicated between the Son of Man and the Holy Ghost. It is a relation of distinction; and yet of close connection. The distinction is that in the Son of Man the revelation of God to men is made in mediated, and, so far, veiled form; therefore may be misunderstood, so that the blasphemer may always have the benefit of the prayer, ' Forgive them, they know not what they do '; but in the Holy Ghost the revelation is made immediately, inwardly, therefore unmistakably; therefore there is no excuse for the blasphemer. At the same time the Holy Ghost is not thought of as above the Son of Man but in Him. The Son of Man is the man who has the Spirit of God in His entire fulness, whose inmost though unrecognized essence is the Holy Spirit, the man whose human appearance is the absolute revelation of God. To this corresponds the fact, obvious in the text, that the blasphemy of the Son of Man is represented as the most heinous of pardonable sins." A. B. Bruce, " The Humiliation of Christ," [2] 1881, p. 227, quotes these statements only unsuccessfully to contravert the view that the passage teaches that " offences against the Son of Man are pardonable, but that is all; such sins form the extreme limit of the forgivable." He supposes that Jesus rather means to say " with characteristic magnanimity " that sins against Himself are easily forgivable, because not more heinous than sins against any other good man, and due to the same general cause; and he adopts the view that Jesus' warning turns precisely on this, — that the Pharisees in their injurious imputations were " *not* sinning against *Him*, but against the Holy Ghost."

H. J. Holtzmann expresses it), " a distinction is made between the Spirit as the higher power (*Instanz*) and Jesus as the human vehicle of the Spirit." A somewhat bizarre writer, on that ground, insists that these passages — which, he considers, represent the original form of the declaration — are a Montanistic interpolation into the Gospels, since (as he is reported) " only Montanism places the revelation of the Spirit, the Paraclete, above that of the Apostles of Christ." We cite this extraordinary opinion, not, as we well might, as an example of the lengths to which this kind of criticism can go, — in principle, it is just as sound criticism as that of many who seem to be pillars, — but in order to introduce Schmiedel's, as it seems to us, instructive rejoinder to it. " Certainly," Schmiedel replies, " Montanism was the first to place the Holy Spirit above Jesus — after Jesus Himself. Some effort is made to form an appropriate idea of Montanism: but of what Jesus thought of Himself, none at all. ' Where elsewhere in the Synoptic tradition can anything similar be found? ' I should have thought we would have been thankful to find it only once. A pearl does not cease to be genuine merely because it exists in only one example. . . ." [69] Possibly. But meanwhile, it is thus allowed that in this interpretation a meaning is assigned to the passage which is unexampled elsewhere in the Synoptic Gospels, and indeed in the entirety of the Christian literature of the first age; a meaning, that is, so unexpected that surely it cannot be entertained unless it is unassailably shown to be the real meaning of the passage. How little that is the case we have already seen. What Schmiedel is actually doing in his interpretation of the passage is, therefore, importing into the Gospels a conception which is wholly alien to them; and also which, as he expressly admits (for this is the very principle of his criticism), stands in direct contradiction to their whole drift. A human Jesus must be found at all hazards, and if violence is required to find Him in the Evangelical tradition, then violence must be used.[70]

[69] " Protestantische Monatshefte," ii. (1898) p. 305.

[70] Into the detailed attempts to account for the divergent forms of the whole passage as given by the three Synoptics, on the Two-Document hypoth-

Meanwhile it is unquestionable that the passage contains difficulties. It is not easy to separate clearly blasphemy of the Son of Man from blasphemy of that Holy Spirit by which He wrought His great works of healing upon the possessed. It is not easy to understand in what blasphemy of the Son of Man is a less heinous sin than blasphemy against the Holy Ghost, or why the one is more pardonable than the other. It is not easy indeed to be perfectly sure precisely in what the un- pardonable blasphemy of the Holy Spirit consists, or whether our Lord means to convict His opponents of having committed it. We may, of course, form conjectures on these matters; and these conjectures will, no doubt, be more or less plausible; and they may seem to be supported with more or less convinc- ingness by this or that assertion or suggestion of the text or context. The passage itself, however, scarcely gives us decisive instruction on these matters; and on most of them opinions may lawfully differ. They are in any event subjects of per- petual investigation and most of them continue to be zealously debated by the commentators.[71] Many commentators, for ex- ample, are eager to make it clear that our Lord does not charge His opponents with having committed the unpardonable sin of blasphemy against the Holy Spirit, but only warns them against committing it.[72] This carries with it, of course, denial

---

esis, in its mechanical interpretation, we do not enter. We cannot look upon a discussion like that of Burton Scott Easton, " The Beelzebul Sections," *The Journal of Biblical Literature*, xxxii. (1913) pp. 57–73 as anything more than highly refined speculation without any possibility of attaining valid results.

[71] A good brief *résumé* of the main discussion may be read in Carl Clemen's " Die christliche Lehre von der Sünde," 1897, pp. 89 ff.

[72] For example, Th. Zahn, " Das Evangelium des Matthäus," 1903, pp. 460–466, closing with the statement (p. 466): " Jesus does not yet treat the Pharisees here as such as have already committed the sin against the Holy Spirit, but as such as need to be warned of this ultimate step which they have it in mind to take." Compare the statement on p. 461: " No doubt the Phari- sees called the Power by which Jesus healed the possessed, an evil spirit, whereas that Power was in fact the Spirit of God; but they did not blaspheme the Spirit for they did not recognize Him in the Power which worked through Jesus. They rather concluded from the behavior of Jesus, which in their judg- ment was godless, lawless, and immoral (ix. 3–11, xii. 2–10) that this man wrought these, in themselves, beneficent and praiseworthy miracles by the

that merely to accuse Jesus of working His healings of demoni-
acs by the aid of Beelzebul, or even of being possessed by Beelzebul, constitutes the unpardonable sin. And the way having
thus been opened, a wide field lies open for conjecture as to
what does constitute that sin. Despite these deeper mysteries,
however, the main implications of the passage are sufficiently
clear, and among these implications this one must rank among
the clearest — that He who authoritatively makes this great
declaration of the relative heinousness of sins, and calmly announces what sins shall and what sins shall not be forgiven,
whether in this world or in that which is to come, does not
mean to proclaim Himself a mere man, when He declares that
he who speaks a word against Him may be forgiven, but not
he who speaks a word against the Holy Spirit. Whatever may
be the reason for treating blasphemy of the Son of Man as
more pardonable than blasphemy of the Holy Spirit, that
reason cannot be found in a sheer difference in the intrinsic
dignity of the two persons.

The judgment of unbelief on Jesus, we have found occasion to remark, is inevitably that He was mad. As inevitably
the judgment of active disbelief on Him must be that He was
wicked. Not only in His own day but throughout all time the
alternatives constantly stare us in the face — *aut Deus aut non
sanus; aut Deus aut non bonus.* If in our own time the latter
alternative has retired somewhat into the background, and that

---

aid of evil spirits, and thus they blasphemed the Son of Man. This blasphemy
would become a blasphemy of the Holy Spirit, however, if they persisted in it,
after Jesus had shown them the irrationality of their inference. When and in the
measure in which they must recognize that the Power by which Jesus heals
is a holy Power, every inimical word against Him becomes a sin against the
Holy Spirit." So also G. Wohlenberg, " Das Evangelium des Markus," 1910,
p. 115: " That the scribes have committed such blasphemy the Lord does not
say. It may even be judged that even their accusation that Jesus had Beelzebul
and cast out the demons through the prince of the demons, or as it is said in
verse 30, that He had an unclean spirit, does not yet necessarily involve that
terrible sin. For the question continually presents itself, how far uncomprehending but well-meant zeal has coöperated here; how far the conscience has
been unpricked, unconcerned, when they so dreadfully accused the Lord." For
earlier writers to the same effect. see C. Clemen, as cited. p. 91 note.

which imposes itself upon the consciousness of contemporary criticism is that between a Divine Jesus and an " ecstatic " Jesus, as it is euphemistically called, — a paranoiac Jesus, as it really would amount to — that is doubtless in part because, in the languid sceptical temper of our times, and their preoccupation with abstract questions of pure history, little occasion or place has been left for the play of the more violent emotions about our historical findings. At bottom, however, disbelief, when it works itself out, must not merely neglect Jesus but condemn Him: and the ravings of a Nietzsche may serve to keep us in mind that the ultimate alternative is always that of the Pharisees and Scribes. Either Jesus has come forth from God, or we can scarcely avoid declaring Him possessed of the Evil One. He makes or mars the world.[73]

[73] Compare the striking closing pages of the fourth of Liddon's Bampton Lectures on " *The Divinity of our Lord, etc.*"

III

JESUS' ALLEGED CONFESSION OF SIN

JESUS' ALLEGED CONFESSION OF SIN[1]

THE pericope of "the rich young ruler" is found in all three of the Synoptic Gospels, and it is associated in all of them with narratives of a common type. In all three it immediately follows the account of Jesus' receiving and blessing little children; and it is clear from Mark's representation (as also indeed from Matthew's[2]) that the incident actually occurred in immediate sequence to that scene. In Luke, these two narratives are immediately preceded by the parable of the Pharisee and Publican praying in the Temple; in Matthew they are immediately succeeded by the parable of the workmen in the vineyard who were surprised that their rewards were not nicely adjusted to what they deemed their relative services. It cannot be by accident that these four narratives, all of which teach a similar lesson, are brought thus into contiguity. It is the burden of them all that the Kingdom of God is a gratuity, not an acquisition; and the effect of bringing them together is to throw a great emphasis upon this, their common teaching.

Perhaps this teaching finds nowhere more pungent intimation than in the declaration of our Lord which forms the core of the account of His reception of the children: " For of such is the kingdom of heaven," (or " of God ": Mt. xix. 14; Mk. x. 14; Lk. xviii. 16). These " little children " were, as we learn from Luke, mere babies (Lk. xviii. 15: τὰ βρέφη), which Jesus held in His arms (Mk. x. 16: ἐναγκαλισάμενος; cf. ix. 36 and also Lk. ii. 28).[3] What Jesus says, therefore, is that those

---

[1] From *The Princeton Theological Review*, xii. 1914, pp. 177-228.

[2] Accordingly, Th. Zahn, " Das Evangelium des Matthaeus ausgelegt," 1903, p. 589, says correctly (on Mt. xix. 16): " The close chronological connection is assured by the καὶ ἰδού, verse 16, after ἐπορεύθη ἐκεῖθεν, verse 15."

[3] Therefore Zahn, pp. 587-588, is quite right when he comments on Matthew's παιδία : " Little children who were still in the arms (therefore, Lk. xviii. 15 βρέφη), were brought by their mothers or nurses to Jesus."

who enter the Kingdom of God are like " infants of days."
Such infants are not to be debarred from coming [4] to Him,
because forsooth they cannot profit by His teaching or profit
Him by their service. It is precisely of such [5] as they that the
Kingdom of God consists. " And verily I say unto you," He
adds, " whosoever shall not receive the Kingdom of God as a
little child, he shall in no wise enter therein " (Mk. x. 15: Lk.
xviii. 17). The meaning is accurately expressed in Alford's
paraphrase (the emphases are his own): " In order for us who
are mature to come to Him, we must cast away all that wherein
our maturity has caused us to differ from them and *become
LIKE THEM*. . . . None can enter God's Kingdom except *as an
infant*." But when Alford comes to explain what " as an infant " means, he loses the thread and thinks of the innocence,
the simplicity, the trustfulness of childhood, or the like.[6] That

[4] T. R. Glover, " The Conflict of Religions in the Early Roman Empire,"
1909, p. 121, remarks: " We are apt to forget that ' come ' is a Greek verb
carrying volition with it." This is scarcely true. Ἔρχομαι expresses rather mere
motion, progress: cf. e.g. Mt. ii. 9, vi. 10, vii. 25, 27, ix. 15, x. 13, xviii. 7, xxiii. 35.

[5] That is, not of infants like those now in His presence, but of people
like those infants in the qualities which had led to their debarring. Zahn, however (p. 588), reasonably argues that in the τῶν τοιούτων there is included
also a τούτων or rather a καὶ τούτων. He soon, however, transforms this
into its opposite, as if he were arguing that in a designated τούτων there was
also a καὶ τοιούτων included: " not only do the little children belong to the
Kingdom and the Kingdom to them, but the Kingdom belongs only to them
and to such as have become like them." Similarly Loisy, " Les Évangiles
Synoptiques," 1908, ii. p. 205. What our Lord says is that the Kingdom consists
not of children, but of those who are like children; actual children are no doubt
included, but we must not reverse the emphasis. Even Calvin (*Inst.* IV, xvi.
7 *ad fin.*), arguing for infant baptism, yields to the temptation to reverse it:
" When He commands that infants should be permitted to come to Him,
nothing is clearer than that He means true infancy. That this may not seem
absurd He adds: ' Of such is the kingdom of heaven.' But if infants must be
included, it cannot be doubtful that by the term ' of such ' there are designated infants themselves and also those who are like them."

[6] It would be difficult to go more astray here than A. Loisy does (p. 205):
" He profits by the occasion to remind them of the moral worth of infants,
and the merit which belongs to the spirit of infancy. . . . Nothing is
opposed to Jesus' having in view infants and those who resemble them in the
spirit of candor and of simplicity." C. G. Montefiore (" The Synoptic Gospels,"
1909, i. p. 243) is better, though still confused: " The child symbolizes or
represents the temper in which the Kingdom must be received. Humble trust,

in which maturity differs from infancy, however, lies just in its self-dependence and power of self-help. We become " as a little child " when, in the words of the revival hymn which was such an offence to James Anthony Froude, " we cast our deadly doing down " and make our appeal on the sole score of sheer helplessness.

Zahn, therefore, strikes a much truer note when he comments: [7] " Over against the fancy (*Dünkel*) of the disciples, who ground their claim that the Kingdom belongs to them on their intelligence and will, Jesus reminds them that they must rather, by renunciation of their own intelligence and will, obtain the receptivity (*Empfänglichkeit*) for the blessings and benefit of the Kingdom which the immature children possess of themselves." And so does Wendt: [8] " But in this very respect, of having no claim, so that they could offer nothing but only wish to have something, Jesus finds the ground for the children being permitted to come to Him, that He might show them His love and give them His blessing. For in this unpretentious receptivity He recognizes the necessary condition which must exist in all who will enter the kingdom of God." " Under this childlike character, He does not understand any virtue of childlike blamelessness, but only the receptivity itself (which is the notion impressively emphasized by Him) on the part of those who do not regard themselves as too good or too bad for the offered gift, but receive it with hearty desire." The emphasis which these expositors throw on " receptivity " as the characteristic of infancy — as if it were an active quality — is not drawn from the text but belongs to the habits of thought derived by them from a Lutheran inheritance. It requires to be eliminated before the meaning of our Lord's enunciation can be purely caught. Infancy is char-

---

a complete lack of assertiveness, no consciousness of ' merit ' or desert, simple confidence and purity, — these are the qualities which Jesus means to indicate in the character of a true child. The Kingdom can only be entered by those who can approach it in such a spirit." New-born babies represent no particular temper, and exemplify no particular spirit: they illustrate a particular condition.

[7] Pp. 588–589.

[8] H. H. Wendt, " The Teaching of Jesus," E. T. ii. pp. 49–50.

acterized by " receptivity " as little as by " blamelessness " or
by " trustfulness "; its characteristic is just helpless need. He
who receives [9] the Kingdom of God " as a little child " receives
it (in this sense) passively; is the pure recipient, not the earner
of its blessings. What our Lord here declares is thus, in brief,
that no one enters the Kingdom of God save as an infant enters
the world, naked and helpless and without any claim upon it
whatever.

No more illuminating comment on our Lord's teaching here
could easily be imagined than that which is supplied by the
immediately succeeding incident, that of the rich young ruler.
No sooner had our Lord announced that " whosoever shall not
receive the Kingdom of God as a little child, he shall in no wise
enter therein," than one appeared before Him bent on making
his way into the Kingdom in quite another fashion. And,
indeed, if any could hope to acquire it for himself, it might
well be supposed to be this eager young man. He had everything
to commend him. He was young, he was rich, he was highly
placed, he was clean. He was accustomed to desire good things,
and, desiring them, he was accustomed to obtain them for himself: and, with the resources at his command, — resources of
youthful energy, wealth, position, moral earnestness — he was
accustomed to obtain them without much difficulty. He had
heard of Jesus, perhaps had heard Him; and he recognized in
Him a good man whose counsel were well worth having. And
he had conceived a commendable desire for the eternal life
which Jesus was proclaiming. What remained but to learn from
this good teacher what needed to be done, in order to obtain
it? It never occurred to this rich and influential youth, accustomed to get what he wanted, but that this good thing
which he now desired might be obtainable at its own proper
price; and was he not prepared and fully able to pay the price
and so to secure it? It seemed to him an easy thing to purchase
eternal life.

[9] Δέχομαι, not λαμβάνω (or αἱρέω) is the word our Lord uses, and despite
the wearing off of the edges of the distinction in usage, the difference remains
fundamentally good that λαβεῖν is taking, δέξασθαι is receiving.

It was our Lord's painful task, in response to the young
man's appeal for guidance, to reveal him to himself in the
shallowness of his nature and outlook; to open his eyes to the
nature of that eternal life which he sought, in its radical difference from the life he was living; and to make it clear to him
that what he had thought so easy to acquire was to be had only
at a great price, a price which he might not be willing to pay,
a price which he might find it was impossible for him to pay.
And it was our Lord's task, further, on the basis of this incident,
to carry home poignantly to the consciousness of His disciples
the lesson He had already taught them in the incident of the
blessing of the little children, that the Kingdom of God is not
a thing into which in any case men can buy their way; that
they stand before it helpless, and can make their way into it
as little as a camel can force itself through the eye of a needle.
It may be conferred by God: it cannot be acquired by
men.[10]

As the result of his conversation, the young man departed
with his countenance fallen,[11] exceeding sorrowful,[12] — the
eternal life which he had expected to reach out his hand and
take was not for him. And the disciples had had borne in upon
them with tremendous force the fundamental fact that salvation [13] in every case of its accomplishment is nothing less

[10] Nothing could be more inapt than to say with Montefiore (1, pp. 243–
244); "Wellhausen points out most aptly how Shakespeare [Rich. II, act v,
scene v] has felt the contrast between this section [on the blessing of the
children] and the section which follows it [on the rich young man]. For *here*
the Kingdom is a gift which one must accept as a child, *there* it is only to be
won by effort and self-denial." In both sections alike the Kingdom is a pure
gift and cannot be earned.

[11] Mk. x. 22, στυγνάσας, full of gloom; cf. Swete's note *in loc.*

[12] Lk. xviii. 23, περίλυπος, hemmed in on all sides by sorrow, so that there
is no escape; cf. "Biblical and Theological Studies by the Members of the
Faculty of Princeton Theological Seminary," 1912, p. 76.

[13] It is worth noting how the terms "eternal life," "the kingdom of God,"
"salvation" are interchanged in the narrative, as an indication of the sense
put upon them by our Lord. In the conversation with the young man, the term
used is "eternal life" (Mt. xix. 17, "life"). But on our Lord's turning to His
disciples (Mt. xix. 23; Mk. x. 23; Lk. xviii. 24) "the Kingdom of God
[heaven]" is substituted for this with no substantial change of meaning. This

than an authentic miracle of divine grace; always and everywhere in the strictest sense impossible with man, and possible only with God, with whom all things are possible. The effect of this teaching, if it was naturally to depress those who sought eternal life by their own efforts, was equally naturally to exhilarate those who were looking to God alone for the blessings of the Kingdom, giving them a higher sense of both their certainty and their value. This surely is the right account to give of Peter's question (Mt. xix. 27; Mk. x. 28; Lk. xviii. 28), with our Lord's response to which the conversation closes. We cannot say, then, with Edersheim: [14] " It almost jars on our ears, and prepares us for still stranger and sadder things to come, when Peter, perhaps as spokesman for the rest, seems to remind the Lord that they had forsaken all to follow Him." Peter rather, his heart swelling with freshly inflamed hope (*spe ex verbis Salvatoris concepta,* remarks Bengel accurately) inquires eagerly (not boastfully but in humble gratitude) into the nature of the blessings which God has in mind for those who have entered the Kingdom.[15] Our Lord meets the inquiry in its own spirit and grants to His followers a splendid vision of their reward, — only closing with words which would leave fixed in their minds the consciousness that all things are reserved to the Divine discretion: " And many shall be last that are first; and first that are last."

There are no substantial differences between the three reports which are given us of this remarkable incident. Each of the Evangelists records details peculiar to himself. Each narrative has its own tone and coloring: Mark's is distinguished by vividness, Luke's by plain straightforwardness, Matthew's

---

in turn in all three narratives (Mt. xix. 25; Mk. x. 26; Lk. xviii. 26) is understood by the disciples to be equivalent to " salvation." " Eternal life " appears again at the end (Mt. xix. 29; Mk. x. 30; Lk. xviii. 30).

[14] " Life and Times of Jesus," [1] ii. p. 343; cf. the even more condemnatory note of Swete on Mk. x. 28, where he seems to suggest that a " tactless frankness " of speech meets us in Mark's report, which Luke already found it desirable to soften, and that Matthew's " what then shall we have " we may hope was never spoken.

[15] Cf. A. Plummer, on Lk. xviii. 28.

by clearness. But it is precisely the same story which is told by them all: the same story in its contents, in its mode of development, in its *dénouement*, in its lesson. Having any one of the three we have it all, presented after the same fashion and with the same force. It has no doubt been common to represent the descriptions of the opening scene, by Mark and Luke on the one hand and by Matthew on the other, as divergent; and this divergence has been magnified, and serious inferences have been drawn from it, derogatory to Matthew's integrity as a historian and injurious to our Lord's dignity as a Divine person and even to His moral perfection. All this rests upon misunderstanding. The wide-spread vogue it has obtained requires, nevertheless, that it shall be carefully looked into.

A simple reading of the opening two verses in the three accounts reveals at once, of course, a formal difference between Mark and Luke on the one side and Matthew on the other in their reports alike of the words in which the young man addressed Jesus and of those in which our Lord responded to his inquiry. In Mark (and Luke) we read that the young man addressed Jesus as " Good Master " and asked Him broadly, " What shall I do that I may inherit eternal life? " In Matthew, he is represented as addressing Him simply as " Master," and asking Him with more exact definition, " What good thing shall I do that I may have life? " Correspondingly, Jesus is represented in Mark (and Luke) as replying, " Why callest thou me good? No one is good except one, God. Thou knowest the commandments . . ."; but in Matthew, " Why askest thou me concerning the good? One there is that is good. But if thou wishest to enter into life, keep the commandments. . . ." We have spoken of these differences as formal; it would seem to be difficult to magnify them into anything more. Though, naturally, a matter of curious interest, they in no way affect the significance of the story itself. Despite them the two narratives, even at this precise point, yield exactly the same general sense and differ only in the details through which this common sense is brought to expression. To make this evident we need only to attend separately to what each mode of telling the story actually places before us.

According to Matthew, then, scarcely had Jesus issued from the house in which He had received and blessed the children,[16] when an individual (there is a slight emphasis upon his being *one* out of the multitude) came to Him, and, addressing Him as " Master " (that is, " Teacher," or " Rabbi "), asked Him, " What good thing shall I do that I may have eternal life? " He is asking, not for general prescriptions of righteousness, but for a particular requirement by doing just which he may secure the eternal life he seeks; and so set is his mind upon this particular good thing that when Jesus refers him to the divine commandments in general, he still demands (verse 18), " Which? " In response to his demand, nevertheless, Jesus points him just to the divine commandments, thus in effect repelling the implication that eternal life can be grounded on anything but that entire righteousness reflected in the law of God; and, behind that, suggesting that it was not instruction in righteousness that the young man needed but the power of a new life. Jesus' reply amounts, thus, to saying: " Why make inquiry concerning the good thing needed? There is One who is good and He has given commandments; keep them." It is the equivalent of, " They have Moses and the Prophets; let them hear them " of Luke xvi. 29. What Jesus actually says is: " Why askest thou me concerning the good? There is One that is good, and,[17] if thou wishest to enter into life, keep His commandments."

The thing to be noted particularly is that no emphasis falls on the enclitic με, and therefore no contrast is intimated between Jesus and the One that is good. The contrast intimated is wholly between the good thing inquired of and the known commandments of God. To avoid the almost inevitable emphasizing of the " me " in a translation, it might be well to omit it altogether for the moment and to paraphrase simply:

[16] So Zahn correctly, p. 589.
[17] It is the continuative δέ, like *autem:* cf. Meyer *in loc.*

"Why dost thou inquire about the good as if that were a matter still in doubt? God, who is goodness itself, has published the eternal rule of righteousness." Keim,[18] it is true, scoffs at the notion that no contrast is drawn between Jesus and God. "But εἶς," he cries, meaning that quite apart from the με the contrast is inherent in the mere declaration that "there is One"—that is to say, only One—"who is good." There is, however, an inadvertence apparent in this. The declaration that "there is One that is good" does set God in contrast with all others: it is to God in His already published will, not to anyone else whatever, that we are to go to learn the law of life. But it does not set God in contrast specifically with Jesus. So soon as it is read as contrasting God specifically with Jesus an emphasis is necessarily thrown on the enclitic με which it will not bear. Jesus is therefore not contrasting Himself here with God. He is only in the most emphatic way pointing to God and His published law as the unique source of the law of life. His own relation to that God is completely out of sight, and nothing whatever is suggested with reference to it. Zahn is accordingly entirely right when he writes:[19] "For the question of the position Jesus assigns Himself between the one good One who is God and men who are evil, little occasion is given by this pedagogic conversation."

Mark, like Matthew, connects the incident of the rich young man closely with that of the blessing of the little children. It was while Jesus was in the act of coming forth from the house (verse 10) in which the blessing of the children had taken place, for His journeying,[20] that an individual from the crowd (εἶς) came running, and fell on his knees, and, addressing Him by the unusual title of "Good Master," demanded of Him what he should do to inherit eternal life. It is the strangeness of the address, "Good Master"—apparently unexampled in extant Jewish literature [21]—which attracts attention here;

[18] "Jesus of Nazara," E. T. v. p. 37, note.
[19] P. 590, note 64.   [20] Cf. B. Weiss *in loc.*
[21] Cf. Edersheim, "Life and Times," ii. p. 339: "In no recorded instance was a Jewish Rabbi addressed as 'Good Master'"; A. Plummer, on Lk. xviii.

and naturally it was this which determined the response of Jesus.[22] It threw into relief — as it would not have done had it been more customary — the levity with which the young man approached Jesus of whom he knew so little, with so remarkable a demand. Jesus' response naturally, therefore, takes the form, " Why callest thou me good? No one is good except one, God. Thou knowest the commandments. . . ." This response at first sight seems in itself to be capable of two constructions. We may either fill out: " Thou art wrong in calling me good; this predicate, in any worthy sense of it at least, belongs to none but God." Or we may fill out rather: " There is a great deal involved, if only you appreciated it, in calling me good; for there is no one that is good but one, that is God." The primary objection to the former view is that it presses the contrast beyond the power of the enclitic $\mu\epsilon$ to bear. For the $\mu\epsilon$ is enclitic here as well as in Matthew, and can be emphasized here as little as there. The emphasis certainly falls not on it, but on the $\dot{\alpha}\gamma\alpha\theta\dot{\alpha}\nu$.[23] The sense is therefore certainly not that the young

19: " There is no instance in the whole Talmud of a Rabbi being addressed as ' Good Master ': the title was absolutely unknown among the Jews. This, therefore, was an extraordinary address, and perhaps a fulsome compliment"; G. Dalman, " The Words of Jesus," E. T. p. 337: " This address was at variance with actual usage, and, moreover, in the mouth of the speaker was mere insolent flattery." F. Spitta, *ZNTW*, ix. (1908) p. 14, strangely wishes to divide the " Good Master " into two independent designations: " If we keep Mark and Luke alone in view, there is to be remarked first of all, with respect to the address to Jesus common to them, $\delta\iota\delta\dot{\alpha}\sigma\kappa\alpha\lambda\epsilon$ $\dot{\alpha}\gamma\alpha\theta\dot{\epsilon}$, that the difficulty adverted to above, of connecting רַבִּי with the predicate טוֹב, is removed if we take $\dot{\alpha}\gamma\alpha\theta\dot{\epsilon}$ as a second address by the side of $\delta\iota\delta\dot{\alpha}\sigma\kappa\alpha\lambda\epsilon$ (cf. von Hofmann on Lk. xviii. 18). By this, of course, the stress on the designation of Jesus as $\dot{\alpha}\gamma\alpha\theta\dot{\alpha}s$ is further strengthened," . . . Lagrange on Mk. x. 17, very properly remarks: " No example is known of a Rabbi being designated thus (רַבִּי טוֹב), but this is no reason for cutting the appellation in two (against Spitta). It is only necessary to note that it exceeds usage and accustomed courtesies."

22 Cf. Edersheim, ii. p. 339: " The strangeness of such an address from Jewish lips giving only the more reason for taking it up in the reply."

23 So Swete *in loc.* correctly: " The emphasis is on $\dot{\alpha}\gamma\alpha\theta\dot{\alpha}\nu$, not on the pronoun. The Lord begins by compelling the enquirer to consider his own words. He had used $\dot{\alpha}\gamma\alpha\theta\dot{\epsilon}$ lightly, in a manner which revealed the poverty of his moral conceptions. From that word Christ accordingly starts. . . . The man is summoned to contemplate the absolute $\dot{\alpha}\gamma\alpha\theta\omega\sigma\dot{\nu}\nu\eta$ which is the attribute of God, and to measure himself by that supreme standard."

man had called specifically *Jesus* good; but that he had called
Jesus specifically *good*. There is no contrast therefore instituted
between Jesus and God. This is the fundamental fact regarding
the passage which must rule its whole interpretation.

The sense need not be, however, that Jesus identifies Himself here with God, though the words are in themselves flexible
to that interpretation: " Why is it that thou dost thus address
me as *good?* Dost thou fully apprehend what is involved in
this? Art thou really aware that I am indeed that God who
alone is good? " It may rather be that Jesus, without implication as to His own real personality, is only directing attention
to God as the only true standard of goodness: " Why dost thou
use this strange address of ' *Good* Master '? Art thou seeking
someone good enough to give sure directions as to eternal
life? Hast thou forgotten God? And dost thou not know His
commandments? " If it be thought that some slight contrast
between Jesus and God is still discoverable, even in this understanding of the passage, and the enclitic με is appealed to in
order to forbid even so much emphasis on Jesus' person, the
remark may be in place here as truly as it was with regard to
Matthew's phrase, that the contrast involved in the words
" No one is good except one, God," is not between God and
Jesus, but between God and all others. There can be imported
into the pasage, in any case, no denial on Jesus' part, either that
He is good or that He is God. It is again merely the " They
have Moses and the Prophets; let them hear them." The whole
emphasis is absorbed in the stress laid upon God's sole right to
announce the standard of goodness. The question of the relation of Jesus to this God does not emerge: there is equally no
denial that He is God, and no affirmation that He is God.[24]

[24] So J. A. Alexander, on Mk. x. 18: " The goodness of our Lord Himself
and His divinity are then not at all in question, and are consequently neither
affirmed nor denied "; Swete: " Viewed in this light the words are seen not
to touch the question of our Lord's human sinlessness, or of His oneness with
the Father "; Wohlenberg: " Whether this predicate does not belong to Him
in its complete and full sense is a question into which our Lord does not
enter." Lagrange: " But it may be said that the most traditional opinion is
that Jesus glorifies His Father without comparing Himself with Him. The
question of His own nature is not raised; in responding to the young man He

The young man is merely pointed to the rule which had been given by the good God as a witness to what it is requisite to do that we may be well-pleasing to Him. He is merely bidden not to look elsewhere for prescriptions as to life save in God's revealed will. The search for a master good enough to lead men to life finds its end in God and His commandments.

Obviously the drift of the conversation in Mark (and Luke) is precisely the same as in Matthew. The two narratives are in substance completely consentaneous.[25] It is not to be supposed that either has reported in full detail all that was said. Actual conversations are ordinarily somewhat repetitious: good reports of them faithfully give their gist, in condensation. It has been said that Jane Austen records the conversations at her dinner-parties with such, not faithfulness but, circumstantiality that her reports bore the reader almost as much as the actual conversations would have done. There is no reason to suppose that the Evangelists aimed at such meticulous particularity in their reports of our Lord's conversations. Not all that He said, any more than all that He did (Jno. xx. 30, xxi. 25), has been recorded. Each selects the line of remark which seems to him to embody the pith of what was said; and the skill and faithfulness with which they have done this are attested by such a phenomenon as now faces us, where, amid even a striking diversity in the details reported, a complete harmony is preserved in the substance of the discourse. Wilhelm Wagner[26] makes himself merry indeed over what he

---

only takes account of the state of his mind. . . . There cannot be drawn from this passage any conclusion for or against Christological doctrine." Cf. also Plummer on Mt. xix. 10 ff.: " The explanation of ' Why callest thou me good? None is good save one, even God,' belongs to the commentators on Mark (see Swete). Suffice it to say here that Jesus was neither questioning His own sinlessness, nor intimates that the rich man ought not to call Him good unless he recognized Him as divine. The rich man could not have appreciated either of these points. Rather He turns his thoughts from his own inadequate standard of what may win eternal life to the Standard of the Divine Goodness."

[25] Cf. Schanz on Lk. xviii. 18: " The *punctum saliens* in both forms is the reference away from Himself and the reference to God. . . . The two differ only in form."

[26] *ZNTW*, viii. (1907) p. 144.

considers the conceit of Olshausen,[27] who recognizes in both
forms of narrative exact historical tradition, and looks upon
each as preserving only fragments of what was said. And, no
doubt, if the state of the case were as Wagner represents it, —
if, that is, the two narratives were mutually contradictory and
exclusive of one another, so that one could not say of them,
Sowohl . . . wie . . . but only *Entweder . . . oder . . .*, Olshausen's treatment of them would be absurd. Since, however,
they are entirely in agreement in substance, Olshausen's assumption is a mere matter of course. Each gives us in any case
only a portion of what was said. It may be plausibly argued,
indeed, that Mark intimates as much by his employment of the
imperfect tense when introducing the words reported from the
lips of the questioner: ἐπηρώτα.[28] We are told, to be sure, that
Mark's imperfects are not significant, that he interchanges
them arbitrarily with aorists, and that therefore no inferences
can be grounded on them.[29] This contention seems, however, to

[27] " Synoptische Erklärung der drei ersten Evangelien," on Mt. xix. 17.

[28] Cf. George Salmon, " The Human Element in the Gospels," 1907, p.
400: " It had occurred to me as possible that Mark's imperfect (ἐπηρώτα)
might be understood to imply that the rich man had put his question more
than once, and that thus there would be no contradiction between Evangelists
who recorded different forms in which the question had been put. But I
am now disposed rather to think that the imperfect tense indicates that the
young man puts a question which he had asked before, and that now, learning
of our Lord's approaching departure, he runs up to ask it once more before our
Lord goes away." The earlier view is certainly the more plausible.

[29] Cf. the discussion on the subject referred to by P. W. Schmiedel,
" Encyclopaedia Biblica," ii. col. 1874, note 1: " Feine, *JPT*, 1887, pp. 45–57, 77 ;
1888, pp. 405 f.; Holtzmann, *ibid.*, 1878, pp. 168–171, with Weiss' reply, pp.
583–585." B. Weiss, in his " Das Marcusevangelium und seine synoptischen
Parallelen," 1872, p. 27, had said of Mark: " The judicious interchange of the
descriptive imperfect, of the vivaciously representative present, and of the
narrative aorist is far from arbitrary; it is conformed with the greatest accuracy
to the whole disposition and intention of the representation, which makes
itself clear precisely by means of its careful observation." H. J. Holtzmann
declares this overdrawn: the imperfect is often employed merely to give
vividness and an autoptic air to the narrative and is " frequently in use by
later writers, especially with verbs of saying, giving, sending." He quotes Alex.
Buttmann (" Grammatik des N. T. Sprachgebrauchs," 1859, p. 173 [E. T. p.
200]) to the effect that the interchange of aorists and imperfects in historical
writing depends only on the caprice of the writer. In reply, Weiss (p. 584)

be overstrained; and in a case — like that now before us — where the present, aorist and imperfect tenses are brought together in close contiguity, their shades of implication can scarcely be wholly neglected. The general fact, however, does not rest upon the interpretation put upon Mark's ἐπηρώτα. It lies in the nature of the case that two accounts of a conversation which agree as to the substance of what was said, but differ slightly in the details reported, are reporting different fragments of the conversation, selected according to the judgment of each writer as the best vehicles of its substance.

An account of the relations of the two narratives quite different from this, it is true, is very commonly given. The representation which for the moment seems to be most widely adopted, looks upon Mark's narrative as the original one, and supposes it to have been closely followed by Luke but fundamentally altered by Matthew under the influence of dogmatic considerations. This view implies an interpretation of the narrative of Mark different from that offered above, as well as a different account of the relations of the narratives of the Evangelists to one another. According to it, Mark represents Jesus as repelling the attribution to Him of the epithet "good," because He is conscious of creaturely imperfection; and thus as, in His creaturely humility, setting Himself over against God in the strongest possible contrast. Matthew then is supposed to have drawn back from this representation as deroga-

---

reiterates his belief that Mark does not use the imperfect without significance. Feine in response, endeavors to show by examples that Mark uses the imperfect quite arbitrarily, often in quite the sense of the aorist (1888, p. 405 f.), and that especially with regard to ἠρώτα which is only a verb of asking. Matthew uses this verb, when it occurs in a historical tense of the finite verb, always in the aorist (seven times) while Mark uses it in the aorist only six times, but in the imperfect fifteen times, often in the imperfect where Matthew in the parallel passage has the aorist. Facts like these only show, however, that in narrating the facts the two writers present them to this extent from a different point of view, and this is what Buttmann means in the passage cited by Holtzmann, — not that the tenses do not differ in their implications but that it is often a mere matter of the way a writer looks at the same facts which is involved. For the matter in general, see the grammarians; beside Buttmann, § 137, 7, also Winer, § 40, 3, d, Blass, § 57, 4, Jelf, § 401, 34.

tory to Jesus' dignity as he conceived it, and to have therefore modified the narrative so that it should no longer imply a repudiation on Jesus' part of either goodness or divinity. That the conception of the drift of Mark's narrative which is assumed in this view is exegetically untenable, we have already endeavored to show. It is already wrecked indeed on the simple enclitic με,[30] which will not allow the contrast between Jesus and God which is its core. That it throws into chief prominence a matter which lies quite apart from the main subject under discussion is also fatal to it. There are, however, general considerations which also quite forbid it. That Matthew should be gratuitously charged with falsifying the text that lay before him in the interests of his doctrinal views is an indefensible procedure. There is no reason to believe Matthew capable of such dishonesty. And why the narrative as it lies in Mark's account should have been less acceptable to Matthew than it was to Mark himself and to Luke remains inexplicable. It is not doubted that the dogmatic standpoint of Matthew was fully shared by Mark and Luke. It is quite certain that, if the meaning put upon Mark's narrative by this conception of it is its true meaning, that fact was wholly unsuspected by either Mark or Luke. And there is no reason to suppose it would have been divined by Matthew either. There can be no doubt that Mark and Luke supposed, when they were narrating this incident, that they were writing down words in full harmony with their reverence for Jesus the Divine Savior, for the expression and justification of which they wrote their Gospels. To attribute to incidents which they record with this intent an exactly contrary significance, a meaning which flatly contradicts their most cherished convictions and the whole tenor of their Gospels, is to charge them with a stupidity in " compiling " their Gospels which is wholly incompatible with the character of the Gospels they have written. A critical theory which is inapplicable except on the assumption of stupidity and dis-

---

[30] The matter is explained by Blass, "Grammar of N. T. Greek," § 48, 3 (p. 165). Perhaps Mt. x. 32–33 may be profitably compared with our present passage.

honesty on the part of such writers as the Evangelists show themselves to be, is condemned from the outset.

Despite its impossibility, however, this theory has of late acquired wide vogue; and it is perhaps worth while to see how it is presented by its chief advocates. We may perhaps permit P. W. Schmiedel to expound it for us. He is speaking at the moment of the Gospel of John and remarks: [31] " And equally unacceptable to this Evangelist would be the record in Mark (x. 17 f.) and Luke, that to the address of a rich man, ' Good Master, what must I do to obtain eternal life? ' Jesus replied: ' Why callest thou me good? No one is good except God alone.' And yet beyond question this reply came from Jesus' lips. How little it could have been invented by any one of His worshippers who write in the Gospels, is shown by Matthew. With him (xix. 16 ff.) the rich man asks: ' Master, what good thing must I do that I may have eternal life? ' And Jesus answers: ' Why askest thou me concerning the good? There is one that is good.' How does Jesus come by these last words? Should He not rather, since He was asked concerning the good, proceed: ' There is one thing that is good '? and that would not only be the sole suitable reply, because of what had preceded, but also because of what follows: for Jesus says further: ' If, however, thou wouldst enter into life, keep the commandments.' Accordingly, in Jesus' view, the good concerning which He was asked, consists in keeping the commandments. How did Matthew come by the words: ' There is one that is good '? Only by having before him as he wrote the text of Mark. Here we

[31] " Das vierte Evangelium gegenüber den drei ersten " (" Religionsgeschichtliche Volksbücher I, 8 and 10), 1906, p. 19. Cf. " Encyclopaedia Biblica," ii. 1901, col. 1847; " In Mark x. 17 f. the answer of Jesus to the question, ' Good Master, what shall I do that I may inherit eternal life? ' is ' Why callest thou me good? None is good, save God only.' In Mt. xix. 16 f. the question runs, ' Master, what good thing shall I do that I may have eternal life? ' and the first part of the answer corresponds: ' Why askest thou me concerning that which is good? ' Very inappropriate, then, is the second part: ' One (masc.) there is who is the good (ὁ ἀγαθός).' Had not Matthew here had before him such a text as that of Mark and Luke, he would certainly, following his own line of thought, have proceeded: ' One (neut.) is the good (τὸ ἀγαθόν),' all the more because the immediate continuation also (verses 17–19), the exhortation to keep the commandments, would have suited so admirably."

have our finger on the way in which Matthew with conscious
purpose altered this text in its opening words, so that it should
no longer be offensive: and on the way in which at the end he
has left a few words of it unaltered, which betray to us the
manner in which the thing has been done." [32] This representation turns on three hinges. They are, first, that, according to
Mark's account, Jesus repels the ascription of goodness to Him
because He is conscious of not deserving it; secondly, that Matthew, offended by this attribution to Jesus of a consciousness
of sinfulness, has deliberately [33] altered the story so as to re-

[32] Cf. also Otto Schmiedel, " Die Hauptprobleme der Leben-Jesu-Forschung," [2] 1906, p. 47: " Here also belongs the passage which has been
mentioned in another place, where Jesus, in Mk. x. 18, said to the rich young
man, ' Why callest thou me good? No one is good except God.' Jesus denies
therefore His absolute sinlessness. Matthew (xix. 17), seeks to efface that."
At the place referred to (p. 27) he had said: " In Mk. x. 18 Jesus says to the
rich young man, ' Why callest thou me good? No man is good except God.'
To Matthew (xix. 17), this statement seemed dangerous to the sinlessness of
Jesus, and so he changed it to: ' Why askest thou me concerning the good
(neuter)?' Now, however, the following: ' No one is good,' &c., naturally no
longer fits on." Cf. also the similar representation by W. Heitmüller in Schiele
and Zscharnack's " Die Religion in Geschichte und Gegenwart," iii. (1912)
col. 359.

[33] Even W. C. Allen declares the differences of Matthew from Mark
" probably intentional " changes, and A. Plummer (" Com. on Mt.," pp. 264–
265) elaborately explains: " It is quite easy to see *why* Mt. has made these
alterations. He could not bring himself to record that Jesus said, ' Why callest
thou Me good? None is good save one, even God.' We have seen how readily
he omits anything which seems to detract from the Divine nature of the
Messiah, such as His asking for information or exhibiting human emotion,
and how he loves to emphasize the wonderful features in His mighty works.
Such a writer would feel that our Lord's reply, as recorded by Mk. was likely
to mislead, and was not likely to be correctly worded; he therefore substitutes
what seems to him to be more probable." Wilhelm Brückner (" Protestantische Monatshefte," iv. 1900, p. 423), arguing that Mark looked upon Jesus
as merely a creature, supposes that he naturally and without hesitation ascribes
to Him the repudiation of the ascription of " Good Master," which Lk. xviii.
18, 19 retains, while at Mt. xix. 16, 17 there is found " a perfectly obvious
tendential alteration." H. J. Holtzmann (" Die Synoptiker," p. 268, cf. p. 88)
also applies to Matthew's action the opprobrious epithet of " tendential." J.
M. Thompson (" Jesus according to S. Mark," 1909, p. 160), considers
Matthew's text " a clumsy attempt to get rid of what seemed to him to be a
difficulty." F. C. Conybeare (*Hibbert Journal*, I, i. [Oct., 1902], pp. 109, 112),
so far improves on this as to attribute this " bit of botching " not to the author

move it; and thirdly, that Matthew has done this so bunglingly as to retain, at an important point, a trait from Mark which is meaningless in his own narrative.[34]

The third of these contentions obviously neutralizes the second. A writer shrewd enough to undertake and so skillfully to begin the dogmatic alterations ascribed to Matthew would be shrewd enough to carry them successfully through. Certainly he would not have deliberately altered Mark's " No one is good except God alone," and yet have altered it so little to his purpose. To have supposed that Matthew, after having taken the trouble to reconstruct the first portion of the conversation of the young man with Jesus in order to adjust it to his own views, should have neglected to reconstruct the second portion of it and have left it in staring contradiction to what he had just written, would have been bad enough. But to suppose that he did not neglect to reconstruct the second portion also, but altered it too, but altered it so bunglingly as to leave it essentially the same in meaning as it was before alteration, and still in crass conflict with his reconstructed version of the former part of the conversation, is past crediting. A critical theory which will not hold unless we suppose not only that Mark and Luke were too stupid to perceive the open meaning of the incident they were recording, but also that Matthew, who was intelligent enough to perceive it and dishonest enough to at-

---

of the Gospel of Matthew but to " an ancient corrector who could not bear even the shadow of an insinuation that the Lord was other than ' without sin.' "

[34] Cf. Wellhausen on Mt. xix. 17: "The εἰς ἀγαθός of his model he has retained, although it no longer makes sense. It should logically be ' There is one thing that is good ' "; A. Plummer, " Com. on Mt.," p. 264, note: " Somewhat illogically he has left εἰς and ἀγαθός unchanged: it should be ἓν and ἀγαθόν : ' one *thing* is good ' "; Montefiore, " The Synopt. Gospels," 1909, ii. p. 694, " Matthew rather awkwardly keeps εἰς ὁ ἀγαθός, which is based on Mark's οὐδεὶς ἀγαθὸς εἰ μὴ εἰς ὁ θεός although the words have really no meaning without the repudiation of ' goodness ' as applied to Jesus." The odd thing is that none of the critics appears to have observed that " One thing is good " could scarcely be said by Jesus in this context, when the young man was inquiring after one good thing that he might do and Jesus was pointing him rather to the comprehensive law: " one thing is good " would be out of the key of the whole conversation.

tempt to adjust it to the view of Jesus common to all three, was yet so stupid that he could not carry the adjustment through — although it required only the substitution of an obvious neuter for a baldly impossibly masculine, — is clearly unworthy of serious consideration. It is very plain that such a theory is violently imposed on the texts and is driven through in the face of impossibilities. We have already seen that it is based on a failure to catch the meaning, natural and easy, of either narrative the relations of which it professes to expound: we perceive now that the explanation it offers of these relations is nothing less than absurd. There is no reason to suppose that Matthew would put a meaning — and, be it remembered, an intrinsically unnatural and linguistically impossible meaning — on Mark's narrative which it is certain that neither Mark nor Luke put on it; there is no justification for imagining that, if he did, he was dishonest enough to attempt to reconstruct the narrative so as to bring it into harmony with his own conception of Jesus (which, be it remembered, was Mark's and Luke's also); there is no propriety in assuming that if he undertook such a task he was capable of botching it as he is, on this theory, represented as doing. Whatever may be the relations of these narratives, it is certain that Matthew's was not made out of Mark's; and assuredly not as a dogmatic revision in the interests of our Lord's sinlessness and deity.[35]

[35] Keim ("Jesus of Nazara," v. p. 37) insists on the priority of Matthew's narrative. In point of fact neither narrative can be derived from the other. And in general, no form of criticism is more uncertain than that, now so diligently prosecuted, which seeks to explain the several forms of narratives in the Synoptics as modifications one of another. P. W. Schmiedel very properly acknowledges ("Encyclopaedia Biblica," ii. col. 1846) that "every assertion, no matter how evident, as to the priority of one Evangelist, and the posteriority of another, in any given passage, will be found to have been turned the other way round by quite a number of scholars of repute." The illustration he gives is characteristic. It is Mk. vi. 3 as compared with Mt. xiii. 55; Lk. iv. 22. "On the one side it is held that Matthew and Luke are here secondary, because they shrink from calling Jesus an artisan; on the other the secondary place is given to Mark because he shrinks from calling Jesus the Son of Joseph." The fundamental fault lies in the primary presupposition that the Evangelists (or their sources) have manipulated their material in the interests of the glorification of Jesus. Omit this unjustified presupposition and no ground

There is no reason, therefore, derivable from this critical speculation why we should desert the natural understanding of Mark's (and Luke's) narrative and its relation to Matthew's which lies on its surface. And our confidence in it will be greatly strengthened, if we will attend for a little to the alternative interpretations of it which have been proposed. These are very numerous and very divergent. They may be arranged, however, in a not unnatural sequence, and we may thus be enabled to survey them without confusion, and to catch their essential significance with some ease.

The interpretation which imposes on Mark's (and Luke's) narrative a repudiation by Jesus of the predicate " good," with its involved contrast of Him with God, was already current among the Arians,[36] and possibly even in certain heretical circles of the second century.[37] It is only natural that it should be widely adopted again in modern Liberal circles. Wilhelm Wagner in an interesting sketch of the history of the interpretation of the passage [38] chooses G. Volkmar as the representative of this mode of interpreting it. In Volkmar's view,[39] what is given expression in Jesus' reply is that in the Kingdom of

remains for either form of conjecture. An (unsuccessful) effort was made long ago by A. Hilgenfeld (" Kritische Untersuchungen über die Evangelien Justins, der Clementinischen Homilien, und Marcions," 1850, pp. 220 f., 362, 426; "Theologische Jahrbücher," 1853, pp. 207, 235 f.; 1857, pp. 414 ff.; cf. *ZWT*, 1863, pp. 361–362, note 3) to discover an older form of text of which both Mk. (and Lk.) and Mt. are modifications in doctrinal interests; cf. also W. Bousset, " Die Evangeliencitate Justins," 1891, pp. 105–106, and (as a curiosity of critical literature) F. C. Conybeare, *Hibbert Journal*, i. (Oct., 1902) pp. 109–112. See the detached note below (note 88).

[36] So we are told explicitly by Athanasius (Migne, " Pat. Graec.," 26, col. 985 C) and Epiphanius (" Pat. Graec.," 42, col. 229) : see also Ambrose (" Pat. Lat.," 16, col. 563) and Augustine (" Pat. Lat.," 42, col. 800) ; and as well the Clementine Homilies (" Pat. Graec.," 2, coll. 404, 405), on which see Dom Chapman, *ZNTW*, ix. (1908).

[37] Marcion is reported by Epiphanius, *H*. 33, 7 (p. 339, cf. p. 315) to have read the passage: " Call me not good; one is good, even God the Father " (but cf. Hippolytus, " Ref. Haer.," viii. 19). See further Hilgenfeld and Bousset as above, note 35), and especially Th. Zahn " Geschichte des Neutestamentlichen Kanons,"[1] ii. 1890, pp. 483 f. See the detached note below (note 88).

[38] *ZNTW*, viii. (1907) p. 156.

[39] Die Evangelien, oder Marcus und die Synopsis," 1870, p. 489.

God proclaimed by Him God is the sole Good, to whom homage
is due. God is the supreme Good, and the adoration of Him the
highest aim of the Kingdom of God. " Jesus is the announcer
and even the King of the Kingdom of God on Earth, but not
the supreme Good itself, which is to be adored. The Son of
Man sought only to lead man to the perfect worship of God."
To make his meaning clearer he adds: " Also He went (Mk.
i. 9) to the baptism of repentance in consciousness of sin
(*sündbewusst*)." Perhaps, however, the spirit of this interpretation is better expressed by no one than by H. J. Holtzmann [40]
who writes: " We see Him who is addressed, in the consciousness of His own incompleteness, in remembrance of His severe
moral battles and conflicts, in prevision of the approaching
tidal-wave of a last and most violent trial, draw back, point
above, and speak the humbly great word: 'Why callest thou
me good? No one is good, except God alone ' (Mk. x. 17-18;
Lk. xviii. 18-19; cf. with this the deflection of Mt. xix. 16-17
which even the dullest eye must recognize as tendential).
There is only one who stands above the world, without vari-
ableness or the necessity of ethical development, the eternally
unchangeable God. By this, Jesus affirmed the fixed and immovable interval which separates Godhead and manhood in
the moral sphere, as in Mk. xiii. 32 = Mt. xxiv. 36 He opens the
same gulf between the two natures in the intellectual sphere.
On both occasions Jesus takes His stand simply on the side of
manhood." He goes on to say that the Lord's prayer, which he
insists was not merely given to His disciples but was prayed
by Jesus in company with His disciples, bears witness to the
same effect, in its petitions for forgiveness and for protecton
from the evil one.[41] Among English writers J. M. Thompson

[40] " Lehrbuch der NT Theologie," ii. 1897, p. 268.

[41] Cf. also F. Barth, " Die Hauptprobleme des Lebens Jesu," [3] 1907, p.
251: " On the one side, Jesus takes His place wholly over against God on the
side of man, and confesses Himself to possess the imperfection of human
nature " — laying no claim to omniscience (Mk. xiii. 32), omnipotence (Mk. x.
40) or moral perfection (Mk. x. 17 f.). This last passage is misinterpreted if
it is made to imply the deity of Christ: " the Christ of dogma would have
spoken thus; the historical Jesus on the other hand refuses the predicate ' good,'
as belonging to God alone."

affords an example of the same general point of view.[42] " The
stress in the last sentence is on ' good ' not ' me,' " he writes,
" but this hardly lessens the force of the passage. It is not
enough to suggest that the young man's idea of goodness
needed correction, and that Jesus would point him from a
wrong to a right meaning of the word. Nor is it Jesus' intention to deny as man any equality with God. The address, ' Good
Master ' contains no such suggestion. Theology is out of place
in this passage, which deals with plain words in a plain way.
There is in fact no adequate alternative to the natural interpretation. Jesus did not think Himself ' good ' in the sense in
which the young man had used the word, and in the sense in
which it would be commonly used of God. . . . If He did not
at this time feel Himself to be good in the sense in which God
is good, neither did He think Himself to be divine in the sense
in which God is divine." " A broad distinction is drawn — a distinction which cannot reasonably be confined to the simple
ground of ' goodness ' — between Jesus and God." Perhaps,
however, no more pungent emphasis has been thrown upon this
view than that thrown upon it by C. G. Montefiore.[43] " The
reply of Jesus," he writes, " is of the utmost significance. It is
obvious that no divine being would or could have answered
thus. Jesus knew Himself to be a man. . . . Yet it is a noble
character which peeps through the fragmentary and one-sided
records — none the less noble because we may be sure that of
Jesus, both in fact and in his own estimate of Himself, the adage was true: ' there is no man that sinneth not.' " [44]

---

[42] " Jesus according to S. Mark," 1909, p. 159, also p. 254.

[43] " The Synoptic Gospels," 1909, i. pp. 246–247.

[44] The attitude of P. W. Schmiedel to the sinlessness of Jesus, and the
bearing of our passage upon it, is revealed in the following words from the
paper contributed by him to the volume called " Jesus or Christ? " printed
as a *Hibbert Journal Supplement* for 1908 (p. 68) : — " As far as Jesus is
concerned, it is certain that all the writers of the New Testament assumed His
sinlessness, even though they speak of it with remarkable infrequency. But
we are surely not at liberty to see a proof in this aspect of the matter, when
we consider the attitude of veneration in which they stood towards Him, and
the kind of being whom they held Him to be " [the meaning is that the
testimony of the New Testament writers is invalid, because from their point

The nerve of this interpretation resides of course in the contention that a repudiation of the epithet " good " is necessarily involved in the question, " Why callest thou me good? " (Mk. x. 18; Lk. xviii. 19). This contention is unjustified: whether the question involves a repudiation of the epithet " good," or is a call to a closer consideration of the implications of the original request, is a matter for the context to determine; and the context very decidedly determines it in the latter sense. Nevertheless the contention is often given very vigorous expression; and by no one is it given more vigorous expression than by Wilhelm Wagner, who writes as follows: [45] " Whoever cannot attribute to Jesus the use of language more to conceal than to reveal His thought, whoever rather holds the opinion that Jesus really meant His words in the sense in which they must be understood by every unprejudiced hearer, — cannot help allowing that Jesus in Mk. x. 18 distinctly distinguishes between God and Himself, and that He just as earnestly rejects the predicate $\dot{a}\gamma a\theta\delta s$ for Himself here, and reserves it for God, as in Mark xiii. 32 he denies knowledge of the day of the Parousia for His own person and ascribes it to the Father alone." Wagner does not admit, however, that in thus repudiating the predicate " good " of Himself, Jesus confesses Himself a sinner. Thus we are advised that it has been found possible to hold to the interpretation of Jesus' response to the young ruler which sees in it a repudiation of the predicate " good," and yet escapes from the ascription of conscious sin to Jesus. There are in fact more ways than one in which this has been attempted. A series of variant interpretations of our passage has thus arisen, differing from one another

---

of view they must have held Him sinless]. " Nor can we regard the passage in the Fourth Gospel (viii. 46) as an expression of Jesus Himself in view of the character of the book in which it stands. All the more importance attaches to Mark x. 18: 'Why callest thou me good? There is none good save God.' It is true that philologists are now proving with much zeal that the original Aramaic word means 'gracious' [*gütig*]; but they do not reflect that Jesus cannot have justly regarded Himself as morally good, if He repudiated even the epithet 'gracious.'"

[45] *ZNTW*, viii. (1907) p. 154.

in the sense put upon the term " good " or in the explanation
offered of Jesus' intention in repudiating that predicate, but
agreeing that He does repudiate it in some sense, not involving
the confession of sin on His part. Some account should be given
of these mediating methods of exposition.

Wagner himself, in company with a considerable number
of recent expositors,[46] wishes to take the term " good " in the
sense, not of moral excellence, but of graciousness, kindness.
This, in itself attractive, suggestion is rendered nugatory,
however, by the unfitness of the address, " Kind Master " as a
preparation for Jesus' reply. Johannes Weiss seems to be right
when he remarks of the ἀγαθέ: " The questioner clearly
wishes to express by it not merely his reverence but also his
conviction that Jesus, as a perfect man, is able to give new life
and particular information as to the way to eternal life." [47]
Jesus' reply puts the sense of moral perfection on the address.
The advantage sought by reading the predicate as " gracious "
rather than " good," is that in that case its repudiation by
Jesus does not imply a confession of sin on His part. " If the
word should be so understood," remarks Dalman, " then there
is no need to inquire in what sense Jesus disclaims sinlessness." [48] " His sinlessness or moral perfection Jesus has, therefore, not denied in our passage," is Wagner's way of putting

[46] For example, G. Dalman, " The Words of Jesus," E. T. p. 337: " The
proper translation is ' Kind Master ' "; J. Wellhausen on Mk. x. 18 (p. 86):
"'Ἀγαθός means less ' sinless ' than ' gracious '"; Karl Thieme, " Die christliche Demut," 1906, pp. 106–107; M. J. Lagrange, on Mk. x. 17: " Goodness
of heart (Schanz, Wellhausen, Spitta) rather than moral perfection (Loisy,
etc); ἀγαθός can mean goodness, it is true, but also the goodness of benevolence (Mt. xx. 15) and this is always the case when in the O. T. it is said that
God is ' good ' (Spitta: cf. W. Wagner, ZNTW, 1907, pp. 143–161) "; F. Spitta,
ZNTW, ix. (1908), pp. 12 ff.; J. Lebreton, " Les Origines du Dogme de la
Trinité," 1910, p. 235, etc. Contra, e.g. Wohlenberg, " Kom. zu Markus," p. 273,
note 89; P. W. Schmiedel as above, note 41. Wagner thinks that Justin Martyr
already took the ' good ' here in the sense of ' kind '; but see on this the note
of J. Moffatt, The Expositor for January 1908, p. 84.

[47] Wagner (p. 159, note) criticises Weiss' use of the word " perfect " instead of " good " in this remark, but on the very next page himself equates
the terms " sinlessness " and " moral perfection." Cf. what Dalman (p. 338)
says in opposition to A. Seeberg's explanation which is similar to that of Weiss.

[48] P. 338.

it.[49] The inquiry of P. W. Schmiedel whether the repudiation
of " kindness " is not also, however, the repudiation of moral
goodness,[50] is here very pertinent; and it is observable that
Wagner at least does not seem prepared with a plausible answer to it. After declaring that, since what is under discussion
is " kindness," Jesus does not deny His sinlessness or moral
perfection, that there is no question raised as to that, he continues:[51] " No doubt, however, He does disclaim the predicate
' kind-gracious ' (Gütig-gnädig) for His own person and reserve it for God. Should this result nevertheless seem to
anyone equally objectionable with Volkmar's exposition, mentioned above, the reply is to be made to him that we must adjust our conception of Jesus to that of the Holy Scriptures and
not vice versa. . . ." No doubt. Therefore the question presses
whether it is easy to believe that the Jesus presented to us, we
do not say broadly in the Holy Scriptures, but in the Synoptic
Gospels, would repudiate the predicate " kind " or " gracious,"
when applied to Him, especially with the energy which is supposed in this interpretation of His words. It does not appear
that the predicate $\dot{a}\gamma a\theta \dot{o}s$ is elsewhere in the Synoptics attributed to Jesus, nor is it, for the matter of that, elsewhere
attributed to God — and it may be a nice question to which
limb of this statement we might consider Mt. xx. 15 a quasi-
exception. But surely it is difficult to suppose that the Synoptists, who attribute " compassion " to Jesus more frequently
than any other emotion, and one of whose number represents
the sponsor of another as summing up Jesus' career as a " go-
ing about, doing good " ($\epsilon\dot{v}\epsilon\rho\gamma\epsilon\tau\hat{\omega}\nu$, Acts x. 38), could have
understood Him to be repelling here the attribution to Him
of " kindness." And surely this repudiation of the predicate
of " kindness " sounds strange upon the lips of the Jesus who is
represented by them as declaring that He had compassion upon
the multitude (Mt. xv. 32; Mk. viii. 2), and as inviting all
those who labor and are heavy laden to come to Him that He
might give them rest (Mt. xi. 28).

Wagner endeavors to ease this difficulty by suggesting that

[49] P. 160.   [50] See above list, note 44.   [51] Pp. 160–161.

like εὐεργέτης, which Jesus forbids His disciples to permit themselves to be called (Lk. xxii. 25), ἀγαθός, " gracious," might have come to be employed almost as a divine attribute; and he connects this suggestion with Jesus' disgust at the " honor-hunger " which characterized " the Scribes and Pharisees " of the time, and which provoked Him to forbid His disciples to be called Rabbi or Leader καθηγητής (Mt. xxiii. 10). This line of thought had already been carried a step further by Karl Thieme,[52] and before him by Karl Heinrich Weizsäcker.[53] These writers [54] threw the whole burden of Jesus' repudiation of the predicate " good " upon His revulsion from Rabbinical vanity, and hence held that " this interdiction of the designation ' Good Teacher ' has nothing at all to do with the self-consciousness of Jesus, but is solely a repulsion of the Rabbinical title." From this point of view, Thieme, who also takes the ἀγαθός in the sense of " gracious," is able to contend that Jesus by no means repudiates that quality for Himself. " According to this interpretation," he writes,[55] " Jesus defended Himself from involvement in the Rabbinical title-seeking. He repelled it from Himself without giving a single thought to whether He Himself had or had not a right to the title of ' gracious.' He did not address Himself here to a solemn deliverance as to His distinction from God, but, painfully af-

[52] " Die christliche Demut," 1906, p. 107.

[53] " Untersuchungen über die evangelische Geschichte," 2 1901, p. 295.

[54] Cf. also J. Lebreton, " Les Origines du Dogme de la Trinité, 1910, pp. 234–235: " It would clearly be a mistake to see in the ' goodness ' in question here, virtue or moral excellence: and when our Savior attributes it exclusively to God, that is not in order to make it understood that God alone is morally perfect, but no doubt only because He alone is Goodness itself, infinitely beneficent and benignant. Applied to a Rabbi — and the interlocutor of Christ saw in Him nothing more — this designation of ' Good Master ' was, as Dalman remarks, an ' insolent flattery ': our Lord repelled it without revealing to an auditor so badly prepared to receive it a property he was far from suspecting. The meaning of the text is very similar to that of a text cited above: ' Call no man here below Father, for you have but one Father, that is God; and have not yourselves called Masters, for you have only one Master, the Christ.' The only difference between the two texts is that in the second (Mk. x. 17) the Christ effaces Himself far more before God His Father."

[55] P. 108.

fected by the extravagances of the rich man, He gave expression to His old aversion to the whole odious behavior of the Pharisees and Scribes, in a quick and sharply spoken word of reprehension. It is therefore rather an emotional declaration from which may be learned how unlike the Pharisees and Scribes He was."

Attractive as this exposition is it is burdened with the insuperable difficulty that Jesus does not, in point of fact, refuse for Himself any of the titles which He forbids His followers to accept. He forbade them to be called Rabbi or Leader; but He claims both titles for Himself (Mt. xxiii. 8 f.). It is not merely in John (xiii. 13) that He vindicates His right to the titles of Master and Lord. Both are put upon His lips with reference to Himself by the Synoptists also (Mk. xiv. 14; Mt. xxvi. 18; Lk. xxii. 11; Mk. xi. 3; Mt. xxi. 3; Lk. xix. 31), and He constantly and without apparent difficulty accepts them both when applied to Him by others. Thieme himself has to acknowledge that "when He was Himself called Rabbi, He found it right, for He was it, He alone and no other in His little flock." [56] If He revolted against the lust for empty titles of the Scribes and Pharisees, that was because those titles were empty for them; they did not rightly belong to or describe them; were mere vanities with no other function than to gratify pride. He would not have His disciples like the Scribes and Pharisees in this. But it does not follow that He would repel these titles when applied to Himself, to whom they rightfully belonged: in point of fact He did not.[57] There is an essential difference between craving vain titles, and accepting just ones. We may be quite sure that Jesus would not have repudiated the ascription of graciousness to Him unless He had felt that it did not rightly describe Him and that He therefore had no right to it.

A far more widely adopted interpretation of the passage,

[56] P. 107.

[57] Cf. R. Stier, "The Words of the Lord Jesus," Fourth American Edition, i. p. 360b, note: "Never has Jesus anywhere said (if He says so here it is the only time) that anyone honored Him too highly; never did He protest against any degree of love, honor, thanksgiving, adoration (Roos, "Die Lehre J. Christi," p. 79)."

seeking the same end, accepts the term ἀγαθός in the sense
of morally good, but distinguishes between the quality of goodness which is proper to man, and that absolute and indeclinable
goodness which belongs to God alone. Jesus, it is said, when He
repels the predicate "good" of Himself, and declares that
God alone is good, means the term good in its highest, its absolute sense, and in no way implies that He is not good as a man
wholly without flaw may be good. Sometimes what is meant
by this is that only God is Good-of-Himself (αὐτοάγαθος),
has the source of His goodness in Himself; men, though wholly
good, can have only a derived goodness, and must owe all their
goodness to the goodness of God. Origen,[58] indeed, would carry
this distinction far beyond the sphere of creaturely relations,
into the Trinitarian relations themselves. According to him
our Lord speaks here not as a man but as the Son Himself, and
yet separates Himself in His goodness as Son from the Father,
the *Fons Deitatis,* from whom is derived all that the Son is.
No other goodness exists in the Son as such save that which
is in the Father; and when the Savior says that "there is none
good save one only, God the Father," He means to declare, not
that He, the Son of God, is not good, but that all the goodness
in Him is of the Father. God alone is primarily good; the Son
and Spirit are good with the goodness of God: while creatures
can be said to be good only catachrestically and have in them
only an accidental, not an essential goodness. It is not of the
subordinationism of Origen, however, that our modern writers
are thinking when they say that our Lord, in denying that He
was good and reserving this predicate to God alone, meant
merely that His goodness was not original with Himself but
derived from God the sole source of goodness. They are thinking of the man Jesus who, they suppose, is here referring His
goodness to the Father, the source of all goodness. An example
of this mode of expounding the passage is supplied by Karl
Ullmann in the earlier editions of his famous book on " The
Sinlessness of Jesus." [59] According to him what Jesus means is,

[58] " De Principiis," I, ii. 13.
[59] " Ueber die Sündlosigkeit Jesu. Eine apologetische Bertrachtung."

" If I am good, I am so only in and by means of God, so far as
I am one with God," and he expounds his own meaning as
follows: " Here, then, ἀγαθός is to be taken in the most pregnant sense: as the ultimate highest source of good, as the absolute good; Jesus is good, but only in His inward complete
communion with God, as the expression of the divine; and in
this sense He demands of the young man: " Thou must rise
above the common human goodness, — and in so far also above
me, considered as a man detached from God, as merely a good
teacher in the sense of the Rabbis and Pharisees — and hold
to the supreme source of all good, and thence there will flow
to thee the good, and eternal life." Another example seems to
be supplied by A. Plummer's comment on Luke xviii. 19. The
young man's defect, he tells us, " was that he trusted too much
in himself, too little in God. Jesus reminds him that there is
only one source of goodness, whether in action (Matthew),
or in character (Mark, Luke), viz., God. He Himself is no
exception. His goodness is the goodness of God working in
Him. ' The Son can do nothing of Himself, but what He seeth
the Father doing. . . . For as the Father hath life in Himself,
even so gave He to the Son also to have life in Himself. . . .
I can of Myself do nothing; as I hear, I judge: and My judgment is righteous, because I seek not my own will but the will
of Him that sent Me ' (Jno. v. 19-30). *Non se magistrum non
esse, sed magistrum absque Deo nullum bonum esse testatur*
(Bede). There is no need to add to this the thought that the
goodness of Jesus was the goodness of perfect development
(see on ii. 52), whereas the goodness of God is that of absolute

---

Hamburg, 1833, p. 112, note; ed. 3, 1836, p. 136. The former of these editions is
called the " second, improved and enlarged edition " on the title page, but
appears to be the first separately printed edition, the treatise having appeared
in the first instance in the " Theologische Studien und Kritiken," i. 1828. Cf.
also Ullmann's " Polemisches in Betreff der Sündlosigkeit Jesu " in the *TSK*
for 1842. An English translation of " The Sinlessness of Christ " (Edinburgh,
1870, newly issued 1902) was made from the seventh German edition. The
passage referred to has been so modified in the later editions that the feature
for which it is cited has disappeared.

perfection (Weiss on Mk. xi. 18)." [60] An extraordinary number
of expositors have retained the fundamental notion of this
interpretation as one, but not the chief, element in their explanations: a clause or two suggesting that the goodness of
Jesus finds its source in God is inserted in the midst of other
matter. The difficulty with it is that there is nothing in the
passage either to suggest or to sustain it. An attempt has, indeed, been made by Karl Wimmer to find a point of attach-
ment for it in what he calls the conditional sense of $\epsilon i \ \mu \acute{\eta}$.
Instead of " No one is good except God," he would render

[60] Similarly, Henri Bois, " La Personne et l'Oeuvre de Jésus " propounds,
and in an article in the *Revue de Théologie et des Questions Religieuses,* xxii.
1 (January, 1913), pp. 40–53, defends the view that Jesus does not indeed confess Himself a sinner yet ranges Himself definitely as subordinate to God in
the moral sphere also. He thinks this view " the golden mean " between the
" rationalistic " view which makes Jesus acknowledge His sinfulness and the
" orthodox " view which makes Him proclaim Himself God, and defends it
in the *Revue* article against strictures by A. Berthoud, " Jésus et Dieu,' 1912.
According to Berthoud (see also *Avant-Garde* for April 15, 1907) Jesus proclaimed Himself *in point of goodness* equal to God. He repels the homage
of which he was made the object, not because He felt Himself unworthy of it,
but because He felt it to be banal. It was not a sense of imperfection which
dictated His response; He speaks rather out of a consciousness of purity without flaw, of perfect holiness. He is thus not assimilating Himself with
men, but proclaiming Himself equal with God — not indeed metaphysically,
but morally. The ideas of immutability, absoluteness, eternity, are not here
in question: goodness is a *moral* conception, and it is from a moral point of
view only that Jesus feels on an equality with God. Bois rightly rejoins that
the moral and metaphysical cannot be thus separated. If Jesus is equal with
God in holiness, He is metaphysically the same with God. He cannot be the
prototype of the moral law, the sole inspirer and source of all good, without
being God, the creator and conservator of the world. Bois does not himself
seem to conceive his own interpretation clearly. He cites *both* Dalman, who
denies that *moral* good is here in question, and Swete who denies that Jesus'
goodness in any sense is here in question, as if they supported him who thinks
that it is precisely of moral good that Jesus is speaking and that He is proclaiming Himself subordinate to the Father precisely with respect to *it.*
" Jesus recognizes," he says, " His subordination over against God even in
the moral point of view, — subordination, which is, however, perfectly compatible with the absence of sin." In this moral subordination of Jesus to God,
he recognizes on the one side that His holiness is positive and not negative;
but declares on the other side that it finds its whole source in God — that
" every idea of the good is in Jesus, an inspiration which He receives from God,
the sole absolute good."

rather, "No one is good if not — that is to say, without, — God"; and then explain this as declaring that goodness cannot exist apart from God. But this is only a curiosity of exegesis.[61]

It has been more common, therefore, to seek the contrast which Jesus is supposed to intimate between His goodness and that of God in the essentially developing character of human goodness as distinguished from the absolute goodness of God. A very clear expression is given to this view by the compressed comment of E. P. Gould: [62] "The reason of this question and of the denial of goodness to any one but God which follows it, is that God alone possesses the absolute good. He is what others become. Human goodness is a growth, even where there is no imperfection. It develops, like wisdom, from childhood to youth, and then to manhood. And it was this human goodness which was possessed by Jesus. See Lk. ii. 52; Heb. ii. 10, v. 8." The longer comment of H. A. W. Meyer on Mark x. 18, which has in substance been retained by B. Weiss through all of his revisions, is perhaps, however, more typical.[63] "Ingeniously and clearly Jesus makes use of the address, διδάσκαλε ἀγαθέ, in order to direct the questioner to the highest moral Ideal in whose commands the solution of the question is given (verse 19). He does this in such a manner that He takes the predicate ἀγαθός in the highest moral sense (against Bleek and Klostermann, according to whom He only denies that man

[61] *TSK*, 1845, p. 128. He argues that εἰ μή is fundamentally conditional, not exclusive, in its meaning; and that, therefore, when Jesus says, "No one is good εἰ μή God," He does not mean that no one except God is good, but that no one without, apart from, God, is good; that the divine goodness is the condition of all other goodness, and all that is good has its ground in God's goodness. Jesus, thus, does not set God over against all others as the only good one, and does not contrast Himself with God, either as not unexceptionally good or as not absolutely good. He only declares that He does not wish to be called good, without the proper recognition that any goodness which belongs to Him has its source in God.

[62] "International Critical Commentary on Mark," Mk. x. 18.

[63] Meyer on Mark, E. T. i. p. 164: We quote from the sixth German edition, which is the first of those prepared by Weiss, p. 152: in ed. 8 (p. 176) which announces itself as revised by Bernhard and Johannes Weiss, it is somewhat compressed; and in ed. 9 in which Johannes Weiss' name falls away again, it remains much as it appears in ed. 8.

as such, and without relation to God can be called good). ' Thou
art wrong in calling me good: this predicate, in its complete
conception, belongs to none save One, God.' Cf. Ch. F. Fritzsche, in " Fritzschior. Opusc.," pp. 78 ff. This declaration, however, is no evidence against the sinlessness of Jesus; rather,
it is the true expression of the distance which human consciousness — even the sinless consciousness as being human — recognizes between itself and the absolute perfection of God (cf.
Dorner, " Jesu sündlose Vollkommenheit," p. 14). For [64] the
human perfection is necessarily a *growing* (*werdende*) one,
and even in the case of Jesus was conditioned by His advancing
development, even though it can respond at every point to the
moral ideal (Lk. ii. 52; Heb. v. 8; Lk. iv. 13, xxii. 28. Cf. Ullmann in the *TSK,* 1842, p. 700); the absolute being-good
that excludes all having become and becoming so (*das absolute,
alles Gewordensein und Werden ausschliessende Gutsein*) pertains only to God who is *verae bonitatis canon et archetypus,*
(Beza)." [65] " Even the man Jesus," adds Meyer (omitted by
Weiss) " had to wrestle until He attained the victory and peace

[64] This important last sentence is retained verbally through the ninth
edition.

[65] Cf. here Paul Feine, " Theologie des NTs," 1910, p. 28: " He, who had
given out of the perfection of His inwardness all the ideal commandments
of the Sermon on the Mount, and had conceived the nature of God out of
the pure ground of His life in an ethical purity hitherto unknown, declines
to be called good. That predicate belongs to God only." He adds in a note:
" It is wrong when many seek to make capital of this declaration in favor of
the contention that Jesus was ethically imperfect. When Jesus says to the rich
young man, ' Why callest thou me good? ' or ' Call me not good ' μή με λέγε
ἀγαθόν as Conybeare, *Hibbert Journal,* Oct. 1902, i. pp. 96–113 represents the
oldest form, after Marcion, the Clementine Homilies, Tatian, Origen, &c., in
Mk. and Lk. xviii. 19), ' No one is good except *one,* God ' — that is as much a
refusal of the address as in the case of the Syro-phoenician woman, Mt. xv.
25 f. As nevertheless in that case, Jesus yet fulfilled the request of the repulsed
one, so there occurs here too in the end an answer to the question, ' *Good*
Master, what shall I do to have eternal life? ' He knows the way, and indeed
He alone, for His answer culminates in the word, ' Come and follow me '
(Mk. x. 21). He could not have said that, in the loftiness of His requirement
for entrance into the Kingdom, had He not been ' good.' We must have an
eye for the antithetical, contrast-loving manner of Jesus. Then we can avoid
such essential misunderstandings as the repulsed young man fell into."

of the cross." Quite similarly E. K. A. Riehm [66] writes: "The emphatic 'No one is good except one, God,' or, as the words stand in Matthew, 'One is good,' does not fit in well with the explanation according to which Jesus does not wish to refuse the predicate 'good' for Himself, but wishes to say only that the young man should not, *from his standpoint,* that, namely, He was only a human teacher, address Him as 'Good Master.' We are of the opinion that Christ wishes the word 'good' to be taken in the absolute sense (cf. the ὁ ἀγαθός) and really refuses the predicate in this sense for His own person, and ascribes it to God only. When so understood, the expression does not at all show that Jesus had any other consciousness than that of essential unity with the God-will, but it does show that He was conscious that in His moral development He had not yet reached the highest stage of absolute perfection, which still was therefore proper to God alone."

Following Wagner's example we may add some further examples of this exposition, taken from dogmaticians. He selects for the purpose R. A. Lipsius and J. Kaftan. The former [67] maintains for Jesus, indeed, a development free from the consciousness of guilt, but nevertheless conceives of Him so humanly as to open a great gulf between His hardly retained integrity and the absolute perfection of God. To wish to deny for Him the possibility of sin or natural temptability, he declares, would abolish the reality of His humanity, for to it the σάρξ of necessity belongs. Jesus was tempted, and that shows that He was not free from inner vacillations and momentary obscurations of His God-consciousness. All of this He no doubt victoriously overcame: but certainly we cannot wonder that He felt impelled to distinguish His goodness, if He so conceived it, from God's absolute goodness. In much the same spirit, Kaftan,[68] will not hear of the attribution of impeccability to Jesus. This would yield, he thinks, only an unmoral

[66] "Lehrbegriff des Hebräerbriefes," 1867, p. 383.
[67] "Lehrbuch der Evangelisch-protestantischen Dogmatik," [2] 1879, pp. 569 f.
[68] "Dogmatik," [3] and [4] 1901, p. 441.

notion of Him, Jesus' sinless perfection was a truly moral condition and receives its content from the uninterrupted moral trial
to which He was subjected. In Mk. x. 18 " the predicate ἀγαθός
applies in its absolute sense to God only, who is ἀπείραστος,
not to man who, while living and walking in the world, remains
always subject to temptation. It we would wish to find expressed in this declaration of Jesus, instead of this, the consciousness of a moral fault attaching to Him, that would come
into contradiction with His testimony with respect to Himself
elsewhere. He is the sinlessly perfect man, but He became such
by His own act and confirmation, by virtue of actual ethical
decision through temptation." If we may appeal to a prophet
of our own, we may find the whole tendency and significance of
this mode of interpreting the passage very clearly expounded
by H. R. Mackintosh.[69] The salutation of the young ruler, he
tells us, Jesus waved back with the uncompromising rejoinder,
' None is good save one, even God.' " And then he continues:
" The words cannot be a veiled confession of moral delin-
quency, which certainly would not have taken this ambiguous
and all but casual form. What Jesus disclaims, rather, is *God's*
perfect goodness. None but God is good with a goodness unchanging and eternal; He only cannot be tempted of evil but
rests for ever in unconditioned and immutable perfection.
Jesus, on the contrary, learnt obedience by the things which He
suffered, being tempted in all points like as we are (Heb. v. 8,
iv. 15). In the sense of transcendent superiority to moral conflict and the strenuous obligation to prove His virtue ever
afresh in face of new temptation and difficulty, He laid no
claim to the absolute goodness of His Father. Which reminds
us emphatically that the holiness of Jesus, as displayed in the
record of His life, is no automatic effect of a metaphysical substance, but in its perfected form the fruit of continuous moral
volition pervaded and sustained by the Spirit. It is at once the
Father's gift and progressively realized in an ethical experience.
This follows from the moral condition of incarnation."

That the goodness of Jesus' human nature was a developing

[69] " The Doctrine of the Person of Christ," 1912, p. 37.

goodness, and was not only not while He was on earth but
never can be the infinite goodness of God is a matter of course.
It is further not inconceivable that in referring to His moral
quality He might on occasion quite readily speak of the moral
quality of His human nature only, as, in a famous instance, in
referring to His knowledge, He has spoken only of His human
mind (Mk. xiii. 32). It is certain, still further, that in speaking
of God's goodness in our present passage He has the absoluteness of His goodness in view. So far we encounter no grounds
of objection to the general line of interpretation which we have
just been illustrating. There is no reason in the nature of the
case why Jesus might not have contrasted His human goodness
with the infinite goodness of God, which is here adverted to.
But neither is there any reason obvious why we should suppose
Him to wish, at this moment and in the midst of the irrelevant
conversation recounted, to interpose a bit of instruction upon
the developing character of His human goodness. The remark
of Fritzsche seems also pertinent: " the words, $\tau\acute{\iota}$ $\mu\epsilon$ $\lambda\acute{\epsilon}\gamma\epsilon\iota\varsigma$
$\dot{a}\gamma a\theta\acute{o}\nu$, do not mean *in what sense* do you call me good? but
why do you call me good? " [70] If this question has, as Fritzsche
also insists, the force of an " objurgation," and means " You
wrongly call me good," it is hard to see how Jesus could have
expected His interlocutor to understand Him as meaning no
more than that His goodness (as respects His human nature)
was not the absolute goodness of Deity. To say, 'You are
wrong in calling me good, because though, even in my human
nature, I am really good, good through and through, good without flaw, I am nevertheless (in my human nature) not good as
the infinite God is good,' would not only be a subtlety which
this interlocutor could not be expected to follow, but as addressed to him inconsequent. If Jesus means to contrast Himself as not good with God as good, He can scarcely mean less in
this context than that He is, in the common sense of the word,
not good; that is, that He is not free from sin. The interpretation which would pare this down to a contrast between immaculate goodness and absolute goodness is a refinement uncon-

[70] " Fritzschiorum Opuscula academica," 1838, p. 79.

formable with the simplicity of the language employed and the directness with which the conversation develops. It is idle to appeal to such passages as Job iv. 18, xv. 15, xxv. 5; for the point is, not that the distinction in question is not real, nor that it cannot be expressed in natural language, but that it is not suggested by the language of the present passage and breaks in upon the course of its development.[71] From the dogmatic point of view this interpretation is of course more acceptable than that which sees in the passage a plain confession of sin. It has moreover the great advantage of not giving us a Jesus wholly out of harmony with the Jesus of the rest of the Synoptic tradition, and even perhaps with the Jesus of the remainder of this very narrative — where He speaks of " following " Him as the foundation of the new life. But from the narrower exegetical point of view it is at a disadvantage in comparison with the other; and yet lies open to all the exegetical objections which are fatal to that view.

Still another modification of the interpretation which supposes Jesus in our passage to repudiate the predicate good, has had large vogue. Jesus, it is said, repudiates this predicate not from His own but from His questioner's point of view. This interpretation, which is very common among the Fathers, is well illustrated by a passage in one of Athanasius' anti-Arian tracts.[72] " And when He says," we read, " ' Why callest thou me good? No one is good except one, God,' God, reckoning Himself among men, spoke this according to His flesh, and with respect to the opinion of him who came to Him. For that one thought Him man only and not God, and the response keeps this opinion in view. For, if you think me a man, He says, and not God, call me not good, for no one is good. For the good does not belong to human nature but to God." It is obvious, that to say that Jesus repudiates the predicate only from the point of view of His interlocutor is to say that He does not really repudiate it at all. It is not strange, therefore, as Montefiore

---

[71] Cf. what R. Stier excellently says in criticism of Oetinger and Ullmann, in " The Words of the Lord Jesus," i. pp. 360b–361b.

[72] Migne, " Pat. Graec.," xxvi. col. 993 A and B.

seems to find it,[73] that "the capable Roman Catholic commentator," Schanz, "who honestly insists on the correct translation of this verse," understanding its repudiation to be meant *ad hominem*, adds that "the words do not exclude ' that Jesus as respects His higher nature, may belong to this divine Being.' "[74] And Olshausen is quite logical when he writes: [75] "The questioner saw in Christ a mere διδάσκαλος. . . . To such a conception, however, the ἀγαθός was not suitable. He [Jesus] repudiates, therefore the name and directs him to Him who is Goodness itself. By this, however, the Lord does not deny that He is Himself just the ἀγαθός, because the true God is reflected in Him as His image; only this teaching could not be dogmatically presented to the young man, but should vitally form itself in his own heart." And Keil: [76] " Jesus, taking this predicate in its full sense, uses this address to direct the young man to God as the Supreme Being, when He replies: ' Why callest thou me good? ' that is, ' Call me not good,' ' no one is good except one, God.' Jesus by no means repudiates goodness or sinlessness by this, but only says that the predicate would not be suitable for Him if He were nothing more than a διδάσκαλος, for which the young man took Him. This question gives no occasion, however, to instruct the young man

[73] i. p. 246.

[74] Schanz's comment on Mk. x. 18 runs as follows: " Jesus makes use of the address διδάσκαλε ἀγαθέ, in order to teach the young man that the word ἀγαθός in its full sense, as the designation of essential, immutable goodness, belongs to God only, so that it is only by conforming to the will of God that blessedness can be attained. Since, however, the young man had addressed Jesus, according to his conception, as a human teacher, even though exalted far above others, Jesus replied to him, as He often does elsewhere, from the standpoint of the questioner (Chrysostom, Jerome, Bede, Euthymius, Theophylact, and all Catholic expositors; Bengel, Olshausen, Ebrard, Keil), an explanation to whom of His Sonship to God was not now in place. No doubt, there must be supplied with οὐδείς not λέγεται but only ἐστί (Krüg. 62, 1, 1, Kühn. 417, 2) and the sense of οὐδείς εἰ μή is nothing else than *nemo nisi*, i.e., ' none but '; but all this does not exclude that Jesus, with respect to His higher nature, can Himself belong to this Divine Being: ' and He does not say, " Except my Father " that you may learn, that He did not ἐξεκάλυψεν Himself to the young man ' (Chrysostom)."

[75] " Biblischer Kommentar," [3] i. 1837, pp. 724 f.

[76] On Mark x. 18.

thoroughly as to His Divine-human nature." This interpretation, therefore, readily passes into the essentially different
one — with which we are on the entirely different ground that
Jesus does not in any sense repudiate the goodness attributed
to Him — which understands Jesus in His response to be really
announcing His deity. The transition from the one to the other
of these interpretations is perhaps indicated by such a comment as that of M. Lepin, who writes as follows: [77] " ' Why
callest thou me good? ' says He to the young man who accosts
Him; ' No man is good except God only.' The young man, no
doubt, saw in the Master only an ordinary Rabbi. Seemingly
Jesus refuses, as due to God alone, a title which is given Him
only as man. Perhaps, however, He does not refuse it absolutely, and wishes discreetly to insinuate to His interlocutor, or
to His disciples, who surrounded Him, that He to whom this
title is given and who, as they well know, thoroughly deserves
it, is not merely man but is God also. There is indeed nothing
to show that our Savior wishes formally to decline such an
attribution; that would indeed be strange and out of keeping
with His usual attitude; had He not said, ' Learn of me, for I
am meek and lowly of heart? ' The turn of expression employed,
' Why callest thou me good? ' seems rather intended to cause
the young man to reflect upon the unconscious bearing of his
appellation. It is thus that on another occasion the Divine
Master asked the Jews, ' Why do the Scribes say that the Christ
is the Son of David? ' Considering the subsequent reflection
made by the Savior, the method employed when He remitted
the sins of the paralytic is recalled: ' God only can forgive sins,
as you say; well, I claim to forgive sins; and thus I prove
my authority to do so! ' Similarly here: ' Thou callest me
good. The title is deserved: thou thyself hast judged me in
comparison with ordinary masters; I therefore do not decline
it; but consider well! there is none that is good but God
alone! ' "

A comment like this brings us to the point of turning away

[77] " Jésus Messie et Fils de Dieu.," [3] 1907, pp. 366 ff. (E. T. " Christ and
the Gospel," 1910, pp. 412 ff.).

altogether from the "objurgatory" interpretation of our Lord's demand, "Why callest thou me good?" It remains therefore only to read the question simply as a question, that is to say as an incitement to inquiry on the part of the questioner.[78] In that case only two lines of interpretation lie open. Either the question, along with the succeeding clause, "no one is good but one, God," is intended to suggest to the interlocutor that Jesus is Himself divine, or else it is intended to turn attention for the moment away from Jesus altogether and focus it on God. The former line of interpretation has been taken by many and was for long indeed the ruling view.[79] As so understood, so far from suggesting that our Lord is neither divine nor good, it is an assertion that He is both good and divine. Ambrose will supply us with a good example of this interpretation.[80] Inveighing against the Arians who make out that our Lord here denies that He is good, he asks that we consider when, where and with what circumspection our Lord speaks here. "The Son of God," he continues, "speaks in the form of man, and He speaks to a Scribe, — to him, that is, who called the Son of God 'Good Master,' but denied Him to be God. What he does not believe Christ adds, that he may believe in

78 A. Plummer, commenting on Lk. xx. 42 (p. 473), suggests that the question there may be intended only to make the Scribe think; and illustrates by a reference to our present passage: "The question 'Why callest thou Me good?' appears to serve a similar purpose. It *seems* to imply that Christ is not to be called good (Mk. x. 18). But it need mean no more than that a young man who addressed Jesus as 'Good Master' ought to reflect as to the significance of such language before making use of it." He compares also Lk. xi. 19 as possibly a similar case.

79 Cf. Schanz on Lk. xviii. 19: "The most of the Fathers, if they do not call the question an ensnaring one (*versuta,* Ambrose; *tentans,* Jerome, Cyril) and therefore look upon the reply as a repulse, *arguta responsio,* assume that it is meant for the young man's instruction as to the deity of Christ. Jesus, it is said, reproves the ruler for calling Him a good teacher instead of a good God." He cites as expressing this latter view, Ambrose, Athanasius, Gregory of Nyssa, Gregory of Nazianzus, Basil, Cyril, Chrysostom, Hilary, Jerome, Augustine, Bede. Cf. A. Plummer, on Lk. xviii. 19 (p. 422, note 1), where Cyril and Ambrose are quoted and Jerome, Basil and Epiphanius referred to (with Maldonatus and Wordsworth among the commentators).

80 "De Fide," II, 1 (Migne, "Patr. Lat.," 16, col. 563; E. T. "Post Nicene Fathers," second series, x. p. 226).

the Son of God, not as a Good Master but as the Good God.
For, if wheresoever the ' One God ' is named, the Son of God
is never separated from the fullness of the Unity, how, when
the one God is declared good is the Only-begotten excluded
from the fullness of the divine goodness? They must therefore
either deny that the Son of God is God, or confess that He is
the good God. With heavenly circumspection, then, He said,
not ' No one is good but the Father only,' but ' No one is good
but God only.' For ' Father ' is the proper name of Him who
begets, but the ' one God ' by no means excludes the Godhead
of the Trinity, and therefore extols the Natures: goodness is
therefore in the nature of God, and in the nature of God is also
the Son of God, and therefore what is predicated is not predicated of the Singularity but of the Unity. Goodness is, then,
not denied by the Lord, but such a disciple is rebuked. For
when the Scribe said, ' Good Master,' the Lord responded,
' Why callest thou me good? ' And that means, ' It is not
enough to call me good whom thou dost not believe to be God.
I do not seek such disciples, who rather believe in a good master according to manhood than according to Godhead the good
God."

It is not easy to turn up a modern comment moving on precisely these lines. Perhaps something like it is intended by
Friedrich Köster, when he writes: [81] " Should it, now, seem as
if Jesus in the words, ' Why callest thou me good,' repels the
predicate of goodness from Himself, it is already remarked by
Wolf (in *Curis* ad h. l.), *Haec quaestio non negantis est, sed
examinantis.* ' Dost thou consider well, when thou callest me
good, that this predicate belongs to God alone? ' It belongs to
Jesus, therefore, only by virtue of His perfect union with the
Father." And Rudolf Stier plays upon the same note amid
others which go to make up his chord, when he writes: [82]
" Christ takes care not to say, *I am not good,* for One only is

[81] *TSK*, 1856, p. 422.
[82] " The Words of the Lord Jesus," i. p. 360b. Cf. p. 361a: " Thou
speakest with too much readiness of *doing* good (I too should not be good as
thou thinkest, if I were a man as thou supposest)."

good, *my Father*. . . . He deals more exactly with the word
than the rationalists, who ' exhaust themselves in phrases, call
Him the best, noblest, most excellent, most perfect, etc.,' and
yet deny His divine dignity. He said then to the young ruler
what He must say still more strongly to these modern pane-
gyrists, not in kindness but in anger: ' Why callest thou me
good? ' He, however, at the same time attests His divinity
(although He does not speak plainly of what is concealed)
when He who knew no sin affirms: ' None is good save One,
that is God.' " In support, he quotes in a note [83] the following
dilemma: " Choose then, ye friends of reason, between these
two conclusions dictated by reason itself. None is good but the
one God; Christ is good; therefore Christ is the one God. Or:
none is good but the one God: Christ is not the one God; therefore Christ *is not good*." The sober and pregnant comment of
Bengel may also find a place here. " Nevertheless," he writes,[84]
" He does not say, I am not good; but, Why dost thou call me
good? Just as in Mt. xxii. 43 He does not deny that He, the
son of David, is, at one and the same time, also the Lord of
David. God is good: there is no goodness without Godhead.
This young man perceived in Jesus the presence of goodness in
some degree: otherwise he would not have applied to Him:
but he did not perceive it in the full extent; otherwise he would
not have gone back from Him. Much less did he recognize His
Godhead. Wherefore Jesus does not accept from him the title
of goodness without the title of Godhead (cf. the ' *Why* call ye
me Lord, Lord,' Lk. vi. 46); and thereby He vindicates the
honor of the Father with whom He is one. See Jno. v. 19. At
the same time He causes a ray of His omniscience to enter into
the heart of the young man, and shows that the young man has
not as yet the knowledge concerning Himself, Jesus Christ,
worthy of so exalted a title, which otherwise is altogether appropriate to Him. Wherefore, He does not say, *There is none
good save one, that is my Father,* but, *There is none good save*

[83] From the " Hom. lit. Correspondenzblatt," 1829, p. 176. He tells us
that the same dilemma is well presented also in a sermon by Nitzsch.
[84] Gnomon, on Mk. x. 18.

one, that is, God.' Our Lord often adjusted His words to the capacity of those who questioned Him (Jno. iv. 22)."

Most recent writers, however, who have come to see that our Lord's question is *non negantis sed examinantis*, have also come to see that His purpose here is not inconsequently to proclaim His own deity, but in accordance with the demands of the occasion to point the young man inquiring after a law of life to Him who had once for all proclaimed a perfect law of life.[85] They have, of course, varying ways of expressing the general understanding of the passage common to them all; and they inevitably bring out its implications and connections with more or less completeness, and with more or less penetration.[86] The emphasis seems to be particularly well distributed in a passage in A. Schlatter's " Theology of the New Testament," [87] and we therefore venture to quote it here. " To him who sought from Him, the Good Master, direction as to the work by which he could secure for himself eternal life, He replied that no one

[85] Cf. J. A. Dorner, " Ueber Jesu Sündlosigkeit," 1862, pp. 13–14. After showing that Jesus had no intention of leading the young man to suppose that he could enter into life apart from Him, or of pointing him away from Himself when He pointed him to God, Dorner continues: " But the first thing he had need of, as Jesus saw from the light, easy way in which he used the word ' good ' was self-knowledge, not the announcement of Christ's mission and dignity, for the understanding of which he still lacked the preconditions; concerning which therefore, in accordance with His method as elsewhere manifested, Jesus meanwhile preserved silence. . . . The purpose of the passage is, therefore, not to deny goodness to the person of Christ, nor to make a positive declaration as to what He is, but to rebuke the frivolous attribution of goodness to a teacher at the cost of reverence to God, and by a striking declaration, which would conquer through its humility, to reveal to the young man his fundamental fault, namely that he took goodness too lightly. That Jesus intended to ascribe sinfulness to Himself is impossible, since that would be out of accord with His other self-expressions as to His redemptive vocation, both in the Synoptics and in John, and with the position He takes in the Kingdom of God. The Evangelists too, as little as the primitive church so understood Him. . . ." Dorner thinks, however, that there is nevertheless intrinsic in the passage a contrast between Jesus' goodness, as human, and God's, as absolute — " since no earthly, creaturely goodness can yet be called perfect, because it is not yet perfected, and is not yet raised beyond temptations and change."

[86] See above, note 24, for some of the commentators of this class.

[87] A. Schlatter, " Die Theologie des NTs," i. 1909, p. 302.

is good except God, but God is really good; and instead of
meeting his wish and Himself giving him a commandment, He
binds him to the divine commandments in their simple clearness. The desire to obtain, instead of them, a new prescription
which should now for the first time assure eternal life, Jesus
calls impious, a denial of God, which is made no better by
being attributed to Him too. To permit Himself to be praised
as good, while at the same time, or even thereby, God's goodness is denied, could not be endured by Jesus. Against this kind
of religion He ever spoke as the Son who defended the goodness
of the Father against every doubt, and hallowed His commandments as perfect. A glorifying of His own dignity at the cost of
God's, a trust in His judgment along with distrust in God's
commandments, an exalting of His own goodness along with
reproaches against God — meant to Him absolute impossibility." No doubt, there are elements in this statement which are
open to criticism. But the main matter comes in it to clear
announcement. Jesus' concern here is not to glorify Himself
but God: it is not to give any instruction concerning His own
person whatever, but to indicate the published will of God as
the sole and the perfect prescription for the pleasing of God.
In proportion as we wander away from this central thought,
we wander away from the real meaning of the passage and misunderstand and misinterpret it.[88]

[88] Detached note on some attempts to discover a more original text
than that transmitted by our Gospels, especially F. C. Conybeare's (see notes
35, 36, 37). — H. J. Holtzmann, " Hand-Commentar zum N. T.," i. " Die Synoptiker,"[3] 1901, p. 88, writes: " This section concerning riches early aroused
doubts on the score of the repudiation of the predicate ' good ' (Mk. verse
18 = Lk. verse 19). Instead of recognizing the distinction between deity and
humanity (see on Mt. vi. 12), which is obliterated by Matthew (verse 18)
in a tendential manner, but is otherwise manifoldly witnessed in the early
ecclesiastical literature (Bousset, " Justin," pp. 105 f.), the patristic exegesis
found here instruction on the deity of Christ as if Jesus' reply presented the
major and the address to Him the minor premises of a syllogism, of which the
reader is expected to draw the conclusion." At the place referred to in this
cautious allusion (" Die Evangeliencitate Justins," &c., 1891, pp. 105–106)
Bousset seeks to show from certain early citations of our passage that there
existed an early form of the text — from which Matthew's text was derived
" by dogmatic adjustment " — in which the latter part of our Lord's response

stood something like what we find in Justin, "Dial." 101 [6]: εἶς ἐστιν ἀγαθὸς ὁ
πατήρ μου ὁ ἐν τοῖς οὐρανοῖς. How the first part of our Lord's reply ran, he
seems to be less sure. He supposes, however, that there lay behind Justin
a form of text in which were combined a repudiation of the address of "Good
Master" and a response to the demand "What shall I do to inherit eternal
life?" — much as we find them combined in the Gospel according to the Hebrews. This text, though an earlier source than our Synoptic Gospels, he does
not consider the original text (p. 106, note 3). The form preserved in Justin,
or something like it, he judges to be more likely to be that. In "Dial." 101 [6]
this stands merely τί με λέγεις ἀγαθόν;

In this discussion Bousset makes no advance upon what Hilgenfeld had
argued a half-century before ("Kritische Untersuchungen über die Evangelien
Justins, der Clementinischen Homilien und Marcians," 1850, pp. 220 f., 362,
426; 'Theologische Jahrbücher," 1853, pp. 207, 235 f.; 1857, pp. 414 ff.; cf.
ZWT, 1863, pp. 361–362, note 3). That the reading attributed to Marcion by
Epiphanius, H, 42,[50] p. 339: μή με λέγεις (p. 315 λέγετε) ἀγαθόν, εἶς ἐστιν ἀγαθὸς ὁ
θεὸς ὁ πατήρ is a divergent text-form and not an interpretation, Hilgenfeld is
sure; and that this text form was in circulation beyond Marcionite, or even
Gnostic, circles he thinks is shown by its occurrence four times in the Clementine Homilies ("Theol. Jhbb.," 1857, p. 415). Our present Matthew-text preserves from this earlier form the positive clause εἶς ἐστιν ὁ ἀγαθός. This positive clause is not to be supposed, therefore, to have been made out of the
negative form found in our Mark and Luke: οὐδεὶς ἀγαθὸς εἰ μὴ εἶς ὁ θεός.
The contrary is the fact: the negative clause (first found in Justin, "Apol.,"
i. 16) is rather a correction of the positive clause in an anti-Gnostic interest.
For the Gnostics interpreted the εἶς ἐστιν ὁ ἀγαθὸς ὁ πατήρ (in which the
ὁ πατήρ is the essential thing) as a distinguishing declaration that the only
good God was the Father of Jesus Christ. The difference between the positive
and the negative forms is, then, far from unimportant; it was of deep polemical
significance. "If this difference seems small, it is nevertheless by means of the
negative turn that the contrast between the perfect God and the imperfection
of all men is made the sole possible interpretation. And if, now, in our present
Matthew-text there is apparent a purpose to exclude the distinction of Jesus
from the perfect goodness of God, we recognize in this just a second alteration
of this expression, at the basis of which lies already the doctrine of the deity
of Christ " ("Theol. Jhbb.," 1857, p. 416). It is an illusion to suppose therefore,
that Matthew is made out of Mark: Matthew preserves a reading earlier than
Mark's which Mark has set aside in an anti-Gnostic interest. But our present
Matthew is a product of a still later revision, — in the interests of the deity
of Christ.

A further attempt is made by F. C. Conybeare (*Hibbert Journal*, i. Oct.,
1902, pp. 109–112) to validate the Marcionic text as underlying all three of the
Synoptics, with the interest shifted now, however, to the opening (instead of
the closing) words of our Lord's reply. The contention in which Conybeare is
particularly interested is that, in the original text, we have not a question but
a categorical injunction: "Call me not good!" And he endeavors to show
that this reading held its ground into the fourth century, not in heretical circles
only, but also, as at least an alternative reading, among the orthodox (Origen,

Athanasius, Didymus, Ephrem). Conybeare does not write with judicial balance or in the spirit of scientific objectivity. He has a thesis to sustain, and pushes matters to such an extreme as to be self-refuting. There would be no reason for entering upon any examination of his contentions except for the fact that some tendency has shown itself of late to accept these speculations whether of Hilgenfeld or of Conybeare as findings of fact, and even to build critical conclusions upon them.

Thus, for example, F. Barth, " Die Hauptprobleme des Lebens Jesu," [3] 1907, p. 251, describing Jesus' testimony to His person, writes as follows: " That Jesus . . . saw Himself compelled to make clear His position with reference to God . . . by a self designation, we see better in proportion as we closely contemplate this position in detail and convince ourselves that it is a thoroughly peculiar, almost an enigmatical one. On the one hand, Jesus takes His place wholly on the side of man, over against God, and confesses Himself to possess the imperfections of human existence. He lays claim to no omniscience, but declares that He does not know the time of the parousia (Mk. xiii. 32); nor to any omnipotence, for it is not His to make determination as to the places of honor in the Kingdom of heaven (Mk. x. 40). We may be most struck, however, that He also seems to repudiate absolute moral perfection in the answer to the rich young man who asked Him, ' Good Master, what shall I do to inherit eternal life? ' (Mk. x. 17 f.; Lk. xviii. 18 f.). Jesus responded: ' Why callest thou me good? No one is good but *one,* God.' . . . The reading: ' Why callest thou me good? ' (or ' Call me not good! ') ' No one is good but one, my Father in heaven ' * is no doubt a Gnostic heightening. It would originally emphasize the contrast with the world-maker, the Jewish God, who is not the Father of Jesus and not good (gracious), but righteous and wrathful. The Catholic counterpart to this is formed by the rare reading: " No one is good except God only who has made all things "; here the sole good one is identified precisely with the world-maker. Still more decisively in contrast with it is the change which the Gospel of Matthew contains. . . ." At the point marked by an asterisk he gives a list of vouchers which certainly show that a reading in which " the Father " or " my Father who is in heaven " took the place of " God " in our Lord's response was in early circulation: but it is not so clear that this reading was manufactured by the Gnostics, though no doubt it was utilized by them; and neither is it clear that the alternative reading in the first clause " Call me not good " is a genuine " various reading." And it is certainly not clear that the readings which Barth enumerates, Justin's and Matthew's, illustrate how readily " uncomfortable readings are pushed out of existence." An even better example of the unjustified use of these textual speculations is supplied by Paul Feine, " Theologie des NTs," 1910, p. 28, note, who, in explaining the meaning of our Lord in His response to the young ruler, incorporates, quite simply, these words: " When Jesus says to the rich young man: ' Why callest thou me good? ' or ' Call me not good ' (μή με λέγε ἀγαθόν, as Conybeare, *Hibbert Journal,* 1902, i. 96–113, represents the oldest form, after Marcion, the Clementine Homilies, Tatian, Origen, etc., in Mk. and Lk. xviii. 19). . . ." A phenomenon like this seems to require that we should subject Conybeare's argument to a sufficiently close scrutiny to bring out its real character.

Conybeare is engaged in seeking out doctrinal modifications of the original text occurring in the text of our Gospels. In the present state of critical opinion it is not unnatural that he fixes at once upon Mt. xix. 17 as an instance. This " bit of botching," as he calls it, however, contrary to the common critical opinion, he attributes not to the author of the Gospel, but, in accordance with his present quest, to an ancient corrector, working on the original text of Matthew " before Matthew was joined in one book with the other two gospels." He is not content however to find " doctrinal modifications " in Matthew's text; he discovers them in the text of Mark and Luke as well. The evidence on which he relies for this discovery, he gives as follows. Marcion, according to Epiphanius, read at Lk. xviii. 19: μή με λέγε ἀγαθόν εἶς ἐστιν ἀγαθὸς ὁ θεὸς ὁ πατήρ. "" Marcion's evidence goes back far behind any other." It is a priori unlikely, from Marcion's philosophical views, that he himself made the reading, " Call me not good." And that he did not make it is put beyond doubt by its appearance in the Clementine Homilies also, where, although it appears rather as a citation from Matthew than from Mark-Luke, it a fortiori argues the presence of the imperative reading in Mark-Luke. All this is borne out by the persistence of the imperative reading in later writings. In the Old Armenian version of a tract of Athanasius', it appears four times, and though in the present Greek text it is found in only one of these places, the editor tells us it occurs in the best manuscripts in another of them; and we may believe that if the best manuscripts were scrupulously followed it would occur in all four of them. It seems to be presupposed in certain passages in the Armenian version of Ephrem's commentary on Tatian's " Diatessaron," " though the actual citations have been conformed to the ordinary text." It seems likewise to be presupposed in some passages in Origen's commentaries " though the text has been conformed either by the scribes or editors of his MSS."

As marshalled by Conybeare there seems to be presented here a considerable body of evidence. This is, however, illusory. The whole of the later evidence, from Origen to Didymus and Ephrem, may be at once dismissed. No question of reading is raised by it but only of interpretation. To suggest that Tatian must have read the imperative in his text because Ephrem, in commenting on this passage, speaks of Christ as " renouncing the appellation of ' good ' " is nothing less than monstrous (cf. Zahn's " Tatians Diatessaron," p. 173). To intimate that Origen must have read the imperative in his text, because he understands the Lord to reject the epithet " good," is so absurd that it reaches almost the level of the sublime. Not only does Origen repeatedly quote the passage and always with the interrogative, not the imperative (e.g. in the first two volumes of the Prussian Academy's edition, I, 9, 5; II, 12, 19; II, 355, 16; in the Commentary on John in the same series, 45, 10; 261, 28); but he explicitly tells us that the interrogative stood in his text of Mark and Luke, — that while Matthew reads, " Why askest thou me concerning the good," " Mark and Luke on the contrary say that the Savior said: ' Why callest thou me good? No one is good except one, God ' " (" Com. in Mt.," Tomus xv. 10; Lommatzsch iii. p. 346). Conybeare's dealing with Athanasius and Didymus, however, is so characteristic and therefore so instructive as regards his methods, that it deserves to be quoted at large and examined in some detail. " Among the writings of Athanasius," he writes, " is one called

'About the Epiphany of the Flesh of the God word and against the Arians,' printed in Migne, "Pat. Graec.," xxvi. coll. 984 ff. The text is cited from Mark or Luke four times, viz., col. 985c, col. 993a and b, col. 1012b. In only one of these passages, 993b, has the imperative, μή με λέγε ἀγαθόν survived the efforts both of editor and copyist to keep it out, and won its way into the printed text. But in 985c the editor, Montfaucon, in his note states that it was so read in the three best MSS. In all four passages the Old Armenian version renders, 'Call thou me not good,' so testifying that the Greek MSS. had it. Probably a more accurate editing of these would show that they have it still. In his treatise on the Trinity (c. 337) Didymus also cites the text in the form 'Call thou me not good,' but with condemnation." Possibly it is Conybeare's predilection for things Armenian which has led him astray with reference to Athanasius' reading. The fact is that Athanasius cites the text of Mark and Luke in the form in which it now finds a place in these Gospels, and never otherwise. It stands in this form, therefore in 993a and 1012b where he is directly citing the text: in 993b he is not making a citation; and in 985c, he is citing the text not directly but from the lips of his Arian opponents. There is no evidence to be derived from these passages, therefore, that the text was read by Athanasius in the form " Call me not good." It will repay us to look at the passages.

In 1012b, Athanasius is directly citing Scripture to support a proposition. He argues: " For unless the Holy Spirit were of the essence (τῆς οὐσίας) of the Only Good (τοῦ μόνου ἀγαθοῦ) He would not be called good, since the Lord prohibits Himself to be called good, in so far as He had become man, saying, ' Why callest thou me good? None is good but one, God.' The Holy Spirit, however, is not forbidden by the Scriptures to be called good, as David says, ' Thy good Spirit shall lead me into the right land.' " What we read in the continuous passage embracing both the references, 993a and b, is this: " And when He says: ' Why callest thou me good? No one is good but one, God,' God, reckoning Himself among men, spoke this according to His flesh, and with respect to the opinion of him who came to Him. For that one thought Him man only and not God, and the response keeps this opinion in view. For, if you think me a man, He says, and not God, call me not good, for no one is good. For the good does not belong to human nature but to God." Obviously the " Call me not good " here is not a citation but a free rendering of the sense of the "Why callest thou me good? " which is immediately before formally cited. The final passage, 985c, is more complicated. Athanasius is talking of his Arian opponents. " And now, these people," he says, " if they knew the Holy Scriptures, would not dare to blaspheme the Creator of all things as a creature and a piece of handiwork. For they distort them to us, saying How can [the Son] be like [the Father], or of the Father's essence, when it is written, As the Father has life in Himself, So He has given also to the Son to have life in Himself. There is, they say, a superiority in the giver above the receiver. And, Why callest thou me good? they say, No one is good but one, God. And again, My God, my God, why hast thou forsaken me? And once more, Of the last day no one knoweth, not even the Son, except the Father. And again, Whom the Father sanctified and sent into the world. And again, Whom the Father raised from the dead. How then, they say, can He that is raised from the dead be like or of the same nature (ὁμοούσιος) with Him that raised Him?" Here is a series of Scriptural texts in use by the Arians and cited from their lips — Jno. v. 26; Mk. x. 18; Mt. xxvii. 47; Mk. xiii. 2; Jno. x. 26; Gal. i. 1. Some of them are quoted with accuracy (Jno. v. 26; Mt. xxvii. 47; Jno. x. 36). But some of them merely reproduce the sense (Gal. i. 1). Mk. x. 18 is printed as an accurate quotation. But the editor tells us in a note (Migne, "Pat. Graec.," xxvi. col. 986) that in some of the MSS. it is read rather: μή με λέγε, φησίν, ἀγαθόν, that is to say, "Call me not, they say, good." It may well be, as Conybeare contends, that this reading should be put into the text. In this context this would not mean that Athanasius so read it in his Mark, but only at the most that the Arians so read it in their Mark. We say "at the most," for there would be little more reason for supposing that even they so read it in their Mark than for supposing that they read also in their Mark (at xiii. 32): περὶ τῆς ἡμέρας τῆς ἐσχάτης οὐδεὶς οἶδεν, οὐδὲ ὁ υἱός. If this is merely a paraphrase of the meaning, that may equally well be so too.

We presume that the "c. 377" attached to the reference to Didymus' treatise on the Trinity is meant to indicate the column in Migne, "Pat. Graec.," where the passage referred to may be found. No such passage, however, is found at that reference. In coll. 349–352, however, there is a passage which we take to be the one intended. Heb. ii. 24 had just been quoted and commented on; and the discourse continues: "The Son also, however, showed that the deity is one, when He said, 'Why callest thou me good? No one is good but one, God'; but that the three hypostases are of equal dignity and of equal power, by the teaching concerning baptism [that is, by Mt. xxviii. 19]. Not responding to the lawyer who questioned Him temptingly, 'Call me not good' but 'Why callest thou me good?' He showed that He too is good equally with the Father, and from His Father's goodness manifests His own, and demonstrates that He is good generated from God. . . ." It is, of course, conceivable that Didymus is referring here to a rival reading of Mk. x. 18 rejected by him. But there is no likelihood of that being the case. On the face of it, what he says is that this reading is not found in Mk. x. 18. We observe in passing that Didymus elsewhere also quotes Mk. x. 18 in the form "Why callest thou me good?" without betraying any consciousness of another reading; e.g. at col. 864: "And the response to the lawyer who temptingly addressed our Lord as a man, 'Good Master' and heard 'Why callest thou me good?' . . . is of this kind."

Thus nothing is left as evidence of the currency of a reading "Call me not good"! but Epiphanius' representation that this was the reading of Marcion's Gospel, supported by the appearance of the passage in this form in the Clementine Homilies. Conybeare seems very sure that Marcion's text read as Epiphanius represents. A glance at the very full note of Zahn at the place ("Geschichte des Neutestamentlichen Kanons,"[1] ii. 1890, pp. 483–484) will show how little this confidence is justified. Zahn himself prints Marcion's text in the hesitant form: τί (or μή) με λέγετε ἀγαθόν; εἷς ἐστὶν ἀγαθός, ὁ (?) θεὸς ὁ πατήρ (?); tells us that it is "variously transmitted"; and suggests that the μή transmitted by Epiphanius may be only a transcriptional error for τί, — unless, he adds, the τί transmitted by Hippolytus is a transcriptional error for μή." We ought not to let it fall out of sight, that there is no evidence for the currency of the phrase "Call me not good," as a reading at Mk. x. 18, Lk. xviii. 19, Mt. xix. 17, earlier than the fourth century, for it seems that the Clementine Homilies should be assigned to that century (cf. Dom Chapman, *ZNTW*, ix. 1908). When Hippolytus ("Refut.," vii. 19) cites this text from a Marcionite book — apparently from Marcion himself — he gives it in the form, τί με λέγετε ἀγαθόν; our own inclination is to suppose that the reading μή με λέγε ἀγαθόν stood in Marcion's Gospel as it was in circulation in the fourth century, but was not original in it. We are led to this view by the circumstance that in the Clementine Homilies too (where this reading occurs four times; iii. 57, xvii. 4, xviii. 1, 3) it seems to appear (xviii. 1) as a Marcionite reading (Zahn, pp. 469, 483). But it is to be observed that in this understanding of the matter, all appeal to the Clementine Homilies as evidence that this reading was in circulation elsewhere than in Marcionite circles, or earlier than the fourth century, is precluded. Conybeare is as sure that Marcion (he would doubtless extend this to the Marcionites as a body) could not have invented the reading "Call me not good" as that it was read by Marcion. One would think a simple reading of Hippolytus' chapter just referred to ("Refut.," vii. 19) would disabuse anyone's mind of this misjudgment. Whether, however, the reading arose by "doctrinal modification" on the part of the Marcionites or by simple transcriptional error as Zahn supposes, is of little moment. The point of importance is that there is no convincing evidence that such a reading was known earlier than the fourth century and no evidence whatever that it ever had any currency outside (later) Marcionite circles and perhaps among the Arians, to whom it was transmitted by the Clementine Homilies; for this is apparently the significance of the Clementine Homilies in this matter — that they formed the connecting link between Marcionite and Arian. It is meaningless, therefore, when Conybeare remarks: "Marcion's evidence goes back far behind any other," though that remark would be inexplicable in any case. It is probably not Marcion's personal evidence that is in question, but only that of the later Marcionites. And were it his personal evidence that was in question, Justin who quotes the text in the interrogative form was his strict contemporary, Tatian but a little younger contemporary, to say nothing of Marcosians and Naasenes with whom Irenaeus and Hippolytus connect the text in its interrogative form. In any case the total direct transmission of the text of the New Testament is not to be treated with this levity. On the face of it, apart from all citations of as early a date as Marcion, the text as set down in the critical editions of the New Testament is older than Marcion and was already in his day in wide circulation in versions as well as in the original Greek. When we speak in terms of relative originality — instead of in those of mere chronology — there is no room for question here. Any history which may be back of our existent manuscript-text of Mark and Luke in this passage (as indeed of that of Matthew too) is not a textual history but a literary history. What emerges from the ruck of confusion into which Conybeare has gratuitously cast the matter is thus simply that there may have been in circulation in heretical circles in the fourth century a reading in Mk. x. 18 or Luke xviii. 19 which substituted an imperative for the interrogatory form. Needless to say such a fact affords no slightest justification for looking upon this form as "the original" form.

IV
JESUS CHRIST

JESUS CHRIST [1]

THE rise of Christianity was a phenomenon of too little apparent significance to attract the attention of the great world. It was only when it had refused to be quenched in the blood of its founder, and, breaking out of the narrow bounds of the obscure province in which it had its origin, was making itself felt in the centers of population, that it drew to itself a somewhat irritated notice. The interest of such heathen writers as mention it was in the movement, not in its author. But in speaking of the movement they tell something of its author, and what they tell is far from being of little moment. He was, it seems, a certain " Christ," who had lived in Judea in the reign of Tiberius (14–37 A.D.), and had been brought to capital punishment by the procurator, Pontius Pilate (q.v.; cf. Tacitus, " Annals," xv. 44). The significance of His personality to the movement inaugurated by Him is already suggested by the fact that He, and no other, had impressed His name upon it. But the name itself by which He was known particularly attracts notice. This is uniformly, in these heathen writers, " Christ," not " Jesus." [2] Suetonius (" Claudius," xxv.) not unnaturally confuses this " Christus " with the Greek name " Chrestus "; but Tacitus and Pliny show themselves better informed and preserve it accurately. " Christ," however, is not a personal name, but the Greek rendering of the Hebrew title " Messiah." Clearly, then, it was as the promised Messiah of the Jews that their founder was reverenced by " the Christians "; and they had made so much of his Messiahship in speaking of Him that

[1] Article " Jesus Christ " from " The New Schaff-Herzog Encyclopedia of Religious Knowledge," vi. pp. 150–160. Pub. N. Y. & Lond., Funk & Wagnalls Co., [1910].

[2] In Josephus, *Ant.* XVIII., iii. 3, XX., ix. 1, " Jesus," " Jesus, surnamed Christ," occur. But the authenticity of the passages is questionable, especially that of the former.

the title " Christ " had actually usurped the place of his personal name, and He was everywhere known simply as " Christ." Their reverence for His person had, indeed, exceeded that commonly supposed to be due even to the Messianic dignity. Pliny records that this " Christ " was statedly worshipped by " the Christians " of Pontus and Bithynia as their God (Pliny, " Epist.," xcvi. [xcvii.] to Trajan). Beyond these great facts the heathen historians give little information about the founder of Christianity.

What is lacking in them is happily supplied, however, by the writings of the Christians themselves. Christianity was from its beginnings a literary religion, and documentary records of it have come down from the very start. There are, for example, the letters of the Apostle Paul (q.v.), a highly cultured Romanized Jew of Tarsus, who early (34 or 35 A.D.) threw in his fortunes with the new religion, and by his splendid leadership established it in the chief centers of influence from Antioch to Rome. Written occasionally to one or another of the Christian communities of this region, at intervals during the sixth and seventh decades of the century, that is to say, from twenty to forty years after the origin of Christianity, these letters reflect the conceptions which ruled in the Christian communities of the time. Paul had known the Christian movement from its beginning; first from the outside, as one of the chief agents in its persecution, and then from the inside, as the most active leader of its propaganda. He was familiarly acquainted with the Apostles and other immediate followers of Jesus, and enjoyed repeated intercourse with them. He explicitly declares the harmony of their teaching with his, and joins with his their testimony to the great facts which he proclaimed. The complete consonance of his allusions to Jesus with what is gathered from the hints of the heathen historians is very striking. The person of Jesus fills the whole horizon of his thought, and gathers to itself all his religious emotions. That Jesus was the Messiah is the presupposition of all his speech of Him, and the Messianic title has already become his proper name behind which His real personal name, Jesus, has retired. This Messiah

is definitely represented as a divine being who has entered the
world on a mission of mercy to sinful man, in the prosecution
of which He has given Himself up as a sacrifice for sin, but has
risen again from the dead and ascended to the right hand of
God, henceforth to rule as Lord of all. Around the two great
facts, of the expiatory death of the Son of God and his rising
again, Paul's whole teaching circles. Jesus Christ as crucified,
Christ risen from the dead as the first fruits of those that
sleep — here is Paul's whole gospel in summary.

Into the details of Christ's earthly life Paul had no occasion to enter. But he shows himself fully familiar with them,
and incidentally conveys a vivid portrait of Christ's personality. Of the seed of David on the human, as the Son of God on
the divine side, He was born of a woman, under the law, and
lived subject to its ordinances for His mission's sake, humbling
Himself even unto death, and that the death of the cross. His
lowly estate is dwelt upon, and the high traits of His personal
character manifested in His lowliness are lightly sketched in,
justifying not merely the negative declaration that " He knew
no sin," but his positive presentation as the model of all perfection. An item of His teaching is occasionally adverted to, or
even quoted, always with the utmost reverence. Members of
His immediate circle of followers are mentioned by name or by
class — whether His brethren according to the flesh or the
twelve apostles whom He appointed. The institution by Him
of a sacramental feast is described, and that of a companion
sacrament of initiation by baptism is implied. But especially
His sacrificial death on the cross is emphasized, His burial, His
rising again on the third day, and His appearances to chosen
witnesses, who are cited one after the other with the greatest
solemnity. Such details are never communicated to Paul's
readers as pieces of fresh information. They are alluded to as
matters of common knowledge, and with the plainest intimation of the unquestioned recognition of them by all. Thus it is
made clear not only that there underlies Paul's letters a complete portrait of Jesus and a full outline of his career, but that
this portrait and this outline are the universal possession of

Christians. They were doubtless as fully before his mind as such in the early years of his Christian life, in the thirties, as when he was writing his letters in the fifties and sixties. There is no indication in the way in which Paul touches on these things of a recent change of opinion regarding them or of a recent acquisition of knowledge of them. The testimony of Paul's letters, in a word, has retrospective value, and is contemporary testimony to the facts.

Paul's testimony alone provides thus an exceptionally good basis for the historical verity of Jesus' personality and career. But Paul's testimony is far from standing alone. It is fully supported by the testimony of a series of other writings, similar to his own, purporting to come from the hands of early teachers of the Church, most of them from actual companions of our Lord and eye-witnesses of His majesty, and handed down to us with credible evidence of their authenticity. And it is extended by the testimony of a series of writings of a very different character; not occasional letters designed to meet particular crises or questions arising in the churches, but formal accounts of Jesus' words and acts.

Among these attention is attracted first by a great historical work, the two parts of which bear the titles of " the Gospel according to Luke " and " the Acts of the Apostles." The first contains an account of Jesus' life from His birth to His death and resurrection; or, including the opening paragraphs of the second, to His ascension. What directs attention to it first among books of its class is the uncommonly full information possessed concerning its writer and his method of historical composition. It is the work of an educated Greek physician, known to have enjoyed, as a companion of Paul, special opportunities of informing himself of the facts of Jesus' career. Whatever Paul himself knew of the acts and teachings of his Lord was, of course, the common property of the band of missionaries which traveled in his company, and could not fail to be the subject of much public and private discussion among them. Among Paul's other companions there could not fail to be some whose knowledge of Jesus' life, direct or derived, was considerable; an example is found, for instance, in John Mark, who had come out of the immediate circle of Jesus' first followers, although precise knowledge of the meeting of Luke and Mark as fellow companions of Paul belongs to a little later period than the composition of Luke's Gospel. In company with Paul Luke had even visited Jerusalem and had resided two years at Cæsarea in touch with primitive disciples; and if the early tradition which represents him as a native of Antioch be accepted, he must be credited with facilities from the beginning of his Christian life for association with original disciples of Jesus. All that is needed to ground great confidence in his narrative as a trustworthy account of the facts it records is assurance that he had the will and capacity to make good use of his abounding opportunities for exact information. The former is afforded by the preface to his Gospel in which he reveals his method as a historian and his zeal for exactness of information and statement; the latter by the character of the Gospel, which evinces itself at every point a sincere and careful narrative resting upon good and well-sifted information. In these circumstances the determination of the precise time when this narrative was actually committed to paper becomes a matter of secondary importance; in any event its material was collected during the period of Paul's missionary activity. It may be confidently maintained, however, that it was also put together during this period, that is to say, during the earlier years of the seventh decade of the century. Confidence in its narrative is strengthened by the complete accord of the portrait of Jesus, which its detailed account exhibits with that which underlies the letters of Paul. Not only are the general traits of the personality identical, but the emphasis falls at the same places. In effect, the Jesus of Luke's narrative is the Christ of Paul's epistles in perfect dramatic presentation, and only two hypotheses offer themselves in possible explanation. Either Luke rests on Paul, and has with consummate art invented a historical basis for Paul's ideal Christ; or else Paul's allusions rest on a historical basis and Luke has preserved that historical basis in his careful, detailed narrative. Every line of Luke's narrative refutes the former and demonstrates the latter supposition.

Additional evidence of the trustworthiness of Luke's Gospel as an account of Jesus' acts and teaching is afforded by the presence by its side of other narratives of similar character and accordant contents. These narratives are two in number and have been handed down under the names of members of the earliest circle of Christians — of John Mark, who was from the beginning in the closest touch with the apostolic body, and of Matthew, one of the apostles. On comparison of these narratives with Luke's, not only are they found to present, each with its own peculiar point of view and purpose, precisely the same conception and portrait of Jesus, but to have utilized in large measure also the same sources of information. Indeed, the entire body of Mark's Gospel is found to be incorporated also in Matthew's and Luke's.

This circumstance, in view of the declarations of Luke's preface, is of the utmost significance for an estimate of the trustworthiness of the narrative thus embodied in all three of the " Synoptic " Gospels. In this preface Luke professes to have had for his object the establishment of absolute " certainty," with respect to the things made the object of instruction in Christian circles; and to this end to have grounded his narrative in exact investigation of the course of events from the beginning. In the prosecution of this task, he knew himself to be working in a goodly company to a common end, namely, the narration of the Christian origins on the basis of the testimony of those ministers of the word who had been also " eye-witnesses from the beginning." He does not say whether these fellow narrators had or had not been, some or all of them, eye-witnesses of some or of all the events they narrated; he merely says that the foundation on which all the narratives he has in view rested was the testimony of eye-witnesses. He does not assert for his own treatise superiority to those of his fellow workers; he only claims an honorable place for his own treatise among the others on the ground of the diligence and care he has exercised in ascertaining and recording the facts, through which, he affirms, he has attained a certainty with regard to them on which his readers may depend. Now, on comparing the narrative of Luke with those of Matthew and Mark, it is discovered that one of the main sources on which Luke draws is also one of the main sources on which Matthew draws and practically the sole source on which Mark rests. Thus Luke's judgment of the value and trustworthiness of this source receives the notable support of the judgment of his fellow evangelists, and it can scarcely be doubted that what it contains is the veritable tradition of those who were as well eye-witnesses as ministers of the Word from the beginning, in whose accuracy confidence can be placed. If the three Synoptic Gospels do not give three independent testimonies to the facts which they record, they give what is, perhaps, better, — three independent witnesses to the trustworthiness of the narrative, which they all incorporate into their own as resting on autoptic testimony and thoroughly deserving of credit. A narrative lying at the basis of all three of these Gospels, themselves written certainly not later than the seventh decade of the century, must in any event be early in date, and in that sense must emanate from the first followers of Christ; and in the circumstances — of the large and confident use made of it by all three of these Gospels — cannot fail to be an authentic statement of what was the conviction of the earliest circles of Christians.

By the side of this ancient body of narrative must be placed another equally, or perhaps, even more ancient source, consisting largely, but not exclusively, of reports of " sayings of Jesus." This underlies much of the fabric of Luke and Matthew where Mark fails, and by their employment of it is authenticated as containing, as Luke asserts, the trustworthy testimony of eye-witnesses. Its great antiquity is universally allowed, and there is no doubt that it comes from the very bosom of the Apostolical circle, bearing independent but thoroughly consentient testimony, with the narrative source which underlies all three of the Synoptists, of what was understood by the primitive Christian community to be the facts regarding Jesus. This is the fundamental fact about these two sources — that

the Jesus which they present is the same Jesus; and that this
Jesus is precisely the same Jesus found in the Synoptic Gospels
themselves, presented, moreover, in precisely the same fashion
and with the emphases in precisely the same places. This
latter could, of course, not fail to be the case since these sources
themselves constitute the main substance of the Synoptic Gospels into which they have been transfused. Its significance is
that the portrait of Jesus as the supernatural Son of God who
came into the world as the Messiah on a mission of mercy to
sinful men, which is reflected even in the scanty notices of him
that find an incidental place in the pages of heathen historians,
which suffused the whole preaching of Paul and of the other
missionaries of the first age, and which was wrought out into
the details of a rich dramatization in the narratives of the
Synoptic Gospels, is as old as Christianity itself and comes
straight from the representations of Christ's first followers.

Valuable, however, as the separation out from the Synoptic
narrative of these underlying sources is in this aspect of the
matter, appeal cannot be made from the Synoptics to these
sources as from less to more trustworthy documents. On the
one hand, these sources do not exist outside the Synoptics; in
them they have "found their grave." On the other hand, the
Synoptics in large part are these sources; and their trustworthiness as wholes is guaranteed by the trustworthiness of
the sources from which they have drawn the greater part of
their materials, and from the general portraiture of Christ in
which they do not in the least depart. Luke's claim in his
preface that he has made accurate investigations, seeking to
learn exactly what happened that he might attain certainty in
his narrative, is expressly justified for the larger part of his
narrative when the sources which underlie it are isolated and
are found to approve themselves under every test as excellent.
There is no reason to doubt that for the remainder of his narrative (and Matthew too for the remainder of his narrative)
not derived from these two sources which the accident of their
common use by Matthew, Mark, and Luke, or by Matthew and
Luke, reveals, he (or Matthew) derives his material from

equally good and trustworthy sources which happen to be used only by him. The general trustworthiness of Luke's narrative is not lessened but enhanced by the circumstance that, in the larger portion of it, he has the support of other evangelists in his confident use of his sources, with the effect that these sources can be examined and an approving verdict reached upon them. His judgment of sources is thus confirmed, and his claim to possess exact information and to have framed a trustworthy narrative is vindicated. What he gives from sources which were not used by the other evangelists, that is to say, in that portion of his narrative which is peculiar to himself (and the same must be said for Matthew, *mutatis mutandis*), has earned a right to credit on his own authentication. It is not surprising, therefore, that the portions of the narratives of Matthew and Luke which are peculiar to the one or the other bear every mark of sincere and well-informed narration and contain many hints of resting on good and trustworthy sources. In a word, the Synoptic Gospels supply a threefold sketch of the acts and teachings of Christ of exceptional trustworthiness. If here is not historical verity, historical verity would seem incapable of being attained, recorded, and transmitted by human hands.

Along with the Synoptic Gospels there has been handed down by an unexceptionable line of testimony under the name of the Apostle John, another narrative of the teaching and work of Christ of equal fulness with that of the Synoptic Gospels, and yet so independent of theirs as to stand out in a sense in strong contrast with theirs, and even to invite attempts to establish a contradiction between it and them. There is, however, no contradiction, but rather a deep-lying harmony. There are so-called Synoptical traits discoverable in John, and not only are Johannine elements imbedded in the Synoptical narrative, but an occasional passage occurs in it which is almost more Johannine than John himself. Take, for example, that pregnant declaration recorded in Matt. xi. 27–28, which, as it occurs also in Luke (x. 21, 22), must have had a place in that ancient source drawn on in common by these two Gospels which comes from the first days of Christianity. All the high teaching of John's Gospel, as has been justly remarked, is but " a series of variations " upon the theme here given its " classical expression." The type of teaching which is brought forward and emphasized by John is thus recognized on all hands from the beginning to have had a place in Christ's teaching; and John differs from the Synoptics only in the special aspect of Christ's teaching which he elects particularly to present. The naturalness of this type of teaching on the lips of the Jesus of the Synoptists is also undeniable; it must be allowed — and is now generally allowed — that by the writers of the Synoptic Gospels, and, it should be added, by their sources as well, Jesus is presented, and is presented as representing Himself, as being all that John represents Him to be when he calls Him the Word, who was in the beginning with God and was God. The relation of John and the Synoptists in their portraiture of Jesus somewhat resembles, accordingly, that of Plato and Xenophon in their portraiture of Socrates; only, with this great difference — that both Plato and Xenophon were primarily men of letters and the portrait they draw of Socrates is in the hands of both alike eminently a sophisticated and literary one, while the Evangelists set down simply the facts as they appealed to them severally. The definite claim which John's Gospel makes to be the work of one of the inner circle of the companions of Jesus is supported, moreover, by copious evidence that it comes from the hands of such a one as a companion of Jesus would be — a Jew, who possessed an intimate knowledge of Palestine, and was acquainted with the events of our Lord's life as only an eye-witness could be acquainted with them, and an eye-witness who had been admitted to very close association with Him. That its narrative rests on good information is repeatedly manifested; and more than once historical links are supplied by it which are needed to give clearness to the Synoptical narrative, as, for example, in the chronological framework of the ministry of Jesus and the culminating miracle of the raising of Lazarus, which is required to account for the incidents of the Passion-Week. It presents no different Jesus from the Jesus of the Synoptists, and it throws the emphasis at the same place — on His expiatory death and rising again; but it notably supplements the narrative of the Synoptists and reveals a whole new side of Jesus' ministry, and if not a wholly new aspect of His teaching, yet a remarkable mass of that higher aspect of His teaching of which only occasional specimens are included in the Synoptic narrative. John's narrative thus rounds out the Synoptical narrative and gives the portrait drawn in it a richer content and a greater completeness.

This portrait may itself be confidently adduced as its own warranty. It is not too much to say with Nathaniel Lardner that " the history of the New Testament has in it all the marks of credibility that any history can have." But apart from these more usually marshaled evidences of the trustworthiness of the narratives, there is the portrait itself which they draw, and this cannot by any possibility have been an invention. It is not merely that the portrait is harmonious throughout — in the allusions and presuppositions of the Epistles of Paul and the other letter-writers of the New Testament, in the detailed narratives of the Synoptists and John, and in each of the sources which underlie them. This is a matter of importance; but it is not the matter of chief moment; there is no need to dwell upon the impossibility of such a harmony having been maintained save on the basis of simple truthfulness of record, or to dispute whether in the case of the Synoptics there are three independent witnesses to the one portrait, or only the two independent witnesses of their two most prominent " sources." Nor is the most interesting point whether the aboriginality of this portrait is guaranteed by the harmony of the representation in all the sources of information, some of which reach back to the most primitive epoch of the Christian movement. It is quite certain that this conception of Christ's person and career was the conception of his immediate followers, and indeed of himself; but, important as this conclusion is, it is still not the matter of primary import. The matter of primary significance is that this portrait thus imbedded in all the authoritative sources of information, and thus proved to be the conception of its founder cherished by the whole of primitive Christendom, and indeed commended to it by that founder himself, is a portrait intrinsically incapable of invention by men. It could never have come into being save as the revelation of an actual person embodying it, who really lived among men. " A romancer," as even Albert Réville allows, " can not attribute to a being which he creates an ideal superior to what he himself is capable of conceiving." The conception of the God-man which is embodied in the portrait which the sources draw of Christ, and which is dramatized by them through such a history as they depict, can be accounted for only on the assumption that such a God-man actually lived, was seen of men, and was painted from the life. The miracle of the invention of such a portraiture, whether by the conscious effort of art, or by the unconscious working of the mythopeic fancy, would be as great as the actual existence of such a person. Of this there is sufficient *a posteriori* proof in the invariable deterioration this portrait suffers in its secondary reproductions — in the so-called " Lives of Christ," of every type. The attempt vitally to realize and reproduce it results inevitably in its reduction. A portraiture which cannot even be interpreted by men without suffering serious loss cannot be the invention of the first simple followers of Jesus. Its very existence in their unsophisticated narratives is the sufficient proof of its faithfulness to a great reality.

Only an outline of this portrait can be set down here. Jesus appears in it not only a supernatural, but in all the sources alike specifically a divine, person, who came into the world on a mission of mercy to sinful man. Such a mission was in its essence a humiliation and involved humiliation at every step of its accomplishment. His life is represented accordingly as a life of difficulty and conflict, of trial and suffering, issuing in a shameful death. But this humiliation is represented as in every step and stage of it voluntary. It was entered into and abided in solely in the interests of His mission, and did not argue at any point of it helplessness in the face of the difficulties which hemmed Him in more and more until they led Him to death on the cross. It rather manifested His strong determination to fulfil His mission to the end, to drink to its dregs the cup He had undertaken to drink. Accordingly, every suggestion of escape from it by the use of His intrinsic divine powers, whether of omnipotence or of omniscience, was treated by Him first and last as a temptation of the evil one. The death in which His life ends is conceived, therefore, as the goal in which His life culminates. He came into the world to die, and every stage of the road that led up to this issue was determined not for Him but by Him: He was never the victim but always the Master of circumstance, and pursued His pathway from beginning to end, not merely in full knowledge from the start of all its turns and twists up to its bitter conclusion, but in complete control both of them and of it.

His life of humiliation, sinking into His terrible death, was therefore not his misfortune, but His achievement as the promised Messiah, by and in whom the kingdom of God is to be established in the world; it was the work which as Messiah he came to do. Therefore, in his prosecution of it, He from the beginning announced himself as the Messiah, accepted all ascriptions to him of Messiahship under whatever designation, and thus gathered up into His person all the preadumbrations of Old-Testament prophecy; and by His favorite self-designation of " Son of Man," derived from Daniel's great vision (vii. 13), continually proclaimed Himself the Messiah he actually was, emphasizing in contrast with His present humiliation His heavenly origin and His future glory. Moreover, in the midst of His humiliation, He exercised, so far as that was consistent with the performance of his mission, all the prerogatives of that " transcendent " or divine Messiah which He was. He taught with authority, substituting for every other sanction His great " But I say unto you," and declaring Himself greater than the greatest of God's representatives whom He had sent in all the past to visit His people. He surrounded Himself as He went about preaching the Gospel of the kingdom with a miraculous nimbus, each and every miracle in which was adapted not merely to manifest the presence of a supernatural person in the midst of the people, but, as a piece of symbolical teaching, to reveal the nature of this supernatural person, and to afford a foretaste of the blessedness of His rule in the kingdom He came to found. He assumed plenary authority over the religious ordinances of the people, divinely established though they were; and exercised absolute control over the laws of nature themselves. The divine prerogative of forgiving sins he claimed for Himself, the divine power of reading the heart He frankly exercised, the divine function of judge of quick and dead he attached to His own person. Asserting for Himself a superhuman dignity of person, or rather a share in the ineffable Name itself, He represented Himself as abiding continually even when on earth in absolute communion with God the Father, and participating by necessity of nature in the treasures of the divine knowledge and grace; announced Himself the source of all divine knowledge and grace to men; and drew to Himself all the religious affections, suspending the destinies of men absolutely upon their relation to His own person. Nevertheless he walked straight onward in the path of His lowly mission, and, bending even the wrath of men to his service, gave Himself in his own good time and way to the death He had come to accomplish. Then, His mission performed, He rose again from the dead in the power of His deathless life; showed Himself alive to chosen witnesses, that He might strengthen the hearts of His people; and ascended to the right hand of God, whence He directs the continued preparation of the kingdom until it shall please Him to return for its establishment in its glorious eternal form.

It is important to fix firmly in mind the central conception of this representation. It turns upon the sacrificial death of Jesus to which the whole life leads up, and out of which all its issues are drawn, and for a perpetual memorial of which he is represented as having instituted a solemn memorial feast. The divine majesty of this Son of God; His redemptive mission to the world, in a life of humiliation and a ransoming death; the completion of his task in accordance with His purpose; His triumphant rising from the death thus vicariously endured;

His assumption of sovereignty over the future development of the kingdom founded in His blood, and over the world as the theater of its development; His expected return as the consummator of the ages and the judge of all — this is the circle of ideas in which all accounts move. It is the portrait not of a merely human life, though it includes the delineation of a complete and a completely human life. It is the portrayal of a human episode in the divine life. It is, therefore, not merely connected with supernatural occurrences, nor merely colored by supernatural features, nor merely set in a supernatural atmosphere: the supernatural is its very substance, the elimination of which would be the evaporation of the whole. The Jesus of the New Testament is not fundamentally man, however divinely gifted: he is God tabernacling for a while among men, with heaven lying about Him not merely in his infancy, but throughout all the days of His flesh.

The intense supernaturalism of this portraiture is, of course, an offense to our anti-supernaturalistic age. It is only what was to be expected, therefore, that throughout the last century and a half a long series of scholars, imbued with the anti-supernaturalistic instinct of the time, have assumed the task of desupernaturalizing it. Great difficulty has been experienced, however, in the attempt to construct a historical sieve which will strain out miracles and yet let Jesus through; for Jesus is Himself the greatest miracle of them all. Accordingly in the end of the day there is a growing disposition, as if in despair of accomplishing this feat, boldly to construct the sieve so as to strain out Jesus too; to take refuge in the counsel of desperation which affirms that there never was such a person as Jesus, that Christianity had no founder, and that not merely the portrait of Jesus, but Jesus Himself, is a pure projection of later ideals into the past. The main stream of assault still addresses itself, however, to the attempt to eliminate not Jesus Himself, but the Jesus of the Evangelists, and to substitute for Him a desupernaturalized Jesus.

The instruments which have been relied on to effect this result may be called, no doubt with some but not misleading

inexactitude, literary and historical criticism. The attempt has
been made to track out the process by which the present witnessing documents have come into existence, to show them
gathering accretions in this process, and to sift out the sources
from which they are drawn; and then to make appeal to these
sources as the only real witnesses. And the attempt has been
made to go behind the whole written record, operating either
immediately upon the documents as they now exist, or ultimately upon the sources which literary criticism has sifted out
from them, with a view to reaching a more primitive and presumably truer conception of Jesus than that which has obtained record in the writings of His followers. The occasion for
resort to this latter method of research is the failure of the
former to secure the results aimed at. For, when, at the dictation of anti-supernaturalistic presuppositions, John is set aside
in favor of the Synoptics, and then the Synoptics are set aside
in favor of Mark, conceived as the representative of " the
narrative source " (by the side of which must be placed —
though this is not always remembered — the second source of
" Sayings of Jesus," which underlies so much of Matthew and
Luke; and also — though this is even more commonly forgotten — whatever other sources either Matthew or Luke has
drawn upon for material), it still appears that no progress
whatever has been made in eliminating the divine Jesus and
His supernatural accompaniment of mighty works — although, chronologically speaking, the very beginning of Christianity has been reached. It is necessary, accordingly, if there
is not to be acknowledged a divine Christ with a supernatural
history, to get behind the whole literary tradition. Working on
Mark, therefore, taken as the original Gospel, an attempt must
be made to distinguish between the traditional element which
he incorporates into his narrative and the dogmatic element
which he (as the mouthpiece of the Christian community) contributes to it. Or, working on the " Sayings," discrimination
must first be made between the narrative element (assumed to
be colored by the thought of the Christian community) and
the reportorial element (which may repeat real sayings of

Jesus); and then, within the reportorial element, all that is too lofty for the naturalistic Jesus must be trimmed down until it fits in with his simply human character. Or, working on the Gospels as they stand, inquisition must be made for statements of fact concerning Jesus or for sayings of his, which, taken out of the context in which the Evangelists have placed them and cleansed from the coloring given by them, may be made to seem inconsistent with " the worship of Jesus " which characterizes these documents; and on the narrower basis thus secured there is built up a new portrait of Jesus, contradictory to that which the Evangelists have drawn.

The precariousness of these proceedings, or rather, frankly, their violence, is glaringly evident. In the processes of such criticism it is pure subjectivity which rules, and the investigator gets out as results only what he puts in as premises. And even when the desired result has thus been wrested from the unwilling documents, he discovers that he has only brought himself into the most extreme historical embarrassment. By thus desupernaturalizing Jesus he leaves primitive Christianity and its supernatural Jesus wholly without historical basis or justification. The naturalizing historian has therefore at once to address himself to supplying some account of the immediate universal ascription to Jesus by his followers of qualities which he did not possess and to which he laid no claim; and that with such force and persistence of conviction as totally to supersede from the very beginning with their perverted version of the facts the actual reality of things. It admits of no doubt, and it is not doubted, that supernaturalistic Christianity is the only historical Christianity. It is agreed on all hands that the very first followers of Jesus ascribed to him a supernatural character. It is even allowed that it is precisely by virtue of its supernaturalistic elements that Christianity has made its way in the world. It is freely admitted that it was by the force of its enthusiastic proclamation of the divine Christ, who could not be holden of death but burst the bonds of the grave, that Christianity conquered the world to itself. What account shall be given of all this? There is presented a problem here, which is insoluble on the naturalistic hypothesis. The old mythical theory fails because it requires time, and no time is at Its disposal; the primitive Christian community believed in the divine Christ. The new " history-of-religions " theory fails because it can not discover the elements of that " Christianity before Christ " which it must posit, either remotely in the Babylonian inheritance of the East, or close by in the prevalent Messianic conceptions of contemporary Judaism. Nothing is available but the postulation of pure fanaticism in Jesus' first followers, which finds it convenient not to proceed beyond the general suggestion that there is no telling what fanaticism may not invent. The plain fact is that the supernatural Jesus is needed to account for the supernaturalistic Christianity which is grounded in him. Or — if this supernaturalistic Christianity does not need a supernatural Jesus to account for it, it is hard to see why any Jesus at all need be postulated. Naturalistic criticism thus overreaches itself and is caught up suddenly by the discovery that in abolishing the supernatural Jesus it has abolished Jesus altogether, since this supernatural Jesus is the only Jesus which enters as a factor into the historical development. It is the desupernaturalized Jesus which is the mythical Jesus, who never had any existence, the postulation of the existence of whom explains nothing and leaves the whole historical development hanging in the air.

It is instructive to observe the lines of development of the naturalistic reconstruction of the Jesus of the Evangelists through the century and a half of its evolution. The normal task which the student of the life of Jesus sets himself is to penetrate into the spirit of the transmission so far as that transmission approves itself to him as trustworthy, to realize with exactness and vividness the portrait of Jesus conveyed by it, and to reproduce that portrait in an accurate and vital portrayal. The naturalistic reconstructors, on the other hand, engage themselves in an effort to substitute for the Jesus of the transmission another Jesus of their own, a Jesus who will seem " natural " to them, and will work in " naturally " with their naturalistic world-view. In the first instance it was the miracles of Jesus which they set themselves to eliminate, and this motive ruled their criticism from Reimarus (1694–1768), or rather, from the publication of the Wolfenbuettel Fragments (q.v.), to Strauss (1835–36). The dominant method employed — which found its culminating example in H. E. G. Paulus (1828) — was to treat the narrative as in all essentials historical, but to seek in each miraculous story a natural fact underlying it. This whole point of view was transcended by the advent of the mythical view in Strauss, who laughed it out of court. Since then miracles have been treated ever more and more confidently as negligible quantities, and the whole strength of criticism has been increasingly expended on the reduction of the supernatural figure of Jesus to " natural " proportions. The instrument relied upon to produce this effect has been psychological analysis; the method being to re-work the narrative in the interests of what is called a " comprehensible " Jesus. The whole mental life of Jesus and the entire course of his conduct have been subjected to psychological canons derived from the critics' conception of a purely human life, and nothing has been allowed to him which does not approve itself as " natural " according to this standard. The result is, of course, that the Jesus of the evangelists has been transformed into a nineteenth-century " liberal " theologian, and no conceptions or motives or actions have been allowed to him which would not be " natural " in such a one.

The inevitable reaction which seems to be now asserting itself takes two forms, both of which, while serving themselves heirs to the negative criticism of this " liberal " school, decisively reject its positive construction of the figure of Jesus. A weaker current contents itself with drawing attention to the obvious fact that such a Jesus as the " liberal " criticism yields will not account for the Christianity which actually came into being; and on this ground proclaims the " liberal " criticism bankrupt and raises the question, what need there is for assuming any Jesus at all. If the only Jesus salvable from the débris of legend is obviously not the author of the Christianity which actually came into being, why not simply recognize that Christianity came into being without any author — was just the crystallization of conceptions in solution at the time? A stronger current, scoffing at the projection of a nineteenth-century " liberal " back into the first century and calling him " Jesus," insists that " the historical Jesus " was just a Jew of his day, a peasant of Galilee with all the narrowness of a peasant's outlook and all the deficiency in culture which belonged to a Galilean countryman of the period. Above all, it insists that the real Jesus, possessed by those Messianic dreams which filled the minds of the Jewish peasantry of the time, was afflicted with the great delusion that He was Himself the promised Messiah. Under the obsession of this portentous fancy He imagined that God would intervene with His almighty arm and set him on the throne of a conquering Israel; and when the event falsified this wild hope, he assuaged his bitter disappointment with the wilder promise that he would rise from death itself and come back to establish his kingdom. Thus the naturalistic criticism of a hundred and fifty years has run out into no Jesus at all, or worse than no Jesus, a fanatic or even a paranoiac. The " liberal " criticism which has had it so long its own way is called sharply to its defense against the fruit of its own loins. In the process of this defense it wavers before the assault and incorporates more or less of the new conception of Jesus — of the " consistently eschatological " Jesus — into its fabric. Or it stands in its tracks and weakly protests that Jesus' figure must be conceived as greatly as possible, so only it be kept strictly within the limits of a mere human being. Or it develops an apologetical argument which, given its full validity and effect, would undo all its painfully worked-out negative results and lead back to the Jesus of the evangelists as the true " historical Jesus."

It has been remarked above that the portrait of Jesus drawn in the sources is its own credential; no man, and no body of men, can have invented this figure, consciously or unconsciously, and dramatized it consistently through such a varied and difficult life-history. It may be added that the Jesus of the naturalistic criticism is its own refutation. One wonders

whether the " liberal " critics realize the weakness, ineffectiveness, inanition of the Jesus they offer; the pitiful inertness they
attribute to him, his utter passivity under the impact of circumstance. So far from being conceivable as the molder of the
ages, this Jesus is wholly molded by his own surroundings, the
sport of every suggestion from without. In their preoccupation
with critical details, it is possible that its authors are scarcely
aware of the grossness of the reduction of the figure of Jesus
they have perpetrated. But let them only turn to portray their
new Jesus in a life-history, and the pitiableness of the figure
they have made him smites the eye. Whatever else may be said
of it, this must be said — that out of the Jesus into which the
naturalistic criticism has issued — in its best or in its worst
estate — the Christianity which has conquered the world could
never have come.

The firmness, clearness, and even fulness with which the
figure of Jesus is delineated in the sources, and the variety of
activities through which it is dramatized, do not insure that
the data given should suffice for drawing up a properly so-called
" life of Jesus." The data in the sources are practically confined
to the brief period of Jesus' public work. Only a single incident
is recorded from His earlier life, and that is taken from His
boyhood. So large a portion of the actual narrative, moreover,
is occupied with His death that it might even be said — the
more that the whole narrative also leads up to the death as the
life's culmination — that little has been preserved concerning
Jesus but the circumstances which accompanied His birth and
the circumstances which led up to and accompanied His death.
The incidents which the narrators record, again, are not recorded with a biographical intent, and are not selected for their
biographical significance, or ordered so as to present a biographical result: in the case of each Evangelist they serve a
particular purpose which may employ biographical details, but
is not itself a biographical end. In other words the Gospels are
not formal biographies but biographical arguments — a circumstance which does not affect the historicity of the incidents they
select for record, but does affect the selection and ordering of

these incidents. Mark has in view to show that this great religious movement in which he himself had a part had its beginnings in a divine interposition; Matthew, that this divine interposition was in fulfilment of the promises made to Israel; Luke, that it had as its end the redemption of the world; John, that the agent in it was none other than the Son of God himself. In the enforcement and illustration of their several themes each records a wealth of biographical details. But it does not follow that these details, when brought together and arranged in their chronological sequence, or even in their genetic order, will supply an adequate biography. The attempt to work them up into a biography is met, moreover, by a great initial difficulty. Every biographer takes his position, as it were, above his subject, who must live his life over again in his biographer's mind; it is of the very essence of the biographer's work thoroughly to understand his subject and to depict him as he understands him. What, then, if the subject of the biography be above the comprehension of his biographer? Obviously, in that case, a certain reduction can scarcely be avoided. This in an instance like the present, where the subject is a superhuman being, is the same as to say that a greater or lesser measure of rationalization, "naturalization," inevitably takes place. A true biography of a God-man, a biography which depicts His life from within, untangling the complex of motives which moved Him, and explaining His conduct by reference to the internal springs of action, is in the nature of the case an impossibility for men. Human beings can explain only on the basis of their own experiences and mental processes; and so explaining they instinctively explain away what transcends their experiences and confounds their mental processes. Seeking to portray the life of Jesus as natural, they naturalize it, that is, reduce it to correspondence with their own nature. Every attempt to work out a life of Christ must therefore face not only the insufficiency of the data, but the perennial danger of falsifying the data by an instinctive naturalization of them. If, however, the expectation of attaining a " psychological " biography of Jesus must be renounced, and even a complete external life can not be pieced together from the fragmentary communications of the sources, a clear and consistent view of the course of the public ministry of Jesus can still be derived from them. The consecution of the events can be set forth, their causal relations established, and their historical development explicated. To do this is certainly in a modified sense to outline " the life of Jesus," and to do this proves by its results to be eminently worth while.

A series of synchronisms with secular history indicated by Luke, whose historical interest seems more alert than that of the other evangelists, gives the needed information for placing such a " life " in its right historical relations. The chronological framework for the " life " itself is supplied by the succession of annual feasts which are recorded by John as occurring during Jesus' public ministry. Into this framework the data furnished by the other Gospels — which are not without corroborative suggestions of order, season of occurrence, and relations — fit readily; and when so arranged yield so self-consistent and rationally developing a history as to add a strong corroboration of its trustworthiness. Differences of opinion respecting the details of arrangement of course remain possible; and these differences are not always small and not always without historical significance. But they do not affect the general outline or the main drift of the history, and on most points, even those of minor importance, a tolerable agreement exists. Thus, for example, it is all but universally allowed that Jesus was born c. 5 or 6 B.C. (year of Rome 748 or 749), and it is an erratic judgment indeed which would fix on any other year than 29 or 30 A.D. for his crucifixion. On the date of His baptism — which determines the duration of his public ministry — more difference is possible; but it is quite generally agreed that it took place late in 26 A.D. or early in 27. It is only by excluding the testimony of John that a duration of less than between two and three years can be assigned to the public ministry; and then only by subjecting the Synoptical narrative to considerable pressure. The probabilities seem strongly in favor of extending it to three years and some months. The decision between a duration of two years and some months and a duration of three years and some months depends on the determination of the two questions of where in the narrative of John the imprisonment of John the Baptist (Mt. iv. 12) is to be placed, and what the unnamed feast is which is mentioned in John v. 1. On the former of these questions opinion varies only between John iv. 1–3 and John v. 1. On the latter a great variety of opinions exists: some think of Passover, others of Purim or Pentecost, or of Trumpets or Tabernacles, or even of the day of Atonement. On the whole, the evidence seems decisively preponderant for placing the imprisonment of the Baptist at John iv. 1–3, and for identifying the feast of John v. 1 with Passover. In that case, the public ministry of Jesus covered about three years and a third, and it is probably not far wrong to assign to it the period lying between the latter part of 26 A.D. and the Passover of 30 A.D.[3]

The material supplied by the Gospel narrative distributes itself naturally under the heads of (1) the preparation (2) the ministry, and (3) the consummation. For the first twelve or thirteen years of Jesus' life nothing is recorded except the striking circumstances connected with His birth, and a general statement of His remarkable growth. Similarly for His youth, about seventeen years and a half, there is recorded only the single incident, at its beginning, of His conversation with the doctors in the temple. Anything like continuous narrative begins only with the public ministry, in, say, December, 26 A.D. This narrative falls naturally into four parts which may perhaps be distinguished as (a) the beginning of the Gospel, forty days, from December, 26 to February, 27; (b) the Judean ministry, covering about ten months, from February, 27 to December, 27; (c) the Galilean ministry, covering about twenty-two months, from December, 27 to September, 29;

[3] Ramsay, Sanday, and Turner prefer 29 A.D. for the date of the crucifixion. Turner's dates are: birth, 7–6 B.C.; baptism, 26 A.D.; ministry, between two and three years; death, 29 A.D. Sanday's dates are: birth —; baptism, late 26 A.D.; ministry, two and a half years; death, 29 A.D. Ramsay's dates are: birth, autumn, 6 B.C.; baptism, early in 26 A.D.; ministry, three years and some months; death, 29 A.D.

(d) the last journeys to Jerusalem, covering some six months, from September, 29 to the Passover of (April) 30. The events of this final Passover season, the narrative of which becomes so detailed and precise that the occurrences from day to day are noted, constitute, along with their sequences, what is here called " the consummation." They include the events which led up to the crucifixion of Jesus, the crucifixion itself, and the manifestations which He gave of Himself after His death up to His ascension. So preponderating was the interest which the reporters took in this portion of the " life of Christ," that is to say, in His death and resurrection, that about a third of their whole narrative is devoted to it. The ministry which leads up to it is also, however, full of incident. What is here called " the beginning of the Gospel " gives, no doubt, only the accounts of Jesus' baptism and temptation. Only meager information is given also, and that by John alone, of the occurrences of the first ten months after His public appearance, the scene of which lay mainly in Judea. With the beginning of the ministry in Galilee, however, with which alone the Synoptic Gospels concern themselves, incidents become numerous. Capernaum now becomes Jesus' home for almost two full years; and no less than eight periods of sojourn there with intervening circuits going out from it as a center can be traced. When the object of this ministry had been accomplished Jesus finally withdraws from Galilee and addresses Himself to the preparation of his followers for the death He had come into the world to accomplish; and this He then brings about in the manner which best subserves His purpose.

Into the substance of Jesus' ministry it is not possible to enter here. Let it only be observed that it is properly called a ministry. He Himself testified that He came not to be ministered unto but to minister, and He added that this ministry was fulfilled in His giving His life as a ransom for many. In other words, the main object of His work was to lay the foundations of the kingdom of God in His blood. Subsidiary to this was His purpose to make vitally known to men the true nature of the kingdom of God, to prepare the way for its advent in their hearts, and above all, to attach them by faith to His person as the founder and consummator of the kingdom. His ministry involved, therefore, a constant presentation of Himself to the people as the promised One, in and by whom the kingdom of God was to be established, a steady " campaign of instruction " as to the nature of the kingdom which He came to found, and a watchful control of the forces which were making for His destruction, until, His work of preparation being ended, He was ready to complete it by offering Himself up. The progress of His ministry is governed by the interplay of these motives. It has been broadly distributed into a year of obscurity, a year of popular favor, and a year of opposition; and if these designations are understood to have only a relative applicability, they may be accepted as generally describing from the outside the development of the ministry. Beginning first in Judea Jesus spent some ten months in attaching to Himself His first disciples, and with apparent fruitlessness proclaiming the kingdom at the center of national life. Then, moving north to Galilee, He quickly won the ear of the people and carried them to the height of their present receptivity; whereupon, breaking from them, He devoted Himself to the more precise instruction of the chosen band He had gathered about Him to be the nucleus of His Church. The Galilean ministry thus divides into two parts, marked respectively by more popular and more intimate teaching. The line of division falls at the miracle of the feeding of the five thousand, which, as marking a crisis in the ministry, is recorded by all four Evangelists, and is the only miracle which has received this fourfold record. Prior to this point, Jesus' work had been one of gathering disciples; subsequently to it, it was a work of instructing and sifting the disciples whom He had gathered. The end of the Galilean ministry is marked by the confession of Peter and the transfiguration, and after it nothing remained but the preparation of the chosen disciples for the death, which was to close His work; and the consummation of His mission in His death and rising again.

The instruments by which Jesus carried out his ministry

were two, teaching and miracles. In both alike He manifested His deity. Wherever He went the supernatural was present in word and deed. His teaching was with authority. In its insight and foresight it was as supernatural as the miracles themselves; the hearts of men and the future lay as open before Him as the forces of nature lay under His control; all that the Father knows He knew also, and He alone was the channel of the revelation of it to men. The power of His " But I say unto you " was as manifest as that of His compelling " Arise and walk." The theme of His teaching was the kingdom of God and Himself as its divine founder and king. Its form ran all the way from crisp gnomic sayings and brief comparisons to elaborate parables and profound spiritual discussions in which the deep things of God are laid bare in simple, searching words. The purport of His miracles was that the kingdom of God was already present in its King. Their number is perhaps usually greatly underestimated. It is true that only about thirty or forty are actually recorded. But these are recorded only as specimens, and as such they represent all classes. Miracles of healing form the preponderant class; but there are also exorcisms, nature-miracles, raisings of the dead. Besides these recorded miracles, however, there are frequent general statements of abounding miraculous manifestations. For a time disease and death must have been almost banished from the land. The country was thoroughly aroused and filled with wonder. In the midst of this universal excitement — when the people were ready to take Him by force and make Him King — He withdrew Himself from them, and throwing His circuits far afield, beyond the bruit and uproar, addressed Himself to preparing His chosen companions for His great sacrifice — first leading them in the so-called " later Galilean ministry " (from the feeding of the 5,000 to the confession at Cæsarea Philippi) to a better apprehension of the majesty of His person as the Son of God, and of the character of the kingdom He came to found, as consisting not in meat and drink but in righteousness; and then, in the so-called " Peræan ministry " (from the confession at Cæsarea Philippi to the final arrival at Jerusalem) specifi-

cally preparing them for His death and resurrection. Thus
He walked straightforward in the path He had chosen, and His
choice of which is already made clear in the account of His
temptation, set at the beginning of His public career; and in
His own good time and way — in the end forcing the hand of
His opponents to secure that he should die at the Passover —
shed His blood as the blood of the new covenant sacrifice for
the remission of sins. Having power thus to lay down His life,
He had power also to take it again, and in due time He rose
again from the dead and ascended to the right hand of the majesty on high, leaving behind Him His promise to come again
in His glory, to perfect the kingdom He had inaugurated.

It is appropriate that this miraculous life should be set
between the great marvels of the virgin-birth and the resurrection and ascension. These can appear strange only when the
intervening life is looked upon as that of a merely human
being, endowed, no doubt, not only with unusual qualities, but
also with the unusual favor of God, yet after all nothing more
than human and therefore presumably entering the world like
other human beings, and at the end paying the universal debt
of human nature. From the standpoint of the evangelical
writers, and of the entirety of primitive Christianity, which
looked upon Jesus not as a merely human being but as God
himself come into the world on a mission of mercy that involved the humiliation of a human life and death, it would be
this assumed community with common humanity in mode of
entrance into and exit from the earthly life which would seem
strange and incredible. The entrance of the Lord of Glory into
the world could not but be supernatural; His exit from the
world, after the work which He had undertaken had been performed, could not fail to bear the stamp of triumph. There is
no reason for doubting the trustworthiness of the narratives at
these points, beyond the anti-supernaturalistic instinct which
strives consciously or unconsciously to naturalize the whole
evangelical narrative. The "infancy chapters" of Luke are
demonstrably from Luke's own hand, bear evident traces of
having been derived from trustworthy sources of information,

and possess all the authority which attaches to the communications of a historian who evinces himself sober, careful, and exact, by every historical test. The parallel chapters of Matthew, while obviously independent of those of Luke — recording in common with them not a single incident beyond the bare fact of the virgin-birth — are thoroughly at one with them in the main fact, and in the incidents they record fit with remarkable completeness into the interstices of Luke's narrative. Similarly, the narratives of the resurrection, full of diversity in details as they are, and raising repeated puzzling questions of order and arrangement, yet not only bear consentient testimony to all the main facts, but fit into one another so as to create a consistent narrative — which has moreover the support of the contemporary testimony of Paul. The persistent attempts to explain away the facts so witnessed or to substitute for the account which the New Testament writers give of them some more plausible explanation, as the naturalistic mind estimates plausibility, are all wrecked on the directness, precision, and copiousness of the testimony; and on the great effects which have flowed from this fact in the revolution wrought in the minds and lives of the apostles themselves, and in the revolution wrought through their preaching of the resurrection in the life and history of the world. The entire history of the world for 2,000 years is the warranty of the reality of the resurrection of Christ, by which the forces were let loose which have created it. " Unique spiritual effects," it has been remarked, with great reasonableness, " require a unique spiritual cause; and we shall never understand the full significance of the cause, if we begin by denying or minimizing its uniqueness."

V

CONCERNING SCHMIEDEL'S " PILLAR-PASSAGES "

CONCERNING SCHMIEDEL'S " PILLAR-PASSAGES "[1]

THE publication by Paul W. Schmiedel in 1901 of the article " Gospels " in the " Encyclopaedia Biblica " marks (we do not say, creates) something very much like an epoch in the history of the criticism of the Gospel-narratives. For more than a century — " from Reimarus to Wrede " — " the quest of the historical Jesus " has been pursued with unflagging industry. That is to say, the energies of a long line of brilliantly endowed scholars, equipped with the instrument of the most extensive and exact erudition, have been exhausted in the effort to discover some historical basis for the " natural " Jesus which their philosophical presuppositions compelled them to assume behind the supernatural Jesus presented in the Gospel-narratives. " Exhausted " is the right word to use here. For precisely what Schmiedel's article advises us of, is the failure of this long-continued and diligently prosecuted labor to reach the results expected of it. After a half-century of somewhat unmethodical investigation, Ferdinand Christian Baur, in the middle of the last century, laid down the reasonable rule by which subsequent research has been governed: " criticism of documents must precede criticism of material."[2]   But the subsequent half-

[1] From *The Princeton Theological Review*, xi. 1913, pp. 195–269.

[2] F. C. Baur, " Kritische Untersuchungen über die kanonischen Evangelien," 1847, Introduction. Strauss had proceeded on the principle that a history which contains narratives of miracles can deserve no credit. Baur raises the question whether this is not a rash conclusion; whether the metaphysical notion of the miraculous is not too abstract a category to be made the test of the entire evangelical history; whether, in a word, some investigation into the origin of the narratives is not called for before a conclusion is drawn against their contents; and whether, therefore, Strauss has not erred in making his criticism so exclusively a criticism of the history to the neglect of criticism of the writings (p. 46). He recognizes a certain naturalness in Strauss' procedure in the state of the documentary criticism of the day. But he con-

century of criticism of documents has issued in certainly nothing to the purpose, and, Schmiedel seems half-inclined to declare, nothing solid at all. The Synoptic problem, he tells us, remains as vexed at the end of it as it was at the beginning. Certain immediate sources of the Synoptics' material it is, of course, easy enough to discern lying behind them, and these are very generally recognized. But behind them in turn stretches a vista of sources, traveling down which the eye becomes weary; and the complications which result when an attempt is made to take these into consideration confound the most promising hypotheses. " The solution of the synoptical problem which appeared after so much toil to have been brought so near," remarks Schmiedel, " seems suddenly to be removed again to an immeasurable distance." [3] " It cannot but seem unfortunate " therefore, he continues, " that the decision as to the credibility of the gospel narratives should be made to depend upon the determination of a problem so difficult and perhaps insoluble as the synoptical is." [4] Consequently he proposes a return to the pre-Tübingen position of criticism of the material independently of the criticism of the documents in which this material is presented. " It would accordingly be a very important gain," he says, " if we could find some means of making " the decision as to the credibility of the Gospel-narratives " in some measure at least independent of " the determination of the Synoptical problem.[5]

The procedure which Schmiedel here proposes is obviously

---

cludes: " The fault of the Straussian work is that it makes the Gospel history the object of criticism without first attaining a solid result with the criticism of the writings " (p. 71). " However natural and in a sense unavoidable the way opened up by Strauss may be, it nevertheless remains undeniable that it is from the very nature of the case impossible to reach an assured result with the criticism of the history, so long as the criticism of the writings is so wavering and uncertain " (p. 72). Cf. Otto Pfleiderer, " The Development of Theology in Germany since Kant," 1890, pp. 224 ff.

[3] " Encyclopaedia Biblica," col. 1868.

[4] *Ibid.*, col. 1872.

[5] *Ibid.*, col. 1872; cf. *Protestantische Monatshefte*, x. (1906) p. 400: " They [his ' pillar-passages '] provide the possibility of establishing very essential traits of the life of Jesus without the question of the origin and the mutual relations of the first three Gospels having to be solved."

revolutionary; so revolutionary that it marks, as we say, something very like an epoch in the history of the criticism of the Gospel-narratives. It is an express return to the methods of Strauss as opposed to the more scientific methods validated once for all by Baur as against Strauss; and in returning to Strauss' methods it returns in a very curious way to Strauss' exact standpoint of unreasoned scepticism with respect to the Gospel-narratives. What it particularly concerns us here to emphasize, however, is that it registers the failure of " literary criticism " of the Gospels as prosecuted during the last half-century, either, as Schmiedel intimates, to accomplish anything of importance, or, in any event, to accomplish anything to the purpose. There are many, no doubt, who will disown Schmiedel's low estimate of the formal results of Synoptical criticism. But no well-informed person will care to deny that for the ultimate purpose for which this criticism has been invoked its failure has been complete. No stratum of tradition has been reached by it in which the portrait of Jesus differs in any essential respect from that presented in the Synoptic Gospels. If the writers of the Synoptic Gospels were (in Schmiedel's phrase) [6] " worshippers of Jesus," no less were those who formed and transmitted to them the tradition on which they ultimately rest (also in Schmiedel's phrase) [7] " worshippers of Jesus." As we go back, and ever farther back, to the very beginnings of any tradition to which literary criticism can penetrate, the purely human Jesus who is assumed to lie behind the Jesus of the

[6] This is the term employed in the English of the " Encyclopaedia Biblica " (e.g. col. 1872), the Preface which Schmiedel contributed to Arno Neumann's " Jesus " (e.g. pp. ix, xviii; here, as elsewhere, the E. T. is referred to), and his lecture on " Jesus in Modern Criticism " (e.g. p. 16) alike; and as all these discussions owe their English clothing to friends of Schmiedel, working under his eye, we should perhaps permit the term to stand. The German term which is rendered (*Verehrung, Verehrer*) we should not suppose necessarily expressed so specific a notion.

[7] Preface to Neumann, p. ix: " The Gospels are, all of them, the work of worshippers of Jesus, and their contents have been handed down through the channel of tradition in like manner by His worshippers "; p. xviii: " This tradition was itself really handed down by worshippers of Jesus." So also W. Heitmüller, in Schiele and Zscharnack's " Die Religion," etc., iii. coll. 357–359.

Gospels still continually eludes us. Accordingly a Pfleiderer frankly despairs of ever recovering Him,[8] and a Wellhausen leaves on his readers a strong impression that his drastic criticism must land us ultimately in the same desperation.[9] Schmiedel's counsel is, in these circumstances, to reverse the established method of the last half-century, and, abandoning the criticism of documents which no longer seems hopeful, to seek to break a way to the assumed purely human Jesus by means of immediate criticism of the historical material itself. And he thinks he can blaze out the road directly to the desired goal.

It ought to be noted in passing that Schmiedel sometimes speaks as if he were not prepared to admit that the attainment of the purely human Jesus, so long sought in vain by literary criticism, were the determining motive of the change of procedure which he suggests.[10] He everywhere speaks, indeed, as if the critical principle which he invokes were quite indifferent to this issue. He even asserts explicitly: "In reality, my foundation-texts were in no sense sought out by me for any purpose whatever; they thrust themselves upon me in virtue of one feature, and one feature only: the impossibility of their having been invented, and their consequent credibility."[11] Except in a purely formal sense, however, this is manifestly absurd. It is its superhuman Jesus with His nimbus of the supernatural which is the sole *skandalon* of the Synoptic narrative, apart from which that narrative would be acknowledged by all as exceptionally trustworthy. "Precisely this," remarks Albert Schweitzer justly, "is the characteristic of the literature of the Life of Jesus at the opening of the twentieth century, — that the purely historical, even in the productions of historical, scientific, professional theology, retires behind the interest

[8] Cf. *The Princeton Theological Review*, iv. (1906) pp. 121–124.

[9] Cf. H. Weinel, "Ist das 'liberale' Jesusbild widerlegt?" 1910, p. 20: "And even now if Wrede and Wellhausen do not really mean that Jesus is a wholly imaginary figure, yet the judgment to which their work leads runs: 'Jesus is for us unknowable (*unerkennbar*).'"

[10] "Encyclopaedia Biblica," col. 1881.

[11] Preface to Neumann, p. xxi.

in the world-view." [12] Schmiedel does not separate from his companions in this. He comes to the criticism of the Gospel-narratives with a definite world-view as the primary pre-supposition of his work; and this world-view is the current anti-supernaturalistic one. There is nothing of which he is surer than that Jesus was merely a man; [13] unless it be that miracles in general do not happen.[14] The only reason why he rejects out of hand the Jesus given him by the Synoptic narratives is that the Jesus given him by the Synoptic narratives is not a mere man. And the precise thing he sets himself to look for behind the Synoptic narratives is evidence of some kind that the real Jesus was, despite the constant testimony of the tradition, nevertheless merely man. "What," he asks, "are the portions of the Gospels which are so persistently objected to?" And he replies: "We find that they are, to say all in a word, those in which Jesus appears as a Divine Being whether in virtue of what He says or in virtue of what He does." [15] There is no other reason why the portrait of Jesus given by the Synoptics should be "objected to." And so firmly set is Schmiedel's reluctance to the admission of the possibility of such a Jesus that he even

[12] "Quest of the Historical Jesus."

[13] *Hibbert Journal* Supplement: *Jesus or Christ?* 1909, p. 66 f.: "Since the divine and human nature cannot be united in Jesus, and since Jesus was undoubtedly man, we have simply to regard his human nature as given. . . ." "Jesus in Modern Criticism," 1907, p. 86: "My religion, moreover, does not require me to find in Jesus an *absolutely perfect* model, and it would not trouble me if I found another person who excelled him, as indeed, in certain respects some have already done. Convinced as I am that he was human, if another should have more to offer me than he had, I should consider this simply another instance of God's bounty and favour." *Ibid.*, p. 6: "It is no less pleasant to note at the same time that the person of Jesus is being explained in a more and more definitely human way by all theological parties, and in a more or less human way even by ultra-conservatives." Cf. "Encyclopaedia Biblica," col. 1881; "Jesus in Modern Criticism," p. 24.

[14] "It would clearly be wrong," he indeed declares ("Encyclopaedia Biblica," col. 1876), "in an investigation such as the present, to start from any such postulate or axiom as that 'miracles' are impossible"; but he is soon found arguing that "even one strongly predisposed to believe in miracles would find it difficult to accept a narrative" like that of Lk. xxiii. 44 ff. because it alleges a darkening of the sun at a time of the month when eclipses do not happen — that is because if it happened at all it must have been by miracle.

[15] Preface to Neumann, p. ix.

goes the length of declaring that were this representation consistent and unbroken, he, for his part, might find it impossible
to defend the actual existence of any Jesus at all.[16] Either a
purely human Jesus or no Jesus at all is the only alternative
that he will admit, prior to entering into any critical inquiry
into the evidence; and the sole object of his criticism is to
discover some evidence of the existence of a purely human
Jesus. The precise significance of his proposed revolution in
critical procedure, therefore, is that it openly recognizes that
literary criticism has failed to discover any evidence of the
existence of a purely human Jesus behind the superhuman
Jesus of the Synoptic narratives, and suggests that another
and more direct way be therefore tried to reach the desired
end.

Schmiedel's criticism brings us, then, to a parting of the
ways. Not only are we justified, therefore, in giving it an
attention which in itself it might not seem to merit, but it is in
a sense required of us to subject it to a sufficiently careful
scrutiny to assure us that we understand exactly what he proposes, and also, if possible, exactly what the significance of
this proposal is.

So far as we are informed, Schmiedel, after a brief incidental suggestion of it in the course of an article in the *Protestantische Monatshefte*, first propounded his new critical
method at some length in the article " Gospels " which was
published in the second volume of the " Encyclopaedia Biblica " in 1901. The commendation of it to a German public
seems in the first instance to have been made by expositions
of it given by his brother, Otto Schmiedel, in 1902 [17] and by

---

[16] " Encyclopaedia Biblica," col. 1881: " If passages of this kind were
wholly wanting in them it would be impossible to prove to a sceptic that any
historical value whatever was to be assigned to the gospels; he would be in a
position to declare the picture of Jesus contained in them to be purely a work
of phantasy, and could remove the person of Jesus from the field of
history. . . ."

[17] " Die Hauptprobleme der Leben Jesu Forschung," von Otto Schmiedel, 1902, § vi, pp. 39–41. The second edition, 1906, repeats this section without change, pp. 46–48.

his pupil, Arno Neumann, in 1904.[18] It was apparently not until 1906 that Schmiedel himself laid it at length before his countrymen, early in that year somewhat incidentally in a tractate on the Gospel of John as compared with the Synoptics,[19] and later more at length in a lecture on the Person of Jesus in modern controversy, which was delivered at the meeting of the Swiss Association for Free Christianity on June 15, 1906, and published in the July number of the *Protestantische Monatshefte,* and afterwards separately.[20] In the same year he returned to its exposition and defence in English in a preface which he wrote for the English translation of Neumann's "Jesus";[21] and in the following year there was issued an English translation of his Swiss lecture.[22] These publications constitute our sources of information with respect to the proposal we are to examine.[23]

In its primary publication[24] Schmiedel explains his suggestion, if succinctly, yet with sufficient clearness. Turning from literary to historical criticism, the investigator finds, he remarks, two lines of procedure open to him — a negative and a positive one. He must on the one hand, "set on one side

[18] "Jesus, wer er geschichtlich war," von Arno Neumann, 1904, "Die Vorfrage," § 5, pp. 16–18. E. T.: "Jesus," 1906, pp. 9–11.

[19] "Das vierte Evangelium gegenüber den drei ersten," von Professor D. P. W. Schmiedel, Zürich, being the 8th and 10th parts of the first series of the well-known "Religionsgeschichtliche Volksbücher," 1906, pp. 16–22, 31 f., 33, 81–83, 85–87.

[20] *Protestantische Monatshefte,* x. (1906) 7, pp. 257–282. "Die Person Jesu im Streite der Meinungen der Gegenwart," Vortrag . . . von D. Paul Wilh. Schmiedel . . . Leipzig, 1906.

[21] "Jesus." By Arno Neumann. Translated by Maurice A. Canney, M.A. With a Preface by Professor P. W. Schmiedel, London: Adam and Charles Black, 1906. The Preface occupies pp. v.–xxviii.

[22] "Jesus in Modern Criticism." A lecture by Dr. Paul W. Schmiedel, Professor of Theology in Zurich. Translated into English (by permission of the publishers of the *Prot. Monatshefte*) by Maurice A. Canney, M.A. London: Adam and Charles Black, 1907.

[23] A "Nachwort über die 'Grundsäulen' eines Lebens Jesu" in reply to an article in the same number (pp. 386–392) by Eduard Hertlein of Jena, entitled, "Neue 'Grundsäulen' eines 'Lebens Jesu'?" was published by Schmiedel in the number of the *Protestantische Monatshefte* for Nov. 1906 (x. 10, pp. 393–400). [24] "Encyclopaedia Biblica," coll. 1872 ff.

everything which for any reason arising either from the substance or from considerations of literary criticism has to be
regarded as doubtful or wrong." On the other hand, " one
must make search for all such data, as from the nature of their
contents cannot possibly on any account be regarded as inventions." Following out the former of these lines of inquiry
with respect to the Synoptic Gospels Schmiedel points out a
number of matters (including their accounts of miraculous
occurrences) in which he considers them clearly untrustworthy.[25] With this negative criticism we are not for the moment concerned. We only note in passing that it is sufficiently
drastic to lead Schmiedel to remark at the close of the sections
devoted to it, " The foregoing sections may have sometimes
seemed to raise a doubt whether any credible elements were to
to be found in the Gospels at all." [26] The method of the positive
investigation is outlined as follows: [27]

" When a profane historian finds before him a historical document which testifies to the worship of a hero unknown to other
sources, he attaches first and foremost importance to those features
which cannot be deduced merely from the fact of this worship, and
he does so on the simple and sufficient ground that they would not
be found in this source unless the author had met with them as
fixed data of tradition. The same fundamental principle may safely
be applied in the case of the gospels, for they also are all of them
written by worshippers of Jesus. We now have accordingly the
advantage — which cannot be appreciated too highly — of being
in a position to recognise something as being worthy of belief even
without being able to say, or even being called on to inquire,
whether it comes from original Mk., from logia, from oral tradition, or from any other quarter that may be alleged. The relative
priority becomes a matter of indifference, because the absolute
priority — that is, the origin in real tradition — is certain. In such
points the question as to credibility becomes independent of the
synoptical question. Here the clearest cases are those in which only
one evangelist, or two, have data of this class, and the second, or
third, or both, are found to have taken occasion to alter these
in the interests of the reverence due to Jesus.

[25] *Ibid.,* coll. 1873–1880.   [26] *Ibid.,* col. 1881.   [27] *Ibid.,* col. 1872.

" If we discover any such points — even if only a few — they guarantee not only their own contents, but also much more. For in that case one may also hold as credible all else which agrees in character with these, and is in other respects not open to suspicion. Indeed the thoroughly disinterested historian must recognise it as his duty to investigate the grounds for this so great reverence for himself which Jesus was able to call forth; and he will then, first and foremost, find himself led to recognise as true the two great facts that Jesus had compassion for the multitude and that he preached with power, not as the scribes (Mt. ix. 36; vii. 29)." [28]

Proceeding after this fashion Schmiedel fixes primarily on five passages which seem to him to meet the conditions laid down; that is to say, they make statements which are in conflict with the reverence for Jesus that pervades the Gospels and therefore could not have been invented by the authors

---

[28] The meaning of these last sentences is practically that, having by the processes of criticism outlined in the preceding paragraph secured a merely human Jesus, Schmiedel now sets himself to present as high a conception of this merely human Jesus as he can without overstepping the bounds of His mere humanity. Consequently he is willing to point to such passages as Mt. vii. 29; Mk. vi. 34; Mt. xi. 28 as " of the same truthful nature " as the " pillar passages," though the principle of their selection is now the opposite one, that they *enhance* the character of Jesus (" Jesus in Modern Criticism," pp. 25–26). He is even on this principle prepared to run directly in the teeth of the principle of his " pillar-passages." Those passages, he says, have thrust themselves upon him because the statements in them are too inconsistent with the reverence in which Jesus was held by the community to represent their view, and must therefore have come from an earlier tradition which is true. But there are passages which in his judgment attribute to Jesus teachings which he refuses to believe were genuinely Jesus' because they are altogether too inconsistent with reverence for Him. There is, for example, the parable of the rich man and Lazarus, in which (in his view) mere poverty is made a virtue, and mere riches a vice (Lk. xvi. 25). There is the parable of the unrighteous steward, in which mere relaxation of financial claims without any consideration of the rights and duties involved is made a shining virtue (Lk. xvi. 1–9). Why not reason that these are obviously fragments of an earlier tradition inconsistent with the worship in which Jesus had come to be held, and demonstrate to us that Jesus was an " Ebionite," a fanatical leveler? But Schmiedel draws back and remarks: " It should be obvious that Jesus cannot have said such things as these " (" Jesus in Modern Criticism," pp. 72–73), arguing against their genuineness after a fashion which sounds very strange on his lips, and raises the question whether he himself really believes in the principle of his " pillar-passages."

of the Gospels, but must have come to them from earlier
fixed tradition; and they are preserved in their crude contradiction with the standpoint of the evangelists, accordingly,
only by one or two of them, while the others, or other, of them,
if they report them at all, modify them into harmony with
their standpoint of reverence.[29] These five passages are: Mk.
x, 17 ff. ("Why callest thou me good? None is good save God
only"); Mt. xii. 31 ff. (blasphemy against the Son of Man
can be forgiven); Mk. iii. 21 (His relations held Him to be
beside Himself); Mk. xiii. 32 ("Of that day and of that hour
knoweth no one, not even the angels in heaven, neither the
Son but the Father"); Mk. xv. 34, Mt. xxvii. 46 ("My God,
my God, why hast thou forsaken me?"). To these he adds four
more which have reference to Jesus' power to work miracles,
viz.: Mk. viii. 12 (Jesus declines to work a sign); Mk. vi. 5 ff.
(Jesus was able to do no mighty works in Nazareth); Mk.
viii. 14–21 ("The leaven of the Pharisees and of Herod" refers
not to bread but to teaching); Mt. xi. 5; Lk. vii. 22 (the signs
of the Messiah are only figuratively miraculous). These nine
passages he calls "the foundation-pillars for a truly scientific
life of Jesus." In his view, they prove, on the one hand, that
"he [Jesus] really did exist, and that the Gospels contain at
least some trustworthy facts concerning him," — a matter
which, he seems to suggest, would be subject to legitimate
doubt in the absence of such passages; and, on the other hand,
that "in the person of Jesus we have to do with a completely
human being, and that the divine is to be sought in him only
in the form in which it is capable of being found in a man."[30]
From them as a basis, he proposes to work out, admitting
nothing to be credible which is not accordant with the non-
miraculous, purely human, Jesus which these passages imply.

The principle of procedure which Schmiedel invokes, it
will be seen, he represents as one which is in universal use in
like circumstances among profane historians. He represents it
as altogether independent of literary criticism and as finding
its chief value in this fact. He represents it further as yielding

[29] "Encyclopaedia Biblica," col. 1881.   [30] *Ibid.*

results which may be confidently depended upon. And he represents these results as totally reversing the portrait of Jesus presented in the documents subjected to this critical scrutiny, substituting for the divine Jesus which they depict a purely human Jesus. All this will become clearer as we attend to the subsequent expositions he has given of his method.

The subject is introduced, in the little book on John,[31] in the course of a discussion of the miracles attributed to our Lord by John. John, it is remarked, represents our Lord as working miracles as "signs"; but we learn from Mk. viii. 11–13 that Jesus refused to give a "sign" to that generation. "And," continues Schmiedel, "He must really have made this declaration; for no one of His reporters would have invented it, since they, each and every one of them, believed that Jesus did work miracles with this purpose." Then he continues:

"In order to place the significance of such passages in its full light, we give them the name of *foundation-pillars of a really scientific life of Jesus*. Every historical investigator, no matter in what field he works, follows the principle to hold for true in the first instance, in any account which testifies to reverence (*Verehrung*, 'worship') for its hero, that which runs counter to this reverence, because that cannot be based on invention. Since we possess a plurality of Gospels we can further observe how in one or more of them such passages are in part transformed, in part wholly omitted, because they were too objectionable precisely to reverence for Jesus. In their original form such passages show, therefore, in the most certain way how Jesus really thought and lived, namely after a fashion which we — with all recognition that there was something divine in Him — must call a genuinely human one. On the other hand, it is only such passages which give assurance that we may, at least in some degree, depend upon the Gospels in which they occur, that is to say the first three Gospels. Were they wholly lacking in them, it would be difficult to withstand the allegation that the Gospels *everywhere* give us only a sacred image painted on a gold ground, and we could therefore not at all know what kind of an appearance Jesus really made, or indeed perhaps even whether He ever existed at all. The 'foundation-pillars' upon

[31] Pp. 16–17.

which, along with the one already mentioned, we can rely in order to obtain a right idea of the miraculous works of Jesus, we speak of at p. 31 f., and in chapter III., paragraphs 18 and 19; and of the remaining ones which are of importance for other aspects of Jesus' nature at pp. 18 f., 19 f., 21, 22, and 23.

"It is self-evident that what we find to be credible in the Synoptics is in no wise confined to these nine ' foundation-pillars.' It belongs to the chief tasks of an historical investigator, from his words and acts, to make the effect (*Erfolg*) which a great historical figure has had intelligible. This effect in Jesus' case is, however, so great that even an investigator who stands entirely cool in His presence must seek out and accept as true everything which is adapted to establish His greatness and to make the reverence felt for Him by His contemporaries intelligible, — it being premised, of course, that it does not contradict the portrait of Jesus obtained from the ' foundation-pillars,' and also does not otherwise rouse well-grounded doubts."

There is perhaps observable in this statement a certain heightening of what was more cautiously expressed in the initial statement, in the " Encyclopaedia Biblica." There, for example, we were told that it was when a historian found himself before a unique document testifying to the worship of a hero unknown to other sources that he resorted to this method of investigating the credibility of his otherwise uncontrollable informant. Here all this qualification falls away and it is spoken of as if this were a universally practised method in all historical research. The general untrustworthiness of the evangelical portrait of Jesus and the closeness of the alternative that we should have no credible account of Jesus and perhaps be left in doubt of his very existence seems also to be somewhat more extremely suggested.

We are in a different atmosphere in the Preface to Arno Neumann's " Jesus." Here Schmiedel is defending his critical method and its results against the strictures of John M. Robertson, who holds that Jesus is a pure myth and that therefore the Gospels cannot contain any credible testimony to His existence. Schmiedel is concerned accordingly to throw into emphasis the positive side of his method, and to make plain that he obtains by it not mere probability but certainty as to Jesus — both as to His existence and as to His true character. He concedes that the Gospels present the appearance of altogether untrustworthy narratives, and that we are, therefore, with them on our hands as our sources of knowledge of Jesus, in a very unfavorable position. But he reasons thus. [32]

" Yet let us examine a little more closely. What are the portions of the Gospels which are so persistently objected to? We find that they are, to say all in a word, those in which Jesus appears as a Divine Being whether in virtue of what He says or in virtue of what He does. And the reason why exception is taken to these passages may be stated thus: The Gospels are, all of them, the work of worshippers of Jesus, and their contents have been handed down through the channel of tradition in like manner by His worshippers; the portions to which exception is taken are open to the suspicion that they are the outcome of these feelings of devotion, and not purely objective renderings of the facts as they actually occurred. But how, let us ask, if the Gospels also contain portions which are absolutely free from any suspicion whatever of this sort? So far as the difficulty just referred to is concerned, these at least may be historical. May be; yet it is also possible that they may not be; plainly, in fact, they cannot be if the person of Jesus is altogether unhistorical. For example: moral precepts which in themselves might justify no suspicion against the historical character of the person to whom they are attributed, could yet very easily be put into the mouth of a purely invented and in no sense historical Jesus.

" Thus we find ourselves still left in the unfavorable position already indicated — unless peradventure, we should be able to find in the Gospels some passages which far from being equally appropriate alike to an invented and to a historical Jesus, should be wholly impossible in the former case. If Jesus is an imaginary person, the things which are, without historical foundation, ascribed to Him are entirely due to the reverence in which He was held. If, accordingly, we find in the Gospels any passages which cannot by any possibility have found their inspiration in the worshipful regard in which He was held, and which in fact are, on the contrary, incompatible with it, they in themselves prove that the Gospels con-

[32] Pp. ix. ff.

tain at least something that has been rightly handed down; for if these passages had not been handed down to the Evangelists and those who preceded them in a manner that made doubt impossible, they would never have found admission into our Gospels at all.

"Such was the underlying thought when in the 'Encyclopaedia Biblica' article *Gospels*, §§ 131, 139 f., I characterized nine passages in the Synoptical Gospels as 'the foundation-pillars for a truly scientific life of Jesus.' I limited myself to so small a number because I desired to include no instance against the evidential value of which any objection could possibly be taken with some hope of success; and further, I, of set purpose, selected only those passages in which it is possible to.show from the text of the Gospels themselves that they are incompatible with the worship in which Jesus came to be held. Thus they are, all of them, found only in one Gospel, or at most two; the second and third, or the third, either omits the passage in question, although, by universal consent, the author who omits must have known at least one of the Gospels in which it occurs, or the source from which it was drawn; or alternatively, he turns it round, often with great ingenuity and boldness, in such a manner that it loses the element which makes it open to exception from the point of view of a worshipper of Jesus."

What is most insisted upon in this statement is that there are sought (and found) in Schmiedel's " pillar-passages " not merely affirmations which are appropriate to a human Jesus, but affirmations which are impossible for a Divine Jésus. Their characteristic is, as Schmiedel expresses it on a later page,[33] that " they are not consistent with the worship in which Jesus had come to be held "; that they " are appropriate only to a man, and could never, by any possibility, have been written had the author been thinking of a demi-god." There are in the Synoptic Gospels, as Schmiedel explains,[34] three classes of " sayings of Jesus (or, to speak more correctly, passages in the Synoptics about Jesus) ": " first, those which are plainly incredible; secondly, those which are plainly credible; and in the third category those which occupy an intermediate position as bearing on the face of them no certain mark either of

[33] P. xvii.   [34] Pp. xiii f.

incredibility or of credibility." This is Schmiedel's way of saying that there are some passages which clearly ascribe a supernatural character to Jesus; some which are clearly inconsistent with a supernatural character in Him; and still some others which do not raise the question of His supernatural character at all. This third class of passages Schmiedel is perfectly willing to accept as transmitting a true tradition: he actually does so accept them. But not on their own credit, but only on the faith of the small class of passages — his "pillar-passages" — which assure him of the actual existence of a merely human Jesus to whom, then, it is natural to ascribe these "indifferent" passages also. For, as he says in his primary statement,[35] and repeats here: [36] "If we discover any such points — even if only a few — they guarantee not only their own contents but also much more. For in that case one may also hold as credible all else which agrees in character with these, and is in other respects not open to suspicion." The fundamental characteristic of the "pillar-passages," without which they would not be "pillar-passages," is, therefore, that they are absolutely irreconcilable with a supernatural Jesus.

The statement in the lecture on "Jesus and Modern Criticism" [37] is made from the same standpoint as that in the Preface to Neumann's "Jesus" and adds very little to it. We are told that "it is of little use merely to say in a vague and general way that the figure of Jesus portrayed in the Gospels could not possibly have been invented." What is of importance is that we should recognize that "the Gospels, though they seem to be very much exposed to doubt, actually contain in themselves the best means of overcoming it."

"All we require to do is to limit the statement that their contents could not have been invented, which in its vague and general form possesses no evidential value, to specific' passages in which it is not open to question. I select nine such passages, and, in order to emphasize their importance, give them a special name; I call them the *foundation-pillars of a really scientific life of Jesus.*

---

[35] "Encyclopaedia Biblica," coll. 1872–1873, § 131.
[36] Neumann, p. xiii.   [37] Pp. 15 ff., 22 ff.

"Now, the important point is that they are chosen on the same principles which guide every critical historian in extra-theological fields. When we make our first acquaintance with a historical person in a book which is throughout influenced by a feeling of worship for its hero, as the Gospels are by a feeling of worship for Jesus, in the first rank of credibility we place those passages of the book which really run counter to this feeling; for we realize that, the writer's sentiments being what they were, such passages cannot have been invented by the author of the book; nor would they have been taken from the records at his service if their absolute truthfulness had not forced itself upon him. In the case of the Evangelists, moreover, we are so fortunate as to be able to note how a record of this kind which runs counter to the author's feeling of worship for Jesus is often incorporated by one or by two of them, while the other has omitted it or has altered it with the clear intention of emphasizing Jesus' higher rank. I have included among my foundation-pillars only such passages as have been passed over or altered by at least one of the three Evangelists. Of course, in the case of almost every one of these, it has already been said once, perhaps often, that it could not be the product of an inventive mind. What scholars had previously neglected to do was to make these passages the starting point for the critical treatment of the life of Jesus. . . .

"*What then have I gained in these nine 'foundation-pillars'?* You will perhaps say, 'Very little.' I reply, 'I have gained just enough.' . . . In a word, I know, on the one hand, that his person cannot be referred to the region of myth; on the other hand, that he was man in the full sense of the term, and that, without of course denying that the divine character was in him, this could be found only in the shape in which it could be found in any human being.

"I think, therefore, that if we knew no more, we should know by no means little about him. But, as a matter of fact, the 'foundation-pillars' are but the starting-point of our study of the life of Jesus. . . . We must, therefore, work upon the principle that, together with the 'foundation-pillars,' and as a result of them, everything in the first three Gospels deserves belief which would tend to establish Jesus' greatness, provided that it harmonizes with the picture produced by the foundation-pillars, and in other respects does not raise suspicion."

Certainly, with four such extended expositions of his method, it would be difficult seriously to misapprehend

Schmiedel's essential meaning. Nevertheless some difficulty has apparently been experienced in grasping at once what we may call the principle of direct contradiction which forms its core. Even Otto Schmiedel, for example, seems to lose hold of it, — although, no doubt he does not profess to do more than to follow his brother's scheme " in its essentials." His version of it runs as follows: [38]

" The criticism of the sources has brought us thus far. I will now make a further attempt, from general considerations which are independent of the search for sources, to find certain points of support to give the necessary certainty to the portrait of the life of Jesus which we are seeking to sketch. We have recognized it as an essential characteristic of the presentations of the lives of the founders of religions and redemptive personalities, that with holy zeal they glorify, and indeed *deify* these personalities. The more this tendency increases the more does the account lose its historical character and become legendary. Let us turn the matter around. If we find in the Gospels passages which declare of Jesus something in contradiction to this tendency to glorification, which, however, have been altered or omitted by *later* Gospels, because they take offence at these human things, at this lack of glorification, then we may with assurance infer from this that these passages which do *not* glorify Jesus are *old* and *authentic*."

He then adduces five examples of such passages, intimating in passing that many more might be produced, and declares of them in the mass that they form the skeleton of what is incontestable and thus provide a solid basis for the Life of Jesus. Three of his five passages, he takes over from P. W. Schmiedel. The two that are added can scarcely be said to preserve perfectly the characteristic feature claimed for the " pillar-passages," — express contradiction of the deity ascribed to Jesus in the historical tradition. They are expounded by Otto Schmiedel thus:

" In the oldest Gospel, Mark, it is continually emphasized that Jesus *forbade* His disciples to make His deeds of healing known.

[38] " Die Hauptprobleme der Leben-Jesu Forschung." [2] 1906, pp. 46 ff.

In the later Gospels this trait retires, and indeed the number and importance of the deeds of healing steadily increases. This last serves for glorification. *Therefore* the representation of Mark, Jesus' horror of being trumpeted as a miracle-worker, is all the more certainly historical. . . ."

" The older Gospels relate, *without* assignment of reasons, that Jesus was betrayed by Judas Iscariot. Luke and John seek all kinds of explanations for this, while the enemies of Christianity mock at the betrayal of the Master by one of His own disciples: all the more certain is it that the betrayal was not invented by Jesus' adherents, but is old and historical."

It does not appear why a divine, no less than a human Jesus, might not, for reasons of His own, forbid His cures to be heralded abroad; or why a divine, no less than a human Jesus, might not be betrayed by one of His own disciples. The stress which P. W. Schmiedel lays on the contradiction to the deity of Jesus in his " pillar-passages," Otto Schmiedel lays rather on modifications by later Gospels of statements in the earlier which struck the Christian feeling of the time as making too little for the glory of Jesus. The alteration or omission of the statements of his " pillar-passages " by one or another of the Gospels had been appealed to by P. W. Schmiedel only as a secondary consideration; it bears the character of a verification of the asserted offensiveness of these passages to the Christian feeling of the day. The hinge of his argument turns on the intrinsic inconsistency of these statements with the deification of Jesus. He infers immediately from this their " uninventibility " by the authors of the Gospels and of the tradition which the Gospels represent, and their consequent originality. The hinge of Otto Schmiedel's argument, on the other hand, turns on the modifications which these statements have suffered at the hands of later Evangelists. From these he infers the relative originality of the simpler statement, and by further consequence the unpretentiousness of Jesus' self-manifestation. The movement of thought in the two cases is not only different but directly opposite. This is particularly apparent in the diverse treatment given by the two writers to the " pillar-passages " which are adduced by both. On Mark vi. 5 f. P. W. Schmiedel writes: [39]

" When He appeared in His native city of Nazareth He was sneered at as one of whom it was known whose son and brother He was, and He was made to feel that a prophet finds no honor in His own country. Now in Mark (vi. 5 f.) we read further: ' And He could not do any mighty work there, except He healed a few sick folk by laying His hands upon them; and He marveled at their unbelief.' He could not. This is another narrative like that of the sign of Jonah; it most certainly would not be found in our Gospels if it had not been handed down by someone who had himself witnessed the occurrences and then been repeated unaltered. How unacceptable it must have been to the later narrators, all of whom, Mark not excepted, were convinced of Jesus' power to work miracles, is shown by Matthew, who (xiii. 58 f.) reports it thus: ' And He *did* there not many mighty works, because of their unbelief.' "

In Otto Schmiedel's hands, we find, on the contrary, this essentially different representation (we do not stop to point out the misreport of what Mark says, or even the remarkable illation): [40]

" In Mk., vi. 5 there stands: In Nazareth Jesus *could* work no miraculous cures because of the lack of faith in His fellow-townsmen. In Mt. xiii. 58: ' He did there *not many* miracles.' It is, therefore, historically certain that Jesus' healing work was *dependent* psychologically on the *trust* of those who sought the healing."

Of Mk. xiii. 32, P. W. Schmiedel, contrasting it with John's ascription of omniscience to Jesus, writes: [41]

" In the Synoptics . . . we find His express declaration (Mk. xiii. 32) that ' of that day,' that is to say that on which He was to return from heaven in order to establish the kingdom of God on earth, ' or of that hour, knoweth no one, not even the angels in heaven, nor yet the Son, but the Father only '; another one of the statements which certainly no one of His worshippers invented. Luke leaves it out altogether; Matthew (according to the probably original text) at least the decisive words ' nor yet the Son.'

[39] " Das vierte Evangelium, etc.," pp. 31–32.   [40] P. 47.
[41] " Das vierte Evangelium, etc.," p. 22.

What we find in Otto Schmiedel is:

" Mk. xiii. 32 says: Time and hour *when* the Son of Man returns
on the clouds of heaven knoweth no one, *not even the Son*. Mt.
xxiv. 36 leaves out ' not even the Son ' as offensive to him. Therefore
these words are *genuine*. Jesus claims for Himself therefore *no*
knowledge of the future."

In the treatment of the remaining passage adduced by them
both a more primary place seems to be given by P. W. Schmiedel to the forms in which it appears in the several Gospels.
This, however, is an illusion, and is due largely to the circumstance that his primary discussion of it happens to be introduced at that point in his argument where he is preoccupied
with the relations of the Gospels to one another.[42] As in the
other cases we quote what he says about it in his booklet on
John's Gospel: [43]

" And equally unacceptable to this Evangelist would be the
record in Mk. (x. 17 f.) and Lk. that Jesus, to the address of a rich
man, ' Good Master, what must I do to obtain eternal life? ' replied:
' Why callest thou me good? No one is good except God alone.' And
yet beyond question, this reply came from Jesus' lips. How little
it could have been invented by anyone of His worshippers, who
drive the pen in the Gospels, Matthew shows. With him (xix. 16 f.),
the rich man says, ' Master, what good thing must I do in order to
have eternal life? And Jesus answers, ' Why askest thou me concerning the good? There is One that is good.' How does Jesus come
here to the six last words? Should He not, since He was asked concerning the good, proceed: ' There is *one thing* that is good? ' And
that would be the only suitable reply not only because of what
had preceded, but also because of what follows; for Jesus says
further, ' If, however, thou wouldst enter into life, keep the commandments.' Accordingly, in Jesus' opinion, the good concerning
which He was asked consists in keeping the commandments. How
did Matthew come to the words, ' There is One that is good? ' Only
by having before him, as he wrote, the language of Mark. Here we
have our finger on the way in which Matthew, with conscious purpose, altered this language in its opening words, so that it should

---

[42] " Encyclopaedia Biblica," col. 1847 (b).   [43] Pp. 19 f.

no longer be offensive, and on the way in which, at the end, he has left a few words of it unaltered, which betray to us the manner in which the thing has been done."

Here also Otto Schmiedel's whole case is summed up in the relations of the Synoptical reports:

" Here also belongs the passage which has been mentioned in another connection,[44] where Jesus, in Mk. x. 18, said to the rich young man, ' Why callest thou me good. No one is good except God.' Jesus denies, therefore, His absolute sinlessness. Mat. xix. 17 seeks to efface this."

The same imperfect grasp upon the exact point of the " pillar-passages " which deflects Otto Schmiedel's treatment of them, has affected also the use made of them by Schmiedel's pupil, Arno Neumann. Neumann does, indeed, quite purely reproduce Schmiedel's point of view in his general statement. After having likened the attempt to get at the true tradition of Jesus' life, to working through a series of geological strata, he raises the question whether this does not " make the whole foundation [of our knowledge of Jesus] precarious, and open a door to all kinds of arbitrary conjecture." He then proceeds:[45]

" It would do so if we did not come upon such elements in the tradition as the worshippers of Jesus would never have preserved unless they had been handed down as facts in the story of Jesus' life, or if we were no longer able to show from the parallel accounts how worship has constantly changed the old data handed down by traditions and adapted them to its own wishes. But we do find sayings and incidents of this description in one or other of the Gospels, be they few or many, and, this being so, we are entitled to draw from them general inferences as to what is credible in the life and work of Jesus. For it is impossible (here every historian will agree) for one who worships a hero to think and speak in such a way as to

[44] Cf. p. 27: " In Mk. x. 18 Jesus says to the rich young man, ' Why callest thou me good? No one is good except God.' To Matthew (xix. 17) this statement seemed to put the sinlessness of Jesus in danger, and so he changed it to, ' Why askest thou me concerning the good (neuter)? ' Now, however, the following, ' No one is good,' etc., naturally no longer fits on."

[45] " Jesus," pp. 9 ff.

contradict or essentially modify his own worship.[46] Statements which do this can be nothing more or less than survivals of the truth, precious fragments which have been covered and well-nigh hidden for ever by the deposits of later times. For this reason a scholar of our own time, Dr. Schmiedel, has called these portions of the tradition, ' foundation-pillars of the life of Jesus.' The existence of such statements is the salvation of the Synoptic Gospels, giving them a definite value of sources.[47] The Gospels cannot be pure sagas or legends when material so intractable is enshrined in them."

Perhaps a certain imperfection in Neumann's appreciation of the stringency of the presumed effect of the " pillar-passages " is already betrayed by the admission of an alternative expression into the phrase declaring it impossible for a worshipping writer to invent or assert anything not merely which contradicts but also which " essentially modifies " his own worship. We perceive clearly his defection from this stringency, however, only when we scan his illustrative passages. He adduces eight of these, two of Schmiedel's being omitted, and a new one added and indeed given the premier place in the list. The two omitted — Mk. viii. 14–21, and Mt. xi. 5 — are both, in Schmiedel's view, " transformed parables " and the inclusion of them in the " pillar-passages " is in any case surprising, so that we need not wonder that Neumann omits them, although perfectly agreeing with Schmiedel that they are " transformed parables." [48] The passage added is, however, as little stringent as any could be. It is Lk. ii. 52 (cf. iv. 16) which " says that Jesus grew in stature in a truly human way." " Had the writer been a worshipper of Jesus as a deity," Neumann comments, " he would have presented Him to us as full-grown," — of which we have no other assurance, however, than this expres-

[46] More literally: " For every historian will pronounce it impossible that one who reverences " (or " worships ") " a hero should invent or assert things which contradict his own reverence " (or " worship "), " or modify it fundamentally."

[47] More literally: " By their presence a certain source-value is preserved to the Synoptic Gospels."

[48] See pp. 76, 86. Neumann calls attention on p. 11, note 1, to his passing them by here, apparently in order to avoid giving the impression that he is correcting Schmiedel.

sion of opinion by Neumann himself, in opposition to the
example of Matthew and Luke, both of whom were "worshippers of Jesus" and both of whom record the story of His infancy. But what most clearly shows us the imperfection of
Neumann's grasp on the peculiarity of the "pillar-passages"
is a remark he adjoins at the end of the list, in which he endeavors to make them do double duty. "All these passages," he
tells us, "are of such a nature as neither the worship of Jesus
in the growing church, nor yet the religious socialism of the
masses, could ever have invented." [49] But why could not a
"religious socialist" believe that Jesus grew up like any other
boy? Or that Jesus refused to work "signs," or indeed that He
could not work miracles; or that He did not know all that the
future had in store for Him or His followers? Or, indeed, that
He was not absolutely without sin, or could be thought by
His kinspeople to be out of His head, or could have felt Himself
deserted by God in the end? Socialists in our own day seem to
have no difficulty in believing such things. Neumann has obviously temporarily lost the exact point of view of the "pillar-
passages," and consequently has confused the argument which
is built upon them. We say he has "temporarily" lost their
point of view; for he immediately recovers it and writes:

"They prove, indeed, that the figure of Jesus was originally a
truly human one, and that we can therefore speak of Him as
"divine," only in the sense that divinity is possible within the
limits of the human."

He was, no doubt, greatly human, and we must of course paint
Him so; but

"There is only one critical limitation that need be added:
the proviso, namely, that construction must be such as will adapt
itself to the adamantine restrictions of the knowledge given in our
foundation texts."

We know much more of Jesus than we can learn from the
"pillar-passages"; but the Jesus we know cannot transcend

[49] The German is perhaps a little more lucid: "The list of passages
which the common reverence of the growing church, or for that matter the
religious socialism of the masses could never have invented."

the Jesus of these fundamental texts. They give us the absolute norm of what Jesus was.

The tendency of Schmiedel's followers to abate a little of the stringency of the idea of the " pillar-passages " means, of course, a tendency, more or less developed, to look at them broadly as passages which do not find their explanation in " the faith of the community " and may therefore very well be (or perhaps we may insist, are most probably, or even quite certainly) genuine traditions; rather than narrowly, as passages which, because they directly contradict the reverence for Jesus which forms the primary bias of the vehicles of the tradition, oral or written, that has preserved for us the memory of Jesus, must therefore necessarily preserve true traditions and give us not only our most reliable knowledge of Jesus but knowledge of Him which is absolutely trustworthy. And this change in point of view, as we cannot have failed to observe, is accompanied by an associated tendency to treat the appeal to such " pillar-passages " not so much as a substitute for literary criticism — though this is the precise thing which commends the appeal to them to Schmiedel himself — as rather as a supplement to it, called in only after it has done its work, to enable us to take a step farther than it can lead us. These tendencies, in proportion as they are yielded to, are tantamount, of course, to desertion of all that is distinctive in Schmiedel's critical method and reversion to the common methods of " Liberal " criticism, which first employs literary criticism in order to ascertain what the oldest sources contain, and then calls in historical criticism, — operating on the single canon that we are to penetrate by its aid behind " the faith of the community " — that we may ascertain what, in that which is transmitted by the sources, is true. It will conduce to a better understanding, both of the general " Liberal " method and of the peculiarity of Schmiedel's method if we bring into view a tolerably full account of the " Liberal " method in one of its most consistent and yet genial recent exponents. We cannot do better for this purpose than turn to the exposition of it by W. Heitmüller, in his interesting article " Jesus Christ " in

Schiele and Zscharnack's "Encyclopaedia," published under the title of "Die Religion in Geschichte und Gegenwart." [50] The circumstances that Heitmüller is writing for a general, educated and not merely a technically theological public, and that Schmiedel's criticism is apparently not wholly out of his thought, only add to the value of his exposition for our purposes.

At the point at which we enter his discussion he is engaged in searching out the trustworthy sources of knowledge of Jesus. He has just outlined the processes by which the evangelical documents are tested. It has been a long and difficult task to penetrate by this criticism to their Sources, and when we have reached these Sources our labors are far from being at an end. Mark and the Discourse-Source are after all not the *ultimate* Sources. The *ultimate* Sources are " the separate narratives and separate declarations or discourses of Jesus to be obtained from these and from the peculiar portions of Matthew and Luke, by the help of critical labor." And then, when we have got these well before us, we have to raise the question whether they give us " immediately historical, utilizable, trustworthy material." " Is the portrait of Jesus, — no, are the separate features of this portrait which look out upon us from these separate fragments — really genuine features? " [51] From the Discourse-Source and Mark (which with Heitmüller is the Narrative-Source), on to John we have found everything in a flux. What was there previous to the Discource-Source and Mark? Were not the same forces which modified the transmission subsequently already at work before these Sources arose? The question requires only to be put for the answer to come clearly back to us.

" These narratives and declarations were taken from the oral tradition of the Christian community and written down about 60 or 70 A.D.; thus they had lived for thirty or forty years in the oral tradition, they were handed on from mouth to mouth, from hand to hand; through how many hands! What lived on further and was preserved was necessarily conditioned in its very substance by the

[50] Vol. iii. 1912, coll. 356 ff.   [51] Col. 356.

nature and the need of the community. Accordingly, we must suppose it at least possible that these separate materials, as they are accessible to us in Mark, say, have been influenced by the faith of the community and those other entities. That means, however, that the ultimate direct Sources which can be reached by us, the separate declarations and narratives, do not, when taken strictly, carry us beyond the portrait of the Christ of the Palestinian community of about 50–70 A.D. To turn aside here from everything else for the sake of brevity, we need only to realize that the community which transmitted orally knowledge of Jesus, stood under the influence of belief in the resurrection of Jesus; how this belief must already have steeped even good reminiscences in an alien, new light! Nay, must we not assume that even for the immediate disciples recollection was disturbed in many points by the influence of the Easter experience and the faith which attaches itself to it? And in point of fact a more careful scrutiny shows that even in this oldest obtainable memorial, of separate declarations and separate narratives, legendary traits are present, that the belief and usage of the community have already exerted their moulding and forming power and activity.[52]

It is in this circumstance that the difficulty of research into the life of Jesus lies. " The starting-point of all further investigation is recognition that the ultimate Direct-Sources carry us only to the portrait of Jesus of the primitive community of about 60 A. D." [53] The question is whether we have any means — any possibility — of getting behind the portrait of Jesus of the community to the actual reality. Some are utterly sceptical of doing so. But this extreme scepticism is unreasonable. It is not difficult to show that the portrait of Christ current in the community of 60 A.D. is not a simply imaginary one.

" That in spite of legendary, mythological elements, in spite of the repainting by the faith of the community, which must be admitted, in this Evangelical representation, there are historical elements in the ultimate sources of which we have spoken, will, in accordance with universally recognized principles, have to be allowed to be certain if *constituents* are found in them which *are not reconcilable* (*vereinbar*) with the faith of the community to which the

---

[52] Coll. 356–357.　　　　　　　[53] Col. 357.

whole portrait belongs. What does not stand in harmony with it can certainly not owe its origin to it. Not a few constituents, now, of this kind are found. They not seldom betray themselves as contradictory to the faith of the community by this — that they are omitted or altered by the later narrators. Let us indicate some of them.[54] In Mk. x. 17 ff. Jesus repudiates the address of ' Good Master ' with the words, ' Why callest thou me good? None is good but God only.' The community looked upon its Lord as sinless; this account is not then the product of their belief. How little the declaration of Jesus pleased the community is shown by its alteration by the later Mt. xix. 16 ff., which formulates the question of the young man thus: ' Master, what good thing must I do? ' and makes Jesus answer: ' Wherefore askest thou me concerning the good? Only One is good.' . . . The Gethsemane scene, Mk. xiv. 32–42 which shows Jesus in deep distress, could never have been invented by the believing community; it glorified Him precisely as one who went of His own will to His death. Luke softens down the account; John omits it. The story of Mk. iii. 21, according to which His own people say of Jesus, ' He is beside Himself,' cannot be understood as an invention of the faith which glorified Jesus: Matthew and Luke pass the story by. The community saw in Peter its chief Apostle: it cannot have invented his shameful denial. The community glorified the disciples: the story of their cowardly flight (Mk. xiv. 50) when Jesus went to His death, was certainly not the product of their fancy: Luke and John suppress this also. It was early the belief of the community (I Cor. xv. 1 ff.) that Jesus died for the sins of men. And yet in the old tradition there are very few declarations in which this belief has found any sort of expression (Mk. x. 45; xiv. 24) ; but there has been preserved on the other hand a parable (Lk. xv. 11 ff.)‚ that of the Lost Son, which is utterly irreconcilable with this dominant idea.[55] These and other observations suffice to prove with

[54] It will be observed that of the six passages here adduced by Heitmüller, two are common to him and Schmiedel (Mk. x. 17; iii. 21), and a third is of the same character (Mk. ix. 22–32, and is, of course, looked upon by Schmiedel in the same light as the others (see " Das vierte Evangelium, etc.," p. 20); a fourth, the Parable of the Lost Son (Lk. xv. 11 ff.) although belonging to another category is, of course, also accepted as genuine by Schmiedel with the same heartiness as by Heitmüller (" Encyclopaedia Biblica," col. 1841); while the two remaining ones concern the sensitivity of the early community for the honor of the Apostles, not of Jesus.

[55] We may ask in passing what ground on Heitmüller's principles there

compelling convincingness that in the community's portrait of Jesus, about 50–70 A.D., there are in any case contained and are recognizable some indubitably genuine original traits. This fact, now, is adapted to strengthen confidence in the tradition in general. For if, as we see here, the community has transmitted declarations and narratives which contradict its own conception, it follows that this community has shown respect for the tradition, and in any case has not set itself simply to suppress what was unpleasant to it. And now, there force themselves on the attentive eye other observations also which operate greatly to strengthen confidence in the oldest tradition." [56]

Heitmüller then proceeds to adduce the Aramaic coloring of the basis of both Mark and the Discourse-Source, their particularity in intimate details, the general tone of the Discourse-Source, the cultivated memories of the men of the day, as conducing to the conclusion that there is much gold mingled with the dross in the tradition.[57] The question is how the gold is to

---

is for assigning Lk. xv. 11 ff. to the oldest tradition, seeing that it occurs neither in Mk. nor in the Discourse-Source. Heitmüller's account of the parables (col. 361) is: "With respect to the apothegms and parables the principle that that will pass for genuine which seems individual, striking and original, will not be wholly rejected, but as a principle which is not decisive, will be applied only with the greatest caution." Cf. Schmiedel, "Encyclopaedia Biblica," col. 1841. From our own point of view, there is of course no reason why the matter peculiar to Luke should not be of as indisputable originality as that which is common to him with Matthew or with Matthew and Mark. Cf. Schmiedel, ibid., col. 1868; and especially Weinel, ZTK, 1910, I. p. 24: "Finally Wellhausen has ventured on the proposition: 'The presupposition is self-evident that we must recognize in the peculiar matter which is found in one of the Evangelists, the latest literary stratum' ("Einleitung, etc.," p. 73). That is true — provided only, precisely in Wellhausen, it does not mean more than it says, provided only there is not continually connected with it an attempt to assign to these passages a lower rank not only literarily but also historically, that is to say with reference to their value as sources. It is however, wholly false to hold a narrative better attested for this reason — that three Evangelists (that means, however, Mark, which the others follow) or that two (that means, however, the Discourse-Source) report it — than if only one (that means another tradition) reports it. That a tradition has been written down say ten years after Mark does not weight it with a presupposition against it."

[56] Coll. 358 ff.
[57] Col. 361.

be extracted. And the answer is that first, by literary criticism, the oldest attainable form of each narrative or declaration is to be established, and then historical criticism is to be called in. At the foundation is to be laid "the material which runs counter to the belief, the theology, the customs, the cultus of the primitive community, or which at least does not completely correspond with it. "We may have," he declares, "unconditional confidence in such material." We may admit, along with this, much that stands in close relation with it, and yet is in harmony with the belief of the community. On the other hand, we must pronounce ungenuine everything which "all too plainly corresponds with the belief, the cultus, and the dogmatic and apologetical needs of the community, or can be explained only from them." Our scrupulosity must be particularly active "against everything that lay especially at the heart of the oldest Christianity" — such as belief in Jesus' messiahship, His approaching return, the whole domain of so-called eschatology, His passion and resurrection, His miraculous power. In this careful and laborious fashion it will be possible to penetrate behind the community's portrait of Christ at about 60 A.D. and approach the truth about Jesus.

The critical methods of Schmiedel and Heitmüller are fundamentally the same; and yet they differ at cardinal points. Heitmüller, as well as Schmiedel, acknowledges the failure of literary criticism to reach a stratum of tradition in which Jesus is other than the divine figure which the Evangelists paint Him; and like Schmiedel he calls in historical criticism to recover some trustworthy traces of a merely human Jesus. He applies this historical criticism, however, only to the Sources which literary criticism has unearthed, and therefore finds his "pillar-passages" not, as Schmiedel does, in any of the Synoptic Gospels indifferently, but all in Mark, which is to him the Narrative-Source.[58] The principle of his "pillar-passages" is not, as with Schmiedel (or at least not so openly), narrowly that they directly contradict the deifying conception of Jesus which dominated the transmitters of the tradition, but more

[58] For exceptions, see above note 55.

broadly that they contradict, or at least do not find their explanation in, the general point of view of the early Christian community; they do not reflect " interests " of that community. Accordingly the evidential value of these " pillar-passages " as witnesses to the real Jesus is hardly as great with Heitmüller as with Schmiedel. With Heitmüller they form no doubt as with Schmiedel the nucleus of " all sound historical knowledge of Jesus," but they scarcely come with the demonstrative force which they take on in Schmiedel's hands, placing beyond all possibility of question both the actual existence and the purely human character of Jesus. From the " pillar-passages " both work outwards to the same general results with respect both to the compass of the transmitted material which may be utilized in forming our picture of Jesus and His life and work; and with respect to the actual portrait of Jesus which is derived from this material as the genuine Jesus of history. The principle of the construction of the real Jesus of history in both writers alike is that of contradiction to the whole mass of the testimony concerning Him, which is set aside on no other ground than that it is possible to find here and there imbedded in it a statement which seems to these writers not perfectly consistent with its general drift. As to the legitimacy of this procedure, particularly when the mass and weight of the testimony is considered, and the number and character of the contradictory passages, we for the moment leave the reader to judge for himself.

Although Schmiedel's critical method has been before the public since 1901, and very fully since 1906, it has as yet been subjected to very little formal criticism. This has been due partly, no doubt, to a feeling that it is only a modification — and that not a very important modification — of the ordinary critical procedure in general use among " Liberal " theologians, and partly to a greater or less failure to apprehend precisely the nature of the modification in the ordinary " Liberal " procedure which it proposes. Perhaps also account should be taken of the circumstance that no separate work has been devoted by Schmiedel himself to the exposition of his proposals, but they have been presented only incidentally in works whose chief concernment lies elsewhere. In reviews of these publications there has been, of course, some expression of opinion upon this portion of their contents also, more or less fully supported by reasoning. Only here and there, however, has there been any extended discussion of the new critical method in its details, except indeed at the hands of the extreme radicals, who deny the very existence of Jesus.[59] It is part of Schmiedel's contention, it will be remembered, that his method supplies a short and easy demonstration of the actual existence of Jesus. This side of his contention has attracted the attention and drawn the fire of those writers who are engaged in an attempt to persuade the public that the whole figure of Jesus is mythical. Little of value in the way of general criticism of Schmiedel's method could be expected from this quarter; and in point of fact these writers usually lose themselves quickly in discussions of the exegesis of the passages adduced by Schmiedel as "pillar-passages," ordinarily in an effort to vacate their literal sense and to impose on them a purely symbolical significance, which would make them part and parcel of the myth of Jesus, the pure product of the invention of His votaries.

"There are no passages in the Gospels," declares W. B. Smith,[60] which testify to a pure humanity for Jesus. It is of course set forth how He teaches, journeys from place to place, how even He sleeps and (in a very transparent parable) hungers, how he works miracles, is arrested, imprisoned, tried, condemned, executed, buried and rises

[59] E.g. John M. Robertson, "Pagan Christs," 1903, pp. 227–238; Friedrich Steudel, "Im Kampf um die Christusmythe," 1910, pp. 88–110; William Benjamin Smith, "Ecce Deus: die urchristliche Lehre des reingöttlichen Jesu," 1911, pp. 104–224 (E. T. under same title, 1912); Arthur Drews, "Die Zeugnisse für die Geschichtlichkeit Jesu," 1911, pp. 212–225 (E. T. "The Witnesses to the Historicity of Jesus," 1912 pp. 144–156). With these writers, no doubt, Eduard Hertlein, *Protestantische Monatshefte*, x. (1906) pp. 386 ff. may be classed for the essence of the matter without danger of great injustice. Cf. also F. Ziller, "Die moderne Bibelwissenschaft und die Krisis der evangelischen Kirche," 1910, pp. 117–118. Schmiedel replies elaborately to Robertson in his preface to Neumann's "Jesus," and to Hertlein in the next number of the *Protestantische Monatshefte*.

[60] "Ecce Deus," p. 199.

again But all this is intended only figuratively; it is only the linen
cloth that is thrown around the divine form of the ' new doctrine ';
it is only the historical projection of a system of religious ideas. The
profound thinkers who invented these parables and symbols were
fully conscious of their real inward meaning, as were also those who
first heard them, and repeated and recorded them."

Nevertheless the broader question is not wholly left to one
side, nor are there lacking in the remarks devoted to it criticisms which, if they do not quite go to the root of the matter,
yet have real validity as against Schmiedel's modes of presenting his argument. It is common to all of these writers, for
example, to point out that this argument proves too much;
that, if it were valid, there are few characters of fiction, professed or mythical, which we should not have to recognize as
having really existed. Thus, Friedrich Steudel urges: [61]

" There is a fatal flaw involved in the whole of the demonstration which Schmiedel essays. It is, no doubt, true that when a
historian portrays a personality the historicity of which is *otherwise established,* most credit will be given to those accounts which
stand in a certain contradiction to the characterization which is
intended to be given of him in general. But it could never be erected
into a universally valid method, to conclude solely from the presence
of such traits in a tradition to the historicity of a personality depicted in it. For in that case, to speak plainly, even a Zeus to whom
his worshippers have imputed all sorts of vicious, human — only
too human — traits must be a historical personality because it
cannot be otherwise understood how his worshippers could have
ascribed to him such human traits. Indeed any contradictory trait
which a critic discovers in the characters of a dramatic poem must,
according to the requirements of Schmiedel's method, bring him to
the view that the poet cannot have been inventing here but must
have had a historical model. Or, to make the application to our
own case, — if the historicity of Jesus, — which, however, is just
the thing that stands in question — *did not stand in question,* then
it could be said that when the writer who deifies Him, nevertheless
adduces human traits, there the historical element lies most certainly before us; but historicity can and may never be concluded

[61] P. 98.

merely from the fact of apparent contradictions within a portrait which on other grounds has become questionable, especially when, as in the case in hand, these contradictions find their simplest and most natural explanation in the dogmatic and literary peculiarity of the sources." [62]

Following out the same line of remark, John M. Robertson [63] directs us to Grote's famous chapter on Greek myths, and cites from it a series of apt sentences in which Grote argues that no trustworthy historical facts can be extracted from such mythical stories. The passage adduced runs in its entirety, as follows: [64]

" The utmost which we accomplish by means of the semi-historical theory, even in its most successful applications, is, that after leaving out from the mythical narrative all that is miraculous or high-colored or extravagant, we arrive at a series of credible incidents — incidents which *may, perhaps,* have really occurred, and against which no intrinsic presumption can be raised. This is exactly the character of a well-written modern novel (as, for example, several among the compositions of Defoe), the whole story of which is such as may well have occurred in real life: it is plausible fiction, and nothing beyond. To raise plausible fiction up to the superior dignity of truth, some positive testimony or positive ground of inference must be shown; even the highest measure of intrinsic probability is not alone sufficient. A man who tells us that, on the day of the battle of Platæa, rain fell on the spot of ground where the city of New York now stands, will neither deserve nor obtain credit, because he can have had no means of positive knowledge; though the statement is not in the slightest degree improbable. On the other hand, statements in themselves very improbable may well deserve belief, provided they be supported by sufficient positive evidence;

[62] Similarly Arthur Drews (" Die Zeugnisse, etc.," p. 221; E. T. p. 152): " If the historicity of Jesus was *otherwise established,* then it would be justifiable to conclude from the presence of such traits to the historical tradition which the author could not evade." On this reasoning, he remarks, we could prove the historicity of Heracles from the presence in his legend of traits which accord very ill with the otherwise noble figure of this hero.

[63] P. 230.

[64] George Grote, " History of Greece," American reprint of the second London ed., 1856, i., p. 429 (Robertson cites London, 1888, i., p. 382).

thus the canal dug by order of Xerxês across the promontory of Mount Athos, and the sailing of the Persian fleet through it, is a fact which I believe, because it is well-attested — notwithstanding its remarkable improbability, which so far misled Juvenal as to induce him to single out the narrative as a glaring example of Grecian mendacity."

The hinge of Grote's position, it will be seen, turns on the distinction between the possible and the actual, the credible and the certified. We may purge a narrative of impossibilities and not make a single step towards authenticating it. " The narrative ceases to be incredible, but it still remains uncertified, — a mere commonplace possibility." [65] " By the aid of conjecture, we get out of the impossible, and arrive at matters intrinsically plausible, but totally uncertified; beyond this point we cannot penetrate without the light of extrinsic evidence, since there is no intrinsic mark to distinguish truth from plausible fiction." [66] In the absence of positive evidence of reality, no superior intrinsic credibility attaching to certain events above others in the same narrative can accredit them as real.

Schmiedel has fairly laid himself open to a rejoinder of this kind by his reprehensible dallying with the suggestion that Jesus may never have really existed. If Heinrich Weinel thinks it necessary to rebuke the levity of his Preface to W. B. Smith's " Der vorchristliche Jesus," [67] what shall we say of his repeated intimation in the exposition of his method of criticism, not merely that the real existence of Jesus is an open question, but even that it is a question which is all but closed, which apart from the "pillar-passages" would be closed, in an adverse

[65] P. 431.

[66] P. 417–418.

[67] " Ist das 'liberale' Jesusbild widerlegt? " 1910, p. 13: " It was not, however, a merely tactical blunder in Schmiedel, to write for the German translation of Smith a Preface in which he not only maintained that it is not easy to refute Smith, but further that Smith's learning is 'by no means at the disposal of every one who works after a strictly scientific fashion'; and in which he speaks of the 'art of his scientific method.' This is simply untruth. And Schmiedel only gets what he deserves, when, despite his protestation that he does not think anything in Smith's construction right, he is everywhere invoked as compurgator — after allowance for the 'theological arabesque.' "

sense? To say that " if passages of this kind were wholly wanting in them, it would be impossible to prove to a sceptic that
any historical value whatever was to be assigned to the Gospels; he would be in a position to declare the picture of Jesus
contained in them to be purely a work of phantasy and could
remove the person of Jesus from the field of history "; [68] or
even, as it is elsewhere perhaps not quite so strongly put,[69] that
" if they were wholly wanting in them, it would be difficult to
withstand the allegation that the Gospels *everywhere* give us
only a sacred image painted on a gold ground, and we could
therefore not at all know what kind of an appearance Jesus
really made, if not indeed even whether He ever existed at
all "; — is of course mere fustian: nobody knows better than
Schmiedel that even were there no Gospels at all the actual
existence of Jesus would be exceptionally attested and altogether beyond question. But the effect of permitting himself
to give utterance to such inconsiderate assertions is to hand
himself over bound hand and foot to his enemies. He has
treated the whole tradition of Jesus as if it were pure myth, and
has represented the task of the historian to be to seek out and
isolate the kernel of fact which lies at the center of this myth.
It is open to anyone to rejoin that this task is hopeless; that on
this pathway we can reach only the plausible, not the attested,
while it is only the attested that can claim to be the actual. It
is ineffective to urge in rebuttal that the statements appealed
to do not range with the merely " credible " elements which
are selected out from the body of the myth by those whom
Grote speaks of as advocates of " the semi-historical theory,"
but have the peculiarity that they could not have been invented by the framers of the myth, because they are inconsistent with its whole substance and must therefore have been
carried over unchanged from the pre-mythical tradition. It is
easy to rejoin (with W. B. Smith) that an impossibility is
attempted here; that no limits can be set to the invention of
man; and it is equally easy to point out (reverting to Grote)

[68] " Encyclopaedia Biblica," col. 1881.
[69] " Das vierte Evangelium, etc.," p. 17.

that what is here claimed as a peculiarity of the "pillar-passages" is a common phenomenon in all divine myths. In them all express inconsistencies abound and in the nature of the case must abound, since human invention is incompetent to the task of consistently dramatizing deity. Let a poet be of the highest genius and do his utmost to realize his picture of the divine actor he is depicting: "If he does not consistently succeed in it, the reason is because consistency in such a matter is unattainable, since, after all, the analogies of common humanity, the only materials which the most creative imagination has to work upon, obtrude themselves involuntarily, and the lineaments of the man are thus seen even under a dress which promises superhuman proportions." [70] And what the most supreme art must fail in — how can we attribute that to the blind working of the mythopoeic fancy? But above all it is pertinent to rejoin that thus the whole ground of the argument has been shifted. It was assumed that the entire story of Jesus is mythical, and it was represented that unless some kernel of truth could be found embedded in this myth the historicity of Jesus could scarcely be defended. It is now assumed that the story of Jesus is, rather, essentially history. We are in effect betrayed into a vicious circle of reasoning; and we assign an underlying reality to statements like those contained in the "pillar-passages" only because we have from the beginning assumed that a reality lay behind our so-called myth and our task was merely to ascertain its nature. If there exists indeed good reason, extraneous to the myth itself which we are investigating, to believe in the actual existence of the hero it celebrates, why undoubtedly *cadit quaestio*. "Grote," even Robertson tells us,[71] "never argued that history proper, the record of a time by those who lived in it, is to be so tried; and he constantly accepts narratives which might conceivably be plausible fictions, — nay, he occasionally accepts tales which appear to some of us to be fictions. It is when we are dealing with myths that he denies our power to discriminate: in history proper he undertakes — at times too confidently — to discrimi-

[70] "History of Greece," i., p. 385.   [71] P. 232.

nate." We must really settle in our minds whether we are dealing with myth in which there may possibly be embedded some historical kernel, or with history which may possibly be encrusted with some mythical adornments, before we can profitably proceed with our criticism.

It is not worth our while to pause here to inquire into the justice of the extreme attitude taken up by Grote with reference to the possibility of extracting matters of fact from pure myths without the aid of extrinsic attestation.[72] This, at the moment, not merely because of the absurdity of treating the tradition of Jesus as if it were pure myth, but because of the absurdity of the proposal to treat it as if it were pure myth coming from Schmiedel. For despite this implication of his suggestion Schmiedel does not really believe that the historicity of the Jesus whose figure is presented to us in the Gospel-narratives is without sufficient attestation apart from the Gospels to render it indisputable. He may minimize the amount and

[72] Grote himself tells us (pp. 408–409 note) that exception was already taken to the extremity of his views as well by an able article in *The Quarterly Review* for October, 1846 (what is meant is volume lxxviii. number clv., June, 1846, pp. 113 ff.), as by Professor Kortüm writing in the "Heidelberger Jahrbücher der Literatur" for 1846. The former contended that "the mythopoeic faculty of the human mind, though essentially loose and untrustworthy, is never creative, but requires some basis of fact to work upon"; the latter similarly that the myths always contain "real matter of fact along with mere conceptions." Grote responds that this may very well be; all that he asserts is that apart from extrinsic attestation we are without criteria for singling out the matters of fact. Robertson refers us to the criticism of Grote's position by Sir Alfred C. Lyall in his "Asiatic Studies," First Series, ed. 2, 1884, pp. 30 ff.; see also Second Series, 1899, pp. 324 ff. The difference between Grote and Lyall seems to reduce actually to something like this: Whether myths are ordinarily a specific product of imagination and feeling distinct in kind from both history and philosophy (as Grote contends), or concretions gathered around a nucleus of fact (as Lyall contends). In the former case they are fundamentally fictions and plausibility in their contents is no evidence of reality. In the latter, they are fundamentally history, however bad history, and the kernel of fact in them may be sought and conceivably found. The difference is, however, only relative; and the real crux is, as Grote insists, Granted that there is a kernel of truth in myths, how are we going to get at it? The Quarterly Reviewer confesses: "We pretend to no key by which we can extract the history from the legend" (p. 119) and Sir Alfred C. Lyall suggests none.

force of this attestation, speaking, for example, of " the meagreness of the historical testimony regarding Him, whether in
canonical writings outside the Gospels, or in profane writers,
such as Josephus, Tacitus, Suetonius, and Pliny. . . ."[73] But
this is only part of the attempt to give an external appearance
of propriety to his dealing with the tradition of Jesus as if it
were, if not pure myth, yet at least almost pure myth; and it
does not in point of fact even so far fairly represent his own
point of view. The plain fact is that Schmiedel comes to the
Gospel narratives with the historicity of Jesus already immovably established on extrinsic grounds, and therefore cannot
properly represent the historicity of Jesus as in any sense dependent on his power to separate out from those narratives on
intrinsic grounds items of information about Jesus which
cannot in the nature of the case be their invention. Whatever
we may think of the validity of the argument that the presence
of such statements in such a narrative can be accounted for
only by the imposition of them upon it by primitive tradition,
so that they must be recognized as preserving fragments of
historical truth, in the actual case before us this argument can
possess only corroborative value with reference to the historicity of Jesus, and acquires primary importance only with reference to the character of the historical Jesus already given. It is
nothing less than a reprehensible misrepresentation of the state
of the case to endeavor to convey an impression that the recognition of the historicity of Jesus is in any sense dependent on
this argument. In point of fact no one is more assured than
Schmiedel that it is quite firmly established altogether apart
from this argument.

Even when we have settled it well in our minds, however,
that we have to do in the Gospel-narratives, not with a myth
in which we may hope to find, perhaps, some relics of tradition,
we have not yet escaped from misleading suggestions of the
state of the case. Schmiedel is very eager to have it understood
that the critical procedure he proposes is the common method

[73] " Encyclopaedia Biblica," col. 1881, cf. Preface to Neumann, pp. vii,
viii; " Jesus in Modern Criticism," p. 14.

of historians. " Every historical investigator," he tells us, therefore, in commending it to us,[74] " in what field soever he may be
working, follows the principle of holding for true, in the first
rank, in any account which testifies to reverence for its hero,
that which runs counter to this reverence, since that cannot
rest on invention." The broad generality of this representation
is not, however, always retained. Sometimes the suggestion is
rather that it is only when the historian makes his " first acquaintance with a historical person in a book which is throughout influenced by a feeling of worship for its hero, as the Gospels are by a feeling of worship for Jesus," that he places " in
the first rank of credibility " those passages of the book which
" run counter to this feeling." [75] Sometimes indeed, as in the
primary statement,[76] we are carried into an even narrower
sphere, and actually read: " When a profane historian finds
before him a historical document which testifies to the worship
of a hero unknown to other sources, he attaches first and foremost importance to those features which cannot be deduced
merely from the fact of this worship, and he does so on the
simple and sufficient ground that they would not be found in
this source unless the author had met with them as fixed data
of tradition." It is amazing to read here farther: " The same
fundamental principle may safely be applied in the case of the
Gospels, for they also are all of them written by worshippers
of Jesus." We get further and further from the actual state of
the case with the narratives of the Gospels, of course, as each of
these limitations is added. Nobody first learns of Jesus from
the Gospel-narratives. To suggest that Jesus is " unknown to
other sources " than the Synoptic Gospels, or that these Gospels
may be treated as if they were a single document, fairly attains
the absurd. If an analogy to the critical method which Schmiedel recommends us to apply to the Gospels can be found in
the practice of " every historical investigator " in the extra-
theological field only in such dissimilar cases as are here indi-

[74] " Das vierte Evangelium," pp. 16–17.
[75] " Jesus in Modern Criticism," p. 16 (German edition, p. 6).
[76] " Encyclopaedia Biblica," col. 1872.

cated, — why, then, there is no analogy. The appearance is very strong that Schmiedel, wishing to appeal to the example of secular historians in support of the critical method he is propounding, and finding among them no exact analogies, except in the very specific case which he alludes to, vacillates between simply claiming the example of secular historians in general, and assigning the case of the Gospel-narratives to the obviously unsuitable category in which he finds in practice the closest analogy to his proposed critical method.

The question having thus been raised it may be interesting to inquire what established methods of research are in use among historians in general which may be thought to present analogies more or less close with the manner of dealing with the Gospel-narratives proposed by Schmiedel. Anything like close analogies we shall, of course, find only among the methods which have been devised for ascertaining what may be regarded as trustworthy in generally untrustworthy accounts, or, to put it baldly, for eliciting the truth from the accounts of partizan writers. The fundamental presupposition of Schmiedel's criticism — as indeed of the whole " Liberal " criticism — is that we have to do in the historical tradition of Jesus with intensely partizan reports. The entire tradition is the product, in Schmiedel's phrase, of " worshippers of Jesus," and has consequently been cast in the moulds of their worship of Jesus; in the phrase of the common " Liberal " criticism it is the work of the primitive Christian community and reflects at every point the beliefs of that community. How, then, do the methodologists deal with bias? Ernst Bernheim describes the general procedure as follows: [77]

" We must keep clearly in view with what particular circle an author has more or less personal relations, of what nation, of what station he is, whether he belongs to a particular political or confessional party, whether he is a one-sided patriot, whether he has had part in the determining of the events which he describes,

[77] " Lehrbuch der historischen Methode und der Geschichtsphilosophie," 1908, p. 509; cf. pp. 485–486, 492–493.

whether he gives accounts of personal enemies or friends. In all these relations there can lie reasons, on the one side, for keeping silence as to, or smoothing over, what is obnoxious, for immoderately emphasizing and praising what is congenial; on the other side for ignoring what is meritorious and emphasizing what is obnoxious. The statements of a writer who is involved in such relations, cannot be taken as absolute matters of fact, without some testing, so far as they may be effected by these relations; and the old methodologists already emphasize strongly enough that a partizan writer deserves unqualified credit only when he relates what is good of his enemies, what is prejudicial of his friends, fellow-partizans, compatriots."

Accordingly, a little later, speaking of the possibility of extracting trustworthy facts out of an untrustworthy narrative he writes: [78]

" It is especially to be observed that there often meet us, in the midst of untrustworthy communications, statements which, precisely in these surroundings, we may hold to be unqualifiedly trustworthy: to wit, when an author who is governed by distinctly marked interests or tendencies, adduces facts, passes judgments, which stand in contradiction with his tendency, since he here involuntarily pays homage to the pure truth, and does not observe, or at least does not heed, the contradiction with his tendency, — as in the case of admissions of defeats, blunders, weaknesses of his own party, or on the other hand in the case of communication of victories, services, virtues of the enemy. The testimony of Lambert of Hersfeld, for example, must be taken as altogether trustworthy when, in involuntary recognition, he relates individual honorable traits of Henry IV, because Lambert is animated throughout by a strong enmity to the King. We can generalize this observation to the effect that statements in general, which have a content obnoxious for the communicator and his personal interests — obnoxious, that is to say, not according to our opinion, but in his own view — are thoroughly trustworthy; for, if it is already for most men difficult to communicate truths which are unfavorable to themselves and those associated with them, it runs entirely counter to human nature falsely to set itself in an unfavorable light."

[78] P. 523–524.

To the important qualifying clause, " obnoxious, that is to say, not according to our opinion, but in his own view," Bernheim attaches a note which tells us that Charles Seignobos, " has rightly emphasized this," in the " Introduction to the Study of History " which he published in collaboration with Langlois.[79] In the passage referred to, Seignobos is pointing out the kinds of statements which, occurring in historical documents, authenticate themselves. Thus, for instance, he tells us,[80] *bona fides* at least may be inferred when the fact stated is " manifestly prejudicial to the effect which the author wished to produce." " In such a case," he remarks, " there is a probability of good faith." But we must take good care to reach our judgments in such matters from the point of view of the writer, not our own. " It is quite possible that the author's notions of his interest or honour were very different from ours." We need not accredit good faith to Charles IX, for example, when he acknowledged that he was responsible for the massacre of St. Bartholomew's day; to us that would be to confess an infamy, to him it was a boast of glory. There are even cases, Seignobos proceeds to intimate, in which more than *bona fides,* — in which truth itself, — may be inferred, viz. when " the fact was of such a nature, that it could not have been stated unless it were true." [81]

" A man does not declare that he has seen something contrary to his expectations and habits of mind unless observation has compelled him to admit it. A fact which seems very improbable to the man who relates it has a good chance of being true. We have, then, to ask whether the fact stated was in contradiction to the author's opinions, whether it is a phenomenon of a kind unknown to him, an action or a custom which seems unintelligible to him; whether it is a saying whose import transcends his intelligence, such as the sayings of Christ reported in the Gospels, or the answers made by Joan of Arc to questions put to her in the course of her trial."

[79] 1898, p. 188.
[80] " Introduction to the Study of History," E. T. 1898, p. 186.
[81] P. 188.

And then the caution is again added that in all such cases we must be very careful to judge according to the ideas of the author, not our own.

That the whole case may be before us we append an additional citation from another writer on general historical method. H. B. George remarks: [82]

"If a particular writer is our only authority for this or that matter, concerning which his sentiments are obvious, it is inevitable that we should feel a tinge of prima facie suspicion that the facts may not be fairly represented. Our belief in his statement will not be quite so confident as if there were separate and independent testimony in support of it, but we have no ground for carrying our mistrust farther. In such a case, as continually when dealing with historical evidence, we must be content with something short of unhesitating assurance." "Internal criticism may indeed suggest that the author was a partisan, and our general knowledge that partisanship is liable to lead authors into misrepresenting facts may reasonably render us suspicious: but no merely internal indications could justify our totally disbelieving the author's specific statements on a matter concerning which, *ex hypothesi*, we have no evidence but his." "The most bigoted partisan may be giving a thoroughly true account of a transaction which is of special importance to the cause that he favors; the most credulous of writers may be telling a perfectly true story, even if it sounds improbable."

The principles of procedure outlined in passages like these are in general those which Schmiedel wishes to invoke in his criticism of the Gospel-narratives. We could almost conjecture that he wrote with the very words of Bernheim in his mind. Nevertheless a different spirit breathes in them from that which animates his procedure. And in attempting to apply such principles to the criticism of the Gospel-narratives, he has been misled into a number of violences in dealing with his material.

In the first place, there is the flagrant absurdity, of which something has already been said, of suggesting that the Synoptic Gospels may be treated as the sole source of our knowledge of Jesus. The evidence, not merely of the existence of Jesus, but

[82] "Historical Evidence," 1909, pp. 84, 96, 95.

of the manner of man he was, quite independent of the Synoptic Gospels, is altogether exceptional, as well in consistency and contemporaneousness, as in sheer amount. This evidence culminates, of course, in the testimony of Paul, though it is by no means confined to his testimony. Schmiedel, it is true, minifies the testimony of Paul; but he cannot deny it, much less can he evacuate it. It only betrays the exigencies of his position when he permits himself to speak regarding it in such studiedly disparaging terms as these: [83]

"If, as Dr. Neumann and the present writer believe, it is possible to show that the genuineness of these Epistles " — the major epistles of Paul — " is unassailable, and that the figure of Jesus cannot be projected back into a period earlier than the Christian era, we shall be justified in regarding the existence of Jesus as historically established. Only, by this we have gained exceedingly little for the construction of a Life of Jesus; the number of data supplied by Paul is but small." [84]

"With reference to the Epistles of the Apostle Paul, which no doubt unquestionably presuppose an actual Jesus, appeal can be made to the fact that according to many investigators they all came into being only in the second century. And if the composition of the most important of them be assigned to the years 50–60 A.D., — which is my view also — nevertheless it must be acknowledged that they relate deplorably little about Jesus, and do not in the least afford a guarantee for all that is commonly regarded as credible about him from the first three Gospels." [85]

If it be borne in mind that the question at issue does not concern the details of the daily life of Jesus, but His very existence and the manner of person He was, the unhappy art of these statements will be apparent. Much more justly Heinrich Weinel not only tells us that Paul's letters " contain so much about Jesus that he is our best and surest witness in the controversy that has just been started afresh about the historicity of the person of Jesus," and that, however few references he

---

[83] Cf. " Encyclopaedia Biblica," col. 1881.
[84] Preface to Neumann, p. viii.
[85] " Die Person Jesu, etc.," p. 6; E. T. " Jesus in Modern Criticism," p. 14.

makes to events in His life, Paul has yet " preserved the picture of Jesus for us very clearly and distinctly," [86] but, addressing himself to the precise point now engaging our attention, says plainly: [87]

" The critical theology has continually emphasized how little we learn of Jesus from Paul. I too myself have formerly placed the matter in this false light. What Paul gives us of Jesus and His words is little, if we measure it by the standard of a Gospel; it is little too if we demand that a Paul shall buttress all his ideas with declarations of Jesus. It is, however, not merely enough to find the existence of Jesus attested in the Epistles of Paul; rather in all important matters the echoes of Jesus' sayings are heard in Paul, and there is not only a whole multitude of details which Paul knows and transmits, but also all the distinguishing traits of the preaching of Jesus and His nature are preserved to us by Paul. There is therefore a great deal, if we do not carry the old prejudice with us to these Epistles which are after all occasional writings and are not written with the express design of informing us of Jesus."

Even Schmiedel's own pupil, Arno Neumann, indeed, rebukes the madness of his teacher, when, in the Introduction to the little Life of Jesus, to the English translation of which Schmiedel contributed a Preface, coming to speak of Paul's testimony to Jesus, he tells us that to give any scientific character to the denial of Jesus' existence, we must first push incontinently out of the path that " historical Rock whose name is Paul." By Paul, the genuineness of whose chief Epistles is indubitable, he adds: [88]

" there are accredited not only the manifestations (*Auftreten*) of Jesus Christ in general, His epoch, the peculiarity of His character, and His death, but also some of His fundamental ideas, His twelve disciples, and the remarkable impression He must have made," —

in a word, the entire fact and figure of Jesus. But that the force of Paul's testimony may be fully appreciated it must be

[86] " St. Paul, the Man and his Work," E. T. 1906, pp. 316, 321: the whole passage should be read.
[87] " Ist das ' liberale ' Jesusbild widerlegt? " 1910, p. 16.
[88] " Jesus, wer er geschichtlich war," 1904, pp. 10–11; E. T. pp. 4–5.

kept in mind that it is original testimony, properly so-called contemporaneous testimony.[89] Paul, it is true, was not himself a companion of Jesus; but he connected himself with the Christian movement in its very earliest days, lived in constant communication with Jesus' immediate disciples, enjoyed the fullest opportunity to learn at first hand all they knew, and wrote under their eye.[90] In a true sense his testimony is theirs; he is in it their mouthpiece; and it is accordingly supported in all its extent by every line of tradition which comes down from them.[91]

The absurdity of treating the Synoptic Gospels as the sole source of our knowledge of Jesus is fairly matched by the absurdity of attempting to treat them as together constituting but a single source of that knowledge, and that a source of the value of which we are ignorant. Schmiedel warns us not to imagine that a narrative which is found in all three of the Synoptic Gospels comes to us therefore accredited by three witnesses; for he says that all are drawing from one source.[92] But he

[89] " Original authorities," according to Bernheim (pp. 413–507), are *strictly* only actual eye-and-ear-witnesses of what is narrated. But as even these must fill out what they relate from the testimony of others, it is usual to widen the notion and to call " contemporary accounts which rest on their own immediate perception and on that of other contemporaries " " original authorities." This is reasonable. On the other hand, E. A. Freeman (" The Methods of Historical Study," 1886, p. 168) unduly extends the notion when he accords the name of " original authorities " to derived accounts in case the original sources are lost. To deserve the name of " original authorities " the element of contemporaneousness must not be wholly lacking.

[90] Accordingly Neumann adds (p. 11; E. T. p. 5): " It is accordingly no impairment of the value of Paul as reporter that he never personally saw Jesus; for certainly there was nothing left lacking to this new convert of the most eager inquiries (I Cor. xi. 23; vii. 10 ff.; II Cor. x. 1; viii. 9, etc.)."

[91] Out of the immense literature of the subject, cf. especially: R. J. Knowling, " The Testimony of St. Paul to Christ," 1905; Th. Zahn, " Einleitung in das N. T.,"[1] ii. pp. 164 ff. (ix. § 48, Anmerkungen 4, 5); R. Drescher, " Das Leben Jesu bei Paulus," 1900; H. J. Holtzmann, in " Die Christliche Welt," xxiv. (1910), coll. 151–160; A. J. Mason, Essays on Some Theological Questions of the Day by Members of the University of Cambridge, edited by H. B. Swete, 1905, pp. 425 ff.; J. G. Machen, " Biblical and Theological Studies by the Members of the Faculty of Princeton Theological Seminary," 1912, pp. 561 ff.

[92] " Encyclopaedia Biblica," col. 1872.

does not take the same trouble to warn us that this one source lies, therefore, distinctly nearer to the events it narrates than any of the three Gospels that have drawn from it; or that the circumstance that they have all drawn so largely from it accredits it as a very excellent source, everywhere depended upon in its own day; or, even, that it is not the only source from which these Gospels draw, — that by its side lies another source, certainly equal in age and value to it, from which two of them at least draw, and by their side lie still other sources from which one or another of them draws, which need not be inferior in either age or value to either of them. If we are to break up the Gospels into their sources and appeal rather to these sources than to the Gospels themselves (which is not the method of procedure which Schmiedel is in act to commend to us, presenting his critical method rather as independent of literary criticism) we do not lose but profit by the process. Instead of three witnesses of about the seventh decade of the century we have now in view quite a number of witnesses, all earlier than the seventh decade of the century, some of them perhaps very much earlier; and all commended to our favorable consideration by their selection as trustworthy sources of information concerning Jesus by writers so earnest and careful as the authors of the Synoptic Gospels, and by the remarkable completeness of their harmony with one another in the portrait of Jesus which they draw, a harmony which extends also to the portrait of Jesus given us by Paul and by all other witnesses which we may be willing to accept as coming to us from the same general period. No fault in the historical criticism of the Gospel narratives could be more gross than the obscuring of the existence or of the impressiveness of this consistent tradition concerning Jesus, stretching back of the Synoptic Gospels to the very beginning of the Christian movement. And nothing requires to be more strongly emphasized than that it is just because of the impressive consent of the whole tradition of Jesus, running back of the Synoptic Gospels to the beginning, that critics whose presuppositions will not permit them to accept this tradition as trustworthy appeal from literary criticism to historical criticism in an endeavor to get behind the consistent tradition to a Jesus unknown to it. The Synoptic Gospels come before us, meanwhile, not as new phenomena relatively to the portrait of Jesus which they embody, but distinctly as merely the bearers of a tradition of the richest and most consistent sort, which from all that appears is aboriginal; in a word, as witnesses of really contemporaneous value to the Jesus who was known by those who companied with Him and could give first-hand information about Him. This great fact is obscured by Schmiedel, by suggesting unreasonably late dates for the composition of the Synoptic Gospels, thus lengthening unwarrantably the interval which separates them from the facts which they narrate; by leaving in the background the richness and trustworthiness of the tradition which bridges this interval; by treating the Synoptic Gospels as "flying leaves" of wholly unknown provenience and value; and by dealing with them as if they were a single unsupported document.

It must not be supposed that Schmiedel speaks dogmatically upon all these matters. That is not his ordinary manner. The whole drift of his reasoning is towards a late date for the Gospels; he seems indeed to wish to cluster them in the last few years of the century.[93] But he is careful to guard his readers against supposing that it would affect his estimate of the value of their contents if they should turn out to be earlier. He says: [94]

"The chronological question is in this instance a very subordinate one. Indeed, even if our Gospels could be shown to have been written from 50 A.D. onwards, or even earlier, we should not be under any necessity to withdraw our conclusions as to their contents; we should, on the contrary, only have to say that the indubitable transformation in the original tradition had taken place much more rapidly than one might have been ready to suppose. The

[93] Otto Schmiedel, who may possibly consider himself the follower of his brother in this matter, gives more distinctly the following dates: Mark, A.D. 80; Matthew 90, with reworking up to 120 or even later; Luke, 100.

[94] "Encyclopaedia Biblica," col. 1894.

credibility of the Gospel history cannot be established by an earlier dating of the Gospels themselves in any higher degree than that in which it has been shown to exist, especially as we know that even in the lifetime of Jesus miracles of every sort were attributed to him in the most confident manner. But as the transformation has departed so far from the genuine tradition, it is only in the interest of a better understanding and of a more reasonable appreciation of the process that one should claim for its working out a considerable period of time."

On the peculiarities of the reasoning of this paragraph we do not feel called upon to comment. Each sentence seems to neutralize its immediate neighbors. But in any event few will be found to agree with Schmiedel that it will make no difference in our estimate of the credibility of the Gospels whether we place their own composition about A.D. 100, and that of their chief sources about 70; or their own composition somewhere around 50, and that of their chief sources — shall we say about 40 or 35, or even earlier? To assert otherwise is indeed to deny a fundamental canon of criticism. For it is quite obvious that if our Gospels were composed from 50 to 70 (it is our own belief that they were composed in the sixties) and rest on sources, to a considerable extent recoverable from them, which come from a period ten or twenty years — or more — earlier, we possess in them in effect contemporaneous testimony. And contemporaneous testimony of such mass and constancy cannot be lightly neglected. It is not easy to believe in a transformation so great as that which is assumed, taking place so rapidly as in this case it must have done; though, of course, this will not appear formidable to Schmiedel who allows that Jesus was looked upon as a supernatural person even in His lifetime, thus admitting in effect that it is not a question of transformation with which we are concerned but a question of the credibility of contemporaneous testimony. From our point of view, at any rate, it is not a matter of indifference whether the Gospels are dated near 100 A.D., or between 50 and 70, and we therefore think it worth while to insist that there is really no reason for removing any of them to a time later than A.D. 70, as even a Harnack has (somewhat tardily) come to see.[95]

No more than the early dates of the Gospels does Schmiedel dogmatically deny the richness of the tradition that lies behind them. He even elsewhere fully recognizes it, investigating with great diligence the sources of the sources and intimating the far-reaching consequences which the recognition of them has upon the literary criticism of the Gospels.[96] But when he comes to consider the credibility of the Gospel narratives he ignores altogether the fulness and constancy of this historical tradition of which they are merely the vehicles. We do not forget that this is in accord with his professed procedure; that precisely what he proposes to do is to turn away from literary criticism and to seek to reach a decision upon the credibility of the narratives by a historical criticism which, wholly independently of literary criticism, works directly upon the transmitted material itself without consideration of the modes or channels of its transmission. But precisely what we are complaining of is the impropriety of this method. It is in essence an attempt to ignore a fundamental fact, the fact, that

[95] Cf. W. P. Armstrong, in "Biblical and Theological Studies by the Members of the Faculty of Princeton Theological Seminary," 1912, pp. 348–349: "With the increasing recognition of the evidence for the early date of the Synoptic Gospels, their sources — of whatever kind and constitution — being still earlier — carry back the witness of the documents to the time of the eye-witnesses. And among these there was no difference of opinion concerning the factual basis which underlies the tradition recorded by the Gospels in concrete and varying forms. To admit with Harnack that the Gospel of Luke was written before 70 A.D. and early in the sixties ("Neue Untersuchungen zur Apostelgeschichte," pp. 81 ff.), is to accept a fact which has an important bearing on the origin of the sources of the Synoptic Gospels, — a fact which makes it difficult, as Harnack himself foresaw ("Die Apostelgeschichte," p. 221, note 2), to regard as legendary their account of supernatural events. For if the Gospels embody the view of Jesus which was current in the primitive Christian community about 60 A.D. — as Heitmüller admits — or earlier — as Harnack's dating of Luke requires — the rejection of their witness cannot be based upon their differences or upon purely historical considerations. Recourse must be had to a principle springing ultimately out of philosophical conceptions by which their unanimous witness to essential features in their portraiture of Jesus may be set aside." Cf. also the accompanying note 180.

[96] "Encyclopaedia Biblica," coll. 1862 ff., §§ 128–129.

is, that the Synoptic Gospels do not stand off in isolation, and cannot be dealt with as if they were, — or even as if they were only possibly — a body of inventions; but are known to rest on a background of copious, consentient and contemporary historical tradition. To lose sight of this fact is to lose sight of the primary fact in the case, and to do violence to the fundamental law of evidence which demands that well-attested facts shall not be treated as unattested facts. What Schmiedel asks of us is to begin our investigation into the credibility of the Synoptic Gospels by abstracting our attention from the primary evidence of their credibility, viz., that they are but vehicles of a copious and unbroken historical tradition which is contemporaneous with the facts which it transmits. Having failed to shake this testimony by literary criticism he proposes — not to allow it its due weight but — to neglect it and direct his assault upon the credibility of the Gospel-narratives to another point!

It is part of this studied disregard of the real conditions of the case, that Schmiedel treats the Synoptic Gospels as documents of entirely unknown provenience and value. Here indeed he becomes even dogmatic. He is quite sure that the Third Gospel, for example, is not the production of Paul's companion, Luke, although he is equally sure that this Gospel and the Book of Acts are from the same pen;[97] he will not concede to Luke even the " we "-sections of Acts, which he considers to come from a different hand from the rest of the book. We take it, however, that — as even a Harnack again has come to perceive[98] — a sober criticism must allow that Acts is all of a piece — " we "-passages and all — and Acts and the Third Gospel are from the same hand, and this hand is that to which a constant historical tradition has from the earliest times ascribed both books, — that of Luke. This being so, the Gospel

---

[97] *Ibid.*, col. 1893.

[98] See especially numbers i., iii., and iv. of Harnack's " New Testament Studies " (Crown Theological Library, xx., xxvii., xxxiii.) ; " Luke the Physician," 1907 ; " The Acts of the Apostles," 1909 ; " The Date of the Acts and of the Synoptic Gospels," 1911.

of Luke is entitled to the credit which belongs to a book by a known author, of known opportunities to inform himself of the subject-matter of which he treats, and of known will and capacity to treat that subject-matter worthily. Luke is known to have been an educated physician, who as a companion of Paul's was exceptionally favorably situated for learning the facts concerning Jesus. Whatever Paul knew, he knew. Whatever was known by other companions of Paul's into contact with whom he came, some of whom (as for example John Mark) had come out of the circle of Jesus' immediate disciples, he knew. He even visited Jerusalem in company with Paul; and resided with him for two years at Caesarea in touch with primitive disciples. What such a writer has given us concerning Jesus, set down in such an obviously painstaking narrative, — especially when it proves to be wholly at one with what is given us by Paul, as well as by his fellow evangelists in equally painstaking narratives, and indeed with the whole previous tradition so far as that tradition can be penetrated, — cannot be treated simply as floating reports.[99]

[99] It may conduce to a better understanding of the trustworthiness of Luke as a biographer if we will look at it in the light of an analogous case. Why is not Luke's relation to the subjects he deals with in his Gospel much the same as that of, say, Mr. Clement R. Shorter to the Brontës? Mr. Shorter did not know the Brontës. But he has diligently sought out the facts from those who knew them, and from those who have described them at first hand. His title page very fairly parallels Luke's prologue: "The Brontës: Life and Letters. Being an attempt to present a full and final record of the lives of the three sisters, Charlotte, Emily and Anne Brontë, from the Biographies of Mrs. Gaskell and others, and from numerous hitherto unpublished Manuscripts and Letters." That is not far from the way Luke might have phrased his title page: "Jesus Christ: Life and Teachings. Being an attempt to present a trustworthy record of His life from the biographies which have been published of Him, and from hitherto unpublished recollections communicated by those who knew Him." Of course, this is second-hand biography; Luke, like Mr. Shorter, belongs to the second generation. But, like Mr. Shorter, he enjoyed exceptional opportunities to learn the truth, and exhibits exceptional zeal in ascertaining and recording the truth of the matters with which he deals. In the circumstances in which he wrote the trustworthiness of his communications, and particularly of the general portraiture he gives of Jesus, is not lessened, — it is perhaps even enhanced — by his secondariness. Mrs. Gaskell's "Life of Charlotte Brontë" cannot be superseded; but Mr. Shorter's account is not inferior in trustworthiness to it. The sources from which Luke drew are, of course, more original

With elements of the actual state of the case like these clearly in mind, we shall know what estimate to place on the extremely sceptical attitude which Schmiedel takes up with reference to the Synoptic narratives. He does not approach them with the deference due to an exceptionally well-attested historical tradition, but with an already active assumption of their untrustworthiness, in the portrait of Jesus which they transmit. Of this assumption no justification is possible and none is attempted. We cannot rank as such the pages in which there are accumulated elements in the Synoptic narratives " which for any reason arising either from the substance or from considerations of literary criticism " seem to Schmiedel " doubtful or wrong; " [100] and which he closes with the words: " The foregoing sections may have sometimes seemed to raise a doubt whether any credible elements were to be found in the gospels at all. " [101] But these sections register the effects, not the cause, of the scepticism with which Schmiedel approaches the Synoptic narratives and form a body of what is little better than special pleading. Nowhere are the Synoptic narratives given the benefit of the presumption which lies in their favor; that is to say, nowhere is any consideration shown to the weight of the historical tradition of which they are but the vehicles, and which confessedly stretches back to the very beginning of the Christian movement. The one aim of all his criticism is to set aside this tradition; the principle he invokes is that of con-

---

than his own narrative; but his narrative resting on these written sources, supplemented by his own inquiries, does not yield in trustworthiness to them. It is, in fact, just these sources themselves, tested and supplemented by competent inquiry in original quarters, and these sources do not lose but increase in value by being incorporated in such a work as Luke's. By all means let us go back to the Narrative-Source, and to the Discourse-Source, and to any other sources we can identify, so far as we can isolate them; but let us not fancy that out of Luke they are more trustworthy than they are in Luke, or that the cement in which Luke imbeds them is less trustworthy than they are — this cement itself is from original sources. It is not merely what Mr. Shorter repeats from Mrs. Gaskell or other formal biographies which is worthy of credit in his book.

[100] " Encyclopaedia Biblica," coll. 1872, 1873–1881; §§ 132–138.
[101] *Ibid.*, col. 1881.

tradiction; and the effect of his criticism is to substitute for the portrait of Jesus handed down by the entire tradition a new portrait related to it as its precise opposite.[102]

It is needless to say that in this extreme scepticism as over against the whole historic tradition Schmiedel receives no encouragement whatever from the general practice of historians. We have only to glance over even the brief extracts we have cited [103] from the methodologists to perceive in how different a spirit historians are accustomed to approach their task. The attitude they commend to us is one of general deference to positive testimony; and if they point out conditions which in particular instances may rightly modify this deference or even neutralize it, and indicate methods of procedure by which, when suspicion is justified, the more trustworthy elements of a tradition may be sifted out, they never suggest an attitude of general scepticism as over against positive testimony; they even expressly deny the propriety of altogether rejecting positive testimony on merely internal grounds. The whole tendency of the recommendations of the methodologists is towards respect to positive testimony, and they test it with a view rather to discovering what we can most completely trust than with a view to disregarding it in principle. Schmiedel, on the contrary, begins with the rejection of the tradition in principle although it is exceptionally copiously and harmoniously attested; and sets himself to seek in it not the most trustworthy elements in a generally trustworthy tradition, on the basis of which the whole positive testimony may be given its rightful coloring and validity; but encysted elements of an underlying truth in contradiction to the whole testimony, on the basis of which he can reverse the tradition and recover the lost truth submerged by it. For a procedure of this sort, applied to a historical tradition such as that embodied in the Synoptic

---

[102] Johannes Weiss, " Jesus von Nazareth, etc.," 1910, pp. 84–85 has some wise words on " the really morbid scepticism " which is too often permitted by modern critics (his example is Wrede) to intrude between the source and the reader.

[103] See above pp. 220–223.

Gospels, supported as that tradition is by a wealth of extraneous testimony such for example as that of Paul, and traceable as it is back to contemporary sources, it is safe to say no support can be found in the recognized practice of secular historians. It is in fact not a historical procedure which is proposed at all; it is pure anti-historism — a bold attempt to pour history into the mould of *a priori* construction. Against such a procedure the methodologists protest with all their strength. No one has less their respect than the critic who — as Bouché-Leclercq expresses it — " after having discredited all his witnesses, claims to put himself in their place, and sees with their eyes something quite different from what they saw." [104] " The one thing which is illegitimate for criticism," remarks H. B. George,[105] " is to assume that it can divine the truth underlying the existing narrative, which it declares to be more or less fabulous." [106]

Certainly it will be admitted that if a historical tradition like that transmitted to us in the narratives of the Synoptic Gospels is to be reversed on the faith of fragments of a rival tradition which, if not older (for there can scarcely be a tradition older than that which confessedly was shared by the immediate disciples of Jesus) is yet truer, imbedded in it like flies in amber, then these fragments of the truer tradition must authenticate themselves with absolute certainty as quite irreconcilable with the tradition which is to be replaced by them. Schmiedel, in point of fact, does not fail to claim this absolute contrariety with the tradition in which they are imbedded for his " pillar-passages." It is because he finds imbedded in the Synoptic narrative occasional statements which run absolutely

[104] Quoted by Seignobos, in Langlois and Seignobos, " Introduction to the Study of History," 1898, pp. 158–159, note 2.

[105] " Historical Evidence," 1909, p. 69. He adds: " It may put forward guesses, and they may seem probable: but nothing can transform them into ascertained facts."

[106] F. J. A. Hort long ago warned us that " criticism is not dangerous except when, as in so much Christian criticism, it is merely the tool for reaching a result not itself believed in on that ground but on the ground of speculative postulates " (" Hulsean Lectures for 1871," 1908, p. 177).

counter to it in its fundamental tendency, and therefore cannot owe their origin to the invention of those to whom this
narrative (immediately or ultimately) is due, that he feels
able to point to them as fragments of an underlying truer tradition which would have perished save for the vitality of these
fragments. They were too firmly established in the minds of the
followers of Jesus to be passed by; and have therefore been
taken up into the growing legend to preserve the memory of
the real Jesus, which it was obliterating. When we come to
scrutinize these relics of truer recollection, however, we are
surprised to note how little they are able to bear the burden
of the argument which is erected upon them. Schmiedel selects
nine of them for special remark. He intimates that these are by
no means all that might be gathered out of the fabric of the
narrative.[107] But it lies in the nature of the case that they are
fairly representative of the whole body; and indeed that they
present the clearest and most convincing instances of the
phenomenon adverted to. Schmiedel himself divides them into
two categories. Five of them, he tells us, " throw light on Jesus'
figure as a whole "; the other four " have a special bearing on
His character as a worker of wonders." [108] To speak more
plainly the five former of them are supposed to stand in irreconcilable contradiction with the deification of Jesus which
had grown up in the Christian community; the latter four are
supposed to stand in equally irreconcilable contradiction with
the ascription of miracles in the strict sense to Jesus, which
had also become the custom of the Christian community. On
the basis of the former five Schmiedel thinks that we are entitled to assert that Jesus was originally fully understood by
His followers to be merely a human being; on the basis of the
latter four that He was equally fully understood by His followers originally to be a wholly non-miraculous man. The two
classes of statements together make it clear that Jesus was
not at first the object of worship by His followers: they are
" not consistent with the worship in which Jesus had come

[107] See e.g., Preface to Neumann, p. xiii.
[108] " Die Person Jesu, etc.," p. 7. E. T. p. 18.

to be held "; they " are appropriate only to a man, and could never by any possibility have been written had the author been thinking of a demi-god." [109]

Now, the singular thing is that some of the "pillar-passages," at least, even with the meaning which Schmiedel puts upon them, do not obviously have the directly contradictory bearing upon the attribution of deity or of the possession of supernatural powers to Jesus, which is ascribed to them, and which is required of them if they are to serve the function put upon them. It is not immediately apparent, for example, that the statement in Mk. iii. 21 to the effect "that his relations held him to be beside himself" [110] contradicts the attribution of deity to Jesus. Why must a divine Jesus be supposed to have been fully understood "in the days of his flesh," even by those nearest to Him? Or, for the matter of that, why should not worshippers of Jesus even invent such a statement? " As if," exclaims Friedrich Steudel,[111] with considerable force, " a poet would depreciate his hero, by representing him as one who was misunderstood in his closest surroundings! " As if, in a word, the tendency of such an incident as is here recorded might not easily be, — on the supposition that it is part and parcel of a mythical account of a divine being for a time on earth — precisely to show His greatness by representing that not only did His enemies accuse Him of working wonders by the power of the Evil One, but His very friends thought Him mad. And certainly Schmiedel himself must have felt some difficulty in including among his " pillar-passages " Mk. xiii. 32 (cf. Mt. xxiv. 36),[112] in which, if Jesus is made to confess that there was at least one thing He did not know, He is at the same time made to range Himself in dignity of being above the angels — and on the side of God in contrast with even the highest of creatures. Upon others of the " pillar-passages " a most unnatural meaning has to be imposed before they can be thought of in that connection. For example, in the narrative connected with Jesus' warning of His

[109] Preface to Neumann, p. xvii.
[110] " Encyclopaedia Biblica," col. 1881; cf. " Das vierte Evangelium," p. 18.   [111] P. 89.   [112] See " Das vierte Evangelium," p. 22.

disciples to beware of "the leaven of the Pharisees and of Herod " (Mk. viii. 15, cf. Mt. xvi. 6), it is only by the most sinuous exegesis that we arrive at the conclusion that the miracles of the feeding of the five thousand and the four thousand (both of which are narrated both by Matthew and by Mark) are only "transformed parables " — though even if they were, that fact would scarcely prove that Jesus never wrought miracles. So, it is not a natural interpretation which reduces Jesus' enumeration of His miraculous works in reply to the inquiry of John the Baptist's message (Mt. xi. 5, Lk. vii. 22) to a series of figurative statements which mean only that He was exercising notable spiritual power among the people — though again, even were that the true interpretation, it would scarcely prove that Jesus wrought no miracles. At the most, it would suggest that He laid greater stress on His spiritual than on His physical miracles; and surely that is obvious enough in any case. It is unreasonable, further, to insist on an interpretation of Jesus' refusal to give a "sign " (Mk. viii. 12 cf. Mt. xvi. 4, and further Mt. xii. 39, Lk. xi. 29) which makes it a categorical declaration on Jesus' part that He would work in no circumstances any sort of miracle, and therefore a confession by Him that He could work no miracle. The context suggests a very different interpretation, and Schmiedel himself is free elsewhere to point out a distinction between miracles as such and miracles as "signs." [113] Similarly, it is an unreasonable interpretation of Jesus' inability to work miracles at Nazareth (Mk. vi. 5: "He could there do no mighty work ") to make it teach that it was never He that worked miracles, but the people themselves by the ardor of their faith; and to infer from this that the real Jesus wrought no other wonders than "faith cures." [114] The narrative itself includes in the broader category

[113] *Ibid.*, pp. 15 ff.

[114] " Encyclopaedia Biblica," §§ 141, 144; e.g., col. 1885: " It is quite permissible for us to regard as historical only those of the class which even at the present day physicians are able to effect by psychical methods . . ."; " Jesus in Modern Criticism," pp. 19 f. The same conclusion is reached on the same grounds by W. Heitmüller, Schiele and Zscharnack's " Die Religion, etc.," iii. 1912, col. 372.

of "mighty works," as of like supernatural character with them, these "faith cures" (if we insist on describing them by this name) which He worked also at Nazareth; attributes these "mighty works" to Him as ordinary acts; [115] and leaves no other interpretation possible than that His "inability" to work these mighty works at Nazareth was a moral and not a natural "inability"; it was unsuitable for Him to do so.[116] Even were it otherwise it still would not be clear why a limitation upon Jesus' power to work miracles imposed by unbelief should argue a general inability in Him to work miracles. Precisely what Jesus meant to imply when He declared that speaking against His person might be forgiven, while blasphemy against the Holy Spirit would not be forgiven (Mt. xii. 31) may be an open question.[117] But it is not obvious that He must have meant that His person was inferior in dignity to that of the Holy Spirit, as Schmiedel assumes; [118] and if He did, it is not obvious that this implies a self-confession of His mere humanity. It may be plausible to argue that He refuses the address "Good Master" (Mk. x. 17) and in doing so spoke

[115] Mk. vi. 2, 5: "Whence hath this man these things — and what mean such mighty works wrought by His hands?" "And He could there do no mighty work save that He laid His hands upon a few sick folk, and healed them."

[116] Cf. H. R. Mackintosh, "The Doctrine of the Person of Jesus Christ," 1912, p. 14: "The verdict passed on Nazareth to the effect that, owing to the unbelief He encountered there, Jesus could work no miracle (Mk. vi. 5), has often been misconstrued. The meaning is not that the people's mistrust deprived Him of Messianic power; it is rather that the ethical conditions of reception being absent, a moral impossibility existed that He should put His power in active operation."

[117] W. Lütgert, "Die Liebe im N. T.," 1905, p. 99, wishes to explain the passage from the general principle that Jesus' anger burns against offenses against God, never against offenses against Himself: "The same simple rule lies at the bottom of the declaration about the blasphemy of the Spirit. What is spoken against the Son of Man. that is, against Him personally, Jesus pardons; what on the other hand is spoken against the Spirit, that is, against God, — that is unpardonable."

[118] "Das vierte Evangelium," p. 33. Cf. the good reply of Karl Thieme, "Die christliche Demut," i. 1906, p. 139, who says that the clause "and whosoever shall say a word against the Son of Man, it shall be forgiven him" here has the same effect as the clause "nor yet the Son" in xxiv. 26, and is "less an offensive minification than a great glorification of Jesus."

out of a human consciousness; but this interpretation of the
passage is by no means to be accepted as certain, or even
probable, — or, we might justly add, even possible.[119] The cry
of dereliction on the cross (Mk. xv. 34) certainly seems the
expression of a human consciousness, though why of a merely
human consciousness does not appear.[120] If then recognition of
Jesus as human is equivalent to denying Him to be divine,
there is a single passage among Schmiedel's nine which clearly
contradicts the ascription of deity to Jesus: and others of them
may, no doubt, be put forward with more or less plausibility in
the same interest, if we are set upon making out an argument
vi et armis. But to advance these passages as definitely inconsistent with the attribution of deity or miracles to Jesus, so
inconsistent that they must be recognized as remnants of a
truer tradition of a merely human, non-miraculous Jesus, and
able to bear the weight of a structure which must supersede the
portrait of the divine, miraculous Jesus drawn in the Synoptic
tradition, and in all other extant tradition, can strike us as
nothing but a counsel of despair.

A further consideration, which has already been hinted at
in passing, requires emphasizing at this point. W. B. Smith has
urged with some persistency that if these " pillar-passages "
are really inconsistent with the Synoptic tradition, the writers
of the Synoptic Gospels are strangely unaware of it. That the
Synoptic Gospels record these statements must, he thinks, at
least be recognized as evidence that their asserted inconsistency
with the fundamental tendency of the Synoptic Gospels is
imaginary. And then Smith adds with force: [121]

" They may seem to *us* what they will; in the view of the
authors of the Gospels, who were worshippers of Jesus, they cer-

[119] Cf. what Karl Thieme has to say, as cited, pp. 106 ff.

[120] Schmiedel himself will not admit that it was a cry of *despair* (" Jesus
in Modern Criticism," p. 50).

[121] " Ecce Deus, etc." (German edit.), p. 179. Cf. the summary on p. 181:
" I permit myself to repeat: The mere fact that a declaration or an act is
ascribed to Jesus by the author of a Gospel is a positive proof that it did not
stand in conscious contradiction to the conception of Jesus held by that
author; and it is moreover not probable that an unconscious contradiction
is present, for these Gospels are very unusually well thought-out works. . . ."

tainly were *not* incompatible with that worship. The ground of this contention is obvious. Had these passages been felt as irreconcilable with worship of Jesus, with the cult of Jesus as a God, they would have been altered, and their disharmony corrected."

It is easy, no doubt, to rejoin that it is by no means inconceivable or even unexampled that inconsistent elements of fact should be preserved in a growing legend; this is, as Bernheim expresses it,[122] the homage which legend pays to truth, and it may easily occur without consciousness, or at least clear consciousness, of it on the part of the writer. As to the harmonizing of these statements with the legend, why, is it not part of Schmiedel's contention that this is precisely what was done, and that we can trace the process in the Synoptic record itself?[123] This rejoinder scarcely, however, meets the objection. The Synoptic Gospels are not simply sections of a growing legend, gradually working its way to the consistent presentation of a germinal conception. They are, each of them, the careful composition of a thoughtful, alert writer alive to his purposes to his finger-tips. And the method by which the supposed progressive harmonization of the incongruous elements of truth with the demands of the legend is detected, is one of extreme untrustworthiness, in the conclusions of which, to speak frankly, no dependence whatever can be placed. The general canon which governs it is justly challenged as without foundation in fact;[124] and the processes by which under this

[122] " Lehrbuch der historischen Methode, etc.," p. 523 (see above pp. 220–222).

[123] Preface to Neumann, p. xi.: " I, of set purpose, selected only those passages in which it is possible to show from the text of the Gospels themselves that they are incompatible with the worship in which Jesus came to be held. Thus, they are, all of them, found only in one Gospel, or at most in two; the second and third, or the third, either omits the passage in question, although, by universal consent, the author who omits must have known at least one of the Gospels in which it occurs, or the source from which it was drawn; or, alternatively, he turns it round, often with great ingenuity and boldness, in such a manner that it loses the element which makes it open to exception from the point of view of a worshipper of Jesus." Cf. " Jesus in Modern Criticism," p. 16; " Das vierte Evangelium," p. 17; " Encyclopaedia Biblica," col. 1872.

[124] Thus, for example, Franz Dibelius, " Das Abendmahl," 1911, remarks

general canon findings are reached in individual cases are
fatally mechanical and confessedly capable of making out an
equally plausible case for any finding desired.[125] After all said,
we must revert to the fundamental canon of all criticism of
this order, emphasized as such by all the methodologists.[126] We
must not impute ourselves to the writers we are criticising, but
must judge of alleged contradictions occurring in their narratives not from our own point of view but from theirs. We
cannot avoid raising the question, therefore, whether the statements declared in Schmiedel's " pillar-passages " to be inconsistent with the historical tradition embodied in the Synoptic
narratives merely seem to us incompatible with the fundamental tendency of that tradition, or are such as must have
been felt by the authors of the Synoptic Gospels themselves to
be contradictory to their fundamental conception of Jesus. In
the former case we may perhaps be in a position to pronounce
the legend of Jesus, as presented in the Synoptic Gospels, not
quite self-consistent; that is our own affair and concerns only
our personal attitude towards the figure of Jesus. It is only in
the latter case that we should be in a position to point to such
passages as evidence of the existence of a better tradition underlying the Synoptic tradition on the basis of which the latter
should be corrected. When this only relevant question is fairly
faced it is by no means impertinent to point out that if the
statements of the " pillar-passages " are really inconsistent
with the historical tradition embodied in the Synoptic Gospels,

---

that the canon of literary criticism, which is uniformly followed, runs:
" Where there are differing accounts, that one deserves the most credit which
is the simplest, that is, commonly, which is the briefest; where important
elements of the one are lacking in another, they are later, interpolated additions " (p. 2); and then he criticises its validity sharply (p. 7).

[125] Schmiedel himself remarks ("Encyclopaedia Biblica," col. 1846)
that "every assertion, no matter how evident, as to the priority of one
evangelist and the posteriority of another in any given passage will be found
to have been turned the other way round by quite a number of scholars of
repute. . . ."

[126] Cf. Bernheim above, p. 222; Langlois and Seignobos, *op. cit.,* pp.
165–166.

it is strange that these Gospels are so completely unconscious of it.

In point of fact the argument based on the "pillar-passages" has been pushed through with very little consideration for the point of view of the Synoptic Gospels, or of the historical tradition they represent. It has been made to run much as follows. The Synoptic Gospels represent a tradition in which worship of Jesus is the dominating feature: they make it their business to present before adoring eyes the figure of a divine, miraculous Jesus: but we find embedded in their narrative statements which present to us the figure of a human Jesus, a Jesus with the limitations that belong to a man: these statements must be as yet unassimilated fragments of a truer tradition: otherwise their presence in this tradition of a divine Jesus would be unaccountable: we must, therefore, base our conception of the real Jesus on these unassimilated fragments, and reject all in the tradition embodied in these Gospels which is inconsistent with them. The underlying assumption is that Jesus must have been either divine or human; so that the discovery of a Jesus who was human abolishes the legend of a Jesus who was divine. The question is never once raised whether, in the sense of the Synoptic tradition, Jesus might not have been both divine and human. If that question were raised and answered in the affirmative, then the inconsistency with the Synoptic tradition of the statements alleged to be found in the "pillar-passages" would at once vanish, and the whole argument founded on it evaporate. At best it would remain only a new mode of putting the common "Liberal" procedure of setting over against one another the divine and human traits ascribed to Jesus in the Gospels and, on the assumption that both cannot be true, choosing the human and rejecting the divine.[127] Its only advantage over the ordinary presentation of that argument would be in its concentration of the evidence of a human Jesus into

[127] Thus, for example, Johannes Weiss ("Jesus von Nazareth," pp. 132–133) enumerates first the divine traits attributed to Jesus in Mark, and then the human traits — and concludes that the divine traits belong to the Jesus of legend and the human to the Jesus of fact. See *The American Journal of Theology,* xv. (1911) pp. 553–555.

a few passages, set forth as its quintessence. It could claim superior validity over the common "Liberal" argument only if it could be shown that the passages in which it concentrates the essence of the argument for a human Jesus present to our view an exclusively human Jesus, that is, a Jesus who is in such a sense human that He cannot also be divine. These matters will require some brief consideration.

That the Jesus of the Evangelists, while truly God and as such claiming our worship, is not exclusively God, but also man, ought not in these days to require argument to prove. Certainly for those who hold the position of Schmiedel with respect to the origin and dating of the Synoptic Gospels, all motive for failure to recognize the divine-human character of the Jesus of these Gospels would seem to be removed. To say no more, the Jesus of Paul is distinctly conceived as a divine person who became man on a mission of mercy for men,[128] and His true humanity is as persistently presupposed as His deity itself. If He is in His essential nature rich, He became poor that by His poverty we might become rich; if He subsists in His proper nature "in the form of God," He did not consider His being on an equality with God so precious but that for the good of men He was willing to take "the form of a servant": He was no less, as concerns His flesh, of Israel, of the seed of David, than He was in His higher nature "God over all, blessed for ever." And Paul does not present this conception as a novelty, a peculiarity of His personal thought, an invention of His own. He tells us distinctly, on the contrary, that it was the common faith of the Christian communities among which he moved: "*for ye know*," says he, "the grace of our Lord Jesus Christ, that although He was rich, yet for your sakes He became poor." What reason is there for doubting that it was the conception of the writers of the Synoptic Gospels, and is the account to give of their frank representation of Jesus now as divine, and now as human, with inextricable intermixture of

[128] Even B. W. Bacon ("Fifth International Congress of Free Christianity and Religious Progress," 1911, p. 268) can speak briefly of "Paul's Christology of incarnation and atonement."

the traits of deity and humanity? Consider only that "pillar-passage," Mk. xiii. 32, which in one breath ascribes to Him an exalted being above all creatures and ignorance of so simple a matter as the time of the occurrence of an earthly event. In point of fact, the historical tradition of Jesus of which the Synoptic Gospels are the bearers, and which stretches back of them as far into the past as literary criticism enables us to penetrate, is the tradition of an exclusively divine Jesus as little as it is the tradition of an exclusively human Jesus; it is distinctly the tradition of a divine Jesus who is living and moving in the flesh. To represent statements in this tradition which emphasize the humanity of Jesus as on that account contradictory to its fundamental tendency is nothing short of absurd. Only if they could be shown to ascribe to Jesus a clearly exclusive humanity could they run athwart the drift of the tradition in which they are embedded.

We are not forgetting the currency of the representation that the two-natured Jesus is a contribution of Paul's to Christian thought. That the Synoptic Gospels are "Pauline" in their conception of Jesus scarcely anybody doubts nowadays. But it is still widely held that they are Pauline because their conception has been moulded by Paul, not, as is more nearly true, because Paul was moulded by the historical tradition of which they are the repositories. In point of fact, however, the two-natured Jesus is aboriginal to Christian thought; and the proof of this lies in that very failure of literary criticism to find a tradition of a Jesus different from its own back of the Synoptic record, which has provoked Schmiedel into seeking such a tradition by the more direct path of immediate historical criticism. The assumption that has ruled "Liberal" criticism for a generation that between Paul and the primitive community there lies a deep gulf and again another between the primitive community and the actual Jesus, must give way before this fact. It is already giving way. Franz Dibelius is but voicing a growing better understanding of the state of the case when he declares roundly that it is quite unjustified, and altogether contrary to historical reality, to assume, as has so long been assumed, "that there are two deep clefts in the history of primitive Christianity, one between Jesus and the Jerusalem community, and the other between the primitive community and Paul; that the theology of Paul — Paulinism — is substantially different from the theology of the primitive community and the theology of the primitive community substantially different from the faith of Jesus; that our whole tradition as to the life and words of Jesus is strongly influenced — ' painted over ' — by the conceptions of Christ of the primitive community and of Paul." [129] Even an Adolf Harnack warns us that the place of Paul in the history of Christian thought was not that of a creator, and that the gospel Paul preached was already preached by the primitive community and coalesces in substance with that of Jesus Himself; so that a crass contrast between what he calls " the first " and " the second " gospels can by no means be erected.[130] It will be observed that the effect of this revulsion from the current opposition of Paul and the primitive community, or of Paul and Jesus, is not exhausted in wiping out the difference between Paul and Jesus which it has been the custom to emphasize; it also wipes out the difference between the early community and Jesus which it has been equally the custom to emphasize. That is to say, it sets aside the canon on which " Liberal " criticism has been accustomed to act when it has assigned a large part of the Gospel tradition to " the Christian community," whose faith, it has been asserted, has been carried back into the historical tradition and imposed on Jesus. There is no evidence, as Dibelius rightly insists, that any such process took place, and, in the absence of that evidence, we may claim even a Weinel as a witness to the impropriety of assuming it. He is telling us how the work of criticism is to be prosecuted. Literary criticism, he

[129] " Das Abendmahl," 1911, p. 8.

[130] " Das doppelte Evangelium im Neuen Testament " (1910) in " Aus Wissenschaft und Leben," ii. 1911, p. 216 (E. T. in *The Proceedings and Papers of the Fifth International Congress of Free Christianity and Religious Progress*, 1911, p. 101). Cf. " What is Christianity? " E. T. 1901, pp. 153–154. Also H. Weinel, " Ist das ' liberale ' Jesusbild widerlegt? " 1910, pp. 15–16; " Seven Oxford Men," " Foundations," 1913, pp. 77, 157.

says, must first be carried to its utmost extent. Its business is
to make clear what the oldest sources contain. After that has
been ascertained, historical criticism is to be called in. Its business is to determine what has been added to the true tradition
in the course of oral transmission. He adds: [131]

" For this, now, the sole canon for distinguishing the genuine
from the non-genuine is the principle that only such traits of the
tradition are to be excluded as not genuine which *can* not come from
an interest of Jesus, but only from an interest of the community.
This principle — as was shown above against Wrede — is not to be
stretched into the different one that wherever the community has an
interest — where, however, no reason forbids that Jesus may have
also had it — the tradition is to be rejected as wholly ungenuine.
Rather — since here it is always a matter of exclusion — proof
must first be adduced that the interest in question can have arisen
only later."

As long, then, as evidence is lacking that the conception of
Jesus as divine was the product of the faith of the community,

[131] *Ibid.,* pp. 30–31. Weinel presents here the common " Liberal " canon
of criticism in its most reasonable form. He rejects it in the sweeping positive
form that everything is to be rejected which can be explained from the
" interests " of the early Christian community, and validates it only in the
narrower negative form that only that is to be rejected which cannot be
explained from an " interest " of Jesus but only from an interest of the
community. In this form, however, it remains still unworkable. It involves,
indeed, circular reasoning: we are to determine what is true of Jesus by
omitting all that is not true of Jesus; and of course we must know what is
true of Jesus before we can determine what is not true of Jesus. We may
search the literature of criticism almost in vain for workable *formal* canons
of criticism. E. A. Abbott does indeed suggest one (" Encyclopaedia Biblica,"
col. 1782, note 2; cf. col. 1788, note 2 and Schmiedel's allusion to it, col. 1872)
in the form that the presence of stumbling-blocks in a narrative is proof of
an early date; and this is a canon which is recognized in general by the
methodologists (cf. E. A. Freeman, " The Methods of Historical Study,"
1886, pp. 128, 136; H. B. George, " Historical Evidence," 1909, p. 165) as
analogous to the rule in Textual Criticism that " preference should be given
to the *difficilior lectio.*" But this canon is very plastic in its application as may
be observed from Abbott's exposition of it on the one hand, and Schmiedel's
reading of it as equivalent to his canon of contradiction on the other (cf.
" Das vierte Evangelium, etc.," p. 86 bottom). Bernheim (*op cit.,* p. 507)
remarks on the slowness of the emergence into recognition in general historical
science " of the great simple maxims of investigation."

we are not only justified in holding that the claims to a divine nature attributed to Jesus by the historical tradition are genuine, but we are bound so to hold.

But, it may be demanded, is not, as Bousset phrases it, faith the foe of fact? [132] And are we not justified in discounting the claims to a divine nature placed on the lips of Jesus by the Christian community, by the mere fact that this community was a worshipper of Jesus and therefore predisposed to represent Him as making the claims which would justify that worship? This is, however, precisely what we have just seen Weinel telling us it is illegitimate to do. The fact that the community believed Jesus to be divine is no proof that Jesus did not Himself also believe that He was divine. It must first be proved (assuming it, is not enough) that Jesus could not have made a claim to divinity, before the otherwise credible representation of the community that He did make such a claim can be set aside. We must not fall into the banality of pronouncing the testimony of earnest men to facts within their knowledge untrustworthy, just in proportion as they have themselves believed these facts and yielded themselves to their influence. Rather, their adherence to these facts, and their manifest profound belief in them, is the strongest testimony to their actuality which they could give us. So far from faith being the foe of fact, faith is the correlate of fact and its proper evidence. " Faith," in other words, as a recent writer puts it,[133] " did not

---

[132] " Was wissen wir von Jesus? " 1904, p. 54: " It has been rightly emphasized that in this regard our first three Gospels are distinguished from the fourth only in degree. Must there not, then, have taken place here a complete repainting from the standpoint of faith? For there is a certain propriety in saying that faith is the foe of history. Where we believe and honor we no longer see objectively."

[133] Hugh R. Mackintosh, " The Doctrine of the Person of Jesus Christ," 1912, p. 8. He continues: " The impulse to select, to fling upon words or incidents a light answering to the later situation of the Church, is natural and intelligible; what is not so is an impulse to deform or to fabricate. ' Fidelity to the historical tradition,' a sympathetic writer [it is of E. F. Scott, " The Fourth Gospel," p. 2 that he is speaking] has said, ' was undoubtedly the chief aim of the Synoptic writers. Their work may here and there bear traces of theological coloring, but their first interest was the facts. Their part was not to interpret, but simply to record.' "

incapacitate the evangelists as narrators; it showed them, rather, how infinitely the life of Jesus deserved narration." "What mandate of historical method," exclaims Johannes Weiss,[134] " tells us that the interested parties [*die Betheiligten*] are to be distrusted under all circumstances? . . . The truly unprejudiced man will say: 'With reference to the nature of a personality we shall always reach ultimately a clearer notion along with these who have surrendered themselves to his influence than with those whom hate has made blind, or who have simply taken no interest in him.' " The matter is placed in a fair light by some remarks of W. Heitmüller's: [135]

" For all particular accounts we are indebted altogether to *Christian* sources, that is, to sources which come from followers of Jesus. It is a sign of the presently reigning anxiety with respect to the knowledge of Jesus and especially a proof of the defective historical training of the oppugners of Jesus, that this fact is regarded as a ground of uneasiness, and, on the other side, as a weapon to be used against the historicity of the Nazarene. Who, on such grounds, doubts the historicity of Socrates, because we are indebted to his votaries (*Verehren*), Plato and Xenophon, for the chief accounts of him? And whence do we have any knowledge of Buddha save from the Buddhist literature? " [136]

In the absence of all positive proof that Jesus was not what His followers represent Him, we must accept Him as what they

---

[134] " Jesus von Nazareth, etc.," 1910, p. 93.

[135] Schiele und Zscharnack's " Die Religion, etc.," iii. 1912, col. 345.

[136] Cf. H. Weinel, " Ist das ' liberale ' Jesusbild widerlegt? " 1910, p. 28. " The whole tradition about Jesus is Christian, — Mark too, even Wellhausen's ' Primitive Mark,' has Christian traits; and what is Christian must be cleared away from the portrait of Jesus before He Himself is found. But, then, only what is in a particular sense Christian. Jesus was certainly no Jew, but something new; what is Christian is to be warded off from Him only so far as it concerns thoughts and ideas and tendencies which only the later community could have." The emphasis upon the word " only " here is strong; see p. 31 (quoted above, p. 247) and also pp. 21–22 when in opposition to Wrede, Weinel declares: " We must give credit to a tradition so long as it is not clearly proved to be impossible." We must not reject tradition *in principle* and demand that historical facts be shown to be *necessary*, before we accept them as *actual*.

represent Him. To refer subjectively to the faith of His followers what they refer objectively to His person, for no other reason than that it would seem to us more natural that He should have been something different — what we choose to think Him rather than what they knew Him to be — is only to be guilty ourselves, in the portrait which we form of Jesus, in an immensely aggravated form, of the fault of which we accuse them.

We have allowed that Schmiedel's "pillar-passages" might be worthy of more consideration as evidence of a contradictory tradition underlying that which alone has survived and become embodied in the Synoptic Gospels, if the Jesus which they bring before us was not merely a Jesus who possessed truly human traits and who sometimes would not work miracles, but a Jesus who was merely a human being and was quite incapable of working miracles in any circumstance. Of such an implication of these "pillar-passages," however, there can be no question, as has already sufficiently appeared. He in whom a truly human soul dwelt (though in conjunction with the Divine Spirit) might well — nay, needs must — have been the subject, as respects that soul, of ignorances (Mk. xiii. 32) and the sense of desolation in the throes of mortal agony (Mk. xv. 34); and might take a secondary place in comparison with the pure Divine Spirit (Mt. xii. 32). Refusal to work miracles in given circumstances and on particular demands cannot be held to carry with it sheer inability to work them in all circumstances (Mk. vi. 5; viii. 12). Even in the instances (Mk. x. 18; vi. 5) in which a certain surface plausibility may attach to the contention that a less than divine Jesus is implied, this plausibility depends upon a particular interpretation which does not do justice to the actual language of the passages. The chief interest which attaches to Schmiedel's "pillar-passages" accordingly lies in the exposure which they supply of the weakness of the case against the consistency of the portraiture of the divine Jesus drawn in the Synoptic narratives. Innumerable passages may be pointed out in which the true humanity of Jesus is presupposed and illustrated; but when passages are sought in

which the true deity of Jesus is denied or excluded, they are discoverable with great difficulty and are verifiable only at the
price of a method of interpreting them which does extreme
violence to them.

Schmiedel is not alone in his failure to unearth such passages. Others, too, have sought for them and have come forward
with as meager a fruitage of their searching in their hands. For
example, H. J. Holtzmann thought that he could adduce a few
passages — they are five in all — in which Jesus ranked Himself in dignity of being distinctly below the Divine. It may be
worth while to place Holtzmann's passages by the side of
Schmiedel's that the weakness of the general case may become
more apparent. What Holtzmann is contending for, is that,
however high the self-estimation may be which is involved in
Jesus' claim to the Messiahship — a claim which Schmiedel
also allows that Jesus certainly made, and against the "presumption" involved in which, to call it by no uglier name, he
also strives to defend his Jesus.[137] He nevertheless distinctly
ranks Himself below the Divine in dignity and thus guards
Himself against the imputation of claiming "superhuman-
hood" (*Uebermenschentum*). The central portion of his
argument runs as follows: [138]

"Let the title of Messiah betoken the highest exaltation of
human self-esteem (*Selbstgefühl*), there is at least given in the
unqualified subordination of the idea of the Messiah to the supreme
idea of God an absolutely sufficient guarantee against a self-glorify-

[137] "Die Person Jesu, etc.," pp. 10–18 (E. T. pp. 28–52). It was in no sense
due to presumption (*Ueberhebung, pride*), he contends, that Jesus held Himself to be the Messiah. He reached that conception of Himself only through
severe struggles (p. 16). Therefore, though in so thinking of Himself, He cannot be cleared of the charge of being a visionary (*Schwärmer*), if this means
only that "He cherished expectations concerning Himself which go too high
and are afterwards not realized," yet these too exalted expectations were not
the product of pride (*Selbstüberhebung*) and He was not a visionary in this
sense. "It certainly is a misfortune that the highest up to which Jesus reached
out in order to fulfil His mission, His belief in His messianic dignity, . . . led
also to expectations such as these, which could never really be fulfilled; but I
do not see that any shadow is cast by this upon His character or His purity"
(p. 17: E. T. p. 51).

[138] H. J. Holtzmann, "Das messianische Bewusstsein Jesu," 1907, pp. 82 f.

ing superhumanness. Immutable facts establish this, such as that sins against the Son of Man are adjudged pardonable, in contrast with sins against the Spirit of God (Mt. xii. 32 = Lk. xii. 10), and that He recognizes as His own not those that call on Him as Lord, but only those that do the will of His Father (Mt. vii. 21–23 = Lk. vi. 46, Mk. iii. 35 = Mt. xii. 50 = Lk. viii. 21).[139] He even indeed declines to be addressed as ' Good Master,' because this would involve assumption of God's exclusive property (Mk. x. 18 = Lk. xviii. 19). It is not His but solely God's concern to dispose of dignities and honors in the Kingdom of Heaven (Mk. x. 40 = Mt. xx. 23). Jesus rather knows Himself (Lk. xxii. 27) with each of His followers as a servant, and when He enforces upon His disciples that all true greatness which avails with God reveals itself in service (Mk. x. 43–45 = Mt. xx. 26–28; Mt. xxiii. 11 = Lk. xxii. 26) this applies to Himself too. These are declarations incapable of being invented (unerfindbare), which surpass in eternal value all that is eschatological, in the mouth of Him whom nevertheless the very next generation exalted to the throne of the Judge of the world (Mt. xxv. 31–34) and in the end made equal with God.[140]

[139] On these passages, cf. Karl Thieme, " Die christliche Demut," i. (1906) p. 137: " But with reference to such judgments on such passages, the question is to be asked whether there are really set over against one another here God and Jesus' ego, a demeanor towards the one and a demeanor towards the other.

" What Jesus brings into opposition to one another is rather two kinds of demeanor towards Himself and His preaching — the one, calling Him ' Lord, Lord,' pleading rights of kinship with Him, giving Him extravagant admiration, envying His mother, and so forth, and not doing what He commands (cf. Lk. vi. 46) ; the other, according obedience to the word of God with which He comes forward, and doing what He announces as the will of God. The general meaning of these declarations is not that Jesus points in any way away from Himself to God, but that He deprecates every manner of relation to Him which does not include the doing of His moral requirements."

[140] It is interesting to observe how little advance has been made on the Arians in this method of argument. Athanasius (Migne, " Patr. Graec." xxvi. col. 985 B, C) tells us that in attempting to discover a less than divine Jesus in the Scriptures they said: " How can [the Son] be like [the Father] or of the Father's essence, when it is written, As the Father has life in Himself, so He has given also to the Son to have life in Himself? There is, they say, a superiority in the giver above the receiver. And, Why callest thou me good? they say, No one is good except one, God. And again, My God, my God, why hast thou forsaken me? And once more, Of the last day no one knoweth, not even the Son, except the Father. And again, Whom the Father sanctified and sent into the world. And again, Whom the Father raised from the dead. How, then,

It was not, however, the next generation which "exalted Jesus to the throne of the Judge of the world," but Jesus Himself; it is involved, to go no farther, in His favorite self-designation of Son of Man. Nor was it merely "in the end" that He was made "equal with God": Jesus Himself placed Himself not only "at the side of God" in contradistinction to all creatures, above the angels of heaven themselves (Mk. xiii. 32, one of Schmiedel's "pillar-passages"), and asserted for Himself an interactive reciprocity with God in knowledge of one another, such as implies His equality with God (Mt. xi. 27, a passage admitted by Schmiedel to be authentic), but also combines His own person as Son with the Father and the Spirit in the One Name which is above every name (Mt. xxviii. 19). The difficulty with Holtzmann as with Schmiedel is only that he cannot think in the terms of the historical tradition of Christianity and is consumed by zeal to get behind the tradition and impose his own forms of thought on the "real" Jesus. The marks of lowliness of spirit which he discovers in Jesus — who, being man, declared Himself to be meek and lowly in heart — seem to him to be inconsistent with a claim for Jesus of a Divine nature for no other reason than that he sets before himself the irreconcilable dilemma, either Divine or human, and never once entertains the wider conception of both Divine and human. And yet it is really undeniable that this is the conception which rules the whole historical tradition of Christianity, underlies the narratives of the Synoptic Gospels as truly as the reasoning of Paul, and provides the one key which will unlock the mysteries of the self-consciousness of Jesus as depicted in the earliest tradition known to us. To tear the elements of this self-consciousness apart, and assign fragments of it to Jesus and other fragments to the "faith of the community" on no other ground than that thus a view of Jesus and of the development of Christian feeling and thinking about Jesus is attained which falls better in with the para-

---

they say, can He that is raised from the dead be like or of the same nature with Him that raised Him?" This is to all intents and purposes Holtzmann before Holtzmann.

digms of our preconceived conceptions of what were "natural," or even of what were possible, is utterly illegitimate
criticism, in the complete absence of evidence for any such
discrimination of facts in the tradition, or for any such development of feeling and thinking concerning Jesus, as is
supposed. We must awake at last to the understanding that
the historical tradition of Jesus is of a Divine-human Jesus
and that this tradition is copious, constant, and to all appearance aboriginal. To break with this tradition is to break with
the entire historical tradition of Jesus, and to cast ourselves
adrift to form a conception of the real Jesus purely *a priori,*
in accordance with our own notions of the fit or the possible,
unaided by the least scrap of historical evidence.

But surely, it will be exclaimed, we must exclude the impossible from our conception of the actual Jesus. Undoubtedly
the impossible cannot have been actual. It is a reasonable
custom of historians therefore to exclude the manifestly impossible from the constructions of the actual which they extract from the testimony before them;[141] though it is worthy
of remark that they recommend a wise wariness in declaring
attested occurrences impossible.[142] Of one thing we may meanwhile be sure, — that what was actual can scarcely be
impossible; and it is not a bad way — among others — of determining what is possible to observe what is actual. The testimony to the actual existence of the supernatural Jesus is
simply overwhelming. Shall we set it all aside on the bald
assumption that the supernatural is impossible? Two remarks fall to be made here. The first is that Schmiedel at least

---

[141] Cf. Langlois and Seignobos, "Introduction to the Study of History,"
1898, pp. 206 ff.: H. B. George, "Historical Evidence," 1909, pp. 138–167.

[142] H. B. George, for example, wishes us to be chary of rejecting all miraculous accounts (though on grounds which only go part of the way) and not
only enunciates the general proposition that "when a statement is made by a
real contemporary, we require something beyond mere intrinsic improbability
to lead us to disbelieve it" (p. 164), but, with his eye directly on miracles, declares that although when the document narrating them is of low credibility
they may be safely neglected, yet when the general credibility of documents
must be rated high, " it becomes more difficult to disparage any statement contained in them, whether it is called miraculous or not " (p. 169).

is committed not to treat the supernatural element in the Synoptical account of Jesus as *a priori* impossible. " It would clearly be wrong," he says,[143] " in an investigation such as the present, to start from any such postulate or axiom as that 'miracles' are impossible," — though, as we have seen, if he does not start from this postulate he soon calls it in as the determining principle of his criticism.[144] The second remark is that the supernatural element cannot be excluded from the life of Jesus except on the ground of its *a priori* impossibility. To all critical efforts to exclude it, it proves absolutely intractable. The whole historical tradition testifies to an intensely supernatural Jesus. It is only on the ground of a philosophical presupposition that the supernatural is impossible that the supernatural Jesus can be set aside.[145] But thus the question as to the supernatural Jesus is shifted into a region other than the historical. Whether the supernatural is possible is a question not of historical criticism but of philosophical world-view. For the present it may be permitted to go at that. It is enough to have made it plain that if the supernatural Jesus is to be displaced from history, it is not on historical grounds that He can be displaced.

[143] " Encyclopaedia Biblica," col. 1876.

[144] " Encyclopaedia Biblica," col. 1878: " Lk. xxiii. 44 f. expressly, and Mk. xv. 33, Mt. xxvii. 45 also to all appearance, allege an eclipse of the sun, a celestial phenomenon which, however, is possible only at the period of New Moon, — i.e., shortly before the 1st of Nisan — and cannot happen on the 15th or 14th of a month," that is to say the phenomenon of the darkening of the sun *cannot* have happened unless it happened *naturally*. Cf. above, note 14.

[145] " For," says Strauss (second " Life of Jesus," 1879, i. p. 19), " if the Gospels are really and truly historical, it is not possible to exclude miracles from the life of Jesus; if, on the other hand, miracles are incompatible with history, then the Gospels are not really historical records."

VI

THE " TWO NATURES " AND RECENT CHRISTOLOGICAL SPECULATION

THE "TWO NATURES" AND RECENT CHRISTOLOGICAL SPECULATION [1]

I. THE CHRISTOLOGY OF THE NEW TESTAMENT WRITINGS

ONE of the most portentous symptoms of the decay of vital sympathy with historical Christianity which is observable in present-day academic circles is the widespread tendency in recent Christological discussion to revolt from the doctrine of the Two Natures in the Person of Christ. The significance of this revolt becomes at once apparent, when we reflect that the doctrine of the Two Natures is only another way of stating the doctrine of the Incarnation; and the doctrine of the Incarnation is the hinge on which the Christian system turns. No Two Natures, no Incarnation; no Incarnation, no Christianity in any distinctive sense. Nevertheless, voices are raised all about us declaring the conception of two natures in Christ no longer admissible; and that very often with full appreciation of the significance of the declaration.

Thus, for example, Johannes Weiss tells us that it is unthinkable that Godhood and manhood should be united in a single person walking upon the earth; that, while no doubt men of ancient time could conceive " that a man might really be an incarnate deity," modern men feel much too strongly the impassable barrier which separates the divine and the human to entertain such a notion.[2] And Paul Wilhelm Schmiedel pronounces it "simply impossible," now that they have awakened to inquire "what is psychologically possible and impossible," for men to submit any longer to a demand that does such violence at once to their intelligence and to their religious experience as the demand " that they should embrace the idea

[1] Reprinted from *The American Journal of Theology*, xv. 1911, pp. 337–361; 546–568.   [2] Christus: Die Anfänge des Dogmas," (1909), p. 88

of a perfect God and a perfect Man as united in the one and indivisible person of a Saviour whom they are longing to revere." Accordingly, since the divine and human nature cannot be united in Jesus, and since " Jesus was undoubtedly man," he continues, we have simply to regard him as man and nothing more.[3] Coming nearer home, William Adams Brown declares that men are no longer to be satisfied with " the old conception of Christ as a being of two natures, one divine and one human, dwelling in a mysterious union, incapable of description, within the confines of a single personality." Such a conception, he thinks, fails to " do justice to the genuine humanity " of Jesus, who " shares our limitations "; and supposes " an impassable gulf between God and man " which requires " a miracle" to bridge it. The only " incarnation" which is real, he asserts, concerns not "a single instance," but the eternal entrance of God " into humanity." [4] These are but examples of numerous deliverances which may differ from one another in the clearness with which they announce the consequences, but do not differ in the decisiveness with which they reject the doctrine of the Two Natures.[5]

The violence of the revolution which is thus attempted is somewhat obscured by the bad habit, which is becoming common, of speaking of the doctrine of the Two Natures as in some sense the creation of the Chalcedonian fathers. Even Albert Schweitzer permits himself to write:

" When at Chalcedon the West overcame the East, its doctrine of the two natures dissolved the unity of the Person, and thereby cast off the last possibility of a return to the historical Jesus. The self-contradiction was elevated into a law. . . . This dogma had first to be shattered before men could once more go out in quest of the historical Jesus, before they could even grasp the thought of His existence." [6]

[3] " Jesus or Christ? " Being the *Hibbert Journal* Supplement for 1909, p. 66.   [4] *Methodist Quarterly Review,* Nashville, Tenn., 1911, p. 44.

[5] Cf. how the subject is dealt with in such widely read dogmatic treatises as Julius Kaftan's " Dogmatik " [3]. [4]. (1901), §§ 42, 44 ff.; and F. A. B. Nitzsch's " Lehrbuch der evangelischen Dogmatik " (1892), §§ 43 ff.

[6] " The Quest of the Historical Jesus," E. T., 1910, p. 3.

By "the historical Jesus" is here meant the merely human Jesus; and it is quite true that the doctrine of the Two Natures interposes an insuperable obstacle to the recognition of such a Jesus as the real Jesus. There is a sense also in which it may be truly said that at Chalcedon the West impressed on the East its long-established doctrine of the Two Natures — a doctrine which had been fully formulated in the West from at least the time of Tertullian. But by this very token it is clear that the doctrine decreed at Chalcedon was nothing new; and if, as is often the case,[7] the further suggestion is conveyed that what was new in it was the "Two Natures" itself, the perversion becomes monstrous.

It was no part of the task of the fathers at Chalcedon to invent a new doctrine, and the doctrine which they formulated had no single new element in it. Least of all was the doctrine of the Two Natures itself new. No one of the disputants in the long series of controversies which led up to Chalcedon, any more than in the equally long series of controversies which led down from it, cherished the least doubt of this doctrine — not even Arius, and certainly not Apollinaris, or Nestorius, or Eutyches, or any of the great Monophysite or Monothelite leaders, or any of their opponents. The doctrine of the Two Natures formed the common basis on which all alike stood; their differences concerned only the quality or integrity of the two natures united in the one person, or the character or effects of the union by which they were brought together. It was the adjustment of these points of difference alone with which the council was concerned, or rather, to speak more precisely, the authoritative determination of the range within which such attempted adjustments might be tolerated in a church calling itself Christian.

It was not to the fourth-century fathers alone, however, that the doctrine of the Two Natures was "given." There

[7] Cf. J. Weiss, "Christus," usw. (1909), p. 88: "A series of inexpressibly complicated and supremely unhappy controversies attached itself to this, until the famous compromise formula [*Beschwichtigungsformel*] of one person in two natures was discovered, which no matter how acutely it may be elaborated can never give satisfaction."

never was a time when it was not the universal presupposition of the whole attitude, intellectual and devotional alike, of Christians to their Lord. The term δύο οὐσίαι may first occur in extant writings in a fragment of Melito's of Sardis [8] (Tertullian, duae substantiae; Origen and later writers generally, δύο φύσεις). But the thing goes back to the beginning.[9] When we read, for example, in Clement of Rome's Letter to the Corinthians, in a passage (xvi) containing echoes of Heb. i. 8 and Phil. ii. 6, that "the Scepter of the Majesty of God, our Lord Jesus Christ, came not in the pomp of arrogance or pride — though he could well have done that — but in lowliness of mind," or in a passage (xxxii) manifestly reminiscent of Rom. ix. 5, that "the Lord Jesus," . . . that Lord Jesus to whom the highest predicates are ascribed (as e.g. in xxxvi) — is "according to the flesh," "of Jacob," the two natures are as plainly presupposed as they are openly asserted in such Ignatian passages as: "There is one Healer, fleshly and spiritual, generate and ingenerate, God in man, true life in death, both of Mary and of God, first passible and then impassible, Jesus Christ our Lord" (Eph. vii. 2), or: "For our God, Jesus Christ, was borne in the womb of Mary, according to a dispensation, of the seed of David, indeed, but also of the Holy Spirit" (xviii. 2). Adolf Harnack, it is true, has made a brilliant attempt to distinguish "adoptionist" as well as "pneumatic" Christologies underlying the Christian tradition. But he has felt himself compelled notably to qualify his original representation;[10] while F. Loofs has quite properly permitted the whole notion to drop out of sight;[11] and R. Seeberg has solidly refuted it.[12] To discover a one-natured Christ, we must turn to the outlawed sects of the Docetists on the one hand, and the Ebionites with their successors, the

[8] Fragment VI, Otto, ix. p. 416.

[9] Cf. F. Loofs, "Herzog Realencyklopädie,"[3] iv. pp. 36, 37: "Melito spoke of δύο οὐσίαι in Christ. The tradition of Asia Minor supplied to him the materials for this: the formula was not derived from it by Melito."

[10] "Grundriss,"[4] p. 44, note.

[11] "Herzog Realencyklopädie,"[3] iv. pp. 23 ff.

[12] "Lehrbuch der Dogmengeschichte"[2] (1908), i. pp. 104 ff.

Dynamistic Montanists, on the other. Whatever else the church brought with it out of the apostolic age, it emerged from that, its formative, epoch with so firm a faith in the Two Natures of its Lord as to be incapable of wavering. "Perfect man" [13] it knew him to be. But the exhortation of Christians to one another ran in such strains as we find in the opening words of the earliest Christian homily that has come down to us: "Brethren, thus ought we to think of Jesus Christ — as of God, as of Judge of quick and dead";[14] and so exhorting one another, they naturally were known to their heathen observers precisely as worshippers of Christ.[15] So fixed in the Christian consciousness was the conception of the Two Natures of the Savior, that nothing could dislodge it. We shall have to come down to the radical outbreak which accompanied the Reformation — Trancendental or Socinian — for the first important defection from it after the early Dynamistic Monarchianism; and it was not until the rise in the eighteenth century of the naturalistic movement known as the Enlightenment that there was inaugurated any widespread revolt from it. It is under the influence of this revolt, which has not yet spent its force, that so many "moderns" have turned away from the doctrine as "impossible."

The constancy with which the church has confessed the doctrine of the Two Natures finds its explanation in the fact that this doctrine is intrenched in the teaching of the New Testament. The Chalcedonian Christology, indeed, in its complete development is only a very perfect synthesis of the biblical data. It takes its starting-point from the New Testament as a whole, thoroughly trusted in all its declarations, and seeks to find a comprehensive statement of the scriptural doctrine of the Person of Christ, which will do full justice to all the elements of its representation. The eminent success which it achieves in this difficult undertaking is due to the cir-

---

[13] Ignatius, ad Symrn. iv. p. 2, ad fin.; Zahn compares the fragment of Melito's alluded to above (note 8): θεὸς γὰρ ὤν ὁμοῦ τε καὶ ἄνθρωπος τέλειος ὁ αὐτός.

[14] 2 Clem. Rom. i. 1.

[15] Plin., Ep. x. p. 96: "carmenque Christo quasi deo dicere secum invicem."

cumstance that it is not the product of a single mind working under a "scientific" impulse, that is to say, with purely theoretical intent, but of the mind, or rather the heart, of the church at large searching for an adequate formulation of its vital faith, that is to say, of a large body of earnest men distributed through a long stretch of time, and living under very varied conditions, each passionately asserting, and seeking to have justice accorded to, elements of the biblical representation which particularly "found" him. The final statement is not a product of the study, therefore, but of life; and was arrived at, externally considered, through protracted and violent controversies, during the course of which every conceivable construction of the biblical data had been exploited, weighed, and its elements of truth sifted out and preserved, while the elements of error which deformed it were burned up as chaff in the fires of the strife. To the onlooker from this distance of time, the main line of the progress of the debate takes on an odd appearance of a steady zigzag advance. Arising out of the embers of the Arian controversy, there is first vigorously asserted, over against the reduction of our Lord to the dimensions of a creature, the pure deity of his spiritual nature (Apollinarianism); by this there is at once provoked, in the interests of the integrity of our Lord's humanity, the equally vigorous assertion of the completeness of his human nature as the bearer of his deity (Nestorianism); this in turn provokes, in the interests of the oneness of his Person, an equally vigorous assertion of the conjunction of these two natures in a single individuum (Eutychianism): from all of which there gradually emerges at last, by a series of corrections, the balanced statement of Chalcedon, recognizing at once in its "without confusion, without conversion, eternally and inseparably" the union in the Person of Christ of a complete deity and a complete humanity, constituting a single person without prejudice to the continued integrity of either nature. The pendulum of thought had swung back and forth in ever-decreasing arcs, until at last it found rest along the line of action of the fundamental force. Out of the continuous controversy of a century there issued a balanced statement in which all the elements of the biblical representation were taken up and combined. Work so done is done for all time; and it is capable of ever-repeated demonstration that in the developed doctrine of the Two Natures (as it is worked out with marvelous insight and delicate precision in such a presentation of it as is given, say, in the " Admonitio Christiana," 1581, written chiefly by Zacharias Ursinus and published in his works) and in it alone, all the biblical data are brought together in a harmonious statement, in which each receives full recognition, and out of which each may derive its sympathetic exposition. This key unlocks the treasures of the biblical instruction on the Person of Christ as none other can, and enables the reader as he currently scans the sacred pages to take up their declarations as they meet him, one after the other, into an intelligently consistent conception of his Lord.

The key which unlocks so complicated a lock can scarcely fail to be its true key. And the argument may be turned around. That all the varied representations concerning our Lord's Person contained in the New Testament fall into harmony under the ordering influence of so simple a hypothesis as that of the Two Natures, authenticates these varying representations as each a fragment of a real whole. It were inconceivable that so large a body of different and sometimes apparently divergent data could synthetize in so simple a unifying conception, were they not component elements of a unitary reality. And this consideration is greatly strengthened by the manner in which these differing or sometimes even apparently divergent data are distributed through the New Testament. They are not parceled out severally to the separate books, the composition of different writers, so that one set of them is peculiar to one writer or to one set of writers, and a set of different import peculiar to another writer or set of writers. They are, rather, pretty evenly distributed over the face of the New Testament, and the most different or apparently divergent data are found side by side in the writings of the same author or even in the same writing. The doctrine of the Two Natures is not merely a synthesis of all data concerning the Person of Christ found in the New Testament; it is the doctrine of each of the New Testament books in severalty. There is but one doctrine of the Person of Christ inculcated or presupposed by all the New Testament writers without exception. In this respect the New Testament is all of a piece. Book may differ from book in the terms in which it gives expression to the common doctrine, or in the fulness with which it develops its details, or with which it draws out its implications. But all are at one in the inculcation or presupposition of the common doctrine of the Two Natures.

It has no doubt required some time for the critical study of the New Testament writings to arrive solidly at this conclusion. But it is at this conclusion, it may fairly be said, that the critical study of the New Testament has at length arrived. The day is gone by in which a number of mutually exclusive Christologies could be ascribed to the writers of the New Testament and set over against one another in crass contradiction. Nowadays, the New Testament is admitted to be Christologically much on a level, and though we still hear of a pre-Pauline, a Pauline, and a post-Pauline Christology, this very phraseology shows the dominance of a single type, and the boundary lines which separate even the varieties which are thus suggested are very indistinct. There are in fact next to no pre-Pauline writings in the New Testament, and therefore no pre-Pauline Christologies are taught in it; and though there are writings in the New Testament which in point of chronological sequence are post-Pauline, it is only with much ado that a post-Pauline Christology in the proper sense of the term can be even plausibly discovered in it. F. C. Baur discriminated three sharply divergent types of Christology among the New Testament writers. To the Synoptists Christ was a mere man, endowed with the Holy Spirit as Messiah; to Paul he was still a man but a deified man; to John he was a God incarnated in a human body. We have to travel far from this before we reach, say, Johannes Weiss. To Weiss the whole New Testament is written under the influence of Paul who introduced the Logos

Christology. Before Paul, men indeed thought of Christ as a deified man; but no New Testament book is written from this standpoint. After Paul, some explication of what is already implicit in Paul took place; but the general lines laid down by Paul are only deepened, not departed from. The Christologies of Peter, Paul, and John are still distinguished; but the distinctions are posited on little or no differences in recorded utterances.

The difficulty in discovering a substantial difference between the Christologies of Paul and John, for example, is fairly illustrated by the straits to which so acute a writer as Johannes Weiss is brought in the effort to establish one. The only such difference he is able to suggest is that the superhuman Being whose incarnation constituted the Two-Natured Christ believed in by both writers alike, is, with Paul, though divine in his nature, yet of subordinate rank to the supreme God, while with John he is the supreme God himself. Unfortunately, however (or, rather, fortunately), when Paul speaks of the superhuman element in the person of his Lord, he does not hesitate to declare him the supreme God in the most exalted sense, and that in language which, for clearness and emphasis, leaves nothing for John to add to it.

He does this, for example, in Rom. ix. 5, where he describes Christ as to his higher nature in these great words: ὁ ὢν ἐπὶ πάντων θεὸς εὐλογητὸς εἰς τοὺς αἰῶνας, ἀμήν. It is instructive to observe how Johannes Weiss deals with such a passage. He is arguing that Paul carefully avoids calling Christ by the high name of "God," although he places Him as "Lord" by the side of God (I Cor. iii. 23, viii. 6); and he adds:[16]

"It is, then, very remarkable that in the present text of Rom. ix. 5 there stands the following doxology, which can be referred only to Christ: 'He who is God over all, be blessed for ever.' If κύριος had stood here we should not have been surprised; that the text should, however, ascribe to Him here a predicate which puts Him altogether in God's place — without any indication of subordination — is inconceivable. Accordingly it has been rightly as-

16 "Christus" (1909), p. 29.

sumed that there is a textual corruption here. It is undoubtedly genuine, however, when, in Jno. xx. 28, Thomas exclaims to the resurrected Christ: ' My Lord and my God.' So also Christ is called God in I Jno. v. 20 and Tit. ii. 13. This is accordant with the dominant Hellenistic mode of thought in these late New Testament writings. The strictly Jewish foundation of the oldest Christianity is no longer so strong; feeling is no longer shocked by the appearance by the side of God of a second Godhead."

Needless to say, however, there is not a scintilla of evidence of textual corruption in Rom. ix. 5; corruption is assumed solely because the assertion of the passage does not fit in with the lowered Christology which Weiss would fain assign to Paul. The allusion to previous writers who have assumed corruption is doubtless to the recent attempt [17] to revive an old emendation proposed by the Socinian controversialists, J. Schlichting and J. Crell. The suggestion is that the words ὁ ὤν be transposed, so as to read ὤν ὁ (Hoekstra would be satisfied with the simple omission of the ὁ).[18] Thus it is thought the last clause of the passage would be brought into parallelism with its predecessors, and the whole would rise to its climax in the assertion that not only do the fathers belong to the Jews, and not only has the Christ (as regards the flesh) sprung from them, but to them belongs also the supreme God himself who is blessed forevermore, Amen. The mere statement of the proposal surely is its sufficient refutation. The variation of the construction in the instance of the Christ from ὤν to ἐξ ὤν, and the limitation of even this assertion with respect to him to his flesh (τὸ κατὰ σάρκα) render the adjunction of such a a clause as the reconstructed form gives us simply incredible. Should Paul, after refusing to declare their own Messiah to

[17] J. Lepsius, "Das Reich Christi" (1904); Strömann, *ZNTW* (1907), p. 319; (1908), p. 80 (A. Bischoff).

[18] Cf. W. C. van Manen, "*Conjecturaal-kritiek* toegepast op den Tekst van de Schriften des Nieuwen Testaments" (1880), p. 262. Van Manen wonders that no one, instead of θεὸς has read ὅς after the analogy of I Tim. iii. 16; but that would scarcely (here any more than at I Tim. iii. 16) mend the matter. Christ would remain ὁ ἐπὶ πάντων and be εὐλογητὸς εἰς τοὺς αἰῶνας; and these predicates import deity at its height.

belong distinctively to the Jews and carefully limiting his relation to them to merely that of issuing from them — and that,
only " according to the flesh " — immediately assert with cli-
matic emphasis that the supreme and eternal God himself is
their peculiar possession? " Is he the God of the Jews only and
not also of the Gentiles? " Paul asks in the same broad context
(Rom. iii. 29), and answers with emphasis, " Yes, of the
Gentiles also "; and by that answer advertises to us that he
could not have written here, in his enumeration of the distinctive privileges of the Jews, that "theirs is the God over all,
blessed forever." The resort to textual emendation to ease the
pressure of the passage fails, thus, as dismally as, according to
Weiss's own confession, the more common resort to artificial
exegesis of it fails — whether this follows the older methods
of varying merely the punctuation so as to throw the obnoxious clause into innocuous isolation as an interjected doxology
to God, or the new suggestion of F. C. Burkitt which would
take the ὁ ὤν as the Tetragrammaton itself, and read the
whole passage as not "description but ascription " — a protestation, calling the Eternal to witness the sincerity of Paul's
great asseveration.[19] It is at least a healthful sign of the times
when Weiss discards all such artificial exegesis; we may even
hope that the day has dawned when it is no longer possible.[20]

[19] *JTS*, v. pp. 451–455.

[20] C. Clemen, " Religionsgeschichtliche Erklärung des N. T." (1909), pp.
261–262, writes: " If even Jesus himself already exalted himself above the
measure of other men by his proclamation of his return to judgment, and this
happened to a still greater extent in the primitive Christian community, yet
it was Paul who first designates him as the Lord in whom all things consist,
and not only sets him side by side with God, but — according to the much
more probable interpretation of Rom. ix. 5 — even gives him the very name."
Even when the reference to Christ is denied, it is frequently admitted that
the exegetical considerations favor it. Thus, M. Brückner, " Die Entstehung
der paulinischen Christologie " (1903), p. 67, allows that " exegetically the
reference to Christ is almost necessary," though, pleading that " grammatical
exegesis cannot always be permitted to give the decision," he decides against
it, on the strange ground that it is " precisely here out of place to emphasize
the divine nature of Christ," as if the fact that the possession of divine nature
by the Messiah who issued from them was not the Jews' supreme glory!
Similarly, Robert B. Drummond writes (*The Academy*, March 30, 1895, No.

It is mere matter of fact that Paul, speaking distinctly οὐ κατὰ
τιμήν, ἀλλὰ κατὰ φύσιν, as the contrast with τὸ κατὰ σάρκα
shows, designates Christ here " God over all, blessed forever."
It were well for us to adjust our theories to this plain fact and
cease to endeavor to brush the fact out of the way of our
theories.

Why so much zeal and ingenuity should be expended in attempting to vacate this declaration of its plain meaning, it is
meanwhile a little difficult to comprehend. If it stood alone
among Paul's utterances [21] it might be natural for those who
wish to contribute another doctrine to him to seek to set it in
some way aside. But so far from standing alone, it is but one
of many declarations running through his epistles, to the
same effect. There is Phil. ii. 6, for example, where, beyond
question, Christ Jesus is asserted to be " on an equality with
God " [22] an assertion, one would think, not easy to reconcile

1195, p. 273): " I must confess for myself that I feel very strongly the grammatical difficulty of the Unitarian interpretation; but, on the other hand, the
improbability of Paul attributing not only deity, but supreme deity (ἐπὶ
πάντων Θεός) to Christ, seems to me so great as to outweigh all other considerations." Why, however, it should be thought " improbable " that Paul should
attribute to Christ in terms the supreme deity he everywhere accords him
in fact does not appear; had Paul held Drummond's views concerning Christ
it would have been a different matter. On Rom. ix. 5 in general, see Dwight,
Journal of the Exegetical Society (1881), p. 22, and Sanday-Headlam, Gifford,
and Zahn, *in loco.*

[21] That it does stand alone in Paul's writings is, of course, the implication of Weiss, and is often explicitly asserted. Thus, for example, E. P. Gould,
" The Biblical Theology of the New Testament " (1900), pp. 93–94, reasons
as follows: " All that can be said in favor of this interpretation, according to
which Jesus is here called God, is that it is a natural explanation, probably
the natural explanation of the passage as it stands, supposing there is nothing
against it. But on the other side is the fact that it stands absolutely alone
in the apostle's writings." Phil. ii. 6 Gould interprets as implying that equality
with God was something the preincarnate Christ did not possess but might
conceivably aspire to (ἁρπαγμός, active). Colossians he denies to Paul.

[22] The interpretation (represented by E. P. Gould; see above note 21;
cf. also M. Brückner, *op. cit.,* pp. 66 ff., who thinks the thing lacking to make
Christ " equal with God " was only " the name and position of ' Lord ' ")
which first insists on the active form of ἁρπαγμός and then represents Christ's
example as consisting on the negative side in a refusal to aspire to equality
with God (Brückner even draws a parallel with Gen. iii. 5–9) is certainly

with the notion that he was a being definitely lower than God. Lietzmann seems therefore to speak very sensibly when he writes in his comment on Rom. ix. 5: " Since Paul represents Christ in Phil. ii. 6 as ἴσα θεῷ there is no reason why he should not, on occasion, call him directly θεός." [23] When he goes on, however, to say: "The decision here, as often, if we are not acting under dogmatic prejudices, is a matter of pure feeling; to me it seems that ὁ ὢν ἐπὶ πάντων θεός is more suitable for the 'Almighty God' the Father of Jesus," he seems to forget that his former remark forbids him to say this feeling could be operative with Paul — which is the only matter *ad rem*. That the writer of Phil. ii. 6 might very well " on occasion " call Christ directly God is made even more clear by the circumstance that he does this very thing in this very passage, and that in the most emphatic manner possible. For that the representation of Christ Jesus as ἐν μορφῇ θεοῦ ὑπάρχων is precisely to call him God is evidenced not merely by the intimation which is immediately given that he who is " in the form of God " is " on an equality with God," but by the connotation of the phraseology itself. It is undeniable that in the philosophico-popular mode of speech here employed, " form " means just that body of characterizing qualities which makes anything the particular thing it is — in a word, its specific character.[24] To say that Christ Jesus is [25] " in the form of

---

wrong. If ἁρπαγμός is to be taken actively the only tolerable sense is something like that given it by J. Ross, *JTS* (1909), pp. 573–574: Christ " did not think that to be on an equality with God spelled rapacity, plundering, self-aggrandizement," that is to say, did not treat the equality which he had with God as an opportunity for self-aggrandizement but made nothing of himself.

[23] " Handbuch zum N. T.," *in loc.*

[24] Cf. J. B. Lightfoot, *in loc.*: " μορφή implies not the external accidents but the essential attributes "; " μορφή must apply to the attributes of the Godhead. In other words, it is used in a sense substantially the same which it bears in Greek philosophy "; " this sense of μορφή as the specific character."

[25] This is the right tense: for ὑπάρχων is not a past participle; and hence already involves that continuance of Jesus " in the form of God " after as well as before he had assumed " the form of a servant," which is one of the chief implications of the whole passage. There is here, in other words, as often in Paul, an explicit assertion of the Two Natures. Cf. E. H. Gifford, " The Incarnation," 1897.

God " is then to say not less but more than to say shortly that he is " God ": for it is to emphasize the fact that he has in full possession and use all those characterizing qualities which make God the particular Being we call " God "; and this mode of expression, rather than the simple term " God," is employed here precisely because it was of the essence of the Apostle's purpose to keep his reader's mind on all that Christ was as God rather than merely on the abstract fact that he was God.

By the side of Phil. ii. 6 there stands also Col. ii. 9, where it is declared that in Christ " there dwelleth all the fulness of the Godhead bodily," that is to say, in plain words, that Christ is an incarnation of the Godhead in all its fulness, which again is a statement rather difficult to harmonize with the notion that its author believed it was something less than God which was incarnated in Christ. And by the side of the whole series of such passages there stands the immense number of instances in which Christ is designated "Lord." For κύριος is not with Paul of lower connotation than θεός. Johannes Weiss does, indeed, in the passage we have quoted from him above,[26] suggest that if only it were κύριος instead of θεός which we found in Rom. ix. 5 we should experience no surprise at the declaration and, presumably, feel no inclination to correct the text; the implication being that Paul might very well call Christ " Lord over all " but not " God over all." " Lord over all " would have meant, however, precisely what " God over all " means,[27] and it is singularly infelicitous to give the im-

[26] Pp. 267–268.

[27] Peter is reported in Acts x. 36 as declaring that Jesus Christ is " Lord of all " and this high designation is sustained by the further announcement in x. 42 that he has been " ordained of God to be the judge of quick and dead," a purely divine function. How, then, can it be said, as is often said, as, e.g., by Schmiedel (" Jesus or Christ? " p. 62), that in Acts x. 38, lying between these two statements of express deity, there " is expressed . . . with noteworthy clearness " the notion that Jesus " had been a man who differed from others merely by reason of his being endowed with divine power " ? On the meaning of " Lord of all " compare G. Dalman, " Der Gottesname Adonaj " (1889), p. 83. Referring to the use of the term " Lord " by Luke to characterize Christ, he writes: " It is the same that Paul uses in Phil. ii. 11 where Jesus appears as the Lord to be recognized in heaven and earth and beneath

pression that Paul in currently speaking of Christ as "Lord"
placed him on a lower plane than God. Paul's intention was
precisely the opposite, viz., to put him on the same plane with
God; and accordingly it is as "Lord" that all divine attributes
and activities are ascribed to Christ and all religious emotions
and worship are directed to him. In effect, the Old Testament
divine names, Elohim on the one hand, and Jehovah and Ad-
honai on the other, are in the New Testament distributed between God the Father and God the Son with as little implication of difference in rank here as there. "Lord," in a word, is
Paul's divine name for Christ; is treated by him as Christ's
proper name — as, in fact, what can scarcely be called anything
else than his inter-trinitarian name and, in this technical
sense, his "personal" name. Accordingly Paul does not enumerate the Persons of the Trinity as our Lord is reported as
doing (Mt. xxviii. 19), according to their relations to one
another, "Father, Son, and Spirit," but according to his own
relation to each in turn, as God, the Lord, the Spirit: "the
grace of the Lord Jesus Christ, and the love of God, and the
communion of the Holy Spirit be with you all" (II Cor.
xiii. 14). The only distinction which can be discerned between
"God" and "Lord" in his usage of the terms is a distinction
not in relative dignity, but in emphasis on active sovereignty.
"God" is, so to speak, a term of pure exaltation; "Lord"
carries with it more expressly the idea of sovereign rulership
in actual exercise. It is probable that Paul's appropriation
specifically of the divine designation "Lord" to Christ was in
part at least occasioned by his conviction that he, as God-man,
has become the God of providence in whose hand is the kingdom, to "reign until he hath put all his enemies under his

---

the earth in a position in which the Old Testament knows God alone. Jesus
is here the πάντων κύριος of Acts x. 36 (cf. מָרֵי כֹלָּא of God, Talm. Nedarim,
22b) which does not lie far from the ἐπὶ πάντων θεός of Rom. ix. 5." Dalman
goes on, to be sure, to say that "the Apostles would have shrunk from designating Jesus by the Hebrew יהוה or אדני, since these expressions too closely
recalled the θεὸς ἀόρατος," and that only Thomas' confession (Jno. xx. 28)
"treads on the boundary line here"; but these remarks are only the unauthorized expressions of Dalman's own prejudices.

feet " (I Cor, xv. 24, etc.; cf. Phil. ii. 9 ff.), or, as it is expressed with great point and fulness in Eph. i. 20–23, He has been seated on the right hand of God, far above any conceivable power and made head over all things for his church. In a word, the term " Lord " seems to have been specifically appropriated to Christ not because it is a term of function rather than of dignity, but because along with the dignity it emphasizes also function.

All this is, of course, well known to Johannes Weiss. He writes:[28]

" To expound the religious significance which the use of the name 'Lord' had for the early Christians, the whole New Testament would need to be transcribed. For in the formula 'our Lord Jesus Christ' the essence of the primitive religion is contained. Obedient subjection, reverence, and holy dread of offending him, a complete sense of dependence on him for all things ('if the Lord will!' I Cor. iv. 19), gratitude and love and trust — in short, everything that man can feel in the presence of God — comes to expression in this term. We can best perceive this in the benedictions at the opening of the epistles. Here 'grace and peace' are invoked or desired 'from God the Father and the Lord Jesus Christ.' What is looked for from God can also be granted by the Lord. This inclusion of God and Christ in a single view which corresponds precisely with their coenthronement is characteristic of the piety of primitive Christianity. As Christians cry 'Abba Father' and pray to him, so there can be no doubt that they also 'prayed' in the strict sense of the word to Christ, not only in loyal adoration, but also in the form of petition. We have particular instances of this 'calling on the Lord' (Rom. x. 12) in Paul (II Cor. xii. 8) and in Stephen (Acts vii. 60). But such prayers were certainly made infinitely more often. Christians stand, therefore, in point of fact, over against Christ, as over against God (cf. 2 Clem. i. 1)."

And again, from Phil. ii. 9 ff. as a starting-point:[29]

" Now not only is this word ($\kappa\dot{v}\rho\iota o s$) known in the general language of Hellenisticism, but it has a special history in the peculiar region of Jewish Hellenisticism. The Jews were taught to substitute

[28] " Christus," usw., (1909), pp. 24–25.
[29] " Christus," usw., (1909), pp. 27 f.

for the proper name of God, Jahwe, in the sacred text the expression Adonai (Lord). The Greek translators of the Old Testament were acting in the correct Jewish fashion when they replaced the name יהוה by κύριος, the frequently occurring combination יהוה האלהם by κύριος ὁ θεός that is, exactly, 'Lord, the God' (so also, Luke i. 32, 68, etc.). The κύριος without an article is felt almost as a proper name. When Luther represents it by 'God, the Lord,' it is on the contrary 'God' that he feels as a proper name. It is from this that the passage in the Epistle to the Philippians may be understood — all the more that there is a reminiscence here of passages like Isa. xlii. 8, xlv. 23: 'I am κύριος ὁ θεός, this is my name, my honor will I not give to another ': ' to me shall every knee bow and every tongue confess God.' This name which God jealously guards as his own prerogative, he has now ceded to Christ, and has thereby publicly proclaimed that all beings shall bow to him and acknowledge him Lord. The transference of the name signifies, according to ancient usage, endowment with the power which the name designates. This passage is only another declaration of the transference to him by God of sovereignty over the world, of His constitution as 'Lord of Lords and King of Kings.' Thus the content of this passage coalesces in substance with what is said in Acts ii. 36 and intimated in I Cor. viii. 5. But whereas it is there to be understood that Christ alone rightly bears the name of κύριος, there is this much more intimated here — that κύριος is not merely a general designation of honor but the name of God become almost Christ's proper name. By this Christ is not merely elevated into a generally divine region: He takes the very place of the omnipotent God. Here, accordingly, κύριος cannot in any case have a weaker meaning than θεός."

Despite, however, such a clear perception of the high connotation of κύριος in the case of Paul (and the whole primitive Christian community), Johannes Weiss endeavors to interpret it, on Paul's lips, as expressive of something short of " God." He asserts (quite in the teeth of the facts, as we have seen) that Paul carefully avoids using the term "God" to denote Christ. Forgetting that with Paul, Christ (because — as nobody doubts — he is a two-natured person) is not only all that God is, but also all that man is, he appeals to

I Cor. iii. 23 to prove that Christ is dependent on God specifically with respect to his divine nature. He even points to I Cor. viii. 6 as implying this manner of subordination. Let us, however, hear him fully on this latter passage. He writes: [30]

"What Paul understands [by the term 'Lord'] may be seen from I Cor. viii. 5. When he here grants that there are, in point of fact, many (certainly only so-called) 'Gods and Lords,' he means to say that there exist many (in his view demonic) beings to whom men render worship and adoration, calling upon them as God or Lord. In contrast with these many 'lords,' particularly perhaps to emperor worship, Christians acknowledge and venerate only the *one* κύριος, Jesus Christ (cf. Deissmann, 'Licht von Osten,' pp. 233 ff.). It would not be impossible — though there is no way certainly to prove it — that in Paul's sense the predicate 'Lords' stands a grade lower than 'Gods,' that he would recognize it as applied only to deified men, heroes, and gods of lower degree. In any event, speaking from the point of view of style, to the word 'Gods' in vs. 5 the 'God the Father' of vs. 6 corresponds; and to the word 'Lords' the 'Lord Jesus Christ.' Now there can be no doubt (and precisely our passage gives a distinct proof of it) that what Paul seeks to do is, in spite of Christ's position by God's side, to subordinate him again to God (so, e.g., II Cor. i. 3 when he calls God not only the Father but also 'the God of our Lord Jesus Christ': cf. Eph. i. 17; Jno. xx. 17). And thus it were possible that he took over all the more readily the name κύριος derived by him from the primitive community, because he could express by it, no doubt, the divine position of Christ and the divine veneration due to him, and yet draw a line by means of which the interval between Christ and God should remain protected."

It certainly is surprising to find Weiss suggesting here that Paul may be using the term "Lord" after a heathen fashion to designate only gods of lower degree; we have just seen him solidly proving that, in its application to Christ, at least, Paul employs it in a sense in which it is not capable of discrimination from "God." For the same reason it is sur-

[30] "Christus," usw., p. 26.

prising to find him suggesting here that one of Paul's motives
in applying to Christ the term "Lord" may perhaps have been
to avoid confounding him with God. And in view of Paul's
doctrine of the Two Natures (which Weiss does not in the
least question) it is still further surprising to find him adducing here the circumstance that Paul sometimes speaks of God
as the "God," as well as the Father, "of our Lord Jesus
Christ" as throwing doubt on his ascription of proper deity
to Christ's divine nature — a procedure which one would think
would have been rendered impossible by the circumstance (to
which Weiss himself calls attention) that the same mode of
speech occurs in John, where, at least, Weiss does not doubt
Christ is simply God. Finally, how little I Cor. viii. 5, 6 itself
can be supposed to suggest the subordination of the "Lord"
Jesus Christ as to His deity to "God" the Father, becomes
evident at once on our noting that the two — the one Lord
Jesus Christ and the one God the Father — are represented
here as together constituting that God of which it is emphatically declared there is but one. For it is precisely in exposition of his energetic assertion in verse 4, in contradiction
of all polytheistic points of view, that "there is no God, except *one*," that Paul declares that Christians recognize that
there is only " one God the Father and one Lord Jesus Christ."
By as much as it is certain that he did not intend to represent
the Christians themselves as polytheists, worshiping, like the
rest, deity in grades, but, in contrast with all polytheists, as
worshipers of but one Deity, it is clear that he did not intend
to assign to Christ the position of a secondary deity. Obviously
to him the "one God the Father" and "the one Lord Jesus
Christ" were in some high and true sense alike included in that
one God who alone is recognized as existing.

This energetic assertion of monotheism by Paul, combined
with a provision within it for at least some kind of dualism,
leads us to revert for a moment to the closing clauses of the
first extract we quoted from Johannes Weiss.[31] There Weiss,
having recognized for the Johannine writings and the Pastoral

[31] Above, pp. 267–268.

Epistles [32] — what he would not recognize for Paul — that in
them Christ is directly called " God " with the fullest meaning,
seeks to account for this by suggesting that these " late New
Testament writings " may have lapsed from the strictness
of Jewish monotheism under the influence of Hellenistic modes
of thought, and thus have been enabled to place a second God
by the side of God the Father in a sense still impossible to
Paul. On the face of it, however, it certainly does not appear
that there has been any falling away from the highest monotheism in their case; monotheism is rather the presupposition of
all their teaching (Jno. v. 44; xvii. 3; I Tim. i. 17; ii. 5; vi. 15).
It is Weiss' method which is again at fault. Whatever conclusion may seem valid to him he obtrudes without more ado upon
the New Testament writers, although their point of view obviously differs from his by a whole diameter. On his frankly Socinian postulates,[33] it may seem clear that where two are God
there cannot be one God only. He therefore at once declares that

[32] For Weiss treats the Pastoral Epistles together as the work of one
author, described as " a pupil of Paul." Even in their case, however, though
admitting their high Christology, Weiss throws out a gratuitous expression of
doubt as to the integrity of the text in which this high Christology finds its
most precise expression. He writes (" Christus," usw., pp. 68–69; Schiele's
" Religion," usw., i. coll. 1732–1733) : " Although, therefore, the author energetically emphasizes that Jesus was *man*, he holds at the same time fast to
his divine origin — yes (if we have the right text), he calls him (Tit. ii. 13)
precisely ' our great God and Savior, Jesus Christ.' But even if we must read
or explain this text otherwise, there is *one* expression, which our author uses
with predilection, that will give us light. He speaks (II Tim. i. 10) of the
' epiphany ' of the Savior. Every Greek reader must have understood this well-
known term in the sense that Jesus Christ is a God appearing in human form
on earth. It was thus that the epiphany of a God was spoken of, when he appeared to men to command perhaps the building of a temple, or the establishment of a festival, or to confer benefactions: thus Antiochus IV of Syria was
called ' Epiphanes ' as a God walking on the earth; and so the expression on
the lips of our author means just *the incarnation of a God."*

[33] Cf. his " Paulus und Jesus " (1909), pp. 4–5, where, describing two forms
of " Christianity," one of which is " Christ-religion " and worships Christ, and
the other is " God-religion " and worships God alone, only permitting itself
to be led by Jesus of Nazareth " to the Father," he adds: " I make no secret
of my profession, in company with the majority of recent theologians, of the
second of these views. . . . But as a historian I must declare it widely different from the dominant view of primitive Christianity, from the Pauline
view."

the monotheism of John and the author of the Pastoral Epistles, who recognize at least two as God, is clearly falling into decay. But the Socinian postulates, dear to Weiss, have not determined the point of view of these writers! Their ascription of
proper deity to Christ, therefore, in no wise imperils the purity
of their monotheism; no monotheism, however strict, could
inhibit the fullest recognition of the proper deity of Christ
with writers whose fundamental thought runs on the lines on
which their thought runs, and the ascription of a purer monotheism than theirs to Paul, on the ground that they look upon
the deity of Christ as proper and supreme, is nothing but a
gratuitous prejudicing of the case. In point of fact, Paul stands
precisely on the same level with them as with respect to the
doctrine of God, so with respect to the doctrine of Christ.
Every line of his epistles is vocal with the cry of Thomas, " My
Lord and my God "; for the Epistle to the Romans as truly as
for the Epistle to Titus, Christ is " our great God and Savior ";
to the Epistle to the Philippians as fully as to the First Epistle
of John, Christ is " the true God," that is to say, he fills out
and perfectly satisfies the whole idea of God — for that is
as distinctly the connotation of ὑπάρχων ἐν μορφῇ θεοῦ as it is
of ὁ ἀληθινὸς θεός.

The attempt to separate Paul's doctrine of Christ from
John's as something essentially different, therefore, utterly
fails. It is much more plausible to expound John's doctrine as
a mere copy of Paul's. There is considerable appearance of
reasonableness, for example, in P. Wernle's representation
that the significance of John's Gospel consists merely in its
"bridging the chasm between Jesus and Paul and transferring
the Pauline gospel back into the discourses and life-delineation
of Jesus." [34] Was it not precisely through this transposition,

[34] "Die Anfänge unserer Religion " [2] (1904), pp. 446–449. Wernle, of
course, does not deny that certain " modifications " were made in Paul's doctrine when it was taken over by John. While the groundwork remains the same,
yet in John the *life* of Christ among men comes more to its rights, alongside
of his death, and is filled with a positive content of divine revelation. The
sole *deviation* from Paul's point of view which he finds in John, however, is
that the earthly life of Jesus is conceived by John more under the category

indeed, he asks, that Paulinism first attained to dominance in the church? The trouble with this representation, however, is twofold: it ascribes distinctively to Paul what was the common doctrine of the whole church; and it credits particularly to John a service which had already been rendered — if it needed to be rendered — by the Synoptics. For the difficulty of construing Paul's Christology in lower terms than that of John is fairly matched by the difficulty of construing the Christology of the other writers of the New Testament in lower terms than that of Paul. The attempt has most frequently been made with respect to the Synoptic Gospels, and among them probably most persistently with respect to Mark. We have often been told that in that " oldest of the Gospels " — the first attempt to sketch a narrative " life of Christ " — we have a portrait of the human Christ, unfalsified as yet by " dogmatic elements." From this ineptitude, it is to be hoped, we have now been conclusively delivered, more especially through its trenchant exposure by Wrede, who, whatever else he did, certainly made it abundantly clear that what we have in the Gospel of Mark is far from what has been called a "primitive document " presenting a " primitive " view of the Person of Christ.[35] The highest astonishment is accordingly being now expressed from every quarter that it could ever have been imagined that documents written in " the sixties," or at least in " the fifties," could fail to reflect the high Christology which, as we know from Paul's letters, was at that time the established faith of the whole Christian community.[36] In any

of exaltation than of humiliation — and this came to John from the Synoptics. He is constrained to add, however: " It must be said, nevertheless, that the Pauline Christology harmonizes admirably with the Johannine supplement, and acquires by it its convincing power." Cf. the sound criticism of Wernle by Jules Lebreton, " Les Origines du dogme de la Trinité " (1910), p. 376: " There is, no doubt, between John and Paul, a basis of identical doctrine which has become the common doctrine of the church; but there are also in the case of each of them doctrinal aspects which are purely individual, and by which they are profoundly distinguished from one another."

[35] Wrede, " Das Messiasgeheimnis in den Evangelien " (1901).

[36] So far, at least, agreement is perfect among writers otherwise of polar divergence. H. Bavinck (" Gereformeerde Dogmatiek," [2] iii. p. 284) remarks:

event the Christology of the Synoptic Gospels is indistinguishable from that of Paul, and this is as true of the Christology
of Mark as of that of Matthew or of Luke. We do not ourselves look upon Mark as " the primitive Gospel "; [37] we do
not even subscribe to the now almost universal opinion that it
is the earliest of our three Synoptics; we agree with Johannes
Weiss in assigning it to 64-68 A.D., but for reasons of our own
we place it quite at the end of this period; we agree with
Harnack in thinking Luke certainly as old as this and much
more likely as old as 63 A.D., or even as 58-60 A.D.; and Matthew, we are sure, is as old as Mark and may very well be as
old as Luke; we should find no serious difficulty, indeed, in
placing both Matthew and Luke early in the "fifties." But
the brevity, and, so to say, relative externality, of Mark naturally suggest it as the particular one of the Synoptics in which

---

" It is the same Christ who meets us throughout the whole New Testament.
How could it be otherwise? The Synoptic Gospels are just as truly apostolic
writings as the letters of Paul and were written even later than Paul's letters;
there is nowhere any suggestion of a controversy among the apostles over
the Person of Christ." J. Weiss says of Mark's Gospel particularly ("Christus,"
usw., p. 74) : " That the evangelist takes his start from a distinct Christology
is certain — how could it be otherwise with a writer who presupposes the work
of Paul and is writing down after the death of the first apostolic generation
the 'Gospel of Jesus Christ' for the practical use of the mission to the
heathen? " And then of the Synoptics at large (p. 73) : " None of their authors
was an eye-witness and all belong to the second generation, whose care it was
to preserve the precious possession which had been intrusted to it "; " they
all start, with respect to the dogmatic-christological positions, no longer at
the standpoint of the first community: the exaltation-Christology has long
[this in the fifties or sixties!] been transcended, and in its place there has
stepped, as with Paul, the Incarnation-Christology."

[37] Cf. J. Weiss, "Jesus von Nazareth" (1910), p. 135: " Mark is anything
but a first draftsman of the tradition; he is rather an eclectic reworker of old
traditions; his book is not a source but a receptacle (Sammelbecken) "; also,
" Das älteste Evangelium " (1903), p. 2: " As firmly as I am convinced that
we have in Mark the oldest Gospel, I can as little agree that it presents the
first and original cast (Niederschlag) of the evangelical tradition. So far as I
can judge, Mark is already a station on the road which ends in John's Gospel,
not the commencement of that road. It is no longer a source but a receptacle
(Sammelbecken). The tradition which precedes it and which has received
literary form in it was no longer fluid and unfixed but had reached already a
relatively fixed shape."

the Christology common to them all is likely to be expressed in, if not its lowest, yet at least its least-elaborated terms; and it is not unnatural, therefore, that it has been scrutinized with especial care with a view to determining the real nature of the synoptic conception of Christ. The result has been to make it perfectly plain that the Synoptic conception of the Person of Christ is just that doctrine of the Two Natures which, as we have seen, is given expression in Paul's Epistles and is everywhere presupposed in them as the established faith of the Christians of the middle of the first century, and of any earlier date to which the retrospective testimony of this body of Epistles may be allowed to extend.

" The Christology of the Gospel of Mark [writes Johannes Weiss] [38] is already given expression in the title: his gospel treats of Jesus Christ (the Son of God, in case these last words are genuine). . . . The particularly designating names of Jesus are for him ' the Son of God ' and ' the Son of Man.' When the evangelist so frequently places the latter of these in the mouth of Jesus as a self-designation, he thus betrays that he no longer possesses any sense of the suitability of this name exclusively for the heavenly Messiah, whether as pre-existent or as exalted. For him it is precisely the Jesus who walks the earth who is no other than the ' heavenly Man,' who came down from heaven, and has been again exalted to heaven (xv. 62), whence he is to come again in the clouds with great power and glory (xiii. 26). Accordingly he makes Jesus call himself the Son of Man even when he is speaking of his earthly activity (ii. 10, 28; x. 45), of his sufferings (e.g., viii. 31), and of his resurrection (ix. 9). He was in this already preceded by the Discourses-source (Mt. xi. 9 = Lk. vii. 34) and Matthew carried still farther this replacement of an ' I ' in the mouth of Jesus by ' the Son of Man ' (cf. Mt. xvi. 13 with Mk. viii. 27). This use of the name is an altogether sufficient proof that, just like Paul, Mark looked upon Jesus as the ' Man ' who came from heaven. Similarly it cannot be doubted that this post-Pauline writer understood, as

[38] " Christus," usw., pp. 75–76, and Schiele's " Religion," usw., i. coll. 1734–1735; cf. the further discussion in " Das älteste Evangelium " (1903), pp. 45 ff., 96 ff., where he particularly shows that from the christological doctrine of John " our Gospel of Mark does not stand far "; that " the Christology of Mark stands much nearer that of John than is commonly allowed," etc.

Paul understood it, the name ' Son of God,' which stood perhaps in
the title of his gospel as the most significant name of dignity — that
is to say, not in the theocratic sense, examined above (pp. 19 ff.), of
him who has been chosen and called to the messianic kingship, but
(p. 34) of him who was the sole one among men that, of his nature,
bears in himself the essence (*Wesen*) of God.

Of course Weiss would distinguish shades of view among the
several writers — the authors of the Gospels severally and
Paul — but his testimony to the main matter is quite distinct;
that, in a word, to the author of Mark, as to all the others of
these writers, Christ was, as he himself puts it, "a divine
being ' incarnated ' — we must already make use of this expression — in a man." [39] And it will be found impossible to
make this divine being, with Mark any more than with Paul,
anything less than the supreme God himself. When Mark
records our Lord himself as testifying that he is, in the hierarchy of being, above even the angels, he places him outside
the category of created beings; and there is no reason to
doubt that with him as truly as with all his Jewish compatriots the Son of God which he repeatedly calls Jesus connoted, as John defines the phrase for us (v. 18), just "equality
with God."

It is not necessary to labor the point. It is undeniable that
the Christ of the whole body of New Testament writers, without exception, is a Two-Natured Person — divine and human;
and indeed this is scarcely any longer denied. Whatever attempts are still made to discriminate between the Christologies of the New Testament writers fall within the limits of
this common doctrine. Wilhelm von Schnehen does not go
one whit beyond the facts of the case when he declares,[40] no
doubt after a fashion and with implications derived from his
own point of view:

" Go back into the history of Christianity as far as you will, you
will nowhere find the least support for the notion that Jesus was

---

[39] " Christus," usw., p. 77.
[40] " Der moderne Jesuskultus " [2] (1907), pp. 10–11.

revered on the ground of his purely human activity and attributes, say as the founder of a religion, as teacher of morals, or even only as religious-ethical example. Understand the content of the word 'gospel' as you may, never has it to do with a mere 'man' Jesus, never does it give to this the central place in Christian worship. For the glad-tidings of the Rabbi of Nazareth, even the adorers of his human personality will not in the end deny this. That it is valid also for the Gospel-writings of the New Testament is equally indubitable. The Jesus of which these writings tell us is through and through not a man but at the very least a super-man. Yes, he is more than that; he is the unique Son of God; the Christ, the coming God-man of the orthodox church. For the Fourth Gospel this is, of course, universally recognized; the Johannine Jesus is an incarnate creative word, the human manifestation of the 'Logos,' who from the beginning was with God and himself was God, whose divine glory was continuously apparent to his disciples, beneath its earthly shell. But the other Gospels also think of nothing so little as telling us of a mere 'man' Jesus, and demanding a believing reverence for such a one. No, the miraculously begotten Son of the Virgin with Luke and Matthew, the Jesus who rose from the dead and ascended into heaven of the First and Third Gospels, is just as little a mere 'natural man' as the Johannine Christ. And as regards finally the Gospel of Mark, Professor Bousset, for example, remarks: 'It is already from the standpoint of faith that the oldest Gospel is written; already for Mark Jesus is not only the Messiah of the Jewish people but' (in consequence of the communication of the Spirit at the baptism!) 'the miraculous, eternal Son of God whose glory shines into this world. And it has been rightly emphasized that in this respect our three first Gospels differ from the Fourth only in degree.'"

The comment which is made on this and similar utterances of recent radicalism, by Richard Grützmacher [41] is eminently justified:

"The immense significance of this acknowledgment can be measured only by one who knows the unnumbered theological and extra-theological attempts of the last century and a half from the extremest left to far into the circle of the mediating theology to

[41] "Ist das liberale Jesusbild modern?" [5] (1907), pp. 29, 30.

obtain from the New Testament itself, or at least from the three first Gospels, a purely human portrait of Jesus, and to eliminate all metaphysical and supernatural content from their expressions. The 'modern' and the church interpretation of the New Testament at the beginning of the twentieth century — to which also in very large measure the later 'Liberalism' gives its adhesion — is in complete accord in this result: that the church-doctrine of the God-man Christ can appeal with full right to the New Testament in its entire compass, and any development beyond that which has taken place is only formal. The allegorizing-dogmatic exegesis of the last hundred and fifty years has been transcended." [42]

That is to say, the doctrine of the Two Natures of Christ is not merely the synthesis of the teaching of the New Testament, but the conception which underlies every one of the New Testament writings severally; it is not only the teaching of the New Testament as a whole but of the whole of the New Testament, part by part. Historically, this means that not only has the doctrine of the Two Natures been the invariable presupposition of the whole teaching of the church from the apostolic age down, but all the teaching of the apostolic age rests on it as its universal presupposition. When Christian literature begins, this is already the common assumption of the entire church. If we wish to translate this into the terms of positive chronology, what must be said is that before the opening of the sixth decade of the first century (for we suppose that I Thess. must be dated somewhere about 52 A.D.), the doctrine of the Two Natures already is firmly established in the church as the universal foundation of all Christian thinking concerning Christ. Such a mere chronological statement, however,

---

[42] Grützmacher very properly, in a note (p. 30), cries out on "the marvelous anachronism and self-deception" of which Julius Kaftan is guilty when he represents that in the portrait of the God-man, "it is the unhistorical interpretation of the New Testament, dominated by ecclesiastical dogma, that is working" ("Jesus und Paulus," p. 59). Over against this he sets A. Kalthoff ("Enstehung," usw., p. 9): "From the ecclesiastical God-man there leads a straight line backward through the epistles and gospels of the New Testament to the Apocalypse of Daniel in which the ecclesiastical type of the portrait of Jesus took its beginning."

hardly does justice to the case. What needs to be emphasized is that there is no Christian literature in existence which does not base itself, as upon an already firmly laid foundation, on the doctrine of the Two Natures. So far as Christian litera- ture can bear testimony, there never has been any other doctrine recognized in the church. This literature itself goes back to within twenty years or so of the death of Christ; and of course — since it did not create but reflects this faith — has a retrospective value as testimony to the faith of Christians.

Nevertheless, men still seek to posit an " earlier," " more primitive," " simpler " view of the Person of Christ, behind this oldest attested doctrine. In another article we shall ask whether it is possible thus to go back of the doctrine of the New Testament writings to a more " primitive " view of the Person of Christ.

II. THE NEW TESTAMENT JESUS THE ONLY REAL JESUS

In a former article [1] we have pointed out that the doctrine of the " Two Natures " is the common presupposition of the whole body of the New Testament writings — a presupposi- tion which is everywhere built upon, and which comes to clear enunciation wherever occasion calls for it. The literature gathered into the New Testament is not only the earliest Christian literature which has come down to us, but goes back to within twenty years or so of the death of Christ; and since it did not create but reflects the faith it expresses, it must be allowed to possess a retrospective significance in its unbroken testimony to the belief of Christians. What the whole Christian community is found to be resting in, with complete assurance, as the truth respecting the person of its founder in, say, 50 A.D. — a time when a large number of his personal followers were doubtless still living, and certainly the tradition of which they were bearers (cf. Lk. i. 2) cannot have become obscured

---

[1] *The American Journal of Theology*, July, 1911, pp. 337 ff.

— can scarcely fail to have been the aboriginal belief of the Christian body. Nevertheless, a determined effort is still made to discover an "earlier," "more primitive," "simpler" view of the person of Christ behind the oldest attested doctrine. There is confessedly no "direct" evidence of the existence of any such "earlier," "more primitive," "simpler" view. "Of the religion of the earliest Jewish-Christian community," says Johannes Weiss, as he enters upon the exposition of "the faith of the primitive community," [2] "we have no *direct* witnesses; for we can, today, no longer consider the Epistles of Peter and James genuine works of the primitive apostles" — largely, it needs to be remembered, because they do not contain the "more primitive" Christology which it is assumed these "primitive apostles" must have cherished. But it is thought that by means of indirect evidence, the existence in the first age of Christianity of an earlier view of Christ than any which has found record in the New Testament may be established. The whole mass of expressions of which the New Testament writers make use in speaking of Christ, is subjected to a searching scrutiny with a view to discovering among them, if possible, "survivals" of an "earlier" mode of thinking of Christ. Weiss accordingly continues:

"For this pre-Pauline epoch also we are first of all directed to the letters of Paul. He occasionally speaks of having received something from the primitive community (I Cor. xv. 3 ff.). But more important still are the numerous elements of the oldest primitive-Christian conceptions which without expressly notifying the fact he carries along in his theology, and which betray themselves to the eye of the investigator as a universal-Christian stratum underlying the more Hellenistically colored specifically-Pauline doctrine. Similarly, all the other documents of the Apostolic and post-Apostolic age contain such old Christian traits, which point back to the standpoint of the oldest community. Thereto we reckon especially the discourses in the first part of Acts. Though they may have come from a later time, yet, precisely in their Christology, they contain very antique conceptions."

[2] "Christus," usw., p. 7.

What is attempted, it will be seen, is on subjective grounds —
there are, in the circumstances, none other available — to
distinguish, among the New Testament deliverances concerning Christ, those which belong to the primitive age from those
which belong to the age when the books were written. The
whole New Testament is doubtless laid under contribution
for this purpose, but the happy hunting-ground of the quest
is found in the early chapters of the Acts and in the Synoptic
Gospels.

It is not without the clearest justification that we have
emphasized the purely subjective grounding of this quest. If
we possessed a single Christian document earlier in date than
those which constitute our New Testament, in which was
taught the special Christology which it is proposed to extract
from our New Testament as an earlier form of belief than
that which the New Testament itself universally commends
to us, there might be some excuse for gathering out of our New
Testament books the sentences and forms of expression which
semed to fall particularly in with the teachings of this earlier
document and pronouncing them survivals of its earlier modes
of thought. But in the absence of any such earlier document,
what reason is there for pronouncing these forms of expression
"survivals"? The touchstone by which their "earlier" character is determined, Weiss tells us, resides in "the searcher's
eye." That is to say, shortly, in the critic's *a priori* paradigms.
The critic comes to his task with a settled conviction, *a priori*
established, that Jesus was a mere man, and must have been
thought of by his followers as a mere man; and sets himself to
search out in the extant literature — which is informed by a
contrary conviction — modes of expression which he can interpret as "survivals" of such an "earlier" point of view.
Meanwhile, there is no evidence whatever that these modes
of expression are "survivals," or that there ever existed in the
Christian community an "earlier" view of the person of
Christ than that given expression in the New Testament
writings. Reinhold Seeberg has quite accurately expounded
the state of the case when, speaking more particularly of Har-

nack's unfortunate attempt to distinguish in primitive Christianity an "adoptionist" and a "pneumatic" Christology, he says:[3]

"Investigators, in my opinion, are as a rule misled by this — that they make the ' historical Jesus ' their starting-point by simple assumption, and treat all expressions which go beyond this as attributes added to him in gradual precipitation on the ground of faith in his resurrection. The historical starting-point is, however, in reality contained in three facts: (1) that Jesus in his earthly life manifested a superhuman self-consciousness; (2) that his disciples were convinced by him, *after* his resurrection, not precisely *by* it, that they had directly experienced and received proof of his divine nature; and (3) that they accordingly honored and proclaimed him as the heavenly Spirit-Lord. These facts are, in my opinion, indisputable, and from these facts as a starting-point — they are simply ' given ' and not deducible — the entire thought-development can be fully explained."

When the study of historical records is approached with a fixed assumption of an opposite point of view to their own as instrument of interpretation, it is not strange if their representations are replaced by a set of contradictory representations. But the "results" thus reached are not in any recognizable sense "historical." They are the product of wresting history in order to fill in a foregone conclusion of abstract thought.[4]

[3] "Lehrbuch der Dogmengeschichte," [2] i. p. 104. Seeberg, of course, only repeats in this what has been clearly pointed out from the beginning. Thus E. K. A. Riehm, " Der Lehrbegriff des Hebräerbriefes (1867), p. 332, remarks: "That it is only on the basis of his well-known false preconception to the effect that the *original* Christian conception of the person of Christ was an Ebionitish one, that Schwegler refers the declarations as to the exaltation of the person of Christ to a mere effort, to a *tendency*, while he refers the declarations as to the likeness of Christ to men to the *tradition*, we note only in passing."

[4] Cf. Albert Schweitzer's characterization of this method of criticism in an analogous field (" The Quest of the Historical Jesus," pp. 330–331): " In order to find in Mark the life of Jesus of which it is in search, modern theology is obliged to read between the lines a whole host of things, and those often the most important, and then to foist them upon the text by means of a psychological conjecture. It is determined to find evidence in Mark of a development of Jesus. . . . Mark knows nothing of any development in

It should not pass without very particular notice that the forms of expression gathered from our New Testament books, out of which is to be fashioned an " earlier " Christology than that presupposed by this literature, do not lie on the face of the New Testament as alien fragments. It is not without significance that Johannes Weiss, after remarking that Paul occasionally puts forward statements as derived by him from "the primitive community," at once adds that, for the purpose of reconstructing the faith of this "earlier community " from Paul's writings, " survivals " in his writings not expressly notified as such are both more numerous and more important. In other words, our New Testament writers who have preserved for us the elements of this " earlier " Christology wholly different from their own, and indeed contradictory to it, have preserved them with the most engaging unconsciousness of their alien character: in point of fact, they have written down these contradictory sentences with no other thought than that they were the just expression of their own proper views; and they betray no sense of embarrassment whatever with respect to them. This is true even — or perhaps we should say, especially — of the extreme case of the record of Peter's christological utterances in the earlier chapters of the Book of Acts. It is quite clear that Luke is wholly unaware that he is recording views of his Lord which differ from his own, which, indeed, are in sharp conflict with his own and, to speak frankly, stultify his entire attitude toward his Lord, for the validation of which his whole great two-part work was written.

Jesus. . . . Another hitherto self-evident point — the historical kernel which it has been customary to extract from the narratives — must be given up, until it is proved, if it is capable of proof, that we can and ought to distinguish between the kernel and the husk. . . . Whatever the results obtained by the aid of the historical kernel, the method pursued is the same; 'it is detached from the context and transformed into something different.' 'It finally comes to this,' says Wrede, ' that each critic retains whatever portion of the traditional sayings can be fitted into his construction of the facts and his conception of historical possibility and rejects the rest.' The psychological explanation of motive and the psychological connection of the events and actions which such critics proposed to find in Mark, simply do not exist. That being so, nothing is to be made out of his account by the application of a priori psychology."

We may well ask whether such unconscious *naïveté* can be attributed to such an alert writer as Luke shows himself to be. Or if with Schmiedel [5] we deny these chapters to Luke and suppose the speeches of Peter "free compositions" of a later author, the *tour de force* which we attribute to this great nameless dramatist rises quite to the level of the miraculous. It is hardly worth while to ask similarly whether Paul, in his fervid expressions of reverence to Christ as "Lord," can be supposed with such simplicity to mix in with his own language, so vividly expressive of this reverence, other forms of speech standing in flat contradiction to all that he was proclaiming, merely because he found them in use in " the primitive community." Surely the Epistle to the Galatians does not encourage us to believe Paul to have been filled with such blind veneration for "the primitive community," that he would be likely to continue to repeat its language in devout subjection to the authority of its modes of statement, though it ran counter to his profoundest convictions and his most fervent religious feelings.

The general point we are endeavoring to make deserves some elaboration with special reference to the Synoptic Gospels. It is particularly behind their narrative that the traces of an earlier conception of the person of Christ than that presented by our whole New Testament — inclusive of these Gospels — are supposed to be discoverable. It is frankly allowed, as we have seen, that the Gospels as they stand present to our view a divine Christ, an incarnated Son of God, who came to earth on a mission, and whose whole earthly life is only an episode in the existence of a Heavenly Being. But it is immediately added that in the narrative put together from this standpoint, there are imbedded elements of an earlier tradition, to which Jesus was a mere man, bounded by all human limitations. And it is assumed to be precisely the task of criticism to identify and draw out these elements of earlier tradition, that we may recover from them the idea formed of Jesus by his real contemporaries and, therefore, presumably, the true conception of him before he was transformed by the

5 " Encyclopaedia Biblica," i. pp. 47–49; see the allusion above, p. 287.

reverent thought of his followers into an exalted Being, to be which he himself made no claim. We say nothing now of purely "literary criticism" — the attempt to ascertain the sources on which our Gospels as literary compositions rest, and from which they draw their materials. For this "literary criticism" in no way advances the discovery of a "more primitive" Christology lying behind that presented by the authors of our Gospels. It would have been a strange proceeding indeed had the authors of our Gospels elected to draw their materials, by preference, from earlier documents presenting a totally different, or, rather, sharply contrasting conception of Jesus from that which they had in heart and mind to commend to their readers; and they are obviously wholly unaware of doing anything of the kind. Happily, we are delivered from the necessity of considering the possibility of such a literary phenomenon. It is no doubt impossible to reconstruct any of the sources which "have found their graves" in our Gospels with full confidence, with respect either to the details of their contents or even to their general compass. But neither the "narrative source" — the so-called *Urmarkus* — which underlies all three of the Synoptics, nor the "discourses-source" — the so-called "Logia" — which underlies the common portions of Matthew and Luke not found also in Mark, on any rational theory of its compass and contents, differs in any respect in its christological point of view from that of the Gospels, so large a portion of which they constitute.[6] We may remark in passing that this carries the evidence for the aboriginality in the Christian community of the two-natured conception of Christ back a literary generation behind the Synoptics themselves; and that surely must bring us to a time which can scarcely be thought to be wholly dominated by Paul's innovating influence. It is enough for us here to note, however, that "literary criticism" does not take us back to documents presenting a "pre-Pauline" Christology. If such

---

[6] We have already seen above (p. 282) Johannes Weiss incidentally noting the use in the "discourses-source" of the "Son of Man," of Christ: of course, the same use occurs in the *Urmarkus,* however it be reconstructed. But the general point is easily demonstrable in detail.

a " pre-Pauline " Christology is to be found in the background
of our Gospels, much coarser methods of reaching it than
"literary criticism" must be employed.

The absurd attempt of P. W. Schmiedel to reverse the conception of Christ transmitted to us by the Gospels, by insisting
that, in the first instance, we must trust only such passages
as are — or rather, as, when torn from their contexts, may be
made to seem — inconsistent with the main purpose of the
evangelists in writing their Gospels, namely, to honor Christ,
is only an unusually crass application of the method which
from the beginning has been common to the whole body of
those who, like him, are in search of evidence in the Gospels
of the existence of a "more primitive" tradition than that
which the Gospels themselves represent. The essence of this
method is the attempt to discover in the Gospel-narrative
elements in the delineation of Jesus which are inconsistent
with the conception of Jesus which it is their purpose to convey; to which unassimilated elements of a different tradition,
preference is at once given in point of both age and trustworthiness. This method is as freely in use, for instance, by
Johannes Weiss, who seems to wish to separate himself from
Schmiedel,[7] as by Schmiedel himself. Let us note how Weiss
deals with the matter:[8]

[7] Or can Weiss not have Schmiedel in mind in writing as follows (" Jesus
von Nazareth," 1910, p. 93): " What mandate of the historical method, however, tells us that the interested parties [die Betheiligten] are to be distrusted
under all circumstances? There no doubt still exist people to whom the
declarations of a pious man are antecedently suspicious. We need not argue
with them; they have been born a century and a half too late. They simply
neglect a moral duty when they deny to those who differ with them the
same bona fides they make claim to for themselves. The truly unprejudiced
man will say: ' With reference to the nature of a personality we shall always
reach ultimately a clearer notion along with those who have surrendered
themselves to his influence than with those whom either hate has made blind,
or who have simply taken no interest in him. It is possible to think the
reverence shown him excessive and to draw back from many things his
friends say of him: yet certain fundamental traits are here most surely to
be found.'"

[8] " Jesus von Nazareth," usw., pp. 132–133. It is perhaps worth while to
observe how Riehm, in a passage which has already been adverted to (" Der
Lehrbegriff des Hebräerbriefes " [1867], pp. 331–332), already deals with this

" The Christology of the evangelist himself [he is speaking of Mark] is very far advanced in the direction of the Johannine; there can be no doubt that Jesus is to him the Son of God, in the sense of a divine being with divine power and divine knowledge from the beginning on. Nothing is hidden from him: his own destiny, the denial, the betrayal, the fate of Jerusalem — he tells it all exactly beforehand. Nothing is impossible to him: the most marvelous healings, like the sudden cure of the withered hand, of leprosy, of blindness, are performed by him without any difficulty; he raises

sort of criticism as applied by Schwegler to the Epistle to the Hebrews: " The two kinds of expression, set side by side, stand in remarkable contrast. Now it is said that the Son as the effulgence of the glory of God possesses the fulness of God's essential glory, then again that like us he partakes of flesh and blood; now that he is eternal and unchangeable, then again that he is like us in all things; now he is exalted high above all men, and even above angels and set in an absolutely unique relation to God, then again he is placed on the level of men and set forth as standing in a human relation to God; there is no trait in the nature of God which is not found also in the nature of the Son, and yet it is only through severe conflicts of suffering that he struggles to attain the highest stage of moral-religious perfection; he upholds all things by the word of his power, and yet he is subjected to the cruelest sufferings and the death of the cross. With an eye on these contrasts it is easy to understand how Schwegler came to the contention (ii. p. 388): ' We perceive still in the Christology of the Epistle to the Hebrews the lack of harmony which belongs to the first beginnings; we meet everywhere with an unreconciled contradiction of the two constitutive elements of the person of Christ, the human and the divine in him, his subordination beneath the Father, and his co-ordination and consubstantiality with the Father. In spite of the visible effort which the author makes to bring the divine in Christ to its highest possible and most specific expression, there presses continually forward the traditional human conception of the person.' This contention is, however, thoroughly false. That it is only on the basis of his well-known false presupposition that the *original* Christian conception of the person of Christ was an Ebionitish one, that Schwegler refers the declarations of the exaltation of the person of Christ to a mere effort, to a *tendency,* while he refers the declarations of the likeness of Christ to men to the *tradition,* we note only in passing. But even apart from this, do these two kinds of declarations really stand in an unreconciled contradiction to one another? The author makes it very clear that in his own consciousness the conciliation of the two modes of conceiving Christ, as the Son of God and as true man, was fully carried out, when in v. 8 he expressly says that the sonship to God and the learning of obedience through suffering in no way (as might be thought) exclude one another. It is accordingly clear to him that Christ *on earth* could be God's Son, and true man *at the same time;* that he was both in *one* person."

a dead person; he walks on the water, and feeds thousands with a
few loaves; he makes the fig tree wither — it is all related as if
nothing else could be expected; we see in these accounts neither the
bold faith to which all is possible nor the enthusiasm of one beside
himself, nor natural intermediation; Jesus can do just anything.
And therefore, to the evangelist, it is nothing singular that at his
death the sun was darkened, and the veil of the temple was rent;
and that he left the grave on the third day — all this follows altogether naturally and of itself from his Christology. But alongside
of these stand other traits: his power rests on the Spirit, which was
communicated to him at baptism; we see how this Spirit struggles
with the spirits (i. 25, iii. 11, v. 6, 8, ix. 25 f.); his miraculous power
is limited by unbelief (vi. 5), he must have faith himself and find
faith in others if he is to help; his dominion over suffering and death
has its limits; he trembles and is afraid, and feels forsaken by God;
he is ignorant of the day and hour; he will not permit himself to be
called ' Good Master '; he prays to the Father like a man, and is
subject to all human emotions, even anger, and to mistake with
reference to his disciples."

The whole art of the presentation is apparent. Weiss would
make it appear that there are two Jesuses in Mark's narrative,
a divine Jesus and a human Jesus; and if we take the one, he
suggests, the other must be left. Mark himself believed in the
divine Jesus; the human Jesus, which he places by His side,
must therefore be the "earlier" Jesus, to which he has been
so accustomed that he cannot away with him even when he
would. The astonishing thing, however, is that Mark is entirely
unconscious of the straits he is in. He records the human traits,
which are supposed to refute the whole portraiture he is endeavoring to draw, with no sense of their incongruity. For,
" we must . . . remember," as Dr. Percy Gardner admonishes
us,[9] " that the three Gospels are not mere colourless biographies, but collections of such parts of the Christian tradition as
most impressed a society which had already begun to seek in
the life of its founder traces of a more than human origin
and nature." They are, to put it more accurately, presentations

[9] " Jesus or Christ? " Being the *Hibbert Journal* Supplement for 1909,
p. 46.

of the salient acts and sayings of Jesus by men who thoroughly believed in the divine Christ, and who wished — as Dr. Gardner says of Paul, the master of two of these evangelists — to "place the human life of Jesus between two periods of celestial exaltation." Why then did these men, of all men, preserve elements of an earlier tradition which contradict their own deepest convictions of the origin and nature of their Lord? Is it because they lacked literary skill to convey the picture they were intent on conveying, and so, as Dr. Gardner puts it, in their attempt to depict the Jesus they believed in, the "human legend was not effaced, but it was supplemented here and there with incongruous elements"? Surely, the day is long since past when our Gospels can be treated thus as *naïve* narratives by childlike hands endeavoring only to set down the few facts concerning Christ which had come to their knowledge. If these elements of "the human legend" were retained, it was, on the contrary, precisely because they presented to the consciousness of these writers no incongruity with their conceptions of the divine Christ; and that is as much as to say that the Jesus whom they were depicting was in their view no less truly human than truly divine. The life of the Master on earth, which they placed between the two periods of celestial exaltation, bore for them the traits of a truly human life.

But as soon as we say this, it is clear that we cannot appeal to the human traits which they ascribe to Jesus as evidence of the existence of an "earlier" Christology than theirs, which looked upon Jesus as merely human. These traits are congruous parts of their own Christology. They are not fragments of an earlier view of Christ's person, persisting as "survivals" in a later view; they are the other half of a consistent christological conception. They supply, therefore, no evidence that there ever existed an earlier Christology than that in which they occupy a necessary place. We may reject, if we please, the Christology of the evangelists, and, rejecting it, insist that Christ was not a divine-human, but simply a human being. But we can get no support for this private, and possibly pious, opinion of our own, from the writings of the evangelists. The human traits, which they all ascribe to Jesus, do not in the least suggest that they, in the bottom of their hearts, or others before them, believed in a merely human Jesus. They only make it manifest that they, and those from whom they derive, believed in a Jesus who was human. The attempt to distort the evidence that they believed in a Jesus who was human, as well as divine, into evidence that they had inherited belief in a merely human Jesus, and unconsciously lapsed into the language of their older and simpler faith, even when endeavoring to commend quite another conception, does violence to every line of their writings; it is not acute historical exposition, but the crassest kind of dogmatic imposition. Because from the critic's own point of view the doctrine of the " Two Natures " involves a psychological impossibility, when he finds the evangelists presenting in their narratives a Jesus who is both divine and human, he proclaims that there are clumsily mixed here two mutually inconsistent Christologies chronologically related to one another as earlier and later; and because from his own point of view a purely divine Jesus were as impossible as a divine-human one, he pronounces that one of these two warring Christologies which makes Jesus a mere man, the earlier, "historical" view, and that one which makes Him divine, a later, "mythical" view. For neither the one nor the other of these pronouncements, however, has he other ground than his own *a priori* prejudice. The divine and the human Jesus of the evangelists do not stand related to one another chronologically, as an earlier and a later view, but vitally, as the two sides of one complex personality; and had there been reason to interpret them as chronologically related there is no reason derivable from the evangelists themselves — or, we may add, from the history of thought in the first years of the Christian proclamation — why the human view of Christ's person should be supposed to be the earlier of the two. From all that appears in these narratives, and from whatever other records we possess, Jesus was, on the contrary, from the beginning understood by His followers to be very God, sojourning on earth. In a word, not only is the doctrine of the "Two Natures" the synthesis of the entire body of christological data embodied in the pages of the New Testament; and not only is it the teaching of all the writers of the New Testament severally; but the New Testament provides no material whatever for inferring that a different view was ever held by the Christian community. The entire Christian tradition, from the beginning, whatever that may be worth, is a tradition of a two-natured Jesus, that is to say, of an incarnated God. Of a one-natured Jesus, Christian tradition knows nothing, and supplies no materials from which He may be inferred.

This determination of the state of the case includes in it, it will be observed, Jesus' own self-testimony. We know nothing of Jesus' self-consciousness, or self-testimony, save as it has been transmitted to us by His followers. The Jesus whom the evangelists have given us testifies to the possession of a self-consciousness which matches perfectly the conception of Jesus which the evangelists are set upon conveying; indeed, the evangelists' conception of Jesus is embodied largely in terms of Jesus' self-testimony. Behind this we can get only by the method of criticism whose inconsequence we have been endeavoring to expose. That "historical Jesus," whom Johannes Weiss (in act of bearing his witness as a historian to the historical validity of the higher Christology) describes as, "so far as we can discern him, seeing his task in drawing his followers into the direct experience of sonship with God, without demanding any place for himself in their piety," [10] has never existed anywhere except in the imaginations of Weiss and his "liberal" fellow-craftsmen. The evangelists know nothing of Him nor does He lurk anywhere in the background of their narratives. The only Jesus of which they have knowledge — or whose figure is traceable in any of their sources — is a Jesus who ranked Himself above all creatures (Mk. xiii. 32, one of Schmiedel's "pillar-passages," of which J. H. Moulton speaks as "that saying of uniquely acknowledged authentic-

---

[10] "Paulus und Jesus" (1909), p. 5.

ity ");[11] who represented Himself as living continuously in an intercourse with God which cannot be spoken of otherwise than as perfect reciprocity (Mt. xi. 25; Lk. x. 22 — a passage which has its assured place in the " discourses-source "); and who habitually spoke of Himself as the " Son of Man " (as witnessed in both the " narrative-source " and the " discourses-source " — of course, with all the implications of heavenly origin, ineffable exaltation, and judgeship of the world — divine traits all — which accompany that designation). It is pure illusion, therefore, for Karl Thieme to think of himself as faithful to the self-consciousness of Jesus, or as casting off only an " apostolical theologoumenon (*Glaubensgedanke*) " — which he considers no fault — when he attaches himself to a merely human Jesus and pronounces all that is more than this " mythological." [12] This merely human " historical Jesus " is a pure invention of the wish that is father to the thought, and would have been, not merely to Paul, as Martin Brückner justly reminds us,[13] but to all the New Testament writers as well, and to Jesus himself, as depicted by them and as discernible in any sense behind their portraiture — just "nonsense."

We cannot withhold a certain sympathy, nevertheless, from men who, caught in the toils of modern naturalism, and unable themselves to admit the intrusion of the supernatural into this world of " causative nexus," are determined to keep the merely human Jesus, whom alone they can allow to have existed, free from at least the grosser illusions concerning His person with which the thought of His followers has been (in their view) deformed. There surely is manifested in this determination — utterly unhistorical as it is, in both spirit and

[11] *Free Church Year-Book and Who's Who* for 1911, cited in *The Expository Times*, May, 1911, p. 339.

[12] *Z.Th.K.*, xviii. (1908) pp. 431, 442.

[13] " Die Entstehung der paulinischen Christologie " (1903), p. 12: " For the Christ, too, is for Paul, a redemptive-*historical* personality. Of course, not in the modern sense. The historical Christ in, say, the sense of the Ritchlian school, would have been for Paul, nonsense. The Pauline Christology had rather to do with the experiences of a heavenly being which have, and should have, an extraordinary significance for humanity."

effect — a strong underlying wish to honor Jesus; to preserve to Him at least his sanity — for that is what it comes to in the essence of the matter. A merely human Jesus, who nevertheless believed Himself to be God, were a portentous figure on which to focus the admiring gaze of the Christian generations. We may well believe that a saving instinct underlies all the more extreme historical skepticism in the modern attempts to construe the figure of Jesus, as it is somewhat grotesquely phrased, "historically." The violence done to historical verity, for example, in denying that Jesus thought and proclaimed Himself the Messiah, receives a kind of — shall we say psychological, or shall we say sentimental? — if not justification, yet at least condonation, when we reflect what it would mean for Jesus, if, not being really the Messiah (and from this naturalistic point of view the whole body of messianic hopes were but a frenzied dream), He nevertheless fancied himself the Messiah and assumed the rôle of Messiah. There may even be pleaded a sort of historical condonation for it; it certainly were inconceivable that such a man as Jesus is historically authenticated as being — His whole life informed, for example, with a gracious humility before God — could have been the victim of such a megalomania.[14]

It is into a perfect labyrinth of inconsistencies and contradictions, in fact, that the assumption that Jesus was a mere man betrays us; and from them there is no issue except by the correction of the primal postulate. The old antithesis *aut Deus, aut non bonus* need, indeed, no longer be pressed; none in these modern days (since Renan) is so lost to historical verisimilitude as to think of charging Jesus with coarse charlatanry (cf. Mt. xxvii. 63). But His integrity is saved only at the cost of His intelligence. If none accuse Him of charlatanry, there are many who are ready to ascribe to Him the highest degree of fanaticism, and a whole literature has grown up in recent years around the matter. There is, indeed, no escape from crediting to Him some degree of "enthusiasm," if He is

[14] This point is admirably elaborated by M. Lepin, "Jésus Messie et Fils de Dieu d'après les Évangiles Synoptiques "[3] (1907), p. 163.

to be considered a mere man. And this, let us understand it
clearly, is to ascribe to Him also, when the character of this
"enthusiasm" is understood, some degree of what we are
accustomed, very illuminatingly, to call "derangement." It
is easy, of course, to cry out, as Hans Windisch, for example,
does cry out, against the antithesis "Either Jesus Christ was
mentally diseased, or He was God-man," as "frightful and
soul-imperiling." [15] It is that; but it offers us, nevertheless, the
sole possible alternatives. Shall we not recognize it as a delusion which argues mental unsoundness when a mere man proclaims himself God? Even D. F. Strauss taught us this much
two generations ago: "If he were a mere man" says he,[16]
"and, nevertheless, cherished that expectation" — the expectation, to wit, of quickly coming on the clouds of heaven
to inaugurate the messianic kingdom — "we cannot help
either ourselves or him. He was, according to our conceptions,
a fanatic (*Schwärmer*)." It is possible, no doubt, sturdily to
deny that Jesus could have harbored these high thoughts of
Himself, or cherished these great expectations. But this is
flatly in the face of the whole historical evidence. It is undeniable that the only Jesus known to history was both recognized
by His followers and Himself claimed to be something much
more than man, and to have before Him a career accordant
with His divine being. Nor can this lowered view of Jesus be
carried through: neither Harnack, nor Bousset, nor Hausrath,
nor Otto has been able, with the best will in the world, to present to us a Jesus free from supernatural elements of self-consciousness.[17] So that it is a true judgment, which Hermann
Werner passes upon their efforts to depict a merely human

---

[15] *Theologische Rundschau*, May, 1911, p. 221. He has in view especially
Ph. Kneib, "Moderne Leben-Jesu-Forschung unter dem Einflusse der Psy-
chiatrie" (1908), and H. Werner, "Die psychische Gesundheit Jesu" (1908),
both of whom press the antithesis.

[16] "Der alte und der neue Glaube," p. 80.

[17] These particular names are adduced only because they happen to be
those singled out by H. Werner for examination in a striking article entitled
"Der historische Jesus der liberalen Theologie — ein Geisteskranker," published in the *N.K.Z.* (May, 1911), xxii. pp. 347–390. He shows in detail that
the Jesus of each of these authors presents symptoms of paranoia.

Jesus: " The historical Jesus of the liberal theology is and
abides a mentally diseased man — as Lepsius strikingly said,
' a tragedy of fanaticism ' (*Schwärmerei*)." [18] If these supernatural claims were " mythical," then either there was no real
Jesus, and His very personality vanishes into the myth into
which all that is historical concerning Him is sublimated, or
the real Jesus was the subject of acute megalomania in His
estimate of Himself.

And here we discover the significance in the history of
thought of the new radicalism which has, in our day, actually
raised the question — a question which has become a " burning " one in Germany, the home of the " merely human Jesus "
— whether " Jesus ever lived." Men like Albert Kalthoff and
Karl Kautsky, Wilhelm von Schnehen and Arthur Drews,
emphasize the fact that the only Jesus known to history
was a divine being become man for human redemption — not
a deified man, but an incarnate God. If this Jesus is a mythological figure — why, there is no " historical Jesus " left. The
zeal for vindicating the actual existence of a " historical
Jesus," which has developed in the circles of German " liberalism " during the past two years, is most commendable. The
task is easy, and the success with which it has been accomplished is correspondingly great. But the real significance,
whether of the attack or the defense, seems to be only slowly
becoming recognized, or at least to have been acknowledged
by those involved most deeply in the conflict. It lies, however,
very much on the surface. Arthur Drews is simply the *reductio
ad absurdum* of David Friedrich Strauss. And the vindication
of the actuality of a " historical Jesus," against the assault of
which Drews has become the central figure, is the definitive
refutation of the entire " mythical theory," which, inaugurated
by Strauss, has been the common foundation on which the
whole " liberal" school has built for two generations. There
is, of course, nothing more certain than that " Jesus lived."
But there is another thing which is equally certain with it;
and that is expressed with irrefutable clearness and force

[18] H. Werner, as above, pp. 383–389.

by Arthur Drews when he declares that "the Jesus of the oldest Christian communities is not, as is commonly thought" — that is to say, in the circles of "liberalism" — "a deified man, but a humanized God." It is impossible to sublimate into myth the whole Jesus of the New Testament testimony, the Jesus of the evangelists, the Jesus of all the evangelical sources which can be even in part isolated and examined, the Jesus, in a word, of the entire historical witness, and retain any Jesus at all. The "mythical Jesus" is not the invention of Drews, but of Strauss, and it is common ground with Drews and all his "liberal" opponents. It is a mere matter of detail whether we say with Weinel that the historical Jesus was a mere man, but a man whom "we know right well — as well as if we could see him still before us today, and were able to hear his voice"; or with Pfleiderer, that He was certainly a mere man, but is so bound up with the legends that have grown up about Him that we can never know anything about His real personality; or with Drews, that there is no reason for supposing that He ever existed at all: a mere matter of detail, indifferent to history, which knows nothing of any Jesus but the divine Jesus. The advent of the new radicalism into the field of discussion cannot fail, however, greatly to clear the air; the merely human Jesus is really eliminated by it from the catalogue of possible hypotheses, and the issue is drawn sharply and singly: Is the divine-human Jesus, who alone is historically witnessed a reality, or a myth? *Tertium non datur.*

Thus we are brought to the final issue. The two-natured Christ is the synthesis of the whole mass of biblical data concerning Christ. The doctrine of the Two Natures underlies all the New Testament writings severally, and it is commended to us by the combined authority of all those primitive followers of Christ who have left written records of their faith. It is the only doctrine of Christ which can be discerned lying back of our formal records in pre-written tradition; it is the aboriginal faith of the Christian community. It is the only alternative to a non-existent Christ; we must choose between a two-natured Christ and a simply mythical Christ. By as much

as " Jesus lived," by so much is it certain that the Jesus who
lived is the person who alone is witnessed to us as having lived
— the Jesus who, being Himself of heavenly origin and superior to the very angels, had come to earth on a mission of
mercy, to seek and save those who are lost, and who, after
He had given His life a ransom for many, was to come again on
the clouds of heaven to judge the world. No other Jesus than
this ever lived. No doubt He lived as man, His life adorned
with all the gracious characteristics of a man of God. But He
cannot be stripped of His divine claims. We have already had
occasion to advert to the gross contradiction which is involved
in supposing that such a man as He was could have preserved
that fine flavor of humility toward God which characterized
His whole life-manifestation and yet have falsely imagined
Himself that exalted being in whose fancied personality He
lived out His life on earth. The trait which made it possible for
Him to put Himself forward as the Fellow of God would have
made the humility of heart and demeanor which informed all
His relations with God impossible. Our modern humanitarians,
of course, gloze the psychological contradiction; but they cannot withhold recognition of the contrast of traits which must
be accredited to any Jesus who can really be believed — even
on their postulates — to have ever existed.[19] Standing before
this puzzle of his life-manifestation, Adolf Harnack writes: [20]

" Only one who has had a kindred experience could go to the
bottom here. A prophet might perhaps attempt to lift the veil; such
as we must be content to assure ourselves that the Jesus who taught
self-knowledge and humility, yet gave to himself, and to himself
alone, the name of the Son of God."

And again: [21]

[19] " What contradictions must Jesus have united in himself on the basis
of the liberal life-picture of him," exclaims H. Werner (*Neue kirchliche
Zeitschrift,* May, 1911, p. 389). " He was at the same time humble and proud,
acute-minded and weak-minded, clear-sighted and blind, sober-minded and
fanatical, with profound knowledge of men and no self-knowledge, clear in
his insight of the present, and full of fantastic dreams of the future. His life
was, as Lepsius strikingly said, ' a tragedy of fanaticism.' "

[20] " Das Wesen des Christentums " (56–60 Tausend, 1908), p. 82.

[21] " Das Christentum und die Geschichte,"[5] p. 10 (E. T. " Christianity
and History," 1896, p. 37).

" But it is of one alone that we know that he united the deepest humility and purity of will with the claim that he was more than all the prophets who were before him, even the Son of God. Of him alone, we know that those who ate and drank with him glorified him, not only as the Teacher, Prophet, and King, but also as the Prince of Life, as the Redeemer, Judge of the world, as the living power of their existence — ' It is not I that live, but Christ in me ' — and that presently a band of the Jew and gentile, the wise and foolish, acknowledged that they had received from the abundance of this one man, grace for grace. This fact which is open to the light of day is unique in history; and it requires that the actual personality behind it should be honored as unique."

In similar vein Paul Wernle, having pointed out that the two elements found in the Gospels are also found in Jesus' own consciousness, exclaims: [22]

" What is astonishing in Jesus is the co-existence of the superhuman self-consciousness with the most profound humility before God. It is the same man that cries, ' All things have been delivered unto me of my Father, and no one knoweth the Father save the Son,' and who replies to the rich young ruler, ' Why callest thou me good, there is none good save God.' Without the former, a man like us; without the latter, a fanatic."

By his last words Wernle apparently fancies that all is said which needs to be said in order to explain the anomaly, when it is said that Jesus takes up " the rôle of Mediator ": we shall no longer be surprised that he claims something on both parts. But the astounding features of the case cannot be so lightly disposed of. When the two elements of it are given each its full validity; when the completeness of Jesus' humility before God is realized on the one side, and the height of His claim reaching to the supreme deity itself, on the other, it is safe to say that such a combination of mental states within the limits of a single nature will be acknowledged to be inconceivable. It is inconceivable that the same soul could have produced two such contradictory states of mind contemporaneously. Could have *produced* them, we say. Should we not add the question

[22] " Die Anfänge unserer Religion " [2] (1904), p. 28.

whether a single soul could even have harbored such contradictory states? Such contradictory states of consciousness could no more dwell together in one unitary conscious spirit than issue from it as its creation. The self-consciousness of Jesus is, in other words, distinctly duplex, and necessarily implies dual centers of self-consciousness. Only in such a conception of the person can the mind rest. If Jesus was both the Son of God, in all the majesty of true deity, and a true child of man, in creaturely humility — if, that is, He was both God and man, in two distinct natures united, however inseparably and eternally, yet without conversion or confusion in one person — we have in His person, no doubt, an inexhaustible mystery, the mystery surpassing all mysteries, of combined divine love and human devotion. If He was not both God and man in two distinct natures combined in one person, the mystery of His personality passes over into a mere mass of crass contradictions which cannot all be believed; which, therefore, invite arbitrary denial on the one side or the other; and which will inevitably lead to each man creating for himself an artificial Jesus, reduced in the traits allowed to Him to more credible consistency — if indeed, it does not directly tempt to His entire sublimation into a highly composite ideal.

It can scarcely be necessary to add that escape from these psychological contradictions, incident to the attempt to construct a one-natured Christ, cannot be had by fleeing to " the discoveries of the new psychology." It is vain to point, for example, to the phenomena of what is commonly spoken of as " multiple personality " as offering a parallel to the duplex consciousness manifested by our Lord. We need not insist on the pathological character of these phenomena, and their distressing accompaniments, marking as they do the disintegration of the normal consciousness; or on the lack of affinity of the special form of mental disease of which they are symptomatic with the paranoia from which Jesus must have suffered, on the hypothesis that He was no more than a man. It is doubtless enough to ask what kind of a super-divine nature this is that is attributed to Him under the guise of a human nature, which is capable of splitting up in its disintegration into supreme Godhood and perfect manhood as its aliquot, perhaps even as aliquant, parts. If the mere fragments of His personality stand forth as God in His essential majesty and man in the height of man's possibilities, what must He be in the unitary integration of His normal personality? Surely no remotest analogy to such a dualism of consciousness can be discovered in the pitiable spectacle of Dr. Morton Prince's "Miss Beaucamp" and her "Sally." [23] If we have here a merely human personality, in dual dissociation, the miraculous multiplication of the loaves and fishes is eclipsed; the fragments are in immeasurable overplus of the supply.

It may seem more hopeful, therefore, to call in " the new psychology " as an aid to the explanation of the mystery of our Lord's person, when the divine nature is not denied. Even if, however, the original nature be conceived as divine, and the man Jesus be interpreted as a dissociated section of the divine consciousness, which maintains itself in its full divinity by its side, what have we given us but a new Docetism, complicated with a meaningless display of contradictory attributes? A special form is sometimes given [24] to this mode of conceiving the matter, however, which, perhaps, should not pass without particular notice. Appeal is made to the curious cases of "alternating personality," occasionally occurring, in which a man suddenly loses all consciousness of his identity and becomes for a time, longer or shorter, practically a different person. Thus, for example, Ansel Bourne, preacher, of Greene, R. I., became suddenly A. J. Brown, confectioner, of Norristown, Pennsylvania, and remained just A. J. Brown for some months with no consciousness whatever of Ansel Bourne, until just as suddenly he became Ansel Bourne again with no consciousness whatever of A. J. Brown.[25] In the light of such instances, we

[23] Morton Prince, " The Dissociation of a Personality. A Biographical Study in Abnormal Psychology " (1906).

[24] As, for example, very recently by D. A. Murray, " Christian Faith and the New Psychology " (1911).

[25] The case is described by William James in his " Principles of Psychology " (ed. 1908), i. pp. 391–393.

aro asked, what psychological obstacle forbids our supposing
that the Divine Being who created the universe and has existed from eternity as the Son of God became for a season a
man with all the limitations of a man? Why may we not, with
psychological justification, look upon Jesus Christ as the infinite God "functioning through a special consciousness with
limited power and knowledge"? Why not explain the man
Jesus, in other words, just as the "alternative personality" of
the Second Person of the Trinity? Such purely speculative
questions may possess attractions for some classes of minds;
but they certainly have no concernment with the Christ of history. The problem which the Christ of history presents is not
summed up merely in the essential identity of the man Jesus
with the God of heaven, but includes the co-existence in that
one person, whom we know as Christ Jesus, of a double consciousness, divine and human. The solution which is offered
leaves the actual problem wholly to one side. In proposing
a merely human Jesus, with a divine background indeed, of
which, however, He is entirely unconscious, it constructs a
purely artificial Jesus of whom history knows nothing: the
fundamental fact about the historical Jesus in His unoccul-
tated divine consciousness.[26]

For the same reason the suggestion which has been made [27]
that the phenomenal Jesus may be allowed to be strictly hu-

---

[26] Therefore even the cautious and strictly limited appeal to the phenomena of multiplex personality by J. Oswald Dykes (*The Expository Times,*
January, 1906, xvii. p. 156) is without effect. He says: " I am far from implying that the analogy between the phenomena of the subliminal life, and the
coexistence in our Lord of divine and human consciousness is either close or
satisfying. The case of incarnate Deity is and must be unique and incomparable. What they do suggest is that within the mysterious depths of a single
personality, there may coexist parallel states of spirit life, one only of which
emerges in ordinary human consciousness. They may serve to repel the
superficial objection that such a dualism is impossible. Within Christ's complex and wonderful constitution, room might be found for a life-activity,
verily His own, yet of which He had on earth no human consciousness, or at
most, it may be, an intermittent and imperfect knowledge; and, if it were so,
the psychology of the human personality has nothing to say against it." The
case supposed is not that of the historical Christ.

[27] By W. Sanday, "Christologies Ancient and Modern" (1910); further

man, and the divine Jesus be sought in what it is now fashionable to call His "subliminal self," is altogether beside the mark. The "subliminal self" is only another name for the subconscious self; and the relegation of the divine in Jesus to the realm of the unconscious definitely breaks with the entire historical testimony. Even if the hypothesis really allowed for a two-natured Christ — which in the form, at least, in which it is put forward, it does not, but presents us with only a man-Christ, differing from His fellow-men only in degree and not at all in kind — it would stand wholly out of relation with the only Christ that ever existed. For the Christ of history was not unconscious, but continually conscious, of His deity, and of all that belongs to His deity. He knew Himself to be the Son of God in a unique sense — as such, superior to the very angels and gazing unbrokenly into the depths of the Divine Being, knowing the Father even as He was known of the Father. He felt within Him the power to make the stones that lay in His pathway bread for His strengthening, and the power (since He had come to save the lost) rather to bruise his feet upon them that He might give His life a ransom for many and afterward return on the clouds of heaven to judge the world. Of this Jesus, the only real Jesus, it cannot be said that His consciousness was "entirely human"; and a Jesus of whom this can be said has nothing in common with the only historical Jesus, in whom His divine consciousness was as constant and vivid as His human.

The doctrines of the Two Natures supplies, in a word, the only possible solution of the enigmas of the life-manifestation of the historical Jesus. It presents itself to us, not as the creator, but as the solvent of difficulties — in this, performing the same service to thought which is performed by all the Christian doctrines.[28] If we look upon it merely as a hypothesis, it com-

---

explained in a more recent pamphlet, called "Personality in Christ and in Ourselves" (1911), in which the incarnation is expressly reduced to the indwelling of the Holy Spirit. Cf. also H. R. Mackintosh, *The Expository Times*, xxi. (August and September, 1910) pp. 486, 553.

[28] Cf. B. F. Westcott, "The Gospel of Life" (1892).

mands our attention by the multiplicity of phenomena which it reduces to order and unifies, and on this lower ground, too, commends itself to our acceptance. But it does not come to us merely as a hypothesis. It is the assertion concerning their Lord of all the primary witnesses of the Christian faith. It is, indeed, the self-testimony of our Lord Himself, disclosing to us the mystery of His being. It is, to put it briefly, the simple statement of " the fact of Jesus," as that fact is revealed to us in His whole manifestation. We may reject it if we will, but in rejecting it we reject the only real Jesus in favor of another Jesus — who is not another, but is the creature of pure fantasy. The alternatives which we are really face to face with are, Either the two-natured Christ of history, or — a strong delusion.

VII

CHRISTLESS CHRISTIANITY

CHRISTLESS CHRISTIANITY [1]

"The Christ Myth" by Arthur Drews was published early in 1909,[2] and before the year was out its author was being requisitioned by dissidents from Christianity of the most incongruous types as a promising instrument for the general anti-Christian propaganda. Few more remarkable spectacles have ever been witnessed than the exploitation throughout Germany in the opening months of 1910 of this hyper-idealistic metaphysician, disciple of von Hartmann and convinced adherent of the "Philosophy of the Unconscious," by an Alliance the declared basis of whose organization is a determinate materialism. As, under the auspices of the *Monistenbund,* he made his progress from city to city, lecturing and debating, he drew a tidal-wave of sensation along with him. A violent literary war was inaugurated. It seemed as if all theological Germany were aroused.

In one quarter there was an ominous silence. The "conservative" theologians looked on at the whole performance with bitter contempt. When twitted [3] with leaving to the "liberals" the whole task of defending the historicity of Jesus against Drews, they replied with much justice that it was none of their fight. The liberals had for two generations been proclaiming the only Jesus that ever existed a myth: why should it cause surprise if some at length were taking the proclamation seriously and drawing the inference — if such a simple recasting of the identical proposition can be called

---

[1] From *The Harvard Theological Review,* v. 1912, pp. 423–473.

[2] Arthur Drews, "Die Christusmythe," Jena, 1909, and many subsequent editions. English translation: "The Christ Myth," by Arthur Drews, Ph.D., Professor of Philosophy in the Techn. Hochschule, Karlsruhe. Translated from the third edition (revised and enlarged) by C. Delisle Burns, M.A. London [1910].

[3] As by the *Christliche Freiheit,* February 13, 1910.

an inference — that therefore no Jesus ever existed? If the Christianity which flowed out from Palestine and overspread the world was not the creation of Jesus, but the spontaneous precipitation of old-world myths from a solution just now, 'as it happened, evaporated past the saturation point, why postulate behind it a shadowy figure, standing in no causal relation to it, without any effective historical connection with it, for whose existence there is therefore neither historical nor logical need? We may not think the language elegant, but we can scarcely pronounce the jibe unprovoked, when Herr Superintendent Doctor Matthes of Kolberg bursts forth in Hengstenberg's old *Evangelical Church-Journal:* [4] " That the wasted, colorless phantom which alone the Liberal theology leaves over of Jesus could not have transformed a world, — that is clear to all the world except the Liberal theologians themselves, who are still always hoping to see their homunculus come forth from the Gilgameshmishmashmush-brine which alone is left in the pantry of the comparative-religionists and which Arthur Drews has served out afresh to the Berliners." That the liberal theology has travailed and brought forth a monstrous birth is not surprising; nor is it surprising that the fruit of its womb should turn and rend it. Let them fight it out; that is their concern; and if the issue is, as seems likely, the end of both, the world will be well rid of them. Why should sane people take part in such a " theological mill " in which " as-yet Christians " and " no-longer Christians " struggle together in the arena with nothing at stake, — for certainly the difference between the reduced Jesus of the one and the no Jesus of the other is not worth contending about? To deny the existence of Jesus is, of course, as Ernst Troeltsch puts it, "silly"; [5] to be asked to defend the actual existence of Jesus is, as Adolf Harnack phrases it, "humiliating." [6] But the artillery which the liberal theologians have hurriedly trained

[4] *Die evangelische Kirchenzeitung,* March 6, 1910.

[5] " Die törichte Frage " (" Die Bedeutung der Geschichtlichkeit Jesu für den Glauben," 1911, p. 2).

[6] " Beschämend " (*Neue Freie Presse,* May 15, 1910, reprinted in " Aus Wissenschaft und Leben," 1911, ii. p. 167).

upon the denial shows how little they can really let it go at
that. It is only the conservative, secure in the possession of
the real Jesus, who can look serenely upon this shameful folly
and with undisturbed detachment watch the wretched comedy
play itself out.

Only the conservative, — and, we may add, the extreme
radical. For there is a radicalism, still calling itself Christian,
so thoroughgoing as to fall as much below concernment with
the question whether Jesus ever lived as conservatism rises
above it. The conservative looks with unconcern upon all the
pother stirred up by the debate on the historicity of Jesus,
because he clearly perceives that it is all (if we may combine
Harnack's and Troeltsch's phraseology) scandalous nonsense,
unworthy of the notice of anyone with an atom of historical
understanding. The radical looks upon it with unconcern because in his self-centered life Jesus has no essential place and
no necessary part to play: the question whether Jesus ever
lived is to him a merely academic one. An interesting episode
in Drews' lecture tour through the Germanic cities brings
this point of view before us with strong emphasis. A discussion
was contemplated at Bremen also, and the *Monistenbund*
there extended an invitation to the local *Protestantenverein*
to take part in it. This invitation was decisively declined, and
the *Protestantenverein* took a good deal of pains to make it
perfectly plain why it was declined. The *Protestantenverein*
was not quite clear in its own mind that the whole business
was not merely an advertising scheme for the benefit of the
Monistenbund; though, to be sure, it could not see what
Monists as Monists have to do with the question whether
Jesus ever lived, more than "whether Socrates ever lived,
or Bacon wrote Shakespeare's plays." The *Protestantenverein,*
moreover, for itself felt entirely assured on good historical
grounds of the historicity of Jesus, and had no interest in
threshing out old straw. But it was on neither of these grounds
that it declined to take part in the debate, but precisely because it was a matter of no importance to it whether Jesus ever
lived or not. " All the theologians of the Bremen *Protestanten-*

verein," they formally explain, " are agreed that the question whether Jesus lived is, as such, not a religious but a historico-scientific question. It would be sad for Christianity as a religion if its right of existence hung on the question whether anybody whatever ever lived, or anything whatever ever occurred, even though it be the greatest personalities and the most important events which are in question. Every true religion lives not because of ' accidental truths of history,' but because of ' eternal truths of reason.' It lives not because of its past, more or less verifiable and always subject to the critical scrutiny of historical science; but because of the vital forces which it every day disengages afresh into the soul from the depths of the unconditioned." All the great religious forces of Christianity — trust in the Living God, elevated moral self-respect, sincere love of men — are quite independent today of all question of the historicity of Jesus, and therefore this question can without fear be left in the hands in which it belongs, — in the hands of untrammelled historical criticism. " Whether Jesus existed or not, is for our religious and Christian life, in the last analysis, a matter of indifference, if only this life be really religious and Christian, and preserve its vital power in our souls and in our conduct." [7]

There is asserted here something more than that religion is independent of Jesus. That was being vigorously asserted by the adherents of the *Monistenbund;* and as for Drews, his " Christ Myth " — like the " Christianity of the New Testament " of his master, von Hartmann, before it — was written, he tells us, precisely in the interests of religion, and seeks to sweep Jesus out of the way that men may be truly religious. With the extremities of this view the members of the Bremen *Protestantenverein* express no sympathy: they are of the number of those who profess and call themselves Christians. What they assert, therefore, is not that religion merely, but distinctively that Christianity is independent of Jesus. They do not declare, indeed, that Christianity, as it has actually

[7] See the whole document in the *Christliche Welt,* April 28, 1910, coll. 402 ff.

existed in the world, has had, in point of fact, nothing to do with Jesus; or that Christians of today — they themselves as Christians — have had or have no relations with Jesus. They are convinced on sound historical grounds of the historicity of Jesus; they recognize that he has played a part in setting the movement called Christianity going; they draw, no doubt, inspiration from his memory. What they cannot allow is that he is essential to Christianity. They are conscious of standing in some such relation to him as that in which an idealistic philosopher stands, say, to a Plato. In point of fact such a philosopher reverences Plato, and derives from him inspiration and impulse, perhaps even instruction. But had there been no Plato, he would be able to do very well without a Plato. So Christians may in point of fact owe not a little to Jesus, and they may be very willing to acknowledge their indebtedness. But Christianity cannot be dependent on Jesus. Though there had been no Jesus, Christianity would be; and were his figure eradicated from history — or even from the mind of man — tomorrow, Christianity would suffer no loss. The sources of its life, the springs of its vitality, lie in itself: it may owe much to a great personality, teaching it, embodying it; it cannot owe to him its being.

The *Protestantenverein* of the good city of Bremen is, of course, not the inventor of this Christless Christianity. It is as old as Christianity itself; and has come to explicit assertion whenever and wherever men have thought of Christianity rather as universal human religion in more or less purity of expression — perhaps in the purest expression yet given to it, or even in its purest possible expression — than as a specific positive religion instituted among men in particular historical circumstances.[8] The classical period of this point of view is, of course, the Enlightenment; and its classical expounder in that period, Gotthold Ephraim Lessing; and the classical treatise in which Lessing propounds it, the tract written in response to Johann Daniel Schumann under the title, " Con-

---

[8] Hermann Reuter, " Geschichte der religiösen Aufklärung im Mittel-alter," 1875, 1877, gives mediaeval instances.

cerning the Proof of Spirit and Power " (1777); in which occurs accordingly its classical crystallization in a crisp proposition, the famous declaration (very naturally quoted by the
theologians of the Bremen *Protestantenverein*) that "accidental truths of history can never be the proof of necessary
truths of reason."

In Lessing's conception, as in that of some before him and
of many after him,[9] Christianity is in its essence simply what
we have learned to know as altruism. He sums it up in what
he calls "the Testament of John," — "Little children, love
one another"; and he refuses to believe that "dogmas," whatever may be said of their probability, or even of their truth,
can enter into its essence. The proximate purpose of the tract,
"Concerning the Proof of Spirit and Power,"[10] is to show that
the "dogmas" of the "Christian religion" cannot be put forward as essential truths, and so far as they are not intrinsically
self-evidencing rest on evidence which is at best but probable.
But the argument itself takes rather the form of an assault on
the trustworthiness of historical testimony in general. Lessing does not deny, in this tract, that truths might conceivably
be commended by authority. If a man actually witnessed
miracles or fulfilments of prophecy, he might no doubt be
brought to subject his understanding to that of him in whom
the prophecies were visibly fulfilled and by whom the miracles were wrought. But this is not our case. We have no miracles or fulfilments to rest on; we have only accounts of
miracles and fulfilments. And "accounts of the fulfilment of
prophecies are not fulfilments of prophecies; accounts of miracles are not miracles." " Prophecies fulfilled before my eyes,

[9] Perhaps the most thoroughgoing expression of it is given by Ludwig
Feuerbach, " The Essence of Christianity," E. T.[2] 1881, p. 209: " He therefore
who loves man for the sake of man, who rises to the love of the species, to
universal love, adequate to the nature of the species, he is a Christian, is
Christ himself." Auguste Sabatier, however, in his ultimate statement, scarcely
falls short of this. Christianity, he tells us, is the religion " of universal redemption by love," that is everybody's love for everybody. (" The Doctrine
of the Atonement and its Historical Evolution," E. T. 1904, p. 134.)

[10] " Ueber den Beweis des Geistes und der Kraft," in Lachmann's edition
of Lessing's " sämtliche Schriften," xiii. pp. 1–8.

miracles worked before my eyes," he explains, " work immediately. Accounts of fulfilments of prophecies and of miracles have to work through a medium which deprives them of all force." "How," he exclaims, " can it be asked of me to believe with the same energy, on infinitely less inducement, the very same incomprehensible truths which people from sixteen to eighteen hundred years ago believed on the strongest possible inducement?" "Or," he demands, with a show of outrage, " is everything that I read in trustworthy history, without exception, just as certain for me as what I myself experience?"

The argumentative force of the representation resides, of course, largely in its exaggerations, — "deprived of *all* force," "without exception." But Lessing skilfully proceeds to cover these exaggerations up by assuming at once an air of the sweetest reasonableness. " I do not know," he remarks, " that anyone ever maintained just that; what is maintained is only that the accounts which we have of these prophecies and miracles are just as trustworthy as any historical truths can be. And then it is added that no doubt historical truths cannot be demonstrated, — yet, nevertheless, we must believe them just as firmly as demonstrated truths." Surely, however, exclaims Lessing, " if no historical truth can be demonstrated, then nothing can be demonstrated *by means* of historical truths, that is, accidental truths of history can never be the proof of necessary truths of reason." " I do not deny at all," he protests, " that prophecies were fulfilled in Christ; I do not deny at all that Christ wrought miracles: but I do deny that these miracles, since their truth has altogether ceased to be evinced by miracles which are still accessible today, since there exist nothing but accounts of miracles (no matter how undenied, how undeniable, they may be supposed to be), can or ought to bind me to the least faith in any other teachings of Christ."

The whole procedure involves at any rate a μετάβασις εἰς ἄλλο γένος. To know that Christ raised a man from the dead, — how does that prove that God has a Son? Suppose I could prove that Christ rose from the dead? How does that prove

that He is God's Son? " In what connection does my inability
to advance anything decisive against the testimony to that
fact stand with my duty to believe something which outrages
my reason? " You tell me that the very Christ who rose from
the dead declared that He was the Son of God, of the same nature with God. Of that declaration, too, we have nothing but
historical evidence. If you say, No, we have inspired evidence,
for the Bible is inspired, — of that, too, we have nothing but
historical evidence! " This, this, is the nasty wide ditch, across
which I cannot get, no matter how often and earnestly I have
tried to leap it. If anybody can help me over it, let him do it,
I beg him, I implore him. He will do me a great charity."
Thus Lessing ends his sinuous argument with a round denial
that " historical evidence " can ever place a fact beyond question. It is a case of general historical skepticism. The only
evidence which can really establish a truth is the truth's own
self-evidence. He breaks off suddenly, therefore, with a recommendation to his readers, divided by disputes over the Gospel
of John, to come together on the Testament of John. " It is,
no doubt, apocryphal, this Testament: but it is not the less
divine for that." Truth is truth wherever we find it. And truth
is truth to us for no other reason than that it finds us.[11]

[11] Otto Kirn, " Glaube und Geschichte," 1900, pp. 9–10, remarks on
Lessing's double point of view and the consequent confusion in his argument:
" The position of the critic appears upon more exact consideration as little
sure. He attacks his adversary at once from two standpoints which are not in
harmony. He asserts with the Wolffian Dogmatism that reason can never
receive its convictions through history. To this standpoint, however, self-
experienced and past facts are alike unimportant and inconclusive, when the
question concerns religious or ethical propositions. Then he comes forward
in the armor of the historical critic, who is ready to let himself be convinced
by facts if only they be certainly established, and authenticated by self-
experienced analogies: the training of his critical judgment forbade him,
however, to draw far-reaching conclusions from facts which ' act through
a medium,' and remain controversial. As a Wolffian he could not openly
concede what as historian of certainly authenticated facts he declared himself
ready to grant. Lessing's vacillation between dogmatic rationalism and critical
empiricism manifests itself in this double attitude towards history: with the
one he belongs to the Enlightenment, with the other he is preparing the way
for a time which would be able to see in history something better than a
source of ' obscure and confused ideas ' (cf. Windelband, " A History of
Philosophy," § 33, 9)."

It was not to be expected that a point of view so natural to the Age of Reason should continue in the same measure to hold the minds of men in the Age of History. But neither was it to be expected that a point of view so deeply rooted in the popular philosophy of the eighteenth century should fail to project itself into the nineteenth, and color the thought of all who in any large degree draw their mental inheritance from the Enlightenment. We are not surprised to find Kant standing in his judgment of history wholly on the ground of Rationalism, or the lately resurrected Fries following closely in Kant's steps. Nor are we really surprised to observe Fichte still determined by the old point of view, and not even Hegel yet emancipated from it.[12] What does surprise us is that at the end of the days a Rudolf Eucken, true child of the Age of History, and, if one could be permitted to judge only from his profound sense of sin and of the need of divine grace for its overcoming, almost persuaded to be a Christian, can still speak through much the same mask. There is a passage in the first edition of his book on " The Truth-contents of Religion," [13] which, though historical in form, fairly expresses his own attitude towards the relation of religious truth to historical fact. Historical criticism, he thinks, has very seriously shattered the historical foundations of Christianity; indeed, the very subjection of these foundations to criticism, he argues, disqualifies them for serving as foundations of faith, however this criticism issues. Then he proceeds:

" But the shaking of the historical foundations of the religious life goes still further: it is not merely that we are compelled to doubt particular items of their contents, it is that history itself no longer seems proper to serve as the foundation of religion. For the thought to which the modern world commits the guidance of life is not disposed to recognize history as a source of eternal truths. Such

[12] A lucid sketch of the history of opinion on the relations of faith and history is given in pp. 1–27 of Otto Kirn's " Glaube und Geschichte," 1900. See also Karl Dunkmann, " Das religiöse Apriori und die Geschichte," 1910, pp. 11–51, and the admirable general account by C. W. Hodge, in the article, " Fact and Theory " in Hastings's " Dictionary of Christ and the Gospels," i. 1908, pp. 562–567, esp. 564–565.

[13] " Der Wahrheitsgehalt der Religion," 1901, pp. 34–35.

a truth must be capable of immediate realization; it must be veri-fiable by every one and at all times; that is possible, however, only where it is grounded in the timeless nature of reason, and is con-tinually verifiable anew thence. An occurrence of the past, on the other hand, no matter how deeply it has been imbedded in the historical connection, and no matter how energetic it may still be in its effects, does not on that account at all become a portion of our life: we cannot experience it immediately, we cannot our-selves even test its validity, we cannot transform it into a personal possession. That, however, according to our conviction, is precisely what is required for fundamental truths of religion. Thus reason and history stand over against one another in sharp opposition, and the grounding, as of all spirituality, so also of religion, on history calls out the strongest opposition. ' Accidental truths of history can never become the proof of necessary truths of reason ' (Les-sing). If life, however, casts off this connection with history, it be-comes nonsense and an unendurable burden to bind the health of man's soul to the voluntary acceptance of historical occurrences, or even of occurrences supported by history. ' That historical belief is a duty and belongs to salvation is superstition ' (Kant). Can such a dissolution of the old blending of reason and history affect and shake any other religion more deeply than Christianity, which is the most historical of all religions? "

Some modifications have been introduced into this passage in the second edition of " The Truth-contents of Religion," [14] but these do not alter its general bearing. It is allowed that the Enlightenment " differentiated too sharply reason and history, the individual life and tradition, and overestimated the power of any present moment of consciousness." But the contention that history can provide no foundation for religious convic-tions is still pronounced true, and the quotations from Lessing and Kant are still approved, and this from Fichte is added: " Let no one assert that it does no harm to cling to such historical beliefs. It is injurious in that subsidiary facts are given equal validity with essential ones, or, indeed, are pre-sented as the essential facts, and consequently the main facts are suppressed and the conscience tormented." With such a

---

[14] Published in 1905: E. T., " The Truth of Religion," 1911, pp. 33–34.

view of history in its relation to religion, of course Eucken cannot find the roots of his religion, which he would still call Christianity, in Christ. "We can honor him," he tells us, " as a leader, a hero, a martyr; but we cannot directly bind our-selves to him, or root ourselves in him: we cannot uncon-ditionally submit to him. Still less can we make him the centre of a worship. To do so, from our point of view, would be nothing less than an intolerable deification of a human being." [15] Eucken thus quite purely carries on the tradition of a non-historical, which is, of course, also in the nature of the case a Christless Christianity.

There is much in the mental state of our times to add strength to this traditional distrust of history as a basis for religious convictions. Modern thought is not yet emancipated from that ingrained individualism which is impatient of all " external authority," and wishes each soul to be a law to itself. The very preoccupation of the age with history has moreover brought with it its nemesis. A wide-spread impres-sion has grown up that in the crucible of historical criticism all historical magnitudes have melted; that the whole past has become uncertain and conjectural, if not absolutely un-knowable; and that nothing solid is left to offer a foundation for faith. Looking upon themselves and all that they have, instinctively, as the product of historical development, men's hold upon even their most precious spiritual possessions has relaxed; everything is in a flux, and all alike, as it is the product of change, so is held to be subject to change. Chris-tianity itself in the universal flow comes to be thought of only as a passing phase of religious thought, as only one among many religions, rising above the rest, if at all, only in degree.

[15] " Können wir noch Christen sein? " 1911, p. 37. Eucken, in this work, asks if we can still be Christians, and answers yes, — but only by remoulding Christianity to fit our new philosophy which will not hear of a divine Re-deemer or an expiatory redemption. " We have asked," he says in his closing words (p. 236), " whether we of today can still be Christians. We reply that not only can we be, but we must be. We can be Christians, however, only if Chris-tianity be recognized to be a world-historical movement still in flux, if it be shaken out of its ecclesiastical petrifaction and placed upon a broader basis. In this are found the task of our time and the hope of the future."

Many have even become surfeited with history, and, suffocated by its load of facts, react from what Nietzsche girds at as " the hypertrophy of history " [16] in the interests of " untrammelled thinking." Meanwhile the broadened historical horizon has dwarfed the significance of isolated historical events, which alone, it is said, are accessible to our observation. The imagination, fed on illimitable stretches of space and endless progressions of time, finds difficulty in attaching supreme importance to this or that historical incident, occurring at but a point of this boundless space and occupying but a moment of this measureless time. If men are disheartened by the uncertainties of history and irritated by its oppressive superfluity, they are even more dispirited by its littleness and insignificance as known to us. With what propriety, it is asked, " can a proposition about the happening of a particular incident at a certain time in a little corner of the earth " be represented as " one of the fundamental verities which every man ought to know and believe for his soul's health?"

This last sentence we have taken from an article by Arthur O. Lovejoy, which very fairly represents the manner in which this general point of view may still be advocated at the opening of the twentieth century. He calls his article, significantly, " The Entangling Alliance of Religion and History "; [17] and, in the course of it, he advances most of the considerations in aversion to this alliance which we have just rapidly summarized from a statement, already doubtless sufficiently summary, by Ernst Troeltsch. [18]

" Since [he argues] religion constitutes a man's ultimate and definitive intellectual and moral reaction upon his experience, and since it presupposes the possession of truths valid and significant for all men, religious belief will naturally affirm only [why ' only '?] truths of a universal and cosmic bearing. It will deal exclusively

[16] " Vom Nutzen und Schaden der Historie für das Leben," in " Unzeitgemässe Betrachtungen," 1874, ii.[2] p. 210.

[17] *Hibbert Journal,* January, 1907, pp. 258–276: cf. esp. p. 269.

[18] Article, " Glaube und Geschichte " in Schiele and Zscharnack," Die Religion, etc.," ii. coll. 1450–1452.

[why ' exclusively '?] with the ' eternal ' verities and ignore contingent and temporal matters-of-fact. . . . Its content will consist of propositions equally pertinent to the interests, and equally accessible to the knowledge [is the equality absolute?] of all such beings, at any time, in any place. . . . It will not make the belief in the occurrence or non-occurrence of specific local and temporal events any part of its essence."

The very spirit of Lessing is here, — even to Lessing's characteristic assumptions of definitions and characteristic exaggerations of statement. It is treated as axiomatic on the one hand that the whole truth-content of religion must be self-evident, and on the other that history can afford us only probabilities. The Deists, it is suggested, were in the essence of the matter right, when they contended that historical propositions are unfitted to enter into the truth-content of religion because, on the one hand, they cannot be universally known, and, on the other, they "do not strictly constitute knowledge at all." No beliefs about happenings, assuredly, can stand the test of the *Quod semper, ubique, et ab omnibus* — if we take the terms strictly; or can the actual occurrence of events be made more than probable, of remote and particularized events more than barely probable, of such events as are " contrary to the usual order " anything but improbable, so improbable that " it becomes at least debatable whether any amount of purely traditional or documentary evidence can offset" the presumption against them. It is recognized that Christianity is implicated, as is no other religion, with history; it is even allowed that its entanglement with historical facts was indispensable to its survival in the environment in which it first found itself struggling; but it is strenuously asserted that the historical elements which have thus become connected with it are not essential to it. The historical data with which it has been most intimately associated are gravely disputable; it is, indeed, " just those incidents which theology has attached the greatest dogmatic weight " which have most decisively " been removed from the sphere of the clearly ascertainable to that of the problematical." It is fortunate, therefore, that their reality is not of the highest importance from the religious point of view. Indeed, "religious history often becomes more available and more useful religiously when it is taken as poetry."

"If we take even the life and character of Jesus, and consider them solely with respect to their inspirational and exemplary value, it is not a question of primary *religious* importance whether that life and character existed in bodily incarnation upon the solid earth of Galilee, or chiefly in the devout imagination of earlier believers. There happen, just now, to be signs of a revival of the theory of the non-historicity of Jesus of Nazareth. . . . Suppose the theory established. . . . There would be some real gain. The Gospels would become more wonderful and more encouraging than before; for the profound wisdom and lofty character found in them would prove to be the expression, not of a single and unique religious genius, but of the spiritual idealism of many humble and unknown men. That a group of men should be able to conceive the hero of the Synoptic Gospels is more inspiring than that one wholly exceptional man should have been that hero — but, for the same reason, doubtless more improbable. In so far, then, as religious history simply affords ideals for our reverence and imitation, the ideals are no worse for their lack of past reality; they were at least the products of some other men's minds, and foreshadowings of possible realities to come, in the human nature of the future. Our feeling with respect to Jesus would undoubtedly be in significant ways altered. . . . But nothing of the deepest religious concernment can be at issue here."

There is much in these remarks which invites criticism. What it concerns us especially to note, however, is that they go beyond the assertion that matters of fact do not enter into the essence of religion, and that Christianity, as it is religion, may be indifferent to them. They seem to suggest that religion may thrive better in an atmosphere of fancy than of reality. Christianity could not only do very well without Jesus; it would perhaps be better off without Jesus. Jesus as a myth might make a stronger religious appeal, might be of a higher religious value, than Jesus as a fact. It would almost seem a pity, religiously speaking, that Jesus ever lived.[19]

All cannot go quite so far as this. It does not appear that even the members of the Bremen *Protestantenverein* go so far. Most are satisfied with pronouncing Jesus unessential to Christianity, indifferent to Christianity, hardly noxious to it. The difference is rooted ultimately in a difference in point of departure. When the point of departure lies in a philosophical system, appeal to historical criticism is essentially in support of conclusions already attained. Most of those who nowadays pursue a line of reasoning substantially the same, begin nevertheless at the opposite pole. Their start is taken from historical criticism, and philosophical considerations are summoned only secondarily and subsidiarily, to give a basis to conclusions already adopted. Precisely the same philosophical assumptions are invoked, but they are not the primary presuppositions of the actual line of thought, and their logic is less prevalent. It is not so much in pride of pure reason and in contempt of history that these reasoners pronounce faith independent of Jesus, although they fall back on pure reason for a standing-ground, and express a hearty distrust in the trustworthiness of historical data. It is rather in timidity in the face of the processes of historical research, and in panic at the aspect of its results, that they seek and find a sheltered position in the independence of faith of historical entities. They are not so much tempted to despise Jesus because He is merely historical as they are tempted to despair of Him for fear He is not historical enough. The Christless Christianity which is springing more and more into view about us, is, in a word, the fruit less of a strong religious mysticism than of a weak historical scepticism, which has become anxious about the religious props on which it has hitherto depended.

It is the historical criticism of the Gospels "from Reimarus to Wrede" which has created the wide-reaching and deeply

---

[19] Lovejoy must not be thought singular in this suggestion: it is found also in the philosophers of whom he serves himself heir — for instance, in Kant and in Fichte; and it is intrinsic to the general point of view.

seated distrust in the historical tradition of Jesus that has of late become so evident. As Paul Wernle himself allows, in the very act of rebuking this distrust as excessive, "to us all it is more or less certain that the evangelists are not Jesus Himself, that they are all already dependent on tradition, and that this tradition has already suffered all kinds of changes, by which the spirit of the disciples has in manifold ways been mingled with the spirit of Jesus." [20] This being so, it is widely felt that no other attitude towards the person of Jesus remains possible except one at best of skepticism. There are in effect a whole series of Jesuses presented to our consideration. There is the dogmatic Christ which the great Christian community has worshipped through the ages with no other thought than that He was assuredly the Jesus Christ of the biblical record. And there is this Jesus Christ of the biblical record which the scientific study of the Bible has split up into several mutually inconsistent personalities. And there is the "historical Jesus" which biblical criticism has hardly and with much variety of interpretation extracted from the presuppositions of the biblical records. Where among these differing Jesuses can faith find a firm footing? The dogmatic Christ, we are told, has evaporated into a myth; the biblical Jesus Christ has been disintegrated into the tesserae out of which its mosaic was formed; the "historical Jesus," itself the product of doubt, remains a doubtful and fluctuating figure. If we are to continue Christians, must we not at least seek for our Christianity a less unstable basis?

The air in critical circles is fairly palpitating with questions like these. The resulting state of mind finds a clearly argued expression in such a treatise as F. Ziller's *Modern Biblical Science and the Crisis of the Evangelical Church.*[21] The thesis maintained is that the progress of scientific study of the Bible has hopelessly shattered the entire basis on which the faith of the Christian church has hitherto rested. The

---

[20] *Christliche Welt*, February 17, 1910, col. 147.

[21] "Die moderne Bibelwissenschaft und die Krisis der evangelischen Kirche," Tübingen, 1910, see esp. pp. 99–100.

results even of textual criticism already bring certain of the most cherished church-doctrines into peril. Literary criticism renders it very difficult to repose any real confidence in the biblical writers. And material criticism has cast into the gravest doubt the facts related by these writers which are most indispensable to the established teaching. Finally, the science of comparative religion has reduced the foundations of the central doctrines and rites of the church to the level of heathen ideas and usages. The conceptions and ideas of the Bible have become only elements in the universal history of religions, and the biblical writings themselves only a particular section of general religious literature. The figure of Jesus has been well-nigh wiped off the page of history: the dogmatic Christ, the product of reflection, of course; and the biblical Jesus Christ, a composition of disparate materials, equally of course; but also in large measure the "historical Jesus" himself, which it has been the object of science to disinter. "The historical Jesus, as we have seen, has been set aside by the scientific study of the Bible down to meager remnants, and the foundation of the dogmatic Christ has been obliterated." Is there then anything left to rest upon except an "ideal Christ," a creation of fancy? Ziller, who, despite the ruin of historical Christianity which he sees about him, would fain remain a Christian, insists that there is. There is not, indeed, the "historical Jesus," doubt-born and incapable of sustaining faith, but there is the "historical Christ," which is not an ideal, but a fact. On this fact faith can stay itself.

" What the altruistic postulates of an inflated egoism, and what the postulates of pure reason cannot avail for, for that neither can those of the 'ideal Christ' avail. That there is such a thing as practised self-renunciation, in contrast to nature; that on the basis of such a self-renunciation there can develop a high world-overcoming life, — this conviction cannot be derived either from the pure reason or from our practical ideals with the certainty that is required by faith, face to face with the known laws of nature. Only a fact can give the certainty for it, and this fact is ' Christ.'

But how is this fact of Christ to be reached? The reply takes the form of an apologue. Ziller writes:

" All the day long, I have had before me a wide mountain-ridge. In the morning, it stood out, deep-blue, in almost menacing nearness; towards noon, in a like-shaped whitish-grey mist on the horizon; and now, in the evening, it throws over the whole landscape the splendor of a golden reflection. Is it really the same mountain through it all? I think so. . . . What I see is merely the effects which it works on my eye by means of the light straining through the changing atmosphere. What, then, if the mountain were no mountain; if it were only the boundless plain which seems to rise in the distance; if it were only cloud-forms deceiving my eyes? My glance sweeps over the meadows, through which my path runs. The brooks which water it come from yonder. The mountain itself I shall, indeed, not reach; its crags I shall not explore; but I believe in the existence of the mountain.[22]

So, he would say, he believes in the existence of the Christ from whom flow the streams of blessing which gladden the plain of human life. Thus, though the " historical Jesus " has been set aside " down to meagre remnants," the "historical Christ abides unshaken for faith." We seek, and we find, Him, however, not in a book, much less in a creed, but " in the entire, constantly developing Christianity in which we believe."

" Out of faith in the Christ vitally active here today, there grows up for us faith in the Christ of the past. The predicates which the past ascribed to him, we can no longer ascribe to him in the same sense, but we know how to value them from the standpoint of our faith; and though we no longer connect the same meaning with them, or though we permit them to be supplanted by others which express for *us* what is highest — we do it in the consciousness that we are only carrying forward a process in which the oldest Christianity has preceded us, and which others in their own fashion will follow us." [23]

Despairing of the "historical Jesus," Ziller, in other words, substitutes for Him, as he says, a " Christ who varies with the

[22] *Christliche Welt,* May 5, 1910, col. 413.   [23] *Ibid.*

changes of human thought." Christianity, transforming itself ceaselessly from age to age, finds for itself ever a transformed Christ, suited to its changed needs. Christ, in a word, grows with His church; and it would be as impossible for the church of today to believe in the Jesus of the first Christians as it would be for us to live today the life of two thousand years ago. It is out of the whole history of Christianity that God speaks to us of today, and Christ would be dead, did He not live on in the life of human development.[24]

We are not concerned for the moment with the validity of this representation. Paul Wernle is unhesitant in declaring it nonsense. It is nonsense, he asserts, to speak of modern critical research as having sapped our confidence in the "historical Jesus." There continue to be, no doubt, as there always have been, skeptical writers; in late years, for example, there are Wellhausen, Wrede, Schweitzer; but they must not be taken too seriously. "I do not find that, in its essential traits, the person of Jesus has even in the least become uncertain or controversial through the investigations of recent years."[25] And how, indeed, could historical science, let us honor it ever so highly, "avail against the voice of a history of nearly two-thousand years' duration in which Jesus and faith in Jesus — I purposely bring them together — have been the greatest of impulsive and constructive forces?" It is greater nonsense still, Wernle declares, to pretend to retain Christ when the historical Jesus has been abandoned. Once convince him that the historical Jesus has been set aside by science, and faith in Christ has no further personal interest to him: faith in God without Christ would then be his only recourse. "This whole separation of Jesus and Christ," he adds, "abandoning the one and retaining the other, is nothing but a miserable product of opportunism. It was the weakest point in the old Liberal Christianity, and it has not been bettered by any new

[24] "Die moderne Bibelwissenschaft, etc.," p. 101. Cf. the very similar representation of Shirley Jackson Case, "The Historicity of Jesus," 1912, pp. 306-307.
[25] *Christliche Welt*, February 17, 1910, col. 149.

grounding. What we retain in our hands when the historical Jesus falls away is just myths and phantasms, which can afford no support to our faith." [26]

Meanwhile, however, we observe Ziller abandoning the "historical Jesus" and clinging to the "historical Christ," who "still lives in the church." In this, he but follows an example set by Schleiermacher,[27] and from his day on imitated by a long series of writers occupying essentially the same position, but differing immensely among themselves in the completeness or incompleteness, on the one hand, of their abandonment of the historical Jesus, and, on the other, of their clinging to a living Christ. At the one extreme we may discover — shall we say even a Martin Kähler? or shall we content ourselves with saying a Wilhelm Herrmann? [28] At the

---

[26] *Christliche Welt*, May 12, 1910, col. 441.

[27] Cf. Otto Kirn, "Glaube und Geschichte," 1900, p. 22: "According to what has been said, we may trace back to Schleiermacher the idea which recurs through the nineteenth century in manifold modifications, that the figure of the Redeemer, ever only uncertainly or indistinctly established by historical research, is lifted, by the experience of his redemptive power continuing in the community, to a certainty and clearness sufficient for faith. The effect of Christ, capable of being experienced by every man seeking redemption, permits (so it is said) the inference to a personality standing at the head of the community, and in union with God, even if we cannot otherwise come to know anything whatever about him that is historically assured."

[28] Cf. what is said of Kähler and Herrmann as representatives of historical skepticism with respect to the "historical Jesus" by Otto Ritschl in an article entitled, "Der geschichtliche Christus, der christliche Glaube, und die theologische Wissenschaft" in the "Zeitschrift für Theologie und Kirche," iii. 1893, pp. 372 f. "There is accordingly at present no Rationalistic tendency, threatening to bring into question the value for theology of historical investigation. It is true, however, that the confidence which has been hitherto overwhelmingly felt in the result of theological historical research is made doubtful by a skeptical mood which seems to be gaining ground with many theologians. . . . To this skeptical mood . . . Kähler has hitherto given the strongest expression." But Herrmann shares Kähler's historical skepticism, "ascribing to historical research the ability to attain only probable judgments." "In spite of these unfavorable judgments as to the capacity of historical science, Kähler and Herrmann are too deeply persuaded of the nature of Christianity as an historical religion not to lay stress on this — that the Christ which historical research cannot reach with its instruments, but is laid hold of now by faith, is the historical Christ. In contrast with him Kähler speaks of the 'so-called historical Jesus' as a creature of phantastic arbitrariness." See also Karl Dunkmann, "Das religiöse Apriori und die Geschichte," 1911, pp. 44–45.

other stand the theologians of the Bremen *Protestantenverein*. Those who gather around the former node, only sit loosely to the "historical Jesus" as He is presented to us in the Gospel narrative, and can in no way do without the "historical Christ," on whom, indeed, their whole religious system hangs. Those who gather around the latter, though they may or may not, for themselves, feel any real doubt that Jesus really lived, yet are quite able to get along wholly without Him in their religious system, whether we call Him Jesus or Christ. It is these latter, accordingly, who are express "Christless Christians."

Perhaps it may be well to keep near home here and select as examples of this truest Christless Christianity only certain prophets of our own.

A very good example is afforded by Douglas C. Macintosh.[29] With the historicity of Jesus, Macintosh has for himself no difficulty; but neither does he feel any imperative need of the living Christ. He finds the historical Jesus useful; the loss of Him would be a great loss, — a sentimental loss, a pedagogical loss, above all a loss to the easy attainment of Christian certitude. He would even, it appears, allow that the Christ-ideal is indispensable — that it is, indeed, precisely the differentia of Christianity; and he does not see his way to accounting for the clearness at least of this ideal without assuming the historical Jesus, and in this sense, therefore, he is prepared to admit that the historicity of Jesus is "historically indispensable." Indispensable, that is, to the historian, not to the Christian. What the Christian must have is the Christ-ideal, not Christ. "Christian faith is trust in the Christ-like God; whether the Christ be regarded as historical fact or mere ideal, it is trust in the God of holy and unselfish love, whose purpose is the spiritual redemption of humanity and who is revealed in the Christ-like everywhere." Was not Jesus Himself — if He existed — a Christian, the first Christian? And was "the historical Jesus" needed for Him as the presupposition of His faith? We cannot distinguish between the

---

[29] *American Journal of Theology*, July, 1911, pp. 362–372; January, 1912, pp. 106–110.

"religion of Jesus" and the "gospel of Christ": the "gospel of Christ" is just the "religion of Jesus." He is not the content of our faith, but only, historically, the first of the series of believers of that particular kind which we call Christian. Say that the series began in another, in a later, than He, and that he is a myth. What essential difference does that make to our faith? The "Christian God-idea" in any case remains; and the "Christian God-idea" is constitutive of Christianity.

"So far as the content of Christianity is concerned, our religion would remain essentially the same, whatever judgment might be rendered upon questions of historical fact.

"The disproof, or rendering seriously doubtful, of the historicity of Jesus would not mean the disappearance of any essential content from the Christian religion.

"It is not incorrect to say that the essence of Christianity is Jesus Christ, if [Oh that 'if'!] it be recognized that it is also possible to set forth the essence of Christianity without reference to the historic Jesus.

"Granted the historicity of Jesus, was not *his* faith fully Christian? And yet *he* could not make that faith rest upon the historicity of a person of ideal character who had gone before him. If then we believe in the historicity of Jesus, we must admit that Christian faith has been possible in the case of one at least who did not believe in the historicity of any ideal Jesus before his day."

"Without the historical Jesus we may find ourselves with less verification of our faith than we thought." That is a loss; but it is not an irreparable loss, since we may find sufficient verification elsewhere. Meanwhile,

"Christianity, while enjoying the advantages of historical verification, has this qualification for being the 'absolute' and universal religion, that its fate is not bound up with the actuality of any one reputed fact of history, even when that 'fact' is the one which surpasses every other fact in its value to humanity."

In a single word, Christ does not form any part of the content of Christianity, and therefore His historicity cannot be indispensable to Christianity. "Spiritual religion is self-dependent," and finds all its resources in itself; it cannot therefore

be dependent " on the religious experience and inner assurance of another, even though that other be the Jesus of
history."

An almost equally good example is supplied by Frank H.
Foster,[30] the stress of whose argument is laid on the general
consideration that our religious relation cannot rest on the uncertainties of history. His particular manner of phrasing his
contention is that "in some important respects it makes no
difference to the modern thinker whether Jesus was a historical person or not," because " no system of truth which shall
dominate the mind and claim authority over the conduct of
man can rest upon the reality of any historical person." "Salvation " is " an inner state of the soul," and therefore cannot
be something "'objectively' secured by the work of a historical person." " Truth is truth " only as it "shines to the
mind by its own light," and therefore " cannot be something
which depends upon the existence of the person who first
spoke it." If " salvation," " truth," were thus dependent on
the historicity of a person, they " would be exposed to every
breath of criticism." They must not be left in that perilous
condition.

" Though Jesus should be proved never to have existed, the truth
which has come down to us, and which we have received because
of its self-evidencing value, and which we have found to work out
such great results in the liberation of our spirits from the thraldom
of sin and the establishment of holy relations with our Heavenly
Father, would still be true, and its effects would remain unaltered.
In this sense, a historical Jesus is unnecessary."

For himself, Foster does not at all doubt that Jesus was an
historical person. He confesses, indeed, that " of no single
historical detail can we be absolutely sure, unless it be his
death by crucifixion "; though, somewhat inconsistently, he
at once draws up a tolerably detailed picture of the real
Jesus and sets Him before us as " a realized ideal," — " a
realized ideal," moreover, let us note, so lofty that none of His
followers could have invented the portraiture. His historicity

[30] *American Journal of Theology,* October, 1911, pp. 584–598.

remains nevertheless unessential, since our real ground, for example, for acknowledging Him sinless, is that this acknowledgment is useful to us — " our final reason for accepting it is its value "; and a " realized ideal " is after all fundamentally an ideal, and owes its existence as such and whatever power it may exert to its erection into an ideal, not to its historical embodiment, if it chances to be historically embodied, in a person. " No system of truth which shall dominate the mind and claim authority over the conduct of men," we will remember, " can rest upon the reality of any historical personality."

It is scarcely necessary to multiply examples further. We may pass from instance to instance; but do not escape from a common circle of ideas. R. Roberts assumes to speak for the class, and may be accepted as doing so, when he announces [31] that " the supreme need of the hour in these matters is the disengagement of religion from its dependence on historical personalities." " Truth is truth," he declares, " whether uttered by Sophocles or Plato in Athens, by Hillel or Jesus in Palestine, by Seneca or Aurelius in Rome." " Religion, too, rests not on inspired or divine personalities, but on the order of the world." " And if, in the inevitable evolution of the not-distant future, Jesus too should disappear from the assured certainties of the world, man would not cease to be religious." P. W. Schmiedel — if we may take advantage of the vogue of his writings in their English form to refer to him here — speaks, with the greater caution of his better scholarship, of the prospect of the elimination of the figure of Jesus from " the assured certainties of the world ": " As a critical historian I can only say that I see no prospect of this." And it is a deeper note of personal appreciation of Jesus — and of indebtedness to Him — which he sounds. But the purport of his declaration is the same.

" My inmost religious convictions would suffer no harm, even if I now felt obliged to conclude that Jesus never lived. It would, of course, be a loss to me, if I could no longer look back and up to him

[31] *Hibbert Journal*, October, 1909, pp. 100–101.

as a historical person; but I should feel assured that the measure of piety which had long become a part of my nature could not be lost, because I could no longer derive it from him." [32]

Always there lie at the basis of the reasoning the twin assumptions of the old Rationalism: the assumption of the adequacy of pure reason to produce out of its own inalienable endowments the whole body of religious truth which it is necessary or possible for reasonable men to embrace, and the assumption of the inadequacy of history to lay a foundation of fact sufficiently assured to supply a firm basis on which the religious convictions and aspirations of reasonable men may rest. And always there is built upon these assumptions the denial that Christianity, — as it is a religion worthy of the acceptance of reasonable men, and actually exerting influence over reasonable men, and supplying the forms in which their religious life is expressed, — can possibly be dependent for its existence or power on any events or personalities in its past history, no matter how prominent a place these events or personalities may actually have occupied in its historical origination or its continued historical manifestation. The immediate motive which leads to this declaration of independence of historical events and personalities may differ from individual to individual: it is perhaps very commonly a feeling of uncertainty as to the actual historicity of the facts and personalities in question, and a desire to protect what is thought of as Christian faith from the danger incident to this uncertainty. The personal attitude of the reasoners towards Jesus may also differ greatly: most commonly, no doubt, a strong sense of indebtedness to Jesus and a deep feeling of reverence to him are preserved. But the general line of argument remains the same. History can give us only probabilities. Religion, therefore, which requires certainties, cannot be dependent on historical facts. Jesus is at best an historical fact. Christianity, therefore, as it is truly religion, cannot possibly be dependent on Jesus. So far accordingly as Christianity is

[32] "Jesus in Modern Criticism," E. T. 1907, p. 85.

truly religion, it must be independent of Jesus.[33] What are we to say to these things?

It can scarcely be expected that at this time of day the ancient debate with Rationalism should be taken up afresh and threshed out over again. Butler's " Analogy " is still extant, with its initial insistence upon probability as the guide of life, and its solid proof of the reasonableness of an historical revelation. It might not even be amiss to invite those to whom matters of fact appear to be intrinsically doubtful, or at least to become at once on occurrence incapable of establishment beyond "reasonable doubt," to bring their philosophy down to earth by a course of reading in such primary text-books as Greenleaf " On Evidence " and Ram " On Facts." Of course man is a religious being, and by the very necessity of his nature will have a religion. We have not needed to wait for W. Bousset to tell us [34] that religion has its seat in the aboriginal disposition of the reason, and we have only to look within ourselves to find it as the central fundamental law of our life. To name none other, John Calvin has told us long ago that, entering into the very constitution of man, and, above all else, distinguishing him from the brute, there is an ineradicable *sensus deitatis,* which — so far from lying inert within him — is a fertile *semen religionis;* and that accordingly all men

[33] Compare the description of this type of thought by Shirley Jackson Case, " The Historicity of Jesus," 1912, pp. 319 f.

[34] In his address at the Berlin Congress of Free Christianity, 1910, under the title, " Die Bedeutung der Person Jesu für den Glauben." History according to Bousset gives us only symbols, which cannot demonstrate, but only illustrate, the eternal ideas that reside in our bosoms. Founders of religions, Jesus among them, as historical entities, have their place among these symbols. Neither the certainty nor the contents of our faith can find its grounding in symbols. On the one hand, as regards Jesus, " What do we know that is historically certain of this Jesus of Nazareth, his life, his teaching and his person? " (p. 4). Yet, on the other, " the portrait of Jesus as it is depicted in the gospels by his immediate community, as romance and truth, remains and will remain more effective than all attempts at historical reconstruction, however exact they may be " (p. 17). Effective, that is, as a symbol; for as Wobbermin (" Geschichte und Historie in der Religionswissenschaft," 1911, pp. 47 f.) points out, Bousset leaves to Jesus no significance as source of religion.

have, and must needs have, religion. It is another question, however, whether this constitutional religion, which man cannot choose but have, is adequate to his need in the situation in which he actually finds himself, a situation which Eucken tells us has been most truly appreciated not by the optimists but the pessimists.[35] It is not obvious, to say the least, that a provision of nature must be competent also for unnatural conditions; that a power of living implies also a *vis naturae medicatrix* which in the presence of disease renders the exhibition of remedies impertinent. Though "pure reason" be sufficient for the religion of pure nature, what warrants the assumption that its sufficiency is unimpaired when nature is no longer pure?

It was the fault of the eighteenth century, in its pride of intellect and virtue, to neglect in its religious theorizing the evil case of man, and to proclaim under the name of "natural religion" an abstract scheme of a few meagre truths of reason as the sum of all religion, and, as such, the whole religious content of Christianity, the presently dominant religion, — which was thus represented as, so far as it was truly religious, "as old as creation." We have passed beyond the possibility of such shallow intellectualism now; we all repeat with avidity Bernhard Pünjer's caustic jibe that the difficulty with this so-called "natural religion" was that it was neither natural nor a religion. But have we bettered things in the essence of the matter? The misery of humanity may be more poignantly present to our consciousness, and even, in a sense, its sin; religion may be more prevalently thought of as "faith," rather than as opinion; the goodness of God may fill the whole horizon of our thought of him, and loving trust in his love form the entire reaction of our souls in his presence. But are we doing justice to that inexpugnable sense of guilt which constitutes the most fundamental and persistent deliverance of our moral consciousness? Shall we hope to soothe it to sleep

[35] See the striking passage on the radical evil which afflicts the human race in "Der Wahrheitsgehalt der Religion," 1st ed., 1901, pp. 72 f.; "The Truth of Religion, 1911, pp. 96 f.

with platitudes about the goodness of God; assurances that God is love, and that love will not reckon with sin? That deep moral self-condemnation which is present as a primary factor in all truly religious experience protests against all attempts merely to appease it. It cries out for satisfaction. No moral deduction can persuade it that forgiveness of sins is a necessary element in the moral order of the world. It knows on the contrary that indiscriminate forgiveness of sin would be precisely the subversion of the moral order of the world. The annulment of guilt is the annulment of the law of righteousness, out of the breach of which guilt arises; and the law of righteousness is only another name for the moral order of the world. There is a moral paradox in the forgiveness of sins which cannot be solved apart from the exhibition of an actual expiation. No appeal to general metaphysical or moral truths concerning God can serve here; or to the essential kinship of human nature to God; or, for the matter of that, to any example of an attitude of trust in the divine goodness upon the part of a religious genius, however great, or to promises of forgiveness made by such a one, or even — may we say it with reverence — made by God himself, unsupported by the exhibition of an actual expiation. The sinful soul, in throes of self-condemnation, is concerned with the law of righteousness ingrained in his very nature as a moral being, and cannot be satisfied with goodness, or love, or mercy, or pardon. He cries out for expiation. And expiation, in its very nature, is not a principle but a fact, an event which takes place, if at all, in the conditions of time and space. A valid religion for sinful man includes in it, accordingly, of necessity an historical element, an actually wrought expiation for its sin. It is the very nerve of Christianity and the essence of its appeal to men — by virtue of which it has won its way in the world — that it provides this historical element and proclaims an actual expiation of human sin. As it has been eloquently put: [36]

[36] Otto Kirn, "Glaube und Geschichte," 1900, pp. 47–48. Cf. the whole passage, pp. 47–50.

" Only the fact that Christ stands out in history as surety of the gracious will of God, that in God's name he punishes sin and calls the sinner to himself, that in holy suffering he endures the lot of sinners in order to convict them of their sin and free them from it, that as the Risen One he brings them the assurance of justification and of eternal life, is able to transform human seeking after salvation into finding. Severed from this fact which forms its very essence, faith is nothing, an empty desire, a question without an answer."

It would be sad for humanity, needing thus above all things an actual expiation that it may have warrant to trust in God's forgiving love, if no such warrant can be given it because of the inability of the human mind to attain certainty with reference to matters of fact. It is, indeed, difficult to see how man could sustain his being and prosecute his common tasks in the world, if matters of fact are intrinsically uncertain, or become immediately uncertain on their occurrence. Man is, after all said, a creature of time and space, and all that he does and all that he experiences takes place in the conditions of time and space, and becomes at once on taking place matter of history. He could acquire no knowledge whatever, the whole discipline of life would be lost to him, if uncertainty were really the mark of the historical. We deceive ourselves, for instance, if we fancy we may distinguish in principle between historical facts as uncertain and scientific facts as certain. As Lessing reminds us, we cannot base certainties on uncertainties; and the material of all the sciences is in point of fact historical. "Every science," observes Eberhard Vischer,[37] "builds its conclusions on the particular experiences which men have had. Every observation in the natural sciences, every experiment, gives us in the first instance not knowledge of what is, but of what at the moment of the observation, of the experiment, the observer experiences. . . .

[37] *Zeitschrift für Theologie und Kirche*, 1898, p. 200, article on " Die geschichtliche Gewissheit und der Glaube an Jesus Christus." Compare also his lecture on " Jesus Christus in der Geschichte," Tübingen, 1912, where the discussion is more popular in form.

An experience had by the scientific observer, therefore an historical fact, is the foundation-stone on which is grounded, as in general the entire conduct of man, so also all scientific attainment." If, then, historical facts are by their very nature uncertain, — "if nothing that befalls man can be certainly known, then all scientific certainty whatever passes into the realm of the impossible."

It may be suspected that the current assumption that historical facts cannot rise above probabilities, derives at least some of its force and persistency from a confusion of two senses of the word "probable." As the opposite of "demonstrative," "probable" refers to the nature of the ground on which the judgment of truth or reality rests; as the opposite of "certain" it refers to the measure of assurance which the grounds on which this judgment rests are adapted to produce. Historical facts may be "only probable" in the one usage and yet not less than "certain" in the other. This ambiguity of the term seems to be reflected in a certain embarrassment which is observable in its use in the present connection. Thus G. B. Foster talks of historical evidence as capable of producing only "probable certainty"; Otto Kirn of it as producing at best only "relative certainty"; while Heinrich von Sybel declares it able to produce "conclusive certainty," — which he then explains by the further declaration that "historical science is capable of attaining to altogether exact knowledge." [38] "Conclusive certainty" is of course pleonastic, and "probable certainty," "relative certainty," are contradictions in terms, the employment of which only bears witness to the feeling of the writers using them that after all historical facts are, or may be, "certain." Let it go at that. In point of fact, there is nothing more certain than a matter of fact: what is, certainly is; and the certainty of demonstration cannot be more sure than the certainty of experience. It is no more sure that two and two make four, than that the two nuts which I have in each hand when brought together are

[38] Ueber die Gesetze des historischen Wissens," 2. Abdruck, 1864, p. 17; or in "Vorträge und Aufsätze," 1874, p. 11.

four, — though I arrive at my certainty in the one case *a priori* by demonstrative reasoning, and in the other *a posteriori* by actual experience. The ground of certainty in both cases is my confidence in my faculties.

It may be urged, to be sure, that history, as commonly spoken of, deals only with past experiences, and it is only present experience which is " certain." But experience does not cease to be experience with the passage of time: and (as it has been well phrased) " reality that has been made " is no less reality than "reality in the making "; "reality once ' made,' is ' made ' for ever." [39] If what is, certainly is, then what has been, just as certainly has been; and its actuality as matter of fact is not in the least disturbed by the irrelevant circumstance that it has occurred at one point of time rather than at another. Indeed, as the writer just cited playfully points out, distance of time may be neutralized by distance in space. To an observer on the dog-star, earthly events which to an observer on earth occurred a generation ago are present-day facts; and by merely stationing ourselves at the proper distance we may recover any occurrence of the past to "immediate perception." We cannot, to be sure, take our post of observation at will in Orion or the Pleiades, but we need not on that account cast the actuality of the actual into doubt or declare ourselves incapable of assuring ourselves of it. If free transportation through the immeasurable reaches of space is denied us, there are other ways of getting at the actualities of the past which we need not on that account deny ourselves.

For one thing, we need not persist in looking at past occurrences as each an isolated event, standing absolutely out of relation with all other events, up to which therefore no lines of approach lead. Past events still live in other vibrations also, besides those which, trembling through the ether, carry notification of their occurrence to the depths of space. Everything that occurs affects everything else that occurs, and history must be conceived not merely as a series of linked

[39] F. R. Tennant, " Historical Fact in Relation to the Philosophy of Religion." *Hibbert Journal,* viii. 1909–1910, p. 173.

chains passing side by side through time; but as one woven network covering the whole past, and running with unbroken web through the present into the illimitable future. Not by one line only but by manifold lines, therefore, we can travel from any point which for the moment may chance to be the present, over the woven pattern of the fabric to any other point, which holds changelessly its proper position in the whole, and its fixed relations to all the other parts of it. Of course, such creatures as we are cannot contemplate the whole pattern in all its details; we are like insects climbing slowly along a thread of some tapestry. There are myriads of occurrences of even the recent past which are gone beyond all hope of recovery. At best we can know a few of the events that have occurred, and them only in part. But the past is not singular in this. We do not know the present, even that present with which we are most intimately concerned, in all of its details, or in any of its details perfectly. We know nothing except in part. Every sparklet of human knowledge shines out from a limitless surrounding of obscurity. But we can yet know truly where we can know only in part. And because we cannot know all the past, we must not therefore fancy that we can know nothing that is past. There are occurrences which stand out so brightly against the enveloping darkness, which have wrought so powerfully on the course of events that have succeeded them, which are connected with us by so many and so deeply marked lines of effects, that we might as well pretend not to be able to see the sun in the heavens as not to be able to perceive them looming in the past, however distant. There are no doubt some who do not see the sun. They are blind.

Whether the origins of the Christian religion belong to this class of outstanding facts — the great peaks rising out of the plain with such prominence that no observer looking over the field of history can miss them — is merely a question of the evidence. This evidence is, however, of the most compelling and varied kind. It is not merely documentary, subject to those processes of testing which we lump together under the name of criticism. It is institutional as well; and it is more than institutional. The seed out of which Christianity has grown may be known, like other seed, by that which has grown out of it: "by their fruits ye shall know them." Christianity itself is a witness to the nature of its origins; and to Christianity must be added the whole world in its development through two thousand years. It is futile to ask, as has been asked with the processes of historical criticism in mind: "Is any one entitled to believe, or to ask others to believe, in specific historical matters of fact except upon historical evidence?"[40] The question is already answered by Lessing in that striking refutation of his own historical skepticism which he gives in his "Axiomata":[41]

"There is still one question over which I cannot wonder enough, which the Herr Pastor puts with a confidence that seems to imply that only one answer is possible. 'Had the New Testament books not been written, and had they not come down to us,' he asks, 'would there have remained in the world a trace of what Jesus did and taught?' God forbid that I should ever think so meanly of Christ's teaching as to dare to answer this question with a No. No, I would not repeat such a No, even had an angel from heaven dictated it to me, to say nothing of a case where it is only a Lutheran pastor who would put it into my mouth. All that occurs in the world leaves traces in the world behind it, even though men can not always point them out at once; and should Thy teaching only, divine Friend of man, which Thou didst command, not to be written but to be preached, have effected nothing, absolutely nothing, from which its origin might be recognized? Should Thy words have been words of life only when transformed into dead letters?"

[40] A. O. Lovejoy, *Hibbert Journal*, v. January, 1907, p. 269. Cf. the much more cautious statement of O. Ritschl, "Zeitschrift für Theologie und Kirche," iii. 1893, p. 376. *Per contra,* cf. Eberhard Vischer, "Jesus Christus in der Geschichte," 1912, pp. 35 f.: had the historical records preserved for us no single intimation of the existence of a Dante, the existence of the Divina Commedia would compel his postulation, and had historical records preserved for us no single intimation of the existence of Jesus Christ, — or, what comes to the same thing, should historical criticism obliterate every existing intimation of his existence, — there are effects about us, quite as palpable as the Divina Commedia, which would compel his postulation.

[41] Lessing's "sämtliche Schriften," Lachmann's ed., xiii. p. 120.

We are not fleeing from the results of historical criticism to take refuge in the argument from effects. We shall appeal, indeed, from a naturalistically biased to an unbiased historical criticism; but we shall have no difficulty in trusting the latter to give us not only an actual Jesus, but a supernatural Christ, and in Him a supernatural redemption. We are only concerned now to point out that even such a vindication of the fact-basis of Christianity on historico-critical grounds does not exhaust the evidence for it; that there is still further evidence of the richest and most varied kind for the origin of Christianity in a supernatural founder; that there is, for example, the evidence from effects, which, resting as it does on the causal judgment, has much of the quality of demonstration.[42] "What then is it," asks a recent writer,[43] "which gives us knowledge of what has been?" "Three things," he answers, "monuments, traditions, effects"; and then he adds another well-known saying of Lessing's: "When the paralytic *experiences* the healing shocks of the electric spark, what does he care whether Nollet or Franklin, or neither of them, is right?"[44] — and concludes: "So may the pious man be of good courage, while the learned are disputing over particular problems of the gospel-history. But as to the presence and as to the nature of the power which then came into the world, he too has a little word to say." He has. And though this "little word" may not be quite the same word which either this writer or Lessing might suggest, it is a word which has supreme value, and which combines with the abundant evidence from other quarters and of other orders to render the facts which belong to the origins of Christianity

[42] The value of the argument from effects in establishing historical facts is expounded at length by Eberhard Vischer as cited above, and applied in detail to the facts of the Christian origins. Cf. the review of the lecture, "Jesus Christus in der Geschichte," in *The Princeton Theological Review* for October, 1912, pp. 654–659.

[43] *Christliche Welt*, February 17, 1910, coll. 162–163.

[44] Axiomata, 1778; Lessing's "sämtliche Schriften," Lachmann's ed., xiii. p. 134. Lessing is in this passage defending this proposition as previously made by him, and denying that he considers this experimental evidence the only convincing evidence of the truth of Christianity.

the most certain of all the facts which have occurred in the world.[45]

We are not absurdly undertaking to prove the historicity of Jesus in ten words. Happily, our present task does not require this proof of us; and happily also, as has already been intimated, the work has been perhaps sufficiently done for us — though in many more than ten words — by a multitude of recent writers who have sprung to the defence of the historicity of Jesus against its denial by the new radicalism most prominently represented at present by Arthur Drews. One of the results of the promulgation of this denial for which we may be thankful has been that some check has been put upon the less guarded expression of historical skepticism on the part of the liberal theologians, and there has been called out some stronger assertion and fuller exposition of the more positive side of their conception of the historical origins of Christianity than it has been usual for them to give.[46] This has been a gain. Much has, no doubt, been left to be desired, but it has been pleasant to see such writers as W. Bousset and Johannes Weiss take up even so far the rôle of " apologists." What we have been attempting to do is merely, by a brief statement of the actual state of the case with reference to the historicity of Jesus, to wash in a background against which the true character and significance of the Christless Christianity which is being exploited about us may be thrown up into clear relief. There really is no occasion for a panic with reference to the historicity of Jesus; and there is no need of such drastic measures as those pursued by the promulgators of our Christless Christianity to allay the rising panic with respect to it. It is only among the old Liberals and — on somewhat different grounds — the members of the school of Ritschl that panic

[45] " Jesus," says Erich Foerster (*Christliche Welt*, 1909, col. 1249), " is a fact in the history of our race, and this fact cannot be eliminated by any dilettantism, however scientifically garnished. He who does not wish to turn his back on all reality must recognize it and adjust himself to it."

[46] Heinrich Weinel, " Ist dast ' liberale ' Jesusbild widerlegt? " 1910, has been particularly candid in chiding his colleagues for their excesses in the one direction and their shortcomings in the other.

here is natural. The mordant criticism of the evangelical
history practised by the old liberals has left them without
defence when this criticism is pressed a step further and the
historicity of Jesus is denied, — requiring, though they do,
the historicity of Jesus not only to account for the origin of
Christianity according to their view of its origin, but to give
distinctiveness and distinction to their conception of what
Christianity is. It has been the peculiarity of the school of
Ritschl, in its effort to preserve Christianity from destruction
by the assaults of historical criticism no less than by those of
philosophy and science, to proclaim the independence of faith
of all historical facts as well as of all metaphysical notions.
What defence have they when the fact of Christ is included
in the facts of which Christianity is independent? Yet "the
fact of Christ" bears with them the whole weight of Christianity.[47] Our Christless Christians have passed beyond all
this. Indifference to Christ may have much the same practical
effects as denial of the existence of Jesus; but it is a specifically different attitude and throws into the foreground specifically different questions. It has no interest in the historicity
of Jesus. It has no interest in the living Christ. Its sole interest
is in Christianity. It does not follow, however, that the historicity of Jesus has no bearing on it; or the nature of the
Jesus who is historical. Conceivably, a real Jesus may be more
difficult to ignore than an imaginary one; especially if the
Jesus that is real is a Jesus whom it is not easy to ignore, who
has brought into the world influences and set at work forces
which cannot be disregarded or escaped. In any event it is
important to approach the consideration of Christless Christianity with a clear understanding that the Christ it would
ignore is not a doubtful Christ but a real Christ, is not an inert
Christ but an active Christ.[48]

[47] On the Ritschlian attitude to historical facts and its sequences cf.
E. Cremer, "Der Glaube und die Thatsachen," in "Greifswalder Studien:
theologische Abhandlungen Hermann Cremer . . . dargebracht," 1895, pp.
261–283; G. Vos, "Christian Faith and the Truthfulness of Bible History,"
in The Princeton Theological Review, iv. 1906, pp. 289–305.

[48] Richard Rothe even a half-century ago sounded a warning against

The particular question raised meanwhile by Christless Christianity is not that of the historicity of Jesus but that of the nature of Christianity, or, as it is fashionable nowadays to phrase it, "the essence of Christianity." It is only when "Christianity" has come to be looked upon as little more than a modern man's "religious reaction upon the whole realm of reality — past and present — available for him," "the total embodiment of the actual religious attainments of modern men in a modern environment" — whatever this "reaction," these "attainments," may chance to be — as it has been described by a not wholly unsympathetic historian,[49] that the question of the indifference of "Christianity" to Jesus can be seriously raised. Douglas C. Macintosh[50] very frankly allows that to all that has hitherto borne the name of Christianity the historicity of Jesus has been indispensable, or, to speak more adequately, the living Jesus has stood at the very centre of thought and faith. To the "early disciples of Jesus," whose faith hinged on the messiahship of Jesus; to "the Greek Christian development," whose entire teaching and trust turned on the reality of a divine incarnation in humanity; to "Christian faith in its mediaeval form, whether Romanist or Protestant," which grounded all its hope in the substitutive sacrifice of the God-man — to all these alike Jesus forms the very core of Christianity. It is only when historical — or if the word pleases better, traditional — Christianity has suffered a sea-change and become "the Christianity of to-day," that it can be contented that "the disproof or rendering seriously doubtful of the historicity of Jesus need not mean the disappearance of any essential content from the Christian religion." The question thus concerns not Christianity in its historical sense, but "our religion," "of to-day"; and it might

attempting to root faith in the *merely* historical Jesus, who lived and died two thousand years ago. "If," he declared, "this Christ is not to be altogether ignored and stricken out of history, if he is to be permitted to play any rôle and to be believed in at all, he must absolutely be conceived also as the *living* Christ."

[49] S. J. Case, as cited, p. 321.
[50] *American Journal of Theology*, xv. July, 1911, pp. 364 f.

perhaps be better phrased, not, Is Christ essential to the Christian faith? but, Is the so-called Christianity of today to which Christ is not essential still Christian?

Ernst Troeltsch has treated the matter more at large and with his wonted thoroughness and candor in a lecture which he has recently published under the title of " The Significance of the Historicity of Jesus for Faith." [51] The question which he here raises is twofold: first, whether it is "still" possible to speak of an inner essential significance of Jesus for faith; and secondly, whether, that being answered in the negative, the historicity of Jesus is therefore indifferent to the " Christianity" which alone remains possible for modern culture. This latter question also Troeltsch answers with a negative, and thus comes forward as the advocate of the indispensableness of Jesus to even the most attenuated faith which still cares to call itself Christian. " So long as there exists a Christianity in any sense whatever it will be bound up with the central place of Christ in worship."

The word "still" in the former member of Troeltsch's question intimates that in his view a change has taken place in men's conception of what Christianity is and imports, and that it is only because of this change that the question suggested can be raised. Troeltsch does not hesitate to speak of this change as a veritable " transformation [52] of Christianity." Formerly Christians have believed in a divine Christ "propitiating God and thus freeing men from the consequences of their infection with original sin." To raise the question of the historicity of Jesus from this standpoint would be simply to call in question the right of Christianity to exist. It is only when we have learned, like David Friedrich Strauss (in his Christian period), to distinguish between the principle of Christianity and the person of Christ, and have come to see that what we call Christianity is just " a particular faith in God, a peculiar knowledge of God, with its corresponding

[51] " Die Bedeutung der Geschichtlichkeit Jesu für den Glauben," Tübingen, 1911. Cf. the review of it in *The Princeton Theological Review* for October, 1912, pp. 647–654.
[52] " Umwandelung," p. 8.

mode of life, or, as it is called, a religious idea, a religious principle," — so that there is no historical redemptive work postulated in the background, — that we may ask ourselves with any meaning whether there exists any necessity for the assumption of an historical Jesus. Even on this ground, however, a negative answer is not to be taken for granted. There even exist some who have come so far, — to whom therefore "redemption is not something once for all completed in the work of Christ, and thereafter only to be applied to individuals, but an occurrence continually completing itself afresh in the action of God on the soul by means of the knowledge of God" wrought by faith, — to whom a negative answer is still impossible. This is because they "connect this redeeming faith-knowledge with the knowledge and recollection of the historical personality of Jesus, although this comes into consideration with them, not in its miraculous element, nor in its particular teachings, but only in the total effect of the religious personality." It is "the later, ecclesiastical Schleiermacher" that Troeltsch has in view here, and especially Ritschl and Herrmann. With them "all notion of a historical redemptive miracle, occurring once for all," indeed, is lacking; but with them also the faith-knowledge that constitutes Christianity is "bound to the historical personality of Christ, by which alone power or certitude is lent it." In this, he contends, there is betrayed lurking at the back of the brain a remnant of the old doctrine of original sin; there persists a notion "of the essential incapacity of men who do not know Christ for hearty faith in God." To such a conception, questioning of the historicity of Jesus were as fatal as to the old orthodoxy itself. Only when we occupy ground which allows no inward necessity for the assumption of an historical Jesus, can we discuss with any meaning whether the historical Jesus is indispensable to Christianity.

Troeltsch himself occupies this ground, and therefore admits that the indispensableness of Jesus to Christianity is to him a legitimate matter of debate. He holds very decided views, however, in the matter. Even on this ground he argues

— and it is the chief purpose of his lecture to argue this — that Christianity cannot get along without Jesus. His argument is based on considerations derived from the history of religions and religious psychology, and amounts in general to the contention that religion is, after all said, a social affair and cannot persist without cultus and communion; while these require a rallying-centre, which must be envisaged as real; and this rallying-centre in the present stage of culture cannot be anything but Jesus Christ. The persistence of even this type of religious belief hangs thus on the historicity of Jesus, and whenever, if ever (Troeltsch thinks they will never), the results of historical research shall prove unfavorable to the historicity of Jesus, then the death-knell of even this type of religious faith is sounded. This is, he assures us, the last word of social-psychological research in the realm of religion.[53]

The question thus defined and debated is, however, little more than an academic one. Troeltsch does not pretend that the extremely attenuated "Christianity" to which alone the question of the indispensableness of the historical Jesus has meaning, possesses vitality as a religion. Individuals may profess it and do profess it; he professes it himself; but the churches in which religious life is rich and powerful, are, he tells us, of a very different faith. We may be interested to know that even in this, its most attenuated form, "Christianity" cannot, in the opinion of one of our chief masters in the psychology and phenomenology of religion, dispense with Jesus. But the real question which presses for an answer is whether this very attenuated "Christianity," in which alone the question of the indispensableness of Jesus to Christianity can with any meaning be raised, possesses any just claim upon the name of Christianity. Its adherents are no doubt prompt in asserting their right to the name. But the allowance of their

[53] " In the central position cf the personality of Jesus, Christianity does not possess a distinguishing peculiarity, separating it from all other religions, and for the first time making redemption possible, but only fulfils a general law of the spiritual life of man after a fashion peculiar to itself " (p. 42).

claim depends upon the prior question of what precisely Christianity is, and what kinds of "transformation" it can suffer without ceasing to be Christianity. If Christianity is only a particular way of conceiving God, with the emotional and volitional accompaniments and consequences of this way of conceiving God, then no doubt a particular way of conceiving God may claim to be Christianity, — that is, if it be the particular way of conceiving God which Christianity is. If Christianity, however, be anything more than just a way of conceiving God, it is hard to see what just claim a mere way of conceiving God can put in to the name.

We should not omit to note in passing that Troeltsch goes a step further than contending that Jesus is indispensable to Christianity even in that attenuated form of so-called Christianity to which he gives his adhesion. He contends that no other form of religion than this attenuated Christianity with Jesus enshrined at its centre can exist in the conditions of modern life. In a word, Jesus is to him indispensable to religion in the conditions of modern life. This is not, to be sure, quite the same as saying with Heinrich Weinel, that "after Jesus it is his religion or none." Troeltsch is not prepared to declare Christianity "the eternal religion," which can never be transcended. But he is prepared to insist that Christianity — of course, in the interpretation of Christianity which commends itself to him — is so bound up with, and gives such competent expression to, the religious side of the civilization of the Mediterranean basin, that so long as that civilization endures, so long must Christianity remain the only religion possible to civilized humanity. It is possible, of course, that the civilization of the Mediterranean basin may after a while be replaced by a still higher civilization; and then, no doubt, there will arise a new form of religious expression conformable to the new civilization. Christianity is thus not pronounced by Troeltsch the final, the absolute religion, but merely the only religion possible to the highest civilization as yet known to man. His defence of the indispensableness of Jesus means, then, only that we cannot in his opinion get along at present without Jesus.[54] After a while — who can tell? — as we advance beyond our present stage of culture, we may advance also beyond Christianity as a possible religion, and beyond the need of Jesus as the religious rallying-point of men.

The question of course springs at once into the mind whether, in thus representing Christianity as merely the natural and therefore necessary religion for the civilization of the Mediterranean basis, and Jesus as indispensable only for the religion belonging to that civilization, — which is not final but may pass away, — Troeltsch has not rendered this Christianity impossible as a religion for himself at least — if not for the Mediterranean basin — and thus emancipated himself from Jesus as the indispensable rallying-point of his religion. He himself certainly thus assumes a standpoint above the Christianity which he conceives as — at least possibly — only a stage in the journey of man towards the absolute religion, and he cannot possibly belong inwardly to its life-world. Can he, then, look to Jesus, the inspiring centre of this life-world, as really indispensable to his own faith? Must he not stand as much above the need of the inspiration of Jesus as he stands above the religious life which Jesus inspires, and so by his own definition exclude himself from the Christian name? [55]

[54] Troeltsch's remarks in this connection provide a useful commentary upon the discussion in his "Die Absolutheit des Christentums und die Religionsgeschichte," 1902. The adherents of Christianity as of all other religions, he tells us there, live in a naïve belief in the absoluteness of their religion, due to failure to compare it with others and a natural estimate of their actual knowledge of the higher life as ultimate and unique. Christianity's claim to absoluteness is, no doubt, the most inwardly free and universal of all; and when Christianity has attained its new form, in which alone it appeals to modern man, it comes near to justification. Troeltsch can even say: "The claim itself" — i.e., to absoluteness — "has nowhere as yet been refuted or surmounted, and no imagination is capable of excogitating such a surmounting; and so it remains that no other foundation is laid for the soul's health of mankind except Jesus Christ" (p. 126). After a while, however, we here learn, it is possible that a new and better foundation may be laid. On the whole matter cf. C. W. Hodge, "The Finality of the Christian Religion," in Biblical and Theological Studies by the Members of the Faculty of Princeton Theological Seminary, 1912, especially pp. 477 f.; also F. X. Kiefl, "Der geschichtliche Christus und die moderne Philosophie," pp. 61–74.

[55] Otto Kirn, "Glaube und Geschichte," 1900, pp. 31–32, speaking of the

In any event, by his refusal to recognize the Christianity to which, he argues, Jesus is indispensable, as "the eternal religion," Troeltsch certainly takes his place among those who deny that Jesus is indispensable to the religion, if not of today, yet of tomorrow.

Meanwhile why should the definition of the essence of Christianity be so vexed? Why should there be so much controversy over the application of the name? There surely ought to be little difficulty in determining what Christianity is. We need not disturb ourselves greatly about the debate which has been somewhat vigorously prosecuted as to whether its definition should be derived from its New Testament presentation or from its whole historical manifestation.[56] Impure as the development of Christianity has been, imperfect as has always been its manifestation, corrupt as has often been its expression, it has always presented itself to the world, as a whole, substantially under one unvarying form. Unquestionably, Christianity is a redemptive religion, having as its fundamental presupposition the fact of sin, felt both as guilt and as pollution, and offering as its central good, from which all other goods proceed, salvation from sin through an historical expiation wrought by the God-man Jesus Christ. The essence of Christianity has always been to its adherents the sinner's experience of reconciliation with God through the propitiatory sacrifice of Jesus Christ. According to the Synoptic tradition Jesus Himself represented Himself as having come to seek and to save that which is lost, and described His salvation as a

---

demand of faith for absoluteness, remarks: " A simply provisional revelation, a merely relative religious truth, an only probable reconciliation with God, and a purely conjectural assurance of salvation, — these are, not merely for a church, but for the religious nature, intolerable ideas. A religion which would see in Christ only a transition point of the religious development of mankind would have, even in an historical judgment, no right whatever to call itself Christian."

[56] J. Weiss, " Jesus von Nazareth," 1910, p. 7: " That the ' essence of Christianity ' is to be found not merely in the New Testament, but in the entire fulness of its historical phenomena, there should today be no longer doubt." Cf. E. Vischer, " Ist die Wahrheit des Christentums zu beweisen? " 1902, p. 16.

ransoming of many by the gift of His life, embodying this conception, moreover, in the ritual act which He commanded His disciples to perform in remembrance of Him. Certainly His first followers with single-hearted unanimity proclaimed the great fact of redemption in the blood of Christ as the heart of their gospel: to them Jesus is the propitiation for sin, a sacrificial lamb without blemish, and all their message is summed up in the simple formula of " Jesus Christ and Him as crucified." Nor has the church He founded ever drifted away from this fundamental point of view, as witness the central place of the mass in the worship of its elder branches, and the formative place of justification by faith in Protestant life.[57] No doubt parties have from time to time arisen who have wished to construe Christianity otherwise. But they have always occupied a place on the periphery of the Christian movement, and have never constituted its main stream.

We can well understand that one swirling aside in an eddy and yet wishing to think of himself as travelling with the current — or even perhaps as breaking for it a new and better channel — should attempt to define Christianity so widely

---

[57] Emil Sulze may be adduced in passing as a witness to this fact. Writing on " Die notwendige Umgegstaltung der evangelischen Glaubenslehre " (*Protestantische Monatsheft*, xi. 1907, pp. 250 f.), he declares that " the greatest danger has been brought, as to the moral life so also to faith in God, by the circumstance that the old Protestantism held fast to the foundation-stone of Catholicism, to the doctrine of the substitutive satisfaction of Christ." He is deeply grieved, therefore, that the Protestant churches of Germany still sing:

> Mein Gewissen beisst mich nicht,
> Moses kann mich nicht verklagen.
> Der mich frei und ledig spricht,
> hat die Schulden abgetragen.

To make it truly " Christian," this verse, he declares, must be transformed into this:

> Klagt mich mein Gewissen an,
> lässt doch Gott mich nicht verzagen,
> stärkt mich auf der Leidensbahn,
> hilft mir Schuld und Strafe tragen.

The antipodal attitudes to redemption of the Old Protestantism and the " transformation " which would fain present itself as a New Protestantism could not be more vividly expressed.

or so vaguely as to make it embrace him also. The attempt has
never been and can never be successful. He is a Christian, in
the sense of the founders of the Christian religion, and in the
sense of its whole historical manifestation as a world-phenomenon, who, conscious of his sin, and smitten by a sense of
the wrath of God impending over him, turns in faith to Jesus
Christ as the propitiation for his sins, through whose blood
and righteousness he may be made acceptable to God and be
received into the number of those admitted to communion
with Him. If we demand the right to call ourselves Christians
because it is by the teaching of Jesus that we have learned
to know God as He really is, or because it is by his example
that we have been led into a life of faithful trust in God, or
because it is by the inspiration of His " inner life," dimly
discerned through the obscuring legends which have grown
up about Him, that we are quickened to a like religious hope
and aspiration, — we are entering claims that have never been
recognized and can never be recognized as valid by the main
current of Christianity. Christianity as a world-movement is
the body of those who have been redeemed from their sins
by the blood of Jesus Christ, dying for them on the cross.
The cross is its symbol; and in its heart sounds the great jubilation of the Apocalypse: " Unto Him that loveth us and
loosed us from our sins by his blood; and he made us to be a
kingdom, to be priests unto his God and Father; to Him be
the glory and the dominion forever and ever. Amen."

A Christianity without redemption — redemption in the
blood of Jesus Christ as a sacrifice for sin — is nothing less
than a contradiction in terms.[58] Precisely what Christianity

[58] It is of course generally recognized that Christianity is in its essence
a religion of redemption. See for example its exposition as such by Eucken,
" The Truth of Religion," E. T. 1911, pp. 10 f., where Christianity is described
as specifically the religion of redemption from sin. But, as Troeltsch expresses it, the idea of redemption has been " transformed " to suit modern
notions. It often happens, therefore, that definitions of Christianity recognize
the specific peculiarity of Christianity in words while evaporating it in meaning. Thus Schleiermacher (" Glaubenslehre," 2te Aufl., § 11) describes Christianity as " a monotheistic form of faith belonging to the teleological tendency
of piety, distinguished from other similar forms of faith essentially by this —

means is redemption in the blood of Jesus. No one need wonder therefore that, when redemption is no longer sought and found in Jesus, men should begin to ask whether there remains any real necessity for Jesus. We may fairly contend that the germ of Christless Christianity is present wherever a proper doctrine of redemption has fallen away or even has only been permitted to pass out of sight. Of course in the meantime some other function than proper redemption may be found for Jesus. We are not insensible, for example, of the importance of the function assigned to Him in, say, the Ritschlian theology; and we quite agree when Troeltsch urges that to the proper Ritschlians, therefore, Jesus is indispensable. But we cannot close our eyes to the artificiality of the Ritschlian construction, and we cannot put away the impression that the indispensable rôle assigned to Jesus, as it rests rather on inherited reverence for His person than on the logic of the system, is, in a word, only an interim-measure. Why should an influence from Jesus be needed to awake man to faith-knowledge? And how could such a creative influence be exerted by a personality so slightly known, or an " inner life " so vaguely discerned through the mists of time? Herrmann, for example, expressly denies that there is any direct communion of the believer with the exalted Christ; everything is mediated through the " community." All this, therefore, will easily fall away and the actual influence which begets faith be assigned, as Otto Ritschl, for instance, does assign it, to the " community," [59] while to Jesus there is left little more than the

that in it everything is referred to redemption accomplished by Jesus of Nazareth." Here the wide genus to which Christianity is assigned is monotheistic religion, and the proximate genus, teleological (that is, ethical monotheistic) religion, while its differentia within this proximate genus is found in the fact that " in it everything is referred to redemption accomplished by Jesus of Nazareth." If they could be read without reference to the special use of terms by their framers, definitions such as this might be taken as loose descriptions of what Christianity really is. They bear witness to the difficulty experienced by writers of a different point of view in escaping from accustomed terminology.

[59] *Zeitschrift für Theologie und Kirche*, iii. 1893, p. 388. In the number of the *Zeitschrift für Theologie und Kirche* for July, 1912 (pp. 244-268), which

rôle of first Christian. And so soon as Jesus becomes merely the first Christian, He at once, as Macintosh justly urges,[60] ceases to be indispensable for subsequent Christians. Why should not they, as well as He, rise out of the void? He may be the first of the series: that is an accident. Being the first of the series He may have set an example which works powerfully through all subsequent time; He may even have left precepts and directions which smooth the path of all who would adventure the Christian walk with Him; above all He may have by His " inner life " of perfect trust in His Father become an inspiration which throbs down all the years. He may, in other words, be exceedingly useful. But indispensable? To be indispensable He must be something more than a teacher, an example, an inspiration. He must be a creator. And to be a creator, He must be and do something far more than the first Christian, living in realization of the fatherhood of God. Whenever Jesus is reduced in His person or work to the level of His " followers," His indispensableness is already in principle subverted and the seeds of a Christless Christianity are planted.

---

has come to hand since this article was sent to the printer, Wilhelm Fresenius subjects Troeltsch's Lecture to a detailed criticism from the Ritschlian standpoint and in the name of the Ritschlians repudiates the representation that the historicity of Jesus is indispensable to faith. Ritschlians mean only, it seems, that they themselves find in Jesus what they need for faith: they do not mean that others may not attain faith by some other way (p. 250). With them " faith rests not on ' historischen ' but on ' geschichtlichen ' facts," that is to say, on genuine " life-experiences "; and (p. 262) " accordingly faith can look quietly on while criticism does its work, and openly accept its results: it could even endure that the unhistoricity of Jesus should be proved — a thing which, to be sure, has not been done and which sober historical criticism, moreover, will scarcely maintain is likely to be done in the future, — but in principle this case would not turn the scale for faith, that is, so long as faith remains conscious that it is of historical (geschichtlichen) nature and the historical (geschichtliche) fact on which it bases itself ultimately, can be neither established nor refuted by historical (historischen) science. According to Fresenius, therefore, it is a matter of indifference to Ritschlians whether there ever was any " historical Jesus " or not: it is only necessary that they should have had a genuine " experience." This is a full-fledged " Christless Christianity."

[60] *American Journal of Theology*, xvi. January, 1912, p. 110.

The application of this principle will, no doubt, carry us far. When Auguste Sabatier, for example, tells us[61] that the whole of Christianity is summed up in the parables of the prodigal son and of the publican, he is intent only on abolishing from Christianity the idea of satisfaction. But does he not by necessary consequence with it abolish also Jesus Himself, so far as His indispensableness to the Christian religion is concerned? In point of fact, these parables have a Jesus in them as little as a satisfaction. Sabatier very naturally teaches us, therefore, that there is no uniqueness in Christ's work, nothing in it " isolated and incomprehensible." "The sufferings and death of the righteous and the good operate in the same way as the passion of Christ upon the conscience of the wicked "; "all God's servants" have stood by the side of Jesus as, along with Him and in the same sense (though not in the same degree), our saviours. We need not, however, journey so far from home for an example. When Horace Bushnell expends the first Part of his "Vicarious Sacrifice" in proving that there is " nothing superlative in vicarious sacrifice, or above the universal principles of right and duty," that in what Christ did, He did " neither more nor less than what the common standard of holiness and right requires," and what was "no way peculiar to him, save in degree," he has already thrown the door wide open for a Christless Christianity.[62] He may himself be preoccupied in vindicating to Jesus some kind of uniqueness, if not in the nature, yet in the effect of His work. But this is not intrinsic to the system, and easily falls away. The assimilation of Christ to His followers in the nature of His work and the kind of effect wrought by it is logically fatal to His indispensableness to the religion of which He is still thought of as the founder.

There are other forms of teaching, also, that have enjoyed great vogue, in which the indispensableness of Jesus is, to say

[61] " The Doctrine of the Atonement, and its Historical Evolution," E. T. 1904, pp. 123–133. Cf. also the review of the book in *The Princeton Theological Review*, iii. 1905, pp. 505–509.

[62] Cf. especially " Vicarious Sacrifice," New York, 1866, p. 107, and 2d ed., i. New York, 1877, p. 107.

the least, not explicit. One such, oddly enough, finds incidental expression in a criticism by Shailer Mathews of Macintosh's separation of Christianity from Christ.[63] Mathews
very properly questions whether the issue raised by Macintosh's reasoning "does not really involve the momentous
question as to whether we are not in the process of evolving
a new phase of religion from historic Christianity"; and as
properly remarks that the retention of the name Christianity
for " what we regard as ideal," even though it is not historically
traceable to Jesus or to Paul, " would not be the first time that
the effort has been made to submerge New Testament teaching in general culture, and in much the same fashion of
substituting dehistoricalized, speculative systems for a Christianity with historical content." He expresses hearty agreement with Macintosh, however, in one thing. It is this: that
" saving faith, in the personal religious sense, does not wait
upon the verdict of the higher criticism as to the historicity
of Jesus." Why? Because, apart from the higher criticism, that
is, apart from all scientific scrutiny of the gospel records,
there is reason enough for trusting our all to Jesus? No. Because Jesus is not necessary to "saving faith, in the personal
religious sense "! " Men are not saved by mere orthodoxy or
heterodoxy," Mathews remarks, — inconsequently, since nobody ever supposed they were. But then he adds positively:
" In the sense that their wills are one with God's, men who
have never heard of Jesus have been and are to be saved."

The doctrine here enunciated is practically the doctrine
which has played a large part in theological controversy —
witness the " Andover debate " of a quarter of a century ago
— under the name of the " essential Christ." According to it,
men can exercise " saving faith " without any knowledge of
Christ; that is to say, as Mathews suggests, their "religious

[63] *American Journal of Theology*, xv., October, 1911, pp. 614–617. For
an uncompromising assertion of the point of view here intimated by Mathews
see J. Warschauer, " Jesus: Seven Questions," 1908, pp. 206–233; " Is Belief
in Him Necessary? " Warschauer has no hesitation in declaring that " there is
no room in a civilized theology for a doctrine which would limit salvation
to those professing any one form of religious belief " (p. 230).

faith, however imperfect," may "possess a quality" that makes them "one with those who through the clearer revelation and deeper certainty given by Jesus also trust God as fatherly and so partake of the divine spirit." In this very prevalent doctrine, there is obviously a very express preparation for a Christless Christianity. In the form given it by Mathews it has indeed already fairly passed over into Christless Christianity. He conceives the function of Jesus to be to induce trust in God as fatherly; and he conceives that men can exercise and do exercise a faith which has this "quality," apart from any action upon them by Jesus. This is already the announcement that Jesus may be dispensed with — all that He is and all that He does — for some. Some attain saving faith without Jesus; some — no doubt, more easily — with Him.[64] More commonly a higher function is attributed to Jesus. He has, it is said, made atonement for sin; on the basis

---

[64] This is not nowadays a rare point of view. Emil Sulze, for example, who is very much afraid the honor due to God shall be accorded to Jesus, gives repeated expression to it. Paul Mehlhorn (*Protestantische Monatshefte,* v. 1901, p. 190) describes Sulze's view, with references to his " Wie ist der Kampf um die Bedeutung der Person und des Wirkens Jesu zu beendigen? " 1901, as follows: " Although now Sulze emphasizes that faith is an immediate work of God in us, so that there are circumstances in which it can arise without the mediation of acquaintance with Christ and the church, yet it would be in his view a terrible loss for the individual if he did not permit himself to be helped forward and given assurance in this matter by history and its pioneering personalities. Just as a German statesman ' who had not formed himself on Stein and Bismarck must remain a pitiable beginner ' (p. 34), so for the clarifying and establishment of our faith, ' the person of every child of God ' is ' for us a means of grace in God's hand,' while Christ is and abides ' by his unique vocation . . . the perfectly unique means of grace for us ' (p. 35)."

Sulze, however, is more hospitable to the idea of the independence of " Christian " faith of Christ than Mathews. Neither complete peace nor complete assurance can be had, he urges, without a free attitude towards Jesus himself. And quite after the manner of Macintosh, he argues: " And is the attitude to God which is here described not the same as that which, according to all that we know of him, was occupied by Christ himself? He did not win love to his Father in Heaven in dependence on an historical person. God himself gave him what he revealed by him " (*Protestantische Monatshefte,* xi. 1907, p. 247). His views as to the dispensability of Jesus are more or less clearly expressed in a number of articles in the *Protestantische Monatshefte.*

of this atonement men may be saved. He has shed down His Spirit, quickening faith in men; their faith, therefore, though exercised in ignorance of Him, has its warrant, and its source, and its effect from Him. Their salvation is accordingly from Christ, and by Christ, and in Christ, though they are ignorant of all this. In proportion as this higher doctrine is approached, in that proportion is the preparation made for a Christless Christianity less explicit. But even in it, there is an implicit preparation for it. A Christ of whom you are unconscious is at best in some sense a Christ who does not exist for you: and if everything He may be for you depends upon your consciousness of him, a Christ of whom you are unconscious does not exist at all for you. A salvation apart from knowledge of Christ is always liable to be conceived as a salvation apart from Christ. In Mathews' construction, though he is in the act of repelling a Christless Christianity, it actually becomes salvation without Christ. He speaks of it only with reference to some. But if some may thus be saved without Christ, why not all? There seems no compelling reason, on Mathews' ground, why Jesus should be proclaimed, or why He should exist, at all.

We may learn from Otto Ritschl [65] that a very similar line of thought may be developed on Ritschlian premises. Ritschl is examining W. Herrmann's doctrine of faith. According to Herrmann, man finds the living God not within himself, where mysticism bids him seek Him, but solely in the personal life of Jesus. Christian faith is thus made to carry with it " a clear consciousness of its conditioning through the personal life of Jesus." This, Ritschl thinks, is too narrow a view. He asks:

" What are we to hold respecting such Christians as lack a clear consciousness of the inner possessions for which they are indebted to Christ? Or is it also deficiency in complete faith when a Christian in prayer to his God and Father seeks and finds firm support in the cares and tasks and strifes of life, without at the same time recalling Christ as the sole revelation of this God; although he has failed in this perhaps only because he lacked the

[65] *Zeitschrift für Theologie und Kirche*, iii. 1893, pp. 380–388.

spiritual energy to grasp the religious conception of God and that of Christ in one and the same prayer-idea? Can we doubt that such Christians have faith in the full sense, because the theoretical consideration leads to conceiving Christian faith in general not apart from a clear consciousness of its conditioning through Christ's personal life? "

It is plain fact, he urges, that the fruits of faith are reaped where this clear consciousness is not present; and it is equally plain fact that this clear consciousness can be present and no fruits of faith show themselves: the question obtrudes itself "whether the conscious but unfruitful or the fruitful but unconscious faith is the more valuable." Clear consciousness must obviously be looked upon as only occasional, as "a special charism"; some have it, in others it is "latent or undeveloped."

" Wherever world-overcoming faith, recognizable in its fruits, is found, it must be referred back to the influence of Christ, whether the believing subject is conscious of this connection or not. On the other hand, it should be recognized, in opposition to Herrmann, that the faith which does not bring with it a clear consciousness of its conditioning through Christ, but which nevertheless is actually conditioned through Christ's operations, is only mediately grounded on the personal life of Jesus. Immediately, however, the ground of such faith is the Christian life practised in the sense of Christ in the community. And only in this also do the vital activities of Christ propagate themselves from generation to generation."

Jesus may have been needed, then, to set the course of Christian life going in the world. After that He may safely be forgotton. There is no obvious reason why He may not be forgotten by the whole Christian community, — why the memory of Him may not fade entirely out of the world, — and still faith be continued through the influence of the faith-exercising community; just as motion once induced in the first of a series of balls in contact with one another may be transmitted to the last ball, though it is touched actually only by the penultimate one. A fully developed Christless Christianity may thus grow out of Christ Himself; if you will only permit us to think of Christ as providing merely the initial impulse and then withdrawing out of sight.

It has been thought worth while to bring into view these remoter tendencies of thought making towards Christless Christianity, that the numerous pathways may be kept in mind along which men may travel, from depreciation of the function of Christ in "redemption," through neglect or forgetfulness of Him, to actual denial of His indispensable place in the religious life of Christians. These pathways, while very direct, are also no doubt often somewhat long. That is to say, the passage from unconsciousness to conscious disregard of Christ is made logically much more quickly than it is practically. From the practical point of view the distance that separates the conscious from the merely virtual denial of the indispensableness of Jesus to faith is beyond doubt immense. The phenomenon which now faces us is that this immense space has been actually overstepped by many about us. There are many still calling themselves Christians who have come to the pass that, not inadvertently or by way of logical implication merely, but in the most heedful manner in the world, and by express declaration, they turn away from Jesus as no longer possessing supreme significance for their religious life. They deliberately pronounce Him unnecessary for their faith, and seek its source and ground and content elsewhere. No doubt, they exhibit differences among themselves. George B. Foster, who surely ought to know, distinguishes two varieties. He says:

" To-day [66] there are two kinds of spirits which dream of a Christianity without Christ: the weak and the strong. The weak are those who have received all the priceless blessings which we possess in Christianity, only at third or fourth hand. They have been refreshed, nourished, led by these blessings — whence they came is of little concern to them. . . . The others are the strong. They know very well that Christianity sprang from Christ. But one does not now need him longer. Were they to be quite frank, they would say that he, not entirely unlike miracles, had come to

[66] " The Finality of the Christian Religion," 2d ed., 1909, p. 331.

be something of a hindrance. . . . But would it not poorly serve the expansion of Christianity, the pervasion of the world with Christianity, and one's own peace and joy in Christianity, to drain off the fountain? Is not their view much the same as if we were to sever the connection of our arteries with the heart whence the blood comes? "

The criticism is apt, from the Christian point of view: apt, though not quite adequate. From the Christian point of view it may very properly be said (though this is far from all that needs to be said) that those who are advising us that Christianity can get along very well without Christ are very much like men sitting by a brookside and reasoning that since we have the brook we do not need the spring from which it flows, and may readily admit the doubt whether there is a spring. If even this criticism does not seem valid to our Christless Christians, that can only be because they no longer occupy the Christian point of view.

The point which needs particular pressing lies, indeed, just here, — that in thus separating themselves from Jesus as the source and ground and content of their faith, they sever themselves from Christianity and proclaim themselves of another religion. By some odd tangle of thought they may still declare themselves Christians, though they no longer hold to Christ or look to Him for redemption from their sins. They have learned, we are told, from David Friedrich Strauss (in his Christian period) to distinguish between the principle of Christianity and the person of Christ. The discovery of this distinction was, we know, with Strauss " the first step which counts" towards we know what end. May we not commend to those who follow him in this first step the example which he set them when he opened his eyes at last and saw whither it really had conducted him?

" Therefore, my conviction is that, if we are not dealing in evasion, if we do not wish to tack and trim, if we do not desire to say Yea, yea, and Nay, nay, — in short, if we speak like honest and candid men, we must confess that we are no longer Christians." [67]

[67] " Der alte und der neue Glaube," 1872, p. 90; cf. p. 143.

Why should there be any hesitation in the matter? A Christianity to which Christ is indifferent is, as a mere matter of fact, no Christianity at all. For Christianity, in the core of the matter, consists in just, " Jesus Christ and Him as crucified." Can he be of the body who no longer holds to the Head?

What is, after all, the fundamental difference between Christianity and other "positive" religions? Does it not turn just on this — that the founders of the other religions point out the way to God while Christ presents Himself as that Way? It is primary teaching that we receive, when we are told:

" Buddha and Confucius, Zarathustra and Mohammed are no doubt the first confessors of the religions which have been founded by them, but they are not the content of these religions, and they stand in an external and to a certain extent accidental relation to them. Their religions could remain the same even though their names were forgotten, or their persons replaced by others. In Christianity, however, it is altogether different. To be sure the notion is occasionally given expression that Christ too does not desire to be the only mediator and He would be quite content that His name should be forgotten, if only His principles and spirit lived on in the community. But others who for themselves have wholly broken with Christianity have in an unpartisan fashion denied and refuted these notions. Christianity stands to the person of Christ in a wholly different relation from that of the religions of the peoples to the persons by whom they have been founded. Jesus is not the first confessor of the religion which bears His name. He was not the first and most eminent Christian, but He holds in Christianity a wholly different place. . . . Christ is Christianity itself; He stands not outside of it but in its centre; without His name, person and work, there is no Christianity left. In a word, Christ does not point out the way to salvation; He is the Way itself." [68]

[68] Herman Bavinck, " Magnalia Dei," p. 312.

VIII
THE TWENTIETH–CENTURY CHRIST

THE TWENTIETH-CENTURY CHRIST [1]

WHAT may very properly be called the Chalcedonian " settlement " has remained until today the authoritative statement of the elements of the doctrine of the Person of Christ.
It has well deserved to do so. For this " settlement " does
justice at once to the data of Scripture, to the implicates of an
Incarnation, to the needs of Redemption, to the demands of
the religious emotions, and to the logic of a tenable doctrine
of our Lord's Person. But this "settlement" is a mere statement of the essential facts, and therefore does nothing to
mitigate the difficulty of the conception which it embodies.
The difficulty of conceiving two distinct natures united in a
single person remains; and this difficulty has produced in
every age a tendency more or less widespread to fall away
from the doctrine, or to explain it away, or decisively to reject
it. Weak during the Middle Ages, this tendency acquired
force in the great intellectual upheaval which accompanied the
Reformation; and then gave birth, amid many other interesting phenomena, to the radical reaction against the doctrine of
the Two Natures which we know as Socinianism. The shallow
naturalism of the Enlightenment came in the next age to the
reinforcement of the movement thus inaugurated, and under
the impulses thus set at work a widespread revolt has sprung
up in the modern church against the doctrine of the Two
Natures.

Germany is today the *præceptor mundi*. And how things
stand in the academical circle of Germany Professor Friedrich Loofs informs us in his recent Oberlin lectures. "The
whole German Protestant theology of the present time," he
tells us, has, "to a certain extent," turned away from the conception of the Two Natures. "In the preceding generation,"

---

[1] From *The Hibbert Journal*, xii. 1914, pp. 583–602.

it seems, " there was still a learned theologian in Germany who thought it correct and possible to reproduce the old orthodox formulas in our time without the slightest modification, viz.: Friedrich Adolph Philippi, of Rostock (1882)." " At present," however, Loofs proceeds, " I do not know of a single professor of evangelical theology in Germany of whom this might be said. All learned Protestant theologians in Germany, even if they do not do so with the same emphasis, really admit unanimously that the orthodox Christology does not do sufficient justice to the truly human life of Jesus, and that the orthodox doctrine of the two natures in Christ cannot be retained in the traditional form. All our systematic theologians, so far at least as they see more in Jesus than the first subject of Christian faith, are seeking new paths in their Christology." No doubt matters have not yet gone so far in lands of English speech; but the drift here, too, is obviously in the same direction, and even among us an immense confusion has come to reign with regard to this fundamental doctrine of the Christian religion.

The alternative of two natures is, of course, one nature: and this one nature must be conceived, naturally, either as Divine or as human. The tendency to conceive of Christ as wholly Divine — so far as it has asserted itself at all — has been rather a religious than a theological tendency, if we may avail ourselves here of this overworked and misleading terminology. It has existed rather as a state of heart, and as a devotional attitude, than as a reasoned doctrine. Nothing has been more characteristic of Christians from the beginning than that they have been " worshippers of Christ." To the writers of the New Testament, the recognition of Jesus as Lord was the mark of a Christian; and all their religious emotions turned to Him. It has been made the reproach of the Evangelists that they — following their sources — were all worshippers of Jesus: and it is precisely on that ground that modern naturalistic criticism warns us that we are not to trust their representations as to His supernatural life on earth. To the heathen observers of the early Christians, their most distinguishing characteristic, which differentiated them from all others, was that they sang praises to Christ as God. A shrewd modern controversialist has even found it possible to contend that the only God the Christians have is Christ. "Christianity," says he, " is pre-eminently the worship of Christ. Far away in the background of existence there may be a power, answering to Indian Brahma or Greek Kronos and conceived as God the Father. But the working, ever-living, ever-active Deity is Christ. He is the creator and preserver of the world, the ruler, redeemer, and judge of men. He and no other is worshipped as God, hymned, prayed to, invoked. To Him have been transferred the attributes of Jehovah. He and no other is the Christian God." If there is some exaggeration here, it is not to be found on the positive side; and G. K. Chesterton is not overstating the matter when he speaks of Christ incidentally as " the chief deity of a civilisation."

This worship of Christ has had, of course, theological results of great importance, some of them even portentous — if, for example, we can with many historians look upon adoration of saints, and especially of the Virgin Mary, as, in part at least, an attempt of the human spirit to supply, outside of the Christ thought of as purely Divine, the human element in the mediatorially conceived Divine relation. But only now and again has it worked back and sought a theological basis for itself by the formal divinitising of the whole Christ. We think here naturally of the Apollinarians, and the Monophysites; but more particularly of confessional Lutheranism, which by its theory of the *communicatio idiomatum* managed to preserve indeed to theology a human nature for Christ, but at the same time to present a purely Divine Christ to our religious emotions. But we shall have to go back to the Gnostic Docetism of the first Christian centuries for any influential effort speculatively to construe Christ as a wholly Divine Being. If men have here and there forgotten the human Christ in their reverence for the Divine Christ, they have shown no great inclination to explain Christ to thought in terms of the purely Divine.

Revolt from the doctrine of the Two Natures means, therefore, nothing more or less than the explanation of Christ in
terms of mere humanity. When we are told by Loofs that
the whole of learned Germany has rejected the doctrine of the
Two Natures, that is equivalent accordingly to being told that
the whole of learned Germany has rejected the doctrine of the
Deity of Christ, and construes Him to its thought as a purely
human being. It may continue to reverence Him; men here
and there may even continue to worship Him. As many of
the older Unitarians found it possible still to offer worship to
Christ, and incorporated in their official hymn-books hymns of
praise to Him as God — such as Bonar's "How shall Death's
Triumph end? " in which Christ is celebrated as " The First
and Last, who was and is," or Ray Palmer's " My Faith looks
up to Thee," in which he is addressed as "Saviour Divine " —
so many of our new German Humanitarians still worship
Christ. Karl Thieme, for example, who righteously rebukes his
fellows for continuing to use such phraseology as "the Godhead," "the Deity," "the Divinity" of Christ, when they
know very well that Jesus is not God but only man, yet
strenuously argues that He is worthy of our worship, because
of what he calls His "representative unity with God." When
asked how his worship of Jesus differs in principle from the
gross hagiolatry of the Church of Rome, Thieme naïvely and
most significantly replies, Why, in this most important respect,
that he worships only *one* such holy one, the Romanists many!
The adoring attitude preserved by men of this class towards
Jesus — whom they nevertheless declare to be mere man —
has called out not unnaturally in wide circles a deep disgust.
They are not unjustly reproached with idolatry, are contemptuously dubbed "Jesusites " — worshippers of the man Jesus;
and occasion has even been taken from their corrupt Jesus-
cult to inaugurate a movement in revolt from Christianity as
a whole, wrongfully identified with them, in the interests of a
pure and non-idolatrous service of God. Men like Wilhelm von
Schnehen and Arthur Drews are thus able to come forward
with the plea that in their philosophical cult alone can be

found true worship, and do not hesitate to declare that the greatest obstacle to pure religión in the world to-day is precisely this idolatrous adoration of Jesus, interpreted as merely a human being. We can only record it to their honour, therefore, when the majority of those who have given up the Deity of our Lord refuse to worship Him, and, while according to Him their admiration and respect, reserve their religious veneration for God alone.

The present great extension of purely humanitarian conceptions of the person of Christ has, of course, not been attained without a gradual development, in the progress of which there has been enunciated a variety of compromising views seeking to mediate between the doctrine of the Two Natures and the growing Humanitarianism. The most interesting of these is that wonderful construction which has been known under the name of Kenotism, from its vain attempt to intrench itself in the declaration of Paul (Phil. ii. 8) that Jesus, being by nature in the form of God, emptied Himself — as our Revised Version unfortunately mistranslates the Greek verb from which the term, Kenosis, is derived — and so became man. The idea is that the Son of God, in becoming man, abandoned His deity, extinguished it, so to speak, by immersing it in the stream of human life. This curious view bears somewhat the same relation to the tendency to think of Christ in terms of pure humanity that the Lutheran Christology bears to the opposite tendency to think of Him in terms of pure deity. As that was an attempt to secure a purely Divine Christ while not theoretically denying His human nature, so this was an attempt to secure a purely human Christ without theoretically denying His Divine nature. In effect it gives us a Christ of one nature and that nature purely human, though it theoretically explains this human nature as really just shrunken deity. Therefore Albrecht Ritschl called it *verschämter Socinianismus* — Socinianism indeed, but a Socinianism differing from the bold Socinianism to which we are accustomed by shyly hanging back and trying to hide itself behind sheltering skirts.

Kenotism differs from Socinianism fundamentally, however, in that Socinianism took away from us only our Divine Christ, while Kenotism takes away also our very God. For what kind of God is this that is God and not God alternately as He chooses, and lays off and on at will those specific qualities which make God the kind of being we call "God," as a king might put off and on his crown, or as a leopard might wish to change his spots but cannot, or an Ethiopian his skin? Of course, this is all — as Albrecht Ritschl again aptly described it, and as Loofs repeats from his lips — "pure mythology"; and the only wonder is that it enjoyed considerable vogue for a while, and, indeed, has not yet wholly passed out of sight on the outskirts of theological civilization. Loofs seems to raise his eyebrows a little as he remarks that, as it has gradually died out in Germany, it has seemed to find supporters in England: "in Sweden, too," he adds, with meticulous conscientiousness, "it was confidently defended as late as 1903 by Oskar Bensow." The English writers to whom he thus refers are men of brilliant parts — such as D. W. Forrest, W. L. Walker, P. T. Forsyth, and latest of all H. R. Mackintosh. But even writers of brilliant parts will not be able to fan the dead embers of this burned-out speculation into life again. The humanitarian theorizers are in search of a true man in Jesus, not a shrivelled God; and no Christian heart will be satisfied with a Christ in whom (we quote Ritschl again) there was no Godhead at all while He was on earth, and in whom (we may add) there may be no manhood at all now that He has gone to heaven. It really ought to be clear by now that there cannot be a half-way house erected between the doctrines that Christ is both God and man and that Christ is merely man. Between these two positions there is an irreducible "either or," and many may feel inclined to adopt Biedermann's caustic criticism of the Kenotic theories, that only one who has himself suffered a kenosis of his understanding can possibly accord them welcome.

On the sinking of the Kenotic sun beneath the horizon, there has been left, however, a certain afterglow hanging behind it. A disposition is discoverable in certain quarters to speak in Kenotic language while recoiling from the Kenotic name; to claim as a Christian heritage the essential features of the Kenotic Christology while declining to lay behind them the precise Kenotic explanation. An isolated early instance of this procedure was supplied by Thomas Adamson, who draws a portrait of Jesus in his "Studies of the Mind in Christ" (1898) which seems to require the assumption of kenosis to justify it, but who vigorously repudiates the attribution of that assumption to him. Much more notable instances are found in such writers as Johannes Kunze of Vienna (now of Greifswald) and Erich Schäder of Kiel, whose formula for the incarnation is that in Jesus Christ the Godhead is "presented in the form of a human life." According to Kunze the Godhead appears in Jesus always as humanly mediated: the two, Godhead and manhood, can never be contemplated apart; all that is human is Divine, and all that is Divine is human. The omnipotence which belongs to His deity appearing in Christ only as humanly mediated, for example, is conditioned on His *prayer;* Jesus could accomplish all things by the power of prevalent prayer! So also with all the Divine attributes; the result being that we have in Jesus phenomenally nothing but a man, but a man who, we are told, is nevertheless to be thought of as the Eternal God.

Similarly, according to Schäder, God in becoming flesh has not at all ceased to be what He was; He has only become it "in another way." In the place of the doctrine of the Two Natures, Schäder places the idea of what he calls "the Being of God in Jesus" — *das Sein Gottes in Jesus* — a phrase which becomes something like a watchword with him. "We have here," he says, "a man before us to whom there is lacking not the least thing that is human, a man who is man in everything, be it what it may"; and yet who is just God become flesh, "having ceased to be nothing which He eternally is," but "having only become it in *another* manner." By what a narrow line this doctrine of "God in human form" is separated from express Kenotism may be observed from the diffi-culties in which Schäder finds himself when he comes to speak of the act by which the mighty transformation, which he postulates in the Son of God, takes place. Here his language is not only distinctly Kenotic, but extremely Kenotic, as-similating him in his subordinationism and transmutationism to what Loofs does not scruple to speak of as the "reckless" teaching of Gess. "Now, God our Father," he writes, "lets it, lets this Son proceed from Himself as man, and *thus* enter into history. This is an almighty act of His love, of His reconciling will": "what is in question here is an almighty transformation of the mode of being of the Logos by God." When we are thus told that, "by God's almighty act, God's eternal Son becomes a weak, developing child," we are not so much reassured as puzzled that we are told in the same breath that thus "He does not cease to be what He was, He only becomes the same thing in another way"; nor are we much helped by having it explained to us that even in His pre-existent state the Son of God, because He was Son, was dependent on God, subordinate to Him, and wrought only God's will — so that even in His pre-existent state He used prayer to God, preserved humility in the Divine presence, and lived in obedience to God. It is only borne strongly in upon us that it is an exceedingly difficult task at one and the same time to evaporate and to preserve the true Deity of Christ.

The fundamental formulas with which Kunze and Schäder operate — that the incarnation consists in "the Being of God in Christ," that "God is in Christ in human form" — reappear in perhaps even more purity in the writings of the late R. C. Moberly. "Christ," he says, "is, then, not so much God *and* man, as God in, and through, and as man." "God, as man, is always, in all things, God *as man*"; "if it is all Divine, it is all human too." So also W. P. Du Bose wishes us not to forget that "God is most God at the moment when He is most love," and not to fail to recognise God "in the highest act of His highest attribute," confusing external pomp with internal nobility — all of which has the appearance at least of being only a way of laying claim to the inheritance of the Kenotists, while avoiding the scandal of the name. Reviewing Du Bose, Professor Sanday falls in with the notions he here expresses, and pronounces it likely that the moderns in their insistence on the single personality of our Lord, which is both Divine and human — and, apparently, Divine only because it is perfectly human, — have made an improvement on the old Two Nature doctrine of the Creeds. We may perceive from this how completely the movement is but a phase of the zealous propaganda for a one-natured Christ, and but propounds a new method of submerging God in man. This method is to proclaim the paradox that God is most God when He ceases to be God — when He becomes man. For this condescension marks the manifestation at its height of the highest of all the activities of God — Love.

But we may perceive here, too, what may also legitimately interest us, a stage in the drifting of Sanday's Christological views towards the apparently humanitarian position at which they seem ultimately to arrive. In earlier writings Sanday had taught with clarity the essentials of the Trinitarian Christology, and had pronounced himself unfavourable to the Kenotic speculations. In this review of Du Bose he falls in, however, with Kenotic modes of expression; and soon afterwards he is found confessing himself in some sense a Kenotist — while, nevertheless, in the act of propounding what seems really to be a merely humanitarian Christology. For Sanday's final suggestion is to the effect that we should think of Christ as the man into whose subconscious being — which is to be conceived as open at the bottom and through that opening in contact with the ocean of Deity which lies beyond — the waves of this ocean of Deity wash with more frequency, fullness, and force than in the case of other men, and so with more frequency, fullness, and force make themselves felt in the upper stratum of His being, His conscious self, also than in the case of other men. At the basis of this suggestion there lies a mystical doctrine of human nature, which makes the subliminal being of every man the dwelling-place of God.

If we only go down deep enough into man's being, we shall find God; and if the tides of the Infinite only wash in high enough, they will emerge into consciousness. Man differs from man, no doubt, in the richness and fullness with which the Divine that underlies his being surges up in him and enters his consciousness; and Jesus differs from other men in being in this incomparably above other men. There is Deity in Him as well as humanity; but not Deity alongside of humanity, but Deity underlying and sustaining His humanity — as Deity underlies and sustains all humanity. The mistake of the orthodox Christology has been to draw the line which divides the Deity and the humanity vertically: let us draw it rather horizontally, "between the upper human medium, which is the proper and natural field of all active expression, and those lower depths which are no less the proper and natural home of whatever is Divine." Thus we shall have a Christ whose life, though, "so far as it was visible, it was a strictly human life," yet "was, in its deepest roots, directly continuous with the life of God Himself." That the same may be said in his measure of every man Sanday expressly affirms, and he as expressly identifies this Divine element which is to be found at the roots of the being of both Christ and all other men with what the Scriptures call "the indwelling of the Holy Spirit." Christ thus becomes just the man in whom the Holy Spirit dwells in greater abundance than in other men. He is not God and man; He is not even God in man; He is man with God dwelling in Him — as, though less completely, God dwells in all men. We have reached here a Christology which substitutes for the incarnation a notion which librates between the two conceptions of the general Divine immanence and the special indwelling of the Holy Spirit. According as the one or the other of these conceptions is given precedence will it find its affinities, therefore, with one or another widely spread form of the humanitarian theorizing now so popular. For there are many about us who, declaring Jesus to be no more than man, wish to explain the Divine that is allowed also to be found in Him on the basis of the Divine immanence; and there are equally many among us who wish to explain it on the basis of the Divine indwelling or inspiration.

Those who occupy the former of these standpoints are prone to speak of Jesus as " a human organism filled with the Divine thought." This conception may be presented in a very crass form, or it may be clothed in very beautiful language and made the vehicle of very fervent expressions of reverence for Christ. " I see," explains James Drummond, "in the beauty of a rose a Divine thought, which is no other than God Himself coming unto manifestation through the rose, so far as the limitations of a rose will permit; but I do not believe that the rose is God, possessed of omniscience, omnipotence, and so forth. . . . So, there are those who have, through the medium of the New Testament and the traditional life of the purest Christendom, looked into the face of Jesus, and seen there an ideal, a glory which they have felt to be the glory of God, a thought of Divine Sonship which has changed their whole conception of human nature, and the whole aim of their life. . . ." Such a conception, we are told by its advocates, is far superior to the " masked God " of current orthodoxy; it " exalts Christ above all men, and gives Him a place at the right hand of God." He was, no doubt, only a man — a human organism — but He was a man whose " attitude of will was such that God could act upon Him as upon no other in the history of humanity." " From the dawn of consciousness the human Christ assumed such an ethical uprightness before God that God could pour Himself out on Christ in altogether exceptional activities." In Him " for the first and only time the Almighty was granted His opportunity with a human soul," and, " as the Master kept Himself in unique ethical surrender to God, God acted upon Him in such a manner as to make the metaphysical relationship also unique. The ethical uniqueness implies and renders inevitable its corresponding metaphysical uniqueness of relation to God." For, we are told, " it is possible for God so to fill a responsive heart with His own spirit that every word of that soul becomes a word of God, that every deed becomes a deed of God, that every feeling reveals the loving heart of God willing to suffer with His children. In short, the life becomes such a life as God Himself would live were it possible for Him to be reduced to human circumstances. God could not suggest any improvement. He would find this soul such an open channel that He could at last pour Himself out to the utmost drop. There would be such complete mutual sympathy that the sorrows of God would become the sorrows of this soul, and the sorrows of this soul the sorrows of God. If in a moment of distress at the onslaught of sin the soul should cry out, 'Why hast Thou forsaken me?' the distress would be as real to God as to the soul, for every sorrow of either God or this soul would cut both ways. The soul would become God's masterpiece. God would throw Himself into its development with such flood that the metaphysical relationship would be beyond anything known to humanity, and beyond anything attainable by humanity. As the supreme work of the Father, and as the supreme response to the ethical cravings of the Father, such a creation could be called in the highest sense the Son of God."

Perhaps we may say that the exaltation of the man Jesus could go little further than this. And we can scarcely fail to observe that we have before us here a movement of thought running on precisely opposite lines from that of the Kenotic theories. In them we were bidden to observe how God could become man; in this we are asked in effect whether it may not be possible to believe that in Jesus Christ man became God. We are naturally reminded at this point that consentaneously with the rise of the Kenotic theories in the middle of the last century there was born also a contradictory theory — that of Isaac A. Dorner — which, with a much more profound meaning, proposed to our thought a solution of the problems of the incarnation which formally reminds us of that just described. Dorner, beginning with the human Jesus, asked us to watch Him become gradually God by a progressive communication to Him of the Divine Being, so that, though at the start He was but man, in the end He should become in the truest and most ontological sense the God-man. The difficulties of such a conception are, of course, insuperable; it would compel us to think of the Godhead as capable of abscission and division, so that it could be imparted piecemeal to a human subject, or of manhood as capable by successive creative acts of being itself transmuted into Godhead. But it was inevitable that this theory, too, should leave some echoes of itself in the confused discord of modern thought.

We hear these echoes in the high christological construction of Martin Kähler. We hear them also in the lower theories of Reinhold Seeberg. According to Seeberg, Jesus Christ is just a man whom the willing God has created as His organ and through whom the personal will of God has so worked that He has become fully one with this personal will of God. " The will of God," he says, " chose the man Jesus for His organ, and formed Him into the clear and distinct expression of His Being. He emphasizes the personal character of the Divine will in Jesus, but he allows no second hypostasis in the Godhead as its Trinitarian background. In his view we can admit the eternal existence of only one thinking and willing Divine personality, though in that one personality there co-existed a threefold tendency of will. That particular tendency of the Divine will-energy which aims at the realization of a church, manifests itself in the man Jesus, and so fully takes possession of Him that in Him it becomes for the first time personal and makes Him really the Son of God. Before God thus created Jesus into His organ there was no second ego standing over against the Father; there pre-existed in the eternal God only the eternal tendency of will to create a church. " What is peculiarly Divine in Christ " is therefore only " the peculiar will-content which we can distinguish from other will-contents, the tendency of the Divine will to the historical realization of salvation." Seeberg thinks that thus he does justice to the Godhead of Christ. He looks upon Him as the Redemptive Will of God forming as organ for itself a human subject and coming to complete personality in it. " Jesus," he says, " in the peculiar contents of His soul is God." " Herrschaft," authority,

therefore belongs to Him; but also "Demut," humility;
but especially "Herrschaft," for is He not the personal Son of
God, the only personal Son of God that ever was or ever will
be? "That ever will be," we say: for the question arises, what
has become of this personal Son of God now that His life on
earth is over and He has ascended where He was before? As
before the "Incarnation" the particular Divine will of salvation was not a Divine personality over against the Father,
but acquired personality only as it flowed into the human
person, Jesus Christ, and formed Him to its organ — has it,
now that this man Jesus has passed away from earth, lost
again its personality and sunk again into merely the tendency
of the Divine will making for salvation? It is Karl Thieme
who asks this question. For ourselves, we may be content with
observing that in Seeberg's construction it is not God, but
only the Divine will of salvation, that becomes incarnate in
Jesus Christ; and that Jesus Christ is therefore not God, but
only, as we say in our loose everyday language, "the very
incarnation" of the Divine will of salvation. We see in Him,
not God, but only the will of God to save men — and this
seems only another way of saying that Christ is not Himself
God, but only the love of God is manifested in and through
Him. What we get from Seeberg, then, is obviously not a doctrine of the incarnation, but only another form of the prevalent doctrine of Divine indwelling or inspiration, and it is
because of this that Seeberg's theory seems to Friedrich Loofs
one of the most valuable of those recently promulgated.

In an interesting passage Loofs selects out of the results of
recent speculation the three conclusions which he considers
the most valuable, and thus reveals to us his own christological
conceptions. These are: "First, that the historical person of
Christ is looked upon as a human personality; secondly, that
this personality, through an indwelling of God or His Spirit,
which was unique both before and after, up to the ending of
all time, became the Son of God who reveals the Father, and
became also the beginner of a new mankind; and, thirdly, that
in the future state of perfection a similar indwelling of God

has to be realized, though in a copied and therefore secondary form, in all people whom Christ has redeemed." The central point in this statement is that Christ is a man in whom God dwells. " The conviction," remarks Loofs in his explanation of his views, "that God dwelt so perfectly in Jesus through His Spirit as had never been the case before, and never will be till the end of all time, does justice to what we teach historically about Jesus, and may, at the same time, be regarded as satisfactorily expressing the unique position of Jesus, which is a certainty to faith." He is willing to admit, indeed, that he does not quite know what the dwelling of the Spirit of God in Jesus means; and, indeed, he is free to confess that he does not understand even what is meant by the "Spirit of God." And he agrees that the formula of the indwelling of the Spirit of God in Jesus is capable of being taken in so low a sense as to destroy all claim of uniqueness for Jesus. He does not feel so well satisfied with it, therefore, as Hans Hinrich Wendt, for example, expresses himself as being. But he knows nothing better to say, and is willing to leave it at that, with the further acknowledgment that he feels himself face to face here with something of a mystery. Loofs is a Ritschlian of the extreme right wing, and in his sense of a mystery in the person of Christ, leaving him not quite satisfied with the definition of His person as a man in whom God uniquely dwells, we perceive the height of christological conception to which we may attain on Ritschlian presupposition.

What Ritschl himself thought of Christ it is rather difficult to determine; and his followers are not perfectly agreed in their detailed interpretation of it. He himself warns us not to suppose him to be unaware of mysteries because he does not speak of them: it is precisely of the mysteries, he says, that he wishes to preserve silence. Meanwhile he is silent of all that is transcendental in Christ, His pre-existence, His metaphysical Godhead, His exaltation — if these things indeed belong to Christ. If Jesus had any transcendent Being other than His phenomenal Being as man, Ritschl says nothing about it. He seems, indeed, to leave no place for it. He speaks, no doubt, of

the "Godhead" of Christ; but by this he means neither to
allow that Christ existed as God before He was man, nor to
attribute a Divine nature to the historical Christ, nor to suggest that He has now been exalted to Divine glory. He means
merely to express his sense that Christ has the value of God for
us — that is to say, that we are conscious that we owe salvation to Him. The "Deity" thus predicated to Him, it is explained, is purely "ethical" and not "metaphysical," and,
moreover, is transferable to His people so that His Church,
viewed as the sphere of His influence, is as Divine as He is.
It is the "calling" of Christ to be the founder of the Kingdom
of God; and in fulfilling this "calling" He fulfils the eternal
purpose of God for the world and mankind. And it is only
because His personal will is thus one with the will of God that
the predicate of Godhead belongs to Him. "Christ is God"
with Ritschl — thus S. Faut sums up the matter — "so far as
He is on the one side the executor, on the other the object of
the Divine will." It all comes, we see, at the best, to the conception that Jesus is the unique Revealer of God and Mediator
of Redemption; and it is in these ideas that the higher class
of Ritschlian thinkers live and move and have their being.
To them Jesus is indeed purely human — "mere man" if
you will, though the adjective "mere" is objected to as
belittling. On the other hand, however, he stands in a unique
relation to God "as the embodiment of God's life in humanity,
and the guarantor of its presence and power; in whom God
verifies Himself to us as Father and Redeemer." There is
indeed no metaphysical Sonship with the Father in question;
Sonship is an ethico-religious idea when applied to Jesus.
When we call Him Son, we do not mean to declare Him God
in a metaphysical sense; we but indicate "His superior mission for humanity as representing and communicating the
Father's life." By His "centrality for the whole human race,
as the one perfect mediator of the Divine life," He is so
identified with God that those who have seen Him may be
said to have seen the Father also. Through Him and Him
only indeed has the Father ever been seen; in Him alone is
"manifested the Father's ideal of humanity and the Father's

purpose of grace toward the sinful." Through Him alone have men or can men come to the knowledge of the Father and to true and full communion with Him. "He is the one supreme Revealer," and "not only utters the thought of God " — who thus speaks through Him — but "incarnates the life of God, which through Him communicates itself to mankind as a redeeming and renewing power."

It is thus, we say, that the highest class of Ritschlian thinkers conceive of Jesus. We must emphasize, however, the words "the highest class." For this sketch of their thought of Jesus goes fairly to the limit of what can be said of Christ's dignity on Ritschlian ground. It not only, of course, gives expression to views which would be deemed impossible by a Schultz, a Harnack, a Wendt, but it transcends also what a Kaftan, a Kattenbusch, a Loofs, a Bornemann might be willing to say. For the whole Ritschlian school Christ is not so much Himself God as the means by which God is made known to us, and the instrument through which we are brought to God — and it is therefore only that they are willing, in a modified sense, to call Him Divine. " The term Divinity, applied to Jesus, expresses at bottom " in Ritschl's usage, says a careful expositor of his thought, " nothing more than the absolute confidence of the believer in the redemptive power of the Saviour." " The Godhead of Christ, therefore," says Gottschick, " expresses the value which the historical reality of this personal life possesses, as the power that produces the new humanity of regenerate and reconciled children of God." It is common, indeed, for Ritschlians, like Herrmann, to repudiate altogether experience of the power of the exalted Christ, and to suspend everything on the impression made by "the historical Christ," — and often, like Otto Ritschl, they mediate this through the Church to such an extent that Jesus appears merely as the starting-point of a movement propagated through the years from man to man; and He may therefore, without fatal loss, be lost sight of altogether. The Ritschlian conception of Christ must take its place as merely another of the numerous forms which the Humanitarianism of our anti-supernaturalistic age manifests.

For the characterizing feature of recent theories of the person of Christ is that they are all humanitarian. The Kenotic theory, which tried to find a middle ground between the God-man and the merely-man Jesus, having passed out of sight, the field is held by pure Humanitarianism. The situation is very clearly revealed in the classification of the possible Christological " schematizations " which Otto Kirn gives us in his " Elements of Evangelical Dogmatics." There are only four varieties of Christology, he tells us, which we need bear in mind as we pass our eye down the labours in this field of all the Christian centuries. These are, in his nomenclature, the Trinitarian, the Kenotic, the Messianic, and the Prophetic Christologies. The former two — the Trinitarian and the Kenotic — allow for a God-man; the first in fact, the second in theory. They are theories of the past. Only the Messianic and the Prophetic are living theories of to-day; and both of these give us merely a man Jesus. They differ only in one respect. Whereas in the Messianic Christology no less than in the Prophetic, Jesus in His self-consciousness as well as in His essential nature belongs to humanity and to humanity only, He is yet held in the Messianic Christology to be God's absolute organ for carrying out His counsel of salvation, and to be endowed for His work by a communication of the Holy Spirit beyond measure, fitting Him for unity with God and constituting Him the head of the community of God. The Prophetic Christology, on the other hand, looks upon Him as merely a religious genius, who in reaction upon His environment has become the unrivalled model of piety and as such the supreme guide to humanity in the knowledge of God and in the religious life. We may conceive of Jesus as the God-endowed man, or as the God-discovering man. In the former case we may see in Him God reaching down to man, to do him good: in the latter man reaching up to God, seeking good. Between these two conceptions we may take our choice: beyond them self-styled " modern thought " will not let us go.

Whether this reduction of Jesus to the dimensions of a mere man marks the triumph of modern christological speculation, or its collapse, is another question. The reduction of Jesus to the dimensions of a mere man was a phase of thought concerning His person which required to be fully exploited. And in that sense a service has been done to Christian thinking by the richness and variety of modern humanitarian constructions. Surely by now every possible expedient has been tried. The result is not encouraging. To him who would fain think of Him as merely a man, Jesus Christ looms up in history as ever more and more a mystery; a greater mystery than the God-man who is discarded in His favour. Say that the union of God and man in one person is intrinsically an incomprehensive mystery. It is nevertheless a mystery which, if it cannot be itself explained, yet explains. Without it, everything else is an incomprehensible mystery: the whole developing history of the kingdom of God, the gospel-record, the great figure of Paul and his great christological conceptions, the rise and growth and marvellous power of nascent Christianity, the history of Christianity in the world, the history of the world itself for two thousand years — your regenerated life and mine, our changed hearts and lives, our assurance of salvation, our deathless hope of eternal life. And yet we are invited to believe Him to have been a mere man, on no other ground than that it is easier to believe him to have been a mere man than a God-man! For that, after all, is what the whole ground of the assertion that Jesus was a mere man ultimately reduces to. It is intrinsically easier to believe in the existence of a mere man than in the existence of a God-man. But is it possible to believe that all that has issued from Jesus Christ could issue from a mere man? Apart from every other consideration, does there not lie in the effects wrought by Him an absolute bar to all humanitarian theories of His Person? The humanitarian interpretation of the Person of Christ is confronted by enormous historical and vital consequences, impossible of denial, which apparently spring from a fact which it pronounces inconceivable; though, apart from this fact, these consequences appear themselves to be impossible of explanation.

IX

THE ESSENCE OF CHRISTIANITY AND THE CROSS OF CHRIST

THE ESSENCE OF CHRISTIANITY AND THE CROSS OF CHRIST[1]

In a recent number of *The Harvard Theological Review,*[2] Professor Douglas Clyde Macintosh of the Yale Divinity School outlines in a very interesting manner the religious system to which he gives his adherence. For "substance of doctrine" (to use a form of speech formerly quite familiar at New Haven) this religious system does not differ markedly from what is usually taught in the circles of the so-called "Liberal Theology." Professor Macintosh has, however, his own way of construing and phrasing the common "Liberal" teaching; and his own way of construing and phrasing it presents a number of features which invite comment. It is tempting to turn aside to enumerate some of these, and perhaps to offer some remarks upon them. As we must make a selection, however, it seems best to confine ourselves to what appears on the face of it to be the most remarkable thing in Professor Macintosh's representations. This is his disposition to retain for his religious system the historical name of Christianity, although it utterly repudiates the cross of Christ, and in fact feels itself (in case of need) quite able to get along without even the person of Christ. A "new Christianity," he is willing, to be sure, to allow that it is — a "new Christianity for which the world is waiting"; and as such he is perhaps something more than willing to separate it from what he varyingly speaks of as "the older Christianity," "actual Christianity," "historic Christianity," "actual, historical Christianity." He strenuously claims for it, nevertheless, the right to call itself by the name of "Christianity."

[1] From *The Harvard Theological Review,* vii. 1914, pp. 538–594.
[2] vii. 1, January, 1914, pp. 16–46.

It is, no doubt, a kind of tribute to Christianity — this clinging to its name to designate a religious system which retains so little of what that name has heretofore been used to express. Clearly, the name "Christianity" has become an honorable one under its old connotation, and has acquired secondary implications which do it credit. Mr. G. K. Chesterton has lately called our attention in his serio-comic way to the extent to which such secondary implications have attached themselves to it in the speech of the common people. The apple-women and charwomen, the draymen and dustmen, it seems, are accustomed to employ it in a sense of which we can only say that it lies somewhere between " sane " and " civilized"; which "signifies that which is human, normal, social, and self-respecting." "Where can I get Christian food? " " Where can I find a Christian bed? " These are natural forms of popular speech with which we are all familiar. And, adds Mr. Chesterton, when the modern idealist puts away wine and war and dons peasants' clothes in imitation of Tolstoy, and parts his hair in the middle as he has seen it parted in paintings of Christ, the democracy will most likely pass its scornful judgment on him by simply demanding, " Why can't he dress like a Christian? " By some such immanent logic " Christianity" has apparently come to mean to Professor Macintosh, " rational," " ethical"; and we can observe him, when wishing to express his vigorous rejection of " a particular theory of redemption " — this " particular theory of redemption " being the Christian doctrine of the Atoning Sacrifice of Christ — merely declaring of it roundly that it is "not only not essential to Christianity, because contrary to reason, but moreover essentially unchristian because opposed to the principles of sound morality." [3]

We certainly feel no impulse to deny that whatever is Christian is rational and moral. And we are profoundly interested in such indications as are supplied by the form of Pro-

---

[3] P. 18. Cf. p. 35, where this judgment is repeated: " being irrational, it cannot be of the essence of Christianity "; not being " rigidly moral," " it must be pronounced essentially unchristian."

fessor Macintosh's declaration, that the general mind has been
so thoroughly imbued with this fact that men instinctively
reason on the subaudition that when we say, " Christian," we
say " rational," " moral." But surely it cannot be necessary to
point out that we may not determine the contents of a historical system after this fashion. Shall we deal so with Buddhism
or Mohammedanism or Mormonism, with Romanism or Calvinism or the new " Liberalism "? If we find doctrines taught
by these systems repugnant to reason and morality, we (so far)
reject these systems. We do not forthwith declare that these
(alleged) irrational and immoral doctrines can therefore have
no place in these systems. We can deal differently with Christianity only on the assumption that Christianity is through
and through and in all its parts in complete accordance with
right reason and sound morality. The assumption is, no doubt,
accordant with fact. But we are not entitled to make it prior
to examination. And the first step in this examination cannot
be taken until the contents of Christianity have been ascertained.

To argue that a doctrine is not Christian because it is not
reasonable or moral, in a word, is to argue in a manifestly
vicious circle. It is to confuse the historical question, What
is Christianity? with the rational question, What is true? And
it can result in nothing other than replacing historical Christianity by a " rational " system of our own, or, to phrase it in
Mr. Chesterton's language, in " turning the Christians into
a new sect, with new doctrines hitherto unknown to Christendom." Nietzsche, Mr. Chesterton reminds us, insisted that
there never was but one Christian, and He was crucified; the
improvement now offered, Mr. Chesterton hints, may consist
in suggesting that perhaps even that single Christian was not
a " Christian." Certainly, the " Christianity " which is constructed on the principle, not that it consists in the religion
founded by Jesus Christ and practised ever since by His followers, taught of Him, but that it shall contain only what
commends itself to our ideas of " reason " and accords with our
ideas of " morality " runs a considerable risk of becoming a

Christianity which stands out of all relation to Christ and to whatever has heretofore passed for Christianity. It offers us, in point of fact, merely a Rationalistic system — taking the term in its broader historical and not in its narrow philosophical significance.

Clearly, Christianity being a historical religion, its content can be determined only on historical grounds. The matter scarcely requires arguing; and we may be permitted, perhaps, at this point to content ourselves with simply referring to the very lucid statement of its elements made by H. H. Wendt in the opening pages of his "System of Christian Doctrine," as also in an earlier pamphlet devoted to the subject. "The Christian religion," remarks Wendt with admirable point [4] —

" is a historically given religion. We cannot by an ideal construction or by deduction from a general notion of religion, determine what constitutes its genuine essence. We must rather seek to determine this essence by such an objective historical examination as we should give it were we dealing with the determination of the essence of some other historical religion."

Again [5]:

" In a scientific presentation of Christian doctrine, as we have already seen, one side of its criticism and positive justification must be directed to the proof that the doctrine presented is also genuinely Christian doctrine. How is this proof to be made? The recognition of the fact that Christianity is an entity which is historically given, and is not to be ideally constructed, is of fundamental importance for answering this question. . . . The question of the genuine Christianity of the Christian doctrine to be presented is, as a matter of principle, not to be confused with the question of the truth and the value of this doctrine. From our incidental conviction of the truth and indispensableness of Christianity there easily arises the assumption that a religious conception, if it is true and valuable, must also be genuinely Christian. But from the scientific standpoint it is self-evident that it must first be proved what conceptions are genuinely Christian, and only then the truth of these Christian

[4] " Die Norm des echten Christentums," 1893, p. 3; cf. p. 23.
[5] " System der christlichen Lehre," i. 1906, pp. 23–24; cf. pp. 3 ff., 42 ff.

conceptions be tested. Even when a capacity for ever-advancing development is recognized for Christianity and for Christian doctrine, the question of the authentic Christianity of any conception presented as Christian remains at bottom a historical one. For the question of what constitutes the ground-type of Christianity and of Christian doctrine, by which it is to be determined whether anything can still pass as Christian or not, is just as certainly to be answered historically as, for example, the question of what belongs to the ground-type of the Buddhist religion and doctrine."

There is really no mystery about the matter. The process by which it is determined what is a truly Christian doctrine (something very different from what is a true Christian doctrine), or what the Christian religion really is, differs in principle in no respect from the process by which we determine what is an old Hellenic doctrine or what Ritschlism really teaches, what is the nature of Islam or what is the essence of the Pragmatic philosophy. In the very nature of the case such questions are purely historical and purely objective in their character, and the answers to them are not in the least advanced by any judgments we may pass upon the rationality or morality of the several doctrines or systems which come under our survey.

The justification which Professor Macintosh offers for permitting his subjective judgments of rationality and ethical value to intrude into the determination of the purely objective question of "What is Christianity?" he draws from a theory, which he very earnestly advocates, of the proper method of procedure in determining "the essence" of "any historical *quantum*." This theory might well have been derived, by the simple process of transferring it to historical quantities, from the metaphysical doctrine of "essence" propounded of late by our Pragmatic philosophers. Out of the general Pragmatic doctrine that "reality must be defined in terms of experience" [6] — or, as even more sharply expressed, that "reality is experience" [7] — these thinkers have evolved the notion that

[6] John Dewey, "Studies in Logical Theory," p. x.
[7] F. C. S. Schiller, "Studies in Humanism," p. 463.

the " essence " of anything is not what it is, but what it is, not
merely to but for me; not that which makes the thing precisely
the thing it is, but that in the thing, whatever it may be, which
I find needful for the realization of a purpose of my own.
" The essence of a thing," says William James,[8] " is that one of
its properties which is so *important for my interests* that, in
comparison with it, I may neglect the rest." Applying this
astonishing doctrine to historical entities, and especially to
Christianity, which is the historical entity in which at the
moment he is interested, Professor Macintosh feels able to
argue that the essence of Christianity is not that in Christianity which makes it the particular thing which we call
Christianity, but that in Christianity which he finds it desirable to preserve in constructing what he considers the ideal
religion. Since the essence, as he tells us with the emphasis
of italics, " is necessarily *what is essential for a purpose,*"
and the right purpose is, of course, the realization of the true
ideal, the essence of the Christian religion is necessarily " that
in the totality of the religious phenomena of Christianity
which is a necessary factor in the realization of the true ideal
for humanity, and of the true ideal for human religion in
particular "; or, varying the language slightly without altering the sense, " whatever in actual phenomenal Christianity
is necessary for the realization of the true ideal of human
spiritual life in general and of human religion in particular."

The odd thing is that Professor Macintosh does not betray
any consciousness of the outstanding fact that, in the process
of his reasoning, he has transmuted the question which he
started out to discuss, namely, What is essential to the retention of Christianity? into the fundamentally different one, in
which he is himself perhaps more deeply interested, of What
in Christianity is it essential that we retain? — namely in
order that we may build up " the ideal religion." Unless we
judge it to be still odder that he does not seem to have considered what would be the effect of the application of this

---

[8] " Text-Book of Psychology," 1892, p. 357; cf. " The Principles of Psychology, 1908," ii. p. 333.

method of determining the essence of a religious system to other religions besides Christianity — although he expressly presents it broadly as the proper method of determining "the essence of the Christian religion, or, for that matter, the essence of any historical *quantum*." If the discovery "in the totality of the religious phenomena of Christianity " of something which we judge "necessary for the realization of the true ideal of human spiritual life in general and of human religion in particular" justifies our calling that particular thing the "essence of Christianity" and ourselves, on the strength of our retention of it, "Christians "; would not the discovery of such an element in " the totality of the religious phenomena " of, say, Mormonism, equally justify us in declaring that element the " essence " of Mormonism and ourselves Mormons on the strength of our retention of it in our ideal religion? And surely we cannot doubt that Mormonism does possess in its composite system, however deeply buried beneath its own *bizarreries,* some truly religious and even some truly Christian elements — from which, indeed, we may believe, it derives whatever vitality it exhibits as a religious system; and certainly we cannot avoid retaining these elements as we build up our ideal religion. Or, if we seem to go too far afield in adducing Mormonism as an example, let us think for a moment of that active Christian sect known as the Seventh-Day Adventists. Undoubtedly, in the "totality of the religious phenomena" exhibited in the life of the members of this sect, there are many elements which must abide in any ideal system of religion. Do these elements therefore constitute the " essence " of Seventh-Day Adventism? And does our retention of them in our ideal construction justify our calling ourselves Seventh-Day Adventists?

It may not be an unpleasing thought to Professor Macintosh that, discerning something of value in each of the great religious movements which have stirred the waters of humanity, and preserving for the purposes of his ideal religion all that he sees in them of value, he may conceive himself to have therefore embraced " the essence " of each of them in turn, and to have thus acquired the right to claim for himself the name of every one of them. It may please him thus to think of himself as at once a Fetishist and a Shamanist, a Brahmanist and a Buddhist, a Confucian and a Mussulman, as well as a Jew and a Christian; perhaps also at once a Romanist and a Protestant, a Pelagian and an Augustinian, an Arminian and a Calvinist — for surely there is *something* of permanent value even in Calvinism, and if so, that is its " essence," and he who holds to the " essence " of Calvinism is surely a Calvinist. We have no wish to deny that Professor Macintosh's claim upon the one name may be as sound as upon another. But we confess to a doubt of the value of so diffused a claim upon names representing movements historically so distinct. And we confess to something more than a doubt of the validity of the method of determining " the essence " of historical entities which may lead to results so very embarrassing.

It must be admitted that the notion of " essence " has not always been dealt with lucidly by the metaphysicians. Cicero, indeed, who introduced the term into the Latin language, defined it very sensibly as " the whole of that by which a thing is, and is what it is " — a definition happily echoed in Locke's " the very being of anything, whereby it is what it is." And that essentially this remains the meaning of the term until today in general philosophical usage, we may be assured by Rudolf Eisler's definition of it. " Essence (οὐσία, *essentia*)," says he,[9] " is, ontologically speaking, that which constitutes the reality (Selbst-Sein) of a thing, its most proper, abiding nature, in distinction from its time-and-space-conditioned, changeable existence." Even an activist like the late Borden P. Bowne [10] without hesitation speaks in the same sense of " essence " as just " the nature of a thing ": " We believe that everything is what it is because of its nature, and that things differ because they have different natures. . . . The nature of a thing expresses the thing's real essence; and we hold that we have no true knowledge of the thing until we grasp its

---

[9] " Wörterbuch der philosophischen Begriffe," [3] 1910, iii. p. 1774.
[10] " Metaphysics," 1882, pp. 59–60.

nature." To him, of course, as Being is just action, and a thing as conceived just a "conceived formula of action," the essence of a thing consists in a law "which gives both its coexistent and its sequent manifestations." But this concerns only his ontology. Under its guidance he writes:

" Now this rule or law which determines the form and sequence of a thing's activities, represents to our thought the nature of a thing, or expresses its true essence. It is in this law that the definiteness of a thing is to be found; and it is under this general form of a law determining the form and sequence of activity that we must think of the nature of the thing." " In the metaphysical sense, the nature of a thing is that law of activity whereby it is not merely a member of a class, but also, and primarily, itself in distinction from all other things." " When then we speak of the nature of a thing under the form of a law, we regard this law as entirely specific and individual and not as universal. The nature has the form of a law but applies only to the single case."

In one word, to Bowne too, the " essence " means just the specific quality of a thing.

Nevertheless already a half-century ago James McCosh could write of "essence": "It is a very mystical word, and a whole aggregate of foolish speculation has clustered round it." [11] He had perhaps been reading the section on "essence" in Hegel's "Phaenomenologie," without the assistance of William Wallace. " Still," he adds hopefully, " it may have a meaning." Whether he could have spoken so hopefully, had he had the discussions of our Twentieth-century Pragmatists before him, we can only conjecture. Certainly they have done what they could to confuse the matter, and it may be a fair question whether under their definitions the term " essence " retains any meaning at all. What is called its " essence " certainly ceases to have any significance for the object whose " essence " it is said to be; and, being transmuted into merely whatever the changing observer in his changing moods may find from time to time in an object utilizable for his varying purposes, has whatever significance it may retain rather for

[11] " The Intuitions of the Mind," [2] 1869, p. 152.

him than for it. We observe in the mean time that the Pragmatists have great difficulty in carrying their discussions of " essence " through consistently on these lines. The real meaning of the term is continually making itself felt, and advertising to the reader the artificiality of the construction which is being commended to him.

William James's discussion is particularly instructive in this respect.[12] Every object, he explains, has an indefinite number of attributes. But we, being finite, cannot attend to all these attributes at once. We must, by the necessity of the case, make a selection. And we shall inevitably make our selection according to our interests. The attribute to which we attend under the influence of an interest at the moment governing our attention, is not more " essential" to the object than any other attribute to which another observer, led by another interest, or ourselves at another time, governed by another interest, may attend. The object " is really *all* that it is " — a statement which seems to assure us that the essence of an object is " really " all that by virtue of which it is what it is, and that is very much the old definition of " essence." But *we* must "attack it piecemeal, ignoring the solid fulness in which the elements of Nature exist, and stringing one after another of them together in a serial way, to suit our little interests as they change from hour to hour." Thus the " essence " of the object may seem to us to be a different attribute at each successive moment. And that leads James to declare with the emphasis of underscoring: " *There is no property* ABSOLUTELY *essential to any one thing. The same property which figures as the essence of a thing on one occasion becomes a very unessential feature upon another." This, however, can only mean that there is no single property among the many which belong to the object " really " which is " absolutely," that is to say, always and in every contingency, essential — to us, for our interests and purposes. Our interests change, and with the change of interest the quality of the object to which we attend also changes. This is not to say, of course, that there are no

[12] " The Principles of Psychology," 1908, ii. pp. 332 ff.

properties of an object which are absolutely, that is indispensably, essential — to it, that is to say to the preservation of its integrity as the very thing that it is. That this cannot be said is already made plain when it is declared that the object "is really all that it is." That little word "really" has confounded all of James's reasoning. And so he proceeds to tell us that "the elements of Nature exist" "in solid fulness"; and that it is only our partial, piecemeal dealing with them that hides this fact from us from time to time. Things, then, have "really" a "solid fulness" of properties by virtue of which they are objectively what they are; and this fact cannot be altered, though it may be obscured, by our habit — it may be a necessary habit — of attending to this "solid fulness" of elements one by one, and emphasizing each as it may meet a transient (or permanent) interest of our own. What things "really" are — that is what is essential *to them;* what in them meets an interest of ours (transient or permanent) — that is what we find essential *for our* (transient or permanent) purposes.

It is quite proper for James to say, therefore, that those properties which we are accustomed to select out of an object in accordance with "our usual purpose," "characterize us more than they characterize the thing." They are, no doubt, properties of the thing, and so far characterize it. But they need not be the particular properties of the thing which are most characteristic of it and form its specific quality. They are only the particular qualities of the thing by virtue of which it is most usually serviceable for us, and which therefore most constantly attract our attention. It is not implied, therefore, that there are no qualities which particularly characterize the thing, make it the thing it is, and so constitute its "essence." It is only recognized that we do not always, or commonly, select these properties for contemplation. When we are making selections of properties in accordance with our interests, we rather commonly, or always, select elements in the object which, because they are essential to *our* purposes, characterize *us* rather than the object. It is passing strange, therefore, that James should now go on to define the "essence *of a thing*," as "that one of its properties which is so *important for my interests* that in comparison with it I may neglect the rest." This, he has told us, is not "really" "the *essence* of the thing"; *that* lies elsewhere, and *this* is only the element in the thing which is essential *to my purpose* — which surely is a very different matter; unless, indeed, our particular purpose at the moment happens to be to determine what the "essence of the thing" is, in which case we may perhaps select out the particular properties which, constituting the essence of the thing, meet also our present purpose.

It is, of course, the Pragmatic point of view which, intruding here so many years before its formal announcement, forces this logical saltation upon James. From this point of view, he despises all questions of "inner essence"[13] as mere hairsplitting abstractions, and insists that "we carve out everything" "to suit our human purposes."[14] Accordingly he suddenly asserts here, without any justification in the preceding discussion, that "the only meaning of essence is teleological." A thing *is* just what it is good for, and, let us add, just what it is good for to me — and now. He has given us no reason, however, to believe that this is the case. He has only given us reason to believe that our interest in things is apt to be focussed on whatever we find serviceable to us, for the moment or permanently. That this is not all that the things are, however, he tells us himself, when he tells us not only that "the properties which are important vary from man to man and from hour to hour" in accordance with the purposes which dominate observation, but in express words that "the reality overflows these purposes at every pore." Surely it cannot be pretended that the properties which constitute the "concrete fact" "vary from man to man and from hour to hour," and are never more than what meets our purposes, which the reality that they constitute "overflows at every pore." And surely it is legitimate to inquire what then these properties are which enter into and constitute this "concrete fact," from

---

[13] Cf. "Pragmatism," 1907, p. 107.　　[14] "Pragmatism," pp. 251 ff.

the richness of which men may select what suits their purposes from time to time, but which in its richness " overflows "
these purposes "at every pore." On the face of it this is the
problem of " the essence " of the " concrete fact " in question.

Except that it seems to show a somewhat more formal
respect for objectivity, F. C. S. Schiller's definition of "essence " [15] does not differ essentially from James's. He speaks,
of course, from his activistic standpoint, to which " the activity is the substance; a thing *is* only in so far as it is active."
"So it is the activity," he explains, "which *makes* both the
'essence' and the 'accidents,' both of which are as it were
'precipitated' from the same process of active functioning."
"The 'essence,'" therefore, he proceeds, "is merely such
aspects of the whole behavior as are selected from among the
rest by reason either of their relative permanence or of their
importance for our purposes." He is recognizing nothing but
activities. Some of these " activities " are " relatively " more
permanent than others. Some of them are more important for
us than others. We are to call either the one or the other of
these sets of " activities" the "essence " of the object under
consideration. Which? The former give us an objective criterion; the latter, a subjective one. Both are activities; but
the latter only are conceived Pragmatically. If the latter be
employed as our criterion, we are fully on William James's
ground. If the former, we seem to be as fully off of it; we seem
to be allowing that the " essence " of a thing is what makes it
persistently (at least " relatively ") the thing that it is, not
what we discover in it serviceable to us — which is what we
shall have if the latter criterion be employed.

How the two criteria — objective and subjective — can be
conciliated, does not appear. Schiller does indeed tell us that
they "are, of course, convergent." And he explains this by
remarking that " a permanent aspect is naturally one which
it is important for us to take into account, while an important
aspect is naturally one which we try to render permanent."
We shall have to take his word for both declaration and ex-

[15] " Humanism " (1903),[2] 1912, p. 225.

planation. An aspect taken into account because it is permanent is surely one selected on grounds relative to the object; it tells us what the object itself is, or, if we prefer that mode of statement, how the object itself behaves. And an aspect taken into account because it is important for us (we assume that it is not significant that the " for us " has dropped out of the second clause) is one selected on grounds relative to us, to " our purposes "; it tells us what we find in the object (or its behavior) which is serviceable to us. How these two criteria can be said to " converge " passes our comprehension — unless indeed we are to think circularly as well as activistically, and conceive that motions in diametrically opposite directions will meet — on the other side of the circle. It must be admitted that Schiller's statement is not free from suggestions of such a circular movement. If an aspect of the behavior of an object under our contemplation is to be held " important for us " because it is permanent, one would think that its observed permanence would precede our interest and determine it; and that, in such a case, we could scarcely say that the " essence " of the object, identified with this permanent aspect of its behavior, is determined by our interest. And yet we are immediately told that we can render permanent an aspect of the behavior of such an object in which we chance to be interested; or at least that we may try to do so, presumably hopefully. One would like to know how he is to go about trying to make permanent an aspect of the behavior of an object under his observation; and if we can render an aspect of it permanent because it is important for us that it should be so, why cannot we create this aspect for ourselves in the first instance, that it may serve our purposes?

We may take it that Schiller's disjunctive is merely another illustration of the difficulty of carrying out the programme of the subjectivation of the "essence," and that it therefore bears witness only to the fact that the " essence " of an object cannot really be conceived merely as that in it which is essential for me — which is of importance for my purposes — but will continue to present itself as that in the object which is essential for it — which is necessary to its integrity, to its remaining the precise thing it is. That is to say, those aspects of the whole behavior of an object which are permanent constitute its "essence," and that quite independently of their "importance for us." It is important, of course, that we should take cognizance of them and adjust our behavior to them, for they constitute reality, that actual environment upon which we react. Hardness, for example, does not enter into the essence of a stone-wall because it serves an interest of ours and can be made serviceable to us. It enters into its essence because it is "there," quite independently of its serving an interest of ours; and it is important for us to recognize that it is "there" because the recognition of realities serves interests of ours, and realities have a very unpleasant fashion of revenging themselves on those who do not recognize them. It is the hardness of the stone-wall which determines our interests, not our interests which determine its hardness; and it would be very difficult to understand how we should go about rendering its hardness permanent, because we found it important for us. We may discover many good reasons, on the other hand, why it would be well for us to render permanent our recognition that a stone-wall is hard. The assumption of an "external world" which ordinary experience makes, as Schiller himself allows, "works splendidly."[16]

It is upon some such flimsy philosophical basis that Professor Macintosh, transferring the matter to the sphere of historical entities, develops his method of determining the "essence" of historical movements. It must be allowed that, in applying to this new class of objects the principles laid down by the metaphysicians, he proceeds with a consistency which fairly puts the metaphysicians to the blush. He is seeking what he indifferently speaks of as a valid "definition," "the real nature," the "essence" of the Christian religion. In order to obtain this, he lays down with great firmness and with the emphasis of italics the general proposition that "the essence," that is, the essence of any "historical *quantum*," "is neces-

[16] "Studies in Humanism," p. 459.

408 CHRISTOLOGY AND CRITICISM

sarily *what is essential for a purpose."* The " unrelieved subjectivity" of this proposition is obvious, and he seeks to mitigate it, but only by insisting that " the controlling purpose "
which is to determine the essence of an object "must be the
right purpose in the given situation." He explains this to mean
that it must be "the purpose to realize what under the circumstances is the true ideal." Thus we obtain what he regards
as two "normative principles" which it is necessary to observe in extracting " the essence " from any historical entity.
They are: " in the first place, the essence must be in the total
actuality "; " and in the second place, the controlling purpose
must be the right purpose." " In short," we read (again in the
emphasis of italics), *" the essence is whatever is both present
in the actual and demanded by the ideal."*

Why the essence of any historical entity must be something
found not only in it but also in our ideal, is not made clear to
us, and we profess ourselves unable to divine. We appear only
to be given a formula by means of which we may get rid of
the historical entity and substitute for it our own ideal; we
are to recognize as the essence of the historical entity nothing
that we do not find in our ideal. Shall Protestant investigators
then declare that the essence of Romanism must be identified
with what is common to Romanism and their ideals? Or Rationalistic investigators declare that the essence of Protestantism is what is common to Protestantism and their ideals?
In that case Romanism is merely defined as really Protestantism, and Protestantism as really Rationalism. The matter is
not relieved by the expedient taken to guard against error.
" To guarantee that what is taken as essential is the real essence," we read, " what is taken as the ideal must be the true
ideal." What is to guarantee that what is taken as the ideal
is the true ideal, we are not told here, but afterwards it is
intimated that "what this true ideal is, must be determined
by a critical philosophy of values," which leaves us in great
concern to know whose " critical philosophy of values " is to
have this decisive function committed to it.

A third normative principle is now, however, invoked.

What is under these rules extracted as the essence of any historical entity must, we are told, "be able to maintain itself after it has been selected and separated from all that is unessential" — that is, we infer, from all that to the investigator seeking the " true ideal " seems harmful to that ideal. Accordingly, " in addition to being the highest common factor of the actual and the ideal, *the essence must be vital enough to persist in separation from all that must be eliminated.*" " The essence of the actual, then " — we reach now the final summing up — " is that element in the actual whose continued existence is demanded by the true ideal, and which can retain its actuality and vitality after the elimination of all objectionable elements from the actual at the demand of that same ideal."

The process of extracting the essence of any historical entity which is commended to us by Professor Macintosh is now before us. It is in brief the following. First, by " a critical philosophy of values," determine independently for yourself what is the true ideal. Next, go to the historical entity in question with this " true ideal " in your hand, and select from this historical entity whatever seems to you fitted to promote the " true ideal." This is " the essence " of that historical entity — provided only that when you discard all in it which is not in your judgment fitted to promote your " true ideal," enough is left to call the essence of anything. If not enough is left, then say that that entity has no " good essence " and discard it *in toto*. Clearly, in this process, the historical entity is nothing; our ideal is everything. We have simply sunk the historical entity in our ideal; and it almost has the look of a concession that it is still allowed that what is called its essence shall actually be found in the historical entity.

Applying this method of extracting the essence of historical entities to the Christian religion, Professor Macintosh has naturally no difficulty in moulding Christianity to his own taste. He tells us that the result reached is that " the Christian religion " must be in essence whatever in actual phenomenal Christianity is necessary for the realization of the true ideal of human spiritual life in general and of human religion in particular." Obviously, then, the contents of "the Christian religion" are not determined by the contents of "actual phenomenal Christianity"—and by this must be understood not merely the Christianity which happens to be actual at any one moment, but any and all Christianity which has ever been actual in the course of its entire history — but by the contents of "the true ideal of human spiritual life in general and of human religion in particular." The "true ideal" of religion — that is, of course, the investigator's ideal of what religion ought to be, determined, no doubt, by his "critical philosophy of values"—is thus simply substituted for Christianity, and given its name. The only connection which this ideal can claim with "actual phenomenal Christianity"—that is, any Christianity which has ever actually existed—will be dependent on the presence in "actual phenomenal Christianity" of elements which are in harmony with it and may, therefore, be preserved. Whatever in "actual phenomenal Christianity" agrees with "the true ideal" of religion is preserved; the rest is discarded; and the total ideal religion, — inclusive, of course, of the elements thus "taken over" from "actual phenomenal religion" because already present in the ideal religion, and also, of course, of all else that is contained in the ideal religion which was not present in "actual phenomenal Christianity," — recieves the name of "the Christian religion." The process is exceedingly simple. "Our religion" is certainly Christianity, because *real* Christianity is, of course, just "our religion." Everything else in "actual phenomenal Christianity" is to be discarded because it is not included in "our religion."

The particular religion to which, under the name of "the ideal religion," Professor Macintosh reduces Christianity by this process, proves, as has been already intimated, to be indistinguishable from that which is generally professed in the circles of so-called "Liberal Christianity." How he arrives at the conviction that this is "the ideal religion" and therefore essential Christianity, he does not fully explain to us. It emerges as such in his pages as the culmination of an exposi-

tion of the fundamentally moral character of Christianity as
he conceives it — a moral character attributed to his "Christianity" because it is an element "common to actual Christianity and to ideal religion." If we understand Professor
Macintosh at this point, he defines Christianity on this ground
as the "religion of moral redemption," and then distinguishes
it from other religions of moral redemption by the particular
quality of the morality of which the redemption wrought by
it consists. Christianity, he says, "is the religion whose ' miracle ' or ' revelation ' consists in the experience of *moral*
'salvation' or 'redemption.' "[17] To the objection that " a
moral element is to be found in other historical religions also,"
he seems to reply that this need not invalidate the claim of
Christianity to be the moral religion by way of eminence — if,
that is, the quality of the morality brought by it to its votaries
may be shown to be superior to that offered by other moral
religions. This he affirms to be the fact, and he fixes on the
term " Christlike " to express the specific quality of specifically
Christian morality. Accumulating emphasis upon this quality
he declares, then, that " Christianity is the religion of deliverance from unchristlikeness to a Christlike morality, through a
Christlike attitude towards a Christlike superhuman reality."
Repeating this with further elaboration, he declares again:
" There is good ground to suppose, then, we take it, that redemption from unchristlikeness to a Christlike morality and
ultimately to a Christlike fellowship with God, accomplished
in the life of men by the activity of the Christlike God in
response to a Christlike dependence and filial attitude on the
part of the individual, is the essence of the Christian religion."

It is important to observe that these statements contain
much more than was prepared for by the preceding argument.
We have travelled very rapidly and very far and have arrived
very unexpectedly at a very definite dogmatic result. Not only
is the character of the morality involved in the Christian " redemption " defined as " Christlike " without sufficient justifi-

[17] The echoes of Rudolf Eucken's language may be noted, but we do not
stop to advert to the matter.

cation or even explanation, so that we get a particular standard of morality, and one, be it observed, quite external to the
subjects of religion, and wholly dependent on the truth of
history for its validity and its very meaning. But we also have
a particular manner — and that a very astonishing manner —
in which the moral revolution asserted to take place in the
subjects of the Christian religion, is wrought, made, without
any, we do not say merely justification, but preparation in the
preceding discussion, a part of the definition of that religion.
It is wrought, we are now suddenly told, " through a Christlike attitude towards a Christlike superhuman reality"; "by
the activity of the Christlike God in response to a Christlike
dependence and filial attitude on the part of the individual."
The essence of the Christian religion is thus made to consist
not merely in the fact that it brings a moral redemption, and
not merely in the specific character of the morality which it
brings, but still further in the particular manner in which this
moral redemption is produced. We do not stop now to press
the question of what is involved with respect to the relation
of Christianity to the historic Christ in the definition of this
morality — and everything else significantly Christian — as
" Christlike." We merely ask the warrant for the particular
manner in which the moral revolution which is declared to be
the essence of Christianity is asserted to be accomplished.
Professor Macintosh gives us none. At a later point, it is true,
we are told that this is involved in " the essence of the Christian gospel," and that this is derived from " the religious example of Jesus." " The Christian evangel," we read, " is the
gospel of the power of God manifesting itself in a Christlike
morality on condition of the cultivation of a life of Christlike religious devotion. It is the gospel of the universal possibility of redemption as a human religious experience, through
following the religious example of Jesus, taking the attitude
of sonship towards the 'God and Father of our Lord Jesus
Christ.' " We have difficulty, however, in accepting mere repetition as justification. And we observe that Professor Macintosh can only profess in any case to be " practically certain "

that the attitude here declared to be of the essence of Christianity on the ground that it was the attitude of Jesus, was
really " the religious attitude of Jesus "; and indeed contends
strenuously that it is not absolutely necessary for the validation of his " Christianity," thus made to hang entirely on the
example of Jesus, that there ever should have been any Jesus
to set this example. Nor have we discovered any reason given
by him justifying the belief that if there was a Jesus and this
was His attitude to God, it is capable of being imitated by us;
or indeed whether, if it were imitable by us, it would have the
effects asserted for it. The upshot of it all is merely that it is
dogmatically declared to us, with no reasons rendered, that
the ordinary " Liberal " construction of Christianity is the
only true Christianity, and its fundamental postulates constitute " the essence of Christianity." On the face of it this declaration rests on nothing more solid than that the ordinary
" Liberal " construction of Christianity seems to Professor
Macintosh the " ideal religion," and it pleases him to call
what he thinks the " ideal religion," " Christianity."

Even Adolf Harnack did better than that. It is quite true,
as Alfred Loisy points out,[18] that Harnack does not speak
really as a historian but as a dogmatician, in those brilliant
lectures in which he advocates his personal religious opinions[19]
under the name of " the essence of Christianity," and which,
Ernst Troeltsch tells us,[20] have become " to a certain degree
the Symbolical Book of all those who follow the historical
tendency in theology." But he had at least the grace to profess
to derive his idea of what Christianity is from historical Christianity, and his argument at least formally runs, that this and

[18] " L'Évangile et l'Église,"[3] 1904, pp. ix f.: " The definition of Christianity according to Harnack — is it that of a historian or only that of a
theologian who takes in history what suits his theology? The theory which is
expounded in the lectures on " The Essence of Christianity " is the same
as that which dominates the learned " History of Dogmas " which the same
author has published. But has he really deduced it from history, or has he
rather only interpreted history according to the theory? "

[19] Loisy, p. v, justly calls the " Wesen des Christentums," " a profession
of personal faith in the form of a historical sketch."

[20] *Die Christliche Welt,* xvii. (1903) 19, col. 444.

nothing else is the essence of the Christianity which was launched into the world by Jesus and has been lived by His followers. He tells us accordingly [21] that it is "a purely historical question" which he undertakes, and that therefore it is to be dealt with absolutely objectively; we are simply to ask what Christianity is without regard to what "position the individual who examines it may take up in regard to it, or whether in his own life he values it or not." His historical point of view is so marked, indeed, that he even declares that though we must start from "Jesus Christ and His Gospel," it is impossible to get "a complete answer to the question, What is Christianity?" "so long as we are restricted to Jesus Christ's teaching alone"; we must look upon Him merely as the root out of which the tree of Christianity has grown. "We cannot form any right estimate of the Christian religion unless we take our stand upon a comprehensive induction which shall cover all the facts of its history." "What is common to all the forms which it has taken, corrected by reference to the Gospel, and, conversely, the chief features of the Gospel, corrected by reference to history, will, we may be allowed to hope, bring us to the kernel of the matter."

We could not easily have fairer historical professions. The pity is that Harnack's actual procedure corresponds so ill with them. He certainly does not approach his task in a purely historical spirit. He brings with him to the investigation of the teaching of Jesus, for example, a whole body of presuppositions, under the influence of which he forces his material into preconceived moulds. And he certainly does not derive his conception of Christianity from an induction from its entire phenomenal manifestation; he simply makes his reconstructed version of Jesus' Christianity the sole Christianity which he will recognize. Troeltsch [22] accordingly is compelled to pronounce Harnack's critics right when they declare that "his *Wesen* is no purely empirical-inductive work, but includes in

---

[21] "Das Wesen des Christentums," 1900, 56–60 thousand, 1908, Lect. 1. E. T. "What is Christianity?" 1901, pp. 7, 8, 10, 11, 15.

[22] As cited, 21, coll. 486 f.

it strong religio-philosophical preconceptions by which it is deeply influenced"; nor can he deny that Harnack treats the gospel of Jesus alone as the essence of Christianity and "works up the details of Jesus' preaching into an idea of Christianity, which he then merely illustrates from the later history of the Church, partly by pointing to departures from it, partly by emphasizing what is consonant with it in further developments." [23] What Harnack invites us to do is thus in point of fact merely to recognize as "the essence of Christianity" the "religion of Jesus" as he has reconstructed it under the influence of his own naturalistic postulates. Before we can follow him we must be assured that what he presents as such was really "the religion of Jesus," and that "the religion of Jesus," in his sense of that phrase, is really Christianity. We do not need to adopt Loisy's standpoint to perceive the justice of his criticisms at these points. And surely a remark like this cuts to the bottom:

" If what is desired is to determine historically the essence of the gospel, the canons of a sound criticism do not permit us to resolve in advance to consider as unessential what we are now inclined to think uncertain or unacceptable. What is essential to the gospel of Jesus is what holds the first and the most considerable place in His authentic teaching, the ideas for which He strove and for which He died, not that merely which we believe to be still vital today. . . . In order to determine the essence of Islam we shall not take, in the teaching of the Prophet and in the Mussulman tradition, what we may consider true and fertile, but what was actually of most importance to Mahomet and his followers, in point of belief, ethics, and worship. Otherwise with a little good will we might discover that the essence of the Koran is the same as that of the Gospels — faith in the clement and merciful God." [24]

It is interesting and not uninstructive to observe in passing the diametrical opposition of the methods by which Har-

[23] Cf. W. Sanday's remarks, "An Examination of Harnack's 'What is Christianity?'" 1901, pp. 16 ff.: "And yet in spite of these explicit promises the criterion that Harnack really proposes throughout his book is his own mutilated version of the teaching of Jesus."

[24] As cited, pp. xiv ff.

nack and Loisy, each, seek to extract the essence of Christianity. If Harnack, having reconstructed from the evangelical narratives a Jesus to fit his naturalistic presuppositions, sees in this reconstructed Jesus at once the entirety of Christianity and will allow nothing to enter into its essence but what he finds in Him, Loisy perceives in the Jesus to which he looks back through the stretches of history only the germ out of which his Christianity has expanded. It is Harnack, it is true, who writes: [25]

" Just as we cannot obtain a complete knowledge of a tree without regarding not only its root and its stem but also its bark, its branches, and the way in which it blooms, so we cannot form any right estimate of the Christian religion unless we take our stand upon a comprehensive induction that shall cover all the facts of its history."

But it is not Harnack's but Loisy's method which this figure suggests. " Why," demands Loisy — [26]

" Why ought the essence of the tree be thought to be contained in a single particle of the germ from which it has proceeded, and why will it not be just as truly and more perfectly realized in the tree as in the seed? Is the process of assimilation by which it makes its growth to be regarded as a change in the essence, virtually contained in the germ; or is it not rather the indispensable condition of its existence, of its preservation, of its advance in a life always the same and incessantly renewed? "

Harnack, he contends,[27]

" does not conceive of Christianity as a seed which has grown — first a potential plant, then an actual plant, identical with itself from the beginning of its evolution to the present moment, and from its root to the tip of its trunk; but as a ripe, or rather, a decayed, nut which must be shelled if its incorruptible kernel is to be reached. And Harnack tears off the shell with so much perseverance that the question arises whether anything will remain at the end."

[25] As cited, p. 11.   [26] As cited, p. xxvi.   [27] As cited, pp. xxix, xxx.

Perhaps with a little idealization, we may represent to ourselves the fundamental ideas embodied in the divergent views
as involving essentially some such conceptions as the following. Harnack wishes to see the essence of Christianity in what
is constant in the entire history of the Church, and just on
that account seeks it in the primitive beginnings of Christianity — in those primitive beginnings, no doubt, as reconstructed by him on the basis of his postulates. He therefore
makes primitive Christianity, the Christianity of Jesus Himself (as he reconstructs it), the standard of all Christianity;
that alone is Christianity which is to be found in the preaching of Jesus. Loisy wishes to view Christianity as a constant
development, as finding its reality not in its germ but in its
full growth. The gospel of Jesus is merely to him the root of
the Church; the Church is the living development of the
gospel; the essence of Christianity is its historical evolution,
which in every part is the necessary outcome of the complex
of circumstances in which it lives.[28]

When he lays aside figures and speaks plainly, Loisy, it
is true, finds difficulty in maintaining himself at these high
levels. At one point, indeed, he seems to work rather with the
ordinary logical conception of " essence " in his mind, according to which " it denotes the common quality or qualities
which are found in all the members of the class." [29] He makes
in effect a genus of Christianity by cutting it up into periods;
and, extracting the characteristic quality of each period in
turn, he compares these together and concludes that what
is common to all is the essence of Christianity and what is
peculiar to each is the differentiation of each period.[30] No
doubt there may be obtained thus a conception of what has
persisted through all ages of Christian history; and this may,

[28] Cf. Troeltsch, as cited, col. 445.

[29] McCosh, as cited, p. 152.

[30] As cited, p. xv: " If common traits have been conserved and developed
from the origin until our day in the Church, these are the traits which constitute the essence of Christianity. At least the historian cannot recognize any
others; he has no right to apply any other method than that which he applies
to any other religion."

in a sense, be called " common Christianity." But what will be
the result, if perchance Christianity has become apostate in
any one age and has recovered itself (" come to itself" like
the Prodigal Son) only after a period of general corruption?
Obviously, at the best, such a method must confound " the
essence of Christianity" with the minimum of Christianity,
and presents no great advantage in this respect over that
thoroughly misleading method of determining what is essential
to Christianity, dear to the hearts of all " indifferentists,"
which seeks it in what is common to all those who in any age
" profess and call themselves Christians " — extension through
space taking here the place of Loisy's extension through time.
What is common to all who call themselves Christians,
whether as extended through time or space, is, of course, just
the minimum of Christianity; otherwise those forms of professed Christianity or those periods of Christian history in
which only the minimum of Christianity is or has been confessed would be excluded. The " essence of Christianity " and
the minimum of Christianity are not, however, synonymous
expressions. If choice were confined to these two, it would be
better to follow Loisy in his ecclesiastical evolutionism and
discover the essence of Christianity in the maximum of Christianity, in Christianity in its fullest growth and vigor.

The evolutionism of Loisy is reproduced in Ernst
Troeltsch, though of course with all the involved tempera-
mental and environmental differences.[31] Troeltsch bids us [32]
keep in mind that the conception involved in the phrase " the
essence of Christianity" is historically inseparably wrapped
up with the modern critical evolutionary point of view. The
Romanist, he says, does not speak of " the essence of Christianity," but of the faith of the Church, and distinguishes
only between the complete knowledge of that faith which is
expected of the clergy and the less explicit knowledge of it

[31] Six articles entitled " Was heist ' Wesen des Christentums,'" published
in *Die Christliche Welt,* xvii. (1903) Nos. 19, 21, 23, 25, 28, 29. These articles
have been reprinted in Troeltsch's "Gesammelte Schriften," ii. 1913, pp.
386–451, but we cite from the articles.

[32] Col. 483.

which may be tolerated in the laity. Nor would old orthodox
Protestantism have used the phrase. It would have said, " the
revelation of the Bible," and have distinguished only between
fundamental and non-fundamental articles. Even for the Enlightenment, the phrase would have had no significance. It
spoke with Locke of "the reasonableness of Christianity"
and rationalized the Bible, making the post-Apostolic Church
responsible for all untenable dogmas. It is with Chateaubriand
and his *Génie du Christianisme* that the notion first emerges
into sight; that is to say, it is a product of Romanticism. And
it is to the German Idealists and especially to the Hegelians
that we owe its development. By it is not meant Christianity
as a whole — this is external appearance — but that which
unfolds itself in the phenomena of Christianity, "the idea
and power" which has dominated Christianity through all its
history and determined its varied phenomenal forms. It is
"the internal spiritual unity" which binds all these phenomenal forms together and which can be reached only by a
process of historical abstraction. Serving himself heir to the
Hegelians (with the necessary corrections),[33] Troeltsch accordingly looks upon Christianity as, like other great coherent
complexes of historical occurrences, the development of an
idea which effloresces progressively, incorporating into itself
and adapting to its uses all alien material which lies in its
path. The isolation of this idea to thought is, in his view, the
discovery of the essence of Christianity. The essence of Christianity is, therefore, an abstract notion by means of which
the whole body of the phenomena which constitute Christian
history is reduced to unity and explained.

It must not be imagined, however, that this wonderful informing idea which is to be distilled from phenomenal Christianity can, in the opinion of Troeltsch, " be simply abstracted
from the whole course and the totality of the manifestations
of Christianity in its historical development." A distinction,
it is asserted, must be drawn between the phenomena which
express the essence and those in which it is suppressed.[34] The

[33] Col. 484.   [34] Col. 534.

historical forms must be subjected to a criticism according
" to the ideal which informs the chief tendency." [35] This ideal
may most conveniently be discovered, Troeltsch thinks, in the
classical expression of Christianity in its origins.[36] But even
there distinctions must be drawn. The primitive age must not
be assumed to be a perfectly unitary complex. We must ask,
What in the primitive age contains what is really classic? No
doubt we shall find this in the figure and preaching of Jesus.
But we must not forget that the figure and preaching of Jesus
must be reconstructed. And for this reconstruction we need
something more than the Synoptic Gospels. We need Paul and
John, and more. " We do not find our foundation in the historical Christ, the Christ after the flesh, but in the spirit of
Christ, which was disengaged by the destruction of the earthly
manifestation in death." [37] The " words of Christ " are not
Christianity; rather faith in Christ and the spirit which proceeds from this faith and operates in the community — this
is Christianity. This spirit, however, did not exhaust its efficiency in the Pauline and Johannine Gospels; the totality of
the Christian development is involved. In it elements continually present themselves, which were, no doubt, present in
the primitive age, and in the light of the later development
may be recognized as having been present in it, but which
certainly only manifest themselves later and in particular
circumstances. " We must recognize them as contained in the
essence of Christianity and as important for the determination of that essence; we must look upon them as effects of the
spirit of Christ: but we do not find them expressed in the
primitive form in itself alone, and indeed cannot even directly
attribute them to it." [38] So clear is it that we cannot derive
the essence of Christianity exclusively from its primitive form;
this essence " cannot be an unchangeable idea which is given
once for all in the teaching of Jesus." Rather —

" the essence must be a somewhat which contains in itself energy
and mobility, productive power of continuous reproduction. It can

[35] Col. 534.   [36] Col. 578–9.   [37] Col. 580.   [38] Col. 581.

certainly not be denoted by a word or a doctrine, but only by an idea which includes in itself from the first mobility and fulness of life; *it must be a self-developing spiritual principle,* a ' germinative principle ' or a seed-thought, as Caird has it, a historical idea in Ranke's sense, that is, not a metaphysical or dogmatic conception, but a spiritual force which contains in itself a life-aim and a life-value, and which unfolds in its consistency and power of adaptation." [39]

The continuity — the unity binding the multiplicity of forms together — is, Troeltsch admits, no doubt, difficult to trace. It cannot lie simply in the preaching of Jesus, as persisting in all forms of Christianity as their basal element; nor yet in an abstract, generic idea common to all varieties of Christianity. It does not consist in any formulated conception, but in a spiritual power embracing in itself many ideas. Nor are we done with it when we are done with historical Christianity. In determining the essence of Christianity we must take in present Christianity as well as past Christianity; yes, and future Christianity too — if we believe in any future for Christianity. Thus from an abstraction, the essence of Christianity becomes an ideal.[40] We cannot avoid transforming it thus if we stand in any vital relation to Christianity. We study its history that we may learn from it. What we thus learn must be applied to the present, and must be projected also into the future. Thus the " divinatorial imagination " of abstraction necessarily passes into that " prognosticational imagination " which presages the further unfolding of the basal idea.

" Determination of essence is modification of essence. It is the extraction of the essential idea of Christianity from history in such a fashion that it shall illuminate the future; and at the same time a vital survey of the present and future world together in this light. The repeated determination of the essence is the repeated historical reorganization of Christianity. This can be avoided by none who seeks the essence of Christianity in a purely historical manner, and at the same time believes in the progressive power of the essence. Only those can take a different course who look upon

[39] Col. 581.   [40] Col. 651 f.

Christianity as an outworn and transcended historical organism
or who understands Christianity from an exclusively supernatural
revelation in the Bible." [41]

This apparently means that Troeltsch is aware that in the
process of extracting "the essence" of Christianity from its
phenomenal manifestation, he is moulding it to his own ideals,
and that he considers this natural to one in his position — one,
that is, who looks upon Christianity as a growth and yet is
concerned for its continuance in the world. We find him a little
later, accordingly, speaking not merely of "the essential
elements of Christianity" but rather of "the abiding and essential elements of Christianity." The notions of "abidingness" and "essentialness" have, however, in themselves nothing in common; and we only confuse ourselves, when we are
seeking to discover the essence of Christianity, if we insist
that what we find "essential" must be what we consider will
be "abiding." We are here very near to employing the term
"essential" again in the sense of "essential to us."

Troeltsch does not glose the essentially subjective character of the method of determining the essence of Christianity
which he proposes, nor does he fail to perceive the danger
which accompanies it of passing, without observing it, beyond
the limits of Christianity into a new religion only loosely
connected with Christianity. [42] These things, he says, simply
must be recognized and faced. Then he continues: [43]

"These remarks show our attitude towards one of the strongest
assaults made of late years upon the Christianity of the essence of
Christianity, as Harnack and his friends understand it. Eduard
von Hartmann, who already somewhat earlier called the so-called
Liberal theology the self-decomposition of Protestantism, will not
permit the left-wing Ritschlians — therefore, above all, Harnack
and those of like mind with him — to pass any longer as Christians.
Their essence of Christianity is, he intimates, the abandonment of
Christianity; and their Christianity is a self-deception due to their
training and sentiment. What they maintain to be Christianity
is their modern religious conviction, which has only a loose connec-

[41] Col. 654.   [42] Col. 682.   [43] Coll. 682–3.

tion with the real spirit of Christianity, and which clings all the more anxiously to a few accidental historical supports. The proof which Hartmann offers of this view is as instructive for the whole question of the essence of Christianity as for the question of the maintenance of its continuity. For him, in a purely historical sense, the essence of Christianity lies in the conception of God-manhood; and he explains this conception in a Pantheistic sense of the unity of the Divine and human spirits; and declares it the great idea of Christianity, which only needs to be separated from the myth of the incarnation of God in Jesus, and to be freed from all theistic-personal traits in the idea of God, to be able to enrich the religion of the future. That means, however, very clearly that Hartmann too will recognize as essence only what has in his eyes a relatively abiding importance; with him too the essential is what is valuable for the future, as he understands it. But because this abiding element can obtain for him its full further significance only by elimination of essential conceptions of historical Christianity, the revelation-significance of Jesus and the personality of God, therefore Christianity, despite it, is for him in its entirety a transcended epoch, and those are already fallen out of the continuity of Christianity who do not make the conception of God-manhood central, but by giving it an externally historical connection with some words of Jesus persuade themselves that an ethical Deism, without significance either for itself or for the future, is the essence of Christianity."

The question raised here, says Troeltsch, cannot be argued; the difference lies in the point of view. But the reader will scarcely be able to agree that a mere strong counter-assertion on the part of Troeltsch and his friends that they know themselves to possess a better objective-historical conception of Christianity than Hartmann, and to preserve with it a personal religious continuity precisely in what is essential to it, is a sufficient refutation of Hartmann's strictures. Their "Christianity" is confessedly not the Christianity of the past; as Troeltsch elsewhere acknowledges,[44] it is not the vital Christianity of the present; and it can become the "Chris-

---

[44] "Die Bedeutung der Geschichtlichkeit Jesu für den Glauben," 1911; cf. *The Harvard Theological Review,* iv. (October, 1912), p. 459.

tianity " of the future (as he also allows) [45] only if Christianity may suffer a sea-change into something possibly richer, but assuredly exceedingly strange — and yet remain Christianity. Whether it can perform this feat is the real question of " the essence of Christianity " as expounded by Troeltsch.

It is, of course, precisely Troeltsch's evolutionism which commends his presentation of " the essence " of Christianity to our evolution-obsessed generation. And a purer evolutionist than he, Edward Caird,[46] reminds us in more direct language that " evolution in human history includes revolution." If we are to distort (as Caird does) Tertullian's *anima naturaliter Christiana* into a prophetic pronouncement that what we call Christianity is the natural production of the human soul, as man struggles slowly towards the " consciousness of himself and of his relation to God," there is no reason why we should not understand that this so-called Christianity, as it reacts on its changing environment, takes on many forms and passes through many phases, connected only as the successive, though varying, expressions of the " growing idea of humanity." And there is no reason why these phases, as they succeed one another, should not advance by a zig-zag motion, which may often seem (and indeed be) retrogression, or should not sometimes even bring contiguous phases into a relation of direct opposition to one another; Caird tells us that the condition of development " is rebellion against the immediate past." Only, then, let it be distinctly understood, Christianity has lost all content. It is no longer a religion, but religion, finding its expression through varied forms: and the forms through which it finds its expression, whether of thought or of sentiment or of practice, are indifferent to it, so only the underlying religious impulse is there. It is only natural, therefore, that Jean Réville, for example, in endeavoring to tell us what " Liberal Protestantism " is — he might just as well have said

---

[45] *Ibid.* Troeltsch speaks of the change which Christianity has passed through in the hands of those who think with him as a " transformation."

[46] Article, " Christianity and the Historical Christ," in *The New World,* VI. xxi. (March, 1897) p. 10.

" Liberal Christianity," he tells us himself — takes much this line.[47] It is not to be denied, of course, that there is a sense in which it may very properly be said that the essence of all religious movements is just religion. It is this primal instinct of human nature which gives its vitality to every form of religion from Fetishism up to — well, just short, let us say, of the religions of revelation, if it be allowed that there is such a thing as revelation. Here we have the thing which all religions have in common, and by virtue of which they live in the world. We may abstract everything else from each of them in turn, and, leaving to each only the pure religious impulse and its products, may plausibly maintain that in this we have " the essence " of every religion which has ever existed or which can ever exist. Only, in that case, it is clear, we must allow that there never has been and never will be at bottom more than one religion. The " essence " of Christianity, so conceived, and the " essence " of Fetishism are the same; and we may, on the ground of holding to its " essence " call ourselves with equal right by either name. In holding the " essence " of one, we hold the " essence " of all. It was under the influence of some such conception that the late Auguste Sabatier lost himself in rapture over what he seemed to himself to see, in the way of real unity in the midst of apparent diversity, in any average congregation of " Christian " worshippers. There is the aged woman who has no other conception of God than the white-bearded old man with eyes like coals of fire she has seen in the pictures in the big Bible on the parlor-table. And there is the young collegian imbued with a pure Deism by his philosophical course at the university. And there is the disciple of Kant who holds that all positive ideas of God are contradictory and who can allow of God only that He is the Unknowable. And there is the proud Hegelian who knows all

[47] " Liberal Christianity," E. T. 1903, p. xi.; cf. p. 200: " The profession of faith of Liberal Protestantism — or of Liberal Christianity, for these two names are interchangeable — is wholly summed up in the single precept: *Thou shalt love the Lord thy God with all thy soul and thy neighbor as thyself.*" It does not trouble itself, however, as to who or what this God is which its ' single precept ' requires it to love " (pp. 64, 76, 120, 194).

about God, and knows Him to be the All Moved by a common
piety all these bow down together and adore. I do not know,
says Sabatier, if there is a spectacle on earth which is more
like heaven! [48]

From such a standpoint, the cry Back to Christ! can have,
as Caird does not fail to remind us, little meaning. The adjective " Christian " is employed to describe the movement which
goes by this name only because that particular movement of
religious development is supposed, in point of fact, to have
taken its temporal beginning in Christ, or to have reached
in the rise of Christianity a decisive — or at least an important
— stage of its development, or merely perhaps to have received from Christ or from the rise of Christianity some impulse, more or less notable, the memory of which is preserved
in the name by which it thus is accidentally designated. It is
in any case an illusion to suppose that we can find in Christ
" the true form " of the movement which is thus more or less
loosely connected with His name; that would be, Caird suggests, " seeking the living among the dead." [49] If we speak of
Him as the " seed " out of which the " plant " of Christianity
has grown, we are merely using tropical language which very
easily may be deceptive. We may imagine that " there is an
implicit fulness in the seed which is not completely repeated
in any subsequent stage in the life of the plant "; but then
we must allow that this fulness in the seed is very " implicit "
indeed; and we should not do amiss to bear in mind that " we
can know what is in the germ only by seeing how it manifests
itself in the plant." We must, in plain words, interpret Christ
from Christianity, not Christianity from Christ. It strikes the
reader with a sense of unreality, therefore, when writers like

---

[48] " Discours sur l'évolution des dogmes," pp. 21–22; cf. the comment
on it by H. Bois, " De la Connaissance Religieuse," 1894, pp. 35 ff. Also Jean
Réville, " Liberal Christianity," E. T. pp. 61 ff.: " You may hold doctrines
most dissimilar and even irreconcilable concerning the essence of God and
God's government of the world, and yet be equally good and faithful disciples
of Christ."

[49] Caird employs the phrase, not directly of the cry Back to Christ! but
illustratively of the parallel cry, Back to Kant!

Troeltsch, committed to an evolutionary view of Christianity, are found laying great stress on primitive Christianity and particularly on the personality and teaching of Jesus. No sooner does Troeltsch establish the "classical" place of primitive Christianity and especially of Jesus for the interpretation of Christianity, to be sure, than he forthwith sets himself to unravelling the coil in which he has thus involved himself. We do not say he succeeds in unravelling it. But that only shows that his evolutionary conception of Christianity is not only inconsistent with the significance he has established for Jesus as not merely the germ out of which it has grown but its Founder; but, being inconsistent with it, is untenable. We can look upon the stress laid upon primitive Christianity, and on the person and teaching of Jesus, by writers of this class, in a word, only as concessions to undeniable fact; fatal concessions to a fact which, when fairly allowed for, refutes their entire point of view. Christianity, clearly, is not a natural evolution of the religious spirit of man, with a more or less accidental connection with the man Jesus; it is a particular religion instituted by Christ and given once for all its specific content by His authority.

The manner in which Troeltsch establishes the "classical" significance of "the person and preaching of Jesus" for the determination of the "essence" of Christianity, is meanwhile worth observing somewhat more closely on its own account. His acknowledgment of the universal recognition of "primitive Christianity and behind primitive Christianity the person and preaching of Jesus" as bearing this "classical" significance is itself a concession of the highest importance. He is, no doubt, dissatisfied with the manner in which the classical significance of primitive Christianity and the person and preaching of Jesus is ordinarily established, because of the involution in it of, as he explains, "the presuppositions of the popular antique supernaturalism" and because of the position of absolute authority in which it leaves primitive Christianity and Jesus. He desiderates, therefore, a new grounding for the acknowledged fact, a grounding which will invoke and issue in nothing which is unacceptable to "the purely human-historical conception." He explains: [50]

" What is in question is a purely historically grounded significance of primitive Christianity for the determination of the essence. Such an one is, of course, actually at hand in the fullest sense, and is easy to point to. The authentic meaning of a historical phenomenon is contained most strongly and purely in its origins; and if such a statement can apply only in a qualified sense to complicated culture-forms like, say, the Renaissance, it certainly applies without quali-fication to the prophetic-ethical religions, which receive their entire life from the personalities of their founders, require their adherents constantly to renew their vitality from the primitive sources, and therefore connect their names and essence in the closest way with their personalities; it especially applies in an unqualified sense to Christianity, which prescribes to its adherents more rigidly than any other religion the continual nourishment of their religious life from contact with the Founder, and in its Christ-mysticism [51] has produced a unique phenomenon which corresponds with especial clearness with this circumstance. Accordingly, it is self-evident that the determination of the essence should adhere before all to the primitive period, and look upon it as the classical age."

We may look askance at some of the things that are said in this extract, but one thing emerges with great emphasis. Chris-tianity certainly did not just " grow up "; it was founded. And subsequently to its founding, it has not "run wild," gone off in this or that direction according as some contentless " in-forming spirit " or " germinal life " within it may have chanced to lead it; it has been held strictly, more strictly than any other religious movement, to its fundamental type, by con-stant references back to its foundations. For whatever reason, on whatever ground, it has kept a constant check upon itself lest it should depart from type, and has shown an amazing power, after whatever aberrations, continually to return to type. Its eye has been fixed not merely in forward gaze but in backward as well. It has manifested a unique capacity of growth, justifying its Founder's comparison of it to the mus-

[50] Col. 579.
[51] On this Christ-mysticism, cf. also J. Réville, as cited, p. 123.

tard-seed and to the leaven; but, after all is said as to the transformations it has suffered, its slacknesses, its degenerations,
its failures, its growth has lain not in the gradual development
of a content for itself, but in the steadily increasing assimilation of its environment to itself. In this respect too it has been
like the mustard-seed and the leaven to which its Founder
compared it; it has grown at the expense of its environment,
not being moulded by it, but moulding it. It has accordingly
remained amid its changing surroundings, and through all the
forms which it has occasionally taken, essentially the same;
and its "nature" is to be ascertained, therefore — like the
"nature" of other stable entities — simply by looking at it.
"Divinational imagination," and "prognosticational imagination" are all very well in their place, and we have no wish to
deny that there is a place for them even in estimating the
meaning and movements of Christianity. But observation is
the proper instrument for the ascertainment of the nature of
stable entities, and in spite of the "varieties of Christianity"
in time and in space, it will broadly suffice for the ascertainment of what Christianity is.

It is clear then, and it may be taken as generally acknowledged, that Christianity is not merely a form which religion has spontaneously taken in the course of developing
culture, but a specific religion which has been "founded,"
and the specific content of which has been once for all imposed upon it at its foundation. It is in the strictest sense of
the terms, a "positive religion," a "historical religion"; and
its content is to be ascertained not by reference to what we
may think "the ideal religion," but by reference to the character given it by its Founder. This is the real meaning of a
procedure like Harnack's, when, after proposing to determine
the nature of Christianity from its total historical manifestation, he really seeks and finds it solely in what he has brought
himself to look upon as "the religion of Jesus." His procedure
here is not in itself wrong. His fault lies primarily in the
critical method by which he ascertains the "religion of Jesus";
or, to speak more exactly, by which he imposes his own ideal

of religion upon Jesus as "the religion of Jesus." Thus he is
led to present as "the religion of Jesus" a religion which is as
different as possible from the actual religion of Jesus, and the
result of that is that he completely separates "the religion of
Jesus" from the religion which He founded, and is compelled,
therefore, to treat Christianity in its entire historical manifestation as a radical departure from "the religion of Jesus";
or, to put it brusquely, as a religion quite distinct from that
which had been introduced into the world by Jesus, although
it has usurped its place and name. In these circumstances,
naturally, he could not fulfil his promise to present Christianity from "a comprehensive induction that should cover
all the facts of its history." He could only present what he had
determined to be "the religion of Jesus" as genuine Christianity, and illustrate from the subsequent history the greatness of its departure from the original type, and the occasional
efforts which have been made to return more or less fully to
it; perhaps also the abiding presence throughout its whole
history of a persistent, if vague, apprehension that some such
religion lay in the background, until at last at the end of the
accumulating centuries, through great throes of labor, the
"Liberal" theology has thrown off the superincumbent accretions and recovered the pure gospel; or, at least, recovered
it in its essence; for the acknowledgment is inevitable that
"the religion of Jesus" in its completeness, just as it lay in
His own mind and heart, was His own, belonged to His time
and circumstances, and cannot be brought back again, in its
completeness, in our day. All we can do is to recover what in
it is of "permanent validity."

In thus setting "the religion of Jesus" and historical
Christianity over against one another in a relation which can
be called nothing less than antipodal (whatever larger or
smaller qualifications may be insisted upon) Harnack is speaking, of course, as the representative of the "Liberal" theology
in general. It has become the traditional historical postulate
of the "Liberal" construction of the early history of Christianity that the "religion of Jesus" was at once overlaid by

the "faith of the primitive community," and this in turn by the dogmatic constructions of Paul. Thus Paul emerges to view as "the second founder" of Christianity, and the Christianity which has propagated itself through the ages is held to derive from him rather than from Jesus.[52] Two deep clefts — between Paul and the primitive community and between the primitive community and Jesus — are imagined to separate historical Christianity from the teaching of Jesus; and across these, we are told, we must somehow find our way if we are to recover the teaching of Jesus, as across them the teaching of Jesus would have had to find its way if it were to determine the development of historical Christianity. It is to this conception of the course of early Christian history that William Wrede gives perhaps somewhat extreme expression when he declares — we avail ourselves of Harnack's words here — that " the second gospel," that is, the teaching of Paul over against " the first gospel," that is, the teaching of Jesus, " is something entirely new, that it, as far as it contains what we call historical Christianity, presents a new religion, in which Jesus Christ Himself has no, or only a most remote, part, and that the Apostle Paul is the founder of this religion." [53] And it is from this point of sight that Wilhelm Bousset, for example, twits " the orthodox " with "basing the truth of their whole system and the form of their faith on a fantastic mythical-dogmatic interpretation of the life of Jesus by Paul." [54]

---

[52] Cf. W. Wrede, "Paulus" (1904), E. T. 1907, pp. 179 ff.: "It follows then conclusively from all this that Paul is to be regarded as *the second founder of Christianity* . . . for Paul it demonstrably was who first . . . introduced into Christianity the ideas whose influence on its history up to the present time has been deepest and most wide-reaching. . . . This second founder of Christianity has even, compared with the first, exercised beyond all doubt the stronger — not the better — influence. . . . Throughout long stretches of church history . . . he has thrust the greater person, whom he meant only to serve, utterly into the background." Cf. pp. 165 f.: " The name ' disciple of Jesus ' has little applicability to Paul, if it is used to denote a historical relation. . . . He stands much further away from Jesus than Jesus Himself stands from the noblest figures of Jewish piety."

[53] Harnack, " Aus Wissenschaft und Leben," ii. 1911, p. 216.

[54] Address on " The Significance of the Personality of Jesus Christ for

One great difficulty — certainly not the only one nor even the greatest one — which stands in the way of this reading of the course of primitive Christian history, arises from Paul's vigorous repudiation of the honor thrust upon him. He emphatically denies that he is the teacher of a new gospel[55] and explicitly represents himself as in his teaching but repeating the common gospel of Christ which had been taught from the beginning; and that especially in those very items in which he is declared to be most violently the innovator. To adduce but a single instance — that with which we are at the moment most immediately concerned — Paul, in the most natural way in the world and with a simplicity which confounds every effort to discredit it, declares that he did not invent but received from his predecessors in the teaching of Christ's gospel the great central fact — it is made the head and front of his offending — " that Christ died for our sins, according to the Scriptures," that is to say, the Christian doctrine of atonement in the blood of Jesus.[56] We may believe, however, that it is rather the insuperable general difficulties which spring at once into sight when an attempt is made to construe Christianity as rather Paulinism — with its involved relegation of Jesus, as Wrede puts it, " utterly into the background " (though He is still inconsequently declared the greater person of the two) — which has caused this construction of primitive Christian history, long dallied with, to begin to crumble just

---

Belief," printed in the *Proceedings and Papers of the Fifth International Congress of Free Christianity and Religious Progress,* 1911, p. 209.

[55] Cf. E. von Dobschütz, *TSK,* 85 (1912), p. 364: " Paul calls his preaching gospel, the gospel; in conflict with the Judaisers, he vigorously denies that there is any other gospel (Gal. i. 6., 2 Cor. xi. 4.) ; another gospel exists just as little as there exists another Jesus." But Wrede (as cited, p. 166) does not hesitate to say there was another Christ: " The being whose disciple and apostle he wished to be was not actually the historical man, Jesus, but another." This contention indeed lies at the very root of the theory expressed by the phrase " the double gospel " in the New Testament.

[56] Wrede can only say in a footnote (p. 112, E. T. p. 168), that " it requires a very literal interpretation of Paul's words to make out that what was delivered to him includes ' died *for our sins* ' " — a remark which is very naturally cited by von Dobschütz (p. 342, note) with a subaudition of derision.

so soon as it has been given clear and unvarnished statement and its logical consequences exhibited. It is not without its significance that a single recent number of a theological journal [57] contains side by side two articles in which the attempt is made to close up again the yawning gulf that has been opened by the speculations of the "Liberal" theology between Jesus and Paul. The circumstance that the two writers proceed to their common end by precisely opposite methods — the one by denying that Paul was a "Paulinist," [58] and the other more reasonably by pointing out that Jesus was Himself very much of a "Paulinist" [59] — only exhibits the more clearly the precise nature of the difficulty which is created by attempting to set Paul in opposition to Jesus and emphasizes the more strongly the intolerableness of the situation induced.

We need not, however, go beyond Harnack himself to learn both the intolerableness and the untenableness of this construction of primitive Christian history. In an address delivered before the Fifth International Congress of Free Christianity and Religious Progress, held at Berlin in the early days of August 1910, under the title of "The Double Gospel in the New Testament," [60] Harnack as decisively as von Dobschütz repels the notion that Paul was the author of a new gospel, and shows as clearly as von Dobschütz that the germ of Paul's teaching is to be found also in that of Jesus, although he still rests rather more than von Dobschütz under the illusion

[57] "Theologische Studien und Kritiken," 85 (1912), Heft 3.

[58] G. Kittel, "Jesus bei Paulus, *TSK*, 85 (1912), pp. 366–402. By a drastic criticism of the text followed up by an artificial exegesis, Kittel manages to deprive Paul of everything which would markedly separate him from the "Liberal" Jesus.

[59] E. von Dobschütz, "Gibt es ein doppeltes Evangelium in Neuen Testament?" pp. 331–366. Von Dobschütz's thesis is that "the contrast between Jesus and Paul, as it has been set forth by the newer theology, especially since the publication of the Volksbücher of Bousset and Wrede, is possible only when the Gospel of Jesus has been greatly reduced and, on the other side, the traits of the preaching of Paul which lead away from the Gospel of Jesus are strongly emphasized in a one-sided manner" (p. 346).

[60] "Aus Wissenschaft und Leben," ii. 1911, pp. 211–224 (E. T. in the *Proceedings and Papers of the Fifth International Congress of Free Christianity and Religious Progress,* 1911, pp. 97–107).

that the gospel of Paul differs from that of Jesus in important particulars.[61] He therefore speaks of " a double gospel " lying side by side in the teaching of the New Testament writers, and indeed persisting side by side throughout the entire history of the Church. The problem of the origin of what he calls " the second gospel," that is, " the preaching that the Son of God descended from heaven, was known as man, through His death and resurrection brought to believers redemption from sin, death, and devil, and thus realized God's eternal counsel of salvation " — just " Paulinism " in the tradition of the " Liberal " theology — he carries back with complete confidence to the beginnings of the Christian community. He says: [62]

" The declaration that Christ ' died for our sins according to the Scriptures ' Paul calls a traditional, therefore a universal Christian article of belief of the first rank; and he says the same of the resurrection of Christ. It is accordingly certain that the original apostles and the Jerusalem community shared this belief and doctrine. This is also attested by the first chapters of the Book of Acts, the trustworthiness of which in this respect is incontestable. The problem must therefore be carried back chronologically from Paul to Jesus' first disciples. They already preached the atoning death (*Sühnetod*) and resurrection of Christ. If they preached them, however, they also of course recognized them as the principle articles, therefore as ' the gospel ' in the gospel, and this is evident in point of fact in the oldest written Gospel which we possess, that is, in that of Mark. The whole work of Mark is so disposed and composed that death and resurrection appear as the aim of the entire presentation. Mark may certainly have been influenced by the Pauline preaching; but the same structure has been given to the Palestinian Gospel of Matthew too; it will not have been new then to the Palestinian Christians."

[61] Therefore von Dobschütz (p. 364) notes: " I must accordingly, however, repel also Harnack's formula of the ' double gospel ' which is found in the New Testament, however much I approve of its purpose to bring the apostolic preaching again to its rights. I think that Paul and the others would have one and all protested against it; they were not conscious of any difference and would have acknowledged none."

[62] Pp. 216 f. (E.T. p. 101).

If Harnack's eyes are still so far holden, that he does not yet see that what Paul found in the primitive disciples they in turn found in Jesus Himself, he is still able to go a certain distance towards the recognition of this great fact also. We find him saying: [63]

"Jesus' proclamation comes so far into consideration here as He preached not only the necessity and actuality of forgiveness of sins, but undoubtedly placed His Person and His Work in relation to it. He not only laid claim to the power to forgive sins, but at the celebration of the Last Supper He brought His death into connection with the deliverance of souls. This may indeed be disputed, but this much is at any rate certain, that attachment to His Person, that is, discipleship, was His own provision. He, however, who attached himself to Him must have found and known Him as somehow 'the Way' to the Father and to all the benefits of the Kingdom ('Come unto me')."

Why these utterances of Harnack's should have aroused the wide-spread interest which they have is a little difficult to understand. Not only do they seem very much a matter of course — and Harnack himself reminds us that they have always been common property (not even Strauss, says he, disputed them, and Baur fully acknowledged them) [64] — but he had himself years ago set them in a clear light and partly in even more suggestive form, in his lectures on *What is Christianity*. "If we also consider," says he there,[65] "that Jesus Himself described his death as a service which he was rendering to many, and that by a solemn act he instituted a lasting memorial of it — I see no reason to doubt the fact — we can understand how this death and the shame of the cross were bound to take the central place." He even calls attention there to that very significant fact, that the death of Christ, being looked upon as a sacrifice — as it confessedly was by His very earliest disciples— "put an end to all blood-sacrifices" [66]; surely not (as Harnack inconsequently suggests) [67] because it showed that blood-sacrifices were in themselves

[63] P. 218 (E. T. p. 103).   [64] "What is Christianity?" p. 156.
[65] P. 160.   [66] Pp. 156 ff.   [67] P. 158.

meaningless (it was itself looked upon as a blood-sacrifice),
but because (as is implied in Harnack's own words) this was
to Jesus' followers the only true blood-sacrifice and left no
room for any other. " This death," he is impelled himself to
write,[68] " had the value of a sacrificial death; for otherwise
it would not have possessed the power to penetrate into that
inner world out of which blood-sacrifices have issued "—
which surely is as much as to say, with the author of the
Epistle to the Hebrews, that it actually cleansed the consciences of men while other sacrifices did not avail to cleanse
them, that it satisfied the demands of the uneasy consciences
of those who were suffering under a sense of their guilt.

That there is something still lacking in these acknowledgments is of course true. Something of what is lacking is
supplied by von Dobschütz's somewhat more hearty recognition of the saving value which Jesus Himself attached to His
death.[69] That He looked upon His death, not as an untoward
accident befalling Him or as a hard necessity breaking off His
work but as an instrument for the accomplishment of His
mission, von Dobschütz shows with sufficient solidity. And

" We have still three declarations in which Jesus expresses Himself to His disciples — certainly only to them — with respect to the
redemptive significance of His death, suggestively, figuratively,
yet sufficiently distinctly; I mean the declaration about ministering and giving His life λύτρον ἀντὶ πολλῶν (Mk. x. 45), the
declaration about the Body and Blood as symbols of the New Covenant (Mk. xiv. 24), and the declaration, transmitted to be sure only
in the Fourth Gospel but certainly original, about the hazarding of
His life in conflict with the adversary who menaces His people (Jno.
x. 11) ; three varying figures, all of which come at last to the recognition by Jesus of His death as necessary for the completion of His
work, viz., for uniting men again with God, by an expiation removing the guilt which separated them, overcoming the Evil One, estab-

[68] P. 99 (German ed.; E. T. pp. 157 f.).

[69] Pp. 352 ff. Harnack is inclined to deny to Jesus the saying recorded
in Mk. x. 45. Mt. xx. 28. especially its last clause (" Zeitschrift für Theologie
und Kirche," 1912, xxii, p. 9) ; of von Dobschütz's three passages, he would
allow therefore only one (Mk. xiv. 24.) to be direct evidence of Jesus' teaching.

lishing the indissoluble covenant relation predicted by the prophets.
I can find no decisive reason for exscinding these three declarations
from the genuine tradition of Jesus. What has been adduced against
them proceeds from *a priori* presuppositions which seem to me unjustified, such as that Jesus could not foresee His death, to say nothing of predicting it. Neither His own dismay at Gethsemane, nor
the conduct of the disciples, their flight and their despair, gives any
justification to such a contention. They remain psychologically
thoroughly intelligible, even with respect to the perception and
salutariness of His death. And then these declarations are, so to
say, necessary for explaining the fact that the Apostolical preaching
from the beginning deals with the redemptive significance of Jesus'
death as with a settled fact, while yet remaining entirely without
clarity as to the ' how ' and seeking after varying explanations,
all of which, however, ultimately move in directions more intimated
than inculcated by these declarations of the Lord."

In order to reach the truth we need only take one step
more and frankly recognize that these declarations are central
to Jesus' conception of His mission.[70] And this step we must
take not less on account of the declarations themselves (Jesus
says expressly that He " came " for the distinct purpose of
" giving His life as a ransom for many " and with great explicitness declares the sacrificial character of His death) than
on account of numerous other less direct but no less real
references to the significance of His mission as redemptive, and
in order that the whole subsequent historical development
may not be rendered unintelligible (the very disposition of
the matter of the Gospels is determined by this presupposition, and the whole preaching of the disciples turns on it as its
hinge). No doubt Jesus is thus implicated in the presentation
of Christianity as specifically a redemptive religion; " an appearance is created," to use Paul Wernle's phrase in an analogous connection, " that Jesus Himself is responsible for the
momentous dogmatic development, and encumbered the
simple, eternal will of God with a minimum of dogma and

[70] Compare the discussion of the matter in *The Princeton Theological
Review*, xi. 2 (April, 1913), pp. 259 ff.

ecclesiasticism " [71]; an appearance, we may add, which is not deceptive, as Wernle would have us believe, and with an amount of " dogma " which cannot justly be called a "minimum." This is, however, only to permit Jesus to come to His rights in the matter of His teaching; and to allow Him to found the religion which He tells us He came to found, and not to insist on thrusting an essentially different one upon Him because we happen ourselves to like it better.[72] These declarations of Jesus as to the redemptive significance of His death cannot be denied to Him; their meaning cannot be eviscerated by studiously minimizing expositions,[73] and they cannot be deprived of their cardinal position in the religion which He founded.[74] In point of fact, Jesus announced His mission as not to the righteous but sinners; and what He offered to sinners was not mere exemption — or if even that word retains too much reminiscence of a price paid, say immunity — but specifically redemption.

In the mind of Jesus as truly as in the minds of His followers, the religion which He founded was by way of eminence the religion of redemption. Perhaps we could have no better evidence of this than the tenacity with which those who would fain retain the name of Christianity while yet repudiating its specific character, cling to the term " redemptive " also as descriptive of the nature of their new Christianity, identified by them with the religion of Jesus. Professor Macintosh, for example, wishes still to describe his new religion as " the religion of moral redemption "; though he discriminates the

[71] " Die Anfänge unserer Religion," [2] 1904, p. 58.

[72] A very pleasantly written exposition of Jesus' relation to " the double gospel " may be found in Lic. theol. Martin Schulze's brochure, " Das Wesen des Christentums," 1897.

[73] We permit ourselves merely to refer here to the treatment of these by James Denney, " The Death of Christ," 1902, pp. 11–60. E. D. Burton's attempt to make " to give His life a ransom for many " mean to give His life, not His death (" Biblical Ideas of Atonement," 1909, pp. 113 ff.) surely requires no refutation.

[74] Cf. what Paul Feine says, " Theologie des Neuen Testaments," 1910, pp. 120 ff.

THE ESSENCE OF CHRISTIANITY

notion which the term connotes with him as its broad sense, as over against "the narrow sense" which it bears in its customary application to Christianity. By "redemption" he means, however, merely "reformation"; and these are not only the narrow and the broad of it; they are specifically different conceptions, and the employment of the two terms as synonyms cannot fail to mislead. For our part, we prefer the perhaps brutal but certainly more unambiguous frankness of William Wrede.[75] He conceives "the religion of Jesus" on the same lines as Professor Macintosh's "Christianity," and roundly denies on that very account that it can strictly be called a religion of redemption, contrasting it with Paul's precisely on this score. He does not deny that "redemption" may have a wider meaning also, according to which we "may say of all real religion that it is and intends to be redemptive." But he knows very well that "it is not of this general truth that we are thinking when we characterize particular religions as religions of redemption." And since in his view the emphasis in the religion of Jesus "falls on individual piety and its connection with future salvation," he remarks simply, that "no one who set out to describe the religion which lives in the sayings and similitudes of Jesus could hit by any chance on the phrase 'religion of redemption,'" while on the other hand, with respect to Paul, "everything . . . is said when we say that he made Christianity the religion of redemption." It tends to obscure the fact that a religion is being ascribed to Jesus which is not in the accepted ("narrow") sense of the word "redemptive," to characterize the religion which is ascribed to Him so emphatically as "redemptive" (in the "wider" sense of the word), especially when it lies on the face of the record that the religion which Jesus founded is a redemptive religion in the narrow sense, that is to say, has the Cross set in its centre.

Its redemptive character has not, then, been imported into Christianity from without, in the course of its development in the world — whether through the instrumentality of Paul or

of some other one. It has constituted its essence as a specific
religion from the beginning; without which it would cease to
be the religion that Jesus founded, and that, retaining the
specific character impressed on it by Him, has borne His name
through the centuries known from it as Christian. Precisely
what Christianity was in the beginning, has ever been through
all its history, and must continue to be so long as it keeps its
specific character by virtue of which it is what it is, is a redemptive religion; or rather that particular redemptive religion which brings to man salvation from his sin, conceived
as guilt as well as pollution, through the expiatory death of
Jesus Christ.

So clear is this that even an observer who approaches the
matter from a very general point of view, and seeks only, as
a student of philosophy, to determine from the outstanding
facts what the real nature of Christianity is, cannot miss it.
Josiah Royce [76] asks himself " what is vital in Christianity? "
using the term " vital " much in the sense which is ordinarily
attached to the term "essential." " That is vital for an organic
type," he explains, illustratively, " which is so characteristic
of that type that, were such vital features changed, the type
in question, if not altogether destroyed, would be changed
into what is essentially another type." In seeking an answer,
he naturally brings the "Liberal" and what he calls the
"Traditional" answers into comparison. " Is Christianity essentially a religion of redemption," he inquires, " in the sense
in which tradition defines redemption? Or is Christianity
simply that religion of the love of God and the love of man
which the sayings and the parables so richly illustrate? " For
the former view, he notes, is pleaded " the whole authority,
such as it is, of the needs and religious experience of the church
of Christian history; the church early found, or at least felt,
that it could not live at all without thus interpreting the person and work of Christ." For the latter is pleaded that " the
doctrine in view seems to be, at least in the main, unknown to

[76] Essay III. in the volume, " William James and Other Essays on the
Philosophy of Life," 1911.

the historic Christ, in so far as we can learn what he taught."
Nevertheless he has no hesitation in rejecting the latter view,
or in ascribing the former to Jesus. "As a student of philosophy, coming in no partisan spirit," he declares, "I must
insist that this reduction of what is vital in Christianity to
the so-called pure gospel of Christ, as he preached it and as
it is recorded in the body of the presumably authentic sayings and parables, is profoundly unsatisfactory." The historic
church was led to support the opposite view, he asserts, by
"a sense of religious values which was a true sense." And
despite what he (erroneously) believes to be the testimony
of the records, he refuses to believe that the "Liberal" view
can fully represent our Lord's own conception of His religion.
He argues:

"For one thing, Christ can hardly be supposed to have regarded
his most authentically reported religious sayings as containing the
whole of his message, or as embodying the whole of his mission.
For, if he had so viewed the matter, the Messianic tragedy in which
his life work culminated would have been needless and unintelligible. For the rest, the doctrine that he taught is, as it stands,
essentially incomplete. It is not a rounded whole. It looks beyond
itself for a completion, which the master himself unquestionably
conceived in terms of the approaching end of the world, and which
the church later conceived in terms of what has become indeed vital
for Christianity." [77]

That one who does not profess to approach the question with
which he deals "as an authority in matters which are technically theological," and who has accordingly been led astray
by those upon whom he was compelled to depend for the statement of the facts — and whose own interpretation, we must
add, of the significance of the conclusion that he reaches leaves
so much to be desired — should yet have seen thus clearly,
and been led to assert thus strongly, that Christianity is, in
its essence, "a redemptive religion" and that "what is most
vital in Christianity is contained in whatever is essential and
permanent about the doctrines of the incarnation and the

[77] P. 141.

atonement," seems a notable testimony to the obviousness of the main facts. Had Royce understood that these elements in the Christian religion which he finds vital to it were not introduced into it by the followers of Christ in their interpretation of His religion, but were inserted into it as its very heart by the Master Himself, we may fancy with what increased emphasis he would have insisted upon them as the very essence of this religion.

Professor Macintosh tells us, to be sure, that if this is Christianity, "he would have to confess not only that he is not a Christian, but that he does not see how he ever could be a Christian." It is a sad confession, but by no means an unexampled one. Every Inquiry Room supplies its contingent of like instances, and Christianity had not grown very old before it discovered that the preaching of Christ crucified was unto the Jews a stumbling-block and unto the Greeks foolishness. The only novel feature in the present situation lies in the proposal that if one cannot or will not accept the Christianity of the crucified Son of God, we shall just call what he can or will accept " Christianity " and let it go at that. This may seem an easy adjustment; but it is attended with the inconvenience of transferring our interest from things to mere names. The thing which has hitherto been known as Christianity appears to remain the same, however we deal with the name by which it has hitherto been known. And that thing enshrines the Cross in its heart. Paul Feine does not in the least exaggerate when, in the opening words of the section in his " Theologie des Neuen Testaments " [78] which speaks of Jesus' own teaching as to His death, he writes:

" It has been the belief and the teaching of the Christian Church of all ages and of all Confessions, that Jesus, the Son of God, in His sacrificial death on the cross wrought the reconciliation of men with God, and by His resurrection begot anew those who believe in Him unto a living hope of eternal life. This belief forms the content of the hymns and prayers of Christian devotion through all the centuries. It filled with new life the dying civilization of Greece and

[78] P. 120.

Rome and conquered to Christianity the youthful forces of the Germanic stock. In the proclamation of Jesus the Divine Saviour who died for us on the Cross, still lies even today the secret of the successes of Christian missions among the heathen. The symbol of this belief greets us in the form of the Cross from the tower of every church, from every Christian grave-stone and in the thousands of forms in which the Cross finds employment in daily life; this belief meets us in the gospel of the great Christian festivals and in the two sacraments of the church."

Enough; there can be no doubt what Christianity has been up to today; and there can be no doubt that what it is now proposed to transfer the name to is an essentially different religion. Have we not had it for a generation past dinned into our ears that it is an essentially different religion? that precisely what Paul did, when he substituted " the religion about Jesus," that is, the religion of the Cross, for "the religion of Jesus," that is, the " Liberal " reconstruction of what Jesus Himself taught, was to introduce a new religion, a religion, to recall Wrede's characterization, more unlike the religion of Jesus than the religion of Jesus was unlike Judaism? [79]

It seems merely frivolous to declare in one and the same breath that Paul introduced an essentially new religion when he supplanted "the simple gospel of Jesus " with the religion of the Cross, and that this new religion of the Cross is not essentially deserted when a return is made from it to "the simple religion of Jesus." The two religions are, in point of fact, essentially different, and no attempt to confuse them under a common designation can permanently conceal this fact. He who looks to be perfected through his own assumption of what he calls a Christlike attitude towards what he calls a Christlike superhuman reality — though he considers that the term "Christlike " may without fatal loss be a merely conventional designation — is of a totally different religion from him who feels himself a sinner redeemed by the blood of a divine Saviour dying for him on the Cross. It may be, as

[79] If Wrede be thought a mere extremist, let the words of Paul Wernle ("Anfänge," 2 1904, p. 112; E. T. i. pp. 158 f.) be considered.

Troeltsch seems to suggest, that "Liberal Christianity" lacks the power to originate a church and can live only as a kind of parasitical growth upon some sturdier stock.[80] It may be that it is not driven by internal necessity to separate itself off from other faiths, on which it rather depends for support. It is otherwise with those who share the great experience of reconciliation with God in the blood of His dear Son. They know themselves to be instinct with a life peculiar to themselves and cannot help forming a community, distinguished from all others by this common great experience. We have quoted the opening words of Feine's remarks on Jesus' teaching as to His sacrificial death. The closing words are worth pondering also. They run: [81]

" Let it be said in closing that in the two declarations of the ransom-price and the cup of the Lord's Supper there lies church-building power. Jesus did not organize His community; He founded no church in His earthly labors. But the Christian Church is an inevitable product of the declaration of the expiatory effect of His death for many. For those who have experienced redemption and reconciliation through the death of Jesus must by virtue of this gift of grace draw together and distinguish themselves over against other communities."

There is indeed no alternative. The redeemed in the blood of Christ, after all is said, are a people apart. Call them " Christians," or call them what you please, they are of a specifically different religion from those who know no such experience. It may be within the rights of those who feel no need of such a redemption and have never experienced its transforming power to contend that their religion is a better religion than the Christianity of the Cross. It is distinctly not within their rights to maintain that it is the same religion as the Christianity of the Cross. On their own showing it is not that.

[80] As cited, col. 681.   [81] As cited, p. 148.

X

APPENDIX
THE SUPERNATURAL BIRTH OF JESUS

THE SUPERNATURAL BIRTH OF JESUS [1]

I have promised the editors of the *American Journal of Theology* to indicate to their readers the answer I think must be given to the question, " Is the doctrine of the supernatural birth of Jesus essential to Christianity? " In addressing myself to fulfil this promise, however, I find myself laboring under a good deal of embarrassment. I am naturally embarrassed, for example, by the narrowness of the space at my disposal. Within the limits allowed me, I can hope to do nothing more than suggest a few of the considerations which weigh with me, and these only in the most cursory manner. I am much more embarrassed, however, by the infelicity of discussing the relation to Christianity, considered as a system of doctrine (that is to say, as a consistent body of truth), of a fact, the historicity of which I am to leave to others to discuss, who may perhaps reach conclusions to which I could by no means assent, whether in kind or merely in degree. I can only say that I have myself no doubt whatever of the fact of the supernatural birth of Jesus, as that fact is recorded in the opening chapters of the gospels of Matthew and Luke. I certainly make no question that additional evidence of tremendous weight is brought to this fact by its place in the system of Christianity, commended as this system as a whole is by the entire body of proof which we call the " Christian evidences." But I do not believe that it needs this additional evidence for its establishment. And I prefer my readers to understand that I proceed to the consideration of its place in the Christian system with it in my hands, not as a hypothesis of more or less probability (or improbability), but as a duly authenticated actual occurrence, recognized as such on its own direct evidence, and bringing as such its own quota of support to the Christian system of which it forms a part.

[1] From *The American Journal of Theology*, x. 1906, pp. 21–30.

I am embarrassed most of all, however, by the ambiguity of the language in which the question I am to discuss is stated. What is "the doctrine of the supernatural birth of Jesus"? What exactly, indeed, is intended by the main term employed? What is a "supernatural birth"? Were the births of Isaac and of John the Baptist "supernatural births"? Or those of Samson and of Samuel? Or those of Jeremiah and of Paul, whom, we are told, the Lord had selected for his own in or from the womb? Is not, indeed, the birth of every good man whom God prepares for some special work for him — certainly by influences beginning in the loins of his ancestors — in some sense supernatural? Nay, no one who believes in Providence can doubt that there is a supernatural element in the birth of every man that comes into the world. It may easily come about, therefore, that one may be found contending earnestly that the "supernatural birth" of Jesus is essential to Christianity, and yet sharply denying that that birth was "supernatural" in the only sense in which it is important to contend for its supernaturalness. What sense, further, we need to ask, is to be attached to the word "essential" here? Is the inquiry, perchance, whether the supernatural birth of Jesus constitutes the very essence of Christianity, so that in this doctrine Christianity is summed up? Or merely whether it enters so into the substance of Christianity that Christianity is not fully stated without it? The crowning ambiguity attaches, however, to the term "Christianity" itself. Is it to be taken subjectively or objectively? Are we asking whether it is possible for a man to commit his soul to Christ as his Savior without a clear knowledge and firm conviction of his Lord's virgin birth? Or are we asking whether any statement of Christianity can be thought complete which omits or ignores this doctrine? Or if it be supposed that this question is already settled by the use of the word "doctrine," we still have to ask what objective "Christianity" it is that we are to have in mind? The Christianity of the New Testament, or of some fragment of the New Testament, arbitrarily torn from its context and interpreted in isolation? The Chris-

tianity of the churches — the historical Christianity embodied
in the authoritative creeds of Christendom; or the Christianity
of a certain school of recent critical speculations — the Christianity of Auguste Sabatier, say, or of Paul Lobstein, or of
Otto Pfleiderer, or of Adolf Harnack?

Were the inquiry a purely historical one, it might no doubt
be soon settled. It admits of no doubt, for example, that, historically speaking, the "supernatural birth of Jesus" forms
a substantial element in the Christianity as well of the New
Testament, taken in its entirety, as of the creeds of the church.
There it stands plainly written in both, and even he who runs
may read it.[2] Of course, it does not stand written on every page
of the New Testament or of the creeds — why should it? And,
of course, it may be thought a debatable question whether it
has been logically or practically as important to historical
Christianity as its prominent confession in the documents
might seem to imply.[3] That it holds no essential place in much
of the "Christianity" current at the opening of the twentieth
century is certainly too obvious for discussion. To the late
Auguste Sabatier, for example, "Christianity" had come to
mean just the altruistic temper; and nobody will imagine the
"supernatural birth of Jesus" — or any kind of birth of Jesus,
for that matter, natural or supernatural or unnatural — essential to the altruistic temper. Must not much the same be
said also of the "Christianity" of Otto Pfleiderer, or of any
form of that at present very fashionable "Christianity" which
supposes the parable of the Prodigal Son, say, to contain a
complete statement of the Christian religion? As there is no
atonement, and no expiation, and no satisfaction, so there is

---

[2] "The church assigns the highest value to the doctrine of the virgin
birth" (Schmiedel, "Encyclopaedia Biblica," col. 2964). It is "a constant and,
we may truly say, universally recognized element in the doctrinal tradition of
the post-apostolic period, for of any important or fruitful opposition to it
the history of doctrine knows nothing" (Hering, "Zeitschrift für Theologie
und Kirche," v. p. 67).

[3] This is the gist of Hering's assault on it; cf. as above, and p. 74: "The
denial of the fact (of the virgin birth) has in all ages been adjudged heresy,
but its positive utilization has been very slight."

no mediator, no Jesus of any kind in the parable of the Prodigal Son. And the " Christianity " which refuses to know anything but the love of God which is there revealed to us, as it has no need of a Jesus, can have no need of a " supernatural birth " for the Jesus whom it totally ignores, or for whom it makes at best but an unessential place.

It is very evident, then, that if we are to ask whether " the doctrine of the supernatural birth of Jesus is essential to Christianity," we must settle it in our minds very clearly at the outset what " Christianity " it is we are talking about. Our answer will be one thing if we are thinking of what many about us are vaguely and vainly calling " Christianity," and perhaps quite another thing if we are thinking of the Christianity of Christ and his apostles, recorded in the New Testament, and drawn from the New Testament by the historical church through all ages. This latter is the only Christianity in which I can personally have more than a historical interest. I shall therefore confine myself to it. For the same reason I shall take " the supernatural birth of Jesus " in its highest sense — that of the truly miraculous birth of Jesus from a virgin mother, without intervention of man. It is in this sense that the " supernatural birth of Jesus " was actual; and this is the only sense, therefore, in which a discussion of it can have a real, as distinguished from a merely academic, interest. Defining thus my terms, the specific question which I shall seek to answer is whether the doctrine of the miraculous birth of Jesus from a virgin mother, taught in the opening chapters of the gospels of Matthew and Luke, forms an element in the Christianity of the New Testament, indispensable in the sense that without it that Christianity would be incompletely stated and left in one important matter defective, and, therefore, liable to misconception, if not open to dangerous assault.

Were I asked to name the three pillars on which the structure of Christianity, as taught in the New Testament in its entirety, especially rests, I do not know that I could do better than point to these three things: the supernatural, the incarnation, redemption. In an important sense, these three things constitute the Christianity of the New Testament; proceeding from the more general to the more specific, they sum up in themselves its essence. What interests us particularly at the moment is that the virgin birth of Jesus takes its significant place and has its significant part to play with respect to each one of them. Without it each one of them would be sheared of some portion of its meaning and value, and would take on a different and weakened aspect.

No one can doubt that the Christianity of the New Testament is supernaturalistic through and through. Whether we have regard to the person of Jesus or to the salvation he brought to men, the primary note of this Christianity certainly is supernaturalism. He who walked the earth as its Lord, and whom the very winds and waves obeyed; who could not be holden of the grave, but burst the bonds of death and ascended into the heavens in the sight of man: he who now sits at the right hand of God and sheds down his gift of salvation through his Spirit upon the men of his choice — it were impossible that such a one should have entered the world undistinguished among common men. His supernatural birth is given already, in a word, in his supernatural life and his supernatural work, and forms an indispensable element in the supernatural religion which he founded.

It would no doubt be difficult — or impossible, if you will — to believe that a natural Jesus had a supernatural origin; or, going at once to the root of the matter, that a natural "salvation" requires a supernatural Redeemer. Much of the Christianity about us today is distinctively, and even polemically, to use von Hartmann's term, "autosoteric"; and he who feels entirely competent to save himself finds a natural difficulty in believing that God must intervene to save him. I fully agree with the adherents of this "autosoteric" Christianity, that from their point of view a supernatural birth for Jesus would be devoid of significance, and therefore incredible. They should with similar frankness allow to me, I think, that to the Christianity of the New Testament, on the other hand, just because it stands as the opposite pole to their "autosoteric Christianity," the supernatural birth of Jesus is a necessity.

This, indeed, they in effect do when they argue that the virgin birth of Jesus is the invention of the Christianity of the New Testament on the basis of the extreme supernaturalism of its conception of Christianity. Thinking of Jesus as they did, we are told, the early Christians could not but postulate for him an origin consonant with what they conceived to be his nature, his powers, his career, the work he came to do, did do, is doing.[4] Nothing could be more true. The supernatural Christ and the supernatural salvation carry with them by an inevitable consequence the supernatural birth. In other words, the supernatural birth of Jesus is an implication of the Christian consciousness — that is, of course, of the supernaturalistic Christian consciousness.[5] And the Christian consciousness in this judgment receives the support of the universal human consciousness. Men have always and everywhere judged that a supernatural man, doing a supernatural work, must needs have sprung from a supernatural source.[6] If there

---

[4] "The conception that our Savior was a son of God born from a virgin was the involuntary, yea the inevitable, reflection of the divinity of Christ in the souls of converted Greeks" (Usener, "Das Weihnachtsfest," p. 75; cf. p. 76: "There could not fail the birth as visible sign that something divine had entered the world"). Cf. Soltau, "The Birth of Jesus Christ," p. 44.

[5] Lobstein, "The Virgin Birth of Christ," 1903, p. 33, argues that the consciousness of the gulf which separates the believer from "the One in whom he has found his Master," leads him instinctively to infer a difference in origin, and thus "the tradition of the miraculous birth of Jesus seems to anticipate the conviction of the believer, merely transferring into the realm of history a truth of which he finds in himself the most conclusive confirmation"; cf. p. 35. What is this but to say that in the logic of the heart the supernatural Redeemer demands for himself a supernatural origin?

[6] "Stories of supernatural birth may be said to have a currency as wide as the world. Heroes of extraordinary achievement or extraordinary qualities were necessarily of extraordinary birth. The wonder or the veneration they inspired seemed to demand that their entrance upon life, and their departure from it, should correspond with the impression left by their total career" (Hartland, "The Legend of Perseus," i. pp. 71, 72). So Origen ("Contra Celsum," i. 37), speaking of the story of Plato's supernatural birth, says: "But this is really a myth, and the simple incitement to imagine this of Plato was that man believes that a man of wisdom and power greater than

had been nothing extraordinary in the coming of the Saviour into the world, a discordant note would have been struck at this point in the "heterosoteric" Christianity of the New Testament, which would have thrown it in all its elements out of tune. To it, it would have been unnatural if the birth of the Savior had been natural, just because it itself in none of its elements is natural, but is everywhere and through all its structure, not, indeed, unnatural or contra-natural, but distinctively supernatural.

The cardinal point upon which the whole of this supernaturalistic Christianity, commended to us by the New Testament, turns, is formed by its doctrine of incarnation. The supernatural Savior, who has come into the world to work a supernatural salvation, could not possibly be conceived by it as of this world. If it would be to "annul Jesus," to imagine that he had not come in the flesh, or that he who had come in the flesh was not the Word of God who in the beginning was with God and was God — God only-begotten who was in the bosom of the Father — it would no less be to "annul him" to imagine that he could owe his coming to earthly causes or collocations. Born into our race he might be and was; but born of our race, never — whether really or only apparently.

There has been a very odd attempt made, to be sure, to set over against one another the doctrines of the pre-existence and of the supernatural birth of our Lord, as if they were mutually exclusive, or at least parallel rather than complementary conceptions. In speaking of such a thing as birth, however, it is obvious that when we say pre-existence we have already said supernatural, and as soon as we have said Deity we have said miraculous. So far as appears, it required the Socinians to teach us that one of these things could be taken and the other left — that any rational mind could suppose a non-supernatural being to be the product of a super-

---

those of the multitude must have had a higher and more divine origin than they." The point of importance is whether the truly supernatural *life and work* are real.

natural birth; while surely only a pronounced pantheist could so confound things that differ as to imagine that for bringing a supernatural being into the world those causes may be thought to suffice by which commonly mere men are produced. Ordinary people may be trusted to continue to judge that, as incarnation means precisely the entrance into the human race of a being not in any sense the product of the forces working in that race, but introduced from without and above, it is in its very essence a supernatural occurrence, and will necessarily bear in its mode of occurrence its credentials as such. It is, indeed, obviously not enough to say that it behooved the Divine Person who became incarnate in Jesus Christ, in entering into a new phase of existence, not to seem then first to begin to be; although to say that is no doubt to say something to the point. Would we do justice to the case, we must go on and affirm that, when the Life itself (which is also the Truth itself) entered into the conditions of human existence, it could not but come, according to its nature, creatively — bringing its own self-existing Life with it, and not making a round-about way so as to appear only now to begin, by way of derivation, to exist. When the Word was made flesh and tabernacled among men, it could not be but that men should behold his glory — a glory as of an only-begotten of the Father, full of grace and truth.

In point of fact, accordingly, it is just in proportion as men lose their sense of the Divine personality of the messianic king who is Immanuel, God with us, that they are found to doubt the necessity of the virgin birth; while in proportion as the realization of this fundamental fact of the Christianity of the New Testament remains vivid and vital with them, do they instinctively feel that it is alone consonant with it that this Being should acknowledge none other father than that Father which is in heaven, from whom alone he came forth to save the world. Accordingly, the adherents of the modern kenosis doctrine of the person of Christ, seeing in Jesus Christ nothing but God (though God shrunk to man's estate), have become the especial defenders of the doctrine of the virgin birth, and at this point the especial opponents of the modern rationalists, with whom otherwise they have so much in common. In contradistinction to both, the Christianity of the New Testament, remembering the two natures — which nowadays nearly everybody forgets — offers us in our Lord's person, not a mere man (perhaps in some sense made God), nor a mere God (perhaps in some sense made man), but a true God-man, who, being all that God is and at the same time all that man is, has come into the world in a fashion suitable to his dual nature, conceived indeed in a virgin's womb, and born of a woman and under the law, but not by the will of the flesh, nor by the will of man, but solely by the will of God who he is.[7]

Not even in the incarnation, however, is the Christianity of the New Testament summed up. Rather, the incarnation appears in it, not for its own sake, but as a means to a farther end — redemption. And it is only in its relation to the New Testament doctrine of redemption that the necessity of the virgin birth of Jesus comes to its complete manifestation. For in this Christianity the redemption that is provided is distinctively redemption from sin; and that he might redeem men from sin it certainly was imperative that the Redeemer himself should not be involved in sin. He would be a bold man, indeed, who would affirm that the incarnation of the Holy One in sinful flesh presents no difficulties to his thought. The sinlessness of Jesus, in the sense of freedom from subjective corruption as well as from overt acts of sin, seems to be involved in the incarnation itself, purely and simply; and, in point of fact, those who imagine it was in principle sinful

[7] Such criticisms as that of Réville, "Histoire du dogme de la divinité de Jésus-Christ" (1869, p. 30; 1904, p. 27), miss the mark and would apply only to the Kenotic perversion: "A pre-existent being who becomes man reduces himself, if you will, to the condition of a human embryo; but he is not conceived by virtue of an act external to himself in the womb of a woman, etc." In the New Testament view of the God-man, as there is no reduction of the Godhead to the level of a human embryo, so there is a true conception of a complete human embryo by an act external to itself. Only, the cause external to this embryo, by virtue of which it is conceived, is the power of the Most High, and not natural fertilization.

flesh which was assumed by the Son of God are prone to represent this flesh as actually cleansed of its sinfulness, either by the act of incarnation itself or by the almighty operation of the Spirit of God as a condition precedent to incarnation. But something more than sinlessness in this subjective sense was requisite for the redemption up to which the incarnation leads. Assuredly no one, resting for himself under the curse of sin, could atone for the sin of others; no one owing the law its extreme penalty for himself could pay this penalty for others. And certainly in the Christianity of the New Testament every natural member of the race of Adam rests under the curse of Adam's sin, and is held under the penalty that hangs over it. If the Son of God came into the world therefore — as that Christianity asserts to be a "faithful saying" — specifically in order to save sinners, it was imperatively necessary that he should become incarnate after a fashion which would leave him standing, so far as his own responsibility is concerned, outside that fatal entail of sin in which the whole natural race of Adam is involved. And that is as much as to say that the redemptive work of the Son of God depends upon his supernatural birth.

I am, of course, well aware that this doctrine of redemption, and as well the doctrine of sin which underlies it, is nowadays scouted in wide circles. With that, however, I have no present concern. I cheerfully admit that to a "Christianity" which knows nothing of race-sin and atonement, the necessity of the supernatural birth of the "Redeemer," if it be recognized at all, must rest on other, and perhaps on less stringent, grounds. But I have not undertaken to investigate the possible place of the supernatural birth of Jesus in the varied forms of so-called "Christianity" prevalent in the modern world, many of which stand in no other relation to the Christianity of the New Testament than that of contradiction. Nor am I to be deterred from recognizing the doctrines of "original sin" and of "satisfaction" as fundamental elements in the Christianity of the New Testament, by the habit which has grown up among those who do not like them, of speaking of them scornfully as "Augustinian" and "Ansel-mic." What rather attracts my attention is that it seems to be universally allowed that, on these "Augustinian" and "Anselmic" presuppositions, the doctrine of the virgin birth of Jesus is an absolutely essential element of Christianity. In so far, then, as it is admitted that the doctrines of "original sin" and of "satisfaction" are constituent elements of the Christianity of the New Testament, it may be taken as acknowledged that the virgin birth of our Lord is confessedly essential to it.[8]

If, then, it cannot be denied that the supernatural birth of Jesus enters constitutively into the substance of that system which is taught in the New Testament as Christianity — that it is the expression of its supernaturalism, the safeguard of its doctrine of incarnation, the condition of its doctrine of redemption — are we to go on and say that no one can be saved who does not hold this faith whole and entire? The question is thoroughly impertinent. We are discussing, not the terms of salvation, but the essential content of the Christian system; not what we must do to be saved, but what it behooved Jesus Christ to be and to do that he might save us. Say that faith is the instrument by which salvation is laid hold upon; the instrument by which the prerequisites of the salvation laid hold of by faith are investigated is the intellect. As it is certain that the only Jesus, faith in whom can save, is the Jesus who was conceived by the Holy Ghost, and born of the virgin Mary, according to the Scriptures, it is equally certain that the act of faith by which he is savingly apprehended involves these presuppositions, were its implicates soundly developed. But our logical capacity can scarcely be made the condition of our salvation.[9] The Scriptures do not encourage us to believe that only the wise are called. They even graciously assure us

---

[8] Cf. Lobstein, *op. cit.*, p. 84; *Cheyne,* "Bible Problems," p. 95; etc.

[9] I have the unwonted felicity of being thoroughly at one in this with Professor Paul Schwartzkopff, who remarks: "The faith which lays hold of the living God in Christ is not necessarily conditioned by the thoroughness with which the intellect grasps its content" ("The Prophecies of Jesus Christ," E. T. p. 3).

that blasphemy itself against the Son may be forgiven. It would surely be unfortunate if weakness of intellect were more fatal than wickedness of heart. On the whole, we may congratulate ourselves that it was more imperative that Jesus, by whom the salvation has been wrought, should know what it behooved him to be and to do that he might save us, than it is that we should fully understand it. But, on the other hand, it will scarcely do to represent ignorance or error as advantageous to salvation. It certainly is worth while to put our trust in Jesus as intelligently as it may be given to us to do so. And it certainly will over and over again be verified in experience that he who casts himself upon Jesus as his divine Redeemer, will find the fact of the virgin birth of this Saviour not only consonant with his faith and an aid to it, but a postulate of it without which he would be puzzled and distressed.

LIST OF OTHER ARTICLES ON CHRISTOLOGY

I. THE DEITY OF CHRIST. ("The Fundamentals" v. i, pp. 21–28.)

II. THE HUMAN DEVELOPMENT OF JESUS. (*The Bible Student*, v. i New Series, January, 1900, pp. 12–19.)

III. ON THE POST-EXILIAN PORTION OF OUR LORD'S GENEALOGY. (*The Presbyterian Review*, v. ii, 1881, pp. 388–397.)

IV. THE RESURRECTION OF CHRIST A FUNDAMENAL DOCTRINE. (*The Homiletic Review*, v. xxxii, 1896, pp. 291–298.)

V. THE RESURRECTION OF CHRIST AN HISTORICAL FACT, EVINCED BY EYE-WITNESSES. (*The Journal of Christian Philosophy*, v. iii, 1884, pp. 305–318.)

VI. CHRISTIANITY AND THE RESURRECTION OF CHRIST. (*The Bible Student and Teacher*, v. viii, 1908, pp. 277–283.)

STUDIES IN
TERTULLIAN AND AUGUSTINE

BY

BENJAMIN BRECKINRIDGE WARFIELD

Professor of Didactic and Polemic Theology
in the Theological Seminary of Princeton
New Jersey, 1887–1921

Baker Books

A Division of Baker Book House Co
Grand Rapids, Michigan 49516

PREFATORY NOTE

REV. BENJAMIN BRECKINRIDGE WARFIELD, D.D., LL.D., Professor of Didactic and Polemic Theology in the Theological Seminary of the Presbyterian Church at Princeton, New Jersey, provided in his will for the collection and publication of the numerous articles on theological subjects which he contributed to encyclopaedias, reviews and other periodicals, and appointed a committee to edit and publish these papers. In pursuance of his instructions, this, the fourth volume, containing his articles on Tertullian and Augustine, has been prepared under the editorial direction of this committee.

The generous permission to publish articles contained in this volume is gratefully acknowledged as follows: Charles Scribner's Sons, for the article entitled "Augustine" taken from "Encyclopaedia of Religion and Ethics," ed. by James Hastings, and for the article entitled "Augustine and the Pelagian Controversy" taken from "A Select Library of the Nicene and Post-Nicene Fathers of the Christian Church," First Series, volume v.

The clerical preparation of this volume has been done by Mr. Johannes G. Vos, to whom the thanks of the committee are hereby expressed.

ETHELBERT D. WARFIELD
WILLIAM PARK ARMSTRONG
CASPAR WISTAR HODGE
Committee.

CONTENTS

I
TERTULLIAN AND THE BEGINNINGS OF THE DOCTRINE OF THE TRINITY

TERTULLIAN AND THE BEGINNINGS OF THE DOCTRINE OF THE TRINITY [1]

FIRST ARTICLE

IT is exceedingly impressive to see Christian Latin literature Athena-like spring at once into being, fully armed, in the
person of an eminently representative man, in whom seem
summed up the promise and potency of all that it was yet to
be. This is what occured in Tertullian, whose advent and career
provide a remarkable illustration of the providential provision
of the right man for the right place. Seldom has one been called
to a great work who was better fitted for it by disposition and
talents as well as by long and strenuous preparation. Ardent in
temperament, endowed with an intelligence as subtle and original as it was aggressive and audacious, he added to his natural gifts a profound erudition, which far from impeding only
gave weight to the movements of his alert and robust mind.
A jurist of note, he had joined to the study of law not only
that of letters, but also that of medicine; born and brought up
in the camp he had imbibed from infancy no little knowledge
of the military art; and his insatiable curiosity had carried him
into the depths of every form of learning accessible to his time
and circumstances, not even excepting the occult literature
of the day. When he gave himself in his mature manhood to the
service of Christianity, he brought in his hands all the spoils of
antique culture, smelted into a molten mass by an almost incredible passion.

The moment when he appeared on the scene was one well
calculated to call out all his powers. It was shortly after the
beginning of the last decade of the second century. Commodus

[1] From *The Princeton Theological Review*, iii. 1905, pp. 529–557; iv. 1906,
pp. 1–36, 145–167.

3

had died and left a trail of civil war behind him, in the midst of which persecution had broken out afresh in Africa. Harassed from without, the African Church was also torn from within by an accumulation of evils; apostasies, heresies, and schisms abounded. Up through the confusion were thrust Tertullian's mighty shoulders, casting off the enemies of the Gospel upon every side. He was not formed for defensive warfare. Even against the persecuting heathenism he took the offensive. Not content with repelling its calumnies and ridiculing the popular hatred of Christianity, he undertook to demonstrate, as a jurist, the illegality of the persecuting edicts, and, as a moralist, the absurdity of the heathen superstitions. He broke out a short and easy way for the refutation of heretics, by which he put them out of court at the start, and then followed them remorselessly into every corner of their reasoning. Within the Church itself he pursued with mordant irony the crowding abuses which had grown up in the Christian life. Of course he had the defects of his qualities. This terrible adversary of others was a terrible adversary also of his own peace. The extremity of his temper made him a prey to the fanatical claims of the Montanists and ultimately drove him beyond even them. He died the head of a new sect of his own.

Meanwhile he had rendered a service to the Church which it is no exaggeration to call inestimable. There is certainly discoverable in the writings of his immediate successors little open recognition of the immensity of the debt which Christianity owed to him. Throughout the whole of the remainder of the third century — a period of some eighty years — his name is not once mentioned. In the Greek Church, indeed, no one but the historian Eusebius seems ever to have heard of him. Even in his own West, Lactantius (305–306) is the first to allude to him, and he does so with obvious depreciation. Jerome, it is true, gives free vent to his admiration for the learning and acuteness, the vehemence and elegance of this " torrent of eloquence," and not only places him formally among the " illustrious men " of the Church, but calls him fondly " our Tertullian." With Hilary and Augustine, however, he has already taken his place definitely in the catalogue of heretics, and thenceforward he found hardly any who were prepared to do him reverence.[2] All this appearance of neglect passing into reprobation, however, is appearance only. Men might carefully avoid speaking of Tertullian; they could not escape his influence. Cyprian, for example, never breathes his name; yet the works of Cyprian are filled with the silent witnesses of the diligence with which he studied his brilliant predecessor; and his secretary told Jerome he never passed a day without reading him, and was accustomed to ask for him in the significant formula, " Hand me the Master." This is not far from a typical instance. " The man was too great a scholar, thinker, writer," remarks Harnack,[3] " and he had done the Western Church too distinguished service during a long series of years for his memory to become effaced."

In modern times the vigor of Tertullian's mind and the brilliancy of his literary gifts have perhaps generally been fully recognized. It is questionable, however, whether the greatness of his initiative in the development of Christian doctrine is even yet estimated at its true value. That many of the streams of doctrinal thought that have flowed down through the Western Church take their rise in him is indeed universally understood. But perhaps it comes to us with a little surprise when Harnack claims for him, for example, that it was he who broke out the road for the formulation of the Christian doctrine of the Trinity. "When the Nicene formulary is praised," says Harnack,[4] " it is always of Athanasius that we think; when the Chalcedonian decree is cited, it is the name of Leo the Great that is magnified. But that Tertullian is in reality the father of the orthodox doctrines of the Trinity and of the Person of Christ, and that in the whole patristic literature there is no treatise that can be compared in importance and

---

[2] The generous but qualified praise of Vincent, " Commonitorium," xviii. [24] stands almost alone by the side of Jerome's.

[3] *Sitzungsberichte der königlich preussischen Akademie der Wissenschaften zu Berlin,* June, 1895, p. 545: ." Tertullian in der Litteratur der alten Kirche."

[4] *Loc. cit.*

influence with his tract "Against Praxeas," it has necessarily been left to the . . . investigation of our own day to exhibit." If such a statement as this can be substantiated it is enough to mark Tertullian out not merely as a man of exceptional gifts and worthy performance, but as one of the greatest forces which have wrought in history.

It is proposed to subject this statement to such testing as is involved in going to the tract "Against Praxeas" and seeking to form a judgment of its value and of the place in the development of the Christian doctrine of the Trinity which it vindicates for its author.

The tract "Against Praxeas," it must be borne in mind from the outset, is not an extended treatise. It is a brief document filling but some fifty pages. Nor is it a calm constructive work in which the author sets himself to develop in its completeness a doctrinal elaboration. It is a vigorous and lively polemic designed to meet an immediate crisis. In other words, it is distinctly an occasional writing, devoted to the refutation of a heresy which was at the moment troubling the churches. Any doctrinal construction which may be found in it is accordingly purely incidental, and rather betrays the underlying conceptions of the writer's mind than forms the calculated burden of the document. If this constructive element, thus emerging, is nevertheless epoch-making for the history of thought, it will redound with peculiar force to the honor of the author. That it so emerges, however, renders it necessary that, for the proper estimate of the tract, we should begin by obtaining a somewhat exact understanding of the circumstances which gave birth to it.

We must not be misled by its title or by the reversion of the discourse now and then to the form of direct address into supposing the tract a personal assault upon Praxeas himself. It is quite clear that Praxeas was a figure resurrected by Tertullian from a comparatively remote past, and given prominence in the discussion, perhaps, as a sort of controversial device. Ter-

tullian, apparently, would represent the teachings he is opposing as a mere recrudescence of an exploded notion, discredited
in its vacillating and weak propounder a generation ago.[5]
Of Praxeas himself we know nothing except what Tertullian
tells us: there is no independent mention of his name in the
entirety of Christian literature. He is represented as an Asian
confessor who was the first to import into Rome the type of
doctrine which Tertullian calls Monarchianism or Patripas-
sianism.[6] Evidently he had made himself felt for a time in
Rome, and among other things had succeeded in reversing the
favorable policy of the Roman bishops with respect to the
Montanists. By this achievement he naturally earned from
Tertullian a twofold scorn. Tertullian bitingly remarks that
thus Praxeas had doubly done the devil's business in Rome —
" he had expelled prophecy and brought in heresy, had exiled
the Paraclete and crucified the Father." [7] His heresy passed
over into Africa — while the people, says Tertullian, slept in
doctrinal simplicity. But God raised up a defender of the truth:
and the heresy was exposed and seemingly destroyed; Praxeas

[5] Even were this motive not operative it would not follow from the use of
Praxeas' name that he and the book were contemporaneous. Josephus controverted Apion and Origen Celsus only after a considerable interval of years. The
same seems to be true of the use of Fronto's name in the " Octavius " of
Minucius Felix. (See Harnack, " Chronologie," ii. p. 326, and note; and compare what is said by Hagemann, " Die Römische Kirche," pp. 235–236.)

[6] Hagemann's attempt (" Die Römische Kirche," pp. 234, sq.) to identify
Praxeas with Callistus is only a part of his general attempt so to manipulate
the facts as to make Callistus the real protagonist for fundamental Christian
truth and Tertullian the real errorist. In the prosecution of this endeavor he
gives to Callistus all that belongs rightfully to Tertullian (and more). He speaks
of him (p. 128) as setting forth " the doctrine of the unity of nature of the
Father and Son and the doctrine of the hypostatic union of the two natures in
Christ, with a completeness of formal development such as they received later
through the instrumentality of the General Councils only after long and bitter
controversies," and as thus more than a hundred years in advance of the
Church at large refuting Arianism and establishing for Rome a triune creed
(see especially pp. 101 and 128). On the other hand, he represents Tertullian
as, under the influence of Hippolytus, so misunderstanding Callistus that, under
the nick-name of Praxeas, he treats his epoch-making orthodox definitions as if
they were Monarchian.

[7] " Against Praxeas," i. Ita duo negotia diaboli Praxeas Romæ procuravit:
prophetiam expulit et hæresim intulit, paracletum fugavit et patrem crucifixit.

himself submitted to correction and returned to the old faith. Apparently this was the end of it all: *exinde silentium,* says Tertullian, with terse significance. But it is the curse of noxious growths that they are apt to leave seeds behind them. So it happened in this case also. The tares had been rooted up and burned. But lo, after so long a time, the new crop appeared, and the last state was unspeakably worse than the first. The tares had everywhere, says Tertullian, shaken out their seed, and now, after having lain hid so long, their vitality had become only too manifest. It is not then an individual that Tertullian is facing; it is a widespread condition. This tract is not an attempt to silence a heretic menacing the peace of the Church; it is an effort to correct a rampant evil already widely spread in the community, by which the very existence of the truth is endangered.

The tones in which Tertullian speaks of the rise of the heresy in the person of Praxeas and of its prevalence at the time of his writing are noticeably different. Then it was an exotic vagary seeking footing in the West and finding none: now it is a native growth, springing up everywhere. The tares had cast their seed, he says, " everywhere " (*ubique*). Nor can he look with comfort on the task of rooting them up. Though he is not the man to lose courage, and reminds himself of the past success, he yet finds his deepest consolation in the assurance that all tares shall be burnt up at the last day. When a man looks forward to the Judgment Day for the vindication of his cause, he is not far from despairing of success here and now. It looks very much as if Tertullian felt himself in a hopeless minority in his defense of what he calls the pristine faith (*pristinum*). He does not conceal the difficulty he experienced in obtaining even a fair hearing for his doctrine. Christians at large were impatient of everything that seemed to their uninstructed minds to imperil their hard-won monotheism. The majority of believers he tells us are ever of the simple, not to say the unwise and untaught (*simplices, ne dixerim imprudentes et idiotæ*); and they were nothing less than terrified (*expavescunt*) by the mention of an " economy " within the being of God by virtue of which the one only God may be supposed to present distinctions within His unity. They continuously cast in the teeth of those who inculcated such doctrines the charge of preaching two or three gods, while they arrogated to themselves alone the worship of the one only true God.

If we are to take this literally, it will mean that Christians at large in Tertullian's day — that is, at the time when he wrote this tract — were suspicious of the doctrine of the Trinity and looked upon it almost as a refined polytheism; that they were inclined rather strongly to some form of Monarchianism as alone comporting with a real monotheism. There are not lacking other indications that something like this may have been the case. Hippolytus, in approaching in the course of his great work " On Heresies " the treatment of the Monarchianism of his day, betrays an even more poignant sense of isolation than Tertullian. He speaks of the promoters of the Monarchian views as bringing great confusion upon believers throughout the whole world.[8] In Rome at least, he tells us, they met with wide consent;[9] and he represents himself as almost single-handed in his opposition to their heresy. In effect it seems to be quite true that through no less than four episcopates — those of Eleutherus, Victor, Zephyrinus and Callistus — the Modalistic theology was dominant and occupied the place indeed of the official faith at Rome. We may neglect here hints in Origen[10] that something of the same state of affairs may have obtained in the Eastern churches also. Enough that it is clear that at the time when Tertullian's tract was written — say during the second decade of the third century[11] — the common sentiment of the West was not untouched by Modalistic tendencies.

It must not be supposed that the mass of the Christian

---

[8] " Philosophumena," ix. 1: μέγιστον τάραχον κατὰ πάντα τὸν κόσμον ἐν πᾶσι τοῖς πιστοῖς ἐμβάλλοντες.

[9] Do., ix. 6.

[10] See Harnack, " History of Dogma," iii. p. 53, note 2; Dorner, " Doctrine of the Person of Christ," Div. I. vol. ii. p. 3.

[11] Harnack (" Chronologie," ii. pp. 285–286, 296) sets the date of the book at c. 213–218.

population, in the West at least — for it is with the West that we have particularly to do — held to a Modalistic theory as a definitely conceived theological formula. What is rather to be said is that the Modalistic formula when warily presented roused in the minds of most men of the time no very keen sense of opposition, while the Trinitarian formula was apt to offend their monotheistic consciousness. This is by no means surprising; and it is partially paralleled by the situation in the East after the promulgation of the Nicene creed. The difficulty in obtaining assent to that symbol did not turn on the prevalence of definitely Arian sentiments so much as upon the indefiniteness of the conceptions current among the people at large and the consequent difficulty experienced by so definite a formula in making its way among them. Men were startled by these sharp definitions and felt more or less unprepared to make them the expression of their simple and somewhat undefined faith. So here, a century before the Nicene decision, the people in the West found similar difficulty with the Trinitarian distinctions. The naïve faith of the average Christian crystallized around the two foci of the unity of God and the Deity of Christ: and the Modalistic formulas might easily be made to appear to the untrained mind to provide simply and easily for both items of belief, and so to strike out a safe middle pathway between the Dynamistic Monarchianism of the Theodotuses and Artemodites, on the one hand, and the subtle constructions of Hippolytus and Tertullian on the other. The one extreme was unacceptable because it did not allow for the true deity of the Redeemer: the other seemed suspicious as endangering the true unity of God.

It is not at all strange, therefore, that the unsophisticated Christian should tremble on the verge of accepting Modalistic Monarchianism, especially when presented, in a guarded form, as a simple and safe solution of a vexing problem. It was thus that it was quick to commend itself; and it was on this ground that it was in its most prudent formulation exploited at Rome as the official faith. When it was brought to Rome, we must remember, it was set over against, not developed Trinitarianism, but rather, on the one side, the crude humanitarianism of the Dynamistic school of Monarchianism which was at the moment troubling the Church there, and, on the other, the almost equally crude emanationism of the Logos speculation, which had held the minds of thinking men for a generation. It was therefore naturally treated as a deliverance from opposite heresies, along whose safe middle way men might walk in the light of the twin truths of the deity of Christ and the unity of God. When Hippolytus assailed it, therefore, he obtained no hearing and was treated as merely another disturber of the Church's peace. His assault did not, indeed, fail of all effect: he rendered it impossible for Modalism to be adopted in its crudest form, and forced modifications in it by which it was given the appearance of more nearly covering the main facts of the revelation of God in the Gospel. But he could by no means turn the thoughts of men into a different channel; neither, indeed, was he capable of digging a channel into which their thoughts might justly flow. The outcome, therefore, was only that Callistus excommunicated both Sabellius and Hippolytus and set forth as the Christian faith a new doctrine which was intended to declare the central truths of the Gospel as understood by men of moderation and balanced judgment. Hippolytus looked on this new doctrine as itself essentially Modalism, with a tendency downward. And Hippolytus was right. But it commended itself powerfully to the age, and that not merely in Rome, but in Africa. It is this refined Modalism of the Roman compromise, which seemed to be threatening to become the Christianity of the West, that Tertullian attacks in his tract " Against Praxeas."

It is not necessary for our present purpose to trace the gradual modifications which the Monarchian teaching underwent from its earliest form as taught at Rome by Noëtus and possibly by Praxeas to its fullest development and most advanced adjustment in the hands of Callistus to the fundamental Church doctrines of God and Christ. Suffice it to say that the modifications by which Callistus sought to " catholicize " Monarchian Modalism, proceeded by according some sort of rec-

ognition to the Logos doctrine on the one hand, and on the
other by softening the crass assertion that it was the Father
who suffered on the cross. Of course no personal distinction
between Father and Son, or God and Logos, was admitted.
But a nominal distinction was accorded, and this distinction
was given quasi-validity by a further distinction of times.
"Callistus says," explains Hippolytus,[12] " that the same Logos
is at once Son and Father, distinguished in name, but really
one individual Spirit, . . . and that the Spirit incarnated in
the virgin is not different from the Father but one and the
same. . . . For that which is seen, which is of course the man
— it is that which is the Son; but the Spirit which is contained
in the Son is the Father, since there are not two Gods, Father
and Son, but one. Now, the Father being in him " — i.e., the
Son, which is the " man " or the " flesh " — " seeing that he
had assumed the flesh, deified it by uniting it with Himself,
and made it one, so that the Father and Son are called one
God, while this person being one cannot be two, and so the
Father suffered along with the Son." Hippolytus adds that Callistus worked out this form of statement because he did not
" wish to say the Father suffered." The point here, therefore,
is that the Son differs from the Father not as the incarnate differs from the unincarnate God, but rather as the incarnating
man differs from the incarnated Spirit. As then the flesh is
properly designated by the " Son " and it is the flesh that suffers, the Father, who is properly the Spirit incarnated in the
" Son," may more exactly be said to have suffered along with
the flesh, i.e., the " Son," than Himself to have endured the
suffering. The suffering was, in other words, in the " flesh ":
the informing " Spirit " only partook in the suffering of the
" flesh " because joined in personal union with it. The artificiality of this construction is manifest on the face of it; as also
is its instability. Hippolytus himself pointed out its evident
tendency to fall back into the lower Dynamistic Monarchianism; since in proportion as the Father as the Spirit and the
Son as the flesh were separated in thought, the reality of the

[12] " Philosophumena," ix. 7.

incarnation was likely to give way in favor of a more or less clearly conceived inhabitation. Thus Jesus would become again only a man in whom God dwelt. The formula of " the Father suffering with the Son " was really, therefore, a mediation toward humanitarianism rather than toward full recognition of the deity of the Son; and it is interesting to observe in the later Arians the reëmergence of the mode of expression thus struck out by Callistus. With them of course it was not a question of the Father but of that " Middle Being " which they called the Son of God; but what they affirm of it is that having taken " man " from the Virgin Mary, it " shared in " the sufferings of this " man " on the cross.[13] The obvious meaning of the Arians will throw light back upon the idea which Callistus meant to convey. This was clearly that the incarnation of the Spirit which was God in the man which was Christ, brought that Spirit into definite relations to the sufferings endured by this man properly in his flesh.

What it concerns us to note here particularly, however, is that it is just this Callistan formula which underlies the Monarchianism which Tertullian is opposing in his tract.[14] The evidence of this is pervasive. It will doubtless be enough to adduce the manifest agreement of his opponents with the Callistan formula in the two chief points to which we have adverted. Tertullian's opponents, it appears, while allowing to the Word a sort of existence, would not admit Him to be a really *substantiva res,* " so that He could be regarded as a *res et persona* " and, being constituted as a second to God the Father, make with the Father " two, Father and Son, God and the Word." [15] They " sought to interpret the distinction be-

[13] At the Synod of Sirmium, A.D. 357. See Hahn, " Bibliothek der Symbole und Glaubensregeln der alten Kirche," [3] § 161. The idea is that the " man " alone " suffers " (*patitur*): the Logos incarnate in the " man " only co-suffers (*compatitur*) with it. The Spirit, say the Arians at Sardica, A.D. 343, " did not suffer, but the man (ἄνθρωπος) which it put on suffered "; because, as it is immediately explained, this is " capable of suffering." Cf. Hahn, " Bibliothek der Symbole und Glaubensregeln der alten Kirche," [3] p. 189.

[14] Cf. Rolffs in the " Texte und Untersuchungen zur Geschichte der altchristlichen Literatur," XII. iv. pp. 94 *sq.*

[15] " Against Praxeas," chap. vii.

tween Father and Son conformably to their own notion, so as
to distinguish between them within a single person, saying that
the Son is the flesh, that is, the man, that is Jesus, but the
Father the Spirit, that is God, that is Christ." [16] Similarly Tertullian's opponents seeking to avoid the charge that they
blasphemed the Father by making him suffer, granted that the
Father and Son were so far two that it was the Son that suffered while the Father only suffered with Him.[17]

The special interest of this for us at the moment lies in a
corollary which flows from it. Tertullian was not breaking out
a new path in his controversy with the Monarchians. He was
entering at the eleventh hour into an old controversy, which
had dragged along for a generation, and was now only become
more acute and more charged with danger to the Church. This,
to be sure, is already implied in his reference to an earlier refutation of Praxeas, and in his representation of the error at
present occupying him as merely a repristination of that old
heretic's teaching. Accordingly, not only is the controversy old,
but it is old to Tertullian. The general fact is evident on every
page of his tract. It is quite clear that Tertullian is not here
forging new weapons to meet novel attacks. On both sides
much acuteness had already been expended in assault and defense [18] and the lines of reasoning had already long been laid
down and even the proofs *pro* and *con* repeatedly urged. The
very exegetical arguments bear on them the stamp of long use
and betray the existence on both sides of a kind of exegetical
tradition already formed. The emergence of this fact throws us
into doubt as to how much even of what seems new and original
in the tract may not likewise be part of the hereditary property
of the controversy. Even the technical terms which Tertullian
employs with such predilection and which are often thought of
as contributions of his own to the discussion, such as οἰκονομία,

[16] Chap. xxvii.

[17] Chap. xxix. "Filius quidem patitur, pater vero compatitur." "Compas-
sus est pater filio."

[18] We are here drawing upon Lipsius' admirable article, "On Tertullian's
Tract Against Praxeas," published in the *Jahrbücher für deutsche Theologie*,
xiii. (1868), pp. 701–724. For the present matter see especially p. 710.

trinitas,[19] for example, need not be new, but may owe it only to accident that they come here for the first time strikingly before us. Indeed, Tertullian does not use them as if they were novelties. On the contrary, he introduces them as well-known terms, which he could freely employ as such. He speaks [20] of " that dispensation which we call the οἰκονομία," that is to say, apparently, "which is commonly so called." And in the same connection he joins the " distribution of the Unity into a Trinity " [21] with the οἰκονομία in such a manner as inevitably to suggest to the reader that this mode of explaining the οἰκονομία belonged to its tradition. Assuredly no reader would derive from the tract the impression that such terms were new coinages struck out to meet the occasion.

Additional point is given to this impression by the circumstance that Tertullian not only puts forward no claim to originality, but actually asserts that his teaching is the traditional teaching of the Church. As over against the novel character of the new-fangled teaching of Praxeas, which falls as such under the prescription which Tertullian was wont to bring against all heresies as innovations and therefore no part of the original deposit of the faith, he sets his doctrine as a doctrine which had always been believed and now much more, under the better instruction of the Paraclete. " We, however, as always, so now especially, since better instructed by the Paraclete, who is the leader into all truth, believe that there is one God indeed, but yet under the following dispensation, which we call the οἰκονομία." [22] An attempt has been made, it is true, to read in this statement a hint that the doctrine of the Trinity was a peculiarity of the Montanists; [23] and to make out that Tertul-

---

[19] Lipsius, as above, p. 721, instances these two terms as " expressions which meet us here for the first time." Both terms appear in Hippolytus' " Contra Noëtum," and if that tract antedates Tertullian's this would be an earlier appearance; and each appears once in earlier literature.

[20] Chap. ii.

[21] Chap. ii. Cf. chap. iii.

[22] Chap. ii.

[23] That Tertullian owed his Trinitarianism to Montanism was already suggested by the younger Christopher Sand in the seventeenth century —

lian means to say only that "we Montanists" have always so
believed. The language, however, will not lend itself to this
interpretation. Tertullian does say that since he became a Mon-
tanist his belief has been strengthened, and elsewhere (chap.
xiii.) he intimates that the Montanists were especially clear
as to the "economy," as he calls the distinction within the
unity of the Godhead. Perhaps he means that special prophetic
deliverances expounding the Trinity in unity had among the
Montanists been added to the traditionary faith. Perhaps he
means only that the emphasis laid by the Montanistic movement, in distinction from the Father and Son, on the activity
and personality of the Paraclete as the introducer of a new
dispensation, had conduced to clearer views of the distinctions
included in the unity of the Godhead. But the very adduction
of this clearer or fuller view as consequent upon his defection
to Montanism, only throws into prominence the fact that the
doctrine itself belonged to his pre-Montanistic period also.
"We as always, so now especially," contrasts two periods and
can only mean that this doctrine dated in his consciousness
from a day earlier than his Montanism. We must understand
Tertullian then as affirming that the doctrine of the Trinity in
unity which he is teaching belongs to the traditionary lore of
the Church. His testimony, in this case, is express that what
he teaches in this tract is nothing new, but only a part of his
original faith.

This testimony is supported by the occurrence in earlier

whose "Nucleus Historiæ Ecclesiasticæ" was one of the works which Bull's
"Defensio" was intended to meet. See Bull, "Defensio Fidei Nicaenæ," II. vii.
7 (E. T. 1851, i. p. 203). It was revived vigorously by the Tübingen School
(Baur, "Die christliche Lehre von der Dreieinigkeit und Menschwerdung
Gottes," i. p. 177, and especially Schwegler, e.g., "Nachapostolischer Zeitalter,"
ii. p. 341). Lipsius, as quoted, p. 719, opposes the notion, but argues that
nevertheless in Africa, at least, there was a connection between Montanism
and Trinitarianism. Besides his own paper in the *Zeitschrift für wissenschaftliche Theologie*, 1866, p. 194, Lipsius refers for information to Ritschl, "Altka-
tholische Kirche," 2d ed. pp. 487 f, and Volckmar, "Hippolyt.," p. 115. Stier
argues the question in his "Die Gottes- und Logos-Lehre Tertullians," p. 93,
note; cf. Dorner, "Doctrine of the Person of Christ," Div. I. ii. p. 20, and
especially p. 448–449.

treatises by Tertullian — notably in his great " Apology " [24] —
of passages in which essential elements of his doctrine are given
expression in his characteristic forms. And it is still further
supported by the preservation of such a treatise by the hand of
another, as Hippolytus' fragment against Noëtus,[25] in which
something similar to the same doctrine is enunciated. It has
been contended, indeed, that Tertullian borrowed from Hippolytus, or that Hippolytus borrowed from Tertullian. And
there may be little decisive to urge against either hypothesis if
otherwise commended. But in the absence of such further commendation it seems much more probable that the two treatises
independently embody a point of view already traditional in
the Church.[26] In any case Hippolytus must be believed to be
stating in essence no other doctrine than that which he had
striven for a generation to impress upon the Roman Church;
and he makes the same impression that Tertullian does of
handling well-worn weapons. Indeed we need bear in mind
nothing more than the most obvious New Testament data
culminating in the baptismal formula, the ritual use of which
kept its contents clearly before the mind of every Christian,
and the prevalence attained throughout the Christian world
by the Logos speculation of the Apologists, to be assured *à
priori* that it was not left either to Hippolytus or to Tertullian
to work out the essential elements of the doctrine of the Trinity in unity. But this compels us to recognize that something
more entered into the naïve faith of the average Christian
man as essential constituents of his Christian confession than
the two doctrines of the unity of God and the deity of the Redeemer. Even the simple Christian could not avoid forming
some conception of the relation of his divine Redeemer to the
Father, and in doing so could not content himself with an absolute identification of the two. Nor could he help extending his
speculation to embrace some doctrine of the Spirit whom he

---

[24] Chap. 21. It seems to have been written about the end of A.D. 197.
[25] " Contra Noëtum." Cf. " Philosophumena," ix.
[26] On Tertullian's relations to the anti-Modalistic writings of Hippolytus,
see Harnack in the *Zeitschrift für die historische Theologie*, 1874, pp. 203 *sq.*

was bound to recognize as God, and yet as in some way neither the Father nor the Son, along with whom He was named in the formula of baptism. In proportion as the believer was aware of the course of the debate that had gone on in the Church, and was affected by the movements which had agitated it from the beginning — all of which touched more or less directly on these points — he would have been driven along a pathway which, in attempting to avoid the heresies that were tearing the Church, could emerge in nothing else than some doctrine of Trinity in unity. The presence of a Trinitarian tradition in the Church is thus so far from surprising that its absence would be inexplicable. There is no reason, therefore, why we should discredit Tertullian's testimony that Christians had always believed in essence what he teaches in his tract " Against Praxeas."

If it is very easy to exaggerate the originality of Tertullian's doctrine as set forth in this tract, however, it is equally easy to underestimate it. Let us allow that Trinitarianism is inherent in the elements of the Gospel, and that, under the influence of the Logos Christology and in opposition to Gnostic emanationism, a certain crude Trinitarianism must have formed a part of the common faith of naïve Christendom. It remains none the less true that men were very slow in explicating this inherent doctrine of Christianity, at least with any clearness or concinnity; and meanwhile they were a prey to numerous more or less attractive substitutes for it, among which the Logos Christology long held the field, and its contradictory, Modalistic Monarchianism, as we have seen, at one time bade fair to establish itself as the common doctrine of the churches. And it remains true, moreover, that no one earlier than Tertullian and few besides Tertullian, prior to the outbreak of the Arian controversy, seem to have succeeded in giving anything like a tenable expression to this potential Trinitarianism. If Tertullian may not be accredited with the invention of the doctrine of the Trinity, it may yet be that it was through him that the elements of this doctrine first obtained something like a scientific adjustment, and that he may not unfairly, therefore, be accounted its originator, in a sense somewhat similar to that in which Augustine may be accounted the originator of the doctrines of original sin and sovereign grace, Anselm of the doctrine of satisfaction, and Luther of that of justification by faith. Whether he may be so accounted, and how far, can be determined only by a careful examination of what he has actually set down in his writings.

When now we come to scrutinize with the requisite closeness the doctrine which underlies Tertullian's enunciations in his tract, " Against Praxeas," we perceive that it is, in point of fact, fundamentally little else than the simple Biblical teaching as to the Father, Son, and Holy Spirit elaborated under the categories of the Logos Christology.

This Logos Christology had been simply taken over by Tertullian from the Apologists, who had wrought it fully out and made it dominant in the Christian thought of the time. Its roots were planted alike in Jewish religion and in Gentile speculation. Its point of origin lay in a conception of the transcendence of God which rendered it necessary to mediate his activity *ad extra* by the assumption of the interposition of intermediate beings. In their highest form, the speculations thus induced gave birth to the idea of the Logos. Under the influence of passages like the eighth chapter of Proverbs and the first chapter of John, the historical Jesus was identified with this Logos, and thus the Logos Christology was, in principle, completed. It will be observed that the Logos Christology was in its very essence cosmological in intention: its reason for existence was to render it possible to conceive the divine works of creation and government consistently with the divine transcendence: it was therefore bound up necessarily with the course of temporal development and involved a process in God. The Logos was in principle God conceived in relation to things of time and space: God, therefore, not as absolute, but as relative. In its very essence, therefore, the Logos conception likewise involved the strongest subordinationism. Its very reason for existence was to provide a divine being who does

the will of God in the regions of time and space, into which
it were inconceivable that the Invisible God should be able
to intrude in His own person. The Logos was therefore necessarily conceived as reduced divinity — divinity, so to speak,
at the periphery rather than at the center of its conception.
This means, further, that the Logos was inevitably conceived
as a protrusion of God, or to speak more explicitly, under the
category of emanation. The affinity of the Logos speculation
with the emanation theories of the Gnostics is, therefore,
close. The distinction between the two does not lie, however,
merely in the number of emanations presumed to have proceeded from the fountain-deity, nor merely in the functions
ascribed to these emanations, bizarre as the developments of
Gnosticism were in this matter. The distinction lies much
more in the fundamental conception entertained of the nature
of the fountain-deity itself, and more directly in the conception developed of the nature of the emanation process and the
relation of the resulting emanations to the primal-deity. The
Gnostic systems tended ever to look upon the source-deity as
a featureless abyss of being, to conceive the process of emanation from it as a blind and necessary evolution, and to attribute to the emanations resulting from this process a high
degree of independence of the primal-deity. In direct contradiction to the Gnostic construction, the Logos speculation
conceived God as personal, the procession of the Logos as a
voluntary act on the part of God, and the Logos itself as, so
to say, a function of the eternal God Himself, never escaping
from the control of His will, or, as it might be more just to say,
from participation in His fullness. The effect of the Gnostic
speculation was to create a hierarchy of lesser divinities,
stretching from the primal abyss of being downward in ever-
widening circles and diminishing potencies to the verge of the
material world itself. The value of the Logos speculation to
the first age of Christianity was that it enabled Christian
thinkers to preserve the unity of God while yet guarding His
transcendence; and to look upon the historical Jesus, identified with the Logos, as very God, the Creator and Governor

of the world, while yet recognizing His subordination to the will of God and His engagement with the course of development of things in time and space. It is probable that it was only by the help of the Logos speculation that Christianity was able to preserve its fundamental confession in the sharp conflict through which it was called to pass in the second century. By the aid of that speculation, at all events, it emerged from this conflict with a firm and clear hold upon both of the fundamental principles of the unity of the Indivisible God and the deity of the historical Jesus, who was, as John had taught in words, the Logos of God; that is to say, as the leaders of the day interpreted the significance of the term, the pretemporal protrusion of the deity for the purpose of creating the world of time and space and the mediating instrument of the deity in all His dealings with the world of time and space.

Tertullian, now, was the heir of this whole Logos construction, and he took it over from the Apologists in its entirety, with his accustomed clearness and even intensity of perception.[27] There was no element in it which he did not grasp with the most penetrating intuition of its significance and of the possibilities of its development at the call of fresh doctrinal needs. The demand for a new application of it came to him in the rise of the Monarchian controversy, and he opposed the Logos doctrine to the new construction with a confidence and a skill in adaptation which are nothing less than astonishing. This seems the precise account to give of the scope of the tract, " Against Praxeas." It is in essence an attempt to adapt the old Logos speculation, which Tertullian had taken over in its entirety from the Apologists, to the new conditions induced by the rise and remarkable success of the Monarchian movement.

[27] The general dependence of Tertullian on the Apologists is very marked. Loofs says justly: " Tertullian's general conception of Christianity is determined by the apologetical tradition " (Herzog, " Realencyklopädie für protestantische Theologie und Kirche," [3] xii. p. 264, line 46); and again: " Novatian and Tertullian were much more strongly influenced than Irenæus by the Apologists: their general conception of Christianity received its color from this influence " (*Sitzungsberichte der königlich preussichen Akademie der Wissenschaften zu Berlin*, June, 1902, p. 781).

Whatever contributions, then, to the development of the doctrine of the Trinity Tertullian was able to make were made
because of the emergence of need for such new adjustments of
the old Logos speculation, and because he met this need with
talents of the first order.

We must not underestimate the significance of the rise and
rapid spread of the Monarchian Christology; or imagine that
it could have filled the place in the history of the late second
and early third centuries which it did, if it had found no justification for itself in the condition of Christian thought at the
time, or had brought no contribution for the Christian thought
of the future. The truth is, the Logos speculation left much to
be desired in the formulation of the Christian doctrines of
God and the Mediator between God and man; and the Monarchian speculation came bearing these very desiderata in its
hands. The Logos Christology put itself forward as the guardian alike of the unity of God and of the deity of Jesus. But the
unity it ascribed to God was, after all, apt to be but a broken
unity, and the deity it ascribed to Jesus was at best but a derived deity. According to it, Jesus was not the God over all
that Paul called Him, but the Logos; and the Logos was not
one with the Father, as John taught, and indeed as Jesus
(who was the Logos) asserted, but an efflux from the Father
— by so much lower than the Father as the possibility of
entrance into and commerce with the world of space and time
implied. Men might very well ask if this construction did justice either to the unity of God or to the deity of Jesus which it
essayed to protect; whether every attempt to do justice on
its basis to the unity of God would not mean disparage-
ment of the perfect deity of Jesus, and every attempt to do
justice to the deity of Jesus would not mean the erection of
the Logos, with whom Jesus was identified rather than with
God, to a place alongside of God, which would involve the
confession of two Gods. By the rise of Monarchianism, in
other words, the traditional Logos construction was put
sharply on its trial. It was demanded of it that it show itself
capable of doing justice to the deity of Jesus, while yet re-

taining in integrity the unity of God, or else give place to a better scheme which by identifying Jesus directly with the One God, certainly provided fully for these two focal conceptions.

The difficulty of the situation into which the assault of Monarchianism brought the Logos Christology, by its insistence that Jesus should be recognized as all that God is, becomes manifest when we reflect that every attempt to elevate the deity that was in Jesus to absolute equality with the God over all seemed to involve in one way or another the abandonment of the entire Logos speculation. The simple identification of Jesus with God would be, of course, the formal abolishment of the Logos speculation altogether. But the attempt to retain the distinction beween God and the Logos, while Jesus as the Logos was made all that God is, seemed only a roundabout way to the same goal. Since the postulation of a Logos turned precisely on the assumption that God in Himself is too transcendent to enter into commerce with the world of space and time, the obliteration of the difference between the Logos and God appeared to reduce the whole Logos hypothesis to an absurdity. Either the primal-deity would need no Logos, or the Logos Himself would require another Logos. The task Tertullian found facing him when he undertook the defense of the Logos Christology over against the Monarchian assault was thus one of no little delicacy and difficulty. It was a task of great delicacy. For the Monarchians did not come forward as innovators in doctrine, but as protestants in the interest of the fundamental Christian doctrines of the divine unity and of the Godhead of the Redeemer against destructive speculations which were endangering the purity of the Christian confession. They embodied the protest of the simple believer against philosophic evaporations of the faith. Above all they were giving at last, so they said, his just due to Christ. It means everything when we hear Hippolytus quoting Noëtus as exclaiming: "How can I be doing wrong in glorifying Christ? " [28] — a cry, we may be sure, which found an echo in

[28] τί οὖν κακὸν ποιῶ, δοξάζων τὸν Χριστόν;

every Christian heart. And it was a task of great difficulty. For what Tertullian had to do was to establish the true and complete deity of Jesus, and at the same time the reality of His distinctness as the Logos from the fontal-deity, without creating two Gods. This is, on the face of it, precisely the problem of the Trinity. And so far as Tertullian succeeded in it, he must be recognized as the father of the Church doctrine of the Trinity.

Of course Tertullian was not completely successful in so great a task. On his postulates, indeed, complete success was difficult to the verge of impossibility. The Logos Christology was, to speak shortly, in its fundamental assumptions incompatible with a developed doctrine of immanent Trinity. Its primary object was to provide a mediating being through which the essentially " Invisible " God could become " visible " — the absolute God enter into relations — the transcendent God come into connection with a world of time and space. To it Jesus must by the very necessity of its fundamental postulates be something less than the God over all. So soon as He was allowed to be Himself all that God is, the very reason for existence of the Logos speculation was removed. Nor was it easy on the assumptions of the Logos Christology to allow a real distinctness of person for the Logos. On its postulates the Logos must be itself God — God prolate — God in reduction — God, as we have said, on the periphery of His Being: but God Himself nevertheless. On every attempt to sharpen the distinction by conceiving it as truly personal rather than gradual, the whole speculation begins to evaporate. The distinction inherent in the Logos speculation may be a distinction of transcendent and immanent, of absolute and relative, of more or less: a distinction between person and person is outside the demands of its purpose. How can a distinct person be the absolute God become relative? And these difficulties reach their climax when we suppose this distinction to be eternal. What function can be conceived for a relative God in the depths of eternity, when nothing existed except God Himself? A meaningless God is just no God at all. Tertullian, in a word, as a convinced adherent of the Logos Christology, was committed to conceptions which were not capable of holding a doctrine of immanent Trinity. The most that could be expected from him would be that he should approach as closely to a doctrine of Trinity as was possible on his presuppositions — that he should fill the conceptions of the Logos Christology, the highest as yet developed in the Church, so full that they should be nigh to bursting: We shall see that he did more than this. But in proportion as he did more than this has he transcended what could legitimately have been expected of him; and we shall be forced to allow that, in his effort to do justice to elements of faith brought into prominence in this controversy, he filled the conceptions of the Logos speculation so full that they actually burst in his hands. The Logos Christology, in other words, was stretched by him beyond its tether and was already passing upward in his construction to something better.

A great deal has been said of Tertullian's failure in perfect consistency: a great deal of his indebtedness to the Monarchians themselves for many of his ideas: a great deal of elements of compromise with his opponents discoverable in his construction. These things are not, however, proofs of weakness, but indications of strength in him. They mean that with all his clearness of grasp upon the Logos Christology, and with all his acuteness in adapting it to meet the problem he was facing, he yet saw the truth of some things for which, for all his acumen, it could not be made to provide — and stretched it to make it cover them also. They mean that he was not misled into the denial of positive elements of truth, always confessed by the Church, by zeal against the body of errorists that had taken them under their especial charge. For it is not quite exact to speak of these elements of truth as accepted by Tertullian at the hands of the Monarchians. They were rather elements of truth embodied in the general Christian confession, hitherto more or less neglected by the theologians, but now thrown into prominence by the presently raging controversy. It is the nemesis of incomplete theories that neglected elements of truth rise up after awhile to vex them. So it happened with the Logos Christology. But Tertullian sought to stretch the Logos Christology to cover these truths, not because they were urged with so much insistence by his opponents — he was not quite the man to meet insistence by yielding: but because they were parts of the Rule of Faith and were universally accepted by Christians as imposed on their belief by the divine Oracles, and he, for his part, was determined to be loyal to the Rule of Faith and to the teaching of Scripture.

There was one thing, in other words, which was more fundamental to Tertullian's thinking than even the Logos Christology. That was the Rule of Faith — the immemorial belief of Christians, grounded in the teaching of the Word of God.[29] The insistence on certain truths by his opponent may have been the occasion of Tertullian's notice of them: his attempt to incorporate them into his construction was grounded in recognition of them as elements in the universal Christian faith. This Rule of Faith had come down to him from " the

[29] This is, briefly, what appears to be the meaning of the Rule of Faith, or the Rule of Truth, in the writings of Tertullian as of the other early Fathers. There has been much discussion among scholars as to the exact relation of the conception to Scripture, on the one hand, and to the Baptismal Creed — what we know as " The Apostles' Creed " — on the other. Kunze, in his " Glaubensregel, Heilige Schrift und Taufbekenntnis," seems greatly to have advanced the matter. It seems clear that the Rule of Faith means the common fundamental faith of the Church, as derived from Scripture and expressed especially in the Baptismal Creed. That is to say, it is (1) the authoritative teaching of Scripture as a whole; (2) but this teaching conceived as the common faith of the whole Church; (3) most commodiously set out in brief in the Apostles' Creed. This may be sharply expressed by saying that the Rule of Faith was supposed to be the Scriptures, and the Creed was supposed to be the Rule of Faith. In the East the consciousness that the Rule of Faith was merely the teaching of the Scriptures as drawn from them and confessed by the Church, in the West the consciousness that the Apostles' Creed was a summary setting forth of the Rule of Faith, tended to rule the usage of the term. Accordingly the tendency was in the East to see most pointedly the Scriptures *through* the Rule of Faith, or, if you will, the Rule of Faith *in* the Scriptures; in the West to see the Apostolicum *in* the Rule of Faith, or, if you will, the Rule of Faith *through* the Apostolicum. On Tertullian's conception of the relation of the Rule of Faith to Scripture see especially Kunze, p. 178.

beginning of the Gospel," as he phrased it; [30] and he recognized it as his first duty to preserve it whole and entire. The Logos Christology had not been able to take up all the items of belief which Christians held essential to their good profession: perhaps it was due to the Monarchian controversy that Christians were enabled to see that clearly. It is to the credit of Tertullian, that seeing it, he sought rather to stretch his inherited Christology to include the facts thus brought sharply to his notice, than to deny the facts in the interest of what must have seemed to him the solidly worked out philosophy of revealed truth. By his sympathetic recognition of these elements of truth he built a wider foundation, on which a greater structure could afterward be raised. To his own consciousness the principle of his doctrine remained ever the data of Scripture embodied in the Rule of Faith and interpreted under the categories of the Logos Christology. Beyond the Logos Christology he did not purposely advance. It remained for him to the end the great instrument for the understanding of Scripture. But it happened to him, as it has happened to many besides him, that the process of pouring so much new wine into old bottles had an unhappy effect upon the bottles. This great adherent of the Logos speculation became the prime instrument of its destruction.

What is true in this matter of Tertullian is true also in his own measure of Hippolytus. Both stood firmly on the Rule of Faith: [31] and the instrument for its interpretation used by each alike was the Logos Christology, which both had adopted in its entirety from the Apologists. This accounts for the similarity of their teachings. The difference of their teachings is due very largely to the unequal ability of the two men.[32] Ter-

[30] He carries back the Rule of Faith to the teaching of Christ ("De Præscriptione," ix. xiii. Cf. xx. xxi. xxvii. etc.).

[31] In Hippolytus the term and its synonyms are of very important occurrence (see Kunze, p. 129), and except in the "Little Labyrinth" the form "Rule of Truth" is the one he employs.

[32] A similar judgment is expressed by Bethune-Baker, "The Meaning of Homoousios in the 'Constantinopolitan' Creed," in "Texts and Studies," J. A. Robinson, ed., vii. 1, pp. 73–74, note.

tullian was much the abler man and succeeded much better in making room in his construction for the elements of truth embedded in the Rule of Faith which the Logos Christology found difficulty in assimilating. Callistus was not without some color of justification in excommunicating Hippolytus as well as Sabellius, as alike with him defective in his teaching. Only, Callistus was incapable of perceiving that it was the Logos Christology, and not the facile methods of Monarchian Modalism, which was seriously seeking to embrace and explain all the facts; that in it alone, therefore, was to be found the promise of the better construction yet to come, toward which it was reaching out honest and eager hands. His own shallow opportunism prevented him from apprehending that what was needed was not denial of all real distinction between God and Logos, Father and Son, and therewith the confounding of the entire process of redemption, but the rescue of this distinction from its entanglement with cosmological speculation, and the elevation of it from a mere matter of degrees of divinity to the sphere of personal individualization, while yet it should be jealously guarded from the virtual division of the Godhead into a plurality of deities. Callistus, the politic ruler of a distracted diocese, intent above all on calming dangerous excitement and discouraging schism, ready to purchase peace at any cost, was not capable of such a feat of sound thinking. Hippolytus was too little independent of his inheritance to be capable of it. Even Tertullian was not capable of carrying through such a task to its end: though he was able to advance it a little stage toward its accomplishment. All the circumstances considered, this was a great achievement, and it could not have been accomplished had not Tertullian united to his zeal in controversy and his acumen in theological construction an essential broad-mindedness, an incorruptible honesty of heart and a sure hold on the essentials of the faith.

That the account thus suggested correctly represents the facts will appear upon a somewhat more detailed investigation of the exact attitude of Tertullian both to the Logos

Christology and to the Rule of Faith. To such an investigation we shall now address ourselves.

Even in his earliest writings there occur passages in which full and convinced expression is given to the speculations of the Logos Christology, from which it appears that from the beginning of his activity as a Christian writer these speculations supplied the molds in which Tertullian's thought ran. When, for example, in the twenty-first chapter of his " Apology," which was written about 197, he undertakes to expound to his heathen readers the deity of Christ,[33] he identifies Him out of hand with the Logos of Zeno and Cleanthes,[34] because, as he says, " we have been taught " (*didicimus*) as follows — whereupon he proceeds to set forth the Logos doctrine, thus declared to be to him the traditionary doctrine of the Church.[35] " We have been taught," says he, that the Logos " was produced (*prolatum*) from God (*ex Deo*) and in [this] production generated, and therefore is called the Son of God and God, because of (*ex*) the unity of the substance, since God also is Spirit. Just as when a ray is put forth (*porrigitur*) from the sun, it is a portion of the whole (*portio ex summa*), but the sun will be in the ray, because it is a ray of the sun, and is not separated from the substance, but stretched out (*non separatur substantia sed extenditur*); so Spirit [is extended] from Spirit and God from God, as light is kindled from light. The *materiæ matrix* (source of the material) remains entire and undiminished (*integra et indefecta*) although you draw out from it

---

[33] " Necesse est igitur pauca de Christo ut deo."

[34] " Your philosophers . . . Zeno . . . Cleanthes . . . and *we too* (et nos autem). . . ."

[35] Kunze, p. 197, has some excellent remarks on the relative places-taken by philosophy and Scripture in the thinking of such men as Irenæus and Tertullian. They wished to be purely Biblical; and the influence of philosophy " was exerted only through the medium of their understanding of the Bible, through the filter of Bible interpretation." " This was true, for example," he adds, " of their Logos theory. As certain as it is that in this matter extra-Christian influences are recognizable, it is equally certain that for Tertullian, and especially for Irenæus, the Logos idea and its corollaries would have formed no part of the regula had they not found word and thing alike in the Scriptures."

many branches of its kind (*traduces qualitatis*): thus also what is derived (*profectum*) from God is God and the Son of God, and the two are one. In this manner, then, He who is Spirit from Spirit and God from God made another individual in mode [of existence], in grade, not in state (*modulo alternum numerum, gradu non statu fecit*), and did not separate from but stretched out from the source (*et a matrice non recessit sed excessit*). This ray of God, then, descended into a certain virgin, as it had always been predicted in times past. . . ."[36]

What we read in the tract " Against Praxeas " embodies the same ideas in the same terms. We must, however, note in more detail how far Tertullian here commits himself to the forms of the Logos speculation. We observe, then, in the first place, that Tertullian with complete conviction shares the fundamental conception out of which the Logos doctrine grows — the conception of the transcendence of God above all possibility of direct relation with a world of time and space. So axiomatic did it seem to him that God in Himself is exalted above direct concernment with the world-process, that when discussing the temporal activities of our Lord, he permits himself to say that such things, hard to believe of the Son and only to be credited concerning Him on the authority of Scripture, could scarcely have been believed of the Father, even if Scripture had explicitly affirmed them of Him.[37] That is to say, the doctrine of the transcendence of God, or as Tertullian phrases it, in Scriptural language which had become traditional in this school, of the " invisibility " of God " in the fulness of His majesty,"[38] stood, as a fixed datum, at the root of Tertullian's whole thought of God. In the second place, we observe that Tertullian shared with equal heartiness the current conception of the Logos as, so to speak, the world-form of God. It was, indeed, only in connection with the world, and as its condition, both with respect to origin and government, that he was accustomed

---

[36] Cf. the parallel statements in " De Præscriptione " 13.

[37] " Against Praxeas," chap. xvi.: " Fortasse non credenda de patre, licet scripta."

[38] Chap. xiv.

to think of a Logos at all. The prolation of the Logos took place, in his view, only for and with the world, as a necessary mediator, to perform a work which God as absolute could not perform. It was " *then*," says Tertullian with pointed emphasis,[39] that the Word assumed " His own form," when God said, " Let there be light! " It was only when God was pleased to draw out (*edere*) into " their own substances and forms " (*in substantias et species suas*) the things He had planned within Himself, that He put forth (*protulit*) the Word, in order that all things might be made through Him.[40] We observe, in the third place, that Tertullian, with equal heartiness, shared the consequent view that the Logos is not God in His entirety, but only a " portion " of God — a " portion," that is, as in the ray there is not the whole but only a " portion " of the sun. The difference seems to be not one of mode only, but of measure. " The Father," he says, " is the entire substance, but the Son is a derivation and portion of the whole." [41] He speaks " of that portion of the whole which was about to retire into the designation of the Son." [42] To Tertullian this idea was self-evident inasmuch as the Logos was to him necessarily produced, or, rather, reduced Divinity — Divinity brought to a level on which it could become creator and principle of the world of time and space.[43] We observe, in the fourth place, that Tertullian also accorded with the current conception in thinking of the prolation of the Logos as a voluntary act of God rather than a necessary movement within the divine essence.

[39] *Loc. cit.*, chap. vii.: " Tunc igitur etiam ipse sermo speciem et ornatum suum sumit, sonum et vocem, cum dixit deus: fiat lux."

[40] Chap. vi.: " Iam, ut primum deus voluit ea, quæ cum sophiæ ratione et sermone disposeuerat intra se, in substantias et species suas edere, ipsum primum protulit sermonem, habentem in se individuas suas, rationem et sophiam, etc. So also chap. xii. " The first statement of Scripture is made, indeed, when the Son had not yet appeared: ' And God said, " Let there be light," and there was light.' Immediately there appears the Word, ' that true light. . . . From that moment God willed creation to be effected in the Word, Christ.' . . ."

[41] Chap. ix.

[42] Chap. xxvi.

[43] The real meaning of this phraseology will be discussed further on in this article.

As there was a time before which the Son was not,[44] so He came into being by the will of God,[45] and remains in being to fulfill the will of God, and at last when He has fulfilled the will of God retires once more into the divine unity.[46] All this, of course, applies only to the prolate Logos.[47] This whole development of the prolate Logos, therefore, is not only a temporal but a temporary expedient, by means of which God, acting voluntarily, accomplishes a work. When this work is accomplished the arrangements for it naturally cease. The Logos mode of existence thus emerges as an incident in the life of God which need not, perhaps, find a necessary rooting in His nature, but only a contingent rooting in His purposes. In the very nature of the case, therefore, the prolate Logos is dependent on the divine will.[48] It is hardly necessary to make a separate fifth observation, therefore, that Tertullian thoroughly shared the subordinationism inherent in the Logos Christology.[49] To him the Son, as prolated Logos, was self-evidently less (*minor*) than the Father, seeing that His prolation occurred by the Father's will, and in order to do His will. He remains subject to His will,[50] and when that will is accomplished returns into the divine

[44] Chap. v.: God was alone " up to the generation of the Son." Cf. chaps. vi. xiii. Cf. " Against Hermog.," iii.: Fuit autem tempus cum . . . Filius non fuit . . . ; and see Bull's long discussion of this passage in his " Denfensio Fidei Nicaenæ," iii. x. (E. T. 1851, pp. 509 f.). The real meaning of this too will be discussed later.

[45] Chap. xvi.: " The Scripture informs us that He who was made less (than the angels) was so affected by another and not Himself by Himself." Cf. chaps. iv. xxiii. The insistence of the Apologists on the origination of the Logos in an act of the will of God was their protest against the blind evolutionism of the Gnostics, and often was but their way of saying that creation was not a necessary process but a voluntary act on God's part; that is to say, it hangs together with their cosmological conception of the Logos. Cf. Hagemann, " Die Römische Kirche," p. 194. On the whole subject compare Dorner, " Doctrine of the Person of Christ," Div. I. ii. p. 460, and Bethune-Baker, " An Introduction to the Early History of Christian Doctrine," p. 159, note,[2] and pp. 194–195.

[46] Chap. iv. Cf. chaps. xxii. xxiii.

[47] The as yet unprolated Logos Tertullian wishes to distinguish from the uttered Logos or Sermo, as the unuttered Logos or Ratio; cf. chap. v.

[48] Cf. Stier, p. 100.

[49] Cf. Stier, p. 71.

[50] Chaps. iv. xvi. xviii.

bosom. The invisible Father alone possesses the fullness of the divine majesty: the Son is visible *pro modulo derivationis* — by reason of the measure of His derivation — and stands related to the Father as a ray does to the sun.[51] He is the *second,* in every sense of the term.

Even such a brief survey as this of the natural forms in which Tertullian's thought ran makes it exceedingly clear that the prime instrument in his hands for the interpretation of the facts of the Christian revelation was just the Logos Christology taken over in its entirety from his predecessors.

But if the Logos Christology thus supplied to Tertullian the forms of thought with which he approached the problems now brought into renewed prominence, the matter of his thinking was derived from another source, and from a source that lay even more deeply embedded in his convictions. If the Logos Christology was the instrument by means of which he sought to interpret the Rule of Faith, the Rule of Faith supplied the matter to be interpreted. The question that was always pressing upon him, therefore, was whether this matter in its entirety could be interpreted by the Logos Christology. Certainly Tertullian must be credited with a loyal effort to preserve all its data in their integrity, as even his most cursory reader will at once perceive; [52] and in making this effort, largely under the

---

[51] Chap. xiv.

[52] The Rule of Faith, which originates in the teaching of Christ and comes to us in the apostolic proclamation, and which is, therefore, " absolutely one, alone, immovable and irreformable," according to " De Vel. Virg.," 1, " prescribes the belief that there is one only God . . . who produced all things out of nothing through His own Word first of all sent forth; that this Word is called His Son . . . was made flesh and . . . having been crucified, rose again the third day, ascended into the heavens, sat at the right hand of the Father; sent instead of Himself the power of the Holy Ghost to lead such as believe on Him " (" De Præscriptione," xiii.). Or as Tertullian sets forth the items in " Against Praxeas," 2, relatively to the matters in hand in that tract, this aboriginal Rule of Faith teaches that " there is one God "; that " this one only God has also a Son, His Word, who proceeded from Himself, by whom all things were made and without whom nothing was made "; and that this Son has " sent also from heaven from the Father, according to His own promise, the Holy Ghost, the Paraclete, the Sanctifier of the faith of those who believe in the Father, and in the Son and in the Holy Ghost." Tertullian obviously looks

influence of the Monarchian controversy, he found himself
compelled to enlarge and modify the contents of the Logos
speculation, in order to embrace the data of the Rule of Faith.

In the first place, the Rule of Faith imposed on Tertullian
the duty of framing a doctrine of the Holy Spirit as well as of
the Son of God. For this, of course, the Logos Christology did
not necessarily provide. But it pointed out a road to it by way
of analogy. The Apologists, accordingly, though they were absorbed in the doctrine of the Logos and did not always know
what to do with the Spirit, yet did not leave the subject
so entirely to one side but that they handed down to their
successors the beginnings of a doctrine of the Spirit framed on
the analogy of this Christology.[53] They had already made it a
matter of traditionary doctrine, for example, that the Spirit
is related to the Son much as the Son is to the Father, and
makes a third alongside of the Father and Son.[54] Tertullian
takes up these somewhat fluid elements of traditional teaching
and gives them sharpness and consistency.[55] He looks upon the
Spirit apparently as a prolation from the Son, as the Son is
from the Father, thus preserving, so to speak, a linear development in the evolution of God: [56] but he carefully preserves the

---

upon the Rule of Faith as originating in the baptismal formula given by our
Lord, and as finding its normal succinct expression in the Baptismal Creed, commonly known as the Apostles' Creed.

[53] On the early opinions as to the Spirit, besides Dr. Swete's book on this
precise subject, see Kahnis, "Lehre vom heiligen Geiste," pp. 168 f.; Nösgen
"Geschichte der Lehre vom heiligen Geiste," chap. i.; Harnack, i. p. 197, note,
and ii. p. 209, note [1]; Scott, "Origin and Development of the Nicene Theology," Lecture V.

[54] Scott, pp. 274, 284. "The doctrine of the Holy Spirit," says Scott, p.
285, note, "was not developed in the second century, but it was plainly present
in the Church, both East and West. The theological statement of the Spirit in
the second century did not use the term *hypostatic;* but all that was meant
later by that term is clearly involved in the teachings of the Apologists and the
anti-Gnostic writers." Tertullian "first called the Spirit 'God,' but he only
uttered what the Church had ever believed."

[55] On Tertullian's doctrine of the Spirit, see Kahnis, pp. 255 f.; Scott, p.
284; Harnack, ii. p. 261, note [4]; Stier, p. 92, note. The most distinctive passages seem to be found in "Against Praxeas," ii. iii. iv. viii. ix. xi. xiii. xxvi. xxx.

[56] This characteristic of the Apologists' construction is its most marked

conception of the Father as *fons deitatis,* and thus frames as his exact formula the assertion that the Spirit, being the third degree in the Godhead, proceeds "from no other source than from the Father through the Son" (chap. iv.). In his familiar figures, as the Father and Son are represented by the root and the stem of the tree, by the fountain and the river, by the sun and its ray, so the Spirit, being "third from God and the Son," is as the fruit of the tree, which is third from the root, or as the stream from the river, which is third from the fountain, or as the apex from the ray, which is third from the sun (chap. viii.).[57] All flows down from the Father through colligated and conjoined grades (*per consertos et conexos gradus,* chap. viii. *ad fin.*), but the immediate connection is of the Father in the Son and the Son in the Paraclete (chap. xxv. *ad init.*), and thus it may be truly said that the Son received the Spirit from the Father and yet Himself shed Him forth — this "Third Name in the Godhead and Third Grade in the Divine Majesty, the Declarer of the One Monarchy of God and yet, at the same time, the Interpreter of the Economy" (chap. xxx.). Under the guidance of the Logos speculation Tertullian thus, in the first instance, conceives the Spirit apparently as a prolation of the Son as the Son is of the Father, and as therefore subordinate to the Son as the Son is to the Father: but nevertheless as ultimately deriving from the *fons deitatis* itself, through the Son, and through the Son subject ultimately to it.[58]

The consistent extension of the Logos speculation to cover the Third divine Person confessed in the Rule of Faith was, however, only a short step toward embracing the data included in that formula under the categories of the Logos speculation. The really pressing problem concerned the relations in which

---

trait, and is therefore frequently noted. Thus Hagemann, p. 139, when speaking of Hippolytus, adverts to the difference between the Church's construction and his, that the one thought of the trinitarian relationships "after the analogy of a circular motion (Kreisbewegung) and the other as *advancing in a straight line.*"

[57] Tertius enim est spiritus a deo et filio, sicut tertius a radice fructus ex frutice, et tertius a fonte rivus ex flumine, et tertius a sole apex ex radio.

[58] Stier, p. 92, note; Harnack, ii. p. 261, note [4].

the Father, Son, and Holy Spirit stand to one another. In the Rule of Faith — in the Baptismal Formula — they appear as coördinate persons, to each of whom true deity is ascribed, or, rather, to all three of whom the Name is attributed in common. Was the Logos speculation capable of taking up these data into itself and doing full justice to them? Tertullian must be credited with a sincere and a fruitful effort to make it do so. So far as the mere inclusion of the data under a single formula is concerned he found little difficulty. His formula is that the Father, Son, and Spirit are one in substance and distinct in person. In this formula he intrenches himself and reiterates and illustrates it with inexhaustible zest. He opens the serious discussion of the tract with a clear enunciation of it drawn out in full detail — crying out against the Monarchian assumption that the unity of the Godhead implies unity of Person, " as if One might not be All in this way also — viz., in All being of One, by unity of substance, while the mystery (*sacramentum*) of the οἰκονομία is still preserved, by which the unity is distributed into a Trinity, ordering (*dirigens*) the three — Father, Son, and Holy Ghost — three, however, not in status but in grade, not in substance but in form, not in power but in aspect (*species*); yet of one substance, and of one status, and of one power, inasmuch as He is one God from whom are reckoned these grades and forms and aspects under the name of the Father and Son and Holy Ghost." This is Tertullian's complete formula of Trinity in unity, which he promises to explicate more fully in the remainder of the treatise. This promise he very fairly fulfills — now repeating the entire statement more or less fully and now insisting on this or that element of it.[59] One of his favorite methods of indicating briefly the combined sameness and distinction is by employing distinctively the neuter and masculine forms of the words. " I and the Father are one," says our Lord; and Tertullian lays stress not only on the plural verb — " I and the Father *are*," not " *am*," one — but on the neuter form of the adjective — " unum," not " unus " — as implying. " not singularity of number but unity

[59] E.g., chaps. iv. viii. ix. xi. xii. xxi. *sq.*

of essence," and the like (chap. xxii.). " These Three," he says again (chap. xxv.), " are unum, not unus, in respect of unity of substance, not singularness of number." So he rings the changes constantly on the unity of substance and distinction of persons.

So far, we shall easily say, so good. For so much the Logos speculation opens the way without straining. It is inherent in it that the divine prolations should be of the very essence of God, while, on the other hand, capable as prolations of acting in some sense as distinct beings. The tug comes when we ask whether this asserted unity of substance provides for the supreme deity of the prolations, so that we can say that Jesus Christ, for example, is all that God is; and whether this asserted distinctness of persons provides for a real individualization of personality, so that each so-called person stands over against the others in permanent distinctness and not in merely apparent and in its very nature temporary objectivation. Certainly the Logos speculation suggests a reduced deity for the prolations, and that in diminishing grades: and a temporal rather than an eternal — whether *a parte ante* or *a parte post* — distinction between them. Does Tertullian see glimpses beyond? In such glimpses beyond we shall discover whatever approach he has made to constructing a doctrine of a real Trinity. The hinge of the problem turns on the answers we shall be compelled to give to five questions: (1) Whether Tertullian by his distinction of " persons " intends a distinction which is really personal in the philosophical sense of that term; (2) whether Tertullian supposes this distinction of persons to have been constituted by the prolations of the Logos and Spirit, which, he teaches, took place in order to the creation and government of the world, or to belong rather to the essential mode of existence of God; (3) whether he succeeds in preserving the unity of God despite the distinction of persons which he teaches; (4) whether he is able to ascribe such deity to Christ as to say of Him that He is all that God is; (5) whether he accords to the Holy Spirit also both complete deity and eternal distinctness of personality. We shall need to look at his response to these five questions in turn.

But we shall reserve this for the Second Article.

SECOND ARTICLE [60]

IN the First Article it was pointed out that any approach which Tertullian may have made toward formulating a doctrine of a really immanent Trinity will be revealed by attending to the responses he makes to five questions. These questions are: (1) Whether he intends a real distinction of persons, in the philosophical sense of the term, by the distinction he makes between the divine " persons "; (2) whether he supposes this distinction of persons to belong to the essential mode of the divine existence, or to have been constituted by those prolations of the Logos and Spirit which, according to his teaching, took place in order to the creation and government of the world; (3) whether he preserves successfully the unity of God in the distinction of persons which he teaches; (4) whether he conceives deity in Christ to be all that it is in the Father; (5) whether he accords to the Holy Spirit also both absolute deity and eternal distinctness of personality. We shall endeavor now to obtain Tertullian's responses to these questions.

(1) The interest with which we seek Tertullian's answer to the first of these questions, great enough in itself, has been largely increased by a suggestion made by Dr. Charles Bigg, which has been taken up and given additional significance by Prof. Adolf Harnack. Dr. Bigg suggested [61] that Tertullian may have borrowed the word " persona " which he applies to the distinctions in the deity, not from the schools, but from the law courts. Harnack added to this the further suggestion [62] that the term " substantia " in Tertullian may well have had a similar origin. On these suppositions it was thought possible

[60] As originally printed in *The Princeton Theological Review,* January, 1906.

[61] " The Christian Platonists of Alexandria," p. 165.

[62] *Theolog. Litteraturzeitung,* 1887, No. 5, p. 110.

that Tertullian by his formula of three persons in one substance may have meant very little more than the Monarchians themselves might supposedly be able to grant. In his " History of Dogma " Harnack returns to the matter [63] with some persistency and, we might almost say, dogmatism. Tertullian he asserts, (iv. p. 144),[64] was not dealing with philosophical conceptions, but employing rather " the method of legal fictions." " It was easy for him," continues Harnack, " by the help of the distinction between ' substance ' and ' person ' current among the jurists, to explain and establish against the Monarchians, not alone the old, ecclesiastical, preëminently Western formula, ' Christus deus et homo,' but also the formula, ' pater, filius et spiritus sanctus — unus deus.' ' Substance ' (Tertullian never says ' Nature ') is, in the language of the jurists, nothing personal; it rather corresponds to ' property ' in the sense of possession, or ' substance ' in distinction from appearance or ' status '; ' Person,' again, is in itself nothing substantial, but rather a subject having legal standing and capable of holding property (*das rechts- und besitzfähige Subject*), who may as well as not possess various substances, as, on the other hand, it is possible that a single substance may be found in the possession of several persons." " Speaking juristically," he remarks again (iv. p. 122),[65] " there is as little to object to the formula that several persons are holders of one and the same substance (property), as to the other that one person may possess unconfused several substances." That is to say, apparently, when Tertullian describes God as " one substance in three persons," we may doubt whether any other conception floated before his mind than that one piece of property may very well be held in undivided possession by three several individuals; and when he speaks of our Lord as one person with two substances, we may question whether he meant more than that the same individual may very well appear in court with two distinct " properties."

[63] See especially E. T. ii. p. 257, note, 282; iv. pp. 57, 122 *sq.*, 144 *sq.*
[64] German 1st ed., 1887, ii. p. 307.
[65] German, as above, p. 288.

The theory certainly lacks somewhat in definiteness of statement,[66] and leaves us a little uncertain whether its application to Tertullian's teaching results in lowering the conception we suppose him to have attached to the term " person " or that we suppose him to have attached to the term " substance." The fact seems to be that Harnack, at least, himself vacillates in his application of it. Despite the passages already quoted, he sometimes speaks as if when Tertullian says that " Father, Son and Holy Ghost are three persons in the unity of the Godhead," we should raise the question whether by " persons " he means anything more than " capacities " — that is, whether the persons were conceived by him as much more than simply " nomina " (Harnack, iv. p. 57; " Against Praxeas," 30), and whether, therefore, his doctrine was not at least as nearly related to Monarchianism as to Nicene Trinitarianism (so Harnack, iv. p. 57, note). On the other hand, when he says that " God and man, two substances, are one Christ," we seem to be expected to raise the question whether by " substance " he means much more than " status, virtus, potestas " — that is, whether he really conceived the individual Jesus Christ as including in Himself two unconfused natures, or only two aspects of being. The sense of confusion produced by this attempt so to state the theory as to make it do double duty — and that, in each instance of its application — is already an indication that it is not easy to adjust it precisely to the facts it is called in to explain. What we are asked to do apparently is not merely to presume that Tertullian derived his nomenclature from the law courts; but to suppose that he was not quite sure in his own mind in what sense he was borrowing it. In other words, we are to suppose that he began by borrowing the terms, leaving the senses in which he should employ them to be fixed afterward; instead of beginning, as he must have done,

[66] Bethune-Baker, in his " The Meaning of Homoousios in the ' Constantinopolitan ' Creed," in " Texts and Studies," J. A. Robinson, ed., vii. 1, pp. 21 *sq.*, and especially in his " An Introduction to the Early History of Christian Doctrine," pp. 138 *sq.*, gives a lucid statement of the theory, and adopts it up to a certain point, but remarks that " the conceptions and expressions of Tertullian were by no means entirely controlled by legal usage. . . ."

with the conceptions to express which he borrowed or framed terms.

The real difficulty with the theory, however, is that it seems to be entirely without support in Tertullian's own usage of the words, and much more in his definitions and illustrations of their meaning. Harnack urges in its support little beyond the two somewhat irrelevant facts that Tertullian is known to have been a jurist, and so might well be familiar with juristic language, and that he used by predilection the term " substance " rather than " nature." [67]   On the other hand, that Tertullian is

---

[67] The introduction of " substance " instead of " nature " appears to' have been due to an attempt to attain greater precision of terminology. Augustine, " De Trinitate," Book VII. chap. vi. § 11 (" Nicene and Post-Nicene Fathers," Series I. iii. p. 112), explicitly testifies that this use of " substance " was of comparatively recent origin: " The ancients also who spoke Latin, before they had these terms, *which have not long come into use,* that is, essence or substance, used for them to say nature. In an earlier treatise, " De Moribus Manichaeorum " (A.D. 388), chap. ii. § 2, Augustine had made the same remark (" Nicene and Post-Nicene Fathers," Series I. iv. p. 70): " Hence is the new word which we now use derived from the word for being — essence namely, or, as we usually say, substance — while, before these words were in use, the word nature was used instead." The whole matter is exhibited again in " De Haer.," xlix.: " The Arians, from Arius, are best known for the error by which they deny that the Father, Son and Holy Spirit are of one and the same nature and substance, or to speak more precisely, essence, called in Greek οὐσία"; and again, in the " Contra Sermon. Arian." xxxvi., " The Arians and Eunomians dub us Homoousiani, because against their error we defend the Father, Son and Holy Spirit by the Greek word ὁμοούσιον, that is, as of one and the same substance, or to speak more precisely, essence, which is called οὐσία in Greek; or, as it is more plainly (planius) expressed, of one and the same nature." That is Nature is the *common* word; Essence the *exact* one but stilted; Substance the nearest natural equivalent of Essence. The word " essentia " was as old as Cicero (Seneca, " Epistulae Morales.," lviii., *ad init.;* cf. Quintilian, " Inst.," 2. 14. 2; 3. 6. 23; 8. 3. 33), but never commended itself to the Roman ear, which esteemed it harsh and abstract: it was left, therefore, to an occasional philosopher to employ and then scarcely without apologies (Seneca, " Epistulae Morales," lviii. § 6; Quintilian, 2. 14, 1. 2). The more concrete " substantia " (apparently a post-Augustan word, cf. Quintilian, 2. 15. 34) became, therefore, the usual term in careful writing. The two are constantly used as exact synonyms: e.g., Apuleius, " De Platone et eius Dogmate," I. vi. writes: " The οὐσίαι which we call essentiæ, [Plato] says are two, by which all things are produced, even the world itself. Of these one is conceived by thought only, the other may be attained by the senses. . . . And *primæ quidem substantiæ vel essentiæ.* . . ." Nature was simply the popular term and was held to be less exact, and

here speaking as the heir of the Apologists and is dealing with conceptions not of his own framing, that, moreover, the whole drift of his discussion is philosophical, and that, above all, his own explanations of his meaning — as, for example, in the illustrations he makes use of — fix on the terms he employs a deeper sense, put this whole theory summarily out of court. It has accordingly made very few converts, and has more than once been solidly refuted.[68] In the aspect of it in which it comes especially before us in our present discussion, it certainly seems impossible to give it a hospitable reception.

If there is anything, indeed, that seems clear in Tertullian's exposition it is that he deals seriously with the personality which he attributes to the three distinctions of the " economy." [69] This is indeed the very hinge on which the whole controversy which he was urging so sharply against the Monarchian conception turns. Whatever care he exhibits in guarding the unity of the divine substance, therefore, by denying that

---

was therefore avoided by careful writers. Harnack's notion that Tertullian's preference of substantia has some deep theological significance seems, therefore, peculiarly unfortunate. For a refutation of it on its merits see Stier, *as cited,* pp. 76 *sq.* Bethune-Baker (" The Meaning of Homoousios in the ' Constantinopolitan ' Creed," in " Texts and Studies," J. A. Robinson, ed., vii. 1, pp. 16 and 65; cf. also *Journal of Theological Studies,* iv. p. 440) also appears to overstrain the distinction between " Substance " and " Nature " in Tertullian and his successors. Their preference for " substantia " is sufficiently accounted for by the greater precision of the word and its freedom from *qualitative* implications (cf. Quintilian's distinction of " substantia " and " qualitas " in 7. 3. 6). The " natura " of a thing suggests implications of kind; " substantia " raises no question of kind and asserts merely reality.

[68] E.g., briefly, by Seeberg, " Lehrbuch der Dogmengeschichte," 1895, i. pp. 85–87; and very copiously by J. Stier, " Die Gottes- und Logos-Lehre Tertullians," 1899, pp. 74–78. Even Loofs says (" Leitfaden zum Studium der Dogmengeschichte," 2d ed. p. 87): " These formulas show that [Tertullian] learned something in the course of his polemics, but are so thoroughly explicable as formalistic reworking of the Apologetic and Asian Tradition, that there is no need to derive them artificially from the juristic usage (against Harnack, ii. p. 288)."

[69] Cf. Dorner, " Doctrine of the Person of Christ," I. ii. p. 59: " As he gazed on the incarnate Logos, he felt certainly convinced of His personality. For it was not a mere impersonal power, but a divine subject, that had become man in Christ," etc. Cf. also p. 24, note 2.

any *separatio,* or *divisio,* or *dispersio* [70] has taken place or could take place in it, is necessarily matched by the equal emphasis he places on the reality of the *distributio, distinctio, dispositio* [71] that has place in it, and by virtue of which He who is eternally and unchangeably one (unum) is nevertheless not one (unus), but three — not, indeed, in status, substance, power, but in grade, form, species, aspect.[72] The point of importance to be noted here is not merely that Tertullian calls these distinctions " persons " (which he repeatedly does),[73] but that he makes them persons by whatsoever designation he marks them. The whole of Scripture, he declares, demands this of its readers: it attests clearly the existence and distinction of the Trinity, and indeed establishes the Rule that He who speaks and He of whom He speaks and He to whom He speaks cannot possibly be the same; nor does it fail to place thus by the first and second the third person also.[74] Only on the basis of this tripersonality of God, he urges, can the plural forms in which

---

[70] Chaps. iii. viii. ix.

[71] Chaps. ix. xiii.

[72] Chap. ii.: " Custodiatur οἰκονομίας sacramentum, quæ unitatem in trinitatem disponit, tres dirigens patrem et filium et spiritum, — tres autem non statu, sed gradu, nec substantia, sed forma, nec potestate, sed specie, — unius autem substantiæ et unius status et unius potestatis."

[73] Bethune-Baker, " An Introduction to the Early History of Christian Doctrine," p. 139, note [2] (cf. " The Meaning of Homoousios in the ' Constantinopolitan ' Creed," in " Texts and Studies," J. A. Robinson, ed., vii. 1, pp. 17–18), remarks, to be sure: " Tertullian seems, however, to avoid the use of *personæ* in this connexion " — that is to say, when " speaking as regards the being of God of one substance and three persons " — " using *tres* alone to express ' the three ' without adding ' persons ' in the case of the Trinity; just as later Augustine, while feeling compelled to speak of three ' persons,' apologized for the term and threw the responsibility for it upon the poverty of the language (" De Trinitate," v. 10, vii. 7–10). Tertullian has the definite expression only when it cannot well be omitted — *e.g.* when supporting the doctrine of the Trinity from the baptismal commission, he writes, ' nam nec semel, sed ter, ad singula nomina in personas singulas tinguimur ' (" Against Praxeas," chap. 26)." There seems, however, to be as frequent use of the term as there would be any reason to expect, and Tertullian explains (ch. xii.) that when he speaks of the distinction as " one " or " another " it is on the ground of " personality." See the long list of passages in Harnack, iv. p. 123.

[74] Chap. xi.

God speaks of Himself in Scripture be explained: [75] and how can one issue what can justly be called a command except to another? " In what sense, however, you ought to understand Him to be another," he adds, " I have already explained — on the ground of personality, not of substance — in the way of distinction not of division." [76]

In this whole discussion, Tertullian's watchword was necessarily *the economy:* and the economy was just the Trinity in the unity. Had he not felt bound to assert the economy, there had been no quarrel between him and the Monarchians, whose watchword was the unity. As it was, he required to begin his polemic against them with the distinct positing of the question: and this involved the distinct enunciation of the doctrine of plural personality in the Godhead. We have always believed and do now still believe, he says,[77] that there is one only God — *but* — and it is in this " but " that the whole case lies — *but* " under the following dispensation, or οἰκονομία, as it is called — that this one God has also a Son, His Word, who proceeded from Himself . . . who also sent from heaven, from the Father, according to His own promise, the Holy Ghost, the Paraclete, the Sanctifier of the faith of those who believe in the Father and in the Son and in the Holy Ghost." This is Tertullian's anti-Monarchian Confession of Faith. His complaint is that men behaved as if the unity of the Godhead could be preserved in no other way than by representing the Father, the Son, and the Holy Ghost as the very selfsame person, thus in their zeal for the unity neglecting the *sacramentum oikonomiae,*[78] which distributes the unity into a Trinity. On the contrary, he insists,[79] although the true God is one only God, He must yet be believed in with His own οἰκονομία — which with its numerical order and distribution of the Trinity is a support to, not a breach of, the true unity; because, he ex-

[75] Chap. xii. *ad init.*

[76] Chap. xii. *ad fin.* Cf. xiii., near the beginning. Cf. Dorner, as cited, Div. I. vol. ii. p. 24, note.[2]

[77] Chap. ii.

[78] Chap. ii.

[79] Chap. iii.

plains,[80] such a Trinity, flowing down from the Father through intertwined and connected steps does not at all disturb the monarchy, while it at the same time guards the state of the economy. Men must not be permitted to extol the monarchy at the expense of the economy, contending for the identity of the Father and Son, whereas the very names, Father and Son, plainly declaring their distinct personality, proclaim the economy [81] — lest under pretense of the monarchy men come to hold to neither Father nor Son, abolishing all distinctions in the interest of their monarchy.[82] Thus the discussion runs on, upholding the economy against the falsely conceived monarchy, to end in the same note [83] — in the declaration that the Son, the second name in the Godhead, and the second degree of the divine Majesty, has shed forth on the Church in these latter days the promised gift, "even the Holy Spirit — the Third Name in the Godhead and the Third Degree of the Divine Majesty, the Declarer of the One Monarchy of God, but at the same time the Interpreter of the *Economy,* to every one who hears and receives the words of the new prophecy; and the ' Leader into all truth,' such as is in the Father, and the Son, and the Holy Ghost, according to the mystery of the doctrine of Christ." To reject the economy is, in effect, he charges, to revert to Judaism — for to Jews not to Christians it belongs " so to believe in one God as to refuse to reckon the Son besides Him, and after the Son the Spirit." [84] The distinctive mark of Christianity to him, thus, is that the unity of God is so held that God is now openly known in His proper names and persons.[85]

Among the passages in which Tertullian exhibits with especial emphasis the distinction which he erects between the Father, Son, and Spirit under the name of persons there is a striking one [86] in which he is replying to the Callistan formula which made the Father not indeed suffer in and of Himself, but

80 Chap. viii. end.   84 Chap. xxxi.
81 Chap. ix.   85 Chap. xxxi.
82 Chap. x.   86 Chap. xxix.
83 Chap. xxx.

participate in the suffering of the Son. He makes his primary appeal here to the impassibility of God as such, and then falls to magnifying the distinction between the Father and the Son. " The Father," he asserts, " is separate from the Son, though not from God." The meaning seems to be that the Son is the name specifically of the incarnated Logos, and the incarnated Logos — as God, indeed, one in substance with the Father — is, as incarnated, something more, viz., flesh as well; and on this side of His being, which is the only side in which He suffered (for the Son, under the conditions of His existence as God, Tertullian allows, is as incapable of suffering as the Father) is not one with God, but separate from Him. The Monarchian might certainly reply that on this showing the Father Himself, if conceived to be incarnate, might be as truly said to share in the sufferings of the Son, or the flesh, as the Son, incarnated, could be said to have suffered. If the sufferings of the flesh were not of the flesh alone, but the incarnated deity stood in some relation to them, this would be, on Tertullian's own showing, as conceivable of the Father, deemed incarnate, as of the Son. Tertullian, therefore, attempts to help his answer out by means of a simile. If a river, he says, is soiled with mud, this miring of the stream does not affect the fountain, though the river flows from the fountain, is identical in substance with it, and is not separated from it: and although it is the water of the fountain which suffers in the stream, yet since it is affected only in the stream and not in the fountain, the fountain is not contaminated, but only the river that has issued from the fountain. We are not concerned now with the consistency of Tertullian: how he could say in one breath that the Son as God is as impassible, being God Himself, as the Father, and in the next that it is the very water from the fountain — the very substance of God in its second distinction — that is affected by the injury which has befallen it. What it concerns us to notice is, that in this illustration Tertullian very much magnifies the distinction between the persons of the Godhead. The Son is so far distinct from the Father that He may be involved in sufferings which do not reach back to or affect the

Father. The stream may be the fountain flowing forth: but the stream is so far distinct from the fountain, that what affects it is no longer felt in the fountain. Here is the individualization of personal life in an intense form, and an indication of the length to which Tertullian's conception of the personal distinction went.

In another passage [87] Tertullian announces the same results without the aid of a figure. He is engaged in discriminating between mere effluxes of power or other qualities from God and the prolation of a real and substantial person: in doing this, he magnifies the distinction between the original source and the prolation. Nothing that belongs to another thing is precisely that thing: and nothing that proceeds from it can be simply identified with it. The Spirit is God, no doubt; and the Word is God; because they proceed from God, from His very substance. But they are not actually the very same as He from whom they proceed. Each is God of God: each is a *substantiva res;* but each is not *ipse Deus;* but only " so far God as He is of the same substance with God Himself, and as being an actually existing thing, and as a portion of the Whole."

In still another passage Tertullian is repelling the Monarchians' scoff that as a word is no substantial thing, but a mere voice and sound made by the mouth, merely so much concussed air, intelligible to the ear as a symbol of thought, but in itself nothing at all: therefore (so they argued) the Word of God — the Logos — is to be conceived not as a substantial thing distinguishable from the Father, but only as a symbol of intelligible meaning. Tertullian reproaches them for being unwilling to allow that the Word is a really substantive being, having a substance of its own — an objective thing and a person — who, by virtue of His constitution as a second to God, makes, with God, two, the Father and the Son, God and the Word. He argues on two grounds that the Logos must have this substantial existence. The one is that He came forth from so great a substance: God who is Himself the fullness of Being, cannot be presumed to prolate an empty thing. The other is

[87] Chap. xxvi.

that He is Himself the author of substantial things: how could He, who was Himself nothing, produce things which are realities, with substantial existence? Whatever else this argument proves, it certainly proves that Tertullian conceived of the distinction between God the Father and God the Son as attaining the dignity of distinct individuality. " Whatever, therefore " — he closes the discussion with these words — " Whatever, therefore, has the substance of the Word, that I designate a Person. I claim for it the name of Son, and, recognizing the Son, I assert His distinction as second to the Father."

(2) It may remain, no doubt, a question whether Tertullian did not conceive this distinction of persons to have been the result of those movements of the divine substance by which successively the Logos and the Spirit proceeded from the fontal source of deity, so that the economy was thought of as superinduced upon a previous monarchy. It is thus, indeed, that he has been commonly understood.[88] In this case, while certainly he would take the personal distinctions seriously, he might be supposed not to look upon them as rooted essentially in the very being of God. God in Himself would be conceived as a monad: God flowing out to create the world and to uphold and govern it, as becoming for these purposes a triad. The " invisible God " would be a monad; the " visible God " — the God of the world-process — would become a triad.

It may be that it was after a fashion somewhat similar to this that Tertullian was naturally inclined to think of God and the distinctions he conceived to exist in His being; that is to say, his thought may have run most readily in the molds of what has come to be called an economic as distinguished from what is known as an immanent Trinitarianism. It was along these lines that the Logos speculation tended to carry him, and his hearty acceptance of that speculation as the instrument with which to interpret the deposit of Christian truth might well lead him to conceive and speak of the Trinitarian distinctions as if they were merely " economical." But the deposit of

[88] So, e.g., Dorner, Hagemann, Harnack, Stier.

truth subjected to interpretation by the Logos speculation was not quite tractable to it, and it is interesting to inquire whether Tertullian betrays any consciousness of this fact — whether in his dealing with the data embedded in the Rule of Faith he exhibits any tendency to carry back the distinction of persons in the Godhead behind the prolations by which the Logos and Spirit proceeded from it for the purpose of producing the world of time and space. So loyal an adherent of the Rule of Faith might well be expected to deal faithfully with its data, and to seek to do something like justice to them even when they appeared to be intractable to his ordinary instrument of interpretation. And so bold a thinker might well be incited by the pressure of such data to ask himself if there were nothing in the *fons deitatis* itself which might be recognized as a kind of prophecy or even as a kind of predetermination of the prolations which ultimately proceeded from it — if the very issue of these prolations do not presuppose in the Godhead itself a certain structure, so to speak, which involved the promise and potency of the prolations to come — if, in a word, the distinctions brought into manifestation by the prolations must not be presumed to have preëxisted in a latent or less manifest form in the eternal monad, out of which they ultimately proceeded.

That some indications exist of such a tendency on Tertullian's part to push the personal distinctions behind the prolations into the Godhead itself is perhaps universally recognized. It is frequently denied, to be sure, that this tendency goes very far. Harnack's form of statement is that it gives to Tertullian's teaching " a strong resemblance to the doctrine of an immanent Trinity, without being such." [89] Tertullian, he says, knew " as little of an immanent Trinity as the Apologists," and his Trinity " only *appears* such, because the unity of the substance is very vigorously emphasized." [90] Johannes Stier holds

---

[89] *Op. cit.,* iv. p. 122.

[90] *Op. cit.,* ii. pp. 260–261. Similarly Loofs remarks: " These formulas anticipate the later orthodoxy: it is all the more necessary to emphasize how strongly subordinationist they are: . . . the ' economical ' trinity here is just as little an eternal one as in the case of the older theologians of Asia Minor " (" Leitfaden zum Studium der Dogmengeschichte," 2d ed., p. 89).

essentially the same opinion. " Of an immanent Trinity in Tertullian," [91] he argues, " there can be no talk, because he is absolutely explicit that a plural personality came into existence for
the purpose of the world. Without the world, the primal unity
would have abided. It is indeed true that the Logos and the
Spirit were immanent in the unity of the divine original essence from the beginning, but nevertheless not — and this is
the point — in a *personal* manner! From the beginning God,
the divine original-essence, was alone; alone precisely as person (cf. " Against Praxeas," chap. v). From this (first) person,
no doubt, absolutely immediately, the Logos (*ratio, sermo*)
was distinguished as *subject,* but not yet as (second) *person* —
he became person only pretemporally-temporally. And as for
the Spirit, the matter is perfectly analogous in His case (cf.
" Against Praxeas," chap. vi). The Trinity of Tertullian is
purely (against Schwane, p. 164, and others) economical, conceived solely with reference to the world; nothing is easier to
see if we have the will to see it (cf. also Gieseler, p. 137; Harnack, i. p. 536; Huber, p. 117)." Nevertheless Harnack not only
can speak of Tertullian as " creating the formulas of succeeding orthodoxy," but can even declare that " the orthodox doctrine of the Trinity already announced its presence even in its
details, in Tertullian." [92] And Stier is forced to acknowledge
that Tertullian came within a single step of an immanent
Trinity.[93] " There needed, we must admit," he remarks, " only
a single step more to arrive at the eternal personal being of the
sermo in God, to establish an eternal, immanent relation between the divine original-essence and His Logos as *two divine
personalities,* to advance thence to the immanent Trinity. But
Tertullian stopped with conceiving the *sermo* from eternity,
it is true, along with the *ratio* — and the discernment of this
already itself means something — but still only as the *impersonal* basis (*Anlage*) of a future *personal sermo.*" The reason of Tertullian's failure to take the last step Stier, like

[91] *Op. cit.,* p. 95, note.
[92] iv. p. 121.
[93] P. 81.

Hagemann [94] and others before him, finds in the fact that Tertullian connected the personal *sermo* so intimately with the world that had he conceived the one as eternal, he must needs have conceived the other as eternal also: and as he was not prepared to think of the world as eternal, neither could he ascribe eternity to the personal Logos (cf. " Against Praxeas," chap. vi. *sq.*).

Possibly there is a *petitio principii* embedded in the terms in which this reason is stated. Tertullian certainly connected the prolate Logos so closely with the world that we could scarcely expect him to separate the two. But whether that involves a similar inseparable connection between the personal Logos and the world is precisely the question at issue. The prolation and the personality of the Logos seem to be for the moment confused by our critics, doubtless because it is judged that the two went together in Tertullian's mind: but this judgment cannot be justified by merely repeating it. Meanwhile we note that it is allowed that Tertullian did conceive the *sermo* as eternally existent along with the *ratio,* and this is rightly re-

[94] "Die Römische Kirche," pp. 173 *sq.* On p. 175 Hagemann writes as follows: " With the last idea " — the idea namely that the *sermo* is inseparable from the *ratio,* and therefore even *before* creation God was not " alone," but His " Word " included in his " reason " was with him — " Tertullian was advancing on the right road to the recognition of the eternal and personal existence of the Word in God. The Word has its ground in the Being of God, falls in the circle of His inner life, is inseparably given with Him. But he had shut himself off from the full and right understanding of the manner itself, by introducing into the investigation from the start the world-idea. He could not maintain, therefore, the full and eternal existence of the Word, without at the same time admitting the full and eternal existence of the world itself; and since this was to him an impossible idea, he could not carry through the former in its whole strictness. To him the Logos hung together with the world, and his conception of the latter was decisive for the conception of the former also. To be sure, he came near to the conviction of the eternity and the full divine nature of the Logos; but just as he was about to reach the goal, the world-idea hinderingly intruded in the way. No doubt it is to be said that his insight in this matter was injuriously affected by too great dependence on the Apologists." Again, on p. 177, summing up: " Enough: in order not to allow also the eternity of the world, he had sacrificed the eternity of the Son and taught, as a progressive realization of the world-idea, so also a progressive hypostatizing of the Logos."

garded as a matter of some significance and as equivalent at
least to the postulation of something in the eternal mode of
existence of God which supplies the basis (*Anlage*) for a future
personal Logos. What this something was Stier does not indeed tell us, contenting himself merely with denying that it
amounted in Tertullian's thought to a *personal* distinction,
prior to the prolation of the Logos. He uses a German term to
designate it — *Anlage* — which might be fairly pressed to
cover all that Tertullian expresses as to his personal Logos,
when he speaks of it as a *distributio, distinctio, dispositio, dis-
pensatio:* and Stier can scarcely mean less than that Tertullian
recognized in the eternal mode of existence of the Godhead
such a distinction, disposition, distribution, dispensation, as
manifested itself in the outgoing from Him of a *portio* into a
truly personal distinction when He was about to create the
world. Less than this would come perilously near to saying
merely that the Son was potentially in the Father before He
actually came into existence from the Father, which, as George
Bull repeatedly points out, is no more than can be said of all
created beings, all of which (according to Tertullian also),
before they were produced actually, preëxisted in the thought
and power of God.[95] By as much as Stier cannot mean that
Tertullian recognized in the original mode of the divine existence no deeper basis for the personal prolation of the Word
than there was for the production of the creature-world, by so

[95] e.g., "Defensio Fidei Nicaenæ," III. ix. 3 (E. T. 1730, p. 419). Dorner
does not shrink from this assimilation of the preëxistence of the Logos and
of the world: to Tertullian, he affirms explicitly. "In the first instance He
has a mere ideal existence in the inner essence of God, like the world-idea
itself" (Div. I. vol. ii. p. 64), and therefore "became a person for the first
time, at, and for the sake of, the creation of the world" (pp. 73–74). "There is
no place," in Tertullian's view, he says, "for a real, hypostatic Sonship in the
inner, eternal essence of God: all that he has tried to point out, is the existence in God of an eternally active potence of Sonship" (p. 63), a "real potence
of Sonship, . . . impersonal but already a personific principle" (p. 69). It
does not appear what purpose these latter phrases serve beyond exhibiting a
possible doubt in Dorner's own mind whether it is quite adequate to Tertullian's thought to represent him as assigning no more real preëxistence to the
Logos than to the world — whether, in other words, the Logos, in his view, did
not exist in some more real form than mere potentiality.

much must he be supposed to mean that Tertullian recognized that the very structure, so to speak, of the Godhead, from all eternity, included in it some disposition by virtue of which the prolation of the Logos, and afterward that of the Spirit, were provided for as manifestations of an eternal distinction in the Godhead. This certainly leaves only a short step to the recognition of an immanent Trinity; so short a step, indeed, that it is doubtful whether it does not lead inevitably on to it. The question is narrowed down at any rate to whether distinctions eternally existent in the Godhead, and afterward manifested in the prolate Logos and the prolate Spirit as truly personal, were conceived as already personal in the eternal mode of existence of God or as made such only by the acts of prolation themselves. We imagine that the average reader of Tertullian, while he will not fail to note how much the prolations meant to Tertullian's thought, will not fail to note, on the other hand, that these prolations rested for Tertullian on distinctions existent in the Godhead prior to all prolation, as the appropriate foundations for the prolations; nor will he fail to note further that Tertullian sometimes speaks of these ante-prolation distinctions in a manner which suggests that he conceived them as already personal.

The whole matter has been solidly argued, once for all, in the tenth chapter of the third book of George Bull's " Defensio Fidei Nicaenæ " (written in 1680, published in 1685). That this notable book is marred by special pleading, and that Bull shows a less keen historical conscience, as Baur puts it,[96]

[96] " Die christliche Lehre von der Dreieinigkeit und Menschwerdung Gottes," i. p. 110, where a sober estimate of the value of the work may be found. Cf. also Schaff, " History of the Christian Church," ii. p. 544. Meier (" Die Lehre von der Trinität," ii. pp. 76–77) looks upon Bull's effort to save the doctrine of the Trinity as a counsel of despair in the midst of a general decline of faith in this doctrine. Under the feeling that the doctrine could not be based on Scripture, since it is nowhere taught explicitly in Scripture, Bull undertook to show that it had for it at least the consistent testimony of antiquity. Even so, however, it was only a curtailed doctrine that he undertook the defense of. " Bull found himself also forced to make concessions; he perceived himself that he could maintain only the consubstantiality and the eternity of the Son, while allowing that differences existed as to special points —

or as we should rather say, a less acute historical sense, than Petavius, his chief opponent in this famous debate, we suppose can scarcely be denied. In the main matter of dispute between these two great scholars, we can but think Petavius had the right of it. The position which Petavius takes up,[97] indeed, appears to involve little more than recognizing that the literary tradition of the Church, prior to the Council of Nice, was committed to the Logos Christology: while Bull undertakes the impossible task, as it seems to us, of explaining the whole body of ante-Nicene speculation in terms of Nicene orthodoxy. The proper response to Petavius would have been to point out that the literary tradition, running through " Athenagoras, Tatian, Theophilus, Tertullian, Lactantius," together with " certain others, such as Origen," [98] is not to be identified at once with the traditionary teaching of the Church, but represents rather a literary movement or theological school of thought, which attempted with only partial success a specific philosophizing of the traditionary faith of the Church. The measure of success which Bull achieved in explaining this literary tradition in harmony with the traditional faith of the Church — which was rather to be sought in the Rule of Faith and the naïve Christian consciousness of the times — is due to the constant refer-

---

es e.g., whether the Son was begotten from the Father as respects substance: and he considers that the ground of the differences among the Fathers which Petavius adduced was due to an attempt to find scholastic definitions among them. In his own faith he reverts to the pre-Augustinian period, . . . and sees himself driven back upon the Logos-idea, . . . and in this driftage we see the beginning of the destruction of the dogma even in the Church itself." It probably is a fact that every attempt to revert from the Augustinian to the Nicene construction of the Trinity marks a stage of weakening hold upon the doctrine itself. With all Bull's zeal for the doctrine, therefore, his mode of defending it is an indication of lack of full confidence in it, and in essence is an attempt to establish some compromise with the growing forces of unbelief. The same phenomenon is repeating itself in our own day: cf. Prof. L. L. Paine's " The Evolution of Trinitarianism," the assault of which on the Augustinian construction of the doctrine is a sequence of a lowered view of the person of Jesus gained from a critical reconstruction of the Bible.

[97] " De Trinitate," I. v. 8, quoted in Bull, " Introduction," 7 (E. T. 1851, p. 9).

[98] This is the enumeration given by Petavius, " De Trinitate," I. v. 8.

ence which the writers with whom he deals made in their thinking to the Rule of Faith, of which they were always conscious as underlying their speculations and supplying the norm to which they strove to make their conclusions as far as possible conform; as well as to the survival in the final product which we know as Nicene theology of such elements of the Logos speculation as could be assimilated by it. He was able, therefore, to show repeatedly that the very men whom Petavius adduced as teachers of the inadequate formula betrayed here and there consciousness of elements of truth for which this formula, strictly interpreted, left no place; and also that language much the same as theirs — and conceptions not far removed from theirs — might easily be turned up in writers of unimpeachable orthodoxy living after the Council of Nice. In both matters he has done good service. It is unfair not to remember that these earlier writers wished to be and made a constant effort to remain in harmony with the Rule of Faith; and that we do not obtain their whole thought, therefore, until we place by the side of their speculative elaborations the elements of truth which they also held, for which these speculations nevertheless made no place. They were in intention, at all events, orthodox; and the failure of their theory to embrace all that orthodoxy must needs confess was an indication rather of the inadequacy of the theory to which they had committed their formal thinking, than of any conscious willingness on their part to deny or neglect essential elements of the truth. And it is useful, on the other hand, to be reminded that their unwearying effort to do justice — as far as their insight carried them — to the whole deposit of the faith bore its appropriate fruit, first, in the gradual, almost unnoted passing of their theory itself into something better, as the Nicene orthodoxy supplanted because transcending it, and next in the projection into the Nicene orthodoxy itself of many of the characteristic modes of thought and forms of expression of the earlier theory — conditioning both the conceptions and the terms used to embody them which entered as constituent elements into the new and better construction. Meanwhile, to fail to appreciate this historic evolution, and to attempt to interpret the inadequate conceptions of the earlier thinkers as only somewhat clumsily expressed enunciations of Nicene orthodoxy, is a grave historical fault, and could not fail to fill Bull's book with expositions which give it as a whole the appearance of an elaborate piece of special pleading. Only when the writer with whom he chances in any given passage to be dealing had become sharply aware — or at least uneasily conscious — of one or another of the elements of truth embodied in the Rule of Faith for which the speculation he had adopted as yet provided no place, and was really striving to take it up into his theory, make even by violence a place for it, and do justice to it, is Bishop Bull's exposition altogether admirable. This is the case with Tertullian in the matter of the eternal distinctions in the Godhead, and the result is that Bishop Bull, in the chapter in which he deals with this subject, has performed a delicate piece of expository work with a skill and a clearness which leave little to be desired.

He begins the discussion by adducing what is perhaps the most striking of the passages in which Tertullian appears explicitly to deny the eternity of the personal distinctions in the Godhead. It is to be found in the third chapter of his treatise against Hermogenes and runs as follows: " Because God is a Father and God is a Judge, it does not on that account follow that, because He was always God, He was always a Father and a Judge. For He could neither have been a Father before the Son, nor a Judge before transgression. But there was a time when there was no transgression, and no Son, the one to make the Lord a Judge, and the other a Father." Here certainly, apart from the context, and that wider context of the author's known point of view, there appears to be a direct assertion that there was a time before which the Son was not: and this falls in so patly with the Logos speculation which assigns a definite beginning to the prolated Logos, that it is easy to jump to the conclusion that Tertullian means to date the origination of the Logos at this time. Such a conclusion would, however, be erroneous; and it is just in the doctrine of the prolation of the Logos at a definite time that the passage finds its juster ex-

planation. It emerges that the term " Son " in Tertullian's nomenclature designates distinctively the prolate Logos. He
therefore asserts nothing in the present passage concerning the
eternity or non-eternity of personal distinctions in the Godhead. He affirms only that God became Father when the Logos
was prolated, seeing that the Logos became Son only at his prolation. Bishop Bull animadverts not unjustly on a tendency of
Tertullian exhibited here to overacuteness in argument and to
readiness to make a point at some cost: but he fairly makes
out his case that in the present instance Tertullian is to be
interpreted in this somewhat artificial sense — as if one should
say there was a time when God was not the Creator, because
creation occurred at a definite point of time, before which
therefore God was existent indeed, but not as Creator.[99] So
God became Father, not when the Logos came into existence,
but when He became a Son. By this neat piece of exposition
Bishop Bull seeks to remove the antecedent presumption
against Tertullian's admission of eternal distinctions in the
Godhead, which would arise from an explicit assertion on his
part that there was a time before which the Logos was not —
that is to say, the prolate Logos. He shows that this is only
Tertullian's way of saying that the Logos was not always
prolate.

He then wisely proceeds at once to a discussion of the principal passage, wherein Tertullian seems to recognize personal
distinctions in the Godhead prior to the prolations of Logos
and Spirit. This is, of course, the very remarkable discussion in
the fifth chapter of the tract, " Against Praxeas," in which Tertullian gives, as it were, a complete history of the Logos.[100] In
this passage Tertullian begins by affirming that " before all
things " — alike before the creation of the world and the generation of the Son, that is to say, the prolation of the Logos —
God was alone (*solus*). He immediately corrects this, however,

99 See above, pp. 30–31.
100 This passage is discussed by Bull in Book III., chap. x., §§ 5–8. At an
earlier point — III. v. 5 — he had expounded the same passage more briefly,
but not less effectively.

by saying that by " alone " he means only that there was nothing extrinsic to God by His side: for not even then was He really alone (*solus*), seeing that He had with Him that which He had within Himself, namely, His Reason. This Reason, he continues, is what the Greeks call the Logos, and the Latins are accustomed to call Sermo — though Sermo is an inadequate translation, and it would be better to distinguish and say that Reason must antedate Speech, and that God rather had Reason with Him from the beginning, while He had Speech only after He had sent it forth by utterance — that is to say, at the prolation. This distinction, however, adds Tertullian immediately, is really a refinement of little practical importance. The main thing is that " although God had not yet sent His Word, He nevertheless already had Him within Himself, with and in Reason itself, as He silently considered and determined with Himself what He was afterward to speak through the Word." Thus even in the silence of eternity, when God had not yet spoken, the Word in its form of Reason was with God, and God was therefore not alone. To illuminate his meaning, Tertullian now introduces an illustration drawn from human consciousness. He asks his readers to observe the movements that go on within themselves when they hold silent converse with themselves; whenever they think, there is a word; whenever they conceive, there is reason. Speaking thus in the mind, the word stands forth as a " conlocutor," in which reason dwells.[101] " Thus," adds Tertullian, " the word is, in some sort, a second within you, by means of which you speak in thinking, and by means of which you think in speaking: this word is another." [102] Now, he reasons, all this is, of course, carried on in God on a higher plane (*plenius*), and it is not venturesome to affirm that " even before the creation of the universe [103] God

[101] There may be a reminiscence here, and there certainly is a parallel, of the passage in Plato's " Sophist," § 263 E, where thought is called " the unuttered conversation of the soul with itself," and we are told that " the stream of thought flowing through the lips is called speech."

[102] " Ita secundus quodammodo in te est sermo, per quem loqueris cogitando, et per quem cogitas loquendo; ipse sermo alius est."

[103] " Ante universitatis constitutionem."

was not alone, seeing that He had within Him both Reason and, intrinsic in Reason, His Word, which He made a second to Himself by agitating it within Himself." This Word, having within Himself Reason and Wisdom, His inseparables, He at length put forth (*protulit*) when it at length pleased Him to create the universe, that is, to draw out (*edere*) into their own substances and kinds the things He had determined on within Himself by means of this very Reason and Word.[104]

Nothing can be clearer than that in this passage Tertullian carries back the distinction manifested by the prolate Logos into the depths of eternity. It already existed, he says, within the silent God before the generation of the Word, that is, before the prolation of the Logos. He explicitly distinguishes its mode of preëxistence from that of things to be created, which " having been thought out and disposed," by means of that Word who was also the Reason of God, existed " in Dei sensu," and only needed to be drawn out in their substances and kinds — whereas He, the Word, from eternity coexisted with God as " a second," " another." All this Bishop Bull points out with great lucidity. He directs attention first to Tertullian's sharp discrimination at the outset between God's eternal existence "alone," so far as external accompaniment is concerned, and his inner companionship — so that He was never " alone," but ever had with Him, i.e., within Him, His " fellow," the Logos.

---

[104] It is interesting to observe how closely Marcellus of Ancyra, in this portion of his system, reproduced the thought of Tertullian in this chapter. To Marcellus, says Loofs (*Sitzungsberichte der königlich preussischen Akademie der Wissenschaften zu Berlin,*" 1902, i. pp. 768–769), "the Logos is eternal. . . . And this Logos of God is without any γένεσις. Before the time of the creation of the world, He was simply in God; the one God, along with whom was nothing, ' had not yet spoken ' (ἡσυχία τις ἦν). When, however, God addressed Himself to create the world, τότε ὁ λόγος προελθὼν ἐγίνετο τοῦ κόσμου ποιητής, ὁ καὶ πρότερον ἔνδον νοητῶς ὀνομάζων αὐτόν. This προέλθειν in sequence to which came in the πρὸς τὸν θεὸν εἶναι of which Jno. i. 1 speaks, did not, however, bring to a close the ἐν θεῷ εἶναι: the Logos remains δυνάμει ἐν τῷ θεῷ, and only ἐνεργείᾳ was He πρὸς τὸν θεόν; προῆλθεν δραστικῇ ἐνεργείᾳ. How this is to be understood, Marcellus — with all sorts of cautions — has illustrated by the analogy of the human Logos: ἓν γάρ ἐστι καὶ ταὐτὸ τῷ ἀνθρώπῳ ὁ λόγος καὶ οὐδενὶ χωριζόμενος ἑτέρῳ, ἢ μόνῃ τῇ τῆς πράξεως ἐνεργείᾳ." This reads (so far) almost like an exposition of the fifth chapter of the tract, " Against Praxeas."

He next calls attention to the fact that by Reason in this context Tertullian does not mean God's faculty of ratiocination, by virtue of which He was rational, but a really subsisting ἔννοια — the *verbum mentis* of the schools. Still further, he animadverts on Tertullian's admission that the distinction he was drawing between the Reason and the Word was not drawn by Christians at large who, translating the Greek word " Logos " in John i. 1, by the Latin *Sermo,* were accustomed to say simply that " the Word was in the beginning," i.e., eternally, and that " with God." In doing this he adverts to Tertullian's admission that he lays little stress on this distinction himself, and is fain himself to allow that the " Word " is coeternal with " Reason " — that is to say, of course, the " inner Word," not yet uttered for the purpose of creation: and further, that he allows that the Word consists of Reason, and existed in this His hypostasis or substance before He became the Word by utterance. Then, arriving at the apex of his argument, he points out that " Tertullian teaches that the Word, even anterior to His mission and going out from God the Father, existed with the Father as a Person distinct from Him." This, (1) because God is said not to be " alone "; but He only is not alone with whom is another person present. If through all eternity God was unipersonal, and there was not in the divine essence one and another, then God was alone. Hence God was not unipersonal, since He is affirmed not to have been alone. (2) Because in the illustration from human experience Tertullian distinguishes between the quasi-personality of the human inner word and the real personality of the divine inner Word. The whole drift of the illustration turns on the idea that " what occurs in man, God's image, is merely the shadow of what occurs really and in very fact in God." Finally, Bull argues that Tertullian clearly identifies the " Reason that coexisted with God from eternity with the Word prolated from Him at a definite point of time, and makes one as much personal as the other, conceiving nothing to have occurred at the prolation but the prolation itself — the Word remaining all the while, because God, unchangeable. This argument is expanded in a supplementary reason which Bull gives for his conclusion by the help of a passage which occurs in the twenty-seventh chapter of the tract, " Against Praxeas." In this passage Tertullian argues that the Word, because God, is " immutabilis et informabilis " — unchangeable and untransformable: since God never either ceases to be what He was or begins to be what He was not. How, then, Bull asks, can Tertullian have believed that the Word, who is God, began to be a person only at His prolation, or, indeed, for that is what is really in question, began at that time only to be at all? [105] From such passages, Bull justly suggests, we may learn that by all that Tertullian says of the prolations of the Logos and Spirit he does not mean to detract in any way from the unchangeableness of the divine persons concerned in these acts: nothing intrinsic was, in his view, either added to or taken from either of the two, seeing that each is the same God, eternal and unchangeable. " Tertullian does indeed teach " — thus Bull closes the discussion — " that the Son of God was made, and was called the Word (*Verbum* or *Sermo*), from some definite beginning; i.e. at the time when He went out from God the Father, with the voice, ' Let there be light,' in order to arrange the universe. But yet that he believed that that very hypostasis, which is called the Word (*Sermo* or *Verbum*) and Son of God, is eternal, I have, I think, abundantly demonstrated." [106]

(3) There has been enough adduced incidentally in the course of the discussion so far, to make it clear that Tertullian in insisting on the distinction of persons in the Godhead — and in carrying this distinction back into eternity — had no inten-

[105] In support of this take such a statement as the following from the thirteenth chapter: " You will find this," says Tertullian, " in the Gospel in so many words: ' In the beginning was the Word, and the Word was with God and the Word was God.' He who was is One: and He with whom He was is another." As it is probable that by the words " in the beginning " Tertullian understood eternity, here is an explicit assertion of a distinction of persons in eternity. Again, in chap. viii., he says: " The Word, therefore, was both in the Father always, as He says, ' I am in the Father,' and with the Father always, as it is written, ' And the Word was with God.' "

[106] E. T. p. 545.

tion of derogating in any way from the unity of God. If in his debate with the Monarchians his especial task was to vindicate the οἰκονομία, the conditions of that debate required of him an equal emphasis on the " monarchy." And he is certainly careful to give it, insisting and insisting again on the unity of that one God whom alone Christians worship. This insistence on the unity of God has come, indeed, to be widely represented as precisely the peculiarity of Tertullian's doctrine of God. Says Loofs: [107] " Tertullian's Logos doctrine waxed into a doctrine of the Trinity (*trinitas* occurs first in him) because Tertullian sought to bring the Apologetic traditions into harmony with the stricter monotheism of the Asiatic theology." Similarly Harnack supposes that Monarchianism exercised a strong influence on Tertullian, " spite of the fact that he is opposing it," and remarks in proof that " no thought is so plainly expressed " by him in his tract, " Against Praxeas " " as this, that Father, Son and Spirit are *unius substantiæ,* that is ὁμοούσιοι"; [108] and again, that " Tertullian in so far as he designated Father, Son, and Spirit as one substance expressed their *unity* as strongly as possible." [109] We may attribute the influence which led Tertullian to lay the stress he did on the unity of God to whatever source we choose, but we must acknowledge that Tertullian himself did not trace it to the Monarchians. Though, no doubt, the necessity he felt upon him not to neglect this great truth was intensified by the fact that it was just with Monarchians that he was contending, yet Tertullian is not himself conscious of indebtedness to them for either his conception of it or his zeal in its behalf. To him it is the very principium of Christianity and the very starting-point of the Rule of Faith. Though he recognizes a monadistic monarchy as rather Jewish than Christian, therefore, and is prepared for a certain pluralism in his conception of God, all this is with him conditioned upon the preservation of the monarchy, and he has his own way of reconciling the monarchy, in which all his Christian

[107] " Leitfaden zum Studium der Dogmengeschichte," p. 88.
[108] iv. p. 57, note: cf. ii., pp. 257, note,[2] 259.
[109] ii. p. 257 note.[2]

thinking is rooted, on the one side, with the economy, which he is zealous to assert, on the other.

This way consists, briefly, in insistence not merely that the three persons, Father, Son, and Spirit, are of one substance, but that they are of one undivided substance. Though there is a *dispositio, distinctio* between them, there is no *divisio, separatio*. It is not enough for him that the Three should be recognized as alike in substance, condition, power.[110] What he insists on is that the Father, Son, and Spirit are inseparable from one another and share in a single undivided substance — that it is therefore "not by way of diversity that the Son differs from the Father, but by distribution: it is not by division that He is different, but by distinction."[111] "I say," he reiterates, they are "distinct, not separate" (*distincte, non divise*)."[112] They are distinguished "on the ground of personality, not of substance — in the way of distinction, not of division,"[113] "by disposition, not by division." The ill-disposed and perverse may indeed press the distinction into a separation, but the procession of the Son from the Father "is like the ray's procession from the sun, and the river's from the fountain, and the tree's from the seed"[114] — and thus the distinction between them may be maintained "without destroying their inseparable union — as of the sun and the ray, and the fountain and the river."[115]

By the aid of such illustrations Tertullian endeavored to make clear that in distinguishing the persons he allowed no division of substance. His conception was that as the sun flows out into its beams while yet the beams remain connected inseparably with the sun, and the river flows out of the fountain but maintains an inseparable connection with it, so the Son and Spirit flow out from the Father while remaining inseparable from Him. There is, in a word, an unbroken continuity of substance, although the substance is drawn out into — if we may speak after the manner of men — a different mold. The con-

---

[110] Chap. ii.
[111] Chap. ix.
[112] Chap. xi.
[113] Chap. xii.; cf. xxi. xxii.
[114] Chap. xxii.
[115] Chap. xxvii.

ception is that the prolation of the Logos — and afterward of the Spirit proximately from the Logos — is rather of the nature of a protrusion than an extrusion: the Godhead is, now, of a new shape, so to speak, but remains the Godhead still in its undivided and indivisible unity. As Tertullian expresses it sharply in the twenty-first chapter of the " Apology ": " Just as when a ray is shot forth (*porrigitur*) from the sun, it is a portion of the whole, but the sun will be in the ray because it is a ray of the sun, and is not separated from the substance but is extended (*extenditur*), so from Spirit [is extended] Spirit, and from God, God, as light is kindled from light. The *materiæ matrix* remains *integra et indefecta,* although you draw out from it a plurality of *traduces qualitatis;* and thus what has come forth (*profectum*) out of God is God, and the Son of God, and the two are one. Similarly as He is Spirit from Spirit and God from God, he is made a second member in manner of existence, in grade not state, and has not receded from the matrix but exceeded beyond it (*et a matrice non recessit sed excessit*)." In a word, the mode of the prolation is a stretching out of the Godhead, not a partition of the Godhead: the unity of the Godhead remains *integra et indefecta.*

The unity of the Godhead is thus preserved through the prolations themselves, which are therefore one in a " numerical unity," as it afterward came to be spoken of — though in Tertullian's usage this language would not be employed, but he would rather say that the persons differ in number, as first, second and third, while the substance remains undivided. It is precisely on the ground that in their view the prolations involved a division and separation of substance that he separates himself from the Valentinians.[116] " Valentinus," says he, " divides and separates his prolations from their author. . . . But this is the prolation of the truth, the guardian of the unity, wherein we declare that the Son is a prolation of the Father without being separated from Him. For God sent forth the Word (as the Paraclete also declares [117]) just as the root puts

[116] Chap. viii.

[117] I.e., this is a doctrine supported by the Montanistic prophecies.

forth the tree, and the fountain the river, and the sun the ray. For these are προβολαί of the substances from which they proceed. . . . But still the tree is not severed from the root, nor the river from the fountain, nor the ray from the sun; and neither the Word separated from God. . . . In like manner the Trinity, flowing down from the Father, through intertwined and connected steps, does not at all disturb the monarchy, while it at the same time guards the state of the economy." [118]

Harnack, therefore,[119] does considerably less than justice to Tertullian's conception, when he represents it as substantially the same as that of Valentinus, differing only in the number of emanations acknowledged — because, as Hippolytus certifies, the Valentinians "acknowledge that the one is the originator of all " and " the whole goes back to one." Nor does he improve matters when he adds in a note that " according to these doctrines, the unity is sufficiently preserved (1) if the several persons have one and the same substance, (2) if there is one possessor of the whole substance, i.e., if everything proceeds from him." Tertullian, on the contrary, is never weary of asseverating that his doctrine of unity demands much more than this — not merely that it is out of the one God that all proceeds — nor merely that what thus comes forth from God is of His substance, so that all of the emanations are of the substance of God — but specifically that this going forth from God of His prolations is merely an *extension* of the Godhead, not a division from it. Thus the unity, he says, is preserved through the prolations; and no separation from God is instituted by the prolations. These abide unbrokenly " portions " of the deity, not fragments broken off from the deity. Nor is Harnack much happier when he goes on [120] to say that Tertullian conceived God up to the prolation of the Logos " as yet . . . the only *person*." According to his explicit exposition of the life of God in eternity, Tertullian held that there never was a time when God was alone, except in the sense that there was no created universe about Him: in the beginning

[118] Chap. viii.   [119] ii. p. 258.   [120] ii. p. 259.

itself that Reason which the common people, simply translating the Greek of John's Gospel, call the Word, was with
Him, though within Him, as Another. Thus in the unity of the
Godhead there always was a distinction of persons, even before,
by the prolations of Son and Spirit, this distinction was manifested *ad extra.*

The distinctions of persons in the Godhead, accordingly,
as Tertullian conceived them, were not created by the prolations of Son and Spirit. These prolations merely brought into
manifestation the distinctions of persons already existing in
the Godhead. Neither did he suppose that these distinctions
would cease on the recession of these prolations back into the
Godhead — as Tertullian anticipates will take place when
their end is served. It is the prolations, not the personal distinctions, which in his thought have a beginning and ending;
and when he teaches that these prolations come forth at the
Father's will, fulfill their purpose and retire back into the Godhead, this cannot in any way affect his doctrine either of the
unity of God or of the Trinity in the unity. In all this process,
rather, he is tracing out only an incident in the life of God, a
temporary outflowing of God to do a specific work. The whole
exposition which Harnack gives of this transaction is colored
by misapprehension of Tertullian's import. It is indeed more
infelicitous than even this circumstance would indicate. No
doubt Tertullian's subordinationism is very marked. Though
he conceives the prolate Logos and the Spirit as truly God,
they are, in his view, God at the periphery of His being, going
forth, in a certain reduction of deity, for the world-work.[121]
But to speak of even the prolate Logos as a " Being which must
be a derived existence, which has already in some fashion a
finite element in itself, because it is the hypostatized Word of
creation, which has an origin "; and to add, " From the stand-

[121] Cf. Dorner, "Doctrine of the Person of Christ," Div. I. vol. ii. pp. 108,
186, 460. Dorner somewhat misses the point by failing to see that Tertullian
recognized the eternity of the personal distinction and so distinguished between the unprolated and the prolated Logos (see below, pp. 69 *sq.*): but even
Dorner perceives that there was some limit to Tertullian's subordinationism:
"An Arian Subordinationism was . . . foreign to his mind " (p. 74; cf. p.
108).

point of humanity this deity is God Himself, *i.e.*, a God whom
men can apprehend and who can apprehend them, but from
God's standpoint, which speculation can fix but not fathom,
this deity is a subordinate, nay, even a temporary one " — is
to go beyond all warrant discoverable in Tertullian's exposition. It is of the very essence of Tertullian's thought that there
was no " finite element " in the Logos, or in the Spirit which
constitutes the third in the Godhead — " as the fruit of the
tree is third from the root, or as the stream out of the river is
third from the fountain, or as the apex of the ray is third from
the sun "; [122] that these prolations are, in a word, nothing
but God Himself extended for the performance of a work —
nothing, if the simile can be allowed, but the hand of God
stretched out for the task of bringing a world into existence
and guiding its course to its destined end. As such the Logos
mediated between God and the world; but to make Tertullian
teach, to use words of Bull's,[123] that " the very nature of the
Son in itself is a mean between God and the creatures," that
is to say, is something distinguishable alike from the supreme
nature of God on the one side, and from the rest of created
beings on the other — is to confound his whole conception.
He not only did not teach that the Logos is a creature of nature
different from that of God, of a derived existence, having an
absolute origin, and destined to reach an end: but he explicitly
teaches the contradictory of these things. The Logos existed
eternally, he asseverates, in God: the prolation of the Logos,
indeed, had a beginning and will have an end; but the Logos
Himself who is prolated, is so far from being a derived existence, which has a finite element in it, and has an origin and
is to make an end — that He is just God Himself prolated,
that is, outstretched like a hand, to His work. And what is
true of the Logos is true of the Spirit. He is not, as the Arians
imagined, the creature of a creature, but just the still further
prolated God — the tips of the fingers of the hand of God.[124]

[122] Chap. viii. *ad fin.*
[123] III. ix. 11 (E. T. p. 503).
[124] Irenæus makes use of the simile of God's hands to explain his conception of the relation of the Son and Spirit to God. Cf. IV. praef. § 4: " Man

(4) With this conception of the relation of the prolations to the divine essence Tertullian was certainly in a position to do complete justice to the deity of our Lord. Had the prolate Logos been to him a "middle substance" — something between God and man in its very nature — then it no doubt would have been impossible for him to do full justice to our Lord's deity as the incarnation of this Logos. But seeing that the Logos was to him God Himself prolated, one in substance with the primal deity itself, no question of the complete deity of the incarnated Logos could arise in his mind. "Nor shall we approximate," he says,[125] "to the opinions of the Gentiles, who, if at any time they be forced to confess God, yet will have other Gods below Him. The Godhead, however, has no gradation, for It is only one" and can, therefore, "in no case be less than Itself." Accordingly he is constant in declaring the Son, as He is God, to be "equal with" the Father.[126] All that is true of the Father, therefore, he would have us understand, is true also of the Son: they are not only of the same substance, but of the same power also; and all the attributes of the one belong also to the other. "The names of the Father," he says [127] — "God Almighty, the Most High, the Lord of Hosts, the King of Israel, He that Is — inasmuch as the Scriptures so teach, these, we say, belonged also to the Son, and in these the Son has come, and in these has ever acted, and thus manifested them in Himself to men. . . . When, therefore, you read Almighty God, and Most High, and God of Hosts, and King of Israel, and He that Is, consider whether there be not indicated by these the Son also, who in His own right is God

. . . was moulded by God's hands, i.e., by the Son and Spirit to whom He said, Let us make," etc. Cf. also IV. 20. 1; V. 1. 3; V. 5. 1; V. 28. 4. At a later date the Sabellians employed the figure of the alternately outstretched and withdrawn arm and hand as a figure of their notion of the successive movements of the divine revelation (Dorner, Div. I, vol. ii. pp. 155, 159, 168). Augustine *in Joannem*, § 53. 2–3, in criticising this Sabellian use of it, recognizes the propriety of the figure in itself.

[125] "Against Hermogenes," vii. (Bull, E. T. pp. 580–581).
[126] "Against Praxeas," chaps. vii. xxii.; "De Resurrectione Carnis," chap. vi.
[127] "Against Praxeas," chap. xvii. (Bull, E. T. p. 198).

Almighty, in that He is the Word of God Almighty." Again,[128] "' All things,' saith He, ' are delivered unto Me of the Father.' . . . The Creator hath delivered all things to Him who is not less than Himself, — to the Son: all things, to wit, which He created by Him, i.e., by His own Word." Accordingly, Tertullian does not hesitate to speak of the Son as God or to attribute to Him all that is true of God. He does not scruple, for example, to apply Rom. ix. 5 to Him — affirming Him in the words of that text to be God over all, blessed for ever.[129]

If it be asked how Tertullian made this recognition of the full equality of the Son with the Father consistent with the subordinationism which he had taken over from the Apologists along with their Logos Christology, the answer appears to turn on the identification of the Son with the prolate Logos. The strong subordination of the Son belongs to Him as prolated, not specifically as second in the Godhead. " It will therefore follow," says Tertullian in an illuminating passage,[130] " that by Him who is invisible, we must understand the Father *in the fullness of His majesty,* while we recognize the Son as visible *by reason of the dispensation of His derived existence (pro modulo derivationis)*; even as it is not permitted us to contemplate the sun in the full amount of his substance which is in the heavens, but we can only endure with our eyes a ray by reason of the tempered condition of this portion which is projected from him to the earth. . . . We declare, however, that the Son also, *considered in Himself,* . . . is invisible, in that He is God, and the Word, and Spirit of God." In this passage it is affirmed that in Himself, because He is God, the Son shares all the qualities of God, and becomes " reduced God," if we can be allowed such a phrase, only *pro modulo derivationis,* that is to say, as the result of the prolation by virtue of which He is extended outwards for the purpose of action in and on the world. This passage will aid us also in apprehending how we are to understand Tertullian when he

[128] " Against Marcion," iv. 25 (Bull, *loc. cit.*).
[129] " Against Praxeas," xiii. xv.
[130] Chap. xiv.

speaks of the Son as a " portion " only of the Godhead. Again
it is, of course, only as prolate Logos that He is so spoken of:
and as prolate Logos He is conceived under the figure of the
ray which as a " portion " of the sun is " tempered " to the
eyes of men. Similarly the prolate Logos is a " portion " of
the Godhead, that is to say, not a separated part or even a
particular part of the Godhead, but the Godhead itself " tempered " for its mission relatively to the world. This " portion "
is not to be conceived, then, as a fragment of Godhead; it is
in and of itself all that God is. Tertullian not only distinctly
affirms this on all occasions, but expressly explains that it is
neither separated from the Godhead nor in anything less than
it, but is " equal to the Father, and has and possesses all that
the Father has." [131] Nay, Tertullian tells us with crisp directness that this " *portio* " of the Godhead is Itself " consort in Its

[131] We are here quoting Bull, II. vii. 5 (E. T. p. 200), where, as well as
pp. 536 *sq.*, the meaning of " portio " is discussed. It is discussed also in Hageman, pp. 182 *sq.*, who suggests, with a reference to *De virg. vel.*, chap. 4, *ad fin.*,
that it is a technical logical term, and imports the " specific " as distinguished
from the " general," in which case the Logos as a *portio* of the deity would
rather be a " particularization " of deity than a " fragment " of deity. Dorner
(Div. I. vol. ii. p. 78) thinks that the employment of such " inappropriate
physical categories of the Son " is due to the " somewhat physical character
of [Tertullian's] view of God," and " should be set rather to the account of
his mode of expression, than of his mode of thought ": it " really disguised
Tertullian's proper meaning " (cf. pp. 121–122). From the manner in which
Tertullian uses the term " portio " it would seem probably to be a technical
term in the Logos Christology and that would imply its currency in the
debates of the day. It is interesting to observe in a " Sermon of the Arians "
in " Augustini Opera Omnia," Migne ed., 1841, viii. coll. 677–684, which was in
circulation in North Africa early in the fifth century what looks very much
like a repudiation of the phraseology by the Arians — for Arianism was very
much only the Logos Christology run to seed, the " left " side of the developing schemes of doctrine. In this document, at chap. 23, it is said: " The Son is
not a part or a portion of the Father, but His own and beloved, perfect and
complete, only-begotten Son. The Spirit is not a part or a portion of the
Son, but the first and highest work (*opus*) of the only-begotten Son of God,
before the rest of the universe." Augustine (" Contra Sermon. Arian.," xxvii. 23)
answers only: " But what Catholic would say the Son is a part of the Father
or the Holy Spirit part of the Son? A thing they [the Arians] think is to
be so denied as if there were a question between us and them on it." It looks
very much as if the whole past history of the use of this phraseology was out
of memory in the opening fifth century.

fullness" (*plenitudinis consors*). "If you do not deny," he
argues with Marcion,[132] "that the Creator's Son and Spirit and
Substance is also His Christ, you must needs allow that those
who have not acknowledged the Father have likewise failed
to acknowledge the Son, seeing that they share the same substance (*per ejusdam substantiæ conditionem*): for if It baffled
men's understanding in Its Plenitude, much more has a portion
of It, especially since It is consort in the Plenitude."[133]

It cannot surprise us, therefore, when we observe Tertullian
representing a distinctive way of designating our Lord as in
part due merely to a desire to be clear and to avoid confusion
in language. He is speaking [134] of the habit of distinguishing
between God the Father and the Son by calling the former
God and the latter Lord. There is no foundation for the distinction, he tells us, in the nature of things. Any one of the
persons of the Godhead may with equal propriety be called
either God or Lord. He " definitely declares that *two* are God,
the Father and the Son, and with the addition of the Holy
Spirit, even *three,* according to the principle of the divine
οἰκονομία, which introduces number." He will never say, however, that there are two Gods or two Lords, yet " not as if,"
he explains, " it were untrue that the Father is God, and the
Son is God, and the Holy Ghost is God, and each is God." This
apparently can only mean that the three are all together the
one God — and, indeed, one of his characteristic phrases is
the famous *deus ambo* or even *tres.*[135] But though Christ is
thus rightly called God, it is best, he thinks, in order to avoid
mistakes, to speak of Him as Lord when the Father is mentioned at the same time, and to call Him God only when
He is mentioned alone. For there is no gradation in the Godhead, as Tertullian elsewhere remarks,[136] although there are
three " grades " in the Godhead: which is as much as to say
that considered in themselves, those who are distinguished as

132 " Against Marcion," iii. 6, *ad fin.*
133 Cf. Bull, II. vii. 6 (E. T. pp. 201 *sq.*).
134 " Against Praxeas," chap. xiii.
135 " Against Praxeas," xiii. *med.*
136 " Against Hermogenes," vii. (quoted above).

first, second, and third — that is to say, in the modes of their existence as source and prolations of the first and second order — are yet consorts in the plenitude of God.[137]

On this basis Tertullian, in developing his doctrine of the person of Christ in the formula of "Deus homo, unus Christus," could strenuously insist on the complete deity as well as perfect humanity of this one divine-human person. And in this insistence we may find the culminating proof that he sought to do full justice to the true deity of Christ. He approaches this subject [138] in the course of a confutation of the Monarchian attempt to find a distinction between Father and Son by understanding the Father to be the divine Spirit incarnated and the Son to be the incarnating flesh. Thus, says Tertullian, while contending that the Father and Son are one and the same, they do, in fact, divide them and so fall into the hands of the Valentinians, making Jesus, the man, and Christ, the inhabiting Spirit, two. Proceeding to expound the true relation between the incarnated Spirit and the incarnating

---

[137] Bull, IV. ii. 5 (E. T. pp. 580–581) treats with great care the apparent contradiction between Tertullian's assertion in "Against Hermogenes," vii., that "the Godhead has no gradations," and the assertion in "Against Praxeas," ii., that the persons of the Godhead are three "not in state but in gradation." Tertullian, Bull tells us, means in the latter passage by "*gradation, order,* but not greater or less Godhead." "For," continues Bull, "whom he acknowledges to be three in gradation, Them he denies to be different in state. But with Tertullian, as we have seen, for a thing not to be different from another in state, means, not to be set under it, but to be on a par and equal to it. Hence in the same passage, presently after, he expressly says, that the three Persons of the Holy Trinity are all of *one power;* and consequently that no One of Them is more powerful or excellent than Another. Therefore the Godhead 'has no gradation,' that is, 'is in no case less than Itself,' as Tertullian distinctly explains himself; yet there are gradations in the Godhead, that is, a certain order of the Persons, of whom One derives His origin from Another; in such wise that the Father is the first Person, existing of Himself; the Son second from the Father, whilst the Holy Ghost is third, who proceeds from the Father through the Son, or from the Father and the Son." This is a very favorable specimen of Bull's reasoning: and Tertullian's language may be made consistent with itself on this hypothesis. On the whole, however, it seems more likely that the real state of the case in Tertullian's thought was that indicated in the text. In the Godhead there are no gradations: but after prolations grades of being are instituted.

[138] Chap. xxvii.

flesh, he next argues that the process of incarnation was not that of a transformation of the divine Spirit into flesh, because God neither ceases to be what He was nor can He be any other thing than what He is. Accordingly when the Word became flesh, this was accomplished not by His becoming transmuted into flesh but by His clothing Himself with flesh. No less is it insupposable, he argues, that the incarnation was accomplished by any mixture of the two substances, divine Spirit and flesh, forming a third substance intermediate between the two.[139] At that rate Jesus would have ceased to be God while not becoming man: whereas the Scriptures represent Him to have been both God and man. Accordingly we must believe that there was no confusion of the two in the person of Jesus, but such a conjunction of God and man that, the property of each nature being wholly preserved, the divine nature continued to do all things suitable to itself, while the human nature, on the other hand, exhibited all the affections that belong to it. Jesus, thus, was in one these two — man of the flesh, God of the Spirit: and in Him coexist two substances, viz., the divine and the human,[140] the one of which is immortal and the other mortal. Throughout this whole discussion the integrity of the divine nature — immortal, impassible, unchangeable — is carefully preserved and its union in the one person Jesus Christ with a human nature, mortal, passible, capable of change, is so explained as to preserve it from all confusion, intermixture or interchange with it. We could not have a clearer exhibition of Tertullian's zeal to do full justice to the true deity of Christ.

(5) It scarcely seems necessary to add a separate detailed statement of how Tertullian conceived of the Holy Spirit.

---

[139] Accordingly we must not understand the phrase " Homo Deo mixtus," which occurs in the " Apology," chap. xxi., to imply that the two substances were " mixed," so as to make a *tertium quid*. What he means to say is only that Jesus Christ was neither man nor God alone, but the two together. Cf. Bethune-Baker, " The Meaning of Homoousios in the ' Constantinopolitan ' Creed," in " Texts and Studies," J. A. Robinson, ed., vii. 1, p. 22, note.

[140] Chap. xxix. *ad init.*

While we cannot say with Harnack [141] that Tertullian exhibits no trace of independent interest in the doctrine of the Spirit, it is yet true that he speaks much less fully and much less frequently of Him than of the Logos,[142] and that his doctrine of the Spirit runs quite parallel with that of the Logos. He has spoken of Him, moreover, ordinarily in connections where the doctrine of the Logos is also under discussion and therefore his modes of thought on this branch of the subject have already been perhaps sufficiently illustrated. The *distinct personality* of the Spirit is as clearly acknowledged as that of the Logos Himself. In the οἰκονομία the unity is distributed not into a duality, but into a trinity, providing a place not for two only but for three — the Father, Son, and Holy Ghost; who differ from one another not in condition, substance, or power but in degree, form, and aspect.[143] And everywhere the third person is treated as just as distinct a personality as the second and first. There is no clear passage carrying this distinct personality back into *eternity*. That Tertullian thought of the personality of the Spirit precisely as he did of that of the Logos is here our only safe guide. On the other hand, there is no lack of passages in which the *unity of substance* is insisted upon relatively to the Spirit also.[144] After explaining that the substance of the Son is just the substance of the Father, he adds: "The same remark is made by me with respect to the third degree, because I believe the Spirit to be from no other source than from the Father through the Son." [145] So again: "The Spirit is the third from God and the Son, as the fruit from the tree is the third from the root, and the stream from the river is third from the fountain, and the apex from the ray is third from the sun. Nothing, however, is separated from the matrix from which it draws its properties; and thus, the

[141] ii. p. 261, note 4.

[142] Cf. Nösgen, " Geschichte der Lehre vom heiligen Geiste," p. 21.

[143] " Against Praxeas," chap. ii. *ad fin.*, cf. chap. iii. near end, chaps. viii. xi. *ad fin.*, xiii. xxx. Cf. Stier, *op. cit.*, p. 92, note.

[144] " Against Praxeas," chaps. ii. *ad fin.*, iii. *ad fin.*, iv. *ad init.*, viii. ix. *ad init.*, etc.

[145] Chap. iv. *ad init.*

Trinity flows down from the Father through *consertos et conexos gradus* and in no respects injures the monarchy while protecting the economy." [146] On this view the *true deity* of the Spirit is emphasized as fully as that of the Logos, and Tertullian repeatedly speaks of Him likewise shortly as God,[147] as " the Third Name in the Godhead and the Third Degree of the Divine Majesty." [148] Accordingly when he " definitely declares that two are God, the Father and the Son," he adds,[149] "and with the addition of the Holy Ghost, even *three,* according to the principle of the divine economy, which introduces number, in order that the Father may not, as you perversely infer, be believed to have Himself been born, and to have suffered." To Tertullian, therefore, the alternative was not the complete deity of the Spirit or His creaturehood; but the unity of Monarchianism or the Trinity in the unity of the economy. He never thinks of meeting the Monarchian assault by denying the full deity of the Spirit, but only by providing a distinction of persons within the unity of the Godhead. The most instructive passages are naturally those in which all three persons are brought together, of which there are a considerable number.[150] To quote but one of these, he explains that " the connection of the Father in the Son, and of the Son in the Paraclete, produces three coherent Persons, [distinct, nevertheless] one from the other: these three are one substance, [*unum*], not one person, [*unus*], as it is said, ' I and my Father are one [*unum*],' in respect of unity of substance not singularity of number." [151] There can, in short, be no question that Tertullian had applied to the Spirit with full consciousness all that he had thought out concerning the Son, and that His doctrine of God was fully settled into a doctrine

---

[146] Chap. viii. *ad fin.*

[147] He seems to be the first in writings which have chanced to come down to us to apply the name " God " to the Spirit; but this is mere accident.

[148] Chap. xxx. *ad fin.*

[149] Chap. xiii. *med.*

[150] E.g., chaps. ii. *ad init., et fin.,* iii. *ad fin.,* viii. *ad fin.,* ix. *ad init.,* xiii. *med.,* xxv. xxx.

[151] Chap. xxv. *ad init.*

of Trinity. His mode of speaking of the Spirit introduces no new difficulty in construing his doctrine — which is something that cannot be said of all his predecessors.

By such expositions as these, Tertullian appears, in seeking to do justice to the elements of doctrine embalmed in the Rule of Faith, fairly to pass beyond the natural reach of the Logos speculation and to open the way to a higher conception. A symbol of this advance may not unfairly be discovered in the frequent appearance in his pages of the new term "Trinity." The Greek equivalent of this term occurs in his contemporary Hippolytus,[152] but scarcely elsewhere, at this early date, to designate the distinctions in the Godhead — unless indeed we account the single instance of its employment by Theophilus of Antioch a preparation for such an application of it.[153] In any event, there is a fine appropriateness in the sudden apparition of the term in easy and frequent use,[154] for the first time, in the pages of an author whose discussions make so decided an approximation toward the enunciation of that doctrine to denote which this term was so soon to become exclusively consecrated. The insistence of Tertullian upon the οἰκονομία in the monarchy — on unity of substance, with all that is implied in unity of substance, persisting in three distinct persons who coexist from eternity — certainly marks out the lines within which the developed doctrine of the Trinity moves, and deserves to be signalized by the emergence into literature of the term by which the developed doctrine of the Trinity should ever afterward be designated.

It is possible that something of the same symbolical significance may attach also to Tertullian's use of his favorite term οἰκονομία. Of course, οἰκονομία is not a new word; but it is used by Tertullian in an unwonted sense — a sense scarcely found

[152] "Contra Noëtum," chap. 14.

[153] "Ad Autol.," ii. 15. Here the term τρίας first occurs in connection with distinctions in the Godhead; and it is customary, therefore, to say that here first it is applied to express the Trinity. So, e.g., Kahnis, Harnack, Loofs, Seeberg. As Nösgen (pp. 13–14) points out, however, it is by no means certain that the word here has any technical import.

[154] E.g., "Against Praxeas," chaps. ii. iii. xi. xii. etc.

elsewhere except in his contemporary Hippolytus,[155] and, perhaps as a kind of preparation for their use of it, in a single passage of Tatian.[156] Tertullian constantly employs it, as we have seen, to designate, as over against the monarchy, the mystery of the Trinity in the unity. There can be no question of its general implication in his pages; but it is, no doubt, a little difficult to determine the precise significance of the term itself which he employs. The fundamental sense of the word is " disposition "; but in its application it receives its form either from the idea of " administration," or from that of " structure." If it is used by Tertullian in the former shade of meaning, its employment by him need not have great significance for his Trinitarian doctrine. He would, in that case, only say by it that the monarchy of God is administered by a disposition of the Godhead into three several personalities, Father, Son, and Holy Ghost, through whom the single Lordship is carried on, as it were, by deputy; while the precise relation of these personalities to one another and to the Godhead itself would be left to the context to discover.

An argument which occurs in the third chapter of the tract, " Against Praxeas," seems to many to suggest that it was in this sense that the term was employed by Tertullian. Tertullian here explains that " monarchy has no other meaning than single and unique rule "; " but for all that," he adds, " this monarchy does not preclude him whose government it is . . . from administering his own monarchy by whatever agents he will ": and much less can the integrity of a monarchy suffer by the association in it of a Son, since it is still held in common by two who are so really one (*tam unicis*). Applying these general principles to the monarchy of God, he argues that this monarchy is therefore by no means set aside by the circumstance that it is administered by means of legions and hosts of angels "; and much less can it be thought to be injured by the participation in it of the Son and Holy Spirit, to whom the second and third places are assigned, but who are in-

[155] " Contra Noëtum," chaps. 8 and 14.
[156] " Ad Græc.," 5.

separably joined with the Father, in His substance. " Do you really suppose," he asks, " that those who are naturally members of the Father's own substance, His congeners,[157] instruments of His might, nay, His power itself, and the entire system of His monarchy, are the overthrow and destruction thereof? " It seems tolerably clear that Tertullian is not here comparing the economy with the administrative agents of a monarchy: with them he rather compares the hosts of angels through whom the divine monarchy is administered. The economy is rather compared to the sharing of the monarchy itself between father and son as co-regents on a single throne. In that case, so far is economy on his lips from bearing the sense of administration that it is expressly distinguished from it, and referred to something in the Godhead deeper than its administrative functions. The illustration, therefore, emphasizes, indeed, the personal distinctions of the economy — they are comparable to the distinction between father and son in a conjoint rule — but it suggests equally the penetration of this distinction behind all matters of administration into the Godhead, the Ruling Being, itself.

Nor is this impression set aside by the implication of the other figures employed by Tertullian to explain the relations of the persons in the Godhead. When he compares them to the root, the tree, and the fruit, or to the fountain, the river, and the stream, or to the sun, the ray, and the apex, his mind seems undoubtedly to be upon the prolated Logos and Spirit; these figures indeed, so constantly upon his lips, seem inapplicable to eternal distinctions, lying behind the prolations. But it must be remembered, first, that these illustrations are not original with Tertullian, but are taken over by him from the Apologists along with their Logos speculation — although they are doubtless developed and given new point by him; next, that the precise point which he adduces them to illustrate is not the whole import of the economy, but the preservation of the unity of substance within the economy of three persons; and finally, that the ordinary engagement of his mind with the

---

[157] *pignora* = pledges of his love, i.e., his close relations.

Trinity of Persons, in what we may call its developed form —
its mode of manifestation in God acting *ad extra* — need not
by any means exclude from his thought a recognition of an
ontological basis, in the structure of the Godhead itself, for
this manifested Trinity. And if in one passage he presses his
illustrations to the verge of suggesting a separation of the Son
from the Father — intimating that the Son may be affected
by the sufferings of the God-man while the Father remains in
impassible blessedness; [158] in another, on the other hand, he
seems expressly to carry back the distinction of persons into
the eternal Godhead itself — affirming that God was never
" alone " save in the sense of independence of all external
existence, but there was always with Him, because in Him,
that other self which afterward proceeded from Him for the
making of the world.[159] The fullest recognition, therefore, that
Tertullian habitually thought of the Trinity in, so to speak,
its developed form — with the Logos and the Spirit prolate
and working in the world — by no means precludes the possibility that the very term οἰκονομία connoted in his hands something more fundamental than a distinction in the Godhead
constituted by these prolations.

And certainly the word was currently employed in senses
that lent it a color which may very well have given it to
Tertullian the deeper connotation of internal structure, when
he applied it to the Godhead. To perceive this, we have only
to recall its application to express the proper adjustment of
the parts of a building, as Vitruvius, for example, uses it,[160]
or to express what we call the disposition, that is the plan or
construction of a literary composition, as it is used, say, by
Cicero, when he speaks of the οἰκονομία *perturbatior* of his
letter,[161] or by Quintilian,[162] when he ascribes to the old Latin
comedies a better οἰκονομία than the new exhibited.[163] A very

---

[158] Chap. xxix.
[159] Chap. v.
[160] " De Architectura," I. ii. 1.
[161] " Ad Att.," vi. 1.
[162] " Inst.," I. viii. 9.
[163] This sense is discussed by Daniel, as below, note [166], under his divi-

interesting instance of the employment of the word in this sense of " structure " occurs in the *Letter of the Church of Smyrna,* giving an account of the martyrdom of Polycarp.[164] The martyrs were so torn by the scourge, says this passage, that " the οἰκονομία of their flesh was visible even so far as the inward veins and arteries." Lightfoot translates here, " *the internal structure and mechanism,*" and refers us to Eusebius' paraphrase, which tells us the martyrs were so lacerated that " the hidden inward parts of the body, both their bowels and their members, were exposed to view." [165] There can be no doubt that this very common usage of the term was well known to Tertullian the rhetorician, and it may very well be that when he adopted it to express the distribution of the Godhead into three persons it was because it suggested to him rather the inner structure, so to speak, of the Godhead itself, than merely an external arrangement for the administration of the divine dominion.

That Tertullian's usage of the term implies as much as this is recognized, indeed, by the most of those who have busied themselves with working out the interesting history of this word in the usage of the Fathers.[166] Dr. W. Gass, for example,

---

sion 4, p. 160, where a number of examples are given. See also Lightfoot, on Eph. i. 10, and the Lexicons.

[164] Chap. ii. See the note of Lightfoot on the passage in his great work on " Ignatius " (II. ii. p. 950).

[165] " Historia Ecclesiastica," iv. 15; McGiffert's Translation, p. 189a.

[166] An account of the several attempts to trace the history of the word is given by Gass in the article referred to in the next note. The more important are: von Cölln in Ersch and Gruber sub. voc. *Œconomia;* H. A. Daniel in his " Tatianus der Apologet," pp. 159 *sq.;* Münscher in his " Dogmengeschichte," iii. pp. 137 *sq.;* Gass's own extended article; and Lightfoot in his posthumously published volume entitled " Notes on Epistles of St. Paul," p. 319 (on Eph. i. 10), with which should be compared his notes on Col. i. 25, Ign. "ad Eph." xviii. (II. i. p. 75), and " Martyr. Polycarp.," ii. (II. ii. p. 950). The discussion of Gass is by far the fullest, but needs the preceding ones to supply the earlier philological development, and Lightfoot's clear statement as a supplement. See also the Bishop of Lincoln's (Kaye's) " Account of the Writings of Justin Martyr," pp. 173, *sq.,* and Baur's " Dreieinigkeit," i. p. 178, note. Hagemann " Die Römische Kirche," pp. 136, 150, 167, 175, etc., as per index) constantly represents the οἰκονομία as (even in Tertullian) merely " the sum of the divine acts which have reference to the government of the world," " the sum of the ex-

after tracing the word up to Tertullian and finding it employed up to that point to express "the outward-going revelatory activity of God, whether creative and organizing or redemptive,"[167] remarks upon the sudden change that meets us in Tertullian. "It has been justly thought remarkable," he continues, "that this same expression is applied by Tertullian to the inner relations of the Godhead itself. He employs 'economy' as an indispensable organon of the Christian knowledge of God, in his controversy with Praxeas." Then, after quoting the passages in the "Against Praxeas," chaps. ii. and iii., he proceeds: "Monarchy and economy are therefore the two interests on the combination and proper balancing of which the Trinitarian conception of God depends; by the former the unity of the divine rule, by the latter the right of an immanent distinction is established, and it is only necessary that the latter principle should not be pressed so far as to do violence to the former." Without laying too much stress on so nice a point, it would seem not unnatural therefore to look upon Tertullian's predilection for the term οἰκονομία as, like his usage of the term *Trinitas*, symptomatic of his tendency to take a deeper view of the Trinitarian relation than that which has in later times come to be spoken of as "merely economical."

We derive thus from our study of Tertullian's modes of statement a rather distinct impression that there is discoverable in them an advance toward the conception of an immanent Trinity. The question becomes at once in a new degree pressing how far this advance is to be credited to Tertullian himself, and how far it represents only modes of thought and even forms of statement current in the Christianity of his

---

ternal revelations of God," "the internal distributions of the original unitary Godhead into a purely divine and a finite substance, and the division of the latter into a graded plurality of beings which make up the pleroma "— which last is the Gnostic way of expressing it.

[167] In an article on "Das patristische Wort οἰκονομία," in Hilgenfeld's *Zeitschrift für wissenschaftliche Theologie*, xvii. (1874), pp. 478 *sq.*

time, which push themselves to observation in his writings only because he chances to be dealing with themes which invite a rather fuller expression than ordinary of this side of the faith of Christians. We shall return to this question in the Third Article.

THIRD ARTICLE [168]

In the First and Second Articles it has been pointed out that there is discoverable in Tertullian's modes of statement a rather distinct advance towards the conception of an immanent Trinity. We wish now to inquire how far this advance is to be credited to Tertullian himself, and how far it represents modes of thought and forms of statement current in his time, and particularly observable in Tertullian only because he chances to be dealing with themes which invited a fuller expression than ordinary of this side of the faith of Christians.

We have already seen that there is a large traditional element in Tertullian's teaching; that even the terms, " Trinity " and " Economy," in which his doctrine of the distinctions within the Godhead is enshrined, are obviously used by him as old and well-known terms; and that he betrays no consciousness of enunciating new conceptions in his development of his doctrine, but rather writes like a man who is opposing old truth to new error. Indeed he openly asserts that this is the case. If we are to take his own point of view in the matter, we cannot hesitate to assert, then, that he has himself made no advance, but is simply enforcing the common Christian faith against the innovations of destructive heresy. Of course this common Christian faith, which he is zealous thus to enforce, is fundamentally the Rule of Faith. But it can scarcely be denied that it is more than this; Tertullian's own view clearly is that his expositions embody also the common understanding of the Rule of Faith. He is not consciously offering any novel constructions of it, or building up on his own account a higher structure upon it. No doubt he is doing his best to state the common faith clearly and forcibly, and to apply its elements tellingly in the controversy in which he was engaged; and he may certainly in so doing have clarified

[168] As originally printed in *The Princeton Theological Review,* April, 1906.

83

it, and even filled it with new significance, not to say developed from it hitherto unsuspected implications. How far, however, this can be affirmed of him can be determined only by some survey of the modes of thought and statement of his predecessors and contemporaries who have dealt with the same doctrines.

What first strikes us when we turn to the Apologists with this end in view is that most of Tertullian's modes of statement can be turned up, in one place or another, in the Apologetic literature. We say " in one place or another " advisedly, for the peculiarity of the case is that they do not all appear in the pages of a single writer, but scattered through the writings of all. Thus if the term $\tau\rho\iota\alpha s$ appears in Theophilus, it is in Tatian that the term $oi\kappa\sigma\nu o\mu\iota a$ meets us in a sense similar to that in which Tertullian uses it. If Athanagoras seems to struggle to carry back the divine relationships into eternity,[169] and Theophilus by the use of the distinction between the $\lambda\delta\gamma os$ $\epsilon\nu\delta\iota\acute{a}\theta\epsilon\tau os$ and the $\lambda\delta\gamma os$ $\pi\rho o\phi o\rho\iota\kappa\delta s$ at least seeks a basis for the distinction of God and His Logos prior to the prolation of the Logos, Justin leaves us uncertain whether he thought of the Logos as having any sort of being before the moment of His begetting. The simile by which the relation of the Logos to God is compared to the relation of the light to the sun is already found in Justin: but it is to Tatian that we must go to discover such a careful exposition of the relation of the Logos to God as the following: " He came into being by way of impartation ($\kappa\alpha\tau\grave{a}$ $\mu\epsilon\rho\iota\sigma\mu\delta\nu$) not of abscission ($\kappa\alpha\tau\grave{a}$ $\acute{a}\pi o\kappa o\pi\acute{\eta}\nu$); for what is cut off is separated from the primitive ($\tau o\hat{v}$ $\pi\rho\acute{\omega}\tau ov$), but what is imparted, receiving its share of the Economy,[170] does not make him from whom it is taken de-

[169] Cf. Bethune-Baker, " An Introduction to the Early History of Christian Doctrine," p. 129.

[170] This is a very obscure phrase: $oi\kappa\sigma\nu o\mu\iota as$ $\tau\grave{\eta}\nu$ $ai\rho\epsilon\sigma\iota\nu$ $\pi\rho o\sigma\lambda\alpha\beta\delta\nu$. Clericus declared that in his day it had never been successfully explained. Daniel (p. 164) explains: " What has arisen through participation, as one light is kindled from another, has of course part in the nature of the thing from which it is derived, and is of the same nature with it; but does not make the thing from which it is taken any poorer in this nature." Baur translates the whole passage thus: " What is cut off is separated from the substance, but what is distinguished as a portion, what by free self-determination receives the œconomy,

ficient." [171] The result is that while we could from fragments, derived this from one and that from another of the Apologists, piece together a statement of doctrine which would assimilate itself to Tertullian's, we could verify this statement from no one of the Apologists, but, on the contrary, elements of it would be more or less sharply contradicted by one or another of them. There are, in other words, hints scattered through the Apologists that men were already reaching out toward the forms of statement that meet us in Tertullian, but only in him are these hints brought together. We assent, therefore, when Harnack [172] says: "We cannot at bottom say that the Apologists possessed a doctrine of the Trinity." Only we must in this statement emphasize both the terms " at bottom " and " doctrine." There are everywhere discoverable in the Apologists suggestions of a Trinitarian mode of thought: but these are not brought together into a formulated doctrine which governed their thinking of the being of God.

The phenomena are such, in one word, as to force us to perceive in the writings of the Apologists — as has been widely recognized by students of their works — a double deposit of conceptions relative to the mode of the divine existence. There is their own philosophical construction, which is, briefly, the Logos speculation. And underlying that, there is the Christian tradition — to which they desired to be faithful and which was ever intruding into their consciousness and forcing from them acknowledgment of elements of truth which formed no part of their philosophical confession of faith. This divided character of the Apologetic mind is by no one more clearly expounded than by the late Dr. Purves in his lectures on " The Testimony of Justin Martyr to Early Christianity." Justin was, as Harnack remarks, [173] " the most Christian among

---

the plurality in the unity, causes no loss to that from which it comes." Bethune-Baker (p. 126) renders: " Receiving as its function one of administration," and explains: " The part of οἰκονομία, administration of the world, revelation."

[171] " Or. c. Gr." 8.

[172] ii. 209, note 1 at the end.

[173] ii. p. 203, note 2.

the Apologists," and this feature in his dealing with doctrine is perhaps especially marked in him: but it is shared also by all his congeners. Dr. Purves fully recognizes that Justin was, in his thinking about God, first of all the philosopher: and that his "own thought strongly *tended away from the doctrine of a Trinity* " [174] — toward a sort of ditheism which embraced a doctrine of "the consubstantiality of the Logos and the Father of all." And yet there crops up repeatedly in his writings testimony to the worship by the Christians of three divine persons. This testimony is particularly remarkable with reference to the Spirit. For "his own theology had really no place for the Spirit," and yet "Justin speaks of the Spirit as not only an object of worship but as the power of Christian life." "Thus Justin," concludes Dr. Purves,[175] "in spite of himself testifies to the threefold object of Christian worship. He even finds in Plato an adumbration of the first, second and third powers in the universe, though in doing so he misunderstands and misinterprets that philosopher. Justin's own conception is vague, or, when not vague, unscriptural in certain important points. . . . But . . . he . . . effectively testifies to the traditional faith of the Church in the Father, Son, and Spirit as the threefold object of Christian worship, and the threefold source of Christian life." What was true of Justin was true, each in his measure, of the other Apologists. "Two conceptions of Deity were struggling with each other " [176] in their minds. Dominated by their philosophical inheritance, they could only imperfectly assimilate the Christian revelation, which therefore made itself felt only in spots and patches in their teaching. What was needed that the Christian doctrine of God should come to its rights was some change in the conditions governing the conceptions of the leaders of Christian thinking by which they might measurably be freed from the philosophical bondage in which they were holden.

The appearance of juster views precisely in the expositions of Tertullian would seem thus to be connected ultimately with

[174] *Op. cit.*, p. 275.   [176] P. 145.
[175] P. 279.

a certain shifting of interest manifested in Tertullian as compared with the Apologists. The Apologists were absorbed
largely in the cosmological aspects of Christian doctrine.[177]
In Tertullian these retire into the background and the soteriological interest comes markedly forward. In their cosmological
speculations, the Apologists, for example, scarcely felt the
need of a Holy Spirit; all that they had clamantly in mind
to provide for, they conceived of as the natural function of
the Logos. Their recognition of the Holy Spirit was therefore
largely conventional and due to allegiance to the Christian
tradition. A new point of view has been attained when Tertullian, out of his soteriological interest, thinks of the Spirit profoundly as the sanctifier of men, the " vicarious power " of the
Logos for applying His redemptive work. This shifting of interest inevitably led to a new emphasis on the distinctive personalities of the three persons of the deity, and to their
separation from the world-process that justice might be done
to their perfect deity as the authors — each in his appropriate sphere — of salvation.[178] It is instructive that in his
" Apology," addressed like the chief works of the Apologists
to the heathen, Tertullian still moves, like them, largely
within the cosmological sphere: whereas in his tract, " Against
Praxeas," addressed to fellow-Christians, the soteriological
point of view comes more to its right. And it is equally instructive that among preceding writers it is in Irenæus who,

[177] General discriminations like this must, of course, not be pressed to extremes. See, e.g., Purves, *op. cit.*, p. 277. Cf. Bethune-Baker, " An Introduction
to the Early History of Christian Doctrine," p. 125.

[178] For the point of view of the text cf., e.g., Nösgen, " Geschichte der
Lehre vom heiligen Geiste," pp. 24 *sq.*: " Precisely with this Church father
[Tertullian] there begins, on the ground of Christian experience, to break
through the recognition of the inner necessity of the Holy Spirit for the nature
of the Triune God. . . . His interest in the third Person of the Trinity hangs
on the fact that the Holy Spirit leads the children of God (credentes agat).
. . . Accordingly it must not be made a reproach to him that he permits the
immanent relation statedly to shine through only as the background of the
self-revelation of the Triune One. . . . It is precisely because he does this
that he first marked out definitely the point of departure from which the
peculiarity of the Holy Spirit as God and as trinitarian Person could be really
grasped." Cf. Kahnis, p. 296.

with emphasis, eschewed philosophy and sought to build up a specifically Biblical doctrine, that we find forms of statement concerning the three persons whom Christians worshiped as the one God most nearly approaching the construction adumbrated by Tertullian. Perhaps it is not too much to say that the supplanting among Christian thinkers of the Logos speculation by a doctrine of immanent Trinity was largely mediated by the shifting of interest from the cosmological to the soteriological aspect of Christian truth, and that in Tertullian we see for the first time clearly marked the beginning of the process by which this change was wrought.

This suggestion receives notable support from a comparison of Tertullian's modes of statement with those of his contemporary Hippolytus, in his treatise, " Against Noëtus " — a treatise which, as it arose out of conditions remarkably like those which called out Tertullian's tract, " Against Praxeas," contains so much that is similar to what we find in that tract that it is hard to shake ourselves entirely free from the illusion that one borrows from the other. Hippolytus' relation as a pupil to Irenæus,[179] whose language in regard to the Trinitarian relationships approaches that of Tertullian most nearly of all previous writers, and from whom Tertullian himself frankly draws, is doubtless another factor of importance in accounting for the resemblance between the two tracts. But as we have already suggested, we are persuaded that this resemblance, so far as it is real, is mainly due to the fact that Tertullian and Hippolytus, alike heirs of the Logos-speculation, and alike determined to do justice to the deposit of truth in the Rule of Faith, were alike called upon in the new conditions of the early third century to uphold the common faith of Christendom against the subtlest form of the Monarchian attack. If this be true, nothing could hold out a better promise of enabling us to discriminate in Tertullian's statements the traditional element from his personal contribution than a comparison of them with those of Hippolytus.

The first thing that strikes us in attempting such a com-

[179] Cf., e.g., Harnack, " Chronologie," ii. pp. 213, 223.

parison is the extent of the common element in the two. We meet in Hippolytus the same terminology which we have found in Tertullian. He, too, employs the term Trinity; [180] and, as well, Tertullian's favorite term, " the Economy " [181] — although perhaps not with the same profundity of meaning; even Tertullian's phrase, " the mystery of the economy." [182] We almost feel ourselves still on Tertullian's ground when we read in Hippolytus: " For who will not say that there is one God? Yet he will not on that account deny the Economy." [183] This feeling is increased by the occurrence in Hippolytus of similar illustrations of the relations of the Logos to the primal Godhead. " But when I say *another*," he remarks, " I do not mean that there are two Gods, but that it is only as light of light, or as water from a fountain, or as a ray from the sun." [184] Even the same proof-texts are employed in the same manner. Thus the declaration in Jno. x. 30, " I and the Father are one," is treated quite in Tertullian's manner. " Understand that He did not say, ' I and the Father *am one,* but *are one.*' For the word *are* is not said of one person, but it refers to *two persons,* and one power." [185] So again, like Tertullian, Hippolytus insists strongly on the true deity of Christ and supports it after much the same fashion. He calls Him " God," [186] " the Almighty," [187] appeals just like Tertullian to Mt. xi. 27, and like Tertullian even applies to Him the great text, Rom. ix. 5, commenting: " He who is over all, God blessed, has been born; and having been made man, He is God for ever." [188] His doctrine of the Person of Christ, moreover, is indistinguishable from Tertullian's. " Let us believe, then, dear brethren," he says, " according to the tradition of the apostles, that God the Word came down from heaven, into the holy Virgin Mary, in order that, taking the flesh from her, and assuming also a human, by which I mean a rational soul, and becoming

---

[180] " Contra Noëtum," chap. 14.
[181] Chaps. 3, 4, 8, 14.
[182] Chap. 4, no fewer than three times.
[183] Chap. 3.
[184] Chap. 11.

[185] Chap. 7.
[186] Chap. 8.
[187] Chap. 6.
[188] Chap. 6.

thus all that man is with the exception of sin, he . . . was manifested as God in a body, coming forth too as a perfect man. For it was not in mere appearance or by conversion, but in truth, that He became man." [189] Underlying and sustaining all these detailed resemblances, moreover, is the great fundamental likeness between the two writers arising from their common application of the Logos speculation to the facts of the Christian tradition, and their common opposition to the Monarchian heresy.

With a little closer scrutiny, however, marked differences between the two writers begin to develop.

In the first place, we observe that Hippolytus does not very well know what to do with the Holy Spirit. He repeats the triune formula with great emphasis: "We cannot otherwise think of one God," he says, "but by believing in truth in Father and Son and Holy Spirit." "The Economy of agreement is gathered up into one God: for God is One: for He who commands is the Father, and He who obeys is the Son, and that which teaches wisdom is the Spirit." [190] "We accordingly see the Word incarnate, and through Him we know the Father, and believe in the Son and worship the Holy Ghost." [191] He manifestly desires to be led in all things by the Scriptural revelation: from no other quarter, he declares, than the oracles of God will he derive instruction in such things, and therefore as they declare to us what the Father wills us to believe, that will he believe, and as He wills the Son to be glorified, so will he glorify Him, and as He wills the Holy Spirit to be bestowed, so will he receive Him.[192] Nevertheless it is quite clear that he can hardly assimilate the Biblical doctrine of the Spirit, and when he comes to speak out his mind upon Him, he makes it apparent that he does not at all think of Him as a person. It is curious to observe, indeed, the circumlocutions he employs to avoid calling Him a person. "I shall not indeed say there are two Gods, but one; two persons, however, while the third economy is the grace of the Holy Spirit. For the Father indeed

[189] Chap. 17.   [191] Chap. 12.
[190] Chap. 14.   [192] Chap. 9.

is one, but there are two persons, because there is the Son also: and then there is the third, the Holy Spirit." [193] From a passage like this, Hippolytus' fundamental thought would seem to have been, like Justin's, a kind of ditheism, somewhat violently transformed into a tritheism under the pressure of the traditional faith.

When we look further we perceive that even this ditheism is far from pure. We observe a notable effort to avoid that clear assertion of substantial unity of the Father and Son which constitutes the very core of Tertullian's doctrine. When the declaration of our Lord in Jno. x. 30, " I and the Father are one," is quoted,[194] Hippolytus' exposition is: " It refers to two persons and one " — not substance, as Tertullian would have said, but — " *power*." And then Hippolytus calls in illustratively Jno. xvii. 22, 23, where our Lord expresses His desire that His disciples may be one, even as He and the Father are one, and asks triumphantly, " Are all [the disciples] one body in respect of substance, or is it that we become one in the power and disposition of likemindedness? " [195] " In the same manner " — thus he applies the illustration — " the Son . . . confessed that He was in the Father in power and disposition." This view of the unity of Father and Son as consisting in unity in mind and power only is consistently preserved throughout; [196] and the revelatory character of the Son is in harmony with this hung, not on His identity with God, but on His character as the *image* of God.[197] Accordingly, we discover that the Logos is not thought by Hippolytus to have been eternally with God, but is assigned an absolute beginning at a definite point of time previous to the creation of the world. Like Ter-

---

[193] Chap. 14. That the personality of the Holy Spirit is here denied is held by Meier, " Die Lehre von der Trinität," i. p. 88; Harnack, E. T. ii. p. 262, note; Nösgen, " Geschichte der Lehre vom heiligen Geiste," p. 20. Cf. also J. Sjöholm, " Hippolytus och Modalismen," Lund: 1898. On the other hand, see Döllinger, " Hippolytus and Callistus," E. T. pp. 193–194, and Hagemann, " Die Römische Kirche," pp. 268 *sq.*

[194] Chap. 7.

[195] τῇ δυνάμει καὶ τῇ διαθέσει τῆς ὁμοφρονίας ἓν γινόμεθα;

[196] E.g., chaps. 8 and 16.

[197] Chap. 7 *ad fin.*

tullian, he tells us that God subsisted from all eternity alone, having nothing contemporaneous with Himself. But he does not, like Tertullian, tell us that though thus existing alone, so far as things external to Himself are concerned, there was within Him another, His fellow, His eternal Word, a second to Him. Quite differently, he tells us that though alone, He was many — a plurality.[198] And then he goes on to explain that this means that God was never "reasonless, or wisdomless, or powerless, or counselless, but all things were in Him and He was the all."[199] In other words, it is not of a personal Logos as the eternal Companion that Hippolytus is thinking, but of the ideal world, the κόσμος νοητός, as constituting an eternal "plurality" of God. Accordingly when in another place[200] he is again describing the origin of the Logos, the eternal existence which he attributes to Him is not an existence as a personal Logos, but only as the "indwelling rationality of the universe." The Logos thus for Hippolytus exists from all eternity only ideally. From this ideal existence He came into real existence for the first time when God, intending to create the world, begat Him "as the Author and Fellow-Counsellor and Framer of the things that are in formation,"[201] and "thus," says Hippolytus,[202] "there appeared another beside Him" — thus and then only. Here it must be remarked is a doctrine of the absolute origination of the Logos by the will of the Father, so that the Logos appears distinctly as a creature of the Father's will.[203]

---

[198] Chap. 10, ad init., αὐτὸς δὲ μόνος ὢν πολὺς ἦν.

[199] οὔτε γὰρ ἄλογος, οὔτε ἄσοφος, οὔτε ἀδύνατος, οὔτε ἀβούλευτος ἦν, πάντα δὲ ἦν ἐν αὐτῷ, αὐτὸς δὲ ἦν τὸ πᾶν.

[200] "Philosophumena," x. 33 (xxix.) — ἐνδιάθετος τοῦ παντός λογισμός.

[201] "Contra Noëtum," chap. 10 — ἀρχηγὸν καὶ σύμβουλον καὶ ἐργάτην.

[202] Chap. 11.

[203] On the extreme emphasis put by Hippolytus on the divine will, cf. Hagemann, "Die Römische Kirche," p. 197: "No one of the earliest representatives of Christian science lays such stress on the will of God as Hippolytus. With great emphasis, often several times in succession in almost identical phrases, he repeats, when speaking of the origin of the Logos or of creation in general, the formula in which he expresses his proposition that the whole revelation of God ad extra is grounded in His will, that He can create or not create,

Nor does Hippolytus in the least shrink from this conception. When explaining that Adam was made a man with the characteristics and limitations of a man, not by inadvertence or because of any limitation of power on God's part, but by design, he says: " The Creator did not wish to make him a God and failed in His aim; nor an angel — be not deceived — but a man. For if He had wished to make thee a God He could have done so: *you have the example of the Logos.*" [204] To Hippolytus, therefore, the Logos is distinctly a created God, whom God made a God because, shortly, He chose to do so. He has indeed preëminence above all other creatures, not only because He was made a God and they were not, but also because He alone of creatures was made by God Himself while all other creatures were made by Him the Logos; and because they all were made out of nothing, while " Him alone God produced from existing things (ἐξ ὄντων)," and, as God alone existed, that means from His own substance.[205] The Logos is therefore only in this sense of the substance of God, that He was framed

---

retain the Logos in Himself or permit Him to proceed out, as He wills. He even speaks once of the Logos himself as a product of the divine will (chap. 13; cf. chaps. 8, 9, 10, 11)." For the fundamental significance of this see above, p. 32 note [45], and the references there given. Natural as this stress on the voluntariness of the divine action, even in the prolation of the Logos, was on the lips of the Apologists in protest against the natural processes of emanation taught by the Gnostics, there underlay it in its application to the prolation of the Logos a view of the relation of the Logos to the Father which scarcely did justice to the real state of the case, and was near to a conception of the Logos as absolutely originating in this act of the divine will, and hence as of creaturely character. This point of view was that of some of the Apologists, and was revived by the Arians. In opposition to it the Nicene Fathers (Athanasius, " Or. cont. Ar.," III. xxx.; " De Decret. Nic. Syn."; Ambrose, " De Fide Chr.," iv. 9) learned to go behind the will of God in the generation of the Logos. There is a sense, of course, in which, as Döllinger points out (" Hippolytus and Callistus," E. T. p. 198), God as voluntary subject does all He does voluntarily; but after all said and done as the Arian contention that the Son owed His being to an act of will on the part of the Father was meant to imply that the Son was a creature, this mode of speech is Arian in tendency and it is best frankly to say — taking will in its natural sense — that the act of eternal generation is not an act of will but a necessary movement in the divine being. (Cf. Dorner, *op. cit.,* Div. I. vol. ii. p. 460.)

[204] " Philosophumena," x. 33. (xxix.).
[205] *Ibid.*

out of the divine substance; although what the process was
by which God thus " begat Him as He willed," Hippolytus declines to inquire as too mysterious for human investigation.[206]
He has no hesitation, however, in speaking of him as a creature
who came into existence at a definite time, is only what His
maker willed, and is God and possessor of the power of God
and therefore almighty only by gift and not by nature.[207]

It is not necessary to pursue this inquiry further. Enough
has been brought out to show that Hippolytus' Trinity consisted in a transcendent God who produced at a definite point
of time a secondary divinity called the Logos, to whom He
subjected all things; and along with these a third something
not very definitely conceived, called by the Church the Holy
Spirit. Here is not one God in three persons; here is rather one
God producing a universe by steps and stages, to the higher of
which divinity is assigned. In other words, we see in Hippolytus a clear and emphatic testimony indeed to a rich deposit of
Christian faith, but overlying and dominating it a personal
interpretation of it which reproduces all the worst defects of
the Logos speculation. In this he forms, despite the surface resemblance of his discussion to Tertullian's, a glaring contrast
with that writer. In Tertullian the fundamental faith of the
Church comes to its rights and is permitted to dominate the
Logos speculation. And it is just in this that his superiority as
a theologian to Hippolytus is exhibited. Hippolytus' thought
remains in all essential respects bound within the limits of the
Logos speculation. Tertullian's has become in all essential respects a logical development of the Church's fundamental
faith. It is therefore that it is he and not Hippolytus who became the Father of the doctrine of an immanent Trinity.

A comparison of Novatian's treatise " On the Trinity " [208]

---

[206] " Contra Noëtum," chap. 16.

[207] Cf. also chap. 6, where Christ is said to have been " appointed almighty
by the Father."

[208] There seems no real reason for doubting the authorship of this book
by Novatian, though Hagemann (pp. 371 sq.) doubts it, and Quarry even ascribes it to Hippolytus. Cf. Harnack, " Chronologie," ii. pp. 396 sq., note 1, and
p. 400, note 2. Harnack dates it c. 240 (p. 399).

will still further strengthen our respect for Tertullian. Novatian seems to have been a diligent student of Tertullian; [209] it
might be presumed, therefore, that in this treatise he has
drawn upon the master whom he honored by his imitation but
never names. Despite, however, Jerome's declaration that the
book is only " a kind of epitome " [210] of Tertullian's work, and
the repetition of this judgment by a whole series of subsequent
writers,[211] we find ourselves doubting whether the presumed
fact is supported by the treatise itself. Novatian goes his own
way, and it is questionable whether there is much common to
his treatise and Tertullian's tract " Against Praxeas," which
may not be best accounted for on the ground of the traditional
elements of belief underlying both.[212] No doubt Novatian must
be supposed to have known Tertullian's treatise and his own
thinking may have been affected by its teaching. But there
seems little or no evidence that he has drawn directly upon it
for his own work. Novatian's tract, unlike those of Tertullian
and Hippolytus, is not in the first instance a piece of polemics
with only incidental positive elements; but is primarily a constructive treatise and only incidentally polemic; moreover, its
polemic edge is turned not solely against Monarchianism, but
equally against tritheism. In point of form it is an exposition
of the Rule of Truth,[213] which requires us to believe in God the

---

[209] Cf. Harnack in the *Sitzungsberichte der königlich preussischen Akademie der Wissenschaften zu Berlin,* 1895, ii. p. 562, and " Chronologie," ii. pp.
399–400.

[210] " De virr. inlust.," chap. 70.

[211] E.g., Loof's " Leitfaden zum Studium der Dogmengeschichte," p. 105:
" There is scarcely a thought that cannot be pointed out in Tertullian." But
Harnack, " Chronologie," ii. pp. 399–400, recognizes that in any event Jerome's
statement is overdrawn, though he finds a real connection between the two
books.

[212] We have the support in this, at least, of Hagemann, " Die Römische
Kirche," p. 379.

[213] Novatian's own phrase is always Rule of Truth, although the title of
his treatise has Rule of Faith, whence Kunze infers that the title is not from
his own hand (" Glaubensregel, Heilige Schrift und Taufbekenntnis," pp.
5–6). Novatian, remarks Kunze (p. 178), makes use of the Roman Baptismal
Creed (Apostolicum), but evidently " only the Trinitarian formula stood to
him as a formula, and we may even say that to him the notion of *regula*

Father and Lord Omnipotent, in the Son of God, Christ Jesus, the Lord our God, and in the Holy Spirit, once promised to the Church; and its disposition follows these three fundamental elements of the faith (chaps. i.–viii.; ix.–xxviii.; xxix.; with a conclusion, xxx.-xxxi.). To its expository task it gives itself with a conscious effort to avoid wandering off into the refutation of heresies, farther than may be necessary to subserve the purpose in view. " I could set forth the treatment of this subject," he remarks on one occasion when a heresy is engaging his attention, " by all the heavenly Scriptures . . . except that I have not so much undertaken to speak against this special form of heresy as to expound the Rule of Truth concerning the person of Christ." [214]

The positive exposition Novatian has set himself to give is very richly worked out and quite justifies Jerome's admiration of the book. In particular the exegetical demonstration of the divinity of Christ which it offers is very thorough and noble and can scarcely find its superior in ancient literature. Alongside of its zeal for the deity of Christ, its zeal for the unity of God burns warmly, and its Trinitarian doctrine seems to be dominated by the interaction of these two factors. The key to the whole is revealed by Novatian himself when he declares our chief duty to be to contend earnestly that Christ is God, but in such a way as not to militate against the Scriptural *fundamentum* that there is but one God.[215] It is indeed tritheism rather than Monarchianism which causes Novatian the deepest anxiety and though he argues stoutly against the latter, it is his opposition to the former which most decisively determines his own forms of statement. Thus, although he exhibits little vital interest in the Logos speculation for its own sake, and writes rather from the standpoint of the traditional

---

veritatis belonged only to it and not to the 'Apostles' Creed'; and to the 'Apostles' Creed' only so far as it is built up upon the Trinitarian formula." This is, however, in effect the essential conception of all the early Fathers: that is to say, the Apostles' Creed to them is not the Rule of Faith, but only a commodious summary of it.

[214] Chap. xxi.
[215] Chap. xxx. near the beginning.

faith, he is thrown back strongly upon the linear development of the Trinity which is the product of the Logos speculation.[216] Laboring to secure the unity of God at all hazards, he feels that he can do this only by emphasizing the origination of the Son; and not attaining to a clear grasp of the conception of eternal generation, he is led to protect the origination of the Son by emphasizing His posteriority to the Father.[217] Amid these ideas, it must be confessed, he somewhat flounders. He is earnestly desirous of doing full justice to the deity of Christ, and he feels that in order to do so he must assimilate Him to the eternal God. But he does not know quite how to do this consistently with a fitting proclamation of the unity of God. Accordingly he tells us, on the one hand, that the Son " was always in the Father " because the " Father was always Father ": but he at once turns to argue, on the other hand, that the Father must in some sense precede the Son, because it is " necessary that He who knows no beginning must precede Him that has a beginning "; and to insist over and over again that there would be two Gods, if there were two who had not been begotten, or two who were without beginning, or two who were self-existent. The doctrine of " eternal generation " is here struggling in the womb of thought: we do not think it quite comes to the birth.

And thus Novatian seems to us to fall back essentially upon the Logos construction, but on the Logos construction so far purified that it is on the point of melting into Nicene orthodoxy. In order to protect the unity of God, in other words, he was led to emphasize not the sameness of the Son and Spirit with God the Father, as Tertullian did with his developed doctrine of the numerical unity of substance, but their difference from Him. The nerve of Novatian's Trinitarianism thus becomes his strong subordinationism. Though he knows and emphasizes the difference between creation and procession,[218] and urges as few others have urged the true divinity of Christ, yet our Lord's deity is to Him after all only a secondary deity. He

216 See above, pp. 34-36.   218 Cf. Harnack, ii. p. 259, note 3.
217 Chap. xxxi.

had a beginning; He was not self-originated; He was the product of His Father's will; He exists but to minister to that will; though He be God, He is not God of Himself, but only because "He was begotten for this special result, that He should be God"; and though He is Lord, He is Lord only because the Father so willed and only to the extent the Father willed.[219] When He says "I and the Father are one," therefore, "He referred to the agreement, and to the identity of judgment, and to the loving association itself, as, reasonably, the Father and Son are one in agreement and love and affection."[220] Tertullian would here have referred to sameness of substance: even Hippolytus would have referred to sameness of power: Novatian's zeal for the unity of God holds him back, and though he believes the Son to be consubstantial with the Father in the sense that as the son of a man is a man so the Son of God is God,[221] yet he must believe also that He is second to the Father in the strongest sense of that word. This subordination of the Son to the Father is repeated, in his view, in the similar subordination of the Spirit to the Son. So clear is it that, with all his good intentions and upward strivings, Novatian remains, in his theoretical construction of the relationships of the three persons he recognized as God, under the Logos speculation and fails to attain the higher standpoint reached by Tertullian. Revolting from the tritheism of Hippolytus, he yet does not know any other way to secure the unity of God but Hippolytus' way — that is, by so sharply emphasizing the subordination of the two objects of Christian worship additional to God the Father as to exalt the Father into the sole Self-Existent, Beginningless, Invisible, Infinite, Immortal, and Eternal One. That he guards this subordination better than Hippolytus is a matter of degree and does not erect a difference of kind between them. Novatian

[219] All these phrases are from chap. xxxi.

[220] Chap. xxvii.

[221] Cf. Bull, iii. 17, E. T. pp. 541 *sq.*, and see Nösgen, p. 26, note 2. Novatian is treated by Bull, especially pp. 131, 297, 479, 528, 582, 597, 607, E. T. The best that can be said for him is there said.

marks, no doubt, the highest level of Trinitarian doctrine attainable along the pathway of subordinationism. That this level is lower than the level attained by Tertullian is only evidence that Tertullian's organizing principle had become no longer subordinationism but equalization. It is, in other words, Tertullian's formula of numerical sameness of essence with distinction of persons, not the formula of the Logos speculation in which the stress was laid on subordinationism,[222] that had in it the promise and potency of the better things to come.

From such comparisons as these we obtain a notion of the nature of the step toward the formulation of the Church's ingrained faith in an immanent Trinity which was made by Tertullian. The greatness of this step is fairly estimable from the fact that Tertullian's statements will satisfy all the points on which Bishop Bull laid stress in his famous effort to show " the consent of primitive antiquity with the fathers of the Council of Nice." These points he sums up in four:[223] " first, that Christ our Lord in His higher nature existed before [His birth of] the most blessed Virgin Mary, and, further, before the creation of the world, and that through Him all things were made; secondly, that in that very nature He is of one substance with God the Father, that is [that] He is not of any created and mutable essence, but of a nature entirely the same with the Father, and consequently very God; thirdly, which is a consequence of this, that He is co-eternal with God the Father, that is, a Divine Person, co-existing with the Father from everlasting; lastly, that He Himself is, nevertheless, subordinate to God the Father, as to His Author and Principle." Tertullian teaches, in other

---

[222] Speaking of the Logos doctrine, Prof. L. L. Paine says truly: " In this view the subordination element is vital, and it became the governing note of the whole Logos-school " (" Evolution of Trinitarianism," p. 31). Where Prof. Paine is wrong is in not perceiving how deeply this subordinationism was contrary to the fundamentals of the Christian faith: and by this failure he is led to do grave injustice alike to Athanasianism — in which he discerns more subordinationism than really existed in it — and to Augustinianism — whose reproach to him is that it is determined to be rid of subordinationism. Prof. Paine, in other words, misconceives both the historical development and its meaning.

[223] Bull, Defensio Fidei Nicaenæ," Conclusion, *ad init.*, E. T. p. 655.

words, the prëexistence, consubstantiality, eternity, and subordination of the Son, and likewise of the Spirit. What, then,
lacks he yet of Nicene orthodoxy? It is this question which
Bishop Bull presses; but, as he presses it, he only makes us
aware that Nicene orthodoxy cannot quite be summed up in
these four propositions. Meeting these four tests Tertullian yet
falls short of Nicene orthodoxy, retaining still too great a
leaven of the Logos speculation. But that he is able to meet
Bull's tests, which none of his predecessors or contemporaries
can meet, indicates the greatness of the step he marks toward
the Nicene orthodoxy.

That we may fairly call Tertullian the father of the Nicene
theology there seems to be wanting nothing but some clear
historical connection between his work and that of the Nicene
fathers. It is over-exigent no doubt to demand an external
proof of connection. The silent influence of Tertullian's discussion supplemented by that of Novatian [224] supplies a sufficient
nexus. But we naturally desire to trace in some overt manifestations the working of this influence. A step toward providing this is afforded by the episode of the " two Dionysii," in
which the Roman Dionysius out of his Western Trinitarian
consciousness corrects and instructs his less well-informed
Alexandrian brother, who had permitted himself to speak of
our Lord after a fashion which betrayed the most unformed
conceptions of the relations of the distinctions in the Godhead.
The letter of Dionysius of Rome (259–269 A.D.) *Against the
Sabellians,* a considerable portion of which has been preserved
by Athanasius in his " Letter in Defense of the Nicene Definition," [225] is very properly appealed to by Athanasius as an
instance of Niceneism before Nice. It seems clearly to be dependent on Tertullian, though, as Harnack puts it, " no single
passage in it can be pointed out which is simply transcribed
from Tertullian, but Dionysius has, rather in opposition to the

---

[224] On the great influence of Novatian's treatise see Bethune-Baker, (" An
Introduction to the Early History of Christian Doctrine," p. 191.

[225] Chap. vi. or §§ 26–27 (" Nicene and Post-Nicene Fathers," Second
Series, iv. pp. 167–168).

formula of Dionysius of Alexandria, developed further in the direction of orthodoxy Tertullian's Trinitarian doctrine." [226] Quite in the Roman manner [227] Dionysius turned the edge of his polemic as much against tritheism as against Monarchianism, and thus, by insisting on " the gathering up of the Divine Triad into a summit," preserved the unity of the common essence and so helped forward to the formulation of the *homoousios.* Similarly by his insistence that the Son was no " creature " ($\pi o \iota \eta \mu a$) and was not "made " ($\gamma \epsilon \gamma o \nu \epsilon \nu a \iota$) but "begotten " ($\gamma \epsilon \gamma \epsilon \nu \nu \eta \sigma \theta a \iota$), he laid the foundations of the Nicene formula of " begotten, not made," which also thus goes back through him to Tertullian. Nothing could be more instructive than the emergence into the light of history of this instance in the latter half of the third century of the greater readiness of the West to deal with the Trinitarian problem than the East.

We need seek no other historical link, however, between Western orthodoxy and the East than that provided by " the great Hosius " himself, who was the channel by means of which the formulas beaten out in the West, primarily by Tertullian, were impressed on the East in the Nicene symbol. We are credibly told by Socrates [228] that Hosius disputed in Alexandria on " substance " ($o \upsilon \sigma \iota a$) and " person " ($\upsilon \pi \delta \sigma \tau a \sigma \iota s$) prior to the Nicene Council; and his dominant influence with the emperor as well as the prominent place he occupied in the Council itself afford sufficient account of the successful issue of that Council in establishing Tertullian's formula of " one substance and three persons " — the $\delta \mu o o \upsilon \sigma \iota o s$ in effect — as the faith of the whole Church. [229] If despite Athanasius' hint that it

[226] *Sitzungsberichte der königlich preussischen Akademie der Wissenschaften zu Berlin,* 1895, ii. p. 563.

[227] Callistus, Novatian, Dionysius.

[228] " Historia," III. vii.

[229] Cf. Harnack, iv. pp. 5, 11 and 50, 121; and *Sitzungsberichte der königlich preussischen Akademie der Wissenschaften zu Berlin,* 1895, ii. p. 564, especially the former references where the matter is argued. See also Gams, " Kirchengeschichte von Spanien," II. i. p. 140. When Socrates (III. vii.) tells us that on Hosius' visit to Alexandria in 324 $\tau \eta \nu$ $\pi \epsilon \rho \iota$ $o \upsilon \sigma \iota a s$ $\kappa a \iota$ $\upsilon \pi o \sigma \tau a \sigma \epsilon \omega s$ $\pi \epsilon \pi o \iota \eta \tau a \iota$ $\zeta \eta \tau \eta \sigma \iota \nu$, we are tempted to see not only a priming of the Alexandrians

was Hosius who " set forth the Nicene Faith," [230] we cannot quite say that Hosius was the " draftsman " of the Nicene Creed,[231] since that Creed was formally framed by a series of amendments out of a formula offered by Eusebius of Cæsarea, yet what is implied in such a statement is essentially true. Hosius was the effective author of the Nicene Creed, and that is as much as to say that in its fundamental assertions that Creed is a Western formulary,[232] and its roots are set in the

for what was to come, by this Westerner, the heir of the Western Trinitarianism, but in the choice of the term " hypostasis " for " person " a reflection of Tertullian's *substantiva res* — especially as we are told that Hosius was on this occasion especially zealous in guarding against Sabellian tendencies. We must not, however, push the details of Socrates' report too far.

[230] " History of the Arians," chap. 42.

[231] Bethune-Baker, " The Meaning of Homoousios in the ' Constantinopolitan ' Creed," in " Texts and Studies," J. A. Robinson, ed., vii. 1, p. 11, note: " That Hosius — for many years previously the most influential bishop in the West, the intimate friend and trusted adviser in ecclesiastical matters of Constantine — was the real ' draftsman ' of the Creed seems certain." Loofs, in Herzog, " Realencyklopädie für protestantische Theologie und Kirche,³ " viii. p. 378: " That Hosius, the confidant of the emperor, was of great influence here [at the Synod of Nice] lay in the nature of the circumstances, . . . and the statement of Athanasius that ' he set forth (ἐξέθετο) the faith at Nice ' (" History of the Arians," § 42), although not exact in its affirmation — for the Nicænum was framed by amendments out of a draft offered by Eusebius of Cæsarea — nevertheless is in essence true." Zahn, " Marcellus von Ancyra," p. 23: " Hosius from the beginning of the Arian controversies exerted the most decisive influence on the course of external events, *i.e.*, on the Emperor. It was due to him that Constantine came forward so positively for the ὁμοούσιος, that Eusebius could speak as if the Emperor were the actual originator of that term. Hosius is said to have raised the question concerning οὐσία and ὑπόστασις on the occasion of his visit to Alexandria, and Athanasius makes his enemies declare of him, ' It was he that set forth the faith at Nice ' (" History of the Arians," § 42) — by which he assigns him not merely a share in the development of the Nicene faith, as Hefele supposes (i. p. 280), but a controlling influence in the debates on the faith which took place at Nice, and that means nothing less than in the choice of the formula." Zahn adds that Socrates' statement of what happened in Alexandria finds support in the independent report of Philostorgius (i. 7), that Alexander had come to an understanding with Hosius as to the ὁμοούσιος before the Synod. It seems clear, in any event, that antiquity thought of Hosius as bearing the prime responsibility for the homoousios in the Nicene Creed.

[232] Loofs, in Herzog, " Realencyklopädie für protestantische Theologie und Kirche,³ " ii. p. 15, line 16: " The Nicænum became what it is under Western

teaching of Tertullian. It was thus given to Tertullian to mark out the pathway in which the Church has subsequently walked and to enunciate the germinal formulas by means of which the Arians were ultimately overcome.

It would be wrong, of course, to derive from these facts, striking as they are, the impression that Tertullian's influence was the only important force operative in the Church for the formation of the doctrine of the Trinity. It would be truer to see in Tertullian and in his definitions only one manifestation of a universally working tendency making steadily toward this end. Wherever the Rule of Faith, which was rooted in the formula of the baptismal commission, formed the fundamental basis of Christian belief, and wherever the data supplied by this Rule of Faith were interpreted in the forms of the Logos speculation, there was constantly in progress a strenuous effort to attain clarity as to the relations of the distinctions in the Name designated by the terms Father, Son, and Holy Ghost. And this is as much as to say that every thinking man in the Church was engaged with all the powers of construction granted to him in working out this problem. Even the Monarchians themselves, to whom in the providence of God it was given to keep poignantly before the eyes of men the items of the faith which were likely to be neglected by the Logos speculation, were yet apt to express themselves more or less in its terms.[233] Accord-

---

influences"; ii. p. 14, line 53: "The positive declarations of the symbol can be historically understood only when we remember that the emperor was a Westerner and . . . was directed by the advice of Western counsellors, especially Hosius"; iv. pp. 45–46: "Only the influence of the West — Constantine (although he understood Greek) had Western counsellors — explains the acts of the Synod of Nice: the characteristic terminology of the Nicænum . . . fits, in its entirety, only Western conceptions."

[233] The same is true also of the Montanists — to whom the function was committed of emphasizing the doctrine of the Spirit in the Church — if we can judge by the example and trust the testimony of Tertullian. Harnack (E. T. iv. pp. 108 *sq.*) is right in assigning to them an important place in the development of the doctrine of the Spirit: he is wrong in the specific function assigned them in this development. If we can judge by the example of Tertullian, the

ingly from the very beginning Christian literature is filled with adumbrations of what was to come. Already in Athenagoras Tertullian's doctrine of eternal pre-prolate distinctions in the Godhead almost came to birth; already in Theophilus Origen's doctrine of eternal generation seemed on the verge of conception. Least of all did the great Alexandrian divines wait for Tertullian's initiative. Origen, for example, his younger contemporary, and at once the calmest and profoundest thinker granted to the Church in the Ante-Nicene age, went his own independent way toward the same great goal. Only, Origen sought the solution of the problem not with Tertullian by separating the Logos from the cosmic processes and thereby carrying the distinctions in the Godhead, freed from all connection with activities *ad extra,* back into the mysteries of the innermost modes of the divine existence, but by pushing the cosmic processes themselves, along with the Logos, back into, if not the immanent, at least the eternal modes of the divine activity. Thus he gave the Church in full formulation the doctrine of the eternal generation of the Son of God, indeed, but along with it also the doctrine of eternal creation: and by his failure to separate the Son from the world, with all that was, or seemed to be, involved in that, he missed becoming the father of the Christian doctrine of the Trinity by becoming instead — well or ill understood, but at least not unnaturally — the father of Arianism. It was not along this pathway that the Church doctrine of the Trinity was to be attained, but rather along that beaten out by the feet of Tertullian.[234] And this, simply because the Church doctrine of the Trinity could not come to its rights within the limits of the Logos specula-

---

effect of their movement was to elevate and deepen the conception of the Spirit and His work.

[234] Harnack (E. T. iv. p. 110), speaking of the development of the doctrine of the Spirit, although he recognizes that in his doctrine of the pretemporal *processio* of the Spirit Origen is in advance of Tertullian, for Tertullian does not teach this *explicitly* (see above, pp. 70–71), yet remarks that " by the ' unius substantiæ,' which he regards as true of the Spirit also, Tertullian comes nearer the views which finally prevailed in the Fourth Century."

tion, and Origen's construction preserved the essential elements of the Logos speculation while Tertullian's prepared the way for transcending it.

To put the matter into somewhat abstract form, the immanent movement of Christian thought, we conceive, took some such course as the following. The Logos speculation laid its stress on the gradations of deity manifested in the Logos and the Spirit, and just on that account did less than justice to the Church's immanent faith in which the Father, Son, and Holy Ghost appeared as equal sharers in the Name. That justice might be done to the immanent faith of the Church, therefore, it was essential that the stress should be shifted from gradations of deity to the equality of the persons of the Godhead. This correction carried with it the confession not merely of the eternity of these persons, but also their unchangeableness, since not only eternity but also unchangeableness is an essential attribute of deity, and must belong to each person of the Godhead if these persons are to be seriously conceived to be equal. That justice might be done to these conceptions, it obviously was not enough, then, that a basis for the prolations should be discovered in the eternal existence form of God, nor indeed merely that personal distinctions underlying these prolations should be carried back into eternity, nor merely that the prolations themselves should be pushed back into eternity. In the last case the eternal prolates must further be conceived as in no sense inferior to the unprolate deity itself, sharers in all its most intimate attributes — not only in its eternity and unchangeableness, therefore, but also in its exaltation, or in the speech of the time, its " invisibility," including self-existence itself. But so to conceive them involved, of course, the evisceration of the entire prolation speculation of its purpose and value — as may be readily perceived by reading in conjunction the chapters of Tertullian (who is still so far under the control of the Logos speculation) in which he argues that " invisibility " is the peculiarity of the Father in distinction from the Son, the very characteristic of the Son being His " visibility," [235] and

[235] " Against Praxeas," chaps. xiv.-xvi.

the discussion of Augustine [236] in which he solidly argues that
the Son and Spirit are, because equally God with the Father,
also equally " invisible " with the Father.[237] The orthodox doctrine of the Trinity could not become complete, in other words,
until, under the pressure of the demand of the Christian consciousness for adequate recognition of the true and complete

[236] " De Trinitate," ii.

[237] There is, of course, a stream of better teaching running through the
very fathers who denied " invisibility " to the prolate Logos in the interests of
the Logos speculation. The passage in Ignatius, " Ad Ephes." (end of chap. iii.)
sets the norm of this better mode of speech. See also Melito, *Frag.*, § 13 (Otto,
" Corpus Apologetarum Christianorum," ix. p. 419), and Tertullian himself
who, despite his elaborate distinction of " the Father from the Son by this
characteristic, that the Son is visible, the Father invisible," nevertheless, " in
the very same book and chapter " — viz., the fourteenth chapter of the tract
" Against Praxeas," remarks " that the Son also, considered in Himself, is invisible " (Bull, IV. iii. 9, E. T. pp. 609 *sq.*). But the doctrine of the like invisibility of the Son with the Father came to its rights only with Augustine. On the
whole subject of the patristic ideas of the " visibility " of the Logos and the
" invisibility " of God as such, the discussions — which certainly involve no
little special pleading — of Bull, Book iv. chap. iii., are well worth consulting. To
the general student of doctrine these discussions of Bull have an additional interest, inasmuch as — although it doubtless would have shocked him to have
had it suggested to him — his defense of the subordinationism of the fathers on
the ground that they conceived it due not to any difference between the Father
and Son in essence or attributes but to an " economy," is equivalent to attributing to the fathers and adopting for himself the essential elements of what
is known in the history of doctrine as the " Covenant Theology " — a theology
that was being taught by many Reformed theologians in Bull's day. When
Bull says of the fathers (IV. iii. 12, E. T. ii. p. 615): " They by no means
meant to deny that the Son of God, equally with the Father, is in His own
nature immeasurable and invisible; but merely intimated this, that all such
appearances of God, and also the incarnation itself, had reference to the
economy which the Son of God undertook " — he has only in other words
enunciated the Covenant idea. When he adds: " Which economy is by no
means suited to the Father, inasmuch as He had not His origin from any beginning, and is indebted for His authorship to none " — apart from his unwonted phraseology, he does not necessarily go beyond the Covenant theologians, who were quick to contend that the terms of " the Covenant " are
themselves grounded in the intrinsic relations of the three Persons. These,
they taught, are such as made it proper and fit that each person should assume
the precise functions He did assume — as, in a word, made it alone suitable
that it should be the Son and Spirit who should be " sent " and not the Father,
and the like. The alternatives, in a word, would appear to be either an Arianiz-
ing subordinationism or the Covenant theology: all other constructions are
half views and inherently unstable.

deity of the Son and Spirit, the whole conception of prolations of deity for specific functions had been superseded by a doctrine of eternally persisting personal distinctions in the Godhead itself. The way was prepared for this historically, no doubt, in large measure, by pushing the idea of prolation back into eternity, as Origen did, where it took the form of a doctrine of eternal generation and procession, and in so doing lost its primary significance and grew nigh to vanishing away — for what is the value of an essential, eternal, and unchangeable prolation of deity which, just because essential, eternal, and unchangeable, can have no inherent relation to activities *ad extra?* But the real goal was attained only when the whole idea of prolation, thus rendered useless and meaningless, had fallen away, and the Logos speculation gave place to something better. And it was Tertullian's definitions, not Origen's speculations, which prepared the way for the attainment of this goal. So that it was not Origen but Tertullian who become the real father of the Christian doctrine of the Trinity.

It is, of course, quite possible to exaggerate the measure in which this revolution of thought is traceable in the pages of Tertullian. It is first discernible in its completeness in the expositions of Augustine two centuries later. But it seems sufficiently clear that the beginnings of the line of development which ended in Augustine are perceptible in Tertullian.[238] Their mark is his insistence on the equality of the Son and Spirit with the Father, an insistence in which he fairly enunciated the great conception afterward embodied in the term *homoousios.* Tertullian, however, still lived and moved and had his being under the spell of the Logos speculation; he did not even perceive, as did Origen, that the notion of prolations before time must give way to the higher conception of eternal generation and procession — much less that even this latter

[238] Even Dorner, who does not perceive that Tertullian had in principle separated the Divine Persons as such from the world-process, yet admits that in his " conception of the Three Persons as inwardly connected (as *consertos, cohærentes*)" Tertullian's view " includes a speculative element, to which the later doctrine of the Church was long in attaining " (" Doctrine of the Person of Christ," Div. I. vol. ii. pp. 76–77).

conception is of doubtful utility. Athanasius himself, indeed, did not perceive this last — and therefore the Nicene doctrine of the Trinity, worked out under his inspiration, still preserves these shells of outlived speculation, the kernel of which has withered away.[239] The phraseology in which they are embodied keeps its place even in the forms of statement of Augustine. The hold which the Logos speculation had on the minds of men is in nothing made more manifest than in such persistence of its forms in subsequent thought, after they had lost all their meaning. In very truth the Logos speculation provided the common ground on which the whole world of fourth century Christian thought still stood; and Arian differed from Athanasian largely only as the left wing differs from the right wing of the same fundamental type of thinking.[240] The merit of Tertullian is that his definitions, though still adjusted to the forms of the Logos speculation, had in them the potency of a better construction and were sure sooner or later to burst the

[239] Cf. the very judicious remarks of Dorner ("Doctrine of the Person of Christ," Div. I. vol. ii. pp. 327 *sq.*) on the survivals in the Nicene construction; see also pp. 184, 203–204, 491.

[240] Cf. Hagemann, p. 134: "When the origin of the Son out of the essence of God is placed in immediate connection with the creation of the world, there is needed in the way of great logical acuteness only a single unimportant step to set the Son in the sense of an Arius alongside of the world, as creature and Creator. No doubt Origen had guarded against this by ascribing not to the Son only but to the world as well an eternal origin: but the latter necessarily fell away as an open contradiction to the Church, and so nothing remained except either to join the Son so essentially with the Father that now the idea of His deity would come to its full rights and He should be recognized as in His Being wholly independent of the origin of the world, by which there would necessarily be raised again the problem of the unity of essence of the Father and the Son; or else so to connect Him with the temporal origin of the world that He should fall thereby out of the circle of the divine life and be conceived as a kind of created God in Plato's sense, as an Under-God by the side of or rather beneath the Father, who would embrace the whole divine world in Himself, the one God over all. Already in the case of Dionysius of Alexandria we have noted in *theory* a tendency to this latter development, even though his faith-consciousness remained free from this evil. In the case of Arius the theory, however, obtained a decisive victory over the faith. . . ." In this passage, we conceive, the essential logical relations of Orthodoxy and Arianism to their common basis in the Logos speculation are lucidly set forth. Cf. Dorner, as cited, pp. 267–280, and pp. 454–455.

shell in which they were artificially confined. In his recognition of the eternity of the personal distinctions in the Godhead apart from all questions of prolation, and in the emphasis he laid upon the equal deity of these persons, he planted fruitful seed which could not fail of a subsequent growth. Men might still cling to the old forms and seek merely to match the downward development which emphasized the distinction of the prolations from the fontal deity until it had degraded them into temporal creatures of the divine will, by emphasizing for themselves rather their eternity and their equality with God.[241] But by this very movement upward it was inevitable that the very idea of prolation, which was the core of the Logos speculation, should lose its significance and be pushed first out of notice and then out of belief — until the whole conception of a linear trinity should disappear and there should emerge the completed Trinitarianism of an Augustine, to whom the persons of the Trinity are not subordinate one to another but coordinate sharers of the one divine essence.

It is, of course, not the close of this process of thought that we see in Tertullian, but its beginning. But in him already appears the pregnant emphasis on the equality rather than the graded subordination of the personal distinctions in the Godhead, by the logical inworking of which the whole change in due time came about. So far as we can now learn it was he first, therefore, who, determined to give due recognition to the elements of the Church's faith embodied in the Rule of Faith, pointed out the road over which it was necessary to travel in order to do justice to the Biblical data. Say that he was in this but the voice of the general Christian consciousness. It remains that it was left to him first to give effective voice to the Christian consciousness, and that it was only by following out the lines laid down by him to their logical conclusion that the great achievement of formulating to thought the doctrine of the triune God was at length accomplished.

[241] Cf. Dorner, as cited, p. 328.

II

AUGUSTINE

AUGUSTINE [1]

1. LIFE. — Aurelius Augustine (the prænomen " Aurelius "
is attested by contemporaries but does not occur in his own
works or in his correspondence) was born of mixed heathen
and Christian parentage November 13, 354 A.D., at Tagaste, a
small municipality in proconsular Numidia. He was taught in
his childhood the principles of Christianity, and great sacrifices
were made to give him a liberal education. From his youth he
was consumed by an insatiable thirst for knowledge, and was
so inflamed by the reading of Cicero's " Hortensius " in his
nineteenth year that he thenceforth devoted his life to the
pursuit of truth. The profession to which he was bred was that
of rhetorician, and this profession he practiced first at Tagaste,
and then successively at Carthage, Rome, and Milan up to the
great crisis of his life (386). In his early manhood he had fallen
away from his Christian training to the Manichæans, who were
the rationalists of the age (373); and subsequently (383) had
lapsed into a general skepticism; but he had already fought his
way out of this, under the influence of the Neo-Platonists, before his conversion to Catholic Christianity took place at Milan
in the late summer of 386. He spent the interval between this
crisis and his baptism (Easter, 387) in philosophical retirement at Cassiciacum, and then, after a short sojourn at Rome,
returned to Africa (autumn, 388) and established at his native
town a sort of religio-philosophical retreat for himself and his
friends. Early in 391 he was almost forcibly ordained presbyter
at Hippo Regius, and nearly five years later (shortly before
Christmas, 395) was raised to the rank of coadjutor-bishop.
From the first he sustained practically the entire burden of the
administration, and, soon succeeding to its sole responsibility,

[1] From " Encyclopaedia of Religion and Ethics," ed. by James Hastings,
ii. pp. 219–224. Used by permission of the publishers, Charles Scribner's Sons.

continued bishop of that second-rate diocese until his death, August 28, 430.

In this simple framework was lived out the life of one who has been strikingly called incomparably the greatest man whom, " between Paul the Apostle and Luther the Reformer, the Christian Church has possessed." [2] We cannot date from him, it is true, an epoch in the external fortunes of the Church in the same sense in which we may from, say, Gregory the Great or Hildebrand. He was not, indeed, without ecclesiastico-political significance. He did much to heal the schisms which tore the African Church. He regenerated the clergy of Africa by his monastic training school. And it must not be forgotten that the two great Gregorys stood upon his shoulders. But his direct work as a reformer of Church life was done in a corner, and its results were immediately swept away by the flood of the Vandal invasion.

2. WRITINGS. — It was through his voluminous writings, by which his wider influence was exerted, that he entered both the Church and the world as a revolutionary force, and not merely created an epoch in the history of the Church, but has determined the course of its history in the West up to the present day. He was already an author when he became a Christian, having published (about 380) an æsthetical study (now lost), on " De pulchro et apto." But his amazing literary productivity began with his conversion. His first Christian writings were a series of religio-philosophical treatises, in which he sought to lay the foundations of a specifically Christian philosophy. These were followed by a great number of controversial works against the Manichæans, Donatists, Pelagians, interspersed with Biblical expositions and dogmatic and ethical studies. The whole was crowned by four or five great books in which his genius finds perhaps its fullest expression. These are his " Confessiones " (397–400), in which he gives an analysis of his religious experience and creates a new *genre* in literary form; the " de Doctrina Christiana " (397–426), in which the

[2] Harnack, " Monasticism and the Confessions of St. Augustine," p. 123.

principles of his Biblical exposition are expounded; the "Enchiridion ad Laurentium" on Faith, Hope, and Charity (421), which contains his most serious attempt to systematize his thought; the "De Trinitate (395–420), in which its final formulation was given to the Christian doctrine of the Trinity; and the "De Civitate Dei" (413–426), in which are laid the foundations of a rational philosophy of history.

He seems to have been himself aware of the significance of the writings into which he had so unstintedly poured himself, and he devoted some of his last years to a careful survey and revision of them in his unique "Retractationes" (426–428), in which he seeks to compact them into an ultimate whole. The influence which they exerted from the beginning is attested no less by the spiteful comments on their volume which escaped from those less well affected to them (e.g., the interpolators of Gennadius), than by the wondering admiration of the better disposed (already, Possidius, "Vita," chap. vii.). In point of fact they entered the Church as a leaven which has ever since wrought powerfully towards leavening the whole mass.

3. INFLUENCE. — (a) *Its extent.* — The greatness of the influence exerted by Augustine is fairly intimated by the suggestion that the division between the Eastern and Western Churches may properly be represented as having been "prepared" by him.[3] No doubt, according to Renan's saying, the building of Constantinople contained in it the prophecy of the division of the Empire, and the division of the Empire the prophecy of the division of the Church. But it was Augustine who imprinted upon the Western section of the Church a character so specific as naturally to bring the separation of the Churches in its train. It must not be inferred, however, that his influence was felt only in the West. The prevailing impression to this effect implies some failure to appreciate not only the extent of the intercourse between the East and the West in Augustine's day, but also the indebtedness of the East to the West for its theological constructions. The interest of the An-

[3] Reuter, "Augustinische Studien," vii. p. 499.

tiochenes in Western Christological thought, as illustrated, for instance, in the "Eranistes" and the correspondence of Theodoret, is only one example of a much wider fact; and in any event, the great doctrines of the Trinity and the Person of Christ, which form almost the entirety of "dogma" in the East, so far from being a gift from the East to the West, as often represented, had their origin in the West, and were thence communicated to the East — the former through the intermediation of "the great Hosius," and the latter through that of Leo the Great. Augustine, through whom — working, no doubt, in full knowledge of what had been done by the Greeks, but in entire independence of them — the doctrine of the Trinity received its completed statement, came too late to affect the Greek construction of this doctrine, and accordingly gave form on this great topic only to the thought of the West. But his Christological conceptions underlay the formulations of Leo, as those of Ambrose underlay his, and through Leo determined the Christological definitions of the East as well as of the West. Accordingly, while the doctrines of the East and the West on the Person of Christ have remained identical, in their doctrines of the Trinity the two sections draw somewhat apart, not only with respect to that perennial bone of contention, the *filioque* clause in the definition of the procession of the Spirit, but in what underlies this difference — their general conception of the relations of the Trinitarian Persons. This in the East is ruled by subtle subordinational inheritances (embedded in the Nicene formulary in the phrase θεὸς ἐκ θεοῦ and its equivalents), while in the West it is dominated by that principle of equalization which found its sharpest assertion in the ascription of αὐτοθεότης to Christ by Calvin, whose construction marks the only new (subordinate) epoch in the development of the doctrine of the Trinity after Augustine. This complete determination of Western thought on the fundamental Christian doctrine of the Trinity fairly illustrates at once the place of Augustine in Western Christian thought, and the effect of his supreme influence there in creating a specifically Western type of Christianity.

It is worth while, no doubt, to distinguish between the actual influence exerted by Augustine in the West, and what may perhaps, in a more external sense, be called the authority enjoyed by his name in the Latin Church. To no other doctor of the Church has anything like the same authority been accorded, and it seemed for long as if his doctrine of grace at least was to be treated as a definitely defined dogma, *de fide* in the Church. Already in 431 Celestine sharply reproved the bishops of Gaul for permitting Augustine's authority to be questioned in their dioceses; and soon afterwards, Gelasius (493) addressed to the bishop of Picenum a similar letter of rebuke for the like carelessness. Subsequent deliverances of Hormisdas (520), and Boniface II (530–531), and John II (534) confirmed the authority thus assigned him; and their encomiums were repeated by many later Roman bishops. It very naturally became, therefore, the custom of the " Augustinians " in the Church of Rome — like Diego Alvarez, Jansen, Noris — to ascribe " irrefragable authority " to his teaching; and the question was gravely debated among the theologians whether a truly plenary authority were really to be attributed to him, or whether he were only to rank as the first of the Church's authorized teachers. The result was very naturally that every tendency of thought in the Church was eager to claim for itself the support of his name; and the extraordinary richness of his mind, and the remarkable variety of, so to say, the facets of his teaching, lent him more than ordinarily to the appeal of numerous and even divergent points of view. The possibility of this was increased by the long period of time covered by his literary activity, and the only gradual crystallization of his thought around his really formative ideas. The Augustine of Cassiciacum or even of the presbyterate was a somewhat different Augustine from the Augustine of the episcopate; and not even at his death had perfect consistency been attained in his teaching. Accordingly the most amazing variety of doctrine, on almost every conceivable subject, throughout the Middle Ages, and later in the Church of Rome, has sought support for itself in some saying or other of his; and both sides of almost every controversy have appealed with confidence to his teaching. Schools of thought which had drifted entirely away from his most fundamental postulates still regarded and represented themselves as " Augustinian "; and the Church of Rome itself, whose whole history since the second Council of Orange (529) has been marked by the progressive elimination of Augustinianism from its teaching, is still able to look upon him as the chief doctor of the Church, upon whom its fabric is especially built. Confusion became so confounded that the Confession of Faith which Pelagius presented to Innocent was inserted quite innocently into the " Libri Carolini," and was even produced by the Sorbonne in 1521 against Luther as Augustine's own.

Obviously this universal deference to the name of Augustine furnishes no accurate measure of his real influence. It supplies, however, a fair general reflection of its extent. In point of fact the whole development of Western life, in all its phases, was powerfully affected by his teaching. This, his unique ascendancy in the direction of the thought and life of the West, is due in part to the particular period in history in which his work was done, in part to the richness and depth of his mind and the force of his individuality, and in part to the special circumstances of his conversion to Christianity. He stood on the watershed of two worlds. The old world was passing away; the new world was entering upon its heritage; and it fell to him to mediate the transference of the culture of the one to the other. It has been strikingly remarked that the miserable existence of the Roman Empire in the West almost seems to have been prolonged for the express purpose of affording an opportunity for the influence of Augustine to be exerted on universal history.[4] He was fortunate even in the place of his birth and formative years; although on the very eve of its destruction, Africa was at this precise moment, in the midst of the universal decadence, the scene of intense intellectual activity — into which he entered with all the force of his ardent

[4] Harnack, " Grundriss der Dogmengeschichte," E. T. " Outlines of the History of Dogma," p. 335.

nature. He gathered up into himself all that the old world had to offer, and re-coining it sent it forth again bearing the stamp of his profound character. It belonged to the peculiarity of his genius that he embraced all that he took up into himself " with all the fibres of his soul "; not, as has been said, " with his heart alone, for the heart does not think, nor with the mind only; he never grasps truth in the abstract, and as if it were dead," [5] but with his whole being, giving himself to it and sending it forth from himself as living truth, driven on by all the force of his great and inspiring personality. Accordingly, when, having tested everything that the old world had to offer and found it wanting, he gave himself at last to Catholic Christianity, it was with no reserves. Catholicism, frankly accepted as such, became his passion, and into the enthusiastic maintenance of it he threw all his forces. It was primarily as a Catholic Christian, therefore, that he thought, and worked, and lived. But the man who threw himself with such zeal into the service of Catholic Christianity was a man who had already lived through many experiences and had gathered much spoil in the process. He had sounded the depths of heresy in its most attractive form and had drunk the waters of philosophy in its culminating development; life in the conventicles of the sects and in the circle of cultured heathenism was alike familiar to him. But, above all the spoil he brought from without, he brought with him himself. He was a man of the highest and most individual genius — intellectual, but far beyond that, religious — who had his own personal contribution to make to thought and life. If we cannot quite allow that there were in very truth many Augustines, we must at least recognize that within the one Augustine there were very various and not always consistent currents flowing, each of which had its part to play in the future. Within the Catholic Christian a philosopher of the first rank was restlessly active; and within both a religious genius of the highest order was working; while for the expression of the resulting complex of feelings and ideas a lit-

[5] Portalié, in Vacant-Mangenot, " Dictionnaire de la Théologie Catholique," i. col. 2453.

erary talent was available second to none in the annals of the Church.

It is no wonder, therefore, that the Western Church has felt the force of his influence in all the main lines of its development, and in no one of its prominent characteristics could it have been without him what it has become. In him are found at once the seed out of which the tree that we know as the Roman Catholic Church has grown; the spring or strength of all the leading anti-hierarchical and mystical movements which succeeded one another through the Middle Ages; at least the promise and pre-formation of the great types of Western philosophical thought; and, above all, the potent leaven of vital religion. Beginning in the first force of its fresh promulgation by overcoming the ingrained rationalism of the popular Christianity expressed in Pelagianism and its daughter movements, it refused to be bound by the compromises of the Council of Orange, compacted though they were into a system by the genius of a Thomas, and given irrefragable authority in the Church of Rome by the decrees of Trent, but manifested its power by outbreak after outbreak, from Gottschalk in the ninth to Jansen in the seventeenth century; and then burst all bonds and issued in the Protestant Reformation in the sixteenth century.

(b) *Augustine as a Church-teacher.* — No doubt it is preeminently as the great Catholic doctor that Augustine stands out on the page of history. To his own consciousness he was just a Catholic Christian; and the whole mass of his teaching was conceived by him as simply the body of Catholic doctrine. It is, accordingly, interesting to observe that it is precisely as the Catholic doctor that he has lived in the hearts of the people. The legends which have gathered around his name picture him preëminently as the expounder of the *principia* of the Christian faith, particularly of the mysteries of the Godhead, who abode continually *in excelsis disputans de gloria excellentissimæ Trinitatis,* and communicated to the Church the results of his high meditations "as he was able" — a note of humility caught from his own habitual tone when speaking of himself.[6] The task to which he consciously gave himself was to apprehend, so far as it was given to him to apprehend, to proclaim, maintain, and defend the Catholic truth; and from this task he never swerved. It was no empty formula with him when he declared, as he repeatedly declared, " This is the Catholic faith, and it is therefore also my faith "; and he was altogether in earnest when he exhorted his readers not to love him more than the Catholic faith, and his critics not to love themselves more than the Catholic truth.[7] The body of Catholic doctrine constitutes thus the traditional element in Augustine's teaching. But, of course, it by no means left his hands precisely as it entered them. Nor did he contribute to it merely intellectual precision and logical completeness; he impressed on it the stamp of his religious fervor, and transmuted its elements into religious entities.

It was particularly in the doctrine of the Church, which he thus took up and transfigured, that he became in a true sense the founder of Roman Catholicism, and thus called into being a new type of Christianity, in which " the idea of the Church became the central power in the religious feeling " and " in ecclesiastical activity," " in a fashion which has remained unknown to the East." [8] This idea of the Church was, to be sure, so little the creation of Augustine that he took it over whole from his predecessors, and in his innermost thought, indeed, never thoroughly homologated it. It was Cyprian, not Augustine, who identified the Church with the episcopate, and to whom the Church outside which there is no salvation was fundamentally the hierarchical institution. It was Gregory the Great who first spoke of the organized Church as the divine *civitas.* To Augustine the Church was fundamentally the *congregatio sanctorum,* the Body of Christ, and it is this Church which he has in mind when he calls it the *civitas Dei,* or the Kingdom of God on earth. He is, however, not carefully observant of the distinction between the empirical and the ideal

---

[6] Cf. Stilting, " Acta Sanctorum," Aug. vi.
[7] " De Trinitate," I. iv. 7; III. *præf.* 2.
[8] Reuter, *op. cit.,* p. 499.

Church, and repeatedly — often apparently quite unconsciously — carries over to the one the predicates which in his
fundamental thought, belonged properly to the other. Thus
the hierarchically organized Church tends ever with him to
take the place of the *congregatio sanctorum*, even when he is
speaking of it as the Kingdom or City of God in which alone
any communion with God is possible here, and through which
alone eternal blessedness with God is attainable hereafter.

In the Donatist controversy, although the distinction between *habere* and *utiliter* or *salubriter habere* is made to do
yeoman service, the conception of the Church as the sole
sphere of salvation, passing into the conception of the Church
as the sole mediatrix of grace, and therefore the sole distribu-
tor of salvation, was necessarily thrown into high emphasis;
and the logic of the situation too directly and too powerfully
identified this Church with the empirical Church for the
deeper-lying conception of the *congregatio sanctorum* to remain in sight. Thus Augustine, almost against his will, became the stay of that doctrine of the Church as the sole instrument at once of true knowledge of the divine revelation and
of saving grace which provides the two *foci* about which the
ellipse of Roman Catholic doctrine revolves. What before him
was matter of assertion became in his hands a religion and
went forth to conquer the world. His profounder conception
of the Church as the *congregatio sanctorum,* and the consequent distinction between the empirical and the ideal Church,
with all its implications with respect to the action of the Sacraments and the effect of ecclesiastical decrees, and even of excommunication, did not indeed remain unobserved or unutil-
ized when occasion demanded. Thus, for example, they came
forward in their .completeness in the arguments of the Im-
perialists in the great controversies of the later eleventh century.[9] These also, and in a truer sense than the Papalists in
that debate, were " Augustinians." But the main stream of
Augustine's influence flowed meanwhile in the traditionalist

[9] Mirbt, "Die Stellung Augustins in der Publicistik des gregorianischen
Kirchenstreits," p. 80.

channel, and gave the world the Church as the authoritative organ of divine truth and the miraculous vehicle of saving grace, through which alone the assured knowledge of the revelation of God could be attained, or the effective operations of His redeeming love experienced. Many of the subsidiary conceptions which fill out the system of Roman Catholic doctrine also find their direct prop in his teaching — its doctrine of merit, the distinctions between precepts and counsels, mortal and venial sins, and particularly the elaborate sacramental system, with its distinction between matter and form, its assertion of *ex opere operato* action, and of the indelible character of baptism and ordination, and even the doctrine of intention. On this side of his teaching the Roman Catholic Church may well be accounted Augustine's monument.

(c) *As a thinker.* — But beneath Augustine the traditionalist lay Augustine the thinker, and as a thinker he gave law not only to the Church but to the world. From the moment of his conversion, to be sure, religion became paramount with him. But this did not quench his philosophical impulse; it only made his specifically a religious philosophy, and himself, to adopt Rudolph Eucken's more precise definition,[10] " the single great philosopher on the basis of Christianity proper the world has had " — in the richness of his thought and poetry of his expression alike, not unworthy of comparison even with his great master Plato.[11] He brought with him into Catholic Christianity not only a sufficient equipment of philosophical knowledge, but a powerful and trained intelligence, and an intellectual instinct which had to find scope. It was in the rôle of Christian philosopher, seeking to give form and substance to fundamental verities from the Christian standpoint, that he first came forward in the service of faith; and though later the religious teacher and defender of the faith seemed likely to swallow up the philosophical inquirer, they never really did so, but

[10] Eucken, " Die Lebensanschauungen der grossen Denker [2], p. 216.

[11] Cf. E. Norden, in " Die Kultur der Gegenwart, i. 8, 1905, p. 394: " Augustine was the great poet of the ancient Church, though just as little as Plato did he write in verse. These two go together as the great poet-philosophers of all time."

his rich and active mind kept continually at work sounding all depths. Thus not only was there imparted to all his teaching an unwonted vitality, originality, and profundity, but " the activities set in motion were not confined to the narrow circle of theological science, but extended, directly or indirectly, to all forms of human life." [12] In every department of philosophical inquiry he became normative for the succeeding centuries; and until the rise of Aristotelianism in the twelfth century and its establishment' in influence by the advocacy of such teachers as Albertus Magnus and Thomas Aquinas, Augustinianism reigned supreme. Throughout the remainder of the Middle Ages it contended masterfully with its great rival, forming many compromises with it, and tending to offset the rationalism into which Aristotelianism was ever degenerating by itself falling into mysticism. It thus became the support of the tendency towards mysticism which prevailed through the Middle Ages, or rather its protection from the pantheism into which, when drawing more directly from Neo-Platonic sources, it was ever liable to deteriorate. From it every Catholic reformer drew his strength, and to it the whole body of reformers before the Reformation made their appeal. From its partial obscuration it emerged at the Renaissance, and burst against into full view in the seventeenth century to lay the foundations of modern thought. Siebeck accordingly bids us see in Augustine " the first modern man "; [13] and, if Eucken questions the exactness of the designation, he is free to allow that the modern world finds in Augustine many points of contact, and, not only in questions of religious philosophy may wisely take its start from him rather than from Luther or Thomas, Schleiermacher or Kant, but in purely philosophical matters will find him in many respects more modern than Hegel or Schopenhauer.[14]

It was in the spheres of psychology and metaphysics that the dominion of Augustine was most complete. He aspired to

[12] Mirbt, *op. cit.*, p. 1.

[13] *Zeitschrift für Philosophie und Pädagogik*, 1888, p. 190.

[14] Eucken, *op. cit.*, p. 249.

know nothing, he tells us, but God and the soul; but these he strove with all his might to know altogether. His characteristic mark as a thinker was the inward gaze; the realities of consciousness were the primary objects of his contemplation; and from them he took his starting point for reflection on the world. Antiquity supplies no second to him in the breadth and acuteness of his psychological observation. And in his establishment of "immediate certainty of inner experience," as Windelband calls it,[15] in "the controlling central position of philosophic thought" he transcended his times and became "one of the founders of modern thought." If he may truly be said to have derived from Plato and Plotinus, in a far truer sense he stood above his Neo-Platonic teachers, and of his lineage have come Descartes and Malebranche and all that has proceeded from the movements of thought inaugurated by them. Even the famous ontological argument for the being of God, and, indeed, the very *cogito, ergo sum* of Descartes, have not merely their material but their formal pre-formation in him. It was not, however, in abstract thought alone, or chiefly, that he made his mark on the ages; his own thinking was markedly concrete, and nothing characterized it more strongly than the firmness of its grasp upon the realities of life, to the understanding and direction of which it was held strictly ancillary.

His impact upon the world might accordingly not unfairly be summed up, from one point of view, in the ethical revolution which he wrought. "In essence," remarks Harnack,[16] "Augustine's importance in the history of the Church and dogma lies in his giving to the West in the place of the Stoic-Christian popular morals, as that was recapitulated in Pelagianism, a religious, specifically Christian ethics, and so strongly impressing this on the Church that at least its formulas maintain up to to-day their supremacy in the whole extent of Western Chris-

---

[15] "A History of Philosophy," pp. 264, 270, 276.

[16] "Dogmengeschichte" [E. T. v. p. 30]; cf. on Augustine's place in the history of ethics, Joseph Mausbach, in "Die Kultur der Gegenwart," i. 4, 1906, p. 526.

tianity." Indeed, we might do worse, in seeking an index of his influence as a thinker, than fix upon the place he has occupied in political theory and practice. The entire political development of the Middle Ages was dominated by him; and he was in a true sense the creator of the Holy Roman Empire. It was no accident that the *De civitate Dei* was the favorite reading of Charlemagne: " he delighted," Einhard tells us (*Vita Caroli*, 24), " in the books of St. Augustine, and especially in those that bear the title ' Of the City of God.' " And in the great struggle between the Empire and the Papacy in the later eleventh century it was expressly to him that the controversialists on both sides made their appeal. No Father is quoted by them as often as he, except, perhaps, Gregory the Great; and no series of documents is cited more frequently than his writings, except, perhaps, the pseudo-Isidorian decretals.[17] Not only do writers like Walram of Naumburg and Wido of Ferrara reflect accurately his conception of the Church, with its emphasis on unity and its vacillation between the ideas of the *congregatio sanctorum* and a hierarchical organization — echoes of which still sound in William of Occam's " Defensor Pacis " and the discussions of the conciliatory party in the Roman Church whose ornament was Gerson — but they made their appeal to Augustine in their endeavors to give validity to their defense " of the State as a Divine institution, of the moral significance and relative independence of the earthly sovereignty, of the necessary concordance of the *Sacerdotium* and *Imperium*," and the like.[18]

On the theoretical side he must be accredited, in this aspect of his thought, with the creation of the science of the Philosophy of History. For the primary significance of the *De civitate Dei* lies in the fact that " in it for the first time an ideal consideration, a comprehensive survey of human history found its expression." [19] No doubt his external position at the division of the ages, when the Old World was dying and the New

---

[17] Mirbt, *op. cit.*, p. 75.

[18] Reuter, *op. cit.*, p. 508.

[19] Seyrich, " Die Geschichtsphilosophie Augustins," 1891, p. 68.

World, under the dominion of Christianity, was struggling into its place, supplied him with incitement for the creation of this new science; and the demands which the times, in the crash of the secular order, made for an apology for Christianity, powerfully determined him to a general historical philosophy. But it was Christianity itself, as the entrance into the world of a renovating force, and his own particular conception of Christianity (leading him to conceive the history of human society no less than the course of the individual life, as the continuous evolution of the divine purpose, and impeling him to interpret all the forces of time as working harmoniously onward towards that faroff divine event to which all creation moves) that gave him not only the impulse to work out a philosophy of history, but the elements of the particular philosophy of history which he actually presents in his epoch-making treatise, which, incomplete and perhaps one-sided as it is, still retains full validity in its fundamental traits.

(d) *As a regilious genius.* — Not even, however, in Augustine the philosopher do we find the Augustine whose influence has wrought most powerfully in the world. The crisis through which he passed at his conversion was a profound religious revolution; and if he gave himself at once to the task of constructing a philosophy, it was distinctively a Christian philosophy he sought to construct, built though it was largely out of Platonic materials: the authority of Christ, he tells us in the earliest of the writings in which this task was prosecuted, ranked with him even above that of reason. And if he devoted all his powers to the exposition and defense of the Catholic faith, it was because he saw in the Catholic faith the pure expression of religion, and poured into the Catholic faith all the fulness of his religious emotion. It is not Augustine the traditionalist, or Augustine the thinker, but Augustine the religious genius, who has most profoundly influenced the world. The most significant fact about him is that he, first among Church teachers, gave adequate expression to that type of religion which has since attached to itself the name of " evangelical "; the religion, that is to say, of faith, as distinct from the religion of works; the religion which, despairing of self, casts all its hope on God, as opposed to the religion which, in a greater or less degree, trusts in itself; in a word — since religion in its very nature is dependence on God — religion in the purity of its conception, as over against a *quasi*-religious moralism. What requires particularly to be noted is that he gave full expression to this type of religion both in its vital and in its thetical aspects — the former most adequately in that unique book in which he reveals his soul, and admits us as spectators to the struggles of his great heart as it seeks to cleanse itself of all trust in itself and to lay hold with the grasp, first of despair, next of discerning trust, and then of grateful love, on the God who was its salvation; and the latter most adequately in that long series of writings in which he expounds, defends, and enforces with logical argument and moving exhortation the fundamental elements of the theology of grace, as against the most direct assailants which that theology has been called upon to meet in the whole history of Christian thought. The great contribution which Augustine has made to the world's life and thought is embodied in the theology of grace, which he has presented with remarkable clearness and force, vitally in his " Confessions," and thetically in his anti-Pelagian treatises.

It would be altogether a mistake to suppose that Augustine consciously discriminated between the theology of grace, which was his personal contribution to Christian thought, and the traditional Catholicism, which he gave his life to defend and propagate. In his own consciousness, the two were one: in his theology of grace he was in his own apprehension only giving voice to the Catholic faith in its purity. Nevertheless, however unconsciously, he worked with it a revolution both in Christian teaching and in Christian life, second in its depth and its far-reaching results to no revolution which has been wrought in Christian feeling and thought in the whole course of its history. A new Christian piety dates from him, in which, in place of the alternations of hope and fear which vex the lives of those who, in whatever degree, hang their hopes on their own merits, a mood of assured trust in the mercy of a gracious God is substituted as the spring of Christian life. And a new theology corresponding to this new type of piety dates from him; a theology which, recalling man from all dependence on his own powers or merits, casts him decisively on the grace of God alone for his salvation. Of course, this doctrine was not new in the sense that it was Augustine's invention; it was the doctrine of Paul, for example, before it was the doctrine of Augustine, and was only recovered for the Church by Augustine, though in that age, dominated in all its thinking by the dregs of Stoic rationalism, it came with all the force of a new discovery. And, of course, Augustine did not discover it all at once. Because his conversion was a vital religious experience, in which the religious relation was realized in thought and life in unwonted purity and power, the fundamental elements of his religious revolution were from the first present in his mind and heart; in his earliest Christian writings he already gives expression to both the formal and the material principles, as we may term them, of the theology of grace. The authority of the divine revelation in and through Christ, embodied in the Scriptures, and the utter dependence of man on God for all good (*potestas nostra Ipse est, da fidem*), are already the most intimate expression of his thought and life. But just because the religious system to which he gave himself on his conversion was taken over by him as a whole, time was requisite for the transfusion of the whole mass by the consistent explication and conscious exposition of the " Augustinianism " implicitly summed up in such maxims. The adjustment went on slowly, although it went on unbrokenly. It required ten years before the revived Paulinism attained even a fully consistent positive enunciation (first in the work, " De diversis quæstionibus ad Simplicianum," A.D. 396); and, though the leaven worked steadily thereafter more and more deeply and widely into his thought, death intervened before all the elements of his thinking were completely leavened. That is the reason why Augustine was both the founder of Roman Catholicism and the author of that doctrine of grace which it has been the constantly pursued effort of Roman Catholicism to neutralize, and which in very fact either must be neutralized by, or will neutralize, Roman Catholicism. Two children were struggling in the womb of his mind. There can be no doubt which was the child of his heart. His doctrine of the Church he had received whole from his predecessors, and he gave it merely the precision and vitality which insured its persistence. His doctrine of grace was all his own: it represented the very core of his being; and his whole progress in Christian thinking consists in the growing completeness with which its fundamental principles applied themselves in his mind to every department of life and thought. In this gradual subjection to them of every element of his inherited teaching, it was inevitable, had time been allowed, that his inherited doctrine of the Church, too, with all its implications, would have gone down before it, and Augustine would have bequeathed to the Church, not "problems," but a thoroughly worked out system of evangelical religion.

(e) *Augustine and Protestantism.* — The problem which Augustine bequeathed to the Church for solution, the Church required a thousand years to solve. But even so, it is Augustine who gave us the Reformation. For the Reformation, inwardly considered, was just the ultimate triumph of Augustine's doctrine of grace over Augustine's doctrine of the Church. This doctrine of grace came from Augustine's hands in its positive outline completely formulated: sinful man depends, for his recovery to good and to God, entirely on the free grace of God; this grace is therefore indispensable, prevenient, irresistible, indefectible; and, being thus the free grace of God, must have lain, in all the details of its conference and working, in the intention of God from all eternity. But, however clearly announced and forcefully commended by him, it required to make its way against great obstacles in the Church. As over against the Pelagians, the indispensableness of grace was quickly established; as over against the Semi-Pelagians, its prevenience was with almost equal rapidity made good. But there advance paused. If the necessity of prevenient grace was thereafter (after the second Council of Orange, 529) the established doctrine of the Church, the irresistibility of this prevenient grace was put under the ban, and there remained no place for a complete "Augustinianism" within the Church, as Gottschalk and Jansen were fully to discover. Therefore, when the great revival of religion which we call the Reformation came, seeing that it was, on its theological side, a revival of "Augustinianism," as all great revivals of religion must be (for "Augustinianism" is but the thetical expression of religion in its purity), there was nothing for it but the rending of the Church. And therefore also the greatest peril to the Reformation was and remains the diffused anti-"Augustinianism" in the world; and, by a curious combination of circumstances, this, its greatest enemy, showed itself most dangerous in the hands of what we must otherwise look upon as the chief ally of the Reformation — that is to say, Humanism. Humanism was the ally of the Reformation in so far as it, too, worked for the emancipation of the human spirit; and, wherever it was religious, it became the seed-plot of the Reformation. But there was a strong anti-"Augustinian" party among the Humanists, and from it emanated the gravest danger which threatened the Reformation. Where this tone of thought was dominant the Reformation failed, because religious depth was wanting. What Spain, for example, lacked, says R. Saint-Hilaire justly, was not freedom of thought, but the Gospel. In the first stages of the Reformation movement in the North, this anti-"Augustinianism" may be looked upon as summed up in Erasmus; and Erasmus, on this very ground, held himself aloof from the Reformation movement, and that movement held itself aloof from him. "I am at present reading our Erasmus," wrote Luther six months before he nailed his theses on the door of the Schloss-Kirche at Wittenberg, "but my heart recoils more and more from him. . . . Those who ascribe something to man's freedom of will regard these things differently from those who know only God's free grace." Do we realize how much we owe to Erasmus and his friends that they remained Roman Catholics, and thus permitted the "Augustinianism" of the Reformation to plant its seed and to bear its fruit?

LITERATURE. — The literature upon Augustine is immense.

An excellent selection from it is given by Loofs at the head of the article " Augustinus " in Herzog, " Realencyklopädie für protestantische Theologie und Kirche," ³ ii. pp. 257 ff., with which should be compared that given by Harnack, "History of Dogma," v. pp. 61 f. The following deal directly with the influence of Augustine: Feuerlein, " Ueber die Stellung Augustins in der Kirchen- und Kulturgeschichte," in von Sybel's " Historische Zeitschrift," 1869, xxii. pp. 270–313; Reuter, " Augustinische Studien," Gotha, 1887, vii. pp. 479–516; Cunningham, " S. Austin and his place in the History of Christian Thought " (Hulsean Lectures for 1885), London, 1886; Schaff, " History of the Christian Church," iii., New York, 1884, § 180, pp. 1016–1028; Eucken, " Die Lebensanschauungen der grossen Denker," Leipzig, 1890 (2nd ed. 1897, pp. 216–250; 4th ed. 1902, pp. 210, etc.) ; Nourrisson, " La Philosophie de Sant Augustin," Paris, 1866, ii. pp. 147–276; Werner, " Die Scholastik des späteren Mittelalters," iii., Vienna, 1883, and " Die Augustinische Psychologie in ihrer mittelalterlich-scholastischen Einkleidung und Gestaltung," *Sitzungsberichte der phil.- hist. Classe der kais. Akademie der Wissenschaften*, Vienna, 1882, pp. 435–494; Siebeck, " Die Anfänge der neueren Psychologie," in *Zeitschrift für Philosophie und Pädagogik*, 1888, pp. 161 f., cf. his " Geschichte der Psychologie "; Ehrle, " Der Augustinismus und der Aristotelismus in der Scholastik gegen Ende des xiii. Jahrhundert," " Archiv für Literatur- und Kirchengeschichte des Mittelalters," 1889, v. pp. 603–635, cf. also *Zeitschrift für Katholische Theologie*, Innsbruck, 1889, xiii. pp. 172–193; Mirbt, " Die Stellung Augustins in der Publicistik des gregorianischen Kirchenstreits," Leipzig, 1888; Koch, " Der heilige Faustus, Bischof von Riez," Stuttgart, 1895, pp. 129–191; Gwatkin, " The Knowledge of God," ² 1908, ii. p. 179; Portalié, " Augustine," in " Catholic Encyclopædia," ii. pp. 84–104, New York, 1907. The text of Augustine is most generally accessible in " Patrologia Latina," xxxii.-xlvii.; and his chief writings are translated in " Nicene and Post-Nicene Fathers," First Series i.–viii., Oxford and New York, 1886–1888.

III

AUGUSTINE'S DOCTRINE OF KNOWLEDGE AND AUTHORITY

AUGUSTINE'S DOCTRINE OF KNOWLEDGE AND AUTHORITY[1]

FIRST ARTICLE

AUGUSTINE marks almost as great an epoch in the history of philosophy as in the history of theology. It was with him that the immediate assurance of consciousness first took its place as the source and warrant of truth. No doubt there had been a long preparation for the revolution which was wrought by his announcement of " the principle of the absolute and immediate certainty of consciousness," as Windelband calls it, and his establishment of it in " the controlling central position of philosophic thought." But the whole preceding development will not account for the act of genius by which he actually shifted the basis of philosophy, and in so doing became " the true teacher of the middle ages," no doubt, but above and beyond that " one of the founders of modern thought."[2] He may himself be said to have come out of Plato, or Plotinus; but in even a truer sense out of him came Descartes and his successors.[3] When he urged men to cease seeking truth without them, and to turn within, since the home of truth is inside of man, he already placed them upon the firm footing which Descartes sought with his *cogito ergo sum*.[4]

[1] From *The Princeton Theological Review*, v. 1907, pp. 353–397.

[2] Windelband, " A History of Philosophy," E. T. pp. 276, 264, 270.

[3] Leder, " Augustins Erkenntnistheorie," p. 76: " If we must see in Plotinus the father of Augustine's Platonism, we may yet recognize it as an especially original service of the Church Father, that he established over against all scepticism the first point of all certitude in self-consciousness. He found in Plotinus no guidance for this: rather by an act of genius he anticipated in it the line of thought which Descartes (1640) made in his *Meditationes* the starting point of his expositions."

[4] " De vera religione," 39.72: " Noli foras ire, in te ipsum redi, in interiore homine habitat veritas."

If Augustine can be said to have had a philosophical master before he fell under the influence of the Neo-Platonists, that master must be discerned in Cicero. And from Cicero he derived rather a burning zeal in the pursuit of truth than a definite body of philosophical tenets or even a philosophical point of view. It is a mistake to think of him as ever surrendering himself to the skepticism of the New Academy. He does, indeed, tell us that, in his disillusionment with Manichaeism and his increasing despair of attaining the truth, the notion sprang up within him that the so-called Academics might after all prove the best philosophers, contending as they did that everything hangs in doubt and truth cannot be comprehended by men.[5] It is not strange that at such moments his thoughts surged in great waves towards their teachings.[6] But he tells us also that he could not commit himself to them; not only because he was repelled by their heathenism,[7] but also because he was shocked by their skepticism.[8] His difficulty at the time lay, in fact, in another quarter. He found no obstacle in the attainment of certitude: but nothing but apodeictic certitude satisfied him. He entertained no doubt, for example, that seven and three make ten; what he demanded was the same kind and degree of certainty he had here, for everything else. In other words, he would not commit himself to any truth for which he did not have ready at hand complete demonstration.

[5] " Confessiones " v. 10. 19.

[6] " De ultilitate credendi," viii. 20: " Saepe mihi videbatur [verum] non posse inveniri, magnique fluctus cogitationum mearum in Academicorum suffragium ferebantur." He proceeds to say that so often as he was thus tempted, he reacted on considering the vivacity, sagacity, perspicacity of the human mind; he could not believe this mind so much incapable of truth as ignorant as yet of the right way of going about its discovery: thus he was led to meditate on the problem of authority. " De beata vita," i. 4: " at ubi discussos eos [Manichaeos] evasi, maxime trajecto isto mari, dui gubernacula mea repugnantia omnibus ventis in mediis fluctibus Academici tenuerunt."

[7] " Confessiones " v. 14. 25: " I utterly refused to commit the healing of my soul to these philosophers, because they knew not the saving name of Christ."

[8] " Confessiones " vi. 4. 6: " I was not so insane as to fancy that not even this " — mathematical truth — " could be comprehended."

Augustine's point of departure was therefore the precise contradictory of that of the Academics. They asserted that we can never get beyond suspense because we lack all criterion of truth. The best we can do is to say that this or that looks like truth; that it is *verisimile* or *probabile:* we can never affirm that it is truth, *verum;* though, of course, we can as little affirm that it is not truth. Lacking all *signum,* we are left in utter and hopeless uncertainty. Augustine, on the contrary, in the apodeictic certainty of, say, mathematical formulas, was in possession of a sure criterion on the basis of which he could confidently assert truth. His difficulty was that he wished to apply this *signum* mechanically to every sphere of truth alike, and could content himself with no other kind of certitude. He was tempted to declare that nothing resting on less cogent grounds is known, or can be known, at all. What he needed yet was to learn that so far from the possession of apodeictic certitude for some things throwing into the shadow of doubt all for which it cannot be adduced, it provides a basis for valid assurance with respect to them, too. On the basis of this *signum* we may obtain in every sphere at least the *verisimile,* the *probabile* — a sufficient approach to truth to serve all practical purposes; or rather truth itself though not truth in its purity, free from all admixture of error. In other words, in every department of investigation there is attainable real and clear, if somewhat roughly measured, knowledge. What we currently call a yard of muslin, for example, though shown by the application of a micrometer not to be an exact yard, is yet by the self-same test just as truly shown to be a yard for all the practical ends for which muslin is used. The possession of a criterion gives validity to the *verisimile;* for who can declare that anything is like the truth unless he has the truth itself in mind with which to compare it and by which to judge it?

It was by a line of reasoning something like this that Augustine overthrew the Academics when, in his retirement at Cassiciacum, in the interval between his conversion and his baptism, he undertook to lay the foundations of a positive

Christian philosophy. It is absurd to talk of a *verisimile*, he urged, unless the standard, the *verum*, is in our possession. And not only is this standard, this *verum*, certainly in the possession of every man and instinctively employed by him; but no one can by any means rid himself of it. Do what we will, we cannot help knowing that the world is either one or not one; [9] that three times three are nine; [10] and the like; that is to say the principles which underlie, say for example, logic and mathematics. And in knowing these things, we know them not only to be true, but to be eternally and immutably true, quite independently of our thinking minds — so that they would be equally true if no human minds had ever existed, and would remain true though the whole human race should perish.[11] With this indefectible certainty of necessary truth the mind unavoidably knows, therefore, the laws of the true, the beautiful and the good,[12] according to which, as its criterion, it judges all of the true, beautiful, and good which is brought into observation in the experience of life. Nor can doubt be thrown upon these things by calling in question the reality of the very mind itself by which they are known, and therefore the validity of its convictions. Rather, the reality of the mind is given in the very act of knowledge: for what is not cannot act. Say even that this act is an act of doubt. If the mind did not exist, it could not even doubt.[13] The act of doubt itself becomes, thus, the credential of certitude. It is impossible even to doubt unless we are, and remember, and understand, and will, and think, and know, and judge: so that he that doubts must not and cannot doubt of these things, seeing that even if he doubts he does them.[14] Even he who says, " I do not know," thereby evinces not only that he exists and that he knows that he exists, but also that he knows what knowing is and that he

[9] " Cont. Acad." iii. 10. 23.

[10] " Cont. Acad." iii. 11. 25.

[11] " Cont. Acad." iii. 11. 25: necesse est, vel genere humano stertente, sit verum. Cf. " De lib. arbit." ii. 8. 21; " De Trinitate, ix. 6.

[12] " De lib. arbit." ii. 8, 9, 10, 15, 16; " De Trinitate," ix. 6; viii. 3; xiv. 15.

[13] " De lib. arbit." ii. 3, 7.

[14] " De Trinitate," x. 10. 14.

knows that he knows it.[15] It is impossible to be ignorant that we are; and as this is certain, many other things are certain along with it, and the confident denial of this is only another way of demonstrating it.

What Augustine is doing in this reasoning, it will be observed, is withdrawing attention from the external world and focusing it upon the inner consciousness. There, there alone, he asserts, can truth be found. Those who seek it without, never attain to it; [16] it is in the inner man that it makes its home, and it can be discovered, therefore, only by those who look within.[17] His polemic is turned upon that Sensationalism in philosophy which had long reigned supreme in the schools, and the dominion of which he was the first to break. In this polemic, he considered himself to be building upon the New Academy, whose mordant criticism of knowledge he persuaded himself was only the negative side of a defense of an essential Platonism which they kept, in its positive side, meanwhile in reserve. In this judgment of fact he was certainly mistaken; the Academy had itself fallen into the prevalent Sensationalism and was itself, therefore, as truly as the Epicurean and Stoic schools of the time the object of his confutation.[18] But to the Sensationalistic maxim that " there is nothing in the intellect which was not beforehand in the senses," by whomsoever taught and in whatsoever forms, he opposes the direct contradiction that truth is to be sought, in the first instance, in the intellect alone. As Robert Browning phrases it, " to know rather consists in opening out a way whence the imprisoned splendor may escape, than in effecting entry for a light supposed to be without." In other words, Augustine came forward as a flaming Rationalist in the philosophical sense of that term; in the sense, that is, in which it describes those thinkers who hold that the " reason " is the fundamental source of

15 " De Trinitate," x. 1. 3.

16 " De vera religione," 49.94: . . . "veritas, ad quam nullo modo perveniunt qui foris eam quaerunt."

17 " De vera religione," 39.72: " noli foras ire, in te ipsum redi, in interiore homine habitat veritas." Cf. " Retractationes," i. 13.

18 Cf. Leder, " Augustins Erkenntnistheorie," p. 35.

knowledge; and, in opposition alike to Sensationalism and Empiricism, which teach respectively that our knowledge is derived exclusively from sensation or experience (that is, sensation and reflection), contend rather that it is the " reason," acting under laws of its own, which supplies the forms of thought without which no knowledge can be obtained either by sensation or by experience.

Arnobius, his·fellow African of a hundred years before, on the basis of the popular Stoicism was as flaming a Sensationalist as Augustine was a Rationalist, and it is interesting to contrast the strong expressions which the two give, each to his own point of view. Arnobius calls to the aid of his exposition the imaginary case of a man secluded from infancy to maturity in a dark cavern, guarded from every possible commerce with the external world. Such an one, he contends, would remain mentally empty; and, if confronted, not with some complicated problem, but with even the simple twice two are four, would stand like a stock or the Marpesian rock, as the saying is, dumb and speechless, understanding nothing.[19] In staring contrast with Arnobius, Augustine sometimes speaks as if contact with the external world and the intrusion of sensible images into the mind were a positive hindrance to the acquisition of knowledge; and as if the mind would do its essential work better if it could do it free from what, in that case, would be conceived as the distractions of sense; as if, in a word, something like the condition in which Laura Bridgman or Helen Keller were found were the most favorable for the development of human intelligence. This exaggeration, however, is no part of his system; and its occasional suggestion serves only to throw into a high light the strength and seriousness of his rationalism.

This rationalism, however, it may be observed, is never pressed to the extreme of conceiving the reason as the creator of its own object. That is to say, it never passes into the Idealism which in more modern times has lain so frequently in its

[19] Arnobius, " Adv. Gent." ii. 20 (American ed. of " The Ante-Nicene Fathers," vi. p. 442).

pathway. To Augustine the world of observation was far from being merely a " psychological phenomenon." Indeed, not only does he recognize the objectivity of the world of sense, but, with all the vigor of his contention that we must look within for truth, he insists equally on the objectivity of even the intelligible world. Man no more creates the world of ideas he perceives within him, than the world of sense he perceives without him. In his assertion that the objects of sensible and intellectual perception alike have indubitable objectivity lies, indeed, one of the main features of Augustine's philosophy.[20] Perhaps we may best catch his general idea, in the distinction he made between the two modes of knowledge — sense perception and intellection — corresponding to the two worlds, sensible and intelligible — if we represent him as thinking of the human soul as existing in a double environment, with both of which it is connected by appropriate organs of perception. On the one hand, it is connected with the sensible world by the external senses; on the other hand, with the intelligible world by the *sensus intimus* which is the intellect.[21] Augustine's notion is, essentially, that the soul, by these two modes of contact with its double environment, is enabled to read off the facts of each. His mode of statement commonly takes the form that as the sensible world impresses itself upon us through the external senses, so the intelligible world impresses itself upon us through the intellect: but we must not press the passivity of the soul to its several impressions which might seem

[20] Cf. Nourrison, " La Philosophie de Sant Augustin," ii. p. 295: " To affirm the certitude of consciousness is, for him, to affirm in the same act the certitude of the external world. . . . It is well to take note of the sagacity with which he distinguishes the phenomenon from the being and thus exonerates the senses from the errors which are commonly attributed to them. Organs and witnesses of what passes, and not of what does not pass, of the phenomenal and not the real, they are not the judges of truth — *judicium veritatis non esse in sensibus*. It is the intellect that knows or the intellect that deceives itself. Its knowledge is certitude. No Scotchman of our day could express it better."

[21] " Cont. Acad." iii. 17. 37: " Platonem sensisse duos esse mundos, unum intelligibilem, in quo ipsa veritas habitaret, istum autem sensibilem, quem manifestum esse nos visu tactuque sentire. Itaque illum verum, hunc verisimilem. . . ."

to be implied in this mode of statement. If, now, these two worlds, the sensible and the intelligible, stood contradictorily over against each other, the soul of man lying between them and invaded by impressions from each, would be in parlous case. Such, however, is not Augustine's conception. The sensible world is not thought of by him as itself independent of the intelligible. It not only has its source in the intelligible world, but derives its whole support and direction from it; and reflects, after its own fashion, its content. It cannot be perceived, therefore, save, so to speak, from the angle of the intelligible world; and in order that it may be understood, the soul must bring to its perception the principles derived from the intelligible world. In a word, the soul is caparisoned for the perception and understanding of the sensible world only by prior perception and understanding of the intelligible world. That is to say, the soul brings over from the intelligible world the forms of thought under which alone the sensible world can be received by it into a mental embrace.

This is, of course, a very developed form of Intuitionalism. According to the Stoics — those Sensationalists *a outrance* — the human mind is in the first instance a *tabula rasa*, on which outer things impress themselves (τύπωσις). But even the Stoics could speak of truths of nature. In their most materialistic development they could find a place in their system for general ideas common to all men (κοιναὶ ἔννοιαι, *communes notiones*), which they not only recognized as real, but valued as the best constituents of human knowledge. As men have practically the same environment, they explained, the sum of the impressions made by surrounding nature upon each, is practically the same as the sum of the impressions made upon all. Hence, peculiar confidence should be put in the ideas common to all men: they are the general teachings of nature, that nature life in conformity with which is the wise man's mark. "Natural ideas" are not foreign, then, to the Stoic system; but when the Stoics spoke of these ideas as "natural," they did not at all mean that they constitute a part of the nature with which man is endowed. Man was not supposed to bring them into life with him, but distinctly to acquire them in the process of living: they are impressed by nature on his soul. The transition is easy, however, from the conception of a body of ideas natural to man in this sense, to a conception of a body of ideas belonging to his nature as such, or, in other words, innate. Along with his reason, it is now said, every man possesses by nature, that is, by his constitution as man, a body of ideas: they belong to his nature as a rational being. In making this step we have definitely passed over from Sensationalism to Rationalism, and have so far approached Augustine's conception. But we have not yet reached it. The doctrine of innate ideas, strictly construed in that form is deistic. These ideas are ours because they have been from the beginning once for all impressed upon our nature by our Maker, who has made us thus and not otherwise — namely, so that by the action of our intellect we become aware of the principles thus made a part of our very structure. Augustine, however, was as little deistic as Sensationalistic in his thinking, and necessarily advanced a step further to a truly theistic Intuitionalism. These ideas, he teaches, are natural to man in the sense that they inhere in his nature as such, and are not impressed on him by external nature; and they are innate in the sense that they belong to his nature from the beginning of his being. But he cannot conceive them merely as impressed on the mind, or rather built into its structure, once for all at its creation. He thinks rather of the soul as constantly dependent on God, who is no more its Creator than its Upholder and Director; and of its intrinsic ideas as, therefore, continuously impressed on it by God. Thus its light is God alone; and the soul, in intellection, bears the same constant relation to God the Illuminator as in ethical action it bears to God the Sanctifier. God, he is never weary of saying, in his own adaptation of a Platonic formula, is at once the Author of all being, the Light of all knowledge, and the Fountain of all good; the God of creation, of truth, of grace: or, otherwise put, the *causa subsistendi,* the *ratio intelligendi,* and the *ordo vivendi.* His ontology of "innate ideas," accordingly, is that they are the immediate product in the soul of God the Illuminator, always present with the soul as its sole and indispensable Light, in which alone it perceives truth.

No doubt there is a Neo-Platonic factor in this construction, and possibly also the modes of expression employed may betray a reminiscence of Stoic τύπωσις — with the source of the impression elevated, however, from nature to nature's God. But we must beware of pushing it out of its theistic sobriety into the regions of an essentially pantheistic mode of thought, whether developed or only implicated. Nothing could be farther from Augustine's meaning than that God, as the Universal Reason and Sole Intelligence, comes to the knowledge of the truth in us, and we in and by Him, so that our knowledge simply coalesces with His. His doctrine of creation, by which the creature is set as an objective somewhat, with powers of its own, over against God the Creator, placed him at a whole diameter's distance from the pantheistic tendencies of Plotinus, otherwise so much his master.[22] But neither does the " ontologism " of William of Paris and Malebranche, Fenelon and Bossuet precisely reproduce his meaning. Augustine does not teach that we contemplate immediately the Divine Being, and in Him the intelligible world, that pleroma of eternal and immutable truths which constitutes the world of divine Ideas.[23] It would be much nearer his meaning to say that we see God in the eternal truths which by our *sensus intimus* we contemplate, than that we see them in Him. Undoubtedly he teaches that the soul has an immediate knowledge of God; and, in a sense, he does identify with God the intelligible world into contact with which the soul is brought by its *sensus intimus*. We should not be far from his meaning, however, if, reverting to a mode of representation we have already employed, we should say that the soul, set in its double environment, the sensible world on the one hand and the intelligible world on the

[22] Cf. Nourrison, *op. cit.*, ii. pp. 301, 334; Grandgeorge, " St. Augustine et le Néoplatonisme," p. 111; Portalié in Vacant-Mangenot, " Dictionaire de Théologie Catholique, i. col. 2330. *Per contra,* however, Ritschl, Loesche, etc.

[23] Cf. Portalié as cited, col. 2335; and Storz, " Philosophie d. hl. Aug.," pp. 65 *sq.*

other, as it knows the sensible world directly through the
senses, so knows God in the intelligible world directly through
the intellect. But God is not identified with the intelligible
world, as it appears in the soul of man, except as its immediate author. He is in the soul of man not *substantialiter* but only
effective; and it is precisely in this that the difficulty of the
conception lies. If we may be permitted to employ theological
conceptions here, we may say that Augustine's ontology of the
intuition by which man attains intelligible truth, embraced
especially two factors: the doctrine of the image of God, and
the doctrine of dependence on God. To put it briefly, man's
power of attaining truth depends, in his view, first of all upon
the fact that God has made man like Himself, Whose intellect
is the home of the intelligible world, the contents of which
may, therefore, be reflected in the human soul; and then, secondly, that God, having so made man, has not left him, deistically, to himself, but continually reflects into his soul the contents of His own eternal and immutable mind — which are
precisely those eternal and immutable truths which constitute
the intelligible world. The soul is therefore in unbroken communion with God, and in the body of intelligible truths reflected into it from God, sees God. The nerve of this view, it
will be observed, is the theistic conception of the constant dependence of the creature on God. This stands midway between
the deistic conception, on the one side, that has no need of God
except for the primal originating of the creature, and supposes
that after that the creature's own powers suffice for all its acts;
and the pantheistic view, on the other side, which substitutes
the divine action for the creature's action and, having no need
of a creature at all, transforms it into a mere simulacrum without reality of being or action. In the Theistic view, there is
postulated the creature as the product of a real creation, by
which it produced a real thing with real activities of its own;
and alongside of this, the real dependence of this creature for
the persistence and use of all its activities on the constant action of God. Applying this conception to the problem of intellection, Augustine conceives the soul as at once active and

acted upon, but as active only because acted upon. It is only in the light of God, the sun of the soul, that the soul is illuminated to see light.

There was nothing novel in the ascription of all human knowledge to the illumination of God. It was not only Numenius who declared all knowledge to be but the kindling of a little light from the great light which lightens the world.[24] Platonist and Stoic alike offered a metaphysical and epistemological basis for such a representation. According to the one, knowledge is recollection; and Cicero had explained this — or explained it away — as meaning that right knowledge is implanted in the soul by God at its creation, and is, therefore, inherent in it; while Plotinus' language on the subject is scarcely distinguishable from Augustine's.[25] According to the other, the human *logos* is but a fraction of the universal *Logos* and reproduces in its thought His normative mind. In the mere matter of forms of statement, therefore, Augustine had harbingering enough. It was, nevertheless, quite a new spirit which informed his declarations, the spirit of a pure theism, derived, not from his philosophical predecessors, but from those Scriptures which themselves also told him of the true light that lighteth every man who cometh into the world.[26] It was the personal God, therefore, whom he spoke of as the " Sun of the soul, by whose illumination alone can intelligible verities be perceived," [27] the " Light of the truth," by which alone is knowledge of the truth awakened in the soul,[28] or — changing the figure only — the inner Monitor and Master of the soul.[29] It was the personal Logos that he had in mind, through whose immanent working all things that exist exist, all things that live live, all things that understand understand. Surely if it

[24] Eusebius, " Praep. Evang.," xi. 18.

[25] Cf. " De civitate Dei," x. 2.

[26] Cf. " Tract. in Joan." ii. 7; " Epist." 120. 4; " De pecc. merit." i. 25, 37, 48.

[27] " Solill.," i. 3.

[28] " De pecc. merit.," i. 25, 37.

[29] " De magistro."

be true even of the body that in Him we live and move and have our being,[30] it must much more be true of the mind, which, having been made in His likeness, lives and moves and has its being in Him in some more excellent, but of course not visible but intelligible way,[31] so that our spiritual illumination comes from the Word of God.[32]

We perceive that the outcome of this conception is that the condition of all knowledge is revelation. Accordingly, our action in seeking knowledge is represented as essentially a consultation of God; God's action in giving us knowledge as essentially a transference of truth to us by a divine imprinting of it on the soul. That mental act which we call understanding, Augustine explains,[33] is performed in two ways: either by the mind or reason within itself, as when we understand that the intellect itself exists; or on occasion of a suggestion from the senses, as when we understand that matter exists: in the first of which two kinds of acts we understand through ourselves, that is, by consulting God [34] concerning that which is within us; while in the second we understand by consulting God regarding that of which intimation is given us by the body and the senses. That is to say, in brief, knowledge of the sensible and of the intelligible alike is God-given, and in both instances is to be obtained only by referring to His teaching. He adds, in another place,[35] that this God who is so consulted, and who, being so consulted, teaches us, is none other than Christ, who dwells in the inner man — that is to say, " the incommutable Virtue of God, and His eternal Wisdom, which every rational soul, indeed, consults, though to each there is given only in proportion to his receptive capacity as determined by his own bad or good will." The divine act of giving, Augustine presents by predilection under the figure of an impressing as by a seal

---

[30] " Epist." 120. 4; " De Trinitate," xiv. 12.
[31] " De Trinitate, xiv. 12.
[32] Cf. " Tract. in Joan.," i.
[33] " Epist." xiii. (to Nebridius) 4.
[34] Deum consulendo.
[35] " De magistro," xi. 38.

or stamp, upon the soul. In what may be thought, perhaps, the classical passage on this subject,[36] he raises the question whence men obtain their knowledge of God and of the moral law. Not from memory, he answers, whether of their former existence in Adam or of any other state. Whence, then? Can we suppose that they can read off these immutable laws from their own mutable natures; these righteous laws from their own unrighteous hearts? " Where, then, do these rules stand written, whence even the unrighteous may recognize what is righteous; whence he that has not may learn what he ought to have? Where can they stand written save in the book of that Light which is called the Truth, whence every righteous law is transcribed, and transferred into the heart of the man who works righteousness, not by a process of transportation, but by a process of imprinting, as the device from a ring while it passes over into the wax, yet does not leave the ring." What the soul receives, therefore, is not the ring itself with its device; certainly not the device in the ring; but the device as impressed upon it from the ring, and the ring only in and through the device. The care which is taken here to represent the process as a transference of the laws without transfusion of the substance may be said to be the characteristic feature of this passage, as it is of the entire teaching of Augustine on the topic. The figure itself is in repeated use by him, and always with the same implication. Nowhere does he permit the reader to suppose either that God in His substance invades the soul, or that the soul sees in God the ideas which constitute the intelligible world: although he insists steadily that these ideas are the ideas that are in God and that he who sees them, therefore, so far sees God — but in a glass darkly. In a word, he preserves the distinctness of the human soul at the same time that he discovers in the intelligible world open to the soul a point of contact with God; and in the soul's perception of the intelligibles a perception at the same time of God, whose existence thus becomes to the soul as intuitively certain as is its own.

[36] " De Trinitate," xiv. 15. 21.

The effect of such an ascription of all human knowledge to a revelation from God is naturally greatly to increase the assurance with which truth is embraced. The ultimate ground of our certitude becomes our confidence in God. In the last analysis, God is our surety for the validity of our knowledge; and that, not merely remotely, as the author of our faculties of knowing, but also immediately as the author of our every act of knowing, and of the truth which is known. We must guard, indeed, against supposing that, in Augustine's view, the human mind is passive in the acquisition of knowledge, or that the acquisition of knowledge is unconditioned by the nature or state of the acquiring soul. We have already had occasion to quote passages in which the contrary is asserted, but we must now emphasize it with some energy. We have been contemplating thus far only Augustine's ontology of knowledge: that we may be sure that we understand him aright we need to attend also to his expositions of its mode. The fundamental principle which rules his thought here may be brought into relation with his favorite figure, if we bear in mind that an impression from a seal is conditioned not only by the device on the seal from which the transference is made, but also by the nature and state of the wax into which it is made — which " takes " the impression, as we say. Suppose, for example, that the wax is not of a quality, or is not in a condition, to take or to retain with exactness or with clearness the device which is impressed upon it? Augustine accordingly insists that, although " every rational mind consults the eternal wisdom," that is to say, by virtue of its very rationality is a recipient of impressions from the divine world of ideas, and thus has the acquisition of truth opened to it, or even, rather, thrust upon it: yet this truth is " actually laid open to it (' unfolded to it,' *panditur*) in each case, only so far as it is able to lay hold of it (' receive it,' ' take it,' *capere*) by reason of (*propter*) its own will, whether evil or good." [37] In the interests of this point of

---

[37] " De magistro," xi. 38; cf. also " De Trinitate," xiv. 15. 21, *ad finem;* " In Psalmos," iv. 8, *med. et fin.* Knowledge, therefore, with Augustine, is conditioned by the will; though we must be careful not to take the term " will "

view, Augustine made, in effect, a distinction between ideas, conceptions and perceptions. The ideas, which are reflections from the divine mind are always shining into the souls of men, unchangeable in the midst of men's multiform changes, whether these changes are due to their natural development from infancy to maturity, and on to old age, or to any other accident of life. But the perception of these ideas by the differing souls of men, or by the same soul in its varying stages or states, and, much more, the conceptions built up upon the foundation of these perceptions by the differing souls, or by the same soul in its varying states — obviously these are very different matters. In these things the soul itself comes into play, and the result will differ as soul differs from soul, or the soul in one of its states differs from itself in another of its states. If the condition of all knowledge, then, is revelation, and therefore all knowledge is in its source divine; yet it is equally true that the qualification of all knowledge is rooted in the human nature that knows, and in the specific state of the human being whose particular knowledge it is. It is in this fact that the varying degrees of purity in which knowledge is acquired by men find their explanation.

The underlying conception here is the very fruitful one that knowledge is not a function of the intellect merely but involves the whole man. There is nothing on which Augustine more strenuously insists; as, indeed, there is nothing upon which from his psychological or ethical point of view it became him more strenuously to insist. His psychological insight was too clear, and his analysis too profound, for him to lose sight of the simplicity of the soul and its consequent engagement

---

in too narrow a sense — as if it always must mean in Augustine the faculty of determination. It is, rather, quite frequently the whole voluntary nature; and what Augustine is really teaching is that the ethical state of the soul conditions knowledge. See the whole subject discussed from different points of view by W. Kahl, " Die Lehre vom Primat des Willens bei Augustinus, Duns Scotus und Descartes," 1886, and O. Zänker, " Der Primat des Willens vor dem Intellekt bei Augustin," in " Beiträge zur Förderung christlicher Theologie," xi. 1907. The literature of the subject is cited by these writers.

as a whole in all its acts; and the demands of his ethical nature
were too clamant and his religious sense too lively to permit
him to forget for an instant the determining effect upon every
movement of the soul of the influences proceeding from them.
Accordingly he does not content himself with declaring that
no one can hope to see the truth without giving to philosophy
his whole self.[38] Applying this conception in detail, he insists
that God accords the truth only to those who seek it *pie, caste
et diligenter*,[39] and urges therefore to a strenuous and devout
pursuit of it, because it is only those who so seek whom God
aids,[40] and the vision of the truth belongs only to those who
live well, pray well, and labor well.[41] The conception includes
more than a contention that for the actual framing of knowledge there is required no less than the action of God reflecting
truth into the soul, an action of the soul's own in embracing
this truth, and prior to that a preparation of the soul for embracing it. It seems to be further implied that the several orders
of truth need different kinds or at least degrees of preparation
for their reception. In proportion as we rise in the scale of
knowledge, in that proportion embracing the truth becomes
difficult and the preparation of the soul arduous. To attain the
knowledge of God, which stands at the apex of achievement,
demands therefore a very special purgation. Drawing near to
Him does not mean journeying through space, for He is everywhere; it means entering into that purity and virtue in which
He dwells.[42] "O God," he prays, "whom no one finds who is

---

[38] "Cont. Acad." ii. 3. 8: "ipsum verum non videbis, nisi in philosophiam
totus intraveris."

[39] "De quantitate animae," xiv. 24.

[40] "De vera religione," x. 20: "intende igitur . . . diligenter et pie,
quantum potes; tales enim adjuvat Deus."

[41] "De ordine," ii. 19. 51.

[42] "De doctrina Christiana," i. 10. 10: "The soul must be purified that it
may have power to perceive that light and to rest in it when it is perceived";
this purification is journeying to God, for it is not by change of place that we
draw near to Him who is everywhere, but by becoming pure and virtuous. Cf.
"De Trinitate," iv. 18. 24: Sinful men need cleansing to be fitted to see eternal
things; "De agone Christiano," xiii. 14: A vicious life cannot see that pure
and sincere and changeless life.

not fully purged." [43] The influence of his Neo-Platonic teachers is here very apparent, and is further manifested in a tendency to represent the purgation of the soul for the higher knowledge as consisting largely in its emancipation from sense. With him as with them knowledge of the truth is constantly spoken of as hanging essentially upon the escape of the soul from entanglement with the sensible.[44] This, as we have seen, is a corollary of his rationalism and was perhaps inevitable with his training. But these expressions which might be almost exactly matched in Plotinus, have in Augustine, nevertheless, an indefinitely deeper implication than in his Neo-Platonic predecessors. With him the purely intellectualistic bearing which they have with them, has noticeably given way to a profoundly ethical one. Though he may still say that " the filth of the soul " " from which filth the more one is cleansed, the more readily he sees the truth," is shortly " the love of anything whatever except God and the soul ";[45] and though, therefore, he may still relatively depreciate all knowledge other than that of God and the soul; yet after all, as he uses these terms, it is of something far more profound than the relative intellectual rank of the several objects of knowledge that he is thinking.

The implications of this general conception carried Augustine very far. Three of the corollaries which flow from it seem especially worthy of attention here. The first of these is that, the human soul being finite, it cannot hope to attain to absolutely perfect knowledge. The second is that, the human soul being subject to development, it can hope to attain to anything like adequate knowledge only by a slow process, and by means of aid from without. The third is that, the human soul in its present condition being sinful, there is a clog upon it in its aspiration to knowledge which it can never in its own strength overcome. In order that we may apprehend Augustine's thought we must therefore attend to his doctrine of mystery as lying at the heart of all our knowledge; to his doctrine

---

[43] " Solil.," i. 3.

[44] " Cont. Acad." II. ii.

[45] " De utilitate credendi," 34.

of authority as the necessary pedagogue to knowledge; and to his doctrine of revelation as the palliative, and of grace as the cure, of the noetic effects of sin.

In his assertion of the certitude of human knowledge, Augustine is far from asserting that the human soul can know everything; or that it can know anything with that perfection of knowledge with which the infinite mind knows all things. It is impossible for the finite intelligence to comprehend in its mental embrace all that is the object of knowledge: it is as impossible for it to penetrate to the bottom of any object of knowledge which it embraces. For it, mystery not only surrounds the circle of knowledge illuminated by its intelligence, with a vast realm of impenetrable darkness; mystery equally underlies all that it knows as an unfathomable abyss which it cannot plumb. We know, then, and can know, only in part; only part of what there is to know, and what we do know only in part. This is true of all our knowledge alike, whether of sensible things or of intelligible things, whether of the world without us or of the world within us, or — in the highest measure — of the world above us, culminating in God, the mystery that surrounds whom dismays the intellect and compels us to exclaim that no knowledge can be had of Him beyond the knowledge of how ignorant we are of Him.[46] Of our very souls themselves, the very selves which know and which are known most intimately of all things, we know next to nothing. Augustine exhorts his somewhat bumptious young correspondent who fancied, apparently, that he knew all that was to be known of the soul, " to understand what he did not understand, lest he should understand nothing at all." [47] For who knows either how the soul comes into existence, or (that impenetrable mystery) how it is related to the body? So far is Augustine from supposing, therefore, that the soul is clothed in omniscience, or that it can know unto perfection any single object of its knowledge, that he rather teaches that all our knowledge rests

---

[46] " De ordine " ii. 18. 47: " cujus (Dei) nulla scientia est in anima, nisi scire quomodo eum nesciat." Cf. " De doctrina Christiana " i. 6. 6.

[47] " De anima et ejus origine," vi. 11. 15.

on mystery and runs up into mystery. What we know we know; and our certitude of that may be complete. But what we do not know surges all about us, an ocean of illimitable extent, and sinks beneath our very knowledge, a bottomless depth. We penetrate with our knowing but a very little way into the knowable before we lose ourselves in profundities which baffle all our inquisition.

The limitation which is placed upon our knowledge by our very nature as finite beings is greatly aggravated by the circumstance that we are not only finite but immature beings. We do not come into existence in the maturity of our powers; indeed, we remain throughout life, or we would better say throughout eternity, creatures whose very characteristic is change, or, to put it at its best, ever-progressing growth. At no given point in this development, of course, are we all that even we shall become. For the attainment, then, in our immaturity, of such knowledge as belongs to us as finite beings, there is obvious need of help from without. In other words, there is place for authority, and its correlate, faith. This is an ordinance of nature. Those who are first infants, then children, and only through the several stages of gradual ripening attain the maturity of their powers, will need at every step of their growth the guidance of those who are more mature than they, that they may accept on their authority, by faith, what they are not yet in a position to ascertain for themselves, by reason. And, as it is inevitable even among mature men, that some should outrun others in the attainment of knowledge; and especially that some should become particularly knowing in this or that sphere of knowledge, to which they have given unusual attention, or for which they have enjoyed uncommon facilities; there will always remain for creatures subject to change and developing progressively in their powers, not only a legitimate but a necessary place for authority on the one hand and for faith on the other. Not, of course, as if faith should, or could, supplant reason, or be set in opposition to reason. On the one hand, a right faith is always a reasonable faith; that is to say, it is accorded only to an authority which com-

mends itself to reason as a sound authority, which it would be
unreasonable not to trust. On the other hand, faith is in its
idea not so much a substitute for reason as a preparation for
reason; and the effort of the wise man should be to transmute
his faith into knowledge, that is to say as his powers become
more and more capable of the performance and opportunity
offers, gradually to replace belief by sight. But in any event
for such creatures as we are, our walk must largely be guided
by faith, and it is only through faith that we can hope to attain
to knowledge.[48]

Now add the factor of sin — sin which enters the soul of
man, already, one would think, sufficiently handicapped in attaining truth by its finiteness and its immaturity, and refracts
and deflects the rays of truth reflected into it from the divine
source, so rendering the right perception of the truth impossible. The finiteness of the soul only so far limits it in the attainment of truth, that, being finite, it cannot know all truth
nor all that is true of what it truly knows: what it does know is
truth, and so far as it is known this truth is truly known. The
immaturity of the soul passes gradually away as its powers
develop, and therefore imposes only a temporary check upon
the attainment of truth — determines that attainment to be a
process of gradual advance instead of an instantaneous achievement. Neither the soul's finiteness, nor its mutability, accordingly, need more than warn us of the limitations of our powers
and induce in us a becoming humility and patience. But the
invasion of the soul by sin is a different matter. Here is a
power which acts destructively upon the soul's native powers
of apprehending truth, blinds the eyes of the mind, distorts its
vision, fills it with illusions, so that it sees awry; and a power

[48] For this doctrine in its highest application, cf., e.g., " De Trinitate " xv.
27. 49: " But if they think they ought to deny that these things are, because
they, with their blind minds, cannot discern them, then those who are blind
from their birth, also, ought to deny that there is a sun. The light shines in
darkness, and if the darkness comprehend it not, let them first be illuminated
by the gift of God, that they may be believers: and let them begin to be
light in comparison with unbelievers; and when this foundation has been laid,
let them look up and see what they believe, that at some time they may be
able to see."

which so far from passing away with time and growth, battens by what it feeds on and increases in its baleful influence until it overwhelms the soul with falsehood. No merely incomplete, or as yet uncompleted, knowledge accordingly results; but just no knowledge at all, or even anti-knowledge, positive error, vanity, and lies; and thus a condition is created which assuredly calls not for humility and patience, but for despair.

The question obtrudes itself whether such a doctrine does not render nugatory all of Augustine's carefully built up theory of the acquisition of knowledge. Granted that normal man may look within and find there impressed upon his very being the forms of thought by which God thinks, in the light of which he may see truth and know it to be divinely certain because certainly divine. Man as we know him is not normal man. Afflicted by the disease of sin which darkens the light that shines into him from God, clouding his vision of truth and deflecting all the activities of his mind — who will give him true knowledge? Surely, whatever may be true of abstract man, sinful man, which is the only man we know, is on this teaching condemned to eternal nescience. Must not Augustine, on his own showing, in the case of actual man, take his place, then, among the skeptics? It certainly is important for the understanding of Augustine's doctrine of knowledge to observe how he meets this obvious criticism.

Of the form in which the criticism itself is often urged, we may find a very instructive example in the formulation of it by Mr. John Owen, who, as an outcome of the very line of reasoning which we have suggested, formally classes Augustine not only among the skeptics, but among the skeptics of the worst order. Simple skepticism, he tells us, affects the basis of knowledge only; Augustine's variety of skepticism undermines the foundations, not only of truth but also of morals. For, according to Augustine, he continues —

By the disobedience of its ancestor the majority of the whole human race has become totally incapacitated for knowing or doing what is right and good. The faculties of every man, both of soul and body, have become perverted and misleading. It is needless to dwell on the theological aspects of this momentous doctrine; our present concern is with its philosophical bearings. We here see, as I have already suggested, the Augustinian theology in intimate relationship with Skepticism. With one voice the Greek Skeptics had declared the senses to be untrustworthy, the reason to be perverted, all the natural powers of man to be insufficient to attain knowledge, and precisely the same conclusions were arrived at by Augustine with the portentous extension of the incapacity to all right and good action. The latter fact renders, in my opinion, Augustine's theological Skepticism much more mischievous than any amount of mere speculative theoretical unbelief could possibly have been. . . . That man with all his efforts is unable to attain truth may conceivably be an unavoidable necessity of the only possible *modus operandi* of his faculties, and therefore the fact may not in the least detract from the beneficence of his Creator; but the moment we make his creation and fall, and perhaps his consequent eternal misery, indissoluble parts of the original intention of Omnipotence concerning him, that moment God is shorn of his attribute of goodness, man becomes the hapless victim of a caprice as unreasonable as it is irresistible, and the creation, so far as the majority of human beings is concerned, is a stupendous act of despotism and cruelty.[49]

We have required to quote so much of Mr. Owen's remarks in order to place his representation fully before us; and we require to say this much to exonerate ourselves from the suspicion of having quoted so much merely in order that we might stultify Mr. Owen's profession of concerning himself solely with the philosophical bearings of Augustine's doctrine of original sin. In point of fact he concerns himself with little except its theological aspects. After having barely remarked that it has philosophical bearings, he lapses at once into an assault on the doctrine on the ground that it contradicts the beneficence of God and indeed transmutes the good God into a cruel demon. We must refuse to be led off from our proper subject by this impertinent display of the *odium theologicum;* and we take note here accordingly merely of Mr. Owen's phil-

[49] John Owen, "Evenings with the Skeptics," ii. p. 196.

osophical criticism that Augustine's doctrine of original sin brings him into intimate relations with Greek skepticism.

Apparently what Mr. Owen means to suggest is that Augustine reached "precisely the same conclusions" with the Greek skeptics, and differed from them only in the grounds upon which he based these conclusions. They contended that human faculties are, as such, incapable of ascertaining truth; he, that human faculties have been so injured by sin as to have become incapable of ascertaining truth. That there is a sense in which this representation is perfectly just is obvious. Augustine did hold that the native depravity of man has noetic as well as thelematic and ethical effects: and that sinful man, as such, is therefore precluded by his sinfulness from that perception of truth which can be only *pie et caste* attained. To him it was therefore axiomatic that the natural man is incapable of attaining to true knowledge, at least in its highest reaches — those reaches in which the deflection of sin would be most apparent. But in his hatred of Augustine's doctrine of original sin, Mr. Owen has failed to observe that Augustine did not leave matters at that point. Where he differs by a whole diameter from the skeptics is that he knows a remedy for the dreadful condition in which human nature finds itself. When the skeptics declared that it belongs to human nature as such to be incapable of knowledge, there was an end of the matter. The condition of man is hopeless: he actually lacks faculty for knowing. Augustine's contention, on the contrary, is that it is knowledge, not nescience, which belongs to human nature as such. And if he finds human nature in a state in which it cannot fulfill its destiny of knowing, he knows how it may be recovered to itself and to the capacity for knowledge which properly belongs to it. In other words, the sinful condition of human nature is viewed by Augustine as abnormal; and all the results of this sinfulness as abnormalities which may be and are to be overcome. That Mr. Owen says nothing at this point of the provisions for overcoming these abnormalities cannot be set down to the credit of his account of Augustine's teaching.

At another point of Mr. Owen's discussion, no doubt, there does occur some suggestion of these provisions, though certainly a very insufficient one. He remarks [50] that " from the earliest history of Christianity the skeptical argument had been employed, for evidential purposes, as an *à priori* justification of divine revelation both in its ethical and intellectual acceptation." And he supports this by remarking further that " by the early Christian Fathers the confessions of ignorance, limitation, &c. on the part of Greek skeptics were put forward to show the necessity of superhuman knowledge." Even this suggestion is introduced, however, not to palliate but to accentuate Augustine's fault — not to point so much to the remedy which he offered for the noetic effects of sin, as to the excess of his " depreciation of human nature." Augustine had so low an opinion " of the intellectual imbecility of humanity," it seems, that he readily accepted the dogma " of the natural depravity of man " " as a complete solution of what would otherwise have been an enigma " to him. Nevertheless, it is not difficult to perceive that the postulation of a divine revelation comes in upon the conception of the sinborn " imbecility of humanity " as a mitigation of its otherwise hopeless condition. The proclamation of the provision of a divine revelation, if on the one hand it implies a need for it, on the other hand asserts a remedy for that need. Nor does the assertion of divine revelation cover the whole provision which Augustine offers for the removal of the natural incapacities of sinful man. He did not confine himself to pointing out a mitigation for the symptom; he sought and found also a remedy for the disease. If the noetic effects of sin might be neutralized by divine revelation, sin itself might be removed by divine grace. It is certainly grossly unfair to Augustine's teaching as to man's condition to focus attention upon the disease under which he holds that man suffers, and withdraw it entirely from the remedy which he asserts has been provided for this disease.

We must not, then, be misled into supposing Augustine

[50] *Op. cit.*, ii. p. 190.

to teach, even by remote implication, that man is hopelessly
sunk in nescience or even in sin. Perfectly true as this is of his
teaching of the condition of man considered in himself alone
and so far as his own powers are concerned, it is considerably
less than half the truth of Augustine's teaching of the condition of man. It means, no doubt, that Augustine, as he
looked upon the virtues of the heathen as little more than
splendida vitia, so looked upon the philosophy of the heathen
as very much a farrago of nonsense. What a multitude of
philosophers there have been, he exclaimed, in effect, and
almost more opinions than philosophers! Who can find any
two of them who perfectly agree? Varro enumerates not less
than two hundred and eighty-eight possible sects. It would
be easier to find a needle in a haystack than truth among these
professional purveyors of truth.[51] But then Augustine knew
something better than heathen thought to which to direct one
in search of truth, as he knew something better than heathen
ethics to which to direct one in search of holiness. His great
word was *revelation;* and behind and above and all through
revelation, there was the greater word still, *grace.* No doubt
this means that he transferred dependence for truth, as for
holiness, from man to God. He did distrust human nature as
he found it. He did consider it in its own strength incapable
of any good thing, and equally of any right thought. He did
cast men back for all good on God's grace, for all truth on
God's teaching. So far writers like Mr. Owen are quite right.
Augustine did believe in the ingrained depravity of man in
his present manifestation on earth; he did believe that this
depravity renders him morally incapable and intellectually
imbecile, if this somewhat exaggerated language pleases us.
But he believed also in the goodness of God; and he believed
that this good God has intervened with His grace to cure
man's moral inability, and with His revelation to rescue man
from his intellectual imbecility.

Nor was this doctrine of revelation and grace as remedies
for man's sinful incapacities and condition a mechanical in-

[51] See " De Civitate Dei," xviii. 41.

trusion of an alien idea into Augustine's general conception. It rather stands in the most direct analogy alike with his whole conception of man's relation to God and with his particular view of man's natural needs and the natural provision for their satisfaction. Even had man not been sinful, Augustine would never have allowed that he was in a position of himself, apart from God, to do any good or to attain any truth. That would have seemed to him a crass deism, of which he would have been incapable. Even sinless man would have been to him absolutely dependent on God, the Author of all being, the Light of all knowledge, the Source of all good. We have seen him openly teaching that man as man can see light only in the Light; that all truth is the reflection into the soul of the truth that is in God; in a word, that the condition of all knowledge for dependent creatures is revelation, in the wider sense of that word. When now he teaches that revelation in a narrower sense and a more objective form is the condition of all right knowledge of higher things for sinful man — a revelation which is an integral part of a scheme of grace for the recovery of sinful man, not only from the effects of his sin but form his sin itself — he is speaking in close analogy with his fundamental theistic conception of the universe. He is but throwing sinful man back afresh on the God on whom men in all states and condition are absolutely dependent.

Similarly, the provision which Augustine makes, in revelation, to meet the sin-bred inability of men to attain right knowledge, is only an extension in a right line of the provision he discovered for meeting man's natural weakness growing out of his finiteness, and especially out of his only gradually attained maturity. In that case, we remember, he pointed to authority as the remedy for as yet ineffective reason. The child is naturally dependent on the authority of its elders, who offer to its faith the truth which its reason is as yet incapable of discovering or authenticating for itself. In every sphere of life we remain dependent on the authority of those who are in this or that or the other department of knowledge better instructed than we; and he who will be taught nothing, but

insists on following his reason alone, is soon at the end of
living in this world. Revelation plays precisely the same rôle
for the mind darkened by sin. The heavenly Father intervenes to meet the needs of sin-blinded souls by offering to
their faith, on the authority of God, the truth which they
are as sinners incapable of ascertaining for themselves. This
is the essence of Augustine's doctrine of revelation. Of course
the condition of man as sinner determines as well the nature
of the truths he needs to know as the manner in which alone
he can come to the knowledge of them: the whole content
of revelation is determined by the needs of those to whom it
is made. But that may be left to one side here. What we are
at present especially concerned with is that the need of revelation and the provision of revelation for sinful man stand in
perfect analogy with the need and provision of instruction for,
say, the immature child. The principle which governs in both
cases is, not that reason is superseded by something better,
but that, in default of reason due to special circumstances,
provision is taken to supply the lack of reason, until reason
may come to its rights. The lame man is supplied with a
crutch until his lameness is healed. Here we have in brief
Augustine's whole doctrine of revelation.

Clear and reasonable, however, as is Augustine's doctrine
of revelation as the remedy for man's sin-bred disability to
know aright, it seems to be very difficult for some writers
to believe that it could have been a reality to him. It is not
rare, therefore, to hear it intimated that he passed all his
days under the torture of gnawing doubt, and flung himself
upon the authority of the Church as some sort of palliation
of his wearing despair. His permanent state of mind regarding
Christianity, we are told, is much that which is exhibited in
a certain class of Romish controversial literature, in which
after every other support for human trust has been sedulously
removed we are ultimately invited to take refuge in the authority of the Church as the sole haven of peace. This representation is given expression, as well as elsewhere, in some
remarks of Prof. Adolf Harnack's, when he comes, in his

" History of Dogma," to deal with Augustine's attitude to
the authority of the Church.[52] Here we are told that Augustine
had become convinced, in his conflict with himself, " of the
badness of human nature," and had been left by Manichæism
" in complete doubt as to the foundations and truth of the
Christian faith." And then:

> His confidence in the rationality of Christian truth had been
> shaken to the very depths, *and it was never restored.* In other words,
> as an individual *thinker* he never gained the subjective certitude
> that Christian truth, and as such everything contained in the two
> Testaments had to be regarded, was clear, consistent and demon-
> strable. When he threw himself into the arms of the Catholic Church,
> he was perfectly conscious that he needed its *authority* not to sink
> in scepticism or nihilism.

Dr. Harnack is too good a scholar to enunciate a historical
judgment utterly without elements of truth. There are elements of truth of great importance even in this judgment,
far from the mark as is the application which is made of them;
and there are even points of great interest in the use which
Dr. Harnack makes of these elements of truth. It is certainly
true that in his experience with the Manichæans Augustine
learned to distrust unaided reason as the source of religious
truth; and discovered that there is a legitimate place for
authority in religion. The Manichæans had promised him a
purely rational religion; he found on testing it that what
they gave him was a mass of irrationalities; and on feeling
out for himself he discovered that unaided reason was inadequate to the task of meeting all the needs of man. There
is truth, therefore, in saying that he once for all discarded
reason as the sole instrument for the acquisition of truth in
the religious sphere, and cast himself on instruction as the
single hope of the soul in its longing after truth. But the
sense in which this is true of Augustine is indefinitely different
from the sense it takes upon itself in Dr. Harnack's representation. Beneath Dr. Harnack's representation there lies

[52] E. T. v. p. 79.

Dr. Harnack's own conception not only of the place of authority in religion, but of the nature of the Christian religion and its relation to authority, and of the nature of the particular source of authority to which he conceives that Augustine fled in his need, and of the rationality of Augustine's act in taking refuge with it. His whole statement, therefore, leaves the impression that Augustine in despair of reason renounced rationality, and gave himself over to an unreasoned authority for guidance; and never again recovered, we will not say objective rationality in his religious views, but even subjective confidence. The very interesting defense of authority in religion — from the historical point of view at least, if not from the intrinsic — with which Dr. Harnack closes his discussion [53] does nothing to modify this impression. It remains the gist of his exposition that Augustine took refuge in authority, because he despaired of reason, and therefore his attitude towards Christianity remained throughout life that of an irrationalist.

Nothing, however, could be less true than this of Augustine's real attitude. His appeal to authority was in his own mind not a desertion of reason but an advance towards reason. He sought truth through authority only because it became clear to him that this was the rational road to truth. It was thus not as an irrationalist, but as a rationalist, that he made his appeal to authority. His breach with Manichæism and his gradual establishment in Christian truth, in other words, was on this side of it merely the discovery that the Christian religion is not a natural religion and is therefore not either excogitable or immediately demonstrable by reason working solely on natural grounds; but is rather a revealed religion and therefore requires in the first instance to be told to us. It is thus in the last analysis, supernaturalism as versus naturalism that he turns to; [54] and this is far from the same

[53] Pp. 82–83.

[54] " De utilitate credendi," 29: " Therefore this so vast difficulty, since our inquiry is about religion, God alone can remedy: nor, indeed, unless we believe both that He is, and that He helps men's minds, ought we even to inquire of the true religion itself."

thing as irrationality as versus rationality — except, indeed,
on the silent assumption that the supernatural is an absurdity,
an assumption which was decidedly not Augustine's. In the
sixth book of the " Confessions " he recounts to us the several
steps by which he rose from the pure naturalism which had
hitherto held him to this Christian supernaturalism. His disillusionment with Manichæism did not at once deliver him
from his naturalistic point of view. He had found the tenets
of the Manichæans irrational. But his rejection of them as
such did not at once entail the adoption of another set of
tenets as rational. His sad experience with them operated
rather to make him chary of committing himself to any
other body of conclusions whatever. He remained in principle
a naturalist *á outrance*. He demanded the apodeictic certainty
of mathematical demonstration for conviction; that is to say,
he still depended for the discovery of truth upon immediate
rational demonstration alone. This alone seemed to him adequate evidence upon which one could safely venture. All this
time, says he, he was restraining his heart from believing anything, and thus in avoiding the precipice was strangling his
soul: what he was demanding was that he should be made as
certain of things unseen as that seven and three make ten.[55]
He goes on to remark that a cure for his distress lay open
before him in faith (*credendo*), had he chosen to take that
road, since thus the sight of his mind might have been purged
for vision of the truth. But as yet he could not enter that
path. It was not long, however, before it began to invite his
feet, slowly but surely. He could not avoid perceiving after
a while that it is the path of nature. He reflected upon the
host of things which he accepted on testimony. He reminded
himself that in it lay the foundation of all history: and that
life itself would soon come to a standstill if we refused to act
on the credit of others. He meditated further upon the strength
of the conviction which testimony produces when its validity
and adequacy are beyond question. As the great place which
faith fills in common life thus became more and more clear

[55] " Confessiones," vi. 4. 6.

to him, he could not escape the query why it should not serve a similar end in higher things. The principle of faith and its correlate authority, having once been recognized, it became, indeed, only a question of time before it should take its proper place in these higher concerns also. And, then, it was only a question of fact whether there existed in the world any adequate authority to guide men into the truth. Thus, says he, the Lord drew him on little by little, with a hand of infinite gentleness and mercy, and composing his heart gradually convinced him that in the Scriptures He had given to men an authority to which their faith is due, and through which they may attain by faith that knowledge of divine things to which they are as yet unable to rise through reason. " And also," he adds, " since we are too weak to search out the truth by mere (liquida) reason, and therefore need the authority of Holy Scriptures, I began to believe God never would have given such surpassing authority to those Scriptures throughout the whole world except that He wished to be believed through them and to be sought by their means." [56] There is depicted for us in this vital narrative, no despairing act of renunciation in which Augustine offered up his intellect a sacrifice upon the altar of faith, and sought peace from insatiable doubt in an arbitrary authority to which by an effort of sheer will he submits. What we see is a gradual advance under the leading of reason itself to a rational theory of authority in religion, on the basis of which rational certitude may be enjoyed in the midst of the weakness of this life.

What has been thus incidentally brought before us, it will be perceived, is Augustine's doctrine of faith and reason. The relations of faith and reason, as thus outlined, remained to him always a matter of sincere and reasoned conviction. We may read them so stated in the books " Against the Academics " and in the books " On the Predestination of the Saints " alike. It will be enough for our purpose, however, to observe how he deals with the matter in two or three treatises which are devoted expressly to elucidating certain aspects of it.

[56] " Confessiones," vi. 4. 8.

Take for example the treatises " On the Profit of Believing "
(A.D. 391) and " On Faith in Things Not Seen " (A.D. 400),
which were written not very far apart in time and in very
similar circumstances. In both of these treatises he begins by
setting himself sharply in opposition to the Sensationalists,
" who fancy," says he,[57] " that there is nothing else than what
they perceive by those five well-known reporters of the body,"
and " essay to measure the unsearchable resources of truth "
by " the deceitful rule " of the " impressions (*plagas*) and
images they have received from these "; whom, in a word,
" folly has so made subject to their carnal eyes that whatsoever they see not through them they think they are not to believe." [58] From this starting point, in both alike, however, the
advance is made at once to the defense of faith as a valid form
of conviction, with respect not only to things not perceived by
the bodily senses, but also to those lying beyond the reach of
the intellect itself.[59] And in both alike the stress of the argument is laid upon the naturalness of faith and its indispensableness in the common life of men.[60] Why should that act of
faith which lies at the very basis of human intercourse be excluded from the sphere of religion — especially in the case of
one, say, of weak intelligence? Must a man have no religion
because he is incapable of excogitating one for himself? [61] Certainly we must not confound faith with credulity: nobody asks
that Christ should be believed in without due evidence that he
is worthy of being believed in.[62] But, on the other hand, it is
just as certain that we shall not attain to any real religion without faith. Say you are determined to have a religion which
you can demonstrate. The very search for it presupposes a
precedent faith that there is a God and that he cares for us;
for surely no one will seek God, or inquire how we should

[57] " De utilitate credendi," 1.
[58] " De fide rerum quae non vid.," 1.
[59] *Ibid.* 2 *sq.*
[60] *Ibid.* 4; " De utilitate credendi," 23.
[61] " De utilitate credendi," 24.
[62] " De fide rerum quae non vid.," 5: cf. " De utilitate credendi," 22 *sq.*, and
25, where the necessary distinctions are drawn.

serve Him, without so much to go on.[63] And where and how will you seek? Perchance you will inquire the way of those who are wise? Who are the wise? How will you determine who are wise in such things? In the manifold disagreements of pretenders to wisdom, it will require a wise man to select the really wise. We are caught in a fatal circle here; we must needs be wise beforehand in order to discriminate wisdom.[64] There is but one outlet; and that outlet is, shortly, revelation. For revelation is a thing which can be validated by appropriate evidence even to those who have not yet attained wisdom; and which, when once trusted on its appropriate grounds, gradually leads us into that wisdom which before was unobtainable. Thus, to man unable to see the truth, a justified authority steps in to fit him to see it; and it is authority alone which can bring such wisdom.[65] This is the reason the Lord has chosen this method of dealing with us. Bringing us a medicine destined to heal our corrupted condition, " he procured authority by miraculous works, acquired faith by authority, drew together numbers by faith, gained antiquity by numbers, confirmed religion by antiquity: so that not only the supremely inept novelty of heresy in its deceitful working, but even the inveterate error of heathenism in its violent antagonism can never root up this religion in any way whatever." [66] Here we have Augustine's golden chain. Miracles, authority, faith, numbers, antiquity, an absolutely established religion: that is the sequence, traveling along which men arrive at a secure conviction which nothing can shake.

We may hear him argue the question with even more specific application to the Christian religion in a notable letter which he wrote about 410 to an eminent courtier and scholar.[67] " The minds of men," he tells us here, " are blinded by the pollutions of sin and the lust of the flesh "; they are therefore lost in the mazes of discussion and are unable to

[63] " De utilitate credendi," 29.
[64] *Ibid.* 28.
[65] *Ibid.* 34.
[66] *Ibid.* 32 *ad fin.*
[67] " Epist." 118 (to Dioscorus), 5. 32–33.

discover the truth of things by reason. Therefore, that men
may have the truth, Christ came — the Truth Itself, in union
with a man — to instruct them in truth. Thus men are given
the truth through faith, in order that "by instruction in
salutary truth they may escape from their perplexities into
the atmosphere of pure and simple truth." That is to say, we
are introduced to truth by Christ's authority, so that, thus
receiving it by faith, we may then be able to defend it by
reason. "The perfection of method in training disciples," we
read, "is, that those who are weak should be encouraged to
enter the citadel of authority, in order that, when they have
been safely placed there, the conflict necessary for their defence may be maintained by the most strenuous use of reason."
"Thus," he adds, "the whole supremacy of authority and
light of reason for regenerating and reforming the human
race has been made to reside in the one saving Name, and in
His one Church." For Christ has "both secured the Church
in the citadel of authority . . . and supplied it with the
abundant armor of equally invincible reason." The former He
has done by means of the "highly celebrated ecumenical councils, and the Apostolic sees themselves" — which is as much
as to say, apparently, that the authority of the Church finds
expression through these organs. And the latter He has done
"by means of a few men of pious learning and unfeigned
spirituality" — that is to say, apparently, these are the organs through which the inherent rationality of Church teaching evinces itself. The entire sense seems, then, to be that what
is taught by the Church on authority, through the appropriate
organs of authority, is equally defended by the Church by
reason, through the appropriate organs of reason. The Church
as the pillar and ground of the truth commends it to faith; the
Church, giving a reason for the faith that is in it, defends
it to reason. The Doctor,[68] in other words, is as truly a manifestation of the Church's inherent life as the Bishop himself:

[68] On the "Doctor" in the early church, see Smith and Cheetham, "Dictionary of Christian Antiquities," 1876, i. p. 385a; and Harnack, in his larger
edition of the "Didaché," 1884, pp. 131 sq.; and in his "Expansion of Christianity," E. T. i. pp. 444 sq.

reasoning is as inadmissibly her function as authoritative definition. Here is certainly an elevation of authority, properly grounded, as a source of conviction; an elevation of faith, properly placed, as a mode of conviction. But here is no depreciation of demonstration and reason to make way for authority and faith. On the contrary, the two are placed side by side, as joint methods and organs for attaining truth; and the contention is merely that to each its own sphere belongs into which the other cannot intrude.

It has seemed most convenient to present in the first instance Augustine's entire doctrine of faith and reason in concrete form, and in its application to the main problem to which he applied it. But having in this way caught a glimpse of it as a whole and in its ultimate bearings, it seems desirable to pause and to glance in some detail at the main elements which enter into it.

Let us first look at the doctrine in its most general aspects. The fact of primary importance to note here is that with Augustine faith and reason are never conceived as antagonists, contradictories, but always as coadjutants, coöperating to a common end. The thing sought is truth: what Augustine has discovered is that there are two modes of mental action by which truth may be laid hold of. It may be grasped by faith, or it may be grasped by reason. " No one doubts," he tells us, " that we are impelled to the acquisition of knowledge by a double impulse — of authority and of reason." [69] And, though we may be so constituted as eagerly to desire " to apprehend what is true not only by faith but by the understanding "; [70] and may, therefore, give to reason the primacy in rank, yet we are bound to acknowledge for faith a priority in time.[71] Granted that faith may seem to be a mode of conviction more suitable for the ignorant multitude than for the instructed few; yet there is no one who does not begin by being ignorant, and there are many things great and good which we could

---

[69] " Cont. Acad.," iii. 20. 43, *ad fin.;* cf. " De ordine," ii. 9. 26, *ad init.*
[70] " Cont. Acad.," *loc. cit.*
[71] " De ordine," *loc. cit.*

never attain were the door not opened to us by faith.[72] Life
is too short to attempt to solve every question for ourselves,
even of those which are capable of being solved. We must be
content to accept many things on faith and leave difficulties
to be dealt with afterwards, or never to be dealt with.[73] And
surely it is the height of folly, because of insoluble difficulties,
to " permit to escape from our hands things which are altogether certain." [74] What is it but pride — which is the destruction of all true knowledge — that leads us to demand that
we shall, as we say, " understand everything "?

Not, of course, as if faith should be lightly or irrationally
accorded. If there is a sense in which faith precedes reason,
there is equally a sense in which reason precedes faith. That
mental act which we call faith is one possible only to rational
creatures; [75] and of course we act as rational creatures in performing it. " If, then," Augustine argues, " it is rational that,
with respect to some great concerns which we find ourselves
unable to comprehend, faith should precede reason; there can
be no question but that the amount of reason which leads us to
accord this faith, whatever that amount may be, is itself anterior to faith." [76] Faith is by no means blind: it has eyes of
its own with which, before it completes itself in giving that
assent which, when added to thinking, constitutes it believing,[77] it must needs see both that to which it assents and that
on the ground of which it assents to it. As we cannot believe
without knowing what it is to which we accord our faith, so
we cannot believe without perceiving good grounds for according our faith. " No one believes anything unless he has

[72] *Ibid.*

[73] " Epist." 102 (to Deogratias; 406 or 408 A.D.) chap. 38: " sunt enim in-
numerabiles [quaestiones] quae non sunt finiendae ante fidem, ne finiatur vita
sine fide."

[74] " De musica," vi. 5. 8.

[75] " Epist." 120 (to Consentius) chap. 3. " etiam credere non possemus,
nisi rationales animas haberemus."

[76] *Ibid.*

[77] " De praedest. sanctt." ii. 5: "Believing is nothing else than cum assensione cogitare "; " Enchirid." 20: " But if assent is taken away, faith too
falls; for sine assensione nihil creditur."

before thought it worthy of belief." [78] Reason, therefore, can
never be "wholly lacking to faith, because it belongs to it to
consider to whom faith should be given." [79] This function of
reason, by which it considers to what men or writings it is
right to accord faith is then precedent to faith; though faith
is precedent to reason in the sense that, an adequate ground
of credit having been established by reason, conviction must
at once form itself without waiting for comprehension to
become perfect.

Our knowledge thus embraces two classes of things: things
seen and things believed. The difference between them is
this: "with respect to things we have seen or see, we are
our own witnesses; but with respect to those which we believe, we are moved to faith by other witnesses." [80] The distinction which Augustine erects between faith and reason, that
is to say, is briefly that faith is distinctively that conviction
of truth which is founded on testimony as over against that
conviction which is founded on sight.[81] All the corollaries
which flow from this distinction were present to his mind.
He is found, for example, pointing out that all so-called knowledge itself rests on faith, so that in the deepest sense an act
of faith precedes all knowledge. And on the other hand — and
it is this point which is of most present interest to us — that
all faith presupposes reason, and is so far from an irrational
act that an unreasonable faith, a faith not founded in a reasonable authority demanding credit on reasonable grounds, is no
faith at all, but mere "credulity," while what is thus un-
warrantedly believed is mere "opinion." [82] As distinguished
from knowledge on the one hand and credulity on the other,
faith is that act of assent which is founded on adequate testi-

[78] "De praedest. sanctt." ii. 5.

[79] "De vera religione," xxiv. 45, also xxv. 46.

[80] "Epist." 147. 3. 8.

[81] "Epist." 147. 2. 7; "De Diversis Quaestionibus lxxxiii.," Quaest. 54.
In "Retractationes," i. 14. 3 he allows that in such distinctions he is employing
the word "knowledge" in a strict rather than a popular sense: in common
speech we say "we know" even what rests on testimony.

[82] "De utilitate credendi," 11. 25; "De mendac.," 3.

mony; and the form of conviction which is so called may be
free from all doubt whatsoever.[83] So far is faith thus from being a cloak for inexhaustible doubt, that doubt is inconsistent
with it and is excluded just in proportion to the firmness of the
grounding of faith, or, we may better say, just in proportion
as faith fulfills its own idea. Its distinction from knowledge
does not turn on the strength of the conviction it describes,
but on the ground of this conviction. We know by sight; we
believe on testimony.

We turn now to the application of this abstract doctrine
of faith to the problem of the Christian religion. In this instance the testimony on which faith rests — on the basis of
which that conviction we call faith is formed — Augustine
supposed to be the testimony of God Himself. The grounds
on which he accepted as such what he took to be a revelation
from God may be assailed as insufficient; and the channels
through which he considered that what he took to be a revelation from God asserts its authority over us, may be subject
to criticism. But we can scarcely refuse to recognize the formal
cogency of his reasoning. If it can be established that God,
condescending to our weakness, has given us a revelation, then,
undoubtedly, that revelation becomes an adequate authority
upon which our faith may securely rest; and, as rational beings, we must accept as true what it commends to us as such,
even though our reason flags in its attempts even to comprehend it, and utterly fails to supply an immediate rational
demonstration of its truth. Here, above everywhere else, faith
obviously must precede reason, and prepare the way for
reason. It is here accordingly that Augustine's insistence on
the priority of faith to reason culminates. It is with this
application in mind that he repeats most assiduously that
" before we understand it, it behooves us to believe "; [84] that
" faith is the starting-point of knowledge "; [85] that we believe

---

[83] " De mendac." 3: " ille qui credit, sentit se ignorare quod credit; quamvis de re quam se ignorare novit, omnino non dubitet; sic enim firme credit.
Qui autem opinatur, putat se scire, quod nescit."

[84] " De Trinitate," viii. 5. 8.

[85] *Ibid.* ix. 1. 1.

that we may know, not know that we may believe. Least of all, in this highest application of faith, does he mean that this faith does not itself rest upon reason, in the sense that it is accorded to an authority which is not justified to reason on valid grounds.[86] What he means is rather that the particular truths commended to us on the authority of a revelation from God, validated as such by appropriate evidence, are to be accepted as truths on that authority, prior to the action of our reason upon them either by way of an attempt fully to comprehend them, or by way of an attempt to justify them severally to our logical reason; and that this act of faith is in the nature of the case a preparation for these efforts of reason. The order of nature is, in other words, first, the validation of a revelation as such on its appropriate grounds; secondly, the acceptance by faith of the contents of this revelation on the sole ground of its authority; and, thirdly, the comprehension by the intellect of the contents of the revelation and the justification of them severally to reason so far as that may prove to be possible to us. This order of procedure Augustine defends against the Manichæans — who were the philosophic naturalists in vogue at the time — from every conceivable point of view and with endlessly varied arguments. The gist of the whole, however, is simply that when a revelation has been validated as such, we owe to the truths commended to us by it immediate credit, on the sole authority of the revelation itself, and neither need nor are entitled to wait until each of these truths is separately validated to us on the grounds of reason before we give our assent to it. In a word, the rational ground on which we accept each truth is the proof that the authority by which it is commended to us is adequate, and not a particular verdict of reason immediately passed upon each several truth. The particular verdict of reason on each several truth must wait on the act of faith by which we honor the general verdict of reason on the validity of the authority; and it may wait endlessly without invalidating or weakening the strength of conviction which we accord to the de-

---

[86] E.g., "Epist." 120. 1. 3 (as quoted above).

liverances of a revelation which has been really validated to us as such.

We may revert, of course, to the prior question, whether the assumed revelation on the authority of which faith is yielded has been soundly validated as such to reason. It is at this point that criticism of Augustine's system of faith becomes possible; and it is at this point that such criticism becomes sharp. We are told that Augustine accepted an alleged revelation on insufficient evidence; and that it is this fact which justifies the suspicion that his acceptance of it and the subjection of his reason to its authority were acts of violence done to his intellect in despair of ever attaining a solid basis in reason for religious conviction. It is quite possible to confuse in such a concrete judgment a number of suggestions, which we should discriminate if we are to form an estimate of the value of the criticism offered. We shall need to ask, for example, if what it is intended to suggest is that the evidence in existence for the reality of the revelation which Augustine accepted as a true revelation from God is insufficient to validate it; or only that the evidence which was actually before Augustine's mind and on which he personally depended in reaching his decision was insufficient. In the latter case we shall need to ask further if what is meant is that the evidence actually before Augustine's mind would be insufficient to convince us — seems to us in itself insufficient to command credit; or that it was actually insufficient to convince Augustine, so that, despite his protestations of conviction, he remained in reality unconvinced and at heart an actual skeptic all his days. It is the last of these propositions, it will be remembered, that Dr. Harnack affirms; although he does not keep it as rigorously separate from the others as would seem desirable. It is surely one thing to say that Augustine is open to criticism for giving credit to the Evidences of Christianity and recognizing the revelatory character of the Christian system; and quite another thing to say that Augustine is open to criticism for the particular conception he entertained of the Christian evidences — the selection he makes of the special items of evidence upon which he personally relies for the validation of the Christian system as a revealed religion; and still quite another thing to suggest that Augustine is open to criticism for his inaccessibility to the evidences of the Christian system as a revelation from God, and for remaining therefore all his life a doubter of the intellect, finding only a precarious peace for his distracted soul in an act of submission to an external authority arbitrarily yielded to in defiance of insatiable skepticism.

It can scarcely be expected that the whole body of the Christian evidences should be subjected to a new critical examination merely because a writer not himself able to look upon them as supplying a satisfactory proof of the divine origin of the Christian religion, blames Augustine for placing upon them a value beyond that which he is himself able to accord. We must be prepared to find those who resist the force of this evidence themselves, despising those who yield to it as superstitious, or even accusing them of intellectual dishonesty. It surely is enough at this point simply to recognize that this not unnatural tendency of the naturalistic mind is not without its influence upon the proneness in some quarters to speak of Augustine as making a sacrifice of his intellect in throwing himself upon authority in matters of religion. One thing is perfectly clear: if Augustine made such a sacrifice he was himself completely unconscious of doing so. He nowhere betrays the state of mind which is here attributed to him. He speaks always in terms of the most complete conviction of the truth of the Christian religion, and rests himself with entire confidence upon the evidences which appealed to him. To go behind his obviously sincere asseverations of security of mind and heart, because we are conscious that, in his place, we should have felt less secure, is to push the biographer's (and critic's) privilege of " imputing himself to his victim " to an unwarrantable extreme. Whatever we may feel Augustine ought to have done; whatever we may feel we, in his place, should have done; it certainly is a matter of historical fact that Augustine confidently accepted the Christian revelation as a genuine revelation, and found for his faith in it abundant justification. No fact in his mental history is more patent, or call it flagrant if you will. When in the closing words of his first Christian composition,[87] in the very act of consecrating himself to a life-long search of truth, he declares that " he certainly would never more give up the authority of Christ, because no stronger could be found," he speaks out of an unmistakably sincere conviction. And the note thus struck so far from fading away swells steadily to the end. Clearly the restless heart had found at last its rest: and rest is the characteristic of his Christian life. A skeptic, intellectual or moral, may be found in any man rather than in Augustine. He who in his despair as, in the crumbling of his former beliefs, he almost gave up hope of ever attaining assurance, yet could not fall in with the Academics because he still knew some things to be indisputably true, and only began to wonder whether the right way to truth was known to man — certainly could not lose his confidence after he had discovered the Way and established himself in it.

It remains a matter of interest of course to determine the nature of the grounds on which Augustine was convinced, or sought to convince others, of the truth of the Christian religion. To do so with any fullness would be, however, to write a section of the history of Apologetics, and would find its importance in that connection. We need not go so far afield in seeking to apprehend Augustine's doctrine of authority in religion. What is of primary importance here is merely to ascertain in a simple manner his conception of the sources, nature, and seat of this authority and the mode of its validation to men. In the Second Article we shall seek to do this with as much completeness as is requisite for our purpose.

[87] " Cont. Acad.," iii. 20. 43. It was the common sentiment of the men of the time: Paulinus of Nola says: " Plurima quaesivi, per singula quaeque cucurri, Sed nihil inveni melius quam credere Christo."

SECOND ARTICLE [88]

IN the First Article we attempted to give a general exposition of Augustine's doctrine of knowledge and authority, which naturally ran up into some account of his doctrine of authority in religion. The more detailed study of this specific subject we were forced, however, to postpone to another occasion. We wish now to take up this topic and to make as clear as possible Augustine's teaching concerning it.

The cardinal facts to bear in mind are that, to speak broadly, with Augustine the idea of authority coalesces with that of revelation, the idea of revelation with that of apostolicity, and the idea of apostolicity with that of Scripture. With him, therefore, the whole question of authority in religion is summed up in the questions whether there is a revelation from God in existence, where that revelation is to be found, and how it is validated to and made the possession of men: while the master-key to these problems lies in the one word apostolicity. Whatever is apostolic is authoritative, because behind the apostles lies the authority of Christ, who chose, appointed, and endowed the apostles to be the founders of His Church; and Christ's authority is the authority of God, whose Son and Revelation He is. The great depository of the apostolic revelation is the Holy Scriptures, and these Scriptures become thus to Augustine the supreme proximate seat of authority in religion. The line of descent is, therefore, briefly, God, Christ, the Apostles, the Scriptures — the Scriptures being conceived as the embodied revelation of God, clothed with His authority as His inspired word, given to us by His accredited messengers, the apostles. Let us see how Augustine expresses himself on each of these points in turn.

On the actual authority of Scripture he certainly expresses himself in no wavering terms. The Holy Scriptures, he tells

[88] *The Princeton Theological Review,* July, 1907, pp. 353–397.

us, have been " established upon the supreme and heavenly
pinnacle of authority " [89] and should therefore always be read
" in assurance and security as to their truth " [90] and all their
statements accepted as absolutely trustworthy.[91] To them
alone among books had he learned to defer this respect and
honor — most firmly to believe that no one of their authors
has erred in any respect in writing: [92] for of these books of the
prophets and apostles it would be wicked [93] to have any doubt
as to their entire freedom from error.[94] " To these canonical
Scriptures only," he repeats,[95] " does he owe that implicit subjection so to follow them alone as to admit no suspicion whatever that their writers could have erred in them in any possible
respect, or could possibly have gone wrong in anything." The
accumulated emphases in such passages, no more than fairly
represent the strength of Augustine's conviction that, as he
puts it in another place, " it is to the canonical Scriptures
alone that he owes unhesitating assent." [96] It is this contention
accordingly in its most positive form which he opposes endlessly to the Manichæans in his long controversy with them.
He points out to Faustus, for example, that a sharp line of
demarcation is drawn between the canonical books of the Old
and New Testaments and all later writings, precisely in point
of authority. The authority of the canonical books, " confirmed
from the time of the apostles by the successions of the bishops
and the propagations of the churches, has been established in
so lofty a position, that every faithful and pious mind submits
to it." Other writings on the contrary, of what sort soever
they may be, may be read " not with necessity of believing

[89] " Epist." 82 (to Jerome), ii. 5: " sanctam Scripturam, in summo et
cœlesti auctoritatis culmine collocatam."

[90] *Ibid.*: " de veritate ejus certus ac securus legam."

[91] *Ibid.*: " veraciter discam."

[92] *Ibid.*: i. 3.

[93] " Nefarium."

[94] *Ibid., ad fin.*

[95] *Ibid.*: iii. 24: " sicut paulo ante dixi, tantummodo Scripturis canonicis
hanc ingenuam debeam servitutem, qua eas solas ita sequar, ut conscriptores
earum nihil in eis omnino errasse, nihil fallaciter posuisse non dubitem."

[96] " De natura et gratia," lxi. 71: " sine ulla recusatione consensum."

but with liberty of judgment." The same truth may indeed be found in some of these which is found in Scripture, but never the same authority, seeing that none of them can be compared with "the most sacred excellence of the canonical Scriptures." From what is said by other books we may accordingly withhold belief, unless indeed it is demonstrated "either by sound reason or by this canonical authority itself"; but "in this canonical eminence of the Holy Scriptures, even though it be but a single prophet, or apostle, or evangelist that is shown to have placed anything in his Scriptures, by this confirmation of the canon we are not permitted to doubt that it is true." [97] Similarly when writing to the Donatist Cresconius,[98] he refuses to treat even Cyprian as indefectible. "For," says he, "we do no injury to Cyprian when we distinguish his books — whatever they may be — from the canonical authority of the divine Scriptures. For not without reason has there been constituted with such wholesome vigilance that ecclesiastical canon to which belong the assured books of the prophets and apostles, on which we do not dare to pass any judgment at all, and according to which we judge with freedom all other writings whether of believers or of unbelievers." In a word, Augustine defends the absolute authority of every word of Scripture and insists that to treat any word of it as unauthoritative is to endanger the whole. This he argues to Jerome [99] and over and over again to the Manichæans, culminating in a most striking passage in which he protests against that subjective dealing with the Scriptures which "makes every man's mind the judge of what in each Scripture he is to approve or disapprove." "This," he sharply declares, "is not to be subject for faith to the authority of Scripture, but to subject Scripture to ourselves: instead of approving a thing because it is read and written in the sublime authority of Scripture, it seems to us written rightly because we approve it.[100]

[97] "Contra Faustum Man.," xi. 5.
[98] II. xxxi. 39.
[99] "Epist." 40. iii. 3.
[100] "Contra Faustum Man.," xxxii. 19.

With no less emphasis Augustine traces the supreme authority which he thus accords to the Scriptures to their apostolicity. Their authority is according to him due in the first
instance to the fact that they have been imposed upon the
Church as its *corpus juris* by the apostles, who were the accredited agents of Christ in founding the Church. In laying
this stress on the principle of apostolicity, he was, of course,
only continuing the fixed tradition of the early Church. From
the beginning apostolicity had been everywhere and always
proclaimed as the mark of canonicity,[101] and apostolicity remained with him the only consciously accepted mark of
canonicity.[102] He says expressly that " the truth of the divine
Scriptures has been received into the canonical summit of authority, for this reason — that they are commended for the
building up of our faith not by anybody you please, but by
the apostles themselves." [103] The proper proof of canonicity is
to him therefore just the proof of apostolicity: and when it
has been shown of a declaration that it has been made by an
apostle, that is to give it supreme authority.[104] Though one
declaration may be from the writings of one apostle and another " from any other apostle or prophet — such is the quality
of canonical authority . . . that it would not be allowable to
doubt of either." [105] To say " canonical " writings accordingly
is to add nothing to speaking of them as genuine writings of the
prophets and apostles.[106] The genuineness of the Christian
Scriptures as documents of the apostolic age is, therefore,
the point of chief importance for him. " What Scriptures can
ever possess weight of authority," he asks with conviction in
his voice, " if the Gospels, if the Apostolic Scriptures, do not
possess it? Of what book can it ever be certain whose it is, if it

[101] This has recently been shown afresh by Kunze, " Glaubensregel, Heilige
Schrift und Taufbekenntnis," 1899, pp. 114 *sq.*, 249 *sq.* Cf. Cramer, " Nieuwe
Bijdragen," etc., iii. 155.

[102] Cf. Kunze, as cited, p. 302.

[103] " Epist." 82 (to Jerome), ii. 7: " non a quibuslibet, sed ab ipsis Apostolis, ac per hoc in canonicum auctoritatis culmen recepta."

[104] " Contra Faustum Man." xi. 5.

[105] *Ibid.*, 6.   [106] *Ibid.*: " vere.'

be uncertain whether those Scriptures are the Apostles', which are declared and held to be the Apostles' by the Church propagated from those very Apostles, and manifested with so great conspicuousness through all nations? "[107] We are not concerned for the moment, however, with the nature of the evidence relied on to prove these books apostolical: what we are pointing out is merely that to Augustine the point of importance was that they should be apostolical, and that this carried with it their canonicity or authority. Their authority was to him rooted directly in their apostolicity.

How completely Augustine's mind was engrossed with the principle of apostolicity as the foundation of authority is illustrated by a tendency he exhibited to treat as in some sense authoritative everything in the Church for which an apostolic origin can be inferred. The best example of this tendency is afforded by what we may call this doctrine of tradition.[108] This doctrine is, in brief, to the effect that where the guidance of the Scripture fails, the immemorial mind of the universal Church may properly be looked upon as authoritative, on the presumption that what has always been understood by the entire Church is of apostolic origin. Repeated expression is given to this position; for example, in his Anti-Donatist treatise " On Baptism " (A.D. 400) where he is seeking to defend the validity of heretical baptism and is embarrassed by Cyprian's rejection of it on the plea that Scripture is silent on the subject. Cyprian's principle, " that we should go back to the

---

[107] " Contra Faustum Man." xxxiii. 6.

[108] To Roman Catholic writers Augustine's doctrine of tradition seems that of the Church of Rome. Cf. Schwane, " Dogmengeschichte der patrist. Zeit," 1895, § 89.9 (pp. 703 sq.), and, though following Schwane closely, yet somewhat more dogmatically, Portalié in Vacant-Mangenot, " Dictionnaire de théologie Catholique, i. col. 2340. Schwane insists that Augustine joins oral Apostolic tradition to Scripture as necessary both for its completeness and for its interpretation, and that with reference to doctrine as well as usages; yet admits that to Augustine the Scriptures occupy the first place in authority and contain all things necessary to salvation, and that with adequate clearness; and that only the Scriptures are inspired and infallible (cf. loc. cit., pp. 713 sq.). Probably even this is assigning to tradition a much greater rôle than Augustine gave it, particularly with reference to doctrine.

fountain, that is to apostolical tradition, and thence turn the
channel of truth to our own times " he of course heartily accepts; [109] he seeks only to turn it against Cyprian. " Let it be
allowed," he says, that the " apostles have given no injunctions " on this point — that is to say, in the canonical Scriptures. It is not impossible, nevertheless, that the custom (*consuetudo*) prevalent in the Church may be rooted in apostolical
tradition. For " there are many things which are held by the
universal Church and are *on that account* (*ob hoc*) fairly
(*bene*) believed to be precepts of the apostles, although they
are not found written," *i.e.*, in the Scriptures: [110] or, as it is put
in an earlier point, " there are many things which are not
found in the letters of the apostles, nor yet in the councils of
their followers, which yet *because they have been preserved
throughout the whole church* (*per universam ecclesiam*) are
believed to have been handed down and commended by
them." [111]

Even when thus arguing for the apostolicity of tradition,
however, Augustine never forgets the superior authority of
Scripture. Perhaps the most instructive passage in this point
of view is one in which he is investigating the value of baptism
of infants. After appealing to the tradition of the universal
Church he proceeds as follows: " And if anyone seeks a divine
authority in this matter — although what is held by the universal Church, and that not as a thing instituted by councils
but as of primitive inheritance (*nec conciliis institutum sed
semper retentum est*) is most properly (*rectissime*) believed
to have been handed down by apostolic authority — we are
able in any case (*tamen*) to form a true conjecture of the
value of the sacrament of baptism in the case of infants from
the circumcision of the flesh . . . " [112] Here, in the very act
of vindicating apostolicity, and therefore authority, for universal primitive custom, language is employed which seems to

[109] " De bapt. contra Donat.," V. xxvi. 37.
[110] *Ibid.*, V. xxiii. 31.
[111] *Ibid.*, II. vii. 12; cf. IV. vi. 9.
[112] *Ibid.*, IV. xxiv. 31.

betray that Augustine was wont to conceive " divine authority " (*auctoritas divina*) the peculiar property of Scripture.
In another Anti-Donatist treatise — the work against the
grammarian Cresconius (*c.* 406) [113] — we read somewhat similarly that " although no doubt no example " of the custom
under discussion " is adduced from the canonical Scriptures,
the truth of these Scriptures is nevertheless held by us in this
matter, since what we do is the *placitum* of the universal
Church, which is commended by the authority of these very
Scriptures; and accordingly since the Holy Scriptures cannot
deceive, whoever is afraid of being led astray by the obscurity
of this question should consult with respect to it that Church
which without any ambiguity is pointed out by the Holy
Scripture."

This care in preserving the superior right of Scripture is
not to be accounted for as due to the exigencies of the controversy with the Donatists. It reappears in more formal form
in purely didactic teaching — in a reply, for instance, which
Augustine made to a series of questions addressed to him by a
correspondent on matters of ritual observance.[114] Here Augustine distinguishes carefully between three varieties of such
observances: those prescribed by Scripture, those commended
by the practice of the universal Church, those of merely local
usage. When an observance is prescribed by the authority of
divine Scripture, no doubt can be admitted but that we must
do precisely as we read.[115] Similarly also only insane insolence
would doubt that we ought to follow the practice of the whole
Church, throughout the world.[116] In matters of varying usage
in different parts of the Church, on the other hand, we must
beware of erecting our own custom into a guide, and should
conform ourselves freely to the custom that obtains in the
Church where we may chance from time to time to be — in

[113] *Op. cit.,* i. 33. 39.

[114] " Epist." 54 and 55 (to Januarius — the 40th of that name in Smith and
Wace, " Dictionary of Christian Biography," — about 400).

[115] " Epist." 54, v. 6: " non sit dubitandum quin ita facere debeamus ut
legimus."

[116] *Ibid.;* " quid . . . tota per orbem frequentat ecclesia."

short, follow Ambrose's wise rule of "doing when we are in Rome as the Romans do." [117] There is nothing that Augustine deprecates more than the arbitrary multiplication of ordinances, by which, he says, the state of Christians which God wished to be free — appointing to them only a few Sacraments and those easy of observance — is assimilated to the burdensomeness of Judaism. He could wish therefore that all ordinances should be unhesitatingly abolished which are neither prescribed by the authority of the Holy Scriptures, nor have been appointed by the councils of bishops, nor have been confirmed by the custom of the universal Church [118] — in which sentence the selection of the terms so that "authority" is ascribed to Scripture alone is not unwitting.

Elsewhere, no doubt, Augustine uses the term "authority" more loosely of the other sources of "custom" also. This is true, for example, of the opening paragraphs of these very letters. Here he carefully draws out the threefold distinction among ordinances, which he applies throughout. The fundamental principle of the discussion on which he is about to enter, he tells us, is that our Lord Jesus Christ has subjected us to an easy yoke and a light burden, laying upon us only few Sacraments and those not difficult of observance. He then adds: "But with respect to those not written but traditional matters to which we hold, observed as they are throughout the whole world, what we are to understand is that they are retained as commended and instituted by the Apostles themselves, or by plenary councils, the authority of which in the Church is very useful." [119] The term "authority" happens to be employed here only of what the context tells us is the least weighty of the three "authorities" to the observances com-

117 *Ibid.*, ii. 3, where a pleasant anecdote is told of Ambrose's advice to Monnica to follow his example in this.

118 "Epist." 55, xix. 35; cf. 27, where the "authority" of the divine Scriptures and the "consent" of the whole Church are brought together.

119 "Epist." 54. 1. 1.: "illa autem quae non scripta sed tradita custodimus, quae quidem toto terrarum orbe servantur, datur intelligi, vel ab ipsis apostolis, vel plenariis conciliis, quorum est in ecclesia saluberrima auctoritas commendata atque statuta retineri."

mended by which we should yield obedience: the Scriptures, universal primitive custom arguing apostolic appointment, and counciliary enactment. We may look somewhat roughly, perhaps, upon these three "authorities" as representing to Augustine respectively the authority of "Scripture," the authority of "tradition," and the authority of "the Church"; and if so, then these three "authorities" — the Scriptures, Tradition, the Church — took rank in his mind in that order. First and above all is the "authority" of Scripture, which is just the infallible Word of God, whose every word is to be believed and every precept obeyed just as it stands written. Then comes the "authority" of immemorial universal tradition, on the presumption that just because it is immemorially universal it may, or must, be apostolic; and if apostolic then also of divine appointment. Last of all comes the "authority" of the Church itself, for which no claim is made of divine infallibility, since that is an attribute of Scripture alone — nor even of such constructive apostolicity as may be presumed of immemorial tradition; but only of righteous jurisdiction and Spirit-led wisdom. Neither the individual bishop, nor any body of bishops assembled in council, up to the whole number in the plenary or ecumenical council, though each and all are clothed with authority appropriate to the place and function of each, is safeguarded from error, or elevated above subsequent criticism and correction. This high altitude of indefectible infallibility is attained by Scripture alone.[120]

An appropriate authority is granted of course to bishops,

[120] Cf. Reuter, "Augustin. Studien, p. 329: "There is not, to my knowledge, to be found in Augustine, any statement giving *un*ambiguous expression to this notion [of the infallibility of the Church]. We read, *Contra Cresconium* ii. 33. 39, 'Since Holy Scripture cannot err'; but I have sought in vain for any declaration corresponding to this with reference to the Church. The assertion, 'Outside the Church, there is no salvation' is nowhere complemented by this other one, 'The Church cannot err.'" Reuter proceeds to say that, although this precise formula does not occur, yet "important premises of it" may be found; but here opinions may lawfully differ. On what follows in the text Reuter, pp. 328 *sq.*, 333 *sq.*, may be profitably consulted; cf. also Schmidt, in Liebner's *Jahrbücher für deutsche Theologie* (1861), vi. pp. 197–255, especially 234 *sq.*

each in his proper sphere: but no one of them is free from error or exempt from testing and correction by the Holy Scriptures. Its own appropriate authority belongs similarly to councils of every grade: but no one of them can claim to have seen truth simply and seen it whole. If the Donatists appealed to Cyprian and his council, for example, Augustine, while ready to yield to Cyprian all the deference that was his due, did not hesitate to declare roundly, " The authority of Cyprian has no terrors for me," [121] and to assert that no council is exempt from error. For, he explains at length,[122] no one " is ignorant that the Holy Canonical Scriptures, as well of the Old as of the New Testament, are contained within their own determined (*certis*) limits, and that they are so set above all later letters of bishops that with respect to them it is not possible to doubt or to dispute whether anything that stands written in them is true or right, while all the letters of bishops which, since the closing of the canon have been written or shall be written, are open to confutation, either by the wiser discourses of some one who happens to be more skilled in the particular matter, or by the weightier authority or more learned prudence of other bishops, or by councils — if there chances to be anything in them that deviates from the truth." And as little is anyone ignorant

---

[121] " De Bapt. contr. Donat." ii. 1. 2: "non me terret auctoritas Cypriani." This does not mean, of course, that he denies all authority to Cyprian; but only that he knows the limits of Cyprian's authority. So, when he says, *op. cit.*, iii. 3. 5. *med:* " No authority (nulla auctoritas), clearly, deters me from seeking the truth," he is not proclaiming an abstract indefeasible liberty in seeking the truth, as A. Dorner (" Augustinus," p. 236) appears to suppose (cf. Reuter, *op. cit.*, p. 335, note 4), but means only to say that Cyprian expressly leaves the path open and does not interpose his authority (whatever that may amount to) to shut off free investigation. Accordingly, he repeats at the end of the paragraph more explicitly: " We have then liberty of investigation conceded to us by Cyprian's own moderate and truthful declaration." The assertion of a zeal for truth which takes precedence of all else, apparently wrongly attributed to this passage, may be more justly found in the remark which occurs in the " Contra Epist. Manich. Fundam." iv. 5, to the effect that " if the truth is so clearly proved as to leave no possibility of doubt, it takes precedence of all things which keep me in the Catholic Church." Cf. Schmidt, as cited above.

[122] *Ibid.*, ii. 3. 4.

" that the councils themselves which are held in the several regions and provinces must without any evasion yield to the authority of plenary councils which are assembled from the whole Christian world; and that even the earlier plenary councils themselves are corrected by later ones, when by some actual trial, what was closed has been opened, and what was hidden has come to light." We perceive accordingly that the limiting phrases in the famous passages in which Augustine declares the Holy Scriptures the sole infallible authority in the world are by no means otiose. He means just what he says when he writes to Jerome, " For I confess to your charity that I have learned to defer this respect and honor to those Scriptural books only (*solis*) which are now called canonical, that I believe most firmly that no one of those authors has erred in any respect in writing " ; [123] or again when he says in another place, " In the writings of such authors" — that is to say Catholic writers — " I feel myself free to use my own judgment, since I owe unhesitating assent *to nothing but the canonical Scriptures.*" [124] A presumptive apostolicity may lend to the immemorial customs of the universal Church an authority which only arrogance can resist; and to the Church which was founded by the apostles, and made by them a depository of the tradition of truth, a high deference is due in all its deliverances: but to the Scriptures alone belongs supreme authority because to them alone belongs an apostolicity which coalesces with their entire fabric. They alone present us with what we may perhaps call " fixed apostolicity."

The ground of this conception of apostolicity as the principle of divine authority lies ultimately in the relation in which the apostles stood to Christ. The apostles, as Christ's accredited agents, empowered by His Spirit for their work, are, in effect, Christ Himself speaking. This idea underlies the entirety of Augustine's reasoning, and is very fully developed in a striking passage which occurs at the close of the first book of the Harmony of the Gospels.[125] He tells us here that our

---

[123] " Epist." 82. 1. 3.   [124] " De natura et gratia," lxi. 71.
[125] " De consensu Evang.," i. 35. 54.

Lord, "who sent the prophets before His own descent, also despatched the apostles after His ascension. . . . Therefore, since these disciples have written matters which He declared and spoke to them, it ought not by any means to be said He has written nothing Himself; for the truth is that His members have accomplished only that which they became acquainted with by the repeated statements of the Head. For all that He was minded to give for our perusal on the subject of His own doings and saying, He commanded to be written by those disciples, whom He thus used as if they were His own hands. Whoever apprehends this correspondence of unity and this concordant service of the members, all in harmony in the discharge of diverse offices under the Head, will receive the account which he gets in the Gospel through the narrative constructed by the disciples, in the same kind of spirit in which he might look upon the actual hand of the Lord Himself, which he bore in that body that He made His own, were he to see it engaged in the act of writing." Apostolicity therefore spells authority because it also spells inspiration: what the apostles have given the Church as its law is the inspired Word of God. The canonical Scriptures are accordingly "the august pen of the Spirit" of God; [126] and in reading them we are, through the words written by their human authors, learning "the will of God in accordance with which we believe these men to have spoken," [127] seeing that it is "the Holy Spirit who with admirable wisdom and care for our welfare has arranged the Holy Scriptures" in all their details, [128] and has spoken in them in perfect foresight of all our needs and perplexities. [129] Accordingly Augustine makes the Lord declare to him, "O man, verily what my Scripture says, I say"; and this is the reason that we may be assured that the Scripture is true — because it is He that is true, or rather the Truth Itself, who has given it

[126] "Confessiones," vii. 21. 27: "venerabilem stilum Spiritus tui."
[127] "De doctrina Christiana," ii. 5. 6.
[128] Ibid., ii. 6. 8.
[129] Ibid., iii. 27. 38: "assuredly the Holy Spirit who through him [the human author] spoke these words, foresaw that this interpretation would occur to the reader. . . ."

forth.[130] Thus the circle of the authority of the Scriptures completes itself. The Scriptures occupy the pinnacle of authority because they are the Word of God, just God's congealed speech to us. We know them to be such because they have been given to us as such by the apostles who were appointed and empowered precisely for the task of establishing the Church of God on earth, and who are therefore the vehicles for the transmission to us of the will of God and the Word which embodies that will.

But have the Scriptures which we have and which have acquired canonical authority in the Church, really been given to us by the apostles as the Word of God? How shall we assure ourselves of these Scriptures that they possess that apostolicity which lends to them their revelatory character and makes them our supreme authority?   The answer returned by Augustine to this question has been most variously conceived, and indeed, out of the several interpretations given it, heterogeneous traditions of his teaching have grown up as discordant at the extremes as the formal principles of Romanism and Protestanism. If we could content ourselves with a simple concrete statement, it doubtless would not be far astray to say briefly that Augustine received the Scriptures as apostolic at the hands of the Church; and that this is the meaning of his famous declaration, " I would not believe the Gospel except I were moved thereto by the authority of the Catholic Church." But the question at once arises whether this appeal to the Church is for conclusive testimony or for authoritative decision. Divergent interpretations at once intervene, and we find ourselves therefore little advanced by our concrete response. The precise question that is raised by these divergent interpretations is whether Augustine validated to himself the Scriptures as apostolic in origin and therefore the revealed Word of God by appropriate evidence, more or less fully drawn out and more or less wisely marshaled; or declined all argument and

---

[130] " Confessiones," xiii. 29. 44: " O Domine, nonne ista Scriptura tua vera est, quoniam tu verax et veritas edidisti eam? . . . O homo, nempe quod Scriptura mea dicit, ego dico."

cut the knot by resting on the sheer enactment of the contemporary Church. In the latter case Augustine would appear as the protagonist of the Romish principle of the supreme authority of the Church, subordinating even the Scriptures to this living authority. In the former he would appear as the forerunner of the Protestant doctrine of the supreme authority of Scripture.

The proper evidence of the apostolicity of the canonical Scriptures is, of course, historical. Apostolicity is a historical conception and its actuality can be established only on historical evidence. When Augustine declares of Scripture that it owes its authority to its apostolicity, he would seem, therefore, already to have committed himself to dependence for the validation of the authority of Scripture upon historical evidence. Many others than the Romanists, however, have found Augustine defective in his teaching or at least in his practice at this point. Neander remarks that Augustine having been brought by Manichæism into doubt as to which were the true documents of the Christian religion, and not being prepared for a historical investigation to determine the truth of the matter, had nothing left him but to fall back upon the tradition of the Church; [131] and this opinion is echoed by Reuter,[132] and sharpened by Harnack.[133] It is to be observed, however, that, when we have suggested that Augustine's dependence was placed wholly on the " tradition of the Church," [134] as Neander phrases it, we have not removed the ground of his conviction out of the sphere of historical judgments. To say " tradition " is indeed only to say " history " over again. And the question at this point is not whether the historical evidence which Augustine rested upon was good historical evidence, but whether he rested upon historical evidence at all, rather than upon the bare authority of the contemporary Church. It will be useful to

---

[131] " Katholismus und Protestantismus " (1863), p. 82.

[132] " Augustinische Studien," p. 491, note 1.

[133] " History of Dogma," v. p. 80; cf. Loofs, " Leitfaden zum Studium der Dogmengeschichte."

[134] " Die Ueberlieferung der kirche."

recall here Augustine's discussion of "tradition" to which we have just had occasion to advert. We will remember that he expressly distinguishes between "tradition" and "Scripture," and decisively subordinates the authority of "tradition" to that of "Scripture." It would certainly be incongruous to suppose him to be at the same moment basing the superior authority of Scripture on the inferior authority of tradition — in any other sense than that in which fact is based upon its appropriate evidence. We should bear in mind, moreover, that his appeal to "tradition" was in the instances brought before us distinctly of the nature of an appeal to testimony, and as such was distinctly discriminated from an appeal to the "Church," speaking, say, through a bishop or a council, and as distinctly preferred to it. His purpose was to validate certain customs prevalent in the Church as incumbent on all. This he does, not directly by asserting as sufficient the authority of the contemporary Church, as if the Church was as such clothed with the right to determine the practice of its adherents by a mere *ipse dixit*. He proceeds, rather, indirectly, by seeking to establish the apostolicity of these customs by an appeal to the immemorial universality of their tradition in the Church. Obviously "tradition" is treated here not as authority, but as evidence; and the "authority" thus validated by tradition is treated as superior to the "authority" of the contemporary Church speaking through whatever channels. It certainly would be incongruous to suppose that he was nevertheless consciously basing the authority of Scripture, which was to him superior to that of even tradition, on the bare authority of the Church, which he defines to be inferior to either. His appeal to the "Church," as by its "authority" moving men to believe the "Gospel" can scarcely be understood otherwise, therefore, than as a broad statement that the Scriptures are validated as apostolic and therefore authoritative in some way by the Church. What is meant, when this is made specific, is, obviously, that the testimony of the whole Church, borne unbrokenly from the beginning, to the apostolicity of the canonical Scriptures is conclusive of the fact.

In his appeals to the " Church " after this fashion Augustine certainly had in mind the Church as a whole, as extended through both space and time; and his fundamental contention is that the testimony of this Church is of decisive weight to the origin of her Scriptures in apostolic gift, and therefore to the authority of the Scriptures as an inspired revelation of the divine will. Such an appeal is distinctly of the nature of an appeal to historical testimony. But the nature of this appeal would not be essentially altered were we to omit consideration of the extension of the Church in time and focus attention on its extension in space alone, as many suppose Augustine to have done. To appeal to the testimony of the universal Church is to adduce historical evidence. Even if we do not accord such weight to this evidence as was obviously accorded to it by Augustine, this difference in our estimate of its conclusiveness should not blind us to its nature. We may smile if we will at the easiness of Augustine's historical conscience, and wonder that he could content himself with testimony so untested. But we ought to recognize that in so doing we are criticising his sense of historical values, not disproving that his resort to the Church was precisely for testimony.

Nor is it very difficult to do serious injustice to Augustine's sense of historical values in a matter of this kind. It is very much a matter of times and seasons. An appeal to the testimony of the universal Church at the close of the nineteenth or at the opening of the twentieth century is not altogether without historical value. But we must not fail to bear in mind that an appeal to the testimony of the universal Church at the close of the fourth or the opening of the fifth century is something very different from an appeal to its testimony at the close of the nineteenth or the opening of the twentieth century. Certainly the testimony of the universal Church at the close of the first or the opening of the second century is still treated in wide circles, as in such a thing as the apostolic gift of the Scriptures, conclusive. And it is not an easy matter accurately to estimate exactly the rate at which the value of this testimony decreases with the lapse of time. Are we so sure that its value had depreciated by the close of the fourth century to such an extent as to render an appeal to the Church as witness-bearer, at that period, absurd? The Church to which the Scriptures were committed by the apostolic college, by whom it was founded and supplied with its corpus juris — is not this Church the proper witness to the apostolicity of the Scriptures it has received from the hands of its apostolic founders? And is it strange that it has always been appealed to for its testimony to this fact? No doubt, as time passed and the years intervening between the commission of the Scriptures to the Church and its witness-bearing to them increased, this testimony became ever weaker as testimony. And no doubt as it became weaker as testimony it naturally took to itself more and more the character of arbitrary authentication. No doubt, further, it was by this slow transmutation of testimony into authentication that the Romish conception of Scripture as dependent upon the Church for its authentication gradually came into being. And no doubt still further the change was wrought practically before it was effected theoretically. Men came practically to rest upon the authority of the Church for the accrediting of Scripture, before they recognized that what they received from the Church was anything more than testimony. The theoretic recognition came inevitably, however, in time. So soon as the defect in the testimony of the Church arising from the lapse of time began to be observed, men were either impelled to cure the defect by an appeal to the Church of the past, that is to say by a historical investigation; or else tempted to rest satisfied with the authority of the living Church. The latter course as the line of easiest resistance, falling in, moreover, as it did, with the increasingly high estimate placed on the Church as mediatrix of religion, was inevitably ultimately taken; and the Romish doctrine resulted. Let it be allowed that in this outline we have a true sketch of the drift of thought through the Patristic Church. It still is not obvious that this development had proceeded so far by the close of the fourth century that Augustine's appeal to the " Church " to authenticate the " Gospel " must be understood as an appeal to the authority strictly so called rather than to the testimony of the Church. On the face of it, it does not seem intrinsically absurd to suppose that Augustine may still at that date have made his appeal to the Church with his mind set upon testimony. And when we come to scrutinize the actual appeals which he made, it seems clear enough that his mind rested on testimony.

Perhaps there is no better way to bring the fact clearly before us than to note the passages quoted by the Romish expositors with a view to supporting their view that Augustine based the authority of the Scriptures immediately upon the dogmatic authority of the Church. Thus, for example, Professor E. Portalié writes as follows: [135]

Above Scripture and tradition is the living authority of the Church. It alone guarantees to us the Scriptures, according to the celebrated declaration in the treatise " Against the Epistle of Manichæus called Fundamental," v. 6: " I indeed would not believe the Gospel except the authority of the Catholic Church moved me." Compare " Against Faustus the Manichæan " xxii. 79; xxviii. 2.

We reserve for the moment comment on " the celebrated declaration " from the " Contra Epist. Manich. Fundam.," and content ourselves with observing that if it indeed implies that Augustine based the authority of Scripture on that of the " living " Church, it receives no support from the companion passages cited. They certainly appeal to the " historical " Church, that is to say adduce the testimony of the Church extended in time rather than the bare authority of the Church extended in space. So clear is this in the latter case [136] that Augustine in it sets the testimony of the Manichæans to the genuineness of their founder's writings side by side, as the same in kind, with the testimony of the Church to the genuineness of the Apostolic writings. I believe, he says, that the book you produce is really Manichæus', because from the days of Manichæus until to-day it has been kept in continuous possession

---

[135] Vacant-Mangenot, " Dictionaire de théologie Catholique," i. col. 2341.

[136] " Contra Faustum Man.," xxviii. 2.

and estimation as his, in the society of the Manichæans: similarly you must believe that the book we produce as Matthew's is his on the same kind of testimony in the Church. To the fixed succession of bishops among the Christians is assigned no different kind of authority than is allowed to the fixed succession of presiding officers among the Manichæans; in both alike this succession is adduced merely as a safeguard for trustworthy transmission. No doubt Augustine represents the testimony of the Church as indefinitely more worthy of credit than that of the Manichæans, but this is a different matter: *gradus non mutant speciem*. Similarly, in the former citation [137] Augustine's appeal is not specifically to the Church of his time, but to the " holy and learned men " who were living in the time of the writers — real or alleged — of the books in question, who, he says, would be in position to know the truth of the matter. Nothing can be clearer in this case either, than that the point of Augustine's argument turns on the validity of the testimony of the Church, not on the dogmatic authority of the Church.

The note struck by these passages is sustained in all Augustine's discussions of the matter and sometimes swells to an even clearer tone. Take for instance the *argumentum ad absurdum* with which he plies Faustus [138] to the effect that we can never be assured of the authorship of any book " if we doubt the apostolic origin of those books which are attributed to the apostles by the Church which the apostles themselves founded, and which occupies so conspicuous a place in all lands." Clearly the appeal to the Church here is for testimony, not for authorization, as is evidenced very plainly in the sequel. For Augustine goes on to contrast the hardiness of the Manichæans in attempting to doubt the apostolicity of books so attested, with their equal hardiness in accepting as apostolic books brought forward solely by heretics, the founders of whose sect lived long after the days of the apostles; and then adduces parallels from classical authors. There are, he tells us, spurious books, in circulation under the

---

[137] " Contra Faustum Man.," xxii. 79.   [138] *Ibid.*, xxxiii. 6.

name of Hippocrates, known to be spurious among other things from the circumstance " that they were not recognized as his at the time when his authorship of his genuine productions was determined." And who doubts the genuineness of these latter? Would not a denial of it be greeted with derision — " simply because there is a succession of testimonies to these books from the time of Hippocrates to the present day, which makes it unreasonable either now or hereafter to have any doubt on the subject." Is it not by this continuity of the chain of evidence that any book is authenticated — Plato's, Aristotle's, Cicero's, Varro's — or any of the Christian authors' — " the belief becoming more certain as it becomes more general, up to our own day "? Is not the very principle of authentication this: the transmission of information from contemporaries through successive generations? How then can anyone be so blinded by passion as " to deny the ability of the Church of the apostles — a community of brethren as numerous as they were faithful — to transmit their writings unaltered to posterity, as the original seats of the apostles have been occupied by a continuous succession of bishops to the present day? " Are we to deal with the apostolic writings differently from the natural dealing we accord day by day to ordinary ones — whether of profane or religious authors? [139]

The matter is not different when at an earlier place in the same treatise [140] he takes up much the same point on which he is arguing in the famous passage " I would not believe the Gospel, etc." When Manichæus calls himself an apostle, he says, it is a shameless falsehood, " for it is well known that this heresy began not only after Tertullian, but after Cyprian." And what evidence can Manichæus or Faustus bring forward,

[139] Cf. *ibid.*, xxxii. 19: " Why not rather submit to the authority of the Gospel which is so well-founded, so confirmed, so generally acknowledged and admired, and which has an unbroken series of testimonies from the Apostles down to our own day, that you may have an intelligent belief? " Cf. also xi. 2, xiii. 4, xxxiii. 6 and 9. Because Augustine was deeply impressed by the catholicity of the Church's testimony (as e.g., " De morr. eccles. cath.," xxix. 61) is no reason why we should fail to see that he is equally impressed by its continuity — that is, by its historical character.

[140] xiii. 4, 5.

which will satisfy anyone not inclined to believe either their
books or themselves? Will Faustus " take our apostles as witnesses? Unless he can find some apostles in life, he must read
their writings: and these are all against him. . . . He cannot
pretend that their writings have been tampered with; for that
would be to attack the credit of his own witnesses. Or if he
produces his own manuscripts of the apostolic writings, he
must also obtain for them the authority of the Churches
founded by the apostles themselves, by showing that they
have been preserved and transmitted by their sanction. It will
be difficult for a man to make me believe him on the evidence
of writings which derive their authority from his own word,
which I do not believe. . . . The authority of our books,
which is confirmed by the agreement of so many nations, supported by a succession of apostles, bishops, and councils, is
against you. Your books have no authority, for it is an authority maintained by only a few and these the worshippers of
an untruthful God and Christ. . . . The established authority
of the Scriptures must outweigh every other: for it derives
new confirmation from the progress of events which happen,
as Scripture proves, in fulfilment of the predictions made so
long before their occurrence." Of course this is a piece of
polemic argumentation, not a historical investigation: but the
gist of the polemic is simply that the Scriptures of the Christians owe their authority to a valid historical vindication of
them as of apostolic origin, while the Scriptures of the Manichæans lack all authority because they lack such a validation.
Augustine does not think of such a thing as simply opposing
the authority of the Church to the Manichæan contentions;
and much less of course does he take a roundabout way to the
same result, by opposing to them the authority of Scriptures
which owe all their authority to the mere *ipse dixit* of the
Church. If he speaks of authority as given to sacred books
only " through the Churches of Christ," it is clear that this
does not mean that these churches communicate to these
Scriptures an authority inherent in the Churches, but only
that it is by their testimony that that supreme authority

which belongs to the Scriptures from their apostolic origin is vindicated to them, as indeed it is confirmed to them by other testimonies also, those, to wit, of miracles and fulfilled prophecy and the consent of the nations and the succession of apostles, bishops, and councils, to confine ourselves to items enumerated here. Surely it cannot be doubted that here also Augustine's appeal to the Church as authenticating the Scriptures is to the Church as a witness, not as an authorizer.

It is natural to turn from this passage immediately to the closely related one in the treatise "Against Manichæus' Epistle called Fundamental," in which the famous words, "I would not believe the Gospel, etc.," occur. If the passage which we have just had before us is rather a piece of sharp polemics than a historical investigation, much more this. Augustine proposes here to join argument with the Manichæans on the pure merits of the question at issue between them. He wishes to approach the consideration of their claims as would a stranger who was for the first time hearing their Gospel: and as they promise nothing less than demonstration he demands that they give him nothing less than demonstration before asking of him assent.[141] He warns them that he is held to the Catholic Church by many bonds, which it will be hard to loosen: so that their task of convincing him on the ground of pure reason will not be an easy one. He has found a very pure wisdom in the Catholic Church — not indeed attained to in this life by more than a few spiritual men, while the rest walk by faith, but nevertheless shining steadily forth for all who have eyes to see it. He has been deeply impressed by the wide extension of the Church. The authority it exercises — " inaugurated by miracles, nourished by hope, augmented by love, established by antiquity " — has very strongly moved him. The unbroken succession of rulers in the Church possesses for him a great weight of evidence. He confesses that the very name of "Catholic" — retained unchallenged amid so many heresies — has affected him deeply. What have the Mani-

141 "Contra Epist. Manich. Fundam.," iii. 3.

chæans to offer him which would justify him in setting aside these and such inducements to remain a Catholic? Nothing but the " promise of the truth " (*sola veritatis pollicitatio*). The " promise " of the truth, observe: not " the truth " itself. If the latter — why, Augustine gives up the contest at once. For he allows without dispute, that if they give him truth itself — so clearly the truth that it cannot be doubted — *that* is something that is to be preferred to all these things which he has enumerated as holding him in the Catholic Church — these and all other things that can be imagined as holding him there. For nothing is so good as truth. But he persistently demands that there must be something more than a " promise " of truth before he can separate himself from the Catholic Church — or rather, as he puts it, before he can be moved " from that faith which binds his soul with ties so many and so strong to the Christian religion." It is, then, we perceive, strict demonstration which Augustine is asking of the Manichæans, and he conducts the argument on that basis.

Turning at once to Manichæus' " Fundamental Epistle " as a succinct depository of nearly all which the Manichæans believe, he quotes its opening sentence: " Manichæus, an apostle of Jesus Christ, by the providence of God the Father." There he stops immediately to demand proof — proof, remember, not mere assertion. You have promised me truth, he says — demonstrated truth: and this is what you give me. Now, I tell you shortly, I do not believe it. Will you prove it to me: or will you, in defiance of the whole claim of the Manichæans, that they ask faith of no man save on the ground of demonstration, simply demand of me belief without clear and sound proof? If you propose proof, I will wait for it. Perhaps you will turn to the Gospel and seek there a testimony to Manichæus. But suppose I do not believe the Gospel? Are you to depend for your proof — you who differentiate yourselves from Christians in this, that while they demand faith, you offer them demonstration and ask belief of nothing until you have demonstrated it — are *you* to depend for your proof on this very faith of the Christians? For observe, my faith in the Gospel rests on the authority of the Catholic Church. And moreover, I find myself in this quandary: the same Church that tells me to believe the Gospel tells me not to believe Manichæus. Choose, then, which you will. If I am to believe the Catholics, then I cannot believe Manichæus — for they tell me not to. If I am not to believe the Catholics, then, you cannot use the Gospel, because, it was out of the preaching of the Catholics that I have been brought to believe the Gospel. Or if you say I am to believe them in this one matter and not in the other — I am scarcely so foolish as to put my faith thus at your arbitrary disposal, to believe or not believe as you dictate, on no assigned ground. It was agreed that you should not ask faith from me without clear proof — according to your universal boast that you demand no belief without precedent demonstration. It is clear, then, that to render such a proof you must not appeal to the Gospel. " If you hold to the Gospel, I will hold to those by whose teaching I have come to believe the Gospel; by their instructions I will put no credit in you whatever. And if by any chance you should be able to find anything really clear as to the apostolicity of Manichæus you will weaken the authority of the Catholics for me, since they instruct me not to believe you; and this authority having been weakened I shall no longer be able to believe the Gospel for it was through them that I came to believe it." The upshot of it is that if no clear proof of Manichæus' apostleship is to be found in the Gospel, I shall credit the Catholics rather than you; while if there is such to be found in the Gospel I shall believe neither them nor you. Where then is your demonstration of the apostleship of Manichæus — that I should believe it? Of course I do not mean I do not believe the Gospel. I do believe it, and believing it I find no way of believing you. You can point out neither in it nor in any other book faith in which I confess, anything about this absurd apostleship of Manichæus. But it is certainly evident that your promise to demonstrate to me your tenets signally fails in this case on any supposition.

This is Augustine's argument in this famous passage. Undoubtedly the exact interpretation of its implications with respect to the seat of authority in Christianity is attended with considerable difficulty. And it is not altogether strange that the Romanists have seized upon it as subordinating the " Gospel " to the " Church ": nor even that they have been followed in this, not merely by extreme rationalists predisposed to every interpretation of a Patristic writer which tends to support their notion that the clothing of Scripture with absolute authority was a late and unhistorical dogmatic development,[142] but also by many scholars intent only upon doing complete justice to Augustine's opinions.[143] There are serious difficulties, however, in the way of this interpretation of the passage. One of them is that it would in that case be out of accord with the entirety of Augustine's teaching elsewhere. It is quite true that elsewhere also he speaks of the authority of the Church, and even establishes the Church on the " summit of authority." But in all such passages he speaks obviously of the Church rather as the instrument of the spread of the saving truth than as the foundation on which the truth rests — in a word, as the vehicle rather than the seat of authority.[144] And in general, as we have already seen, Augustine's allusions to the Church as " the pillar and ground of the truth " throw the stress on its function of witness-bearing to the truth rather than found the truth on its bare *ipse dixit*. It is scarcely likely that he has spoken in a contrary sense in our present passage. We must not permit it to fall out of sight that Augustine's point of view in this passage is that of one repelling the Manichæan claim of strict demonstration of the truth of their teaching. His rejoinder amounts to saying that they cannot ground a demonstration upon a Gospel accepted only on faith.

[142] Cf. e.g., H. J. Holtzmann, " Kanon und Tradition " (1859), pp. 2, 3.

[143] Cf. e.g., Harnack, " History of Dogma," v. 80; Loofs, " Leitfaden zum Studium der Dogmengeschichte "; Dorner, " Augustinus "; Kunze, " Glaubenslehre," etc.

[144] Portalié, as cited, col. 2413, adduces in proof that Augustine places the Church " above even Scripture and tradition," *De utilitate credendi*, xvii. 35, comparing " Epist." 118, 32.

The contrast at this point is not between the weakness of the basis on which they accept their tenets and the incomparable weight of the authority of the Church on which Christians accept the " Gospel." On the contrary, the contrast is between the greatness of their claims to demonstration and the weakness of its basis — nothing but the " Gospel " which is accepted on " authority " not on " demonstration " — on " faith " not on " reason " — in effect, on " testimony," not on " sight." In a word, the " authority of the Church " is adduced here not as superlatively great — so great that, in the face of it, the Manichæan claims must fall away let them be grounded in what they may; but rather as incongruously inadequate to support the weight the Manichæan must put on it if he is to build up his structure of demonstration. The Manichæan undertakes a demonstration, scorning a faith that rests on authority: and then actually wishes to rest that demonstration on a premise which has no other basis than a faith that rests on authority. He cannot *demonstrate* that Manichæus was an Apostle of Christ on the testimony of a " Gospel " which itself is accepted on the *authority* of the Catholic Church: " authority " being used here in its contrast with " reason," not with " testimony," and in pursuance of Augustine's general contention that all religious truth must begin with faith on authority and not with demonstration on reason. This being the case, so far is the passage from predicating that Augustine esteemed the " authority " of the Church as " the highest of all " as the Romish contention insists,[145] that its very gist is that the testimony of the Church is capable of establishing only that form of conviction known as " faith " and therefore falls hopelessly short of " demonstration."

Such being the case we cannot be surprised that in all ages there has been exhibited a tendency among those more or less emancipated from the Romish tradition to deny that even this famous passage asserts the supreme authority of the contemporary Church. Striking instances may be found

[145] Cf. Portalié, as cited, col. 2341 and col. 2413.

for example in William Occam [146] and Marsilius of Padua [147] in the fourteenth century and in John Wessel [148] in the fifteenth: and examples are not wanting throughout the whole period of papal domination.[149] Of course the early Protestant controversialists take their place in this series. With them the matter was even less than with William Occam and Marsilius a merely academical question. In their revolt from the dogmatic authority of the Church and their appeal to the Scriptures alone as the sole source and norm of divine truth, they were met by the citation of this passage from Augustine. As on its theological side the Reformation was precisely an " Augustinian " revival, the adduction of Augustine's authority in behalf of the subjection of Scripture to the Church, was particularly galling to them and amounted to a charge that they were passing beyond the limits of all established Christianity. They were indeed in no danger, in casting off the authority of the Church, of replacing it with the authority of any single father. Doubtless Luther spoke a little more brusquely than was the wont of the Reformers, in the well-known assertion: " Augustine often erred; he cannot be trusted: though he was

[146] Occam explains that the " ecclesia quae majoris auctoritatis est quam evangelista, est illa ecclesia cujus auctor evangelii pars esse agnoscitur " (Goldasti mon. tom. 1. fol. 402). That is to say, he understands the Church here as projected through time, and as including even Jesus Himself: the historical not the contemporary Church. But he takes " authority " strictly. Cf. Neander, " General History of the Christian Religion and Church," E. T. v. p. 40.

[147] Marsilius explains: " Dicit autem Augustinus pro tanto se credere evangelio propter ecclesiae catholicae auctoritatem, quia suae credulitatis initium inde sumpsit, quam Spiritu Sancto dirigi novit: fides enim quandoque incipit ex auditu " — in which he anticipates the general Protestant position. Cf. (quite fully) Neander, op. cit., E. T. v. pp. 27–28.

[148] De Potestate Ecclesiastica (Opp. p. 759): " We believe in the Gospel on God's account, and on the Gospel's account in the Church and the Pope; not in the Gospel on the Church's account: wherefore that which Augustine says (" Contra Epist. Manich. Fundam.," chap. 6), concerning the Gospel and the Church, originis de credendo verbum est, non comparationis aut praeferentiae. For the whole passage and others of like import, see Gieseler, " Lehrbuch der Kirchengeschichte," 1829, II, part 3, sect. 5, § 153, p. 495; E. T. " Ecclesiastical History," 1868, iii. 468; and cf. Schmidt, Jahrbücher für die Theologie, (1861), vi. 235.

[149] Cf., for example, the instances mentioned by Chamier, below.

good and holy, yet he, as well as other fathers, was wanting in the true faith." But the essential opinion here expressed was the settled judgment of all the Reformers and is by no means inconsistent with their high admiration of Augustine or with their sincere deference to him. The gist of the matter is that though they looked upon Augustine as their great instructor, esteeming him indeed the greatest teacher God had as yet given His Church; and felt sure, as Luther expressed it, that " had he lived in this century, he would have been of our way of thinking "; they yet knew well that he had not lived in the sixteenth century but in the fourth and fifth and that in the midst of the marvelous purity of his teaching there were to be found some of the tares of his time growing only too richly. Ready as they were to recognize this, however, they were not inclined to admit without good reason that he had erred so sadly in so fundamental a matter as that at present before us; and they did not at all recognize that the Romanists had made good their assertion that Augustine in saying that " he would not believe the Gospel except as moved thereto by the authority of the Catholic Church " was asserting the Romish theory that the authority of the Church lies behind and above all other authorities on earth — that, as even Schwane puts it, the Church is the representative of God on earth and its authority alone can assure us of the reality of a divine revelation.

Already at the Leipzig disputation with Eck, Luther had been triumphantly confronted with this statement of Augustine's; and in his " Resolutions " on that debate he suggests that Augustine was only giving what was historically true in his own case.[150] Augustine had himself been led to believe the Gospel through the ministration of the Church; and he adduces this fact only that he might bring to bear upon his heretical readers the impressive testimony of the whole Church, which was, of course, of much more moving weight than his own personal witness could be. As a matter of fact,

[150] See Köstlin, " The Theology of Luther," E. T. ii. pp. 224, 255, and especially i. pp. 320–321.

comments Luther, the Gospel does not rest on the Church, but contrariwise, the Church on the Gospel. It was not Luther's way to say his say with bated breath. This is the way he expresses his judgment in his " Table Talk ": [151] " The Pope . . . to serve his own turn, took hold on St. Augustin's sentence, where he says, *evangelio non crederem,* &c. The asses could not see what occasioned Augustin to utter that sentence, whereas he spoke it against the Manicheans, as much as to say: I believe you not, for ye are damned heretics, but I believe and hold with the Church, the spouse of Christ." It seemed to Luther, in other words, quite one thing to say that the credit of the Church ought to be higher than that of the Manichæans, and quite another to teach that the authority of the Church was needed to give authority to the Gospel. Perhaps the consentient opinion of the Reformers in this matter is nowhere better stated, in brief form, than in the Protestant " Objections " to the Acts of Ratisbon, which were penned by Melanchthon. [152] " Although therefore," we read here, " the conservation of certain writings of the Prophets and Apostles is the singular work and benefit of God, nevertheless there must be recognized that diligence and authority of the Church, by which it has, in part testified to certain writings, in part by a spiritual judgment separated from the remaining Prophetic and Apostolic Scriptures those that are unworthy and dissentient. Wherefore Augustine commends to us the authority of the primitive Church, [153] receives the writings that are approved by the Catholic consent of the primitive Church; (and) repudiates the later books of the Manichæans. Accordingly he says: ' *I would not believe the Gospel except the authority of the Catholic Church moved me.*' He means that he is moved by the consentient testimony of the primitive Church, not to doubt that these books were handed down from

[151] " Of the Fathers," near the beginning (chap. DXXX.). Augustine's statement is invoked in the bull, *Exsurge Domine,* published by Leo X in 1520 against Luther.

[152] *Corpus Reformatorum,* iv. 350. A French version is given in the Brunswick ed. of Calvin's works, v. 564 (*Corpus Reformatorum,* v. 33).

[153] " Auctoritatem primae Ecclesiae."

the Apostles and are worthy of credit (*fide*)." In a word, according to Melanchthon, Augustine is to be read as appealing to the testimony of the Church not as asserting its authority.

In the same line follow all the Reformers, and much the same mode of statement may be read, for example, in Butzer, or Calvin, or Bullinger, or Peter Martyr. "I will not now remember," writes Bullinger,[154] "how by manifest words the standard-bearers of that see do write, that the canonical scripture taketh her authority of the church, abusing this sentence of the ancient father St. Augustine, ' I would not have believed the Gospel, if the authority of the holy Church had not moved me.' . . ." How they abused it Peter Martyr tells us more fully: [155] "But they say that Augustine writes ' Against the Epistola Fundamenti,' ' I would not believe the Gospel except the authority of the Church moved me.' But Augustine wished to signify by these words nothing else than that much is to be attributed to the ministry of the Church which proposes, preaches, and teaches the Gospel to believers. For who of us came to Christ or believed the Gospel except as excited by the preaching of the Gospel which is done in the Church? It cannot be inferred from this, however, that the authority of the Gospel hangs on the Church in the minds of the auditors. For if that were true, long ago the Epicureans and Turks had been persuaded. . . ." As was to be expected it was Calvin who gives us the solidest piece of reasoning upon the subject. The gist of what he says is that Augustine was not setting forth the source whence the Gospel derives its authority, but the instrument by which men may be led to recognize that authority. The unbeliever, he remarks, may well be brought to trust the Gospel by the consent of the Church; but the believer's trust in the Gospel finds its authority not in the Church, but in the Gospel itself, and this is logically prior to that of the Church, though no doubt, it may be chronologically recognized last by the inquirer. The Church may thus

154 " Decades," v. 2 (Parker Soc. ed. v. p. 67).
155 " Loci Communes," Zurich, 1580, i. 251 (iii. 3. 3).

bring us to the Gospel and commend the Gospel to us; but when we have accepted the Gospel our confidence in it rests on something far more fundamental than the Church. Augustine, he insists, " did not have in mind to suspend the faith which we have in the Scriptures on the will and pleasure (*nutu arbitriove*) of the Church, but only to point out, what we too confess to be true, that those who are not yet illuminated by the Spirit of God, are by reverence for the Church brought to docility so as to learn from the Gospel the faith of Christ; and that the authority of the Church is in this way an introduction, by which we are prepared for the faith of the Gospel." Augustine is perfectly right, then, he continues, to urge on the Manichæans the universal consent of the Church as a *reason* why they should come believingly to the Scriptures, but the *ground* of our faith in the Scriptures as a revelation of truth is that they are from God.[156]

The Protestant scholastics, of course, developed what had by their time become the traditional Protestant contention, and defended it against the assaults of the Romish controversialists. Who first invented the philological argument that Augustine uses in this sentence the imperfect for the pluperfect " in accordance with the African dialect " — so that he says, not " I would not believe the Gospel," but, historically, " I would not have believed the Gospel " — we have not had the curiosity to inquire. If we may trust the English version of the " Decades," Bullinger already treats the tense as a pluperfect. Musculus,[157] who devotes a separate section of his *Locus de Sacris Scripturis* to the examination of Augustine's declaration lays great stress on this particular point, that in it *non crederem* is used for *non credidissem;* and Musculus is gen-

[156] " Institutes," i. 7. 3. Calvin very appositely points out that Augustine in the immediately preceding context represents the proper course to be to " follow those who invite us first to believe what we are not yet able to see, that, being made able by this very faith, we may deserve to understand what we believe, our mind being now inwardly strengthened and illuminated not by men but by God Himself." In these words, Calvin remarks, Augustine grounds our confidence in the Gospel on the internal operation of God Himself upon our minds. Cf. below, note 175.

[157] " Loci Communes," Basle, 1560, pp. 181–183 (Locus xxi).

erally cited by later writers upon it. This is true, for example, of both Whitaker and Chamier, who with Stillingfleet may be mentioned as offering perhaps the fullest and best discussions of the whole matter. Whitaker [158] devotes a whole chapter to it, and after adducing the arguments of Peter Martyr, Calvin, and Musculus, affirms that " it is plain that he (Augustine) speaks of himself as an unbeliever, and informs us how he first was converted from a Manichæan to be a Catholic, namely, by listening to the voice of the Church " — in which remark he appears to us to be quite wrong. Chamier's [159] treatment, which also fills a whole chapter, is exceedingly elaborate. He begins by calling attention to the singularity of the passage, nothing precisely to the same effect being adducible from the whole range of Augustine's writings. Then he cites the opinions of eminent Romanists divergent from the current Romish interpretation — those of John, Cardinal of Torre Cremara, Thomas Valden, Driedo, Gerson, who represent Augustine as assigning only a *declarative* authority to the Church, or as speaking not of the "living" but of the "historical" Church. " Augustine," says Driedo, " speaks of the Catholic Church which was from the beginning of the Christian faith ": " by the Church," says Gerson, " he understands the primitive congregation of those believers who saw and heard Christ and were his witnesses." All these are good staggers towards the truth, says Chamier: but best of all is the explanation of the passage which is given by Petrus de Alliaco, himself a cardinal, " in the third article, of the first question on the first of the sentences." In the judgment of this prelate Augustine's meaning is not that the Church was to him a *principium theologicum,* by which the Gospel was theologically proved to him to be true, but only a " moving cause " by which he was led to the Gospel — much " as if he had said, ' I would not believe the Gospel unless moved thereto by the holiness of the Church, or by the miracles of Christ: in which (forms of statement) though

---

[158] " Disp. on Holy Scripture " (1610), iii. 8 (Parker Society, E. T. p. 320).
[159] " Panstrat. Cathol." (Geneva, 1926), i. pp. 198 *sq.* (I. i. 7. 10).

a cause is assigned for believing the Gospel, there is no
principium prius set forth, faith in which is the cause why
the Gospel is believed." In a word, as it seems, Petrus de
Alliaco is of the opinion that Augustine's appeal to the Church
is to its testimony rather than to its authority. This opinion,
now, continues Chamier, is illustrated and confirmed by
weighty considerations brought forward by Protestant writers
— whereupon he cites the arguments of Peter Martyr, Calvin,
Musculus, Whitaker, and through them makes his way into
a detailed discussion of the passage itself in all its terms.
Rivaling Chamier's treatment in fullness if not equaling it
in distinction is that given the passage in Stillingfleet's "Rational Account of the Grounds of the Protestant Religion," [160]
under the three heads of (1) the nature of the controversy in
which Augustine was engaged; (2) the Church by whose authority he was moved; and (3) the way and manner in which
that Church's authority moved him — certainly a logically
complete distribution of the material. The whole argument of
scholastic Protestantism is brought before us in its briefest
but certainly not in its most attractive form, however, in the
concise statement given in De Moor's Commentary on John
Marck's Compend.[161] According to this summary: (1) The
Papists in adducing this passage to support their doctrine of
the primary authority of the Church deceive themselves by
a twofold fallacy — (A) They draw a general conclusion from
a particular instance: it does not follow that because Augustine did not believe the Gospel except as moved by the authority of the Church, therefore no one can believe the Gospel
whom the authority of the Church does not move; (B) They
misunderstand Augustine, as if he were speaking of himself
at the time of his writing, instead of at the time of his conversion. "For where he says, ' I would not believe were I not
moved' he is employing, as the learned observe, an African
mode of speech, familiar enough to Augustine, in which the

---

[160] i. 7; "Works" (1709), iv. pp. 210 *sq.*

[161] "De Moor in J. Marck. Compend.," (1761), i. p. 160 (chap. ii. 7. *ad
fin.*).

imperfect form is used for the pluperfect." . . . " His meaning then is not that believers should depend on the authority
of the Church, but that unbelievers should take their start
from it "; and in this sense he elsewhere speaks often enough.
(2) Augustine is not speaking here of *auctoritas praecipiens,
juris et imperii* (injunctionary authority, with a legal claim
upon us for obedience) "as the Papists insist, — as if Augustine would have believed solely because the Church pronounced
belief to be due": but of *auctoritas dignitatis* (the authority
of observed desert), "which flows from the notable manifestations of Divine Providence observable in the Church, —
such as miracles, antiquity, common consent (chap. iv.), and
which may lead to faith though it is incapable of implanting
it in the first instance." (3) " What is noted here, then, is the
external motive of faith, but not at all the infallible *principium
credendi,* which he teaches in the fourth chapter is to be sought
in the truth alone. . . . And it is to be noted that the fathers
elsewhere rightly hold that the Holy Scriptures are superior
in authority both *in se* and *quoad nos* to the Church. . . ."

Of course it is observable enough from this survey, that
the interest of the Protestant scholastics was far more in the
dogmatic problem of the seat of authority in Christianity,
than in the literary question of the precise meaning of Augustine's words. We must bear in mind that the citations we have
made are taken not from studies in literary history but from
dogmatic treatises; and that their authors approach the particular question upon which we are interrogating them from
a dogmatic point of view, and in a doctrinal interest. There
would be a certain unfairness in adducing these citations in
a connection like the present, therefore, were there any real
occasion to defend the tone in which they are couched. This
is by no means the case. We need not hesitate to recognize
nevertheless at once that some of the reasoning employed
by them to support their interpretation will scarcely bear
scrutiny. It is a counsel of despair, for example, to represent
Augustine as employing — " in accordance with the usage of
the African dialect " — the imperfect in a pluperfect sense.

We may readily confess that the supposition does violence to the context of the passage itself, which requires the imperfect sense; it seems clearly to be the offspring of a dogmatic need rather than of a sympathetic study of the passage. And we are afraid the same must be said of the general conception of the meaning of the passage which has probably given rise to this philological suggestion — viz., that it is a historical statement of Augustine's own experience and means merely that he himself was led by the Church's authority to the Gospel. He is not writing his autobiography in this passage, but arguing with the Manichæans; and he is not informing them of what had been true of his own manner of conversion but confounding them by asserting what in a given case he, as a reasonable man, would do. There are elements enough of doubtful validity in the argument of the Protestant scholastics, therefore — as there could not fail to be in the circumstances. But it is quite another question whether their general conception of the passage is not truer than that of their Romish opponents, and whether they do not adduce sound reasons enough for this general conception to support it adequately. It is a matter of common experience in every department of life — and not least in judicial cases, where the experience has been crystallized into a maxim to the effect that it is best to announce decisions and withhold the reasons — that the decisions of men's judgment are often far better than the reasons they assign for them: and it may haply prove true here too, that the position argued for by the Protestant scholastics is sounder than many of the arguments which they bring forward to support it.

It must be confessed, meanwhile, that modern Protestant opinion does not show so undivided a front as was the case during the scholastic period. The majority of Protestant scholars, historical investigators as well as dogmatic systematizers, do, indeed, continue to defend the essential elements of the interpretation for which the Protestant scholastics contended; but even these ordinarily adopt a different line of argument and present the matter from a somewhat different point of

view; and there are many recent Protestant scholars, and they
not invariably those deeply affected by the rationalism of
the day, who are inclined to revert more or less fully to the
Romish interpretation. Even Dr. W. G. T. Shedd, who reproduces more of the scholastic argument than is now usual,[162]
shows the effect of the change. Even he quotes Hagenbach [163]
approvingly to the effect that Augustine " merely affirms " " a
subjective dependence of the believer upon the authority of
the Church universal, but not an objective subordination of
the Bible itself to this authority "; though he proceeds to
weaken the " subjective dependence of the believer upon the
authority of the Church " so as to leave room for a " private
judgment." What in his view Augustine is asserting is the
duty of the individual to respect the authority of the Church,
because the " Church universal had an authority higher than
that of any one member," and it is therefore unreasonable
for the individual, or a heretical party, to " oppose their private judgment to the catholic judgment." Or rather, what he
supposes Augustine to affirm is — as he fortunately weakens
the statement in the next sentence — " the greater probability
of the correctness of the Catholic Mind, in comparison with
the Heretical or Schismatic Mind, and thereby the *authority*
of the Church in relation to the individual, without dreaming,
however, of affirming its absolute *infallibility*, — an attribute
which he confines to the written revelation." Augustine's notion of " ecclesiastical authority " is by this expedient reduced
to " the natural expectation of finding that the general judgment is a correct one," coupled with " the right of private
judgment; the right to examine the general judgment and
to perceive its correctness with his own eyes." Thus, Dr. Shedd
supposes, " Augustine adopts the Protestant, and opposes the
Papal theory of tradition and authority." " The Papist's
method of agreeing with the catholic judgment," he explains,
" is passive. He denies that the individual may intelligently

[162] " History of Christian Doctrine," i. pp. 144–150. Cf. S. Baumgarten:
' Untersuchung. theol. Streitigkeiten," iii. pp. 2, 8.
[163] " Dogmengeschichte," § 119.

verify the position of the Church for himself, because the Church is *infallible,* and consequently there is no possibility of its being in error. The individual is therefore shut up to a mechanical and passive reception of the catholic decision. The Protestant, on the other hand, though affirming the high probability that the general judgment is correct, does not assert the infallible certainty that it is. It is conceivable and possible that the Church may err. Hence the duty of the individual, while cherishing an antecedent confidence in the decisions of the Church, to examine these decisions in the light of the written word, and to convert this presumption into an intelligent perception, or else demonstrate its falsity beyond dispute. ' Neither ought I to bring forward the authority of the Nicene Council,' says Augustine (" Contra Maximianum Arianum " II. xiv. 3), ' nor you that of Ariminum, in order to prejudge the case. I ought not to be bound (*detentum*) by the authority of the latter, nor you by that of the former. Under the authority of the Scriptures, not those received by particular sects, but those received by all in common, let the disputation be carried on, in respect to each and every particular.' " [164]

What strikes one most in these remarks of Dr. Shedd is that they begin by attributing to Augustine a doctrine of the authority of the Church universal over the individual, which forbids the individual to oppose his private judgment to the catholic judgment: proceed to vindicate to the individual a private judgment in the sense of a right to examine the general judgment that he may perceive its correctness with his own eyes — that is to say to an active as distinguished from a merely passive agreement with the catholic judgment: and end by somehow or other supposing that this carries with it the right to disagree with and reject the catholic judgment on the basis of an individual judgment. The premise is that it is not reasonable to erect the individual judgment against the catholic judgment: the conclusion is that it is the duty of the individual to subject the catholic judgment to his per-

[164] *Op. cit.,* pp. 148–149.

sonal decisions: the connecting idea is — that the individual
ought to be able to give an active and not merely a passive reception to the catholic decision. The logic obviously halts.
But it seems clear that what Dr. Shedd is striving to do is to
give due validity to what he considers Augustine to assert in his
famous declaration, viz., this, that the individual is subjectively under the authority of the Church; and yet at the same
time to vindicate for Augustine a belief in the right of private
judgment. He wishes to do justice to the conception of " authority " which he supposes Augustine to have had in mind in
this expression, without doing injustice to Augustine's obvious
exercise of freedom of opinion under the sole authority of the
Scriptures. It cannot be said that he has fully succeeded,
although there is much that is true in his remarks, considered
as an attempt to give a general account of Augustine's estimate of the authority of the Church. But it is of no great
importance for our present inquiry whether he has fully succeeded in this particular effort, or not; since, as has already
been pointed out, Augustine does not seem to intend in this
passage to place the individual subjectively under the " authority of the Church "; but appears to employ the term
" authority " in an entirely different sense from that which it
bears in such phrases — the sense namely in which it is the
synonym of " testimony " and the ground of " faith," in distinction from the " demonstration " of " reason " which is the
ground of that form of conviction which he calls " knowledge."

From another point of view of importance Dr. Shedd's instinct has carried him very near to the truth. We refer to the
recognition that informs his discussion that Augustine did
make more of the Church and of the authority of the Church
than the Protestant scholastics were quite ready to admit.
It is probably the feeling that this is the case which accounts
for much of the tendency among recent scholars to concede
something to the Romish interpretation of Augustine's doctrine of the authority of the Church. It certainly cannot easily
be denied that Augustine does declare in this passage, that
the credit we accord the Gospel hangs on the credit we give

the Church. In this particular passage, this no doubt means no more than that we are dependent on the Church to accredit to us the Gospel; that it is from the Church's hands and on her testimony that we receive the Gospel as apostolic and divine. But, if we raise the broader question of Augustine's attitude towards the Church in its relation to the reception of the truth it cannot be successfully contended that it was solely as a *motivum credibilitatis* that he reverenced the Church. To him the Church was before all else the institute of salvation, out of which there is no salvation. And although it may be difficult to find expressed in language parallel to this crisp *extra ecclesiam nulla salus,* that outside of the Church there can be no right knowledge of God, it nevertheless certainly belongs to the very essence of his doctrine that outside of the Church there can be no effective knowledge of God. The Scriptures may be the supreme authority for faith, and it may be true, therefore, that wherever the Scriptures go, the salvatory truth will be objectively conveyed; but it is equally true that with Augustine this Word of truth will exert no saving power save in and through the Church.[165] As the Church is the sole mediatrix of grace and that not merely in the sense that it is through her offices alone that men are brought once for all to God, but also in the sense that it is through her offices only that all the saving grace that comes to men is conveyed to them — so that we are with Christ only when we are with His body the Church, and it is only in the Church that communion with God can be retained as well as obtained — it follows that the Word, however well known it may be and however fully it may perform its function of making known the truth of God, profits no man spiritually save in the Church.[166] It seems to be implicated in this that it is part of Augustine's teaching that the revealed truth of God, deposited in the Holy Scriptures, will not profit men

[165] The distinction between " habere " and " utiliter habere " or " salubriter habere " was made to do yeoman's service as regards baptism, in the Donatist controversy.

[166] Cf. A. Dorner, " Augustinus," pp. 233 *sq.,* and H. Schmidt, in *Jahrbücher für die Theologie* (1861), vi. 233.

even intellectually so that they may come by it to know God save in communion with the Church. Certainly he would never allow that an adequate knowledge could be obtained of that truth which must be chastely and piously sought and the key to which is love — access to which is closed to all but the spiritual man — outside the limits of that Church the supreme characteristic of which is that in it and in it alone is the love of God shed abroad in our hearts by the Holy Spirit which He has given unto us.[167]

The reverence which Augustine accordingly shows to the teaching of the Church is both great and sincere. It is no meaningless form when he opens his treatise on the " Literal Interpretation of Genesis " [168] or his great work on " The Trinity " [169] with a careful statement of the faith of the Church on the topics to be dealt with, to stand as a norm of teaching beyond which it would be illegitimate to go [170] — declaring moreover with complete simplicity, "This is my faith, too, since it is the Catholic faith." [171] There can be no question therefore that he accorded not merely a high value but also a real authority to the teaching of the Church, an authority which within its own limits may well be called a " dogmatic authority." But it needs also to be borne in mind that the organs of this authority were not conceived by him as official but vital — those called of God in the Church to do the thinking and teaching for the Church; [172] that the nature of this authority is never conceived by him as absolute and irreformable but always as relative and correctible — no teaching from any source is to be accepted unhesitatingly as above critical examination except that of the Scriptures only; and that as to its source this authority is not thought of by him

---

[167] " De unitate eccles." ii. 2: " The members of Christ are linked together by means of love that belongs to unity, and by means of it are made one with their Head."

[168] " De Gen. ad Lit. imperf.," *ad init.*   [169] " De Trinitate," i. 4. 7.

[170] " De Gen. ad Lit. imperf.," i. 1: " catholicae fidei metas; . . . praeter fidem catholicae disciplinae "; 2: " as the Catholic discipline commands to be believed."   [171] " De Trinitate," i. 4. 7, *ad fin.*

[172] " Epist." 118, v. 32: " armed with the abundant weapons of reason, by means of a comparatively few devoutly learned and truly spiritual men."

as original but derived, dependent upon the Scriptures upon which it rests and by which it is always to be tested and corrected. The Catholic faith as to the Trinity, for example, which is also his faith because it is the Catholic faith, is the faith that has been set forth, not by the organized Church on its own authority, but by "the Catholic expounders of the Divine Scriptures," intent upon teaching "according to the Scriptures" [173] and therefore only on the authority of these Scriptures. If there can be no question, therefore, that Augustine accorded a "dogmatic authority" to the Church, there can be no question either that the "dogmatic authority" he accorded to the Church was subordinated to the authority of the Scriptures, and was indeed but the representation of that authority in so to speak more tangible form. This, it is obvious, is in complete harmony with what we have already had occasion to note, in the matter of Christian observances, as to the relative authority Augustine accorded to the Scriptures, Tradition, the Church — in descending series. Only, it is to be noted that the dogmatic authority of the Church of which we are now specifically speaking expresses itself not merely, and not chiefly, through conciliar decrees, but rather through the vital faith of the people of God, first assimilated by them from the Scriptures, and then expressed for them by the appropriate organs of the expression of Christian thought, which in general are the Doctors of the Church. Such being the case, there can no question be raised whether or not the Church may be conceived as the supreme seat of authority in the dogmatic sphere. In many cases the proximate seat of authority it doubtlessly is; but never the ultimate seat of authority. That belongs with Augustine ever and unvaryingly to the Holy Scriptures,[174]

[173] "De Trinitate," i. 4. 7, *ad init.*

[174] "Epist." 164, iii. 6, offers a typical mode of statement: "And with respect to that first man, the father of the human race, that [Christ] loosed him from hell almost the whole Church agrees; and it is too considered that the Church does not believe this in vain — whencesoever it has been handed down, although the authority of the Canonical Scriptures is not expressly adducible for it (etiamsi canonicarum Scripturarum hinc expressa non proferatur auctoritas)."

witnessed to by the Church as given to it by the apostles as the infallible Word of God, studied and expounded by the Church for its needs, and applied by it to the varying problems which confront it with the measure of authority which belongs to it as the Church of God, the pillar and ground of the truth.

It is, however, in a deeper sense than even this that Augustine thought of the Church in relation to the acquisition of the knowledge of the truth. With Augustine the Church as it is the mediatrix of divine grace, is also the mediatrix of divine knowledge. As such the Church holds a position of the very highest significance between the supreme seat of authority, the Holy Scriptures, and the souls of men. Only in and through the Church can a sound as well as a saving knowledge of the contents of the Scriptures be hoped for; only in and through the Church can the knowledge of God enshrined in the Holy Scriptures avail for the illumination of the intellect with true knowledge of God, no less than for the sanctification of the soul for true communion with God. But, it must be remembered that in speaking thus, Augustine is thinking of the Church not mechanically as an organized body acting through official organs, say the hierarchy, but vitally, as the *congregatio sanctorum* acting through its vital energies as a communion of love. The Church in which alone according to Augustine true knowledge of God is to be had is fundamentally conceived as the Body of Christ. And this is as much as to say that the essence of his doctrine of the authority of the Church would not be inaptly expressed by the simple and certainly to no Christian thinker unacceptable formula, that it is only in Jesus Christ that God can be rightly known. The Church of Christ is the Body of Christ, and this Body of Christ is the real subject of the true knowledge of God on earth: it is only therefore as one is a member in particular of this Body that he can share in the knowledge of God, of which it is the subject. This is the counterpart in Augustine of that doctrine of the *Testimonium Spiritus Sancti* which was first formulated by Calvin and from him became the corner stone of the Protestant doctrine of authority: and it differs from that doctrine only because and as Augustine's doctrine of "the means of grace" differs from the Protestant.[175]

Augustine's doctrine of the Church is a fascinating subject on which it is difficult to touch without being carried beyond the requirements of our present purpose. Perhaps enough has already been said to indicate sufficiently for the end in view the place which the Church holds in Augustine's doctrine of authority. In the sin-bred weakness of humanity, the Church mediates between the divine revelation deposited in the Holy Scriptures and the darkened mind of man; and thus becomes a paedagogue to lead men to the truth. It is in the Church that the truth is known; and this not merely in the sense that it is in the hands of the Church that the Scriptures are found, those Scriptures in which the whole Truth of God is indefectibly deposited; but also in the sense that it is in the Church alone that the mysteries of the faith, revealed in the Scriptures, are comprehended: that it is only in the participation of the graces found in her that men may hope to attain to the vision which is the possession solely of saints. The true knowledge of God belongs to the fellowship of His people, and out of it cannot be attained. And therefore, although Augustine knows of many things which bind him to the Catholic Church and the adduc-

---

[175] On Augustine's conception of the Church as a communion of saints, see the fifth of Reuter's "Augustinische Studien"; and compare Schmidt as above cited, especially from p. 233. On Augustine's relation to the Protestant doctrine of the "testimony of the Holy Spirit" see Pannier, "Le Témoignage du Saint-Esprit" (1893), pp. 67–68. After citing "Tract. iii. in Ep. Joan. ad Parthos," ii. 13; "De Trinitate," iii. 1–2; "Confessiones," vi. 5, and xi. 3, he adds: "There certainly is not yet here the whole of the witness of the Holy Spirit. . . . But St. Augustine has the intuition of a mysterious work which is wrought in the soul of the Christian, of an understanding of the Bible which does not come from man, but from a power external to him and superior to him; he urges the rôle which the direct correspondence between the Book and the reader must play in the foundation of Christian certitude. In this, as on so many other points, Augustine was the precursor of the Reformation, and a precursor without immediate continuers." In point of fact Augustine is just as clear as the Reformers that earthly voices assail only the ears, and that cathedram in coelo habet qui cordia docet ("Tract. iii. in Ep. Joan. ad Parthos," ii. 13). He differs from them only in the place he gives the Church in communicating that grace out of which comes the preparation of the mind to understand, as well as of the heart to believe, and of the will to do.

tion of which as undeniable credentials giving confidence to those who hold to that Church, he thinks should impress any hearer — such as the consent of peoples and nations, the just authority it enjoys among men, the unbroken succession of its rulers from the beginning, and the very name of Catholic — yet the real thing which above all others held him to the Catholic Church was, as he was well aware, that there was to be found in it "the purest wisdom" (*sincerissima sapientia*). He needs indeed to confess that to the knowledge of this wisdom only a few spiritual men (*pauci spirituales*) attain in this life, and even they (because they are men) only very partially (*ex minima quidem parte*), though without the least uncertainty (*sine dubitatione*).[176] The crowd (*turba*) meanwhile walk even in the Church, by faith — since their characteristic is, not vivacity of intellect, but simplicity in believing — the Church performing its function to them in holding out the truth to them to be believed. So that even the crowd are made in the apprehension of faith — each according to his ability — to share in the truth of which the Church is the possessor. All the time, however, there is in the Church and in it alone for the few spiritual men both the fullness of truth to be known and the opportunity to know it. The underlying idea is clearly that for the knowledge of the truth there are requisite two things — the revelation of the truth to be apprehended and the preparation of the heart for its apprehension: and that these two things can be found in conjunction only in the Church. Our thought reverts at once to Augustine's fundamental teaching that the remedy for the disabilities of sinful men is to be found in the twofold provision of Revelation and Grace. In the Church these two provisions meet, and it is therefore only in the Church that the sin-born disabilities of men can be cured: and only in the Church that men, being sinful, can attain to that knowledge of divine things in which is life.

By this construction, it will not fail to be perceived, Augustine sets the Church over against the world — or, as he would have phrased it, the glorious city of God over against

[176] "Contra Epist. Manich. Fundam.," i. 4, 5.

the earthly city — as the sole sphere in which true knowledge (*sapientia*) is found. Thus there is introduced a certain dualism in the manifestation of human life on earth. Two classes of men are marked off, separated one from another as darkness is separated from light. In the one, at the best only broken lights can play; because it is the natural development of sin-stricken humanity alone that it can offer. In the other may be found the steady shining of that true light which shall broaden more and more to the perfect day. The dualism of this conception of human life is resolved, however, by two considerations. In observing human life in its dualistic opposition we are observing it only in its process of historic development. The dualism is constituted by the invasion of the realm of darkness by the realm of light: and it exists only so long as the conquest of the darkness by the light is incomplete. A temporary dualism is the inevitable result of the introduction of any remedial scheme which does not act immediately and all at once. In the city of God — the Church of God's saints — we perceive the progress of the correction of the sin-born disabilities of men. Again the opposition of nature and the supernatural as the principles of the opposing kingdoms, must not be pressed to an extreme. With Augustine, as we have seen, all knowledge, even that which in contrast with a higher supernatural, may rightly be called natural knowledge, is in source supernatural: all knowledge rests ultimately on revelation. The problem to him was not, therefore, how to supplant a strictly natural knowledge by a strictly supernatural knowledge: but how to restore to men the power to acquire that knowledge which we call natural — how to correct sin-bred disabilities so that the general revelation of God may be reflected purely in minds which now are blinded to its reflection by sin. For this end, a special revelation, adapted to the needs of sin-disabled minds, is called in. Special revelation is not conceived here, then, as a substitute for general revelation, but only as a preparation for its proper assimilation. The goal is still conceived as the knowledge of God by direct vision; and special revelation is presented only as spectacles through which the blind may trace out the way to the cure. The intervention of God by a special revelation works, therefore, harmoniously into the general scheme of the production of knowledge of God through general revelation. The conception is that man being a sinner, and unable to profit by general revelation, God intervenes creatively by special revelation and grace — by special revelation enabling him to walk meanwhile until by grace he is once more prepared to see the Light in its own light. Special revelation, given through the prophets and apostles, is embodied in the Scriptures and brought to bear on man by the Church, in which is found the grace to heal men's disabilities. The Church therefore sets up in the world a city of God in which, and in which alone, man may live free from the disabilities that clog all action in the earthly city.

If we cry out that the remedy is incomplete, the answer is that it were better to say that the cure it is working is as yet uncompleted. So long as grace has not wrought its perfect work in our souls, there remains a dualism in all the functioning of our souls; so long as grace has not wrought its perfect work in the world there will remain a dualism in the world. But when grace has wrought its perfect work, then, as sin has been removed, the need of special revelation falls away, nay the need of all the instrumentalities by which grace is wrought falls away — the Church, the Scriptures, Christ the Mediator Himself — and God alone suffices for the soul's requirements. The end to which all is directed and in which all issues is not the destruction of nature but the restoration of nature: and when nature is restored, there is no longer need of the remedies. "There is nothing," says Augustine with emphasis, "that ought to detain us on the way" in our aspiration to God, in whom alone can we find our rest. And to put the sharpest possible point upon the remark he at once proceeds to apply it to our Lord Himself, who, says he, " in so far as He condescended to be our Way," wished not " to hold us " — the reference being possibly to Jno. xx. 17 — " but rather to pass away, lest we should cling weakly to temporal things, even though they had been put on and worn by Him for our salvation, and not rather press rapidly through them and strive to attain unto Himself who has freed our nature from the bondage of temporal things and set it down at the right hand of His Father." [177] The whole soteriological work of our Lord, in other words, is viewed by Augustine as a means to the end of our presentation, holy, and without spot, to the Father, and therefore as destined to fall away with all means when the end is attained.[178] When the Mediatorial Christ is viewed thus as instrument, of course the lower means also are so considered. Augustine, even, in a passage in the immediate neighborhood of what we have just quoted, speaks as if a stage of development might be attained even in this life in which the Scriptures, say, might fall out of use as a lame man healed would no longer need his crutch. " A man," says he,[179] " supported by faith, hope and love, and retaining these unshakenly, does not need the Scriptures except for instructing others." He adduces certain solitaries as examples: men in whom I Cor. xiii. 8 is already fulfilled — who "by means of these instruments " (as they are called) have had built up within them so great an edifice of faith and love that they no longer require their aid. So clear is it that by him all the means put in action by grace to cure the sin-bred disabilities of man were strictly conceived as remedies which, just because they work a cure, provide no substitutes for nature but bring about a restoration of nature.[180]

[177] " De Doctrina Christiana," i. 34, 38.

[178] Th. Bret, " La Conversion de S. Augustine " (Geneva, 1900), p. 64, generalizes as follows " We remark, however, that Augustine is affirmative only in what concerns the activity of Christ as reconciler. The rôle of eternal mediator, of perpetual friend, between the individual and God, was never clearly understood by Augustine. For him Christ came to restore man to his true condition, but, that once attained, the rôle of Saviour passed into the background. The sinner once cleansed of his sins, and placed in an atmosphere of the grace of God, found himself directly united with the Father without the intervention of the Son." This is only very partially correct; and its incorrectnesses touch on some important elements of Augustine's teaching. But it contains the essential matter.

[179] " De Doctrina Christiana," i. 39. 43.

[180] The general conception — but guarded from the fancy that attainment in this life can proceed so far as to be freed from the necessity of means

Augustine's whole doctrine thus becomes a unit. Man is to find truth within himself because there God speaks to him. All knowledge rests, therefore, on a revelation of God; God impressing on the soul continually the ideas which form the intellectual world. These ideas are taken up, however, by man in perception and conception, only so far as each is able to do so: and man being a sinner is incapacitated for their reception and retention. This sinful incapacity is met in the goodness of God by revelation and grace, the sphere of both of which is the Church. The Church is therefore set over against the world as the new Kingdom of God in which sinful man finds restoration and in its gradual growth we observe the human race attaining its originally destined end. The time is to come when the Kingdom of God shall have overspread the earth, and when that time comes, the abnormalities having been cured, the normal knowledge of God will assert itself throughout the redeemed race of man. Here, in a single paragraph, is Augustine's whole doctrine of knowledge and authority.

— is among the inheritances of Augustinians until this day. Cf., e.g., A. Kuyper, "Encyc. of Sacred Theology," E. T. pp. 368 *sq.;* and especially H. Bavinck, "Gereform. Dogmatiek," i. pp. 389 *sq.,* where the necessary cautions are noted. The misapprehensions of Harnack ("History of Dogma," E. T. v. pp. 99–100) will be obvious.

IV

AUGUSTINE AND HIS " CONFESSIONS "

AUGUSTINE AND HIS "CONFESSIONS"[1]

THERE is probably no man of the ancient world, of whose outward and inward life alike we possess such full and instructive knowledge as of Augustine's. His extraordinarily voluminous literary product teems with information about himself: and the writings of his contemporaries and successors provide at least the usual quota of allusions. But in his case these are supplemented by two remarkable books. For the whole earlier portion of his experiences, up to and including the great crisis of his conversion, we have from his own hand a work of unique self-revelation, in which he becomes something more than his own Boswell. And for the rest of his career, comprising the entire period of his activity as a leader in the Church, we have an exceptionally sober and trustworthy narrative from the hand of a pupil and friend who enjoyed a close intimacy with him for an unbroken stretch of nearly forty years. He is accordingly the first of the Christian fathers, the dates of whose birth and death we can exactly determine, and whose entire development we can follow from — as we say — the cradle to the grave.

The simple facts of his uneventful external life are soon told. He was born of mixed heathen and Christian parentage, in the small African municipality of Thagaste, on the thirteenth of November, 354. Receiving a good education, he was trained to the profession of rhetorician and practiced that profession successively at Thagaste, Carthage, Rome, and Milan, until his conversion, which took place at the last-named city in the late summer of 386. Baptized at Easter, 387, he returned to Africa in the autumn of 388, and established at his native town a sort of religio-philosophical retreat for himself and his friends. Here he lived in learned retirement until early in 391,

[1] From *The Princeton Theological Review*, iii. 1905, pp. 81–126.

when he was ordained a presbyter at Hippo — the sacred office being thrust upon him against his will, as it was later upon his followers, John Calvin and John Knox. Five years later (shortly before Christmas, 395), he was made coadjutor-bishop of Hippo, and from the first sustained practically the entire burden of its administration. He continued bishop of that second-rate sea-side town, until his death on August 28, 430, meanwhile having revolutionized the Church of Africa by his ceaseless labors and illuminated the world by his abundant writings. In this humble framework was lived a life the immediate products of which seemed washed out at once by the flood of disasters which instantly overwhelmed the African provinces, and with them the African Church which it had regenerated; but the influence of which is, nevertheless, not yet exhausted after a millennium and a half of years.

I. POSSIDIUS' PORTRAIT OF AUGUSTINE

The "Life" by Possidius is much briefer than we could have wished, but it presents a clear outline of Augustine's life drawn by the hand of one who worked in the full consciousness that he was handing down to posterity the record of a career which was of the first importance to the world. Augustine's literary activity by means of which he freed the Church from her enemies and built her up in the knowledge and service of God; Augustine's labors for the Church's peace by means of which he healed the schisms that divided the African community; Augustine's regeneration of the clergy of Africa through his monastic training-school: these are the points on which Possidius lays the greatest stress. In the meanwhile, however, he does much more than sum up for us what Augustine was doing for the Church and the world; though in doing this, he was speaking with a wisdom beyond his own knowledge, inasmuch as in a broader field than Africa Augustine has been a determining factor in precisely the matters here emphasized. He also paints for us a touchingly sincere portrait of the personality of his beloved master and enables us to see him at his daily work, submerged under superabundant labors, but always able to lift his heart to God, and already enjoying his rest with Him even in the midst of the clangor of the warfare he was ever waging for His Church and His truth.

Even as a presbyter, we read, he began to reap the fruit of his labors:

Alike at home and in the Church, he gave himself unstintedly to teaching and preaching the word of salvation with all confidence, in opposition to the heresies prevalent in Africa, especially to the Donatists, Manicheans and Pagans — now in elaborated books, and again in unstudied sermons — to the unspeakable admiration and delight of the Christians who as far as in them lay spread abroad his words. And thus, by God's help, the Catholic Church began to lift up its head in Africa, where it had long lain oppressed under luxuriating heresies, and especially under the Donatists, who had rebaptized the greater part of the people. And these books and tractates of his, flowing forth by the wonderful grace of God in the greatest profusion, instinct with sweet reasonableness and the authority of Holy Scripture, the heretics themselves, with the greatest ardor, vied with the Catholics in hearkening to, and moreover every one who wished and could do so brought stenographers and took notes even of what was spoken. Thus the precious doctrine and sweet savour of Christ was diffused throughout all Africa, and even the Church across the sea rejoiced when she heard it — for, even as when one member suffers all the members suffer with it, so when one member is exalted all the members rejoice with it.[2]

The labors he thus began as a presbyter, we are told, he but completed as bishop, the Lord crowning his work for the peace of the Church with the most astonishing success:

And more and more, by the help of Christ, was increased and multiplied the unity of peace and the fraternity of the Church of God. . . . And all this good, as I have said, was both begun and brought to a completion by this holy man, with the aid of our bishops.[3]

But alas! while man may propose it is God that disposes. Scarcely had this hard-won *pax ecclesiæ* been attained, when

[2] "Sancti Augustini Vita Scripta a Possidio Episcopo," chap. vii .
[3] Chap. xiii.

the Vandal invasion came and with it the ruin of the land. As the fabric he had built up fell about him, the great builder passes away also, and Possidius draws for us the picture of his last days with a tenderness of touch which only a true friend could show: [4]

We talked together very frequently and discussed the tremendous judgment of God enacted under our eyes, saying, " Just art Thou, O God, and Thy judgment is righteous." Mingling our grief and groans and tears we prayed the Father of mercies and Lord of all consolation to vouchsafe to help us in our trouble. And it chanced on a day as we sat at the table with him and conversed, that he said, " Bear in mind that I am asking God in this our hour of tribulation, either to deign to deliver this town from the enemy that is investing it, or, if that seems not good to Him, to strengthen His servants to submit themselves to His will, and in any event to take me away from this world to Himself." Under his instruction it became therefore our custom thereafter, and that of all connected with us, and of those who were in the town, to join with him in such a prayer to God Almighty. And behold, in the third month of the siege, he took to his bed, afflicted with a fever; and thus fell into his last illness. Nor did the Lord disappoint His servant of the fruit of his prayer. . . . Thus did this holy man, his path prolonged by the Divine bounty for the advantage and happiness of the Church, live seventy and six years, almost forty of which were spent in the priesthood and bishopric. He had been accustomed to say to us in familiar conversation, that no baptised person, even though he were a notable Christian and a priest, should depart from the body without fitting and sufficient penitence. So he looked to this in his last sickness, of which he died. For he ordered that those few Psalms of David called Penitential should be written out, and the sheets containing them hung upon the wall where he could see them as he lay in bed, in his weakness; and as he read them he wept constantly and abundantly. And that he might not be disturbed, he asked of us who were present, some ten days before he departed from the body, that no one should come in except at those hours when the physicians visited him or when food was brought him. This wish was, of course, observed, and he thus had all his time free for prayer. Unintermittently, up to the outbreak of this last illness, he had zealously and energetically preached

[4] Chaps. xxviii. xxix. xxxi.

in the church the Word of God, with sanity of mind and soundness of judgment. And now, preserved to a good old age, sound in all the members of his body, and with unimpaired sight and hearing, and with us, as it is written, standing by and watching and praying, he fell asleep with his fathers, having been preserved to a good old age: and we offered a sacrifice to God for the peaceful repose of his body and buried him.

His library, the biography proceeds, he left to the Church; and his own books, who that reads them can fail to read in them the manner of man he was? He adds: [5]

But I think that those could profit more from him who could hear and see him speaking as he stood in the church, especially if they were not ignorant of his walk among men. For he was not merely a learned scribe in the kingdom of heaven, bringing out from his treasury things new and old, and one of those merchantmen who, having found a pearl of great price, went and sold all that he had and bought it; but he was also of those to whom it is written, " So speak and so do," and of whom the Saviour says, " Whosoever shall do and teach men thus, he shall be called great in the kingdom of heaven.

What a testimony is this to Augustine's daily life before his companions! And how pathetic is this companion's parting request of his readers:

Pray with me and for me, that I may both in this world become the emulator and imitator of this man with whom for almost forty years, by God's grace, I lived in intimacy and happiness, without any unpleasant disagreement, and in the future may enjoy with him the promises of God Almighty.

II. The " Confessions " of Augustine

It is, however, to his own " Confessions," of course, that we will turn if we would know Augustine through and through. This unique book was written about 397–400, say about a dozen years after Augustine's conversion and shortly after his ordination as bishop of Hippo — at a time when he was al-

[5] Chap. xxxi.

ready thoroughly formed in both life and thought. There is laid bare to us in it a human heart with a completeness of self-revelation probably unparalleled in literature.

Jean Jacques Rousseau, to be sure, claims this distinction for his own " Confessions." " I have entered on a performance," says he, " which is without example, whose accomplishment will have no imitator. I mean to present my fellow-mortals with a man in all the integrity of nature; and this man shall be myself." Rousseau has at least the merit of perceiving what many have not recognized, that his book cannot be considered to belong to the same class of literature with Augustine's. But what we wish now to emphasize is that even as an unveiling of the soul of a man, which it makes its sole object, Rousseau's performance falls far behind Augustine's searching pages, although, as we shall see, self-revelation was in these merely an incidental effect. The truth is, Rousseau did not see deeply enough and could not command a prospect sufficiently wide to paint all that is in man, even all that is in such a man as he essayed to portray. Quite apart from the interval that separates the two souls depicted, Rousseau's conception of self-revelation rose little above exhibiting himself with his clothes off. To his prurient imagination nakedness, certainly unadorned and all the better if it were unadorning, appeared the most poignant possible revelation of humanity. It seemed to him, essential scandal-monger that he was, that he needed but to publish on the housetop all his " adventures " to enable the whole world to say of him in the Roman proverb, *Ego te intus et in cute novi;* and he was only too pleased to believe that the world, on so seeing his inward disposition at least if not his outward life, would be convinced that it agreed well with " loose Natta's." [6] He could feel no sympathy with Augustine's cry, " I became a mighty puzzle to myself." [7] The shallow self he knew only too well absorbed his entire attention and his one engagement was in presenting this self to the gaze of the public. What lay beneath the surface he passed by with

[6] Persius, " Satt.," iii. 30.

[7] " Confessiones," iv. 4. 9.: " factus eram ipse mihi magna quæstio."

the unconsciousness of an essentially frivolous nature.[8] No wonder that an air of insincerity hangs over the picture he has drawn. There will be few readers who will easily persuade themselves that what they read all happened, or happened as it is set down; they will rather be continually haunted with the suspicion that they are perusing not a veracious autobiography but a piccaroon novel. The interval that divides the " Confessions " of Rousseau from the " Adventures of Gil Blas of Santillane " is, in any case, narrower than that which separates it from the " Confessions " of Augustine.

It must be confessed, it is true, that, if not the sincerity, at least the trustworthiness of the portrait Augustine draws of himself also has not passed wholly unquestioned. It has of late become quite the mode, indeed, to remind us that the " Confessions " were written a dozen years after the conversion up to which their narrative leads; and that in the meanwhile the preceding period of darkness had grown over-black in Augustine's eyes, and as he looked back upon it through the intervening years he saw it in distorted form and exaggerated colors.[9] His is accordingly represented as " a prominent example

[8] James Russell Lowell, " Prose Works," 1891, ii. p. 261: " Rousseau cries, ' I will bare my heart to you! ' and throwing open his waistcoat, makes us the confidants of his dirty linen."

[9] See, e.g., Boissier, " La Fin du Paganisme," i. p. 293; Harnack, " Monasticism and the Confessions of Augustine," pp. 132, 141; Reuter, " Augustinische Studien," p. 4; Loofs, Herzog " Realencyklopädie für protestantische Theologie und Kirche," [3] ii. pp. 260–261, and especially pp. 266–267. Cf. also Gourdon, " Essai sur la Conversion de Saint Augustin," Cahors, 1900. R. Schmid in an article entitled " Zur Bebehrungsgeschichte Augustins " in the *Zeitschrift für Theologie und Kirche,* 1897, vii. pp. 80–96, has made the fact and extent of failure of the " Confessions" in trustworthiness the subject of a special study. No one doubts, he remarks, the subjective sincerity of the " Confessions "; and its objective trustworthiness can come into question only in minutiæ. The conclusion at which he arrives is that only in two points are the " Confessions " open to correction in their representation. Augustine was not led to give up his professorship by his conversion, but these two things fell together only by accident; and he still wished after conversion for a comfortable life, an *otium cum dignitate,* and loved to teach. " Thus in reality there remains, so far as the ' Confessions ' do not correct themselves — that is, permit the history to be seen through the veil of later reflections thrown over it — very little over. But even a little is, here, much. . . . In the main matter, however, the ' Con-

of a tendency frequently found in religionists of an effusive type, to exaggerate their infirmities in order to enhance their merits in having escaped them, or by way of contrasting present attainment with former unworthiness, just as a successful merchant sometimes boasts that he began his career with only sixpence in his pocket." [10] We are warned, therefore, not to take his descriptions of his youthful errors and of his fruitless wanderings in search of truth at the foot of the letter. A recent writer, for example, condemns all current biographies of Augustine because, as he says, they "all are constructed on the perverse type which is followed by Augustine himself in his seductive ' Confessions,' " in which he " is sternly bent on magnifying his misdeeds." Blinded by " the glare of his new ideal," as leading ecclesiastic and theologian of the West, his psychic perspective was foreshortened and he hopelessly misrepresented his unregenerate youth. " The truth seems to be," we are told, " that the book is a kind of theological treatise and work of edification. The Bishop of Hippo takes the rhetorician as an ' awful example ' of nature without God. To point his dogmatic antithesis of nature and grace, philosophy and Christianity, nothing could be more forceful than his own career painted as darkly as conscience would permit. . . . But the fallacy of it all for us, reducing its value as a human document, is that Augustine examines his earlier life from a false point of view." [11]

Despite the modicum of truth resident in the recognition by the writer last quoted that the book is not formally an autobiography, but, as he terms it, " a kind of theological treatise and work of edification," this whole representation is fundamentally wrong. The judgment that Augustine passed on the misdeeds not merely, but the whole course, of his youth was

---

fessions' remain in the right — that it was a revolutionary inward experience, which brought him completely into the road on which he sought and found God and himself " (p. 96).

[10] See John Owen, " Evenings with the Sceptics," ii. p. 139.

[11] Joseph McCabe, " St. Augustine and His Age," pp. v., 24, 39, 41, 54, 69, 70, 195–198.

naturally essentially different at the time when he wrote his
" Confessions " from what it had been during the life which is
passed in review in them. He does not leave us to infer this —
he openly declares it; or rather it is precisely this change of
judgment which it is one of the chief purposes of the " Confessions " to signalize. We could hardly ask a man after he has
escaped from what he has come to look upon as the sty to write
of his mode of life in it from the point of view of one who loves
to wallow in the mire. It is, however, something very like this
that is suggested by our critics as the ideal of autobiographical
narration. At least we read: " About the year 400, when they
[the " Confessions "] were written, Augustine had arrived at a
most lofty conception of duty and life; he commits the usual
and inevitable fallacy of taking this later standard back to illumine the ground of his early career. In the glare of his new
ideal, actions which probably implied no moral resistance at
the time they were performed, cast an appalling shadow." [12]
And again: " There is no trace in the ' Confessions ' that his
conscience had anything to say at the time." [13]

Surely there is laid here a most unreasonable requirement
upon the historian. We may or may not accord with the judgment that Augustine passes upon his early life. We may or
may not consider that he who takes his knowledge of Augustine's youth from the " Confessions " must guard himself from
accepting from them also the judgment they pass on the course
of that youth as well as on the separate events that entered
into it. For example, we may or may not believe that Augustine was right in attributing the passions of anger and jealousy manifesting themselves in infancy to the movements of
inherent corruption derived from our first parents, or in representing the childish escapade of robbing a pear tree as an exhibition of a pure love of evil, native in men as men. But any
such differences of moral standpoint of which we may be conscious, between ourselves and the Augustine who wrote the
" Confessions," are one thing; and the trustworthiness of the
record he has given us, whether of the external occurrences of

[12] *Op. cit.*, p. 24. [13] *Ibid.*, p. 41.

his youth or of the inner movements of his soul during that period of restless search, which knew no rest because it had not yet found rest in God, is quite another thing. It is not merely the transparent sincerity of the " Confessions" which impresses every reader; it is the close and keen observation, the sound and tenacious memory, the sane and searching analysis that equally characterize them. " Observation, indeed," says Harnack, with eminent justice, " is the strong point of Augustine. . . . What is *characteristic* never escapes him " — and that is especially true of the secret movements of the heart.[14] The reader feels himself in the hands of a narrator not only whose will but whose capacity as well both to see and to tell the truth he cannot doubt. There is spread over the whole the evidence no more of the most absolute good faith than of the utmost care to distinguish between fact and opinion — between what really was and what the writer could wish had been. You may think " there is a morbid strain in the book "; you may accuse its author of "making a stage-play of his bleeding heart "; you may judge him " in many places overstrained, unhealthy, or even false." [15] All this will depend on the degree in which you feel yourself in sympathy with his standpoint. But " there is a look of intense reality on every page," as a careful student has put it; [16] and as you read you cannot doubt that here is not merely a sincere but a true record of the experiences of a soul, which you may — nay, must — trust as such without reserve.

It is important, however, in order that we may appraise the book properly, to apprehend somewhat more exactly than perhaps is common precisely what Augustine proposed to himself in it. It is inadequate to speak of it simply either broadly as an autobiography, or more precisely as a *vie intime*. Not to emphasize just here the decisive consideration that only nine of

[14] *Op. cit.,* pp. 128, 131. Cf. also T. R. Glover, "Life and Letters in the Fourth Century," p. 195.

[15] Harnack, *op. cit.,* p. 132.

[16] A. F. West, " Roman Autobiography, Particularly Augustine's Confessions," in *The Presbyterian and Reformed Review,* xii. No. 46 (April 1901) p. 183.

its thirteen books have any biographical content, it lies quite
on the face of the narrative that even the biographical material provided in these nine books is not given with a purely
biographical intent. Augustine is not the proper subject either
of the work as a whole, or even of those portions of it in
which his life-history is depicted. What he tells us about himself, full and rich and searching as it is, nevertheless is incidental to another end than self-portraiture, and is determined
both in its selection and in its mode of treatment by this end.
In sending a copy of the book, almost a generation later, to a
distinguished and admiring friend who had asked him for it,
he does indeed speak of it frankly as a mirror in which he himself could be seen; and, be it duly noted, he affirms that he
is to be seen in this mirror truly, just as he was. " Accept," he
writes to his correspondent [17] — " accept the books of my Confessions which you have asked for. Behold me therein, that you
may not praise me above what I am. Believe there not others
about me, but me myself, and see by means of myself what I
was in myself; and if there is anything in me that pleases you,
praise with me there Him whom I wish to be praised for me —
for that One is not myself. Because it is He that made us
and not we ourselves; nay, we have destroyed ourselves, but
He that made us has remade us. And when you find me there,
pray for me that I be not defective but perfected." Similarly in his " Retractations," [18] he says simply that the first
ten books were " written about himself "; but he does not
fail to declare also of the whole thirteen that " they praise
the just and good God with respect both of his evil and his
good and excite the human intellect and affection toward
Him." This, he says, was their effect on himself as he wrote
them, and this has been their effect on those that have read
them.

From such passages as these we perceive how Augustine
uniformly thought of his " Confessions " — not as a biography
of himself, but, as we have commended a rather blind com-

[17] " Epist." 231, to Count Darius (§ 6).
[18] ii. 6: " a primo usque ad decimum de me scripti sunt."

mentator for seeing, rather as a book of edification, or, if you will, a theological treatise. His actual subject is not himself, but the goodness of God; and he introduces his own experiences only as the most lively of illustrations of the dealings of God with the human soul as He makes it restless until it finds its rest in Him. Such being the case the congeners of the book are not to be found in simple autobiographies even of the most introspective variety. The "Confessions" of Rousseau, of Hamann, of Alfred de Musset — such books have so little in common with it that they do not belong even in the same literary class with it. Even the similarity of their titles to its is an accident. For Augustine does not use the term "Confessions" here in the debased sense in which these writers use it; the sense of unveiling, uncovering to the sight of the world what were better perhaps hidden from all eyes but God's which see all things; but in that higher double sense in which we may speak of confessing the grace of God and our humble dependence on Him, a sense compounded of mingled humility and praise.

The real analogues of Augustine's "Confessions" are to be found not then in introspective biographies whose sole purpose is to depict a human soul, but in such accounts of spiritual experiences as are given us in books like John Newton's "Authentic Narrative," although the scope of this particular narrative is too narrow to furnish a perfect analogy. At the head of his narrative Newton has written this text: "Thou shalt remember all the way, by which the Lord thy God led thee through this wildness"; and the same text might equally well be written at the head of Augustine's "Confessions." We might almost fancy we hear Augustine explaining his own purpose when we hear Newton declaring that with him it was a question "only concerning the patience and long-suffering of God, the wonderful interposition of His providence in favor of an unworthy sinner, the power of His grace in softening the hardest heart, and the riches of His mercy in pardoning the most enormous and aggravated transgressions." Perhaps, however, the closest analogy to Augustine's "Confessions," among books, at least, which have attained anything like the same popular influence, is furnished by John Bunyan's "Grace Abounding to the Chief of Sinners." Bunyan's purpose is precisely the same as Augustine's — to glorify the grace of God. He employs also the same means of securing this end — an autobiographical account of the dealings of God with his soul. "In this relation of the merciful working of God upon my soul," says Bunyan, "it will not be amiss if, in the first place, I do, in a few words, give you a hint of my pedigree and manner of bringing up; that thereby the goodness and bounty of God toward me may be the more advanced and magnified before the sons of men." Just so Augustine, also, gave what he gave of "his pedigree and manner of bringing up"; and what he gave of his youthful wanderings in error and in sin; and what he gave of his struggles to find and grasp, to grasp and cling to what of good he saw and loved: only that "the goodness and bounty of God toward him might be the more advanced and magnified before the sons of men." We have said that the interval that divides Rousseau's "Confessions" from the "Adventures of Gil Blas of Santillane," is less than that which separates them from Augustine's. We may now say that the interval that divides Augustine's "Confessions" from the "Pilgrim's Progress" is less than that which separates them from any simple autobiography — veracious and searching autobiography though a great portion of it is. For the whole concernment of the book is with the grace of God to a lost sinner. It is this, and not himself, that is its theme.

This fundamental fact is, of course, written large over the whole work, and comes not rarely to explicit assertion. "I wish to record my past foulnesses and the carnal corruptions of my soul," says Augustine, "not because I love them, but in order that I may love Thee, O my God. For love of Thy love do I do this thing, — recollecting my most vicious ways in the bitterness of my remembrance, that Thou mayest become my Joy, Thou never-failing Joy, Thou blessed and sacred Joy; and collecting myself from the dissipation in which I was torn to pieces, when turned from Thee, the One, I was lost among the

many." [19] " To whom do I relate this? . . . And why? Just
that I and whosoever may read this may consider out of what
depths we are to cry unto Thee. And what is nearer to Thy ears
than a confessing heart and a life of faith? " [20] " Accept the sacrifice of my confessions from the hand of my tongue which
Thou didst form and hast prompted that it may confess to Thy
name. Heal all my bones and let them say, Lord, who is like
unto Thee? . . . Let my soul praise Thee that it may love
Thee, and let it confess to Thee Thy mercies that it may
praise Thee." [21] " Why, then, do I array before Thee the narrations of so many things? . . . That I may excite my affection toward Thee, and that of those who read these things, so
that we all may say, ' Great is the Lord and highly to be
praised.' " [22] In these last words we observe that as he approaches the end of the book, he is still bearing in mind the
words which he set at its beginning; [23] and by thus reverting
to the beginning, he binds the whole together as one great
volume of praise to the Lord for His goodness to him in leading him to His salvation. Accordingly he adds at once: " Therefore, we are manifesting our affection to Thee, in confessing
to Thee our miseries and Thy mercies toward us, in order that
Thou mayest deliver us altogether since Thou hast made a
beginning, and we may cease to be miserable in ourselves
and become blessed in Thee, since Thou hast called us to
be poor in spirit, and meek and mourners, and hungerers,
and thirsters after righteousness, and merciful and pure in
heart and peacemakers." [24] Here the theme of the " Confessions " is clearly set before us. It is the ineffable goodness of
God, which is illustrated by what He has done for Augustine's miserable soul, in delivering it from its sins and distresses and bringing it out into the largeness of the divine
life and knowledge.

It is, obviously, only from this point of view that the unity
of the book becomes apparent. For we must not fancy that

[19] ii. 1. 1.   [22] xi. 1. 1.
[20] ii. 3. 5.   [23] i. 1. 1.
[21] v. 1. 1.   [24] xi. 1. 1.

when Augustine has brought to a completion the narrative of
the wonderful dealings of God with him, by which he was led
to repentance, he has ended his "confessions"; to which he attaches the last four books therefore purely mechanically, without any rational bond of connection with their predecessors.
To his consciousness, throughout the whole extent of these
books, he continues to sound the voice of his confessions: and
if we search in them for it we shall find the same note ringing
in them as in the others. "Behold," he cries,[25] "Thy voice is
my joy: Thy voice surpasses the abundance of pleasures. . . .
Let me confess unto Thee whatsoever I have found in Thy
books, and let me hear the voice of praise and drink Thee in
and consider the wonderful things of Thy law, even from the
beginning, in the which Thou didst make the heaven and the
earth, down to the everlasting kingdom of Thy Holy City, that
is with Thee." Not the least of the mercies that Augustine
wished to confess to God that he had received from His hand
was the emancipation of His intellect, and the freeing of his
mind from the crudities with which it had been stuffed; and
it is this confession that he makes, with praises on his lips, in
these concluding books. The construction of the work, then, is
something like the following: first Augustine recounts how
God has dealt with him in bringing him to salvation (books
i.–ix.); then what he has under the divine grace become, as a
saved child of God (book x.); and finally what reaches of
sound and satisfying knowledge have been granted to him in
the divine revelation (books xi.–xiii.): and all to the praise
of the glory of His grace. Body, heart, mind, all were made for
God: all were incited to seek Him and to praise Him: and all
were restless, therefore, until at last they found their rest in
Him. Elsewhere than in Him had happiness, peace, knowledge
been sought, but nowhere else had they been found. The
proud was cast down: and he that exalted himself inevitably
fell. But they whose exaltation God becomes — they fall not
any more forever. This is the concluding word of the "Confessions."

[25] xi. 2. 3, *ad fin.*

Only in proportion as this, the true character of the book, is apprehended, moreover, does its true originality become evident. Even were it possible to think of it merely as an introspective autobiography, it would no doubt be epoch-making in the history of literary form. In an interesting paper on "Roman Autobiography," [26] Prof. A. F. West points out that this species of composition was especially Roman. "Autobiography, as well as satire," he remarks, "should be credited to the Romans as their own independent invention." "The appearance of Augustine's 'Confessions,' in 399 or 400," he continues, "dates the entrance of a new kind of autobiography into Latin literature — the autobiography of introspection, the self-registered record of the development of a human soul." It was characteristic of Augustine's genius that, in a purely incidental use of it, he invented an entirely new literary form and carried it at a stroke to its highest development. No wonder that Harnack falls into something like enthusiasm over this accomplishment.

The significance of the "Confessions," says he, "is as great on the side of form as on that of content. Before all, they were a literary achievement. No poet, no philosopher before him undertook what he here performed; and I may add that almost a thousand years had to pass before a similar thing was done. It was the poets of the Renascence, who formed themselves on Augustine, that first gained from his example the daring to depict themselves and to present their personality to the world. For what do the "Confessions" of Augustine contain? The portrait of a soul — not psychological disquisitions on the Understanding, the Will, and the Emotions in Man, not abstract investigations into the nature of the soul, not superficial reasonings and moralizing introspections like the "Meditations" of Marcus Aurelius, but the most exact portraiture of a distinct human personality, in his development from childhood to full age, with all his propensities, feelings, aims, mistakes; a portrait of a soul, in fact, drawn with a perfection of observation that leaves on one side the mechanical devices of psychology, and pursues the methods of the physician and the physiologist.[27]

[26] *Presbyterian and Reformed Review*, xii. No. 46 (April, 1901), p. 183.
[27] *Op. cit.*, pp. 127–128.

Obviously Harnack is thinking of the first nine books only. Otherwise he could scarcely speak so absolutely of the absence from the "Confessions" of "psychological disquisitions." For what is the great discourse on "Memory," embodied in the tenth book, but a psychological disquisition of the most penetrating kind, to say nothing now of the analysis of the idea of "Time," broached in the eleventh book? The achievement which he signalizes is, therefore, only part of the achievement of the book, and if Augustine in it has incidentally become the father of all those who have sought to paint the portrait of a human soul, what must be said of the originality of his performance when understood in its real peculiarity — as the dramatic portraiture of the dealing of divine grace with a sinful soul in leading it through all its devious wanderings into the harbor of salvation? Not in the poets of the Renascence — not even in Goethe's "Faust" in which Harnack strangely seeks the nearest literary parallel to the "Confessions" — can it now find its tardy successors. We must come down to the Reformation — perhaps to the "second Reformation" as the men of the seventeenth century loved to call their own times, and after that to that almost third Revolution which was wrought by the "Evangelical Revival" or "Great Awakening" — before we discover its real successors; and we must look through all the years, perhaps in vain, to find any successor worthy to be placed on a level with it.

We must avoid exaggeration, however, even with respect to the novelty of the book. Perhaps if we eliminate the question of value and think merely of the literary species which it so uniquely represents, it can scarcely be said that Augustine's performance was absolutely without forerunners, or remained absolutely without successors "for a thousand years." The greatness of its shining may blind our eyes unduly to lesser points of light, which, except for the glare of its brilliancy, might be seen to stud the heavens about it. A recent writer, for example, claims for a tractate of Cyprian's — the treatise or letter "To Donatus" — the honor of having pointed out the way in which Augustine afterward walked. He says:

Finally,[28] a great novelty appears in this little book. The pages on the conversion of Cyprian, which mark almost the advent of a new species of literature, directly herald the "Confessions" of St. Augustine. For a long time, a very profane manner of life, a passionate taste for pleasure, along with a sort of instinctive defiance of Christianity; subsequently, up to the very eve of the decisive event, incapacity to believe in the renewal promised in baptism, a very clear perception of the obstacles which a life so worldly opposed to so sudden a revolution; then, after many hesitations, grace, as startling as a clap of thunder, revolutionizing the whole being in its profoundest depths, to turn it toward a new destiny; and in the recollection left by this miraculous transformation, a fixed determination to refer all to God, to turn confession into acts of thankfulness: such are in Cyprian the essential traits that mark the steps of conversion. And these are precisely the ideas that dominate the "Confessions" of Augustine.

In effect, we have in this affected, mincing tract of Cyprian's, hidden as its lessons well-nigh are under the shadow of its rhetorical virtuosity, what may be called the beginnings of the Autobiography of Conversion — unless we prefer to penetrate yet a hundred years further back and see its beginnings in the beautiful description with which Justin Martyr opens his "Dialogue with Trypho" of how he found his way through philosophy to Christ. Both narratives have much in their substance that is fitted to remind of Augustine's. But both are too brief; the one is too objective and the other too affected; neither is sufficiently introspective or sufficiently searching to justify their inclusion in the same class with their great successor. A better claim, many will think, might be put in for the spiritual history which Hilary of Poictiers gives of his own former life in the splendid Latin of the first fifteen sections of his treatise "On the Faith" or, as it is commonly called, "On the Trinity." It is the story of a naturally noble soul, seeking and gradually finding more and more perfectly the proper aim of life as it rises to the knowledge first of the God of philosophy and then of the God of revelation, and ulti-

[28] Monceaux, "Hist. Lit. de l'Afrique Chrét.," II., "S. Cyprien et son temps," p. 266.

mately attains assured faith in the God and Father of our Lord Jesus Christ. Did it not move so exclusively on the intellectualistic plane, without depth of experimental coloring, its dignity of language and high eloquence might, despite its brevity, justify us in esteeming it no unworthy forerunner of the "Confessions."

Such predecessors, interesting as they are and valuable as marking the channels in which the new Christian literature naturally flowed, can hardly be thought of as having opened the way for Augustine — partly because their motive is too primarily autobiographical. Similarly he had few immediate successors who can be said to follow closely in his steps. Perhaps the "Eucharisticos Deo" of Paulinus of Pella — in which he essays to praise God for His preservation of him and for His numerous kindnesses through a long and eventful life — may not unfairly be considered a typical instance of such spiritual autobiographies as the next age produced. This poem is assuredly not uninteresting, and to the student of manners it has its own importance; but as a history of a soul it lacks nearly everything that gives to the "Confessions" their charm. That some resemblance should be discernible between the picture Augustine draws of his life and that which such writers draw of their own was unavoidable, since he and they were alike men and Christians and were prepared to thank God for making them both. But the resemblance ends very much at that point. The sublime depths and heights of Augustine and all that has made him the teacher of the world in this his most individual book is wanting, as well in his successors as in his predecessors. He had to wait for Bunyan before there was written another such spiritual "autobiography," or to be more precise, another such history of God's dealings with a soul: and even the "Grace Abounding" stands beside the "Confessions" only *longe intervallo*.

The attractiveness of the "Confessions" obviously lurks, not in its style, but in its matter — or rather in the personality that lies behind both style and matter and gives unity, freshness, depth, brilliancy to both matter and style. Harnack is

quite right when he remarks that the key to the enduring influence of the book is found in the fact that we meet a person
in it — a person " everywhere richer than his expression ": [29]
that we feel a heart beating behind its words and perceive that
this is a great heart, to whose beating we cannot but attend.
Nevertheless the form of the " Confessions " is itself not without its fascination, and its very style has also its allurement.
His rhetorical training had entered, to be sure, into Augustine's very substance and the false taste with which he had
been imbued had become a second nature with him. Even in
such heart-throes as express themselves in this book, he could
not away with the frivolous word-plays, affected assonances,
elaborate balancing of clauses and the like that form the hall-
mark of the sophistic rhetoric of the times. It has been remarked that " rhetorician as Augustine was, and master of
several styles, he had a curious power of dropping his rhetoric
when he undertook in homilies and commentaries to interpret
Scripture." [30] Unfortunately, he also had a curious facility of
dropping into offensive rhetorical tricks in the midst of the
most serious discussions, or the most moving revelations of
feeling. Apart from these occasional lapses — if lapses so frequent can be called occasional — the very form given this book
as a sustained address to God is wearisome to many. M. Boissier [31] remarks that the transports and effusions with which
Augustine addresses himself to God " end by seeming to us
monotonous." Harnack thinks the book too long and too alien
to modern thought ever to enter into really literary use in its
entirety: and therefore welcomes the preparation of abridge-
ments of it. [32] Prof. West [33] finds in it " ineptitudes and infelici-
ties " which can be expected to shrink and permit " the central
power " of the book to appear only for him who reads it in its
original Latin. The merely English reader, he remarks, can

[29] *Op. cit.*, i. p. 136.

[30] E. W. Watson, *Classical Review*, February, 1901, p. 65, quoted in
Glover, *op. cit.*, p. 195, note.

[31] *Op. cit.*, p. 292.

[32] *Theolog. Literaturzeitung*, 1903, No. 1, 12.

[33] As cited, pp. 184–185.

scarcely hope to find it very interesting. "The unchecked rhetoric, the reiterated calls on God, varied and wearisome, the
shrewd curiosity in hunting down subtleties to their last hiding-
places, the streaks of inane allegorizing,[34] and sometimes the
violent bursts of feeling, — these are the things that frighten
away readers and prevent them from reaching the real delights of the book."

It is difficult to draw up a catalogue of such defects without exaggeration: and in the present case an exaggerated impression, both with respect to quantity and quality, is almost
certain to be conveyed. After all said, the "Confessions" are
an eminently well and winningly written book. There is even
in the mere style a certain poetic quality that gives it not
merely character but beauty. Harnack justly speaks of "the
lyricism of the style." There is certainly present in it, as Dr.
Bigg points out,[35] something of "the same musical flow, the
same spiritual refinement and distinction" that characterizes
the "Imitation of Christ." It is not, indeed, as Dr. Bigg justly
adds, either "so compact or so highly polished" as the "Imitation of Christ": "St. Augustine cannot give the time to
cut each word as if it were an individual diamond, as a Kempis
did." But Augustine more than compensates for this deficiency
in preciosity by his greater richness, depth, and variety. There
is nothing effeminate in Augustine's style, nothing over-filed,
nothing cloying or wearisome. Here, too, indeed, it is true, as
it generally is, that the style is the man. And Augustine is
never an uninteresting person to meet, even through the medium of the written, or even of the translated, page. No more
individual writer ever lived: and the individuality which was
his was not only powerful and impressive, but to an almost
unexampled degree profound, rich, and attractive. Harnack
is right; the charm of the "Confessions" is that they are
Augustine's and that he draws his readers into his life by

[34] Are these found to any appreciable extent outside the Thirteenth
Book?

[35] Introduction to his version, published in Methuen's series, called the
"Library of Devotion," 3d ed., 1900, p. 5.

them. Here are reflected, as in a mirror, the depth and tenderness of his ardent nature, the quickness and mobility of
his emotions and yet, underlying all, his sublime repose. He
who reads shares the conflicts and the turmoils depicted:
but he enters also into the rest the writer has found with
God.

It is in this fact that the unique attractiveness of the book
as a " work of edification " resides — an attractiveness which
has made it through a millennium and a half the most widely
read of all books written in Latin, with the possible exception
of the " Æneid " of Virgil.[36] He who reads these pages enters
as in none other into the struggles of a great soul as it fights its
way to God, shares with it all its conflict, and participates at
last with it in the immensity of its repose. As he reads, that
great sentence that sounds the keynote of the book and echoes
through all its pages, echoes also in his soul: " Thou hast made
us for Thyself, O Lord, and our heart is restless till it finds its
rest in Thee." The agonizing cry becomes his also, " O by Thy
loving-kindness, tell me, O Lord my God, what Thou art to
me: say unto my soul, *I am thy Salvation.*" And there likewise becomes his the childlike prattle of the same soul, stilled
in praise now that it has found God its salvation, as it names
over to itself as its dearest possession the sweet names by
which its God has become precious to it, " O Lord, my God,
my Light, my Wealth, my Salvation! " What is apt to escape
us who have, after so many years, entered into the heritage
which Augustine has won for us is that it was really he who
won it for us — that in these groans and tears into which we
so readily enter with him as we read, and in this hard-earned
rest in God into which we so easily follow him, he was breaking out a pathway not only for his own but for our feet. For
here is the astonishing fact that gives its supreme significance
to this book: it is the earliest adequate expression of that type
of religion which has since attached to itself the name of
" evangelical "; and, though the earliest, it is one of the fullest,
richest, and most perfect expressions of this type of religion

[36] Glover, *op. cit.,* p. 195.

which has ever been written. Adolf Harnack, realizing the immense significance of the appearance in Augustine of this new type of religion, consecrates a whole chapter in his "History of Dogma" to "The Historical Position of Augustine as Reformer of Christian Piety," as a preparation for the due exposition of his doctrinal teaching. In this chapter he makes many true and striking remarks; but he hardly exhibits a just appreciation of the intimate relation which subsists between Augustine's peculiar type of piety and his peculiar type of doctrine. Harnack, in fact, speaks almost as if it were conceivable that one of these could have come into existence apart from the other. The truth is, of course, that they are but the joint products in the two spheres of life and thought of the same body of conceptions, and neither could possibly have arisen without the other. If before Augustine alternating hope and fear were the characteristic sentiments of Christians and the psychological form of their piety was therefore unrest, while in Augustine the place of hope and fear is taken by trust and love, and unrest gives way to profound rest in God, this was because pre-Augustinian Christianity was prevailingly legalistic, and there entered into it a greater or less infusion of the evil leaven of self-salvation, while Augustine, with his doctrine of grace, cast himself wholly on the mercy of God, and so, as the poet expresses it,

> Turned fear and hope to love of God.
> Who loveth us.

The fact of the matter is that pre-Augustinian Christian thinking was largely engrossed with Theological and Christological problems and with Augustine first did Christian Soteriology begin to come to its rights. It was not he first, of course, who discovered that man is a sinner and therefore depends for his salvation on the grace of God; but in him first did these fundamental Christian truths find a soil in which they could come to their richest fruitage in heart and life, in thought and teaching. And here lies the secret of his profound realization (on which Harnack lays so much stress) that Christian happiness consists in "comforted remorse" (getrösteter Sünden-schmerz).[37] Before him men were prone to conceive them-selves essentially God's creatures, whose business it was to commend themselves to their Maker: no doubt they recognized that they had sinned, and that provision had been made to relieve them of the penalty of their sins; but they built their real hope of acceptance in God's sight more or less upon their own conduct. Augustine realized to the bottom of his soul that he was a sinner and what it is to be a sinner, and therefore sought at God's hands not acceptance but salvation. And this is the reason why he never thought of God without thinking of sin and never thought of sin without thinking of Christ. Be-cause he took his sin seriously, his thought and feeling alike traveled continually in this circle, and could not but travel in this circle. He thus was constantly verifying afresh the truth of the Savior's declaration that he to whom little is forgiven loves little, while he loves much who is conscious of having received much forgiveness: and as his trust increased and his love grew ever greater he realized better and better also that other saying that there is joy in heaven over one sinner that repents more than over ninety and nine righteous persons which need no repentance. So he came to understand that the heights of joy are scaled only by him who has first been miser-able, and that the highest happiness belongs only to him who has been the object of salvation. Self-despair, humble trust, grateful love, fullness of joy — these are the steps on which his own soul climbed upward: and these steps gave their whole color and form both to his piety and to his teaching. In his doctrine we see his experience of God's seeking and saving love toward a lost sinner expressing itself in propositional form; in his piety we see his conviction that the sole hope of the sinner lies in the free grace of a loving God expressing itself in the forms of feeling. In doctrine and life alike he sets before us in that effective way which belongs to the discoverer, the religion of faith as over against the religion of works — the religion

[37] "Lehrbuch der Dogmengeschichte," iii. p. 59; E. T. "History of Dogma," v. p. 66.

which despairing of self casts all its hope on God as over against the religion that to a greater or less degree trusts in itself: in a word, since religion in its very nature is dependence on God, religion in the purity of its conception as over against a quasi-religious moralism. It is to the fact that in this book we are admitted into the very life of Augustine and are permitted to see his great heart cleansing itself of all trust in himself and laying hold with the grasp first of despair, then of discerning trust and then of grateful love upon the God who was his salvation, that the "Confessions" owe their perennial attractiveness and their supreme position among books of edification. In them Augustine uncovers his heart and lets us see what religion is in its essence as it works in the soul of one who has, as few have, experienced its power. He has set himself determinedly in this book to exhibit the grace of God in action. Elsewhere he has expounded it in theory, defended it against its assailants, enforced it with logical argument and moving exhortation. Here he shows it at work, and at work in his own soul.

It was only in his effort to show us the grace of God as it worked upon his own soul, that Augustine was led to set before us his life-history through all the formative years of his career — until, after long wandering, he at last had found his rest in God. This is the meaning and this is the extent of the autobiographical element in the "Confessions." Nine of the thirteen books are devoted to this religious analysis of his life-history; and although, of course, the matter admitted and its treatment alike are determined by the end in view, yet Augustine's analysis is very searching and the end in view involves a very complete survey of all that was especially determining in his life-development. In these pages we can see, therefore, just what Augustine was, and just how he became what he became. And the picture, almost extreme in its individuality as it is, is nevertheless as typical as it is individual. It is typical of the life of the ancient world at its best: for in his comprehensive nature Augustine had gathered up into himself and given full play to all that was good in the culture of the ancient world. And it is typical of what Christian experience is at its best: for in Augustine there met in unusual fullness and fought themselves out to a finish all the fundamental currents of thought and feeling that strive together in the human heart when it is invaded by divine grace, and is slowly but surely conquered by it to good and to God. It may repay us to run over the salient elements in this life-history as here depicted for us.

III. The Augustine of the "Confessions"

Augustine came into being at the "turn of the ages," just as the old world was dying, and the new was being born. He was the offspring of a mixed marriage, itself typical of the mixed state of the society of the times. His father, a citizen of importance but of straitened means, in a small African town, remained a heathen until his gifted son had attained his middle youth: [38] he appears to have been a man of generally jovial disposition, liable to fits of violent temper, possessing neither intellectual endowments nor moral attainments to distinguish him from the mass of his contemporaries: but he appreciated the promise of his son, and was prepared to make sacrifices that opportunity might be given for his development. His mother, on the other hand, was one of nature's noblewomen, whose naturally fine disposition had been further beautified by grace. Bred a Christian from her infancy, her native sensibility had been heightened by a warm piety: and her clear and quick intellect had been illuminated by an equally firm and direct conscience. Under her teaching her son was imbued from his infancy with a sense of divine things which never permitted him to forget that there is a God who governs all things and who is unchangeably good, or to find satisfaction in any teaching in which the name of Jesus Christ was not honored. He thus grew up in the nurture of the Lord,[39] but with the divided mind

[38] He became a catechumen shortly before Augustine's sixteenth year ("Confessiones," ii. 3. 6. Cf. ix. 9. 22). He died soon afterward.

[39] Cf. "De duabus anim.," i. 1: "The seeds of the true religion wholesomely implanted in me from boyhood."

which almost inevitably results from the divided counsels of a mixed parentage.

As his gifts more and more exhibited themselves worldly ambition took the helm and every nerve was strained to advance him in his preparation for a great career. His early piety, which had been exhibited in frequent prayer as a schoolboy [40] and in an ardent desire for baptism during an attack of dangerous illness,[41] more and more fell away from him, and left him, with his passionate temperament inherited from his father, a prey to youthful vices. An interval of idleness at home, in his sixteenth year (A.D. 370), brought him his great temptation, and he fell into evil ways; and these were naturally continued when, to complete his education, he went next year up to Carthage, that great and wicked city. But this period of unclean life was happily of short duration, lasting at the most only a couple of years. By the time Augustine had reached his seventeenth birthday (autumn of 371) we find him already attached to her who was to be the companion of his life for the next fourteen years, in a union which, though not marriage in the highest sense, differed from technical marriage rather in a legal than in a moral point of view. Though he himself, later at least, did not look upon such a union as true marriage,[42] it was esteemed its equivalent not only in the best heathen society of the time, but even in certain portions of the Church, perhaps up to his own day by the entire Church; [43] and it served to screen him from the multitudinous temptations to vice that

[40] "Confessiones," i. 9. 14: "For even as a boy I began to pray to Thee, my Help and my Refuge; to call upon Thee I burst the bonds of my tongue and prayed to Thee — child as I was, how passionately! — that I might not be flogged at school."   [41] "Confessiones," i. 11.

[42] "Confessiones," iv. 2. 2.: "One not joined to me in lawful wedlock"; x. 30. 41: "Thou hast commanded me to abstain from concubinage." Cf. "Apost. Constt.," viii. 32: "A believer who has a concubine — if she be a slave, let him cease, and take a wife legitimately: if she be free, let him take her as his legitimate wife; and if he does not, let him be rejected."

[43] Cf. the canons of the Council of Toledo of 400, can. 17: "Only let him be content with one woman, whether wife or concubine." Cf. Herzog, "Realencyclopädie für protestantische Theologie und Kirche ³," x. p. 746, and *The Princeton Theological Review,* i. No. 2 (April, 1903), pp. 309–10.

otherwise would have beset him. " I was faithful to her," he says.[44]

It was an overmastering and lofty ambition, not fleshly lust, that constituted the real power in his life, and these years of preparation at Carthage were years of strenuous labor, during which Augustine was ever growing toward his higher ideals. Already in his nineteenth year (373) he was incited to lay aside his lower ambitions by the reading of a book of Cicero's, since lost,[45] which had been designed to inflame the heart of the reader with a love of philosophy and which wrought so powerfully on Augustine that he resolved at once to make pure truth thenceforward the sole object of his pursuit.[46] During this whole period he must be believed to have remained nominally Christian; and perhaps we may suppose him to have continued in the formal position of a catechumen.[47]

He seems to have been a frequenter of the Church services,[48] and he speaks of himself as having been during this time under the dominance of " a certain puerile superstition " which held him back from the pursuit of truth.[49] Accordingly, when the " Hortensius " stirred his heart to seek wisdom and yet left him unsatisfied, because the name of Jesus which, as he says, he had " sucked in with his mother's milk," was not mentioned in it, he turned to the Scriptures in apparently the first earnest effort to seek their guidance he had made since his earliest youth. But the lowly Scriptures — especially as read in the rough Old Latin Version — had nothing to offer to the finical rhetorician, and his eyes were holden that he could not penetrate their meaning: he was offended by their servant-form and — seeking wisdom, not salvation — turned from them in disgust. He had reached a crisis in his life, and the result was that he formally broke with Christianity.

[46] Cf. especially " Solil.," iv. 2. 2. 17.

[45] His " Hortensius."   [46] Cf. especially " Solil." iv. 2. 2. 17.

[47] " De utilitate credendi," i. 2: " sed de me quid dicam, qui iam catholicus christianus eram? "

[48] " Confessiones," iii. 3. 5. According to " Contra Epist. Manich. Fundam," viii. 9, *ad fin.*, he had been accustomed to enjoy the Easter festival and missed it sadly when he became a Manichæan.   [49] " De beata vita," 4.

It was eminently characteristic of Augustine both that throughout his years of indulgence and indifference he had maintained his connection with the Church, and that he broke with it when, having sloughed off his grosser inclinations, he turned to it in vain for the satisfaction of his higher aspirations. Essential idealist that he was, throughout the years in which he was entangled in lower aims the Church had stood for him as a promise of better things: now he felt that his spirit soared above all it had to offer him. But in breaking with the Church, he could not break with his conception of God as the good Governor of the world, nor with his devotion to the name of Jesus Christ. So he threw himself into the arms of the Manichæans. The Manichæans were the rationalists of the day. Professing the highest reverence for Christ and continually bearing His name on their lips, they yet set forth, under his cloak, a purely naturalistic system. The negative side of their teaching included a most drastic criticism of the Christian Scriptures, while on the positive side they built up a doctrine of God which seemed to separate Him effectually from all complicity with evil, and a doctrine of man which relieved the conscience of all sense of unworthiness and responsibility for sin, while yet proposing a stringent ascetic ideal. In all these aspects its teaching was attractive to the young Augustine, who, on fire with a zeal for wisdom, despised all authority, and, conscious of moral weaknesses, wished to believe neither God nor himself answerable for them. He not only, therefore, heartily adopted the Manichæan system, but entered apparently with enthusiasm into its propagation.

The change nearly cost him the chief saving external influence of his life — intercourse with his godly mother. Terrified by his open repudiation of Christianity and his ardent identification of himself with one of its most dangerous rivals for the popular favor, she forbade him her house, and was only induced to receive him back into the family circle when she became convinced that his defection was not hopeless. Monnica has been made the object of much severe and, as it seems

to us, scarcely intelligent criticism for her action on this occasion. It has been sneeringly remarked, for example, that she did
not object very much to Augustine's cherishing a concubine,
but did object violently to his cherishing a heresy. " She seems
to have accepted his companion without a murmur," says a
recent writer,[50] " but the descent into heresy was an unpardonable depth." We shall raise no question here of the validity of
Bacon's dictum, that " it is certain that heresies and schisms
are of all others the greatest scandals; yea, more than corruption of manners." In any event the antithesis is unwisely
chosen. We have seen that no great moral obliquity attached
to such concubinage as Augustine's, which was, in fact, only
an inferior variety of marriage: and though, no doubt, this
entanglement was deeply regretted by Monnica, whose ambition for her son had earlier forbidden her providing him with a
wife, yet it is quite likely that she saw no reason seriously to
reprobate a relation which not only the law of the State, but
probably that of the Church, too, acknowledged as legitimate.
On the other hand, it is unfair not to recognize the immense
change which Augustine's step wrought in his attitude to the
religion which was his mother's very life. He may have been
up to this moment both indifferent and even of evil life. But he
had remained at least formally a Christian; he was still a
catechumen; and there was ever hope of repentance. Now he
had formally apostatized. He had not only definitively turned
his back on Christianity, but was actively assailing it with
scorn and ridicule, and that with such success that he was
drawing his circle of friends away with him.[51] It was, says Augustine,[52] " because she hated and detested the blasphemies of
his error " that she had broken off fellowship with him. Surely
his mother's horror is not inexplicable; and it is to be remembered that her attitude of renunciation of intercourse was at
once reversed on the reintroduction of hope for her son into

[50] McCabe, *op. cit.*, p. 66.

[51] In the " De duabus anim.," chap. ix., Augustine tells of the effect his
easy victory over the ignorant Catholics had in hardening him in his error.

[52] " Confessiones," iii. 11. 19.

her heart. Nor did she ever cease to pursue him with her tears and her prayers.[53]

Despite the eagerness with which he cast himself into the arms of the Manicheans and the zeal with which he became their advocate, Augustine had had very little grounding in the debatable questions that lay at the base of the system. His studies in literature and the rhetorical art had been formal rather than philosophical. His sudden discovery in the teachings of the Manicheans, of the " wisdom " he had been inflamed to seek, was therefore liable to a rude shock of awaking when his studies in the liberal sciences, on which he now zealously entered, should begin to bear fruit. It was not, in effect, long before the sagacity of the good bishop's advice to Monnica, that he should not be plied with argument but left to the gradual effects of his own reading and meditation to open his eyes, began to manifest itself. He remained nine years — from the end of his nineteenth to the beginning of his twenty-ninth year (373–383) — in the toils of the Manichean illusion, exercising in the interval his function of teacher, first at Thagaste and then at Carthage. But by the end of this period the doubts which had early in it began to insinuate themselves, first as to the mythological elements, and then as to the whole structure of the system, had fulfilled themselves. He seems to have been no longer inwardly a Manichean when he went to Rome in the spring of 383, though throughout his one year's stay at that city he remained in outer connection with the sect. When he left Rome for Milan in the late spring of 384, as his thirtieth year was running its course, he left his Manicheism definitively behind him. Nothing had come, however, to take its place. His

[53] It is probably not necessary to revert here to the fact that Manichæism was not merely under the ban of the Church, but also under that of the State — that it was crime as well as heresy. The " severe and bloody laws enacted against them by Valentinian, A.D. 372, Theodosius, A.D. 381," repeating, possibly, the earlier proscription of Diocletian, A.D. 287 (see Stokes, " Smith & Wace," *op. cit.*, iii. p. 799), do not seem to have been executed with sufficient vigor in Africa to have made the profession of the heresy very dangerous (cf. Stokes as above: and Loofs, Herzog, " Realencyklopädie für protestantische Theologie und Kirche,[3] " ii. pp. 262, ll. 37 ff).

own experiences combined with his philosophical reading to cast his mind into a complete state of uncertainty, not to say of developed skepticism. He was half-inclined to end the suspense by adopting out of hand the opinions of " those philosophers who are called Academics, because they taught we must doubt everything, and held that man lacks the power of comprehending any truth." [54] But he revolted from committing the sickness of his soul to them, " because they were without the saving name of Christ." [55] And so, no longer a Manichean and yet not a Catholic, he hung in the balance, and " determined therefore to be a catechumen in the Catholic Church, commended to him by his parents, until something assured should come to light by which to steer his way." [56] Thus he reverted to the condition of his youth, but in a state of mind unspeakably different.

So far as his outward fortunes were concerned Augustine was now at last in a fair way to realize the ambitions which had been the determining force in his life. [57] Driven from Thagaste by a burning heart, racked with grief for a lost friend; and then successively from Carthage and Rome by chagrin over the misbehavior of his pupils; he cannot be said hitherto to have attained a position of solid consequence. Whatever reputation he may have acquired as a teacher, whatever applause he may have gained in the practice of his art, whatever triumphs he may have secured in public contests, [58] all were by the way, and left him still a " viator " rather than a " consummator." At Milan, however, as Government Professor of Rhetoric, he had at last secured a post which gave him assured social standing and influence, and in the fulfillment of the official duties of which he was brought into pleasant contact with the highest civic circles and even with the court itself. Now for the first time all that he had hoped and striven for seemed within his reach. His mother and brother came to him out of Africa; the circle of his old intimates gathered around him; new friends

---

[54] " Confessiones," v. 10. 19.
[55] " Confessiones," v. 14. 25.
[56] " Confessiones," v. 14. 25.

[57] Cf. Loofs, *op. cit.*, pp. 265 ff.
[58] Cf. " Confessiones," iv. 2. 3; iv. 3. 5.

of wealth and influence attached themselves to him. It appeared no difficult matter to obtain some permanent preferment — through his host of influential friends a governorship might easily be had; and then a wife with a little money to help toward expenses could be taken; and the height of his desire would be reached.[59] Things were set in train to consummate this plan; a suitable maiden was sought and found and the betrothment concluded; [60] and everything was apparently progressing to his taste.

But, as so often happens, as the attainment of what had been so long and eagerly sought drew nigh, it was found not to possess the power to satisfy which had been attributed to it.[61] At no period of his life, in fact, was Augustine so far removed from complacency with himself and his situation, inward and outward, as at this moment. His whole mental life had been thrown into confusion by the growth of his skeptical temper, and he had been compelled to see himself deprived of all rational basis for his intellectual pride. And now the very measures taken to carry his ambitious schemes to their fruition reacted to rob him of whatever remnants of moral self-respect may have remained to him. The presence in his household of his concubine was an impediment to the marriage he was planning: and accordingly she was, as he expresses it,[62] torn from his side, leaving a sore and wounded place in his heart where it had adhered to hers. This was bad enough: but worse was to follow. Finding the two years that were to intervene before his marriage irksome, he took another concubine to fill up the interval. He could conceal from himself no longer his abject slavery to lust. And he was more deeply shamed still by the contrast into which his degrading conduct brought him with others whom he had been accustomed to consider his inferiors. His discarded concubine to whom his heart still clung

[59] vi. 11. 19, *ad fin.*: " amicorum maiorum copia "; " præsidatus "; " cum aliqua pecunia."

[60] vi. 13. 23.

[61] Cf. Loofs, *op. cit.*, p. 265, and Bret, " La Conversion de St. Augustine," pp. 68–69.

[62] vi. 15. 25.

set him a better example; but, as he says, he could not imitate even a woman. The iron entered his soul; and his pride, intellectual and moral, was preparing for itself a most salutary fall. No doubt the precarious state of his health at this moment added something to increase his dejection. Possibly on account of the harshness of the northern climate of Milan, he had been seized with a serious affection of the chest, which required rest at least from his labors, and possibly threatened permanently his usefulness as a rhetorician. It tended at all events to cause deep searchings of heart in which he was revealed to himself in all his weakness.

Simultaneously with the growth of his better knowledge of himself, there was opening up to him also a better knowledge of Christianity. Received with distinguished kindness by Ambrose on coming to Milan and drawn by the fame of his oratory, he was accustomed to frequent the preaching services, with a view to estimating Ambrose's rhetorical ability. But as he listened, the matter of the discourses began also to reach his conscience, and he gradually learned not only that the absurdities of belief — such as, for example, that God had a physical form like a man's — which the Manicheans had charged upon the Catholics, but that the whole scheme of the baneful Biblical criticism he had learned from them lacked foundation. His prejudices having thus been removed he soon came to perceive that the Catholics had something to say for themselves worth listening to, and that there was an obvious place for authority in religion. By this discovery his mind was made accessible to the evidences of the divine authority of the Christian Scriptures, and he turned with new zest to them for instruction. Another discovery in his thirty-first year contributed powerfully to open his mind to their meaning. This was nothing less than the discovery of metaphysics. Up to this time Augustine's learning had been largely empirical and his thought was confined to crassly materialistic forms. Now the writings of the Neo-Platonists came into his hands and revealed to him an entirely new world — the world of spirit. Under these new influences his whole mental life was revolutionized: he passed from his divided mind with a bound, and embraced with all the warmth of his ardent nature the new realities assured to him at once by the authority of Scripture and the authentication of reason. To all intents and purposes he was already on the intellectual side a Christian, and needed but some determining influence to secure the decisive action of his will, for his whole life to recrystallize around this new center.

This determining influence was brought him apparently by means of a series of personal examples. These were given especial power over him by the self-contempt into which he had fallen through his discovery of his moral weakness. There was first the example of the rhetorician Victorinus, the story of whose conversion was related to him by Simplicianus, whom Augustine had consulted for direction in his spiritual distress. By this narrative Augustine was inflamed with an immense emulation to imitate his distinguished colleague, but found himself unable to break decisively with his worldly life. Then came the example of Anthony and the Egyptian monks, related to him by a fellow-countryman, Pontianus, on a chance visit; and with this the example also of their imitators in the West. This brought on the crisis. "A horrible shame," he tells us, "gnawed and confounded his soul" while Pontianus was speaking. "What is the matter with us?" he cried to Alypius. "What is it you hear? The unlearned rise and take heaven by storm, and we with all our learning, see how we are wallowing in flesh and blood! Are we ashamed to follow where they lead the way? Ought we not rather to be ashamed not to follow at once?" [63] We all know the story of the agony of remorse that seized him and how release came at length through a child's voice, by which he was led at last to take up the book that lay on the table and read; reading, he found strength to make the great decision that changed his whole life. It is a story which must not be told, however, except in Augustine's own moving words.[64]

[63] "Confessiones," viii. 8. 19.
[64] "Confessiones," viii. 8. 19; 11. 25; 12. 28–30.

There was a little garden to our lodging of which we had the use. . . . Thither the tumult of my heart drove me, where no one could interrupt the fierce quarrel which I was waging with myself, until it should reach the issue known to Thee but not to me. . . . Thus was I sick and tormented, reproaching myself more bitterly than ever, twisting and writhing in my chain, until it should be entirely broken, since now it held me but slightly — though it held me yet. . . . And I kept saying in my heart, " O let it be now! let it be now! " and as I spoke I almost resolved — I almost did it, but I did it not. . . . So when searching reflection had drawn out from the hidden depths all my misery and piled it up in the sight of my heart, a great tempest broke over me, bearing with it a great flood of tears. . . . And I went further off . . . and flung myself at random under a fig tree there and gave free vent to tears; and the flood of my eyes broke forth, an acceptable sacrifice to Thee. And not indeed in these words, but to this purport, I cried to Thee incessantly, " But Thou, O Lord, how long? How long, O Lord? Wilt Thou be angry forever? O remember not against us our iniquities of old! " I felt myself held by them: I raised sorrowful cries: " How long, How long? To-morrow, and to-morrow? Why not now, why not this instant, end my wickedness? "

I was speaking thus and weeping in the bitterest contrition of heart, when lo, I heard a voice, I know not whether of boy or girl, saying in a chant and repeating over and over: Take and read, Take and read. At once with changed countenance I began most intently to think whether there was any kind of game in which children chanted such a thing, but I could not recall ever hearing it. I choked back the rush of tears and rose, interpreting it no otherwise than as a divine command to me to open the book and read whatever passage I first lighted upon. For I had heard of Anthony, that he had received the admonition from the Gospel lesson which he chanced to come in upon, as if what was read was spoken to himself: " Go, sell all that thou hast and give to the poor, and thou shalt have treasure in heaven: and come, follow me "; and was at once converted by this oracle to Thee. So I returned quickly to the place where Alypius was sitting, for I had laid down the volume of the apostle there when I left him. I seized it, opened it, and read in silence the passage on which my eyes first fell: " Not in rioting and drunkenness, not in chambering and wantonness, not in strife and envying; but put ye on the Lord Jesus Christ, and make not provision for the flesh, to fulfil the lusts thereof." No further did I wish to read: nor was there need. Instantly, as I reached the end of this sentence, it was as if the light of peace was poured into my heart and all the shades of doubt faded away. . . . For Thou didst convert me to Thyself in such a manner that I sought neither a wife nor any hope of this world — taking my stand on that Rule of Faith on which Thou didst reveal me to my mother so many years before.

Thus there was given to the Church, as Harnack says,[65] incomparably the greatest man whom "between St. Paul the Apostle and Luther the Reformer the Christian Church has possessed"; and the thankful Church has accordingly made a festival of the day on which the great event occurred — according this honor of an annual commemoration of their conversions only to Paul and Augustine among all her saints, "thus seeming to say," as Boissier remarks,[66] "that she owes almost an equal debt of gratitude to each." But it would be more in accordance with Augustine's own heart to say, Thus a soul was brought to its God, and made so firmly His that throughout a long life of service to Him it never knew the slightest wavering of its allegiance. It is easy to make merry over the impure elements that entered into the process of his conversion. It is easy to point scornfully to the superstition which made out of the voice of a child at play a message from heaven; and which resorted to the sacred volume as to a kind of book of divination. It is easy to exclaim that after all Augustine's "conversion" was not to Christianity but to Monachism [67] — with its entire ascetic ideal, including its depreciation of woman and its perversion of the whole sexual relation. It is easy to raise doubts whether the conversion was as sudden or as complete as Augustine represents it: to trace out the steps that led up to it with curious care and to lay stress on every hint of incompleteness of Christian knowledge or sentiment which may plausibly be brought forward from his writings of the immediately suc-

[65] "Monasticism and the Confessions of Augustine," E. T. p. 123.

[66] "La Fin du Paganisme," i. p. 291.

[67] Loofs says Augustine "was converted, because he permitted himself to be shamed — by Monachism" (*op. cit.*, p. 267, l. 31).

ceeding months.[68] But surely all this is to confuse the kernel
with the husk. Of course, the conversion was led up to by a
gradual approach, and Augustine himself analyzes for us with
incomparable skill the progress of this preparation through all
the preceding years. And, equally of course, there was left a
great deal for him to learn after the crisis was past: and he does
not conceal from us how much of a babe in Christ he was and
felt himself to be as he emerged new-born from the stress of the
conflict. And of course, in the preparation for it and in the
gradual realization of its effects in his thought and life alike,
and even in the very act itself by which he gave himself to
God, there were mingled elements derived from his stage of
Christian knowledge and feeling, from the common sentiments
of the time, which powerfully affected him, and from his own
personality and ingrained tendencies. But these things, which
could not by any possibility have been absent, not only do not
in any respect derogate from the reality or the profundity of
the revolution then accomplished — the reality and profundity
of which are attested by his whole subsequent life [69] — but do
not even detract from the humanity or attractiveness of the
narrative or of the personality presented to us in it. He must
be sadly lacking not only in dramatic imagination, but in human sympathy as well, who can find it strange that in the stress
of his great crisis, when his sensibilities were strained to the
breaking point, Augustine could see the voice of heaven in the

[68] So especially Harnack and Boissier: they are sufficiently though briefly
answered by Wörter, " Die Geistesentwickelung des hl. Aurelius Augustinus bis
zu seiner Taufe," Paderborn, 1892, pp. 63 *sq.*

[69] Even Loofs, who is quite ready to correct the " Confessions " by what
he deems the testimony of the treatises emanating from the period just after
the conversion, is free to admit that a revolutionary crisis did take place in
Augustine's life at this time, and that, therefore, the " Confessions," in describing such a crisis, give us a necessary complement to what we could derive from
these treatises. He says (Herzog, " Realencyclopädie für protestantische Theologie und Kirche [3]," p. 267) that there must have happened *something* between
Augustine's adoption of Neo-Platonism at a time when he still lived in concubinage and his decisive revulsion from all sexual life, witnessed in the " Soliloquies " (i. 17), which will account for the great change: and this *something*
the " Confessions " alone give us. This is a testimony to the historicity of the
" Confessions " of the first value.

vagrant voice of a child; or should have followed out the hint
thus received into his heated imagination and committed his
life, as it were, to the throw of a die. Surely this is as psychologically true to life as it is touching to the sensibilities: and
in no way, in the circumstances, can it be thought derogatory
to either the seriousness of his mind or the greatness of his
character. And how could he, in the revulsion from what he
felt his special sin, fail to be carried in the swing of the pendulum far beyond the point of rest, in his estimate of the relation
that could safely obtain between the sexes? The appearance of
such touches of human weakness in the story contributes not
only to the narrative the transparent traits of absolute truth
and to the scene depicted a reality which deeply affects the
heart of the reader, but to the man himself just that touch of
nature which " makes the whole world kin." In such traits as
these we perceive indeed one of the chief elements of the charm
of the " Confessions." The person we meet in them is a person,
we perceive, who towers in greatness of mind and heart, in the
loftiness of his thought and in his soaring aspirations, far above
ordinary mortals: and yet he is felt to be compacted of the
same clay from which we have ourselves been molded. If it
were not so obviously merely the art of artless truth, we should
say that herein lies, more than in anything else, the art of the
" Confessions." For it is the very purpose of this book to give
the impression that Augustine himself was a weak and erring
sinner, and that all of good that came into his life was of God.

It is especially important for us precisely at this point to recall our minds to the fact that to give such an impression is the
supreme purpose of the " Confessions." This whole account of
his life-history which we have tried to follow up to its crisis in
his conversion is written, let us remind ourselves, not that we
may know Augustine, but that we may know God: and it shows
us Augustine only that we may see God. The seeking and saving grace of God is the fundamental theme throughout. The
events of Augustine's life are not, then, set forth in it *simpliciter*. Only such events of his life are set down as manifest how
much he needed the salvation of God and how God gradually

brought him to that salvation: and they are so set down and so
dealt with as to make them take their places, rightly marshaled, in this great argument. This is the account to give of
that coloring of self-accusation that is thrown over the narrative which is so offensive to some of its readers; as if Augustine
were set upon painting his life in the blackest tints imaginable,
and wished us to believe that his " quiet and honest youth "
and strenuous and laborious manhood, marked as they really
were by noble aspiration and adequate performance, were
rather " all sin ": nay, that the half-instinctive acts of his infancy itself and the very vitality of his boyish spirits were but
the vents which a peculiarly sinful nature formed for itself. In
these traits of the narrative, however, Augustine is not passing
judgment on himself alone, but in himself on humanity at large
in its state of sin and misery. By an analysis of his own life-
history he realizes for himself, and wishes to make us realize
with him, what man is in his sinful development on the earth,
that our eyes may be raised from man to see what God is in His
loving dealing with the children of men. We err, if from the
strong, dark lines in which he paints his picture we should infer
that he would have us believe that in his infancy, youth, or
manhood he was a sinner far beyond the sinfulness of other
men. Rather would he say to us in his Savior's words: " Nay,
but except ye repent ye shall all likewise perish." But we
should err still more deeply, should we fancy that he meant
us to suppose that it was due to any superiority to other men
on his part that God had sought him out and granted to him
His saving grace. He knew his own sinfulness as he knew the
sinfulness of no other man, and it was his one burning desire
that he should in his recovery to God recognize and celebrate
the ineffableness of the grace of God. The pure grace of God is
thus his theme throughout, and nowhere is it more completely
so than in this culminating scene of his conversion. The human elements that enter into the process, or even into the
act itself by which he came to God, only heightened the clearness of his own perception that it was to the grace of God
alone that he owed his recovery, and he would have them

similarly heighten the clearness with which his readers perceive it with him.[70]

With his conversion, therefore, the narrative of the " Confessions " culminates and practically ends. There follows, indeed, another book of narration in which he tells us briefly of
his preparation for baptism and of the baptism itself and its
meaning to him; but chiefly of his mother and of that remarkable conversation he held with her at Ostia in which they fairly
scaled heaven together in their ardent aspirations; and then
of how he laid her away with a heart full of appreciation of her
goodness and of his loss. And then, in yet another book, he
undertakes to tell us not what he was, but what he had become,
but quickly passes into such searching psychological and ethical
analyses that the note of autobiography is lost. Not in this
book, then, is the revelation of what Augustine had become to
be found; it is rather given us by means of the narrative which
fills the first nine books, in the judgment he passes there on his
former self and in the cries of gratitude he raises there to God
for the great deliverance he had wrought in his soul. We see
without difficulty that this new Augustine who is writing is a
different Augustine from him whom he depicts in the narrative: we see that it is even a different Augustine from him
whom he leaves with us at the end of the narrative — after his
conversion, and his emergence from his country retreat for
baptism, and his return to his native Africa. And yet we see also
that the making of this new Augustine was in essence completed at the point where the narrative leaves him. Whatever
development came after this came in the processes of natural
growth, and argues no essential change.

IV. The Development of Augustine

It is convenient to draw a distinction between what we may
call, by a somewhat artificial application of the terms, the

[70] Augustine's testimony that it was to the grace of God that he owed his
conversion is drawn out at some length by T. Bret, " La Conv. d. St. Augustine," pp. 60–66. See also Wörter, *op. cit.*, especially the summary, pp. 62 ff.

making and the development of Augustine. Under the former term we may sum up the factors that coöperated to make the man who emerged from the crisis of his conversion just the man he was; and by the latter we may designate the gradual ripening of his thought and life after he had become a Christian to their final completeness. The factors that enter into his " making," in this sense, are exhibited to us in his own marvelous analysis in the vital narrative of the " Confessions." It is in the mirror of the works which he composed through the course of his busy life that we must seek the manner of man he was when he entered upon his Christian race and the man he became as he pressed forward steadily to his goal. Soundly converted though he was, it was yet the man who had been formed by the influences which had worked upon him through those thirty eager years who was converted: and his Christianity took form and color from the elements he brought with him to it.

An interesting indication of the continued significance to him of those old phases of his experience is discoverable in his setting about, at once upon his conversion, to refute precisely those systems of error in the toils of which he had himself been holden, and that in the reverse order in which he had passed through them. And that is as much as to say that he attacked them in the order in which they may be supposed to have been still living memories to him. It was during the very first months after his conversion, and even before his baptism, that his treatise " Against the Academics " was written. And before the year was out his first work against the Manichæans was published, inaugurating a controversy which was to engage much of his time and powers for the next ten years.[71] This very polemic reveals the completeness with which he had outgrown these phases of belief, or rather of unbelief: there is no trace in it of remaining sympathy with them, and his entanglement in them is obviously purely a matter of memory.

[71] On the place in his works of a polemic against Polytheism — which would be going back to the very beginning — see Naville, " Saint-Augustin," etc., pp. 70–71, note.

He entered at this time into no such refutation of Neo-platonism: this was reserved for the teeming pages of the "City of God." Rather it was as a Neo-platonic thinker that Augustine became a Christian; and he carried his Neo-platonic conceptions over into Christianity with him. This is not to say, however, as has been said, that his thinking "was still essentially Neo-platonic," and "his Christianity during this period was merely Neo-platonism with a Christian stain and a Christian veneering." [72] Much less is it to say, as also has been said, that what we call his "conversion" was a conversion not to Christianity but merely to Neo-platonic spiritualism, while actual Christianity was embraced by him only some years later on [73] — if indeed it was ever fully assimilated, for still others insist that his thinking remained "essentially Neo-platonic" throughout his life, or at least a complete Neo-platonic system lay always in his mind alongside his superinduced Christianity, unassimilated and unassimilable by it.[74] All this is the gravest kind of exaggeration. An analysis of Augustine's writings composed during his retreat at Cassiciacum while he was awaiting baptism, presents to our observation already a deeply devout and truly Christian thinker, although it reveals the persistence in his thought and in his modes of expression alike, of conceptions and terms derived from his engrossment with Neo-platonic forms of thought and speech, which in his later writings no longer appear.[75]

The reality of a gradual development of Augustine's thought is already indicated by this circumstance, and it remains only to fix its course with such precision as may be attainable and to determine its stages and its rate of progress. It has become quite common to mark off in it quite a series of definite changes.

[72] Loofs, Herzog, "Realencyclopädie für protestantische Theologie und Kirche [3]," p. 270, l. 31.

[73] L. Gourdon, *op. cit.,* pp. 45–50, 83.

[74] Harnack, "History of Dogma" (E. T.), V. chap. iv.

[75] Such an analysis, brief but admirably done (except that justice is not done to the *Christianity* of this period of Augustine's life), may be found in Loofs' article, Herzog, "Realencyclopädie für protestantische Theologie und Kirche [3]," pp. 270, line 11; 274, line 8. See also Wörter, *op. cit.*

Thus we read [76] that it was only "on his entrance upon a clerical career," that is, only on his ordination as presbyter in 391, that Augustine entered upon a new phase of thought, marked by increasing knowledge of the Scriptures and deepening Church feeling; and only on his consecration as bishop, late in 395, that he at length attained in principle that complete system of thought which we know as "Augustinianism." Even greater detail is sometimes attempted with respect to the development of the preëpiscopal period. The presbyterial period (391–395) is appropriately called "the last section of his apprenticeship," and the preceding four or five years are subdivided into the period between conversion and baptism in which the first place is given to reason and the effort is to conciliate religion with philosophy; and the period from baptism to ordination in which the first place is given to Scripture and the effort has come to be to conciliate philosophy with religion. [77] Four successive epochs in Augustine's thought are thus distinguished, marked by the progressive retirement of philosophy — Neo-platonism in this case — and the progressive advancement of Scripture to its rightful place as primary source of divine knowledge: and these four epochs are sharply divided from one another by external occurrences in Augustine's life — his baptism, ordination as presbyter, and consecration as bishop.

It is scarcely possible to avoid the impression that the scheme of development thus outlined suffers from overprecision and undue elaboration. We are struck at once by the rapidity of the movement which is supposed to have taken place. Augustine's conversion occurred in the late summer of 386: the treatise "On Divers Questions to Simplicianus," in which it is allowed on all hands that "Augustinianism" appears, in principle, in its completeness, was written before the end of 396. Only ten years are available, then, for a development which is supposed to run through four well-marked

---

[76] Loofs, Herzog, "Realencyclopädie für protestanische Theologie und Kirche ³," loc. cit., pp. 270, 279.

[77] Nourisson, "La philos. de St. Augustine," i. pp. 33–34.

stages. The exact synchronism of the periods of development
with changes of importance in the external conditions of Augustine's life raises further suspicion: there seems to be nothing either in the external changes fitted to produce the internal
ones, or in the internal changes to produce the external ones.
We begin to wonder whether the assumed internal " development " may not be largely an illusion produced merely by the
gradual shifting of interest, accompanied by the natural adjustments of emphasis, which was inevitable in the passage of a
layman to official positions in the Church of increasing responsibility. Color is given to this suggestion by the actual series
of treatises proceeding from each of these periods of Augustine's
life. When Augustine connected himself with the Church in
386, and entered the arena of discussion, he entered it not as
an accredited teacher clothed with ecclesiastical authority, but
in the rôle of Christian philosopher. His earliest writings bear
entirely this character; and it does not appear that writings on
the same themes and with the same end in view, if proceeding
from him later in life, would not have assimilated themselves
closely to these in tone and character. The shifting of the
emphasis to more positive Christian elements in the later
treatises belonging to his lay period, follows closely the change
in the subjects which he treated. His polemic against the Manichæans, already begun in Rome, continued during his residence
in Thagaste to absorb his attention. This controversy still
largely occupied him through his presbyterial period: but already not only was the Donatist conflict commenced, but his
positive expositions of Scripture began to take a large place
in his literary product. Speaking now from the point of view
of an official teacher of the Church, it is not strange that a
stronger infusion of positive elements found their way into
his works. In his episcopal period purely thetical treatises enter
into the product in important proportions, and the anti-Mani-
chæan polemic gave way first to the anti-Donatist, and after
412 to the anti-Pelagian, both of which were favorable to the
fuller expression of the positive elements of his Christian doctrine — the one in its ecclesiastical and the other in its indi-

vidualistic aspects. On a survey of the succession of treatises we acquire a conviction that such a series of treatises could not fail to give the impression of a developing doctrinal position such as is outlined by the expositors, whether such a development was actual or not. In other words, the doctrinal development of Augustine as drawn out by the expositors may very well be and probably is largely illusory. Its main elements may be fully accounted for by the different occasions and differing purposes on and for which the successive treatises were written.

We must, then, look deeper than this gradual change from treatises of thoroughly philosophical tenor to treatises of thoroughly Christian contents before we can venture to affirm a marked doctrinal growth in Augustine from 386 to 396 and beyond. On seeking to take this deeper view we are at once struck by two things. The first of these is that the essence of " Augustinianism " as expounded in the treatises of the episcopal period is already present in principle in the earliest of Augustine's writings and, indeed, from the first constitutes the heart of his teaching. The second is that the working of this " Augustinianism " outwards, so as to bring all the details of teaching into harmony with itself, was, nevertheless, a matter of growth — and a growth, we may add, which had not reached absolute completeness, we do not say merely, until Augustine had obtained his episcopacy in 396, but when he laid down his pen and died in 430. Augustine's great idea was the guiding star of his life from the very beginning of his Christian career. It more and more took hold of his being and extruded more and more perfectly the remainders of inconsistent thinking. But up to the end it had not, with absolute completeness, adjusted to itself his whole circle of ideas. An attempt must now be made at least to illustrate this suggestion.

What is the essence of " Augustinianism " ? Is it not that sense of absolute dependence on God which, conditioning all the life and echoing through all the thought, produces the type of religion we call " evangelical " and the type of theology we call " Augustinian " ? This is the keynote of the " Confessions," and gives it at once its evangelical character and its

appeal to the heart of the sinner. It is summed up in the famous prayer: "Command what Thou wilt, and give what Thou
commandest" — hearing which, Pelagius, representative of
anti-Augustinianism at its height, recognized in it the very
heart of Augustinianism and was so incensed as to come nearly
to blows with him who had rashly repeated it to him. Now it
is notable that this note is already struck in the earliest class
of Augustine's writings. "Command, I beg," he prays in the
"Soliloquies" (i. 5) — "Command and ordain, I beg, whatsoever Thou wilt; but heal and open my ears. . . . If it is by
faith that those who take refuge in Thee find Thee, give faith."
When exhorted to believe — if, indeed, that is in our power —
his pious response is: "Our power He Himself is." These great
words, "*Da fidem*," "*Potestas nostra Ipse est*," sum up in
themselves implicitly the whole of "Augustinianism"; and
they need only consistent explication and conscious exposition
so as to cover the entirety of life and thought, to give us all
that "Augustinianism" ever gave us.

It may still, indeed, be asked whether the note they strike is
the fundamental note of these earlier writings and whether
such expressions constitute as large an element in them as
might be expected from Augustine. On the whole, we think,
both questions must be answered in the affirmative. But
this answer must be returned with some discrimination. It is
not meant, of course, that the substance of these books is made
up of such sentences, even in the sense in which this is true,
say, of the "Confessions." What is meant is that these books,
being of an entirely different character from, say, the "Confessions," and written to subserve an entirely different purpose,
yet betray this fundamental note throbbing behind the even
flow of their own proper discourse, and thus manifest themselves as the product of a soul which was resting wholly upon
its God. We must profess our inability fully to understand the
standpoint of those who read these earliest books as the lucu-
brations of a Neo-platonic philosopher throwing over the mere
expression of his thoughts a thin veil of Christian forms.
Plainly it is not the philosopher, only slightly touched by

Christianity, that is speaking in them, but the Christian theologian, who finds all his joy in the treasures he has discovered in his newly gained faith. Through the Socratic severity of their philosophical discourse — which is, after all, but the stillness after the storm — there continually breaks the undercurrent of suppressed emotion. The man who is writing has obviously passed through severe conflicts and has only with difficulty attained his present peace. He has escaped from the bonds of superfluous desires, and, the burden of dead cares being laid aside, now breathes again, has recovered his senses, returned to himself.[78] There is no direct reference made to the conversion that had so lately transformed him into a new man, but the consciousness of it lies ever in the background and it is out of its attainment that he now speaks.[79]

We may be sure that when this man gives himself up after passing through such a crisis to philosophical discourses, it is not because there lies nothing more than these abstract reasonings deep in his heart, but because he has a conscious end of importance to serve by them. The end he has set before him in them certainly is not, as Harnack supposes, merely to " find himself " after the turmoil of the revolution he has experienced, to clarify to his own thinking his new religio-philosophical position. There is indication enough that he does not speak his whole heart out. He is rather seeking, as Boissier hints, to serve the religion to which he has at last yielded his heart and his life. In breaking with the world had he taken an irrational step? Had he sacrificed his intellect in bowing to authority? No, he would have all men know he is rather just entering now upon the riches of his inheritance — in which, moreover, all that he has really gained from the best thought of the world has its proper place and its highest part to play. He is, in a word, not expounding here the Neo-platonic philosophy in Christian terms: he is developing the philosophy of Christianity in terms of the best philosophic thought of the day — serving himself as a Christian heir to the heritage of the ages.

[78] " Cont. Acad.," ii. 2. 4, *ad init.*
[79] Cf. " Cont. Acad.," ii. 2. 5.

The task he had set himself [80] was to construct a Christian philosophy out of Platonic materials. Nor will the notion that he was at the outset so keen an advocate of the hegemony of reason that he was unprepared to submit his thought to the authority of Christ and of the Scriptures which He has given us, bear investigation: it shatters itself not only against the whole tone of the discussion, but also against repeated express declarations. In the very earliest of his books he tells us, for example, that to him the authority of Him who says "Seek and ye shall find" is greater than that of all philosophy; [81] and he sets the authority of Christ over against that of reason with the declaration that it is certain that he shall never fall away from it, because he cannot find a stronger.[82]

Although, however, he had thus firmly from the beginning laid hold of what we may call both the formal and the material principles of his theology — the authority of the divine revelation in and through Christ, embodied in the Scriptures, and the utter dependence of man on God for all good; it does not in the least follow that he had already drawn out from Scripture all that was to be believed on its authority or worked out all the implications of his profound sense of absolute dependence on God. The explication of the teaching of Scripture and the realization of the implications of his fundamental principle of dependence on God constituted, on the contrary, precisely his life-work, on which he was just entering. As we read on from book to book we do not fail to feel, even within the limits of his lay life, a gradual deepening and widening of his knowledge of Scripture, and under the influence of this growing knowledge, a gradual modification of his opinions philosophical and theological alike, and even a gradual change in his very style.[83]

[80] Cf. Naville, *op. cit.*, p. 69.

[81] "Cont. Acad.," ii. 3. 9.

[82] *Ibid.*, iii. 20. 43. For this point of view see especially R. Schmid's paper in the *Zeitschrift für Theologie und Kirche*, 1897, vii. p. 94.

[83] Cf. Naville, *op. cit.*, p. 70: "Beyond doubt, when we study in their chronological succession the works of these five years, we perceive the rôle of Scripture gradually to increase. The author, we feel, has immersed himself in the study of Scripture. He has acquired a knowledge of it, of ever-increasing

His earliest writings certainly contain indications enough of
crudities of thought which were subsequently transcended.
We do not need to advert here to such peripheral matters as his
confession that he cannot understand why infants are baptized.[84] Despite the passion of his dependence on God and the
vigor of his reference to God alone of all that is good, he had
not throughout this whole period learned to exclude the human initiative from the process of salvation itself. "God does
not have mercy," he says,[85] "unless the will has preceded."
"It belongs to us to believe and to will, but to Him to give to
those that believe and will the power to do well, through the
Holy Spirit, through whom love is shed abroad in our hearts."[86]
"God has not predestinated any one except whom He foreknew would believe and answer His call."[87] Thus his zeal for
free will which burned warmly throughout this whole period
of his life, did not expend itself merely in its strong assertion
over against the notion of involuntary sin,[88] but was carried
over also into the matter of salvation. No doubt this zeal was
in large measure due to the stress of his conflict with Manicheism, which colored the thought of the whole period: but
what it concerns us here to note especially is that it was possible for him to hold and proclaim these views of human initiative in salvation although the center of his thought and feeling alike lay in the great confession: "Our power He Himself
is." It is quite clear that throughout this period his most central ideas had not yet succeeded in coming fully to their rights.
He had not yet attained to a thorough understanding of himself as a Christian teacher.

depth. His very style becomes modified under its influence. No doubt, also,
the idea of the Church is more and more emphasized up to the book on the
True Religion, in which Augustine expressly undertakes to expound the faith
of the Catholic Church. Finally the philosophical thought itself undergoes on
some points alterations, which we shall point out." This is all very justly said.

[84] "De quantitate animae," 36. 80.
[85] "De diversis quaestionibus lxxxiii." 68. 5.
[86] "Exposito quarumdam propositionum ex Epistola ad Romanos," 61.
[87] *Ibid.*, 55.
[88] E.g., "De vera religione," 14. 27.

It is well to focus our attention on the particular instance of as yet unformed views which we have adduced. For it happens that with reference to it we have the means of tracing the whole process of his change of view; and it is most instructive. It was indeed just at the opening of his episcopal period that the change took place; but it stood in no direct connection with this alteration in his external status. Nor was it the result of any controversial sharpening of his sight: it is characteristic of Augustine's life that his views were not formed through or even in controversy, but were ready always to be utilized in controversies which arose after their complete formation. It was the result purely and simply of deeper and more vital study of Scripture.

The corrected views find their first expression in the first book of the work " On Divers Questions to Simplicianus," which was written in 396, the same year in which he was made bishop. The " questions " discussed in this book were Rom. vii. 7–25 and Rom. ix. 10–29. In the "Retractations " [89] he says relatively to the latter " question ": " Later in this book the question is taken from that passage where it says, ' But not only so, but Rebecca also having conceived of one, even our father Isaac ' — down to where it says, ' Except the God of Sabaoth had left us a seed we had been made a Sodom and had been like unto Gomorrah.' In the solution of this question, we struggled indeed for the free choice of the human will; [90] but the grace of God conquered: otherwise the apostle could not have been understood to speak with obvious truth when he says, ' For who maketh thee to differ? and what has thou that thou didst not receive? But if thou didst receive it why dost thou glory, as if thou hadst not received it? ' It was because he wished to make this clear that the martyr Cyprian set forth the whole meaning of this passage by saying: ' We are to glory in nothing because nothing is ours ' " (*Cypr.*, lib. 3, testim. 4). Driven thus by purely exegetical considerations — working, no doubt, on a heart profoundly sensible of its utter dependence

[89] ii. 1. 1.

[90] " Laboratum est quidem pro libero arbitrio voluntatis humanæ."

on God — Augustine was led somewhat against his will to recognize that the "will to believe" is itself from God. Accordingly, in this " question " he teaches at length that whether man
despises or does not despise the call does not lie in his own
power.[91] For, he reasons, " if it lies in the power of him that is
called not to obey, it is possible to say, ' Therefore it is not of
God that showeth mercy, but of man that willeth and runneth,'
because the mercy of him that calls is in that case not enough
unless it is followed by the obedience of him that is called." [92]
No, he argues, " God has mercy on no one in vain: but so calls
him on whom He has mercy — after a fashion He knows will
be congruous to him — that he does not repulse Him that
calls." [93]

At a much later time, Augustine details to us the entire
history of this change of view.[94] The whole passage is well
worth reading, but we can adduce only the salient points here.
His earlier view he speaks of as merely an unformed view. He
"had not yet very carefully inquired into or sought out the
nature of the election of grace of which the apostle speaks "
in Rom. x. 1–5. He had not yet thought of inquiring whether
faith itself is not God's gift. He did not sufficiently carefully
search into the meaning of the calling that is according to God's
purpose. It was chiefly I Cor. iv. 7 that opened his eyes. But
here we will listen to his own words: " It was especially by this
passage that I myself also was convinced, when I erred in a
similar manner " — with the Semi-Pelagians, that is — " thinking that the faith by which we believe in God is not the gift of
God, but that it is in us of ourselves, and that by it we obtain
the gifts of God whereby we may live temperately and
righteously and piously in this world. For I did not think that
faith was preceded by God's grace — so that by its means
might be given us what we might profitably ask — except in
the sense that we could not believe unless the proclamation of
the truth preceded; but to consent after the Gospel had been

[91] " De diversis quaestionibus ad Simplicianum," i. 2. 12.
[92] *Ibid.*
[93] *Ibid.*, 13.   [94] " De prædest. sanctt.," iii. 7.

preached to us, I thought belonged to ourselves, and came to us from ourselves."

That it was precisely at the beginning of his episcopate that he attained to his better and more consistent doctrine on this cardinal point, thus giving its completed validity for the first time to his fundamental principle of utter dependence on God, was obviously a pure accident. And there is a single clause in the expression he gives to his new doctrine on this the first occasion of its enunciation which exhibits to us that even yet he had not worked it out in its completeness. " But him on whom He has mercy," we read, "He calls, *in the manner that He knows will be congruous to him,* so that he will not repulse the Caller." [95] About this clause there was much disputation a thousand years later between the Jansenists and the Congruists. As it stands in the text it is only a chance clause, in no way expressive of Augustine's developed thought, in which undoubtedly the grace of God is conceived as creative. Indeed, immediately before it occurs the declaration that " the effect of the Divine mercy can by no means be abandoned to the powers of man, as if, unless man willed it, God would vainly have exercised His mercy," the doctrine suggested by which is scarcely wholly congruous with the notion of " congruous grace." What the clause indicates to us is not, therefore, a determinate teaching of Augustine's, but rather the fact that he had not even yet very carefully inquired into the nature of the operation of God which he called grace, and was liable to suggest inconsistent views of its mode of operation in immediately contiguous sentences. Was it the *quâ* or merely a *sine quâ non* of salvation? To this question his fundamental principle of absolute dependence on God, that God alone is " our power," had a very decisive reply to give: and he was destined to find that reply and to announce it with great decision. But as yet he had not been led to think it out with precision. In important respects his view remained still unformed.

This instance of the gradual elaboration even of Augustine's most fundamental conceptions is only one of many that

[95] " De diversis quaestionibus ad Simplicianum," i. 2. 13.

could be adduced. Another striking illustration is offered by the slow clarification of his doctrine of predestination — purely again under the influence of deeper study of Scripture.[96] The totality of Augustine's development consists, in a word, of ever fuller and clearer evolution of the contents of his primary principle of complete dependence on God, in the light of ever richer and more profound study of Scripture: and we can follow out this development quite independently of external influences, which in his case never conditioned his thought, but only gave occasion to its fuller expression. It might fairly be said that his entire growth is simply a logical development of his fundamental material principle of dependence on God under the guidance of his formal principle of the authority of Scripture. One of the most striking results of this was that he learned little or nothing of primary moment from the controversies in which he was constantly engaged: but rather met them with already formed convictions. No doubt his conceptions were brought out in more varied and even in part clearer and stronger expression during the course of these controversies: but in point of mere fact they were in each case already formed and had been formally announced before the controversies arose. If Loofs says of Athanasius, for example, that he did not make the Nicænum, but the Nicænum made him; he is compelled to say, on the contrary, of Augustine, that he was not formed in the Pelagian controversy, but his preformation was the occasion of it. "Pelagianism," he remarks,[97] perhaps with some slight exaggeration, "was first of all nothing but a reaction of the old moralistic rationalism against the monergism of grace that was exalted by Augustine's type of piety." Of course, we are not to imagine that on this showing Augustine had from the first nothing to learn: or even that he ultimately worked out his fundamental principle perfectly into all the details of his teaching. We have already intimated that a

---

[96] "Expositio quarumdam propositionum, etc.," 60. The matter is sufficiently expounded by Loofs, Herzog, "Realencyclopädie für protestantische Theologie und Kirche ³," p. 276, line 21.

[97] Leitfaden zum Studium der Dogmengeschichte ²," § 53, p. 210.

process of growth is traceable in him and that the process of his growth to a perfect elaboration of his principle was never completed. Had it been, Harnack could not say of him that he bequeathed to posterity only "problems."

In very fact, there remained to the end, as the same writer puts it, " two Augustines," which is as much as to say, that he embraced in his public teaching inconsistent elements of doctrine.[98] It is indeed quite possible by attending alternately to one element of his teaching alone to draw out from his writings two contradictory systems: and this is just what has been done in the vital processes of historical development. To him as to their founder both Romanist and Protestant make their appeal.[99] The specific estimate which the Catholic places on the *unitas ecclesiæ* goes back to him, who it was that gave that compactness and far-reaching elaboration to the doctrine of the Church and its Sacraments which rendered the immense structure of Catholicism possible. It was equally he who by his doctrine of grace contributed the factor of positive doctrine by which the Reformation was rendered possible; for the Reformation on its theological and religious side was just an Augustinian revival. Two children were thus struggling in the womb of his mind. There can be no doubt which was the child of his heart. His doctrine of the Church he had received whole from his predecessors and himself gave it only the sharpness and depth which insured its vitality. His doctrine of grace was all his own, his greatest contribution to Christian thought. He was pleased to point out how this element of it and that had found broken expression in the pages of his great predecessors. He was successful in showing that all the true religious life of the Church from the beginning had flowed in the channels determined by it. But after all it was his, or rather it was he

[98] Harnack, "Dogmengeschichte," iii. p. 90 (E. T. "History of Dogma," v. p. 102); cf. Schaff, "Saint Chrysostom and Saint Augustin," p. 154.

[99] And not Romanist and Protestant alone: in a finely conceived passage Loofs, Herzog, "Realencyclopädie für protestantische Theologie und Kirche 3," ii. p. 277 outlines Augustine's position as the spring out of which many different waters flow. Cf. also his "Leitfaden zum Studium der Dogmengeschichte," § 46 (p. 176).

himself translated into forms of doctrine. It represented the very core of his Christian being: by it he lived; and his whole progress in Christian thinking is only the increasing perfection with which its fundamental principle applied itself in his mind to every department of Christian thought and life. Everything else gave way gradually before it, and it was thus that his thought advanced steadily toward a more and more consistent system.

But his doctrine of the Church and Sacraments had not yet given way before his doctrine of grace when he was called away from this world of partial attainment to the realms of perfect thought and life above. It still maintained a place by its side, fundamentally inconsistent with it, limited, modified by it, but retaining its own inner integrity. It is the spectacle of collectivism and individualism striving to create a *modus vivendi;* of dependence on God alone, and the intermediation of a human institution endeavoring to come to good understanding. It was not and is not possible for them to do so. Augustine had glimpses of the distinction between the invisible and the visible Church afterward elaborated by his spiritual children: he touched on the problem raised by the notions of baptismal regeneration and the necessity of the intermediation of the Church for salvation in the face of his passionately held doctrine of the free grace of God, and worked out a sort of compromise between them. In one way or another he found a measure of contentment for his double mind. But this could not last. We may say with decision that it was due only to the shortness of human life; to the distraction of his mind with multifarious cares; to the slowness of his solid advance in doctrinal development — that the two elements of his thought did not come to their fatal conflict before his death. Had they done so, there can be no question what the issue would have been. The real Augustine was the Augustine of the doctrine of grace.[100] The whole history of his inner life is a history of the

[100] Cf. Reuter, "Augustinische Studien," Studies First and Second; e.g., p. 102: "It was not the idea of the Church as the institute of grace that was dominant in his later years, but that of predestinating grace"; "the doctrine

progressive extension of the sway of this doctrine into all the chambers of his thought; of the gradual subjection to it of every element of his inherited teaching. In the course of time — had time been allowed — it was inevitable that his inherited doctrine of the Church also would have gone down before it, and he would have bequeathed to the Church not " problems " but a thoroughly worked-out system of purely evangelical religion.

No doubt it was the weakness of Augustine that this was not accomplished during the span of his six and seventy years. But it was a weakness in which there abode an element of strength. No facile theorizer he. Only as the clearly ascertained teaching of the Word slowly and painfully acquired moved him, did he move at all. Steadily and surely his thought worked its way through the problems presented to it; solidly but slowly. He left behind him, therefore, a structure which was not complete: but what he built he built to last. Had he been granted, perhaps, ten years longer of vigorous life, he might have thought his way through this problem also. He bequeathed it to the Church for solution, and the Church required a thousand years for the task. But even so, it is Augustine who gave us the Reformation. For what was the Reformation, inwardly considered, but the triumph of Augustine's doctrine of grace over Augustine's doctrine of the Church?

---

of predestinating grace was the fundamental principle of his religious consciousness. *It* must be unconditionally maintained, while all else must give way to it."

V

AUGUSTINE AND THE PELAGIAN CONTROVERSY

AUGUSTINE AND THE PELAGIAN CONTROVERSY [1]

I. The Origin and Nature of Pelagianism

It was inevitable that the energy of the Church in intellectually realizing and defining its doctrines in relation to one another, should first be directed towards the objective side of Christian truth. The chief controversies of the first four centuries and the resulting definitions of doctrine concerned the nature of God and the person of Christ; and it was not until these theological and Christological questions were well upon their way to final settlement, that the Church could turn its attention to the more subjective side of truth. Meanwhile she bore in her bosom a full recognition, side by side, of the freedom of the will, the evil consequences of the fall, and the necessity of divine grace for salvation. Individual writers, or even the several sections of the Church, might exhibit a tendency to throw emphasis on one or another of the elements that made up this deposit of faith that was the common inheritance of all. The East, for instance, laid especial stress on free will: and the West dwelt more pointedly on the ruin of the human race and the absolute need of God's grace for salvation. But neither did the Eastern theologians forget the universal sinfulness and need of redemption, or the necessity, for the realization of that redemption, of God's gracious influences; nor did those of the West deny the self-determination or accountability of men. All the elements of the composite doctrine of man were everywhere confessed; but they were variously emphasized, according to the temper of the writers or the controversial demands of the times. Such a state of affairs, however, was an invita-

[1] From "A Select Library of the Nicene and Post-Nicene Fathers of the Christian Church," First Series, v. pp. xiii.–lxxi. Used by permission of the publishers, Charles Scribner's Sons.

tion to heresy, and a prophecy of controversy; just as the simultaneous confession of the unity of God and the deity of Christ, or of the deity and the humanity of Christ, inevitably carried in its train a series of heresies and controversies, until the definitions of the doctrines of the Trinity and of the person of Christ were complete. In like manner, it was inevitable that sooner or later someone should arise who would do so one-sidedly emphasize one element or the other of the Church's teaching as to salvation, as to throw himself into heresy, and drive the Church, through controversy with him, into a precise definition of the doctrines of free will and grace in their mutual relations.

This new heresiarch came, at the opening of the fifth century, in the person of the British monk, Pelagius. The novelty of the doctrine which he taught is repeatedly asserted by Augustine,[2] and is evident to the historian; but it consisted not in the emphasis that he laid on free will, but rather in the fact that, in emphasizing free will, he denied the ruin of the race and the necessity of grace. This was not only new in Christianity; it was even anti-Christian. Jerome, as well as Augustine, saw this at the time, and speaks of Pelagianism as the "heresy of Pythagoras and Zeno";[3] and modern writers of the various schools have more or less fully recognized it. Thus Dean Milman thinks that "the greater part" of Pelagius' letter to Demetrias "might have been written by an ancient academic";[4] and Bishop Hefele openly declares that their fundamental doctrine, that "man is virtuous entirely of his own merit, not of the gift of grace," seems to him "to be a rehabilitation of the general heathen view of the world," and compares with it Cicero's words:[5] "For all the blessings of life, we have to re-

[2] "On the Merits and Remission of Sins," iii. 6, 11, 12; "Against Two Letters of the Pelagians," iv. 32; "The Unfinished Work Against Julian," i. 2; "On Heresies," 88; and often elsewhere. Jerome found *roots* for the theory in Origen and Rufinus (*Letter* 133. 3), but this is a different matter. Compare "On Original Sin," 25.

[3] Preface to Book iv. of his work on Jeremiah.

[4] "History of Latin Christianity," 1899, i. p. 166, note [2].

[5] "De Natura Deorum," iii. 36.

turn thanks to the Gods; but no one ever returned thanks to God for virtue." [6] The struggle with Pelagianism was thus in reality a struggle for the very foundations of Christianity; and even more dangerously than in the previous theological and Christological controversies, here the practical substance of Christianity was in jeopardy. The real question at issue was whether there was any need for Christianity at all; whether by his own power man might not attain eternal felicity; whether the function of Christianity was to save, or only to render an eternity of happiness more easily attainable by man.[7]

Genetically speaking, Pelagianism was the daughter of legalism; but when it itself conceived, it brought forth an essential deism. It is not without significance that its originators were " a certain sort of monks "; that is, laymen of ascetic life. From this point of view the Divine law is looked upon as a collection of separate commandments, moral perfection as a simple complex of separate virtues, and a distinct value as a meritorious demand on Divine approbation is ascribed to each good work or attainment in the exercises of piety. It was because this was essentially his point of view that Pelagius could regard man's powers as sufficient to the attainment of sanctity — nay, that he could even assert it to be possible for a man to do more than was required of him. But this involved an essentially deistic conception of man's relations to his Maker. God had endowed His creature with a capacity (*possibilitas*) or ability (*posse*) for action, and it was for him to use it. Man was thus a machine, which, just because it was well made, needed no Divine interference for its right working; and the Creator, having once framed him, and endowed him with the *posse*, henceforth leaves the *velle* and the *esse* to him.

At this point we have touched the central and formative principle of Pelagianism. It lies in the assumption of the plenary ability of man; his ability to do all that righteousness

[6] " A History of the Councils of the Church," (E. T.) ii. p. 446, note [3].

[7] Compare the excellent statement in Thomasius' " Die Christliche Dogmengeschichte," i. p. 483.

can demand — to work out not only his own salvation, but also his own perfection. This is the core of the whole theory; and all the other postulates not only depend upon it, but arise out of it. Both chronologically and logically this is the root of the system.

When we first hear of Pelagius, he is already advanced in years, living in Rome in the odour of sanctity,[8] and enjoying a well-deserved reputation for zeal in exhorting others to a good life, which grew especially warm against those who endeavoured to shelter themselves, when charged with their sins, behind the weakness of nature.[9] He was outraged by the universal excuses on such occasions — " It is hard! " " it is difficult! " " we are not able! " " we are men! " — " Oh, blind madness! " he cried: " we accuse God of a twofold ignorance — that He does not seem to know what He has made, nor what He has commanded — as if forgetting the human weakness of which He is Himself the Author, He has imposed laws on man which He cannot endure." [10] He himself tells us [11] that it was his custom, therefore, whenever he had to speak on moral improvement and the conduct of a holy life, to begin by pointing out the power and quality of human nature, and by showing what it was capable of doing. For (he says) he esteemed it of small use to exhort men to what they deemed impossible: hope must rather be our companion, and all longing and effort die when we despair of attaining. So exceedingly ardent an advocate was he of man's unaided ability to do all that God commanded, that when Augustine's noble and entirely scriptural prayer — " Give what Thou commandest, and command what Thou wilt " — was repeated in his hearing, he was unable to endure it; and somewhat inconsistently contradicted it with such violence as almost to become involved in a strife.[12] The powers of man, he held, were gifts of God; and it was, there-

[8] " On the Proceedings of Pelagius," 46; " On the Merits and Remission of Sins," iii. 1; " Epist." 186, etc.

[9] " On Nature and Grace," 1.

[10] Pelagius' " Epistle to Demetrias," 16.

[11] *Ibid.*, 2.

[12] " On the Gift of Perseverance," 53.

fore, a reproach against Him as if He had made man ill or evil, to believe that they were insufficient for the keeping of His law. Nay, do what we will, we cannot rid ourselves of their sufficiency: "whether we will, or whether we will not, we have the capacity of not sinning." [13] "I say," he says, "that man is able to be without sin, and that he is able to keep the commandments of God; " and this sufficiently direct statement of human ability is in reality the hinge of his whole system.

There were three specially important corollaries which flowed from this assertion of human ability, and Augustine himself recognized these as the chief elements of the system.[14] It would be inexplicable on such an assumption, if no man had ever used his ability in keeping God's law; and Pelagius consistently asserted not only that all might be sinless if they chose, but also that many saints, even before Christ, had actually lived free from sin. Again, it follows from man's inalienable ability to be free from sin, that each man comes into the world without entailment of sin or moral weakness from the past acts of men; and Pelagius consistently denied the whole doctrine of original sin. And still again, it follows from the same assumption of ability that man has no need of supernatural assistance in his striving to obey righteousness; and Pelagius consistently denied both the need and reality of divine grace in the sense of an inward help (and especially of a prevenient help) to man's weakness.

It was upon this last point that the greatest stress was laid in the controversy, and Augustine was most of all disturbed that thus God's grace was denied and opposed. No doubt the Pelagians spoke constantly of "grace," but they meant by this the primal endowment of man with free will, and the subsequent aid given him in order to its proper use by the revelation of the law and the teaching of the gospel, and, above all, by the forgiveness of past sins in Christ and by

---

[13] "On Nature and Grace," 57.

[14] "On the Gift of Perseverance," 4; "Against Two Letters of the Pelagians," iii. 24; iv. 2 *sq*.

Christ's holy example.[15] Anything further than this external
help they utterly denied; and they denied that this external
help itself was absolutely necessary, affirming that it only rendered it easier for man to do what otherwise he had plenary
ability for doing. Chronologically, this contention seems to
have preceded the assertion which must logically lie at its
base, of the freedom of man from any taint, corruption, or
weakness due to sin. It was in order that they might deny
that man needed help, that they denied that Adam's sin had
any further effect on his posterity than might arise from his
bad example. " Before the action of his own proper will," said
Pelagius plainly, " that only is in man which God made." [16]
" As we are procreated without virtue," he said, " so also without vice." [17] In a word, " Nothing that is good and evil, on account of which we are either praiseworthy or blameworthy, is
born with us — it is rather done by us; for we are born with
capacity for either, but provided with neither." [18] So his later
follower, Julian, plainly asserts his " faith that God creates
men obnoxious to no sin, but full of natural innocence, and
with capacity for voluntary virtues." [19] So intrenched is free
will in nature, that, according to Julian, it is " just as complete
after sins as it was before sins; " [20] and what this means may
be gathered from Pelagius' definition in the " Confession of
Faith," that he sent to Innocent: " We say that man is always
able both to sin and not to sin, so as that we may confess that
we have free will." That sin in such circumstances was so common as to be well-nigh universal, was accounted for by the
bad example of Adam and the power of habit, the latter being
simply the result of imitation of the former. " Nothing makes
well-doing so hard," writes Pelagius to Demetrias, " as the

[15] " On the Spirit and Letter," 4; " On Nature and Grace," 53; " On the
Proceedings of Pelagius," 20, 22, 38; " On the Grace of Christ," 2, 3, 8, 31, 42,
45; " Against Two Letters of the Pelagians," iv. 11; " On Grace and Free Will,"
23–26, and often.   [17] *Ibid.*
[16] " On Original Sin," 14.   [18] *Ibid.*
[19] " The Unfinished Work Against Julian," iii. 82.
[20] Do. i. 91; compare do. i. 48, 60; ii. 20. " There is nothing of sin in man,
if there is nothing of his own will." " There is no original sin in infants at all."

long custom of sins which begins from childhood and gradually brings us more and more under its power until it seems to
have in some degree the force of nature (*vim naturæ*)." He is
even ready to allow for the force of habit in a broad way, on
the world at large; and so divides all history into progressive
periods, marked by God's (external) grace. At first the light of
nature was so strong that men by it alone could live in holiness. And it was only when men's manners became corrupt
and tarnished nature began to be insufficient for holy living,
that by God's grace the Law was given as an addition to mere
nature; and by it " the original lustre was restored to nature
after its blush had been impaired." And so again, after the
habit of sinning once more prevailed among men, and " the
law became unequal to the task of curing it," [21] Christ was
given, furnishing men with forgiveness of sins, exhortations to
imitation of the example and the holy example itself.[22] But
though thus a progressive deterioration was confessed, and
such a deterioration as rendered desirable at least two supernatural interpositions (in the giving of the law and the coming
of Christ), yet no corruption of nature, even by growing habit,
is really allowed. It was only an ever-increasing facility in imi-
tating vice which arose from so long a schooling in evil; and all
that was needed to rescue men from it was a new explanation
of what was right (in the law), or, at the most, the encouragement of forgiveness for what was already done, and a holy example (in Christ) for imitation. Pelagius still asserted our continuous possession of " a free will which is unimpaired for
sinning and for not sinning; " and Julian, that " our free will is
just as full after sins as it was before sins; " although Augustine does not fail to twit him with a charge of inconsistency.[23]

The peculiar individualism of the Pelagian view of the
world comes out strongly in their failure to perceive the effect
of habit on nature itself. Just as they conceived of virtue as a
complex of virtuous acts, so they conceived of sin exclusively

[21] " On Original Sin," 30.
[22] " On the Grace of Christ," 43.
[23] " The Unfinished Work," i. 91; compare 69.

as an act, or series of disconnected acts. They appear not to have risen above the essentially heathen view which had no notion of holiness apart from a series of acts of holiness, or of sin apart from a like series of sinful acts.[24] Thus the will was isolated from its acts, and the acts from each other, and all organic connection or continuity of life was not only overlooked but denied.[25] After each act of the will, man stood exactly where he did before: indeed, this conception scarcely allows for the existence of a " man " — only a willing machine is left, at each click of the action of which the spring regains its original position, and is equally ready as before to reperform its function. In such a conception there was no place for character: freedom of will was all. Thus it was not an unnatural mistake which they made, when they forgot the man altogether, and attributed to the faculty of free will, under the name of "*possibilitas*" or "*posse*," the ability that belonged rather to the man whose faculty it is, and who is properly responsible for the use he makes of it. Here lies the essential error of their doctrine of free will: they looked upon freedom in its *form* only, and not in its *matter;* and, keeping man in perpetual and hopeless equilibrium between good and evil, they permitted no growth of character and no advantage to himself to be gained by man in his successive choices of good. It need not surprise us that the type of thought which thus dissolved the organism of the man into a congeries of disconnected voluntary acts, failed to comprehend the solidarity of the race. To the Pelagian, Adam was a man, nothing more; and it was simply unthinkable that any act of his that left his own subsequent acts uncommitted, could entail sin and guilt upon other men. The same alembic that dissolved the individual into a succession of voluntary acts, could not fail to separate the race into a heap of uncon-

[24] Dr. Matheson finely says (*Expositor*, i. ix. 21, 1879), " There is the same difference between the Christian and the Pagan idea of Prayer as there is between the Christian and Pagan idea of sin. Paganism knows nothing of sin, it knows only of sins: it has no conception of the principle of evil; it comprehends only a collection of evil acts." This is Pelagianism too.

[25] Compare Schaff, " History of the Christian Church," iii. 804; and Thomasius' " Die Christliche Dogmengeschichte," i. 487–488.

nected units. If sin, as Julian declared, is nothing but will, and the will itself remained intact after each act, how could the individual act of an individual will condition the acts of men as yet unborn? By "imitation" of his act alone could (under such a conception) other men be affected. And this carried with it the corresponding view of man's relation to Christ. He could forgive us the sins we had committed; He could teach us the true way; He could set us a holy example; and He could exhort us to its imitation. But He could not touch us to enable us to will the good, without destroying the absolute equilibrium of the will between good and evil; and to destroy this was to destroy its freedom, which was the crowning good of our divinely created nature. Surely the Pelagians forgot that man was not made for will, but will for man.

In defending their theory, as we are told by Augustine, there were five claims that they especially made for it.[26] It allowed them to praise as was their due, the creature that God had made, the marriage that He had instituted, the law that He had given, the free will which was His greatest endowment to man, and the saints who had followed His counsels. By this they meant that they proclaimed the sinless perfection of human nature in every man as he was brought into the world, and opposed this to the doctrine of original sin; the purity and holiness of marriage and the sexual appetites, and opposed this to the doctrine of the transmission of sin; the ability of the law, as well as and apart from the gospel, to bring men into eternal life, and opposed this to the necessity of inner grace; the integrity of free will to choose the good, and opposed this to the necessity of divine aid; and the perfection of the lives of the saints, and opposed this to the doctrine of universal sinfulness. Other questions, concerning the origin of souls, the necessity of baptism for infants, the original immortality of Adam, lay more on the skirts of the controversy, and were rather consequences of their teaching than parts of it. As it was an obvious fact that all men died, they could not admit that Adam's death was a consequence of sin lest they should

[26] "Against Two Letters of the Pelagians," iii. 25, and iv. at the beginning.

be forced to confess that his sin had injured all men; they
therefore asserted that physical death belonged to the very nature of man, and that Adam would have died even had he not
sinned.[27] So, as it was impossible to deny that the Church
everywhere baptized infants, they could not refuse them baptism without confessing themselves innovators in doctrine;
and therefore they contended that infants were not baptized
for forgiveness of sins, but in order to attain a higher state of
salvation. Finally, they conceived that if it was admitted that
souls were directly created by God for each birth, it could not
be asserted that they came into the world soiled by sin and
under condemnation; and therefore they loudly championed
this theory of the origin of souls.

The teachings of the Pelagians, it will be readily seen, easily welded themselves into a system, the essential and formative elements of which were entirely new in the Christian
Church; and this startlingly new reading of man's condition,
powers, and dependence for salvation, it was, that broke like
a thunderbolt upon the Western Church at the opening of the
fifth century, and forced her to reconsider, from the foundations, her whole teaching as to man and his salvation.

II. The External History of the Pelagian Controversy

Pelagius seems to have been already somewhat softened by
increasing age when he came to Rome about the opening of the
fifth century. He was also constitutionally averse to controversy; and although in his zeal for Christian morals, and in
his conviction that no man would attempt to do what he was
not persuaded he had natural power to perform, he diligently
propagated his doctrines privately, he was careful to rouse no
opposition, and was content to make what progress he could
quietly and without open discussion. His methods of work sufficiently appear in the pages of his "Commentary on the Epistles of Saint Paul," which was written and published during

[27] This belongs to the earlier Pelagianism; Julian was ready to admit
that death came from Adam, but not sin.

these years, and which exhibits learning and a sober and correct but somewhat shallow exegetical skill. In this work, he manages to give expression to all the main elements of his system, but always introduces them indirectly, not as the true exegesis, but by way of objections to the ordinary teaching, which were in need of discussion. The most important fruit of his residence in Rome was the conversion to his views of the Advocate Cœlestius, who brought the courage of youth and the argumentative training of a lawyer to the propagation of the new teaching. It was through him that it first broke out into public controversy, and received its first ecclesiastical examination and rejection. Fleeing from Alaric's second raid on Rome, the two friends landed together in Africa (A.D. 411), whence Pelagius soon afterwards departed for Palestine, leaving the bolder and more contentious [28] Cœlestius behind at Carthage. Here Cœlestius sought ordination as a presbyter. But the Milanese deacon Paulinus stood forward in accusation of him as a heretic, and the matter was brought before a synod under the presidency of Bishop Aurelius.[29]

Paulinus' charge consisted of seven items,[30] which asserted that Cœlestius taught the following heresies: that Adam was made mortal, and would have died, whether he sinned or did not sin; that the sin of Adam injured himself alone, not the human race; that new-born children are in that state in which Adam was before his sin; that the whole human race does not, on the one hand, die on account of the death or the fall of Adam, nor, on the other, rise again on account of the resurrection of Christ; that infants, even though not baptized, have eternal life; that the law leads to the kingdom of heaven in the same way as the gospel; and that, even before the Lord's coming, there had been men without sin. Only two fragments of

[28] " On Original Sin," 13.

[29] Early in 412, or, less probably, according to the Ballerini and Hefele 411.

[30] See " On Original Sin," 2, 3, 13; " On the Proceedings of Pelagius," 23. They are also given by Marius Mercator (Migne, " Patrologia Latina," xlviii. 69, 70), and the fifth item (on the salvation of unbaptized infants) omitted — though apparently by an error.

the proceedings of the synod in investigating this charge have come down to us; [31] but it is easy to see that Cœlestius was contumacious, and refused to reject any of the propositions charged against him, except the one which had reference to the salvation of infants that die unbaptized — the sole one that admitted of sound defence. As touching the transmission of sin, he would only say that it was an open question in the Church, and that he had heard both opinions from Church dignitaries; so that the subject needed investigation, and should not be made the ground for a charge of heresy. The natural result was that, on refusing to condemn the propositions charged against him, he was himself condemned and excommunicated by the synod. Soon afterwards he sailed to Ephesus, where he obtained the ordination which he sought.

Meanwhile Pelagius was living quietly in Palestine, whither in the summer of 415 a young Spanish presbyter, Paulus Orosius by name, came with letters from Augustine to Jerome, and was invited, near the end of July in that year, to a diocesan synod, presided over by John of Jerusalem. There he was asked about Pelagius and Cœlestius, and proceeded to give an account of the condemnation of the latter at the synod of Carthage, and of Augustine's literary refutation of the former. Pelagius was sent for, and the proceedings became an examination into his teachings. The chief matter brought up was his assertion of the possibility of men living sinlessly in this world; but the favor of the bishop towards him, the intemperance of Orosius, and the difficulty of communication between the parties arising from difference of language, combined so to clog proceedings that nothing was done; and the whole matter, as Western in its origin, was referred to the Bishop of Rome for examination and decision. [32]

Soon afterwards two Gallic bishops — Heros of Arles, and Lazarus of Aix — who were then in Palestine, lodged a formal accusation against Pelagius with the metropolitan, Eulogius

[31] Preserved by Augustine, "On Original Sin," 3, 4.

[32] An account of this synod is given by Orosius himself in his "Apology for the Freedom of the Will."

of Cæsarea; and he convened a synod of fourteen bishops which met at Lydda (Diospolis), in December of the same year (415), for the trial of the case. Perhaps no greater ecclesiastical farce was ever enacted than this synod exhibited.[33] When the time arrived, the accusers were prevented from being present by illness, and Pelagius was confronted only by the written accusation. This was both unskilfully drawn, and was written in Latin which the synod did not understand. It was, therefore, not even consecutively read, and was only head by head rendered into Greek by an interpreter. Pelagius began by reading aloud several letters to himself from various men of reputation in the Episcopate — among them a friendly note from Augustine. Thoroughly acquainted with both Latin and Greek, he was enabled skilfully to thread every difficulty, and pass safely through the ordeal. Jerome called this a "miserable synod," and not unjustly: at the same time it is sufficient to vindicate the honesty and earnestness of the bishops' intentions, that even in such circumstances, and despite the more undeveloped opinions of the East on the questions involved, Pelagius escaped condemnation only by a course of most ingenious disingenuousness, and only at the cost both of disowning Cœlestius and his teachings, of which he had been the real father, and of leading the synod to believe that he was anathematizing the very doctrines which he was himself proclaiming. There is really no possibility of doubting, as any one will see who reads the proceedings of the synod, that Pelagius obtained his acquittal here either by a "lying condemnation or a tricky interpretation"[34] of his own teachings; and Augustine is perfectly justified in asserting that the heresy was not acquitted, but the man who denied the heresy,[35] and who would himself have been anathematized had he not anathematized the heresy.

However obtained, the acquittal of Pelagius was yet an accomplished fact. Neither he nor his friends delayed to make

[33] A full account and criticism of the proceedings are given by Augustine in his "On the Proceedings of Pelagius."

[34] "On Original Sin," 13, at the end.

[35] "On the Proceedings of Pelagius," 59, 60, sq.

the most widely extended use of their good fortune. Pelagius
himself was jubilant. Accounts of the synodal proceedings were
sent to the West, not altogether free from uncandid alterations; and Pelagius soon put forth a work " In Defence of Free
Will," in which he triumphed in his acquittal and " explained
his explanations " at the synod. Nor were the champions of the
opposite opinion idle. As soon as the news arrived in North
Africa, and before the authentic records of the synod had
reached that region, the condemnation of Pelagius and Cœlestius was re-affirmed in two provincial synods — one, consisting
of sixty-eight bishops, met at Carthage about midsummer of
416; and the other, consisting of about sixty bishops, met soon
afterwards at Mileve (Mila). Thus Palestine and North Africa
were arrayed against one another, and it became of great importance to obtain the support of the Patriarchal See of Rome.
Both sides made the attempt, but fortune favored the Africans.
Each of the North-African synods sent a synodal letter to Innocent I, then Bishop of Rome, engaging his assent to their
action: to these, five bishops, Aurelius of Carthage and Augustine among them, added a third " familiar " letter of their own,
in which they urged upon Innocent to examine into Pelagius'
teaching, and provided him with the material on which he
might base a decision. The letters reached Innocent in time for
him to take advice of his clergy, and send favorable replies on
Jan. 27, 417. In these he expressed his agreement with the
African decisions, asserted the necessity of inward grace, rejected the Pelagian theory of infant baptism, and declared
Pelagius and Cœlestius excommunicated until they should return to orthodoxy. In about six weeks more he was dead: but
Zosimus, his successor, was scarcely installed in his place before Cœlestius appeared at Rome in person to plead his cause;
while shortly afterwards letters arrived from Pelagius addressed to Innocent, and by an artful statement of his belief
and a recommendation from Praylus, lately become bishop of
Jerusalem in John's stead, he attempted to enlist Rome in his
favor. Zosimus, who appears to have been a Greek and therefore inclined to make little of the merits of this Western con-

troversy, went over to Cœlestius at once, upon his profession of willingness to anathematize all doctrines which the pontifical see had condemned or should condemn; and wrote a sharp and arrogant letter to Africa, proclaiming Cœlestius "catholic," and requiring the Africans to appear within two months at Rome to prosecute their charges, or else to abandon them. On the arrival of Pelagius' papers, this letter was followed by another (September, 417), in which Zosimus, with the approbation of the clergy, declared both Pelagius and Cœlestius to be orthodox, and severely rebuked the Africans for their hasty judgment. It is difficult to understand Zosimus' action in this matter: neither of the confessions presented by the accused teachers ought to have deceived him, and if he was seizing the occasion to magnify the Roman see, his mistake was dreadful. Late in 417, or early in 418, the African bishops assembled at Carthage, in number more than two hundred, and replied to Zosimus that they had decided that the sentence pronounced against Pelagius and Cœlestius should remain in force until they should unequivocally acknowledge that "we are aided by the grace of God, through Christ, not only to know, but to do what is right, in each single act, so that without grace we are unable to have, think, speak, or do anything pertaining to piety." This firmness made Zosimus waver. He answered swellingly but timidly, declaring that he had maturely examined the matter, but it had not been his intention finally to acquit Cœlestius; and now he had left all things in the condition in which they were before, but he claimed the right of final judgment to himself. Matters were hastening to a conclusion, however, that would leave him no opportunity to escape from the mortification of an entire change of front. This letter was written on the 21st of March, 418; it was received in Africa on the 29th of April; and on the very next day an imperial decree was issued from Ravenna ordering Pelagius and Cœlestius to be banished from Rome, with all who held their opinions; while on the next day, May 1, a plenary council of about two hundred bishops met at Carthage, and in nine canons condemned all the essential features of Pelagianism. Whether this simultaneous action was the result of skilful arrangement, can only be conjectured: its effect was in any case necessarily crushing. There could be no appeal from the civil decision, and it played directly into the hands of the African definition of the faith. The synod's nine canons part naturally into three triads.[36] The first of these deals with the relation of mankind to original sin, and anathematizes in turn those who assert that physical death is a necessity of nature, and not a result of Adam's sin; those who assert that new-born children derive nothing of original sin from Adam to be expiated by the laver of regeneration; and those who assert a distinction between the kingdom of heaven and eternal life, for entrance into the former of which alone baptism is necessary. The second triad deals with the nature of grace, and anathematizes those who assert that grace brings only remission of past sins, not aid in avoiding future ones; those who assert that grace aids us not to sin, only by teaching us what is sinful, not by enabling us to will and do what we know to be right; and those who assert that grace only enables us to do more easily what we should without it still be able to do. The third triad deals with the universal sinfulness of the race, and anathematizes those who assert that the apostles' (1 John i. 8) confession of sin is due only to their humility; those who say that "Forgive us our trespasses" in the Lord's Prayer, is pronounced by the saints, not for themselves, but for the sinners in their company; and those who say that the saints use these words of themselves only out of humility and not truly. Here we see a careful traversing of the whole ground of the controversy, with a conscious reference to the three chief contentions of the Pelagian teachers.[37]

The appeal to the civil power, by whomsoever made, was, of course, indefensible, although it accorded with the opinions of the day, and was entirely approved by Augustine. But it was the ruin of the Pelagian cause. Zosimus found himself forced either to go into banishment with his wards, or to desert their

---

[36] Compare Canon Bright's *Introduction* in his "Select Anti-Pelagian Treatises of St. Augustine," p. xli.

[37] See above, pp. 293–294, and the passages in Augustine cited in note 16.

cause. He appears never to have had any personal convictions on the dogmatic points involved in the controversy, and so, all the more readily, yielded to the necessity of the moment. He cited Cœlestius to appear before a council for a new examination; but that heresiarch consulted prudence, and withdrew from the city. Zosimus, possibly in the effort to appear a leader in the cause he had opposed, not only condemned and excommunicated the men whom less than six months before he had pronounced " orthodox " after a " mature consideration of the matters involved," but, in obedience to the imperial decree, issued a stringent paper which condemned Pelagius and the Pelagians, and affirmed the African doctrines as to corruption of nature, true grace, and the necessity of baptism. To this he required subscription from all bishops as a test of orthodoxy. Eighteen Italian bishops refused their signature, with Julian of Eclanum, henceforth to be the champion of the Pelagian party, at their head, and were therefore deposed, although several of them afterwards recanted, and were restored. In Julian, the heresy obtained an advocate, who, if aught could have been done for its re-instatement, would surely have proved successful. He was the boldest, the strongest, at once the most acute and the most weighty, of all the disputants of his party. But the ecclesiastical standing of this heresy was already determined. The policy of Zosimus' test act was imposed by imperial authority on North Africa in 419. The exiled bishops were driven from Constantinople by Atticus in 424; and they are said to have been condemned at a Cilician synod in 423, and at an Antiochian one in 424. Thus the East itself was preparing for the final act in the drama. The exiled bishops were with Nestorius at Constantinople in 429; and that patriarch unsuccessfully interceded for them with Cœlestine, then Bishop of Rome. The conjunction was ominous. And at the ecumenical synod at Ephesus in 431, we again find the " Cœlestians " side by side with Nestorius, sharers in his condemnation.

But Pelagianism did not so die as not to leave a legacy behind it. " Remainders of Pelagianism "[38] soon showed them-

[38] Prosper's phrase.

selves in Southern Gaul, where a body of monastic leaders attempted to find a middle ground on which they could stand, by allowing the Augustinian doctrine of assisting grace, but retaining the Pelagian conception of our self-determination to good. We first hear of them in 428, through letters from two laymen, Prosper and Hilary, to Augustine, as men who accepted original sin and the necessity of grace, but asserted that men began their turning to God, and God helped their beginning. They taught [39] that all men are sinners, and that they derive their sin from Adam; that they can by no means save themselves, but need God's assisting grace; and that this grace is gratuitous in the sense that men cannot really deserve it, and yet that it is not irresistible, nor given always without the occasion of its gift having been determined by men's attitude towards God; so that, though not given on account of the merits of men, it is given according to those merits, actual or foreseen. The leader of this new movement was John Cassian, a pupil of Chrysostom (to whom he attributed all that was good in his life and will), and the fountain-head of Gallic monasticism; and its chief champion at a somewhat later day was Faustus of Rhegium (Riez).

The Augustinian opposition was at first led by the vigorous controversialist, Prosper of Aquitaine, and, in the next century, by the wise, moderate, and good Cæsarius of Arles, who brought the contest to a conclusion in the victory of a softened Augustinianism. Already in 431 a letter was obtained from Pope Cœlestine, designed to close the controversy in favor of Augustinianism, and in 496 Pope Gelasius condemned the writings of Faustus in the first index of forbidden books; while, near the end of the first quarter of the sixth century, Pope Hormisdas was appealed to for a renewed condemnation. The end was now in sight. The famous second Synod of Orange met under the presidency of Cæsarius at that ancient town on the 3d of July, 529, and drew up a series of moderate articles which received the ratification of Boniface II in the following year.

[39] Augustine gives their teaching carefully in his " On the Predestination of the Saints," 2.

In these articles there is affirmed an anxiously guarded Augustinianism, a somewhat weakened Augustinianism, but yet a distinctive Augustinianism; and, so far as a formal condemnation could reach, semi-Pelagianism was suppressed by them in the whole Western Church. But councils and popes can only decree; and Cassian and Vincent and Faustus, despite Cæsarius and Boniface and Gregory, retained an influence among their countrymen which never died away.

III. AUGUSTINE'S PART IN THE CONTROVERSY

Both by nature and by grace, Augustine was formed to be the champion of truth in this controversy. Of a naturally philosophical temperament, he saw into the springs of life with a vividness of mental perception to which most men are strangers; and his own experiences in his long life of resistance to, and then of yielding to, the drawings of God's grace, gave him a clear apprehension of the great evangelic principle that God seeks men, not men God, such as no sophistry could cloud. However much his philosophy or theology might undergo change in other particulars, there was one conviction too deeply imprinted upon his heart ever to fade or alter — the conviction of the ineffableness of God's grace. Grace — man's absolute dependence on God as the source of all good — this was the common, nay, the *formative* element, in all stages of his doctrinal development, which was marked only by the ever growing consistency with which he built his theology around this central principle. Already in 397 — the year after he became bishop — we find him enunciating with admirable clearness all the essential elements of his teaching, as he afterwards opposed them to Pelagius.[40] It was inevitable, therefore, that although he was rejoiced when he heard, some years later, of the zealous labors of this pious monk in Rome towards stemming the tide of luxury and sin, and esteemed him for his devout life, and

[40] Compare his work written this year, " On Several Questions to Simplicianus." For the development of Augustine's theology, see the admirable statement in Neander's " General History of the Christian Religion and Church," E. T. ii. 625 *sq*.

loved him for his Christian activity, he yet was deeply troubled when subsequent rumors reached him that he was "disputing against the grace of God." He tells us over and over
again, that this was a thing no pious heart could endure; and
we perceive that, from this moment, Augustine was only biding
his time, and awaiting a fitting opportunity to join issue with
the denier of the Holy of holies of his whole, I will not say
theology merely, but life. " Although I was grieved by this,"
he says, " and it was told me by men whom I believed, I yet
desired to have something of such sort from his own lips or in
some book of his, so that, if I began to refute it, he would not
be able to deny it." [41] Thus he actually excuses himself for not
entering into the controversy earlier. When Pelagius came to
Africa, then, it was almost as if he had deliberately sought his
fate. But circumstances secured a lull before the storm. He
visited Hippo; but Augustine was absent, although he did not
fail to inform himself on his return that Pelagius while there
had not been heard to say " anything at all of this kind." The
controversy against the Donatists was now occupying all the
energies of the African Church, and Augustine himself was a
ruling spirit in the great conference now holding at Carthage
with them. While there, he was so immersed in this business,
that, although he once or twice saw the face of Pelagius, he
had no conversation with him; and although his ears were
wounded by a casual remark which he heard, to the effect " that
infants were not baptized for remission of sins, but for consecration to Christ," he allowed himself to pass over the matter,
" because there was no opportunity to contradict it, and those
who said it were not such men as could cause him solicitude
for their influence." [42]

It appears from these facts, given us by himself, that Augustine was not only ready for, but was looking for, the coming
controversy. It can scarcely have been a surprise to him when
Paulinus accused Cœlestius (412); and, although he was not a
member of the council which condemned him, it was inevitable

[41] " On the Proceedings of Pelagius," 46.
[42] " On the Merits and Remission of Sins," iii. 12.

that he should at once take the leading part in the consequent controversy. Cœlestius and his friends did not silently submit to the judgment that had been passed upon their teaching: they could not openly propagate their heresy, but they were diligent in spreading their plaints privately and by subterraneous whispers among the people.[43] This was met by the Catholics in public sermons and familiar colloquies held everywhere. But this wise rule was observed — to contend against the erroneous teachings, but to keep silence as to the teachers, that so (as Augustine explains [44]) " the men might rather be brought to see and acknowledge their error through fear of ecclesiastical judgment than be punished by the actual judgment." Augustine was abundant in these oral labors; and many of his sermons directed against Pelagian error have come down to us, although it is often impossible to be sure as to their date. For one of them (170) he took his text from Phil. iii. 6–16, " as touching the righteousness which is by the law blameless; howbeit what things were gain to me, those have I counted loss for Christ. . . ." He begins by asking how the apostle could count his blameless conversation according to the righteousness which is from the law as dung and loss, and then proceeds to explain the purpose for which the law was given, our state by nature and under law, and the kind of blamelessness that the law could produce, ending by showing that man can have no righteousness except from God, and no perfect righteousness except in heaven. Three others (174, 175, 176) had as their text 1 Tim. i. 15, 16, and developed its teaching, that the universal sin of the world and its helplessness in sin constituted the necessity of the incarnation; and especially that the necessity of Christ's grace for salvation was just as great for infants as for adults. Much is very forcibly said in these sermons which was afterwards incorporated in his treatises. " There was no reason," he insists, " for the coming of Christ the Lord except to save sinners. Take away diseases, take away wounds, and there is no reason for medicine. If the great Physician came from heaven,

---

[43] " Epist." 157. 22.

[44] " On the Proceedings of Pelagius," 46.

a great sick man was lying ill through the whole world. That
sick man is the human race " (175, 1). " He who says, ' I am
not a sinner,' or ' I was not,' is ungrateful to the Saviour. No
one of men in that mass of mortals which flows down from
Adam, no one at all of men is not sick: no one is healed without the grace of Christ. Why do you ask whether infants are
sick from Adam? For they, too, are brought to the church; and,
if they cannot run thither on their own feet, they run on the
feet of others that they may be healed. Mother Church ac-
commodates others' feet to them so that they may come, others' heart so that they may believe, others' tongue so that they
may confess; and, since they are sick by another's sin, so when
they are healed they are saved by another's confession in their
behalf. Let, then, no one buzz strange doctrines to you. *This*
the Church has always had, has always held; this she has received from the faith of the elders; this she will perseveringly
guard until the end. Since the whole have no need of a physician, but only the sick, what need, then, has the infant of
Christ, if he is not sick? If he is well, why does he seek the physician through those who love him? If, when infants are
brought, they are said to have no sin of inheritance (*peccatum
propaginis*) at all, and yet come to Christ, why is it not said in
the church to those that bring them, ' Take these innocents
hence; the physician is not needed by the well, but by the sick;
Christ came not to call the just, but sinners ' ? It never has
been said, and it never will be said. Let each one therefore,
brethren, speak for him who cannot speak for himself. It is
much the custom to intrust the inheritance of orphans to the
bishops; how much more the grace of infants! The bishop protects the orphan lest he should be oppressed by strangers, his
parents being dead. Let him cry out more for the infant who,
he fears, will be slain by his parents. Who comes to Christ has
something in him to be healed; and he who has not, has no
reason for seeking the physician. Let parents choose one of
two things: let them either confess that there is sin to be
healed in their infants, or let them cease bringing them to the
physician. This is something else than to wish to bring a well

person to the physician. Why do you bring him? To be baptized. Whom? The infant. To whom do you bring him? To Christ. To Him, of course, who came into the world? Certainly, he says. Why did He come into the world? To save sinners. Then he whom you bring has in him that which needs saving?"[45] So again: "He who says that the age of infancy does not need Jesus' salvation, says nothing else than that the Lord Christ is not *Jesus* to faithful infants; i.e., to infants baptized in Christ. For what is *Jesus? Jesus* means saviour. He is not Jesus to those whom He does not save, who do not need to be saved. Now, if your hearts can bear that Christ is not *Jesus* to any of the baptized, I do not know how you can be acknowledged to have sound faith. They are infants, but they are made members of Him. They are infants, but they receive His sacraments. They are infants, but they become partakers of His table, so that they may have life."[46] The preveniency of grace is explicitly asserted in these sermons. In one he says, "Zacchaeus was seen, and saw; but unless he had been seen, he would not have seen. For 'whom He predestinated, them also He called.' . . . In order that we may see, we are seen; that we may love, we are loved. 'My God, may His pity prevent me!'"[47] And in another, at more length: "His calling has preceded you, so that you may have a good will. Cry out, 'My God, let Thy mercy prevent me' (Ps. lix. 10). That you may be, that you may feel, that you may hear, that you may consent, His mercy prevents you. It prevents you in all things; and do you too prevent His judgment in something. In what, do you say? In what? In confessing that you have all these things from God, whatever you have of good; and from yourself whatever you have of evil" (176. 5). "We owe therefore to Him that we are, that we are alive, that we understand: that we are men, that we live well, that we understand aright, we owe to Him. Nothing is ours except the sin that we have. For what have we that we did not receive?" (1 Cor. iv. 7) (176. 6).

It was not long, however, before the controversy was driven

[45] "Sermon" 176. 2.   [46] "Sermon" 174. 7.   [47] Do.

out of the region of sermons into that of regular treatises. The
occasion for Augustine's first appearance in a written document bearing on the controversy, was given by certain questions which were sent to him for answer by " the tribune and
notary " Marcellinus, with whom he had cemented his intimacy at Carthage, the previous year, when this notable official was presiding, by the emperor's orders, over the great conference of the Catholics and Donatists. The mere fact that
Marcellinus, still at Carthage, where Cœlestius had been
brought to trial, wrote to Augustine at Hippo for written answers to important questions connected with the Pelagian
heresy, speaks volumes for the prominent position he had already assumed in the controversy. The questions that were
sent, concerned the connection of death with sin, the transmission of sin, the possibility of a sinless life, and especially infants' need of baptism.[48] Augustine was immersed in abundant
labors when they reached him: [49] but he could not resist this
appeal, and that the less as the Pelagian controversy had already grown to a place of the first importance in his eyes. The
result was his treatise, " On the Merits and Remission of Sins
and on the Baptism of Infants," consisting of two books, and
written in 412. The first book of this work is an argument for
original sin, drawn from the universal reign of death in the world
(2–8), from the teaching of Rom. v. 12–21 (9–20), and chiefly
from the baptism of infants (21–70).[50] It opens by exploding
the Pelagian contention that death is of nature, and Adam
would have died even had he not sinned, by showing that the
penalty threatened to Adam included physical death (Gen. iii.
19), and that it is due to him that we all die (Rom. viii. 10, 11;
1 Cor. xv. 21) (2–8). Then the Pelagian assertion that we are

[48] " On the Merits and Remission of Sins," iii. 1.

[49] Do., i. 1. Compare " Epist." 139.

[50] On the prominence of infant baptism in the controversy, and why it
was so, see " Sermon " 165. 7 sq. " What do you say? ' Just this,' he says, ' that
God creates every man immortal.' Why, then, do infant children die? For if
I say, ' Why do adult men die? ' you would say to me, ' They have sinned.'
Therefore I do not argue about the adults: I cite infancy as a witness against
you," and so on, eloquently developing the argument.

injured in Adam's sin only by its bad example, which we imitate, not by any propagation from it, is tested by an exposition of Rom. v. 12 *sq.* (9–20). And then the main subject of
the book is reached, and the writer sharply presses the Pelagians with the universal and primeval fact of the baptism of
infants, as a proof of original sin (21–70). He tracks out all
their subterfuges — showing the absurdity of the assertions
that infants are baptized for the remission of sins that they
have themselves committed since birth (22), or in order to
obtain a higher stage of salvation (23–28), or because of sin
committed in some previous state of existence (31–33). Then
turning to the positive side, he shows at length that the Scriptures teach that Christ came to save sinners, that baptism is
for the remission of sins, and that all that partake of it are
confessedly sinners (34 *sq.*); then he points out that John iii.
3, 5, on which the Pelagians relied, cannot be held to distinguish between ordinary salvation and a higher form, under
the name of "the kingdom of God" (58 *sq.*); and he closes
by showing that the very manner in which baptism was administered, with its exorcism and exsufflation, implied the infant to be a sinner (63), and by suggesting that the peculiar
helplessness of infancy, so different not only from the earliest
age of Adam, but also from that of many young animals, may
possibly be itself penal (64–69). The second book treats, with
similar fulness, the question of the perfection of human righteousness in this life. After an exordium which speaks of the
will and its limitations, and of the need of God's assisting
grace (1–6), the writer raises four questions. First, whether it
may be said to be possible, by God's grace, for a man to attain
a condition of entire sinlessness in this life (7). This he answers in the affirmative. Secondly, he asks, whether any one
has ever done this, or may ever be expected to do it, and answers in the negative on the testimony of Scripture (8–25).
Thirdly, he asks why not, and replies briefly because men are
unwilling, explaining at length what he means by this (26–
33). Finally, he inquires whether any man has ever existed,
exists now, or will ever exist, entirely without sin — this ques-

tion differing from the second inasmuch as that asked after the attainment in this life of a state in which sinning should cease, while this seeks a man who has never been guilty of sin, implying the absence of original as well as of actual sin. After answering this in the negative (34), Augustine discusses anew the question of original sin. Here after expounding from the positive side (35–38) the condition of man in paradise, the nature of his probation, and of the fall and its effects both on him and his posterity, and the kind of redemption that has been provided in the incarnation, he proceeds to answer certain cavils (39 sq.), such as, " Why should children of baptized people need baptism? " — " How can a sin be remitted to the father and held against the child? " — " If physical death comes from Adam, ought we not to be released from it on believing in Christ? " — and concludes with an exhortation to hold fast to the exact truth, turning neither to the right nor left — neither saying that we have no sin, nor surrendering ourselves to our sin (57 sq.).

After these books were completed, Augustine came into possession of Pelagius' " Commentary on Paul's Epistles," which was written while he was living in Rome (before 410), and found it to contain some arguments that he had not treated — such arguments, he tells us, as he had not imagined could be held by any one.[51] Unwilling to re-open his finished argument, he now began a long supplementary letter to Marcellinus, which he intended to serve as a third and concluding book to his work. He was some time in completing this letter. He had asked to have the former two books returned to him; and it is a curious indication of his overworked state of mind, that he forgot what he wanted with them: [52] he visited Carthage while the letter was in hand, and saw Marcellinus personally; and even after his return to Hippo, it dragged along, amid many distractions, slowly towards completion. Meanwhile, a long letter was written to Honoratus, in which a section on the grace of the New Testament was incorporated.[53] At

---

[51] " On the Merits and Remission of Sins," iii. 1.
[52] " Epist." 139. 3.   [53] " Epist." 140.

length the promised supplement was completed. It was professedly a criticism of Pelagius' " Commentary," and therefore naturally mentioned his name; but Augustine even goes
out of his way to speak as highly of his opponent as he can [54] —
although it is apparent that his esteem is not very high for his
strength of mind, and is even less high for the moral quality
that led to his odd, oblique way of expressing his opinions.
There is even a half sarcasm in the way he speaks of Pelagius'
care and circumspection, which was certainly justified by the
event. The letter opens by stating and criticising in a very
acute and telling dialectic, the new arguments of Pelagius,
which were such as the following: " If Adam's sin injured
even those who do not sin, Christ's righteousness ought likewise to profit even those who do not believe " (2–4); " No
man can transmit what he has not; and hence, if baptism
cleanses from sin, the children of two baptized parents ought
to be free from sin "; " God remits one's own sins, and can
scarcely, therefore, impute another's to us "; and " if the soul
is created, it would certainly be unjust to impute Adam's alien
sin to it " (5). The stress of the letter, however, is laid upon
two contentions — 1. That whatever else may be ambiguous
in the Scriptures, they are perfectly clear that no man can
have eternal life except in Christ, who came to call sinners to
repentance (7); and 2. That original sin in infants has always
been, in the Church, one of the fixed facts, to be used as a basis
of argument, in order to reach the truth in other matters, and
has never itself been called in question before (10–14). At this
point, the writer returns to the second and third of the new
arguments of Pelagius mentioned above, and discusses them
more fully (15–20), closing with a recapitulation of the three
great points that had been raised; viz., that both death and
sin are derived from Adam's sin by all his posterity; that infants need salvation, and hence baptism; and that no man
ever attains in this life such a state of holiness that he cannot
truly pray, " Forgive us our trespasses."

Augustine was now to learn that one service often entails

[54] " On the Merits and Remission of Sins," iii. 1, 5.

another. Marcellinus wrote to say that he was puzzled by what
had been said in the second book of this work, as to the possibility of man's attaining to sinlessness in this life, while yet
it was asserted that no man ever had attained, or ever would
attain, it. How, he asked, can that be said to be possible which
is, and which will remain, unexampled? In reply, Augustine
wrote, during this same year (412), and sent to his noble
friend, another work, which he calls " On the Spirit and the
Letter," from the prominence which he gives in it to the words
of 2 Cor. iii. 6.[55] He did not content himself with a simple, direct answer to Marcellinus' question, but goes at length into
a profound disquisition into the roots of the doctrine, and
thus gives us, not a mere explanation of a former contention,
but a new treatise on a new subject — the absolute necessity
of the grace of God for any good living. He begins by explaining to Marcellinus that he has affirmed the possibility while
denying the actuality of a sinless life, on the ground that all
things are possible to God — even the passage of a camel
through the eye of a needle, which nevertheless has never
occurred (1, 2). For, in speaking of man's perfection, we are
speaking really of a work of God — and one which is none the
less His work because it is wrought through the instrumentality of man, and in the use of his free will. The Scriptures, indeed, teach that no man lives without sin, but this is only the
proclamation of a matter of fact; and although it is thus contrary to fact and Scripture to assert that men may be found
that live sinlessly, yet such an assertion would not be fatal
heresy. What is unbearable, is that men should assert it to be
possible for man, unaided by God, to attain this perfection.
This is to speak against the grace of God: it is to put in man's
power what is only possible to the almighty grace of God (3,
4). No doubt, even these men do not, in so many words, exclude the aid of grace in perfecting human life — they affirm
God's help; but they make it consist in His gift to man of a
perfectly free will, and in His addition to this of commandments and teachings which make known to him what he is to

[55] " Sermon " 163 treats the text similarly.

seek and what to avoid, and so enable him to direct his free will to what is good. What, however, does such a "grace" amount to? (5). Man needs something more than to know the right way: he needs to love it, or he will not walk in it; and all mere teaching, which can do nothing more than bring us knowledge of what we ought to do, is but the letter that killeth. What we need is some inward, Spirit-given aid to the keeping of what by the law we know ought to be kept. Mere knowledge slays; while to lead a holy life is the gift of God — not only because He has given us will, nor only because He has taught us the right way, but because by the Holy Spirit He sheds love abroad in the hearts of all those whom He has predestinated, and will call and justify and glorify (Rom. viii. 29, 30). To prove this, he states to be the object of the present treatise; and after investigating the meaning of 2 Cor. iii. 6, and showing that "the letter" there means the law as a system of precepts, which reveals sin rather than takes it away, points out the way rather than gives strength to walk in it, and therefore slays the soul by shutting it up under sin — while "the Spirit" is God's Holy Ghost who is shed abroad in our hearts to give us strength to walk aright — he undertakes to prove this position from the teachings of the Epistle to the Romans at large. This contention, it will be seen, cut at the very roots of Pelagianism: if all mere teaching slays the soul, as Paul asserts, then all that what they called "grace" could, when alone, do, was to destroy; and the upshot of "helping" man by simply giving him free will, and pointing out the way to him, would be the loss of the whole race. Not that the law is sin: Augustine teaches that it is holy and good, and God's instrument in salvation. Not that free will is done away: it is by free will that men are led into holiness. But the purpose of the law (he teaches) is to make men so feel their lost estate as to seek the help by which alone they may be saved; and will is only then liberated to do good when grace has made it free. "What the law of works enjoins by menace, that the law of faith secures by faith. What the law of works does is to say, 'Do what I command thee'; but by the law of faith we say to God, 'Give me what thou commandest.'" (22).[56] In the midst of this argument, Augustine is led to discuss the differentiating characteristics of the Old and New Testaments; and he expounds at length (33–42) the passage in Jer. xxxi. 31–34, showing that, in the prophet's view, the difference between the two covenants is that in the Old, the law is an external thing written on stones; while in the New, it is written internally on the heart, so that men now wish to do what the law prescribes. This writing on the heart is nothing else, he explains, than the shedding abroad by the Holy Spirit of love in our hearts, so that we love God's will, and therefore freely do it. Towards the end of the treatise (50–61), he treats in an absorbingly interesting way of the mutual relations of free will, faith, and grace, contending that all co-exist without the voiding of any. It is by free will that we believe; but it is only as grace moves us, that we are able to use our free will for believing; and it is only after we are thus led by grace to believe, that we obtain all other goods. In prosecuting this analysis, Augustine is led to distinguish very sharply between the faculty and use of free will (58), as well as between ability and volition (53). Faith is an act of the man himself; but only as he is given the power from on high to will to believe, will he believe (57, 60).

By this work, Augustine completed, in his treatment of Pelagianism, the circle of that triad of doctrines which he himself looked upon as most endangered by this heresy [57] — original sin, that imperfection of human righteousness, the necessity of grace. In his mind, the last was the kernel of the whole controversy; and this was a subject which he could never approach without some heightened fervor. This accounts for the great attractiveness of the present work — through the whole fabric of which runs the golden thread of the praise of God's ineffable grace. In Canon Bright's opinion, it " perhaps, next to the ' Confessions,' tells us most of the thoughts of that

---

[56] See this prayer beautifully illustrated from Scripture in *On the Merits and Remission of Sins*, ii. 5.

[57] See above, p. 293.

'rich, profound, and affectionate mind' on the soul's relations to its God." [58]

After the publication of these treatises, the controversy certainly did not lull; but it relapsed for nearly three years again, into less public courses. Meanwhile, Augustine was busy, among other most distracting cares ("Epist." 145. 1), still defending the grace of God, by letters and sermons. A fair illustration of his state of mind at this time may be obtained from his letter to Anastasius (145), which assuredly must have been written soon after the treatise "On the Spirit and the Letter." Throughout this letter, there are adumbrations of the same train of thought that filled this treatise; and there is one passage which may almost be taken as a summary of it. Augustine is so weary of the vexatious cares that filled his life, that he is ready to long for the everlasting rest, and yet bewails the weakness which allowed the sweetness of external things still to insinuate itself into his heart. Victory over, and emancipation from, this, he asserts, "cannot, without God's grace, be achieved by the human will, which is by no means to be called free so long as it is subject to enslaving lusts." Then he proceeds: "The law, therefore, by teaching and commanding what cannot be fulfilled without grace, demonstrates to man his weakness, in order that the weakness, thus proved, may resort to the Saviour, by whose healing the will may be able to do what it found impossible in its weakness. So, then, the law brings us to faith, faith obtains the Spirit in fuller measure, the Spirit sheds love abroad in us, and love fulfils the law. For this reason the law is called a schoolmaster under whose threatening and severity 'whosoever shall call on the name of the Lord shall be delivered.' But 'how shall they call on Him in whom they have not believed?' Wherefore, that the letter without the Spirit may not kill, the life-giving Spirit is given to those that believe and call upon Him; but the love of God is poured out into our hearts by the Holy Spirit who is given to us, so that the words of the same apostle, 'Love is the fulfilling of the law,' may be realized. Thus the law

[58] As referred to above, note 36.

is good to him that uses it lawfully; and he uses it lawfully, who, understanding wherefore it was given, betakes himself, under the pressure of its threatening, to liberating grace. Whoever ungratefully despises this grace by which the ungodly is justified, and trusts in his own strength for fulfilling the law, being ignorant of God's righteousness, and going about to establish his own righteousness, is not submitting himself to the righteousness of God; and therefore the law is made to him not a help to pardon, but the bond of guilt; not because the law is evil, but because 'sin,' as it is written, ' works death to such persons by that which is good.' For by the commandment, he sins more grievously, who, by the commandment, knows how evil are the sins which he commits." Although Augustine states clearly that this letter is written against those " who arrogate too much to the human will, imagining that, the law being given, the will is, of its own strength, sufficient to fulfill the law, though not assisted by any grace imparted by the Holy Ghost, in addition to instruction in the law " — he refrains still from mentioning the names of the authors of this teaching, evidently out of a lingering tenderness in his treatment of them. This will help us to explain the courtesy of a note which he sent to Pelagius himself at about this time, in reply to a letter he had received some time before from him; of which Pelagius afterwards (at the Synod of Diospolis) made, to say the least of it, an ungenerous use. This note,[59] Augustine tells us, was written with "tempered praises " (wherefrom we see his lessening respect for the man), and so as to admonish Pelagius to think rightly concerning grace — so far as could be done without raising the dregs of the controversy in a formal note. This he accomplished by praying from the Lord for him, those good things by which he might be good forever, and might live eternally with Him who is eternal; and by asking his prayers in return, that he, too, might be made by the Lord such as he seemed to suppose he already was. How Augustine could really intend these prayers to be understood as an admonition to Pelagius

[59] " Epist." 146. See " On the Proceedings of Pelagius," 50, 51, 52.

to look to God for what he was seeking to work out for himself, is fully illustrated by the closing words of this almost contemporary letter to Anastasius: "Pray, therefore, for us," he writes, "that we may be righteous — an attainment wholly beyond a man's reach, unless he know righteousness, and be willing to practise it, but one which is immediately realized when he is perfectly willing; but this cannot be in him unless he is healed by the grace of the Spirit, and aided to be able." The point had already been made in the controversy, that, by the Pelagian doctrine, so much power was attributed to the human will, that no one ought to pray, "Lead us not into temptation, but deliver us from evil."

If he was anxious to avoid personal controversy with Pelagius himself in the hope that he might even yet be reclaimed, Augustine was equally anxious to teach the truth on all possible occasions. Pelagius had been intimate, when at Rome, with the pious Paulinus, bishop of Nola; and it was understood that there was some tendency at Nola to follow the new teachings. It was, perhaps, as late as 414, when Augustine made reply in a long letter,[60] to a request of Paulinus' for an exposition of certain difficult Scriptures, which had been sent him about 410.[61] Among them was Rom. xi. 28; and, in explaining it, Augustine did not withhold a tolerably complete account of his doctrine of predestination, involving the essence of his whole teaching as to grace: "For when he had said, 'according to the election they are beloved for their father's sake,' he added, 'for the gifts and calling of God are without repentance.' You see that those are certainly meant who belong to the number of the predestinated. . . . 'Many indeed are called, but few chosen'; but those who are elect, these are called 'according to His purpose'; and it is beyond doubt that in them God's foreknowledge cannot be deceived. These He foreknew and predestinated to be conformed to the image of His Son, in order that He might be the first born among many brethren. But 'whom He predestinated, them He also called.' This calling is 'according to His purpose,' this calling is 'without repentance,'" etc., quoting Rom. viii. 30–31. Then continuing, he says, "Those are not in this vocation, who do not persevere unto the end in the faith that worketh by love, although they walk in it a little while. . . . But the reason why some belong to it, and some do not, can easily be hidden, but cannot be unjust. For is there injustice with God? God forbid! For this belongs to those high judgments which, so to say, terrified the wondering apostle to look upon."

Among the most remarkable of the controversial sermons that were preached about this time, especial mention is due to two that were delivered at Carthage, midsummer of 413. The former of these [62] was preached on the festival of John the Baptist's birth (June 24), and naturally took the forerunner for its subject. The nativity of John suggesting the nativity of Christ, the preacher spoke of the marvel of the incarnation. He who was in the beginning, and was the Word of God, and was Himself God, and who made all things, and in whom was life, even this one "came to us. To whom? To the worthy? Nay, but to the unworthy! For Christ died for the ungodly, and for the unworthy, though He was worthy. We indeed were unworthy whom He pitied; but He was worthy who pitied us, to whom we say, For Thy pity's sake, Lord, free us! Not for the sake of our preceding merits, but for Thy pity's sake, Lord, free us; and for Thy name's sake be propitious to our sins,' not for our merit's sake. . . . For the merit of sins is, of course, not reward, but punishment." He then dwelt upon the necessity of the incarnation, and the necessity of a mediator between God and "the whole mass of the human race alienated from Him by Adam." Then quoting 1 Cor. iv. 7, he asserts that it is not our varying merits, but God's grace alone, that makes us differ, and that we are all alike, great and small, old and young, saved by one and the same Saviour. "What then, some one says," he continues, "even the infant needs a liberator? Certainly he needs one. And the witness to it is the mother that faithfully runs to church with the child to be baptized. The witness is Mother Church herself, who receives

[62] "Sermon" 293.

the child for washing, and either for dismissing him [from this life] freed, or nurturing him in piety. . . . Last of all, the tears of his own misery are witness in the child himself. . . . Recognize the misery, extend the help. Let all put on bowels of mercy. By as much as they cannot speak for themselves, by so much more pityingly let us speak for the little ones " — and then follows a passage calling on the Church to take the grace of infants in their charge as orphans committed to their care, which is in substance repeated from a former sermon.[63] The speaker proceeded to quote Matt. i. 21, and apply it. If Jesus came to save from sins, and infants are brought to Him, it is to confess that they, too, are sinners. Then, shall they be withheld from baptism? " Certainly, if the child could speak for himself, he would repel the voice of opposition, and cry out, ' Give me Christ's life! In Adam I died: give me Christ's life; in whose sight I am not clean, even if I am an infant whose life has been but one day in the earth.' " " No way can be found," adds the preacher, " of coming into the life of this world except by Adam; no way can be found of escaping punishment in the next world except by Christ. Why do you shut up the one door? " Even John the Baptist himself was born in sin; and absolutely no one can be found who was born apart from sin, until you find one who was born apart from Adam. " ' By one man sin entered into the world, and by sin, death; and so it passed through upon all men.' If these were my words, could this sentiment be expressed more expressly, more clearly, more fully? "

Three days afterwards,[64] on the invitation of the Bishop of Carthage, Augustine preached a sermon professedly directed against the Pelagians,[65] which takes up the threads hinted at in the former discourse, and develops a full polemic

---

[63] " Sermon " 176. 2.

[64] The inscription says, " V Calendas Julii," i.e., June 27; but it also says, " *In natalis martyris Guddentis,*" whose day appears to have been July 18. Some of the martyrologies assign 28th of June to Gaudentius (which some copies read here), but possibly none to Guddene.

[65] " Sermon " 294.

with reference to the baptism of infants. He began, formally enough, with the determination of the question in dispute. The Pelagians concede that infants should be baptized. The only question is, for what are they baptized? We say that they would not otherwise have salvation and eternal life; but they say it is not for salvation, not for eternal life, but for the kingdom of God. " The child, they say, although not baptized, by the desert of his innocence, in that he has no sin at all, either actual or original, either from himself or contracted from Adam, necessarily has salvation and eternal life even if not baptized; but is to be baptized for this reason — that he may enter into the kingdom of God, i.e., into the kingdom of heaven." He then shows that there is no eternal life outside the kingdom of heaven, no middle place between the right and left hand of the judge at the last day, and that, therefore, to exclude one from the kingdom of God is to consign him to the pains of eternal fire; while, on the other side, no one ascends into heaven unless he has been made a member of Christ, and this can only be by faith — which, in an infant's case, is professed by another in his stead. He then treats, at length, some of the puzzling questions with which the Pelagians were wont to try the catholics; and then breaking off suddenly, he took a volume in his hands. " I ask you," he said, " to bear with me a little: I will read somewhat. It is St. Cyprian whom I hold in my hand, the ancient bishop of this see. What he thought of the baptism of infants — nay, what he has shown that the Church always thought — learn in brief. For it is not enough for them to dispute and argue, I know not what impious novelties: they even try to charge us with asserting something novel. It is on this account that I read here St. Cyprian, in order that you may perceive that the orthodox understanding and catholic sense reside in the words which I have been just now speaking to you. He was asked whether an infant ought to be baptized before he was eight days old, seeing that by the ancient law no infant was allowed to be circumcised unless he was eight days old. A question arose from this as to the day of baptism — for concerning the origin of sin there was no question; and therefore from this thing of which there was no question, that question that had arisen was settled." And then he read to them the passage out of Cyprian's letter to Fidus, which declared that he, and all the council with him, unanimously thought that infants should be baptized at the earliest possible age, lest they should die in their inherited sin, and so pass into eternal punishment.[66] The sermon closed with a tender warning to the teachers of these strange doctrines: he might call them heretics with truth, but he will not; let the Church seek still their salvation, and not mourn them as dead; let them be exhorted as friends, not striven with as enemies. " They disparage us," he says, " we will bear it; let them not disparage the rule [of faith], let them not disparage the truth; let them not contradict the Church, which labours every day for the remission of infants' original sin. This thing is settled. The errant disputer may be borne with in other questions that have not been thoroughly canvassed, that are not yet settled by the full authority of the Church — their error should be borne with: it ought not to extend so far, that they endeavour to shake even the very foundation of the Church! " He hints that although the patience hitherto exhibited towards them is " perhaps not blameworthy," yet patience may cease to be a virtue, and become culpable negligence: in the mean time, however, he begs that the catholics should continue amicable, fraternal, placid, loving, long suffering.

Augustine himself gives us a view of the progress of the controversy at this time in a letter written in 414.[67] The Pelagians had everywhere scattered the seeds of their new error; and although some, by his ministry and that of his brother workers, had, "by God's mercy," been cured of their pest, yet they still existed in Africa, especially about Carthage, and were everywhere propagating their opinions in subterraneous whispers, for fear of the judgment of the Church. Whenever

[66] The passage is quoted at length in " On the Merits and Remission of Sins," iii. 10. Compare " Against Two Letters of the Pelagians," iv. 23.
[67] " Epist." 157. 22.

they were not refuted, they were seducing others to their following; and they were so spread abroad that he did not know where
they would break out next. Nevertheless, he was still unwilling to brand them as heretics, and was more desirous of healing them as sick members of the Church than of cutting them
off finally as too diseased for cure. Jerome also tells us that
the poison was spreading in both the East and the West, and
mentions particularly as seats where it showed itself the islands
of Rhodes and Sicily. Of Rhodes we know nothing further;
but from Sicily an appeal came to Augustine in 414 from one
Hilary,[68] setting forth that there were certain Christians about
Syracuse who taught strange doctrines, and beseeching Augustine to help him in dealing with them. The doctrines were
enumerated as follows: " They say (1) that man can be without sin, (2) and can easily keep the commandments of God
if he will; (3) that an unbaptized infant, if he is cut off by
death, cannot justly perish, since he is born without sin; (4)
that a rich man that remains in his riches cannot enter the
kingdom of God, except he sell all that he has; . . . (5) that
we ought not to swear at all; " (6) and, apparently, that the
Church is to be in this world without spot or blemish. Augustine suspected that these Sicilian disturbances were in some
way the work of Cœlestius, and therefore in his answer [69] informs his correspondent of what had been done at the Synod
of Carthage (412) against him. The long letter that he sent
back follows the inquiries in the order they were put by Hilary. To the first he replies, in substance, as he had treated the
same matter in the second book of the treatise, " On the Merits
and Remission of Sins," that it was opposed to Scripture, but
was less a heresy than the wholly unbearable opinion that this
state of sinlessness could be attained without God's help.
" But when they say that free will suffices to man for fulfilling the precepts of the Lord, even though unaided to good
works by God's grace and the gift of the Holy Spirit, it is to
be altogether anathematized and detested with all execrations.
For those who assert this are inwardly alien from God's grace,

---

[68] " Epist." 156.   [69] " Epist." 157. 22.

because being ignorant of God's righteousness, like the Jews of whom the apostle speaks, and wishing to establish their own, they are not subject to God's righteousness, since there is no fulfilment of the law except love; and of course the love of God is shed abroad in our hearts, not by ourselves, nor by the force of our own will, but by the Holy Ghost who is given to us." Dealing next with the second point, he drifts into the matter he had more fully developed in his work " On the Spirit and the Letter." " Free will avails for good works," he says, " if it be divinely aided, and this comes by humble seeking and doing; but when deserted by divine aid, no matter how excellent may be its knowledge of the law, it will by no means possess solidity of righteousness, but only the inflation of ungodly pride and deadly arrogance. This is taught us by that same Lord's Prayer; for it would be an empty thing for us to ask God ' Lead us not into temptation,' if the matter was so placed in our power that we would avail for fulfilling it without any aid from Him. . . . For this free will is free in proportion as it is sound, but it is sound in proportion as it is subject to divine pity and grace. For it faithfully prays, saying, ' Direct my ways according to Thy word, and let no iniquity reign over me.' For how is that free over which iniquity reigns? But see who it is that is invoked by it, in order that it may not reign over it. For it says not, ' Direct my ways according to free will because no iniquity shall rule over me,' but ' Direct my ways according to Thy *word, and let no iniquity rule over me.*' It is a prayer, not a promise; it is a confession, not a profession; it is a wish for full freedom, not a boast of personal power. For it is not every one ' who confides in his own power,' but ' every one who calls on the name of God, that shall be saved.' ' But how shall they call upon Him,' he says, ' in whom they have not believed? ' Accordingly, then, they who rightly believe, believe in order to call on Him in whom they have believed, and to avail for doing what they receive in the precepts of the law; since what the law commands, faith prays for."
" God, therefore, commands continence, and gives continence; He commands by the law, He gives by grace; He commands

by the letter, He gives by the spirit; for the law without grace makes the transgression to abound, and the letter without the spirit kills. He commands for this reason — that we who have endeavoured to do what He commands, and are worn out in our weakness under the law, may know how to ask for the aid of grace; and if we have been able to do any good work, that we may not be ungrateful to Him who aids us." The answer to the third point traverses the ground that was fully covered in the first book of the treatise " On the Merits and Remission of Sins," beginning by opposing the Pelagians to Paul in Rom. v. 12–19: " But when they say that an infant, cut off by death, unbaptized, cannot perish since he is born without sin — it is not this that the apostle says; and I think that it is better to believe the apostle than them." The fourth and fifth questions were new in this controversy; and it is not certain that they belong properly to it, though the legalistic asceticism of the Pelagian leaders may well have given rise to a demand on all Christians to sell what they had, and give to the poor. This one of the points, Augustine treats at length, pointing out that many of the saints of old were rich, and that the Lord and His apostles always so speak that their counsels avail to the right use, not the destruction, of wealth. Christians ought so to hold their wealth that they are not held by it, and by no means prefer it to Christ. Equal good sense and mildness are shown in his treatment of the question concerning oaths, which he points out were used by the Lord and His apostles, but advises to be used as little as possible lest by the custom of frequent oaths we learn to swear lightly. The question as to the Church, he passes over as having been sufficiently treated in the course of his previous remarks.

To the number of those who had been rescued from Pelagianism by his efforts, Augustine was now to have the pleasure of adding two others, in whom he seems to have taken much delight. Timasius and James were two young men of honorable birth and liberal education, who had, by the exhortation of Pelagius, been moved to give up the hope that they had in this world, and enter upon the service of God in an

ascetic life.[70] Naturally, they had turned to him for instruction, and had received a book to which they had given their
study. They met somewhere with some of Augustine's writings, however, and were deeply affected by what he said as to
grace, and now began to see that the teaching of Pelagius
opposed the grace of God by which man becomes a Christian.
They gave their book, therefore, to Augustine, saying that it
was Pelagius', and asking him for Pelagius' sake, and for the
sake of the truth, to answer it. This was done, and the resulting book, " On Nature and Grace," sent to the young men, who
returned a letter of thanks [71] in which they professed their
conversion from their error. In this book, too, which was written in 415, Augustine refrained from mentioning Pelagius by
name,[72] feeling it better to spare the man while not sparing
his writings. But he tells us, that, on reading the book of Pelagius to which it was an answer, it became clear to him beyond
any doubt that his teaching was distinctly anti-Christian; [73]
and when speaking of his own book privately to a friend, he
allows himself to call it " a considerable book against *the heresy* of Pelagius, which he had been constrained to write by
some brethren whom he had persuaded to adopt his fatal error,
denying the grace of Christ." [74] Thus his attitude towards the
persons of the new teachers was becoming ever more and
more strained, in despite of his full recognition of the excellent motives that might lie behind their " zeal not according
to knowledge." This treatise opens with a recognition of the
zeal of Pelagius, which, as it burns most ardently against
those who, when reproved for sin, take refuge in censuring
their nature, Augustine compares with the heathen view as
expressed in Sallust's saying, " The human race falsely complains of its own nature," [75] and which he charges with not being according to knowledge, and proposes to oppose by an

[70] " Epist." 177.; and 179. 2.
[71] " Epist." 168. " On the Proceedings of Pelagius," 48.
[72] " On the Proceedings of Pelagius," 47; and " Epist." 186. 1.
[73] Compare " On Nature and Grace," 7; and " Epist." 186. 1.
[74] " Epist." 169. 13.
[75] " On Nature and Grace," 1. Sallust's " Jugurthine War," 1, *ad init.*

equal zeal against all attempts to render the cross of Christ of none effect. He then gives a brief but excellent summary of the more important features of the catholic doctrine concerning nature and grace (2–7). Opening the work of Pelagius, which had been placed in his hands, he examines his doctrine of sin, its nature and effects. Pelagius, he points out, draws a distinction, sound enough in itself, between what is " possible " and what is " actual," but applies it unsoundly to sin, when he says that every man has the *possibility* of being without sin (8–9), and therefore without condemnation. Not so, says Augustine; an infant who dies unbaptized has no possibility of salvation open to him; and the man who has lived and died in a land where it was impossible for him to hear the name of Christ, has had no possibility open to him of becoming righteous by nature and free will. If this be not so, Christ is dead in vain, since all men then might have accomplished their salvation, even if Christ had never died (10). Pelagius, moreover, he shows, exhibits a tendency to deny the sinful character of all sins that are impossible to avoid, and so treats of sins of ignorance as to show that he excuses them (13–19). When he argues that no sin, because it is not a substance, can change nature, which is a substance, Augustine replies that this destroys the Saviour's work — for how can He save from sins if sins do not corrupt? And, again, if an act cannot injure a substance, how can abstention from food, which is a mere act, kill the body? In the same way sin is not a substance; but God is a substance — yea, the height of substance, and only true sustenance of the reasonable creature; and the consequence of departure from Him is to the soul what refusal of food is to the body (22). To Pelagius' assertion that sin cannot be punished by more sin, Augustine replies that the apostle thinks differently (Rom. i. 21–31). Then putting his finger on the main point in controversy, he quotes the Scriptures as declaring the present condition of man to be that of spiritual death. " The truth then designates as *dead* those whom this man declares to be unable to be damaged or corrupted by sin,

— because, forsooth, he has discovered sin to be no substance!" (25). It was by free will that man passed into this
state of death; but a dead man needs something else to revive
him — he needs nothing less than a Vivifier. But of vivifying
grace, Pelagius knew nothing; and by knowing nothing of a
Vivifier, he knows nothing of a Saviour; but rather by making
nature of itself able to be sinless, he glorifies the Creator at the
expense of the Saviour (39). Next is examined Pelagius' contention that many saints are enumerated in the Scriptures as
having lived sinlessly in this world. While declining to discuss
the question of fact as to the Virgin Mary (42), Augustine
opposes to the rest the declaration of John in 1 John i. 8, as
final, but still pauses to explain why the Scriptures do not
mention the sins of all, and to contend that all who ever were
saved under the Old Testament or the New, were saved by the
sacrificial death of Christ, and by faith in Him (40–50). Thus
we are brought, as Augustine says, to the core of the question,
which concerns, not the fact of sinlessness in any man, but
man's ability to be sinless. This ability Pelagius affirms of all
men, and Augustine denies of all " unless they are justified by
the grace of God through our Lord Jesus Christ and Him crucified " (51). Thus, the whole discussion is about grace, which
Pelagius does not admit in any true sense, but places only in
the nature that God has made (52). We are next invited to
attend to another distinction of Pelagius', in which he discriminates sharply between the nature that God has made,
the crown of which is free will, and the use that man makes of
this free will. The endowment of free will is a " capacity " ; it
is, because given by God in our making, a necessity of nature,
and not in man's power to have or not have. It is the right use
of it only, which man has in his power. This analysis, Pelagius illustrates at length, by appealing to the difference between the possession and use of the various bodily senses. The
ability to see, for instance, he says, is a necessity of our nature; we do not make it, we cannot help having it; it is ours
only to use it. Augustine criticises this presentation of the
matter with great sharpness (although he is not averse to the

analysis itself) — showing the inapplicability of the illustrations used — for, he asks, is it not possible for us to blind ourselves, and so no longer have the ability to see? and would not many a man like to control the " use " of his " capacity " to hear when a screechy saw is in the neighborhood? (55); and as well the falsity of the contention illustrated, since Pelagius has ignored the fall, and, even, were that not so, has so ignored the need of God's aid for all good, in any state of being, as to deny it (56). Moreover, it is altogether a fallacy, Augustine argues, to contend that men have the " ability " to make every use we can conceive of our faculties. We *cannot* wish for unhappiness; God *cannot* deny Himself (57); and just so, in a corrupt nature, the mere possession of a *faculty of choice* does not imply the ability to use that faculty for not sinning. " Of a man, indeed, who has his legs strong and sound, it may be said admissibly enough, ' whether he will or not, he has the capacity of walking ' ; but if his legs be broken, however much he may wish, he has not the ' capacity.' The nature of which our author speaks is corrupted " (57). What, then, can he mean by saying that, whether we will or not, we have the capacity of not sinning — a statement so opposite to Paul's in Rom. vii. 15? Some space is next given to an attempted rebuttal by Pelagius of the testimony of Gal. v. 17, on the ground that the " flesh " there does not refer to the baptized (60–70); and then the passages are examined which Pelagius had quoted against Augustine out of earlier writers — Lactantius (71), Hilary (72), Ambrose (75), John of Constantinople (76), Xystus — a blunder of Pelagius, who quoted from a Pythagorean philosopher, mistaking him for the Roman bishop Sixtus (77), Jerome (78), and Augustine himself (80). All these writers, Augustine shows, admitted the universal sinfulness of man — and especially he himself had confessed the necessity of grace in the immediate context of the passage quoted by Pelagius. The treatise closes (82 *sq.*) with a noble panegyric on that love which God sheds abroad in the heart, by the Holy Ghost, and by which alone we can be made keepers of the law.

The treatise " On Nature and Grace " was as yet unfinished, when the over-busy [76] scriptorium at Hippo was invaded by another young man seeking instruction. This time it was a zealous young presbyter from the remotest part of Spain, " from the shore of the ocean " — Paulus Orosius by name, whose pious soul had been afflicted with grievous wounds by the Priscillianist and Origenist heresies that had broken out in his country, and who had come with eager haste to Augustine, on hearing that he could get from him the instruction which he needed for confuting them. Augustine seems to have given him his heart at once; and, feeling too little informed as to the special heresies which he wished to be prepared to controvert, persuaded him to go on to Palestine to be taught by Jerome, and gave him introductions which described him as one " who is in the bond of catholic peace a brother, in point of age a son, and in honour a fellow-presbyter — a man of quick understanding, ready speech, and burning zeal." His departure to Palestine gave Augustine an opportunity to consult with Jerome on the one point that had been raised in the Pelagian controversy on which he had not been able to see light. The Pelagians had early argued,[77] that, if souls are created anew for men at their birth, it would be unjust in God to impute Adam's sin to them. And Augustine found himself unable either to prove that souls are transmitted (*traduced,* as the phrase is), or to show that it would not involve God in injustice to make a soul only to make it subject to a sin committed by another. Jerome had already put himself on record as a believer in both original sin and the creation of souls at the time of birth. Augustine feared the logical consequences of this assertion, and yet was unable to refute it. He therefore seized this occasion to send a long treatise on the origin of the soul to his friend, with the request that he would consider the subject anew, and answer his doubts.[78] In this treatise he

---

[76] For Augustine's press of work just now, see " Epist." 169. 1, 13.

[77] The argument occurs in Pelagius' " Commentary on Paul," written before 410, and is already before Augustine in " On the Merits and Remission of Sins," iii. 5.   [78] " Epist." 166.

stated that he was fully persuaded that the soul had fallen into sin, but by no fault of God or of nature, but of its own free will; and asked when could the soul of an infant have contracted the guilt, which, unless the grace of Christ should come to its rescue by baptism, would involve it in condemnation, if God (as Jerome held, and as he was willing to hold with him, if this difficulty could be cleared up) makes each soul for each individual at the time of birth? He professed himself embarrassed on such a supposition by the penal sufferings of infants, the pains they endured in this life, and much more the danger they are in of eternal damnation, into which they actually go unless saved by baptism. God is good, just, omnipotent: how, then, can we account for the fact that " in Adam all die," if souls are created afresh for each birth? " If new souls are made for men," he affirms, " individually at their birth, I do not see, on the one hand, that they could have any sin while yet in infancy; nor do I believe, on the other hand, that God condemns any soul which He sees to have no sin; " " and yet, whoever says that those children who depart out of this life without parting of the sacrament of baptism, shall be made alive in Christ, certainly contradicts the apostolic declaration," and " he that is not made alive in Christ must necessarily remain under the condemnation of which the apostle says that by the offence of one, judgment came upon all men to condemnation." " Wherefore," he adds to his correspondent, " if that opinion of yours does not contradict this firmly grounded article of faith, let it be mine also; but if it does, let it no longer be yours." [79] So far as obtaining light was concerned, Augustine might have spared himself the pain of this composition: Jerome simply answered [80] that he had no leisure to reply to the questions submitted to him. But Orosius' mission to Palestine was big with consequences. Once there, he became the accuser of Pelagius before John of Jerusalem, and the occa-

[79] An almost contemporary letter to Oceanus (" Epist." 180, written in 416) adverts to the same subject and in the same spirit, showing how much it was in Augustine's thoughts. Compare " Epist." 180. 2, 5.

[80] " Epist." 172.

sion, at least, of the trials of Pelagius in Palestine during the summer and winter of 415 which issued so disastrously, and ushered in a new phase of the conflict.

Meanwhile, however, Augustine was ignorant of what was going on in the East, and had his mind directed again to Sicily. About a year had passed since he had sent thither his long letter to Hilary. Now his conjecture that Cœlestius was in some way at the bottom of the Sicilian outbreak, received confirmation from a paper which certain catholic brethren brought out of Sicily, and which was handed to Augustine by two exiled Spanish bishops, Eutropius and Paul. This paper bore the title, " Definitions Ascribed to Cœlestius," and presented internal evidence, in style and thought, of being correctly so ascribed.[81] It consisted of three parts, in the first of which were collected a series of brief and compressed " definitions," or " ratiocinations " as Augustine calls them, in which the author tries to place the catholics in a logical dilemma, and to force them to admit that man can live in this world without sin. In the second part, he adduced certain passages of Scripture in defence of his doctrine. In the third part, he undertook to deal with the texts that had been quoted against his contention, not, however, by examining into their meaning, or seeking to explain them in the sense of his theory, but simply by matching them with others which he thought made for him. Augustine at once (about the end of 415) wrote a treatise in answer to this, which bears the title of " On the Perfection of Man's Righteousness." The distribution of the matter in this work follows that of the treatise to which it is an answer. First of all (1–16), the " ratiocinations " are taken up one by one and briefly answered. As they all concern sin, and have for their object to prove that man cannot be accounted a sinner unless he is able, in his own power, wholly to avoid sin — that is, to prove that a plenary natural ability is the necessary basis of responsibility — Augustine argues *per contra* that man can entail a sinfulness on himself for which and for the deeds of which he remains responsible, though he is no longer able to avoid sin; thus ad-

[81] See " On the Perfection of Man's Righteousness," 1.

mitting that for the race, plenary ability must stand at the root
of sinfulness. Next (17–22) he discusses the passages which
Cœlestius had advanced in defence of his teachings, viz., (1)
passages in which God commands men to be without sin, which
Augustine meets by saying that the point is, whether these
commands are to be fulfilled *without God's aid*, in the body of
this death, while absent from the Lord (17–20); and (2) passages in which God declares that His commandments are not
grievous, which Augustine meets by explaining that all God's
commandments are fulfilled only by *Love*, which finds nothing
grievous; and that this love is shed abroad in our hearts by the
Holy Ghost, without whom we have only fear, to which the
commandments are not only grievous, but impossible. Lastly,
Augustine patiently follows Cœlestius through his odd " oppositions of texts," explaining carefully all that he had adduced, in an orthodox sense (23–42). In closing, he takes up
Cœlestius' statement, that " it is quite possible for man not to
sin even in word, if God so will," pointing out how he avoids
saying " if God give him His help," and then proceeds to distinguish carefully between the differing assertions of sinlessness that may be made. To say that any man ever lived, or will
live, without needing forgiveness, is to contradict Rom. v. 12,
and must imply that he does not need a Saviour, against Mt.
ix. 12, 13. To say that after his sins have been forgiven, any
one has ever remained without sin, contradicts 1 Jno. i. 8 and
Mt. vi. 12. Yet, if God's help be allowed, this contention is
not so wicked as the other; and the great heresy is to deny the
necessity of God's constant grace, for which we pray when we
say, " Lead us not into temptation."

Tidings were now (416) beginning to reach Africa of what
was doing in the East. There was diligently circulated everywhere, and came into Augustine's hands, an epistle of Pelagius'
own " filled with vanity," in which he boasted that fourteen
bishops had approved his assertion that " man can live without sin, and easily keep the commandments if he wishes," and
had thus " shut the mouth of opposition in confusion," and
" broken up the whole band of wicked conspirators against

him." Soon afterwards a copy of an "apologetical paper," in which Pelagius used the authority of the Palestinian bishops against his adversaries, not altogether without disingenuousness, was sent by him to Augustine through the hands of a common acquaintance, Charus by name. It was not accompanied, however, by any letter from Pelagius; and Augustine wisely refrained from making public use of it. Towards midsummer Orosius came with more authentic information, and bearing letters from Jerome and Heros and Lazarus. It was apparently before his coming that a controversial sermon was preached, only a fragment of which has come down to us.[82] So far as we can learn from the extant part, its subject seems to have been the relation of prayer to Pelagianism; and what we have, opens with a striking anecdote: "When these two petitions — 'Forgive us our debts as we also forgive our debtors,' and 'Lead us not into temptation' — are objected to the Pelagians, what do you think they reply? I was horrified, my brethren, when I heard it. I did not, indeed, hear it with my own ears; but my holy brother and fellow-bishop Urbanus, who used to be presbyter here, and now is bishop of Sicca," when he was in Rome, and was arguing with one who held these opinions, pressed him with the weight of the Lord's Prayer, and "what do you think he replied to him? 'We ask God,' he said, 'not to lead us into temptation, lest we should suffer something that is not in our power — lest I should be thrown from my horse; lest I should break my leg; lest a robber should slay me, and the like. For these things,' he said, 'are not in my power; but for overcoming the temptations of my sins, I both have ability if I wish to use it, and am not able to receive God's help.'[83] You see, brethren," the good bishop adds, "how malignant this heresy is: you see how it horrifies all of you. Have a care that you be not taken by it." He then presses the general doctrine of prayer as proving that all good things come from God, whose aid is always necessary to us, and is always attainable by prayer; and closes as follows: "Consider, then, these things, my brethren,

[82] Migne's Edition of Augustine's Works, vol. v. Coll. 1719–1723.
[83] Compare the words of Cicero quoted above, p. 290.

when any one comes to you and says to you, ' What, then, are we to do if we have nothing in our power, unless God gives all things? God will not then crown us, but He will crown Himself.' You already see that this comes from that vein: it is a vein, but it has poison in it; it is stricken by the serpent; it is not sound. For what Satan is doing today is seeking to cast out from the Church by the poison of heretics, just as he once cast out from Paradise by the poison of the serpent. Let no one tell you that this one was acquitted by the bishops: there was an acquittal, but it was his confession, so to speak, his amendment, that was acquitted. For what he said before the bishops seemed catholic; but what he wrote in his books, the bishops who pronounced the acquittal were ignorant of. And perchance he was really convinced and amended. For we ought not to despair of the man who perchance preferred to be united to the catholic faith, and fled to its grace and aid. Perchance this was what happened. But, in any event, it was not the heresy that was acquitted, but the man who denied the heresy." [84]

The coming of Orosius must have dispelled any lingering hope that the meaning of the council's finding was that Pelagius had really recanted. Councils were immediately assembled at Carthage and Mileve, and the documents which Orosius had brought were read before them. We know nothing of their proceedings except what we can gather from the letters which they sent [85] to Innocent at Rome, seeking his aid in their condemnation of the heresy now so nearly approved in Palestine. To these two official letters, Augustine, in company with four other bishops, added a third private letter,[86] in which they took care that Innocent should be informed on all the points necessary to his decision. This important letter begins almost abruptly with a characterization of Pelagianism as inimical to the grace of God, and has grace for its subject throughout. It

[84] Compare the similar words in " Epist." 177. 3, which was written, not only after what had occurred in Palestine was known, but also after the condemnatory decisions of the African synods.

[85] " Epist." 175 and 176.

[86] " Epist." 177. The other bishops were Aurelius, Alypius, Evodius, and Possidius.

accounts for the action of the Palestinian synod, as growing out of a misunderstanding of Pelagius' words, in which he seemed to acknowledge grace, which these catholic bishops understood naturally to mean that grace of which they read in the Scriptures, and which they were accustomed to preach to their people — the grace by which we are justified from iniquity, and saved from weakness; while he meant nothing more than that by which we are given free will at our creation. " For if these bishops had understood that he meant only that grace which we have in common with the ungodly and with all, along with whom we are men, while he denied that by which we are Christians and the sons of God, what Catholic priest could have patiently listened to him — or even have borne him before his eyes? " The letter then proceeds to point out the difference between grace and natural gifts, and between grace and the law, and to trace out Pelagius' meaning when he speaks of grace, and when he contends that man can be sinless without any really inward aid. It suggests that Pelagius be sent for, and thoroughly examined by Innocent, or that he should be examined by letter or in his writings; and that he be not cleared until he unequivocally confessed the grace of God in the catholic sense, and anathematized the false teachings in the books attributed to him. The book of Pelagius which was answered in the treatise " On Nature and Grace " was enclosed, with this letter, with the most important passages marked: and it was suggested that more was involved in the matter than the fate of one single man, Pelagius, who, perhaps, was already brought to a better mind; the fate of multitudes already led astray, or yet to be deceived by these false views, was in danger.

At about this same time (417), the tireless bishop sent a short letter [87] to a Hilary, who seems to be Hilary of Norbonne, which is interesting from its undertaking to convey a characterization of Pelagianism to one who was as yet ignorant of it. It thus brings out what Augustine conceived to be its essential features. " An effort has been made," we read, " to raise a certain new heresy, inimical to the grace of Christ, against the

[87] " Epist." 178.

Church of Christ. It is not yet openly separated from the Church. It is the heresy of men who dare to attribute so much power to human weakness that they contend that this only belongs to God's grace — that we are created with free will and the possibility of not sinning, and that we receive God's commandments which are to be fulfilled by us; but, for keeping and fulfilling these commandments, we do not need any divine aid. No doubt, the remission of sins is necessary for us; for we have no power to right what we have done wrong in the past. But for avoiding and overcoming sins in the future, for conquering all temptations with virtue, the human will is sufficient by its natural capacity without any aid of God's grace. And neither do infants need the grace of the Saviour, so as to be liberated by it through His baptism from perdition, seeing that they have contracted no contagion of damnation from Adam." [88] He engages Hilary in the destruction of this heresy, which ought to be " concordantly condemned and anathematized by all who have hope in Christ," as a " pestiferous impiety," and excuses himself for not undertaking its full refutation in a brief letter. A much more important letter was sent off, at about the same time, to John of Jerusalem, who had conducted the first Palestinian examination of Pelagius, and had borne a prominent part in the synod at Diospolis. He sent with it a copy of Pelagius' book which he had examined in his treatise " On Nature and Grace," as well as a copy of that reply itself, and asked John to send him an authentic copy of the proceedings at Diospolis. He took this occasion seriously to warn his brother bishop against the wiles of Pelagius, and begged him, if he loved Pelagius, to let men see that he did not so love him as to be deceived by him. He pointed out that in the book sent with the letter, Pelagius called nothing the grace of God except nature; and that he affirmed, and even vehemently contended, that by free will alone, human nature was able to suffice for itself for working righteousness and keeping all God's commandments; whence any one could see that he opposed the grace of God of which the apostle spoke in Rom. vii. 24, 25,

[88] " Epist." 178.

and contradicted, as well, all the prayers and benedictions of the Church by which blessings were sought for men from God's grace. " If you love Pelagius, then," he continued, " let him, too, love you as himself — nay, more than himself; and let him not deceive you. For when you hear him confess the grace of God and the aid of God, you think he means what you mean by it. . . . But let him be openly asked whether he desires that we should pray God that we sin not; . . . whether he proclaims the assisting grace of God, without which we would do much evil; . . . whether he believes that even children who have not yet been able to do good or evil are nevertheless, on account of one man by whom sin entered into the world, . . . in need of being delivered by the grace of Christ." If he openly denies such things, Augustine would be pleased to hear of it.

Thus we see the great bishop sitting in his library at Hippo, placing his hands on the two ends of the world. That nothing may be lacking to the picture of his universal activity, we have another letter from him, coming from about this same time, that exhibits his care for the individuals who had placed themselves in some sort under his tutelage. Among the refugees from Rome in the terrible times when Alaric was a second time threatening the city, was a family of noble women — Proba, Juliana, and Demetrias [89] — grandmother, mother, and daughter — who, finding an asylum in Africa, gave themselves to God's service, and sought the friendship and counsel of Augustine. In 413 the granddaughter " took the veil " under circumstances that thrilled the Christian world, and brought out letters of congratulation and advice from Augustine and Jerome, and also from Pelagius. This letter of Pelagius seems not to have fallen into Augustine's way until now (416): he was so disturbed by it that he wrote to Juliana a long letter warning her against its evil counsels.[90] It was so shrewdly phrased, that, at first sight, Augustine was himself almost persuaded that it

---

[89] See " A Select Library of the Nicene and Post-Nicene Fathers of the Christian Church," First Series, i. p. 459, and the references there given. Compare Canon Robertson's vivid account of them in his " History of the Christian Church," 1904, ii. pp. 18, 145.   [90] " Epist." 188.

did somehow acknowledge the grace of God; but when he compared it with others of Pelagius' writings, he saw that here, too,
he was using ambiguous phrases in a non-natural sense. The
object of his letter (in which Alypius is conjoined, as joint author) to Juliana is to warn her and her holy daughter against
all opinions that opposed the grace of God, and especially
against the covert teaching of the letter of Pelagius to Demetrias.[91] "In this book," he says, "were it lawful for such an one
to read it, a virgin of Christ would read that her holiness and
all her spiritual riches are to spring from no other source than
herself; and thus before she attains to the perfection of blessedness, she would learn — which may God forbid! — to be ungrateful to God." Then, after quoting the words of Pelagius, in
which he declares that "earthly riches came from others, but
your spiritual riches no one can have conferred on you but
yourself; for these, then, you are justly praised, for these you
are deservedly to be preferred to others — for they can exist
only from yourself and in yourself," he continues: "Far be it
from any virgin of Christ to listen willingly to statements like
these, who understands the innate poverty of the human heart,
and therefore declines to be adorned otherwise than by the gifts
of her spouse. . . . Let her not listen to him who says, 'No
one can confer them on you but yourself, and they cannot exist
except from you and in you: ' but to him who says, 'We have
this treasure in earthen vessels, that the excellency of the power
may be of God, and not of us.' . . . And be not surprised that
we speak of these things as yours, and not from you; for we
speak of daily bread as ' ours,' but yet add ' give it to us,' lest
it should be thought it was from ourselves." Again, he warns
her that grace is not mere knowledge any more than mere nature; and that Pelagius, even when using the word "grace,"
means no inward or efficient aid, but mere nature or knowledge
or forgiveness of past sins; and beseeches her not to forget the
God of all grace from whom (Wisdom viii. 21) Demetrias had
that very virgin continence which was so justly her boast.

[91] Compare "On the Grace of Christ," 40. In the succeeding sections, some
of its statements are examined.

With the opening of 417, came the answers from Innocent to the African letters.[92] And although they were marred by much boastful language concerning the dignity of his see, which could not but be distasteful to the Africans, they admirably served their purpose in the satisfactory manner in which they, on the one hand, asserted the necessity of the " daily grace, and help of God," for our good living, and, on the other, determined that the Pelagians had denied this grace, and declared their leaders Pelagius and Cœlestius deprived of the communion of the Church until they should " recover their senses from the wiles of the Devil by whom they are held captive according to his will." Augustine may be pardoned for supposing that a condemnation pronounced by two provincial synods in Africa, and heartily concurred in by the Roman bishop, who had already at Jerusalem been recognized as in some sort the fit arbiter of this Western dispute, should settle the matter. If Pelagius had been before jubilant, Augustine found this a suitable time for his rejoicing.

About the same time with Innocent's letters, the official proceedings of the synod of Diospolis at last reached Africa, and Augustine lost no time (early in 417) in publishing a full account and examination of them ("On the Proceedings of Pelagius "), thus providing us with that inestimable boon, a full contemporary history of the chief events connected with the controversy up to this time. This treatise, which is addressed to Aurelius, bishop of Carthage, opens with a brief explanation of Augustine's delay heretofore, in discussing Pelagius' defence of himself in Palestine, as due to his not having received the official copy of the Proceedings of the Council at Diospolis (1–2a). Then Augustine proceeds at once to discuss at length the doings of the synod, point by point, following the official record step by step (2b–45). He treats at large here eleven items in the indictment, with Pelagius' answers and the synod's decision, showing that in all of them Pelagius either explained away his heresy, taking advantage of the ignorance of the judges of his books, or else openly repudiated or anathematized

[92] " Epist." 181, 182, 183, among Augustine's letters.

it. When the twelfth item of the indictment was reached (41b–
43), Augustine shows that the synod was so indignant at its
character (it charged Pelagius with teaching that men cannot
be sons of God unless they are sinless, and with condoning sins
of ignorance, and with asserting that choice is not free if it depends on God's help, and that pardon is given according to
merit), that, without waiting for Pelagius' answer, it condemned the statement, and Pelagius at once repudiated and
anathematized it (43). How could the synod act in such circumstances, he asks, except by acquitting the man who condemned the heresy? After quoting the final judgment of the
synod (44), Augustine briefly characterizes it and its effect
(45) as being indeed all that could be asked of the judges, but
of no moral weight to those better acquainted than they were
with Pelagius' character and writings. In a word, they approved his answers to them, as indeed they ought to have
done; but they by no means approved, but both they and he
condemned, his heresies as expressed in his writings. To this
statement, Augustine appends an account of the origin of
Pelagianism, and of his relations to it from the beginning,
which has the very highest value as history (46–49); and then
speaks of the character and doubtful practices of Pelagius (50–
58), returning at the end (59–65) to a thorough canvass of the
value of the acquittal which he obtained by such doubtful
practices at the synod. He closes with an indignant account of
the outrages which the Pelagians had perpetrated on Jerome
(66).

This valuable treatise is not, however, the only account of
the historical origin of Pelagianism that we have, from Augustine's hands. Soon after the death of Innocent (March 12,
417), he found occasion to write a very long letter [93] to the
venerable Paulinus of Nola, in which he summarized both the
history of, and the arguments against, this "worldly philosophy." He begins by saying that he knows Paulinus has loved
Pelagius as a servant of God, but is ignorant in what way he

---

[93] "Epist." 186, written conjointly with Alypius.

now loves him. For he himself not only has loved him, but
loves him still, but in different ways. Once he loved him as
apparently a brother in the true faith: now he loves him in
the longing that God will by His mercy free him from his
noxious opinions against God's grace. He is not merely following report in so speaking of him: no doubt report did for a
long time represent this of him, but he gave the less heed to it
because report is accustomed to lie. But a book of his [94] at last
came into his hands, which left no room for doubt, since in it
he asserted repeatedly that God's grace consisted of the gift
to man of the capacity to will and act, and thus reduced it to
what is common to pagans and Christians, to the ungodly and
godly, to the faithful and infidels. He then gives a brief account
of the measures that had been taken against Pelagius, and
passes on to a treatment of the main matters involved in the
controversy — all of which gather around the one magic word
of " the grace of God." He argues first that we are all lost — in
one mass and concretion of perdition — and that God's grace
alone makes us to differ. It is therefore folly to talk of deserving the beginnings of grace. Nor can a faithful man say that he
merits justification by his faith, although it is given to faith;
for at once he hears the words, " What hast thou that thou
didst not receive? " and learns that even the deserving faith
is the gift of God. But if, peering into God's inscrutable judgments, we go farther, and ask why, from the mass of Adam, all
of which undoubtedly has fallen from one into condemnation,
this vessel is made for honor, that for dishonor — we can only
say that we do not know more than the fact; and God's reasons are hidden, but His acts are just. Certain it is that Paul
teaches that all die in Adam; and that God freely chooses, by
a sovereign election, some out of that sinful mass, to eternal
life; and that He knew from the beginning to whom He would
give this grace, and so the number of the saints has always been
fixed, to whom he gives in due time the Holy Ghost. Others, no
doubt, are called; but no others are elect, or " called according

[94] The book given him by Timasius and James, to which " On Nature and
Grace " is a reply.

to his purpose." On no other body of doctrines, can it be possibly explained that some infants die unbaptized, and are lost. Is God unjust to punish innocent children with eternal pains? And are they not innocent if they are not partakers of Adam's sin? And can they be saved from that, save by the undeserved, and that is the gratuitous, grace of God? The account of the Proceedings at the Palestinian synod is then taken up, and Pelagius' position in his latest writings is quoted and examined. "But why say more?" he adds. . . . "Ought they not, since they call themselves Christians, to be more careful than the Jews that they do not stumble at the stone of offence, while they subtly defend nature and free will just like philosophers of this world who vehemently strive to be thought, or to think themselves, to attain for themselves a happy life by the force of their own will? Let them take care, then, that they do not make the cross of Christ of none effect by the wisdom of words (1 Cor. i. 17), and thus stumble at the rock of offense. For human nature, even if it had remained in that integrity in which it was created, could by no means have served its own Creator without His aid. Since then, without God's grace it could not keep the safety it had received, how can it without God's grace repair what it has lost?" With this profound view of the Divine immanence, and of the necessity of His moving grace in all the acts of all his creatures, as over against the heathen-deistic view of Pelagius, Augustine touched in reality the deepest point in the whole controversy, and illustrated the essential harmony of all truth.[95]

The sharpest period of the whole conflict was now drawing on.[96] Innocent's death brought Zosimus to the chair of the Roman See, and the efforts which he made to re-instate Pelagius and Cœlestius now began (September, 417). How little the

[95] Compare also Innocent's letter ("Epist." 181) to the Carthaginian Council, chap. 4, which also Neander, "History of the Christian Religion and Church," E. T. ii. 646, quotes in this connection, as showing that Innocent "perceived that this dispute was connected with a different way of regarding the relation of God's providence to creation." As if Augustine did not see this too!

[96] The book addressed to Dardanus, in which the Pelagians are confuted, but not named, belongs about at this time. Compare "Retractations," ii. 49.

Africans were likely to yield to his remarkable demands, may be seen from a sermon [97] which Augustine preached on the 23d of September, while Zosimus' letter (written on the 21st of September) was on its way to Africa. The preacher took his text from John vi. 54–66. "We hear here," he said, "the true Master, the Divine Redeemer, the human Saviour, commending to us our ransom, His blood. . . . He calls His body food, and His blood drink; and, in commending such food and drink, He says, 'Unless you eat My flesh, and drink My blood, ye shall have no life in you.' . . . What, then, is this eating and drinking, but to live? Eat life, drink life; you shall have life, and life is whole. This will come — that is, the body and blood of Christ will be life to every one — if what is taken visibly in the sacrament is in real truth spiritually eaten and spiritually drunk. . . . But that He might teach us that even to believe in Him is of gift, not of merit, He said, . . . 'No one comes to Me, except the Father who sent Me draw him.' *Draw* him, not *lead* him. This violence is done to the *heart,* not the flesh. Why do you marvel? Believe, and you come; love, and you are drawn. Think not that this is harsh and injurious violence; it is soft, it is sweet; it is sweetness itself that draws you. Is not the sheep drawn when the succulent herbage is shown to him? And I think that there is no compulsion of the body, but an assembling of the desire. So, too, do you come to Christ; wish not to plan a long journey — when you believe, then you come. For to Him who is everywhere, one comes by loving, not by taking a voyage. . . . And even after you have come, and are walking in the right way, become not proud, lest you perish from it: . . . 'happy are those that confide in Him,' not in *themselves,* but in *Him.* We are saved by grace, not of ourselves: it is the gift of God. . . . Why do I continually say this to you? . . . It is because there are men who are ungrateful to grace, and attribute much to unaided and wounded nature. It is true that man received great powers of free will at his creation; but he lost them by sinning. He has fallen into death; he has been made weak; he has been left half dead in the way, by

[97] "Sermon" 131, preached at Carthage.

robbers; the good Samaritan passing by . . . has lifted him up upon his ass, and borne him to the inn. Why should we boast? . . . But I am told that it is enough that sins are remitted in baptism. But does the removal of sin take away weakness too? . . . What! will you not see that after pouring the oil and the wine into the wounds of the man left half dead by the robbers, . . . he must still go to the inn where his weakness may be healed? . . . Nay, so long as we are in this life we bear a fragile body; . . . it is only after we are redeemed from all corruption that we shall find no sin, and receive the crown of righteousness. Grace, that was hidden in the Old Testament, is revealed in the New. Even though the Jew may be ignorant of it, why should Christians be enemies of grace? why presumptuous of themselves? why ungrateful to grace? For, why did Christ come? Was not nature already here — that very nature by the praise of which you are beguiled? Was not the law here? But the apostle says, ' If righteousness is of the law, then is Christ dead in vain.' What the apostle says of the law, that we say to these men about nature: if righteousness is by nature, then Christ is dead in vain. What then was said of the Jews, this we see repeated in these men. They have a zeal for God: I bear them witness that they have a zeal of God, but not according to knowledge. For, being ignorant of God's righteousness, and wishing to establish their own, they are not subject to the righteousness of God. My brethren, share my compassion. Where you find such men, wish no concealment; let there be no perverse pity in you: where you find them, wish no concealment at all. Contradict and refute, resist, or persuade them to us. For already two councils have, in this cause, sent letters to the Apostolic See, whence also rescripts have come back. The cause is ended: would that the error might some day end! Therefore we admonish so that they may take notice, we teach so that they may be instructed, we pray so that their way be changed." Here is certainly tenderness to the persons of the teachers of error; readiness to forgive, and readiness to go all proper lengths in recovering them to the truth. But here is also absolute firmness as to the truth itself, and a

manifesto as to policy. Certainly, on the lines of the policy
here indicated, the Africans fought out the coming campaign.
They met in council at the end of this year, or early in the
next (418); and formally replied to Zosimus, that the cause
had been tried, and was finished, and that the sentence that
had been already pronounced against Pelagius and Cœlestius
should remain in force until they should unequivocally
acknowledge that "we are aided by the grace of God through
Christ, not only to know, but to do, what is right, and that
in each single act; so that without grace we are unable to have,
think, speak, or do anything belonging to piety (Migne, " Patrologia Latina," x. col. 1723)." As we may see Augustine's hand
in this, so, doubtless, we may recognize it in that remarkable
piece of engineering which crushed Zosimus' plans within the
next few months. There is, indeed, no direct proof that it was
due to Augustine, or to the Africans under his leading, or to the
Africans at all, that the State interfered in the matter; it is even
in doubt whether the action of the Empire was put forth as a
rescript, or as a self-moved decree: but surely it is difficult to
believe that such a *coup de théâtre* could have been prepared
for Zosimus by chance; and as it is well known, both that Augustine believed in the righteousness of civil penalty for heresy, and invoked it on other occasions, and defended and used
it on this, and that he had influential friends at court with
whom he was in correspondence, it seems, on internal grounds,
altogether probable that he was the *Deus ex machinâ* who let
loose the thunders of ecclesiastical and civil enactment simultaneously on the poor Pope's devoted head.

The " great African Council " met at Carthage, on the 1st
of May, 418; and, after its decrees were issued, Augustine remained at Carthage, and watched the effect of the combination of which he was probably one of the moving causes. He
had now an opportunity to betake himself once more to his
pen. While still at Carthage, at short notice, and in the midst
of much distraction, he wrote a large work, in two books which
have come down to us under the separate titles of " On the
Grace of Christ," and " On Original Sin," at the instance of an-

other of those ascetic families which formed so marked a feature in those troubled times. Pinianus and Melania, the daughter of Albina, were husband and wife, who, leaving Rome amid the wars with Alaric, had lived in continence in Africa for some time, but now in Palestine had separated, he to become head of a monastery, and she an inmate of a convent. While in Africa, they had lived at Sagaste under the tutelage of Alypius, and in the enjoyment of the friendship and instruction of Augustine. After retiring to Bethlehem, like the other holy ascetics whom he had known in Africa, they kept up their relations with him. Like the others, also, they became acquainted with Pelagius in Palestine, and were well-nigh deceived by him. They wrote to Augustine that they had begged Pelagius to condemn in writing all that had been alleged against him, and that he had replied in the presence of them all, that "he anathematized the man who either thinks or says that the grace of God whereby Christ Jesus came into the world to save sinners is not necessary, not only for every hour and for every moment, but also for every act of our lives," and asserted that "those who endeavor to disannul it are worthy of everlasting punishment." [98] Moreover, they wrote that Pelagius had read to them, out of his book that he had sent to Rome,[99] his assertion "that infants ought to be baptized with the same formula of sacramental words as adults." [100] They wrote that they were delighted to hear these words from Pelagius, as they seemed exactly what they had been desirous of hearing; and yet they preferred consulting Augustine about them, before they were fully committed regarding them.[101] It was in answer to this appeal, that the present work was written; the two books of which take up the two points in Pelagius' asseveration — the theme of the first being "the assistance of the Divine grace towards our justification, by which God co-operates in all things for good to those who love Him, and whom He first

[98] "On the Grace of Christ," 2.

[99] The so-called "Confession of Faith" sent to Innocent after the Synod of Diospolis, but which arrived after Innocent's death.

[100] "On Original Sin," 1.

[101] Do., 5.

loved, giving to them that He may receive from them " —
while the subject of the second is " the sin which by one man
has entered the world along with death, and so has passed upon
all men." [102]

The first book, " On the Grace of Christ," begins by quoting
and examining Pelagius' anathema of all those who deny that
grace is necessary for every action (2 sq.). Augustine confesses
that this would deceive all who were not fortified by knowledge of Pelagius' writings; but asserts that in the light of them
it is clear that he means that grace is always necessary, because we need continually to remember the forgiveness of our
sins, the example of Christ, the teaching of the law, and the
like. Then he enters (4 sq.) upon an examination of Pelagius'
scheme of human faculties, and quotes at length his account
of them given in his book, " In Defence of Free Will," wherein
he distinguishes between the *possibilitas* (*posse*), *voluntas*
(*velle*), and *actio* (*esse*), and declares that the first only is
from God and receives aid from God, while the others are entirely ours, and in our own power. Augustine opposes to this
the passage in Phil. ii. 12, 13 (6), and then criticises (7 sq.)
Pelagius' ambiguous acknowledgment that God is to be praised
for man's good works, because the capacity for any action on
man's part is from God, by which he reduces all grace to the
primeval endowment of nature with " capacity " (*possibilitas,
posse*), and the help afforded it by the law and teaching. Augustine points out the difference between law and grace, and
the purpose of the former as a pedagogue to the latter (9 sq.),
and then refutes Pelagius' further definition of grace as consisting in the promise of future glory and the revelation of
wisdom, by an appeal to Paul's thorn in the flesh, and his experience under its discipline (11 sq.). Pelagius' illustrations
from our senses, of his theory of natural faculty, are then
sharply tested (16); and the criticism on the whole doctrine
is then made and pressed (17 sq.), that it makes God equally
sharer in our blame for evil acts as in our praise for good ones,
since if God does help, and His help is only His gift to us of

[102] " On the Grace of Christ," 55.

ability to act in either part, then He has equally helped to the evil deeds as to the good. The assertion that this " capacity of either part " is the fecund root of both good and evil is then criticised (19 *sq.*), and opposed to Mt. vii. 18, with the result of establishing that we must seek two roots in our dispositions for so diverse results — covetousness for evil, and love for good — not a single root for both in nature. Man's "·capacity," it is argued, is the root of nothing; but it is capable of both good and evil according to the moving cause, which, in the case of evil, is man-originated, while, in the case of good, it is from God (21). Next, Pelagius' assertion that grace is given according to our merits (23 *sq.*) is taken up and examined. It is shown, that, despite his anathema, Pelagius holds to this doctrine, and in so extreme a form as explicitly to declare that man comes and cleaves to God by his freedom of will alone, and without God's aid. He shows that the Scriptures teach just the opposite (24–26); and then points out how Pelagius has confounded the functions of knowledge and love (27 *sq.*), and how he forgets that we cannot have merits until we love God, while John certainly asserts that *God loved us first* (1 Jno. iv. 10). The representation that what grace does is to render obedience *easier* (28–30), and the twin view that prayer is only relatively necessary, are next criticised (32). That Pelagius never acknowledges real grace, is then demonstrated by a detailed examination of all that he had written on the subject (31–45). The book closes (46–55) with a full refutation of Pelagius' appeal to Ambrose, as if he supported him; and exhibition of Ambrose's contrary testimony as to grace and its necessity.

The object of the second book — " On Original Sin " — is to show, that, in spite of Pelagius' admissions as to the baptism of infants, he yet denies that they inherit original sin and contends that they are born free from corruption. The book opens by pointing out that there is no question as to Cœlestius' teaching in this matter (2–8), as he at Carthage refused to condemn those who say that Adam's sin injured no one but himself, and that infants are born in the same state that Adam was in before the fall, and openly asserted at Rome that there is no sin *ex traduce*. As for Pelagius, he is simply more cautious and mendacious than Cœlestius: he deceived the Council at Diospolis, but failed to deceive the Romans (5–13), and, as a matter of fact (14–18), teaches exactly what Cœlestius does. In support of this assertion, Pelagius' " Defence of Free Will " is quoted, wherein he asserts that we are born neither good nor bad, " but with a capacity for either," and " as without virtue, so without vice; and previous to the action of our own proper will, that that alone is in man which God has formed " (14). Augustine also quotes Pelagius' explanation of his anathema against those who say Adam's sin injured only himself, as meaning that he has injured man by setting a bad " example," and his even more sinuous explanation of his anathema against those who assert that infants are born in the same condition that Adam was in before he fell, as meaning that they are *infants* and he was a *man!* (16–18). With this introduction to them, Augustine next treats of Pelagius' subterfuges (19–25), and then animadverts on the importance of the issue (26–37), pointing out that Pelagianism is not a mere error, but a deadly heresy, and strikes at the very center of Christianity. A counter argument of the Pelagians is then answered (38–45), " Does not the doctrine of original sin make marriage an evil thing? " No, says Augustine, marriage is ordained by God, and is good; but it is a diseased good, and hence what is born of it is a good nature made by God, but this good nature in a diseased condition — the result of the Devil's work. Hence, if it be asked why God's gift produces any thing for the Devil to take possession of, it is to be answered that God gives his gifts liberally (Mt. v. 45), and makes men; but the Devil makes these men sinners (46). Finally, as Ambrose had been appealed to in the former book, so at the end of this it is shown that he openly proclaimed the doctrine of original sin, and here too, before Pelagius, condemned Pelagius (47 *sq.*).

What Augustine means by writing to Pinianus and his family that he was more oppressed by work at Carthage than anywhere else, may perhaps be illustrated from his diligence in preaching while in that capital. He seems to have been almost constantly in the pulpit, during this period " of the sharpest conflict with them," [103] preaching against the Pelagians. There is one series of his sermons, of the exact dates of which we can be pretty sure, which may be adverted to here — Sermons 151 and 152, preached early in October, 418; Sermon 155 on October 14, 156 on October 17, and 26 on October 18; thus following one another almost with the regularity of the days. The first of these was based on Rom. vii. 15–25, which he declares to contain dangerous words if not properly understood; for men are prone to sin, and when they hear the apostle so speaking they do evil, and think they are like him. They are meant to teach us, however, that the life of the just in this body is a war, not yet a triumph: the triumph will come only when death is swallowed up in victory. It would, no doubt, be better not to have an enemy than even to conquer. It would be better not to have evil desires: but we have them; therefore, let us not go after them. If they rebel against us, let us rebel against them; if they fight, let us fight; if they besiege, let us besiege: let us look only to this, that they do not conquer. With some evil desires we are born: others we make, by bad habit. It is on account of those with which we are born, that infants are baptized; that they may be freed from the guilt of inheritance, not from any evil of custom, which, of course, they have not. And it is on account of these, too, that our war must be endless: the concupiscence with which we are born cannot be done away as long as we live; it may be diminished, but not done away. Neither can the law free us, for it only reveals the sin to our greater apprehension. Where, then, is hope, save in the superabundance of grace? The next sermon (152) takes up the words in Rom. viii. 1–4, and points out that the inward aid of the Spirit brings all the help we need. " We, like farmers in the field, work from without: but, if there were no one who worked from within, the seed would not take root in the ground, nor would the sprout arise in the field, nor would the shoot grow strong and become a tree, nor would branches and fruit and leaves be

[103] " On the Gift of Perseverance," 55.

produced. Therefore the apostle himself distinguishes between the work of the workmen and of the Creator (1 Cor. iii. 6, 7). . . . If God give not the increase, empty is this sound within your ears; but if he gives, it avails somewhat that we plant and water, and our labor is not in vain." He then applies this to the individual, striving against his lusts; warns against Manichean error; and distinguishes between the three laws — the law of sin, the law of faith, and the law of deeds — defending the latter, the law of Moses, against the Manicheans; and then he comes to the words of the text, and explains its chief phrases, closing thus: "What other do we read here than that Christ is a sacrifice for sin? . . . Behold by what ' sin ' he condemned sin: by the sacrifice which he made for sins, he condemned sin. This is the law of the Spirit of life which has freed you from the law of sin and death. For that other law, the law of the letter, the law that commands, is indeed good; ' the commandment is holy and just and good: ' but ' it was weak by the flesh,' and what it commanded it could not bring about in us. Therefore there is one law, as I began by saying, that reveals sin to you, and another that takes it away: the law of the letter reveals sin, the law of grace takes it away." Sermon 155 covers the same ground, and more, taking the broader text, Rom. viii. 1–11, and fully developing its teaching, especially as discriminating between the law of sin and the law of Moses and the law of faith; the law of Moses being the holy law of God written with His finger on the tables of stone, while the law of the Spirit of life is nothing other than the same law written in the heart, as the prophet (Jer. xxxi. 33) clearly declares. So written, it does not terrify from without, but soothes from within. Great care is also taken, lest by such phrases as, " walk in the Spirit, not in the flesh," " who shall deliver me from the body of this death? " a hatred of the body should be begotten. " Thus you shall be freed from the body of this death, not by having no body, but by having another one and dying no more. If, indeed, he had not added, ' of this death,' . . . perchance an error might have been suggested to the human mind, and it might have been said, ' You see that God does not wish us

to have a body.' But He says, ' the body of this death.' Take
away death, and the body is good. Let our last enemy, death,
be taken away, and my dear flesh will be mine for eternity. For
no one can ever ' hate his own flesh.' Although the ' spirit lusts
against the flesh, and the flesh against the spirit,' although
there is now a battle in this house, yet the husband is seeking
by his strife not the ruin of, but concord with, his wife. Far be
it, far be it, my brethren, that the spirit should hate the flesh
in lusting against it! It hates the vices of the flesh; it hates the
wisdom of the flesh; it hates the contention of death. This corruption shall put on incorruption — this mortal shall put on
immortality; it is sown a natural body; it shall rise a spiritual
body; and you shall see full and perfect concord — you shall
see the creature praise the Creator." One of the special interests of such passages is to show, that, even at this early date,
Augustine was careful to guard his hearers from Manichean
error while proclaiming original sin. One of the sermons which,
probably, was preached about this time (153), is even entitled,
" Against the Manicheans openly, but tacitly against the Pelagians," and bears witness to the early development of the
method that he was somewhat later to use effectively against
Julian's charges of Manicheanism against the catholics.[104]
Three days afterwards, Augustine preached on the next few
verses, Rom. viii. 12–17 (156), but can scarcely be said to have
risen to the height of its great argument. The greater part of
the sermon is occupied with a discussion of the law, why it
was given, how it is legitimately used, and its usefulness as a
pedagogue to bring us to Christ; then of the need of a mediator; and then, of what it is to live according to the flesh, which
includes living according to merely human nature; and the
need of mortifying the flesh in this world. All this, of course,
gave full opportunity for opposing the leading Pelagian errors;
and the sermon is brought to a close by a direct polemic against
their assertion that the function of grace is only to make it

[104] Compare, below, pp. 376–384. Neander, in the second volume (E. T.)
of his " History of the Christian Religion and Church," p. 659, discusses the
matter in a very fair spirit.

more easy to do what is right. " With the sail more easily, with the oar with more difficulty: nevertheless even with the oar we can go. On a beast more easily, on foot with more difficulty: nevertheless progress can be made on foot. It is not true! For the true Master who flatters no one, who deceives no one — the truthful Teacher and very Saviour to whom the most grievous pedagogue has led us — when he was speaking about good works, i.e., about the fruits of the twigs and branches, did not say, 'Without me, indeed, you can do something, but you will do it more easily with me;' He did not say, 'You can make your fruit without me, but more richly with me.' He did not say this! Read what He said: it is the holy gospel — bow the proud necks! Augustine does not say this: the Lord says it. What says the Lord? 'Without me you can do *nothing' !*" On the very next day, he was again in the pulpit, and taking for his text chiefly the ninety-fourth Psalm.[105] The preacher began [106] by quoting the sixth verse, and laying stress on the words " our Maker." "No Christian," he said, "doubted that God had made him, and that in such a sense that God created not only the first man, from whom all have descended, but that God to-day creates every man — as He said to one of His saints, ' Before that I formed thee in the womb, I knew thee.' At first He created man apart from man; now He creates man from man: nevertheless, whether man apart from man, or man from man, ' it is He that made us, and not we ourselves.'. . . Nor has He made us and then deserted us; He has not cared to make us, and not cared to keep us. . . . Will He who ' made us without being asked, desert us when He is besought?' But is it not just as foolish to say, as some say or are ready to say, that God made them men, but they make themselves righteous? . . . Why, then, do we pray to God to make us righteous? . . . The first man was created in a nature that was without fault or flaw. He was made righteous: he did not make himself righteous; what he did for himself was to fall and break his righteousness. God permitted it, as if He had said, ' Let him desert Me; let him find

[105] English version, xcv.; see verse 6.
[106] " Sermon " 26.

himself; and let his misery prove that he has no ability without Me.' In this way God wished to show man what free will was worth without God. O evil free will without God! . . . Behold, man was made good; and by free will man was made evil! When will the evil man make himself good by free will deserting God? When good, he was not able to keep himself good; and now that he is evil, is he to make himself good? . . . Nay, behold, He that made us has also made us 'His people' (Ps. xciv. 7, Eng. Vers. xcv. 7). Nature is common to all, but grace is not. It is not to be confounded with nature; but if it were, it would still be gratuitous. For certainly no man, before he existed, deserved to come into existence. And yet God has made him, and that not like the beasts or a stock or a stone, but in His own image. Who has given this benefit? . . . He gave it who was in existence: he received it who was not. And only He could do this, who calls the things that are not as though they were: of whom the apostle says that 'He chose us before the foundation of the world.' We have been made in this world, and yet the world was not when we were chosen. Ineffable! wonderful! They are chosen who are not: neither does He err in choosing, nor choose in vain. He chooses, and has elect whom He is to create to be chosen: He has them in Himself, not indeed in His nature, but in His prescience. Let us not, then, glory. If we are men, He made us. If we are believers, He made us this too. . . . He who sent the Lamb to be slain has, out of wolves, made us sheep. This is grace. And it is an even greater grace than that grace of nature by which we were all made men." " I am continually endeavouring to discuss such things as these," said the preacher, " against a new heresy which is attempting to rise; because I wish you to be fixed in the good, untouched by the evil. . . . For, disputing against grace in favor of free will, they became an offence to pious and catholic ears. They began to create horror; they began to be avoided as a fixed pest; it began to be said of them, that they argued against grace. And they found such a device as this: . . . 'Because I defend man's free will, and say that free will is sufficient in order that I may be righteous,' says one, ' I do not

say that it is without the grace of God.' The ears of the pious
are pricked up, and he who hears this, already begins to rejoice:
'Thanks be to God! He does not defend free will without the
grace of God! There is free will, but it avails nothing without the grace of God.' If, then, they do not defend free will
without the grace of God, what evil do they say? Expound
to us, O teacher, what grace you mean? 'When I say,' he says,
'the free will of man, you observe that I say "of man"?'
What then? 'Who created man?' God. 'Who gave him free
will?' God. 'If, then, God created man, and God gave man
free will, whatever man is able to do by free will, to whose
grace does he owe it, except to His who made him with free
will?' And this is what they think they say so acutely! You
see, nevertheless, my brethren, how they preach that general
grace by which we were created and by which we are men;
and, of course, we are men in common with the ungodly, and
are Christians apart from them. It is this grace by which we
are Christians, that we wish them to preach, this that we wish
them to acknowledge, this that we wish — of which the apostle says, 'I do not make void the grace of God, for if righteousness is by the law, Christ is dead in vain.'" Then the
true function of the law is explained, as a revealer of our sinfulness, and a pedagogue to lead us to Christ: the Manichean
view of the Old Testament law is attacked, but its insufficiency
for salvation is pointed out; and so we are brought back to
the necessity of grace, which is illustrated from the story of
the raising of the dead child in 2 Kings iv. 18–37 — the dead
child being Adam; the ineffective staff (by which we ought
to walk), the law; but the living prophet, Christ with his
grace, which we must preach. "The prophetic staff was not
enough for the dead boy: would dead nature itself have been
enough? Even this, by which we are made, although we nowhere read of it under this name, we nevertheless, because it
is given gratuitously, confess to be grace. But we show to you
a greater grace than this, by which we are Christians. . . .
This is the grace by Jesus Christ our Lord: it was He that
made us, — both before we were at all, it was He that made us,

and now, after we are made and fallen, it is He that has made us righteous, — and not we ourselves." There was but one mass of perdition from Adam, to which nothing was due but punishment; and from that mass vessels have been made unto honor. " Rejoice because you have escaped; you have escaped the death that was due, — you have received the life that was not due. 'But,' you ask, 'why did He make me unto honor, and another unto dishonor?' . . . Will you who will not hear the apostle saying, 'O man, who art thou that repliest against God?' hear Augustine? . . . Do you wish to dispute with me? Nay, wonder with me, and cry out with me, 'Oh the depth of the riches! ' Let us both be afraid, — let us both cry out, ' Oh the depth of the riches! ' Let us both agree in fear, lest we perish in error."

Augustine was not less busy with his pen, during these months, than with his voice. Quite a series of letters belong to the last half of 418, in which he argues to his distant correspondents on the same themes which he was so iterantly trying to make clear to his Carthaginian auditors. One of the most interesting of these was written to a fellow-bishop, Optatus, on the origin of the soul.[107] Optatus, like Jerome, had expressed himself as favoring the theory of a special creation of each at birth; and Augustine, in this letter as in the paper sent to Jerome, lays great stress on so holding our theories on so obscure a matter as to conform to the indubitable fact of the transmission of sin. This fact, such passages as 1 Cor. xv. 21 *sq.*, Rom. v. 12 *sq.*, make certain; and in stating this, Augustine takes the opportunity to outline the chief contents of the catholic faith over against the Pelagian denial of original sin and grace: that all are born under the contagion of death and in the bond of guilt; that there is no deliverance except in the one Mediator, Christ Jesus; that before His coming men received him as promised, now as already come, but with the same faith; that the law was not intended to save, but to shut up under sin and so force us back upon the one Saviour; and that the distribution of grace is sovereign. Au-

[107] " Epist." 190.

gustine pries into God's sovereign counsels somewhat more freely here than is usual with him. " But why those also are created who, the Creator foreknew, would belong to damnation, not to grace, the blessed apostle mentions with as much succinct brevity as great authority. For he says that God, 'wishing to show His wrath and demonstrate His power, endured with much longsuffering vessels of wrath fitted unto destruction' (Rom. ix. 22). . . . Justly, however, would he seem unjust in forming vessels of wrath for perdition, if the whole mass from Adam were not condemned. That, therefore, they are made on birth vessels of anger, belongs to the punishment due to them; but that they are made by re-birth vessels of mercy, belongs to the grace that is not due to them. God, therefore, shows his wrath — not, of course, perturbation of mind, such as is called wrath among men, but a just and fixed vengeance. . . . He shows also his power, by which he makes a good use of evil men, and endows them with many natural and temporal goods, and bends their evil to admonition and instruction of the good by comparison with it, so that these may learn from them to give thanks to God that they have been made to differ from them, not by their own deserts which were of like kind in the same mass, but by His pity. . . . But by creating so many to be born who, He foreknew, would not belong to his grace, so that they are more by an incomparable multitude than those whom he deigned to predestinate as children of the promise into the glory of His Kingdom — He wished to show by this very multitude of the rejected how entirely of no moment it is to the just God what is the multitude of those most justly condemned. And that hence also those who are redeemed from this condemnation may understand, that what they see rendered to so great a part of the mass was the due of the whole of it — not only of those who add many others to original sin, by the choice of an evil will, but as well of so many children who are snatched from this life without the grace of the Mediator, bound by no bond except that of original sin alone." With respect to the question more immediately concerning which the letter was written, Augustine explains that he is willing to accept the opinion that souls are created for men as they are born, if only it can be made plain that it is consistent with the original sin that the Scriptures so clearly teach. In the paper sent to Jerome, the difficulties of creationism are sufficiently urged; this letter is interesting on account of its statement of some of the difficulties of traducianism also — thus evidencing Augustine's clear view of the peculiar complexity of the problem, and justifying his attitude of balance and uncertainty between the two theories. "The human understanding," he says, "can scarcely comprehend how a soul arises from a parent's soul in the offspring; or is transmitted to the offspring as a candle is lighted from a candle and thence another fire comes into existence without loss to the former one. Is there an incorporeal seed for the soul, which passes, by some hidden and invisible channel of its own, from the father to the mother, when it is conceived in the woman? Or, even more incredible, does it lie enfolded and hidden within the corporeal seed?" He is lost in wonder over the question whether, when conception does not take place, the immortal seed of an immortal soul perishes; or, does the immortality attach itself to it only when it lives? He even expresses the doubt whether traducianism will explain what it is called in to explain, much better than creationism; in any case, who denies that God is the maker of every soul? Isaiah (lvii. 16) says, "I have made every breath"; and the only question that can arise is as to method — whether He "makes every breath from the one first breath, just as he makes every body of man from the one first body; or whether he makes new bodies indeed, from the one body, but new souls out of nothing." Certainly nothing but Scripture can determine such a question; but where do the Scriptures speak unambiguously upon it? The passages to which the creationists point only affirm the admitted fact that God makes the soul; and the traducianists forget that the word "soul" in the Scriptures is ambiguous, and can mean "man," and even a "dead man." What more can be done, then, than to assert what is certain, viz., that sin is propagated, and leave what is uncertain in the doubt in which God has chosen to place it?

This letter was written not long after the issue of Zosimus' "Tractoria," demanding the signature of all to African orthodoxy; and Augustine sends Optatus "copies of the recent letters which have been sent forth from the Roman see, whether specially to the African bishops or generally to all bishops," on the Pelagian controversy, "lest perchance they had not yet reached" his correspondent, who, it is very evi--dent, he was anxious should thoroughly realize "that the authors, or certainly the most energetic and noted teachers," of these new heresies, "had been condemned in the whole Christian world by the vigilance of episcopal councils aided by the Saviour who keeps His Church, as well as by two venerable overseers of the Apostolical see, Pope Innocent and Pope Zosimus, unless they should show repentance by being convinced and reformed." To this zeal we owe it that the letter contains an extract from Zosimus' "Tractoria," one of the two brief fragments of that document that have reached our day.

There was another ecclesiastic in Rome, besides Zosimus, who was strongly suspected of favoring the Pelagians — the presbyter Sixtus, who afterwards became Pope Sixtus III. But when Zosimus sent forth his condemnation of Pelagianism, Sixtus sent also a short letter to Africa addressed to Aurelius of Carthage, which, though brief, indicated a considerable vigor against the heresy which he was commonly believed to have before defended,[108] and which claimed him as its own.[109] Some months afterwards, he sent another similar, but longer, letter to Augustine and Alypius, more fully expounding his rejection of "the fatal dogma" of Pelagius, and his acceptance of "that grace of God freely given by Him to small and great, to which Pelagius' dogma was diametrically opposed." Augustine was overjoyed with these developments. He quickly replied in a short letter [110] in which he expresses the delight

---

[108] See "Epist." 194. 1.

[109] See "Epist." 191. 1.

[110] "Epist." 191.

he has in learning from Sixtus' own hand that he is not a defender of Pelagius, but a preacher of grace. And close upon the heels of this he sent another much longer letter,[111] in which he discusses the subtler arguments of the Pelagians with an anxious care that seems to bear witness to his desire to confirm and support his correspondent in his new opinions. Both letters testify to Augustine's approval of the persecuting measures which had been instituted by the Roman see in obedience to the emperor; and urge on Sixtus his duty not only to bring the open heretics to deserved punishment, but to track out those who spread their poison secretly, and even to remember those whom he had formerly heard announcing the error before it had been condemned, and who were now silent through fear, and to bring them either to open recantation of their former beliefs, or to punishment. It is pleasanter to recall our thoughts to the dialectic of these letters. The greater part of the second is given to a discussion of the gratuitousness of grace, which, just because grace, is given to no preceding merits. Many subtle objections to this doctrine were brought forward by the Pelagians. They said that "free will was taken away if we asserted that man did not have even a good will without the aid of God"; that we made "God an accepter of persons, if we believed that without any preceding merits He had mercy on whom He would, and whom He would He called, and whom He would He made religious"; that "it was unjust, in one and the same case, to deliver one and punish another"; that, if such a doctrine is preached, "men who do not wish to live rightly and faithfully, will excuse themselves by saying that they have done nothing evil by living ill, since they have not received the grace by which they might live well"; that it is a puzzle "how sin can pass over to the children of the faithful, when it has been remitted to the parents in baptism"; that "children respond truly by the mouth of their sponsors that they believe in remission of sins, but not because sins are remitted to *them,* but because they believe that sins are remitted in the church or in baptism to

[111] " Epist." 194.

those in whom they are found, not to those in whom they do not exist," and consequently they said that "they were unwilling that infants should be so baptized unto remission of sins as if this remission took place in them," for (they contend) "they have no sin; but they are to be baptized, although without sin, with the same rite of baptism through which remission of sins takes place in any that are sinners." This last objection is especially interesting,[112] because it furnishes us with the reply which the Pelagians made to the argument that Augustine so strongly pressed against them from the very act and ritual of baptism, as implying remission of sins.[113] His rejoinder to it here is to point to the other parts of the same ritual, and to ask why, then, infants are exorcised and exsufflated in baptism. "For, it cannot be doubted that this is done fictitiously, if the Devil does not rule over them; but if he rules over them, and they are therefore not falsely exorcised and exsufflated, why does that prince of sinners rule over them except because of sin?" On the fundamental matter of the gratuitousness of grace, this letter is very explicit. "If we seek for the deserving of hardening, we shall find it. . . . But if we seek for the deserving of pity, we shall not find it; for there is none, lest grace be made a vanity if it is not given gratis, but rendered to merits. But, should we say that faith preceded and in it there is desert of grace, what desert did man have before faith that he should receive faith? For, what did he have that he did not receive? and if he received it, why does he glory as if he received it not? For as man would not have wisdom, understanding, prudence, fortitude, knowledge, piety, fear of God, unless he had received (according to the prophet) the spirit of wisdom and understanding, of prudence and fortitude, of knowledge and piety and the fear of God; as he would not have justice, love, continence, except the spirit was received of whom the apostle says, 'For you did not receive the spirit of fear, but of virtue, and love, and

---

[112] It appears to have been first reported to Augustine, by Marius Mercator, in a letter received at Carthage. See "Epist." 193. 3.

[113] As, for example, in "On the Merits and Remission of Sins," etc., i.

continence: ' so he would not have faith unless he received the spirit of faith of whom the same apostle says, ' Having then the same spirit of faith, according to what is written, " I believed and therefore spoke," we too believe and therefore speak.' But that He is not received by desert, but by His mercy who has mercy on whom He will, is manifestly shown where he says of himself, ' I have obtained mercy to be faithful.' " " If we should say that the merit of prayer precedes, that the gift of grace may follow, . . . even prayer itself is found among the gifts of grace " (Rom. viii. 26). " It remains, then, that faith itself, whence all righteousness takes beginning; . . . it remains, I say, that even faith itself is not to be attributed to the human will which they extol, nor to any preceding merits, since from it begin whatever good things are merits: but it is to be confessed to be the gratuitous gift of God, since we consider it true grace, that is, without merits, inasmuch as we read in the same epistle, ' God divides out the measure of faith to each' (Rom. xii. 3). Now, good works are done by man, but faith is wrought in man, and without it these are not done by any man. For all that is not of faith is sin " (Rom. xiv. 23).

By the same messenger who carried this important letter to Sixtus, Augustine sent also a letter to Mercator,[114] an African layman who was then apparently at Rome, but who was afterwards (in 429) to render service by instructing the Emperor Theodosius as to the nature and history of Pelagianism, and so preventing the appeal of the Pelagians to him from being granted. Now he appears as an inquirer: Augustine, while at Carthage, had received a letter from him in which he had consulted him on certain questions that the Pelagians had raised, but in such a manner as to indicate his opposition to them. Press of business had compelled the postponement of the reply until this later date. One of the questions that Mercator had put concerned the Pelagian account of infants sharing in the one baptism unto remission of sins, which we have seen Augustine answering when writing to Sixtus. In this

[114] " Epist." 193.

letter he replies: " Let them, then, hear the Lord (Jno. iii. 36). Infants, therefore, who are made believers by others, by whom they are brought to baptism, are, of course, unbelievers by others, if they are in the hands of such as do not believe that they should be brought, inasmuch as they believe they are nothing profited; and accordingly, if they believe by believers, and have eternal life, they are unbelievers by unbelievers, and shall not see life, but the wrath of God abideth on them. For it is not said, ' it *comes* on them,' but ' it *abideth* on them,' because it was on them from the beginning, and will not be taken from them except by the grace of God through Jesus Christ, our Lord. . . . Therefore, when children are baptized, the confession is made that they are believers, and it is not to be doubted that those who are not believers are condemned: let them, then, dare to say now, if they can, that they contract no evil from their origin to be condemned by the just God, and have no contagion of sin." The other matter on which Mercator sought light concerned the statement that universal death proved universal sin: [115] he reported that the Pelagians replied that not even death was universal — that Enoch, for instance, and Elijah, had not died. Augustine adds those who are to be found living at the second advent, who are not to die, but be " changed"; and replies that Rom. v. 12 is perfectly explicit that there is no death in the world except that which comes from sin, and that God is a Saviour, and we cannot at all "deny that He is able to do that, now, in any that he wishes, without death, which we undoubtingly believe is to be done in so many after death." He adds that the difficult question is not why Enoch and Elijah did not die, if death is the punishment of sin; but why, such being the case, the justified ever die; and he refers his correspondent to his book " On the Baptism of Infants " [116] for a resolution of this greater difficulty.

It was probably at the very end of 418 that Augustine wrote a letter of some length [117] to Asellicus, in reply to one

[115] Compare " On Dulcitius' Eight Questions," question 3.
[116] That is, " On the Merits and Remission of Sins," etc., ii. 49 *sq.*
[117] " Epist." 196.

which he had written on "avoiding the deception of Judaism," to the primate of the Bizacene province, and which that ecclesiastic had sent to Augustine for answering. He discusses in this the law of the Old Testament. He opens by pointing out that the apostle forbids Christians to Judaize (Gal. ii. 14–16), and explains that it is not merely the ceremonial law that we may not depend upon, "but also what is said in the law, ' Thou shalt not covet ' (which no one, of course, doubts is to be said to Christians too), does not justify man, except by faith in Jesus Christ and the grace of God through Jesus Christ our Lord." He then expounds the use of the law: " This, then, is the usefulness of the law: that it shows man to himself, so that he may know his weakness, and see how, by the prohibition, carnal concupiscence is rather increased than healed. . . . The use of the law is, thus, to convince man of his weakness, and force him to implore the medicine of grace that is in Christ." " Since these things are so," he adds, " those who rejoice that they are Israelites after the flesh, and glory in the law apart from the grace of Christ, these are those concerning whom the apostle said that ' being ignorant of God's righteousness, and wishing to establish their own, they are not subject to God's righteousness; ' since he calls ' God's righteousness ' that which is from God to man; and ' their own,' what they think that the commandments suffice for them to do without the help and gift of Him who gave the law. But they are like those who, while they profess to be Christians, so oppose the grace of Christ, that they suppose that they fulfil the divine commands by human powers, . . . and, ' wishing to establish their own,' are ' not subject to the righteousness of God,' and so, not indeed in name, but yet in error, Judaize. This sort of men found heads for themselves in Pelagius and Cœlestius, the most acute asserters of this impiety, who by God's recent judgment, through his diligent and faithful servants, have been deprived even of catholic communion, and, on account of an impenitent heart, persist still in their condemnation."

At the beginning of 419, a considerable work was published by Augustine on one of the more remote corollaries which the Pelagians drew from his teachings. It had come to his ears, that they asserted that his doctrine condemned marriage: " If only sinful offspring come from marriage," they asked, " is not marriage itself made a sinful thing? " The book which Augustine composed in answer to this query, he dedicated to, and sent along with an explanatory letter to, the Comes Valerius, a trusted servant of the Emperor Honorius, and one of the most steady opponents at court of the Pelagian heresy. Augustine explains [118] why he has desired to address the book to him: first, because Valerius was a striking example of those continent husbands of which that age furnishes us with many instances, and, therefore, the discussion would have especial interest for him; secondly, because of his eminence as an opponent of Pelagianism; and, thirdly, because Augustine had learned that he had read a Pelagian document in which Augustine was charged with condemning marriage by defending original sin. [119] The book in question is the first book of the treatise " On Marriage and Concupiscence." It is, naturally, tinged, or rather stained, with the prevalent ascetic notions of the day. Its doctrine is that marriage is good, and God is the maker of the offspring that comes from it, although now there can be no begetting and hence no birth without sin. Sin made concupiscence, and now concupiscence perpetuates sinners. The specific object of the work, as it states it itself, is " to distinguish between the evil of carnal concupiscence, from which man, who is born therefrom, contracts original sin, and the good of marriage " (i. 1). After a brief introduction, in which he explains why he writes, and why he addresses his book to Valerius (1–2), Augustine points out that conjugal chastity, like its higher sister-grace of continence, is God's gift. Thus copulation, but only for the propagation of children, has divine allowance (3–5). Lust, or "shameful concupiscence," however, he teaches, is not of the essence, but only an accident, of marriage. It did not

[118] " On Marriage and Concupiscence," i. 2.
[119] Compare the Benedictine Preface to " The Unfinished Work."

exist in Eden, although true marriage existed there; but arose from, and therefore only after, sin (6–7). Its addition to marriage does not destroy the good of marriage: it only conditions the character of the offspring (8). Hence it is that the apostle allows marriage, but forbids the " disease of desire " (1 Thess. iv. 3–5); and hence the Old Testament saints were even permitted more than one wife, because, by multiplying wives, it was not lust, but offspring, that was increased (9–10). Nevertheless, fecundity is not to be thought the only good of marriage: true marriage can exist without offspring, and even without cohabitation (11–13), and cohabitation is now, under the New Testament, no longer a duty as it was under the Old Testament (14–15), but the apostle praises continence above it. We must, then, distinguish between the goods of marriage, and seek the best (16–19). But thus it follows that it is not due to any inherent and necessary evil in marriage, but only to the presence, now, of concupiscence in all cohabitation, that children are born under sin, even the children of the regenerate, just as from the seed of olives only oleasters grow (20–24). And yet again, concupiscence is not itself sin in the regenerate; it is remitted as guilt in baptism: but it is the daughter of sin, and it is the mother of sin, and in the unregenerate it is itself sin, as to yield to it is even to the regenerate (25–39). Finally, as so often, the testimony of Ambrose is appealed to, and it is shown that he too teaches that all born from cohabitation are born guilty (40). In this book, Augustine certainly seems to teach that the bond of connection by which Adam's sin is conveyed to his offspring is not mere descent, or heredity, or mere inclusion in him, in a realistic sense, as partakers of the same numerical nature, but concupiscence. Without concupiscence in the act of generation, the offspring would not be a partaker of Adam's sin. This he had taught also previously, as, e.g., in the treatise " On Original Sin," from which a few words may be profitably quoted as succinctly summing up the teaching of this book on the subject: " It is, then, manifest, that that must not be laid to the account of marriage, in the absence of which even marriage would still have existed. . . .

Such, however, is the present condition of mortal men, that the connubial intercourse and lust are at the same time in action. . . . Hence it follows that infants, although incapable of sinning, are yet not born without the contagion of sin, . . . not, indeed, because of what is lawful, but on account of that which is unseemly: for, from what is lawful, nature is born; from what is unseemly, sin " (42).

Towards the end of the same year (419), Augustine was led to take up again the vexed question of the origin of the soul — both in a new letter to Optatus,[120] and by the zeal of the same monk, Renatus, who had formerly brought Optatus' inquiries to his notice — in an elaborate treatise entitled " On the Soul and its Origin," by way of reply to a rash adventure of a young man named Vincentius Victor, who blamed him for his uncertainty on such a subject, and attempted to determine all the puzzles of the question, though, as Augustine insists, on assumptions that were partly Pelagian and partly worse. Optatus had written in the hope that Augustine had heard by this time from Jerome, in reply to the treatise he had sent him on this subject. Augustine, in answering his letter, expresses his sorrow that he has not yet been worthy of an answer from Jerome, although five years had passed away since he wrote, but his continued hope that such an answer will in due time come. For himself, he confesses that he has not yet been able to see how the soul can contract sin from Adam and yet not itself be contracted from Adam; and he regrets that Optatus, although holding that God creates each soul for its birth, has not sent him the proofs on which he depends for that opinion, nor met its obvious difficulties. He rebukes Optatus for confounding the question of whether God makes the soul, with the entirely different one of how he makes it, whether *ex propagine* or *sine propagine*. No one doubts that God makes the soul, as no one doubts that He makes the body. But when we consider how he makes it, sobriety and vigilance become necessary lest we should unguardedly fall into the Pelagian heresy. Augustine defends his attitude of uncertainty, and enumerates the

[120] " Epist." 202, *bis*. Compare " Epist." 190.

points as to which he has no doubt: viz., that the soul is spirit, not body; that it is rational or intellectual; that it is not of the nature of God, but is so far a mortal creature that it is capable of deterioration and of alienation from the life of God, and so far immortal that after this life it lives on in bliss or punishment for ever; that it was not incarnated because of, or according to, preceding deserts acquired in a previous existence, yet that it is under the curse of sin which it derives from Adam, and therefore in all cases alike needs redemption in Christ.

The whole subject of the nature and origin of the soul, however, is most fully discussed in the four books which are gathered together under the common title of " On the Soul and its Origin." Vincentius Victor was a young layman who had recently been converted from the Rogatian heresy; on being shown by his friend Peter, a presbyter, a small work of Augustine's on the origin of the soul, he expressed surprise that so great a man could profess ignorance on a matter so intimate to his very being, and, receiving encouragement, wrote a book for Peter in which he attacked and tried to solve all the difficulties of the subject. Peter received the work with transports of delighted admiration; but Renatus, happening that way, looked upon it with distrust, and, finding that Augustine was spoken of in it with scant courtesy, felt it his duty to send him a copy of it, which he did in the summer of 419. It was probably not until late in the following autumn that Augustine found time to take up the matter; but then he wrote to Renatus, to Peter, and two books to Victor himself, and it is these four books together which constitute the treatise that has come down to us. The first book is a letter to Renatus, and is introduced by an expression of thanks to him for sending Victor's book, and of kindly feeling towards and appreciation for the high qualities of Victor himself (1–3). Then Victor's errors are pointed out — as to the nature of the soul (4–9), including certain far-reaching corollaries that flow from these (10–15), as well as, as to the origin of the soul (16–30); and the letter closes with some remarks on the danger of arguing from the silence of Scripture (30), on the self-contradictions of Victor (34), and

on the errors that must be avoided in any theory of the origin
of the soul that hopes to be acceptable — to wit, that souls
become sinful by an alien original sin, that unbaptized infants
need no salvation, that souls sinned in a previous state, and
that they are condemned for sins which they have not committed but would have committed had they lived longer. The
second book is a letter to Peter, warning him of the responsibility that rests on him as Victor's trusted friend and a clergyman, to correct Victor's errors, and reproving him for the uninstructed delight he had taken in Victor's crudities. It opens
by asking Peter what was the occasion of the great joy which
Victor's book brought him? could it be that he learned from
it, for the first time, the old and primary truths it contained?
(2–3); or was it due to the new errors that it proclaimed —
seven of which he enumerates? (4–16). Then, after animadverting on the dilemma in which Victor stood, either of being
forced to withdraw his violent assertion of creationism, or else
of making God unjust in His dealings with new souls (18), he
speaks of Victor's unjustifiable dogmatism in the matter (19–
21), and closes with severely solemn words to Peter on his responsibility in the premises (22–23). In the third and fourth
books, which are addressed to Victor, the polemic, of course,
reaches its height. The third book is entirely taken up with
pointing out to Victor, as a father to a son, the errors into
which he has fallen, and which, in accordance with his professions of readiness for amendment, he ought to correct. Eleven
are enumerated: 1. That the soul was made by God out of
Himself (3–7); 2. That God will continuously create souls
forever (8); 3. That the soul has desert of good before birth
(9); 4. (contradictingly) That the soul has desert of evil before birth (10); 5. That the soul deserved to be sinful before
any sin (11); 6. That unbaptized infants are saved (12); 7.
That what God predestinates may not occur (13); 8. That
Wisd. iv. 11 is spoken of infants (14); 9. That some of the man-
sions with the Father are outside of God's kingdom (15–17);
10. That the sacrifice of Christ's blood may be offered for the
unbaptized (18); 11. That the unbaptized may attain at the

resurrection even to the kingdom of heaven (19). The book closes by reminding Victor of his professions of readiness to correct his errors, and warning him against the obstinacy that makes the heretic (20–23). The fourth book deals with the more personal elements of the controversy, and discusses the points in which Victor had expressed dissent from Augustine. It opens with a statement of the two grounds of complaint that Victor had urged against Augustine; viz., that he refused to express a confident opinion as to the origin of the soul, and that he affirmed that the soul was not corporeal, but spirit (1–2). These two complaints are then taken up at length (2– 16 and 17–37). To the first, Augustine replies that man's knowledge is at best limited, and often most limited about the things nearest to him; we do not know the constitution of our bodies; and, above most others, this subject of the origin of the soul is one on which no one but God is a competent witness. Who remembers his birth? Who remembers what was before birth? But this is just one of the subjects on which God has not spoken unambiguously in the Scriptures. Would it not be better, then, for Victor to imitate Augustine's cautious ignorance, than that Augustine should imitate Victor's rash assertion of errors? That the soul is not corporeal, Augustine argues (18–35) from the Scriptures and from the phenomena of dreams; and then shows, in opposition to Victor's trichotomy, that the Scriptures teach the identity of " soul " and " spirit " (36–37). The book closes with a renewed enumeration of Victor's eleven errors (38), and a final admonition to his rashness (39). It is pleasant to know that Augustine found in this case, also, that righteousness is the fruit of the faithful wounds of a friend. Victor accepted the rebuke, and professed his better instruction at the hands of his modest but resistless antagonist.

The controversy now entered upon a new stage. Among the evicted bishops of Italy who refused to sign Zosimus' " Epistola Tractoria," Julian of Eclanum was easily the first, and at this point he appears as the champion of Pelagianism. It was a sad fate that arrayed this beloved son of his old friend against

Augustine, just when there seemed to be reason to hope that the controversy was at an end, and the victory won, and the plaudits of the world were greeting him as the saviour of the Church.[121] But the now fast-aging bishop was to find, that, in this "very confident young man," he had yet to meet the most persistent and most dangerous advocate of the new doctrines that had arisen. Julian had sent, at an earlier period, two letters to Zosimus, one of which has come down to us as a "Confession of Faith," and the other of which attempted to approach Augustinian forms of speech as much as possible; the object of both being to gain standing ground in the Church for the Italian Pelagians. Now he appears as a Pelagian controversialist; and in opposition to the book "On Marriage and Concupiscence," which Augustine had sent Valerius, he published an extended work in four thick books addressed to Turbantius. Extracts from the first of these books were sent by some one to Valerius, and were placed by him in the hands of Alypius, who was then in Italy, for transmission to Augustine. Meanwhile, a letter had been sent to Rome by Julian,[122] designed to strengthen the cause of Pelagianism there; and a similar one, in the names of the eighteen Pelagianizing Italian bishops, was addressed to Rufus, bishop of Thessalonica, and representative of the Roman see in that portion of the Eastern Empire which was regarded as ecclesiastically a part of the West, the design of which was to obtain the powerful support of this important magnate, perhaps, also, a refuge from persecution within his jurisdiction. These two letters came into the hands of the new Pope, Boniface, who gave them also to Alypius for transmission to Augustine. Thus provided, Alypius returned to Africa. The tactics of all these writings of Julian were essentially the same; he attempted not so much to defend Pelagianism, as to attack Augustinianism, and thus literally to carry the war into Africa. He insisted that the corruption of nature which Augustine

---

[121] Compare "Epist." 195.

[122] Julian afterwards repudiated this letter, perhaps because of some falsifications it had suffered; it seems to have been certainly his.

taught was nothing else than Manichæism; that the sovereignty of grace, as taught by him, was only the attribution of " acceptance of persons," and partiality, to God; and that his doctrine of predestination was mere fatalism. He accused the anti-Pelagians of denying the goodness of the nature that God had created, of the marriage that He had ordained, of the law that He had given, of the free will that He had implanted in man, as well as the perfection of His saints.[123] He insisted that this teaching also did dishonor to baptism itself which it professed so to honor, inasmuch as it asserted the continuance of concupiscence after baptism — and thus taught that baptism does not take away sins, but only shaves them off as one shaves his beard, and leaves the roots whence the sins may grow anew, and need cutting down again. He complained bitterly of the way in which Pelagianism had been condemned — that bishops had been compelled to sign a definition of dogma, not in council assembled, but sitting at home; and he demanded a rehearing of the whole case before a lawful council, lest the doctrine of the Manichæans should be forced upon the acceptance of the world.

Augustine felt a strong desire to see the whole work of Julian against his book " On Marriage and Concupiscence " before he undertook a reply to the excerpts sent him by Valerius; but he did not feel justified in delaying obedience to that officer's request, and so wrote at once two treatises, one an answer to these excerpts, for the benefit of Valerius, constituting the second book of his " On Marriage and Concupiscence "; and the other, a far more elaborate examination of the letters sent by Boniface, which bears the title, " Against Two Letters of the Pelagians." The purpose of the second book of " On Marriage and Concupiscence," Augustine himself states, in its introductory sentences, to be " to reply to the taunts of his adversaries with all the truthfulness and scriptural authority he could command." He begins (2) by identifying the source of the extracts forwarded to him by Valerius, with Julian's work against his

[123] Compare " Against Two Letters of the Pelagians," iii. 24; and see above, p. 293.

first book, and then remarks upon the garbled form in which he is quoted in them (3–6), and passes on to state and refute Julian's charge that the Catholics had turned Manichæans (7–9). At this point, the refutation of Julian begins in good earnest, and the method that he proposes to use is stated; viz., to adduce the adverse statements, and refute them one by one (10). Beginning at the beginning, he quotes first the title of the paper sent him, which declares that it is directed against "those who condemn matrimony, and ascribe its fruit to the Devil" (11), which certainly, says Augustine, does not describe him or the Catholics. The next twenty chapters (10–30), accordingly, following Julian's order, labor to prove that marriage is good, and ordained by God, but that its good includes *fecundity* indeed, but not *concupiscence*, which arose from sin, and contracts sin. It is next argued, that the doctrine of original sin does not imply an evil origin for man (31–51); and in the course of this argument, the following propositions are especially defended: that God makes offspring for good and bad alike, just as He sends the rain and sunshine on just and unjust (31–34); that God makes everything to be found in marriage except its *flaw*, concupiscence (35–40); that marriage is not the cause of original sin, but only the channel through which it is transmitted (41–47); and that to assert that evil cannot arise from what is good leaves us in the clutches of that very Manichæism which is so unjustly charged against the Catholics — for, if evil be not eternal, what else was there from which it could arise but something good? (48–51). In concluding, Augustine recapitulates, and argues especially, that shameful concupiscence is of sin, and the author of sin, and was not in paradise (52–54); that children are made by God, and only marred by the Devil (55); that Julian, in admitting that Christ died for infants, admits that they need salvation (56); that what the Devil makes in children is not a substance, but an injury to a substance (57–58); and that to suppose that concupiscence existed in any form in paradise introduces incongruities in our conception of life in that abode of primeval bliss (59–60).

The long and important treatise, " Against Two Letters of the Pelagians," consists of four books, the first of which replies to the letter sent to Rome, and the other three to that sent to Thessalonica. After a short introduction, in which he thanks Boniface for his kindness, and gives reasons why heretical writings should be answered (1–3), Augustine begins at once to rebut the calumnies which the letter before him brings against the Catholics (4–28). These are seven in number: 1. That the Catholics destroy free will; to which Augustine replies that none are " forced into sin by the necessity of their flesh," but all sin by free will, though no man can have a righteous will save by God's grace, and that it is really the Pelagians that destroy free will by exaggerating it (4–8); 2. That Augustine declares that such marriage as now exists is not of God (9); 3. That sexual desire and intercourse are made a device of the Devil, which is sheer Manichæism (10–11); 4. That the Old Testament saints are said to have died in sin (12); 5. That Paul and the other apostles are asserted to have been polluted by lust all their days; Augustine's answer to which includes a running commentary on Rom. vii. 7 *sq.*, in which (correcting his older exegesis) he shows that Paul is giving here a transcript of his own experience as a typical Christian (13–24); 6. That Christ is said not to have been free from sin (25); 7. That baptism does not give complete remission of sins, but leaves roots from which they may again grow; to which Augustine replies that baptism does remit all sins, but leaves concupiscence, which, although not sin, is the source of sin (26–28). Next, the positive part of Julian's letter is taken up, and his profession of faith against the Catholics examined (29–41). The seven affirmations that Julian makes here are designed as the obverse of the seven charges against the Catholics. He believed: 1. That free will is in all by nature, and could not perish by Adam's sin (29); 2. That marriage, as now existent, was ordained by God (30); 3. That sexual impulse and virility are from God (31–35); 4. That men are God's work, and no one is forced to do good or evil unwillingly, but is assisted by grace to good, and incited by the Devil to evil (36–

38); 5. That the saints of the Old Testament were perfected in righteousness here, and so passed into eternal life (39); 6. That the grace of Christ (ambiguously meant) is necessary for all, and all children — even those of baptized parents — are to be baptized (40); 7. And that baptism gives full cleansing from all sins; to which Augustine pointedly asks, "What does it do for infants, then?" (41). The book concludes with an answer to Julian's conclusion, in which he demands a general council, and charges the Catholics with Manichæism.

The second, third, and fourth books deal with the letter to Rufus in a somewhat similar way, the second and third books being occupied with the calumnies brought against the Catholics, and the fourth with the claims made by the Pelagians. The second begins by repelling the charge of Manichæism brought against the Catholics (1–4), to which the pointed remark is added, that the Pelagians cannot hope to escape condemnation because they are willing to condemn another heresy; and then defends (with less success) the Roman clergy against the charge of prevarication in their dealing with the Pelagians (5–8), in the course of which all that can be said in defense of Zosimus' wavering policy is said well and strongly. Next the charges against Catholic teaching are taken up and answered (9–16), especially the two important accusations that they maintain fate under the name of grace (9–12), and that they make God an " accepter of persons " (13–16). Augustine's replies to these charges are in every way admirable. The charge of " fate " rests solely on the Catholic denial that grace is given according to preceding merits; but the Pelagians do not escape the same charge when they acknowledge that the "fates" of baptized and unbaptized infants do differ. It is, in truth, not a question of "fate," but of *gratuitous bounty;* and " it is not the Catholics that assert fate under the name of grace, but the Pelagians that choose to call divine grace by the name of ' fate ' " (12). As to " acceptance of persons," we must define what we mean by that. God certainly does not accept one's " person " above another's; He does not give to one rather than to another because He sees something to please Him in one rather than an another: quite the opposite. He gives of His bounty to one while giving all their due to all, as in the parable (Mt. xx. 9 *sq.*). To ask why He does this, is to ask in vain: the apostle answers by not answering (Rom. ix.); and before the dumb infants, who are yet made to differ, all objection to God is dumb. From this point, the book becomes an examination of the Pelagian doctrine of prevenient merit (17–23), concluding that God gives all by grace from the beginning to the end of every process of doing good. 1. He commands the good; 2. He gives the desire to do it; and, 3. He gives the power to do it: and all, of His gratuitous mercy. The third book continues the discussion of the calumnies of the Pelagians against the Catholics, and enumerates and answers six of them: viz., that the Catholics teach, 1. That the Old Testament law was given, not to justify the obedient, but to serve as cause of greater sin (2–3); 2. That baptism does not give entire remission of sins, but the baptized are partly God's and partly the Devil's (4–5); 3. That the Holy Ghost did not assist virtue in the Old Testament (6–13); 4. That the Bible saints were not holy, but only less wicked than others (14–15); 5. That Christ was a sinner by necessity of His flesh (doubtless, Julian's inference from the doctrine of race-sin) (16); 6. That men will begin to fulfill God's commandments only after the resurrection (17–23). Augustine shows that at the basis of all these calumnies lies either misapprehension or misrepresentation; and, in concluding the book, enumerates the three chief points in the Pelagian heresy, with the five claims growing out of them, of which they most boasted, and then elucidates the mutual relations of the three parties, catholics, Pelagians, and Manicheans, with reference to these points, showing that the catholics stand asunder from both the others, and condemn both (24–26). This conclusion is really a preparation for the fourth book, which takes up these five Pelagian claims, and, after showing the catholic position on them all in brief (1–3), discusses them in turn (4–19): viz., the praise of the creature (4–8), the praise of marriage (9), the praise of the law (10–11), the praise of free will (12–16), and the praise of the saints (17–18). At the end, Augustine calls on the Pelagians to cease to oppose the Manichæans, only to fall into as bad heresy as theirs (19); and then, in reply to their accusation that the Catholics were proclaiming novel doctrine, he adduces the testimony of Cyprian and Ambrose, both of whom had received Pelagius' praise, on each of the three main points of Pelagianism (20–32),[124] and then closes with the declaration that the " impious and foolish doctrine," as they called it, of the Catholics, is immemorial truth (33), and with a denial of the right of the Pelagians to ask for a general council to condemn them (34). All heresies do not need an ecumenical synod for their condemnation; usually it is best to stamp them out locally, and not allow what may be confined to a corner to disturb the whole world.

These books were written late in 420, or early in 421, and Alypius appears to have conveyed them to Italy during the latter year. Before its close, Augustine, having obtained and read the whole of Julian's attack on the first book of his work " On Marriage and Concupiscence," wrote out a complete answer to it [125] — a task that he was all the more anxious to complete, on perceiving that the extracts sent by Valerius were not only all from the first book of Julian's treatise, but were somewhat altered in the extracting. The resulting work, " Against Julian," one of the longest that he wrote in the whole course of the Pelagian controversy, shows its author at his best: according to Cardinal Noris's judgment, he appears in it " almost divine," and Augustine himself clearly set great store by it. In the first book of this noble treatise, after professing his continued love for Julian, " whom he was unable not to love, whatever he [Julian] should say against him " (35), he undertakes to show that in affixing the opprobrious name of Manichæans on those who assert original sin, Julian is incriminating many of the most famous fathers, of both the Latin and Greek Churches.

124 To wit: Cyprian's testimony on original sin (20–24), on gratuitous grace (25–26), on the imperfection of human righteousness (27–28), and Ambrose's testimony on original sin (29), on gratuitous grace (30), and on the imperfection of human righteousness (31).

125 Compare " Epist." 207, written probably in the latter half of 421.

In proof of this, he makes appropriate quotations from
Irenæus, Cyprian, Reticius, Olympius, Hilary, Ambrose, Gregory Nazianzenus, Basil, John of Constantinople.[126] Then he
argues, that, so far from the Catholics falling into Manichæan
heresy, Julian plays, himself, into the hands of the Manichæans
in their strife against the Catholics, by many unguarded statements, such as, e.g., when he says that an evil thing cannot
arise from what is good, that the work of the Devil cannot be
suffered to be diffused by means of a work of God, that a root
of evil cannot be placed within a gift of God, and the like.
The second book advances to greater detail, and adduces the
five great arguments which the Pelagians urged against the
Catholics, in order to test them by the voice of antiquity. These
arguments are stated as follows (2): " For you say, ' That we,
by asserting original sin, affirm that the Devil is the maker of
infants, condemn marriage, deny that all sins are remitted in
baptism, accuse God of the guilt of sin, and produce despair of
perfection.' You contend that all these are consequences, if
we believe that infants are born bound by the sin of the first
man, and are therefore under the Devil unless they are born
again in Christ. For, ' It is the Devil that creates,' you say, ' if
they are created from that wound which the Devil inflicted on
the human nature that was made at first.' ' And marriage is
condemned,' you say, ' if it is to be believed to have something
about it whence it produces those worthy of condemnation.'
' And all sins are not remitted in baptism,' you say, ' if there
remains any evil in baptized couples whence evil offspring are
produced.' ' And how is God,' you ask, ' not unjust, if He, while
remitting their own sins to baptized persons, yet condemns
their offspring, inasmuch as, although it is created by Him, it
yet ignorantly and involuntarily contracts the sins of others
from those very parents to whom they are remitted? ' ' Nor can
men believe,' you add, ' that virtue — to which corruption is
to be understood to be contrary — can be perfected, if they
cannot believe that it can destroy the inbred vices, although,
no doubt, these can scarcely be considered vices, since he does

[126] That is, Chrysostom.

not sin, who is unable to be other than he was created.' " These
arguments are then tested, one by one, by the authority of the
earlier teachers who were appealed to in the first book, and
shown to be condemned by them. The remaining four books
follow Julian's four books, argument by argument, refuting
him in detail. In the third book it is urged that although God
is good, and made man good, and instituted marriage which is,
therefore, good, nevertheless concupiscence is evil, and in it the
flesh lusts against the spirit. Although chaste spouses use this
evil well, continent believers do better in not using it at all. It
is pointed out, how far all this is from the madness of the
Manichæans, who dream of matter as essentially evil and coeternal with God; and shown that evil concupiscence sprang
from Adam's disobedience and, being transmitted to us, can be
removed only by Christ. It is shown, also, that Julian himself confesses lust to be evil, inasmuch as he speaks of remedies
against it, wishes it to be bridled, and speaks of the continent
waging a glorious warfare. The fourth book follows the second
book of Julian's work, and makes two chief contentions: that
unbelievers have no true virtues, and that even the heathen
recognize concupiscence as evil. It also argues that grace is not
given according to merit, and yet is not to be confounded with
fate; and explains the text that asserts that " God wishes all
men to be saved," in the sense that " all men " means " all that
are to be saved, since none are saved except by His will." [127]
The fifth book, in like manner, follows Julian's third book, and
treats of such subjects as these: that it is due to sin that any
infants are lost; that shame arose in our first parents through
sin; that sin can well be the punishment of preceding sin;
that concupiscence is always evil, even in those who do not
assent to it; that true marriage may exist without intercourse;
that the " flesh " of Christ differs from the " sinful flesh " of
other men; and the like. In the sixth book, Julian's fourth
book is followed, and original sin is proved from the baptism
of infants, the teaching of the apostles, and the rites of exorcism and exsufflation incorporated in the form of baptism.

[127] Compare " On Rebuke and Grace," 44.

Then, by the help of the illustration drawn from the olive and the oleaster, it is explained how Christian parents can produce unregenerate offspring; and the originally voluntary character of sin is asserted, even though it now comes by inheritance.

After the completion of this important work, there succeeded a lull in the controversy, of some years duration; and the calm refutation of Pelagianism and exposition of Christian grace, which Augustine gave in his " Enchiridion," [128] might well have seemed to him his closing word on this all-absorbing subject. But he had not yet given the world all he had in treasure for it, and we can rejoice in the chance that five or six years afterwards drew from him a renewed discussion of some of the more important aspects of the doctrine of grace. The circumstances which brought this about are sufficiently interesting in themselves, and open up to us an unwonted view into the monastic life of the times. There was an important monastery at Adrumetum, the metropolitan city of the province of Byzacium,[129] from which a monk named Florus went out on a journey of charity to his native country of Uzalis about 426. On the journey he met with Augustine's letter to Sixtus [130] in which the doctrines of gratuitous and prevenient grace were expounded. He was much delighted with it, and, procuring a copy, sent it back to his monastery for the edification of his brethren, while he himself went on to Carthage. At the monastery, the letter created great disturbance: without the knowledge of the abbot, Valentinus, it was read aloud to the monks, many of whom were unskilled in theological questions; and some five or more were greatly offended, and declared that free will was destroyed by it. A secret strife arose among the brethren, some taking extreme grounds on both sides. Of all this, Valentinus remained ignorant until the return of Florus, who was attacked as the author of all the trouble, and who felt it

[128] See " A Select Library of the Nicene and Post-Nicene Fathers of the Christian Church," Series I. iii. pp. 237 *sq.*

[129] Now a portion of Tunis.

[130] " Epist." 194.

his duty to inform the abbot of the state of affairs. Valentinus applied first to the bishop, Evodius, for such instruction as would make Augustine's letter clear to the most simple. Evodius replied, praising their zeal and deprecating their contentiousness, and explaining that Adam had full free will, but that it is now wounded and weak, and Christ's mission was as a physician to cure and recuperate it. " Let them read," is his prescription, " the words of God's elders. . . . And when they do not understand, let them not quickly reprehend, but pray to understand." This did not, however, cure the malcontents, and the holy presbyter Sabrinus was appealed to, and sent a book with clear interpretations. But neither was this satisfactory; and Valentinus, at last, reluctantly consented that Augustine himself should be consulted — fearing, he says, lest by making inquiries he should seem to waver about the truth. Two members of the community were consequently permitted to journey to Hippo, but they took with them no introduction and no commendation from their abbot. Augustine, nevertheless, received them without hesitation, as they bore themselves with too great simplicity to allow him to suspect them of deception. Now we get a glimpse of life in the great bishop's monastic home. The monks told their story, and were listened to with courtesy and instructed with patience; and, as they were anxious to get home before Easter, they received a letter for Valentinus [131] in which Augustine briefly explains the nature of the misapprehension that had arisen, and points out that both grace and free will must be defended, and neither so exaggerated as to deny the other. The letter of Sixtus, he explains, was written against the Pelagians, who assert that grace is given according to merit, and briefly expounds the true doctrine of grace as necessarily gratuitous and therefore prevenient. When the monks were on the point of starting home, they were joined by a third companion from Adrumetum, and were led to prolong their visit. This gave him the opportunity he craved for their fuller instruction: he read with them and explained to them not only his letter to Sixtus,

[131] " Epist." 214.

from which the strife had risen, but much of the chief literature of the Pelagian controversy,[132] copies of which also were
made for them to take home with them; and when they were
ready to go, he sent by them another and longer letter to
Valentinus, and placed in their hands a treatise composed for
their especial use, which, moreover, he explained to them. This
longer letter is essentially an exhortation " to turn aside
neither to the right hand nor to the left " — neither to the left
hand of the Pelagian error of upholding free will in such a
manner as to deny grace, nor to the right hand of the equal
error of so upholding grace as if we might yield ourselves to
evil with impunity. Both grace and free will are to be proclaimed; and it is true both that grace is not given to merits,
and that we are to be judged at the last day according to our
works. The treatise which Augustine composed for a fuller
exposition of these doctrines is the important work " On Grace
and Free Will." After a brief introduction, explaining the occasion of his writing, and exhorting the monks to humility and
teachableness before God's revelations (1), Augustine begins
by asserting and proving the two propositions that the Scriptures clearly teach that man has free will (2–5), and, as
clearly, the necessity of grace for doing any good (6–9). He
then examines the passages which the Pelagians claim as teaching that we must first turn to God, before He visits us with His
grace (10–11), and then undertakes to show that grace is not
given to merit (12 sq.), appealing especially to Paul's teaching and example, and replying to the assertion that forgiveness is the only grace that is not given according to our merits
(15–18), and to the query, " How can eternal life be both of
grace and of reward? " (19–21). The nature of grace, what it
is, is next explained (22 sq.). It is not the law, which gives only
knowledge of sin (22–24), nor nature, which would render
Christ's death needless (25), nor mere forgiveness of sins, as
the Lord's Prayer (which should be read with Cyprian's comments on it) is enough to show (26). Nor will it do to say that
it is given to the merit of a good will, thus distinguishing the

[132] " Epist." 215. 2 sq.

good work which is of grace from the good will which precedes
grace (27–30); for the Scriptures oppose this, and our prayers
for others prove that we expect God to be the *first mover,* as
indeed both Scripture and experience prove that He is. It is
next shown that both free will and grace are concerned in the
heart's conversion (31–32), and that love is the spring of all
good in man (33–40), which, however, we have only because
God first loved us (38), and which is certainly greater than
knowledge, although the Pelagians admit only the latter to be
from God (40). God's sovereign government of men's wills is
then proved from Scripture (41–43), and the wholly gratuitous
character of grace is illustrated (44), while the only possible
theodicy is found in the certainty that the Lord of all the earth
will do right. For, though no one knows why He takes one and
leaves another, we all know that He hardens judicially and
saves graciously — that He hardens none who do not deserve
hardening, but none that He saves deserve to be saved (45).
The treatise closes with an exhortation to its prayerful and
repeated study (46).

The one request that Augustine made, on sending this
work to Valentinus, was that Florus, through whom the controversy had arisen, should be sent to him, that he might converse with him and learn whether he had been misunderstood,
or himself had misunderstood Augustine. In due time Florus
arrived at Hippo, bringing a letter [133] from Valentinus which
addresses Augustine as "Lord Pope" (*domine papa*), thanks
him for his "sweet" and "healing" instruction, and introduces Florus as one whose true faith could be confided in. It is
very clear, both from Valentinus' letter and from the hints
that Augustine gives, that his loving dealing with the monks
had borne admirable fruit: "none were cast down for the
worse, some were built up for the better." [134] But it was reported to him that some one at the monastery had objected to
the doctrine he had taught them, that "no man ought, then,
to be rebuked for not keeping God's commandments; but only

[133] "Epist." 216.
[134] "On Rebuke and Grace," 1.

God should be besought that he might keep them." [135] In other
words, it was said that if all good was, in the last resort, from
God's grace, man ought not to be blamed for not doing what
he could not do, but God ought to be besought to do for man
what He alone could do: we ought, in a word, to apply to the
source of power. This occasioned the composition of yet another treatise " On Rebuke and Grace," [136] the object of which
was to explain the relations of grace to human conduct, and especially to make it plain that the sovereignty of God's grace
does not supersede our duty to ourselves or our fellow-men. It
begins by thanking Valentinus for his letter and for sending
Florus (whom Augustine finds well instructed in the truth),
thanking God for the good effect of the previous book, and
recommending its continued study, and then by briefly expounding the Catholic faith concerning grace, free will, and
the law (1–2). The general proposition that is defended is that
the gratuitous sovereignty of God's grace does not supersede
human means for obtaining and continuing it (3 sq.) This is
shown by the apostle's example, who used all human means for
the prosecution of his work, and yet confessed that it was
" God that gave the increase " (3). Objections are then answered (4 sq.) — especially the great one that " it is not my
fault if I do not do what I have not received grace for doing "
(6); to which Augustine replies (7–10), that we deserve rebuke for our very unwillingness to be rebuked, that on the same
reasoning the prescription of the law and the preaching of the
gospel would be useless, that the apostle's example opposes
such a position, and that our consciousness witnesses that we
deserve rebuke for not persevering in the right way. From this
point an important discussion arises, in this interest, of the
gift of perseverance (11–19), and of God's election (20–24);
the teaching being that no one is saved who does not persevere,
and all that are predestinated or " called according to the pur-

[135] " Retractations," ii. 67. Compare " On Rebuke and Grace," 5 sq.

[136] On the importance of this treatise for Augustine's doctrine of predestination, see Wiggers' " Augustinianism and Pelagianism," E. T. p. 236, where
a sketch of the history of this doctrine in Augustine's writings may be found.

pose " (Augustine's phrase for what we should call " effectual calling ") will persevere, and yet that we coöperate by our will in all good deeds, and deserve rebuke if we do not. Whether Adam received the gift of perseverance, and, in general, the difference between the grace given to him, (which was that grace by which he could stand) and that now given to God's children (which is that grace by which we are actually made to stand), are next discussed (26–38), with the result of showing the superior greatness of the gifts of grace now to those given before the fall. The necessity of God's mercy at all times, and our constant dependence on it, are next vigorously asserted (39–42); even in the day of judgment, if we are not judged " with mercy " we cannot be saved (41). The treatise is brought to an end by a concluding application of the whole discussion to the special matter in hand, *rebuke* (43–49). Seeing that rebuke is one of God's means of working out his gracious purposes, it cannot be inconsistent with the sovereignty of that grace; for, of course, God predestinates the means with the end (43). Nor can we know, in our ignorance, whether our rebuke is, in any particular case, to be the means of amendment or the ground of greater condemnation. How dare we, then, withhold it? Let it be, however, graduated to the fault, and let us always remember its purpose (46–48). Above all, let us not dare hold it back, lest we hold back from our brother the means of his recovery, and, as well, disobey the command of God (49).

It was not long afterwards (about 427) when Augustine was called upon to attempt to reclaim a Carthaginian brother, Vitalis by name, who had been brought to trial on the charge of teaching that the beginning of faith was not the gift of God, but the act of man's own free will (*ex propria voluntatis*). This was essentially the semi-Pelagian position which was subsequently to make so large a figure in history; and Augustine treats it now as necessarily implying the basal idea of Pelagianism. In the important letter which he sent to Vitalis,[137] he first argues that his position is inconsistent with the prayers of the Church. He, Augustine, prays that Vitalis may

[137] " Epist." 217.

come to the true faith; but does not this prayer ascribe the origination of right faith to God? The Church so prays for all men: the priest at the altar exhorts the people to pray God for unbelievers, that He may convert them to the faith; for catechumens, that He may breathe into them a desire for regeneration; for the faithful, that by His aid they may persevere in what they have begun: will Vitalis refuse to obey these exhortations, because, forsooth, faith is of free will and not of God's gift? Nay, will a Carthaginian scholar array himself against Cyprian's exposition of the Lord's Prayer? for he certainly teaches that we are to ask of God what Vitalis says is to be had of ourselves. We may go farther: it is not Cyprian, but Paul, who says, "Let us pray to God that we do no evil" (2 Cor. xiii. 7); it is the Psalmist who says, "The steps of man are directed by God" (Ps. xxxvii. 23). "If we wish to defend free will, let us not strive against that by which it is made free. For he who strives against grace, by which the will is made free for refusing evil and doing good, wishes his will to remain captive. Tell us, I beg you, how the apostle can say, 'We give thanks to the Father who made us fit to have our lot with the saints in light, who delivered us from the power of darkness, and translated us into the kingdom of the Son of His love' (Col. i. 12, 13), if not He, but itself, frees our choice? It is, then, a false rendering of thanks to God, as if He does what He does not do; and he has erred who has said that 'He makes us fit, etc.' . . . The grace of God, therefore, does not consist in the nature of free-will, and in law and teaching, as the Pelagian perversity dreams; but it is given for each single act by His will, concerning whom it is written," — quoting Ps. lxviii. 9. About the middle of the letter, Augustine lays down twelve propositions against the Pelagians, which are important as communicating to us what he thought, at the end of the controversy, were the chief points in dispute. "Since, therefore . . . ," he writes, "we are Catholic Christians: 1. We know that new-born children have not yet done anything in their own lives, good or evil, neither have they come into the miseries of this life according to the deserts of some previous life, which

none of them can have had in their own persons; and yet, because they are born carnally after Adam, they contract the
contagion of ancient death, by the first birth, and are not freed
from the punishment of eternal death (which is contracted by
a just condemnation, passing over from one to all), except they
are by grace born again in Christ. 2. We know that the grace of
God is given neither to children nor to adults according to our
deserts. 3. We know that it is given to adults for each several
act. 4. We know that it is not given to all men; and to those
to whom it is given, it is not only not given according to the
merits of works, but it is not even given to them according to
the merits of their will; and this is especially apparent in
children. 5. We know that to those to whom it is given, it is
given by the gratuitous mercy of God. 6. We know that to
those to whom it is not given, it is not given by the just judgment of God. 7. We know that we shall all stand before the
tribunal of Christ, and each shall receive according to what
he has done through the body, — not according to what he
would have done, had he lived longer, — whether good or evil.
8. We know that even children are to receive according to what
they have done through the body, whether good or evil. But
according to what 'they have done' not by their own act, but
by the act of those by whose responses for them they are said
both to renounce the Devil and to believe in God, wherefore
they are counted among the number of the faithful, and have
part in the statement of the Lord when He says, 'Whosoever shall believe and be baptized, shall be saved.' Therefore also, to those who do not receive this sacrament, belongs
what follows, 'But whosoever shall not have believed, shall
be damned' (Mk. xvi. 16). Whence these too, as I have said,
if they die in that early age, are judged, of course, according to what they have done through the body, i.e., in the time
in which they were in the body, when they believe or do not
believe by the heart and mouth of their sponsors, when they
are baptized or not baptized, when they eat or do not eat the
flesh of Christ, when they drink or do not drink His blood, —
according to those things, then, which they have done through

the body, not according to those which, had they lived longer, they would have done. 9. We know that blessed are the dead that die in the Lord; and that what they would have done had they lived longer, is not imputed to them. 10. We know that those that believe, with their own heart, in the Lord, do so by their own free will and choice. 11. We know that we who already believe act with right faith towards those who do not wish to believe, when we pray to God that they may wish it. 12. We know that for those who have believed out of this number, we both ought and are rightly and truly accustomed to return thanks to God, as for his benefits." Certainly such a body of propositions commends their author to us as Christian both in head and heart: they are admirable in every respect; and even in the matter of the salvation of infants, where he had not yet seen the light of truth, he expresses himself in a way as engaging in its hearty faith in God's goodness as it is honorable in its loyalty to what he believed to be truth and justice. Here his doctrine of the Church ran athwart and clouded his view of the reach of grace; but we seem to see between the lines the promise of the brighter dawn of truth that was yet to come. The rest of the epistle is occupied with an exposition and commendation of these propositions, which ranks with the richest passages of the anti-Pelagian writings, and which breathes everywhere a yearning for his correspondent which we cannot help hoping proved salutary to his faith.

It is not without significance, that the error of Vitalis took a semi-Pelagian form. Pure Pelagianism was by this time no longer a living issue. Augustine was himself, no doubt, not yet done with it. The second book of his treatise " On Marriage and Concupiscence," which seems to have been taken to Italy by Alypius, in 421, received at once the attention of Julian, and was elaborately answered by him, during that same year, in eight books addressed to Florus. But Julian was now in Cilicia, and his book was slow in working its way westward. It was found at Rome by Alypius, apparently in 427 or 428, and he at once set about transcribing it for his friend's use. An opportunity arising to send it to Africa before it was finished, he forwarded to Augustine the five books that were ready, with an urgent request that they should receive his immediate attention, and a promise to send the other three as soon as possible. Augustine gives an account of his progress in his reply to them in a letter written to Quodvultdeus, apparently in 428.[138] This deacon was urging Augustine to give the Church a succinct account of all heresies; and Augustine excuses himself from immediately undertaking that task by the press of work on his hands. He was writing his " Retractations," and had already finished two books of them, in which he had dealt with two hundred and thirty-two works. His letters and homilies remained, and he had given the necessary reading to many of the letters. Also, he tells his correspondent, he was engaged on a reply to the eight books of Julian's new work. Working night and day, he had already completed his response to the first three of Julian's books, and had begun on the fourth while still expecting the arrival of the last three which Alypius had promised to send. If he had completed the answer to the five books of Julian which he already had in hand, before the other three reached him, he might begin the work which Quodvultdeus so earnestly desired him to undertake. In due time, whatever may have been the trials and labors that needed first to be met, the desired treatise " On Heresies " was written (about 428), and the eighty-eighth chapter of it gives us a welcome compressed account of the Pelagian heresy, which may be accepted as the obverse of the account of catholic truth given in the letter (217) to Vitalis.[139] But the composition of this

[138] " Epist." 224.

[139] The account given of Pelagianism is as follows: " They are in such degree enemies of the grace of God, by which we have been predestinated into the adoption of sons by Jesus Christ unto Himself (Eph. i. 5), and by which we are delivered from the power of darkness so as to believe in Him, and be translated into His kingdom (Col. i. 13) — wherefore He says, ' No man comes to Me, except it be given him of my Father' (Jno. vi. 65) — and by which love is shed abroad in our hearts (Rom. v. 5), so that faith may work by love: that they believe that man is able, without it, to keep all the Divine commandments, — whereas, if this were true, it would clearly be an empty thing that the Lord said, ' Without Me ye can do nothing' (Jno. xv. 5).

work was not the only interruption which postponed the completion of the second elaborate work against Julian. It was in

When Pelagius was at length accused by the brethren, because he attributed nothing to the assistance of God's grace towards the keeping of His commandments, he yielded to their rebuke, so far as not to place this grace above free will, but with faithless cunning to subordinate it, saying that it was given to men for this purpose; viz., that they might be able more easily to fulfil by grace, what they were commanded to do by free will. By saying, 'that they might be able more easily,' he, of course, wished it to be believed that, although with more difficulty; nevertheless men were able without divine grace to perform the divine commands. But that grace of God, without which we can do nothing good, they say does not exist except in free will, which without any preceding merits our nature received from Him; and that He adds His aid only in that by His law and teaching we may learn what we ought to do, . . . but not in that by the gift of His Spirit we may do what we have learned ought to be done. Accordingly, they confess that knowledge by which ignorance is banished is divinely given to us, but deny that love by which we may live a pious life is given; so that, forsooth, while knowledge, which, without love, puffeth up, is the gift of God, love itself, which edifieth so that knowledge may not puff up, is not the gift of God (1 Cor. viii. 11). They also destroy the prayers which the Church offers, whether for those that are unbelieving and resisting God's teaching, that they may be converted to God; or for the faithful, that faith may be increased in them, and they may persevere in it. For they contend that men do not receive these things from Him, but have them from ourselves, saying that the grace of God, by which we are freed from impiety, is given according to our merits. Pelagius was compelled, no doubt, to condemn this by his fear of being condemned by the episcopal judgment in Palestine; but he is found to teach it still in his later writings. They also advanced so far as to say that the life of the righteous in this world is without sin, and the Church of Christ is perfected by them in this mortality, to the point of being entirely without spot or wrinkle (Eph. v. 27); as if it were not the Church of Christ, that, in the whole world, cries to God, 'Forgive us our debts.' (Mt. vi. 12.) They also deny that children, who are carnally born after Adam, contract the contagion of ancient death from their first birth. For they assert that they are born so without any bond of original sin, that there is absolutely nothing that ought to be remitted to them in the second birth, yet they are to be baptized; but for this reason, that, adopted in regeneration, they may be admitted to the kingdom of God, and thus be translated from good into better, — not that they may be washed by that renovation from any evil of the old bond. For although they be not baptized, they promise to them, outside the kingdom of God indeed, but nevertheless, a certain eternal and blessed life of their own. They also say that Adam himself, even had he not sinned, would have died in the body, and that this death would not have come as a desert to a fault, but as a condition of nature. Certain other things also are objected to them, but these are the chief, and also either all, or nearly all, the others may be understood to depend on these." (" On Heresies," 88.)

the providence of God that the life of this great leader in the battle for grace should be prolonged until he could deal with semi-Pelagianism also. Information as to the rise of this new form of the heresy at Marseilles and elsewhere in Southern Gaul was conveyed to Augustine along with entreaties, that, as " faith's great patron," he would give his aid towards meeting it, by two laymen with whom he had already had correspondence — Prosper and Hilary.[140] They pointed out [141] the difference between the new party and thoroughgoing Pelagianism; but, at the same time, the essentially Pelagianizing character of its formative elements. Its representatives were ready, as a rule, to admit that all men were lost in Adam, and no one could recover himself by his own free will, but all needed God's grace for salvation. But they objected to the doctrines of prevenient and of irresistible grace; and asserted that man could initiate the process of salvation by turning first to God, that all men could resist God's grace, and no grace could be given which they could not reject, and especially they denied that the gifts of grace came irrespective of merits, actual or foreseen. They said that what Augustine taught as to the calling of God's elect according to His own purpose was tantamount to fatalism, was contrary to the teaching of the fathers and the true Church doctrine, and, even if true, should not be preached, because of its tendency to drive men into indifference or despair. Hence, Prosper especially desired Augustine to point out the dangerous nature of these views, and to show that prevenient and coöperating grace is not inconsistent with free will, that God's predestination is not founded on foresight of receptivity in its objects, and that the doctrines of grace may be preached without danger to souls.

Augustine's answer to these appeals was a work in two books, " On the Predestination of the Saints," the second book of which is usually known under the separate title of " The Gift of Perseverance." The former book begins with a careful dis-

---

[140] Compare " Epist." 225. 1, and 156. It is, of course, not certain that this is the same Hilary that wrote to Augustine from Sicily, but it seems probable.
[141] In " Epist." 225 and 226.

crimination of the position of his new opponents: they have
made a right beginning in that they believe in original sin, and
acknowledge that none are saved from it save by Christ, and
that God's grace leads men's wills, and without grace no one
can suffice for good deeds. These things will furnish a good
starting-point for their progress to an acceptance of predestination also (1–2). The first question that needs discussion in
such circumstances is, whether God gives the very beginnings
of faith (3 *sq.*); since they admit that what Augustine had
previously urged sufficed to prove that faith was the gift of
God so far as that the increase of faith was given by Him, but
not so far but that the beginning of faith may be understood to
be man's, to which, then, God adds all other gifts (compare
43). Augustine insists that this is no other than the Pelagian
assertion of grace according to merit (3), is opposed to Scripture (4–5), and begets arrogant boasting in ourselves (6).
He replies to the objection that he had himself once held this
view, by confessing it, and explaining that he was converted
from it by 1 Cor. iv. 7, as applied by Cyprian (7–8), and expounds that verse as containing in its narrow compass a sufficient answer to the present theories (9–11). He answers,
further, the objection that the apostle distinguishes faith from
works, and works alone are meant in such passages, by pointing to Jno. vi. 28, and similar statements in Paul (12–16).
Then he answers the objection that he himself had previously
taught that God acted on foresight of faith, by showing that he
was misunderstood (17–18). He next shows that no objection
lies against predestination that does not lie with equal force
against grace (19–22) — since predestination is nothing but
God's foreknowledge of and preparation for grace, and all questions of sovereignty and the like belong to grace. Did God
not know to whom he was going to give faith (19)? or did he
promise the results of faith, works, without promising the
faith without which, as going before, the works were impossible? Would not this place God's fulfilment of his promise
out of His power, and make it depend on man (20)? Why are
men more willing to trust in their weakness than in God's

strength? do they count God's promises more uncertain than their own performance (22)? He next proves the sovereignty of grace, and of predestination, which is but the preparation for grace, by the striking examples of infants, and, above all, of the human nature of Christ (23–31), and then speaks of the twofold calling, one external and one " according to purpose " — the latter of which is efficacious and sovereign (32–37). In closing, the semi-Pelagian position is carefully defined and refuted as opposed, alike with the grosser Pelagianism, to the Scriptures of both Testaments (38–42).

The purpose of the second book, which has come down to us under the separate title of " On the Gift of Perseverance," is to show that that perseverance which endures to the end is as much of God as the beginning of faith, and that no man who has been " called according to God's purpose," and has received this gift, can fall from grace and be lost. The first half of the treatise is devoted to this theme (1–33). It begins by distinguishing between temporary perseverance, which endures for a time, and that which continues to the end (1), and affirms that the latter is certainly a gift of God's grace, and is, therefore, asked from God: which would otherwise be but a mocking petition (2–3). This, the Lord's Prayer itself might teach us, as under Cyprian's exposition it does teach us — each petition being capable of being read as a prayer for perseverance (4–9). Of course, moreover, it cannot be lost, otherwise it would not be " to the end." If man forsakes God, of course it is he that does it, and he is doubtless under continual temptation to do so; but if he abides with God, it is God who secures that, and God is equally able to *keep* one when drawn to Him, as He is to *draw* him to Him (10–15). He argues anew at this point, that grace is not according to merit, but always in mercy; and explains and illustrates the unsearchable ways of God in His sovereign but merciful dealing with men (16–25), and closes this part of the treatise by a defense of himself against adverse quotations from his early work " On Free Will," which he has already corrected in his " Retractations." The second half of the book discusses the objections that were being urged against the preaching of predestination (34–62), as if it opposed and enervated the preaching of the Gospel. He replies that Paul and the apostles, and Cyprian and the fathers, preached both together; that the same objections will lie against the preaching of God's foreknowledge and grace itself, and, indeed, against preaching any of the virtues, as, e.g., obedience, while declaring them God's gifts. He meets the objections in detail, and shows that such preaching is food to the soul, and must not be withheld from men; but explains that it must be given gently, wisely, and prayerfully. The whole treatise ends with an appeal to the prayers of the Church as testifying that all good is from God (63–65), and to the great example of unmerited grace and sovereign predestination in the choice of one human nature without preceding merit, to be united in one person with the Eternal Word — an illustration of his theme of the gratuitous grace of God which he is never tired of adducing (66–67).

These books were written in 428–429, and after their completion the unfinished work against Julian was resumed. Alypius had sent the remaining three books, and Augustine slowly toiled on to the end of his reply to the sixth book. But he was to be interrupted once more, and this time by the most serious of all interruptions. On the 28th of August, 430, with the Vandals thundering at the gates of Hippo, full of good works and of faith, he turned his face away from the strifes — whether theological or secular — of earth, and entered into rest with the Lord whom he loved. The last work against Julian was already one of the most considerable in size of all his books; but it was never finished, and retains until today the significant title of " The Unfinished Work." Augustine had hesitated to undertake this work, because he found Julian's arguments too silly either to deserve refutation, or to afford occasion for really edifying discourse. And certainly the result falls below Augustine's usual level, though this is not due, as is so often said, to failing powers and great age; for nothing that he wrote surpasses in mellow beauty and chastened strength the two books, " On the Predestination of the Saints,"

which were written after four books of this work were completed. The plan of the work is to state Julian's arguments in
his own words, and follow it with his remarks; thus giving it
something of the form of a dialogue. It follows Julian's work,
book by book. The first book states and answers certain calumnies which Julian had brought against Augustine and the
Catholic faith on the ground of their confession of original sin.
Julian had argued, that, since God is just, He cannot impute
another's sins to innocent infants; since sin is nothing but evil
will, there can be no sin in infants who are not yet in the use
of their will; and, since the freedom of will that is given to
man consists in the capacity of both sinning and not sinning,
free will is denied to those who attribute sin to nature. Augustine replies to these arguments, and answers certain objections that are made to his work " On Marriage and Concupiscence," and then corrects Julian's false explanations of certain
Scriptures from Jno. viii., Rom. vi., vii., and 2 Tim. The
second book is a discussion of Rom. v. 12, which Julian had
tried, like the other Pelagians, to explain by the " imitation " of Adam's bad example. The third book examines the
abuse by Julian of certain Old Testament passages — in Deut.
xxiv., 2 Kings xiv., Ezek. xviii. — in his effort to show that God
does not impute the father's sins to the children; as well as his
similar abuse of Heb. xi. The charge of Manichæism, which was
so repetitiously brought by Julian against the Catholics, is then
examined and refuted. The fourth book treats of Julian's strictures on Augustine's " On Marriage and Concupiscence " ii.
4–11, and proves from 1 Jno. ii. 16 that concupiscence is evil,
and not the work of God, but of the Devil. He argues that the
shame that accompanies it is due to its sinfulness, and that
there was none of it in Christ; also, that infants are born obnoxious to the first sin, and proves the corruption of their origin
from Wisd. x. 10, 11. The fifth book defends " On Marriage and
Concupiscence " ii. 12 sq., and argues that a sound nature could
not have shame on account of its members, and the need of
regeneration for what is generated by means of shameful concupiscence. Then Julian's abuse of 1 Cor. xv., Rom. v., Mt.

vii. 17 and 33, with reference to " On Marriage and Concupiscence " ii. 14, 20, 26, is discussed; and then the origin of evil, and God's treatment of evil in the world. The sixth book traverses Julian's strictures on " On Marriage and Concupiscence " ii. 34 *sq.*, and argues that human nature was changed for the worse by the sin of Adam, and thus was made not only sinful, but the source of sinners; and that the forces of free will by which man could at first do rightly if he wished, and refrain from sin if he chose, were lost by Adam's sin. He attacks Julian's definition of free will as " the capacity for sinning and not sinning" (*possibilitas peccandi et non peccandi*); and proves that the evils of this life are the punishment of sin — including, first of all, physical death. At the end, he treats of 1 Cor. xv. 22.

Although the great preacher of grace was taken away by death before the completion of this book, yet his work was not left incomplete. In the course of the next year (431) the Ecumenical Council of Ephesus condemned Pelagianism for the whole world; and an elaborate treatise against the pure Pelagianism of Julian was already in 430 an anachronism. Semi-Pelagianism was yet to run its course, and to work its way so into the heart of a corrupt church as not to be easily displaced; but Pelagianism was to die with the first generation of its advocates. As we look back now through the almost millennium and a half of years that has intervened since Augustine lived and wrote, it is to his " Predestination of the Saints " — a completed, and well-completed, treatise — and not to " The Unfinished Work," that we look as the crown and completion of his labors for grace.

IV. The Theology of Grace

The theology which Augustine opposed, in his anti-Pelagian writings, to the errors of Pelagianism, is, shortly, the theology of grace. Its roots were planted deeply in his own experience, and in the teachings of Scripture, especially of that apostle whom he delights to call " the great preacher of grace," and to follow whom, in his measure, was his greatest desire. The grace of God in Jesus Christ, conveyed to us by the Holy Spirit and evidenced by the love that He sheds abroad in our hearts, is the center around which this whole side [142] of His system revolves, and the germ out of which it grows. He was the more able to make it thus central because of the harmony of this view of salvation with the general principle of his whole theology, which was theocentric and revolved around his conception of God as the immanent and vital spirit in whom all things live and move and have their being. [143] In like manner, God is the absolute good, and all good is either Himself or from Him; and only as God makes us good, are we able to do anything good.

The *necessity of grace* to man, Augustine argued from the condition of the race as partakers of Adam's sin. God created man upright, and endowed him with human faculties, including free will; [144] and gave to him freely that grace by which he was able to retain his uprightness. [145] Being thus put on probation,

[142] This is a necessary limitation, for there is another side — a churchly side — of Augustine's theology, which was only laid alongside of, and artificially combined with, his theology of grace. This was the *traditional* element in his teaching, but was far from the determining or formative element. As Thomasius truly points out ("Die Christliche Dogmengeschichte," i. p. 495), both his experience and the Scriptures stood with him above tradition.

[143] It is only one of the strange assertions in Professor Allen's "Continuity of Christian Thought," that he states that "the Augustinian theology rests upon the transcendence of Deity as its controlling principle" (p. 3), which is identified with a tacit assumption of deism (p. 171), and explained to include a localization of God "as a physical essence in the infinite remoteness," "separated from the world by infinite reaches of space" (p. 1). As a matter of mere fact, Augustine's conception of God was that of an immanent Spirit, and his tendency was consequently distinctly towards a pantheistic rather than a deistic view of His relation to His creatures. Nor is this true only "at a certain stage of his career" (p. 6), which is but Professor Allen's attempt to reconcile fact with his theory, but of his whole life and all his teaching. He, no doubt, did not so teach the Divine immanence as to make God the author of the *form* as well as the *matter* of all acts of His creatures, or to render it impossible for His creatures to turn from Him; this would be to pass the limits that separate the conception of Christian immanence from pure pantheism, and to make God the author of sin, and all His creatures but manifestations of Himself.   [144] "On Rebuke and Grace," 27, 28.

[145] "On Rebuke and Grace," 29, 31 *sq.*

with divine aid to enable him to stand if he chose, Adam used his free choice for sinning, and involved his whole race in his fall.[146] It was on account of this sin that he died physically and spiritually, and this double death passes over from him to us.[147] That all his descendants by ordinary generation are partakers in Adam's guilt and condemnation, Augustine is sure from the teachings of Scripture; and this is the fact of original sin, from which no one generated from Adam is free, and from which no one is freed save as regenerated in Christ.[148] But how we are made partakers of it, he is less certain: sometimes he speaks as if it came by some mysterious unity of the race, so that we were all personally present in the individual Adam, and thus the whole race was the one man that sinned; [149] sometimes he speaks more in the sense of modern realists, as if Adam's sin corrupted the nature, and the nature now corrupts those to whom it is communicated; [150] sometimes he speaks as if it were due to simple heredity; [151] sometimes, again, as if it depended on the presence of shameful concupiscence in the act of procreation, so that the propagation of guilt depends on the propagation of offspring by means of concupiscence.[152] However transmitted, it is yet a fact that sin is propagated, and all mankind became sinners in Adam. The result of this is that we have lost the divine image, though not in such a sense that no lineaments of it remain to us; [153] and, the sinning soul making the flesh corruptible, our whole nature is corrupted, and we are unable to do anything of ourselves truly good.[154] This includes, of course, an injury to our will.

[146] " On Rebuke and Grace," 28.

[147] " On the City of God," xiii. 2, 12, 14; " On the Trinity," iv. 13.

[148] " On the Merits and Remission of Sins," i. 15, and often.

[149] " Against Two Letters of the Pelagians," iv. 7; " On the Merits and Remission of Sins," iii. 14, 15.

[150] " On Marriage and Concupiscence," ii. 57; " On the City of God," xiv. 1.

[151] " Against Two Letters of the Pelagians," iv. 7.

[152] " On Original Sin," 42.

[153] " Retractationes," ii. 24.

[154] " Against Julian," iv. 25, 26. Compare Thomasius' " Die Christliche Dogmengeschichte," i. pp. 501 and 507.

Augustine, writing for the popular eye, treats this subject in popular language. But it is clear that he distinguished, in his thinking, between will as a faculty and will in a broader sense. As a mere faculty, will is and always remains an indifferent thing [155] — after the fall, as before it, continuing poised in indifferency, and ready, like a weathercock, to be turned whithersoever the breeze that blows from the heart ("will," in the broader sense) may direct.[156] It is not the faculty of willing, but the man who makes use of that faculty, that has suffered change from the fall. In paradise man stood in full ability: he had the *posse non peccare*, but not yet the *non posse peccare;* [157] that is, he was endowed with a capacity for either part, and possessed the grace of God by which he was able to stand if he would, but also the power of free will by which he might fall if he would. By his fall he has suffered a change, is corrupt, and under the power of Satan; his will (in the broader sense) is now injured, wounded, diseased, enslaved — although the faculty of will (in the narrow sense) remains indifferent.[155] Augustine's criticism of Pelagius' discrimination [158] of "capacity " (*possibilitas, posse*), "will " (*voluntas, velle*), and "act " (*actio, esse*), does not turn on the discrimination itself, but on the incongruity of placing the *power, ability* in the mere capacity or possibility, rather than in the living agent who "wills" and "acts." He himself adopts an essentially similar distribution, with only this correction;[159] and thus keeps the faculty of will indifferent, but places the power of using it in the active agent, man. According, then, to the character of this *man,* will the use of the free will be. If the man be holy he will make a holy use of it, and if he be corrupt he will make a sinful use of it: if he be essentially holy, he cannot (like God Himself) make a sinful use of his will; and if he be enslaved to sin, he cannot make a good use of it. The last is the present con-

---

155 " On the Spirit and Letter," 58.
156 " On the Merits and Remission of Sins," ii. 30.
157 Cf. " On Rebuke and Grace," 29–32.
158 " On the Grace of Christ," 4 *sq.*
159 " On the Predestination of the Saints," 10.

dition of men by nature. They have free will; [160] the faculty by which they act remains in indifferency, and they are allowed to use it just as they choose: but such as they cannot desire and therefore cannot choose anything but evil;[161] and therefore they, and therefore their choice, and therefore their willing, is always evil and never good. They are thus the slaves of sin, which they obey; and while their free will avails for sinning, it does not avail for doing any good unless they be first freed by the grace of God. It is undeniable that this view is in consonance with modern psychology: let us once conceive of "the will" as simply the whole man in the attitude of willing, and it is immediately evident, that, however abstractly free the "will" is, it is conditioned and enslaved in all its action by the character of the willing agent: a bad man does not cease to be bad in the act of willing, and a good man remains good even in his acts of choice.

In its nature, grace is assistance, help from God; and all divine aid may be included under the term — as well what may be called natural, as what may be called spiritual, aid.[162] Spiritual grace includes, no doubt, all external help that God gives man for working out his salvation, such as the law, the preaching of the gospel, the example of Christ, by which we may learn the right way; it includes also forgiveness of sins, by which we are freed from the guilt already incurred; but above all it includes that help which God gives by His Holy Spirit, working within, not without, by which man is enabled to choose and to do what he sees, by the teachings of the law, or by the gospel, or by the natural conscience, to be right.[163] Within this aid are included all those spiritual exercises which we call regeneration, justification, perseverance to the end — in a word, all the divine assistance by which, in being made Christians, we are made to differ from other men. Augustine

[160] " Against Two Letters of the Pelagians," i. 5. " Epist." 215. 4, and often.
[161] " Against Two Letters of the Pelagians," i. 7. Compare i. 5, 6.
[162] " Sermon " 26.
[163] " On Nature and Grace," 62. " On the Grace of Christ," 13. " On Rebuke and Grace," 2 *sq.*

is fond of representing this grace as in essence the writing of
God's law (or of God's will) on our hearts, so that it appears
hereafter as our own desire and wish; and even more prevalently as the shedding abroad of love in our hearts by the
Holy Ghost, given to us in Christ Jesus; therefore, as a change
of disposition, by which we come to love and freely choose,
in coöperation with God's aid, just the things which hitherto
we have been unable to choose because in bondage to sin.
Grace, thus, does not make void free will: [164] it acts through
free will, and acts upon it only by liberating it from its bondage to sin, i.e., by liberating the agent that uses the free will,
so that he is no longer enslaved by his fleshly lusts, and is enabled to make use of his free will in choosing the good; and
thus it is only by grace that free will is enabled to act in good
part. But just because grace changes the disposition, and so
enables man, hitherto enslaved to sin, for the first time to desire and use his free will for good, it lies in the very nature of
the case that it is *prevenient*.[165] Also, as the very name imports, it is necessarily *gratuitous;* [166] since man is enslaved to
sin until it is given, all the merits that he can have prior to it
are bad merits, and deserve punishment, not gifts of favor.
When, then, it is asked, *on the ground of what,* grace is given,
it can only be answered, " on the ground of God's infinite
mercy and undeserved favor." [167] There is nothing in man to
merit it, and it first gives merit of good to man. All men alike
deserve death, and all that comes to them in the way of
blessing is necessarily of God's free and unmerited favor. This
is equally true of all grace. It is preëminently clear of that
grace which gives faith, the root of all other graces, which is
given of God, not to merits of good will or incipient turning
to Him, but of His sovereign good pleasure.[168] But equally
with faith, it is true of all other divine gifts: we may, indeed,

---

[164] " On the Spirit and Letter," 52; " On Grace and Free Will," 1 *sq.*
[165] " On the Spirit and Letter," 60, and often.
[166] " On Nature and Grace," 4, and often.
[167] " On the Grace of Christ," 27, and often.
[168] " On the Grace of Christ," 34, and often.

speak of "merits of good" as succeeding faith; but as all these merits find their root in faith, they are but "grace on grace," and men need God's mercy always, throughout this life, and even on the judgment day itself, when, if they are judged without mercy, they must be condemned.[169] If we ask, then, why God gives grace, we can only answer that it is of His unspeakable mercy; and if we ask why He gives it to one rather than to another, what can we answer but that it is of His will? The *sovereignty* of grace results from its very gratuitousness:[170] where none deserve it, it can be given only of the sovereign good pleasure of the great Giver — and this is necessarily inscrutable, but cannot be unjust. We can faintly perceive, indeed, some reasons why God may be supposed not to have chosen to give His saving grace to all,[171] or even to the most;[172] but we cannot understand why He has chosen to give it to just the individuals to whom He has given it, and to withhold it from just those from whom He has withheld it. Here we are driven to the apostle's cry, "Oh the depth of the riches both of the mercy and the justice of God!"[173]

The *effects of grace* are according to its nature. Taken as a whole, it is the re-creative principle sent forth from God for the recovery of man from his slavery to sin, and for his reformation in the divine image. Considered as to the time of its giving, it is either *operating* or *coöperating* grace, i.e., either the grace that first enables the will to choose the good, or the grace that coöperates with the already enabled will to do the good; and it is, therefore, also called either *prevenient* or *subsequent* grace.[174] It is not to be conceived of as a series of disconnected divine gifts, but as a constant efflux from God; but

[169] "On Rebuke and Grace," 41.

[170] "On Grace and Free Will," 30, and often.

[171] "On the Gift of Perseverance," 16; "Against Two Letters of the Pelagians," ii. 15.

[172] "Epist." 190 (to Optatus) 12.

[173] "On the Predestination of the Saints," 17, 18.

[174] "On Grace and Free Will," 17; "On the Proceedings of Pelagius," 34, and often.

we may look upon it in the various steps of its operation in men, as bringing forgiveness of sins, faith, which is the beginning of all good, love to God, progressive power of good working, and perseverance to the end.[175] In any case, and in all its operations alike, just because it is power from on high and the living spring of a new and re-created life, it is *irresistible* and *indefectible*.[176] Those on whom the Lord bestows the gift of faith working from within, not from without, of course, have faith, and cannot help believing. Those to whom perseverance to the end is given must persevere to the end. It is not to be objected to this, that many seem to begin well who do not persevere: this also is of God, who has in such cases given great blessings indeed, but not *this* blessing, of perseverance to the end. Whatever of good men have, that God has given; and what they have not, why, of course, God has not given it. Nor can it be objected, that this leaves all uncertain: it is only unknown to us, but this is not uncertainty; we cannot know that we are to have any gift which God sovereignly gives, of course, until it is given, and we therefore cannot know that we have perseverance unto the end until we actually persevere to the end;[177] but who would call what God does, and knows He is to do, uncertain, and what man is to do certain? Nor will it do to say that thus nothing is left for us to do: no doubt, all things are in God's hands, and we should praise God that this is so, but we must coöperate with Him; and it is just because it is He that is working in us the willing and the doing, that it is worth our while to work out our salvation with fear and trembling. God has not determined the end without determining the appointed means.[178]

Now, Augustine argues, since grace certainly is gratuitous, and given to no preceding merits — prevenient and antecedent to all good — and, therefore, sovereign, and bestowed

[175] Compare Thomasius' "Die Christliche Dogmengeschichte," i. p. 510.
[176] "On Rebuke and Grace," 40, 45; "On the Predestination of the Saints," 13.
[177] "On Rebuke and Grace," 40.
[178] "On the Gift of Perseverance," 56.

only on those whom God selects for its reception; we must, of course, believe that the eternal God has foreknown all this from the beginning. He would be something less than God, had He not foreknown that He intended to bestow this prevenient, gratuitous, and sovereign grace on some men, and had He not foreknown equally the precise individuals on whom He intended to bestow it. To foreknow is to prepare beforehand. And this is *predestination*.[179] He argues that there can be no objection to predestination, in itself considered, in the mind of any man who believes in a God: what men object to is the gratuitous and sovereign grace to which no additional difficulty is added by the necessary assumption that it was foreknown and prepared for from eternity. That predestination does not proceed on the foreknowledge of good or of faith,[180] follows from its being nothing more than the foresight and preparation of grace, which, in its very idea, is gratuitous and not according to any merits, sovereign and according only to God's purpose, prevenient and in order to faith and good works. It is the sovereignty of grace, not its foresight or the preparation for it, which places men in God's hands, and suspends salvation absolutely on his unmerited mercy. But just because God is God, of course, no one receives grace who has not been foreknown and afore-selected for the gift; and, as much of course, no one who has been foreknown and afore-selected for it, fails to receive it. Therefore the number of the predestinated is fixed, and fixed by God.[181] Is this fate? Men may call God's grace fate if they choose; but it is not fate, but undeserved love and tender mercy, without which none would be saved.[182] Does it paralyze effort? Only to those who will not strive to obey God because obedience is His gift. Is it unjust? Far from it: shall not God do what He will with His own undeserved favor? It is nothing

---

[179] "On the Predestination of the Saints," 36 *sq.*

[180] "On the Gift of Perseverance," 41 *sq.*, 47.

[181] "On Rebuke and Grace," 39. Compare 14.

[182] "On the Gift of Perseverance," 29; "Against Two Letters of the Pelagians," ii. 9 *sq.*

but gratuitous mercy, sovereignly distributed, and foreseen and provided for from all eternity by Him who has selected us in His Son.

When Augustine comes to speak of *the means of grace,* i.e., of the channels and circumstances of its conference to men, he approaches the meeting point of two very dissimilar streams of his theology — his doctrine of grace and his doctrine of the Church — and he is sadly deflected from the natural course of his theology by the alien influence. He does not, indeed, bind the conference of grace to the means in such a sense that the grace must be given at the exact time of the application of the means. He does not deny that "God is able, even when no man rebukes, to correct whom He will, and to lead him on to the wholesome mortification of repentance by the most hidden and most mighty power of His medicine." [183] Though the Gospel must be known in order that man may be saved [184] (for how shall they believe without a preacher?), yet the preacher is nothing, and the preachment is nothing, but God only that gives the increase.[185] He even has something like a distant glimpse of what has since been called the distinction between the visible and invisible Church — speaking of men not yet born as among those who are "called according to God's purpose," and, therefore, of the saved who constitute the Church [186] — asserting that those who are so called, even before they believe, are "already children of God, enrolled in the memorial of their Father with unchangeable surety," [187] and, at the same time, allowing that there are many already in the visible Church who are not of it, and who can therefore depart from it. But he teaches that those who are thus lost out of the visible Church are lost because of some fatal flaw in their baptism, or on account of post-baptismal sins; and that those who are of the "called

[183] "On Rebuke and Grace," 8.

[184] "On the Predestination of the Saints," 17, 18; if the Gospel is not preached at any given place, it is proof that God has no elect there.

[185] "On the Merits and Remission of Sins," etc., i. 37.

[186] "On Rebuke and Grace," 23.

[187] Do., 20.

according to the purpose " are predestinated not only to salvation, but to salvation by baptism. Grace is not tied to the
means in the sense that it is not conferred save in the means;
but it is tied to the means in the sense that it is not conferred
without the means. Baptism, for instance, is absolutely necessary for salvation: no exception is allowed except such as save
the principle — baptism of blood (martyrdom),[188] and, somewhat grudgingly, baptism of intention. And baptism, when
worthily received, is absolutely efficacious: " if a man were to
die immediately after baptism, he would have nothing at all
left to hold him liable to punishment." [189] In a word, while
there are many baptized who will not be saved, there are none
saved who have not been baptized; it is the grace of God
that saves, but baptism is a channel of grace without which
none receive it.[190]

The saddest corollary that flowed from this doctrine was
that by which Augustine was forced to assert that all those
who died unbaptized, including infants, are finally lost and
depart into eternal punishment. He did not shrink from the
inference, although he assigned the place of lightest punishment in hell to those who were guilty of no sin but original
sin, but who had departed this life without having washed
this away in the " laver of regeneration." This is the dark
side of his soteriology; but it should be remembered that it
was not his theology of grace, but the universal and traditional
belief in the necessity of baptism for remission of sins, which
he inherited in common with all of his time, that forced it
upon him. The theology of grace was destined in the hands of
his successors, who have rejoiced to confess that they were
taught by him, to remove this stumbling-block also from
Christian teaching; and if not to Augustine, it is to Augustine's theology that the Christian world owes its liberation
from so terrible and incredible a tenet. Along with the doc-

---

[188] " On the Soul and its Origin," i. 11; ii. 17.
[189] " On the Merits and Remission of Sins," etc., ii. 46.
[190] On Augustine's teaching as to baptism, see the Rev. James Field Spalding's " The Teaching and Influence of Augustine," pp. 39 *sq*.

trine of infant damnation, another stumbling-block also, not so much of Augustinian, but of Church theology, has gone. It was not because of his theology of grace, or of his doctrine of predestination, that Augustine taught that comparatively few of the human race are saved. It was, again, because he believed that baptism and incorporation into the visible Church were necessary for salvation. And it is only because of Augustine's theology of grace, which places man in the hands of an all-merciful Saviour and not in the grasp of a human institution, that men can see that in the salvation of all who die in infancy, the invisible Church of God embraces the vast majority of the human race — saved not by the washing of water administered by the Church, but by the blood of Christ administered by God's own hand outside of the ordinary channels of his grace. We are indeed born in sin, and those that die in infancy are, in Adam, children of wrath even as others; but God's hand is not shortened by the limits of His Church on earth, that it cannot save. In Christ Jesus, all souls are the Lord's, and only the soul that itself sinneth shall die (Ezek. xviii. 1–4); and the only judgment wherewith men shall be judged proceeds on the principle that as many as have sinned without law shall also perish without law, and as many as have sinned under law shall be judged by the law (Rom. ii. 12).

Thus, although Augustine's theology had a very strong churchly element within it, it was, on the side that is presented in the controversy against Pelagianism, distinctly anti-ecclesiastical. Its central thought was the absolute dependence of the individual on the grace of God in Jesus Christ. It made everything that concerned salvation to be of God, and traced the source of all good to Him. "Without me ye can do nothing," is the inscription on one side of it; on the other stands written, "All things are yours." Augustine held that he who builds on a human foundation builds on sand, and founded all his hope on the Rock itself. And there also he founded his teaching; as he distrusted man in the matter of salvation, so he distrusted him in the form of theology. No other of the

fathers so conscientiously wrought out his theology from the
revealed Word; no other of them so sternly excluded human
additions. The subjects of which theology treats, he declares, are such as " we could by no means find out unless we
believed them on the testimony of the inspired Scriptures." [191]
" Where Holy Scripture gives no certain testimony," he
says, " human presumption must beware how it decides in
favor of either side." [192] " We must first bend our necks to
the authority of the Holy Scriptures," he insists, " in order
that we may each arrive at understanding through faith." [193]
And this was not merely his theory, but his practice.[194]
No theology was ever, it may be more broadly asserted,
more conscientiously wrought out from the Scriptures. Is it
without error? No; but its errors are on the surface, not of
the essence. It leads to God, and it came from God; and in the
midst of the controversies of so many ages it has shown itself
an edifice whose solid core is built out of material " which
cannot be shaken." [195]

[191] " On the Soul and its Origin," iv. 14.
[192] " On the Merits and Remission of Sins," etc., ii. 59.
[193] " On the Merits and Remission of Sins," i. 29.
[194] Compare " On the Spirit and the Letter," 63.
[195] On the subject of this whole section, compare Reuter's " Augustinische
Studien," which has come to hand only after the whole was already in type,
but which in all essential matters — such as the formative principle, the
sources, and the main outlines of Augustine's theology — is in substantial
agreement with what is here said.

CALVIN AND CALVINISM

BY

BENJAMIN BRECKINRIDGE WARFIELD

*Professor of Didactic and Polemic Theology
in the Theological Seminary of Princeton
New Jersey, 1887–1921*

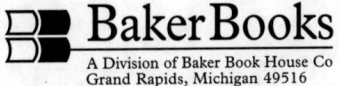
BakerBooks

A Division of Baker Book House Co
Grand Rapids, Michigan 49516

Copyright 1932 by
Oxford University Press
New York, Inc.

Reprinted 2003 by
Baker Book House Company

Set of Ten Volumes
ISBN: 0-8010-9645-6

Printed in the United States of America

For information about academic books, resources for
Christian leaders, and all new releases available from
Baker Book House, visit our web site:
http://www.bakerbooks.com

PREFATORY NOTE

Rev. Benjamin Breckinridge Warfield, D.D., LL.D., Professor of Didactic and Polemic Theology in the Theological Seminary of the Presbyterian Church at Princeton, New Jersey, provided in his will for the collection and publication of the numerous articles on theological subjects which he contributed to encyclopaedias, reviews, and other periodicals, and appointed a committee to edit and publish these papers. In pursuance of his instructions, this, the fifth volume, containing his articles on Calvin and Calvinism, has been prepared under the editorial direction of this committee.

The generous permission to publish articles contained in this volume is gratefully acknowledged as follows: Lamar and Whitmore, Agents, for the article taken from *The Methodist Quarterly Review,* Funk and Wagnalls Company for the article taken from " The New Schaff-Herzog Encyclopedia of Religious Knowledge," and The Board of Christian Education of the Presbyterian Church in the U. S. A. for the article taken from the Memorial Edition of " Calvin's Institutes."

In addition to the articles on Calvin and Calvinism published in this volume, there remain to be mentioned three addresses in commemoration of the four hundredth anniversary of the birth of Calvin: " John Calvin the Theologian "; " The Theology of Calvin "; " Present-Day Attitude to Calvinism." These addresses have been published in pamphlet form under the title "Calvin as a Theologian and Calvinism Today," at Philadelphia by The Presbyterian Board of Publication, and at Edinburgh by The Hope Trust.

The clerical preparation of this volume has been done by Mr. John E. Meeter, to whom the thanks of the committee are hereby expressed.

Ethelbert D. Warfield
William Park Armstrong
Caspar Wistar Hodge
Committee.

CONTENTS

I

JOHN CALVIN: THE MAN AND HIS WORK

JOHN CALVIN: THE MAN AND HIS WORK [1]

JOHN CALVIN was born on the tenth of July, 1509, at Noyon, in Picardy. His boyhood was spent under the shadow of the "long, straight-backed" cathedral which dominates his native town. His mother, a woman of notable devoutness, omitted no effort to imbue her son with her own spirit. His father, a successful advocate and shrewd man of affairs, holding both ecclesiastical and civil offices, stood in close relations with the cathedral chapter, and seems to have been impressed with the advantages of a clerical life. At all events, he early devoted his promising son to it. According to the bad custom of the times, a benefice in the cathedral was assigned to the young Calvin at an early age, and to it was afterwards added a neighboring curacy; thus funds were provided for his support. His education was conducted in companionship with the youthful scions of the local noble house of Montmor, and began, therefore, with the training proper to a gentleman. As changing circumstances dictated changes of plan, he was educated, first as a churchman, then as a lawyer, and through all and most abundantly of all as a man of letters. He was an eager student, rapidly and solidly mastering the subjects to which he turned his attention, and earning such admiration from his companions as to be esteemed by them rather a teacher than a fellow-pupil. His youth was as blameless as it was strenuous. It is doubtless legendary, that the censoriousness of his bearing earned for him from his associates the nickname of "The Accusative Case." But serious-minded he undoubtedly was, dominated by a scrupulous piety and schooled in a strict morality which brooked with difficulty immorality in his associates; an open-minded, affectionate young man, of irreproachable life

[1] From *The Methodist Review*, Quarterly edited by Gross Alexander, October, 1909 (lviii. pp. 642–663). Reprinted in pamphlet form, 1909, Publishing House of the M. E. Church, South.

and frank manners; somewhat sensitive, perhaps, but easy to be entreated, and attracting not merely the confidence but the lasting affection of all with whom he came into contact.

At the age of twenty-two this high-minded young man is found established at Paris as a humanist scholar, with his ambition set upon literary fame. His début was made by the publication of an excellent commentary on Seneca's treatise " On Clemency " (April, 1532), in which a remarkable command of the whole mass of classical literature, a fine intelligence, and a serious interest in the higher moralities are conspicuous. A great career as a humanist seemed opening before him, when suddenly he was " converted," and his whole life revolutionized. He had always been not only of an elevated ethical temper, but of a deeply religious spirit; but now the religious motive took complete possession of him and directed all his activities. " Renouncing all other studies," says Beza, " he devoted himself to God." He did not, indeed, cease to be a " man of letters," any more than he ceased to be a man. But all his talents and acquisitions were henceforth dedicated purely to the service of God and His gospel. Instead of annotating classical texts, we find him now writing a Protestant manifesto for the use of his friend Nicholas Cop (November 1, 1533), a detailed study of the state of the soul after death (1534), and, in his enforced retirement at Angoulême (1534), making a beginning at least with a primary treatise on Christian doctrine, designed for the instruction of the people as they came out into the light of the gospel — which, however, when driven from France, he was destined to publish from his asylum at Basle (spring of 1536), in circumstances which transformed it into " at once an apology, a manifesto, and a confession of faith." It is interesting to observe the change which in the meantime had come over his attitude toward his writings. When he sent forth his commentary on Seneca's treatise — his first and last humanistic work — he was quivering with anxiety for the success of his book; he wanted to know how it was selling, whether it was being talked about, what people thought of it. He was proud of his performance; he was zealous to reap the fruits of his labor; he was eager for his legitimate reward. Only four years have passed, and he issues his first Protestant publication — it is the immortal " Institutes of the Christian Religion " in its " first state " — free from all such tremors. He is living at Basle under an assumed name, and is fully content that no one of his acquaintance shall know him for the author of the book which was creating such a stir in the world. He hears the acclamations with which it was greeted with a certain personal detachment. He has sent it forth not for his own glory, but for the glory of God; he is not seeking his own advantage or renown by it, but the strengthening and the succoring of the saints. His sole joy is that it is doing its work. He has not ceased to be a " man of letters," we repeat; but he has consecrated all his gifts and powers as a " man of letters " without reserve to the service of God and His gospel.

What we see in Calvin, thus, fundamentally is the " man of letters " as saint. He never contemplated for himself, he never desired, in all his life he never fully acquiesced in, any other vocation. He was by nature, by gifts, by training — by inborn predilection and by acquired capacities alike — a " man of letters "; and he earnestly, perhaps we may even say passionately, wished to dedicate himself as such to God. This was the life which he marked out for himself, from which he was diverted only under compulsion, and which he never in principle abandoned. It was only by " the dreadful imprecation " of Farel that he was constrained to lay aside his cherished plans and enter upon the direct work of the reformation of Geneva (autumn of 1536). And when, after two years of strenuous labor at this uncongenial employment, he was driven from that turbulent city, it came to him only as a release. Once more he settled down at Basle and applied himself to his beloved studies. It required all of Bucer's strategy as well as entreaties to entice him away from his books to an active ministry at Strasburg; and he yielded at last only when it was made clear to him that there would be leisure there for literary labors. That leisure he certainly not so much found as made for himself. His little conventicle of French refugees quickly became under his hand a model church. His lectures at the school attracted ever wider and wider attention. As time passed, he was called much away to conferences and colloquies, where as "the Theologian," as Melanchthon admiringly called him, he did important service. But it was at Strasburg that his literary activity as a Protestant man of letters really began. There he transformed his "little book" of religion — the "Institutes" of 1536, which was not much more than an extended catechetical manual — into an ample treatise on theology (August, 1539). There, too, he inaugurated the series of his epoch-making expositions of Scripture with his noble commentary on Romans (March, 1540). Thence, too, he sent out his beautiful letter to Sadoleto, the most winningly written of all his controversial treatises (September, 1539). There, too, was written that exquisite little popular tract on the Lord's Supper, which was the instruction and consolation of so many hundreds of his perplexed fellow-countrymen (published in 1541). It caused Calvin great perturbation when these fruitful labors were broken in upon by a renewed call to Geneva. It was with the profoundest reluctance that he listened to this call, and he obeyed it only under the stress of the sternest sense of duty. Returning to Geneva was to him going "straight to the cross": he went, as he said, "as a sacrifice slain unto God" — "bound and fettered to obedience to God." He was not the man to take up a cross and not bear it; and this cross, too, he bore faithfully to the end. But neither was he the man to forget the labor of love to which he had given his heart. Hence the unremitting toil of his pen, with which he wore out the days and nights at Geneva; hence the immensity of his literary output, produced in circumstances as unfavorable as any in which a rich literary output was ever produced. Even "on this rack" Calvin remained fundamentally the "man of letters."

It requires fifty-nine quarto volumes to contain the "Works of John Calvin" as collected in the great critical edition of Baum, Cunitz, and Reuss. Astonishing for their mere mass, these "works" are still more astonishing for their quality.

They are written in the best Latin of their day, elevated, crisp, energetic, eloquent with the eloquence of an earnest and sober spirit — almost too good Latin, as Joseph Scaliger said, for a theologian; or in a French which was a factor of importance in the creation of a worthy French prose for the discussion of serious themes. The variety of their literary form runs through the whole gamut of earnest discourse, from lofty discussion and pithy comment laden with meaning, to burning exhortation, vehement invective, and biting satire. The whole range of subjects proper to a teacher of fundamental truth, who was also both a churchman and a statesman, a minute observer of the life of the people, and a student of the forces by which peoples are moved, is treated, and never without that touch of illumination which we call genius.

At the head of the list of his writing stands, of course, his great dogmatic treatise — the " Institutes of the Christian Religion." In a very literal sense this book may indeed be called his life-work. It was the first book he published after he had " devoted himself to God," and thus introduces the series of his works consecrated to the propagation of religion. But from its first appearance in the spring of 1536 to the issue of its definitive edition in 1559 — throughout nearly a quarter of a century — Calvin was continually busy with it, revising, expanding, readjusting it, until from a simple little handbook, innocent of constructive principle, it had grown into a bulky but compact and thoroughly organized textbook in theology. The importance to the Protestant cause of the publication of this book can hardly be overstated. It is inadequate praise to describe it, as the Roman Catholic historian, Kampschulte, describes it, as " without doubt the most outstanding and the most influential production in the sphere of dogmatics which the Reformation literature of the sixteenth century presents." This goes without saying. What demands recognition is that the publication of the " Institutes " was not merely a literary incident but an historical event, big with issues which have not lost their importance to the present day. By it was given to perplexed, hard-bestead Protestantism an adequate positive programme for its Reformation. As even a not very friendly critic is compelled to bear witness, in this book Calvin at last raised banner against banner, and sounded out a ringing *sursum corda* which was heard and responded to wherever men were seeking the new way. "The immense service which the *Institutes* rendered to the 'Evangelicals,'" expounds this critic — it is M. Buisson in his biography of Sebastien Castellion, and he is thinking particularly of the "Evangelicals" of France though, *mutatis mutandis,* what he says has its application elsewhere too — "was to give a body to their ideas, an expression to their faith." Protesting against superstitious and materialistic interpretations of doctrine and worship, "their vague aspirations would, undoubtedly, have issued in nothing in the Church or out of it." What they needed, and what the "Institutes" did for them, was the disengagement of a principle "from this vortex of ideas," and the development of its consequences. "Such a book," continues M. Buisson, "is equally removed from a pamphlet of Ulrich von Hutten, from the satire of Erasmus, from the popular preaching, mystical and violent, of Luther: it is a work of a theologian in the most learned sense of the term, a religious work undoubtedly, penetrated with an ethical inspiration, but before all, a work of organization and concentration, a code of doctrine for the minister, an arsenal of arguments for simple believers: it is the *Summa* of Reformed Christianity." "The author's concernment is far more to bring out the logical force and the moral power of his own doctrine than to descant on the weak points of the opposing doctrine. What holds his attention is not the past but the future — it is the reconstruction of the Church." What wonder, then, that it has retained its influence through all succeeding time? As the first adequate statement of the positive programme of the Reformation movement, the "Institutes" lies at the foundation of the whole development of Protestant theology, and has left an impress on evangelical thought which is ineffaceable. After three centuries and a half, it retains its unquestioned preëminence as the greatest and most influential of all dogmatic treatises. "There," said Albrecht Ritschl, pointing to it, "There is the masterpiece of Protestant theology."

Second only to the service he rendered by his "Institutes" was the service Calvin rendered by his expositions of Scripture. These fill more than thirty volumes of his collected works, thus constituting the larger part of his total literary product. They cover the whole of the New Testament except II and III John and the Apocalypse, and the whole of the Old Testament except the Solomonic and some of the Historical books. It was doubtless in part to his humanistic training that he owed the acute philological sense and the unerring feeling for language which characterize all his expositions. A recent writer who has made a special study of Calvin's Humanism, at least, remarks: " In his sober grammatico-historical method, in the stress he laid on the natural sense of the text, by the side of his deep religious understanding of it — in his renunciation of the current allegorizing, in his felicitous, skillful dealing with difficult passages, the humanistically trained master is manifest, pouring the new wine into new bottles." Calvin was, however, a born exegete, and adds to his technical equipment of philological knowledge and trained skill in the interpretation of texts a clear and penetrating intelligence, remarkable intellectual sympathy, incorruptible honesty, unusual historical perception, and an incomparable insight into the progress of thought, while the whole is illuminated by his profound religious comprehension. His expositions of Scripture were accordingly a wholly new phenomenon, and introduced a new exegesis — the modern exegesis. He stands out in the history of biblical study as, what Diestel, for example, proclaims him, " the creator of genuine exegesis." The authority which his comments immediately acquired was immense — they " opened the Scriptures" as the Scriptures never had been opened before. Richard Hooker — "the judicious Hooker " — remarks that in the controversies of his own time, " the sense of Scripture which Calvin alloweth " was of more weight than if " ten thousand Augustines, Jeromes, Chrysostoms, Cyprians were brought forward." Nor have they lost

their value even to-day. Alone of the commentaries of their
age the most scientific of modern expositors still find their
profit in consulting them. As Professor A. J. Baumgartner,
who has set himself to investigate the quality of Calvin's
Hebrew learning (which he finds quite adequate), puts it,
after remarking on Calvin's " astounding, multiplied, almost
superhuman activity " in his work of biblical interpretation:
" And — a most remarkable thing — this work has never grown
old; these commentaries whose durable merit and high value
men of the most diverse tendencies have signalized, — these
commentaries remain to us even to-day, an astonishingly rich,
almost inexhaustible mine of profound thoughts, of solid and
often ingenious interpretation, of wholesome exposition, and at
the same time of profound erudition."

The Reformation was the greatest revolution of thought
which the human spirit has wrought since the introduction of
Christianity; and controversy is the very essence of revolutions. Of course Calvin's whole life, which was passed in the
thick of things, was a continuous controversy; and directly
controversial treatises necessarily form a considerable part of
his literary output. We have already been taught, indeed, that
his fundamental aim was constructive, not destructive: he
wished to rebuild the Church on its true foundations, not to
destroy its edifice. But, like certain earlier rebuilders of the
Holy City, he needed to work with the trowel in one hand and
the sword in the other. Probably no more effective controversialist ever wrote. " The number of Calvin's polemical treatises," remarks an unfriendly critic, " is large; and they are all
masterpieces in their kind." At the head of them, in time as
well as in attractiveness, stands his famous " Letter to Cardinal
Sadoleto," written in his exile at Strasburg for the protection
from an insidious foe of the Church which had cast him out.
Courteous, even gentle and deferential in tone, and yet cogent,
conclusive, in effect, it perfectly exemplifies the precept of
suaviter in modo, fortiter in re. Others are, no doubt, set in a
different key. The critic we have just quoted (E. F. Bähler)
tells of the one he thinks " the harshest and bitterest of all,"

the " Defense Against the Calumnies of Peter Caroli." " The letter to Sadoleto," he remarks, " was certainly written in a good hour; the contrary must be said of the present book. From the point of view of literary history, the *Defense,* no doubt, merits unrestricted praise. The elegant, crisp style, the skill with which the author not only casts a moral shadow upon his opponent, but brands him as an unsavory person not to be taken seriously, while over all is poured the most sovereign disdain, brings to the reader of this book, now almost four hundred years old, such æsthetic pleasure that it is only with difficulty that he recalls himself to righteous indignation over the gross unfairness and open untruthfulness which the author permits himself against Caroli." No doubt Calvin often spoke in harsh terms of his opponents; they were harsh things they were seeking for him; and the contest in which he was engaged was not a sparring match for the amusement of the onlookers. Nor need it be asserted that he was infallible; though " even his enemies will admit," as even Mark Pattison allows, " that he knows not how to decorate or disguise a fact." Between the suavity of the " Letter to Sadoleto " and the furiousness of the " Defense Against Caroli," a long list of controversial writings of very varying manners range themselves. A frankness of speech characterizes them which never balks at calling a spade a spade; we meet in them with depreciatory, even defamatory, epithets which jar sadly on our modern sensibilities. These are faults not of the man, but of the times: as we are reminded by M. Lenient, the historian of French satire, of all figures of rhetoric euphemism was the least in use in the sixteenth century. But none of Calvin's controversial tracts fails to be informed from beginning to end with a loftiness of purpose, to be conducted with a seriousness and directness of argument, and to be filled with a solid instruction, such as raise them far above the plane of mere partisan wrangle and give them a place among the permanent possessions of the Church.

Fault was found with him in his own day — as, for example, by Castellion — for permitting himself the use of satire in religious debate. This was not merely a result of native tem-

perament with him, but a matter of deliberate and reasoned
choice. Of course he had nothing in common with the mere
mockers of the time — des Périers, Marot, Rabelais — whose
levity was almost as abominable to him as their coarseness. Satire to him was a weapon, not an amusement. The
proper way to deal with folly, he thought, was to laugh at
it. The superstitions in which the world had been so long entangled were foolish as truly as wicked; and how could it be,
he demanded, that in speaking of things so ridiculous, so intrinsically funny, we should not laugh at them " with wide-
open mouth " ? Of course this laugh was not the laugh of pure
amusement; and as it gained in earnestness it naturally lost
in lightness of touch. It was a rapier in Calvin's hands, and its
use was to pierce and cut. And how well he uses it! The Sorbonne, for example, issued a series of " Articles," declaring the
orthodox doctrine on the points disputed by the Protestants.
Calvin republishes these " Articles," and subjoins to each of
them a quite innocent-looking " Proof," conceived perfectly
in the Sorbonnic manner, but issuing in each case in a hopeless
reductio ad absurdum. Thus: " It is proved, moreover, that
vows are obligatory from their being dispensed and loosed:
the Pope could not dispense vows were it not for the power of
the keys, and hence it follows that they bind the conscience,"
— truly as fine a specimen of *lucus a non lucendo* as one will
find in a day's search. It is only rarely that the mask is dropped
a moment and a glimpse given of the mocking eyes behind —
as thus: " But that our masters, when congregated in one body,
are the Church, is proved from this, that they are very like the
ark of Noah — since they form a herd of all sorts of beasts."
The matter is indeed in general so subtly managed that perhaps the " Antidote," which in each instance follows on the
" Proof," was not altogether unnecessary. There is no such subtlety in what is, perhaps, the best known of Calvin's satirical
pieces — his " Admonition, Showing the Advantage which
Christendom Might Derive from an Inventory of Relics." Here
we have a simple, straightforward enumeration of the relics
exposed in various churches for the veneration of the people.

The effect is produced by the incongruity, which grows more and more monstrous, of the reduplication of these relics. "Everybody knows that the inhabitants of Tholouse think that they have got six of the bodies of the apostles. Now, let us attend to those who have had two or three bodies. For Andrew has another body at Malfi, Philip and James the Less have each another body at the Church of the Holy Apostles, and Simeon and Jude, in like manner, at the Church of St. Peter. Bartholomew has also another in the church dedicated to him at Rome. So here are six who each have two bodies, and also, by way of a supernumerary, Bartholomew's skin is shown at Pisa. Matthias, however, surpasses all the rest, for he has a second body at Rome, in the church of the elder Mary, and a third one at Treves. Besides, he has another head, and another arm, existing separately by themselves. There are also fragments of Andrew existing at different places, and quite sufficient to make up half a body." And so on endlessly; and of course monotonously — which, however, is part of the calculated effect. As M. Lenient remarks, " his pitiless calculations give to a mathematical operation all the piquancy of a *bon mot*, and the irony of numbers destroys the credit of the most respected pilgrimages." It is, however, in such a tract as the " Excuse of the Nicodemites " that Calvin's satire is found at its best, as he rails at those weak Protestants who were too timid to declare themselves. " His pen," says M. Lenient, " was never more light or incisive. Moralist and painter after the fashion of La Bruyère, he amuses himself sketching all these profiles of effeminate Christians, with their slacknesses, their compromises of conscience, their calculations of selfishness, and indifferent lukewarmness." Literature this all is, doubtless, and good literature; and by virtue of it " Calvinistic satire " — Calvin, Beza, and Viret were its first masters — has a recognized place in the history of French satire. But it is not primarily or chiefly literature, and it had its part to play among the moral and religious forces which Calvin liberated for the accomplishment of his reforming work.

Perhaps enough has been said to suggest how Calvin ful-

filled his function as reformer by his literary labors. There
were, of course, other forms of his literary product which
have not been mentioned — creeds and catechisms, Church
ordinances and forms of worship, popular tracts and academic
consilia. We need not stop to speak of them particularly. Of
one other product of his literary activity, however, a special
word seems demanded. Calvin was the great letter-writer of
the Reformation age. About four thousand of his letters have
come down to us, some of them almost of the dimensions of
treatises, many of them practically theological tractates, but
many of them also of the most intimate character in which he
pours out his heart. In these letters we see the real Calvin,
the man of profound religious convictions and rich religious
life, of high purpose and noble strenuousness, of full and freely
flowing human affections and sympathies. In them he rebukes
rulers and instructs statesmen, and strengthens and comforts
saints. Never a perplexed pastor but has from him a word of
encouragement and counsel; never a martyr but has from him
a word of heartening and consolation. Perhaps no friend ever
more affectionately leaned on his friends; certainly no friend
ever gave himself more ungrudgingly to his friends. Had he
written these letters alone, Calvin would take his place among
the great Christians and the great Christian leaders of the
world.

It is time, however, that we reminded ourselves that Calvin's work as a reformer is not summed up in his literary activities. A "man of letters" he was fundamentally; and a
"man of letters" he remained in principle all his life. But he
was something more than a "man of letters." This was his
chosen sphere of service; and he counted it a cross to be compelled to expend his energies through other channels. But this
cross was laid upon him, and he took it up and bore it. And
the work which he did under the cross was such that had we no
single word from his pen, he would still hold his rank among
the greatest of the Reformers. We call him "the Reformer of
Geneva." But in reforming Geneva he set forces at work which
have been world-wide in their operation and are active still

to-day. Were we to attempt to characterize in a phrase the peculiarity of his work as a reformer, perhaps we could not do better than to say it was the work of an idealist become a practical man of affairs. He did not lack the power to wait, to make adjustments, to advance by slow and tentative steps. He showed himself able to work with any material, to make the best of compromises, to abide patiently the coming of fitting opportunities. The ends which he set before himself as reformer he attained only in the last years of his strenuous life. But he was incapable of abandoning his ideals, of acquiescing in half measures, of drifting with the tide. Therefore his whole life in Geneva was a conflict. But in the end he made Geneva the wonder of the world, and infused into the Reformed Churches a spirit which made them not only invincible in the face of their foes, but an active ferment that has changed the face of the world. Thus this "man of letters," entering into life with his ideals, was "the means," to adopt the words of a critic whose sympathy with those ideals leaves much to be desired, "of concentrating in that narrow corner" of the world "a moral force which saved the Reformation"; or rather, to put it at its full effect, which "saved Europe." "It may be doubted," as the same critic — Mark Pattison — exclaims in extorted admiration, "if all history can furnish another instance of such a victory of moral force."

When Calvin came to Geneva, he tells us himself, he found the gospel preached there, but no Church established. "When I first came to this Church," he says, "there was as good as nothing here — *il n'y avoit quasi comme rien*. There was preaching, and that was all." He would have found much the same state of things everywhere else in the Protestant world. The "Church" in the early Protestant conception was constituted by the preaching of the Word and the right administration of the sacraments: the correction of the morals of the community was the concern not of the Church but of the civil power. As a recent historian — Professor Karl Rieker — rather flippantly expresses it: "Luther, when he had preached and sowed the seed of the Word, left to the Holy Spirit the care of producing the fruit, while with his friend Philip he peacefully drank his glass of Wittenberg beer." Calvin could not take this view of the matter. " Whatever others may hold," he observed, " we cannot think so narrowly of our office that when preaching is done our task is fulfilled, and we may take our rest." In his view the mark of a true Church is not merely that the gospel is preached in it, but that it is " followed." For him the Church is the " communion of saints," and it is incumbent upon it to see to it that it is what it professes to be. From the first he therefore set himself strenuously to attain this end, and the instrument which he sought to employ to attain it was, briefly — Church discipline. It comes to us with a surprise which is almost a shock to learn that we owe to Calvin all that is involved, for the purity and welfare of the Church, in the exercise of Church discipline. But that is the simple truth, and so sharp was the conflict by which the innovation won a place for itself, and so important did the principle seem, that it became the mark of the Reformed Churches that they made " discipline " one of the fundamental criteria of the true Church. Moreover, the application of this principle carried Calvin very far, and, indeed, in its outworking gave the world through him the principle of a free Church in a free State. It is ultimately to him, therefore, that the Church owes its emancipation from the State, and to him goes back that great battle-cry which has since fired the hearts of many saints in many crises in many lands: " The Crown Rights of King Jesus in His Church."

Censorship of manners and morals was not introduced by Calvin into Geneva. Such a censorship, often of the most petty and galling kind, was the immemorial practice not only of Geneva but of all other similarly constituted towns. It was part of the recognized police regulations of the times. Calvin's sole relation to this censorship was through his influence — he never bore civil office or exercised civil authority in Geneva, and, indeed, acquired the rights of citizenship there only late in life — gradually to bring some order and rationality into its exercise. What Calvin introduced — and it was so revolu-

tionary with respect both to the State and to the Church that
it required eighteen years of bitter struggle before it was established — was distinctively *Church* discipline. The principles on which he proceeded were already laid down in the
first edition of his " Institutes " (spring of 1536). And when he
came to Geneva in the autumn of 1536 he lost no time in seeking to put them into practice. Already at the opening of 1537
we find a document drawn up by him in the name of the ministers of Geneva before the Council, in which the whole new conception is briefly outlined. This great charter of the Church's
liberties — for it is as truly such as the " Magna Charta "
is the charter of British rights — opens with these simple and
direct words: " It is certain that a Church cannot be said to be
well ordered and governed unless the Holy Supper of our Lord
is frequently celebrated and attended in it, and that with such
good regulation that no one would dare to present himself at
it except with piety and deep reverence. And it is therefore
necessary for the Church to maintain in its integrity the discipline of excommunication, by which those should be corrected who are unwilling to yield themselves amiably and in
all obedience to the holy Word of God." In the body of the
document the matter is argued, and three things are proposed:
First, that it be ascertained at the outset who of the inhabitants of the town wished " to avow themselves of the Church
of Jesus Christ." For this, it is suggested that a brief and comprehensive Confession of Faith be prepared, and " all the inhabitants of your town " be required to " make confession and
render reason of their faith, that it may be ascertained which
accord with the Gospel, and which prefer to be of the kingdom
of the Pope rather than of Jesus Christ." Secondly, that a catechism be prepared, and the children be diligently instructed
in the elements of the faith. And thirdly, that provision be
made by the appointment of " certain persons of good life and
good repute among all the faithful, and likewise of constancy
of spirit and not open to corruption," who should keep watch
over the conduct of the Church members, advise with them,
admonish them, and in obstinate cases bring them to the at-

tention of the ministers, when, if they still prove unamenable, they are " to be held as rejected from the company of Christians," and " as a sign of this, rejected from the communion of the Lord's Supper, and denounced to the rest of the faithful as not to be companied with familiarly." By this programme Calvin became nothing less than the creator of the Protestant Church. The particular points to be emphasized in it are two. It is purely *Church* discipline which is contemplated, with none other but spiritual penalties. And the Church is for this purpose especially discriminated from the body of the people — the State — and a wedge is thus driven in between Church and State which was bound to separate the one from the other.

In claiming for the Church this discipline, Calvin, naturally, had no wish in any way to infringe upon the police regulations of the civil authorities. They continued, in their own sphere, to command his approval and coöperation. He has the clearest conception of the limits within which the discipline of the Church must keep itself, and expressly declares that it is confined absolutely to the spiritual penalty of excommunication. But he just as expressly suggests that the State, on its own part, might well take cognizance of spiritual offenses; and even invokes the aid of the civil magistrate in support of the authority of the Church. " This," he says to the Council, after outlining his scheme for the appointment of lay helpers — in effect elders — in the exercise of discipline, — " this seems to us a good way to introduce excommunication into our Church, and to maintain it in its entirety. And beyond this correction the Church cannot proceed. But if there are any so insolent and abandoned to all perversity that they only laugh at being excommunicated, and do not mind living and dying in such a condition of rejection, it will be for you to consider how long you will .endure and leave unpunished such contempt and such mockery of God and His Gospel." This is not requiring the State to execute the Church's decrees: the Church executes her own decrees, and its extremest penalty is excommunication. It is only recognizing that the State as well as the Church may take account of spiritual offenses. And particularly it is declaring that while the Church by her own sanctions protects her own altars, it is the part of the State by its own sanctions to sustain the Church in protecting its altars. Calvin has not risen to the conception of the complete mutual independence of Church and State: his view still includes the conception of an "established Church." But the "established Church" which he pleads for is a Church absolutely autonomous in its own spiritual sphere. In asking this he was asking for something new in the Protestant world, and something in which lay the promise and potency of all the freedom which has come to the Reformed Churches since.

Of course Calvin did not get what he asked for in 1537. Nor did he get it when he returned from his banishment in 1541. But he never lost it from sight; he never ceased to contend for it; he was always ready to suffer for its assertion and defense; and at last he won it. The spiritual liberties which he demanded for the Church in 1536, for the assertion of which he was banished in 1538, for the establishment of which he ceaselessly struggled from 1541, he measurably attained at length in 1555. In the fruits of that great victory we have all had our part. And every Church in Protestant Christendom which enjoys to-day any liberty whatever, in performing its functions as a Church of Jesus Christ, owes it all to John Calvin. It was he who first asserted this liberty in his early manhood — he was only twenty-seven years of age when he presented his programme to the Council; it was he who first gained it in a lifelong struggle against a determined opposition; it was he who taught his followers to value it above life itself, and to secure it to their successors with the outpouring of their blood. And thus Calvin's great figure rises before us as not only in a true sense the creator of the Protestant Church, but the author of all the freedom it exercises in its spiritual sphere.

It is impossible to linger here on the relations of this great exploit of Calvin's, even to point out its rooting in his fundamental religious conceptions, or its issue in the creation of a spirit in his followers to the efflorescence of which this modern world of ours owes its free institutions. We cannot even stop to indicate other important claims he has upon our reverence. We say nothing here, for example, of Calvin the preacher — the "man of the Word" as Doumergue calls him, pronouncing him as such greater than he was as "man of action" or "man of thought," as both of which he was very great — who for twenty-five years stood in the pulpit of Geneva, preaching sometimes daily, sometimes twice a day, a word the echoes of which were heard to the confines of Europe. We say nothing, again, of his reorganization of the worship of the Reformed Churches, and particularly of his gift to them of the service of song: for the Reformed Churches did not sing until Calvin taught them to do it. There are many who think that he did few things greater or more far-reaching in their influence than the making of the Psalter — that Psalter of which twenty-five editions were published in the first year of its existence, and sixty-two more in the next four years; which was translated or transfused into nearly every language of Europe; and which wrought itself into the very flesh and bone of the struggling saints throughout all the "killing times" of Protestant history. The activities of Calvin were too varied and multiplex, his influence in numerous directions too enormous, to lend themselves to rapid enumeration. We can pause further only to say a necessary word of that system of divine truth which, by his winning restatement and powerful advocacy of it, he has stamped with his name, and with his eye upon which a Roman Catholic writer of our day — Canon William Barry — pronounces Calvin "undoubtedly the greatest of Protestant divines, and, perhaps, after St. Augustine, the most persistently followed by his disciples of any western writer on theology."

It has become very much the custom of modern historians to insist that Calvin's was not an original but only a systematizing genius. Thus, for example, Reinhold Seeberg remarks: "His was an acute and delicate but not a creative mind." "As a dogmatician, he furnished no new ideas; but with the most delicate sense of perception he arranged the dogmatic ideas at hand in accordance with their essential character and their historical development." "He possessed the wonderful talent of comprehending any given body of religious ideas in its most delicate refinements and giving appropriate expression to the results of his investigations." Accordingly, he did not leave behind him "uncoined gold, like Luther," or "questionable coinage, like Melanchthon," but good gold well minted — and in this lies the explanation of the greatness of his influence as a theologian. The contention may very easily be overpressed. But at its basis there lies the perception of a very important fact; perhaps we may say the most important fact in the premises.

Calvin was a thoroughly independent student of Scripture, and brought forth from that treasure-house things not only old but new; and if it was not given to him to recover for the world so revolutionizing a doctrine as that of Justification by Faith alone, the contributions of his fertile thought to doctrinal advance were neither few nor unimportant. He made an epoch in the history of the doctrine of the Trinity: by his insistence on "self-existence" as a proper attribute of Son and Spirit as well as of the Father, he drove out the lingering elements of Subordinationism, and secured to the Church a deepened consciousness of the co-equality of the Divine Persons. He introduced the presentation of the work of Christ under the rubrics of the threefold office of Prophet, Priest, and King. He created the whole discipline of Christian Ethics. But above all he gave to the Church the entire doctrine of the Work of the Holy Spirit, profoundly conceived and wrought out in its details, with its fruitful distinctions of common and efficacious grace, of noëtic, aisthetic, and thelematic effects, — a gift, we venture to think, so great, so pregnant with benefit to the Church as fairly to give him a place by the side of Augustine and Anselm and Luther, as the Theologian of the Holy Spirit, as they were respectively the Theologian of Grace, of the Atonement, and of Justification.

Nevertheless, despite such contributions — contributions

of the first order — to theological advance, it is quite true — and it is a truth deserving the strongest emphasis — that the system of doctrine which Calvin taught, and by his powerful commendation of which his greatest work for the world was wrought, was not peculiar to himself, was in no sense new, — was, in point of fact, just " the Gospel " common to him and all the Reformers, on the ground of which they spoke of themselves as " Evangelicals," and by the recovery of which was wrought out the revolution which we call the Reformation. Calvin did not originate this system of truth; as " a man of the second generation " he inherited it, and his greatest significance as a religious teacher is that by his exact and delicate sense of doctrinal values and relations and his genius for systematic construction, he was able, as none other was, to cast this common doctrinal treasure of the Reformation into a well-compacted, logically unassailable, and religiously inspiring whole. In this sense it is as systematizer that he makes his greatest demand on our admiration and gratitude. It was he who gave the Evangelical movement a theology.

The system of doctrine taught by Calvin is just the Augustinianism common to the whole body of the Reformers — for the Reformation was, as from the spiritual point of view a great revival of religion, so from the theological point of view a great revival of Augustinianism. And this Augustinianism is taught by him not as an independent discovery of his own, but fundamentally as he learned it from Luther, whose fertile conceptions he completely assimilated, and most directly and in much detail from Martin Bucer into whose practical, ethical point of view he perfectly entered. Many of the very forms of statement most characteristic of Calvin — on such topics as Predestination, Faith, the stages of Salvation, the Church, the Sacraments — only reproduce, though of course with that clearness and religious depth peculiar to Calvin, the precise teachings of Bucer, who was above all others, accordingly, Calvin's master in theology. Of course he does not take these ideas over from Bucer and repeat them by rote. They have become his own and issue afresh from him with a new

exactness and delicacy of appreciation, in themselves and in
their relations, with a new development of implications, and
especially with a new richness of religious content. For the
prime characteristic of Calvin as a theologian is precisely the
practical interest which governs his entire thought and the religious profundity which suffuses it all. It was not the head
but the heart which made him a theologian, and it is not
the head but the heart which he primarily addresses in his
theology.

He takes his start, of course, from God, knowledge of whom
and obedience to whom he declares the sum of human wisdom.
But this God he conceives as righteous love — Lord as well as
Father, of course, but Father as well as Lord; whose will is, of
course, the *prima causa rerum* (for is He not God?), but whose
will also it will be our joy as well as our wisdom to embrace
(for is He not our Father?). It was that we might know ourselves to be wholly in the hands of this God of perfect righteousness and goodness — not in those of men, whether ourselves
or some other men — that he was so earnest for the doctrine
of predestination: which is nothing more than the declaration of the supreme dominion of God. It was that our eternal felicity might hang wholly on God's mighty love — and
not on our sinful weakness — that he was so zealous for the
doctrine of election: which is nothing more than the ascription
of our entire salvation to God. As he contemplated the majesty
of this Sovereign Father of men, his whole being bowed in
reverence before Him, and his whole heart burned with zeal for
His glory. As he remembered that this great God has become
in His own Son the Redeemer of sinners, he passionately gave
himself to the proclamation of the glory of His grace. Into His
hands he committed himself without reserve: his whole spirit
panted to be in all its movement subjected to His government
— or, to be more specific, to the " leading of His Spirit." All
that was good in him, all the good he hoped might be formed
in him, he ascribed to the almighty working of this Divine
Spirit. The " glory of God alone " — the " leading of the
Spirit " (or, as a bright young French student of his thought

has lately expressed it, *la maitrise*, the "mastery," the control, of the Spirit), — became thus the twin principles of his whole thought and life. Or, rather, the double expression of the one principle; for — since all that God does, He does by His Spirit — the two are at bottom one.

Here we have the secret of Calvin's greatness and the source of his strength unveiled to us. No man ever had a profounder sense of God than he; no man ever more unreservedly surrendered himself to the Divine direction. "We cannot better characterize the fundamental disposition of Calvin the man and the reformer," writes a recent German student of his life — Bernhard Bess — "than in the words of the Psalm: 'What is man, that thou art mindful of him? and the son of man, that thou visitest him?' After that virtuoso in religion of ancient Israel, no one has spoken of the majesty of God and the insignificance of man with such feeling and truth as Calvin. The appearance which Luther's expressions often give, as if God exists merely for man's sake, never is given by Calvin. God is for him the almighty will which lies behind all that comes to pass. What comes to pass in the world serves no doubt man, the Church, and salvation; but this is not its ultimate end, but the revelation of the glory and the honor of God." If there is anything that will make a man great, surely it is placing himself unreservedly at the disposal of God and seeking not only to do nothing but God's will, but to do all God's will. This is what Calvin did, and it is because he did this that he was so great.

He was, of course, not without his weaknesses. He had no doubt a high temper, though to do him justice we must take the term in all its senses. He did not in all things rise superior to the best opinion of his age. We have seen, for example, that he was in full accord with his time in its extension of the cognizance of the civil courts to spiritual offenses; and it was by the consent of his mind to this universal conviction of the day that he was implicated in that unhappy occurrence — the execution of Servetus. But to do him justice here we must learn to speak both of his connection with that occur-

rence and of Servetus himself in quite other terms than the
reckless language with which a modern writer of repute speaks
when he calls Calvin " the author of the great crime of the age
— the murder of the heroic Servetus." Servetus, that " fool
of genius," as a recent writer, not without insight, characterizes him, was anything but an heroic figure. The " crime " of
his " murder," unfortunately, had scores of fellows in that
age, in which life was lightly valued, and it was agreed on all
hands that grave heresy and gross blasphemy were capital
offenses in well-organized states. And Servetus was condemned
and executed by a tribunal of which Calvin was not a member, with which he possessed little influence, and which rejected his petition against the unnecessary cruelty of the
penalty inflicted.

" There are people," remarks Paul Wernle, who is certainly under the influence of no glamour for Calvin or Calvinism — " There are people who have been told at school
that Servetus was burned through Calvin's fault, and are therefore done with this man. They ought to remember that had they
lived at the time, they would in all probability have joined
in burning him. It is not so easy to be done with the man who
was the most luminous and penetrating theologian of his time
and the source from which flowed that *power* which Protestantism showed in Scotland, France, England, Holland. We
are all glad, no doubt, that we did not live under his rod; but
who knows what we would all be, had not this divine ardor
possessed him? Concentrated, well-directed enthusiasm —
that is his essence; it was himself, first of all, whom he consumed in his zeal; his rule at Geneva was no more rigorous
than the heroism was glorious with which he compacted half
the Protestantism of Europe into a power which nothing
could break. Calvin was in very truth the soul of the battling
and conquering Reformed world; it was he who fought on
the battlefields of the Huguenots and the Dutch, and in the
hosts of the Puritans. In scarcely another of the Reformers is
there to be seen such thoroughness, absoluteness. And yet
what moderation, what real dread of every kind of excess;

with what deference and tact did he know how to speak to the great! If you would know the man, how he lived with and for God and the world, read first of all in the *Institutes* the section *On the Life of the Christian Man.* It is the portrait of himself. And then for his religious individuality add the sections *On Justification* and *On Predestination,* where will be found what is most profound, most moving in his life of faith."

Such a man was John Calvin; and such was the work he did for God and His Kingdom on earth. Adolf Harnack has said that between Paul the Apostle and Luther the Reformer, Augustine was the greatest man God gave His Church. We may surely add that from Luther the Reformer to our day God has given His Church no greater man than John Calvin.

II

CALVIN'S DOCTRINE OF THE KNOWLEDGE OF GOD

CALVIN'S DOCTRINE OF THE KNOWLEDGE OF GOD [1]

THE first chapters of Calvin's "Institutes" are taken up with a comprehensive exposition of the sources and guarantee of the knowledge of God and divine things (Book I. chs. i.–ix.). A systematic treatise on the knowledge of God must needs begin with such an exposition; and we require no account of the circumstance that Calvin's treatise begins with it, beyond the systematic character of his mind and the clearness and comprehensiveness of his view. This exposition therefore makes its appearance in the earliest edition of the "Institutes," which attempted "to give a summary of religion in all its parts," redacted in orderly sequence; that is to say, which was intended as a textbook in theology. This was the second edition, published in 1539, which was considered by Calvin to be the first which at all corresponded to its title. In this edition this exposition already stands practically complete. Large insertions were made into it subsequently, by which it was greatly enriched as a detailed exposition and validation of the sources of our knowledge of God; but no modifications were made in its fundamental teaching by these additions, and the ground plan of the exposition as laid down in 1539 was retained unaltered throughout the subsequent development of the treatise.

We may observe in the controversies in which Calvin had been engaged between 1536 and 1539 a certain preparation for writing this comprehensive and admirably balanced statement, with its equal repudiation of Romish and Anabaptist error and its high note of assurance in the face of the scepticism of the average man of the world. We may trace in it the fruits of his eager and exhaustive studies prosecuted in the interval,

[1] From *The Princeton Theological Review,* vii. 1909, pp. 219–325.

as pastor, professor, and Protestant statesman; and especially
of his own ripening thought as he worked more and more into
detail his systematic view of the body of truth. But we can
attribute to nothing but his theological genius the feat by
which he set a compressed apologetical treatise in the forefront of his little book — for the "Institutes" were still in
1539 a little book, although already expanded to more than
double the size of their original form (edition of 1536). Thus
he not only for the first time supplied the constructive basis
for the Reformation movement, but even for the first time in
the history of Christian theology drew in outline the plan of a
complete structure of Christian Apologetics. For this is the
significance in the history of thought of Calvin's exposition of
the sources and guarantee of the knowledge of God, which
forms the opening topic of his "Institutes." "Thus," says Julius
Köstlin, after cursorily surveying the course of the exposition,
"there already rises with him an edifice of Christian Apologetics, in its outlines complete (*fertig*). With it, he stands, already in 1539, unique (*einzig*) among the Reformers, and among
Christian theologians in general up to his day. Only as isolated building-stones can appear in comparison with this, even
what Melanchthon, for example, offered in the last elaboration of the *Loci* with reference to the proofs for the existence
of God." [2] In point of fact, in Augustine alone among his
predecessors do we find anything like the same grasp of the
elements of the problem as Calvin here exhibits; and nowhere
among his predecessors do we find these elements brought together in a constructive statement of anything like the completeness and systematic balance which he gave to it.

At once on its publication, however, Calvin's apologetical
construction became the property of universal Christian
thought, and it has entered so vitally into Protestant, and
especially Reformed, thinking as to appear now-a-days very
much a matter of course. It is difficult for us to appreciate

[2] Article on "Calvin's Institutio, nach Form und Inhalt, in ihrer geschichtlichen Entwickelung," printed in the *Theologische Studien und Kritiken* for
1868, p. 39. Köstlin's whole account of the origin of these sections in the edition
of 1539 is worth reading (pp. 38–39).

its novelty in him or to realize that it is not as native to every Christian mind as it now seems to us the inevitable adjustment of the elements of the problems raised by the Christian revelation. Familiar as it seems, therefore, it is important that we should apprehend it, at least in its outlines, as it lies in its primary statement in Calvin's pages. So only can we appreciate Calvin's genius or estimate what we owe to him. A very brief abstract will probably suffice, however, to bring before us in the first instance the elements of Calvin's thought. These include the postulation of an innate knowledge of God in man, quickened and developed by a very rich manifestation of God in nature and providence, which, however, fails of its proper effect because of man's corruption in sin; so that an objective revelation of God, embodied in the Scriptures, was rendered necessary, and, as well, a subjective operation of the Spirit of God on the heart enabling sinful man to receive this revelation — by which conjoint divine action, objective and subjective, a true knowledge of God is communicated to the human soul.

Drawn out a little more into detail, this teaching is as follows. The knowledge of God is given in the very same act by which we know self. For when we know self, we must know it as it is: and that means we must know it as dependent, derived, imperfect, and responsible being. To know self implies, therefore, the co-knowledge with self of that on which it is dependent, from which it derives, by the standard of which its imperfection is revealed, to which it is responsible. Of course, such a knowledge of self postulates a knowledge of God, in contrast with whom alone do we ever truly know self: but this only the more emphasises the fact that we know God in knowing self, and the relative priority of our knowledge of two objects of knowledge which we are conscious only of knowing together may for the moment be left undetermined. Meanwhile, it is clear than man has an instinctive and ineradicable knowledge of God, which, moreover, must produce appropriate reactions in his thought, feeling, and will, whence arises what we call religion. But these reactions are conditioned by the state of the soul which reacts. Although, then, man cannot avoid possessing a knowledge of God, and this innate knowledge of God is quickened and developed by the richest manifestations of God in nature and providence, which no man can escape either perceiving or so far apprehending, yet the actual knowledge of God which is framed in the human soul is affected by the subjective condition of the soul. The soul, being corrupted by sin, is dulled in its instinctive apprehension of God; and God's manifestation in nature and history is deflected in it. Accordingly the testimony of nature to God is insufficient that sinful man should know Him aright, and God has therefore supernaturally revealed Himself to His people and deposited this revelation of Himself in written Scriptures. In these Scriptures alone, therefore, do we possess an adequate revelation of God; and this revelation is attested as such by irresistible external evidence and attests itself as such by such marks of inherent divinity that no normal mind can resist them. But the sin-darkened minds to which it appeals are not normal minds, but disordered with the awful disease of sin. What is to give subjective effect in a sin-blinded mind to even a direct revelation from God? The revelation of God is its own credential. It needs no other light to be thrown upon it but that which emanates from itself: and no other light can produce the effect which its own splendor as a revelation of God should effect. But all fails when the receptivity is destroyed by sin. For sinners, therefore, there is requisite a repairing operation upon their souls before the light of the Word itself can accredit itself to them as light. This repairing operation on the souls of sinful men by which they are enabled to perceive light is called the testimony of the Holy Ghost: which is therefore just the subjective action of the Spirit of God on the heart, by virtue of which it is opened for the perception and reception of the objective revelation of God. The testimony of the Spirit cannot, then, take the place of the objective revelation of the Word: it is no revelation in this strict sense. It presupposes the objective revelation and only prepares the heart to respond to and embrace it. But the objective revelation can take no effect on the unprepared heart.

What the operation of the Spirit on the heart does, then, is to implant, or rather to restore, a spiritual sense in the soul by which God is recognized in His Word. When this spiritual sense has been produced the necessity of external proofs that the Scriptures are the Word of God is superseded: the Word of God is as immediately perceived as such as light is perceived as light, sweetness as sweetness — as immediately and as inamissibly. The Christian's knowledge of God, therefore, rests no doubt on an instinctive perception of God native to man as man, developed in the light of a patefaction of God which pervades all nature and history; but particularly on an objective revelation of God deposited in Scriptures which bear in themselves their own evidence of their divine origin, to which every spiritual man responds with the same strength of conviction with which he recognizes light as light. This is the basis which Calvin in his " Institutes " places beneath his systematic exposition of the knowledge of God.

The elements of Calvin's thought here, it will readily be seen, reduce themselves to a few great fundamental principles. These embrace particularly the following doctrines: the doctrine of the innate knowledge of God; the doctrine of the general revelation of God in nature and history; the doctrine of the special revelation of God and its embodiment in Scriptures; the doctrine of the noëtic effects of sin; the doctrine of the testimony of the Holy Spirit. That we may do justice to his thought we must look in some detail at his treatment of each of these doctrines and of the subordinate topics which are necessarily connected with them.

I. Natural Revelation

That the knowledge of God is innate (I. iii. 3), naturally engraved on the hearts of men (I. iv. 4), and so a part of their very constitution as men (I. iii. 1), that it is a matter of instinct (I. iii. 1, I. iv. 2), and every man is self-taught it from his birth (I. iii. 3), Calvin is thoroughly assured. He lays it down as incontrovertible fact that " the human mind, by natural instinct itself, possesses some sense of a deity "

(I. iii. 1, *ad init. et ad fin.;* 3 — *sensus divinitatis* or *deitatis*),[3] and defends the corollaries which flow from this fact, that the knowledge of God is universal and indelible. All men know there is a God, who has made them, and to whom they are responsible. No savage is sunk so low as to have lost this sense of deity, which is wrought into his very constitution: and the degradation of men's worship is a proof of its ineradicableness — since even such dehumanization as this worship manifests has not obliterated it (I. iii. 1). It is the precondition of all religion, without which no religion would ever have arisen; and it forms the silent assumption of all attempts to expound the origin of religion in fraud or political artifice, as it does also of all corruptions of religion, which find their nerve in men's incurable religious propensities (I. iii. 1). The very atheists testify to its persistence in their ill-concealed dread of the deity they profess to despise (I. iv. 2); and the wicked, strive they ever so hard to banish from their consciousness the sense of an accusing deity, are not permitted by nature to forget it (I. iii. 3). Thus the cases alike of the savages, the atheists, and the wicked are made contributory to the establishment of the fact, and the discussion concludes with the declaration that it is by this innate knowledge of God that men are discriminated from the brutes, so that for men to lose it would be to fall away from the very law of their creation (I. iii. 3, *ad fin.*).[4]

[3] " Institutes," I. iii. 1: Quemdam inesse humanae menti, et quidem naturali instinctu, divinitatis sensum, extra controversiam ponimus; iii. 3, *ad init.:* " This indeed with all rightly judging men will always be assured, that there is engraved on the minds of men *divinitatis sensum, qui deleri numquam potest* "; iii. 3, *med.:* vigere tamen ac subinde emergere quem maxime extinctum cuperent, *deitatis sensum;* iv. 4, *ad fin.:* naturaliter insculptum esse deitatis sensum humanis cordibus; iv. 4, *ad fin.:* manet tamen semen illud quod revelli a radice nullo modo potest, aliquam esse divinitatem. The phraseology by which Calvin designates this " natural instinct " (*naturalis instinctus;* iii. 1, *ad init.*) varies from *sensus divinitatis* or *sensus deitatis* to such synonyms as: *numinis intelligentia, dei notio, dei notitia.* It is the basis on the one hand of whatever *cognitio dei* man attains to and on the other of whatever *religio* he reaches; whence it is called the *semen religionis.*

[4] That the knowledge of God is innate was the common property of the Reformed teachers. Peter Martyr, " Loci Communes," 1576, *praef.,* declares that *Dei cognitio omnium animis naturaliter innata*[*est*]. It was thrown

If the knowledge of God enters thus into the very idea of humanity and constitutes a law of its being, it follows that it is given in the same act of knowledge by which we know ourselves. This position is developed at length in the opening chapter. The discussion begins with a remark which reminds us of Augustine's familiar contention that the proper concern of mankind is the knowledge of God and the soul; to which it is added at once that these two knowledges are so interrelated that it is impossible to assign the priority to either. The knowledge of self involves the knowledge of God and also profits by the knowledge of God: the better we know ourselves the better we shall know God, but also, we shall never know ourselves as we really are save in contrast with God, by whom is supplied the only standard for the formation of an accurate judgment upon ourselves (I. i. 2). In his analysis of the mode of the implication of the knowledge of God in the knowledge of self, Calvin lays the stress upon our nature as dependent, derived, imperfect, and responsible beings, which if known at all must be known as such, and to be known as such must be known as over against that Being on whom we are dependent, to whom we owe our being, over against whom our imperfection is manifest, and to whom we are responsible (I. i. 1). As we are not self-existent, we must recognize ourselves as " living and moving " in Another. We recognize ourselves as products, and in knowing the product know the cause; thus our very endowments, seeing that they distil to us by drops from heaven, form so many streams up which our minds must needs travel to their Fountainhead. The perception of our imperfec-

---

into great prominence in the Socinian debate, as the Socinians contended that the human mind is natively a *tabula rasa* and all knowledge is acquired. But in defending the innate knowledge of God, the Reformed doctors were very careful that it should not be exaggerated. Thus Leonh. Riissen, " F. Turretini Compendium . . . auctum et illustratum," 1695, i. 8, remarks: " Some recent writers explain the natural sense of deity (*numinis*) as *an idea of God impressed on our minds*. If this idea is understood as an innate *faculty* for knowing God after some fashion, it should not be denied; but if it expresses an *actual and adequate representation of God from our birth*, it is to be entirely rejected." (Heppe, " Die Dogmatik der evangelisch-reformirten Kirche," 1861, p. 4.)

tions is at the same time the perception of His perfection; so
that our very poverty displays to us His infinite fulness. Our
sense of dissatisfaction with ourselves directs our eyes to Him
whose righteous judgment we can but anticipate; and when in
the presence of His majesty we realize our meanness and in the
presence of His righteousness we realize our sin, our perception of God passes into consternation as we recognize in Him
our just Judge.

The emphasis which Calvin places in this analysis upon
the sense of sin and the part it plays in our knowledge of God,
at once attracts attention. It is perhaps above everything the
" miserable ruin " in which we find ourselves, which compels
us, according to him, to raise our eyes towards heaven, spurred
on not merely by a sense of lack but by a sense of dread: it
is only, he declares, when we have begun to be displeased with
ourselves that we energetically turn our thoughts Godward.
This is already an indication of the engrossment of Calvin in
this treatise with practical rather than merely theoretical problems. He is less concerned to show how man as man attains to
a knowledge of God, than how man as he actually exists upon
the earth attains to it. In the very act of declaring that this
knowledge is instinctive and belongs to the very constitution
of man as such, therefore, he so orders the exposition of the
mode of its actual rise in the mind as to throw the emphasis
on a quality which does not belong to man as such, but only
to man as actually existing in the world — in that "miserable
ruin into which we have been plunged by the defection of the
first man " (I. i. 1). Man as unfallen, by the very necessity of
his nature would have known God, the sphere of his being, the
author of his existence, the standard of his excellences; but
for man as fallen, Calvin seems to say, the strongest force compelling him to look upwards to the God above him, streams
from his sense of sin, filling him with a fearful looking forward
to judgment.

It is quite obvious that such a knowledge of God as Calvin
here postulates as the unavoidable and ineradicable possession of man, is far from a mere empty conviction that such

a being as God exists. The knowledge of God which is given in our knowledge of self is not a bare perception, it is a conception: it has content. " The knowledge of ourselves, therefore," says Calvin (I. i. 1, *ad fin.*), " is not only an incitement to seek after God, but becomes a considerable assistance towards finding God." The knowledge of God with which we are natively endowed is therefore more than a bare conviction that God is: it involves, more or less explicated, some understanding of what God is. Such a knowledge of God can never be otiose and inert; but must produce an effect in human souls, in the way of thinking, feeling, willing. In other words, our native endowment is not merely a *sensus deitatis,* but also a *semen religionis* (I. iii. 1, 2; iv. 1, 4; v. 1). For what we call religion is just the reaction of the human soul to what it perceives God to be. Calvin is, therefore, just as insistent that religion is universal as that the knowledge of God is universal. " The seeds of religion," he insists, " are sown in every heart " (I. iv. 1; cf. v. 1); men are propense to religion (I. iii. 2, *med.*); and always and everywhere frame to themselves a religion, consonant with their conceptions of God.

Calvin's ideas of the origin and nature of religion are set forth, if succinctly, yet with eminent clearness, in his second chapter. Wherever any knowledge of God exists, he tells us, there religion exists. He is not speaking here of a competent knowledge of God such as redeemed sinners have in Christ. But much less is he speaking of that mere notion that there is such a being as God which is sometimes called a knowledge of God. It may be possible to speculate on " the essence " of God without being moved by it. But certainly it is impossible to form any vital conception of God without some movement of intellect, feeling, and will towards Him; and any real knowledge of God is inseparable from movements of piety towards Him. Piety means reverence and love to God; and the knowledge of God tends therefore to produce in us, first, sentiments of fear and reverence; and, secondly, an attitude of receptivity and praise to Him as the fountain of all blessing. If man were not a sinner, indeed, such would be the result: men, knowing

God, would turn to Him in confidence and commit themselves
without reserve to His care — not so much fearing His judgments, as making them in sympathetic loyalty their own (I. ii.
2). And herein we see what pure and genuine religion is: " it
consists in faith, united with a serious fear of God, comprehending a voluntary reverence, and producing legitimate worship agreeable to the injunctions of the law " (I. ii. 2, *ad fin.*).[5]

The definition of religion to which Calvin thus attains is
exceedingly interesting, and that not merely because of its
vital relation to the fundamental thought of these opening
chapters, but also because of its careful adjustment to the
state of the controversy in which he was engaged as a leader
of the Reformation. In the first of these aspects, as we have
already pointed out, religion is with him the vital effect of the
knowledge of God in the human soul; so that inevitably religions will differ as the conceptions of God determining our
thought and feeling and directing our life differ. In the estate
of purity, the knowledge of God produces reverence and trust:
and the religion of sinless man will therefore exhibit no other
traits but trust and love. In sinful man, the same knowledge
of God must produce, rather, a reaction of fear and hate —
until the grace of God intervenes with a message of mercy.
Sinful man cannot be trusted, therefore, to form his own religion for himself, but must in all his religious functioning
place himself unreservedly under the direction of God in His
gracious revelation. In its second aspect, then, we perceive
Calvin carefully framing his definition so as to exclude all
" will-worship " and to prepare the way for the condemnation of the " formal worship " and " ostentation in ceremonies "
which had become prevalent in the old Church. The position he
takes up here is essentially that which has come down to us
under the name of " the Puritan principle." Religion consists,
of course, not in the externalities of worship, but in faith, united
with a serious fear of God, and a willing reverence. But its

[5] En quid sit pura germanaque religio, nempe *fides,* cum serio *Dei timore*
coniuncta; ut timor et *voluntariam reverentiam* in se contineat, et secum
trahat *ligitimum cultum,* qualis in Lege praescribitur.

external expression in worship is not therefore unimportant, but is to be strictly confined to what is prescribed by God: to " legitimate worship, agreeable to the injunctions of the law " (I. ii. 2, *ad fin.*). This declaration is returned to and expounded in a striking section of the fourth chapter (I. iv. 3; cf. I. v. 13), where Calvin insists that " the divine will is the perpetual rule to which true religion is to be conformed," and asserts of newly invented modes of worshipping God, that they are tantamount to idolatry. God cannot be pleased by showing contempt for what He commands and substituting other things which He condemns; and none would dare to trifle in such a manner with Him unless they had already transformed Him in their minds into another and different Being: and in that case it is of little importance whether you worship one god or many.[6]

From this digression for the sake of asserting the " Puritan," that is, the " Reformed," principle with reference to acceptable worship, it is already apparent that Calvin did not suppose that men have been left to the *notitia Dei insita* for the framing of their religion, although he is insistent that therefrom proceeds a propensity to religion which already secures that all men shall have a religion (I. ii. 2). On the contrary, he teaches that to the ineradicable revelation of Himself which He has imprinted on human nature, God has added an equally clear and abundant revelation of Himself externally to us. As we cannot know ourselves without knowing God, so neither can we look abroad on nature or contemplate the course of

---

[6] The significance and relations of " the Puritan principle " of absolute dependence on the Word of God as the source of knowledge of His will, and exclusive limitation to its prescriptions of doctrine, life, and even form of Church government and worship, are suggested by J. A. Dorner, " Hist. of Protest. Theol.," 1871, i. p. 390, who criticizes it sharply from his " freer " Lutheran standpoint. But even Luther knew how, on occasion, to invoke " the Puritan principle." Writing to Bartime von Sternberg, Sept. 1, 1523, he says: " For a Christian must do nothing that God has not commanded, and there is no command as to such masses and vigils, but it is solely their own invention, which brings in money, without helping either living or dead " (" The Letters of Martin Luther " (selected and translated) by Margaret A. Currie, 1908, p. 115).

events without seeing Him in His works and deeds (I. v.). Calvin is exceedingly emphatic as to the clearness, universality, and convincingness of this natural revelation of God. The whole world is but a theatre for the display of the divine glory (I. v. 5); God manifests Himself in every part of it, and, turn our eyes whichever way we will, we cannot avoid seeing Him; for there is no atom of the world in which some sparks of His glory do not shine (I. v. 1). So pervasive is God in nature, indeed, that it may even be said by a pious mind that nature is God (I. v. 5) — though the expression is too readily misapprehended in a Pantheistic (I. v. 5) or Materialistic (I. v. 4) sense to justify its use. Accordingly, no man can escape this manifestation of God; we cannot open our eyes without seeing it, and the language in which it is delivered to us penetrates through even the densest stupidity and ignorance (I. v. 1). To every individual on earth, therefore, with the exclusion of none (I. v. 7), God abundantly manifests Himself (I. v. 2). Each of the works of God invites the whole human race to the knowledge of Him; while their contemplation in the mass offers an even more prevalent exhibition of Him (I. v. 10). And so clear are His footsteps in His providence, that even what are commonly called accidents are only so many proofs of His activity (I. v. 8).

In developing this statement of the external natural revelation of God, Calvin presents first His patefaction in creation (I. v. 1–6) and then His patefaction in providence (I. v. 7–9), and under each head lays the primary stress on the manifestations of the divine wisdom and power (I. v. 2–5, wisdom; 6, power; 8, wisdom and power). But the other attributes which enter into His glory are not neglected. Thus, under the former caption, he points out that the perception of the divine power in creation " leads us to the consideration of His eternity; because He from whom all things derive their origin must necessarily be eternal and self-existent," while we must postulate goodness and mercy as the motives of His creation and providence (I. v. 6). Under the second caption, he is particularly copious in drawing out the manifestations of the divine benignity and beneficence — of His clemency — though

he does not scruple also to point to the signs of His severity
(I. v. 7, cf. 10). From the particular contemplation of the
divine clemency and severity in their peculiar distribution
here, indeed, he pauses to draw an argument for a future life
when apparent irregularities will be adjusted (I. v. 10).

The vigor and enthusiasm with which Calvin prosecutes
his exposition of the patefaction of God in nature and history
is worth emphasising further. He even turns aside (I. v. 9)
to express his special confidence in it, in contrast to *a priori*
reasoning, as the "right way and the best method of seeking
God." A speculative inquiry into the essence of God, he suggests, merely fatigues the mind and flutters in the brain. If
we would know God vitally, in our hearts, let us rather contemplate Him in His works. These, we shall find, as the Psalmist points out, declare His greatness and conduce to His praise.
Once more, we may observe here the concreteness of Calvin's
mind and method, and are reminded of the practical end he
keeps continually in view.[7] So far is he from losing himself
in merely speculative elaborations or prosecuting his inquiries
under the spur of "presumptuous curiosity," that the practical religious motive is always present, dominating his thought.
His special interest in the theistic argument is, accordingly,
due less to the consideration that it rounds out his systematic
view of truth than to the fact that it helps us to the vital
knowledge of God. And therefore he is no more anxious to set
it forth in its full force than he is to point out the limitations
which affect its practical value.[8] In and of itself, indeed, it has

---

[7] Cf. P. J. Muller, "De Godsleer van Zwingli en Calvijn," 1883, p. 8:
"If Zwingli follows more the *a priori*, Calvin follows the *a posteriori* method";
and E. Rabaud, "Hist. de la doctrine de l'inspiration, etc.," 1883, p. 58: "his
lucid and, above everything, practical genius."

[8] It is this distribution of Calvin's interest which leads to the impression that he lays little stress on "the theistic proofs." On the contrary, he
asserts their validity most strenuously: only he does not believe that any
proofs can work true faith apart from "the testimony of the Spirit," and
he is more interested in their value for developing the knowledge of God
than for merely establishing His existence. Hence P. J. Muller is wrong
when he denies the one to affirm the other, as, e.g., in his "De Godsleer van
Zwingli en Calvijn," 1883, p. 11: "Neither by Zwingli nor by Calvin are

no limitations; Calvin is fully assured of its validity and analyses its data with entire confidence; to him nothing is more certain than that in the mirror of His works God gives us clear manifestations both of Himself and of His everlasting dominion (I. v. 11). But Calvin cannot content himself with an intellectualistic contemplation of the objective validity of the theistic argument. So dominated is he by practical interests that he actually attaches to the chapter in which he argues this objective validity a series of sections in which he equally strongly argues the subjective inability of man to receive its testimony. Objectively valid as the theistic proofs are, they are ineffective to produce a just knowledge of God in the sinful heart. The insertion of these sections here is the more striking in that they almost seem unnecessary in view of the clear exposition of the noëtic effects of sin which had been made in the preceding chapter (ch. iv.) — although, of course, there the immediate reference was to the *notitia Dei insita,* while here it is to the *notitia Dei acquisita.*

Thus, however, our attention is drawn very pointedly to Calvin's doctrine of the disabilities with reference to the knowl-

---

proofs offered for the existence of God, although some passages in their writings seem to contain suggestions of them. The proposition, ' God exists,' needed no proof either for themselves, or for their coreligionists, or even against Rome. The so-called cosmological argument has no doubt been found by some in Zwingli (Zeller, *Das theolog. Syst. Zwingli's* extracted from the *Theol. Jahrbücher,* Tübingen, 1853, p. 33; [or p. 126 in the *Th. Jahrb.*]), and the physico-theological in Calvin (Lipsius, *Lehrbuch der ev. prot. Dogmatik,* ed. 2, 1879, p. 213); but it would not be difficult to show that we have to do in neither case with a philosophical deduction, but only with a means for attaining the complete knowledge of God." Though Calvin (also Zwingli) makes use of the theistic proofs to develop the knowledge of God, it does not follow that he (or Zwingli) did not value them as proofs of the existence of God. And we do not think Muller is successful (pp. 12 *sq.*) in explaining away the implication of the latter in Zwingli's use of these theistic arguments, or in Calvin's (p. 16). Schweizer, " Glaubenslehre der ev.-ref. Kirche," 1844, i. p. 250, finds in Calvin's citation of Cicero's declaration that there is no nation so barbarous, no tribe so degraded, that it is not persuaded that a God exists, an appeal to the so-called *historical* argument for the divine existence (cf. the use of it by Zwingli, " Opera," Schuler und Schultess ed., 1832, iii. p. 156): but Calvin's real attitude to the theistic argument is rather to be sought in the implications of the notably eloquent ch. v.

edge of God which are induced in the human mind by sin. He has, as has just been noted, adverted formally to them twice in these opening chapters of his treatise — on the earlier occasion (ch. iv.) with especial reference to the revelation of God made in the constitution of human nature, and on the later occasion (ch. v. §§ 11–15) with especial reference to the revelation of God made in His works and deeds. Were man in his normal state, he could not under this double revelation, internal and external, fail to know God as God would wish to be known. If he actually comes short of an adequate knowledge of God, therefore, this cannot be attributed to any shortcomings in the revelation of God. Calvin is perfectly clear as to the objective adequacy of the general revelation of God. Men, however, do come short of an adequate knowledge of God; and that not merely some men, but all men: the failure of the general revelation of God to produce in men an adequate knowledge of Him is as universal as is the revelation itself. The explanation is to be found in the corruption of men's hearts by sin, by which not merely are they rendered incapable of reading off the revelation of God which is displayed in His works and deeds, but their very instinctive knowledge of God, embedded in their constitution as men, is dulled and almost obliterated. The energy with which Calvin asserts this is almost startling, and matches in its emphasis that which he had placed on the reality and objective validity of the revelation of God. Though the seeds of religion are sown by God in every heart, yet not one man in a hundred has preserved even these seeds sound, and in no one at all have they grown to their legitimate harvest. All have degenerated from the true knowledge of God, and genuine piety has perished from the earth (I. iv. 1). The light which God has kindled in the breasts of men has been smothered and all but extinguished by their iniquity (I. iv. 4). The manifestation which God has given of Himself in the structure and organization of the world is lost on our stupidity (I. v. 11). The rays of God's glory are diffused all around us, but do not illuminate the darkness of our mind (I. v. 14). So that in point of fact, "men who are taught only by nature, have no certain, sound or distinct knowledge, but are confined to confused principles; they worship accordingly an unknown God " (I. v. 12, *fin.*): " no man can have the least knowledge of true and sound doctrine without having been a disciple of the Scriptures " (I. vi. 2, *ad fin.*): " the human mind is through its imbecility unable to attain any knowledge of God without the assistance of the Sacred Word " (I. vi. 4, *ad fin.*).

Calvin therefore teaches with great emphasis the bankruptcy of the natural knowledge of God. We must keep fully in mind, however, that this is not due in his view to any inadequacy or ineffectiveness of natural revelation, considered objectively.[9] He continues to insist that the seeds of religion are sown in every heart (I. v. 1, *ad init.*); that through all man's corruption the instincts of nature still suggest the memory of God to his mind (I. v. 2); that it is impossible to eradicate that sense of the deity which is naturally engraved on all hearts (I. iv. 4, *ad fin.*); that the structure and organization of the world, and the things that daily happen out of the ordinary course of nature, that is under the providential government of God, bear a witness to God which the dullest ear cannot fail to hear (I. v. 1, 3, 7, esp. II. vi. 1); and that the light that shines from creation, while it may be smothered, cannot be so extinguished but that some rays of it find their way into the most darkened soul (I. v. 14). God has therefore never left Himself without a witness; but, " with various and most abundant benignity sweetly allures men to a knowledge of Him, though they persist in following their own ways, their pernicious and fatal errors " (I. v. 14). The sole cause of the failure of the natural revelation is to be found, therefore, in the corruption of the human heart. Two results flow from this fact. First, it is not a question of the extinction of the knowledge of God, but of the corruption of the knowledge of God. And secondly, men are without excuse for their cor-

[9] P. J. Muller, " De Godsleer van Zwingli en Calvijn," 1883, pp. 18 *sq.*, does not seem to bear this in mind, although he had clearly stated it in his " De Godsleer van Calvijn," 1881, pp. 13–25.

ruption of the knowledge of God. On both points Calvin is insistent.

He does not teach that all religion has perished out of the earth, but only that no "genuine piety" remains (I. iv. 1, *ad init.*): he does not teach that men retain no knowledge of God, but no "certain, sound or distinct knowledge" (I. v. 12, *ad fin.*). The seed of religion remains their inalienable possession, "but it is so corrupted as to produce only the worst fruits" (I. iv. 4, *ad fin.*). Here we see Calvin's judgment on natural religion. Its reality he is quick to assert: but equally quickly its inadequacy — and that because not merely of a negative incompleteness but also of a positive corruption. Men have corrupted the knowledge of God; and perhaps Calvin might even subscribe the declaration of a modern writer that men's religions are their worst crimes.[10] Certainly Calvin paints in dark colors the processes by which men form for themselves conceptions of God under the light of nature, or rather, in the darkness of their minds, from which the light of nature is as far as lies in their power excluded. "Their conceptions of God are formed, not according to the representations He gives of Himself, but by the invention of their own presumptuous imaginations" (I. iv. 1, *med.*). They set Him far off from themselves and make Him a mere idler in heaven (I. iv. 2); they invent all sorts of vague and confused notions concerning Him, until they involve themselves in such a vast accumulation of errors as almost to extinguish the light that is within them (I. iv. 4); they confuse Him with His works, until even a Plato loses himself in the round globe (I. v. 11); they even endeavor to deny His very existence (I. v. 12), and substitute demons in His place (I. v. 13). Certainly it is not surprising, then, that the Holy Spirit, speaking in Scripture, "condemns as false and lying whatever was formerly wor-

[10] Cf. F. C. Baur, "Die christliche Lehre von der Dreieinigkeit, etc.," iii. 1843, p. 41: "From this point of view"—he is expounding Calvin's dôctrine —"the several manifestations in the history of religions are conceived not as stages in the gradually advancing evolution of the religious consciousness, but as inexcusable, sinful aberrations, as wilful perversions and defacements of the inborn idea of God."

shipped as divine among the Gentiles," nay, "rejects as false every form of worship which is of human contrivance," and "leaves no Deity but in Mount Zion " (I. v. 13). The religions of men differ, doubtless, among themselves: some are more, some less evil; but all are evil and the evil of none is trivial.

Are men to be excused for this, their corruption of the knowledge of God? Are we to listen with sympathy to the plea that light has been lacking? It is not a case of insufficient light, but of an evil heart. Excuses are vain, for this heart-darkness is criminal. If we speak of ignorance here, we must remember it is a guilty ignorance; an ignorance which rests on pride and vanity and contumacy (I. iv. 1), an ignorance which our own consciences will not excuse (I. v. 15). What! shall we plead that we lack ears to hear what even mute creatures proclaim? that we have no eyes to see what it needs no eyes to see? that we are mentally too weak to learn what mindless creatures teach? (I. v. 15). We are ignorant of what all things conspire to inform us of, only because we sinfully corrupt their message; their insufficiency has its roots in us, not in them; wherefore we are without excuse (I. iv. 1; v. 14–15). Our " folly is inexcusable, seeing that it originates not only in a vain curiosity, but in false confidence, and an immoderate desire to exceed the limits of human knowledge " (I. iv. 1, *fin.*). "Whatever deficiency of natural ability prevents us from attaining the pure and clear knowledge of God, yet, since that deficiency arises from our own fault, we are left without any excuse " (I. v. 15, *ad init.*).

The natural revelation of God failing thus to produce its legitimate effects of a sound knowledge of God, because of the corruption of men's hearts, we are thrown back for any adequate knowledge of God upon supernatural activities of God communicating His truth to men. It is accordingly in an assertion and validation of these supernatural revelatory operations of God that Calvin's discussion reaches its true center. To this extent his whole discussion of natural revelation — in its inception in the implantation in man of a *sensus deitatis,* in its culmination in the patefaction of God in His works and deeds, and in its failure through the sin-bred blindness of humanity — may be said to be merely introductory to and intended to prepare the way for his discussion of the supernatural operations of God by which He meets this otherwise hopeless condition of humanity sunk in its corrupt notions of God. These operations obviously must meet a twofold need. A clearer and fuller revelation of God must be brought to men than that which is afforded by nature. And the darkened minds of men must be illuminated for its reception. In other words, what is needed, is a special supernatural revelation on the one hand, and a special supernatural illumination on the other. It is to the validation of this twofold supernatural operation of God in communicating the knowledge of Himself that Calvin accordingly next addresses himself (chs. vi.–ix.).

One or two peculiarities of his treatment of them attract our notice at the outset, and seem to invite attention, before we enter into a detailed exposition of the doctrine he presents. It is noticeable that Calvin does not pretend that this supernatural provision of knowledge of God to meet men's sin-born ignorance is as universal in its reach as the natural revelation which it supplements and, so far as efficiency is concerned, supersedes. On the contrary, he draws it expressly into a narrower circle. That general revelation " presented itself to all eyes " and " is more than sufficient to deprive the ingratitude of men of every excuse, since," in it, " God, in order to involve all mankind in the same guilt, sets an exhibition of His majesty, delineated in the creatures, before them all without exception " (I. vi. 1, *init*.). But His supernatural revelation He grants only " to those whom He intends to unite in a more close and familiar connection with Himself " (*ibid*.); " to those to whom He has determined to make His instructions effectual " (I. vi. 3) ; in a word, to " the elect " (I. vi. 1; vii. 5 near end). In dealing with the supernatural revelation of God, therefore, Calvin is conscious of dealing with a special operation of the divine grace by means of which God is communicating to those He is choosing to be His people the saving knowledge of Himself. It is observable also that, in speaking

of this supernatural revelation, he identifies it from the outset
distinctly with the Scriptures (ch. vi.). This is in accordance
with the practical end and engrossment which, as we have already had occasion to note, dominate his whole discussion. He
was not unaware that the special revelation of God antedates the Scriptures: on occasion he speaks discriminatingly
enough of this revelation in itself and the Scriptures in which
it is embodied. But his mind is less on the abstract truth than
on the concrete conditions which surrounded him in his work.
Whatever may have been true ages gone, to-day the special
revelation of God coalesces with the Scriptures, and he does
not occupy himself formally with it except as it presents itself
to the men of his own time. The task which he undertakes,
therefore, is distinctly to show that men have in the Scriptures
a special revelation of God supplementing and so far superseding the general revelation of God in nature; and that God
so operates with this His special revelation of Himself as to
overcome the sin-bred disabilities of man.

In this state of the case we may perhaps be justified in
leaving at this point the logical development of his construction and expounding Calvin's teaching more formally under
the heads of his doctrine of Holy Scripture and his doctrine
of the Testimony of the Holy Spirit.

II. Holy Scripture

First, then, what was Calvin's doctrine of Holy Scripture?

Under the designation of " Scripture " or " the Scriptures "
Calvin understood that body of writings which have been
transmitted to us as the divinely given rule of faith and life.
In this body of writings, that is to say, in " the Canon of
Scripture," he included all the books of the Old Covenant
which were recognized by the Jewish Church as of divine gift,
and as such handed down to the Christian Church; and all the
books of the New Covenant which have been given the Church
by the Apostles as its authoritative law-code. Calvin's attitude
towards the canon was thus somewhat more conservative than,

say, Luther's. He knew of no such distinction as that between Canonical and Deutero-Canonical Books, whether in the Old or the New Testament. The so-called " Apocryphal Books " of the Old Testament, included within the canon by the decrees of Trent, he rejected out of hand: the so-called " Antilegomena" of the New Testament he accepted without exception.[11]

The representations which are sometimes made, to the effect that he felt doubts of the canonicity of some of the canonical books or even was convinced of their uncanonicity,[12] rest

[11] Cf. J. Cramer, *Nieuwe Bijdragen op het gebied van Godgeleerdheid en Wijsbegeerte,* iii. 1881, p. 102: " By the Scripture or the Scriptures he [Calvin] understood the books of the Old and New Testaments which have been transmitted to us by the Church as canonical, as the rule of faith and life. The Apocrypha of the O. T. as they were determined by the Council of Trent, he excludes. They are to him indeed *libri ecclesiastici,* in many respects good and useful to be read; but they are not *libri canonici* ' ad fidem dogmatum faciendam' (*Acta Synodi Tridentinae, cum antidoto,* 1547)." In a later article, " De Roomsch-Katholieke en de Oud-protestantsche Schriftbeschouwing," 1883, p. 36, Cramer declares that by the Scriptures, Calvin means "nothing else than the canon, established by the Synods of Hippo and Carthage, and transmitted by the Catholic Church, with the exception of the so-called Apocrypha of the O. T.," etc. Cf. Leipoldt, " Geschichte des N. T. Kanons," ii. 1908, p. 149: " We obtain the impression that it is only for form's sake that Calvin undertakes to test whether the disputed books are canonical or not. In reality it is already a settled matter with him that they are. Calvin feels himself therefore in the matter of the N. T. canon bound to the mediæval tradition." Cf. also Otto Ritschl, " Dogmengeschichte des Protestantismus," i. 1908, pp. 70, 71, to the same effect.

[12] Cf. e.g. J. Pannier, " Le témoignage du Saint-Esprit," 1893, pp. 112 *sq.*: " One fact strikes us at first sight: not only did Calvin not comment on the Aprochryphal books, for which he wrote a very short preface, which was ever more and more abridged in the successive editions, but he did not comment on all the Canonical books. And if lack of time may explain the passing over of some of the less important historical books of the Old Testament, it was undoubtedly for a graver reason that he left to one side the three books attributed to Solomon, notably the Song of Songs. ' In the New Testament there is ordinarily mentioned only the Apocalypse, neglected by Calvin undoubtedly for critical or theological motives analogous to those which determined the most of his contemporaries, but it is necessary to note that the two lesser epistles of John are also lacking, and that in speaking of the large epistle Calvin always expresses himself as if it were the only existing one' (Reuss, *Revue de Théologie* de Strasbourg, vi. 1853, p. 229). In effect, at the very time when he was defending particularly the au-

50   CALVIN AND CALVINISM

on a fundamental misconception of his attitude, and are wrecked on his express assertions. No doubt he has not left us commentaries on all the Biblical Books, and no doubt his omission to write or lecture on certain books is not to be explained merely by lack of time, but involves an act of selection on his part, which was not unaffected by his estimate of the relative importance of the several books or by his own spiritual sympathies.[13] He has also occasionally employed a current expres-

---

thority of the Scriptures against the Council of Trent, when he was dedicating to Edward VI, the King of England, his Commentaries on the ' Epistles which are accustomed to be called Canonical ' (1551), he included in the Canon only the First Epistle of Peter, the First Epistle of John, James and, at the very end, the Second Epistle of Peter and Jude." — Reuss, however, in his " History of the Canon of the Holy Scriptures in the Christian Church " (1863, E. T. 1884), greatly modifies the opinion here quoted from him: " Some have believed it possible to affirm that he [Calvin] rejected the Apocalypse because it was the only book of the N. T., except the two short Epistles of John, on which he wrote no commentary. But that conclusion is too hasty. In the *Institutes,* the Apocalypse is sometimes quoted like the other Apostolic writings, and even under John's name. If there was no commentary, it was simply that the illustrious exegete, wiser in this respect than several of his contemporaries and many of his successors, understood that his vocation called him elsewhere " (p. 318). He adds, indeed, of II and III John: " It might be said with more probability that Calvin did not acknowledge the canonicity of these two writings. He never quotes them, and he quotes the First Epistle of John in a way to exclude them: *Joannes in sua canonica, Instit.* iii. 2. 21; 3. 23 (*Opp.* ii. 415, 453)." But this opinion requires revision, just as that on the Apocalypse did, as we shall see below. Cf. further, in the meantime: Reuss, " Hist. of the Sacred Scriptures of the N. T.," 1884, ii. p. 347, and S. Berger, " La Bible au seizième siècle," 1879, p. 120, who expresses himself most positively: " Calvin expresses no judgment on the lesser Epistles of St. John. But we remark that he never cites them and that he mentions the First in these terms: ' As John says in his canonical.' This word excludes, in the thought of the author, the two other Epistles attributed to this Apostle."

[13] This may have been the case with the Apocalypse, which not only Reuss, as we have seen, but Scaliger thought him wise not to have entered upon; and which he is — perhaps credibly — reported to have said in conversation he did not understand (cf. Leipoldt's " Geschichte des N. T. Kanons," ii. 1908, p. 148, note). But how impossible it is to imagine that this implies any doubt of the canonicity or authority of the book will be quickly evident to anyone who will note his frequent citation of it in the same fashion with other Scripture and alongside of other Scripture (e.g. *Opp.* i. 736 = ii. 500; i. 953 = ii. 957; i. 1033 = ii. 1063; i. 1148; ii. 88, 859; v. 191, 196, 532; vi. 176; vii.

sion, such as, for example, "the Canonical Epistle of John," [14] when speaking of I John, which, if strictly interpreted, might be thought to imply denial of the genuineness of certain books of the canon — such as II and III John — and not merely the momentary or habitual neglect of them; just as the common use of the term "the Apostle" of Paul might be said, if simi-

---

29, 118, 333; xxxi. 650), sometimes mentioning it by name (vii. 469; i. 733 = ii. 497), sometimes by the name of John (i. 715 = ii. 492, viii. 338 [along with I John]), sometimes by the name of both "John" and "the Apocalypse" (ii. 124, vii. 116, xxx. 651, xlviii. 122), and always with reverence and confidence as a Scriptural book. He even expressly cites it under the name of Scripture and explicitly as the dictation of the Spirit: vii. 559, "Fear not, says the Scripture (Eccles. xviii. 22). . . . Again (Rev. xxii. 11) . . . and (John xv. 2) "; i. 624: "Elsewhere also the Spirit testifies . . ." (along with Daniel and Paul). Cf. also such passages as ii. 734, "Nor does the Apocalypse which they quote afford them any support . . ."; xlviii. 238: "I should like to ask the Papists if they think John was so stupid that . . . etc. (Rev. xxii. 8) "; also vi. 369; v. 198.

[14] We use the simple expression "the Epistle of John"; the apparently, but only apparently, stronger and more exclusive, "the Canonical Epistle of John," which Calvin employs, although it would be misleading in our associations, is its exact synonym. Those somewhat numerous writers who have quoted the form "the *Canonical* Epistle of John" as if its use implied the denial of the *canonicity* of the other epistles of John forget that this was the ordinary designation in the West of the Catholic Epistles — "the Seven Canonical Epistles" — and that they are all currently cited by this title by Western writers. The matter has been set right by A. Lang: "Die Bekehrung Johannis Calvins" (II. i. of Bonwetsch and Seeberg's "Studien zur Geschichte der Theologie und der Kirche," 1897, pp. 26–29). On the title "Canonical Epistles" for the Catholic Epistles, see Lücke, *SK*. 1836, iii. pp. 643–650; Bleek, "Introd. to the N. T.," § 202 at end (vol. ii. 1874, p. 135); Hilgenfeld, "Einleitung in d. N. T.," 1875, p. 153; Westcott, "Epp. of St. John," 1883, p. xxix.; Salmond, Hastings' BD. i. 1898, p. 360. In 1551, Calvin published his "Commentarii in Epistolas Canonicas" — that is on the Catholic Epistles; also his "Commentaire sur l'Épistre Canonique de St. Jean," i.e. on "the Epistle of John"; also his "Commentaire sur l'Épistre Canonique de St. Jude." Calvin does not seem ever to have happened to quote from II and III John. The reference given in the Index printed in *Opp.* xxii., viz., III John 9, *Opp.* xb. 81, occurs in a letter, not by Calvin but by Christof Libertetus to Farel. Cf. J. Leipoldt, "Geschichte des N. T. Kanons" (2nd Part, Leipzig, 1908), p. 148, note 1: "The smaller Johannine Epistles Calvin seems never to have cited. He cites I John in *Inst.* III. ii. 21 by the formula: dicit Johannes in sua canonica. Nevertheless it is very questionable whether inferences can be drawn from this formula as to Calvin's attitude to II and III John." He adds a reference to Lang as above.

larly strictly pressed, to imply that there was no other Apostle
but he. It is also true that he expresses himself with moderation when adducing the evidence for the canonicity of this
book or that, and in his modes of statement quite clearly betrays his recognition that the evidence is more copious or
more weighty in some cases than in others. But he represents
the evidence as sufficient in all cases and declares with confidence his conclusion in favor of the canonicity of the whole
body of books which make up our Bible, and in all his writings
and controversies acts firmly on this presupposition. How, for
example, is it possible to contend that some grave reason connected with doubts on his part of their canonical authority
underlies the failure of Calvin to comment on " the three books
attributed to Solomon, particularly the Song of Songs," [15] in
the face of the judgment of the ministers of Geneva with regard to Castellion, which is thus reported by Calvin himself
over his signature.[16] " We unanimously judged him one who
might be appointed to the functions of the pastor, except for
a single obstacle which opposed it. When we asked him, according to custom, whether he was in accord with us on all
points of doctrine, he replied that there were two on which
he could not share our views: one of them . . . being our in-
scribing the Song of Solomon in the number of sacred books.
. . . We conjured him first of all, not to permit himself the
levity of treating as of no account the constant witness of
the universal Church; we reminded him that there is no book
the authenticity of which is doubtful, about which some discussion has not been raised; that even those to which we now
attach an undisputed authenticity were not admitted from the
beginning without controversy; that precisely this one is
one which has never been openly repudiated. We also exhorted
him against trusting unreasonably in his own judgment, espe-

[15] Pannier, as cited, p. 113.

[16] *Opera*, xi. 674–676: cf. Buisson, " Castellion," 1892, i. pp. 198–199.
Buisson discusses the whole incident and quotes from the minutes of the
Council before which Castellion brought the matter: the point of dispute
is there briefly expressed thus: " Moss [r] Calvin recognizes as holy, and the
said Bastian repudiates " (p. 197) the book in question.

cially where nothing was toward which all the world had not been aware of before he was born. . . . All these arguments having no effect on him, we thought it necessary to consider among ourselves what we ought to do. Our unanimous opinion was that it would be dangerous and would set a bad precedent to admit him to the ministry in these circumstances. . . . We should thus condemn ourselves for the future to raise no objection to another, should one present himself and wish similarly to repudiate Ecclesiastes or Proverbs or any other book of the Bible, without being dragged into a debate as to what is and what is not worthy of the Holy Spirit." [17] Not merely the firmness with which Calvin held to the canonicity of all the books of our Bible, but the importance he attached to the acceptance of the canonical Scriptures in their integrity, is made perfectly clear by such an incident; and indeed so also are the grounds on which he accepted these books as canonical.

These grounds, to speak briefly, were historico-critical. Calvin, we must bear in mind, was a Humanist before he was a Reformer,[18] and was familiar with the whole process of determining the authenticity of ancient documents. If then he re-

[17] Calvin employs all these " three books attributed to Solomon " freely as Scripture and deals with them precisely as he does with other Scriptures. As was to be expected, he cites Proverbs most frequently, Canticles least: but he cites them all as Solomon's and as authoritative Scripture. " ' I have washed my feet' says the believing soul in Solomon . . ." is the way he cites Canticles (*Opp.* i. 778, ii. 589). " They make a buckler of a sentence of Solomon's, which is as contrary to them as is no other that is in the Scriptures " (vii. 130) is the way he cites Ecclesiastes. He indeed expressly contrasts Ecclesiastes as genuine Scripture with the Apocryphal books: " As the soul has an origin apart, it has also another preëminence, and this is what Solomon means when he says that at death the body returns to the earth from which it was taken and the soul returns to God who gave it (Eccl. xii. 7). For this reason it is said in the Book of Wisdom (ii. 23) that man is immortal, seeing that he was created in the image of God. This is not an authentic book of Holy Scripture, but it is not improper to avail ourselves of its testimony as of an ancient teacher (*Docteur ancien*) — although the single reason ought to be enough for us that the image of God, as it has been placed in man, can reside only in an immortal soul, etc." (vii. 112, written in 1544).

[18] Cf. A. Bossert, " Calvin," 1906, p. 6: " Humanist himself as well as profound theologian . . ."; Charles Borgeaud, " Histoire de l'Université de Genève," 1900, p. 21: " Before he was a theologian, Calvin was a Humanist. . . ."

ceived the Scriptures from the hands of the Church, not indulging himself in the levity of treating the constant witness
of the universal Church as of no account, he was nevertheless
not disposed to take " tradition " uncritically at its face value.
His acceptance of the canon of the Church was therefore not
a blind but a critically mediated acceptance. Therefore he discarded the Aprocrypha: and if he accepted the Antilegomena
it was because they commended themselves to his historico-
critical judgment as holding of right a place in the canon. The
organon of his critical investigation of the canon was in effect
twofold. He inquired into the history of the books in question.
He inquired into their internal characteristics. Have they
come down to us from the Apostolic Church, commanding
either unbrokenly or on the whole the suffrages of those best
informed or best qualified to judge of their canonical claims?
Are they in themselves conformable to the claims made for
them of apostolic, which is as much as to say, divine origin?
It was by the application of this twofold test that he excluded
the Apocrypha of the Old Testament from the canon. They
had in all ages been discriminated from the canonical books,
and differ from them as the writing of an individual differs
from an instrument which has passed under the eye of a notary
and been sealed to be received of all.[19] Some Fathers, it is true,

[19] Cf. the Preface he prefixed to the Apocryphal Books (for the history
of which, see *Opera,* ix. 827, note): " These books which are called Apocryphal have in all ages been discriminated from those which are without
difficulty shown to be of the Sacred Scriptures. For the ancients, wishing to
anticipate the danger that any profane books should be mixed with those
which certainly proceeded from the Holy Spirit, made a roll of these latter
which they called ' Canon '; meaning by this word that all that was comprehended under it was the assured rule to which we should attach ourselves.
Upon the others they imposed the name of Apocrypha; denoting that they
were to be held as private writings and not authenticated, like public documents. Accordingly the difference between the former and latter is the
same as that between an instrument, passed before a notary, and sealed
to be received by all, and the writing of some particular man. It is true
they are not to be despised, seeing that they contain good and useful doctrine. Nevertheless it is only right that what we have been given by the
Holy Spirit should have preëminence above all that has come from men."
Cf., in his earliest theological treatise, the " Psychopannychia " of 1534–1542
(*Opp.* v. 182), where, after quoting Ecclus. xvii. 1 and Wisd. ii. 23 as " two

deemed them canonical; even Augustine was of that way of thinking, although he had to allow that opinions differed widely upon the matter. Others, however, could admit them to no higher rank than that of " ecclesiastical books," which might be useful to read but could not supply a foundation for doctrine; among such were Jerome and Rufinus.[20] And, when we observe their contents, no sane mind will fail to pass judgment against them.[21] Rome may, indeed, find her interest in defending them, for she may discover support in them for some of her false teachings. But this very fact is their condemnation. " I beg you to observe," he says of the closing words of II Maccabees, where the writer sets his hope in his own works: " I beg you to observe how far this confession falls away from the majesty of the Holy Spirit " [22] — that is to say, from the constant teaching of Holy Scripture.

And it was by the application of the same two-fold test that he accredited the Antilegomena of the New Testament as integral parts of the canon. In the Preface which he has prefixed to II Peter, for example, he notes that Eusebius speaks of some who rejected it. " If it is a question," he adds, " of yielding to the simple authority of men, since he [Eusebius] does not name those who brought the matter into doubt, no necessity seems to be laid on us to credit these unknown

sacred writers," he adds: " I would not urge the authority of these writers strongly on our adversaries, did they not oppose them to us. They may be allowed, however, some weight, if not as canonical, yet certainly as ancient, as pious, and as received by the suffrages of many. But let us omit them and let us retain . . ." etc. In the " Psychopannychia " his dealing with Baruch on the other hand is more wavering. On one occasion (p. 205) it is quoted with the formula, " sic enim loquitur propheta," and on another (p. 227), " in prophetia Baruch " corrected in 1542. In the " Institutes " of 1536 he quotes it as Scripture: " alter vero propheta scribit " (*Opp.* i. 82) — referring back to Daniel. This is already corrected in 1539 (i. 906; cf. ii. 632). In 1534–1536, then, he considered Baruch canonical: afterwards not so. His dealing with it in v. 271 (1537), vi. 560 (1545), vi. 638 (1546) is *ad hominem*.

[20] " Acta Synodi Tridentinae, cum antidoto " (1547), *Opp.* vii. 365–506.

[21] " Vera ecclesiae reformandae ratio," *Opp.* vii. 613: quae divinitus non esse prodita, sani omnes, saltem ubi moniti fuerint, iudicabunt.

[22] " Acta Synodi Tridentinae, cum antidoto," *Opp.* vii. 413: Quantum, obsecro, a Spiritus Sancti maiestati aliena est haec confessio!

people. And, moreover, he adds that afterwards it was generally received without contradiction. . . . It is a matter agreed
upon by all, of common accord, that there is nothing in this
Epistle unworthy of Saint Peter, but that, on the contrary,
from one end of it to the other, there are apparent the force,
vehemence and grace of the Spirit with which the Apostles were
endowed. . . . Since, then, in all parts of the Epistle the majesty of the Spirit of Christ is clearly manifest, I cannot reject
it entirely, although I do not recognize in it the true and natural phrase of Saint Peter." [23] To meet the difficulty arising
from the difference of the style from that of I Peter, he therefore supposed that the Epistle is indeed certainly Peter's, since
otherwise it would be a forgery, a thing inconceivable in a book
of its high character,[24] but was dictated in his old age to some
one of his disciples, to whom it owes its peculiarities of diction.
Here we have an argument conducted on the two grounds of
the external witness of the Church and the internal testimony
of the contents of the book: and these are the two grounds on
which he everywhere depends. Of the Epistle of Jude he says: [25]
" Because the reading of it is very useful, and it contains nothing that is not in accord with the purity of the Apostolic doctrine; because also it has long been held to be authentic by
all the best men, for my part, I willingly place it in the number
of the other epistles." In other cases the external evidence of
the Church is not explicitly mentioned and the stress of the
argument is laid on the Apostolic character of the writing as
witnessed by its contents. He receives Hebrews among the
Apostolic Epistles without difficulty, because nowhere else
is the sacrifice of Christ more clearly or simply declared and
other evangelical doctrines taught: surely it must have been
due to the wiles of Satan that the Western Church so long

[23] This is translated from the French version, ed. Meyrueis, iv. 1855, p. 743.
The Latin is the same, though somewhat more concise: nihil habet Petro
indignum, ut vim spiritus apostolici et gratiam ubique exprimat . . . eam
prorsus repudiare mihi religio est.

[24] Haec autem fictio indigna esset ministro Christi, obtendere alienam
personam.

[25] Ed. Meyrueis, iv. p. 780.

doubted its canonicity.[26] James seems to him to contain nothing unworthy of an Apostle of Christ, but to be on the contrary full of good teaching, valuable for all departments of Christian living.[27] For the application of this argument he of course takes his start from the Homologoumena, which gave him the norm of Apostolic teaching which he used for testing the other books. It must not be supposed that he received even these books, however, without critico-historical inquiry: but only that the uniform witness of the Church to their authority weighed with him above all grounds of doubt. It was, in a word, on the ground of a purely scientific investigation that Calvin accredited to himself the canon. It had come down to him through the ages, accredited as such by the constant testimony of its proper witnesses: and it accredited itself to critical scrutiny by its contents.[28]

[26] *Ibid.,* iv. p. 362.

[27] *Ibid.,* iv. p. 694. Latin: mihi ad epistolam hanc recipiendam satis est, quod nihil continet Christi apostolo indignum.

[28] Cf. J. Cramer, as cited, p. 126: " It was thus, in the first place, as the result of scientific investigations that Calvin fixed the limits of the canon . . . not *a priori,* but *a posteriori,* that he came to the recognition of the canonicity of the Biblical books." But especially see the excellently conceived passage on pp. 155–6, to the following effect: " What great importance Calvin attaches to the question whether a Biblical book is *apostolic!* If it is not apostolic, he does not recognize it as canonical. To determine its apostolicity, he appeals not merely to the ecclesiastical tradition of its origin, but also and principally to its contents. This is what he does in the case of all the antilegomena. The touchstone for this is found in the homologoumena. That he undertakes no investigation of the apostolic origin of these latter is a matter of course. This, for him and for all his contemporaries, stood irreversibly settled. The touchstone employed by Calvin is a scientific one. The *testimonium Spiritus Sancti* no doubt made its influence felt. But without the help of the scientific investigation, this internal testimony would not have the power to elevate the book into a canonical book. That Calvin was treading here in the footprints of the ancient Church will be understood. The complaint sometimes brought against the Christians of the earliest centuries is unfounded, that they held all writings canonical in which they found their own dogmatics. No doubt they attached in their criticism great weight to this. But not less to the question whether the origin of the books was traceable back to the apostolical age, and their contents accorded with apostolic doctrine, as it might be learned from the indubitably apostolic writings. So far as science had been developed in their day, they employed it in the formation of the canon. . . ." In a later article Cramer says: " In the determina-

The same scientific spirit attended Calvin in his dealing with the text of Scripture. As a Humanist he was familiar with the processes employed in settling the texts of classical authors; and naturally he used the same methods in his determination of the text of the Biblical books. His practice here is marked by a combination of freedom and sobriety; and his decisions, though often wrong, as they could not but be in the state of the knowledge of the transmission of the New Testament text at the time, always manifest good sense, balance, and trained judgment. In his remarks on the pericope of the adulteress (John viii. 1–11), we meet the same circle of ideas with which we are familiar from his remarks on the Antilegomena: "because it has always been received by the Latin Churches and is found in many of the Greek copies and old writers, and contains nothing which would be unworthy of an apostolical spirit, there is no reason why we should refuse to take our profit from it." [29] He accepts the three-witness passage of I John v. 7. "Since the Greek codices do not agree with themselves," he says, "I scarcely dare reach a conclusion. Yet, as the context flows most smoothly if this clause is added, and I see that it stands in the best codices and those of the most approved credit, I also willingly adopt it." [30] When puzzled by

---

tion of the compass of Scripture, he [Calvin], like Luther, took his start from the writings which more than the others communicated the knowledge of Christ in His kingdom and had been recognized always by the Church as genuine and trustworthy. Even if the results of his criticism were more in harmony than was the case with those of the German reformer with the ecclesiastical tradition, he yet walked in the self-same critical pathway. He took over the canon of the Church just as little as its version and its exegesis without scrutiny " (" De Roomsch-Katholieke en de Oud-protestansche Schriftbeschouwing," 1883, pp. 31–32). Cramer considers this critical procedure on Calvin's part inconsistent with his doctrine of the testimony of the Spirit, but (p. 38) he recognizes that we cannot speak of it as the nodding of Homer: " It is not here and there, but throughout; not in his exegetical writings alone, but in his dogmatic ones, too, that he walks in this critical path. We never find the faintest trace of hesitation."

[29] Comment on John viii. 1 (Meyrueis' ed. of the Commentaries, ii. 1854, p. 169).

[30] Comment on I John v. 7 (Meyrueis' ed. of the Commentaries, iv. 1855, p. 682).

difficulties, he, quite like the Humanist dealing with a classical text, feels free to suggest that there may be a " mendum in voce." This he does, for example, in Mat. xxiii. 35, where he adduces this possibility among others; and still more instructively in Mat. xxvii. 9, where he just as simply assumes " Jeremiah " to be a corrupt reading [31] as his own editors assume that the " Apius " which occurs in the French version of the " Institutes " in connection with Josephus is due to a slip of his translators, not of his own — remarking: " It is evident that it cannot be Calvin who translated this passage." [32] His assurance that it cannot be the Biblical writer who stumbles leads him similarly to attribute what seems to him a manifest error to the copyists. It is only, however, in such passages as these that he engages formally in textual emendation. Ordinarily he simply follows the current text, although he is, of course, not without an intelligent ground for his confidence in it.[33] As we cursorily read his commentaries we feel ourselves in the hands of one who is sanely and sagely scrutinizing the text with which he is dealing from the point of view of a scholar accustomed to deal with ancient texts, whose confidence in its general integrity represents the well-grounded conclusion of a trained judgment. His occasional remarks on the text, and his rare suggestion of a corruption, are indicia of the alertness of his general scrutiny of the text and serve to assure us that his acceptance of it as a whole as sound is not merely inert ac-

[31] Quomodo Jeremiae nomen obrepserit, me nescire fateor, nec anxie laboro; certe Jeremiae nomen errore positum esse pro Zacharia res ipsa ostendit; quia nihil tale apud Jeremiam legitur (*Opera,* xlv. 749).

[32] *Opera,* iii. 100, note 3.

[33] Cf. J. Cramer, as cited, pp. 116–117: " Calvin does not largely busy himself with textual criticism. He follows the text which was generally received in his day. It deserves notice only that he exercises a free and independent judgment and recognizes the rights of science." Cramer adduces his treatment of I John v. 7 and proceeds: " He comes forward on scientific grounds against the Vulgate. The decree of Trent that this version must be followed as ' authentical,' he finds silly; and reverence for it as if it had fallen down from heaven, ludicrous. ' How can anyone dispute the right to appeal to the original text? And what a bad version this is! There are scarcely three verses in any page well rendered ' (*Acta Synod. Trident.,* etc., pp. 414–416)."

quiescence in tradition, but represents the calm judgment of an instructed intelligence.

Now, these sixty-six books of canonical Scriptures handed down to us, in the singular providence of God,[34] in a sound text which meets the test of critical scrutiny, Calvin held to be the very Word of God. This assertion he intended in its simplest and most literal sense. He was far from overlooking the fact that the Scriptures were written by human hands: he expressly declares that, though we have received them from God's own mouth, we have nevertheless received them " through the ministry of men." [35] But he was equally far from conceiving that the relation of their human authors to their divine author resembled in any degree that of free intermediaries, who, after receiving the divine word, could do with it what they listed.[36]

[34] "Institutes," I. viii. 10. Cf. I. vi. 2–3.

[35] I. vii. 5, *ad init.:* " We have received it from God's own mouth by the ministry of men."

[36] It is quite common to represent Calvin as without a theory, at least an expressed theory, of the relation of the divine and human authors of Scripture. Thus J. Cramer, as cited, p. 103, says: " How we are to understand the relation of the divine and human activities through which the Scriptures were produced is not exactly defined by Calvin. A precise theory of inspiration such as we meet with in the later dogmaticians is not found in him." Cramer is only sure that Calvin did not hold to the theory which later Protestants upheld: " It is true that Calvin gave the impulse [from which the later dogmatic view of Scripture grew up], more than any other of the Reformers. But we must not forget that here we can speak of nothing more than the impulse. We nowhere find in Calvin such a magical conception of the Bible as we find in the later dogmaticians. It is true he used the term ' dictare ' and other expressions which he employs under the influence of the terminology of his day, but on the other hand — in how many respects does he recognize the *human* factor in the Scriptures! " (p. 142). Similarly Pannier, as cited, p. 200: " In any case Calvin has not written a single word which can be appealed to in favor of *literal* inspiration. What is divine for him, if there is anything specifically divine beyond the contents, the brightness of which is reflected upon the container, is the *sense* of each book, or at most of each phrase, — never the employment of each word. Calvin would have deplored the petty dogmatics of the *Consensus Helveticus,* which declares the vowel points of the Hebrew text inspired, and the exaggerations of the

On the contrary, he thought of them rather as notaries (IV. viii. 9), who set down in authentic registers (I. vi. 3) what was dictated to them (*Argumentum in Ev. Joh.*).[37] They wrote, therefore, merely as the organs of the Holy Ghost, and did not speak *ex suo sensu,* not *humano impulsu,* not *sponte sua,* not *arbitrio suo,* but set out only *quae coelitus mandata fuerant.*[38] The diversity of the human authors thus disappears for Calvin before the unity of the Spirit, the sole responsible author of Scripture, which is to him therefore not the *verba Dei,* but emphatically the *verbum Dei.*[39] It is *a Deo* (" Institutes," I. vii. 5); it has " come down to us from the very mouth of God " (I. vii. 5); [40] it has " come down from heaven as if the living words of God themselves were heard in it " (I. vii. 1); [41] and " we owe it therefore the same reverence which we owe to God Himself, since it has proceeded from Him alone, and there is nothing human mixed with it " (Com. on II Tim. iii. 16).[42] According to this declaration the Scriptures are altogether divine, and in them, as he puts it energetically in another place, " it is God who speaks with us and not mortal

---

theopneusty of the nineteenth century." Yet nothing is more certain than that Calvin held both to " verbal inspiration " and to " the inerrancy of Scripture," however he may have conceived the action of God which secured these things.

[37] Cf. Otto Ritschl, " Dogmengeschichte des Protestantismus," 1908, i. p. 63: " If we may still entertain doubts whether Bullinger really defended the stricter doctrine of inspiration, it certainly is found in Calvin after 1543. He may have merely taken over from Butzer the expression *Spiritus Sancti amanuenses;* but it is peculiar to him that he conceives both the books of the Old Testament inclusively as contained in the historical enumerations, and those of the New Testament, as arising out of a verbal dictation of the Holy Spirit."

[38] These phrases are brought together by J. Cramer (as cited, pp. 102–3) from the Comments on II Tim. iii. 16 and II Pet. i. 20.

[39] Cf. Pannier, as cited, p. 203: " The Word of God is for him one, *verbum Dei,* and not *verba Dei.* The diversity of authors disappears before the unity of the Spirit." [40] Ab ipsissimo Dei ore ad nos fluxisse.

[41] E coelo fluxisse acsi vivae ipsae Dei voces illic exaudirentur.

[42] Hoc prius est membrum, eandem scripturae reverentiam deberi quam Deo deferimus, quia ad eo solo manavit, nec quidquam humani habet admistum.

men " (Com. on II Pet. i. 20).[43] Accordingly, he cites Scripture everywhere not as the word of man but as the pure word
of God. His " holy word " is " the scepter of God "; every
statement in which is " a heavenly oracle " which " cannot
fail " (Dedicatory Epistle to the " Institutes," *Opp.* ii. 12):
in it God " opens His own sacred mouth " to add His direct
word to the voice of His mute creatures (I. vi. 1). To say
" Scripture says " and to say " the Holy Ghost says " is all one.
We contradict the Holy Spirit, says Calvin — meaning the
Scriptures — when we deny to Christ the name of Jehovah or
anything which belongs to the majesty of Jehovah (I. xiii. 23).
" The Holy Spirit pronounces," says he, . . . " Paul declares
. . . the Scripture condemns . . . wherefore it is not surprising if the Holy Spirit reject " — all in one running context,
meaning ever the same thing (I. v. 13): just as in another context he uses interchangeably the " commandments of Christ "
and the " authority of Scripture " of the same thing (Dedicatory Letter).

It may be that Calvin has nowhere given us a detailed discussion of the mode of the divine operation in giving the
Scriptures. He is sure that they owe their origin to the divine
gift (I. vi. 1, 2, 3) and that God has so given them that they
are emphatically His word, as truly as if we were listening to
His living voice speaking from heaven (I. vii. 1): and, as we
have seen, he is somewhat addicted to the use of language
which, strictly taken, would imply that the mode of their gift
was " dictation." The Scriptures are " public records " (I. vi.
2), their human authors have acted as " notaries " (IV. viii. 9),
who have set down nothing of their own, but only what has
been dictated to them, so that there appears no admixture of
what is human in their product (on II Tim. iii. 16).[44] It is not

[43] Justa reverentia inde nascitur, quum statuimus, Deum nobiscum loqui,
non homines mortales.

[44] The account of Calvin's doctrine of inspiration given by E. Rabaud,
" Histoire de la doctrine de l'inspiration . . . dans les pays de langue française,"
1883, pp. 52 *sq.,* is worth comparing. Calvin's thought on this subject, he tells
us, was more precise and compact than that of the other Reformers, although
even his conception of inspiration was far from possessing perfectly firm
contours or supplying the elements of a really systematic view (p. 52). He

unfair to urge, however, that this language is figurative; and that what Calvin has in mind is not to insist that the mode of inspiration was dictation, but that the result of inspiration is

---

was the first, nevertheless, to give the subject of Sacred Scripture a fundamental, theoretic treatment, led thereto not by the pressure of controversy, but by the logic of his systematic thought: for his doctrine of inspiration (not yet distinguished from revelation) is one of the essential bases, if not the very point of departure of his dogmatics (p. 55). To him "the Bible is manifestly the word of God, in which He reveals Himself to men," and as such "proceeds from God." "But" (pp. 56 sq.) "the action of God does not, in Calvin's view, transform the sacred authors into machines. Jewish verbalism, Scriptural materialism, may be present in germ in the ideas of the *Institutes* — and the cold intellects of certain doctors of the Protestant scholasticism of the next century developed them — but they are very remote from the thought of the Reformer. Chosen and ordained by God, the Biblical writers were subject to a higher impulse; they received a divine illumination which increased the energy of their natural faculties; they understood the Revelation better and transmitted it more faithfully. It was scarcely requisite for this, however, that they should be passive instruments, simple secretaries, pens moved by the Holy Spirit. Appointed but intelligent organs of the divine thought, far from being subject to a dictation, in complete obedience to the immediate will of God, they acted under the impulsion of a personal faith which God communicated to them. 'Now, whether God was manifested to men by visions or oracles, what is called celestial witnesses, or ordained men as His ministers who taught their successors by tradition, it is in every case certain that He impressed on their hearts such a certitude of the doctrine, that they were persuaded and convinced that what had been revealed and preached to them proceeded from the true God: for He always ratified His word so as to secure for it a credit above all human opinion. Finally, that the truth might uninterruptedly remain continually in vigor from age to age, and be known in the world, He willed that the revelations which He had committed to the hands of the Fathers as a deposit, should be put on record: and it was with this design that He had the Law published, to which He afterwards added the Prophets as its expositors' (*Institutes,* I. vi. 2). These few lines resume in summary form the very substance of Calvin's doctrine of inspiration. We may conclude from it that he did not give himself to the elaboration of this dogma, with the tenacity and logical rigor which his clear and above all practical genius employed in the study and systematization of other points of the new doctrine. We shall seek in vain a precise declaration on the mode of revelation, on the extent and intensity of inspiration, on the relation of the book and the doctrine. None of these questions, as we have already had occasion to remark, had as yet been raised: the doctors gave themselves to what was urgent and did not undertake to prove or discuss what was not yet either under discussion or attacked. The principle which was laid down sufficed them. God had spoken — this was the faith which every consciousness of the time received without repugnance, and against

as if it were by dictation, viz., the production of a pure word of God free from all human admixtures. The term " dictation " was no doubt in current use at the time to express rather the effects than the mode of inspiration.[45] This being allowed, it is all the more unfair to urge that, Calvin's language being in this sense figurative, he is not to be understood as teaching that the effect of inspiration was the production of a pure word of God, free from all admixture of human error. This, on the contrary, is precisely what Calvin does teach, and that with the greatest strenuousness. He everywhere asserts that the effects of inspiration are such that God alone is the responsible author of the inspired product, that we owe the same reverence to it as to Him Himself, and should esteem the words as purely His as if we heard them proclaimed with His living voice from heaven; and that there is nothing human mixed with them. And he everywhere deals with them on that assumption. It is true that men have sought to discover in Calvin, particularly in his " Harmony of the Gospels," acknowledgments of

---

which no mind raised an objection. To search out how He did it was wholly useless: to undertake to prove it, no less so " (p. 58). There is evident in this passage a desire to minimize Calvin's view of the divinity of Scripture; the use of the passage from I. vi. 2 as the basis of an exposition of his doctrine of inspiration is indicative of this — whereas it obviously is a very admirable account of how God has made known His will to man and preserved the knowledge of it through time. The double currents of desire to be true to Calvin's own exposition of his doctrine and yet to withhold his *imprimatur* from what the author believes to be an overstrained doctrine, produces some strange confusion in his further exposition.

[45] Cf. J. Cramer, as cited, p. 114: " How Calvin conceives of this *dictare* by the Holy Ghost it is difficult to say. He borrowed it from the current ecclesiastical usage, which employed it of the *auctor primarius* of Scripture, as indeed also of tradition. Thus the Council of Trent uses the expression *dictante Spiritu Sancto* of the unwritten tradition inspired by the Holy Spirit." Otto Ritschl, " Dogmengeschichte des Protestantismus," i. 1908, p. 59, argues for taking the term strictly in Calvin. It is employed, it is true, in contemporary usage in the figurative sense, of the deliverances of the natural conscience, for example; and some Reformed writers use it of the internal testimony of the Spirit. Calvin also himself speaks as if he employed it of Scripture only figuratively — e.g. *Opp.* i. 632: verba *quodammodo* dictante Christi Spiritu. Nevertheless, on the whole Ritschl thinks he meant it in the literal sense.

the presence of human errors in the fabric of Scripture.[46] But these attempts rest on very crass misapprehensions of Calvin's efforts precisely to show that there are no such errors in the fabric of Scripture. When he explains, for example, that the purpose " of the Evangelists " — or " of the Holy Spirit," for he significantly uses these designations as synonyms — was not to write a chronologically exact record, but to present the general essence of things, this is not to allow that the Scriptures err humanly in their record of the sequences of time, but to assert that they intend to give no sequences of time and therefore cannot err in this regard. When again he suggests that an " error " has found its way into the text of Mat. xxvii. 9 or possibly into Mat. xxiii. 35, he is not speaking of the original, but of the transmitted text; [47] and it would be hard if he were not permitted to make such excursions into the region of textual criticism without laying himself open to the charge of denying his most assured conviction that nothing human is mixed with Scripture. In point of fact, Calvin not only asserts the freedom of Scripture as given by God from all error, but never in his detailed dealing with Scripture allows that such errors exist in it.[48]

[46] Cf., e.g., J. Cramer, as cited, pp. 114–116, whose instances are followed in the remarks which succeed. Cf. also p. 125. How widespread this effort to discover in Calvin some acknowledgment of errors in Scripture has become may be seen by consulting the citations made by Dunlop Moore, *The Presbyterian and Reformed Review*, 1893, p. 60: he cites Cremer, van Oosterzee, Farrar. Cf. even A. H. Strong, " Syst. Theol.," ed. 1907, vol. i. p. 217, whose list of " theological writers who admit the errancy of Scripture writers as to some matters unessential to their moral and spiritual teaching " requires drastic revision. Leipoldt (" Geschichte des N. T. Kanons," ii. 1908, p. 149) says: " Fundamentally Calvin holds fast to the old doctrine of verbal inspiration. His sound historical sense leads him, here and there, it is true, to break through the bonds of this doctrine. In his harmony of the Gospels (*Commentarii in harmoniam ex Mat., Mk., et Lk. compositam*, 1555), e.g., Calvin shows that the letters are not sacred to him; he moves much more freely here than Martin Chemnitz. But in other cases again Calvin draws strict consequences from the doctrine of verbal inspiration. He ascribes, e.g., to all four Gospels precisely similar authority, although he (with Luther and Zwingli) considers John's Gospel the most beautiful of them all."

[47] This is solidly shown, e.g., by Dunlop Moore, as cited, pp. 61–62: also for Acts vii. 16.

[48] Despite his tendency to lower Calvin's doctrine of inspiration with

If we ask for the ground on which he asserts this high doctrine of inspiration, we do not see that any other reply can be given than that it was on the ground of the teaching of Scripture itself. The Scriptures were understood by Calvin to claim to be in this high sense the word of God; and a critical scrutiny of their contents brought to him nothing which seemed to him to negative this claim. There were other grounds on which he might and did base a firm confidence in the divine origin of the Scriptures and the trustworthiness of their teach-

---

respect to its effects, J. Cramer in the following passage (as cited, pp. 120–121) gives in general a very fair statement of it: "We have seen that Calvin, although he has not given us a completed theory of inspiration, yet firmly believed in the inspiration of the entirety of Scripture. It is true we do not find in him the crass expressions of the later Reformed, as well as Lutheran, theologians. But the foundation on which they subsequently built — though somewhat onesidedly — is here. We cannot infer much from such expressions as ' from God,' ' came from God,' ' flowed from God.' Just as in Zwingli, these expressions were sometimes in Calvin synonyms of ' true.' Thus, at Titus ii. 12, he says he cannot understand why so many are unwilling to draw upon profane writers, — ' for, since all truth is from God (a Deo), if anything has been said well and truly by profane men, it ought not to be rejected, for it has come from God (a Deo est profectum).' More significant are such expressions as, ' nothing human is mixed with Scripture,' ' we owe to them the same reverence as to God,' God ' is the author of Scripture ' and as such has ' dictated ' (dictavit) all that the Apostles and Prophets have written, so that we ' must not depart from the word of God in even the smallest particular,' etc. All this applies not only to the Scriptures as a whole, not merely to their fundamental ideas and chief contents, but to all the sixty-six books severally. In contra-distinction from the Apocrypha, they have been given by the Holy Spirit (Préface mise en tête des livres apocryphes de l'Ancien Test.: Opp. ix. 827). The book of Acts ' beyond question is the product of the Holy Spirit Himself,' Mark ' wrote nothing but what the Holy Spirit gave him to write,' etc. To think here merely of a providential direction by God, in the sense that God took care that His people should lack nothing of a Scriptural record of His revelation — is impossible. For, however often Calvin may have directed attention to such a ' singularis providentiae cura ' (Inst., I. vi. 2, cf. I. viii. 10; Argumentum in Ev. Joh.) with respect to Scripture, he yet saw something over and above this in the production of the sacred books. He looked upon them as the writings of God Himself, who, through an extraordinary operation of His Spirit, guarded His amanuenses from all error as well when they transmitted histories as when they propounded the doctrine of Christ. Thus to him Scripture (naturally in its original text) was a complete work of God, to which nothing could be added and from which nothing could be taken away."

ing as a revelation from God. But there were no other grounds on which he could or did rest his conviction that these Scriptures are so from God that there is nothing human mixed with them, and their every affirmation is to be received with the deference which is due to the living voice of God speaking from heaven. On these other grounds Calvin was led to trust the teaching of the Scriptures as a divine revelation: and he therefore naturally trusted their teaching as to their own nature and inspiration.

Such, then, are the Scriptures as conceived by Calvin: sixty-six sacred books, " dictated " by God to His " notaries " that they might, in this " public record," stand as a perpetual special revelation of Himself to His people, to supplement or to supersede in their case the general revelation which He gives of Himself in His works and deeds, but which is rendered ineffective by the sin-bred disabilities of the human soul. For this, according to Calvin, is the account to give of the origin of Scripture, and this the account to give of the function it serves in the world. It was because man in his sinful imbecility was unable to profit by the general revelation which God has spread before all eyes, so that they are all without excuse (I. vi. 1), that God in His goodness gave to " those whom He intended to unite in a more close and familiar connection with Himself," a special revelation in open speech (I. vi. 1). And it was because of the mutability of the human mind, prone to errors of all kinds, corrupting the truth, that He committed this His special revelation to writing, that it might never be inaccessible to " those to whom He determined to make His instructions effectual " (I. vi. 3). In Calvin's view, therefore, the Scriptures are a documentation of God's special revelation of Himself unto salvation (I. vi. 1, *ad init.*); but a documentation cared for by God Himself, so that they are, in fine, themselves the special revelation of God unto salvation in documentary form (I. vi. 2, 3). The necessity for the revelation documented in them arises from the blindness of men in their sin: the necessity for the documentation of this revelation arises from the instability of men, even when taught of God.

We must conceive of special revelation, and of the Scriptures
as just its documentation, therefore, as not precisely a cure, but
rather an assistance to man dulled in his sight so as not to be
able to perceive God in His general revelation. "For," says
Calvin, "as persons who are old, or whose eyes have somehow
become dim, if you show them the most beautiful book, though
they perceive that something is written there, can scarcely read
two words together, yet by the aid of spectacles will begin to
read distinctly — so the Scripture . . ." etc. (I. vi. 1). The
function of Scripture thus, as special revelation documented,
is to serve as spiritual spectacles to enable those of dulled spiritual sight to see God.

Of course, the Scriptures do more than this. They not only
reveal the God of Nature more brightly to the sin-darkened eye;
they reveal also the God of Grace, who may not be found in
nature. Calvin does not overlook this wider revelation embodied in them: he particularly adverts to it (I. vi. 1). But he
turns from it for the moment as less directly germane to his
present object, which is to show that without the "spectacles"
of Scripture, sinful man would not be able to attain to a sound
knowledge of even God the Creator. It is on this, therefore,
that he now insists. It was only because God revealed Himself
in this special, supernatural way to them, that our first fathers
— "Adam, Noah, Abraham and the rest of the patriarchs" —
were able to retain Him in their knowledge (I. vi. 1). It was
only through this special revelation, whether renewed to them
by God, or handed down in tradition, "by the ministry of
men," that their posterity continued in the knowledge of God
(I. vi. 2). "At length, that the truth might remain in the
world in a continual course of instruction to all ages, God determined that the same oracles which He deposited with the
patriarchs, should be committed to public records" — first
the Law, then the Prophets, and then the books of the New
Covenant (I. vi. 2). It is now, therefore, only through these
Scriptures that man can attain to a true knowledge of God.
The revelation of God in His works is not useless: it makes
all men without excuse; it provides an additional though lower

and less certain revelation of God to His people — to a consideration of which all should seriously apply themselves, though they should principally attend to the Word (I. vi. 2). But experience shows that without the Word the sinful human mind is too weak to reach a sound knowledge of God, and therefore without it men wander in vanity and error. Calvin seems to speak sometimes almost as if the Scriptures, that is special revelation, wholly superseded general revelation (I. v. 12, *ad fin.*; vi. 2, *ad fin.*; 4, *ad fin.*). More closely scrutinized, it becomes evident, however, that he means only that in the absence of Scripture, that is of special revelation, the general revelation of God is ineffective to preserve any sound knowledge of Him in the world: but in the presence of Scripture, general revelation is not set aside, but rather brought back to its proper validity. The real relation between general and special revelation, as the matter lay in Calvin's mind, thus proves to be, not that the one supersedes the other, but that special revelation supplements general revelation indeed, but in the first instance rather repeats and by repeating vivifies and vitalizes general revelation, and flows confluently in with it to the one end of both, the knowledge of God (I. vi. 2). What special revelation is, therefore — and the Scriptures as its documentation — is very precisely represented by the figure of the spectacles. It is aid to the dulled vision of sinful man, to enable it to see God.

The question forcibly presents itself, however, whether "spectacles" will serve the purpose here. Has not Calvin painted the sin-bred blindness of men too blackly to encourage us to think it can be corrected by such an aid to any remainders of natural vision which may be accredited to them? The answer must be in the affirmative. But this only opens the way to point out that Calvin does not present special revelation, or the Scriptures as special revelation documented, as the entire cure, but places by the side of it the *testimonium Spiritus Sancti*. Special revelation, or Scripture as its documented form, provides in point of fact, in the view of Calvin, only the objective side of the cure he finds has been provided by God. The subjective side is provided by the *testimonium Spiritus Sancti.* The spectacles are provided by the Scriptures: the eyes are opened that they may see even through these spectacles, only by the witness of the Spirit in the heart. We perceive, then, that in Calvin's view the figure of the spectacles is a perfectly just one. He means to intimate that special revelation alone will not produce a knowledge of God in the human soul: that something more than external aid is needed before it can see: and to leave the way open to proceed to point out what further is required that sinful man may see God. Sinful man, we say again: for the whole crux lies there. Had there been no sin, there would have been no need of even special revelation. In the light of the splendid revelation of Himself which God has displayed in the theatre of nature, man with his native endowment of instinctive knowledge of God would have bloomed out into a full and sound knowledge of Him. But with sinful man, the matter is wholly different. He needs more light and he needs something more than light — he needs the power of sight.[49] That we may apprehend Calvin's thought, therefore, we must turn to the consideration of his doctrine of the Testimony of the Spirit.

III. The Testimony of the Spirit

What is Calvin's doctrine of the Testimony of the Spirit? The particular question which Calvin addresses himself to when he turns to the consideration of what he calls the testi-

---

[49] In I. v. 14 Calvin says that the Apostle in Heb. xi. 3, "By faith we understand that the worlds were framed by the Word of God" wishes to intimate that "the invisible divinity *was represented* indeed by such displays of His power, but that we have no eyes *to perceive it* unless they are illuminated through faith by the inner revelation of God" (Invisibilem divinitatem *repraesentari* quidem talibus spectaculis, sed ad illam *perspiciendam* non esse nobis oculos, nisi interiore Dei revelatione per fidem illuminentur). Here he distinguishes between the external, objective representation, and the internal, subjective preparation to perceive this representation. God is objectively revealed in His works: man in his sins is blind to this revelation: the interior operation of God is an opening of man's eyes: man then sees. The operation of God is therefore a palingenesis. This passage is already in ed. 1539 (i. 291); the last clause (nisi . . .) is not, however, reproduced in the French versions of either 1541 or 1560 (iii. 60).

mony of the Spirit concerns the accrediting of Scripture, not the assimilation of its revelatory contents. The reader cannot fail to experience some disappontment at this. The whole development of the discussion hitherto undoubtedly fosters the expectation, not, indeed, of an exclusive treatment of the assimilation of special revelation by sinful man — for both problems are raised by it and the two problems are at bottom one and their solution one — but certainly of some formal treatment of it, and indeed of such a treatment of the double problem that the stress should be laid on this. Calvin, however, is preoccupied with the problem of the accrediting of Scripture. This is due in part, doubtless, to its logical priority: as he himself remarks, we cannot be "established in the belief of the doctrine, till we are indubitably persuaded that God is its Author" (I. vii. 4, *ad init.*). But it was rendered almost inevitable by the state of the controversy with Rome, who intrenched herself in the position that the Protestant appeal to Scripture as over against the Church was inoperative, seeing that it is only by the Church that the Scriptures can be established in authority: for who but the Church can assure us that these Scriptures are from God, or indeed what books enter into the fabric of Scripture, or whether they have come down to us uncorrupted? As a practical man writing to practical men for a practical purpose, Calvin could not fail, perhaps, to give his primary attention to the aspect of the problem he had raised which was most immediately pressing. But this scarcely prepares us for the almost total neglect of its other aspect, with the effect that the construction of his general doctrine is left with a certain appearance of incompleteness. Not really incomplete; for the solution of the one problem is, as we have already suggested, the solution of the other also; and even the cursory reader — or perhaps we may say especially the cursory reader — may well be trusted to feel this as he is led on through the discussion, particularly as there are not lacking repeated suggestions of it, and the discussion closes with a direct reference to it and a formal postponement of the particular discussion of the other aspect of the double problem to a later portion of the treatise. " I pass over many things for the present," says

Calvin, "because this subject will present itself for discussion in another place. Only, let it be known here that that alone is true faith which the Spirit of God seals in our hearts. And with this one reason every reader of docility and modesty will be satisfied" (I. vii. 5, near the end). That is as much as to say, This whole subject is only one application of the general doctrine of faith; and as the general doctrine of faith is fully discussed at another place in this treatise, we may content ourselves here with the somewhat incomplete remarks we have made upon this special application of that doctrine; we only need to remind the reader that there is no true faith except that which is begotten in the soul by the Holy Spirit.

We can scarcely wonder that Calvin contents himself with this simple reference of the topic now engaging his attention, as a specific case, to the generic doctrine of faith, when we pause to realize how nearly this simple reference of it, as a species to its genus, comes to a sufficient exposition of it. We shall stop now to signalize only two points which are involved in this reference, the noting of which will greatly facilitate our apprehension of Calvin's precise meaning in his doctrine of the testimony of the Spirit to the divinity of Scripture. This doctrine is no isolated doctrine with Calvin, standing out of relation with the other doctrines of his system: it is but one application of his general doctrine of faith; or to be more specific, one application of his general doctrine of the function of the Holy Spirit in the production of faith. Given Calvin's general doctrine of the work of the Holy Spirit in applying salvation, and his specific doctrine of the *testimonium Spiritus Sancti* in the attestation of Scripture, and in the applying of its doctrine as well, was inevitable. It is but one application of the general doctrine that there is no true faith except that which the Spirit of God seals in our hearts. For Calvin in this doctrine — and this is the second point we wish to signalize — has in mind specifically "true faith." He is not asking here how the Scriptures may be proved to be from God. If that had been the question he was asking, he would not have hesitated to say that the testimony of the Church is conclusive of the fact. He does say so. " The universal judgment of the Church " (I. vii. 3, *fin.*) he represents as a very useful argument, " the consent of the Church " (I. viii. 12, *init.*) as a very important consideration, in establishing the divine origin of the Scriptures: although, of course, he does not conceive the Church as lending her authority to Scripture " when she receives and seals it with her suffrage," but rather as performing a duty of piety to herself in recognizing what is true apart from her authentication, and treating it with due veneration (I. vii. 2, *ad fin.*). For what is more her duty than " obediently to embrace what is from God as the sheep hear the voice of the shepherd " ? [50] Were it a matter of proving the Scriptures to be the Word of God, Calvin would, again, have been at no loss for rational arguments which he was ready to pronounce irresistible. He does adduce such arguments and he does pronounce them irresistible. He devotes a whole chapter to the adduction of these arguments (ch. viii.) — such arguments as these: the dignity of the subject-matter of Scripture — the heavenliness of its doctrine and the consent of all its parts — (§ 1), the majesty of its style (§ 2), the antiquity of its teaching (§ 3), the sincerity of its narrative (§ 4), its miraculous accompaniment, circumstantially confirmed (§§ 5, 6), its predictive contents authenticated by fulfilment (§§ 7, 8), its continuous use through so many ages (§§ 9–12), its sealing by martyr blood (§ 13): and these arguments he is so far from considering weak and inconclusive (I. viii. 13, *med.*) that he represents them rather as capable of completely vindicating the Scriptures against all the subtleties of their calumniators (*ibid.*). Nay, he declares that the proofs of the divine origin of the Scriptures are so cogent, as " certainly to evince, if there is a God in heaven, that He is the

[50] In his response to the Augsburg Interim (" Vera Ecclesiae reformandae ratio," 1549, *Opp.* vii. 591–674) he allows it to be the *proprium ecclesiae officium* to *scripturas veras a suppositiis discernere;* but only that *obedienter amplectitur, quicquid Dei est,* as the sheep hear the voice of the shepherd. It is nevertheless *sacrilega impietas ecclesiae judicio submittere sacrosancta Dei oracula.* See J. Cramer, as cited, p. 104, note 3. Cramer remarks in expounding Calvin's view: " By the approbation she gives to them " — the books of Scripture — " the Church does not make them authentic, but only yields her homage to the truth of God."

author of the Law, and the Prophecies, and the Gospel " (I. vii.
4, near the beginning); as to extort with certainty from all
who are not wholly lost to shame, the confession of the divine
gift of the Scriptures (*ibid.*).[51] " Though I am far from possessing any peculiar dexterity " in argument " or eloquence," he
says, " yet were I to contend with the most subtle despisers of
God, who are ambitious to display their wit and their skill in
weakening the authority of Scripture, I trust I should be able
without difficulty to silence their obstreperous clamor " (*ibid.*).
But objective proofs — whether the conclusive testimony of
witnesses, or the overwhelming evidence of rational considerations — be they never so cogent,[52] he does not consider of
themselves capable of producing " true faith." And it is " true
faith," we repeat, that Calvin has in mind in his doctrine of
the *testimonium Spiritus Sancti.* If it seemed to him a small
matter that man should know that God is if he did not know
what God is, it equally seemed to him a small matter that man
should know what God is, in the paradigms of the intellect, if
he did not really know this God in the intimacy of communion
which that phrase imports. And equally it seemed to him utterly unimportant that a man should be convinced by stress of

[51] It would require that we should be wholly hardened (nisi ad perdi-
tam impudentiam obduruerint) that we should not perceive that the doctrine of Scripture is heavenly, that we should not have the confession wrung
from us that there are manifest signs in Scripture that it is God who speaks
in and through it (extorquebitur illis haec confessio, manifesta signa loquentis
Dei conspici in Scriptura ex quibus pateat coelestem esse eius doctrinam) —
I. vii. 4.

[52] The exact relations of the "proofs" to the divinity of Scripture,
which Calvin teaches, was sufficiently clear to be caught by his successors.
It is admirably stated in the Westminster Confession of Faith, i. 5. And we
may add that the same conception is stated also very precisely by Quenstedt:
" These motives, as well internal as external, by which we are led to the
knowledge of the authority of Scripture, make the theopneusty of Sacred
Scripture probable, and produce a certitude which is not merely conjectural
but moral . . . they do not make the divinity of Scripture infallible and
altogether indubitable." (" Theologia didactico-polemica, sive Systema theologicum," Lipsiae, 1715, Pars prima, pp. 141–2.) That is to say, they are not
of the nature of *demonstration,* but nevertheless give moral certitude: the
testimony of the Spirit is equivalent to demonstration — as is the deliverance of any simply acting sense.

rational evidence that the Scriptures are the Word of God, unless he practically embraced these Scriptures as the Word of God and stayed his soul upon them. The knowledge of God which Calvin has in mind in this whole discussion is, thus, a vital and vitalizing knowledge of God, and the attestation of Scripture which he is seeking is not an attestation merely to the intelligence of men, compelling from them perhaps a reluctant judgment of the intellect alone (since those convinced against their will, as the proverb has it, are very apt to remain of the same opinion still), but such an attestation as takes hold of the whole man in the roots of his activities and controls all the movements of his soul.

This is so important a consideration for the exact apprehension of Calvin's doctrine that it may become us to pause and assure ourselves of the simple matter of fact from the language which Calvin employs of it in the course of the discussion. We shall recall that from the introduction of the topic of special revelation he has in mind and keeps before his readers' mind its destination for the people of God alone. The provisions for producing a knowledge of God, consequent on the inefficiency of natural revelation, Calvin is careful to explain, are not for all men, but for " the elect " (I. vi. 1), or, as they are more fully described, " those whom God intends to unite in a more close and familiar connection with Himself " (*ibid.*), " those to whom He determines to make His instructions effectual " (I. vi. 3). From the first provisions of His supernatural dealings, therefore, He " intends to make His instructions effectual." More pointedly still he speaks of the *testimonium Spiritus Sancti* as an act in which " God deigns to confer a singular power on His elect, whom He distinguishes from the rest of mankind " (I. vii. 5).[53] This singular power, now, is

---

[53] Cf. Pannier, as cited, pp. 207–8: " We see that this understanding of the Scriptures, this capacity to receive the testimony of the Spirit, is not, according to Calvin, possible for all; and that, less and less . . . He continually emphasises more and more the incapacity of man to persuade another of it, without the aid of God; but he emphasises still more progressively the impossibility of obtaining this aid if God does not accord it first. 1550 (I. viii. at end): ' Those who wish to prove to unbelievers by arguments

nothing else but "saving faith," and Calvin speaks of it in all the synonymy of "saving faith." He calls it "true faith" (I. vii. 5), "sound faith" (I. vii. 4), "firm faith" (I. viii. 13), "the faith of the pious" (I. vii. 3), "the certainty of the pious" (I. vii. 3), "that assurance which is essential to true piety" (I. vii. 4), "saving knowledge" (I. viii. 13), "a solid assurance of eternal life" (I. vii. 1). It is the thing which is naturally described by this synonymy which Calvin declares is not produced in the soul except by the testimony of the Holy Spirit. This obviously is nothing more than to declare that that faith which lays hold of Christ unto eternal life is the product of the Holy Spirit in the heart, and that it is one of the exercises of this faith to lay hold of the revelation of this Christ in the Scriptures with assured confidence, so that it is only he who is led by the Spirit who embraces these Scriptures with "sound faith," that is, "with that assurance which is essential to true piety" (I. vii. 4). What Calvin has in mind, in a word, is simply an extended comment on Paul's words: "the natural man receiveth not the things of the Spirit of God . . . but he that is spiritual judgeth all things" (I Cor. ii. 14, 15).[54]

---

that the Scriptures are from God are inconsiderate; for this is known *only to faith.*' 1559 (I. vii. *in fine*): The mysteries of God are not understood, *except by those to whom it is given.* . . . It is quite certain that the witness of the Spirit does not make itself felt except to believers, and is not *in itself* an apologetic means with respect to unbelievers. . . . The *natural* man receiveth not spiritual things."

[54] Cf. Pannier, as cited, pp. 195–6: "First let us recall this, — for Calvin this testimony of the Holy Spirit is only one act of the great drama which is enacted in the entire soul of the religious man, and in which the Holy Spirit holds always the principal rôle. While the later dogmatists make the Holy Spirit, so to speak, function mechanically, at a given moment, in the pen of the prophets or in the brain of the readers, Calvin sees the Holy Spirit constantly active in the man whom He wishes to sanctify, and the fact that He leads him to recognize the divinity and the canonicity of the sacred books is only one manifestation, — a very important one, no doubt, but only a particular one, — of His general work." It is only, of course, the Lutheran and Rationalizing dogmatists who, constructively, subject the action of the Spirit to the direction of man — whether by making it rest on the application of the "means of grace" or on the action of the human will. Calvin and his followers — the Reformed — make the act of man depend on the free and sovereign action of the Spirit.

Calvin does not leave us, however, to gather from general remarks referring it to its class or to infer from its general effects, what he means by the testimony of the Spirit of God to the divinity of Scripture, but describes for us its nature and indicates the mode of its operation and specific effects with great exactitude.[55] He tells us that it is a " secret " (I. vii. 4),

[55] J. Cramer, as cited, pp. 122–3, somewhat understates this, but in the main catches Calvin's meaning: " Calvin does not, it is true, tell us in so many words precisely what this *testimonium Sp. S.* is, but it is easy to gather it from the whole discussion. He is thinking of the Holy Spirit, who, as the Spirit of our adoption as children, leads us to say Amen to the Word which the Father speaks in the Holy Scriptures to His children. He even says expressly in *Inst.* I. vii. 4: ' As if the Spirit was not called " seal " and " earnest " just because He confers faith on the pious.' But more plainly still, and indeed so that no doubt can remain, we find it in Beza, the most beloved and talented pupil of Calvin, who assuredly also in his conception of Scripture was the most thoroughly imbued with the spirit of his teacher. In his reply to Castellion, Beza says: ' The testimony of the Spirit of adoption does not lie properly in this, that we believe to be true what the Scriptures testify (for this is known also to the devils and to many of the lost), but rather in this, — that each applies to himself the promise of salvation in Christ of which Paul speaks in Rom. viii. 15, 16.' Accordingly a few lines further down he speaks of a ' testimony of adoption and free justification in Christ.' In the essence of the matter Calvin will have meant just this by his testimony of the Holy Spirit. . . ." Beza's words are in his " Ad defensiones et reprehensiones Seb. Castellionis " (" Th. Bezae Vezelii Opera," i. Geneva, 1582, p. 503): Testimonium Spiritus adoptionis non in eo proprie positum est ut credamus verum esse quod Scriptura testatur (nam hoc ipsum quoque sciunt diaboli et reprobi multi), sed in eo potius ut quisque sibi salutis in Christo promissionem applicet, de qua re agit Paulus, Rom. viii. 15, 16. . . . That it was generally understood in the first age that this was the precise nature of the witness of the Spirit is shown by its definition in this sense not only by the Reformed, but by the Lutherans. For example, Hollaz defines thus: " The testimony of the Holy Spirit is the supernatural act (*actus supernaturalis*) of the Holy Spirit by means of the Word of God attentively read or heard (His own divine power having been communicated to the Scriptures) by which the heart of man is moved, opened, illuminated, turned to the obedience of faith, so that the illuminated man out of these internal spiritual movements truly perceives the Word which is propounded to him to have proceeded from God, and gives it therefore his unwavering assent." (" Examinis theologici acroamatici univers. theologiam thet. polem.," Holmiae et Lipsiae, 1741, p. 125.) The Lutheranism of this definition resides in the clauses: " By means of the Word of God " . . . " His own divine power having been communicated to the Scriptures " . . . which make the action of the Holy Spirit to be from out of the Word, in which He dwells *intrinsicus*. But the nature of the testi-

" internal " (I. vii. 4; viii. 13), " inward " (I. vii. 5) action of
the Holy Spirit on the soul, by which the soul is " illuminated "
(I. vii. 3, 4, 5), so as to perceive their true quality in the Scriptures as a divine book. We may call this " an inward teaching "
of the Spirit which produces " entire acquiescence in the Scriptures," so that they are self-authenticating to the mind and
heart (I. vii. 5); or we may call it a " secret testimony of the
Spirit," by which our minds and hearts are convinced with a
firmness superior to all reason that the Scriptures are from
God (I. vii. 4). In both instances we are using figurative language. Precisely what is produced by the hidden internal operation of the Spirit on the soul is a new spiritual sense (*sensus*,
I. vii. 5, *med.*), by which the divinity of Scripture is perceived
as by an intuitive perception. " For the Scripture exhibits as
clear evidence of its truth, as white and black things do of their
color, and sweet and bitter things of their taste " (I. vii. 2,
end); and we need only a sense to discern its divine quality to
be convinced of it with the same immediacy and finality as
we are convinced by their mere perception of light or darkness,
of whiteness or blackness, of sweetness or bitterness (*ibid.*).
No conclusions based on " reasoning " or " proofs " or founded
on human judgment can compare in clearness or force with
such a conviction, which is instinctive and immediate, and finds
its ultimate ground and sanction in the Holy Spirit who has
wrought in the heart this spiritual sense which so functions
in recognizing the divine quality of Scripture. Illuminated
by the Spirit of God, we believe, therefore, not on the ground
of our own judgment, or on the ground of the judgment of
others, but with a certainty above all human judgment, by
a spiritual intuition.[56] With the utmost explicitness Calvin so
describes this instinctive conviction in a passage of great
vigor: " It is, therefore," says he, " such a persuasion as re-

---

mony of the Spirit is purely conceived as an act of the Holy Spirit by which
the heart of man is renewed to spiritual perception, in the employment of
which he perceives the divine quality of Scripture.

[56] Supra humanum iudicium, certo certius constituimus (non secus ac
si ipsius Dei numen illic intueremur) hominum ministerio, ab ipsissimo Dei
ore ad nos fluxisse (I. vii. 5).

quires no reasons; such a knowledge as is supported by the highest reason and in which the mind rests with greater security and constancy than in any reasons; in fine, such a sense as cannot be produced but by a revelation from heaven" (I. vii. 5).[57] Here we are told that it is a *persuasio,* or rather a *notitia,* or rather a *sensus.* It is a persuasion which does not require reasons — that is to say, it is a state of conviction not induced by arguments, but by direct perception: it is, that is to say, a knowledge, a direct perception in accord with the highest reason, in which the mind rests, with an assurance not attainable by reasoning; or to be more explicit still, it is a sense which comes only from divine gift. As we have implanted in us by nature a sense which distinguishes between light and darkness, a sense which distinguishes between sweet and bitter, and the verdict of these senses is immediate and final; so we have planted in us by the creative action of the Holy Spirit a sense for the divine, and its verdict, too, is immediate and final: the spiritual man discerneth all things. Such, in briefest outline, is Calvin's famous doctrine of the testimony of the Spirit.

MODE OF THIS TESTIMONY

Certain further elucidations of its real meaning and bearing appear, however, to be necessary, to guard against misapprehension of it. When we speak of an internal testimony of the Holy Spirit, it is evident that we must conceive it as presenting itself in one of three ways. It may be conceived as of the nature of an immediate revelation to each man to whom it is given. It may be conceived as of the nature of a blind conviction produced in the minds of its recipients. It may be conceived as of the nature of a grounded conviction, formed in their minds by the Spirit, by an act which rather terminates immediately on the faculties, enabling and effectively persuading them to reach a conviction on grounds presented

[57] Talis ergo est persuasio quae rationes non requirat; talis notitia, cui optima ratio constet: nempe in qua securius constantiusque mens quiescit quam in ullis rationibus; talis denique sensus, qui nisi ex coelesti revelatione nasci nequeat (I. vii. 5).

to them, than produces the conviction itself, apart from or
without grounds. In which of these ways did Calvin conceive
the testimony of the Spirit as presenting itself? As revelation, or as ungrounded faith, or as grounded faith?

Certainly not the first. The testimony of the Spirit was
not to Calvin of the nature of a propositional "revelation"
to its recipients. Of this he speaks perfectly explicitly, and
indeed in his polemic against Anabaptist mysticism insistently. He does indeed connect the term "revelation" with
the testimony of the Spirit, declaring it, for example, such
a sense (*sensus*) as can be produced by nothing short of "a
revelation from heaven" (I. vii. 5, *med.*). But his purpose
in the employment of this language is not to describe it according to its nature, but to claim for it with emphasis a
heavenly source: he means merely to assert that it is not
earth-born, but God-wrought, while at the same time he intimates that in its nature it is not a propositional revelation,
but an instinctive "sense." That he did not conceive of it as a
propositional revelation is made perfectly clear by his explicit
assertions at the opening of the discussion (I. vii. 1, *init.*),
that we "are not favored with daily oracles from heaven,"
and that the Scriptures constitute the sole body of extant revelations from God. It is not to supersede nor yet to supplement these recorded revelations that the testimony of the
Spirit is given us, he insists, but to confirm them (I. ix. 3): or,
as he puts it in his polemic against the Anabaptists, "The office of the Spirit which is promised us is not to feign new and
unheard-of revelations, or to coin a new system of doctrine,
which would seduce us from the received doctrine of the Gospel, but to seal to our minds the same doctrine which the
Gospel delivers" (I. ix. 1, *fin.*).

In this polemic against the Anabaptists (ch. ix.) he gives
us an especially well-balanced account of the relations which
in his view obtain between the revelation of God and the
witness of the Spirit. If he holds that the revelation of God is
ineffective without the testimony of the Spirit, he holds
equally that the testimony of the Spirit is inconceivable with-

out the revelation of God embodied in the Word. He even declares that the Spirit is no more the agent by which the Word is impressed on the heart than the Word is the means by which the illumination of the Spirit takes effect. " If apart from the Spirit of God " we " are utterly destitute of the light of truth," he says (I. ix. 3, *ad fin.*), equally " the Word is the instrument by which the Lord dispenses to believers the illumination of the Spirit." So far as the knowledge of the truth is concerned, we are as helpless, then, without the Word as we are without the Spirit, for the whole function of the Spirit with respect to the truth is, not to reveal to us the truth anew, much less to reveal to us new truth, but efficaciously to confirm the Word, revealed in the Scriptures, to us, and efficaciously to impress it on our hearts (I. ix. 3). This Calvin makes superabundantly plain by an illustration and a didactic statement of great clearness. The illustration (I. ix. 3) is drawn from our Lord's dealings with His two disciples with whom after His rising He walked to Emmaus. " He opened their understandings," Calvin explains, " not that rejecting the Scriptures they might be wise of themselves, but that they might understand the Scriptures." Such also, he says, is the testimony of the Spirit to-day: for what is it — and this is the didactic statement to which we have referred — but an enabling of us by the light of the Spirit to behold the divine countenance in the Scriptures that so our minds may be filled with a solid reverence for the Word (I. ix. 3)? Here we have the nature of the testimony of the Spirit, and its manner of working and its effects, announced to us in a single clause. It is an illumination of our minds, by which we are enabled to see God in the Scriptures, so that we may reverence them as from Him.

Other effect than this Calvin explicitly denies to the testimony of the Spirit, and he defends his denial from the charge of inconsistency with the stress he has previously laid upon the necessity of this testimony (I. ix. 3). It is not to deny the necessity of this work of the Spirit, he argues, to confine it to the express confirmation of the Word and of the revelation

contained therein. Nor is it derogatory to the Spirit to confine
His operations now to the confirmation of the revealed Word.
While on the other hand to attribute to Him repeated or new
revelations to each of the children of God, as the mystics do,
is derogatory to the Word, which is His inspired product. To
lay claim to the possession of such a Spirit as this, he declares,
is to lay claim to the possession of a different Spirit from that
which dwelt in Christ and the Apostles — for their Spirit honored the Word — and a different Spirit from that which was
promised by Christ to His disciples — for this Spirit was " not
to speak of Himself." It is to lay claim to a Spirit for whose
divine mission and character, moreover, we lack all criterion —
for how can we know that the Spirit that speaks in us is from
God, save as He honors the Word of God (I. ix. 1 and 2)? From
all which it is perfectly plain not only that Calvin did not conceive the testimony of the Spirit as taking effect in the form of
propositional revelations, but that he did conceive it as an operation of God the Holy Spirit in the heart of man which is so
connected with the revelation of God in His Word, that it
manifests itself only in conjunction with that revelation.

Calvin's formula here is, The Word and Spirit.[58] Only in
the conjunction of the two can an effective revelation be made
to the sin-darkened mind of man.[59] The Word supplies the ob-

[58] Köstlin, as cited, pp. 412–13, especially 413, note a, adverts to this with
a reference to Dorner, " Gesch. d. protest. Theologie," p. 377, who makes it
characteristic of Calvin in distinction from Zwingli to draw the outer and
inner Word more closely together. The justice of Dorner's view, which would
seem to assign to Calvin in his doctrine of the Word as a means of grace a
position somewhere between Zwingli and Luther, may well be doubted. According to Dorner, Calvin " modified the looser connection between the outward and inward Word held by Zwingli and connected the two sides more
closely together." " In reference, therefore, to the principle of the Reformation," he continues, " with its two sides, Calvin is still more than Zwingli, of
one mind and spirit with the German Lutheran Reformation " (E. T. i. 1871,
p. 387). Again (i. p. 390): " The double form of the *Verbum Dei externum*
and *internum,* held by Zwingli, gives place indeed in Calvin to a more inward
connecting of the two sides; the Scriptures are according to him not merely
the sign of an absent thing, but have in themselves divine matter and
breath, which makes itself actively felt." We do not find that Calvin and
Zwingli differ in this matter appreciably.

[59] Cf. his response to Sadolet (1539), *Opp.* v. 393: tuo igitur experimento

jective factor; the Spirit the subjective factor; and only in the union of the objective and subjective factors is the result accomplished. The whole objective revelation of God lies, thus, in the Word. But the whole subjective capacitating for the reception of this revelation lies in the will of the Spirit. Either, by itself, is wholly ineffective to the result aimed at — the production of knowledge in the human mind. But when they unite, knowledge is not only rendered possible to man: it is rendered certain. And therefore it is that Calvin represents the provision for the knowledge of God both in the objective revelation in the Word and in the subjective testimony of the Spirit as destined by God not for men at large, but specifically for His people, His elect, those " to whom He determined to make His instructions effectual " (I. vi. 3). The Calvinism of Calvin's doctrine of religious knowledge comes to clear manifestation here; and that not merely because of its implication of the doctrine of election, but also because of its implication of Calvin's specific doctrine of the means of grace. Already in his doctrine of religious knowledge, we find Calvin teaching that God is known not by those who choose to know Him, but by those by whom He chooses to be known: and this simply because the knowledge of God is God-given, and is therefore given to whom He will. Men do not wring the knowledge of God from a Deity reluctant to be known: God imparts the knowledge of Himself to men reluctant to know Him: and therefore none know Him save those to whom He efficaciously imparts, by His Word and Spirit, the knowledge of Himself. " By His Word and Spirit " — therein is expressed already the fundamental formula of the Calvinistic doctrine of the " means of grace." In that doctrine the Spirit is not, with the Lutherans,. conceived as in the Word, conveyed and applied wherever the Word goes: nor is the Word, with the mystics, conceived as in the Spirit always essentially present wherever He is present in His power as a Spirit of revelation and truth. The two are severally contemplated, as separable factors, in the

disce non minus importunum esse spiritum iactare sine verbo, quam futurum sit insulsum, sine spiritu verbum ipsum obtendere.

one work of God in producing the knowledge of Himself which
is eternal life in the souls of His people; separable factors
which must both, however, be present if this knowledge of
God is to be produced. For it is the function of the Word to set
before the soul the object to be believed; and it is the function
of the Spirit to quicken in the soul belief in this object: and
neither performs the work of the other or its own work apart
from the other.

It still remains, however, to inquire precisely how Calvin
conceived the Spirit to operate in bringing the soul to a hearty
faith in the Word as a revelation from God. Are we to understand him as teaching that the Holy Spirit by His almighty
power creates, in the souls of those whom God has set upon to
bring to a knowledge of Him, an entirely ungrounded faith in
the divinity of the Scriptures and the truth of their contents,
so that the soul embraces them and their contents with firm
confidence as a revelation from God wholly apart from and in
the absence of all *indicia* of their divinity or of the truth of
their contents? So it has come to be very widely believed; and
indeed it may even be said that it has become the prevalent
representation that Calvin taught that believers have within
themselves a witness of the Spirit by which they are assured of
the divinity of Scripture and the truth of its contents quite
apart from all other evidence. The very term, " the testimony
of the Spirit," is adduced in support of this representation, as
setting a divine witness to the divinity of Scripture over
against other sources of evidence, and of course superseding
them: and appeal is made along with this to Calvin's strong
assertions of the uselessness and even folly of plying men with
" the proofs " of the divine origin of Scripture, seeing that, it
is said, in the absence of the testimony of the Spirit such
"proofs" must needs be ineffective, and in the presence of
that effective testimony they cannot but be adjudged unnecessary. What can he mean, then, it is asked, but that the testimony of the Holy Spirit is sufficient to assure us of the divinity of Scripture apart from all *indicia,* and does its work
entirely independently of them?

The sufficient answer to this question is that he can mean
— and in point of fact does mean — that the *indicia* are wholly
insufficient to assure us of the divinity of Scripture apart from
the testimony of the Spirit; and effect no result independently of it. This is quite a different proposition and gives rise
to quite a different series of corollaries. Calvin's dealing with
the *indicia* of the divinity of Scripture has already attracted
our attention in one of its aspects, and it is quite worthy of
renewed scrutiny. We have seen that he devotes a whole chapter to their exposition (chap. viii.) and strongly asserts their
objective conclusiveness to the fact of the divine origin of
Scripture (I. vii. 4). Nor does he doubt their usefulness whether
to the believer or the unbeliever. The fulness and force of his
exposition of them is the index to his sense of their value to
the believer: for he adduces them distinctly as confirmations
of believers in their faith in the Scriptures (I. viii. 1, 13), and
betrays in every line of their treatment the high significance he
attaches to them as such. And he explicitly declares that they
not only maintain in the minds of the pious the native dignity
and authority of Scripture, but completely vindicate it against
all the subtleties of calumniators (I. viii. 13). No man of sound
mind can fail to confess on their basis that it is God who
speaks in Scripture and that its doctrine is divine (I. vii. 4).
It is a complete misapprehension of Calvin's meaning, then,
when it is suggested that he represents the *indicia* of the divinity of Scripture as inconclusive or even as ineffective.[60] Their

[60] There is a certain misapprehension involved, also, in speaking of
Calvin *subordinating* the *indicia* to the witness of the Spirit, as if he conceived them on the same plane, but occupying relatively lower and higher
positions on this plane. The witness of the Spirit and the *indicia* move in
different orbits. We find Köstlin, as cited, p. 413, accordingly speaking not
quite to the point, when he says: " He subordinated to the power of this one,
immediate, divine testimony, all those several criteria by the pious and
thoughtful consideration of which our faith in the Scriptures and their contents may and should be further mediated. Even miracles, as Niedner has
rightly remarked (*Philosophie- und Theologiegeschichte*, p. 341, note 2),
take among the evidences for the divinity of the Biblical revelation, 'nothing
more than a coördinate ' place: we add in passing that Calvin introduces them
here only in the edition of 1550, and then enlarges the section which treats
of them in the edition of 1559. He does not, however, put a low estimate on

conclusiveness could not be asserted with more energy than he asserts it: nor indeed could their effectiveness — their effectiveness in extorting from the unbeliever the confession of the divinity of Scripture and in rendering him without excuse in refusing the homage of his mind and heart to it — in a word, will he, nill he, convincing his intellect of its divinity; their effectiveness also in confirming the believer in his faith and maintaining his confidence intact. This prevalent misapprehension of Calvin's meaning is due to neglect to observe the precise thing for which he affirms the *indicia* to be ineffective

such criteria; he would trust himself — as he says in an addition made in the edition of 1559 (xxx. 59) — to silence with them even stiff-necked opponents; but this certainty which faith should have, can never be attained, says he, by disputation, but can be wrought only by the testimony of the Spirit." The question between the testimony of the Spirit and the *indicia* is not a question of which gives the strongest evidence; it is a question of what each is fitted to do. The *indicia* are supreme in their sphere; they and they alone give objective evidence. But objective evidence is inoperative when the subjective condition is such that it cannot penetrate and affect the mind. All objective evidence is in this sense subordinate to the subjective change wrought by the Spirit: but considered as objective evidence it is supreme in its own sphere. The term "subordinate" is accordingly misleading here. For the rest, it is true that Calvin places the miracles by which the giving of Scripture was accompanied rather among the objective evidences of their divinity than at their apex: but this is due not to an underestimation of the value of miracles as evidence, but to the very high estimate he placed on the internal criteria of divinity, by which the Scriptures evidence themselves to be divine. And above all we must not be misled into supposing that he places miracles below the testimony of the Spirit in importance. Such a comparison is outside his argument: miracles are part of the objective evidence of the deity of Scripture; the testimony of the Spirit is the subjective preparation of the heart to receive the objective evidence in a sympathetic embrace. He would have said, of course — he does say — that no miracle, and no body of miracles, could or can produce "true faith": the internal creative operation of the Spirit is necessary for that. And in that sense the evidence of miracles is subordinated to the testimony of the Spirit. But this is not because of any depreciation of the evidential value of miracles; but because of the full appreciation of the deadness of the human soul in sin. The evidential value of miracles, and their place in the objective evidences of the divine origin of the Scriptures, are wholly unaffected by the doctrine of the testimony of the Spirit; and the strongest assertions of their valuelessness in the production of faith, apart from the testimony of the Spirit, do not in the least affect the estimate we put on them, as objective evidences.

and the precise reason he assigns for this ineffectiveness. There is only one thing which he says they cannot do: that is to produce "sound faith" (I. vii. 4), "firm faith" (I. viii. 13) — that assurance which is essential to "true piety" (I. vii. 4). And their failure to produce "sound faith" is due solely to the subjective condition of man, which is such that a creative operation of the Holy Spirit on the soul is requisite before he can exercise "sound faith" (I. vii. 4; I. viii. 13). It is the attempt to produce this "sound faith" in the heart of man, not renewed for believing by the creative operation of the Holy Spirit, which Calvin pronounces preposterous and foolish. "It is acting a preposterous part," he says, "to endeavor to produce *sound faith* in the Scriptures by disputations": objections may be silenced by such disputations, "but this will not fix in men's hearts *that assurance which is essential to true piety*"; for religion is not a matter of mere opinion, but a fundamental change of attitude towards God (I. vii. 4). It betrays, therefore, great folly to wish to demonstrate to infidels that the Scriptures are the Word of God, he repeats in another place, obviously with no other meaning, "since this cannot be known without faith," that is, as the context shows, without the internal working of the Spirit of God (I. viii. 13, end).

That Calvin should thus teach that the *indicia* are incapable of producing "firm faith" in the human heart, disabled by sin, is a matter of course: and therefore it is a matter of course that he should teach that the *indicia* are ineffective for the production of "sound faith" apart from the internal operation of the Spirit correcting the sin-bred disabilities of man, that is to say, apart from the testimony of the Spirit. But what about the *indicia* in conjunction with the testimony of the Spirit? It would seem to be evident that, on Calvin's ground, they would have their full part to play here, and that we must say that, when the soul is renewed by the Holy Spirit to a sense for the divinity of Scripture, it is through the *indicia* of that divinity that it is brought into its proper confidence in the divinity of Scripture. In treating of the *indicia,* Calvin

does not, however, declare this in so many words. He sometimes even appears to speak of them rather as if they lay
side by side with the testimony of the Spirit than acted
along with it as co-factors in the production of the supreme
effect. He speaks of their ineffectiveness in producing sound
faith in the unbeliever: and of their value as corroboratives
to the believer: and his language would sometimes seem to
suggest that therefore it were just as well not to employ them
until after faith had formed itself under the testimony of the
Spirit (I. viii. 1, 13). Of their part in forming faith under the
operation of the testimony of the Spirit he does not appear
explicitly to speak.[61]

[61] Cf. Köstlin, as cited, pp. 413–415: "We find in Calvin the afore-
mentioned several criteria set alongside of this witness of the Spirit, and
indeed especially those which are internal to the Scriptures themselves, such
as their elevation above all merely human products, which cannot fail to
impress every reader, etc. It would certainly be desirable to trace an inner
connection between this impression made by the character, by the style of
speech, by the contents of Scripture, and that supreme immediate testimony of
the Spirit for it. Assuredly God Himself, the Author of Scripture, works
upon us also in such impressions, which we analyse in our reflecting human
consideration, and in our debates strive to set before opponents; and we feel,
on the other side, a need to analyse, as far as is possible for us, even the supreme witness of the Spirit, in spite of its immediacy, and to relate it with
our other experiences and observations with respect to Scripture, so as to
become conscious of the course by which God passes from one to the other.
Calvin, however, does not enter into this; he sets the two side by side and
over against one another: 'Although (Scripture) conciliates reverence to
itself by its own supreme majesty, it does not seriously affect us, until it is
sealed to our hearts by the Spirit' (XXIX. 295; XXX. 60; ed. 3, I. vii. 5): he
does not show the inner relation of one to the other. He does not do this even
in the edition of 1559, where he with great eloquence speaks more fully of the
power with which the Word of the New Testament witnesses manifests its
divine majesty. The witness of the Spirit comes forward with Calvin thus
somewhat abruptly. By means of it the Spirit works true faith, which the
Scripture, even through its internal criteria, cannot establish in divine certainty; and indeed He does not work it in the case of all those — and has no
intention of working it in the case of all those — to whom the Scripture is
conveyed with its criteria, but, as the section on Predestination further
shows, only in the case of those who have been elected thereto from all
eternity. Here we are already passing over into the relation of the Calvinistic
conception of the Formal Principle or the Authority of Scripture, to its conception of the means of grace. In this matter the Lutheran doctrine stands
in conflict with it. But with reference to what we have been discussing, we

Nevertheless, there are not lacking convincing hints that there was lying in his mind all the time the implicit understanding that it is through these *indicia* of the divinity of Scripture that the soul, under the operation of the testimony of the Spirit, reaches its sound faith in Scripture, and that he has been withheld from more explicitly stating this only by the warmth of his zeal for the necessity of the testimony of the Spirit which has led him to a constant contrasting of this divine with those human " testimonies." Thus we find him repeatedly affirming that these *indicia* will produce no fruit *until* they be confirmed by the internal testimony of the Spirit (I. vii. 4, 5; viii. 1, 13): " Our reverence may be conciliated by its internal majesty [the Scripture's], but it never seriously affects us, *till* it is confirmed by the Spirit in our hearts " (I. vii. 5). " *Without this certainty,* . . . in vain will the authority of Scripture be either defended by arguments or established by the consent of the Church, or of any other supports: since, unless the foundation be laid, it remains in perpetual suspense " (I. viii. 1). The *indicia* " are *alone* not sufficient to produce firm faith in it [the Scriptures], *till* the heavenly Father, discovering His own power therein, places its authority above all controversy " (I. viii. 13). It is, however, in his general teaching as to the formation of sound faith in the divinity of Scripture that we find the surest indication that he thought of the *indicia* as co-working with the testimony of the Spirit to this result. This is already given, indeed, in his strenuous insistence that the work of the Spirit is not of the nature of a revelation, but of a confirmation of the revelation deposited in the Scriptures, especially when this is taken in connection with his teaching that Scripture is self-authenticating. What the Spirit of God imparts to us, he says, is a *sense* of divinity: such a sense discovers divinity only where

---

do not find that the Lutheran dogmaticians, when they come to occupy themselves more particularly with the *testimonium Spiritus Sancti* to the Scriptures, dealt more vitally with its relation to the operation of these criteria on the human spirit. No doubt, in Luther's own conception this was more the case: but he gave no scientific elaboration of it."

divinity is and only by a perception of it — a perception which of course rests on its proper *indicia*. It is because Scripture " exhibits the plainest evidence that it is God who speaks in it " that the newly awakened *sense* of divinity, quickened in the soul, recognizes it as divine (I. vii. 4). The senses do not distinguish light from darkness, white from black, sweet from bitter — to use Calvin's own illustration (I. vii. 2) — save by the mediation of those *indicia* of light and darkness, whiteness and blackness, sweetness and bitterness, by which these qualities manifest themselves to the natural senses; and by parity of reasoning we must accredit Calvin as thinking of the newly implanted spiritual sense discerning the divinity of Scripture only through the mediation of the *indicia* of divinity manifested in Scripture. To taste and see that the Scriptures are divine is to recognize a divinity actually present in Scripture; and of course recognition implies perception of *indicia*, not attribution of a divinity not recognized as inherent. Meanwhile it must be admitted that Calvin has not at this point developed this side of his subject with the fulness which might be wished, but has left it to the general implications of the argument.

OBJECT TESTIFIED TO

Closely connected with the question of the mode in which Calvin conceived the testimony of the Spirit to be delivered, is the further question of the matters for which he conceived that testimony to be available. On the face of it it would seem that he conceived it directly available solely for the divinity of the Scriptures and therefore for the revelatory character of their contents. So he seems to imply throughout the discussion, and, indeed, to assert repeatedly. Nevertheless, there is a widespread impression abroad that he appealed to it to determine the canon of Scripture too,[62] and indeed also to estab-

[62] Cf. Köstlin, as cited, p. 417: " The certainty that the Scriptures really possess such authority, rests for us not on the authority of the Church, but just on this testimony of the Spirit. Calvin's reference here is even to the several books of Scripture: he is aware that the opponents ask how, without a decree of the Church, we are to be convinced what book should be re-

lish the integrity of its text. This impression is generally, though not always, connected with the view that Calvin conceived the mode of delivery of the testimony of the Spirit to be the creation in the soul of a blind faith, unmotived by reasons and without rooting in grounds; and it has been much exploited of late years in the interests of a so-called " free " attitude towards Scripture, which announces itself as following Calvin

---

ceived with reverence, what should be excluded from the canon; he himself adduces in opposition to this, even here, nothing else except the *testimonium Spiritus:* the entirety of Scripture seems to him to be equally, so to say, *en bloc,* divinely legitimated by this." So also Pannier, as cited, p. 202: " The question of canonicity never presented itself to the thought of Calvin, except in the second place as a corollary of the problem of the divinity (I. vii. 1). If the Holy Spirit attests to us that a given book is divine, He in that very act attests that it forms a part of the rule of faith, that it is canonical. Nowhere has Calvin permitted, as his successors have done, a primary place to be taken by a theological doctrine which became less capable of resisting the assaults of adversaries when isolated from the practical question. Perhaps, moreover, he did not render as exact an account as we are able to render after the lapse of two centuries, of the wholly new situation in which the Reformation found itself with respect to the canon, or of the new way in which he personally resolved the question." Accordingly, at an earlier point Pannier says: " It is true that the faculty of recognizing the Word of God under the human forms included for Calvin, and especially according to the Confession of Faith of 1559, the faculty of determining the canonicity of the books. This is a consequence secondary but natural, and so long as they maintained the principle, the Reformed doctors placed themselves in a false position when they showed themselves disposed to abandon the consequences to the criticisms of their opponents " (p. 164). Cf. J. Cramer, *Nieuwe Bijdragen,* iii. p. 140: " But you must not think . . . of an *immediate* witness of the Spirit to the particular parts of the Holy Scriptures. The old theologians did not think of that. They conceived the matter thus: The *testimonium Spiritus Sancti* gives witness *directly* to the religio-moral contents of Scripture only. Since, however, the religio-moral contents must necessarily have a particular form, and the dogmatic content is closely bound up with the historical, neither the chronological nor the topographical element can be separated out, etc.— therefore the *testimonium Spiritus Sancti* gives to the total content of Scripture witness that it is from God." This, after all, then, is not to appeal to the *testimonium Spiritus Sancti,* directly to authenticate the canon; but to construct a canon on the basis of a testimony of the Spirit given solely to the divinity of Scripture, the movement of thought being this: All Scripture given by inspiration of God is profitable; this Scripture is given by inspiration of God; accordingly this Scripture belongs to the category of profitable Scripture, that is to the canon.

when it refuses to acknowledge as authoritative Scripture any portion of or element in the traditionally transmitted Scriptures which does not spontaneously commend itself to the immediate religious judgment as divine. Undoubtedly this is to reverse the attitude of Calvin towards the traditionally transmitted Scriptures, and it is difficult to believe that two such diametrically contradictory attitudes towards the Scriptures can be outgrowths of the same principal root. In point of fact, moreover, as we have already seen, not only does Calvin not conceive the mode of the delivery of the testimony of the Spirit to be by the creation of a blind and unmotived faith, but, to come at once to the matter more particularly in hand, he does not depend on the testimony of the Spirit for the determination of canonicity or for the establishment of the integrity of the text of Scripture. So far from discarding the *via rationalis* here, he determines the limits of the canon and establishes the integrity of the transmission of Scripture distinctly on scientific, that is to say, historico-critical grounds. In no case of his frequent discussion of such subjects does he appeal to the testimony of the Spirit and set aside the employment of rational and historical argumentation as invalid or inconclusive; always, on the contrary, he adduces the evidence of valid tradition and apostolicity of contents as conclusive of the fact. It is hard to believe that such a consequent mind could have lived unconsciously in such an inconsistent attitude towards a question so vital to him and his cause.[63]

[63] Reuss, in the sixteenth chapter of his " History of the Canon of the Holy Scriptures," E. T. 1884, expounds Calvin, with his usual learning and persuasiveness, as basing the determination of the canon solely on the testimony of the Spirit. But the exposition falls into two confusions: a confusion of the authority of Scripture with its canonicity, and a confusion of the divine with the apostolic origin of Scripture. Of course, Calvin repelled the Romish conception that the authority of Scripture rests on its authentication by the Church and its tradition (p. 294), but that did not deter him from seeking by a historical investigation to discover what especial books had been committed by the apostles to the Church as authoritative. Of course, he founded the sure conviction of the divine origin of the Scriptures on the witness of the Spirit of God by and with them in the heart, but that did not prevent his appealing to history to determine what these Scriptures which were so witnessed were in their compass. Accordingly even Reuss has to admit that it

So far as support for the impression that Calvin looked to the testimony of the Spirit to determine for him the canon of Scripture and to assure him of its integrity is derived from his writings, it rests on a manifest misapprehension of a single passage in the " Institutes," and what seems to be a misassignment to him of a passage in the old French Confession of Faith.

The passage in the " Institutes " is a portion of the paragraphs which are devoted to repelling the Romish contention that " the Scriptures have only so much weight as is conceded to them by the suffrages of the Church; as though the eternal and inviolable truth of God depended on the arbitrary will of men " (I. vii. 1). " For thus," Calvin says — and this is the passage which is appealed to — " For thus, dealing with the Holy Spirit as a mere laughing stock (*ludibrio*), they ask, Who shall give us confidence that these [Scriptures] have come from God, — who assure us that they have reached our time safe and intact, — who persuade us that one book should be received reverently, another expunged from the number (*numero*) — if the Church should not prescribe a certain rule for all these things? It depends, therefore, they say, on the Church, both what reverence is due to Scripture, and what books should be inscribed (*censendi sint*) in its catalogue (*in eius catalogo*) " (I. vii. 1). This passage certainly shows that the Romish controversialists in endeavoring to prove that the authority of Scripture is dependent on the Church's suffrage, argued that it is only by the Church that we can be assured even of the contents of Scripture and of its integrity — that its very

---

is exceedingly difficult to carry through his theory of Calvin's theoretical procedure consistently with Calvin's observed practice. In point of fact, the Reformers, and Calvin among them, did not separate the Apocrypha from the Old Testament on the sole basis of the testimony of the Spirit: they appealed to the evidence of the Jewish Church (p. 312). Nor did they determine the question of the New Testament antilegomena on this principle: this, too, was with them " a simple question of historical criticism " (p. 316) — although Reuss here (p. 318) confuses Calvin's appeal to the internal evidence of apostolicity with appeal to " religious intuition." In a word, Reuss's exposition of Calvin's procedure in determining the canon rests on a fundamental misconception of that procedure.

canon and text rest on the Church's determination. But how
can it be inferred that Calvin's response to this argument
would take the form: No, of these things we can be assured by
the immediate testimony of the Spirit? In point of fact, he
says nothing of the kind, and the inference does not lie in the
argument. What he says is that the Romish method of arguing is as absurd as it is blasphemous, a mere cavil (I. vii. 2),
as well as derogatory to the Holy Spirit. The Holy Spirit, he
says, assures us that in the Scriptures God speaks to us. To
bid us pause on the ground that it is only the Church who
can assure us that this or that book belongs to the body of the
Scriptures, that the text has been preserved to us intact and
the like, is to interpose frivolous objections, and can have
no other end than to glorify the Church at the expense of
souls. Accordingly, he remarks that these objectors are without concern what logical difficulties they may cast themselves
into: they wish only to prevent men taking their comfort out
of the direct assurance by the Spirit of the divinity of the
Scriptures. He repudiates, in a word, the entire Romish argument: but we can scarcely infer from this, that his response
to it would be that the immediate witness of the Spirit provides us with direct answers to their carping questions. It
is at least equally likely from the mere fact that he speaks
of these objections as cavils (I. vii. 2) and girds at the logic
of the Romish controversialists as absurd, that his response
would be that the testimony of the Spirit for which he was
contending had no direct concernment with questions of canon
and text.

The passage in the Confession of La Rochelle, on the other
hand, does certainly attribute the discrimination of the canonical books in some sense — in what sense may admit of debate
— to the testimony of the Spirit. In the third article of this
Confession there is given a list of the canonical books.[64] The
fourth article, then, runs as follows: "We recognize these

---

[64] "All this Holy Scripture is comprised in the canonical books of the
Old and New Testaments, the number (*le nombre*) of which is as follows"
. . . the list ensuing. See *Opp.* ix. 741.

books to be canonical and the very certain rule of our faith, not so much by the common accord and consent of the Church, as by the inward witness and persuasion of the Holy Spirit, who makes us distinguish them from the other ecclesiastical books, upon which, though they may be useful, no article of faith can be founded." This article, however, was not the composition of Calvin, but was among those added by the Synod of Paris to the draft submitted by Calvin.[65] Calvin's own article " On the Books of Holy Scripture," which was expanded by the Synod into several, reads only: " This doctrine does not derive its authority from men, nor from angels, but from God alone; we believe, too (seeing that it is a thing surpassing all human sense to discern that it is God who speaks), that He Himself gives the certitude of it to His elect, and seals it in their hearts by His Spirit." [66] In this fine statement we find the very essence of the teaching of the " Institutes " on this subject; the ideas and even the phraseology of which are reproduced.

We may learn, therefore, at most, from the Confession of La Rochelle, not that Calvin, but that some of his immediate followers attributed in some sense the discrimination of the canonical books to the witness of the Spirit. Other evidences of this fact are not lacking. The Belgian Confession, for example, much like that of La Rochelle, declares of the Scriptural books, just enumerated (Art. v.): " We receive all these books alone, as holy and canonical, for the regulation, foundation and establishment of our faith, and we fully believe all that they contain, not so much because the Church receives and approves them, but principally because the Spirit gives witness to them in our hearts that they are from God, and also because they are approved by themselves; for the very blind can perceive that the things come to pass which they predict." Perhaps, however, we may find a more instructive instance still in the words of one of the Protestant disputants in a con-

[65] *Opp.* ix., *prolg.*, pp. lvii.–lx.: cf. Dieterlen, " Le Synode général de Paris," 1873, pp. 77, 89; Pannier, as cited, pp. 126–7; and for a brief précis, Müller, " Bekenntnisschriften der reform. Kirche," 1903, p. xxxiii.

[66] *Opp.* ix. 741.

ference held at Paris in 1566 between two Protestant ministers
and two doctors of the Sorbonne.[67] To the inquiry, How do you
know that some books are canonical and others Apocryphal,
the Protestant disputant (M. Lespine) answers: " By the
Spirit of God which is a Spirit of discrimination, by whom all
those to whom He is communicated are illuminated, so as to
be made capable of judging and discerning spiritual things
and of recognizing (*cognoistre*) and apprehending the truth
(when it is proposed to them), by the witness and assurance
which He gives to them in their hearts. And as we discriminate light and darkness by the faculty of sight which is in the
eye; so, we can easily separate and recognize (*recognoistre*)
truth from falsehood, and from all things in general which
can be false, absurd, doubtful or indifferent, when we are invested with the Spirit of God and guided by the light which
He lights in our hearts." M. Lespine had evidently read his
Calvin; though there is a certain lack of crisp exactness in
his language which may raise doubt whether he has necessarily
reproduced him with precision. Clearly his idea is that the
Spirit of God in His creative operation on the hearts of
Christ's people has implanted in them — or quickened in them
— a spiritual sense, which recognizes the stamp of divinity
upon the books which God has given to the Church, and so
separates them out from all others and thus constitutes the
canon. This is to attribute the discrimination of the canonical
books to the witness of the Spirit not directly but indirectly,
namely, through the intermediation of the determination of the
books which are of divine origin, which, then, being gathered
together, constitute the canon, or divinely given rule of our
faith and life. This conception of the movement of the mind
in this matter became very common, and was given very
clear expression, for example, by Jurieu, in a context which
bears as evident marks of reminiscences of Calvin as do M. Lespine's remarks. " That grace which produces faith in a soul,"

---

[67] " Actes de la dispute et conference tenue à Paris ès mois de juillet et
aoust 1566 " (Strasbourg, 1566), printed in the *Biblioth. de la Soc. de l'Hist. du
Prot. franc.* We draw from the account of it in Pannier, as cited, pp. 141 *sq.*

says he,[68] " does not begin . . . by persuading it that a given
book is canonical. This persuasion comes only afterwards and
as a consequence. It gives to the consciousness a taste for the
truth: it applies this truth to the mind and heart; it proceeds
from this subsequently that the believer believes that a given
book is canonical, because the truths which ' find ' him are
found in it. In a word, we do not believe that which is contained in a book to be divine because this book is canonical.
But we believe that a given book is canonical because we have
perceived that what it contains is divine. And we have perceived this as we perceive the light when we look on the fire,
sweetness and bitterness when we eat." Whether we are to
attribute this movement of thought, however, to Calvin, is another question.[69] There is no hint of it in his writings.

It is not even obvious that this precise movement of
thought is the conception which lay in the mind of the authors
of the additional articles in the Confession of La Rochelle and
of the similar statement in the Belgian Confession. The interpretation of these articles is particularly interesting, as they
both undoubtedly came under the eye of Calvin and their
doctrine was never disavowed by him. It is not, however, altogether easy, because of a certain ambiguity in the use of the
term " canonical." It is on account of the ambiguity which attends the use of this term that in speaking of their teaching we
have guardedly said that they appear to suspend the canonicity
of the Scriptural books in some sense directly on the testimony

[68] " Le vray systeme de l'Eglise et la véritable analyse de la foy," 1686,
III. ii. 453. Pannier, as cited, quotes this, pp. 167–168.

[69] As we have seen, it is attributed to Calvin by both Pannier and Cramer.
Pannier (p. 203) remarks that " if Calvin was not able to appreciate in all its
purity " the new situation with regard to the canon into which the Reformation brought men, " it was even less incumbent on him to render account of
the personal attitude which he himself took up with reference to it." " It is
his successors only who, in adopting his conclusions (except that they apply
them more or less), have asked themselves how they reached them, and have
reconstructed the reasoning which no doubt Calvin himself had unconsciously
followed." Is not this a confession that after all the view in question was not
Calvin's own view? At least not consciously to himself? But Pannier would
say, no doubt, either this was Calvin's view or he appealed to the testimony of
the Spirit directly to authenticate the canon.

of the Spirit. This ambiguity may be brought sharply before us by placing in juxtaposition two sentences from Quenstedt in which the term " canonical " is employed, obviously, in two differing senses. " We deny," says he, " that the catalogue of canonical books is an article of faith, superadded to the others [articles of faith] contained in Scripture. Many have faith and may attain salvation who do not hold the number of canonical books. If the word 'canon' be understood of the *number* of the books, we concede that such a catalogue is not contained in Scripture." " These are two different questions," says he again, " whether the Gospel of Matthew is canonical, and whether it was written by Matthew. The former belongs to saving faith; the latter to historical knowledge. For if the Gospel which has come down to us under the name of Matthew had been written by Philip or Bartholomew, it would make no difference to saving faith." In the former extract the question of canonicity is removed from the category of articles of faith; in the latter it is made an integral element of saving faith. The contradiction is glaring — unless there be an undistributed middle. And this is what there really is. In the former passage, where Quenstedt is engaged in repelling the contention that there are articles of faith that must be accepted by all, which are not contained in Scripture — in defending, in a word, the Protestant doctrine of the sufficiency or perfection of Scripture — he uses the terms " canon," " canonical " in the purely technical sense of the extent of Scripture. In the latter passage, where he is insisting that the authority of Scripture as the Word of God hangs on its divine, not on its human, author, he uses the term " canonical " in the sense of " divinely given." The term " canonical " was current, then, in the two senses of "belonging to the list of authoritative Scriptures," " entering into the body of the Scriptures," and " God-given," " divine." In which of these two senses is it used in the Gallican and Belgian Confessions? If in the former, then these Confessions teach that the testimony of the Spirit is available directly for the determination of the canon: if in the latter, then they teach no such thing, but only that it is on the testimony of the Spirit that we are assured of the divine origin and character of these books.

That the Gallican Confession employs the term in the latter of these senses, seems at least possible when once attention is called to it, although regard for the last clause of the statement, " who makes us distinguish them from the other ecclesiastical books," etc., prevents the representation of this interpretation as certain. Its declaration, succeeding the catalogue of the books given in the third section, is obviously intended to affirm something that is true of them already as a definite body of books before the mind. " We recognize *these* books," it says, " to be canonical and the very certain rule of our faith." That is to say, to this body of books we ascribe the quality of canonicity and recognize their regulative character. What would seem, then, to be in question is a quality belonging to a list of books already determined and in the mind of the framer of the statement as a whole. The same may be said of the Belgian Confession. It, too, has already given a list of the canonical books, and now proceeds to affirm something that is true of " all of these books and them only." The thing affirmed is that they are " holy and canonical," where the collocation suggests that " canonical " expresses a quality which ranges with " holy." We cannot help suspecting, then, that these early confessions use the term " canonical " not quantitatively but qualitatively, not extensively but intensively; and in that sense it is the equivalent of " divine." [70]

[70] The following is the account of the treatment of the question of the canon in these creeds, given by J. Cramer (" De Roomsch-Katholieke en de Oud-protestantsche Schriftbeschouwing," 1883, pp. 48 *sq.*) : " And on what now, does that authority rest? This question, too, is amply discussed in the Reformed Confessions, and that, as concerns the principal matter, wholly in the spirit of Calvin. Only, more value is ascribed to the testimony of the Church. No doubt the authority of the Scriptures is not made to rest on it; but it is permitted an important voice in the question of the canon. When it is said that ' all that is said in the Holy Scriptures is to be believed *not so much* because the Church receives them and holds them as canonical, but especially because the Holy Spirit bears witness to them in our heart that they are from God,' a certain weight is attributed to the judgment of the Church. This appears particularly from the way in which the canonical books are spoken of

Even the inference back from them to Calvin that he may have supposed that the testimony of the Spirit is available to determine the canon becomes therefore doubtful: and no other reason exists why we should attribute this view to him. We cannot affirm that the movement of his thought was never from the divinity of Scripture, assured to us by the testimony of the Spirit, to the determination of the limits of the canon: but we have no reason to ascribe this movement of thought to him except that it was adopted by some of his successors.

On the other hand, Calvin constantly speaks as if the only thing which the testimony of the Spirit assures us of in the case of the Scriptures is the divinity of their origin and contents: and he always treats Scripture when so speaking of it as a definite entity, held before his mind as a whole.[71] In these

in distinction from the Apocryphal books. In enumerating the Bible books, the Belgian Confession prefixes the words: ' Against which nothing can be said ' (Art. iv.). By this apparently is meant, that against the canonicity of these books, from a historical standpoint, with the eye on the witness of the Church, nothing can be alleged (a thing not to be said of the Apocrypha). In the same spirit the Anglican Articles, when speaking of the books of the Old and New Testaments, says that ' Of their authority there has never been any doubt in the Church.' I will not raise the question here how that can be affirmed with the eye on the Antilegomena. It shows, however, certainly that much importance is attached to the ecclesiastical tradition. The fundamental ground, however, why the Scriptures of the Old and New Testaments are to be held to be the Word of God is sought in the Scriptures themselves, and, assuredly, in the testimony which the Holy Spirit bears to their divinity in the hearts of believers. Like Calvin, the Confessions suppose that thus they have given an immovable foundation to the divine authority of the Scriptures, and have taken an impregnable position over against Rome, which appealed to the witness of the Catholic Church. . . ." Calvin, however, allowed as much to the testimony of the Church — external evidence — as is here allowed, and the very adduction of its testimony shows that sole dependence was not placed on the testimony of the Spirit for the canonicity of a book: what it is appealed to for is the divinity of the canonical books.

[71] So even Köstlin perceives, as cited, p. 417: " The entirety of Scripture appeared to him divinely legitimated by the *testimonium Spiritus,* altogether, so to say, *en bloc.* . . . The declarations of Calvin as to the Word spoken by the prophets and apostles, which they rightly asserted to be God's Word, pass without hesitation over into declarations as to the Holy Scriptures, as such, and that in their entirety; with the proposition ' the Law and the Prophets and the Gospel have emanated from God ' is interchanged the proposition ' the Scripture is from God,' — and the witness of the Spirit assures us of it." So also Pan-

circumstances his own practice in dealing with the question of canonicity and text, makes it sufficiently clear that he held their settlement to depend on scientific investigation, and appealed to the testimony of the Spirit only to accredit the divine origin of the concrete volume thus put into his hands. The movement of his thought was therefore along this course:

---

nier (pp. 203–204): " Everything goes back to his considering things not in detail but *en bloc*. The Word of God is for him one, *verbum Dei*, not *verba Dei*. The diversity of the authors disappears before the unity of the Spirit. The same reasoning applies to each single book as to the whole collection. All the verses hold together; and if one introduces us to the knowledge of salvation we may conclude that the book is canonical. Given the collection, it is enough in practice, since all the parts are of a sort, to establish the value of one of them to guarantee the value of all the others. It is certain that the critical theologian and the simple believer even yet proceed somewhat differently in this matter; the simplest and surest method is that of the humble saint, and Calvin was very right not to range himself among the theologians at this point. ' The just shall live by faith.' This affirmation seemed to him a revealed truth: he concluded from it that the whole epistle to the Romans is inspired; some remarks of this kind in other passages of the Epistles, of the Gospels, and the canonicity of the New Testament is established. The same for the Old Testament. The Second Epistle of Peter and the Song of Songs thus go with the rest. The human testimonies, internal and external criteria, useful for confirming the other parts of a book of which a passage has been recognized as inspired, are insufficient to expel from the canon a book which the witness of the Spirit has not recognized as opposed to the doctrine of salvation." We quote the whole passage to give Pannier's whole thought: but what we adduce it for is at present merely to signalize the admission it contains that Calvin dealt with the Scriptures in the matter of the testimony of the Spirit, so to speak, " in the lump " — as a whole. Pannier cites apparently as similar to Calvin's view, Gaussen, " Canon," ii. p. 10: " This testimony, which every Christian has recognized when he has read his Bible with vital efficacy, may be recognized by him only in a single page; but this page is enough to spread over the book which contains it an incomparable brightness." That is, Calvin, like the simple believer, has a definite book — the Bible — in his hands and treats it as all of a piece — of course, in Calvin's case, not without reasonable grounds for treating it as all of a piece: in other words, the canon was already determined for him before he appealed to the testimony of the Spirit to attest its divinity. Cf. Cramer (p. 140) as quoted above. Cramer is quite right *so far*, therefore, when he says (pp. 156–157) : " Although we determine securely by means of the historical-critical method what must be carried back to the apostolical age and what accords with the apostolical doctrine, we have not yet proved the divine authority of these writings. This hangs on this, — whether the Holy Spirit gives us His witness to them. On this witness alone rests our assurance of faith, not on the force of a historical-critical demonstration." This, so far as appears, was Calvin's method.

first, the ascertainment, on scientific grounds, of the body of
books handed down from the Apostles as the rule of faith and
practice; secondly, the vindication, on the same class of
grounds, of the integrity of their transmission; thirdly, the
accrediting of them as divine on the testimony of the Spirit.
It is not involved in this that he is to be considered to have
supposed that a man must be a scholar before he can be a
Christian. He supposed we become Christians not by scholarship but by the testimony of the Spirit in the heart, and he had
no inclination to demand scholarship as the basis of our Christianity. It is only involved in the position we ascribe to him
that he must be credited with recognizing that questions of
scholarship are for scholars and questions of religion only for
Christians as such. He would have said — he does say — that
he in whose heart the Spirit bears His testimony will recognize
the Scriptures whenever presented to his contemplation as
divine, will depend on them with sound trust and will embrace
with true faith all that they propound to him. He would doubtless have said that this act of faith logically implicates the determination of the " canon." But he would also have said — he
does in effect say — that this determination of the canon is a
separable act and is to be prosecuted on its own appropriate
grounds of scientific evidence. It involves indeed a fundamental misapprehension of Calvin's whole attitude to attribute to him the view that the testimony of the Spirit determines immediately such scientific questions as those of the
canon and text of Scripture. The testimony of the Spirit was
to him emphatically an operation of the Spirit of God on the
heart, which produced distinctively a spiritual effect: it was
directed to making men Christians,[72] not to making them theologians. The testimony of the Spirit was, in effect, in his view,
just what we in modern times have learned to call " regenera-

[72] Calvin would certainly have subscribed to these words of Pannier, as
cited, p. 164: The most of the Catholics " have always strangely misapprehended
the illumination which, according to the Reformed, the least of believers is
capable of receiving and of applying to the reading of the Bible. It is a question, not as they suppose, of becoming theologians, but of becoming believers, of having not the plenitude of knowledge, but the certitude of faith."

tion " considered in its noëtic effects. That "regeneration" has noëtic effects he is explicit and iterative in affirming: but that these noëtic effects of "regeneration" could supersede the necessity of scientific investigation in questions which rest for their determination on matters of fact — Calvin would be the last to imagine. He who recognized that the conviction of the divinity of Scripture wrought by the testimony of the Spirit rests as its ground on the *indicia* of the divinity of Scripture spiritually discerned in their true weight, could not imagine that the determination of the canon of Scripture or the establishment of its text could be wholly separated from their proper basis in evidence and grounded solely in a blind testimony of the Spirit alone: which indeed in that case would be fundamentally indistinguishable from that "revelation" which he rebuked the Anabaptists for claiming to be the recipients of.

THE TESTIMONY AND THE RELIGIOUS LIFE

When we clearly apprehend the essence of Calvin's doctrine of the testimony of the Spirit to the divinity of Scripture to be the noëtic effects of "regeneration" we shall know what estimate to place upon the criticism which is sometimes passed upon him that he has insufficiently correlated his doctrine of the testimony of the Spirit with the inner [73] religious

[73] Cf. Köstlin, as cited, pp. 415–416. After raising the question of the relation of the witness of the Spirit to the inner experience of the Christian, and the relative priority of the two — and remarking that in case the vital process is conceived as preceding the witness of the Spirit to the divinity of the Scriptures, it will be hard not to allow to the Christianized heart the right and duty of criticism of the Scriptures (where the fault in reasoning lies in the term *process*), Köstlin continues: "We touch here on the relation between the formal and material sides of the fundamental evangelical principle. And we think at once of the relation in which they stood to one another in Luther's representation, by which his well-known critical attitude, with respect, say, to the Epistle of James, was rendered possible. Calvin, too, now has no wish to speak of a witness of the Spirit merely with reference to the Scriptures, and is far from desiring to isolate that witness of the Spirit for the Scriptures. He comes back to it subsequently, when speaking of faith in the saving content of the Gospel, declaring that the Spirit seals the contents

life of the Christian, has given too separate a place to the Spirit's witness to Scripture, and thus has overestimated the formal principle of Protestantism in comparison with the material principle,[74] with the effect of giving a hard, dry, and

---

of the Word in our hearts (1539, XXIX. 456 *sq.*, 468 *sq.;* further in 1559, III. 2 [In Köstlin's pagination, given here, XXIX. refers to the " Corpus Ref." as a whole; III. 2 stands for " Institutes," Book III. chap. ii., or XXX. 397 *sq.*]). He also inserted in the section on the Holy Scriptures and the witness of the Spirit to them, in 1550, an additional special sentence, in which he expressly refers to his intention to speak further on such a witness of the Spirit in a later portion of the treatise, and declares of faith in general, that there belongs to it a sealing of the divine Spirit (XXIX. 296 [1559, I. vii. 5, near end]). In any event he must have recurred to such a Spiritual testimony for the assurance of individual Christians of their personal election. But in the first instance — and this again is precisely what is characteristic for Calvin — he nevertheless treats of the doctrine of the divine origin and the divine authority of the Scriptures, and of the witness of the Spirit for them, wholly apart. The presentation proceeds with him in such a manner, that the Spirit first of all fully produces faith in this character of the Scriptures, and only then the Bible-believing Christian has to receive from the Scriptures its contents, in all its several parts, as divinely true, — though, no doubt, this reception and this faith in the several elements of the truth are by no means matters of human thought, but are rather to be performed under the progressive illumination and the progressive sealing of these contents in the heart by the Holy Spirit. Even though he, meanwhile, calls that the ' truth ' of the Scriptures, which we come to feel in the power of the Spirit, he means by this in the section before us, an absolute truth-character, which must from the start be attributed to the Scriptures as a whole, and will be experienced in and with the divinity of the Scriptures in general. So the matter already stands in the edition of 1539 . . . (XXIX. 292 *sq.*)." Accordingly Calvin teaches that the Scriptures in all their parts are of indefectible authority, and should be met in all their prescriptions with unlimited obedience (p. 418), because it is just God who speaks in them. Then: " With Dorner (*Geschichte der protest. Theologie,* p. 380) — and even more decisively than he does it — we must remark on all this: ' The formal side of the protestant principle remains with Calvin an over-emphasis, in comparison with the material, and with this is connected that he sees in the Holy Scriptures above all else the revelation of the will of God which he has dictated to man through the sacred writers.' And this tendency came ever more strongly forward with him in the successive revisions of the *Institutes.* His conception of the formal principle thus left no room for such a criticism as Luther employed on the several parts of the canon." Later Lutheranism, however, Köstlin concludes by saying, adopted Calvin's point of view here and even exaggerated it.

[74] " The formal side of the Protestant principle retains with Calvin the ascendency over the material; and with this is connected the fact that he sees in the Holy Scriptures chiefly the revelation of the will of God, which

legalistic aspect to Christianity as expounded by him. With
Luther, it is said, everything is made of Justification and the
liberty of the Christian man fills the horizon of thought; and
this is because his mind is set on the "faith" out of which
all good things flow and by which everything — Scripture
itself — is dominated. With Calvin, on the other hand,
with his primary emphasis on the authority of Scripture,
accredited to us by a distinct act of the Holy Spirit, the
watchword becomes obedience; and the horizon of thought is
filled with a sense of obligation and legalistic anxiety as to
conduct.

How Calvin could have failed to correlate sufficiently
closely the testimony of the Spirit with the inner Christian
life, or could have emphasized the formal principle of Protestantism at the expense of the material, when he conceived
of the witness of the Spirit as just one of the effects of "regeneration," it is difficult to see. So to conceive the testimony of
the Spirit is on the contrary to make the formal principle of
Protestantism just an outgrowth of the material. It is only
because our spirits have been renewed by the Holy Spirit that
we see with convincing clearness the *indicia* of God in Scripture, that is, have the Scriptures sealed to us by the Spirit as
divine. It is quite possible that Calvin may have particularly
emphasized the obligations which grow out of our renewal by
the Holy Spirit and the implantation in us of the Spirit of
Adoption whereby we become the sons of God — obligations
to comport ourselves as the sons of God and to govern our-

he has prescribed to men through the sacred writers." — Dorner, "Hist. of
Protest. Theology," i. 1871, p. 390. Cf. p. 387: "The formal principle is, according to him, the norm and source of dogma, whilst he does not treat faith,
in the same way as Luther, as a source of knowledge for the dogmatical structure, that is to say, as the mediative principle of knowledge." Hence Dorner
complains (p. 390) of the more restricted freedom which Calvin left "for the
free productions of the faith of the Church in legislation and dogma," and
instances his treatment of "the Apostolic Age as normative for all times, even
for questions of Church constitution," and the little room he left for destructive Biblical criticism. Cf. what is said above of Calvin's adoption of "the
Puritan principle" (pp. 38 *sq.*).

selves by the law of God's house as given us in His Word; while
Luther may have emphasized more the liberty of the Christian
man who is emancipated from the law as a condition of salvation and is ushered into the freedom of life which belongs to
the children of God. And it is quite possible that in this difference we may find a fundamental distinction between the two
types of Protestantism — Lutheran and Reformed — by virtue
of which the Reformed have always been characterized by a
strong ethical tendency — in thought and in practice. But it
is misleading to represent this as due to an insufficient correlation on Calvin's part of the testimony of the Spirit to the
divinity of Scripture with the inner Christian life. It would be
more exact to say that Calvin in this correlation thinks especially of what in our modern nomenclature we call "regeneration," while the mind of his Lutheran critics is set more upon
justification and that "faith" which is connected with justification. With Calvin, at all events, the recognition of the Scriptures as divine and the hearty adoption of them as the divine
rule of our faith and life is just one of the effects of the gracious
operation of the Spirit of God on the heart, renewing it into
spiritual life, or, what comes to the same thing, one of the
gracious activities into which the newly implanted spiritual
life effloresces.

Whether we should say also that it was with him the first
effect of the creative operation of the Spirit on the heart, the
first act of the newly renewed soul, requires some discrimination. If we mean logically first, there is a sense in which we
should probably answer this question also in the affirmative.
Calvin would doubtless have said that it is in the Scriptures
that Christ is proposed to our faith, or, to put it more broadly,
that Christ is the very substance of the special revelation documented in the Scriptures, and that the laying hold of Christ by
faith presupposes therefore confidence in the revelation the
substance of which He is — which is as much as to say the embracing of the Scriptures in firm faith as a revelation from God.
If the Word is the vehicle through which the knowledge of
Christ is brought to the soul, it follows of itself that it is only

when our minds are filled with a solid reverence for the Word, when by the light of the Spirit we are enabled and prevalently led to see Christ therein, that we can embrace Christ with a sound faith: so that it may truly be said that no man can have the least true and sound knowledge of Christ without learning from Scripture (cf. I. ix. 3; I. vi. 2). In this sense Calvin would certainly have said that our faith in Christ presupposes faith in the Scriptures, rather than that we believe in the Scriptures for Christ's sake. But if our minds are set on chronological sequences, the response to the question which is raised is more doubtful. Faith in the revelation the substance of which is Christ and faith in Christ the substance of this revelation are logical implicates which involve one another: and we should probably be nearest to Calvin's thought if, without raising questions of chronological succession, we should recognize them as arising together in the soul. The real difference between Calvin's and the ordinary Lutheran conception at this point lies in the greater profundity of Calvin's insight and the greater exactness of his analysis. The Lutheran is prone to begin with faith, which is naturally conceived at its apex, as faith in Jesus Christ our Redeemer; and to make everything else flow from this faith as its ultimate root. For what comes before faith, out of which faith itself flows, he has little impulse accurately to inquire. Calvin penetrates behind faith to the creative action of the Holy Spirit on the heart and the new creature which results therefrom, whose act faith is; and is therefore compelled by an impulse derived from the matter itself to consider the relations in which the several activities of this new creature stand to one another and to analyse the faith itself which holds the primacy among them (for trust is the essence of religion, chap. ii.), into its several movements. The effect of this is that " efficacious grace " — what we call in modern speech " regeneration " — takes the place of fundamental principle in Calvin's soteriology and he becomes preëminently the theologian of the Holy Spirit. In point of fact it is from him accordingly that the effective study of the work of the Holy Spirit takes its rise, and it is only in the channels cut by him and at the hands

of thinkers taught by him that the theology of the Holy Spirit
has been richly developed.[75]

[75] Cf. the Introduction to the English Translation of Kuyper's "The
Work of the Holy Spirit," 1900, especially pp. xxxiii.–iv. Cf. what Pannier,
pp. 102–104, says of Calvin's general doctrine of the work of the Spirit and the
relation borne to it by his particular doctrine of the testimony of the Spirit
to Scripture. "If we pass beyond the two particular chapters whose contents
we have been analysing and seek in the *Institutes* from 1536 to 1560 for
other passages relating to the Holy Spirit, we shall see Calvin insisting ever
more and more and on all occasions — as in the Commentaries — upon these
diverse manifestations of the Holy Spirit, and presenting them all more or
less as *testimonies*. He constantly recurs to the natural incapacity of man
and the necessity of divine illumination in his mind, and especially in his
heart, for the act of faith. It is from this point of view that he brings together
the ideas of the Spirit and the Word of God in the definition of faith: ' It is a
firm and certain knowledge of the good will of God towards us: which, being
grounded in the free promise given in Jesus Christ, is revealed to our heart
by the Holy Spirit.' He introduces the same ideas in his introductory remarks
on the Apostles' Creed, and they lie at the basis of the explication he gives
of the Third Article in all its forms, . . . e.g., in the ed. of 1560: ' In sum, He
is set before us as the sole fountain from which all the celestial riches flow
down to us. . . . For it is by His inspiration that we are regenerated into celestial life, so as no longer to govern or guide ourselves, but to be ruled by His
movement and operation; so that if there is any good in us, it is only the
fruit of His grace. . . . But since *faith is His prime master-piece*, the most of
what we read in the Scriptures of His virtue and operation relates itself to
this faith, by which He brings us to the brightness of the Gospel, in a manner which justifies calling Him the King by whom the treasures of the kingdom
of heaven are offered to us, and His illumination may be called the longing
of our souls.' From these quotations it is made plain that the witness of the
Holy Spirit which at the opening of the *Institutes* in 1539 appeared as the
means of knowledge, was thenceforward nevertheless considered, in the progress of the work, as the *means of grace*, and that taking his start from this
point of view, Calvin discovered ever more widely extending horizons, so as
at the end to speak particularly of the Holy Spirit in at least four different
connections, but always — even in the first — in direct and constant relation
to faith, with respect to its origin, and with respect to its consequences; and
by no means almost exclusively with respect to assurance of the authority of
the Scriptures." The progress which Pannier supposes he traces in Calvin's
doctrine of the work of the Spirit seems illusory: the general doctrine of the
work of the Spirit is already pretty fully outlined in 1536. But the relating
of the testimony of the Spirit to Scripture to Calvin's general doctrine of faith
as the product of the Spirit is exact and important for the understanding of
his teaching. From beginning to end, Calvin conceived the confidence of the
Christian in Scripture, wrought by the Holy Spirit, as one of the exercises of
saving faith. Calvin is ever insistent that all that is good in man comes from
the Spirit — whether in the sphere of thought, feeling, or act. " It is a notion

It is his profound sense of the supernatural origin of all that is good in the manifestations of human life which constitutes the characteristic mark of Calvin's thinking: and it is this which lies at the bottom of and determines his doctrine of the witness of the Holy Spirit. He did not doubt that the act of faith by which the child of God embraces the Scriptures as a revelation of God is his own act and the expression of his innermost consciousness. But neither did he doubt that this consciousness is itself the expression of a creative act of the Spirit of God. And it was on this account that he represented to himself the act of faith performed as resting ultimately on " the testimony of the Spirit." Its supernatural origin was to him the most certain thing about it. That language very much resembling his own might be employed in a naturalistic sense was, no doubt, made startlingly plain in his own day by the teaching of Castellion. Out of his pantheising rationalism Castellion found it possible to speak almost in Calvin's words. " It is evident," says he, " that the intention and secret counsels of God, hidden in the Scriptures, are revealed only to believers, the humble, the pious, who fear God and have the Spirit of God." If the wicked have sometimes spoken like prophets, they have nevertheless not really understood what they said, but are like magpies in a cage going through the forms of speech without inner apprehension of its meaning.[76] But Castellion meant by this nothing more than that sympathy is requisite to understanding. Since his day multitudes more have employed Calvin's language to express little more than this; and

---

of the natural man," he says on John xiv. 17 (1553: xlvii. 329–330), " to despise all that the Sacred Scriptures say of the Holy Spirit, depending rather on his own reason, and to reject the celestial illumination. . . . For ourselves, feeling our penury, we know that all we have of sound knowledge comes from no other fountain. Nevertheless the words of the Lord Jesus show clearly that nothing can be known of what concerns the Holy Spirit by human sense, but He is known only by the experience of faith." " No one," says he again (" Institutes " of 1543, i. 330), " should hesitate to confess that he attains the knowledge of the mysteries of God only so far as he has been illuminated by God's grace. He that attributes more knowledge to himself is only the more blind that he does not recognize his blindness."

[76] *Opp.* xiv. 727–733 (Pannier, as cited, p. 120).

have even represented Calvin's own meaning as nothing more than that the human consciousness acquires by association with God in Christ the power of discriminating the truth of God from falsehood. Nothing could more fundamentally subvert Calvin's whole teaching. The very nerve of his thought is, that the confidence of the Christian in the divine origin and authority of Scripture and the revelatory nature of its contents is of distinctively supernatural origin, is God-wrought. The testimony of the Spirit may be delivered through the forms of our consciousness, but it remains distinctively the testimony of God the Holy Spirit and is not to be confused with the testimony of our consciousness.[77] Resting on the language of Rom. viii. 16, from which the term "testimony of the Spirit" was derived, he conceived it as a co-witness along with the witness of our spirit indeed, but on that very account distinguishable from the witness of our spirit. This particular point is nowhere discussed by him at large, but Calvin's general sense is perfectly plain. That there is a double testimony he is entirely sure — the testimony of our own spirit and that of the Holy Spirit: that these are though distinguishable yet inseparable, he is equally clear: his conception is therefore that this double testimony runs confluently together into one. This is only as much as to say afresh that the testimony of the Holy Spirit is not delivered to us in a propositional revelation, nor by the creating in us of a blind conviction, but

[77] The classical instance of this confusion is supplied by the teaching of Claude Pajon (1626–1685), who, in accordance with his general doctrine that "without any other grace than that of the Word, God changes the whole man, from his intellect to his passions," explained the "testimony of the Spirit" as nothing else than the effect of the *indicia* of divinity in Scripture on the mind. The effect of these "marks" is a divine effect, because it is wrought in prearranged circumstances prepared for this effect: *facit per alium facit per se*. The conception is essentially deistic. It is no small testimony to the cardinal place which the doctrine of "the testimony of the Spirit" held in the Reformed system of the seventeenth century that Pajon still taught it; and it is no small testimony to its current conception as just "regeneration" that Pajon too identified it with regeneration, explained, of course, in accordance with his fundamental principle that all that God works He works through means. See on the whole matter Jurieu, "Traitté de la Nature et de la Grace," 1688, pp. 25, 26, who quotes alike from Pajon and his followers.

along the lines of our own consciousness. In its essence, the act of the Spirit in delivering His testimony, terminates on our nature, or faculties, quickening them so that we feel, judge, and act differently from what we otherwise should. In this sense, the testimony of the Spirit coalesces with our consciousness. We cannot separate it out as a factor in our conclusions, judgments, feelings, actions, consciously experienced as coming from without. But we function differently from before: we recognize God where before we did not perceive Him; we trust and love Him where before we feared and hated Him; we firmly embrace Him in His Word where before we turned indifferently away. This change needs accounting for. We account for it by the action of the Holy Spirit on our hearts; and we call this His " testimony." But we cannot separate His action from our recognition of God, our turning in trust and love to Him and the like. For this is the very form in which the testimony of the Spirit takes effect, into which it flows, by which it is recognized. We are profoundly conscious that of ourselves we never would have seen thus, and that our seeing thus can never find its account in anything in us by nature. We are sure, therefore, that there has come upon us a revolutionary influence from without; and we are sure that this is the act of God. Calvin would certainly have cried as one of his most eloquent disciples cries to-day: " The Holy Spirit is God, and not we ourselves. What we are speaking of is a Spirit which illuminates our spirit, which purifies our spirit, which strives against our spirit, which triumphs over our spirit. And you say this Spirit is nothing but our spirit? By no means. The Holy Spirit, the Spirit of God — this is God coming into us, not coming from us." [78] It is with equal energy that Calvin declares the supernaturalness of the testimony of the Spirit and repels every attempt to confound it with the human consciousness through which it works. To him this testimony is just God Himself in His intimate working in the human heart, opening it to the light of

[78] Doumergue, " Le problème protestant," 1892, p. 46 (Pannier, as cited, p. 192).

the truth, that by this illumination it may see things as they really are and so recognize God in the Scriptures with the same directness and surety as men recognize sweetness in what is sweet and brightness in what is bright. Here indeed lies the very hinge of his doctrine.[79]

It has seemed desirable to enter into some detail with respect to Calvin's doctrine of the testimony of the Spirit, not only because of its intrinsic interest, but also because of its importance for understanding Calvin's doctrine of the knowledge of God and indeed his whole system of truth, and for a

[79] Pannier, as cited, pp. 188 *sq.*, is quite right in insisting on this. After quoting D. H. Meyer ("De la place et du rôle de l'apologétique dans la théologie protestante," in the *Revue de théologie et des quest. relig.*, Jan., 1893, p. 1) to the effect that "the witness of the Holy Spirit in the heart of Christians is not a subjective phenomenon . . . it is an objective thing and comes from God," — he continues: "Now this objective character of the witness of the Holy Spirit is precisely what appears to make it 'incomprehensible' to our modern theologians (so A. E. Martin, *La Polemique de R. Simon et de J. Le Clerc*, 1880, p. 29: 'This intervention of the Holy Spirit distinct from the individual consciousness appears to us incomprehensible'). We are not speaking of those who venture to pretend that Calvin identifies the witness of the Holy Spirit with 'the intimate feeling' of each Christian. When one takes his place by the side of Castellion he may lawfully say, For me as for him 'the inspiration of the Holy Ghost confounds itself with consciousness; these revelations made to the humble are nothing more than the intuitions of a moral and religious sense fortified by meditation' (Buisson, *Castellion,* i. p. 304, cf. p. 201: 'Castellion placed above the tradition of the universal Church his own sense, his own reason, or rather, let us say it all at once, for it is the foundation of the debate, his consciousness'). But when one invokes the real fathers of the real Reformation, ah, please do not take for theirs the very opinions they combat. To make of the testimony of the Holy Spirit the equivalent of the testimony of the human spirit, of the individual consciousness, is to deny the real existence and the distinct rôle of the Holy Spirit, is to show that we have nothing in common with the faith expounded by Calvin so clearly, and defended through a century against the attacks of the Catholics as one of the essential bases of the Reformed theology and piety." Again, Pannier is quite right in his declaration (p. 214): "What we deny is that our reason — moral consciousness, religious consciousness, the term is of no importance — can, of itself, *make us see* the divinity of the Scriptures. It is this which *sees* it; but it is the Holy Spirit which *makes us see it*. He is not the inner eye for seeing the truth which is outside of us, but the supernatural hand which comes to open the eye of our consciousness — an eye which is, no doubt, divine in the sense that it too was created by God, but which has been blinded by the consequences of sin."

proper estimate of his place in the history of thought. His doctrine of the testimony of the Spirit is the keystone of his doctrine of the knowledge of God. Men endowed by nature with an ineradicable *sensus deitatis,* which is quickened into action and informed by a rich revelation of God spread upon His works and embodied in His deeds, are yet held back from attaining a sound knowledge of God by the corruption of their hearts, which dulls their instinctive sense of God and blinds them to His revelation in works and deeds. That His people may know Him, therefore, God lovingly intervenes by an objective revelation of Himself in His Word, and a subjective correction of their sin-bred dullness of apprehension of Him through the operation of His Spirit in their hearts, which Calvin calls the Testimony of the Holy Spirit. Obviously it is only through this testimony of the Holy Spirit that the revelation of God, whether in works or Word, is given efficacy: it is God, then, who, through His Spirit, reveals Himself to His people, and they know Him only as taught by Himself. But also on this very account the knowledge they have of Him is trustworthy in its character and complete for its purpose; being God-given, it is safeguarded to us by the dreadful sanction of deity itself. This being made clear, Calvin has laid a foundation for the theological structure — the scientific statement and elaboration of the knowledge of God — than which nothing could be conceived more firm. There remained nothing more for him to do before proceeding at once to draw out the elements of the knowledge of God as they lie in the revelation so assured to us, except to elucidate the *indicia* by which the Christian under the influence of the testimony of the Spirit is strengthened in his confidence that the Scriptures are the very Word of God, and to repudiate the tendency to neglect these Scriptures so authenticated to us in favor of fancied continuous revelations of the Spirit. The former he does in a chapter (chap. viii.) of considerable length and great eloquence, which constitutes one of the fullest and most powerful expositions of the evidence for the divine origin of the Scriptures which have come down to us from the Reformation age. The latter he does in a briefer chapter (chap. ix.), of crisp polemic quality, the upshot of which is to leave it strongly impressed on the reader's mind that the whole knowledge of God available to us, as the whole knowledge of God needful for us, lies objectively displayed in the pages of Scripture, which, therefore, becomes the sole source of a sound exposition of the knowledge of God.

This strong statement is not intended, however, to imply that the Spirit-led man can learn nothing from the more general revelation of God in His works and deeds. Calvin is so far from denying the possibility of a " Natural Theology," in this sense of the word, that he devotes a whole chapter (chap. v.) to vindicating the rich revelation of God made in His works and deeds: though, of course, he does deny that any theology worthy of the name can be derived from this natural revelation by the " natural man," that is, by the man the eyes of whose mind and heart are not opened by the Spirit of God — who is not under the influence of the testimony of the Spirit; and in this sense he denies the possibility of a " Natural Theology." What the strong statement in question is intended to convey is that there is nothing to be derived from natural revelation which is not also to be found in Scripture, whether as necessary presupposition, involved implication or clear statement; and that beside that documented in Scripture there is no supernatural revelation accessible to men. The work of the Spirit of God is not to supplement the revelation made in Scripture, far less to supersede it, but distinctively to authenticate it. It remains true, then, that the whole matter of a sound theology lies objectively revealed to us in the pages of Scripture; and this is the main result to which his whole discussion tends. But side by side with it requires to be placed as a result of his discussion secondary only to this, this further conclusion, directly given in his doctrine of the testimony of the Spirit — that only a Christian man can profitably theologize. It is in the union of these two great principles that we find Calvin's view of the bases of a true theology. This he conceives as the product of the systematic investigation and logical

elaboration of the contents of Scripture by a mind quickened
to the apprehension of these contents through the inward operations of the Spirit of God. It is on this basis and in this
spirit that Calvin undertakes his task as a theologian; and what
he professes to give us in his " Institutes " is thus, to put it
simply, just a Christian man's reading of the Scriptures of
God.

The Protestantism of this conception of the task of the
theologian is apparent on the face of it. It is probably, however, still worth while to point out that its Protestantism does
not lie solely or chiefly in the postulate that the Scriptures are
the sole authoritative source of the knowledge of God —
" formal principle " of the Reformation though that postulate
be, and true, therefore, as Chillingworth's famous declaration
that " the Bible and the Bible only is the religion of Protestants " would be, if only Chillingworth had kept it to this
sense. It lies more fundamentally still in the postulate that
these Scriptures are accredited to us as the revelation of God
solely by the testimony of the Holy Spirit — that without this
testimony they lie before us inert and without effect on our
hearts and minds, while with it they become not merely the
power of God unto salvation, but also the vitalizing source of
all our knowledge of God. There is embodied in this the true
Protestant principle, superior to both the so-called formal and
the so-called material principles — both of which are in point
of fact but corollaries of it. For it takes the soul completely
and forcibly out of the hands of the Church and from under
its domination, and casts it wholly upon the grace of God. In
its formulation Calvin gave to Protestantism for the first time,
accordingly, logical stability and an inward sense of security.
Men were no more puzzled by the polemics of Rome when
they were asked, You rest on Scripture alone, you say: but
on what does your Scripture rest? Calvin's development of the
doctrine of the testimony of the Spirit provided them with
their sufficient answer: " On the testimony of the Spirit of
God in the heart." Here we see the historical importance of
Calvin's formulation of this doctrine. And here we see the ex-

planation of the two great facts which reveal its historical importance, the facts, to wit, that Calvin had no predecessors in the formulation of the doctrine, and that at once upon his formulation of it it became the common doctrine of universal Protestantism.

IV. HISTORICAL RELATIONS

The search for anticipations of the doctrine of the testimony of the Spirit among the Fathers and Scholastics [80] reveals only such sporadic assertions of the dependence of man on the inward teaching of the Holy Spirit for the knowledge or the saving knowledge of God as could not fail in the speech of a series of Christian men who had read their Bibles. A sentence of this kind from Justin Martyr,[81] another from Chrysostom,[82] two or three from Hilary of Poitiers,[83] almost exhaust

[80] See especially P. Du Moulin, " Du Iuge des controverses traitté," 1636, pp. 294 sq., and cf. Pannier, as cited, pp. 64–68.

[81] "Dialogue with Trypho," vii. ("Opera," ed. Otto. I. ii. 32): οὐ γὰρ συνοπτὰ οὐδὲ συννοητὰ πᾶσίν ἐστιν, εἰ μή τῳ θεὸς δῷ συνιέναι, καὶ ὁ Χριστὸς αὐτοῦ: "these things cannot be perceived or understood by all, but only by the man to whom God and His Christ have given it to understand them."

[82] "In Cap. v. et vi. Genes. homil. xxi." (Migne, liii. 175): Διάτοι τοῦτο προσήκει ἡμᾶς ὑπὸ τῆς ἄνωθεν χάριτος ὁδηγουμένους, καὶ τὴν παρὰ τοῦ ἁγίου Πνεύματος ἔλλαμψιν δεξαμένους οὕτως ἐπιέναι τὰ θεῖα λόγια. Οὐδὲ γὰρ σοφίας ἀνθρωπίνης δεῖται ἡ θεία Γραφὴ πρὸς τὴν κατανόησιν τῶν γεγραμμένων, ἀλλὰ τῆς τοῦ Πνεύματος ἀποκαλύψεως . . . : "For we must be led by the grace from above, and must receive the illumination of the Holy Spirit, to approach the divine oracles; for it is not human wisdom but the revelation of the Holy Spirit that is needed for understanding the Holy Scriptures." It will be perceived that it is more distinctly the understanding of the Scriptures than the reception of them as from God which is in question with both Justin and Chrysostom.

[83] "De Trinitate," ii. 34: Animus humanus, nisi per fidem donum Spiritus hauserit, habebit quidem naturam Deum intelligendi, sed lumen scientiae non habebit; iii. 24: non enim concipiunt imperfecta perfectum, neque quod ex alio subsistit, absolute vel auctoris sui potest intelligentiam obtinere, vel propriam; v. 21: neque enim nobis ea natura est, ut se in coelestem cognitionem suis viribus efferat. A Deo discendum est quid de Deo intelligendum sit; quia non nisi se auctore cognoscitur. . . . Loquendum ergo non aliter de Deo est, quam ut ipse ad intelligentiam nostram de se locutus est. (For these citations see Migne, "Patro. Lat.," x. 74–75; x. 92; x. 143.) Hilary certainly teaches that for such creatures as men there can be no knowledge of God except it be God-taught: but it is not so clear that he teaches that for sinful

what the first age yields. It is different with Augustine. With his profound sense of dependence on God and his vital conviction of the necessity of grace for all that is good in man, in the whole circle of his activities, he could not fail to work out a general doctrine of the knowledge of God in all essentials the same as Calvin's. In point of fact, as we have already pointed out, he did so. There remain, however, some very interesting and some very significant differences between the two.[84] It is interesting to note, for instance, that where Calvin speaks of an innate *sensus deitatis* in man, as lying at the root of all his knowledge of God, Augustine, with a more profound ontology of this knowledge, as at least made explicit in the statement, speaks of a continuous reflection of a knowledge of Himself by God in the human mind.[85] There is here, however, probably only a difference in fulness of statement, or at most only of emphasized aspect. On the other hand, it is highly significant that, instead of Calvin's doctrine of the testimony of the Spirit, Augustine, in conformity with the stress he laid upon the " Church " and the " means of grace " in the conference of grace, speaks of the knowledge of God as attainable only " in the Church." [86] Accordingly, in him also and his successors there are to be found only such anticipations specifically of the doctrine of the testimony of the Spirit as are afforded by the increased frequency of their references to the dependence of man for all knowledge of God and divine things on grace and the inward teaching of the heavenly Instructor. The voice of men may assail our ears, says Augustine, for instance, but those remain untaught " to whom that inward unction does not speak, whom the Holy Spirit does not inwardly

creatures there must be a special illapse of the Spirit that such as they may know God — may perceive Him in His Word and so recognize that Word as from Him and derive a true knowledge of Him from it. It is this soteriological doctrine which is Calvin's doctrine of the Holy Spirit's testimony: not that ontological one.

[84] Cf. article: " Augustine's Doctrine of Knowledge and Authority," in *The Princeton Theological Review* for July and October, 1907.

[85] *Ibid.*, pp. 360 *sq.*

[86] *Ibid.*, pp. 571 *sq.*

teach ": for " He who teaches the heart has His seat in heaven." [87] Moses himself, yea, even if he spoke to us not in Hebrew but in our own tongue, could convey to us only the knowledge of what he said: of the truth of what he said, only the Truth Himself, speaking within us, in the secret chamber of our thought, can assure us though He speaks neither in Hebrew nor in Greek nor in Latin, nor yet in any tongue of the barbarians, but without organs of voice or tongue and with no least syllabic sound.[88] Further than this men did not get before the Reformation: [89] nor did the first Reformers themselves get further. No doubt they discerned the voice of the Spirit in the Scriptures, as the Fathers did before them; and in a single sentence, written, however, after the " Institutes " of 1539 (viz., in 1555), Melanchthon notes with the Fathers that the mind is " aided in giving its assent " to divine things " by the Holy Spirit." [90] Zwingli here stands on the same plane with his brethren. He strongly repels the Romish establishment of confidence in the Scriptures on the *ipse dixit* of the Church, indeed: and asserts that those who sincerely search the Scriptures are taught by God, and even that none acquire faith in the Word except as drawn by the Father, admonished

[87] " Tract. iii. in Ep. Joan. ad Parthos," ii. 13 (Migne, xxxv. 2004). Again: " There is, then, I say, a Master within that teacheth: Christ teacheth; His inspiration teacheth. Where His inspiration and His unction are not, in vain do words make a noise from without."

[88] " Confessions," xi. 3 (Migne, xxxii. 811). Cf. vi. 5 (Migne, xxxii. 723).

[89] Pannier, *loc. cit.*, says: " The whole of the testimony of the Holy Spirit is not yet here. Only once is the Holy Spirit Himself named [in these passages from Augustine] in a formal way. But Augustine has the intuition of a mysterious work wrought in the soul of the Christian, of an understanding of the Bible which comes not from man but from a power exterior and superior to him; and he sets forth the rôle which this direct correspondence between the book and the reader may play in the foundation of Christian certitude. In this, as in so many other points, Augustine was the precursor of the Reformation, and a precursor without immediate followers: for except a couple of very vague and isolated hints in Salvianus (*De Provid.*, iii. 1) and Gregory the Great († 604, *Homil. in Ezek.*, I. x.), nothing further is found on this subject through ten centuries: it comes into view again at the approach of the new age, when thought aspired to free itself from the Scholastic ruts, with Biel († 1495, *Lib. iii. Sent.* dist. 25, dub. 3) and Cajetan († 1534, *Opera*, II. i. 1)."

[90] " Loci," ed. 1555 (" Corpus Ref.," xxi. 605).

by the Spirit, taught by the unction — as, says he, all pious men have found.[91] But such occasional remarks as this could not fail wherever the Augustinian conception of grace was vitally felt; and show only that the doctrine of the testimony of the Spirit was always implicit in that doctrine.[92]

[91] " De vera et falsa religione ": Cum constet verbo nusquam fidem haberi quam ubi Pater traxit, Spiritus monuit, unctio docuit . . . hanc rem solae piae mentes norunt. Neque enim ab hominum disceptatione pendet, sed in animis hominum tenacissime sedet. Experientia est, nam pii omnes eam experti sunt. " Articles of 1523 " (Niemeyer, " Collectio confessionum in eccles. ref. publ.," 1840, p. 5) : Art. xiii. Verbo Dei quum auscultant homines pure et sinceriter voluntatem Dei discunt. Deinde per Spiritum Dei in Deum trahuntur et veluti transformantur. " Von Klarheit und Gewüsse des Worts Gottes " (" Werke," Schuler und Schulthess, 1828, i. 81; or " Werke " in " Corp. Ref.," i. 382) : " The Scriptures . . . came from God, not from man; . . . and the God who has shined into them will Himself give you to understand that their speech comes from God." Cf. the interesting biographical account of how he came to depend on the Scriptures only, on p. 79 (or " Corp. Ref.," i. 379).

[92] E. Rabaud, " Hist. de la doctr. de l'inspiration," etc., 1883, pp. 32–33, 42–43, 47 sq., 50, expounds the earlier Reformers as in principle standing on the doctrine of the testimony of the Spirit. With respect to the interpretation of Scripture he remarks: " The hermeneutical principle of the witness of the Holy Spirit (if we may speak of it as a principle) is common to all the Reformers. Luther only, without being ignorant of it, makes no use of it. Besides responding to the polemic needs, it responded to the aspirations of the faith and of the piety of simple men, better than rational demonstrations " (p. 50, note 4). " In a general way," he remarks, pp. 32–33, " Luther considered the Bible as the sole incontestable and absolute authority. Here is the solid foundation of the edifice, the impregnable citadel in which he shut himself in order to repel victoriously all attacks. It is for him, in truth, a religious axiom, a postulate of faith, and not a dogma or a theory; it is revealed to his believing soul independently of all intellectual activity. Thus Luther, trusting in the action of the Holy Spirit, operating through the Scriptures, does not pause to prove its authority, nor to establish it dialectically: it imposes itself; a systematic treatment is not needed. More and more as circumstances demanded it, he gave reasons for his faith and his submission. Poor arguments to modern thinking, but in his times, and commended by his vibrant eloquence and powerful personality, possessing a power of persuasion very impressive. . . . It seemed idle to Luther, we may say, to enter into an argument to establish what was evident to him. He did not attempt, therefore, to prove the authority of the Bible — he asserted it repeatedly in warm words, . . . in passionate declarations, but rarely if ever proceeds by a formal demonstration." Raising the question of Zwingli's doctrine of the mode and extent of inspiration (p. 47), he remarks: " No more than the others does Zwingli respond to these questions, which had not yet been raised. God has spoken: the Bible contains His word: that is enough. The divinity of

The same remark applies to the first edition of Calvin's "Institutes" (1536) also, though with a difference. This difference — that, if we cannot say that the doctrine of the internal testimony of the Spirit to the divinity of the Scriptures is found there already in germ [93] any more than we can say the same of the Augustinian Fathers, and the criticism passed [94] on the adduction of Melanchthon's single sentence in this reference to the effect that he speaks rather " of the action of the Holy Spirit with reference to the object of faith, that is to say, to the contents of the Word of God " than " with reference to the divinity of the Scriptures themselves," is valid also for Calvin's first edition; yet it is certainly true that the general doctrine of the internal testimony of the Spirit comes much more prominently forward in even the first edition of the " Institutes " than in any preceding treatise of the sort — that much more is made in it than in any of its predecessors of the poverty of the human spirit and the need and actuality of the prevalent influence of the Spirit of God that man may have — whether in knowledge or act — any good thing. We shall have to go back to Augustine to find anything comparable to the conviction and insight with which even in this his earliest work Calvin urges these things. Calvin's whole thought is already dominated by the conception of the powerlessness of the human soul in its sin in all that belongs to the knowledge

---

the Bible is once more a fact, an axiom, so much so that he does not dream of establishing it dialectically or of defending it."

[93] So Pannier, as cited, p. 63: " Like all the other essential parts of the Reformed Dogmatics, the doctrine of the internal testimony of the Holy Spirit is found in germ in the first edition of the *Institutes,* although still without any development. It is almost possible to deny that it exists there, as has been done with predestination. Nevertheless, if the doctrine is not yet scientifically formulated, it may yet be perceived to preëxist necessarily as an essential member of the complete body of doctrine which is slowly to grow up." When Pannier comes, however (pp. 72–77), to expound in detail the germs of the doctrine as they lie in the edition of 1536, it turns out that there is not only no full development of the doctrine in that edition, but also no explicit mention of it, as it is applied to the conviction which the Christian has of the divinity of Scripture; so that it preëxists in this edition only as implicit in its general doctrine of the Spirit and His work.

[94] By Pannier, p. 69.

of God which is salvation, and its entire dependence on the sovereign operations of the Holy Spirit: and in this sense it may be said that the chapters in the new " Institutes " of 1539 in which he develops this doctrine of the noëtic effects of sin and their cure by objective revelation, documented in Scripture, and subjective illumination wrought by the Holy Spirit, lay implicitly in his doctrine of man's need and its cure by the indwelling Spirit which pervades the " Institutes " of 1536. There he already teaches that the written law was required by the decay of our consciousness of the 'law written on the heart; that to know God and His will we have need to surpass ourselves; that it is the Spirit dwelling in us that is the source of all our right knowledge of God; and that it is due to the power of the Spirit alone " that we hear the word of the Holy Gospel, that we accept it by faith, and that we abide in this faith " (p. 137, or *Opp.* i. 72). With eminent directness and simplicity he already there tells us that " our Lord first teaches and instructs us by His Word; secondarily confirms us by His Sacraments; and thirdly by the light of His Holy Spirit illuminates our understandings and gives entrance into our hearts both to the Word and to the Sacraments, which otherwise would only beat upon our ears and stand before our eyes, without penetrating or operating beneath them " (p. 206, or *Opp.* i. 104). There is, in other words, very rich teaching in the " Institutes " of 1536 of the entire dependence of sinful man on the Spirit of God for every sound religious movement of the soul: but there is no development of the precise doctrine of the testimony of the Holy Spirit to the divinity of the Scriptures. It is not merely that the term *testimonium Spiritus Sancti* does not occur in this early draft, or occurs only once, and then not in this sense: [95] it is that the

[95] Pannier, as cited, p. 77, notes that " the words: *testimonio Spiritus Sancti* occur only a single time, at the end, and in the old sense of — ' by the divinely inspired Scriptures.' " He refers to the ed. of 1536, p. 470, that is, *Opp.* i. 228: and notes that this passage was dropped in the edition of 1559 (*Opp.* iv. 796, note 5). The passage runs: " Thus Hezekiah is praised *by the testimony of the Holy Spirit* " — that is, obviously, " by the inspired Scriptures " — " for having broken up the brazen serpent which Moses had made by Divine command."

thing is not explicated and is present only as implicated in the general doctrine of grace, which is very purely conceived.

It was left, then, to the edition of 1539 to create the whole doctrine at, as it were, a single stroke.[96] For, as we have already had occasion to note, Calvin's whole exposition of the doctrine of the testimony of the Spirit to the divinity of Scripture appears all at once in its completeness in the second edition of the "Institutes," the first edition which he issued as a textbook on theology, that of 1539. This exposition was reproduced without curtailment or alteration in all subsequent editions, and is thereby given the great endorsement of Calvin's permanent approval: while the additions which are made to it in the progressive expansion of the treatise, while large in amount, are devoted to guarding it from the misapprehension that the necessity it asserted for the testimony of the Spirit in any way detracted from the objective value of the *indicia* of the divinity of Scripture, rather than to modifying the positive doctrine expounded. The additions within the limits of chapter vii. consist essentially of the insertion of the discussion of Augustine's doctrine in § 3 and of the caveat with reference to the underestimation of the *indicia* in § 4, while practically the whole of chapter viii. — all except the opening sentence — is of later origin. If we will omit the first sentence of chapter vii., the whole of §§ 3 and 4, with the exception of the sentence near the beginning of the latter, which begins: "Now if we wish to consult the true intent of our conscience" — and the beginning and end of § 5, retaining only the central passage beginning: "For though it conciliate our reverence . . ." down to the words: "Superior to the power of any human will or knowledge," and also the two striking sentences, beginning with: "It is such a persuasion" and ending with "a just ex-

---

[96] Köstlin, as cited, p. 411, strongly states these facts. The whole of the discussion on the sources and norms of religious truth "is altogether lacking in the original form" of the "Institutes": "Calvin worked out this section for the first time for the edition of 1539": but it is found here already thoroughly done, "in all its fundamental traits already complete and mature." He adds that the Lutheran dogmatists (as well as the Reformed) at once, however, took up the construction of Calvin and made it their own.

plication of the subject " — we shall have substantially the text of the edition of 1539, needing only to add the two opening sentences of chapter viii. and the major part of chapter ix. It will at once be seen that the edition of 1539 contains the entire positive exposition of the doctrine of the testimony of the Spirit as retained by Calvin to the end.

The formulation of this principle of the testimony of the Spirit by Calvin in 1539 had an extraordinary effect both immediate and permanent.[97] Universal Protestantism perceived in it at sight the pure expression of the Protestant principle and the sheet-anchor of its position. The Lutherans as well as the Reformed adopted it at once and made it the basis not only of their reasoned defence of Protestantism, but also of their structure of Christian doctrine and of their confidence in Christian living.[98] To it they both continued to cling so long and so far as they continued faithful to the Protestant principle itself. It has given way only as the structure of Protestantism has itself given way in reaction to the Romish position, or, more widely, as the structure of Christian thought has given way in rationalizing disintegration. No doubt it has undergone at the hands of its various expounders, from time to time, more or less modification, and in its journeyings to the

[97] The history of the doctrine among the Reformed is touched on by A. Schweizer, " Glaubenslehre," i. § 32; among the old Lutherans by Klaiber, " Die Lehre der altprotestantischen Dogmatiker von dem test. Sp. Sancti " in the *Jahrbücher für d. Theologie*, 1857, pp. 1–54. Its history among French theologians is traced by Pannier, as cited, Part iii. pp. 139–181, cf. 186–193: his notes on the history outside of France (pp. 181–185) are very slight. On pp. 161–163 Pannier essays to gather together, chiefly, as it appears, from the scattered citations in the Protestant controversialists of the seventeenth century (p. 162, note 2), the hints which appear in the Romish writers, mainly Jesuits of the early seventeenth century, of recognition of the internal work of the Holy Spirit illuminating the soul. These bear more or less resemblance to the Protestant doctrine of the testimony of the Spirit. Some of the passages he cites are quite striking, but do not go beyond the common boundaries of universal Christian supernaturalism.

[98] In his brief remarks on the subject in his " Dogmengeschichte des Protestantismus," i. 1908, pp. 178 *sq.*, Otto Ritschl seeks to discriminate between the Reformed and Lutherans in their conception of the testimony of the Spirit; but his discrimination touches rather the application than the essence of the matter.

ends of the earth, has suffered now and again some sea-change — sometimes through sheer misapprehension, sometimes through sheer misrepresentation, sometimes through more or less admixture of both. A spurious revival of the doctrine was, for example, set on foot by Schleiermacher in his strong revulsion from the cold rationalism which had so long reigned in Germany to a more vital religious faith; and sentences may be quoted from his writings which, when removed out of the context of his system of thought, almost give expression to it.[99] But after all, his revival of it was rather the revival of sub-

---

[99] Some of them are cited, e.g., by Schweizer, *op. cit.*, followed, e.g., by Pannier, as cited (p. 186, note 1) — such as: "Faith is already presupposed when a peculiar authority is conceded to Scripture," — "The recognition of what is canonical comes into existence only gradually and progressively, since the sense for the truly Apostolic is a gracious gift which grows up only gradually in the Church," — "Faith cannot be established in unbelievers by the Scriptures, so that their divine authority is in the first instance proved from merely rational considerations." — There is much that is true and well said in such remarks, and they enrich the writings of Schleiermacher and his followers with a truly spiritual element. But at bottom the central position occupied is vitiated by the use of "faith" as an "undistributed middle," and the remarks of writers of this type do not so much tend to exalt the place of saving faith as to depress the authority of Scripture, by practically denying the existence or validity of *fides humana*. That attitude towards the Scriptures which gladly and heartily recognizes them as the Word of the Living God, and with all delight in them as such, seeks to subject all thought and feeling and action to their direction, certainly is, if not exactly a product of "true faith," yet (as the Westminster Confession defines it) an exercise of true faith, and a product of that inward creative operation of the Holy Spirit from which all true faith comes: that keen taste for the divine which is the outgrowth of the spiritual gift of discrimination — the "distinguishing of things that differ" which Paul gives a place among Christian graces — is assuredly a "gift of grace" which may grow more and more strong as the Christian life effloresces; and such a taste for the divine cannot be awakened in unbelievers by the natural action of the Scriptures or any rational arguments whatever, but requires for its production the work of the Spirit of God *ab extra accidens*. But it is a totally different question whether the peculiarity of Scripture as a divine revelation can call out no intellectual recognition in the minds of inquiring men, but must remain wholly hidden and produce no mental reaction conformable to its nature, until true faith has already been born in the heart: whether there are no valid tests of what is apostolical except a spiritual sense for the truly apostolical which can only gradually grow up in the Church; whether the unbeliever may not be given a well-grounded intellectual conviction of the apostolic origin, the canonical author-

jectivity in religion than of the doctrine of the testimony of the Spirit as the basis of all faith: and it has borne bitter fruit in a widespread subjectivism, the mark of which is that it discards (as "external") the authority of those very Scriptures to which the testimony of the Spirit is borne. Not in such circles is the continued influence of the doctrine of the testimony of the Spirit to be sought or its continued advocacy to be found. If we would see it in its purity in the modern Church we must look for it in the hands of true successors of Calvin — in the writings, to name only men of our own time, of William Cunningham [100] and Charles Hodge [101] and Abraham Kuyper [102] and Herman Bavinck.[103]

As we have already had occasion to note, the principle of the testimony of the Spirit as the true basis of our confidence in the Scriptures as the Word of God was almost from the hands of Calvin himself incorporated into the Reformed Creeds. We have already pointed out the sharpness and strength of its expression in the Gallican (1557–1571) and Belgian (1501–1571)

---

ity, and the divine character of Scripture by the presentation to him of rational evidence which, however unwillingly on his part, will compel his assent. The question here is not whether this *fides humana* is of any great use in the spiritual life: the question is whether it is possible and actual. We may argue, if we will, that it is not worth while to awake it — though opinions may differ there: but how can we argue that it is a thing inherently impossible? To say this is not merely to say that reason cannot save, which is what Calvin said and all his followers: it is to say that salvation is intrinsically unreasonable — which neither Calvin nor any of his true followers could for a moment allow. Sin may harden the heart so that it will not admit, weigh, or yield to evidence: but sin, which affects only the heart subjectively, and not the process of reasoning objectively, cannot alter the relations of evidence to conclusions. Sin does not in the least degree affect the cogency of any rightly constructed syllogism. No man, no doubt, was ever reasoned into the kingdom of heaven: it is the Holy Spirit alone who can translate us into the kingdom of God's dear Son. But there are excellent reasons why every man should enter the kingdom of heaven; and these reasons are valid in the forum of every rational mind, and their validity can and should be made manifest to all.

[100] "Theological Lectures," etc., New York, 1878, pp. 317, 320 *sq.*

[101] "The Way of Life," 1841; also "Systematic Theology," as per Index.

[102] "Encyclopædie, etc.," ii. 1894, pp. 505 *sqq.*

[103] "Gereformeerde Dogmatiek," ed. 1, i. pp. 142–145, 420–422, 490–491.

Confessions, and it finds at least the expression of suggestion in the Second Helvetic Confession (1562). It was not, however, merely into the Confessions of the Reformation age that it was incorporated. It is given an expression as clear as it is prudent, as decided as it is comprehensive, in that confession of their faith which the persecuted Waldenses issued after the massacres of 1655; [104] and it is incorporated into the Westminster Confession of Faith (1646) in perhaps the best and most balanced statement it has ever received — the phraseology of which is obviously derived in large part from Calvin, either directly or through the intermediation of George Gillespie,[105]

[104] Written, no doubt, by Léger, moderator at the time of " the Table," and preserved for us in his " Histoire générale des églises évangéliques des vallées de Piédmont," 1669, i. p. 112 (cf. p. 92). See Pannier, as cited, p. 133.

[105] Dr. A. F. Mitchell ("The Westminster Assembly, its History and Standards," the Baird Lecture for 1882, ed. 2, 1897, p. 441, note), following Prof. J. S. Candlish (*Brit. and For. Ev. Rev.*, 1877, p. 173), is " very sure " that Gillespie has here " left his mark on the Confession." The " Miscellany Questions," in the xxi. of which occurs the passage from Gillespie from which the Confession is supposed to have drawn, was a posthumous work, published in 1649; but a number of the papers of which it is made up have the appearance of being briefs drawn up by Gillespie for his own satisfaction, or as preparations for speeches, or possibly even as papers handed in to committees, during the discussions of the Westminster Assembly. The language in question, however, whether in Gillespie or in the Confession, is so strongly reminiscent of Calvin, that the possibility seems to remain open that the resemblance between Gillespie and the Confession is due to their common relation to Calvin. Here is the passage in Gillespie (" Presbyterian Armoury " ed., vol. ii. pp. 105–106): " The Scripture is known to be indeed the Word of God by the beams of divine authority it hath in itself, and by certain distinguishing characters, which do infallibly prove it to be the Word of God; such as the heavenliness of the matter; the majesty of the style; the irresistible power over the conscience; the general scope, to abase man and to exalt God; nothing driven at but God's glory and man's salvation; the extraordinary holiness of the penmen of the Holy Ghost, without respect to any particular interests of their own, or of others of their nearest relations (which is manifest by their writings); the supernatural mysteries revealed therein, which could never have entered into the reason of men; the marvellous consent of all parts and passages (though written by divers and several penmen), even where there is some appearance of difference; the fulfilling of prophecies; the miracles wrought by Christ, by the prophets and apostles; the conservation of the Scriptures against the malice of Satan and fury of persecutors; — these and the like are characters and marks which evidence the Scriptures to be the Word of God; yet all these cannot beget in the soul a full persua-

but the substance of which was but the expression of the firmly
held faith of the whole body of the framers of that culminating Confession of the Reformed Churches.

" We recognize the divinity of these sacred books," says
the Waldensian Confession (chap. iv.), " not only through the

---

sion of faith that the Scriptures are the Word of God; this persuasion is from
the Holy Ghost in our hearts. And it hath been the common resolution of
sound Protestant writers (though now called in question by the sceptics of this
age [the allusion being to " Mr. J. Godwin in his Hagiomastix "]) that these
arguments and infallible characters in the Scripture itself, which most certainly prove it to be the Word of God, cannot produce a certainty of persuasion in our hearts, but this is done by the Spirit of God within us, according
to these Scriptures, I Cor. ii. 10–15; I Thes. i. 5; I John ii. 27; v. 6–8, 10;
John vi. 45." — Whatever may be the immediate source of the Confessional
statement, Calvin is clearly the real source of Gillespie's statement. — For the
essence of the matter Gillespie's discussion is notably clear and exact, particularly with reference to the relation of the *indicia* to the testimony of the
Spirit, a matter which he strangely declares had not to his knowledge been
discussed before. The clarity of his determinations here is doubtless due to
the specific topic which he is in this Question investigating, viz., the validity
of the argument from marks and fruits of sanctification to our interest in
Christ: a parallel question in the broader soteriological sphere to the place of
indicia in our conviction of the divinity of Scripture, which he therefore uses
illustratively for his main problem. " It may be asked," he remarks, " and
it is a question worthy to be looked into (though I must confess I have
not read it, nor heard it, handled before), How doth this assurance by marks
agree with or differ from assurance by the testimony of the Holy Spirit? May
the soul have assurance either way, or must there be a concurrence of both
(for I suppose they are not one and the same thing) to make up the assurance? " (p. 105). He proves that they are " not one and the same thing ";
and then shows solidly that for assurance there " must be a concurrence of
both." " To make no trial by marks," he says, " and to trust an inward testimony, under the notion of the Holy Ghost's testimony, when it is without
the least evidence of any true gracious marks, this way (of its own nature, and
intrinsically, or in itself) is a deluding and ensnaring of the conscience "
(p. 105). That is to say, a blind confidence and conviction, without cognizable grounds in evidence cannot be trusted. Again and very clearly: " So
that, in the business of assurance and full persuasion, the evidences of graces
and the testimony of the Spirit, are two concurrent causes or helps, both
of them necessary. Without the evidence of graces, it is not a safe nor a well-
grounded assurance " (p. 106). It remains only to add that while arguing this
out in the wider soteriological sphere, Gillespie appears to take it as a matter of course in the accrediting of the Scriptures as divine — giving that case,
in the course of his argument, as an illustration to aid in determining his
conclusion.

testimony of the Church, but principally through the eternal
and indubitable truth of the doctrine which is contained in
them, through the excellence, sublimity, and majesty of the
pure divinity (*du tout divine*) which are apparent in them,
and through the operation of the Holy Spirit which makes us
receive with deference the testimony which the Church gives
to them, which opens our eyes to receive the rays of the celestial light which shines in the Scriptures, and so corrects our
taste that we discern this food by the divine savor which it
possesses." The dependence of this fine statement on Calvin's
exposition is evident; but what is most striking about it is the
clarity with which it conceives and the fulness with which
it expounds the exact mode of working of the testimony of
the Spirit and its relation to the *indicia* of divinity in Scripture, through which, and not apart from or in opposition to
which, it performs its work. So far from supposing that the witness of the Spirit is of the nature of a new and independent
revelation from heaven or works only a blind faith in us, setting thus aside all evidences of the divinity of Scripture, external and internal alike, this careful statement particularly
explains that our faith in the divinity of Scripture rests, under
the testimony of the Spirit, on these evidences as its ground,
but not on these evidences by themselves, but on them as
apprehended by a Spirit-led mind and heart — the work of the
Spirit consisting in so dealing with our spirit that these evidences are, under His influence, perceived and felt in their
real bearing and full strength.

An even more notable statement of the whole doctrine
is that incorporated into the Westminster Confession (i. 4,
5), and in a more compressed form into the Larger Catechism
(Q. 4). "The authority of the Holy Scripture, for which it
ought to be believed and obeyed," says the Confession, "dependeth not upon the testimony of any man or church, but
wholly upon God (who is truth itself) the author thereof;
and therefore it is to be received, because it is the Word of
God. We may be moved and induced by the testimony of the
Church to a high and reverent esteem of the Holy Scripture;

and the heavenliness of the matter, the efficacy of the doctrine, the majesty of the style, the consent of all the parts, the scope of the whole (which is to give all glory to God), the full discovery it makes of the only way of man's salvation, the many other incomparable excellencies, and the entire perfection thereof, are arguments whereby it doth abundantly evidence itself to be the Word of God; yet notwithstanding, our full persuasion and assurance of the infallible truth, and divine authority thereof, is from the inward work of the Holy Spirit, bearing witness by and with the Word in our heart." In the Larger Catechism this is reduced to the form: "The Scriptures manifest themselves to be the Word of God, by their majesty and purity; by the consent of all the parts, and the scope of the whole, which is to give all glory to God; by their light and power to convince and convert sinners, to comfort and build up believers unto salvation; but the Spirit of God bearing witness by and with the Scriptures in the heart of man, is alone able fully to persuade it that they are the very Word of God." The fundamental excellence of this remarkable statement (for the full understanding of which what is said of "faith" in chapter xiv. of the Confession and Question 72 of the Catechism should be compared with it — just as Calvin referred his readers to his later discussion of "faith" for further information on the topic of the testimony of the Spirit) is the care with which the several grounds on which we recognize the Scriptures to be from God are noted and their value appraised, and that yet the supreme importance of the witness of the Spirit is safe-guarded.[106] The external testimony of the Church is noted and its value pointed out: it moves and induces us to a high and reverent esteem for Scripture. The internal testimony of the characteristics of the Scriptures themselves is noted and its higher value pointed out: they "abundantly evidence" or "manifest" the Scriptures "to be the

[106] For the meaning of the Confession's statement, supported by illustrative excerpts from its authors, see *The Presbyterian and Reformed Review*, iv. 1893, pp. 624–32; and cf. W. Cunningham, "Theological Lectures," New York, 1878, pp. 320 *sq.*, and *The Presbyterian Quarterly*, January, 1894, pp. 19 *sq.*

Word of God." The need and place of the testimony of the Spirit is then pointed out in the presence of this "abundant evidencing" or "manifesting": it is not to add new evidence — which is not needed — but to secure deeper conviction — which is needed; and not independently of the Word with its evidencing characteristics, but "by and with the Word" or "the Scriptures." What this evidence of the Spirit does is "*fully* to persuade us" that "the Scriptures are the very Word of God," — to work in us "*full* persuasion and assurance of the infallible truth and divine authority" of the Word of God. It is a matter of completeness of conviction, not of grounds of conviction; and the testimony of the Spirit works, therefore, not by adding additional grounds of conviction, but by an inward work on the heart, enabling it to react upon the already "abundant evidence" with a really "full persuasion and assurance." Here we have the very essence of Calvin's doctrine, almost in his own words, and with even more than his own eloquence and precision of statement.

What Calvin has given to the Reformed Churches, therefore, in his formulation of the doctrine of the Testimony of the Spirit is a fundamental doctrine, which has been as such expounded by the whole body of their theologians, and incorporated into the fabric of their public Confessions, so that it has been made and continues to be until to-day the officially declared faith of the Reformed Churches in France and Holland, Switzerland, Italy, Scotland, and America, wherever the fundamental Reformed Creeds are still professed.

III

CALVIN'S DOCTRINE OF GOD

CALVIN'S DOCTRINE OF GOD[1]

HAVING expounded in the opening chapters of the " Institutes " the sources and means of the knowledge of God, Calvin naturally proceeds in the next series of chapters (I. x. xi. xii. xiii.) to set forth the nature of the God who, by the revelation of Himself in His Word and by the prevalent internal operation of His Spirit, frames the knowledge of Himself in the hearts of His people. He who expects to find in these chapters, however, an orderly discussion of the several topics which make up the *locus de Deo* in our formal dogmatics, will meet with disappointment. Calvin is not writing out of an abstract scientific impulse, but with the needs of souls, and, indeed, also with the special demands of the day in mind. And as his purpose is distinctively religious, so his method is literary rather than scholastic. In the freedom of his literary manner, he had permitted himself in the preceding chapters repeated excursions into regions which, in an exact arrangement of the material, might well have been reserved for exploration at this later point. To take up these topics again, now, for fuller and more orderly exposition, would involve much repetition without substantially advancing the practical purpose for which the " Institutes " were written. Calvin was not a man to confound formal correctness of arrangement with substantial completeness of treatment; nor was he at a loss for new topics of pressing importance for discussion. He skillfully interposes at this point, therefore, a short chapter (chap. x.) in which under the form of pointing out the complete harmony with the revelation of God in nature of the revelation of God in the Scriptures — the divine authority of which in the communication of the knowledge of God he had just demonstrated — he reminds his readers of all that he had formerly said of the nature

[1] From *The Princeton Theological Review,* vii. 1909, pp. 381–436.

and attributes of God on the basis of natural revelation, and takes occasion to say what it remained necessary to say of the same topics on the basis of supernatural revelation. Thus he briefly but effectively brings together under the reader's eye the whole body of his exposition of these topics and frees his hands to give himself, under the guidance of his practical bent and purpose, to the two topics falling under the rubric of the doctrine of God which were at the moment of the most pressing importance. His actual formal treatment of the doctrine of God thus divides itself into two parts, the former of which (chaps. xi. xii.), in strong Anti-Romish polemic is devoted to the uprooting of every refuge of idolatry, while the latter (chap. xiii.), in equally strong polemic against the Anti-trinitarianism of the day, develops with theological acumen and vital faith the doctrine of Trinity in Unity.

It is quite true, then, as has often been remarked, that the "Institutes" contain no systematic discussion of the existence, the nature, and the attributes of God.[2] And the lack of formal, systematic discussion of these fundamental topics, may, no doubt, be accounted a flaw, if we are to conceive the "Institutes" as a formal treatise in systematic theology. But it is not at all true that the "Institutes" contain no sufficient indication of Calvin's conceptions on these subjects: nor is it possible to refer the absence of formal discussion of them

---

[2] Cf. Köstlin, "Calvin's Institutio," etc., in *Studien und Kritiken*, 1868, i. pp. 61–2: "On the other hand — and this is for us the most important matter, — there is not given there any comprehensive exposition of the attributes, especially not of the ethical attributes of God, nor is any such afterwards attempted." Again, iii. p. 423: "We cannot present and follow out the doctrine of the *Institutio* on the divine nature and the divine attributes, and their relations, as a whole, as we can its doctrine of the Trinity, because Calvin himself, as we have mentioned already, has nowhere presented them as a whole." Cf. also P. J. Muller, "De Godsleer van Zwingli en Calvijn," 1883, p. 11: "Neither by Zwingli nor by Calvin are there offered proofs of the existence of God" (cf. p. 16). Again, "De Godsleer van Calvijn," 1881, p. 26: "A doctrine of the nature of God as such we do not find in Calvin." *Ibid.*, p. 38: "We find nowhere in Calvin a special section which is devoted particularly to the treatment of God's attributes"; "since he gives no formal doctrine of the attributes, we find in him also no classification of the attributes."

either to indifference to them on Calvin's part or to any peculiarity of his dogmatic standpoint,[3] or even of his theological method.[4] The omission belongs rather to the peculiarity of
this treatise as a literary product. Calvin does not pass over all
systematic discussion of the existence, nature, and attributes
of God because from his theological standpoint there was nothing to say upon these topics, nor because, in his theological
method, they were insignificant for his system; but simply because he had been led already to say informally about them all
that was necessary for the religious, practical purpose he had
in view in writing this treatise. For here as elsewhere the key
to the understanding of the " Institutes " lies in recognizing
their fundamental purpose to have been religious, and their
whole, not coloring merely, but substance, to be profoundly religious — in this only reflecting indeed the most determinative trait of Calvin's character.

It is important to emphasize this, for there seems to be
still an impression abroad that Calvin's nature was at bottom cold and hard and dry, and his life-manifestation but
a piece of incarnated logic: while the " Institutes " themselves
are frequently represented, or rather misrepresented — it is
difficult to believe that those who so speak of them can have
read them — as a body of purely formal reasoning by which
intolerable conclusions are remorselessly deduced from a set
of metaphysical assumptions.[5] Perhaps M. Ferdinand Brune-

[3] As Köstlin, for example, has suggested, as cited, p. 423, followed by
P. J. Muller in his earlier work, " De Godsleer van Calvijn," 1881, pp. 10, 46.

[4] So P. J. Muller expresses himself in his later volume — " De Godsleer
van Zwingli en Calvijn," 1883, p. 46 — modifying his earlier view: " Köstlin
asks if it does not belong to Calvin's dogmatic standpoint that he does not
venture to seek after a bond between the several elements which come forward
in God's many-sided relation to men. This question can undoubtedly be answered in the affirmative, although we should rather speak here of the peculiarity of Calvin's *method*." That is to say, Muller here prefers to refer the
phenomenon in question to Calvin's *a posteriori* method rather than to his
theological standpoint.

[5] André Duran, " Le Mysticisme de Calvin," 1900, p. 8, justly says: " The
Institutes are remarkable precisely for this: the absence of speculation. It is
especially with the heart that Calvin studies God in His relations with men;
and it is by the heart that he attains to complete union of man with God."

tière may be looked upon as a not unfair representative of the
class of writers who are wont so to speak of the " Institutes." [6]
According to him, Calvin has " intellectualized " religion and
reduced it to a form which can appeal only to the " reasonable," or rather to the " reasoning " man. " In that oratorical
work which he called *The Institutes,*" M. Brunetière says,
" if there is any movement . . . it is not one which comes
from the heart . . . and — I am speaking here only of the
writer or the religious theorizer, not of the man — the insensibility of Calvin is equalled only by the rigor of his reasoning.
. . ." The religion Calvin sets forth is " a religion which consists essentially, almost exclusively, in the adhesion of the intellect to truths all but demonstrated," and commends itself
by nothing " except by the literalness of its agreement with a
text — which is a matter of pure philology — and by the solidity of its logical edifice — which is nothing but a matter of pure
reasoning." To Calvin, he adds, " religious truth attests itself
in no other manner and by no other means than mathematical
truth. As he would reason on the properties of a triangle, or of
a sphere, so Calvin reasons on the attributes of God. All that
will not adjust itself to the exigencies of his dialectic, he contests or he rejects . . . Cartesian before Descartes, rational
evidence, logical incontradiction are for him the test or the
proof of truth. He would not believe if faith did not stay itself
on a formal syllogism. . . . From a ' matter of the heart,' if
I may so say, Calvin transformed religion into an ' affair of
the intellect.' "

We must not fail to observe, in passing, that even M. Brunetière refrains from attributing to Calvin's person the hard insensibility which he represents as the characteristic of his religious writings — a tribute, we may suppose, to the religious
impression which is made by Calvin's personality upon all

For a satisfactory discussion of the " heart in Calvin's theology " see E. Doumergue, " Jean Calvin," etc., iii. 1905, pp. 560–563. Compare also the third address in Doumergue's " L'Art et le sentiment dans l'oeuvre de Calvin," Geneva,
1902.

    [6] " Discours de combat," 1903, pp. 135–140.

who come into his presence, and which led even M. Ernest Renan, who otherwise shares very largely M. Brunetière's estimate of him, to declare him "the most Christian man of his age." [7] Nor can we help suspecting that the violence of the invectives launched against the remorseless logic of the "Institutes" and of Calvin's religious reasoning in general, is but the index of the difficulty felt by M. Brunetière and those who share his point of view, in sustaining themselves against the force of Calvin's argumentative presentation of his religious conceptions. It is surely no discredit to a religious reasoner that his presentation commends his system irresistibly to all "reasonable," or let us even say "reasoning" men. A religious system which cannot sustain itself in the presence of "reasonable" or "reasoning" men, is not likely to remain permanently in existence, or at least in power among reasonable or reasoning men; and one would think that the logical irresistibility of a system of religious truth would be distinctly a count in its favor. The bite of M. Brunetière's assault is found, therefore, purely in its negative side. He would condemn Calvin's system of religion as nothing but a system of logic; and the "Institutes," the most systematic presentation of it, as in essence nothing but a congeries of syllogisms, issuing in nothing but a set of logical propositions, with no religious quality or uplift in them. In this, however, he worst of all misses the mark; and we must add he was peculiarly unfortunate in fixing, in illustration of his meaning, on the two matters of the "attributes of God" as the point of departure for Calvin's dialectic and of the intellectualizing of "faith" as the height of his offending.

In Calvin's treatment of faith there is nothing more striking than his determination to make it clear that it is a matter not of the understanding but of the heart; and he reproaches

[7] "Études d'histoire religieuse," ed. 7, 1864, p. 342: "l'homme le plus chrétien de son siècle." It must be borne in mind that this is not very high praise on M. Renan's lips; and was indeed intended by him to be depreciatory. We need not put an excessive estimate on Calvin's greatness, he says in effect; he lived in an age of reaction towards Christianity and he was the most Christian man of his age: his preëminence is thus accounted for.

the Romish conception of faith precisely because it magnifies
the intellectual side to the neglect of the fiducial. "We must
not suppose," it is said in the Confession of Faith drawn up
for the Genevan Church,[8] either by himself or by his colleagues
under his eye, "that Christian faith is a naked and mere knowledge of God or understanding of the Scriptures, which floats in
the brain without touching the heart. . . . It is a firm and
solid confidence of the heart." Or, as he repeats this elsewhere,[9]
"It is an error to suppose that faith is a naked and cold
knowledge.[10] . . . Faith is not a naked knowledge,[11] which
floats in the brain, but draws with it a living affection of the
heart." [12] "True Christian faith," he expounds in the second edition of the "Institutes," [13] . . . "is not content with a
simple historical knowledge, but takes its seat in the heart of
man." "It does not suffice that the understanding should be
illuminated by the Spirit of God if the heart be not strengthened by His power. In this matter the theologians of the Sorbonne very grossly err, — thinking that faith is a simple consent to the Word of God, which consists in understanding, and
leaving out the confidence and assurance of the heart." "What
the understanding has received must be planted in the heart.
For if the Word of God floats in the head only, it has not yet
been received by faith; it has its true reception only when
it has taken root in the depths of the heart." Again, to cite
a couple of passages in which the less pungent statement of
the earlier editions has been given new point and force in the
final edition of the "Institutes": "It must here be again observed," says he,[14] "that we are invited to the knowledge of

---

[8] "Instruction et confession de foy dont on use en l'eglise de Genève"
(*Opp.* xxii. 47). The Strasburg editors assign it to Calvin's colleagues; Doumergue ("Jean Calvin," ii. 1902, pp. 236–251) to Calvin.

[9] "Vera Christianae pacificationis et ecclesiae reformandae ratio," 1549
(*Opp.* vii. 598–600).

[10] nudam frigidamque notitiam.

[11] nudam notitiam.

[12] vivum affectum qui cordi insideat.

[13] Ed. of 1539: the quotations are made from the French version of
1541, pp. 189, 202, 204. See *Opp.* iii. 15, 53, 57.

[14] I. v. 9.

God — not a knowledge which, content with empty speculation, floats only in the brain, but one which shall be solid and
fruitful, if rightly received by us, and rooted in the heart."
"The assent we give to God," he says again,[15] "as I have already indicated and shall show more largely later — is rather
of the heart than of the brain, and rather of the affections than
of the understanding." [16] It is quite clear, then, that Calvin did
not consciously address himself merely to the securing of an
intellectual assent to his teaching, but sought to move men's
hearts. His whole conception of religion turned, indeed, on this:
religion, he explained, to be pleasing to God, must be a matter
of the heart,[17] and God requires in His worshippers precisely
heart and affection.[18] All the arguments in the world, he insists, if unaccompanied by the work of the Holy Spirit on the
heart, will fail to produce the faith which piety requires.[19]

This scarcely sounds like a man to whom religion was simply a matter of logical proof.

And so far is he from making the attributes of God, metaphysically determined, the starting-point of a body of teaching deduced from them by quasi-mathematical reasoning — as
one would deduce the properties of a triangle from its nature as a triangle — that it has been made his reproach that
he has so little to say of the divine nature and attributes, and
in this little confines himself so strictly to the manifest *indicia*
of God in His works and the direct teaching of Scripture, refusing utterly to follow "the high priori" road either in determining the divine attributes or from them determining the
divine activities. Thus, his doctrine of God is, it is said, no
doubt notably sober and restrained, but also, when compared
with Zwingli's, for example — equally notably unimportant.[20]

[15] III. ii. 8.
[16] Cordis esse magis quam cerebri, et affectus magis quam intelligentiae.
[17] fidem et veritatem cordis.
[18] cor et animum (*Opp.* vi. 477, 479).
[19] I. vii. 4.
[20] Cf. P. J. Muller, "De Godsleer van Zwingli en Calvijn," 1883, p. 111:
"A theologian like Calvin, Zwingli was not; but still in the history of the
doctrine of God the pages devoted to Zwingli are more important than

It is confessed, however, that it is at least thoroughly religious;
and in this is found, indeed, its fundamental characteristic.
Precisely where Calvin's doctrine differs from Zwingli's markedly is that he constantly contemplated God religiously, while
Zwingli contemplated him philosophically — that to him God
was above and before all things the object of religious reverence, while to Zwingli he was predominatingly the First Cause,
from whom all things proceed.[21] " It is not with the doctrine
of God," says the historian whose representations we have
been summarizing, " but with the *worship* of God that Calvin's first concern was engaged. Even in his doctrine of God
— as we may perceive from his remarks upon it — religion

those devoted to Calvin. The *loci de Trinitate, de Creatione,* and *de Lapso*
apart, Zwingli's system is undeniably more coherent than that of Calvin,
in which we miss the bond by which the several parts are joined. On the
other hand, however, we miss in Zwingli's doctrine of God precisely what
constitutes the value of a doctrine of God for the *theologian,* that is to say,
its religious character. We do not find in Zwingli as in Calvin a recoil from
the consequences of his own reasoning, which leads necessarily to the ascription to God of the origination of evil, or sin, just because God is *not* with
him as with Calvin conceived above everything as the object of religious
reverence, but rather as the object of speculative thought."

[21] Cf. P. J. Muller, " De Godsleer van Zwingli en Calvijn," 1883, p. 6: " If
the doctrine of God for the theologian is determined by its religious character, the contemplation of God as the object of religious reverence will
take a higher place with him than the merely philosophical contemplation
of God as the ultimate cause. Since it is not to be denied — as the following
exposition will show — that with Zwingli God is speculatively contemplated
much more as the ultimate cause than as the object of religious reverence,
we may conclude that — so far as religious value is concerned — Zwingli's
doctrine of God must be ranked below Calvin's." Again (p. 21): " In the
nature of the case Calvin's conceptions of the nature of God must be very
sober. For to him, God was very predominantly the object of religious reverence, and he could not therefore do otherwise than disapprove of the attempt
to penetrate into the nature of the Godhead (I. v. 9). With Zwingli, on the
contrary, in whose system God is preëminently conceived as the ultimate
cause, the doctrine of the nature of God must form one of the most important sections of the doctrine of God." Once more (p. 23): " Calvin, whose
pride it was to be a ' Biblical theologian,' does not follow the method of the
philosophers, — the aprioristic method. He is therefore sober in his conceptions of the nature of God, since he had noted that in the Scriptures God
speaks little of His nature, that He may teach us sobriety " — quoting I. xiii.
1: *ut nos in sobrietate contineat, parce de sua essentia* [*Deus*] *disserit.*

stands ever in the foreground (I. ii. 1). Before everything else Calvin is a religious personality. The Reformation confronts Catholicism with a zeal to live for God. With striking justice Calvin remarked that 'all alike engaged in the worship of God, but few really reverenced Him, — that there was everywhere great ostentation in ceremonies but sincerity of heart was rare' (I. ii. 2). *Reverence* for God was the great thing for Calvin. If we lose sight of this a personality like Calvin cannot be understood; and it is only by recognizing the religious principle by which he was governed, that a just judgment can be formed of his work as a dogmatician. . . ." [22] Again, Calvin "considers the knowledge of the nature and of the attributes of God more a matter of the heart than of the understanding; and such a knowledge, he says, must not only arouse us to ' the service of God, but must also awake in us the hope of a future life ' (I. v. 10). In his extreme practicality — as the last remark shows us — Calvin rejected the philosophical treatment of the question. The Scriptures, for him the source of the knowledge of God, he takes as his guide in his remarks on the attributes. . . ." [23] Still again, " Already more than once have we had occasion to note that when Calvin treats of God, he does this as a *believer,* for whom the existence of God stands as a fixed fact; and what he says of God, he draws from the Scriptures as his fundamental source, finding his pride in remaining a *Biblical* theologian, and whenever he can, taking the field against the *philosophico more interpretari* of the Scriptural texts (see e.g. I. xvi. 3). His doctrine of God has the *practical* end of serving the needs of his fellow-believers. It is also noteworthy that he closes every stage of the consideration with an exhortation to the adoration of God or to the sur-

[22] Cf. P. J. Muller, " De Godsleer van Calvijn," 1881, p. 117.

[23] Cf. P. J. Muller, " De Godsleer van Zwingli en Calvijn," 1883, pp. 46, 47. The author of the anonymous Introduction to the edition of the " Institutes " in French, published by Meyrueis et Cie, Paris, 1859, p. xii., says similarly: " Of a mind positive, grave, practical, removed from all need of speculation, very circumspect, not expressing its thought until its conviction had attained maturity, taking the fact of a divine revelation seriously, Calvin learned his faith at the feet of the Holy Scriptures . . ."

render of the heart to Him. Of the doctrine of the Trinity he
declares that he will hold himself ever truly to the Scriptures,
because he desires to do nothing more than to make what
the Scriptures teach accessible to our conceptions *planioribus
verbis,* and this will apply equally to the *whole* of his doctrine
of God." [24] In a word, nothing can be clearer than that in his
specific doctrine of God as well as in his general attitude to religious truth Calvin is as far as possible from being satisfied
with a merely logical effect. When we listen to him on these
high themes we are listening less to the play of his dialectic
than to the throbbing of his heart.

It was due to this his controlling religious purpose, and to
his dominating religious interest, that Calvin was able to
leave the great topics of the existence, the nature, and the attributes of God, without formal and detailed discussion in his
" Institutes." It is only a matter, we must reiterate, of the
omission of formal and detailed discussion; for it involves not
merely a gross exaggeration but a grave misapprehension to
represent him as leaving these topics wholly to one side, and
much more to seek to account for this assumed fact from some
equally assumed peculiarity of Calvin's theological point of
view or method. Under the impulse of his governing religious
interest, he was able to content himself with such an exposition of the nature and attributes of God, in matter and form,
as served his ends of religious impression, and was under no
compulsion to expand this into such details and order it into
such a methodical mode of presentation as would satisfy the
demands of scholastic treatment. But to omit what would be
for his purpose adequate treatment of these fundamental elements of a complete doctrine of God would have been impossible, we do not say merely to a thinker of his systematic
genius, but to a religious teacher of his earnestness of spirit. In
point of fact, we do not find lacking to the " Institutes " such
a fundamental treatment of these great topics as would be appropriate in such a treatise. We only find their formal and
separate treatment lacking. All that it is needful for the Chris-

[24] P. J. Muller, " De Godsleer van Calvijn," 1881, pp. 103–104.

tian man to know on these great themes is here present. Only, it is present so to speak in solution, rather than in precipitate: distributed through the general discussion of the knowledge of God rather than gathered together into one place and apportioned to formal rubrics. It is communicated moreover in a literary and concrete rather than in an abstract and scholastic manner.

It will repay us to gather out from their matrix in the flowing discourse the elements of Calvin's doctrine of God, that we may form some fair estimate of the precise nature and amount of actual instruction he gives regarding it. We shall attempt this by considering in turn Calvin's doctrine of the existence, knowableness, nature, and attributes of God.

We do not read far into the "Institutes" before we find Calvin presenting proofs of the existence of God. It is quite true that this book, being written by a Christian for Christians, rather assumes the divine existence than undertakes to prove it, and concerns itself with the so-called proofs of the divine existence as means through which we rather obtain knowledge of what God is, than merely attain to knowledge that God is. But this only renders it the more significant of Calvin's attitude towards these so-called proofs that he repeatedly lapses in his discussion from their use for the former into their use for the latter and logically prior purpose. That he thus actually presents these proofs as evidences specifically of the existence of God can admit of no doubt.[25]

[25] P. J. Muller's view is different, as may be seen from the following extracts: "Neither by Zwingli nor by Calvin are there offered proofs of the existence of God, although there are particular passages in their writings which seem to recall them. The proposition 'That God exists' needed neither for themselves nor for their fellow-believers, nor even against Rome, any proof. It has been thought indeed that the so-called cosmological argument is found in Zwingli, the physico-theological argument in Calvin (Lipsius, *Lehrb. der ev. prot. Dogmatik,* ed. 2, 1879, p. 213). But it would not be difficult to show that in the case of neither have we to do with a philosophical deduction, but only with an aid for attaining a complete knowledge of God" ("De Godsleer van Z. en C.," 1883, p. 11, cf. p. 14). In a note Prof. Muller adverts to the possible use by Calvin, I. iii. 1, of "the so-called historical argument." "If Zwingli gives us no proof of God's existence, the same is true of Calvin. It is true that the physico-theological argument has been discovered

If, for example, he adduces that *sensus deitatis* with which all men, he asserts, are natively endowed, primarily as the germ which may be developed into a profound knowledge of God, he yet does not fail explicitly to appeal to it also as the source of an ineradicable conviction, embedded in the very structure of human nature and therefore present in all men alike, of the existence of God. He tells us expressly that because of this *sensus divinitatis,* present in the human mind by natural instinct, all men without exception (*ad unum omnes*) know (*intelligant,* perceive, understand) "that God exists" (*Deum esse*), and are therefore without excuse if they do not worship Him and willingly consecrate their lives to Him (I. iii. 1). It is to buttress this assertion that he cites with approval Cicero's declaration [26] that "there is no nation so barbarous, no tribe so savage, that there is not stamped on it the conviction that there is a God." [27] Thus he adduces the argument of the *consensus gentium* — the so-called "historical" argument — with exact appreciation of its true bearing, not directly as a proof of the existence of God, but directly as a proof that the conviction of the divine existence is a native endowment of human nature, and only through that indirectly as a proof of the existence of God. This position is developed in the succeed-

---

in the *Institutes.* Yet as he wrote over the fifth chapter of the first book, 'That the knowledge of God is manifested in the making and continuous government of the world,'—it is already evident from this that he did not intend to argue from the teleology of the world to the existence of God as its Creator, Sustainer, and Governor, but that he wished merely to point to the world as to 'a beautiful book,'—to speak in the words of our [Netherlandish] Confession (Art. ii.),—'in which all creatures, small and great, serve as letters to declare to us the invisible things of God.' Here, too, we have accordingly to do simply with a means for a rise to a fuller *knowledge* of God" (*Do.,* p. 16). "The Scholastics may indeed—although answering the inquiry affirmatively—begin with the question, Is there a God? Such a question cannot rise with Calvin. The Reformer, assured of his personal salvation, the ground of which lay in God Himself, could also for his co-believers leave this question to one side. Practical value attached only to the inquiry how men can come to know God, of whose existence Calvin entertained no doubt" ("De Godsleer van Calvijn," 1881, p. 11).

[26] ut ethnicus ille ait (the allusion is to Cicero, "De natura deorum," i. 16).

[27] Deum esse.

ing paragraph into a distinct anti-atheistic argument. The existence of religion, he says, presupposes, and cannot be accounted for except by, the presence in man of this "constant persuasion of God" from which as a seed the propensity to religion proceeds: men may deny "that God exists," [28] "but will they, nill they, what they wish not to know they continually are aware of." [29] It is a persuasion ingenerated naturally into all, that "some God exists" [30] (I. iii. 3), and therefore this does not need to be inculcated in the schools, but every man is from the womb his own master in this learning, and cannot by any means forget it. It is therefore mere detestable madness to deny that "God exists" (I. iv. 2).[31] In all these passages Calvin is dealing explicitly, not with the knowledge of what God is, but with the knowledge that God is. It is quite incontrovertible, therefore, that he grounds an argument — or rather the argument — for the existence of God in the very constitution of man. The existence of God is, in other words, with him an "intuition," and he makes this quite as plain as if he had devoted a separate section to its exposition.

Similarly, although he writes at the head of the chapter in which he expounds the revelation which God makes of Himself in His works and deeds: "That the knowledge of God is manifested in the making of the world and its continuous government" (chap. v.), he is not able to carry through his exposition without occasional lapses into an appeal to the patefaction of God in His works as a proof of His existence, rather than as a revelation of His nature. The most notable of these lapses occurs in the course of his development of the manifestation of God made by the nature of man himself (I. v. 4), where once more he gives us an express anti-atheistic argument. "Yea," he cries, "the earth is supporting to-day many monstrous beings, who without hesitation employ the very seed of divinity which has been sown in human nature

[28] qui Deum esse negent.

[29] velint tamen nolint, quod nescire cupiunt, subinde sentiscunt.

[30] imo et naturaliter ingenitam esse omnibus hanc persuasionem, esse aliquem Deum.

[31] negantes Deum esse.

for eclipsing of the name of God. How detestable, I protest, is this insanity, that a man, discovering God a hundred times in his body and soul, should on this very pretext of excellence deny that God exists! [32] They will not say that it is by chance that they are different from brute beasts; they only draw over God the veil of 'nature,' which they declare the maker of all things, and thus abolish (*subducunt*) Him. They perceive the most exquisite workmanship in all their members, from their countenances and eyes to their very finger nails. Here, too, they substitute 'nature' in the place of God. But above all how agile are the movements of the soul, how noble its faculties, how rare its gifts, discovering a divinity which does not easily permit itself to be concealed: unless the Epicureans, from this eminence, should like the Cyclops audaciously make war against God. Is it true that all the treasures of heavenly wisdom concur for the government of a worm five feet long, and the universe lacks this prerogative? To establish the existence of a kind of machinery in the soul, correspondent to each several part of the body, makes so little to the obscuring of the glory of God that it rather illustrates it. Let Epicurus tell what concourse of atoms in the preparation of food and drink distributes part to the excrements, part to the blood, and brings it about that the several members perform their offices with as much diligence as if so many souls by common consent were governing one body." "The manifold agility of the soul," he eloquently adds (I. v. 5, *med.*), "by which it surveys the heavens and the earth, joins the past to the future, retains in memory what it once has heard, figures to itself whatever it chooses; its ingenuity, too, by which it excogitates incredible things and which is the mother of so many wonderful arts; are certain insignia in man of divinity. . . . Now what reason exists that man should be of divine origin and not acknowledge the Creator? Shall we, forsooth, discriminate between right and wrong by a judgment which has been given to us, and yet there be no Judge in heaven? . . . Shall we be thought the inventors of so many useful arts, that we may defraud

[32] Deum esse neget.

God of His praise — although experience sufficiently teaches us
that all that we have is distributed to us severally from elsewhere? . . ." Calvin, of course, knows that he is digressing
in a passage like this — that " his present business is not with
that sty of swine," as he calls the Epicureans. But digression
or not, the passage is distinctly an employment of the so-called
physico-theological proof for the existence of God, and advises
us that Calvin held that argument sound and would certainly
employ it whenever it became his business to develop the arguments for the existence of God.

The proofs for the existence of God on which we perceive
Calvin thus to rely had been traditional in the Church from
its first age. It was precisely upon these two lines of argument
that the earliest Fathers rested. " He who knows himself," says
Clement of Alexandria, quite in Calvin's manner, " will know
God." [33] " The knowledge of God," exclaims Tertullian, " is
the dowry of the soul." [34] " If you say, ' Show me thy God,' "
Theophilus retorts to the heathen challenge, " I reply, ' Show
me your man and I will show you my God.' " [35] The God who
cannot be seen by human eyes, declares Theophilus,[36] " is beheld and perceived through His providence and works ": we
can no more surely infer a pilot for the ship we see making
straight for the harbor, than we can infer a divine governor
for the universe tending straight on its course. " Those who
deny that this furniture of the whole world was perfected by
the divine reason," argues the Octavius of Minucius Felix,[37]
" and assert that it was heaped together by certain fragments
casually adhering to each other, seem to me to have neither
mind, nor sense, nor, in fact, even sight itself." " Whence comes
it," asks Dionysius of Alexandria, criticizing the atomic theory

[33] " Paed.," III. i. ed. Stählin, i. 1905, p. 235; cf. E. T. in the " Ante-
Nicene Christian Library ": " Clement of Alexandria," i. 1867, p. 273. Cf.
" Strom.," V. xiii.; " Protrep.," vi.

[34] " Adv. Marc.," i. 10: E. T. " The Ante-Nicene Fathers," iii. 1903, p.
278. Cf. " De test. animae," vi.: E. T. op. cit., p. 179.

[35] " Ad Autol.," i. 2: E. T. " Ante-Nicene Fathers," ii. 1903, p. 89.

[36] Do., i. 5: E. T. op. cit., p. 90.

[37] Chap. xvii.: E. T. " Ante-Nicene Fathers," iv. 1902, p. 182.

quite in Calvin's manner,[38] that the starry hosts — " this multitude of fellow-travellers, all unmarshalled by any captain, all
ungifted with any determination of will, and all unendowed
with any knowledge of each other, have nevertheless held their
course in perfect harmony? " Like these early Fathers, Calvin
adduces only these two lines of evidence: the existence of God
is already given in our knowledge of self, and it is solidly attested by His works and deeds. Whether, had we from him a
professed instead of a merely incidental treatment of the topic,
the metaphysical arguments would have remained lacking in
his case as in theirs,[39] we can only conjecture; but it seems very
possible that as foreign to his *a posteriori* method (cf. I. v. 9)
they lay outside of his scheme of proofs. Meanwhile, he has
in point of fact adverted, in the course of this discussion, only
to the two arguments on which the Church teachers at large
had depended from the beginning of Christianity. He states
these with his accustomed clearness and force, and he illuminates them with his genius for exposition and illustration; but
he gives them only incidental treatment after all. In richness
as well as in fulness of presentation he is surpassed here by
Zwingli,[40] and it is to Melanchthon that we shall have to go

[38] " Adv. Epic.," iii.: E. T. " Ante-Nicene Fathers," vi. 1899, p. 88.

[39] H. C. Sheldon, " History of Christian Doctrine," i. 1886, p. 56:
" Metaphysical proofs of the existence of God, such as those adduced by
Augustine, Anselm, and Descartes, were quite foreign to the theology of
the first three centuries." But in the next age they had already come in; cf.
Sheldon, p. 187: " We find a new class of arguments, something more in the
line of the metaphysical than anything which the previous centuries brought
forward. Three writers in particular aspired to this order of proofs; viz.,
Diodorus of Tarsus, Augustine, and Boëthius." Augustine is the real father of
the ontological argument: but Augustine only chronologically belonged to
the old world; as Siebeck puts it, he was " the first modern man."

[40] Cf. P. J. Muller, " De Godsleer van Zwingli en Calvijn," 1883, pp. 11–16,
where a very interesting account is given of Zwingli's handling of the theistic
proofs — though Prof. Muller thinks that Zwingli employs them not to establish the existence of God but to increase our knowledge of God. With Zwingli
all knowledge of God rests at bottom on Revelation, which is his way of
saying what Calvin means by his universal *sensus deitatis*. Zwingli says, on
his part, that " a certain seed of knowledge of God is sown [by God] also
among the Gentiles " (iii. 158). But he argues with great force and in very
striking language, that all creation proclaims its maker. Cf. A. Baur, " Zwinglis

to find among the Reformers a formal enumeration of the
proofs for the divine existence.[41]

Theologie," i. 1885, pp. 382–383: "In the doctrine of God, Zwingli distinguishes
two questions: first that of the nature, and secondly that of the existence of
God. The answer to the first question surpasses the powers of the human
mind; that of the second, does not." That the knowledge of the existence of
God, which "may be justified before the understanding" (Muller, p. 13), does
not involve a knowledge of His nature, Zwingli holds, is proved by the wide
fact of polytheism on the one hand and the accompanying fact, on the other,
that natural theism is always purely theoretical (Baur, p. 383).

[41] In the earliest "Loci Communes" (1521) there was no *locus de Deo* at
all. In the second form (1535–1541) there was a *locus de Deo,* but it was not
to it but to the *locus de Creatione* that Melanchthon appended some arguments for the existence of God, remarking ("Corp. Ref.," xxi. 369): "After
the mind has been confirmed in the true and right opinion of God and of Creation by the Word of God itself, it is then both useful and pleasant to seek
out also the vestiges of God in nature and to collect the arguments (*rationes*)
which testify that there is a God." These remarks are expanded in the final
form (1542 +) and reduced to a formal order, for the benefit of "good
morals." The list ("Corp. Ref.," xxi. 641–643) consists of nine "demonstrations, the consideration of which is useful for discipline and for confirming
honest opinions in minds." "The first is drawn from the order of nature itself,
that is from the effects arguing a maker. . . . The second, from the nature of
the human mind. A brute thing is not the cause of an intelligent nature. . . .
The third, from the distinction between good and evil . . . and the sense of
order and number. . . . Fourthly: natural ideas are true: that there is a God,
all confess naturally: therefore this idea is true. . . . The fifth is taken, in
Xenophanes, from the terrors of conscience. . . . The sixth from political society. . . . The seventh is . . . drawn from the series of efficient causes. There
cannot be an infinite recession of efficient causes. . . . The eighth from final
causes. . . . The ninth from prediction of future events." "These arguments,"
he adds, "not only testify that there is a God, but are also *indicia* of providence. . . . They are perspicuous and always affect good minds. Many others
also could certainly be collected; but because they are more obscure, I leave
off." . . . G. H. Lamers, "Geschiedenis der Leer aangande God," 1897, p. 179
[687], remarks: "It should be noted that Melanchthon always when speaking of God, whether as *Spirit* or as *Love,* wishes everywhere to ascribe the
highest value to God's ethical characteristics. Even the particulars, nine in
number, to which he (Doedes, *Inleiding tot de Leer van God,* p. 191) points
as proofs that God's existence must be recognized, show that ethical considerations especially attract him." More justly Herrlinger, "Die Theologie
Melanchthons," 1879, comments on Melanchthon's use of the "proofs" as
follows: "The natural knowledge of God, resting on an innate idea and awakened especially by teleological contemplation of the world, Melanchthon
makes in his philosophical writings, particularly in his physics, the object of
consideration, so that we may speak of the elements of a natural theology

That this God, the conviction of whose existence is part
of the very constitution of the human mind and is justified by
abundant manifestations of Himself in His works and deeds,
is knowable by man, lies on the face of Calvin's entire discussion. The whole argument of the opening chapters of the
" Institutes " is directed precisely to the establishment of this
knowledge of God on an irrefragable basis: and the emphasis
with which the reality and trustworthiness of our knowledge
of God is asserted is equalled only by the skill with which the
development of our native instinct to know God into an actual
knowledge of Him is traced (in chap. i.), and the richness with
which His revelation of Himself in His works and deeds is illustrated by well-chosen and strikingly elaborated instances
(in chap. v.). Of course, Calvin does not teach that sinful man
can of himself attain to the knowledge of God. The noëtic
effects of sin he takes very seriously, and he teaches without
ambiguity that all men have grossly degenerated from the true
knowledge of God (chap. iv.). But this is not a doctrine of the
unknowableness of God, but rather of the incapacitating effects
of sin. Accordingly he teaches that the inadequateness of the
knowledge of God to which alone sinners can attain is itself a
sin. Men's natures prepare them to serve God, God's revelations
of Himself display Him before men's eyes: if men do not know
God they are without excuse and cannot plead their inculpating sinfulness as exculpation. God remains, then, knowable

---

in him " (p. 168). Melanchthon heaps up these arguments, enumerating nine
of them, in the conviction that they will mutually strengthen one another.
Herrlinger thinks that, as they occur in much the same order in more of
Melanchthon's writings than one, they may be arranged on some principle —
possibly beginning with particulars in nature and man, proceeding to human
association, and rising to the entirety of nature (p. 392). He continues (p. 393) :
" Clearly enough it is the teleological argument which in all these proofs is
the real nerve of the proof. Melanchthon accords with Kant, as in the high
place he gives this proof, so also in perceiving that all these proofs find their
strength in the ontological argument, in the innate idea of God, which is the
most direct witness for God's existence. 15. 564; ' The mind reasons of God
from a multitude of vestiges. But this reasoning would not be made if there
were not infused (insita) into the mind a certain knowledge (notitia) or
πρόληψις of God.' Similarly, De Anima, 13. 144, 169." The relation of the proofs
to the innate sensus deitatis here indicated, holds good also for Calvin.

to normal man: it is natural to man to know Him. And if in point of fact He cannot be known save by a supernatural action of the Holy Spirit on the heart, this is because man is not in his normal state and it requires this supernatural action of the Spirit on his heart to restore him to his proper natural powers as man. The " testimony of the Holy Spirit in the heart " does not communicate to man any new powers, powers alien to him as man: it is restorative in its nature and in principle merely recovers his powers from their deadness induced by sin. The knowledge of God to which man attains through the testimony of the Spirit is therefore the knowledge which belongs to him as normal man: although now secured by him only in a supernatural manner, it is in kind, and, so far as it is the product of his innate *sensus deitatis* and the revelation of God in His works and deeds, it is in mode also, natural knowledge of God. Calvin's doctrine of the noëtic effects of sin and their removal by the " testimony of the Spirit," that is to say, by what we call " regeneration," must not then be taken as a doctrine of the unknowableness of God. On the contrary it is a doctrine of the knowableness of God, and supplies only an account of why men in their present condition fail to know Him, and an exposition of how and in what conditions the knowableness of God may manifest itself in man as now constituted in an actually known God. When the Spirit of God enters the heart with recreative power, he says, then even sinful man, his blurred eyes opened, may see God, not merely that there is a God, but what kind of being this God is (I. i. 1; ii. 1; v. 1).

Of course, Calvin does not mean that God can be known to perfection, whether by renewed man, or by sinless man with all his native powers uninjured by sin. In the depths of His being God is to him past finding out; the human intelligence has no plumbet to sound those profound deeps. " His essence " (*essentia*), he says, " is incomprehensible (*incomprehensibilis*); so that His divinity (*numen*) wholly escapes all human senses " (I. v. 1, cf. I. xi. 3); and though His works and the signs by which He manifests Himself may " admonish men of His incomprehensible essence " (I. xi. 3), yet, being men, we are not *capax Dei;* as Augustine says somewhere, we stand disheartened before His greatness and are unable to take Him in (I. v. 9).[42] We can know then only God's glory (I. v. 1), that is to say, His manifested perfections (I. v. 9), by which what He is to us is revealed to us (I. x. 2). What He is in Himself, we cannot know, and all attempts to penetrate into His essence are but cold and frigid speculations which can lead to no useful knowledge. " They are merely toying with frigid speculations," he says (I. ii. 2), " whose mind is set on the question of what God is (*quid sit Deus*), when what it really concerns us to know is rather what kind of a person He is (*qualis sit*) and what is appropriate to His nature (*natura*) " (I. ii. 2).[43] We are to seek God, therefore, " not with audacious inquisitiveness by attempting to search into His essence (*essentia*), which is rather to be adored than curiously investigated; but by contemplating Him in His works, in which He brings Himself near to us and makes Himself familiar and in some measure communicates Himself to us " (I. v. 9). For if we seek to know what He is in Himself (*quis sit apud se*) rather than what kind of a person He is to us (*qualis erga nos*) — which is revealed to us in His attributes (*virtutes*) — we simply lose ourselves in empty and meteoric speculation (I. x. 2).

The distinction which Calvin is here drawing between the knowledge of the *quid* and the knowledge of the *qualis* of God; the knowledge of what He is in Himself and the knowledge of what He is to us, is the ordinary scholastic one and fairly repeats what Thomas Aquinas contends for (" Summa Theol.," i. qu. 12, art. 12), when he tells us that there is no knowledge of God *per essentiam,* no knowledge of His nature, of His *quidditas per speciem propriam;* but we know only *habitudinem ipsius ad creaturas.* There is no implication of nominalism here; nothing, for example, similar to Occam's declaration that we can know neither the divine essence, nor

[42] " In Psalmos," 144: illum non possumus capere, velut sub eius magnitudine deficientes.

[43] We cannot know the quiddity of God: we can only know His quality: that is, to say what His essence is, is beyond our comprehension, but we may know Him in His attributes.

the divine quiddity, nor anything intrinsic to God, nor anything that God is *realiter*. When Calvin says that the Divine attributes describe not what God is *apud se*, but what kind of a person He is *erga nos*,[44] he is not intending to deny that His attributes are true determinations of the divine nature and truly reveal to us the kind of a person He is; he is only refusing to speculate on what God is apart from His attributes by which He reveals Himself to us, and insisting that it is only in these attributes that we know Him at all. He is refusing all *a priori* methods of determining the nature of God and requiring of us to form our knowledge of Him *a posteriori* from the revelation He gives us of Himself in His activities. This He insists is the only knowledge we can have of God, and this the only way we can attain to any knowledge of Him at all. Of what value is it to us, he asks (I. v. 9), to imagine a God of whose working we have had no experience? Such a knowledge only floats in the brain as an empty speculation. It is by His attributes (*virtutes*) that God is manifested; it is only through them that we can acquire a solid and fruitful knowledge of Him. The only right way and suitable method of seeking Him, accordingly, is through His works, in which He draws near to us and familiarizes Himself to us and in some degree communicates Himself to us. Here is not an assertion that we learn nothing of God through His attributes, which represent only determinations of our own. On the contrary, here is an assertion that we obtain through the attributes a solid and fruitful knowledge of God. Only it is not pretended that the attributes of God as revealed in His activities tell us all that God is, or anything that He is in Himself: they only tell us, in the nature of the case, what He is to us. Fortunately, says Calvin, this is what we need to know concerning God, and we may well eschew all speculation concerning His intrinsic nature and content ourselves with knowing what He is in His relation to His

[44] Cf. the passage in ed. 2 and other middle editions in which, refuting the Sabellians, he says that such attributes as strength, goodness, wisdom, mercy, are " epithets " which " show *qualis erga nos sit Deus*," while the personal names, Father, Son, Spirit, are " names " which " declare *qualis apud semetipsum vere sit* " (*Opp*. i. 491).

creatures. His object is, not to deny that God is what He seems
— that His attributes revealed in His dealings with His creatures represent true determination of His nature. His object is
to affirm that these determinations of His nature, revealed
in His dealings with His creatures, constitute the sum of our
real knowledge of God; and that apart from them speculation will lead to no solid results. He is calling us back, not
from a fancied knowledge of God through His activities to the
recognition that we know nothing of Him, that what we call
His attributes are only effects in us: but from an *a priori* construction of an imaginary deity to an *a posteriori* knowledge
of the Deity which really is and really acts. This much we
know, he says, that God is what His works and acts reveal
Him to be; though it must be admitted that His works and acts
reveal not His metaphysical Being but His personal relations
— not what He is *apud se,* but what He is *quoad nos.*

Of the nature of God in the abstract sense, thus — the *quiddity* of God, in scholastic phrase — Calvin has little to say.[45]

[45] Cf. P. J. Muller, " De Godsleer van Calvijn," 1881, p. 26: " A doctrine
of the nature of God as such we do not find in Calvin." To teach us modesty,
Calvin says, God says little of His nature in Scripture, but to teach us what
we ought to know of Him he gives us two epithets — immensity and spirituality (p. 29). Again, " De Godsleer van Zwingli en Calvijn," 1883, pp. 30–31:
" The little that Calvin gives us on this subject (the Divine Essence) limits
itself to the remark that God's essence is ' immense and spiritual ' (I. xiii. 1),
' incomprehensible to us ' (I. v. 1)." Again, p. 38: " If the aprioristic method
[as employed by Zwingli] is thus not favorable to the development of a doctrine of the Trinity, Calvin's aposterioristic method is on the other hand the
reason that his conceptions of the nature of God — apart from the Trinity
— are of less significance than Zwingli's. Since oûr understanding, according
to Calvin, is incapable of grasping *what* God is, it is folly to seek with arrogant curiosity to investigate God's nature, ' which is much rather to be
adored than anxiously to be inquired into ' (*On Romans,* i. 19: ' They are
mad who seek to discover what God is '; *Institutes,* I. ii. 2: ' The essence of
God is rather to be adored than inquired into '). If we nevertheless wish
to solve the problem up to a certain point, let this be done only by means
of the Scriptures in which God has revealed His nature to us so far as it
is needful for us to know it. The warning he gives us is therefore certainly
fully comprehensible, — that ' those who devote themselves to the solving of
the problem of what God is should hold their speculations within bounds;
since it is of much more importance for us to know *what kind of a being God
is* ' (I. ii. 2). How can a man who cannot understand his own nature be able

But his refusal to go behind the attributes which are revealed to us in God's works and deeds, affords no justification to us for going behind them for him and attributing to him against his protest developed conceptions of the nature of the divine essence, which he vigorously repudiates. Calvin has suffered more than most men from such gratuitous attributions to him of doctrines which he emphatically disclaims. Thus, not only has it been persistently asserted that he reduced God, after the manner of the Scotists, to the bare notion of arbitrary Will, without ethical content or determination,[46] but the con-

---

to comprehend God's nature? ' Let us then leave to God the knowledge of Himself: and ' — so Calvin says — ' we leave it to Him when we conceive Him as He has revealed Himself to us, and when we seek to inquire with reference to Him nowhere else than in His Word ' (I. xiii. 21). . . ."

[46] This is fast becoming the popular representation. Cf. e.g. Williston Walker, " John Calvin," 1906, p. 149: " Thus he owed to Scotus, doubtless without realizing the obligation, the thought of God as almighty will, for motives behind whose choice it is as absurd as it is impious to inquire." Again, p. 418: " Whether this Scotist doctrine of the rightfulness of all that God wills by the mere fact of His willing it, leaves God a moral character, it is perhaps useless to inquire." But Calvin does not borrow unconsciously from Scotus: he openly repudiates Scotus. And Calvin is so far from representing the will of God to be independent of His moral character, that he makes it merely the expression of His moral character, and only inscrutable *to us*. Cf. also C. H. Irwin, " John Calvin," 1909, p. 179: " Holding as he did the theory of Duns Scotus, that a thing is right by the mere fact of God willing it, he never questioned whether a course was or was not in harmony with the Divine character, if he was once convinced that it was a course attributed to God in Scripture." But Calvin did not hold that a thing is made right by the mere fact that God wills it but that the fact that God wills it (which fact Scripture may witness to us) is proof enough to us that it is right. The vogue of this remarkable misrepresentation of Calvin's doctrine of God is doubtless due to its enunciation (though in a somewhat more guarded form) by Ritschl (*Jahrbb. für deutsche Theologie*, 1868, xiii. pp. 104 *sq.*). Ritschl's fundamental contention is that the Nominalistic conception of God, crowded out of the Roman Church by Thomism, yet survived in Luther's doctrine of the enslaved will and Calvin's doctrine of twofold predestination (p. 68), which presuppose the idea of " the groundless arbitrariness of God " in His actions. Calvin was far from adopting this principle in theory or applying it consistently. He is aware of and seeks to guard against its dangers (p. 106); but his doctrine of a double predestination (in Ritschl's opinion) proceeds on its assumption: " In spite of Calvin's reluctance, we must judge that the idea of God which governs this doctrine comes to the same thing as the Nominalistic *potentia absoluta* " (p. 107). The same line of reasoning may be read also

tradictory conceptions of a virtual Deism [47] and a developed
Pantheism [48] have with equal confidence been attributed to
him. To instance but a single example, Principal A. M. Fairbairn permits himself to say that " Calvin was as pure, though
not as conscious and consistent a Pantheist as Spinoza." [49] As-

---

in Seeberg, " Text-Book of the History of Doctrines," § 79, 4 (E. T. ii. 1905,
p. 397), who also is compelled to admit that this conception of God is both
repudiated by Calvin and is destructive of his " logical structure "! For a
sufficient refutation of this whole notion see Max Scheibe's " Calvin's Prädestinationslehre," 1897, pp. 113 *sq.* " Calvin," says Scheibe, " could therefore very
properly repudiate the charge of proceeding on the Scoto-nominalistic idea
of the *potentia absoluta* of God. . . . With Calvin, on the contrary, the conception of the will of God as the highest causality has the particular meaning
that God is not determined in His actions by anything lying outside of Himself, . . . while it is distinctly not excluded that God acts by virtue of an inner
necessity, accordant with His nature."

[47] Cf. e.g. A. V. G. Allen, " The Continuity of Christian Thought," 1884,
p. 299: " The God who is thus revealed is a being outside the framework of
the universe, who called the world into existence by the power of His will.
Calvin positively rejected the doctrine of the divine immanence. When he
spoke of that ' dog of a Lucretius ' who mingles God and nature, he may have
also had Zwingli in his mind. In order to separate more completely between
God and man, he interposed ranks of mediators. . . ." Also, p. 302: " In
some respects the system of Calvin not merely repeats but exaggerates the
leading ideas of Latin Christianity. In no Latin writer is found such a determined purpose to reject the immanence of Deity and assert His transcendence
and His isolation from the world. In his conception of God, as absolute arbitrary will, he surpasses Duns Scotus. . . . The separation between God and
humanity is emphasized as it has never been before, for Calvin insists, dogmatically and formally, upon that which had been, to a large extent, hitherto,
an unconscious though controlling sentiment." Prof. Allen had already represented the Augustinian theology as " resting upon the transcendence of
Deity as its controlling principle," — which he explains as a " tacit assumption " of Deism (pp. 3, 171).

[48] Cf. Principal D. W. Simon, " Reconciliation by Incarnation," 1898, p.
282, where he speaks of " the Pantheism . . . with which Calvin is logically
chargeable — strongly as he might resent the imputation — when he says:
' Nothing happens but what He has knowingly and willingly decreed '; ' All
the changes which take place in the world are produced by the secret agency
of the hand of God '; ' Not heaven and earth and inanimate creatures only,
but also the counsels and wills of men are so governed as to move exactly in
the course which He has destined.' " To Dr. Simon providential government of
the world implies pantheism!

[49] " The Place of Christ in Modern Theology," 1893, p. 164. Even H. M.
Gwatkin, " The Knowledge of God," etc., 1906, ii. p. 226, having spoken of

tonishing as such a declaration is in itself, it becomes more astonishing still when we observe the ground on which it is based. This consists essentially in the discovery that the fundamental conception of Calvinism is that " God's is the only efficient will in the universe, and so He is the one ultimate causal reality " [50] — upon which the certainly very true remark is made that " the universalized Divine will is an even more decisive and comprehensive Pantheism than the universalized Divine substance." [51] The logical process by which the Calvinistic conception of the sovereign will of God as the *prima causa rerum* — where the very term *prima* implies the existence and reality of " second causes " — is transmuted into the Pantheising notion that the will of God is the sole efficient cause operative in the universe; or by which the Calvinistic conception of God as the sovereign ruler of the universe whose " will is the necessity of things " is transmuted into the reduction of God, Hegelian-wise, into pure and naked will [52] — although it has apparently appealed to many, is certainly very obscure. In point of fact, when the Calvinist spoke of God as the *prima causa rerum* (the phrase is cited from William Ames [53]) he meant by it only that all that takes place takes place in accordance with the divine will, not that the divine will is the only efficient cause in the universe; and when Calvin quotes

---

Calvin as " taking over from the Scotists " his conception of God as " sovereign and inscrutable will," adds that he needed only to suppose further that " the divine will " is " necessitated as well as inscrutable " to have taught a Pantheistic system. But as he thus allows Calvin did not suppose this, and had just pointed out that Calvin explains that God is not an " absolute and arbitrary power," we probably need not look upon this language as other than rhetorical: it certainly is not true to the facts in either of its members.

[50] P. 164. Cf. p. 430. It is Amesius to whom Dr. Fairbairn appeals to justify this statement: but he misinterprets Amesius.

[51] P. 168.

[52] Cf. Baur, " Die christliche Lehre von der Dreieinigkeit," iii. 1843, pp. 35 *sq.*

[53] " Medulla," I. vii. 38: " Hence the will of God is the first cause of things. ' By thy will they are and were created ' (Apoc. iv. 11). But the will of God, as He wills to operate *ad extra,* does not presuppose the goodness of the object, but by willing posits and makes it good."

approvingly from Augustine — for the words are Augustine's [54] — that " the will of God is the necessity of things," so little is either he or Augustine making use of the words in a Pantheistic sense that he hastens to explain that what he means is only that whatever God has willed will certainly come to pass, although it comes to pass in " such a manner that the cause and matter of it are found in " the second causes (*ut causa et materia in ipsis reperiatur*).[55]

Calvin beyond all question did cherish a very robust faith in the immanence of God. " Our very existence," he says, " is subsistence in God alone " (I. i. 1). He even allows, as Dr. Fairbairn does not fail to inform us, that it may be said with a pious meaning — so only it be the expression of a pious mind — that " nature is God " (I. v. 5, end).[56] But Dr. Fairbairn

[54] The phrase is quoted by Dr. Fairbairn (p. 164) as Calvin's, to support the assertion that he was " as pure . . . a pantheist as Spinoza." But it is cited by Calvin (III. xxiii. 8) from Augustine. The matter in immediate discussion is the perdition of the reprobate.

[55] III. xxiii. 8.

[56] Cf. Muller, " De Godsleer van Zwingli en Calvijn," 1883, p. 26: "Accordingly also Pliny was right — according to Zwingli (*De Provid. Dei Anamnema*, iv. 90) — in calling what he calls God, nature, since the learned cannot adjust themselves to the conceptions of God of the unununderstanding multitude; inasmuch as by nature he meant the power which moves and holds together all things, and that is nothing else but God." Again, on the general question of the charge of Pantheism brought against Zwingli, pp. 26–28: " As is well known, it has been supposed that there is a pantheistic element in Zwingli's *Anamnema*. It cannot be denied that there are some expressions which sound Spinozistic; and for those who see Pantheism in every controversion of fortuitism, Zwingli must of necessity be a Pantheist. Yet if we are to discover Spinozism in Zwingli, we can with little difficulty point to traces of Spinozism also in Paul. Such a passage as the following, for example, would certainly have been subscribed by Paul: ' If anything comes to pass by its own power or counsel, then the wisdom and power of our Deity would be superfluous there. And if that were true, then the wisdom of the Deity would not be supreme, because it would not comprehend and take in all things; and his power would not be omnipotent, because then there would exist power independent of God's power, and in that case there would be another power which would not be the power of the Deity ' (*Opp*. vi. 85). In any case, Zwingli cannot be given the blame of standing apart from the other Reformers on this point. Calvin certainly recognizes (*Inst*. I. v. 5) that — so it occurs, simply — ' it may be said out of a pious mind that nature is God '; (cf. *Zwingli*, vi. a. 619: ' Call God Himself Nature, with the philosophers, the principle from

neglects to mention that Calvin adds at once, that the expression is " crude and unsuitable " (*dura et impropria*), since " nature is rather the order prescribed by God "; and, moreover, noxious, because tending to " involve God confusedly with the inferior course of His works." He neglects also to mention that the statement occurs at the end of a long discussion, in which, after rebuking those who throw an obscuring veil over God, retire Him behind nature, and so substitute nature for Him — Calvin inveighs against the " babble about some sort of hidden inspiration which actuates the whole world," as not only " weak " but " altogether profane," and brands the speculation of a universal mind animating and actuating the world as simply jejune (I. v. 4 and 5). Even his beloved Seneca is reproved for " imagining a divinity transfused through all parts of the world " so that God is all that we see and all that we do not see as well (I. xiii. 1), while the Pantheistic scheme of Servetus is made the object of an extended refutation (II. xiv. 5–8). To ascribe an essentially Pantheistic conception of God to Calvin in the face of such frequent and energetic repudiations of it on his own part [57] is obviously to miss his meaning altogether. If he " may be said to have anticipated Spinoza in his notion of God as *causa immanens*," and " Spinoza may be said . . . to have perfected and reduced to philosophical consistency the Calvinistic conception of Deity " [58] — this can mean nothing more than that Calvin was not a Deist. And in point of fact he repudiated Deism with a vehemence equal to that which he displays against Pantheism. To rob God of the active exercise of His judgment and providence, shutting Him up as an

which all things take their origin, from which the soul begins to be '); although he adds the warning that in matters of such importance ' no expressions should be employed likely to cause confusion.' Danaeus (*Lib.* i. 11 of his *Ethices Christ. lib. tres*) marvels that those who would fain bear the name of Christians, should conceive of God and nature as two different hypostases, since even the heathen philosophers (and like Zwingli, he names Seneca) more truly taught that ' the nature by which we have been brought forth is nothing else than God. . . .' "

[57] Cf. instances in addition at I. xiv. 1, I. xv. 5.
[58] Fairbairn, *op. cit.*, pp. 165–166.

idler (*otiosum*) in heaven, he characterizes as nothing less than
"detestable frenzy," since, says he, "nothing could less comport with God than to commit to fortune the abandoned government of the world, shut His eyes to the iniquities of men
and let them wanton with impunity " (I. iv. 2).[59]

Calvin's conception of God is that of a pure and clear
Theism, in which stress is laid at once on His transcendence
and His immanence, and emphasis is thrown on His righteous government of the world. "Let us bear in mind, then,"
he says as he passes from his repudiation of Pantheism, "that
there is one God, who governs all natures " (I. v. 6, *ad init.*),
" and wishes us to look to Him, — to put our trust in Him, to
worship and call upon Him " (I. v. 6); to whom we can look
up as to a Father from whom we expect and receive tokens of
love (I. v. 3). So little is he inclined to reduce this divine
Father to bare will, that he takes repeated occasion expressly
to denounce this Scotist conception. The will of God, he says,
is to us indeed the unique rule of righteousness and the supremely just cause of all things; but we are not like the
sophists to prate about some sort of "absolute will " of God,
"profanely separating His righteousness from His power,"
but rather to adore the governing providence which presides
over all things and from which nothing can proceed which is
not right, though the reasons for it may be hidden from us
(I. xvii. 2, end). "Nevertheless," he remarks in another place,
after having exhorted his readers to find in the will of God a
sufficient account of things — "nevertheless, we do not betake ourselves to the fiction of absolute power, which, as it is
profane, so ought to be deservedly detestable to us; we do not
imagine that the God who is a law to Himself is *exlegem*, . . .
the will of God is not only pure from all fault, but is the su-

[59] Cf. I. xvi. 1: "To make God a momentaneous creator, who entirely
finished all His work at once, were frigid and jejune," etc. Also the Genevan
Catechism of 1545 (*Opp.* vi. 15–18): The particularization of God's creator-
ship in the creed is not to be taken as indicating that God so created His
works at once that afterwards He rejects the care of them. It is rather so to
be held that the world as it was made by Him at once, so now is conserved
by Him; and He is to remain their supreme governor, etc.

preme rule of perfection, even the law of all laws " (III. xxiii.
2, end).[60] In a word, the will of God is to Calvin the supreme
rule for us, because it is the perfect expression of the divine
perfections.[61]

Calvin thus refuses to be classified as either Deist, Pantheist, or Scotist; and those who would fain make him one or
the other of these have nothing to go upon except that on the
one hand he does proclaim the transcendence of God and
speaks with contempt of men who imagine that divinity is
transfused into every part of the world, and that there is a portion of God not only in us but even in wood and stone (I. xiii.
1, 22); and on the other he does proclaim the immanence of
God and invites us to look upon His works or to descend within
ourselves to find Him who " everywhere diffuses, sustains, animates and quickens all things in heaven and in earth," who,

[60] It is not uncommon for historians of doctrine who are inclined to represent Calvin as enunciating the Scotist principle, therefore, to suggest that
he is scarcely consistent with himself. Thus, e.g., H. C. Sheldon, " History of
Christian Doctrine," 1886, ii. pp. 93–94: " Some, who were inclined to extreme
views of the divine sovereignty, asserted the Scotist maxim that the will of
God is the absolute rule of right. Luther's words are quite as explicit as those
of Scotus. . . . ' The will of God,' says Calvin . . . (*Inst.* III. xxiii. 2). . . .
Calvin, however, notwithstanding this strong statement, suggests after all
that he meant not so much that God's will is absolutely the highest rule of
right, as that it is one which we cannot transcend, and must regard as binding on our own judgment; for he adds, ' We represent not God as lawless,
who is a law to Himself.' " Cf. Victor Monod, " Le problème de Dieu," 1910,
p. 44: " Calvin was assuredly not himself a Scotist; but his disciples were."
Again: " It was in the Calvinistic logic to place God above the moral law
itself, and Calvin was not always able to resist this tendency."

[61] " The goodness of God," says Calvin (" Institutes," II. iii. 5), " is so
united with His divinity that it is as much a necessity to Him to be good as to
be God." Again (*Opp.* viii. 361) : " It would be easier to separate the light of the
sun from its heat, or its heat from its fire, than to separate the power of God
from His righteousness." Cf. Bavinck, " Geref. Dogmatiek," ii. 1897, p. 226,
who, after remarking on Calvin's rejection of the Scotist notion of *potentia
absoluta*, as a " profane invention " — adducing " Institutes," III. xxiii. 1, 5;
I. xvi. 3; II. vii. 5; IV. xvii. 24; " Comm. in Jes.," xxiii. 9, " in Luk.," i. 18, adds:
" The Romanists on this account charge Calvin with limiting and therefore
denying God's omnipotence (Bellarmine, *De gratia et lib. arbitrio*, iii. chap.
15). But Calvin is not denying that God can do more than He actually does,
but only opposing such a *potentia absoluta* as is not connected with His Being
or Virtues, and can therefore do all kinds of inconsistent things."

" circumscribed by no boundaries, by transfusing His own vigor into all things, breathes into them being, life and motion " (I. xiii. 14); while still again he does proclaim the will of God to be inscrutable by such creatures as we are and to constitute to us the law of righteousness, to be accepted as such without murmurings or questionings. In point of fact, all these charges are but several modes of expressing the dislike their authors feel for Calvin's doctrine of the sovereignty of the divine will, which, following Augustine, he declares to be " the necessity of things ": they would fain brand this hated conception with some name of opprobrium, and, therefore, seek to represent Calvin now as hiding God deistically behind His own law, and now as reducing Him to a mere stream of causality, or at least to mere naked will.[62] By thus declining alternately to contradictories they show sufficiently clearly that in reality Calvin's doctrine of God coincides with none of these characterizations.

The peculiarity of Calvin's conception of God, we perceive, is not indefiniteness, but reverential sobriety. Clearing his skirts of all Pantheistic, Deistic, Scotist notions — and turning aside even to repudiate Manichaeism and Anthropomorphism (I. xiii. 1) — he teaches a pure Theism which he looks upon as native to men (I. x. 3). The nature of this one God, he con-

[62] A flagrant example may be found in the long argument of F. C. Baur, " Die christl. Lehre von der Dreieinigkeit," iii. 1843, pp. 35 ff., where he represents the Calvinistic doctrine of election and reprobation as postulating in God a schism between mercy and justice which can be reduced only by thinking of Him as wholly indifferent to good and evil, and indeed of good and evil as a non-existent opposition. If justice is an equally absolute attribute with God as grace, he argues, then evil and good are at one, in that reality cannot be given to the attribute in which the absolute being of God consists without evil. Evil has the same relation to the absolute being of God as good; and " God is in the same sense the principle of evil as of good "; and " as God's justice cannot be without its object, God must provide this object " (pp. 37–38). " But if evil as well as the good is from God, then on that very account evil is good: thus good and evil are entirely indifferent with respect to each other, and the absolute Dualism is resolved into the same absolute arbitrariness (*Willkür*) in which Duns Scotus had placed the absolute Being of God " (p. 38). This, however, is not represented as Calvin's view, but as the consequence of Calvin's view — as drawn out in the Hegelianizing dialectic of Baur.

ceives, can be known to us only as He manifests it in His works (I. v. 9); that is to say, only in His perfections. What we call the attributes of God thus become to Calvin the sum of our knowledge of Him. In these manifestations of His character we see not indeed what He is in Himself, but what He is to us (I. x. 2); but what we see Him to be thus to us, He truly is, and this is all we can know about Him. We might expect to find in the "Institutes," therefore, a comprehensive formal discussion of the attributes, by means of which what God is to us should be fully set before us. This, however, as we have already seen, we do not get.[63] And much less do we get any metaphysical discussion of the nature of the attributes of God, their relation to one another, or to the divine essence of which they are determinations. We must not therefore suppose, however, that we get little or nothing of them, or little or nothing to the point. On the contrary, besides incidental allusions to them throughout the discussion, from which we may glean much of Calvin's conceptions of them, they are made the main subject of two whole chapters, the one of which discusses in considerable detail the revelation of the divine perfections in His works and deeds, the other the revelation made of them in His Word. We have already remarked upon the skill with which Calvin, at the opening of his discussion of the doctrine of God (chap. x.), manages, under color of pointing out the harmony of the description of God given in the Scriptures with the conception of Him we may draw from His works, to bring all he had to say of the divine attributes at once before the reader's eye. The Scriptures, says he, are in essence here merely a plainer (I. x. 1) republication of the general revelation given of God in His works and deeds: they "contain nothing" in their descriptions of God, "but what may be known from the contemplation of the creatures" (I. x. 2, *med.*). And he illustrates this remark by quoting from Moses (Ex. xxxiv. 6), the

[63] Cf. P. J. Muller, "De Godsleer van Zwingli en Calvijn," 1883, p. 40: "Neither in Zwingli nor in Calvin do we meet with a formal 'doctrine of the attributes' or with a classification of the attributes. No doubt it happens that both occasionally name a number of attributes together; and have something to say of each attribute in particular."

Psalms (cxlv.) and the prophets (Jer. ix. 24), passages in which God is richly described, and remarking on the harmony of the perfections enumerated with those which he had in the earlier chapter (v.) pointed out as illustrated in the divine works and deeds. This comparison involves a tolerably full enumeration and some discussion of the several attributes, here on the basis of Scripture, as formerly (chap. v.) on the basis of nature. He does not, therefore, neglect the attributes so much as deal with them in a somewhat indirect manner. And, we may add, in a highly practical way: for here too his zeal is to avoid "airy and vain speculations" of what God is in Himself and to focus attention upon what He is to us, that our knowledge of Him may be of the nature of a lively perception and religious reaction (I. x. 2, *ad init. et ad fin.*).

In a number of passages Calvin brings together a plurality of the attributes — his name for them is "virtues" [64] — and even hints at a certain classification of them. One of the most beautiful of these passages formed the opening words of the first draft of the "Institutes," but fell out in the subsequent revisions — to the regret of some, who consider it, on the whole, the most comprehensive description of God Calvin has given us. [65] It runs as follows: "The sum of holy doc-

[64] *Virtutes Dei,* I. ii. 1; v. 7, 9, 10; x. 2. In xiii. 4, *med.,* he uses the term *attributa.* In xiii. 1, speaking of the divine spirituality and immensity, he used *epitheta.*

[65] Köstlin, as cited, pp. 61–62: " On the other hand, — and this is the most important for us, — there is not given in the *Institutes* any comprehensive presentation of the attributes, especially of the ethical attributes of God, nor is any such attempted anywhere afterwards; the first edition, which began with some comprehensive propositions about God as infinite wisdom, righteousness, mercy, etc., rather raises an expectation of something more in the later, more thoroughly worked out editions of the work: but these propositions fell out of the first edition and were never afterward developed." In the intermediate editions (1543–1550) this paragraph has taken the form of: " Nearly the whole sum of our wisdom — and this certainly should be esteemed true and solid wisdom — consists in two facts: the knowledge of God and of ourselves. The one, now, not only shows that there is one God whom all ought to worship and adore, but at the same time teaches also that this one God is the source of all truth, wisdom, goodness, righteousness, justice, mercy, power, holiness, so that we are taught that we ought to expect and seek all these things from Him, and when we receive them to refer them to Him with

trine consists of just these two points, — the knowledge of God and the knowledge of ourselves. These, now, are the things which we must keep in mind concerning God. First, we should hold fixed in firm faith that He is infinite wisdom, righteousness, goodness, mercy, truth, power (*virtus*), and life, so that there exists no other wisdom, righteousness, goodness, mercy, truth, power, and life (Baruch iii.; James i.), and wheresoever any of these things is seen, it is from Him (Prov. xvi.). Secondly, that all that is in heaven or on earth has been created for His glory (Ps. cxlviii.; Dan. iii.; and it is justly due to Him that everything, according to its own nature, should serve Him, acknowledge His authority, seek His glory, and obediently accept Him as Lord and King (Rom. i.). Thirdly, that He is Himself a just judge, and will therefore be severely avenged on those who depart from His commandments, and are not in all things subject to His will; who in thought, word, and deed have not sought His glory (Ps. vii.; Rom. ii.). In the fourth place that He is merciful and long-suffering, and will receive into His kingdom, the miserable and despised who take refuge in His clemency and trust in His faithfulness; and is ready to spare and forgive those who ask His favor, to succor and help those who seek His aid, and desirous of saving those who put their trust in Him (Ps. ciii.; Is. lv.; Ps. xxv., lxxxv.)." In the first clause of this striking paragraph we have a formal enumeration of God's ethical attributes, which is apparently meant to be generically complete — although in the course of the paragraph other specific forms of attributes here enumerated occur; and all of them are declared to exist in God in an infinite mode. The list contains seven items: wisdom; righteousness; goodness (clemency); mercy (long-sufferingness); truth; power; life.[66] If we compare this list with the enumera-

---

praise and gratitude. The other, however, by manifesting to us our weakness, misery, vanity and foulness, first brings us into serious humility, dejection, diffidence and hatred of ourselves, and then kindles a longing in us to seek God, in whom is to be found every good thing of which we discover ourselves to be so empty and lacking."

[66] In the list which takes the place of this in the middle editions of the "Institutes," the order is different (and scarcely so regular), and "life" is

tion in the famous definition of God in the Westminster
"Shorter Catechism" (Q. 4),[67] we shall see that it is practically the same: the only difference being that Calvin adds to
the general term "goodness" the more specific "mercy," af-
fixes "life" at the end, and omits "holiness," doubtless considering it to be covered by the general term "righteousness."

If just this enumeration does not recur in the "Institutes"
as finally revised, something very like it evidently underlies
more passages than one. Even in the first section of the first
chapter, which has taken its place, we have an enumeration
of the "good things" (*bona*) in God which stand opposed to
our "evil things" (*mala*), that brings together wisdom, power,
goodness, and righteousness: for in God alone, we are told, can
be found "the true light of *wisdom*, solid *power* (*virtus*),
a perfect affluence of all *good* things, and the purity of *righteousness*" (I. i. 1). In the opening section of the next chapter we have two enumerations of the divine perfections, obviously rhetorical, and yet betraying an underlying basis of
systematic arrangement: the later and fuller of these brings together power, wisdom, goodness, righteousness, justice, mercy
— closing with a reference to God's powerful "protection."
God, we are told, "sustains this world by His immense *power*
(*immensa potentia*), governs it by His *wisdom*, preserves it by
His *goodness*, rules over the human race especially by His
righteousness and *justice* (*iudicium*), bears with it in His
mercy, defends it by His *protection* (*praesidium*)." The most
complete enumerations of all, however, are given, when, leaving the intimations of nature, Calvin analyses some Scriptural
passages with a view to drawing out their descriptions of the
divine perfections. His analysis of Exod. xxxiv. 6 is particularly
full (I. x. 2). He finds the divine eternity and self-existence
embodied in the name Jehovah; the divine strength and power
(*virtus et potentia*) expressed in the name Elohim; and in the

---

omitted, while "justice" is added to "righteousness," and "sanctity" appended at the end, and "potentia" substituted for "virtus": "truth; wisdom; goodness; righteousness; *justice;* mercy; (power); *holiness*."

[67] "Wisdom, power, holiness, justice, goodness, and truth."

description itself an enumeration of those virtues which describe God not indeed as He is *apud se,* but as He is *erga nos* — to wit, His clemency, goodness, mercy, righteousness, justice, truth. The strongest claim which this passage has on our interest, however, is the suggestion it bears of a classification of the attributes. The predication to God of eternity and self-existence (*αὐτουσία*) evidently is for Calvin something specifically different from the ascription to Him of those virtues by which are described not what He is *apud se,* but what He shows Himself to be *erga nos.* They in a word belong rather to the quiddity of God than to His *qualitas.* In a subsequent passage (xiii. 1) we have a plainer hint to the same effect. There we are given " two epithets " which we are told are applied by Scripture to the very " essence " of God, in its rare speech concerning His essence — immensity and spirituality.[68] It seems quite clear, then, that Calvin was accustomed to distinguish in his thought between such epithets, describing what God is *apud se,* and those virtues by which He is manifested to us in His relations *erga nos.* That is to say, he distinguishes between what are sometimes called His physical or metaphysical and His ethical attributes: that is to say, between the fundamental modes of the Divine Being and the constitutive qualities of the Divine Person.[69]

If we profit by this hint and then collect the attributes of the two classes as Calvin occasionally mentions them, we shall in effect reconstruct Calvin's definition of God.[70] This

[68] Quod de immensa et spirituali Dei essentia traditur in Scripturis . . . parce de sua essentia disserit, duobus tamen illis quae dixi epithetis. . . .

[69] See the distinction very luminously drawn out by J. H. Thornwell, " Works," i. 1871, pp. 168–169.

[70] Perhaps as near as Calvin ever came to framing an exact definition of God *apud se,* is the description of God in the middle edd. of the " Institutes," vi. 7 (*Opp.* i. 480), summed up in the opening words: " That there is one God of eternal, infinite and spiritual essence, the Scriptures currently declare with plainness." The *essence* of God then is eternal, infinite and spiritual. Cf. " Adv. P. Caroli Calumnias " (*Opp.* vii. 312): " The one God which the Scriptures preach to us we believe in and adore, and we think of Him as He is described to us by them, to wit, as of eternal, infinite and spiritual essence, who also alone has in Himself the power of existence from Himself and bestows it upon His creatures."

would run somewhat as follows: There is but one only true God,[71] a self-existent,[72] simple,[73] invisible,[74] incomprehensible [75] Spirit,[76] infinite,[77] immense,[78] eternal,[79] perfect,[80] in His Being, power,[81] knowledge,[82] wisdom,[83] righteousness,[84] justice,[85] holiness,[86] goodness,[87] and truth.[88] In addition to these more general designations, Calvin employs a considerable number of more specific terms, by which he more precisely expresses his thought and more fully explicates the contents of the several attributes. Thus, for example, he is fond of the term "severity" [89] when he is endeavoring to give expression to God's attitude as a just judge to the wicked; and he is fond of setting in contrast with it the corresponding term "clemency" [90] to express His attitude towards the repentant sinner. It is especially the idea of "goodness" which he thus draws out into its several particular manifestations. Beside the term

[71] unicus et verus Deus, I. ii. 2; unicus Deus, xii. 1; xiii. 2; xiv. 2; unus Deus, ii. 1; v. 6; x. 3; xii. 1; verus Deus, x. 3; xiii. 2; unitas Dei, xiii. 1, etc.

[72] a se ipso principium habens, v. 6; αὐτουσία, x. 2; αὐτουσία, id est a se ipso existentia, xiv. 3.

[73] simplex Dei essentia, xiii. 2; simplex et individua essentia Dei, xiii. 2; una simplexque Deitas, "Adv. Val. Gent." (*Opp.* ix. 365).

[74] invisibilis Deus, I. v. 1; II. vi. 4 (made visible in Christ, so also II. ix. 1); invisibilis I. xi. 3 (of Holy Spirit).

[75] incomprehensibilis, v. 1; xi. 3 (in xiii. 1 apparently used for immensa).

[76] spiritualis Dei essentia, xiii. 1; spiritualis natura, xiii. 1.

[77] in Deo residet bonorum infinitas, i. 1 (cf. ed. 1, i. *ad init.* [p. 42], infinitas).

[78] eius immensitas, xiii. 1; immensitas, xiii. 1; immensa Dei essentia, xiii. 1.

[79] aeternitas, v. 6; x. 2; xiii. 18; xiv. 3; aeternus [Deus], v. 6.

[80] exacta iusticiae, sapientiae, virtutis eius perfectio, i. 2.

[81] potentia, ii. 1; v. 3, 6, 8; x. 2; immensa potentia, ii. 1; omnipotentia, xvi. 3; omnipotens, xvi. 3; virtus, i. 1, 3; v. 1, 6, 10; x. 2; virtus et potentia, x. 2.

[82] notitia, III. xxi. 5; praescientia, III. xxi. 5.

[83] sapientia, i. 1, 3; ii. 1; v. 1, 2, 3, 8, 10; mirifica sapientia, v. 2.

[84] iustitia, ii. 1; v. 10; x. 2; xv. 1; III. xxiii. 4; iustitiae puritas, i. 1; iustitia iudiciumque, ii. 1.

[85] iudicium, ii. 2; x. 2; iustitia iudiciumque, ii. 1; iustus iudex, ii. 2.

[86] sanctitas, x. 2; puritas, i. 3; divina puritas, i. 2.

[87] bonitas, ii. 1; v. 3, 6, 9, 10; x. 1, 2; xv. 1; bonus, ii. 2.

[88] veritas, x. 2; Deus verax, III. xx. 26.

[89] severitas, ii. 2; v. 7, 10; xvii. 1.

[90] clementia, v. 7, 8, 10; x. 2.

"clemency" he sets the still greater word "mercy," or "pity," [91] and by the side of this again he sets the even greater word "grace," [92] while the more general idea of "goodness" he develops by the aid of such synonyms as "beneficence" [93] and "benignity," [94] and almost exhausts the capacity of the language to give expression to his sense of the richness of the Divine goodness.[95] God is "good and merciful" (ii. 2), "benign and beneficent" (v. 7), "the fount and source of all good" (ii. 2), their fecund "author" (ii. 2), whose "will is prone to beneficence" (x. 1), and in whom dwells a "perfect affluence," nothing less than an "infinity," of good things. And therefore he looks upwards to this God not only as our Lord (ii. 1) the Creator (ii. 1), Sustainer (ii. 1), and Governor (ii. 1) of the world — and more particularly its moral governor (ii. 2), its "just judge" (ii. 2) — but more especially as our "defender and protector," [96] our Father [97] who is also our Lord, in whose "fatherly indulgence" [98] we may trust.

There is in the "Institutes" little specific exposition of the manner in which we arrive at the knowledge of these attributes. The works of God, we are told, illustrate particularly His wisdom (v. 2) and His power (v. 6). But His power, we are further told, leads us on to think of His eternity and His self-existence, "because it is necessary that He from whom everything derives its origin, should Himself be eternal and have the ground of His being in Himself": [99] while we must

[91] misericordia, ii. 1; x. 2; misericors, ii. 2 (bonus et misericors).

[92] gratia, v. 3.

[93] beneficus, v. 7; voluntas ad beneficentiam proclivis, x. 1; Dei favor et beneficentia, xvii. 1.

[94] benignitas, v. 7; benignus et beneficus, v. 7.

[95] bonus et misericors, ii. 2; benignus et beneficus, v. 7; bonorum omnium fons et origo, ii. 2; bonorum omnium autor, ii. 2; voluntas ad beneficentiam proclivis, x. 1; bonorum omnium perfecta affluentia, i. 1; in Deo residet bonorum infinitas, i. 1.

[96] tutor et protector, ii. 2.

[97] Dominus et Pater, ii. 2.

[98] paterna indulgentia, v. 7.

[99] v. 6: iam ipsa potentia nos ad cogitandam eius aeternitatem deducit; quia aeternum esse, et a se ipso principium habere necesse est unde omnium trahunt originem.

posit His goodness to account for His will to create and preserve the world.[100] By the works of providence God manifests
primarily His benignity and beneficence; and in His dealing
with the pious, His clemency, with the wicked His severity [101]
— which are but the two sides of His righteousness: although,
of course, " His power and wisdom are equally conspicuous." [102]
It is precisely the same body of attributes which are ascribed
to God in the Scriptures,[103] and that not merely in such a passage as Ex. xxxiv. 6, to which we have already alluded, but
everywhere throughout their course (x. 1, *ad fin.*). Psalm cxlv.,
for example, so exactly enumerates the whole list of God's perfections that scarcely one is lacking. Jeremiah ix. 24, while not
so full, is to the same effect. Certainly the three perfections
there mentioned are the most necessary of all for us to know —
the divine " mercy in which alone consists all our salvation;
His justice, which is exercised on the wicked every day, and
awaits them more grievously still in eternal destruction; His
righteousness, by which the faithful are preserved and most
lovingly supported." Nor, adds Calvin, is there any real omission here of the other perfections — " either of His truth, or
power, or holiness, or goodness." " For how could we be assured, as is here required, of His righteousness, mercy and
justice, unless we were supported by His inflexible veracity?
And how could we believe that He governs the world in justice
and righteousness unless we acknowledged His power? And
whence proceeds His mercy but from His goodness? And if all
His ways are justice, mercy, righteousness, certainly holiness
also is conspicuous in them." The divine power, righteousness,
justice, holiness, goodness, mercy, and truth are here brought
together and concatenated one with the others, with some indication of their mutual relations, and with a clear intimation
that God is not properly conceived unless He is conceived in
all His perfections. Any description of Him which omits more
or fewer of these perfections, it is intimated, is justly chargeable with defect. Similarly when dealing with those more fundamental " epithets " by which His essence is described (xiii.

[100] *Do.*   [101] v. 7.   [102] v. 8.   [103] x. 2.

1), he makes it plain that not to embrace them all in our
thought of God, and that in their integrity, is to invade His
majesty: the fault of the Manichaeans was that they broke up
the unity of God and restricted His immensity.[104]

There is no lack in Calvin's treatment of the attributes,
then, of a just sense of their variety or of the necessity of
holding them all together in a single composite conception
that we may do justice in our thought to God. He obviously
has in mind the whole series of the divine perfections in clear
and just discrimination, and he accurately conceives them as
falling apart into two classes, the one qualities of the divine
essence, the other characteristics of the divine person — in a
word, essential and personal attributes: and he fully realizes
the relation of these two classes to each other, and as well the
necessity of embracing each of the attributes in its integrity in
our conception of God, if we are to do any justice whatever to
that conception.

What seems to be lacking in Calvin's treatment of the
attributes is detailed discussion of the notion imbedded in each
several attribute and elaboration of this notion as a necessary
element in our conception of God. Calvin employs the terms
unity, simplicity, self-existence, incomprehensibility, spirituality, infinity, immensity, eternity, immutability, perfection,
power, wisdom, righteousness, justice, holiness, goodness, benignity, beneficence, clemency, mercy, grace,[105] as current terms

---

[104] I. xiii. 1: Certe hoc fuit et Dei unitatem abrumpere, et restringere
immensitatem.

[105] These are fairly brought together by P. J. Muller, " De Godsleer van
Calvijn," 1881, pp. 39–44. The third section of the " Instruction " (French, 1537)
or " Catechism " (Latin, 1538) is almost a complete treatise in brief on the attributes. As in the " Institutes," on which this " Catechism " is based, the attributes derived from the study of the Divine Works are first enumerated and
then those derived from the Word. As to the former, Calvin says: " For we
contemplate in this universe of things, the *immortality* of our God, from which
has proceeded the commencement and origin of all things; His *power*
(*potentia*) which has both made and now sustains so great a structure
(*moles,* machine); His *wisdom,* which has composed and perpetually governs so great and confused a variety in an order so distinct; His *goodness,*
which has been the cause to itself that all these things were created and now
exist; His *justice,* which wonderfully manifests itself in the defense of the

bearing well-understood meanings, and does not stop to develop their significance except by incidental remarks.[106] The
confidence which he places in their conveyance of their meaning seems to be justified by the event; although, no doubt,
much of the effect of their mere enumeration is due to the remarkable lucidity of Calvin's thought and style: he uses his
terms with such consistency and exactness, that they become
self-defining in their context. We are far, then, from saying
that his method of dealing with the attributes, by mere allusion as we might almost call it, is inadequate for the practical
religious purpose for which he was writing: and certainly it
is far more consonant with the literary rather than scholastic
form he gives his treatise. When we suggest, then, that from
the scholastic point of view it seems that it is precisely at this
point that Calvin's treatment of the attributes falls somewhat
short of what we might desire, we must not permit to slip
out of our memory that Calvin expressly repudiates the scholastic point of view and is of set purpose simple and practical.[107]

---

good and the punishment of the wicked; His *mercy,* which, that we may be
called to repentance, endures our wickedness with so great a clemency " (*Opp.*
v. 324–325).

[106] Observe the admirable discussion of the omnipotence of God after
this incidental fashion in " Institutes," I. xvi. 3.

[107] Cf. P. J. Muller, " De Godsleer van Calvijn," 1881, p. 45: " No doubt
we should expect a doctrine of the attributes, when we hear him say that
God has revealed Himself in His *virtutes,* but we should bear in mind
that Calvin (although not always free himself from philosophical influences)
renounces philosophical treatment of theological questions, and is extremely
practical, so that it is to him, for example, less important to seek a connection between the several attributes, than to point out what we may learn
from them not so much of God, as for ourselves and our lives." — So, also,
" De Godsleer van Zwingli en Calvijn," 1883, pp. 46–47: " Calvin does not recommend such a ' knowledge of God ' as merely ' raises an idle speculation in
the brain,' but such an one ' as should be firm and fruitful also in consequences,
which can be expected only of the knowledge which has its seat in the
heart ' (I. v. 9). He considers the knowledge of the nature and of the attributes of God more a matter of the heart than of the understanding; and such
knowledge not only must arouse us to ' the service of God, but must also
plant in us the hope of a future life ' (I. v. 10). In his extreme practicality —
as the last remark shows us — Calvin rejected the philosophical treatment of
the question. The Scriptures, for him the fountain of the knowledge of God,
he takes as his guide in his remarks on the attributes." Compare what Lob-

He does not seek to obtain for himself or to recommend to others such a knowledge of God as merely " raises idle speculation in the brain "; but such as " shall be firm and fruitful " and have its seat in the heart. He purposely rejects, therefore, the philosophical mode of dealing with the attributes and devotes himself to awakening in the hearts of his readers a practical knowledge of God, a knowledge which functions first in the fear (*timor*) of God and then in trust (*fiducia*) in Him.

And here we must pause to take note of this two-fold characterization of the religious emotion, corresponding, as it does in Calvin's conception, to the double aspect in which God is contemplated by those who know Him. God is our Lord, in whose presence awe and reverence become us; God is our Father, to whom we owe trust and love. Fear and love — both must be present where true piety is: for, says Calvin, what " I call piety (*pietas*) is that reverence combined with love of God, which a knowledge of His benefits produces " (I. ii. 1). In the form he has given this statement the element of reverence (*reverentia*) appears to be made the formative element: piety is reverence, although it is not reverence without love. But if it is not reverence in and of itself but only the reverence which is informed by love, love after all may be held to become the determining element of true piety. And Calvin does not hesitate to declare with the greatest emphasis that the apprehension of God as deserving of our worship and adoration — in a word as our Lord — *simpliciter,* does not suffice to produce true piety: that is not born, he says, until " we are persuaded that God is the fountain of all that is good and cease to seek for good elsewhere than in Him " (*ibid.*); that is to say, until we apprehend Him as our Father as well as our Lord. " For," adds he, " until men feel that they owe everything to God,

---

stein says in his " Études sur la doctrine Chrétienne de Dieu," 1907, p. 113: " The passages of Calvin's *Institutes* devoted to the idea of the divine omnipotence are inspired and dominated by the living interest of piety, which gives to their discussions a restrained emotion and a warmth to which no reader can remain insensible."

that they are cherished by His paternal care, that He is the author to them of all good things and nothing is to be sought out of Him, they will never subject themselves to Him in willing obedience (*observantia, reverent* obedience); or rather I should say, unless they establish for themselves a solid happiness in Him they will never devote themselves to Him without reserve truly and heartily (*vere et ex animo totos*)." And then he proceeds (I. ii. 2) to expound at length how the knowledge of God should first inspire us with fear and reverence and then lead us to look to Him for good. The first thought of Him awakes us to our dependence on Him as our Lord: any clear view of Him begets in us a sense of Him as the fountain and origin of all that is good — such as in anyone not depraved by sin must inevitably arouse a desire to adhere to Him and put his trust (*fiducia*) in Him — because he must recognize in Him a guardian and protector worthy of complete confidence (*fides*). " Because he perceives Him to be the author of all good, in trial or in need," he proceeds, still expounding the state of mind of the truly pious man, " he at once commits himself to His protection, expectant of His help; because he is convinced that He is good and merciful, he rests on Him in assured trust (*fiducia*), never doubting that a remedy is prepared in His clemency for all his ills; because he recognizes Him as Lord and Father, he is sure that he ought to regard His government in all things, revere His majesty, seek His glory, and obey His behests; because he perceives Him to be a just judge, armed with severity for punishing iniquities, he keeps His tribunal always in view, and in fear restrains and checks himself from provoking His wrath. And yet, he is not so terrified by the sense of His justice, that he wishes to escape from it, even if flight were possible: rather he embraces Him not less as the avenger of the wicked than as the benefactor of the pious, since he perceives it to belong to His glory not less that there should be meted out by Him punishment to the impious and iniquitous, than the reward of eternal life to the righteous. Moreover, he restrains himself from sinning not merely from fear of punishment, but be-

THE DOCTRINE OF GOD

cause he loves and reverences God as a father (*loco patris*) and honors and worships Him as Lord (*loco domini*), and even though there were no hell he would quake to offend Him."

We have quoted this eloquent passage at length because it throws into prominence, as few others do, Calvin's deep sense not merely of reverence but of love towards God. To him true religion always involves the recognition of God not only as Lord but also as Father. And this double conception of God is present whether this religion be conceived as natural or as revealed. " The knowledge of God," says he (I. x. 2, *ad fin.*), " which is proposed to us in the Scriptures is directed to no other end than that which is manifested to us in the creation: to wit, it invites us first to the fear of God, then to trust in Him; so that we may learn both to serve Him in perfect innocence of life and sincere obedience, and as well to rest wholly in His goodness." That is, in a word, the sense of the divine Fatherhood is as fundamental to Calvin's conception of God as the sense of His sovereignty. Of course, he throws the strongest conceivable emphasis on God's Lordship: the sovereignty of God is the hinge of His thought of God. But this sovereignty is ever conceived by him as the sovereignty of God our Father. The distinguishing feature of Calvin's doctrine of God is, in a word, precisely the prevailing stress he casts on this aspect of the conception of God. It is a Lutheran theologian who takes the trouble to make this plain to us. " The chief elements which are dealt with by Calvin in the matter of the religious relation," he says, " are summed up in the proposition: God is our Lord, who has made us, and our Father from whom all good comes; we owe Him, therefore, honor and glory, love and trust. We must, so we are told in the exposition of the Decalogue in the first edition of the *Institutes,* just as we are told in Luther's Catechism — we must ' fear and love ' God. . . . [But] we find in the *Institutes,* and, indeed, particularly in the final edition, expressions in which the second of these elements is given the preference. . . . We may find, indeed, in Luther and the Lutherans, the element of fear in piety still more emphasized

than in Calvin. . . ." [108] In a word, with all his emphasis on
the sovereignty of God, Calvin throws an even stronger emphasis on His love: and his doctrine of God is preëminent
among the doctrines of God given expression in the Reformation age in the commanding place it gives to the Divine
Fatherhood. " Lord and Father " — fatherly Sovereign, or sovereign Father — that is how Calvin conceived God.

It was precisely because Calvin conceived of God not only
as Lord, but also as Father, and gave Him not merely his
obedience but his love, that he burned with such jealousy for
His honor. Everything that tended to rob God of the honor due
Him was accordingly peculiarly abhorrent to him. We cannot
feel surprised, therefore, that he devotes so large a portion of
his discussion of the doctrine of God to repelling that invasion of the divine rights which was wrought by giving the
worship due to Him alone to others, and particularly to idols,
the work of man's own hand. His soul filled with the vision of
the majesty of a God who will not give His glory to another,
and his heart aflame with a sense of the Fatherly love he was
receiving from this great God, the Lord of heaven and earth,
he turned with passionate hatred from the idolatrous rites into
which the worship of the old Church had so largely degenerated, and felt nothing so pressingly his duty as to trace out the
fallacies in the subtle pleas by which men sought to justify
them to themselves, and so far as lay within him to rescue
those who looked to him for guidance from such dreadful profanation of the divine majesty. As a practical man, with his
mind on the practical religious needs of the time, this " brutal
stupidity " of men, desiring visible figures of God — who is an
invisible Spirit — corrupting the divine glory by fabricating
for themselves gods out of wood, or stone, or gold, or silver, or
any other dead stuff, seemed to him to call for rebuke as little
else could. The principle on which he proceeds in his rebuke
of idolatry is expressed by himself in the words, that to attribute to anything else than to the one true God, anything that
is proper to divinity is " to despoil God of His honor and to

[108] Köstlin, as cited, pp. 424–425.

violate His worship." [109] So deeply rooted is the jealousy for
the divine honor given expression in this principle not only in
Calvin's thought, but in that of the whole tendency of thought
which he represents, that it may well be looked upon as a determinative trait of the Reformed attitude — which has therefore been described as characterized by a determined protest
against all that is pagan in life and worship. [110]

Certainly the zeal of Calvin burned warmly against the
dishonor he felt was done to God by the methods of worshipping Him prevalent in the old Church. God has revealed Himself not only in His Word, but also in His works, as the one
only true God. But the vanity of man has ever tended to corrupt the knowledge of God and to invent gods many and lords
many, and not content with that, has sunk even to the degradation of idolatry — fabricating gods of wood or stone,

[109] I. xii. 1: Quod autem priore loco posui, tenendum est, nisi in uno
Deo resideat quidquid proprium est divinitatis, honore suo ipsum spoliari,
violarique eius cultum.

[110] Cf. Schweizer, " Glaubenslehre d. rf. Kirche," i. 1844, p. 16: " Only an
essentially complete survey of the particular Reformed dogmas can lead to
the fundamental tendency to which they all belong. This can be represented
as a dominating protest against all that is pagan." P. 25: " Protestation against
the deification of the creature is therefore everywhere the dominating, all-
determining impulse of Reformed Protestantism." (Cf. pp. 40, 59, and the
exposition there of how this principle worked to prevent all half-measures
and inconsequences in the development of Reformed thought.) Cf. also
Scholten, " De Leer der Hervormde Kerk," 1870, ii. pp. 12, 13: " Schweizer
finds the characteristic of the Reformed doctrine in the Biblical principle of
man's entire dependence on God, together with protestation on the ground
of original Christianity against any heathenish elements which had seeped
into the Church and its teaching. That in the opposition of the Reformed to
Rome, such an aversion to all that is heathenish exhibited itself, history tells
us, and cannot be denied." P. 17: " The maintenance of the sovereignty of
God is the point from which, with the Reformed, everything proceeds. Hence
as well their protest against the pagan element in the Romish worship. . . ."
Pp. 150–151: " What led Luther to repudiate the intercession and adoration
of Mary and the saints was primarily the conviction that the saints are sinners and their intercession and merits, therefore, cannot avail us, cannot cover
our sins before God. Zwingli and Calvin take their starting point here, from
the conception of *God* and deny that the love of *God* can be dependent
on any intercession, and reject the worship of Mary and the honoring of the
saints as a deification of creatures, and an injury to the sovereignty of God "
(cf. also pp. 139–140; 16 *sq.*).

gold or silver, or some other dead stuff. It is, of course, not idolatry in general, but the idolatry of the Church of Rome that Calvin has his eye particularly upon, as became him as a practical man, absorbed in the real problems of his time. He therefore particularly animadverts upon the more refined forms of idolatry, ruthlessly reducing them to the same level in principle with the grossest. God does not compare idols with idols, he says, as if one were better and another worse: He repudiates all without exception — all images, pictures, or any other kind of tokens by which superstitious people have imagined He could be brought near to them (I. xi. 1, end). He embraces all forms of idolatry, however, in his comprehensive refutation; he even expressly adverts to the "foolish subterfuge" (inepta cautio) of the Greeks, who allow painted but not graven images (I. xi. 4, end). Or rather he broadens his condemnation until it covers even the false conceptions of God which we frame in our imaginations (I. xi. 4, ad init.), substituting them for the revelations He makes of Himself: for the "mind of man," he says, "is, if I may be allowed the expression, a perpetual factory of idols" (I. xi. 8). Thus he returns to "the Puritan conception" which we have seen him already announcing in former chapters, and proclaims as his governing principle (I. xi. 4, med.) that "all modes of worship which men excogitate from themselves are detestable." [111]

He does not content himself, however, with proclaiming and establishing this principle. He follows the argument for the use of images in worship into its details and refutes it item by item. To the plea that "images are the books of the illiterate" and by banishing them he is depriving the people of their best means of instruction, he replies that no doubt they do teach something, but what they teach is falsehood: God is not as they represent Him (§§ 5–7). To the caveat that no one worships the idols, but the deity through the idols, that they are never called "gods" and that what is offered them is δουλεία, not λατρεία — he replies that all this is distinction

[111] Ut hoc fixum sit, detestabiles esse omnes cultus quos a se ipsis homines excogitant.

without difference; the Jews in their idolatry reasoned in a
similar manner, and it is easy to erect a distinction between
words, but somewhat more difficult to establish a real difference in fact (§§ 9–11). To the reproach that he is exhibiting a
fanaticism against the representative arts, he rejoins that such
is far from the case; he is only seeking to protect these arts
from abusive application to wrong purposes (§§ 12, 13). And
finally to the appeal to the decisions of the Council of Nice of
786–787 favorable to image-worship, he replies by an exposure
of the " disgusting insipidities " and " portentous impiety " of
the image-worshipping Fathers at that Council (§§ 14 *sq.*).
The discussion is then closed (chap. xii.), with a chapter in
which he urges that God alone is to be worshipped and only in
the way of His own appointment; and above all that His glory
is not to be given to another. Thus the ever-present danger
of idolatry, as evidenced in the gross practices of Rome, is
itself invoked to curb speculation on the nature of the Godhead and to throw men back on the simple and vitalizing
revelation of the word of a God like us in that He is a spiritual
person, but unlike us in that He is clothed in inconceivable
majesty. These two epithets — immensity and spirituality —
thus stand out as expressing the fundamental characteristics of
the divine essence to Calvin's thinking: His immensity driving
us away in terror from any attempt to measure Him by our
sense; His spirituality prohibiting the entertainment of any
earthly or carnal speculation concerning Him (I. xiii. 1).

In the course of this discussion there are three matters
on which Calvin somewhat incidentally touches which seem
too interesting to be passed over unremarked. These are what
we may call his philosophy of idolatry, his praise of preaching, and his recommendation of art.

His philosophy of idolatry (I. xi. 8, 9) takes the form of a
psychological theory of its origin. While allowing an important
place in the fostering and spread of idolatry to the ancient
customs of honoring the dead and superstitiously respecting
their memory, he considers idolatry more ancient than these
customs, and the product of debased thoughts of God. He

enumerates four stages in its evolution. First, the mind of
man, filled with pride and rashness, dares to imagine a god
after its own notion; [112] and laboring in its dullness and sunk in
the crassest ignorance, naturally conceives a vain and empty
spectre for God. Next, man attempts to give an outward form
to the god he has thus inwardly excogitated; so that the hand
brings forth the idol which the mind begets. Worship follows
hard on this figment; for, when they suppose they see God in
the images, men naturally worship Him in them. Finally, their
minds and eyes alike being fixed upon the images, men begin to
become more imbruted, and stand amazed and lost in wonder
before the images, as if there were something of divinity inherent in them. Thus easy Calvin supposes to be the descent
from false notions of deity to the superstitious adoration of
stocks and stones, and thus clearly and reiteratedly he discovers the roots of idolatry in false conceptions of God and proclaims its presence in principle wherever men permit themselves to think of God otherwise, in any particular, than He
has revealed Himself in His works and Word.

As we read Calvin's energetic arraignments of the sinfulness of our deflected conceptions of God — the essential idolatry of the imaginary images we form of Him — and our duty
diligently to conform our ideas of God to the revelations of
Himself He has graciously given us, we are reminded of an
eloquent picture which the late Professor A. Sabatier once
drew [113] of a concourse of professing Christians coming together
to worship in common a God whom each conceives after his
own fashion. Anthropomorphists, Deists, Agnostics, Pantheists
— all bow alike before God and worship, says Prof. Sabatier;
and the worship of one and all is acceptable, equally acceptable, to God. Not so, rejoins M. Bois: [114] and there is not a less
admirable spectacle in the world than this. Calvin was of
M. Bois's opinion. To his thinking we have before us in such a

[112] pro captu suo.

[113] In his " Esquisse d'une philosophie de la religion," 1897, pp. 303–304.
The chapter of which this is a part was published separately in a slightly different form in 1888, with the title: " La vie intime des dogmes et leur puissance
d'évolution."   [114] H. Bois: " De la connaissance religieuse," 1894, p. 36.

concourse only a company of idolaters — each worshipping not the God that is but the god who in the pride of his heart he has made himself. And to each and all Calvin sends out the cry of, Repent! turn from the god you have made yourself and serve the God that is!

It is in the midst of his response to the specious plea that images are the books of the illiterate and the only means of instruction available for them that Calvin breaks out into a notable eulogy on preaching as God's ordained means of instructing His people (I. xi. 7). Even though images, he remarks, were so framed that they bore to the people a message which might be properly called divine — which too frequently is very far from the case — their childish suggestions (*naeniae*) are little adapted to convey the special teaching which God wishes to be taught His people in their solemn congregations, and has made the common burden of His Word and Sacraments — from which it is to be feared, however, the minds of the people are fatally distracted as their eyes roam around to gaze on their idols. Do you say the people are too rude and ignorant to profit by the heavenly message and can be reached only by means of the images? Yet these are those whom the Lord receives as His own disciples, honors with the revelation of His celestial philosophy, and has commanded to be instructed in the saving mysteries of His kingdom! If they have fallen so low as not to be able to do without such " books " as images supply, is not that only because they have been defrauded of the teaching which they required? The invention of images, in a word, is an expedient demanded not by the rudeness of the people so much as by the dumbness of the priests. It is in the true preaching of the Gospel that Christ is really depicted — crucified before our eyes openly, as Paul testifies: and there can be no reason to crowd the churches with crucifixes of wood and stone and silver and gold, if Christ is faithfully preached as dying on the cross to bear our curse, expiating our sins by the sacrifice of His body, cleansing us by His blood and reconciling us to God the Father. From this simple proclamation more may be learned than from a thousand crosses.

Thus Calvin vindicates to the people of God their dignity as
God's children taught by His Spirit, their right to the Gospel
of grace, their capacity under the instruction of the Spirit to
receive the divine message, and the central place of the preaching of the atonement of Christ in the ordinances of the sanctuary.

It seems the more needful that we should pause upon Calvin's remarks on art in this discussion long enough to take in
their full significance, that this is one of the matters on which
he has been made the object of persistent misrepresentation.
It has been made the reproach of the Reformation in general
and of Calvinism in particular that they have morosely set
themselves in opposition to all artistic development, while
Calvin himself has been inveighed against as the declared
enemy of all that is beautiful in life. Thus, for example, Voltaire in his biting verse has explained that the only art which
flourished at Geneva (where men cyphered but could not
laugh) was that of the money-reckoners: and that nothing was
sung there but the antique concerts of " the good David " in
the belief " that God liked bad verses." Even professed students of the subject have passionately assailed Calvin as insensible to the charms of art and inimical to all forms of artistic expression. Thus, M. D. Courtois, the historian of sacred
music among the French Reformed, permits himself, quite
contrary to the facts in the sphere of his own especial form of
art, to say that Calvin "nourished a holy horror for all that
could resemble an intrusion of art into the religious domain ";
and M. E. Müntz, who writes on " Protestantism and Art,"
exclaims that " in Calvin's eyes beauty is tantamount to idolatry "; while M. O. Douen, the biographer of Clément Marot,
brands Calvin as " anti-liberal, anti-artistic, anti-human, anti-
Christian." The subject is too wide to be entered upon here in
its general aspects. Professor E. Doumergue and Dr. A. Kuyper
have made all lovers of truth their debtors by exposing to the
full the grossness of such calumnies.[115]

[115] See: A. Kuyper, " Calvinisme en de Kunst," 1888; " Calvinism," Stone
Lectures for 1898–1899, Lecture v.; E. Doumergue, " L'Art et le sentiment dans

In point of fact Calvin was a lover and fosterer of the arts, counting them all divine gifts which should be cherished, and expressly declaring even of those which minister only to pleasure that they are by no means to be reckoned superfluous and are certainly not to be condemned as if forsooth they were inimical to piety. Even in the heat of this arraignment of the misuse of art-representations in idolatry which is at present before us, we observe that he turns aside to guard himself against being misunderstood as condemning art-representations in general (§ 12). The notion that all representative images are to be avoided he brands as superstition and declares of the products both of the pictorial and of the sculptural arts that they are the gifts of God granted to us for His own glory and our good. "I am not held," he says, "in that superstition, which considers that no images at all are to be endured. I only require that since sculptures and pictures are gifts of God, the use of them should be pure and legitimate; lest what has been conferred on us by God for His own glory and for our good, should not only be polluted by preposterous abuse, but even turned to our injury." Here is no fanatical suspicion of beauty: no harsh assault upon art. Here is rather the noblest possible estimate of art as conducive in its right employment to the profit of man and the glory of the God who gives it. Here is only an anxiety manifested to protect such a noble gift of God from abuse to wrong ends. Accordingly in the "Table or brief summary of the principal matters contained in this Institution of the Christian religion," which was affixed to the French edition of 1560, the contents of this section are described as follows: "That when idolatry is condemned, this is not to abolish the arts of painting and sculpture, but to require that the use of both shall be pure and legitimate; and we are not to amuse ourselves by representing God by some

l'oeuvre de Calvin," 1902 (the second "Conference" is on "Painting in the Work of Calvin"); "Jean Calvin," etc., ii. 1902, pp. 479–487; "Calvin et l'art" in *Foi et Vie*, 16 March, 1900. Cf. also H. Bavinck, "De Algemeene Genade," 1894; also article "Calvin and Common Grace" in *The Princeton Theological Review*, 1909, vii. pp. 437–465.

visible figure, but only such things as may be objects of sight." [116] Calvin, then, does not at all condemn art, but only pleads for a pure and reverent employment of art as a high gift of God, to be used like all others of God's gifts so as to profit man and glorify the Great Giver.

If we inquire more closely what he held to be a legitimate use of the pictorial arts, we must note first of all that he utterly forbids all representations of God in visible figures.[117] This prohibition he rests on two grounds: first, God Himself forbids it; and secondly, " it cannot be done without some deformation of His glory," — in which we catch again the note of zeal against everything which detracts from the honor of God. To attempt the portraiture of God is, thus, to Calvin, not merely to disobey God's express command, but also to dishonor Him by an unworthy representation of Him, which is essential idolatry. Highly as he esteemed the pictorial arts, as worthy of all admiration in their true sphere, he condemned utterly pressing them beyond their mark, lest even they should become procurers to the Lords of Hell. We note secondly that he dissuaded from the ornamentation of the churches with the products of the representative arts (I. xi. 13); but this on the ground not of the express commandment of God or of an inherent incapacity of art to serve the purposes contemplated, but of simple expediency.[118] Experience teaches us, he says, that to set up images in the churches is tantamount to raising the standard of idolatry, because the folly of man is so great that it immediately falls to offering them superstitious worship. And a deeper reason lies behind, which would determine his judgment even if this peril were not so great. The Lord has Himself ordained living and expressive images of His grace for His temples, by which our eyes should be caught and held — such ceremonies as Baptism and the Lord's Sup-

[116] *Opp.* iv. 1195. Cf. the parallel remark in the " Genevan Catechism " of 1545 (*Opp.* vi. 55): " It is not to be understood then, that all sculpture and painting are forbidden, in general; but only all images which are made for divine service or for honoring Him in things visible, or in any way abusing them in idolatry. . . ."

[117] Deum effingi visibile specie nefas esse putamus.   [118] expediat.

per — and we cannot require others fabricated by human ingenuity; and it seems unworthy of the sanctity of the place to intrude them. There is, of course, an echo here of Calvin's fundamental " Puritan principle " with reference to the worship of God: his constant and unhesitating contention that only that worship which is ordained by Himself is acceptable to God. Had God desired the aid of pictorial representations to quicken the devotions of His people He would have ordained them: to employ them is in principle to despise the provisions He has made and to invent others — and we may be sure inadequate if not misleading ones — for ourselves.

This is not the place to inquire into Calvin's positive theory of art-representation. It is worth while, however, as illustrating the wide interests of the man, to note that he has such a theory and betrays the fact that he has it and somewhat of the lines on which it runs, in incidental remarks, even in such a discussion as this. It emerges, for example, that he would confine the sphere of the representative arts to the depicting of objects of sight (*ea sola quorum sint capaces oculi*) — of such things as the eye sees. Of these, however, he discovers two classes — " histories and transactions " on the one side, " images and forms of bodies " on the other.[119] The former may be made useful for purposes of instruction or admonition, he thinks; the latter, so far as he sees, serve only the ends of delectation. Both are, however, alike legitimate, if only they be kept to their proper places and used for their proper ends; for the delectation of man is as really a human need as his instruction. So little does Calvin then set himself with stern moroseness against all art-representation, that he is found actually forming a comprehensive theory of art-representation and pleading for its use, not only for the profit, but also for the pleasure of man.

It remains to speak of Calvin's doctrine of the Trinity.

[119] A. Bossert, " Calvin," 1906, pp. 203–204, after quoting this statement of Calvin's adds: " It is the program of Dutch painting," in this repeating what E. Doumergue in his " Conference " on " Painting in the Work of Calvin " (as cited, pp. 36–51) had fully set forth.

IV
CALVIN'S DOCTRINE OF THE TRINITY

CALVIN'S DOCTRINE OF THE TRINITY [1]

WHEN Calvin turns, in his discussion of the doctrine of God, from the Divine Being in general to the Trinity (chap. xiii.), he makes the transition most skillfully by a paragraph (§ 1) which doubtless has the design, as it certainly has the effect, of quickening in his readers a sense of the mystery of the divine mode of existence.[2] The Scriptures, he tells us, speak sparingly of the divine essence. Yet by two " epithets " which they apply to it, they effectually rebuke not only the follies of the vulgar but also the subtleties of the learned in their thought of God. These epithets are " immensity " and " spirituality "; and they alone suffice at once to check the crass and to curb the audacious imaginations of men. How dare we invade in our speculations concerning Him either the spirituality or the immensity of this infinite Spirit, conceiving Him like the Pantheists as an impersonal diffused force, or like the Manichæans limiting His immensity or dividing His unity? Or how can we think of the infinite Spirit as altogether like ourselves? Do we not see that when the Scriptures speak of

---

[1] From *The Princeton Theological Review*, vii. 1909, pp. 553–652.

[2] Something like Calvin's mode of transition here is repeated by Triglandius when he arrives at this topic in his " Antapologia " (c. v.). " That God is most simple in His essence," writes Triglandius, " eternal, infinite, and therefore of infinite knowledge and power, has been sufficiently demonstrated in the preceding chapter. Whence it is clear that He is one and unique. But Scripture sets before us here a great mystery, namely that in the one unique essence of God, there subsist three hypostases, the first of which is called the Father, the second the Son, the third the Holy Spirit. An arduous mystery indeed, and one simply incomprehensible to the human intellect; one, therefore, not to be measured by human reason, nor to be investigated by reasons drawn from human wisdom, but to be accredited solely from the Word of God; by going forward as far as it leads us, and stopping where it stops. Whenever this rule is neglected the human reason wanders in a labyrinth and cannot discern either end or exit " (in " Refutatio Apologiae Remonstrantium," p. 76).

Him under human forms they are merely employing the artless art of nurses as they speak to children? All that we can
either say or think concerning God descends equally below His
real altitude. Calvin thus prepares us to expect depths in the
Divine Being beyond our sounding, and then turns at once to
speak of the divine tripersonality, which he represents as a
mysterious characteristic of the divine mode of existence by
which God is marked off from all else that is. " But " — this is
the way he puts it (xiii. 2, *ad init.*) — " He points Himself out
by another special note also, by which He may be more particularly defined: for He so predicates unity of Himself that
He propones Himself to be considered distinctively in three
Persons; and unless we hold to these there is nothing but a
bare and empty name of God, by no means (*sine*) the true
God, floating in our brain."

That we may catch the full significance of this remarkable
sentence we should attend to several of its elements. We must
observe, for example, that it ranges the tripersonality of God
alongside of His immensity and spirituality as another special
" note " by which He is more exactly defined. The words are:
" But He designates Himself also by *another* special note, by
which He may be more particularly distinguished," — the *another* referring back to the " epithets " of immensity and spirituality.[3] The tripersonality of God is conceived by Calvin,

---

[3] We must not fancy, however, that Calvin conceived the personal distinctions in the Godhead as mere " epithets," that is, that he conceived the
Trinity Sabellianwise as merely three classes of attributes or modes of manifestation of God. He does not say that the tripersonality of God is another
" epithet " but another " note " along with His immensity and spirituality —
that is to say, another characteristic fact defining God as differing from all
other beings. He explicitly denies that the personal distinctions are analogous
in kind to the qualities of the divine essence. He says: " Yet in that one
essence of God we acknowledge the Father, with His eternal Word and
Spirit. In using this distinction, however, we do not imagine three Gods, as
if the Father were some other entity (*aliud quiddam*) than the Word, nor yet
do we understand them to be mere epithets (*nuda epitheta*) by which God
is variously designated, according to His operations; but, in common with
the ecclesiastical writers, we perceive in the simple unity of God these three
hypostases, that is, subsistences, which, although they coexist in one essence,
are not to be confused with one another. Accordingly, though the Father is

therefore, not as something added to the complete idea of God, or as something into which God develops in the process of His existing, but as something which enters into the very idea of God, without which He cannot be conceived in the truth of His being. This is rendered clearer and more emphatic by an additional statement which he adjoins — surely for no other purpose than to strengthen this implication — to the effect that " if we do not hold to these [the three Persons in the divine unity], we have nothing but a naked and empty name of God, by no means the true God, floating in our brain." According to Calvin, then, it would seem, there can be no such thing as a monadistic God; the idea of multiformity enters into the very notion of God.[4] The alternative is to suppose that he is speaking here purely *a posteriori* and with his mind

---

one God with His Word and Spirit, the Father is not the Word, nor the Word the Spirit." — " Adversus P. Caroli Calumnias," *Opp.* vii. 312. And again in refuting the Sabellians he expressly draws the distinction: " The Sabellians do indeed raise the cavil that God is called now Father, now Son, now Spirit in no other sense than He is spoken of as both strong and good, and wise and merciful; but they are easily refuted by this, — that it is clear that these latter are epithets which manifest what God is *erga nos,* while the others are names which declare what God really is *apud semetipsum.*" — " Institutes," ed. 2, and other middle edd., *Opp.* i. 491.

    [4] The idea of " multiformity," not of " multiplicity " — which would imply *composition.* Hence Calvin, I. xiii. 2, *ad fin.,* declares that it is impious to represent the essence of God as " multiplex "; and at the beginning of that section he warns against vainly dreaming of " a triplex God," and defines that as meaning the division of the simple essence of God among three Persons. The same warning had been given by Augustine, " De Trinitate," VI. vii. 9: " Neither, because He is a Trinity, is He to be therefore thought to be triplex; otherwise the Father alone, or the Son alone, would be less than the Father and Son together, — although it is hard to see how we can say, either the Father alone, or the Son alone, since both the Father is with the Son and the Son with the Father always inseparably." That is to say, God is not a compound of three deities, but a single deity which is essentially trinal. This mode of statement became traditional. Thus Hollaz says: " That is triune which, one in essence, has three modes of subsistence; that is triplex which is compounded of three. We say God is triune; but we are forbidden by the Christian religion to say He is triplex " (in " Examinis Theol. Acroam.," 1741, p. 297). Again: " We may speak of the trinal, but not of the triple deity." Note also Hase's " Hutterus Redivivus," 1848, pp. 166–167; and Keckermann, " Syst. S. S. Theol.," 1615, p. 21.

absorbed in the simple fact that the only true God is actually a Trinity: so that he means only to say that since the only God that is, is, in point of fact, a Trinity, when we think of a divine monad we are, as a mere matter of fact, thinking of a God which has no existence — which is a mere naked and empty name, and not the true God at all. The simplicity of Calvin's speech favors this supposition; and the stress he has laid in the preceding discussion upon the necessity of conceiving God only as He reveals Himself, on pain of the idolatry of inventing unreal gods for ourselves, adds weight to it. But it scarcely seems to satisfy the whole emphasis of the statement. The vigor of the assertion appears rather to invite us to understand that in Calvin's view a divine monad would be less conceivable than a divine Trinity, and certainly suggests to us that to him the conception of the Trinity gave vitality to the idea of God.[5]

This suggestion acquires importance from the circumstance that the Reformers in general and Calvin in particular have been sometimes represented as feeling little or no interest in such doctrines as that of the Trinity. Such doctrines, we are told, they merely took over by tradition from the old Church, if indeed they did not by the transference of their interest to a principle of doctrinal crystallization to which such doctrines were matters of more or less indifference, positively prepare for their ultimate discarding. Ferdinand Christian Baur, for example, points out that the distinctive mark of the Reformation, in contrast with Scholasticism with its prevailing dialectic or intellectualistic tendency, was that it was a deeply religious movement, in which the heart came to its rights and everything was therefore viewed from the standpoint of the great

[5] So in his "Instruction" or "Catechism" of 1537 and 1538 (*Opp.* v. 337 or xxii. 52), Calvin says: "The Scriptures, and pious experience itself, show us in the absolutely simple essence of God, the Father, the Son, and the Holy Spirit; so that our intelligence is not able to conceive the Father without at the same time comprehending the Son in whom His living image is repeated, and the Spirit in whom His power and virtue are manifested." Cf. the Commentary on Gen. i. 26: "I acknowledge that there is something in man which refers to the Father and the Son and the Spirit" — the exact meaning of which, however, is not apparent (see below, note 54, p. 225).

doctrines of sin and grace.[6] He then seeks to apply this observation as follows: "The more decisively Protestantism set the central point of its dogmatic consciousness in this portion of the system, the more natural was the consequence that even such doctrines as that of the Trinity were no longer able to maintain the preponderating significance which they possessed in the old system; and although men were not at once clearly conscious of the altered relation — as, in point of fact, they were not and could not be — it is nevertheless the fact that the doctrines which belong to this category attracted the interest of the Reformers only in a subordinate degree; and, without giving themselves an exact account of why it was so, men merely retained with reference to them the traditional modes of teaching — abiding by these all the more willingly that they could not conceal from themselves the greatness of the difference which existed between them and their opponents in so many essential points."[7] They no doubt set themselves in opposition to the more radical spirits of their time who, taking their starting point from the same general principles, were led by their peculiarities of individuality and relations, of standpoint and tendency, to discard the doctrine of the Trinity altogether. But they could not stem the natural drift of things. "How could the Protestant principle work so thoroughgoing an alteration in one part of the system, and leave the rest of it unaffected?"[8] And what was to be expected except that the polemic attitude with reference to the ecclesiastical doctrine of the Trinity, which was at first confined to small parties outside the limits of recognized Protestantism, should ultimately become a part of Protestantism itself?[9]

In accordance with this schematization, Baur represents Melanchthon as, in the first freshness of his Reformation-consciousness, passing over in his "Loci" such doctrines as that of the Trinity altogether as incomprehensible mysteries of God which call rather for adoration than scrutiny;[10] and,

---

[6] "Die christliche Lehre von der Dreieinigkeit," iii. 1843, pp. 6–7.
[7] Pp. 9–10.   [9] Pp. 10–11.
[8] P. 10.   [10] P. 20.

though he returned to them subsequently, doing so with a difference, a difference which emphasized their subordinate and indeed largely formal place in his system of thought.[11] While as regards Calvin, he sees in him the beginnings of a radical transformation of the doctrine of the Trinity. Calvin does, indeed, like Melanchthon, present the doctrine as the teaching of Scripture, and attaches himself to the ecclesiastical definitions of it as merely a republication of the Scriptural doctrine in clearer words. " We perceive, however, that he does not know how to bring the doctrine itself out of its transcendental remoteness into closer relations with his religious and dogmatic consciousness. Instead, therefore, of speculatively developing the Trinitarian relation as the objective content of the idea of God, out of itself, he rather repels the whole conception as a superfluity which leads to empty speculation (*Inst.*, I. xiii. 19 and 20), or else where he enters most precisely into it, inclines to a mode of apprehending it in which the ecclesiastical *homoousia* is transmuted into a rational relation of subordination." [12] " The intention was to retain the old orthodox doctrine unchanged; but it was internally, in the new consciousness of the times, already undermined, since there was no longer felt for it the same religious and dogmatic interest, as may be seen from the whole manner in which it is dealt with in these oldest Protestant theologians. Men could no longer find their way in the old, abstract form of the dogma. A new motive impulse must first proceed from the central point of the Protestant consciousness. The first beginnings of a transformation of the dogma are already discoverable in Calvin, when he locates the chief element of the doctrine of the Trinity in the practical consciousness of the operations in which the Son and Spirit make themselves known as the peculiar principles of the divine life (I. xiii. 13, 14), and finds the assurance of the election in which the finite subject has the consciousness of his unity with God solely in the relation in which the individual stands to Christ." [13] That is to say, if we understand Baur aright, the new construction of the Trinity already foreshadowed in Calvin was

---

[11] Pp. 24 *sq.*					[12] Pp. 42–43.					[13] Pp. 44–45.

to revolve around Christ; but around Christ as God-man conceived as the mediating principle between God and man, the unity of the finite and infinite, bearing to us the assurance that what God is in Himself that also He must be for the finite consciousness — in which mode of statement we see, however, a great deal more of Baur's Hegelianism than of Calvin's Protestantism.

So far as this representation implies that Calvin's interest in the doctrine of the Trinity was remote and purely traditional, it is already contradicted, as we have seen, by the first five lines of his discussion of the subject (I. xiii. 2, *ad init.*) — if, that is, as we have seen some reason to believe, he really declares there that vitality is given to the idea of God only by the Trinitarian conception of Him. It is indeed contradicted by itself. For the real meaning of the constitutive place given in Calvin's thought of the Trinity to " the practical consciousness of the operations in which the Son and Spirit make themselves known as the peculiar principles of the divine life," is that the doctrine of the Trinity did not for him stand out of relation to his religious consciousness but was a postulate of his profoundest religious emotions; was given, indeed, in his experience of salvation itself.[14] For him, thus, certainly in no less measure than it had been from the beginning of Christianity, the nerve of the doctrine was its implication in the experience of salvation, in the Christian's certainty that the Redeeming Christ and Sanctifying Spirit are each Divine Persons. Nor did he differ in this from the other Reformers. The Reformation movement was, of course, at bottom a great revival of religion. But this does not mean that its revolt from Scholasticism was from the doctrines " of God, of His unity and His trinity, of the mystery of creation, of the mode of the incarnation "[15]

---

[14] In the "Catechism" of 1537, 1538 (*Opp.* v. 337 or xxii. 52) he says: "Scripture and *pious experience itself* show us in the absolutely simple essence of God, the Father, the Son and the Holy Spirit."

[15] This is Melanchthon's enumeration of the doctrines which he will not enter into largely in his "Loci." Cf. Augusti's ed. of 1821, p. 8, as quoted by Baur, p. 20: " Proinde non est, cur multum operae ponamus in locis supremis de Deo, de unitate, de trinitate Dei, de mysterio creationis, de modo incarna-

themselves, but from the formalism and intellectualism of the
treatment of these doctrines at the hands of the Scholastic
theologians. When Melanchthon demands whether, when
Paul set down a compendium of Christian doctrine in his
Epistle to the Romans, he gave himself over to philosophical disquisitions (*philosophabatur*) " on the mysteries
of the Trinity, on the mode of the incarnation, on active
and passive creation," and the like, we must not neglect
the emphasis on the term "*philosophical disquisitions.*" [16]
Melanchthon was as far as possible from wishing to throw
doubt upon either the truth or the importance of the doctrines of the Trinity, the Incarnation, Creation. He only wished
to recall men from useless speculations upon the mysterious
features of these doctrines and to focus their attention no
doubt on the great central doctrines of sin and grace, but also
on the vital relations of such doctrines as the Trinity, the Incarnation, and Creation to human needs and the divine provision for meeting them. The demand of the Reformers, in a
word, was not that men should turn away from these doctrines,
but that they should accord their deepest interest to those elements and aspects of them which minister to edification rather

---

tionis." How little Melanchthon was intending to manifest indifference to these
doctrines is already apparent from the word *supremis* here. Baur's comment
is: " It is precisely with these doctrines which the dialectic spirit of speculation of the Scholastics regarded as its peculiar object, and on which it expended
itself with the greatest subtlety and thoroughness, — with the doctrines of
God, of His unity and trinity, of creation, incarnation, etc., — that Melanchthon would have so little to do, that he did not even make a place for them
in his *Loci*, and that not on the ground that it did not belong to the plan
of that first sketch of Protestant dogmatics to cover the whole system, but
on the ground of the objective character of those doctrines, as they appeared
to him from the standpoint determined by the Reformation " (p. 20). Even
so, however, there is not involved any real underestimate of the importance
of these doctrines, but only a reference of them to a place in the system less
immediately related to the experience of salvation. Nor must we forget the
origin of the " Loci " in an exposition of the Epistle to the Romans and its
consequent lack of all systematic form, or completeness.

[16] " Loci," as above, p. 9, quoted by Baur, p. 21. The point of Melanchthon's remark is that Paul did not give himself over to philosophical disquisition on abstruse topics, but devoted himself single-heartedly to applying the
salvation of Christ to sinning souls.

than to curious questions that furnish exercise only to intellectual subtlety. Any apparent neglect of these doctrines which may seem to be traceable in the earliest writings of the Reformers was, moreover, due not merely to their absorption in the proclamation of the doctrine of grace, but also to the broad fact that these doctrines were not in dispute in their great controversy with Rome, and therefore did not require insisting upon in the stress of their primary conflict. So soon as they were brought into dispute by the radicals of the age, we find the Reformers reverting to them and reasserting them with vigor: and that is the real account to be given of the increased attention given to them in the later writings of the Reformers, which seems to those historians who have misinterpreted the relatively small amount of discussion devoted to them in the earlier years of the movement, symptomatic of a lapse from the purity of their first love and of a reëntanglement in the Scholastic intellectualism from which the Reformation, as a religious movement, was a revolt. In point of fact, it marks only the abiding faith of the Reformers in doctrines essential to the Christian system, but not hitherto largely asserted and defended by them because, shortly, there was not hitherto occasion for extended assertion and defense of them.

In no one is the general attitude of the Reformers to the doctrine of the Trinity more clearly illustrated than in Calvin. The historian of Protestant Dogmatics, Wilhelm Gass, tells us that " Calvin's exposition of the Trinity is certainly the best and most circumspect which the writings of the Reformers give us: surveying as it does the whole compass of the dogma and without any loss to the thing itself wisely avoiding all stickling for words." [17] That this judgment is quoted by subsequent expounders of Calvin's doctrine of the Trinity,[18] surprises us only in so far as so obvious a fact seems not to need the authority of Gass to support it. Apart, however, from the superiority

---

[17] " Geschichte der protestantischen Dogmatik," i. 1854, p. 105.

[18] Köstlin, *Theologische Studien und Kritiken*, 1868, p. 420; Muller, " De Godsleer van Zwingli en Calvijn," 1883, p. 31.

of Calvin's theological insight, by which his treatment of the
doctrine of the Trinity is made not only " the best and most
circumspect which the writings of the Reformers have given
us," but even one of the epoch-making discussions of this great
theme, Calvin's whole dealing with the doctrine of the Trinity
supplies an exceptionally perfect reflection of the attitude of
the Reformers at large to it. At one with them in his general
point of view, the circumstances of his life forced him into a
fulness and emphasis in the exposition of this doctrine to
which they were not compelled. The more comprehensive character of the work, even in its earliest form, coöperated with
the comparative lateness of the time of its publication [19] and
his higher systematic genius, to secure the incorporation into
even the first edition of Calvin's " Institutes " (1536) not
only of a Biblical proof of the doctrine of the Trinity, argued
with exceptional originality and force, but also of a strongly
worded assertion and defense of the correctness and indispensableness of the current ecclesiastical formulation of it. No
more than the earlier Reformers, however, was Calvin inclined
to confound the essence of the doctrine with a particular mode
of stating it; nor was he willing to confuse the minds of infantile Christians with the subtleties of its logical exposition.
The main thing was, he insisted, that men should heartily believe that there is but one God, whom only they should serve;
but also that Jesus Christ our Redeemer and the Holy Spirit
our Sanctifier is each no less this one God than God the Father
to whom we owe our being; while yet these three are distinct
personal objects of our love and adoration.[20] He was wholly
agreed with his colleagues at Geneva in holding that " in the
beginning of the preaching of the Gospel," it conduced more
to edification and readiness of comprehension to refrain from

[19] For example, Servetus' " De Trinitatis erroribus " appeared in 1531,
and his " Dialogi de Trinitate " in 1532.

[20] " Institutes," I. xiii. 5, *ad init.:* " I could wish that they [the technical
terms by which the Trinity is expressed and guarded] were buried, indeed, if
only this faith stood fast among all: that the Father and the Son and the
Spirit are one God; and yet neither is the Son the Father, nor the Spirit the
Son, but they are distinct by a certain property."

the explanation of the mysteries of the Trinity, and even from
the constant employment of those technical terms in which
these mysteries are best expressed, and to be content with declaring clearly the divinity of Christ in all its fulness, and
with giving some simple exposition of the true distinction between the Father, Son, and Holy Spirit.[21] He acted on this
principle in drawing up the formularies of faith with which he
provided the Church at Geneva immediately after his settlement there, and he vigorously defended this procedure when it
was called in question by that " theological adventurer," as he
has been not unjustly called,[22] Peter Caroli. This, of course,
does not mean that he was under any illusions as to the indispensableness to the Christian faith of a clear as well as a
firm belief in the doctrine of the Trinity, or as to the value for
the protection of that doctrine of the technical terms which had
been wrought out for its more exact expression and defense in
the controversies of the past. He was already committed to an
opposite opinion by his strong assertions in the first edition of
his " Institutes " (1536), which he retained unaltered through
all the subsequent editions; and the controversies in which he
was contemporaneously embroiled — with Anabaptists, Anti-

[21] Cf. their defense of themselves, *Opp.* xi. 6.

[22] Philip Schaff, "History of the Christian Church," vii. 1892, p. 351:
" A more serious trouble was created by Peter Caroli, a doctor of the Sorbonne, an unprincipled, vain, and quarrelsome theological adventurer and
turncoat. . . . He [Caroli] raised the charge of Arianism against Farel and
Calvin at a synod in Lausanne, May, 1537, because they avoided in the Confession the metaphysical terms *Trinity* and *Person*, (though Calvin did use
them in his *Institutio* and his Catechism,) and because they refused, at Caroli's
dictation, to sign the Athanasian Creed with its damnatory clauses, which
are unjust and uncharitable." See also Schaff's " Creeds of Christendom," i.
1881, p. 27, note 1: " Calvin, who had a very high opinion of the Apostles'
Creed, depreciates the Nicene Creed, as a ' *carmen cantillando magis aptum,
quam confessionis formula*' (*De Reform. Eccles.*)." It would not, however,
be easy to crowd more erroneous suggestions into so few words than Dr.
Schaff manages to do here. Calvin did not have difficulty with the metaphysical terminology of the doctrine of the Trinity; he did not object to the damnatory clauses in the Athanasian Creed; he did not depreciate the Nicene Creed.
Nor is the passage in which he speaks of the Nicene Creed as more suitable
for a song than a creed to be found in the tract, " De vera ecclesiae refor-
matione."

trinitarians, "theological quacks" — were well calculated to
fix in his mind a very profound sense of the importance of stating this doctrine exactly and defending it with vigor. He was
only asserting, as strongly as he knew how, the right of a
Christian teacher, holding the truth, to avoid strife about words
and to use his best endeavors to "handle aright the word of
truth." He never for one moment doubted, we do not say the
truth merely, but also the importance for the Christian system,
of the doctrine of the Trinity. He held this doctrine with a
purity and high austerity of apprehension singular among its
most devoted adherents. As we have seen, he conceived it not
only as the essential foundation of the whole doctrine of redemption, but as indispensable even to a vital and vitalizing
conception of the Being of God itself. He did not question even
the importance of the technical phraseology which had been
invented for the expression and defense of this doctrine, in
order to protect it from fatal misrepresentation. He freely confessed that by this phraseology alone could the subtleties of
heresy aiming at its disintegration be adequately met. But he
asserted and tenaciously maintained the liberty of the Christian teacher, holding this doctrine in its integrity, to use it
in his wisdom as he saw was most profitable for the instruction of his flock — not with a view to withdrawing it in its entirety or in part from their contemplation or to minimizing its
importance in their sight or to corrupting their apprehension
of it, but with a view to making it a vital element in their faith;
first perhaps more or less implicitly — as implied in the very
core of their creed — and then more or less explicitly, as they
were able to apprehend it; but never as a mere set of more or
less uncomprehended traditional phrases. To him it was a great
and inspiring reality: and as such he taught it to the babes of
the flock in its most essential and vital elements, and defended
it against gainsayers in its most complete and strict formulation.

The illusion into which it is perhaps possible to fall in the
case of the earlier Reformers, by which this double treatment
of the doctrine of the Trinity is supposed to represent consecu-

tive states of mind, is impossible in the case of Calvin. Circumstances compelled him to deal with the doctrine after both fashions contemporaneously. None can say of him, as Baur says of Melanchthon — in our belief wrongly interpreting the phenomena — that he first passed by the doctrine of the Trinity unconcernedly and afterwards reverted to the Scholastic statement of it. At the very moment that Calvin was insisting on teaching the doctrine vitally rather than scholastically, he was equally insisting that it must be held in its entirety as it had been brought into exact expression by the ecclesiastical writers.

Calvin began his work at Geneva on the fifth day of September, 1536, and among the other fundamental tasks with which he engaged himself during the winter of 1536 and 1537 was the drawing up of his first catechism, the "*Instruction* used in the Church at Geneva*," as it is called in its French form, which was published in 1537, or the "Catechismus sive Christianae Religionis Institutio," as it is called in the Latin form, which was published early (March) in 1538. Along with this Catechism, there had been prepared in both languages also a briefer "Confession of Faith," written, possibly, not by Calvin himself, but by his colleagues in the Genevan ministry, or, to be more specific, by Farel,[23] but certainly in essence Calvin's, and related to the Catechism very much as the Catechism was related to the "Institutes" of 1536; that is to say, it is a free condensation of the Catechism. In this Confession of Faith, although it was the fundamental documentation of the faith of the Genevan Church to which all citizens were required to subscribe, there is no formal exposition of the doctrine of the Trinity at all: the unity of God alone is asserted (§ 2), and it is left to the mere recitation of the Apostles' Creed, which is incorporated into it (§ 6), supported only by a rare (§ 15) reference to Jesus as God's Son, to suggest the Trinity. Even in

[23] So the Strasburg editors and also A. Lang ("Die Heidelberger Katechismus," 1907, pp. xxxv.–xxxvi.; "Johannes Calvin," 1909, pp. 38 and 208). Doumergue ("Jean Calvin," ii. 1902, pp. 236–251) agrees with Rilliet ("Le Cat. fran. de Calvin, publié en 1537," 1878, pp. lii.–lvii.) in assigning it to Calvin himself.

the Catechism [24] the statement of the doctrine, although explicit and precise, and supported by equally explicit assertions of the uniqueness of our Lord's Sonship ("He is called Son of God, not like believers, by adoption and grace, but true and natural and therefore sole and unique, so as to be distinguished from the others," p. 53, cf. pp. 45–46, 53, 60, 62), and of His true divinity ("His divinity, which He had from all eternity with the Father," p. 53), is far from elaborate. It is confined indeed very much to the assertion of the fact of the Trinity — although even here it is suggested that it enters by necessity into our conception of God; and even this assertion is made apparently only because it seemed to be needed for the understanding of the Apostles' Creed. In the general remarks on this Creed, before the exposition of its several clauses is taken up (p. 52), we read as follows: " But in order that this our confession of faith in the Father, Son and Holy Spirit may trouble no one, it is necessary first of all to say a little about it. When we name the Father, Son and Holy Spirit we by no means imagine three Gods; but the Scriptures and pious experience itself show us in the absolutely simple (*tres-simple*) essence of God, the Father, His Son and His Spirit. So that our intelligence is not able to conceive the Father without at the same time comprehending the Son in whom His living image is repeated, and the Spirit, in whom His power and virtue are manifested. Accordingly, we adhere with the whole thought of our heart to one sole God; but we contemplate nevertheless the Father with the Son and His Spirit." There is certainly here a clear and firm assertion of the fact of the Trinity; we may even admire the force with which, in so few words, the substance of the doctrine is proclaimed, and it is also suggested that it has its roots planted not only in Scripture but in Christian experience, and indeed is involved in a vital conception of God. Calvin assuredly was justified in pointing to it, when

[24] *Opp.* xxii. 33–74. The Latin edition of this Catechism (*Opp.* v. 317–354) was not printed until 1538, but it must have been prepared contemporaneously with the French, since it was quoted by Calvin in the debate with Caroli as early as February, 1537 (see Bähler, " Petrus Caroli und Johannes Calvin," in the *Jahrbuch für schweizerische Geschichte*, xxix. 1904, p. 64, note).

the calumnies raised by Caroli were spread abroad and men were acquiring a suspicion that his " opinion concerning the personal distinctions in the one God dissented somewhat (*non nihil*) from the orthodox consent of the Church," as a proof that he had from the first taught the Church at Geneva " a trinity of persons in the one essence of God." [25] But it is perhaps not strange that this should seem to some very little to say on the fundamental doctrine of the Trinity in a statement of fundamental doctrines which extends to some forty-two pages in length.[26] In its brevity it may perhaps illustrate almost as strikingly as the entire omission of all statement of the doctrine from the accompanying Confession (except as implied in the repetition of the Apostles' Creed) the feeling of Calvin and his colleagues that the elaboration of this doctrine belongs rather to the later stages of Christian instruction, while for babes in Christ it were better to leave it implicit in their general religious standpoint (seeing that it is implicated in the experience of piety itself) than to clog the unformed Christian mind with subtle disputations about it. Meanwhile, at the very moment when Calvin and his colleagues were preparing these primary statements of faith, in which no or so small a space was given to the doctrine of the Trinity, they were also vigorously engaged in confuting and excluding from the Genevan Church impugners of that doctrine. For from the very beginning of his work at Geneva Calvin was brought into conflict with that anti-trinitarian radicalism the confutation of which was to draw so heavily upon his strength in the future. There were already in the early spring of 1537 Anabaptists to confute and banish, among whom was that John Stordeur whose widow was afterwards to become Calvin's wife.[27] And there was to

[25] Preface to the Latin Translation, which was issued, in fact, precisely to meet these calumnies, which had obtained an incredible vogue (*Opp.* v. 318).

[26] We may compare, however, the brevity with which the doctrine of the Trinity is dealt with in the Westminster Confession and Shorter Catechism.

[27] So Colladon tells us, *Opp. Calvini*, xxi. 59; the registers of the Council of Geneva read the name, " Jehan Tordeur." See N. Weiss, *Bulletin de la société de l'histoire du protestantisme français*, lvi. 1907, pp. 228–229.

deal with just before their appearance that poor half-crazy
fanatic Claude Aliodi — once Farel's colleague at Neuchâtel
— who had as early as 1534 been denying the preëxistence of
Christ, and was in the spring of 1537 at Geneva, teaching his
anti-trinitarian heresies.[28]
Calvin's exact attitude on the doctrine of the Trinity and
its teaching was, moreover, just at this time forced into great
publicity by the assaults made upon the Genevan pastors by
one of the most frivolous characters brought to the surface
by the upheaval of the Reformation.[29] It was precisely at this

[28] Cf. Doumergue, "Jean Calvin," ii. 1902, pp. 241–242. Herminjard,
"Correspondance," etc., ed. 2, iii. 1878, Index (note especially pp. 172–175,
notes 1, 5, 7). Cf. also the clear brief account of E. Bähler, "Petrus Caroli und
Johannes Calvin" (in the *Jahrbuch für schweizerische Geschichte*, xxix. 1904),
pp. 73 *sq.*

[29] The Strasburg editors (*Calvini Opera*, vii. p. xxx.) characterize Caroli
as "vir vana ambitione agitatus, opinionibus inconstans, moribus levis." Doumergue's judgment upon him is embodied in these words: "Unhappily his
character was not as high as his intelligence, and if the new ideas attracted
him they did not transform him" (ii. 1902, p. 252). He quotes Douen's characterization of him as "a bold and adventurous spirit badly balanced, and
more distinguished by talents than by rectitude of conduct" (p. 253, note 2).
Kampschulte ("Johann Calvin," i. 1869, p. 162) contents himself with calling
him "a man of restless spirit and changeable principles" — who (p. 295) was
not above playing on occasion a dishonorable part. A. Lang's ("Johannes
Calvin," 1909, p. 40) characterization runs: "Acute but also weak in character and self-seeking." The inevitable rehabilitation of Caroli has been
undertaken by Eduard Bähler, Pastor at Thierachern in Switzerland, in a
long article entitled "Petrus Caroli und Johannes Calvin: Ein Beitrag
zur Geschichte und Kultur der Reformationszeit," published in the twenty-
ninth volume of the *Jahrbuch für schweizerische Geschichte* (1904, pp. 39–
168). Bähler's thesis is that Caroli belonged really to that large semi-
Protestant party in the French Church which found its inspiration in Faber
Stapulensis and its spiritual head in William Briçonnet, Bishop of Meaux;
occupying thus a middle ground he could rest content neither in the Roman
nor in the Protestant camp — and from this ambiguous position is to be
explained all his vacillations and treacheries. Granting the general contention and its explanatory value up to a certain point, it supplies no defense
of Caroli's character and conduct, which Bähler's rehabilitation leaves where
it found them. Cf. A. Lang's estimate of Bähler's lack of success: "There remains clinging to Caroli enough of wretched frivolity and of the most deplorable inconstancy. How great over against him stands out particularly Farel!"
("Johannes Calvin," 1909, p. 209). On Caroli the historians of the Protestant
movement in Metz should be consulted, e.g., Dietsch, "Die evang. Kirche von

time (January, 1537) that Peter Caroli, who was at the moment giving himself the airs of a bishop as " first pastor " at Lausanne, conceived the idea of avenging himself upon the pastors of Geneva for what he thought personal injuries by bringing against them the charge of virtual Arianism. That the charge received an attention which it did not deserve was, no doubt, due in part to an old suspicion which had been aroused against Farel by the calumnies of Claude Aliodi.[30] These were founded on the circumstance that in his " Sommaire " (1524–1525), Farel — with a purely paedagogical intent, as he explained in a preface prefixed to the edition of 1537–1538, because he believed the doctrine of the Trinity too difficult a topic for babes in faith — had passed over the doctrine of the Trinity, just as the Genevan pastors did again in their Confession of 1537.[31] It is difficult for us, in any event, however, at this late date, to understand the hearing which a man like Caroli obtained for his calumnies. The whole Protestant world was filled with suspicions of the orthodoxy of the Genevan pastors. It was whispered from one to another — at Bern, Basle, Zurich, Strasburg, Wittenberg — that they were strangely chary of using the terms " Trinity," " Person," — that they were even " heady " in their refusal to employ them in their popular formularies. It was widely reported that they were beginning to fall into Arianism, or rather into that worst of all errors (*pessimus error*) which Servetus the Spaniard was spreading abroad. Not only was a local crisis thus created, which entailed personal controversies and synods and decisions, but a widely spread atmosphere of distrust was produced, which demanded the most careful and prompt attention. All the spring and summer Calvin was occupied in writing letters hither and thither, correcting the harmful rumors

---

Metz," pp. 68–77, and Winkelmann, " Der Anteil der deutschen Protestanten an den kirchlichen Reformbestrebungen in Metz bis 1543," in the *Jahrbuch der Gesellschaft für lothringische Geschichte und Altertumskunde,* ix. 1897, pp. 229 *sq.*

[30] Cf. Doumergue, " Jean Calvin," ii. 1902, p. 258, note; and Bähler, " Petrus Caroli und Johannes Calvin," p. 73.

[31] Cf. Bähler, as cited, p. 71.

which had, as he said, been set going by "a mere nobody" (*homo nihili*), urged on by "futile vanity."[32] And after the conferences and synods and letters, there came at length treatises. The result is that all excuse is taken away for any misapprehension of Calvin's precise position.

Throughout the whole controversy — in which Calvin was ever the chief spokesman, coming forward loyally to the defense of his colleagues, who, rather than he, were primarily struck at — two currents run, as they run through all his writings on the Trinity, and not least through his chapter (I. xiii.) on that subject in the "Institutes." There is everywhere manifested not only a clear and firm grasp of the doctrine, but also a very deep insight into it, accompanied by a determination to assert it at its height. Along with this there is also manifest an equally constant and firm determination to preserve full liberty to deal with the doctrine free from all dictation from without or even prescription of traditional modes of statement. There is nothing inconsistent in these two positions. Rather are they outgrowths of the same fundamental conviction: but the obverse and reverse of the same mental attitude. At the root of all lies Calvin's profound persuasion that this is a subject too high for human speculation and his consequent fixed resolve to eschew all theoretical constructions upon it, and to confine himself strictly to the revelations of Scripture. On the one hand, therefore, because he appealed to Scripture only, he refused to be coerced in his expression of the doctrine by present authority or even the formularies of the past; on the other, because he trusted Scripture wholly, he was insistent in giving full validity to all that he found there. It was the purity of his Protestantism, in other words, which governed Calvin's dealing with this doctrine; giving it an independence which is not yet always understood and has afforded occasion once and again for comment upon his attitude which betrays a somewhat surprising inability to enter into his mind.[33]

---

[32] Doumergue, ii. 1902, pp. 266–268.

[33] An old instance is supplied by Bellarmine, who, on Caroli's testimony, seeks to intimate that Calvin's refusal at the Council of Lausanne to sign the

For the matter, which has been thus vexed, was perfectly simple. Calvin refused to subscribe the ancient creeds at Caroli's dictation, not in the least because he did not find himself in accord with their teaching, but solely because he was determined to preserve for himself and his colleagues the liberties belonging to Christian men, subject in matters of faith to no other authority than that of God speaking in the Scriptures. He tells us himself that it was never his purpose to reject these creeds or to detract from their credit; [34] and he points out that he was not misunderstood even by Caroli to be repudiating their teaching; but Caroli conceded that what he did was — in Caroli's bad Latin, or as Calvin facetiously calls it, "his

Creeds resembled the conduct of the Arians at the Council of Aquileia (" Controversia de Christo," ii. 19, near middle, in " Opp. Omnia," Paris, i. 1870, p. 335). " Calvin," he says, " is not unlike the Arians in this: for at the Council of Aquileia, St. Ambrose never could extort from the two Arian heretics that they should say that the Son is very God of very God; for they always responded that the Son is the very Only-begotten, Son of the very God, and the like, but never that He is very God of very God, although they were asked perhaps a hundred times. And that from Calvin at the Council of Lausanne, it could never be extorted that he should confess that the Son is God of God, Petrus Caroli, who was present, reports in his letter to the Cardinal of Lorraine." Bellarmine is blind to the fact that Calvin was ready to confess all that the Creeds contained to the exaltation of the Son and *more*, while the Arians would not confess so much. Even F. W. Kampschulte (" Johann Calvin," u. s. w., ii. 1899, p. 171) permits himself to say that Calvin " in the controversy with Caroli expresses himself on the Athanasian symbol in a very dubious way (*in sehr bedenklichem Masse*)," and adds in a note: " It was not groundlessly that he was upbraided with this by his later opponents. ' Calvin waxes angry and employs the same taunts as the anti-trinitarians against the Symbol of Athanasius and the Council of Nice, when his opinion touching the Trinity is brought under discussion.' Cf. F. Claude de Saintes, *Declaration d'aucuns atheismes de la doctrine de Calvin*, Paris, 1568, p. 108." Cf. on Kampschulte, Doumergue, " Jean Calvin," ii. 1902, p. 266. We have already had occasion to point out the uncomprehending way in which Dr. Schaff speaks of the matter (above, p. 199, note 22), in which, however, he is only the type of a great crowd of writers.

[34] " Adv. P. Caroli calumnias," *Opp.* vii. 315: Calvino quidem et aliis propositum nequaque erat symbola abiicere aut illis derogare fidem. Compare what he writes on Oct. 8, 1539, to Farel of the discussion at Strasburg: Quamquam id quoque diluere promtum erat, nos non respuisse, multo minus improbasse, sed ideo tantum detrectasse subscriptionem, ne ille, quod captaverat, de ministerio nostro triumpharet (Herminjard, vi. 1883, p. 53).

Sorbonnic elegance " — " neither to credit nor to discredit them." [35] He considered it intolerable that the Christian teacher's faith should be subjected to the authority of any traditional modes of statement, however venerable, or however true; and he refused to be the instrument of creating a precedent for such tyranny in the Reformed Churches by seeming to allow that a teacher might be justly treated as a heretic until he cleared himself by subscribing ancient symbols thrust before him by this or that disturber of the peace. There were his writings, and there was his public teaching, and he was ready to declare plainly what he believed: let him be judged by these expressions of his faith in accordance with the Word of God alone as the standard of truth. Accordingly, when he first confronted Caroli in behalf of the Genevan ministers, he read the passage on the Trinity from the new Catechism as the suitable expression of their belief. And when Caroli cried out, " Away with these new Confessions; and let us sign the three ancient Creeds," Calvin, not without some show of pride, refused, on the ground that he accorded authority in divine things to the Word of God alone.[36] " We have professed faith in God alone," he said, " not in Athanasius, whose Creed has not been

[35] " Adv. P. Caroli calumnias," *Opp.* vii. 316: ego neque credo neque discredo. So Calvin tells Farel that Caroli had reported at Strasburg not that Calvin and his colleagues had denied the teaching of the three Symbols, but: nos vero non tantum detrectasse [subscriptionem], sed vexasse multis cachinnis symbola illa quae perpetua bonorum consensione authoritatem firmam in Ecclesia semper habuerunt (Herminjard, vi. 1883, p. 52). And, when writing to the Pope, what Caroli charges the Protestant preachers with doing is " ridiculing, satirizing, defaming " the symbols and denying not their truth but their authority: eoque devenisse ut concilii Niceni et divi Athanasii symbola maiori ex parte riderent, proscinderent, proculcarent, et ab ecclesia legitima umquam fuisse recepta negarent (Herminjard, iv. ed. 2, 1878, p. 249). Compare below, note 37, p. 209.

[36] Cf. A. Lang (" Johannes Calvin," 1909, p. 41): " There shows itself here Calvin's self-reliance and independence as over against every kind of ecclesiastical tradition. . . . Thus, in the Confession which he adduced at Lausanne in his and his colleagues' names, he explains: ' We cannot seek God's majesty anywhere except in His Word; nor can we think anything about Him except with His Word, or say anything of Him except through His Word.' . . . ' A religious Confession is nothing but a witness to the faith which abides in us; . . . therefore it must be drawn only from the pure fountain of Scripture.' "

approved by any properly constituted Church." [37] His meaning is that he refused to treat any human composition as an authoritative determination of doctrine, from which we may decline only on pain of heresy: that belongs to the Word of God alone. At the subsequent Council of Lausanne he took up precisely the same position, and addressing himself more, as he says,[38] *ad hominem* than *ad rem*, turned the demand that he

[37] *Opp.* xb. 83–84 (Herminjard, iv. ed. 2, 1878, pp. 185–186) : " Ad haec Calvinus, nos in Dei unius fidem iurasse respondit, non Athanasii cuius Symbolum nulla unquam legitima ecclesia approbasset." Doumergue (" Jean Calvin," ii. 1902, p. 256) renders correctly : " Nous avons jure la foi en un seul Dieu, et non en Athanase, dont le symbole n'a été approuvé par aucune Église légitime." Williston Walker (" John Calvin," 1906, p. 197), missing the construction, renders misleadingly : " We swear in the faith of the one God, not of Athanasius, whose creed no true church would ever have approved." So also A. Lang (" Johannes Calvin," 1909, p. 40) : " Wir haben den Glauben an den einen Gott beschworen, aber nicht an Athanasius, dessen Symbol eine wahre Kirche nie gebilligt haben würde." Perhaps worst of all, James Orr, " The Christian View of God and the World," 1893, p. 309, note : " We have sworn to the belief in One God, and not to the creed of Athanasius, whose symbol a true Church would never have had admitted." Calvin is not declaring the Athanasian Creed unworthy of the approbation of any true church; he is recalling the fact that it is a private document authorized by no valid ecclesiastical enactment. For Caroli's account of what Calvin said, see above, note 35, end. Nevertheless, the Athanasian Creed had attained throughout the Western Church a position of the highest reverence (for the extent of its " reception and use " see Ommaney, " A Critical Dissertation on the Athanasian Creed," 1897, pp. 420 *sq.*), and was soon to be " approbated " by the Protestant Churches at large. Zwingli in the " Fidei Ratio " (1530) and Luther in the Smalcald Articles (1537) had already placed it among the Symbols of the Churches, whose authority they recognized: and the " Formula Concordiae " and many Reformed Confessions, beginning with the Gallican, were soon formally to accord it a place of authority in the Protestant Churches. See Loofs, " Athanasianum," in Herzog, " Realencyklopädie," ed. 3, ii. p. 179; Schaff, " Creeds of Christendom," ed. 1, i. p. 40; E. F. Karl Müller, " Die Bekenntnisschriften der reformierten Kirche," Index *sub voc.*, " Athanasianum "; Ménégoz, as cited in note 42. Calvin found at Strasburg that the manner in which he had spoken of the Creeds was offensive to his colleagues there. He writes to Farel (Herminjard, vi. 1883, p. 53) : " It was somewhat harder to purge ourselves in the matter of the Symbols: for this was what was offensive (*odiosum*), that we repudiated them, though they ought to be beyond controversy, since they were received by the suffrages of the whole Church. It was easy to explain that we did not disapprove, much less reject them, but only declined to subscribe them that he [Caroli] might not enjoy the triumph over our ministry which he longed for. Some odium, however, always remained."

[38] *Opp.* vii. 316: non tam ad rem quam ad hominem.

should express his faith in the exact words of former formularies into ridicule. He was, he tells us, in what he said about
the Creeds just " gibing " [39] Caroli. Caroli had attempted to recite the Creeds and had broken down at the fourth clause of the
Athanasian Symbol.[40] You assert, Calvin said, that we cannot
acceptably confess our faith except in the exact words of these
ancient symbols. You have just pronounced these words from
the Athanasian Creed: "Which faith whosoever doth not
hold cannot be saved." You do not yourself hold this faith:
and if you did, you could not express it in the exact words of
the Creed. Try to repeat those words: you will infallibly again
stick fast before you get through the fourth clause. Now what
would you do, if you should suddenly come to die and the
Devil should demand that you go to the eternal destruction
which you confess awaits those who do not hold this faith whole
and entire, meaning unless you express this your faith in these
exact terms? And as for the Nicene Creed — is it so very certain it was composed by that Council? One would surely suppose those holy Fathers would study conciseness in so serious
a matter as a creed. But see the battology here: "God of
God, Light of Light, very God of very God." Why this repetition — which adds neither to the emphasis nor to the expres-
siveness of the document? Don't you see that this is a song,
more suitable for singing than to serve as a formula of confession? [41] We may or may not think Calvin's pleasantry happy.
But we certainly cannot fail to marvel when we read in even
recent writers that Calvin refused to sign the Athanasian
Creed because of its damnatory clauses, " which are unjust and
uncharitable," and that he " depreciated the Nicene Creed." [42]

[39] iocatus est (ibid., p. 315).

[40] " When he had recited three clauses of the Athanasian Symbol, he was
not able to recite the fourth . . ." (ibid., p. 311, top).

[41] Ibid., pp. 315–316. This manner of speaking of the Nicene Creed also
impressed the Strasburg theologians unfavorably. Calvin writes to Farel Oct.
8, 1539 (Herminjard, vi. 1883, p. 54): " I had to give satisfaction about the bat-
tologies. I could not by any effort convince them that there is any battology
there. I admitted, however, that I should not have so spoken if I had not
been compelled by that man's wickedness."

[42] Schaff: see p. 199 above, note 22. E. Ménégoz is therefore in the essen-

According to his own testimony, he did nothing of the kind: he "never had any intention of depreciating (*abiicere*) these creeds or of derogating from their credit." [43] His sole design was to make it apparent that Caroli's insistence that only in the words of these creeds could faith in the Trinity be fitly expressed was ridiculous.

Calvin's refusal to be confined to the very words of the old formulas in his expression of the doctrine of the Trinity did not carry with it, therefore, any unwillingness to employ in his definition of the doctrine the terms which had been beaten out in the Trinitarian controversies of the past. These terms he considered rather the best expressions for stating and defending the doctrine. That they were unwilling to employ them had indeed been made the substance of one of the charges brought by Caroli against the Genevan pastors. But the refutation of this calumny, so far as Calvin himself was concerned, was easy. He had only to point to the first edition of the "Institutes" (1536), in which he had not only freely used the terms in question, but had defended at large the right and asserted the duty of employing them, as the technical language by which alone the doctrine of the Trinity can be so expressed as to confound heretical misconstructions. When, then, Caroli expressed his wonder at "the pertinacity with which

---

tials of the matter right, when he expresses his wonder that men can suppose that the circumstances that Calvin "once refused to obey an injunction to sign the Symbol," or "pronounced a judgment unfavorable to the literary form of this document" — M. Ménégoz is confusing for the moment the Athanasian and Nicene Creeds — prove that "in the depths of his heart he held these anathemas in aversion" ("Publications diverses sur le Fidéisme," 1900, pp. 276–277). He adds with equal justice: "It is an infelicitous idea to appeal to Calvin as a witness that Protestantism, though receiving the Catholic Symbols, had no intention of approving their anathemas. And it is a historical error to imagine that the Reformers would have accepted these Symbols, if they had not firmly believed them, if they had felt any scruples, or cherished any mental reservations regarding the damnatory clauses. There was no paltering in a double sense in that age. There was no practice of 'economy.' . . . If the Protestants had felt any hesitation about the anathemas, they would have said so without ambiguity, and they would have purely and simply discarded the Symbols. Nothing would have been easier."

[43] *Opp.* vii. 315.

Calvin refused the terms ' Person,' ' Trinity,' " Calvin replied
flatly that neither he nor Farel nor Viret ever had the smallest
objection to these terms. " The writings of Calvin," he adds,
" testify to the whole world that he always employed them
freely, and even reprehended the superstition of those who
either disliked or avoided them." [44] That the Genevan pastors
passed them by in their Confession, and refused to employ
them when this was violently demanded of them, he explains,
was due to two reasons. They were unwilling to consent to such
tyranny as that when a matter has been sufficiently and more
than sufficiently established, credit should be bound to words
and syllables. But their more particular reason was, he adds,
that they might " deprive that madman of the boast he had
insolently made." " For Caroli's purpose was to cast suspicion
on the entire doctrine of men of piety and to destroy their influence." [45] Though they felt to the full, therefore, the value
of these terms, not only for confounding heresy, but also for
consolidating churches in a common confession, when their
use was contentiously demanded of them they followed a high
example and refused to give place, in the way of subjection,
even for an hour.

Calvin's attitude to the employment of this technical language is sufficiently interesting in itself to repay a pause to
observe it. As we have intimated, it is fully set forth already
in the first edition of the " Institutes " (1536) in a very interesting passage, which is retained without substantial alteration throughout all the subsequent editions. The position of
this passage in the discussion of the doctrine of the Trinity,
however, is changed in the final edition from its end (as in all
the earlier editions) to its beginning. In the final edition,
therefore, it appears as a preface to the discussion of the substance of the doctrine (I. xiii. 3–5), and it is strengthened in
this edition by an introductory paragraph (§ 2), in which an
attempt is made to vindicate for one of these technical terms
direct Biblical authority. Calvin finds the term " Person " in
the ὑπόστασις of Heb. i. 3; and insists, therefore, that it, at

[44] *Opp.* vii. 318.   [45] " Adv. P. Caroli calumnias ": *Opp.* vii. 318.

least, is not of human invention (*humanitus inventa*). The argument in which he does this is too characteristic of him and too instructive, not only as to his attitude towards the terms in question, but also as to his doctrine of the Trinity and his exegetical methods, to be passed over in silence. We must permit ourselves so much of a digression, therefore, as will enable us to attend to it.

What Calvin does, in this argument, is in essence to subject the statement of Heb. i. 3 that the Son is " the very image of the hypostasis of God " — the χαρακτὴρ τῆς ὑποστάσεως αὐτοῦ — to a strict logical analysis. The term ὑπόστασις, he argues, must designate something the Son is not: for He could scarcely be said to be the *image* of something He is. When we say *image,* we postulate two distinct things: the thing imaged and the thing imaging it. If the Son is the *image* of God's hypostasis, then, the hypostasis of God must be something which the Son does not *share;* it must be rather something which He is *like.* The Son *shares* the Divine essence: hence hypostasis here cannot mean essence. It must be taken then in its alternative sense of " person ": and what the author of the Epistle says, therefore, is that the Son is exactly like the Father in person; His double, so to speak. This Epistle, therefore, expressly speaks here of two Persons in the Godhead, one Person which is imaged, another which precisely images it. And the same reasoning may be applied to the Holy Spirit. There is Biblical warrant, therefore, for teaching that there are three hypostases in the one essence of God — " therefore, if we will give credit to the Apostle's testimony, there are in God three hypostases, " — and since the Latin " person " is but the translation of the Greek " hypostasis," it is mere fastidiousness to balk at the term " person." If anyone prefers the term " subsistence " as a more literal rendering, why, let him use it: or even " substance," if it be taken in the same sense. The point is not the vocable but the meaning, and we do not change the meaning by varying the synonyms. Even the Greeks use " person " (πρόσωπον) interchangeably with " subsistence " (ὑπόστασις) in this connection.

It is not likely that this piece of exegesis will commend itself to us. Nor indeed is it likely that we shall feel perfect satisfaction in the logical analysis, even as a piece of logical analysis. After all, the Son is not the image of the Father in His Personality — if we are, like Calvin, to take the Personality here in strict distinction from the Essence. What the Son differs from the Father in is, rather, just in His "Personality," in this sense: as Person He is the Son, the Father the Father, and what we sum up under this "Fatherhood" and "Sonship" is just the distinguishing "properties" by which the two are differentiated from each other. That concrete Person we call the Son is exactly like that concrete Person we call the Father; but the likeness is due to the fact that each is sharer in the identical essence. After all, therefore, the reason why the Son is the express image of the Father is because, sharing the divine essence, He is in His essence all that the Father is. He is the repetition of the Father: but the repetition in such a sense that the one essence in which the likeness consists is common to the two, and not merely of like character in the two. The fundamental trouble with Calvin's argument is that it seeks a direct proof for the Trinitarian constitution of the Godhead from a passage which was intended as a direct proof only of the essential deity of the Son. What the author of the Epistle to the Hebrews had in mind was not to reveal the relation of the Son to the Father in the Trinity — as a distinct hypostasis in the unity of the essence; but to set forth the absolute deity of the Son, to declare that He is all that God is, the perfect reflection of God, giving back to God when set over against Him His consummate image. The term "hypostasis" is not indeed to be taken here, in the narrow sense, as "essence": but neither is it to be taken, in the abstract sense, as "person." It means the concrete person, that is to say, the whole substantial entity we call God; which whole substantial entity is said to be in the Son exactly what it is in the Father. Nothing is said directly as to the relation of the Son to the Father, as distinct persons in the Trinity; the whole direct significance of the declaration is exhausted in the assertion that this "Son" differs in no single particular from "God": He is God in the full height of the conception of God.

It is not, however, the success or lack of success of Calvin's exegesis which most interests us at present. It is rather two facts which his exegetical argument brings before us with peculiar force. The one of them is that the developed doctrine of the Trinity lay so firmly entrenched in his mind that he makes it, almost or perhaps quite unconsciously, the major premise of his argument. And the other is that he was so little averse to designating the distinctions in the Godhead by the term "persons" that that term was rather held by him to have definite Biblical warrant. His argument that ὑπόστασις in this passage cannot mean "essence," but must mean "person," turns on this precise hinge — that the Father and Son are numerically one in essence, and can be represented as distinct only in person: "For since the essence of God is simple and indivisible (*simplex et individua*) Him — who contains in Himself the whole of it, not in apportionment or in deflection, but in unbroken perfection (*integra perfectione*) — it would be improper or rather inept to call its image." In other words, the doctrine of the Trinity in its complete formulation is the postulate of his argument. And the outcome of the argument is that the Epistle to the Hebrews distinctly sets the Father and Son over against each other as distinguishable "Persons," employing this precise term, ὑπόστασις, to designate them in their distinction. "Accordingly," says Calvin, "if the testimony of the Apostle obtains credit, it follows that there are in God three hypostases." This term as the expression of the nature of the distinctions in the Godhead is therefore not a "human invention" (*humanitus inventa*) to Calvin, but a divine revelation.

Since, then, the Bible had obtained credit with Calvin, he could not object to the use of the term "person" to express the distinctions in the Trinity. But he nevertheless takes over from the earlier editions, in which the discovery of the term in Heb. i. 3 is not yet to be found, a defense of the use of

this term on the assumption that it is not Biblical. And this
defense is in essence the assertion of the right and the exposition of a theory of interpretation. There are men, says Calvin,
who cry out against every term framed according to human
judgment (*hominum arbitrio confictum nomen*) and demand
that our words as well as our thoughts concerning divine things
shall be kept within the limits of Scripture example. If we
use only the words of Scripture we shall, say they, avoid many
dissensions and disputes, and preserve the charity so frequently
broken in strifes over "exotic words." Certainly, responds
Calvin, we ought to speak of God with not less religion than
we think of Him. But why should we be required to confine
ourselves to the exact words of Scripture if we give the exact
sense of Scripture? To condemn as "exotic" every word not
found in so many syllables in Scripture, is at once to put
under a ban all interpretation which is not a mere stringing
together of Scriptural phrases. There are some things in Scripture which are to our apprehension intricate and difficult. What
forbids our explaining them in simpler terms — if these terms
are held religiously and faithfully to the true sense of Scripture, and are used carefully and modestly and not without
occasion? Is it not an improbity to reprobate words which express nothing but what is testified and recorded by the Scriptures? And when these words are a necessity, if the truth is
to be plainly and unambiguously expressed — may we not
suspect that the real quarrel of those who object to their
use is with the truth they express; and that what they are
offended by is that by their use the truth has been made
clear and unmistakable (*plana et dilucida*)? As to the terms
in which the mystery of the Trinity is expressed — the term
Trinity itself, the term Person, and those other terms which the
tergiversations of heretics have compelled believers to frame
and employ that the truth may be asserted and guarded — such
as *homoousios,* for example — no one would care to draw sword
for them as mere naked words. Calvin himself would be altogether pleased to see them buried wholly out of sight — if only
all men would heartily receive the simple faith, that the

Father, Son, and Spirit are one God and yet neither is the Son
the Father, nor the Spirit the Son, but they are each distinguished by a certain property (I. xiii. 5). But that is just
the trouble. Men will not accept the simple faith, but palter
in a double sense. Arius was loud enough in declaring Christ
to be God — but wished to teach also that He is a creature and
has had a beginning: he was willing to say Christ is one with
the Father, if he were permitted to add that His oneness is the
same in kind as our own oneness with God. Say, however,
the one word ὁμοούσιος — " consubstantial " — and the mask
is torn from the face of dissimulation and yet nothing whatever
is added to the Scriptures. Sabellius was in no way loath to
admit that there are in the Godhead these three — Father,
Son, and Holy Spirit; but he really distinguished them only
as attributes are distinguished. Say simply that in " the unity
of God a trinity of persons subsists," and you have at once
quenched his inane loquacity. Now, if anyone who does not like
the words will ingenuously [46] confess the things the words
stand for — cadit quaestio: we shall not worry over the words.
" But," adds Calvin significantly, " I have long since learned
by experience, and that over and over again, that those who
contend thus pertinaciously about terms, are really cherishing
a secret poison; so that it is much better to bear their resentment than to consent to use less precise and clear language
for their behoof " (I. xiii. 5, ad fin.). Golden words! How
often since Calvin has the Church had bitter cause to repeat
them! When we read, for example, William Chillingworth's
subtle pleas for the use of Scriptural language only in matters of faith; his eloquent asseverations — " The Bible, I say,
the Bible only is the religion of Protestants "; his loud railing at " the vain conceit, that we can speak of the things of
God better than in the words of God," " thus deifying our
own interpretations and tyrannously enforcing them upon
others " — we know what it all means: that under this cloak
of charity are to lie hidden a multitude of sins. When we hear
Calvin refusing to swear in the words of another, we must not

[46] non fraudulenter.

confuse his defense of personal right with a latitudinarianism like Chillingworth's. If he said, It is the Word of God, not
the word of Athanasius, to which I submit my judgment, he
said equally, The sense of Scripture, not its words, is Scripture. No ambiguous meanings should be permitted to hide behind a mere repetition of the simple words of Scripture, but all
that the Scripture teaches shall be clearly and without equivo-
cation brought out and given expression in the least indeterminate language.[47]

Calvin's interest was, in other words, distinctly in the substance of the doctrine of the Trinity rather than in any particular mode of formulating it. It rested on the terms in which
it was formulated only because, and so far as, they seemed essential to the precise expression and effective guarding of the
doctrine. This was consistently his attitude from the beginning. Already in the " Institutes " of 1536, as we have seen, he
had given this attitude an expression so satisfactory to himself
that he retained the sections devoted to it until the end. It is
indeed astonishing how complete a statement of the doctrine
of the Trinity itself was already incorporated into this earliest
edition of the " Institutes," and how clearly in that statement
all the characteristic features of Calvin's treatment of the doctrine already appear. The discussion was no doubt greatly expanded in its passage from the first to the last edition. In the

[47] Dorner's account of Calvin's attitude to these questions is not quite
exact either in the motive suggested, or in the precise action ascribed to
him, though it recognizes Calvin's contribution to a better understanding
of the doctrine (" Doctrine of the Person of Christ," E. T. II. ii. 1862, p. 158,
note 1): " Even Calvin, about the time of his dispute with Caroli, asserted
the necessity of a developing revision of the doctrine of the Trinity. On this
ground he declined pledging himself to the Athanasian Creed, and wished
to cast aside the terms ' persona,' ' Trinitas,' as scholastic expressions. At
the same time he was so far from being inclined towards the Antitrinitarians,
that he wished to carry out the doctrine of the Trinity still more completely.
He saw clearly that in the traditional form of the doctrine, the Son had not
full deity, because aseity (aseitas) was reserved to the Father alone, who
thus received a preponderance over the Son, and was identified with the
Monas, or the Divine essence. The Antitrinitarians, with whom he had to
struggle, usually directed their attacks on this weak point of the dogma, and
deduced therefrom the Antitrinitarian conclusions."

first edition (1536) it occupies only five columns in the Strasburg edition; these have grown to fifteen and a half columns in the middle editions and to twenty-seven and a half (of which eleven and a half are retained from the earlier editions and sixteen are new) in the final edition of 1559. That is to say, its original compass was tripled in the middle editions and almost doubled again in the final edition, where it has become between five and six times as long as in the first draft.[48] And in this process of expansion it has not only gathered increment but has suffered change. This change is not, however, in the substance of the doctrine taught or even in the mode of its formulation or the language in which it is couched or in the general tone which informs it. It is only in the range and the governing aim of the discussion.

The statement in the first edition is dominated by a simple desire to give guidance to docile believers, and therefore declines formal controversy and seeks merely to set down briefly what is to be followed, what is to be avoided on this great subject. Positing, therefore, at the outset that the Scriptures teach one God, not many, but yet not obscurely assert that the Father is God and the Son is God and the Holy Spirit is God; Calvin here at once develops, by combining Eph. iv. 5 and Mat. xxviii. 19, a Biblical proof of the Trinity which in its strenuous logic reminds us of the analytical examination of Heb. i. 3 which we have already noted. Paul, he says, connects together one baptism, one faith and one God; but in Matthew we read that we are to be baptized in the name of the Father and of the Son and of the Holy Spirit — and what is that but to say that the Father and the Son and the Holy Spirit are together the one God of which Paul speaks?[49] This is supported

---

[48] The "Institutes" as a whole were about doubled in length from the first edition (1536) to the second (1539), and again about doubled in the last edition (1559), so that the last edition (1559) is about four times as long as the first (1536). The treatment of the Trinity was, therefore, a little more expanded than the volume as a whole.

[49] This argument is retained in the later editions and appears in its final form in the ed. of 1559, I. xiii. 16. In its earliest statement it runs thus (1536, pp. 107–108: Strasburg ed., p. 58): "Paul so connects these three things, God, faith and baptism, that he reasons from one to the other (Eph. 4). So that,

by Jeremiah's (xxiii. 33) designation of the Son by "that name which the Jews call ineffable"[50] and other Scriptural evidence

---

because there is one faith, thence he demonstrates that there is one God; because there is one baptism, thence he shows that there is one faith. For since faith ought not to be looking about hither and thither, neither wandering through various things, but should direct its view towards the one God, be fixed on Him and adhere to Him; it may be easily proved from these premises that if there be many faiths there should be many Gods. Again because baptism is the sacrament of faith, it confirms to us His unity, seeing that it is one. But no one can profess faith except in the one God. Therefore as we are baptized into the one faith, so our faith believes in the one God. Both that therefore is one and this is one, because each is of one God. Hence also it follows that it is not lawful to be baptized except into the one God, because we are baptized into faith in Him, in whose name we are baptized. Now, the Scriptures have wished (Mat. at end) that we should be baptized into the name of the Father and of the Son and of the Holy Ghost, at the same time that it wishes all to believe with one faith in the Father, the Son and the Holy Spirit. What is that, truly, except a plain testimony that the Father, Son and Holy Spirit are one God? For if we are baptized in their name, we are baptized into faith in them. They are therefore one God, if they are worshipped in one faith."

[50] *Opp.* i. 58. This awkward periphrasis suggests that, when the "Institutes" were written — in 1534–1535 — Calvin had no convenient expression at hand for the Tetragrammaton. This conjecture is supported by the circumstance that "Jehovah" does not seem to occur in the first edition; it is lacking even in the Preface to the First Commandment, where the customary *Dominus* takes its place. Already in the spring of 1537, however (*Opp.* vii. 314; ix. 704, 708, 709; xb. 107, 121) it is used familiarly; and thenceforward throughout Calvin's life. During his sojourn at Basle (1535) Calvin had studied Hebrew with Sebastian Münster (Baumgartner, "Calvin Hébraïsant," 1889, p. 18), and it was doubtless from him that he acquired the pronunciation "Jehovah" (see Münster on Ex. vi. 3 in "Critici Sacri," Amsterdam ed., 1698, i. 107, 108; Frankfort ed., i. 447; cf. 32). From his own comment on Ex. vi. 3 we may learn the clearness of Calvin's conviction that "Jehovah" is the right pronunciation: "It would be tedious to enumerate all the opinions on the name 'Jehovah.' It is certainly a foul superstition of the Jews that they dare not either pronounce or write it, but substitute 'Adonai' for it. It is no more probable that, as many teach, it is unpronounceable because it is not written according to grammatical rule. . . . Nor do I assent to the grammarians who will not have it pronounced because its inflection is irregular. . . ." How fixed the pronunciation "Jehovah" had become at Geneva by 1570 is revealed by an incident which occurred at the "Promotions" at the Academy that year. The Hebrew Professor, Corneille Bertram, having declared in response to an inquiry that "Adonai" not "Jehovah" was to be read, was rebuked therefor and compelled to apologize: "This M. de Bèze and all the Company found ill-said, and remonstrated with him for agitating

that our Lord is one God with the Father and the Spirit. He has in mind to prove both elements in the doctrine of the Trinity, the unity of God and the true distinction of persons, and therefore introduces these citations with the words: " There are extant also other clear (*luculenta*) testimonies, which assert, in part, the one divinity of the three, and in part their personal

this curious and idle question, and for affirming an opinion which very many great men of this age, of good knowledge, piety, and judgment, have held to be absurd, superstitious and merely Rabbinic " (*Reg. Comp.*, 31 May, 1570, cited by Charles Borgeaud, " Histoire de l'Université de Genève," 1900, p. 228). — The history of the pronunciation " Jehovah " has not been adequately investigated. See, however, G. F. Moore, " Notes on the Name יהוה," A. J. T., 1908, xii. pp. 34–52; A. J. S. L., 1909, xxv. pp. 312–318; 1911, xxviii. pp. 56–62. It has become the scholastic tradition to say that it was introduced by Peter Galatin, confessor of Leo X, and first appears in his " De Arcanis Catholicae Veritatis," ii. 10 (the first of two chapters so numbered) which was first published in 1516 (cf. Buhl's " Gesenius' Lexicon," ed. 13, 1899, p. 311, " about 1520 "; Brown, Driver, Briggs, " Hebrew and English Lexicon," 1906, p. 218a, 1520; Kittel, " Herzog," 3 viii. pp. 530–531, 1518; Davidson, Hastings' B. D., art. " God," 1520; A. J. Maclean, Hastings' One Vol. B. D., 1909, p. 300a, 1518; A. H. McNeile, " Westminster Commentary on Exodus," 1908, p. 23, 1518; Oxford English Dictionary, *sub voc.*, 1516; and Moore, *op. cit.*, 1518: cf. the very strong statement of Dillmann, " Alttest. Theologie," 1895, p. 215). But this tradition is simply reported from mouth to mouth, from Drusius' tract on the Tetragrammaton (" Critici Sacri," Amsterdam ed., vol. I. part ii. pp. 322 *sq.*: also in Reland, " Decas. Exercitationum . . . de vera pronuntiatione nominis Jehova," 1707). Since Drusius no one seems to have made any independent effort to ascertain the facts, except F. Böttcher, " Ausführliches Lehrbuch der Hebräischen Sprache," i. 1866, § 88 (p. 49, note 2). In copying Drusius the scholars have failed to note that he himself points out in a later note, inserted on p. 355, that the form " Jehovah " (Porchetus' form is Johova, not Jehova) occurs already in Porchetus, A.D. 1303: and it has been pointed out also that it occurs in Raimund Martini's " Pugio Fidei," which was written about 1270 (Böttcher's suggestion that it may be an interpolation in the " Pugio Fidei " does not seem convincing, although Moore agrees with him here, *op. cit.*). It is not unlikely that Galatin, who draws heavily on Martini either directly or through Porchetti, may have derived it from him: and in any event he uses it not as a novel invention of his own, but as a well-known form. The origin and age of the pronunciation are accordingly yet to seek. The words of Dr. F. Chance (*The Athenæum*, No. 2119, June 6, 1868, p. 796) are here in point: " There is no doubt, I think, that the letters *jhvh* were from the very introduction of the Hebrew points pointed as they now are . . . and if so, surely anybody that read what he had before him must have *read* Jehovah. If the word were never so *written* before the sixteenth century, it was probably because up to that time Hebrew was studied by very few people, except by

distinctions." [51] Then comes the defense of the technical words
by which the truth of the Trinity is expressed and protected,
of which we have already spoken. The enlarged and readjusted
treatment of the topic for the second edition of 1539 seems to
have been composed under the influence of the controversy
with Caroli. It is marked at least by the incorporation of a
thorough proof of the Godhead of the Father, Son and Spirit,
of the unity of their essence, and of the distinction between
them, and a coloring apparently derived from this controversy is thrown over the whole discussion, in which liberty to
formulate the doctrine in our own words and the value of the
technical terms already in use are equally vigorously asserted.
The material of 1539 remains intact throughout the middle
editions (1543, 1550), although some short quotations from
Augustine (§§ 16, 20) and from Jerome and Hilary (§ 24)
were introduced in 1543. But it is very freely dealt with in the
final edition (1559). Only some two-thirds of it (eleven and
a half columns out of fifteen and a half) is preserved in that
edition, while sixteen new columns are added: about three-
fifths of the whole is thus new.[52] Moreover, whole sections are

Jews who could not write this holiest of God's names, and by Gentiles who,
having learned their Hebrew from Jews, followed their example in substituting for it in reading and writing, Adonai, the Lord, etc." — No doubt the
vogue of the form in the middle of the sixteenth century is due, not to its
accidental occurrences in Galatin's book, but to the progress of Hebrew scholarship in sequence to the revival of letters, which looked upon the Jewish refusal to pronounce the name as mere superstition and attached an exaggerated importance to the Massoretic pointing. The debate about the proper
pronunciation of the name is, in any event, a Humanistic phenomenon, and
the form "Jehovah" is found in use everywhere where Hebrew scholarship
penetrated, until it was corrected by this scholarship itself. Reuchlin indeed
appears not to have used it; nor Melanchthon. But it is used by Luther
(1526–1527 and 1543, though not in his Bible), and by Matthew Tyndale in
his Pentateuch of 1530, and so prevailingly by Protestant scholars that Romish
controversialists were tempted to represent it as an impiety (so Genebrardus)
of the "Calviniani et Bezani" following the example of Sanctes Pagninus
(who, according to MS. but not printed copies did indeed use it).

[51] *Opp.* i. 58.

[52] The most notable additions are the argument on ὑπόστασις in Heb. i. 3
(§ 2); the definition of "person" (§ 6); and the whole polemic against Servetus and Gentilis (§§ 22 to end). These sections contain nine of the sixteen
new columns.

omitted (§§ 10 and 15), a new order of arrangement is adopted, and much minor alteration is introduced. In this recasting and expansion of the discussion the chief place in the formative forces determining its form and tone is taken by the attack of the radical Antitrinitarians. The existence of these Antitrinitarian scoffers is recognized, indeed, from the first: they are explicitly adverted to already in the edition of 1536 as "certain impious men, who wish to tear our faith up by the roots": it is quite clear, indeed, that Servetus' teachings were already before his mind at this date. But it is only for the final edition (1559) that their assault assumes the determining position at the basis of the whole treatment: and it is only in this edition that Servetus, for example, is named. Now, Calvin not only arrays against them the testimony of Scripture in a developed polemic, but adjusts the whole positive exposition of the doctrine to its new purpose, shaping and phrasing its statements and modifying them by added sentences and clauses. The result is a polemic the edge of which is turned no longer against those who may have doubted Calvin's orthodoxy, as was the case in 1539, but rather against those who have essayed to bring into doubt or even openly to deny the mysteries which enter into the Christian doctrine of the Trinity. The sharp anti-scholastic sentences which are permitted to remain, serve to give a singular balance to the discussion, and to make it clear that the polemic against the Antitrinitarians has in view vital interests and not mere matters of phraseology.

The disposition of the material in this its final form follows the lines of its new dominant interest. The discussion opens, as we have seen, with a paragraph designed to bear in on the mind a sense of the mystery which must characterize the divine mode of existence (§ 1). This is immediately followed by an announcement of the Trinitarian fact and a defense of the technical terms used to express and protect it (§§ 2–5). After this introduction the subject itself is taken up (§ 6, *ad init.*) and treated in two great divisions, by way first of positive statement and proof (§§ 6–20) and by way secondly of polemic defense (§§ 21 to end). The positive portion opens with a careful definition of what is meant by the " Trinity " (§ 6) and is prosecuted by an exhibition of the Scriptural proof of the doctrine in three sections: first the proof of the complete deity of the Son (§§ 7–13), then the proof of the deity of the Spirit (§§ 14–15), and then the proof of the Trinitarian distinctions, which includes a dissertation on the nature of these distinctions on the basis of Scripture (§§ 16–20). The polemic phase of the discussion begins with some introductory remarks (§ 21) and then defends in turn the true personality of the Son against Servetus (§ 22) and His complete deity against its modern impugners, Valentinus Gentilis being chiefly in mind (§§ 23–29).

This comprehensive outline is richly filled in with details, all of which are treated, however, with a circumspection and moderation which illustrate Calvin's determination to eschew human speculations upon this high theme and to confine himself to the revelations of Scripture, only so far explicated in human language as is necessary for their pure expression and protection.[53] We observe, for example, that he introduces no proofs or illustrations of the Trinity derived from metaphysical reasoning or natural analogies. From the example of Augustine it had been the habit throughout the Middle Ages to make much of these proofs or illustrations, and the habit had passed over into the Protestant usage. Melanchthon, for example, gave new currency alike to the old ontological speculations which under the forms of subject and object sought to conceive the Logos as the image of Himself which the thinking Father set over against Himself, and to the human analogies by which the Trinitarian distinctions were fancied to be illustrated, such, for example, as the distinctions between the intellect, sensibility and will in man. Calvin held himself aloof from all

[53] Cf. Köstlin, *Studien und Kritiken*, 1868, p. 419, who speaks of " the circumspect, cautious moderation with which Calvin confines himself to the simplest principles of the Church conception and refuses to pass beyond the simple declarations of Scripture to a dogmatic formulation, much more to scholastic questions and answers, one step farther than seemed to him to be demanded for the protection of the Godhead of the Redeemer and of the Holy Spirit from the assaults of old and new enemies."

such reasoning, doubting, as he says (§ 18), "the value of
similitudes from human things for expressing the force of the
Trinitarian distinction," and fearing that their employment
might afford only occasion to those evil disposed for calumny
and to those little instructed for error.[54] What he desired was
a plain proof from Scripture itself of the elements of the doctrine, freed from all additions from human speculation. This
proof he attempted, in outline at least, to set down in his pages.
It is interesting to observe how he conducts it.

He begins, as we have already pointed out, with a plain
statement of what he means by the Trinity (§ 6). Such a
"short and easy definition" (*brevis et facilis definitio*) had
been his object from the outset (§ 2, *ad init.*), and it was in
fact in order to obtain it that he entered upon the defense,
which fills the first sections, of the term and conception of
"Person" as applied to the distinctions in the Godhead. Reverting to it after this defense, he carefully defines (§ 6) what
he means by "Person" in this connection, viz., "a subsistence in the Divine essence, which, related to the others, is yet
distinguished by an incommunicable property." What he has
to prove, therefore, he conceives to be that in the unity of the
Godhead there is such a distinction of persons; or, as he phrases
it, in a statement derived from Tertullian, that "there is in
God a certain disposition or economy, which makes no difference, however, to the unity of the essence"; or, as he puts
it himself a little later on (§ 20, *ad init.*), that "there is understood under the name of God, a unitary and simple essence,

[54] Cf. I. xv. 4, *ad fin.* Cf. Commentary on Genesis, i. 26, where, speaking
of the human faculties, he remarks: "But Augustine, beyond all others,
speculates with excessive refinement for the purpose of fabricating a trinity in
man. For in laying hold of the three faculties of the soul enumerated by
Aristotle, the intellect, the memory and the will, he afterwards out of one
trinity derives many. If any reader, having leisure, wishes to enjoy such
speculations, let him read the tenth and fourteenth books of *The Trinity*,
also the eleventh book of *The City of God*. I acknowledge indeed that there is
something in man which refers to the Father, and the Son, and the Spirit;
and I have no difficulty in admitting the above distribution of the faculties,
. . . but a definition of the image of God ought to rest on a firmer basis
than such subtleties." For the later Reformed attitude, see Heppe, "Die Dogmatik der ev.-ref. Kirche," 1861, pp. 85 *sqq.*

in which we comprise three persons or hypostases." In order to prove this doctrine, it would be necessary to prove that while God is one, there are three persons who are God, and Calvin undertakes the proof on that understanding. He does not pause here, however, to argue the unity of God at length, taking that for the moment for granted, though he reverts to it in the sequel to show that the distinction of persons which he conceives himself to have established in no respect infringes on it (§ 19), and indeed in his polemic against Valentinus Gentilis very fully vindicates it from the objections of the Arianisers and Tritheists (§§ 23 sq.). His proof resolves itself, therefore, into the establishment of the distinctions in the Godhead; and in order to do this he undertakes to prove first that the Son and the Holy Spirit are each God, and then to show that the Scriptures explicitly recognize that there is such a distinction in the Godhead as their divinity (taken in connection with the Divine unity) implies.

The proof of the deity of the Son is very comprehensive and detailed, and is drawn from each Testament alike. The Word of God, by which, as God "spake," He made the worlds, it is argued, must be understood of the substantial Word, which is also called in Proverbs, Wisdom (§ 7); and must accordingly be understood as eternal. In connection with this, the whole scheme of temporal prolation as applied to the Son is sharply assaulted. It is impious to suppose that anything new can ever have happened to God in Himself (in se ipso), and there is "nothing less tolerable than to invent a beginning for that Word, who both was always God and afterwards became the maker of the world" (§ 8). To this more general argument is brought the support of a number of Old Testament passages, which, it is contended, advert to the Son with declarations of His deity: such as the Forty-fifth Psalm, "Thy throne, O God, is for ever and ever"; Is. ix. 6, "His Name shall be called Mighty God, Father of Eternity"; Jer. xxiii. 6, "The Branch of David shall be called Jehovah our Righteousness" (§ 9). And then the phenomena connected with the manifestations of the Angel of Jehovah are adduced in corroboration

(§ 10). The New Testament evidence is marshalled under two heads: the divine names are applied to Christ by the New Testament writers (§ 11), and divine works and functions are assigned to Him (§§ 12–13). Not only are Old Testament passages which speak of Jehovah applied to Christ in the New Testament (Is. viii. 14, Rom. ix. 33; Is. xlv. 23, Rom. xiv. 10, 11; Ps. lxviii. 18, Eph. iv. 8; Is. vi. 1, Jno. xii. 41), but these writers themselves employ the term "God" in speaking of Christ (Jno. i. 1, 14; Rom. ix. 5; I Tim. iii. 16; I Jno. v. 20; Acts xx. 28; Jno. xx. 28), and the like. And what divine work do not the New Testament writers credit Him with, either from His own lips or theirs? They represent Him as having been co-worker with God from all eternity (Jno. v. 17), as the upholder and governor of the world (Heb. i. 3), as the forgiver of iniquities (Mat. ix. 6) and the searcher of hearts (Mat. ix. 4). They not only accredit Him with mighty works, but distinguish Him from others who have wrought miracles, precisely by this — these others wrought them by the power of God, He by His own power (§ 13a). They represent Him as the dispenser of salvation, the source of eternal life and the fountain of all that is good: they present Him as the proper object of saving faith and trust, and even of worship and prayer (§ 13b).

The deity of the Spirit is similarly argued on the ground of certain Old Testament passages (Genesis i. 2; Is. xlviii. 16) where the Spirit of God seems to be hypostatized; of the divine works attributed to Him, such as ubiquitous activity, regeneration, and the searching of the deep things of God on the one hand and the bestowing of wisdom, speech and all other blessings on men on the other; and finally of the application of the name God to Him in the New Testament writings (e.g., I Cor. iii. 16, vi. 19; II Cor. vi. 16; Acts v. 3; xxviii. 25; Mat. xii. 31).

Having thus established the deity of the Son and the Spirit, Calvin turns to the passages which elucidate their deity to us by presenting to us the doctrine of the Trinity. These are all in the New Testament, as was natural (suggests Calvin), because the advent of Christ involved a clearer revelation of God and therefore a fuller knowledge of the personal distinctions in His being (§ 16). The stress of the argument here is laid upon Eph. iv. 5 in connection with Mat. xxviii. 19, which were already expounded at length, as we have seen, in the first edition of the " Institutes," and are here only strengthened and clarified by a better statement. As we are initiated by baptism into faith in the one God and yet baptism is in the name of the Father, the Son and the Holy Spirit, argues Calvin, it is " solidly clear " that the Father, Son and Spirit are this one God; whence it is perfectly obvious that " there reside (*residere*) in the essence of God three Persons, in whom the one God is cognized " (*cognoscitur*); and " since it remains fixed that God is one not many, we can only conclude that the Word and the Spirit are nothing other than the essence of God itself." The Scriptures, however, he proceeds (§ 17), no more thus identify the Son and Spirit with God than they distinguish them — distinguish, not divide them. He appeals to such passages as Jno. v. 32, viii. 16, 18, xiv. 16, " another "; [55] xv. 26, viii. 16, " proceeding," " being sent ": but this part of the subject is lightly passed over on the ground that the passages already adduced themselves sufficiently show that the Son possesses a " distinct property " by which He is not the Father — for, says he, " the Word could not have been *with* God unless He had been another than the Father, neither could He have had His glory *with* the Father, unless He was distinct from Him ": the distinction noted in which passages it is plain, further, is not one which could have begun at the incarnation, but must date from whatever point He may be thought to have begun to be " in the bosom of the Father " (Jno. i. 18). The determination that there is a personal distinction between Father and Son and Holy Spirit leads Calvin to inquire what this distinction carries with it. He finds it to be Scriptural to say that " to the Father is attributed the *principium agendi,* as fountain and source of all things; to the Son, wisdom, counsel and the actual dispensation of things to be done; but to the

[55] In ed. 1 (1536) he remarks (*Opp.* i. 59) that " that the Holy Spirit is ' another ' than Christ is proved by more than ten passages from the Gospel of John (John xiv. xv.)."

Spirit is assigned the power and efficiency (*virtus et efficacia*) of the action " — that is to say, if we may be permitted to reduce the definitions to single words, the Father is conceived as the Source, the Son as the Director, the Spirit as the Executor of all the divine activities; the Father as the Fountain, the Son as the Wisdom emerging from Him, the Spirit as the Power by which the wise counsels of God are effectuated (§ 18).[56] Only now when this argument is finished and his conclusion drawn (§ 19) does Calvin pause formally to point out that "this distinction in no way impedes the absolutely simple unity of God" — since the conception is that the "whole nature (*natura*) is in each hypostasis," while "each has its own propriety." " The Father," he adds, " is *totus* in the Son, and the Son *totus* in the Father" — as Christ Himself teaches in Jno. xiv. 10. We are here, however, obviously passing beyond the proof to the exposition of the Trinity — a topic which occupies some later sections (§§ 19 and 20).

It will have already become apparent from the citations incidentally adduced that in his doctrine of the Trinity Calvin departed in nothing from the doctrine which had been handed down from the orthodox Fathers. If distinctions must be drawn, he is unmistakably Western rather than Eastern in his conception of the doctrine, an Augustinian rather than an Athanasian.[57] That is to say, the principle of his construction of the

[56] This passage is already found in ed. 1 (1536) (*Opp.* i. 62): " The Persons are so distinguished by the Scriptures that they assign to the Father the *principium agendi,* and the fountain and origin of all things; to the Son the wisdom and *consilium agendi;* to the Spirit the *virtus et efficacia actionis;* whence also the Son is called the Word of God, not such as men speak or think, but eternal and unchangeable, as emerging in an ineffable manner from the Father."

[57] Cf. L. L. Paine, " The Evolution of Trinitarianism," 1900, p. 95: " It is a remarkable fact that the Protestant Reformation only increased the prestige of Augustine. . . . The question of the Trinity was not a subject of controversy and the Augustinian form of trinitarian doctrine became a fixed tradition. The Nicene Creed, as interpreted by the Pseudo-Athanasian Creed, was accepted on all sides and passed into all the Protestant Confessions. It is to be noted that Calvin insisted on the use of the term 'person' as the only word that would unmask Sabellianism. He also held to numerical unity of essence. This would seem to indicate that Calvin believed that God was

Trinitarian distinctions is equalization rather than subordination. He does, indeed, still speak in the old language of refined subordinationism which had been fixed in the Church by the Nicene formularies; and he expressly allows an " order " of first, second and third in the Trinitarian relations. But he conceives more clearly and applies more purely than had ever previously been done the principle of equalization in his thought of the relation of the Persons to one another, and thereby, as we have already hinted, marks an epoch in the history of the doctrine of the Trinity. That he was enabled to do this was a result, no doubt, at least in part, of his determination to preserve the highest attainable simplicity in his thought of the Trinity. Sweeping his mind free from subtleties in minor matters, he perceived with unwonted lucidity the main things, and thus was led to insist upon them with a force and clearness of exposition which throw them out into unmistakable emphasis. If we look for the prime characteristics of Calvin's doctrine of the Trinity, accordingly, we shall undoubtedly fix first upon its simplicity, then upon it consequent lucidity, and finally upon its elimination of the last remnants of subordinationism, so as to do full justice to the deity of Christ. Simplification, clarification, equalization — these three terms are the notes of Calvin's conception of the Trinity. And, of course, it is the last of these notes which gives above all else its character to his construction.[58]

---

one Being in three real persons, and, if so, he must have allowed that in God nature and person are not coincident. Yet he nowhere raises the question, and I am inclined to think he was not conscious of any departure from the views of Augustine." Calvin does, however, repeatedly raise the question whether " nature " and " person " are coincident and repeatedly decides that they are, in the sense that the person is the whole nature in a personal distinction. " The whole nature (*tota natura*) " is affirmed to be " in each hypostasis (*in unaquaque hypostasi*)," though there is present to each one its own propriety (I. xiii. 19). Hence there is no such thing as " a triplex God," as " the simple essence of God being divided among the three Persons " (xiii. 2); the essence is not multiplex, and the Son contains the whole of it in Himself (*totam in se*), etc. (*ibid.*).

[58] It is the same thing that is meant by G. A. Meier, " Lehre von der Trinität, etc.," 1844, ii. pp. 58–59, where, after remarking that the Reformed were prone to emphasize especially the unity of God (which involves what

The note of simplification is struck at the outset of the discussion when Calvin announces it as his intention to seek " a short and easy definition which shall preserve us from all error " (I. xiii. 2, *ad init.*). What the short and easy definition which he had in mind included is suggested when he tells us later (20) that " when we profess to believe in one God, under the name of God is to be understood the single and simple essence in which we comprehend three persons or hypostases." He accordingly expresses pleasure in the definition of Tertullian, when properly understood, that " there is in God a certain disposition or economy, which in no respect derogates from the unity of the essence " (6, *ad fin.*); and frankly declares that for him the whole substance of the doctrine is included in the simple statement " that the Father and the Son and the Spirit are one God; and yet neither is the Son the Father nor the Spirit the Son, but they are distinct by a certain property " (5). Similar simple forms of statement are thickly scattered through the discussion. " God so predicates Himself to be one," he says at its outset, " that He propones Himself to be dis-

---

we have called " equalization "), he proceeds: " External circumstances early led to the sharp emergence of this peculiarity. In the controversy with Gentilis, who maintained that the essential being of the Son was from the Father, Calvin was compelled to contend that in His Godhead and in His nature, the Son is of Himself, and without principium, and only in His personal subsistence, has His principium in the Father.[1] Catholic theologians, especially Petau, have charged him with heresy for this, though he was only enunciating with increased sharpness the conviction of the Church, and rightly recalling that otherwise a plurality of Gods would be introduced.[2] " At the points indicated the following notes are added. " 1. ' Since the name Jehovah is used in the passages cited above, it follows that the Son of God is with respect to His deity solely of Himself.' *Val. Gentilis impietatum brevis explic.* (*Calv. Opp.*, Amstel. 1667, viii. p. 572). ' The essence of the Son has no principium, but the principium of the Person is God Himself ' (*loc. cit.*, p. 573). ' We concede that the Son takes origin from the Father, so far as He is Son, but it is an origin not of time, nor of essence, . . . but of order only ' (*l. c.*, p. 580)." " 2. ' Unless moreover the Son is God along with the Father, a plurality of Gods will necessarily be brought in ' (*Ep. ad. Fratres Polonos*, p. 591). Accordingly Calvin called the " Deus de Deo " a " hard saying." Against him see Petau, *De theol. dogm.*, II. *lib.* iii. c. 3, §§ 2, 3. On the other hand, Bellarmine acknowledges that in the maintenance of the αὐτοθεότης of the Son there is no real departure from the doctrine of the Church."

tinctly considered in three Persons " (2, *ad init.*). " There truly
subsist in the one God, or what is the same thing, in the unity
of God," he says again, "a trinity of Persons " (4, *ad fin.*).
" There are three *proprietates* in God " (*ibid.*). " In the one
essence of God, there is a Trinity of Persons," and these are
" consubstantial " (5, *ad fin.*). " In the divine essence there
exist three Persons, in whom the one God is cognized " (16).
" There is a Trinity of Persons contained in the one God, not
a trinity of Gods " (25). It is quite clear, not only from the
frequency with which he lapses into such brief formulas, but
also from the distinctness with which he declares that they contain all that is essential to the doctrine of the Trinity (e.g., § 5),
that in Calvin's habitual thought of the Trinity it lay summed
up in his mind in these simple facts: there is but one God; the
Father, the Son, the Spirit is each this one God, the entire divine essence being in each; these three are three Persons, distinguished one from another by an incommunicable property.[59]

Calvin's main interest among the elements of this simple
doctrine of the Trinity obviously lay in his profound sense
of the consubstantiality of the Persons. Whatever the Father
is as God, that the Son and the Spirit are also. The Son — and,
of course, also the Spirit — contains in Himself the whole essence of God, not part of it only nor by deflection, but in complete perfection (§ 2). What the Father is, reappears therefore
in its totality (*se totum*) in the Son and in the Spirit. This is
a mere corollary of their community in the numerically one
essence. If the " entire nature " (*tota natura*, § 19) is included
in each, it necessarily carries with it all the qualities by which
it is made this particular nature which we call divine. Calvin

---

[59] Cf. "Adv. P. Caroli calumnias" (*Opp.* vii. 312): "Yet in that one
essence of God we acknowledge the Father with His eternal Word and
Spirit. In using this distinction, however, we do not imagine three Gods, as
if the Father were some other thing than the Son, nor yet do we understand
them to be naked epithets, by which God is variously designated from His
actions; but, along with the ecclesiastical writers, we perceive in the simple
unity of God these three hypostases, that is subsistences, which although
they coexist in one essence are not to be confused with each other. Accordingly, though the Father is one God with His Word and Spirit, the Father is
not the Word, nor the Word the Spirit."

is accordingly never weary of asserting that every divine attribute, in the height of its meaning, is manifested as fully in the Son — and, of course, also in the Spirit — as in the Father. In this indeed lay for him the very nerve of the doctrine of the Trinity. And in it, consistently carried out, lies the contribution which he made to the clear apprehension and formulation of that doctrine. For, strange as it may seem, theologians at large had been accustomed to apply the principle of consubstantiality to the Persons of the Trinity up to Calvin's vigorous assertion of it, with some at least apparent reserves. And when he applied it without reserve it struck many as a startling novelty if not a heretical pravity. The reason why the consubstantiality of the Persons of the Trinity, despite its establishment in the Arian controversy and its incorporation in the Nicene formulary as the very hinge of orthodoxy, was so long in coming fully to its rights in the general apprehension was no doubt that Nicene orthodoxy preserved in its modes of stating the doctrine of the Trinity some remnants of the conceptions and phraseology proper to the older prolationism of the Logos Christology, and these, although rendered innocuous by the explanations of the Nicene Fathers and practically antiquated since Augustine, still held their place formally and more or less conditioned the thought of men — especially those who held the doctrine of the Trinity in a more or less traditional manner. The consequence was that when Calvin taught the doctrine in its purity and free from the leaven of subordinationism which still found a lurking place in current thought and speech, he seemed violently revolutionary to men trained in the old forms of speech and imbued with the old modes of conception, and called out reprobation in the most unexpected quarters.

Particular occasion of offense was given by Calvin's ascription of " self-existence " (aseity, αὐτοουσία) to the Son, and the consequent designation of Him by the term αὐτόθεος. This term, which became famous in later controversy as designating Calvin's doctrine of Christ, seems, however, to have come forward only in the latest years of his life, in the dispute with Valentinus Gentilis (1558, 1561); and indeed to be rather Gentilis' word than Calvin's. Calvin, indeed, does not appear to have himself employed it, but only to have reclaimed it for Christ (and the Spirit) when Gentilis asserted that it was exclusively God the Father who could be so designated. " The Father alone," said Gentilis, " is αὐτόθεος, that is, essentiated by no superior divinity; but is God a se ipso "; " the λόγος of God is not that one αὐτόθεος whose λόγος it is; neither is the Spirit of God that immense and eternal Spirit whose Spirit it is." [60] Such assertions, declares Calvin, are against all Scripture, which makes Christ very God: for "what is more proper to God than to exist (vivere), and what else is αὐτοουσία than this? " [61] But the thing represented by the term — " self-existence " — Calvin asserts of Christ from the beginning of his activity as a Christian teacher. It does not seem to be explicitly declared of Christ that He is self-existent, indeed, in the first edition of the " Institutes " (1536), although it is already implied there too, not only in the general vigor with which the absolute deity of Christ is asserted with all its implications, but also in the identification of Christ with Jehovah, which was to Calvin the especial vehicle of his representation of Him as the self-existent God. " That name which the Jews call ineffable is attributed to the Son in Jeremiah " (Jer. xxiii. 33),[62] he already here tells us. In the spring of the following year,[63] however, at the councils held within a few days of one another respectively at Lausanne and Bern, our Lord's self-existence was fairly enunciated in so many words in the statement of his faith which Calvin made in rebuttal of the charges of Caroli. He begins with a very clear exposition of the doctrine of the Trinity, and then comes to speak of what peculiarly concerns

---

[60] " Expositio impietatis Valentini Gentilis," 1561 (Opp. ix. 374, 380).

[61] Ibid., Preface, p. 368. Cf. Beza in his Life of Calvin, who speaks of Gentilis under the year 1558 and describes him as wishing to make the Father alone αὐτόθεος (Opp. xxi. 154). These four references (ix. 368, 374, 380; xxi. 154) are all that are given in the Index to the Strasburg ed. (xxii. 493 — this word does not occur in the Index of xxiii. sq.) of Calvin's works under the word αὐτόθεος.

[62] Opp. i. 58, at bottom of column.   [63] May 14 and 31, 1537.

Christ, adverting especially to His two natures. " For," he
continues, " before He assumed flesh He was the eternal Word
itself, begotten by the Father before the ages, very God, of one
essence, power, majesty with the Father, and indeed Jehovah
Himself, *who has always had it of Himself that He should be
and has inspired the power of subsisting in others.*" [64] Caroli
at once seized upon this declaration, and complained that
therein " Christ was set forth as Jehovah, as if He had His
essence of Himself (*a se ipso*)." [65] From this beginning rose the
controversy. For in this one of his " calumnies " Caroli found
some following, and Calvin was worried by petty attacks upon
this element of his teaching through a series of years.[66]

Calvin apparently was somewhat astonished by the pother
which was raised over an assertion which seemed to him not
only a very natural one to make, but also a very necessary one
to make if the true deity of our Lord is to be defended. He
calls this particular one of Caroli's assaults the " most atrocious " of all his calumnies, and he betrays some irritation at
the repetition of it by others. One effect of it was, however, to
make him see that, although it might seem to him a matter of
course to speak of Christ as the self-existent God, it was not a
matter which could be taken for granted, but needed assertion and defense. He inserted, therefore, in the " Institutes "
of 1539 (second edition) a clear declaration on the subject,
which, with only the adduction of some additional support
chiefly drawn from Augustine (inserted in 1543 and 1559),
was retained throughout the subsequent editions. " More-

[64] *Opp.* vii. 314: qui a se ipso semper habuit ut esset, et aliis subsistendi virtutem inspiravit. Cf. ix. 707; xb. 107, 121. Cf. Ruchat, " Histoire de la
reformation de la Suisse," 1835 *sq.*, v. pp. 27–28; Bähler, as cited, p. 78; and
also Merle D'Aubigné, " History of the Reformation in Europe in the Time of
Calvin," E. T. vi. 1877, p. 316.

[65] *Ibid.*, p. 315.

[66] *Ibid.*, p. 322: " But the most atrocious calumny of all is where he im-
pugns this statement: that Christ always had it of Himself that He should
be; in which he has been followed by some others, men of no account, who,
however, worry good men with their improbity; in the number of whom is a
certain rogue (*furcifer*) very like himself (Caroli), who calls himself Cortesius."

over," says he in this passage, " the absolutely simple unity of
God is so far from being impeded by this distinction, that it
rather affords a proof that the Son is one God with the Father,
because He possesses one and the same Spirit with Him: while
the Spirit is not another Being diverse from the Father and the
Son, because He is the Spirit of the Father and of the Son. For
in each hypostasis the whole nature is understood, along with
that which is present to each one as His propriety. The Father
is as a whole (*totus*) in the Son, the Son as a whole in the
Father, as He Himself also asserts: ' I in the Father and the
Father in me '; and that one is not separated from another by
any difference of essence is conceded by the ecclesiastical writers.[67] By this understanding the opinions of the fathers are to
be conciliated, which otherwise would seem altogether at odds
with one another. For they teach now that the Father is the
principium of the Son; and now they assert that the Son has
from Himself (*a se ipso*) both divinity and essence.[68] When,
however, the Sabellians raise a cavil that God is called now
Father, now Son, now Spirit, in no way differently from His
being named both strong and good and wise and merciful, they
may easily be refuted from this, — that these manifestly are

[67] References to Augustine and Cyril are given in the margin: and in
1543 the following is inserted here in the text: "' By these appellations which
denote distinctions,' says Augustine, ' what is signified is a reciprocal relation;
not the substance itself which is one.' "

[68] In 1543 there was added: " and therefore is one principium with the
Father. The cause of this diversity, Augustine explains well and perspicuously in another place, speaking as follows: ' Christ with reference to Himself
(*ad se*) is called God; with reference to the Father (*ad patrem*) is called
Son.' And again ' The Father *ad se* is called God, *ad filium* is called Father.
What is called Father *ad filium* is not the Son; what is called Son *ad patrem*
is not the Father: what is called Father *ad se,* and Son *ad se* is the same God.'
When therefore we speak *simpliciter* of the Son without respect to the Father,
we well and properly assert Him to be *a se,* and therefore call Him the unique
principium. When, however, we are noting the relation in which He stands
to the Father, we properly make the Father the principium of the Son."
To this there is further added in 1559: " To the explication of this matter
the fifth book of Augustine's *De Trinitate,* is wholly devoted. It is far safer
to rest in that relation which he teaches, than by more subtly penetrating
into the divine mystery to wander through many vain speculations." And
with these words the paragraph closes in 1559.

epithets which show what God is with respect to us, while the others are names which declare what He is really with respect to Himself. Neither ought anyone to be moved to confound the Spirit with the Father and the Son, because God announces Himself as a whole to be a Spirit (Jno. iv. 24). For there is no reason why the whole essence of God should not be spiritual, and in that essence the Father, Son and Spirit be comprehended. And this very thing is made clear by the Scriptures. For as we hear God called a Spirit in them, so also we hear the Holy Spirit spoken of, and that both as God's Spirit and as from God." [69]

Calvin was not permitted, however, to content himself with this brief positive declaration. A running fire was kept up upon his assertion of self-existence for Christ by two pastors of Neuchâtel and its neighboring country, Jean Chaponneau (Capunculus) and Jean Courtois (Cortesius) — the latter of whom had married the daughter of Chaponneau's wife.[70] Calvin was disposed at first to treat their criticism lightly, but was ultimately driven to give it serious attention. Writing to the Neuchâtel ministers regarding certain articles which Courtois had drawn up — with the help, as was understood, of Chaponneau — Calvin remarks that he sees no reason for supposing them directed as a whole against him. One of them, however, he recognizes as having him in view — that one in which, " as from a tripod," the writer pronounces heretics those who say that " Christ, as He is God, is *a se ipso.*" " The answer," he declares, "is easy. First let him tell me whether Christ is true and perfect God. Unless he wishes to parcel out the essence of God, he must confess that the whole of it is in Christ. And Paul's words are express: that ' in Him dwelleth the fulness of the Godhead.' Again I ask, ' Is that fulness of

[69] *Opp.* i. 490–491.

[70] See Haag, "La France protestante," *sub nom.,* "Chaponneau," ed. 2, iii. p. 1084: " Shortly afterwards Chaponneau married; he married a widow whose daughter soon became the wife in turn of the Pastor John Courtois, known by some disputes that he had with Calvin. Chaponneau no more than his son-in-law hesitated to enter the lists with Calvin. The quarrel had its rise from a question relating to the person of Jesus. . . ."

the Godhead from Himself or from some other source?' But
he will object that the Son is of the Father. Who denies it?
That I, for one, have not only always acknowledged, but even
proclaimed. But this is where these donkeys deceive themselves: because they do not consider that the name of Son
is spoken of the Person, and therefore is included in the predicament of relation, which relation has no place where we are
speaking simply (*simpliciter*) of the divinity of Christ." [71]
In support of this distinction he then quotes Augustine, and
proceeds to cite Cyril on the main point at issue — passages to
which we shall revert in the sequel. This letter was written at
the end of May, 1543, and later in the year we find Calvin
holding a conference with Courtois, the course of which he reports to the Neuchâtel ministers in a letter written in November.[72] Courtois went away, however, still unconvinced, and
Calvin found himself compelled not many months later (opening of 1545) to write to the Neuchâtel pastors again at length
on the subject, under considerable irritation.[73] "This," he here
declares, "is the state of the controversy (*status controver-
siae*): Whether it may be truly predicated of Christ, that He is,
as He is God, *a se ipso*? This Capunculus denies. Why? Because the name of Christ designates the Second Person in the
Godhead, who stands in relation to the Father. I confess that
if respect be had to the Person, we ought not so to speak. But
I say we are not speaking of the Person but of the essence. I
hold that the Holy Spirit is the real (*idoneum* = proper) author of this manner of speaking, since He refers to Christ all
the declarations in which αὐτοουσία is predicated of God, as
in other passages, so in the first chapter of the Epistle to the
Hebrews. . . . He [Capunculus] contends that Christ, because He is of the substance of the Father, is not *a se ipso*,
since He has a principium from another. This I allow to him
of the Person. What more does he want? . . . I confess that

---

[71] *Opp.* xi. 560, Letter 474.

[72] *Opp.* xi. 652, Letter 521.

[73] *Opp.* xii. 16, Letter 607; cf. the letter of Capunculus, *Opp.* xi. 781, Letter
590.

the Son of God is of the Father. Accordingly, since the Person
has a cause (*ratio*), I confess that He is not *a se ipso*. But when
we are speaking, apart from consideration of the Person, of
His divinity or simply of the essence, which is the same thing,
I say that it is rightly predicated of Him that He is *a se ipso*.
For who, heretofore, has denied that under the name of Jehovah, there is included the declaration of αὐτοουσία? . . ."

It was, however, in his " Defense Against the Calumnies of
Peter Caroli," which was sent out in 1545 in reply to a new
"libel" put forth by Caroli early that year,[74] that Calvin
speaks most at large on this subject, gathering up into this
one defense, indeed, all the modes of statement and forms of
argument he had hitherto worked out. He regards Caroli's
strictures upon his assertion of Christ's self-existence as the
most atrocious of all his calumnies, and prefixes to his discussion of them a citation of his own explanation of the matter,
which he calls a " brief and naked explication." This runs as
follows: " When we are speaking of the divinity of Christ all

[74] The " Defensio " was pseudonymously published under the name of
Nicholas des Gallars, Calvin's secretary. Bähler, as cited, pp. 153 *sq.*, judges
it very unfavorably and sharply criticises the advantage taken of its pseudony-
mity and its inaccuracies, as well as its harshness of tone. " The number of
Calvin's polemical writings," says he, " is great, and they are all master-
works of their order. No other, however, surpasses the *Defensio* in harshness
and bitterness. It is all in all, scarcely a happy creation of Calvin's. . . . From
the standpoint of literary history the *Defensio* indisputably deserves unrestricted praise. The elegant, crisp style, the skill with which the author
not only morally annihilates his opponent, but puts upon him the stamp of
an impertinent person not to be taken seriously, and permeates all with the
most sovereign scorn, makes the reading of this book, now nearly four hundred
years old, an aesthetic enjoyment, which obscures the protest of righteous
indignation at the startling injustices and glaring untruths which the author
has permitted himself against Caroli. No doubt Calvin's conduct, if it cannot
be excused, may yet to a certain degree be understood, when we reflect that
Caroli, through almost ten years, had brought to the Reformer of Geneva incessant annoyances and the most bitter mortification, and by his accusations
had imperilled his life-work as perhaps no other antagonist had been able to
do " (p. 159). Compare the more measured censure of A. Lang (" Johannes
Calvin," 1909, p. 42) of the harshness of tone and opprobrious language used
towards Caroli, in contrast with the high praise given the three Reformers
— " when, although it was questionless written by Calvin himself, it was published in the name of his amanuensis, Nicholas des Gallars."

that is proper to God is rightly ascribed to Him, because respect is there had to the Divine essence and no question is
raised as to the distinction which exists between the Father and
the Son. In this sense it is true to say that Christ is the One
and Eternal God, existing of Himself (*a se ipso existentem*).
Nor can it be objected to this statement — what certainly is
also taught by the ecclesiastical writers — that the Word or
Son of God is of the Father (*a Patre*), even with respect to His
eternal essence; since there is a notation of Persons, when
there is commemorated a distinction of the Son from the
Father. But what I have been speaking of is the divinity, in
which is embraced not less the Father and the Spirit than the
Son. So Cyril, who is often wont to call the Father the principium of the Son, holds it in the highest degree absurd for
the Son not to be believed to have life and immortality of
Himself (*a se ipso*). He also teaches that if it is proper to the
ineffable nature to be self-existent (*a se ipsa*), this is rightly
ascribed to the Son. And moreover in the tenth book of his
Thesaurus, he argues that the Father has nothing of Himself
(*a se ipso*) which the Son does not have of Himself (*a se
ipso*)." [75] From this beginning, he proceeds to elucidate the
whole subject, drawing freely upon all that he had previously
written upon it. The note of the discussion is given in the
words: "I assert both truths — both that Christ is of the
Father as He is the second Person, and that He is of Himself
(*a se ipso*) if we have respect to the Divine essence *simpliciter*" [76] — a declaration which he supports from the Fathers,
particularly Augustine, thus: "Similarly Augustine (*Sermo*
38 'de tempore'): 'Those names which signify the substance . . . or essence of God, or whatever God is said to be
in Himself (*ad se*), belong equally to all the Persons. There is
not, therefore, any name of nature which can so belong to the
Father that it may not belong also to the Son, or Holy Spirit.'"
The whole is brought to a conclusion by a passage the substance
of which we have already had before us, but which seems worth
quoting again that its force may be appreciated in its new

[75] *Opp.* vii. 322.   [76] *Opp.* vii. 323.

setting: " I confess that if respect be had to the Person we ought not so to speak, but I say we are not speaking of the Person but of the essence. I hold that the Holy Spirit is the real author of this manner of speaking, since He refers to Christ all the declarations in which αὐτοουσία is predicated of God, as well in other passages, as in the first chapter of the Epistle to the Hebrews. . . . They contend that Christ, because He is of (ex) the substance of the Father, is not of Himself (a se ipso), since He has His principium from another. This I allow to them of the Person. What more do they ask? I acknowledge, then, that the Son of God is of the Father, and when we are speaking of the Person I acknowledge that He is not of Himself. But when, apart from consideration of the Person, we are speaking of His divinity, or which is the same thing simpliciter of the essence, I say that it is truly predicated of it that it is a se ipso. For who hitherto has denied of the name Jehovah, that it includes the declaration of αὐτοουσία? When, then, they object that the Son is of the Father, that I not only willingly acknowledge, but have even continually proclaimed. But here is where these donkeys are in error — that they do not consider that the name of Son is spoken of the Person, and is therefore contained in the predication of relation; which relation has no place when we are talking of Christ's divinity simpliciter. And Augustine discourses eloquently on this matter " . . . quoting the passages from Augustine to which we have already made reference.[77]

That Calvin let the paragraph he had prepared on this subject for the second edition of his " Institutes " (1539) stand practically unchanged — strengthened only by a couple of passages cited from Augustine — in the editions of 1543 and 1550, may be taken as indication that he supposed that what he had brought together in his " Defense Against the Calumnies of Caroli " (1545), incorporating as it does the essence of former expositions and defenses, was a sufficient exposition of the subject and defense of his point of view. In the meantime, how-

[77] *Opp.* vii. 323–324.

ever, the troubles in the Italian church in Geneva had broken
out, culminating after a while in the controversies with Valentinus Gentilis (1558), in which new occasion was given for
asserting the self-existence of Christ, and this brought it
about that something more on this subject was incorporated
into the " Institutes " of 1559. The positive statement was
left, indeed, much as it had been given form in the " Institutes "
of 1539 (§ 19): but in the long defense of the doctrine of the
Trinity against Gentilis and his congeners with which the discussion of the doctrine closes in this edition much more is
added on the self-existence of Christ. As over against these
opponents the especial point in the doctrine of the Trinity
which required defense was the true deity of the second and
third Persons. On this defense Calvin entered *con amore,* for he
ever showed himself, as he had himself expressed it, a " detester
as sacrilegious of all who have sought to overturn or to minimise or to obscure the truth of the divine majesty which is in
Christ." [78] The God whom Isaiah saw in the Temple (vi. 1), he
says, John (xii. 41) declares to have been Christ; the God
whom the same Isaiah declares shall be a rock of offense to the
Jews (viii. 14) Paul pronounces to be Christ (Rom. ix. 33); the
God to whom the same Isaiah asserts every knee shall bow
(xlv. 23), Paul tells us is Christ (Rom. xiv. 11); the God whom
the Psalmist proclaims as laying the foundations of the earth
and whom all angels shall worship (Ps. cii. 25, xcvii. 7) the
Epistle to the Hebrews identifies with Christ (i. 6, 10). Now,
continues Calvin, in every one of these passages it is the name
" Jehovah " which is used, and that carries with it the self-
existence of Christ with respect to His deity.[79] " For if He is
Jehovah, it cannot be denied that He is the same God who elsewhere cries through Isaiah (xliv. 6), ' I, I am, and besides me
there is no God.' We must also weigh," he adds, " that declaration of Jeremiah (x. 11): ' the gods which have not made
the heaven and the earth shall perish from the earth which is

[78] *Opp.* vii. 314.

[79] *Opp.* ii. 110; " Institutes," 1559, I. xiii. 23: nam quum ubique ponatur
nomen Iehovae, sequitur deitatis respectu ex se ipso esse.

under heaven '; while on the other hand it must be acknowledged that it is the Son of God whose deity is often proved
by Isaiah from the creation of the world. But how shall the
Creator who gives being to all things not be self-existent (*ex
se ipso*) but derive His essence from another? For whoever
says the Son is essentiated by the Father, denies that He is of
Himself (*a se ipso*). But the Holy Spirit cries out against this
by naming Him Jehovah." " The deity, therefore, we affirm,"
he says a little later,[80] " to be absolutely self-existent (*ex se
ipsa*). Whence we acknowledge the Son, too, as He is God, to
be self-existent (*ex se ipso*), when reference to His Person is
not present: while, as He is Son, we say He is of the Father.
Thus the essence is without principium; but the principium
of the Person is God Himself."

It does not seem necessary, however, to multiply citations.
Enough have already been adduced, doubtless, to illustrate
the clearness, iterance and emphasis with which Calvin asserted the self-existence of Christ as essential to His complete deity; and at least to suggest his mode of conceiving
the Trinity in accordance with this emphasis on the absolute
equality, or rather, let us say, identity of the three Persons
of the Godhead in their deity. His conception involved, of
course, a strongly emphasized distinction between the essence
and the Personality. In essence the three Persons are numerically one: the whole essence belongs to each Person: [81] the
whole essence, of course, with all its properties, which are
only its peculiarities as an essence and are inseparable from
it just because they are not other substances but only qualities. In person, however, the three Persons are numerically
three, and are as distinct from one another as the distinguishing qualities by which one is the Father, another the Son
and the third the Spirit. In these facts Calvin found the essence of the doctrine of the Trinity, and in accordance with his
professed purpose to find a brief and easy definition of the

[80] P. 113: I. xiii. 25.
[81] Cf. I. xiii. 2: The Son contains in Himself the whole essence of God:
not a part of it only, nor by deflection only, but in *integra perfectione*.

Trinity we may say that in these facts are summed up all he held to be necessary to a doctrine of the Trinity.

Nevertheless Calvin's conception of the Trinity, if we cannot exactly say necessarily included, yet in point of fact included, more than this. It included the postulation of an " order " in the Persons of the Trinity, by which the Father is first, the Son second, and the Spirit third. And it included a doctrine of generation and procession by virtue of which the Son as Son derives from the Father, and the Spirit as Spirit derives from the Father and the Son. Perhaps this aspect of his conception of the Trinity is nowhere more succinctly expressed than in a passage in the eighteenth section of this chapter (xiii.). Here he explicitly declares that " although the eternity of the Father is the eternity of the Son and Spirit also, since God could never be without His Wisdom and Power, — and in eternity there is no question of first and last — it is nevertheless not vain or superfluous to observe an *order* [in the three Persons], since the Father is enumerated as the first, next the Son *ex eo,* and afterwards the Spirit *ex utroque.* For everyone's mind instinctively inclines to consider God first, then the Wisdom emerging from Him, and finally the Power by which He executes the decrees of His counsel. For this reason the Son is said to come forth (*exsistere*) from the Father (*a Patre*), the Spirit alike from the Father and the Son." The intimations which are here brought together are often repeated. Thus, for example: " For since the properties in the Persons bear an order, so that in the Father is the *principium et origo* . . . the *ratio ordinis* is held, which, however, in no respect derogates from the deity of the Son and Spirit " (§ 20). Again: " But from the Scriptures we teach that *essentialiter* there is but one God, and therefore the essence as well of the Son as of the Spirit is unbegotten (*ingenitam*). Yet inasmuch as (*quatenus*) the Father is first in order and has begotten His own Wisdom *ex se,* He is justly (as we have just said) considered the *principium et fons* of the whole divinity " (§ 25). Again, although he " pronounces it a detestable figment that the essence is the property of the Father alone as if He were the *deificator* of the Son," he yet " acknowledges that *ratione ordinis et gradus,* the *principium divinitatis* is in the Father " (§ 24). " The Father is the fountain of the deity, not with respect of the essence, but the order " (§ 26). And because the Father is thus the *fons et principium deitatis* (§ 23) from whom (*ex eo,* § 18) there have come forth (*exsistere,* § 18) the Son and afterwards from the Son along with the Father the Spirit (§ 18, *ex utroque*), there is involved here a doctrine of an eternal generation of the Son and procession of the Spirit. Both are repeatedly asserted. Of the Son, for example, we read: " It is necessary to understand that the Word was begotten of the Father (*genitum ex Patre*) before time (*ante saecula*) " (§ 7); "we conclude again, therefore, that the Word, before the beginning of time, was conceived (*conceptum*) by God " (§ 8); " He is the Son of God, because He is the Word begotten of the Father (*genitus a Patre*) before the ages (*saecula*) " (§ 23); " He is called the Son of God, . . . inasmuch as He was begotten of the Father (*genitus ex Patre*) before the ages (*saecula*) " (§ 24).[82]

Although such passages, however — and they are very numerous, or we may perhaps better say, pervasive, in Calvin's discussion of the Trinity — make it perfectly plain that he taught a doctrine of order and grade in the Persons of the Trinity, involving a doctrine of the derivation — and that, of course, before all time — of the second and third Persons from the first as the fountain and origin of deity, it is important for a correct understanding of his conception that we should attend to the distinctions by which he guarded his meaning. Of course, he did not teach that the essence of the Son or of the Spirit is the product of their generation or procession. It had been traditional in the Church from the begin-

[82] Already in the *first* edition of the "Institutes" this phraseology is fixed; *Opp.* i. 64: "By which we confess that we believe in Jesus Christ, who, we are convinced, is the unique Son of God the Father, not like believers by adoption and grace only, but naturally as begotten from eternity by the Father." So p. 62: "The Word of the Father — not such as men speak or think, but eternal and unchangeable, as emerging in an ineffable manner from the Father."

ning of the Trinitarian controversies to explain that generation and procession concerned only the Persons of the Son and
Spirit; [83] and Calvin availed himself of this traditional understanding. " The essence, as well of the Son as of the Spirit, is
unbegotten (*ingenitam*) " (§ 25). " The essence of the Son has
no *principium*, but God Himself is the *principium* of His Person " (§ 25). The matter does not require elaboration here,
both because this is obviously the natural view for Calvin to
present and hence goes without saying, and because his mode
of presenting and arguing it has been sufficiently illustrated
in passages already cited.[84] There is another distinction he ap-

[83] Cf. De Moor, " In Marckii Compend.," i. 1761, p. 775: " The Nicene
fathers had reference to nothing but the personal order of subsistence when they
said the Son is ' God of God, Light of Light '; while, considered absolutely
and essentially, the Son is the same God with the Father." This is expressed
by Dr. Shedd with his wonted clearness and emphasis as follows (" A History
of Christian Doctrine," 1873, i. pp. 339 *sq.*): " The Nicene Trinitarians rigorously confined the ideas of ' Sonship ' and ' generation ' to the hypostatical
character. It is not the essence of the Deity that is generated, but a *distinction* in that essence. And, in like manner, the term ' procession ' applied to
the Holy Spirit pertains exclusively to the third hypostasis, and has no application to the substance of the Godhead. The term ' begotten ' in the Nicene
trinitarianism is descriptive only of *that which is peculiar to the second Person, and confined to Him.* The Son is generated with respect only to His
Sonship, or, so to speak, His individuality (ἰδιότης), but is not generated
with respect to His essence or nature. . . . The same *mutatis mutandis* is true
of the term ' procession.' . . . Thus, from first to last, in the Nicene construction of the doctrine of the Trinity, the terms ' beget,' ' begotten,' and ' proceed,' are confined to the hypostatical distinctions, and have no legitimate
or technical meaning, when applied to the Trinity as a whole, or, in other
words, to the Essence in distinction from the hypostasis." . . . Calvin was
fully entitled to avail himself of this distinction, as he fully did so.

[84] His later Trinitarian controversies with Gentilis and his companions
brought out many strong assertions precisely in point. For example, in the
discussion in the " Institutes " (I. xiii. 23 *sq.*), he defines the precise thing he
wishes to refute as the representation of the Father as " the sole essentiator "
who " in forming the Son and the Spirit has transfused His own deity into
them " (§ 23); to whom therefore alone the " essence of God belongs " and to
whom as " essentiator " the Son and Spirit owe their essence. In opposition
to this he declares that " although we confess that in point of order and
degree the *principium divinitatis* is in the Father, we nevertheless pronounce
it a detestable figment that the essence is the property of the Father alone,
as if He were the deificator of the Son; because in this way either the essence
would be multiplex or the Son would be called God only in a titular and

pears to have made, however, which is not so clear. Although he taught that the Son was begotten of the Father, and of course begotten before all time, or as we say from all eternity, he seems to have drawn back from the doctrine of " eternal generation " as it was expounded by the Nicene Fathers. They were accustomed to explain " eternal generation " (in accordance with its very nature as "eternal"), not as something which has occurred once for all at some point of time in the past — however far back in the past — but as something which is always occurring, a perpetual movement of the divine essence from the first Person to the second, always complete, never completed.[85] Calvin seems to have found this conception difficult, if not meaningless. In the closing words of the discussion of the Trinity in the " Institutes " (I. xiii. 29, *ad fin.*) he classes it among the speculations which impose unnecessary burdens on the mind. "For what is the profit," he asks, " of disputing whether the Father always generates (*semper generet*), seeing that it is fatuous to imagine a continuous act of generating (*continuus actus generandi*) when it is evident that

---

imaginary sense. If they allow that the Son is God but second from the Father, then the essence will be in Him *genita et formata,* which is in the Father *ingenita et informis* " (§ 24, near end). " We teach from the Scriptures," he explains (§ 25, beginning) " that there is one God in point of essence (*essentialiter*), and therefore the essence of both Son and Spirit is *ingenita.* But inasmuch as the Father is first in order and has begotten from Himself (*genuit ex se*) His own Wisdom, He is rightly considered, as I have just said, the *principium et fons totius divinitatis.* Thus God indefinitely is *ingenitus;* and the Father with regard to His Person also is *ingenitus.*" Calvin's weapon against the tritheists, therefore, was precisely that the essence of God, whether in the first, second or third Person, is not generated: that it is only the Person which is generated, and that, strictly speaking, only the Person of the Son — the Person of the Father being ingenerate, and it being more proper to speak of the Person of the Spirit as " proceeding." This is merely, however, the traditional representation, utilized by Calvin, not a new view of his own.

85 Cf. Sheldon, " History of Christian Doctrine," 1886, i. p. 202: " Like Origen, the Nicene fathers seem to have conceived of the generation, not as something accomplished once for all, but as something parallel with the eternal life of the Son, ever complete and ever continued." Also, Shedd, " A History of Christian Doctrine," i. 1864, p. 317: " Eternal generation is an immanent perpetual activity in an ever existing essence."

248 CALVIN AND CALVINISM

three Persons have subsisted in God from eternity?" His meaning appears to be that the act of generation must have been completed from all eternity, since its product has existed complete from all eternity, and therefore it is meaningless to speak of it as continually proceeding. If this is the meaning of his remark, it is a definite rejection of the Nicene speculation of "eternal generation." But this is very far from saying that it is a rejection of the Nicene Creed — or even of the assertion in this Creed to the effect that the Son is "God of God." We have just seen that Calvin explicitly teaches the "eternal generation" of the Son, in the sense that He was begotten by the Father before all time. It manifestly was a matter of fixed belief with him. He does indeed refuse to find proof texts for it in many of the passages which it had been the custom to cite in evidence of it.[86] But he does not therefore feel that he lacks adequate proof of it. There is one argument for it, he tells us, which seems to him worth a thousand distorted texts. "It is certain that God is not a Father to men except through the intercession of that only begotten Son, who alone rightly vindicates to Himself this prerogative, and by whose beneficence it derives to us. But God always wished to be called upon by His people by His name of Father: whence it follows that there was already then in existence the Son through whom that relationship was established."[87] That the Son is "God of God"

[86] Of this Scholten, "De Leer der Hervormde Kerk," ed. 4, ii. p. 237 (cf. i. p. 24, ii. p. 229) makes great capital. In the middle edd. of the "Institutes," i. 483, however, Calvin in the very act of discarding these texts as proof asserts his firm belief in the fact of the Divine Sonship of our Lord, as is immediately to be shown. On Calvin's clear-sightedness and critical honesty in dealing with such texts Baumgartner has some good remarks ("Calvin Hébraïsant," 1889, pp. 37, 38). He illustrates the scandal it created at the time among those accustomed to rely on these texts by citing Aegidius Hunnius' book with the portentous title: Calvinus judaizans, hoc est: Judaicae glossae et corruptelae quibus Johannes Calvinus illustrissima Scripturae sacrae loca et testimonia de gloriosa trinitate, deitate Christi et Spiritus Sancti, cumprimis autem vaticinia prophetarum de adventu Messiae, nativitate ejus passione et resurrectione, ascensione in coelos et sessione ad dextram Dei, detestandum in modum corrumpere non exhorruit. Addita est corruptelarum confutatio (Wittemberg: 1593).

[87] Middle edd. of "Institutes," *Opp.* i. 483.

he is therefore as fully convinced as the Nicene Fathers themselves. When, then, he criticises the formulas of the Nicene Creed, " God of God, Light of Light, very God of very God," as repetitious, this is a criticism of the form, not of the content of this statement.[88] And when he speaks of the " Deus de Deo " of the Creed as a " hard saying " (dura locutio), he by no means denies that it is " true and useful," in the sense its framers put on it, in the sense, that is, that the Son has His *principium* merely as Son in the Father, but only means that the form of the statement is inexact — the term " Deus " requiring to be taken in each case of its occurrence in a nonnatural personal sense — and that, being inexact, it is liable to be misused in the interests of a created God, in the sense of Gentilis, and must therefore be carefully explained.[89] His

[88] *Opp.* vii. 315, where it is explicitly declared that he had no intention of derogating from the symbol: cf. p. 316.

[89] Preface to the " Expositio impietatis Valen. Gentilis," 1561 (*Opp.* ix. 368) : " But the words of the Council of Nice run: Deum esse de Deo. A hard saying (*dura locutio*), I confess; but for removing its ambiguity no one can be a more suitable interpreter than Athanasius, who dictated it. And certainly the design of the fathers was none other than to maintain the origin which the Son draws from the Father in respect of Person, without in any way opposing the sameness of the essence and deity in the two, so that as to essence the Word is God *absque principio*, while in Person the Son has His principium from the Father." Petavius' criticism is therefore wide of the mark when (" De Trinitate," III. iii. 2, ed. Paris, 1865, pt. ii. p. 523; cf. also Bellarmine, " De Christo," Preface of his " Opera," i. p. 244) he declares that Calvin " speaks rashly and altogether untheologically (temere et prorus ἀθεολογήτως) when he calls this locution ' hard,' because he supposes that Christ, as He is God is *a se ipso*, i.e., αὐτόθεος." But Calvin (who certainly does believe that Christ is self-existent God and therefore may properly be called αὐτόθεος), does not find the locution *Deus de* (or *ex*) *Deo* " hard " (*dura*) on that account: he thoroughly believes both in the θεὸς ἐκ θεοῦ of the Creed and in the αὐτοθεότης of Christ, and found no difficulty whatever in harmonizing them. When he pronounces this locution " harsh " his mind is on the possibility of its misuse by the Antitrinitarians as if it meant that the Son was *made God* by the Father. When, therefore, Petavius adds (§ 3, p. 524): " So then, the locution, *God is from God*, is not only true but useful (*proba*) and consentaneous to Christian teaching; not as the Autotheani and Calvinists ignorantly babble, *hard* " — he says no more for the substance of it than Calvin had himself said in the very passage in which he called the locution " harsh," — that is to say, that it expresses an important truth, this, to wit, that the Son draws His origin, with respect to His Person, from the Father. No doubt

position is, in a word, that of one who affirms the eternal generation of the Son, but who rejects the speculations of the
Nicene Fathers respecting the nature of the act which they
called "eternal generation." It is enough, he says in effect, to
believe that the Son derives from the Father, the Spirit from
the Father and the Son, without encumbering ourselves with
a speculation upon the nature of the eternally generating act
to which these hypostases are referred. It is interesting to observe that Calvin's attitude upon these matters is precisely repeated by Dr. Charles Hodge in his discussion in his "Systematic Theology." [90] It seems to be exactly Calvin's point of
view to which Dr. Hodge gives expression when he writes: " A
distinction must be made between the Nicene Creed (as amplified in that of Constantinople) and the doctrine of the Nicene
Fathers. The creeds are nothing more than the well-ordered arrangement of the facts of Scripture which concern the doctrine
of the Trinity. They assert the distinct personality of the
Father, Son and Spirit; their mutual relation as expressed by
these terms; their absolute unity as to substance or essence,
and their consequent perfect equality; and the subordination
of the Son to the Father, and of the Spirit to the Father and
the Son, as to the mode of subsistence and operation. These
are Scriptural facts, to which the creeds in question add nothing; and it is in this sense that they have been accepted by the
Church Universal. But the Nicene Fathers did undertake in
a greater or less degree to explain these facts. These explanations relate principally to the subordination of the Son and
Spirit to the Father, and to what is meant by generation, or
the relation between the Father and the Son. . . . As in reference to the subordination of the Son and Spirit to the Father,
as asserted in the ancient creeds, it is not to the fact that ex-

---

Calvin may also suggest that there might wisely have been chosen a less
ambiguous way of saying this than the "harsh" locution *Deus de Deo* — which
certainly is capable of being misunderstood as teaching that the Son owes His
divinity to the Father — as Gentilis taught. See below, note 94.

[90] "Systematic Theology," i. 1874, pp. 462 *sq.* On pp. 466, 467 he gives
a very clear statement of Calvin's position, of which he expresses full approval.

ception is taken, but to the explanation of that fact, as given by the Nicene Fathers, the same is true with regard to the doctrine of Eternal Generation."

The circumstance that Dr. Charles Hodge, writing three centuries afterwards (1559–1871), reproduces precisely Calvin's position may intimate to us something of the historical significance of Calvin's discussion of the Trinity. Clearly Calvin's position did not seem a matter of course, when he first enunciated it. It roused opposition and created a party. But it did create a party: and that party was shortly the Reformed Churches, of which it became characteristic that they held and taught the self-existence of Christ as God and defended therefore the application to Him of the term αὐτόθεος; that is to say, in the doctrine of the Trinity they laid the stress upon the equality of the Persons sharing in the same essence, and thus set themselves with more or less absoluteness against all subordinationism in the explanation of the relations of the Persons to one another. When Calvin asserted, with the emphasis which he threw upon it, the self-existence of Christ, he unavoidably did three things. First and foremost, he declared the full and perfect deity of our Lord, in terms which could not be mistaken and could not be explained away. The term αὐτόθεος served the same purpose in this regard that the term ὁμοούσιος had served against the Arians and the term ὑπόστασις against the Sabellians. No minimizing conception of the deity of Christ could live in the face of the assertion of aseity or αὐτοθεότης of Him. This was Calvin's purpose in asserting aseity of Christ and it completely fulfilled itself in the event. In thus fulfilling itself, however, two further effects were unavoidably wrought by it. The inexpugnable opposition of subordinationists of all types was incurred: all who were for any reason or in any degree unable or unwilling to allow to Christ a deity in every respect equal to that of the Father were necessarily offended by the vindication to Him of the ultimate Divine quality of self-existence. And all those who, while prepared to allow true deity to Christ, yet were accustomed to think of the Trinitarian relations along the lines of the traditional Nicene orthodoxy, with its assertion of a certain subordination of the Son to the Father, at least in mode of subsistence, were thrown into more or less confusion of mind and compelled to resort to nice distinctions in order to reconcile the two apparently contradictory confessions of αὐτοθεότης and of θεὸς ἐκ θεοῦ of our Lord. It is not surprising, then, that the controversy roused by Caroli and carried on by Chaponneau and Courtois did not die out with their refutation; but prolonged itself through the years and has indeed come down even to our own day. Calvin's so-called innovation with regard to the Trinity has, in point of fact, been made the object of attack through three centuries, not only by Unitarians of all types, nor only by professed Subordinationists, but also by Athanasians, puzzled to adjust their confession of Christ as " God of God, Light of Light, very God of very God " to the at least verbally contradictory assertion that in respect of His deity He is not of another but of Himself.

The attack has been especially sharp naturally where the assailants were predisposed to criticism of Calvin on other grounds, as was the case, for example, with Romanists, Lutherans and afterward with Arminians. As was to be expected, it is found in its most decisive form among the Romanists, and we are afraid we must say with Gomarus that with them it seems to have been urged in the first instance, rather because of a desire to disparage Calvin and the Calvinists than in any distinct doctrinal interest.[91] The beginning of the assault seems to have been made by Genebrardus, who " in the first book of his treatise on the Trinity, refutes what he calls the heresy of those denominated *Autotheanites,* that is of those who say that Christ is God of Himself (*a se ipso*), not of the Father, attributing this heresy to Calvin and Beza and in the Preface to his work [mistakenly] surmising that Francis Stancarus was the originator of it." [92] The way thus opened, however, was

[91] " Diatribe de Christo αὐτοθεῷ," printed by Voetius, in " Selectae Disputationes Theologicae," Part i. 1648, p. 445: calumniandi potius libidine quam erroris cum Arianis societate.

[92] We are quoting from Bellarmine, " De Christo," II. cap. xix. *ad init.* (his " Opera," i. p. 333). Cf. the opening words of Petavius' discussion, " De

largely followed by the whole crowd of Romish controversialists, the most notable of whom in the first age were probably
Anthony Possevinus, Alphonsus Salmeron, William Lindanus,
Peter Canisius, Dionysius Petavius,[93] all of whom exhaust the
resources of dialectics in the endeavor to fix upon Calvin and
his followers a stigma of heresy in the fundamental doctrine of
the Trinity. A more honorable course was pursued by probably the two greatest Romish theologians of the time, Gregory of Valentia and Robert Bellarmine. Although in no way
disinclined to find error in the teaching of Calvin and the Calvinists, these more cautious writers feel compelled to allow that
Calvin in his zeal to do full justice to the deity of Christ has
not passed beyond Catholic truth, and blame him therefore
only for inaccuracy of phrase. Gregory of Valentia, whom Gomarus calls " the Coryphaeus of Papal theologians," speaking
of the error of the Autotheanites, remarks: " Genebrardus has
attributed this error to Calvin (*Inst.*, I. xiii), but, in point of
fact, if he be read attentively, it will be seen that he [Calvin]
meant merely that the Son, as He is indeed essentially God,
is *ex se*, and is *ex Patre* only as He is a Person: and that is
true. For although the Fathers and Councils assert that He is
Deus ex Deo most truly, by taking the term [God] personally,
so that it signifies the Person itself at once of the Father and of

---

Trinitate," VI. xi. 5 (his " Opera," iii. p. 251): " With respect to more recent writers, there exists a far from small altercation of the Catholics with
heretics, especially with Calvin, Beza and their crew (*asseclis*). For Genebrardus in the first book of his " De Trinitate " very sharply upbraids (*insecta-
tur*) them and gives them the name *autotheanites*, because they say the Son
has His divinity and essence of Himself; an error mentioned also by William
Lindanus."

[93] Voetius, " Dispt.," i. pp. 453, 454, gives an account of the opponents of
the Reformed ascription of ᾿αὐτοθεότης to Christ. There are three classes:
Romanists, Lutherans, and Arminians, to which he adds as fourth and fifth
classes Peter Caroli, and the Antitrinitarians (Crell and Schlichting). The
Romanists he subdivides into two classes, those who find that Calvin taught
heresy and those who object to his language only. The latter sub-class includes only Bellarmine and Gregory of Valentia. Under the former, however,
he enumerates a long list of writers with exact references. Cf. also De Moor,
" In Marck. Comp.," i. 1761, pp. 773-774 (V. x.).

the Son; [94] nevertheless the Son, as He is essentially God, that is, as He is that one, most simple Being which is God, is not from another, because as such He is an absolute somewhat. If this were all that were meant by the other heretics who are called 'Autotheanites,' there would be no occasion for contending with them. For it was in this sense that Epiphanius, *Haer.* 69, seems to have called the Son αὐτοθεός." [95] Bellarmine's candor scarcely stretches so far as Gregory's. While he too feels compelled to allow that Calvin's meaning is catholic, he yet very strongly reprobates his mode of stating that meaning and declares that it gives fair occasion for the strictures which have been passed upon him. " When," says he, " I narrowly look into the matter itself, and carefully consider Calvin's opinions, I find it difficult to declare that he was in this error. For he teaches that the Son is of Himself (*a se*), in respect of essence, not in respect of Person, and seems to wish to say that the Person is begotten by the Father [but] the essence is not begotten or produced, but is of itself (*a se ipsa*); so that if you abstract from the Person of the Son the relation to the Father, the essence alone remains, and that is of itself (*a se ipsa*)." But on the other hand Bellarmine thinks " that Calvin has undoubtedly erred in his manner of expressing himself, and given occasion to be spoken of as he has been spoken of by our [the Romish] writers." This judgment is supported by the following specifications: " For he [Calvin] says, *Inst.*, I. xiii. 19: ' The ecclesiastical writers now teach that the Father

[94] That is to say, the phrase " God of God " is interpreted to mean " God the Son, of God the Father " — God in the first instance meaning (not the essence but) the Person of the Son, and in the second instance (not the essence but) the Person of the Father. Only on this supposition, as Gregory allows, can the phrase " God of God " be applied to Christ in exactness of speech. That is to say, Gregory finds the phrase as inexact as Calvin does when he calls it a *dura locutio.*

[95] We repeat the passage from Gomarus' citation in Voetius' " Disputat.," i. 1648, p. 448. Gomarus cites Gregory, " Ad summae Thomae," part i. disp. 2, quaest. 1, punct. 1, p. 718. The passage is found also, however, in Gregory's treatise " De Trinitate," ii. 1 (to which Voetius refers us, p. 454, adding appropriate references also to i. 22 and ii. 17). See Gregorii de Valentia " . . . de rebus fidei hoc tempore controversis Libri," Paris, 1610, p. 205, first column, B and C.

is the principium of the Son, now assert that the Son has both divinity and essence of Himself (*a se ipso*).' And below this: 'Accordingly, when we speak of the Son *simpliciter* without respect to the Father, we may well and properly assert that He is of Himself (*a se*).' And in the twenty-third section, speaking of the Son, 'How,' he asks, 'shall the creator who gives being to all things not be of Himself (*a se ipso*), but derive His essence from another?' And in his letter to the Poles and in his work against Gentilis, Calvin frequently asserts that the Son is αὐτόθεος, that is, God of Himself (*a se ipso*), and [declares] the expression in the Creed 'God of God, Light of Light' an improper and hard saying." [96]

The gravamen of Bellarmine's charges we see from a later passage (p. 334b, near bottom) turns on Calvin's assertion that " the Son has [His] essence from Himself (*a se*)." This, Bellarmine declares, is to be "repudiated *simpliciter*," as he undertakes to demonstrate, on the grounds that it is repugnant to Scripture, the definitions of the Councils, the teaching of the Fathers, and reason itself, and as well to Calvin's own opinions; and is not established by the arguments which Calvin adduces in its behalf. In Bellarmine's view, however, in so speaking Calvin merely expressed himself badly: he really meant nothing more than that the Son with respect to His essence, which is His as truly as it is the Father's, is of Himself (*a se ipso*). He thinks this is proved by the fact that Calvin elsewhere speaks in terms which infer his orthodoxy in the point at issue. He speaks of the Son, for example, as begotten of the Father, which would be meaningless, if He does not receive His nature, or essence, from the Father, since " it is not a mere relation which is called the Son, but a real somewhat subsisting in the divine nature," and the Son is " not a mere propriety but an *integra hypostasis*." He even plainly says in so many words (I. xiii. 28) that the essence is communicated from the Father to the Son: " If the difference is in the essence, let them reply whether He has not shared it (*communicaverit*) with the Son. . . . It follows that it is wholly and al-

96 *Op. cit.*, p. 334a.

together (*tota et in solidum*) common to the Father and Son."
And he does not embrace the errors which would flow from
ascribing to the Son His essence of Himself: for example, he
ascribes but a single essence to the Persons of the Trinity, and
he does not distinguish the essence from the Persons *realiter*
but only *ratione*.

Petavius does not find it possible to follow Bellarmine in
this exculpating judgment. For his part, he willingly admits
that Calvin sometimes speaks inconsistently with himself,
but he cannot doubt that he means what he says, when he
declares that the Son has His essence not from the Father but
from Himself — and this is a thing which, says he, is not only
false, but impious to say, and cannot be affirmed by any Catholic. For it stands to reason, he argues, that everyone " has his
essence from him by whom he is begotten; since generation is
just the communication of the nature, — whether, as in created things, in kind, or, as in the divine production of the
Word, in number. It is indeed impossible to form any conception of generation without the nature, and some communication of the essence, occurring to the mind." [97] The whole question of Calvin's orthodoxy, between these writers, it will be
seen, turns on their judgment as to his attitude towards the
doctrine of "eternal generation." Bellarmine judges that, on
the whole, though he has sometimes expressed himself inconsistently with regard to it, Calvin soundly believes in the doctrine of "eternal generation"; and therefore he pronounces
him orthodox. Petavius judges that, though he sometimes expresses himself in the terms of the doctrine of "eternal generation," Calvin does not really believe in it; and therefore he
pronounces him heretical. To both authors alike the test of
orthodoxy lies in conformity of thought to the Nicene speculation, and they cannot conceive of a sound doctrine of the Trinity apart from this speculation and all the nice discriminations and adjustments which result from it.[98] And it can

[97] *Op. cit.,* p. 252a.
[98] It is interesting to observe how constantly the argument hangs formally on the suppressed premise of the Nicene doctrine of generation.

scarcely be denied that Calvin laid himself open to suspicion
from this point of view. The principle of his doctrine of the
Trinity was not the conception he formed of the relation of the
Son to the Father and of the Spirit to the Father and Son, expressed respectively by the two terms "generation" and
"procession": but the force of his conviction of the absolute
equality of the Persons. The point of view which adjusted everything to the conception of "generation" and "procession" as
worked out by the Nicene Fathers was entirely alien to him.
The conception itself he found difficult, if not unthinkable;
and although he admitted the facts of "generation" and "procession," he treated them as bare facts, and refused to make
them constitutive of the doctrine of the Trinity. He rather
adjusted everything to the absolute divinity of each Person,
their community in the one only true Deity; and to this we
cannot doubt that he was ready not only to subordinate, but
even to sacrifice, if need be, the entire body of Nicene speculations. Moreover, it would seem at least very doubtful if Calvin, while he retained the conception of "generation" and
"procession," strongly asserting that the Father is the *principium divinitatis*, that the Son was "begotten" by Him before all ages and that the Spirit "proceeded" from the Father

---

Thus Bellarmine argues (p. 334b) that "those who assert that the Son
has His essense *a se ipso* err because they are compelled either (1) to make
the Son ingenerate *and the same person with the Father*, or (2) to mul-
ply the essences, or at least (3) to distinguish the essence from the person *realiter* and so introduce a quaternity." As Calvin does none of these
things, he is pronounced orthodox in meaning. But the point now to be illustrated lies in the assumption under (1) that to make the Son ingenerate is
to make Him the same person with the Father. It does not occur to Bellarmine as possible that one should deny the Son to be generated and yet not
make Him the same person with the Father, while holding free from (2)
and (3). Similarly, when replying to Danaeus, who asks: "If He is not God
a se, how is He God?" Petavius (p. 256) declares that so to speak is perfidious
and ignorant — "for," says he, "it either robs the Son of His deity or denies
that He is God begotten of the Father." The one seems to him as intolerable
as the other. Neither Bellarmine nor Petavius seems fairly to have faced the
possibility of a doctrine of a true Trinity of Persons in one essence which did
not hang on the doctrine of "eternal generation," which seemed to them, thus,
equipollent with the doctrine of the Trinity.

and Son before time began, thought of this begetting and procession as involving any communication of essence. His conception was that, because it is the Person of the Father which begets the Person of the Son, and the Person of the Spirit which proceeds from the Persons of the Father and Son, it is precisely the distinguishing property of the Son which is the thing begotten, not the essence common to Father and Son, and the distinguishing property of the Spirit which is the product of the procession, not the essence which is common to all three persons. Of course, he did not hold, as Bellarmine phrases it, that " the Son is a mere relation," " a mere property ": the Son was to him too, as a matter of course, " *aliquid subsistens in natura divina,*" " *integra hypostasis.*" But he did hold that Sonship is a relation and that the Son differs from the Father only by this property of Sonship which is expressed as a relation (I. xiii. 6); and it looks very much as if his thought was that it is only in what is expressed by the term Sonship that the second Person of the Trinity is the Son of the Father, or, what comes to the same thing, has been begotten of the Father. His idea seems to be that the Father, Son and Spirit are one in essence, and differ from one another only in that property peculiar to each, which, added to the common essence, constitutes them respectively Father, Son and Spirit; and that the Father is Father only as Father, the Son, Son only as Son, or what comes to the same thing, the Father begets the Son only as Son, or produces by the act of generation only that by virtue of which He is the Son, which is, of course, what constitutes just His Sonship.

The evidence on which Bellarmine relies for his view that Calvin taught a communication of essence from Father to Son is certainly somewhat slender. If we put to one side Bellarmine's inability to conceive that Calvin could really believe in a true generation of the Son by the Father without holding that the Son receives His essence from the Father, and his natural presumption that Calvin's associates and pupils accurately reproduced the teaching of their master — for there is no doubt that Beza and Simler, for example, understood by

generation a communication of essence — the evidence which
Bellarmine relies on reduces to a single passage in the " Institutes " (I. xiii. 23). Calvin there, arguing with Gentilis, opposes to the notion that the Father and Son differ in essence,
the declaration that the Father " shares " the essence together
with the Son, so that it is common, *tota et in solidum,* to the
Father and the Son. It may be possible to take the verb " communicate " here in the sense of " impart " rather than in that of
" have in common," but it certainly is not necessary and it
seems scarcely natural; and there is little elsewhere in Calvin's
discussion to require it of us. Petavius points out that the sentence is repeated in the tract against Gentilis — but that carries us but a little way. It is quite true that there is nothing
absolutely clear to be found to the opposite effect either. But
there are several passages which may be thought to suggest a
denial that the Son derives His essence from the Father. Precisely what is meant, for example, when we are told that the
Son " contains in Himself the simple and indivisible essence
of God in integral perfection, not *portione aut deflexu,*" is no
doubt not clear: but by *deflexu* it seems possible that Calvin
meant to deny that the Son possessed the divine essence by impartation from another (I. xiii. 2). It is perhaps equally questionable what weight should be placed on the form of the statement (§ 20) that the order among the Persons by which the
principium and *origo* is in the Father, is produced (*fero*) by
the " proprieties "; or on the suggestion that the more exact
way of speaking of the Son is to call Him " the Son of the
Person " (§ 23) — the Father being meant — the term God
in the phrase " Son of God " requiring to be taken of the Person of the Father. When it is argued that " whoever asserts
that the Son is essentiated by the Father denies that He is self-
existent " (§ 23), and " makes His divinity a something abstracted from the essence of God, or a derivation of a part from
the whole," the reference to Gentilis' peculiar views of the
essentiation of the Son by the Father, i.e., His creation by the
Father, seems to preclude a confident use of the phrase in the
present connection. Nor does the exposition of the unbegot-

tenness of the essence of the Son and Spirit as well as of the
Father, so that it is only as respects His Person that the Son
is of the Father (§ 25) lend itself any more certainly to our
use. A survey of the material in the " Institutes " leads to the
impression thus that there is singularly little to bring us to a
confident decision whether Calvin conceived the essence of
God to be communicated from the Father to the Son in " generation " and from the Father and Son to the Spirit in " procession." And outside the " Institutes " the same ambiguity
seems to follow us. If we read that Christ has " the fulness
of the Godhead " of Himself (*Opp*. xi. 560), we read equally
that the Fathers taught that the Son is " of the Father even
with respect to His eternal essence " (vii. 322), and is of the
substance of the Father (vii. 324). In this state of the case
opinions may lawfully differ. But on the whole we are inclined
to think that Calvin, although perhaps not always speaking
perfectly consistently, seeks to avoid speaking of generation
and procession as importing the communication of the Divine
essence; so that Petavius appears to be right in contending
that Calvin meant what he says when he represents the Son
as " having from Himself both divinity and essence " (I. xiii.
19).

   We have thought it worth while to dwell with some fulness on this matter, because, as we have suggested already, it
is precisely in this peculiarity of Calvin's doctrine of the Trinity that the explanation is found of the widespread offense
which was taken at it. Men whose whole thought of the Trinity lived, moved and had its being in the ideas of generation
and procession, that is, in the notion of a perpetual communication of the Divine essence from the Father as the *fons deitatis* to the Son, who is thereby constituted the Son, and from
the Father and Son to the Spirit, who is thereby constituted
the Spirit, could not but feel that the Trinity they had known
and confessed was taken away when this conception was conspicuous only by its absence, or was at best but remotely suggested, and all the stress was laid on the absolute equality of
the Father, Son and Holy Spirit. Such a conception of the

Trinity would inevitably appear to them to savor of Sabellianism or of Tritheism, according as their minds dwelt more on the emphasis which was laid upon the numerical unity of the essence common to all the Persons or on that which was laid upon the distinctness of the Persons. Dissatisfaction with Calvin's Trinitarian teaching was therefore not confined to Romish controversialists seeking ground of complaint against him, but was repeated in all whose thought had run strictly in the moulds of Nicene speculation. Despite an occasional defender like Meisner or Tarnov,[99] the Lutheran theologians, for example, generally condemned it. Many, like Tilemann Heshusius and Aegidius Hunnius and, later, Stechmannus, hotly assailed it, and the best that could be hoped for at Lutheran hands was some such firm though moderately worded refusal of it as is found, for example, in John Gerhard's " Loci Theologici." " The Greek doctors," he tells us,[100] " call only the Father αὐτόθεος καὶ αὐτοούσιος, not because there is a greater perfection of essence in the Father than in the Son, but because He is ἀγένητος and *a se ipso* and does not have deity through generation or spiration. Bucanus, *Loc.* i, *De Deo*, p. 6, responds thus: ' The Son is *a se ipso* as He is God; from the Father as He is Son.' This he got from Calvin, who, Book I, c. xiii, § 25, writes: ' The Son as He is God we confess is *ex se ipso*, considered apart from His Person, but as He is Son we say that He is of the Father; thus His essence is without principium, but of His Person God is Himself the principium.' We are not able, however, to approve these words, but confess rather with the

---

[99] It is to be hoped that modern Lutherans in general will subscribe the excellent remarks of Prof. Milton Valentine, " Christian Theology," 1906, i. 309: " Emphasis must . . . be laid on the attribute of *aseity* as belonging to the whole Godhead, to the divine Being as such. . . . It cannot therefore be allowable to think of God as originating the Trinality of the Godhead, as though there was a time when He was not Tripersonal in His Being. . . ." Accordingly he ascribes self-existence to the Son (pp. 321–322). A. Ritschl, " Justification and Reconciliation," iii. E. T. 1900, p. 470, represents "theological tradition," which at least includes Lutheran tradition, as " expressly excluding aseity " in its representations of the Deity of Christ.

[100] Ed. Cotta, i. Tubingen, 1762, pp. 291–292 (Loc. IV. pars ii. cap. v. § 179).

Nicene Creed that 'the Son is begotten of the Father, God of God, Light of Light,' and follow the saying of Christ, Jno. v. 26 . . . Prov. viii. 24. . . . Zacharias Ursinus [101] therefore is right to separate from his preceptor here, writing in *Catech.*, p. II. q. 25, p. 179: ' The Son is begotten of the Father; that is, He has the Divine Essence in an ineffable manner communicated to Him from the Father.' D. Lobechius, *disp.* 3 *in Augustinum Conf.* th. 26, says: ' The essence should be considered in a two-fold way, either with respect to itself or with respect to its own being, or else with respect to its communication: it has no principium with respect to its own being; but with respect to its communication we say that the essence has as its principium, to be from the Father in the Son, for it has been communicated from the Father to the Son.' " Nevertheless, Gerhard, of course, does not deny that, when properly explained, the Son may fitly be called αὐτόθεος; since that would be tantamount to denying His true divinity. Accordingly he writes elsewhere: [102] " The term is ambiguous: for it is either opposed to communication of the divine essence and in that sense we deny that Christ is αὐτόθεος, because He receives the essence by eternal generation from the Father; or it is opposed to the inequality of the Divine essence, and in that sense we concede that Christ is αὐτόθεος. Gregory of Valentia, *De Trinitate*, i. 22: ' The Son as He is a Person is from another; as the most simple being, is not from another.' Christ is verily and in Himself God (*vere et se ipso Deus*), but He is not of Himself (*a se ipso*) God." One would think Gerhard was skating on very thin ice to agree with Gregory of Valentia — who agrees with Calvin and uses his very mode of statement — and yet not agree with Calvin.

[101] It must not be supposed, however, that Ursinus separated himself from Calvin as to the self-existence of the Son as He is God: his language is: " the Son is begotten of the Father, of the essence of the Father, but the essence of the Son is not begotten, but, existent of itself (*a se ipsa existens*), is communicated to the Son at His begetting (*nascenti*) by (*a*) the Father." " And what is said concerning the generation of the Son," he adds, " is to be understood also of the procession of the Spirit " (" Loci," p. 542).   [102] iii. Tubingen, 1764, p. 395 (Locus IV. cap. v. § 67).

The subordinationism [103] of the Arminians was of quite a different quality from that of the Lutherans. The dominant note which the Lutheran Christology sounded was the majesty of Christ; nothing that tended to exalt Christ could be without its appeal to Lutherans; they drew back from Calvin's assertion of His αὐτοθεότης only in the interests of the traditional Nicene construction of the Trinity. The Arminians had, on the other hand, a distinct tendency to the proper subordinationism of the Origenists; and in the later members of the school, indeed, there was present a strong influence from the Socinians. To them, of course, the Father alone could be thought of as αὐτόθεος and the Son was conceived as in His very nature, because God only by derivation, less than the Father. As in his whole theological outlook, Arminius himself was here better than his successors. He fairly saves his orthodoxy, indeed; but he emphatically denies the αὐτοθεότης of the Son. The Son

[103] Cf. H. Bavinck, " Geref. Dogmatiek," ed. 1, ii. p. 263. Remarking that the tendency which finds its typical form in Arianism, has manifested itself in various forms in the Church for centuries: " First of all in the form of Subordinationism: the Son is to be sure eternal, generated out of the essence of the Father, no creature, and not made of nothing; but He is nevertheless inferior to or subordinated to the Father. The Father alone is ὁ θεός, πηγή θεότητος, the Son is θεός, receives His nature by communication from the Father. This was the teaching of Justin, Tertullian, Clement, Origen, etc., also of the Semi-Arians, Eusebius of Caesarea and Eusebius of Nicomedia, who placed the Son ἐκτὸς τοῦ πατρός and declared Him ὁμοιοούσιος with the Father; and later of the Remonstrants (Conf. Art. 3; Arminus Op. theol. 1629, pp. 232 sq.; Episcopius, Instit. theol. IV. sect. ii. c. 32; Limborch, Theol. Christ. II. c. xvii. § 25), of the Supranaturalists (Bretschneider, Dogm., i.⁴ pp. 602 sq.; Knapp, Glaubenslehre, i. p. 260; Muntinghe, Theol. Christ. pars theor. § 134 sq., etc.), and of very many theologians of recent times (Frank, Syst. d. chr. Wahr., i. pp. 207 sq.; Beck, Chr. Gl. ii. pp. 123 sq.; Twesten, ii. p. 254; Kahnis, i. pp. 353, 398; van Oosterzee, ii. § 52; Doedes, Ned. Gel. 71 sq.).'' Cf. also H. C. Sheldon, " History of Christian Doctrine," ii. 1886, p. 97: " The Arminians, while they held to the doctrine of three Divine Persons in the Godhead, diverged from the current teaching on the subject by an express emphasis upon the subordination of the Son and the Spirit. Arminius was not specially related to this development, and contented himself with denying, in opposition to Calvin's phraseology, the propriety of attributing self-existence to the Son. But Episcopius, Curcellaeus, and Limborch were very pronounced in the opinion that a certain preëminence must be assigned to the Father over the Son and the Spirit."

may just as well be called Father, he intimates, as be represented as " having His essence *a se ipso* or *a nullo* "; and the
employment of such language cannot be justified by saying
that to affirm that the Son of God, as God, has His essence
a se ipso, is only to say that the divine essence is not *ab aliquo:*
there can, in fact, be no reason for calling the Son αὐτόθεος.[104]
On the other hand, nevertheless, he recognizes that the word
αὐτόθεος may be taken in two senses. It may describe the one
to whom it is applied either merely as *vere et se ipso* God, or
else as God *a se.* In the former usage it is as applied to the Son
tolerable; in the latter not.[105] He argues that we must distinguish between saying that the essence which the Son has is
from none, and that the Son which has this essence is from
none: " for," says he, " the Son is the name of a person, which
has a relation to the Father, and therefore cannot be defined
or contemplated apart from this relation; while the essence, on
the other hand, is an absolute somewhat." [106] " To contend,"
he urges, " that to say ' He is God ' and ' He has His essence
from none ' are equivalent statements, is to say either that the
Father alone is God, or else that there are three collateral
Gods." He cheerfully allows that neither of these assertions
expresses the meaning of Calvin or Beza: but he contends that
they use misleading language when they call Christ αὐτόθεος
and he appeals to Beza's admission, when excusing Calvin,
that " Calvin had not strictly observed the discrimination between the particles *a se* and *per se.*"

The gravitation of Arminianism was, however, downward;
and we find already taught by Episcopius, no longer a certain
subordination in order among the Persons of the Trinity in the
interests of the Nicene doctrine of " eternal generation " and
" procession," but rather a generation and procession in the interests of a subordination in nature among the Persons of the

104 " Declaratio sententiae suae ad ordines Holl. et Westfr.," in " Opera
Theol.," 1635, pp. 100–101. See E. T. " Works," translated by James Nichols,
London, i. 1825, pp. 627–631.
105 " Resp. ad xxxi. Articulos," in " Opera," p. 131 (E. T. " Works," ii.
1828, pp. 29–32).
106 *Ibid.,* p. 132.

Trinity. " It is certain " from Scripture, says he, " that this
divinity and the divine perfections are to be attributed to these
three persons, not collaterally and coördinately, but subordinately." " This subordination," he adds, " should be carefully
attended to, because of its extremely great usefulness, since by
it not only is there fundamentally overthrown the τριθεότης
which collateralism almost necessarily involves, but also the
Father's glory is preserved to Him unimpaired." Wherefore,
he continues, " they fall into perilous error who contend that
the Son is αὐτόθεος, in such a manner that as He is God He is
of Himself, as He is Son of the Father; because from this point
of view, the true subordination between the Father and the
Son is taken away." [107] It is scarcely necessary to pause to point
out with Triglandius [108] that to say that the Son and Spirit are
not collaterally or coördinally divine with the Father is to say
they are not equally divine with Him, and to say that it is
injurious to the Father's glory to call the Son αὐτόθεος, even
as He is God, is to say that He is inferior to the Father even in
His essence. No doubt Episcopius says in the same breath that
" one and the same divine nature " is to be attributed to the
three Persons. But this is not easy to conciliate with his argument, except on the supposition that in saying " one and the
same nature," his thought wavered somewhat between numerical oneness and specific oneness,[109] or else that he conceived the
relation of the several Persons to this one nature to differ
among themselves — one possessing it of Himself, the others
by derivation from — shall we even suggest, by favor of? —
another.

The path thus opened by Episcopius was eagerly walked
in by his successors. All that may be thought to be latent in
Episcopius came to light in Curcellaeus. We will, however,
permit another hand to describe to us his teaching with regard
to the Trinity. " If you take his own account," writes Robert

107 Cf. Episcopius' theologial works, printed at Amsterdam, 1650–1665;
espec. his " Instit. Theolog.," lib. iv. § 11, de Deo, capp. 32–36. But we cite
from Triglandius.
108 Triglandius, " Antapologia," cap. v. pp. 77 sq.
109 Cf. Triglandius, pp. 579, 580.

Nelson, in his " Life of Dr. George Bull," [110] there would be no man more orthodox and catholic " than Curcellaeus is " in the doctrine of the Trinity, as also in that of the Incarnation of Christ. And he insisted, that both from the pulpit and from the chair, he had always taught and vindicated that faith, into which he had been baptized, and which he had publicly professed in the congregation, according to the form generally received; and did even teach and vindicate the same at that very time, when the charge of Anti-trinitarianism was brought against him. Yea, he expressed so great a zeal for the orthodox doctrine in this great fundamental, as he would seem forward to seal the truth thereof, even with his blood; if, as he said, God would vouchsafe him this honor. Notwithstanding all this, it is notoriously known, and that from his own very Apology, that he was no less an enemy to the Council of Nice than his master before him, if not more than he; that he was no friend at all to the use of the word 'Trinity'; that he so explained himself concerning that mystery as to assert no more than a ' specifical unity ' in the divine Persons; that he defended the cause of Valentinus Gentilis, beheaded at Bern in Switzerland for Tritheism, maintaining his doctrine to have been the same with that of the primitive Fathers, particularly of Ignatius, Justin Martyr, Irenaeus, Athenagoras, Tertullian, and Clemens Alexandrinus; that he impeached the common (which he called the Modern and Scholastic) doctrine of the Trinity for approaching so very near Sabellianism, as hardly to be distinguished from it, and charged it to be a thousand years younger than that which was taught by Christ and His apostles; that he exploded the notion of consubstantiality, in the sense in which it is now generally taken, when applied to the Father and Son; that he was very much afraid to have his mind perplexed with the ' divine relations,' or with the manner of 'generation' and 'procession' in the Deity, or with modes of 'subsistence' and 'personalities,' or with 'mutual consciousness,' and the like; and therefore was for discarding at once all such terms and phrases as are not ' expressly legiti-

[110] London, 1713, pp. 290 *sq.*

mated' by the sacred writers; that he fully believed the Godhead of the Father to be more excellent than that of the Son,
or of the Holy Ghost, even so far as to look upon this superiority as a thing unquestionable, and to appeal to the consentient
testimony of the primitive Church for evidence; and lastly
that he took care to recommend Petavius, and the author of
Irenicum Irenicorum,[111] a learned physician of Dantzick . . .
to the perusal of his readers, for the sake of that collection of
testimonies which is to be found in them, as wherein they
might easily find ' an account of the primitive faith ' concerning these great articles." A subordinationism like this, of course,
could not endure Calvin's Trinitarianism, of which the corner-
stone was the equality of the Persons in the Trinity — which
equality it was that was safeguarded by the ascription of
αὐτοθεότης to Christ.

Indeed, this ascription was equally unacceptable to a subordinationism of far less extreme a type than that of Curcellaeus and his Remonstrant successors. It is the biographer of
George Bull to whom we have appealed to bring Curcellaeus'
trinitarian teaching before us: and George Bull is perhaps the
best example of that less extreme, convinced, no doubt, but
well-guarded, subordinationism which we have now in mind
— the subordinationism which entrenched itself in the Nicene
definitions and the explanations of the Nicene Fathers, interpreted, however, rather from the tentative and inadequate constructions out of which they were advancing to a sounder and
truer trinitarianism, than from this sounder and truer trinitarianism of which they were the expression. It can scarcely
be doubted that Bull's subordinationism owed much to the
Arminian movement, from the extremes of which, on this
point at least, he drew back. The Arminianism flowing in from
the continent had been a powerful co-factor in the production
of that Catholic reaction of seventeenth century England of
which Bull was, in its post-Restoration days of triumph, one of
the representatives and ornaments. It is interesting to note
that the " Theological Institutes " of Episcopius, at the time

[111] Daniel Zwicker. See "Allgem. deutsche Biog.," xlv. 1900, p. 533.

that Bull was contemplating writing his " Defence of the Ni-
ceno Creed," was " generally in the hands of students of divinity in both universities, as the best system of Divinity that had
appeared," [112] and that Bull himself speaks of Episcopius with
high respect in all except his attitude towards the Nicene Fathers.[113] Indeed, when he comes to state the subordinationism
which he professes to defend as commended by Catholic antiquity, he avails himself of Episcopius' precise phrase, declaring that all " the Catholic Doctors, those that lived before and
those that lived after the Council of Nice," " with one consent
have taught that the divine Nature and Perfections do agree
to the Father and Son, not collaterally or coördinately, but
subordinately." [114] But the particular form which Bull's subordinationism took was determined, naturally, by that special
appeal which the neo-Catholic party to which he belonged
made to primitive antiquity, by which he was led — with some
insular exaggeration of the importance of his own position —
to suppose that the design of Petavius in his exposition of the
unformed trinitarianism of the ante-Nicene Fathers was to
help " the cause of the Pope " by showing that " there is very
little regard to be had to the Fathers of the three first ages, to
whom the Reformed Catholics " — that is to say, the Catholiz-
ing party of the Church of England — " generally do appeal." [115] Whatever may be said of this conjecture, it cannot
be doubted that Bull's design was to show that the appeal to
the " first three ages " yielded in the matter of the Trinity the
self-same doctrine which the Nicene Fathers formulated. In
order to do this, however, he was compelled to saddle upon the
Nicene doctrine a subordinationism which, of the very essence
of the Logos Christology of the second and third centuries, was
in the Nicene construction happily in the act of being tran-

[112] Nelson, as cited, p. 301.
[113] " Defence," Proem., § 5. Ralph Cudworth was at the moment teaching
a doctrine of the Trinity indistinguishable from that of Episcopius and his
followers.
[114] Nelson, p. 315, Bull, Sect. iv. cap. i. § 1 (E. T. Oxford, 1852, p. 557, in
the " Library of Anglo-Catholic Theology ").
[115] Nelson, p. 287: Bull, Proem, § 8.

scended. In the interests of this subordinationism Calvin's equalization of the Son with the Father through the ascription to Him of αὐτοθεότης was necessarily distasteful to Bull. That the Son is " very God " and in that sense may fitly be called αὐτοθεός he is, indeed, frank to allow, for he is himself, with all the Fathers, a true and firm believer in the Godhead of Christ: but that the Son is αὐτόθεος, " God of Himself," he repudiates with decision as inconsistent with " catholic consent " which pronounces Him rather θεὸς ἐκ θεοῦ. For, depending here on Petavius, he will not allow that it is possible to say " that the Son is from God the Father, as He is Son, and not as He is God; that He received His Person, not His essence, or Divine Nature, from the Father "; on the ground that begetting means just communication of essence.[116] It is a little amusing to see Bull, from his Anglican tripod, as Calvin would himself have said, patronizing Calvin. He graciously allows that Calvin has deserved well of us " for the good service which he rendered in purging the Church of Christ from the superstition of popery "; but he " earnestly exhorts pious and studious youths to beware of a spirit from which have proceeded such things " as Calvin's unreverential allusions to the Nicene Creed, which he had dared to speak of as containing harsh expressions and " vain repetitions." [117] " Even the zeal of Mr. Bull " thus, as his admiring biographer tells us, " hath not here hindered him from treating with esteem the author of so dangerous an opinion " as that Christ is God of Himself, the self-existent God, " while at the same time he is confuting it, for the sake of some laudable qualifications which he discerned in him, and was endeavoring to excuse him as well as the matter could bear, against the insults of the most learned writer of his whole order, so famous for learning " [118] — by which we suppose Nelson means to intimate that Bull defended Calvin against injurious imputations of Petavius; though we have failed to observe this feature of Bull's discussion.

In England, too, however, the downward movement ful-

[116] " Defence of the Nicene Faith," IV. i. 7 sq.
[117] Ibid., § 8.   [118] Nelson, pp. 319 sq.

filled itself. After Bull came Samuel Clarke and his fellow
Arians in the established Church, matched by the Socinian
drift among the dissenters. To these, naturally, Calvin's αὐτόθεος was as far beyond the range of practical consideration as it
was to Crell [119] or Schlichting,[120] who did him the honor to express their dissent from it. Clarke, however, may claim from us
a moment's notice, not so much on his own account, as for the
sake of a distinction which Waterland was led to make in refuting him. Clarke was willing to admit that the Son may have
been begotten of the essence of the Father, though he wished
it to be allowed that it was equally possible that He may have
been made out of nothing. " Both are worthy of censure," he
said,[121] " who on the one hand affirm that the Son was made
out of nothing, or on the other affirm that He is self-existent
substance." In his response, Waterland exhibits afresh the difficulties which lie in wait for those who take their starting-
point from even the measure of subordinationism which is embalmed in the language of the Nicene formularies, when they
seek to do justice to the full deity of Christ. In the interests of
the Nicene doctrine of eternal generation, he proposes to distinguish between necessary existence and self-existence, and,
denying the latter, to claim only the former for the Son. The
Second Person of the Godhead, he says, participates in the one
substance of the Godhead, and is therefore necessarily existent; but He participates in it by communication from the
Father, not of Himself, and therefore He is not self-existent.
" We say," he explains,[122] " the Son is not self-existent, meaning He is not unoriginate. You " — that is, Clarke — " not only
say the same, but contend for it, meaning not necessarily existing." " Self-existence as distinct from necessary existence, is
expressive only of the order and manner in which the perfections are in the Father, and not of any distinct perfection." [123]

[119] " Tract. de uno Deo Patre," Book I. sect. ii. cap. 2.
[120] " Contra Meisnerum."
[121] " On the Trinity," 1712, Part ii. § 14, p. 276. Cf. ii. § 5. An interesting
account of Clarke may be found in Nelson, as cited, pp. 322 sq.
[122] " Vindication," etc., Q. xiii. (Cambridge, 1721, p. 207).
[123] " Second Defense," Q. iii. (London, 1723, p. 172).

That is to say, in Waterland's view, the Son is all that the Father is, but not in the same manner: the Father is all that He is in this manner, viz., that He is it of Himself; the Son, in this manner, viz., that He is it of the Father. Both are necessarily all that they are, and therefore both are necessarily existent: but only the Father is all that He is of Himself, and therefore self-existence can be predicated of Him alone. What is really declared here is obviously only that the generation of the Son is a necessary and not a voluntary movement in the divine nature: and all that is affirmed is therefore merely that the existence of the Son is not dependent on the divine will. Is this all that need be affirmed, however, in order to vindicate to the Son true deity? We must bear in mind that it is not impossible to conceive creation itself as necessary: the history of theology has not been a stranger to the idea that the world is the eternal and necessary product of the divine activity. In order to vindicate true deity to the Son it is not sufficient, therefore, to affirm that He is equally with the Father " necessary in respect of existence." [124] That might be true of Him even were He a creature. What must be affirmed of Him if we would recognize His true deity is not merely that He could not but exist, but that the ground of His existence is in Himself. It is self-existence, not necessary existence, in other words, which really imports deity, and it is a degradation of this great and fundamental attribute to attempt to reduce it to a mere synonym of " ingenerate." It is rather the synonym of necessary existence as applied to deity, describing this necessary existence in its deeper significance and implications. The artificial distinction which Waterland wishes to make between the two as applied to the Son, seems thus merely an invention to " save the face " of the Nicene doctrine of " generation." Let us admit, says he, in effect, that the Son is equally with the Father " necessary in respect of existence." That is, of course, " self-existent " according to the proper significance of the term in its application to a Divine Being. But let us agree to say that we will not use the term " self-existence " but " neces-

[124] *Ibid.*

sarily existing " in this sense, and will reserve " self-existence "
for another sense, distinct from " necessary existence." Now,
" as distinct from necessary existence," " self-existence " can
express only " the order and manner in which the perfections
are in the Father " and not " any distinct perfection." Granted.
If we are to use the term " self-existence " to express some other
idea than self-existence — then it may express something
which the self-existing, i.e., necessarily existing God who is the
Son is not. But then it remains true that this necessarily existing God who is the Son is at this very moment confessed to be
the self-existent God — under its synonym of " necessarily
existent." In a word, if we will agree to use the term " self-
existent " in the sense of " ingenerate " — which it does not in
the least mean — we may, of course, deny that the Son who
is " generate " is " self-existent ": but if we employ that term
in the sense of " necessarily existent," — which is just what it
means in the full reach of that term as applied to God — why,
then we must say that the Son is " self-existent." To put the
thing in a nutshell: the Nicene doctrine that the generation of
the Son and the procession of the Spirit are necessary movements in the divine essence and not voluntary acts of God the
Father, carries with it the ascription of necessary existence, in
the sense of that term applicable to God, that is of " self-
existence," to the Son and Spirit and requires that each
be spoken of as αὐτόθεος. To deny to them the quality of
αὐτοθεότης is thus logically to make them creatures of the Father's power, if not of His will; by which their true deity is
destroyed. Thus the tendency among the so-called strict Nicenists to deny to our Lord that He is, as God, a se ipso betrays
a lurking leaven of subordinationism in their thought. It indicates a tendency to treat the Nicene doctrine of eternal generation, not, as it was intended by its framers, as the safeguard of the absolute equality of the Son with the Father, but
rather as the proclamation of the inferiority of the Son to the
Father: the Son because generate must differ from the ingenerate Father — must differ in this, that He cannot be, as
is the Father, self-existent God, which is, of course, all one

with saying that He is not God at all, since the very idea of God includes the idea of self-existence.[125]

It was, therefore, a very great service to Christian theology which Calvin rendered when he firmly asserted for the second and third persons of the Trinity their αὐτοθεότης. It has never since been possible for men to escape facing the question whether they really do justice to the true and complete deity of the Son and Spirit in their thought of the Trinitarian distinctions. It has not even been possible since for men who heartily believe in the deity of the Son and Spirit to refuse to them the designation of αὐτοθεός. They may have distinguished, indeed, between αὐτόθεος and αὐτοθεός — Self-Existent God and Very God — and allowed the latter to the second and third Persons while withholding the former.[126] But

[125] De Moor, " In Marck. Compend.," i. 1761, p. 772, seems to prefer the word " independence " for the expression of the aseity of God and of the Son as God : " By parity of reasoning, it is certain that if the Son be *true* God, He is *independent* God ; for independence is easily first among the attributes of God, and is inseparable from the essence of God. . . . And this being true, the title αὐτόθεος or αὐτοθεός (for the theologians accent it differently) cannot be denied to the Son, nor to the Spirit, as if this title were suitable to the Father only." . . . " By independence," he continues, " God is, as we have seen at chap. iv. § 20, *a se* in the negative sense, not in the sense of a proper causality of Himself, and it is this that the title αὐτοθεός expresses. 1. If then the Son is the supreme and independent God He is αὐτοθεός. 2. And since the reality of the Divine essence cannot exist without independence, the Son would not be true God unless He was at the same time αὐτοθεός. 3. If the Father be acknowledged to be αὐτοθεός, the Son must also be such, unless the Son be denied to be the same God with the Father and a plurality of Gods is erected, a numerical plurality of divine essences. For the same God and the same Divine essence cannot at the same time be *a se ipso* and not *a se ipso*. The Son is not, of course, αὐτουιός, *Son a se ipso;* but He certainly is αὐτοθεός, *God a se ipso.* He is of the Father relatively to His being Son, but He is *a se* considered absolutely as He is God : as He has the Divine essence existing *a se,* and not divided or produced by another essence ; but not as if having that essence *a se ipso.* He is ' God *a se* '; not, ' He is *a se,* God,' or, what is the same thing, He is not Son *a se.*"

[126] The debate on the αὐτοθεότης of the Son caused the theologians to enter into long disquisitions on the force of αὐτός in composition and the proper sense or senses of αὐτόθεος. Voetius, for example (pp. 449–451) argues that αὐτός in composition has five senses. It either (1) emphasises singularity ; or (2) distinguishes as κατ' ἐξοχήν ; or (3) means *a se;* or (4) *per se,* intrinsically, essentially ; or (5) *per se* and operating with a proper and sufficient principial

in the very act of drawing such a distinction, they have emphasized the true deity of the second and third Persons, and have been deterred from ascribing αὐτοθεότης to them in the sense of self-existence only by confusing it with " ingeneration." It is, however, a part of the heritage, particularly of the Reformed Churches, that they have learned from Calvin to claim for Christ the great epithet of αὐτόθεος: [127] and their characteristic mark has therefore become the strength of the emphasis which they throw on the complete deity of the Lord. Whatever differences may have existed among them have not concerned the true deity of Christ, but rather the attitude taken by their teachers towards the Nicene speculation of " eternal generation." Concerning this speculation differences early manifested themselves. Immediate successors of Calvin, such as Theodore Beza and Josiah Simler, were as firm and exact in their adhesion to it as Calvin was dubious with reference to it. " The Son," says Beza, " is of the Father by an ineffable communication from eternity of the whole nature." [128] " We deny not," says Simler, " that the Son has His essence

---

force, producing somewhat. Accordingly it is improper to assume that theologians always mean the *third* sense, when they employ the term αὐτόθεος. Any one of five senses may be intended: (1) God κατ' ἐξοχήν; (2) The only, sole God; (3) God essentially, not by participation, *per se* and not *per accidens, in se* and essentially, not in some external respect or denomination; (4) God *a se* and not *ab alio*, ἄναρχος, that is to say, καὶ ἀναίτιος; (5) God, the *primus agens, primus motor*, dependent on none, but the first cause.

[127] Voetius, " Disp.," i. 1648, p. 460, gives a characteristic list of Reformed doctors who previous to himself (1648) had taught that Christ is properly to be called αὐτόθεος — lest anyone should think that the αὐτοθεότης of Christ had been proclaimed only by one here and there, zealous for their own notion or loving novelty, rather than by all in the necessary defense of the common truth. His list includes, besides Calvin, Beza, Simler, the whole mass of representative Reformed teachers: Danaeus, Perkins, Keckermann, Trelcatius, Tilenus, Polanus, Wollebius, Scalcobrigius, Altingius, Grynaeus, Schriverius, Zanchius, Chamierus, Zadeel, Lectius, Pareus, Mortonus, Whittaker, Junius, Vorstius, Amesius, Rivetus. Heppe, " Dogmat. d. ev.-ref. Kirche," 1861, p. 84, records: " And moreover the Son is as such not created or made by God, or adopted out of favor or on account of desert, but He is according to His nature God the Son, and is therefore like the Father and the Holy Spirit veritably αὐτοθεός."

[128] " Axiomat. de Trinitate," Axiom 14.

from God the Father; what we deny is a begotten essence." [129]
And no less or less prejudiced an authority than Bellarmine
pronounces these declarations " Catholic." [130] Indeed, despite
the influence of Calvin, the great body of the Reformed teachers remained good Nicenists. But they were none the less, as
they were fully entitled to be, good " Autotheanites " also.
They saw clearly that a relation within the Godhead between
Persons to each of whom the entire Godhead belongs, cannot
deprive any of these Persons of any essential quality of the
Godhead common to them all.[131] And they were determined
to assert the full and complete Godhead of them all. Of course,
there have been others, on the other hand, who have followed
Calvin in sitting rather loosely to the Nicene tradition. Examples of this class are furnished by Trelcatius, Keckermann,
Maccovius.[132] Keckermann, for example, while not denying
that many have preferred to say that " the Son has His essence
communicated from the Father," yet considers that this can
be said only in a modified sense and must be accompanied by
certain important explanations — for, says he, " it is false if
spoken of the essence considered absolutely, since the Son (as
also the Holy Spirit) has this *a se ipso.*" For himself he prefers,

[129] " Epist. ad Polon." or " Lib. de Filio Dei."

[130] *Op. cit.,* p. 334b.

[131] Cf. the remark of De Moor, " In Marck. Compend.," i. 1761, p. 775:
" Distinctions in *mode of subsistence,* and the personal order which flows from
this, cannot affect the equality of essence; and inferiority and inequality cannot consist with numerical oneness of essence."

[132] Cf. Voetius, as cited, p. 465: " Trelcatius, *Loc. Com.,* and Keckermann, *Syst. Theol.,* seem to deny the communication of the essence: and
Maccovius, in his *Metaphysica,* c. 8, follows them, when, against Arminius,
he determines that not the essence, but the personality, is communicated from
the Father." " Strictly speaking, however, we must say," adds Voetius, " that
the Person is begotten by the communication of the essence: though these
authors are to be excused because they took the word ' communication ' too
physically and had Valentinus Gentilis in view." Voetius' own view is expressed
in the " maxims " (p. 461) that: " The essence *in divinis* neither begets nor is
begotten, but the person of the Father begets *in, de* and *ex* His essence which
is the same with the essence of the Son ": " the essence may therefore be said
to be communicated, given, by the Father, and received, and had, by the Son
from that communication or gift. Briefly, the Person of the Father begets the
Person of the Son by the communication of the essence."

therefore, to say that "the second mode of existence in the Trinity, which is called the Son, . . . is communicated from the Father." [133] This is, as we have seen, apparently Calvin's own view, while the more advanced position still which rejects, or at least neglects, the conception of " communication " altogether, whether of essence or of mode of existence,[134] although

[133] "Systema SS. Theologiae," Hanoviae, 1615, p. 54.

[134] This position was taken by Herman Alexander Roëll, professor at Franeker, at the end of the seventeenth century. The idea of "eternal generation" he held to be wholly unscriptural and at war with the perfect nature of God — whether as Father or as Son. The designation of the Second Person of the Trinity as Son he at first found to rest on His consubstantiality with the Father ("By the words 'Son' and 'Generation' is signified, in emphasis, that the Second Person has the same essence and nature with the First, and has coëxisted with Him from eternity," — " De Generatione Filii," 1689, p. 5), but afterwards to be expressive rather of His divine mission, and the clear relation existing between God the Sender and God the Sent. A good account is given of his views by Ypeij and Dermout, " Geschiedenis der Nederlandsche Hervormde Kerk," ii. 1822, pp. 544 sq. The idea of Herman Muntinghe, professor at Hardewijk and later at Groningen, at the end of the next century (see Ypeij and Dermout, iv. 1827, pp. 271 sq.) was similar. Much the same notions were introduced into the Congregational churches of New England by Nathaniel Emmons. " We feel constrained to reject the eternal generation of the Son, and the eternal procession of the Holy Ghost, as such mysteries as cannot be distinguished from real absurdities, and as such doctrines as strike at the foundation of the true doctrine of three equally divine persons in one God " (" Works," iv. 1842, p. 114). " The Scripture teaches us that each of the divine persons takes His peculiar *name* from the peculiar *office* which He sustains in the economy of redemption. . . . The first person assumes the name of Father, because He is by office the Creator or Author of all things, and especially of the human nature of Christ. The second person assumes the name of Son and Word, by virtue of His incarnation and mediatorial conduct. . . . The third person in the Trinity is called the Holy Ghost on account of His peculiar office as Sanctifier " (p. 109). This view became thereafter the common view among the New England churches, finding its complete expression in Moses Stuart (" Letters on the Eternal Generation of the Son," 1822) and Horace Bushnell (" God in Christ," 1849). Cf. George P. Fisher, " Discussions in History and Theology," 1880, p. 273: " Hopkins was the last to hold to the Nicene doctrine of the primacy of the Father and the eternal Sonship of Christ. The whole philosophy of the Trinity, as that doctrine was conceived by its great defenders in the age of Athanasius, when the doctrine was formulated, had been set aside. It was even derided; and this chiefly for the reason that it was not studied. Professor Stuart had no sympathy with or just appreciation of the Nicene doctrine of the generation of the Son." It should be noted, however, that the " eternal primacy " of the Father and the " eternal generation " of the Son do not necessarily go together. Neither Roëll nor

it cannot find an example in Calvin, may yet be said to have had its way prepared for it by him. The direct Scriptural proof which had been customarily relied upon for its establishment he destroyed, refusing to rest a doctrinal determination on " distorted texts." He left, therefore, little Biblical basis for the doctrine of " eternal generation " except what might be inferred from the mere terms " Father," " Son " and " Spirit," and the general consideration that our own adoption into the relation of sons of God in Christ implies for Him a Sonship of a higher and more immanent character, which is His by nature and into participation in the relation of which we are admitted only by grace.[135] Certainly other explanations of these facts are

---

Emmons, for example, while decidedly denying the " eternal generation " of the Son, doubted that the Father is first in the Trinity, not only in office but also in order — as Emmons (p. 137) expresses it, is " the head of the sacred Trinity." They do deny, however, that the Father is superior to the Son in nature; and they take their starting point from the absolute deity of the Son, in the interests of which it is largely that they deny the doctrine of " eternal generation." When Dr. Fisher (p. 273) says, " The eternal fatherhood of God, the precedence of the Father, is as much a part of the orthodox doctrine of the Trinity as is the divinity of the Son," by the orthodox doctrine of the Trinity he means the doctrine as it was formulated by " the Nicene Fathers who framed the orthodox creed." The rejoinder lies ready at hand that the Nicene Fathers overdid the matter from the point of view of " the precedence of the Father," and left the way open for doing less than justice to " the divinity of the Son " — which therefore requires reassertion and better guarding. In point of fact, it is around these two foci — " the precedence of the Father," which in its exaggeration becomes Arianism, and " the divinity of the Son," which in its exaggeration becomes Sabellianism — that the Trinitarian constructions have revolved. The Trinitarian problem is, to find a mode of statement that does full justice to both. To do this it must of course be carefully ascertained from Scripture in what sense " the Father " has " precedence " of the Son; and in what sense the Son is God. Roëll and Emmons deny that the Scriptures accord such " precedence " to the Father as is expressed by the phrase " God of God ": they affirm that the Scriptures ascribe absolute deity to the Son. On the New England doctrine of the Trinity from Emmons down see L. L. Paine, " The Evolution of Trinitarianism," 1900, pp. 104 sq.

135 Cf. the striking passage, already alluded to in part, which is found in the middle editions of the " Institutes," at the opening of the discussion (Opp. i. 482–483): " But since everything follows from the proof of the divinity [of the Son], we shall lay our chief stress on the assertion of that. The Ancients, whose idea was that the Son existed (exstitisse) by eternal generation from the Father, endeavored to prove it by the testimony of Isaiah (Is. liii. 8), ' Who shall declare His generation? ' But it is clear that they were under an illusion

possible; [136] and the possibility — or preferability — of other
explanations was certain sooner or later to commend itself to
some. Nothing, meanwhile, could illustrate more strikingly the

---

in citing this text. For the prophet does not speak there of how the Father
generated the Son but by how numerous a posterity His kingdom should be
increased [so 1539: but 1550 *sq.*: " but through how long a period His kingdom should endure "]. Neither is there much force in what they take from
the Psalms: ' from the womb before the morning star have I begotten Thee ';
for that version is by no means consonant with the Hebrew, which runs thus
(Ps. cx. 3): ' From the womb of the morning is to thee the dew of thy nativity.' The argument, then, which seems to have special plausibility, is taken
from the words of the Apostle in which it is taught that the worlds were
made by the Son; for unless there had already been a Son, His power could
not have been put forth. But little weight can attach to this argument either,
as appears from similar formulas. For none of us would be affected if anybody
sought to take the word ' Christ ' back to that time, in which Paul says that
' Christ ' was tempted by the Jews (I Cor. x. 9) [where Calvin evidently
reads " Christ "]. For its particular application belongs properly to the humanity [of Christ]. Similarly, because it is said (Heb. xiii. 8) that ' Jesus
Christ ' was yesterday, is to-day, and shall be forever, if anybody should
contend that the name of ' Christ ' belonged to Him always, he has accomplished nothing. What do we do but expose the holy and orthodox doctrines
of religion to the cavils of heretics, when we contort texts after this fashion,
which, when taken in their proper sense, serve our cause either not at all or
very little? To me, however, this one argument is worth a thousand for confirming my faith in the eternity of the Son of God. For it is certain that God
is not a Father to men, except through the intercession of that only begotten
Son, who alone rightly vindicates this prerogative to Himself, and by whose
favor it comes to us. But God always wished to be worshipped by His people
under the name of Father; from which it follows that already then [i.e.,
semper] He was Son, through whom that relationship is established." Similarly
in his Commentaries he explains Micah v. 1, 2 of the eternal decree of God, not
of the eternity of the generation of Christ: and on Ps. ii. 7 prefers to follow
Paul (Acts xiii. 33) to referring it to the eternal generation of Christ by " subtly
philosophizing on the word ' to-day.' " In the New Testament he follows the
rule (with few exceptions) " that the writers of the New Testament, and especially Jesus Himself, speak of Christ not as the absolute Logos but as the
God-man. . . . Especially in the Gospel of John, the declarations of Jesus
concerning Himself are expounded not out of an absolute logos-consciousness
but out of the theanthropic consciousness of Jesus, so that after John i. 14
there is no further reference to the Logos ἄσαρκος or to the *nuda divinitas*
Christi except only in Jno. viii. 58 and xvii. 5 " (Scholten, " De Leer der Hervormde Kerk," ed. 4, ii. p. 231; cf. p. 229 and i. p. 24). Similarly of the Holy
Spirit (p. 236) he refuses to get proof for His trinitarian relation either from
Jno. xiv. 16 or I Cor. ii. 10.

[136] As, for example, that the terms " Son," " Spirit " are not expressive

vitality of the ecclesiastical tradition than that in such a state of the case the Nicene construction of the Trinity held its ground: held its ground with Calvin himself in its substantial core, and with the majority of his followers in its complete speculative elaboration. We are astonished at the persistence of so large an infusion of the Nicene phraseology in the expositions of Augustine, after that phraseology had really been antiquated by his fundamental principle of equalization in his construction of the Trinitarian relations: we are more astonished at the effort which Calvin made to adduce Nicene support for his own conceptions: and we are more astonished still at the tenacity with which his followers cling to all the old speculations.[137]

The repeated appeals which he makes to the Fathers is, as we have just hinted, a notable feature of Calvin's discussion of the Trinity and especially of his defense of his construction of the Trinitarian relationships. The citations he drew from the

---

of " derivation " (by " generation " or " spiration ") but just of " consubstantiality." The Son is the repetition of the Father; the Spirit is the expression of God. So Roëll in his first view; and even Stuart remarks, justly: " The Hebrew idiom calls him the son of any person or thing, who exhibits a resemblance in disposition or character " (*op. cit.*, p. 105). More broadly, W. Robertson Smith (" The O. T. in the Jewish Church," ed. 1, p. 427) remarks: " Among all Semites membership in a guild is figured as sonship." That is to say, in the Semitic view, sonship denotes broadly oneness of kind, class; more specifically likeness; at the height of its meaning, consubstantiality; and does not suggest derivation. As the son of a man is a man, the Son of God is God. It is the Indo-European consciousness which imparts to the terms Son, Spirit the idea of derivation.

137 When during the first weeks of its sessions, the Westminster Assembly was engaged on the revision of the Thirty-nine Articles, and Article viii. on the Three Creeds came up for discussion, objection was made to the ἐκ θεοῦ clauses. It does not appear that there was any pleading for the subordinationist position: the advocates for retaining the Creeds rather expended their strength in voiding the credal statement of any subordinationist implications. Thus Dr. Featley's reply to the current objection was that " although Christ is God of God, it doth not therefore follow that the deity of the Son is from the deity of the Father, . . . as it does not follow *quia Deus passus est ergo Deitas passa est*, or *quia Maria mater Dei, ergo est Maria mater deitatis* " (see his speech printed in his " Dippers Dipt," London, 1651, pp. 187–189). Were this taken literally it would explain the Sonship of our Lord wholly from the side of His humiliation and identify His filiation with the incarnation.

Fathers for this purpose were naturally much striven over. One instance seems worth scrutinizing, as on it was founded an accusation that Calvin did not know the difference between the two Latin prepositions " *ad* " and " *a*," or else chose to "play to the gallery," which he counted upon not to know it. That the best Latinist of his day, whose Latin style is rather classical than mediæval, could fail to feel the force of the common prepositions of that language is, of course, absurd: that a reasoner conspicuous for his fair-mindedness in his argumentation could have juggled with ambiguous phrases is even more impossible. An attentive reading of the passages in question will, as was to be expected, quickly make it clear that it is not Calvin but his critics who are at fault. Bellarmine, arguing that the reasons which Calvin assigns for calling our Lord αὐτόθεος are not valid, adduces his appeal to the passages in which Augustine remarks that our Lord " is called Son, with reference to the Father (*ad patrem*) and God with reference to Himself (*ad seipsum*)." " But," he adds, in rebuttal, " it is not the same thing to say that the Son is God *ad se,* and that He is God *a se.*" " For," he somewhat superfluously argues, " the first signifies that the name of God is not relative and yet belongs to the Son: and this Augustine says and says truly, for although the Son is a relative, it is nevertheless a relative which exists, is divine, and accordingly includes the essence which is absolute. But [to say] that the Son is God *a se* signifies that the Son of God is not the Son of God, but is unbegotten, which Augustine never said, but Calvin falsely attributes to him." [138] " It is either," writes Petavius,[139] improving even on Bellarmine, " a remarkable piece of chicanery or else a remarkable hallucination in Calvin, when he seems to take as equivalents these two terms *ad se* and *a se:* as also these two, *ad alium* and *ab alio,* which " [i.e., *ad se* and *ad alium*] " Augustine makes free use of in explaining the mystery of the Trinity." Then, after quoting Calvin's citation of Augustine, he concludes: " Unless Calvin had supposed *ad se* to be the same as *a se,* and *ad alium* to be the same as *ab alio,* he would not have employed

---

[138] *Op. cit.,* p. 335.   [139] *Op. cit.,* p. 252.

these passages from Augustine." [140] In point of fact, however,
Calvin does not confuse "ad" and "a" and he does not cite
Augustine's use of the one as if he had employed the other.
His citations are not intended to show that Augustine taught
that the Son is not of the Father but of Himself: but only to
show that we may — or rather must — speak in a twofold

[140] We suppose Arminius scarcely intended to repeat Bellarmine's and
Petavius' accusation of confusion between *a se* and *ad se* when ("Works,"
E. T. ii. 1828, p. 32) he remarks on the modified manner in which αὐτοθεὸς is
used when applied to Christ, and adds: "But their explanation does not agree
with the phraseology they employ. For this reason Beza excuses Calvin, and
openly confesses 'that he had not with sufficient strictness observed the difference between these particles *a se* and *per se.*'" The remark of Beza is referred to his "Praef. in Dialog. Athanasii." We have not access to Beza's edition
of this Pseudo-Athanasian tractate and cannot assure ourselves of his meaning. We assume that he was not criticizing Calvin's philological equipment but
his doctrinal construction; and we suspect that what he says is that Calvin
in insisting that Christ is God *a se ipso* was not sufficiently carefully dis-
guishing between saying He is God *per se* — in and of Himself, and that He
is God *a se* — from Himself. In that likely case Beza is only explaining the
differences between himself and Calvin which are expressed in Calvin's denial
that the Son has His essence from the Father and Beza's affirmation that He
has His essence from the Father. Calvin here, he says, is not sufficiently considering the difference between being God *a se* and being God *per se.* In this
case Beza's distinction is much like Waterland's between self-existent and
necessarily-existent God and makes αὐτοθεότης mean merely ingenerateness;
and we note that if our conjecture is right, there is involved a testimony from
Beza that Calvin's real thought of the Trinity denied the communication of
essence from Father to Son. In his letter to Prince Radziwil on "The Unity of
the Divine Essence and the three Persons subsisting in it," against the Polish
Unitarians, Beza declares ("Tractat. Theolog.," 1582, i. p. 647) that it is inept
to say that "the Father alone is αὐτόθεος, that is, as they interpret it, has
His Being *a se ipso* and therefore can be called God," — and gives his reason:
"For to be *a se* and *ab alio,* do not constitute different kinds of nature; and
therefore the Father cannot on that ground be said to be the sole and unique
God, nor ought He to be, but rather the sole and unique Father, as the Son is
sole and unique because 'only-begotten.'" Can we really say that "to be *a se*
and *ab alio* do not constitute different kinds of nature (*aliam naturae speciem*)? If the contrast is that of self-existing and derived Being it can scarcely
be said. But if the contrast is between ingenerate and generate Being — it is
true enough. Every father and son are consubstantial, and the very point of
the usage of Father and Son in this connection seems to be to assert their consubstantiality. Beza has this latter contrast in view and only means to say
that the ascription of αὐτοθεότης to the Son is in no way interfered with by
the fact that He is "generate" — for the generate and the generator are ever
the same in kind.

way of the Son, absolutely, to wit, as He is in Himself and relatively, as He is with reference to the Father. It is his own statement, not Augustine's, when he proceeds to say that when we thus speak of our Lord absolutely as He is in Himself, we are to say that He is *a se*, and only when we speak of Him relatively as He is with reference to the Father are we to speak of Him as *a Patre*. It is marvellous that anyone could confuse this perfectly clear argument: more marvellous still that, on the ground of such a confusion, anyone should venture to charge Calvin with gross ignorance of the meaning of the simplest Latin words or else of " remarkable chicanery " in his use of Latin texts. Here is what Calvin actually says: " By these appellations, which denote distinction, says Augustine, that is signified by which they are mutually related to one another: not the substance itself by which they are one. By which explanation, the sentiments of the ancients which otherwise might seem contradictory may be reconciled with one another. For now they teach that the Father is the principium of the Son; and now they assert that the Son has His divinity and essence alike of Himself, and is therefore one principium with the Father. The cause of this diversity is elsewhere well and perspicuously explained by Augustine when he speaks as follows: Christ is called God with respect to Himself, He is called Son with respect to the Father. And again, the Father is called God with respect to Himself, with respect to the Son He is called Father. What is called Father with respect to the Son is not the Son; what is called Son with respect to the Father is not the Father: what is called Father with respect to Himself and Son with respect to Himself is God. When, then, we speak of the Son, simply, without respect to the Father, we rightly and properly assert that He is of Himself; and we therefore call Him the sole (*unicum*) principium; but when we are noting the relation in which He stands to the Father, we justly make the Father the principium of the Son." [141] A simple reading of the passage is enough to refute the suggestion that Calvin makes Augustine assert that Christ is " of Him-

[141] " Institutes," I. xiii. 19.

self " when he is merely asserting that Christ is God when
considered with respect to Himself and not relatively to the
Father. If a matter so clear in itself, however, can be made
clearer by further evidence, it is easy enough to adduce direct
evidence. For Calvin has incorporated into the "Institutes"
here material he uses often elsewhere. And in more than one
of these instances of its use elsewhere, he distinctly tells us
that he did not understand Augustine in these passages to be
asserting the aseity of the Son. We may take, for example, a
letter to the Neuchâtel pastors, written in November, 1543,
with respect to Cortesius, with whom he had been having a
discussion on our Lord's aseity — or as Calvin puts it, περὶ
αὐτοουσίας Christi. In the course of the discussion, he says,
"we came to that difficulty that he did not think he could
speak of the essence of Christ without mention of the person.
I opposed to this first the authority of Augustine, who testifies that we can speak in a twofold way (bifariam) of Christ,
as He is God — according to relation, that is, and simply (simpliciter). And that the discussion might not be prolonged, I
adduced certain passages of Cyril, where in so many words
(dissertis verbis) he pronounces on what we were discussing." [142] That is to say, the passages of Augustine were appealed to not as direct witness to the αὐτοουσία of Christ, but
only to prove the subordinate point that we can speak of our
Lord in a twofold way: the passages from Cyril alone "expressly" declare on the point at issue. The declaration that
Cyril was adduced as pronouncing on the point itself in so
many words, is a declaration that Augustine was not so adduced.

In his assertion of the αὐτοθεότης of the Son Calvin, then,
was so far from supposing that he was enunciating a novelty
that he was able to quote the Nicene Fathers themselves as asserting it "in so many words." And yet in his assertion of it
he marks an epoch in the history of the doctrine of the Trinity. Not that men had not before believed in the self-existence
of the Son as He is God: but that the current modes of stating

[142] *Opp.* xi. 653.

the doctrine of the Trinity left a door open for the entrance
of defective modes of conceiving the deity of the Son, to close
which there was needed some such sharp assertion of His absolute deity as was supplied by the assertion of His αὐτοθεότης.
If we will glance over the history of the efforts of the Church
to work out for itself an acceptable statement of the great
mystery of the Trinity, we shall perceive that it is dominated
from the beginning to the end by a single motive — to do full
justice to the absolute deity of Christ. And we shall perceive
that among the multitudes of great thinkers who under the
pressure of this motive have labored upon the problem, and to
whom the Church looks back with gratitude for great services,
in the better formulation of the doctrine or the better commendation of it to the people, three names stand out in high
relief, as marking epochs in the advance towards the end in
view. These three names are those of Tertullian, Augustine and
Calvin. It is into this narrow circle of elect spirits that Calvin
enters by the contribution he made to the right understanding
of the doctrine of the Trinity. That contribution is summed
up in his clear, firm and unwavering assertion of the αὐτοθεότης
of the Son. By this assertion the ὁμοουσιότης of the Nicene Fathers at last came to its full right, and became in its fullest
sense the hinge of the doctrine.

V

CALVIN'S DOCTRINE OF THE CREATION

CALVIN'S DOCTRINE OF THE CREATION [1]

In developing his system, Calvin proceeds at once from the doctrine of God to an exposition of His works of creation and providence (I. xiv.–xv. and xvi.–xviii.). That he passes over the divine Purpose or Decree at this point, though it would logically claim attention before its execution in creation and providence, is only another indication of the intensely practical spirit of Calvin and the simplicity of his method in this work. He carries his readers at once over from what God is to what God does, reserving the abstruser discussions of the relation of His will to occurrences for a later point in the treatise, when the reader's mind, by a contemplation of the divine works, will be better prepared to read off the underlying purpose from the actual event. The practical end which has determined this sequence of topics governs also the manner in which the subject of creation, now taken up (chaps. xiv.–xv.), is dealt with. There is no discussion of it from a formal point of view: the treatment is wholly material and is devoted rather to the nature of the created universe than to the mode of the Divine activity in creating it. Even in dealing with the created universe, there is no attempt at completeness of treatment. The spiritual universe is permitted to absorb the attention; and what is said about the lower creation is reduced to a mere hint or two introduced chiefly, it appears, to recommend the contemplation of it as a means of quickening in the heart a sense of God's greatness and goodness (xiv. §§ 20–22).

It is quite obvious, in fact, from the beginning, that Calvin's mind is set in this whole discussion of creation primarily on expounding the nature of man as a creature of God; and all else that he incorporates into it is subsidiary to this. He is

[1] From *The Princeton Theologial Review*, xiii. 1915, pp. 190–255, continuing the series of articles published in the *Review* during 1909 (pp. 27–284 of this volume).

writing for men and bends all he is writing to what he conceives to be their practical interests. He does not reach the actual discussion of man as creature, to be sure (chap. xv.), until after he has interposed a long exposition of the nature of angels and demons (xiv. 3–12, and 13–19). But this whole exposition is cast in a form which shows that angels and demons are interesting to Calvin only because of the high estimate he places upon the topic for the practical life of man; and it is introduced by a remark which betrays that his thought was already on man as the real subject of his exposition and all he had to say about other spiritual creatures was conceived as only preliminary to that more direct object of interest. " But before I begin to speak more fully concerning the nature of man," he says quite gratuitously at the opening of the discussion (xiv. 3, *ad init.*), " something should be inserted (*inserere*) about angels." What he actually says about angels, good and bad, in the amount of space occupied by it, is more than what he says about man; but it stood before his mind, we observe, as only " something," and as something, be it noted, " inserted," before the real subject of his discourse was reached. In his own consciousness what Calvin undertakes in these chapters is to make man aware of his own nature as a creature of God, and to place him as a creature of God in his environment, the most important elements of which he conceives to be the rest of the intelligent creation.

It is not to be inferred, of course, from the lightness with which Calvin passes over the doctrine of creation itself in this discussion that he took little interest in it or deemed it a matter of no great significance. That he does not dwell more fully on it is due, as we have said, to the practical nature of his undertaking, and was rendered possible by the circumstance that this doctrine was not in dispute.[2] All men in the circles which

[2] Cf. P. J. Muller, " De Godsleer van Zwingli en Calvijn," 1883, pp. 50–51: " Although the importance of the doctrine of creation is felt by the two reformers, yet we seek in vain in Zwingli as well as in Calvin for a definite theory of creation. . . . The reason why the doctrine of creation was not developed by them in the same degree as that of providence, must no doubt be sought in the fact that this dogma did not at the time give occasion to any polemic."

he was addressing were of one mind on it, and there were sources of information within the reach of all which rendered it unnecessary for him to enlarge on it.[3] That he had a clear and firm conception of the nature of the creative act and attributed importance to its proper apprehension is made abundantly plain; and is emphasized by his consecration of the few remarks he gives professedly to the topic to repelling assaults upon its credibility drawn from the nature of the Divine Being (xiv. 1–2).

In his conception of creation Calvin definitely separated himself from all dualistic,[4] and especially from all pantheistic [5] elements of thought by sharply asserting that all substantial existence outside of God owes its being to God, that it was created by God out of nothing, and that it came from God's hand very good. His crispest definition of creation he lets fall incidentally in repelling the pantheistic notion that, as he scornfully describes it, " the essence of the Creator is rent into fragments that each may have a part of it." " Creation," he says, " is not the transfusion, but the origination out of nothing, of essence." [6] " God," says he again, " by the power of His Word and Spirit created out of nothing, the heavens and the earth," that is to say, all that exists, whether celestial

---

Also, " De Godsleer van Calvijn," 1881, p. 51: " We cannot think it strange that Calvin, as a Biblical theologian, will know nothing of any other theory of creation than that which is given us in the Scriptures."

[3] I. xiv. 20: He refers his readers to Moses, as expounded particularly by Basil and Ambrose, " since it is not my design to treat at large of the creation of the world."

[4] Cf. I. xiv. 3, where he inveighs against " Manichaeus and his sect," who attributed to God the origin of good things only, but referred evil natures to the devil. The sole foundation of this heresy, he remarks, is that it is nefarious to ascribe to the good God the creation of any evil thing: but this is inoperative as " there is nothing in the universe which has an evil nature," — " since neither the pravity nor the malice of either man or devil, or the sins that are born from them, are of nature, but rather of corruption of nature."

[5] Cf. I. xv. 5: " To rend the essence of the Creator so that everything should possess a part, is the extremity of madness."

[6] I. xv. 5, *med.*: creatio autem non transfusio est, sed essentiae ex nihilo exordium.

or terrestial.[7] Firmly stated as this doctrine of creation is, however, so as to leave us in no doubt as to Calvin's conception,[8] the elements of it are little elaborated. There is no attempt for example to validate the doctrine of creation *ex nihilo* whether on Biblical [9] or on such rational grounds as we find appealed to by Zwingli, who argues that creation *ex materia* implies an infinite series whether the material out of which the creation is made be conceived as like or unlike in kind to that which is made from it.[10] As we have seen, Calvin does argue, however, (like Zwingli), that creation in its very nature is

[7] I. xiv. 20: Deum verbi ac Spiritus sui potentia ex nihilo creasse coelum et terram. Cf. Genevan Catechism, 1545, *Opp.* vi. 15, 16: Per coelum et terram an non quidquid praeterea creaturarum exstat, intelligis? Imo vero; sed his duobus nominibus continentur omnes, quod aut coelestes sint omnes aut terrenae.

[8] Cf. P. J. Muller, " De Godsleer van Calvijn," 1881, p. 53: " Calvin's doctrine of creation is in brief, this: God created the world out of nothing in six days through His Word, i.e. through His Son."

[9] In his Commentary on Gen. i. 1, however, he does argue that the Bible teaches that creation is *ex nihilo,* the weight of the argument being made to rest on the use of בָּרָא, which he sharply discriminates from יָצַר. Cf. Baumgartner, " Calvin Hebraïsant," 1889, pp. 50, 51: " Richard Simon has pointed, as a proof that Calvin was not strong in Hebrew, to the fact that he understands the בָּרָא of Gen. i. 1 in the sense of ' creation *ex nihilo.*' But here again R. Simon has been misled by his party-spirit, for the modern lexicographers are far from pronouncing Calvin's interpretation wrong " (e.g. Gesenius, " Thesaurus," i. p. 236). The most recent view will scarcely allow that the specific idea of creation *ex nihilo* is expressed in בָּרָא but recognizes that the ideas of novelty, extraordinariness, effortlessness are expressed in it, and that thus it may be said to lay a basis for the doctrine in question: cf. Franz Böhl, " Alttestamentliche Studien Rudolf Kittel zum 60. Geburtstag dargebracht," 1913, pp. 42–60, and Skinner, " Genesis," 1910, pp. 14, 15. Calvin does not understand Heb. xi. 3 of creation *ex nihilo,* but interprets it as the manifestation of the Invisible God in the visible works of His hands, " that we have in this visible world a conspicuous image of God "; " thus the same truth is taught here as in Rom. i. 20, where it is said that the invisible things of God are made known to us by the creation of the world, they being seen by His works." This is the burden of the Argument to the Commentary on Gen. i. and its echoes are heard in " Institutes," I. xiv. 1.

[10] " Opera " (Schuler u. Schulthess), iv. pp. 86 *sq.*: Zwingli argues that, if the preëxisting stuff is the same in kind as the thing created, we have an infinite series of worlds: if of a different kind, we have an infinite series of materials. Hence the world is not *ex materia,* but *ex causa,* which is as much as to say *ex nihilo.*

" origination of essence," so that he would have subscribed
Zwingli's declaration: " This is the definition of creation: to be
out of nothing." [11] He does not even dwell upon the part which
the Son takes in the creating, although he does not leave this
important matter unmentioned, but declares that " the worlds
were created by the Son " (I. xiii. 7), and that God created the
heavens and earth " by the power of His Word and Spirit "
(I. xiv. 20), thus setting the act of creation in its Trinitarian relation. It is, however, rather in the preceding chapter where
he adduces the share they took in creation in proof of the deity
of the Son and the Spirit that Calvin develops this fact. There
he urges that " the power to create and the authority to command were common to the Father, Son, and Spirit," as is
shown, he says, by the words " Let us make man in our image "
of Genesis i. 26; and he argues at length from the creation-narrative of Genesis and the Wisdom passage in Proverbs, no less
than from Heb. i. 2, 3, that it was through the Son that God
made the worlds.[12] On one thing, however, he manages to insist
despite the sketchiness with which he treats the whole subject.

[11] *Ibid.,* iv. p. 87: he defines creation as " esse e nihilo; vel: esse quod
prius non fuit; attamen non ex alio tamquam ex materia."

[12] I. xiii. 24; I. xiii. 7; cf. Commentary on Heb. i. 2: " By Him . . . the
world was created, since He is the eternal Wisdom of God, which was the director of all His works from the beginning. Hence too we gather that Christ
is eternal, for He must needs be before the world has been made by Him."
Cf. also Commentary on Gen. i. 3: " Since He is the Word of God, all things
have been created by Him." And see especially the passage in the first edition
of the " Institutes " (1536), at the beginning of the comment on the " second
part of the Symbol " (*Opp.* i. 64), where, after declaring on the basis of
Heb. i. that " since God the Son is the same God with the Father " He is
" the creator of the heavens and the earth," he proceeds to explain that the
habit of alluding to the Father nevertheless peculiarly as the " creator of the
heavens and the earth " is due to " that distinction of properties, already
stated, by which there is referred to the Father the *principium agendi,* so
that He Himself is indeed properly said to act (*agere*), yet through His Word
and Wisdom — yet in His Power." " But," he adds, " that the action in the
creation of the world was common to the three Persons is made clear by that
word (Gen. i.): ' Let us make man in our image and likeness ' by which there
is not expressed a deliberation with angels, nor a colloquy with Himself, but
a summoning of His Wisdom and Power." Cf. P. J. Muller, " De Godsleer
van Calvijn," 1881, pp. 51–52; " De Godsleer van Zwingli en Calvijn," 1883,
p. 53.

This is that whatever came from the divine hands came from them good. " It is monstrous," he declares,[13] " to ascribe to the good God the creation of any evil thing," and we may not admit that there is in the whole world anything evil in its nature,[14] but must perceive that in all that He has made God has displayed His wisdom and justice. Wherever evil has appeared, then, whether in man or devil, it is not *ex natura*, but *ex naturae corruptione* (I. xiv. 3), not *ex creatione* but *ex depravatione* (I. xiv. 16, *ad init.*). We must beware, therefore, lest in speaking of evil as natural to man, we should seem to refer it to the author of nature, whether we more coarsely conceive it as in some measure proceeding from God Himself, or, with more appearance of piety, ascribe it only to " nature." We cannot attribute to God what is in the most absolute sense alien to His very nature, and it is equally dishonoring to Him to ascribe any intrinsic depravity to the " nature " which comes from His hands.[15]

Calvin expressly disclaims the intention of expounding in detail the story of the creation of the world,[16] and judges it sufficient to refer his readers to the account given by Moses, along with the comments perhaps of Basil and Ambrose, for instruction in the particulars of its history (I. xiv. 20, *ad init.*; cf. I. xiv. 1). He lets fall, however, a few remarks by the way, which enable us to perceive his attitude towards the narrative of Genesis. Needless to say he takes it just as he finds it written. The six days he, naturally, understands as six literal days; and, accepting the *prima facie* chronology of the Biblical narrative, he dates the creation of the world something less than six thousand years in the past. He does not suppose, however, that Moses has included in his story anything like an exhaustive account of all that was created. The instance of angels,

---

[13] I. xiv. 3, *med.*: nefas esse adscribi bono Deo ullius rei malae creationem.

[14] *Do.*: aliquam esse in mundi universitate malam naturam.

[15] I. xiv. 16 and I. xv. 1: Quidquid damnabile . . . est a Deo alienissimum: Cuius in contumeliam recideret, si quid vitii inesse naturae probaretur.

[16] I. xiv. 20, *ad fin.*: creationem enarrare.

of whose origin Moses gives no history, is conclusive to the contrary. Moses, writing to meet the needs of men at large, accommodated himself to their grade of intellectual preparation, and confines himself to what meets their eyes.[17] On the other hand Calvin will not admit that the created universe can be properly spoken of as infinite. God alone is infinite; and, "however wide the circuit of the heavens may be, it nevertheless has some dimension."[18] He frankly conceives of the created universe as geocentric,[19] or more properly as anthropocentric. "God Himself," he declares, "has demonstrated by the very order of creation, that He made all things for the sake of man."[20] For, before making man, "He prepared everything which He foresaw would be useful or salutary for him" (I. xiv. 22). It was "for human use that He disposed the motions of the sun and stars, that He filled the earth, the waters, the air with living creatures, that He produced an abundance of all kinds of fruits which might be sufficient for food — thus acting the part of a provident and sedulous father of a family and showing His wonderful goodness towards us" (I. xiv. 2).

Two difficulties which arise out of the consideration of the infinitude of God in connection with His creative work, Calvin finds sufficiently important to pause even in so rapid a sketch to deal with. These concern the relation of the idea of creation to that of eternity on the one hand, and the description of the creation as a process on the other. Both of these also, however, he treats rather from a practical than a theoretical point of view.

He does not even hint at the metaphysical difficulty which has been perennially derived from the Divine eternity and immutability, that a definite creation implies a change in God —

---

[17] I. xiv. 3, *ad init.*: vulgi ruditati se accommodans . . . populariter loquens.

[18] I. xiv. 1: certe quantumvis late pateat coelorum circuitus, est tamen aliqua eius dimensio.

[19] Cf. the Argt. to the Commentary on Gen. i.: "The circle of the heavens is finite, and the earth, like a little globe, is placed in the center."

[20] I. xiv. 22: omnia se hominis causa condere. Cf. Commentary on Gen. iii. 1: "the whole world which had been created for the sake of man."

the difficulty which Wollebius so neatly turns by the remark
that "creation is not the creator's but the creature's passage
from potentiality to actuality." [21] The difficulty to which he
addresses himself is the purely popular one, which, with a view
to rendering the idea of a definite act of creation on God's part
incredible, asks what God was doing all those ages before He
created the world (I. xiv. 1). His response proceeds in general
on the principle of answering a fool according to his folly, although it is directed to the serious purpose of recalling men's
minds, from fruitless attempts to fathom the mysteries of
infinity, to a profitable use of the creation-narrative as a mirror
in which is exhibited a lively image of God. [22] The gist of this
response seems to be summed up in a sentence which occurs in
the Argument to his Commentary on the first chapter of
Genesis — which runs very much parallel to the discussion
here. "God," he says, "being wholly sufficient for Himself,
did not create a world of which He had no need, until it pleased
Him to do so." He does not disdain, however, before closing, to
advert, under the leading of Augustine, [23] even to the metaphysical consideration that there is no place for a question of
"time when" in our thought of that act of God by which time
began to be. We might as well inquire, Augustine had reasoned,
why God created the world *where* He did, as why He created it
only *when* He did. We may puzzle ourselves with the notion
that there is room in infinite space for an infinite number of
finite universes as readily as with the parallel notion that there
was opportunity in eternal time for the creation of an infinite
series of worlds before ours was reached. The truth is, of
course, that, as there is no space outside of that material world
the dimensions of which when abstractly considered constitute
what we call "space"; so there is no time outside that world
of mutable existence from which we abstract the notion of
succession and call it "time." "If they say," reasons Augustine, "that the thoughts of men are idle, when they conceive

[21] "Compendium Theologiae Christ.," Oxford, 1657, p. 36 (I. v.).

[22] This point is very fully elaborated in the Argument to the Commentary on Gen. i. and in the comment on Heb. xi. 3.

[23] "City of God," xi. 5.

of infinite places, since there is no place beside the world, we
reply that, by the same showing, it is vain to conceive of past
times of God's rest, since there is no time before the world."
Utilizing Augustine's remarks Calvin warns his readers against
vainly striving to press " outside of the world " (*extra mundum*) by " the boundaries of which we are circumscribed," and
exhorts them to seek in " the ample circumference of heaven
and earth " and the certainly sufficient space of " six thousand
years " material for meditating on the glory of God who has
made them all. The primary matter for us to observe in this
discussion is the persistence with which Calvin clings to the
practical purpose of his treatise, so as even in connection with
such abstruse subjects to confine himself to the " practical
use " of them. But it is not illegitimate to observe also the hints
the discussion supplies of his metaphysical opinions. His doctrines of " space " and " time " are here suggested to us. Clearly,
he holds that what we call " space " is only an abstraction from
the concrete dimensions of extended substance; and what we
call " time," an abstraction from the concrete successions of
mutable being. " Space " and " time," therefore, were to him
qualities of finite being, and have come into existence and will
pass out of existence with finite being. To speak of " infinite "
space or " infinite " time contains accordingly a *contradictio
in adjecto*.

Perhaps it may not be improper to pause here a moment to
observe in passing the employment of humor by Calvin in his
discussions. It is rather a mordant bit of humor which appears
here, it is true — this story of the " pious old man " who when
a " scoffer " demanded of him what God had been doing before He created the world, replied, " Making hell for inquisi-
tive people " (*fabricasse inferos curiosis*); and moreover it is
borrowed — ultimately — from Augustine.[24] But though bor-

[24] " Confessions," XI. xii. 14: " Behold, I answer to him who asks ' What
was God doing before He made heaven and earth ' — I answer not, as a
certain person is reported to have done facetiously (avoiding the pressure of
the question), ' He was preparing hell,' saith he, ' for those who pry into mysteries.' It is one thing to perceive, another to laugh — these things I answer
not. Far more willingly would I have answered, ' I know not what I know not',

rowing a story of Augustine's, Calvin does not follow Augustine in his attitude towards it. Augustine declines to commend such a response, because, says he, he would shrink from making a laughing-stock of anyone who brings forward a profound question; while Calvin approves it as a fit answer to a scoffer who raises frivolous objections.[25] And mordant though it is, it provides an instance of that use of humor in argument which was a marked trait of Calvin's manner — and which reveals to us an element of his character not always fully recognized. As this humor manifests itself in his writings — which are predominantly controversial in tone — it is sufficiently pungent. The instance before us is a fair sample of it; and we have already had occasion to note another characteristic instance — his rallying of Caroli in the matter of the ancient creeds.[26] His "Very useful Notice of the great profit which would accrue to Christianity if there should be made an inventory of all the holy bodies and relics which are to be found in Italy, France, Germany, Spain and other kingdoms and nations" (1543) might almost be said to reek with similar instances. He became quickly famous for his biting pen and was solemnly reproved by Sebastian Castellion for employing such weapons and encouraging others in the use of them. He not only, however, approved Beza's and Viret's satirical polemics and heartily enjoyed them — commending them to his friends as full of delightfulness — but he even develops a theory

---

than that I should make him a laughing-stock who asks deep things, and gain praise as one who answers false things." The Argument to the Commentary on Genesis i. runs parallel to the opening paragraphs of this chapter in the "Institutes"; and we are there told that Calvin borrows this anecdote immediately, not from Augustine, but from "The Tripartite History," — that is to say, the "Historiae Ecclesiasticae Tripartitae Epitome," Cassiodorus' revision of the translation made at his instance of the histories of Socrates, Sozomen and Theodoret by Epiphanius Scholasticus (for whom see Smith and Wace, "Dict. of Christ. Biography," ii. 1880, p. 159). This book supplied the mediaeval Church with its knowledge of post-Eusebian church history.

[25] Ac scite pius ille senex quum protervus quispiam . . . per ludibrium quaereret.

[26] See above, p. 210.

of the use of humor in instruction, and of the nature of true facetiousness. " Many — or perhaps we may say, most — men," he says, " are much more readily helped when they are instructed in a joyous and pleasant manner than otherwise. . . . Those who have the gift to teach in such a manner as to delight their readers, and to induce them to profit by the pleasure they give them, are doubly to be praised." " He who wishes to use humor," he adds, however, " ought to guard himself from two faults," — he must neither be forced in his wit, nor must he descend to scurrility.

But his cutting satire was only one manifestation of a special talent for pleasantry which characterized all his intercourse. Laughter, he taught, is the gift of God: and he held it the right, or rather the duty, of the Christian man to practise it in its due season. He is constantly joking with his friends in his letters,[27] and he eagerly joins with them in all the joys of life. " I wish I were with you for half a day," he writes to one of them, " to laugh with you." [28] In a word, contrary to a general impression, Calvin was a man of a great freshness and jocundness of spirit; and so little was he inclined to suppress the expression of the gayer side of life that he rather sedulously cultivated it in himself and looked with pleasure on its manifestation in others. He enjoyed a joke hugely,[29] with that open-mouthed laugh which, as one of his biographers phrases it,[30] belonged to the

[27] E.g., xi. 321 (iocari quam serio conqueri).
[28] xii. 578.
[29] In his youthful work as a humanist — the Commentary on Seneca's " De clementia " — he betrays the readiness of his laughter by his comments on the amusing matters that come before him. In the comment on I. vii. (*Opp.* v. 62) he expresses his sense of the ridiculousness of the soothsayer's solemn mummery and quotes Cato's remark " that it was wonderful that every soothsayer did not laugh whenever he met a fellow soothsayer." On I. x. (*Opp.* v. 84), speaking of the apotheoses of the Roman emperors, he adds: " The rites and ceremonies by which the emperors were consecrated are set forth by Herodianus in his iv. Book; and I am never able to refrain from laughter when I read that passage. The religion of the Romans was as ridiculous as this . . ." Calvin enjoyed his reading and responded to the matter he read with an emotional movement.
[30] Doumergue, " Jean Calvin," iii. 1905, pp. 535–540, where the whole subject is admirably illustrated. See also Doumergue, " L'art et le sentiment dans

men of the sixteenth century. And he knew even how to smile at human folly wishing that the people might not be deprived of their pleasures [31] and might even be dealt with indulgently in their faults. When his students misbehaved, for example, he simply said he thought they ought to have some indulgence and should be accorded the right to be sometimes foolish.[32]

That the work of creation should be thought to occupy time was as much a matter of scoffing from the evil-disposed as that it should take place in time. Why should the omnipotent God take six days to make the world? Did He perhaps find it too hard a task for a single effort? [33] This cavil, too, Calvin deals with purely from the practical point of view, not so much undertaking to refute it as recalling men's minds from it to dwell on the condescension of God in distributing His work into six days that our finite intelligence might not be overwhelmed with its contemplation; and on the goodness of God in thus leading our thoughts up to the consideration of the rest of the seventh day; and above all on the paternal care of God in so ordering the work of bringing the world into being as to prepare it for man before He introduced him into it. In drawing the mind thus away from the cavil, Calvin does not, however, fail to meet the difficulty itself, which was adduced. His response to it, is, in effect, to acknowledge that God perfected the world by process (*progressus,* I. xiv. 2); but to assert that this method of performing His work was not for His own sake, but for ours; so that, so far is this progressive method of producing the world from being unworthy of God, because " alien from His power," [34] that it rather illustrates His higher at-

---

l'oeuvre de Calvin," Geneva, 1902, the third Conference, pp. 61–67. On Calvin's use of satire, see C. Lenient, " La Satire en France, ou la Littérature militante au XVIe siècle," 1877, i. pp. 107 *sq.,* especially pp. 175 *sq.* Cf. also the first article in this volume, pp. 11 *sqq.*

[31] xii. 348: non posse negari omnia oblectamenta.

[32] *Opp.* xb. 441.

[33] I. xiv. 2: Hic etiam obstrepit humana ratio, quasi a Dei potentia alieni fuerint tales progressus.

[34] I. xiv. 2: a Dei potentia alieni.

tributes — His paternal love, for example, which would not create man until He had enriched the world with all things necessary for his happiness. Considered in Himself, " it would have been no more difficult " for God " to complete at once the whole work in all its items in a single moment, than to arrive at its completion gradually by a process of this kind." [35]

It should be observed that in this and similar discussions founded on the progressive completion of the world, Calvin does not intend to attribute what we may speak strictly of as progressive creation to God. With Calvin, while the perfecting of the world — as its subsequent government — is a process, creation, strictly conceived, tended to be thought of as an act. " In the beginning God created the heavens and the earth ": after that it was not " creation " strictly so called, but " formation," gradual modelling into form, which took place. Not, of course, as if Calvin conceived creation deistically; as if he thought of God as having created the world-stuff and then left it to itself to work out its own destiny under the laws impressed on it in its creation. A " momentary Creator, who has once for all done His work," was inconceivable to him: and he therefore taught that it is only when we contemplate God in providence that we can form any true conception of Him as Creator.[36] But he was inclined to draw a sharp distinction in kind between the primal act of creation of the heavens and the earth out of nothing, and the subsequent acts of moulding this created material into the forms it was des-

[35] I. xiv. 22: quum nihilo difficilius esset, uno momento totum opus simul omnibus numeris complere, quam eiusmodi progressione sensim ad complementum pervenire.

[36] I. xvi. 1. Cf. the Genevan Catechism of 1545 (*Opp*. vi. 15–16, 17–18) where the question is asked why God is called in the Creed only Creator of heaven and earth, when " tueri conservareque in suo statu creaturas," is " multo praestantius " than just to have once created them. The answer is that by this particularizing of creation, it is not intended to imply that " God so created His works at one time (*semel*) that He afterwards rejects the care of them." On the contrary, He upholds and governs all He made; and this is included in the idea of His creation of them all. Cf. also the " Confession des Escholiers " of 1559 (*Opp*. ix. 721–722) where we read: " I confess that God created the world at once (*semel*), in such a manner as to be its perpetual governor. . . ."

tined to take; and to confine the term "creation," strictly
conceived, to the former. Hence in perhaps the fullest statement of his doctrine of creation given us in these chapters (I.
xiv. 20), he expresses himself carefully thus: "God, by the
power of His Word and Spirit created out of nothing (*creasse
ex nihilo*) the heavens and the earth; thence produced (*pro-
duxisse*) every kind of animate and inanimate thing, distinguished by a wonderful gradation the innumerable variety of
things, endowed each kind with its own nature, assigned its
offices, appointed its place and station to it, and, since all
things are subject to corruption, provided, nevertheless, that
each kind should be preserved safe to the last day." "Thus,"
he adds, "He marvellously adorned heaven and earth with
the utmost possible abundance, variety and beauty of all
things, like a great and splendid house, most richly and abundantly constructed and furnished; and then at last by forming
(*formando*) man and distinguishing him with such noble
beauty, and with so many and such high gifts, he exhibited in
him the noblest specimen of His works." [37] It is God who has
made all things what they are, he teaches: but, in doing so,
God has acted in the specific mode properly called creation
only at the initial step of the process, and the result owes its
right to be called a creation to that initial act by which the
material of which all things consist was called into being from
non-being. "Indigested mass" as it was, yet in that world-stuff
was "the seed of the whole world," and out of it that world
as we now see it (for "the world was not perfected at its very
beginning, in the manner it is now seen" [38]) has been evoked
by progressive acts of God: and it is therefore that this world,
because evoked from it, has the right to be called a creation.

The distinction which Calvin here draws, it is to be observed, is not that which has been commonly made by Reformed divines under the terms, First and Second Creation, or

[37] It is worth while to observe here how Calvin betrays his sensibility to
the glory and beauty of nature (cf. also I. v. 6; *Opp.* xxix. 300). See the remarks of E. Doumergue, "Jean Calvin," iv. 1910, p. 105.

[38] These phrases occur in the Commentary on Genesis i.

in less exact language Immediate and Mediate Creation. This
distinction posits a sequence of truly creative acts of God
throughout the six days, and therefore defines creation, so as
to meet the whole case, as that act " by which God produced
the world and all that is in it, partly *ex nihilo,* partly *ex materia naturaliter inhabili,* for the manifestation of the glory of
His power, wisdom and goodness "; [39] or more fully, as that
" first external work of God, by which in the beginning of
time, without suffering any change, by His own free will, He
produced by His sole omnipotent command *immediate per se*
things which before were not, from simple non-being to being
— and that, either *ex nihilo,* or *ex materia* which had afore
been made *e nihilo,* but is *naturaliter inhabili* for receiving the
form which, created out of nothing, the Creator induces into
it." [40] It is precisely this sequence of truly creative acts which
Calvin disallows; and he so expresses himself, indeed, as to
give it a direct contradiction. Perhaps as distinct a statement
of his view as any is found in his comment on Genesis i. 21,
where the term " create " is employed to designate the divine
production of the animals of the sea and air, which, according to verse 20, had been brought forth by the waters at the
command of God. " A question arises here," remarks Calvin,
" about the word ' created.' For we have before contended that
the world was made of nothing because it was ' created ': but
now Moses says the things formed from other matter were
' created.' Those who assert that the fishes were truly and
properly ' created ' because the waters were in no way suitable
(*idoneae*) or adapted (*aptae*) to their production, only resort

[39] Joannes Wollebius, *op. cit.,* p. 35.
[40] Amand. Polanus, " Syntagma theologiae christianae," Hanov., 1525, v.
2. Cf. Gisb. Voetius, " Disp.," i. 1648, p. 554: " Creation may be distinguished
. . . into first and second. The first is the production of a thing *ex nihilo,* and
in this manner were produced the heavens, the elements, light; and every day
there are so produced human souls, so far as they are spiritual in essence.
The second is the production of the essential or accidental form, in *prae-
subjecta sed indisposita plane materia,* and that by the immediate operation
of the divine power; and in this manner were produced the works of the
five days as also many miraculous works in the order of nature as now constituted."

to a subterfuge; for the fact would remain, meanwhile, that the material of which they were made existed before, which, in strict propriety, the word does not admit. I therefore do not restrict 'creation' [here] to the work of the fifth day, but rather say it[s use] refers to (hangs from, *pendet*) that shapeless and confused mass which was, as it were, the fountain of the whole world. God, then, is said to have 'created' the seamonsters and other fishes, because the beginning of their 'creation' is not to be reckoned from the moment in which they received their form, but they are comprehended in the universal matter (*corpus, corpore*) which was made out of nothing. So that with respect to their kind, form only was then added to them; 'creation' is nevertheless a term used truly with respect to the whole and the parts."

Calvin's motive in thus repudiating the notion of "Mediate Creation" is not at all chariness on his part with respect to the supernatural. It is not the supernaturalness of the production of the creatures which the waters and earth brought forth which he disallows; but only the applicability to their production of the term "creation." On verse 24, he comments thus: "There is in this respect a miracle as great as if God had begun to create out of nothing these things which He commanded to proceed from the earth." Calvin's sole motive seems to be to preserve to the great word "create" the precise significance of to "make out of nothing," and he will not admit that it can be applied to any production in which preëxistent material is employed.[41] This might appear to involve the view that after the creation of the world-stuff recorded in Genesis i. 1, there was never anything specifically new produced by the divine power. And this might be expressed by saying that, from that point on, the divine works were purely works of providence, since the very differentia of a providential work is that it is the product proximately of second causes. Probably this would press Calvin's contention, however, a little too far: he would scarcely say there was no immediacy in the divine action in the productions of the five days of "creation,"

[41] See above, note 9.

or indeed in the working of miracles. But we must bear in mind that his view of providence was a very high one, and he was particularly insistent that God acted through means, when He did act through means, through no necessity but purely at His own volition. Second causes, in his view, are nothing more than " instruments into which God infuses as much of efficiency as He wishes," and which He employs or not at His will (I. xvi. 2). " The power of no created thing," says Calvin, " is more wonderful or evident than that of the sun. . . . But the Lord . . . willed that light should exist . . . before the sun was created. A pious man will not make the sun, then, either the principal or the necessary cause of the things which existed before the sun was created, but only an instrument which God uses because He wishes to; since He could without any difficulty at all do without the sun and act of Himself." [42] The facility with which Calvin sets aside the notion of " mediate creation " is then due in no sense to desire to remove the productions of the five days of " creation " out of the category of divine products, but is itself mediated by the height of his doctrine of providence.[43]

[42] I. xvi. 2; cf. also the Commentary on Gen. i. 3.

[43] Cf. Köstlin, *TSK*, 1868, p. 427: " In the section of edition 2b (vol. xxix. 510) on God as the Almighty Creator there should be particularly noted the emphasis with which Calvin maintains, in spite of the mediation of the divine activity through creaturely instruments, yet the dependence of these instruments, and the absolute independence of God with respect to them. And in ed. 3 (vol. xxx. 145 *sq.,* 150; Lib. I. c. xvi. §§ 2, 7) there are given still stronger expositions of this. God, says Calvin, bestows on the instruments powers purely in accordance with His own will, and governs them; and God could work what He works through them, say through the sun, just as easily without them, purely by Himself. God, he says, in ed. 3, lets us be nourished ordinarily by bread; and yet according to Scripture, man does not live by bread alone, for it is not the abundance of food but the divine blessing which nourishes us; and on the other hand (Isaiah iii. 1) He threatens to break the staff of bread." " We have here already," adds Köstlin, " the general premises for the special use which God, according to Calvin, makes of the Word and of the Sacraments for His saving work." Would anybody but a Lutheran have ever thought of the " means of Grace " in this connection? Nevertheless it is not bad to be reminded that the Reformed doctrine of the " means of Grace " has its analogue in the Reformed doctrine of providence: it is a corollary of the fundamental notion of God as the Independent One.

It is important further that we should not suppose that Calvin removed the production of the human soul out of the category of immediate creation, in the strictest sense of that term. When he insists that the works of the days subsequent to the first, when "in the beginning God created the heavens and the earth," were not strictly speaking " creations," because they were not productions *ex nihilo,* he is thinking only of the lower creation, inclusive, no doubt, of the human body; all this is made out of that primal " indigested mass " which sprang into being at the initial command of God. The soul is a different matter; and not only in the first instance, but in every succeeding instance, throughout the whole course of human propagation, is an immediate creation *ex nihilo.* Moses, he tells us, perfectly understood that the soul was created from nothing; [44] and he announces with emphasis (" Institutes," I. xv. 5), that it is certain that the souls of men are " no less created than the angels," adding the decisive definition: "now, creation is the origination of essence *ex nihilo.*" It is thus with the lower creation alone in his mind that Calvin insists that all that can justly be called by the high name of " creation " was wrought by God on the first day, in that one act by which He created, that is called into being out of nothing, the heavens and the earth.

It should scarcely be passed without remark that Calvin's doctrine of creation is, if we have understood it aright, for all except the souls of men, an evolutionary one. The " indigested mass," including the " promise and potency " of all that was yet to be, was called into being by the simple *fiat* of God. But all that has come into being since — except the souls of men alone — has arisen as a modification of this original world-stuff by means of the interaction of its intrinsic forces. Not these forces apart from God, of course: Calvin is a high theist, that is, supernaturalist, in his ontology of the universe and in his conception of the whole movement of the universe. To him God is the *prima causa omnium* and that not merely in the sense that all things ultimately — in the world-stuff —

[44] Commentary on Malachi i. 2–6 (*Opp.* xliv. 401).

owe their existence to God; but in the sense that all the modifications of the world-stuff have taken place under the directly upholding and governing hand of God, and find their account ultimately in His will. But they find their account proximately in " second causes "; and this is not only evolutionism but pure evolutionism. What account we give of these second causes is a matter of ontology; how we account for their existence, their persistence, their action — the relation we conceive them to stand in to God, the upholder and director as well as creator of them. Calvin's ontology of second causes was, briefly stated, a very pure and complete doctrine of *concursus,* by virtue of which he ascribed all that comes to pass to God's purpose and directive government. But that does not concern us here. What concerns us here is that he ascribed the entire series of modifications by which the primal "indigested mass," called "heaven and earth," has passed into the form of the ordered world which we see, including the origination of all forms of life, vegetable and animal alike, inclusive doubtless of the bodily form of man, to second causes as their proximate account. And this, we say, is a very pure evolutionary scheme. He does not discuss, of course, the factors of the evolutionary process, nor does he attempt to trace the course of the evolutionary advance, nor even expound the nature of the secondary causes by which it was wrought. It is enough for him to say that God said, " Let the waters bring forth. . . . Let the earth bring forth," and they brought forth. Of the interaction of forces by which the actual production of forms was accomplished, he had doubtless no conception: he certainly ventures no assertions in this field. How he pictured the process in his imagination (if he pictured it in his imagination) we do not know. But these are subordinate matters. Calvin doubtless had no theory whatever of evolution; but he teaches a doctrine of evolution. He has no object in so teaching except to preserve to the creative act, properly so called, its purity as an immediate production out of nothing. All that is not immediately produced out of nothing is therefore not created — but evolved. Accordingly his doctrine of evolution is entirely unfruitful. The whole process takes place in the limits of six natural days. That the doctrine should be of use as an explanation of the mode of production of the ordered world, it was requisite that these six days should be lengthened out into six periods — six ages of the growth of the world. Had that been done Calvin would have been a precursor of the modern evolutionary theorists. As it is, he only forms a point of departure for them to this extent — that he teaches, as they teach, the modification of the original world-stuff into the varied forms which constitute the ordered world, by the instrumentality of second causes — or as a modern would put it, of its intrinsic forces. This is his account of the origin of the entire lower creation.[45]

Of this lower creation he has, however, as has already been pointed out, very little to say in the discussion of the creature which he has incorporated in the " Institutes " (I. xiv. 20–22). And what he does say is chiefly devoted to the practical end of quickening in our hearts a sense of the glory and perfections of its Maker, whose wisdom, power, justice and goodness are illustrated by it, and of raising our hearts in gratitude to Him for His benefits to us. These are the two things, he says, which a contemplation of what is meant by God being the Creator of heaven and earth should work in us: an apprehension of His greatness as the Creator (§ 21) and an appreciation of His care for us His creatures, in the manner in which He has created us (§ 22). More than to suggest this, the scope of his treatise does not appear to him to demand of him; as it does not permit him to dwell on the details of the history of creation — for which he therefore contents himself with referring his readers to the narrative of Genesis, with the

<hr>

[45] H. Bavinck in the first of his Stone Lectures (" The Philosophy of Revelation," 1909, pp. 9–10) remarks: " The idea of development is not a production of modern times. It was already familiar to Greek philosophy. More particularly Aristotle raised it to the rank of the leading principle of his entire system by his significant distinction between *potentia* and *actus*. . . . This idea of development aroused no objection whatever in Christian theology and philosophy. On the contrary, it received extension and enrichment by being linked with the principle of theism." Calvin accordingly very naturally thought along the lines of a theistic evolutionism.

comments of Basil and Ambrose. He pauses, therefore, only to insert the comprehensive statement of the elements of the matter which has already been cited, and which asserts that " God by the power of His Word and Spirit created out of nothing the heavens and the earth " and afterwards moulded this created material into the ordered world we see around us, which also He sustains and governs; in which, then, He has placed man, up to whom all the rest has tended and in whom He has afforded the culminating manifestation of His creative power (§ 20). The main items of his teaching as to the physical universe may therefore be summed up in the propositions that it owes its existence absolutely to the Divine power; [46] that it was created out of nothing; that it was perfected through a process of formation which extended through six days; that it was made and adorned for the sake of man, and has been subjected to him; and that it illustrates in its structure and in all its movements the perfections of its Maker.

It is to the spiritual universe that Calvin turns with predilection, and the greater portion of the fourteenth chapter is devoted accordingly to a thoroughly Biblical account of angelic beings, good and bad (§§ 3–19). The careful Scripturalness of this account deserves emphasis. Calvin himself emphasizes it, and even permits himself to fall into a digression here, in order to expound at some length the proper attitude of the theological teacher to Scripture (I. xiv. 4). His design is to transmit plainly and clearly what the Scriptures teach,[47] and not to pass beyond the simple doctrine of Scripture in anything.[48] He therefore warns his readers against speculations as to " the orders " of angels, asking them to consider carefully the meagreness of the Scriptural foundation these have; [49] and holds the Pseudo-Dionysius up as a terrible example of mis-

---

[46] Commenting on Ps. cxlviii. 5 (*Opp.* xxxii. 434), he remarks: " The pronoun *He* is therefore emphatic, as if the prophet would say that the world is not eternal as profane men dream, nor is produced by some concurring atoms, but this beautiful order which we see suddenly stood forth (*exstitisse*) on the mandate of God." Cf. also *Opp.* xxxi. 327.

[47] I. xiv. 3: diserte et explicate . . . tradamus quae . . . docet scriptura.

[48] I. xiv. 4, end: ex simplici scripturae doctrina.

[49] I. xiv. 8, *ad init.*: viderint quale habeant fundamentum.

placed subtlety and acuteness in such matters (I. xiv. 4). Whereas Paul, who was actually rapt beyond the third heavens sealed his lips and declared it not lawful for a man to speak of the hidden things which he saw, Dionysius who never had such an experience writes with a fulness and confidence of detail which could be justified only if he had come down from heaven and was recounting what he had had the privilege of observing carefully with his own eyes. Such prating of things of which we can really know nothing is unworthy of a theologian, says Calvin; " for it is the part of the theologian not to amuse the ear with empty words, but to confirm the conscience by teaching what is true, certain, profitable." [50] And, " since the teaching of the Spirit is invariably profitable (*utiliter*), but in matters which are of less moment for edification, either He is altogether silent or touches on them only lightly and cursorily, it is our business cheerfully to remain ignorant of what is of no advantage to us." [51] There are two rules therefore which the modest and sober man will certainly bear in mind in the whole business of teaching religion. One is, in obscure matters, neither to speak nor to think, nor even to desire to know, anything more than what has been given us in the Word of God. The other is, in reading Scripture, to tarry for prolonged investigation and meditation only on what conduces to edification, and not to indulge curiosity or fondness for useless things.[52] Practising what he preaches, Calvin endeavors therefore in all he has to say of angels to hold to the limit which the rule of piety prescribes, lest by indulging in

[50] I. xiv. 4: Theologo autem non garriendo aures oblectare, sed vera, certa, utilia docendo, conscientias confirmare propositum est.

[51] I. xiv. 3: Et certe, quum utiliter semper nos doceat Spiritus, in quibus vero parum est momenti ad aedificationem, vel subticeat prorsus, vel leviter tantum et cursim attingat: nostri quoque officii est, libenter ignorare quae non conducunt.

[52] I. xiv. 4: Ne longior sim, meminerimus hic, ut in tota religionis doctrina, tenendam esse unam modestiae et sobrietatis regulam, ne de rebus obscuris aliud vel loquamur, vel sentiamus, vel scire etiam appetamus quam quod Dei verbo fuerit nobis traditum. Alterum, ut in lectione scripturae, iis continenter quaerendis ac meditandis immoremur quae ad aedificationem pertinent, non curiositati aut rerum inutilium studio indulgeamus.

speculation beyond measure he should lead the reader astray from the simplicity of the faith (I. xiv. 3, end). There are many things about angels, indeed, which it may be a matter of regret to some that the Scriptures have not told us (I. xiv. 16). But surely we ought to be content with the knowledge which the Lord has given us, especially as, passing by frivolous questions, His wish has been to instruct us in what conduces to solid piety, the fear of His name, true confidence and the duties of holiness (I. xiv. 4). If we are not ashamed to be His disciples, how can we be ashamed to follow the method He has prescribed (§ 4)? Nay, will we not even abhor those unprofitable speculations from which He recalls us, and rest in comfort in the simple Scriptural teaching, which with respect to good angels consoles us and confirms our faith by making us see in them the dispensers and administrators of the Divine goodness towards us, guarding our safety, assuring our defence, directing our ways, and protecting us by their care from evil (§ 6, *ad init.*) — with respect to evil angels, warns us against their artifices and contrivances and provides us with firm and strong weapons to repel their attacks (§ 13, *ad init.*)?

In accordance with these views of our relation to Scripture as a source of and guide to knowledge, Calvin's whole discussion of angels is not only kept close to Scripture, but is marked by the strongest practical tendency. Perhaps what strikes the reader most forcibly upon the surface of the discussion is the completeness of the faith which it exhibits in the real existence of angelic beings and the concernment of man with them. We will recall the vividness of Luther's similar faith. Perhaps we may say that the supernaturalistic tone of the conceptions of the Reformers is in nothing more visible than in their vital sense of the spiritual environment in which human life is cast. To them angels and demons were actual factors in men's lives, to be counted upon and considered in our arrangement and adjustments as truly as our fellow men.[53] Denial of their

---

[53] Zwingli seems to have been an exception, and to have looked upon the ascription of all events to the action of angels and especially to that of devils as inconsistent with the doctrine of providence: he twits Luther with ascrib-

reality as substantial existences was indeed prevalent enough to require notice and refutation. Calvin's refutation of it is, of course, derived entirely, however, from Scripture, and he recognizes that, therefore, it can have no force for those who do not believe in the Scriptures. He does not consider that it is on that account useless. He designs it to fortify pious minds against such madness and to call back the slothful and incautious to a more sober and better regulated mode of life. For those who believe in the Scriptural revelation, it must be confessed that his argument is complete and final, adducing as it does in the clearest way the chief Biblical evidence for the actual existence and activity of these superhuman intelligences (I. xiv. 9 and 19).

Calvin, then, teaches in accordance with Scripture, that angels are not "qualities or inspirations without substance, but real spirits." [54] He calls them "spirits," "minds," and as such defines them as beings whose characterizing qualities are "perception and intelligence." [55] His intention is to represent them as purely spiritual beings; and therefore he incidentally remarks that "it is certain" that they "have no form." [56] As "celestial spirits" (I. xiv. 5), they are of higher powers than man, and receive in Scripture designations by which their dignity is indicated: Hosts, Powers, Principalities, Dominions, Thrones, even "Gods" — not of course as if they were really

---

ing everything to "the poor devil" and asks what then becomes of universal providence ("Opera," Schuler u. Schulthess, iib. p. 27). Cf. P. J. Muller, "De Godsleer van Zwingli en Calvijn, 1883, p. 77, note. But Luther, remarks Muller, could believe in the determining providence of God, " *und wenn die welt voll teufel wär.*" How it strikes a modern of the moderns may be learned from William Wrede's remark ("Paul," E. T. 1907, p. 95): "Angels, in our time, belong to children and to poets; to Paul and his age they were a real and serious quantity."

[54] I. xiv. 9: ex quibus [Scripturis] clarissime evincitur re vera esse spiritus naturae subsistentis; . . . non qualitates aut inspirationes sine substantia sed veros spiritus. Note also § 19: non motiones aut affectiones mentium, sed magis revera, quod dicuntur, mentes, vel spiritus sensu et intelligentia praeditos. Cf. *Opp.* xlv. 271.

[55] I. xiv. 19: sensu et intelligentia praeditos.

[56] I. xiv. 8: forma spiritus carere certum est. Cf. *Opp.* xl. 659: quoniam angeli carent corporibus.

"Gods" or ought to be worshipped, but "because in their ministry, as in a glass, they represent in some degree divinity to us." [57] "The preëminence (*praestantia*) of the angelic nature has," to be sure, "so impressed the minds of many" that they have felt it would be an injury to angels to degrade them, as it were, under the control of the One only God; and thus there has been invented for them a certain kind of divinity (I. xiv. 3). They are of course like God: for they were made in the image of God.[58] They are, however, just creatures of God, His servants who execute His commands.[59] Moses, it is true, in the history of creation, does not give any account of their creation: but that history does not pretend to be complete, but limits itself to the visible creation, and it is easy to collect from his subsequent introduction of angels as God's ministers that He is their maker.[60] So a matter of course does this seem to Calvin, that he does not stop here to adduce specific Scriptural assertions of the origination of angels by creation. These however he emphasizes elsewhere. Thus for example, in his commentary on the passage, he expounds Col. i. 16 as follows: "Because Paul wished to make this assertion" — that all things were created in the Son — "particularly of angels, he now mentions the invisible things: not only, then, the heavenly creatures visible to our eyes, but also the spiritual ones (*spirituales*) have been made (*conditae*) by the Son of God." The inferiority of angels to Christ, he proceeds to remark (in his commentary on the next verse), is manifested in the four points: First, "because they were created (*creati*) by Him; secondly, because their creation (*creatio*) is referred to Him as its legitimate end; thirdly, because He always existed

[57] I. xiv. 5. Cf. *Opp.* xlii. 455; lii. 86.

[58] I. xv. 3, end: "Neither is it to be denied *angelos ad Dei similitudinem creatos esse*, since our highest perfection, as Christ testifies (Mat. xxii. 30), will be to become like them."

[59] I. xiv. 3: [Moses] angelos Dei ministros inducit, colligere facile licet eorum esse conditorem, cui suam operam et officia impendunt. Cf. 4: angelos sane, quum Dei sint ministri ad iussa eius exsequenda ordinati, esse quoque illius creaturas, extra controversiam esse debet. Again 16: quum a Deo conditus sit diabolus. Cf. *Opp.* xxxiii. 206; lv. 334.

[60] I. xiv. 3: eorum conditor. Cf. *Opp.* xxxv. 466, to the same effect.

before they were created (*crearentur*); fourthly, because it is He who sustains them by His power and conserves them in their condition." [61] Creation in and of itself means with Calvin, as we have seen, absolute origination of essence, and he therefore teaches that the angels have been, like all other creatures, created out of nothing. It is to be held, he says, as a thing certain that the souls of men and angels alike " have been created " — adding at once: " Now creation is not transfusion but the origination out of nothing of essence." [62]

The questions of when they were created and how their creation is to be related to Moses' narrative Calvin puts aside as frivolous. Moses narrates that the earth was perfected, and the heavens were perfected with all their hosts (Gen. ii. 1): that is certainly broad enough to cover the fact of their creation — why make anxious inquisition as to the day, in which besides the stars and planets, these other more hidden (*recon-*

[61] *Opp.* lii. 85–86. The assertion of Psalm cxlviii. 5 (*Opp.* xxxii. 434) he apparently confines to " creaturis sensu carentibus ": but on the first verse he incidentally remarks of the angels that " they were created (*conditi sunt*)." Cf. the assertions of the creation of the angels, good and bad, *Opp.* xxx. 316; xxxiii. 206. In the exposition of the Symbol, in the " Institutes," of 1543, he comments on the words " Creator of heaven and earth " thus (chap. vi. §§ 28 and 29): " Under the names of heaven and earth all celestial and terrestial things are comprehended, as if God were said to be the Creator of all things without exception. This is found more clearly expressed in the Nicene Creed, where He is called the Maker of all things visible and invisible. That was done probably on account of the Manichees, who imagined two principles, God and the Devil; and attributed to God the creation of good things, indeed, but referred evil natures to the Devil as their author," — and so on as in the " Institutes " of 1559, I. xiv. 3. Then in § 29: " God then is in the first place said to have created the heavens and all that is contained in the heavens. But in that order are the celestial spirits, as well those who have persisted by obedience in their integrity, as those who by defection have fallen into ruin," etc. — explaining that the fact that Moses does not mention this in the history of creation in no respect throws it into doubt. Cf. the " Confession des Escholiers," 1559 (*Opp.* ix. 721–722): " I confess that God created not only the visible world, that is the heaven and the earth, and whatever is contained in them, but also the invisible spirits, some of whom have persisted in obedience to God, and some by their own sin have been precipitated into destruction."

[62] I. xv. 5: animas ergo . . . creatas esse non minus quam angelos, certo statuendum est. Creatio autem non transfusio est, sed essentiae ex nihilo exordium.

diti) celestial hosts began to be? [63] The very language in which he repels the question, however, as it certainly suggests that Calvin conceived of the entire creation, inclusive of the angelic hosts, as a systematized whole, seems also to hint that he himself thought of the creation of this unitary whole as taking place at the one creative epoch, if such language can be pardoned. If so, then in his instinctive thought on this subject — on which, however, he laid no stress — he followed the scholastic opinion, as expounded, say, by Thomas Aquinas rather than that of the Greek Fathers, who interposed an immense interval between the creation of the spiritual and the subsequent creation of the corporeal universe.[64] It is doubtless, however, a mistake to press his language to imply that he thought of the creation of the angels as taking place on the same day with the stars and planets, that is to say, on the fourth day. More probably he thought of them as produced as part of the general creation of the " heavens and earth," that is to say on the first day,[65] and this became the traditional view in the Reformed Churches. " When were the angels created? " asks

[63] I. xiv. 4: terram esse perfectam, et coelos perfectos cum omni exercitu eorum, narrat Moses (Gen. ii. 1). Quid attinet anxie precontari quoto die, praeter astra et planetas, alii quoque magis reconditi coelestes exercitus esse coeperint?

[64] Aquinas, " Summa," Pars I. qu. lxi. art. 3, argues: " Angels are a part of the universe. For they do not constitute in themselves a universe; but unite along with the corporeal creation in a universe. This appears from the relation of one creature to another. For the mutual relation of things is the good of the universe. But no part is perfect, when separated off into a whole by itself. It is not therefore probable that God, ' whose works are perfect,' as is said in Deut. xxxii, created the angelic creation off to itself before the other creatures." Jerome, on the other hand, following the Greeks, exclaims on the multitudinous ages which intervened between the creation of the angels and that of man. It is interesting to observe Dante following Aquinas and making the creation of the angels simultaneous with that of the universe at large, the fall of the evil angels being delayed but twenty seconds after their creation (cf. Maria Rossetti's " Shadow of Dante," 1886, pp. 14, 15), and Milton following Jerome and putting the creation of angels aeons before that of man.

[65] So he seems to say explicitly in the middle editions of the " Institutes " (first in 1543), vi. § 29 (*Opp.* i. 497): " First then God is said to have created the heavens and all that the heavens contain. But in this order are the celestial spirits, whether those who by obedience remained in their integrity, or those who by defection fell into ruin."

Bucanus, and answers, " Not before the ages, for the Son of God alone was existent before the ages: whence it follows that they were made in the beginning of all things. On what day, however, cannot certainly be defined, though it may be gathered with probability from the history of Moses that they were created on the first day, in which the heavens, the inhabitants of which they are, were created; wherefrom they are called the ' angels of heaven.' " [66] " The first day of the creation," says Wollebius,[67] " is illustrious for three works," the first of which is " the creation of the angels with the highest heaven (the heaven called that of the blessed) "; for, he argues, " the creation of the angels can be referred to no better time than the first day, because when God laid the foundations of the earth, it was already celebrated by them (Job xxxviii. 7) " — an argument which is repeated by others, as for example by Ván Mastricht,[68] who reasons in general that " it is certain that they were not created before the first day of creation since before that there was nothing but eternity, . . . and it is equally certain that they were not created after man, whom they seduced." [69] Doubtless some such reasoning as this was before Calvin's mind also, although it is clear that he did not take it so seriously.

On another matter of speculative construction, however, he was not so much inclined to an attitude of indifference. This concerned the distribution of angels into ranks and orders. We have already had occasion to note his reprobation of the Pseudo-Dionysius for his empty speculations on the " celestial hierarchy " (I. xiv. 4). He returns to the general matter later (I. xiv. 8) to express the opinion that data are lacking in Scripture to justify an attempt " to determine degrees of honor among angels, to distinguish the respective classes by their

[66] " Instit. Theolog.," Geneva, 1625, Loc. vi. 4, p. 61.
[67] " Compend. Theolog. Christ.," ed. Oxford, 1657, p. 36.
[68] " Theoretico-practica theol.," Amstel., 1724, III. vii. 4, p. 340.
[69] Heppe, " Dog. d. ev.-ref. Kirche," 1861, p. 149, adds that this is also the teaching of the Leiden Synopsis, Riissen, Wendelinus and of the Reformed in general. Cocceius ("Summa Theol.," xvi. 12) thought of the day when the waters above and below the firmament were separated.

insignia, or to assign its place and station to each." His positive attitude here is due, of course, to the comparison instituted
by the Romanists between the celestial and the ecclesiastical
hierarchies,[70] which he wishes to discredit. Here too he set the
fashion for the Reformed theology. Quite in this sense Van
Mastricht [71] remarks that "the Reformed recognize, indeed,
that there is some order among the angels, not only because
God their Maker is a God of order . . . but because the various names of the angels seem to suggest an order to us (Col. i.
16, Eph. iii. 10, cf. Ezek. ix. 3, Is. vi. 2, I Thes. iv. 16, Gen. iii.
24, Jude 9) while the disjunctive particle, εἴτε θρόνοι, εἴτε
κυριότητες (Col. i. 16), seems especially to confirm some
order among angels, to say nothing of the existence of some
order among the evil spirits themselves (Mat. xii. 24). But
they believe it is not possible for men in this imperfection to
determine what the order among the angels is." If this seems
to allow a little more than Calvin does, it is to go a little
further than he does in denial on the other hand, to contend
with Hyperius that there are no permanent distinctions among
angels " by virtue of which some angels are always preëminent,
others always subordinate," or even with Bucanus, that there
are no distinctions in nature among the angels but only differences in office. Surely these determinations are open to
Calvin's rebuke of pretensions to knowledge which we do not
possess, and contrast sharply with the sobriety with which
Calvin abides by the simple statements of Scripture, allowing
that there are some hints in Scripture of ranks among angels
(I. xiv. 8; cf. 14) and contending only that these hints are insufficient to enable us to develop a complete theory of their
organization.

In holding back from the temptation to speculate on the
organization of the angelic hosts, however, Calvin betrays no
tendency to minify their numbers, and he of course recognizes
the great distinction between good and bad angels. The num-

[70] Cf. a similar rejection of the efforts to determine the numbers and
orders of angels in *Opp.* li. 158.
[71] As cited, III. vii. 30 (p. 348).

bers of both are very great. Of the good angels, he tells us, " we hear from the mouth of Christ of many legions (Mat. xxvi. 53), from Daniel of many myriads (Dan. vii. 10); Elisha's servant saw numerous chariots; and when it is said that they encamp around about those that fear God (Ps. xxxiv. 8), a great multitude is suggested " (I. xiv. 8). When he comes to speak of evil angels his language takes on an even increased energy. He speaks of " great crowds " (*magnas copias*) of them, and even with the exaggerating emphasis of deep conviction of the " infinite multitude " of them (I. xiv. 14). Though these two hosts stand now arrayed against each other they are in origin and nature one; for the evil spirits are just good spirits gone wrong. The fundamental facts which Calvin most insists upon with respect to what he calls " devils " (*diaboli*) are that they are creatures of God and were therefore once good — " for it is impious (*nefas*) to ascribe to the good God the creation of any evil thing " [72] — and that they have become evil by corrupting the good nature with which God endowed them.[73] Their evil, says he crisply, is " not from creation but from depravation." [74] " At their original creation they were angels of God, but they destroyed themselves through degeneration." [75] To ascribe to God, their Creator, the evil they have acquired by their defection and lapse, would be to ascribe to Him what above all things is most alien from Him; [76] and thus far the Manichaeans are right — for the good God cannot have created any evil thing (I. xiv. 3, as above). The Scriptural evidence of the fall

[72] I. xiv. 3: nefas esse adscribi bono Deo ullius rei malae creationem.

[73] I. xiv. 3: " The orthodox faith . . . does not admit that any evil nature exists in the universe of the world; since neither the pravity and malice whether of man or devil or the sins which proceed from them, came from nature but from the corruption of nature; nor has anything at all come into being from the beginning in which God has not given a specimen of His wisdom and righteousness."

[74] I. xiv. 16: quum a Deo conditus sit diabolus, hanc malitiam quam eius naturae tribuimus, non ex creatione sed ex depravatione esse meminerimus.

[75] *Do.:* contenti simus hoc breviter habere de diabolorum natura: fuisse prima creatione angelos Dei, sed degenerando se perdidisse et aliis factos esse instrumenta perditionis.

[76] I. xiv. 16: quod est ab eo alienissimum.

of the "devils" Calvin states with great brevity but with sufficient point. He adduces II Peter ii. and Jude 6 as a clear statement: and I Timothy v. 21 as a tacit implication; and he argues that when our Lord (Jno. viii. 44) declares that when Satan "speaketh a lie he speaketh of his own," and adds as a reason "because he abode not in the truth," He implies that he had once been in the truth and issued from it by an act of his own (I. xiv. 16). In his other writings he returns repeatedly to these conceptions and always with the greatest directness and force of statement. "The devils," says he, "have been angels of God but they did not retain the condition in which they were created but have fallen by a horrible fall, so as to become the examples of perdition." [77] "The devils were created by God as well as the angels, but not as they now are. We must always reserve this, — that the evil which is in the devils proceeds from themselves. . . ." [78] "For we know that the devil is evil not by nature, nor from his original creation (*creationis origine*), but by the fault of his own defection." [79]

It is worth while to dwell on these deliverances, because they contain not merely Calvin's doctrine of devils, but also, so far, his doctrine of the origin of evil. This includes, we already perceive, a vigorous repudiation of the notion that God can be in any way the author of evil. The Augustinian doctrine that *omne esse est bonum* is explicitly reaffirmed. God is good and it is impious to suppose that He may have created anything evil (*malum*). But as God is the author of all that is, everything that has come into being is in its nature good. There is, therefore, no such thing in the universe as an evil

[77] Sermon xvi. on Job iv. (*Opp.* xxxiii. 206).
[78] Sermon iv. on Job i. (*Opp.* xxxiii. 60).
[79] Commentary on I Jno. iii. 8 (*Opp.* lv. 334). Cf. farther *Opp.* xxx. 316 ("Hom. 71 on I Sam. xix."): "Just as when we call the good angels spirits of God, not because they have the same essence with God, but because they were formed and created (*formati et creati sunt*) by Him, so also it is to be thought of devils whose origin was the same with the good angels. For they were not created evil as we see them today, and with that evil with which the Scriptures depict them, but they were corrupted and alienated from God by their departure from their original state; just as, we know, man too fell away from his purity into his present misery."

nature (*mala natura*). All that is evil arises (I. xiv. 3) not from
naturo (*ox natura*) but from corruption of naturc (*ex naturae
corruptione*). This corruption has been introduced by the free
action of the creature: it is (I. xiv. 16) not " of creation " but
" of depravation," — a depravation of which the creature itself
is the cause (*cuius ipse sibi causa*). To put it all in a nutshell,
— evil according to Calvin has its source not in the creative
act of God but in the deflected action of the creaturely will.
Such an assertion takes us, of course, only a little way towards a theodicy: but it is important that as we pass we should
note as a first step in Calvin's theodicy that he very energetically repudiates the notion that God, who is good, can be,
as Creator, the author of any evil thing. All that comes from
His hands is "very good."

As the angels owe their existence to God, so of course they
subsist in Him. They were not brought into being to stand,
deistically, over against God, sufficient to themselves: like all
the rest of His creatures their dependence on God is absolute.
Nothing can be ascribed to them as if it belonged to them apart
from Him. They are, indeed, immortal: but this is so far from
meaning that it is beyond the power of God to destroy them,
that it rather means merely that it is the will of God to sustain
them in endless being. In themselves considered, like all other
creaturely existences, they are mortal.[80] " We know," remarks
Calvin,[81] " that angels are immortal spirits, for God has created
them for this condition, that they shall never be destroyed any
more than the souls of men shall perish. . . . The angels are
immortal because they are sustained by power from on high,
and God maintains them — He who is immortal by nature and
the fountain of life is in Him, as says the Psalmist (xxxvi. 10).
. . . The angels are not stable save as God holds their hand.
They are no doubt called Mights and Powers; but this is because God executes His power by them and guides them.

[80] *Opp.* xlviii. 594: " As they have not always existed, so they are capable
of reaching their end." Cf. *Opp.* xxxiii. 365, and xxxviii. 152.
[81] *Opp.* xxxiii. 206–207 (Sermon xvi. on Job iv.). Cf. *Opp.* xxxiii. 365, and
liii. 92.

Briefly, the angels have nothing in themselves by reason of which they may glory in themselves. For all that they have of power and stability they possess from God. . . ." In all their activities, accordingly, angels are but the instruments of God, although, to be sure, they are " the instruments in which God especially (*specialiter*) exhibits the presence of His divinity (*numinis*) " (I. xiv. 5). We must not think of them, then, as interposed between us and God, so as to obscure His glory; nor must we transfer to them what belongs to God and Christ alone (I. xiv. 10) — worshipping them, perchance,[82] or at least attributing to them independent activities. The splendor of the divine majesty is indeed reflected in them; [83] but the glory by which they shine is a derived glory, and it would be preposterous to allow their borrowed brightness to blind us to its source. In all their varied activities they must be considered merely " the hands of God, which move themselves to no work except under His direction." [84]

Some question may arise as to the wideness of the sphere of activity in which angels are employed as " the hands of God." There is at least a *prima facie* appearance that Calvin thought of them as the instruments through which the entirety of God's providential work is administered. He dwells especially, to be sure, on their employment as " the dispensers and administrators of the divine beneficence " towards His people (I. xiv. 6); but he appears to look upon this as only the culminating instance of a universal activity. When he says that they are " God's ministers ordained for the execution of His laws," [85] we may indeed hesitate to press the language. But three several spheres of activity of increasing comprehensiveness seem to be distinguished, when he tells us God " uses their service for the protection of His people, and by means of them both dispenses His benefits among men and executes also the

---

[82] I. xiv. 10: the cult of angels in the Church of Rome led Calvin to be particularly insistent against their worship. Cf. *Opp.* vi. 83, vii. 653.

[83] I. xiv. 10: in eis fulgor divini numinis refulgeat.

[84] I. xiv. 12: si non ut eius manus a nobis considerantur, quae nullum ad opus nisi ipso dirigente se moveant.

[85] I. xiv. 4: Dei ministri ad iussa eius exsequenda ordinati.

rest of His works." [86] And the whole seems summed up in a
phrase when he tells us again that God " exercises and administers His government in the world through them." [87] The universal reach of their activities appears to be explicitly asserted
in the comprehensive statement that God " uses their ministry and service for executing all that He has decreed." [88] It
certainly would appear from such broad statements that Calvin looked upon the angels as agents through which God carries on His entire providential government.

The question is not unnaturally raised whether by this conception Calvin does not remove God too far from His works,
interposing between Him and His operations a body of intermediaries by which He is separated from the universe after
the fashion of a false transcendenceism. [89] It is quite plain that

---

[86] I. xiv. 9: quorum obsequio utitur Deus ad suorum protectionem, et per
quos tum sua beneficia inter homines dispensat, tum reliqua etiam opera
exsequitur.

[87] I. xiv. 5: imperium suum in mundo.

[88] I. xiv. 5, *ad init.*: ad exsequenda omnia quae decrevit. Cf. Heidegger's
threefold distribution of angelic functions: in praeconio laudum eius, necnon
in regimine mundi, ecclesiae imprimis ministrant (as cited by Heppe:
" Dogmat. d. ev.-ref. Kirche," 1861, p. 146).

[89] " It deserves remark," says P. J. Muller (" De Godsleer van Zwingli en
Calvijn," 1883, p. 77), " that Calvin answers the question why God makes
use of angels, after a fashion which more or less affects the immanence of
God. He points to the multiplicity of our dangers, to our weakness, and to
our liability to *trepidatio* and *desperatio*. Now God not merely promises us
His care; but He even appoints an ' innumerable multitude of protectors,
whom He has commissioned to keep watch over us '; so that we may ' feel
ourselves without danger, no matter what evil threatens, so long as we are
under this protection and care ' (I. xiv. 11), — a mode of conception to which
he does not, however, hold, since he looks upon all things and man as well
rather as immediately dependent on God Himself and on His care alone."
Muller quotes Zwingli (" Opera," iib. p. 27) as complaining of Luther's attribution of all evils to the devil as if there were no such thing as the providence
of God. " How is it," asks Zwingli, " that to you the poor devil must have
done everything, as no man can do in my house? I thought the devil was
already overcome and judged. If the devil is now a powerful lord in the
world, as you have just said, how can it be that all things shall be worked
out through God's providence? " In both Zwingli's and Muller's cases the
antithesis is not exact. All things can be worked out by God's providence
and yet the Devil be the author of all that is evil; because the Devil himself
may be — and is — an instrument of God's providence. God's use of angels

Calvin did not so conceive the matter. So far from supposing that the execution of the works of providence through the medium of angels involves the absence of God from these works, he insists that they are only the channels of the presence of God. "How preposterous it is," he exclaims, "that we should be separated from God by the angels when they have been constituted for the express purpose of testifying the completer presence of His aid to us" (I. xiv. 12). Are we separated from the works of our hands because it is by our hands that they are wrought? And the angels, if rightly conceived, must be thought of just as the hands of God — the appropriate instruments, not which work instead of Him, but by which He works (I. xiv. 12). He, therefore, once for all dismisses "that Platonic philosophy" which interposes angels between God and His world, and even asks us to seek access to God through the angels, as if we had not immediacy of access to Him. "For this is the reason they are called Angels of Power or Powers," he remarks in another place; [90] "not that God, resigning His power to them, sits idle in heaven, but because, by acting powerfully in them, He magnificently manifests His power to us. They therefore act ill and perversely who assign anything to angels as of themselves, or who so make them intermediaries between us and God that they obscure the glory of God as if it were removed to a distance; since rather it manifests itself as present in them. Accordingly the mad speculations of Plato are to be shunned as instituting too great a distance between us and God. . . ." In his view, therefore, the angels do not stand between God and the world to hold them apart but to draw them together as channels of operation through which God's power flows into His works.

If he were asked whether he does not, by this interposition of angels between God and His works, infringe on the concep-

---

in His providence is no injury to His immanent working, because they are the instruments of His immanent working; and Calvin does not depart from the one notion while emphasizing the other, because they are not mutually exclusive notions but two sides of one idea.

[90] Commentary on Jno. v. 4 (*Opp.* xlvii. 105–106).

tion of the Divine immanence and raise doubt as to God's immanent activity, Calvin would doubtless reply that he does not " interpose " the angels between God and His works, but conceives them as just " the hands of God " working; and that he, of course, conceives God as immanent in the angels themselves, so that their working is just His working through them, as His instruments. We must not confuse the question of the method of God's immanent activity with that of the fact of that activity. The suggestion that God carries on His providential government through the agency of angels is only a suggestion of the method of His immanent working and can raise doubt of the reality of His immanent working only on the supposition that these angels stand so over against God in their independence as to break — so to speak — His contact with His works. This is Deism, and is therefore of course inconsistent with the Divine immanence; but it has nothing to do with the question whether He employs angels in which He is immanent in His operations. In any event God executes His works of providence through the intermediation of second causes; for this is the very definition of a work of providence. The discovery that among these second causes there are always personal as well as impersonal agencies to be taken into account, can raise no question as between immanence and transcendence in God's modes of action — unless personal agents are conceived to be, as such, so independent of God as to exclude in all that is performed by their agency the conception of His immanent working. And in that case what shall we say of the Divine immanence in the sphere of human life and activity? In a word, Calvin's conception that all the works of God's providence are wrought through the intermediation of angels excludes the immanence of God in His world as little as the recognition of human activities excludes the immanence of God in history.

The real interest of his conception does not lie, therefore, in any bearing it may be supposed to have on his view of the relation of God to the universe — it leaves his view on that point unaffected — but in the insight it gives us into Calvin's pneumatology. We have already had occasion to note the vividness of his sense of the spiritual environment in which our life is cast. We see here that he conceived the universe as in all its operations moving on under the guiding hand of these superhuman intelligences. This is as much as to say that there was no dualism in his conception of the universe: he did not set the spiritual and physical worlds, or the earthly and supramundane worlds, over against one another as separate and unrelated entities. He conceived them as all working together in one unitary system, acting and interacting on one another. And he accustomed himself to perceive beneath the events of human history — whether corporate or individual — and beneath the very operations of physical nature — not merely the hand of God, upholding and governing; but the activities of those " hands of God " who hearken to His voice and fulfil His word, and whom He not only charges with the care of His " little ones," and the direction of the movements of the peoples, but makes even " winds " and a " flaming fire."

To the question why God thus universally operates through the instrumentality of subordinate intelligences, Calvin has no answer, in its general aspects, except a negative one. It cannot be that God needs their aid or is unable to accomplish without them what He actually does through them. If He employs them, " He certainly does not do this from necessity, as if He were unable to do without them; for whenever He pleases, He passes them by and accomplishes His work by nothing but His mere will; so far are they from relieving Him of any difficulty by their aid " (I. xiv. 11). These words have their application to the whole sphere of angelical activities, as indeed they have to the entire body of second causes (I. xvi. 2), but they are spoken directly only of the employment of angels as ministers to the heirs of salvation. It is characteristic of Calvin that he confines his discussion of the subject to this highest function of angelic service, as that which was of special religious value to his readers, and that to which as a practical man seeking practical ends it behooved him particularly to address himself. In this highest sphere of angelic operation he is not without even a positive response to the query why God uses angels to perform IIis will. It is not for His sake but for the sake of His people; it is, in fact, a concession to their weakness. God is able, certainly, to protect His people by the mere nod of His power; and surely it ought to be enough for them and more than enough that God declares Himself their protector.[91] To look around for further aid after we have received the promise of God that He will protect us, is undeniably wrong in us.[92] Is not the simple promise of the great God of heaven and earth sufficient safeguard against all dangers? But we are weak; [93] and God is good — full of leniency and indulgence [94] — and He wishes to give us not only His protection but the sense of His protection. Dealing with us as we are, not as we ought to be, He is willing to appeal to our imagination and to comfort us in our feeling of danger or despair by enabling us to apprehend, in our own way, the presence of His grace. He, therefore, has added to His promise that He will Himself care for us, the further one that " we shall have innumerable escorts to whom He has given charge to secure our safety " (§ 11). Like Elisha, then, who, when he was oppressed by the numerous army of the Syrians, was shown the multitude of the angels sent to guard him, we, when terrified by the thought of the multitude of our enemies, may find refuge in that discovery of Elisha's: " There are more for us than against us."

In insisting upon this particular function of angels above all others, Calvin feels himself to be, as a Biblical theologian, simply following the lead of Scripture. For, intent especially on what may most make for our consolation and the confirmation of our faith, the Scripture lays its stress, he tells us, on angels as the dispensers and administrators of the Divine beneficence towards God's people; and " reminds us that they guard our safety, undertake our defence, direct our ways, and

[91] I. xiv. 11: illud quidem unum satis superque esse deberet, quod Dominus asserit se nostrum esse protectorem.

[92] Do.: perperam id quidem fieri a nobis fateor, quod post illam simplicem promissionem de unius Dei protectione, adhuc circumspectamus unde veniat nobis auxilium.

[93] Do.: imbecilitas, mollities, fragilitas, vitium.

[94] Do.: pro immensa sua clementia et facilitate.

exercise solicitude that no harm shall befall us " (I. xiv. 6).
These great provisions are universal, he tells us, and belong
" to all believers " without exception. Every follower of Christ
has, therefore, pledged to his protection the whole host of the
angels of God. In the interests of the greatness of this pledge,
Calvin enters the lists against the idea of " guardian angels,"
which had become the settled doctrine of the old Church (I.
xiv. 7), not indeed with the sharpness and decision which afterwards obtained in the Reformed Churches,[95] but yet with an
obvious feeling that this notion lacks Scriptural basis and offers
less than what the Scriptures provide for the consolation and
support of God's people. If it is to be accepted at all, Calvin
wishes it to be accepted not instead of, but alongside of, what he
feels to be the much greater assurance that the whole body of
angels is concerned with the protection and salvation of everyone of the saints. " Of this indeed," he remarks, " we may be
sure — that the case of each one of us is not committed to
one angel alone, but that all of them with one consent watch
over our salvation " (I. xiv. 7). This being a settled fact, he
does not consider the question of " guardian angels " worth
considering: if " all the orders of the celestial army stand
guard over our salvation," he asks, what difference does it
make to us whether one particular angel is also told off to act
as our particular guardian or not? But if any one wishes to
restrict the protection granted us by God to this one angel —
why that is a different matter: that would be to do a great
injury to himself and to all the members of the Church, by
depriving them of the encouragement they receive from the
divine assurance that they are compassed about and defended
on all sides in their conflict by the forces of heaven.[96]

[95] Cf. Voetius, " Disput.," i. 1648, p. 900, who remarks that most of the Reformed (including himself) deny the existence of guardian angels, adding:
" We embrace the opinion of Calvin in *Instit.* I. xiv. 7, and *Com. on Psalms*
(91) and *on Matthew* (18), and of the other Reformers, who reject this opinion
as vain and curious, and we think that something in this matter has adhered
to the ancient fathers from the Platonic theology and the mythological theology
of the Gentiles."

[96] This last sentence is new to the latest edition of the " Institutes."
We may note in passing that Calvin both in the " Institutes " and in his
commentary on the passage, understands Mat. xviii. 10 of " the angels of

What Calvin has to say about the evil spirits — the " devils " as he calls them is determined by the same practical purpose which dominates his discussion of the good angels. He begins, therefore, with the remark that " almost everything which Scripture transmits concerning devils, has as its end that we should be solicitous to guard against their snares and machinations, and may provide ourselves with such arms as are firm and strong enough to repel the most powerful enemies " (§ 13, *ad init.*). He proceeds by laying stress on the numbers, the malice, and the subtlety of these devils; and by striving in every way to awaken the reader to a realizing sense of the desperation of the conflict in which he is engaged with them (§§ 13–15). The effect is to paint a very vivid picture of the world of evil, set over against the world of good as in some sense its counterfeit,[97] determined upon overturning the good, and to that end waging a perpetual war against God and His people.[98] He then points out that the evil of these dreadful beings is of themselves, not of God — coming not from creation but from corruption (§ 16) — and closes with two sections upon the relation they sustain to God's providential government. To these closing sections (§§ 17 and 18), it will repay us to devote careful attention. In them Calvin resolves the dualism which is introduced into the universe by the intrusion of evil into it, by showing that this evil itself is held under the control of God and is employed for His divine purposes; and he does this in such a manner that we scarcely know whether to admire most the justice of the conceptions or the precision and clearness of the language in which they are given expression.[99]

little children " (cf. " Institutes," I. xiv. 7, 9), which seems certainly wrong. Cf. art. " Little Ones " in Hastings' " Dict. of Christ and the Gospels."

[97] I. xiv. 14, end: " For just as the Church and the Society of the Saints have Christ as head, so the faction of the impious and impiety itself is depicted to us with its prince, who holds there supreme dominion." Cf. *Opp.* xxxv. 35; liii. 339.

[98] I. xiv. 15, beginning: Hoc quoque ad perpetuum cum diabolo certamen accendere nos debet, quod adversarius Dei et noster ubique dicitur. Cf. the whole paragraph and especially its closing words.

[99] Cf. the definition given of demons by Voetius, " Disp.," i. 1648, p. 911,

The first of these sections asserts the completeness of the control which God exercises over the devils. It is true that Satan is at discord and strife with God: [100] he is by nature — that is, acquired nature — wicked (*improbus*) and every propension of his will is to contumacy and rebellion; of his own accord he does nothing, therefore, which he does not mean to be in opposition to God (§ 17). But he is, after all, but a creature of God's and God holds him in with the bridle of His power and controls his every act. Although, therefore, every impulse of his will is in conflict with God, he can do nothing except by God's will and approval.[101] So it is uniformly represented in Scripture. Thus we read that Satan could not assault Job until he had obtained permission so to do; [102] that the lying spirit by which Ahab was deceived was commissioned from the Lord; [103] that the evil spirit which punished Saul for his sins was from the Lord; [104] that the plagues of Egypt, sent by God as they were, were wrought, nevertheless, by evil angels.[105] And thus Paul, generalizing, speaks of the blinding of unbelievers both as the " work of God " and the " operation of Satan," meaning of course that Satan does it only under the government of God.[106] " It stands fast, therefore," Calvin concludes, " that Satan is under God's power, and is so governed by God's will (*nutu*) that he is compelled to render God obedience. We may say certainly that Satan resists God, and his works are contrary to God's works; but we at the same time assert that this repugnancy and this strife are dependent on God's permission. I am not now speaking of his will (*voluntate*), nor yet of his efforts (*conatu*), but only of the results

---

summing up what is more broadly taught by Calvin in the brevity of a definition. A demon, says he, " is an angel, created in integrity, who, subjected on account of his own defection to endless evil and misery, serves, even though unwillingly, the providence and glory of God."

[100] I. xiv. 17: discordia et pugna cum Deo.
[101] nisi volente et annuente Deo, nihil facere posse.
[102] nisi impetrata facultate.
[103] a Domino amandatus.
[104] spiritus Domini malus.
[105] per angelos malos.
[106] opus Dei — operatio Satanae.

(*effectu*). For the devil is wicked by nature and has not
the least propension towards obedience to the divine will,
but is wholly bent on contumacy and rebellion. What he
has from his own iniquity, therefore, is that he desires and
purposes to oppose God: by this depravity he is stimulated
to try to do those things which he thinks in the highest degree inimical to God. But God holds him bound and curbed
by the bridle of His power, so that he can carry out only
those things which are divinely permitted to him, and thus,
will he nill he, he obeys his Creator, seeing that he is compelled to perform whatever service God impels him to "
(§ 17, end).

This important passage appears first in the edition of the
" Institutes " published in 1543; but its entire substance was in
Calvin's mind from the beginning. It is given expression, first,
in the course of the broader discussion of the relation of God's
providence to the evil acts of men and devils incorporated into
the second chapter (*De Fide*) of the first edition of the " Institutes " (1536).[107] " Thus, the affliction of Job," Calvin there
declares, " was the work of God and of the devil; and yet the
wickedness of the devil must be distinguished from the righteousness of God; for the devil was endeavoring to destroy Job,
God was testing him (Job i. and ii.). So Assur was the rod of
the Lord's anger, Sennacherib the axe in His hand (Is. x.); all
called, raised up, impelled by Him, in a word His ministers.
But how? While they were obeying their unbridled lust, they
were unconsciously serving the righteousness of God (Jer.
xxvii.). Behold God and them, the authors of the same work,
but in the same work the righteousness of God and their
iniquity manifested! " The same line of thought is much more
completely worked out, and very fully illustrated from the
instance of Job, as a part of the discussion of man's sinfulness
in the presence of the machinations of evil and the providence
of God, which was incorporated into the second edition of the
" Institutes " (1539) and retained from it throughout all the
subsequent editions — in the final edition forming the opening

[107] *Opp.* i. 61.

sections of the discussion of " How God works in the hearts of men " (II. iv. 1–2).[108]

Much the same line of thought is developed again in the full discussion of the providence of God which appears in the tract against the Libertines, which was published in 1545. Speaking here of the particular providence of God, Calvin proceeds as follows: [109] " It is furthermore to be noted that not only does God serve Himself thus with the insensible creatures, to work and execute His will through them; but also with men and even with devils. So that Satan and the wicked are executors of His will. Thus He used the Egyptians to afflict His people, and subsequently raised up the Assyrians to chastise them, when they had sinned; and others in like manner. As for the devil, we see that he was employed to torment Saul (I Sam. xvi. 14, xviii. 10), to deceive Ahab (I Kings xxii. 22), and to execute judgment upon all the wicked whenever they require it (Ps. lxxviii. 49); and on the other hand to test the constancy of God's people, as we see in the case of Job. The Libertines, now, meeting with these passages, are dumfounded by them and without due consideration conclude that, therefore, the creatures do nothing at all. Thus they fall into a terrible error. For not only do they confound heaven and earth together but God and the devil. This comes from not observing two limitations which are very necessary. The first is that Satan and wicked men are not such instruments of God that they do not act also of their own accord. For we must not imagine that God makes use of a wicked man precisely as He does of a stone or of a piece of wood. He employs him rather as a reasonable creature according to the quality of the nature He has given him. When, then, we say that God works by means of the wicked, this does not forbid that the wicked work also on their own account. This Scripture shows us with even remarkable clearness. For while, on the one hand, it declares that God shall hiss (Is. v. 26), and as it were sound the drum to call the infidels to arms and shall harden or inflame their hearts — yet, on the other, it does not leave out of account their own thought and will, and attributes

[108] *Opp.* i. 351; ii. 225.   [109] *Opp.* vii. 188–190.

to them the work they do by the appointment of God. The second limitation which these unhappy men disregard is that there is a very real distinction between the work of God and that of a wicked man when he serves as the instrument of God. For it is by his own avarice, or his own ambition, or his own jealousy, or his own cruelty, that a wicked man is incited to do what he does; and he has no regard to any other end. And it is according to the root, which is the affection of the heart, and to the end which it seeks, that the work is qualified; and so it is rightly accounted wicked. But God has an entirely contrary purpose. It is to execute His righteousness, to save and conserve the good, to employ His goodness and grace towards the faithful, to chastise the ill-deserving. Here, then, lies the necessity of distinguishing between God and men, so as to contemplate in the same work God's righteousness, goodness, judgment, and, on the other side, the malice of the devil or of the wicked. Let us take a good and clear mirror in which to see all that I am saying. When Job heard the news of the loss of his goods, of the death of his children, of the many calamities which had fallen on him, he recognized that it was God who was visiting him, and said, ' The Lord has given, the Lord has taken away.' And, in truth, it was so. But was it not also the devil who had brewed this pottage? Was it not the Chaldeans who had spoiled his goods? Did he commend the thieves and brigands, and excuse the devil, because his affliction had come to him from God? Certainly not. He well knew there was an important distinction to be observed here. And so he condemns the evil, and says ' Blessed be the name of the Lord.' Similarly David, when he was persecuted by Shimei, no doubt said that he had received this from the Lord (II Sam. xvi. 11), and saw that this wretch was a rod by which God was chastising him. But while he praised God, he did not omit to condemn Shimei (I Kings ii. 9). We shall return to this at another place. For the present let it suffice to hear this: that God so uses His creatures and makes them serve His providence, that the instrument which He employs may often be bad; that His turning the malice of Satan or of bad men to good does not in the least excuse their evil or make their work other than bad and to be condemned, seeing that every work receives its quality from the intention with which it is done. . . . On the contrary, we must needs observe that the creatures do their works here in their own degree, and these are to be estimated as good or bad according as they are done in obedience to God or to offend Him. All the time, God is above, directing everything to a good end, and turning the evil into good, or, at least, drawing good out of what is evil, acting according to His nature, that is in righteousness and equity; and making use of the devil in such a manner as in no way to mix Himself with him so as to have anything in common with him, or to entangle Himself in any evil association, or to efface the nature of what is evil by His righteousness. It is just like the sun which, shining on a piece of carrion and causing putrefaction in it, contracts no taint whatever from the corruption, and does not by its purity destroy the foulness and infection of the carrion. So God deals in such a manner with the deeds of the wicked that the holiness which is in Him does not justify the infection which is in them, nor is contaminated by it."

We have thought it desirable to quote at some length one of the more extended passages in which Calvin develops the doctrine announced in the section before us, although it leads us somewhat away from the single point here to be emphasized, into the mysteries of the divine providence. This broader view once before us, however, we may return to emphasize the single point which now concerns us — Calvin's teaching of the absolute control of the evil spirits by God. This seemed to Calvin to lie so close to the center of Christian hope and life that he endlessly repeats it in his occasional writings, and has even incorporated an assertion of it in his Catechism (1545).[110] "But what shall we think of the wicked and of devils," he there asks — " are they, too, subject to God? " And he answers: " Although God does not lead them by His Spirit, He nevertheless holds them in check as with a bridle, so that they cannot move save as He permits them. And He even makes them

110 *Opp.* vi. 17, 18; cf. vii. 188 *sq.*

ministers of His will, so that He compels them to execute unwillingly and against their determination what seems good to
Him." The recognition of this fact seemed to him essential even
to an intelligent theism, which, he urges, certainly requires
that God should be conceived not less as Governor than as Creator of all things — as, indeed, the two things go together. " If,
then, we imagine," he writes,[111] " that God does not govern all,
but that some things come about by fortune, it follows that
this fortune is a goddess who has created part of the world, and
that the praise is not due to God alone. And it is an execrable
blasphemy if we think that the devil can do anything without the permission of God: that is all one with making him
creator of the world in part." " Now Satan," says he again,[112]
" is also subject to God, so that we are not to imagine that
Satan has any principality except what is given him by God;
and there is good reason why he should be subject to Him since
he proceeds from Him. The devils were created by God as
well as the angels, but not such as they are. It is necessary that
we always reserve this, — that the evil which is in the devils
proceeds from themselves." [113]

Calvin was not the man, however, to insist on the control
of the devils by God without consideration of the ends for
which this control was exercised. He therefore follows up his
assertion of this control (§ 17) with a discussion of the use
God makes of "unclean spirits" (*immundi spiritus*) (§ 18).
This use, he tells us, is twofold. They are employed to test, try,
exercise and develop the faithful. And they are employed to

---

[111] *Opp.* xxxv. 152 (Sermon cxxx. on Job xxxiv.).

[112] *Opp.* xxxiii. 60 (Sermon iv. on Job i.).

[113] Cf. also *Opp.* xxx. 178; xxxvi. 338; xl. 309; xlv. 269; xlviii. 594, where it
is the ascended Christ who is affirmed (as God of providence) to hold the
devils in check so that they do nothing save by His will. Also the statement
in the " Confession des Escholiers " of 1559 (*Opp.* ix. 723–724): " And although
Satan and the reprobate endeavor to throw everything into confusion to such
an extent that the faithful themselves doubt the right order of their sins, I
recognize nevertheless that God, as the Supreme Prince and Lord of All, turns
the evil into good, and governs all things by a certain secret curb, and moder-
ates them in a wonderful way, which we ought with all submission of mind
to adore, since we are not able to comprehend it."

punish the wicked. On the latter of these he dwells as little as its faithful presentation permitted. Those whom God "does not design to enroll in His own flock," he tells us, He delivers over to the control of Satan as the minister of the divine vengeance; and he pictures in a few burning words the terribleness of their fate. On the employment of Satan and his angels for the profit of God's people he dwells more at length and with evident reminiscence of his own Christian experience. "They exercise the faithful with fighting," he tells us, "they assail them with snares, harass them with assaults, push them in combat, even fatigue them often, confuse, terrify, and sometimes wound them." Yet they never, he adds, "conquer or overcome them." God's children may often be filled with consternation, but they are never so disheartened that they cannot recover themselves; they may be struck down by the violence of the blows they receive, but they always rise again; they may be wounded, but they cannot be slain; they may be made to labor through their whole lives, but in the end they obtain the victory.

There are several things that are thrown out into a high light in this discussion which it will repay us to take notice of. We observe, first of all, Calvin's view of the Christian life as a conflict with the powers of evil. "This exercise," he says, or we might perhaps almost translate it "this drill" (*exercitium*) — it is the word for military training — "is common to all the children of God." We observe, next, his absolute confidence in the victory of God's children. The promise that the seed of the woman shall crush the head of Satan belongs not only to Christ, but to all His members; and, therefore, he can categorically deny that it is possible for the faithful ever to be conquered or overcome of evil. The dominion of Satan is over the wicked alone, and shall never be extended to the soul of a single one of the faithful. We observe again that Calvin conceives the victory as therefore complete already in principle for every one who is in Christ. "In our Head indeed," he declares, "this victory has always been full and complete (*ad plenum exstitit*); because the prince of the world had nothing in Him." And we observe, finally, that he holds with clear conviction that it will never be complete for any of us in this life. We labor here throughout the whole course of life (*toto vitae curriculo*) and obtain the victory only in the end (*in fine*). The fulfilment of the promise of crushing the head of Satan is only "begun in this life," the characteristic of which is that it is the period of conflict (*ubi luctandum est*): it is only after this period of conflict is over (*post luctam*) that it shall be completely fulfilled. It is only in our Head that the victory is now complete: in us who are members, it appears as yet only in part: and it is only when we put off our flesh, according to which we are liable to infirmity, that we shall be filled with the power of the Holy Spirit. In these several considerations we have outlined for us very vividly Calvin's conception of the life which we now live in the flesh, a life of faith and hope, not of full attainment: a life filled with conflict, but with the sure promise of victory.

The preoccupation of Calvin's mind with man throughout his whole discussion of creation is very strikingly illustrated by his absorption, even while discussing angels and devils, with human relations and human problems. What he is apparently chiefly concerned about is that men shall understand and take their comfort out of the assurance that angelic hosts encamp about them for their protection, and angelic messengers are busied continually with their direction; that men shall understand and take their admonition from the certainty that numerous most subtle and malignant unseen foes lie in wait continually for their souls. We have pointed out that Calvin's conception of the universe was frankly anthropocentric. We see that this anthropocentrism of thought embraced in it the spiritual as well as the physical universe. He does not say, indeed, that these higher spiritual existences exist purely for man: he only says that for our consolation and the confirmation of our faith the Scriptures insist principally on their employment for the dispensing and administering of God's kindness to His people. Here is no speculative investigation into the final cause of angels. Here is only a practical reference to those

functions of angels which it most concerns us to know. But he
does teach of course (on the basis of Col. i. 16) that the very
creation of angels is referred to Christ as its end: and it might
be contended that in this declaration there lie the beginnings of
a " gospel of creation " by which all things without exception
which have been brought into being are set forth as ancillary
to the great end of the redemption of the human race. A certain amount of confirmation may be found for this contention
in the unitary conception which, as has been pointed out, Calvin cherished of the universe as a systematized whole. Meanwhile we have no formal discussion from him of the final cause
of angels, and not even (at this place, at all events) any guiding hints of how he would resolve such a question. Least of all
have we here any such discussion as meets us in many of his
followers of the final cause of the devil,[114] although the elements of such a discussion are involved in any theodicy, and
cannot escape suggestion in any attempt to deal seriously
with the great problem of evil. Calvin, therefore, has not failed
to suggest them; but not directly in our present context, where
he contents himself with assuming the existence of evil in the
spiritual world, declaring its origination by the creature
and asserting the divine control of it and utilization of it in
God's government of the world.[115] For what may penetrate

[114] Few of them, however, have been able to say so much so well in such
few words as Voetius, " Disp.," i. 1648, p. 922: " Final causes of the devil as
such ought not to be assigned, because evil has no end. But although the *opus*
(as we say) in and of itself has no end, the *operans Deus* has — who has made
everything for Himself (*propter seipsum*, Prov. xvi. 4). For to a fixed end He
both created him in the state of integrity, and permitted his fall, and left him
in his fallen state, and ordained his malice to multiplex good. His ultimate
end is therefore the glory of God; the subordinate use of the devil is as an
instrument of divine providence, in this life for plaguing men, the pious for
their discipline only, the impious for their punishment and undoing; after this
life, for torturing the impious. Thus God in both raises a trophy to the honor
of His blameless glory."

[115] A brief statement of how Calvin habitually thought of devils may
be found in his tract against the Libertines (xii.: *Opp.* vii. 181–182): " The
Scriptures teach us that the devils are evil spirits who continually make war
on us, to draw us to perdition. And as they are destined to eternal damnation,
they continually strive to involve us in the same ruin. Likewise that they
are instruments of the wrath of God, and executioners for the punishment of

into the problem more deeply than this, we shall have to go elsewhere.

Meanwhile, having expounded at some length the nature of the spiritual, and more briefly the nature of the physical, environment of man, Calvin is now able to turn definitely to the subject which had really been occupying his thoughts throughout the entire discussion of creation — man, considered as a creature of God. The ruin which has been wrought in man by sin, he postpones for a later discussion; here he concerns himself only with the nature of man as such. Not of course as if he were inviting an idle contemplation of something which no longer exists and therefore cannot deeply concern us. But with a twofold practical object in view. In the first place, that we may not attribute to God, the author of our nature, those natural evils which we perceive in ourselves, in our present condition. And next, that we may properly estimate the lamentable ruin into which we have fallen, by seeing it as it really is — as a corruption and deformity of our proper nature. With these ends in view he invites us to attend to a *descriptio integrae naturae,* that is to an account of the constitution and nature of man as such (I. xv. 1).

Man, in his view, owes his origin, of course, to the productive energy of God (I. xv. 5) and is spoken of by Calvin as among all the works of God, " the most noble and supremely admirable example of the Divine righteousness and wisdom and goodness." [116] His peculiarity among the creatures of God is that he is of a duplex nature. For that man consists of two disparate elements — soul and body — ought, in Calvin's opin-

---

unbelievers and rebels, blinding them and tyrannizing over them, to incite them to evil (Job i. 6, 12; ii. 1, 7; Zech. iii. 1; Mat. iv. 1; Lk. viii. 29, xxii. 31; Acts vii. 51, xxvi. 18; II Cor. ii. 11; I Thes. ii. 18; Jno. viii. 44; xiii. 2; I Jno. iii. 8)."

[116] I. xv. 1, *ad init.:* inter omnia Dei opera nobilissimum ac maxime spectabile est iustitiae eius, et sapientiae, et bonitatis specimen. Cf. Commentary on Gen. i. 26: " If you rightly weigh all circumstances man is among other creatures a certain preëminent specimen of divine wisdom, justice and goodness, so that he is deservedly called by the ancients μικρόκοσμος , ' a world in minature.' " Calvin seems to be speaking with regard only to the other *visible* creatures.

ion, to be beyond controversy.[117] On the one side, then, man takes hold of lower nature — " he was taken from earth and clay "; [118] and this surely ought to be a curb to our pride. On the other side — which is " the nobler part " of man [119] — he is an immortal spirit dwelling in this earthly vessel as a domicile; and in this he may justly glory as a mark of the great goodness of his Maker.[120] Calvin, we perceive then, is a dichotomist, and that not merely inadvertently but with an express rejection of the trichotomistic schematization. He recognizes some plausibility in the arguments advanced to distinguish between the sensitive and rational souls in man; but he finds that there is really no substance in them and advises that we draw off from such questions as frivolous and useless.[121]

Of the bodily nature of man, Calvin has (here at least) little to say. He is not insensible to the dignity of the human form and carriage, celebrating it in a familiar classical quotation; [122] and he admits that by as much as it distinguishes and separates us from brute animals by that much it brings us nearer to God.[123] Though he insists that the image of God is properly spiritual,[124] and that even though it may be discerned

[117] I. xv. 2, *ad init.*: porro hominem constare anima et corpore, extra controversiam esse debet. Cf. *Opp.* vii. 113–114 (1544) : " We hold then, in conformity with the whole teaching of God that man is composed and consists of two parts: that is to say of body and soul."

[118] I. xv. 1, end: ex terra et luto sumptus fuit.

[119] I. xv. 2: quae nobilior eius pars est.

[120] I. xv. 1, end: fictoris sui.

[121] I. xv. 6: qui plures volunt esse animas in homine, hoc est sensitivam et rationalem, . . . repudiandi nobis sunt.

[122] From Ovid, " Metam.," Lib. i.

[123] I. xv. 3. Cf. Commentary on Genesis ii. 7 where he finds in the very way in which man was formed, gradually and not by a simple fiat, a mark of his excellence above the brutes. " Three stages," he says, " are to be noted in the creation of man: that his dead body was formed out of the dust of the earth; that it was endued with a soul whence it should receive vital motion; and that on this soul God engraved His own image, to which immortality is annexed."

[124] In accordance with Augustine's declaration (" De Trinitate," xii. 7 [12]) : Non secundum formam corporis homo factus est ad imaginem Dei, sed secundum rationalem mentem. (Cf. " De Gen. ad lit.," vi. 27 (38) : imaginem [Dei] in spiritu mentis impressam. . . .)

sparkling in these external things it is only as they are informed by the spirit; [125] he yet in this very statement seems in
some sense to allow that it does "sparkle" at least in these
external things, and indeed says plainly that "there is no part
of man including the body itself, in which there is not some
luminous spark of the divine image." [126] What he objected to
in Osiander's view accordingly was not that he allowed to the
body some share in the divine image but that he placed the
image of God "promiscuously" and "equally" in the soul and
body.[127] Calvin might allow it to extend even to the body, but
certainly he would not admit that it had its seat there in equal
measure as in the soul. The only proper seat of the image of
God was to him indeed precisely the soul itself,[128] from which
only it might shine into the body.[129]

[125] I. xv. 3: modo fixum illum maneat, imaginem Dei, quae in his externis
notis conspicitur vel emicat, spiritualem esse.

[126] "Institutes," I. xv. 3. Cf. A. S. E. Talma, "De Anthropologie van
Calvijn," 1882, who thinks Calvin speaks somewhat waveringly about the
body.

[127] Promiscue tam ad corpus quam ad animam.

[128] So he says in the "Psychopannychia" (Opp. v. 180) that in the body,
mirabile opus Dei, prae caeteris corporibus creatis, apparet, nulla tamen
eius imago (in eo) effulget, and reasons out the matter at length in Opp. vii.
112 (1544): "Now where will it be that we shall find this image of God, if
there is no spiritual essence in man on which it may be impressed? For as
to man's body it is not there that the image of God resides. It is true that
Moses afterwards adds (Gen. ii. 7) that man was made a living soul, — a
thing said also of beasts. But to denote a special excellence, he says that God
inspired the power of life into the body He had formed of dust. Thus, though
the human soul has some qualities common to those of beasts, nevertheless
as it bears the image and likeness of God it is certainly of a different kind.
As it has an origin apart, it has also another preëminence and this is what
Solomon means when he says that at death the body returns to the dust from
which it is taken, and the soul returns to God who gave it (Eccl. xii. 7). For
this reason it is said in the Book of Wisdom (ii. 23) that man is immortal,
seeing that he was created in the image of God. This is not an authentic book
of Holy Scripture but it is not improper to avail ourselves of its testimony as
of an ancient teacher (Docteur ancien) — although the single reason ought
to be enough for us that the image of God, as it has been placed in man, can
reside only in an immortal soul, if we understand its contents as Paul expounds it, that is to say, that we are like God in righteousness and true holiness."

[129] Sermons on Daniel, Opp. xli. 459.

He even, indeed, permits himself to speak of the body as a
" prison " from which the soul is liberated at death; [130] though
this is doubtless merely a classical manner of speech, adhered
to without intentional implication of its corollaries,[131] whenever at least his mind is not consciously on " the body of this
death," that is, specifically, the sinful body. In contrast with
the soul, he never tires indeed of pouring contempt upon the
body as a mere lump of clay, which is sustained and moved
and impelled solely by the soul which dwells in it.[132] Dust in its
origin, it shall in accordance with its nature, in obedience to
the curse of God, return to dust,[133] although of course afterwards it shall be raised again in virtue of Christ's redemption;
but here we are speaking again of the body, not as it is in itself,
but as it is under sin, subject on the one hand to the death from
which it was wholly free in the state of integrity [134] and to the

[130] I. xv. 2: ubi soluta est a carnis ergastulo anima; nisi animae cor-
porum ergastulis solutae manerent superstites. In his early tract (1534) against
soul-sleeping, he rings the changes on this idea: ex hoc corporis ergastulo;
corpus animae est carcer; terrena habitatio compedes sunt; post dissolutam
compagem corporis; exuta his vinculis, etc. (Opp. v. 195–196).

[131] This is clearly the case in his early tract, " Psychopannychia," 1534,
Opp. v. 195–196, where the body is " a lump of clay," " a weight of earth,
which presses us down and so separates us as by a wall from God ": and it
is only when the load of the body is put off that " the soul set free from impurities is truly spiritual (vere spiritualis) so as to consent to the will of God
and no longer to yield to the tyranny of the flesh rebelling against Him."

[132] Opp. v. 195: tanta est vis animae, in massa terrae sustinenda, mo-
venda, impellenda; the soul is on the contrary by nature agile (natura agilis).

[133] Opp. v. 204: Is vero pulvis est, qui formatus est de limo terrae: ille
in pulverem revertitur, non spiritus, quem aliunde quam e terra acceptum
Deus homini dedit.

[134] Commentary on Gen. ii. 17: " He was wholly free from death; his
earthly life no doubt would have been only for a time; yet he would have
passed into heaven without death." On Gen. iii. 19: " When he had been
raised to so great a dignity that the glory of the divine image shone in him,
the earthly origin of the body was almost obliterated. Now however, despoiled of his divine and heavenly excellence, what remains but that by his
very departure out of life, he should recognize himself to be earth? Hence
it is that we dread death, because dissolution, which is contrary to nature,
cannot naturally be desired. The first man, to be sure, would have passed to
a better life had he remained upright; but there would have been no separation
of the soul from the body, no corruption, no kind of destruction, in short, no
violent change."

redemption by which it is recovered from the death incurred by sin. Though then our bodies are in themselves, under sin, mere carcasses, yet as " members of Christ " they cannot " sink into putrefaction without hope of resurrection " (III. xxv. 7). They may be " wretched corpses," but they do not cease to be " temples of the Holy Ghost," and God " wishes to be adored in them." " We are the altars at which He is worshipped, in our bodies and in our souls." [135] Hence, as well as for other reasons, Calvin has much to say of the duty of a proper care of the body — of its health and even of its cleanliness. If God deigns to dwell in us we should endeavor to walk in purity of body as well as of soul, to keep our bodies in decency, not to afflict them with austerities, or to neglect them in disease, but so to regulate our lives that we shall be able to serve God, and be in suitable condition to do good.[136]

Even the body, it must be borne in mind, was not according to Calvin created to be the prey of death. In his commentary on Gen. ii. 16 he tells us that had man not sinned, his earthly life indeed would have ceased but only to give way to a

[135] Sermons on Deuteronomy, *Opp.* xxvii. 19, 20.

[136] Sermons on Deut., *Opp.* xxviii. 101; Sermons on I Tim., *Opp.* liii. 533–536. Cf. in general on Calvin's doctrine of the body, E. Doumergue, *Princeton Theological Review,* Jan., 1909 (vii. 1), pp. 93–96, where he brings out the salient points in opposition to the representations of Martin Schulze's " Meditatio Futurae Vitae, ihr Begriff und ihre herrschende Stellung im System Calvins," 1901, pp. 7 *sq.* In his address on " Calvin le prédicateur de Genève," delivered at the celebration at Geneva of the 400th anniversary of Calvin's birth (July 2, 1909), Doumergue briefly sums up his contentions here: " Oh! no doubt the body is a *tent,* a *prison* and worse still in the vehement language of our preacher. But at the same time, ' there is no part of the body in which some sparkle of the divine image is not to be found shining.' It is the ' temple of the Holy Spirit,' ' the altar ' on which God would be adored. . . . And it is in a sort of canticle that Calvin celebrates its resurrection. . . . ' What madness it would be to reduce this body to dust without hope. No, the body of St. Paul, which has borne the marks of Jesus Christ, which has magnificently glorified Him, will not be deprived of the reward of the crown.' — Accordingly what care we should take of this body! Care for the health is a religious duty: ' God does not wish that men should kill themselves,' and to abstain from the remedies which are offered is a ' diabolical pride.' — Health and cleanliness: here is the whole of modern hygiene, which is to be nowhere more scrupulous or splendid than with the peoples which have been most strictly taught in the school of the preacher of Geneva, — the Scotch and Dutch " (p. 21).

heavenly life for the whole man.[137] That man dies is due therefore entirely to sin. Without sin the body itself would have
been immortal. Its *exinanitio* is as much due to sin as the *male-
dictio* which falls on the soul.[138] By Adam's sin death entered
into the world[139] and thus alienation from God for the soul,
and return to dust for the body. And therefore by the redemption in Christ there is purchased for the soul restoration to
communion with God and for the body return from the dust,
in order that the whole man, soul and body, may live forever
in the enjoyment of the Divine favor. The body is not in and of
itself therefore, although the lower part of man and uniting
him with the lower creation, an unworthy element of human
nature. All that is unworthy in it comes from sin.[140]

The " nobler part "[141] of man, the " soul," or as it is alternatively called, the " spirit,"[142] differs from the body not
merely in nature but in origin. In its nature, Calvin conceives
it as distinctively percipient substance: whose " very nature,
without which it cannot by any means exist, is movement, feeling, activity, understanding."[143] From the metaphysical point
of view Calvin defines it as " an immortal, yet created essence,"[144] and he is at considerable pains to justify each element of this definition.

In opposition to the notion that the soul is but a breath

[137] terrena quidem vita illi fuisset temporalis; but, in coelum tamen sine
interitu et illaesus migrasset.

[138] Nunc mors ideo horrori nobis est: primum quia quaedam est exinanitio, quoad corpus: deinde quia Dei maledictionem sentit anima.

[139] On Rom. v. 12.

[140] Cf. Talma, as cited, pp. 37–40.

[141] I. xv. 2: nobilior pars: praecipua pars.

[142] Anima . . . interdum spiritus vocatur (I. xv. 2, *ad init.*). He repeatedly investigates in his occasional works the Biblical usage of the terms
" soul " and " spirit." E.g. in his early work, " Psychopannychia," *ad init.* (*Opp.*
v. 178 *sq.*), and towards the end of the tract against the Anabaptists (*Opp.* vii.
111). Cf. Talma, as cited, p. 34.

[143] " Psychopannychia," *Opp.* v. 184: " If any confess that the soul
lives, and deprive it at the same time of all sensation (*sensu*), they just imagine a soul with nothing of soul about it; or they tear away the soul from
itself; quum eius natura, sine qua consistere ullo modo nequit, sit moveri,
sentire, vigere, intelligere; and (as Tertullian says) animae anima, sensus sit."

[144] I. xv. 2, *ad init.*: animae nomine essentiam immortalem, creatam
tamen intelligo, quae nobilior eius pars est.

(*flatus*) or power (*vis*) divinely infused into bodies, but itself lacking essence (*quae tamen essentia careat*),[145] he affirms that it is a substantial entity distinct from the body, incorporeal in its own nature (*substantia incorporea*),[146] and therefore incapable of occupying space, and yet inhabiting the body as its domicile "not only that it may quicken all its parts,[147] and render its organs fit (*apta*) and useful for their activities, but also that it may hold the primacy (*primatum*) in the government of the life of man," whether in concerns of this life or in those of the life to come (§ 6). The substantiality of the soul as an essence distinct from the body he considers to be clear on its own account, and on the testimony of Scripture as well.[148] The powers with which the soul is endowed, he urges, transcend the capacities of physical substance, and themselves afford therefore ample proof that there is "hidden in man something which is distinct from the body." [149] Here is conscience, for example, which, discriminating between good and evil, responds to the judgment of God. "How shall an affection without essence [150] penetrate to the tribunal of God and strike terror into itself from its guilt"; or fear of a purely spiritual punishment afflict the body? Here is the knowledge of God itself. How should an evanescent activity (*evanidus vigor*) rise to the fountain of life? Here is the marvelous agility of the human mind, traversing heaven and earth, and all the secret places of nature; here are the intellect and memory gathering into themselves all the ages, arranging everything in proper order and even forecasting the future from the past; here is the intellect, conceiving the invisible God and the angels, which have nothing in common with the body, apprehending what is right, and just, and honest, things to which no bodily sense is related: must there

[145] I. xv. 2.

[146] I. xv. 6.

[147] Cf. "Psychopannychia," *Opp.* v. 180: essentiam immortalem, quae in homine vitae causa est.

[148] I. xv. 2: et res ipsa et tota scriptura ostendit.

[149] I. xv. 2: clare demonstrat latere in homine aliquid a corpore separatum.

[150] I. xv. 2: motus sine essentia — the expression is just in view of modern phenomenalistic psychology.

not be something essentially distinct from the body which is the seat of such intelligence (§ 2)? It is upon the Scriptural argument for the distinctness of the soul, however, that Calvin especially dwells; and he has, of course, no difficulty in making it perfectly plain that from beginning to end the Scriptures go on the assumption of the distinctness and even the separability of the soul from the body (§ 2, *ad fin.*).

This whole argument was inserted into the " Institutes " for the first time in the preparation of the last edition (1559). But it is old ground for Calvin. It was already traversed by him with great fulness in his youthful tract against the advocates of Soul-Sleep (1534), the main contention of which is that the soul " is a substance and lives after the death of the body, endowed with sense and intelligence." [151] Ten years later (1544) it was gone over again somewhat more concisely in his " Brief Instructions to arm all good Christians against the errors of the common sect of the Anabaptists," among whose errors was the contention that " souls, departed from the body, do not live until the resurrection," whether because the soul was conceived, not as " a substance or as a creation having essence, but only as the power which man has to breathe, move and perform the other acts of life, while he is living," or because, while it was conceived as " an essential creature," it was thought to sleep " without feeling or knowledge " until the judgment day. As over against the former and extremer type of Anabaptism he undertakes to demonstrate that " souls have an essence of their own " [152] " given to them by God." [153] The richness of the Scriptural material at Calvin's disposal is fairly illustrated by the fact that in these three Scriptural arguments, although some of it is employed more than once, yet much of it is in each case drawn from different passages.

It is interesting to observe that Calvin conceives himself to establish the immortality of the soul in establishing its dis-

[151] *Opp.* v. 177.

[152] *Opp.* vii. 111–112: que les ames ont une essense propre.

[153] *Opp.* vii. 112: l'ame humaine a une essense propre qui luy soit donnée de Dieu.

tinct substantiality. In the argument in the " Institutes," the
two topics of the essentiality and the immortality of the soul
are treated so completely as one, that the reader is apt to be a
little confused by what seems their confusion (I. xv. 2). Calvin's idea seems to be that if it be clear that there is " something in man essentially distinct from the body," the subject
of all these great powers of intellect, sensibility and will, it
will go of itself that this wonderful somewhat will survive
death. This point of view is perhaps already present to his
mind in the " Psychopannychia," although there he more
clearly distinguishes between the proof " that the soul or spirit
of man is a substance distinct from the body," and the proof
that the soul remains in existence after the death of the body,
representing the latter specifically as the question of the immortality of the soul [154] — although it does not seem obvious
that even the question of the survival of the crisis of death
is quite the same question as that of immortality. His method
seems in point of fact to be the result of a more fundamental
conception. This fundamental conception which underlies his
whole point of view seems to be that a spiritual substance is,
as uncompounded, naturally immortal. On that presupposition the proof that there is a spiritual substance in man is the
proof of his immortality. Of course this assumption is not to
be understood to mean that Calvin imagined that any creatures of God whether men or angels are so immortal in and
of themselves, that God cannot destroy them or that they
exist otherwise than " in Him," and by virtue not only of His
purpose in constituting them as He has constituted them, but
of His constant upholding power.[155] It means only that Calvin

[154] *Opp.* v. 184.

[155] Accordingly Calvin in his " Psychopannychia " (*Opp.* v. 222) says
plainly: " When we say that the spirit of man is immortal we do not affirm
that it is able to stand against the hand of God or to subsist apart from His
power." In his Commentary on I Tim. vi. 16 he explains the declaration that
God alone has immortality to refer not to His having immortality *a seipso* but
to His having it *in potestate:* accordingly, he says, immortality does not belong
to creatures save as it is planted in them by the inspiration of God: nam si
vim Dei quae indita est hominis animae tollas, statim evanescet: naturae
immortalitas does not belong to souls or angels. Similarly in his " Responsio

supposed that in constituting them spirits God has constituted them for immortality and given them natures adapted for and implicating their endless existence. The proof that there is an uncompounded spirit in man, therefore, is in his view already a proof of immortality.

It must not be inferred, however, that Calvin always relies solely on this indirect proof of the immortality of the soul. More direct proofs are found elsewhere in the " Institutes " — as for example, in the chapter on the witness of the works and deeds of God to Him (I. v. 10), where a digression is made to point out that the apparent inequality of the moral government of the world suggests the hypothesis of a further life for its rectification. But the simplicity with which he as a Biblical theologian relies on the Scriptures precluded the development by Calvin of an extended or a complete argument for immortality on general considerations. On his view of the disabilities of the human mind induced by sin, he would not look for such

---

contra Pighium de Libero Arbitrio " (*Opp.* vi. 361) he denies that the soul of man is in this sense *per se* immortal: nam et eo modo neque animam per se immortalem esse concedimus. The exception however proves the rule, and the use of this as an argument against Pighius *ex concessu*, suggests that there is a sense in which otherwise than *eo modo*, the soul is *per se* immortal. Pighius had asserted that " mortality and corruption are ex conditione, non vitio naturae." " What is his proof? " asks Calvin, and supplies it thus: " Since the body is thus from its principia out of which it is compounded and from the nature of composition." " But by that argument," rejoins Calvin, " it might be proved that the body would be obnoxious to death even after the resurrection; and that the soul is now mortal. For from what principium has the soul sprung except nothing? " " No doubt," he adds, " if we should say that that perfection which God conferred on man from the beginning did not so belong to nature that he had it *per se* and *ex se*, I would freely accept this opinion. For not even do we concede that the soul is after that fashion *per se* immortal. And this is what Paul teaches when he attributes immortality to God alone (I Tim. vi. 16). Nevertheless we do not on that account confess the soul to be mortal: for we do not estimate its nature from the first power (*virtute*) of the essence, but from the perpetual condition which God has imparted to His creatures." Cf. the tract against the Libertines (*Opp.* vii. 180): " St. Paul, they say, calls God alone immortal (I Tim. vi. 16). I fully agree with St. Paul. But he means that God alone has this privilege of Himself and of His own nature, so that He is the source of immortality. But what He has of Himself He communicated to our souls by His grace, when He formed them in His image."

an argument among the heathen. The heathen philosophers, he tells us accordingly, having no knowledge of the Scriptures, scarcely attained to a knowledge of immortality. Almost no one of them, except Plato, roundly asserts the soul to be an immortal essence. Certain other Socratics reach out towards such a conception indeed; but they are all in more or less doubt and cannot teach clearly what they only half believe. Nevertheless Calvin is persuaded that there is ineradicably imprinted on the heart of man a desire for the celestial life, and also some knowledge of it (I. xv. 6). No man can escape then from some intimations of immortality. And after the heart has been quickened by grace and the intellect illuminated by the workings of the Spirit, proofs of it will abundantly suggest themselves.[156]

Now, this immortal substance, alternately called soul and spirit, which constitutes the animating or governing principle in the human constitution, Calvin is insistent, is an immediate creation of God. He insists upon this, not merely in opposition to the notion that it is no thing at all, but a mere " breath " or " power," but with equal strenuousness in opposition to that " diabolical error " which considers the soul a derivative (*traducem*) of the substance of God — seeing that this would make " the divine nature not only subject to change and passions, but to ignorance also, to depraved desires, to weakness and every kind of vice " (I. xv. 5) . . . " rending the essence of the Creator that every one may possess a part of it." No, says he, " it is to be held as certain that souls are created " and

---

[156] Cf. the remarks of Talma, as cited, p. 35: " But still all men, according to Calvin too, have a certain sense of their immortality. By their alienation from the Father of lights, the light in men is not so wholly extinguished that they are incapable of this sense. . . ." Talma sums up: " It is very certain that Calvin has not fully and finally proved the existence and immortality of the human soul. But this is not his purpose. His object was not so much to refute the error of those who denied these two things, as to strengthen his believing readers in their faith. And for this end the popular presentation of the grounds on which the two things rest was sufficient." On the difference between the human soul and the souls of animals according to Calvin, see Talma, p. 36.

" creation is not transfusion of essence, but the origination of it from nothing " (§ 5). This " origination of the soul out of nothing," which alone can be called " creation," he insists on, again, not merely with reference to the origin of the first soul,[157] but also with reference to every soul which has come into existence since. It is horrible, says he, that it should be thrown into doubt by men who call themselves Christians, whether the souls of men are a true created substance.[158] Calvin's doctrine of the creation of the soul is thrown up into contrast, therefore, on the one side with his view that all else which was brought into being during the creative week, after the primal creation of the indigested mass of the world-stuff on the first day, was proximately the product of second causes; and on the other side, with his belief in the production of the body by ordinary generation in the case of all the descendants of Adam. The soul of the first man stands out as an exception in the midst of mediately produced effects, as the one product of God's direct creative power in the process of the perfecting of the creative scheme. And the souls of the descendants of this first man stand out in contrast with their bodily forms, as in every case also products of God's direct creative activity. In creating souls (*in creandis animabus*), he says, " God does not use the instrumentality of man (*non adhibet hominum operam*)." [159] " There is no need," he says again, " to resort to that old figment of some (*figmentum*), that souls come into being (*oriantur*) *ex traduce*." [160] " We have not come of the race of Adam," he says yet again, " except as regards the body." [161] And not only does he thus over and over again through his writings sharply assert creationism as over against traducian-

---

[157] Cf. e.g. Commentary on Mal. i. 2–6 (*Opp.* xliv. 401): " Moses understands that man's soul was created from nothing. We are born by generation, and yet our origin is clay, and the chief thing in us, the soul, is created from nothing."

[158] *Opp.* vii. 180.

[159] On Heb. xii. 9.

[160] On Gen. iii. 6 (*Opp.* xxiii. 62).

[161] Sermon on Job xiv. 4 (*Opp.* xxxiii. 660).

ism, but he devotes a whole section of the " Institutes " to the question and formally rejects the whole traducian conception.[162]

In its nature, as we have seen, this " immortal and yet created essence " which vitalizes and governs the human frame, is defined by Calvin as percipient substance, whose very nature it is to move, feel, act, understand; which is, in a word, characteristically sensibility.[163] When we attend to Calvin's conception of the soul from this point of view we are in effect observing his psychology: and, of course, he develops his psychology with his eye primarily upon the nature of man in his state of integrity — or rather, let us say, in his uncorrupted condition (I. xv. 1). " When definitions are to be given," he remarks in another place,[164] " the nature of the soul is accustomed to be considered in its integrity." He develops it also, however, under the influence of a strong desire to be clear and simple. Subtleties in such matters he gladly leaves to the philosophers, whose speculations he has no desire to gainsay as to either their truth or their usefulness; for his purposes, however, which look to building up piety, a simple definition will suffice.[165] It is naturally upon the questions which cluster

[162] II. i. 7. Two subordinate points in Calvin's doctrine of creation may be worth noting here. He remarks in passing while commenting on Numbers xvi. 22 (*Opp.* xxv. 222) that it may be collected from that passage that each man has his separate soul: and that by this " is refuted the prodigious delusion of the Manichaeans that all souls are so infused *ex traduce* by the Spirit of God that there should still be one spirit." He returns often to this. Commenting on Job iii. 16 (*Opp.* xxxiii. 162) he teaches that God breathes the soul into the creature at the moment when it is conceived in its mother's womb.

[163] *Opp.* v. 184: sensus.

[164] " Responsio contra Pighium de Libero Arbitrio " (*Opp.* vi. 285): " It is sufficiently clear that [in Basil's remarks here under consideration] the nature of the soul is considered in its integrity; as it is accustomed to be in giving definitions."

[165] Talma, as cited, p. 43, remarks: " The whole manner in which Calvin deals here (*Inst.,* I. xv. 6) with the . . . faculties of the soul is remarkable. The style loses the liveliness, the progress of thought its regularity; and the whole makes the impression that Calvin did not feel fully at home in this field. . . ." Talma notes that the discussion of the faculties of the soul is not found in the " Institutes " of 1536, but is already very full in

around the Will that Calvin's chief psychological interest focuses. We must, however, leave the whole matter of Calvin's psychology and his doctrine of the Will to another occasion. We must postpone also an exposition of his doctrine of the image of God. A survey of these two topics remains in order to complete our exposition of his doctrine of the creature.

the edition of 1539. (Cf. Doumergue, " Jean Calvin," iv. 1910, p. 109, for Calvin's psychology.)

VI

CALVINISM

CALVINISM [1]

1. MEANING AND USES OF THE TERM

CALVINISM is an ambiguous term in so far as it is currently employed in two or three senses, closely related indeed, and passing insensibly into one another, but of varying latitudes of connotation. Sometimes it designates merely the individual teaching of John Calvin. Sometimes it designates, more broadly, the doctrinal system confessed by that body of Protestant Churches known historically, in distinction from the Lutheran Churches, as " the Reformed Churches " (see " Protestantism "); but also quite commonly called " the Calvinistic Churches " because the greatest scientific exposition of their faith in the Reformation age, and perhaps the most influential of any age, was given by John Calvin. Sometimes it designates, more broadly still, the entire body of conceptions, theological, ethical, philosophical, social, political, which, under the influence of the master mind of John Calvin, raised itself to dominance in the Protestant lands of the post-Reformation age, and has left a permanent mark not only upon the thought of mankind, but upon the life-history of men, the social order of civilized peoples, and even the political organization of states. In the present article, the term will be taken, for obvious reasons, in the second of these senses. Fortunately this is also its central sense; and there is little danger that its other connotations will fall out of mind while attention is concentrated upon this.

On the one hand, John Calvin, though always looked upon by the Reformed Churches as an exponent rather than as the creator of their doctrinal system, has nevertheless been both

[1] From " The New Schaff-Herzog Encyclopedia of Religious Knowledge," edited by Samuel Macauley Jackson, D.D., LL.D., ii. pp. 359–364 (copyright by Funk and Wagnalls Company, New York, 1908).

reverenced as one of their founders, and deferred to as that particular one of their founders to whose formative hand and systematizing talent their doctrinal system has perhaps owed most. In any exposition of the Reformed theology, therefore, the teaching of John Calvin must always take a high, and, indeed, determinative place. On the other hand, although Calvinism has dug a channel through which not merely flows a stream of theologial thought, but also surges a great wave of human life — filling the heart with fresh ideals and conceptions which have revolutionized the conditions of existence — yet its fountain-head lies in its theological system; or rather, to be perfectly exact, one step behind even that, in its religious consciousness. For the roots of Calvinism are planted in a specific religious attitude, out of which is unfolded first a particular theology, from which springs on the one hand a special church organization, and on the other a social order, involving a given political arrangement. The whole outworking of Calvinism in life is thus but the efflorescence of its fundamental religious consciousness, which finds its scientific statement in its theological system.

2. FUNDAMENTAL PRINCIPLE

The exact formulation of the fundamental principle of Calvinism has indeed taxed the acumen of a long series of thinkers for the last hundred years (e.g., Ullmann, Semisch, Hagenbach, Ebrard, Herzog, Schweizer, Baur, Schneckenburger, Güder, Schenkel, Schöberlein, Stahl, Hundeshagen; for a discussion of the several views cf. H. Voigt, " Fundamentaldogmatik," Gotha, 1874, pp. 397–480; W. Hastie, " The Theology of the Reformed Church in its Fundamental Principles," Edinburgh, 1904, pp. 129–177). Perhaps the simplest statement of it is the best: that it lies in a profound apprehension of God in His majesty, with the inevitably accompanying poignant realization of the exact nature of the relation sustained to Him by the creature as such, and particularly by the sinful creature. He who believes in God without reserve, and is determined

that God shall be God to him in all his thinking, feeling, willing — in the entire compass of his life-activities, intellectual,
moral, spiritual, throughout all his individual, social, religious
relations — is, by the force of that strictest of all logic which
presides over the outworking of principles into thought and
life, by the very necessity of the case, a Calvinist. In Calvinism, then, objectively speaking, theism comes to its rights;
subjectively speaking, the religious relation attains its purity;
soteriologically speaking, evangelical religion finds at length its
full expression and its secure stability. Theism comes to its
rights only in a teleological conception of the universe, which
perceives in the entire course of events the orderly outworking of the plan of God, who is the author, preserver, and governor of all things, whose will is consequently the ultimate
cause of all. The religious relation attains its purity only when
an attitude of absolute dependence on God is not merely temporarily assumed in the act, say, of prayer, but is sustained
through all the activities of life, intellectual, emotional, executive. And evangelical religion reaches stability only when the
sinful soul rests in humble, self-emptying trust purely on the
God of grace as the immediate and sole source of all the efficiency which enters into its salvation. And these things are the
formative principles of Calvinism.

3. Relation to Other Systems

The difference between Calvinism and other forms of theistic thought, religious experience, evangelical theology is a
difference not of kind but of degree. Calvinism is not a specific
variety of theism, religion, evangelicalism, set over against
other specific varieties, which along with it constitute these
several genera, and which possess equal rights of existence with
it and make similar claims to perfection, each after its own
kind. It differs from them not as one species differs from other
species; but as a perfectly developed representative differs
from an imperfectly developed representative of the same species. There are not many kinds of theism, religion, evangeli-

calism, among which men are at liberty to choose to suit at will their individual taste or moot their special need, all of which may be presumed to serve each its own specific uses equally worthily. There is but one kind of theism, religion, evangelicalism; and the several constructions laying claim to these names differ from each other not as correlative species of a broader class, but as more or less perfect, or more or less defective, exemplifications of a single species. Calvinism conceives of itself as simply the more pure theism, religion, evangelicalism, superseding as such the less pure. It has no difficulty, therefore, in recognizing the theistic character of all truly theistic thought, the religious note in all actual religious activity, the evangelical quality of all really evangelical faith. It refuses to be set antagonistically over against any of these things, wherever or in whatever degree of imperfection they may be manifested; it claims them in every instance of their emergence as its own, and essays only to point out the way in which they may be given their just place in thought and life. Whoever believes in God; whoever recognizes in the recesses of his soul his utter dependence on God; whoever in all his thought of salvation hears in his heart of hearts the echo of the *soli Deo gloria* of the evangelical profession — by whatever name he may call himself, or by whatever intellectual puzzles his logical understanding may be confused — Calvinism recognizes as implicitly a Calvinist, and as only requiring to permit these fundamental principles — which underlie and give its body to all true religion — to work themselves freely and fully out in thought and feeling and action, to become explicitly a Calvinist.

4. CALVINISM AND LUTHERANISM

It is unfortunate that a great body of the scientific discussion which, since Max Goebel (" Die religiöse Eigenthümlichkeit der lutherischen und der reformirten Kirchen," Bonn, 1837) first clearly posited the problem, has been carried on somewhat vigorously with a view to determining the funda-

mental principle of Calvinism, has sought particularly to bring
out its contrast with some other theological tendency, commonly with the sister Protestant tendency of Lutheranism. Undoubtedly somewhat different spirits inform Calvinism and
Lutheranism. And undoubtedly the distinguishing spirit of
Calvinism is rooted not in some extraneous circumstance of
its antecedents or origin — as, for example, Zwingli's tendency
to intellectualism, or the superior humanistic culture and predilections of Zwingli and Calvin, or the democratic instincts of
the Swiss, or the radical rationalism of the Reformed leaders
as distinguished from the merely modified traditionalism of
the Lutherans — but in its formative principle. But it is misleading to find the formative principle of either type of Protestantism in its difference from the other; they have infinitely
more in common than in distinction. And certainly nothing
could be more misleading than to represent them (as is often
done) as owing their differences to their more pure embodiment
respectively of the principle of predestination and that of justification by faith. The doctrine of predestination is not the
formative principle of Calvinism, the root from which it
springs. It is one of its logical consequences, one of the
branches which it has inevitably thrown out. It has been
firmly embraced and consistently proclaimed by Calvinists because it is an implicate of theism, is directly given in the religious consciousness, and is an absolutely essential element in
evangelical religion, without which its central truth of complete dependence upon the free mercy of a saving God can not
be maintained. And so little is it a peculiarity of the Reformed
theology, that it underlay and gave its form and power to the
whole Reformation movement; which was, as from the spiritual point of view, a great revival of religion, so, from the doctrinal point of view, a great revival of Augustinianism. There
was accordingly no difference among the Reformers on this
point: Luther and Melanchthon and the compromising Butzer
were no less jealous for absolute predestination than Zwingli
and Calvin. Even Zwingli could not surpass Luther in sharp
and unqualified assertion of it: and it was not Calvin but Me-

lanchthon who gave it a formal place in his primary scientific statement of the elements of the Protestant faith (cf. Schaff, "Creeds," i. 1877, p. 451; E. F. Karl Müller, "Symbolik," Erlangen and Leipzig, 1896, p. 75; C. J. Niemijer, "De Strijd over de Leer der Praedestinatie in de IXde Eeuw," Groningen, 1889, p. 21; H. Voigt, "Fundamentaldogmatik," Gotha, 1874, pp. 469–470). Just as little can the doctrine of justification by faith be represented as specifically Lutheran. Not merely has it from the beginning been a substantial element in the Reformed faith, but it is only among the Reformed that it has retained or can retain its purity, free from the tendency to become a doctrine of justification on account of faith (cf. E. Böhl, "Von der Rechtfertigung durch den Glauben," Leipzig, 1890). Here, too, the difference between the two types of Protestantism is one of degree, not of kind (cf. C. P. Krauth, "The Conservative Reformation and its Theology," Philadelphia, 1872). Lutheranism, the product of a poignant sense of sin, born from the throes of a guilt-burdened soul which can not be stilled until it finds peace in God's decree of justification, is apt to rest in this peace; while Calvinism, the product of an overwhelming vision of God, born from the reflection in the heart of man of the majesty of a God who will not give His glory to another, can not pause until it places the scheme of salvation itself in relation to a complete world-view, in which it becomes subsidiary to the glory of the Lord God Almighty. Calvinism asks with Lutheranism, indeed, that most poignant of all questions, What shall I do to be saved? and answers it as Lutheranism answers it. But the great question which presses upon it is, How shall God be glorified? It is the contemplation of God and zeal for His honor which in it draws out the emotions and absorbs endeavor; and the end of human as of all other existence, of salvation as of all other attainment, is to it the glory of the Lord of all. Full justice is done in it to the scheme of redemption and the experience of salvation, because full justice is done in it to religion itself which underlies these elements of it. It begins, it centers, it ends with the vision of God in His glory: and it sets itself before all things to render to God His rights in every sphere of life-activity.

5. SOTERIOLOGY OF CALVINISM

One of the consequences flowing from this fundamental attitude of Calvinistic feeling and thought is the high supernaturalism which informs alike its religious consciousness and its doctrinal construction. Calvinism would not be badly defined, indeed, as the tendency which is determined to do justice to the immediately supernatural, as in the first, so also in the second creation. The strength and purity of its belief in the supernatural Fact (which is God) saves it from all embarrassment in the face of the supernatural act (which is miracle). In everything which enters into the process of redemption it is impelled by the force of its first principle to place the initiative in God. A supernatural revelation, in which God makes known to man His will and His purposes of grace; a supernatural record of this revelation in a supernaturally given book, in which God gives His revelation permanency and extension — such things are to the Calvinist almost matters of course. And, above all, he can but insist with the utmost strenuousness on the immediate supernaturalness of the actual work of redemption itself, and that no less in its application than in its impetration. Thus it comes about that the doctrine of monergistic regeneration — or as it was phrased by the older theologians, of " irresistible grace " or " effectual calling " — is the hinge of the Calvinistic soteriology, and lies much more deeply embedded in the system than the doctrine of predestination itself which is popularly looked upon as its hall-mark. Indeed, the soteriological significance of predestination to the Calvinist consists in the safeguard it affords to monergistic regeneration — to purely supernatural salvation. What lies at the heart of his soteriology is the absolute exclusion of the creaturely element in the initiation of the saving process, that so the pure grace of God may be magnified. Only so could he express his sense of man's complete dependence as sinner on the free mercy of a saving God; or extrude the evil leaven of Synergism (q.v.) by which, as he clearly sees, God is robbed of His glory and man is encouraged to think that he owes to some power, some act of choice, some initiative of his own, his participation in that salvation which is in reality all of grace. There is accordingly nothing against which Calvinism sets its face with more firmness than every form and degree of autosoterism. Above everything else, it is determined that God, in His Son Jesus Christ, acting through the Holy Spirit whom He has sent, shall be recognized as our veritable Saviour. To it sinful man stands in need not of inducements or assistance to save himself, but of actual saving; and Jesus Christ has come not to advise, or urge, or induce, or aid him to save himself, but to save him. This is the root of Calvinistic soteriology; and it is because this deep sense of human helplessness and this profound consciousness of indebtedness for all that enters into salvation to the free grace of God is the root of its soteriology that to it the doctrine of election becomes the *cor cordis* of the Gospel. He who knows that it is God who has chosen him and not he who has chosen God, and that he owes his entire salvation in all its processes and in every one of its stages to this choice of God, would be an ingrate indeed if he gave not the glory of his salvation solely to the inexplicable elective love of God.

6. Consistent Development of Calvinism

Historically the Reformed theology finds its origin in the reforming movement begun in Switzerland under the leadership of Zwingli (1516). Its fundamental principles are already present in Zwingli's teaching, though it was not until Calvin's profound and penetrating genius was called to their exposition that they took their ultimate form or received systematic development. From Switzerland Calvinism spread outward to France, and along the Rhine through Germany to Holland, eastward to Bohemia and Hungary, and westward, across the Channel, to Great Britain. In this broad expansion through so many lands its voice was raised in a multitude of confessions; and in the course of the four hundred years which have elapsed since its first formulation, it has been expounded in a vast body of dogmatic treatises. Its development has naturally been much richer and far more many-sided than that of the sister system of Lutheranism in its more confined and homogeneous environment; and yet it has retained its distinctive character and preserved its fundamental features with marvelous consistency throughout its entire history. It may be possible to distinguish among the Reformed confessions, between those which bear more and those which bear less strongly the stamp of Calvin's personal influence; and they part into two broad classes, according as they were composed before or after the Arminian defection (*ca.* 1618) and demanded sharper definitions on the points of controversy raised by that movement (see "Arminius, Jacobus, and Arminianism"; "Remonstrants"). A few of them written on German soil also bear traces of the influence of Lutheran conceptions. And, of course, no more among the Reformed than elsewhere have all the professed expounders of the system of doctrine been true to the faith they professed to expound. Nevertheless, it is precisely the same system of truth which is embodied in all the great historic Reformed confessions; it matters not whether the document emanates from Zurich or Bern or Basel or Geneva, whether it sums up the Swiss development as in the second Helvetic Confession, or publishes the faith of the National Reformed Churches of France, or Scotland, or Holland, or the Palatinate, or Hungary, Poland, Bohemia, or England; or republishes the established Reformed doctrine in opposition to new contradictions, as in the Canons of Dort (in which the entire Reformed world concurred), or the Westminster Confession (to which the whole of Puritan Britain gave its assent), or the Swiss Form of Consent (which represents the mature judgment of Switzerland upon the recently proposed novelties of doctrine). And despite the inevitable variety of individual points of view, as well as the unavoidable differences in ability, learning, grasp, in the multitude of writers who have sought to expound the Reformed faith through these four centuries — and the grave departures from that faith made here and there among them — the great stream of Reformed dogmatics has flowed essentially unsullied, straight from its origin in Zwingli and Calvin to its debouchure, say, in Chalmers and Cunningham and Crawford, in Hodge and Thornwell and Shedd.

7. Varieties of Calvinism

It is true an attempt has been made to distinguish two types of Reformed teaching from the beginning; a more radical type developed under the influence of the peculiar teachings of Calvin, and a (so-called) more moderate type, chiefly propagating itself in Germany, which exhibits rather the influence, as was at first said (Hofstede de Groot, Ebrard, Heppe), of Melanchthon, or, in its more recent statement (Gooszen), of Bullinger. In all that concerns the essence of Calvinism, however, there was no difference between Bullinger and Calvin, German and Swiss: the Heidelberg Catechism is no doubt a catechism and not a confession, but in its presuppositions and inculcations it is as purely Calvinistic as the Genevan Catechism or the catechisms of the Westminster Assembly. Nor was the substance of doctrine touched by the peculiarities of method which marked such schools as the so-called Scholastics (showing themselves already in Zanchius, d. 1590, and culminating in theologians like Alsted, d. 1638, and Voetius, d. 1676); or by the special modes of statement which were developed by such schools as the so-called Federalists (e.g., Cocceius, d. 1669, Burman, d. 1679, Wittsius, d. 1708; cf. Diestel, "Studien zur Föderaltheologie," in *Jahrbücher für deutsche Theologie*, x. 1865, pp. 209–276; G. Vos, "De Verbondsleer in de Gereformeerde Theologie," Grand Rapids, 1891; W. Hastie, "The Theology of the Reformed Church," Edinburgh, 1904, pp. 189–210). The first serious defection from the fundamental conceptions of the Reformed system came with the rise of Arminianism in the early years of the seventeenth century (Arminius, Uytenbogaert, Episcopius, Limborch, Curcellæus); and the Arminian party was quickly sloughed off under the condemnation of the whole Reformed world. The five points of its "Remonstrance" against the Calvinistic system (see "Remonstrants ") were met by the reassertion of the fundamental doctrines of absolute predestination, particular redemption, total depravity, irresistible grace, and the perseverance of the saints (Canons of the Synod of Dort). The first important modification of the Calvinistic system which has retained a position within its limits was made in the middle of the seventeenth century by the professors of the French school at Saumur, and is hence called Salmurianism; otherwise Amyraldism, or hypothetical universalism (Cameron, d. 1625, Amyraut, d. 1664, Placæus, d. 1655, Testardus, d. *ca.* 1650; see " Amyraut, Moïse "). This modification also received the condemnation of the contemporary Reformed world, which reasserted with emphasis the importance of the doctrine that Christ actually saves by His spirit all for whom He offers the sacrifice of His blood (e.g., Westminster Confession, Swiss Form of Consent).

8. Supralapsarianism and Infralapsarianism

If " varieties of Calvinism " are to be spoken of with reference to anything more than details, of importance in themselves no doubt, but of little significance for the systematic development of the type of doctrine, there seem not more than three which require mention: supralapsarianism, infralapsarianism, and what may perhaps be called in this reference, postredemptionism; all of which (as indeed their very names import) take their start from a fundamental agreement in the principles which govern the system. The difference between these various tendencies of thought within the limits of the system turns on the place given by each to the decree of election, in the logical ordering of the " decrees of God." The supralapsarians suppose that election underlies the decree of the fall itself; and conceive the decree of the fall as a means for carrying out the decree of election. The infralapsarians, on the other hand, consider that election presupposes the decree of the fall, and hold, therefore, that in electing some to life God has mankind as a *massa perditionis* in mind. The extent of the

difference between these parties is often, indeed usually, grossly
exaggerated: and even historians of repute are found repre
senting infralapsarianism as involving, or at least permitting,
denial that the fall has a place in the decree of God at all: as if
election could be postposited in the *ordo decretorum* to the de-
decree of the fall, while it was doubted whether there were any
decree of the fall; or as if indeed God could be held to conceive men, in His electing decree, as fallen, without by that
very act fixing the presupposed fall in His eternal decree. In
point of fact there is and can be no difference among Calvinists
as to the inclusion of the fall in the decree of God: to doubt
this inclusion is to place oneself at once at variance with the
fundamental Calvinistic principle which conceives all that
comes to pass teleologically and ascribes everything that actu-

9. POSTREDEMPTIONISM

ally occurs ultimately to the will of God. Accordingly even the
postredemptionists (that is to say the Salmurians or Amyraldians) find no difficulty at this point. Their peculiarity consists
in insisting that election succeeds, in the order of thought, not
merely the decree of the fall but that of redemption as well,
taking the term redemption here in the narrower sense of the
impetration of redemption by Christ. They thus suppose that
in His electing decree God conceived man not merely as fallen
but as already redeemed. This involves a modified doctrine of
the atonement from which the party has received the name
of Hypothetical Universalism, holding as it does that Christ
died to make satisfaction for the sins of all men without exception *if* — if, that is, they believe: but that, foreseeing that
none would believe, God elected some to be granted faith
through the effectual operation of the Holy Spirit. The indifferent standing of the postredemptionists in historical Calvinism is indicated by the treatment accorded it in the historical
confessions. It alone of the " varieties of Calvinism " here mentioned has been made the object of formal confessional condemnation; and it received condemnation in every important

Reformed confession written after its development. There are, it is true, no supralapsarian confessions: many, however, leave the questions which divide supralapsarian and infralapsarian wholly to one side and thus avoid pronouncing for either; and none is polemically directed against supralapsarianism. On the other hand, not only does no confession close the door to infralapsarianism, but a considerable number explicitly teach infralapsarianism which thus emerges as the typical form of Calvinism. That, despite its confessional condemnation, postredemptionism has remained a recognized form of Calvinism and has worked out a history for itself in the Calvinistic Churches (especially in America) may be taken as evidence that its advocates, while departing, in some important particulars, from typical Calvinism, have nevertheless remained, in the main, true to the fundamental postulates of the system. There is another variety of postredemptionism, however, of which this can scarcely be said. This variety, which became dominant among the New England Congregationalist churches about the second third of the nineteenth century (e.g., N. W. Taylor, d. 1858; C. G. Finney, d. 1875; E. A. Park, d. 1900; see "New England Theology"), attempted, much after the manner of the "Congruists" of the Church of Rome, to unite a Pelagian doctrine of the will with the Calvinistic doctrine of absolute predestination. The result was, of course, to destroy the Calvinistic doctrine of "irresistible grace," and as the Calvinistic doctrine of the "satisfaction of Christ" was also set aside in favor of the Grotian or governmental theory of atonement, little was left of Calvinism except the bare doctrine of predestination. Perhaps it is not strange, therefore, that this "improved Calvinism" has crumbled away and given place to newer and explicitly anti-Calvinistic constructions of doctrine (cf. Williston Walker, in *AJT*, April, 1906, pp. 204 *sqq.*).

10. Present Fortunes of Calvinism

It must be confessed that the fortunes of Calvinism in general are not at present at their flood. In America, to be sure, the controversies of the earlier half of the nineteenth century compacted a body of Calvinistic thought which gives way but slowly: and the influence of the great theologians who adorned the Churches during that period is still felt (especially Charles Hodge, 1797–1878, Robert J. Breckinridge, 1800–1871, James H. Thornwell, 1812–1862, Henry B. Smith, 1815–1877, W. G. T. Shedd, 1820–1894, Robert L. Dabney, 1820–1898, Archibald Alexander Hodge, 1823–1886). And in Holland recent years have seen a notable revival of the Reformed consciousness, especially among the adherents of the Free Churches, which has been felt as widely as Dutch influence extends, and which is at present represented in Abraham Kuyper and Herman Bavinck, by a theologian of genius and a theologian of erudition worthy of the best Reformed traditions. But it is probable that few " Calvinists without reserve " exist at the moment in French-speaking lands: and those who exist in lands of German speech and Eastern Europe appear to owe their inspiration directly to the teaching of Kohlbrügge. Even in Scotland there has been a remarkable decline in strictness of construction ever since the days of William Cunningham and Thomas J. Crawford (cf. W. Hastie, " The Theology of the Reformed Church," Edinburgh, 1904, p. 228). Nevertheless, it may be contended that the future, as the past, of Christianity itself is bound up with the fortunes of Calvinism. The system of doctrine founded on the idea of God which has been explicated by Calvinism, strikingly remarks W. Hastie (" Theology as Science," Glasgow, 1899, pp. 97–98), " is the only system in which the whole order of the world is brought into a rational unity with the doctrine of grace. . . . It is only with such a universal conception of God, established in a living way, that we can face, with hope of complete conquest, all the spiritual dangers and terrors of our time. . . . But it is deep enough and large enough and divine enough, rightly understood, to confront them and do battle with them all in vindication of the Creator, Preserver, and Governor of the world, and of the Justice and Love of the Divine Personality." See " Five Points of Calvinism."

BIBLIOGRAPHY: The Reformed Confessions have often been collected; the fullest collection is E. F. K. Müller, "Die Bekenntnisschriften der reformierten Kirche," Leipzig, 1903. For English readers the most convenient is Schaff, "Creeds," iii. (i. contains a history of creeds). An older collection is H. A. Niemeyer, "Collectio Confessionum in ecclesiis reformatis publicatarum," Leipzig, 1840. Consult also: M. Schneckenburger, "Vergleichende Darstellung des lutherischen und reformirten Lehrbegriffs," Stuttgart, 1855; G. B. Winer, "Comparative Darstellung des Lehrbegriffs der verschiedenen christlichen Kirchenparteien," Leipzig, 1837 (ed. 2) and 1882 (ed. 4), English translation, Edinburgh, 1873; and the various works on Symbolics, especially E. F. K. Müller, "Symbolik," Erlangen and Leipzig, 1896. Attempts more or less successful have been made to present the Reformed system from the writings of its representative theologians. For examples of these consult: A. Schweizer, "Die Glaubenslehre der evangelischreformirten Kirche," 2 vols., Zurich, 1844–1847; J. H. Scholten, "De Leer der Hervormde Kerk in hare Grondbeginselen," 2 vols., Leiden, ed. 4, 1870; H. Heppe, "Die Dogmatik der evangelisch-reformirten Kirche," Elberfeld, 1861; cf. B. de Moor, "Commentarius perpetuus in Johannis Marckii compendium theologiæ christianæ," 7 vols., Leyden, 1761–1774.

For the "principle" of Calvinism consult: H. Voigt, "Fundamentaldogmatik," pp. 397–480, Gotha, 1874; W. Hastie, "The Theology of the Reformed Church in its Fundamental Principles," Edinburgh, 1904; cf. Scholten and Schneckenburger, *ut sup.*, where lists of the literature are given. A good history of the Reformed theology is still a desideratum. Sketches have been given in: W. Gass, "Geschichte der protestantischen Dogmatik," Berlin, 1854–1867; G. Frank, "Geschichte der protestantischen Theologie," 3 vols., Leipzig, 1862–1875; J. A. Dorner, "Geschichte der protestantischen Theologie," Munich, 1867, English translation, 2 vols., Edinburgh, 1871. Contributions have been made by: C. M. Pfaff, "Introductio in historiam theologiæ literariam," i. pp. 258 *sqq.*,

Tübingen, 1724; B. Pictet, "Theologia christiana," 2 parts, Leiden, 1733–1734; J. G. Walch, " Bibliotheca theologica selecta," i. 211 sqq., Jena, 1757–1768; A. Toplady, "Historic Proof of the Doctrinal Calvinism of the Church of England," 2 vols., London, 1774; A. Ypey (Ijpeij), " Beknopte letterkundige Geschiedenis der System. Godgeleerd." (Utrecht?), 1793–1798; A. Schweizer, " Die protestantischen Centraldogmen in ihrer Entwicklung innerhalb der reformirten Kirche," Zurich, 1854; J. H. Scholten, ut sup., i. 67 sqq.; H. Heppe, " Die confessionelle Entwicklung der altprotestantischen Kirche Deutschlands," Marburg, 1854; idem, " Dogmatik des deutschen Protestantismus im sechzehnten Jahrhundert," Gotha, 1857; W. Cunningham, " The Reformers and the Theology of the Reformation," Edinburgh, ed. 2, 1866; idem, " Historical Theology," 2 vols., Edinburgh, ed. 2, 1864; J. H. A. Ebrard, " Christliche Dogmatik," i. 44, Königsberg, 1862; J. Walker, " The Theology and Theologians of Scotland," Edinburgh, 1872; C. Sepp, " Het Godgeleerd Onderwijs in Nederland . . . 16e en 17e eeuw," Leiden, 1873–1874; A. Milroy, in " The Church of Scotland, Past and Present," ed. R. H. Story, London, n.d.; idem, "Scottish Theologians and Preachers, 1610–1638," Edinburgh and London, 1891. Consult also on the general subject: A. Kuyper, " Calvinism," New York, 1898 (an admirable statement, summing up a series of brochures in Dutch); J. A. Froude, " Calvinism," New York, 1871, and in " Short Studies on Great Subjects," second series, New York, 1871; J. L. Girardeau, " Calvinism and Evangelical Arminianism," Columbia, 1890; B. B. Warfield, " The Significance of the Westminster Standards as a Creed," New York, 1898; E. W. Smith, " The Creed of Presbyterians," New York, 1901. Some of the chief Calvinistic dogmatists find mention in the text; a list of the more important is given in Heppe and Schweizer, ut sup., at the beginning. The series may be fairly represented by the following names: Calvin, Ursinus, Zanchius, Polanus, Alsted, Voetius, Burman, Turretin, Heidegger, Van Mastricht. The brief compends of Bucanus ("Institutiones theologicæ," Geneva, 1609), Wollebius ("Compendium

theologiæ," Amsterdam, 1648), Ames (" Medulla theologica,"
Amsterdam, 1656, English translation, London, 1642), and
Marck (" Compendium theologiæ," Amsterdam, 1705) present
the system in briefest form. The more recent theologians are
indicated in the text.

VII

ON THE LITERARY HISTORY OF
CALVIN'S " INSTITUTES "

From an Original Painting

CHRISTIA

NAE RELIGIONIS INSTI-
tutio,totam ferè pietatis summã,& quic
quid est in doctrina salutis cognitu ne-
cessarium, complectens : omnibus pietatis studiosis lectu dignissi-
mum opus,ac re-
cens edi-
tum

PRAEFATIO AD CHRI
stianissimum REGEM FRANCIAE, qua
hic illi pro confessione fidei
offertur.

IOANNE CALVINO
Nouiodunensi autore.

BASILEAE,
M. D. XXXVI.

First Edition of the INSTITUTES — Title Page

ON THE LITERARY HISTORY OF CALVIN'S " INSTITUTES "[1]

JOHN CALVIN was born on the tenth of July, 1509. " The Institutes of the Christian Religion " was thrown off in the first draft in 1534 or 1535, but did not finally leave its author's hands in its definitive edition until a quarter of a century afterwards, in the late summer of 1559. The four hundredth anniversary of Calvin's birth is, therefore, also the three hundred and fiftieth of the completion of the " Institutes," and may be fitly marked by the issue of a new edition of the " Institutes " in English.

Certainly the publication of this great work in its completed shape is well worth commemorating on its own account. It was the first serious attempt to cast into systematic form that body of truth to which the Reformed Churches adhered as taught in the Holy Scriptures; and as such it met a crisis and created an epoch in the history of those Churches. In the immense upheaval of the Reformation movement, the foundations of the faith seemed to many to be broken up, and the most important questions to be set adrift; extravagances of all sorts sprang up on every side; and we can scarcely wonder that a feeling of uneasiness was abroad, and men were asking with concern for some firm standing-ground for their feet. It was Calvin's " Institutes " which, with its calm, clear, positive exposition of the evangelical faith on the irrefragable authority of the Holy Scriptures, gave stability to wavering minds, and confidence to sinking hearts, and placed upon the lips of all a brilliant apology, in the face of the calumnies of the enemies of the Reformation.[2]

[1] From Calvin's "Institutes of the Christian Religion," Allen's translation, memorial edition, 1909; i. pp. i.–xlvi. Reprinted in pamphlet form, 1909, Presbyterian Board of Publication, Philadelphia. (Cf. also *The Presbyterian and Reformed Review,* x. 1899, pp. 193–219.)

[2] Cf. T. M. Lindsay, " A History of the Reformation," New York, 1907,

As the fundamental treatise in the development of a truly evangelical theology its mission has stretched, however, far beyond its own day. All subsequent attempts to state and defend that theology necessarily go back to it as their starting-point, and its impress upon the history of evangelical thinking is ineffaceable. Even from the point of view of mere literature, it holds a position so supreme in its class that every one who would fain know the world's best books, must make himself familiar with it. What Thucydides is among Greek, or Gibbon among eighteenth-century English historians, what Plato is among philosophers, or the Iliad among epics, or Shakespeare among dramatists, that Calvin's " Institutes " is among theological treatises. " The *Institutes* of Calvin," says Dr. William Cunningham, to whom will be conceded the right to an opinion on such a matter, " is the most important work in the history of theological science, that which is more than any other creditable to its author, and has exerted directly or indirectly the greatest and most beneficial influence upon the opinions of intelligent men on theological subjects. It may be said to occupy in the science of theology, the place which it requires both the *Novum Organum* of Bacon and the *Principia* of Newton to fill up in physical science, — at once conveying, though not in formal didactic precepts and rules, the finest idea of the way and manner in which the truths of God's Word ought to be classified and systematized, and at the same time actually classifying and systematizing them, in a way that has not yet received any very material or essential improvement." [3] We should indeed be scarcely flying beyond the mark if we gave enthusiasm itself the reins and adopted as sober criticism the famous distich of the Hungarian reformer and poet, Paul Thuri, which — so the editors of the great Brunswick edition

---

ii. pp. 156–157, 159; and especially the fine pages in F. Buisson, " Sébastien Castellion," 1892, i. pp. 96 *sq.*, on the effect of the publication of this book, " at once an apology, a manifesto and a confession of faith," in 1536.

[3] " The Reformers and the Theology of the Reformation," second edition, 1866, p. 295.

tell us [4] — many of the old owners and readers of the "Institutes" have written lovingly on its front:

> Præter apostolicas post Christi tempora chartas,
> Huic peperere libro sæcula nulla parem.[5]

It is this, in effect, which the greatest scholar of Calvin's own age did — that Joseph Scaliger (1520–1609) whose caustic

[4] "Corpus Reformatorum," xxix.: "Ioannis Calvini Opera," i. Brunswick, 1863, p. xxi. note 1.

[5] This famous distich was first mentioned by Thuri's countryman and fellow-student at the feet of Stephen Szegedinus, Matthew Skaricza, in his "Vita et Obitus Stephani Szegedini," prefixed to Szegedinus' "Loci Communes Theologiæ Sinceræ," published at Basle, 1585, and at least four times subsequently. Skaricza, who was Reformed pastor at Kevi, visited Geneva and wrote before 1571. He tells how, at his request, Beza showed him, "under the simple sod, the grave of the great Calvin, who had commanded that he should be buried thus without any monument" — and, after praising Calvin's doctrine of the Lord's Supper and the general adamantine character of his reasoning, proceeds: "And especially what work was ever more vigorous, more acute, more exact than the *Institutes,* whether it be the language or the matter that you consider and weigh? So that our Paul Thuri has not unjustly said, *Præter,*" etc. Thence probably the distich was derived by Gerdesius ("Scrinium Antiquarium," II. i. 1750, p. 451) and Du Buc ("Institutiones Theologicæ," 1630, præf.). Du Buc, in apologizing for writing, enumerates his predecessors in the field of Protestant dogmatics: such as, he says, the works of those great theologians, Melanchthon, Musculus and Peter Martyr, and "that truly golden *Institutes of the Christian Religion* of John Calvin's concerning which Paul Thuri said most truly, *Præter,*" etc. The essential facts concerning Thuri (one of five of the name who achieved fame in Hungary in the sixteenth century) are summed up in the epitaph written by his son, the learned poet, George Thuri:
> "Thurunum genuit, docuit Viteberga Philippo
> Doctore, ossa tenet Szantovia, Astra animam."
Having studied (1551) at Tur (where there is still a strong Reformed church and a gymnasium) under Szegedinus (whom he calls a second Cicero), and afterward (1553) at Wittenberg, he became a professor at the Reformed School at Tolna (1556–1560), where (1557) he wrote his book, "Idea Christianorum Ungaricorum sub Tyrannide Turcica," which lay in MS. until it was published by Molnár at Oppenheim in 1616. In 1560 he became pastor at Sajo Szent Péter, and finally (after 1565) at Szántó, where he died in 1574 or 1575. While at the former place he engaged in the controversy between the Reformed and Lutherans, and while at the latter in the great controversy with the Unitarians. He enjoyed a high reputation as a poet and is ranked by Lotichius among the best Latin poets of the age. Notices of him are generally accessible

criticisms have made so many scholars writhe. " Oh, what a
good book Calvin's *Institutes* is," he exclaims; " Oh, what a
great man! There is none of the ancients to compare with him.
. . . Calvin stands alone among theologians." [6] And, indeed,
it is none other than this that the Strasburg editors of Calvin's
works have done. Certainly among the most widely learned
and least extravagant of the scholars of our day, they yet do
not scruple to adopt Thuri's expression into the well-weighed
language of their prolegomena, and to repeat it as their deliberate judgment upon the merits of the " Institutes." Among
the other reasons which have led them to devote their time
and labor to an edition of Calvin's works, they tell us, is the
unique preëminence and high authority enjoyed by this Ly-
curgus of the Reformed Churches. They continue:

" For, though Luther was supremely great as a man and Zwingli
was second to none as a Christian citizen, and Melanchthon well deserves the appellation of the most learned of teachers, Calvin may
justly be called the leader and standard-bearer of theologians. For
who will not marvel at his command of language and letters, at his
control of the entire sphere of learning? The abundance of his learning, the admirable disposition of his material, the force and validity of his reasoning in dogmatics, the acuteness and subtlety of
his mind, and the alternating gay and biting saltness of his polemics, the felicitous perspicuity, sobriety and sagacity of his exegetics, the nervous eloquence and freedom of his parænetics, his incomparable legislative prudence and wisdom in the constitution,
ordering and governing of the churches — all this is fully recognized among men of learning and candor. Even among Romish controversialists themselves, there is none to-day possessed of even a
moderate knowledge of these matters or endowed with the least
fairness in judgment, who does not admire the richness of his reasoning and ideas, the precision of his language, the weight and

---

in Bod, " Historia Hungarorum Ecclesiastica " (Lugduni, 1888, i. p. 263) and in
Andr. Schmal, " Adversaria," 1863, p. 125 (in " Monumenta Evangelicorum
Aug. Conf. in Hungaria Historica," ii. 1863).

[6] " Scaligerana," being the second part, with separate pagination, of
" Prima Scaligerana, nusquam antehac edita cum praefatione T. Fabri,"
Groningæ, 1669, p. 41.

clearness of his diction, whether in Latin or French. All these qualities are, of course, present in his other writings, but they are especially striking in that immortal *Institutes of the Christian Religion,*
which beyond all controversy far excels all expositions of the kind
that have been written from the days of the apostles down, including, of course, Melanchthon's *Loci Theologici;* and which captivates
even to-day the learned and candid reader, even though he may be
committed to different opinions, and wrests from him an unwilling
admiration." [7]

So estimating the "Institutes," it is no wonder that these
learned editors wished to begin their edition with this work.
This is how they explain their procedure:

"In undertaking a new collection of the works of John Calvin,
of immortal memory — a body of writings worthy of his great name
— we have determined to begin with the *Institutes of the Christian
Religion.* That work does not, to be sure, hold the first place among
his writings in the order of composition, though very few of them
preceded it: but none of them is superior to it in the fame it enjoys.
It has often happened that a book distinguished by the great applause of men has afterwards fallen into neglect through the harsher
judgment or the careless indifference of a later time; often, too,
that one which reached few minds at first, and almost escaped notice, has, as time proceeded, emerged from obscurity and is daily
celebrated with increasing praise. But with regard to this book, seized
upon from its very cradle with great and widespread avidity, and
scrutinized by its very adversaries with a zeal born of envy,
its glory has abided the same, intact now through three centuries,
without the least diminution or fading, despite the frequent changes
which successive schools of theology have introduced into the treatment of Christian doctrine. If it were the custom of our time, as it
was formerly, to collect at the beginning of volumes eulogies pronounced on their writers by various authors, we could gather here a
great harvest of laudations, and time and paper would fail us
before the material at our disposal would be exhausted." [8]

[7] "Corpus Reformatorum," xxix. ("Calvini Opera," i.), pp. ix. x. Cf. Cunningham, as cited, p. 299.

[8] *Ibid.,* p. xxi. Those who would see the omission of the Strasburg editors
partly supplied may consult Calvin's "Commentary on Joshua" as published
by the Calvin Translation Society, Edinburgh, 1854, pp. 376–464. Compare
Schaff, "History of the Christian Church," vii. 1892, pp. 272–295.

I

One of the marvels connected with this remarkable book is the youth of its author when it was written. It is true we do not know with certainty precisely when it was written. But, as the colophon of the first edition tells us, it was published at Basle in March, 1536, and the Prefatory Letter to the King of France, which was written, as we know, some time after the book itself, is dated on the 23d of the preceding August. In the opening words of this preface, Calvin explicitly declares that when the work was written he had no thought of presenting it to Francis. " When I first put hand to this work," he says, " nothing was less in my thoughts, most illustrious king, than to write a book which should be presented to your Majesty. My intention was only to inculcate some elementary truths, by which those interested in religion might be trained to true piety — and at this task I toiled chiefly for our French, multitudes of whom I saw to be hungering and thirsting after Christ, but very few to be possessed of even a slight knowledge of Him. That this was my purpose, the book itself shows by its simple and elementary manner of teaching." It would seem natural to suppose, therefore, that the book was composed some weeks or possibly even months before the middle of 1535 — perhaps even in 1534.

There are not lacking some further considerations which support this supposition. A direct statement to this effect is made, indeed, by an almost contemporary author — Florimond de Raemond (1540–1602), counsellor of the Parlement of Bordeaux, who wrote from the Romish point of view a " Histoire de la naissance, progrez et decadence de l' hérésie de ce siècle " (Paris, 1605, and again 1623). His statements are, to be sure, scarcely worthy of credence when unsupported; but when, as in the present case, they are corroborative of what is otherwise probable, they may be worth attention. He represents Calvin as, on leaving Paris, sojourning three years at Angoulême — a manifest error [9] — and continues as follows:

[9] Cf. Schaff, " History of the Christian Church," vii. 1892, p. 323, note 2.

" Angoulême was the forge where this new Vulcan beat out the strange opinions which he afterwards published; for it was there that he wove to the astonishment of Christendom the fabric of his *Institutes,* which may be called the Koran or rather the Talmud of Heresy, being, as it is, a mass of all the errors that have ever existed in the past, or ever will exist, I verily believe, in the future. . . . He was commonly called the Greek of Claix, from the name of his patron, the curé of Claix, because he made a constant parade of his Greek, without, to be sure, knowing very much of it. . . . This Greek of Claix, then, held in high esteem and reputation, and loved by all who loved letters, would weave into his speech remarks about religion and continually drop piquant words against the authority and traditions of the church. He enjoyed the favor of many persons of authority, especially of Anthony Chaillou, Prior of Bouteville, who has since been called the Pope of the Lutherans, and of the Abbé de Bassac, two men of letters, eager to gather together all the good books they could meet with, and of the Sieur de Torsac, brother of President la Place, who afterwards became the historian of Calvinism. Calvin was often with these two, in the company of du Tillet also. Their rendezvous was in a house outside the town of Angoulême, named Girac, where the Prior of Bouteville ordinarily made his dwelling. There he entertained them with the sketches for his *Institutes,* laying open to them all the secrets of his theology, and read to them the chapters of his book as he composed them, laboring so assiduously on it that he often passed entire nights without sleeping and whole days without eating. It is a pleasure to me to follow step by step the course of this man fatal to our France, and to touch upon all the details of his training, because no one has written it down before. And as I have taken the trouble to inform myself of the truth, I make no complaint of the trouble of writing it." [10]

This picture of Calvin working out his treatise in his retirement at Angoulême seems rather overdrawn. It is quite clear, moreover, not only that the author has wrongly given to Angoulême the whole three years that extended between Calvin's flight from Paris late in 1533 and his arrival in Geneva late in July, 1536, but also that he has in mind the " Institutes," not

[10] Pp. 883 *sq.* of book cited, ed. of 1623, as extracted by Reuss, " Calvini Opera," iii. p. xii.

as first published in the spring of 1536, but in the elaborated form which it took only later. That the book may have been written at Angoulême, where Calvin seems to have spent the greater part of the year from the autumn of 1533 to the autumn of 1534, in the house of his wealthy friend, Louis du Tillet, is in itself, however, certainly possible. And such a supposition may account for Beza's placing it, in the chronological list of Calvin's works which he published immediately after Calvin's death, directly after his first work, the commentary on Seneca's " De clementia," which was published in April, 1532, and before his next book, the " Psychopannychia," which was written in 1534.[11] It may, indeed, be said that Beza was certainly laboring under a misapprehension as to the date of the *publication* of the " Institutes," and that it is due to this error that he so places it in his catalogue, and not to the influence of knowledge on his part that the book was *written* earlier than the date of its publication. He certainly says in the first edition of his " Life of Calvin " that Calvin " left France in 1534, and had his first *Institutes* printed *that same year* at Basle, as an apology addressed to King Francis, first of the name, in behalf of the poor persecuted believers upon whom the name of Anabaptists was imposed in order to excuse the persecution of the Gospel in the eyes of the Protestant princes." And he was certainly wrong in so saying — as is evident, were there nothing else to show it, from the fact that the persecutions in question did not begin until early in 1535. Nevertheless, it is not clear that knowledge on Beza's part that the " Institutes " was *written* in 1534 may not be rather the cause of his error here as to the date of its publication; an error of which he seems subsequently to have become aware, as he suppressed the whole passage in the second edition of his book.[12]

Whatever support may come from these doubtful passages, however, the main ground for supposing that the " Institutes "

[11] The " Psychopannychia " was written in Orleans in 1534, but not published until 1542; see Reuss, " Calvini Opera," xb. 38; Doumergue, " Jean Calvin," i. 1899, pp. 466, 584, etc.; W. Walker, " John Calvin," 1906, p. 123.

[12] For this whole matter see Reuss, " Calvini Opera," iii. p. xvii.; Doumergue, " Jean Calvin," i. 1899, p. 593.

was composed at some point earlier than the middle of 1535, when the Introductory Epistle was written, must be drawn from the pointed discrimination that is made by both Calvin and Beza between the writing and the publishing of the book — as determined by wholly different motives, arising out of changing circumstances, and, therefore, arguing different times. As we have seen, this is plainly asserted in the opening words of the Epistle itself, where his motives in *writing* his " Institutes " are declared by Calvin himself. This account is supplemented by the full account of his motives in *publishing* the book, given in that precious autobiographical fragment which is included in the Preface to his Commentary on the Psalms. It will be wise to have this pretty fully before us, as it will be of use in the discussion of more than one point in the history of the " Institutes."

" Leaving my native country, France," says Calvin, " I in fact retired into Germany, expressly for the purpose of being able there to enjoy in some obscure corner the repose which I had always desired, and which had been so long denied me. But lo! whilst I lay hidden at Basle, and known only to a few people, many faithful and holy persons were burnt alive in France; and the report of these burnings having reached foreign nations, they excited the strongest disapprobation among a great part of the Germans, whose indignation was kindled against the authors of such tyranny. In order to allay this indignation, certain wicked and lying pamphlets were circulated, stating that none were treated with such cruelty but Anabaptists and seditious persons, who, by their perverse ravings and false opinions, were overthrowing not only religion, but also all civil order. Observing that the object which these instruments of the court aimed at by their disguises was not only that the disgrace of shedding so much innocent blood might remain buried under the false charges and calumnies which they brought against the holy martyrs after their death, but also that afterwards they might be able to proceed to the utmost extremity in murdering the poor saints without exciting compassion toward them in the breasts of any, it appeared to me, that unless I opposed them to the uttermost of my ability, my silence could not be vindicated from the charge of cowardice and treachery. This was the consideration which induced me to publish my *Institutes of the Christian Religion*. My objects were, first, to prove that these reports were false and calumnious, and thus to vindicate my brethren, whose death was precious in the sight of the Lord; and next, that as the same cruelties might very soon after be exercised against many unhappy individuals, foreign nations might be touched with at least some compassion toward them and solicitude about them. When it was then published, it was not that copious and labored work which it now is, but only a small treatise, containing a summary of the principal truths of the Christian religion; and it was published with no other design than that men might know what was the faith held by those whom I saw basely and wickedly defamed by those flagitious and perfidious flatterers. That my object was not to acquire fame, appeared from this, that immediately afterwards I left Basle, and particularly from that fact that nobody there knew that I was the author. Wherever else I have gone, I have taken care to conceal that I was the author of that performance; and I had resolved to continue in the same privacy and obscurity, until at length William Farel detained me at Geneva, not so much by counsel and exhortation, as by a dreadful imprecation, which I felt to be as if God had from heaven laid His mighty hand upon me to arrest me." [13]

The plain implication of this passage is that Calvin had the manuscript of his " Institutes " by him, and was led to publish it as an apologetical document by the malignant aspersions on the character of the saints slain in France as if they were a body of mere fanatics; by reading it the world would know the sort of doctrine held by the French martyrs. How long he had had it by him we have no means of certainly divining; but the persecutions in France had begun early in 1535, and it does not seem as if the book could have been so spoken of if it had been written subsequently to this. Whether, however, it was written in Angoulême in 1534 or in Basle in 1535 makes little difference. Calvin was born July 10, 1509. His dedicatory letter to Francis I is dated August 23, 1535 — twenty-six years afterwards. The " Institutes " was beyond question written, then, before he had completed his twenty-sixth year, and pos-

[13] Calvin Society translation, i. 1845, pp. xli. xlii.

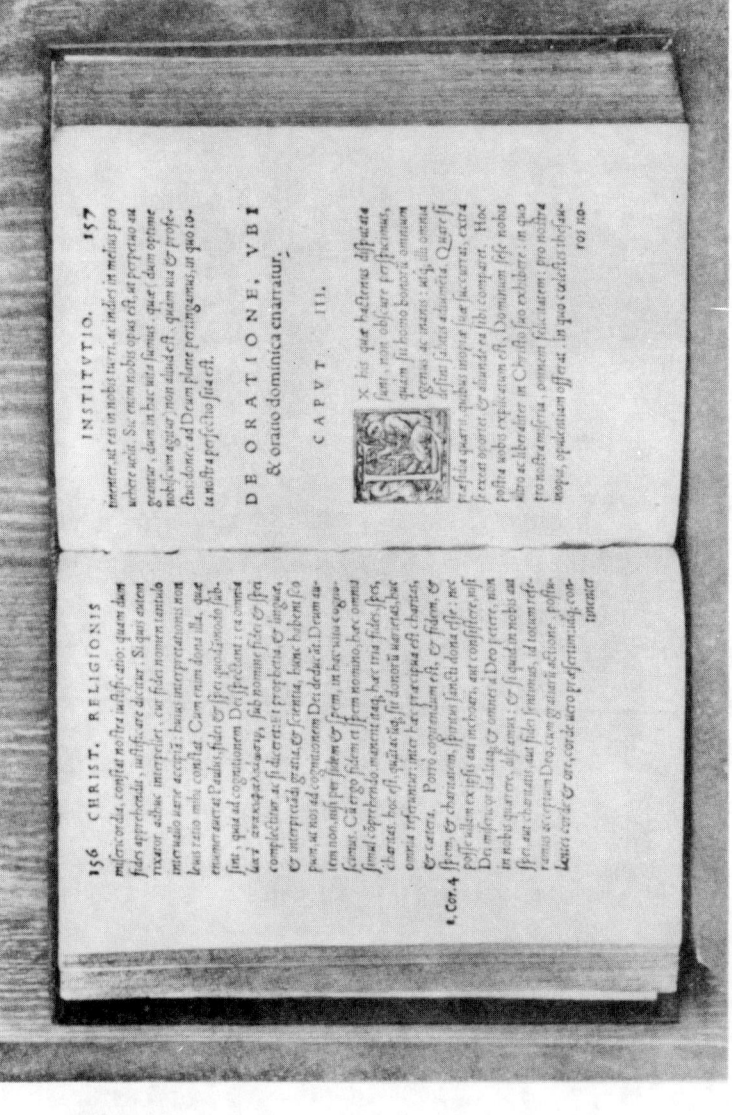

First Edition of the Institutes — Specimen Page

sibly before he had completed his twenty-fifth year. It was in the hands of the public before he had completed his twenty-seventh year.

II

In estimating the nature of this performance, there are two other facts which we should take into consideration, one of an enhancing, the other of a moderating character. We must bear in mind, on the one hand, that the young Calvin's book had practically no predecessors, but broke out a new path for itself; but also, on the other hand, that when it was first given to the public it was far from being the complete treatise in dogmatic theology which we know, but was, as he himself describes it, in the extract already quoted from the Preface to his Commentary on the Psalms, doubtless with some exaggeration of its unimportance, not " densum hoc et laboriosum opus, quale nunc exstat, sed breve duntaxat enchiridion " — " seulement un petit livret contenant sommairement les principales matieres " — " a brief handbook," a " little booklet." From that small beginning it grew under his hand from edition to edition, and was transformed from a short handbook on religion for the people into a scientific treatise in dogmatic theology for students of theology.

When we say it had " practically no predecessors," we do not mean to obscure the fact that before it certain attempts had been made to set forth the fundamental articles of the Christian religion as the Protestants conceived them. As a matter of fact, Calvin's " Institutes " was preceded by three such earlier attempts, two of which at least were of considerable importance. The very nature of the Reformed movement imposed on the Protestant party the necessity of giving a definite account of itself. As Reuss admirably puts it,[14] such a declaration of principles was necessary in the face of adversaries armed with an authority consecrated by ten centuries, and charging the new movement with blasphemy, with the de-

---

[14] " Calvini Opera," iii. pp. vii. *sq.*, from which the substance of this whole paragraph is derived.

struction of all order, human and divine, with the overthrow
of the whole social fabric; it was necessary in the face of troubled friends who gave the reform their sympathy, but were
frightened at the uproar it caused and the very efforts which
were required to sustain it; it was necessary, above all, in the
face of the radical party which always accompanies the advance
of the great movements which agitate humanity, and is always
ready to compromise the good cause and to alienate those who
judge things according to their first results. It was inevitable,
therefore, that even the very first steps of the Reformation
should produce attempts to state in some methodical way the
recovered truths of the Gospel.

The first Protestant Dogmatics accordingly saw the light
scarcely four years after Luther nailed up his theses on indulgences (1521). It did not, indeed, come from the hand of
Luther himself; but it came from the hand of his chief helper
in the Gospel, the saintly and learned Melanchthon. Thus,
as Reuss says, " the first attempt to formulate the evangelical
doctrine according to the methods of the schools was the work
of a young professor of the humanities scarcely twenty-three
years old, who by this publication laid the foundations of
Lutheran dogmatics and impressed on them the direction which
they did not cease to follow for a whole century." The " Loci
Theologici " of Melanchthon in its first form scarcely exceeded
in size one of our catechisms, and, owing its composition to a
course of lectures on the Epistle to the Romans given to a private class, followed in its order the emergence of the topics in
that epistle, and thus lacked all systematic arrangement.[15] But
it was written in a classic style of great simplicity, which de-

[15] Cf. Dr. William Cunningham, " Reformers," etc., ed. 2, 1866, pp. 295–296:
" The first edition of Melanchthon's *Commonplaces* — the only one published before Calvin produced the first edition of his *Institutes* — was not to
be compared to Calvin's work, in the accuracy of its representation of the doctrines of Scripture, in the fulness and completeness of its materials, or in the
skill and ability with which they were digested and arranged: and in the
subsequent editions, while the inaccuracy of its statements increased in some
respects rather than diminished, it still continued, to a considerable extent, a
defective and ill-digested work, characterized by a good deal of prolixity and
wearisome repetition."

served its great popularity, and was gradually wrought by its author into an ever-improving arrangement of topics. Four years after the publication of Melanchthon's "Loci Theologici," the far better ordered and more penetrating work of Zwingli appeared (1525), entitled "Commentarius de vera et falsa religione," written at the solicitation of the Italian and French refugees, and, like Calvin's "Institutes," introduced with a noble dedicatory letter to Francis I. Of much less importance than either of these is the manual of William Farel — the first theological treatise written in the French language — entitled "Sommaire briefue declaration daucuns lieux fort necessaires a ung chascun Chrestien pour mettre sa confiance en Dieu et ayder son prochain," etc., a treatise distinguished by simplicity of language, a truly Biblical popularity, and a pervasive application to the Christian life.[16] Whether Calvin was acquainted with these works or not, we have no direct evidence to show. It may be assumed. But in any event he wrote with independence, and with an unexcelled command of this special field which showed itself ever greater with each new edition.

Were indeed the comparison with his predecessors made only with the first edition of Calvin's "Institutes," his superiority, though marked, would be less great. But the first edition of the "Institutes" was, as we have said, only the first stage in a development,[17] and was a less satisfactory stage to

---

[16] Farel's "Sommaire" was published first in 1524, an edition no exemplar of which remains: the second edition was published in 1534, and has been reprinted by Baum in 1867.

[17] On the editions of the "Institutes" published during Calvin's life, see Reuss, "Calvini Opera," i. p. xxii. and iii. p. xxviii. In the former place, he says: "Ten times in all, so far as we know, the *Institutes* came from the press in its Latin form during the author's life, first at Basle, then at Strasburg and Geneva. These editions differ among themselves variously and may be distributed into three families, or, as one would say to-day, recensions. In the first of these we place only the *Princeps*, published ' per Thomam Platterum et Baltharsarem Lasium,' at Basle, in 1536. The second is represented by six issues "— belonging certainly together, but distributed into three subfamilies, viz., (1) 1539, (2) 1543 and 1545, (3) 1550, 1553, 1554. The third family is introduced by Stevens' second edition, that of 1559, mere copies of which are the two editions of 1561. In the latter place Reuss presents this same classification

its author than to any of his readers. He himself speaks almost with contempt of his own production. In the Preface to the second edition, which was published in 1539, he says: " In the first edition of this work of ours, because I had not the least expectation of that success which God in His goodness has given it, I had, for the greater part, performed my office perfunctorily, as is customary in trivial undertakings (*in minutis operibus*)." Accordingly the title of this second edition, on which he had bestowed much labor and for the late appearance of which he apologizes, is made to run: " Institutio Christianae Religionis nvnc uere demum suo titulo respondens." In it the text is swelled to something more than double its original bulk; and its character is so changed that the reworked volume is put forth as a totally new book with a different purpose from that had in view when it was first composed. The book was *written,* as we are told in the Dedicatory Letter to Francis I, solely to supply rudimentary instruction in religion to the neglected multitudes, and was, therefore, " composed in a simple and elementary form, suitable for instruction." It was *published,* as we are told in the Preface to the Psalms, to exhibit to the world what the French Protestants really believed, and to render incredible the calumnies by which their judicial murder was excused. It was now *revised* or rather *elaborated,* in order to fit it to be a text-book in theology. " I may add," continues Calvin in his Preface, " that my object in this labor " of reworking the " Institutes " " was this: so to prepare and train candidates in sound theology for the reading of the divine Word that they might both have an easy introduction to it and proceed in it with unfaltering step, seeing I have endeavored to give such a summary of religion in all its parts, and have digested it into such an order as to make it not difficult for any one who is rightly acquainted with it, to ascertain what he ought properly to look for in Scripture, and also to what head he ought to refer whatever is contained in it." In other words, Calvin now designed his " Institutes " to be a doctrinal intro-

---

in tabular form, adding the editions of the French version in their places. See below, pp. 387-388; also pp. 392-394.

duction to the study of the Scriptures; and he goes on to explain that the fact that this book was accessible would enable him, when commenting on Scripture, to pass over doctrinal points without long discussion. To this conception he kept, throughout the labor of subsequent revision. For not even the enlarged "Institutes" of 1539 satisfied him. Six additional revisions were made by him before what we may call the definitive edition of 1559 was reached. In this the "Institutes" appears not only once more doubled in length — now about five times the size of the "booklet" of 1536 [18] — but entirely altered in arrangement, and presenting, at last, that excellent disposition of its material in which it has come down to us, and by which it has won the unalloyed admiration of subsequent ages.[19]

In the Preface to this edition, Calvin, speaking of the labor he had expended in bringing the book as first published to a worthier form, says: " This I attempted not only in the second edition, but in every subsequent one the work has received some improvement. But though I do not regret the labor previously expended, I never felt satisfied until the work was arranged in the order in which it now appears." On the title-page, accordingly, we read: " Institutio Christianae Religionis, in libros quatuor nunc primum digesta, certisque distincta capitibus ad aptissimam methodum: aucta etiam tam magna accessione ut propemodum opus novum haberi possit." The first edition was divided into six chapters — on the Law, Faith, Prayer, the Sacraments, Spurious Sacraments and Christian

[18] In the Brunswick edition the "Institutes" of 1536 occupies about 220 columns; the edition of 1559 about 1086.

[19] Even the Jesuit, Cornelis Schultingh (1540–1604), says ("Bibliotheca Catholica contra Calvinianam theologiam," 1602; cf. Gerdes, "Scrinium Antiquarium," II. i. 1750, pp. 469 sq., and Bayle, "Historical and Critical Dictionary," v. ed. 2, 1738, pp. 86–88, E. T.) that the method of the book is so fine and artistic that it is worthy of comparison on this score with the "Institutes" of Justinian, which the lawyers justly consider the most methodical of books. "Calvin," says he, "seems to me from the moment when he began to write on to the end of his life to have bent all his zeal and all his labor and powers to elaborating and enriching these "Institutes," so that they might perfectly set forth his theology." For Schultingh see Migne's "Nouvelle Encyc. Theol.," 2d Series, iii. col. 1046; and especially Bayle, as just cited, who remarks on the prevailing extravagance of his language.

Liberty, the first three chapters being essentially expositions
of the Decalogue, the Apostles' Creed and the Lord's Prayer,
while the concluding three treated the matters chiefly in dispute at the time. As the material grew, these six chapters were
increased partly by division, partly by insertion of additional
topics, to seventeen in the second edition and twenty-one in
subsequent editions, but remained somewhat artificially ordered. With the edition of 1559, however, a totally new arrangement was introduced, which reduced the whole to a simple and
beautiful order — redacted into four books, each with its own
chapter divisions (from seventeen to twenty-five), subdivided
into sections. These four books treat in turn of the Father,
Son, and Holy Ghost, and the Holy Catholic Church — " of
the knowledge of God the Creator," " of the knowledge of God
the Redeemer," " of the mode of receiving the grace of Christ,"
and " of the external means of salvation." The order was suggested by the consecution of topics in the Apostles' Creed, and
follows what is called the Trinitarian method of arrangement,
or the order of God's revelation as Father, Son and Holy Ghost.
The discovery of this simple principle of arrangement gave the
final touch to the " Institutes " as a work of art and permitted
it to make its due impression upon the mind of the reader.
What kind of impression it makes on a spirit sensitive to form
and artistic effect, Mr. Peter Bayne may teach us. " The *Institutes*," he says, " are in all, save material form, a great religious
poem, as imaginative in general scheme, and as sustained in
emotional heat, as *Paradise Lost,* though, of course, not to
be compared, for beauty of language or picturesqueness of detail, with Milton's poem. Calvin treats, in four successive
books, of Christ the Creator, Christ the Redeemer, Christ the
Inspirer, and Christ the King; if he had written in verse,
avoided argumentative discussion, and called his work *The
Christiad,* it would have been the most symmetrical epic in
existence." [20]

[20] " The Chief Actors in the Puritan Revolution," second edition, 1879,
pp. 15, 16. Some such poem as Bayne here suggests Calvin did write — his
" Epinicion Christo Cantatum " (" Opera," v. 423–428) — in sixty-one distichs

INSTITVTIO CHRI-
stianæ religionis, in libros qua-
tuor nunc primùm digesta, totidéque distincta capitibus, ad aptissimam
methodum : aucta etiam tam magna accessione vt propemodùm opus
nouum haberi possit.

IOHANNE CALVINO AVTHORE.

Oliua Roberti Stephani.

GENEVAE.
M. D. LIX.

Definitive Edition of the INSTITUTES — Title Page

It was only, then, in 1559 that the " Institutes " as we know the book was finished. Throughout the whole quarter of a century from the stay in Angoulême in 1534 to the appearance of this, its eighth edition, it was in a true sense in the making, and not until its appearance in this form was it completed. The changes it had undergone since its composition were immense — quintupling its size, revolutionizing its arrangement, changing its very purpose and proposed audience. And yet through all these changes it remained in a true sense the same book, and bore in its bosom precisely the same message. In the case of others of the great writers of the Reformation period, Reuss strikingly remarks, their several publications may mark the stations of their gradual growth in knowledge or conviction; in Calvin's case the successive editions mark only stages in the perfection of his exposition of principles already firmly grasped and clearly stated: [21]

" The masterpiece of Calvin offers in this respect an interest altogether peculiar. We have seen . . . how often it was reworked, how in each rewriting it was enriched and transformed, how from the little sketch it had been at first it ended by becoming a thick volume, how the simple popular outline was changed into a learned

---

written at Worms in 1541, " for his private solace, not for publication." But he did not consider himself a poet. He says of himself : " Quod natura negat, studii pius efficit ardor, Ut coner laudes, Christe, sonare tuas." (Cf. Schaff, vii. 1892, p. 380.)

[21] Almost the sole mark of undeveloped Protestant ideas to be found in the first edition of the "Institutes" is the quotation (" Calvini Opera," i. 82) of Baruch ii. 18, with the formula, " Alter vero propheta scribit," the reference in the " alter " going back to a quotation from Daniel. In the edition of 1539 this has become (i. 906; cf. ii. 632) : " Verissime enim simul ac sanctissime scriptum est, a quocunque tandem sit, quod ab incerto autore scriptum, prophetae Baruch tribuitur." It may be worth noting that in the " Psychopannychia " (written in 1534 but published in 1542) there seems to be some wavering as to Baruch. On one occasion (" Calvini Opera," v. 205) it is quoted with the formula, " sic enim loquitur propheta," and on a subsequent one (p. 227) with " in prophetia Baruch," altered in ed. 1545, to " hanc sententiam plane confirmat oratio, quae est in libro Baruch (saltem qui eius nomine inscribitur)." (Cf. Beveridge's translation of " Institutes," i. p. xxxii.). Cf. " Calvini Opera," v. 271 (1537) ; vi. 560 (1543) ; vi. 638 (1546) where the dealing with Baruch is *ad hominem*.

system, and nevertheless, through all these metamorphoses, which left no single page unaffected, the idea, the theological conception, remained the same, the principles never varied. Its adversaries, in whose eyes change was in itself the worst of errors, vainly strove to discover variations in the doctrine taught in this book. Calvin added, developed, defined — he did not retrench or retract anything. And it was before he had finished his twenty-sixth year that he found himself in full possession of all the productive truths of his theology and never afterwards, during a life of thought and of incessant mental labor, did he find in his work either principles to abjure or elements fundamentally to alter." [22]

III

Another of the notable facts about the " Institutes " is that it was published by its author in two languages — Latin and French. The honor of priority has been a matter of perennial dispute between the two. The earliest French edition, copies of which have as yet to come to light, however, is that of 1541; and it speaks of itself in such a manner as apparently to exclude an earlier French edition, and certainly to exclude a French original for the work. It bears on the title-page the declaration that the book was " composed in Latin by John Calvin and translated into French by the same." And in the Preface the following explicit statement occurs: " Seeing, then, how necessary it was in this manner to aid those who desire to be instructed in the doctrine of salvation, I have endeavored, according to the ability which God has given me, to employ myself in so doing, and with this view have composed the present book. And first I wrote it in Latin (*et premierement l'ay mis en latin*), that it might be serviceable to all studious persons, of what nation soever they might be; and afterwards (*puis apres*), desiring to communicate any fruit that might be in it to my French countrymen, I translated it into our own

---

[22] " Calvini Opera," iii. p. xi.; cf. Cunningham, " Reformers," as cited, p. 294, and the quotation from Beza's " Abstersio Calumniarum," p. 263, note. Compare also what Dr. A. M. Fairbairn says in " The Cambridge Modern History," New York, ii. 1904, p. 363: " Few men may have changed less; but few also have developed more."

tongue (*l'ay aussi translaté en nostre langue*)." It is, of course, true that the mere fact that no copy of an earlier French edition has as yet turned up does not in itself exclude the possibility that such a one may be some day chanced upon; and it may even be allowed that the language just quoted may possibly be pressed to refer to the Latin edition of 1539 alone — which Calvin considered the first edition worthy of the name,[23] and of which the French is certainly a translation. But in the absence of any trace of an earlier French edition, we submit, the natural implication of the words is that the Latin " Institutes " is the fundamental and the French the derived " Institutes."

We are pointed, indeed, to certain facts which are said to imply an earlier French edition. But these seem capable of plausible explanation without this assumption. The most important of them consist of passages from Calvin's own writings, notably the autobiographical passage in the Preface to his Commentary on the Psalms, where he says that when he published his " Institutes " nobody at Basle knew that he was the author of the book, and a sentence in a letter to Francis Daniel, written on the 13th October, 1536, in which he speaks of contemplating " a French edition of our little book." It is argued with respect to the former passage that it must mean that the first edition of the " Institutes " was published anonymously, and that this cannot be said of the Latin edition of 1536, since it bore Calvin's name conspicuously on its front; therefore the reference must be to a previous French issue, published without the name of its author appearing. A careful reading of the passage, however, will convince us that this explanation cannot stand. The ignorance ascribed to the people of Basle as to Calvin's authorship of the book is evidently represented as continuing until Calvin had left that city, and

[23] So, e.g. J. Vielles, " Un problème de bibliographie " in the Montauban *Revue de Théologie*, 1895, p. 127: " That proves nothing in favor of the edition of 1541 [being the first French edition], seeing that that edition is only the translation *word for word* of the Latin edition of 1539. It only amounts to saying: ' I have composed a new edition of the *Institutes* in 1539. I have myself translated this book in 1541.' "

as shared by others outside the city at a later date; in any event, therefore, the Latin edition published before he left Basle comes into account, and it is plain that it is not anonymous publication that he is speaking of, but cautious conduct on the part of the author — perhaps with a reference to the further fact that he lived in Basle under an assumed name.[24] The statement in the letter to Daniel, on the other hand, does seem to show that already in the autumn of 1536 Calvin was contemplating a French version of " his little book ";[25] and this is a very interesting piece of information; but it is clear enough that, for some reason, the project was abandoned or perhaps we should better say was fulfilled only in the edition of 1541. In any event, the reference cannot point to an *original* edition of the " Institutes " in French, as it distinctly speaks of the project as of a French edition of an already existent Latin *libellus*.[26] It would seem, then, pretty certain that the French editions of the " Institutes " begin with that of 1541, which is a close rendering of the Latin of 1539.

The first French edition of the " Institutes," then, that of 1541, is a careful translation by Calvin himself (as the title-page and Preface alike inform us) of the second Latin edition of 1539. The subsequent revisions of the Latin text repeat themselves in editions of the French — the Latin of 1543 (repeated in 1545) in the French of 1545; the Latin of 1550 (repeated in 1553 and 1554) in the French of 1551 (repeated in 1553 and 1554); and, finally, the definitive Latin of 1559 (re-

---

[24] So both Reuss (" Opera Calvini," i. p. xxvi.) and Beveridge (i. 1845, pp. xiii. *sq*.), apparently independently. Cf. Doumergue, " Jean Calvin," i. 1899, p. 591.

[25] The passage is discussed by Reuss in " Opera Calvini," iii. pp. xxi. xxii.

[26] The latest effort to revive the belief in a French first edition is made by J. Vielles in the article mentioned above, in the *Revue de Théologie*, March, 1895, pp. 126–129. He bases his case on three facts: the place given by Beza to the " Institutes " in his list of Calvin's works; Beza's statement that Calvin published his " Institutes " in the same year he left France, viz., in 1534; and the statement in the second edition of " La France Protestante " (column 519), that " Calvin did not put his name to his *Institutes*, but so strong an interest was awakened that people were not slow in recognizing the author " — a statement doubtless derived by misunderstanding from the Preface to the Psalms.

peated twice in 1561) in the French of 1560 (repeated twice in 1561, three times in 1562, and again in 1563 and 1564). There is a remarkable fact about the final, French edition, however, which requires notice. The former editions had repeated, with only the necessary revisions, the original translation of 1541. But the definitive edition of the Latin of 1559 evidently seemed to Calvin a new beginning — increased as it was to nearly twice the bulk of its immediate predecessor; it announces itself, indeed, on its title-page, as " augmented by such additions that it could almost be considered a new work." [27] So looking upon it, Calvin began an entirely new translation of it — a translation corresponding to nothing in the previous editions even in the parts and phrases where the Latin had not been changed. This new translation was continued, however, only to the seventh chapter of the first book. The rest of the volume (except those portions of it merely taken over from the earlier editions — about half of the whole) is by another hand than Calvin's, as its frequent inexactitudes and even occasional misapprehensions of the Latin text show. It would seem that Calvin did not even oversee the proofs of this portion — nearly the whole — of the volume. The French translation of the completed " Institutes " cannot, therefore, be treated, as it often is treated, as a second original,[28] but, in large part, must take its secondary rank as a mere translation of the " Institutes." Its primary value lies only, like other versions, in its giving the great book which it represents a wider circulation and a greater influence than it could have had in its Latin form alone.

[27] The title-page runs: Institutio Christianae religionis, in libros quatuor nunc primum digesta, certisque distincta capitibus, ad aptissimam methodum: aucta etiam tam magna accessione ut propemodum opus novum haberi possit.

[28] Beveridge, therefore, is entirely mistaken when he says (Introductory Notice to his translation, i. 1845, p. li.): " Calvin in preparing it [the French translation of 1562] combined the double character of Author and Translator," and " has occasionally availed himself of his privilege in this respect, and sunk the Translator in the Author," so that " the French edition of 1562 partakes somewhat of the character of an original work, and becomes indispensable in translating the *Institutes* into any other language." It is a good enough translation, but not in any sense a second original.

The French " Institutes " being, of course, in contents, only a reproduction of the Latin " Institutes," adds nothing to its significance for the history of thought, or for the development of theology. It must not be rashly concluded, however, that it, therefore, possesses in itself little importance. It holds a very great place, for instance, in the history of French literature and even in the development of the French language as a literary vehicle. And, above all, it is the visible symbol and evidence of one of the greatest achievements of the Reformation movement — the popularization of religious thought. The Latin " Institutes " was for the learned; the French " Institutes " was made for the unlearned, and the marvel of marvels is that it found or made for itself apparently a great constituency.[29] Who could have believed that in the middle of the sixteenth century a body of vernacular readers could be created so numerous and so avid of theological instruction as to take up in the twenty-five years between 1541, when the first French edition of the " Institutes " was published, and 1566, no less than twenty-one editions of this theological treatise? During Calvin's lifetime, we perceive, the publication of a new edition of the " Institutes " in French was almost an annual affair.

We require to add, however, that after his death, its publication stopped abruptly. Three editions were published, indeed, in 1565, and another in 1566; but then the series comes to an end. Only a single edition was published in the seventeenth century (1609), until as it drew near its close a French pastor at Bremen, Charles Icard by name, began the publica-

[29] Compare Reuss, " Calvini Opera," iii. p. xxv.: " The Reformers had very strong motives for writing in the language of the people, or, at least, for having their works, written in defense of the cause they had embraced, translated into it. If the learned and men of letters could be gained only by speaking the language most familiar to them, another medium was necessary for reaching the masses, for taking hold upon the middle classes already filled with a desire for instruction, for the satisfaction of the religious needs which contemporary society had begun to feel more and more generally. To attain this end the Reformers chose at once the surest and the most legitimate means, — instruction by the living word and by the written word in the common speech. Thus they became, without the least purely literary intention, the fathers and creators of the modern language, in all the lands where the religious reformation took root."

tion of a new French version, or, perhaps we should rather say, a renewed French version.[30] The first Book of this new version appeared in 1696, the second in 1697, the whole not until 1713, in a fine folio; it was reprinted at Geneva in three octavo volumes in 1818. The publication of Icard's version in 1713 alone, however, breaks the barrenness of the eighteenth century. And the nineteenth has only a little better record. Icard's version was reissued, as we have seen, in 1818. The French " Institutes " was, of course, given a place, and that in the best of forms for the student, in the great Brunswick edition of Calvin's " Opera " prepared by the Strasburg theologians, Baum, Cunitz, and Reuss (1865). But of hand editions for popular use, there seem to have been only three issues in the nineteenth century. The earliest of these, in two handsome octavo volumes, was printed at Paris by Charles Meyrueis and Company in 1859, with an interesting Introduction.[31] It has especial claims upon our attention, as it was frankly published not so much to meet a demand as to fulfill a duty of love, and partly by the aid of an appropriation for the purpose voted by " the

---

[30] The anonymous editor of the Meyrueis edition, 1859, writes (p. xiv.): " In 1696 Charles Icard, pastor at Bremen, published the two first books, and completed the work in 1713, dedicating the work to the King of Prussia. Icard had the unhappy idea of wishing to retouch (*rajeunir*) Calvin's style, and yet it is this edition which was reprinted at Geneva, in 1818, 3 vols., 8vo." It should be borne in mind, however, that Calvin is only in a very remote degree responsible for the French style of the completed " Institutes."

[31] Institution de la Religion Chrestienne, nouvellement mise en quatre livres: et distinguée par chapitres, en ordre et méthode bien propre: augmentée aussi de tel accroissement qu'on la peut presque estimer un livre nouveau. Par Jehan Calvin. Nous avons aussi adjousté deux indices, l'un des matières principales; l'autre, des passages de l'Escriture, exposez en icelle, recueillis par A. Marlorat. Paris: Librairie de Ch. Meyrueis et Compagnie, Rue de Rivoli 174, 1859, 2 vols., 8vo. The publisher tells us, p. ii., that in the preparation of this edition, designed to be, in a sense, the definitive edition for the nineteenth century, no pains were spared to secure accuracy of text: " One has no idea," he remarks, " of the inaccuracy of the old editions. The one we have selected for copy, the best " [he unfortunately does not tell us which he selected], " was nevertheless crowded (*criblée*) with errors; errors of printing, erroneous citations, erroneous references to passages, inaccuracies of all kinds. To give only one example, in about four thousand citations of the Scriptures which have been verified, about a thousand have been found inexact and have been corrected."

Presbyterian Committee of Publication at Philadelphia." [32] In 1888 a new edition in two octavo volumes was published at Geneva, "revised and corrected from the edition of 1560 by Frank Baumgartner"; and later this has been placed on the market compacted into a single large volume.[33]

Of course, it is possible, or rather altogether likely, that the early editions of the French " Institutes," which followed one another so rapidly, were small editions, while the modern editions have been large editions. There may be less disparity in the number of copies issued in the nineteenth century as compared with the sixteenth, than in the number of editions. But, after all allowances of this sort are made, the appearance remains strong that Calvin's theology has found fewer eager readers among his compatriots — whether in France or Geneva — in the nineteenth than it did in the sixteenth century. Calvin's theology, we say, not Calvin's French; for we must bear in mind, as we have already pointed out, that the French of the " Institutes " as it has been circulated since 1560 is not Calvin's. There can confidently be attributed to Calvin himself only the French of the first French edition of 1541.[34] As the book grew under his hand, the French text grew *pari passu* with the Latin text, but the rendering of the successive additions may quite possibly have been left to the labors of others. And this may be one of the reasons why, when the definitive Latin edition was published in 1559, Calvin, as we have seen, began to make an entirely new French version of it. Had he completed this new version, no doubt his place in the history

[32] P. i.: " Without the aid long generously afforded by the Presbyterian Committee of Publication at Philadelphia it would have been impossible to undertake and to bring to a happy ending the work " of republishing Calvin's " Commentaries " and "Institutes."

[33] Nouvelle édition, revue sur celle de 1560, par Frank Baumgartner. Préface de L. Durand, prof. Un vol. gr. in 8vo, imprimé sur deux colonnes avéc caractéres neufs.

[34] Reuss (" Calvini Opera," iii. p. xxi.) remarks: " Only the first French edition of the *Institutes* " was translated by Calvin himself; and again (p. xxv.), " We have reached the result that there can be attributed to the author himself with entire confidence, only the first redaction of the French text, as it appeared in 1541; perhaps also the remarkable and altogether exceptional fragment of the earlier chapters of the last edition published in 1560."

of French letters and in the development of the French language might have been much more distinguished than it is. For not only was the "Institutes" of 1559–1560 a greater book than the "Institutes" of 1539–1541 — more thoroughly worked out, more symmetrically developed, more finely ordered — but Calvin had in the course of the intervening twenty years been steadily perfecting his French style and purifying his French vocabulary.[35]

Even on the basis of the French "Institutes" of 1541 alone, however, Calvin takes his place in the first rank of French prose writers.[36] The "Institutes" of Calvin, says M. Ferdinand Brunetière,[37] is "one of the great books of French prose, and

[35] Cf. what is said by A. Bossert, "Calvin," 1906, pp. 211 *sqq.*: "Calvin sought above everything to persuade, but he was no stranger to the effort to speak well, although this effort is less apparent in the discourses taken down from his lips than in the words written by his hand or from his dictation. If he observed the excellencies of the style of others, why should he disdain them for himself? In the midst of his multiplied labors he yet found time to correct his *Institutes* from edition to edition, in order to keep up with the progress of the language. A detailed comparison of the editions of 1541 and 1560 would be an interesting contribution to the history of the French language in the sixteenth century. It would, of course, be necessary to take account, in the comparison, only of the earlier pages of the edition of 1560 which alone were prepared by him. The corrections that Calvin made in his text consist especially in replacing a Latin word or turn of speech by a French equivalent. All have not been sanctioned by usage, not all indeed are felicitous; but the principle which dictated them is worthy of remark." Bossert gives a brief list of variations in language between the editions of 1541 and 1560, which well illustrate his remarks. We may be pardoned for reminding ourselves, however, that too little of the French of the edition of 1560 is Calvin's to justify the expectations which Bossert cherishes from a detailed comparison of the editions.

[36] The "Bibliophile Jacob" (Paul Lacroix) in 1842, regretting that Calvin's French works (as distinguished from those translated into French, often by the hands of others) were inaccessible, undertook to bring the chief of them together in a single small volume: "Œuvres Françoises de J. Calvin, recuellies pour la première fois." The "Institutes"—"that master-work of theological science, religious philosophy and style"—is omitted from this collection, because of its bulk—"although it contains the best pages of French which Calvin wrote in different varieties of dialectic."

[37] "L'Œuvre littéraire de Calvin," in the *Revue des Deux Mondes* for Oct. 15, 1900 (pp. 898–923); E. T. *The Presbyterian and Reformed Review*, July, 1901 (xii. pp. 392–414), pp. 400 and 412. On Calvin's place in the history of French literature Reuss speaks with notable caution ("Calvini Opera," iii.

the first, in point of time, of which we can say that the proportions, the arrangement, and the construction are monumental "; in a word, it is " the first of our books which we can call classic." This position it achieves, he suggests, by virtue of the greatness of its conception, the dignity of its plan, the unity of its treatment, the close concatenation of its thought, its rhetorical grace, the sustained gravity of its style, rising even to majesty, and the purity of its language. To dwell only on the last-mentioned quality, in the purity of his French style Calvin was far in advance of his age. A Latinist of the severest taste, instead of carrying over his Latin into his French, as did most of the writers of the day, he carried over instead the purity of his taste.

" In the schools of that time," writes A. Bossert,[38] " either a barbarous Latin was spoken, or an unpolished French, or a mixture of the two, the type of which is given by Rabelais in the speeches of Janotus demanding in the name of the Parisians the restoration of the bells of Nôtre Dame. Those who wished to speak the mothertongue correctly, affected to use only Frenchified Latin words, or as Olivétan puts it, ' obscure and unaccustomed barbarous terms, which are peeled off from the Latin.' Calvin writes in turn and with equal facility in Latin and in French, in Latin when he addresses himself to the learned, or the theologians, in French when he wishes to be read by all the world. But he keeps the two languages rigorously apart; he does not permit one to encroach on the other. . . . The French prose of his day, when it was applied to serious subjects, was modeled on the Latin period, and was naturally filled with Latin words of which it only gradually freed itself. Calvin, so pure a Latinist when he wrote in Latin, is in his French style the least Latinizing of the great prose writers of the Renaissance. Much more than his contemporary Rabelais, more even than Montaigne, who came forty years later, he approaches the prose of the seventeenth century. From the point of view of the development of the language,

---

pp. xxiii.–xxv.) : but even he remarks that he " is justly regarded as one of the best French writers of his time and his *Institutes* as one of the greatest monuments of French prose of that age."

[38] " Calvin," pp. 200 *sq.;* 213.

he rises out of the chronological sequence and takes his place immediately before Pascal." [39]

IV

The French version, although addressed to a popular audience, had the disadvantage of appealing only to a single nationality. After all, the real extension of the influence of the "Institutes" lay in the hands of the Latin original, which made its appeal to every educated circle in the civilized world. Wings were given to it by the nobility of its form and the unwonted elegance of its language. For Calvin's Latin is as fine in its way as his French; and the Latin "Institutes," too, deserves to be called a classic. Scaliger speaks of it as almost too good in its Latinity for a theologian; [40] and, indeed, its Latinity is not that of a theologian, but that of a humanist. Modeled, as all of the Latin of the day was, on Cicero, its basis is the Ciceronian period; but the Ciceronian period appears in it emancipated from its too carefully calculated balance, and given a new rapidity of movement and an energetic brevity to which all superfluity of words is alien. " To say that the language of Calvin is clear, sharp, precise, is not enough," remarks Bossert,[41] " it is striking and expressive; it abounds in original turns and happy forms."

The demand for the book seems to have been from the first very large. Perhaps edition did not follow edition with quite the same rapidity as was the case with the French version, but the difference is not great; the editions were themselves, no doubt, larger — at least more copies of the Latin editions have survived until our day — and they continued to be published

[39] A. M. Fairbairn, " The Cambridge Modern History," ii. 1904, p. 376, may be compared. For the literature of the subject see A. Erichson, " Bibliographia Calviniana," 1900, pp. 136–138, and cf. the short list in " The Cambridge Modern History," ii. p. 783. Paul Lacroix opens the preface to his collection of Calvin's French writings with a striking paragraph in which he seeks to bring out the precise characteristics of Calvin's French style in comparison with that of Rabelais, Amyot, and Montaigne.

[40] " Prima Scaligerana," Groningen, 1669, p. 39: Calvinus, solidus theologus et doctus, styli sat purgati et elegantioris quam theologum deceat.

[41] A. Bossert, " Calvin," Paris, 1906, p. 209; cf. p. 201.

after the publication of the French version had ceased. Ten or twelve editions were issued in Calvin's lifetime,[42] the most beautiful of which were those of 1553 and 1559 from the press of Robert Stevens; and although his death did not cause a temporarily increased demand for them to spring up as it apparently did for the French — of which there were published no less than three editions in 1565 and another in 1566 — yet they went steadily on: 1568, 1569, 1576 (twice), 1577, 1585, 1586, 1590, 1592 (twice), 1602, 1606, 1607, 1609, 1612, 1617, 1618, 1637, 1654, 1667 — quite to the middle of the seventeenth century. We are struck, as we look over the list, by the completeness with which the Genevan presses monopolized the supply of the world. The first edition (1536) was, of course, printed at Basle, where Calvin had found refuge in his flight from France; and the second, third and fourth (1539, 1543, 1545) were printed at Strasburg, whither Calvin had retired when driven from Geneva in 1538. But by 1550 the " Institutes " had come back to Geneva with Calvin and they had come to stay. One subsequent edition was printed at Strasburg (1561), but except that, none during Calvin's life were printed elsewhere than at Geneva (six editions). After his death, Geneva still remained the center whence the " Institutes " issued. Three editions were soon to be printed at Lausanne (1576, 1577, 1586); otherwise the whole series up to 1637, sixteen in all, was printed at Geneva — with one exception. This single exception interests us very much, for it is the only edition of the " Institutes " in Latin which has ever been printed on English-speaking soil. It was issued at London in 1576 from the printing house of Thomas Vautrollier, a learned Huguenot who had come to England from Paris or Rouen, and with many vicissitudes, in London or in Edinburgh, now basking in the royal favor, now suffering under the inquisition of the Star Chamber, carried on the printer's trade

---

[42] When Reuss says ten, he is omitting from the enumeration the variant form of the edition of 1539 which bears " Alcuin " instead of " Calvin " on the title-page; and the variant form of the edition of 1554, which bears no imprint on the title-page. A facsimile of the title-page of the edition of 1539 " Autore Alcuino," may be seen in Beveridge, i. *ad init.*

until his death, somewhere about 1587.[43] The last edition printed in Geneva came from the press in 1637. From that day to this, no edition of the Latin "Institutes" has been published on the scene of the author's life-work, where also the book was given its final form and sent out appropriately clothed in the splendid typography of Robert Stevens. From that day, to be sure, the Latin "Institutes" has been printed anywhere but seldom. In 1654 the splendid Elzevir edition appeared and this was reprinted in the ninth volume of the fine Amsterdam edition of Calvin's works (1667). After that no further editions were issued until the nineteenth century, when (1834, reprinted 1846) Tholuck published his admirable hand-edition which has supplied readers ever since. Last of all, in 1863–1864, the great critical edition of Baum, Cunitz and Reuss, forming the first two volumes of their splendid edition of Calvin's works, was published at Brunswick, reprinted in a separate issue in 1869.

On the whole, Calvin's "Institutes" has been given a worthy external presentment. Even the first edition, though it was the work of an unknown man, is a very pretty little book — a little book, for, though it is an octavo in the folding of the sheets, the block of type (excluding headline and catchword) measures only $2\frac{5}{8}$ by $4\frac{1}{2}$ inches. The type of the "Epistola Nuncupatoria" (pp. 3–41) is a really fine Roman; while that of the "Institutes" itself (pp. 42–514) is a sufficiently good italic.[44] The two fine folio editions published by Robert Stevens (the second Genevan edition, 1553, and the definitive edition — the fourth Genevan — 1559) are among the notable specimens of the printer's art. The former of these, Reuss praises as the most splendid of all, with its ample page, elegant type and wonderful accuracy in printing. But the latter is splendid enough worthily to close the career of the distinguished printer whose last work it was — for Robert Stevens

---

[43] A sketch of Vautrollier (by George Stronach) is included in the (English) "Dictionary of National Biography" (edited by Sidney Lee), lviii. 1899, pp. 189 sq., with references to further sources of information.

[44] This use of italic type was introduced by Aldus, followed first by Colines.

died only a few days after this edition was finished. It is a
beautiful folio, the block of type (exclusive of headline, there
being no catch-word) measuring 5¾ by 10⅝ inches, printed in an
elegant, bold Roman character, with the notes in the outer
side-margin. Among the splendid editions of the " Institutes "
must be mentioned also the great Leiden folio of 1654, which
gathered into itself all the adventitious matter that — chiefly
in the form of indices and arguments — had grown up gradually around the " Institutes " as aids to its more ready use, evidently intending itself to stand as the final edition of the
book. This indeed it, in fact, remained for a hundred and eighty
years. The " Institutes " in the Amsterdam " Opera " of 1667
is a literal reprint of it — reproducing even its " admonition
to the reader, about this edition " (but omitting Beza's life of
Calvin which also is found in ed. 1654) — and no other edition
was published until Tholuck's hand-edition appeared in 1834.
This great Leiden edition was the work of the famous printers,
John and Daniel Elzevir, but it occurs also with no less than
five other imprints, only the title-page being changed and the
dedication to Professor Heidanus omitted. The explanation of
this odd circumstance is that it was a custom of the times to
issue portions of an edition in the names of the several booksellers who handled it. Thus this noble edition was sent out
not only in the name of its real printers, but also severally in
those of Adrianus Wijngaerden, David Lopez de Haro, Franciscus Haack, Petrus Leffen, and Franciscus Moyard.[45]

There are few modern books which have received the honor
of having had expended upon them all the art of two such
printers as Stevens and Elzevir. And they merely stand at the
head of a list which includes with them many another printer
of note.[46]

[45] Cf. C. Sepp, "Voor de Letterkundige Geschiedenis van Calvijn's Institutio" in *Godgegleerde Bijdragen,* xlii. 1868, p. 865. Reuss says he possessed also copies of the Mill-Kuster New Testament, 1710, with a like variety
of imprints — from Amsterdam, Rotterdam, Leiden.

[46] On the printers of Calvin see Appendix No. xv., in the first volume of
Doumergue, "Jean Calvin," 1899 (pp. 596–608).

Definitive Edition of the Institutes — Specimen Page

V

Calvin intended the "Institutes" (in its later form) as a textbook in theology. It quickly took its place as such, not only among the students at Geneva, but throughout the Reformed world. Francis Junius, in commending it to his pupils at Leiden, used to tell them that he himself had devoted two entire years to its study.[47] Kaspar Olevianus at Heidelberg and Herborn based his theological lectures upon it, going over one book each year and thus completing the course in four years. What Olevianus was doing in Germany the professors at both Oxford and Cambridge were doing in England. A no doubt somewhat hysterical Jesuit observer of the day, himself not altogether insensible to the excellencies of the book, complains that prelections on the "Institutes" constituted the fundamental training in theology at both universities.[48] Even in faraway Hungary it was serving a similar purpose. It was by reading the first edition (1536) of the "Institutes" that Mathias Biró of Déva [49] was brought to the acceptance of the

[47] Schultingh, in his exaggerating way, declares that everybody in Holland, clerical and lay, down to the very laborer (*usque ad infimum aurigam et nautam*), was deeply versed in "the Calvinian theology," studying the "Institutes" day and night, and deciding all controversies from it as if it were a treasure fallen from heaven.

[48] "The books of the *Institutes* are so highly valued in England that exact English versions of them are kept in the several churches for reading, and in both universities there, when the philosophical course is finished, prelections on them are above everything else given to the future theologians" (Schultingh). "What wonder," asks the high-church historian H. O. Wakeman with similar regret (" An Introduction to the History of the Church of England," ed. 7, 1904, p. 330) — "what wonder was it when all was vague and indeterminate, when learning was depressed and libraries destroyed, that men eagerly turned to the one Protestant treatise which contained a logical and simple system of theology, and that the Institutes of Calvin became the acknowledged text-book of the English universities, the mould in which the religious opinions of the English clergy for half a century were formed?" Cf. W. Walker, "John Calvin," 1906, p. 391. Nelson in his "Life of Dr. George Bull," London, 1713, tells how, in the decadence in the later seventeenth century, Calvin's "Institutes" gave way in the universities to Episcopius'.

[49] For him see Bod, "Historia Hungararum Ecclesiastica," Leiden, 1888, i. pp. 237 *sq*. Prof. Francis Balogh says: "The *Institutes,* the fundamental work of Calvin, in Hungary, as everywhere else, produced a great effect upon

Reformed faith, and his summary of Christian doctrine — " A
Short Explanation of the Ten Commandments, the Creed, the
Lord's Prayer, and the Seals of the Creed " — the first doctrinal treatise, written in Hungary (1538), seems to have been
at least inspired by the " Institutes "; while the " Catechism "
of the protagonist of the Reformed faith of the next generation, Péter Juhász — or as he Græcized his name, Peter
Melius [50] — published in 1562 (ed. 2, 1569) as a textbook for
the use of schools, was expressly modeled upon and even drawn
from the " Institutes." [51]

If we may look upon Juhász' " Catechism " as a sort of
abridgment of the " Institutes," it provides us with the earliest
example of a type of literature which, in the interests of sound
instruction in the fundamentals of religion, soon became quite
common. Unless, indeed, we prefer to consider as the first
abridgment of the " Institutes " Calvin's own earliest " Catechism," so-called, which was published in its French form in
1537 and in its Latin form in 1538, to serve as a " book of instruction " for the infant church of Geneva. The first professed
abridgment of the " Institutes," formally set forth as such, was
probably, however, the " Institutionis Christianæ Religionis
a Jo. Calvino conscriptæ compendium " by Edmund Bunney,[52]

the mind. It caught Dévai, too, and afterward he became the first messenger of the Helvetic Reformation " (" History of the Reformed Church
of Hungary," § 11, in *The Reformed Church Review,* Fourth Series, x. 1906,
p. 311). Huszár Gál wrote to Bullinger, Oct. 26, 1557, " Domini Johannis Calvini scripta plurismum imitantur."

[50] For him see Bod, as cited, pp. 256–257.

[51] The book is an 8vo of 9½ sheets, containing 76 unnumbered leaves,
having the following title: Catekismus. Az Egész Keresztieni tudomannac
fundamentoma es sommaja a szent irasbol ezue szedettetett, es megemendal-
tott. Calvinus Janus irassa szerint. Az Somogi Melius Petertol. Jaroljatoc en
hozzam fiaim, hallgassatok engemet, az Urnak felelmere tanitlac en titeket.
Psal. 34. Döbröczönbe MDLXII. That is to say: Catechism. Outline and
Sum of the Whole Christian Knowledge from Holy Scripture, collected and
emended. After the writings of John Calvin. By Peter Melius of Somogy.
" Come, ye children, hearken unto me; I will teach you the fear of the
Lord," Psalm 34. Debreczen, MDLXII.

[52] An account of Edmund Bunney, with references to sources of information, is given in the (English) " Dictionary of National Biography," vii.
1886, pp. 271–272.

published at London by the Huguenot printer Vautrollier in
1579 and reprinted at Antwerp in 1582, and in an English translation in 1580, as follows: "Edm. Bunnie, his abridgment of
Calvin's Institutes, translated by Edw. May ": London, For
William Norton, 1580.[53] This abridgment was, however, very
soon superseded by another, also of English origin. This was the
"Institutionis Christianæ Religionis a Joanne Calvino conscriptæ Epitome, in qua adversariorum objectionibus respon-
siones annotantur, per G. Launæum," London, Vautrollerius,
1583, reprinted in 1584. The author, Guillaume Delaune,[54] was
a learned pastor of the French church in London, and his book
was printed by the learned Huguenot printer, Vautrollier. As
Delaune's object was to make the contents of the "Institutes"
accessible to wider circles than would or could approach it in
its original form, he was very eager to have his abridgment
put into English, a task which he could not himself undertake
as he was not "thoroughly acquainted with our language."
It was, therefore, distributed into four hands to do the translating; but in the end the whole was rendered into English by
Christopher Fetherstone, and published as "An Abridgement
of the Institvtion of Christian Religion written by M. Ihon
Caluin. Wherein briefe and sound aunsvveres to the obiections of the aduersaries are set dovvne. By VVilliam Lawne
minister of the word of God. Faithfullie translated out of
Latine into English by Christopher Fetherstone, Minister of
the word of God." Edinburgh: Thomas Vautrollier, 1585
(24°, pp. [32] 398 [30]). New editions of this English version
were issued in 1586 and 1587: it was even revived in the nineteenth century and republished by different printers in 1837,
1853, and in an undated edition. Delaune stood in close relations with Holland and had been vainly sought as a professor

[53] "This abridgment of Calvin's *Institutes*," we read in the article on
Bunney in the "Dictionary of National Biography," just cited, "was translated
into English by Edward May, 1580, 8vo, but had not so much vogue as the
abridgment by William Lawne, 1584, translated by C. Fetherstone, 1585."

[54] See the notice of him in the (English) "Dictionary of National Biography," xiv. 1888, p. 315, *sub nom.* "Delaune, William." Further references are
given at the end of the article.

at Leiden. It is not surprising, therefore, that a Dutch version of his book was published in 1594,[55] the work of Joris (i.e., George) de Raedt, pastor of the Hoedekenskerke in South Beveland, which was reprinted in 1611, 1650, 1739, 1837. Almost contemporaneously with Delaune's book (1586) Olevianus issued at Herborn his own " Institutionis religionis Christianae epitome ex Institutiones Joh. Calvini excerpta " to serve as a succinct handbook for his students; [56] and there appeared at the same place, the same year, the German " Summa der wahren christlichen Religion." At about the same time must have appeared also the first issue of Johannes Piscator's " Aphorismi doctrinae Christianae maximam partem ex Institutione Calvini excerpti," the earliest edition of which listed by Steubing was printed at Herborn in 1589, and the earliest edition of which listed by Erichson not until 1605.[57] Three editions of it at any rate had already appeared when Henry Holland [58] in 1596 issued his English version of it, " Aphorismes of Christian religion or a verie compendious

---

[55] Institutie ofte onderwijsinghe in de Christelijke religie, uittreksel door G. Delaunay, vert. door Joris de Raed. Amsterdam, 8 *min.*

[56] Cf. J. H. Steubing, in Illgen's *Zeitschrift für die historische Theologie,* iv. 1841, pp. 83, 87, 97.

[57] Steubing (Illgen's *Zeitschrift für die historische Theologie,* iv. 1841, p. 132) gives the following editions: Herborn, 1589, 1592; Siegen, 1597; Herborn, 1599, 1600, 1611, 1619 (= ed. 9), 1622, 1626, 1627. Erichson adds: Herborn, 1605, and Oxford, 1630. Holland tells us, however, that three editions had been published before 1596, and Bayle (*sub nom.* "Schultingius," E. T. v. 1738, p. 86) says the book was first published in 1586. In 1622 Piscator published an expanded commentary on his "Aphorisms": "Johan. Piscatoris Exegesis, sive Explicatio, Aphorismorum Doctrinæ Christianæ " (Herborn, 1622, reprinted 1650) at the end of which is printed a series of *Tabellæ,* reducing the Aphorisms to tabular form. These *Tabellæ* were prepared by Piscator's son Philippus Ludovicus, who, in a Dedication to a friend, dated January 12, 1622, reminds him how, when they were studying theology together at Heidelberg, eight years before — that is in 1614 — he had privately studied " aphorismos locorum communium, qui vocantur, à patre meo Joh. Piscatore ex Calvini Christiana institutione in certos ordines congestos," and drawn up these tables. Piscator began his work at Herborn in 1584, and doubtless drew up these Aphorisms then; they were probably first printed in 1586.

[58] For Holland see the (English) " Dictionary of National Biography," xxvii. 1891, pp. 140–141. His book was dedicated to Dr. Goodman, dean of Westminster.

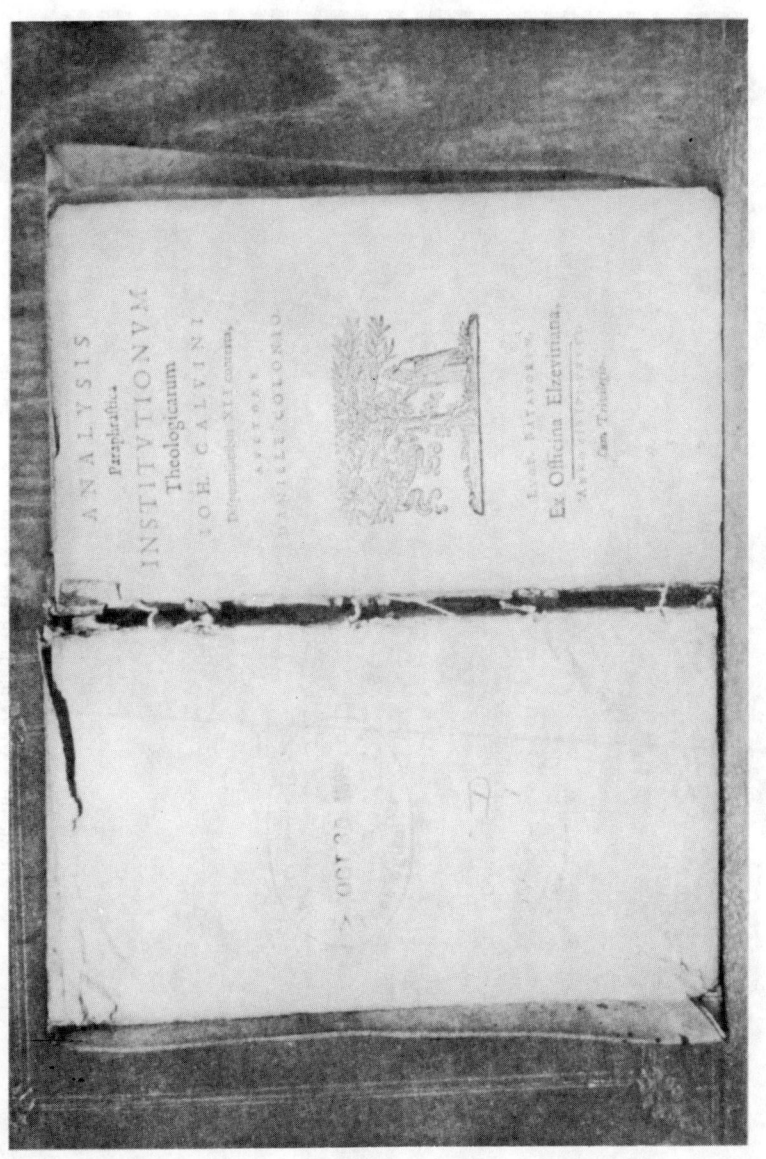

Colonius' Abridgment of the Institutes — Title Page

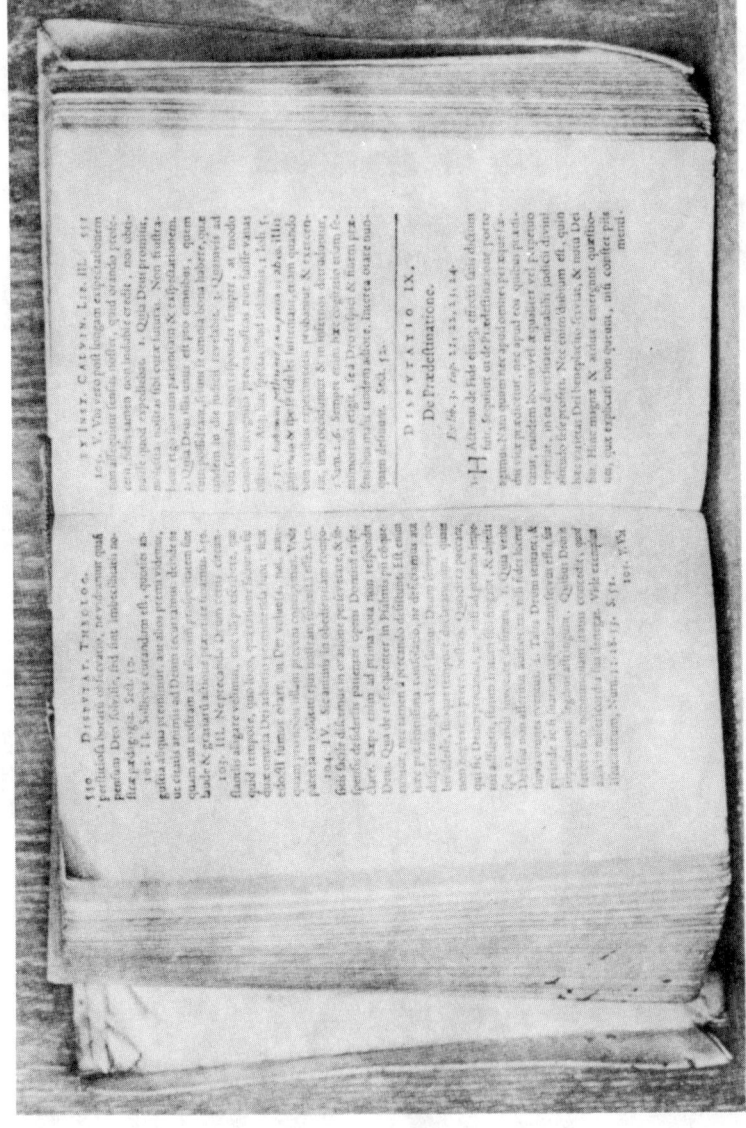

Colonius' Abridgment of the Institutes — Specimen Page

abridgement of M. I. Caluin's Institutions, set forth in short sentences methodically by M. I. Piscator, and now engleshed according to the author's third and last edition " (London, Field, 1596). A new edition of this version, to which was added Calvin's " letter to Francis I in defence of the Reformation," was published at London as late as 1844. Possibly, the little book in German which appeared at Herborn in 1600 may also be connected with Piscator's Aphorisms: " Kurtzer Bericht von den fürnembsten Artickeln der wahren Christlichen Religion, auss den vier Büchern der Institution J. Calvini in ein Büchlein zusamen gezogen." It is a new book, however, which Joh. Jezler, Rector and Pastor at Schafhausen, published in 1610 under the title, " Schediasmus succinctus lemmatibus universum complectens Christianismum, desumpta ex solida Joh. Calvini de Relig. Chr. Instit., quo sublevari potest non tam memoria quam intellectus eam legentium."

The abridgments of the " Institutes " reach their culmination in the admirable " Analysis paraphrastica " of Daniel Colonius, rector of the Walloon College at Leiden, which was published, first, in quarto in 1628,[59] and then in a beautiful duodecimo from the Elzevir press in 1636. Colonius was born at Metz in 1566 and died of the plague at Leiden in 1635: his daughter Sara (Van Ceulen) was married in 1625 to Bonaventura Elsevier who, with his nephew Abraham, was head of the Elzevir firm at the time of Colonius' death.[60] The issue of this beautiful edition of his book the following year (1636) was thus apparently an act of pious commemoration of the dead author. In any event it affords as fine a specimen of the minute Elzevir typography as the edition of the " Institutes " of 1654 provides of the larger style.[61] The title-page runs: " Analysis paraphrastica Institutionum theologicarum Ioh. Calvini disputationibus XLI contexta, avctore Daniele Colonio. Lugd. Bata-

[59] This edition seems to be very rare. There is a copy of it in the Bodleian Library at Oxford (" Catalog. libr. impr. Bibl. Bodleianae " [1843], i. 578).

[60] See Sepp, *Godgeleerde Bijdragen*, xliii. 1869, p. 485, note 1.

[61] Cf. Ch. Pieters, " Annales de l'imprimerie Elseverienne," p. 95: " This edition is printed with great care and is in one of the prettiest of the Elzevirs, though it is omitted in a great number of catalogues."

vorum. Ex Officina Elzeveriana. Anno MDCXXXVI. Cum Privilegio " (12mo, pp. [8] 950). The text is apparently exactly reproduced from the edition of 1628. The dedication to Daniel Heinsius is repeated, as also the *approbatio* of the Faculty of Theology at Leiden signed by Polyander as dean *protempore*, and dated the 6 July, 1628. The character of the work itself is very well described by its title: it is an excellent paraphrastic analysis of the " Institutes," and well adapted to aid the student in mastering the contents of the great work, to study which day and night Colonius advises him in some verses inscribed, " In Calvini Institutiones ":

> Aureus hic liber est, hunc tu studiosa juventus,
> Si cupis optatam studiorum attingere metam,
> Noctes atque dies in succum verte legendo.

It was not for two hundred years after the publication of Colonius' Paraphrastic Analysis that a fresh attempt was made to set forth the gist of the " Institutes " in condensed form. H. P. Kalthoffs' " Christliche Unterweisung in einem kernhaften Auszug," however, was published at Elberfeld in 1828, and was reprinted in 1831 (Barmen) under the title: " Catechismus der Christlichen Lehre." In 1837 there appeared in London, " Christian Theology, selected and systematically arranged " by Samuel Dunn; reprinted in 1843 and translated into Welsh in 1840: " Duwinyddiaeth Cristionogol, a ysgrifenwyd yn wreiddiol gan J. Calvin . . . gan S. Dunn ac a gymreigiwyd gan Evan Meredith (Ievan Grygg). Crughywel, Williams." In 1903 there appeared from the printing house of J. H. Kok, Kampen, " Calvijn's Institutie of onderwijzing in den Christlijken Godsdienst. Een uittreksel door G. Elzenga." These are the latest abridgments of the " Institutes " which have met our eye.

VI

The object of the abridgments of the " Institutes " was to bring the contents of the book within the reach of wider circles of students; and the zeal with which vernacular versions of these abridgments were published — in German, Dutch, most numerously in English, even in Welsh — bears witness to the eagerness with which the "Institutes" was sought by a constituency to which Latin was, at best, a difficult medium. The important task of diffusing the knowledge of the "Institutes" among this class of readers was not left, however, to versions of abridgments of it alone. The book itself was fortunate in securing translation almost at once into most of the languages of Europe.[62] And, we may add, it was fortunate in the translators it secured. Translations are not ordinarily undertaken by men of high powers of original expression. Such a task is usually left to literary talents of distinctly the second rank. Only when some other and deeper impulse than a literary one is present do men of great gifts of expression turn to such work. This deeper impulse was in operation in the case of the "Institutes." Its earlier translators were all men of mark, seriously engaged in propagating the truths to which the "Institutes" gave such uniquely attractive expression; and their versions were not mere mechanical pieces of work but were informed with vitality and gave the book a place, therefore, in the literatures of the several tongues into which they transfused it.

These translations, we have said, began very early. The Italian version, indeed, did not wait even for the definitive edition of the "Institutes" (1559), but (depending mainly on the French) appeared as early as 1557. It was the work of Giulio Cæsare Paschali, an excellent poet, who subsequently (1592) published a metrical Italian version of the Psalms.[63]

[62] These translations are, of course, enumerated in A. Erichson's "Bibliographia Calviniana," in vol. lix. of the Brunswick ed. of "Calvini Opera" and, with additions, separately printed, Berlin, 1900. See also the lists in Haag, "La France Protestante," ed. 2, 1881, iii. col. 553; and Henry, "Leben Calvins," III. ii. 1844, pp. 185–188. When Stähelin, "Johannes Calvin," i. 1863, p. 59, says, "It has been translated into all the languages of Europe, as well as into Arabic, if the notices of the bibliographers are accurate," the exaggeration is pardonable.

[63] A brief account of him (by Escher) may be found in Ersch and Gruber, "Encyklopädie," III. xiii. 1840, p. 3. The following is the notice in Bayle (English ed., London, 1737, sub nomine): "Paschali (Giulio Cæsare) was one of those Italians who left their country in the sixteenth century for the

It was introduced by a dedicatory letter addressed to Galeazzo
Caraccioli, Marquis of Vico, one of the band of nobles who
formed the nucleus of the Protestant church at Naples.[64] So
soon, however, as the "Institutes" was completed and its
definitive edition (1559) published, the rendering of it into the
vernaculars of Europe began apace. The Dutch version was
first in the field. In less than eighteen months after the publication of the definitive Latin edition (August, 1559) the Dutch
version left the press (December 5, 1560, is the date of the
preface), published in two forms, the one bearing no indication of place, but known to have been published at Emden,
the other issued at Dort, by Verhaghen.[65] The translator signs
his preface by the initials "I. D.," and seems otherwise unknown. Next in turn to the Dutch comes the English version
(1561 and six times repeated before 1600). It was the work of
a very capable man, Thomas Norton (1532–1584), a ripe
scholar, able jurist, wise statesman, ardent reformer and no
mean poet, most generally known, doubtless, as co-author with
his friend Thomas Sackville of "The Tragedie of Gorbuduc,"

---

sake of the Protestant religion. He was a good poet in his mother-tongue,
and published the Psalms in Italian verse at Geneva in the year 1592. He
was then sixty-five years of age. He added to it a collection of *Rime
Spirituali*, and the first canto of an epic poem entitled *Universo*. This poem
was finished and contained in thirty-two cantos the whole history of Moses,
from the creation of the world to the entry of the Israelites into the land
of Canaan. I do not think he ought to be distinguished from the *Giulio
Cæsare P.* who caused to be printed at Geneva in 1557 in 4to his Italian version
of Calvin's *Institutes,* and dedicated it to Galeas Carraciol, Marquis del Vico.
The epistle dedicatory is dated from Geneva, the 4th of August, 1558." Henry
("Leben Calvins," III. ii. 1844, p. 185) adds that his translation of the "Institutes" depends largely on the French and that he translated several others
of the works of the Reformers into Italian — Viret's and others. For the suspicions of his orthodoxy and other details, see F. Buisson, "Sébastien Castellion," ii. 1892, p. 125, note 2.

[64] See Herzog, "Realencyklopädie," ed. 3, (and "The New Schaff-Herzog
Encyclopedia,") *sub nom.* Also McCrie, "Reformation in Italy," 1833, pp. 148
and 484 *sqq.;* "The Cambridge Modern History," ii. 1904, pp. 387 *sqq.*

[65] The book is a small folio of 735 pages, two columns to the page. The
Dedicatory Letter to Francis I is omitted on account of the great size of the
book. Le Long in the Catalogue of his books indicates the place of publication as Emden.

a piece which plays a part in the history of the English drama.[66] The theological faculty at Heidelberg gave its united care to the preparation of a German version, which was published at that place in 1572. In 1597 a Spanish version appeared from the pen of Cypriano de Valera, one of the most notable of the Spanish literary reformers, and the translator of the Spanish Bible which is still in use by Spanish-speaking Protestants.[67] A Bohemian version also was made before the end of the century by the learned scholar and hymnologist Jiřík Strejc, or Georg Vetter in the Germanized form of his name (ordained priest in the *Unitas Fratrum* 1567, died 1599),[68] the manuscript of which is still preserved in the " Mährisches Landesarchiv " at Brünow.[69] It was not printed, however, until early in the next century (1617, by Johann Opsimates) and then apparently only partially (the first two books).[70] To these versions was added in 1624 a Hungarian

[66] A full account is given of him (by Sidney Lee) in the (English) " Dictionary of National Biography," xli. *sub nom.*

[67] An account of Cypriano de Valera may be found in " The Spanish Protestants and Their Persecution by Philip II," by Señor Don Adolfo de Castro, E. T. by T. Parker, London, 1851, chap. xviii. (pp. 263–268). Also in C. A. Wilkens, " Geschichte des spanischen Protestantismus im sechzehnten Jahrhundert," ed. 2, 1897, pp. 159–163, especially p. 161 where other references are given. Cf. also McCrie, " Reformation in Spain," Index.

[68] For Strejc see E. De Schweinitz, " History of the Unitas Fratrum," 1885, p. 411. For his Calvinism, see E. Charvériat, " Les affaires religieuses en Bohême au seizième Siècle," 1886, pp. 237–238.

[69] This book is duly listed in the Catalogue of the works of Calvin which have been translated into the language of Austria-Hungary, printed by Prof. D. Dr. Georg Loesche at the end of his " Luther, Melanthon und Calvin in Österreich-Ungarn," 1909, p. 357. He announces that Dr. V. Tardy of Prague promises that the unpublished two books are soon to be printed.

[70] The book is a very rare one. There is a copy in the Royal Public Library at Dresden, a description of which has been kindly furnished by the Chief Librarian, Herr P. E. Richter, also by Dr. J. Th. Müller of Herrnhut. Another copy was in the possession of the late Lic. Theol. Fr. Šebesta, and is now owned by his son, Pastor John Šebesta. Jungmann, " Historie literatury čezké," 2, wydany, W. Praze, 1849, iv. No. 1346, enters the book, and under No. 1894 mistakenly enters it again, giving as title the opening words of the preface. He seems to have had before him only the Dresden copy. This copy lacks the title-page of Book I. That of Book II. remains and begins: " Skladu Welikého zbožj, Mandrosti Nebeské," and ends: " Ad. Jana Opsimatesa. W

translation made by Albert Molnár " for the edification of the Hungarian nation in divine truth," which recites on its title-page that the book had already been translated into " French, English, Dutch, Italian, German, Bohemian and other languages " — truly enough, if we may understand by the " other languages " only the Spanish, which seems to be the only " other language " into which the " Institutes " had been rendered. A Greek version of the " Institutes," printed at Frankfort in 1618, has, indeed, been spoken of, and even an Arabic one; [71] but no copies of them seem to be accessible to attest their reality.[72] Later, in 1626, there was published a Polish translation, not indeed of the " Institutes," but of a portion of it — the portion of it which deals with the very controverted subject of the sacraments. This excerpt had been given separate publication in German at Heidelberg in 1572, and again at Neustadt a. d. Hardt in 1592: it was now rendered into Polish by Blastus Kmita and published at Lubeck.[73]

poslednjm neyhorssjm Wěku." That is: " The Great Treasure of Heavenly Wisdom. . . . Published by John Opsimates, In the last and worst age." The general title of the book is generally given: " Knihy čtyry skladu velikého zboží mandrosti nebeské "; that is, " Four Books of the Great Treasure of Heavenly Wisdom," and this may very likely have stood on the general title-page. It is without indication of place of publication or date, but it is confidently assigned to 1617. The paper measures 290 x 195 mm.; the printed space 215 x 150 mm.; the print is disposed in double columns. The translation is exact (from ed. 1559).

[71] " Finally," we read in Haag, " La France Protestante," ed. 2, iii. col. 553, " it is said that the *Institutes* has been translated also into Bohemian, into Greek, and even into Arabic."

[72] Erichson, as cited, p. 68, says: " A Greek translation of the *Institutes* which Dorn in his *Bibl. Theol. Crit.*, ii. 784, says was published at Frankfort on the Main, in 1618, exists in none of the libraries, whether in the West or the East to which I have access."

[73] The titles of the Polish and German tracts alike may be seen in Erichson as cited, under their years. Among the portions of the " Institutes " published separately should be mentioned the chapters " De prædestinatione et providentia Dei," " De libertate christiana," and " De vita hominis christiani " extracted by Crespin, the Genevan printer, in 1550 from the edition of the "Institutes " published that year, followed in 1552 by a similar extract: " Disputatio de cognitione hominis " (chap. ii. of that edition). In 1594 an English translation by J. Shutte of the chapter on the Christian Life (chap. xxi.) was published under the title: " A Treatise of Christian Life." In 1693 there

The versions of the " Institutes " in the languages of southern Europe, which ultimately remained Catholic, naturally have only a brief history. It does not appear, for example, that the Italian version of 1557 was ever reissued. The Spanish version of 1597 also has apparently been reprinted only in 1858 and that as " an antiquity " — as part of the " Reformistas antiquos españoles " issued by B. B. Wiffen and Luis de Usoz y Rio (xiv., 2 parts, Madrid, 8vo).[74] Evil fortune also followed the Bohemian translation. We have seen that, although from the hand of one of the most influential scholars of the *Unitas Fratrum*, a member of the executive council, and the author of a metrical version of the Psalms upon the model of Marot's, Strejc's version lay in manuscript for years and never was more than half printed. It was not until the end of the nineteenth century that a renewed attempt was made to provide the Bohemians with the " Institutes " in their own tongue; and this attempt met with a similar fate. The maker of the new version was Lic. Theol. František Šebesta, an author of note, who at the time of his death was pastor at Hustopeč in Moravia.[75] Only two books of his version, however, were published (1890, 1895), his death (July 22, 1896) bringing his

appeared at Amsterdam, the " Traité de la justification par J. Calvin, traduit du latin de son Institution par Jean de Labrune," and a new edition of this was issued in 1705. The significance of the extract on Predestination is adverted to by A. F. Mitchell, Baird Lecture on " The Westminster Assembly," ed. 2, p. 519; of that on the Christian Life may be gathered from the remarks of E. Doumergue, *Princeton Theological Review*, January, 1909, vii. p. 97; of that on the sacraments is obvious in view of the controversies of the time.

[74] A description of this series, which extends to twenty volumes (the fourteenth of which contains the " Institutes "), is given by Wilkens in Brieger's *Zeitschrift für Kirchengeschichte*, ix. pp. 341–390 (especially pp. 370–372).

[75] František Šebesta was born Dec. 14, 1844, at Klobouky, Moravia, and educated at the Gymnasium at Teschen, Silesia. For two years he acted as assistant to Kohlbrügge at Elberfeld; then he was pastor 1868–1880 at Mykolčice, in Moravia, where he organized the church; he repeated this at Hustopeč in 1881 and remained pastor there till his death July 22, 1896, having in the meanwhile established stations at Břeclav and Hodonin. His literary product was large; it included a History of the Christian Church, a Dogmatic for the House and School, a Life of Farel, and especially a metrical version of the Psalms.

work to a sudden close as he was engaged on the third book.[76] The Hungarian version of 1624 [77] also has remained unreprinted until to-day. Its translator, Albert Molnár,[78] was one of the greatest scholars of his time, long resident in Germany where he served as professor in the school at Oppenheim. Like so many others of the early translators of the "Institutes" — Paschali, Norton, Strejc — he was a poet and, indeed, gave (1607) the Hungarian Church the version of the Psalms which continues in use up to to-day. His rendering of the "Institutes" remains one of the great monuments of Hungarian literature, but has, of course, long passed out of use. Nothing has come, however, to take its place, although there has lately (1903) been published, by the "Hungarian Protestant Literary Society," at Budapest a version of the first edition of the "Institutes" (1536) by Charles Nagy, formerly professor in the Reformed Faculty at Kolozsvár, with the aid as revisers of Louis Eröss, formerly professor at Debreczen, and Dr. George

[76] The two parts were published separately (8vo, pp. xx., 119, and 183) without Preface or Introduction. The title-page of the first part, which is a general title, runs as follows: Joannis Calvini, theologi magni, Institutio Christianæ Religionis. — Jana Kalvína, Bohoslovce velikého Učení Náboženství Křesťanského. Z jazyka Latinského přeložil Lic. Theol. F. Šebesta, Farář V Hustopeči. V Pardubicich. Nákladem Firmy F. Hoblik, 1890.

[77] The Hungarian title is given with sufficient fulness by Erichson (see also Loesche, p. 359). It runs: "Instruction in the Christian Religion and True Faith, which John Calvin wrote in Latin. And afterward was translated into French, English, Dutch, Italian, Bohemian, and other languages; but now translated by Albert Molnár into the Hungarian tongue for the edification of the Hungarian nation in Divine Truth. Together with useful and complete Indices. Printed in Hanover at the expense of Daniel and David Anbrius and Kelemen Sleikius, 1624." It is a 4to of 1538 pages with 24 pages of preliminary matter and at the end 17 unnumbered leaves of Index. It is dedicated to Prince Gabriel Bethlen.

[78] Molnár was born at Szenczi in 1574, and is hence called Albert Molnár Scenczi. An account of him, enumerating his publications, may be seen in Bod, as cited, ii. pp. 278-279. He was educated in Germany, particularly at Heidelberg. Besides his version of the "Institutes" and his translation of the Psalms, he busied himself with the version of the Hungarian Bible, that is to say the version of Kaspar Károlyi first published in 1590 and remaining till to-day in general use. Molnár's revisions were not very extensive, and his Bible was printed first at Hanover (1608) and then at Oppenheim (1612). Cf. F. Balogh in Herzog,[3] Art. "Bibelübersetzungen," No. 15 (p. 176 of the separate reprint, "Urtext und Übersetzungen der Bibel," 1879).

Bartók, Reformed Bishop of Transylvania.[79] This work was prepared in accordance with the commission of Domakos Szász, Reformed Bishop of Transylvania, who set aside in 1898 a thousand florins for the purpose. Thus, the first edition of the " Institutes " has been rendered into Hungarian alone, with one exception, of vernacular languages. The exception is the German, not even the French having it in their own tongue. The German version bears this title: " Joh. Calvins christliche Glaubenslehre nach der ältesten Ausgabe vom Jahr 1536 zum erstenmal ins Deutsche übersetzt von Bernhard Spiess " (Wiesbaden, 1887, 8vo, pp. xvi., 432).

A richer history has been wrought out by the Dutch, German and English " Institutes."

As we have noted, the first Dutch version appeared in twin issues at Emden and Dort, as early as 1560, with no other indication of the personality of the translator than is supplied by the initials " I. D.," with which the preface is signed. Because of the great bulk of the book, the " long epistle of Calvin to the King of France " was omitted from this edition, as from its repetition, Dort, 1566; it was inserted, however, in the new issue printed at Dort by C. Jans and P. Verhaghen in 1578, as was also Marolatus' Index. The edition issued at Leiden by Jan Paedts and Jan Bouwensz in 1593 is also a reprint of the version of 1560. At this point, however, a new hand comes in, that of Charles Agricola, a native apparently of Antwerp — from which place he is at least registered as a student at Heidelberg in 1572 — and from 1592 to 1624 minister at Rijnsburg. His work seems to have been rather a revision of the earlier version than an entirely new translation. It was first issued by Paedts Jacobsz and Bouwensz in a small folio of 286 pages, double columns, in 1602. It contains as a kind of supplement to the " Institutes " also a Dutch version of Calvin's " Supplex exhortatio " for a needed reformation — a separate print of which seems to have been simultaneously issued. Agricola's

---

[79] Kalvin János, A. Keresztyén Vallás Alapvonalai (Institutio Religionis Christianæ). Az 1536-íki elsö latin kiadás után. Forditotta Nagy Károly, ny. r. tanár a Kolozsvári ev. ref. theol. fakultáson. — Budapesten: 1903.

version was repeated, Rotterdam 1610, Dort 1610, Amsterdam 1614, 1617, Dort 1617, Amsterdam 1645. Then comes another change. In 1650 there appeared from the press of P. van Ravensteyn at Amsterdam a very noble Dutch edition of the " Institutes," in folio, to which was added not merely the " Supplex exhortatio " but certain others of Calvin's works; a fine portrait of Calvin engraved by Vischer formed the frontispiece. The version of the " Institutes " here printed was a new one from the hand of William Corsman, minister from 1622 to his death in 1646 at Baardwijk; and it is spoken of as of the highest quality both as a rendering of Calvin's thought and for the purity and force of its handling of the Dutch language. It appears to have been reprinted in 1739; and certainly a new edition of it, with a preface by Dr. A. Kuyper — also a folio — was issued in 1889 by van Schenk Brill at Doesburg. Occasion was taken from the publication (in 1864) of the " Institutes " in the great Brunswick edition, to make yet another new translation, which was issued — the first part in 1865, the second in 1867, and the whole afresh in 1889–1891 — from the press of G. Ph. Zalsman at Kampen. The translation, we are told, was done " by Wyenberg, under the oversight of de Cock," and it is described as very competently done.

The German translation of the " Institutes " undertaken by the theologians of Heidelberg was first published, as we have seen, at Heidelberg (Meyer) in folio form, in 1572. It was reissued at the same place in 1582, in the same form; and then in quarto in 1597 at Hanau (Cäsar und Anthoni), and in 1608 at Heidelberg (Steinmeyer). As also has already been noted, there was simultaneously with the issue of the first edition (1572) published separately the portion of the Fourth Book containing Calvin's doctrine of the sacraments; and several issues in German were made of abridgments of the " Institutes." A modern German version by F. A. Krummacher, of Elberfeld, was begun in 1823, when the first two books were published at Elberfeld. The completed work was published in two octavo volumes in 1834. We have already noted the translation of the first edition of the " Institutes " (1536) into German, by B. Spiess (1887) — the first translation ever made of the first edition of the "Institutes " into a modern tongue.[80]

VII

We naturally feel a special interest in the English translations. The "Institutes" has been thrice translated into English: by Thomas Norton (1561, and often afterwards: London, 1562, 1574, 1578, 1582, 1587, 1599, 1611, 1634; Glasgow, 1762), by John Allen (London, 1813, 3 vols.; 2nd ed., London, 1838, 2 vols.; 3d ed., London, 1844, 2 vols.; 1st American edition, 1816, 3 vols.; 6th Am. ed. n. d., but 1841–1842, 2 vols.), and by Henry Beveridge (Edinburgh, 1845–1846, 3 vols.; 2nd ed., 1863, 2 vols.). Besides these versions of the complete "Institutes," at least four abridgments of the "Institutes" have been printed in English: Edward May's version of Edmund Bunney's "Compendium" (1580); C. Fetherstone's version of Laune's "Epitome" (1585, 1586, 1587, 1600, 1837, 1853, n. d.); Henry Holland's version of Piscator's "Aphorismes" (1596, 1844); and S. Dunn's "Selection" (1837).

Norton's translation of the whole work, early as it was, was yet almost preceded by a still earlier one. A note from "The Printers to the Reders," printed on the reverse of the title-page of the edition of 1561, which is identified as Norton's only by the initials "T. N." with which the last page of the book is signed, tells us of a previous translation which had been made, but was not published. Here is the note in full:

"Wheras some men haue thought and reported it to be a faulte and negligence in vs for that we haue so long kept backe from you this boke being so profitable a woorke for you, namely sithe maister John Dawes had translated it and deliuered it into our handes more than a twelve-moneth past: you shall understande for our excuse in that behalfe, that we could not wel imprinte it soner. For we haue ben by diuerse necessarie causes constrayned with our earnest entreatance to procure an other frende of oures to translate it whole

---

[80] An article on "Die deutsche Ausgabe von Calvin's Institutio," by W. G. Goeters, which we have not seen, was printed in the *Reformierte Kirchenzeitung* for 1907 (xxx. No. 29).

agayn. This translation, we trust, you shal woll allow. For it hath
not only ben faythfully done by the translater himself, but also
hath ben wholly perused by such men, whoes iugement and credit
al the godly learned in Englande well knowe and esteme. But sithe
it is now come foorth, we pray you accept it, and use it. If any
faultes haue passed us by ouersight, we beseche you let us haue
your patience, as you haue had our diligence."

The bare allusion we are given to it rouses our curiosity as to
why Maister Dawes' translation was set aside; certainly the
Preface is a model document — it seems to take the reader into
full confidence, and yet says nothing derogatory to any one.

No one better fitted for the task of retranslating the book
could easily have been found at any rate than Thomas Norton.
His name appears for the first time on the title-page of the
third edition, while to the fourth he prefixes a nobly written
Preface — " T[homas] N[orton,] the Translator to the
Reader " — in which is included an account of how he was led
to translate the book, of the care he took to do a proper piece
of work in the translating, and of the subsequent means
adopted to perfect the printed text. After a brief account of
Calvin and his purpose in the "Institutes," the Preface continues: [81]

" So great a iewel was meete to be made most beneficiall, that is
to say, applied to most common vse. Therefore in the very beginning of the Queenes Maiesties most blessed reigne, I translated it
out of Latine into English, for the commoditie of the Church of
Christ, at the speciall request of my deere friends of worthy memo-
rie *Reginald Wolfe* [82] and *Edward Whitchurch*,[83] the one her Maiesties Printer for the Hebrew, Greeke and Latin toongs, the other her
Highnes Printer of the bookes of common praier. I performed my
worke in the house of my said friend *Edward Whitchurch*, a man

[81] The quotations are made from the edition of 1599.
[82] The printers of the first edition were " Reinolde Vvolfe and Richarde
Harison."
[83] Whitchurch, " the Calvinistic printer," was Norton's wife's stepfather.
Norton's first wife was Margery, Archbishop Cranmer's third daughter, and
his second wife her cousin, Alice, daughter of Edmund Cranmer, Archdeacon
of Canterbury.

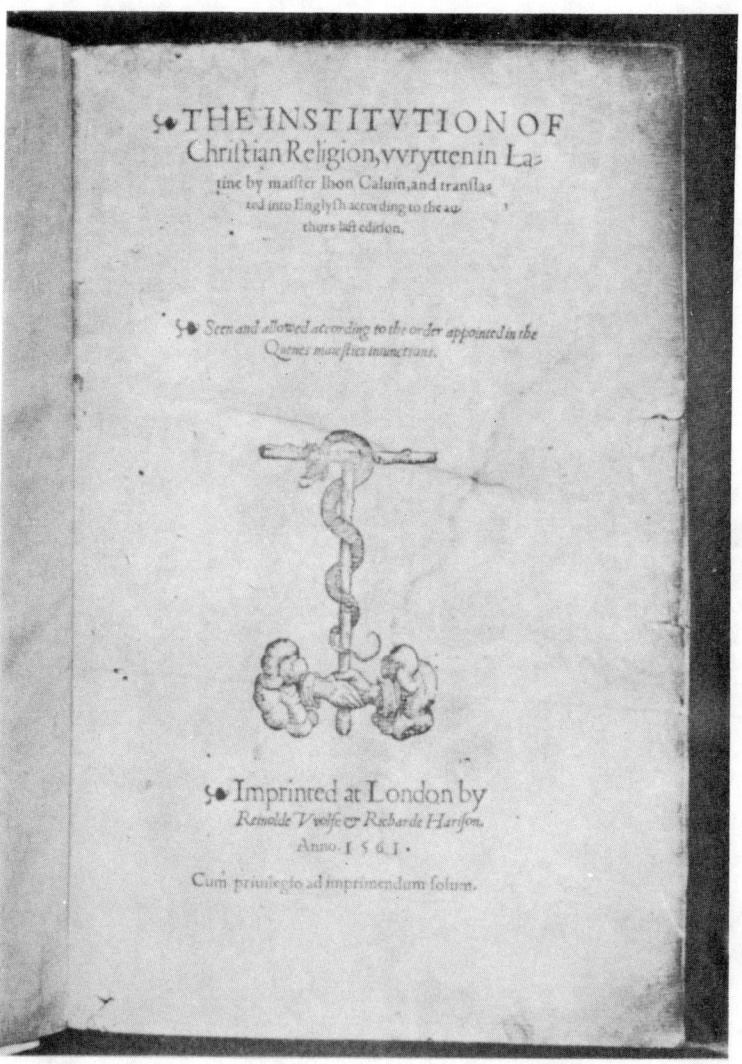

ꝏ THE INSTITVTION OF
Chriſtian Religion, vvrytten in La-
tine by maiſter Ihon Caluin, and tranſla-
ted into Englyſh according to the authors laſt edition.

ꝏ Seen and allowed according to the order appointed in the
Quenes maieſties iniunctions.

ꝏ Imprinted at London by
Reinolde Vvolfe & Richarde Harison.
Anno. 1 5 6 1 .

Cum priuilegio ad imprimendum ſolum.

First Edition of the English INSTITUTES — Title Page

well knowen of vpright hart and dealing, an ancient zealous Gos-
peller, as plaine and true a friend as euer I knew liuing, and as desirous to do any thing to common good, specially by the aduaunce-
ment of true religion."

He then explains why he chose the method of literal rather
than of paraphrastic translation and continues:

" In the doing hereof, I did not only trust mine owne wit or
abilitie, but examined my whole doing from sentence to sentence
throughout the whole booke with conference and ouerlooking of
such learned men, as my translation being allowed by their iudgement, I did both satisfie mine owne conscience that I had done
truly, and their approouing of it might be a good warrant to the
reader, that nothing should herein be deliuered him but sound,
vnmingled, and vncorrupted doctrine, euen in such sort as the author himselfe had first framed it. All that I wrote, the graue, learned,
and vertuous man M. *Dauid Whitehead* [84] (whome I name with
honorable remembrance) did among other, compare with the Latine,
examining euery sentence throughout the whole booke."

The care taken to bring the text of the book in its new editions
to greater correctness in the printing being next noted, the
Preface concludes thus:

" Thus on the Printers behalfe and mine, your ease and commoditie (good Readers) is prouided for. Now resteth your owne
diligence for your owne profit in studying it. To spend many words
in commending the worke it selfe, were needelesse: yet thus much
I thinke I may both not vntruly and not vainly say, that though
many great learned men haue written bookes of common places of
our religion, as *Melanchton, Sarcerius,* [85] and other, whose works are
very good and profitable to the Church of God: yet by the consenting iudgement of those that vnderstande the same, there is none to
be compared to this worke of *Caluine,* both for his substantiall suf-
ficiencie of doctrine, the sound declaration of truth in articles of
our religion, the large and learned confirmation of the same, and

[84] He had been nominated both to an Irish bishopric and to the See of
Canterbury.

[85] Erasmus Sarcerius (1501–1559), Lutheran divine, lived in Nassau and
afterwards in Leipzig. His works are voluminous and include a " Loci communes theologiæ."

the most deepe and strong confutation of all olde and new heresics: so that (the holy Scriptures excepted) this is one of the most profitable bookes for all students of Christian diuinitie. Wherein (good Readers) as I am glad for the glorie of God, and for your benefite, that you may haue this profite of my trauell, so I beseech you let me haue this vse of your gentlenesse, that my doings may be construed to such good ende as I haue meant them: and that if anything mislike you by reason of hardnesse, or any other cause that may seeme to be my default, you will not foorthwith condemne the worke, but reade it ofter: in which doing you will finde (as many haue confessed to me that they haue founde by experience) that those things which at the first reading shall displease you for hardnesse, shall be found so easie as so harde matter woulde suffer, and for the most part more easie than some other phrase which shoulde with greater loosenesse and smoother sliding away deceiue your vnderstanding. I confesse in deede it is not finely and pleasantly written, nor carieth with it such delightfull grace of speech as some great wise men haue bestowed vppon some foolisher things, yet it conteineth sound truth set foorth with faithfull plainnesse without wrong done to the authors meaning: and so if you accept and vse it, you shall not faile to haue great profite thereby, and I shall thinke my labour very well imployed."

We have quoted largely from this Preface, because it appears to us an admirable document, altogether worthy of its place in the forefront of the "Institutes" and of the hand of its author, one of the most notable figures in the literary world of his day. Born in 1532, bred to the law, in which profession he gained high distinction, Thomas Norton lived on terms of intimacy with the leaders of the religious Reformation in England, and did his part to further it by voice and pen. A ripe scholar, he prepared translations of some of the best books in circulation expository of Christian truth,[86] and sent forth a number of writings of his own. A " wise, bold and eloquent " member of Parliament, he championed there the movements

---

[86] His translation of Nowell's " Larger " Catechism, along with a sermon of Nowell preached before Parliament Jan. 11, 1563, was edited for the Parker Society by G. E. Corrie (1853) : " Dictionary of National Biography," xli. 1895, pp. 243 sqq. Cf. Schaff, " Creeds," etc., i. 1877, p. 657; Jacob, " The Lutheran Movement in England," p. 332; Churton's " Life of Nowell," p. 183.

Of the manner howe to receiue

of death, bicause he hath offended against the maiestie of God. Therefore these our futile arguters do stumble, for that they marke not this saing of James, that he which sinneth in one, is made gylty of al, bicause he that hath forbidden to kil, hath also forbidden to steale, &c. Therfore it ought to seeme no absurditie when we saie that death is the wise rewarde of euery sinne, bicause thei are euery one worthy of the wise bypleasure and vengeance of God. But thou shalt reason foolishly, if on ye contrarie side thou gather that by one good worke man may be reconciled to God, whiche with many sinnes deserueth his wrathe.

The. rix. Chapter.

Of Christian libertie.

Now we must entreate of Christian libertie: the declaration wherof he must not omit whose purpose is to comprehend in an abridgment the summe of the doctrine of the Gospel. For it is a thing principally necessarie, & without ye knowledg wherof conscience dare in a maner enterprise nothing without doubting, then stumble and start back in many things, then alway stagger & tremble: but specially it is an appendant of iustification, and auaileth not a litle to the vnderstanding of the strength therof. Yea thei that earnestly feare God, shal hereby receiue an incomparable frute of that doctrine which the wicked & Lunaticall men do pleasantly taunt with their scoffes, because in ye spiritual darkenesse wherewyth thei be taken, euery wanton railing is lawful for them. Wherfore it shal now come foorth in fit reason: & it was profitable to differ to this place ye plainer discoursing of it. (for we haue already in diuers places lightly touched it) because so sone as any mention is brought in of Christian libertie, then either filthy lustes do boyle, or mad motions do arise, vnlesse these wanton wittes be timely met withall, whiche doe otherwise most naughtily corrupte the best thinges. For, some men by pretense of this libertie, shake of all obedience of God, and breake foorth into an vnbridled licentiousnesse: and some men disdaine it, thinking that by yt all moderation, order and choise of thinges is taken away. What shold we here do, brings compassed in suche narrowe streightes. Shall wee bidde Christian libertie farewell, and so cutt of all fit occasion for suche perilles. But as we haue saide, vnlesse ye be fast holden, neither Christ, nor the truthe of the Gospel, nor the inward peace of the soule is rightly knowen. Rather we must endeuoure that so necessarie a part of doctrine be not suppressed, and yet that in the meane time those fonde obiections may be mette withall whiche are wont to rise thereupon.

Christian libertie, as I thinke consisteth in three partes. The firste, that the consciences of the faithful, when the affiance of their iustification before God is to be sought, may raise & aduaunce theselues aboue the lawe, and forget the whole righteousnesse of the lawe. For sithe the lawe (as we haue already in an other place declared) leaueth no man righteous: either we are excluded from all hope of iustificatio, or we muste be loosed from the lawe, and so that there be no regarde at al hadde of workes. For whoso thinketh that he must bring somwhat be it neuer so litle of good workes to obteine righteousnesse, he can not apointe any ende or measure of them, butte maketh him selfe better to the whole lawe.

that tended to the religious settlement of the land on the lines of a complete reformation. Possessed of a poetic gift, he contributed some twenty-eight translations of Psalms to Sternhold and Hopkins' collection,[87] as well as wrought for the advancement of more secular species of English poetry. In every way he seemed glad to use his high powers freely in the cause of religion. Assuredly, we will say Calvin's "Institutes" was introduced by fit hands to its English public; and the excellence of the performance seems to be attested by the rapidly repeated issue of editions of the translation during the latter years of the sixteenth century, and its long-continued hold on the religious public.

It was not until the early years of the nineteenth century that Norton's was superseded by a modernized translation. This was made by John Allen, and appeared first in 1813. John Allen [88] was a layman like Thomas Norton — a nonconformist school-teacher, born at Truro, in Cornwall, 1771, and for thirty years master of a private school at Hackney, near London, where he died in 1839. His principal work was a treatise on "Modern Judaism" (1816), though he published also a "Memoir of Major General Burn" (1815), and a translation of some sermons of D. de Superville (1816) and William Owtram's "Two Dissertations on Sacrifice" (1817). He tells us in the Preface to his translation of the "Institutes," that one of the circumstances which led him to publish it was "the recent controversy respecting Calvinism, commenced by Dr. Tomline, the present Bishop of Lincoln." His interest in that controversy had already been shown by the anonymous publication in 1812 of a reply to Tomline's "Refutation of the Charge of Calvinism against the Church of England," which appeared in 1811. Allen's book bore the title, "The Fathers, the Reformers, and the Public Formularies of the Church of

---

[87] For his place in the history of English poetry, cf., besides the references given by Sidney Lee, the "Cambridge History of English Literature," iii. pp. 51, 324, 342; Baker's "Biographia Drammatica"; Ellis' "Specimens of Ancient Poetry," ii. p. 136.

[88] See the (English) "Dictionary of National Biography," *sub nom.*, and additional references there given.

England in Harmony with Calvin and against the Bishop of Lincoln."

It does not predispose the reader favorably to Allen's work that he speaks with scant appreciation of Norton's translation — though that, perhaps, was not unnatural in the Preface of a work designed to supersede it. This Preface is plainly written, and gives an appreciative account of the book being rendered, and a statement of the translator's method of translating — which, declining both " a servile adherence to the letter " and " a mere attention to the ideas and sentiments," " aimed at a medium between servility and looseness, and endeavored to follow the style of the original as far as the respective idioms of the Latin and English would admit." The translation is certainly so far successful that it conveys with plain directness the meaning of the original author, and so far, at least as we have observed, never either misses it or obscures it.

If Allen is chargeable with underestimating the merits of his predecessor's work, he certainly was called on to repay his fault a hundredfold by the treatment he received at the hands of his successor — Henry Beveridge.[89] Beveridge simply passes

---

[89] Henry Beveridge was born June 19, 1799, at Dunfermline; acted as tutor in the family of Mr. Erskine (afterwards Earl of Buchan) from 1821; was licensed as probationer of the Church of Scotland, 1827, but never took a charge; served as an elder in the church at Tonyburn for a number of years and sat as an elder in the Assembly of 1837; was called to the bar in 1838, but never practised the profession; died March 18, 1863. The greater portion of his life was given to literary labor: as a young advocate he reported the cases decided in Court of Session for the *Scottish Jurist* (1838 sq.); he contributed largely (1848 sq.) to the *Imperial Gazetteer* and the " Popular Encyclopædia," published by Messrs. Blaikie & Son, of Glasgow (1848 sq.); and he served as editor of *The Banner of Ulster* of Belfast (1855–1857). His chief original work was a " Comprehensive History of India," 3 vols. (1858–1862); and he made the translation of the first three volumes of Merle D'Aubigné's " History of the Reformation " (1844 sq.). He published also a translation of Pascal's " Provincial Letters " (1857). He became connected with the Calvin Translation Society early in its history, and besides editing for it Fetherstone's translation of the " Commentary on Acts " (1844), and Rosdell's translation of that on " Romans " (1844), he translated for it the following: " On the Necessity of Reforming the Church " (1843), " Tracts Relating to the Reformation " (3 vols., 1844), " Institutes " (3 vols., 1845), " Four Sermons, Commentary on Joshua " (1854).

by Allen's translation without any mention at all. Allen's judgment on Norton's translation, however, Beveridge repeats with interest — the gravamen of his charge turning on its excessive literalness. " Instead of the pure English of the period at which he wrote," he remarks, " the utmost he could give was English words in a Latin idiom. In this way the translation, which must often have seemed rugged and harsh to his contemporaries, has become in great measure unfit for modern use." Beveridge, for his part, avoiding " overstraining after such scrupulosity as Norton aimed at," hopes that, in his own translation " the true meaning of the Author has been given in plain English, and so made accessible to every class of readers." Beveridge's translation was issued by the Calvin Translation Society [90] in 1845, and has probably superseded in Britain the earlier work of Allen.

Meanwhile, however, already in 1816, Allen's translation had been reissued in America as the " First American from the last London Edition," bearing the imprint: " Philadelphia: Published by Philip H. Nicklin, and by Hezekiah Howe, New Haven. William Fry, Printer, 1816." And in 1841 and 1842,[91] the Presbyterian Board of Publication at Philadelphia had stereotyped a somewhat revised edition of Allen's translation, issuing it as the sixth American edition. This has accordingly become the most accessible translation in America. The edition of the Presbyterian Board was brought out at the expense of the First and Second Presbyterian churches of Baltimore, of which the Revs. John C. Backus and Robert J. Breckinridge were then pastors, and was introduced by a Preface written by Dr. William M. Engles, then editor of the Board. How far the revision of the text extended we have not been careful to investigate. Dr. Engles says: " Under the direction of the Executive Committee of the Board, the translation has been diligently compared throughout with the original Latin and

[90] It was founded in 1842 and issued its first installment of translations in 1843.

[91] So we were kindly informed by Dr. Willard M. Rice, Recording Clerk of the Board, who was connected with the Board for a half century.

French, and various corrections have been made to convey the meaning of the author more distinctly and accurately. This laborious duty has been performed by a member of the Publishing Committee." This " member of the Publishing Committee " was Mr. Joseph Patterson Engles (1793–1861), a man of varied and high culture, master of the Classical Institute at Philadelphia from 1817 to 1845, and from 1845 to his death publishing agent of the Board. He was, perhaps, most widely known as the editor of an American reprint, with many corrections, of the so-called " Polymicrion Greek Testament " (1838, and often afterwards), and was a man who, by habits of exact accuracy and by thorough classical scholarship, was eminently fitted to correct a translation from the Latin.[92]

It should not pass without notice that all three of the later rehandlings of the English " Institutes " plume themselves on their use of the French text — treating it as a second original, of equal or almost equal authority, as a witness to Calvin's meaning, with the Latin. Allen says:

" After the greater part of the work had been translated, he [the translator] had the happiness to meet with an edition in French, of which he has availed himself in translating the remainder, and in the revision of what he had translated before. Every person, who understands any two languages, will be aware that the ambiguity of one will sometimes be explained by the precision of another; and, notwithstanding the acknowledged superiority of the Latin to the French in most of the qualities which constitute the excellence of a language, the case of the article is not the only one in which Calvin's French elucidates his Latin."

Beveridge says:

" Constant use has also been made of the last French translation, revised by Calvin himself, and printed at Geneva in 1562. The Latin text is in general perfectly clear, and where there is a com-

[92] See, especially for his work on the Greek Testament, I. H. Hall, " A Critical Bibliography of the Greek New Testament as Published in America," 1883, pp. 14 sq. A brief notice of him also occurs in the " Encyclopædia of the Presbyterian Church," sub nom. Dr. Rice writes: " His revision of the Institutes was thorough and laborious. Some of the proof sheets passed under my eye and gave evidence of the care with which it was done."

petent knowledge of the language, there is little danger of mistaking the meaning. Ambiguities, however, do occur, and it was considered that there could not be a more legitimate and effectual mode of explaining them than to make the Author his own expositor, and hold the meaning to be what he himself has made it, in his vernacular tongue. It has already been observed, that Calvin, in his translation, occasionally avails himself of his privilege as Author. Due attention has been paid to the changes thus made on the original, any difference of meaning or of expression which seemed deserving of notice being given in footnotes. In this respect it is hoped that the present Translation possesses a very decided advantage."

Dr. Engles says:

" The translation has been diligently compared throughout with the original Latin and French," etc.

This use of the French, except in the first few pages of the first book (to the seventh chapter), as already pointed out, is liable to some danger when carried through uncritically. For the rest of the book, that alone is certainly Calvin's which has been preserved from the first French translation (1541). The text is composed, as Reuss puts it, " of fragments of the old translation, where the Latin text remains the same (although there, too, the changes are somewhat frequent), and a new translation of the complementary additions which form nearly half the text. . . . Here," he adds, " we meet with not only a great number of inexactitudes, omissions, meaningless and embarrassing additions, but even passages where it is evident that the translator did not even understand the Latin text." Striking examples of this are given by Reuss. It is obvious that an uncritical use of this French translation, as in all its parts of equal authority for Calvin's meaning with the Latin original, is scarcely a commendation of a version; and we need no further evidence that, so far as it was used at all, it must have been used uncritically by our English translators, than the fact that though each of them compared the French diligently with the Latin, no one of them discovered those glaring faults in the French which render it impossible to attribute it to Calvin's own hand.

It would be interesting to compare the texts of the several English translations, with a view to discovering how far the later translations are really independent of the earlier, and which represent the original most faithfully, clearly and happily. We cannot undertake that task now; but we can at least give a specimen of their rendering of a typical passage, from which we may, perhaps, catch something of the flavor of each. Here is the opening section of the treatise in its three English forms (Book I. chap. i. § 1):

NORTON, 1599.	ALLEN, 1813.	BEVERIDGE, 1845.
The whole summe in a maner of all our wisedome, which onely ought to be accounted true and perfect wisedome, consisteth in two partes, that is to say, the knowledge of God, and of our selues. But where as these two knowledges be with many bondes linked togither: yet whether goeth before or engendreth the other, it is hard to discerne. For, first no man can looke vpon himselfe, but he must needes by and by turne all his senses to the beholding of God, in whom he liueth and is mooued: bicause it is plaine, that those giftes wherewith we be indued, are not of our selues, yea, euen that we haue being is nothing els but an essense in the one God. Finally, by these good things that are as by dropmeale powred into vs from heauen, we are led as it were by certaine streames to the spring head. And so by our owne needinesse, better appeereth that infinite plentie of good things that abideth in God. Specially that miserable ruine, whereinto the fall of the first man hath throwne vs, compelleth vs to lift vp our eies, not onely being foodelesse	True and substantial wisdom principally consists of two parts, the knowledge of God, and the knowledge of ourselves. But, while these two branches of knowledge are so intimately connected, which of them precedes and produces the other, is not easy to discover. For, in the first place, no man can take a survey of himself but he must immediately turn to the contemplation of God, in whom he "lives and moves;" since it is evident that the talents which we possess are not from ourselves, and that our very existence is nothing but a subsistence in God alone. These bounties, distilling to us by drops from heaven, form, as it were, so many streams conducting us to the fountain-head. Our poverty conduces to a clearer display of the infinite fulness of God. Espe- cially, the miserable ruin, into which we have been plunged by the defec- tion of the first man, compels us to raise our eyes towards heaven, not only as hungry	Our wisdom, in so far as it ought to be deemed true and solid wisdom, consists almost entirely of two parts: the knowl- edge of God and of our- selves. But as these are connected together by many ties, it is not easy to determine which of the two precedes, and gives birth to the other. For, in the first place, no man can survey himself without forthwith turning his thoughts towards the God in whom he lives and moves; because it is perfectly obvious, that the endowments which we possess cannot possibly be from ourselves; nay, that our very being is nothing else than subsistence in God alone. In the second place, those blessings which un- ceasingly distil to us from heaven, are like streams conducting us to the fountain. Here, again, the infinitude of good which resides in God becomes more apparent from our poverty. In par- ticular, the miserable ruin into which the revolt of the first man has plunged us, compels us to turn our eyes upwards; not only that while hungry and

NORTON, 1599.

and hungrie, to craue
from thence that which we
lacke, but also being
awakened with feare, to
learne humilitie. For
as there is found in man
a certaine worlde of all
miseries, and since we haue
beene spoyled of the diuine
apparell, our shamefull
nakednesse discloseth an
infinite heape of filthie
disgracements: it must
needes be that euery man be
pricked with knowledge in
conscience of his owne vn-
happinesse to make him come
at the least vnto some knowledge of God. So by the vnderstanding of our ignorance,
vanitie, beggerie, weakenesse,
peruersnesse, and corruption,
we learne to reknowledge
that no where else but in the
Lord abideth the true light
of wisedome, sound vertue, perfect abundance of all good
things, and puritie of righteous-
nes. And so by our owne
euils we are stirred to consider the good things of God:
and we cannot earnestly aspire toward him, vntill we
begin to mislike our selues.
For of all men what one is
there, that would not willingly rest in himselfe?
yea, who doth not rest, so
long as he knoweth not himselfe, that is to say, so long
as he is contented with his
owne giftes, and ignorant or
vnmindfull of his owne
miserie? Therefore euery
man is by the knowledge
of himselfe, not onely pricked
forward to seeke God, but
also led as it were by the
hand to finde him.

ALLEN, 1813.

and famished, to seek
thence a supply for our
wants, but,
aroused with fear, to
learn humility. For,
since man is subject to
a world of miseries,
and has
been spoiled of his divine
array, this melancholy
exposure discovers an
immense mass of
deformity:
every one, therefore, must be
so impressed with a
consciousness of his own infelicity, as to arrive
at some knowledge
of God. Thus a sense
of our ignorance,
vanity, poverty, infirmity,
depravity, and corruption,
leads us to perceive and acknowledge that in the Lord
alone are to be found true
wisdom, solid strength, perfect goodness,
and unspotted right-
eousness; and so, by our imperfections, we are excited to a
consideration of the perfections
of God. Nor can we really aspire toward him, till we have
begun to be displeased with
ourselves. For who would
not gladly
rest satisfied with himself?
where is the man not ac-
tually absorbed in self-
complacency, while he remains
unacquainted with his true
situation, or content with his
own endowments, and ignorant
or forgetful of his own misery?
The knowledge of ourselves,
therefore, is not only an incitement to seek after God, but
likewise a considerable
assistance towards finding him.

BEVERIDGE, 1845.

famishing we may
thence ask
what we want,
but being aroused by fear
may learn humility. For
as there exists in man something like a world of misery,
and ever since we were
stript of the divine
attire our naked shame
discloses an
immense series of
disgraceful properties,
every man,
being stung by the
consciousness of his own
unhappiness, in this way
necessarily obtains at least
some knowledge
of God. Thus,
our feeling of ignorance, vanity, want, weakness, in short,
depravity and corruption,
reminds us, that in the Lord,
and none but He,
dwell the true light
of wisdom, solid virtue,
exuberant goodness.
We are accordingly urged
by our own evil things to
consider the good things of
God; and, indeed, we cannot
aspire to Him in earnest until
we have begun to be displeased
with ourselves. For what man
is not disposed to rest
in himself? Who, in fact,
does not thus rest, so long
as he is unknown to him-
self; that is, so long as he is
contented with his own
endowments, and uncon-
scious or unmindful
of his misery? Every per-
son, therefore, on coming
to the knowledge of himself,
is not only urged to seek
God, but is also led as by
the hand to find him.

So far as one may judge from so brief an extract, it would
seem that Allen's version is entirely independent of Norton's,
and that Beveridge worked with his predecessors' versions
before him, indeed, but with a conscious effort to give a
fresh rendering of the original. Any one of the three would

appear to provide a plain and sufficiently clear and faithful rendering of the original, while the "perfect version," or the version which conveys the sense of delight and satisfaction with which Calvin's Latin affects the reader, is yet to seek.

THE WESTMINSTER ASSEMBLY
AND ITS WORK

BY

BENJAMIN BRECKINRIDGE WARFIELD

Professor of Didactic and Polemic Theology
in the Theological Seminary of Princeton
New Jersey, 1887–1921

Baker Books
A Division of Baker Book House Co
Grand Rapids, Michigan 49516

PREFATORY NOTE

Rev. Benjamin Breckinridge Warfield, D.D., LL.D., Professor of Didactic and Polemic Theology in the Theological Seminary of the Presbyterian Church at Princeton, New Jersey, provided in his will for the collection and publication of the numerous articles on theological subjects which he contributed to encyclopaedias, reviews, and other periodicals, and appointed a committee to edit and publish these papers. In pursuance of his instructions, this, the sixth volume, containing his articles on the Westminster Assembly and its Work, has been prepared under the editorial direction of this committee.

The clerical preparation of this volume has been done by Mr. John E. Meeter, to whom the thanks of the committee are hereby expressed.

Ethelbert D. Warfield
William Park Armstrong
Caspar Wistar Hodge
Committee.

CONTENTS

OTHER ARTICLES ON THE WESTMINSTER ASSEMBLY AND ITS WORK

I

THE WESTMINSTER ASSEMBLY
AND ITS WORK

THE WESTMINSTER ASSEMBLY
AND ITS WORK

First Article [1]

The " Westminster Assembly of Divines " derives its name from the ancient conventual church of Westminster Abbey, situated in the western district of the county of London. It was convened in the most ornate portion of this noble fabric, the Chapel of Henry VII, on the first day of July, 1643; but, as the cold weather of autumn came on, it was transferred (October 2, 1643) to a more comfortable room (the so-called " Jerusalem Chamber ") in the adjoining Deanery. In that room it thereafter sat, not merely to the end of the 1163 numbered sessions, during which its important labors were transacted (up to February 22, 1649), but through some three years more of irregular life, acting as a committee for the examination of appointees to charges and applicants for licensure to preach. It ultimately vanished with the famous " Long Parliament " to which it owed its being. The last entry in its Minutes is dated March 25, 1652.[2]

The summoning of the Westminster Assembly was an important incident in the conflict between the Parliament and the King, which was the form taken on English soil by the ecclesiastico-political struggle by which all Europe was convulsed during the seventeenth century. It was the difficult task of that century to work out to its legitimate issue what had been auspiciously begun in the great revolution of the preceding period; to secure from disintegration what

[1] Originally printed in *The Princeton Theological Review,* vi. 1908, pp. 177–210.

[2] In the ordinance convening the Assembly, it is commissioned to sit " during this present Parliament, or until further order be taken by both the said houses."

had been won in that revolution; to protect it from reaction; and to repel the destructive forces set in motion against it by the counter-reformation. The new Protestantism was, during this its second age, cast into a crucible in the heats of which it everywhere suffered serious losses, even though it emerged from them, wherever it survived, in greater compactness and purity. The form which the struggle took in England was determined by the peculiar course the Reformation movement had followed in that country. There, on its official side, the Reformation was fundamentally a contest between the King and the Pope. The purpose which Henry VIII set before himself was to free the State from foreign influences exerted by the Pope through the Church; and his efforts were directed, with great singleness of aim, to the establishment of his own authority in ecclesiastical matters to the exclusion of that of the Pope. In these efforts he had the support of Parliament, always jealous of foreign interference; and was not merely sustained but urged on by the whole force of the religious and doctrinal reform gradually spreading among the people, which, however, he made it his business rather to curb than to encourage. The removal of this curb during the reign of Edward VI concealed for a time the evils inherent in the new powers assumed by the throne. But with the accession of Elizabeth, who had no sympathy whatever with religious enthusiasm, they began to appear; and they grew ever more flagrant under her successors. The authority in ecclesiastical matters which had been vindicated to the throne over against the Pope, was increasingly employed to establish the general authority of the throne over against the Parliament. The Church thus became the instrument of the crown in compacting its absolutism; and the interests of civil liberty soon rendered it as imperative to break the absolutism of the King in ecclesiastical affairs as it had ever been to eliminate the papacy from the control of the English Church.

The controversy was thus shifted from a contest between Pope and King to a contest between King and Parliament.

And as the cause of the King had ever more intimately allied itself with that of the prelatical party in the Church, which had grown more and more reactionary until under the leading of Laud (1573–1645) it had become aggressively and revolutionarily so,[3] the cause of Puritanism, that is of pure Protestantism, became ever more identical with that of the Parliament. When the parties were ultimately lined up for the final struggle, therefore, it was King and prelate on the one side, against Parliament and Puritan on the other.[4] The main issue which was raised was a secular one, the issue of representative government over against royal absolutism. This issue was fought to a finish, with the ultimate result that there were established in England a constitutional monarchy and a responsible government. There was complicated with this issue, however, also the issue, no doubt, at bottom, of religious freedom over against ecclesiastical tyranny, for it was impatience with ecclesiastical tyranny which gave its vigor to the movement. But the form which was openly taken by the ecclesiastical issue was rather that of a contest between a pure Protestantism and Catholicizing reaction. It was in the mind of neither of the immediate contestants in the main conflict to free the Church from the domination of the State: they differed only as to the seat of the civil authority to which the Church should be subject — whether King or Parliament. This fundamental controversy lay behind the conflict over the organization of the subject Church and the ordering of its forms

[3] "Laud's real influence was derived from the unity of his purpose. He directed all the powers of a clear, narrow mind and a dogged will to the realization of a single aim. His resolve was to raise the Church of England to what he conceived to be its real position as a branch, though a reformed branch, of the great Catholic Church throughout the world. . . . The first step in the realization of such a theory was the severance of whatever ties had hitherto united the English Church to the Reformed Churches of the Continent. . . . His policy was no longer the purely conservative policy of Parker and Whitgift; it was aggressive and revolutionary " (J. R. Green, " Short History of the English People," New York, 1877, pp. 499–502).

[4] As Mr. J. A. R. Marriott, " The Life and Times of Lucius Cary, Viscount Falkland," 1907, p. 248, puts it: " On the side of King Charles all the Romans and Anglicans; on that of ' King Pym ' all the many varieties of Puritanism."

of worship — matters which quickly lost their importance, therefore, when the main question was settled. It can occasion little surprise, accordingly, that, when the heats of conflict were over and exhaustion succeeded effort, the English people were able to content themselves, as the ultimate result on the ecclesiastical side, with so slight a gain as a mere act of toleration (May 24, 1689).

This struggle had reached its acutest stage when "the Long Parliament" met, on the third of November, 1640. Profoundly distrustful of the King's sincerity, and determined on its own behalf to be trifled with no longer, Parliament was in no mood for compromises with respect whether to civil or to ecclesiastical affairs. On the ecclesiastical side it was without concern, indeed, for doctrine. It was under no illusions, to be sure, as to the doctrinal significance of the Catholic reaction, and it was fully sensible of the spread of Arminianism in high places.[5] But although there were not lacking hints of such a thing, Tract No. 90 had not yet been written,[6] and the soundly Reformed character of the Church of England as well in its official Articles of Religion as in its general conviction was not in dispute. John Milton accurately reflects the common sentiment of the day when he declares that "in purity of Doctrine" English Churchmen "agreed with their Brethren," that is, of the other Reformed Churches, while yet in discipline, which is "the execution and applying of Doctrine home," they were "no better than a Schisme, from all the Reforma-

---

[5] Cf. the Resolutions on Religion of February 24, 1629; reprinted in Gee and Hardy, "Documents Illustrative of English Church History," 1896, pp. 521 *sqq.*

[6] A precursor of Tract No. 90, however, had been published in 1634 by "Franciscus a Sancta Clara," a pervert to Romanism of the name of Davenport, entitled "God, Nature, Grace, or a Treatise on Predestination, the Deserts and Remission of Sin, etc., — *ubi ad trutinam fidei Catholicæ examinatur confessio Anglicana et ad singula puncta quid teneat, qualiter differat, excutitur,*" etc. . . . A new edition of this Tract was called for in 1635. The reactionary divines meanwhile were already acting on such a theory. For the state of the case in the later years of James's reign see Bishop Carleton's "Examination of Bishop Montague's Appeal," pp. 5, 49, 94.

tion, and a sore scandall to them."[7] What the nation in Commons assembled was determined to be rid of in its Church establishment was, therefore, briefly, " bishoprics " and " ceremonies " — what Milton calls " the irreligious pride and hateful tyranny of Prelates" and the " sencelesse ceremonies " which were only " a dangerous earnest of sliding back to Rome." The Convocation of 1640, continuing illegally to sit after the dissolution of the "Short Parliament," had indeed endeavored to protect the established organization of the Church. It had framed a canon, requiring from the whole body of the clergy the famous " et cetera oath," a sort of echo and counterblast to the " National Covenant " which had been subscribed in Scotland two years before (February 28, 1638). By this oath every clergyman was to bind himself never to give his consent " to alter the government of this Church by archbishops, bishops, deans, and archdeacons, etc., as it stands now established, and as by right it ought to stand."[8] It was even thought worth while to prepare a number of petitions for Parliament with the design of counteracting the effect of this act of convocation. The most important of these, the so-called " London " or " Root and Branch " petition, bore no fewer than 15,000 signatures; and the personal attendance of some 1500 gentlemen of quality when it was presented to Parliament lent weight to its prayer. This was to the effect that " the government of archbishops and lord bishops, deans, and archdeacons, etc." (the same enumeration, observe, as in the " et cetera oath ") " with all its dependencies, roots and branches, may be abolished, and all laws in their behalf made void, and the government according to God's word may be rightly placed amongst us."[9] Parliament, however, was in no need of prodding for this work, though it was for various reasons disposed

[7] Cf. " Of Reformation touching Church-Discipline in England," 1641, p. 7; or W. T. Hale's edition, 1916, p. 8.

[8] Wilkins, iv. p. 549; reprinted in Gee and Hardy, " Documents Illustrative of English Church History," 1896, p. 536.

[9] Rushworth, " Historical Collections," iv. 1692, p. 93; reprinted in Gee and Hardy, pp. 537 *sq.*

to proceed leisurely in it. The obnoxious Act of Convocation was at once taken up and rebuked. But even the Root and Branch Petition, which was apparently ready from the beginning of the session,[10] was not presented until December 11, and after its presentation was not taken into formal consideration by the House until the following February. As was natural, differences of opinion also began to manifest themselves, as to precisely what should be done with the bishops, and as to the precise form of government which should be set up in the Church after they had been dealt with. There is no reason to doubt the exactness of Baillie's information [11] that the Commons were by a large majority of their membership for erecting some "kind of Presbyteries," and "for bringing down the Bishop in all things, spiritual and temporal, so low as can be with any subsistance." In Parliament as out of it the great majority of leading men had become Presbyterian in their tendencies, and the Independents were for the present prepared to act with them. But there was very little knowledge abroad among the members of Parliament of what Presbytery really was,[12] and even the most convinced Presbyterians doubted the feasibility of setting up the whole Presbyterian system at once, while an influential party still advocated what Baillie calls [13] a "calked Episcopacie." [14] It still hung in the

[10] Baillie, "Letters and Journals," ed. Laing, 1841–1842, i. pp. 273 *sq.*
[11] Baillie, i. p. 303.
[12] Baillie, ii. p. 117.
[13] Baillie, i. p. 287.
[14] The views of this party find full expression in what Mr. Marriott (" The Life and Times of Lucius Cary, Viscount Falkland," 1907, p. 197) calls Falkland's "powerful speech" in opposition to the "Root and Branch Bill." It is printed by Mr. Marriott, pp. 198–204. Falkland was a typical example of the party, says Mr. Marriott (p. 248), which "anti-Laudian but not anti-Episcopal" felt strongly the evils of the Laudian reaction but were devoted to the traditional settlement of the Church. "He is a great Stranger in Israel," said he in a speech of February 8, 1641 (Marriott, pp. 181–182), "who knows not this kingdom hath long labored under many and great oppressions, both in Religion and Liberty; and his acquaintance here is not great, or his ingenuity less, who doth not both know and acknowledge that a great, if not a principal cause of both these have been some Bishops and their adherents. Mr. Speaker, a little search will serve to find them to have been the destruction

balance, therefore, whether bishops should be utterly abolished; and any hesitation which may have existed in the Commons was more than matched in the House of Lords. Above all it never entered the thought of Parliament to set up in the Church any manner of government whatever over which it did not itself retain control.[15] The result was that actual legislation dragged. Abortive bill after abortive bill was brought in; now simply to deprive the prelates of secular functions, and again to abolish the whole Episcopal system. It was not until the autumn of 1641 (October 21), that at length a bill excluding

---

of Unity, under pretense of Uniformity; to have brought in Superstition and Scandal, under the Titles of Reverence and Decency; to have defiled our Church by adorning our Churches; to have slackened the strictness of that Union which was formerly between us, and those of our Religion, beyond the Sea, . . ." and the like. The remedy, however, for these evils, he insisted, was not to take away bishops but to reduce them to their proper place and functions as spiritual officers of a spiritual body. He expresses the opinion (Marriott, p. 200) that the utter destruction of bishops was not desired by "most men," and that the petitions before Parliament were misleading, "because men petition for what they have not, and not for what they have," and the like. Yet he betrays his conviction (p. 203) that "the Scotch government" is in store for England. Similarly Baxter ("Reliquiae Baxterianae," Sylvester ed., London, 1696, I. ii. p. 146) tells us that Presbytery was "but a stranger" in England, and "though most of the ministers (then) in England saw nothing in the Presbyterian way of *practice,* which they could not cheerfully concur in, yet it was but few that had resolved on their *Principles.*" He adds: [the] "most (that ever I could meet with) were against the *Jus Divinum* of Lay Elders, and for the moderate Primitive Episcopacy."

15 It was this "trenchant secularity" of Parliament — its ingrained Erastianism — which afterwards made it so earnest and persistent for the government of the Church by a Parliamentary Commission. It was in this direction that its thoughts turned at the beginning of its discussion of the settlement of the Church (see the lucid account of the debates on the Root and Branch Bill given by Shaw, "A History of the English Church, during . . . 1640–1660," 1900, i. pp. 90 *sq.,* and cf. Fiennes's speech, pp. 35–36); and from this determination it never receded. Mr. Marriott ("Falkland," as cited, p. 208) remarks so far justly: "The fact is that the dominant sentiment of the Long Parliament as regards the Church was neither Episcopalian, Presbyterian nor Independent; it was Erastian. Amid infinite variety of opinions, two conclusions more and more clearly emerged: first, that there must be some form of ecclesiastical organization; and secondly, that whatever the form might be, its government must be strictly controlled by Parliament." In their Erastianism Falkland and Fiennes were wholly at one.

the bishops from secular activities was passed by the Commons to which the assent of the Lords was obtained (February 5, 1643);[16] and not until another year had slipped away that, under Scotch influence (August, 1642), a bill was finally passed (January 26, 1643) abolishing prelacy altogether.

Alongside of these slowly maturing efforts at negative legislation there naturally ran a parallel series of attempts to provide a positive constitution for the Church after the bishops had been minished or done away. It was recognized from the beginning that for this positive legislation the advice of approved divines would be requisite.[17] Preparation for it took, therefore, much the form of proposals for securing such advice. From all sides, within Parliament and without it alike, the suggestion was pressed that a formal Synod of Divines should be convened to which Parliament should statedly appeal for counsel in all questions which should occasionally arise in the process of the settlement of the Church. And from the beginning it was at least hinted that, in framing its advice, such a Synod might well bear in mind wider interests than merely the internal peace of the Church of England; that it might, for example, consider the advantage of securing along with that a greater harmony with the other Reformed Churches, particularly the neighboring Church of Scotland. It was accordingly

[16] This bill was also passed by the King by a commission ("Lords' Journal," iv. p. 580), and therefore on any ground became a law of the Realm ("Statutes," v. 138; 16 Car. i. c. 27), taking effect February 13, 1642. It may be read in Gee and Hardy, p. 564.

[17] The most notable early attempt to secure such advice was probably that taken by the Lords March 1, 1641, in the appointment of what has come to be known as Bishop Williams' Committee. See the full account of this Committee in Shaw's "History of the English Church, etc.," 1900, i. pp. 65 sqq.; ii. pp. 287–294; cf. A. F. Mitchell, "The Westminster Assembly" (Baird Lecture for 1882), ed. 2, 1897, pp. 100 sqq. Similarly, in its discussion of the "Ministers' petition and remonstrance" in February, 1641, the Commons sought the advice of divines in its committee. The desirability of a standing Assembly of Divines for giving stated advice to Parliament was adverted to by more than one speaker in the course of the discussion of the Root and Branch Bill which was introduced on May 27, 1641: on the government to be set up after the abolishing of the prelates the debaters felt the need of advice from such a body.

with this wider outlook in mind that the proposition was given explicit shape in "the Grand Remonstrance" which was drawn up in the Commons on November 8, 1641, and, having been passed on November 22, was presented to the King on December 1. This document began by avowing the intention of Parliament to "reduce within bounds that exorbitant power which the prelates had assumed unto themselves," and to set up a juster "discipline and government in the Church." It proceeded thus (§ 186): "And the better to effect the intended reformation, we desire there may be a general synod of the most grave, pious, learned, and judicious divines of this island; assisted with some from foreign parts, professing the same religion with us, who may consider of all things necessary for the peace and good government of the Church, and represent the results of their consultations unto the Parliament, to be there allowed of and confirmed, and receive the stamp of authority, thereby to find passage and obedience throughout the kingdom." [18] In pursuance of this design, the Commons engaged themselves desultorily from the ensuing February (1642) in preparations for convening such a Synod. The names of suitable ministers to sit in it were canvassed; selection was made of two divines from each English and one from each Welsh county, two from the Channel Islands and from each University, and four from London; [19] and a bill was passed through both Houses (May 9 to June 30, 1642) commanding the Assembly so constituted to convene on July 1, 1642.[20] The King's assent failing, however, this bill lapsed, and was superseded by another to the same general effect, and that by yet another, and yet another, which went the same way, until finally a sixth bill was prepared, read in the Commons as an ordinance on May 13, 1643, and having been agreed to by the Lords on June 12, 1643, was put into effect without

[18] Rushworth, iv. 1692, pp. 438 *sqq.*, especially p. 450; cf. Gee and Hardy, pp. 553 *sqq.*, especially pp. 561 *sq.*

[19] "Commons' Journal," ii. pp. 524, 535, 539, 541.

[20] "Lords' Journal," v. p. 84; "Commons' Journal," ii. pp. 571, 572, 575, 579, 589, 595, etc.

the King's assent. By this ordinance,[21] the Divines, in number 121, supplemented by ten peers and twenty members of the House of Commons (forty being a quorum) were required "to meet and assemble themselves at Westminster, in the Chapel called King Henry the VII's Chapel, on the first day of July, in the year of our Lord One thousand six hundred and forty-three," and thereafter "from time to time [to] sit, and be removed from place to place" and to "confer and treat among themselves of such matters and things, touching and concerning the Liturgy, Discipline, and Government of the Church of England, or the vindicating and clearing of the doctrine of the same from all false aspersions and misconstructions, as shall be proposed unto them by both or either of the said Houses of Parliament, and no other; and to deliver their opinions and advices of, or touching the matters aforesaid, as shall be most agreeable to the word of God, to both or either of the said Houses, from time to time, in such manner and sort as by both or either of the said Houses of Parliament shall be required; and the same not to divulge, by printing, writing, or otherwise, without the consent of both or either House of Parliament."

The prominence given in this ordinance to the reorganization of the government of the Church of England as the primary matter upon which the Assembly thus instituted should be consulted was inherent in the nature of the case, but should not pass without specific notice. And, we should further note, next to the reorganization of the government of the Church the reform of its liturgy was, as was natural in the circumstances, to be the Assembly's care. Doctrinal matters lay wholly in the background. In the heading of the ordinance it is described with exactness as an ordinance "for the calling of an Assembly of learned and godly Divines, and others, to be consulted with by the Parliament, for the settling of the Govern-

---

[21] Rushworth, v. (III. ii.), 1692, pp. 337 *sqq.*: it is printed in the preliminary materials gathered at the opening of the Scottish editions of the Confession of Faith; also in the opening pages of A. F. Mitchell, "The Westminster Assembly," ed. 2, 1897, pp. xiii.–xvi.

ment and Liturgy of the Church of England "; while it is only added as something clearly secondary in importance that its labors may be directed also to the " vindicating and clearing of the doctrine of the said Church from false aspersions and interpretations." In the body of the ordinance the occasion of calling such an Assembly is detailed. It was because " many things remain in the Liturgy, Discipline, and Government of the Church, which do necessarily require a further and more perfect reformation than as yet hath been attained "; and more specifically because Parliament had arrived at the determination that the existing prelatical government should be taken away as evil, " a great impediment to reformation and growth of religion, and very prejudicial to the state and government of this kingdom." The prime purpose for calling the Assembly is therefore declared to be " to consult and advise " with Parliament, as it may be required to do, in the Parliament's efforts to substitute for the existing prelatical government of the Church, such a government " as may be most agreeable to God's holy word, and most apt to procure and preserve the peace of the Church at home, and nearer agreement with the Church of Scotland, and other Reformed Churches abroad." It is a clearly secondary duty laid on it also " to vindicate and clear the doctrine of the Church of England from all false calumnies and aspersions." It has already been pointed out, that this emphasis on the reformation first of the government and next of the liturgy of the Church, merely reflects the actual situation of affairs. The doctrine of the Church of England was everywhere recognized as in itself soundly Reformed, and needing only to be protected from corrupting misinterpretations; its government and worship, on the other hand, were conceived to be themselves sadly in need of reformation, in the interests of adjustment to the will of God as declared in Scripture, and of harmonizing with the practice of the sister Reformed Churches. Of these sister Reformed Churches, that of Scotland is particularly singled out for mention as the one into " a nearer agreement " with the government of which it were especially desirable that the new government of the Church of England should be brought. But this appears on the face of the ordinance merely as a measure of general prudence and propriety — there is nothing to indicate that any formal uniformity in religion with Scotland was to be sought. It was with the reorganization of the Church of England alone that Parliament was at this time concerned; and the Assembly called "to consult and advise" with it in this work, had no function beyond the bounds of that Church.

What is of most importance to observe in this ordinance, however, is the care that is taken to withhold all independent powers from the Assembly it convened and to confine it to a purely advisory function. Parliament had no intention whatever of erecting by its own side an ecclesiastical legislature to which might be committed the work of reorganizing the Church, leaving Parliament free to give itself to the civil affairs of the nation. What it proposed to do, was simply to create a permanent Committee of Divines which should be continuously accessible to it, and to which it could resort from time to time for counsel in its prosecution of the task of reconstituting the government, discipline, and worship of the Church of England.[22] Parliament was determined to hold the entire power, civil and ecclesiastical alike, in its own hands; and it took the most extreme pains to deny all initiation and all jurisdiction to the Assembly of Divines it was erecting,[23] and to limit it strictly to supplying Parliament with advice upon specific propositions occasionally submitted to it. The ordinance is described in its heading as an ordinance for the calling of an Assembly " to be consulted with by the Parliament." And in the body of the ordinance the function of the Divines is described as " to consult and advise of such matters and

[22] " This is no proper Assemblie," remarks Baillie (ii. p. 186), meaning that it has no such powers as belonged to the Scottish General Assembly, " but a meeting called by the Parliament to advyse them in what things they are asked." As Dr. Leishman puts it, the Westminster Assembly " in the language of our time was rather a Parliamentary Commission " (" The Westminster Directory, etc.," 1901, p. x.).

[23] Cf. e.g. the explicit action of the Lords to this effect, " Lords' Journal," vi. p. 84, to which the closing words of the Ordinance are conformed.

things, touching the premises " — that is to say, the Liturgy, Discipline, and Government of the Church, together with the clearing and vindicating of its doctrine — " as shall be proposed unto them by both or either of the Houses of Parliament, and to give their advice and counsel therein to both or either of the said Houses, when, and as often as they shall be thereunto required." And again, with perhaps superfluous but certainly significant emphasis, in the empowering clauses, the assembled Divines are given " power and authority, and are hereby likewise enjoined, from time to time during this present Parliament, or until further order be taken by both the said Houses, to confer and treat among themselves of such matters and things, touching and concerning the Liturgy, Discipline, and Government of the Church of England, or the vindicating and clearing of the doctrine of the same from all false aspersions and misconstructions, as shall be proposed unto them by both or either of the said Houses of Parliament, and no other "; and are further enjoined " to deliver their opinions and advices of, or touching the matters aforesaid, as shall be most agreeable to the word of God, to both or either of the said Houses, from time to time, in such manner and sort as by both or either of the said Houses of Parliament shall be required; and the same not to divulge, by printing, writing, or otherwise, without the consent of both or either House of Parliament." To make assurance trebly certain the ordinance closes with this blanket clause: " Provided always, That this Ordinance, or any thing therein contained, shall not give unto the persons aforesaid, or any of them, nor shall they in this Assembly assume to exercise any jurisdiction, power, or authority ecclesiastical whatsoever, or any other power than is herein particularly expressed." The effect of these regulations was of course to make the Westminster Assembly merely the creature of Parliament. They reflect the Erastian temper of Parliament, which, intent though it was upon vindicating the civil liberty of the subject, never caught sight of the vision of a free Church in a free State, but not unnaturally identified the cause of freedom with itself and would have felt it a betrayal of liberty not to have retained all authority, civil and ecclesiastical alike, in its own hands as the representatives of the nation. With it, the great conflict in progress was that between King and Parliament; and what it was chiefly concerned with was the establishment of Parliamentary government. In its regulations with respect to the Westminster Assembly, however, it did not go one step beyond what it had been accustomed to see practised in England with regard to the civil control of ecclesiastical assemblies. The effect of these regulations was, in fact, merely to place this Assembly with respect to its independence of action, in the same position relatively to Parliament, which had been previously occupied by the Convocations of the Church of England relatively to the crown, as regulated by 25 Henry VIII (1533/4), c. 19, revived by 1 Eliz. (1558/9), c. 1. s. z., and expounded by Coke, " Reports," xiii. p. 72.[24] And it must be borne in mind that stringent as these regulations were, they denied to the Assembly only initiation and authority: they left it perfectly free in its deliberations and conclusions.[25] The limitation of its discussions to topics committed to it by Parliament, moreover, proved no grievance, in the face of the very broad com-

[24] Even the Thirty-nine Articles (Art. xxi.) declare that " General Councils may not be gathered together but by the commandment and will of princes." This was the " law of creeds " in England. Baillie (i. pp. 95–96) even tells us that when the question was mooted in Scotland whether a lawful Assembly might be held without or in opposition to the will of the Crown, he was himself in grave doubt, and could find no example of a National Assembly meeting against the will of the supreme magistrate, rightly professing, either in antiquity or among the Reformed Churches. Scotland soon supplied him with an example. The doubts of Baillie in Scotland, the attitude of Parliament in England, are incident to the principle of establishment, and it would seem can finally be rid of only in free churches. We must bear in mind, however, that from the beginning the Scotch Church claimed and exercised autonomy in *spiritualia*.

[25] The independence of the spirit of the Assembly is illustrated by the conflict which arose between the Assembly and Parliament in the matter of the exclusion of the scandalous from the Lord's Supper and in the much broader matter of the autonomy of the Church. In these matters, the Assembly exceeded its commission and offered unsought advice to Parliament, much to the distaste of that body; and even declined to act on the determinations of Parliament.

mitments which were ultimately made to it; and its incapacity to give legal effect to its determinations — which it could present only as " humble advices " to Parliament — deprived them of none of their intrinsic value, and has in no way lessened their ultimate influence.

In pursuance of this ordinance, and in defiance of an inhibitory proclamation from the King, the Assembly duly met on July 1, 1643. It was constituted in the Chapel of Henry VII after there had been preached to its members in the Abbey by Dr. William Twisse, who had been named by Parliament prolocutor to the Assembly, a sermon which was listened to by a great concourse, including both Houses of Parliament. Sixty-nine members were in attendance on the first day; and that seems to have thereafter been the average daily attendance.[26] No business was transacted on this day, however, but adjournment was taken until July 6: and it was not until July 8 that work was begun, after each member had made a solemn protestation " to maintain nothing in point of doctrine but what ' he believed ' to be most agreeable to the Word of God, nor in point of discipline, but what may make most for God's glory and the peace and good of his church." The first task committed to the Assembly was the revision of the Thirty-nine Articles, and it was engaged upon this labor intermittently until October 12, at which date it had reached the sixteenth Article.[27] That the Assembly was

[26] Baillie, ii. p. 108: " Ordinarlie there will be present above three-score of their divines."

[27] The House of Commons three years afterwards (December 7, 1646) sent an order to the Assembly asking to have sent up to it "all that they have done upon the Nine-and-thirty Articles," its purpose being to employ them in its negotiations with the King. After some demurring, and after attaching to them an explanatory preface, the Divines sent them up on April 29, 1647. For its own use Parliament omitted the Preface and Article viii. on the Creeds; and they were printed in this form in a tract entitled " The Four Bills, sent to the King to the Isle of Wight to be passed," which was published March 20, 1648. It is in this Parliamentary form that they have usually been reprinted, e.g. in Peter Hall's " The Harmony of Protestant Confessions," 1844, Appendix i. pp. 505–512; Neal's " History of the Puritans," ii. 1849, Appendix vii. pp. 454–457; Stoughton's " Ecclesiastical History of England," ii. (" The Church of the Commonwealth ") 1867, Appendix iii. pp. 528–

thus put for its first work upon the least pressing of the tasks which were expected of it — "the vindicating and clearing of the doctrine of the Church of England from all false aspersions and misconstructions" — may have been due to the concurrence of many causes. It may have been that in its engrossment with far more immediately pressing duties than even the settlement of the future government of the Church of England, Parliament had had no opportunity to prepare work for the Assembly. Beyond question, however, the main cause was the premonition of that change in the posture of affairs by which the work of the Assembly was given a new significance and a much wider range than were contemplated when it was called, and an international rather than a merely national bearing. It was natural that Parliament should hold it back from its more important labors until the arrangements already in progress for this change in the scope of its work were perfected. It is not necessary to suppose that the determinations of the Assembly were essentially altered — or that Parliament supposed they would be — by the change in the bearing of its work to which we allude. It is quite true that in the course of the debates which were subsequently held, sufficient confusion of mind was occasionally exhibited on the part of many in the Assembly to make us thankful that these debates were actually regulated by the firm guidance of men of experience in the matters under discussion.[28] But the known convic-

---

535. The lacking Preface and Art. viii. are printed by Drs. Mitchell and Struthers, " Minutes of the Sessions of the Westminster Assembly of Divines," 1874, Appendix i. pp. 541–542. The complete text, with all the changes made by the Divines marked, may be found in Appendix iv. pp. 343–348 of E. Tyrrell Green's " The Thirty-nine Articles and the Age of the Reformation," London, 1896.

[28] Cf. Baillie, ii. p. 177 (May 9, 1644), who, after remarking on the wide differences of opinion which emerged in the course of debate, cries out: " Had not God sent Mr. Henderson, Mr. Rutherford, and Mr. Gillespie, among them, I see not that ever they could have agreed to any settled government." The task of establishing a Presbyterian government in a Church without any experience of it, in the face of violent Independent and Erastian opposition, was no light one: and it was altogether natural that the English divines whose Presbyterianism was purely theoretical, illuminated by no

tions of the members of the Assembly, evidenced in their printed works no less than in the debates of the Assembly, render it altogether unlikely that had they been called upon, as it was at first contemplated they should be, to advise Parliament unassisted and merely with respect to the settlement of the Church of England, they would have failed to fight their way to conclusions quite similar to those they actually reached.[29] Nevertheless the alteration of the bearing of their work from a merely national to international significance, obviously not only gave it a far wider compass than was at first contemplated, but quite revolutionized its spirit and threw it into such changed relations as to give it a totally different character.

This great change in the function which the Assembly was to serve, was brought about by the stage reached by the civil conflict in the summer of 1643. The Parliamentary cause had sunk to its lowest ebb; and it had become imperative to obtain the assistance of the Scots. But the assistance of the Scots could be had only at the price of a distinctively ecclesiastical alliance. The Scotch had been far greater sufferers than even the English from the absolutism which had been practised by the Stuart Kings in ecclesiastical matters. Not content with asserting and exercising original authority in the ecclesiastical affairs of England, these monarchs had asserted and were ever increasingly exercising the same absolutism in the ecclesiastical affairs of Scotland also; and had freely employed the ecclesiastical instruments at their service in England in order

---

practice, should have been much disabled by varying views among themselves as to the best methods of procedure.

[29] Even Dr. Shaw allows ("A History of the English Church, etc.," i. p. 3) that "it is probable that, without the necessity of calling in Scotch aid, and of adopting the Solemn League and Covenant, the Long Parliament would have resolved upon a system of Church government that might be called Presbyterian." And when he adds "though in a sense very different from that usually conveyed by the term," this caution need not be objected to: it is clear enough that the English, even in the Assembly and much more in Parliament, had much to learn as to what the Presbyterianism which they were intent on setting up was and what it carried with it. Scotch influence was necessary, however, not to make them Presbyterians, but to make them intelligent Presbyterians.

to secure their ends in Scotland. But the relations of Church and State in Scotland were not quite the same as those which obtained in England.[30] In the northern kingdom, from the beginning of the Reformation, the ideal of a free Church in a free State had been sedulously cherished and repeatedly given effect; and the government of the Church was in representative courts which asserted and exercised their own independent spiritual jurisdiction. The interference of the King with the working of this ecclesiastical machinery was, therefore, widely resented as mere tyranny. And as it was employed precisely for the purpose of destroying the ecclesiastical organization which had been established in the Church of Scotland, and of assimilating the Scottish Church in government and mode of worship (doctrine was not in question[31]) to the model of the Church of England, which was considered by the Scots far less pure and Scriptural than their own, it took the form also of religious persecution. No claim could be put in here, as was put in in England, that the royal prerogative was exercised only for conserving the ancient settlement of the Church. It was employed precisely for pulling down what had been built up, and was, therefore, not only tyrannical in form but revolutionary in its entire effect. Add that it was understood that the in-

---

[30] Cf. the "Information from the Estates of the Kingdom of Scotland to the Kingdom of England," 1640: "The second error ariseth from not knowing our laws and so measuring us with your line. . . . We neither know nor will examine if according to your laws these may be accounted derogatory to royal authority. But it is most sure and evident by all the registers and records of our laws . . . that we have proceeded at this time upon no other ground than our laws and practice of this kingdom never before questioned, but inviolably observed as the only rule of our government." The whole matter is judiciously stated by Dr. A. F. Mitchell in his Baird Lectures on "The Westminster Assembly," ed. 2, pp. 289–291; cf. W. Beveridge, "A Short History of the Westminster Assembly," 1904, pp. 116–122, note on "Spiritual Independence"; also Thomas Brown, "Church and State in Scotland," 1891, pp. 114 *sqq.;* J. Macpherson, "The Doctrine of the Church in Scottish Theology," 1903, Lectures 5 and 6.

[31] Cf. the Aberdeen Articles of 1616, which the Westminster Divines did not disdain to use in perfecting their own symbol. On these Articles, cf. C. G. M'Crie, "The Confessions of the Church of Scotland," 1907, pp. 27–35. The Articles may be read in the "Booke of the Universall Kirk of Scotland," pp. 1132–1139.

strument, if not the instigator, of this persecuting tyranny had
come in late years to be a foreign prelate aggressively bent even
in England on a violently reactionary policy, to which that
nation was unalterably averse, and in Scotland balking apparently at nothing which promised to reduce the Church there
to the same Catholicizing model which he had set himself to
establish and perpetuate in England, and it will be apparent
how galling the situation had become. Chafing under such
wrongs, Scotland needed only a spark to be set on fire. The
spark was provided in the spring of 1637, by the imposition
upon the Church of Scotland by the mere proclamation of the
King — " without warrant from our Kirk," as say the Scottish
Commissioners — of a complete new service-book designed to
assimilate the worship of the Scottish Church as closely as
possible to that of England, or, as Milton expresses it from
the English Puritan point of sight,[32] " to force upon their
Fellow-Subjects, that which themselves are weary of, the
Skeleton of a Masse-Booke." [33] When the book was read in the
Cathedral Church of St. Giles, Edinburgh, July 23, 1637,
however " incontinent," says Baillie,[34] " the serving-maids be-

[32] Cf. " Of Reformation . . . in England," 1641, p. 69; or Hale's ed.,
1916, p. 58.

[33] " Ar we so modest spirits, and so towardly handlit in this matter,"
exclaims Baillie, when the imposition of the service-book was in progress,
" that ther is apeirance we will imbrace in a clap such a masse of novelties "
(" Letters," i. p. 1).

[34] i. p. 18. James Gordon's account is as follows: " A number of the
meaner sorte of the people, most of them waiting maides and women, who
use in that towne for to keepe places for the better sorte, with clapping of
their handes, cursings and outcryes, raised such ane uncoth noyse and hub-
bubb in the church, that not any one could either heare or be hearde " (" History of Scots Affairs, from 1637 to 1641," 3 vols., Spalding Club, Aberdeen,
1841, i. p. 7). Cf. Balcanquhal, " A Large Declaration concerning the late
Tumults in Scotland from their first Original, etc.," London, 1639, p. 23. To
understand this scene we must bear in mind the division which obtained in
Scotland of the Sabbath service into the Reader's and the Minister's Service.
The Minister often entered the church only when his own part of the service
began; and it had become the custom of " the better sorte " also to enter at
that time. Meanwhile their places were kept for them by their maids. The
congregation for the first half of the service was, therefore, chiefly made
up of " waiting maides."

gan such a tumult, as was never heard of since the Reformation in our nation"; and thus "the serving-maids in Edinburgh" — symbolized in the picturesque legend of Jennie Geddes and her stool, which has almost attained the dignity of history — "began to draw down the Bishop's pride, when it was at the highest." [35] The movement thus inaugurated ran rapidly forward: as Archbishop Spottiswoode is said to have exclaimed, "all that they had been doing these thirty years past was thrown down at once." The Scots immediately reclaimed their ecclesiastical, and, in doing that, also their civil liberties; eradicated at once every trace of the prelacy which had been imposed on them, and restored their Presbyterian government; secured the simplicity of their worship and reinstated the strictness of their discipline; and withal bound themselves by a great oath — "the National Covenant" [36] — to the perpetual preservation of their religious settlement in its purity.

The Scots to whom the English Parliament made its appeal for aid in the summer of 1643, were, then, "a covenanted nation." They were profoundly convinced that the root of all the ills they had been made to suffer through two reigns, culminating in the insufferable tyranny of the Laudian domination, was to be found in the restless ambition of the English prelates; and they had once for all determined to make it their primary end to secure themselves in the permanent peaceful possession of their own religious establishment. The Parliamentary Commissioners came to them, indeed, seeking aid in their political struggle and with their minds set on a civil compact: they found the Scots, however, equally determined that any bond into which they entered should deal primarily with the ecclesiastical situation and should be fundamentally a religious engagement. "The English," says Baillie,[37] "were for a civill League, we for a religious Covenant." The Scots, indeed, had

[35] Baillie, i. p. 95.

[36] The National Covenant is printed in the current editions of the Scottish "Confession of Faith."

[37] ii. p. 90.

nothing to gain from the alliance which was offered them, unless they gained security for their Church from future English
interference; while on the other hand by entering into it they
risked everything which they had at such great cost recovered
for themselves. Their own liberties were already regained; the
cause of Parliament in England, on the contrary, hung in the
gravest doubt. It really was an act of high chivalry, to call it
by no more sacred name, for them to cast in their lot at this
crisis with the Parliament; and more than one Scot must have
cried to himself during the ensuing years, "Surelie it was a
great act of faith in God, and hudge courage and unheard of
compassion, that moved our nation to hazard their own peace,
and venture their lives and all, for to save a people so irre-
coverablie ruined both in their owne and all the world's
eyes." [38] On the other hand, the Scots demanded nothing more
than that the Parliament should explicitly bind itself to the
course it was on its own account loudly professing to be following, and had already declared, in the ordinance (for example) by which it had called to its aid an advisory council of
Divines,[39] to be the object it was setting before itself in the
reconstruction of the English Church. All that was asked of
the Parliament, in point of fact, was, thus, that it should give
greater precision, and binding force under the sanction of a
solemn covenant, to its repeatedly declared purpose. That the
Parliamentary Commissioners boggled over this demand, especially if it were in the effort to keep "a doore open in England
to Independencie," [40] was scarcely worthy of them, and boded
ill for the future. That they yielded in the end and the Scots
had their way may have been, no doubt, the index of their

[38] So Baillie soliloquizes ("Letters," ii. pp. 99–100): and so all men at the
time judged, as even Mr. J. A. R. Marriott allows. "Baillie is justified," says
he ("The Life and Times of Lucius Cary, Viscount Falkland," 1907, p. 303)
"in taking credit for the Scots in coming to the assistance of a ruined cause."

[39] "Such a government shall be settled in the Church as may be . . .
most apt to procure and preserve . . . nearer agreement with the Church of
Scotland, and other Reformed Churches abroad." This already promised in
effect the establishment of a Presbyterian system in England.

[40] So Baillie, ii. p. 90; cf. also G. Burnet, "The Memoirs of the . . .
Dukes of Hamilton, etc.," 1677, p. 237.

necessities; but it would seem to have been already given in the logic of the situation. To hold out on this issue were to stultify the whole course of the Long Parliament heretofore. The result was, accordingly, "the Solemn League and Covenant."

By this pact, the two nations bound themselves to each other in a solemn league and covenant, the two terms being employed apparently as designating the pact respectively from the civil and the religious sides. This "league and covenant" was sworn to in England by both Houses of Parliament, as also by their servant-body, the Assembly of Divines, and in Scotland by both the civil and religious authorities; and then was sent out into the two countries to be subscribed by the whole population. By the terms of the engagement made in it, the difference in the actual ecclesiastical situations of the contracting parties was clearly recognized, and that in such terms as to make the actual situation in Scotland the model of the establishment agreed upon for both countries. The contracting parties bound themselves to " the *preservation* of the reformed religion in the Church of Scotland, in doctrine, worship, discipline, and government, against our common enemies," on the one hand; and on the other to "the *reformation* of religion in the kingdoms of England and Ireland,[41] in doctrine, worship, discipline, and government, according to the word of God and the example of the best reformed Churches"; to the end that thereby "the Churches of God in the three kingdoms" might be brought "to the nearest conjunction and uniformity in religion, confession of faith, form of Church government, directory for worship and catechizing." [42] According to the terms of this engagement, therefore, the Parliament undertook, in the settlement of the Church

[41] The inclusion of Ireland in the new church-system is to be observed: so that from the Treaty of Edinburgh, November 29, 1643, we hear always of "the three kingdoms" in this connection. (Cf. Shaw, "A History of the English Church, etc.," i. p. 121, note 2.)

[42] Rushworth, v. 1692, pp. 478 *sq*. The "Solemn League and Covenant" is also printed in the ordinary Scotch editions of the "Confession of Faith"; and in Gee and Hardy, pp. 569 *sqq*.

of England on which it was engaged, to study to bring that Church to the nearest possible " conjunction and uniformity " with the existing settlement of the Church of Scotland, and that in the four items of Confession of Faith, Form of Church Government, Directory for Worship, and Catechizing; and these four items were accordingly currently spoken of thereafter as " the four points or parts of uniformity." [43] By this

[43] No doubt the engagement does not in so many words bind the English to the adoption of " the Presbyterian system," and no doubt it was with a view to preserving to them a certain liberty of action that they insisted on inserting the clause "according to the Word of God," and on defining the variety of prelacy which was condemned; but much too much has been made of these things (cf. Gardiner, " History of the Great Civil War," i. 1888, pp. 270 *sq*.). After all the engagement bound the contracting nations to the preservation of the ecclesiastical establishment in Scotland, and to the reformation of the ecclesiastical establishment in England according to the Scotch model, so far as the Word of God permitted, and it was fully understood that whatever this saving clause denoted it had reference to details rather than to principles. It must be admitted, however, that there soon developed a disposition to treat this saving clause as permitting liberty in the settlement of the English Church, so far as the Scriptures allowed it: and to those who were able to persuade themselves that no schedule of church government was derivable from Scripture, this liberty stretched very far. We may observe how the matter was viewed by the Parliamentary contractors, as clearly as elsewhere, no doubt, from certain words of Browne, when rebuking the Assembly (April 30, 1646) for its attitude with respect to the *jus divinum*. " It is much pressed," said he, " for the point of the Covenant. We all agree that the Word of God is the rule and must be the rule; but say there be no positive rule in the Word, are we by the Covenant bound to follow the practice of Reformed Churches in case it be against the fundamental law of the kingdom? You must interpret the Covenant so as that all parts may stand. We are bound to maintain the liberties of Parliament and kingdom. If I do any act against this I am a breaker of the Covenant " (Mitchell and Struthers, " Minutes," pp. 454 *sq*.) That is to say, Browne is so convinced that there is no divine prescription as to the government of the Church and that the sole judge in ecclesiastical things is the State, and that, as Rudyard put it on the same occasion, " the civil magistrate is a church officer in every Christian commonwealth " to whom in England all jurisdiction is reserved, that he cannot admit that the Covenant with its " according to the Word of God " imposes any form of government whatever. He has more difficulty with the adjoined phrase, " and the example of the best Reformed Churches," and in point of fact merely repudiates its binding force when inconsistent with English law — as if the very purpose of the Covenant were not to establish a new law in England. That the Covenant bound all parties to preserve the Presbyterian establishment in Scotland, no man doubted.

engagement there was given obviously not only a wholly new
bearing to the work of the Assembly of Divines which had
been convened as a standing body of counsellors to the Parliament in ecclesiastical affairs, and that one of largely increased
significance and heightened dignity; but also a wholly new
definiteness to the work which should be required of it, with
respect both to its compass and its aim. Whatever else Parliament might call on the Assembly to advise it in, it would now
necessarily call on it to propose to it a new Form of Church
Government, a new Directory for Worship, a new Confession
of Faith, and a new Catechetical Manual. And in framing these
formularies the aim of the Assembly would now necessarily
be to prepare forms which might be acceptable not merely to
the Church of England, as promising to secure her internal
peace, and efficiency, but also to the Church of Scotland as
preserving the doctrines, worship, discipline, government already established in that Church. The significance of the
Solemn League and Covenant was, therefore, that it pledged
the two nations to uniformity in their religious establishments
and pledged them to a uniformity on the model of the establishment already existing in the Church of Scotland.

The taking of the Solemn League and Covenant by the
two nations, on the one side marked the completeness of the
failure of the ecclesiastical policy of the King, and on the other
seemed to promise to the Scots the accomplishment of a dream
which had long been cherished by them. The broader ecclesiastical policy consistently pursued by the throne throughout
the whole Stuart period had been directed to the reduction of
the religion of the three kingdoms to uniformity.[44] The model
of this uniformity, however, was naturally derived from the
prelatical constitution of the Church of England, to which the
Stuart monarchs had taken so violent a predilection; and that,
in the later years of their administration when the policy of
" thorough " was being pushed forward, as interpreted in an

[44] Cf. the expression given to this policy in the Preface to " The Book of
Common Prayer," which was thrust upon the Scottish Church in 1637 (Professor Cooper's edition, Edinburgh and London, 1904, pp. 7–8).

extremely reactionary spirit. No one could doubt that important advantages would accrue from uniformity in the religious establishment of the three kingdoms; and the Scots, taking a leaf out of their adversaries' book, began early to press for its institution in the reconstructed Church, on the basis, however, of their own Presbyterianism. Their motive for this was not merely zeal for the extension of their particular church order, which they sincerely believed to be *jure divino;* but a conviction that only so could they secure themselves from future interference in their own religious establishment from the side of the stronger sister-nation. They had no sooner recovered their Presbyterian organization, and simplicity of worship, therefore, than they began to urge the reformation of the sister-church on their model. The Scottish peace-commissioners, for example, took up to London with them, in the closing months of 1640,[45] a paper drawn up by Alexander Henderson, in which they set forth their " desires concerning unity in religion," and " uniformity of Church government as a special mean to conserve peace in his majesty's dominion." [46] In this paper they declared that it is " to be wished that there were one Confession of Faith, one form of Catechism, one Directory for all the parts of the public worship of God, and for prayer, preaching, administration of sacraments, etc., and one form of Church government, in all the Churches of his majesty's dominions." Here we see enumerated the precise schedule of uniformity which was afterwards undertaken under the sanction of the Solemn League and Covenant, the items being arranged climactically in the order of ascending immediate importance. For the Commissioners recognized that it was uniformity of Church Government which was most imperatively required; and equally frankly urged that this uniformity of Church Government should be sought by the common

[45] Cf. the letter of Alexander Balfour, from Newcastle, 29 December, 1640, printed in Laing's ed. of Baillie's " Letters," ii. p. 473.

[46] The document is printed in the Appendix to Hetherington's " History of the Westminster Assembly," ed. 4, pp. 382 *sq.* Cf. Mitchell, Baird Lectures on " The Westminster Assembly," ed. 2, p. 105 and note.

adoption by both nations of the Presbyterian system. The propriety of such a demand they argued on the grounds that the Presbyterian system was the system in use in all other Reformed Churches; that the English prelatical system had been the source of much evil; that the Reformed Churches were clear that their system is *jure divino,* while the *jus divinum* was not commonly claimed for Episcopacy; [47] and above all, that the Scotch were bound by oath, not lately taken in wilfulness but of ancient obligation, to the Presbyterian system, while the English were free to recast their system, and indeed were already bent on recasting it. This paper was handed in to the Lords of the Treaty on March 10, 1641, with little apparent immediate effect. Indeed, there seems to have been even a disposition to resent its suggestions. The whole matter was put to one side by the Parliament with a somewhat grudging word of thanks to Scotland for wishing uniformity of Church Government with England, and a somewhat dry intimation that Parliament had already taken into consideration the reformation of Church Government and would proceed in it in due time as should " best conduce to the glory of God and peace of the Church." [48] This response was accordingly embodied in the treaty of August 7, 1641,[49] to the effect that the desire expressed for " a conformity of Church Government between the two Nations " was commendable; " and as the Parliament hath already taken into consideration the reformation of Church Government, so they will proceed therein in due time as shall best conduce to the glory of God and peace of the Church and of both Kingdomes."

Nevertheless the suggestion ultimately bore fruit. It was

----

[47] The *jus divinum* seems to have been first claimed for Episcopacy by Bancroft in the reign of Elizabeth, but was finding many supporters at the time when Henderson's paper was drawn up, though these supporters still constituted only a party. The difference between the two parties in this matter was urged by Falkland (Marriott, p. 203): only "some bishops pretended to *jure divino,*" but this is the essence of " the Scotch Government."

[48] Cf. Shaw, *op. cit.,* i. pp. 128–130.

[49] Cf. Makower, " Constitutional History and Constitution of the Church of England," E. T. 1895, p. 78, note 37.

repeated by Henderson to the Scottish Assembly, meeting at the end of July next ensuing, in a proposition that the Scotch Church, by way of holding out the olive branch, should itself draw up a new " Confession of Faith, a Catechisme, a Directorie for all the parts of the publick worship, and a Platforme of Government, wherein possiblie England and we might agree." [50] This proposal met so far with favor that Henderson was himself appointed to take the labor in hand, with such help as he should choose to call to his side. On further consideration, however, he himself judged it best to await the issue of affairs in England; [51] fully recognizing that the adoption of purely Scottish forms by both nations was not to be hoped for, but if uniformity was ever to be attained, " a new Forme must be sett downe for us all, and in my opinion some men sett apairt sometime for that worke." [52] Accordingly, when, as the outbreak of open war between the Parliament and the King became imminent in the midsummer of 1642, Parliament addressed a letter to the Scottish Assembly declaring " their earnest desyre to have their Church reformed according to the word of God," [53] and their well-grounded hope of accomplishing this task if war could be averted — all of which was interpreted, and was intended to be interpreted, by an accompanying letter " from a number of English ministers at London " in which it was asserted that " the desire of the most godly and considerable part " among them was for the establishment in England of the Presbyterian Government, " which hath just and evident foundation both in the Word of God and religious reason "; and, referring directly to the Scottish proposal, " that (according to your intimation) we may agree in one Confession of Faith, one Directorie of Worship, one publike Catechisme, and form of Government " [54] — the Assembly natu-

[50] Baillie, " Letters," i. p. 365; cf. p. 376.

[51] Baillie, ii. pp. 1, 2, 24.

[52] Henderson's letter in Baillie, ii. p. 2.

[53] Baillie, ii. p. 45.

[54] Acts of Assembly, 1642 (July 22): " Acts of the General Assembly of the Church of Scotland, 1638–1842," Church Law Society edition, Edinburgh, 1843, p. 66.

rally responded [55] by reiterating its desire for this unifying settlement and renewing " the Proposition made by " its Commissioners in 1641 " for beginning the work of Reformation at the Uniformity of Kirk-Government." " For what hope," the Assembly argues, " can there be of Unity in Religion, of one Confession of Faith, one Form of Worship, and one Catechism, till there be first one Form of Ecclesiastical Government?" The response of Parliament,[56] satisfactory if a little reserved, intimated the expected meeting of the reforming Synod on November 5, and asked the appointment of some Scottish delegates " to assist at " it; [57] a request which was immediately complied with, and the Commissioners named, who, a year later, after the adoption of the Solemn League and Covenant, went up in somewhat different circumstances, and with a somewhat different commission.[58] Meanwhile the Scots assiduously kept their proposals for the institution of uni-

[55] This letter is printed in Rushworth, v. 1692, pp. 387 *sqq.*

[56] Rushworth, v. 1692, pp. 390 *sqq.*

[57] Baillie, " Letters," ii. p. 55.

[58] These Commissioners were eight in number, and were fairly representative of the Church of Scotland, in the two parties into which it was then divided with respect to its sympathies with the old order in Scotland or with " the movement party in the South," that is, the Puritans. Robert Douglas, Alexander Henderson, Robert Baillie, with the Earl of Cassilis and Lord Maitland, belonged to the one side; Samuel Rutherford, George Gillespie, and Archibald Johnston of Warriston to the other (cf. Leishman, " The Westminster Directory," 1901, p. ix.). Douglas and Cassilis never went up to London on their commission, which Dr. Leishman supposes to have been due to the King's veto on the Assembly, as both were strong royalists (as cited, p. x.). In the case of Douglas, at least, this seems hardly likely, in view of his position in the Commission of the General Assembly, and his letters recorded in its Minutes. Dr. Mitchell rather has the truth, when he writes (*op. cit.,* pp. 129–130): " Robert Douglas, the silent, sagacious, masterful man, . . . could not be spared from the duties of leadership at home, but he assisted and cheered them by his letters, maintained good understanding between them and the Church in Scotland, and in their absence came to occupy a place among his brethren almost as unique as that of Calvin among the presbyters of Geneva." The notices of his colleagues in Baillie's " Letters," which are always appreciative and affectionate, exhibit a complete harmony among the Commissioners at London; and the " Records of the Commissions of the General Assemblies of the Church of Scotland," published by Drs. Mitchell and Christie (1892), reveal an equal harmony between the Commissioners in London and the Commission in Edinburgh under the guidance of Douglas.

formity of religious constitution in the two nations forward,[59] and the course of events finally threw the game into their hands, when the Commissioners of Parliament appeared in Edinburgh in August, 1643, seeking Scottish aid in their extremity, and swore the Solemn League and Covenant as its price. By this compact the two nations bound themselves precisely to the punctual carrying out of the program proposed by the Scottish Commissioners in 1640–1641.

The Solemn League and Covenant, it must be borne in mind, was no loose agreement between two Churches, but a solemnly ratified treaty between two nations. The Commissioners who went up to London from Scotland under its provisions, went up not as delegates from the Scottish Church to lend their hand to the work of the Assembly of Divines, but as the accredited representatives of the Scottish people, to treat with the English Parliament in the settlement of the details of that religious uniformity which the two nations had agreed with one another to institute. They might on the invitation of the English Parliament be present at the sessions of the advisory Assembly it had convened, and give it their advice throughout all the processes of its deliberations. And it is obvious that their presence there would much advance the business in hand, by tending to prevent proposals of a hopelessly one-sided character from being formulated. It would seem obvious also that it was eminently fitting that Scotch counsels should be heard in the deliberations of a body to which, under whatever safeguards, was in point of fact committed the task of preparing the drafts of formularies which it was hoped might prove acceptable to both Churches — especially when thirty members of the English Parliament, the party of the other part to this treaty, were members of the body. But the proper task of the Scotch Commissioners lay not in the Assembly of Divines, but outside of it. It was their function, speaking broadly, to see that such formularies were proposed to the two contracting nations for the reducing of their church estab-

[59] Baillie, ii. p. 84; and cf. the correspondence with the King in Rushworth, ed. 1692, III. ii. (vol. v.), pp. 393 sq.

lishments to uniformity, as would be acceptable to the Church
of Scotland which they represented, and would fulfil the provisions of the Solemn League and Covenant under the sanction
of which they were acting.[60] And if the Assembly of Divines
were utilized, as it in point of fact was utilized, to draw up
these draft formularies, it was the business of the Scottish
Commissioners to see that the Divines did their work in full
view of the Scottish desires and point of view, and that the
documents issued from their hands in a form in which the
Church of Scotland could adopt them. In the prosecution of
these their functions as Treaty Commissioners, their immediate relations were not with the Assembly of Divines but with
the Parliament or with whatever commissioners the Parliament might appoint to represent it in conference with them.
They could treat with or act directly upon the Assembly of
Divines only at the request of Parliament, to treat with which
they were really commissioned; and only to the extent which
Parliament might judge useful for the common end in view.
A disposition manifested itself; it is true, on their appearing
in London, to look upon them merely as Scotch members of
the Assembly of Divines, appointed to sit with the Divines
in response to a request from the English Parliament. This
view of their functions they vigorously repudiated. They were
perfectly willing, they said,[61] to sit in the Assembly as indi-

[60] The General Assembly (" Acts " for 1643, pp. 89–90, 90–92), addressing
the *Parliament of England,* informs it that the Scottish Commissioners have
been " nominated and elected " " to repair unto the Assembly of Divines and
others of the Church of England, now sitting at Westminster, to propound,
consult, treat, and conclude with them . . . in all such things. . . ." Here the
Assembly of Divines and the Scotch Commissioners are looked upon as the
two parties by whose consultings together the contemplated agreements are
to be reached. Addressing the *Assembly of Divines,* however, the General
Assembly only informs them that Commissioners had been appointed " to
repair to your Assembly " without defining to what ends. It is to *Parliament*
that the Assembly speaks as to the other contracting party.

[61] This " willingness " was not, however, spontaneous. Henderson tells us
(Baillie's " Letters," ii. p. 483) that the Commissioners, " against their formar
resolution, were, by their friends and for the good of the cause, persuaded
to joyne " with the Assembly. Baillie's own very lucid account runs as follows (ii. p. 110): " When our Commissioners came up, they were desyred to sitt

viduals and to lend the Divines in their deliberations all the aid in their power, if the Parliament invited them to do so. But as Commissioners for their National Church, they were Treaty Commissioners, empowered to treat with the Parliament itself. Accordingly a committee of Parliament was appointed (October 17–20, 1643) to meet statedly with them and consult with them, to which was added a committee from the Divines; and it was through this " Grand Committee " that the work of the Assembly on the points of uniformity was directed.[62] As they were requested by Parliament also " as private men " to sit in the Assembly of Divines they occupied a sort of dual position relatively to the Assembly,[63] and this has been the occasion of some misunderstanding and even criticism of their varied lines of activity. The matter

---

as members of the Assemblie; but they wiselie declyned to doe so: but since they came up as Commissioners for our National Church to treat for Uniformitie, they required to be dealt with in that capacitie. They were willing, as private men, to sit in the Assemblie, and upon occasion to give their advyce in poynts debated; but for the Uniformitie, they required a committee might be appointed from the Parliament and Assemblie to treat with them thereanent. All these, after some harsh enough debates, was granted: so once a week, and whyles ofter, there is a committee of some Lords, and Commons, and Divines, which meets with us anent our commission." For this committee see p. 102.

[62] " Commons' Journal," iii. p. 278; " Lords' Journal," vi. p. 265; Lightfoot's " Journal," p. 27 (xiii. 1824, of his " Works "). Cf. Baillie, ii. pp. 102, 110; and for the completeness with which they were from the first recognized and dealt with as Treaty Commissioners apart from the Assembly cf. instances in Rushworth, III. ii. (vol. v.), p. 371, ed. 1692.

[63] Cf. the speech of George Gillespie in the General Assembly, August 6, 1647 (Baillie's " Letters," iii. Appendix, p. 450). " Ye know we have acted in a double capacity according to our Commission: We have gone on in a way of treating with the Committee of Parliaments and Divines jointly, and have given in many Papers, as concerning the Officers of the Kirk excluding scandalous persons from the Kirk Sacrament, the growth of Heresies, and such things, as in your judgment and ours, was defective among them. We have acted in another capacity, debating with and assisting the Assembly of Divines their debates. . . ." Lord Warriston thus expresses his relation to the Assembly of Divines: " I am a stranger . . . having a commission both from that Church and State, and at the desire of this kingdome assisting to your debats." (Speech to the Assembly of Divines, May 1, 1646, in " Records of the Commissions of the General Assemblies of the Church of Scotland," edited by Mitchell and Christie, i. 1892, p. 92.)

is, however, perfectly simple. In all its work looking to the preparation of a basis for the proposed uniformity, the Assembly really did its work under the direction proximately not of the Parliament but of " the Grand Committee," and the results of its labors were presented, therefore, not merely to Parliament, but, also, through its Commissioners, to the Scottish Assembly. The Scotch Commissioners as members of " the Grand Committee " had therefore an important part in preparing the work of the Divines for them in all that concerned the uniformity; and as present at the deliberations of the Divines were naturally concerned to secure for their own proposals favorable consideration, and did their best endeavors to obtain such results as they might as Commissioners of the Scotch Church recommend to its approval. Throughout everything they acted consistently as the Commissioners of the Scotch Church, seeking the ends which they were as such charged with securing. They were not members of the Assembly of Divines, were present at its meetings and took part in its deliberations only by express invitation and frankly as the agents of the Scotch Church, and possessed and exercised no voice in the determinations of the body.[64]

By the Solemn League and Covenant, therefore, the work of the Assembly of Divines was revolutionized, and not only directed to a new end but put upon a wholly new basis. Its proceedings up to the arrival of the first of the Scottish Commissioners in London, on September 15, 1643, and the taking of the Covenant on September 25th, must be regarded simply as " marking time." The Parliament perfectly understood before the first of July, what was before it; and it could never have imagined that the revision of the Thirty-nine Articles upon which it had set the Assembly could prove an acceptable Confession of Faith for the two Churches. The employment of the Assembly in that labor was but an expedient to occupy it

[64] The fact that the Scotch Commissioners did not vote in the divisions of the Divines is made evident in various ways, and is confirmed by the absence of their names from all the recorded votes of the Assembly (see e.g. " Minutes," p. 252). Cf. in general the note of Dr. Mitchell in his Baird Lectures (2d ed.), pp. 180–181.

innocuously until its real work under the new conditions could be begun. With the coming of the Scotch Commissioners, however, the real work of the Assembly became possible, and was at once committed to it. Already on September 18, there was referred to it from the Commons the consideration of a discipline and government apt to procure nearer agreement with the Church of Scotland and of a new liturgical form, and from the 12th of the October following,[65] when the Lords had concurred, the Assembly was engaged, with many interruptions, no doubt, but in a true sense continuously, and even strenuously, upon the " four things mentioned in the Covenant, viz.: the Directory for Worship, the Confession of Faith, Form of Church Government, and Catechism." [66] And when " the debating and perfecting " of these four things were over, the real work of the Divines was done, and the last of the Scotch Commissioners accordingly, having caused a formal Minute to that effect to be entered on the records of the Assembly, felt able to take leave of the Assembly and return home.[67] As an advisory committee to the Parliament of England, many other tasks were laid on the Assembly, some of which had their close connection with its work on the points of uniformity, and some of which had no connection with it at all. And the life of the Assembly was prolonged as such a committee for many months after its whole work on " the uniformity " had been completed. But its significant work lies decidedly in its preparation of a complete set of formularies — Confession, Catechisms, Platform of Government, Directory for Worship — which it proposed to the contracting nations as a suitable basis for a uniform church establishment in the three kingdoms.

In the Second Article [68] some account will be given of the work of the Divines in the preparation of these formularies.

[65] The order of the Commons was passed September 18 and at once communicated to the Assembly: but the Lords concurred only on October 12. See the facts drawn out by Shaw, " A History of the English Church," i. pp. 153–154.

[66] " Minutes," Session 936, October 15, 1647, p. 484.

[67] " Minutes," p. 484.

[68] Below, pp. 36–72.

Second Article [69]

IN THE First Article some account was given of the calling of the Westminster Assembly and of its historical meaning. It was pointed out that its really significant work was the preparation of formularies designed to serve the Churches of the three kingdoms as a basis for uniform establishments. Some account of its work on these so-called " four parts of uniformity " is now to be given.

Of these " four parts of uniformity " the one which was at once the most pressing and the most difficult for the Assembly was the preparation of a platform of government for the Churches. Both Parliament and Assembly were, indeed, fairly committed to the Presbyterian system under solemn sanction; and the majority of the members of both bodies were sincerely Presbyterian in conviction.[70] But sincerity and consistency are very different matters; and so soon as the details of church organization were brought under discussion, a bewildering variety of judgments was revealed. The Scots, though prepared to yield in the interest of harmony all that it was possible to yield, perhaps more than it was altogether wise to yield, were yet peremptory for a really Presbyterian establishment, as they were bound to be under the engagements of the National Covenant and were fully entitled to be under those of the Solemn League and Covenant. In this they were supported by the overwhelming majority of the Assembly. It fell, indeed, to the lot of the Scots to hold back the English Presbyterians from precipitate and aggressive action. It was their policy to obtain if possible a settlement not so

[69] Originally printed in *The Princeton Theological Review,* vi. 1908, pp. 353–391.

[70] Baillie, writing in 1645, says (ii. p. 320) : " The bodie of the Parliament, City, and Countrey are for the Presbyterie." Cf. i. p. 287, of December, 1640: " The farr greatest part are for our discipline."

much imposed by a majority as at least acceptable to all.[71]
They therefore gave themselves not merely to conciliate the
minor differences which emerged in the debate — on the part
of those, for example, who preferred a mixed Presbyterian and
Episcopal system (Twisse, Gataker, Gouge, Palmer, Temple)
— but even " to satisfy " the small but able band of Independents in the Assembly (Goodwin, Nye, Burroughs, Bridge, Car-
ter, Caryl, Phillips, Sterry), who wished all authoritative government in the Church to stop with the congregation. The
Independents, on their part, adopted an obstructive policy,
and set themselves not only to obtain every concession it was
possible to wring from the majority, but to delay the adoption
of its scheme of Presbyterian government, and if possible, to
defeat its establishment altogether. They were supported in
this policy by the Erastians who, though not largely represented in the Assembly (Lightfoot, Coleman, Selden), were
dominant in Parliament,[72] which accordingly showed itself

[71] For example, with respect to the office of ruling elders, Baillie tells
us (ii. pp. 110, 111; cf. p. 116) of the procedure thus: " Sundrie of the ablest
were flat against the institution of any such officer by divine right. . . .
The most of the synod was in our opinion. . . . There was no doubt but
we would have carried it by far most voices; yet because the opposites were
men verie considerable, above all gracious and learned little Palmer, we
agreed upon a committee to satisfie, if it were possible, the dissenters. . . .
All of them were ever willing to admitt Elders in a prudentiall way. . . .
We trust to carie at last, with the contentment of sundrie once opposite, and
silence of all, their divyne and scripturall institution." Again, more generally
(ii. p. 122): " We doubt not to carie all in the Assemblie and Parliament
clearlie according to our mind; but if we carie not the Independents with us,
there will be ground laid for a verie troublesome schisme. Alwayes " [i.e. never-
theless] " it's our care to use our outmost endeavor to prevent that dangerous [evil]."

[72] Baillie (ii. p. 307) remarks: " The most part of the House of Commons, especiallie the lawyers, whereof they are many, and divers of them
very able men, are either half or whole Erastians, believing no Church-
government to be of divine right, bot all to be a humane constitution, depending on the will of the magistrates." Again (p. 336), he tells us
that (in 1646) two-thirds of Parliament was made up of worldly men
who would have no ecclesiastical discipline if they could avoid it, Erastians, and Erastianizing lawyers, together with a small but influential
band of Independents. Cf. also pp. 250, 265, 267, 277, 315. Very properly
Baillie remarks therefore, that " the power of the Parliament in ecclesias-

ultimately averse to establishing any church government possessed of independent or final jurisdiction even in spiritual matters.[73] In the vain hope of escaping the schism threatened by the Independents and of avoiding an open breach with the Erastian Parliament, the Presbyterian majority in the Assembly proceeded slowly with their platform of government, contenting itself meanwhile with debating and voting a series of detached propositions, which were moreover couched in the simplest and most comprehensive language, while they postponed for the present framing a systematic statement. This delay was, however, itself as great an evil as could have been encountered; and as the differences it was hoped to conciliate were such as in their nature were not subject to " accommodation," the Assembly was compelled in the end to report its scheme of government, which it had thus reduced to its lowest terms and in so doing shorn of much of its strength and attractiveness, in the face of the protest of the Independents and to a determinedly Erastian Parliament.[74]

The first portion of the Assembly's work presented to Parliament was the " Directory for Ordination " which was sent up on April 20, 1644.[75] This was followed the ensuing autumn (November 8 and December 11, 1644) by certain " Propositions concerning Church Government," compacted out of the several separate declarations upon points of government which had from time to time been voted by the Assembly in the course

---

tick affairs " was the greatest of the questions which were to be determined (ii. p. 205).

[73] The position of Parliament laid down in the resolution with respect to the Convocation of 1640, passed December 15, 1640, *nullo contradicente*, gives a fair expression to its fundamental attitude towards all religious conventions, which was adhered to throughout. " The Clergy of England, Convented in any Convocation, or Synod, or otherwise, have no Power to make any Constitutions, Canons, or Acts, whatsoever, in Matter of Doctrine, Discipline, or otherwise, to bind the Clergy, or the Laity, of this Land, without common Consent of Parliament." (" Commons' Journal," ii. p. 51; cf. " Lords' Journal," iv. p. 273, Rushworth, iii. p. 1365.)

[74] " The Pope and the King," says Baillie (ii. p. 360), " were never more earnest for the headship of the Church than the pluralitie of this Parliament."

[75] " Commons' Journal," iii. p. 466; " Lords' Journal," vi. p. 525.

of its debates, now gathered together and thrown into some semblance of order. It must be confessed that the work of collecting and ordering these propositions was somewhat carelessly done. Now and then, for example, in transferring them from the Minutes clauses are retained which have no proper meaning in their new setting. We are told, for instance, that "the pastor is an ordinary and perpetual officer in the church, prophesying of the time of the Gospel"; and it is only from the *vidimus* of the votes of the Assembly preserved by Gillespie that we learn that the clause "prophesying of the time of the Gospel," here sheer nonsense, was a comment on Jer. iii. 15–17 which was on this ground adduced as a proof-text for the proposition "that there is such an ordinary and perpetual officer in the church as a pastor." [76] Again there is enumerated among the offices of a pastor as if it were an independent function, "to dispense other divine mysteries"; and we have to go to Gillespie's *vidimus* to learn that the Assembly meant just the Sacraments (along with the benediction) and no "other divine mysteries" by this phrase. [77] The document nevertheless

[76] "The Form of Presbyterian Church Government": "The pastor is an ordinary and perpetual officer in the Church, prophesying of the time of the Gospel." "Votes passed in the Assembly of Divines," etc., p. 3 of "Notes of Debates and Proceedings, etc.," 1846, in Gillespie's "Works," ii. 1846: "That there is such an ordinary and perpetual office in the church as a pastor, proved, Jer. iii. 15–17 (prophesying of the time of the gospel), 1 Pet. v. 2–4."

[77] "The Form, etc." "It belongs to his office, To pray for and with his flock. . . . To read the scriptures publickly. . . . To feed the flock, by preaching of the word. . . . To catechise. . . . To dispense other divine mysteries. To administer the sacraments. To bless the people from God. . . . To take care of the poor. And he hath also a ruling power over the flock as a pastor." In the "Votes," p. 3 (Gillespie, ii.): "That which the pastor is to do from God to the people," is distributed under the heads of "Reading," "Preaching" and "the dispensation of other divine mysteries"; and then "That which the pastor is to perform in the behalf and name of the people to God" is taken up and distributed into praying, ruling and caring for the poor. Under "Preaching" is subsumed both preaching and catechising; and under the general head of "the dispensation of other divine mysteries" we have the following two specifications: "That it is the office of a pastor to feed the flock by the dispensation of other divine mysteries, proved by 1 Cor. iv. 1, 2: the administration of the sacraments, Matt. xxviii. 19, 20; Mark xvi. 15, 16; 1 Cor. xi. 23–25, with 1 Cor. x. 16. That he is to bless the people from God, Num. vi. 23–26, with Rev. i. 4, 5 (where the same blessings and persons from

contains a firm enough, though cautiously worded, presentation of the essentials of the Presbyterian system; and was therefore followed, of course, by a protest from the Independent members of the Assembly, which naturally occasioned a reply from the Assembly itself. These documents were later (1648) published together under the title, " The Reasons Presented by the Dissenting Brethren Against Certain Propositions Concerning Church Government, together with the Answers of the Assembly of Divines to these Reasons of Dissent "; and republished in 1652 under the new title, " The Grand Debate concerning Presbytery and Independency by the Assembly of Divines convened at Westminster by authority of Parliament."

The " Propositions " themselves, to which the " Directory for Ordination " was adjoined, so as to form a single document, were dealt with very freely by Parliament. Intent only on the practical settlement of the Church while it preserved to itself all ecclesiastical as well as civil authority, Parliament on the one hand, undertook to extract from " The Propositions " only so much of a practical directory as would enable the Church to go on; and on the other, precipitated the Assembly of Divines into what threatened to become endless debates on the *jus divinum* of the details of the Presbyterian system and the autonomy of the Church and particularly the right of the Church in the exercise of its own spiritual jurisdiction to exclude the scandalous from participation in the Lord's Supper.[78] In these debates, and in the whole conduct of its negotia-

---

whom they came are expressly mentioned), and Isa. lxvi. 21, where, under the names of priests and Levites, to be continued under the gospel, are meant evangelical pastors, who therefore are, by office, to bless the people, Deut. x. 8; 2 Cor. xiii. 14; Eph. i. 2." The " other divine mysteries " are therefore just the Sacraments and benediction; they are enumerated as other than " reading " and " preaching " the Word.

[78] Parliament was in no sense averse to a Presbyterian settlement. What it was unalterably opposed to was a *jus divinum* settlement of any kind. It was of the strongest conviction, in even its most Puritan element, that the Church derived all its authority and jurisdiction from the State; and it identified the State with itself. As Nathaniel Fiennes, son of Lord Saye, put it in the debates of February, 1641: " By the law of the land not only all

tions with Parliament during this dispute, the Assembly manifested the highest dignity, firmness, and courage. If Parliament utterly refused to set up a series of ecclesiastical courts with independent jurisdiction even in purely spiritual matters, and insisted on reserving to itself, or to secular committees established by and directly responsible to it, the review of even such spiritual functions as the determination of fitness to receive the Sacrament of the Lord's Supper,[79] the Assembly on

---

ecclesiastical jurisdiction, but also all superiority and pre-eminence over the ecclesiastical state is annexed to the Imperial crown of this realm, and may be granted by commission under the Great Seal to such persons as his Majesty shall think meet." Parliament, acting as the ultimate source of authority, was to set up a government for the Church: and the government was to be the Parliament's government through and through. What government the Parliament would set up was from the first determined to be the Presbyterian. " Nor shall we need," said D'Ewes in May, 1641, " to study long for a new Church government, having so evident a platform in so many reformed churches." Only, it was Presbyterian government, not *jure divino,* but " in a prudentiall way " which was steadily contemplated. Accordingly when the " Propositions concerning Church Government " came up to Parliament this was the rock on which it struck. Parliament was very willing to order the churches on the Presbyterian model, but not to erect independent judicatories, founded in a divine right, and exercising their functions uncontrolled by Parliament. " We passed proposition 3, about which there had been some dispute among the divines," says Whitaker (" Diary," p. 371), " with this alteration, leaving out the words, ' that the Scriptures doth hold forth,' and resolving it thus, that many several congregations may be under one Presbyterial Government." Cf. " Commons' Journal," iv. pp. 20 and 28. And when the question of the administration of the Sacrament of the Lord's Supper and the exclusion of the scandalous from it, came up, Parliament absolutely refused to commit to the church officers, in congregational or classical assemblies, the determination of what sins should be accounted scandals excluding from the Sacrament, and insisted upon itself making an enumeration of such scandals, and reserving in all other cases appeal to itself. It thus intruded into the very *penetralium* of the *spiritualia* and raised with the Assembly the precise question which Calvin had raised in Geneva in the matter of Berthelier. It was on this point that the sharpest conflict between Parliament and Assembly took place.

[79] In the Elizabethan Articles of 1563, while it is asserted that " the superiority of government of all estates, and in all causes, as well ecclesiastical as temporal, within this realm " appertains to the throne, yet " the administration of the word and sacraments " is expressly excluded from the sweep of this supremacy. Parliament in 1645 was unwilling to permit even the administration of the Sacraments to remain in the unreviewed power of the ecclesiastical authorities. On the other hand, of course, the Westminster

its part respectfully but firmly protested against such an intrusion of the secular arm into spiritual things, and refused to be
a party to any ecclesiastical arrangement which denied to the
Church what it deemed its divinely prescribed rights and responsibilities. It took for its motto the ringing phrase, " The
Crown rights of Jesus Christ," and declared that on His shoulders the government is, and that all power in heaven and
earth has been given Him, and, ascended far above all heavens,
He has received gifts for His Church and has given to it officers necessary for its edification and the perfecting of His
saints. It showed itself, in the noble words of Warriston,
" tender, zealous and carefull to assert Christ and his Church
their priviledge and right . . . that Christ lives and reigns
alone over and in his Church, and will have all done therin
according to his Word and will, and that he hes given no
supreme headship over his Church to any Pope, King, or
Parliament whatsoever." [80] On the matter of the spiritual juris-

Divines in their insistence on the autonomy of the Church, were claiming far
more independence of action for the Church than the Acts of Supremacy no
less of the Elizabethan settlement than of that of Henry VIII allowed. The
Erastian temper of Parliament, which was inclined to push the traditional
control of the Church by the civil powers to extremes, was met thus by an
anti-Erastian principle in the Assembly to which the old settlement seemed
unendurable. There was no wish on the part of the Westminster Divines, to
be sure, to take from the magistrate what is his. " We do not rob the magistrate of that which is his," says Gillespie (" Aaron's Rod," p. xvi.), " by giving unto Christ that which is Christ's.' " I do not plead against ' the power
of the sword,' when I plead for ' the power of the keys.' " But they were
determined that the magistrate should not take from Christ that which
is His. " Is it so small a thing," asked Warriston in his speech of May 1st
(see infra), " to have the sworde that they must have the keyes also? " This
the Divines could not in conscience acquiesce in. On the Long Parliament's
assumption of the entire ecclesiastical jurisdiction, see Dr. Shaw, " A History of the English Church during . . . 1640–1660,"'i. 1900, pp. 227 sqq. (" the
unscrupulous and revolutionary seizure by the Parliament of every part of the
domain of ecclesiastical jurisdiction which had hitherto in whole or part
belonged peculiarly to the spiritual courts," p. 236). Dr. Shaw, on the other
hand, seems to consider the Parliament justified in refusing to commit to the
ecclesiastical courts unreviewed powers in determining the scandals excluding from the Sacrament; which surely is a very remarkable position to take
up in these later days — or at least it seems so to " the clerical mind."

[80] Speech of Lord Warriston in the Assembly, May 1, 1646, in the breach

diction of the Church, the Assembly remained unmoved and insisted that Christ has instituted in the Church a government and governors ecclesiastical distinct from the civil magistrates.[81] Meanwhile, realizing that it was of the first importance to get the framework of the Presbyterian government established and in operation, the Divines under the leadership of Alexander Henderson, passing by these doctrinal matters for the moment, had drawn up a " Practical Directory for Church Government," which they had presented to Parliament July 7, 1645. In this document, which avoided as far as possible all questions of principle, very full and definite expositions were given of the actual framework of Presbyterian government. It commended itself in this aspect of it to Parliament and was ultimately in large part adopted by it in an ordinance passed on August 29, 1648, and was published in this somewhat diluted shape as " The Form of Church Government to be used in the Church of England and Ireland."

In Scotland this document was never formally approved, as the earlier " Propositions," which were approved by the General Assembly of the Church of Scotland, were never ratified by the English Parliament. Thus neither became of authority in both Churches. The modified Presbyterianism set up by the

---

of privilege matter, printed in Mitchell and Christie, " Records of the Commissions of the General Assemblies of the Church of Scotland," i. 1892, pp. 92–98 (see p. 94). Cf. W. Morison, " Johnston of Warriston," 1901, pp. 97 *sqq.*

[81] " I am confident," said Warriston (see Mitchell and Christie, p. 97) to the Assembly, ". . . yee will all look and hold out the maine, Christs kingdome distinct from the kingdomes of the earth." This was said May 1, 1646. On the 6th of the previous March, the proposition " that Jesus Christ as King and Head of His Church hath appointed an ecclesiastical government in His Church in the hand of Church Officers distinct from the civil government " (" Minutes," p. 193), had been brought in for discussion; and it was vigorously debated with Coleman as the leader of the dissent until his death, at the end of March, and then against Lightfoot through April. On July 7th it was passed with Lightfoot alone dissenting. Ultimately it was made the first paragraph of chapter xxx. of the " Confession of Faith," in the wording: " The Lord Jesus, as king and head of his church, hath therein appointed a government in the hand of church officers, distinct from the civil magistrate." This chapter was not accepted by Parliament.

Long Parliament in England, under the direction of the one
document, moreover, was soon swept away; while the other
document, approved indeed by the Scottish General Assembly but never ratified by the Estates of the Scottish Parliament, though it has held its place among the formularies of
the Scottish churches until to-day, has been largely superseded in the churches deriving their descent from them. The
permanent influence of the labors of the Westminster Assembly in the great matter of church organization — supposed
at the time, as they were, to be its most important, as they certainly were its most pressing and its most difficult labors —
has been largely unofficial and somewhat indirect. It has
doubtless been exerted nearly as powerfully, indeed, through
such treatises as " The Grand Debate," already mentioned, or
the " Jus Divinum Regiminis Ecclesiastici," published by some
of the ministers of London at the end of 1646, but supposed to
incorporate the Assembly's answers to the *jus divinum* queries
propounded to it by Parliament, as through their formal advices to Parliament. Indeed, it is questionable whether the
really great works of individual members of the Assembly on
these topics, such as Gillespie's " An Assertion of the Government of the Church of Scotland " (1641) and " Aaron's Rod
Blossoming " (1646), Rutherford's " Due Right of Presbytery " (1644), and Henderson's " The Government and Order
of the Church of Scotland " (1641, and again 1690), must not
be conceived the chief vehicles of this influence. The most that
can be said for the formal work of the Assembly in this field
is that it gave ungrudgingly an immense amount of self-deny-
ing labor to preparing advices for the use of Parliament in
settling the government of the Church of England on a Presbyterian model, but was prevented by the circumstances in
which it did its work from doing full justice in these documents
either to its own clear and strong convictions or to the system
with which it was dealing.

Next to the elaboration of a new scheme of government
for the Church of England which should bring it into harmony
with the established government of the Church of Scotland,

the most pressing task committed to the Assembly of Divines was the preparation of a new form of worship to take the place of " The Book of Common Prayer " now to be abolished, by which the modes of worship in the Church of England should be conformed " to the example of the best Reformed Churches." The prosecution of this task was attended with no such difficulties as beset the formulation of the scheme of government. There existed no doubt differences enough in usage and preference among the several parties in the Assembly in this region of church life also; and these differences ranged all the way from a distaste among the Independents to all prescriptions in worship to a predilection in the case of some of the English churchmen for a complete liturgy.[82] But they were less deeply rooted and more easily conciliated in a middle way than the differences by which they were divided in the matter of church government. The work of formulating forms of worship acceptable to all was, therefore, pushed through comparatively rapidly, and the whole " Directory for the Publique Worship of God throughout the Three Kingdoms of England, Scotland, and Ireland " was sent up to Parliament by the end of 1644. By an ordinance of Parliament, dated January 3d, [4th], 1645, it was established in England and Wales to " be henceforth used, pursued, and observed, . . . in all Exercises of the Publique Worship of God, in every Congregation, Church, Chappell, and place of Publique Worship "; and a month later it was approved and established in Scotland by Acts of Assembly (February 3d) and the Estates of Parliament (February 6th). After some slight adjustments it was printed and put into circulation in both countries during the ensuing spring (the English edition bears on its title-page the date 1644, but that is " old style "). As is indicated by the title, the book is not " a straight liturgy," but a body of agenda and paradigms. Some of these paradigms, to be sure, are so full that they are capable of being transmuted into liturgical forms by a mere transposition of their clauses into the mode of direct address, but they were not intended to be

[82] Cf. Baillie, ii. pp. 122 sq., 242.

so employed and are too compressed to lend themselves read-ily to such use.[83]

The first draft of the document was prepared by a sub-committee of the Great Treaty Committee, and, as in the case of the " Practical Directory for Church Government," it was largely the work of the Scots.[84] The suggestions for the prayers of the Sabbath-day service, and for the administration of the Sacraments, were in the first instance their work; [85] and they ultimately had the drawing up also of the suggestions for preaching and for catechizing.[86] Naturally, therefore, there is much in the book which is derived from Scottish usage. The Sabbath service, for example, is in its general structure practi-cally identical with that of the " Book of Common Order " (commonly called " Knox's Liturgy "), and the materials for the consecration prayer in the directory for celebrating the Lord's Supper are mainly derived from the same source. But, on the other hand, the latter part of this same prayer and the concluding thanksgiving are more reminiscent of the English " Book of Common Prayer." [87] The book as a whole, in fact, does not so much follow Scottish as offer a compromise be-tween Scottish and Puritan usage. Acquiescence in this com-promise must have cost the Scots a great effort, as it was, in effect, a reversal of a deliberate policy which had been adopted by the Scottish Church. After the recovery of its purity of worship consequent upon the outbreak of 1637, the Scottish Church was considerably disturbed by the intrusion of certain

[83] See the Preface to the document (Leishman, " The Westminster Di-rectory," pp. 9–14), and compare Marshall's explanation in the MS. " Minutes," ii. folio 286b, as quoted by Mitchell in his Baird Lectures, ed. 2, p. 240.

[84] Baillie, ii. pp. 117, 131.

[85] Baillie, ii. pp. 131, 140.

[86] Baillie, ii. p. 148.

[87] The directory for the thanksgiving after Sermon has been attributed to Dr. Edward Reynolds, from whom came also the General Thanksgiving which was added to " The Book of Common Prayer " after the Restoration (cf. E. Cardwell, " Synodalia," 1842, p. 658; Procter and Frere, " A New His-tory of the Book of Common Prayer," 1901, p. 428; E. H. Eland, " The Lay-man's Introduction to the Book of Common Prayer," 1896, p. 135; L. Pullan, " The History of the Book of Common Prayer," 1905, Index, p. 330).

" novations " into its worship, which were really Puritan customs, seeping in, no doubt, in part, from England, but mainly
brought in by returning Scottish emigrants to Ulster. These
" novations " were made the subject of earnest conference at the
General Assembly of 1641, and again at that of 1643; and, in
order to meet the peril which they appeared to threaten, it
was determined at the latter Assembly that " a Directorie for
the worship of God " should " be framed and made ready, in
all the parts thereof, against the next General Assembly "
(that of 1644), Henderson, Calderwood, and Dickson being
charged with the drafting of it. This whole undertaking was
naturally superseded, however, by the inauguration of the
broader attempt to introduce, through the mediation of the
Westminster Assembly, a common Directory for the three
kingdoms. But the odd effect of this supersession was that the
" novations " for the exclusion of which from the Church of
Scotland the first undertaking was set on foot, were in large
measure constituted the official usage of the Church by the
new Directory. By the very conditions of its formulation this
Directory became a compromise between the Scottish and the
Puritan modes of worship rather than a bar to the introduction into Scotland of Puritan modes of worship.

By these " novations " the use of " read prayers," [88] and
even of the Lord's Prayer, in public worship, was discountenanced, as was also the use of the Gloria Patri, and of the
Apostles' Creed in the administration of the Sacraments, and
the habit of the minister to bow in silent prayer upon entering the pulpit. No one of these usages, on which the Scots
laid much stress, except the use of the Lord's Prayer, is prescribed by the Directory; but as none of them are proscribed
either, the Scots were able to " save their face " by attaching
to the Act by which the Assembly adopted the Directory the
proviso: " That this shall be no prejudice to the order and
practice of this Kirk, in such particulars as are appointed by

---

[88] On the other hand, *extemporary* prayers had been prohibited on pain
of deprivation in the Canons which had been imposed on the Scottish Church
during the tyranny of Charles (1637). This question was a burning one.

the Books of Discipline and Acts of General Assemblies, and
are not otherwise ordered and appointed in the Directory."
By a supplementary Act of the same Assembly, however, they
voluntarily laid aside — " for satisfaction of the desires of the
reverend Divines in the Synod of England, and for uniformity
with that Kirk, so much endeared to us " — the " lawful custom " of " the Minister's bowing in the pulpit." [89] Of more im-

[89] Leishman, "The Westminster Directory," 1901, pp. 164, 168–169. The
objection (Baillie, "Letters," ii. pp. 122–123) of the English Puritans (and
the Scotch innovators, too; for this was one of "the three nocent ceremonies"
objected to by them) to the minister's private prayer in the pulpit, seems to
have been made insistent by an abuse of it by the prelatical party "to bow
to the east and the altar" (Baillie, ii. p. 258). It appears, however, to rest
ultimately on a maxim widely adopted by the Puritans, "that all private
worship in the time and place of public worship is to be discharged." The
Puritans, therefore, consistently objected also to private prayers by the
people on assembling for worship, and to private praying by the recipients of
the Lord's Supper before and after participation. Cf. Baillie's letter to his
colleagues in opposition to this sentiment, printed as Appendix E to Dr.
Leishman's edition of "The Westminster Directory," pp. 188 *sqq.;* cf. also
Dr. Leishman's notes, pp. 86, 132. Dr. Leishman thinks that the clause in the
Directory, "Let all enter the assembly, not irreverently, but in a grave and
seemly manner, taking their seats or places *without adoration, or bowing
themselves* towards one place or other" (p. 16), does not forbid the offering of private prayer before the service has begun, but only superstitious
recognition of sacred places in the sanctuary (p. 86). But it is clear that private praying on the part of late comers is forbidden in the clause: "If any,
through necessity, be hindered from being present at the beginning, they
ought not, when they come into the Congregation, to betake themselves to
their private devotions, but reverently to compose themselves to join with the
assembly in that Ordinance of God which is then in hand" (p. 17). Perhaps
we may say the exception proves the rule, and the prohibition of private devotions to late comers, that they may not be inattentive to the public worship, implies the approval of private devotions for early comers, before
public worship has begun. But we must have in mind also the general sentiment against such private devotions in public places. In Gillespie's notes of
the debates in the sub-committee concerning the Directory ("Notes of
Debates and Proceedings," etc., p. 102, in "Works," ii. 1846) we read: "Some
debate was about the clause forbidding private adoration at coming into the
church," which seems to imply that the purpose was to forbid all such adoration. But then it is added: "Mr. Marshall, Mr. Palmer, and others said,
This is very necessary for this church, for though the minister be praying,
many ignorant people will not join in it, till they have said over the Lord's
prayer," which seems to suggest that late comers were at least conjointly and
perhaps chiefly in mind.

portance than any of these usages, at least for the conduct of the public services, was the loss by the Scots, through the Westminster Directory, of the office of " Reader." From the Reformation down, the former or liturgical portion of the Scottish Sabbath service — the opening prayer, the lessons from Scripture, and the singing of a Psalm — had been conducted by a " Reader," the Minister taking charge of the services, and indeed commonly entering the church, only when he ascended the pulpit to preach. The Westminster Divines found no Scriptural warrant for the office of " Reader," and, much against the wishes of the Scots, enacted that the Minister should conduct the entire service. " Reading of the Word in the Congregation," they set down in their Directory, " being part of the Public Worship of God (wherein we acknowledge our dependence upon Him, and subjection to Him), and one means sanctified by Him for the edifying of His people, is to be performed by the Pastors and Teachers." [90] The only exception they would allow was that they permitted candidates for the ministry occasionally to perform the office of reading, as also that of preaching, on permission of their Presbyteries.

On the other hand, besides the general structure of the services, as already noted, Scottish usage was followed in the Directory in many important points. This was particularly

[90] Leishman, " The Westminster Directory," 1901, p. 17. The " Teacher " or " Doctor " was a coördinate officer with the " Pastor," which the Divines (again without the cordial assent of the Scots) found provided for in the Scriptures: " The Scripture doth hold out the name and title of teacher, as well as of the pastor; who is also a minister of the Word, as well as the pastor, and hath power of administration of the sacraments " (" Propositions for Church Government "). With respect to the difference about the " Reader," Baillie writes (" Letters," ii. pp. 122–123): " Here came the first question, about Readers: the Assemblie has past a vote before we came, that it is a part of the Pastor's office to read the Scriptures; what help he may have herein by these who are not pastors, it is not yet agitat. Always [nevertheless] these of best note about London are now in use, in the desk, to pray, and read in the Sunday morning four chapters, and expone some of them, and cause sing two Psalms, and then to goe to the pulpit to preach. We are not against the ministers reading and exponing when he does not preach; bot if all this work be laid on the minister before he preach, we fear it put preaching in a more narrow and discreditable roume than we would wish."

true in the regulations for the celebration of the Sacraments. The Baptismal service, for example — although the Creed, the Lord's Prayer, and godparents were omitted — yet followed in general the Scotch order; and it was thought a great gain for the Scots when, in opposition to practically the universal English custom, they got it ordained that Baptism was never to be administered in private, but always in " the place of Public Worship, and in the face of the Congregation." It was over the mode of celebrating the Lord's Supper, however, that the most strenuous debates were held. The manner of celebrating that rite prevalent among the Independents, seemed to the Scots to be bald even to irreverence; while many of the details of the Scottish service were utterly distasteful to the extremer Puritans. In the end, things were ordered fairly to the satisfaction of the Scots, although in one matter which they thought of very great importance, they were ultimately compelled to content themselves with an ambiguous rubric. This concerned the place and manner of the reception of the elements. The Scots were insistent for their own custom, in which the communicants arranged themselves at the table and served one another with the elements as at an actual meal. This usage was, after strenuous debate, at last ordered: but the rubric was subsequently so changed that it ultimately read, merely: " The Table . . . being so conveniently placed, that the Communicants may orderly sit about it, or at it." Accordingly the Scotch Assembly, in adopting the Directory, added this proviso: " That the clause in the Directory of the Administration of the Lord's Supper, which mentioneth the Communicants sitting about the Table, or at it, be not interpreted as if, in the judgment of this Kirk, it were indifferent, and free for any of the Communicants not to come to, and receive at the Table; or as if we did approve the distributing of the Elements by the Minister to each Communicant, and not by the Communicants among themselves." In a supplementary Act the Assembly further laid down a series of details for the administration of this Sacrament. It was in accordance with the Scottish usage, also, that in a concluding section, the Directory abolished all

Festival days, and affirmed that " there is no day commanded in Scripture to be kept holy under the Gospel but the Lord's Day, which is the Christian Sabbath." [91]

A document formed as this was by a series of compromises was not very likely to command the hearty loyalty of any section of its framers. We are not surprised, therefore, that it was much neglected in England, though in Scotland it gradually made its way against ancient custom and ultimately very much molded the usages of the churches. Even in Scotland, however, this gradually perfected assimilation to the Directory has of late suffered from some reaction; and in some of the churches deriving their formularies from the Scottish Church, the Directory was early superseded by new models of their own.[92] At this distance of time we may look upon it dispassionately; and, so viewed, it can scarcely fail to commend itself as an admirable set of agenda, in spirit and matter alike well fitted to direct the public services of a great Church. It is notable for its freedom from petty prescriptions and " superfluities " and for the emphasis it places upon what is specifically commanded in the Scriptures. Its general tone is lofty and spiritual; its

[91] This fact is adverted to by the House of Commons in the short account they gave to the Scotch Commissioners in January, 1644, of what it had already accomplished, that the Assembly in Scotland might be informed: " The Book of Common Prayer, and Festival Days, commonly called Holidays, are, by ordinance of Parliament, taken away; and a Directory for Public Worship established by the same Ordinance " (" Commons' Journal," iv. pp. 11, 12). How strong the Scotch feeling on these matters was may be observed from Rutherford's letter of September 23, 1637, to his parishioners at Anworth, in which he exhorts them to stand fast in the faith he had taught them (Bonar's edition, Letter 68; ed. of 1692, Letter 148 of Part i.). Here he warns them that " no day (besides the sabbath, which is of his own appointment) should be kept holy and sanctified with preaching and the public worship of God, for the memory of Christ's birth, death, resurrection and ascension; seeing such days so observed are unlawful, wil-worship, and not warranted in Christ's word." With respect to the Lord's Supper he warns them, " that ye should in any sort forbear the receiving the Lord's Supper, but after the form that I delivered it to you, according to the example of Christ our Lord, that is, that ye should sit as banquetters, at one table with our King, and eat and drink, and divide the elements one to another."

[92] E.g. the American Presbyterian Churches, for whose Directory and its relations to the Westminster Directory, see L. F. Benson, in *The Presbyterian and Reformed Review*, viii. 1897, pp. 418–443.

conception of acceptable worship is sober and restrained and at the same time profound and rich; the paradigms of prayers which it offers are notably full and yet free from overelaboration, compressed and yet enriched by many reminiscences of the best models which had preceded them; and it is singular among agenda for the dominant place it gives in the public worship of the Church to the offices of reading and preaching the Word.[93] To both of these offices it vindicates a place, and a prominent place, among the parts of public worship, specifically so called, claiming for them distinctively a function in inducing and expressing that sense of dependence on God and of subjection to Him in which all religion is rooted and which is the purest expression of worship; and thus justifying in the ordering of the public services of the churches the recognition of the Word as a means, perhaps we should say the means, of grace. It expends as much care upon the minister's proper performance of the offices of reading and preaching the Word, therefore, as upon his successful performance of the duty of leading the congregation in prayer and acceptably administering to it the Sacraments. The paragraph on the Preaching of the Word is in effect, indeed, a complete homiletical treatise, remarkable at once for its sober practical sense and its profound spiritual wisdom, and suffused with a tone of sincere piety, and of zeal at once for the truth and for the souls which are to be bought with the truth.

One of the sections of the Directory is given to the Singing of Psalms, and declares it " the duty of Christians to praise God publickly, by Singing of Psalms together in the Congregation, and also privately in the family." This rubric manifestly implied the provision of a Psalm Book, and it was made part of the function of the Assembly in preparing a basis for uniformity of worship in the Churches of the three kingdoms, to supply them with a common Psalm Book. The way was prepared for this by the submitment to the Assembly by the

[93] In this it had a worthy forerunner in Cartwright's " Directory," a copy of which was found in his study in 1585 when he was arrested. It was reprinted in 1644 and a modern edition has been published by Principal Lorimer.

House of Commons on November 20, 1643, of the query whether " it may not be useful and profitable to the Church, that the Psalms set forth by Mr. Rouse, be permitted to be publickly sung." The result of the Assembly's examination of Mr. Rouse's version (first printed in 1643) was to recommend it, after it had been subjected to a thorough revision at its own hands, to Parliament as a suitable Psalm Book for the Church (autumn of 1645). The Commons accordingly ordered the book printed in this revised form (it appeared in 1646, i.e. February, 1647), and (April 15, 1646) issued an order establishing it as the sole Psalm Book to be used in the Churches of England and Wales, though the House of Lords never concurred in this order. The Scotch Assembly subjected the book to a still further and more searching revision, and by an act passed in 1649 (ratified by the Estates of Parliament in 1650) approved it in this new form for use in the Scottish churches. It is in this Scottish revision alone (printed in 1650), in which they can only by courtesy continue to bear the name of Francis Rouse as their author, that these Psalms have passed into wide use.[94]

To the punctual completion of " the third part of uniformity," that is to say, the preparation of a new Confession of Faith for the contracting Churches, the Divines were urged by no immediately pressing necessity in the situation of the Church of England. The existing Thirty-nine Articles were recognized by them as a soundly Reformed Creed, the doctrine of which required only to be vindicated and cleared from the false interpretations which the reactionary party was already endeavoring to foist upon it. With the internal needs of the Church of England alone in view, they might possibly have felt contented with a simple revision of these Articles, somewhat more thorough than that they had been engaged upon early in their labors.[95] The duty of preparing an entirely new Creed was imposed on them solely by the Solemn League and

[94] On the Scottish Psalter see especially J. Laing in the Appendix to his edition of Baillie's " Letters," iii. 1842, pp. 525–556.

[95] Compare what they say in the Preface to their revision of the Articles (" Minutes," pp. 541–542).

Covenant, by which a common Confession of Faith was made one of the bases of the uniformity in religion which the contracting nations had bound themselves to institute. It was not supposable that either Church would be content simply to accept and make its own the existing Creed of the other. Indeed, neither Church possessed a Creed which it could seriously propose to the other as suitable to the purpose or adequate to the needs of the times. The old Scotch Confession of 1560, breathing as it does the fervor of the Reformation era and full of noble expressions as it is, is too much of an occasional document, too disproportionate in its development of its topics, and too little complete in its scope or precise in its phraseology to serve as the permanent expression of the faith of a great and comprehensive Church; and the new Confession brought forward by the prelatical party in 1616, though sound in doctrine and in parts finely wrought out, suffered from the same defects. The Scots themselves recognized that they had no Creed which they could ask the English to adopt as the common Confession of the unified Churches, and therefore, when contemplating seeking such unification had it in mind to undertake the preparation of a new Creed for the purpose.[96] There was greater reason for the English to feel similarly with regard to their own formularies. The Thirty-nine Articles had, in their past experience, proved an inadequate protection against the most dangerous doctrinal reactions. It was therefore that the ecclesiastical authorities had been compelled to put forth, a half-century earlier, those " orthodoxal assertions " which have come down to us under the name of the Lambeth Articles (1595). It had long been the desire of the Puritans that these Articles should be set alongside of the Thirty-nine Articles, as an authoritative exposition of their real meaning. This desire had been given expression at the Hampton Court Conference (1604), and had been met in the Church of Ireland by the incorporation of the Lambeth Articles along with the Thirty-nine Articles into those Irish Articles of 1615, to which we may be sure the Westminster Divines would have

[96] Baillie's " Letters," i. p. 365, cf. p. 376; ii. pp. 1, 2, 24.

turned rather than to the Thirty-nine Articles, had they
thought of recommending the simple adoption of an existing
Creed as the doctrinal standard of the unified Churches, and
which indeed they did make the basis of their own new Creed.
Since the necessity of a new Creed was a result of the new
conditions brought about by the Solemn League and Covenant, therefore, these conditions imposed an absolute necessity
for the preparation of such a document; and as time passed
on the demand for the accomplishment of the task became
ever more urgent. The " woeful longsomeness " of the Assembly in all its work was bringing the fulfilment of the engagements into which the nations had entered into jeopardy, and
the Scots, who had paid the price of the Covenant on the faith
of the fulfilment of its provisions, not unnaturally began uneasily to urge their more speedy fulfilment. It was accordingly
under pressure from Scotland that the Divines at length entered actively upon the accomplishment of this " third part of
uniformity." [97]

It must not be inferred, however, from their slowness in
entering upon it, that the work of drawing up a Confession of
Faith was one uncongenial to the Assembly of Divines; or one
for which its members possessed little native fitness or had
made little direct preparation; or one which presented for them
special difficulties. On the contrary, there was no work committed to them for which they were more eminently qualified,
or in which they acquitted themselves with more distinguished
success; nor was there any work committed to them in the
prosecution of which they were less impeded by differences
among themselves. The deep-seated antagonisms which divided them into irreconcilable parties, lay in the region of
church organization and government. Doctrinally they were in
complete fundamental harmony, and in giving expression to
their common faith needed only to concern themselves to state
it truly, purely, and with its polemic edges well-turned out
towards the chief assailants of Reformed doctrine, in order to

[97] Lightfoot, xiii. p. 305 — August 20, 1644; Baillie, ii. pp. 220, 221 —
August 18, 1644; " Minutes," p. 77, of April 9, 1645.

satisfy the minds of all. There were indeed differences among
them in doctrine, too; but these lay for the most part within
the recognized limits of the Reformed system, and there was
little disposition to press them to extremes or to narrow their
Creed to a party document. To the Amyraldians, of whom there
was a small but very active and well-esteemed party in the
Assembly (Calamy, Seaman, Marshall, Vines), there was denied, to be sure, the right to modify the statement of the *ordo
decretorum* so as to make room for their " hypothetical universalism " in the saving work of Christ (cf. the Confession, iii.
6, viii. 5, 8). But the wise plan was adopted with respect to the
points of difference between the Supralapsarians, who were
represented by a number of the ablest thinkers in the Assembly (Twisse, Rutherford), and the Infralapsarians, to which
party the great mass of the members adhered, to set down in
the Confession only what was common ground to both, leaving the whole region which was in dispute between them entirely untouched. This procedure gives to the Confession a
peculiar comprehensiveness, while yet it permits to its statements of the generic doctrine of the Reformed Churches a directness, a definiteness, a crisp precision, and an unambiguous
clarity which are attained by few Confessional documents of
any age or creed. In its third chapter, for example, in which
the thorny subject of " God's Eternal Decree " falls for treatment, the Westminster Confession has attained, by this simple
method, the culmination of the Confessional statement of this
high mystery. Everything merely individual and as well everything upon which parties in the Reformed Churches are divided with respect to this deep doctrine, is carefully avoided,
while the whole ground common to all recognized Reformed
parties is given, if prudent, yet full and uncompromising
statement.

The architectonic principle of the Westminster Confession
is supplied by the schematization of the Federal theology,
which had obtained by this time in Britain, as on the Continent, a dominant position as the most commodious mode of
presenting the *corpus* of Reformed doctrine (so e.g. Rollock,

Howie, Cartwright, Preston, Perkins, Ames, Ball, and cf. Dickson's "Sum of Saving Knowledge" and Fisher's "Marrow of Modern Divinity," both of which emanated from this period and were destined to a career of great influence in the Scottish theology). The matter is distributed into thirty-three comprehensive chapters. After an opening chapter "Of the Holy Scripture" as the source of divine truth — which is probably the finest single chapter in any Protestant Confession and is rivalled in ability only by the chapter on Justification in the Tridentine Decrees — there are successively taken up the topics of God and the Trinity, the Divine Decree, Creation, Providence, the Fall and Sin, and then God's Covenant with Man, and Christ the Mediator of the Covenant, while subsequent treatment is given to the stages in the *ordo salutis* in the order first of the benefits conferred under the Covenant (Vocation, Justification, Adoption, Sanctification) and then of the duties required under the Covenant (Faith, Repentance, Good Works, Perseverance, Assurance). Then come chapters on the Law, Christian Liberty, Religious Worship, Oaths and Vows, followed by others on the relations of Church and State, the Church and the Sacraments, and the rubrics of Eschatology. All the topics of this comprehensive outline are treated with notable fulness, with the avowed object not merely of setting forth the doctrine of the Churches with such clearness and in such detail as to make it plain to all that they held to the Reformed faith in its entirety,[98] but also to meet and exclude the whole mob of errors which vexed the time.[99] In the

[98] "It being necessary that the Protestant Churches Abroad, as well as the People of this Kingdom at Home, may have Knowledge how that the Parliament did never intend to innovate Matters of Faith" ("Lords' Journal," viii. p. 558).

[99] An order sent to the Divines from the House of Commons July 22, 1646, urges the hastening of the Confession, and Catechism, "because of the great use there may be of them in the Kingdom, both for the suppressing of errors and heresies, and for informing the ignorance of the people." The Divines themselves say in a petition presented to Parliament, in October, 1646: "The Confession being large, and as we conceive, requisit so to be, to setle the orthodox doctrine according to the Word of God and the Confession of the best Reformed Churches, so as to meet with common errouris" ("Records of the Commissions of the

prosecution of their work as practical pastors protecting and indoctrinating their flocks, the Divines had acquired an intimate acquaintance with the prevailing errors and a remarkable facility in the formulation of the Reformed doctrine in opposition to them, which bore rich fruit in their Confessional labors. The main source of their Confessional statements was, thus, just the Reformed theology as it had framed itself in their minds during their long experience in teaching it, and had worked itself out into expression in the prosecution of their task as teachers of religion in an age of almost unexampled religious unrest and controversy. This work, however, had not been done by them in isolation. It had been done, on the contrary, in the full light of the whole body of Reformed thought. It is idle, therefore, to inquire whether they depended for guidance in the scholastic statement of their doctrine on British or on Continental masters. The distinction was not present to their minds; intercourse between the British and the Continental Reformed was constant, and the solidarity of their consciousness was complete. The vital statement of Reformed thought ripened everywhere simultaneously in the perfect interaction which leaves open no question of relative dependence. The Federal mode of statement, for example, came forward and gradually became dominant throughout the Reformed world at about the same time; and the Westminster Confession owes its preëminence among Reformed Confessions, not only in fulness but also in exactitude and richness of statement, merely to the fact that it is the ripest fruit of Reformed creed-making, the simple transcript of Reformed thought as it was everywhere expounded by its best representa-

---

General Assemblies of the Church of Scotland," 1646–1647, edited by A. F. Mitchell and James Christie, p. 82). Cf. the speech of George Gillespie in the General Assembly, August 6, 1647 (Baillie's "Letters," ed. Laing, iii. Appendix, p. 451): "The Confession of Faith is framed, so as it is of great use against the floods of heresies and errors that overflow that land; nay, their intention of framing of it was to meet with all the considerable Errors of the present tyme, the Socinian, Arminian, Popish, Antinomian, Anabaptistian, Independent errors, etc. The Confession of Faith sets them out, and refutes them, so far as belongs to a Confession."

tives in the middle of the seventeenth century. So representative is it of Reformed theology at its best, that often one might easily gain the illusion as he read over its compressed sections that he was reading a condensed abstract of some such compend as Heppe's "Dogmatik der evangelisch-reformirten Kirche."

In giving form and order to their statement of the Reformed faith, however, it was but natural for the Westminster Divines to take their starting point from the formularies in most familiar use among themselves. The whole series of Reformed Confessions, as well as all the best Reformed dogmaticians, were drawn upon to aid them in their definitions, and it is possible to note here and there traces of their use. But it was particularly the Irish Articles of 1615, which are believed to have been prepared by Usher, to which they especially turned. From these Articles they derived the general arrangement of their Confession, the consecution of topics through at least its first half, and a large part of the detailed treatment of such capital Articles as those on the Holy Scripture, God's Eternal Decree, Christ the Mediator, the Covenant of Grace, and the Lord's Supper. These chapters might almost be spoken of as only greatly enriched revisions of the corresponding sections of the Irish Articles. Nothing, however, is taken from the Irish Articles without much revision and enrichment, for which every available source was diligently sought out and utilized. There are traces, minute but not therefore the less convincing or significant, for example, of the use for the perfecting of the statements of the Confession, of even the Aberdeen Articles of 1616 and of the Assembly's own revision of the Thirty-nine Articles. So minutely was every phrase scrutinized and every aid within reach invoked.

The work of formulating the Confession of Faith was begun in Committee as early as the midsummer of 1644 (August 20).[100] But it was not until the following spring (April 25, 1645) [101] that any of it came before the Assembly; and not

[100] Lightfoot, xiii. 1824, p. 305; "Minutes," pp. lxxxvi. *sq.*
[101] Baillie, ii. p. 266.

until the next midsummer (July 7, 1645) that the debates upon it in the Assembly began. Time and pains were lavishly expended on it as the work slowly progressed. By the middle of 1646 the whole was substantially finished in first-draft, and the review of it begun. The first nineteen chapters were sent up to the House of Commons on September 25, 1646, and the entire work on December 4. Proof-texts from Scripture were subsequently added, and the book supplied with them was placed in the hands of Parliament on April 29, 1647. Immediately on its completion the book was carried to Scotland, and by an Act of the General Assembly of 1647, ratified by the Estates of Parliament February 7, 1649, it was constituted the official Creed of the Church of Scotland. Meanwhile action on it dragged in the English Parliament. It was not until June 20, 1648, that, curtailed of chapters xxx. and xxxi., on " Church Censures " and " Synods and Councils," and certain passages in chapters xx. (" of Christian Liberty and Liberty of Conscience "), xxiii. (" of the Civil Magistrate "), and xxiv. (" of Marriage and Divorce "), it was approved by Parliament and printed under the title of " Articles of the Christian Religion "; and not until March 5, 1660, after the interval of the Protectorate, that it was declared by the so-called " Rump Parliament " to be " the public Confession of the Church of England," only to pass, of course, out of sight so far as the Church of England was concerned in the immediately succeeding Restoration.

The book was not one, however, which could easily be relegated to oblivion. Thrust aside by the established Church of England, it nevertheless had an important career before it even in England, where it became the Creed of the Non-Conformists. The Independents, at their Synod, met in 1658 at the Savoy, adopted it in the form in which it had been published by Parliament (1648), after subjecting it to a revision which in no way affected its substance; and the Baptists, having still further revised it and adjusted it to fit their particular views on Baptism, adopted it in 1677. By both of the bodies it was transmitted to their affiliated co-religionists in America, where it worked out for itself an important history.[102] It was of course also transmitted, in its original form, by the Scotch Church to the Churches, on both sides of the sea, deriving their tradition from it, and thus it has become the Confession of Faith of the Presbyterian Churches of the British dependencies and of America. In the latter it has been adapted to their free position relatively to the State by means of certain alterations in the relevant chapters, and in some of the Churches it has been subjected to some other revisions. It has thus come about that the Westminster Confession has occupied a position of very widespread influence. It has been issued in something like 200 editions in Great Britain and in about 100 more in America.[103] It was rendered into German as early as 1648 (reprinted, somewhat modified, in Böckel's " Bekenntnisschriften der evangelisch-reformirten Kirche," 1847) ; and into Latin in 1656 (often reprinted, e.g. Niemeyer's " Collectio Confessionum," Appendix, 1840, and Schaff, " Creeds of Christendom," 1878) ; and into Gaelic in 1725 (often reprinted). More recently it has been translated into Hindustani (1842), Urdu (1848), German (1858), Siamese (1873), Portuguese (1876), Spanish (1880 and again 1896–1897), Japanese (1880), Chinese (1881), Arabic (1883), Gujurati (1888), French (1891), as well as into Benga, Persian, and Korean (as yet in MS.). It thus exists to-day in some seventeen languages [104] and is professed by perhaps a more numerous body than any other Protestant creed.[105]

---

[102] Cf. Williston Walker, "The Creeds and Platforms of Congregationalism," New York, 1893; Underhill, "Confessions of Faith . . . illustrative of the History of the Baptist Churches of England in the 17th Century," London, 1854; *The Presbyterian and Reformed Review,* Philadelphia, xiii. 1902, pp. 380 *sqq.* (pp. 368 *sqq.* of this volume).

[103] *Presbyterian and Reformed Review,* October, 1901, xii. pp. 614–659; January, 1902, xiii. pp. 60–120; October, 1902, xiii. pp. 551–587.

[104] Cf. *Presbyterian and Reformed Review,* April, 1902, xiii. pp. 254–276 (pp. 361 *sqq.* of this volume).

[105] Cf. the statistics in the article " Puritaner, Presbyterianer," in Herzog.³ Also J. N. Ogilvie, "The Presbyterian Churches," 1897 and 1925; Henry Cowan, "The Influence of the Scottish Church in Christendom," Baird Lecture for 1895, London, 1896.

The labors of the Divines upon the " fourth part of uniformity," that is to say, in the preparation of a Catechism for the unified Churches, reached a similarly felicitous result. The Westminster Assembly was eminently an assembly of catechists, trained and practised in the art.[106] Not only were its members pupils of masters in this work, but not fewer than a dozen of themselves had published Catechisms which were in wide use in the churches (Twisse, White, Gataker, Gouge, Wilkinson, Wilson, Walker, Palmer, Cawdrey, Sedgewick, Byfield, and possibly Newcomen, Lyford, Hodges, Foxcroft). A beginning was made at a comparatively early date towards drawing up their Catechism; but this labor was successfully completed only after all the other work of the Assembly had been accomplished. In the earlier notices of work on the Catechism it is not always easy to distinguish between references to the preparation of the Directory for Catechising or the Directory for Worship and references to the preparation of the Catechism itself. But as early as November 21, 1644, Baillie speaks of " the Catechise " as already drawn up; and on the 26th of December following, as nearly agreed on in private in its first draft. And we learn from the " Minutes " (p. 13) that on December 2, 1644, a committee was appointed " for hastening the Catechism," and that this committee was augmented on February 7th following (p. 48). On August 5, 1645, the material of this Catechism was under debate in the Assembly itself; and by August 20 it would seem to have been so far nearing completion that a committee was appointed to " draw up the whole draught " of it. Nothing, however, came of this work. It appears, in effect, that one or two false starts were made upon the Catechism before the Divines got down to their really productive work upon it. After midsummer of 1645 we hear nothing about the Catechism for a year, when, writing July 14, 1646, Baillie tells us that all that had been hitherto accomplished was set aside and a new beginning made. " We made, long agoe," he writes, " a prettie progress in the Cate-

[106] Cf. Mitchell, Baird Lectures on " The Westminster Assembly," ed. 2, p. 419, and the passage quoted from Heppe, p. 81.

chise; but falling on rubbes and long debates, it wes laid aside till the Confession wes ended, with resolution to have no matter in it but what wes expressed in the Confession, which should not be debated over againe in the Catechise."

Accordingly, the Confession being now finished and in process of review, the new Catechism [107] was taken up (September 11), and from September 14, 1646, to January 4, 1647, was rapidly passed through the Assembly up to the questions which dealt with the Fourth Commandment. This, however, was only another false start. In the prosecution of this work, the Assembly became convinced that it was attempting an impossible feat; as the Scottish Commissioners express it,[108] it was essaying "to dress up milk and meat bQth in one dish." It therefore again called a halt and "recommitted the work, that tuo formes of Catechisme may be prepared, one more exact and comprehensive, another more easie and short for new beginners." [109] Recommencing on this new basis, the "Larger Catechism" began to be debated on April 15, 1647, and was finished on the 15th of the following October, and sent up to Parliament on October 22. The "Shorter Catechism" was taken up on August 5, 1647, seriously taken in hand October 19, began to come into the Assembly on October 21, and was finished November 22 and sent up to Parliament November 25, 1647. The proof-texts for both Catechisms occupied the Assembly from November 30, 1647, to April 12, 1648, and were presented to Parliament April 14, 1648. The "Shorter Catechism" was approved by Parliament on September 22–25, 1648, and issued under the title, "The Grounds and Principles of Religion, contained in a Shorter Catechism (according to the Advice of the Assembly of Divines sitting at West-

[107] An order from the Commons to hasten the Catechism had come in on July 22, 1646.

[108] Writing to the Commission of the General Assembly. See the published records of the Commission, i. p. 187.

[109] *Do.*: cf. "Minutes" for January 14, where the order for preparing the *two* Catechisms is noted and it is added that in the preparation of them, eye is to be had "to the Confession of Faith, and to the matter of the Catechism already begun" (p. 321). Cf. also Gillespie's account in his speech in the General Assembly, August, 1647 (Baillie's "Letters," iii. Appendix, p. 452).

minster), to be used throughout the Kingdom of England and Dominion of Wales." The " Larger Catechism," however, although passed by the Commons on July 24, 1648, stuck in the House of Lords and never received its authorization. In Scotland, both were approved by acts of the General Assembly of 1648, ratified by the Estates of Parliament, February 7, 1649; but no mention is made of them in the reëstablishment of Presbytery after the Revolution. In the later history of the Westminster formularies, the " Larger Catechism " has taken a somewhat secondary place; but no product of the Divines has been more widely diffused or has exercised a deeper influence than their "Shorter Catechism." It at once became in Scotland the textbook in religion in the schools, and has held that position up to to-day; and for a long period it was scarcely less popular in Non-Conformist England than in Scotland. From both sources it was transmitted to their affiliated Churches in America; and in the extension of the mission work of the several Presbyterian Churches in the nineteenth century its use has been diffused throughout the world.

The tracing of the sources of the Westminster Catechisms is rendered exceptionally difficult not merely by the amazing fecundity in catechetical manuals of the British Churches of the immediately preceding and contemporary periods, but also by the obvious independence of the Westminster Divines in giving form to their catechetical formularies, and their express determination to derive the materials for them, as far as possible, from their own Confession of Faith. The contents of the first Catechism taken in hand by them — the Catechism of 1644–1645 — have not been transmitted to us. We may infer, however, from the meager details which have found record, that it was probably based on the Catechism of Herbert Palmer, published in 1640 under the title of " An Endeavour of Making Christian Religion Easie " (5th edition, 1645). The matter of the second Catechism prepared by the Assembly — that of the autumn of 1646 — is preserved for us in the Minutes, so far as it was debated and passed by the Assembly.[110]

[110] It has been extracted and printed in consecutive form by W. Car-

It professedly derives its material as far as possible from the Assembly's Confession of Faith, but as it covers in large part ground not gone over in the Confession, much of its material must have an independent origin. Palmer's Catechism still seems to underlie it, but supplies no material for its exposition of the Commandments; and the influence of the manuals of Usher seems discernible. Much the same must be said of the sources of the Catechisms which the Assembly completed, " Larger " and " Shorter." The doctrinal portion of the " Larger Catechism " is very much a catechetical recension of the Assembly's Confession of Faith; while in its ethical portion (its exposition of the Ten Commandments) it seems to derive most from Usher's " Body of Divinity " and Nicholl's and Ball's " Catechisms "; and in its exposition of the Lord's Prayer to go back ultimately through intermediary manuals to William Perkins' treatise on the Lord's Prayer. The " Shorter Catechism " is so original and individual in its form, that the question of its sources seems insoluble, if not impertinent. It in the main follows the outline of the " Larger Catechism "; but in its modes of statement it now and again varies from it and in some of these variations reverts to the Catechism of the autumn of 1646. In their striking opening questions both Catechisms go back ultimately to the model introduced by Calvin, possibly but certainly not probably through the intermediation of Leo Judae.[111] Perhaps of all earlier Catechisms the little manual of Ezekiel Rogers most closely resembles the " Shorter Catechism " in its general plan and order; but there is little detailed resemblance between the two. After all said, the " Shorter Catechism " is a new creation, and must be considered in structure and contents alike the contribution to the catechetical art of the Westminster Divines themselves. No other Catechism can be compared with it in its concise, nerv-

---

ruthers in his " The Shorter Catechism of the Westminster Assembly of Divines, . . . with Historical Account and Bibliography," London, 1897.

[111] Leo Judae: " *Q.* Dic, sodes, ad quem finem homo creatus est? *R.* Ut optimi maximi ac sapientissimi Dei Creatoris majestatem ac bonitatem agnoscamus, tandemque illo Æternum fruamur."

ous, terse exactitude of definition, or in its severely logical
elaboration; and it gains these admirable qualities at no expense to its freshness or fervor, though perhaps it can scarcely
be spoken of as marked by childlike simplicity. Although set
forth as "milk for babes" and designed to stand by the side
of the "Larger Catechism" as an "easie and short" manual
of religion "for new beginners," it is nevertheless governed by
the principle (as one of its authors — Seaman — phrased it),
"that the greatest care should be taken to frame the answer
not according to the model of the knowledge the child hath, but
according to that the child ought to have." Its peculiarity, in
contrast with the "Larger Catechism" (and the Confession of
Faith), is the strictness with which its contents are confined
to the very quintessence of religion and morals, to the positive
truths and facts which must be known for their own behoof by
all who would fain be instructed in right belief and practice.[112]
All purely historical matter, and much more, all controversial
matter — everything which can minister merely to curiosity,
however chastened — is rigidly excluded. Only that is given
which, in the judgment of its framers, is directly required for
the Christian's instruction in what he is to believe concerning
God and what God requires of him. It is a pure manual of personal religion and practical morality.

To whom among the Westminster Divines we more especially owe these Catechetical manuals — and particularly the
"Shorter Catechism" — we have no means of determining.
It is, of course, easy to draw out from the records of the Assembly the names of the members of the committees to which
the preparation of the materials for them was entrusted. But

[112] Accordingly the course of salvation alone is traced in questions 20–
38 with no reference whatever to the career or end of those not elected to
everlasting life. The theory is that the catechumen is interested, or ought to
be, exclusively in what has been done for him and what he is to expect.
This is the account to give of the fact which seems strange to some (see
Mitchell, Baird Lectures, ed. 2, p. 450) that there is no reference here to the
future retribution of the lost. This is only a portion of a larger fact. The
Catechism proceeds on the presumption that the catechumen is a child of
God and gives only what the child of God needs to know of the dealings of
God with him and the duties he owes to God.

this seems to carry us a very little way into the problem. On the whole, Herbert Palmer, who bore the reputation, as Baillie tells us, of being " the best catechist in England," appears to have been the leading spirit in the Assembly in all matters concerned with catechetics: and he apparently served on all important committees busied with the Catechisms up to his death, which occurred, however (August 13, 1647), before the " Shorter Catechism " seems to have been seriously taken in hand. We have no direct evidence to connect him with the authorship of this Catechism, only the first — evidently a purely preliminary — report upon which he was privileged to be the medium of making, and the contents of which certainly show much less resemblance to those of his own manual than there is reason to believe was exhibited by the earliest Catechism undertaken by the Assembly. There is still less reason, of course, to connect with its composition the name of Dr. John Wallis, Palmer's pupil and friend, who attended the committee charged with its review as its secretary (from November 9, 1647), and whose mathematical genius has been thought to express itself in the clear and logical definitions which characterize the document. Dr. Wallis' close connection with the " Shorter Catechism," in the minds of the contemporary and following generations, appears to be mainly due to the publication by him at once on its appearance (1648) of an edition of it broken up into subordinate questions according to the model of the treatise of his friend and patron, Palmer. Still less have we evidence to connect the Scotch Commissioners directly with the composition of the " Shorter Catechism." The record may give us reason to infer that the earliest Catechism undertaken by the Assembly may have been in the first instance drafted by the Scots.[113] But we lack even such faint

113 How far this first draft may be represented by " The New Catechisme according to the forme of the Kirk of Scotland," published by the Scots in 1644 (reprinted in Mitchell's " Catechisms of the Second Reformation," 1886) we have no means of determining: but there is reason to believe that if this document was prepared by the Scots as a draft for the consideration of the Assembly, it was much departed from in the Assembly's work, which seems rather to have taken its start from Palmer's Catechism.

suggestions in the case of the Catechisms which were ultimately prepared. Indeed, these Catechisms, and especially the "Shorter," are precisely the portion of the Assembly's constructive work, in the composition of which the Scotch Commissioners appear to have had the least prominent part. Henderson had died before the Confession of Faith was finished; Baillie left immediately after its completion; Gillespie in the midst of the work on the "Larger Catechism"; while Rutherford, who alone remained until the "Shorter Catechism" was under way, judged that his presence until the completion of the "Larger Catechism" justified the declaration that the Scots had lent their aid to the accomplishment of all "the 4 things mentioned in the Covenant,"[114] which is as much as to say that he looked upon the completion of the "Shorter Catechism" as largely a matter of routine work unessential to the main task of the Assembly.[115] It does not follow, of course, that the Scots had nothing to do with the composition of the "Shorter Catechism." We do not know how fully its text had been worked out before any of it was brought before the Assembly, or how hard it rested on previous work done in committee or in the Assembly, or to whom the first essays in its composition were due. Of course, the Scots served with all committees up to the moment of their departure, and may have had much to do with the framing of the drafts of documents with which we have no explicit evidence to connect their

[114] "Minutes," October 15, 1647. Before he actually took his leave (November 9), the Shorter Catechism, which ran rapidly forward, was on the point of completion. See the "Minutes" for November 8, when the Commandments, Lord's Prayer, and Creed were ordered to be added to the Catechism.

[115] It would seem that the Shorter Catechism was not seriously taken in hand until October 19, 1647, and that as late as September 29, 1647, it could still seem doubtful in Scotland whether the Divines would not content themselves with the Larger Catechism. On that date the Commission at Edinburgh, acting on the assumption that there might be no Shorter Catechism prepared by the Divines, appointed a committee of its own to draw up a primary Catechism for use in Scotland. (See "Records of the Commissions of the General Assemblies, etc.," edited by Mitchell and Christie, i. 1892, p. 306.) The Assembly of Divines was already disintegrating and it was hard to get together a quorum.

names. But they appear to have had less to do with giving the
Catechisms their final form than was the case with the other
documents prepared by the Divines for the use of the united
Churches. The Catechisms come to us preëminently as the
work of the Assembly, and we are without data to enable us to
point to any individual or individuals to whom we can confidently assign their characteristic features.

With the completion of the Catechisms, the work of the
Assembly under the engagement of the Solemn League and
Covenant was done. The Scots, as we have seen, caused a Minute to this effect to be entered upon the records of the Assembly (October 15, 1647), reciting that some of them had given
assistance to the Divines throughout the whole of their labors
looking to uniformity. And on the return to Scotland of Rutherford, the last of the Scots to leave London, the Commission
of the General Assembly dispatched a letter to the Assembly
of Divines (November 26, 1647) — with whom it joins in the
address "the Ministers of London, and all the other well-
affected brethren of the Ministrie in England" — which accurately reflects the state of affairs relatively to the work of the
Divines at the end of the year 1647. In this letter the Scots express their unwavering purpose to abide by the Covenant they
had sworn, and exhort their English brethren to do the same,
noting at the same time the difficulties they saw besetting the
way, and recommending in view of them diligence in the fear
of God. In pursuance of its covenant engagement, the letter
goes on to declare, the Scottish Church had approved and ratified the "Directory for Worship" "being about tuo yeares
agoe agreed vpon by the Assemblies and Parliaments of both
kingdomes," and the "Doctrinal Part of Church Government" — that is, the "Propositions for Church Government"
of 1644 — "agreed vpon by the reverend and learned Assemblie of Divines"; and had also approved the "Confession of
Faith" "as sound and orthodox for the matter, and agreed
vnto on their part that it be a part of the Vniformity, and a
Confession of Faith for the Churches of Christ in the three
kingdomes"; while it purposed to consider and expected to

approve the " Directory of Church Government," the " Catechism," and the new " Paraphrase of the Psalms " at the next
Assembly, to meet in the summer of 1648. From this statement we perceive how far Scotland had outrun England in fulfilling the terms of their mutual engagement, and how uneasy
the northern kingdom was becoming over the ever growing
prospect that they would never be fully met in England. Meanwhile all the work of the Divines for uniformity was done;
there remained only the completion of the proof-texts for the
Catechisms, with the completion of which their entire function, as enlarged and given international significance by the
provisions of the Solemn League and Covenant, was performed. We find the Assembly, therefore, on the day on which
Rutherford took his leave of it, appointing a committee " to
consider of what is fit to be done when the Catechism is
finished " (November 9, 1647). For a time the Assembly turned
back to the controversies of the great days of its past, with the
Independents and the Erastians; to its responses to the *jus
divinum* queries; [116] and especially to its answers to the reasons of the Dissenting brethren against the Presbyterian system of government, which it now prepared for publication
(1648, and again 1652). It had ceased to have any further
function, however, than that of a standing advisory board to
Parliament; and as the significance of Parliament decreased
(" Pride's purge," December 6, 1648, was the precursor of the
end, which came in 1653) its own importance necessarily fell
with it. It became increasingly difficult to get a quorum together; and its work dwindled into the mere task of an examining committee for vacant charges, until it passed out of
existence with the Parliament from which it derived its being.

What the Divines could do for the institution of the proposed uniformity of religion in the three kingdoms, we see,
then, had been done and well done, by the beginning of 1648.
The institution of uniformity on the basis formulated by them

[116] These queries had been laid aside " till the Confession and Catechise
were ended " (Baillie, " Letters," ii. pp. 379, 388), so that to return to them
at this point was only to carry out a long-determined plan.

did not lie within their powers. That was a matter of treaty engagement between the two nations. We have seen that the Scotch were in no way backward in the fulfilment of their part of the engagement. The same cannot be said for England. The political situation was very different at the opening of 1648 from what it had been in midsummer of 1643; and Parliament was now perhaps little inclined, and, to do it justice, was certainly little able, to carry out all it had felt constrained to promise five years before.[117] The rise of Independency to political power and the usurpation of the army were the supersession of the Covenant and all its solemn obligations: and after the usurpation came ultimately, not the restoration of Parliamentary government and Presbyterianism, but the restoration of monarchy and prelacy. The dream of an enforced uniformity of religion in the three kingdoms on a Presbyterian basis, under the inspiration of which the Divines had done their constructive work, had vanished; and so far

---

[117] What was done by Parliament, however, was not little, though it was done slowly and proved not lasting. This is how it is sketched by a not very friendly hand: "The years 1640–60 witnessed the most complete and drastic revolution which the Church of England has ever undergone. Its whole structure was ruthlessly demolished — Episcopacy, the Spiritual Courts, Deans and Chapters, Convocation, the Book of Common Prayer, the Thirty-nine Articles, and the Psalter; the lands of the Bishops and of the Deans and Chapters were sold, and the Cathedrals were purified or defiled. On the clean-swept ground an entirely novel Church system was erected. In place of Episcopal Church Government a Presbyterian organization was introduced, and a Presbyterian system of ordination. For the Spiritual Courts were substituted Presbyterian Assemblies (Parochial, Classical and Provincial), acting with a very real censorial jurisdiction, but in final subordination to a parliamentary committee sitting at Westminster. Instead of the Thirty-nine Articles the Confession of Faith was introduced, and the Directory in place of the Book of Common Prayer. New Catechisms and a new metrical version were prepared, a parochial survey of the whole country was carried out, and extensive reorganization of parishes effected. Finally, the equivalent of a modern ecclesiastical commission (or let us say of Queen Anne's Bounty Scheme) was invented, a body of trustees was endowed with considerable revenues for the purpose of augmenting poor livings, and for years the work of this ecclesiastical charity and reorganization scheme was earnestly pursued. There is hardly a parallel in history to such a constitutional revolution as this. . . ." (W. A. Shaw, "A History of the English Church during . . . 1640–1660," i. 1900, pp. vii.–viii.).

as the successful issue of their labors depended on alliance with a friendly state, their work, as regards England at least, had failed. But this alliance was not the strength of the Assembly, but its weakness. Its work was not in character political, but religious; and its product needed no imposition by the civil power to give it vitality. Whatever real authority the formularies it had framed possessed, was inherent in them as sound presentations of truth, not derived from extraneous sources. And by the inherent power of their truth they have held sway and won a way for themselves to the real triumph of the voluntary adhesion of multitudes of Christian men. It is honor enough for the Westminster Assembly that it has provided this multitude of voluntary adherents with a practicable platform of representative government on Scriptural lines, and a sober and sane directory of worship eminently spiritual in tone; and above all, with the culminating Reformed Confession of Faith, and a Catechism preëminent for the exactness of its definitions of faith and the faithfulness of its ethical precepts.

II

THE MAKING OF THE WESTMINSTER CON-
FESSION, AND ESPECIALLY OF ITS CHAP-
TER ON THE DECREE OF GOD

II

THE MAKING OF THE WESTMINSTER CON-FESSION, AND ESPECIALLY OF ITS CHAP-TER ON THE DECREE OF GOD [1]

It is the purpose of this article to give as clear a view as possible of the process by which the Westminster Confession was made. In prosecuting this purpose two tasks present themselves. One concerns the modes of procedure of the Assembly in framing the Confession; the other the course of the debates by which it was beaten out. We shall attempt to give some account of both matters. The latter offers so wide a field, however, that we shall be constrained to deal with it by sample — and, for reasons which will readily suggest themselves at the present juncture, we shall select the third chapter of the Confession as the sample to be dealt with. We shall therefore try first to trace the formal procedure of the Assembly in framing the whole Confession, and to obtain some adequate conception of the labor and time that was expended on it; and then, taking up the third chapter, we shall essay to reconstruct as fully as may be a picture of the actual work of the Assembly in producing it.[2]

[1] From *The Presbyterian and Reformed Review*, xii. 1901, pp. 226–283.

[2] The fundamental authority for the study of the work of the Assembly for the period covered by it is, of course, the volume of its " Minutes " edited by Drs. A. F. Mitchell and John Struthers, and published by William Blackwood and Sons in 1874. Along with this Dr. Mitchell's Baird Lectures for 1882 on " The Westminster Assembly: Its History and Standards " (ed. 2, Philadelphia, 1897), should be consulted. Next to the " Minutes " the fullest source of information is Robert Baillie's " Letters and Journals," edited by Mr. David Laing, Edinburgh, 1841–1842. A very painstaking study of the whole constructive work of the Assembly has recently been published by Dr. Wm. A. Shaw in his " History of the English Church during the Civil Wars and under the Commonwealth, 1640–1660," 2 vols., London, New York, and

I. How the Confession was Made

The amount of time consumed directly on the preparation of the Confession of Faith was certainly very great. But even this does not completely represent the pains expended on this task. To estimate that fairly, there should also be taken into account the time and care given formally to other subjects, which yet necessarily conduced indirectly to the perfecting of the final statement of doctrine. Nearly all the labors of the body, from its coming together on July 1, 1643 till the completion of the Shorter Catechism on April 12, 1648, may without exaggeration be said to have had a doctrinal side; and much time was spent in direct doctrinal discussion. None of this discussion that was precedent to or contemporary with the formulation of the propositions incorporated into the Confession was lost labor with respect to it. There were in particular three or four of the tasks of the Assembly, however, which bore so immediately on its preparation for framing the Confession that they deserve especial mention in this connection.

Among these the first in time to occupy its attention was the revision of the Thirty-nine Articles to which it was set on first coming together.[3] This was the main work of the Assembly from the 8th of July to the 12th of October, 1643, and it necessarily led to a somewhat thorough review, at the very outset of its labors, of the doctrines of God and the Trinity, the Person and Work of Christ, the Scriptures and Rule of Faith, Original Sin and the Freedom of the Will, Justification and

---

Bombay: Longmans, Green & Co., 1900 — a book simply packed with facts. The present article was unfortunately written before Dr. Shaw's book came into our hands. But we have carefully compared it with the account he has given (in pages 357–367 of his first volume) and examined the data afresh in the light of his narrative — not without profit to ourselves, or, occasionally, correction of details in Dr. Shaw's narrative. Where our account differs from Dr. Shaw's, therefore, it is to be understood that the difference is not unintentional.

[3] See the full and very interesting account of this work given by Dr. Mitchell, "The Westminster Assembly," ed. 2, pp. 150 *sqq.* Cf. Dr. Briggs's article in the *Presbyterian Review* for January, 1880.

Sanctification — the main topics on which the first sixteen Articles touch. Lightfoot's " Journal " contains very little record of the debates that were held in the course of this revision,[4] and we should perhaps be in danger of underestimating their reach and thoroughness, had not some fuller intimation of them been preserved in the manuscript Minutes and some specimens of their nature in the published speeches of Dr. Featley. It is evident that very careful and thoroughgoing work was done, of which the text of the revised Articles themselves gives but meager suggestion. All this told afterward on the formulation of these same topics in the Confession of Faith. " The keen and lengthened debates," remarks Dr. Mitchell, " which occurred in the discussions on these Articles could not fail to prepare the way for a more summary mode of procedure in connection with the Confession of Faith. The proceedings then were more summary, or at least more summarily recorded, just because the previous discussions on the more important doctrines of the Protestant system, and especially on that of Justification by Faith, had been thorough and exhaustive, and pretty fully recorded." [5] There does not even lack evidence that in framing the very language of the Confession, regard was had to the *minutiæ* of the work done on this former occasion. Now and again little points of phraseology, for example, are taken over into the Confessional statements from the revised Articles,[6] such as serve to show that the Divines kept their former labors fully in mind in the prosecution of their later, and were perfecting their work in full view of all that had previously been done.[7]

---

[4] He notes the emergence of the matter only on July 8, 10, 11, 12, 15, 17, 18, 27, 28, August 1, 18, and October 12.

[5] " The Westminster Assembly," pp. 150 *sq.* Cf. Shaw, i. pp. 147 *sq.*

[6] Thus: Art. i. Old and Revised Artt. and Conf. of Faith: " of one substance " (Irish: " of one and the same substance "). Art. ii. Old and Revised Artt. and Conf. of Faith: " very and eternal God " (Irish: " true and eternal God "). Especially the following: Art. ii. Revised Artt. and Conf. of Faith: " and *the* manhood " (Old Artt. and Irish omit " the "); Art. x. Revised Artt. and Conf. of Faith: " or [to] prepare " (Old Artt. and Irish: " and prepare ").

[7] The text of the Westminster revision of the first fifteen Articles of the Church of England may be found in Hall's " Harmony of Protestant Con-

Of far less importance, but perhaps worth mentioning in this connection, was the work done by the Assembly in the spring of 1645, in defining for the House of Commons " the particulars of that ignorance and scandal for which persons should be excluded from the sacrament." [8] At this time, also, though in a more summary manner, the Assembly had occasion, prior to its entrance on the actual preparation of the Confession, to review in a systematic exhibit all the chief topics of a dogmatic system.[9]

Many topics which touched on the subjects treated in parallel portions of the Confession were also debated in the preparation of the Form of Government; and, we may be sure, this was not without consciousness on the part of the debaters that their investigations would bear double fruit. We meet, for example, on May 6, 1645, before any part of the Confession had come before the Assembly, a note like this: " Debate whether to bring this under the head of government or a Confession of Faith." And accordingly the proposition thus debated was in substance actually incorporated into the subsequently framed Confession.[10] Similarly the long debates on the *jus divinum* cannot fail to have borne fruit both for the Government and for such chapters of the Confession as that on " The Church and Church Censures," then in process of framing.

Finally the labors of the Assembly in preparing its Cate-

---

fessions," 1844, Appendix i. pp. 505–512; Neal's " History of the Puritans," ii. 1849, Appendix vii. pp. 454–457; Stoughton's " Ecclesiastical History of England," ii. (" The Church of the Commonwealth "), 1867, Appendix iii. pp. 528–535; but correctly as to the 8th Article only in E. Tyrrell Green's " The Thirty-nine Articles and the Age of the Reformation," London, 1896, Appendix iv. pp. 343–348. Mr. Green marks all the changes made in the text. For the Preface and revised Article viii., see especially Mitchell and Struthers, " Minutes," pp. 541–542. Cf. Schaff, " Creeds of Christendom," i. 1877, pp. 653 *sq.*

[8] A good account is given by Shaw, " History of the English Church," i. 1900, pp. 259–261. Cf. " Journals of Commons," iv. pp. 89 *sq.*, etc., and Minutes of Assembly for March 1, 5, 21, 24, 28, April 2 (4?), 21 (August 14), 1645.

[9] For some indication of the nature of these topics see below, p. 85.

[10] Chapter xxiii. § 3.

chism, so far as they were carried on before the Confession left its hands, were of course of use to it in preparing the Confession also. In some sense, these labors began indeed as early as December, 1643: but the matter incorporated into the Catechism does not seem to have come before the Assembly itself earlier than September 14, 1646, from which date until January 4, 1647, the substance of the original Catechism was reported as far as that project was prosecuted by the Assembly.[11] During this period the Assembly was in the process of its review of the text of the Confession, and had reached a portion of it for which the debates upon the Catechism could afford little or no aid.[12] The scrutiny of the substance of doctrine for the Catechism therefore could serve as a help in the formulation of the Confession only in so far as the members of the Committee at work on the Catechism were moulding their opinions by it. In the general Assembly the influence was the other way about. In fact, Baillie tells us that on the reporting of the first matter for the Catechism, the Assembly fell on such " rubbes and long debates " that it was purposely " laid aside till the Confession wes ended, with resolution to have no matter in it but what wes expressed in the Confession, which should not be debated over againe in the Catechise." [13] The subject is nevertheless worth mentioning here as indicating afresh how repeatedly the Divines were, in committee or in full house, led to go over the whole series of doctrinal state-

[11] See especially Mitchell, " The Westminster Assembly," pp. 420 *sqq.,* but compare Shaw, i. p. 369, note. References may be found in the Minutes on December 2, 1644, February 7, 1645, May 12, 13, August 1, 4, 5, 19, 20, and September 11. Then especially September 14 (1646), 15, 17, 22, 23, 24, November 27, 30, December 1, 2, 7, 10, 11, 14, 15, 16, 17, 18, 28, 31, and January 4 and 14, 1647, on which last day the order was given to intermit the preparation of the Catechism on which the Assembly had hitherto been working and to cast the material into two Catechisms. The text of this " first Catechism," so far as it is recorded in the Minutes, has been put together by Mr. Wm. Carruthers, in his admirable " The Shorter Catechism of the Westminster Assembly of Divines," in *facsimile,* London, 1897, pp. 21–26.

[12] When the first propositions from the Catechism were reported the Assembly had just passed chapter xvii. of the Confession (though one or two immediately preceding chapters were not yet passed).

[13] " Letters," ii. p. 379: July 14, 1646.

ments either prior to or parallel with their work in formulating the Confession: all of which repeated reviews of the matter to be placed in the Confession of course were of use in its formulation for that purpose.

If there ever was a document, therefore, whose contents might be expected to exhibit that genius, the essence of which consists, we are told, in *taking pains*, it assuredly is the Westminster Confession of Faith. And when we read its exquisitely balanced phrases, and are moved with admiration for the perfection of the guarding which it gives to its doctrinal propositions on this side and that, we are reaping the benefit of these repeated reviews which the Assembly was forced to give the whole matter, perhaps even more than of the minute scrutiny it lavished on the formulation of it on the final occasion of its actual incorporation into the Confession. And when, after this, and in the light of all the experience gained by such repeated reviews of the material, first the Larger Catechism and then the Shorter Catechism were elaborated, it is not at all strange that a precision of definition was attained which has called forth such praises as these documents, and especially the Shorter Catechism, have received from the most varied quarters.

The framing of a new Confession of Faith was a portion of the task that devolved on the Westminster Assembly through the provisions of the Solemn League and Covenant, by which an engagement was entered into for bringing " the Churches of God in the three kingdoms to the nearest conjunction and uniformity in religion, confession of faith, form of Church government, directory for worship and catechising." [14] The prosecution of the work of uniting the two

[14] It is with reference to this engagement that the following Minute, entered immediately after the completion of the (Larger) Catechism, October 15, 1647, must be read: " Upon a motion made by Mr. Rutherford, it was *Ordered* — That it be recorded in the Scribes' books, ' The Assembly hath enjoyed the assistance of the Honble Reverend and learned Commissioners from the Church of Scotland in the work of the Assembly '; during all the time of the debating and perfecting of the 4 things mentioned in the Cove-

Churches in a common Confession of course involved the substitution of a new Confession, agreed upon by both Churches, for those previously in use, whether in Scotland or in England; it accordingly rendered the revision of the Thirty-nine Articles, on which the Assembly had been engaged during the first months of its labors, no longer *ad rem*. No doubt the persistency of the Commons in securing the insertion into the " Ordinance " calling the Assembly of a clause setting forth as one of the objects in view the procuring of a " nearer agreement with the Church of Scotland," [15] although more particularly referring to the point of " Government," affected in some degree the whole work of the Assembly and bore fruit even in its revision of the Thirty-nine Articles. But the particular instructions given regarding the revision of these Articles limited the Assembly to " vindicating and clearing " them " from all false calumnies and aspersions," and the Assembly itself looked upon this work accordingly as " relating only to the Church of England." [16] When now, on the 25th of September, 1643, the Solemn League and Covenant was taken, the whole situation was changed. Parliament was now committed to that policy of uniformity in religion for the whole country

---

nant, viz., the Directory for Worship, the Confession of Faith, Form of Church Government, and Catechism, some of the Reverend and learned Divines Commissioners from the Church of Scotland have been present in and assisting to this Assembly." There is no question here of a farewell to the Assembly: but of a record of covenanted work completed. Rutherford's leavetaking was made on November 9 subsequent. The relation of the Scottish Commissioners to the Assembly and its work is not always fully understood: it is lucidly explained by Dr. Mitchell in his " The Westminster Assembly," ed. 2, pp. 180–181, note. They were not members of the Assembly and cast no vote in it: they took part in its debates only as private persons on its invitation. They were representatives of the Church of Scotland coördinate as a body with the Assembly as a whole, which represented the Church of England, and conferring with it as a whole on the common formularies.

[15] See Shaw, i. p. 127, note, and cf. the " Ordinance " itself as printed in most Scotch editions of the Confession of Faith and in Dr. Mitchell's " The Westminster Assembly," pp. xiii. *sqq.*

[16] So it says in its Preface prefixed to the portion of the Thirty-nine Articles it had revised, when this was sent up to the Commons. See the Preface in " Minutes," pp. 541–542.

for which the Scots had been unwearyingly pressing ever since their Peace Commissioners had gone up to London early in 1641, and the Assembly considered its work on the Articles as entirely set aside by the subsequent order, as it itself expresses it, " to employ us in framing a Confession of Faith for the three kingdoms, according to our Solemn League and Covenant." [17] It was only with great reluctance and with protestations of their insufficiency that it placed in the hands of the Parliament, when subsequently required to do so, the Articles so far as they had been revised by it.[18]

Nevertheless, the severer task of forming a new Confession of Faith for the whole kingdom was not at once entered upon. A still more severe and, in the judgment of all alike, a still more pressing task required attention first — the framing of a unifying " Government " for the Churches of the whole kingdom. This great labor was begun on October 12, 1643, and consumed the energies and time of the Assembly for many months. The first motion toward undertaking the new Confession was made apparently on Tuesday morning, August 20, 1644. Sir Archibald Johnston of Warriston, lately arrived from Scotland, appeared in the Assembly on August 14, bringing letters from the General Assembly; and in presenting them he emphasized " the general desire of all the nation of Scotland for the hastening of the work in hand " — that is, the work of completing the uniformity in all its parts in accordance with the Solemn League and Covenant. In his response Dr. Burgess added his voice to Warriston's: and " Mr. Henderson also spake to the same purpose, of forwarding and hastening our work. Whereupon it was ordered, that the grand committee should meet to-morrow." [19] The report from the Grand Com-

[17] Preface to Thirty-nine Articles, as above. Cf. Mitchell, " The Westminster Assembly," p. 185.

[18] Mitchell, " The Westminster Assembly," p. 161.

[19] Lightfoot, " Works," ed. Pitman, xiii. 1824, p. 303. Baillie's (" Letters," ii. pp. 220–221) account is as follows: " So soon as my Lord Warriston came up, we resolved on the occasion of his instructings, and the letters of our Generall Assemblie, both to ourselves and to this Assemblie, which he brought, to quicken them a little, who had great need of spurrs. My Lord Warriston

mittee came in on August 20, and contained five resolutions designed for expediting the work. The second of these proposed "a committee to join with the commissioners of Scotland, to draw up a confession of faith." No order, however, was as yet come from Parliament "to enable us to such a thing," [20] and the proposition, therefore, caused some debate; but it was at last determined upon, and a committee of nine, consisting of Drs. Temple, Gouge and Hoyle, Messrs. Gataker, Arrowsmith, Burroughs, Burgess, Vines and Goodwin, was appointed to take the work in hand.[21] Two weeks later, Lightfoot tells us further, "Dr. Temple, chairman of the committee for the drawing up of a confession of faith, desired, that that committee might be augmented." [22] This also was done, and there

---

very particularlie declared in the Assemblie the passionate desires both of our Parliament, Assemblie, armies, and whole people, of the performance of the Covenanted Uniformitie; and withall we called for a meeting of the grand committee of Lords, Commons, Assemblie, and us; to whom we gave a paper penned, notablie well, by Mr. Henderson, bearing the great evills of so long a delay of settling religion, and our earnest desyres that some wayes might be found out for expedition. This paper my Lord Say took to deliver to the House of Lords, Mr. Solicitor also for the House of Commons, and a third copy was given to Mr. Marshall, to be presented to the Assemblie. . . . Also we have the grand committee to meet on Monday, to find out wayes of expeditione; and we have gotten it to be the work of the Assemblie it-selfe, to doe no other thing till they have found out wayes of accellerating; so by God's help we expect a farr quicker progress than hitherto."

[20] Lightfoot, as above, p. 305.

[21] Lightfoot, "Works," xiii. p. 305. The Assembly's own Minute runs: "A Committee to join with the Commissioners of the Church of Scotland to prepare matter for a joint Confession of Faith.

R. neg. 12.	R. affirmat. 9 [to be a Committee].	
Dr. Gouge.	Mr. Burges.	
Mr. Gataker.	Mr. Vines.	
Mr. Arrowsmith.	Mr. Goodwin.	or any 5
Dr. Temple.	Dr. Hoyle.	of them."
Mr. Burroughs.		

See "Minutes," pp. lxxxvi. sq.

[22] Lightfoot, p. 308. The Assembly's own Minute for September 4 runs: 'Report from the Committee for the Confession of Faith. They desire an addi-tion of those persons to the said Committee — Ordered — Mr. Palmer, Mr. Newcomen, Mr. Herle, Mr. Reynolds, Mr. Wilson, Mr. Tuckney, Dr. Smith, Mr. Young, Mr. Ley, Mr. Sedgwicke, be added to the Committee for the Con-fession of Faith " (p. lxxxvii.).

were added the names of Dr. Smith and Messrs. Palmer, New-comen, Herle, Reynolds, Wilson, Tuckney, Young, Ley, and Sedgewick. Baillie congratulates himself that thus the prepara-tion of the Confession had been " put in severall the best hands that are here," and that "the heads of it being distribute among many able hands, it may in a short time be so drawn up, as the debates of it may cost little time." [23]

It was not until the next summer, nevertheless, that any portion of the Confession came before the Assembly.[24] In the spring it seems to have been taken up in earnest, but progress was still slow.[25] Baillie informs us under date of April 25, 1645, that some reports had already been made to the Assembly.[26] We hear of it in the Minutes for the first time, however, on Monday, April 21,[27] and then after a fashion that hints of pres-sure brought on the Assembly for completing the work. The Scotch Commissioners, returning on April 9 from their visit to the Assembly of the Kirk of Scotland,[28] had had presented by the Grand Committee to the Houses of Parliament and the As-sembly of Divines alike a paper setting out the satisfaction of

[23] " Letters," ii. pp. 232, 248.

[24] On December 26, 1644, Baillie tells us why the work on the Confession was delayed: " If the Directorie and Government were once out of our hands, as a few days will put them, then we will fall on our great question of Ex-communication, the Catechise, and Confession. There is here matter to hold us long enough, if the wrangling humour which long predomined in many here did continue. . . . I think we must either passe the Confession to another season, or, if God will help us, the heads of it being distribute among many able hands, it may in a short time be so drawn up, as the debates of it may cost little time. All this chalking is on the supposition of God's singular assistance, continuing such a disposition in the Assemblie and Parliament as hes appeared this moneth or two bypast " (ii. p. 248).

[25] It was not until July that any part of the text got before the Assembly. Baillie (ii. p. 275), writing apparently early in June (Shaw, i. p. 190), can still speak of the Assembly as only " beginning to take the Confession of Faith and Catechise to our consideration," and on the 5th September (ii. p. 315) says, " We are goeing on languidlie with the Confession of Faith and Catechisme."

[26] " Letters," ii. p. 266.

[27] References to the Minutes are of course all to the volume published in 1874 by Drs. Mitchell and Struthers. References are equally easily verifiable whether made by pages, dates, or numbers of sessions — and therefore we shall not burden the footnotes with details.

[28] " Minutes," p. 77. Cf. pp. 28 *sq.*

their Kirk with the parts of the Uniformity already prepared, and urging that " it is with no less zeal and earnestness desired and expected by that whole Kirk and kingdom, that the remanent parts of Uniformity be expedited." [29] Stress was especially laid in this paper on the completion of the Form of Government; but when the paper came before the Commons (on April 14) it found that body engaged on matters of doctrine,[30] and its immediate fruit was accordingly an action to hasten on the preparation of the " Confession of Faith." A paper had been sent up from the Divines to both Houses on March 6 looking to the " preserving the sacraments pure," and both Houses had taken up the matter at once. The debate in the Commons from March 25 took the form of determining the particulars of ignorance and scandal which should exclude from the Lord's Supper. Several communications were passed between the House, sitting in committee, and the Divines by means of which it was determined what should be defined as " a competent measure of understanding " — " concerning God the Father, Son and Holy Ghost," " concerning the state of man by the creation, and by his fall," " the redemption of Jesus Christ, etc.," " the ways and means to apply Christ, etc.," " the nature and necessity of faith, etc.," " repentance, etc.," " the nature and use of the Sacraments, etc.," " the condition of man after this life, etc." [31] The report of the Grand Committee embodying these findings was made to the Commons on the 17th of April, and on the same day a Committee was appointed to draft an ordinance in the terms of the findings.[32] Simultaneously the House voted to desire the Assembly

[29] This paper was brought into the Assembly on April 14: it is given by Dr. Mitchell from the " Journals of the House of Lords," vii. pp. 317, 318, on pp. 80–81, note, of the " Minutes."

[30] See a full account of the work of the Houses in this matter in Shaw's " History of the English Church during the Civil Wars and under the Commonwealth," i. 1900, pp. 257 *sqq.*

[31] Shaw, as above, i. pp. 259–261. " Minutes," p. 71 (March 21 and 24), p. 74 (March 28), p. 75 (April 2), p. 76? (April 4).

[32] Shaw, i. pp. 260–261, citing " Commons' Journal," iv. p. 114, April 17. The names of the Committee are given by Shaw, p. 261, note.

with all convenient speed to resolve upon a Confession of Faith for the Church of England and present it to the House.[33] In this we may doubtless see the combined effects of the pressure brought to bear on the House by the letter from Scotland and its own sense of need arising from its labors in defining censurable ignorance. There are entries in the Minutes of the Assembly for April 18 which may be taken as indicating the reception of this order by that body.[34] In this case it would seem that Messrs. Seaman, Tuckney, Burroughs, Young, Whitaker, Rayner, Vines, and Delamarch were appointed " to consider of this order," and were instructed to meet that afternoon and report at the next meeting. In any event the order was already in process of being obeyed at this next meeting, Monday, April 21. Apparently the Committee appointed on April 18 then reported that the best way to meet the immediate needs of Parliament would be to place in its hands a revised edition of the Thirty-nine Articles, to serve until a Confession of Faith could be prepared. Accordingly it was ordered that the Committee in whose charge the revision of the Thirty-nine Articles had formerly been, or perhaps the new Committee of April 18,[35] should " consider how far they or any of them may be useful to be recommended to both Houses of Parliament for the present, till a Confession of Faith can be drawn up by this Assembly "; and further, that "the Committee for Confession of Faith do meet on Wednesday, in the afternoon."

Nothing further appears until Friday, May 9,[36] when, a new order having meanwhile been received from Parliament for

---

[33] Shaw, i. p. 358, citing " Commons' Journal," iv. p. 113.

[34] So Shaw, i. p. 358.

[35] The language is: " That the Thirty-nine Articles be reviewed by the former Committee, and the Committee to consider &c. . . . R. — To be referred to one Committee." Hence apparently *two* Committees are in view: but finally the whole matter was committed to *one*. *Which* one is not clear.

[36] On Tuesday, May 6, when the propositions as to the Civil Magistrate in the Government were under debate, question was raised whether a proposed form of statement should be placed in the Government or in " a Confession of Faith."

dispatch,[37] it was ordered " that the Assembly consider on Monday morning the best way to expedite the Confession of Faith, . . . and that the two Committees for the Confession of Faith be put into one." What two Committees were here united we have no means of ascertaining. We have heard hitherto of only one Committee to which the " preparing matter " for a Confession of Faith was committed (August 20, 1644), and which was subsequently (September 4) augmented; and even on April 21, as we have just seen, " the Committee for Confession of Faith " is spoken of quite simply as if there were but one, and between that entry and the present one there is no allusion in the Minutes to the matter.[38] But Baillie, though in the previous autumn speaking of " a Committee " to which the Confession of Faith had been referred, under date of April 25, says, " The Catechise and Confession of Faith are put in the hands of severall committees." [39] It is probably easiest to suppose that in the meanwhile another Committee, additional to that of August 20–September 4, 1644, had been appointed.[40] At all events, in accordance with the provision of May 9, the Assembly on Monday, May 12, proceeded to make further arrangements for " expediting the Confession of Faith." The report in the Minutes of what was done is somewhat obscure. But it appears that besides reading and debating " the report of the Confession of Faith," there was an additional " debate about the Committee for drawing up the Confession "; and it was determined that " the first draught of the Confession of Faith shall be drawn up by a Committee of a few "; which Committee was then constituted — apparently of the following members: Drs. Temple and Hoyle,

---

[37] Shaw, i. p. 358, quoting " Commons' Journal," iv. p. 133: " Minutes " for May 8 (p. 90).

[38] The Confession of Faith is mentioned in the interval only on May 6 (as above, p. 78, and p. 86, note 36), and then only incidentally and indeterminately.

[39] As cited, ii. p. 266.

[40] Shaw, i. p. 358, supposes the Committee " to have subdivided " and to be now reunited. It is possible, of course, that the two parts (that appointed August 20 and that appointed September 4) had been sitting as separate Committees and were only now combined.

Messrs. Gataker, Harris, Burgess, Reynolds and Herle. This
Committee is then instructed to meet that same afternoon;
and the Scotch Commissioners " are desired to be assisting to
this Committee."

The question arises whether this Committee was additional
to the former Committee or Committees (of August 20, September 4, 1644, and May 9, 1645), or was a substitute for it
or them. Dr. Mitchell supposes the former, and looks upon
this new Committee as erected in order to receive the material
collected by the already existing Committee, or Committees,
and to digest it into more formal shape before it was finally
submitted to the Assembly.[41] There are certain serious difficulties, however, in the way of this supposition. And these
are greatly increased by a subsequent act of the Assembly's.
On Friday, July 11, 1645, it was ordered — " Monday morning
to divide the body of the Confession of Faith to the three Committees." Accordingly on the next Monday — July 14 — we
hear of a " debate about dividing of heads of confession ": but
the matter was not concluded on that day. On the following
Wednesday — July 16, 1645 — we read of a " report made
from the Committee of the heads of Confession," and it was
ordered: " The first Committee to prepare the Confession of
Faith upon these heads: God and the Holy Trinity; God's decrees, Predestination, Election, etc.; the works of Creation
and Providence; Man's Fall "; " The Second Committee: Sin,
and the punishment thereof; Free will; the Covenant of
Grace; Christ our Mediator "; " The Third Committee: Effectual Vocation; Justification; Adoption; Sanctification ";
" Those three Committees to meet to-morrow in the afternoon "; " If they think fit to leave out any of those heads,
or add any other, they are to make report to the Assembly."
Dr. Mitchell supposes with obvious justice that the three large
Committees into which the Assembly was permanently divided for the preparing of its business [42] are referred to in these
orders; and that " the material prepared by the previous small

[41] " The Westminster Assembly," ed. 2, Philadelphia, 1897, pp. 367 *sq.*
[42] Concerning them see Mitchell, " The Westminster Assembly," p. 147.

committee" was "handed over to these larger committees, and further discussed and elaborated by them before being brought into the Assembly." This seems altogether reasonable in itself, and is fully borne out by the subsequent proceedings. But certainly, under this supposition, it becomes very unlikely that the earlier Committee or Committees (of August 20, September 4, 1644, and May 9, 1645) still continued in existence — if for no other reason than the complicated process which would in that case be involved in getting the several parts of the Confession before the Assembly. First the Committee of August 20–September 4, 1644, would collect the material; then the Committee of May 12, 1645, with the aid of the Scotch Commissioners, would digest it; then the large Committee required thereto on July 16, would further digest it; and only then would it reach the Assembly. Surely this complication of process throws something in the scale to justify us in looking on the Committee of May 12 as a substitute for that of August 20–September 4, rather than additional to it.[43] In that case we must suppose that the Assembly had sought at first to get along with only one Committee, which should prepare the matter of the Confession for its discussion; that that first appointed (August 20, 1644), augmented on September 4, 1644, and again perhaps on May 9, 1645, had proved too large and unwieldy for rapid work, and was superseded by a smaller one, May 12, 1645 — the members of which were, however (with one exception, viz., Mr. Harris), taken from the earlier Committees. Subsequently, for the better digesting of the material, it was ordered (July 11 and 16, 1645) that the reports of the Committee should in the first instance be submitted to one or the other of the three great Committees into which the Assembly was divided for the preparation of its business, and be by them actually brought before the whole body.

There are, to be sure, not lacking some difficulties in the way of the supposition of even this very natural and workable

[43] Shaw, i. p. 358, also seems to look upon the Committee of May 12, 1645, as a substitute for the former Committee.

arrangement. Among them the chief are that in the action of May 9 we read (as we have seen) of its being ordered, " that the two Committees for the Confession of Faith be put into one "; and in the action of July 4 we read of " the sub-Committee for the Confession of Faith," as if there were still divisions in the Committee; and again on July 18 we read of a " report concerning God, by Dr. Temple " being put in — although Dr. Temple was not a member of the First great Committee to which this topic was assigned, but of the Third great Committee, while, on the other hand, he was a member of the Committee of May 12, and as representing it had " made report of that part of the Confession of Faith touching the Scriptures " on July 7 — i.e., before the distribution of the heads to the three great Committees had been made. These difficulties do not, however, seem to be insuperable. We have already offered a suggestion in explanation of the mention of two Committees on May 9. The term " Sub-Committee " in the action of July 4 need not be pressed: it may be, and probably is, only a designation of the Committee of May 12, called Sub-Committee possibly because of its small size in comparison with the three great Committees; or it may be thought not impossible that the work on the topics of God and the Scriptures may actually have been done by a Sub-Committee of that Committee. It seems further, on closer examination, that Dr. Temple made the report of July 18 on " God," as well as that of July 7 on " The Scriptures," in consequence of the order of July 4 " that the *sub-Committee* for the Confession of Faith shall make report to the Assembly on Monday morning of what is in their hands *concerning God and concerning the Scriptures* " — so that these two topics were accounted as in that manner already before the Assembly, though in the interval between this and July 18, when the " report concerning God, by Dr. Temple," was — not made, but — " read and debated," provision had been made for another course to be subsequently pursued. It is not an insuperable objection to this solution of the difficulty that in the distribution of the heads of the Confession to the three Committees on July 16, the head on " Scripture " is not assigned to the first Committee — doubtless as already fully before the house — while the head on "God and the Holy Trinity" is so assigned, as if it were not yet — at least in full — before the house. There are so many things we do not know about the precise course of action that a plausible supposition such as we have suggested may be allowed to be probable, even though we cannot explain all the details. And it is to be observed that when the report on this topic came from the first Committee on July 23, it was not of " God and the Holy Trinity," but " of the article of the Trinity." It may be taken as likely then that the original Committee of May 12 reported as required on the two topics, " The Scriptures " and " God," and that the first report from the great Committee was on " the Trinity " only.

This construction receives further support from other circumstances. We hear nothing of "Committees," but only of a " Committee " on the Confession between the dates May 9, when the " two Committees " were " put into one," and July 16, when the three great Committees were charged with the Confession, while afterwards this is no longer so — as e.g. on August 20 we read of " the Committees for the Confession of Faith." We hear no more of reports from Dr. Temple on the Confession after those on the " Scriptures " of July 7 and on " God " of July 18. At the very next session — July 23 — we read rather: " Report made from the Committee of the article of the Trinity," and afterwards, on August 29: " Report from the first Committee concerning God's decrees "; " Report made by the second Committee of Christ the Mediator "; " Debate on the report of the first Committee of God's decree "; on September 3, " Report from the first Committee about adding the word ' absolutely ' "; " Debate about the 2d Committee's report of Christ the Mediator," and so on.[44] This mode of reference varied only to such forms as the following. On

[44] Reports from *First* Committee, " Minutes," pp. 129, 130, 150, 151, 164, 166, 167, 171, 192. Reports from *Second* Committee, " Minutes," pp. 130, 131, 150, 161, 162, 166, 167. Reports from *Third* Committee, " Minutes," pp. 165, 173.

September 8, "Dr. Gouge offered a report of an addition, though the Committee was not a full number, but 7 " — Dr. Gouge being a member of the First Committee, and possibly at this time its chairman.[45] On September 9, "Dr. Stanton made report additional of Christ the Mediator.[46] Mr. Prophet made report of Effectual Calling"[47] — Dr. Stanton having been from the first chairman of the Second Committee and Mr. Prophet being a member of the Third, the several Committees to which these topics had been assigned on July 16. A note in the proceedings for November 18 (sess. 537) gives the whole state of the case very clearly: "Dr. Gouge [made] report from First Committee of Creation. Mr. Whitakers from the Second Committee, of the Fall of Man, of Sin, and the Punishment thereof. The Third Committee made no report." In the presence of such clear declarations, supported by a number of incidental references accordant with them (such as have been set down in the footnotes), we need not hesitate to say that the several heads of the Confession were obviously reported directly to the Assembly by the three great Committees, even though there remain a few instances where a reference occurs not easily explicable.

The most striking of these are those instances in which we read of a topic of the Confession being reported by a member who does not seem to have been a member of the great Com-

[45] The detailed history of the large Committees is obscure: see Mitchell, " The Westminster Assembly," ed. 2, pp. 148 *sq.* Dr. Burgess was the first chairman of the First Committee, but he had in the meanwhile been in disgrace (p. 181) and during his suspension a new chairman must needs have been chosen. Cf. January 29, 1646, " Mr. Coleman made report of Christian Liberty " (cf. p. 104), Mr. Coleman being also a member of the First Committee: March 5, " Report from Dr. Gouge about the Church."

[46] Cf. November 12: "Dr. Stanton [made] report from second Committee "; December 5: " Report from Dr. Stanton of the Sacraments in general " (cf. pp. 164, 167); but December 29: " Mr. Calamy made report of Baptism."

[47] Cf. November 20: " Mr. Prophet brought in a report from the Third Committee," etc.; March 5, 1646: " Mr. Prophet made report of Religion and Worship," etc.; but December 2, 1645: " Report from Mr. Cheynell of Justification " — Mr. Cheynell being also a member of the Third Committee; January 1, 1646: " Dr. Wincop made report from the Third Committee about the Law of God."

mittee to which this topic was assigned. On one occasion, for example, Dr. Gouge is spoken of as reporting on a topic not belonging to the First, but to the Second Committee: December 15, 1645, " Dr. Gouge made report about Free-will." Dr. Gouge may have been acting here, however, as representing not the original Committee which reported this subject to the Assembly, but a special Committee to which it or some part of it had been recommitted. Color is lent to this suggestion by three facts.   First, the recommitment of special points to special Committees was not uncommon with the Assembly; instances may be noted on pp. 183, 184, 187, 208, 217, 218, 219 of the "Minutes."   Secondly, the note here is made in immediate conjunction with a case of recommitment. The Minutes proceed: " Mr. Arrowsmith made report of that committed concerning the Sacraments." The Sacraments constituted a topic belonging to the Second Committee, indeed, of which Mr. Arrowsmith was a member, and so this case may be only partially parallel. More clearly similar is the instance of November 7, when we read: " Report made by Mr. Reynolds about Reprobation " — evidently in pursuance of the order of November 6: " The paragraph concerning Reprobation referred to the Committee, to make report tomorrow morning." Mr. Reynolds was not, however, a member of the First Committee to which this topic belonged, but of the Second: [48] and thus this would seem to be a case of reference to a special Committee. The matter is plainer still in another instance. We read in the Minutes for March 10, 1646: " Mr. Seaman made report of Christian Liberty and Liberty of Conscience " — a topic belonging to the First Committee

[48] Mr. Reynolds was, however, a member of the Committee of September 4, 1644, and also of that of May 12, 1645: and it is, of course, conceivable that it was to this fundamental Committee that the topic was recommitted. The case would not be so simple in the instances of Mr. Gouge and Mr. Arrowsmith; they were both members of the Committee of August 20, 1644, but not of that of May 12 — which in our view had been substituted for it. In Mr. Seaman's case, just to be mentioned, it is clear that it was to a special Committee that the recommitment was made, and he was moreover not a member of any of the Committees of August 20, September 4, 1644, May 12, 1645.

while Mr. Seaman was a member of the Second. The original
report on Christian Liberty, however, was made on January
29, and not by Mr. Seaman but by Mr. Coleman — a member
of the First Committee. The subject was debated on that day,
and again on February 10, 12, 16, when it was resolved: " That
this whole head of Christian Liberty shall be recommitted ";
and further, " This shall be recommitted to a select Committee " — whose members are then named with Mr. Seaman at
their head (p. 187). It is, of course, from this Committee that
Mr. Seaman reported on March 10. It should, however, be
borne in mind that we cannot implicitly trust the lists of
names given in the schedule which Dr. Mitchell prints of the
members of the three great Committees at the date nearest
to the time when the Assembly was busied with the Confession. For example, we read in the Minutes of January 29,
1646: " Mr. Dury made report from the Second Committee
of Church Offices and Censures." But the name of Mr. Dury
does not occur on the roll of the members of the Second Committee, nor indeed on any of the three rolls. A similar instance
is found in this same note of January 29: " Mr. Newcomen,
Mr. Dury, Mr. Delmy, Dr. Temple, Dr. Gouge, added to the
Committee for report about the Law; to report to-morrow
morning." The reference is not to the original Third Committee, which had reported the chapter on the Law at least as
early as January 7, but to a special Committee appointed
January 12 to consider the propositions under debate concerning the meaning of the terms " ceremonial " and " judicial."
Of the names given in this additional list, two — Messrs. Dury
and Delmy — have no place in Dr. Mitchell's lists of the three
Committees.   Thirdly, it may be added that it does
not appear likely that Dr. Gouge's report on December 15,
1645, represents the first report to the Assembly on the topic
of Free Will. A month before (on November 18) it had been
represented to the Assembly that the Second Committee had
finished all the heads of the Confession that had been committed to it; and this representation was made the occasion of
a new distribution of heads to the three Committees. In the

interval, before December 15, topics from this second distribution had been reported from the Second Committee (e.g., December 1, on the Lord's Supper; December 5, " Of the Sacraments in general "). It does not seem likely that these would be reported before report had been made of material lying ready for report before these topics were undertaken.

In the light of the facts, therefore, it seems certain that the several heads of the Confession were reported immediately from the three great Committees to the Assembly, and that therefore there was no Committee for further digesting their material intermediating between them and the Assembly. It is not safe to differ on such a matter from Dr. Mitchell, but, on the whole, it appears to us likely also that the small Committee appointed on the 12th May, 1645, was substituted for the earlier Committee or Committees (of August 20–September 4, 1644, and perhaps again in the ensuing winter), and that the mode of procedure was that the small Committee of May 12, 1645 — consisting of seven, a quorum of which was five — first drew up the heads of the Confession with the aid of the Commissioners of the Church of Scotland: and that these were then distributed by the Assembly among the three great Committees for thorough digesting: whence they came back finally to the Assembly for discussion and ordering.

The first two of these " heads " had, to be sure, according to our supposition, already been reported to the Assembly by the small Committee, before it had been determined to distribute the heads between the three great Committees. In the Minutes of the session for Friday, July 4, 1645, we read: " Debate about the Confession of Faith. That the sub-Committee for the Confession of Faith shall make report to the Assembly on Monday morning of what is in their hands concerning God and concerning the Scriptures." Accordingly on Monday, July 7, we read: " Dr. Temple made report of that part of the Confession of Faith touching the Scriptures. It was read, debated." We hear no more of the report on the head " God," to be sure, until July 18 — before which date the distribution to the great Committees had been made. But what we read there is not that Dr. Temple made report on this topic, but: "Report concerning God, by Dr. Temple, read and debated"; while subsequently we read (July 23): "Report made from the Committee of the article of the Trinity." Whatever may be the right explanation of these phrases, the reports of the subsequent heads of the Confession were not made by Dr. Temple, but as we have seen from the First, Second, or Third Committee, or some one of their representatives. This series begins, if not on July 23, at least on August 29, with a notice of a report from the First Committee on God's decrees and from the Second Committee on Christ the Mediator. Thereafter the heads were reported one by one from the several Committees to which their digesting had been from time to time committed.[49]

The consideration given in the Assembly itself to the several heads was very careful and the scrutiny of every clause and word searching. Recommitments, ordinarily at least to special Committees, were frequent: final dissent on the part of individuals was sometimes entered. In a word, time, pains, and scrupulous care were not spared for perfecting the instrument. Thus the work went slowly on, until near the middle of 1646, at which time, though the work was not yet completed, the attention of the Assembly was withdrawn by the Parliament to other matters. During the course of these long-continued and searching debates, it was inevitable that many alterations should be entered in the drafts of the several heads as they were first laid before the Assembly. It was felt by the Assembly from the first that provision should be made to have the text and alterations properly adjusted. As early as July 8, 1645, therefore, we find this order: "That Mr. Reynolds, Mr. Herle, Mr. Newcomen be desired to take care of the wording of the Confession of Faith, as it is voted in the Assembly from

[49] There were four distributions — July 16, 1645, November 18, 1645, February 23, 1646 — to which should be added the supplementary distribution of August 19, 1646.

time to time, and to report to the Assembly when they think fit there should be any alteration in the words. They are first to consult with the Commissioners from the Church of Scotland, or one of them, before they report to the Assembly." Of this Committee we hear nothing more: it doubtless did the work committed to it and saw to it that the amendments made were fitted properly into their places and that all went smoothly. As the work advanced, another Committee of similar but apparently somewhat enlarged powers was appointed. This was done on December 8, 1645: "*Ordered* — Mr. Tuckney, Mr. Reynolds, Mr. Newcomen, Mr. Whitakers, a Committee to review the Confession of Faith as it is finished in the Assembly." Apparently it was not contemplated that reports should be made from this Committee in the meantime; but rather that it should quietly prepare matter for the further consideration of the Assembly in a final review of its work. At all events, after the stress of interruption was over and the Confession was completed (at least substantially), we find this Committee reporting (June 17, 1646). The note runs: "Report was made from the Committee about 'the perfecting of the Confession of Faith'" — and at once it is "*Ordered* — That Mr. Arrowsmith be added to the Committee for [perfecting] the Confession of Faith.[50] Upon a debate about the 'reading of the Report again,' it was *Resolved* upon the Q., 'Not to be read again entire, but in parts.' It was debated, and the Assembly began with the Scriptures; and part of that head was ordered." From this it would seem that the report of the Committee on "the perfecting of the Confession of Faith" consisted of the presentation of a perfected copy; that this was read first entire; and then ordered to be again read in parts. On June 19, 1646, it is further ordered, "That the Committee for wording and methodizing of the Confession of Faith shall have liberty, as they see things imperfect, to complete them; and to make report unto the Assembly."

Under the guidance of this Committee the Assembly thus went again over the whole Confession. This work was not done

[50] Mr. Cawdry was added also, September 1, 1646.

perfunctorily.[51] It was begun on June 17, 1646: immediately after determining, as has been already mentioned, to review the Confession in parts, it is noted: " The Assembly began with the Scriptures; and part of that head was ordered. *Ordered* — To proceed in the debate where we left." Accordingly in the Minutes of the next day (June 18) we read: " The Assembly proceeded in the debate of the Confession of Faith concerning ' the Scriptures '; and upon debate the whole head concerning the Scriptures was ordered; and it is as followeth. . . . The Assembly proceeded in the debate of the Article concerning ' God and the Holy Trinity '; and upon debate that head also was ordered; and it is as followeth. . . . The Assembly proceeded in debate of the Article ' Of God's Eternal Decree '; and upon debate part of it was ordered. Upon debate about the last clause of it, concerning the handling of this doctrine, it was *Resolved* upon the Q., To refer this till to-morrow morning." The next day accordingly: " The Assembly proceeded in the debate of the Confession of Faith; and upon debate, that head ' of God's Eternal Decree ' was ordered and is as followeth. . . ." Similarly chapters iv. and v. were passed on the same day; part of chapter vi. on June 22, and the remainder of chapter vi., and chapters vii. and viii. on June 25. Chapter ix., " of Free Will," gave apparently more trouble. We read in the Minutes of June 29: " Report was made by Mr. Tuckney ' of Free Will.' It was read, and also some additionals to the Article ' of the Fall of Man.' The additionals were debated, and ordered to be added. The Assembly debated the Report ' of Free Will '; and upon debate about the first branch of it concerning ' the natural liberty in the Will,' it was *Resolved* upon the Q., To be recommitted." In the Minutes of the next day (June 30) accordingly we read: " Report was made from the Committee of the proposition concerning Free Will recommitted. It was read and debated, and the whole Article assented to. It is as followeth. . . ." On the same day chapter x. was passed upon. After this, work

[51] Compare Baillie's account of the care expended on this review, ii. pp. 400–403: the passages are extracted below, pp. 119–120.

on the Confession was intermitted for nearly a month, and was not resumed until a message was received from Parliament desiring the early completion of the Confession (July 22).[52] On July 23 chapters xi. and xii. were passed: and on the next day, July 24, the interrupted work of framing the first draft of the Confession was also resumed, the Second Committee bringing in its reports on chapters xviii. and xxxii. The time of the Assembly was thereafter largely absorbed in framing the remainder of the first draft: and it is not until September 14 that we meet with the next note bearing on the review: on that date chapter xvii. was passed upon in its perfected form, and on September 15 chapter xviii., while on this latter date also: " Report was made from the Committee for perfecting the Confession of Faith ' of the Law.' It was read and debated, and upon debate much of it was assented to, the rest referred to the Committee." On September 16, chapters xiii. and xiv. were passed upon; on the 17th the rest of chapter xix.; on September 18, chapter xv. On September 21, chapter xvi. was passed; an addition was proposed to it on the 22d by Mr. Prophet, concerning which the Assembly — " *Resolved* upon the Q., Not to take this paper now read into debate "; nevertheless on September 23 its consideration was pressed on the attention of the Assembly again, whereupon it was " *Resolved* upon the Q., This proposition shall not be added." On the same day chapter xiii., on Sanctification, was taken up renewedly and certain alterations proposed by a Committee appointed for the purpose were entered into it. The same afternoon Mr. Whitaker sought to secure a similar review of a clause in chapter iii., but unsuccessfully.

Thus the framing of the first draft of the latter portion of the Confession and the perfecting of that portion of it already drawn up went on side by side. The House of Commons was meanwhile still pressing for its completion and in response to

---

[52] This order was " due to the letter from the Assembly of the Kirk in Scotland of the 18th of June, read in the Lords on the 9th of July (L. J., viii., 425; C. J., iv., 621) " — Shaw, i. p. 360. A letter from the Church of Scotland was delivered also to the Assembly, July 8.

an order received September 18,[53] chapters xv.–xix. were completed and passed upon September 25, and the first nineteen chapters sent up to Parliament. Chapters xx. and xxi. were passed October 30; chapter xxii. November 6; chapter xxiii. November 9; xxvii. and xxviii. November 10; xxix. November 16; xxv. November 17; xxvi. November 20; xxx. xxxi. xxxii. and xxxiii. November 26. On November 26, 1646, the following note was spread on the Minutes: " The Confession of Faith was finished this day, and by order of the Assembly the Prolocutor gave thanks, in the name of the Assembly, to the Committee that had taken so good [or " great "] pains in the perfecting of the Confession of Faith."

Even this exhibition of the work done in bringing the Confession to its present form is not, however, a complete account of the pains expended on it. On September 18, 1646, there seems to have been made an unsuccessful effort to establish yet another Committee for the reviewing of the whole Confession, after this second passage of it through the Assembly. We read: " Upon a motion to appoint a Committee to consider of the Confession of Faith, what errors are not obviated in it, and to that end that there be a review of the Articles of England and Ireland, it was *Resolved* upon the Q., There shall be no Committee to consider of the reviewing of the Articles what errors are not obviated in them." The meaning of this is perhaps elucidated by the form in which it stands in the other draft of the Minutes, lapping here with the printed copy and called Fascicle iii. by the editors: " A new Committee to consider of all the errors unobviated in several Confessions of England, Ireland and Scotland, to give in the catalogue of these errors to the Committee for the wording. *R.* — No Committee to consider of the reviewing Articles what errors are not obviated in them." That is to say, apparently, what was proposed was a Committee to see that all that was erroneous in earlier Confessions had been fitly dealt with in the new Confession: the anxiety seems to have been that no erroneous ex-

[53] The order was made on September 16 (" Commons' Journal," iv. p. 670; Shaw, i. p. 361), and received on September 18 (" Minutes," pp. 285–286).

pressions, however slight and intrenched in the earlier Confessions, should escape correction in this new one.

Though this effort failed, there was, however, a new reviewing made of the text of the Confession that bore fruit for its perfecting. This was accomplished in the process of its transcription. Over this transcription Dr. Burgess had the oversight. He made report September 21, 1646, " of the Confession of Faith transcribed, so much of it as the Assembly had perfected. It was read, and upon debate it was *Resolved* upon the Q., ' The several heads of the Confession of Faith shall be called by the name of Chapters.' *Resolved* upon the Q., That the several sections be distinguished by figures only." Thus was inaugurated what was really a second revision of the Confession — a passage of it through the Assembly for the third time. By September 25, as we have seen, nineteen chapters had passed through this third scrutiny, and were ordered sent up to the Parliament. Subsequently to that we find repeated instances in which Dr. Burgess moves certain alterations or additions to the already completed chapters — which do or do not commend themselves to the Assembly: e.g. on November 20 he moves certain additions to chapter xxi., which had been passed on October 30; on November 23, to chapter xxii., which had been passed on November 6; and an addition was made to chapter xxi. on that same day, doubtless on his motion. This process of improvement continues even after the entry made on November 26, celebrating the completion of the Confession, i.e. during the whole process of its official transcription. Thus on November 27 we read: " Dr. Burges moved for some alterations in the Confession of Faith in some words, which were assented to." And again on December 1, " Upon a motion for an alteration in the chapter of Censures in the Confession of Faith, it was *Resolved* upon the Q., There shall be no alteration." Indeed, the onerousness of Dr. Burgess' work of overseeing the transcription was recognized at this session by the order: " That the brethren that drew up the Confession of Faith " — that is, as we should conjecture, either the Committee appointed May 12, 1645, to frame the first draft (Messrs. Gataker, Harris, Temple, Burgess, Reynolds, Hoyle, Herle) or else the perfecting Committee (Messrs. Tuckney, Reynolds, Newcomen, Whitaker, Arrowsmith and Cawdry) appointed December 8, 1645, and augmented June 17, 1646, and September 1, 1646 — " do assist Dr. Burges in reading over the Confession of Faith with one of the scribes." On December 3 a number of changes in chapters xix. xxi. xxii. xxix. xxxi. were proposed by Dr. Burgess, and either accepted or rejected, and the Committee was required further to " consider of that which is propounded concerning the chapter of the Civil Magistrate." Other changes were debated on December 4, and Dr. Burgess' final report was made, whereupon it was " *Ordered* — That thanks be returned to the Assessor, Dr. Burges, for his great pains in transcribing the Confession of Faith, which was done by the Prolocutor. *Resolved* upon the Q., This " [i.e. the transcribed and finally adjusted copy of the Confession of Faith] " shall be presented to both Houses of Parliament by the whole Assembly. The Confession of Faith as it was presented is as followeth. . . ." Here we reach the really final act in the Assembly's preparation of the text of the Confession. Nothing remained now but the printing of it, and on receiving from Parliament an order to that effect, it was (December 10) " *Ordered* — That the Scribes take care of the exact printing of the Confession of Faith."

The work of preparing proof-texts for the Confession was undertaken somewhat reluctantly by the Assembly, as a consequence of an order from the House of Commons of October 9, 1646, and reported in the Assembly on October 12. It was felt that the demand for proof-texts was only an expedient of " the retarding partie " in Parliament (as Baillie calls it) to delay the completion of the business: and it was feared that the attempt to add the texts would (as Baillie expressed it) " prove a very long business, if not dexterouslie managed," though, no doubt, it would be " for the advantage and strength of the work." [54] A Committee was, however, at once appointed

[54] Baillie, " Letters," ii. p. 403, iii. p. 2. See the text below, pp. 119, 120.

to advise the Assembly "how obedience may be yielded" to this order, and their report, adopted October 13, set forth that to append full proofs to so large a Confession would require a volume, and could scarcely be necessary, inasmuch as what was set forth in the Confession was for its substance "received truths among all churches," and the only question about it concerned "the manner of expression or the fitness to have it put into the Confession." What the Assembly explicitly asked, however, was only time, not absolute reprieve for the task.[55] Parliament was inexorable, and the work was fairly begun on January 6, 1647 (Wednesday). We read: "*Ordered* — That Mr. Wilson, Mr. Byfield, Mr. Gower, be a Committee to prepare Scriptures for the Confession of Faith." On the very next day the Scriptures for the first chapter were reported, and those for the first paragraph were debated. The work was continued steadily thereafter. The proof-texts of the first chapter were completed on January 15: and meanwhile those for the other chapters were being reported — those for chapter ii. having been brought in on January 8, and for chapter iii. on January 13. On Friday, March 5, 1647, the texts for the final chapters were reported, and the Assembly "*Ordered* — That thanks be returned to the Committee for the Scriptures, for their great pains and diligence in that business; which was accordingly done by the Prolocutor. *Ordered* — That Mr. Burges, Dr. Smith, Mr. Calamy, Mr. Palmer, Mr. Seaman, Mr. Strickland, Mr. Spurstow, Mr. Case, Mr. Scudder, and Dr. Hoyle, or any three of them, shall be a Committee to join with the Committee for the Scriptures, to review the Scriptures. They are to meet on Thursday next in the afternoon. The care of this Committee is referred to Mr. Scudder." These resolutions mark the completion of the proof-texts, however, only in the Committee. At this time the Assembly's consideration of them had reached no further than the twentieth chapter. It was not until April 5, 1647, that the work was completed by the As-

[55] The answer of the Assembly to the requisition is printed by Dr. Mitchell in "The Westminster Assembly," ed. 2, 1897, pp. 377 *sq.*: the rejoinder of the House in the "Minutes," 1874, p. 295.

sembly. On that date the note is entered in the Minutes: " The Confession was finished."

It was not even then " finished," however, except in first draft; and it was ordered that the report of the reviewing Committee should now go through the three large Committees, and so come to the Assembly — the work to be begun on the next day. There was an effort made at the same time to have some explanatory declaration added with reference to the proper use of the proof-texts, but this was unsuccessful. The action in full was as follows: " Upon a motion by Mr. Seaman that something be annexed by way of caution to show how the proofs are to be applied, it was *Resolved* upon the Q., There shall be no further debate about cautions to be added about the proofs of Scripture. *Resolved* upon the Q., That the Review of the Confession of Faith be considered of by the three Committees of the Assembly. *Ordered* — That the Committees appointed for the Review of the Confession make report to-morrow morning what they have done about it." It would seem that it was impracticable for the three Committees to report the next day, however, and the expedient appears to have been adopted — in this approximating to the manner in which the text of the Confession itself was first taken up — of having the Committee of Review report the first portion of the texts directly to the Assembly, while the remainder should come to it only through the large Committees. This is at least what appears to be implied by the entry for April 6: " Mr. Scudder made report of the Review of the proofs of the Confession of Faith for the seven first chapters and part of the 8th; and upon debate of it, it was assented to as the proofs are entered in the margin of the Confession of Faith. *Ordered* — That the rest of the 8th chapter, and chapters 9th to the 17th be referred to the First Committee to review; and from chapter 8th to the 25th to the Second Committee, and from chapter 26th to the end of the Confession to the Third Committee." On the succeeding days, April 7, 8, 9, 12, 13, the reports of these Committees for the several sections were brought in and the proof-texts passed by the Assembly. On the 15th

April it was "*Ordered* — That Mr. Wilson, Mr. Gower, and Mr. Wallis do draw up, in the margin of two books of the Confession of Faith, the Scriptures, to be presented to the Parliament." An order having been received from Parliament to send up the texts (April 22), this was done on April 26, 1647, and they were presented to both Houses on April 29.[56]

Thus the Confession of Faith passed in its completed form out of the hands of the Assembly, and the history of the attempt to create a common Confession of Faith for Great Britain properly closes. All the world knows the subsequent fortunes of the product of such long-continued labors. The text of the first nineteen chapters, it will be remembered, was sent up preliminarily to the two Houses of Parliament: they were presented to the House of Commons September 25, 1646, and to the House of Lords, October 1. On December 4 the completed text went to the Commons, and on the 7th of that month to the Lords. Already by November 4, 1646, the first nineteen chapters had passed the House of Lords in the exact form in which they had been sent up by the Assembly: the remainder was passed by them February 16, 1647. In the Commons, however, the matter dragged. The first nineteen chapters were passed perfunctorily on October 6, 1646, and taken up for debate in the Grand Committee on October 9: and then things stopped. Despite prodding from the Lords, the Commons awaited the reception of the proof-texts before they would do anything. On the 29th April, 1647, " the Scriptures " were handed to them, but the commencement of the debate was still postponed until May 19, and their review of the whole was not completed until March 17, 1648. On the 22d of that month a conference was held with the Lords concerning the changes introduced by the Commons, all of which the Lords assented to except that on " Marriage," and this being made known on June 3 to the Commons, the amended Confession

[56] For a history of the proof-texts of the Confession, see Dr. Samuel T. Lowrie's article in *The Presbyterian Review*, July, 1888 (ix. pp. 443 *sqq.*), and his reports in the " Minutes " of the General Assembly for 1891 (pp. 129 *sqq.*), and 1894 (pp. 157 *sqq.*), or in the " Digest " of 1898 (pp. 21 *sqq.*).

was ordered printed on June 20, 1648. This edition omits the whole of chapters xxx. and xxxi., and also the fourth paragraph of chapter xx. and part of the fourth and the whole of the fifth and sixth paragraphs of chapter xxiv., together with the last clause of the fourth paragraph of chapter xxiii., besides making some unimportant alterations in that paragraph. " Further than this," remarks Mr. Shaw, " the Long Parliament never got in its review of the celebrated Confession." [57] It was indeed taken up again by " the Rump " in 1560, and on March 2 agreed to as reported from the Assembly " in all the chapters except the 30th and 31st," and by an Act passed March 5 declared to be " the public Confession of Faith of the Church of England." But, as Mr. Shaw remarks, " needless to say that the enactment was perfectly futile and unregarded."

Meanwhile, the Confession as presented to Parliament and printed without proofs in January, 1647, was carried at once to Scotland by Baillie, and presented to the Commission of the General Assembly; and doubtless the edition of the same with proofs, printed in the spring, reached Scotland before the meeting of the Assembly. At all events, it was in this form that, having been carefully considered in the Assembly of that year, it was passed by an approving Act, *nemine contradicente,* at its twenty-third session. This Act was ratified by the Scottish Parliament, February 7, 1649: and after the evil days of 1661, again in 1690. Thus it comes about that the Confession of Faith of the Church of Scotland is in all respects the Confession as framed by the Assembly of Divines, and that the real history of the creation of the Confession closes with its labors, and may neglect all that was done in Parliament.

For the better apprehension of the progress of the various chapters of the Confession through the hands of the Assembly of Divines we append a tabular statement of the work done upon each: [58]

[57] As cited, i. p. 365.

[58] We have taken the idea of this tabular statement from Shaw (i. pp. 367 *sqq.*), who prints such an one; and we at first intended simply to quote Shaw's table. But on examination the accuracy of his presentation appeared

Chapter I. — " The sub-Committee for the Confession of Faith "
was instructed on Friday, July 4, 1645, to " make report to the
Assembly on Monday morning of what is in their hands con-
cerning . . . the Scriptures." Accordingly on Monday, July 7,
" Dr. Temple made report of that part of the Confession of
Faith touching the Scriptures. It was read, debated." It was
debated on July 7, 11, 14, 15, 16, 17, 18. It was debated in review June 17, 18, 1646. The Scriptural proofs were reported
January 7,[59] 1647, and debated January 7, 8, 11, 12, 13, 14, 15:
and reviewed April 6, 1647. It was debated in the House of
Commons on the 19th and 28th May, 1647 (" Journals of the
House of Commons," v. pp. 177, 189) ; and the respited § 8 again
debated and accepted, 17th March, 1648 (ibid., v. p. 502).

Chapter II. — " The sub-Committee for the Confession of Faith "
was instructed on Friday, July 4, 1645, to " make report to the
Assembly on Monday morning of what is in their hands concerning God. . . ." Meanwhile on July 16, it was " Ordered —
The first Committee to prepare the Confession of Faith upon
these heads: God and the Holy Trinity. . . ." Nevertheless on
July 18, the " report concerning God " was made by Dr. Temple,
the chairman of " the sub-Committee." This was debated July
18 and 23, and on the latter date it is noted that a report was
" made from the Committee," i.e. obviously the First Great
Committee, " of the article of the Trinity." Clearly " the propositions concerning God " were reported in accordance with the
order of July 4 from the " sub-Committee for the Confession
of Faith," and the " article of the Trinity," in accordance with
the disposition of the heads made on July 16, by the First Committee.[60] The whole " Article concerning ' God and the Holy
Trinity ' " was reviewed June 18, 1646. The Scriptural proofs
were reported on January 8, 1647, and debated and ordered on
the 18th: and reviewed April 6. It was debated in the House of
Commons, May 28, 1647 (" Journals, etc.," v. p. 189).

---

scarcely adequate, and we have made out the whole afresh — deriving, of
course, such aid from Shaw as we could. Where our table differs from Shaw's,
therefore, it differs wittingly.

[59] See also " Minutes," p. 473.

[60] From Baillie also (ii. p. 344) we learn that the Articles " God " and
" Trinity " when first passed were two separate Articles. See below, p. 118.

Chapter III. — On July 16, 1645, it was " *Ordered* — The first Committee to prepare the Confession of Faith upon . . . God's decrees, Predestination, Election, etc." On August 29 — " Report from the first Committee concerning God's decrees " — and debate at once began. Debates were held on August 29, September 2, 3, [8], 9, 11, October 3, 17, 20, 21, 22, 23, 24, [30?], 31, November 3, 6, 7, 11. It was debated in review June 18, 19, 1646, and an additional debate was held on September 23, 1646. The Scriptural proofs were reported January 13, 1647, and debated and ordered January 19, 20, 21: they were reviewed April 6. The chapter was debated in the House of Commons, May 28, 1647 (" Journals," v. p. 189).

Chapter IV. — On July 16, 1645, it was " *Ordered* — The first Committee to prepare the Confession of Faith upon . . . the works of Creation and Providence." On November 17, there was made a " report from the first Committee concerning Creation." It was debated on November 18, 19, 20, on the latter date the note running: " The Assembly proceeded in the debate of the report of Creation, and finished." It was reviewed June 19, 1646. The Scriptural proofs were reported on January 15, 1647, and debated and ordered on January 21 and 28; they were reviewed April 6. The chapter was debated in the House of Commons, October 2, 1647 (" Journals," v. p. 323).

Chapter V. — On July 16, 1645, it was " *Ordered* — The first Committee to prepare the Confession of Faith upon . . . the works of Creation and Providence." On November 27, there was " report made from the First Committee about Providence." It was debated November 28, December 2 and 4: and reviewed and ordered June 19, 1646. The Scriptural proofs were debated on January 28, 29, and February 1; and they were reviewed April 6, 1647. The chapter was debated in the House of Commons, October 2, 1647 (" Journals," v. p. 323).

Chapter VI. — On July 16, 1645, it was " *Ordered* — The first Committee to prepare the Confession of Faith upon . . . Man's Fall ": and again, " The second Committee: Sin, and the punishment thereof." How the two topics were got together we are not informed. On November 17, 1645, there was made a

" report concerning Fall of Man, Sin, and the Punishment thereof." This was debated November 20, 21. The review was introduced June 19, 1646, and debated and ordered June 22 and 25: and additions were made June 29. The Scriptural proofs were debated and ordered February 2, 1647: and reviewed April 6.

Chapter VII. — On July 16, 1645, it was " *Ordered* — The second Committee [to prepare the Confession of Faith upon] . . . the Covenant of Grace." It was reported before October 9, at which date " the Assembly proceeded in the debate of the report concerning the Covenant[s]." [61] It was debated further October 10, 17, November 6, 14, 17, December 23, 1645; and reviewed and ordered June 25, 1646. The Scriptural proofs were reported January 21, 1647, and debated and ordered February 3 and 5.

Chapter VIII. — On July 16, 1645, it was " *Ordered* — The second Committee [to prepare the Confession of Faith upon] . . . Christ our Mediator." On August 29 following, there was " report made by the second Committee of Christ the Mediator." It was debated September 2, 3, 4, 8, 9, 11, 12, 15, 16, and November 14, 1645: and reviewed June 25, 1646. The Scriptural proofs were debated and ordered February 8, 1647, and reviewed April 6 and 7, 1647.

Chapter IX. — On July 16, 1645, it was " *Ordered* — The second Committee [to prepare the Confession of Faith upon] . . . Free-will." On December 15 next, " Dr. Gouge made report about Free-will," [62] and on the 17th this report was debated. It was reviewed and ordered June 29, 30, 1646. The Scriptural proofs were reported February 2, 1647, and debated and ordered on February 9: they were reviewed April 8.

Chapter X. — On July 16, 1645, it was " *Ordered* — The third Committee [to prepare the Confession of Faith upon] Effectual

[61] Why the bracketed " s " appears in the printed " Minutes " is not obvious. The " s " is arbitrarily present or absent in the allusions in the " Minutes."

[62] Why it is not likely that this is the first report of chapter ix. made to the Assembly is explained above, pp. 94–95.

Vocation." On September 9 following, " Mr. Prophet made report of Effectual Calling." It was debated September 17, 25, 29 (30), November 6, 13: and reviewed and ordered June 30, 1646. The Scriptural proofs were reported February 3, 1647, and debated and ordered February 9: they were reviewed April 8.

Chapter XI. — On July 16, 1645, it was " *Ordered* — The third Committee [to prepare the Confession of Faith upon] . . . Justification." On December 2 next, there was made " report from Mr. Cheynell of Justification." It was debated December 3, (5), 8, 9, 10, (11), 16; and reviewed and ordered July 23, 1646. The Scriptural proofs were reported February 4, 1647, and debated and ordered February 10, 11: they were reviewed April 8.

Chapter XII. — On July 16, 1645, it was " *Ordered* — The third Committee [to prepare the Confession of Faith upon] . . . Adoption." On November 20 next, " Mr. Prophet brought in a report from the Third Committee about Adoption." It was reviewed and ordered July 23, 1646. The Scriptural proofs were reported February 5, 1647: debated and ordered February 11; and reviewed April 8.

Chapter XIII. — On July 16, 1645, it was " *Ordered* — The third Committee [to prepare the Confession of Faith upon] . . . Sanctification." On November 20 following, " Mr. Prophet brought in a report from the Third Committee . . . about Sanctification." It was debated November 24: and reviewed and ordered September 16 and 23, 1646. The Scriptural proofs were reported February 5, 1647, and debated February 12: they were reviewed April 8.

Chapter XIV. — On the 19th August, 1646, it was " *Resolved* upon the Q., These heads of Faith, Repentance, and Good Works shall be referred to the three Committees in their order to prepare something upon them for the Confession of Faith." [63] From August 21 to August 31 inclusive the Assembly sat only as a Grand Committee, lacking a quorum for a formal meeting:

[63] It will be noted that these three chapters were apparently afterthoughts; they were, to all appearance, not contemplated in the first planning of the Confession.

during this time the report on Saving Faith was reviewed.[64] This report was formally called up in the Assembly, September 4. It was debated September 9, and reviewed and ordered September 16. The Scriptural proofs were reported February 12, 1647: they were reviewed April 8.

Chapter XV. — This chapter also was ordered to be prepared (by the Second Committee) August 19, 1646 (see under chapter xiv. *ad init.*). On September 9, " Dr. Stanton made Report of the Article concerning Repentance." It was debated September 10, 17, 18, at the last of which sessions it was ordered: on September 25, it was finally passed. The Scriptural proofs were debated February 12, 1647: and reviewed April 8.

Chapter XVI. — This chapter also was ordered to be prepared (by the Third Committee) August 19, 1646 (see under chapter xiv. *ad init.*). On September 3, 1646, " Report was made by Dr. Temple ' of Good Works.' " It was debated September 9, 18, 21, and ordered: the matter was reopened September 22, 23; and the perfected chapter passed September 25. The Scriptural proofs were debated and ordered February 15, 1647: and reviewed April 8.

Chapter XVII. — On November 18, 1645, there was referred " to the First Committee, Perseverance. . . ." On December 19 following, there was made " Report from the First Committee of Perseverance." It was debated December 29, 1645; and reviewed September 14, 1646, and finally passed September 25. The Scriptural proofs were debated and ordered February 17, 1647, and reviewed April 8.

Chapter XVIII. — On February 23, 1646, it was " *Ordered* . . . To the Second Committee, — Certainty of Salvation. . . ." It was reported from the Second Committee July 24, 1646, and " *Ordered* — This to be the title — ' Of the Certainty of Salvation.' " It was debated July 24 and 30, and September 14, 15, and assented to under the title, " Of Assurance of Grace and Salvation "; and finally passed September 25. The Scriptural proofs

[64] " Minutes," p. 271.

were debated on February 17 and 18, and reviewed April 7, 1647.

Chapter XIX. — On November 18, 1645, there was referred " to the Third Committee, the Law. . . ." On January 1, 1646, " Dr. Wincop made report from the Third Committee about the Law of God." It was debated on January 7, 9, 12, 13, 29, February 2 and 9, 1646; also in the Grand Committee during the interval in the Assembly's meetings August 21–31, and in the Assembly September 1, 2, 3, 4, 15, 17, and finally passed September 25, 1646. A slight alteration was further made on December 3. The Scriptural proofs were debated and ordered on February 19 and 22, 1647.

Chapter XX. — On November 18, 1645, there was referred " to the First Committee, . . . Christian Liberty. . . ." It was debated January 29, 1646, February 9, 10, 11, 12, 16, (23), March (4), 10,[65] 26,[66] 27,[67] 30, 31,[68] and again September 23, 24, 25, October 1, 7, 8, 9, 12, 13, 14, 15, 16, 20, 21, 30. The Scriptural proofs were debated and ordered February 25, 26, 1647, March 2, 3, 4, 5, 11, 12. This chapter was debated in the House of Commons on the 4th February, 1648, and § 4 respited until chapter xxx. was under consideration (" Journals," v. p. 455).

Chapter XXI. — On November 18, 1645, there was referred " to the Third Committee, . . . Religion, Worship. . . ." And on February 23, 1646, it was " *Ordered* — To the First Committee, in chief heads, — Christian Sabbath. . . ." On March 5, 1646, " Mr. Prophet made report of Religion and Worship," and on March 9, there was made " Report of the Sabbath." " Religion and Worship " was debated March 9,[69] 10 (when the title was changed to " of Religious Worship "),[70] 20,[71] 26,[72] when the subject is recorded as finished. The topic " Of the Sabbath " was debated April 6 (when the title was set as " Of the Sabbath day "). On October 12 the two heads reappeared together: " Mr. Tuckney made report ' of Religious Worship and Sabbath-day ' ";

[65] Cf. also p. 205.
[66] Cf. p. 436.
[67] Cf. p. 437.
[68] Cf. p. 439.

[69] Cf. also p. 205.
[70] P. 205.
[71] Cf. p. 434.
[72] Cf. p. 435.

but it does not appear further that they constituted a single chapter. On October 30, " the Assembly debated the Chapter ' of Religious Worship '; and upon debate it was assented to . . ."; and there were further debates on November 20 and 23, and a slight correction was ordered on December 3. Report of Scriptural proofs for the 21st chapter was made February 18, 1647. The process by which the two chapters were reduced to one is obscure. It was debated in the House of Commons on February 4, 1648 (" Journals," v. p. 455).

Chapter XXII. — On January 8, 1646, there was made a " Report of a Lawful Oath by Mr. Prophet." Mr. Prophet was chairman of the Third Committee, but no such " head " had been recorded among the " heads " distributed to this Committee: perhaps it had emerged into a separate topic in the discussions of the head of " worship " assigned to the Third Committee on November 18, 1645.[73] It was debated January 13, 15, 16, 19, 20, 21, 1646: and in review, October 12 (" of Lawful Oaths and Vows "), November 3, 6: while on November 23 and December 3 additional adjustments were made. The Scriptural proofs were reported February 18 and reviewed April 12, 1647. It was debated in the House of Commons, 4th February, 1648 (" Journals," v. p. 455).

Chapter XXIII. — On February 23, 1646, it was " *Ordered* — To the First Committee, in chief heads . . . the Civil Magistrate." It was reported to the Assembly, March 26, 1646, and debated April (23), 24, 27, [and possibly again October (12), 13, 14, 15, 20, although these debates probably belong to chapter xx.]. It was passed November 9, while further adjustments were made on December 3, 4. The Scriptural proofs were debated on March 3, and reviewed April 12, 1647. It was debated in the House of Commons, 4th February, 1648 (" Journals," v. p. 456).

Chapter XXIV. — On February 23, 1646, it was " *Ordered* — To the First Committee, in chief heads, — . . . Marriage and Di-

---

[73] See what is said of the topic, " Lies and Equivocations," at the end of this tabular statement (p. 116, N. B.). Is it possible that this chapter was developed out of that topic? It is against this supposition that different Committees seem concerned.

vorce." On June 17 next, " Report was made ' of Marriage ' ":
and the report was taken up July 23, and debated August 3 and
4 — apparently under the simple title " Of Marriage." Accordingly on August 10, " Dr. Gouge made Report ' of Divorce,' "
which under the title " Of Divorce " was taken up and debated
September 10, 11. The two were, however, reported on October
12 as constituting one " head," and were so debated November
9, 10, 11, and so passed. The Scriptural proofs were reported
on March 3, 1647. The chapter was debated in the House of
Commons, February 4, 11, and March 3, 1648 (" Journals," v.
pp. 456, 461, 478).

Chapter XXV. — On November 18, 1645, there was referred " to
the First Committee . . . the Church. . . ." When we next hear
of it, it is already in process of debate, February 16, 1646: the
debate continues February 23, 26, 27, March 2, (3, 4), 5 [6, 9,[74]
13,[75] 16, 17, 18, 19, (20), (26), April 3, 7, 8, 10, 13, 14, 15, 16,
17],[76] 20, 21, 22.[77] It was taken up in review November 13, 1646,
and ordered on the 17th. The Scriptural proofs were reported
March 3, 1647. The chapter was debated in the House of Commons, March 10, 1648 (" Journals," v. p. 489).

Chapter XXVI. — On November 18, 1645, there was referred " to
the First Committee . . . the Communion of Saints." On February 17, 1646, there was made a " Report of the Committee of
the Communion of Sacraments " (sic) : and debate was entered
upon on it March 3, and continued March 4, 5. It was resumed
for review November 13, 17, 19, 20. The Scriptural proofs were
reported March 3, 1647, and reviewed April 7. It was debated
in the House of Commons, March 10, 1648 (" Journals," v. p.
490).

[74] Cf. also p. 204.

[75] Cf. also p. 206.

[76] The material developed in the debates recorded on the dates contained within these square brackets entered very little into the formation
of chapter xxv. Part of it was incorporated into chapter xxx.

[77] The debates on the *jus divinum* which took place on May (1), 4, 5,
7, 8, 15, 18, 19, (25), 28, June 1, 2, 5, 8, 10, 11, 12, 15, July 6, 7, 10, 17, did
not, of course, directly concern chapter xxv., but rather were in preparation
of the answer of the Assembly to certain Parliamentary "Questions." See
Baillie's account as given on p. 118, below; and compare Shaw, i. pp. 308 *sqq.*
But the material thus gathered indirectly bore fruit for this chapter also.

Chapter XXVII. — On November 18, 1645, there was referred " to the Second Committee . . . Sacraments. . . ." The report was called for December 2, 1645, and given in December 5. It was debated December 11, 12, 15, 16, 24, 25, and recalled for review November 10, 1646. The Scriptural proofs are not referred to in the Minutes. It was debated in the House of Commons, March 10, 1648 (" Journals," v. p. 490).

Chapter XXVIII. — On November 18, 1645, there was referred " to the Second Committee . . . Baptism. . . ." On December 29 following, " Mr. Calamy made report of Baptism." Debate was held on the chapter, January 1, 2, 5, 6, 8, 9, 16, (19), 21, 26, 1646; and again September 11; and on November 10 it was reviewed and ordered. No record of the adding of the Scriptural proofs. It was debated in the House of Commons, March 10, 1648 (" Journals," v. p. 490).

Chapter XXIX. — On November 18, 1645, there was referred " to the Second Committee . . . the Lord's Supper." On December 1 following, there was made a " Report from the Second Committee of the Lord's Supper ": debate was " proceeded in " December 26: again it was taken up November 11, 12, 13, 1646, and on November 16 ordered. On December 3 some slight adjustments of language were made. The Scriptural proofs were reported March 5, 1647. The chapter was debated in the House of Commons, March 10, 1648 (" Journals," v. p. 491).

Chapter XXX. — On November 18, 1645, there was referred " to the Second Committee, Officers and Censures of the Church. . . ." On January 29, 1646, " Mr. Dury made report from the Second Committee of Church Officers and Censures." It was debated April 23,[78] and recalled for review November 13, 23, 26, and at this last date ordered. An alteration was again proposed December 1. The Scriptural proofs were reported March 5, 1647, and voted April 2, 1647 (" Minutes," p. 345, note 1).

Chapter XXXI. — On November 18, 1645, there was referred " to the Second Committee . . . Councils or Synods. . . ." It was reported to the Assembly, August 4, 1646, and debated August

[78] See above under chapter xxv. (note 76).

5, 6, 7, 10, 11, 13, 14, 17, 19, 20: and again in review November 13 and 26, when it was ordered. On December 3 alterations were debated. The Scriptural proofs were reported March 5, 1647, debated and ordered April 2 (p. 345, note 1), and reviewed April 13.

Chapter XXXII. — On February 23, 1646, it was " *Ordered* — . . . To the Second Committee, . . . the State of the Soul after death. To the Third Committee, — The Resurrection. . . ." The former was reported July 24, 1646, and debated July 31. The latter was reported August 4, and debated September 4. On November 26, 1646, " the Assembly debated ' of the State of Man after death ': and upon debate it was assented to. . . ." How or when the two were united does not appear. The Scriptural proofs for the chapter were reported March 5, 1647, and voted April 5 (p. 345, note 2.) It was debated in the House of Commons, March 10, 1648 (" Journals," v. p. 491).

Chapter XXXIII. — On February 23, 1646, it was " *Ordered* — . . . To the Third Committee, . . . the Last Judgment, Life Eternal." The topic was debated in the Grand Committee during the interval in the meetings of the Assembly, August 21–31, 1646, and was debated in the Assembly September 4, and again on review November 26, when it was ordered. The Scriptural proofs were reported March 5, 1647, and voted April 5 (p. 345, note 2). It was debated in the House of Commons, March 10, 1648 (" Journals," v. p. 491).

N. B. — In the third distribution of the " heads," made February 23, 1646, the topic " Lies and Equivocations " was assigned to the Second Committee. This topic does not emerge again by report to the Assembly, and there is no such chapter in the completed Confession. Possibly it was found that the material to be dealt with in it was sufficiently covered in chapter xxii., " Of Lawful Oaths and Vows " (see above, chapter xxii., note 73).[79]

[79] Shaw (i. p. 372) mentions the topic *Dedication to God*, which is reported as debated January 2, 1646, as " if not represented by Article XII " (Adoption), probably a subsequently omitted Article. Possibly, however, it signalizes only a debate on one phase of Baptism, in immediate contiguity with which it is mentioned.

To this statement we append the chief references to the work of the Assembly on the Confession made in Baillie's " Letters ":

Under date of August 18, 1644 (ii. 1841, p. 220), Baillie recounts the coming of Warriston and the efforts for expedition (see the text above, note 19, p. 82), and under date of August 28 (p. 224) he recounts the progress thus far made in the work of " the Covenanted Uniformitie." Direct mention of the Confession begins in the Publick Letter of October, 1644: " The Confession of Faith is referred to a committee to be put in severall the best hands that are here " (p. 232). Under date of November 21 he writes: " What remains of the Directorie . . . will soon be dispatched. The Catechise is drawn up, and, I think, shall not take up much tyme. I feare the Confession of Faith may stick longer " (p. 242). Under date of December 26: " If the Directorie and Government were once out of our hands, as a few days will put them, then we will fall on our great question of Excommunication, the Catechise, and Confession. There is here matter to hold us long enough, if the wrangling humour which long predomined in many here did continue; but, thanks be to God, that is much abated, and all inclines toward a conclusion. . . . I think we must either passe the Confession to another season, or, if God will help us, the heads of it being distribute among many able hands, it may in a short time be so drawn up, as the debates of it may cost little time " (p. 248). Under date of April 25, 1645: " The Catechise and Confession of Faith are put in the hands of severall committees, and some reports are made to the Assemblie concerning both. We expect not so much debate upon these, as we have had in the Directorie and Government " (p. 266). Under date of May 4, 1645: " Our next work will be the Confession and Catechisme, upon both which we have allreadie made some entrance " (p. 272). In an undated letter printed immediately after the one just quoted from: " We are at a point with the Government; and beginning to take the Confession of Faith and Catechise to our consideration " (p. 275). Under date of July 8, 1645: " Mr. Henderson . . . and Mr. Rutherfoord are gone this day to Epsom waters: so long as anything is to doe here, he cannot be away. I hope the rest of us may ere long be well spared, if once we had through the Catechise and a part of the Confession " (p. 296). Under date of July 8: " Since my last, with our former post, July 1st, we have, thanks be to God, at last finished the whole body of Government. . . . Since, we have entered on the Confession of Faith; as yet I cannot pronounce of the length or shortness of our proceedings therein " (p. 300). In an undated public letter belonging doubtless to August, 1645: " In the Assemblie we have gone through a part of the Catechisme, and a part of the Confession of Faith; but . . . many [hindrances,] when least we expect them, comes in our way . . ." (p. 306). Under date of September 5: " In the Assemblie we are goeing on languidlie with the Confession of Faith and Catechisme " (p. 315). Under date of November 25: " In the Assemblie, we are goeing on with the Confession of Faith. We had long and tough debates about the Decrees of election; yet thanks to God all is gone right according to our mind " (p. 325). " We go on daily in some proposition of the Confession of Faith: till this be ended we will not take in any more of the Catechise " (p. 326). In an undated letter belonging to January 15, 1646: " We are going on in the Assemblie with the Confession, and could, if need were, shortly end it " (p. 336). In an undated letter ascribed by Dr. Laing to about January 20, 1646, he says: " We goe on in the Assemblie with prettie speed now in our Confession of Faith. We have past the heads of Scripture, God, Trinity, Decrees, Providence, Redemption, Covenant, Justification, Sanctification, Free-will, Sacraments in generall, a part of Perseverance, and of the Lord's Supper " (p. 344). Under date of January 31, 1646: " We proceed but slowlie in the Confession of Faith " (p. 348). In February, 1646: " However we wait daylie on the Assemblie, yet our progresse in the Confession of Faith is but slow . . . yet we hope, by God's grace, ere long to end the Confession " (p. 349). Cf. March 17, 1646 (p. 360). Under date of June 26, 1646: " The Parliament's questions have retarded us much: without them we had ended the Confession of Faith " (p. 377). Under date of July 14, 1646: " I have put some of my good friends, leading men in the House of Commons, to move the Assemblie to lay aside our questions " [" some very captious questions of the Parliament, about the clear scripturall warrant for all the punctilioes of the Government," sent in, as Baillie thinks, just " to keep all things from any conclusion " (p. 378)] " for a time, and labour that which is most necessar, and all are crying for, the perfecting of the Confession of Faith and Catechise. If this motion take, I hope we shall end shortly our Confession, for there is but a few articles now to goe through: it will be a very gracious and satisfac-

torie Confession when yow see it " (p. 379). Under date of August
13, 1646: " In the Assemblie we were like to have stucken many
moneths on the questions; and the Independents were in a way to
gett all their differences debated over againe. I dealt so with Mr.
Rous and Mr. Tate, that they brought us ane order from the House
to lay aside the questions till the Confession and Catechise were
ended. Many took it for a trick of the Independents and Erastians
for our hurt; but I knew it wes nothing less. We are now near an
end of our Confession: we stick in the article of Synods, upon the
proposition of their coercive power, or their power to excommunicat.
If this were over, we apprehend no more long debates on the Confession " (p. 388). Under the date of August 18, 1646: " In the
Assemblie we are returned to the Confession of Faith, and are
drawing towards the end of it " (p. 390). Under date of September
22, 1646: " We have ended the Confession of Faith for the matter,
and have perfyted the most half of it, nyneteen chapters; the other
seventeen, I hope, in ten or twelve days will be perfyted, and so all
be sent up to the Houses. It will be, I hope, a very sweet and ortho-
doxe peice, much better than any Confession yet extant, if the
House of Commons mangle it not to us " (p. 397). Under date of
October 2, 1646: " The Assemblie obleidged themselves by promise
to sitt before and after noon for some tyme; but now, thinking they
have satisfied the Houses, by sending up the half of the Confession,
the first nineteen heads, they are relapsed into their former negligence. So we will be able few days in a week to make ane Assemblie; for if there be ane fewer than forty, it is no meeting; and
though the rest of the heads be also past, yet, in the review, the
alteration of words, and the methodizeing, takes up so much time,
that we know not when we shall end. Besides that we have some
additionalls, especially one proposition, about libertie of conscience,
wherein the Independents offer to keep us long and tough debates;
for long agoe they have laid downe in this their maske, and pleads
for a libertie weell near universall " (pp. 400, 401). Under date of
October 13, 1646: " Our Assemblie for one twenty dayes posted
hard; bot since hes gotten into its old pace. The first halfe, and more,
of the Confession we sent up to the House; the end of these who
called for it, wes the shuffling out the Ordinance against Errors; yet
our friends hes carried to goe on with that; but others hes carried
the putting of Scriptures to the margin of the Confession, which
may prove a very long business, if not dexterouslie managed. It

will yet be a fortnight before the other halfe of it be ready; for sundry necessar but scabrous propositions were added in the review" (p. 403). Under date of October 27, 1646: ". . . before the Assemblie end the Confession; for that long I purpose to stay, though my permission to goe were come" (p. 406). Under date of December 1, 1646: "With much adoe we have gone through, at last, the rest of our Confession: the first part I sent, to yow three only, in Mr. David's letter, long agoe; the whole will goe up to the House one of these dayes, and so to the presse. It's generally taken here for a very gracious and brave peece of worke" (p. 411). About Christmas, 1646: "Our Assemblie, with much adoe, at last have wrestled through the whole Confession, and all is now printed. The House of Commons requires to put Scripture to it before they take it to consideration; and what time that will take up, who knows?" (p. 415). Under date of January 26, 1647: "The third point [of Uniformity], the Confession of Faith, I brought it with me [to Scotland], now in print, as it wes offered to the Houses by the Assemblie, without considerable dissent of any. It's much cryed up by all, even many of our greatest opposites, as the best Confession yet extant; it's expected the Houses shall pass it, as they did the Directorie, without much debate. Howbeit the retarding partie hes put the Assemblie to add Scriptures to it, which they omitted only to eschew the offence of the House, whose practice hitherto hes been, to enact nothing of religion on divine right or scripturall grounds, but upon their owne authoritie alone. This innovation of our opposites may weell cost the Assemblie some time, who cannot doe the most easie things with any expedition; but it will be for the advantage and strength of the work" (iii. p. 2). Cf. June 2, 1647 (pp. 5, 6). Speech in the General Assembly at Edinburgh, August 6, 1647: "Right Honourable and Reverend, yow remember, that all your ecclesiastick desyres from your brethren of England, that all the commissions and instructions laid upon us your servants, were only for the obtaining of Uniformitie in four particulars, — in the Worship of God, in the Government of the Church, in a Confession of Faith, and Catechisme. . . . In your third desyre, the Lord made our successe no less prosperous; a large Confession of Faith is perfyted with farr greater unanimitie than any living could have hoped for, among so many learned divines, in so distempered a place and distracted a season. I am confident, if the judgment of many my wiser do not deceave, this piece

of work is so fine and excellent, that whenever yow shall be pleased
to look upon it, the sight of it shall draw from the most censorius
eye, a good acceptation " (p. 11; cf. p. 12). Under date of September 1, 1647, giving account of the Scotch General Assembly: "We
agreed . . . after much debate in the Committee, to the Confession
of Faith " (p. 20).

A word in conclusion as to the title of the volume thus prepared is perhaps not out of place. The Assembly of Divines
quite constantly speak of it in their Minutes, from the beginning, as " a Confession of Faith," or, after it was begun, " the
Confession of Faith." The term was doubtless derived from
the Solemn League and Covenant, which enumerates, among
the items in which uniformity should be sought between the
two nations, " Confession of Faith." Meanwhile, however, the
work of its preparation was prosecuted without formally setting upon a title for the completed book. On the 3d of September, 1646, as it was approaching completion, it was " *Ordered*
— The Committee for the perfecting of the Confession of Faith
do prepare a title for it "; and on September 24 this duty was
apparently laid specifically on Dr. Burgess. On September 25
the report upon the title came in, " and it was *Ordered* — This
to be the title: ' To the Honble the House of Commons assembled in Parliament, The humble Advice of the Assembly of Divines, now by authority of Parliament sitting at Westminster,
concerning part of a Confession of Faith.' " To the completed
Confession also a like title was assigned: and it was under
this title that the Confession was printed in the first instance.
The title thus suggested, however, did not meet with the approval of the House of Commons. It seemed to it, as Rushworth tells us,[80] that nothing was practically a Confession
which did not take the form of " I confess " at the beginning
of each section, and, moreover, that it were well to keep up
the usage established by the Thirty-nine Articles; and so they
altered the title to " Articles of Faith agreed upon by both
Houses of Parliament," or rather to " Articles of Christian re-

[80] See Mitchell in " Minutes," p. 416.

ligion approved and passed by both Houses of Parliament after
advice had with the Assembly of Divines " — under which
latter title they published the Confession with the slight alterations they had made in it, in the summer of 1648.[81] The adoption of the earlier title by the Church of Scotland in its previous action, together with the failure of the whole movement
in England, has secured that the work has lived under the simple title of " The Confession of Faith ": and it is as such that
it is known among all the Churches which still adhere to it.

II. The Formulation of the Third Chapter

The third chapter of the Confession of Faith, having been
prepared in first draft by the Committee appointed for that
service (May 12, 1645), passed through the hands of the First
Great Committee (July 16, 1645) to the Assembly. It was reported from this Committee on August 29, 1645 (Friday), and
the Assembly at once entered into debate upon it. Debate is
mentioned as being held upon it August 29, September 2, 3,
[8], 9, 11, October 3, 17, 20, 21, 22, 23, 24, [30], 31, November
3, 6, 7, 11. In the meantime portions of the chapter were twice,
at least, (September 3 and November 6) recommitted —
doubtless (for such seems to have been the Assembly's custom)
to special Committees: and on five occasions (September [8],
9, 11, October 3, 17, 21) the original Committee brought in
additional reports. In the subsequent reviewing of the Confession as passed, the third chapter was debated again on
Thursday and Friday, June 18, 19, 1646, before it was finally
ordered. It appears, further, that Mr. Whitaker, a member of
the Committee of Review, appointed December 8, 1645, but
acting apparently on his own behalf alone on this occasion,
moved an additional alteration in the chapter on September
23, 1646, and this naturally caused some further debate. The
text was now, however, finally passed from. The proof-texts
for the chapter were debated on January [13], 19, 20, 21, 1647,

---

[81] Mitchell in " Minutes," p. 416, and in " The Westminster Assembly,"
pp. 378–379, and 526; Shaw, i. p. 365.

and after having been considered by the reviewing Committee appointed March 5, 1647, were finally passed on by the Assembly, April 6, 1647. Thus the text of the third chapter occupied the attention of the Assembly some part of at least twenty separate days, besides all the time given to it in the various Committees through whose hands it or parts of it passed. The proof-texts similarly occupied the Assembly on some parts of at least four days in addition to the care given to them in Committee. It would not be excessive to say, in a word, that a good portion of a month's public labor was given to this chapter by the Assembly; and certainly much more than this was expended on it by its Committees.

The debates upon the chapter which are signalized in the Minutes seem to have been especially careful and persistent: [82] and they are perhaps unusually fully reported. We are not able to trace them in full, to be sure, or even to ascertain all the points on which they turned. But it is presumable that those mentioned explicitly were of more importance than those passed over without so much as an indication of the points on which they turned; and doubtless those recorded in some detail were the most important of all. If we may assume so much, we are not without some hint as to the matters about which most interest was felt, and the phraseology of which was framed most carefully and in the fullest light. As is usual in such cases, the real work of creating the chapter was of course done in Committee; and the chapter as finally passed by the Assembly is obviously substantially what in the first instance was reported by the Committee. The notes of debate are sufficient to certify us of that natural and almost inevitable fact. But they also certify us that it was not passed by the Assembly without the most careful scrutiny or without many adjustments and alterations, so that as passed it represents clearly the deliberate and reasoned judgment of the Assembly as a whole.

[82] Baillie says (November 25, 1645; ii. p. 325): "We had long and tough debates about the Decrees of election; yet thanks to God all is gone right according to our mind."

This will at once be made evident by merely noting the special points on which debate is signalized. They concern the title of the chapter (August 29); the phrasing of the first section in no less than six separate particulars (August 29); the whole form of statement of the latter half of the second section (September 3 and 11); the statement of reprobation in section three (November 3, 1645, and September 23, 1646); the whole fabric and especially the retention of a particular phrase of the fifth section (October 3 and 17, 1645); the entire structure of the sixth section (October 20, 21), and, above all, the assertion of its last clause (October 22, 23, 24, 30, 31); the mode of statement of section seven (November 6, 7, 11); and at least the phraseology of section eight (June 18, 1646). It must be borne in mind that this is but a partial list of the topics debated; the precise topic debated is not always mentioned when the fact of a debate on chapter iii. is, nevertheless, recorded; and there is no reason to believe that when it is mentioned it is always done with completeness. The record is enough, however, to assure us that the debate was both extremely searching and very comprehensive. This chapter did not leave the Assembly's hands, we may feel sure, without having been conformed in every particular to the Assembly's belief and even taste.

This will become even more apparent if we will attend to the details debated, so far as the record enables us to follow them. It is quite clear that the report brought in by the Committee, while framed with independence and special theological knowledge and skill, was yet based upon the Irish Articles, and in places followed them very closely — though elsewhere breaking away from them and striking out a new path. The knowledge of this fact will enable us now and again to reconstruct the form of the language in the original report, and so to follow the lines of the debate somewhat more closely than would otherwise be possible from the meager hints of the record.

1. For example, when we are told in the Minutes of August 29, 1645, that debate on this chapter was first joined " upon

the title," we shall be wise to remind ourselves that the title of the corresponding Article in the Irish Articles ran: " Of God's Eternal Decree and Predestination "; and that it is therefore extremely likely that it was reported to the Assembly in some such form. We note accordingly with interest that in the distribution of the heads of the Confession to the three great Committees which was made on July 16, this head reads " God's decrees, Predestination, Election, etc." It is altogether likely, therefore, that when this chapter came to the Assembly it bore a title somewhat like that of the Irish Articles, " Of God's Eternal Decree and Predestination," and that the Assembly curtailed this to the simpler " Of God's Eternal Decree "; although, of course, it is possible, on the other hand, that it was the simpler title that it bore, and what happened in the Assembly was that it was queried whether the longer title of the earlier Articles were not better restored. This Irish title was not exactly tautological; for in the prevailing speech of the time the term " Predestination " was commonly limited to the soteriological decree, so that in the Irish title the collocation really is equivalent to " of God's general and special decree," or " of God's cosmical and soteriological decree." Even the threefold enumeration made in the designation of the topic in the act distributing the heads of the Confession to the Committees, would not be incapable of defense on the ground of progressive advance from the more general to the more specific. It was not uncustomary at the time, however, to look upon the word " Predestination " as so much a synonym of " Election," that it embodied all its precious connotations — a fact which underlies the discrimination between the terms " predestinate " and " foreordain " as used in the third and fourth sections, which otherwise would be puzzling. However accordant with current usage it was, it might well have seemed, therefore, desirable to avoid the formal and unexplained treatment of Predestination as a more inclusive word than Election. Even the Irish heading might seem, indeed, to some, although not essentially tautological, yet to bear so nearly the formal appearance of tautology as to be offensive to the severer taste represented in the Assembly. The choice of the brief and simple " Of God's Eternal Decree " surely seems, in any event, to do the Assembly credit: it is as terse and simple as all the rest of its work and may be looked upon as a fair indication of its temper and taste alike.

We might be tempted to suppose that in the debate on the title of the chapter another point would be raised — whether the singular or plural form should be used — " Of God's Eternal Decree," or " Of God's Eternal Decrees." [83] On October 20, when the sixth section of the chapter was under discussion, a question involved in this difference was under debate, and some difference of opinion on the matter was developed. There is no hint, however, that the question was raised when the title of the chapter was under discussion; and the very occurrence and especially the nature of the subsequent debate render it difficult to suppose that the same subject had already been threshed out so short a while before. It seems altogether likely that the debate on the title was confined, therefore, to its compass, and that the form " Of God's Eternal Decree " was simply adopted, without question raised, from the Irish Articles. How little importance was attached to the difference between the singular and plural forms is evident not only from the subsequent debate, in which indifference to it is manifested by the strongest Calvinists in the body and it is generally treated as a question of language rather than of things; but also from the circumstance that though the singular form is consistently maintained in the Confession, the plural is equally consistently maintained in the Catechisms, both Larger and Shorter.[84]

[83] In the interesting discussion published in pp. 185 *sq.* of his " Theology of the Westminster Symbols," 1900, Dr. Edward D. Morris appears to suggest something like this. " An interesting discussion," he says, " seems to have arisen in the Assembly respecting the use of the singular or the plural term, decree or decrees, in the exposition of this general doctrine." There is, however, no indication of any such discussion having occurred on the title: the debate adverted to by Dr. Morris was upon the sixth section and concerned directly another matter — as will be seen below. The Westminster Divines obviously attached very little importance to this mere matter of phraseology.

[84] The loosely kept notes which we have of the Minutes are too carelessly

2. Our knowledge that the Irish Articles underlay the draft sent in to the Assembly is of yet more aid to us in understanding the debates that are noted as having taken place on the first section of the chapter (August 29, 1645). These are hinted at in the Minutes as follows: " Debate about the word ' counsel,' about those words ' most holy wise,' and about those words ' his own.' Debate about that word ' time,' about the word ' should.' Debate about the transposing." Not all these words occur in the section as passed: but they are explicable from the Irish Articles. We need only to assume that the first half of the section as at first reported was more similar to the Irish Articles than it became in the course of the debate. It probably ran as follows: " God from all eternity did, by the most holy and wise counsel of His own will, freely and unchangeably ordain whatsoever in time should come to pass." In the process of the debate the word " counsel " was scrutinized and retained; the adjectives " holy " and " wise " were transposed; " His own " was scrutinized and retained; and the last clause after careful scrutiny of its phraseology was exchanged to the simpler " whatsoever comes to pass." Thus the form that was adopted was arrived at: " God from all eternity did, by the most wise and holy counsel of His own will, freely and unchangeably ordain whatsoever comes to pass." That the changes thus made were improvements we can scarcely doubt: the order " wise and holy " is the order of nature as well as climax, in its progress from the intellectual to the moral perfections; while the new concluding clause is not only simpler and free from apparent but fictitious limitation, but avoids raising puzzling questions as to what are to be classed as pre- or extra-temporal and what as temporal acts.[85]

---

written to offer any testimony in such a matter. If we have counted correctly, the third chapter is mentioned more or less formally by name ten times in the " Minutes." In five the plural is used (pp. 114, 126, 127, 322, 323); in five the singular (pp. 126, 129, 130, 245, 246).

[85] In the Larger Catechism, Q. 12, the words " in time " are retained: " God's decrees are the wise, free and holy acts of the counsel of His will,

What is intended by " the transposing," debate on which
is noted, we have no means of confidently determining. It may
concern simply the transposition of the adjectives " wise " and
" holy," which we have already referred to. It may, on the
other hand, concern some other transposition of words as
originally reported of which we have no knowledge — or indeed
some transposition of the words as given us which was not
carried out. We note that the concluding words " but rather
established " stand in the Irish Articles " but established
rather ": possibly the reference is to this. It seems most probable, however, that it refers to a transposition to a new section of the clause excluding dependence of the decree on the
Divine foresight, to the likelihood of which we shall recur
when speaking of the following section — which, as we shall
see, was originally a part of this section.

3. The second section of the Confession has nothing parallel to it in the Irish Articles, which reserve the guarding of the
independence of God's decree until they are dealing with
specific or soteriological predestination (§ 14). Without this aid
we find ourselves naturally in difficulties as we essay to reconstruct its original form. The chief notes in the Minutes
concerning it are found in the entries for September 3 and
September 11. The former reads: " Report from the first Committee about adding the word ' absolutely ' — debated. Absolutely without *any* [not being moved thereunto by any] [86]
foresight of anything without himself as a condition moving
him thereunto. *Ordered* — This recommitted." The latter
reads: " Report from the morning Committee that they think
the former vote of the Assembly sufficient to print? the conditional decree."

It is at least evident from these notes that the framing of
this section cost the Assembly some trouble. The new report

---

whereby, from all eternity, He hath, for His own glory, unchangeably foreordained whatsoever comes to pass in time, especially concerning angels and
men."

[86] The words here placed in brackets stand in the Minutes *above* the
line.

from the digesting Committee as to adding the word "absolutely" is proof that there had already been puzzled discussion of the section. The recommitment of the matter, doubtless (as was the wont of the Assembly) to a special Committee, exhibits its dissatisfaction with its work so far. Probably between September 3 and September 11 the matter had again been before the Assembly, and the adjustment made which gives us our present section: for the report of September 11 appears to have come from a Committee meeting that morning, and seems to close the matter by recommending the treatment of a so-called "conditional decree," as it then stood, for passage for printing. Certainly the adjustment that was made was a good deal of a triumph: we do not indeed know the wording of the whole section as originally reported, or at any former stage of the debate — but the phrasing as ultimately agreed on is obviously a much finer piece of work than anything could have been of which the phraseology of the note of September 3 was a part. Is it too much to conjecture that this clause, for which no appropriate place can be found in section 2 as passed, was originally only a part of the first section — coming, perhaps, in between the first and second clauses of that section? In that case the sentence would have read: " God from all eternity did, by the most wise and holy counsel of His own will, freely and unchangeably ordain whatsoever comes to pass, without any foresight of anything without Himself as a condition moving Him thereunto: yet so as thereby, etc." The stages of procedure would, in that case, be as follows: First, it was sought to strengthen the statement by inserting " absolutely " before "without." Then it was queried whether the " any " might not be better omitted. Then a new phraseology was tried: instead of " absolutely without foresight of anything," it was proposed to read " not being moved thereunto by any foresight of anything." It was finally seen that the trouble lay deeper than any adjustment of mere phraseology could cure; that the proposed addition to the Irish statement at this point hopelessly overweighted the sentence. The knot was then happily cut by relieving the sentence of the addition altogether and erecting a new section, which then it was comparatively easy to phrase happily. And, as we have already hinted, perhaps it is this transposition that was debated, but not determined, on August 29.

It is so far in favor of this general supposition that it is altogether likely that an attempt would first be made to include the whole doctrine of the general or cosmical decree in one section, as had been done in the Irish Articles; and the relieving of the heavy sentence which thence resulted would be apt to be an afterthought. And it seems to be brought, in this general sense at least, out of the region of conjecture into that of ascertained fact by a note in the Minutes of September 8: "Dr. Gouge offered a report of an addition, though the Committee was not a full number, but 7. He read it; but the Assembly thought not fit to meddle with it, because they were not a Committee. The addition was, without respect to anything foreseen, to be added after freely and unchangeably." These words occur in the first section, which, accordingly, it was proposed to read thus: "God from all eternity did, by the most wise and holy counsel of His own will, freely and unchangeably, without respect to anything foreseen, ordain whatsoever comes to pass." The proposal brought by Mr. Gouge is evidently a substitute for the heavy clause that was debated and recommitted on September 3, and accordingly that clause too was a part of the first section.

The main result, in any event, of our scrutiny of the section is to advertise to us the importance which was attached by the Assembly to the proper guarding of the doctrine of the decree. This they sought to accomplish by adding in some fit way to the statement of the Irish Articles a clause explicitly affirming the independence of the decree — or, as has actually resulted in the event, fully setting forth the relation of the decree to the divine knowledge.

4. So far as the Minutes record, there was very little debate on sections 3 and 4, which, again, together represent a single section in the Irish Articles (§ 12). We read indeed in the notes for October 3: " Report additional to the article of Predestina-

tion. Debate about it." It is possible that this may refer to section 3, in which the term " predestinated " occurs for the first time, and in which the thing, as currently defined (of specific or soteriological predestination), for the first time emerges. On the other hand, however, the term may be used in a still narrower sense and the reference be to section 5, where the doctrine of election is discussed in its details. And it is almost equally possible that it is used in its broadest sense and refers to the chapter as a whole. The sequence of notices runs as follows: August 29, 1645, " Debate on the report of . . . God's decree "; September 2, " proceed in the debate of the report of decrees "; September 9, " report concerning God's decree "; September 11, " proceed in the debate about the decree "; October 3, " report additional to the article of Predestination "; October 17, " debate upon the report . . . concerning Predestination " [when § 5 was debated]; November 6, " the paragraph concerning Reprobation referred to the Committee, to make report to-morrow morning "; November 7, " Report made . . . about Reprobation "; November 11, " Debate the report of Reprobation " [when § 7 was debated]. The appearance is rather strong that under the term " Predestination " the portion of the chapter that treats of soteriological predestination, or more particularly §§ 3–6, was intended.

There can be little doubt that the entry in the Minutes of November 3, " Debate about leaving out those words, ' foreordained to everlasting death,' " refers to section 3: though it is, of course, not absolutely impossible (though most unlikely) that coming in at this late point in the debate, it may refer to a phrase originally in section 7, and omitted as the result of this debate. The likelihood of its reference to section 3 is moreover distinctly increased by an entry at a much later date — after the Confession, in fact, had been completed, and was ready to be sent up to Parliament. In the Minutes for September 23, 1646, we read: " Mr. Whitakers moved an alteration in these words in the chapt[er] of Predestination, viz., ' and some ordained to everlasting death.' [87] It was debated, and

[87] Dr. Mitchell notes that in the additional copy of the Minutes lapping

upon debate it was *Resolved* upon the Q., The words shall stand
without alteration. Mr. Whitakers enters his dissent." It can
scarcely be doubted that the words in which Mr. Whitaker
desired some alteration are the closing words of section 3; and
the suggestion will perhaps present itself that he was only persisting at this final opportunity in pressing the desire of those
who wished these words omitted in the earlier debate (November 3, 1645). It certainly is not said that Mr. Whitaker wished
the words omitted, but only that "he moved an alteration
in these words" — and what alteration he desired we have
no means of ascertaining. And it would appear that he met
with little or no support for his proposition. The Assembly
not only rejected his motion, but he alone entered dissent. But
it is at least not impossible that he was here only carrying to
its latest stage the debate of November 3 for the omission of
these words.

In that case, we should learn that there were some in the
Assembly — or perhaps only one, as Mr. Whitaker is alone in
his dissent on September 23, 1646, and may have been equally
alone in the contention of November 3, 1645 — who desired
that the doctrine of reprobation should not be so sharply
stated in section 3. What their — or his — reasons for so desiring were, we do not know.[88] But we should equally learn
that the Assembly was not only decided, but we may say un-

---

at this part, which he calls Fascicle iii., the words stand: "and some *foreordained* to everlasting death."

[88] Whitaker was a high Calvinist (see below, p. 136), but beyond that we
know too little of his personal opinions to permit ourselves any conjectures
as to his position on the special point here raised. He left little in print behind him: Brook ("Lives of the Puritans," 1813, iii. pp. 190 *sqq.*) supposes
that only a few occasional sermons were published by him, and names only
three. He was a Cambridge Master of Arts, and a good scholar and unremitting in his labors as a preacher. See also Mr. Lupton's notice in the "Dictionary of National Biography," *sub nom.* It is illustrative of how little even the
best scholars keep in mind the most important matters of Puritan (Presbyterian) history in England that Mr. Lupton can print such a sentence as
this: "When the Westminster assembly of divines was convened in June 1643,
he was one of the first members elected, and in 1647 was appointed moderator." Yet he had Brook's notice before his eyes (p. 191).

usually decided in its determination to have the doctrine of reprobation clearly asserted in this its appropriate place in the Confession. We must not fail to observe that the matter was pressed to a vote, to the sharpest of decisions, and to a recorded dissent: and we must not fail to note the significance of this. Says Dr. Mitchell: [89] " So far as appears from the minutes, the various articles of the Confession were passed by the Assembly all but unanimously. On some occasions, when dissent was indicated even by one or two of the members, the wording of the article they objected to was so modified as to satisfy them. The main occasions on which this policy was not followed were on 4th September 1645, with regard to Dr. Burgess's dissent from the resolution of the Assembly to leave out the word ' Blessed,' retained both in the English and Irish Articles, before the name of the Virgin mother of our Lord; on 23d September 1646, with regard to Mr. Whitaker's dissent from the words ' foreordained to everlasting death '; and on 21st October 1646, with regard to the dissent of several of the Independents from the insertion in a Confession of Faith of certain parts of § 3, chap. xxiii." We must esteem the clear and firm statement of the doctrine of foreordination to death, therefore, a matter which the Assembly deemed of the highest importance. When it was proposed to omit the words (November 3, 1645) the proposition was defeated: and when, at the eleventh hour, Mr. Whitaker returned to the charge and proposed at least some alteration in the words, it was resolved shortly, " The words shall stand without alteration," and Mr. Whitaker was left to enter his dissent. It is very clear that the Assembly by a very large majority — doubtless, in this case too, practically unanimously — deemed that important concerns were guarded by these words.

It is noteworthy that no debates and no dissents are noted on section 4.

5. Only the slightest hint of debate on section 5 is preserved. We have already observed the possibility, but hardly probability, of the notice of debate on " the article of Predes-

[89] " The Westminster Assembly," ed. 2, 1897, p. 373.

tination " mentioned on October 3, 1645, referring to the fifth section. If that be set aside we have only the entry of October 17: " Report from the first Committee concerning Predestination. . . . Debate upon the report of the first Committee concerning Predestination. Debate about those words, ' unto everlasting glory,' whether they be not superfluous." The words were retained — to the enrichment of the statement. But the raising of the question of their superfluity is another indication of the severe terseness of the style given by the Assembly to this chapter — in contrast with the greater elaborateness, if not exactly elaboration, of the language of the underlying Irish Articles.

6. It was about the sixth section, however — the section in which is concentrated the *ordo salutis* of the Westminster Divines — that debate most gathered. From before October 20 to October 31 the Assembly was occupied with this great statement, and every element of it was subjected to the closest scrutiny. Especially did the discussion expand around the three points of the unity of the decree and the relation respectively of the decrees concerning the fall and redemption to the decree of election. We do not know precisely when debate on this section was first begun. The first notice of it (October 20) runs already: " Proceed in the debate about permission of man's fall; about ' the same decree.' " Nor can we reconstruct in its entirety the original form of the section. It seems to have begun somewhat thus: " As God hath appointed the elect unto glory, so hath He, to bring this to pass, ordained by the same decree to permit man to fall, etc."; and the debate first turned on the phrase " the same decree," and then on the phrase " to bring this to pass." To meet the objection to the former phrase, for which he would not contend — for, said he, " when that word is left out, is it not a truth, and so every one may enjoy his own sense " — Mr. Gillespie proposed that the statement should be modified so as to read: " As God hath appointed the elect unto glory, so hath He for the same end ordained to permit man to fall." This involved, however, the retention, in other language, of the idea involved in the phrase " to bring

this to pass," which the Assembly was not disposed to insist on. A formula offered by Mr. Reynolds on October 21 accordingly found more favor. It runs as follows: " As God hath appointed the elect unto glory, so hath He by the same eternal and most free purpose of His will fore-ordained all the means thereunto, which He in His counsel is pleased to appoint for the executing of that decree; wherefore they who are endowed with so excellent a benefit, being fallen in Adam, are called in according to God's purpose." This formula preserves the mention of the fall of Adam, as had just been ordered, but also the phrase " the same decree," which had been debated but the omission of which was not yet determined fully on, and meets by a happy turn the determination that the words " to bring this to pass " should not stand. Whether, however, this formula was simply (as we have presumed) the original formula, modified to meet these orderings, or an entirely new one wrought out by Mr. Reynolds himself, we have no sure means of determining. Immediately after the entry, " *Mr. Reynolds* offered something," with the text as given above, it is added, " *Mr. Chambers* offered something " — but no hint is given of what it was, possibly because the differing reception given to the propositions of the two advertised the scribe that it was Mr. Reynolds' and not Mr. Chambers' offering that would form the basis of subsequent debate. In any event, Mr. Reynolds' paper appears to register the results of the debate so far, and to lay the basis for further advance.

So far, we may say then, two things had been settled about this section: it should mention the fall of Adam and it should not insist on emphasizing the unity of the divine decree. In both matters the decision had been arrived at in the interest of what we may call, perhaps, comprehension — though this must be understood, of course, as a generic Calvinistic and not universalistic Christian comprehension. The Assembly had been led in this policy by the strictest Calvinists in the body. The sharp assertion of the sameness of the decree ordaining both the end and the means (for it was on this point of the unity of the decree alone that the debate turned) was advocated by Mr. Seaman, who seems to be most concerned about the possible misapprehension of the omission; by Mr. Whitaker, who takes the high ground that it is true, and therefore would best be expressed — an indication, by the way, of the sound Calvinism of the man who later was so strenuous to have some alteration (we know not what, but surely from this we can infer no anti-Calvinistic one) made in the last words of the third section; and by Mr. Palmer, who fears to be brought into a worse snare by leaving it out than could arise from inserting it. Mr. Seaman urged that " if those words ' in the same decree ' be left out, will involve us in a great debate "; that " all the odious doctrine of Arminians is from their distinguishing of the decrees, but our divines say they are one and the same decree "; that the censure the Remonstrants lay under for making two decrees concerning election would lie equally against making two decrees of the end and means. Mr. Whitaker simply urged that with reference to time all decrees are " *simul* and *semel: in eterno* there is not *prius* and *posterius* "; that though the conceptions of the Divines were very various about the decrees, there was no reason why the truth should not be frankly asserted. The other side was taken by men like Rutherford, Gillespie, Gouge, Reynolds, and Calamy. They did not deny the truth meant to be expressed in the phrase " the same decree," but rather unanimously affirmed it. But the keynote of their discussion was expressed by Gillespie when he said, " When that word is left out, is it not a truth, and so every one may enjoy his own sense," and by Reynolds when he remarked, " Let not us put in disputes and scholastical things into a Confession of Faith." Obviously it was generic Calvinism they were intent on asserting and not any particular variety of it. And this is given point to by another incident of the debate. Besides the mere phrase " the same decree," its sameness was asserted in the original draft by the concatenation of the clauses. We do not know precisely how its language ran at first; but apparently it was, as we have seen, something like this: " As God hath appointed the elect unto glory, so hath He, to bring this to pass, ordained by the same decree to permit man to fall " — and so on enumerating the several steps in the *ordo decretorum*. " I question," remarked Mr. Calamy, " that ' to bring this to pass '; we assert *massa pura* in this. . . . I desire that nothing may be put in one way or other; it makes the fall of man to be *medium executionis decreti*." It was in the same sense that Rutherford wished to amend by saying simply " God also hath decreed." " It is very probable but one decree," he added, " but whether fit to express it in a Confession of Faith. . . ." A remark of Gillespie's would seem to show that he was not quite willing to yield in this matter; let there be no dispute indeed about a word, he seems to say — but the matter involved is another thing: " Say, ' For the same end God hath ordained to permit man to fall.' . . . This shows that in *ordine naturæ* God ordaining man to glory goes before His ordaining to permit man to fall." The appearance is that Gillespie desired the Confession to be committed not indeed to the supralapsarian position — for that occupies narrower ground than his words need to imply — but to the inclusion of the fall of Adam explicitly in the means to glorification.

Counsels of moderation thus prevailing as the result of this debate of Monday (October 20), the Assembly listened on Tuesday morning (October 21) to the " report made from the first Committee sitting before the Assembly "; and resolved " that mention be made of man's fall," and " that those words ' to bring this to pass ' shall not stand." This is to say, it resolved to include man's fall within the decree of God, but not to assert it to be means to the end of glorification. It was then that Mr. Reynolds' statement as already quoted was brought before them and the debate commenced afresh from this new beginning. By what process this statement was ultimately reduced to the exquisite formula that was finally passed we are not informed. Considerable adjustment was needed. The first sentence required the omission not only of the word " same," but also of its whole concluding clause: " which He in His counsel is pleased to appoint for the executing of that decree " — a redundancy which must have been intolerable to this tersely speaking Assembly. Similarly, while the structure of

the second section is adopted, and, of course, the happy phrase
— cutting all knots — " being fallen in Adam," the language
is wholly recast in the interests of clear and succinct statement: thus the long clause (derived from the Thirty-nine
Articles) " who are endowed with so excellent a benefit " gives
way to the simple " who are elected "; and the Scriptural
" called according to God's purpose " to the more technical
" effectually called," with an additional definition of that unto
which they are called and by what divine agency. Thence the
statement proceeds through the items of the *ordo salutis*. So
far as we can trace it, this is the history of the formulation of
this beautiful section — wise in its insertions and omissions
alike.

There remains, however, a very important clause of the
section about which apparently the keenest and certainly the
most fully reported of all the debates on this chapter was held
— the final sentence of the section, which affirms: " Neither
are any other redeemed by Christ, effectually called, justified,
adopted, sanctified, and saved, but the elect only." The discussion of this statement was formally ordered at the close of the
session on Tuesday, October 21, 1645: " *Ordered* — To debate
the busin[ess] about Redemption of the elect only by Christ
to-morrow morning." The debate, begun Wednesday morning,
October 22, and continued at least to October 31, constitutes
one of the most notable debates reported in the Minutes, and
certifies us that the closing sentence of the sixth section is
one of the most deliberate findings of the Assembly.

The protagonist in the debate was Mr. Calamy, who opened
it with the enunciation of what is known as the " Hypothetical
Universalistic " *schema* — a well-guarded expression of this
theory, certainly, and even, perhaps, a somewhat modified expression of it, but also a clearly-cut and fully developed enunciation of universal redemption with limited application. " I
am far from universal redemption in the Arminian sense," he
said; " but that that I hold is in the sense of our divines in
the Synod of Dort, that Christ did pay a price for all, — absolute intention for the elect, conditional intention for the repro-

bate in case they do believe, — that all men should be *salva-biles, non obstante lapsu Adami* . . . that Jesus Christ did not only die sufficiently for all, but God did intend, in giving of Christ, and Christ in giving Himself, did intend to put all men in a state of salvation in case they do believe." Again, " The Arminians hold that Christ did pay a price for this intention only, that all men should be in an equal state of salvation. They say Christ did not purchase any impetration. . . . This universality of R[edemption] " — that is, of course, that which he, in opposition to this Arminian construction, advocates — " doth neither intrude upon either doctrine of special election or special grace." Still again: " In the point of election, I am for special election; and for reprobation, I am for *massa corrupta*. . . . Those to whom He . . . by virtue of Christ's death, there is *ea administratio* of grace to the reprobate, that they do wilfully damn themselves." If we were to take these statements just as they stand, we should probably be obliged to say that Calamy's position was characterized by the following points: 1. It denied the Arminian doctrine of a universal redemption for all men alike, without exception, on condition of faith, which faith is to be man's own act by virtue of powers renewed through a universal gift of sufficient grace. 2. It denied equally the Amyraldian doctrine of a universal redemption for all men alike, without exception, on condition of faith, which faith, however, is the product of special grace given to the elect alone, so that only the elect can fulfil the condition. 3. It affirmed a double intention on Christ's part in His work of redemption — declaring that He died absolutely for the elect and conditionally for the reprobate. Theologically his position, which has its closest affinities with the declarations of the English Divines at Dort, was an improvement upon the Amyraldian; but logically it was open, perhaps, to all the objections which were fatal to it as well as to others arising from its own lack of consistency.

Both sets of objections were made to tell upon it in the debate. For example, the fundamental objection to all schemes of conditional redemption, that it is inapplicable to more than a moiety of the human race, was early pressed upon him with telling effect. Mr. Palmer asked subtly, " I desire to know whether he will understand it *de omni homine*," i.e. whether Christ died for *every* man — of all sorts and in all conditions — only *conditionally* on the exercise of faith. Mr. Calamy must have felt hard pressed indeed when he answered simply, " *De adultis.*" Where, then, shall those that die in infancy appear? On the other hand, Mr. Reynolds struck a deadly blow at the peculiar form which Mr. Calamy had given his doctrine when he remarked that to assert that Christ, besides dying absolutely for the elect, died also conditionally for the reprobate — in case they do believe — is to say He died for them " upon a condition that they cannot perform, and God never intends to give them." It cannot seem strange to us, therefore, that Mr. Calamy was not able to preserve in the debate his somewhat artificial middle position, and is found arguing roundly for universal redemption of all and several, without distinction, at least in the Amyraldian sense.

To Calamy's aid in the debate there came Messrs. Seaman, Marshall, and Vines: while he was opposed by Palmer, Reynolds, Gillespie, Rutherford, Wilkinson, Burgess, Lightfoot, Price, Goodwin, and Harris. In the early part of the first day the debate turned on the *ordo decretorum*. Gillespie held it firmly to this broader question, and from that point of view — that " there is a concatenation of the death of Christ with the decrees " — asked significantly " *a parte post* what follows upon that conditional redemption." On the authority of the Dordrechtan Divines, to whom Calamy had appealed, Reynolds explained that " the Synod intended no more than to declare the sufficiency of the death of Christ; it is *pretium in se,* of sufficient value to all, — nay, ten thousand worlds," and that " to be salvable is a benefit, and therefore belongs only to them that have interest in Christ." Later in the day the debate turned rather on the Scriptural argument, and Calamy rested his case on the two texts, John iii. 16 and Mark xvi. 15. From the former he argued that it was on account of the love of God for the world at large, not for the elect only, that Christ

came — as the " whosoever believeth " sufficiently indicates.
From the latter he argued that a universal redemption is
requisite to give verity to the universal offer. Those who essayed to answer him exhibit minor differences, especially in
the detailed exegesis of John iii. 16. Gillespie and Rutherford
understand that when it is said God so loved the world, it is
the elect scattered everywhere in the world that are intended;
Lightfoot and Harris understand that " the world " in contradistinction from the Jews is meant; and Price very wisely remarks that even if mankind at large be meant it does not at
all follow that Christ died equally and alike for every individual — there is no inconsequence in saying that it was because of His love for the world that He gave His very life for
the multitudes He chose out of this world to save. However
the term " the world " be taken, therefore, the result of the
debate showed that no conclusion could be drawn from this
text to the universality of redemption. As to Mark xvi. 15,
Rutherford pointed out at once that the argument that the
universality of the offer of the Gospel necessarily inferred
precedent universality of redemption as its ground was obviously unsound inasmuch as it proved too much — the same
argument is equally applicable to, say, justification. The promise of justification is as much included in the Gospel as the
promise of redemption: shall we say, then, that we cannot
preach the Gospel to all except on the supposition of a precedent universal justification? To this Mr. Seaman could reply
only by repeating the shibboleth that what Christ did was to
make all men only salvable, as Adam had made all men damnable — which one cannot believe was much of an aid to the
cause he was advocating, as it involved a seriously low view
of the effect of Adam's fall as well as of Christ's redemption:
surely there were few in the Assembly who would assent to the
proposition that the whole effect of Adam's sin was to render
men liable to be condemned, instead of bringing them under
actual condemnation, and the whole effect of Christ's work
was to render men capable of salvation, instead of actually
saving them. Gillespie, however, as was usual with that bril-

liant young man, put his finger here, too, on the technical flaw in Calamy's reasoning by insisting on the distinction between the *voluntas decreti* and *voluntas mandati:* " The command doth not hold out God's intentions; otherwise God's command to Abraham concerning sacrificing of his son. . . ." Mr. Marshall, who with Mr. Vines gave a support to Mr. Calamy which was evidently as effective and wise as that of Mr. Seaman seems the opposite, acutely replies to this that " there is not only a *mandatum* but a promise " — but obviously this was a good rejoinder rather than a solid distinction. The weight of the debate was clearly on the side of the proposition proposed, and on that score alone we cannot feel surprise that it was retained in the Confession.

The interest of the debate to us lies in the revelation which it gives us of the presence in the Assembly of an influential and able, but apparently small, body of men whose convictions lay in the direction of the modified Calvinism which had been lately promulgated by Cameron and Amyraut for the express purpose of finding a place for a universal redemption in the Calvinistic system. For the origin of this party Dr. Mitchell [90] would point us to English sources: but Baillie especially mentions Amyraut in this connection; [91] and it would seem that it was Amyraut and Cameron — both of whom Gillespie mentions in this debate — whom men had especially in mind during the discussion; and it would seem further to be clear that while the adherents of this universalistic view of the atonement in the Assembly held it with British moderation, and were not prepared to go all lengths with the French Divines who had lately promulgated it with such force, they yet looked upon them as of their school and sought support from them. The result of the debate was a refusal to modify the Calvinistic statement in this direction — or perhaps we should

[90] " Minutes," pp. lv. *sqq.*

[91] And his " Letters " have a number of references to the Amyraldian controversy and the pressing need of a telling refutation of Amyraut, which cannot mean anything else than that it was from him that the Assembly felt that the dissenting opinions emanated.

rather say the definitive rejection of the Amyraldian views and the adoption of language which was precisely framed to exclude them. Dr. Mitchell, reviving an old contention, suggests indeed that unless the clause of the Confession in question be read disjunctively rather than, as it is actually phrased, conjunctively, it will not operate for the exclusion of Amyraldians.[92] It is not clearly obvious, however, that the word "and" here binds the several items of the enumeration so closely together as to make it appear that all that is affirmed is only that the whole of this process takes place in the case of the elect only: the natural sense of the clause is clearly that no one of the transactions here brought together is to be affirmed of the non-elect. And this impression is increased by the broader context, not to speak of the parallel passages in viii. 3 and 5.[93] It might seem somewhat more to the point, possibly, to recall that in this section the language is so ordered as to seem to deal with the actual *ordo salutis* rather than directly with the *ordo decretorum*. It is asserted that the *ordo salutis* is the result of the decreeing of the means by which the elect are brought to glory. But what is subsequently asserted is that none but the elect are (actually) redeemed by Christ, effectually called, etc. — the mind being abstracted for the moment from the intention to the performance. The Westminster Amyraldians — if we may venture so to call them — had, of course, freely admitted the distinction between the elect and non-elect in the application: it was only in the impetration that they disputed it: and it might perhaps seem to them possible to confess that though Christ had died for all, the merits of His death had actually been applied only to some, and to contend that only this is actually expressed by saying that

[92] "Minutes," p. lvii. This contention, together with the other expedients which have been made use of by advocates of universal atonement to explain away the Confessional statement, is judiciously examined by Dr. Cunningham in his "Historical Theology," ii. 1864, pp. 327 *sq.*

[93] Dr. Cunningham remarks that the followers of Cameron made their contention that they were not condemned by the Synod of Dort turn precisely on the fact that nothing exactly like these clauses occurs in its "Canons" (*op. cit.,* p. 329, note).

none but the elect " *are* redeemed by Christ." Even this, however, appears more subtle than satisfactory; and in any event
it would seem quite obvious that the Assembly intended to
state in this clause with adequate clearness their reasoned and
deliberate conviction that the decree of election lies behind the
decree of the gift of Christ for redemption, and that the latter
is to be classed as one of the means for the execution of the
decree of election. This is the definite exclusion of the Amyraldian view, and anything that can be made really consistent
with this conception of the *ordo decretorum* will be found to
differ fundamentally from Amyraldism.[94]

7. We first hear of the seventh section in the Assembly on
November 6, 1645; but then after such a fashion as to suggest
that it had already been before the Assembly and perhaps may
have been already somewhat debated. We read simply: " The
paragraph concerning Reprobation referred to the Committee,
to make report to-morrow morning." This was doubtless a special Committee, according to the wont of the Assembly in
such instances. On November 7 accordingly we read: " Report
made by Mr. Reynolds about Reprobation." Then again on
November 11 we read: " Debate the report of Reprobation.
. . . Debate about that ' sovereign power.' " This is all that
the Minutes tell us about the passage of this important section through the Assembly: and this tells us practically nothing, except that it was carefully scrutinized and debated. We
may conjecture that the debate on the words " sovereign
power " turned on the query whether something more or other

[94] These debates are discussed with the care and prudence habitual to
him by Dr. Mitchell, pp. lii. *sqq.* of his Introduction to the " Minutes ";
and he says the best and most that can be said in favor of the view that
Amyraldism is not peremptorily excluded by the statements finally agreed
on. They are also discussed in somewhat the same spirit by Dr. E. D. Morris,
op. cit., pp. 187 *sqq.,* with which should be compared the remarks on pp. 382 *sqq.*
Dr. Morris, though claiming for the Amyraldians a right of existence under
the " symbol," seems to be unable to free himself of the suspicion that the
letter of the symbol scarcely justifies it. We should heartily accord with
such a conclusion — in both its elements. We have already referred to Dr.
Cunningham's discussion of the meaning of the Symbolic declarations (" Historical Theology," ii. 1864, pp. 327 *sq.*).

than " power " might not wisely be indicated at this point: but this is mere conjecture, and we learn only that the retention of the phrase just as it now stands was not inadvertent but deliberate. The section is one of those which, though it has a point of suggestion in the Irish Articles, yet as it stands is the independent product of the Assembly: and it certainly does credit to the Assembly by the combined boldness and prudence, faithfulness, and tenderness of its sonorous language.[95]

[95] At p. 813 of Dr. E. D. Morris' " Theology of the Westminster Symbols," 1900, we read the following sentences: " Some of the members [of the Westminster Assembly] held with Calamy (Minutes, 153) that by virtue of the death of Christ there is an administration of grace even to the reprobate, so that they in rejecting such grace do willfully damn themselves as a massa corrupta. It is a fact of considerable significance that, in deference to this opinion, it was proposed and somewhat debated in the Assembly to omit any statement respecting reprobation. This would have been in harmony with the course pursued in the framing of most of the continental symbols, which are quite silent respecting the relation of the divine decree to those who reject the divine grace. The statement in the Confession finally agreed upon, (Ch. III. vii.) simply declares that God, in the exercise of his sovereign power or dominion over his creatures passes by the wicked and unbelieving, and ordains them to dishonor and wrath *for their sins,* to the praise of his glorious justice." This seems to say that the omission of the seventh section of chapter iii. was proposed and debated in the Assembly: and indeed the omission of all statements respecting reprobation. There is nothing in the Minutes or, so far as known to us, in any witnessing document to justify such an affirmation. It would seem that Dr. Morris has fallen into an error here — possibly through a misinterpretation of the entries in the Minutes of propositions and debates concerning the language of iii. 3 — of which we have spoken above (pp. 130 *sqq*). This misinterpretation would be rendered easier by the circumstances that the former of these entries occurs in the Minutes for November 3, and is noted by Dr. Mitchell on the margin as a " debate on reprobation," while in the immediately next Minute we have a reference to " the paragraph concerning Reprobation," doubtless referring to § 7, which was certainly under debate November 11. Nevertheless it is very plain that it is § 3 that was debated on November 3: and even if that were not so, there is no ground for Dr. Morris' statement that " it was proposed and somewhat debated in the Assembly to omit any statement respecting reprobation." To desire an " alteration in the words 'and some [fore-] ordained to everlasting death,'" or even the omission " of those words, 'fore- ordained to everlasting death'" — the extent of the notices of the proposals and debates in question — is, certainly, something extremely different from proposing and debating the omission of " any statement respecting reproba-

8. There is no debate signalized on section 8 in its first
passage through the Assembly. But when the chapter came
back again from the perfecting Committee — June 18, 1646 —
we read: " The Assembly proceeded in debate of the Article
' of God's Eternal Decree '; and upon debate part of it was ordered. Upon debate about the last clause of it, concerning the
handling of this doctrine, it was *Resolved* upon the Q., To refer
this till to-morrow morning." We find nothing, however, on
the subject in the Minutes for June 19 beyond this: " The Assembly proceeded in the debate of the Confession of Faith;
and upon debate, that head ' of God's Eternal Decree ' was ordered, and is as followeth. . . ." We are therefore only certified
concerning this admirable section that it was the object of the
care of the Assembly itself up to the last moment, without
being informed what precisely in the course of its stately march
engaged its latest attention.

From this survey, by means, as it were, of specimen bits of
the debates during which the third chapter of the Confession as
we have it was beaten out, we may obtain some sort of idea of
the labor and care expended on it by the Assembly. The survey is certainly calculated to enhance our idea of the deliber-
ateness of its formulation. We have here no hasty draft, rushed
through the body at breakneck speed and adopted at the end
on the credit of the Committee that had drafted it. The third
chapter of the Confession is distinctly the work of the Assembly itself, and comes to us as the well-pondered and thoroughly adjusted expression of the living belief of that whole
body. The differences that existed between the members were
not smoothed over in ambiguous language. They were fully
ventilated. Room was made for them when they were consid-

tion." It is probably safe to say that the attribution to any Westminster
man of a suggestion to omit all reference to reprobation from the Confession would have struck him as a calumny injurious to the soundness of his
faith if not of his intelligence. With reference to the attitude of the other
Reformed symbols to reprobation see *The Presbyterian and Reformed Review,* xiii. 1901, pp. 49–128, especially pp. 121–126: the doctrine of reprobation is certainly not left without " any statement " in the " most " of them.

ered unimportant and mere *apices logici:* but when they concerned matters of moment, after full discussion, the doctrine of the Assembly — well-reasoned and fully thought out — as distinguished from that of individuals, was embodied clearly and firmly in the document. The document as it stands is thus emphatically the Confession of Faith of the Westminster Assembly. We cannot say that this or that clause represents this or that party in the Assembly. There were parties in the Assembly, and they were all fully heard and what they said was carefully weighed. But no merely party opinion was allowed a place in the document. When it came to voting the statements there to be set down, the Assembly as such spoke; and in speaking it showed itself capable of speaking its own mind. It is doing only mere justice to it, therefore, to read the document as the solemn and carefully framed expression of its reasoned faith.

In the appended text (to follow on the succeeding pages) we have given, in the middle column, as nearly as we can make it out, the form in which the third chapter came before the Assembly from its Committee, marking in footnotes the chief amendments which were made in it in the process of reducing the earlier draft to the form in which it left the Assembly and has come down to us. In order that the relations of this first reported text to the Irish Articles, on the one hand, and the completed Westminster Confession, on the other, may be easily apprehended, we have printed these two texts alongside of it, and we have sought so to present them that the eye may easily unravel the historical connections involved.

THE TEXT OF THE THIRD CHAPTER

IRISH ARTICLES (1615) [96] III. OF GOD'S ETERNAL DECREE AND PREDESTINATION	COMMITTEE'S PROPOSAL OF GOD'S ETERNAL DECREE [AND PREDESTINATION] [97]	WESTMINSTER CONFESSION [98] OF GOD'S ETERNAL DECREE
(11) God, from all eternity, did, by his unchangeable counsel, ordain whatsoever in time should come to pass: yet so as thereby no violence is offered to the wills of the reasonable creatures, and neither the liberty nor the contingency of the second causes is taken away, but established rather.	[1] God from all eternity, did by the most holy [and] wise [1] counsel [2] of his [own] [2] will freely and unchangeably [3] ordain whatsoever in time should come [5] to pass, [2] without any foresight of anything without himself as a condition moving him thereunto: [6] yet so, as thereby neither is God the author of sin, nor is violence offered to the will of the creatures, nor is the liberty or contingency of second causes taken away but established rather.	1. GOD FROM ALL ETERNITY DID, by the most wise and holy COUNSEL of his own will, freely and unchangeably ORDAIN WHATSOEVER COMES TO PASS; YET SO AS THEREBY neither is God the author of sin, NOR IS VIOLENCE OFFERED TO THE WILL OF THE CREATURES, NOR IS THE LIBERTY OR CONTINGENCY OF SECOND CAUSES TAKEN AWAY, BUT RATHER ESTABLISHED. 2. Although God knows whatsoever may or can come to pass upon all supposed conditions, yet hath he not decreed any thing because he foresaw it as future, or as that which would come to pass upon such conditions.
(12) By the same eternal counsel, God hath predestinated some unto life, and reprobated some unto death: of both which there is a certain number, known only to God, which can neither be increased nor diminished.	[3] By the decree of God, for the manifestation of his glory, some men and angels are predestinated unto everlasting life, and others foreordained to everlasting death. [7] [4] These angels and men, thus predestinated and foreordained, are	3. BY the decree of God, for the manifestation of his glory, SOME men and angels are PREDESTINATED UNTO everlasting LIFE, and others foreordained TO everlasting DEATH. 4. These angels and men, thus predestinated and fore-

[96] This exhibit is taken without change from the Rev. E. Tyrrell Green's treatise on " The Thirty-nine Articles and the Age of the Reformation " (London [1896]), pp. 354–355. Phrases in italics are derived from the Thirty-nine Articles: those in thick-faced type from the Lambeth Articles. About 58 per cent. of the Irish Articles is taken from Art. xvii. of the Thirty-nine Articles, and about 15 per cent. from the Lambeth Articles: leaving about 27 per cent. of new matter.

[97] Possibly the title read originally as in the Irish Articles, and in the debate the last two words, here bracketed, were omitted.

[98] Phrases in italics are derived from the Thirty-nine Articles: those in thick type from the Lambeth Articles: those in small capitals from the Irish Articles. Phrases derived proximately from the Irish Articles and ultimately from the Thirty-nine Articles will therefore be found set in italic capitals: those derived proximately from the Irish Articles and ultimately from the Lambeth Articles in thick capitals. About 28 per cent. of the chapter is derived matter, about 72 per cent. being original. All but a trace of the derived matter is taken from the Irish Articles: and the material thus taken from the Irish Articles is about evenly divided between material original with them, and material ultimately derived from the Thirty-nine or Lambeth Articles — about 10 per cent. of the whole having each of these three sources for its origin.

IRISH ARTICLES (1615)	COMMITTEE'S PROPOSAL	WESTMINSTER CONFESSION
	particularly and unchangeably designed, and their number is so certain and definite, that it cannot be either increased or diminished.	ordained, are particularly and unchangeably designed; and their **NUMBER IS** so **CERTAIN** and definite that it **CANNOT BE EITHER INCREASED OR DIMINISHED.**
(13) *Predestination to life is the everlasting purpose of God, whereby, before the foundations of the world were laid, he hath constantly decreed in his* secret *counsel to deliver from curse and damnation those whom he hath chosen in Christ out of mankind, and to bring them by Christ unto everlasting salvation, as vessels made to honour.* (14) **The cause moving God to predestinate unto life, is not the foreseeing of faith, or perseverance, or good works, or of anything which is in the person predestinated, but only the good pleasure of God himself.** For all things being ordained for the manifestation of his glory, and his glory being to appear both in the works of his mercy and of his justice, it seemed good to his heavenly wisdom to choose out a certain number, towards whom he would extend his undeserved mercy, leaving the rest to be spectacles of his justice. (15) Such as are predestinated unto life, *be called according unto God's purpose (his Spirit working in due season), and through grace they obey the calling, they be justified freely, they be made sons of God by adoption, they be made like the image of his only-begotten Son Jesus Christ, they walk religiously in good works, and at length by God's mercy they attain to everlasting felicity.*	[5] Those of mankind that are predestinated unto life, God, before the foundation of the world was laid, according to his eternal and immutable purpose, and the secret counsel and good pleasure of his will, hath chosen in Christ unto everlasting glory,[8] out of his mere free grace and love, without any foresight of faith or good works, or perseverance in either of them, or any other thing in the creature, as conditions, or causes moving him thereunto; and all to the praise of his glorious grace.	5. Those of mankind that are *predestinated unto life,* God, *BEFORE THE FOUNDATION OF THE WORLD WAS LAID,* according to his *ETERNAL* and immutable *PURPOSE, AND THE SECRET COUNSEL* and **GOOD PLEASURE** of his will, *HATH CHOSEN IN CHRIST, UNTO EVERLASTING* glory, out of his mere free grace and love, **WITHOUT ANY FORESIGHT OF FAITH OR GOOD WORKS, OR PERSEVERANCE** in either of them, **or** any other thing in the creature, as conditions, or causes moving him thereunto; and all to the praise of his glorious grace.
But such as are not predestinated to salvation shall finally be condemned for their sins.	[6] As God hath appointed the elect unto glory, so hath he to bring this to pass,[9] by the same decree,[10] ordained to permit man to fall; [and such as are predestinated unto life effectually to call to faith in Christ by his Spirit working in due season, to justify, adopt, sanctify, and to keep by his power through faith unto salvation [11]].[12] Neither are any other redeemed by Christ, effectually called, justified, adopted, sanctified, and saved, but the elect only.[13]	6. As God hath appointed the elect unto glory, so hath he, by the eternal and most free purpose of his will, foreordained all the means thereunto. *Wherefore they who are* elected, being fallen in Adam, are redeemed by Christ, *ARE* effectually *CALLED* unto faith in Christ *BY HIS SPIRIT WORKING IN DUE SEASON; ARE JUSTIFIED, ADOPTED,* sanctified, and kept by his power through faith unto salvation. Neither are any other redeemed by Christ, effectually called, justified, adopted, sanctified, and saved, but the elect only.
	[7] The rest of mankind, God was pleased, according to the unsearchable counsel of his own will, whereby he extendeth or withholdeth mercy as he pleaseth, for the glory	7. The rest of mankind God was pleased, according to the unsearchable counsel of his own will, whereby he extendeth or withholdeth mercy as he pleaseth, for the glory of his

IRISH ARTICLES (1615)	COMMITTEE'S PROPOSAL	WESTMINSTER CONFESSION
	of his sovereign power [14] over his creatures, to pass by, and to ordain them to dishonour and wrath for their sin, to the praise of his glorious justice.	sovereign power over his creatures, to pass by, and to ordain them to dishonor and wrath FOR THEIR SIN, to the praise of his glorious justice.
(16) *The godly consideration of predestination and our election in Christ, is full of sweet, pleasant, and unspeakable comfort to godly persons, and such as feel in themselves the working of the Spirit of Christ, mortifying the works of the flesh, and their earthly members, and drawing up their minds to high and heavenly things: as well because it doth greatly confirm and establish their faith of eternal salvation to be enjoyed through Christ, as because it doth fervently kindle their love towards God. And, on the contrary side, for curious and carnal persons lacking the Spirit of Christ, to have continually before their eyes the sentence of God's predestination is* **very dangerous.** **(17)** *We must receive God's promises in such wise as they be generally set forth unto us in holy Scripture: and in our doings, that will of God is to be followed which we have expressly declared unto us in the word of God.*	[8] The doctrine of this high mystery of predestination is to be handled with special prudence and care, that men attending to the will of God revealed in his word, and yielding obedience thereunto, may, from the certainty of their effectual vocation, be assured of their eternal election. So shall this doctrine afford matter of praise, reverence, and admiration of God, and of humility, diligence, and abundant consolation to all that sincerely obey the gospel.[15]	8. The doctrine of this high mystery of predestination is to be handled with special prudence and care, that men *ATTENDING THE WILL OF GOD REVEALED IN HIS WORD,* and yielding obedience thereunto, may, from the certainty of their effectual vocation, be assured of their eternal election. So shall this doctrine afford matter of praise, reverence, and admiration of God; and of humility, diligence, and abundant consolation to all that sincerely obey the gospel.

[1] Amended to "most wise and holy."

[2] Debates signalized on these words, but details not given.

[3] Moved to insert here "without respect to anything foreseen," and omit corresponding clause below: "without . . . thereunto."

[4] "in time" omitted.

[5] "should come" amended to "comes."

[6] After several attempts to adjust this clause, "without . . . thereunto," viz.: (1) by prefixing "absolutely"; (2) by omitting "any"; (3) by modifying so as to read "not being moved thereunto by any foresight of anything without himself"; (4) by transferring in a shortened form to just after "unchangeably" (see note 3) — it was removed from this place and expanded into a new section (§ 2) of the completed Confession.

[7] Omission of the words "foreordained to everlasting death" proposed but refused: Mr. Whitaker proposed some alteration in them, which being refused, he entered his dissent.

[8] The words "unto everlasting glory" were challenged, as perhaps superfluous, but retained.

[9] Ordered not to express "to bring this to pass." Mr. Gillespie proposed to substitute for the clause "so hath he . . . to permit man to fall": "For the same end God hath ordained to permit man to fall"; but it did not prevail.

[10] Ordered not to assert "the same decree."

[11] The bracketed portion is conjectural, to fill out the section according to the original opening: it is derived from the Irish Article.

[12] Mr. Reynolds proposed the following form, which supplied the basis on which the final form was made (the italicized words were altered in making out the final form): "As God hath appointed the elect unto glory, so hath he by the *same*[a] eternal and most free purpose of his will, foreordained all the means thereunto, *which he in his counsel is pleased to appoint for the executing*

of that decree;[b] wherefore they who are *endowed with so excellent a benefit*,[c] being fallen in Adam, are[d] called *in*[e] *according to God's purpose,*"[f] etc. ([a]) "same" was omitted. ([b]) This clause was omitted. ([c]) This clause, derived from Art. xvii. of the Thirty-nine Articles, changed into "elected." ([d]) "redeemed by Christ, are" was inserted here. ([e]) It is uncertain whether "in" here is a mere slip due to a mixture of the two expressions "according to" and "in accordance with," or whether the word "Christ" has fallen out inadvertently after it. ([f]) "called according to God's purpose" was altered to "effectually called unto faith in Christ."

[13] Much debate was held over this final clause, but it was retained decisively.

[14] "sovereign power" perhaps challenged but retained.

[15] Debate signalized on this section but no details given.

III

THE WESTMINSTER DOCTRINE OF HOLY SCRIPTURE

THE WESTMINSTER DOCTRINE OF
HOLY SCRIPTURE [1]

THERE is certainly in the whole mass of confessional literature no more nobly conceived or ably wrought-out statement
of doctrine than the chapter " Of the Holy Scripture," which
the Westminster Divines placed at the head of their Confession and laid at the foundation of their system of doctrine.
It has commanded the hearty admiration of all competent
readers. Dean Stanley thinks that no council or synod has ever
argued and decided any single theological question with an
ability equal to that shown by the great theologians in their private treatises. But he immediately adds: " The nearest approaches to it are the chapters on Justification in the Decrees
of Trent, and on the Bible in the Westminster Confession." [2]
Dr. Schaff considers it " the best Protestant counterpart of the
Roman Catholic doctrine of the rule of faith," and remarks:
" No other Protestant symbol has such a clear, judicious,
concise, and exhaustive statement of this fundamental article
of Protestantism." [3] Such a statement of a fundamental doctrine is a precious heritage, worthy not only to be cherished
but understood. That it may be at once highly praised
and seriously misunderstood has been made sufficiently evident in the course of certain recent controversies. But apart
from all reference to recent controversies, it cannot be otherwise than useful to subject so admirable a statement of doctrine to a close scrutiny, with a view to obtaining as clear an
understanding of its true purport as possible. Something of
this kind is attempted in this article. And that the formulas

[1] From *The Presbyterian and Reformed Review,* iv. 1893, pp. 582–655.

[2] *Contemporary Review,* for August, 1874, p. 499 (as quoted by Dr.
Schaff).

[3] " The Creeds of Christendom," i. 1877, p. 767.

may be looked at discolored as little as possible by the haze
which may rise from the years that have intervened since their
composition, an effort is made to place them in their historical
setting and to illustrate them from discussions contemporary
with themselves.

I. The Preparation of the Chapter

" If any chapter of the Westminster Confession of Faith,"
says Dr. Mitchell, " was framed with more elaborate care than
another, it was that which treats ' Of the Holy Scripture.' It
was considered paragraph by paragraph — almost clause by
clause — by the House of Commons as well as by the Assembly
of Divines, before it was finally passed; and its eighth paragraph was deemed worthy to be made the subject of a special
conference between certain Members of the House and the
Divines of the Assembly." [4] The meager Minutes of the Assembly scarcely enable us to trace this careful work. As early as
the 20th August, 1644, a Committee, consisting of Drs. Gouge,
Temple, and Hoyle, Messrs. Gataker, Arrowsmith, Burroughs,
Burgess, Vines, and Goodwin, together with the Scotch Commissioners, was appointed " to prepare matter for a joint
Confession of Faith." [5] A fortnight later (September 4), Dr.
Smith and Messrs. Palmer, Newcomen, Herle, Reynolds, Wil-
son, Tuckney, Young, Ley, and Sedgewick were added to the
Committee or constituted an additional Committee.[6] Baillie

[4] " Report of Proceedings of the First General Presbyterian Council,"
at Edinburgh, 1877, Appendix vi. p. 371.

[5] Lightfoot (" Works," ed. Pitman, xiii. 1824, p. 305) says: " ' Mr. *Palmer*
reported from the grand committee, desiring this . . . (2) A committee to
join with the commissioners of Scotland, to draw up a confession of faith.
. . .' Hereupon we fell to choose a committee. . . . There was some debate
about the matter, because we have no order yet to enable us to such a thing:
and, at last, when it was resolved, there was some debate about the number:
and, at last, nine were fixed by vote."

[6] We are quoting here from Dr. Mitchell's " The Westminster Assembly:
its History and Standards," the Baird Lecture for 1882, Philadelphia, 1884,
pp. 357 *sq.* (ed. 2, 1897, pp. 367 *sq.*). Compare the excerpts in Mitchell and
Struthers, " Minutes," 1874, pp. lxxxvi.–lxxxvii. Lightfoot (as above, p. 308),
under date of Wednesday, September 4, says: " The first thing done was, that
Dr. *Temple,* chairman of the committee for the drawing up of a confession of

was therefore justified in writing in October: " The Confession of Faith is referred to a committee, to be put in severall the best hands that are here." [7] How much of the matter was prepared by this Committee we do not know. On November 21, Baillie reports that though " the Catechise is drawn up," he fears " the Confession . . . may stick longer "; [8] while on December 26 he thinks " that we must either passe the Confession to another season, or, if God will help us, the heads of it being distribute among many able hands, it may in a short time be so drawn up, as the debates of it may cost little time." [9] By April 25, 1645, some reports concerning the Confession had been made to the Assembly,[10] and on the 4th of May Baillie writes: " Our next work will be the Confession and Catechisme, upon both which we have alreadie made some entrance." [11] Accordingly, on the 12th of May, 1645, " the report of the Confession of Faith " was " read and debated," [12] and a Committee was appointed to draw up the first draft of the Confession. This Committee consisted apparently of Drs. Temple and Hoyle, Messrs. Gataker, Harris, Burgess, Reynolds, Herle, and the Scotch Commissioners. On July 7, the first report was made: " Dr. Temple made report of that part of the Confession of Faith touching the Scriptures. It was read, debated." [13] This chapter on the Scriptures occupied the attention of the Assembly thenceforward until July 18; but it is impossible to trace more than the general outlines of their work. On the 11th of July it is recorded: " Debate about the Scriptures where we left; about the knowledge of the divine authority of the Scripture." [14] From this we may learn that the Assembly had got as far as the fifth section by this date. From the note on the 14th of July [15] we learn that the statement about the necessity of the inward illumination of the Spirit for the saving understanding

---

faith, desired, that that committee might be augmented: which was done accordingly."

[7] " Letters and Journals," ed. Laing, ii. 1841, p. 232.

[8] " Letters," ii. p. 242.

[9] P. 248.

[10] P. 266.

[11] P. 272.

[12] " Minutes," p. 91.

[13] P. 110.

[14] P. 111.

[15] P. 113.

of the Scriptures was not a part of the original draft, but was inserted by the Assembly in the debate. It was debated on this day and on July 15, when also the word " saving " was added, confining this necessity to " the *saving* understanding " of the Word.[16] The debate was continued on the 16th of July and on the 17th of July, on which latter occasion section 9 was before the house: " Proceed in the debate about ' literal sense.' " [17] The last notice of the continuance of the debate is that of the 18th of July.[18]

Early in January, 1647, the proof-texts were added to the first chapter of the Confession. Those for the first paragraph on January 7; [19] for the second on January 8; for the third, fourth, and part of the fifth on January 11; for the rest of the fifth on January 12; for the sixth and seventh on January 14, and for the rest on January 15.[20]

In the meantime, on July 8, 1645, Messrs. Reynolds, Herle, and Newcomen had been appointed " to take care of the wording of the Confession of Faith, as it is voted in the Assembly from time to time, and to report to the Assembly when they think fit there should be any alteration in the words," after having consulted with at least one of the Scotch Commissioners.[21] And on December 8, 1645, it was ordered that Messrs. Tuckney, Reynolds, Newcomen, and Whitaker be a Committee " to review the Confession of Faith as it is finished in the Assembly." [22] The final phrasing of this chapter was, therefore, due to these Committees, or this Committee, for it is probable that it was all one Committee.[23] Its final form was debated and approved by the Assembly on June 17 and 18, 1646.[24]

The outline of their labors undoubtedly bears out the statement that great care was taken in the composition of the chapter, but apparently not that any special or unusual discussion

[16] P. 113.

[17] P. 114.

[18] P. 115.

[19] Pp. 319 and 473.

[20] Pp. 319–322.

[21] P. 110.

[22] P. 168.

[23] Mitchell, " The Westminster Assembly," 1884, p. 358 (ed. 2, 1897, p. 368).

[24] " Minutes," p. 245.

was given to it. There are no great debates recorded concerning it; and the Divines seem to have been more than usually at one concerning its propositions. We are surprised, indeed, by the rapidity and unanimity with which they did their work. The whole first draft passed through the Assembly between July 7 and 18: and debates are signalized only on the knowledge of the divine authority of the Scriptures (§ 5), the need of supernatural illumination for the saving understanding of the Word (§ 6), and the literal sense of Scripture (§ 9). To these may be added the conference with the House of Commons on section 8. The impression is very strong that, in the case of this chapter at least, Baillie's prevision proved correct and the Confession came before the Assembly in a form that roused little discussion and cost but little time in debate.

II. The Sources of the Chapter

It belonged to the historical situation of the Westminster Divines that their doctrinal work should take much the form of a consensus of the Reformed theology. That theology had grown to its maturity during the controversies of the first century of its life. Everywhere there was a strongly felt desire for a comprehensive and universally acceptable creed statement of the Reformed faith, which would unify the scattered Churches and supersede or supplement the multitude of Confessions which had been produced in the first age of the Reformation; and this desire had already found expression in collections and harmonies of the Confessions. The special history of the British Churches — including the Anglo-Catholic and Arminianizing irruption under the leading of Laud — brought to the aid of this general tendency of the times both the impulse to seek support from the universal faith of other Reformed Churches and the necessity of vindicating unity of belief with them. It was in the nature of the case, therefore, that the Westminster Divines placed consciously before themselves as their dominant purpose, the task " of setting forth the whole scheme of Reformed doctrine in harmonious development, in a form of which their country should have no cause to be ashamed in the presence of any of the sister Churches of the continent." Dr. Mitchell does not overstate the matter when he represents the Westminster Assembly as having been " called together chiefly for two purposes: viz., first, to vindicate the doctrine of the Church of England from misrepresentation, and to show that it was in harmony with that of the other Reformed Churches; and, second, to effect such changes on her polity and worship as would bring her into closer union with the Church of Scotland and the Reformed Churches on the Continent." [25] To this, indeed, it was practically bound by the ordinance by which it was called, which set forth as its purpose " the settling of the Government and Liturgy of the Church of England, and . . . vindicating and clearing of the doctrine of the said Church from false aspersions and interpretations," reference being had (as is explicitly stated in its first paragraph) to securing " nearer agreement with the Church of Scotland and other Reformed Churches abroad "; while the Solemn League and Covenant included the vow that they would " endeavor to bring the Churches of God in the three kingdoms to the nearest conjunction and uniformity in religion, confession of faith " and catechising, as well as in government and worship.

THE FUNDAMENTAL SOURCE

This conscious reference in the work of the Assembly to the Reformed theology in general, while it adds interest to a search after the sources of its doctrinal statements, renders it almost impossible, in the chapter on the Scriptures at least, to determine them with any exactness. The difficulty is greatly increased by the circumstance that the Reformed theologians, whether on the Continent or in Britain, did not write in ignorance or independence of one another; so that it is a matter of merely literary interest to determine who was the originator of arguments or modes of statement that are common to all, or through what precise channels they came into the Confes-

[25] " Minutes," p. xxvii.

sion of Faith. No reader of the Puritan literature of the seventeenth century will fail to observe how hard it leans upon the great Reformed divines of the Continent — freely appropriating from them lines of argument, forms of expression and points of view, while also, no doubt, freely adapting them to its own purposes. The consequence is that the sources of the several sections of the Confession of Faith can with almost equal readiness be found in Ball or Du Buc, in Cartwright or Calvin, according as we choose to look near or far for them. There is scarcely a leading divine of the first three-quarters of a century of Reformed theology, who has written at large on the Scriptures, from whom statements may not be so drawn as to make them appear to be the immediate sources of some of the Westminster sections. For example the following sentences from Calvin might very well lie as the basis of the first section:

" Ergo quanquam hominum ingratitudinem satis superque omni patrocinio spoliat fulgor ille qui in coelo et in terra omnium oculis ingeritur, . . . aliud tamen et melius adminiculum accedere necesse est quod nos probe ad ipsum mundi creatorem dirigat. Itaque non frustra verbi sui lumen addidit, quo innotesceret in salutem. . . . Nec frustra eodem remedio nos in pura sui notitia continet; quia mox alioqui diffluerent etiam qui videntur prae aliis firmi stare. . . . Tandem ut continuo progressu doctrinae veritas saeculis omnibus superstes maneret in mundo, eadem oracula quae deposuerat apud patres, quasi publicis tabulis consignata esse voluit. . . . Sed quoniam non quotidiana e coelis redduntur oracula, et scripturae solae exstant quibus visum est Domino suam perpetuae memoriae veritatem consecrare: non alio iure plenam apud fideles autoritatem obtinent, quam ubi statuunt e coelo fluxisse, ac si vivae ipsae Dei voces illic exaudirentur." [26]

This is but to say that the chief source of the Westminster doctrine of Holy Scripture is the general teaching of the Reformed theology; and it is better for us to recognize this at the out-

[26] "Institutio," I. vi. 1 and 2; vii. 1: "Opera Calvini," ed. Baum, Cunitz, and Reuss, ii. pp. 53, 54, and 56.

set than to lose ourselves in the perhaps vain task of endeavoring to find the proximate origin of its several clauses.

That we may realize how entirely the Westminster teaching on Scripture is the common possession of the Reformed theology, it will be well to draw out the Reformed doctrine on the subject in its salient points. In order to do this we shall purposely rely on Heppe's statement, because it is framed out of the Continental divines only, and will serve, therefore, to advise us, in the most pointed way, of the unity of the faith in Britain and abroad. This course is naturally attended, no doubt, with the incidental difficulty that Heppe has not been able to retain so perfect an objectivity in stating the Reformed doctrine that his own conceptions do not sometimes enter into his statement and color the doctrine of his authorities. When this personal equation is allowed for, however, it ceases to be a disadvantage; the essential agreement of the Westminster Confession with the general Reformed doctrine of Scripture becomes all the more striking when it is seen to be so conspicuous even from Heppe's statement of the latter. The following is a translation of Heppe's outline, with the omission, of course, of the passages from representative Reformed theologians, which he gives in his notes in support of the several statements: [27]

Conf.
of Faith,
I. 1a.

" The consciousness that there is a God and that it is his duty to worship Him, is a natural and essential possession of man. This innate knowledge of God, the *notitia Dei insita*, frames itself in man, by the action of his reason and conscience, into the *notitia acquisita*. Hence there is a *religio naturalis*. Reason causes man to apprehend the idea of God immanent to it, and teaches him to rise by inference from the visible world, as the work of God, to its invisible author and ruler. At the same time, conscience teaches man to apprehend God as Him who loves and rewards what is good, abhors and punishes what is wicked, and to whom he is absolutely responsible. Man's natural knowledge of God, therefore (as distinguished from what it becomes through revelation), most completely shapes

[27] Heppe, " Die Dogmatik der evangelisch-reformirten Kirche," 1861, pp. 1 *sqq.*

itself through this — that man looks upon himself as the image of
God.

"This natural knowledge of God is, no doubt, insufficient for
attaining eternal blessedness. For man, who is convicted of his
sinfulness by his conscience, learns by this, indeed, that God punishes wickedness, but from himself knows nothing of what God's
gracious purpose with the sinner may be. The *religio naturalis* is,
therefore, not *salutaris,* and avails only to render man, if he does
not receive revelation, inexcusable. Moreover, man cannot of himself apprehend what he apprehends of God by reason and conscience
as it ought to be apprehended. Nevertheless, what natural religion
teaches of God, although it is incomplete, is true and also useful;
for, on the one side, every excuse is taken from man, as over against
God, if he does not believe in God and keep His law; and, on
the other hand, the natural man who seeks peace with God by the
religio naturalis will the more joyfully and thankfully receive the
revelation of God's grace when it is imparted to him; and the regenerate man who has received the gracious revelation, and believes
it, will be able then the better to understand and comprehend the
natural revelation of God.

"Since man knows himself in his conscience as breaker of God's
command, and, therefore, guilty before God, and yet, through his
natural knowledge of God, apprehends God only as righteous Judge
of the good and bad, it follows that the *religio naturalis* can afford
man no peace with God, and that it cannot be a sufficing *religio* in
itself or for man. It itself points above itself, in that it awakens in
man the need of and the longing for a revelation, through which
he may first rightly understand what it means that a God exists,
and through which he may apprehend that God can be the God even
of the sinner, that God wishes to be sought by the sinner and how
He will be found by the sinner. Thus only as faith in revelation does
religion become what it should be, according to its conception: not
a knowledge of God, nor yet an observance of the divine commandment in itself, but a determination of immediate self-consciousness,
a feeling (Schleiermacher) which rests on the experience of God as
absolute love.

*   *   *   *   *   *   *

"Since theology is to recognize and present what belongs to natural religion too, a distinction may be drawn between *articuli sim-*

Conf.
of Faith,
I. 1b.

plices (*puri*), which rest simply on revelation, and *articuli mixti*, in the presentation of which reason also has its material part. Only we must hold fast to the fact that the fundamental doctrines of theology (of the Trinity, of the fall of the human race, of the Redeemer, of the true blessedness and of the only way to it) can be apprehended only out of revelation, and that, therefore, the holy Scriptures are of absolute authority in all the sections of the system of doctrine.

" The sole source and norm of all Christian knowledge is Holy Scripture, i.e. the sum of the contents of all those books which God has caused to be written through prophets, evangelists and apostles. *Scriptura S. est verbum Dei, autore Spir. S. in veteri test. per Mosen et prophetas, in novo vero per evangelistas et apostolos descriptum atque in libros canonicos relatum, ut de Deo rebusque divinis ecclesiam plene et perspicue erudiat, sitque fidei et vitae norma unica ad salutem* (Heidegg., ii. 6). To Holy Scripture belong, therefore, only those books which were written by prophets and apostles, i.e. by such men as God has illuminated in a special manner by His Spirit, in order to make use of them as instruments of revelation. Since these books have been recognized and numbered from antiquity down by a canon of the Church as prophetic and apostolic, they are called *canonical*. The writings preserved and handed down with them, which are not of prophetic or apostolic origin, are called, on the other hand, *apocryphal* books. *Libri apocryphi sunt et dicuntur, qui nec prophetas nec apostolos habent auctores* (Wendel., *Coll.*, p. 44). Such apocryphal books occur, however, only in the Old Testament, as an appendix to it. For those books of the New Testament which were looked upon by the Reformers, and in part by their disciples, as apocryphal (i.e. as not proceeding from the apostles) . . . , have long been recognized and received by the Church as canonical.

" These canonical books of the Old and New Testament not only contain the Word of God, but are themselves God's written Word; for their penning was brought about by special and immediate agency of the Holy Spirit, who incited the authors to the writing, suggested to them the thoughts and words which should be penned, and guarded them from every error in the writing — that is, the canonical books were *inspired* by the Holy Ghost to their authors, in both contents and form. Upon this unparalleled peculiarity of the origin of Holy Scripture — i.e. upon its

I. 2a, 3.

I. 2b.

divinity — rest its peculiar properties (to wit, *proprietates, quibus divinitas eius sufficienter declaratur* [L. Croc., *Synt.*, iv. 1]). These are: *auctoritas et certitudo, sufficientia et perfectio, necessitas* and *perspicuitas.*

"The divinity or the inspired character of the Holy Scriptures
represents itself to the believer primarily as the property of its
AUTHORITY. *Auctoritas s. scripturae est dignitas et excellentia soli*
sacrae scripturae prae omnibus aliis scriptis competens, qua est et
habetur authentica i.e. *infallibiliter certa, sic ut necessitate abso-* I. 4, 5.
luta ab omnibus ei sit credendum atque obtemperandum propter auc-
torem Deum (Polan., i. 14). By virtue of this the Holy Scriptures
are the principle of the whole of theology, the exclusive norm
of Christian doctrine, and the infallible judge of all controversies;
and that in such a manner that all that is contained in the language
(*Wortlaut*) of Scripture, or follows by indubitable consequence I. 8, 10.
from it, is dogma, while what is contrary to it is error, and everything else, even if it does not contradict Holy Scripture, is indifferent for the soul's welfare. This authority, i.e. its divinity and
authenticity, rests in no sense (not even *quoad nos*) on the recognition of the Church, but wholly and only upon the Scripture itself, I. 4.
which as God's Word is αὐτοπίστος and ἀνυπεύθυνος. The sole witness which certifies Christians of the divinity and authority of the
Holy Scriptures with absolute assurance, is, therefore, the witness
which Scripture bears to itself, or God to it in the conscience of the
believer, to wit, the witness of the Holy Spirit. This is given to
the believer in the fact that the longing for salvation which fills him
obtains complete satisfaction by means of the Holy Scriptures, I. 5.
that the Spirit of God which quickens him recognizes itself in the
Holy Scriptures, and that his own life of faith finds itself promoted
by them more and more and in ever more quickening manner.
On this very account, however, the divinity and authority of the
Scriptures can be apprehended only by Christians. . . . Other evidences which are used for the proof of the divine authenticity of
the Scriptures have value for Christians, therefore, only in so far
as they can be used for the defense of the authority of Scripture
externally. Among them belong the witness of the Church, which
delivers the Holy Scripture to the individual Christian as the
Word of God, recognized by it as such in all ages (which tradition,
nevertheless, has no more value than the witness of heretics, Jews
and heathen, which likewise attests that the Holy Scripture was

recognized by the Church from the beginning as God's Word), as well as the fulfilled prophecies of Holy Scripture (especially the destruction of Jerusalem and the earlier divine guidance and the later dispersion of the Jewish people) and the miracles, through the performance of which the writers of Holy Scripture are attested, by God Himself, as men of God.

" Since the authority of Scripture coincides with the authority of God, it is absolute authority. Nevertheless, there is a distinction drawn in the contents of Scripture in the matter of authority. Inasmuch as, to wit, all that Scripture records is absolutely certain historical truth, *auctoritas s. authentia historica* belongs to it; inasmuch, however, as it contains the absolutely divine rule of faith and life, *auctoritas s. authentia normativa* belongs to it: whence it appears that the *auctoritas historica* extends further than the *auctoritas normativa*. The former belongs to the whole contents of Scripture; the latter, on the other hand, only to a part of it, since what Scripture reports as to the works, words and thoughts of the devil and the godless has certainly *auctoritas historica*, but no *auctoritas normativa*.

" On the divinity of the Holy Scriptures rests further their PERFECTION. *Perfectio scripturae est perfectio partium, qua omnia fidei et morum capita continet, et graduum, qua omnes gradus revelationis* (Burm., 45). With respect to the purpose of Scripture, its perfection presents itself as *sufficiency*, since Scripture contains all that is needful for man, in order that he may be able so to learn God's nature and will as well as himself, that thereby his consciousness of sin shall be awakened and the salvation which he needs be mediated to him. Yet this is not to say that Scripture presents all truths in express words, but that it (*implicite* or *explicite*) reveals the truth in a perfection which leads the believer into all truth, since it instructs man in all that it is necessary for him to know for the attainment of eternal life. A distinction is to be drawn between the *perfectio essentialis*, according to which Holy Scripture contains sufficingly the truths of revelation which are necessary for the attainment of eternal salvation, and the *perfectio integralis*, according to which the Holy Writings have been so preserved by God's grace from destruction and corruption, that no canonical book and no essential part of one has been lost. Of a tradition which may increase the doctrinal contents of Scripture, therefore, the Christian has no need. Only for the organization,

I. 6.

I. 8.

discipline and worship of the Church can tradition come into consideration.

" Just as essentially as the properties of *perfectio* and *sufficientia* belongs also that of NECESSITAS to the Scriptures, since the Scriptures, on account of the weakness of the human heart and the power of error which rules in the world, are necessary for the preservation   I. 1. in the earth of the pure knowledge of revealed truth. Scripture is necessary, therefore, not only for the well-being, but especially for the very being of the Church, which would pass out of existence if it had not an absolutely certain record of the revealed truth. Nevertheless, it must be observed that the necessity of Scripture is not an absolute one, but a *necessitas ex hypothesi dispositionis*, since, had it been the good pleasure of God, He could have preserved the pure knowledge and conviction of His truth, even without the means of a Holy Scripture.

" If now the Scriptures are necessary for the attainment of eternal life and for the preservation of the Church on earth, in like manner must their most essential contents be presented with sufficient clearness to be understood by even the unlearned man who reads the Scriptures with believing heart as one seeking salvation. Therefore there belongs to the Scriptures the property of PERSPI-   I. 7. CUITAS, *qua, quae ad salutem sunt scitu necessaria, in scriptura ita perspicue et clare sunt explicata, ut ab indoctis quoque fidelibus, devote et attente legentibus intelligi possint* (Wendel., *Proleg., cap.* 3). By this is, however, not to be understood that all the several words and sentences of Scripture are clear beyond doubt; rather is the perspicuity of Scripture to be referred only to the fundamental doctrines of revelation affecting salvation, which are contained in it; and it must be further noted that the true knowledge of them is possible only to the reader who is seeking salvation, while others can obtain at the best only a theoretical and purely external knowledge of the truths of faith. For just as the brute can perceive the body but not the spirit of man, because he himself has none, so also the unspiritual man can see and understand, no doubt, the letters but not the spirit of Scripture.

" Neither does the perspicuity of Scripture exclude the necessity of interpreting it. *Interpretatio S. Scripturae est explicatio veri sensus et usus illius, verbis perspicuis instituta, ad gloriam Dei et aedificationem ecclesiae* (Pol., i. 45).

" It likewise follows from the divinity of the Scriptures, that the interpretation of those passages which present difficulties is not to be made dependent on some other judge, as possibly on the authority of the Church, but only on the Spirit of God, the work

I. 9. of whom alone Scripture is, or on itself. Since now all doctrines, the knowledge of which is necessary for eternal life, are presented in Scripture with undoubtable clearness for those who read it with believing mind, i.e. according to the *regula fidei et caritatis*, it follows that the darker passages of Scripture are to be interpreted according to the indubitably clear ones, or according to the *analogia fidei* which rests on these: *Analogia fidei est argumentatio a generalibus dogmatibus, quae omnium in ecclesiae docendorum normam continet* (Chamier, i. 17). It is to be held fast at the same time, that not only what stands in the express language of Scripture,

I. 6. but also what flows from that by necessary consequence, is to be recognized as Scriptural content (*Schriftinhalt*) and revealed truth.

" In the interpretation of Scripture two things are included which, indeed, are expressed in the very idea of it, viz.: (1) The *enarratio veri sensus Scripturae;* and (2) the *accommodatio ad usum* (Pol., i. 45).

" The true sense of Scripture, which interpretation has established, can always be only single, and, in general, only the real, literal sense, the *sensus literalis*, which is either *sensus literalis simplex* or *sensus literalis compositus*. The former is to be firmly held

I. 9. as a rule; the latter, on the other hand, is to be recognized wherever Scripture presents anything typically; and only when the *sensus literalis* would contradict the *articuli fidei* or the *praeceptis caritatis*, where therefore Scripture itself demands another interpretation of its words, is the figurative meaning of them, the *sensus figuratus*, to be sought. Besides this, the allegorical interpretation has its right in the application of the language of Scripture to the manifold relations of life in the *accommod. ad usum*.

" For the right interpretation of Scripture there are, of course, requisite all sorts of human preparations, knowledges, fitnesses (general and spiritual training, knowledge of languages and history, etc.) ; but the essential qualification is, nevertheless, faith and life in communion with the Holy Ghost, who teaches us to understand the complete harmony of Scripture, even in the apparent contraditions of Scripture (in the ἐναντιοφανή). For the Holy Spirit leads all those who are of believing heart, and who call on Him for the purpose of receiving enlightenment only from Him, into all truth. Therefore the believer has the comfort of knowing that God really grants him the true understanding of Scripture, and that the true knowledge of the Word will be preserved forever on earth by God's gracious care."

Even so brief an abstract as this, framed for a far different purpose, illustrates the fact that no single assertion is made in the first chapter of the Confession which is not the common faith of the whole Reformed theology; and this could be vindicated, if there were need to do so, to the minutest detail. A fair case could be made out — if the anachronism of two centuries did not stand in the way — that Heppe's statement was the source of the Westminster chapter. A statement drawn up, from its most representative Continental teachers, by one heartily in accord with all the details of Reformed doctrine, would even more conspicuously show the minuteness and completeness of the relation. The great source of this chapter is, therefore, the recognized Reformed theology of the time.

THE PROXIMATE SOURCES

The most important proximate source of the chapter on Holy Scripture, as it is also the main proximate source, as Dr. Mitchell has shown,[28] of the whole Confession, was those Irish Articles of Religion which are believed to have been drawn up by Usher's hand, and which were adopted by the Irish Convocation in 1615. As no doubt can exist as to this fact, so, says Dr. Mitchell,[29] " as little doubt can be entertained in regard to the design of the framers in following so closely in the footsteps of Ussher and his Irish brethren. They meant to show him and others like him, who had not had the courage to take their place among them, that though absent they were not forgotten nor their work disregarded. They meant their Confession to be

[28] See Mitchell, " The Westminster Assembly," 1884, pp. 376 *sq.* (ed. 2, 1897, pp. 386 *sq.*) ; also " Minutes," pp. xlvii. *sqq.*

[29] " The Westminster Assembly," 1884, pp. 379–380 (ed. 2, 1897, pp. 389–390).

in harmony with the *consensus* of the Reformed Churches, and especially of the British Reformed Churches, as that had been expressed in their most matured symbol. They desired it to be a bond of union, not a cause of strife and division, among those who were resolutely determined to hold fast by ' the sum and substance of the doctrine ' of the Reformed Churches — the Augustianism so widely accepted in the times of Elizabeth and James." Accordingly we might expect that in framing this chapter, too, while resting primarily on the Irish Articles, the Westminster Divines would not neglect the earlier Reformed creeds; and that they actually did their work in full view of what had been done in the way of creed-expression of the doctrine of Scripture before them, Dr. Mitchell shows elsewhere by means of a carefully framed parallel statement of the creeds on this subject.[30] So much of this as seems needful for our purpose, we borrow:

EARLIER CONFESSIONS	WESTMINSTER CONFESSION	IRISH ARTICLES OF 1615
We know God by two means. First, by the creation, and preservation, and government of the whole world . . . by which the invisible things of God may be seen and known unto us, namely, his everlasting power and Godhead, as Paul the apostle speaketh, Rom. i. 20, which knowledge sufficeth to convince all men, and make them without excuse. But much more clearly and plainly he afterwards revealed himself unto us in his holy and heavenly word, so far forth as is expedient for his own glory, and the salvation of his in this life ["The Belgic Confession," 1561].	I. Although the light of nature, and the works of creation and providence, do so far manifest the goodness, wisdom, and power of God, as to leave men inexcusable; yet are they not sufficient to give that knowledge of God, and of his will, which is necessary unto salvation; therefore it pleased the Lord, at sundry times, and in divers manners, to reveal himself, and to declare that his will unto his church; and afterwards, for the better preserving and propagating of the truth, and for the more sure establishment and comfort of the church against the corruption of the flesh, and the malice of Satan and the world, to commit the same wholly unto writing; which maketh the Holy Scripture to be most necessary; those former ways of God's revealing his will unto his people being now ceased.	I. The ground of our religion, and the rule of faith and all saving truth, is the word of God, contained in the Holy Scripture.
["The French Confession" like the Belgic, but far more brief.]		

[30] " Report of Proceedings of the First General Presbyterian Council," held at Edinburgh, 1877, Appendix vi. pp. 371 *sqq.*

EARLIER CONFESSIONS	WESTMINSTER CONFESSION	IRISH ARTICLES OF 1615
All this Holy Scripture is contained in the canonical books of the Old and New Testament, the catalogue whereof is this: [Catalogue follows] ["The French Confession," 1559].	II. Under the name of Holy Scripture, or the word of God written, are now contained all the books of the Old and New Testament, which are these:	II. By the name of Holy Scripture, we understand all the canonical books of the Old and New Testaments, viz.:

OF THE OLD TESTAMENT		**OF THE OLD TESTAMENT**

Genesis,	Ecclesiastes,	The five books	Ecclesiastes,
Exodus,	The Song of	of Moses,	Song of Solomon,
Leviticus,	Songs,		
Numbers,	Isaiah,		Isaiah,
Deuteronomy,	Jeremiah,		Jeremiah:
			Prophecy and
Joshua,	Lamentations,	Joshua,	Lamentations,
Judges,	Ezekiel,	Judges,	Ezekiel,
Ruth,	Daniel,	Ruth,	Daniel,
1 Samuel,	Hosea,	The 1st and 2d	The twelve less
2 Samuel,	Joel,	of Samuel,	Prophets.
1 Kings,	Amos,	The 1st and 2d	
2 Kings,	Obadiah,	of Kings,	
1 Chronicles,	Jonah,	The 1st and 2d	
2 Chronicles,	Micah,	of Chronicles,	
Ezra,	Nahum,	Ezra,	
Nehemiah,	Habakkuk,	Nehemiah,	
Esther,	Zephaniah,	Esther,	
Job,	Haggai,	Job,	
Psalms,	Zechariah,	Psalms,	
Proverbs,	Malachi.	Proverbs,	

OF THE NEW TESTAMENT		**OF THE NEW TESTAMENT**

The Gospels		The Gospels	
according to	1 To Timothy,	according to	
Matthew,	2 To Timothy,	Matthew,	Timothy (two),
Mark,	To Titus,	Mark,	
Luke,	To Philemon,	Luke,	Titus,
John,	The Epistle to	John,	Philemon,
The Acts of the	the Hebrews,	The Acts of the	Hebrews,
Apostles,	The Epistle of	Apostles,	
Paul's Epistles	James,	The Epistle of	The Epistle of
to the Romans,	The 1st and 2d	Paul to the	James,
1 Corinthians,	Epistles of	Romans,	
2 Corinthians,	Peter,	Corinthians	St. Peter (two),
Galatians,	The 1st, 2d and	(two),	
Ephesians,	3d Epistles of	Galatians,	St. John (three),
Philippians,	John,	Ephesians,	
Colossians,	The Epistle of	Philippians,	
1 Thessalonians,	Jude,	Colossians,	St. Jude,
		Thessalonians	
2 Thessalonians,	The Revelation.	(two),	The Revelation of St. John.

We acknowledge these books to be canonical; that is, we account them as the rule and square of our faith ["French Confession," 1559].	All which are given by inspiration of God, to be the rule of faith and life.	All which are acknowledged to be given by inspiration of God, and in that regard to be of most certain credit and highest authority.

EARLIER CONFESSIONS	WESTMINSTER CONFESSION	IRISH ARTICLES OF 1615
We furthermore make a difference between the holy books and those which they call apocryphal: for so much as the apocryphal may be read in the church, and it is lawful also so far to gather instructions out of them as they agree with canonical books; but their authority and certainty is not such as that any doctrine touching faith or Christian religion may safely be built upon their testimony; so far off is it, that they can disannul or impair the authority of the other ["Belgic Confession"].	III. The books commonly called Apocrypha, not being of divine inspiration, are no part of the canon of the Scripture; and therefore are of no authority in the church of God, nor to be any otherwise approved, or made use of, than other human writings.	III. The other books, commonly called apocryphal, did not proceed from such inspiration, and therefore are not of sufficient authority to establish any point of doctrine; but the church doth read them as books containing many worthy things, for example of life and instruction of manners.
We believe that the word contained in these books came from one God; of whom alone, and not of men, the authority thereof dependeth ["French Confession"].	IV. The authority of the Holy Scripture, for which it ought to be believed and obeyed, dependeth not upon the testimony of any man or church, but wholly upon God (who is truth itself), the author thereof; and therefore it is to be received, because it is the word of God.	
Therefore without any doubt we believe those things which are contained in them; and that not so much because the church receiveth and alloweth them for canonical, as for that the Holy Ghost beareth witness to our consciences that they came from God; and most of all for that they also testify and justify by themselves this their own sacred authority and sanctity, seeing that even the blind may clearly behold, and as it were feel the fulfilling and accomplishment of all things which were foretold in these writings ["Belgic Confession"].	V. We may be moved and induced by the testimony of the church to an high and reverent esteem of the Holy Scripture; and the heavenliness of the matter, the efficacy of the doctrine, the majesty of the style, the consent of all the parts, the scope of the whole (which is to give all glory to God), the full discovery it makes of the only way of man's salvation, the many other incomparable excellencies, and the entire perfection thereof, are arguments whereby it doth abundantly evidence itself to be the word of God; yet, notwithstanding, our full persuasion and assurance of the infallible truth, and divine authority thereof, is from the inward work of the Holy Spirit, bearing witness by and with the word in our hearts.	
We believe also that the Holy Scripture doth most perfectly contain all the will of God, and	VI. The whole counsel of God, concerning all things necessary for his own glory,	VI. The Holy Scriptures contain all things necessary to salvation, and are able to in-

that in it all things are abundantly taught, whatsoever is necessary to be believed of man to attain salvation. Therefore seeing the whole manner of worshipping God, which God requireth at the hands of the faithful, is there most exquisitely and at large set down, it is lawful for no man, although he have the authority of an apostle, no, not for any angel sent from heaven (as St. Paul speaks, Gal. i. 8), to teach otherwise than we have long since been taught in the Holy Scripture. For seeing it is forbidden that any one should add or detract anything to or from the word of God, thereby it is evident enough that this holy doctrine is perfect and absolute in all points and parcels thereof; and therefore no other writings of men, although never so holy, no custom, no multitude, no antiquity, nor prescription of times, nor personal succession, nor any councils, and, to conclude, no decrees or ordinances of men, are to be matched or compared with these divine Scriptures, and this bare truth of God; for so much as God's truth excelleth all things [" Belgic Confession "].

man's salvation, faith, and life, is either expressly set down in Scripture, or by good and necessary consequence may be deduced from Scripture: unto which nothing at any time is to be added, whether by new revelations of the Spirit, or traditions of men. Nevertheless we acknowledge the inward illumination of the Spirit of God to be necessary for the saving understanding of such things as are revealed in the word; and that there are some circumstances concerning the worship of God, and government of the church, common to human actions and societies, which are to be ordered by the light of nature and Christian prudence, according to the general rules of the word, which are always to be observed.

struct sufficiently in all points of faith that we are bound to believe, and all good duties that we are bound to practise.

VII. All things in Scripture are not alike plain in themselves, nor alike clear unto all; yet those things which are necessary to be known, believed, and observed, for salvation, are so clearly propounded and opened in some place of Scripture or other, that not only the learned, but the unlearned, in a due use of the ordinary means, may attain unto a sufficient understanding of them.

V. Although there be some hard things in the Scriptures (especially such as have proper relation to the times in which they were first uttered, and prophecies of things which were afterwards to be fulfilled), yet all things necessary to be known unto everlasting salvation are clearly delivered therein; and nothing of that kind is spoken under dark mysteries in one place, which is not in other places spoken more familiarly and plainly to the capacity both of learned and unlearned.

VIII. The Old Testament in Hebrew (which was the native language of the people of God of old), and the New Testa-

EARLIER CONFESSIONS | WESTMINSTER CONFES-SION | IRISH ARTICLES OF 1615

ment in Greek (which at the time of the writing of it was most generally known to the nations), being immediately inspired by God, and by his singular care and providence kept pure in all ages, are therefore authentical; so as in all controversies of religion the church is finally to appeal unto them. But because these original tongues are not known to all the people of God who have right unto, and interest in the Scriptures, and are commanded, in the fear of God, to read and search them, therefore they are to be translated into the vulgar language of every nation unto which they come, that the word of God dwelling plentifully in all, they may worship him in an acceptable manner, and, through patience and comfort of the Scriptures, may have hope.

IV. The Scriptures ought to be translated out of the original tongues into all languages for the common use of all men; neither is any person to be discouraged from reading the Bible in such a language as he doth understand, but seriously exhorted to read the same with great humility and reverence, as a special means to bring him to the true knowledge of God, and of his own duty.

We acknowledge that interpretation of Scriptures for authentical and proper which, being taken from the Scriptures themselves (that is, from the phrase of that tongue in which they were written, they being also weighed according to the circumstances, and expounded according to the proportion of places, either of like or unlike, also of more and plainer), accordeth with the rule of faith and charity, and maketh notably for God's glory and man's salvation ["Latter Swiss Confession"].

IX. The infallible rule of interpretation of Scripture is the Scripture itself; and therefore, when there is a question about the true and full sense of any Scripture (which is not manifold, but one), it must be searched and known by other places that speak more clearly.

Wherefore we do not contemn the holy treatises of the fathers, agreeing with the Scriptures; from whom, notwithstanding, we do modestly dissent, as they are deprehended to set down things merely strange, or altogether contrary to the same. . . . And according to this order we do account of the decrees and canons of councils. Wherefore we suffer not ourselves in con-

X. The Supreme Judge, by which all controversies of religion are to be determined, and all decrees of councils, opinions of ancient writers, doctrines of men, and private spirits, are to be examined, and in whose sentence we are to rest, can be no other but the Holy Spirit speaking in the Scripture.

troversies about religion, or matters of faith, to be pressed with the bare testimonies of fathers, or decrees of councils; much less with received customs, or with the multitude of men being of one judgment, or with prescription of long time. Therefore in controversies of religion or matters of faith, we cannot admit any other judge than God himself pronouncing by the Holy Scriptures what is true, what is false, what is to be followed, or what is to be avoided. So we do not rest but in the judgments of spiritual men, drawn from the word of God [" Latter Swiss Confession "].

Our knowledge that the Westminster Divines did make use of the Irish Articles, both in determining the general outline of the Confession and (in places) its more detailed phraseology, helps us to perceive that it underlay their work in this chapter too. But it is no more clear that they used it than that they used it very freely and only so far forth as served their purpose; they looked to it for advice, not authority.

In one of the passages of this chapter, the rich phraseology of which has been much admired, and to which the Irish Articles have no corresponding section, Dr. Candlish [31] has discovered the traces of a Scotch hand. He points out that section 5 bears so close a resemblance to a passage in Gillespie's " Miscellany Questions " [32] as to suggest that the two came from the same pen.[33] Dr. Mitchell takes up the hint and feels sure that we may here trace Gillespie's authorship.[34] We place the two in parallel columns:

[31] *British and Foreign Evangelical Review* for January, 1877, p. 173.

[32] Chapter xxi. pp. 105–106, ed. 1844 (in " The Presbyterian's Armoury," ii. 1846).

[33] Gillespie's work was published posthumously in 1649, but may have been composed during the Assembly.

[34] " The Westminster Assembly," 1884, pp. 429 *sq.* (ed. 2. 1897, p. 441).

CONFESSION OF FAITH

"The heavenliness of the matter, the efficacy of the doctrine, the majesty of the style, the consent of all the parts, the scope of the whole (which is to give all glory to God), the full discovery it makes of the only way of man's salvation, the many other incomparable excellencies, and the entire perfection thereof, are arguments whereby it doth abundantly evidence itself to be the word of God."

GILLESPIE

"The Scripture is known to be indeed the word of God by the beams of divine authority which it hath in itself . . . such as the heavenliness of the matter; the majesty of the style; the irresistible power over the conscience; the general scope, to abase man and to exalt God; nothing driven at but God's glory and man's salvation; . . . the supernatural mysteries revealed therein, which could never have entered into the reason of men; the marvellous consent of all parts and passages (though written by divers and several penmen), even where there is some appearance of difference, . . . these, and the like, are characters and marks which evidence the Scriptures to be the word of God."

There is much here that belongs to the commonplaces of the time, and almost as close parallels to section 5 may be derived from the writings of several others of the Westminster Divines. Nevertheless the phraseology seems too closely similar for there not to have been some literary connection.

How closely the Westminster Confession held itself to the theological thought of its day may be illustrated from another parallel which we shall immediately give, in which the Confession is placed side by side with two of the chief popular dogmatic handbooks of the age. Ball's " Catechism " was in everybody's hand and is a very fair representative of the Puritan trend of thought. The " Body of Divinity," published by Downame in 1645, under Archbishop Usher's name, may not have been before the framers of this chapter before their work was well on its way.[35] The parallelism is so close, however, that it

[35] Exactly when the "Body of Divinity" was published is difficult to determine. Parr says, simply, during Usher's stay in Wales. Elrington helps us to come a little nearer. He tells us that Usher left Oxford in the spring of 1645 ("Life," etc., in his edition of Usher's "Works," i. 1864, p. 242) and was back in London in June, 1646. The date of Usher's letter to Downame repudiating responsibility for the work is May 13, 1645 (Elrington, p. 249); but this letter is apparently an answer to one which only contemplated publishing the book. It cannot be certain, however, that it was not already published when Usher wrote. On the other hand, the Committee on the Confession of Faith was first appointed as early as August 20, 1644; the actual drafting of the Confession was, however, committed to a Committee only on May 12, 1645. The first report of the chapter on the Scriptures was made on July 7, 1645. On the whole, it is not impossible that the "Body of Divinity" may have

is hard to believe that it did not affect some of the matter or even the phraseology. If not, the closeness of the parallels is a pointed indication of the great indebtedness of the Confession to the same general sources from which Usher drew the material for his " commonplace book." In any case, this parallel will measure for us the accord of the Westminster doctrine of Scripture with the current doctrine of the times among the pronounced Protestant party in England.[36]

BALL, "A Short Treatise containing all the Principal Grounds of Christian Religion," 15th impression, London, 1656.	CONFESSION OF FAITH	USHER, "The Sum and Substance of the Christian Religion," London, 1702.
P. 49: "The Gentiles by nature have the law written in their hearts."	I. i. a: "Although the light of nature, and the works of creation and providence, do so far manifest the goodness, wisdom, and power of God, as to leave men inexcusable;"	Pp. 3, 4: "By what means hath God revealed himself? By his divine **works** and by his holy word. . . . What be the divine works whereby God hath shewed himself? **The creation and preservation** of the world and all things therein. . . . What use is there of the knowledge obtained by the works of God? There is a double use. The one **to make men void of excuse;** as the Apostle teacheth, Rom. i. 20, and so it is sufficient unto condemnation. The other is to further unto salvation, and that by preparing and inducing men to seek God, if happily, by groping they may find him (as the Apostle sheweth, Acts xvii. 27), whereby they are made more apt to acknowledge him when he is perfectly revealed in his word. . . ." Cf. p. 23: "That this knowledge of God is to be had partly by his **works,** viz., so much as may serve to convince man and **make him inexcusable."**

been published in time to affect the draft. Nor is it impossible that it may have been known to the drafters in manuscript.

[36] Some of the phraseology, which seems specially suggestive of the relation of the Confession to Ball and Usher, has been put into broad-faced type, to attract the eye. In quoting, it may be added, certain liberties have been taken: the punctuation and orthography have not been followed strictly, and Scripture passages have been noted — when not passed over — in our usual way.

BALL

P. 46: "In respect of substance, the word of God was always necessary, without which we could (1) neither know, nor (2) worship God aright."

P. 4: "He sendeth us to his word alone for direction, how to attain salvation, Isa. viii. 20, Luk. x. 26; therefore none but he can reveal the way how we should obtain that everlasting inheritance, Psalm xvi. 11, Prov. ii. 6, 9."

P. 51: "Faith and obedience is the way to happiness, and the whole duty of man is faith working by love, which man could not learn of himself."

Pp. 5, 6: "What understand you by the word of God? By the word of God we understand the will of God revealed unto man being a reasonable creature, teaching him what to do, believe, and leave undone, Deut. xxix. 29. . . . Hath not this word been diversly made known heretofore? This word of God hath heretofore been diversly made known, Heb. i. 1, as (1) By inspiration, II Chr. xv. 1, Isa. lix. 21, II Pet. i. 21. (2) By ingraving in the heart, Rom. ii. 14. (3) By visions; Num. xii. 6, 8, Acts x. 10, 11, Apoc. i. 10. (4) By dreams, Job xxxiii. 14, 15, Gen. xl. 8. (5) By Urim and Thummim, Num. xxvii. 21, I Sam. xxx. 7, 8. (6) By signs, Gen. xxxii. 24, Exo. xiii. 21. (7) By audible voice, Exo. xx. 1, 2, Gen. xxii. 15. And lastly by writing, Exo. xvii. 14."

P. 7: "Why was the truth delivered to the church in writing? The truth of God was delivered to the church in writing, (1) That it might be

CONFESSION OF FAITH

I. i. b: "yet are they not sufficient to give that knowledge of God, and of his will, which is necessary unto salvation;"

[Cf. X. iv.]

I. i. c: "therefore it pleased the Lord, at sundry times, and in divers manners, to reveal himself, and to declare that his will unto his church;"

I. i. d: "and afterwards, for the better preserving and propagating of the truth, and for the more sure establishment and comfort of the church

USHER

P. 4: "Are not the works of God sufficient to give knowledge of the only true God and the way unto everlasting happiness? They may leave us without excuse, and so are sufficient unto condemnation; but are not able to make us wise unto salvation. Because of things which are necessary unto salvation, some they teach but imperfectly, others not at all, as the distinction of the persons in the Godhead, the fall of man from God, and the way to repair the same." Cf. p. 1: "May a man be saved by any religion? No, but only by the true, as appeareth by John xvii. 3."

P. 4: "Where then is the saving knowledge of God to be had perfectly? In his holy word. For God, 'according to the riches of his grace, hath been abundant towards us in all wisdom and understanding, and hath opened unto us the mystery of his will, according to his good pleasure, which he hath purposed in himself,' as the Apostle teacheth, Ephes. i. 7, 8, 9. What course did God hold in the delivery of his word unto men? In the beginning of the world he delivered his word by revelation and continued the knowledge thereof by *tradition*, while the number of his true worshippers was small. . . . Were these revelations in times past delivered all in the same manner? No. For (as the Apostle noteth, Heb. i. 1) 'at sundry times and in divers manners God spake in times past, unto the Fathers by the Prophets.' The divers kinds are set down in Num. xii. 6, and I Sam. xxviii. 6, and may be reduced to these two general heads: Oracles and Visions."

P. 4: "But after he chose a great and populous nation, in which he would be honoured and served, he caused the same to be committed to writing for

BALL	CONFESSION OF FAITH	USHER

preserved pure from corruption; (2) That it might be better conveyed to posterity; (3) That it might be an infallible standard of true doctrine; (4) That it might be the determiner of all controversies; (5) That our faith might be confirmed, beholding the accomplishment of things prophesied; And (6) for the more full instruction of the church, the time of the Messias either drawing nigh, or being come." P. 46: "Without which, error in doctrine and manners is unavoidable."

against the corruption of the flesh, and the malice of Satan and the world, to commit the same wholly unto writing;"

all ages to the end of the world. . . . Yet so that in half that time, God's will was also revealed without writing, extraordinarily, and the Holy Books indited one after another, according to the necessity of the times; but in this last half, the whole canon of the Scriptures being fully finished, we and all men, unto the world's end, are left to have our full instruction from the same, without expecting extraordinary revelations, as in times past."

P. 46: "In respect of the manner of revealing in writing, the Scriptures were necessary ever since it pleased God after that manner to make known his will, and so shall be to the end of the world."

I. i. e: "which maketh the Holy Scripture to be most necessary;

those former ways of God's revealing his will unto his people being now ceased."

P. 5: "Where then is the word of God now certainly to be learned? Only out of the book of God contained in the Holy Scriptures; which are the only certain testimonies unto the church of the word of God.

"Why may not men want the Scriptures now, as they did at the first from the creation until the time of Moses, for the space of 2513 years? First, because then God immediately by his voice and Prophets sent from him, taught the church his truth; which now are ceased." P. 4: "But in this last half, the whole canon of the Scriptures being fully finished, we and all men unto the world's end, are left to have our full instruction from the same, without expecting extraordinary revelations as in times past."

P. 6: "What call you the word of God? The Holy Scripture, immediately inspired, which is contained in the books of the Old and New Testament." Pp. 7, 8: "What is it to be immediately inspired? To be immediately inspired, is to be as it were breathed, and to come from the Father by the Holy Ghost, without all means. Were the Scriptures thus inspired? Thus the Holy Scriptures in the originals were inspired both for matter and words. What are the books of the Old Testament? Moses

I. ii : "Under the name of Holy Scripture, or the word of God written,

are now contained all the books of the Old and New Testament, which are these:

[Catalogue.]

P. 5: "What is Scripture then? The word of God written by men inspired by the Holy Ghost for the perfect building and salvation of the church; or holy books written by the inspiration of God to make us wise unto salvation. If the Scriptures be written by men, which are subject unto infirmities; how can it be accounted the word of God? Because it proceeded 'not from the will or mind of man,' but 'holy men' set apart by God for that work, spake and writ 'as they were moved by the

BALL

and the Prophets. What mean you by the books of the Old Testament? All the books of Holy Scripture, given by God to the church of the Jews." P. 9: "Which are the books of the New Testament? Matthew, Mark, Luke and the rest as they follow in our Bibles." P. 1: "What ought to be the chief and continual care of every man in this life? To glorify God and save his soul." P. 4: "Whence must we take directions to attain hereunto? Out of the word of God alone."

CONFESSION OF FAITH

All which are given by inspiration of God, to be the rule of faith and life."

USHER

Holy Ghost.' Therefore God alone is to be accounted the *Author* thereof, who inspired the hearts of those holy men, whom he chose to be his secretaries; who are to be held only the *instrumental causes* thereof. . . ." P. 10: "What books are the Holy Scriptures; and by whom were they written? First, the books of the Old Testament, in number nine and thirty, . . . written by Moses and the Prophets, who delivered the same to the church of the Jews. Secondly, the books of the New Testament, in number seven and twenty, written by the Apostles and Evangelists, who delivered them to the church of the Gentiles."
[Catalogue, pp. 11, 14.]

I. iii.: "The books commonly called Apocrypha, not being of divine inspiration, are no part of the canon of the Scripture; and therefore are of no authority in the church of God, nor to be any otherwise approved, or made use of, than other human writings."

Pp. 11, 12: "Are there no other canonical books of the Scripture of the Old Testament besides these that you have named? No; for those other books which papists would obtrude unto us for canonical, are apocryphal, that is to say, such as are to lie hid when there is proof to be made of religion. How prove you that these apocryphal books are no part of the canonical Scriptures? First, they are not written first in Hebrew, the language of the church before Christ, which all the books of the Old Testament were originally written in. Secondly, **they were never received into the canon of Scripture by the church** of the Jews before Christ (to whom alone in those times the oracles of God were committed, Rom. iii. 2), nor read and expounded in their synagogues. See *Josephus Contra Appion, lib.* i. and *Eusebius, lib.* iii. 10. Thirdly, the Jews were so careful to keep Scripture entire as they kept the number of the verses and letters; within which is none of the Apocrypha. Fourthly, the Scripture of the Old Testament was written by Prophets, . . . But Malachi

BALL   CONFESSION OF FAITH   USHER

was the last Prophet, after whom all the Apocrypha was written. Fifthly, they are not authorized by Christ and his Apostles who do give testimony unto the Scriptures. Sixthly, by the most ancient Fathers and Councils of the primitive churches after the Apostles, . . . they have not been admitted for trial of truth. . . . Seventhly, there is no such constant truth in them as in the canonical Scriptures. For every book of them hath falsehoods in doctrine or history."

Pp. 44, 45: "What is the divine authority of Holy Scripture? Such is the excellency of the Holy Scripture above all other writings whatsoever, that it ought to be credited in all narrations, threatenings, promises, or prophesies, and obeyed in all commandments. Whence hath it this authority? **From God the author thereof**, he being of incomprehensible wisdom, great goodness, absolute power and dominion, and truth that can neither deceive or be deceived. Doth the authority of the Scripture wholly depend upon God? **The authority of the Scripture doth only and wholly depend upon God the author of it.** May not one part of Scripture be preferred before another? Though one part may be preferred before another, in respect of excellency of matter and use, yet in authority and certainty, every part is equal. Is any other writing of equal authority to the Scripture? Only Scripture is of divine authority."

I. iv.: "The authority of the Holy Scripture, for which it ought to be believed and obeyed, dependeth not upon the testimony of any man or church, but wholly upon God (who is truth itself), the author thereof; and therefore it is to be received, because it is the word of God."

P. 15: "The authority of these holy writings, inspired by God, is highest in the church, as the authority of God; whereunto no learning or decrees of angels or men, under what name or color soever it be commended, may be accounted equal, . . . neither can they be judged or sentenced by any."

P. 10: "Reason or witnesses of men; unto which it is unmeet that the word of God should be subject, as papists hold, when they teach that the Scriptures receive their authority from the church. For by thus hanging the credit and authority of the Scriptures on the church's sentence, they make the church's word of more credit than the word of God. Whereas the Scriptures of God cannot be judged or sentenced by any; and God only is a worthy witness of himself, in his word, and by his Spirit; which give mutual testimony one of the other, and work that assurance of faith in his children, that no human demonstrations can make, nor any persuasions or enforcements of the world can remove.'

P. 9: "How may it be proved that these books are the word of God immediately inspired by the Holy Ghost to the Prophets and Apostles? First, by the testimony of the church; sec-

I. v. a: "We may be moved and induced by the testimony of the church to an high and reverent esteem of the Holy Scripture;"

P. 6: "How may it appear therefore, that this book which you call the book of God, and the Holy Scripture, is the word of God indeed and not men's policies? By the constant testi-

BALL   CONFESSION OF FAITH   USHER

ondly, CONSTANCY OF THE SAINTS; thirdly, MIRACLES WROUGHT TO CONFIRM THE TRUTH; and fourthly, BY THE ANTIQUITY THEREOF." P. 15: "What understand you by the church? By the church we understand not the pope, whom the papists call the church virtual; nor his bishops and cardinals met in general council, whom they call the church representative; but the whole company of believers, who have professed the true faith; whether those who received the books of holy Scripture from the Prophets and Apostles, or those who lived after." Pp. 16–18: "How is this testimony of the church considered? The testimony of the church is considered, (1) Of the Jews; (2) Of the Christians. What books did the Jews receive? The church of the Jews professed the doctrine and received the books of the Old Testament, and testified of them that they were divine. What things give force to this testimony? To the testimony of the Jews, these things give force. (1) To them were committed the oracles of God. (2) In great misery they have constantly confessed the same. . . . (3) Notwithstanding the high Priests and others persecuted the Prophets while they lived, yet they received their writings as prophetical and divine. (4) Since obstinacy is come to Israel, notwithstanding their great hatred to the Christian religion, the holy Scripture of the Old Testament is kept pure and uncorrupt amongst them, even in those places which do evidently confirm the truth of Christian religion. What books did the Christian church receive? The Christian church hath embraced the doctrine of God, and received the books both of the Old and New Testament. What things give weight to this testimony? To the testi-

mony of men in all ages, from them that first knew these penmen of the Holy Ghost with their writings, until our time; and reasons taken out of the works themselves, agreeable to the quality of the writers. Both which kinds of arguments the Holy Scriptures have as much and far more than any other writings. Wherefore, as it were extreme impudence, to deny the works of Homer, Plato, Virgil, Tully, Livy, Galen, and such like, which the consent of all ages have received and delivered unto us; which also by the tongue, phrase, matter, and all other circumstances agreeable, are confirmed to be the works of the same authors whose they are testified to be: so it were more than brutish madness to doubt of the certain truth and authority of the Holy Scriptures, which no less but much more than any other writings, for their authors, are testified and confirmed to be the sacred word of the ever-living God. Not only testified (I say) by the uniform witness of men in all ages, but also confirmed by such reasons taken out of the writings themselves, as do sufficiently argue the Spirit of God to be the author of them. For we may learn out of the testimonies themselves (as David did, Psl. cxix. 152) that God hath established them forever." P. 9: . . . "The church of the Jews until the coming of Christ in the flesh, embraced all the former writings of the Prophets as the book of God. Christ himself appealeth unto them as a sufficient testimony of him, John v. 39. The Apostles and Evangelists prove the writings of the New Testament by them: and the catholic church of Christ, from the Apostles' time unto this day, hath acknowledged all the said writings, both of the Old and New Testaments, to be the undoubted word of God. Thus have we the testimony both of

BALL · CONFESSION OF FAITH · USHER

mony of Christians, two things give force: (1) Their great constancy. (2) Their admirable and sweet consent: for in other matters we may observe differences in opinion, in this a singular and wonderful agreement. How many ways is this testimony of Christians considered? This testimony of Christians is considered three ways: (1) Of the universal church, which from the beginning thereof, until these times, professing the Christian religion to be divine, doth also profess that these books are of God. (2) Of the several primitive churches, which first received the books of the Old Testament, and the Epistles written from the Apostles, to them, their pastors, or some they knew; and after delivered them under the same title to their successors, and other churches. (3) Of the pastors and doctors, who (being furnished with skill, both in the tongues and matters divine) upon due trial and examination have pronounced their judgment and approved them to the people committed to their charge. Of what force is this testimony? This testimony of the church is of great weight and importance: (1) It is profitable to prepare the heart and to move it to believe. (2) It is of all human testimonies (whereby the author of any book that hath, is, or shall be extant, can be proved) the greatest, both in respect of the multitude, wisdom, honesty, faithfulness of the witnesses; and the likeness, constancy and continuance of the testimony itself. (3) But this testimony is only human. (4) Not the only, nor the chief whereby the truth and divinity of the Scripture is confirmed. (5) Neither can it be the ground of divine faith and assurance."

[The other items mentioned in the first question quoted are then treated in similar manner.]

the old church of the Jews, God's peculiar people and first-born, to whom the oracles of God were committed, and the new of Christians: together with the general account which all the godly at all times have made of the Scriptures, when they have crossed their natures and courses, as accounting it in their souls, to be of God; and the special testimony of martyrs who have sealed the certainty of the same, by shedding their blood for them. Hereunto also may be added the testimony of those who are out of the church; heathens, out of whom many ancient testimonies are cited, to this purpose by *Josephus contra Appion*, Turks, Jews, (who to this day acknowledge all the books of the Old Testament) and heretics, who labor to shroud themselves under them."

BALL	CONFESSION OF FAITH	USHER

BALL

P. 21: "How else may it be proved that these books are the word of God? BY THE style, efficacy, sweet consent, admirable doctrine, excellent end AND THE WITNESS OF THE SCRIPTURE ITSELF." P. 23: "These things declare the majesty of the style." P. 27: "The efficacy of this doctrine doth powerfully demonstrate the divinity thereof." P. 31: "The sweet and admirable consent which is found in all and every part of Scripture cannot be ascribed to any but to the Spirit of God, each part so exactly agreeing with itself and with the whole." P. 35: "The matter treated of in Holy Scripture is divine and wonderful." P. 38: "The end of the Scripture is divine, viz. (1) The glory of God: and (2) The salvation of man, not temporal but eternal." Pp. 39, 40: "These arguments are of great force, whether they be severally or jointly considered; and do as strongly prove that the Christian religion is only true, as any other reason can, that there was, is, or ought to be any true religion. . . . The testimony of the Scripture itself . . . is (1) most clear, (2) certain, (3) infallible, (4) public, and (5) of itself worthy credit."

CONFESSION OF FAITH

I. v. b: "and the heavenliness of the matter, the efficacy of the doctrine, the majesty of the style, the consent of all the parts, the scope of the whole (which is to give all glory to God), the full discovery it makes of the only way of man's salvation, the many other incomparable excellencies, and the entire perfection thereof, are arguments whereby it doth abundantly evidence itself to be the word of God;"

USHER

Pp. 6, 7, 8: "Let me hear some of those reasons which prove that God is the author of the Holy Scriptures. . . . Fourthly, the matter of the Holy Scripture being altogether of heavenly doctrine, . . . declareth the God of heaven to be the only inspirer of it. Fifthly, the doctrine of the Scripture is such as could never breed in the brains of man. . . . Sixthly, the sweet concord between these writings and the perfect coherence of all things contained in them. . . . For there is a most holy and heavenly consent and agreement of all parts thereof. . . . Seventhly, a continuance of wonderful prophecies. . . . Eighthly, the great majesty, full of heavenly wisdom and authority, such as is meet to proceed from the glory of God, shining in all the Holy Scriptures: yea, oftentimes under great simplicity of words, and plainness and easiness of style. . . . Ninthly, in speaking of matters of the highest nature, they . . . absolutely require credit to be given to them. . . . Tenthly, the end and scope of the Scriptures, is for the advancement of God's glory and the salvation of man's soul. . . . Eleventhly, the admirable power and force that is in them to convert and alter men's minds." . . . etc.

BALL

Pp. 40 *sq.*: "Is this testimony of force to open the eyes or assure the heart? No, for the external light of arguments, and testimonies brought to confirm and demonstrate, must be distinguished from the inward operation of the Holy Ghost, opening our eyes to see the light shining in the Scripture and to discern the sense thereof. These reasons may convince any, be he never so obstinate: but are they sufficient to persuade the heart thereof? No; the testimony of the Spirit is necessary and

CONFESSION OF FAITH

I. v. c: "yet, notwithstanding, our full persuasion and assurance of the infallible truth and divine authority thereof, is from the inward work of the Holy Spirit, bearing witness by and with the word in our hearts."

USHER

P. 9: "Are these motives of themselves sufficient to work saving faith, and persuade us fully to rest in God's word? No. Besides all these, it is required, that we have the Spirit of God, as well to open our eyes to see the light, as to seal up fully unto our hearts that truth which we see with our eyes. For the same Holy Spirit that inspired the Scriptures, inclineth the hearts of God's children to believe what is revealed in them, and inwardly assureth them, above all reasons and arguments, that

BALL   CONFESSION OF FAITH   USHER

only all-sufficient for this purpose. Why is the testimony of the Spirit necessary? Because by nature we are blind in spiritual things. Though therefore the Scripture be a shining light, yet unless our eyes be opened, we cannot see it, no more than a blind man doth the sun. Why is the testimony of the Spirit all-sufficient? (1) Because the Spirit is the author of supernatural light and faith. (2) By the inspiration thereof were the Scriptures written. (3) The secrets of God are fully known unto, and effectually revealed by, the Spirit. (4) The same law which is written in the Scriptures, the Spirit doth write in the hearts of men that be indued therewith. For which reasons it must needs be that the testimony of the Spirit is all-sufficient to persuade and assure the heart that the Scriptures are the word of God."

these are the Scriptures of God." . . . P. 10: " This testimony of God's Spirit in the hearts of his faithful, as it is proper to the word of God, so is it greater than any human persuasions grounded upon reason or witnesses of men: unto which it is unmeet that the word of God should be subject, as papists hold, when they teach that the Scriptures receive their authority from the church," etc. [as above on I. iv.].

Pp. 47–49: "Whatsoever was, is, or shall be necessary or profitable to be known, believed, practised or hoped for, that is fully comprehended in the books of the Prophets and Apostles. . . . The perfection of the Scripture will more plainly appear, if we consider, (1) That religion for the substance thereof, was ever one and unchangeable. (2) The law of God, written by Moses and the Prophets, did deliver whatsoever is needful for, and behoveful to the salvation of the Israelites. (3) Our Saviour 1. Made known unto his Disciples the last and full will of his heavenly Father, and 2. What they received of him they faithfully preached unto the world, and 3. The sum of what they preached is committed to writing. (4) There is nothing necessary to be known of Christians, over and above that which is found in the Old Testament, which is not plainly, clearly and fully set down, and

I. vi. a: "The whole counsel of God, concerning all things necessary for his own glory, man's salvation, faith, and life, is either expressly set down in Scripture, or by good and necessary consequence may be deduced from Scripture: unto which nothing at any time is to be added, whether by new revelations of the Spirit, or traditions of men."

P. 15: "Since God hath appointed the Holy Scriptures, which bear witness of Christ, to be written for our learning: He will have no other doctrine pertaining to eternal life to be received, but that which is consonant unto them, and hath the ground thereof in them. Therefore unto them only is the church directed for the saving knowledge of God." Also: "The books of Holy Scripture are so sufficient for the knowledge of Christian religion, that they do most plentifully contain all doctrine necessary to salvation. They being perfectly profitable to instruct to salvation in themselves, and all other imperfectly profitable thereunto, further than they draw from them. Whence it followeth that we need no unwritten verities, no traditions, or inventions of men, no canons of Councils, no sentences of Fathers, much less decrees of popes, for to supply any supposed defect of the written

BALL

to be gathered out of the writings of the Apostles and Evangelists. . . . In the whole body of the Scripture, all doubts and controversies are perfectly decided, and every particular book is sufficiently perfect for the proper end thereof. What use is to be made hereof? Unwritten traditions, new articles of faith, and new visions and revelations are now to be rejected."

Pp. 49, 50: "To a natural man the Gospel is obscure, accounted foolishness. . . . Things necessary to salvation are so clearly laid down that the simplest, indued with the Spirit, cannot be altogether ignorant of the same. . . . But to them that are in part illightened many things are obscure and dark."

P. 49: "In themselves the whole Scripture is easy, for such excellent matter could not be delivered in more significant and fit words. But all things in Scripture are not alike manifest. . . . Things necessary to salvation are so clearly laid down that the simplest, indued with the Spirit, cannot be altogether ignorant of the same. . . ." Pp. 56–57: "What be the means to find out the true meaning of the Scriptures? . . . (1) Conference of one place of Scripture with another. . . . (2) Diligent consideration of the scope. (3) And circumstances of the place. . . . (4) Consideration of the matter

CONFESSION OF FAITH

I. vi. b: "Nevertheless we acknowledge the inward illumination of the Spirit of God to be necessary for the saving understanding of such things as are revealed in the word;"

I. vi. c: "and that there are some circumstances concerning the worship of God, and government of the church, common to human actions and societies, which are to be ordered by the light of nature and Christian prudence, according to the general rules of the word, which are always to be observed."

I. vii. a: "All things in Scripture are not alike plain in themselves, nor alike clear unto all; yet those things which are necessary to be known, believed, and observed, for salvation, are so clearly propounded and opened in some place of Scripture or other, that not only the learned, but the unlearned, in a due use of the ordinary means, may attain unto a sufficient understanding of them."

USHER

word, or for to give us a more perfect direction in the worship of God, and the way of life, than is already expressed in the canonical Scriptures." P. 17: "It ought to be no controversy amongst Christians, that the whole Scriptures of the Old and New Testament doth most richly and abundantly contain all that is necessary for a Christian man to believe and to do for eternal salvation."

P. 18: "All which are dark and difficult unto those whose eyes the God of this world hath blinded. But unto such as are by grace enlightened and made willing to understand, howsoever some things remain obscure to exercise their diligence, yet the *fundamental doctrines* of faith and precepts of life are all plain and perspicuous."

P. 18: "There are some things hard in the Scriptures that have proper relation to the time in which the Scripture was written and uttered, which are prophesies of things to be fulfilled hereafter; which if we never understand, we shall be never the worse for the attaining of everlasting salvation. . . . For all doctrine necessary to be known unto eternal salvation, is set forth in the Scriptures most clearly and plainly, even to the capacity and understanding of the simple and unlearned." P. 19: "These matters indeed are above human reason: and therefore are we to bring faith

BALL   CONFESSION OF FAITH   USHER

whereof it doth entreat. . . . (5) And circumstances of persons, times and places. . . . (6) Also consideration whether the words be spoken figuratively or simply. . . . (7) And knowledge of the arts and tongues wherein the Scriptures were originally written. . . . (8) But always it is to be observed that obscure places are not to be expounded contrary to the rule of faith set down in plainer places of the Scripture."

to believe them, not human reason to comprehend them. But they are delivered in Scripture in as plain terms as such matter can be." "The whole doctrine of salvation is to be found so plain that it needeth no commentary. And commentaries are for other places that are dark; and also to make more large use of Scripture than a new beginner can make of himself; which we see necessary in all human arts and sciences."

P. 54: "The Scriptures were written in Hebrew and Greek."
P. 6: "The Holy Scripture, immediately inspired, which is contained in the books of the Old and New Testament." Pp. 7, 8: "To be immediately inspired is to be as it were breathed, and to come from the Father by the Holy Ghost, without all means." "Thus the Holy Scriptures in the originals were inspired, both for matter and words."

I. viii. a: "The Old Testament in Hebrew (which was the native language of the people of God of old), and the New Testament in Greek (which at the time of the writing of it was most generally known to the nations), being immediately inspired by God,"

P. 10: "What language were the books of the Old Testament written in? In Hebrew: which was the first tongue of the world, and the most orderly speech; in comparison of which all other languages may be condemned of barbarous confusion; But chosen specially, because it was the language at that time best known unto the church (teaching that all of them should understand the Scriptures). Only some few portions by the later prophets were left written in the Chaldean tongue (understood by God's people after their carrying away into Babylon)." P. 14: "In what language were the books of the New Testament written? In Greek, because it was the most common language, best known then to Jews and Gentiles; teaching that all kingdoms should have the Scriptures in a language which they understand."
[On Inspiration, see above, on I. ii., and cf. p. 10, where the aboriginality of the Hebrew vowel points is defended.]

I. viii. b: "and by his singular care and providence kept pure in all ages,

P. 8: "The marvellous preservation of the Scriptures. Though none in time be so ancient, nor none so much oppugned; yet God hath still by his Providence preserved them and every part of them."
Pp. 20, 21: "Although in the Hebrew copies there hath been observed by the Masorites, some very few differences of

BALL | CONFESSION OF FAITH | USHER

words, by similitude of letters and points; and by the learned in the Greek tongue, there are like diversities of readings noted in the Greek text of the New Testament, which came by fault of writers: yet in most by circumstance of the place, and conference of other places, the true reading may be discerned. And albeit in all it cannot. . . . yet this diversity or difficulty can make no difference or uncertainty in the sum and substance of Christian religion; because the Ten Commandments, and the principal texts of Scripture on which the Articles of our faith are grounded, the sacraments instituted, the form of prayer taught (which contain the sum or substance of Christian religion) are without all such diversity of reading. . . . so plainly set down . . . that no man can make any doubt of them, or pick any quarrel against them." P. 20: "**The original languages . . . in them only the Scriptures are for the letter to be held authentical.** And as the water is most pure in the fountain or spring thereof: so the right understanding of the words of the Holy Scriptures is most certain in the original tongues of Hebrew and Greek in which they were first written and delivered to the church. . . . All translations are to be judged, examined, and reformed according to the text of the ancient Hebrew and original Chaldee . . . and the Greek text. . . . Consequently that the vulgar Latin, etc."

(middle column) are therefore authentical;

so as in all controversies of religion the church is finally to appeal unto them."

Pp. 52 *sq.*: "**Doth the knowledge of the Scriptures belong unto all men?** Yes, all men are not only allowed, but exhorted and commanded to read, hear and understand the Scripture. . . . (1) Because the Scriptures teach the way of life, (2) Set forth the duties of every man in his place and estate of life,

I. viii. c: "But because these original tongues are not known to all the people of God who have right unto, and interest in the Scriptures, and are commanded, in the fear of God, to read and search them, therefore they are to be translated into the vulgar language of every nation unto which they

P. 20: ". . . Out of which languages they must be truly translated for the understanding of them that have not the knowledge of those tongues." P. 22: "The Holy Scriptures are reverently and profitably to be read and heard of all sorts and degrees of men and women; and therefore to be truly trans-

BALL

(3) Are the ground of faith, (4) The epistle of God sent to his Church, (5) His testament wherein we may find what legacies he hath bequeathed unto us, (6) The sword of the Spirit, (7) Being known and embraced, they make a man happy, but (8) Being neglected or contemned, they plunge men into all misery. . . . All men of what age, estate, quality or degree soever, ought to acquaint themselves with the word of God." P. 54: "The Scriptures were written in Hebrew and Greek, how then should all men read and understand them? They ought to be translated into known tongues and interpreted. . . . (1) Because the Prophets and Apostles preached their doctrines to the people and nations in their known languages, (2) Immediately after the Apostles' times, many translations were extant, (3) All things must be done in the congregation unto edifying, I Cor. xiv. 26, but an unknown tongue doth not edify, and (4) All are commanded to try the spirits."

Pp. 55–57: "Is the sense of Scripture one or manifold? Of one place of Scripture, there is but one proper and natural sense, though sometimes things are so expressed, as that the things themselves do signify other matters, according to the Lord's ordinance. Are we tied to the exposition of the Fathers? We are not necessarily tied to the exposition of Fathers or Councils for the finding out of the sense of Scripture. Who is the faithful interpreter of the Scripture? The Holy Ghost speaking in the Scripture is the only faithful interpreter of the Scripture. What be the means to find out the true meaning of the Scriptures? The means to find out the true meaning of the Scriptures, are (1) Conference of one place of Scripture with another. . . . (8) But always it is to be

CONFESSION OF FAITH

come, that the word of God dwelling plentifully in all, they may worship him in an acceptable manner, and through patience and comfort of the Scriptures, may have hope."

I. ix.: "The infallible rule of interpretation of Scripture, is the Scripture itself; and therefore, when there is a question about the true and full sense of any Scripture (which is not manifold, but one), it must be searched and known by other places that speak more clearly."

USHER

lated out of the original tongues into the language of every nation which desireth to know them. For the lay people as well as the learned must read the Scriptures or hear them read, both privately and openly, so as they may receive profit by them: and consequently in a tongue they understand." P. 23: "It were happy if they could understand the Hebrew and Greek; but, howsoever, they may read translations."

P. 20: "What assurance may be had of the right understanding the Holy Scriptures? For the words, it is to be had out of the original text, or translations of the same: for the sense or meaning, only out of the Scriptures themselves (Nehem. viii. 8), which by places plain and evident, do express whatsoever is obscure and hard touching matters necessary to eternal salvation." P. 21: "Why must the true sense or meaning of the Scriptures be learned out of the Scriptures themselves? Because the Spirit of God alone is the certain interpreter of his word, written by his Spirit." (I Cor. ii. 11, II Pet. i. 20, 21.) "The interpretation therefore must be by the same Spirit by which the Scripture was written: of which Spirit we have no certainty upon any man's credit,

BALL

CONFESSION OF FAITH

USHER

observed that obscure places are not to be expounded contrary to the rule of faith set down in plainer places of the Scripture."

but only so far forth as his saying may be confirmed by the Holy Scripture. What gather you from hence? That no interpretation of holy Fathers, popes, Councils, custom or practice of the church, either contrary to the manifest words of the Scripture, or containing matters which cannot necessarily be proved out of the Scriptures are to be received as an undoubted truth. How then is Scripture to be interpreted by Scripture? According to the *analogy of faith* (Rom. xii. 6), and the scope and circumstances of the present, place; and conference of other plain and evident places, by which all such as are obscure and hard to be understood, ought to be interpreted. For there is no matter necessary to eternal life which is not plainly and sufficiently set forth in many places of Scripture; by which other places . . . may be interpreted."

I. x.: "The Supreme Judge, by which all controversies of religion are to be determined, and all decrees of councils, opinions of ancient writers, doctrines of men, and private spirits, are to be examined, and in whose sentence we are to rest, can be no other but the Holy Spirit speaking in the Scripture."

P. 15: "These Holy Scriptures are the rule, the line, the square, the light, whereby to examine and try all judgments and sayings of men and angels. . . . All traditions, revelations, decrees of Councils, opinions of doctors, &c., are to be embraced so far forth as they may be proved out of the divine Scriptures, and not otherwise. So that from them only, all doctrine concerning our salvation must be drawn and derived: that only is to be taken for truth, in matters appertaining to Christian religion, which is agreeable unto them; and whatsoever disagreeth from them is to be refused." Also: "The authority of these holy writings, inspired of God, is highest in the church, as the authority of God; whereunto no learning or decrees of angels or men, under what name or color soever it be commended, may be accounted equal, neither can they be judged or sentenced by any."

III. The Contents of the Chapter

As the Confession accords with the fundamental idea and ordinary practice of the Reformed theology, in beginning its exposition of doctrine with the doctrine of Holy Scripture, as the root out of which all doctrine grows, because the Scriptures are the fountain from which all knowledge of God's saving purpose and plan flows; so in stating the doctrine of Scripture it follows the logical and natural order of topics which had been wrought out by and become fixed in the Reformed theology. First, the necessity of the Scriptures is asserted and exhibited (section 1). Then Scripture is defined, both extensively, or in relation to its general contents, in other words as to the Canon, and intensively, or in relation to its essential character, in other words as to its inspiration; and this definition is applied to the exclusion of the apocryphal books (sections 2 and 3). Then the three great properties of Scripture are taken up: its authority (sections 4 and 5), its completeness or perfection (section 6), and its perspicuity (section 7). The chapter closes with a statement of certain important corollaries, as to the use that is to be made of Scripture, with especial reference to its transmission, whether in the originals or translations, to its interpretation, and to its final authority in controversies (sections 8, 9, and 10).

In somewhat greater detail, the scheme of the chapter is, therefore, the following:

I. The Necessity of Scripture, § 1.
   1. Reality and Trustworthiness of Natural Revelation.
   2. Insufficiency of Natural Revelation.
   3. Reality and Importance of Supernatural Revelation.
   4. Its complete Commitment to Inspired Scriptures.
   5. Consequent Necessity of Scripture.
II. The Definition of Scripture, §§ 2 and 3.
   1. Extensively: The Canon, § 2a.
   2. Intensively: Inspiration, § 2b.
   3. Exclusively: The Apocrypha, § 3.
III. The Properties of Scripture, §§ 4–7.

1. The Authority of Scripture, §§ 4 and 5.
   A. The Source of the Authority of Scripture, § 4.
   B. The Proof of the Authority of Scripture, § 5.
      (a) The Reality and Value of the *External* Evidence.
      (b) The Reality and Value of the *Internal* Evidence.
      (c) The Necessity and Function of the *Divine* Evidence.
2. The Perfection of Scripture, § 6.
   A. Absolute Objective Completeness of Scripture, for the purpose for which it is given.
   B. Need of Spiritual Illumination for its full use.
   C. Place for Christian Prudence and Right Reason.
3. The Perspicuity of Scripture, § 7.
   A. Diversity in Scripture in Point of Clearness.
   B. Clear Revelation of all Necessary Truth.
   C. Accessibility of Saving Truth by Ordinary Means.
IV. The Use of Scripture, §§ 8–10.
   1. In Relation to Its Form and Transmission, § 8.
      A. Primary Value and Authority of the Originals.
         (a) The immediate Inspiration of the Hebrew and Greek Scriptures.
         (b) Their Providential Preservation in Purity.
      B. The Right, Duty, and Adequacy of Translations.
   2. In Relation to Interpretation, § 9.
      A. Scripture Alone the Infallible Interpreter of Scripture.
      B. The Single Sense of Scripture.
   3. In Relation to Controversies, § 10.
      A. Scripture the Supreme Judge in Controversy.
      B. Scripture the Test of all Other Sources of Truth.

Within this scheme, the common Reformed doctrine of Scripture is developed with great richness and beauty of thought and expression. We shall seek to outline the matter of the statement as briefly as possible.[37] To this outline we

[37] Formal expositions of this chapter may be found in Shaw's (Whitburn, 1845; Philadelphia, 1846), Hodge's (Philadelphia, 1869), and Macpherson's (Edinburgh, 1881) commentaries on the Confession. The first is the most practical, the second the most doctrinal, and the third the most historical. See also an article by Dr. James S. Candlish, on "The Doctrine of the Westminster Confession on Scripture," in *The British and Foreign Evangelical Review,* for 1877; the chapters on the Internal Evidence and the Testimony of the Spirit, in Dr. Cunningham's "Theological Lectures"; and Dr. Alexander F.

shall add (under each head, successively) a few illustrative extracts from the writings of the members of the Westminster Assembly, which may serve to enable the reader to enter more readily into the atmosphere of their symbolical statements. These extracts could be almost indefinitely increased in number, but it is hoped that enough are given to serve the purpose in view.

THE NECESSITY OF SCRIPTURE

I. First, then, the Confession expounds the necessity of Scripture, in a paragraph which has always been admired, no less for the chaste beauty of its language than for the justness of its conception.

The paragraph opens with the recognition of the reality and trustworthiness of the natural revelation of God. The scope of this natural revelation is briefly defined as embracing " the goodness, wisdom, and power of God." This is afterwards more fully stated in chapter xxi. 1: " The light of nature showeth that there is a God, who hath Lordship and sovereignty over all; is good, and doeth good unto all; and is therefore to be feared, loved, praised, called upon, trusted in, and served with all the heart, and with all the soul, and with all the might." The effect of this natural revelation, in rendering men inexcusable for not yielding God the service which is His due, is pointed out. Then its insufficiency " to give that knowledge of God, and of His will, which is necessary unto salvation " is explained. This fundamental point, also, is returned to at a later place in the Confession (x. 4), when, in exact harmony with what is here said, it is declared that " men not professing the Christian religion " cannot " be saved in any other way whatsoever, be they never so diligent to frame their lives according to the light of nature, and the law of that religion they do profess." The parallel question and answer of the Larger Catechism (Q. 60) still further exhibits the care of the framers

---

Mitchell's remarks in his lecture on " The Westminster Confession " in his Baird Lectures on " The Westminster Assembly," and in his Introduction to the " Minutes of the . . . Westminster Assembly."

of the Confession to hold forth the Gospel of the grace of God as the only saving power on earth. " Q. Can they who have never heard the Gospel, and so know not Jesus Christ, nor believe in Him, be saved by living according to the light of nature? A. They who, having never heard the Gospel, know not Jesus Christ, and believe not in Him, cannot be saved, be they never so diligent to frame their lives according to the light of nature, or the laws of that religion which they profess; neither is there salvation in any other but in Christ alone, who is the Saviour only of His body, the Church."

It was because of this insufficiency of the natural revelation, that (so the Confession teaches) God in His goodness was led to give a supernatural revelation to His Church, of " His will which is necessary unto salvation." The manner of this supernatural revelation is suggested; it was in parts and by stages, i.e. progressive — " at sundry times and in divers manners." Nor was the goodness of God exhausted in merely making known the saving truth unto men; he took means to preserve the knowledge of it and to propagate it. The Confession teaches that " for the better preserving and propagating of the truth, and for the more sure establishment and comfort of the Church against the corruptions of the flesh, and the malice of Satan and of the world," God, after revealing Himself and His will necessary unto salvation, was pleased " to commit the same wholly unto writing." This declares the written Scriptures to be, at least in part, subsequent to the revelation of God's will; and so far distinguishes them from, and makes them, in this sense, the record of, revelation; a " record," however, made by God Himself, since it was He who committed the revelation to writing. The importance and value of such a commitment to writing is also moderately and winningly stated. It is not affirmed that it was necessary for God to commit His revelation to writing, in order to do justice to man on the one side, or in order to prevent the truth from perishing utterly on the other. It was a matter of " good pleasure " for Him to fix His revelations in writing as truly as it was for Him to give them at all. It was only for " the *better* preserving and propagating of the truth, and for the *more* sure establishment and comfort of the Church " that He committed His revelations wholly to writing. Had they been left unwritten and been committed for safe-keeping and transmission to the native powers of men, they might possibly have been (in some form or other) by God's good providence preserved and propagated, but not so well, so surely, or so safely as in written form. Inspiration is in order to the accurate preservation and wide propagation of the truth, not in order to its very existence, nor (had God chosen so to order it) to its persistence.[38]

All this is the groundwork for the proof of the necessity of the Scriptures. This comes in the further declaration: " Which maketh the Holy Scripture to be most necessary; those former ways of God's revealing His will unto His people being now ceased." The necessity of Scripture is thus made to rest on the insufficiency of natural revelation and the cessation of supernatural revelation — the record of which latter Scripture is declared to be, though a record of such sort that it is itself a revelation of God, since it was God and not merely man who committed His will " wholly unto writing." By this statement the Scriptures are contrasted, not with revelation as something different in kind and quality from it, but with *other forms* of revelation, as being themselves a substantive part of God's revelation: " *Those former ways* of God's revealing His will unto His people being now ceased." Among the ways in which

[38] Mr. Macpherson, in his useful " The Westminster Confession of Faith," Edinburgh, 1881, in " Handbooks for Bible Classes " edited by M. Dods and A. Whyte, properly says (p. 31): " That the written word should take the place of oral revelations handed down, or frequently renewed by direct divine utterances, is not viewed as in itself necessary." This is what the Confession says. But the inferences which Mr. Macpherson founds on this are not just, and are contradicted by the Confession itself and by as many of its authors as have written on this subject. He has confused the two widely different questions, of the necessity of the Scriptures in the sense of whether it was necessary for God to commit His revelations to writing, and the necessity of the Scriptures in the sense of whether the knowledge of the Scriptures, as the only trustworthy record of those revelations, is necessary to salvation now, when the revelations themselves have ceased. The Confession denies the former necessity and affirms the second. Mr. Macpherson, by confusing the two, mistakenly interprets the Confession as denying both.

God has revealed His will, the Scriptures thus are set forth as one way; and as the complete, permanent, and final way, in no respect subordinate to the other ways, except in the matter of time. And their necessity is made to rest on nothing else than that they are the permanent embodiment and sole divinely safeguarded and, indeed, only trustworthy, extant form in which the revelation of God and of His will which is necessary to salvation exists. They are, therefore, something more than the " record " of revelation — they are the revelation itself fixed in written form for its better preservation and propagation. And they are something more than useful — they are necessary, since this alone saving revelation is extant now only in their pages.

" Now that God by the works of his Creation and Providence in the world, doth teach and convince men, and so in that general way call men, is plain, *Rom.* i. . . . So then, the whole world, in the excellent harmony of it, doth necessarily teach a God. . . . This invitation *Paul* considers of in his Sermon at *Athens, Acts* xvii. 27. . . . Now there have been some of old, yea, and many in these days, that would stretch these Texts too far, as if the invitation by the creatures, were immediately saving, or that men might obtain salvation by looking into these: They have not been afraid to say, That by the Sun and Stars we may come to be effectually called, as well as by the Apostles, and the preaching of the Gospel: But how senselesse and absurd is this? For

" First, *This invitation and call by the creatures, doth not, nor cannot reveal anything of Christ, the onely cause of salvation:* Without Christ there is no Salvation; Now how is it possible by the Creatures, in a natural way of discourse, that ever we should come to know or believe in a Christ? . . .

" Secondly, *The call by the creatures is not saving, because it discovers not the way of Salvation, no more than the cause;* viz., *Faith:* As Christ is wholly a Supernatural object, and by revelation, so is faith the way to come to him, the hand to lay hold on him, onely by revelation . . . where then there is no Christ, nor no faith, there must necessarily be no call to salvation.

" Thirdly, *This call could not be saving, for the furthest and utmost effect it had upon men, was onely outwardly to reform their lives:* It restrained many from gross sins, and kept them in the exercises of temperance and justice, and such Moral vertues. . . . But you may say, To what purpose is this call of God by the Creatures, and the work of his providence, if it be not to salvation? Yes, it is much every way:

" First, *Hereby even all men are made inexcusable:* As the Apostle urgeth, God had not left them without a witness or testimony. . . . Men therefore are made inexcusable by this way; they cannot say, God hath left them without any conviction or manifestation of himself: No, the creatures they call, all the works of Gods justice and Gods mercy, they call; and then conscience, which is implanted in every man, the dictates and reasonings thereof, they also call: Thus there will be enough to clear God, and to stop every mans mouth.

" Secondly, Gods purpose in these calls, is to restrain sin, and to draw men on further then they do: There is no man that hath no more than this remote and confuse call, that doth what he may do, and can do; He doth not improve, no, not that natural strength that is in him: (I do not say) to spiritual good things; for so he hath no natural strength: but to such objects as by nature he might: He willfully runneth himself in the committing of sins, against his conscience and knowledge; he doth with delight and joy, tumble himself in the mire and filth of sin: Now God calleth by these natural ways, to curb and restrain him, to put a bound to these waves: For if there were not these general convictions, no Societies, no Commonwealths could consist." — A. Burgess, " Spiritual Refining: or a Treatise of Grace and Assurance," London, 1652, pp. 692–694.

" As for that dangerous opinion, that makes Gods calling of man to repentance by the Creatures, to be enough and sufficient, we reject, as that which cuts at the very root of free grace: A voyce, indeed, we grant they have, but yet they make like *Pauls* Trumpet, an uncertain sound; men cannot by them know the nature of God and his Worship, and wherein our Justification doth consist." — A. Burgess, " Spiritual Refining, etc.," London, 1652, p. 588.

" For to maintain (as some do) that a man may be saved in an ordinary course (I meddle not with extraordinary dispensations, but leave the secrets of God to himself) by any Religion whatsoever, provided he live according to the principles of it, is to turn the

whole world into an *Eden;* and to find a Tree of life in every garden, as well as in the paradise of God " (p. 71). He argues " the insufficiency of all exotick doctrines," from the failure of pagan philosophy to find saving truth (pp. 72 *sqq.*). " The Scriptures . . .
contain the minde of Jehovah. Somewhat of *his nature* we may
learn from the *creatures,* but should have known little or nothing
of *his will,* had not canonical *Scripture* revealed it " (pp. 86, 87).
There are " six several acts " through which men come by nature
to know God — " *respicere, prospicere, suspicere, despicere, inspi-
cere,* and *circumspicere* " (p. 120): " But notwithstanding all this,
as it fared with the wise men from the east, who, although they
were assured by the appearance of a *star* that a King of the Jews
was born, yet needed the *prophets* manuduction to give them notice
who he was, and where they might finde him: so though natural
reason improved can make it appear *that there is* a God, yet there
is a necessity of Scripture-revelation to inform us *who and what
he is,* in regard of his Essence, Subsistence, and Attributes " (p.
128). — JOHN ARROWSMITH, " A Chain of Principles," Cambridge,
1659.

   " There are two great Gifts that *God* hath given to his people.
The *Word Christ,* and the *Word of Christ:* Both are unspeakably
great; but the first will do us no good without the second " (pp. 55,
56). . . . " If the Word of God be of such invaluable excellency,
absolute necessity, and of such admirable use, . . . Blessed be
God who hath not only given us the book of the Creatures, and
the book of Nature to know himself and his will by; but also, and
especially the book of the Scriptures, whereby we come to know
those things of God, and of Christ, which neither the book of Nature nor of the Creatures can reveal unto us. Let us bless God,
not only for revealing his Will in his Word, but for revealing it by
writing. Before the time of *Moses,* God discovered his Will by immediate Revelations from Heaven. But we have a surer word of
Prophesie, 2 *Pet.* i. 19, surer (to us) than a voice from Heaven. For
the Devil (saith the Apostle) *transforms himself into an Angel of
light.* He hath his apparitions, and revelations. . . . And if God
should now at this day discover his way of Worship, and his Divine
Will by revelations, how easily would men be deceived, and mistake
Diabolical Delusions, for Divine Revelations? and therefore let us
bless God for the written Word, which is surer and safer (as to
us) than an immediate Revelation: There are some that are apt

to think, that if an Angel should come from heaven, and reveal God's will to them, it would work more upon them than the written Word; but I would have these men study the conference between *Abraham* and *Dives*, Luke xvi. 27, 28, 29, 30, 31. *Habent Mosen et Prophetas*, etc. *They have Moses and the Prophets*; if they will not profit by them, neither would they profit by any that should come out of Hell, or down from Heaven to them: for it is the same God that speaks by his written Word, and by a voice from Heaven. The difference is only in the outward cloathing; and therefore if Gods speaking by writing, will not amend us, no more will Gods speaking by a voice. *O bless God exceedingly for the written Word!* Let us cleave close to it, and not expect any Revelations from Heaven of new truths but say with the Apostle, *Gal.* i. 8, 9 " (pp. 90–93). — EDWARD CALAMY, " The Godly Mans Ark, etc.," seventh ed., London, 1672.

" Though Humane Reason be a Beam of Divine Wisdom, yet if it be not enlightened with an higher Light of the Gospel, it cannot reach unto the things of God as it should. . . . For though Reason be the Gift of God, yet it doth proceed from God as he is God, and General Ruler of the World: But the Gospel, and the Light thereof, did proceed from the Father, by the Son, to the Church, *Rev.* xxii. 1. . . . *John* i. 17, 18. Though Reason be the Gift of God, and a Beam of the Wisdom of God; yet it cannot sufficiently discover a mans Sins unto him; . . . And as meer Humane Reason cannot make a sufficient discovery of Sin, so it cannot strengthen against Sin, and Temptation. . . . Though the Light of Reason be good, yet it is not a saving Light. . . . 'Tis Revelation-Light from the Gospel, that doth bring to Heaven: meer Humane Reason cannot do it." — WILLIAM BRIDGE, " Scripture-Light, the Most Sure Light," London, 1656, pp. 32, 33.

" It is true, that the very light of nature, which God hath planted in every man, will discover unto him some of the chief heads of the duties, that he requires of him, as to love the Lord with all our hearts, and to fear, and serve him, *Deut.* x. 12. And to serve one another through love, *Gal.* v. 13. But in what particular services we are to express our piety to God, or love to men, what can man prescribe or imagine? " (p. 13). " Whatsoever was impossible to be known by any creature, or to be found out by discourse of naturall reason, that must of necessity be discovered and made known by God himself. But it will appear, as evidently as the very light, that most of the grounds of faith, which the Scripture proposeth unto us, are such as neither eye hath seen, nor eare heard, nor ever entered into mans heart, 1 *Cor.* ii. 9, and therefore could never be either revealed or discovered by man. Wherefore, seeing we finde them discovered in the Scriptures, we can doe no lesse then acknowledge them to be the word of God " (p. 25). The necessity for a *written* word is argued under the following heads (marginal analysis) : " 1. As the most easie way to make it publike. 2. As the safest way to prevent corruption. 3. As the best way to win credit to his Word. 4. And as the most honorable " (pp. 67, 68). —JOHN WHITE, " A Way to the Tree of Life," London, 1647.

" But yet the whole world in the frame thereof, was sufficient evidence of the *Eternall power and Godhead, Rom.* i. 20, and *Psal.* xix. 1. *The heavens declare the glory of God, and the firmament sheweth his handy worke.* And albeit *Aristotle,* the greatest of Philosophers, maintained the eternity thereof without beginning; yet he confesseth ingeniously in his Book *De cœlo,* that all that went before him maintained *mundum genitum esse;* neither was his discourse of power to raze out that naturall instinct hereof, which seems to be graven in the hearts of men, and was the chiefe ground of that universall acknowledgment of a divine power supreame. Now as God made himself known by his works so I nothing doubt but herewithall it was their duty to know him, and according to their knowledge to serve him and glorifie him, in acknowledgment of his glorious nature, so farre as they took notice of it; But as for a rule whereby they should worship him, I know none that God had given them, or that they could gather from contemplation of the creatures. And surely the knowledge of God, as a Creator only, is nothing sufficient to salvation; but the knowledge of him as a Redeemer: And therefore *seeing the World by wisdome knew not God in the wisdome of God, it pleased God by the foolishnesse of Preaching to save them that believe,* 1 *Cor.* i. 21. And the Gentiles are set forth unto us in Scripture, as such *who knew not God,* 1 *Thes.* iv. 5; 2 *Thes.* i. 8. And had they means sufficient without, and ability sufficient within to know him? How could it be that none of them should know him? . . . Yet were they inexcusable (and thus farre their knowledge brought them, *Rom.* i. 20) in changing *the glory of the incorruptible God, to the similitude of the image of a corruptible man, and of birds, and of fourefooted beasts, and of creeping things.* . . . Yet what shall all such knowledge profit a man, if he be ignorant in the knowledge of him as a redeemer? " (pp. 188, 189). " And yet I see no great need of Christ, if it be in the power of an Heathen man to know what it is to please God, and to have an heart to please him; For certainly as many as know what it is to please God, and have an heart to please him, God will never hurt them, much lesse damne them to hell. Yet the Apostle telleth us, that *they that are in the flesh cannot please God* . . ." (p. 190). " No question but *The word of God is the sword of the spirit, Ephes.* vi., *And the Law of the Lord is a perfect Law, converting the soule, Psal.* xix. And it seemes to be delivered in opposition to the Book of the creatures, as if he had said, though *The Heavens declare the glory of God, and the firmament sheweth his handy work*, yet this is the peculiar prerogative of the Book of God's word, and the Doctrine contained therein, that *it converteth the soule:* and upon this is grounded the great preferment of the Jews above the Gentiles, *chiefely that unto them were committed the Oracles of God* " (p. 194). — WILLIAM TWISSE, " The Riches of Gods Love, etc.," Oxford, 1653 (written 1632, see p. 258).

THE DEFINITION OF SCRIPTURE

II. Having thus exhibited the indispensableness of the written form of God's revealed will, which is known under the name of Holy Scripture, the Confession naturally proceeds to define this Holy Scripture, which has been shown to be necessary. The designation used for it is determined by the precedent statement: " Holy Scripture or the Word of God written." God's revelation of Himself and of His will is the Word of God; the Scriptures are this revelation wholly committed unto writing; and, therefore, they are appropriately called " the Word of God written."

The definition of them is framed, first, extensively by the enumeration of the writings which constitute the volume called " Holy Scripture or the word of God written." These are first designated generally as " all the books of the Old and New Testament "; and then to prevent all mistake they are enumerated, one by one, by name. Of these books it is then affirmed, by way of intensive definition, that they are, one and all, in their entirety, " given by inspiration of God, to be the rule of faith and life." The definition having thus been made quantitatively and qualitatively, i.e. both as to the canon and as to inspiration, it is finally applied to the exclusion of " the books commonly called Apocrypha," which, "not being of divine inspiration," " are no part of the canon of the Scripture." They are, therefore, declared, in accord with the ordinary Reformed doctrine, to be " of no authority in the Church of God, nor to be any otherwise approved, or made use of, than other human writings."

In this definition of Scripture the fact of inspiration is very sharply asserted as the distinguishing characteristic of Scripture. " All the books of the Old and New Testament," in their entirety, are declared to be " given by inspiration of God "; and only because they are thus, as wholes and in all their parts, " of divine inspiration," are they " part of the canon of the Scripture " and of " authority in the Church of God." It is due to this fact of inspiration that they are not of the category of " human writings," to which category the " books commonly called Apocrypha " are ascribed, expressly because they are not " of divine inspiration." Here is a strong assertion of the fact of inspiration as the distinguishing characteristic of Scriptural books; but here is no definition of inspiration. The thing in definition is Scripture, not inspiration, and inspiration is the defining, not the defined fact.

The last clause of the second section, " All which are given by inspiration of God, to be the rule of faith and life," is not, therefore, to be taken as a formal definition of inspiration, although it is an express assertion of inspiration; and much less is it to be read as if it were intended to limit inspiration to matters of faith and practice. It is not a definition of inspiraton, but part of the definition of Scripture; and what it affirms is that " all the books of the Old and New Testaments " just enumerated in detail, and, therefore, severally and in their entirety, have been fitted by inspiration to be in their entirety, without discrimination of parts or elements, " the rule of faith and life." Inspiration is asserted to be pervasive, to belong to all the books enumerated without exception, and to all their parts and elements without discrimination; and its result is said to be that it fits these books to be "the rule of faith and life," that is, constitutes them parts of the "canon of the Scripture." Accordingly, the Apocrypha are immediately afterwards excluded from "the canon of the Scripture" on the express ground that they are not of "divine inspiration," but "human writings." The fact of inspiration is asserted, its pervasiveness, and its effect in making the books of which it is affirmed divine and not "human" books; but no definition of it is here given.

The misinterpretation of this clause, which would use it as a definition of inspiration, in the hope of confining inspiration in the definition of the Confession to matters of faith and practice, moreover, is discredited as decisively on historical as on exegetical grounds. This view was not the view of the Westminster Divines. It had its origin among the Socinians and was introduced among Protestants by the Arminians. And it was only on the publication, in 1690, of the "Five Letters concerning the Inspiration of the Holy Scriptures, translated out of the French," which are taken from Le Clerc, that it began to make a way for itself among English theologians.[39]

But, although this special passage presents no formal definition of the nature of inspiration, the Confession by no means leaves its own conception of the nature of inspiration undefined. Already in the first section it had declared that it was God who constituted Scripture by Himself committing His will wholly unto writing, thereby making another way of revelation in addition to those other supernatural ways formerly used by Him. And in the third section this inspiration, so strongly affirmed in the second section as the characteristic of all the books of the Old and New Testaments, is declared to make these books divine and not human writings. In conformity with this, the Confession subsequently declares that the Biblical books have "God (who is truth itself)" for their "author" (§ 4), that they are "immediately

[39] See the interesting historical sketch in Cunningham's "Theological Lectures," 1878, pp. 304 *sq.*

inspired by God " (§ 8), so that they are " the very Word of
God " (Larger Catechism, Q. 4), that they are of " infallible
truth and divine authority " (§ 5), and are to be believed to
be true by the Christian man in everything that is revealed
in them (xiv. 2). As the historical meaning of the word " Inspiration," conferred on the Scriptures in our present section,
is not doubtful, so neither is the meaning of these phrases,
further describing its Confessional sense. For example, the
phrase, to be " immediately inspired," which is used in section
8, is of quite settled and technical connotation. We may find
it, for instance, in Calov (" Syst. loc. theol.," i. p. 463): " Nec
ea tantum credenda verissima, quae ad fidem et mores spec-
tantia in Scriptura traduntur, sed etiam alia quaecunque in
eadem occurrentia, quam ab immediato divino impulsu profecta sint." Or, in Hollaz (" Examinis Theologici, etc.," p. 94):
" Inspiratio diuina, qua res et verba dicenda non minus, quam
scribenda prophetis atque apostolis a spiritu sancto immediate
suggesta sunt." Or, if this seems to be going too far afield, we
may find it in the plainest of English in John Ball, the Puritan
catechist, held in the highest honor by all the Westminster
men. " What is it to be immediately inspired? " he asks in
his " A Short Treatise, etc." (15th ed., 1656, pp. 7 and 8), and
answers: " To be immediately inspired, is to be as it were
breathed, and to come from the Father by the Holy Ghost,
without all means." And again: " Were the Scriptures thus
inspired? A. Thus the Holy Scriptures in the Originals were
inspired both for matter and words." The Westminster Confession contains in itself, therefore, the material by which we
may be assured that the inspiration, which it affirms in our
present sections to be the characteristic of all the Biblical
books, was conceived by it as constituting the Scriptures in
the most precise sense, the very Word of God, divinely trustworthy and divinely authoritative in all their parts and in all
their elements alike.

" 29 Q. *From whence must wee learne to know God and serve
him rightly?* 29 A. To know God, and to serve him rightly, wee

must be taught out of Gods Word. 30 Q. *Which book is Gods Word?*
30 A. The Bible or the Scripture of the Old and New Testament is
the very word of God." — HERBERT PALMER, " An Endeavour of
Making the Principles of Christian Religion . . . plaine and easie,
etc.," London, 1644, p. 7.

" The only rule of faith and obedience is the written Word of
God, contained in the Bible or the Scriptures of the Old and New
Testament." — FIRST DRAFT OF CATECHISM OF WESTMINSTER AS-
SEMBLY (" Minutes," p. 281, for September 14, 1646).

" . . . *Hebrew.* (In which tongue the Prophets left their doctrine as the Canon of the Church)." " For the Original Copies, I
must subscribe to that of *Canus* a Papist, who tells us, *That we
are not to receive into the holy Canon both for the Old and New
Testament, but such books as the Apostles did allow, and deliver
over to the Church of Christ."* — RICHARD CAPEL, " Remains, etc.,"
London, 1658, pp. 37 and 65.

" So that the Spirit of God inspired certain persons, whom he
pleased, to be the revealers of his will, till he had imparted and
committed to writing what he thought fit to reveal under the Old
Testament; and when he had completed that, the Holy Ghost departed, and such inspirations ceased. And when the gospel was to
come in, then the Spirit was restored again, and bestowed upon
several persons for the revealing farther of the mind of God, and
completing the work he had to do, for the settling of the gospel, and
penning of the New Testament: and that being done, these gifts
and inspirations cease, and may no more be expected, than we may
expect some other gospel yet to come " (p. 371). " From these men's
[those that companied with Christ] sermons and relations, many
undertook to write gospels, partly for their own use, and partly for
the benefit of others: which thing though they did lawfully and
with a good intent, yet because they did it not by inspiration, nor
by divine warrant; albeit what they had written, were according
to truth, yet was the authority of their writings but human, and not
to be admitted into the divine canon " (p. 19). — JOHN LIGHT-
FOOT, " Works," ed. Pitman, iii. 1822.

" The word λόγια , whereby heathen writers had been wont to
express their oracles . . . was enfranchised by the holy Ghost,
and applied to the books of Scripture to intimate (as I conceive)
that these books were to be of like use to Christians, as those oracles
had been to Infidels " (p. 86). " These Scripture-Oracles differ from

and excel those other. . . . I. In point of perspicuity. . . . II. In point of piety. . . . III. In point of veracity. . . . IV. In point of duration. . . . V. In point of authority. . . . Scripture is of divine authority: *Holy men of God* (saith *Peter*) *spake as they were moved by the Holy Ghost.* They wrote accordingly. *All Scripture,* saith *Paul, was given by inspiration of God.* It is not more true that they are oracles for their use, then that they have God for their authour " (pp. 95–103). " I answer, Although the pen-man did not, the inditer, *viz.* the Holy Ghost did exactly know whose names were written in the book of life, and whose were not. Now he it was that in the history of the *Acts* suggested and dedicated to his secretary both matter and words " (p. 299). — JOHN ARROWSMITH, " A Chain of Principles," Cambridge, 1659.

" The Scripture, and the Word of God is [the Rule of Lawfulness or Unlawfulness], it is the only Rule whereby I may, and must make up my Judgment of Lawfulness, and Unlawfulness; it is that only which doth stamp Lawfulness upon an Action " (p. 32). " Now this Duty is urged, and amplified; urged by divers Arguments: some taken from the excellency of the Word it self. First, It is λόγος προφητικός, a Word of Prophesie, or a Prophetical Word, written by Divine Inspiration; the same that is spoken of in verse 20 [2 Peter i.], called *Prophesie of Scripture.* Secondly, It is λόγος βεβαιότερος, a more sure Word: Some think the Comparative, is put for the Superlative. . . . But I take it rather to be meant Comparatively; for the Word of God written, is surer than that Voyce which they heard in the Mount (whereof he spake in the former Verse). More sure is the Word written, than that Voyce of Revelation; not *ratione veritatis,* not in regard of the Truth uttered, for that Voyce was as true as any word in the Scripture; but more sure, *ratione manifestationis,* more certain, setled, and established " (pp. 1, 4). " *What must we do, that we may take heed, and attend unto Scripture?* . . . First, for your knowledg in, and understanding of the Scripture, and the written Word of God, ye must, [1.] Observe, keep, and hold fast the Letter of it; for though the Letter of the Scripture be not the Word alone, yet the Letter with the true sense and meaning of it, is the Word. The Body of a Man, is not the Man; but the Body and Soul together, make up the whole Man: the Soul alone, or the Body alone, is not the Man. So here; though the Letter of the Scripture alone, do not make up the Word; yet the Letter, and sense together, do; and if ye destroy the Body, ye destroy the Man; so if ye destroy the Letter of the Scripture, you do destroy the Scripture; and if you deny the Letter, how is it possible that you should attain to the true sense thereof, when the Sense lies wrapped up in the Letters, and the words thereof? . . . [2.] If you would have the true knowledg, and understand the Scripture, and so behold this great Light in its full glory and brightness; you must diligently enquire into the true sense and meaning of it: for the true sense and meaning, is the soul thereof " (pp. 46, 47). — WILLIAM BRIDGE, " Scripture-Light, The Most Sure Light," London, 1656.

" These holy writings are the Word of God himself, who speaks unto us in and by them. Wherefore when we take in hand the Book of the Scriptures, we cannot otherwise conceive of our selves, then as standing in God's presence, to hear what he will say unto us " (p. 1). " Of the pen-men of the Scriptures, that they were holy men, inspired and guided in that work infallibly and wholly, by the Spirit of God " (p. 57). " Who the most of these holy men were, it is well known to the Church, the titles of their Books bearing their names. . . . And that the rest, whose names are either concealed, or doubtful, were such likewise, will be evident to any indifferent person that shall consider two things. . . . It addes something to the estimation of the Scriptures, that they were written by such holy men, as we have formerly mentioned . . . but that which procures unto them divine reverence, which ought to make all hearts stoop unto them, is that they were written by the direction of the holy Spirit, the Spirit of truth, especially if we throughly consider what manner of direction it was which was given unto these holy Pen-men of these sacred Oracles, in the composing thereof. The Apostle, 2 *Pet.* i. 20, 21, describes that kinde of assistance of the holy Ghost, in the delivery of the Scriptures, two ways. *First*, by way of negation, that they were neither of private interpretation, nor came by the wil of man. *Secondly*, he describes the same assistance affirmatively, testifying that they spake as they were moved by the holy Ghost. In the former of these, wherein he expresseth this manner of delivering the Scriptures by way of negation, the Apostle excludes the working of the naturall faculties of mans minde altogether. . . . So that both the understanding, and will of man, as farre as they were meerly naturall, had nothing to doe in this holy work, save onely to understand, and approve that which was dictated by God himselfe, unto those that wrote it from his mouth, or the suggesting of his Spirit. . . . For

we may not conceive that they were moved in writing these Scriptures, as the pen is moved by the hand that guides it, without understanding what they did; For they not onely understood, but willingly
consented to what they wrote. . . . But the Apostles meaning is,
that the Spirit of God moved them in this work of writing the
Scriptures, not according to nature, but above nature, shining into
their understandings clearly, and fully, by an heavenly and supernaturall light, and carrying and moving their wils thereby with
a delight, and holy embracing of that truth revealed, and with a
like desire to publish and make known the secrets and counsels
of God, revealed unto them, unto his Church. Yea, beyond all this,
the holy Ghost not only suggested unto them the substance of that
doctrine which they were to deliver and leave upon record unto
the Church, . . . but besides hee supplied unto them the very
phrases, method, and whole order of those things that are written
in the Scriptures, . . . Thus then the holy Ghost, not only assisted
holy men in penning the Scriptures, but in a sort took the work out
of their hand, making use of nothing in the men, but of their understandings to receive and comprehend, their wils to consent unto,
and their hands to write downe that which they delivered " (pp.
57–61). — JOHN WHITE, " A Way to the Tree of Life," London,
1647.

   " All the Scriptures are θεόπνευστοι by Divine inspiration; and
therefore the breathings of Gods spirit, are to be expected in this
Garden: and those commands of attending to the Scripture onely,
and to observe what is written, is a plain demonstration that God
hath tyed us to the Scriptures onely: so that as the child in the
womb liveth upon nourishment conveighed by the Navel cleaving
to it, so doth the Church live onely upon Christ by the Navel of
the Scripture, through which all nourishment is conveighed." —
A. BURGESS, " Spiritual Refining, etc.," London, 1652, p. 132.

   " It is certain that all Scripture is of Divine inspiration, and
that the holy men of God spake as they were guided by the Holy
Ghost. . . . It transcribes the mind and heart of God. A true Saint
loveth the Name, Authority, Power, Wisdom, and goodness of God
in every letter of it, and therefore cannot but take pleasure in it.
It is an Epistle sent down to him from the God of Heaven " (p. 55).
" The Word of God hath God for its Author, and therefore must
needs be full of Infinite Wisdom and Eloquence, even the Wisdom
and Eloquence of God. There is not a word in it, but breathes out

God, and is breathed out by God. It is (as *Irenæus* saith) κανων τῆς πίστεως ἀκλινὴς, an invariable rule of Faith, an unerring and infallible guide to heaven. It contains glorious Revelations and Discoveries, no where else to be found " (p. 80). " Before the time of *Moses*, God discovered his Will by immediate Revelations from Heaven. But we have a surer word of Prophesie, 2 *Pet.* i. 19, surer (to us) than a voice from Heaven. . . . For it is the same God that speaks by his written Word, and by a voice from Heaven " (pp. 91–93). — EDWARD CALAMY, " The Godly Mans Ark," seventh ed., London, 1672.

" If *Solomon* mistooke not. (And how could hee mistake in that, which the spirit himselfe dictated vnto him)." — CORNELIUS BURGESS, " Baptismall Regeneration of Elect Infants," Oxford, 1629, p. 277 (quoting from Proverbs).

" The Apocrypha speaks for itself, that it is not the finger of God, but the work of some Jews. Which got it so much authority among Christians; because it came from them, from whom the lively oracles of God indeed came also. But the Talmud may be read to as good advantage, and as much profit, and far more." — JOHN LIGHTFOOT, " Works," ed. Pitman, ii. p. 9. " The words of the text are the last words of the Old Testament, — there uttered by a prophet, here expounded by an angel: there concluding the law, and here beginning the gospel. . . . Thus sweetly and nearly should the two Testaments join together, and thus divinely would they kiss each other, but that the wretched Apocrypha doth thrust in between. . . . It is a thing not a little to be admired, how this Apocrypha could ever get such place in the hearts and in the Bibles of the primitive times, as to come to sit in the very centre of them both. . . . But it is a wonder, to which I could never yet receive satisfaction, that in churches that are reformed, they have shaken off the yoke of superstition, and unpinned themselves from off the sleeve of former customs, or doing as their ancestors have done, — yet in such a thing as this, and of so great import, should do as first ignorance, and then superstition, hath done before them. It is true, indeed, that they have refused these books out of the canon, but they have reserved them still in the Bible: as if God should have cast Adam out of the state of happiness, and yet have continued him in the place of happiness." — JOHN LIGHTFOOT, " Works," ed. Pitman, vi. pp. 131, 132.

III. Having thus defined Scripture as the very Word of God given by divine inspiration, and, therefore, not a human, but a divine book, the Confession proceeds next to exhibit the properties that belong to it as such (§§ 4–7).

The Authority of Scripture

1. The first property of a divine book to be adduced is, naturally, its authority (§§ 4–5). (A) Just because the book is God's Book, revealing to us His will, it is authoritative in and of itself; and it ought to be believed and obeyed, not on the ground of any borrowed authority, lent it from any human source, but on the single and sufficient ground of its own divine origin and character, "because it is the Word of God," and "God (who is truth itself)" is "the author thereof" (§ 4). So the Confession asserts, in unison with the whole body of Protestant theology, not as if it held that Scripture is to be believed and obeyed as God's Word before we know it to be such, but as basing its right to be believed and obeyed on its divine origin and character already established by definition in the preceding sections. Because inspired, Scripture is the Word of God; and because the Word of God, it exercises lawful authority over the thought and acts of men.

"The former Position being once granted, that the Scriptures are Gods Word, no man can question their Authority, whether that be of him or no." — JOHN WHITE, "A Way to the Tree of Life," London, 1647, p. 45.

"Scripture is of divine authority. . . . It is not more true that they are oracles for their use, then that they have God for their authour." — JOHN ARROWSMITH, "A Chain of Principles," Cambridge, 1659, p. 103.

"The Scripture resolves our faith on *Thus saith the Lord*, the only authoritie that all the Prophets alledge, and *Paul*, 1 *Thes.* ii. 13. . . ." — SAMUEL RUTHERFORD, "A Free Disputation against pretended Liberty of Conscience," London, 1649, p. 364.

"The Scriptures are to be believed for themselves, and they

need not fetch their credit from any thing else. . . . They are the truth. . . . The reason of the Scriptures' credibility is, because they are the word of God. . . . It is not proper to say, We believe Scriptures are Scriptures, because of the church, without distinguishing upon believing. . . . We may satisfy this by an easy distinction, betwixt believing that Scripture is Scripture, and believing that the church all along hath taken them for Scripture. . . . We believe the church owns the Scriptures; but he is but a poor Christian, that believes the Scriptures are the Scriptures upon no other account. . . . God gives his word; and whether men will hear, or whether they will forbear, it is, and will be, the word of God for ever." — JOHN LIGHTFOOT, " Works," ed. Pitman, vi. pp. 56, 62, 63, 351.

(B) But men are not so constituted as readily to yield faith and obedience even to lawful authority. Their minds are blinded, and their consciences dulled, and their wills enslaved to evil. The Confession accordingly devotes a paragraph of unsurpassed nobility of both thought and phrase to indicating how sinful men may be brought to full conviction of and practical obedience to the infallible truth and divine authority of the Scriptures. The value of the external testimony of the Church is recognized: the assurance of the Church that they are the very Word of God may move and induce us to a high and reverent esteem for the Holy Scriptures. The greater value of the witness of the Scriptures themselves, in form and contents, to their supernatural origin is affirmed and richly illustrated: by the miracle of Scripture itself, it abundantly evidences itself to be the Word of God. " Abundant evidence " one must suppose to be sufficient; and objectively it is sufficient and more than sufficient; and this is what the Confession means to affirm. But, according to the Reformed theology, man needs something more than evidence, however abundant, to persuade and enable him to believe and obey God's Word; he needs the work of the Holy Spirit accompanying the Word, *ab extra incidens*. And, therefore, the Confession proceeds to point out that something more is needed, besides this abundant evidence, to work within us a " full persuasion and assurance of the infallible truth and divine authority " of God's Word — to lead us to commit ourselves wholly to it, trusting its every word as true and obeying its every command as authoritative. What is needed is, in ordinary language, a new heart; in the Confession's language, " the inward work of the Holy Spirit bearing witness by and with the Word in our hearts."

This beautiful statement of the Confession has sometimes of late been strangely misunderstood. It is no more than to say, what every Reformed thinker must be ready to say, that faith in God's Word is not man's own work, but the gift of God; and that man needs a preparation of the spirit, as well as an exhibition of the evidences, in order to be persuaded and enabled to yield faith and obedience. If this be not true the whole Reformed system falls with it. It is, then, neither to be misunderstood as mysticism, on the one hand, as if " the testimony of the Holy Spirit " were to be expected to work faith in the Word apart from or even against the evidences; nor, on the other hand, is it to be explained away in a rationalizing manner as if it meant nothing more than that the Holy Spirit, as the immanent spring of all life and activity, is operative in all human thought. It is simply the Reformed doctrine of faith, stated here in explanation of the origin of faith in the Scriptures. It is, therefore, naturally returned to in the chapter on Saving Faith (chapter xiv.). The first half of the second section of that chapter is nothing more than a restatement of the declaration here: " By this faith " — which (§ 1) " is the work of the Spirit of Christ " in the heart — " a Christian believeth to be true, whatsoever is revealed in the Word, for the authority of God Himself speaking therein; and acteth differently, upon that which each particular passage thereof containeth; yielding obedience to the commands, trembling at the threatenings, and embracing the promises of God for this life, and that which is to come." The only difference between the two passages is that difference of form which springs necessarily from the difference in general subject; here the subject is the Scriptures, and we are told how men are brought to a full faith in them — there the subject is faith, and we are told how this faith acts with reference to the Scriptures. Both passages alike, however, speak simply of that *fides generalis,* which is a topic treated at large in all Reformed systems; [40] and both ascribe, in harmony with all Reformed thought, this *fides generalis* to the testimony of the Holy Spirit, without which no evidences would suffice to awaken it.

" Q. What special proofs are there that the Scriptures of the Old and New Testament are the very Word of God? A. The Scriptures are [specially] [41] proved to be the very Word of God by their majesty and holiness of doctrine, and the fulfilling of the prophecies, by their exalting God and debasing man, and yet offering him sufficient means of comfort and salvation, and by their light and power in convincing and converting.

" [Q. May not all these excellencies and perfections be found in other books besides the Scriptures? A. No words or writings of men have all these excellencies and perfections in them but as they agree unto and are taken from the Scriptures.] [41]

" 5 Q. Are all these proofs sufficient of themselves to persuade a man to believe that the Scriptures are the Word of God? A. It is only the Spirit of God that makes any proofs effectual to assure the soul of this truth, that the Scriptures are the Word of God." — ORIGINAL DRAFT OF CATECHISM, " Minutes," pp. 281–283.

" It is a right, a safe, a sure way to seek after and to enjoy assurance of our interest in Christ, and in the covenant of grace, by

40 For example, and most accessibly, in Dr. Charles Hodge's " Systematic Theology," 1874, iii. p. 95. See the same distinction in the extract from John White quoted below, p. 220, under the terms of General and Particular Objects of Faith. The difficulty which Prof. H. P. Smith has found in conceiving the doctrine of *fides generalis* (" Inspiration and Inerrancy," 1893, p. 230) is as astonishing as the mystical sense read into our section by Dr. C. A. Briggs, although all the Westminster men do their best to guard against it. Dr. Briggs's representation that the position of the Westminster Confession has been " abandoned " by the Presbyterian Church is only an indication of his misapprehension of it. The exact method indicated by the Confession is taken, for example, by Dr. Charles Hodge in his " The Way of Life "; and one must have read the " Systematic Theology " of the same author to little purpose who has not met with such explicit affirmations of this doctrine of the Confession as those made at i. p. 129 and iii. pp. 60, 68, 69, 74. Dr. William Cunningham's exposition of the matter, in chapters xxii.-xxv. of his " Theological Lectures," again, might have been written by George Gillespie.
41 The words enclosed in brackets were subsequently omitted.

the marks and fruits of sanctification. . . . All thy marks will leave thee in the dark if the Spirit of grace do not open thine eyes that thou mayest know the things which are freely given thee of God. Hagar could not see the well, though she was beside it, till her eyes were opened. Marks of grace are useless, undiscernible, unsatisfactory to the deserted and overclouded soul. . . . Whereas, to make no trial by marks, and to trust an inward testimony, under the notion of the Holy Ghost's testimony, when it is without the least evidence of any true gracious mark, this way (of its own nature, and intrinsically, or in itself) is a deluding and ensnaring of the conscience.

" Quest. But it may be asked, and it is a question worthy to be looked into (though I must confess I have not read it, nor heard it handled before), How doth this assurance by marks agree with, or differ from assurance by the testimony of the Holy Ghost? May the soul have assurance either way, or must there be a concurrence of both (for I suppose they are not one and the same thing) to make up the assurance?

" Ans. For answer whereunto I shall first of all distinguish a twofold certainty, even in reference to the mind of man, or in his conscience (for I speak not here de certitudine entis, but mentis): the one may be called ἀσφάλεια, when the conscience is in tuto, may be secure; needeth not fear and be troubled. The Grecians have used the word ἀσφάλεια when they were speaking of giving security and assurance by safe conducts, or by pledges, or by sureties, or the like (H. Steph. in Thes. Ling. Gr., tom. 3, p. 1173). The other is πληροφορια, a full persuasion, when the soul doth not only steer a right and safe course, and needeth not fear danger, but saileth before the wind, and with all its sails full. So there is answerably a double uncertainty, the one may be called ἀποριὰ, when a man is in himself perplexed and difficulted, and not without cause, having no grounds of assurance; when a man doth doubt and hesitate concerning a conclusion, because he hath no reasons nor arguments to prove it; when a man is in a wilderness where he can have no way, or shut up where he can have no safe escaping. The other is ἐποχή, which is a doubting that ariseth not from want of arguments, or from the inextricable difficulty of the grounds, but from a disease of the mind, which makes it suspend or retain its assent, even when it hath sufficient grounds upon which it may be assured. Now it is the evidence of signs of marks of grace which giveth that first kind of certainty, and removeth that first kind of uncertainty; but it is the testimony of the Spirit of the Lord which giveth the second kind of certainty, and removeth the second kind of uncertainty. Take two or three similes for illustration.

" The Scripture is known to be indeed the word of God, by the beams of divine authority which it hath in itself, and by certain distinguishing characters, which do infallibly prove it to be the word of God; such as the heavenliness of the matter; the majesty of the style; the irresistible power over the conscience; the general scope, to abase man and to exalt God; nothing driven at but God's glory and man's salvation; the extraordinary holiness of the penmen of the Holy Ghost, without respect to any particular interests of their own, or of others of their nearest relations (which is manifest by their writings); the supernatural mysteries revealed therein, which could never have entered into the reason of men; the marvellous consent of all parts and passages (though written by divers and several penmen), even where is some appearance of difference; the fulfilling of prophecies; the miracles wrought by Christ, by the prophets and apostles; the conservation of the Scriptures against the malice of Satan and fury of persecutors; — these, and the like, are characters and marks which evidence the Scriptures to be the word of God; yet all these cannot beget in the soul a full persuasion of faith that the Scriptures are the word of God; this persuasion is from the Holy Ghost in our hearts. And it hath been the common resolution of sound Protestant writers (though now called in question by the sceptics of this age (Mr. J. Godwin in his Hagiomastix)) that these arguments and infallible characters in the Scripture itself, which most certainly prove it to be the word of God, cannot produce a certainty of persuasion in our hearts, but this is done by the Spirit of God within us, according to these scriptures, 1 Cor. ii. 10–15; 1 Thess. i. 5; 1 John ii. 27; v. 6–8, 10; John vi. 45. . . .

" I heartily yield that the Spirit of the Lord is a Spirit of revelation, and it is by the Spirit of God that we know the things which are freely given us of God, so that without the Comforter, the Holy Ghost himself, bearing witness with our spirit, all our marks cannot give us a plerophory or comfortable assurance; but this I say, that that which we have seen described by the Antinomians as the testimony of the Spirit of the Lord, is a very unsafe and unsure evidence, and speaks beside, yea, contrary, to the written word. . . . But it is another which is here in question, for clearing whereof observe, that the efficient cause, or revealing evidence, which makes us believe and be assured, is one thing, the *objectum formale fidei,* or that for which we believe and are assured, is another thing. In human sciences, a teacher is necessary to a young student, yet the student doth not believe the conclusions because his teacher teacheth him so, but because these conclusions follow necessarily from the known and received principles of the sciences; and although he had never understood either the principles or the conclusions without the help of a teacher, yet he were an ill scholar who cannot give an account of his knowledge from demonstration, but only from this, that he was taught so. In seeking a legal assurance or security we consult our lawyers, who peradventure will give us light and knowledge of that which we little imagined; yet a man cannot build a well-grounded assurance, nor be secure, because of the testimony of lawyers, but because of the deeds themselves, charters, contracts, or the like. So we cannot be assured of our interest in Christ without the work of the Holy Ghost, and his revealing evidence in our hearts; yet the ground and reason of our assurance, or that for which we are assured, is not his act of revealing, but the truth of the thing itself which he doth reveal unto us from the word of God." — GEORGE GILLESPIE, "A Treatise of Miscellany Questions," chapter xxi. 1649: Edinburgh reprint, 1844, pp. 104–110, in "The Presbyterian's Armoury," ii. 1846.

"Scripture is of divine authority. . . . It is not more true that they are oracles for their use, then that they have God for their authour. Many large volumes have been written for to make good this assertion. It is a thing wherein the Spirit of God, who indited the Scripture, gives such abundant satisfaction to the spirit of godly men, as to make other arguments, though not useless, yet to them of less necessity; He alone bearing witness to the divinity of holy writ, and to the truth of his own testimony, so putting a final issue to that controversie. But because there is need of other reasons for the conviction of other men, I have produced certain arguments elsewhere" [in "Tactica Sacra," *lib.* 2, *cap. ult.*], "and shall here make an addition of two more, which are not mentioned in that discourse, one from consent, another from continuance" (pp. 103, 104). Under "consent," he continues: "Writings of men differ exceedingly one from another, which made *Seneca* say, *Phi-*

*losophers would then be all of one minde when all clocks were
brought to strike at one and the same time.* Yea it is hard finding
an author that doth not differ from himself more or less, if he
write much, and at various seasons. But here is a most harmonious
consent. The word since written fully agrees with that which in
former times was delivered to the Patriarchs, and transmitted by
word of mouth. As the Word *God* is the same to-day, yesterday and
for ever, although not incarnate till the fulness of time came, and
then *made flesh: So the word of God,* although till *Moses* received
a command to put it in writing, there wanted that kinde of incarnation, was for substance the same before and after. And as the *written word* agreed with the *unwritten,* so doth one part of that which
is written harmonize with another. The two Testaments, Old and
New, like the two breasts of the same person give the same milk.
As if one draw water out of a deep well with vessels of different
mettal, one of brass, another of tin, a third of earth, the water may
seem at first to be of a different colour; but when the vessels are
brought near to the eye, this diversity of colours vanisheth, and
the waters tasted of have the same relish: So here, the different
style of the historiographers from Prophets, of the Prophets from
Evangelists, of the Evangelists from Apostles may make the truths
of Scripture seem of different complexions till one look narrowly
into them and taste them advisedly, then will the identity both of
colour and relish manifest it self " (pp. 104–106). — JOHN ARROW-
SMITH, " A Chain of Principles," Cambridge, 1659.

The passage in " Tactica Sacra " referred to above, opens by
stating that Protestants and Papists agree in believing that the
" Sacred Volume is the word of God and not of man," but differ
as to the *ultimate* ground of faith — as to " quidnam illud sit in
quod ultimò resolvitur ista fides, id est, quod sistit credulitatem
nostram, ità ut quando illuc pervenitur non opus sit ulteriore scru-
tinio " (p. 206). In order to elucidate the matter, he distinguishes a
" triplex principium " of the faith we owe to the divine authority
of the Scriptures: " unum *Introductivum*, alterum *Argumentativum*,
tertium, verò *Productivum.*" (1) The Introducing source of faith is the
testimony of the Church: " It may happen, and often does happen,
that the testimony of the church is the introducing source of faith,
i.e. that some believe the Scriptures to be the very word of God by
means of the church as the first to point them to it, but not on account of the church as the palmary basis of assent, but rather on the

Scripture's own account" ("*per Ecclesiam*, ut primum indicem," not "*propter Ecclesiam* ut palmarium assensûs argumentum," but "*propter Se*," p. 207). (2) The Probative source of faith is defined as "ipsius Scripturæ genius et indoles, sive innata" (p. 210). As light makes both other things and itself manifest, so the Scriptures. He lays stress especially on these three qualities as eminently proving Scripture to be the word of God — the majesty of the style, the sublimity of the matter, and the efficacy of the doctrine. (3) The Producing source of faith in the Scriptures is "the operation of the Holy Spirit and it alone." "Let the church testify all it is able to; let the Scripture shine with its own inherent light all it is wont to; if nevertheless, there be present no operation of the Holy Ghost, touching the heart with its own afflatus so that it may recognize the divinity that shines in the sacred volume, Divine Faith will still be absent; the testimony of the church cannot produce more than human faith, nor can the genius of Holy Scripture itself produce more than theological opinion" (p. 212). He then summons to the support of his teaching Calvin ("Institutes," I. vii. 4), Chamier (*lib.* VI. *De Canone, cap.* i. § 7), Whitaker ("Opera," *in fol., tom.* i. pp. 10, 78) and Baronius (p. 212), and defends himself from the charge of enthusiasm or mysticism. — JOHN ARROWSMITH, "Tactica Sacra," Cambridge, 1657 (Amsterdam ed. of 1700, pp. 206–212).

"It must be considered that at present, we have nothing to doe with Atheists, Pagans, Jews, or Turks, that deny the Scriptures, either wholly, or in part, so far are they from acknowledging them to be Gods word; but onely with such persons, as admitting and allowing them to be the word of God, doe yet want some clearer light, and fuller evidence, to work into their hearts a more certain perswasion, and more feeling impression of that truth whereof they are convinced, that all that is within them, even their whole heart, may not onely bow and stoop, but be wholly thrown down, and laid flat on the earth before this mighty scepter of the kingdom of Christ. Wherefore, we shall not need to bring in all the arguments that are used and taken up by others, to prove the Scriptures to be Gods word, but passing by amongst them such as are more obscure and farther deduced, shall content our selves with such plain evidences of this truth, as may be best understood of the simple, and appear at the first view, as being lively characters imprinted on the face and body of this sacred Book, by that divine

Spirit that composed it" (pp. 7, 8). . . . The arguments adduced are: 1. That the Scriptures are a law to the church, and " neither could nor were fit to be given by any other than by God himself "; 2. " That the holy Scriptures appear evidently to be the word of God." Under the latter: " The marks, or notes, by which the holy Scriptures are evidently discovered to be Gods word, are divers, of which we shall for the present content our selves with three only, and those which are most easie to be discerned. The first is, the style and phrase of speech, wherein the Scriptures apparently differ from all other writings, composed by men. The second is, the subjects or matter which the Scriptures handle, which are many times beyond the compasse of mans reason to finde out, and therefore must be revealed by God himself. The third evidence, is taken from the wonderfull effectuall power, which the Scriptures appear to have upon the hearts of men, in terrifying, comforting, subduing, and renuing them " (p. 18). These marks are then developed at large. Subsequently he develops the difference between Historical and Justifying faith: " Amongst Divines, Faith is commonly taken for a full perswasion of any truth upon Divine testimony. . . . The cause of faith is . . . the Spirit of Grace flowing unto a regenerate man from Christ his head. . . . And here we meet with the first difference between Historicall, and Justifying Faith, that they proceed from different causes, the one being infused by the spirit of Christ, dwelling in us, the other the effect onely of naturall reason, further inlightned (at the most) by the assistance of that Spirit. . . . The kind of assurance which true faith is built upon, we call an evidence. . . . How justifying faith hath an evidence of the things which it apprehends, we have seene: Historicall wants this evidence . . . as having no further assurance of what it beleeves, then that which Reason suggests, which may rather be tearmed a conviction that such things must be, then an evidence what they be. . . . To cleare this truth fully, we must consider the different testimonies, upon which justifying and historicall faith are built. For we shall find that true faith is built upon a Divine, the other upon a Humane testimony. . . . We call that a Divine testimony which is given of the Spirit of God to that spirit which is within a regenerate person. For unto any testimony two things are required, *First*, the manifesting, and presenting that which is to be credited, or beleeved: *Secondly*, an ability in him to whom it is witnessed to understand it. . . . It is evident then that true Faith is grounded upon a Divine testimony. In the next place we must make it appear, that Historicall faith relies onely upon an humane testimony. Now it cannot be denied that the truths of Divine mysteries though they cannot be found out by mans reason, . . . yet are they all consonant to right reason: and it is as evident that the testimony of reason, is an humane testimony. I say then, that historicall faith rests not upon the evidence or demonstration, but upon the reasonablenesse of divine truths, which therefore mans reason cannot but assent unto. . . . It is evident, that an Historicall faith beleeving these things for the Reasonablenesse of them, is but meerely upon an Humane Testimonie. Nay, if he should goe a steppe further and beleeve any thing that is written in the Scriptures, for the Testimony of the Scriptures, yet still he beleeves upon an Humane testimony, because he beleeves the Scriptures themselves upon Humane testimony, as upon the generall consent of the Church which receives the Scriptures, as the Word of God; or upon the probability and reasonablenesse of the things therein delivered; lastly, upon the observation of the Truth of those holy writings in most things, which makes them beleeved to be true in all. . . . We see then a wide Difference between Justifying, and Historicall faith, in the cause, subject and ground of Assurance; we shall finde no lesse in the Object. Now the generall Object of Faith, we know, is Gods Word and Promise, which onely is a sure ground to build Faith upon, as being the Word of the God of truth, *Deut*. iii. 2, 4, who cannot lye, *Tit*. i. 2, or denie himselfe, 2 *Tim*. ii. 13, or change his minde, *Num*. xxiii. 19. So that his Word must needs be Everlasting, *Psal*. cxix. 144, founded for ever, *v*. 132, upon two unfailing foundations, his Everlasting Truth, and unresistable Power. But the particular Object of justifying Faith is Gods Promise of Reconciliation, and Salvation by Christ, in whom onely we are Justified, *Rom*. iii. 24. In these Promises, both generall, and particular, an Historicall faith may beleeve both the truth, and the goodnesse of them: But the goodnesse of them to himselfe in particular he beleeves not, which a justifying Faith assents unto, and embraceth " (pp. 90–99). — JOHN WHITE, " A Way to the Tree of Life," London, 1647.

" In your first and main part, concerning the *Scriptures*, your discourse beares a comely suitablenesse to the nature and scope of that subject also. For as the Historicall beleefe of their authority, end, and use, is the foundation of all: so your demonstrations thereof are formed out of, and framed into a congeniall Harmony and consonancy to right Reason, and containe a naturall Genealogy and story of divine Truth about them . . . which way of setting forth divine Truths, as it carries with it the greatest conviction, and (as your selfe (in that forementioned Treatise) expresse it) begets faith Historicall, which hath for its ground a rationality, and consonancy to reason; so it is made use of by the holy Ghost, as a blessed subservient to that which you make the immediate proper cause of saving Faith, *The Demonstration of the Spirit.*" — THOMAS GOODWIN, in the letter " To the Author," prefixed to John White's " A Way to the Tree of Life," 1647, as above.

" The only preaching of the word, it alone without the Spirit, can no *more make an hair white or black, or draw us to the Son, or work repentance in sinners, then the sword of the Magistrate can work repentance.* . . . What can preaching of *man* or *angel* doe without God, is it not God and God only who can open the heart? " — SAMUEL RUTHERFORD, " A Free Disputation, etc.," p. 351.

" And that this light in the word is manifested unto us, 1. By the manuduction and ministry of the church, pointing unto the star, which is seen by its own light. 2. Because we bring not such an implanted suitableness of reason to scripture, as we do to other sciences . . . therefore, to proportion the eye of the soul to the light of the word, there is required an act of the spirit opening the eyes, and drawing away the vail, that we may discern the voice of Christ from strangers: for having the mind of Christ, we do, according to the measure of his spirit in us, judge of divine truths as he did." — EDWARD REYNOLDS, " Works," 1826, v. p. 154.

" Q. How are we assured that the Scripture is Gods Word? A. Not onely by the *Testimony* of the Church, which cannot *universally* deceive, but *especially* by the Testimony of the *Spirit*, working strange and supernaturall effects in us by the Word, giving us such joy, contentment, and satisfaction touching spirituall and eternall things, by way of tast and feeling, as is not possible for humane reason to doe: *Joh.* iv. 42; *Joh.* vi. 68, 69; 1 *Thes.* i. 5; 2 *Pet.* i. 18, 21; 2 *Cor.* iv. 6." — W. LYFORD, " Principles of Faith and Good Conscience, etc.," fifth ed., Oxford, 1658, p. 2.

" There remains one Question to be resolved, 'for the close of this whole matter (namely) *Into what then is our Faith finally resolved, and whereupon doth it stay it selfe, seeing the fore mentioned things, the Church, the Spirit, Reason and Providence, though their help and Ministery be needfull, yet our Faith is not built upon them, as hath been shewed?*

" The Authority and Truth of God speaking in the Scripture, is that upon which our Faith is built, and doth finally stay it selfe; the Ministery of the Church, the Illumination of the Spirit, the right use of Reason, are the choicest helps, by which we believe, by which we see the Law and will of God; But they are not the Law it selfe; the Divine Truth and Authority of Gods Word, is that which doth secure our Consciences.

" To the grounding of Faith it is necessary, that we know, first, what is the truth revealed, for else we cannot believe it, nor rest upon an unknown Truth; Secondly that God hath indeed revealed and declared those truths; and then the soul resteth upon it, as a sure Anchor of faith and hope. . . . If you ask further, How I know that God hath revealed them? I answer, by a two-fold certainty; one of Faith, the other of Experience; First I do infallibly by faith believe the Revelation, not upon the credit of any other Revelation but for it selfe, the Lord giving Testimony thereunto, not only by the constant Testimony of the Church, which cannot universally deceive, nor only by miracles from heaven, bearing witnesse to the Apostles doctrine, but chiefly by its own proper divine light, which shines therein. The truth contained in Scripture is a light, and is discerned by the Sons of light: It doth by its own light perswade us, and in all cases, doubts, and questions, it doth clearly testifie with us, or against us; which light is of that nature, that it giveth Testimony to it selfe, and receiveth Authority from no other, as the Sun is not seene by any light but his own, and we discerne sweet from sowre by its own Taste. And the meanes for opening our eyes to see this light (whereby our consciences are assured that we rest in God,) are diverse: first, some private, as Reading, Prayer, conference of places, consent of Churches in all Ages, Helps of learning, and reason sanctified. Secondly, some publike, as the Ministery of the Word. . . . Thirdly, But the chiefe helpe, to shew me and assure me of this light, is the Holy Spirit, given to Gods children, in, and by the use of the former meanes to open our understandings, to enlighten our mindes, that we may know and believe the words of this life, and the things which are freely given unto us of God; In which light thus shewn unto us, Faith staieth it selfe, without craving any further testimony or proofe, in the same manner that the Philosopher proveth, that with the same sense we see, and are assured we see: Thus I know by the certainty of Faith, resting upon its object, that the Doctrine of Scripture is from God: This is a certainty in respect of the understanding.

" 2. Whereunto adde, that other certainty of experience, which is a certainty in respect of the Affections and of the spirituall man, This is the spirits Seale set to Gods truth, (namely) the light of the word; when it is thus shewen unto us, it doth worke such strange and supernaturall effects upon the soul . . . so that the things apprehended by us in Divine knowledge, are more certainly discerned in the certainty of experience, than anything is discerned in the light of naturall understanding. . . . And thus much of my first doctrine; the supreame and divine Authority of the Scripture, to determine in all matters of faith, and practice." — WILLIAM LYFORD, " The Plain Mans Senses Exercised, etc.," London, 1657, pp. 37–40.

" And now we will draw towards the main conclusion, *How a simple Countrey-man is to believe our Bible to be the Word.* Doctor *Jackson,* and Master *John Goodwin* have set downe many, and many excellent things, but they flie so high, that they are for Eagles. . . . Now all the considerations these great Sophies have, and let there be as much more added to them, yet they will not do the work, till they come to the testimony of the spirit: They may and do work, and acquire in us an humane faith, which may stand free from actual hesitation, and doubting, but not from possible dubitation, for lay them all together, yet they may deceive, or be deceived. . . . So that when we have all done, and got all the help we can to rest on the Scriptures, the work is not done, till we by the Spirit of God have this sealed by infused faith in our souls that these books (which we have translated) are the very words of God. . . . Well then, though all humane reasons, the consent of all the world, will not help us to that faith in the Word, which will help us to heaven, yet they are a preparation, and such a preparation to this faith infused, that we cannot ordinarily look for faith infused, but by the way of this faith which is gotten by the arguments, reasons, considerations, convictions, and helps wrought by the Argumentations, and considerations proposed by men which do work (as most often it doth) in us an acquired humane faith free from actual (though not from possible) mistake and doubting. This may be and is, a faire meanes to bring us to look on the Scripture without any actual question made of it as the Word of God. And then by the use of the

Word to attain to a Divine faith, which is infallible by reason of the Divine infallible truth rightly conceived and believed by it." — RICHARD CAPEL, " Remains, etc.," London, 1658, pp. 69–73.

The Completeness of Scripture

2. The second property of Holy Scripture which the Confession adduces is its perfection or completeness (§ 6). Here the absolute objective completeness of Scripture for the great and primary purpose for which it is given is affirmed; and the necessity of any supplement to it is denied, with reference especially to the " new revelations " of the sectaries and the " traditions " of Rome. It is not affirmed that the Scriptures contain all truth, or even all religious truth; or that no other truth, or even religious truth, is attainable or verifiable by man through other sources of knowledge. This would be inconsistent with the frank recognition in section 1 of the light of nature as a real and trustworthy source of knowledge concerning God. There is only a strong assertion of the completeness and the finality of the Scriptural revelation of truth, for the specific purpose for which Scripture is given. God may give men knowledge concerning Him through the forms of the reason; and the amount of knowledge so attainable, as outlined by the Confession in the first section, is asserted to be enough to render men inexcusable for withholding from God the worship and service which is His due. The memory of the revelations which He may have supernaturally given to men in the past may be, more or less fully or purely, preserved in historical records or institutions; and this is especially true of those revelations which He has embodied in the institution, and in the institutions, of the Church which He has established in the world: the truths so preserved will exert their power over men's consciences, when conveyed to their knowledge by the ordinary testimony of men or by the offices and testimony of the Church. The Confession does not deny either the existence or the value of truth so obtained or so preserved for man. But it does deny the need of such sources of knowledge

to supplement what is set down in Scripture, in order to instruct us what "man is to believe concerning God and what duty God requires of man." It does affirm the absolute objective completeness of Scripture as a guide to the service of God, to faith, and to life. And it does deny that aught in the way of truth required by God to be believed, or in the way of duty required by Him to be performed, in order that we may attain salvation, is to be added from any other source whatever to what is revealed in Scripture.

This, it is to be observed, is to make Scripture something more than *a* rule of faith and practice; something more than *the* rule of faith and practice, in the sense of merely the fullest and best extant rule; something more even than *a sufficient* rule of faith and practice. It is to make it the *only* rule of faith and practice, to which nothing needs to be added to fit it to serve as our rule, and to which nothing is to be added to make it altogether complete as our authoritative law. It contains not only enough to serve all the purposes of a rule of faith and practice, but all that is to be laid as the authoritative law of life on the consciences of Christians. Therefore, the Larger Catechism defines (Q. 3): "The Holy Scriptures of the Old and New Testament are the Word of God, the *only* rule of faith and obedience"; and the Shorter Catechism: "The Word of God, which is contained in the Scriptures of the Old and New Testaments, is the *only* rule to direct us how we may glorify and enjoy Him." One of the chief effects of this declaration of the Confession is, therefore, to protect the people of God from the tyranny of human requirements, which lay upon men's consciences burdens that God has not laid upon them, and that are too grievous to be borne. It is the doctrinal basis of the subsequent assertions that "good works are only such as God hath commanded in His holy Word, and not such as, without the warrant thereof, are devised by men out of blind zeal, or upon any pretence of good intention" (xvi. 1); and that "God alone is Lord of the conscience, and hath left it free from the doctrines and commandments of men which are in anything contrary to His Word, or beside it in matters of faith and worship: so that to believe such doctrines, or to obey such commandments out of conscience, is to betray true liberty of conscience " (xx. 2). In a word, the Confessional doctrine of the sufficiency or completeness of Scripture is the charter of liberty of conscience; God's prescriptions for faith and conscience are required to be received with humility of heart, and none but God's.

It must be observed, however, that the teachings and prescriptions of Scripture are not confined by the Confession to what is " expressly set down in Scripture." Men are required to believe and to obey not only what is " expressly set down in Scripture," but also what " by good and necessary consequence may be deduced from Scripture." This is the strenuous and universal contention of the Reformed theology against Socinians and Arminians, who desired to confine the authority of Scripture to its literal asseverations; and it involves a characteristic honoring of reason as the instrument for the ascertainment of truth. We must depend upon our human faculties to ascertain what Scripture *says;* we cannot suddenly abnegate them and refuse their guidance in determining what Scripture *means.* This is not, of course, to make reason the ground of the authority of inferred doctrines and duties. Reason is the instrument of discovery of all doctrines and duties, whether " expressly set down in Scripture " or " by good and necessary consequence deduced from Scripture ": but their authority, when once discovered, is derived from God, who reveals and prescribes them in Scripture, either by literal assertion or by necessary implication. The Confession is only zealous, as it declares that only Scripture is the authoritative rule of faith and practice, so to declare that the whole of Scripture is authoritative, in the whole stretch of its involved meaning. It is the Reformed contention, reflected here by the Confession, that the sense of Scripture is Scripture, and that men are bound by its whole sense in all its implications. The reëmergence in recent controversies of the plea that the authority of Scripture is to be confined to its expressed declarations, and that human logic is not to be trusted in divine things, is, therefore, a direct denial of a fundamental position of Reformed theology, explicitly affirmed in the Confession, as well as an abnegation of fundamental reason, which would not only render thinking in a system impossible, but would discredit at a stroke many of the fundamentals of the faith, such e.g. as the doctrine of the Trinity, and would logically involve the denial of the authority of all doctrine whatsoever, since no single doctrine of whatever simplicity can be ascertained from Scripture except by the use of the processes of the understanding. It is, therefore, an unimportant incident that the recent plea against the use of human logic in determining doctrine has been most sharply put forward in order to justify the rejection of a doctrine which is explicitly taught, and that repeatedly, in the very letter of Scripture; if the plea is valid at all, it destroys at once our confidence in all doctrines, no one of which is ascertained or formulated without the aid of human logic.

It is further to be observed that the Confession, in asserting the perfection or completeness of Scripture, forgets neither the subjective disabilities of fallen man, nor his needs outside the sphere of " things necessary for God's glory, man's salvation, faith and life," in which sphere alone Scripture is asserted to be objectively complete or perfect. The Confession explicitly recognizes the " inward illumination of the Spirit of God " as necessary to man's " saving understanding of such things as are revealed in the Word." And it as explicitly recognizes that there are " circumstances concerning the worship of God and government of the Church, common to human actions and societies, which are to be ordered by the light of nature and Christian prudence."

While strenuously asserting the completeness of the Scriptural revelation of faith and duty, considered objectively, it adopts the principle, " *credo ut intelligam*," and as clearly asserts that a preparation of spirit is necessary to its saving understanding. As the Minutes of the Assembly show, the word " saving " is significant here. It is not denied that men, in the exercise of their natural powers of understanding, may attain to a knowledge from Scripture of what is revealed in Scripture.

It is only denied, as Dr. James S. Candlish admirably phrases it,[42] that it is possible to attain, without the Spirit's illumination, " such a knowledge as is not merely intellectual and inoperative, but accompanied with a relish and love for the truth, and leading to a life of holy obedience."

And while jealously guarding the uniqueness of the authority of Scripture in divine things, and its completeness in the sphere of faith and duty, the Confession equally clearly asserts that its prescriptions do not cover in detail every circumstance "concerning the worship of God and government of the Church." All that is in Scripture, by express statement or necessary implication, must be obeyed; and all that must be obeyed is in Scripture; but outside of and beyond what Scripture prescribes, there is a sphere of what may properly be done in worshiping God and governing His Church in which the principle of Christian liberty reigns, and in which the ordering is left to the light of nature and Christian prudence. How wide this sphere is, may be a matter of dispute: it is enough that the Confession explicitly recognizes its existence; and specifies " circumstances concerning the worship of God and government of the Church " as matters which fall within it. The limitation it suggests is that these circumstances are such as are " common to human actions and societies "; which probably means that the Church, as a society in the world, is free to take such order for its activities and government as are open to other human societies, though always, of course, because it is a divine society and under a divinely given charter, with regard to " the general rules of the Word, which are always to be observed."

Unless the declaration here be pressed beyond all bounds, no inconsistency will emerge with the position taken in chapter xxi. 1, that " the acceptable way of worshiping the true God is instituted by Himself, and so limited by His own revealed will, that He may not be worshiped according to the imaginations and devices of men, or the suggestions of Satan, under

[42] " The Doctrine of the Westminster Confession on Scripture," in *The British and Foreign Evangelical Review,* xxvi. 1877, p. 174.

any visible representation or any other way not prescribed in the Holy Scripture." Much less will inconsistency emerge with the teaching of chapters xxx. and xxxi. that " the Lord Jesus, as King and Head of His Church, hath therein appointed a government," established offices, and authorized synods. On the contrary, the same provision for the prudent regulation of worship and government which is here made, is there repeated, it being expressly set forth as one of the duties of synods and councils, " to set down rules and directions for the better ordering of the public worship of God, and government of His Church " — which appears to be an authoritative commentary on our present passage. A distinction apparently is intended to be drawn between " a way of worship " and the " ordering of worship ": the ordination of the former, in strong anti-Romish polemic, is reserved to God, while the latter alone is placed in the sphere of the prudent and reasonable regulation of the Church itself. The extreme position is excluded that nothing is to be done in the ordering of God's house except what is warranted by explicit provisions of the Word; but a sharp line of distinction is drawn between the duty of conforming in all things to the provisions of the Word and the liberty to be exercised outside of and beyond these provisions.

There is an inferential application of this declaration to the affairs of daily life also, which it may be wise for us to note. " In other words," says Dr. Alexander F. Mitchell, in his Lecture on " The Westminster Confession of Faith," [43] " the Westminster divines were so far from holding, as the earlier Puritans are accused of doing, that one must have an express text of Scripture for everything he says or does in common life; that they directly assert there are circumstances in regard both to the worship of God, and the government of His Church, for which no such sanction is to be sought, but which are left to be regulated by the dictates of reason and Christian prudence, if only care is taken that all be done decently and in order; and, while they directly grant this much, they leave it clearly to be inferred, farther, that merely human actions and the doings of

[43] Third ed., Edinburgh, 1867, p. 48.

civil societies, are to be regulated in the same way, or, as they elsewhere have it, according to justice, faithfulness, and truth."

" Chapter **XX.** *That necessary consequences from the written word of God do sufficiently and strongly prove the consequent or conclusion, if theoretical, to be a certain divine truth which ought to be believed, and, if practical, to be a necessary duty which we are obliged unto, jure divino.*

" This assertion must neither be so far enlarged as to comprehend the erroneous reasonings and consequences from Scripture which this or that man, or this or that church, apprehend and believe to be strong and necessary consequences (I speak of what *is*, not of what is *thought to be* a necessary consequence) : neither yet must it be so far contracted and straitened as the Arminians would have it, who admit of no proofs from Scripture, but either plain explicit texts, or such consequences as are *nulli non obviæ*, as neither are, nor can be, controverted by any man who is *rationis compos* (see their *Præf. ante Exam. Cens.*, and their *Examen*, cap. 25, p. 283) ; by which principle, if embraced, we must renounce many necessary truths which the reformed churches hold against the Arians, Antitrinitarians, Socinians, Papists, because the consequences and arguments from Scripture brought to prove them are not admitted as good by the adversaries.

" This also I must, in the second place, premise, that the meaning of the assertion is not that human reason, drawing a consequence from Scripture, can be the ground of our belief or conscience; for although the consequence or argumentation be drawn forth by men's reasons, yet the consequent itself, or conclusion, is not believed nor embraced by the strength of reason, but because it is the truth and will of God, which Camero, *Præl.*, tom. i. p. 364, doth very well clear. . . .

" Thirdly, Let us here observe with Gerhard, a distinction between corrupt reason and renewed or rectified reason. . . . It is the latter, not the former reason, which will be convinced and satisfied with consequences and conclusions drawn from Scripture, in things which concern the glory of God, and matters spiritual or divine.

" Fourthly, There are two sorts of consequences which Aquinas, part 1, quest. 32, art. 1, distinguisheth: 1. Such as make a sufficient and strong proof, or where the consequence is necessary and certain. . . . 2. By way of agreeableness or convenience. . . . This latter sort are in divers things of very great use; but for the present I speak of *necessary* consequences." He next proves his point: 1. From the example of Christ and His Apostles. 2. From the custom of the people of God. 3. " If we say that necessary consequences from Scripture prove not a *jus divinum*, we say what is inconsistent with the infinite wisdom of God; for although necessary consequences may be drawn from a man's word which do not agree with his mind and intention, and so men are oftentimes ensnared by their words; yet (as Camero well noteth) God being infinitely wise, it were a blasphemous opinion to hold that anything can be drawn by a certain and necessary consequence from his holy word which is not his will." . . . . 4. That great absurdities follow from the denial of this principle. 5. That the principle is conceded and acted on by those who deny it. 6. We would by denying it, deny " to the great God that which is a privilege of the little gods, or magistrates." — GEORGE GILLESPIE, " A Treatise of Miscellany Questions," 1649 (Edinburgh reprint of 1844, pp. 100–103, in " The Presbyterian's Armoury," vol. ii.).

" Now things may be contained in Scripture, either expresly, and in plain tearms, or by consequence drawn from some grounds that are delivered in Scripture, and one of these two ways all grounds of faith, or rules of practise, are to be found in these holy writings " (p. 65). . . . " two conclusions. The *first* is acknowledged by all men without contradiction, which is, *That there can be no infallible interpreter of the Scriptures but God himselfe.* The *second*, though it be somewhat more questioned, yet is as true as it in all points, namely, *That every Godly man hath in him a spirituall light*, by which he is directed in the understanding of Gods mind revealed in his word in all things needfull to salvation " (p. 161). — JOHN WHITE, " A Way to the Tree of Life," London, 1647.

" But you will say unto me, Now it is given by those holy apostles and prophets, and laid up in the Scriptures, may not all men, or any man, understand it? No; for as you have it in 2 Pet. i. 20, the Scripture is not of private interpretation (and he speaks especially of the gospel), that is, it is not in the power of any man's understanding to apprehend or know the meaning of the word. ' But,' saith he, ' holy men of God spake as they were moved by the Holy Ghost '; and, therefore, as the Scripture was written by the Holy Ghost, so it must be the Holy Ghost that must interpret it. Take all the wise men in the world, they are not able to understand one Scripture: it is but private interpretation. The Holy Ghost, therefore, the same Spirit that guided the holy apostles and prophets to write it, must guide the people of God to know the meaning of it; and as he first delivered it, so must he help men to understand it." — Thomas Goodwin, "Works," ed. Nichol, iv. 1862, p. 295.

"But Secondly, and more practically: If you would so understand the Scripture, that you may take heed thereunto, as to a Light shining in your dark state: then, First: you must go to God for the Spirit; for without it, ye cannot understand the Mind of God in the Scripture. . . . And seeing God hath promised to give this Spirit unto them that ask it, go unto God for the same. Secondly: Take heed of a worldly, fleshly mind; fleshly sins do exceedingly blind the mind from the things of God." — William Bridge, "Scripture-Light, the Most Sure Light," London, 1656, p. 52.

"It is the spirit of wisdom and revelation, which both openeth the heart to the word, giving an understanding to know the scriptures, and openeth the scriptures to the heart; for he takes of Christ's, and sheweth it unto us. . . . The spirit doth not reveal truth unto us, as he did in the primitive patefaction thereof to the prophets and apostles, — by divine and immediate inspiration, or in a way of simple enthusiasm: but what he reveals, he doth it by and out of the scriptures, which are the full and perfect rule of faith and obedience; as Christ opened to his disciples in the scriptures the things which concerned himself (*Luke* xxiv. 27)." — Edward Reynolds, "Works," v. 1826, pp. 152, 153.

The Perspicuity of Scripture

3. The third property of Scripture adduced, is its perspicuity (section 7): and here again the Confession is no less precise and guarded than clear and decided in its assertions. The perspicuity of Scripture is sharply affirmed, in the sense that the saving truth is declared to be placed in Scripture within the reach of all sincere seekers after it. But the limitations of its perspicuity are very fully and carefully stated. It is only "those things which are necessary to be known, believed, and observed, for salvation" that are said to lie perspicuously in Scripture. Even these things are not said to be plainly delivered on every occasion in which they fall to be mentioned or treated in Scripture; but only "in some place of Scripture

or other." Nor is it even stated that they all are anywhere so clearly propounded and opened as that they may easily be understood unto perfection; but only so as that " a sufficient understanding of them " may be attained. Nor yet are they affirmed to be equally understandable by all; but only that they are so clearly spread on the face of Scripture that every man, learned or unlearned, may attain a sufficient understanding of them to secure his salvation and peace. The variety of Scripture is here fully recognized — its frequent obscurities, its difficulties, its problems, and its profound depths darkening to all human gaze. The variety of mental acumen and teachableness of heart brought to the study of Scripture, is sufficiently recognized. But the fact that the Scriptures, despite all their obscurities, are a people's book, is sharply and decisively asserted; and with it the right of the unlearned man to them, and his capacity to make full use of them for the' main purpose for which they were given; and as well, the openness of the Scriptures to the " due use of the ordinary means." In a word there is combined here an adequate recognition of the profundity of the Scriptures and their occasional obscurity, with an equally clear assertion of the popular character of the Word of God as a message to every one of His children.

We must not overlook, in passing, that it is by " a due use of the ordinary means " that the learned and unlearned alike are said to be able to attain a sufficient knowledge of the saving message of Scripture. By the phrase, " a due use of the ordinary means," not only is the need of an infallible interpreting Church denied; but also all dependence on extraordinary revelations, the " inner light " of the mystical sectaries, and the like, is excluded. Within the " ordinary means " is included that " inward illumination of the Spirit of God," which is declared to be necessary to the saving understanding of Scripture in section 6, and which is here declared to be an ordinary endowment of the children of God. Within them is included all the religious and gracious means which God has placed at the disposal of His people, in the establishment of His Church and its teaching functions. But in this phrase is also included

the implication that Scripture is to be interpreted, as other
books are interpreted, in the ordinary processes and by means
of the ordinary implements of exegesis. There is included here,
therefore, the charter of a sound and rational system and
method of exposition; and we are accordingly not surprised to
find the Westminster Divines dealing constantly in their extant
writings with the question of "how to read the Scriptures,"
and laying down well-considered and reasonable canons of interpretation.

" The word is perspicuous, and hath ' notas insitas veritatis ' in
all necessary truth, as being written not for scholars only, but for
vulgar and illiterate men." — EDWARD REYNOLDS, " Works," v.
1826, p. 154.

" Scripture is so framed, as to deliver all things necessary to salvation in a clear and perspicuous way. There are indeed some obscure
passages in it to exercise our understandings, and prevent our lothing
of overmuch plainness and simplicity: yet whatsoever is needfull
for us to satisfie hunger, and nourish our souls to life eternal, is so
exprest (I do not say that it may be understood, but so) as men
that do not wilfully shut their eyes against the light, cannot possibly but understand it." — JOHN ARROWSMITH, " A Chain of Principles," Cambridge, 1659, p. 96.

" As it is a ful, and sufficient Light; so is it a cleer Light, a Light
that shineth; . . . not that there are no hard things therein, and difficulties; where is the man that ever was able to untie al the knots and
difficulties of Scripture? *Pauls* Epistles have their hard things to be
understood, even in the Eyes of *Peter*, Epist. 2. Chap. 3. Verse 16.
Yet what Truth is in all the Scripture, which is necessary to Salvation, but doth lie plain and cleer? . . . Deut. xxx. 11, 12, 13, 14.
Ro. x. 6, etc. . . . 1 Cor. ii. 16. Surely therefore this Light is a
cleer, and a shining light " (p. 14). " *Is there then no use of Reason,*
and of the Light thereof? Yea, much: Not only in Civil things; but
in the things of God, comparing Spiritual things, with Spiritual. Did
not Christ himself make use of Reason to prove the Resurrection:
. . . So the Apostles after him. Surely therefore, we are not so to
adhere to the Letter of the Scripture, as to deny the use of our
Reason in finding out the true sense and meaning of the Scripture.
. . . Reason is of great use, even in the things of God: and wel hath

he said, *Contra Rationem nemo sobrius*" (p. 33). [Clear rules for interpreting Scripture are laid down, pp. 50 *sq.*] — WILLIAM BRIDGE, " Scripture-Light, the Most Sure Light," London, 1656.

" It is true that this inward light, or anointing (as Saint *John* calls it) may be much cleered and enlarged by such helps as God is pleased to afford us, by the ministery of his word, by private conferences, and reading of godly mens writings, which are therefore to be made full use of diligently and constantly." [Good and sound rules for interpreting follow on pp. 164 *sq.*] — JOHN WHITE, " A Way to the Tree of Life," p. 163.

" Thus they fly from the Word written, to their owne revelations; which (as *Melanchthon* doth truly and wisely observe) doth draw after it three maine and mischievous conclusions. 1. A losse of the certainty of the doctrine of the Law, and the Articles of our faith. 2. An utter uncertainty of Christian consolations. 3. An extinction and destruction of true faith, and the exercises of faith: whereas there are now no revelations (sith all is written,) nor no need of any extraordinary revelations to expound the Word, but ordinary only, to expound the Scripture by the Scripture, and so give the sense, comparing places with places " (pp. 245, 246). " That one meaning of the Word is plaine, and a plaine heart shall have a plaine answer from God by his Spirit, *which is which* " (p. 243). — RICHARD CAPEL, " Tentations," (The fourth Part), London, 1655.

THE USE OF SCRIPTURE

IV. On the basis of this exposition of what Scripture is, in its origin and characteristics, the Confession next propounds certain important corollaries as to its use, with especial reference, as we have seen, to its form and transmission in text and translation, to its interpretation, and to its final authority in controversies (sections 8–10). These sections contain the application of the principles laid down in the preceding sections, to the burning practical questions raised by the very existence of the Reformed religion. Their declarations enunciate the fundamental principles of Protestantism: that the appeal for doctrine is not to be to the Latin Vulgate, but to the original Scriptures; that the people have right to the Scriptures in the vernacular; that Scripture, and not an infallible interpreting

Church, is the Supreme Interpreter of Scripture; and that
Scripture and not the Church is the Supreme Judge in religious
controversy. There is a true sense in which the whole preceding portion of the chapter was written in order to furnish firm
groundwork for these three closing sections.

The Transmission of Scripture

1. The object of the first of these sections (section 8) is to indicate the proper place in the Church of God, both of the original Scriptures and of translations of them into vernacular
tongues. The originals are asserted to be the only final appeal in
the defining and defense of doctrine. The translations are asserted to be competent channels for the transmission of saving
truth to the people at large.

In both matters, the impelling motive of the Confessional
statement was, of course, the contentions of the Church of
Rome, which on the one hand declared that the Latin Vulgate
was to be held " pro authentica " in all " public reading, disputation, preaching, and exposition "; and on the other, discountenanced the free use by the people of the Scriptures in
vernacular versions. In defense of both contentions, the Romanist controversialists made much of the uncertainties in
the transmission of Scripture, pointing to the various readings
in the original text and to the mistranslations in the versions,
with the general design of leaving the impression that the
Scriptures have been to such a degree corrupted in their transmission that no one can safely commit himself to their teaching, except under the safeguard of an infallible Church attesting and assuring of the truth.[44] The Westminster Divines were
the more driven formally to oppose this assertion of the practical loss of the divine Scriptures under the errors of transmission, that it had been taken up by the sectaries of the day in
their plea for toleration: how absurd, it was argued, to punish

[44] It is somewhat amusing to find a modern controversialist pointing to
the repetition of this stock argument of the Jesuits by Richard Simon
(1678), as its origination (Professor George F. Moore, D.D., in The Independent for March 30, 1893).

a man for not believing in the divine authority of Scripture, when you have no certainty that you have the true inspired Scripture in this or that passage appealed to. In opposition to both bodies of opponents alike, the Confession affirms the providential preservation of the inspired Scriptures in purity in the originals, and the adequate purity of the Word of God in translations.

The necessity of looking upon the original Scriptures only as " authentical," that is, authoritative in the highest sense,[45] and appealing to them alone as final authorities " in all controversies of religion," is based by the Confession on the fact that these original Scriptures, and they alone, are the *inspired* Bible. The Confession uses the strongest phrase of technical theological terminology to express their divine origin: " Being *immediately inspired* by God." It thereby points to the originals as the very Word of God, authoritative, as such, in every one of their deliverances of whatever kind. The possibility of appealing to the original Scriptures, as we now have them, as the Word of God, is based on the further fact that they have been " by God's singular care and providence kept pure in all ages." The Confession thus distinguishes between the autographic text of sacred Scripture, which it affirms was " immediately inspired by God," and its subsequent transmission in copies, over the course of which it affirms, not that an inspiring activity of God, but that a *providential care* of God has presided, with the effect that they have been kept pure and retain full authority in religious controversy. This distinction cannot be overlooked or explained away; it was intentional, as is proved by the controversies of the day in which the framers of the Confession were actively engaged.[46]

[45] Such appears to the present writer to be its sense here. Compare the word in the Oxford Dictionary, edited by Dr. Murray. It is obviously used here with direct reference to the deliverance of the Council of Trent on the Vulgate, where too the meaning is disputable. Professor Candlish (in *The British and Foreign Evangelical Review* of 1877, p. 176) takes it here as " attested as a correct copy of the author's work," which he thinks is the point mainly in view in this context.

[46] It is surprising, therefore, that Professor E. D. Morris writes: " As a

When it is affirmed that the transmission has been "kept pure," there is, of course, no intention to assert that no errors have crept into the original text during its transmission through so many ages by hand-copying and the printing press; nor is there any intention to assert that the precise text "immediately inspired by God," lies complete and entire, without the slightest corruption, on the pages of any one extant copy. The difference between the infallibility or errorlessness of immediate inspiration and the fallibility or liability to error of men operating under God's providential care alone, is intended to be taken at its full value. But it is intended to assert most strongly, first, that the autographs of Scripture, as immediately inspired, were in the highest sense the very Word of God and trustworthy in every detail; and, next, that God's singular providential care has preserved to the Church, through every vicissitude, these inspired and infallible Scriptures, diffused, indeed, in the multitude of copies, but safe and accessible. "What mistake is in one copy is corrected in another," was the proverbial philosophy of the time in this matter; and the assertion that the inspired text has "by God's singular care and providence been kept pure in all ages," is to

---

Professor in a Theological Seminary, it has been my duty to make a special study of the Westminster Confession of Faith, as I have done for twenty years; and I venture to affirm that no one who is qualified to give an opinion on the subject, would dare to risk his reputation on the statement that the Westminster divines ever thought of the original manuscripts of the Bible as distinct from the copies in their possession" (*The Evangelist* [newspaper], No. 2379, for January 26, 1893). Yet they explicitly make this distinction. When one who has given so much time to the study of the Confession could make this mistake, it is the less surprising that others, with less extended opportunity for learning the doctrine of the Confession, could share it (cf. e.g. Dr. Teunis S. Hamlin, in *The Evangelist* for February 16, 1893; Dr. Simon T. McPherson, *do.*, and in pamphlet form; Dr. Henry Van Dyke, in pamphlet entitled, "The Bible As It Is," 1893). But it is a source of mortification that such an obvious error should be given permanent record in the "Minutes" of the General Assembly, by the repetition of it in a protest to the action of the Assembly of 1893, signed by a number of names. This may give future historians the impression that the study of the Westminster Confession, to say nothing of the Westminster Divines, had fallen into some desuetude in the American Church, towards the end of the nineteenth century.

be understood not as if it affirmed that *every* copy has been kept pure from all error, but that the genuine text has been kept safe in the multitude of copies, so as never to be out of the reach of the Church of God, in the use of the ordinary means. In the sense of the Westminster Confession, therefore, the multiplication of copies of the Scriptures, the several early efforts towards the revision of the text, the raising up of scholars in our own day to collect and collate MSS., and to reform the text on scientific principles — of our Tischendorfs and Tregelleses, and Westcotts and Horts — are all parts of God's singular care and providence in preserving His inspired Word pure.

No doubt the authors of the Confession were far from being critics of the nineteenth century: they did not foresee the course of criticism nor anticipate the amount of labor which would be required for the reconstruction of the text of, say, the New Testament. Men like Lightfoot are found defending the readings of the common text against men like Beza; as there were some of them, like Lightfoot, who were engaged in the most advanced work which up to that time had been done on the Biblical text, Walton's " Polyglott," so others of them may have stood with John Owen, a few years later, in his strictures on that great work; and had their lot been cast in our day it is possible that many of them might have been of the school of Scrivener and Burgon, rather than of that of Westcott and Hort. But whether they were good critics or bad is not the point. It admits of no denial that they explicitly recognized the fact that the text of the Scriptures had suffered corruption in process of transmission, and affirmed that the " pure " text lies therefore not in one copy, but in all, and is to be attained not by simply reading the text in whatever copy may chance to fall into our hands, but by a process of comparison, i.e. by criticism.[47] The affirmation of the Confession includes the two

---

[47] Dr. Mitchell (Lecture on "The Westminster Confession of Faith," as cited, p. 48) says justly: "It does not, at first sight, look as if they were afraid of sound criticism, or meant to commit themselves to oppose its progress, when they thus vindicate for the originals of the Old and New

facts, therefore, first that the Scriptures in the originals were immediately inspired by God; and secondly that this inspired text has not been lost to the Church, but through God's good providence has been kept pure, amidst all the crowding errors of scribes and printers, and that therefore the Church still has the inspired Word of God in the originals, and is to appeal to it, and to it alone, as the final authority in all controversies of religion.

The defense of the right of the people to translations of Scripture in their mother tongue, is based by the Confession on the universality of the Gospel and the inability of the people at large to read and search the Scriptures in the original tongues. In making good this right, the competence of translations to convey the Word of God to the mind and heart is vigorously asserted; and as well the duty of all to make diligent use of translated Scripture, to the nourishing of the Christian life and hope. The sharp distinction that is drawn between the inspired originals and the uninspired translations is, there-

---

Testament Scriptures the place which was their due, and it was the least a council of thoughtful divines, meeting after that of Trent, could do to indicate dissent from its decrees respecting the Latin Vulgate. There were scholars in the Westminster Assembly who knew more about the state of the text than of late they have got credit for, and even those of them who were less skilled in such studies, with the common Hebrew and Greek Bibles of the age, nay, with the common English Bibles (which contained references to some various readings among their marginal annotations), were not left in total ignorance of the existence of such readings, and, therefore, when they asserted, that by God's singular care and providence the originals had been kept ' pure,' they could not mean to ignore the existence of various readings." But what they did mean, Dr. Mitchell seems to us less accurately to divine. They meant to assert that the various readings in the several copies did not prevent the preservation of the text absolutely pure in the multiplicity of copies; not that the text has been, despite various readings, kept adequately pure in every copy — which no doubt is also true, within certain limits. Dr. Briggs recognizes that: " The Westminster divines . . . knew, as well as we know, that there were variations of reading and uncertainties and errors in the Greek and Hebrew texts in their hands. The great Polyglotts had settled that " (" The Bible, the Church, and the Reason," 1892, p. 76). It might not be a bad thing for those who find difficulty in apprehending the attitude of the Westminster Divines on this subject, to consult Walton's " Prolegomena " and his " Considerator Considered," as the best sources of

fore, not permitted to blind men to the possibility and reality of the conveyance in translations, adequately for all the ordinary purposes of the Christian life and hope, of that Word of God which lies in the sense of Scripture, and not in the letter save as in a vessel for its safe conduct. When exactness and precision are needed, as in religious controversies, then the inspired originals only can properly be appealed to. But just because of the doctrine of the perspicuity of Scripture, as set forth in section 7, and that of its perfection, as set forth in section 6, translations suffice for all ordinary purposes, and enable those who truly seek for it to obtain a thorough knowledge of what is " necessary to be known, believed, and observed, for salvation." The use of translations is, thus, vindicated by the Confessional doctrine of the properties of Scripture.

But something more than the right of translations is here vindicated. The duty of making translations " into the vulgar language of every nation " under heaven, is laid upon the consciences of the people of God — a duty to which the great

---

information as to the knowledge of the times. In the latter, for example, we read such passages as these: " The whole *Prolegom. 7.* is spent in proving that the *Original Texts* are *not corrupted either by Jews, Christians or others, that they are of Supream authority in all matters, and the rule to try all translations by, That the copies we now have are the true transcripts of the first αὐτόγραφα written by the sacred Pen-men. That the speciall providence of God hath watched over these books, to preserve them pure and uncorrupt against all attempts of Sectaries, Hereticks and others, and will still preserve them to the end of the world, for the end for which they were at first written. That the errors or mistakes which may befall by negligence or inadvertency of Transcribers or Printers, are in matters of no concernment (from whence various readings have risen) and may by collation of other copies and other means there mentioned be rectified and amended*" (London, 1659, p. 14). " I do not onely say, that all *saving fundamentall truth* is contained in the Originall Copies, but that all revealed truth is still remaining entire; or, if any error or mistake have crept in, it is in matters of no concernment, so that not onely no matter of faith, but no considerable point of Historicall truth, Prophesies or other things, is thereby prejudiced, and that there are means left for rectifying any such mistakes where they are discovered " (p. 66). " To make one Copy a *standard* for all others, in which no mistake in the least can be found, he cannot, no Copy can plead this privilege since the first αὐτόγραφα were in being " (p. 68). So Walton, too, is among the prophets. These remarks might have been penned by Rutherford or Capel. Compare Usher, above, pp. 187–188.

Bible Societies are a part of the splendid response. And the duty of that personal searching of and feeding upon the Scriptures out of which alone a vigorous Christian life can be nourished, is laid upon the individual heart. The characteristic of Westminster piety is distinctly set forth as Bible piety; and everything is said here which could be said, to secure that the teachings of those who should acquire the right to teach under the sanction of this document, should be purely Bible teaching, and that the life of those who should live under it should draw its springs from a personal, vital, and constant contact with " the Word of God, which liveth and abideth forever."

" If you will dispute in Divinity, you must be able to produce the Scriptures in the Original Languages. *For no Translation is simply Authentical, or the undoubted word of God. In the undoubted word of God there can be no error. But in Translations there may be, and are errors. The Bible translated therefore is not the undoubted Word of God, but so far only as it agreeth with the Original* " (p. 1). " They [the Anabaptists] can alledge no Scripture but that which is translated into their Mother-tongue, in which there may be and are some errors; for, though the Scriptures be the infallible Word of God, yet the Translators were men subject to error, and they sometimes mistook " (p. 15). To the Anabaptist objection: " *Though we cannot prove the Letter to be well translated, that matters not much, for the Letter of the Scripture is not Scripture,*" Featley answers: " That is blasphemy, I pray take notice of it, he denieth the letter of the Text to be Scripture. (Anabaptist.) *The letter of the Word of God is not Scripture, without the revelation of the Spirit of God: the Word revealed by the Spirit is Scripture. (D. Featley.)* Very fine Doctrine; if God reveal not to us the meaning of the Scripture, is not the letter of the Text Scripture? By this reason, the greatest part of the *Revelation,* and other difficult Texts of Scripture should not be Scripture, because God hath not revealed to us the meaning of them " (p. 16). — DANIEL FEATLEY, " The Dippers dipt," London, 1660.

Usher, in his " Catholica Assertio Integritatis Fontium " (1610), lays down the propositions: — 1. " Ea editio quæ ab ipso Spiritu Sancto profecta est, et a Prophetis atque Apostolis Ecclesiæ primum tradita, pro authentica agnoscenda est; normaque esse debet, ad quam translationes humana industria elaboratæ examinari debeant " (p. 211). 2. These fountains are not so contaminated as to have lost their αἰθεντἐια for their normative function (p. 213).

The argument for the preservation of Scripture in integrity is drawn from providence, *a priori* applied (p. 215): it is not likely that God would have suffered the words of such illustrious Prophets and Apostles to be generally falsified; merely profane writings have been preserved through longer periods. And the argument may be made *a fortiori:* God's providence is over all His works, least of all will it fail with the " divina oracula, præcipuum manus opus ejus," and thus it is incredible that " utriusque Testamenti verba a Sancto ipsius Spiritu dictata ita corrumperentur, ut amissa primæva αἰθεντἐια . . ." (p. 216). He argues further against the *possibility* of a *perfect* translation (pp. 216–218). — JAMES USHER, " Works," ed. Elrington, xiv. 1864, pp. 211–218.

" To believe the Scriptures (which we are bid to search) whether in the Originals, or in the English translations, to be the Word of God (that is) to contain in them the Mind and Will of God, concerning Mans Salvation, is a necessary foundation of Christian Religion, that is, of our Faith, and worship of our Profession and Practise. . . . Obj. *Yea, but to believe the English scriptures, or the Bible translated into English to be the word of God; This is no foundation of Christian Religion.* This is but an old piece of *Popery* in an *Independent* dresse. . . . For answer hereunto, I lay down these two Conclusions: First, that Divine Truth in English, is as truly the Word of God, as the same Scriptures delivered in the Originall, Hebrew or Greek; yet with this difference, that the same is perfectly, immediately, and most absolutely in the Originall Hebrew and Greek, in other Translations, as the vessels wherein it is presented to us, and as far forth as they do agree with the Originalls: And every Translation agreeing with the Originall in the matter, is the same Canonicall Scripture that Hebrew or Greek is, even as it is the same Water, which is in the Fountain, and in the Stream; we say this is the Water of such or such a Well, or Spring, because it came from thence; so it is in this business, when the Apostles spake the wonderfull works of God in the languages of all Nations (that were at *Jerusalem*) wherein they were born; the Doctrine was the same to all, of the same truth and Divine Authority in the severall Languages: And this Doctrine is the Rule we seek for, and the foundation upon which our Religion is grounded, and it is all one thing, whether it be brought to my understanding in Welch, or English, or Greek, or Latine: All Language, or Writing, is but the Vessell, the Symbole, or Declaration of the Rule, not the Rule it self: It is a certain form or means by which the divine Truth cometh unto us, as things are contained in their words, and because the Doctrine and matter of the Text is not made known unto me but by words, and a language which I understand; therefore I say, the Scripture in English is the rule and ground of my Faith; whereupon I relying, have not a humane, but a Divine Authority for my Faith. Even as an *unbeliever* coming to our Sermons, is *convinced of all*, and *judged of all*, and he will acknowledge the Divine Truth of God, although by a humane voice in preaching, it be conveyed unto him, so we enjoy the infallible Doctrine of the Scripture, though by a mans Translation it be manifested unto me. . . .

 " *O, but I cannot believe them to be true, because the Translators were not assisted immediately by the holy Ghost.*

 " Such extraordinary assistance is needfull to one, that shall indite any part of Scripture, but not to a Translator, for a man by his skill in both Languages, by the ordinary helps of prayer and industry is able to open in the English tongue, what was before lockt up in the Originall Hebrew, or Greek. As a Spanish or Danish Embassadour, delivers his Message, and receives his answer by an Interpreter. — The interpreter needs not any inspiration, but by his skill in both languages, and his fidelity, he delivers the true mind of one Nation to another: So it is in this case, the Translator is Gods interpreter to a strange people.

 " *Oh! But by the often change and variable Translations, it seems that some have erred.* . . .

 " We do not say that this or that Translation is the Rule and Judge, but the Divine Truth translated; the knowledge whereof is brought to us in the Translation, as the vessell, wherein the Rule is presented to us, as is above said." — WILLIAM LYFORD, " The Plain Mans Senses Exercised," London, 1657, pp. 46–51.

 " Now by Scripture is meant the Word of God written. Written then, Printed now; . . . It is consented unto by all parties, that the *Translators* and *Transcribers* might erre, being not *Prophets,* nor indued with that *infallible* spirit in *translating,* or *transcribing,* as *Moses* and the *Prophets* were in their Original writings. The tentation lies on this side, . . . Sith there are no *Prophets,* no *Apostles,* no nor any *infallible* spirits in the *Church,* how can we build on the foundation of the Prophets and Apostles now, sith the Scriptures in their translated Copies are not free from all possible corruptions, in the Copies we have either by *transcribers* or *translators.* . . . For the Originals, though we have not the Primitive Copies written by the finger of God in the Tables, or by *Moses* and the *Prophets* in the *Hebrew,* or by the Apostles, and the rest in the Greek for the New Testament, yet we have Copies in both languages, which Copies vary not from the Primitive writings in any matter which may stumble any. This concernes onely the learned, and they know that by consent of all parties, the most learned on all sides amongst Christians do shake hands in this, that God by his providence hath preserved them uncorrupt. What if there be variety of readings in some Copies? and some mistakes in writing or Printing? this makes nothing against our doctrine, sith for all this the fountaine runs clear, and if the fountain be not clear all translations must needs be muddie. . . .

" For if an Ambassadour deliver his minde by an *Interpreter,* are not the words of the *Interpreter* the words of the *Ambassadour?* Right, say you, if the *Interpreter* do it truely: So, say I, a Translation, is a translation no further then he doth translate, and interpret truely: for a false translation, so farre as it is false, is no translation. . . . God being in his providence very careful, that his Church shall not want sufficient provision for their soules, hath ever, doth, and will ever so assist Translators, that for the main they shall not erre. I am of minde, that there was never any Christian Church, but the Lord did so hold the hands, and direct the pens of the translators, so that the translations might well be called the Word of God, . . . subject I confesse to some errour, but not such errour, but that it did serve to help the Church to faith, for the salvation of their souls. . . .

" I cannot but confesse that it sometimes makes my heart ake, when I seriously consider what is said, *That we cannot assure our selves that the Hebrew in the Old Testament, and the Greek in the New, are the right Hebrew and Greek, any further then our Masters and Tutors, and the General consent of all the Learned in the world do so say, not one dissenting.* But yet say these, *since the Apostles, there are no men in the world but are subject to deceive, and to be deceived. All infallibility* in matters of this nature having long since left the world. . . . And to the like purpose is that observation, *That the two Tables written immediately by Moses and the Prophets, and the Greek Copies immediately penned by the Apostles, and Apostolical men are all lost, or not to be made use of, except by a very few. And that we have none in Hebrew or Greek, but what are transcribed. Now transcribers are ordinary men, subject to mistake, may faile, having no unerring spirit to hold their hands in writing.*

" These be terrible blasts, and do little else when they meet with a weak head and heart, but open the doore to Atheisme and quite to fling off the bridle, which onely can hold them and us in the wayes of truth and piety: this is to fill the conceits of men with evil thoughts against the Purity of the Originals: And if the Fountains run not clear, the *Translation cannot be clean.* . . . It is granted that translators were not led by such an infallible spirit as the Prophets, and Apostles were. . . . Well then, as God committed the Hebrew Text of the Old Testament to the Jewes, and did and doth move their hearts to keep it untainted to this day: So I dare lay it on the same God, that he in his providence is so with the Church of the *Gentiles*, that they have and do preserve the Greek Text uncorrupt, and clear: As for some scapes by Transcribers, that comes to no more, than to censure a book to be corrupt, because of some scapes in the printing, and 'tis certaine, that what mistake is in one print, is corrected in another. . . . Therefore I make no question, but the sweet providence of God hath held the hearts, and hands, and pens of translators, so in all true Churches in all times, that the *virnacular*, and *popular* translation into mother tongues, have been made pure, without any considerable tincture of errour to endanger the soules of his Church. For what if Interpreters and Translators were not Prophets, yet God hath and doth use so to guide them, that they have been, are, and shall be preserved from so erring in translating the Scriptures, that the souls of his people may have that which will feed them to eternal life, that they shall have sufficient for their instruction, and consolation here, and salvation hereafter. . . . *Translations are sufficient with all their mistakes to save the Church.* I will deliver this in the words of Master Baine (Spiritual armory. 263, 264). *Faith cometh by hearing of the word from a particular Minister, who by confession of all is subject to errour; As God hath not immediately and infallibly assisted Ministers, that they cannot erre at all, so we know that he is in some measure with them, that they cannot altogether erre. A Translation that erreth cannot beget faith, so farre forth as it erreth, The word Translated, though subject to errour, is Gods Word, and begetteth, and increaseth faith, not so farre forth, as man through frailty erreth, but as he is assisted through speaking, and translating to write the truth.* So he, This gives full satisfaction to me, and I hope it will to others." — RICHARD CAPEL, " Remains," London, 1658, pp. 3, 12–13, 19–20, 29–33, 38–40, 43, and 79–83.

" But to goe on, That cannot be the way of God which necessarily inferreth the darkeness, inevidence, and inextricable difficultie of understanding the Scriptures. But such is the way of Libertie of Conscience. . . . For Master *John Goodwin,* undeniably the learnedst and most godly man of that way, hath said in a marginall note, of men for piety and learning, I cannot admire enough.

" *The Vindicators call the denying of Scriptures to be the word of God a damnable Heresie, and we have no certainty that the Scriptures of the Old and New Testament which we now have, either the English translation, or the Originall of Hebrew and Greek copies are the word of God. So then holding the Scriptures to be the Word of God in either of these two senses, or significations of the words* (either translations, or originall) *can with no tolerable pretext or colour be called a foundation of Christian Religion, unlesse their foundations be made of the credit, learning and authoritie of men.*

" Because there is need to wonder, by the way, at this, Let the reader observe, that Libertines resolve all our faith, and so the certaintie of our salvation on Paper and Inke; and Mr. *John Goodwin* will allow us no foundation of faith, but such as is made of grammars and Characters, and if the Scripture be wrong pointed, or the Printer drunke, or if the translation slip, then our faith is gone: Whereas the meanes of conveying the things beleeved may be fallible, as writing, printing, translating, speaking, are all fallible meanes of conveying the truth of old and new Testament to us, and yet the Word of GOD in that which is delivered to us is infallible, 1. For let the Printer be fallible, 2. The translation fallible. 3. The Grammer fallible. 4. The man that readeth the word or publisheth it fallible, yet this hindreth not but the truth it self contained in the written word of God is infallible; . . . Now in the carrying of the doctrine of the Prophets and Apostles to our knowledge, through Printers, translators, grammer, pens, and tongues of men from so many ages, all which are fallible, we are to look to an unerring and undeclinable providence, conveying the Testament of Christ, which in it self is infallible and begs no truth, no authoritie either from the Church as Papists dreame, or from Grammer, Characters, Print-

ers, or translator, all these being adventitious, and yesterday accidents to the nature of the word of God, and when Mr. *Goodwin* resolves all our faith into a foundation *of Christian Religion* (if I may
call it Religion, *made of the credit, learning and authority of men,*
he would have *mens learning and authoritie* either the word of God,
or the essence and nature thereof, which is as good as to include the
garments and cloathes of man, in the nature and definition of a man,
and build our faith upon a paper foundation, but our faith is not bot-
tomed or resolved upon these fallible meanes. . . .

 " The Scripture resolves our faith on, *Thus saith the Lord,* the
only authoritie that all the Prophets alledge, and *Paul,* 1 Thes. ii. 13.
*For this cause also thanke we God without ceasing because when ye
received the word of God which ye heard of us, ye received it not as
the word of man* (made of mens credit and learning as Mr. Goodwin
saith), *but (as it is in truth) the word of God.*

 " Weak, dry, and saplesse should be our faith, all our *patience
and consolation of the Scriptures,* Rom. xv. 4, all our hope on the
word of God, Ps. cxix. 49, 50, 52, 54, 55, all our certainty of faith, if
it were so as Mr. Goodwin averreth. But we have βεβαιότερον λόγον
a more sure word of prophesie, surer than that which was heard on
the Mount for our direction, and the establishing of our faith, 2 Pet.
i. 19, Joh. v. 39. . . . Undoubtedly Christ appealeth to the Scriptures as to the onely Judge of that controversie, between him and the
*Jewes, whether the Son of Mary was the eternall Son of God, and the
Saviour of the world,* he supposed the written Scriptures which came
through the hands of fallible Printers and Translatours, and were
copies at the second, if not at the twentieth hand from the first copy
of *Moses* and the Prophets, and so were written by sinfull men, who
might have miswritten and corrupted the Scripture, yet to be a judge
and a rule of faith, and fit to determine that controversie and all
others, and a Judge *de facto,* and actually preserved by a divine
hand from errours, mistakes and corruptions, else Christ might, in
that, appealed to a lying Judge, and a corrupt and uncertaine witnesse; and though there be errours of number, genealogies, etc. of
writing in the Scripture, as written [48] or printed, yet we hold providence watcheth so over it, that in the body of articles of faith, and
necessary truths, we are certaine with the certainty of faith, it is that
same very word of God, having the same speciall operations *of enlightening the eyes, converting the soule, making wise the simple,*

[48] I.e. Manuscript.

as being lively, *sharper than a two-edged sword*, full of divinity, life, Majesty, power, simplicity, wisdome, certainty, etc. which the Prophets of old, and the writings of the Evangelists, and Apostles had.

" Mr. *Goodwins* argument makes as much against Christ, and the Apostles, as against us, for they could never in all their Sermons and Writings so frequently, bottome and found the faith on καθὼς γέγραπται *as it is written in the Prophets, as David saith, as Isaiah saith,* and *Hosea, as Daniel saith, as Moses and Samuel, and all the Prophets beare witnesse,* if they had had no other certainty, *that the writings of the Prophets,* that came to their hands, *was the very word of God,* but *the credit, learning and authority of men,* as Mr. *Goodwin* saith, for sure Christ and the Apostles, and Evangelists, had not the authentick and first copies of *Moses* and the Prophets, but only copies written by men, who might mistake, Printers and Translators not being then, more then now, *immediately inspired Prophets,* but fallible men, and obnoxious to failings, mistakes, and ignorance of ancient Hebraismes, and force of words; and if ye remove an unerring providence, who doubts but men might adde a לא or subtract, and so vitiate the fountaine sense? and omit points, change consonants, which in Hebrew and Greek, both might quite alter the sense: . . . May not *reading, interpunction, a parenthesis, a letter, an accent,* alter the sense of all fundamentalls in the Decalogue? of the principles of the Gospel? and turne the Scripture in all points (which Mr. Doctour [Jeremy Taylor] restricts to some few darker places, whose senses are off the way to heaven, and lesse necessary) in a field of Problemes, and turne all beleeving into degladiations of wits? all our comforts of the Scriptures into the reelings of a Windmill, and phancies of seven Moons at once in the firmament? this is to put our faith and the first fruits of the Spirit, and Heaven and Hell to the Presse. But though Printers and Pens of men may erre, it followeth not *that heresies should be tolerated,* except we say, 1 That our faith is ultimately resolved upon characters, and the faith of Printers. 2 We must say, we have not the cleare and infallible word of God, because the Scripture comes to our hand, by fallible means, which is a great inconsequence, for though *Scribes, Translators, Grammarians, Printers,* may all erre, it followeth not that an [un-]erring providence of him that hath seven eyes, hath not delivered to the Church, the Scriptures containing the infallible truth of God. Say that *Baruch* might erre in writing the Prophesie of *Jeremiah,* it followeth not that the Prophesie of *Jeremiah,* which we have, is not the infallible word of God; if all *Translatours* and *Printers* did then alone watch over the Church, it were something, and if there were not *one with seven eyes* to care for the Scripture. But for *Tradition, Councells, Popes, Fathers,* they are all fallible means, and so far forth to be beleeved, as they bring Scripture with them." — SAMUEL RUTHERFORD, " A Free Disputation Against pretended Liberty of Conscience," London, 1649, pp. 360–366, 370–371.

" How can we hold, and keep fast, the Letter of the Scripture, when there are so many Greek Copies of the New Testament? and those diverse one from another? " " Yes, well: For though there are many received Copies of the New Testament; yet there is no material difference between them. The four Evangelists do vary in the Relation of the same thing; yet because there is no contradiction, or material variation, we do adhere to al of them, and deny none. In the times of the Jews, before Christ, they had but one Original of the Old Testament; yet that hath several readings: there is a Marginal reading, and a Line reading, and they differ no less than eight hundred times the one from the other; yet the Jews did adhere to both, and denied neither; Why? Because there was no material difference. And so now, though there be many Copies of the New Testament; yet seeing there is no material difference between them, we may adhere to all: For whoever wil understand the Scripture, must be sure to keep, and hold fast the Letter, not denying it " (p. 47). [By " material " difference, Bridge means, not difference of moment, but difference in matter or in sense, as the opposite to difference in letter. For his teaching as to the importance of the letter see the quotation above, p. 206: " Though the Letter of the Scripture be not the Word alone, yet the Letter with the true sense and meaning of it, is the Word. . . . So if ye destroy the Letter of the Scripture, you do destroy the Scripture; and if you do deny the Letter, how is it possible that you should attain to the true sense thereof, when the Sense lies wrapped up in the Letters, and the words thereof? . . . If you would have the true knowledg, and understand the Scripture, and so behold this great Light in its full glory and brightness; you must diligently enquire into the true sense and meaning of it: for the true sense and meaning, is the soul thereof " (pp. 46, 47).] — WILLIAM BRIDGE, " Scripture-Light, the Most Sure Light," London, 1656.

" Consider how many copies were abroad in the world. The Old

Testament was in every synagogue: and how many copies would men take of the New? So that it is impossible, but still Scripture must be conveyed " (vi. p. 61). " Admirable is their [the Masorites'] pains, to prove the text uncorrupt, against a gainsaying Papist. . . . So that, if we had no other surety for the truth of the Old Testament text, these men's pains, methinks, should be enough to stop the mouth of a daring Papist " (iv. p. 20). " It was their great care and solicitousness . . . to preserve the text in all purity. . . . Yet could they not, for all their care, but have some false copies go up and down amongst them, through heedlessness or error of transcribers. . . . To which may be added, that the same power and care of God, that preserves the church, would preserve the Scriptures pure to it: and he that did, and could, preserve the whole, — could preserve every part, so that not so much as a tittle should perish " (iii. pp. 405–408). — JOHN LIGHTFOOT, " Works " (ed. Pitman).

" The antient Jews preserved the letter of Scripture entire, but lost the sense; as the Papists now keep the text, but let go the truth " (p. 93). " Yet the bible hath been continued " [in spite of persecution] " still by the over-ruling hand of heaven " (p. 107). — JOHN ARROWSMITH, " A Chain of Principles," Cambridge, 1659.

The Interpretation of Scripture

2. Out of the same properties of Scripture follows also, logically, the Confessional doctrine of the interpretation of Scripture. This cuts off at once the greater part of the difficulty of interpretation, by declaring that Scripture has but one sense; and puts the chief instrument of interpretation in the hands of every Bible reader, by declaring that Scripture is its own interpreter, and that more obscure Scriptures are to be explained by plainer Scriptures. Of course, it is not meant that thus all difficulties of Scripture are cleared up; the Confession is not so immediately concerned here with the detailed scientific exposition of Scripture as with its practical and doctrinal use. What is intended is to affirm, in accord with the doctrines of the perfection and perspicuity of Scripture as set forth in sections 6 and 7, that the plain man, by paying heed to the clear passages of Scripture and by passing provisionally over those of doubtful interpretation, may come to a full and saving

knowledge of its teaching in all " things which are necessary to be known, believed, and observed, for salvation." If he stumbles upon dark statements, yet " in some place of Scripture or other " the saving doctrines may be found " so clearly propounded and opened " that he may obtain " a sufficient understanding of them." And this rule, thus commended to the plain man seeking light, is commended also to the scholar seeking his way through the obscurities of the letter. Human learning may give him aid; parallel passages alone will give him infallible guidance: and while the one is not to be neglected, certainly to the other he may be required docilely to bow. Of course, the rule here set forth is that which is known as " interpreting by the analogy of faith," and its foundation is the assumption of the common authorship of Scripture by God, who is truth itself. If we once allow the Confessional doctrine of the divine authorship of Scripture, it becomes only reasonable that we should not permit ourselves to interpret this divine author into inconsistency with Himself, without compelling reason. This is the Confession's standpoint; and from this standpoint the rule to interpret Scripture by Scripture is more than reasonable — it is necessary.

Having quoted Rom. xi. 2: " God hath not cast away his people whom he foreknew," Arrowsmith adds: " The infallible meaning whereof may be gathered from that in Peter, *Elect according to the foreknowledge of God the Father* (1 Pet. i. 2). And more plainly yet in verse the seventh and eighth of the same chapter." — JOHN ARROWSMITH, " A Chain of Principles," Cambridge, 1659, p. 333.

" The same Scripture hath but one intire Sense. Indeed Papists tel us, that one Scripture hath many Senses; but the Protestants hold, That there is but one Sense of a Scripture, though divers applications of it. . . . Though the sense of the Scripture be but one intire sense, yet somtimes the Scripture is to be understood Literally, sometimes Figuratively, and Metaphorically (but alwaies Spiritually, for when it is taken Literally, it is taken Spiritually) for saies the Apostle; *If thy Brother offend thee, heap coals of fire upon his head:* that is not to be taken Literally, but Metaphorically " (pp. 48, 49). " Something you must do by way of Observation; something by way of Practice. [1.] As for Observation, in case you be able, you must consult the Original. . . . If you would understand the true sense and meaning of a controverted Scripture; then look wel into the Coherence, the Scope, and the Context thereof. . . . If you would understand the Scripture rightly, then compare one Scripture with another. . . . And be sure that you swerve not from the proportion of Faith " (pp. 50, 51). — WILLIAM BRIDGE, " Scripture-Light, the Most Sure Light," London, 1656.

" There are that make many senses of Scripture, but upon no sufficient ground, whereas it is apparent, there can be but one true and right sense. Yet we grant that some places may have a proper sense, or a mysticall or allegoricall, as it is called, *Gal.* iv. 24. But if we weigh it well, there is but one sense of the words, which is proper, the other is the sense of the Type expressed by those words, which represents unto us some mysticall thing. . . . Such Allegoricall senses of Scripture, we must not easily admit, unless the Scripture it self warrant them." Neither must we " obtrude our Allegories upon others, as the sense of the Holy Ghost, much less to build upon them any ground of faith, or rule of life." — JOHN WHITE, " A Way to the Tree of Life," London, 1647, pp. 167, 168.

" The same Spirit which assureth an honest heart, that the Bible is the Word of God, will guide him to finde out the right sense of the Word. The sense of the Law is the Law; and of the Word of God there is but *one* sense: it is the easier found out, because there is but *one* sense." — RICHARD CAPEL, " Tentations," (The fourth Part), London, 1655, p. 243.

The Finality of Scripture

3. The whole exposition of the doctrine of Scripture is appropriately closed (section 10) with the assertion that the Holy Spirit, who speaks in every part of Scripture, is the Supreme Judge in all controversies of religion. This is, of course, nothing more than the application of the property of authority laid down in section 4, to the use of Scripture, which is here in discussion. But there is a sense in which, as Turrettin reminds us, this is the palmary point in the whole controversy as to the Scriptures. For with both the Romanist and the Enthusiast, everything else of the Protestant doctrine of

Scripture which was brought into dispute — its authority, integrity, purity, perspicuity, or perfection — was brought into dispute only that Scripture might be declined as the Supreme Judge in controversies of religion. The Confession therefore most fitly closes its statement with a perfectly explicit affirmation that religious controversies are to be decided, not on the ground of " decrees of councils, opinions of ancient writers, doctrines of men, and private spirits," under whatever names they may masquerade in the changing modes of speech which the passage of years brings to controversies — whether as traditions, deliverances of reason, the voice of immanent divinity, the " testimony of the Spirit," the " Christian consciousness," private or corporate, or the consensus of scholarship — but on the ground of the unrepealable " Thus said the Lord " of Scripture itself. By this indisputable authority all other assumed authorities are to be tested, and in its " sentence we are to rest."

The mode of expression is worth our notice. The Supreme Judge is not said to be Scripture, but " the Holy Spirit speaking in Scripture." It is not, however, to be imagined that a distinction is here drawn between the Scriptures and the Holy Spirit speaking in them. The phraseology is determined by the form which the controversy with Rome had taken. The Romanists distinguished between the Rule and the Judge, and were ready to allow the Scriptures to be the Rule, though an incomplete Rule, but asserted that a Judge was also required to apply the Rule; and this Judge they argued must be a present and living one. The Protestants rejoined that the Holy Spirit who speaks in Scripture is a Living and the sole Supreme Judge. This language cannot be interpreted, therefore, as if it instituted a distinction between Scripture as a whole and that part of it in which the Holy Spirit speaks, so that it is only affirmed that He speaks somewhere in Scripture, and His utterances are to be sought out from the mass of human speech in or under which they are buried, and only they held to be authoritative. Nor yet can it be read as if it were intended to say that the Holy Ghost speaks in Scripture only when, by His power, its words are driven home to our hearts and consciences and so " find us "; so that then, and then only, is Scripture a judge in controversies, when our spirits recognize its words as utterances of God. The passage deals with the objective right of Scripture to rule, not with the subjective recognition of that right on our part. Nor, even yet can it be read as Dr. Candlish appears to read it,[49] as if the phrase were intended to express the twofold fact that Scripture is given by the Holy Spirit and our eyes opened to its meaning by the same Spirit; so that it is He, the combined inspirer and illuminator, who is the Judge in all controversies. In accordance with the whole context of this chapter, and with the ordinary Protestant usage as well,[50] the phrase must be read as asserting that, as a matter of fact, whenever and wherever Scripture speaks, that is the Holy Ghost speaking; and as a matter of duty, every controversy in religion shall be held to be settled by the Word of Scripture, and every other assumed authority shall be brought to the test and sentence of the decisive " It is written."

Nevertheless, the choice of this phrase, as has already been hinted, is not without significance. As Dr. Candlish points out in the article already quoted, Chillingworth, in his " The Religion of Protestants a Safe Way to Salvation," sought to meet the demand of Romish controversialists for a living Judge by suggesting that the Bible is not a dead rule, but the Judge's sentence put on record, and, being plain in all things necessary, is all that we require. The Confession seems to go a step further, and to declare that the living Spirit speaks in His Word, which is " quick and powerful, and sharper than any two-edged sword." If this is all that Dr. Candlish means by his language criticised above, then doubtless it is true that the Spirit is conceived of as more than the Word; but it needs to be recognized that it is wholly as in the Word that He is here spoken of, and

[49] *British and Foreign Evangelical Review*, 1877, pp. 178, 179. Cf. Featley, above, p. 242.

[50] E.g. Turrettin, Loc. ii., qu. 20 (in his " Institutio Theologiæ Elenc."), where *Scriptura* and *Deus in Scriptura loquens* are used convertibly as the *supremus et infallibilis controversiarum Judex.*

not as also in the heart, and that the representation is that the Word of God acts as a living thing because the Spirit is in it, and speaks out from it His decisions in all controversies. The words of Scripture, in brief, are not dead words, but are instinct with life.

" The scriptures . . . are the alone rule of all controversies." " So then the only light by which differences are to be decided, is the word, being a full canon of God's revealed will: for the Lord doth not now, as in former times, make himself known by dreams, or visions, or any other immediate way." — EDWARD REYNOLDS, " Works," v. 1826, pp. 152, 153.

" The Scripture makes it self the judge and determiner of all questions and controversies in religion." — SAMUEL RUTHERFORD, " A Free Disputation, etc.," London, 1649, p. 361.

" The holy Scripture is called ' a more sure word ' than that voice of God which came from heaven concerning his well-beloved Son, 2 Pet. i. 17–19, and so by parity of reason, if not *a fortiori*, the written word of God is surer than any voice which can speak in the soul of a man, and an inward testimony may sooner deceive us than the written word can; which being so, we may and ought to try the voice which speaks in the soul by the voice of the Lord which speaks in the Scripture." — GEORGE GILLESPIE, " A Treatise of Miscellany Questions," chapter xxi. 1649: Edinburgh reprint, 1844, p. 110, in " The Presbyterian's Armoury," ii. 1846.

" ' How may Christians inquire of God in their doubtings, as Israel did . . . in theirs? ' I must answer briefly, and that in the words of God himself, ' To the law and to the testament ': to the written word of God, ' Search the Scriptures.' . . . There is now no other way to inquire of God, but only from his word." — JOHN LIGHTFOOT, " Works," ed. Pitman, vi. p. 286.

Such is the doctrine of Holy Scripture taught in the Westminster Confession. If it be compared in its details with the teachings of Scripture, it will be found to be but the careful and well-guarded statement of what is delivered by Scripture concerning itself. If it be tested in the cold light of scientific theology, it will commend itself as a reasoned statement, remarkable for the exactness of its definitions and the close concatenation of its parts. If it be approached from the point of view of vital religion, it will satisfy the inquirer by presenting him with a formula in which he will discover all the needs of his heart and life met and safeguarded. Numerous divergences from it have been propounded of late years, even among those who profess the Westminster doctrine as their doctrine. But it has not yet been made apparent that any of these divergences can commend themselves to one who would fain hold a doctrine of Scripture which is at once Scriptural and reasonable, and a foundation upon which faith can safely build her house. In this case, the old still seems to be better.

IV

THE DOCTRINE OF INSPIRATION OF
THE WESTMINSTER DIVINES

THE DOCTRINE OF INSPIRATION OF THE WESTMINSTER DIVINES [1]

" CONTROVERSIALISTS in general," says the late Principal
Cunningham, in one of his essays, " have shown an intense and
irresistible desire to prove that their peculiar opinions are supported by the Fathers, or by the Reformers, or by the great
divines of their own church, and have often exhibited a great
want both of wisdom and of candor in the efforts they have
made to effect this object." This device has in no sphere of
doctrinal discussion been made more use of than in recent
controversies concerning the inspiration of the Scriptures.
" The theory of a literal inspiration and inerrancy was not held
by the Reformers," is the first remark which Dr. Schaff makes
in a recent incidental attempt to controvert this doctrine, [2]
and it is the first remark that falls to be made by most writers
of his school. It was so good and learned a man as Tholuck
who has, as Professor Pieper points out, [3] " *sit venia verbo* —
deceived a whole generation of scientific . . . theologians "
into so unhistorical an assertion. Tholuck misquoted and misinterpreted Luther in the article on inspiration in the first
edition of Herzog's " Encyclopaedia," and has been copied ever
since.

A certain palliation may be admitted for this particular
error. There is a difference between the Reformers' treatment
of Scripture and that of the theologians of the seventeenth century, a difference arising from the differing points of view from
which they approach the subject. The Reformers, striving for
very life, had little time or heart to do more than to insist on

[1] From *The Presbyterian Quarterly,* viii. 1894, pp. 19–76.

[2] *The Independent,* July 20, 1893.

[3] *The Presbyterian and Reformed Review* for January, 1893, pp. 261–
263.

the sole divine authority of Scripture, and the facts involved
in and underlying that authority. The Systematists of the
seventeenth century, intrenching a position already won,
sought to give these facts an indefectible foundation in a special theory of the mode of inspiration, the theory of dictation.
The Reformers, though using language conformable to, or even
suggestive of, the theory of dictation, do not formally present
that theory, as do the Systematists of the seventeenth century,
as the fixed ground-work of their doctrine of Scripture. They
were concerned rather with the facts which the seventeenth
century writers put this theory forward to explain and safeguard; and their thinking concerning Scripture appears, indeed, to be rooted in a theory of *concursus* or *synergism* rather
than in one of *dictation*. Observing this, over-eager controversialists may be possibly misled into supposing that the Reformers were no more strenuous as to the facts involved — the
facts as to the plenary or verbal inspiration and infallibility or
inerrancy of the Scriptures — than as to the theory of the
mode of inspiration which would best safeguard these facts.
It is a prodigious historical blunder so to suppose. The fully
developed theory of dictation as applied to inspiration seems
to be a product of seventeenth century thought; but the Reformers are as strenuous as the Quenstedts and Buxtorfs as to
the facts of detailed divine authority and inerrancy which that
theory was intended to secure.Yet one can at least conceive
how such a blunder can be made, especially by men who are
accustomed to assert that it is only on a theory of verbal dictation that detailed divine authority and inerrancy can be defended for the Scriptures. For us to understand the origin of
their error, gross as it is, it is only necessary to suppose that
they imagine the doctrines of verbal inspiration and inerrancy
to be corollaries of the theory of dictation, instead of the theory
of dictation to be, as it was historically, an attempt to supply
for these necessary doctrines a firm and impregnable basis.

It is otherwise with the desperate contention which has
lately been put forth by Dr. Briggs that the seventeenth century divines themselves were adherents of the modern " lib-

eral " doctrine of Scripture. Such a contention as this, as the French say, brings us stupefaction. Pressed with the obvious fact that the Westminster Confession teaches the verbal or plenary inspiration and infallibility or inerrancy of the original Scriptures, Dr. Briggs seeks on the one hand to explain away the obvious meaning of the document, and on the other to undermine it by the round assertion that the British theologians of the Westminster age did not believe the doctrine of the verbal inspiration and inerrancy of Scripture. He has given himself repeatedly to the justification of this extraordinary assertion — the assertion, in effect, that the Reformed theologians of Britain were in violent (though assuredly unconscious) opposition to their brethren on the Continent, in the most fundamental postulate of their system. The most formal attempt to supply proof for it is to be found, however, in two sections in " Whither? " [4] entitled respectively " Verbal Inspiration " and " Inerrancy of the Scriptures," where Dr. Briggs represents the doctrines so described as " false doctrines," which are not only extra-confessional, but wholly shift the ground of confessional doctrine. These assertions he supports by quotations from seventeenth century and especially Westminster divines.

As to verbal inspiration, he presents a catena of six quotations under the caption: " We shall give the opinions of a few Presbyterians of the seventeenth century on this subject, in order to show how far modern divines have departed from the Westminster doctrine of the Bible." It is perhaps not altogether clear to what immediate antecedent the words " this subject " here refer. The subject of the section is " verbal inspiration," and the subject of the immediately preceding sentences is the outcry of certain modern divines against rationalizing critics for destroying the " scholastic theory of verbal inspiration." In any event, the catena of citations is meant to show that the Scriptures were not esteemed by the men who influenced the formulation of the Westminster doctrines of the Bible, as inspired in their " verbal expression " — a mode of statement

[4] Pp. 64–68 and 68–73 (1889).

which Dr. Briggs for himself also declares to be "entirely false." The doctrine of the inerrancy of the Scriptures, he declares to come "into conflict with the historical faith of the Church," on the basis of two quotations. One of these, from Rutherford, is introduced by the statement: "The Westminster divines did not teach the inerrancy of the original autographs. The saintly Rutherford thus expresses their views." The other is from Baxter and is introduced with the statement: "Richard Baxter was the leading Presbyterian of his time. He knew what he was about in his warning" — which is then quoted.

In all these quotations, without exception, Dr. Briggs falls into what has been called the "Fallacy of Quotations," which a recent writer describes as one of the most dangerous of fallacies, because one of the most difficult to detect. It "consists," this writer continues, "in alleging passages from well-known authors as proving some disputed point, when they do not prove it at all, but something resembling it as far as words go, though quite different from it in reality."[5] It may perhaps be worth our while to exhibit the fallacy of these quotations. It might indeed be safely left to the general impossibility of the position asserted, to refute even so formal a presentation of proof. But as it appears that men unacquainted with the history of the doctrine of inspiration, and specifically with the writings of the Puritan divines, may be and have been misled; and as it is in any case a matter of considerable interest to observe how tolerably careful and logically exact writers can be misunderstood and made to testify against their fundamental convictions; it may be useful to subject Dr. Briggs's proof-passages to a sufficiently close scrutiny at least fully to understand them.

DR. BRIGGS'S QUOTATIONS EXAMINED

Let us take up the catena on verbal inspiration first, and (on the principle of *ex pede Herculem*), let us begin with the

[5] R. F. Clarke, S. J., in *The Nineteenth Century*, for January, 1893, p. 85, while reviewing Mr. Mivart on "The Happiness in Hell."

last quotation. It is from John Ball's " Catechism," a famous
work of great repute among the Puritans, and reads as follows:

" The testimonie of the Spirit doth not teach or assure us of the
Letters, syllables, or severall words of holy Scripture, which are
onely as a vessell, to carry and convey that heavenly light unto us,
but it doth seale in our hearts the saving truth contained in those
sacred writings into what language soever they be translated."

In adducing this as a proof that the seventeenth century
divines did not believe in verbal inspiration, Dr. Briggs has
obviously been misled by his own point of view. For there is a
single assumption on which such a passage might seem to assert that only the matter of Scripture is inspired, or, at least,
that we can be assured only of so much — the assumption that
the sole conclusive evidence that the Scriptures are the word
of God, is the witness of the Holy Spirit in the heart. But
though this may be Dr. Briggs's point of view, it is not John
Ball's. The very object of the passage quoted is rather to guard
against this overworking of the testimony of the Spirit: it is
one of six rules which are given professedly " to prevent mistaking " in the use of this evidence. The immediately succeeding rule warns us that " the Spirit doth not lead them in whom
it dwelleth, absolutely and at once into all truth, but into all
truth necessary to salvation, and by degrees " (p. 43); and
one of the previous ones warns us not to forget that it is " private, not publique; testifying only to him that is endued therewith " (p. 42). Ball's object, thus, is not to suggest that the
Scriptures are not verbally inspired, but only to deny that this
can be proved by " the testimonie of the Spirit." By other
forms of testimony, however (he teaches), it can be proved;
and resting upon them as giving a " certainty of the mind,"
he unhesitatingly teaches verbal inspiration. Let us hear his
statement of it:

" *Q.* What call you the word of God?
A. The holy Scripture immediately inspired, which is contained
in the Books of the Old and New. Testament.
Q. What is it to be immediately inspired?

A. To be immediately inspired, is to be as it were breathed, and to come from the Father by the Holy Ghost, without all means.

Q. Were the Scriptures thus inspired?

A. Thus the holy Scriptures in the Originals were inspired both for matter and words " (pp. 6–8).[6]

Examination of the other quotations given in this catena would lead to similar results. Let us take the first. It is drawn from William Lyford's " Plain Mans Senses Exercised," and runs as follows:

" All language or writing is but the vessel, the symbol, or declaration of the rule, not the rule itself. It is a certain form or means by which the divine truth cometh unto us, as things are contained in words, and because the doctrine and matter of the text is not made unto one, but by words and a language which I understand; therefore I say, the Scripture in English is the rule and ground of my faith, and whereupon I relying have not a humane, but a divine authority for my faith."

Here, again, the fault in quotation arises from the fact that a passage is given in which the writer is not speaking to the specific subject for which he is quoted. Lyford is not here discussing directly the matter of inspiration at all, but is arguing the widely different question of the value of translations of Scripture — whether the word of God, that is, as he defines it (p. 46), " the Mind and Will of God," is so competently conveyed in translations that the unlearned may have in them a divine foundation for faith. But though he holds that " Divine Truth in English, is as truly the Word of God, as the same Scriptures delivered in the Originall, Hebrew or Greek," he feels bound to add: " yet with this difference, that the same is perfectly, immediately, and most absolutely in the Originall Hebrew and Greek, in other Translations, as the vessels wherein it is presented to us, and as far forth as they do agree with the Originalls " (p. 49). The difference between the originals and the translations arises from the fact that " the

[6] Cf. John Ball's " Catechism," entitled " A Short Treatise, etc.," fifteenth impression, London, 1656.

Translators were not assisted immediately by the Holy Ghost," while " such extraordinary assistance is needfull to one, that shall indite any part of Scripture " (p. 50).[7] With all his tendency to defend the value of translations, therefore, he does not assimilate the inspiration of the originals to the divine element common to the two.

This enhancement of translations is carried, perhaps, a step. higher by another of Dr. Briggs's witnesses, Richard Capel, whom we may take as our third example, representing the middle of the catena. The following is the passage which Dr. Briggs quotes:

" Now, what shall a poor unlearned Christian do, if he hath nothing to rest his poore soul on? The originals he understands not; if he did, the first copies are not to be had; he cannot tell whether the Hebrew or Greek copies be the *right Hebrew* or the *right Greek*, or that which is said to be the *meaning of the Hebrew or Greek,* but as men tell us, who are not *prophets and may mistake*. Besides, the transcribers were men and might err. These considerations may let in Atheisme like a flood."

The effect of this quotation is somewhat spoiled, as Dr. Briggs gives it, by the omission of the italicizing (restored here),[8] which indicates words borrowed by Capel from his opponent. For Capel is not stating his own view here, as the unwary reader of this extract only might be misled into believing, but controverting another's view. He is inveighing against the carelessness of the welfare of human souls which is shown by those who dwell upon the uncertainties of copies and the fallibilities of scribes and translators, as if the saving word of God did not persist through all these dangers. It is this mode of procedure which he says " may let in Atheisme like a flood "; the passage quoted by Dr. Briggs being a positing of difficulties which he at once sets himself " to help " by laying down a series of contrary propositions. Accordingly he had said at an earlier point (pp. 38–40):

[7] See William Lyford's " The Plain Mans Senses Exercised, etc.," London, 1657.

[8] From Capel's " Remains," London, 1658, pp. 76–77.

" I cannot but confesse that it sometimes makes my heart ake, when I seriously consider what is said, *That we cannot assure our selves that the Hebrew in the Old Testament, and the Greek in the New, are the right Hebrew and Greek, any further then our Masters and Tutors, and the General consent of all the Learned in the world do so say, not one dissenting,* . . . All infallibility in matters of this nature having long since left the world. . . . And to the like purpose is that observation, *That the two Tables written immediately by Moses and the Prophets, and the Greek Copies immediately penned by the Apostles, and Apostolical men are all lost, or not to be made use of, except by a very few. And that we have none in Hebrew or Greek, but what are transcribed. Now transcribers are ordinary men, subject to mistake, may faile, having no unerring spirit to hold their hands in writing.*

" These be terrible blasts, and do little else when they meet with a weak head and heart, but open the doore to Atheisme, and quite to fling off the bridle, which onely can hold them and us in the wayes of truth and piety: this is to fill the conceits of men with evil thoughts against the Purity of the Originals: And if the Fountains run not clear, *the Translation cannot be clean.*"

Capel's purpose, in a word, is not to depreciate the infallibility of the autographs, but to vindicate the general purity of the transmission in copies and translations. The originals were in his view " the dictates of the Spirit," and their writers being " indued with the infallible Spirit," " might not erre." [9] His tendency was thus not to lower the autographs towards the level of the translations, but to elevate the translations, so far as may be, towards the originals, claiming, in effect, for them a kind of secondary (providential) inspiration. Accordingly, although he would confess that the transmitters of Scripture had " no unerring spirit to hold their hands in writing," he yet asserted that God so assists them " that for the main they shall not erre," and that God does " so hold the hands, and direct the pens of the translators, so that the translations might well be called the Word of God " (p. 31). No student of the history of doctrine need be told that the affinities

[9] Cf. " Remains," pp. 12, 38, 43, 55.

of this view are with the highest, even the most mechanical theory of inspiration.[10]

The remaining three quotations in the catena on verbal inspiration, taken from Poole, Vines, and Wallis, are of precisely similar character to those already investigated, and we need not spend time in showing what must now be obvious to every careful reader, that they do not bear at all on the point in support of which they are quoted. Let us turn rather to the passages quoted to prove that the " Westminster divines did not teach the inerrancy of the original autographs." The first of these is from Samuel Rutherford, who proves to be only another representative of the same type of thought that Capel stands for. Indeed, if the reader will read the long passage given in " Whither? " with an eye to the italics which mark the phraseology borrowed from John Goodwin, whom Rutherford is here refuting, or the longer passage given in " The Bible, the Church, and the Reason " (pp. 221, etc.), with the same care, he will not fail to catch a hint of Rutherford's high doctrine. And if he should read with those passages the preceding and succeeding contexts, and the intervening omissions, so as to catch the drift of the whole argument, he would scarcely be able to repress his astonishment that Dr. Briggs could have so misapprehended his author. Rutherford here, in a word, is almost bitterly attacking Goodwin's assertions of the fallibility of the transmission of Scripture; over against which he posits an " unerring and undeclinable providence " (p. 363) presiding over it. So far is he from suggesting that the autographs are not inerrant that he is almost ready to assert that all the copies and translations are inerrant too. He evidently feels himself to be making a great concession, and to be almost straining the truth, when he admits (p. 366) that there may be " errours of number, genealogies, etc., of writing in the Scripture, as written " [i.e. in the manuscript form] " or printed." Though God has used means which, considered in themselves, are fallible in transmitting the Scriptures, yet He has not left the transmission to their fallibility, but has added

[10] Cf. Ladd, " Doctrine of Sacred Scripture," ii. 1883, pp. 182 *sq.*

an unerring providence, keeping them from slipping. He urges that Goodwin's argument " makes as much against Christ, and the Apostles, as against us," for they too had but copies of the Old Testament, the scribes and translators of which were " then [no] more then now, *immediately* inspired *Prophets*," and were consequently liable to error; so that " if ye remove an unerring providence, who doubts but men might adde . . . or subtract, and so vitiate the fountaine sense? and omit points, change consonants, which in the Hebrew and Greek, both might quite alter the sense? " Yet both Christ and the apostles appeal to the Scriptures freely, with such phrases as " as David saith " and the like, staking their trustworthiness on the true transmission. Nor will he allow the argument that it is the inerrancy of the quoters, not of the text quoted, which is our safeguard in such cases. This, he says, presumes " that Christ and the Apostles might, and did finde errours, and misprintings even in written [i.e. manuscript] Scripture, which might reduce the Church in after ages to an invincible ignorance in matters of faith, and yet they gave no notice to the Church thereof " (p. 367).

To Rutherford, therefore, all the Scriptures, whether in matters fundamental or not, were written by God (p. 373); he quotes them with the formula, " The Holy Ghost saith " (pp. 353, 354 *bis*); he declares that the writers of the New Testament were " immediately inspired " (p. 368), a phrase of quite technical and unmistakable meaning; represents it as the part of an apostate to deny " all the Scriptures to be the word of God " (p. 349); and looks upon them as written under an influence which preserved them from error and mistake (pp. 362, 366, etc.), and as constituting a more sure word than an immediate oracle from heaven (p. 193). In the immediately preceding words to those which Dr. Briggs extracts, he declares that " The Scripture resolves our faith on, *Thus saith the Lord*," which is " the only authoritie that all the Prophets alledge, and *Paul* "; and adds that, if it were so as Mr. Goodwin averred, " all our certainty of faith " would be gone; wherefore he praises God that " we have βεβαιότερον λόγον *a more sure word of Prophesie,* surer then that which was heard on the Mount for our direction, and the establishing of our faithe." [11]

It is an interesting indication of the universality of high views of inspiration, that John Goodwin, Rutherford's adversary in this treatise, himself held them. So far as the points we are here interested in are concerned, indeed, the dispute was little more than a logomachy, since Rutherford and his friends admitted that the providential preservation of Scripture is not so perfect but that some errors have found their way into the several copies, and that the translations are only in a derived sense the word of God, and only so far forth as they truly represent the originals; while Goodwin was ready to allow that God's providence is active in preserving the manuscript transmission substantially pure, and that the truth of God is adequately conveyed in any good translation. In Goodwin's reply to his assailants it is made abundantly apparent that he, too, believed in the inerrancy of the autographs, his objection to calling copies and translations the word of God, in every sense, turning just on this — that no one extant copy or translation is errorlessly the word of God.[12]

But what about Richard Baxter? Dr. Briggs tells us that he " was the leading Presbyterian of his time," and that " he knew what he was about in his warning," which is quoted as Dr. Briggs's final proof that " the Westminster divines did not teach the inerrancy of the original autographs." But the passage that is quoted has again really nothing to do with the inerrancy of the autographs. It is only one of Baxter's frequently repeated statements of his sound apologetical position as to the relative value of different portions of Scripture, and the relative importance of the sense and the letter. It is partly on account of his firm grasp and clear expression and defence of this apologetical position, that we think of Baxter as one of

[11] For these references see Rutherford's " A Free Disputation, etc.," London, 1649.

[12] See his " The Divine Authority of the Scriptures, etc.," London, 1648, pp. 8, 9, 11, 12, 13.

the wisest and soundest writers on the subject of Scripture in his day. Here is the passage:

" And here I must tell you a great and needful truth, which, . . . Christians fearing to confess, by overdoing tempt men to Infidelity. The Scripture is like a man's body, where some parts are but for the preservation of the rest, and may be maimed without death: The sense is the soul of the Scripture; and the letters but the body, or vehicle. The doctrine of the Creed, Lord's Prayer, and Decalogue, Baptism and the Lord's Supper, is the vital part, and Christianity itself. The Old Testament letter (written as we have it about Ezra's time) is that vehicle which is as imperfect as the Revelation of these times was: But as after Christ's incarnation and ascension, the Spirit was more abundantly given, and the Revelation more perfect and sealed, so the doctrine is more full and the vehicle or body, that is, the words are less imperfect and more sure to us; so that he that doubteth of the truth of some words in the Old Testament, or of some circumstances in the New, hath no reason therefore to doubt of the Christian religion, of which these writings are but the vehicle or body, sufficient to ascertain us of the truth of the History and Doctrine."

This is admirably said, we say, and despite the fact that it is requoted by Dr. Briggs in " The Bible, the Church, and the Reason," to show that Baxter allows errors in the Scriptures, it really has no bearing on that question. Not that it is at all doubtful what attitude Baxter held on that question. He has been frequently misunderstood and misquoted, but most gratuitously. He did not for a moment doubt the verbal inspiration and autographic inerrancy of Scripture. It is one thing to refuse to make the verbal inspiration of Scripture the ground of all religion; another to deny its reality or importance: and it is the former of these that Baxter did, and the latter that Dr. Briggs says he did. Baxter's chief works are accessible to all in Duncan's London edition of his practical writings, published in 1830, so that we may content ourselves here with the adduction of a passage or two, which will put his position on the exact point at issue beyond doubt, leaving it to the interested student to work out the details for himself. This is Baxter's pervasive testimony:

" Those that affirm that it was but the doctrine of Christianity that was sealed by the Holy Ghost, and in which they were infallible, but that their writings were in circumstantials, and by passages, and method, and words, and other modal respects, imperfect and fallible as other good men's, (in a less degree,) though they heinously and dangerously err, yet do not destroy, or hazard the christian religion by it " (xx. p. 95).

" Though the apostles were directed by the Holy Ghost in speaking and writing the doctrine of Christ, so that we know they performed their part without errors, yet the delivering down of this speech and writings to us is a human work, to be performed by the assistance of ordinary providence " (xx. p. 115).

" All the credit of the Gospel and christian religion doth not lie on the perfect freedom of the Scriptures from all error: but yet we doubt not to prove this their perfection against all the cavils of infidels, though we can prove the truth of our religion without it " (xx. p. 118).

" All that the holy writers have recorded is true, (and no falsehood in the Scripture, but what is from the error of scribes and translators) " (xv. p. 65).

" No error or contradiction is in it, but what is in some copies, by the failing of preservers, transcribers, printers, or translators " (xxi. p. 542).

" If Scripture be so certainly true, then those passages in it that seem to men contradictory, must needs be true; for they do but seem so, and are not so indeed " (xx. p. 27).

THE REAL WESTMINSTER DOCTRINE

The Westminster doctrine of inspiration has probably emerged before this from the confusion into which Dr. Briggs's unfortunate quotations would immerse it. Doubtless it will be more satisfactorily visible, however, if we adjoin a clear and succinct statement of it from the pen of some representative writer. Probably no one man has a better right to be quoted as an exponent of the doctrine of the Westminster divines as a body, on this subject, than " the Patriarch of Dorchester,"

John White. He was chosen by them at the outset of their labors to serve as one of the two assessors, whose activity was expected to supplement the little public capacity of Twisse. His book " Directions for the Profitable Reading of the Scriptures "[13] was introduced to the world by one of the leading Westminster divines, Dr. Thomas Goodwin, in a glowing eulogy. And Baxter[14] names it among the works on the divine authority of the Scriptures which he especially recommends to the English reader. It is, therefore, a truly representative book. We cannot do better than to adduce White's general statement as a fair representation of the prevalent view of his time. He founds his remarks on II Pet. i. 20, 21, and writes as follows:

" The Apostle . . . describes that kinde of assistance of the holy Ghost, in the delivery of the Scriptures, two ways. *First,* by way of negation, that they were neither of private interpretation, nor came by the wil of man. *Secondly,* he describes the same assistance affirmatively, testifying that they spake as they were moved by the holy Ghost.

" In the former of these, wherein he expresseth this manner of delivering the Scriptures by way of negation, the Apostle excludes the working of the naturall faculties of mans mind altogether: *First,* the understanding, when he denies that the Scripture is of any private interpretation, or rather of mens own explication, that is, it was not expressed by the understanding of man, or delivered according to mans judgement, or by his wisdome. So that not onely the matter or substance of the truths revealed, but the very forms of expression were not of mans devising, as they are in Preaching, where the matter which men preach is not, or ought not to be the Ministers own that preacheth, but is the Word of truth, 2 *Tim.* ii. 15. but the tearms, phrases, and expressions are his own. *Secondly,* he saith, that it came not by the will of man, who neither made his own choice of the matters to be handled, nor of the forms and manner of delivery. So that both the understanding, and will of man, as farre as they were meerly naturall, had nothing to doe in this holy work, save onely to understand, and approve that which was dictated by God him-

---

[13] " A Way to the Tree of Life: Discovered in Sundry Directions, etc.," London, 1647.
[14] " Practical Works," xxii. 1830, p. 335.

selfe, unto those that wrote it from his mouth, or the suggesting of
his Spirit.

" Again, the work of the Holy Ghost in the delivery of the Scriptures is set down affirmatively, when the Pen-men of those sacred
writings are described, to speak as they were moved or carried by
the holy Ghost, a phrase which mûst be warily understood. For we
may not conceive that they were moved in writing these Scriptures,
as the pen is moved by the hand that guides it, without understanding what they did: For they not onely understood, but willingly consented to what they wrote, and were not like those that
pronounced the Devils Oracles, rapt and carried out of themselves
by a kinde of extasie, wherein the Devill made use of their tongues
and mouths, to pronounce that which themselves understood not.
But the Apostles meaning is, that the Spirit of God moved them in
this work of writing the Scriptures, not according to nature, but
above nature, shining into their understandings clearly, and fully,
by an heavenly and supernaturall light, and carrying and moving
their wils thereby with a delight, and holy embracing of that truth
revealed, and with a like desire to publish and make known the
secrets and counsels of God, revealed unto them, unto his Church.

" Yea, beyond all this, the holy Ghost not only suggested unto
them the substance of that doctrine which they were to deliver and
leave upon record unto the Church, (for so far he usually assists
faithfull Ministers, in dispensing of the Word, in the course of their
Ministery) but besides hee supplyed unto them the very phrases,
method, and whole order of those things that are written in the
Scriptures, whereas he leaves Ministers in preaching the Word, to
the choice of their own phrases and expressions, wherein, as also in
some particulars which they deliver, they may be mistaken, although in the main fundamentals which they lay before their hearers, and in the generall course of the work of their Ministery, they
do not grossly erre. Thus then the holy Ghost, not only assisted holy
men in penning the Scriptures, but in a sort took the work out of
their hand, making use of nothing in the men, but of their understandings to receive and comprehend, their wils to consent unto, and
their hands to write downe that which they delivered. When we say,
that the holy Ghost framed the very phrase and style wherein
the Scriptures were written, we mean not, that he altered the phrase
and manner of speaking, wherewith custome and education had acquainted those that wrote the Scriptures, but rather speaks his own

words, as it were in the sound of their voice, or chooseth out of their words and phrases such as were fit for his own purpose. Thus upon instruments men play what lesson they please, but the instrument renders the sound of it more harsh or pleasant, according to the nature of it self. Thus amongst the Pen-men of Scriptures, we finde that some write in a rude and more unpolished style, as *Amos;* some in a more elegant phrase, as *Isay.* Some discover art and learning in their writings, as S. *Paul;* others write in a more vulgar way, as S. *James.* And yet withall the Spirit of God drew their naturall style to an higher pitch, in divine expressions, fitted to the subject in hand." (Pp. 59–62.)

It is almost pathetic to observe White's efforts to mitigate the effects of his somewhat mechanical conception of the mode of inspiration in the matter of the style of the authors. Others made similar efforts and sometimes with more success. But the time had not yet come when the true *concursus* of inspiration, by which we may see that every word of Scripture is truly divine and yet every word is as truly human, had become the common property of all. In this, too, White is a fair exponent of his day, and reminds us anew that so far from denying verbal inspiration and the inerrancy of Scripture, the tendency to error of the time was in the opposite direction; and in the strenuousness of its assertion of the fact of an inspiration which extended to the expression and secured infallibility, it was ever in danger of conceiving its mode after a mechanical fashion. That this was the ruling attitude of the middle of the seventeenth century among the Continental theologians, whether Reformed or Lutheran, everybody acknowledges. It is clear from what we have seen that the English Puritans and Scotch Presbyterians were not an isolated body cut off from the currents of thought of their day; but were in harmony with the best theologizing and highest conceptions of their Continental brethren.

With this result we might fairly close the present discussion as, in a sense, formally complete. We are loath to leave the subject, however, without completing it still further by adjoining a tolerably full exposition of the doctrine of inspiration as it was held by some one of the Westminster men, who was more of a Biblical scholar than a dogmatist. In such a one, if in any one, we might expect to find a different view as to the origin and character of the Bible from that which had become the common property of the Protestant systematists of the day. No one offers himself for such a study more favorably than John Lightfoot, who was probably the greatest Biblical scholar that took any large part in the discussions of the Assembly, and who does not appear to have busied himself much with studies in technical dogmatics. If in any one, in him we might expect, then, to find that lowered view of Scripture which Dr. Briggs declares to belong especially to Biblical scholars, and wishes us to think characteristic of the Westminster men. Certainly Lightfoot's distinguished services to Biblical study should make him an honored teacher to even our later and, we would fain believe, wiser age; while his general eminence, ability, and learning will give us increased confidence in appealing to him to tell us just what was the doctrine of inspiration recognized by students of the Bible in his day as Scriptural.

A subordinate interest in ascertaining Lightfoot's attitude towards and thought of Scripture is added by the facts that Dr. Briggs thinks highly of him as an exegete,[15] and has included his name among those to whom he bids us look for a lower and (in his view) truer doctrine of inspiration than that which esteems the Scriptures as in the fullest sense the utterances of God, and as such free from all error.[16] " The Westminster divines," Dr. Briggs writes in the latter of these passages, " knew as well as we do that the accents and vowel-points of the Hebrew text then in their possession did not come down from the original autographs, pure and unchanged. They were not in the original autographs at all. . . . They knew, as well as we know, that there were variations of reading and uncertainties and errors in the Greek and Hebrew texts in their hands. . . . They knew that there were errors of citation and

---

[15] " Biblical Study," 1883, p. 344.
[16] " The Bible, the Church, and the Reason," 1892, p. 96.

of chronology and of geographical statement in the text of Scripture. Luther and Calvin, Walton and Lightfoot, Baxter and Rutherford, and a great company of Biblical scholars recognized them, and found no difficulty with them." There are some things about this passage, indeed, which might justify one in paying it no attention. It is not clear from it just what is intended to be asserted as to Lightfoot's view of Scripture and its fallibility. Is it of Scriptures " as God gave them," or of the Scriptures " as we have them " that Dr. Briggs means his final assertion to be taken? The company in which Lightfoot is here placed is certainly a company who did not recognize errors of any sort in the genuine " text of Scripture," [17] but

---

[17] This has been sufficiently shown as to Baxter and Rutherford above. For Luther, see *The Presbyterian and Reformed Review* for April, 1893, pp. 249–266. For Calvin, see *The Presbyterian and Reformed Review* for January, 1893, pp. 49–70. We have been less careful to ascertain the exact opinions of Bryan Walton on this subject; but a somewhat close familiarity with the " Prolegomena " to his Polyglot and with his reply to John Owen's ill-considered attack upon it, leads us very strongly to doubt whether he held any lower view of Scripture than that of his fellows in this list. He represents himself to have " laboured to assert the *purity, integrity,* and *supream authority* of the *Originall Texts,*" and speaks of the matters more especially alluded to by Dr. Briggs thus: " The *Hebrew* points, (that is, the *modern forms* now used, not the *vowels* and *accents* themselves, which are acknowledged to be coeve with the other Letters, and that the reading of the Text was never arbitrary, but the same before and after the punctuation) were devised and fixed by the *Masorites* about five hundred years after *Christ.*" " The whole *Prolegom.* 7. is spent in proving that the *Original Texts* are not *corrupted either by Jews, Christians or others, that they are of Supream authority in all matters, and the rule to try all translations by, That the copies we now have are the true transcripts of the first* ἀυτόγραφα *written by the sacred Pen-men. That the speciall providence of God hath watched over these books, to preserve them pure and uncorrupt against all attempts of Sectaries, Hereticks and others, and will still preserve them to the end of the world, for the end for which they were at first written. That the errors or mistakes which may befall by negligence or inadvertency of Transcribers or Printers, are in matters of no concernment (from whence various readings have risen), and may by collation of other copies and other means there mentioned be rectified and amended.*" " I do not onely say, that all *saving fundamentall truth* is contained in the Originall Copies, but that all revealed truth is still remaining entire; or, if any error or mistake have crept in, it is in matters of no concernment, so that not onely no matter of faith, but no considerable point in Historicall truth, Prophesies or other things, is thereby prejudiced, and that there are means left for rectify-

labored to explain all apparent inaccuracies which the enemies
of the Bible pretended to find in it — not however without
" finding difficulty with them." Moreover, Dr. Briggs himself
has elsewhere recognized the fact that Lightfoot held the highest conceivable doctrine of verbal inspiration. " Relying upon
these " — i.e. apparently the book Zohar and other Cabbalistic
writing — he tells us,[18] " the elder Buxtorf with his great
authority misled a large number of the most prominent of the
Reformed divines of the continent to maintain the opinion of
the divine origin and authority of the Massoretic vowel points
and accents. In England, Fulke, Broughton, and Lightfoot
adopted the same opinion. These rabbinical scholars exerted,
in this respect, a disastrous influence upon the study of the
Old Testament." Were our impulse to be taken from Dr.
Briggs's representations, therefore, we might be a little puzzled to know what we are bidden to look into Lightfoot to find.
He is, however, worthy of our study for his own sake, and for the
sake of the history of the doctrine of inspiration in Britain in
the Westminster age; and one of the incidental results of our
study will be to inform us which of Dr. Briggs's Lightfoots is
the true one — the Lightfoot who freely recognized errors in
the text of Scripture, or the Lightfoot who held that even the
Hebrew vowel points and accents were from God. At all events,
we invite our readers to a tolerably full exposition of Lightfoot's doctrine of inspiration as a proper close to our study of
the doctrine as held by the Westminster men. We shall make
this exposition by means of a copious series of quotations from
Lightfoot's works,[19] arranged in an order which will bring his
doctrine of Scripture before us in something of a systematic
form.

---

ing any such mistakes where they are discovered." (" The Considerator Considered," 1659, pp. 2, 11, 14, 66.)

[18] " Biblical Study," 1883, p. 142.

[19] Quotations will be designated according to the volume and page in
Pitman's octavo edition of Lightfoot's " Works."

Lightfoot's Doctrine of Scripture

The *canon of Scripture,* according to Lightfoot's conception, was *determined, both in its extent and its details, by the
inspiration of God,* Scripture being nothing other than the
revelation of God's will to man. He says:

" So that the Spirit of God inspired certain persons, whom he
pleased, to be the revealers of his will, till he had imparted and committed to writing what he thought fit to reveal under the Old Testament; and when he had completed that, the Holy Ghost departed,
and such inspirations ceased. And when the gospel was to come in,
then the Spirit was restored again, and bestowed upon several persons for the revealing farther of the mind of God, and completing
the work he had to do, for the settling of the gospel, and penning of
the New Testament: and that being done, these gifts and inspirations
cease, and may no more be expected, than we may expect some other
gospel yet to come " (iii. 371).

The Scriptures are thus the product of the energy of God operating on certain selected men endowed for their production.
It follows, of course, that they contain all the will of God.

" When the inspired penmen had written all that the Holy Ghost
directed to write, ' all truth ' was written " (iii. 369).

And it follows equally that no further revelations are to be
expected.

" Now was the whole will of God revealed and committed to writing, and from henceforth must vision, and prophecy, and inspiration,
cease for ever. These had been used and imparted all along, for the
drawing up of the mind of God into writing " (iii. 368).

On this latter matter he was led to speak fully and repeatedly
in opposition to the " new spirits " of the sectaries of his day.
Thus he writes in another place when commenting on Judges
xx. 27:

" ' How may Christians inquire of God in their doubtings, as
Israel did, here and elsewhere, in theirs? ' I must answer briefly, and
that in the words of God himself, ' To the law and to the testament ':

to the written word of God, 'Search the Scriptures.' As you might
appeal to Balaam to bear witness concerning the blessedness of
Israel, whereas he was called forth to curse them; — so, for the
proof of this matter, — viz. that there is now no other way to inquire
of God, but only from his word, — you may appeal to those very
Scriptures, that they produce, that would maintain that there are
revelations and inspirations still, and that God doth still very often
answer his people by them. . . . To speak fully to this matter, I
should clear this, — I. That, after God had completed and signed
the Scripture-canons, Christians must expect revelations no more.
. . . II. I should show, that the Scripture containeth all things necessary for us to know or to inquire of God about " (vi. 286–287).

He did speak " fully to this matter " in his disputation for
the Doctor's degree, delivered in 1652, in which he defended
the thesis, *Post Canonem Scripturæ consignatum, non sunt
novæ Revelationes expectandæ* (v. 455 *sqq.*). As to the sealing
of the canon, he treats the three matters of the canon that is
sealed, and the time and the mode of its sealing. The *time* of
the close of the canon, he teaches, was determined by the withdrawal of the inspiring Spirit; which also determines the *mode*
in which it was done: " quod nempe ipsa ultimi calami, per
ultimum hunc Spiritus Sancti amanuensem, Scriptis inspiratis
appositio, fuerit ipsissima consignatio " (p. 457). The canon
had been written at the impulse of God, through instruments
selected from time to time for the revelation of His will; and as
they wrote it, it gradually grew to its completion.

" Prophetæ sancti, et divino Spiritu afflati, in unoquoque sæculo a
Deo ad conscribendum sacrum canonem ordinati et edocti, ab impiis
et nefariis hominibus licet pro ludibrio et derisu haberentur, a piis
tamen et Deum timentibus pro veris prophetis et habiti sunt, et
honorati. Quæcunque ergo illi ex dictamine Spiritus Sancti con-
scripserant, in manus piorum hominum ab ipsis tradita, pro divino
verbo et canone ab illis recepta, æstimata et servata " (v. 457).

So, too, with the New Testament: " When the last of the
theopneustic writers had applied the last pen to his writings,
the canon was, as it was completed, so also by this very act,

sealed " (p. 457). Thus " the New Testament grew gradually, just as the Old Testament had grown " (pp. 457–458). The whole truth was therefore written, the canon of Scripture sealed, and revelations were no longer to be expected, " cùm . . . scripsissent illi omnia ea, quæ ab iis scribi voluit Spiritus Sanctus " (p. 458). This happened, as a matter of fact, when John wrote the Apocalypse, which Lightfoot makes the latest-written of New Testament books, while yet placing its composition before the destruction of Jerusalem. He says:

> " The last of those celestial writers was John the Evangelist and Apocalyptist. He wrote the Apocalypse last of all his writings; and when it was completed as a crown, the canon of the New Testament was perfected and sealed, and that of the whole Scripture as well " (p. 459).

It necessarily results from this doctrine of the canon, as we have already seen, not only that no new revelations are to be expected, but also that it is to Scripture itself, and to it alone, that we are to go for spiritual guidance; and that we are to treat it with due reverence and to approach it with all confidence:

> " Divinæ Scripturæ oracula pro oraculo colimus, extra quod nihil vel sciscitandum, vel expectandum, vel æstimandum, quod ad fidem pertineat, aut mores, aut bonam conscientiam. Sacrosanctum hunc canonem veneramur, ut verum, solum, perfectum omnium fidei articulorum penuarium, perfectam omnium actionum nostrarum regulam et normam " (p. 460). " Illi [i.e. Pontificii] ' ecclesiam ' statuunt, nos ' ipsam Scripturam ': atque hoc non sine summa ratione, ac summa ipsius Scripturæ autoritate. Ad hoc nempe oraculum, quasi ab ipso Dei digito, diriguntur homines ad omnia quærenda et cognoscenda, quæ ad Deum cognoscendum, et ad salutem acquirendam, faciunt " (p. 461). " At nos firmissimum habemus verbum Scripturæ, ad omnia hæc, quae nobis scitu opus est, detegenda, et aptum, et datum " (v. 462).

Inspiration having been thus made the principle of the canon, it becomes at once *the criterion of canonical books*. An instructive passage occurs when Lightfoot is commenting on the prologue of Luke's Gospel:

" From these men's sermons and relations, many undertook to write gospels, partly for their own use, and partly for the benefit of others: which thing though they did lawfully and with a good intent, yet because they did it not by inspiration, nor by divine warrant; albeit what they had written, were according to truth, yet was the authority of their writings but human, and not to be admitted into the divine canon. But Luke had his intelligence and instructions ' from above ' (ἄνωθεν, ver. 3.) " (iii. 19).

This criterion is applied of course, however, especially to *the exclusion of the apocryphal books:*

" The Apocrypha speaks for itself, that it is not the finger of God, but the work of some Jews. Which got it so much authority among Christians; because it came from them, from whom the lively oracles of God indeed came also. But the Talmud may be read to as good advantage, and as much profit, and far more " (ii. 9).

" The words of the text are the last words of the Old Testament, — there uttered by a prophet, here expounded by an angel: there concluding the law, and here beginning the gospel. . . . Thus sweetly and nearly should the two Testaments join together, and thus divinely would they kiss each other, but that the wretched Apocrypha doth thrust in between. . . . It is a thing not a little to be admired, how this Apocrypha could ever get such place in the hearts and in the Bibles of the primitive times, as to come to sit in the very centre of them both. . . . But it is a wonder, to which I could never yet receive satisfaction, that in churches that are reformed, they have shaken off the yoke of superstition, and unpinned themselves from off the sleeve of former customs, or doing as their ancestors have done, — yet in such a thing as this, and of so great import, should do as first ignorance, and then superstition, hath done before them. It is true, indeed, that they have refused these books out of the canon, but they have reserved them still in the Bible: as if God should have cast Adam out of the state of happiness, and yet have continued him in the place of happiness " (vi. 131–132).

The *unity* of the canon which is touched on in the last extract is in another place largely dwelt upon. He is commenting on Luke ix. 30, 31:

" Remember that Moses here is the law, and Elias the prophecy; and you have here an emblem of the Scriptures, which is, that ' lex

atque omnis prophetarum chorus Christi prænotat passionem.' . . .
Marcion, the heretic, did once maintain, that the Old Testament was
given by one God, and the New by another; the Old, by a God of
cruelty, — the New, by a God of mercy. . . . If he will but take
the Bible and read, he himself shall evince his own conscience of
this truth, — that both Testaments breathe from one Spirit; that
both mainly aim at one thing; though the letter of the Old be different from the letter of the New, as death from life, yet, that the
Spirit of both is the same, as there is a life under death; that the Old
is the New under a cloud, and the New is the Old with sunshine; that
not only upon this mount, but even throughout the Old Testament,
Moses and Elias, law and prophecy, talk to Christ, ' and speak of
his decease, which he should accomplish at Jerusalem.' . . .

" Moses's law is the ground of all divinity; so was it to Israel,
so must it be to us: the rest of the Old Testament was a divine exposition of Moses's law; so was it to Israel, so must it be to us. The
New Testament is a sweet commentary upon both; so should it be to
us, and so in time shall it be to Israel. God, when he had left in writing as much as his divine wisdom knew to be necessary for Israel's
salvation under the law; and when the Holy Ghost (for his familiar
expressions) ceased from Israel, and departed; when now they had
neither vision nor prophecy to instruct them, till he should come
who should seal vision and prophecy, — God, by his last prophet,
sends them back to remember the law of Moses. . . . These [the
five books of Moses, the Prophets, and the Hagiographa] were
Israel's evangelists, instructing them concerning Christ, and all
things of Christian religion necessary for their salvation. And all
these were not only written for them, but also for us, upon whom the
ends of the world are come; even as they, so must we, lay herein
Moses and Elias, law and prophets, the groundwork of all our religion, and in Christ, or the gospel, finish it: in the law to make the
seed-plot of all doctrines necessary to salvation; in the prophets, to
water it, — and in the gospel, to gather the increase. God himself
hath showed thee, O man, what is good; and what the law doth require of thee in the manner of reading of Scripture, even by his matter of writing it. As Moses, or the law, begins, so the gospel ends; and
as Elias, or prophecy, ends, so the gospel begins; ' Atque in se solvitur,' God rolling the Scripture even in itself, and showing us Moses,
and Elias, and Christ, talking together on the outside of the tabernacle; much more do they within. . . . Thus God, even by his own

method, hath showed thee, O man, what is good, and what method
the Lord requireth of thee in thy reading of the Scriptures; he
brought Moses and Elias to talk to Christ in Scripture, even before
Christ came; he set Moses, and Elias, and Christ, to talk together
in person upon this mountain; and he hath left Christ to talk with
Moses and Elias in Scripture again ever since, and ' Quos Deus conjunxit, nemo separet '; and ' those whom God hath thus joined together, let no man put asunder.' As oft as thou takest the Scripture
in hand to read, thou goest up into a mountain to see Christ in glory;
if Moses and Elias talk not to him there, if thou seest him in glory,
thou seest more than did his own disciples. Thou mayest hear them
talk together if thou wilt; for God hath put them together " (vi.
200–205).

The *nature of the inspiration* which Lightfoot thus made
the principle of the canon of Scripture must already have appeared in general outline in the extracts which have been
given. We have seen him speaking of it as a special gift to
specifically chosen men: " The Spirit of God inspired certain
persons, whom he pleased, to be the revealers of his will " (iii.
371), who, therefore, wrote what He directed to be written (iii.
369), at His dictation (v. 457). The Scriptures are thus naturally looked upon as the " drawing up of the mind of God into
writing " (iii. 368), and the writers as the " amanuenses " of
the Spirit (v. 457); their work is the " finger of God " (v. 461,
ii. 9), and God's oracle, He having " committed to writing what
he thought fit to reveal " (iii. 371), or " left in writing as much
as his divine wisdom knew to be necessary " (vi. 203). Let us
look a little more narrowly at Lightfoot's conceptions thus
brought before us. In his doctorate thesis, of which we have
already spoken, he dwelt largely on the two contentions,
that inspiration was a gift to specially chosen men, and
that it was specifically different both from sanctifying grace
and that illumination of the Spirit common to Christians
by which God leads them into truth, and which may be
loosely called " revelation." We may have new illumination
of Scripture doctrine, he taught, but not by immediate revelation, but only through deeper study of Scripture; we are

certainly given the same Spirit of wisdom and of revelation which the apostles possessed, but not to make new revelations through us, but only to quicken divine knowledge in us through the medium of the word; we are to have to the end of time the guidance of the Spirit, but not by means of direct revelations of duty to us, but only through the prescriptions of the written word — for, "nos firmissimum habemus verbum Scripturæ, ad omnia hæc, quæ nobis scitu opus est, detegenda, et aptum, et datum " (v. 462). This distinction is necessarily much emphasized in opposition to the pretensions of the sectaries of the day to " inner light." It is very strongly asserted in the following passage:

" I might observe, ' obiter,' how great diversity there is betwixt the spirit of prophecy and revelation, and the Spirit of grace and holiness. The same Spirit, indeed, is the author of both; but there is so much diversity in the thing wrought, that a Balaam, a Caiaphas, have the spirit of prophecy, who are as far from having the Spirit of sanctification, as the east is from the west, hell from heaven " (vii. 308).

The need of revelations is superseded by the gift of the Scriptures, for —

" As the great Prophet, he [Christ] teacheth his church himself, by giving of the Scriptures, and instructing his holy ones by his Spirit " (vi. 261).

The whole case is argued at length at vi. 235 *sqq.,* from which we extract as much as will serve our purpose:

" For the prosecuting this argument, you must distinguish between the false pretence to the Spirit of sanctification, and to the spirit of revelation. By the former, men deceive themselves, — by the latter, others. . . . I shall strip this delusion naked, and whip it before you, by observing these four things: — I. No degree of holiness whatsoever doth necessarily beget and infer the spirit of revelation, as the cause produceth the effect. . . . I clear this. . . . First; From the nature of the thing. The Spirit of holiness and revelation are far different; therefore, the one is not the cause of the other. . . . 1. They are impartible to different subjects: — holiness, only to holy men; the spirit of revelation, sometimes to wicked men. So it was imparted to Balaam; so likewise to Judas and Caiaphas. 2. They are bestowed upon different ends: — holiness for the good of him that hath it; revelation, for the benefit of others. 3. They are of different manners and operations. The Spirit of sanctification changeth the heart; Paul is a Saul no more: revelation doth not; Judas is a Judas still. 4. They are of a different diffusion in the soul: sanctification is quite through, — revelation, only in, the understanding. 5. They are of different effects: sanctification never produceth but what is good; revelation may produce what is evil; knowledge puffeth up. . . . II. The spirit of revelation is given indeed to saints, but means little that sense, that these men speak of, but is of a clean different nature. — The apostle prays, Ephes. i. 17, ' That God would give unto them the spirit of wisdom and revelation in the knowledge of him.' And God gives this spirit; but in what sense? Not, to foresee things to come; not to understand the grammatical construction of Scripture without study; not to preach by the Spirit: but the apostle himself explains, ver. 18: ' The eyes of their understanding being enlightened; that ye may know, what is the hope of his calling, and what the riches of the glory of his inheritance in the saints.' So that the revelation, given to the saints, is this, — that God reveals the experience of those things, that we have learned before in the theory from Scripture, — a saving feeling of ' the hope of his calling, and the riches of the glory of his inheritance.' Here let me speak three things: — 1. To feel the experience of grace, is not by new light, that was never known before, but by application of what was known before. . . . As common grace is called grace, because it is above the ordinary working of nature, — so this is called revelation, because above the work of common light. 2. How do men come to assurance of pardon and salvation? Not by the spirit of revelation in their sense; not by any immediate whispers from heaven; but another way: as in Rom. xv. 4, . . . In Scripture is your comfort, and in your own conscience; and in them is your assurance. A saint makes this holy syllogism: — Scripture, major, ' He that repents, believes, loves God, hath the pardon of his sins.' Conscience, minor, ' Lord, I believe; Lord, I love thee.' Saint, from both, makes the conclusion, ' Therefore, I am assured of the pardon of my sins, and my salvation.' . . . 3. I may add, A saint in heaven finds nothing, but what he knew before in little. . . . III. There is no promise in Scripture, whereupon the spirit of revelation is to be expected after the fall of Jerusalem. . . . At the fall of Jerusalem, all Scripture was written, and God's full will revealed; so that there was no farther need of prophecy and revelation. . . . IV. The standing ministry is the ordinary method, that God hath used for the instruction of his church." (vi. 236–242, cf. vi. 211.)

The common *distinction between revelation and inspiration, in the stricter senses of those words,* which confines the former to the direct impartation of truth from God, and the latter to the divine work of securing the correct communication or record of the truth, is not drawn by Lightfoot. The obvious distinction which this usage of the words is intended to express, is not, however, overlooked by him; he draws it in his own way as follows:

" But we may observe a double degree in rapture; as inspired men may be considered under a double notion; viz. those that were inspired with prophecy, or to be prophets and to preach, — and those that were inspired to be penmen of divine writ, which was higher. John [in Revelation] hath both . . ." (iii. 334).

This may not mean, precisely, that " inspiration " is a higher notion than " revelation " in the now current senses of those words: but it does mean that there was a superadded grace of the Spirit above the impartation of the truth, when it was granted to one to fix the truth in written form for the instruction of all ages. The dignity of Scripture as the word of God fixed in written form, is the underlying conception; and Lightfoot is never weary of insisting on this. Take but a single example. When commenting on John v. 39, he says:

" In what he addeth, ' They are they that testify of me,' the emphasis may not be passed unobserved. He saith not only, ' they testify of me,' but ' they are they that do it ': as intimating, that the Scriptures are the great, singular, and intended, witnesses of Christ, the fullest and the highest testimony of him (As, 2 Pet. i. 19). . . . And thus doth Christ read unto us, 1. The dignity of the Scriptures, as his choicest witness. 2. The end of them, himself. 3. Their work, to bring men to him. And, 4. The fruit of all, eternal life " (v. 273).

Upon this conception of the origin of Scripture, *the matter of it is looked upon as a dictation from heaven*. This comes out repeatedly. For example, when speaking of the prologue of Luke's Gospel, he writes:

" He maketh his own undertaking of the like nature with theirs, when he saith, It seemed good ' to me also ': — but he mentioneth these their writings, as only human authorities (undertaken without the injunction of the Holy Ghost), which his divine one was to exclude. . . . Verse 3: ' It seemed good to me also, having had perfect understanding of all things *from above*.' For so might Ἄνωθεν be best translated; and so it signifieth, John, iii. 3. 31, and xix. 11; James i. 17, &c. And, thus taken, it showeth Luke's inspiration from heaven, and standeth in opposition to the many gospels mentioned ver. 1; — which were written from the mouths and dictating of men, ver. 2; but his intelligence for what he writeth, was ' from above ' " (iv. 114–115).

Here inspiration is made to include an injunction from God to write, and the reception from above of what is to be written; so that the writing is " from the mouth and dictating " of God. This is the conception everywhere cropping out more or less fully, e.g.:

" Now, why the three evangelists should be so unanimously silent in so great a matter, for so long a time, needs not be questioned, since the Holy Ghost hath provided, that, by a fourth, that should be supplied which they had omitted " (iv. 386).

" Neither can I see, nor dare I think of, any such superiority and inferiority in the writings of the evangelists " (iv. 429).

On I Kings xv. 14: " A human chronicler is not able to say, ' Such a one's heart was perfect with God '; because he is not able to discern, what the heart is. He writes the story of a man's actions; he cannot write the story of his heart, because he cannot know it. But he that held the pen, and wrote these sacred chronicles, the Holy Ghost, saw the carriage of all actions, saw the secret frame and temper of all hearts; and he was able to give judgment of them, whether they were good or evil; and he could not but give true judgment " (v. 376). . . . " That his heart was so, is confirmed by the mouth of two witnesses, the Book of Kings and Chronicles; and the mouth of the Holy Ghost hath spoken it twice over, here and there; and his word is truth, and no falsehood in it " (v. 378).

The conception here is of course not merely an inspiration of the matter of Scripture, but such a divine gift of Scripture that it is *in its matter and form alike, down to its words and even letters, from God.* This is constantly illustrated in Lightfoot's writings. Take such a passage as the following as an instance. He is speaking of Balaam, in II Peter ii. 15, and animadverts on the fact that he is called the " son of Bosor," whereas the Old Testament has it " son of Beor." He says:

" Those that are apt to tax the originals of Scripture of corruption and interpolation, may chance to think it is so here; and that some carelessness or unhappy dash of the pen made it Bosor here, when it should have been Beor." He then adduces the Chaldee sentence in Jer. x. 11, saying that it " came not into the Chaldee tongue by chance, or any inadvertency, but by sacred wisdom," and so it is here. " The change of the name *Beor* into *Bosor* relishes of the Chaldee language too, . . . And our apostle doth neither mistake himself in so pronouncing the name, nor hath any transcriber miswritten it after him; but he uttered it according to the Chaldee idiom and propriety; and, by this very word, gives intimation, that he was in Chaldea, when he wrote this Epistle." From this he draws three observations, of which the second and third are the following: " Secondly; That no tittle in Scripture is idle, but ought to have its consideration; according to the saying of the Jews, ' That there is no tittle in Scripture, but even mountains of matter hang upon it ': and, as our Saviour saith, ' one jot or tittle of the law shall not perish '; so, not one jot or tittle in Scripture, but hath its weight. Here is one poor letter, which, one would think, was crept in by some oversight, yet that carries with it matter of important and weighty consideration. Thirdly; How necessary human learning is for the understanding and explaining of Scripture, which is so much cried down and debased by some . . ." (vii. 79–81).

There are a number of points brought out in this extract which should interest us. We perceive that Lightfoot was not unfamiliar with the science of textual criticism, though he himself was a critic of conservative tendency. We see that he was zealous for the value and necessity of human learning in the interpretation of Scripture, as over against the enthusiasts who expected to accomplish all by the inner aid of the Holy Ghost. But our present concern is to observe that his doctrine of inspiration led him to attribute everything in Scripture to the Holy Spirit, whose inspiring influence extended to the very words, and even to the several letters in them. To Lightfoot *the Spirit of God was, in the highest and strictest sense, the author of Scripture;* and therefore everything in it, down to the very letters, was held to be significant and important. Let us observe, somewhat in detail, how he deals with Scripture under this conception. One of the commonest of his locutions is to quote the Scriptures as the words of the Holy Ghost. Here are a few scattered examples which will exhibit his usage:

" Search and study the Scriptures, because it is the Scriptures, the writing of God, . . ." (vii. 207).

" The Holy Ghost, that gave the Scriptures, . . ." (vii. 212).

" The Holy Ghost hath spoken . . . Rev. xiii. 2, . . ." (vii. 109).

" The Holy Ghost, in that story, bids us look on him," i.e. Cain (vii. 339).

" And the Holy Ghost doth point, as it were, with the finger," quoting Rev. vii. (vii. 356).

" And here the Holy Ghost, to hint his distaste of such idolatry, blots out his children, to the third, nay, fourth, generation, out of the line and genealogy of our Saviour " (vii. 357).

" In reading of the New Testament, never take your eye off the Old; for the New is but again that in plainer phrase. God himself hath taught us by the writing of the Scripture, what is the best way to read: for he hath folded the two Testaments together; so that, as the law begins, so the gospel ends; and as the prophets end, so the gospel begins; as if calling upon you to look still for the one in the other " (ii. 43–44).

" Notwithstanding, the Holy Ghost would conclude the story of their offering altogether " (ii. 125).

" The Holy Ghost doth tell us, when it was that he [Hezekiah] began his reign . . ." (ii. 258).

" The Holy Ghost setteth a special mark upon these forty years of his [Jeremiah's] prophesying, Ezek. iv. 6 " (ii. 275).

" And the Holy Ghost tells us," Psalm lxxiii. 5, 6 (v. 292).

" When you rehearse this, ' The Holy Catholic Church,' in the Creed, — let your thoughts first recoil to your Bibles, and see how the Holy Ghost pictures them there. . . . Nay, yet the divine limner lays on more precious colours " (vi. 51–52).

" And so I have given you the sense of this place; and, as I conceive, the very sense of the Holy Ghost " (vi. 175).

" As it was foretold by the Holy Spirit in the prophets, . . . so was it also foretold by the same Spirit, . . ." (vi. 230).

" And thus you have the words unfolded to you, and I hope according to the meaning of the Holy Ghost " (vi. 260).

" For so doth the Holy Ghost himself explain it," Rev. xix. 8, and vii. 14 (vi. 296).

" It is not unprofitable to observe, how the Holy Ghost, at the story of great actions, doth oft intimate the Trinity. ' Let *us* make man.' — ' Let *us* confound their language.' And, at Gen. xviii, you read of three men, that stood by Abraham, who are called afterwards Jehovah. And, at the setting of the service of the tabernacle, the form of blessing that was prescribed to the priests to use, intimated a Trinity. . . . But to spare more instances, at Christ's entry into the ministry, the Trinity is at his baptism; and now, at the end of it, he proclaims it, and enjoins it to be professed at every baptism " (vi. 405).

" The Holy Ghost intendeth, in this book [the Acts], to show . . . The Holy Ghost should tell us. . . . The Holy Ghost, which in all the Bible never . . . no, not when he was intentionally writing of . . . should do it now, when he is purposely upon a story of . . ." (viii. 71).

" The second Psalm, which owns not its author in the title, the Holy Ghost ascribeth here to David " (viii. 74).

" That the Holy Ghost, reckoning the porters as they were disposed after the return," I Chron. ix. 23, 24 (ix. 231).

This constant usage exhibits the fact that, to Lightfoot, to say the Scripture says, was equivalent to saying the Holy Ghost says: the two locutions were convertible. This identification of the Scripture and the Holy Spirit comes out very plainly in cases where he passes from the one to the other mode of speech, as it were, unconsciously. Thus when speaking of the anticipation in the narrative at Joshua xv. 8, he says it was " because *the Holy Ghost* . . . would take special notice of . . . ," while just below, on the same page, with reference to a similar difficulty, his mode of speech is that it was " because *the text* would give account of their whole inheritance together, now it is speaking of it " (ii. 141). Hence also such passages as the following:

" *The Holy Ghost* hath given a close intimation, that Uzziah's befel him in the last year of his reign, and not before, 2 Kings, xv. 50 . . . Why, here is the hint that *the Holy Ghost* giveth of the time of Uzziah's being struck leprous . . . for here, *by this very expression*, is showed; . . . and *the text* plainly expresseth the occasion, . . ." (ii. 247–248).

" Therefore, *the Holy Ghost,* in the New Testament, sets himself to speak to this thing, and to show who these ' sons of God ' are. *John* shows who are, and who are not . . . (John, i. 12, 13) . . . *The Holy Ghost* sets the regeneration, in opposition to natural generation " (v. 323).

" Unless the *Spirit of Christ himself in Scripture* tell us . . ." (vi. 10).

" Behold, a greater than Aristotle is here, and sets me a copy, — and that is *the Holy Ghost in the mouth of Joshua;* Josh. xxiv. 19, ' Ye cannot serve the Lord ' (*saith Joshua*) " (vii. 211).

" The *evangelist hath done it* [i.e. written Acts] with a divine pen." " How sparing *the Holy Ghost* hath been through all that book, to express the circumstance of the time, with the relation of the things " (viii. pp. iv. and v.).

No wonder then that Lightfoot calls the Scriptures " the divine oracles," and cautions men not to pick and choose among them or read their own fancies into them (vii. 288): to him *they were all, in all their elements and parts, the utterances of the Holy Ghost.* Observe how he ascribes every element and detail of Scripture to the Holy Spirit.

Is he studying the *chronology* of the Bible? It is cared for by the Spirit:

" For the Holy Ghost reckons by round sums," — quoting Daniel xii. 12, 13 (vii. 217).

" The Holy Ghost draws up a chronicle of times from the creation to the redemption, . . ." (vii. 221).

" See how the Holy Ghost reckons the year of the flood, . . ." (ii. 4).

" The Spirit hath given undoubted helps," to draw up a chronological order (ii. 4).

" Now the Holy Ghost reckoneth from that date, rather than from any other, because, . . ." (ii. 244).

" For I cannot but conclude, that the Holy Ghost, naming the several years of these kings hitherto, intendeth . . ." (ii. 326).

" Here is the standard of time that the Holy Ghost hath set up in the New Testament; unto which, as unto the fulness of time, he hath drawn up a chronicle-chain from the creation: and from which, as from a standing mark, we are to measure all the times of the New Testament, if we would fix them to a creation date " (iii. 34).

" When he shall also see (and that, I suppose, not without admiration) the wondrous and mysterious, and yet, always, instructive style and manner of accounting, used by the Holy Ghost, in most sacred majestickness, and challenging all serious study and reverence " (iv. 98).

" The Holy Ghost chooseth rather to reckon by holy Jotham in the dust, than by wicked Ahaz alive " (iv. 108).

" The Jews reckoned their year by the lunary months. . . . This computation made their years to fall eleven days short of the year of the sun: and this the Holy Ghost seemeth to hint and to hit upon, when, in reckoning the time of Noah's being in his ark, he bringeth him in on the seventeenth day of the second month, and bringeth him out on the seven-and-twentieth day of the same month, on the next year; and yet intendeth him there but an exact and complete year of the sun, but reckoned only by lunary months " (iv. 135–136).

Or is it a question of *the order of the narrative?* This, too, in all its flexions, is attributed directly to the Holy Ghost. In the preface to the " Harmony, &c., of the New Testament," for example, he writes:

" I shall not trouble the reader with any long discourse, to show, how the Scripture abounds with transposition of stories; how the

Holy Ghost doth, eminently, hereby show the majesty of his style and divine wisdom; how this is equally used in both Testaments; what need the student of Scripture hath carefully to observe those dislocations; and what profit he may reap, by reducing them to their proper time and order" (iii. p. vi.).

So, elsewhere:

" The Holy Spirit hath, in divers places, purposely and divinely, laid stories and passages out of their proper places, for special ends " (ii. 3).

" The same Spirit, that dictated both the Testaments, hath observed this course in both the Testaments alike: laying texts, chapters, and histories, sometimes out of the proper place, in which, according to natural chronical order, they should have lain. And this is one of the majesticknesses, wherewithal the Holy Ghost marcheth and passeth through the Scriptures. Not that these dislocations are imperfections, — for they ever show the greatest wisdom: nor that to methodize these transposed passages, is to correct the method of the Holy Ghost; — for it is but to unknot such difficulties, as the Holy Ghost hath challenged more study on: nor that it is desirable, that our Bibles should be pointed in such a methodized way, and such Bibles only to be in common use, — for the very posture of the Bible, as it now lieth, seemeth to be divine, and that the rather from Luke xxiv. 44 . . ." (ii. p. lxii.).

Accordingly, in his detailed explanations of the order of Scripture, he uniformly ascribes it to the Holy Ghost, and seeks a divine reason for it. For example:

" The Holy Ghost, as soon as he hath related how Shimei had obtained his pardon, comes and relates this conference betwixt David and Mephibosheth;" . . . giving us a " hint, by this strange placing of this story." . . . " This is not done at random and by any oversight, as if the Holy Ghost had forgot himself, as we poor fumbling creatures are many times lost in our tale; but the sacred Spirit hath purposely thus methodized the story with such a dislocation, for our own more narrow observation and clearer instruction . . ." (vii. 203).

" But about this we need not much to trouble ourselves; since, as to the understanding of the stories themselves, there can be little illustration taken from their time. . . . We shall not, therefore, offer to dislocate the order of the stories, from that wherein they lie; the Holy Ghost, by the intertexture of them, rather teaching us, that some of them were contemporary, than any way encouraging us to invert their order " (iii. 207, on Acts xii. and xiii.).

Arranging Exod. xviii. between Num. x. 10, 11, he says: " Now, that the Holy Ghost might show that Jethro, . . ." (ii. 127).

" Now the reason why the Holy Ghost hath laid these stories, which came to pass so soon, in so late a place, may be supposed to be this . . ." (ii. 150).

" But the Holy Ghost hath laid it in the beginning of his [Solomon's] history, that . . ." (ii. 199).

" Because the Holy Ghost would mention all Solomon's fabrics together . . ." (ii. 201).

Jer. xxxix. 15–18 is placed after the story of the taking of the city, though Jeremiah prophesied it before, " because, when the Holy Ghost hath showed the safety of Jeremiah in the destruction, he would also show the safety of Ebed-melech, according to Jeremiah's prophecy " (ii. 296).

The institution of the Sabbath is mentioned before the fall of Adam, " partly, because the Holy Ghost would mention all the seven days of the first week together . . ." (vii. 378–379).

The principle thus employed in the matter of the order of the narrative is extended to *all the phenomena of Scripture* which may cause the reader difficulty; they are all part of the majesty of Scripture, and occur by design of the Holy Ghost for good and sufficient reason. Thus we are told in a comment on II Peter iii. 15, 16:

" He citeth Paul's Epistle to the Hebrews, and giveth an honourable testimony to that, and to the rest of his Epistles: but acknowledgeth, that, in some places, they are hard to be understood, and were misconstrued by some unlearned and unstable ones, to their own ruin; yet neither doth he nor Paul, who was yet alive and well knew of this wresting of his Epistles, clear or amend those difficulties, but let them alone as they were: for the Holy Ghost hath so penned Scripture as to set men to study . . ." (iii. 327).

" It became the Holy Ghost, the penner of Scripture, to write in a majesty." . . . " If the Holy Ghost wrote the Scriptures, we must needs conclude, that he wrote them like the Holy Ghost, in a divine majesty . . ." (vii. 212).

Just because, however (as this last extract expresses it), the Holy Ghost is " the penner of Scripture," who " wrote the Scriptures " in His own way, not merely the special disposition of the matter and the general contents and mode of presentation is from Him, but *the very style is determined by the Holy Ghost*. This is very clearly brought out in a passage parallel to one already quoted, based on Peter's commendation of Paul's epistles:

" The Holy Ghost hath purposely penned the Scriptures so as to challenge all serious study of them," — quoting Matt. xxiv. 15 . . . " Peter tells us, that there are divers things in Paul's Epistles hard to be understood; and why did the Holy Ghost dictate them so hard by Paul? . . . . Because the Holy Ghost hath penned Scripture so as to challenge all serious study. He could have penned all so plain, that he that runneth, might have read them; but he hath penned them in such a style, that he that will read them, must not run and read, but sit down and study " (vii. 208).

" Observe that passage, Matt. i. 8; and see whether the style of the Holy Ghost do not hint the very same thing " . . . " These and other things of the like nature, may be observed in the very style and dialect the Holy Ghost useth in Scripture. Whereby he setteth a brand upon idolatry, . . ." (vii. 357).

The " style and dialect " of Scripture is the Holy Ghost's, because He dictated Scripture. Accordingly, *the very words of Scripture are the words of the Holy Ghost*. This is, of course, capable of copious illustration:

" The helps, that it [i.e. Scripture] affords for explaining of itself, are various. The first to be looked after, is the ' language ': the Spirit of God, upon the same occasions, using the same words in the original " (ii. 3).

" The Holy Spirit seldom or never using these [i.e. other languages than Hebrew or Greek, as, e.g. Chaldee], but intimating something of note, if our eyes be but serious." For example, in Hosea v. 5, " He [i.e. the Spirit] useth the Chaldee form, to teach where that affliction and seeking must be " (ii. 3).

"Abijah is also called 'Abijam'; and his mother is called both 'Maachah' and 'Michah'; and his grandfather, by his mother's side, is called 'Absalom' and 'Uriel.' Such changes of names are frequent in Scripture: and sometime so altered by the Holy Ghost, purposely to hint something to us concerning the person; and sometimes so altered by the people, among whom such persons lived, . . ." (ii. 209).

"The Virgin had obtained the highest earthly favour that ever mortal did, or must, do, — to be the mother of the Redeemer: and the Holy Ghost useth a singular word to express so much." — Luke i. 28: iv. 161.

On the word "repentance": "The word which the Holy Ghost hath left us in the original Greek, μετανοεῖτε, is exceeding significant and pertinent to that doctrine and occasion." . . . "Now, the Holy Ghost, by a word of this significancy, doth give the proper and true character of repentance, both against the misprisions which were taken up concerning it, by their traditions in those times, and those also that have been taken up since." (v. 156–157).

"So, when the Holy Ghost proclaimeth in the words of the text," John v. 16 (vi. 331).

The *very letters are from the Spirit.* We have already quoted from vii. 79–81, a passage so asserting with reference to the spelling of "Bosor" in II Peter ii. 15 (see above, p. 290). The following is a similar one. Speaking of Ezra ix. and x. he says:

"This matter was done in the seventh year of Darius, . . . as the text seemeth to carry it on; unless, by the strange writing of the word לדריוש ver. 16, the Holy Ghost would hint Darius's tenth. — Let the learned judge" (ii. 324).

Indeed, Lightfoot goes further, and *attributes directly to the Holy Spirit the very pointing of the Hebrew text,* as it stands in the current copies:

"It cannot pass the eye of him, that readeth the text in the original, but he must observe it, how, in [Deut.] chap. xxix., ver. 29, the Holy Ghost hath pointed one clause, לנו ולבנינו 'to us and to our children belong the revealed things,' after an extraordinary and unparalleled manner; to give warning against curiosity in prying into

God's secrets; and that we should content ourselves with his revealed will " (ii. 137).

He expresses disbelief in the vowels and accents having been
invented by the Massoretes (iv. 20), and argues their antiquity
(iv. 50), adducing our Lord's declaration that not " one iota
shall pass away " as evidence that the vowels were there in
His day, and urging that it would be beyond the skill of man
to point the Ten Commandments, the " pricking " of which
would puzzle the world. At a later point he expresses himself
on the last matter thus:

" I omit the exquisiteness of the pricking of this piece of Scripture of the commandments extraordinarily: some special thing is
in it " (iv. 84).

He even doubts if " the marginals," i.e. the various readings
placed by the Massoretes in the margin of the Hebrew Bible,
" are not only human corrections " (iv. 21; cf. xi. 103).

The primary fact in Lightfoot's doctrine of Scripture is,
then, that it is God's word, in such a sense that the Divine
Spirit is the author of it in its minutest detail. On this hangs
all his thought concerning the Scriptures. It is because they
are divine that they are *authoritative*. The authority of Scripture is to him incontestable, and is allowed by Christ Himself,
though He was God. In commenting on Matt. iv. 4, " It is
written," he writes:

" This is the first speech, that proceeded from our Saviour's
mouth, since his entrance into his ministerial function, that is upon
record; and, though it be very short, yet is it very material for observation of these things: —

1. That the first word, spoken by Christ in his ministerial office,
is an assertion of the authority of Scripture.

2. That he opposeth the word of God, as the properest encoun-
terer against the words of the devil.

3. That he allegeth Scripture, as a thing undeniable and uncon-
troulable by the devil himself.

4. That he maketh the Scripture his rule, though he had the fulness of the Spirit above measure " (iv. 362).

This authority of the Scriptures *rests on nothing else than on their divine origin and character.*

" The Scriptures are to be believed for themselves, and they need not fetch their credit from anything else. Dan. x. 21. . . . They are the truth. — See John v. 39. . . . Observe the bent of Christ's discourse. . . . He concludes in Scripture, as the most undeniable testimony. . . . See also 2 Peter i. 17–19. . . . A voice from heaven might possibly deceive; the Jews feigned such; but the word of prophecy is sure; that is a ' more sure word.' The reason of the Scriptures' credibility is, because they are the word of God: 1 Thess. ii. 13. . . . They received it as the word of God. How knew they that? From the Scriptures themselves. — Therefore it is said, that they are the formal object of faith, as well as the material. They contain what is to be believed, and the reason why to believe them; and that is especially twofold: — I. The majesty of the Spirit of God speaking in them. II. Their powerful working. I. The majesty of the Spirit of God speaking in them such things, as man cannot speak. . . . 1. How impossible is it for man to reveal the deep mysteries of salvation, i.e. the mind of God! 1 Cor. ii. 16. . . . In Scripture we have it; and ver. 7–9 of that chapter. 2. The majesty of the Spirit in Scripture appears, in that it reveals the very thoughts, and commands the very heart of man (Heb. iv. 12). . . . 3. The majesty of the Scriptures appears, in that it discovers the very subtilties of Satan. . . . Thus doth the Scripture reveal itself to be the very word of God, by its divine majesty, wherein it speaketh, — and by the wisdom, wherein it shows itself. II. In its powerful working; breaking hearts, converting souls, conquering the kingdom of Satan. . . . Thousands of experiences have showed, what the divine word of God in Scripture can do against him [that is, the devil]. And thus do they evidence themselves to be the word of God, and so to be believed for themselves, because they are the word of God " (vi. 56–59).

After asking whether the Church gives us the Scriptures, and answering that the Church of Rome rather sought to hinder us from having the Scripture, he continues:

" No, it was the work of the Lord, and the mercy of the Lord; and it is marvellous in our eyes. . . . As far as we owe our receiving of Scripture to men, we are least beholden to the Romish Church.

They put us off with a Latin translation, barbarous and wild. But we have a surer word, the sacred Hebrew, and divine Greek. And the Hebrew we owe to the Jews, and the Greek to the Greek Church, rather than the Roman. ' Unto them (the Jews) were committed the oracles of God.' And from them we received the Old Testament: and not from them neither; for could they have prevented, we had not had it. Consider how many copies were abroad in the world. The Old Testament was in every synagogue: and how many copies would men take of the New? So that it is impossible, but still Scripture must be conveyed. Could all the policy of Satan have hindered, he had done it: for the word of God is his overthrow; so that it was owing to a divine hand. And our faith stands not on the church to believe the Scriptures; but God hath carried the authority of them from age to age " (vi. 61).

" It is not proper to say, We believe Scriptures are Scriptures, because of the church, without distinguishing upon believing. As Austin's, ' Non credidissem Scripturis,' &c. ' I had not believed the Scriptures, had not the church told me '; that is, while he was unconverted. But we may satisfy this by an easy distinction, betwixt believing that Scripture is Scripture, and believing that the church all along hath taken them for Scripture. . . . A good soul desires to build up itself by the rule of faith and life. He finds, that the church hath counted Scripture so; and that he believes. But as yet he believes not they are Scriptures upon that account: but he reads, studies, meditates on them, finds the divine excellency, sweetness, power of them; and then he believes they are the word of God. And that now is not for the church's sake, but for themselves. The church of England, in the thirty-nine articles, hath determined such books canonical. Why? Because the church hath ever held them so? That is some furtherance to their belief, but not the cause of it. They first believed the church held them so, but they saw cause and reason in the books themselves to believe they were so . . . so we believe the church owns the Scriptures; but he is but a poor Christian, that believes the Scriptures are the Scriptures upon no other account " (vi. 62–63).

" God gives his word; and whether men will hear, or whether they will forbear, it is, and will be, the word of God forever. And if men will not believe it, God will not be beholden to them to believe it: let them believe it at their own peril. A Papist will not believe the divine authority of the Scriptures for themselves; God and the Scripture will never be beholden to him to believe it: . . . but let him look to it, if he do not believe it. . . . When God gave the Scriptures, he never intended they should stand at the courtesy of every curious carping atheist, whether they should be of authority, and be believed or no: but God gives them in their divine authority and majesty: and laid them a sure foundation in Sion, elect, precious, and glorious; that he, that will build upon them, may build and prosper. But if any cross, or quarrelsome, or wilfully blind, Bayard, will stumble at them, where he might walk plain, — let him take his own hazard, and stumble, and fall, and be broken, and snared, and taken: while, in the mean while, the foundation of God remaineth sure, and the divine Scriptures will be the divine Scriptures, and retain their truth and Author, when such a wretch is dashed all to pieces. . . . ' God will be God, whether thou wilt or no ': as Scripture will be Scripture, whether thou believest it or no " (vi. 351–352).

That is, as Lightfoot held the doctrine of inspiration which was universally taught by the Reformed theologians of his day, so he held likewise the common Reformed doctrine of the authority of Scripture, founded on its divine origin and character. The extracts we have just given teach the precise doctrine taught in the Confession of Faith, i. 4 and 5, and constitute an excellent commentary on those sections, from the pen of one of the Westminster men.

To him and them, the Bible, and the Bible only, is the religion of Protestants. We have found him so saying in his Doctorate disputation:

" Illi [pontificii] ' ecclesiam ' statuunt, nos ' ipsam Scripturam ': atque hoc non sine summa ratione, ac summa ipsius Scripturæ autoritate. Ad hoc nempe oraculum, quasi ab ipso Dei digito, diriguntur homines ad omnia quærenda et cognoscenda, quæ ad Deum cognoscendum, et ad salutem acquirendam, faciunt " (v. 461).

So again he writes:

" The other [i.e. the Church of Rome] brags of antiquity, universality, visibility, succession, and other bravadoes; whereas the Protestant church hath but this to glory of (and it is enough), That she is built upon the prophets and apostles. Ingenious was that picture: in one scale you see all the trinklements of Popery, and the pope and friars hanging on; in the other, the Protestants put the Bible, and it outweighs. This is the glory and sure friend of a church, to be built upon the Holy Scriptures, although there be no visibility of that church to the eyes of men at all. . . . That church that is built more on traditions and doctrines of men, than on the word of God, is no true church, nor religion. . . . The foundation of the true church of God is Scripture " (vi. 44–45).

The *infallible truth of Scripture* which is thus strongly insisted on is treated everywhere as a first principle (see above, pp. 289–290):

" It is not all, to believe the thing is true; but farther to believe so, as the soul may have advantage. Take one instance: one of the first things in religion to be believed is, ' That the Scriptures are the word of God, and divinely true.' This, who believes not? The devil himself cannot deny it: nay, he cited Scripture, as the word of God, to our Saviour. And there are thousands in hell, that never made a doubt of this. Therefore, the believing of this must have a farther reach, that the soul may receive benefit upon so believing " (vi. 50).

" Whosoever speaks not according to the truth of God in Scripture, he is but a liar, and the truth is not in him. You understand, that I speak of things of faith and religion. In historical, natural, civil, moral things, we deny not, but that they [20] speak much truth. But that is to be tried by our reading and reason. But in the things of divine concernment, there is no truth, but that of Scripture, or what speaks agreeable to it " (vi. 59).

This is, of course, the common Reformed doctrine of the *completeness, perfection, or sufficiency of the Scriptures* as taught in the Westminster Confession, i. 6, or Q. 2 of the Shorter Catechism. In full harmony with these formularies, Lightfoot teaches:

[20] " They," i.e. " men," according to the context. Lightfoot is not confining the truth of Scripture to matters of " faith and religion," but confining the truth which men may acquire apart from Scripture to matters of history, nature, etc. There is truth to be had outside of Scripture on these matters, but Scripture is the sole rule of faith and practice.

" The Scriptures contain all things needful for faith and life; as that in Isaiah viii. 19, 20 . . . so may I say also in this case; if they say to you, Seek to councils, fathers, canons, determinations of the church, — ' To the law, and to the testimony '; to Scripture and holy writ, that contains every thing you need to inquire after for salvation; what to be believed, and what to be done. . . . Whithersoever you need to walk for the pleasing of God, doing your duty to men, or to your own souls, the word of God is a light sufficient. . . . Prophecy was then ceasing. People might complain, ' What shall we do for instruction? ' — Why, go to the word of God, which you have in your hands, to the law of Moses, that will teach you. — Dives desires Abraham to send one from the dead to teach his brethren, that they might escape that place of torment. No, that needs not: Moses and the prophets will teach all things needful. . . . The Apostle speaks this fully, 2 Tim. iii. 16, 17 " (vi. 54–55).

He, of course, also held and teaches the common Reformed doctrine of the *perspicuity of Scripture*. " Scripture," he tells us, " is plain " (vi. 10). But he is more concerned, in opposition to the sectaries of the time, with the other side of this doctrine — the need of careful *interpretation*. In harmony with the Confession of Faith, i. 9, he holds that Scripture is to be interpreted by Scripture: " But the Scripture, which is ever the sure expositor of itself " (iv. 215). And he lays down several rules of interpretation, as e.g.: " The Scripture word is to be interpreted according to the Scripture idiom " (iv. 217); " It is the best rule to come to the understanding of the phrases of Scripture, to consider, in what sense they were taken in that country, and among that people, where they were written " (vi. 414). Here are two sound and scholarly rules which Lightfoot, the Talmudist, was especially bound to dwell on. The scholar Lightfoot is also very naturally concerned to show against the sectaries, the need of human learning in interpreting Scripture. He says, for example:

" The greatest difficulties of the Scripture lie in the language: for unlock the language and phrases, and the difficulty is gone. And, therefore, they, that take upon them to preach by the Spirit, and to expound the Scripture by the Spirit, let them either unlock to me the Hebrew phrases in the Old Testament, and the Greek in the New, that are difficult and obscure, — or else they do nothing. Now, to attain to the meaning of such dark and doubtful phrases, the way is not so proper to put on them a sense of our own, as to consider what sense they might take them in, to whom, and among whom, the things were spoken and written in their common speech " (vi. 335).

In expounding John x. 22, 23, he goes into the whole question of *the need of human learning in interpreting Scripture,* very fully:

" To the expounding of which, the very way that I must go, cannot but mind me to observe this to you: — *That human learning is exceeding useful, nay, exceeding needful, to the expounding of Scripture.* The text gives the rise of this observation, and it gives the proof of it. Here is the mention of the feast of dedication, and not one tittle else in all the Scripture concerning it. And so there is the bare mention of Solomon's porch; and, indeed, it is mentioned once again, in Acts iii. 11; but neither here nor there any more than the bare name. Certainly, the Holy Ghost would never have mentioned these things, if he would not have had us to have sought to know what they meant. But how should we know them? The Scripture gives not one spark of light to find them out; but human learning holds out a clear light of discovery. . . . Here is a text fallen into our hands occasionally (a thousand others of the like nature might be produced); let any of those that deny human learning to be needful in handling of divinity, but expound me this text without the help of human learning, and I shall then think there is something in their opinion. Two things lead them into this mistake: — 1. Because they conceive the New Testament (which part of the Bible Christians have most to deal withal) is so easy of itself, that it needs no pains or study to the expounding of it. 2. And the less, Because, say they, the Spirit reveals it to the saints of God, and so they are taught of God, and can teach others. Give me leave, partly for our settlement in the truth about this point, and partly for the stopping the mouths of such gainsayers, out of many things that might be spoken, to commend these four to you: —

"I. *That, in the time when prophecy flourished, the standing ministry, that was to teach the people, were not prophets, but priests and Levites, that became learned by study.* . . . It is but a wild thing now, when prophecy has ceased so many hundreds years ago, to refuse learning and a learned ministry, and to seek instruction, we know not of whom.

"II. *There is no ground in Scripture to believe, nor promise to expect, that God doth, or ever will, teach men the grammatical or logical construction of the Scripture-text.* — It is true, indeed, that he gives to a gracious saint, ' the spirit of wisdom and revelation in the knowledge of Christ'; as it is Ephes. i. 17. But how? Revealing to him, by experimental feeling, that which he knew, indeed, before in Scripture, but only by bare theory. As, for example, — a man, before his conversion, knows, by reading and hearing, what faith and repentance are in their definitions; but, when he comes to be converted, the Spirit of grace reveals these to him in feeling and experience. And farther, revelation, as to the understanding of Scripture, there is not the least groundwork in Scripture whereupon to expect it.

"III. *When God had committed the New Testament to writing, he had revealed all that he would reveal to men on earth, of his will and way of salvation.* . . .

"IV. *The main difficulty of the New Testament requires study to unfold it, rather than revelation.* . . . The main difficulty of the New Testament is in the language; unlock that clearly, and the sense ariseth easy. . . . Now, certainly, it is more likely to obtain understanding of languages by study, than to attain it by revelation; unless any one will yet expect that miraculous gift of tongues, — which, I suppose, there is none will make himself so ridiculous, as to say he expects " (vi. 210–212).

On the *preservation, or the integrity, of the Scripture-text,* Lightfoot also teaches the ordinary Reformed doctrine, as it is formulated, for instance in the Confession of Faith, i. 8. He was conservative, as a critic of the text; but as the fellow-worker of Walton in the preparation of the great Polyglot, he was in no ignorance of the facts as to the transmission of Scripture. He knew that no one copy of Scripture was perfect; but he believed that the correct text could not be lost. " Consider," he says:

" Consider how many copies were abroad in the world. The Old Testament was in every synagogue: and how many copies would men take of the New? So that it is impossible, but still Scripture must be conveyed. Could all the policy of Satan have hindered, he had done it: for the word of God is his overthrow; so that it was owing to a divine hand " (vi. 61).

But though it was by the " singular providence " of God alone that Scripture has been preserved pure, yet God has accomplished its preservation through means, and we can observe the suitability of the means to the end. When speaking of the scribes, he tells us of the care they exercised in the preservation of the text:

" They were the men, that took upon them to copy the Bible for those, that desired to have a copy. For so great and various is the accuracy and exactness of the Scripture text in the mystical and profound significances of letters, vowels, and accents, that it was not fit that every one should offer to transcribe the original, or that every vulgar pen should copy things of so sublime speculation. Therefore, there was a peculiar and special order of learned men among the Jews, whose office it was to take care of the preservation of the purity of the text, in all Bibles that should be copied out, that no corruption or error should creep into the original of the sacred writ: . . . some set apart for this office, which required profound learning and skill; — namely, to be the copiers of the Bible, when any copy was to be taken; or, at least, to take care, that all copies, that should be transcribed, should be pure and without corruption . . ." (iv. 222).

He praises the work of the Massoretes, and looks upon their methods and exactness as the guarantee of the text. Apropos of the *nun inversum,* at Num. x. 35, he remarks concerning such phenomena:

" If they show nothing else, yet this they show us, — that the text is punctually kept, and not decayed; when these things (that, to a hasty, ignorant beholder, might seem errors) are thus precisely observed in all Bibles " (iv. 19).

" Admirable is their [the Massoretes'] pains, to prove the text uncorrupt, against a gainsaying Papist. . . . So that, if we had no other surety for the truth of the Old Testament text, these men's pains, methinks, should be enough to stop the mouth of a daring Papist " (iv. 20).

The marginal readings may, no doubt, " seem to tax the text of so many errors." But these readings are only variant readings of different copies; and though Lightfoot is inclined to doubt if " these marginals are not only human corrections," yet he treats them with sobriety:

" A second question might follow concerning Keri and Kethib: and a suspicion might also arise, that the text of the law was not preserved perfect to ' one jot and one tittle,' when so many various readings do so frequently occur. Concerning this business, we will offer these few things only . . . It is, therefore, very probable, that the Keri and Kethib were compacted from the comparing of the two copies of the greatest authority, that is, the Jewish and the Babylonian: which when they differed from one another in so many places in certain little dashes of writing, but little or nothing at all as to the sense, — by very sound counsel they provided, that both should be reserved, so that both copies might have their worth preserved, and the sacred text its purity and fulness, while not ' one jot ' nor ' one tittle ' of it perished " (xi. 103–104).

That this result was attained, he thinks is attested by our Lord in Matt. v. 18. For though he considers it plain that our Saviour " did not only understand the bare letters, or the little marks that distinguish them " in this declaration, yet —

" It appears enough hence, that our Saviour also so far asserts the uncorrupt immortality and purity of the holy text, that no particle of the sacred sense should perish, from the beginning of the law to the end of it " (xi. 99–100).

He argues stoutly that the Jews could not, in the nature of the case, have corrupted the Scripture:

" 1. It was their great care and solicitousness . . . to preserve the text in all purity and uncorruptness. . . . 2. Yet could they not, for all their care, but have some false copies go up and down amongst them, through heedlessness or error of transcribers. . . . 3. In every synagogue, they had a true copy: and it was their

care every where to have their Bíble as purely authentic as possible.
. . . 4. Had they been ever so desirous to have imposed upon Christians, by falsifying the text, they could not possibly do it. For —

" First," every synagogue having a true copy, and many Jews being converted, it could not be done. " Secondly," there were so many learned men in the Christian Church that detection would have been certain.

" 5. To which may be added, that the same power and care of God, that preserves the church, would preserve the Scriptures pure to it: and he that did, and could, preserve the whole, — could preserve every part, so that not so much as a tittle should perish" (iii. 405–408).

We have already remarked that Lightfoot was a very conservative textual critic. He speaks somewhat impatiently of the bold critics, " that are apt to tax the originals of Scripture of corruption and interpolation " (vii. 79); who, whenever for want of knowledge they are " not able to clear the sense," " have been bold to say the text is corrupt, and to frame a text of their own heads " (iii. p. xvi.). And he consistently refuses to assume a textual corruption, at Matt. xxvii. 9 for example, in order to ease the difficulty of the text (iii. 157 and xi. 344). An example of his methods and powers *as a textual critic* may be found in the several passages where he discusses Mark i. 2 (iv. 246 and xi. 377). In the former of these passages he argues against the reading " in Isaiah " on five grounds; and in the latter he conjectures as to the origin of the various readings, that the Jewish Christians introduced the reading " in Isaiah " in order to conform the mode of quotation to the Talmudic rules of quoting. His use of internal evidence is exhibited again, in a comment on Acts iii. 20, " Which before was preached unto you ":

" The very sense of the place confirmeth this reading: for though Beza saith, that all the old Greek copies that ever he saw, — as, also, the Syriac, Arabic, and Tertullian, — read it, προκεχειρισμένον , ' fore-ordained '; yet, the very scope and intention of Peter's speech, in this place, doth clearly show, that it is to be read, προκεκηρυγμένον, ' which before was preached to you,' — namely, by Moses, or the law; and by all the prophets " (viii. 66).

The same qualities and methods as a critic came out in several defences of the genuineness of the pericope of the adulteress intruded into John's Gospel (iii. 112; vi. 302–303; xii. 312). In the former passage he says:

"The Syriac wants this story: and Beza doubts it; a man always ready to suspect the text, because of the strangeness of Christ's action, writing with his finger on the ground: ' Mihi, ut ingenue loquar (saith he) vel ob hunc ipsum locum suspecta est hæc historia.' Whereas it speaks the style of John throughout, and the demeanour of the scribes and Pharisees, and of Christ, most consonantly to their carriage all along the gospel " (iii. 112).

In another place he accounts for its omission as follows:

"There is hardly any commentator upon the gospel, or this chapter, but he will tell you, that this story of the adulterous woman was wanting, and left out of some Greek Testaments in ancient times, as appears by this, — that some of the fathers, setting themselves to expound this Gospel, make no mention at all of any part of this story. So Nonnus, turning all this Gospel into Greek verse, hath utterly left out this whole story; and so hath the Syriac New Testament, first printed in Europe; and so, Jerome tells us, did some old Latin translations. When I cast with myself, whence this omission should proceed, I cannot but think of two passages in Eusebius. The one is in his third book of Ecclesiastical History, the very last clause in that book, — where he relates, that one Papias, an old tradition-monger, as he characters him, did first bring in this story of the adulterous woman, out of a book called the ' Gospel according to the Hebrews.' For so is that passage of Eusebius commonly understood. The other is in his fourth book of the Life of Constantine; where he relates, that Constantine ' enjoined him, and committed to his trust, to get transcribed πεντήκοντα σωμάτια' . . . Now, if Eusebius believed, that this story was introduced by Papias, as he seems to do, — you may well conclude, that he would be sure to leave out this story, in all his ' fifty copies,' . . . as having no better authority, than the introduction of it by such a man. Or, if the ages before Eusebius were of the same belief with him in this matter, you may see, why this story might also be wanting in those times. But I shall not trouble you about this matter, which is now past all dispute. For I believe, it is hardly possible in all the world, to find now a printed New Testament, either in the original Greek, or in any other language, either eastern or western, wherein this story is not inserted without any question. Nor had the thing been ever disputed, if the story itself had been searched to the bottom; for then, of itself, it would have vindicated its own authority, to be evangelical and divine " (vi. 302–303).

It is apparent that, though of an extremely conservative temper, Lightfoot was a remarkably well-furnished and able critic for his day. The school of criticism to which he would belong, indeed, has scarcely advanced beyond him in either resources or capacities since his time; and all that was known of the state of the text or of materials for its study in his day was in his easy control.

The difficulties of Scripture formed, in a sense, the main matter of Lightfoot's studies. He has, indeed, formally treated the subject in a single sermon only (vii. 201–216). But all his Talmudic studies were undertaken and are justified by the light which he hoped and found that they would throw upon the obscurities of the Biblical text; and his several expository treatises are specially busy with expounding the difficult passages of Scripture. In fact, his chief interest, after the determination of what may be called the background of the Scriptural revelation — the chronology, topography, geography, historical consecution, and the like, of the Biblical story — seems to have been what he would call the " clearing of scruples " in the text of Scripture. There is hardly a difficulty which had been started, from a harmonistic, chronological, or historical point of view, which he has not treated, sometimes more than once. In a study of his doctrine of Scripture, his treatment of these Scriptural difficulties cannot be neglected. On the contrary, they exhibit his conception of Scripture in action; and a review of them will enable us to look upon his conception of Scripture in the most searching light that can be thrown upon it.

Lightfoot is very far from denying that *difficulties exist in Scripture*. If he is at fault in any respect here, it is in exaggerating their number and their intractableness. Nevertheless, he does not allow that these difficulties are really errors of Scripture, or even blemishes on the divine face of Scripture. Not only are all of them capable of satisfactory explanation; but each several one of them has been purposely introduced into Scripture by the Holy Ghost for a high and good end, and this end is discoverable by the careful and diligent student. The difficulties of Scripture are thus transferred from blots into beauties; from obstacles into aids to faith; from marks of human infirmity into examples of divine wisdom. In the preface to his " Harmony, etc., of the New Testament " (iii. pp. vi.–viii., xvi.), he speaks as follows on the general subject:

" I shall not trouble the reader with any long discourse, to show, how the Scripture abounds with transposition of stories; how the Holy Ghost doth, eminently, hereby show the majesty of his style and divine wisdom: how this is equally used in both testaments; what need the student hath carefully to observe those dislocations; and what profit he may reap, by reducing them to their proper time and order. . . .

" I have not set myself to comment; but, in a transient way, to hint the clearing of some of the most conspicuous difficulties, — and that, partly, from the text itself, — and, partly, from Talmudical collections. . . . Multitudes of passages are not possibly to be explained, but from these records. For, since the scene of the most actings in it, was among the Jews, — the speeches of Christ and his apostles were to the Jews, — and they Jews, by birth and education, that wrote the Gospels and Epistles; it is no wonder if it speak the Jews' dialect throughout; and glanceth at their traditions, opinions, and customs, at every step. . . . Though it be penned in Greek, it speaks in the phrase of the Jewish nation, among whom it was penned, all along; and there are multitudes of expressions in it, which are not to be found but there, and in the Jews' writings, in all the world. They are very much deceived, that think the New Testament so very easy to be understood, because of the familiar doctrine it containeth, — faith and repentance. It is true, indeed, that it is plainer as to the matter it handleth, than the Old, because it is an unfolding of the Old: — but for the attaining of the understanding of the expressions that it useth in these explications, you must go two steps farther than you do about the Old; — namely, to observe where, and how, it useth the Septuagint's Greek, as it doth very commonly; — and where it useth the Jews' idiom, or reference thereunto, which indeed it doth continually. . . . The greatest part of the New Testament might be observed to speak in such reference to something or other commonly known, or used, or spoken, among the Jews; and even the difficultest passages in it, might be brought to far more facility than they be, if these references were well observed. There are divers places, where commentators, not able to clear the sense for want of this, have been bold to say the text is corrupt, and to frame a text of their own heads; whereas the matter, skilfully handled in this way, might have been made plain " (iii. pp. vi. vii. viii. xvi.).

In his sermon on the " Difficulties of Scripture," he tells us that the Holy Ghost purposely introduced difficulties into Scripture to challenge serious study of them; that they are all capable of solution; and that it is our business, and it will be our profit, to search out the solutions and their lessons.

" The Holy Ghost," he says, " hath purposely penned the Scriptures so as to challenge all serious study of them." . . . " Peter tells us, that there are divers things in Paul's Epistles hard to be understood; and why did the Holy Ghost dictate them so hard by Paul? . . . Because the Holy Ghost hath penned Scripture so as to challenge all serious study. He could have penned all so plain, that he that runneth, might have read them; but he hath penned them in such a style, that he that will read them, must not run and read, but sit down and study " (vii. 208).

Accordingly these difficulties, which belong to the majesty of the Scriptures (vii. 212), both can be and are to be understood, for —

" God never writ the difficulties of the Scripture only to be gazed upon and never understood; never gave them as a book sealed, and that could never be unsealed " (vii. 216).

They may be great and numerous, so great that the Old and New Testament may now and again seem to be " directly contrary," " as if the two Testaments were fallen out, and were not at unity among themselves " (vii. 210). Yet this is but an incitement to the discovery of the underlying unity, and Lightfoot has nothing but scorn for those who

" have taken upon them[selves] to pick out some places in the Bible, which, they say, are past all possibility of interpreting or understanding " (vii. 211).

These principles are repeatedly insisted upon. After enumerating such difficulties in another place, he continues thus:

" For resolution of such ambiguities, when you have found them, the text will do it, if it be well searched. . . . This way, attained to, will guide you itself in what else is agreeable to profitable reading; as in marking those things that seem to be contradictions in the text, or slips of the Holy Ghost (in which always is admirable wisdom), . . . Strange variations, yet always divine. . . . Admirable it is to see, how the Holy Spirit of God in discords hath shewed the sweet music. But few men mark this, because few take a right course in reading of Scripture. Hence, when men are brought to see flat contradictions (as unreconciled there may be many in it), they are at amaze, and ready to deny their Bible. A little pains right spent will soon amend this wavering, and settle men upon the Rock; whereon to be built is to be sure " (ii. 8, 9).

In Peter's reference to the difficulties in Paul's epistles, he thinks he sees a proof of the intentional character of them:

" He citeth Paul's Epistle to the Hebrews, and giveth an honourable testimony to that, and to the rest of his Epistles: but acknowledgeth, that, in some places, they are hard to be understood, and were misconstrued by some unlearned and unstable ones, to their own ruin; yet neither doth he nor Paul, who was yet alive and well knew of this wresting of his Epistles, clear or amend those difficulties, but let them alone as they were: for the Holy Ghost has so penned Scripture as to set men to study " (iii. 327).

A few examples of his dealing with these difficulties will be instructive. The following are some *Old Testament cases:*

" Divers psalms in the original are alphabetical; but few of them have the alphabet true, for some reason or other admirably divine: so one letter, in Jeremy's alphabetic Lamentations, is altered constantly, for secret and sweet reason " (ii. 39).

" Men frame intricacies and doubts to themselves here [Gen. xi. on the age, birth, and call of Abraham], where the text is plain, if it be not wrested " (ii. 88). He proceeds to solve the several difficulties.

On II Kings xxiv. 8, 9, and II Chron. xxxvi. 9, as to the age of Jehoiachin when he began to reign: " Now, in expressions that are so different, propriety is not to be expected in both; but the one to be taken properly, and that is, that he was eighteen years old when he began to reign; and the other, that he was the son of the eighth year, or fell in the lot of the eighth year, after any captivity of Judah had begun: for the beginning of his reign was in the eighth year of Nebuchadnezzar; and in the eighth year of the seventy of captivity. And so the Holy Ghost dealeth here, as he doth about Ahaziah, as was observed there " (ii. 288–289).

Accordingly, when speaking of II Kings viii. 26, as compared with II Chron. xxii. 2, he had said: " The original meaneth thus, ' Ahaziah was the son of the two-and-forty years,' — namely, of the house of Omri, of whose seed he was, by the mother's side; and he walked in the ways of that house, and came to ruin at the same time with it " (ii. 227).

Whatever we may think of the reasonableness of such harmonizing, its serious presentation exhibits Lightfoot's conviction of the harmonizable character of the whole Old Testament text, and shows how far he was from readiness to allow that it contained errors.

Let us note now a few *cases from the New Testament:*

" Only there is some difference betwixt Matthew and Luke, in relating the order of the temptations: which Matthew having laid down in their proper rank, . . . Luke, in the rehearsing of them, is not so much observant of the order (that being fixed by Matthew before), as he is careful to give the full story; and so to give it, as might redound to the fullest information. As our mother Eve was tempted by Satan, . . . so, by these, had it been possible, would the same tempter have overthrown the seed of the woman. . . .

Luke, for our better observing of this parallel, hath laid the order of these temptations answerable to the order of those " (iii. 41; cf. iv. 348).

On Luke v. 1–12; Matt. iv. 18–22; Mark i. 16–20: " In the order of Luke, there is some difficulty: — 1. He relateth the calling of these disciples differently from the relation given by the other. . . . They say, he called James and John at some distance beyond Peter and Andrew; but he carrieth it, as if he called them all together. But this is not contrariety, but for the more illustration; they all speak the same truth, but one helps to explain another. . . . 2. A second scruple in the order of Luke is this, — that he hath laid the two miracles of casting out a devil in Capernaum-synagogue, and the healing of Peter's mother-in-law, before the calling of these disciples; which, apparently, by this evangelist, were after. But the reason hereof may be conceived to be, especially, this . . . having an eye, in that his relation, rather to the place than to the time. And so we shall observe elsewhere, that the very mention of a place doth sometimes occasion these holy penmen to produce stories out of their proper time, to affix them to that their proper place " (iii. 52–53). " And thus the scope of his [Luke's] method is plain. And here again we see an example of what was said before, — namely, that the mention of a place doth oftentimes occasion these holy penmen, to speak of stories out of their proper time, because they would take up the whole story of that place all at once, or together " (iii. 58).

As to the Gadarene miracle: " The main doubt lies in this; that, whereas Mark and Luke speak but of one possessed, Matthew speaks of two. So I observe, that Matthew speaks of two blind men begging at Jericho, whereas Mark speaketh but of one; and so likewise Matthew speaks of both the thieves mocking Christ, whereas Luke speaks but of one of them so doing." He gives several possible views of the harmony and then continues: " But, the other examples adduced, where Matthew speaking of two, Mark and Luke speak but of one, it is plain and satisfactory, that these two latter, writing after Matthew, and he having given the story before them, numbering the persons concerned in it, — they have not been curious so much to specify the number of persons, on whom the miracles were wrought, which he had done before, as careful to record the miracle done, — that none of Christ's workings might be left unrecorded, as to the nature of the thing done " (iii. 84).

As to the place of singing the hymn at the Passover: " Which, indeed, is neither contrariety nor diversity of story, but only variety of relation for the holding out of the story more complete" (iii. 151).

On Mark's " third " hour and John's " sixth ": " Mark, therefore, in that calculation of the time, takes his date from the first time that Pilate gave him up to their abusings; and his phrase may be taken of so comprehensive an intimation, as to speak both the time of his first giving up, ' at the third hour ' of the day, and the time of his nailing to his cross, ' the third hour ' from that. And, much after the same manner of account that our Saviour's six hours' suffering, from Pilate's first giving him up, to his dying, are reckoned, so the four hundred and thirty years of sojourning of the children of Israel in Egypt (Exod. xii.), are computed; namely, the one half before they came into Egypt, and the other half after " (iii. 163).

On the inscriptions on the cross: " In the expression of which, the variety of the evangelists shows their style, and how when one speaks short, another enlargeth, and what need of taking all together to make up the full story. . . . Their variety is only in wording this for the reader's understanding " (iii. 165).

On Luke v. and its parallels: " Now, though there seem to be these different, yea, contrary circumstances in the evangelists' relation, yet is the story but one and the same, but only related more largely by Luke than by the other " (v. 149).

One of the most common internal difficulties in the Scriptures arises from what Lightfoot calls " *transposition and dislocation of times and texts.*" Of this he speaks as follows:

" The same Spirit, that dictated both the Testaments, hath observed this course in both the Testaments alike: laying texts, chapters, and histories, sometimes out of the proper place, in which, according to natural chronical order, they should have lain. And this is one of the majesticknesses, wherewithal the Holy Ghost marcheth and passeth through the Scriptures. Not that these dislocations are imperfections, — for they ever show the greatest wisdom: nor that to methodize these transposed passages, is to correct the method of the Holy Ghost; — for it is but to unknot such difficulties, as the Holy Ghost hath challenged more study on: nor that it is desirable, that our Bibles should be pointed in such a methodized way, and such Bibles only to be in common use, — for the very posture of the Bible, as it now lieth, seemeth to be divine. . . ." (ii. p. lxii.).

An example or two should be given also of Lightfoot's mode of dealing with *historical difficulties* in Scripture:

Of Cyrenius: " Either Cyrenius came twice into Syria to lay taxations, as Funccius concludeth; or else Josephus faileth here, as he doth not seldom elsewhere, in chronology " (iv. 193).

Of Theudas, more fully: " This were a very ready and easy interpretation of these words of Gamaliel, if this great scruple did not lie in the way: — namely, that this Theudas, mentioned by Josephus, was about the fourth or fifth year of Claudius; but this Theudas, mentioned by Gamaliel, was before Judas the Galilean, which was in the days of Augustus. There is a great deal of ado among expositors what to make of these two stories, so like in substance, but so different in time. Some conceive, that Josephus hath missed his chronology, and hath set Theudas's story many years later than it fell out. Others refuse Josephus's story, as not applicable to this Theudas of Gamaliel (though they hold that he hath spoken true in it), because the time is so different; but they think Gamaliel's Theudas was some of those villains, that so much infested Judea in the times of Sabinus and Varus, — Joseph. Ant. lib. 17. cap. 12; though Josephus hath not there mentioned him by name. A third sort conceive that Gamaliel's Theudas was not before Judas the Galilean, who rose about the birth of Christ, but a long while after, — namely, a little before Gamaliel speaketh these words: and they render πρὸ ἡμερῶν in the strict propriety, — namely, that it was but ' a few days before '; and μετὰ τοῦτον, not ' *post eum,*' ' after him,' — but ' *praeter eum,*' ' besides him.' In these varieties of opinions and difficulties, it is hard to resolve which way to take; and it is well that it is a matter of that nature, that men may freely use their conjectures in it, and be excusable " (viii. 82–83). He goes on to give it as his own opinion that Josephus' and Gamaliel's Theudas are not the same, but two different men; the second possibly a disciple of the other. This was published in 1645. In a posthumous book he adopts another opinion, as follows: " Josephus makes mention of one Theudas, an impostor, whose character indeed agrees well enough with this of ours; but they seem to disagree in time. . . . Those that are advocates for Josephus, do imagine there might be another Theudas, besides him that he mentions: and they do but imagine it, for they name none. I could instance, indeed, in two more of that name; neither of which agrees with this of Gamaliel, or will afford any light to the chronology of Josephus. . . . Can we suppose now, that Gamaliel could have either of these Theudases in his eye? Indeed, neither the one nor the other has any agreeableness with that character, that is given of this Theudas, about whom we are inquiring. That in Josephus is much more adapted; and grant only that the historian might slip in his chronology, and there is no other difficulty in it. Nor do I indeed see, why we should give so much deference to Josephus in this matter, as to take such pains in vindicating his care or skill in it. We must (forsooth) find out some other Theudas, or change the stops in the verses, or invent some other plaster for the sore, — rather than Josephus should be charged with the least mistake; to whom yet, both in history and chronology, it is no unusual thing to trip or go out of the road of truth. I would therefore think, that the Theudas in Josephus is this same in Gamaliel; only that the historian mistook in his accounts of time, and so defaced a true story by false chronology " (viii. 401–403).

The difficulties that arise from *the quotation of the Old Testament in the New* furnished Lightfoot, naturally, much material for the exercise of his harmonistic skill. We give a few examples of his dealing with them.

With reference to *the application of the Old Testament passages* in the New:

On Matt. ii. 15 and 18: " The two allegations produced here out of the Old Testament . . . are of that fulness, that they speak of two things apiece, and may very fitly be applied unto them both, and show that the one did resemble or prefigure the other " (iv. 231). " The Holy Ghost, therefore, doth elegantly set forth this lamentation, by personating Rachel " (iv. 232).

On Acts i. 16: " Now the application of these places so pertinently and home to Judas, showeth the illumination and knowledge, that the breathing and giving of the Holy Ghost had wrought in the disciples " (viii. 36).

With reference to the New Testament dealing with *Old Testament facts:*

Commenting on Acts vii. 4 and 7: " The Holy Ghost, indeed, hath ascribed the conduct of this journey to Terah, . . . This clause [Acts vii. 7] is here alleged [21] by Stephen, as if it had been spoken to Abraham; whereas it was spoken to Moses four hundred years after. But the Holy Ghost useth to speak short in known stories; as Matt. i. 12; 1 Chron. i. 36; Mark i. 2, 3, &c." (viii. 110, 111; cf. 112).

On Luke xi. 51, on Zecharias, son of Berachias, whom he identi- fies with Zechariah, son of Jehoiada, referring to II Chron. xxiv. (cf. xi. 288): " If any one hesitate about the changing of the name, let him say by what name he finds Jehoiada recited in that cata- logue of priests set down in 1 Chron. vi. . . . If by another name, you will say (supposing he be also called Barachias) he was then a man of three names. This indeed is no unusual thing with that na- tion for some to have more names than one: nay, if you will believe the Jewish doctors, even Moses himself had no less than ten " (xii. 123).

With reference to *the freedom of quotation* by the writers of the New Testament from the Old:

" The evangelists and apostles, when they take on them to cite any text from the Old Testament, are not so punctual to observe the exact and strict form of words, as the pith of them, or sense of the place, as might be instanced in many particulars; so that the difference of the words would not prejudice the agreement in sense, were there not so flat difference [between Mark i. 2 and its Old Testament original] of person as *me* and *thee*." He then argues that this variation is intentional, not " to cross or deny," but to explain and illustrate: " The majesty of Scripture doth often show itself, in requoting of places, in this, — that it allegeth them in difference of words and difference of sense; yea, sometimes in contrariety. . . . Wherein the Holy Ghost, having penned a thing in one place, doth, by variety of words and sense, enlarge and expound himself in an- other " (iv. 247–248).

On Luke i. 17, from Malachi: " But, first, The Holy Ghost is

[21] The reader will, of course, remember that " alleged " means " adduced " or " quoted," not " affirmed," " asserted."

not so punctual to cite the very letter of the prophet, as to give the sense " (iv. 155).

On Matt. ii. 6, he notes the differences and undertakes to investigate them clause by clause. On the substitution in the first clause of " in the land of Juda," for " Ephratah," he remarks: " First; there are that give this general answer to all the differences in this quotation, that the scribes and the evangelist tie not themselves to the very words of the prophet, but only think it enough to render his sense. And this answer may be very well entertained, and give good satisfaction, especially since that, in allegations from the Old Testament, it is usual with the New so to do, — but that the difference between the text and the quotation is so great, that it is not only diverse, but even contrary. Some, therefore, Secondly, . . ." attribute the change to the error of the scribes, whom the evangelist accurately represents; but Lightfoot rejoins that the scribes knew their Bible too well to fall into such an error . . . " Thirdly; Whereas some talk of a Syriac edition, which the Jews used at that time more than the Hebrew, and which had this text of Micah as the evangelist hath cited it . . ." he objects that this rests on two unsupported conjectures, and finally determines as follows: . . . " The scribes, or the evangelists, or both, did thus differently quote the prophet, neither through forgetfulness, nor through the misleading of an erroneous edition, but purposely, and upon a rational intent " — viz., to convey their meaning better to Herod. The variation in the second clause, " but not the least," is met by an exegesis of the Hebrew, showing it to be consonant; then, " The text of the prophet, then, being rendered in this interpretation, this allegation of the evangelist will be found, not to have any contrariety to it at all, but to speak, though not in the very same words, yet to the very same tenor and purpose . . . And thus doth the evangelist express the prophet's mind, though he tie not his expression to his very words, alleging his text to its clearest sense, and to the easier apprehension of the hearer . . ." The change in the third clause, " princes," is shown to be, with a difference of words, the same sense; and so with the fourth clause: " But here again doth he differ from the letter of prophet, but cometh so near the sense, that the difference is as no difference at all " (iv. 225–231).

On Matt. iv. 10, where " only " is inserted: " But, first, our Saviour applies the text close to the present occasion. . . . Our Saviour doth reduce it to such a particular, as was most pertinent and agreeable to the thing in hand. And so parallels might be showed in great variety; where one place of Scripture, citing another, doth not retain the very words of the portion cited, but doth, sometimes, change the expression to fit the occasion: as Matthew, ii. 23, translates Netzer, — ' a branch,' in Isa. xi. 1, — ' a man of Nazareth.' . . . Secondly; Although the word *only* be not in the Hebrew text, yet is it in the Septuagint, . . . and it is most ordinary for the evangelists to follow that copy. And that translation hath warrantably added it, seeing (as Beza well observeth) so much is included in the emphatical particle *hun;* and is also understood by comparing other places " (iv. 346).

The complication of the problem of New Testament *quotation, through the use of the Septuagint,* alluded to in the last extract, is always kept in mind by Lightfoot. Thus:

" The apostle there [in Heb. xi. 21] follows the LXX; that, in their unpricked Bibles, read ' matteh,' ' a rod,' for ' mittah,' ' a bed ' " (ii. 107).

One of the most striking cases of the New Testament's agreement with the Septuagint text concerns the insertion of a second Cainan in the genealogical tables, which appears also in Luke's genealogy of our Lord. This is repeatedly referred to by Lightfoot:

On Gen. xi. 11, 13: " Arphaxad. . . . The Septuagint makes him the father of Cainan, which never was in being; and yet is that followed by St. Luke, for special reason " (ii. 90).

On Luke iii. 36, he speaks of the insertion of Cainan, of there being no mention of him in the Old Testament genealogies; " nor, indeed," he adds, " was there ever any such a man in the world at all "; and remarks that it is easy to see that Luke obtained him out of the Septuagint. Then he adds: " But when this is resolved, the greater scruple is yet behind, — of his warrantableness so to do, and of the purity of the text, where it is so done." " And from hence [the Septuagint] hath St. Luke, without controversy, taken in Cainan into this genealogy, — a man that never was in the world; but the warrantableness of this insertion will require divers considerations to find it out." He sets forth that the Seventy were forced to translate the Bible against their will, and did it as

ill as they could, using an "unpricked Bible" as one device
to mislead; and that they inserted the "said name," Cainan, as
one of their tricks. God used the Septuagint "as the key for
admission of the heathen, and as a harbinger to the New Testament." Luke writes with a universal interest and intent. Now,
he argues:

"This being the intent of the pedigree's placing here, as the very
placing of it doth inevitably evince, it is not only warrantable, but
also admirably divine, that Luke taketh in Cainan from the seventy. For, first, writing for heathens, he must follow the heathens'
Bible in his quotations. Secondly, In genealogies, he was to be a
copier, not a corrector. Thirdly, and chiefly, In following this insertion of the Seventy, he embraceth not their error, but divinely
draweth us to look at their intent.

"When Jude mentioneth Michael's striving with Satan about
the body of Moses, he approveth not the story as true, which he
knew to be but a Talmudic parable; but, from the Jews' own authors, he useth this as an argument against them, and for their instruction.

"So, though Luke, from the Seventy, the Bible of the heathen,
have alleged Cainan the son of Arphaxad, he allegeth it not as the
truth more than the Hebrew; but, from the Septuagint's own authority, or from the matter which they inserted in distaste of the
calling of the heathen, he maketh comfortable use and instruction
to the heathen concerning their calling. . . . Thus are the censers
of Korah and his company, though ordained for an evil end by them,
yet reserved in the sanctuary for a good by the command of God"
(iv. 325–330).

The same argument, in essence, is repeated much more fully
in another passage; and as the matter is important to help
us to estimate Lightfoot's methods, we shall quote it pretty
much at large. He is sure that Luke here follows the Septuagint:

"I cannot be persuaded by any arguments, that this passage concerning Cainan, was in Moses's text, or, indeed, in any Hebrew
copies, which the Seventy used . . . But now if this version be so
uncertain, and differs so much from the original, — how comes it
to pass, that the evangelists and apostles should follow it so ex-

actly, and that even in some places, where it does so widely differ from the Hebrew fountain?

"*Ans.* I. It pleased God to allot the censers of Korah, Dathan, and Abiram, to sacred use, because they were so ordained and designed by the first owners: — so doth it please the Holy Ghost to determine that version to his own use, being so primarily ordained by the first authors. . . . So the Greek version designed for sacred use, as designed for the Holy Bible, — so it was kept and made use of by the Holy Ghost.

"II. Whereas the New Testament was to be wrote in Greek, and come into the hands chiefly of Gentiles, — it was most agreeable, — I may say, most necessary, for them, to follow the Greek copies, as being what the Gentiles were only capable of consulting; that so they, examining the histories and quotations that were brought out of the Old Testament, might find them agreeing with, and not contradicting, them. . . .

"III. . . . *Object.* But the clause, that is before us (to omit many others), is absolutely false: for there was neither any Cainan the son of Arphaxad; nor was Jesus the son of any Cainan, that was born after the flood.

"*Ans.* I. There could be nothing more false as to the thing itself, than that of the apostle, when he calleth the preaching of the gospel μωρίαν, 'foolishness,' 1 Cor. i. 21; and yet, according to the common conceptions of foolish men, nothing more true. So neither was this true in itself, that is asserted here; but only so in the opinion of those, for whose sake the evangelist writes. Nor yet is it the design of the Holy Ghost to indulge them in any thing, that was not true; but only would not lay a stumbling-block at present before them. 'I am made all things to all men, that I might gain some.'

"II. There is some parallel with this of St. Luke and that in the Old Testament, 1 Chron. i. 36: 'The sons of Eliphaz, Teman, and Omar, and Zephi, and Gatam, and Timnah, and Amalek.' Where it is equally false, that Timnah was the son of Eliphaz, — as it is, that Cainan was the son of Arphaxad. But far, far, be it from me to say, that the Holy Ghost was either deceived himself, or would deceive others! Timnah was not a man, but a woman; not the son of Eliphaz, but his concubine; not Amalek's brother, but his mother, Gen. xxxvi. 12. Only the Holy Ghost teacheth us, by this shortness of speech, to recur to the original story, from whence those things are taken, — and there consult the determinate explication of the whole matter: which is frequently done by the same Holy Spirit, speaking very briefly in stories well known before.

" The Gentiles have no reason to cavil with the evangelist in this matter; for he agrees well enough with their Bibles. And if the Jews, or we ourselves, should find fault, he may defend him from the common usage of the Holy Ghost, in whom it is no rare and unusual thing, in the recital of stories and passages well enough known before, to vary from the original, and yet without any design of deceiving, or suspicion of being himself deceived; but according to that majesty and authority that belongs to him, dictating and referring the reader to the primitive story, from whence he may settle and determine the state of the matter, and inquire into the reasons of the variation. St. Stephen imitates this very custom, while he is speaking about the burial of the patriarchs, Acts vii. 15, 16; being well enough understood by his Jewish auditory, though giving but short hints in a story so well known.

" III. It is one thing to dictate from himself, — and another thing to quote what is dictated from others, as our evangelist in this place doth. And when as he did, without all question, write in behalf of the Gentiles, being the companion of him, who was the first apostle of the Gentiles, — what should hinder his alleging according to what had been dictated in their Bibles?

" When the apostle names the magicians of Egypt, Jannes and Jambres, 2 Tim. iii. 9, he doth not deliver it for a certain thing, or upon his credit assure them, that these were their very names, but allegeth only what had been delivered by others, what had been the common tradition amongst them, well enough known to Timothy, a thing about which neither he nor any other would start any controversy.

" So when the apostle Jude speaks of Michael contending with the devil about the body of Moses, he doth not deliver it for a certain and authentic thing; and yet is not to be charged with any falsehood, because he doth not dictate of his own,. but only appeals to something that had been told by others, using an argument with the Jews, fetched from their own books and traditions."

In IV. he argues that if fault is to be found for adding Cainan, it is to be found with the Seventy and not with Luke. (xii. pp. 55–62.)

In estimating the meaning of such a passage as this, we must remember that, for our present purpose, the question is not whether Lightfoot succeeds in saving the credit of the sacred writers, on the grounds which he alleges; but whether he considered himself to succeed in doing so. We are not investigating the real value of his arguments; but the value which he placed upon them. We may possibly ourselves think that the method which he here adopts, and the explanations which he offers, will leave the New Testament writers chargeable with faults and errors, which impinge upon their infallibility; but it is quite evident that Lightfoot did not think so. On the basis of the explanation which we have just quoted, he felt able to say that there " never was in the world " such a man as Cainan mentioned in Luke's genealogy of Christ, that the story of Michael's striving with Satan for Moses' body was " but a Talmudic parable," that Jannes and Jambres were but invented names of the Egyptian magicians; and yet to declare in the same breath that the whole of the books which make mention of them, in all their parts and words and letters, were the dictation of the Holy Ghost, who is incapable of error. He declares that Luke's following the Septuagint in the insertion of Cainan was " not only warrantable, but admirably divine," and that in doing so " he embraceth not the error, but divinely draweth us to look at the intent." In such matters the Holy Ghost acts " according to that majesty and authority that belongs to him "; and the sacred writers are not to be " charged with any falsehood " on their account.

The principles on which Lightfoot bases these explanations are those of accommodation and of the *argumentum ex concessis*. He supposes that the sacred writers, in making use of such material, do it in order to avoid arousing the opposition of their readers or to refute and convince them out of their own mouths; and that this use of such material does not commit the sacred writers to its truth. There can be no question that the *argumentum ex concessis* is a legitimate form of argument; and none that the sacred writers make use of it: and if Lightfoot can succeed in subsuming the present instances under this argument, he has no doubt succeeded in his explanations of them. The point of doubt is whether these are cases of this

kind of argument. He held that they are. He argues this indeed
with iterated persistency. Let us gather some of the chief passages together:

"Whence had the apostle their names [Jannes and Jambres]?
From the common-received opinion and agreement of the Jewish
nation, that currently asserted, that the magicians of Egypt were
called by these names. . . . So that the apostle takes up these two
names, neither by revelation, as certainly asserting that the sorcerers of Egypt were of these names; but, as he found the names
commonly received by the Jewish nation, so he useth them.

"Such a passage is that of the apostle Jude, about ' Michael
contending with the devil about the body of Moses ': which he
neither speaketh by inspiration,[22] nor by way of certain assertion,
— but only citing a common opinion and conceit of the nation,
he takes an argument from their own authors and concessions "
(vii. 90).

Commenting on Jude, 9th verse, elsewhere: " Not that ever such
a dispute was betwixt Michael or Christ, and the devil about
Moses's body; but the Jews have such a conceit and story, and we
meet it in their writings; and the apostle useth an argument from
their own saying to confute their doing " (vii. 179).

" In citing the story of ' Michael the archangel contending with
the devil about the body of Moses,' he doth but the same that Paul
doth in naming Jannes and Jambres; namely, allege a story, which
was current and owned among the nation, though there were no
such thing in Scripture; and so he argueth with them from their
own authors and concessions. . . . His alleging the prophecy of
Enoch, is an arguing of the very like nature; as citing and referring
to some known and common tradition, that they had among them,
to this purpose. . . . And in both these he useth their own testimonies against themselves; as if he should thus have spoken at
large: ' " These men speak evil of dignities," whereas they have
and own a story for current, that even " Michael the archangel "
did not speak evil of the devil, when he was striving with him about
the body of Moses, &c. And whereas they show and own a prophecy
of Enoch, of God coming in judgment, &c.; why, these are the very

[22] Lightfoot's use of " inspiration " as equivalent to " revelation " just
above, must not deceive us into supposing that he means that Jude did not
do this under the inspiration of the Holy Ghost. See the further passages, and
compare above, for his use of the word " inspiration."

men, to whom such a matter is to be applied,' &c. It is no strange thing, in the New Testament, for Christ and the apostles to deal and argue with the Jews upon their own concessions " (iii. 328–329).

This " useful principle of interpreting " is further illustrated in connection with a former passage (vii. 178) by an exposition of Acts vii. 53, where Lightfoot translates " *unto* the disposition of angels."

" As if Stephen did rub their own opinion upon them, as is frequently done by the apostles, and that his meaning should be this: ' You say, and conceive, that the very receiving of the law did translate and dispose them, that heard it, into the very predicate and state of angels; and yet this brave law you have not kept. The law, that, you conceit, made others angels . . . hath had no good effect upon you at all; for ye have not kept it ' " (vii. 178–179).

He then cites another case of the apostles arguing thus, " to confute them from their own opinions and tenets," viz., I Cor. xi. 10, which, indeed, may be a case in point.

Whether we can follow Lightfoot in looking upon all these cases as cases of arguments *ex concessis* or not, we can at least understand that his thinking so gave him an explanation of them which enabled him to contend at the same time that the facts involved were not true, and yet that the Biblical writers were absolutely infallible or inerrant: they did not put them forward as facts. And on this general principle, he was inclined to deal with all testimonies borrowed by the writers of the Bible from sources of authority among their readers; in such cases they were " copiers, not correctors." Thus:

" Jacob goeth down into Egypt with seventy souls. . . . The Septuagint have added five more . . . from 1 Chron. vii. 14. 20, &c.; followed by St. Luke, Acts, vii. 14 " (ii. 104).

Matthew took " the latter end of his genealogy," and Luke " the beginning of his," from the " public registers," " having then the civil records to avouch for them, if they should be questioned " (iv. 172–173).

So Matthew took Rahab's marriage to Salmon, " from ancient records " (iv. 174; cf. 177).

There are other instances also in which Lightfoot's explanations may not seem to us to be satisfactory or indeed suitable. For example, there is a case of quite extreme application of *the principle of accommodation* in his explanation of the parable of the rich man and Lazarus. He supposes that Christ framed the parable according to the common Greek opinion as to Elysium and Tartarus; which empties the whole mass of details in the story of its value as a revelation of the future state. And there is a case also in which two inconsistent explanations are offered, the latter of which suggests something very similar to the modern critical *theory of " re-working,"* — though, of course, with a difference. He is discussing Psalm lxxxix. which he considers to be by Ethan, son of Zerah, " penned many years before the birth of Moses," in the " bondage and affliction of Egypt "; and he raises the difficulty that David is often mentioned in it, to answer it thus:

"*Answer.* 1. This might be done prophetically; as Samuel is thought to be named by Moses, Psalm xcix. 6: for that Psalm, according to a rule of the Hebrews, is held to have been made by him. 2. It will be found in Scripture, that when some holy men, endued with the Spirit of God, have left pieces of writings behind them, indited by the Spirit, — others, that have lived in after-times, endued with the same gift of prophecy, have taken those ancient pieces in hand, and have flourished upon them, as present, past, or future occasions did require. To this purpose, compare Psalm xviii. and 1 Sam. xxii.; Obadiah, and Jer. xlix. 14; and 1 Chron. xvi., and Psalm xcvi., and cv.; and 2 Pet. ii., and the Epistle of St. Jude, ver. 18. So this piece of Ethan being of incomparable antiquity, and singing of the delivery from Egypt, — in after-times, that it might be made fit to be sung in the temple, it is taken in hand by some divine penman, and that groundwork of his is wrought upon, and his song set to a higher key; namely, that whereas he treated only of the bodily deliverance from Egypt, it is wound up so high as to reach the spiritual delivery by Christ; and, therefore, David is so often named, from whence he should come " (ii. 356–357).

In these passages we have probably Lightfoot at his worst. Acute, learned, full of expedients, and always reverently bearing in mind, before all things, that the Scriptures are literally the word of God, in which there can be no error; he yet is overtaken by the fault which so often attends the harmonist, and overreaches himself with unnatural subtleties which raise more difficulties than they lay. It would be a blunder to suppose that this type of explanation is characteristic of Lightfoot. Were our purpose to estimate his ability and his resources as a harmonist, there would be quite a different body of examples to be adduced, far more characteristic of him and far more worthy of his great learning and good judgment. But as our object is to investigate his attitude towards Scripture, we have been forced to adduce rather those instances that have fallen under our eye, in which his dealings with Scripture might be misapprehended by a careless reader as involving the admission of errors in the text of Scripture. It will be only fair, however, that we shall set over against these instances of overstrained subtlety at least one example of his more satisfactory exposition; and we shall choose for this his treatment of that *crux* of interpreters — Matt. xxvii. 9. He discusses this text twice, and to the same effect in both instances; we quote the substance of both passages:

" And here a quotation of Matthew hath troubled expositors so far, that divers have denied the purity of the text . . . whereas those words are not to be found in Jeremiah at all; but in Zechariah they are found. Now Matthew speaks, according to an ordinary manner of speaking, used among the Jews, and by them would, easily and without cavil, be understood, though he cited a text of Zechariah, under the name of Jeremy: for the illustration of which matter, we must first produce a record of their own." He proceeds to quote the well-known passage in *Bava Bathra* fol. 14, f. 2, on the order of the books in the Old Testament, in which the " Prophets " stand thus: Jeremiah, Ezekiel, Isaiah, the Twelve, and continues: " And thus, in their Bibles of old, Jeremiah came next after the Book of Kings, and stood first in the volume of the prophets. So that Matthew's alleging of a text of Zechariah, under the name of Jeremy,

doth but allege a text out of the volume of the prophets, under his
name that stood first in that volume: and such a manner of speech
is that of Christ (Luke, xxiv. 44) . . . in which he follows the
general division that we have mentioned, — only he calleth the
'whole third part,' or 'hagiographa,' by the title 'the Psalms,' because the Book of Psalms stood first of all the books of that part.
In that saying, Matt. xvi. 14, . . . there is the same reason, why
Jeremiah alone is named by name, — viz. because his name stood
first in the volume of the prophets; and so came first in their way,
when they were speaking of the prophets" (iii. 157–158).

    "How much this place hath troubled interpreters, let the famous
Beza, instead of many others, declare: 'This knot hath hampered
all the most ancient interpreters; in that the testimony here is
taken out of Zechariah, and not from Jeremiah; so that it seems
plainly to have been ἁμάρτημα μνημονικὸν, "a failing of memory,"
as Augustine supposes in his third book, "De consensu evangelis-
tarum," chapter the seventh; as also Eusebius in the twentieth book
Ἀποδείξεω , "of demonstration." But if any one had rather impute
this error to the transcribers, or (as I rather suppose) to the unskilfulness of some person, who put in the name of "Jeremiah,"
where the evangelist had writ only, as he often doth in other places,
Διὰ τοῦ προφήτου, "by the prophet," — yet we must confess, that
this error hath long since crept into the Holy Scriptures, as Jerome
expressly affirms,' &c.

    "But (with the leave of so great men) I do not only deny, that
so much as one letter is spurious, or crept in without the knowledge
of the evangelist, but I do confidently assert that Matthew wrote
'Jeremy,' as we read it, — and that it was very readily understood
and received by his countrymen. We will transcribe the following
monument of antiquity out of the Talmudists, and then let the
reader judge" . . . quoting Bab. *Bava Bathra*, folio 14, 2. . . .
"You have this tradition, quoted by David Kimchi in his preface
to Jeremiah. Whence it is very plain, that Jeremiah, of old, had
the first place among the prophets: and hereby he comes to be mentioned above all the rest, Matt. xvi. 14, because he stood first in
the volume of the prophets, therefore he is first named. When,
therefore, Matthew produceth a text of Zechariah under the name
of Jeremy, he only cites the words of the volume of the prophets
under his name, who stood first in the volume of the prophets. Of
which sort is that also of our Saviour, Luke xxiv. 44; 'All things

must be fulfilled, which are written of me in the law, and the
prophets, and the Psalms.' ' In the Psalms '; that is, in the Book
of Hagiographa, in which the Psalms were placed first " (xi. 344–
345).

Surely this is a very admirable specimen of harmonizing.
The fact appealed to is an indisputable one; [23] and the usage
of quoting a section of the Scriptures by the name of its first
book is shown to be a New Testament usage. The only fault
to be found with the treatment is that Lightfoot is a little too
sure that his explanation is the only possible one. Plausible and
satisfactory as it is, we should rather see the whole case put
in a properly apologetical form, and their full weight allowed
to all the possibilities; somewhat thus: 1. It is not absolutely
certain that Matthew wrote " Jeremiah," and not " Zechariah." 2. It is not certain that a passage in Zechariah might
not be properly quoted under the title " Jeremiah." 3. It is
not certain that a passage in Jeremiah might not have been
intended, as well as the passage in Zechariah which supplies
some of the words cited. But we are not now discussing the
errorlessness of the Scriptures, but Lightfoot's obviously firmly-
held belief that they are errorless. And it is clear that he found
no error in the citation in Matt. xxvii. 9, which has been in
all time, and is now afresh in our day, made to do duty as the
plainest of all the errors found in Scripture.

Here we may bring our study of Lightfoot to a close. It is
perfectly evident that his fundamental conception of Scripture
was that it is the Book of God, the " dictates of the Holy
Spirit," of every part and every element of which — its words
and its very letters — God is Himself the responsible author.
It is perfectly evident that he would have considered it blasphemy to say that there is anything in it — in the way of
falseness of statement, or error of inadvertence — which would
be unworthy of God, its Author, who as Truth itself, lacks

[23] Compare Ryle, " The Canon of the Old Testament," 1892, pp. 226 *sqq.*,
for the commonness and the antiquity — Ryle thinks the originality — of the
order appealed to by Lightfoot.

neither truthfulness nor knowledge. It is perfectly evident, in a word, that he shared the common doctrine of Scripture of the Reformed dogmaticians of the middle of the seventeenth century. It is perfectly evident also, we may add, that his doctrine of Scripture is generally that of the Westminster Confession; and that he could freely and with a good conscience vote for every clause of that admirable — the most admirable extant — statement of the Reformed doctrine of Holy Scripture. It is a desperate cause indeed, which begins by misinterpreting that statement, and then seeks to bolster this obvious misinterpretation by asserting that men like Lightfoot, and Rutherford, and Lyford, and Capel, and Ball, and Baxter, did not believe in the doctrines of verbal inspiration and the inerrancy of Scripture. If they did not believe in these doctrines, human language is incapable of expressing belief in doctrines. Is it not a pity that men are not content with corrupting our doctrines, but must also corrupt our history?

V

THE PRINTING OF THE WESTMINSTER CONFESSION

THE PRINTING OF THE WESTMINSTER CONFESSION [1]

I. IN BRITAIN

THE history of the printing of the Confession of Faith presents some rather curious features. It was no less than four times privately printed — once in part and thrice in whole — before it was published. It was first published not in England where it had been made, but in Scotland. It probably had been published in no less than three editions, before its publication was authorized by the legislative body by the direction of which it was drawn up, and to which it was presented only as " humble advice." It has always continued to be published — with the single exception of the normative edition issued by Parliament (June, 1648) — not in the form authorized by that body, but in the form in which it was set forth prior to that authorization. Though its use has extended to the very ends of the British Empire, its publication for that Empire up to to-day continues very much a Scotch monopoly. Only a single edition [2] has been issued in England since the early years of the

---

[1] This was published in five instalments in *The Presbyterian and Reformed Review:*

I. " In Britain ": xii. 1901, of the *Review,* pp. 606–659, of which pp. 606–614 are here printed (pp. 337–347).

II. " In the United States ": xiii. 1902, pp. 60–120, of which pp. 60–70 are printed below (pp. 347–361).

III. " In Translation ": xiii. 1902, pp. 254–276, of which pp. 254–259 are given below (pp. 361–367).

IV. " In Modification ": xiii. 1902, pp. 380–426, of which pp. 380–386 are given below (pp. 368–376).

V. " Appendices ": xiii. 1902, pp. 551–587.

[2] The pamphlet edition is referred to, published by Mr. Wm. Carruthers recently, through the Publishing Office of the Presbyterian Church of England. See *The Presbyterian and Reformed Review,* xii. 1901, pp. 658–659, No. 137.

eighteenth century (1717).[3] It has never been printed in Ireland. It has never been printed in the Dominion of Canada. No Welsh translation of it has ever been made. Some vernacular versions of it have, to be sure, been issued in India — which are, however, with one exception (made by missionaries of the Irish Presbyterian Church), the work of American missionaries. With the exception of these, throughout all the colonies and dependencies of Great Britain, it is only in Victoria and New Zealand[4] that the Confession of Faith has even up to to-day been put into print. As the vigorous bodies of Presbyterians planted in these several lands all trace their origin back to Scotland, so they still draw the needed supply of their symbolical books from the printing presses of Scotland.

The manner in which the Confession of Faith first got into print deserves a full description. Its first issues were private editions, printed strictly for the use of the bodies concerned with its formulation or authorization. The earliest of them contained only its first nineteen chapters. These were sent up to the House of Commons, September 25, 1646, in response to an order issued September 16, and received by the Assembly of Divines September 18. They were read in the House on Friday, October 9, and ordered to be printed, after the Divines should have " put in the margin the proofs out of the Scripture to confirm what they have offered to the House in such places as they shall think it most necessary." This order was brought to the Assembly by Mr. Tate on October 12, and a Committee was appointed " to consider of this order how obedience may be yielded thereto." On the next day the Committee reported, deprecating the requirement of the addition of proof-

---

[3] Such editions as those of " Edinburgh, Robert Seton; and Whittaker & Co., London, 1855 "; " Glasgow and London, 1859 "; " London, Edinburgh and New York, T. Nelson & Sons, 1859 and 1860," are scarcely exceptions to this statement. Neither are the editions of Shaw's Exposition, " Blackie & Son, London and Glasgow, 1877 "; and Hodge's Commentary, " London: T. Nelson & Sons, Edinburgh and New York, 1870."

[4] See *The Presbyterian and Reformed Review*, xii. 1901, pp. 656–658, Nos. 132, 133, 135.

texts before printing. This was made known forthwith to the House of Commons, whereupon it was " *Resolved,* etc., That five hundred copies of the Confession of Faith be forthwith printed for the service of the Houses, without annexing of the texts of Scripture for the present: Yet, notwithstanding, the House does expect that the Divines should send in the texts of Scripture with all convenient speed." This reply was brought by Mr. Marshall to the Assembly on October 14, and it was forthwith " *Ordered* — That the scribes do take care of the exact printing of the Confession of Faith." Accordingly the first nineteen chapters of the Confession were at once put to press and appeared duly in a small quarto volume under the title, " The humble advice of the Assembly of Divines, Now by Authority of Parliament, sitting at Westminster, Concerning part of a Confession of Faith, Presented by them lately to both Houses of Parliament."

Meanwhile the Divines continued their labors on the remaining chapters, and by November 26 were able to record in their Minutes, " The Confession of Faith was finished this day," and to resolve that " the whole Confession of Faith shall be transcribed and read in the Assembly, and sent up to both Houses of Parliament." By December 4 this final reading and adjustment of the text was completed, and on that day it was sent up to the Commons, and on December 7 to the Lords. On December 10 an order was brought from the House of Commons directing that 600 copies of it, and no more, be printed for the service of the two Houses and the Assembly, and that the care of the printing be devolved on the Assembly. It was accordingly ordered, as in the earlier instance concerning the first nineteen chapters, " that the Scribes take care of the exact printing of the Confession of Faith." The work was prosecuted so rapidly that Baillie could write on December 24, 1646, " All is now printed," and was able to carry up the printed book with him to Scotland, and to present it to the Commission of the General Assembly at their January meeting (January 21). It is a small quarto volume bearing the title, " The Humble Advice of the Assembly of Divines, Now by authority of Parliament sitting at Westminster, concerning a Confession of Faith, presented by them lately to both Houses of Parliament."

The work of preparing proof-texts in pursuance of the order of the House of Commons was fairly set on foot on January 6, 1647, and on April 5 following the entry was made again in the Minutes, " The Confession was finished," i.e. in Committee. It was not until the 26th, however, that the proof-texts could be ordered to be sent to the Houses; they were presented to them on April 29. On the same day the Commons ordered, " That six hundred copies, and no more, of the Advice of the Assembly of Divines concerning the Confession of Faith, with the quotations and texts of Scripture annexed, presented to this House, and likewise six hundred copies of the proceedings of the Assembly of Divines upon the Nine-and-thirty Articles of the Church of England, be forthwith printed for the service of both Houses and of the Assembly of Divines; and the printer is enjoined at his peril not to print more than six hundred copies of each, or to divulge or publish any of them. It is further *Ordered* — That no person presume to reprint, divulge, or publish the said Advice or proceedings, or any part of them, till further order be taken by both or either of the Houses of Parliament." This order was on the same day (April 29, 1647) reported to the Assembly of Divines, and it would appear that the work was carried through, in obedience to it, " with all speed as may be." The resultant volume was a small quarto similar to the former issues, and bearing the title, " The humble Advice of the Assembly of Divines, Now by Authority of Parliament sitting at Westminster, Concerning a Confession of Faith, with the Quotations and Texts of Scripture annexed, Presented by them lately to both Houses of Parliament."

As we have already seen, the second of these issues — the complete Confession without proof-texts — was carried up to Scotland by Baillie, who left London probably in the last week of December, 1646 (before the 2d of January, 1647); and was presented to the General Assembly's Commission at their January meeting (January 21). The third issue — the complete

Confession with proofs — had found its way to Scotland before the meeting of the General Assembly, which convened on August 4, 1647. Probably it was brought up by Gillespie, who took his leave of the Westminster Assembly on July 16. At the third session of this General Assembly a Committee was appointed " for examining the Confession of Faith, Rouse's Paraphrase, Catechisme, etc., and to receive any scruples and objections, and to report "; and an invitation was given at the fourth session to " all that had objections against any thing in the Confession, to repaire to the Committee "; while at the fifth session (August 9) there was passed an " Act for Printing 300 Copies of the advise of the Assemblie of Divines in England, Concerning a Confession of Faith, for the use of the Members of the Assembly." This volume, also a small quarto, was accordingly printed by the King's printer, Evan Tyler, with the same title as before — " The Humble Advice of the Assembly of Divines . . . concerning a Confession of Faith, etc." — and bearing the order of the General Assembly of the Church of Scotland providing for the printing of " three hundred copies and no more." It must have appeared during the sessions of the General Assembly, at the twenty-third session of which, August 27, 1647, an act of approbation of the Confession was passed.

So far the Confession had issued from the press only as a privately printed and, presumably, carefully guarded pamphlet. By the Act of the General Assembly of August 27, however, it had become the public Confession of Faith of the Church of Scotland. It was naturally, therefore, at once published. The first published edition was equally naturally a reprint of the copy printed for the use of the Scottish Assembly. It also bears the imprint of Evan Tyler, at Edinburgh, 1647; and like its privately printed predecessor it is a small quarto of fifty-six pages. Meanwhile matters dragged in the English Parliament, which had busied itself with a review of the text of the Confession that had resulted in some slight changes dictated by the growing Independent influence; and it was not until the 20th of June, 1648, that it was " *Ordered* — That the

Articles of Christian Religion " (the Parliament's new name for the document) " . . . be forthwith printed and published "; while on the next day it was " *Resolved,* That the texts of Scripture be printed with the *Articles of Faith.*" Not till midsummer of 1648, therefore (June 27 at the earliest), was the Confession, under this new title and with certain alterations of text, consisting chiefly in the omission of chapters xxx. and xxxi. and parts of chapters xx. and xxiv., with some less important changes in chapter xxiii., published by the authority of Parliament. It is far from unlikely that there had already appeared in the interval not only a Scotch edition, bearing the imprint of " Edinburgh, 1648," but without the name of printer or publisher, which is notable as the first edition which contains in a single volume the Confession and the Catechisms; but also a London edition of the Confession by itself, printed in 1648 for Robert Bostock, under the old title of " The Humble Advice of the Assembly of Divines, etc." It is certain, in any case, that this Parliamentary edition came into the world as an untimely birth, and that all subsequent editions derive from the Scotch edition of Evan Tyler as their *editio princeps,* and not from the authorized Parliamentary " Articles of Christian Religion." Already in 1649 even the earlier title, " The Humble Advice to both Houses of Parliament," had given way to the simpler " The Confession of Faith . . . agreed upon by the Assembly of Divines at Westminster," to which is added in the Scotch editions (and by 1652 in the English also), " And now appointed by the Generall Assembly of the Kirk of Scotland to be a part of Uniformity in Religion between the Kirks of Christ in the three Kingdoms." [5]

[5] Principal Lee remarks on the incongruity of this statement persisting in the title of the Confession after the hope of the institution of such uniformity had long since passed away (" Additional Memorial, etc.," Edinburgh, 1826, pp. *134 *sq.*, where also other anomalies of this kind are recited). The better form, " Of public authority in the Church of Scotland," seems to have been introduced first in Dunlop's " Collection," 1719, and in the normative edition of Lumisden & Robertson, 1728. The " Collection " of Lumisden & Robertson, 1725, however, retained the old form, which naturally persists therefore in its reprints as well as in some other copies at least

The book thus put into the hands of the public proved a very popular one, and became at once the object of a great demand. Before the end of the seventeenth century, at least as many as forty separate editions had been printed, seventeen of which were English and twenty-three Scotch; and, besides, translations had been made into both German (1648) and Latin (1656), and of the Latin version at least nine editions had been issued. By the time its first century was completed these forty editions had been at least doubled, and there had been added to the extant versions an Irish (Gaelic) translation (1725), which had already attained its second edition (1727), and was almost ready for its third (1756). The large popular call for the book, attested by the rapidity with which edition thus followed edition, is further illustrated by what may be called the evolution of the volume in which it was contained. This was such as to adapt it more and more to popular use and fit it ever more fully to meet purely popular needs.

As at first published the volume contained nothing but the bare text of the Confession of Faith, accompanied by supporting references to the Scriptures. Thus the reader was " remitted to the Bible " for even the matter of the proofs: which, as Dunlop truly says in the Advertisement to his critical edition,[6] was " troublesome to him, and in so far equivalent to the not printing the Scriptures at all." It was inevitable, therefore, that in the better adaptation of the book to popular use these references should be expanded into the adduction at large of the proof-passages themselves. It is rather odd that this was first done in a translation — in that early German version (1648) whose authors speak feelingly of the Confession as " a tractate rich in all particulars of the divine wisdom and teaching, drawn almost word for word from the Holy Scriptures," and as " a brief compend of the wholesome Word," out of which " shines brightly and clearly the light of the truth, for the comforting and strengthening of believing hearts." It

---

as late as 1785. (See *The Presbyterian and Reformed Review,* xii. 1901, pp. 641–644 and 647–649, Nos. 57, 58, 62, 63, 66, 90, 96, 97, 102.)

[6] Edinburgh: James Watson, 1719, p. clx.

was not till ten years later (in the Rothwell editions of 1658) that the same extension was made in English, " for the benefit," it is quaintly said, " of masters of families ": on the same occasion, for the further lessening the labor of using these texts, an attempt was made to point their lessons by emphasizing what was thought to be the salient words in them. By whom this expansion of the texts was done is not known: but the texts as thus first extended held the ground up to 1719, when for the first time they were subjected to critical scrutiny and reduced to more precise and scholarly shape by William Dunlop for his notable " Collection " — the earliest attempt (and it may almost be said the last as yet) to produce a scientific as distinguished from a popular edition of the Confession of Faith.

Meanwhile the volume was attracting to itself similar documents, and was ever growing in compass. Two principles of development early exhibited themselves. The one (and the weaker) tended toward making out of it a more complete ecclesiastical manual. The other (and more powerful) tended to make of it an ever more richly furnished popular book of religion. The two Catechisms were early added, as documents too closely similar to the Confession to be kept apart from it. The first edition containing them appeared at Edinburgh in 1648, and by 1649 they may be said to have already established themselves as its inseparable companions. Already in 1649 there was added to these three documents the Divines' " Humble Advice concerning Church Government and Ordination of Ministers " (Bostock's second edition [1649]; see also the London editions of 1650, 1651, and again 1658). But the force of the stream was setting in the other direction: in 1650 " The Sum of Saving Knowledge " first appears in the volume (Edinburgh: Gedeon Lithgow), and at the same time the Directory for Family Worship and the Solemn League and Covenant (the same, alternative copies; cf. London and Edinburgh editions of 1652). After a while the two streams united, and, after the fashion of popular books, the effort of publishers seemed to be to supply as comprehensive a collection as possible. Examples of these developed editions may be found in the Dutch-printed edition of 1679, and the so-called "fifth" London edition of 1717 — the latter of which characteristically boasts on the title-page that it contains "all the other additions that have hitherto been printed." [7] The former of these two issues already contains, besides the Confession and Catechisms, the Sum of Saving Knowledge, the National and Solemn Covenants, the Acknowledgment of Sins, the Directory for Public Worship, Propositions concerning Church Government, and the Directions for Private Worship. The latter contains, in addition to these, the Ordinance for calling the Assembly of Divines together, the Vow taken by its members, the Advice on the ordination of ministers, and certain brief notes, including the Parliamentary order for the reëstablishment of Presbytery in England, etc. In 1728 this evolution completed itself in an edition printed at Edinburgh by Thomas Lumisden and John Robertson, which is the first to contain the precise series of documents which have since become the invariable contents of the standard Scottish editions of "The Confession of Faith."

The regular contents of the Scottish editions, thus attained, embraces the following documents: — 1. Preliminary matter, consisting of two introductory letters and a number of Ordinances and Acts. The introductory letters are (a) the Commendatory Letter "to the Christian Reader, especially Heads of Families," signed by forty-four Puritan Divines, and (b) "Mr. Thomas Manton's Epistle to the Reader." The Ordinances and Acts include: (a) The Ordinance of the Lords and Commons, July 12, 1643, convening the Westminster Assembly; (b) the Act of the Scottish Assembly, August 19, 1643, appointing Commissioners to the Westminster Assembly; (c) the Promise and Vow taken by the Members of the Westminster Assembly; (d) a List of the Divines who met at that Assembly, and of the Commissioners of the Church of Scotland; (e) the Act of the Scottish Assembly, August 27, 1647, approving the Confession of Faith; (f) the Acts of Parliament, February 7, 1649, and 7th June, 1690, ratifying the

[7] As does also the so-called "fourth" edition, Edinburgh, 1708.

Standards. 2. The Text of the Confession and Catechisms. 3. Adjoined matter, viz.: (a) The Sum of Saving Knowledge, with the Practical Use thereof; (b) the National Covenant; (c) the Solemn League and Covenant; (d) the Acknowledgment and Engagement; (e) the Directory for Public Worship; (f) the Form of Presbyterial Church Government; (g) the Directory for Family Worship. Lastly, 4. The "Table." That the main contents of the volume — the Confession and Catechisms — may not be lost amid the accretions gathered about them, it is usual to put them into larger type than that used for the preliminary and adjoined matter, although the opening Commendatory Letter and the Form of Government are also ordinarily accorded the honor of this larger type.

Since the publication of the edition of 1728 little has been done for the Confession of Faith on British ground. The critical work of Dunlop in 1719 had prepared the definitive text and the final form of the proof-texts and even of the " Table " — i.e., so to speak, had done the textual work. The edition of 1728 set finally, so to say, the canon of the collection. The British Churches holding to this Confession have ever since been content to do no more than repeat without intentional change the results thus registered for them. A single set of stereotyped plates — not quite of a sort to leave nothing to be desired on the score of either beauty or accuracy [8] — now suplies the whole world of British Presbyterianism with its " Confessions of Faith." The only exception to this that needs be recognized probably is the carefully edited reprint of the text of the edition of May, 1647, along with the variations of the Parliamentary edition of 1648, which Mr. William Carruthers has issued in a small pamphlet through the press of the Presbyterian Church of England. Even the edition published at Melbourne for the Presbyterians of Victoria — almost a unique attempt among the British Colonial Churches to supply their

---

[8] Samples of errors in current editions are given by Mr. Carruthers in the edition recorded at No. 137. They all occur in this stereotyped text, though some of them are not in Dunlop, e.g. those in ix. 1; xxii. 7. Add the error in Larger Catechism, 105: " Trusting in *un*lawful means."

own demand [9] — proves to be from the same plates. The same languidness has taken the place also of the early zeal to provide versions of the Confessions for peoples of other tongues. The Scottish missionaries seem not to have been accustomed to give the Confession to their converts in their several languages. Even in the British dependencies they have left this to others. As far as we are informed only a single missionary translation of the Confession has been prepared in our day by British hands — the Gujarati version made by the missionaries of the Irish Presbyterian Church. Scotch Presbyterians seem to have come to look upon their Confession much as they do on the sun and the rain — as a Divine blessing with which they have nothing to do but to receive and enjoy it, not without "some murmurings and disputings."

There have come under our notice something less than one hundred and fifty British editions of the Confession of Faith. The time through which our search has been protracted has been too limited and the circumstances under which it has been carried on too unfavorable for us to venture to hope that we have met with more than, say, about half the whole number. We print the list therefore merely as notes toward a bibliography of the Westminster Confession.[10]

II. IN THE UNITED STATES

The Westminster Confession was slow in finding its way into print in America. This was not because it was distasteful to the American Churches: the Puritanism of the Colonists was doctrinally the same as that of England, and they gave a hearty welcome to this Puritan formulary. It was due in the first instance to the lack of facilities in the Colonies at that early day for printing: and afterward to the Independency of the New England Churches, which naturally preferred the

[9] No other Colonial edition is known to us except one published in New Zealand.

[10] For this list of 137 British editions see *The Presbyterian and Reformed Review,* xii. 1901, pp. 614–659.

" Savoy Declaration," put out by the English Congregationalists in 1658, to the original " Westminster Confession," now
become distinctively the creed of the Scottish Presbyterians.

When the Westminster Confession was first given to the
public (1647), there was but a single printing press in the
Colonies. This had been brought out in 1638 and set up at
Cambridge, where from the beginning of 1639 it had been
kept busy, under the supervision of the Rev. Henry Dunster,
the first President of Harvard College. The actual printer up
to about 1649 was one Stephen Day, who had come out with
the press in 1638 for the purpose of operating it, but whose
works do not accredit him as a skilled handicraftsman. He was
succeeded in 1649 by Samuel Green, the first of a family of
printers who for many years carried on their work in New
England; but he was apparently without training in the art,
and only gradually acquired ability to turn out good work.
A new press and equipment were sent out, indeed, during the
course of the years 1654–1658 by the Corporation for Propagating the Gospel among the Indians, and in 1660 the same
Corporation sent out the first skillful printer to come to New
England, Marmaduke Johnson — to assist Samuel Green in
printing the Indian Bible. By these accessions the Cambridge
establishment was greatly improved in capacity and efficiency.
It enjoyed an absolute monopoly in the Colonies until 1674,
when John Foster's press was set up in Boston; and indeed
during the latter portion of this period it was protected in this
monopoly by a law which forbade printing within the jurisdiction of the General Court of Massachusetts, " except in Cambridge " (1664). In none other of the Colonies was a press established for yet ten years more. In these circumstances, the
reprinting of British books in America was not to be thought of.
American books were rather customarily sent to England to
be put into type, and the best that could be done in America
was to overtake in some form or other the absolutely necessary
local demands. Accordingly when the Cambridge Synod of
1646–1648 had done its work, only its " Platform of Church
Discipline " — which was original with it — was printed (and

exceedingly rudely printed) by Samuel Green (1649) at Cambridge; while the Confession of Faith adopted by it — which was accepted from the hands of the Westminster Assembly — was expected to be imported from abroad.

The Westminster Confession, it will be remembered, though previously privately printed (in whole or in part) three times in London for the use of members of Parliament and the Assembly itself, and once in Edinburgh for the use of the members of the Scottish Assembly, was not published until after the rising of the Scottish Assembly in the latter part of August, 1647, and then only in Edinburgh and without authorization from the English Parliament. It was not until June 20, 1648, that the Parliamentary edition was given to the world; and the earlier issue in that same year at Edinburgh and London of what must be looked upon as surreptitious editions can have antedated this but a few weeks. It may be held as quite certain, therefore, that no copies of the Confession had found their way to New England by October 27, 1647, when the General Court of Massachusetts added to the duties with which the Cambridge Synod, in session that year, were already charged, the additional task of preparing a Confession of Faith; and appointed a Committee to draw up a draft of it against the next meeting of the Synod. Before the Synod reconvened, however (midsummer, 1648), copies of the Westminster Confession had arrived, though not (we may feel sure) copies of the Parliamentary issue of June 20th of that year: and it proved so satisfactory to the delegates that the Synod was enabled to decline the labor of preparing a Confession of its own in favor of a simple acceptance of this. The story is told by John Cotton in the Preface to the " Platform." We read:

" Having perused the publick confession of faith, agreed upon by the Reverend assembly of Divines at Westminster, and finding the summ and substance thereof (in matters of doctrine) to express not their own judgements only, but ours also: and being likewise called upon by our godly Magistrates, to draw up a publick confession of that faith, which is constantly taught, and generaly professed amongst us, wee thought good to present unto them, and with them to our churches, and with them to all the churches of Christ abroad, our professed and hearty assent and attestation to the whole confession of faith (for substance of doctrine) which the Reverend assembly presented to the Religious and Honorable Parlamēt of England: Excepting only some sections in the 25 30 and 31. Chapters of their confession, which concern points of controversie in church-discipline; Touching which wee refer our selves to the draught of church-discipline in the ensueing treatise. The truth of what we here declare, may appear by the unanimous vote of the Synod of the Elders and messengers of our churches assembled at Cambridg, the last of the sixth month, 1648: which joyntly passed in these words; *This Synod having perused, and considered (with much gladness of heart, and thankfullness to God) the cōfession of faith published of late by the Reverend Assembly in England, doe judge it to be very holy, orthodox, and judicious in all matters of faith: and doe therefore freely and fully consent thereunto, for the substance thereof. Only in those things which have respect to church government and discipline, wee refer our selves to the platform of church-discipline, agreed upon by this present assēbly: and doe therefore think it meet, that this confession of faith, should be cōmended to the churches of Christ amongst us, and to the Honoured Court, as worthy of their due consideration and acceptance.* However, wee may not conceal, that the doctrine of vocation expressed in *Chap, 10. S. 1.* and summarily repeated *Chap, 13. & 1.* passed not without some debate. Yet considering, that the term of vocation, and others by which it is described, are capable of a large, or more strict sense, and use, and that it is not intended to bind apprehensions precisely in point of order or method, there hath been a generall condescendency thereunto."

The Court acquiescing in this decision and desiring to incite the languid churches to make their returns to its request for their judgment, by a vote passed June 19, 1650, desired.

" yᵗ euery church will, by the first oppertunity, take order for the p'cureinge of that booke, published by the synod at London, concerninge the doctrine of the gosple, that the churches may consider of that booke, also, as soone as they can be gotten."

This, it will be observed, is an order for a wholesale importation of copies of the Westminster Confession. We cannot press the phraseology that designates the volume to be imported as " that booke, *published by the synod* at London." The whole language of the order is popular and general, rather than technically precise: and as a matter of fact no edition of the Confession of Faith was in the strict sense "published by the synod at London." The Parliamentary edition of 1648, entitled "Articles of Christian Religion," was adjusted to Independent opinion, and would doubtless have been most acceptable to the feelings of Congregationalist New England: but there is no reason to believe that this edition was especially in the mind of the Court, as it certainly was not in the mind of the Synod, seeing that they made exception to Articles not contained in this edition: and the early printed copies of the Confession which have been preserved in the libraries of New England to our day are not of this edition. By 1650 some thirteen issues of the Confession had already been made in Britain; but besides the privately printed issues and the Parliamentary edition of 1648, only three of these had been published at London, viz., the two Bostock editions of 1648 and 1649 and an edition of 1650. It was probably from these editions that the Massachusetts Churches were expected to supply themselves; though doubtless they actually purchased whatever editions were most easily procurable in the London markets. These were all, of course, at least ultimately, of Scotch origin. The authors of the Preface to the " Savoy Declaration " in 1658 make it a matter of complaint that " that Copy of the Parliaments, followed by us, is in few mens hands; the other as it came from the *Assembly,* being approved of in *Scotland,* was printed and hastened into the world before the *Parliament* had declared their Resolutions about it; which was not till *June* 20. 1648. and yet hath been, and continueth to be the Copy (ordinarily) onely sold, printed and reprinted for these *eleven* years."

So things went on for a generation until the Reforming Synod of 1679 and 1680 met at Boston, charged, among other things, with the task of setting forth the faith of the new generation. In the interval the English Independents had issued (1658) their modification of the Westminster Confession — the so-called " Savoy Declaration " — based on the Parliamentary " Articles of Christian Religion " of 1648; and it was but natural that the New England Congregationalists should now wish to give their adherence rather to this than to the unaltered Confession of Westminster. This was rendered the more inevitable by the fact that Mather and Oates, the two leading members of the Committee appointed by the Synod to draw up a Confession of Faith, had been in England in 1658, and were on terms of personal friendship with the Independent Divines who had framed the " Savoy Declaration." Accordingly it was the Savoy Declaration, only slightly but significantly altered (and that in a sense the direct opposite to the mind of the British Independents in the point of the relation of the Civil Magistrate to the Church) that was reported to the Synod May 12, 1680. On June 11, 1680, the General Court ordered it published: and it appeared in the same year at Boston, from the press of John Foster, and was several times reprinted subsequently. The Churches of Connecticut adopted the same document at the Saybrook Synod of 1708. They say:

" We agree that the Confession of faith owned and Consented unto by the Elders and Messengers of the Chhs assembled at Boston In New England May 12 1680 being the Second Session of that Synod be Recomended to the Honble the Gen^{ll} Assembly of this Colony at the next Session for their Publick testimony thereto as the faith of the Chhs of this Colony."

In October of that year the General Court of Connecticut accordingly enacted this Confession as the Confession of Faith of Connecticut, and this it continued legally to be until 1784. At its next session, May, 1709, the Court provided for its printing. It appeared at New London in 1710 — the first book printed in Connecticut — and again in 1760; and it has repeatedly been published subsequently. Thus the " Savoy Declaration," which exerted no influence and wrought out no history in England, was given, in a slightly modified form, life and influence in America, and even bade fair entirely to supersede in this land the original Westminster Confession.

In these circumstances it is not strange that the Westminster Confession in its unaltered form had to wait until near the close of the first quarter of the eighteenth century before it found its way into print in America. The circumstances which secured its printing in the first instance even then are obscure. Possibly there had arisen a demand for it among New England Congregationalists themselves; it is certain that it was the Westminster Confession, and not the Savoy modification of it, which was in use among the English Independents of the time; [11] and there is no reason why many in New England may not have wished (to say nothing more) to have in their hands the formularies of their English brethren. It is of course possible, however, on the other hand, that the demand which it was sought to supply by the publication of the book arose from the Presbyterian Scotch-Irish, who were now beginning to make themselves felt as an element in our Colonial life. In any event, the earliest American-printed edition of the Westminster Confession we have met with, is an octavo volume of 161 pages containing the Confession and Larger Catechism (the Shorter Catechism being omitted, doubtless, because otherwise fully accessible), printed in Boston in 1723 by the eminent printer Samuel Kneeland, for the still more eminent bookseller Daniel Henchman, who was probably the most enterprising American publisher prior to the Revolution. As the title-page suggests, it is taken not from the current Scotch editions, but from that rather peculiar series, published chiefly though not exclusively at London, which began with the Rothwell issues of 1658, and proceeded in subsequent issues called the " [second edition]," 1658, " third edition," 1688, " fifth edition," 1717, all published in London — while the two forms of the so-called " fourth edition " alone of the series are Scotch (Glasgow, 1675, Edinburgh, 1708). This cir-

[11] Neal, " History of the Puritans," ii. 1849, p. 178.

cumstance undoubtedly raises a degree of probability for the Congregationalist origin of this edition.

It can hardly be doubted, on the other hand, that the second American edition which we have met with, was called out by a purely Presbyterian demand. This was issued in 1745 at Philadelphia, from the press of Benjamin Franklin, and was a finely manufactured 16mo volume of 588 pages, following the type of the normative Edinburgh edition of Lumisden and Robertson of 1728, and containing all the documents included in that edition and ever subsequently constituting the fixed contents of Scotch editions. It came from the press, it will be observed, the year of the formation of the Synod of New York, and it may well be that the disruption of the Synod of Pennsylvania, and the controversies out of which that disruption grew and which had been disturbing the Church since 1740, were the occasion of its preparation. That only these two editions were issued in America until, as the century was drawing to a close (1789, 1799), the two greater Presbyterian bodies established in this country began to publish their amended editions of the Confession, is readily accounted for by the continued dependence of Presbyterians at large on Scotland for their supply of Confessions. This dependence is attested by the very large number of Scotch Confessions bearing dates in the eighteenth century which are found scattered through America to-day. There are even traces of prominent pastors acting as something like regular importing agencies for greater or smaller communities, and busying themselves with seeing that the Confession of Faith was circulated as widely as possible among their own and contiguous flocks. Benjamin Chestnut,[12] for example, seems to have added this to the many other good works by which he fulfilled the office of a bishop for the whole of South Jersey. Some of the smaller branches of Presbyterianism in America to this day seek much or all of their supply abroad, though reprints of the Scotch book, containing the whole series of documents which have found their way into it, have also continued to be issued in America up to to-day.

[12] See for him, Dr. Alfred Nevin's " Presbyterian Encyclopædia," *sub nom.*

The real history of the publication of the Westminster Confession in America begins thus in 1789. The infancy of Presbyterianism in the New World, and even its lusty youth, was then already a thing of the past; and it was celebrating the attainment of its majority by constituting a General Assembly and preparing a complete Constitution for its future direction. The Doctrinal Standards embodied in this Constitution were borrowed from those prepared by the Westminster Assembly, with only such alterations in their teaching as to the relation of the civil magistrate to the Church and to spiritual things, as were thought necessary to adapt them to a free Church in a free State. But the American Church looked upon them, as thus adjusted, as distinctively its own Standards, in contradistinction to the Standards of the Church of Scotland, and consistently spoke of them and acted toward them as such. The whole process of the framing of a Constitution was begun by raising a Committee, which was instructed to " take into consideration the Constitution of the church of Scotland and other Protestant churches, and agreeably to the general principles of Presbyterian government, to compile a system of general rules for the government of the Synod, and the several Presbyteries under their inspection, and the people in their communion." And the completed series of documents was set forth, at the end, as unitedly composing " the Constitution of the Presbyterian Church in the United States of America," thus consciously differentiated from all other Churches in Christendom. The printing of this distinctive Constitution was in these circumstances a matter of course: and for a while the Assembly retained the publication and diffusion of it entirely in its own hands. There were issued in this way, directly by the Assembly, four editions — one in 1789 from the press of Thomas Bradford (a new impression was issued in 1792), one in 1797 from the press of Robert Aitken, one in 1806 from the press of Jane Aitken, and one in 1815 through the publishing house of W. W. Woodward. There were 1000 to 1500 copies issued in the first of these editions, possibly increased by another 1000 by its second impression;

4000 copies in the second; 5000 in the third; and doubtless quite as many more in the fourth. The book had meanwhile been improved, by a careful and expert revision and the adjunction of proof-texts, in the second edition; and by exquisite typographical skill in the third. Meanwhile the demand for it had become sufficiently great to tempt private enterprise, and " unauthorized editions," the ventures of booksellers on their own account, began to appear as early as 1801. In these circumstances the Assembly was led after the issue of its fourth edition (1815), to adopt the new policy of committing the publication of its " Constitution " to private initiative, only reserving the right of revision and certification of the text as issued, and claiming a percentage on the value of the issues. From 1821, when the first edition under this new arrangement appeared, until 1839, when it was receded from, there were sent forth at least fifteen editions, all except the first of which (Finley, 1821) appear to come from a single set of stereotyped plates. How many copies were thus put into circulation we can only conjecture; but we presume 20,000 would be a low estimate.

In 1838 the great division of the Church into Old and New School bodies took place, and each division went its own way in the publication of the " Constitution " common to the two. The Old School branch at once withdrew the general permission to booksellers to print its book, and placed it exclusively in the hands of the Board of Publication, which it had adopted from the Synod of Philadelphia (1839). Stereotyped plates were at once made; and a new set again in 1853 — a somewhat unfortunate set, from the point of view of accuracy of text. From these the Board issued during the years intervening between the Division and Reunion (1870) no less than 80,000 copies, besides 2000 copies of an *edition de luxe*. In the same period it issued also 37,000 copies of the Confession in a cheaper (pamphlet) form; and 2750 copies of a German translation of it. During this same period there had been issued under the auspices of the New School branch of the Church at least six editions (from 1845); and at least three issues had been put forth by private enterprise. Moreover, the new division of the Church consequent on the Civil War had created a vigorous Church in the Southern States, which had put forth a first edition of its Standards, early in the '60s, of some 20,-000 copies. After the reunion of the Old and New School Churches in 1870, the old plates of the Board of Publication were continued in use to supply the united Church, and 40,500 copies were printed from them up to 1891, when they were happily supplanted by a carefully corrected new set, from which there have already been printed, up to 1900, 10,000 copies. To these must be added 500 copies of the *edition de luxe* issued in 1884; 1000 copies of the German version, issued in 1872–1873 and 1891, and 50,250 issues of the Confession in pamphlet form. The grand total of copies put out by the Board of Publication from 1839 to 1900 thus aggregates no fewer than 224,000 copies. To this must be added 35,818 copies issued by the Southern Church, as well as those issued between 1839 and 1870 by the New School branch and private enterprise. So that it can scarcely be thought excessive to suppose that more than 325,000 copies of the Confession have been put into circulation by the Presbyterian Church since 1840: and perhaps it would not much overshoot the mark to say that throughout its whole history, from 1789 to 1900, there have been put into circulation not many fewer than a half-million copies of the Confession of Faith in the form given it by the Presbyterian Church in the United States of America.

What the Presbyterian Church in the United States of America did for its " Constitution " in 1789, that the Associate Reformed Church did for its in 1799. The first edition of its Constitution, containing the Confession of Faith as modified by the Associate Reformed Synod to the same general effect as had been done by the sister Church ten years before, appeared in that year, and introduced a new series of issues of the Confession of Faith which still continues to be put forth to-day — both in simple reprints of the original Associate Reformed book (still issued by the Associate Reformed Synod of the South), and in the form given it by the United Presbyterian Church in issues beginning in 1859. We have met with only seven editions of the Associate Reformed book; and with only five editions of the United Presbyterian book. But we cannot suppose these to do more than represent a series of much more numerous issues which have escaped our search; and we cannot doubt that a very considerable addition to the total number of copies put into circulation by the American press has been contributed by this series of editions.

The purpose for which the Westminster Confession of Faith has been printed in America has ever been distinctly an ecclesiastico-practical one. Very little scientific interest has intruded itself in the preparation of either the text or its accompaniments. The first editions issued by the several Churches have apparently been taken from whatever texts lay conveniently at hand. In the case of the Southern Presbyterian Church this was unfortunately the unusually inaccurate text then (since 1853) current in the Presbyterian Church in the United States of America; in the case of the other Churches it was the current British texts of the time. Now and then, however, an effort has been made to produce a corrected text. An early instance of this is afforded by the text of the edition of 1797 (Robert Aitken), in which important textual corrections were made. A very notable instance is supplied by the care taken in correcting the text by the Committee of the New School Assembly to which was committed the task of preparing the edition issued by that body in 1850 +. And the editions published by the Presbyterian Board of Publication and Sabbath-School Work since 1891 are the product of a very exact scrutiny and reach the high-water mark of accuracy of printing in the American editions. But even in this text there are conserved a number of readings which have originated rather in printers' slips than in ecclesiastical revisions, and which have been retained in the revised text apparently as distinctively American readings. One would think that it would be better to restore the text in all points, where direct ecclesiastical warrant for change cannot be adduced, to the text of the *princeps* — i.e. the edition of Evan Tyler of 1647.

The history of the accompaniments of the text runs parallel with that of the text itself. The proof-texts, for example, in the reprints of the British editions made for the smaller branches of the Church, and as well in the editions deriving from the Associate Reformed book of 1799, do not intentionally vary from those of Westminster, and are taken uncriticised from the current British editions. The first edition of the Constitution of the Presbyterian Church of the United States of America was printed without proof-texts. And when, shortly afterward, it was proposed to add them, the work was characteristically undertaken as if it were an independent enterprise of a new Church. There was no reference made to the Westminster proofs in the initiation of the work or in the appointment of the Committee to prepare the new texts; and no open profession was made on the part of the Committee of having based their work on the Westminster proofs, or indeed of having even consulted them. It was only when the new proofs were submitted to a new Committee for revision that directions were given that they should be compared with the Westminster proofs. The new proofs cannot, however, be *a posteriori* spoken of as prepared in independence of the Westminster proofs: nor can they be thought an improvement upon the Westminster proofs. A peculiar feature connected with them is the inclusion among them of certain footnotes, of an expository or even argumentative character. Some of these — particularly that on the word " man-stealing " in the 142d Question of the Larger Catechism — were of inordinate length and polemic in character, and subsequently gave trouble and were officially removed from the margin of the Standards in 1816. Nevertheless, these hastily prepared and unsatisfactory proof-texts — with only the removal of the above-mentioned objectional notes, accomplished in 1816 — held their place in the Standards of the Presbyterian Church in the United States of America from 1797 to 1896, and still hold their place in the Standards of the Presbyterian Church of the United States until to-day. Since 1896 they have been replaced in the Standards of the former of these two Churches by a new and much improved set of proofs, which were prepared by a Committee appointed in 1888, and were approved by the Assembly in 1894. In the whole period from 1789 to 1896, moreover, the Shorter Catechism as published in the "Constitution" of these Churches was unprovided with proof-texts, a note advising the reader to turn for them to the corresponding Questions of the Larger Catechism. The current form of the Westminster proofs was accustomed to be printed with the Shorter Catechism as separately published by these Churches. Since 1896, however, the Shorter Catechism as published by the Presbyterian Church in the United States of America has been provided with its own appropriate texts, prepared by the Committee of 1888–1894.

After a history of about a century and three-quarters, at the opening of the twentieth century the Westminster Confession is still in wide circulation in America, and is accessible in several forms. Copies of the British edition are still imported, especially perhaps those issued by T. Nelson & Sons, with a New York as well as British imprint. Reprints of the Scotch book are still made by the Associate Presbyterian Board of Publication, with a Philadelphia imprint, but doing business at Eau Claire, Pa. The old Associate Reformed book is still issued by the Publication Committee of the Associate Reformed Synod of the South, at Atlanta, Ga. But especially three great publishing houses are engaged in supplying a large Presbyterian public with the Confession of Faith, in several different forms: the Presbyterian Board of Publication and Sabbath-School Work, at Philadelphia; the Presbyterian Committee of Publication, at Richmond, Va.; and the United Presbyterian Board of Publication, at Pittsburgh, Pa. From these three houses several thousands of copies of the Confession are put into circulation annually. Little has been done in the meantime to supply the multitudinous foreign population that has crowded to our shores with the Westminster Confession of Faith in their own tongues. A German translation was published by the Presbyterian Board of Publication in 1858, and is still kept on sale. A Spanish translation, based on an earlier one published in Mexico, is now issued at Albuquerque, N. M. But what are these among so many? American Presbyterian missionaries have, on the other hand, been especially faithful in translating and circulating the Confession among the peoples to whom they have carried the Gospel: but this is not the place to speak of these rather numerous versions made and printed outside of the United States.

In the search we have been able to make we have met with some eighty-eight editions of the Confession of Faith printed in the United States. We suppose ourselves to have catalogued almost a complete list of the editions issued by the Presbyterian Church in the United States of America. We cannot suppose ourselves to have been so fortunate, however, in the case of the issues of other Churches: no doubt we have missed quite the half of these. We are able to print, therefore, nothing more than notes toward a bibliography of the American editions.[13]

III. In Translation

The history of the diffusion of the Westminster Confession by means of translation is sufficiently obscure, but by no means lacking in points of curious interest. The work was certainly begun betimes. The Westminster Confession was not published until the autumn of 1647 (in Edinburgh); and not until the next spring did a surreptitious edition of it appear in London, while the authorized Parliamentary edition lingered until midsummer. Within a year of its first appearance, and so hot on the heels of its first publication in London that it must be treated as contemporaneous with the Parliamentary edition itself, a German translation had already appeared in Germany (1648). And by the opening of the next year (January 18, 1649) — before any further effort had been made to circulate the Confession in English [14] — official steps were already taken looking to

[13] See for these 88 American editions *The Presbyterian and Reformed Review*, xiii. 1902, pp. 71–120.

[14] The only editions published prior to 1649 were the first Scotch of 1647, an Edinburgh edition of 1648, the first London of 1648, and the Parliamentary of 1648.

the preparation of a Latin version, which, however, did not appear until several years afterwards (1656). But with this first burst of enthusiasm the primitive zeal for translation seems to have exhausted itself. It was not until the Confession was three-quarters of a century old that it was given the clothing of yet another speech (Gaelic, 1725), and after that all effort so to diffuse it ceased for more than a century. Toward the latter half of the nineteenth century, however, it once more showed a tendency to find its way into the divers tongues of the earth; and by the close of the first two hundred and fifty years of its life it was to be read in at least fifteen different languages.

It is remarkable how little is discoverable of the origin of the earlier versions. Of the German version of 1648 absolutely nothing seems to be known except what can be inferred from the unique copy of it that has been preserved in the Royal Library of Berlin. Without father, without mother, this Melchizedek of versions simply is: it had passed entirely out of the memory of men when it was brought to light again by the description given by Niemeyer in 1840 of the only remaining copy of it. Similarly all record of the making of the Latin version of 1656 has perished: only the initials " G. D.," at the foot of the little preface which introduces it, remain to quicken conjecture as to the personality of the scholar who was so much afraid that his reputation for writing fluent Latin would be spoiled by the spissitude of the material with which he had in this case to deal, his capacity for rhetorical ornament be thrown into doubt by the exceeding gravity of its style. These two versions differ from the whole series of their successors, moreover, in that they can scarcely be thought the product of missionary zeal, but were rather intended, probably, to give information to their Continental brethren of the teaching of the Churches of Britain. The first properly so-called missionary version — that is, the first version the sole purpose of which was to extend the distinctly ecclesiastical use of the Confession — was the " Irish " translation of 1725, which was prepared by the Synod of Argyle, at the instance of the General

Assembly of the Church of Scotland, for the benefit of the Gaelic-speaking Scots. It was also the last version prepared by the Church of Scotland or under its auspices: and indeed the last but one which has hitherto emanated from a British source. Missionaries of the Irish Presbyterian Church have in our own day put forth a version in one of the languages of India (Gujarati, 1888): but with this exception it seems that there has been no translation of the Confession made by British hands since 1725.

The task of giving the Confession to the world in its several languages has been taken up since 1842, however, with some energy by the American Presbyterians; and eleven versions have been made by them during the last sixty years. One of these has been intended to meet needs arising on the home field itself — the German version of 1858. The rest are the product of distinctly foreign-mission zeal and mark so far the planting of the Church in virgin soil. Two are, to be sure, into languages which have long ago learned to speak with a Christian accent — Portuguese and Spanish. But the remainder are incursions into heathen precincts, and offer this textbook of pure and undefiled Christian truth to the study of those to whom Christianity itself is a novelty. These all are the product of American workers, lisping no doubt in these strange tongues; but by the grace of God they may plant seed which shall hereafter bear a harvest of Christian thinking, by means of which whole nations may be blessed.

The eleven versions prepared by American missionaries during the last sixty years are, in the order of their date, the following: Hindustani, 1842; Urdu, 1848; German, 1858; Siamese, 1873; Portuguese, 1876; Spanish, 1880; Japanese, 1880; Chinese, 1881; Arabic, 1883; Benga, 188–; Persian, 189–. Some of them, such as the Spanish and Portuguese and Urdu, have already been thoroughly revised, and either sent forth or at least prepared to be sent forth in better literary form for wider influence. Several are being diligently used in the instruction of ministers of the Word. And though some of them, such as notably the Japanese, have been permitted to fall into desuetude, and others have scarcely yet been launched (such as the Arabic, Persian, and Benga), it is to be hoped that root will ultimately be taken by all and that many more will shortly be added to their number. The Presbyterian Churches owe it to their own sincerity to see that their doctrinal Standards, embodying, as they profess to believe, the very truth of God which is revealed in the Scriptures, are put in the possession of all whom they can reach with their propaganda. Otherwise, how shall they give an account of the " talents " entrusted to them?

Meanwhile it is something that the Westminster Confession now exists in some fifteen languages. It is true many of the more cultured and influential languages are lacking from this list. There does not seem to exist any version of the Westminster Confession in Dutch or French or Italian or any of the tongues of northern or eastern Europe. It must needs be confessed, further, that the versions that exist in the languages of culture are not always couched in the language of culture, and can proffer little claim to a place in the " literature " of those languages. How different in this respect is the history of the translation, say, of Calvin's " Institutes." Every version of the " Institutes " was literature, the product of a master in the idiom in which he worked: the Italian poet Giulio Cæsare Paschali; the English scholar, jurist, and statesman Thomas Norton; the Spanish *litterateur* Cypriano de Valera; the Dutch scholar Charles Agricola; the Bohemian hymnist George Strejc — these names are but examples of the class: in every tongue the " Institutes " flowed out from the hands of master craftsmen. On the other hand, the translations of the Confession have almost never proceeded from writers " to the manner born." For the most part they are the work of foreigners, handling the language with stiff and inflexible — often, no doubt, with bungling — fingers.

We may even go farther and note that the several versions of the Confession have ordinarily failed to find entrance not merely into the literature but even into the regular channels of the book-trade of the several languages into which it has been rendered. The experience of Niemeyer, astonishing as it

is, and in his case indicative chiefly of the disgraceful insular-
ity of German scholarship a half-century ago, would be more
legitimately the experience of the average seeker after knowledge in most of the book-marts of the world. He had published his "Collectio confessionum in ecclesiis reformatis
publicatarum" (Leipzig, 1840) without the Westminster formularies; and he actually tells us in the Preface to an Appendix
he added nine months later, for the purpose of including
them, that he had sought them in vain and had "taken it
very hard" that he could never lay his hand on a single exemplar of the Westminster Confession! Of course he needed
only to send to Edinburgh or to Philadelphia to get a cartload
of exemplars of current issues; and a man of learning, engaged
in the scientific study of symbolics, ought to have known that.
And his friend Reboulius seems to have had no difficulty in
turning up even in the Royal Library of Berlin a German and
three Latin copies, which appear to have been lying there for
the inspection of any one who cared to look at them. But the
incident certainly illustrates how little the Westminster Confession had found its way into the channels of ordinary information and trade of the Germany of 1840 — though there
had been in existence for two hundred years a German translation, and a "literary" version at that. There has been a
Spanish version in existence since 1880, a Portuguese one
since 1876; but the chances of a Spanish or Portuguese reader
coming accidentally across a copy in the most frequented book-
shops of Madrid or Lisbon — or shall we not even say of
Mexico or Rio de Janeiro? — or even succeeding in "unearth-
ing" a copy by diligent inquiry in the most enterprising book-
shops of these cities, would probably be very small. The Westminster Confession may exist at the opening of the twentieth
century in fifteen languages; but it is another matter whether
it can be said to be very much in evidence in these fifteen languages, or even, in any broad sense of the word, accessible in
them. Or, perhaps we should rather say, in any one of them
— even in English. We were credibly told, a couple of years ago,
that a copy of it was sought in vain in the largest book-shops

of Glasgow! It is obviously very easy to overestimate the significance of the existence of the Westminster Confession in fifteen languages.

It is also very easy to underestimate it. That it has found its way into these languages, for the most part, without finding its way into their literature or book-marts is a feature of its history which it shares with the Scriptures themselves, and, indeed, is paralleled by the mode of entrance of Christianity itself into the world. It belongs, in short, to the " servant-form " of Christianity. Christianity has always propagated itself by appeal, in the first instance, to the humble, whose interest has been in content rather than form: and its " literature," in the first instance, has in every race sought none of the ornaments of literary elaboration to give it wings. The very characteristic of the first literature of Christianity, in the eyes of the philologist,[15] is just its " formlessness ": and it was all the product of alien pens. The same has been true of it ever since, as it has found entrance into this or that land. It is the idea that seeks to make its way into the mind of a nation first of all; and this idea is planted as seed, in the first instance, in the hearts of the humble who occupy no great place in the world. It is only after a while, when it takes root and grows, that it blossoms spontaneously into beauty. It has been, therefore, not only inevitable but fully in accord with the fitness of things — with that " servant-form " which our Lord Himself took when he came into the world and offered Himself to the babes and sucklings — that the Confession too has only struggled into other languages, transferring itself into new tongues by the painful efforts of men born aliens to them; and has been put into circulation only among those simple ones who have by their very simplicity been prepared for it. Thus and thus only will it ever find a path into a nation's heart. And it should not in the least discourage us to see it only thus making its way in the world.

What seems discouraging is that several of the fourteen translations which have been made of the Confession do not

[15] See Eduard Norden's " Die antike Kunstprosa," Leipzig, ii. 1898, *ad init.*

seem, for one reason or another, to be receiving that opportunity to plant themselves in the hearts of even the " simple " which alone we expect or crave for them. The Latin version of course was not intended for popular use and is now no longer in any sort of circulation. The old German version has perished, and only a single exemplar of it is known to remain in existence; while the modern German version (1858) is practically confined in its use to the German-speaking Presbyterians of the United States. The Japanese version has been given no real opportunity of life, and is no longer to be had. The Siamese version is almost out of print. The Arabic, Persian, and Benga versions have never been published; and although the two latter are locally in use they can hardly be said to have been given to the world. The use of the Gaelic version must necessarily grow less and less extensive. There remain only the versions in Spanish and Portuguese, Chinese, Hindustani, Urdu and Gujurati, for which we can hope for a future of growing usefulness. An increase of zeal may add new ones or resuscitate old ones — such as the Japanese and Siamese — but at the moment there are, after all, only seven or eight versions (including the German and Gaelic) which are really " in circulation." Even after the comparatively energetic work of the last sixty years, the Presbyterian Churches have no reason to blame themselves for undue zeal in propagating their professed doctrines by means of translations of their Confession.

In the following notes [16] we have brought together the information we have been able to gather as to the translations of the Confession. We have included in the list even those versions which have, because produced either in Britain or the United States, been already mentioned in the lists of editions published in these countries. Thus the list contains the full series of versions brought to our attention. There may well be others which have escaped our search: but it is likely that we have been able to include nearly all.[17]

[16] See for these *The Presbyterian and Reformed Review,* xiii. 1902, pp. 259–276.

[17] Few of these translations are to be found in the collections of editions of the Confession. We have been indebted for our knowledge of them, there-

IV. In Modification

It is not merely in its pure form, as it came from the hands of the Assembly of Divines, that the Westminster Confession has been put into circulation. Perhaps we may even say that during these later years it is not in its pure form that it has been most widely influential. If we wish to attain a complete view of the extent of its dissemination we must attend therefore as well to the modifications of it which have been published. With the nature of these modifications we have here nothing directly to do. We have merely to note the formal fact that modified forms of the Westminster Confession have been produced and sent out into the world.

These modified forms are not very numerous; but they began to be made very early in the history of the document, and they have usurped its place in the case of a very large portion of its constituency. Indeed, it was only in a modified form that the Westminster Confession received the authorization of the very body at whose behest it was prepared. That it was put into circulation in an unmodified form at all was due to the Scotch Church " stealing a march," so to speak, on the English Parliament. And it might almost be said that it is only in a modified form that it is in use to-day outside the limits of immediate Scotch influence. In all the large American Presbyterian Churches, for example, it is not the Westminster Confession precisely as the Assembly of Divines framed it, but the Westminster Confession in some respects modified, that has been adopted as their standard of faith. We must certainly bear in mind that there are modifications and modifications. Some may merely touch the periphery of the circle of doctrines which the document teaches, and may affect even its

---

fore, mostly to the missionaries by whom they are used, and our thanks are due to them for their readiness to supply both copies of the books and information about them. We have tried to give credit for these courtesies, in general, as we have spoken of each version in turn. But it has been impossible to do justice to the kindness we have experienced or even to mention the names of all who have extended it.

external form in only a minute manner. Some, while introducing a considerable amount of change in its form, may penetrate
very little or not at all into the substance of its doctrine. Others may profoundly affect its whole point of view and revolutionize its whole teaching. As a matter of fact, the Westminster Confession has been made the subject of modifications of
all these sorts. But it is chiefly the less serious varieties of modification that have been introduced into it; and it is in its most
slightly modified forms that its wider influence has been gained.

The production of modified forms of the Westminster Confession is of course the result of the existence from the very
time of its publication of bodies of Christians who felt that it
was expected of them to adopt it as the expression of their
faith, but who found it in this or that point unacceptable to
them, and were led to cut the knot by so far modifying it as
to adapt it to their uses. It must be remembered that the Westminster Confession was the product of a national, or perhaps
it would be speaking more properly to say of an international,
movement. It was not the construction of a chance body of
Christians voluntarily gathered together with a view to formulating their peculiar tenets. It was drawn up by a Synod
appointed by the Parliament of England and assisted by delegates from Scotland, the task of which was to prepare a scheme
of uniformity in religion for the Three Kingdoms. It came into
the world, therefore, as a national Confession. As such it was
adopted by the Church of Scotland, and as such it was published by the Parliament of England. It was impossible for any
body of Christians in the Three Kingdoms to avoid attending
to it.

Moreover, it did in effect express the reasoned faith of the
great mass of British Protestants. It was impossible for any
body of them to refuse to take some account of it without
bringing their orthodoxy under the suspicion of their brethren.
A certain moral pressure was thus brought to bear upon the
Protestant bodies of Great Britain and its colonies by the confessed excellence and generally representative character of the
document, which almost compelled them to give it at least a

modified acceptance. But fairly representative as it was of the substance of the general Protestant faith, there were minor points of teaching in the document against which this or the other party was bearing passionate protest. It was the very essence of the Independent contention that was struck at in the Westminster doctrine of Church organization and government. And what was the distinction of the Christian congregations who spoke of themselves as those "baptized upon profession of their faith," except their peculiar views on the subjects and mode of baptism? As it was inevitable that these Christians should have to face the unspoken demand that they should orient themselves with respect to the Westminster Confession, it was equally inevitable that they should wish to set forth forms of it in which their peculiar views should find recognition or at least meet with no open contradiction. Thus, from the first, Independent and Baptist recensions of the Westminster Confession, at least, were foregone conclusions — unless, indeed, the document should fall dead from the press. And the early production of these recensions is the proof that, despite the untoward turn of circumstances which rendered impossible of attainment the main object of the Assembly of Divines — the institution of uniformity of religion in the Three Kingdoms on a sound Reformed basis — the Westminster Confession did not fall dead from the press. Every great branch of Non-Conformists in England adjusted itself to it and gave it, in a form adapted to its special opinions on minor matters, the cordial testimony of public acceptance. Thus the Westminster Confession in its substance became in fact practically the common Confession of the entirety of British non-prelatical Christianity.

The earliest modification of the Westminster Confession was the work of the English Parliament itself, acting in the Independent interest, and was produced even before the Confession was authoritatively published in England. It was thus and thus only in fact that the Confession was offered to the English Churches by the constituted authorities. The edition of the Confession published by Parliament at the end of

June, 1648, under the title of "Articles of Christian Religion, Approved and Passed by both Houses of Parliament, After Advice had with the Assembly of Divines, by Authority of Parliament sitting at Westminster" — the only edition of the Confession published by the authority of the State — is in effect the Independent recension of the Confession. The growing Independent influence had sufficed to secure that all that was offensive to that party should be exscinded from the document before it was put forth as the lawfully ordained public Confession of Faith of the Church of England. The chief bone of contention here concerned, of course, the organization of the churches into a Church, provided with a series of courts clothed with authoritative jurisdiction. With this was involved the whole subject of Church discipline. And more remotely there came to be connected with it the question of a limited toleration, not so much of divergencies in doctrine as of differences in Church organization, government, and forms of worship. To meet the case thus raised the Parliament simply struck out of the document the whole series of sections treating of Church government and discipline. Other changes were made: but they were minor and in a true sense incidental.

It was accordingly upon this Parliamentary recension that the Independent Divines built when, ten years later (1658), they met at the Savoy to frame a Declaration of their faith. They introduced many minor variations in phraseology, recast a whole chapter — that on Repentance — and indeed inserted a whole new chapter — on the Gospel; and here and there they sharpened or heightened the expression of the doctrines taught in the document. But only in the two points of Church government and "discipline" and of "toleration" did they modify greatly its teaching. Their modified Confession had little prolonged circulation or influence, it is true, among the Independent Churches of England; these are found generally continuing to use the unaltered Westminster formularies. But in the New World it made for itself a richer history. Adopted both by the Massachusetts (1680) and Connecticut (1708) Churches as their standard of belief, it constituted for many years the public Confession of American Congregationalists, and indeed lighted the pathway of these Churches down almost to our own day. It is interesting to observe, however, that the American Congregationalists in adopting the Savoy recension resiled from its introduction into the document of the principle of " toleration," thus bidding us to take note that its introduction by the English Independents was rather incident to their position than a settled principle of Independent belief. Independents suffering disabilities and Independents in position to inflict disabilities for religion's sake, took opposite views of the relation of the civil magistrate to religious teaching. It was reserved to Presbyterians, after all, to make the " intolerant " teaching of the Westminster Confession a really constraining ground for modifying the document. The Independent modifications turned, as on their hinge, rather on matters concerned with Church courts: all else was incidental to this and liable to variations and the shadows cast by turning.

Meanwhile the English Baptists had been defining their relation to the Westminster Confession and had published a modification of it of their own (1677). As good Independents, they naturally took their start from the Savoy Declaration (1658), still further interpolating and filing it, and, of course, incorporating into it their own views as to baptism. It cannot be said that this Baptist recension exhibits quite the same degree of skill and learning that characterized the work done by the Savoy Synod: but it does exhibit equal fervor of religious feeling and equal devotion to the Reformed faith. In it the influence of the Independent recension of the Westminster Confession attained its height, and through it perhaps the Westminster teaching itself has reached its widest dissemination. For no more than its parent document did this Baptist recension remain the property of its English framers: it too crossed the sea, and in 1742 became the standard expression of the faith of the American Baptists, who have grown into a great host. If the Westminster Divines had done nothing else than lay down the lines upon which the great Baptist denomi-

nation has built its creed, its influence on the Christian faith
and life of the masses would have been incalculably great.

In the new conditions of political life in free America the
definition of the Westminster Confession of the relations of the
civil magistrate to the Church could not fail to be thrown forward into a fierce light. As we have seen, the English Independents had already, somewhat incidentally, exscinded the
" intolerant " features of the Confession and had been followed
in this by the Baptists: though the American Congregationalists, occupying themselves the seat of the civil magistrate, had
restored the objectionable principle. The fact is that in the
seventeenth century " toleration " was rather a sentiment of
the oppressed than a reasoned principle of Christian ethics:
while unrestricted " religious liberty " had scarcely risen on the
horizon of men's thoughts. Whatever was done toward freeing
the Westminster Confession from " intolerant principles " in
that age was therefore fitful and unstable, and rather a measure of self-protection than the consistent enunciation of a
thoroughly grasped fundamental principle. Thus it happened
that the American Presbyterians were the first to prepare
modifications of the Westminster Confession which turned on
the precise point of the duty of universal toleration, or rather
of the fundamental right of unrestricted religious liberty. The
first of these modifications in the interests of the principle of
religious freedom and the equality of all forms of religious
faith before the law, was that made by the Presbyterian
Church in the United States of America in 1789. The Associate
Reformed Church followed in the same pathway in 1799; and
the United Presbyterian Church has continued this testimony
in its own way ever since its formation in 1858. Thus it has
come about that practically the whole body of American Presbyterians has cleansed the Westminster Confession from every
phrase which could by any form of interpretation be made to
favor intolerance and has substituted the broadest assertion
of religious liberty.

It will have been observed that no one of the modifications
thus far adverted to in any way affected the scheme of doctrine

of the Confession. The Independents, Baptists, American Presbyterians alike gave the heartiest assent to the Reformed faith as set forth in this Confession; and it was only because they recognized in its form of sound words the expression of their fundamental belief that they busied themselves with adjusting it in minor matters to their opinions and practices. The opening nineteenth century saw the rise, however, in what was then the extreme western portion of the United States, of a body of Christians who by inheritance were so related to the Westminster Confession that they found it difficult to discard it altogether, but who in their fundamental theology had drifted away from the Reformed faith, to which it gives so clear and well-compacted an expression. By this combination of circumstances there was produced at last a modification of the Westminster Confession, which was directed not to the adjustment of details of teaching that lay on the periphery of its system of doctrine, but to the dissection out of it of its very heart. An Arminianized Westminster Confession is something of a portent: yet it is just this that the Cumberland Presbyterians sought to frame for themselves (1814), and to which, having in a fashion framed it, they clung for nearly three-quarters of a century.

Of course the Confession thus formed was never satisfactory even to its framers. To Arminianize the Westminster Confession with any thoroughness would leave to it only the general literary tone of its phraseology and its outlying definitions of secondary importance, while all that is really distinctive of it as a Confession of Faith would be extirpated. It required, however, about seventy years for the Arminian leaven placed in the Confession by the Cumberland Presbyterians to leaven the whole lump. The first reworking they gave it, though definitely directed to eliminating from it its formative doctrine — the Reformed doctrine of the sovereignty of God — left the larger part of the document intact. Every direct statement of the doctrine of the divine aetermination of human destiny was expunged, but the general tone of the document remained untouched. The result was felt by the Cumberland Presbyterians themselves to be eminently unsatisfactory. They perceived that the casting out of what they called " the boldly defined statements " of foreordination was insufficient for their end, and only succeeded in bringing the document into conflict with itself; for, as they truly said, " the objectional doctrine with its logical sequences pervaded the whole system of theology formulated in that book." They perceived equally that their own Arminianizing principle was not given its full logical development by the substitution of statements announcing it for the Reformed statements expunged from the Confession. It was thus inevitable that the Confession prepared by them in 1814 should sooner or later be further " modified," and the revolution then begun be made complete. The time seemed to be ripe for this early in the ninth decade of the century: and in 1883 an entirely new Confession was adopted by the Cumberland Presbyterians which is so drastic a " modification " of the Westminster Confession as to retain nothing of its most distinctive character and very little even of its secondary features. In this document " modification " has stretched beyond its tether and become metamorphosis.

In the course of the two hundred and fifty years that have elapsed since its formulation the Westminster Confession has thus been sent out into the world in some half-dozen modifications. Some of these modifications concern so small a portion and so subordinate an element in the document that it becomes doubtful whether the publications in which they are embodied should not be rather treated as editions than as modifications of it. The Parliamentary edition of 1648 and the Confessions of the American Presbyterian Churches belong to this class: and we have accordingly listed them among the editions of the Westminster Confession in the bibliographies published in *The Presbyterian and Reformed Review* for October, 1901, and January, 1902. That we include them also in the list of modifications presently to be given is in the interests of a complete enumeration of these modifications in one place, and need create no confusion. Others of these modifications, while so far transforming the document that they cannot be treated as mere editions of it, are yet fully conservative of the whole system of doctrine taught in it and retain its general structure and the greater part of its very phraseology. In this class belong the Savoy Declaration of 1658 and its descendants in the Boston Confession of 1680 and the Saybrook Confession of 1708, on the one hand, and in the Baptist Confession of 1677 on the other. The Cumberland Presbyterian recensions stand in a class by themselves as an extreme case of modification, striking at the very heart of the Confession and able to result in nothing other than its destruction.

In the following notes [18] we have brought together as full an account of these several modifications as seemed necessary in order to trace the diffusion of the Westminster Confession in the new forms thus given it. We have not attempted to record all the editions in which the several modifications have been issued; but have contented ourselves with referring the reader, when possible, to sources of information in which they can be traced. Only in the case of the Cumberland Presbyterian Confessions, whose history has not hitherto been thoroughly worked out, have we sought fulness of record.

[18] For these see *The Presbyterian and Reformed Review*, xiii. 1902, pp. 387–426.

VI

THE FIRST QUESTION OF THE WEST-
MINSTER SHORTER CATECHISM

THE FIRST QUESTION OF THE WEST-
MINSTER SHORTER CATECHISM[1]

No Catechism begins on a higher plane than the Westminster "Shorter Catechism." Its opening question, "What
is the chief end of man?" with its answer, "Man's chief end
is to glorify God and to enjoy Him forever" — the profound
meaning of which Carlyle said grew to him ever fuller and
richer with the years — sets the learner at once in his right
relation to God. Withdrawing his eyes from himself, even from
his own salvation, as the chief object of concern, it fixes them
on God and His glory, and bids him seek his highest blessedness in Him.

The Shorter Catechism owes this elevated standpoint, of
course, to the purity of its reflection of the Reformed consciousness. To others, the question of questions might be, What
shall I do to be saved? and it is on this plane that many, or
rather most, of the Catechisms even of the Reformation begin.
There is a sort of spiritual utilitarianism, a divine euthumia,
at work in this, which determines the whole point of view.
Even the Heidelberg Catechism is not wholly free from this
leaven. Taking its starting point from the longing for comfort,
even though it be the highest comfort for life and death, it
claims the attention of the pupil from the beginning for his
own state, his own present unhappiness, his own possibilities
of bliss. There may be some danger that the pupil should acquire the impression that God exists for his benefit. The Westminster Catechism cuts itself free at once from this entanglement with lower things and begins, as it centers and ends,
under the illumination of the vision of God in His glory, to
subserve which it finds to be the proper end of human as of
all other existence, of salvation as of all other achievements.

[1] From *The Princeton Theological Review,* vi. 1908, pp. 565–587.

To it all things exist for God, unto whom as well as from whom all things are; and the great question for each of us accordingly is, How can I glorify God and enjoy Him forever?

When we ask after the source of this question and answer, therefore, it is an adequate response to point simply to the Reformed consciousness. It is not merely in this place that this consciousness comes to peculiarly clear expression in the Westminster formularies, which the time and circumstances of their composition combined to make the most complete and perfect exposition of the Reformed mode of conception as yet given confessional expression. It is interesting, however, to go behind this general response and seek to trace the influences by which the literary form of this expression of the Reformed consciousness has been determined. If we ask after its source, in this sense, it is quite evident that we must say that its proximate source is the corresponding question and answer in the Larger Catechism, the preparation of which immediately preceded that of the Shorter Catechism, and a simple — and often most felicitous — condensation of which the Shorter Catechism, in its general structure and specific statements, is largely found to be. The question in the Larger Catechism takes the form, " What is the chief and highest end of man? " and the answer, correspondingly, " Man's chief and highest end is to glorify God, and fully to enjoy Him forever." This differs from the statement of the Shorter Catechism only by an expansion of the simple idea by means of phrases which, while meant to strengthen and enrich, perhaps rather weaken the effect — illustrating aptly Emerson's dictum concerning the fat and the sinew of speech.

The ultimate source of the declaration is almost as easily identified as its proximate source. This must undoubtedly be found in John Calvin, who, in his " Institutes " and in his " Catechisms " alike, placed this identical idea in the forefront of his instruction. One of the first duties to which Calvin addressed himself on coming to Geneva was to provide the Church there with a brief compend of religious truth, drawn up on the basis of his " Institutes," which had been published the year before. This compend was already in 1537 made public in its French form,[2] and it was rendered into Latin in the spring of the following year.[3] Its first section bears the heading: "That all men are born to know God";[4] and its first paragraph runs as follows: "Since there is no one of men to be found, no matter how barbarous and altogether savage, who is not touched by some religious notion,[5] it is clear that *we are all created to this end, that we should know the majesty of our Creator; and knowing Him, should hold Him in esteem, and honor Him with all fear, love and reverence."* [6] And its last paragraph runs as follows: "It is necessary, then, that *the principal care and solicitude of our life should be to seek God and to aspire to Him with all affection of heart and not to rest anywhere save in Him."* [7] However catechetical in intention, this document, it will be perceived, was not at all what we know as a catechism in form. It requires mention here, however, as the foundation-stone in the edifice of Reformed catechetics; although it was soon supplanted in Geneva itself by the document which has for three hundred and fifty years been known affectionately throughout the whole Reformed world as "Calvin's Catechism." This new formulary was published in French and Latin in 1545 and entered at once upon a worldwide mission. Translated into Italian, Spanish, English, German, Dacian-Roumanian, Hungarian, and even Greek and Hebrew (including German-Hebrew), it rapidly penetrated every

[2] "Instruction et confession de foy dont on use en leglise de Geneve" ("Opera," ed. Baum, Cunitz, and Reuss, xxii. pp. 5–74).

[3] "Catechismus sive christianae religionis institutio ecclesiae Genevensis, etc." ("Opera," v. pp. 313–362).

[4] In the Latin: "born for religion."

[5] Latin: "sense."

[6] We have rendered the French; the Latin — which was more broadly known — runs as follows: Quum nemo hominum reperiatur, quamlibet barbarus sit, ac toto pectore efferatus, qui non aliquo afficiatur religionis sensu: nos in hunc finem creatos omnes esse constat, ut maiestatem agnoscamus creatoris nostri, agnitam suspiciamus, omnique et timore, et amore, et reverentia colamus.

[7] The Latin runs: Haec igitur praecipua vitae nostrae cura et sollicitudo sit oportet, Deum quaerere et ad eum omni animi studio adspirare, nec alibi nisi in ipso acquiescere.

corner of the Reformed world. At least thirteen editions of it in English had been printed before the Westminster Assembly convened. This is the way its opening questions stand in the old-English translation: "What is the Principall and chief end of mans life? To know God. What moveth thee to say so? *Because he hath created us, and placed us in this world to set foorth his glory in us:* And it is good reason that we employ our whole life to his glorie, seeing he is the beginning and fountaine thereof. What is then *the chief felicitie of man? Even the self same;* I meane to know God, and to have his glorie shewed foorth in us. Why doest thou call this mans chiefe felicitie? Because that without it, our condition or state were more miserable than the state of brute beastes. Hereby then wee may evidently see, that there can no such miserie come unto man, as not to live in the Knowledge of God? That is most certaine. But what is the true and right knowledge of God? When a man so knoweth God, that he giveth him due honor. Which is the way to honor God aright? It is to put our whole trust and confidence in him; to studie to serve him in obeying his wil; to call uppon him in our necessities, seeking our salvation and all good thinges at his hand; and finally to acknowledge both with hearte and mouth that he is the lively fountaine of all goodnesse." [8] Here the knowledge of God is presented as the chief end and highest good of man; [9] and this knowledge of God is resolved into the glorification of God in us,[10] which again is resolved into our trusting Him, appealing to Him, seeking salvation in Him and finding all good things in Him. That is as much as to say that we exist but to glorify and enjoy Him. What is common to both forms of Calvin's catechetical instruction is, thus, that they alike open with the declaration

[8] We have quoted from Dunlop's "Collection," ii. 1722, pp. 141–142, retaining the inconsistent orthography but making use of italics to suit our own purpose. The Catechism is printed also in Bonar's "Catechisms of the Scottish Reformation," 1866, pp. 1–92. The French and Latin texts may be consulted in Calvin's "Opera," vi. pp. 1–160.

[9] Latin: praecipuus finis; summum bonum. French: la principale fin de la vie humaine; le souverain bien des hommes.

[10] Latin: quo glorificetur in nobis. French: poûr estre glorifié en nous.

that men have been created for the very end of knowing God, and in knowing Him of glorifying Him, and in glorifying Him of finding their happiness in Him. Here is the root which has borne the fruit of the opening question of the Westminster Catechism.

The late Dr. A. F. Mitchell has, indeed, suggested that we may go behind even Calvin. " The first question or interrogation," he says,[11] " which does not seem to have appeared in the former draft of the committee, is taken from the old English translation of Calvin's Catechism, ' What is the principal and chief end of man's life? ' " But the source of the answer to this question he does not consider so simple. " The answer to this question," he suggests, " may be said to combine the answers to Question 3rd in the Catechisms of Calvin and Ames, ' To have his glory showed forth in us,' and ' in the enjoying of God,' and it may have been taken from them; or the first part may have been taken from Rogers, Ball, or Palmer, and the second from one of the earliest catechisms of the Swiss Reformation, viz., that of Leo Judæ, published at Zürich before 1530." If this answer goes back to a period before 1530, it goes, of course, behind Calvin, the earliest of whose Catechisms was not published before 1537, and the first edition of whose " Institutes " itself not before 1536.

It is quite tempting indeed to refer it to Leo Judae's Latin Catechism, the citation from which given by Dr. Mitchell is strikingly like the Shorter Catechism definition. It runs as follows and Dr. Mitchell is fully justified in speaking of it as important in this connection: " Q. Tell me, please, for what end was man created? A. That we may recognize the majesty and goodness of God, the Creator, all good, all great, all wise; *and finally enjoy Him forever.*"[12] But quite apart from the reference of the Shorter Catechism definition to this response

[11] " The Westminster Assembly " (Baird Lecture for 1882), ed. 2, Philadelphia, 1897, p. 432.

[12] Q. Dic, sodes, ad quem finem homo creatus est? R. Ut optimi maximi ac sapientissimi Dei Creatoris majestatem ac bonitatem agnoscamus, tandemque illo aeternum fruamur.

as its source, Dr. Mitchell's dating is at fault. We do indeed owe to Leo Judae the first important Catechism produced by Reformed Switzerland. This was not, however, his Latin Catechism from which Dr. Mitchell quotes, but his Larger German Catechism,[13] which does not contain anything corresponding to these words. Nor was even it published "before 1530," but not before January, 1534,[14] while the Shorter German Catechism (1541) [15] followed upon the Latin Catechism and derives from it. The Latin Catechism [16] was prepared for the use of the youth in the Latin School at Zurich, and Leo Judae quite frankly explains, in a dedication prefixed to it addressed to Johannes Fries, the rector of that school, that he has freely used in compiling it, "certain *Institutes* of the Christian religion lately (*nuper*) composed by John Calvin," that is to say, Calvin's earlier Catechism, which was published under this

[13] "Catechismus. Christliche klare vnd einfalte ynleitung in den Willenn vnnd in die Gnad Gottes, darinn nit nur die Jugedt sunder ouch die Eltern vnderricht, wie sy jre kind in den gebotten Gottes, inn Christlichem glouben, vnd rechtem gebätt vnderwysen mögind. Geschriben durch Leonem Jude, diener des worts der kilchen Zürych."

[14] It contains a preface by Bullinger, dated January 3, 1534. On Leo Judae's Catechisms see C. Pestalozzi (1860), in ix. 1 of Hagenbach's "Leben und ausgewählte Schriften der Väter und Begründer der reformirten Kirche," ii. 10, pp. 56–63, with the relevant notes on pp. 101–103; M. A. Gooszen, "De Heidelbergsche Catechismus. Textus Receptus met toelichtende Teksten," 1890, pp. 35 *sqq.;* A. Lang, "Der Heidelberger Katechismus und vier verwandte Katechismen," 1907, pp. xx.–xxxv.

[15] "Der kürtzer Catechismus. Ein kurtze Christenliche underwysung der jugend in erkanntnusz vnnd gebotten Gottes, im glouben, im gebätt, und anderen notwendigen dingen, von den Dieneren desz worts zu Zürych gestelt in fragens wysz. — Getruckt zu Zürych by Augustin Friesz, im Jar als man zalt M. D. XLI." It was prepared in accordance with a request from the Zurich Synod of October, 1534 (Pestalozzi, pp. 60 and 102), and although a long, is yet in comparison with the earlier Catechism, a brief document. A. Lang (pp. xxxii. *sq.*) argues that it must have been published as early as 1535 and thus predates the Latin Catechism. But his reasons are not convincing and the phenomena appear to be best accounted for by assuming that both documents were in course of preparation simultaneously and influenced each other. The earliest known issue is from 1541.

[16] "Catechismus. Brevissima Christianae religionis formula, instituendae juventuti Tigurinae catechizandisque rudibus aptata, adeoque in communem omnium piorum utilitatem excusa. Tiguri apud Christophorum Froschoverum."

title. On the strength of the word " lately " in this dedication, it has been usual to assign this Latin Catechism to 1538, or at latest 1539.[17] There can be no question, therefore, that Leo Judae derives the sentence which Dr. Mitchell quotes from him from Calvin's first Catechism, which he here reduces to catechetical form [18] and redacts to suit his purpose. What interests us most is to observe how, in doing so, he falls upon a form of words which was almost exactly repeated by the Westminster Divines a century later. For the rest, it is also interesting to observe how the same ideas appear in the Shorter German Catechism which was in preparation simultaneously with this Latin Catechism, although it seems not to have been published until a couple of years later. Here they are very much expanded, but preserve the same tone. The Catechism opens with the question, " Since thou art a rational creature, that is to say, a human being, tell me who made thee? " to which the answer is returned: " God made me." Then follows: " How and whereto? " " When I had no existence, He made me, out of goodness and grace, moved thereto by nothing but His unspeakable goodness, that I might be partaker of His great riches and all His goods." [19] And after a lengthy and very beautiful exposition of what it is to be made in God's image, the question is returned to (Q. 7): " To what end did God make thee? — that thou shouldst be always here in this world? " and the answer is given: " The end for which man was created is God, — that he should learn to know Him, love Him alone above all things, and, after this time, enjoy Him forever, in eternal life. Wherefore I should with my heart rise

[17] Pestalozzi, p. 103; Gooszen, p. 43; Lang, p. xxxii.

[18] Leo Judae put it into the form of question and answer, which, it will be remembered, Calvin had not done (cf. Pestalozzi, pp. 62–63). It will be borne in mind that the two German Catechisms appeared in German only: there was no Latin version of them (cf. Pestalozzi, p. 101).

[19] Leermeister: Diewyl du ein vernünfftige creatur vnd geschöpfft, namlich, ein mensch bist, so sag mir wär hat dich geschaffen? Kind: God hat mich geschaffen. (2) L.: Wie, vnd warzu? K.: Do ich nüt vnn nienen was, hat er mich vsz siner güte vnd gnad erschaffen, darzu jn nüt bewegt hat dann sin vnuszsprächliche güte, dasz ich siner grossen rychtagen vnd aller siner güteren teilhafft wurde (Lang, p. 55).

above all creatures, and cling alone to God my Creator." [20]
Certainly, if Leo Judae rests on Calvin, he knows how to give
the richest expression to the thoughts derived from Calvin,
and quite justifies his own description of himself as a bee
which, going from flower to flower, gathers the honey for himself. By this beautiful description of the destination of man
we are prepared to arrive shortly (Q. 18) at this equally beautiful definition of God, which also has its roots in Calvin: Q. 18.
" Tell me what is God? " A. " God is an inexpressible, inexhaustible fountain of all that is good. What we lack we should
seek in Him alone; of what afflicts us we should complain to
Him alone; to Him alone should we flee in all times of need,
in Him alone should we seek help, comfort, shelter and defence. As He has promised to be our God, that is that He will
give us all that is good and save us from all that is evil, we
should hold and recognize Him as such and trust Him for it." [21]

It is not to be imagined, of course, that these ideas were
the invention of Calvin. They were the property of every
Christian heart and especially of all who had learned in the
school of Augustine — which is as much as to say of all the
leaders of the Reformation movement, whether of high or of
low degree. It could not be but that they should find some
expression, therefore, apart from Calvin, and even before
Calvin, in the numerous catechetical manuals which the new
teachers prepared for the instruction of the people. We find,
therefore, among the large number of catechisms which begin
with questions bringing out what it is to be a Christian, now

[20] L.: Zu was end hat dich Gott geschaffen? solt du allweg hie syn in
diser wält? K.: Das end darzu der mensch geschaffen ist, ist Gott, den sol er
lernen erkennen, jn ob allen dingen allein lieben, vnnd jn nach disem zyt in
ewigem läben ewigklich niessen. Darumm sol ich alle creaturen mit dem
hertzen überstygen, vnn Gott minem schöpffer allein anhangen (Lang, p. 57).
[21] Gott ist ein vnuszsprächlicher vnerschöpfflicher brunn alles guten.
Was vns manglet söllend wir by jm allein suchen: was vns truckt söllend
wir jm allein klagen, zu jm allein söllend wir in allen nöten louffen, by
jm allein söllend wir hilff, trost, schutz vnn schirm suchen. Wie er uns
verheiszt er wölle vnser Gott syn, das ist, er wölle vns alles guts geben,
vnd alles übels ledig machen, also söllend wir jn darfür haben vnn erkennen,
vnd söllend jm des vertruwen, Psal. lxxxj. xcj. (Lang, pp. 59–60).

and then one which carries back the thought to creation itself
and begins with making an effort to explain to the people what
it is to be a creature of God. " A little book in questions and
answers " was printed, for example, somewhere in the middle
of the 'twenties (1522–1526), by a certain Petrus Schultz, possibly for the people of Lemgo — but we really know nothing
of the man or his flock — which opens as follows: " What art
thou? I am a creature. What is a creature? What is made out
of nothing. Who made thee? He who is almighty and eternal.
For what did He make thee? For His kingdom and to do His
will." [22] About the same time — or a little later — a schoolmaster of Rothenburg, Valentin Ickelsamer by name, was
printing beautiful dialogues for the instruction of children in
the great art of knowing themselves and living worthily. One
of these, a dialogue between Margaret and Anna, opens thus: [23]
" Margaret: What art thou? Anna: A rational creature of
God, a human being. M.: How didst thou become a human
being and come into existence? A.: God made me and placed a
living soul in my flesh, that in this house of exile,[24] born on
the earth, it might long after God its creator and apprehend
Him." [25] Sometimes the two lines of thought are united, with
more or less felicity. Thus no less a man than Johannes Brenz,
in no less a book than that which has sometimes (though, of
course, with only relative accuracy) been called " the first
Protestant Catechism " — the " Fragstück des Christlichen
Glaubens " of 1528, designed for young children, and hence
called the " Catechismus Minor " — begins thus: " What art
thou? According to the first birth, I am a rational creature or

[22] F. Cohrs, " Die evangelischen Katechismusversuche vor Luthers Enchiridion " (in the " Monumenta Germaniae Paedagogica," edited by Karl
Kehrbach, vols. xx.–xxiv.), vol. ii. (XXI.), 1900, p. 211. Cohrs says (p. 209):
" Of no catechism do we know so little as of that of Petrus Schultz. We
neither know anything certain of the life of the author . . . nor do we know
anything of either where it was printed or where it was used."

[23] Cohrs, as cited, i. (XX.), pp. 138–139. Ickelsamer holds an honorable
place in the history of German pedagogy. See Vogel, " Leben und Verdienste
V. Ickelsamers," Leipzig, 1894.

[24] Elends: " exile " or " misery." Is there some Origenism here?

[25] sich nach Gott jrem schöpffer sehnen vnd jn erkennen solte.

human being, made by God; [26] but according to the new birth, I am a Christian." [27] And this opening is almost exactly repeated in a later Catechism of Kaspar Gräter's (1537): "What art thou, my dear child? According to the first birth I am a rational creature or human being, made by God, but according to the new birth, I am a Christian"; [28] as also, in a still later one by Johann Meckhart (*circa* 1553 +): "What art thou, my child? According to the first birth, I am a rational creature, a human being, made by God, but according to the second [29] and new birth, I am a Christian." [30] In Bartholomeus Rosinus' "Short Questions and Answers," printed in Regensburg in 1581, this double answer still stands, but is diverted from its original purpose and conformed in both elements to the current soteriological motive: "Dear child, what art thou? By reason of [31] the bodily birth, I am a condemned sinner, but by reason of the spiritual re-birth, I am a saved Christian." [32] We may perhaps look upon this as a reminiscence of the old Brentzian formula, rephrased under the influence of the prevalent method of catechizing. Other examples of the mixture of the two motives may be found in the Catechisms of Kaspar Loener (1529) and Jacob Other (1532), in both of which the idea of the likeness of God is emphasized. The former of these begins as follows: "What art thou? I am a Christian man and a child of God. Whence is man? God made man out of the earth, after His image. How is man God's image? When he is righteous. What man, however, is righteous? He who does righteousness and avoids unrighteousness." [33] The latter be-

[26] The close resemblance of this to the opening of Valentin Ickelsamer's dialogue should not pass unobserved.

[27] Cohrs, iii. 1901, p. 146.

[28] Reu, "Quellen zur Geschichte des Katechismus-Unterrichts" (in "Quellen zur Geschichte des kirchlichen Unterrichts," I. edited by Reu), vol. i. 1904, p. 315. On Brenz and Gräter and the relation of their Catechisms see also Cohrs, iii. pp. 130 *sqq.*, and ii. pp. 313, 316.

[29] andern.

[30] Reu, p. 820.

[31] halben.

[32] Reu, p. 743.

[33] Cohrs, iii. p. 471.

gins as follows: "What art thou? I am a human being. How dost thou know this? Thus, that I am unrighteous, a sinner and nothing worth. Who made thee? God the Almighty who made the heavens and earth and all things. How did He make thee? After His image. What is the image of God? It is righteousness, holiness, truth, eternal joy and blessedness." [34] Instances such as these of the utilization of the conception which dominates Calvin's Catechisms are clearly more interesting than significant. It may possibly be that Leo Judae knew some of these earlier efforts to prepare spiritual food for the babes of the flock. He was a very busy bee and ranged far for his honey: Bullinger, in the preface he prefixed to Leo Judae's earliest Catechism, tells us that "he did not despise the work of other true and learned servants in the Gospel of Christ"; and "made no shame of transcribing and adopting from them into his own what he found most suitable, as indeed not only the most learned of the ancient doctors did, but also the holy prophets." One would like to think he may have known the dialogues of Valentin Ickelsamer, and one can scarcely doubt that he knew the Smaller Catechism of Brenz: and if he knew them he may well have more or less drawn from them. But it is clear that his main source for these questions, not only in his Latin, but also in his Shorter German Catechism, was Calvin. And we can scarcely suppose that Calvin, who obviously is going his own way, was influenced by these earlier manuals.

Calvin, then, it is evident, is the ultimate source of the opening question and answer of the Westminster Shorter Catechism. If Leo Judae is to come into consideration at all, it is only as an intermediary between Calvin and the Westminster formularies. Leo Judae is not, however, the only intermediary which must come into consideration when we begin to ask whether the language of the Westminster Catechisms may not be modified by some of Calvin's successors. There are, for example, the series of Catechisms which were published by John à Lasco in London, and which present very interesting

[34] Reu, i. p. 362.

modifications of Calvin's treatment of this topic. Three of these are of interest to us. The first was prepared by Laski for the Friesian Church as early as 1546, but was first printed, in Dutch, by Jan Utenhove, an elder of the Foreign Church of London, in 1551. The second — a much briefer one — was the production on Laski's model of another of Laski's London helpers, Marten Microen (Micronius), and was first printed, in Dutch, at London in 1552. The third, which was in effect an abridgement of the Catechism of 1551, was prepared for the Church at Embden and was first printed in the autumn of 1554, continuing in use until our own day.[35] The opening words of the first of these Catechisms,[36] which we may call the Friesian Catechism, run as follows: " Why has God created man and endowed him with such great gifts of understanding above all other creatures? That he might learn to know aright his God and Creator, love, fear, laud and praise Him and so become sharer in all His goods." [37] In the second, Micronius', or, as we may perhaps call it distinctively, the London Catechism,[38] they run: " Whereto hast thou been created by God and placed in the world? In order that my life long I may know and serve God according to the right teaching, and finally may live with Him in heaven forever." [39] And in the third, or, as we may call it, the Embden Catechism,[40]

[35] For à Lasco's Catechisms see Lang, pp. xxxix. *sqq.;* Gooszen, pp. 55 *sqq.*

[36] " De Catechismus, oft Kinder leere, diemen te Londen, inde Duytsche ghemeynte, is ghebruyckende . . . Ghedruct tot Londen, by Steuen Myerdman. An. 1551." Printed by A. Kuyper, " Joannis à Lasco Opera," ii. 1866, pp. 340 *sqq.*

[37] Kuyper, p. 355: Dat hi sijnen God eñ Schepper recht soude leeren bekennen, beminnen, vreesen, louen ende prijsen, ende alder sijnder goedē deelachtich wesē soude.

[38] " De kleyne Catechismus, oft Kinder-leere der Duytscher Ghemeynte, van Londen, de welcke nu hier ende daer verstroyt is. — Ghemaeckt door Marten Micron. . . . Ghedruckt by Gellium Ctematium. Anno 1559." Printed by A. Lang, pp. 117–149.

[39] Op dat ick God mijn leuen lanck, ten rechten leere kennen ende dienen: enn eyndelick met hem inden hemel leue in der eewicheyt.

[40] " Catechismus effte Kinderlehre, tho nütte der Jöget in Ostfriesslandt dorch de Deners des hilligen Godtlicken Wordes tho Embden. Appet korteste vernatet. Ghedruckt te Embden by? Anno MDLIV. Octob. 10." It is printed by Kuyper, ii. pp. 495–543.

they run: " Whereto hast thou been created a man? That I should be an image of God, and should know, praise and serve my God and Creator." [41] What is most striking in these Catechisms is that in both of the forms which were issued in London for the use of the Dutch Church there — as in Leo Judae's Latin Catechism — the two items of glorifying and enjoying God are brought together: man is on earth primarily to know and serve God, but also to become partaker in His glory and to live with Him forever. It is clear that already by the middle of the sixteenth century there was a tradition growing up in the Catechetical manuals deriving from Calvin's fundamental statement to emphasize these two items: as indeed faithfulness to Calvin's statement required should be done. We need not feel surprise, then, that Dr. A. F. Mitchell [42] is able to quote Italian and Spanish examples the language of which comes very close indeed to that of the Westminster Catechisms. " To what end was man created? " is asked in the Italian one; and the answer is: " To know and love God and enjoy Him forever "; [43] and the Spanish answer is almost as striking.[44]

We are naturally more interested, however, in the tradition as it manifested itself in England and Scotland, where, as we have seen, Calvin's Catechism was much used, and indeed in Scotland formed part of the recognized formularies of the Church. This tradition is very rich, and takes many variations upon itself in the hands of the several teachers who attempted to draw up manuals for the instruction of youth. In Scotland, from the Reformation down, there was in use in the grammar schools a " Summula Catechismi," designed for the training in piety of the youths gathered there, which is supposed to have been the work of Andrew Simpson, master of the grammar school of Perth both before and after the Refor-

[41] Kuyper, p. 501: Dat ick ein Bildt Gades scholde syn, unde mynen Godt unde Schepper scholde erkennen lauen unde denen.

[42] " Catechisms of the Second Reformation," 1886, p. 3.

[43] A che fine è creato l'huomo? Per conoscer, amar et goder eternamente Deo — Gagliardi (p. 3). Gagliardi's Catechism dates from the 16th century (Mitchell, " Catechisms," p. xx.).

[44] Para servir a Dios en esta vida e despues della gozarle en la otra eternamente (Mitchell, " Catechisms," p. 3).

mation and first Protestant minister of Dunbar.[45] Its opening
questions run: " Who created man? God. How did He create
him? Holy and sound and with dominion over the world. For
what end was he created? To serve God." [46] Less richly the
shorter form of John Craig's Catechism begins by asking,
" What are we by nature? " and after answering, " The Children of God's Wrath," proceeds, " Were we thus created of
God? " to respond, " No, for he made us to his own image." [47]
The essence of the matter, however, is still preserved there.
The tradition of Andrew Simpson's manual, however, appears
to dominate Scottish Catechetics: his method of putting things
at least reasserts itself in the Westminster period in a couple
of documents issued almost or quite with authority in the
Scottish Church. " The A, B, C, or A Catechisme for yong
children appoynted by act of the church and councell of Scotland To be learned in all families and Lector Schooles in the
said Kingdome " seems to have first appeared in 1641. It opens
thus: " Who made man? God. In what estate made he him?
Perfectly holy in body and soule." [48] The " New Catechisme
according to the Forme of the Kirk of Scotland " — which, as
Dr. Mitchell says,[49] " was published in England, just before
the Assembly entered on this part of its labors " — that is, in
1644 — " and (I can hardly doubt) in the hope that it might
tend to facilitate them " — begins thus: " Who made the
Hevins and the Earth, and all things conteined in them? God.
Whereof was man created? Of the earth. To what end was he
made? To serve God." [50]

The English tradition takes a slightly different form and
keeps closer, on the whole, to Calvin's example. In most of

[45] It will be found perhaps in its best form in Dr. Bonar's " Catechisms
of the Scottish Reformation," 1866, pp. 287–298: and also in Dunlop's " Collection," ii. pp. 378–382; cf. ix. in the Table of Contents.

[46] Quis hominem creavit? Deus. Qualem creavit eum? Sanctum et sanum,
mundique dominum. In quem usum creatus est? Ut Deo inserviret.

[47] Bonar, p. 275; Dunlop, ii. p. 368.

[48] Mitchell, " Catechisms," pp. 267 *sq.*

[49] P. xxxiv.

[50] Mitchell, pp. 277 *sq.*

the manuals which begin, after the fashion of Calvin's Catechisms and the best Reformed tradition, with the end of man's
existence, the stress is laid on the glorifying of God: and when
there is an addition to this it ordinarily takes the form of
reference to the securing of salvation. Occasionally the soteriological motive seems to absorb all interest. Thus, for example,
in Dr. William Whittaker's " Short Sum of Christianity delivered by way of Catechism " (London, 1630) we read: " What is
the only thing whereunto all our endeavors ought to be directed? To seek everlasting felicity or salvation in this life,
that we may fully enjoy it in the life to come. What is salvation? Perfect happiness of soul and body forever." [51] More frequently we have the glorification of God set forth alone as the
end of all human existence. Thus, for example, in Dawson's
" Short Questions and Answeares, etc.," of 1584, the opening
question and answer are: " Wherefore hath God made, sanctified, and preserved you? To seek His glory, Romans xi. 30 ";
and in a list of " Articles very necessarie to be knowen of
all yong schollers of Christe's School " appended to " Certaine
Necessarie Instructions meet to be taught the yonger sort before they come to be partakers of the Holy Communion,"
emanating obviously from the same Puritan circles, the first
is " that the end of our creation is to glorify God." More striking still, considered as a forerunner of the Westminster Catechisms, are the first question and answer in another formulary
published in London in 1584, under the title of: " The Ground
of Christianity, composed in a dialogue between Paul and
Titus, containing all the principall poyntes of our Salvation
in Christ." These run: " What is the chiefest duety of a Christian man in this life? The chiefest duety of man, and not of
man onely, but of all the creatures in the world in their nature,
is to set forth the glory of God." The very method of statement of the Westminster formularies is here.[52] Later examples
of the same mode of statement are provided by Paget's
" Summe of Christian Religion " and Openshaw's " Summe of

[51] Mitchell, p. lxxxii.
[52] For all three of these instances, see Mitchell, p. lxxix.

Christian Religion ": " Wherefore hath God made . . . you?
To seek His glory." [53] When there is a double statement it is
sometimes, to be sure, in the form given it by Thomas Sparks
in his " A Brief and Short Catechism, etc.": " To what end
hath he made man? To the setting forth of his own glorie, and
that man should serve him." [54] But more frequently, as we
have said, at least in seventeenth century documents, the double statement draws together the glorifying of God and the
salvation of the soul. One of the most influential of the Catechisms of this type was undoubtedly the Short Catechism of
John Ball, which was published in his early ministry, and had
reached its nineteenth impression in 1642 and its forty-fifth in
1657. Its opening question and answer are: " What ought to be
the chiefe and continuall care of every man in this life? To
glorifie God and save his soule." [55] Similarly we read in William

[53] Mitchell, p. 3.
[54] Mitchell, p. lxxix.
[55] Mitchell, p. 65. It is, no doubt, requisite to distinguish between Ball's
" A Short Catechism containing the Principles of Religion," and his larger
manual, called " A Short Treatise containing all the Principal Grounds of
Christian Religion." It is the latter which is perhaps commonly meant when
" Ball's *Catechism*" is spoken of: but it is the former and briefer compend
which is quoted here. The larger treatise, however, is simply the smaller one
expanded. Incorporating the whole of the smaller one, it follows up each
question with additional ones designed to develop more fully its contents.
It therefore begins with the same question and answer: " What ought to be
the chief and continual care of every man in this life? To glorifie God and save
his soul." Then, after developing what is meant by God's glory, it is asked
(in the seventh question), " What is it then to glorifie God? " and answered,
" To glorifie God is inwardly in heart and outwardly in word and action to
acknowledge God to be such an one as he hath revealed himself." Afterward
(in the ninth question) it is asked, " What is it to take care of our salvation? " and answered, " To take care of our salvation is so to live here, that
we may live with the Lord hereafter." In the next question the reasons why
we should take care of our sálvation are adduced, among which stand: " (6)
The soul came from God, and is after a restlesse manner carried to seek
and desire communion with God. (7) A desire to be happy is naturally planted
in the heart of all men by God himself," and especially " (8) God is infinite
in goodness, the highest of all things that are to be desired. Therefore we
should earnestly set our affections upon things that are above and infinitely
desire the enjoying of God's presence in heaven." It may be questioned
whether we need to look beyond this larger form of Ball's Catechism to ex-

Syme's " Sweet Milk of Christian Doctrine " (1617): " What is the chief and principal end of our being, etc.? That we may glorify God, and work out our own salvation." [56] And again, in " A Short Catechism for Householders," published in London, 1624: " What should be the chief desire and endeavour of every Christian in this life? To seek the glory of God and to obtain happiness and salvation of his own soul." [57] No two Catechisms, probably, are of more significance for the preparation of the Westminster Catechisms than those of Herbert Palmer (ed. 1, 1640; ed. 4, 1644; ed. 6, 1645) and of Ezekiel Rogers (1642). The former of these was not only the work of that member of the Westminster Assembly who had most to do with its catechetical labors, but obviously supplied a starting point for them. And the latter, Dr. Mitchell thinks, is on the whole, in its general structure, most like the Westminster Shorter Catechism of all earlier manuals. Both belong to the class we have now under view. Palmer's begins: " What is a man's greatest businesse in this world? A man's greatest businesse in this world is to glorifie God and save his owne soule. How shall a man come to glorifie God and save his owne soule? They that will glorifie God and save their own soules must needs learn to know God and believe in him and serve him." [58] Here is again the very flavor of the Westminster Catechisms. Rogers' begins: " Wherefore hath God given to man a reasonable and an immortall soul? That he above all other creatures should seek God's glory and his own salvation. Where is he taught how this is to be done? In the Scriptures or Word of God." [59]

There was tradition enough, then, beneath the Westminster Divines as they sat down to frame the first question and answer of their Catechisms: and we cannot fail to see that they were floating on the bosom of this tradition. The tradi-

---

plain the language of the opening question of the Westminster Catechism and its answer. It is all here in substance. The tenth edition of this Catechism was published in 1635, the eleventh in 1637, the fifteenth in 1656.

[56] Mitchell, p. 3. [57] Mitchell, p. lxxxiv.
[58] Mitchell, p. 99. [59] Mitchell, p. 55.

tion does not, however, quite account for their first question and answer. They must themselves be taken into consideration for that. The third question and answer of Calvin's Catechism was undoubtedly in their minds, and from it they no doubt directly derived the question. It would seem that they got the first half of the answer directly from Palmer. But the second half of his answer they improve on. Whence did they draw their improvement? From the third question of William Ames's Catechism, " in the enjoying of God " — as Dr. Mitchell thinks possible? [60] Or " from an Italian catechism of the sixteenth century," as Dr. Mitchell thought worth suggesting in 1886? [61] Or from Leo Judae, as he thought more likely in 1897? [62] Of the three suggestions the most plausible seems to us to be William Ames, whose work was certainly in the hands of the Divines, and may have suggested this heightening and broadening of the current: " and to save his soul." But, in any event, this heightening and broadening conception was already present in Calvin's Catechism; and it may very well be that there was no conscious dependence here on any intermediary, but that the Westminster Divines simply did what Leo Judae, Gagliardi, and Ames had done before them — found a felicitous brief expression for Calvin's thought. Or, if we must seek some intermediary between Calvin and the Westminster Divines, it would seem enough to bear in mind that Ball's " A Short Treatise " was in the hands of all the members of the Assembly, and provided them with language which asserted it to be the chief duty of man " to glorify God " and " infinitely to desire the enjoyment of God's presence in heaven."

The peculiarity of this first question and answer of the Westminster Catechisms, it will be seen, is the felicity with which it brings to concise expression the whole Reformed conception of the significance of human life. We say the whole Reformed conception. For justice is not done that conception if we say merely that man's chief end is to glorify God. That

---

[60] " The Westminster Assembly," ed. 2, p. 432: " Catechisms," p. xx.

[61] " Catechisms," p. xx., meaning Gagliardi: see above, p. 391.

[62] " The Westminster Assembly," ed. 2, p. 432.

certainly: and certainly that first. But according to the Reformed conception man exists not merely that God may be glorified in him, but that he may delight in this glorious God. It does justice to the subjective as well as to the objective side of the case. The Reformed conception is not fully or fairly stated if it be so stated that it may seem to be satisfied with conceiving man merely as the object on which God manifests His glory — possibly even the passive object in and through which the Divine glory is secured. It conceives man also as the subject in which the gloriousness of God is perceived and delighted in. No man is truly Reformed in his thought, then, unless he conceives of man not merely as destined to be the instrument of the Divine glory, but also as destined to reflect the glory of God in his own consciousness, to exult in God: nay, unless he himself delights in God as the all-glorious One.

Read the great Reformed divines. The note of their work is exultation in God. How Calvin, for example, gloried and delighted in God! Every page rings with this note, the note of personal joy in the Almighty, known to be, not the all-wise merely, but the all-loving too. Take, for example, such a passage as the exposition of what true and undefiled religion is, which closes the second chapter of the First Book of the " Institutes." He who comes really and truly to know God, we are here told, rejoices that God is the governor of all things, and flees to Him as his guardian and protector, putting his whole trust in Him. " Because he knows Him to be the author of all good things, whenever he is in distress or want, he flees at once to His protection, sure of His aid; because he is persuaded that He is good and merciful, he relies on Him with assured confidence, doubting not that in His clemency there is prepared a remedy for all his ills; because he recognizes Him as his Lord and Father, he is determined to acknowledge His government in everything, to revere His majesty, to promote His glory, to obey His mandates; because he perceives Him to be a just judge whose severity is armed for the punishment of iniquities, he keeps His tribunal always in view and in fear restrains himself from provoking His wrath. But he is not so terrified by the sense of His justice as to wish to withdraw from it, even were escape possible: he rather loves Him not less as the punisher of the wicked than as the benefactor of the good, since he understands that it belongs to His glory not less that punishment should be visited upon the impious and abandoned than that the reward of eternal life should be conferred on the righteous. And moreover, it is not alone from dread of punishment that he restrains himself from sinning, but because he loves and reverences God as his Father, and honors and worships Him as his Lord, and even though there were no such thing as hell would abhor offending Him."

It is not, however, Calvin who first strikes this note, and there is another in whose thought God is even more constantly present — Calvin's master, Augustine. This is the burden, for example, of Augustine's " Confessions," and its classical expression is to be found in that great sentence which sums up the whole of the teaching of that immortal book: " Thou hast made us for Thyself, O Lord: and our heart is restless till it finds its rest in Thee." For there is nothing the soul can need which it cannot find in God. " Let God," he exhorts in another of those great sentences which stud his pages — " Let God be all in all to thee, for in Him is the entirety of all that thou lovest." And then, elaborating the idea, he proceeds: " God is all in all to thee: if thou dost hunger He is thy bread; if thou dost thirst He is thy drink; if thou art in darkness, He is thy light; . . . if thou art naked, He is thy garment of immortality, when this corruption shall put on incorruption and this mortal shall put on immortality." [63] Delight in God, enjoyment of God — this [64] is the recurrent re-

[63] " Tract. xiii. in Ev. Johan. 5 ": Totum sit tibi Deus, quia horum quae diligis totum tibi est.

[64] Cf. J. Martin, " Saint Augustin," 1901, p. 238: " To enjoy God, *frui Deo*, is an expression which Augustine adopted from the very beginning of his teaching. He employed it continually: he said ' The soul organizes its life in such a fashion as to be able to enjoy God: for it is thus that it is happy ' (*De diversis Quæst. lxxxiii*. [388–395], Q. xxx.: Migne, vi. 20)." " The sense of *frui* is clear in itself: Augustine defines it thus: ' Quid enim est aliud quod dicimus frui, nisi præsto habere quod diligis ' (*De lib. arbitr*. I. iii. 4, Migne, i.

frain of all Augustine's speech of God: delight in God here, enjoyment of God forever.[65] Would we know the way of life, he tells us — in words which his great pupil was to repeat after him — we must come to know God and ourselves, God in His love that we may not despair, ourselves in our unworthiness that we may not be proud.[66] And would we know what the goal is — what is that but the eternal enjoyment of this God of love? " When he who is good and faithful in these miseries shall have passed from this life to the blessed life, then will truly come to pass what is now wholly impossible — that a man may live as he will. For he will not will to live evilly in the midst of that felicity, nor will he will anything that shall be

---

1312)." In the treatise " De beata vita," ii. 10, Migne, i. 964, he says that " the really happy man ' enjoys God.' The perfect satisfaction of souls, that is to say, the happy life, consists in knowing perfectly and devoutly by what we are led to the truth, what truth we should enjoy, and by what means we are joined to the sovereign mode." Cf. Reuter, " Augustinische Studien," 1887, pp. 464–465, where also some criticisms are offered. In Augustine's view, Reuter tells us, God is the transcendent τέλος not only for knowledge, but for all action. " Ipse omnis appetitionis finis " (" De civ. Dei," X. iii.). As the " summum bonum " he is the sole " res " to be *enjoyed:* all else is to be *used.* " The things of the world have no end of their own; their end is realized through the overcoming of (independent) existence by means of man, stand-ing between God and the world, to whom is given as his end the *enjoyment* of the ' Res ' which God is."

   [65] Cf. E. Portalié (Vacant-Mangenot's " Dictionnaire de Théologie Catho-lique," i. 1903, col. 2454): " The other fathers have exalted the majesty of the power of the Creator. Augustine is the first to be ravished by the *beauty* of God; *rapiebar ad te decore tuo (Confess.,* VII. xvii. 23). . . . No man has ever written on this subject pages so inflamed. This beauty, ' always old and always new,' inspires the enraptured flights of the *Soliloquies,* and the passion-ate cries of the *Confessions.* ' Then saw I, in spirit, O my God, Thy invisible beauties in the visible things Thou hast summoned from nothing.' And after contemplating them his soul preserves through life a glowing memory of love: *redditus solitis non meum ferebam nisi amantem memoriam,* etc. *(Confess., ibid.).* To other minds the spectacle of the world reveals the *exist-ence* of God; but for him, in this sublime appeal to all created things, it is on the *beauty* of God that he interrogates them. Their response is an invita-tion to love God: ' but the heaven and the earth and all that in them is, lo! from every quarter they bid me love Thee ' *(Confess.,* X. xv. 8). And he adds that to interrogate them he has only to look upon them: their own beauty is their response."

   [66] " De Trinitate," iv. 1, 2.

lacking, nor shall there be anything lacking which he shall have willed. Whatever shall be loved will be present; and nothing will be longed for which shall not be there. Everything which will be there will be good, and the Supreme God will be the supreme good, and will be present for those to enjoy who love Him; and what is the most blessed thing of all is that it will be certain that it will be so forever." [67]

The distinction of the opening question and answer of the Westminster Shorter Catechism is that it moves on this high plane and says all this in the compressed compass of a dozen felicitous words: " Man's chief end is to glorify God and to enjoy Him forever." Not to enjoy God, certainly, without glorifying Him, for how can He to whom glory inherently belongs be enjoyed without being glorified? But just as certainly not to glorify God without enjoying Him — for how can He whose glory is His perfections be glorified if He be not also enjoyed?

[67] " De Trinitate," XIII. vii. 10.

8

PERFECTIONISM

VOLUME II

BY

BENJAMIN BRECKINRIDGE WARFIELD

Professor of Didactic and Polemic Theology
in the Theological Seminary of Princeton
New Jersey, 1887–1921

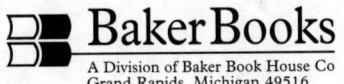 Baker Books

A Division of Baker Book House Co
Grand Rapids, Michigan 49516

PREFATORY NOTE

Rev. Benjamin Breckinridge Warfield, D.D., L.L.D., Professor of Didactic and Polemic Theology in the Theological Seminary of the Presbyterian Church at Princeton, New Jersey, provided in his will for the collection and publication of the numerous articles on theological subjects which he contributed to encyclopaedias, reviews and other periodicals, and appointed a committee to edit and publish these papers. In pursuance of his instructions, this, the eighth volume, containing his articles on Perfectionism in America and England has been prepared under the editorial direction of this committee.

The generous permission to publish articles contained in this volume is gratefully acknowledged as follows: Pittsburgh-Xenia Theological Seminary for the article taken from *Bibliotheca Sacra*, and Union Theological Seminary, Richmond, Virginia, for the article taken from *The Union Seminary Review*.

The clerical preparation of this volume has been done by Mr. Thomas T. Holloway, Jr., to whom the thanks of the committee are hereby expressed.

Ethelbert D. Warfield
William Park Armstrong
Caspar Wistar Hodge
Committee.

CONTENTS

v

I

OBERLIN PERFECTIONISM

OBERLIN PERFECTIONISM [1]

I. THE MEN AND THE BEGINNINGS

OBERLIN COLLEGE [2] had its origin in what seemed a wild dream that formed itself in 1832 in the mind of John J. Shipherd, home-missionary pastor of the little Presbyterian church in the village of Elyria, Ohio. As the scheme floated before his imagination, it was perhaps not very dissimilar to one of those communistic enterprises which were springing up throughout the country in the wake of the excitement aroused by Robert Owen. To that extent Shipherd may be accounted a brother spirit to John H. Noyes. But he had not the courage of conviction, to call it by no harsher name, which drove Noyes on in his reckless course. When he came to draw up the Oberlin " Covenant," he faltered. He provided only that " we will hold and manage our estates personally, but pledge as perfect a community of interest as though we held a community of property." By so narrow a margin Oberlin appears to have escaped becoming a decent Oneida Community: or rather, we should say, by so narrow a margin Oberlin appears to have escaped the early end which has befallen all communistic enterprises which wish to be decent; for communism and decency cannot exist together. [3]

Apart from this one point, the persistency of Shipherd's purpose and the energy of his will were incapable of faltering. By the end of 1833, he had some nine square miles of virgin

[1] Reprinted from *The Princeton Theological Review*, xix. 1921, pp. 1–63, 225–288, 451–493, 568–619.

[2] Compare: J. H. Fairchild, " Oberlin: Its Origin, Progress and Results," 1871, and " Oberlin: the Colony and the College," 1883; W. G. Ballantine, " Oberlin Jubilee, 1833–1883," 1884; D. L. Leonard, " The Story of Oberlin," 1898.

[3] Cf. D. L. Leonard, " The Story of Oberlin," 1898, pp. 87 ff., for some account of Shipherd's communistic leaning.

forest in hand; the beginnings of a colony already settled on
it, pledged to high thinking and hard living (not only no alco-
hol or tobacco, but also no coffee, no tea, no condiments); a
large boarding-school building erected; efficient teachers at
work in it, and a body of pupils, which numbered forty-four
by the end of the session, gathered at their feet. There was of
course only an " Academy " at first. But Shipherd's plan embraced also from the beginning a " College " and a " Theological Seminary "; and already early in 1834, there was a Board
of Trustees in being, operating under a charter, couched in
broad terms, which spoke of an " Oberlin Collegiate Institute."
And by the autumn of that year there was a freshman class
ready to enter at the opening of the next session (in the
spring) " the collegiate department " of this Institute. Summer was term-time at Oberlin, winter vacation. Late in November, accordingly, Shipherd started out, armed with a commission from the Board of Trustees to obtain the means to
make the step forward now become necessary. What he sought
was money and a President. But like Saul, seeking the asses,
he found much that he was not looking for. He found a whole
Theological Seminary — President, professors, pupils and endowment — all complete; and he brought it all back with him
to Oberlin in the spring of 1835.

Shipherd always contended that he was supernaturally
guided in this quest. And Asa Mahan, the President whom he
found, fully agreed with him. Up to the end of his long life,
Mahan constantly insisted that he was supernaturally called
to the Presidency of Oberlin College, not in the providential
sense in which this phrase is ordinarily employed, but with
as immediate a supernaturalism as that with which Saul or
David was designated king over Israel.[4] Shipherd, having
money and a President to find, naturally should have gone
east where money and Presidents were to be found. But he
discovered himself going south instead. " An irresistible impression " drove him without any clear intelligence justifying
his action, in the wrong direction. So he reached Cincinnati

[4] Cf. Asa Mahan, " Autobiography," 1882, pp. 190 ff.

instead of New York, and found — Mahan; who, everybody
in Cincinnati told him, was the very person he was seeking.
He thought so too; and with the more confidence that he
could see now that he had been divinely guided to him. Mahan
had a whole Theological Seminary ready for removal to Oberlin. There had been an abolitionist organization among the
students of Lane Theological Seminary, which the Trustees of
that institution had endeavored to suppress. The result was
that the students had withdrawn from the Seminary, practically in a body; and, housed near by, were endeavoring to continue their theological education independently, with only the
aid of John Morgan, who had been tutor in the preparatory
department at Lane and had withdrawn with the students.
Mahan had been the single member of the Board of Trustees
who had taken the students' part; and he now proposed that
they, with Morgan, should go with him to Oberlin, thus completing at a stroke the three-storied structure proposed for
that institution.

Excited by these bewildering occurrences, Shipherd, taking
Mahan with him, proceeded east to complete his mission. He
now, however, no longer sought money and a President, but
money and a Professor of Theology. The office was offered on
the way to Theodore G. Weld, the young abolitionist agitator,
who had had much to do with the students' revolt at Lane and
who was their idol. He pointed them rather to Charles G.
Finney; and to Finney, then pastor of the Broadway Tabernacle Congregationalist Church, New York, accordingly they
went. They found him depressed in body and spirit, with a
feeling that the bow of his strength was broken and his evangelistic days were over; [5] and quite ready to listen to their proposal if only the necessary financial provision could be made.
This was managed with the help of his friend, Arthur Tappan,
who was always ready to multiply good works. One condition,

[5] Preface (probably written about 1834) to his "Sermons on Important
Subjects," 1836, p. iv.: "My health has been such as to render it probable that
I shall never be able to labor as an evangelist again." Preface to his "Lectures
on Revivals of Religion" (1835), ed. 2, 1835, p. iii.: "I am now a Pastor, and
have not sufficient health to labor as an Evangelist."

however, was made by all — Tappan and Finney and Mahan and the Lane students alike. There was to be no color line drawn at Oberlin. The whole enterprise was near to wrecking on this condition. It was only with the greatest difficulty and in the end by a majority of only one vote, and that on an ambiguously worded resolution, that the Trustees were brought to comply with it. It was however thus complied with; and so Shipherd was able to bring his Theological Seminary to Oberlin in the spring of 1835.

The end of woes, however, was not yet. The New York backers of the enterprise failed; and it found itself plunged into the greatest financial straits. The students who had come from Lane proved a little difficult — some of them perhaps quite impossible — as from their antecedents it was to be anticipated they would.[6] His colleagues found Mahan himself something more than a little difficult.[7] Finney bristled with eccentricities.[8] Fads were exaggerated into fanaticisms, foibles

[6] When Asa Mahan, "Autobiography," p. 231, speaks of the lugubrious tone of their Christianity, some discount may properly be made on account of his natural zeal against a "miserable-sinner Christianity." Though they were "from among the brightest converts" of the great revivals, he says, "their common experience was represented in the words: ' Where is the blessedness I knew, when first I saw the Lord?'" Speaking of their tone of mind while still at Lane (pp. 239 ff.), he says: "Several of the most talented among them" refused to go to church saying they could "receive no benefit from the discourses of Dr. Beecher or any other pastor in the city." "They understood the whole subject." They did go to chapel, "and there listened to one of the feeblest preachers I ever knew," and openly said that feeble as they were, his sermons were as useful to them as any others in the city could be. "Of these young men," he remarks, "every one, as far as I could learn, afterwards made shipwreck of the faith. Only one or two of them entered the ministry at all, and they soon after left it, under the influence of some of the absurdities that then obtained."

[7] D. L. Leonard, "The Story of Oberlin," 1898, pp. 40–41: "Certain faults and infirmities of his had wrought not a little damage." Again, pp. 274–275: "His spirit was radical, positive and aggressive, and while he made many warm friends and admirers, others not a few were stirred to disfavor and antagonism. . . . Certain serious defects, however, attended his career, which in particular his associates in the faculty found it increasingly difficult to endure. After long forbearance and as a last resort it was determined to draw up a paper setting forth the facts in the case, to be signed by all and presented to the trustees."

[8] For example, Leonard, as cited, p. 35: "With the advent of Mr. Finney,

into gospels. There were some who, worn out with the wrangle, left — "in a very unhappy frame," as the historian says.[9] Most stayed on, and rasped along. Meanwhile Finney and Mahan, with the valuable assistance of John Morgan and Henry Cowles — who completed the theological faculty — were preaching, with the greatest power and effect, the duty, the privilege, the possibility of a holy walk. The circumstances in which they found themselves imposed this particular topic upon them as, in a very distinct sense, their peculiar message; and they delivered it with great elaboration and persistency. As they pressed on in their more and more intensified exhortations, it came about that they were preaching just the duty and attainability of a life of perfect holiness, though they themselves had not faced the fact.

It required to be forced on their recognition by pressure from without. This came in the summer and autumn of 1836 as the second year of the Theological Seminary was drawing to a close. Under the exhortations of their preceptors the students perceived that precisely what was required of them was perfection. They put the question; and at length — though not until the ensuing winter — received the affirmative answer. We are assisting here at the birth of Oberlin Perfectionism. Once born, it proved a very vigorous and very exacting child. Its exposition and defense absorbed a very large part of the energies of the staff of theological instructors. It was Mahan who took the lead and made himself first and last its chief expounder. Finney, however, was first on the field. Spending the winter of 1836–1837 in New York, as was his custom during his early years at Oberlin, and preaching there a series of " Lectures to Professing Christians " — his new engrossment — he preached two of them on " Christian Perfection,"

---

it began to be taught that a strict Graham diet was the only one either hygienic or truly Christian, while meat and all condiments were to be eschewed." Compare p. 210.

    [9] Leonard, as cited, pp. 35, 242, 261. J. P. Cowles is alluded to, whose views, we are told, " were at so many points so opposed to those of his associates, and who felt constrained to speak and act just as he felt, that his resignation was requested." He left Oberlin in 1839.

the first public proclamation of Oberlin Perfectionism. A semi-monthly newspaper — *The Oberlin Evangelist* — the first number of which appeared on the first of November, 1838, was established under the editorship of Henry Cowles, for the main purpose of propagating the new doctrine. In it there were at once printed certain articles on the all-absorbing topic, out of which books by Finney, Mahan and Cowles were soon gathered together.[10] Wherever Oberlin was heard of, it was Oberlin Perfectionism which was heard of first.[11]

The Oberlin Professors, we see, did not bring perfectionism to Oberlin. They brought an ultraistic temper [12] and the " New Divinity." And the " New Divinity," here too, as it had previously done in Central and Western New York, begot perfectionism out of its own loins. Oberlin was only an extension of Western New York into the wilds of Northern Ohio, and it repeated in its religious history, as it reproduced in its mental quality, the characteristic features of its stock. John Morgan [13] and Henry Cowles,[14] were not Western New York men. But they had both fallen under influences of the same general character, the one in contact with Lyman Beecher at Cincinnati, the other under the instruction of N. W. Taylor at Yale; and had received the same stamp. The situation was domi-

---

[10] An address of Mahan's published in the first number, was utilized as the core of a small book by him, called " Christian Perfection " (early in 1839), which at once became the chief vehicle of the doctrine.

[11] Asa Mahan, " Autobiography," p. 261: " The college early became, principally through its President and Professor of Theology, the visible representative of the doctrine of the Higher Life."

[12] What was understood at the time by the phrase " religious ultraism," then very current, may be conveniently read in an admirable printed sermon of W. B. Sprague's bearing that title (Albany, 1835). Cf. also D. R. Goodwin, " On Religious Ultraism," in *The Literary and Theological Review*, iii. 1836, pp. 56–66, completed by " Radical Opinions," same journal, pp. 253–265.

[13] Born at Cork, Ireland, 1802; graduated at Williams College, 1826; taught at New York; Preparatory School Teacher at Lane. Cf. Calvin Durfee, " Williams Biographical Annals," 1871, p. 429.

[14] Born at Norfolk, Connecticut, 1803; graduated at Yale College, 1826; studied in Yale Divinity School 1826–1828; pastor for seven years in Northern Ohio. Cf. D. L. Leonard, " The Story of Oberlin," pp. 279 ff.; " The New Schaff-Herzog Encyclopedia," and " Appletons' Cyclopædia of American Biography," *sub nom.*

nated in any case, however, by Finney and Mahan, both Western New York men, both " New Divinity " men, and both men of aggressive spirit and radical temper. Their previous lives, though springing out of the same soil, had run on very different lines, and it is rather remarkable to see them converge at Oberlin in a common end.

The details of Finney's early life which are current seem to rest altogether on his own recollections. He does not profess that these were complete, and there is some reason to suspect that they were not always altogether accurate. The main facts which he gives us [15] are that he was born in Warren, Litchfield Co., Connecticut, August 29, 1792; that two years afterwards the family removed to Brothertown, Oneida Co., New York; whence, however, while Finney was still so young a child that he retained no recollection of it, they were compelled, by the settlement of certain tribes of Indians there, to move to Hanover (subsequently renamed Kirkland), then a part of the large township of Paris, in the same county. There the boy grew up and went to school, until he was about sixteen years of age (Finney says he does not remember the exact date), when the family moved again — to Henderson, Jefferson Co., New York, a hamlet a little south of Sackett's Harbor. At this new home he taught school for something like four years. Then, when he was " about twenty years old," or " soon after he was twenty years of age," he went back to his ancestral home, Warren, Connecticut, and spent some four years there and in New Jersey, in study and teaching. Returning thence to his parents, he soon afterward entered the law-office of Benjamin Wright at Adams, New York, and began the study of law. This, he says, was in 1818.

It is a little difficult to form a vivid picture of the actual life of the boy within this framework. It was a raw frontier life; and there seem to have been few cultural and no religious ameliorations afforded him by his home associations. There

---

[15] " Memoirs of Rev. Charles G. Finney, written by Himself," 1876, pp. 4 ff.; P. H. Fowler, " Historical Sketch of Presbyterianism within the Bounds of the Synod of Central New York," 1877, p. 258.

may be some reason to believe that his father, like Lyman Beecher's, pursued the trade of a blacksmith; [16] and it is certain that the household, like that in which Beecher was bred, was without church connections.[17] Indeed, Finney not only represents the household as without religion, but broadens out the representation until the impression is conveyed that no "religious privileges were accessible to him in the community." This is a, perhaps not unnatural, exaggeration. Looking back upon his youth, barren of religious impressions, he transferred to his surroundings much that belonged only to himself, and thus transmuted his fault into his misfortune. Even in the frontier districts in which he lived not only Christian people but Christian churches could be found by those who desired to be associated with them; and not only unlettered itinerants and absurd exhorters but also learned ministers and faithful pastors could be met with by those who sought them out. The particular region in which Finney's boyhood was spent was indeed peculiarly well supplied with opportunities for religious culture. Clinton was but a short two-miles away, and Clinton was already a center of religious influence. There seems also to have been an organized religious society in his own hamlet with so excellent a minister as P. V. Bogue at the head of it.[18]

[16] David W. Bartlett, in the sketch of Finney in his "Modern Agitators, or Pen-Portraits of Living American Reformers," 1855, p. 152, says that as a boy Finney "found considerable time to wield the sledge at his father's anvil," taking thus "his first lesson in moulding the hot iron to a desired shape." His authority for the statement is not given.

[17] "Memoirs," p. 4: "My parents were neither of them professors of religion, and, I believe, among our neighbors there were very few religious people." Compare Lyman Beecher's "Autobiography," edited by Charles Beecher, i. p. 78.

[18] See the "Journal of the Rev. John Taylor, on a Mission through the Mohawk and Black River Country, in the year 1802," printed in E. B. O'Callaghan, "The Documentary History of the State of New York," iii. 1850, p. 1112. "Most of the churches in this part of the world are on the presbyterian plan. The church at Clinton is, however, congregational. Mr. Norton has a church containing 240 members; and this people is considered to be the most harmonious, regular, and pious of any in the northern part of the State of New York. In this town, or rather parish, is an academy, which is in a flourishing state. A Mr. Porter, an excellent character, and a preacher, is preceptor. They have one usher, and about 60 scholars. This institution prom-

The difficulty with Finney's early religious training was not that he lacked opportunity but that he lacked desire for it.

Things naturally were different when the family left this favored region (about 1808) and made a new home for itself in the backwoods of Jefferson County. There was practically no settled ministry at that time in this region; [19] and the young school-teacher passed some four years here without easy access to the stated means of grace. Returning thence to civilization and religious privileges he was able to sit, however, Sabbath after Sabbath, in the choir-gallery of good Peter Starr's church at Warren, Connecticut, unmoved to any spiritual response by his pastor's faithful preaching.[20] Meanwhile changes were taking place in Jefferson County. A revival had swept through that region in 1815.[21] Settled churches were being established. A Presbyterian church at Sackett's Harbor which in 1816 had called to its pastorate Samuel Finley Snowden, a man of the

ises fair to be of great service to this part of the country. Piety is very much encouraged in it — and some young gentlemen have become preachers who have received education in it. There are in the town a few Universalists, and one small Baptist church, but not a sufficient number to have any influence. In the society of Paris, of which Clinton is a part, Mr. Steele is pastor; he is said to be a good, and reputable man — he has a respectable congregation. In Hanover, a society of Paris, Mr. Bogue is Pastor." Cf. Fowler, as cited, p. 180. The church at Clinton was organized in 1791 by Jonathan Edwards the younger; Asahel Strong Norton was installed pastor of it in 1793 " and remained there for forty years, upheld by grace and the support of an unwavering faithfulness, an unerring judgment, an unspotted character and a blameless life " (Fowler, p. 90). For a biographical sketch of Bogue see Fowler, pp. 464–465. After a successful ministry at Winchester, Conn. (from 1791), he was employed in New York by the Missionary Society of Connecticut (from 1798), " and then accepted a call to Hanover, (now Kirkland) Oneida County, where he was equally successful for a number of years, and after that took charge of the church in Vernon Center." This appears to extend Bogue's pastorate at Kirkland through most of Finney's residence there.

[19] Fowler, as cited, p. 180: " That region also suffered long from the want of means of grace. A minister who visited it in 1816, relates: ' To the north as far as the St. Lawrence and east to Champlain, there are probably not six gospel ministers ' — an extent of country including the quarter of the State of New York. . . . And a little later, a missionary writes, ' we could not hear of any minister in St. Lawrence county, and there are very few on the Black River.' "

[20] " Memoirs," pp. 6 ff.; G. Frederick Wright, " Charles Grandison Finney," 1891, p. 4.   [21] Fowler, p. 180.

highest quality, was formally organized in the early months of 1817.[22] A Congregational church, soon to become Presbyterian, was organized at Adams.[23] When Finney returned to his father's house in 1816, or somewhat later, it was no longer to a community in which the stated means of grace were inaccessible, and no longer to a household to which the grace of God was a stranger. A brother had given himself to God during his absence.[24] If he himself still knew nothing of the grace of God, that could only be because he did not wish to know anything of it. We are glad to be told that he was not in any sense vicious: [25] he was, however, in every sense godless. It was not that he had no contact with religion. If he had not a praying mother, he had a praying sweetheart who did not cease to bear him on her heart before God; [26] and it is obvious

[22] For biographical notice of Snowden, see Fowler, pp. 647 ff., and J. F. Hageman, "History of Princeton and its Institutions," 1879, ii. pp. 94 ff. Cf. W. B. Sprague, "Annals of the American Pulpit," iii. p. 341. He was dismissed by the Presbytery of Oneida, to take charge of the church at Sackett's Harbor in 1816 but the formal organization of the church did not take place until February 17, 1817.

[23] In the "Minutes of the General Assembly of the Presbyterian Church in the U. S. A." for 1819 these two churches stand side by side in the Presbytery of St. Lawrence: Sackett's Harbor, Samuel F. Snowden, and Adams North Congregational Church, Edward W. Rosseter. We quote from the "Minutes" of 1819, since there are no statistical tables in those of the immediately preceding years.

[24] In his "Lectures on Systematic Theology," ed. of 1851, p. 429, Finney relates this incident: "I well recollect, when far from home, and while an impenitent sinner, I received a letter from my youngest brother, informing me that he was converted to God. He, if he was converted, was, as I supposed, the first and the only member of the family who then had a hope of salvation. I was at the time, and both before and after, one of the most careless sinners, and yet on receiving this intelligence, I actually wept for joy and gratitude, that one of so prayerless a family was likely to be saved."

[25] Hiram Mead, *The Congregational Quarterly*, January, 1877, p. 3: "It is a remarkable fact, which he has not thought worthy of notice, that in spite of his lack of religious advantages, he never became reckless or vicious. As a young man, he was spirited, and, no doubt, sometimes rough and hilarious; but, considering his associations, he was exceptionally conscientious and highminded."

[26] G. F. Wright, as cited, p. 37, tells us that Finney's sweetheart (her home was at Whitestown, only a few miles from Kirkland) "had been deeply interested in praying for Finney's conversion in the days of his impenitence."

from his own narrative that he was repeatedly more or less affected by the religious appeal. If he did not know God it was because he refused to have God in his knowledge. He was not ignorant of Christianity; he was, as a contemporary puts it " a great opposer of the Church before his conversion." [27] Or, as the historian phrases it, he was " without godliness and with the spirit of a sceptic and scoffer." [28]

When Finney, yielding to the persuasions of his invalid mother who wished him to remain near her, gave up his purpose of further pursuing his literary education, and entered the law-office of Benjamin Wright (afterwards Wright and Wardwell) at Adams, in 1818 (he was then twenty-six years old), he seemed to have come to his own. He was peculiarly endowed for the work of an advocate, and we are not surprised to learn that he loved his profession and was successful in its practice from the very first. An indelible impression was left upon his mind by his legal studies, and his habits of thought and modes of public speech were fixed for life during the four short years of his practice at the bar. He was not to be left, however, to the peaceful prosecution of his chosen profession. He was already suffering under a certain amount of religious uneasiness; and the circumstances of his life in Adams did not permit him to escape from the daily appeal of religion to him. Religion had always been within his reach — the difference was only comparative. " Up to this time," [29] he says, " I had never enjoyed *what might be called* religious privileges ": " I had never lived in a praying community, *except* during the periods when I was attending the high school in New England ": " At Adams, for the first time, I sat *statedly, for a length of time,* under an educated ministry ": " I had never, until this time, lived where I could attend a *stated* prayer meeting." The qualifications, which have been

[27] E. H. Snowden in *The Baltimore Literary and Religious Magazine,* May, 1838, p. 236. Snowden (son of S. F. Snowden, mentioned above) had been a pastor at Brownville where he says both Finney and Burchard had labored — disastrously to the church. Cf. Finney's " Memoirs," pp. 7–11.

[28] D. L. Leonard, " The Story of Oberlin," p. 128.

[29] " Memoirs," pp. 6–8. The italics are ours.

thrown up to attention by italicizing them, deserve the most marked emphasis. It is only by regarding them that we obtain a view of the true state of the case. What happened to Finney at Adams was that he was no longer permitted to neglect religion. The young pastor of the Presbyterian church there, George W. Gale, was a man of force and a pastor of parts. He never permitted this fine young lawyer, who was scoffing at religion, but was clearly not easy in his mind about it, to escape beyond its influence. He made him leader of the choir and so secured his constant attendance at the church. He was in the habit, Finney naïvely says, " of dropping in at our office frequently, and seemed anxious to know what impression his sermons had made on my mind," — apparently not dreaming that that was not vanity on Gale's part, but good pastoral work. Finney found himself going not merely to church but to prayer-meeting. He says in his old age that he does not recollect having ever attended a prayer-meeting before: and now he wished to do so, partly from curiosity, and partly from an uneasiness of mind on the subject which he could not well define.[30] He got a Bible, the first he had ever owned; and took to reading it, at first under cover of interest in Biblical law, but soon with deeper concern. He did not easily yield; he was a harsh critic of his pastor's sermons and of the prayers of Christians. But Gale's zeal did not flag; and we may be sure he saw clearly enough the signs of the coming end.

Precisely how the end came, we are not quite sure. Finney tells us, " I was brought face to face with the question whether I would accept Christ." [31] " On a Sabbath evening in the autumn of 1821," he says, " I made up my mind that I would settle the question of my soul's salvation at once." [32] So closely is his account confined to his own subjective experiences that the reader is tempted to suppose that there were no objective occurrences by which they were brought about. In point of fact Finney's conversion took place in a great revival; and it

[30] Tract on " Prevailing Prayer."
[31] " Memoirs," p. 11.
[32] P. 12.

was currently supposed that his final step was the result of the exhortations of Jedediah Burchard.[33] Ever since his return to the West he had been living in the presence of revival conditions. The revival of 1815 already mentioned as sweeping over this region, had been followed by others without intermission. Sixty-five converts were added to the little church at Adams in 1819, at the opening of Gale's ministry there. Seventy were added to the church at Sackett's Harbor in 1820. In 1821 the whole region was stirred to its depths; from eight hundred to a thousand converts were reported from Jefferson County — no fewer than seventy or eighty from Finney's home hamlet, Henderson. In Adams itself one of the churches received forty-four new members and the other sixty or seventy.[34] It was in these stirring scenes that Finney's conversion took place. He gives us a very detailed account of his experiences in it.[35] The most notable feature of these experiences is their supernaturalism; a supernaturalism not wholly in keeping with his strenuous subsequent insistence on the "make yourself a new heart" of the "New Divinity"; there is imbedded in them a most poignant experience of express inability.[36] The account of them, written in his old age, is more or less adjusted to his subsequent modes of thought,[37]

[33] For example, Joseph I. Foot (*The Literary and Theological Review,* March, 1838, p. 70) when speaking of the fanatical teaching of John Truair, continues: "Over the fields where Truair had recently sown the seeds, the Rev. J. Burchard soon passed, whose subsequent labors in the vicinity are said to have brought forth the Rev. C. G. Finney." A more favorable opinion of Truair is expressed by Fowler, as cited, pp. 664–665, and as favorable an account of Burchard as could be given may be found in the same work, pp. 278–281. Burchard was at the time still a layman, resident at Sackett's Harbor, and zealously holding lay services there and at Adams.

[34] Fowler, as cited, p. 190, drawing the details from *The Utica Christian Repository,* of the time. The general fact is safeguarded by the report of the Presbytery of St. Lawrence itself, which mentions revivals as occurring at Watertown, Sackett's Harbor, Adams, first and second, Lorraine, and Rodman.

[35] "Memoirs," chapter ii.

[36] Lyman H. Atwater, *The Presbyterian Quarterly and Princeton Review,* October, 1876, p. 706 remarks on this, while G. F. Wright, pp. 9–10, seeks to explain it away.

[37] G. F. Wright, as cited, p. 6, speaking of interpreting Finney's conversion says: "The difficulty of such an interpretation is also somewhat

and closes with a couple of odd paragraphs in which he "improves" his conversion by representing it as impressing then and there indelibly on his mind his later doctrines of justification *in foro conscientiæ* rather than *in foro Dei*, and of its issue in sinlessness. " I could not feel a sense of guilt or condemnation, by any effort that I could make. . . . My sins were gone; and I do not think I felt any more sense of guilt than if I never had sinned. . . . I felt myself justified by faith; and, so far as I could see, I was in a state in which I did not sin. Instead of feeling that I was sinning all the time, my heart was so full of love that it overflowed. . . . I could not feel that I was sinning against God. Nor could I recover the least sense of guilt for my past sins." [38] He adds: " Of this experience I said nothing that I recollect, at the time, to anybody; that is, of this experience of justification."

Finney emerged from his conversion a new man: the " sceptic and scoffer " had become the believer and zealous propagandist. His devotion to the legal profession fell away at once with his old man; he assumed immediately the new profession of bringing men to Christ. A judicial case on which he was engaged came up for trial the morning after his conversion. " I have a retainer from the Lord Jesus Christ to plead His cause, and I cannot plead yours," [39] he said to his astonished client. And at once he went out on the streets to compel them to come in. It is not possible to obtain a connected view of his activities during the two years between the outstanding dates of his conversion in the autumn of 1821 and his licensure by the Presbytery of St. Lawrence on Dec. 30, 1823. His biographer says that " about as much mystery hangs over the first

---

increased by the fact that, in the Memoirs written by himself, Finney has accompanied his narrative by numerous doctrinal disquisitions, in which those familiar with the controversies of the time readily detect the result of subsequent years of reflection interjecting their later theology in the narrative of early experience." " It is extremely improbable," he declares, " that the theological system defended in his later life burst upon his mind at the outset in such complete form as his own narrative would imply."

[38] " Memoirs," p. 23; cf. p. 18.
[39] " Memoirs," p. 24.

year and a half of Finney's life subsequent to his conversion
as that which shrouds the corresponding period of the apostle
Paul's renewed life." [40] The comparison, to be sure, is not very
apt; but it is true that although we know many details of
Finney's activities during this period and its general character
is clear, our knowledge of it remains confused. The account
Finney gives of himself after his conversion loses itself in unordered details; and his dates give us no guidance, being all
wrong. He makes it perfectly plain, however, that he at once
gave himself to active Christian work, which centered in the
church at Adams, but reached out also at least to his old
home at Henderson; there he had the happiness of bringing
his parents to Christ. From another account,[41] we learn that
he "actively engaged in the same school-house labors" which
were being carried on by Jedediah Burchard, as a layworker,
from his center at Sackett's Harbor.

In the midst of these activities, he was taken under the
care of Presbytery of St. Lawrence with a view to the gospel
ministry, at a meeting held at Adams, June 25, 1823, and was
"directed to pursue his studies under the direction of Rev.
Messrs. Gale and Boardman." [42] It would not have been
easy to find better men for this service.[43] They were both
men of sufficient learning, great force of character, and skill
in dealing with men. The whole work apparently, however,
fell into the hands of Gale, who was also Finney's pastor,[44]
and with whom he was already in consultation. There was
no mental sympathy between the two young men — Gale was

[40] G. F. Wright, as cited, p. 19.
[41] Fowler, as cited, p. 190.
[42] Fowler, p. 258; G. F. Wright, p. 20.
[43] There are biographical sketches of both in Alfred Nevin's "Encyclopædia of the Presbyterian Church," 1884, *sub nomm.*, and in Fowler, as cited,
pp. 190, 467 and 552 respectively. For Gale see also Martha F. Webster,
"Seventy-five Significant Years; The Story of Knox College, 1837–1912," 1912,
pp. 1 ff.
[44] "Memoirs," p. 46: "They appointed my pastor to superintend my
studies." On p. 140 accordingly he calls Gale simply, "my theological teacher,"
and on p. 153, with meticulous care, explains that Gale "by direction of the
Presbytery, had attended somewhat to my theological studies."

now in his thirty-fourth year and Finney in his thirty-first:
each was conscious of native power, and was tenacious of his
opinions; and the so-called instruction appears to have degenerated into a constant wrangle. Finney brought to Gale the
unordered Pelagianism of the man in the street, strengthened
and sharpened by the habits of thought picked up in the law-
courts; and he used Gale merely as an anvil on which to beat
his own views into shape. His attitude at first was one of
mere denial; he rejected with decision, not to say violence,
the evangelical system which Gale sought to inculcate. The
positive construction naturally came more slowly. "My views
took on a positive type but slowly. At first I found myself
unable to receive his peculiar views; and then gradually
formed views of my own in opposition to them, which appeared to me to be unequivocally taught in the Bible." [45] We
do not know when his views were fully formed. When they
were, they had run into the mold of the "New Divinity" in
the special form in which it was being taught at the moment
in New Haven. There are some who think this result purely
accidental: Finney, a great original thinker, reproduced for
himself without any connection with him whatever, what
N. W. Taylor was teaching with such revolutionary effect in
New Haven.[46] So far as the fundamental principle and general
substance of his thought are concerned no doubt this is the
true account to give of its origin. Pelagianism, unfortunately,
does not wait to be imported from New Haven, and does not
require inculcating — it is the instinctive thought of the natural man. But Finney's thought ran not merely into the general mold of Pelagianism, but into the special mold of the
particular mode of stating Pelagianism which had been worked
out by N. W. Taylor. The historian of New England Theology

[45] "Memoirs," p. 54.

[46] For example, A. T. Swing, *The Bibliotheca Sacra,* July, 1900, p. 465:
"What in New England had been gradually evolved from Old Calvinism
through two generations of theological reformers was substantially wrought
out independently of them by President Finney's rational revolt ("Memoirs,"
pp. 7, 42–60), which was so closely connected with his conversion as to be
practically inseparable from it."

feels compelled therefore to say that "independent as it was, and vigorously as its author had impressed upon it the marks of his own pronounced individuality," Finney's theology "may be dismissed in the one word 'Taylorism.'"[47] There were "various underground currents," he says,[48] which "set from New Haven westward, and some of them bore theological ideas into the region where Finney was." We do not need, however, to raise question as to the channels of communication by which Taylorism was brought to Finney. Intercourse between Connecticut and Western New York was constant; Finney received part of his education in Connecticut and his was the common case; all the ministers of his acquaintance were trained in the East and came from the East and maintained connection with the East; and Taylorism was, at the moment, the vogue. What we need more particularly to ask ourselves is only, how far at this early date Finney's views had crystallized into distinctly Taylorite shape. According to his own representation in his "Memoirs" they had already done so, at least in general, at the opening of his ministry; and certainly we cannot trace any other type of teaching in any account we have of his work. We know no other Finney than the Taylorite Finney.

On the 30th of December 1823, only six months after he had been taken under the care of the Presbytery, Finney was licensed to preach the Gospel at a meeting of the Presbytery of St. Lawrence held at Adams. He tells us that the Presbytery dealt gently with him and avoided raising questions on which he differed from it. Having now become a minister, he entered at once upon his ministerial labors in the northern part of Jefferson County — Evans Mills and Antwerp — as a missionary in the employment of the Female Missionary Society of the Western District of New York. As such a man naturally would be, he was successful in his labors from the start. He was ordained on his field, July 1, 1824, at a meeting of the

[47] Frank H. Foster, "A Genetic History of the New England Theology," 1907, p. 467.
[48] P. 453.

Presbytery at Evans Mills; and seems to have contemplated settling at that place in a permanent pastorate. He was drawn off, however, into further evangelistic labors, and prosecuted them unbrokenly in Jefferson and St. Lawrence counties up to the autumn of 1825. During these two years he lived the ordinary life of a frontier missionary, witnessing the same kinds of incidents — some of them bizarre enough — making the common experiences, but reaping more than ordinarily rich a harvest. According to his representations the matter of his preaching was constantly the " New Divinity " — pressed on his hearers with the pungency of expression, extremity of statement, and polemical vehemence, which belonged to his natural temperament.

This period was brought to a close, and the greatest episode of Finney's life inaugurated, by an unforeseen occurrence. He visited the Synod of Utica, of which he was a member, in October, 1825,[49] and on beginning his return journey home was waylaid by G. W. Gale, his " theological teacher," as he calls him here,[50] and induced to turn aside to preach at Western. Gale had been compelled by ill health to resign his charge at Adams in 1823, shortly before Finney left that place, and was now engaged on a farm at Western in laying the foundations of what was to be an eminently successful and indeed famous Manual Labor Institution, the parent of many less successful similar ventures. This preaching at Western broadened out into seven years (1825–1832) of probably the most spectacular revival activity the country has ever witnessed. That Finney felt himself to have taken a decisive step forward in entering upon this work — to have advanced to a new stage in his career — may be indicated by his transferring his presbyterial membership from the Presbytery of St. Lawrence to that of Oneida.[51] He had turned his back on frontier work: henceforth

---

[49] G. F. Wright, as cited, p. 46, erroneously says " October 1826." Fowler, as cited, p. 202, says " the last of September, 1825." Finney himself (" Memoirs," p. 140) says it was in October.

[50] " Memoirs," p. 140.

[51] In the " Minutes of the General Assembly," for 1825, Finney is listed as a W. C. of the Presbytery of St. Lawrence. In the " Minutes " for 1828,

his labors lay in the towns and cities of this rich and populous region, with their established churches and organized religious activities — and beyond. In his " Memoirs " [52] he marks the transition by pausing to note that " at this place commenced that series of revivals, afterward called ' the Western Revivals.' " Lyman Beecher calls them by the more designative name of " the Oneida denunciatory revivals." [53] They may have owed the feature which won them this designation, and much else about them that brought them into disrepute, in part at least to the circumstance that they were an invasion of the backwoods into civilization. Here was this young man, but two years a minister, but four a Christian, with no traditions of refinement behind him, and no experience of preaching save as a frontier missionary, suddenly leading an assault upon the churches. He was naturally extravagant in his assertions, imperious and harsh in his bearing, relying more on harrowing men's feelings than on melting them with tender appeal. " Force," says the judicious observer whom we are here drawing upon — " force was his factor, and ' breaking down ' his process." [54] And in exercising this force he did not shrink from denunciations which bordered on the defamatory, or from the free use of language which can be characterized no otherwise than as coarse and irreverent.

All this was no doubt to be expected in the circumstances; and it was to be expected also no doubt that Finney should give himself of set purpose to stir up a commotion; and, having the assistance of a band of able coadjutors, that he should succeed in doing so to an incredible extent. The whole region was stricken with religious excitement, and nothing was permitted to stand in the way of fanning this excitement into ever hotter flames. Parishes were invaded without invitation,

---

he is listed as a W. C. of the Presbytery of Oneida. These lists were at that time printed only every three years: there are none therefore for 1826 and 1827.

[52] P. 144.

[53] " Autobiography," edited by Charles Beecher, ii. p. 345.

[54] Fowler, as cited, p. 264.

churches divided, opposing ministers "broken down," or even
driven from their pulpits, the people everywhere set and kept
on edge. Finney was under no illusions as to the nature of
this excitement or as to its dangers. He did not confound it
with a movement of grace. It was only an instrument which
he used to attract popular attention to the business he had
in hand. It served him in other words as a means of " advance publicity." " It seems sometimes to be indispensable,"
he says,[55] " that a high degree of excitement should prevail for
a time, to arrest public and individual attention, and to draw
people off from other pursuits to attend to the concerns of
their souls." This function served, the excitement is so little of
further value that it becomes noxious; it now draws the mind
off from the religion to prepare the way for which it is invoked,
and if it were long continued, in " the high degree in which it
is sometimes witnessed," it could end in nothing but insanity.
Nevertheless Finney permitted himself to play with this fire;
and it is a question whether his chief work in this region consisted in much else than in kindling it. Certainly the characteristic feature of these "Western Revivals " lies in the immensity of the religious excitement engendered by them; and
it is matter of discussion until to-day whether their chief
results are not summed up in this effect. That many souls
were born again and became ultimately the support and stay
of the churches of the region, nobody doubts. As little does
anybody doubt that grave evils also resulted, the effects of
which have been overcome only with difficulty and through
the lapse of time. There is room for difference only in the
relative estimate placed on these two opposite effects.

One reason why many were converted in these revivals
was that there were very many to be converted; and the character of this large unconverted multitude accounts, no doubt,
in part also for their accessibility to a revival of this type.
The churches were in a depressed state and this meant both
an abnormally low condition of Christian life within them,
and an abnormally large mass of indifference or worse without

[55] " Views of Sanctification," 1840, p. 19.

them: an abnormal reaction was to be expected, and was indeed inevitable. Asa Mahan tells us,[56] that, observing these things, he had formed the distinct impression, before the revival came, that they must have a great and general revival of religion, or the churches would soon become extinct. "My reasons for that conviction," says he, "were two-fold: the general and embittered opposition to religion itself, and the appalling neglect of religious services, on the part of the unconverted outside the churches, on the one hand; and the utter worldliness and indifference to the interests of souls and the cause of religion itself on the part of professors of Christianity, on the other." "No one," he adds, "not personally acquainted with the facts as they were can conceive how appalling these two aspects of the moral and religious state of the community then appeared." The harvest was ripe and waiting for the sickle. It must be borne in mind, also, that a very large proportion of those swept into the churches by the excitement of the revival were not really converted, as their subsequent history only too clearly proved. Joseph Ives Foot, writing in 1838, is constrained to say: [57] "During ten years, hundreds, and perhaps thousands, were annually reported to be converted on all hands; but now it is admitted, that his (Finney's) real converts are comparatively few. It is declared, even by himself, that 'the great body of them are a disgrace to religion'; as a consequence of these defections, practical evils, great, terrible, and innumerable, are in various quarters rushing in on the Church."

It is very true that Finney could not conceal the instability of his converts from himself. Later he found a reason for it. It was because he had brought them only into traditional Christianity, and not into perfectionism. "While I inculcated the common views," he says,[58] meaning the common views as

---

[56] "Autobiography," 1882, p. 221.

[57] *The Literary and Theological Review,* March, 1883, p. 39. For Foot see W. B. Sprague, "Annals of the American Pulpit," iv. 1858, pp. 669 ff., and the "Memoir" by his brother, George Foot, mentioned by Sprague.

[58] "Lectures on Systematic Theology," ed. of 1851, p. 619.

to an as yet imperfect sanctification, "I was often instrumental in bringing Christians under great conviction, and into a state of temporary repentance and faith " — it is thus that he speaks of his entire evangelistic work up to 1836! — "but," he continues, "falling short of urging them up to a point, where they would become so acquainted with Christ as to abide in him, they would of course soon relapse again into their former state. I seldom saw, and can now understand that I had no reason to expect to see, under the instruction which I then gave, such a state of religious principle, such steady and confirmed walking with God among Christians, as I have seen since the change in my views and instructions." There lies in this passage an affecting acknowledgment of the failure of his early evangelistic labors to produce permanent results. One of the odd things connected with it, however, is that Finney fancies that, had he preached perfectionism, the effect might have been different — meaning that the perfectionism of his converts would have protected them from sinning. In point of fact, though he did not himself preach perfectionism, his preaching made perfectionists, as more than one witness testifies; [59] and his preaching of perfectionism could scarcely have done more than that. Yet the results were as we have seen. Jedediah Burchard roundly asserts that all revivals produce a crop of perfectionists, having in mind of course, the type of revival known to him. Finney does not go as far as that, but is willing to allow that revivals — again of course revivals such as he fomented — are commonly accompanied by a certain amount of what he would call fanaticism. In a tract written in his old age, called "Hindrances to Revivals,"

[59] Take for example the following words of Joseph I. Foot (*The Literary and Theological Review*, March, 1838, p. 70): "These doctrines, with a corresponding system of measures, were driven like a hurricane through the churches . . . Hundreds and thousands . . . were led to believe themselves converted, and were immediately driven into the church. . . . Many of his (Finney's) spiritual progeny, under the abilities of his system [that is, under his teaching of a Pelagian ability of will], and the several influences which acted upon them, soon manifested their fatherhood [Pelagian] and declared themselves to be perfect. . . ."

he declares that he has seldom seen a revival in which a bitter, denunciatory, faultfinding spirit did not make its appearance sooner or later, and that to a considerable extent. His account of this phenomenon is that when the Spirit of God is poured out on a people, Satan pours himself out on them too.

The phenomenon, however, will admit of another explanation, especially when we learn that in propagating these revivals everything was bent to the production of the excited state of feeling that was aimed at, and all ordinary Christian duties were in abeyance — absorbed in the one duty of exaltation of feeling. Thus, for example, Josephus Brockway [60] tells us that it was noted by all during the revival excitement at Troy in 1826–1827, that the whole charitable work of the churches fell away and even the Sabbath Schools were neglected: all manifestations of Christian love stopped: there was nothing, he says, but " a machine put in motion by violence, and carried by power." Even the Bible was thrust aside. " For a long time, during the high state of feeling," he writes, [61] " (when, indeed, feeling was made a substitute for every christian duty,) the Bible must not be introduced at all, into any social meeting, from one month's end to another. And while the exhortation was often reiterated, ' come, brethren, pray now, but don't make any *cold* prayers,' it was evidently held, although I do not say it was publicly expressed, that reading of the Bible was too cold a business for a Revival spirit. No time must be wasted in reading or singing, but the whole uninterruptedly devoted to praying with this faith and particularity, so vastly important." We are witnessing here a sustained effort to push excited feeling on to the breaking point.

To the breaking point, of course, it came, all over the region which the revivals covered; and despite those who had been brought into a sure hope of eternal life — absolutely a large number, let us believe — the last stage of the region as such was worse than the first. It is the calm judgment of a

[60] " A Delineation of the Characteristic Features of a Revival of Religion in Troy, in 1826 and 1827," 1827, p. 47.

[61] *Ibid.*, p. 28.

man of affairs and of letters, seeking to put on record an
observed social and religious phenomenon, which we have in
the following statement of facts by the editor of *The New
York Commercial Advertiser:* [62] " Look at the present condition of the churches of Western New York, which have become, in truth, ' a people scattered and peeled.' The time has
not come to write the ecclesiastical history of the last ten
years. And yet somebody should chronicle the facts now,
lest in after times the truth, however correctly it may be preserved by tradition, should not be believed. . . . The writer
entertains no doubt, that many true conversions have occurred
under the system to which he is referring. But as with the
ground over which the lightning has gone, scorching and
withering every green thing, years may pass away before the
arid waste of the church will be grown over by the living
herbage." If any corroboration of this testimony were needed,
it would be supplied by that of the workers in these revivals
themselves. James Boyle writes to Finney himself December
25, 1834: [63] " Let us look over the fields where you and others
and myself have labored as revival ministers, and what is now
their moral state? What was their state within three months
after we left them? I have visited and revisited many of these
fields, and groaned in spirit to see the sad, frigid, carnal, contentious state into which the churches had fallen — and fallen
very soon after our first departure from among them." No
more powerful testimony is borne, however, than that of Asa
Mahan, who tells us [64] — to put it briefly —that everyone who
was concerned in these revivals suffered a sad subsequent
lapse: the people were left like a dead coal which could not be
reignited; the pastors were shorn of all their spiritual power;
and the evangelists — " among them all," he says, " and I was
personally acquainted with nearly every one of them — I can-

[62] William L. Stone, " Matthias and His Impostures," 1835, pp. 314–315.
The " system " to which Colonel Stone is referring is the revival system in
practice in Western and Central New York. For Stone, see Appletons'
" Cyclopædia of American Biography," *sub nom.*

[63] Cited in *The Literary and Theological Review,* March, 1838, p. 66.

[64] " Autobiography," 1882, pp. 227–231.

not recall a single man, brother Finney and father Nash excepted, who did not after a few years lose his unction, and become equally disqualified for the office of evangelist and that of pastor." [65]

Thus the great "Western Revivals" ran out into disaster. Although it belongs to Finney's earlier missionary labors it is a typical instance of their effects which Ebenezar Hazard Snowden gives us from his own parish. "Both Mr. Finney and Burchard," he says, "made special efforts in Brownville, where I was afterwards settled. Mr. Wells, the pastor who was before beloved by every man woman and child, was as a result obliged to give up his charge about the time Mr. Finney was there. Such a course was pursued as exasperated a great portion of the respectable members of the congregation, and they immediately set up an Episcopal church which they have attended ever since." [66] As a consequence of such occurrences Finney's ministrations became no longer acceptable, and his preaching no longer effective in the very region in which he had once swayed men like a wind among the reeds. Over and over again, when he proposed to revisit one of the churches, delegations were sent him or other means used, to prevent what was thought of as an affliction. P. H. Fowler [67] quite unintentionally supplies us with a pungent instance of the decay of Finney's acceptibility as a preacher in this region, of which

[65] P. 229.

[66] *The Baltimore Literary and Religious Magazine*, May, 1838, pp. 236–237. — Snowden adds about Burchard: " Mr. Burchard's meeting there, was equally disastrous in its results. He assumed the airs of a commander, and would turn off about so many every day, and announce them to be converted. Some of those who then became members, never entered the church afterwards. Some became perfectionists, and of the remainder many were expelled. One of the elders remarked to me, that the church lost much of its vitality at that time." Snowden, born in 1799, brought up in Oneida Co., graduated at Hamilton College, 1818, admitted to the bar at Utica, joined his father's church at Sackett's Harbor about the time Finney was joining the church at the neighboring town of Adams: he was pastor at Brownville in 1836–1837. See the " Princeton Theological Seminary Biographical Catalogue," 1909, *sub nom.* p. 56; and especially the " Necrological Report presented to the Alumni Association of Princeton Theological Seminary, May 7, 1895," 1895, pp. 294–295.

[67] As cited, p. 284.

he was himself cognizant. Finney came back in 1855 to Rome, the scene of one of his greatest triumphs in 1826,[68] Now, however, his preaching elicited no response. He has himself told us of it,[69] and attributes what seemed to him the otherwise inexplicable coldness of his reception, to the fault of the pastor. This Fowler declares to have been very erroneous and very unjust. He himself ascribes it to a change in fashions in preaching. Finney preached, he says, just as he did in 1826, with the same ability, earnestness, force. But this kind of preaching was *passé* — and " his old friends in Utica, where considerable religious interest existed, deemed it unwise to invite him there." This kind of preaching was not *passé*, however, in other regions. It was still capable of oppressing men's souls elsewhere. But not again here — even after a generation had passed by these burnt children had no liking for the fire.

The offence of Finney's preaching attached both to its manner and to its matter; and it attached not to his preaching only but to his whole manner of conducting revivals, and not to his person only but to the whole bevy of assistants who gathered around him in prosecuting them.[70] It belonged to the

---

[68] " Memoirs," p. 159.

[69] " Memoirs," p. 434.

[70] Marquis L. Worden, (in William Hepworth Dixon's " Spiritual Wives," ii. pp. 81–82) tells us who some of these were: " Revivals prevailed in the neighborhoods and region round about Manlius, and through the country in which the New Measure Evangelists, such as Luther Meyrick, Horatio Foote, and James Boyle led the way." How Foote preached we shall let Josephus Brockway (" A Delineation, etc.," 1827, pp. 57–58) tell us. He is speaking of his preaching in the Troy revivals, 1826–1827. " I went to Mr. Foote, a would-be minister, who was no small occasion of offence and disgust, nor ought I, perhaps, to be delicate in saying, he was no improper object of contempt. He preached, what some called a sermon, in which he attempted to show that no man could get to heaven, without having lived a perfect life. I went to him with objections to his sermon, showing them to elder Cushman as I went. One of his positions was, ' That man's hope ain't worth a groat that isn't founded on obedience.' — To which I objected, that man's hope is good for nothing that is not founded on the merits of Christ, and evinced by obedience. Another of his statements was, ' Sinners never can be saved, and whoever has preached that sinners can be saved, has preached what is not true.' To which I objected; Christ came to save sinners, and there was none in our world to be saved, but sinners. . . ." Foote's teaching is of course just

movement itself and constituted its characteristic. We have
seen Lyman Beecher using the epithet "denunciatory" in
describing these revivals, and it may provisionally serve as
well as another word to intimate their peculiarity. It was as
if the day of judgment had come and the instruments of vengeance were abroad, with whips of scorpions, lashing the people into the Kingdom of God. Everywhere, naturally, there
was wailing and gnashing of teeth. The denunciation indulged
in was constant and unmeasured. It was not confined to the
preaching: denunciatory praying was practiced as diligently
as denunciatory preaching. Diverted from their ostensible purpose as petitions to the Almighty, prayers were employed
merely as means of exciting the audience. Sometimes the effect
aimed at can only be characterized as direct hysteria. At
others, usurping the place of preaching, the prayer became an
assault on the hearer; and that not merely with a more or less
general reference, but, under the protection of the form of
petition, with a particularizing of the precise individual intended and a detailed description of his faults, which would
scarcely have been tolerated in preaching. People were " prayed
at " rather than " prayed for," with the mind obviously set
more on moving them than on moving God.[71]

Pelagian Perfectionalism in its purity — and it was preached in the Troy revival as part of its official presentation. Finney has the grace, it is true, to be
a little ashamed of it; but he will not repudiate it. " In the midst of the revival," he writes in his " Memoirs," (p. 204), " it became necessary that I
should leave Troy for a week or two, and visit my family at Whitesboro. While
I was gone, Rev. Horatio Foote was invited by Dr. Beman to preach. I do not
know how often he preached; but this I recollect, that he gave great offence
to the already disaffected members of the church. He bore down upon them
with the most searching discourses, as I learned." He wishes to roll the responsibility of inviting Foote over on Beman: but he himself endorses him.
Foote appears in the " Minutes of the General Assembly " from 1825, when
he is a Licentiate of the Presbytery of Cayuga, to 1854, when he is a
stated supply at Redford and resides at Ripley, Ohio. He disappears from
the " Minutes " without ever having held a settled pastorate.

[71] Asahel Nettleton ("Letters of the Rev. Dr. Beecher and Rev. Mr.
Nettleton, on the 'New Measures' in Conducting Revivals of Religion,"
1828, p. 35) gives the following as the substance of what had been communicated to him on this subject by men on the ground. "There are various

We are observing here only one item in a system of practices which formed the characteristic feature of these revivals,
and which soon came to be known collectively as "the new
measures." [72] These "new measures" of course were much
spoken against; but all opposition to them was sternly stamped
out. There was no more highly esteemed minister in this
region than William Raymond Weeks, who was at the time
serving the Congregational church at Paris Hill.[73] A Pastoral Letter issued by the ministers of the Oneida Association
of which he was a member, warning the members of the
churches under its care against the new practices, was composed by him; [74] and naturally also, in writing to his friends
in the East, he expressed with some decision (for that belonged
to his character) his opinion of the evils he saw being thus thrust
upon the people. As a result not only was he driven in the end
out of his pulpit, but his memory has been sedulously defamed
ever since. Fifty years after, Finney was still speaking with
undeserved contempt of him,[75] and he and Henry Davis,[76]
President at the time of Hamilton College — whose crime also

---

errors in the mode of conducting revivals in this region, which ought to be
distinctly pointed out. That on the prayer of faith. The talking to God as a
man talks to his neighbor, is truly shocking — telling the Lord a long
story about A. or B., and apparently with no other intent than to produce
a kind of stage effect upon the individual in question, or upon the audience generally. This mouthing of words, those deep and hollow tones, all
indicate that the person is speaking into the ears of man, and not to God. I
say nothing of the nature of the petitions often presented; but *the awful
irreverence of the manner!*" — On the "particularity" used with reference
to individuals in public prayer, see Brockway, as cited, pp. 22–28.

[72] Sprague, "Annals etc.," iv. pp. 473–474: "His situation was now
rendered very unpleasant by the introduction of what were technically
called the 'new measures' in connection with revivals of religion; and he
therefore removed. . . ."

[73] Biographical notice in W. B. Sprague, "Annals, etc.," iv. pp. 473–476;
P. H. Fowler, as cited, pp. 673–675, 85, 261, 274; "Appletons' Cyclopædia of
American Biography," *sub nom.*

[74] "Pastoral Letter of the Ministers of the Oneida Association to the
Churches under their care, on the Subject of Revivals of Religion," 1827.

[75] "Memoirs," p. 144.

[76] Biographical notice in Sprague, as cited, pp. 224 ff.; Fowler, as cited,
pp. 505–510; Appleton, as cited, *sub nom.*

was " opposition to the revivals " — seem to be the only ones
among the multitude of ministers who have worked in Central
New York discussed by P. H. Fowler in his history, whom he
has dealt with with obvious injustice. The Pastoral Letter
which was the head and front of Weeks' offending, is not only
a perfectly inoffensive but an eminently judicious document,
expressed in entirely temperate language. It is absolutely free
from personalities, and equally free from rasping particularizing. Framed in general terms, it merely enumerates the kinds of
practices, which may possibly be met with in revivals of religion, that lovers of God and their own souls would do well
to avoid. It might be read through without divining that it
was directed against any particular movement: and one would
suppose that its serious and quiet cautions would be accepted
by all as an excellent road-book for the wayfarer through a
troubled land. That the participants in " the Western Revivals " were quick to declare that their own portrait was depicted may cause us some surprise; and more, that their
resentment was occasioned not by their looking upon the portrait drawn as a caricature of them, but by the painter's intimation that he himself considered it ugly. We clearly have, in
this calm enumeration of things to be avoided in revivals, a
trustworthy outline sketch of how " the Western Revivals "
were being carried on.

The phrase " new measures " soon however, acquired a sense
of rather narrower compass, in which it embraced only those
of the new practices which might be conceived as means employed to produce the effect sought.[77] As these came to be more

[77] Besides the " Pastoral Letter of the Oneida Association " and the
" Letters of Drs. Beecher and Nettleton," consult on " the New Measures "
especially: Andrew Reed and James Matheson, " A Narrative of the Visit
to the American Churches by the Deputation from the Congregational Union
of England and Wales," 1835, ii. pp. 1–50 (by Reed); C. Hodge, *The Biblical
Repertory and Theological Review*, October, 1835, pp. 601–615; Albert B. Dod,
ibid., pp. 626–674; and J. W. Nevin, " The Anxious Bench," 1843. Finney
tells us (" Memoirs," p. 288) that he made little or no use of " the Anxious
Seat " until the Rochester Revivals of 1831. G. F. Wright (pp. 100–101),
while properly recognizing its use as falling in with Finney's dogmatic
scheme, errs in supposing that the opposition to it turned on a notion in

fully known, they astonished, distressed, appalled the friends
of revivals everywhere; and most of all, as was natural, those
who felt themselves to stand in particularly close connection
with the churches of Central New York — such as the clergy
of Connecticut. Asahel Nettleton, the most esteemed "revival
minister" of the day, took the lead in an effort to abate the
evil.[78] Others — notably Lyman Beecher [79] — joined themselves
to him. Many — Griffin, Porter, Nott, Tucker, Cornelius —
visited Troy where Finney was then holding revival services,
that they might observe "the new measures" for themselves.
They came away more shocked than before. Letters were
written.[80] And finally a conference was arranged — "the New
Lebanon Convention," held July 18–26, 1827 — in which the
"Eastern brethren" endeavored to bring their "Western
brethren" to reason.[81] The attempt was in vain; and the fundamental reason why it was in vain is not difficult to discern.
The axe was not laid to the root of the tree. The "new measures" were not arbitrary practices due to nothing but a coarse
and depraved taste, the correction of which might be easily
managed and need work no great change in principle. They
belonged to the very essence of the revival as conceived by its
promoters. It was in them that its heart expressed itself. They
were in a word the natural and inevitable effect of the doctrine

---

the minds of Finney's opponents that "there was little natural connection
between the means used for the persuasion of men and their conversion."
A simple reading of their discussions will show that their objections turned
on quite other considerations.

[78] See Bennet Tyler, "Memoir of the Life and Character of Rev. Asahel
Nettleton, D.D.," 1844, chapter xii. pp. 245–270, "His opposition to new
measures."

[79] See "Autobiography," edited by his son, Charles Beecher, 1865, ii.
chapter 12: "New Measures," pp. 89–108.

[80] See especially, "Letters of the Rev. Dr. Beecher and Rev. Mr. Nettleton, on the 'New Measures' in Conducting Revivals of Religion. With a
Review of a Sermon, by Novanglus," 1828.

[81] Finney gives an account of the New Lebanon Convention from his
point of view in the sixteenth chapter of his "Memoirs," pp. 202–225;
G. F. Wright devotes to it a chapter in his life of Finney, pp. 57–95. It will
be found described from their point of view in the lives of Nettleton and
Beecher, as referred to above.

on which the revival was based. For what was new in this revival was not merely the particular "measures" by which it was prosecuted — that might be a merely surface phenomenon — but the particular doctrine on which it was founded, of which the measures employed were only the manifestation. This was a Pelagian revival. That was its peculiarity: and everything else connected with it was merely the expression of this.

That it was "the new measures" rather than the Pelagianism of "the Western Revivals" which in the first instance at least offended the Eastern brethren is no doubt due in part to the general fact that it is always external things which first meet the eye. The external things in this instance were shocking in themselves; and their rooting in a doctrinal cause was often felt but vaguely or not at all. Pelagianizing modes of thought, derived from the same general source from which Finney had himself drunk — the "New Divinity" taught at New Haven — were moreover widely diffused among the New England clergy themselves. Men of this type of thinking might be offended by Finney's practices on general grounds, but could scarcely be expected, for that very reason, to assign them as to their cause to a doctrine common to his and their own thinking. And that the more that there were as yet no adequate means of ascertaining what the doctrinal basis of Finney's preaching was. Only his actual hearers were in any real sense informed of his teaching. When a little later he began to publish lectures and sermons the scales fell from men's eyes. The discerning had no difficulty then in seeing the correlation between his practices and his doctrines, or in clearly understanding that the phenomena of his revivals which gave most offence were merely the natural consequences of the fundamental fact that they were Pelagian revivals.

Accordingly Albert B. Dod is found writing: [82] "We recollect that it was matter of surprise to many when the conjunction took place between the coarse, bustling fanaticism of

[82] *The Biblical Repertory and Theological Review*, October, 1835, pp. 656–657.

the New Measures and the refined, intellectual abstractions of the New Divinity. — It was a union between Mars and Minerva, — unnatural, and boding no good to the church. But our readers will have observed that there is a close and logical connection between Mr. Finney's theology and his measures. The demand created for the one by the other, and the mutual assistance which they render, are so evident, that we will spend no time in the explanation of them." And Charles Hodge: [83] " That the new measures and the new divinity should have formed an intimate alliance, can surprise no one aware of their natural affinity. . . . No better method therefore could be devised to secure the adoption of the new doctrines, than the introduction of the new measures. The attempt has accordingly been made. The cold, Pelagian system of the new divinity has been attached to the engine of fanaticism." These writers, it will be observed, do not assert that such practices as are summed up in the " new measures " may not exist — have not existed — apart from a determinate Pelagian system: what they affirm is that it is in such practices that a Pelagian system naturally expresses itself if it seeks to become aggressively evangelistic, and that in them we may perceive the Pelagian system running out into its appropriate methods. Joseph Ives Foot describes Finney's revivals therefore frankly from this point of view.[84] " These doctrines, with a corresponding system of measures, were driven like a hurricane through the churches. To resist this operation was to resist God. Conscientious Christians gave place, till they should see what it was. Timorous ones were attached to his triumphal car, while the bold and the ignorant seized the reins and the whip; and hundreds and thousands under these various influences, were led to believe themselves converted, and were immediately driven into the church. These scenes were called *revivals;* and thus the very name of the operations of divine grace was

---

[83] *The Biblical Repertory and Theological Review,* October, 1835, p. 614.

[84] *The Literary and Theological Review,* March, 1838, p. 70, article entitled, " Influence of Pelagianism on the Theological Course of Rev. C. G. Finney, developed in his Sermons and Lectures."

brought into suspicion." It is from the same point of view that Charles D. Pigeon writes with a somewhat broader reference: [85] "We look upon the course of Mr. Finney as particularly instructive. He of all others has taught the New Haven theology in its greatest purity and has ventured to push its principles to their legitimate results. Those parts of New York which have been the scene of his labours, are giving, and will long continue to give the most instructive lessons as to the nature of that system of doctrine, and its influence on individual character and religious institutions." And it is still from the same point of view that Samuel J. Baird places at the head of the very instructive chapter in which he gives an account of "the Western Revivals" the descriptive title of "Practical Pelagianism," and brings the chapter to a close with these words: [86] "Such were the fruits, widely realized in Western New York, from the New Haven theology. They were its legitimate and proper results. The good taste, common sense, and piety, of many of the disciples of that school, may revolt from these exhibitions, and pause before adopting them, in their full development. But the practical system of Finney, Burchard, Myrick, and their compeers, was deduced, from the theology of New Haven, by a logic, which no ingenuity can evade."

It will not have escaped observation that the writers we have last quoted assume that "the Western Revivals" were already generally understood to have been far from successful, as judged by their ultimate fruits. That indeed was the case. We have already seen that Finney himself came in the end to a recognition of this unhappy fact. It will cause no surprise that he should become wearied with this unfruitful work. Already in 1832 he was looking back upon this portion of his career as a closed page of doubtful success, and was consciously seeking a new phase of activity. He was yet to do a great deal of evangelistic work; but, although he threw the circle of his labors wider and wider, even across the seas, he thought of

[85] *The Literary and Theological Review*, March, 1838, p. 70, editor's note.
[86] "A History of the New School," 1868, pp. 217–234.

himself as no longer an evangelist — he had become a pastor.[87] His own account of the change is as follows.[88] " I had become fatigued, as I had labored about ten years as an evangelist, without anything more than a few days or weeks of rest, during the whole period. . . . We had three children, and I could not well take my family with me, while laboring as an evangelist. My strength, too, had become a good deal exhausted; and on praying and looking the matter over, I concluded that I would accept the call from the Second Free church, and labor, for a time at least, in New York." By this action Finney became a part of a movement then making in the Presbyterian churches of New York to reach the people by the establishment of " free " churches, that is, churches with no pew-rentals and otherwise adapted to attract and hold the unchurched masses.[89] In this way he gave to his pastorate a genuinely evangelistic character.

The church over which he was settled was a Presbyterian church, and Finney had always been a Presbyterian. It was in the Presbyterian Church that he was converted, licensed, ordained; it was under its authorization that he had pursued his whole work as an evangelist, and the region in which he had pursued his chief revivalistic enterprises was a distinctively Presbyterian region: and now he was settled as pastor over a Presbyterian church. But Finney was nothing less than a Presbyterian. The church of which he was pastor — as were all the Free Presbyterian Churches — was under the care of the Third Presbytery of New York, an " elective-affinity " Presbytery, as little Presbyterian as anything could be which was willing to bear the name. Still, there was friction over matters of discipline and the like; and Finney felt uncom-

---

[87] " Memoirs," p. 94: " I have been a pastor now for many years — indeed, ever since 1832." How completely Finney felt he had broken with his past we have already seen (above p. 5 and note 5).

[88] Pp. 318–319.

[89] An interesting " History of the Free Churches in the City of New York," by one of the prime movers in their establishment, Lewis Tappan, may be read in the appendix to Reed and Matheson's " Narrative of the Visit to the American Churches, etc.," 1835, ii. pp. 341–353.

fortable in his harness. His friends accordingly built a new church for him — the " Broadway Tabernacle " — which they organized as a Congregationalist church. Of this church he took charge in the autumn of 1834. He did not take his dismission from the Presbytery, however, until the spring of 1836, after he had been at Oberlin for a year, and was on the point of returning thither for his second session.[90] What led him thus tardily to sever his connection with a church with which he had so little in common we can only conjecture. Perhaps the process of writing his theological lectures at Oberlin quickened his consciousness both as to the significance of matters of faith in church relations and as to the complete dissonance of his own beliefs with those of the Presbyterian Church of which he was still an accredited teacher.

He had not been left without pointed reminders of the falseness of the position which he occupied. So soon as his " Sermons on Various Subjects " (1834) and " Lectures on Revivals of Religion " (1835) had been published this had become glaring and created an open scandal. He was called upon publicly to withdraw from a church in which he was so patently out of place. Albert B. Dod, for example, in July, 1835, closes his review of his " Sermons on Various Subjects " with an expression of thanks to him " for the substantial service he has done the church " in them, " by exposing the naked deformity of the New Divinity," and then adds: " He can render her still another, and in rendering it perform only his plain duty, by leaving her communion, and finding one within which he can preach and publish his opinions without making war upon the standards in which he has solemnly professed his faith." [91]

[90] The records of the Third Presbytery of New York concerning Finney's case tell that, " on the 14th of February, 1832, the Second Free Church (Chatham Chapel), composed chiefly of members from the First Free Church, was organized, and on the 28th of September the Rev. Charles G. Finney was installed pastor. . . . On the 2d of March, 1836, Dr. Finney was released " (S. D. Alexander, " The Presbytery of New York, 1738 to 1888," 1887, p. 107). This Second Free Church became a Congregational Church June 13, 1836, and Asa Mahan tells us (" Autobiography," p. 230) that Finney's immediate successor in the pulpit made shipwreck of his faith.

[91] *The Biblical Repertory and Theological Review,* July, 1835, p. 527.

In closing, in the following October, his review of the "Lectures on Revivals of Religion," Dod returns to the subject and insists on Finney's duty to leave the church. " It is an instructive illustration of the fact that fanaticism debilitates the conscience," he now says,[92] " that this man can doubt the piety of any one who uses coffee, and call him a *cheat*, who sends a letter to another on his own business, without paying the postage, while he remains, apparently without remorse, with the sin of broken vows upon him. In this position we leave him before the public. Nor will we withdraw our charges against him, until he goes out from among us, for he is not of us." We know nothing, of course, of the effect of such challenges on Finney's action; but it is to be noted that he withdrew from the Church immediately (within six months) after they were made. Perhaps it should be added as illustrating the lightness with which Finney regarded the obligations of his doctrinal professions, that, according to his own account, he had originally incurred those obligations without informing himself of what he was committing himself to. In describing his licensure,[93] he records: " Unexpectedly to myself they asked me if I received the confession of faith of the Presbyterian church. I had not examined it — that is, the large work containing the catechism and confession. This had made no part of my study. I replied that I received it for substance of doctrine, so far as I understood it. But I spoke in a way that plainly implied, I think, that I did not pretend to know much about it. However, I answered honestly, as I understood it at the time." Amid the curiously interlaced qualifications and explanations of this statement, it only emerges that Finney was not unaware of the character of his action. Under its cover, he for a dozen years flouted the doctrines he had been placed by it under obligation to propagate.

During all these dozen years Finney had been a wanderer on the face of the earth, doing the work of an evangelist. Even during the four years of his stay in New York, he did not stay

---

[92] *The Biblical Repertory and Theological Review*, October, 1835, p. 674.
[93] " Memoirs," p. 51.

in New York. He had accepted the pastorate offered to him there as a means toward securing a more settled mode of existence; and in impaired health and depression of spirits he was obviously still longing for peace and a quiet life. It was in this mood that the proposal to go to Oberlin found him; and it was in this mood that he accepted it. He was in the prime of life, and the event shows that his amazing vigor was unimpaired. His real career was indeed just opening before him; forty years remained to him in which he was " Oberlin's central spiritual force and most eminent representative." [94] The pulpit, the lecture hall, the press, were now the instruments with which he wrought, and with all alike he wrought with the hand of a master-workman. It is possible, to be sure, to exaggerate here. " In intellectual insight into the deepest realities of religion, in originality of treatment and in logical power," writes Albert Temple Swing,[95] " President Finney is to be ranked side by side with Edwards. They are the two greatest American theologians." This is only one of those provincial judgments which Oliver Wendell Holmes satirizes when he says that every village has, somewhere on its lawns, the biggest tree in the world. We must manage to see over the rim of the dell within the limits of which our experiences are wrought out. But certainly it must be recognized that Finney was " the greatest mind and the regulating force in the development of Oberlin theology." [96] He was blessed with coadjutors of a high order of talent. But it was to him that, above all others, Oberlin owed the measure of greatness which it achieved.

[94] D. L. Leonard, " The Story of Oberlin," 1898, p. 60; cf. pp. 276–277: " Beyond comparison his was the chief personal force upon the colonial tract. The pulpit was the throne from which Sunday after Sunday, for more than a generation, he swayed vast audiences. . . . For forty years his lectures on theology were given, and in addition, 1851–1858, he filled the chair of intellectual and moral philosophy. For fifteen years, 1851–1865, he was Oberlin's executive head. . . . Through his sermons, lectures and letters published in *The (Oberlin) Evangelist* and elsewhere a vast influence was wielded. Some of his books sold literally by the hundred thousand."

[95] *The Bibliotheca Sacra,* July, 1900, pp. 480–481.

[96] Frank Hugh Foster, " A Genetic History of the New England Theology," 1907, p. 453.

The contrast between the pictures of the religious conditions obtaining in Central and Western New York during the
first quarter of the nineteenth century, received from the accounts which Finney and Asa Mahan respectively give of their
early years, is nothing less than startling. The two lives ran on
very closely parallel lines. Both men spent their early boyhood
in Oneida County — in hamlets only a few miles distant from
one another. The later youth of both was passed in the wilder
West. Yet the religious conditions in which the two grew up
are described by them very differently. All the religious advantages which Finney represents himself as lacking, Mahan
represents himself as possessing. He was born and bred in a
pious household, and surrounded on all sides by religious influences. His father, to be sure, was not, in his son's judgment
at least, a thoroughly consecrated man. But his mother was
a deeply religious woman with an aura of devoutness hanging
always about her. It was a Bible-reading, praying family, in
which the religious books that to Finney were inaccessible
lay always at hand. The Church was at the door, and the
ministrations of the sanctuary were constantly enjoyed: if
there was formal preaching only on alternate Sabbaths, service
was held every Sabbath; and when sermons were not preached
by ministers, they were read by laymen. The house was the
resort of itinerant ministers, and the whole neighborhood was
full of Christian people ready to give Christian succor. One
rubs his eyes and wonders if this can be the same country-
side in which Finney found little that pretended to be religious, and nothing that pretended to be religious that was
not also absurd. To such an extent, it seems, does varying
personality color the aspect of surroundings, and even by a
process of selection mold them into harmony with itself.

Mahan was a few years Finney's junior, and, although he
found his way into the ministry at a somewhat younger age
than Finney, he had had a shorter — and a far less stirring
and notable — ministerial experience than Finney, when they
came together at Oberlin. He was born November 9, 1799,[97] at

[97] So Mahan himself repeatedly says (e.g. " Out of Darkness into Light,"
1874, edition of 1888, p. 1; " Autobiography," 1882, p. iii.). On the other hand

Vernon, Oneida County, New York, a hamlet some sixteen
miles west of Utica and about half that distance from Kirkland, Finney's boyhood home, with which it had easy communication over the famous " Genesee Turnpike." [98] Here he
was bred in what he calls [99] " ' the straitest sect ' of the Calvinistic faith," and was surrounded both in his home and in
the church life into which he was carried as a matter of course,
with constant religious influences. These had no more effect
upon him, however, than that he grew up a boy of good
habits and excellent character. When he was about twelve
years of age the family removed to the West — to Orangeville,
Wyoming County, four miles from Warren and some forty
miles southwest of Rochester. The change of residence, however, brought no essential change in the boy's inner life or
his external carriage. He lived in his new home, too, as a
member of a religious household would be expected to live,
taking part in all the religious activities of the community;
but withal, he was still destitute of religious experiences of
his own. He was known, however, as a young man of sterling
character and irreproachable conduct. And so it came about,
that when his own schooling was completed, he was " on
account of " his " well-known attainments and moral reputation," [100] " selected to teach school in one of the most Christian, moral and intelligent districts in all the region round."
Here, when he had entered by a few months into his eighteenth
year (1816), he was led during the progress of a revival, to
give his heart to God.[101] His conversion, as he describes it,
was as distinctively supernaturalistic as Finney's: " if not
miraculous, yet altogether supernatural," [102] is the somewhat

the Encyclopædias (" Appletons' Cyclopædia of American Biography," " Johnson's Universal Cyclopædia," " The New Schaff-Herzog Encyclopedia of Religious Knowledge ") uniformly give the date as 1800.

[98] For this turnpike and its significance see in O'Callaghan's " The Documentary History of the State of New York," ii. pp. 1142, 1165 ff. For the state
of things west of Utica in 1792, see p. 1131.

[99] " Out of Darkness into Light," p. 9.

[100] " Out of Darkness into Light," p. 28.

[101] P. 9.

[102] " Autobiography," p. 50.

odd phrase with which he describes it, drawing at the same
time a parallel between it and that of Colonel Gardiner, understood by him to be the result of a miraculous intervention.[103] He represents himself [104] as praying "that I might be
kept from ever returning to that state of alienation from Him
in which my life had been spent." And, "I had no sooner pronounced these words," he says, "than I was consciously encircled in 'the everlasting arms.'" This was a prayer for
"perseverance" and it seems to be implied that it was granted
and that a pledge was given him of its granting, in a tangible
response.[105] Whatever else may be said of this, it was not, any
more than Finney's, a conversion according to the Pelagianizing prescriptions of the "New Divinity."

For some months after his conversion, Mahan tells us,[106]
his "spiritual state was rather of a *negative* than *positive*
character"; by which he appears to mean that his thoughts
were rather on the privileges that his new relation to God
had brought him than on service. That, however, was soon
corrected; and he gave himself with diligence not only to prepare himself for the ministry but to improve his opportunities
to bring souls to Christ. In consequence, not only did he have
trophies to show, in the favorable situation in which he was
at the time, but having removed for his next winter's teaching
to a very ungodly neighborhood, he built up a church there
of from thirty to fifty members.[107] As years passed on, however, he lost the "inward peace and joy in God which the
first love had induced,"[108] and passed into a condition which

---

[103] "Autobiography," pp. 53–57.

[104] "Out of Darkness into Light," p. 13.

[105] On p. 28 however he seems to assign his attainment of assurance
of "perseverance" to a somewhat later, though apparently not greatly
later, date: "At length, I attained to a full assurance that I was, not only
then an accepted servant of Christ, but should have grace to continue such
even unto the end. In this assurance, I have done service for Christ up to
the present. Not a shadow of doubt rests upon my mind that I am His for
eternity." On this basis he rejects the "moment by moment" teaching of
most Higher Life teachers and declares that according to Scripture we are
"to exercise present faith" both for "present" and for "future sanctification."

[106] P. 18.   [107] P. 20.   [108] P. 90.

he speaks of as "twilight," and in which he continued for no less than eighteen years — in fact up to his discovery of "perfection" as the proper state of the Christian, at Oberlin, in 1836. "Twilight" is merely his name, accordingly, for the condition of the "ordinary Christian." He does not think of denying that this "dim twilight of a semi-faith" is a "genuine form of Christian experience," as genuine a form of it as "the sunlight" itself.[109] In both states alike he had sin, and understood that every deliberate sin committed deserved death. But the two states were characterized by different "*sentiments and expectations*" with reference to sin.[110] In the one he expected to sin: in the other he had no expectation of sinning. And, he adds,[111] "in each my experience fully accorded with my faith" — a sentence which contradictorily to the preceding statement, seems to assert the enjoyment in the later state of actual "perfection." It was "in the twilight" then that he lived out his life up to his great experience at Oberlin. He soon set his heart, however, on the ministry and began active preparation for it. There were two years of preparatory study; then four years at Hamilton College from which he was graduated in 1824; and then three years at Andover Seminary, from which he was graduated in 1827. Henry Davis was President of Hamilton College during his time; at Andover he came under the instruction of Leonard Woods and Moses Stuart — from the latter of whom he learned at least how to deal with the seventh chapter of Romans so that it would interpose no obstacle to his later theories. He paints the general conditions at Andover in almost as dark colors as John Humphrey Noyes does a few years later. He does not hint at any improprieties of conduct: "There was nothing morally impure about it." But he found no great spirituality: "Never was I in an atmosphere less morally and spiritually vitalising than that which encircled us during those three years."[112]

Leaving Andover, he became a candidate under the charge

---

[109] "Autobiography," p. 281; cf. "Out of Darkness into Light," p. 98.
[110] P. 284.
[111] P. 285.   [112] "Autobiography," p. 144.

of the Presbytery of Oneida, occupying himself meanwhile in " agencies and miscellaneous ministerial duties," as he puts it.[113] Soon, however, he found himself back in the West, and " commenced work in the city of Rochester, with the expectation of organising a new church there."[114] " Just as the organisation was being effected," however, he says, " I was suddenly stricken down by an attack of inflammatory rheumatism in both knees and ankles and my left wrist." He was taken to his father's house in Orangeville, (" where," says he, " my youth had been spent "); but even in his illness he could not be idle. He found the church there in a most deplorable state.[115] He caused himself to be carried to it Sunday after Sunday in a chair, and preached from the chair " for about three months." The result was a revival in which he had the happiness of seeing his own father brought to Christ. " Among the converts was my aged father. He had professed religion from my childhood, but was manifestly a total stranger to the grace of God."[116] When he was able to undertake regular work again, he became " pastor elect of the Congregational church in Pittsford, near Rochester,"[117] and duly appears in the Minutes of the General Assembly for 1830 as a member of the Presbytery of Rochester and pastor at Pittsford.[118] His tenure of this charge was, however, very brief. He had already

[113] P. 155.

[114] P. 167.

[115] This was probably in 1828. The church at Orangeville after a period of vacancy had enjoyed the service of a Stated Supply in 1826, and was vacant again in 1827 and 1828, obtaining a Stated Supply in 1829 (" Minutes of the General Assembly," volume for 1826–1829, pp. 63, 182, 284, 460).

[116] " Autobiography," p. 168.

[117] " Autobiography," p. 167. Pittsford, Monroe Co., N. Y., eight miles southeast of Rochester.

[118] His record in the " Minutes " runs thus: 1829 (his first appearance), licentiate of the Presbytery of Oneida; 1830, pastor at Pittsford, Presbytery of Rochester; 1831, W. C. Presbytery of Rochester; 1832, S. S. Sixth Church at Cincinnati; 1833, W. C. of the Presbytery of Cincinnati (the Sixth Church vacant); 1834, S. S. Sixth Church, to which are assigned 134 'members — the only statistics of the church's membership in the entries; 1835, Asa Mahan's name no longer appears, and Herman Norton is given as pastor of the Sixth Church.

left it in time to be reported to the General Assembly of 1831 as without charge; and by August, 1831 he had removed to Cincinnati to take the oversight of a new venture, called then the Sixth Presbyterian Church, but soon afterward to become the Vine Street Congregationalist Church. He "commenced labours" with this church, he tells us,[119] on "August 29th, 1831, and resigned May 1st, 1835" — serving it therefore somewhat less than four years. The church consisted at the beginning of only sixteen members [120] "who lived in the city and worshipped with us"; but towards the end of his stay with it, it was largely increased: seventy-two were added on examination in 1834, and in the course of eight months' time upwards of a hundred. Throughout the whole period of Mahan's stay with it, it worshiped in a hired hall, "and," he adds, "a very plain one" at that. He was never really settled over it as its pastor, and even his service to it as "stated supply" does not seem to have been uninterrupted.[121]

These details have been recited in order that the extent and nature of Mahan's ministerial experience before going to Oberlin in 1835 may be estimated. From his graduation at Andover in 1827 to his arrival at Oberlin some eight years had elapsed, but little more than half of these had been spent in the actual care of a church, and for barely a single year had he sustained the office of pastor. In determining the value of his experiences, such work as he did at Rochester in gathering together the nucleus of a church, and at Orangeville in leading a revival movement, must not be underestimated. Immediately on settling in Cincinnati, also, he was elected a Trustee and a member of the Prudential Board of Lane Seminary, and this brought him into active participation in the broader work of the church; and indeed thrust him at once into the focus of the most hotly debated national question of the day — that which concerned slavery. With it all it must be said,

[119] "Autobiography," p. 163.
[120] "Autobiography," p. 164.
[121] In the "Minutes" of 1833 Mahan is listed as without charge and the church as vacant.

however, that his ministerial experience had been exceedingly small and very narrow.

Meanwhile he had not maintained intact the faith in which he was bred. That was, he tells us — speaking of course from the New England point of view [122] — "'the straitest sect' of the Calvinistic faith." From the very beginning of his personal religious life, however, this hereditary Calvinism had begun to crumble. Of the imputation of Adam's sin,[123] he declares that "subsequently to my conversion, I never for a moment entertained that sentiment"; and he adds [124] that he "quite early" adopted the "universal atonement." [125] In a broader statement, he informs us that from the commencement of his ministry he "rejected the Old School and Hopkinsian theories, and adopted and became a zealous advocate of that of divine efficiency." Perhaps his drift had not gone much further than this when he went to Oberlin. His going to Oberlin marks, however, the beginning of a completer revolution in his faith, a revolution which he represents, in a statement which defines it by the widest limits, as carrying him "from the extreme bounds of Calvinism" — that is the way he expressed the faith in which he had been bred — "to the quite opposite pole of the evangelical faith" — which is his description of his ultimate point of view.[126] This ultimate point of view he describes again as "the antipodes of all the peculiarities of that [the Calvinistic] faith." [127] His mind here is chiefly on

[122] "Autobiography," p. 320.

[123] P. 199.

[124] P. 200.

[125] In later life he distinguished between *three* opinions on the extent of the Atonement, e.g. "Christian Perfection" (1844), pp. 126–127: — (1) *Limited* Atonement, "Christ died for a part only of the human race — the elect," (2) *General* Atonement, "Christ died for no individuals of our race in particular, but for all in general," (3) *Special* Atonement, "Christ . . . died for *every man in particular*" — so much for each that it might seem to him that it was for him alone that he died. It is the third that Mahan makes his own. But he modified it so as to escape universal salvation by saying that although Christ died for each, he avails only for those who accept him. We do not get the full flavor of this fervent individualism of Christ's death until we recall that the theory of atonement held is the Rectoral!

[126] "Autobiography," p. viii.   [127] P. 320.

the question of liberty and ability, and, accordingly, he expresses elsewhere the revolution in faith which he suffered as changing "fundamentally my life-long and fondly cherished beliefs, and" repudiating "utterly the doctrine of necessity, and" adopting "that of liberty." [128] What he means is that he rejected the whole conception of natural and moral inability and adopted in its stead a doctrine of plenary ability; [129] or, to put it more sharply, that he now took up with the notion that obligation is limited by ability, a notion which, he rightly says, compelled an entire reconstruction of his theology. [130] It seems to be clear enough that this fundamental step was already taken before going to Oberlin; so that he began his work there, like Finney and his other colleagues, as a zealous preacher of the "New Divinity." There is no reason to doubt therefore the accuracy of James H. Fairchild's representation, [131] that all the "founders" of Oberlin, including John J. Shipherd, and not only Finney, but Mahan and Morgan and Cowles, held to "New School views," in the sense that they insisted upon "the doctrine of human ability." "These men," he says, and obviously very truly, "were all earnest preachers of human ability, and of the personal, voluntary responsibility of the sinner for everything about him that can be reckoned as sin."

It is Fairchild also who reminds us [132] that the gathering of a body of such men as these in a place like Oberlin, necessarily concentrated the immense personal power which they represented, specifically on the cultivation of the spiritual life. Out in the wide world their energies had been intensely directed to the conversion of sinners: here, in this narrow sphere, where "there was only here and there a sinner to be converted," they were naturally diverted to the perfecting of the saints. Men were set to the intensive cultivation of their Christian life; and the preachers pressed upon them with all

[128] "Autobiography," p. 204.
[129] Pp. 203–204.
[130] P. 214.
[131] *The Congregational Quarterly*, April, 1876, p. 237.
[132] As cited, p. 238.

the insistence that had been employed in the whirlwind revivals from which they had come, the duties of examining
themselves whether they were in Christ and of immediate
completion of their entire consecration to His service. " It
was not a rare thing," says Fairchild, " for a large portion of
the congregation, after a searching sermon by Prof. Finney
or Pres. Mahan, to rise up in acknowledgment that they had
reason to apprehend that they were deceived as to their Christian character, and to express their determination not to rest
until their feet were established upon the Rock." It is almost
incredible that the preachers did not realize from the beginning that what they were demanding from their hearers
was sheer perfection; and that what they were preaching was
mere perfectionism. Perfection was men's duty, and all that
was duty was practicable — for obligation and ability are coextensive. But we must remember that these were somewhat
reckless men, who made it a virture not to count costs; and
who were accustomed to tear every passion to tatters and to
lash every dawning emotion into excesses with unmeasured
invective; pursuing their conceived ends without regard to
the inevitable consequences of the means employed. There is
no reason why we should not believe them when they tell us
that they were unaware that they were demanding perfection
of their hearers as an achievable duty, until their eyes were
opened to it by their hearers themselves. One of the odd circumstances connected with the situation was that Finney and
Mahan knew perfectly well what perfectionism was. They
had lived with it in Central and Western New York: their
companions in their evangelistic work there had preached it
in their presence: their followers had often rushed headlong
into it. They themselves had kept their skirts free from it;
partly, no doubt, because of their engrossment with the prior
matter of conversion; more, no doubt, because of the mystical
and antinomian form taken by " the New York Perfectionism," which was abhorrent to them as preachers of righteousness. But they could not help knowing that perfectionism lay
at their door; and yet they drove on, preaching an essential
perfectionism without, they say, being aware of it.

Perfectionism lay at their door even in the literal, physical sense. Oberlin was not so isolated as to be insensible to what was going on in Central and Western New York, or even in its own immediate neighborhood, in the Western Reserve of Ohio. Its settlers were recruited from the class in which "New York Perfectionism" was prevalent; and they did not shed their memories or break off their lines of communication when they came to Oberlin. The students of theology, to whom the appeals of the preachers were most frequently addressed, were themselves the products — Mahan says the best products — of "the Western Revivals," and could not fail to be familiar with their constant accompaniments. Even if we lacked direct evidence of contact, therefore, we could not assume that Oberlin Perfectionism arose wholly apart from connection with the wide-spread perfectionist movement which preceded it. In point of fact direct evidence is not lacking. We know that, in the quarters in which perfectionist tendencies first showed themselves at Oberlin, not only was the earlier movement known, but the Putney literature was read and an impulse derived from it to repeat the experiences described in it. It served, for instance, "to raise the question of obligation as to the degree of holiness which Christians might attain,"[133] in the summer of 1836 (the second session of the Theological Seminary), for a body of young men associated in a missionary society and earnestly engaged upon their spiritual culture in preparation for their prospective work. They rejected with decision the antinomian features of the teaching they found in this literature; but, under its influence, they advanced, along the lines of the "New Divinity" common to it and themselves, to a full conviction of the duty and possibility of completely putting away sin. A fervid consecration meeting was held by them, in which they solemnly bound themselves not to grieve their Master by any further sinning. "They left the meeting" — so one of their number records[134] — "feeling that they were pledged to a life of entire obedience, chiefly from the side of duty — the obliga-

[133] Fairchild, as cited, pp. 238–239.
[134] We are quoting from D. L. Leonard, "The Story of Oberlin," p. 238.

tion and the possibility of it." Very naturally, and very truly, a report went around that "the missionary society had all become Perfectionists." We gather that the step they had taken met, for the moment, with but imperfect — certainly not with universal — sympathy, although it was the only logical outcome of the searching preaching to which they were listening day by day. It was a straw, however, showing which way the wind was blowing; and by the time the session then in progress ended, the wind was blowing a gale.

The preaching itself was growing ever more fervid and insistent. Mahan represents himself as burdened in spirit over the low state of Christian living, and earnestly seeking light on the great problem of Christian attainment. One day, he visited one of his associates, and they together sought guidance in the Word. The conversation turned on the passage, "The love of Christ constraineth us." "While thus employed,"[135] he says, "my heart leaped up in ecstacy indescribable, with the exclamation, ' I have found it.' " What he had found was that Christ is all in all. All in all; for in Him is to be had not merely our justification, but also our sanctification: the one is as truly a gift of grace, as exclusively a work of God, as the other, and is to be had on the same condition.[136] " The highway of holiness was now, for the first time rendered perfectly distinct to my mind. . . "[137] We may perhaps express what he found in the two words, " Jesus only." In Him, he perceived, we obtain all we need; and we must go to Him for it all, and receive it all by a direct act of faith. He had known hitherto what to do when a sinner asked, What shall I do to be saved? He would say, Go to Christ in faith. But he had not known that precisely the same answer is to be given to the believer who wishes to be delivered from his low plane of living. He had been accustomed to instruct such "to confess his sins, put them away, renew his purpose of obedience, and go forward with a fixed resolution to do the

[135] " Christian Perfection " (1839), ed. 7, 1844, p. 185.
[136] " Autobiography," p. 324.
[137] " Christian Perfection," p. 187.

entire will of God." [138] He now saw that that was "a fundamental mistake." "We are not only to be 'justified by the
faith of Christ'; but to be sanctified also by 'the faith that is
in Him.'" We cannot be justified by faith, and be sanctified by
"resolves": you must "cease wholly from man and from yourself, and trust Christ universally." Along with this new light on
Christ as all in all, he now saw also the necessity of the work of
the Spirit. And he considers it remarkable that "the doctrine of
Christ as our 'wisdom, righteousness, sanctification and redemption,' and 'the promise of the Spirit,' as the great central
truths of the gospel," should have been presented to his mind
at one and the same time.[139] Of course, however, they necessarily go together because they are only two aspects of the
supernaturalness of salvation.

For exactly what happened to Mahan in this great experience — this experience which he always looked back upon
as pivotal for his life — was the rediscovery of the supernaturalness of salvation. In this aspect of it, it was a reaction
from the emphasis which, as a preacher of the " New Divinity,"
he had been placing on " ability," and a return to what he
calls " universal " dependence on the grace of Christ. He says
himself [140] that the teaching stands in contrast with his talk,
" in " his " ignorance," of " human ability to do all that is
required of us," and with the consequent trust he had put in
his " own resolutions." This seems a confession that in teaching
according to the formulas of the " New Divinity " he had
been walking in a Pelagian path: and, so far as there was now
a reaction from that bad way of thinking, he had turned his
face to the light, and ceasing from self-sufficiency had put
his dependence in God. This reaction, most commendable in
itself, was nevertheless, as actually experienced by him, at
once insufficient and excessive. He still reserved faith entirely
to man; he wished to exclude human effort only from the
walk in Christ. And like all Christians of his class he could

[138] " Out of Darkness into Light," p. 140.
[139] P. 147.
[140] P. 141.

not conceive of truly concursive activities. He operated with
an unconditioned either — or: either works or grace; either
effort or trust. As he had formerly allowed no place for faith
in sanctification, so now he did not wish to allow any place for
effort in sanctification. He seems not to be able to understand
that we must both " work and pray," as the popular maxim puts
it; both believe and labor; he wishes us to " cast all the responsibility " on Christ after a fashion which smacks more of
mysticism than the Gospel.[141] Meanwhile the reader is filled
with amazement that this discovery of the supernaturalness of
salvation should have seemed something new to Mahan. Bred
in "' the straitest sect' of Calvinism," did he have to wait for
this moment to learn that Christ is all in all; that in Him
we have by faith all that we can need; that He is made to us
sanctification as well as justification — yes, all that is included
in redemption?

Naturally this great discovery did not remain inoperative
in Mahan's life. In the act of so learning Christ, he so experienced Christ — and this constituted his " second conversion,"
in which he seemed to himself to rise into a higher plane of
Christian living, and passed, as he loves to express it, from
" twilight " into the full light of Christian experience. It is
interesting to observe, as he explicitly tells us, that when he
communicated his new experience to Finney, it found a ready
welcome with him, and was repeated in his experience. " When
my associate, then Professor Finney," he relates in one characteristic account,[142] " became aware of the great truth that by
being 'baptized with the Holy Ghost' we can 'be filled with
all the fulness of God,' he of course sought that baptism with
all his heart and with all his soul, and very soon obtained what
he sought." Finney also received therefore at this time " the

---

[141] In his " Autobiography," pp. 289 ff., he tells us that the great difference between the two points of view which had been successive in his
life turned on sanctification. In the one justification is held to be by faith,
while sanctification is by hard labor; in the other both justification and
sanctification are purely of faith, both are wrought by God alone and when
we claim either by faith — " our responsibility is at an end."

[142] " Out of Darkness into Light," p. 180.

second blessing "; and not Finney only; the doctrine, the experience, was contagious. Of course it was carried at once also into the preaching and gave it an added insistence, an increased ardor. These men and their preaching — whatever they or it had been before — now became definitely perfectionist, though that was not yet recognized. Mahan explains their position by the use of the contrasting adverbs " theoretically " and " practically." [143] They had become " practically " perfectionists, he says, but not yet "theoretically " so. By this he does not seem to mean here primarily that they had become perfect and did not yet know it — although it is not clear that that too does not lie in his meaning — but that they had adopted and were preaching perfectionist doctrine, but had not yet come to see clearly that this was what they had done. The way he expresses it at large is this: " The redemption of Christ was then presented to my mind as a full and perfect redemption. I felt that in Christ I was 'complete,' that in him every demand of my being was met, and perfectly met. In this light I presented him to others." But it was only " by subsequent reflection, however, that I became aware that the principles which I had practically adopted necessarily involved the doctrine of Christian perfection." We are not now concerned with the defects of Mahan's logical processes. The discovery of the supernaturalness of salvation does not involve exclusion of the consumption of time in the realization of all that is included in it. But we have now merely to note that this was not perceived; and accordingly what Mahan and his colleagues had come to believe and were now fervidly preaching was the possibility and duty of the immediate enjoyment of all that Christ had bought for His people, at least in the spiritual sphere, without remainder. That is perfectionism.

With the leaven of perfectionism already working among the students and preaching of this character proceeding with ever increasing insistence, the end might easily have been foreseen. During the autumn of 1836 a series of revival meet-

[143] *The American Biblical Repository,* October, 1840, pp. 425–426.

ings were held at Oberlin, by which the whole community, citizens and students, was profoundly moved. At most of these Mahan was the preacher; and at one of them, held just after the close of the academic session, he preached a powerful sermon, enforcing with great urgency the topic now always in his heart and on his lips, the duty of a higher consecration. A young man in the audience, just graduated from the theological department — Sereno Wright Streeter was his name [144] — rose and asked with solemn earnestness that his religious instructors, Finney and Mahan, would tell him plainly to what extent he might hope to be delivered from sinning; whether he could expect to receive really entire sanctification on faith. "When we look to Christ for sanctification," he asked,[145] "what degree of sanctification may we expect from Him? May we look to Him to be sanctified wholly, or not?" "I do not recollect that I was ever so shocked and confounded at any question before or since," says Mahan.[146] "I felt, for the moment, that the work of Christ among us would be marred, and the mass of minds around us rush into Perfectionism." An answer, definite and decided, could not be avoided; but it could be postponed — especially as the end of the session had arrived which brought with it the time for the scattering of both teachers and taught. No answer was attempted, therefore, at the moment, but a promise was given that the matter would be carefully canvassed and an answer returned in due season.

Thus the Oberlin teachers were compelled fairly to face the question of perfectionism. They gave themselves diligently to its solution. Finney was accustomed at this time to

[144] See "General Catalogue of Oberlin Seminary," 1898, *sub nom.* He was graduated with the first theological class that was graduated and ordained at Oberlin, October 10, 1836.

[145] Mahan, "Christian Perfection," p. 188. The exact form of the question is given differently in the various reports, but the substance always remains the same. Cf. Mahan's "Autobiography," p. 323; Fairchild, as cited, pp. 239–240; Wright, "Charles Grandison Finney," p. 204; Leonard, as cited, p. 239.

[146] "Christian Perfection," p. 188.

spend the winter — vacation-time at Oberlin — in New York, preaching in the "Broadway Tabernacle." On this occasion Mahan accompanied him. They explored the Scriptures together; and, says Mahan,[147] "after looking prayerfully at the testimony of Scripture, in respect to the provisions and promises of divine grace, we were constrained to admit, that but one answer to the above question could be given from the Bible; and the greatest wonder with me is, that I have been so long a 'master of Israel and have never before known these things.'" But they did not confine themselves to the appeal to Scripture. They sought guidance also from those who had been perfectionists before them. It was naturally on the Methodists that their glance was first cast and lingered longest — for were not the Methodists the type of evangelical perfectionists? Finney found their idea of sanctification unacceptable, because it seemed to him "to relate almost altogether to states of the sensibility," [148] and he elsewhere declares with decision that their notion that less is required of us under the Gospel than was required under the law is inadmissible. Nevertheless, he pronounced Wesley's "Plain Account of Christian Perfection" — the acquaintance of which he made at this time — though marred by some expressions (he thinks merely expressions) to which he should object, "an admirable book," which he wishes every member of his church would read.[149] By the side of Wesley's "Christian Perfection" he places the "Memoir of James Brainerd Taylor" — which he also wishes "every Christian would get" "and study." He had read the most of it he says, "three times within a few months." This same collocation of Wesley and Taylor meets us also incidentally in a passage of Mahan's: he speaks of "such men as John Wesley and James B. Taylor, who believed that by the grace of Christ applied to 'cleanse them from all sin,' they had 'been made perfect in love.'"

[147] "Christian Perfection," p. 189.
[148] "Memoirs," p. 340.
[149] "Lectures to Professing Christians," ed. 1880, pp. 358–359.

What is odd about this is that it was just these two books
which John Humphrey Noyes read in the autumn of 1834 —
two years earlier — when he was making his way also to
perfectionism. And Finney repeats the same gossip which
Noyes repeats, to the effect that Taylor's biographers had
suppressed the most perfectionistic passages in his letters.
We have seen that perfectionism did not show itself among
the students of Oberlin apart from influences derived from
the earlier perfectionism of New York, or apart specifically
from the teachings of J. H. Noyes. It was much more a matter
of course that Finney and Mahan did not arrive at their
perfectionism in ignorance of these prior movements. We are
scarcely prepared, however, for the emphasis which they
seem to place on their knowledge of them; or for what seems
very much like a tendency to apologize in part at least for
them. " I have read their publications," says Finney,[150] " and
have had much knowledge of them as individuals." He cannot give assent to "many of their views"; he repudiates
the imputation to him of their "peculiarities"; especially
he turns with reprobation from their " antinomianism." But
he adds at once that they are not all antinomians — " some
of their leading men " are not; and although " there are still
a number of important points of difference " between them
and the orthodox church, the points of agreement are very
numerous.[151] Similarly Mahan sees in all the perfectionist
movements of the recent past a divine preparation for what
was to come in them; and adopting them, along with the
Methodists, as their own, adds:[152] " Some outside the Methodist denomination had ' entered into rest ' before we did." It
is not merely misery that loves company; and the desire to
discover precedents is ordinarily strong enough to lead us
to take them where we can find them. It is meanwhile clear
enough that Finney's and Mahan's sense of solidarity with
perfectionists as such was strong. It was strongest, of course,

[150] P. 346.
[151] "Views of Sanctification," 1840, pp. 134 ff.
[152] "Out of Darkness into Light," 1888, p. 195.

with the Methodists, from whom they derived most — among other things the terms by which they expressed their new doctrine. " The *terms* by which we designated it," says Mahan,[153] "were those by which it had been presented since the times of Wesley and Fletcher, namely, Christian Perfection, Entire Sanctification, and Full Salvation." The *thing* expressed by these terms they would not admit they got from the Methodists. What they offered they got direct from the Scriptures — though this affirmation naturally can be overpressed. " I gave myself earnestly," says Finney,[154] " to search the Scriptures, and to read whatever came to hand upon the subject, until my mind was satisfied that an altogether higher and more stable form of Christian life was attainable, and was the privilege of all Christians. . . . I was satisfied that the doctrine of sanctification in this life, and entire sanctification, in the sense that it was the privilege of Christians to live without known sin, was a doctrine taught in the Bible, and that abundant means were provided for the securing of that attainment." The doctrine thus described as derived from the Scriptures has in any case somewhat close affinities with the Methodist doctrine.[155]

No sooner was the Oberlin doctrine of perfection conceived than it was published. Finney was the first to publish it. He was in New York during the winter months of 1836–1837 for the purpose of preaching in the " Broadway Tabernacle." Preoccupied with the subject of the Christian walk, he delivered to his congregation a series of " Lectures to Professing Christians," which were printed as they were delivered in *The New York Evangelist,* and soon afterward (1837) were

---

[153] " Autobiography," p. 367.

[154] " Memoirs," pp. 340–341.

[155] The Methodist books were very diligently read, not only the fundamental treatises of Wesley and Fletcher, but such biographies as those of Hester Ann Rogers and William Carvosso (cf. J. S. Fairchild, *The Congregational Quarterly,* April, 1876, p. 242); and the Methodist commentators — particularly Adam Clarke — were very much deferred to (cf. Finney, " Views of Sanctification "). Along with them the support of other perfectionists. like Robert Barclay, was welcomed.

gathered into a volume.[156] Two of these lectures were devoted
to the subject of " Christian Perfection." In this first exposition of Oberlin perfectionism there are naturally seen lying
in the background all the characteristic traits of Finney's
theological thinking. All virtue consists in disinterested benevolence; nothing is sinful but voluntary action; we have
no obligation beyond our ability — we can do all that we
ought to do, and what, for any reason whatever, we cannot
do, we no longer, in any sense whatever, ought to do: it is
such conceptions as these which form the substructure. On
this basis a perfectionism is developed which already bears
the fundamental character that ever afterwards marked the
Oberlin doctrine. What is taught is a perfection that consists
in complete righteousness, but in righteousness which is adjusted to fluctuating ability. Enoch Pond, in reviewing the
lectures, rejoices to find that the perfection taught — in
contrast with the Wesleyan doctrine of a so-called " evangelical
perfection " — requires the perfect fulfilment of the law of
God.[157] But, as W. E. Boardman — discriminating later the
" Oberlinian " from the Wesleyan doctrine — points out, what
is really distinctive of " Oberlinian " perfection is the " view
of the claims of the law as graduated to the sinner's ability." [158]
This teaching is already here. But the more fundamental idea
that perfection is the fulfilment of the law is more dwelt upon.
The lectures are thus given the aspect of insisting on perfect
righteousness, and point is given to this insistence by an open
polemic against the Wesleyan conception. " No part of the
obligation of the law is discharged," it is said: [159] " the Gospel
holds those who are under it to the same holiness as those
under the law." The definition of Christian Perfection is given
crisply as " perfect obedience to the law of God "; and this is
explained as requiring that " we should do neither more nor
less than the law of God prescribes." " This," it is added,[160] " is
being, morally, just as perfect as God."

[156] " Lectures to Professing Christians " (1837), Oberlin, 1880.
[157] *The American Biblical Repository*, January, 1839, pp. 44 ff.
[158] " The Higher Christian Life," 1859, p. 41.
[159] P. 342.   [160] P. 341.

When Finney undertakes to show that this perfection is attainable in this life, his argument runs on the familiar lines.[161] He pleads that God wills our perfection; that all the promises and prophecies of God respecting our sanctification have perfect sanctification in view; that this is the great blessing promised throughout the Bible; and the very object for which the Holy Spirit is given. Every one of these propositions is true; and none of them is to the point. The whole point at issue concerns the process by which the believer is made perfect; or perhaps we would better say, whether it is by a process that he is made perfect. Avoiding the hinge of the argument, Finney endeavors to impale his readers on dilemmas.[162] " If it is not a practicable duty to be perfectly holy in this world, then it will follow that the devil has so completely accomplished his design of corrupting mankind, that Jesus Christ is at fault, and has no way to sanctify His people but by taking them out of the world." " If perfect sanctification is not attainable in this world, it must be either from a want of motives in the Gospel, or a want of sufficient power in the Spirit of God." It would be a poor reader indeed who did not perceive at once that such dilemmas could be applied equally to every evil with which man is afflicted — disease, death, the uncompleted salvation of the world. If it is not a practicable thing.to be perfectly well in this world, then Jesus Christ has been vanquished by the Devil and has no way to make His people well except by taking them out of the world. If freedom from death is not attainable in this world, then it must be due to want of sufficient power in the Spirit of God. If the world does not become at once the pure Kingdom of God in which only righteousness dwells, then we must infer either a want of sufficient motives in the Gospel or a want of sufficient power in the Son of God. There have been people who reasoned thus: the point of interest now is, that it was not otherwise that Finney reasoned — and that accounts for many things besides his perfectionism. It is a simple matter of fact that the effects of redemption, in the individual and in the world at large, are realized, not all at once, but through a long

[161] Pp. 346 ff.   [162] P. 352.

process: and that their complete enjoyment lies only "at the end."

A certain lack of logical coherence is discernable in other features of these lectures also. Finney was too good a Pelagian readily to homologate Quietistic conceptions: it is not for the Pelagian to say, "Cast thy dreadful doing down": doing is with him rather the beginning, and middle, and end of all things. Yet we have already seen Mahan imbuing him with his newly-found notion (borrowed ultimately from the Wesleyans) that sanctification is to be attained immediately by an act of faith, and indeed also with his mystical Quietistic explanation of how this sanctification is brought about by faith. We noted at the time that it was interesting to observe this, and the interest seems to us to be enhanced when we observe the doctrine enunciated — so far as it is enunciated — in the context of these lectures. Finney the Pelagian denies that Christ in His Spirit can work on man otherwise than by bringing motives to action to bear on him — in a word by persuading him himself to act. Whatever man does, then, in the way of obeying the law — perfect obedience to which constitutes his perfection — he must himself do: it cannot be done for him or in him or through him by another; no other can affect him otherwise than by presenting motives to action to him. We should like to know then exactly what Finney means when he rebukes those who seek sanctification "by their own resolutions and works, their fastings and prayers, their endeavors and activity, instead of taking right hold of Christ by faith, for sanctification, as they do for justification." [163] What he says is that we may — must — attain to sanctification — or, as entire sanctification is meant, to perfection, that perfection which is perfect obedience to the law of God — immediately by an act of faith, without any resolution or effort on our part to obey the law, or apparently, any activity on our part in obeying it. "Faith," he says, "will bring Christ right into the soul, and fill it with the same spirit" — note the small s — "that breathes through Him-

[163] P. 362.

self." We greatly wonder how "faith" does all this, and note only that it is faith that does it, not Christ: Christ supplies only the model to which faith conforms us. For light on this dark question, however, we shall have to go elsewhere.

Finney's inconcinnity is not occasional merely but constant. Take another instance.[164] He is arguing that the power of habit need not inhibit perfection, since it does not inhibit conversion. The power of habit is a thing that may be overcome. As he argues this point, however, he raises in our minds a previous question — the question whether God can save at all. The answer he supplies is yes, sometimes; and sometimes, no — at least "consistently with his wisdom," a phrase which does not vacate but only locates His inability. Of man in his natural state we must recognize, he says, that "selfishness has the entire control of the mind, and . . . the habits of sin are wholly unbroken." And this condition of course presents an obstacle to salvation — an obstacle, he says, "so great, in all cases, that no power but that of the Holy Ghost can overcome it." It is indeed, he adds, "so great, in many instances, that God himself cannot consistently with his wisdom, use the means necessary to convert the soul." Men then, it seems, may be so set in their wickedness that no "power" — the term is misleading; God uses no power in the transaction except the power of persuasion — which God, being wise, is willing to use upon them will avail for their salvation. Finney says this is the actual case "in many instances." These men, clearly, then, are unsalvable. God, so long as he remains the wise God, cannot save men so sunk in sin. We have thus reached the astonishing conclusion that men may be too sinful to be saved. They are saved, or they are not saved, according to their determination in sin. Moderately sinful souls can be saved, very sinful souls are beyond the possibilities of salvation. This no doubt is good Pelagian doctrine: it is not Paul's doctrine or Christ's. We are surprised to find it here where Finney had started out to prove that evil habits cannot inhibit the attainment of per-

[164] P. 353.

fection, because they do not inhibit the attainment of conversion. We have ended by proving that " in many instances "
they can and do inhibit the attainment of conversion; and
that, whether we are converted or not does not depend therefore on God who in many cases is helpless in the face of our
sinfulness, but on the degree of our sinfulness.

In his " Lectures on Systematic Theology," [165] Finney makes
the following remarks concerning the lectures we have been
considering. " These lectures were soon spread before thousands
of readers. Whatever was thought of them, I heard not a word
of objection to the doctrine from any quarter. If any was
made, it did not, to my recollection, come to my knowledge."
He is often inexact in his historical statements; and perhaps
we should not wonder that he is inexact here too. In point of
fact the lectures received the normal attention of reviewers;
and it is difficult to believe that the strictures made on them
were not at the time brought to the author's attention. *The
Quarterly Christian Spectator,* the organ of Finney's own
party, gives them, it is true, only passing mention. But this
passing mention is not without its significance. Its object is
apparently to read Finney a lecture, as the *enfant terrible* of
the " New Divinity " party, and to serve notice on him that
he was expected to keep within the bounds and to content
himself with repeating the shibboleths appointed for him. " On
the subject of *Christian Perfection,"* we read,[166] " we think
Mr. Finney is not always sufficiently guarded, and though we
do not believe he means anything more than we should fully
admit — the possibility and duty of obedience to God in all
things commanded — yet we fear he may be liable to misconstruction and injure the consciences of many weak, but pious
persons." The note of irritation here is unmistakable: in the
sequence of obligation, ability, actualization, could not Finney,
like the rest of them, be satisfied with the first two without
pushing on inconsiderately to the third? So far then from
there having been no word of objection to the teaching of the

[165] Ed. 1, ii., 1847, p. 170; ed. 2, 1851, p. 571.
[166] *The Quarterly Christian Spectator,* June, 1837, p. 342.

lectures spoken from any quarter, they were objected to from all quarters. And, naturally, the reviewers "from the other side" did not content themselves with passing mention but subjected them to reasoned criticism. This was done, for example, by Joseph Ives Foot in a trenchant article in *The Literary and Theological Review*,[167] which was given the uncompromising title of "Influence of Pelagianism on the Theological Course of Rev. C. G. Finney, developed in his Sermons and Lectures." It was done also by Enoch Pond in a prudent article published in *The American Biblical Repository*.[168] And although it was not done in a subsequent article on current works on perfectionism published in the same journal by N. S. Folsom,[169] it was made plain that that was only because the writer considered that it had been already sufficiently done by Pond. Pond as a good New Englander goes so far with Finney that he is glad to allow "the attainableness" of perfection by the Christian, or, as he phrases it, "its metaphysical attainableness"; but like *The Quarterly Christian Spectator* he wishes to stop right there and deny that it is ever "attained actually." On the ground of the current New England doctrine, which postulated "natural ability" for all that can be required, the whole question reduced itself thus for him to one of mere fact, and he argues it on that understanding.

[167] March, 1838, pp. 38 ff. See particularly pp. 52 ff.
[168] January, 1839, pp. 44 ff.
[169] July, 1839, p. 143.

II. MAHAN'S TYPE OF TEACHING

WE have given more space to the earliest presentation of
the Oberlin doctrine of perfection than it intrinsically deserves.
This, partly, because it was its first presentation; but more
because, despite its brevity and the colloquial looseness of its
language, it was in more than a temporal sense the forerunner
of a whole group of others which shortly followed it. For
nearly two years, it is true, it stood alone. Then, at the close
of 1838, *The Oberlin Evangelist* was founded to be, above
everything else, the organ of the doctrine. And early in 1839
the book was published which has the best right of all to be
considered the representative statement of the Oberlin Doctrine at this stage of its development. This is Mahan's
" Christian Perfection." [170] The nucleus of this book was a sermon first preached in Oberlin and afterwards widely published
and especially printed by request in *The New York Evangelist*
(in November 1838).[171] The " series of discourses " of which
it professes to be further made up were delivered in the
Marlboro Chapel, Boston, where Mahan was supplying the
pulpit during the illness of the pastor.[172] The book ran through
many editions and enjoyed a very wide circulation.[173] During

[170] " Scripture Doctrine of Christian Perfection; With Other Kindred
Subjects, Illustrated and Confirmed in a Series of Discourses Designed to
Throw Light on the Way of Holiness," 1839. We cite it always from the
seventh edition, 1844, but the pagination of all editions after the first is the
same.

[171] On this sermon, see D. L. Leonard, " The Story of Oberlin," 1898,
p. 253: " In September (1838) President Mahan gave his famous perfection
address before the Oberlin Society of Inquiry, which was printed the next
month in the [*Ohio*] *Observer* (published at Hudson) filling ten columns,
and a month later still appeared in the first issue of *The Oberlin Evangelist*
[November, 1838], about the same time also in the leading eastern papers.
The Hudson " organ " invites its readers to peruse the same and send on
the results of their thinking. Which thing they do so abundantly that for a
long period well-nigh every number is redolent of reviews and refutations."
Hudson was the seat of the rival Western Reserve College.

[172] Compare N. S. Folsom, " Review of Mahan on Christian Perfection,"
in *The American Biblical Repository* for July, 1839, p. 143.

[173] The tenth edition was published in 1849. We have seen no later.

the same year Henry Cowles' little booklet on " The Holiness of Christians in the Present Life " was reprinted " with some revision " from *The Oberlin Evangelist;* and in 1840 the much more considerable volume by Finney, entitled " Views of Sanctification " was reproduced from the same journal. A pamphlet by Charles Fitch, pastor of the Free Presbyterian Church at Newark, New Jersey, bearing the same title as Finney's volume — " Views of Sanctification " — preceded that volume by a year (1839). It deserves to be included in this group of writings, because, although its author was not connected with Oberlin, he teaches the same doctrine as the Oberlin writers; and although he does this perhaps more attractively than they do themselves, he does it obviously in immediate dependence on them.[174] All this group of writings not only teach the same doctrine, but teach it after the same fashion, employing common definitions, a common logical method, the same supporting Scriptures, expounded on the same principles and applied with the same argumentative peculiarities; there has clearly been the closest collusion between them. Each writer has an individuality of his own, of course, and shows it in his use of the common material. But this does not abate the essential oneness of their conception

[174] Fitch's pamphlet was occasioned by an inquiry into his teaching instituted by his Presbytery, which resulted in asking him to withdraw from its fellowship (cf. Leonard, as cited, p. 256). Along with it should be cited: " An Appeal, together with a Brief Account of the Sentiments of Five Members of the Free Presbyterian Church of Newark, New Jersey, termed by their Opponents Modern Perfectionists," Newark, 1840 — although the perfectionism of the writers of this pamphlet is more of the New York variety. Fitch's pamphlet was answered by William R. Weeks: " A Letter to the Rev. Charles Fitch on his Views of Sanctification," 1840; and it is supposed to be included (along with Mahan's and Finney's writings) in the basis of Leonard Wood's discussion, " The Doctrine of Perfection " in the January and April numbers for 1841 of *The American Biblical Repository.* Fitch was the youngest son of Ebenezer Fitch, first President of Williams College, and there is a very brief notice of him in C. Durfee's " Williams Biographical Annals," 1871, p. 385. He was born in 1799; was graduated from Williams College in 1818; studied at Princeton Theological Seminary, 1818–1821. An outline of his life may be found in the " Princeton Thelogical Seminary Biographical Catalogue," 1909, p. 40. He appears to have been as extreme in his views on the Second Advent as in those on Sanctification.

and mode of presentation. They all obviously come from one
mint; and there seems good reason to believe that the dominant influence producing this uniformity was Mahan's. It
is only fair to speak of this phase of Oberlin Perfectionism, therefore, as the period of the ascendency of Mahan's
thought.

At this stage of its development, Oberlin Perfectionism
would not be inaptly described as Wesleyan Perfectionism
grafted on the stock of the New Divinity — Wesleyan Perfectionism so far modified as to adjust it to the paradigms
of the New Divinity. As the New Divinity was primarily
an ethical scheme and Wesleyan Perfectionism primarily a
religious doctrine, this process might be not unjustly described as so far a process of " religionizing " the New Divinity.
Mahan took the lead in this work. That was the significance
of his rediscovery of the supernaturalness of salvation as
already described; of his conjoint vision of Christ as the soul's
all in all and of the Spirit who baptizes the soul with power;
of his suspension of everything on the simple act of faith.
This was no ephemeral enthusiasm with him. It was a profound spiritual revolution which reversed all the currents of
his being and determined the course of his subsequent life.
From this time to the end of his life, a half a century later,
he knew nothing but the twin doctrines he acquired in this
moving religious experience — the doctrines of Christian Perfection and the Baptism of the Spirit; and he gave himself to
their exposition and propagation with an unwearied constancy
which his readers may be tempted sometimes to think wearisome persistency.[175] He infected his colleagues with these doctrines; but they never took the place in their theology which
they did in his. In the succeeding adjustments it became thus
his function to emphasize the new doctrines to the utmost;

[175] In his " Autobiography," 1882, p. 321, he says that for the forty-six
years preceding that date, the one theme of his life had been " the two great
doctrines " of Christian Perfection and the Baptism of the Holy Ghost. This
is only one of many such statements; and the fact asserted is absolutely true
— the " Autobiography " itself, for example, shows him to have been simply
possessed by these two ideas.

it was the function of Finney, say, on the other hand, to see that in the engrafting of the new doctrines on the stock of the New Divinity the concepts of the New Divinity suffered no loss. This brings about a certain difference in tone — not exactly in teaching — between the two writers. Mahan's "Christian Perfection" and Finney's "Views of Sanctification" teach the same general doctrine, and they teach it with the same clearness of conviction. But in the one the main interest has shifted from the New Divinity to Perfectionism — though the concepts of the New Divinity are not abandoned; in the other it remains with the New Divinity — though the concepts brought in by Perfectionism are welcomed. Perhaps it would be too much to say that the emphasis differs: what differs is not so much the emphasis as the concernment, and that seems to be rooted less in a difference in the convictions than in the temperament of the two writers.

The perfectionism of this stage of Oberlin Perfectionism, as we have said, is fundamentally Wesleyan. It was not merely the " terms " which were retained from the Wesleyan doctrine, as Mahan tells us; but so far the thing.[176] What was taught was the immediate attainment of entire sanctification by a special act of faith directed to this end. Justification was presupposed as already enjoyed. There were accordingly two kinds of Christians, a lower kind who had received only justification, and a higher kind who had received also sanctification. This is all Wesleyan, although, of course, it is not all that is

[176] Mahan finds it possible, therefore, when speaking in general terms, to describe his doctine in language derived from Wesley. When telling us in the opening discourse of his "Christian Perfection" (p. 13) what the thing is of which he is to speak he says: "It is, in the language of Mr. Wesley, 'In one view, purity of intention, dedicating all the life to God. It is the giving God all the heart; it is one desire and design ruling all our tempers. It is devoting, not a part, but all our soul, body, and substance to God. In another view, it is all the mind that was in Christ Jesus, enabling us to walk as He walked. It is the circumcision of the heart from all filthiness, from all inward as well as outward pollution. It is the renewal of the heart in the whole image of God, the full likeness of him that created it. In yet another, it is loving God with all our heart, and our neighbor as ourselves.'" This is the loose language of metaphor: but it indicates a conscious as well as real connection with Wesley.

Wesleyan.[177] When this doctrine was transferred into a New
Divinity setting, the primary effort was to adjust to the new
setting the conception of the content of the perfection thus
attained. The New Divinity was a Pelagian scheme; a scheme
of ethics; it was therefore essentially legalistic and could not
conceive of perfection otherwise than as perfect obedience to
law — the law of God. It could not homologate therefore the
Wesleyan idea of an "evangelical obedience," graciously accepted of believers in lieu of the "legal obedience" they were
not in a position to render. Of anything else, as constituting perfection, than complete obedience to the law of God, the Oberlin men would hear nothing. But they had their own way of
reaching the same relaxing result which the Wesleyans had
reached. They defined the content of the law, obedience to
which constitutes perfection, as just "love"; and although this
language meant with them something different from what it
meant with the Wesleyans, it is not clear that they were able
to give it any greater ethical content. Supposing them successful, however, in pouring into the concept of love, objectively,
the whole content of righteousness ideally viewed, they did not
in any case require this content for the love by which a man is
made perfect. To be perfect, he does not require to love as God
loves — in whose love all righteousness is embraced — or as
the angels love, or as Adam loved, or even as any better man
than he loves. He only requires to love as he himself, being
what he is, and in the condition in which he finds himself, can
love. If he loves all he can love in his present condition, he is

[177] Despite the dependence of the Oberlin doctrine of perfection on
the Wesleyans, the remarks of S. B. Canfield, "An Exposition of the Peculiarities, Difficulties and Tendencies of Oberlin Perfectionism," 1841, p. 83,
are perfectly just: — "The Wesleyan doctrine of 'Christian Perfection' is
not only different in itself from the Oberlin theory, but held in connection
with different views of native depravity — of the heart — of moral agency
— of the nature of sanctification. . . . Those Methodists who have been at
the pains to analyze the Oberlin system regard it as differing very widely
from their own. A writer in *The Christian Advocate and Journal* of June
19, (1840) after making various strictures upon the Oberlin theory, says:
'It is not the Arminian theory. It is Pelagian Perfectionism, and the truth
will suffer loss, if we permit the public to be misled by the supposition that
their theory and ours are the same.'"

perfect. No matter how he came into his present condition; suppose if you will that he came into it by a long course of vice, or by some supreme act of vice, it makes no difference. His obligation is limited by his ability; we cannot say, he ought to do more than he can do; if he does all he can do, he has no further obligation, he is perfect. The moral idiot — Finney does not hesitate to say it — is as perfect as God is: being a moral idiot, he has no moral obligation; when he has done nothing at all he has done all that he ought to do: he is perfect.[178] God Himself cannot do more than all He ought

[178] In a long note, pp. 12–16 of his "Lectures on Systematic Theology," Finney notes some grave objections which had been brought against his doctrine; among others this one, — that "the more ignorant and debilitated a person is, . . . the less the law would require of him"; so that he could extinguish his obligation by committing violence upon himself, and through his wickedness become perfectly holy — that is completely observant of all that is required of him. This assault does not lead Finney in any way to modify his doctrine; and indeed he could not modify it, seeing that it is a mere corollary of his fundamental doctrine of moral accountability. "God so completely levels his claims . . . to the present capacity of every human being, however young or old, however maimed, debilitated, or idiotic," he reiterates, "as, to use the language or sentiment of Prof. Hickok, of Auburn Seminary, uttered in my hearing, that 'if it were possible to conceive of a *moral pigmy*, the law requires of him nothing more, than to use whatever strength he has, in the service and for the glory of God'" (p. 14). It is quite clear that Finney is entangled here in some ambiguities. He very properly distinguishes between a fault and the effects of a fault. But there is a further ambiguity latent in the conception of "demoralization," which leads him astray. He treats the term as implying that "to demoralize" is to make *un*moral, not *im*moral: and so supposes that we cease to be moral agents in proportion as we become wicked. The source of his difficulty lies in his doctrine of "natural ability," which leads him to scale down obligation to fit decreasing ability. "If a man should annihilate himself," he asks, "would not he thereby set aside his moral obligation to obey God? . . . Should he make himself an idiot, would he not thereby *annihilate* his *moral agency?*" "The truth is," he answers himself, "that for the time being, a man may destroy his moral agency, by rendering himself a lunatic or an idiot; and while this lunacy or idiotcy continues, obedience to God is naturally impossible, and therefore not required" (p. 15). A moral agent cannot annihilate himself; neither can he annihilate his moral agency. He exists everlastingly and so long as he exists he is a moral agent, possessing a moral character and acting in accordance with it. If his moral character is bad, it inhibits good action, but does not in the least lessen obligation to it. If the wickedness becomes absolute the inhibition to good action becomes absolute; but the obligation to good remains absolute also. When J. L. Wilson said in the course of Lyman

to do; and when He has done all He ought to do, He is no
more perfect than the moral idiot is — although what He has
done is to fulfil all that is ideally righteous and the moral
idiot has done nothing.

In this conception the law of God, complete obedience to
which is perfection, is made a sliding scale.[179] It is not that
perfect rule, which as the Greeks say, like a straight-edge,
straight itself, measures both the straight and the crooked;
but a flexible line which follows the inequalities of the surface
on which it is laid, not molding it, but molded by it. Obligation here is interpreted in terms of ability with the result that
each man becomes a law to himself, creating his own law;
while the objective law of God, the standard of holiness in
all, is annulled, and there are as many laws, as many standards
of holiness, as there are moral beings. To object on this basis
to the Wesleyan doctrine of "evangelical obedience" on the
ground that it supposes a relaxation of the universal obligation of the law, is fatuous. There is no such thing as a universal
obligation of the law to be relaxed; or indeed as a universal
law, binding on all alike, to create a universal obligation. Each

---

Beecher's trial that "moral obligation does not require any ability whatever,"
the phraseology may be open to objection, but the thing intended is true. The
fact is that Finney and his fellows did not believe in moral agents; they
believed in moral volitions.

[179] George Duffield (Finney, "Lectures on Systematic Theology," p. 979)
tellingly arraigns Finney's teaching "that moral law requires nothing more
than honesty of intention," and "that sincerity or honesty of intention is moral
perfection" (so Finney explicitly, pp. 138, 295). "By this rule," says Duffield,
Finney's teaching "graduates the claims of the law of God, so as to make
it a most convenient sliding scale, which adapts itself to the ignorance and
weakness of men. It utterly perverts men's notions of that high and absolute
perfection which the law demands, and makes moral perfection a variant
quantity, changing continually, not only in different persons, but in the same
individual. It reasons as follows, namely: Moral law respects intention only.
Honesty of intention, or sincerity, is moral perfection. But light, or knowledge
of the ultimate end, is the condition of moral obligation. Consequently, the
degree of obligation must be just equal to the mind's honest estimate of the
value of the end! Thus, to love God with all the heart, soul, mind, and
strength, means nothing more than 'that the thoughts shall be expended in
exact accordance with the mind's honest judgment of what is at every
moment the best economy for God.'"

man's obligation is exhausted in the law which his own ability creates for him; and as soon as the Wesleyans remind us that in their view " evangelical obedience " is accepted primarily because it alone is within the capacity of men to render — " legal obedience " being beyond their power — the Oberlin objector is dumb; that is just his own doctrine. Except for this — that, not content with this general adjustment of the requirements of the law to the moral capacity of sinful men, he pushes the principle to such an extreme as to adjust them in detail to the moral capacity of each individual sinner, all the way down to moral idiocy; with the effect of making our sin the excuse for our sin, until we may cease to be sinners altogether by simply becoming sinful enough. Of course he does not really believe this. If he had really believed it, we should not have found Finney troubling to argue — as we have found him arguing [180] — that the ingrained habit of evil need not inhibit the attainment of perfection — that would be a matter of course; or that men may become so wicked that they cannot be saved — that would be absurd. He would only have needed to point out that the acquisition of unconquerable habits of evil, by progressively destroying obligation, renders perfection ever easier of acquisition by constantly reducing the content of the perfection to be acquired; and that one of the surest roads to salvation is therefore to become incurably wicked.

One of the most striking features of these earlier presentations of the Oberlin doctrine — though not of them only — is the strenuousness with which they insist that they are not arguing for the " actual attainment " of " entire sanctification," " perfection," but only for its " attainability." An unpleasant impression is sometimes produced that an attempt is being made to escape from the real question at issue by a logical trick. The contention made this impression on its New England critics, and called out from them, from that point of view, somewhat sharp words of rebuke. Nobody, they say, doubts the attainability of perfection; the only question in

[180] " Lectures to Professing Christians," p. 353.

dispute is whether it is ever attained. We have already seen
this position taken up by Enoch Pond in criticising Finney's
" Lectures to Professing Christians." " The question between
us," he says,[181] " is simply one of *fact*. The perfectionist asserts,
not only that Christians *ought* to be perfect in the present life,
but that they often *are* so; — not only that perfection is metaphysically attainable, but that, in frequent instances, it is
actually attained." N. S. Folsom, in reviewing Mahan's " Christian Perfection " goes so far as to express a sense of outrage at
the impression, created by his mode of stating the question,
that none but the Oberlin men believe in " the attainableness
of entire sanctification in this life." This doctrine, he asserts,
is, on the contrary, admitted on all hands. The editor of *The
New York Evangelist* in remarking on Mahan's primary perfectionist sermon, when it was first printed in that journal,
allows it; Enoch Pond has just expressed his agreement with
it. At the basis of every exhortation to be holy, lies " the
metaphysical truth that perfection in holiness is attainable."
To give the impression that anybody doubts this, is not to
argue fairly; it is to play the sophist.[182] Leonard Woods, in his
comprehensive discussion of the Oberlin arguments up to the
date of his writing, echoes this protest.[183] He and his friends,
he declares, hold as decidedly as Mahan does — he takes Mahan as his example — " that, in the common acceptation of
the term, complete holiness is *attainable* in the present life."
" When we assert that a thing is *attainable*, or *may* be attained," he explains, " our meaning is, that a proper use of
means will secure it; that we shall obtain it, if we do what
we ought; and that, if we fail of obtaining it, truth will require us to say we *might* have obtained it, and that our failure
was owing altogether to our own fault." There surely is not included in the assertion of the attainableness of anything the
assertion that we have done all we ought and therefore have
actually attained it; attainability and actual attainment are

---

[181] *The American Biblical Repository,* January, 1839, p. 47.

[182] *Ibid.,* July, 1839, p. 144.

[183] *Ibid.,* January, 1841, pp. 174 ff.

different things and the proof of the one has no tendency
to prove the other. Whatever was the purpose of the
Oberlin men, then, in their insistence that they were contending not for the actual attainment but only for the attainability of perfection, it actually had the controversial value
to them that it threw their New England opponents into
confusion.

The ultimate ground of this confusion cannot, however,
be laid at the door of the manner in which the Oberlin men
preferred to frame their argument. It lay in the ambiguities
of the New England doctrine of "natural ability." Accordingly
W. D. Snodgrass [184] very properly criticizes Woods' use of
language in representing perfection as "attainable," only
never "attained." This language is founded on the current
New England distinction between "natural" and "moral"
ability; and is intended to assert that we are commanded to
be perfect, that full provision for our perfection is made, that
it is our duty to be perfect, and that there is no reason why
we are not perfect except that we will not strive to be perfect
with the energy requisite to attain it. This is supposed to be
justly expressed by saying that perfection is attainable, but
will never actually be attained. Perhaps the words may bear
that sense. It is not their natural sense. Snodgrass very justly
says that to say that perfection is attainable is just to say that
it is practicable for us to be perfect; and yet those who employ
this language fully recognize that it is not practicable for us
to be perfect. Say that nothing but a "will not" stands in the
way. This "will not" is a fixed, an unvarying, incorrigible
"will not." It is really a "can not"; and a perfection to which
we cannot attain is not an attainable perfection. He might
have added that Woods himself knew perfectly well that the
"will not" affirmed in the case is really a "can not." [185] If he
denies a "natural inability," he confesses a "moral inability,"
an inability which "results from moral causes"; and he is

[184] "The Scripture Doctrine of Sanctification Stated, and Defended
against the Error of Perfectionism," 1841, pp. 30 ff.
[185] *The American Biblical Repository,* October, 1840, pp. 474 ff.

unable to deny that this is a real inability.[186] God, he himself says, with the emphasis of italics, *"cannot* lie" (p. 475); "the unrenewed sinner *cannot* call forth the affection of love to God, and so be subject to his law" (p. 477). Assuredly he is right, then, in saying that there is an important sense in which men "cannot obey" God (p. 478); and if he contends at the same time that there is also an important sense in which they *can* obey God, we will not fail to observe that he is compelled to allow that their moral inability to obey "prevents obedience as certainly and effectually as a *natural impossibility* could" (p. 482). In these circumstances it would seem to be eminently misleading to speak of things as attainable, on the ground of "natural ability," the attainment of which is inhibited by "moral inability."

Let us remind ourselves moreover that the matters which fall under discussion here are of the order of what the Bible calls "things of the Spirit," things which are not to be had at all except as imparted by the Holy Ghost; and that it is therefore peculiarly infelicitous to speak of them as "attainable," merely on the ground of "natural ability." In so speaking of them, we seem gravely in danger of forgetting the dreadful

[186] The situation among the parties dividing theological thought in New England is vividly brought before us in a letter of Lyman Beecher's to N. W. Taylor of April 25, 1835, printed in Beecher's "Autobiography" (ii. p. 344). The New Divinity represented by Beecher and Taylor (as by Finney and Mahan) denied all inability, and all "physical" operation of God, and confined the divine operation in man to suasion: the older school (Woods, Tyler, Nettleton) drew back and in one way or another affirmed these things. Beecher declares that what lay "at the foundation of revolt in Woods, and Tyler and Nettleton" was "the doctrine of a physical execution of God's decrees and of physical regeneration — in short, of moral government by direct omnipotence." This, he says, tends to go back to the "natural inability of Old Calvinism in the Emmons and Burton form." On the other hand he deprecates preaching free-agency in a form which "avails to save by its own actual sufficiency, without the Holy Ghost." The Holy Ghost is to be necessary but is permitted to act only suasively, inducing men to save themselves by a free agency quite capable of doing all the saving, if only it can be persuaded to do it. Man is naughty and requires correction — not reconstruction of nature, but correction of manners; he is perfectly able to behave properly if he will; it is inducements alone that he needs. This in a nutshell is the whole New Divinity System.

evil of sin as the corruption of our whole nature, and the absolute need of the Spirit's free action in recovering us from
this corruption. The unregenerate man cannot believe; the
regenerate man cannot be perfect; because these things are
not the proper product of their efforts in any case but are conferred by the Spirit, and by the Spirit alone. It is good to see
Mahan in some degree recognizing this fundamental fact; and
indeed founding one branch of his argument upon it. It is not
enough, however, to say that perfection is attainable only
"through the Spirit." Mahan says that, and then goes on to
give it the Pelagianizing turn that the believer nevertheless
"attains" perfection, by employing the Spirit to do this work
for him. The Scriptures do not thus subordinate the Spirit's
action to that of man; they do not think of the gifts of the
Spirit as "attained," but as "conferred." Snodgrass is incapable of such a *bêtise* and rightly emphasizes the supernatural nature of sanctification, as of regeneration, and of salvation
at large. We do not sanctify ourselves by our own power;
we do not even sanctify ourselves by using the Spirit as the
instrument by which alone we can accomplish this great result.
It is God who sanctifies us; and our activities are consequent
at every step on His, not His on ours. Though he fails to rise
to the height of the Scriptural supernaturalness of sanctification, however, Mahan's reference of it to the Holy Spirit, acting at the behest of man, nevertheless recognizes the supernaturalness of the actual process of the sanctifying work; and
enables us to see what he and (so far as they shared his views)
his colleagues meant when they spoke of the attainableness of
perfection. They were not thinking in terms of "natural ability"; they were prepared to assert that the so-called "natural
ability" of the New England divines is no ability at all. They
were not arguing for a "metaphysical attainability" of perfection; they were talking religion, not metaphysics. They were
clear, to be sure, that any perfection which should ever be
achieved by any man must be achieved through his "natural
ability," that is to say through the action of those powers
which belong to him as a moral being and are inseparable

from him as a moral agent; but they were equally clear that
no man of himself would ever employ those powers with the
energy, and diligence and singleness of purpose requisite to
reach the high goal of perfection, and that therefore actual
perfection is the product of the Spirit of God. They had no interest in affirming and arguing the "attainability" of perfection in the sense in which their New England critics took the
phrase. They were as free as those critics were to declare that
that "attainability" did not infer attainment, and was a barren notion unillustrated by a single case of attainment under
it. What they were interested in affirming was that God in
His grace had made provision in the Gospel of His Son and the
baptism of the Spirit to transmute that natural "will not"
which, despite the so-called "natural ability" results in every
child of man in a real "can not," into a glorious "can." What
they were concerned to assert was a real practicable "attainability" due to the provisions of God's grace which placed
within the reach of every believer at his option an actualized
perfection. And the establishment of this attainability rightly
seemed to them a much greater fact than the establishment of
the actual attainment of perfection by these or those. They
did not fail to assert this actual attainment of perfection. Perhaps the establishment of the attainability of perfection would
have been difficult had there been no "samples" to adduce.
But they sought to keep the evidence for actual attainment
in the subordinate position of an additional argument for its
attainability. If it has been actually attained, it will be hard
to deny that it is attainable.

There is a noticeable difference among the several Oberlin
writers in the relative interest they show in the different elements which enter into their common teaching. Finney, to
whom the New Divinity was the Gospel, dwelt proportionately
more fully on the conception of "natural ability," which constituted the basis on which any and all holiness must be built.
Mahan, who had come to see the Gospel in the supernaturalness
of salvation, naturally threw the stress of his discussion on it.
Henry Cowles writes with such brevity as to discourage seek-

ing to ascertain the niceties of his particular way of looking at the common doctrine. It is perhaps enough to note that he states it with some sharpness of outline. The vital question to which he addresses himself, he declares to be, not "whether any mere man on earth has ever attained absolute and confirmed perfection," but "has God given us such moral powers and made such provisions in Providence and Grace for our aid, that real death to sin, victory over the world, and living by faith in constant obedience to all the known will of God, are *objects of rational effort, the duty and privilege of every Christian.*" [187] There are many loose ends left in this statement and the matter is not bettered when a little later,[188] repeating it, he proceeds to reduce the notion of perfection which he is ready to affirm to be attainable. It is no heavenly perfection, but an earthly one, including "such service and obedience as man is able to render in the present state." On this purely relative holiness he lays the greatest stress, and brings his discussion to a close, accordingly, by remarking [189] that his object in writing is to express his full conviction that "God has made provision for the attainment in the present life of all the holiness which he requires, and which the present state admits." That says so little that it practically says nothing at all. God has only made provision for the attainment of this holiness: He does not secure its attainment — that is left to us. And the holiness attainable is only what "the present state admits of." That might be said of the devils in hell. The only point of interest is, not whether we may attain "all the holiness our present state admits of" — that might be no holiness at all. It is whether we may be *holy*.

To these propositions little more than hinted at by Cowles, Finney gives the definiteness of dogmatic statement. When he comes, in his "Views of Sanctification," to the point where he discusses the attainableness of "entire sanctification," [190] he

---

[187] "Holiness of Christians in the Present Life," 1840, p. 8.
[188] Pp. 14 ff.
[189] P. 86.
[190] Pp. 59 ff.

lays down the fundamental proposition "that entire and permanent sanctification is attainable in this life." This he at once pronounces "self-evident" — on the ground of "natural ability." "To deny this," he affirms, "is to deny that a man is able to do as well as he can." And, he declares, "the very language of the law" bears out the assertion, because, in requiring us to love the Lord our God with all *our* heart, and the rest, it levels "its claims to the capacity of the subject, however great or small." If there were a moral pigmy, he would be required to love God up to his pigmy strength. If we morally mutilate ourselves, we may no doubt be answerable for doing it; but having thus reduced our powers, we would have lessened our responsibility to the law, and could be entirely sanctified on this lower ground. "An angel is bound to exercise an angel's strength; a man, the strength of a man; and a child, the strength of a child." "Now," he sums up, "as entire sanctification consists in perfect obedience to the law of God, and as the law requires nothing more than the right use of whatever strength we have; it is of course forever settled that a state of entire and permanent sanctification is attainable in this life on the ground of natural ability." This he says is New School doctrine and necessary New School doctrine. Ability limits obligation, hence there is no obligation where there is no ability — hence (it is but an identical proposition) it is possible for every man to do all that is required of him (not all that may be required of another man); and that is to be perfect. After all this exploitation of "natural ability," however, Finney turns and says that we have on this line of reasoning arrived at only an abstract possibility. Whether this abstract possibility is ever realized in fact, must be the subject of further inquiry. A second proposition is therefore laid down.[191] It is this: "The provisions of grace are such as to render its actual attainment [entire and permanent sanctification] in this life the object of reasonable pursuit." This proposition he transmutes into the question, "Is this state attainable as a matter of fact before death; and if so, when,

[191] P. 61.

in this life, may we expect to attain it?" — and submits the
inquiry to the arbitrament of the Scriptures. Thus even Finney
suspends the actual attainment of entire sanctification on
grace, not nature; and seeks the evidence for it therefore in
Scripture.

The vigor with which the Oberlin men asserted that they
were primarily interested in the attainability, not in the actual
attainment, of perfection, not only led to misunderstanding,
but sometimes, it must be acknowledged, has an odd appearance in itself. To the man in the street the affirmation of the attainability of perfection seems to derive all its value from the
promise it holds out for its actual attainment. And it is very
clear that the Oberlin men were not contending for the barren
attainability of the New Divinity, unillustrated by examples
of attainment and indeed incapable of being so illustrated.
Theirs is an attainability, they said, which can be realized in
fact; and which, they affirmed, had been, is, and will be realized
in numerous cases in fact. What they affirmed was, not that we
must posit merely an inoperative attainability in order to
ground accountability for the universal non-attainment of perfection; but that we must assert an operative attainability
which realizes itself constantly in attainment. They have
advanced here beyond the New Divinity; and they have it
chiefly at heart to validate their difference from it, which becomes the main matter at issue precisely because it carries
with it the affirmation of attainment as its corollary. The
Oberlin men thought themselves to have laid their hands on
a factor in the problem, which, as they said, had been neglected by the New Divinity, and which, in their view, transformed the barren "attainability" which served no other
purpose than to ground accountability, into an operative
"attainability" of possible and ready accomplishment.

This new factor was nothing less than the factor of grace.
The New Divinity, they said, operated with "natural ability"
only; and, as obligation is, as it taught, limited by ability, was
bound to affirm that the perfection required of man is "attainable" by him; otherwise he would not be obligated by it, and

would be perfect, that is, all that he could be required to be, without it. But this " attainability " is only the postulate of accountability and affirms only that man could be perfect if he would, leaving the undoubted fact that he will not untouched — and in strict logic this will not ought to be expressed in terms of can not. In point of fact, man, standing in the conditions in which he finds himself, with an ingrained disposition to evil governing his conduct, can not be perfect, despite all the underlying " natural ability " to be perfect which can be ascribed to him. You may prefer to say that this " cannot " is only a " certainly will not," but this choice of soft words to express it does not alter the hard fact.

Now, the Oberlin men were altogether willing to say that *this* attainability never passes into attainment. This was not the attainability for which they were contending and which they looked upon as the issue at stake. Mahan says plainly enough, one would think,[192] that " our natural ability . . . may exist in all its fulness, with the absolute certainty that no attainments at all in holiness will be made." " This is in fact," he adds, " true of all fallen spirits, and with all mankind in the absence of the influence of the grace of the gospel." There is, he says, another kind of " attainability," however, over and above that grounded in " natural ability," and that is what they are contending for, and the appearance of logomachy given to their reasoning by their opponents rests on neglect to note this fact. They are contending for a real, concrete, and not merely a theoretical, abstract attainability; not common to all men, but peculiar to those under " the influence of the gospel." The opponents of the Oberlin teaching have uniformly assumed that there were but two parts to the question brought into debate. Is perfect holiness attainable? Is it actually attained? As both parties agreed in an affirmative answer to the first question, they declared the only issue concerned the second. Stop, said the Oberlin men; the first question is ambiguous and hides in it two separate ones, on one of which we are agreed and on the other not. And the question

---

[192] *The American Biblical Repository*, October, 1840, p. 410.

hidden in it, on which we are not agreed, is the crux of the whole matter. What do you mean by saying that perfect holiness is attainable? Do you mean that we have "natural ability" to obtain it if we will — though most certainly we will not? Or do you mean that perfection has now in the gospel been brought by the grace of God within our practicable reach, and relying on that grace we may in the power of Christ through His Spirit actually attain it? There are in point of fact, says Mahan at this place,[193] three, not two questions raised: " 1. What is the natural ability of men? or, have men natural ability to yield perfect obedience to the commands of God? . . . 2. Are we authorized, in view of the provisions and promises of divine grace, together with the other teachings of inspiration, to expect to attain to a state of perfect holiness in this life? 3. Do the Scriptures teach us that any *have attained,* or *will attain* to a state of entire sanctification in this life? " The opponents of the Oberlin doctrine, he now adds, overlook entirely the second question, "in respect to which we are at issue."

It is precisely on this second question, however, that the Oberlin men lay the whole stress of the argument, says Mahan. " Every thing is said as a means to one end — the determination of the great question, To what degree of holiness do the Scriptures authorize us to *expect* to attain in this life? That which is practicable to us on the ground of our natural ability, is in one sense attainable. That which is rendered practicable, not on the ground of natural ability, but by the provisions of divine grace, is attainable in a different and higher sense of the term. It is in this last sense, that the term is used by me." The reaction here from the Pelagianizing conceptions which ruled the New Divinity we have already called attention to, but it is good to dwell on it. An appeal is made from nature to grace.[194] An attempt is made to ground a doctrine of per-

193 Pp. 410–411.
194 Leonard Woods, *The American Biblical Repository,* January, 1841, p. 170, says: "I am glad to see, that, as Mr. Mahan has come to entertain more exalted views of the gracious provisions of the gospel for the sanctification of believers, he has ceased to give such prominence, as he formerly

fection in the great fact that grace overcomes the disabilities
of nature, and to point to the sufficiency in Christ for what
" natural ability " cannot do. Thus the debate is carried away
from the natural powers of men, to the provisions of the gospel, and becomes at once a purely Biblical one. Do the Scriptures represent God in Christ as providing for the immediate
sanctification of his people? That becomes the sole question of
real interest, and as such the Oberlin men treat it. It would be
inexplicable, of course, if such provision has been made, that it
should be illustrated by no single example. It becomes important therefore to show that there have been, are and will be
perfect saints in this world. But this takes the secondary place
of illustration and verification.[195] The main matter remains

---

did, to the ability, or free-will, of man, and has expressly renounced it, as
furnishing any ground of hope for sinners, or any spring of holiness to
Christians, and has been brought to rely wholly on the grace of Christ, and
to look to him for the whole of salvation." There is overstatement here.
Mahan renounced human free will only as the *immediate* ground of hope
and source of holiness in the Christian. He retained it as the *ultimate* ground
of our hope and source of our holiness; for he suspended the action of the
Spirit on our faith, not our faith on the action of the Spirit. He remained
fundamentally therefore Pelagian.

[195] They betray a tendency indeed to underestimate its importance.
They do, it is true, argue at length that many have been perfect — Paul, John,
Isaiah, and perhaps, on the basis of Rev. xiv. 3–5, 144,000 and certainly an
indefinite number of souls of the Old and New Covenants (Mahan, " Christian
Perfection," pp. 37 ff.; Finney, " Lectures on Systematic Theology," 1851, chapter lxi.). But Mahan explains that the Oberlin people did not concern themselves
so much with " mere personal attainments " (the " mere " should be noted)
as with the " revealed privileges of the sons of God." " The question, what
attainments we have made," he explains (" Out of Darkness into Light," p. 357)
" lies wholly between our consciences and our God. The question, what are
our revealed privileges, is to be settled, not by an appeal to the conscious or
visible attainments of any individual or class of individuals, but wholly and
exclusively by reference ' to the law and to the testimony.' " Though arguing
that many had been wholly sanctified, Finney did not in 1837 (" Lectures to
Professing Christians," p. 358) claim to be himself wholly sanctified: " I do
not myself profess now to have attained perfect sanctification." In 1840 (" Views
of Sanctification," p. 9) he even seems to deprecate anyone making such a
profession, though apparently only on the ground that such a profession
would be sure to be misunderstood. " Nothing is more clear than that in
the present vague unsettled views of the church upon this question, no individual could set up a claim to having attained this state without being a

the witness of Scripture to the gracious purpose of God. And the whole matter being thus referred to the Scriptures, the Oberlin men adduce the provisions made in the Gospel for the attainment of perfection, the promises of perfection given to Christians, the commands to them to be perfect, the prayers for their perfection which are recorded, and the like — a very impressive showing, which beyond question proves what Mahan, indeed, declares it is solely intended to prove — that Christians are to seek after perfection "with the expectation of obtaining it." The mistake that Mahan makes lies in his supposing that this means that perfection may be attained by any Christian, at any time, all at once; that it lies at the disposal of Christians, to be had for the taking; and not rather that it may be and is attainable only through so long a curriculum of preparation that a lifetime may well be none too long for its accomplishment. We are to seek it with the expectation of attaining it; he that seeks it will certainly find it; but the attainment is a great task — and it delays its coming. The attainment of perfection in other words, is not an act but a work: and this is the real point of difference between the parties to the debate — whether the perfection which is provided for, promised, commanded, urged to, is a gift received all at once, or an attainment acquired through a long-continued effort. That it is supernatural, not natural, in its origin and nature was a great discovery for the Oberlin men to make in the Pelagianizing atmosphere in which they were immersed. But its supernatural origin and nature do not in the least prejudice the question whether it comes all at once or only as the final crown of a life of "working out our salvation in fear and trembling." We are brought here, however, to perceive the important part played in the early Oberlin scheme by the doctrines of "Sanctification by faith," and the "Baptism of the Holy Ghost."

It appears that the whole body of the Oberlin teachers of

---

stumbling block to the church." In a later section he says that he would be in danger of being a stumbling block to himself. Is perfection then a gift both difficult to verify and perilous to possess?

perfection were entirely at one, from the start, in declaring
that sanctification is by faith. Time was required, however,
to bring them into even measurable harmony in their conceptions of how faith brings about this sanctification which is to
be had only "by" it. Finney himself seems inclined at first
to represent faith as the immediate producing cause of sanctification. No doubt his fundamentally Pelagian type of thinking was peculiarly embarrassing to him when he came to deal
with a thing like faith, which, in its very nature, looks outward from self and seeks something from another. Even in his
early teaching faith is the indispensable condition, he would
say, of the "reception of Christ," "the eternal life," "the holiness of the soul." But at this early stage of his teaching this language seems merely the repetition of a shibboleth. There
seems no particular reason why "Christ" should be "received," and certainly no reason why "the holiness of the
soul" should wait for His "reception." For faith, according to
Finney, is itself a holy exercise, both in kind and degree all the
confidence of the heart, working by love, that God does or
can require. That is to say, like all other holy exercises, it is a
perfectly holy exercise; and, as there is nothing about us,
morally considered, but our exercises, in exercising faith we are
perfectly holy. We are already therefore perfectly holy before
Christ is received, who is nevertheless designated "the holiness of the soul." And as S. B. Canfield [196] pertinently asks, if
we may previously to the reception of "the holiness of the
soul," put forth one holy exercise, and that one perfectly holy,
why may we not put forth two, or three, or ten thousand?
If we may enter into perfection without Christ, why may we
not abide in it without Christ? The fact seems to be that
Finney's fundamentally Pelagian mode of thinking, already
run to seed in his doctrine of "the simplicity of moral action,"
— the origin of which it is customary (apparently erroneously)
to date in 1841 — has betrayed him here into a conception of
man which makes him sufficient for himself, and leaves no

[196] "An Exposition of the Peculiarities, Difficulties and Tendencies of
Oberlin Perfectionism," p. 45.

need for either Christ or the Holy Spirit to make him perfect. The doctrines of Christ and the Holy Spirit appear thus as only ornamental superstructures to the system. How he employs them as such may be illustrated by a remark like this: "Faith would instantly sanctify your heart, sanctify all your doings, and render them, in Christ Jesus, acceptable to God." [197] What is the effect of the insertion of the words " in Christ Jesus?" If our heart and all our doings are already sanctified, are they not already acceptable to God? " They are," remarks Canfield,[198] " (by the supposition) as free from *moral defilement* . . . as Christ's own 'doings.'" Since faith "instantly" sanctifies our heart and all our doings, *ex opere operato*, what place is left for the sanctifying Christ? The instantaneousness of the sanctifying action of faith, is much insisted on and should not be passed by unmarked.[199] If you will only believe, says Finney, " this will at once bring you into entire sanctification." [200] The exercise of faith is manifested holiness; holiness is not a subsequent result flowing from faith — it and faith are the same thing. " Let it be distinctly noted, then," Canfield comments,[201] " that according to the principles of ' Oberlin Perfectionism,' entire sanctification is *conditioned* on *previous* perfection. To *become* sinlessly perfect, you must go to the Saviour *already perfect*." It cannot even be said that, though we make ourselves perfect, we must depend on Christ to keep us perfect. He does not, according to " Oberlin Perfectionism," keep us perfect — we may fall. And if we continue perfect that is because we preserve our faith: permanent en-

[197] Quoted by Canfield, p. 45, from *The Oberlin Evangelist,* i. p. 19. This seems to carry the notion back to 1839.

[198] P. 45.

[199] In "Views of Sanctification," 1840, pp. 168 f., Finney says: "Full faith in the word and promise of God, naturally, and certainly, and immediately produces a state of entire sanctification." " This result is instantaneous on the exercise of faith, and in this sense sanctification is an instantaneous work." " The sense in which I use the term entire sanctification," he says in this context, " includes all that is implied in perfect obedience to the law of God." Immediately on exercising faith we have kept the whole law of God.

[200] Cf. also *The Oberlin Evangelist,* ii. p. 57, referred to by Canfield, p. 46.

[201] P. 47.

tire sanctification is conditioned on permanent faith, just as
simple entire sanctification is conditioned on simple faith. We
must keep ourselves perfect as a condition of Christ's keeping
us perfect. "Permanent, entire sanctification is *conditioned*
(according to this view) *on itself*! You shall be perfect as long
as you shall continue to be perfect." [202]

Approaching the subject in another passage from a different angle — in the midst of a long description (there are
thirty-five numbered affirmations) of what entire sanctification is not [203] — Finney tells us that "entire sanctification does
not imply the same degree of faith" in everybody. It does not,
for example, imply the same degree of faith in us, sinners,
"that might have been exercised but for our ignorance and
past sin." It requires a lower degree of faith to make a sinner
perfectly holy than is required to make a saint perfectly holy:
and the worse sinners we are the lower is the degree of faith
that is required to make us perfectly holy. It does not resolve
this paradox to observe that Finney is obviously confusing here
the degree of faith exercised, and the amount of knowledge
which is possessed of the object on which faith rests. What he
really means to say, however, is that the less knowledge we
have of God and divine things, the less faith is required of us
that we may be perfect. The proposition on which he relies for
support runs: "We cannot believe any thing about God of
which we have no evidence or knowledge," and therefore, "entire sanctification implies . . . nothing more than the heart's
faith or confidence in all the truth that is perceived by the
intellect." The deflecting influence here is derived from his doctrine that as obligation is limited by ability, he who does all
he can (being what he is) is as perfect as God Himself. On this
ground he declares that: "Perfection in a heathen would imply
much less faith than in a christian. Perfection in an adult would
imply much more and greater faith than in an infant. And
perfection in an angel would imply much greater faith than in
a man, just in proportion as he knows more of God than man."
Our attention is attracted for the moment by the suggestion

[202] Canfield, p. 48.   [203] "Views of Sanctification," p. 29.

that perfection is conceivable in a heathen. This is not a slip. Finney fully means it. " The heathen," he explains, " are not under obligation to believe in Christ, and thousands of other things of which they have no knowledge." Not being under obligation to believe in Christ, of course they can be perfect without believing in Him. If they have " heart's faith or confidence in all the truth that is perceived by their intellect," they will not be kept from being perfect by lack of faith in Christ of whom they have no knowledge. Perfection clearly is not conceived as the product of Christ in the heart and life of him who believes in Him. It is not Christ but faith that makes us perfect, and it apparently does not much matter what the object is on which the faith rests. The faith of a fetich-worshipper (provided it embraces all he knows) is as efficacious to produce perfection in him as the faith of a John or a Paul. We see how loosely Finney sits to the fundamental proposition for which, under Mahan's influence, he argues, that the effective attainability of perfection is a gift of God in the provisions of the gospel.

All this leaves us quite in the dark as to how faith sanctifies us. That faith sanctifies us wholly, and that instantaneously on our exercising it, quite independently of what we believe, whether much or little (so only it be all we know), we are told with some emphasis. But we are not told how faith does this extraordinary thing. Henry Cowles offers himself to us for this time of need.[204] He has a chapter on " the Bible doctrine concerning faith as a means of holiness," in which he describes in a very attractive way the sufficiency and richness of the provision in Christ for the believer's sanctification. But he does not deal with the matter exhaustively, and what he omits is unfortunately the gist of the matter. He does not tell us that it is by faith that we are united with Christ, and, having received forgiveness of sin and a title to eternal life, are granted the Holy Spirit as a power within us, not ourselves, making for righteousness. He deals in his next chapter with the work of the Spirit as Sanctifier; and does not

[204] " Holiness of Christians in the Present Life," 1840, pp. 39 ff., 90 ff.

there mention the reception of Him as a result of our faith.
But though he does not give an exhaustive account of the
part played by faith in our sanctification, what he does say
is true and important, and errs only by defect — although it is
by a great defect. There is a two-fold function ascribed to
faith in our sanctification. Through it we obtain true and
vivid views of what Jesus is — and are sanctified "by the
influence of his character contemplated." And by it we turn
to Him for His "aid in the divine life," and so take "the attitude of suppliants, and recipients at his feet, and he does
sustain us." If the concluding clause here seems to promise
relief from the bald Pelagianizing of the rest, we are the more
disappointed to discover that promise unfulfilled in a later
passage. We *walk* by faith, we there read; we *live* by faith;
and " 'the life which I now live in the flesh, I live,' not by
self-moved holy impulses, but 'by the faith of the Son of
God who loved me and gave himself for me.' " The unnecessary opposition of "self-moved holy impulses," and "faith"
may seem to point to a mystical doctrine of the indwelling
Christ superseding our activities. But no — Cowles explains
thus: "My belief that the Son of God did thus love me, and
give himself for me, works love in my soul, and constrains
me to live to him who thus lived and even died for me." There
is nothing supernatural about it, then, at all. "Christ lives in
me by faith," means only that a belief in Christ lives in me;
and it is not Christ but this belief which is the dynamic of my
activities. Accordingly Cowles proceeds at once to say that
what Paul teaches is that "Christ lived within him," "*in this
sense,* viz.: his belief of certain great truths in respect to
Christ, through the Spirit impressing those truths upon his
heart [we wish we knew how he supposes the Spirit to do
this!], constrains him to live wholly for Christ." "Love of
Christ, produced through the Spirit [how?] by believing these
things, now reigns in his soul, and controls his life." Has not
the phrase, "through the Spirit" an awkward appearance
here? Somehow, we know not how, it was in some way,
we know not in what way, "through the Spirit," that the

love of Christ was produced "by believing these things";
and this love which we have to Christ constrains us to
follow after Him. Pelagius himself could scarcely have said
less.

That some such ideas as these were present to the mind
of Finney also seems to be implied in a passage in the "Lectures on Systematic Theology." [205] His fundamental contention," he says, "are by faith alone " — meaning that both are
attained by faith alone." "Both justification and sanctification," he says, "are by faith alone " — meaning that both are
surely enjoyed by the believer, but that each is attained by
an act of faith of its own. He is no longer prepared to assert,
however, that the faith by which sanctification is attained is
itself the immediately producing cause of sanctification. On
the contrary he proceeds to guard against that notion. "But
let me by no means be understood," he writes, "as teaching
sanctification by faith, as distinct from and opposed to sanctification by the Holy Spirit, or Spirit of Christ, or which is the
same thing, by Christ our sanctification, living and reigning
in the heart." Again and with even more precision of statement: " Faith is rather the instrument or condition, than the
efficient agent that induces a state of present and permanent
sanctification. Faith simply receives Christ, as king, to live
and reign in the soul. It is Christ, in the exercise of his different offices, and appropriated in his different relations to the
wants of the soul, by faith, who secures our sanctification."
This assertion is the direct contradiction of what we have formerly seen Finney affirming. In the former affirmations, faith
was the immediately producing cause of our sanctification.
In this it only entrusts the production of our sanctification to
Christ, and Christ Himself undertakes and carries through
the work of our sanctification. How He does it is explained
in the following words: " This he does by Divine discoveries
to the soul of his Divine perfections and fulness. The condition of these discoveries is faith and obedience." Our sanctification, secured by faith and obedience, is wrought by Christ,

[205] Ed. of 1851, pp. 635 ff. The passage occurs also in the first edition, 1847.

whose offices in working it are the precise thing that we secure by faith and obedience.

We ought not to neglect to notice the intrusion of the words " and obedience " into this statement. It is unexpected — and unauthorized. We had just been told that " the state of sanctification is attained by faith alone." We are now told that it is secured by " faith and obedience." We had just heard faith alone designated the " condition " of our sanctification. We now hear that its " condition " is " faith and obedience." And we are a little puzzled to understand how obedience can be the condition of obedience — for sanctification in Finney's definition of it is nothing but obedience. We are again very near to saying: We can become holy by becoming holy. All this, however, by the way. The main affirmation here is that the way in which Christ, who it is that sanctifies us, sanctifies us is — by making discoveries to the soul of His divine perfections and fulness. The real efficient agent of our sanctification is then no more Christ than faith; one is as little the " condition or instrument " of it as the other: the immediate, effective cause of our sanctification is the vision of the glory of Christ granted the soul. We are told, it is true, that Christ lives and reigns in the souls of those who receive Him by faith, and, living and reigning in them, exercises His different offices there: but nothing is meant beyond His making Himself known to these souls in His glory, and in His relations to the soul's varied wants. And nothing happens until the soul, moved by this great vision into action, sanctifies itself. Christ does nothing to it except make Himself known to it. We are sanctified by revelation, not by renewal: Christ brings instruction, not power. The efficiency of the inducement here particularly intimated is now argued [206] on the ground that man, as sinner, is the victim of a one-sided development of his sensibilities. He is lob-sided. All he needs is that the spiritual world should be revealed and made real to him. This can be done only by the Holy Spirit who takes the things of Christ and shows them to us. What we need in order

[206] Pp. 636 ff.

to become entirely sanctified may be summed up in three
things. We must have "natural ability" to do the whole will
of God — and that we all have. We must have sufficient
knowledge to reveal to us our whole duty — and that also
we all have, because nothing is duty until we know it as such.
But we must have also "sufficient knowledge or light," "to
reveal to us clearly the way or means of overcoming any and
every difficulty or temptation that lies in our way." This "is
proffered to us upon condition that we receive the Holy Spirit,
who offers himself as an indwelling light and guide, and who
is received by simple faith." Our sanctification is here conditioned on faith in the Holy Spirit and is wrought by Him as
"light and guide" — we need only to have the way pointed
out, we are quite competent of ourselves to walk in it. There
is a long list of the functions of the Holy Spirit as "light and
guide": nothing is intimated but various forms of "knowledge."

There is an appearance at a little later point,[207] it is true,
that something more may be acknowledged. "The Holy Spirit
sanctifies us," we are here told, "only by revealing Christ to
us as our sanctification. He does not speak of himself, but
takes of the things of Christ and shows them to us." It is Christ
who is our real Sanctifier, or rather our Sanctification. And
Finney proceeds now to magnify Him in this office. He does not,
to be sure, admit that Christ "does something to the soul
that enables it to stand and persevere in holiness in its own
strength"; "He does not change the structure of the soul." [208]
This language is only Finney's customary way of denying that
Christ does what He Himself says He does — make the tree
good that the fruit may be good. In point of fact Christ does
precisely what is intended to be denied here. He does do something to the soul that enables it to stand and persevere in
holiness in its own strength —though not all at once. The
sanctified Christian will do holiness in his own strength in the
same sense that a holy angel does — or that the sun attracts
the earth in its own strength, or that it is with its own sweet-

[207] P. 644.   [208] P. 643.

ness that honey is sweet. But sanctified Christians in this full
sense do not exist on earth; and no creature of God is independent of Him, in whom we all live and move and have our
being. What Finney means is to reject altogether all "physical" sanctification; although "physical sanctification" is of
course all the sanctification that is real sanctification. Permit
him, however, to repudiate that, and he seems willing to go
pretty far — if we can speak of anything as far which falls
short of that. Christ, he says, "watches over" the soul — but
that is sufficiently external. He also, however, he says, "works
in it to will and to do continually" — and now we begin to take
notice. This is less, to be sure, than that transforming of the
soul's ethical character which the Scriptures ascribe to Him;
but it appears at least to imply control. It seems to ascribe to
Christ not merely a plying of the soul with motives, but a
determining of its action under these motives. And when we
read: "He rules in and reigns over the soul," "in so high a
sense, that he, as it were, develops his own holiness in us," —
we are almost ready to rejoice with trembling. We do not quite
know what the words "develops his own holiness in us" are
intended to mean; as indeed Finney himself did not, as the
qualifying "as it were" seems to imply. The words may bear
the perfectly good sense that Christ produces in us a holiness
just like His own. They may become, however, a rather crass
mystical suggestion, as if Christ transferred His holiness to us
or shared it with us. And there is other mystical language employed in the context. We read that He "swallows us up, . . .
enfolds, if I may so say, our wills and our souls in his." What
is it to have not only our wills but our very souls "swallowed
up," "enfolded" in Christ's? Our souls swallowed up in His
soul, enfolded in His soul! This language, however, is not only
qualified by the inserted "if I may so say," suggesting that
it is not really meant, but is incorporated into a sentence which
wholly empties it of the meaning that it might seem naturally
to carry. What is said is, that Christ "*as it were* swallows us
up, so enfolds, *if I may so say,* our wills and our souls in his,
that we are willingly led captive by him." (The italics are

ours.) We drop at once from the mystical heights, and discover that all that is intended is that "we will and do as he
wills within us" — that is, obey Him. And having started to
drop, we drop still lower when we read the next sentence,
which reduces again the working in us to will and to do to a
mere matter of inducement: "He charms the will into a universal bending to his will." Control has become only a "charming." And now comes the end: "He becomes our sanctification
only in so far forth as we are revealed to ourselves, and he
revealed to us, and as we receive him and put him on." "What!
has it come to this!" — we borrow this exclamation from
Finney with our apologies — that after all the apparent promise of a real sanctifying operation in us — after all the even
mystical language employed to describe it — we have nothing
left in our hands but "revelation"? Christ reveals us to ourselves and Himself to us; and then, we, induced by this revelation, "receive him," and "put him on." What Christ gives is
revelation; we do the rest.

Despite all this elaborate relegation of the whole sanctifying work to ourselves, Finney continues strenuously to insist
that sanctification is by faith alone; as truly so as justification. His meaning apparently is that the "revelation" under
the inducement of which we sanctify ourselves, is secured
by faith, so that ultimately it is through faith that we are
sanctified. He is willing to allow accordingly one difference
between the relation of justification and sanctification respectively to their procuring acts of faith. Both are "brought
about by grace through faith"; but "it is true, indeed, that
in our justification our own agency is not concerned, while
in our sanctification it is." [209] This somewhat notable admission of the part played by our own activities in the process
of sanctification, need not be, but is, a recognition of sanctification as self-wrought. It affirms therefore a very great difference in the relations of justification and sanctification to their
respective procuring acts of faith. In the one case faith
secures from God a decree of justification. In the other faith

[209] "Lectures on Systematic Theology," Ed. of 1851, p. 745.

secures from God only inducements under which we sanctify ourselves. Meanwhile Finney speaks now and again in very misleading language of the relation of sanctification to works "of law." Whatever is said to an inquirer, he says on one occasion,[210] " that does not clearly convey the truth, that both justification and sanctification are by faith, without works of law, is law, and not gospel." There can, of course, be no such thing as sanctification "without works of law." In Finney's own phrase, sanctification is just " obedience, for the time being, to the moral law." How can " obedience to law " take place " without works of law "? Justification can be " without works of law " because justification is not law-keeping on our own part, but acceptance of us as righteous by God: and when it is said to be without " works of law," what is meant is that the ground of our acceptance as righteous is found not in our own obedience to the law, but in that of another rested on by us in faith. When, on the other hand, it is said that sanctification is by faith "without works of law," — that, to speak frankly, is mere nonsense. The phrase might have meaning if what was intended were that, as sanctification is an issue of justification, and justification is by faith without works of law, we obtain our sanctification ultimately by faith " without works of law." That is true; but what we obtain in sanctification is just " works of law " — for sanctification is, as Finney rightly tells us, obedience to the moral law. This obedience to the moral law, now, cannot possibly be, in any case, the immediate effect of faith. We do not obey by faith, but by works. Faith by its very nature, rests on something outside of ourselves; obedience is the product of something which works within us. Another's righteousness can form the basis of our pardon; another's righteousness cannot form the content of our holiness. Another can supply the ground of our acceptance with God: another cannot supply our personal conformity to the requirements of the law. We may entrust our sanctification to another, just as we entrust our justification to another. We do. But the effect is wrought differently in

[210] P. 631.

the two cases: in the one case without us and in the other within us. And unless we are willing to admit that Christ works in us, conforming us to the law, we cannot speak of sanctification as by faith: and even in that case we cannot speak of it as "without works of law." It is not secured by "works of law," but it consists of "works of law," apart from which it does not exist.

Into this closed circle of Pelagian conceptions Mahan breaks with his assertion of the supernaturalness of salvation. It is as an assertion of the supernaturalness of the whole of salvation, that he understands the declaration that our sanctification as well as our justification is by faith, by faith alone. Faith, in its very nature, is a commitment, an entrusting to another; and its results must be brought about therefore by the action of this other. Sanctification by faith is thus only another way of saying sanctification by Christ through His Spirit, on whom it is that faith rests. This is the precise contradictory of sanctification by our own activities, and it is only paltering in a double sense, according to Mahan, to explain that Christ, through His Spirit, sanctifies us, by presenting the motives to sanctification to us so strongly as to call out our self-activities effectively to that end. The motives which induce us to commit our sanctification to Christ would induce us to sanctify ourselves if that were possible to us under the mere influence of motives: in point of fact they do induce us to sanctify ourselves, in the only way in which we can sanctify ourselves, namely by committing our sanctification to Christ. The committal of our sanctification to Christ in faith is a confession that we cannot sanctify ourselves; and the prescription of this method of sanctification by the Scriptures is their testimony that we cannot sanctify ourselves. The main facts in the case accordingly are that we are incapable of sanctifying ourselves, and that it is precisely because we are incapable of sanctifying ourselves that sanctification is by faith, that is to say, by Christ in response to the commitment of it to Him. Here we have the foundation of Mahan's reasoning. Some of the corollaries which he draws from it are, that because this sanctification is wrought by Christ alone, it may be and is immediate, instantaneous and complete. His perfectionism is thus distinctively a supernatural perfectionism. Christ's people may be perfect, precisely because it is Christ the Lord who makes them perfect, and not they themselves.

There are some passages in Mahan's "Christian Perfection" which seem to imply that Christ's sanctifying work [211] is conceived by him as accomplished simultaneously with the act of justification and in response to the same exercise of faith by which justification is obtained. In one of these,[212] he represents it as "the grand mistake, into which the great mass of Christians appear to have fallen, in respect to the gospel of Christ," that they expect "to obtain *justification*, and not, at the same time, and to the same extent, *sanctification*, by faith in Christ." Attention is naturally attracted, first of all to the phrase "to the same extent" — a mode of speech repeated elsewhere, as, for instance in the sentence: [213] "If Christ should justify, and not to the same extent sanctify his people, he would save them *in*, and not *from* their sins." It seems at first sight to be implied that justification like sanctification is a progressive work, and that the two proceed *pari passu*, and therefore always coexist in the same measure: we are always sanctified just so far as we are justified and cannot be justified beyond the measure in which we are sanctified.[214] Closer scrutiny makes it clear, however, that

---

[211] Both Mahan and Finney sometimes use the word "work" of sanctification in contrast with "act," used of justification, apparently out of mere reminiscence of this distinction of usage in the Shorter Catechism, but not reproducing that distinction. They mean by "work" to distinguish sanctification as a production, from justification which is only an action. Cf. e.g. Mahan, "Autobiography," pp. 292–293.

[212] P. 100.

[213] P. 21.

[214] Canfield as cited, pp. 52 ff., does not fail to put his finger on the passages in Mahan's "Scripture Doctrine of Christian Perfection" (pp. 27, 123 of ed. of 1839), in which he insists that Christ must sanctify His people "to the same extent" that He justifies them. He rightly points out that it is absurd to speak of a gradual or incomplete justification. He expounds Mahan's teaching,

this is not Mahan's meaning. He is not insisting that justification must be as progressive as sanctification; but, just the contrary, that sanctification must be as instantaneously complete as justification. He means to say that it is absurd to suppose that we are completely justified all at once — as we certainly are — and not to suppose that we are completely sanctified at the same time: and it is as wicked as it is absurd, since then we should be asserting that we are saved *in* and not *from* our sins. This, however, is all the more strongly to assert the absolute coetaneousness of justification and sanctification in its completeness; and compels us not only to give its full validity to the phrase " at the same time," but to throw a strong emphasis upon it. Justification and sanctification in its completeness are thus affirmed in the most uncompromising way to take place together.

It is of course true that it is by one and the same act of faith that we receive Christ both as our justification and as our sanctification, and that we cannot have Him as the one without having Him as the other: we cannot take Him in one of his offices as our Mediator, and reject Him in another. Had that been Mahan's assertion he would have been only repeating an elementary teaching of the universal Reformed faith. When he asserts, however, that by this single act of faith we not only obtain both justification and sanctification, but obtain them both at once in their utmost completeness, he asserts more than either the Reformed faith or his own better judgment permits. On the ground here taken, if the believer be not perfectly sanctified from the very moment of his justification, that is, of his believing, he is, in the sense here conveyed, saved *in* his sin. If he has a single sin remaining, and that the tiniest that a sin can be and yet remain a sin — he is saved *in* his sin. What is really declared then is

---

however, as that " *complete* justification and *entire* sanctification are *simultaneous* — that justification is not *complete,* until sanctification is *entire,*" — and that no one can be an heir of eternal life unless he is entirely sanctified. Only the perfectly sanctified can say: There is, therefore, now no condemnation.

that every believer is perfect, in the sense that he is freed from all sin from the moment of his believing. That carries with it the consequence that no one is a believer — that no one is justified — that no one is saved in any sense, to whom there clings a single, even the tiniest sin. Christ's salvation is *from* sin and never *in* sin. Now Mahan does not in the least believe that. He is only for the moment caught in the meshes of his own chop-logic, and is reasoning on a submerged premise, assumed not only without but against proof — that sanctification takes place all at once and occupies no time. If sanctification occupies time, then it does not follow that because sins still occur in a Christian's life, he is not in Him who saves *from* sin and not *in* sin; it follows only that his salvation *from* sin is not yet completed. At the moment Mahan is commenting on Rom. viii. 3, 4 — " that the righteousness of the law might be fulfilled in us." " To have this righteousness fulfilled in us," he comments, " implies, that it be *perfectly accomplished in us,* or, that we are brought into *perfect conformity to the moral rectitude required by the law.* This is declared to be one of the great objects of Christ's death." Nothing truer could be said. But then he adds: " Such conformity, then, is practicable to the Christian, or Christ failed to accomplish one of the prime purposes of his redemption." And at once the submerged premise confuses the reasoning and vitiates the conclusion. Both too little and too much is said. It is too little to say that perfect conformity to the moral rectitude required by the law is practicable to the Christian. It is assured to him. He not only may have it; he certainly will have it. There is no question of Christ's failing to accomplish this prime purpose of His redemption. It will be accomplished. But too much is said when it is implied that the Christian can enjoy this prime purpose of redemption, in its absolute completeness, at any moment he wishes, without regard to its nature, or the method — the laws if you will — of its conference. This is a blessing in the conference of which time is consumed; and it is not to be had without the expenditure of time-consuming effort. To suggest that the Christian is warranted in concluding that Christ has failed to accomplish one of the prime purposes of His redemption, if he finds himself *not yet* in possession of this blessing in its fullest extent, is a sad piece of reasoning. To intimate that we may have all that Christ has purchased for us, in all its fulness, all at once, at the moment of believing, is not merely to confound all human experience, but to go beyond what Mahan has found it possible to believe himself. For after all, Mahan does not believe what he here asserts — that all who believe in Christ are immediately in that act of faith both perfectly justified and perfectly sanctified.

One indication that he does not believe it may be found in passages, lying side by side with those just quoted, in which he develops a conception of the relation of faith to the blessings obtained by it, which is quite incongruous to what he here asserts. In one of these [215] he is discussing the difference between perfect and imperfect faith. This he finds not in a difference in the degree of confidence the two exhibit — as if trust and distrust were mixed in them in different proportions — but in the breadth of their reference. " In consequence of ignorance of the perfect fulness of Christ's redemption in all respects," we may be found reposing " confidence in one, and not in every feature of Christ's character as a Savior." Our confidence in Him may be full confidence, from the intensive point of view, but far from full from the extensive point of view. We entrust to Him utterly what we entrust to Him, but we do not entrust to Him all we ought to entrust to Him. The illustration given is precisely this: " The mind . . . may repose full confidence in Christ as a *justifying*, but not as a *sanctifying* Savior." We may then receive justification and not sanctification. These two are not necessary concomitants, the inseparable co-products of one act of faith. They are severally products of different acts of faith and are sought and enjoyed each for itself. There is indeed a wider implication behind this — that we seek by faith and receive the several benefits which Christ bestows

[215] " Christian Perfection," p. 114.

on His people one by one, as we appeal to Him for each.
And behind that lies the deeper implication still that salvation is not a unit, but may be broken up into fragments and
granted piecemeal; and therefore also may be enjoyed by
this or that individual only in this or that part. He that has
only partial faith, that is to say faith for only part of the
things which are to be had in Christ, may be saved only in
part, that is, may receive only part of salvation. We may be
justified, for example, and not sanctified. One would like to
know what the state of such a man is. Being justified, his sins
are all pardoned; he is accepted in God's sight; and the reward of eternal life is given him. We suppose this means,
in common parlance, that he will "go to heaven." And indeed, where else would one go, against whom the law of
God brings no charge, and for whom it bears witness
that he is righteous? But not having been sanctified, he
must go to heaven a corrupt and polluted, though not
guilty, wretch. And we are brought up short by the fundamental principle that without holiness no man shall see the
Lord.

It is of course in part a defective view of justification itself
which produces these remarkable results. Corruption is the
very penalty of sin from which we are freed in justification;
holiness is the very reward which is granted us in justification. It is therefore absurd to suppose that sanctification can
fail where justification has taken place. Sanctification is but
the execution of the justifying decree. For it to fail would be
for the acquitted person not to be released in accordance with
his acquittal. It is equally absurd to speak of a special
" sanctifying faith " adjoined to " justifying faith "; " justifying faith " itself necessarily brings sanctification, because
justification necessarily issues in sanctification — as the
chains are necessarily knocked off of the limbs of the acquitted man. The Scriptures require of us not faiths but
faith. Mahan, on the other hand, is very much inclined to
make a hobby of the notion that we must have a special
faith for every particular benefit received of Christ. " Per-

fect faith," he asserts,[216] " is a full and unshaken confidence in Christ, as in all respects, at all times, and in every condition, a full and perfect Savior, a Savior able and willing to meet every possible demand of our being." That is true, and well-said: that is in its nature the faith which every Christian has and lives by. But must all the sides and aspects of Christ's saving activities be explicated in our knowledge or else we do not get them? Does our enjoyment of them absolutely depend on our explication of them in our knowledge and the direction of our faith to each and every one of them separately? That is the tendency of Mahan's treatment of the matter. We must not go to Christ, he tells us,[217] as a Savior in general, expecting Him to save us from our sins. We must take our sins to Him one by one. " From our sins Christ does not and cannot save us, unless by faith we thus " — that is distributively — " appropriate the provisions of his redemption." So strongly is the notion of the exercise of faith distributively pressed, that Mahan is even ready to say,[218] that no blessing will be received — for example the blessing of sanctification — if it be applied for in a general way. This is the reason, he says, that " Christians apply to Christ for sanctification, etc., almost without success. Their object is commonly general and undefined, and nothing specific is presented." We must come to Christ with a specific need in our hearts and one of His specific promises in our hands, and do this over and over again, until we work through all our needs and all His promises. We seem far enough away, in this presentation of the way of life, from the notion asserted in the passages formerly adduced, that perfect sanctification accompanies justification as its inseparable concomitant, else Christ would save us *in*, not *from* our sins: that we must in other words at once on believing be saved *from all* our sins on pain of implicating Christ in their continuance.

However Mahan may have endeavored to conciliate for himself such conflicting lines of thought, he emerges into the open with the clear and firm conviction that justification and

[216] As cited, p. 114.   [217] P. 134.   [218] P. 157.

sanctification are two distinct and separable benefits to be sought and obtained by two distinct and separable acts of faith. This is already apparent in the full exposition which he gives us of the theoretical foundation of his doctrine of perfection, in the fourth discourse of his "Christian Perfection." [219] He speaks freely here of our being made perfect by divine grace — even of our being made perfect by the indwelling Christ — after a fashion which seems to bear a more mystical than Pelagian implication. But the two tendencies are not to him irreconcilable. Everything is made to depend on the human will; and man may therefore be said to work out his own perfection. But it appears that he does this not directly but indirectly — by handing it over to grace or to the indwelling Christ to work it out for him. Accordingly Christ is represented as saying to the believer, " I will secure you in a state of perfect and perpetual obedience to every command of God, and in the full and constant fruition of his presence and love "; and as promising, " All this will I do in perfect consistency with the full, and free, and uninterrupted exercise of your own voluntary agency." [220] What the believer is to do is " to make a full surrender " of himself to Christ. This includes "an actual reception of Christ, and reliance upon him for all these blessings, in all their fulness — a surrender of your whole being to him, that he may accomplish in you all the ' exceeding great and precious promises ' of the new covenant." [221] And we are told that " when this is done — when there is that full and implicit reliance upon Christ, for the entire fulfillment of all that he has promised — he becomes directly responsible for our full and complete redemption." By a complete surrender to Him we voluntarily put ourselves into His hands, and He thereafter assumes " all the responsibility." [222] " Christ is now present in your

[219] Pp. 77 ff.

[220] P. 78.

[221] P. 89.

[222] Canfield, pp. 67 ff., adduces this statement of Mahan's and analogous ones of Finney's, and remarks that it is involved, of course, that we can never sin again. If Christ becomes " directly responsible for our full and complete

heart, and ready to confer all this purity and blessedness
upon you, if you can believe that he is able and willing to do
it for you, and will cast your entire being upon his faithfulness." [223] " If . . ." It is all primarily in our hands and rests
on our will. But when we have met that " if," then it is all in
Christ's hands and He will do it all. "We learn" hence,
Mahan explains,[224] "how to understand and apply such
declarations of Scripture as the following — 'Wash you,
make you clean'; 'Make to yourselves a new heart and a
new spirit'; 'Let us cleanse ourselves from all filthiness
of the flesh and spirit,' etc." "The common impression seems
to be," he says, "that men are required to do all this, in the
exercise of their own unaided powers; and because the sinner
fails to comply, grace comes in, and supplies the condition in
the case of Christians." That is not his view. His view is that
grace is always standing ready to do the work, if only we will
draw on it for it. We are not required to do it ourselves; we
are required to do it by means of grace, which is put at our
disposal for the purpose. The fountain, whose waters cleanse
from sin, is set open: it is our business to descend into it and
wash. " The sinner is able to make to himself a 'new heart
and a new spirit,' because he can instantly avail himself of
proffered grace." It is really his own act: *facit per alium, facit
per se*. Grace is but the instrument he uses to accomplish his
result. "He does literally 'make to himself a new heart and
a new spirit,' when he yields himself up to the influence of
that grace. The power to cleanse from sin lies in the blood
and grace of Christ; and hence, when the sinner 'purifies

redemption" — is "pledged," "to produce in us perfect and perpetual obedience," — to "'sanctify us wholly, and preserve our whole spirit, soul, and body,
blameless unto the coming of our Lord Jesus Christ,'" (in the sense Mahan
put on these words) — how can we possibly sin again? Yet Mahan within
four pages can write: "We can 'abide in Christ,' and thus bring forth the
fruit required of us. If by unbelief we separate ourselves from Christ, we of
necessity descend, under the weight of our own guilt and depravity, down the
sides of the pit, into the eternal sepulchre " (pp. 92–93).
[223] P. 90.
[224] P. 91.

himself by obeying the truth through the spirit,' the glory of his salvation belongs, not to him, but to Christ." [225] The validity of this inference is more than questionable: Christ in this view is but the instrument with which the sinner works. Meanwhile, however, it is made very plain that Christ and Christ only does or can do the work; and as the application is expressly made to the work of sanctification, the immediate supernaturalness of sanctification and its direct dependence on faith and faith alone are clearly asserted. "Herein also lies the ability of the creature to obey the commands of God, addressed to us as redeemed sinners. . . . We can ' abide in Christ,' and thus bring forth the fruit required of us." [226] The way we bear fruit is to apply to Christ for it.

We may perhaps be advanced in apprehending Mahan's conception by attending to a passage in which he undertakes to discriminate between what he calls the antinomian, the legal and the evangelical spirits. The antinomian spirit, he says, looks to Christ for justification now, and satisfied with that, does not bother itself at all about sanctification. The legal spirit has two forms. In its extremest form — the form in which it appears in the ancient Pharisee and "modern moralist " — it seeks both to justify and to sanctify itself by its own efforts. In its milder form it looks to Christ for justification and depends on its own efforts for sanctification. The evangelical spirit looks to Christ for both justification and sanctification through faith alone. He differentiates himself here from the antinomian through his zeal for sanctification: he is concerned for personal holiness and earnestly seeks it. He differentiates himself on the other hand from the "legalist," by the means he uses to obtain this longed-for holiness. The "legalist " seeks it "by personal efforts "; he seeks it "by faith." This is as much as to say that the "legalist " seeks it in himself and expects to draw it out of himself by strenuous strivings; while Mahan seeks it in Christ and expects to receive it from Christ on faith. We do not stop to point out the injustice of setting sanctification by effort and sanctification by faith in mutually

[225] P. 92.   [226] P. 92.

exclusive opposition to one another. If there be any who, having looked to Christ for their justification, then expect to sanctify themselves altogether apart from Christ, they present in their own persons a very odd contradiction. How can they, united to Christ by faith, act in their attempts to be holy, altogether out of relation with Christ, into union with whom they have come? Their efforts to be holy are themselves part of the sanctifying effects of the faith by which they are united with Christ — not all of it nor even the main part of it, but a part of it. Effort and faith cannot in themselves be set in crass opposition to one another, as if where the one is the other cannot be. They rather go together in a matter like sanctification which consists in large part of action. But that is not the matter which it concerns us most at the moment to take note of. The matter for us to note now is that by setting himself in opposition to those who " expect sanctification from personal effort," and by the very inconsiderateness of this opposition, it is made the clearer that Mahan thinks of himself as teaching that sanctification is obtained not at all by " personal effort," but by faith alone, and is the work of Christ exclusively, into which no other work of man enters except faith alone.[227]

In a later writing,[228] Mahan tells us explicitly that, when

---

[227] This is of course a Quietistic attitude. John Woodbridge ("Theological Essays: Reprinted from the Princeton Review," 1846, pp. 413–414) deals admirably with Mahan's Quietism. The illustrative passages quoted from Mahan ("Scripture Doctrine of Christian Perfection," pp. 189, 190, 191) are excellently chosen and the comments are telling (p. 414). "It is manifest from the inspired volume that we are to come to Christ, not for the purpose of saving ourselves the trouble of a personal warfare, but that we may engage in such a warfare with good motives, with becoming zeal, with persevering energy, and with success. . . . When Christ works in us, both to will and to do, of his own good pleasure, it is that sustained, quickened by his power, we may work out our own salvation with fear and trembling." " Yet, after all," he continues, " it is not intended by the writers to whom we refer, to ascribe all holiness to divine agency. Their meaning appears to be, that Christ will sanctify us wholly, if we look to him for such a blessing; yet there is no provision in their system to secure the act of looking itself. Man begins to turn, and God completes the sanctification of man."

[228] "Out of Darkness into Light," 1875, p. 37.

he was first converted, he "knew Christ well in the sphere of justification, or the pardon of sin, but knew nothing of Him in that of our sanctification, and had never heard of Him, or thought of Him, as 'the Son of God who baptizes with the Holy Ghost.'" "Of the idea of 'the life of faith,' and of the life revealed in the words, 'I in them, and Thou in me, that they may be made perfect in one,' I was as ignorant as an unborn babe." If we were compelled to take these words in their general, ordinary meaning, the statement made in them would be sheerly incredible. Mahan intends them only in the sense of his own special doctrines of sanctification and the baptism of the Spirit. In that case they amount only to saying that he had not yet elaborated his peculiar views on the subject, when he was first converted — as how should he? He therefore proceeds to plead that young converts should be taught at once that entire sanctification is to be had immediately from Christ on going to Him for it — just as full justification has been had. His meaning is, that they should not be permitted uselessly to expend their strength in seeking to hew out sanctification for themselves, when the only way in which it can be obtained is from Christ by faith alone. A very striking enforcement of this counsel is found in a passage in his "Autobiography"[229] in which he sharply criticizes Finney's methods of dealing with converts "before he learned the way of the Lord more perfectly." He wished "to induce among believers *permanence* in the Divine life." But he knew no way to do it, it is said, except to insist on "the renunciation of sin, consecration to God, and purpose of obedience." He worked along this line with the utmost zeal and to the permanent injury of his converts. Years afterward, his converts at the Chatham Street Chapel, New York, had "never recovered from the internal weakness and exhaustion which had resulted from the terrible discipline through which Mr. Finney had carried them." "And this," Mahan adds, "was all the good that had resulted from his efforts." The same method, he says, had the same effect on

[229] P. 246.

Finney's first pupils at Oberlin. He was prescribing effort:
the only right way is the way of faith.

It should be carefully noted that it is involved in these
criticisms that, in Mahan's view, sanctification is not merely
not by effort but by faith, but also not by the act of faith by
which justification is received, but by a subsequent act of
faith all its own. He is speaking of those already converted,
and of their sanctification as a subsequent transaction. This is
not a matter of little concern to him. He is insistent that
sanctification follows conversion. He is found indeed sharply
inveighing against those who say that all Christians have
received "the baptism of the Holy Ghost" at the time of
their conversion, and in doing so makes it plain enough that
"the baptism of the Holy Ghost," which with him is a condition of the influx of the grace that sanctifies the soul, is a
distinct and subsequent enduement to converting grace. He
repels the accusation that, as we have received this baptism
at conversion, there is "no such promise as you speak of,"
"in reserve for us now." He insists that no matter what they
once received, Christians are obviously in sore need of such
an enduement now. He argues formally that Christ makes
"prior obedience the express condition of this reception of
'the Comforter'" — with the meaning that it must therefore be not an initial gift but one that comes in the course of
Christian living. He declares: " Does not inspiration speak expressly of two classes of converted persons, — of the one class
as 'spiritual,' and the other as 'yet carnal,' — the one as
made, and the other as not yet made, 'perfect in love,' — the
one as having, and the other as not having, 'fellowship' with
the Father and with His Son Jesus Christ, — the one as having received, and the other as not having received, the Holy
Ghost since they believed — and of the 'joy' of the one class
as being, and of the other as not being, 'full.' " [230]

There is a passage in the " Autobiography " [231] in which
Mahan's doctrine of sanctification is set forth in quite a systematic form, and which may well serve therefore as a norm

[230] " Out of Darkness into Light," 1875, pp. 317–318.   [231] Pp. 292 ff.

for the interpretation of more scattered expositions. " Sanctification," we here read, " is a gift of grace in the same sense,
and attainable on the same condition, that justification is.
Justification is an *act* of God, an act by which our sins are
remitted, and we restored to a legal standing before Him,
as if we had never sinned. Sanctification, on the other hand,
is a *work* [232] wrought in us by the Holy Spirit, ' a renewing of
the Holy Ghost' by which ' the body of sin is destroyed,'
that is, evil dispositions and tendencies are ' taken out of
our flesh,' and we are made ' partakers of a Divine nature.'
We have no more direct and immediate agency in sanctification than we have in justification. Each, with equal exclusiveness, is, I repeat, a gift of grace, and each is vouchsafed
on the same condition as the other. . . . To comply with
the condition is our part in the transaction. The condition
being complied with, our responsibility in the matter is at an
end." Having cited Ezek. xxxvi. 25–27, he proceeds: " Three
great blessings, in all fulness, are here specifically promised;
namely, full and perfect cleansing from all sinful dispositions,
tendencies, and habits; an equally full and perfect renewal,
' the gift of a new spirit,' and ' a heart of flesh,' in the place
of the heart of stone which ' had been taken out of the flesh ';
and the ' gift of the Holy Ghost,' by Whose indwelling the
believer is ' endued with power' for every good word and
work, and perfected in his obedience to God's statutes and
judgments." Here is a complete negative and positive explication of what sanctification is. Negatively, everything
sinful is eradicated from the believer — including every sinful
disability he may be supposed to have. Positively, holiness is
infused into him, carrying with it power to every good word
and work. " Every item " of this transformation " is the exclusive work of God." Our part in sanctification is " to come
to God by Jesus Christ, to have these things done for us." [233]
" Sanctification and justification being both in common, and
with the same exclusiveness, gifts of God, the one is just as

---

[232] For Mahan's use of the term, see note 211.
[233] P. 294.

instantaneous as the other." [234] The Scriptures do indeed speak of " growth in grace," but that is " quite another thing " from a process of becoming holy: it is the expansion and development of the already holy person. " First, the healing, restoration to health, or sanctification; then growth, 'growth in grace,' " — a growth this, that is not merely progressive but eternal. The note struck here is the note of a supernatural, instantaneous, entire transformation — a transformation which is " total " not only in the extensive sense but in the intensive sense. For one of the most notable features of it is the emphasis with which it is declared that the transformation is a transformation of nature and not merely of activities. " The body of sin is destroyed "; and that is defined as meaning that " evil dispositions and tendencies are 'taken out of our flesh ' ": a " full and perfect cleansing " is made " from all sinful dispositions, tendencies, and habits." A new heart is placed within us: and we are made " partakers of a Divine nature." A work like this cannot well be called other than " physical."

It is important to observe that the " physical " salvation which is thus taught is strictly reserved for the second stage of salvation, and is a result of the second conversion. There is a curious passage in " Out of Darkness into Light " [235] in which this is explained to us. Here it is taught that, when we have been " through the Spirit " " convicted of sin," and have " exercised genuine ' repentance toward God, and faith toward our Lord Jesus Christ,' " strange to say, nothing has been wrought in us by His Spirit. We have taken up a new attitude, and that is all. We have done our duty — exercised repentance and faith — and that is the whole of it. God responds to this repentance and faith, it is true, by granting us pardon: but that takes place outside of us, and remains outside of us — we remain ourselves precisely as before. " As far as his *voluntary* activities are concerned," Mahan remarks, the believer " is now in a state of supreme obedience to the will of God." But he adds: " His old propensities, dispositions, temper, and tendencies, however, remain as they were, and remain to war

[234] P. 294.   [235] Pp. 270 ff.

against this new-born purpose of obedience." Nothing has happened to the believer in himself: he has turned to God, but this has brought no change to his inner self. If left in this condition — and Mahan says the majority of believers are left in this condition — the believer cannot sustain himself in his newly assumed attitude. He lapses from his first love, lives on a low plane, falls, and falls again. There is apparently attributed to him a power to retain the faith he has conceived; but, being left to himself, he can retain it only with a feeble hold. What we wonder at is that he can be supposed to retain it at all. " Open and gross immoralities excepted," we read,[236] " the convert carries with him into the Christian life the same propensities, dispositions, and temper that he had before his conversion, and these, when strongly excited, overcome him as they did before." The convert in his own strength can avoid open and gross immoralities; but, nothing having happened to him within, he is unable to resist the impulses which arise from his unaffected " old man." It is a curious condition this, and one cannot see that there can be attributed to it anything that can justly be thought of as a state of salvation. We are told that the believer has escaped the penalties due to his sins — is a pardoned man: but he remains in precisely the same inward condition in which he was before. He is still in the condition of the natural man seeking to reform himself.

But now a second step can be taken. Christ may be apprehended " as the Mediator of the new covenant " — to employ a favorite phrase of Mahan's; that is, the convert may seek and obtain from Christ " the baptism of the Holy Ghost," and thus receive the Spirit for " the work of universal renovation." The Spirit now takes away the heart of stone and gives the convert a heart of flesh — a new heart and a new spirit; writes the law in his inward parts — and the rest. This is " an all-cleansing, all-renovating, and all-vitalising process," and, in contrast with " the washing of regeneration," is called " the renewing of the Holy Ghost." The convert is now, his old man being crucified, imbued with a new " divine nature," and

[236] P. 271.

"filled with the Holy Ghost." The old propensities, dispositions, tempers and lusts are gone; and the Christian is free.
"What a melancholy reflection it is," Mahan exclaims,[237]
"that most believers advance no further in the Christian life
than 'the washing of regeneration,' are ignorant of Christ as
the Mediator of the new covenant, and, consequently, have no
experience of 'the renewing of the Holy Ghost.'" Is it not a
more melancholy reflection still that a Christian teacher can
so cut Christ's great salvation up into sections as to imagine
that a sinner can sincerely repent of his sins, and cast himself
in faith on Christ for salvation — and then not receive it?
According to Mahan this is the condition in which most
Christians find themselves. Their salvation has been wholly
intermitted after the first step.

We see that one of the things which Mahan has greatly
at heart, in urging to this second step, is that the Christian may
be relieved from his old evil propensities and thus be freer to
fight, in the Christian warfare, against external enemies. Up
to the reception of "the second blessing" the old evil propensities remain and are the constant source of sin. It is useless
to strive against them — we cannot eradicate them: though,
as we have just seen, we can do what seems on the whole not
a little in the way of repressing their worst movements, and
Mahan accordingly characterizes this condition as one, not of
darkness, but of "twilight." He is not counselling, however,
inert acceptance of them; he is only recommending rightly
directed efforts — we must strive not ourselves to conquer
them, but to obtain their eradication at the hands of Christ.
In one of the passages in which he describes most fully what
he means by this,[238] he is speaking directly of "religious joy,"
but he expressly makes the attainment to this "religious
joy" rest on the same principles as the attainment of holiness,[239] and we may use the description of the method of the
attainment of the one therefore equally well of the attainment of the other. We can have it, he says, only on the

[237] P. 273.
[238] "Out of Darkness into Light," pp. 339–345.   [239] P. 343.

condition "that, with all sincerity, earnestness, and tireless perseverance, 'God shall for this be inquired of by you to do it for you.'" This is one of the phrases which he loves to repeat; and the enforcement of the duty inculcated by it he makes one of his chief concerns. If we wish any blessing we must inquire of the Lord for it, and we must do this with all strenuousness. "When you are told," then, he explains, "not to make any efforts to banish your cares or sorrows, or to induce religious peace and joy, you receive wise and healthful advice." These things do not come "at the bidding of our wills, but at the bidding of Christ." We must strive after them — but we must strive after them from the hands of Christ. It is wrong, then, "when inquirers are told, . . . as they frequently are, not to think anything about their feelings, nor to give themselves any concern about them one way or the other." The truth is [240] "that our emotions, as well as our moral states" — it is here that our own interest for the moment focuses — "should be the objects of reflection, faith, and prayer. The divine direction is this: — 'Be careful for nothing; but in everything by prayer and supplication, with thanksgiving, let your requests be made known unto God.' . . . The promises pertaining to our peace are as really the objects of faith and prayer as those pertaining to our justification and sanctification." Striving thus in the right way, we may be rid of our evil propensities, rid of them not in part, or merely in their activities, but altogether. Mahan knows, for he has tried it. "As a witness for Christ," he says,[241] "I would say that, were there a perfect oblivion of the facts of my life prior to the time when I thus knew my Saviour, I should not, from present experiences, ever suspect that these old dispositions, which once tyrannised over me, had ever existed." And one of the things that render it important to be rid of them is that then we are free to contend against external temptations with no traitor in the camp. For though perfected now, we are not free from temptations. And we shall need to strive against them with all our might.

[240] P. 344.　　　　　[241] P. 275.

At this point in the discussion Mahan introduces a warning against what he represents as an extreme position taken
up by some in his own camp, which surprises us very much.[242]
" I hear much said," he says, " about receiving Christ as our
present sanctification " which must be accepted with caution.
If we have nothing in view but salvation from actual sin —
we may, of course, expect immediate relief on believing. But
" when we inquire of Him, as the Mediator of the new covenant, to do for us all that is promised in that covenant,
the case is different." And the difference in the case apparently consists in this — we must leave the fulfillment of all
that for which we believe to God's own good time and way.
We may, like the disciples, have to tarry for " the promise of
the Spirit." After all, then, entire sanctification is not the
immediate and complete response to faith. It may come
gradually, in instalments. We may expect salvation " from
actual sin " at once. But " heart-searching may precede the
final cleansing, searching for God with all the heart must
precede the finding of Him, and waiting and praying may
precede, we cannot tell how long, the baptism of power."
There is an appearance of excessive analysis here. Salvation
from actual sin, final cleansing, finding of God, baptism of
power — and there are others. There is for example the distinction which is at once made between the " presence " of
Christ in the heart and His " manifestation " there. It seems
that Christ may dwell in us, and yet dwell there after some
otiose fashion — not occupying Himself with us. We obtain
His indwelling by faith: His manifestation of Himself within
us awaits His own pleasure. The effort seems to be to safeguard to some degree the divine sovereignty. When we do
our part, that does not compel His doing His part — at least,
at once: He will do it, no fear as to that; but He will do it
when and as He will. " Faith on our part does not of itself
give us rest. The rest of faith is what Christ gives ' after we
have believed.' " *Gives* — an emphasis is laid on this. We
do not by faith take it: Christ gives it. We must conceive

[242] Pp. 277–279.

then, it seems, of our second act of faith as securing for us
the indwelling of Christ, who brings, of course, His benefits
with Him; and then of His conferring these benefits one by
one at His own discretion, but always in response, we infer
from other passages already cited, to acts of faith claiming
them. This notion of the indwelling Christ forms apparently
the culmination of Mahan's conception of the saving process.
At the end of his book, " Out of Darkness into Light," [243] he
has a chapter on " Christ in us, and Christ for us," a phrase
in which, he thinks, the whole gospel is summed up. He declines [244] to explain the " sense " and " form " in which
" Christ dwells and lives in believers," on the ground that
no one who has not experienced it can understand it. He outlines, however, some of the blessings which this indwelling
brings. We shall, possessing it, have union, fellowship, and
intercommunion with Him, in kind the same as obtains between Christ and the Father. " Christ will so completely control and determine our mental and moral states and activities,
and so completely transform our whole moral characters after
His own image, that the Father will love us as he does Christ "
— that is, of course, with the love of complacency, since we are
then perfect; our love to Christ " will, in our measure, be rendered as perfect as His is to us "; " our content under all the
allotments of Providence " will be as perfect as His; our peace
and joy as constant and full; and our love for our fellow-
Christians " will be the same in kind as that which exists
between Christ and the Father " — and the like. In a word,
although we cannot tell what the indwelling of Christ is, we
know it by its effects; and these effects are so described as to
show that we are by it assimilated to Christ. By His dwelling within us Christ makes us like Himself.

Now, there are two conditions of obtaining this high gift.
The first of these is that " we must . . . through faith in
Christ, in the varied relations in which He is for us, as a Saviour from sin, be brought into a state of full present consecration to Christ, and obedience to His commandments." We

[243] Pp. 327–338.   [244] Pp. 332–333.

must, in other words, receive Christ in all that He is " for us."
We must already be loving Christ and keeping his words;
Christ will not make His abode in any but loving hearts and
obedient spirits. Certainly this seems to say that the indwelling
Christ does not make us " perfect," but finds us " perfect."
The second condition is that we must have already received
the " Comforter," " to enlarge our capacities to receive Christ
and the Father." That is to say not only is perfection but
also what Mahan calls " the baptism of the Holy Spirit " presupposed. " Christ and the Father," we are told, " can dwell
within us but upon the condition that the Spirit shall first
'strengthen us with might in the inner man'; shall 'take of
the things of Christ, and show them unto us,' and shall ' show
us plainly of the Father.' " " Remember," we are told more
broadly, " that this promise can be fulfilled in your experience
but upon the condition that you shall love and obey Christ,
as the disciples did, and ' the Holy Ghost shall fall upon you
as He did upon them at the beginning.' " It is clear from a
passage like this that to Mahan the twin pillars on which the
highest structure of salvation rests are " perfection " and " the
baptism of the Spirit "; and these, we will remember, he repeatedly tells us are the great doctrines to the promulgation
of which he gave his life.

In the earliest of his perfectionist books — the " Scripture
Doctrine of Christian Perfection " of 1839 — the doctrine of
the " Baptism of the Spirit " is not developed. The last of the
discourses included in the book, however, deals with the work
of the Spirit in sanctification under the caption of " The Divine
Teacher," and this caption fairly conveys the conception of the
mode of His sanctifying work which is presented in the discussion. He is directly described in it as follows: He " enlightens the intellect, and carries on the work of sanctification in
the heart, by the presentation of truth to the mind." [245] And
again we are told [246] that " the Spirit sanctifies by presenting
Christ to the mind in such a manner, that we are transformed into his image." These phrases are so external that it

[245] P. 164.   [246] P. 172.

is necessary to remind ourselves that it is the work of the indwelling Spirit which is spoken of. He is spoken of in such a fashion as to imply that His presence in the heart is conceived as a supernatural fact, and His action as a supernatural action. But His action is spoken of exclusively as of the nature of "enlightening"; it is as "the divine teacher" alone that he is presented. It appears to be intended distinctly to deny that the mode of His action is of the nature of what is called "physical," and to confine its effects to such as are wrought by the truth. We are left, however, in darkness as to how the indwelling Spirit is thought to enlighten the mind, or, as that is here explained, to present truth or to present Christ to the mind. It does not seem to be meant that the Spirit reveals new truth to the mind, or reveals to it the old truths afresh. His action does not appear to be conceived as, in the strict sense revelatory, but rather as in its nature clarifying and enforcing: he gives clearness and force and effectiveness to the things of Christ. He makes Christ, in all that Christ is as our sanctification, vivid and impressive to us. What puzzles us is how He does it. Surely not by an effect on the truth itself with which He deals; or on Christ Himself whom He presents. Must not His operation terminate on the mind itself, affecting it in such a manner that it sees the truth in a new light and the Christ in His preciousness, and goes out to and embraces it and Him? And what is that but a "physical" effect? In subsequent discussions this ambiguity is left still imperfectly resolved. In the opening pages of "Out of Darkness into Light," [247] for example, we read this sentence: "According to the express teachings of inspiration, we know, and can know, divine truth in none of its forms but through a divine insight imparted to us through the Spirit." This is of course true, and would call for no remark except in a writer of this type. In such a one, it leaves us wondering how this insight can be thought to be imparted, especially when we read further and learn that all knowledge imparted thus by the Spirit is absolute knowledge. We may have beliefs of greater or less degrees of "conscious

[247] 1875, p. 5.

certainty" with "the teaching of the Spirit"; but when He illuminates the soul, we have not *beliefs* but *knowledge,* and that in the form of absolute knowledge.[248] On the basis of the religious psychology prevalent at Oberlin, it is exceedingly difficult to understand what the process of illumination can be which produces this effect. It seems to involve the assumption of an effect wrought by the Spirit on the man himself, that is on his heart, which cannot be called anything but "physical," and that seems to demand such a "physis" for man as is susceptible to such an operation. Mahan goes on to say [249] that by an action of the Spirit he was himself "made absolutely conscious that God had pardoned and accepted" him. "I was as absolutely — I could not tell how — assured of this, as I was that I existed at all." That is a familiar mode of speech among mystical perfectionists, and is called by Mahan "the witness of the Spirit." It seems to be represented as merely an ungrounded conviction; the ground of it is assumed to be the Spirit; and the guarantee of this assumption appears to be merely the absoluteness of the conviction. So explained, it falls within the category of revelations, and we observe Mahan, on a later page,[250] laying claim to special supernatural experiences which fall in nothing short of particular revelations. In this he but followed in the steps of those "New York Perfectionists" from whom he seeks fundamentally to separate himself, and of whom such experiences were characteristic. Perhaps we ought to state here also that the fanaticism of "faith cure" — "prayer cure," Mahan calls it [251] — was fully shared by both him and Finney.

The special doctrine of "the Baptism of the Spirit," under that name, seems to have been given vogue among the Oberlin coterie first by John Morgan, who published in *The Oberlin Quarterly Review* for 1845 and 1846, two essays on "Holiness Acceptable to God," and "The Gift of the Holy Ghost," respectively.[252] The latter of these works out the doctrine substan-

---

[248] P. 7.   [249] P. 17.   [250] P. 229.
[251] Pp. 248–254, where a number of typical instances are described.
[252] Subsequently reprinted at Oberlin, 1875.

tially as subsequently taught at Oberlin, with great clearness and force of presentation.[253] Mahan's first formal discussion of it appears in his book bearing the title, "The Baptism of the Holy Ghost," which was not published until 1870.[254] The doctrine is set forth in outline in the opening pages of the volume. First a very welcome and no doubt much needed testimony is borne to the fact "that whenever any of the leading characteristics of 'the new man' are referred to in the Bible, they are specifically represented as induced by the *indwelling presence, special agency and influence of the Holy Spirit.*"[255] This is true and important — the most important fact in the premises; we are sanctified by the Spirit whom God has given to dwell in us, and otherwise not. But next it is affirmed, as if it were equally true and equally important, that this gift of the spirit for our sanctification is an after-gift, granted to believers subsequently to their becoming believers. "This indwelling presence of the Spirit in our hearts . . . is distinctly revealed, as promised to us, and given to us, AFTER [emphasis his] we have, through His convicting power, 'repented of sin, and believed in Christ.'" There is a sense, of course, in which it is to be said that the work of the indwelling Spirit in sanctifying the soul, follows upon His act in regenerating it, by which we are converted, and, being converted, are justified. But this is not what Mahan means; he is not analyzing the unitary salvation into its distinguishable stages but dividing it into separable parts. Consequently he goes on [256]

[253] See the excellent accounts of Morgan's discourse by James H. Fairchild, *The Congregational Quarterly,* April, 1876, p. 253, and Frank H. Foster, "A Genetic History of the New England Theology," p. 456.

[254] In his "Autobiography," p. 150, Mahan speaks of this book with a certain amount of pride. "Every discourse in that book," he says, "two or three of the last excepted, was prepared and delivered as a part of a regular course of theological lectures to a class of theological students, and was sent to the publisher just as prepared and delivered." He says the delivery of the lectures produced a revival in the institution, Adrian College, Michigan, of which he was then President. His latest exposition of the doctrine (which pervades all his later writings) will be found in the "Autobiography," pp. 353–364. It does not differ from that in "The Baptism of the Holy Ghost."

[255] Pp. 10 ff.

[256] "The Baptism of the Holy Ghost," pp. 13 ff.

to affirm as the third element in his doctrine, that "the indwelling presence and power of the Spirit, 'the baptism of the Holy Ghost,' are, according to the express teachings of inspiration, to be sought and received by faith in God's word of promise, on the part of the believer, *after* he has believed; just as pardon and eternal life are to be sought by the sinner *prior* to justification." That is to say, the gift of the Spirit is not a result of justification, inseparably involved in it, but an independent gift to be obtained by an independent act of faith. The sinner seeks pardon and eternal life *prior* to his justification, by one act of faith; he then *after* his justification seeks the gift of the Spirit by another, similar but distinct act of faith. "If this promise is not embraced by faith, the gift, 'the sealing and earnest of the Spirit,' will not be vouchsafed." We believe for justification and get it; and if we are content with that, we get that alone. But the way is open to us, to believe for the baptism of the Spirit, too, and if we do so, we get that, too. If we do not take this second step we shall remain merely justified and shall not receive the Spirit. A very inadequate conception of justification of course underlies this notion. Mahan identifies it here with "pardon and eternal life," but is obviously thinking of "pardon," as merely, in the most limited and external sense, relief from penalty incurred, and of "eternal life" as merely the extension of this relief indefinitely. Even so, however, it is difficult to understand how he can imagine that this benefit can be received and continue to be enjoyed alone. Is it conceivable that a child of God, pardoned of all his sin, can remain just as he was before his pardon; can abide forever an unchanged sinner?

It cannot be said that it is made overly clear precisely what are the effects of the baptism of the Holy Ghost. This is apparently partly because these effects are conceived very comprehensively — as bringing for example blessings personal to the individual who receives it, and also blessings through him to others; as including thus both the gift of holiness, and that of power. In one passage, for example, the effects of the baptism are described thus: [257] "Now the special mission of the Spirit is to take truth in all its forms — truth as revealed in both Testaments, and to render it most effective for our sanctification, consolation, fulness of joy, and through us for the sanctification and edification of the Church, and the salvation of men." He who has received this baptism is accordingly marked out from other men, especially, by these two characteristics — he is holy, and he has power with men for the conversion of their souls and the establishment of them in holiness. It makes men on their own part perfect and in their Christian relations a source of perfection for others. Mahan is very much interested in the second of these effects: the baptism of the Holy Ghost is a baptism with power and conveys to its recipients a mysterious effectiveness in the propagation of the gospel and the winning of souls. We are naturally most interested in the former of them; the baptism of the Holy Ghost is the *rationale* of perfection, the efficient cause of our "entire sanctification." [258] There is a curious passage [259] in which it is likened to a kind of divine house-cleaning of the soul. Just as the housewife in her annual house-cleaning brings to light much dust and dirt that have been hidden from sight, and all seems in confusion and disorder, though this very confusion and disorder is but the preparation for universal order and purity: so, we are told, the Holy Spirit as He takes possession of the heart often discloses forms of internal corruption, "secret faults," evil tendencies and habits, emotive insensibilities unsuspected before — though this is only prepara-

---

[257] P. 77.

[258] In "Out of Darkness into Light," p. 315, Mahan remarks that the mistake, as it seemed to him of very many who teach the doctrine of the higher life, "is the fact that they do not set forth, as the immutable condition of entering into and continuing in that life, that we must receve 'the promise of the Spirit in our hearts.'" This at least fixes Mahan's conception of the relation of the Baptism of the Spirit to perfection — it is its "condition." At the bottom of this contention there lies a healthful supernaturalism. Our faith does not itself work the miracle of the Christian life: that is wrought by God the Holy Ghost. There may be something left to be desired when we inquire after the manner of His working this effect.

[259] P. 118.

tory to the enduement of power. Perhaps in comparing the baptism of the Spirit specifically to the housewife's "annual housecleaning," Mahan drops a hint that it is not conceived as a process which is done once for all, but as one which may be repeated. Elsewhere, somewhat surprisingly, he seems to intimate this. At least we read of its being "renewed," "often renewed," — perhaps, however, here in the sense of relaying rather than reënaction.[260] He certainly teaches that after we have received it we may lose it again,[261] and that leaves the way open for its "renewal" in the strictest sense. "With the Spirit in our hearts," he says, and he means it of this supernatural gift received in the Baptism of the Holy Ghost, "we need not sin, but we may sin. We may even 'grieve' and 'quench' the Holy Spirit of God." He instances men who, having had this great gift, have lost it: "who have attained the highest forms of the Higher Life," and "afterwards 'make shipwreck of the faith.'" He warns us that it is possible that Christ may, for our sins, "take" our "part out of the Book of Life."

Perhaps it ought to be explicitly stated that Mahan does not think of God ever bestowing this great gift of the baptism of the Spirit spontaneously. It must be obtained by us. What God does is merely to put it within our reach. It depends on us, then, whether we obtain it. "All who receive this baptism," he says,[262] "do so in consequence of a previous compliance with the conditions on which God has promised the blessing." He must be inquired of by believers to do it for them. He never grants it unless He is inquired of with all the heart and all the soul. We must previously be keeping His word and preparing the way for His coming; and, then, seek it with all the heart. Mahan's supernaturalism thus rests on a very express naturalism. We must take the initiative; and indeed it sometimes looks as if we must do much more — as if we must first have the blessing that we may get the blessing, as if we must be perfect in order to acquire perfection. At any rate, it is clear that God never blesses any except those who first "ago-

[260] P. 102.   [261] Pp. 124, 127, 128.   [262] P. 111.

nize " for the blessing. It is an indispensable prerequisite to the reception of the Baptism of the Spirit, we are told, that the mind be " brought to realize a deep, inward want, ' an aching void within ' — a soul-necessity, which must be met." [263] " Our Methodist brethren," it is added, " formerly denominated this state, ' being convicted for sanctification.' "

It is an inconvenience to Mahan that he has to depend for the Scriptural ground of his doctrine of the baptism of the Spirit on passages which teach that the Spirit is given to all believers. He is compelled to transmute this into the very different representation that He is at the disposal of all believers. " While all who believe become thereby entitled to this promise," he says,[264] " its fulfillment is to be sought by faith, after we have believed; just as pardon is to be sought in conversion." " The promise," he elaborates the comparison, " is just as absolute in one case as in the other. There is nothing which God so desires to bestow upon sinners as pardon, and with it eternal life. There is no gift he is more willing to bestow upon believers than this divine baptism." Only, God does not say that all sinners have pardon and eternal life; that this is the characteristic of sinners that they have pardon and eternal life. And He does say that all believers have the Spirit; that it is their very characteristic that they have the Spirit. Only those who are led by the Spirit of God are sons of God: " if any man have not the Spirit of Christ, he is none of His."

There are, to be sure, the charismatic passages, and perhaps the most amusing instance of the inconvenience which the Scriptures he is compelled to depend upon occasion Mahan, is afforded by one of these — Acts xix. 2 ff. This is so much the main passage on which he relies in proof of his cardinal contention that the baptism of the Spirit is a subsequent benefit, sought and received by a special act of faith, " after we believe," that he weaves it into the statement of his doctrine with an iteration that becomes irksome. We have already met with more than one instance of the emphatic employ-

[263] P. 96.   [264] P. 51.

ment which he makes of it. It has of course no bearing on the subject in any case; for its reference is to the charismatic and not to the sanctifying Spirit. But Mahan, although protesting [265] against confounding the two things, finds himself compelled to draw the primary support for his doctrine of the sanctifying Spirit from the charismatic passages — Acts xix. 1–6; viii. 14–17; x. 44–47.[266] The point now made, however, is that even when thus perverted from its real reference and violently applied to the sanctifying Spirit, the passage in question is so far from serving Mahan's purpose that it bears precisely the contrary meaning to that which he attributes to it. So eager is he in his employment of it that he adduces it even in the preface to his book on " The Baptism of the Holy Ghost," [267] with the emphasis of italics: " Paul put this important question to certain believers, when he first met them, to wit: ' Have ye received the Holy Ghost *since* ye believed? ' Does not this question imply that the promise of the Spirit awaits the believer *after* conversion? " And of course, when he comes formally to expound his doctrine,[268] he exploits the same passage: " We learn that the gift of the Spirit was not expected *in,* but *after* conversion: ' Have ye received the Holy Ghost *since* ye believed? ' " It would be a curious speculation to inquire into the effect it would have had on his constructions, had Mahan learned that what Paul really said was, " Did ye receive the Holy Spirit when ye believed? " At all events, since the wrong doctrine not only seeks support from the wrong reading of the text, but to a very extraordinary degree is dependent on it and apparently is even largely derived from it, it is a pity that Mahan did not look beyond the language of the Authorized English Version in seeking the meaning of the text. It is true that he did not have the Revised Version to set him right. But he had his Greek Testament; and he had his Alford, whom he repeatedly quotes when it serves his occasion — but not on this occasion. His Alford would have told him that " the aorist should be faithfully rendered:

---

[265] P. 113.
[266] Chapter iii.

[268] Pp. 37 ff.
[268] Pp. 37 ff.

not as E. V., 'Have ye received the Holy Ghost since ye believed?' but ' *Did ye receive the Holy Ghost when ye became
believers?* ' " Indeed Alford would even have argued the question for him, pointing out that not only the grammar but also
the sense of the passage requires this rendering. The matter
is made the more absurd that Eph. i. 13, which is not a charismatic passage, is repeatedly quoted [269] in support of Acts xix.
2 ff. and is stumbled over in the same fashion. From it is extracted, indeed, such nonsense as this [270]: — " When the creature believes in Christ, he ' sets to his seal that God is true.'
When God gives his Spirit, that is his seal. . . ." But, he argues, unfortunately the two do not go together; we may give
our seal to God long before He vouchsafes His to us. What
the Apostle really says is of course, that we were sealed " on
believing " — intimating that the sealing occurred at once on
our believing, and that it occurs, therefore to all that believe.
The sealing of the Spirit belongs according to their very nature
as such, to all Christians. It is not a special privilege granted
after a while to some; but at once to all. Alford would have
set Mahan right here, too. He renders the passage: " in whom,
on your believing, ye were sealed," and remarks that " this
use of the aorist marks the time when the act of belief first
took place." [271]

[269] Pp. 38, 40, 115.

[270] P. 40.

[271] Similarly H. C. G. Moule, " Ephesian Studies," 1900, p. 35: " *In whom
also, on believing, you were sealed with the Spirit of the Promise, the Holy*
One; the gifts and power of the Paraclete were made yours at once on your
union with the Christ of God." He adds, to be sure, in a note: " Those gracious
gifts may indeed need the believer's constantly advancing *use,* and his growing discovery of what they are. But in covenant provision they are *his at once*
' in Christ.' " This, however, does not affect the testimony of this passage
against the " second blessing."

III. THE DEVELOPMENT OF THE OBERLIN
TEACHING

When we have obtained some insight into Mahan's doctrines of "Christian Perfection," and "the Baptism of the Holy Spirit," we have already seen into the heart of his theology. It is on these things that he most constantly and strenuously dwelt in his religious instruction. There were other elements of his teaching, however — not altogether unconnected with these, and therefore not altogether untouched in what has preceded — to which we must give some particular attention if we would know Mahan in his peculiarity as a religious teacher, and especially in his distinction from his colleagues at Oberlin. He makes no secret that there were some things in which he differed from Finney, although, very naturally, he minimizes their importance. They were not things, he tells us in a curious passage,[272] in which perfectly sanctified people may not differ without fault. Paul and Barnabas differed in some things, he says, and " on a very few questions in Moral Philosophy and Theology, Brother Finney and myself have arrived at opposite conclusions." " Yet each," he adds, " has the same assurance as before, that the other is ' full of faith, and of the Holy Ghost.' " " We differ just where minds under the influence of the purest integrity, and the highest form of divine illumination, are liable to differ." It would almost seem as if it were a virtue to differ on these things. One of the things on which they thus faultlessly differed, was the ground of moral obligation; which does not strike us as an unimportant matter. Mahan represented at Oberlin what Finney calls by the ugly name of " rightarianism." We are glad that the thing is not as bad as the name. It means, indeed, just that Mahan defended at Oberlin intuitive morality against Finney's teleological system — which is no morality at all. Effects of this difference naturally are traceable throughout the whole range of their teaching. Another matter of difference between them, far from unimportant whether in itself or in

[272] " The Baptism of the Holy Ghost," pp. 124–125.

its results, has already been incidentally touched upon. This is the morality of our dispositions and propensities. Finney denied that any moral character attached to the affectional movements as such; only the will and its volitions are properly speaking moral. In asserting the contrary Mahan necessarily gave a totally different complexion to his doctrine of sin and of salvation from sin.

No more than Finney did he, to be sure, acknowledge any doctrine of " original sin." Sin, says he,[273] is " exclusively a *personal* matter, a state of the inner man, a form of voluntary moral activity." The soul becomes sinful, " not from necessity, but choice." We derive no sin from our ancestry, near or remote; and we have no form or degree of merit or demerit which does not attach to us personally and to no one else but us. " Personal criminality " and nothing else is sin to us. But however we have become sinful, we are all entirely sinful. All sin consists in alienation and estrangement from God, His character, His will, and the law of duty; and this alienation and estrangement from all the claims of God and of His moral law, affects all our moral movements. In all forms of our moral activity, whether externally right or wrong, this estrangement is total. " No moral act of " our " unregenerate life " is " prompted by that motive and intent which render such act morally virtuous, or such that the conscience or God can regard, or ought to regard, as an act of obedience to the divine will and the law of duty." Surely this positive fact of universal sinfulness in all our moral activities cannot be given negative statement otherwise than in terms of inability to good. Mahan will not go so far as that. But he allows that though we may see the good and approve it, we cannot do it. There is always " a total failure ' to *do* that which is good ' — the good to do which there is a readiness to will." [274] He avoids the word " inability," but he is compelled to recognize some sort of a " human impotence " to good; a " self-impotence," a " total self-impotence." He even rebukes the preachers of the revival

---

[273] " Out of Darkness into Light," pp. 13–15.
[274] *Ibid.*, pp. 104–105.

of the early thirties for their purely Pelagian teaching on ability; this was, he says,[275] " a leading cause of the ultimate decline of those revivals." It was a better teaching, to be sure, he declares, than the old New England doctrine of a so-called " natural ability " wholly neutralized by a " moral inability " — which left no ability at all. But in reacting from this the revivalists reacted too far and left no disability at all.

It is plain matter of fact, however, that we are dependent on God's grace for holy choices, or, at least, for holy executions. " We are free agents: but the freedom which we and all creatures possess is a dependent one. . . . Light and grace are provided and rendered available; by availing ourselves of these we ' may stand perfect and complete in all the will of God.' We are free to avail, or not to avail, ourselves of this light and grace. Refusing or neglecting to do this, we have no available power for anything but sin." " We have no available power "; what is that but inability? An inability overcome, indeed, by " light and grace "; but how overcome by " light and grace "? Mahan says they are " made available." But he does not tell us how their being " made available " overcomes our previous inability " for anything but sin." Surely the mere proffering of them to us cannot overcome this inability. What Mahan tells us is, however, just that. He tells us that we have power to accept or reject proffered grace as we will; but naturally no power to perform without grace what can be performed only with grace. Grace is the instrument for working certain effects: we must use it if we wish those effects. But what enables us, who are unable to use it — for we can do nothing but sin and to use grace surely is no sin — to use it although we are unable to do so? Mahan is silent. Or rather he deserts his doctrine of inability to good, and substitutes for it a doctrine of absolute ability — but with it a complementary doctrine of right instrumentation. We are perfectly able to do what is right — to love God, to serve Him, to be perfect; but of course we are not able to do any of these things except we use the proper instruments for their performance.

[275] " Autobiography," pp. 244–245.

We are perfectly able to cut down a tree, but not with our finger nails; we are perfectly able to drive a spike home, but not with our naked fists. If we will consent to use an axe and hammer, we can easily perform these tasks. Mahan very truly says: "Teaching the doctrine of ability as an absolute and not dependent power, tends to induce, not faith in God and His grace, but self-assurance, self-dependence, and the pride of self-sufficiency and self-righteousness." He wishes then to teach something else than "ability as an absolute power." He apparently supposes that he is teaching ability dependent for its exercise on grace. He is not. He is teaching grace dependent for its operation on ability. We use grace, not grace us. The whole truth is that Mahan has raised the problem of ability and inability, and then — has dodged it. He has left us with man on our hands "impotent" to good: and as he has not made it quite plain to us why he is impotent to good, so he has not given us any ground whatever to believe, that, being impotent to good, he is quite able at his option to avail himself of God's proffered grace and by it work all good. Clearly these problems can find no solution except in the frank postulation on the one hand of the sinfulness of human nature disabling it for good, and on the other of recreative grace recovering it to good.

When he comes to deal with the doctrine of salvation from sin, Mahan gets still deeper into his problem. He is no longer able to escape ascribing to unregenerate man a sinful "nature" which determines his actions; or to the saving Spirit a "physical" effect on this nature by which it is made good and the proximate source of our renewed activities. When God takes the stony heart out of our flesh and gives us a heart of flesh, he says,[276] what is really meant is "a fundamental change and a renewal of our propensities." "We are," he says, "by nature 'children of wrath,' 'prone to evil as the sparks are to fly upward.'" When God makes the change He promises, "we have 'a new heart,' and 'a new spirit,' 'a divine nature,' which impels us to love and obedience, just as our old nature impelled

[276] "Out of Darkness into Light," pp. 267–268.

us to sin." Referring to the "works of the flesh," of Gal. v. 19 ff., he remarks that "behind all these forms of sin, 'works of the flesh,' lie certain propensities, dispositions, and tempers, which, when touched by corresponding temptations, set on fire burning and 'warring lusts' and evil passions, and these induce the sins and crimes above designated." "These old propensities, dispositions, and tempers are taken away, and in this state, new ones of an opposite nature are given," and "under our renovated propensities, and new dispositions, tendencies, and tempers, or 'divine nature,' it becomes just as easy and natural for us to bear 'the fruits of the Spirit' as it was, under our old ones, to work 'the works of the flesh.'" The subject is pursued and similar phraseology repeated indefinitely. "'By nature,'" we read,[277] "— that is, under the influence of our old nature, or propensities, dispositions, and tempers, we are 'children of wrath,' and 'bring forth fruit unto death.' Under the dispositions, tempers, and tendencies of our new or 'divine nature,' we are just as naturally 'children of God,' and 'have our fruit unto holiness.'" We are to reckon ourselves dead unto sin, "because 'our old man,' our old propensities, dispositions, and tempers, is crucified, 'put to death' with Him, that the 'body of sin,' our old and evil nature, 'might be destroyed, that henceforth we should not serve sin.'" While the old nature remains, we are told, we cannot help sinning; similarly when the new nature is given we cannot help being holy. Sometimes, it is true, a note of "may" rather than "must" is struck. "Because that, through the Spirit of Christ dwelling in us, 'the body of sin,' our old and evil propensities, 'may be destroyed,' and 'the old man may be crucified with Him,' and we may 'through the law of the Spirit of Christ Jesus,' be 'made free from the law of sin and death,' we should indeed cease to 'live after the flesh,' should be 'not in the flesh but in the Spirit'; and should 'reckon ourselves dead indeed unto sin, but alive unto God through Jesus Christ our Lord.'" But this phraseology appears to be preserved only for purposes of exhortation, and its apparent

[277] Pp. 268–270.

suggestion that the effect lies in our own power is fully corrected when the speech takes a didactic form. " Such language," we read,[278] " implies more than this, that his old propensities, ' the body of sin,' ' the old man,' is yet living and warring in the soul, but, by the grace of Christ, are held in subjection. Mere subjection is not death. What the Apostle undeniably intended to teach is this: that his propensities, dispositions, and temper had been so renovated that the world, with its affections and lusts, had no more power over him than they have over the dead. Christ, on the other hand, lived in him, and occupied all his affections, and held undisputed control over all his activities." This certainly suggests a " physical " change wrought in us by the Spirit of God, by which our governing dispositions are changed: and that as certainly implies that we are governed by our dispositions, whether evil or good.

At an earlier point,[279] discussing the phrase " divine nature " in II Pet. i. 4, Mahan remarks: " The words ' the divine nature,' imply, as all will admit, not only the holiness and blessedness of the divine mind, but also that divine *disposition* or nature in God which induces His holiness and blessedness. For us to become possessed of this ' divine nature ' implies not only present holiness and blessedness such as God possesses, but a divine disposition in us, a new and divine nature, which induces and prompts us to holiness, just as God's nature prompts Him to the same. In our old or unrenewed state, we not only sinned, but had a nature or dispositions, which prompted us to sin. In Christ, we not only obey the divine will, but receive from Him, as the Mediator of the New Covenant, a new or ' divine nature,' which prompts us to purity and obedience, just as our old dispositions prompted us to sin." A tendency appears here to think of the new nature imparted to us as if it were a separate entity implanted within us: and this is identified with the Holy Spirit whose coming into our hearts brings " the disposition " of Christ with Him. In commenting [280] on the words: " God sends the Spirit of His Son

---

[278] P. 270.   [279] Pp. 128–129.   [280] P. 130.

into our hearts," the phrase is employed: " the *Spirit,* or disposition, of His Son." This corresponds to a mystical tendency which shows itself elsewhere in Mahan's writings and forms a connecting link between him and the " New York Perfectionists " who preceded him. Apart from the suggestion of this special conception of the nature of the " new nature " imparted to us, however, there appears to be here a real recognition of the existence in us of a substrate of our activities, having moral quality itself, and so conditioning our moral activities as to determine their moral quality. " We are not only saved from the actual sins that are in the world," we read, " but . . . the evil propensities and tempers, ' the law in our members,' which induces sin, are taken from us." This certainly seems to posit a law in our members, underlying and determining our activities. We receive, we read again, " not only deliverance from sinning, but ' the death of the old man,' or " — as it is now explained — " the crucifixion of all those tempers and dispositions which induce sin." There are, then, permanent tendencies in us, which determine our activities to be sinful. On the positive side, we receive " new and divine tendencies " which naturally induce the opposite virtues — " not only actual obedience to the divine will, but ' a divine, nature,' which prompts and constrains obedience in all its forms." Are we not to give validity to the phrases " *naturally* induce," " *constrains* " here? And then it is added in a general summary: " It is as much the nature of ' the new man,' or the promptings of his new and divine tendencies, to be pure in heart and life, as it was that of ' the old man ' to ' obey the law of sin.' " Surely a " physical " corruption, and a " physical " holiness, and a physical change from the one to the other is taught here.

This teaching forms the foundation for Mahan's doctrine of the " sanctification of the sensibility," to which we have already had occasion to advert, and which was a peculiarity of his teaching among his fellows. James H. Fairchild [281] very properly tells us that it appears " to involve a supernatural

[281] *The Congregational Quarterly,* April, 1876, pp. 241–242.

and almost mechanical action upon our human nature, restoring it to its normal state before the fall, — all, however, in response to our faith." The words, " All, however, in response to our faith," mark the limits beyond which Mahan would not go in ascribing salvation to God; and, with that, the gross inconsistency of his thinking. For, as we have seen, he ascribes to the evil dispositions which constitute the " old man " just as much determining power over our activities, making them evil, as he ascribes to the good dispositions constituting our new man, making our activities good. And yet he supposes that while still under the dominance of the " old man " we may at will turn to Christ in saving faith. More: immediately upon the heels of his exposition of the determining effects on conduct of our " propensities, dispositions, temper and tendencies," [282] he speaks of the man who has believed for pardon but not yet for holiness, being " as far as his *voluntary* activities are concerned . . . in a state of supreme obedience to the will of God," while yet (since the " physical " change comes only with the " second blessing ") all these " old propensities, dispositions, temper, and tendencies " remain as they were and remain at war against this new-born purpose of obedience. If validity be given to the preceding exposition, this is nonsense: if validity be given to this assertion, that exposition is without significance. Whatever Mahan teaches as to a supernatural action on the human soul of the Spirit of God — an action which Fairchild looks upon as " almost mechanical " — he has no intention whatever of suspending human salvation on anything else than human volition; a volition which at bottom he conceives as acting in complete independence of any as well subjective as objective determinants. Mahan's whole discussion of " the sanctification of the sensibility," therefore, with its suggestions of controlling dispositions lying behind our activities and of a consequent " physical " change in our sanctification, must be looked upon as a mere tendency of thought running athwart his most fundamental convictions and capable therefore of having validity given to it only so far as it

[282] " Out of Darkness into Light," p. 271.

can be made consistent with a doctrine of the will, and of the dependence of salvation on the will, with which it is in essential disharmony.

Fairchild, in his notice of this excursion of Mahan's thought, proceeds to tell us how Finney stood in the matter. " Pres. Finney," he says, " while not disclaiming this idea entirely, and sometimes presenting facts and experiences which were in harmony with it, insisted more upon the moral power of Gospel truth upon the believer's heart. He found deliverance from temptation and from the power of sin in the views which the Spirit gives of Christ. The truth as it is in Jesus was to him the power of God unto salvation. ' Sanctify us through the truth ' was the burden of his prayer and of his teaching; and this was the prevalent idea with the other leaders of thought here." That is to say Finney dallied a little with the idea of " the baptism of the Spirit," but did not really adopt it; he continued to confine the work of the Spirit to illumination and to deny all recreative functions to Him: He is our Guide, not our Regenerator. There is nothing strange in Finney's failure to assimilate this idea: what is surprising is that he could dally with it even for a moment. That he did do so is probably only an illustration of that hospitality which he was ever showing to the notions of his colleagues, by which he was led to assimilate them as far as his fundamental teaching permitted him to do so, without, however, ever really modifying his fundamental teaching to accommodate them. A striking instance of how he dealt with them, apparently adopting them with heartiness and really transforming them into the image of his own thought, is afforded by his treatment of this very doctrine of the Baptism of the Holy Ghost, at a dramatic moment of his own life. Mahan's book bearing that title was published in 1870. The National Council of Congregational Churches met at Oberlin in 1871, and, making much of Finney in his hale old age (he was in his eightieth year), invited him to address it. He did so, and, on request, continued his discussion on the following Sabbath. The subject he chose to speak on was the Baptism of the Holy Ghost; and his treatment of

the theme ran on the lines laid down in Mahan's recently published book. He followed up his address with some letters
printed in *The Independent,* and afterwards put into tract
form. In the first of these (called " Power from on High ") he
outlines the doctrine of the baptism of the Spirit for power, as
he had outlined it at the Council; and it might almost have
been simply transcribed from Mahan. This baptism of the
Holy Ghost, he declares, is the indispensable condition of performing the work given us by Christ to do; Christ has expressly promised it to the whole Church; the condition of
receiving it is to continue in prayer and supplication until we
receive it; it is not to be confounded with the peace which
comes to the justified state — it is not peace but power; Christ
gives peace but promises power — and we must not rest in
conversion but go on to this second blessing which is at our
disposal. A second letter now followed, in which the doctrine is
given a somewhat new turn. The blessing conferred on the
Apostles at Pentecost by the baptism of the Spirit is first reduced to " the power to fasten *saving impressions* upon the
minds of men," the power " to savingly impress men." And
then in his effort to define precisely what this power consists
in, Finney comes to this: — " It was God speaking in and
through them. It was a power from on high — God in them
making a saving impression upon those to whom they spoke."
And then he still further teaches that the power was not conferred at Pentecost alone, and not alone on the Apostles. It is
still conferred: he himself has received it. He has often converted men by so chance a word that he had no remembrance
of having spoken it, or even by a mere look. He illustrates this
with anecdotes from his own life, such as are found in the
" Memoirs " which he had recently completed. It is a sufficiently odd doctrine which he here enunciates, a kind of new
Lutheranism with the evangelist substituted for the Word.
The Holy Ghost is represented, not, as in the Reformed doctrine, as accompanying the word preached *extrinsecus accedens*
— " the Lord opened Lydia's heart," " Paul may plant and
Apollos water, the Lord gives the increase "; and not as in the

Lutheran doctrine as intrinsic in the Word spoken, acting out
from the Word on the heart of the hearer; but as intrinsic in
the evangelist speaking. By a mere gaze, without a word
spoken, Finney says he reduced a whole room-full of factory
girls to hysteria. As the Lutheran says God in the Word works
a saving impression, Finney says God in the preacher works a
saving impression. Not the Word, but the preacher is the
power of God unto salvation. The evangelist has become a
Sacrament. The letters were continued after an interval. There
was another descriptive one ("The Enduement of the
Spirit") in which the anecdote of the preaching in "Sodom"
related in the "Memoirs" is repeated. Then there was one
called "Power from on High: Who May Expect the Enduement?" in which he explains that "all Christians, by virtue
of their relation to Christ, may ask and receive this enduement
of power to win souls to Him," adding that it comes "*after
their first faith*," and as an "instantaneous" gift. In another,
"Is It a Hard Saying?" he defends his assertion that those
without this power are disqualified for office in the Church.
And finally, "Enduement of Power from on High" considers
the conditions upon which this enduement of power can be
obtained. It is a pathetic sight to observe the aged Finney after
a long life of insistence that it is only by the power of truth
that men can be brought to Christ, clothing at the end the
evangelist himself with supernatural powers and representing
him as fitted for his functions only by the possession of these
supernatural powers. It is an odd instance of the invention of a
supernaturally endowed priesthood to mediate between God
and man, when God is not permitted Himself to act immediately on the heart; and it seems to bear witness to a deeply-
lying conviction in the human soul that its salvation will not
be accomplished without a supernatural intervention somewhere. The pragmatic refutation of the Pelagian construction
of salvation is not a mean one. It will not work; and no one
really believes that it will work. The supernaturalism thrown
out at the window is very apt to creep back through some
chink or other.

The form given to the Oberlin doctrine of perfection in the first stage of its development did not remain its permanent form. It was distinctly taught in essentially this form, it is true, throughout his long life, by Asa Mahan, to whose influence apparently the first shaping of the doctrine was mainly due. And Henry Cowles seems never to have advanced much beyond this mode of conceiving it. But it was not long before, in its general apprehension, it suffered a sea-change which gave it a totally new character. This was due to the dominating place given in Oberlin thinking, from 1841 on, to what is called the doctrine of "the simplicity of moral action." This was not a new doctrine. It lay, as corollary, too near to the teleological ethics inherited by Oberlin from the New England theology, for it not to have had attention drawn to it before. Frank H. Foster has shown that it is very clearly alluded to in certain arguments of Nathaniel Emmons,[283] and indeed that it was already more than hinted at by Samuel Hopkins: "Every moral action is either perfectly holy or perfectly sinful." [284] It was a settled presupposition of Finney's thought from at least the beginning of 1839, although he recalls a time when he had not yet recognized it.[285] But it seems to have been left

[283] "A Genetic History of the New England Theology," pp. 463–464.
[284] *Ibid.*
[285] John C. Lord, *The Biblical Repertory and Princeton Review,* April, 1841, pp. 238–239, expounds the doctrine on the basis of a passage from *The Oberlin Evangelist,* i. 1839, p. 42, where Finney says that he was himself formerly of the opinion that an "exercise might be put forth, in view of several motives," or partake of "the complex character of the motives that produced it," but is now persuaded that "this philosophy is false." His present view is expressed thus: "It seems to be a very general opinion, that there is such a thing as imperfect obedience to God, (i.e.) as it respects one and the same act. . . . But I cannot see how an imperfect obedience, relating to one and the same act, can be possible. *Imperfect* OBEDIENCE! What can be meant by this, but *disobedient* OBEDIENCE! a *sinful* HOLINESS. Now, to decide the character of any act, we are to bring it into the light of the law of God. If agreeable to this law, it is obedience — it is right — *wholly right.* If it is, in *any respect,* different from what the law of God requires, it is disobedience — it is wrong — *wholly wrong.*" Lord's own summary of Finney's teaching is admirable: "He admits that obedience may be imperfect in respect to its constancy, but never in regard to degree; and insists that if a Christian, at any given moment, has any holiness, it must be perfect both in kind and degree,

to two of the theological students at Oberlin of the class of
1842, to bring it out of comparative neglect, announce it as of
primary importance, enforce it by extended reasoning, and
make it a determining factor in Oberlin thinking.

It is interesting to observe the part taken by the students
at Oberlin in formulating its doctrine of perfection. We have
already seen that, had the students not intervened, the Oberlin
professors might never have discovered that they were in fact
teaching a doctrine of perfection. And we see them intervening
here again to bring into full recognition and use a fundamental
principle of Oberlin thinking which appeared to be in danger
of being neglected. In neither instance was there a new discovery made. In both instances what we are called upon to
observe is the fresh young minds of the students, in working
on the material given to them, throwing up into clear view
elements of necessary implication which were being left by
their teachers out of sight. Finney, writing in 1847, felicitates
himself on the method of instruction pursued at Oberlin, by
which the students were made fellow workers with the
teachers; and handsomely acknowledges the benefit he had
received from his students' activity. " I . . . owe not a little
to my classes," he says,[286] " for I have availed myself to the
uttermost of the learning and sagacity and talent of every
member of my classes in pushing my investigations." The
particular members of his classes to whose sagacity he owes
not indeed his knowledge of the doctrine of " the simplicity of
moral action," but its elevation to the commanding place it
at once took in Oberlin thinking, were two brothers, Samuel D.
and William Cochran.

It was William Cochran, a brilliant young man who afterwards served a few years as a professor at Oberlin, until cut

---

and the individual of course, for the time being, wholly sanctified. The whole
scope of the argument amounts to this: that the soul is nothing but its exercises: that there are no permanent dispositions; that character is what the
exercises of the individual, at any given moment, may happen to be, and that
these fluctuating states are always perfect for good or evil, both in kind and
degree."

[286] " Lectures on Systematic Theology," ii. 1847, p. v.

off by an untimely death in 1847, who brought the subject into
public discussion. This he did in an address delivered before
the Society of Inquiry in the spring of 1841 and repeated the
following autumn, at Commencement, before the Society of
Alumni. Permanency was given to this address by its publication in *The Oberlin Evangelist*,[287] and Cochran afterwards developed his views at greater length in the pages of *The Oberlin
Quarterly Review*.[288] From this time on the doctrine of " the
simplicity of moral action " became a characteristic feature of
Oberlin theology. The leading instructors and preachers of the
time, with " the possible exception of Henry Cowles " embraced it at once; and " especially by the consistent and unvarying advocacy of President Fairchild " it was propagated
through a succeeding generation as the only genuine Oberlin
teaching.[289]

The essence of this doctrine is briefly explained by Fairchild [290] as follows: " The doctrine maintains the impossibility
of a divided heart in moral action. The sinner, in his sin, is
utterly destitute of righteousness, and the good man, in his
obedience, is completely, entirely obedient: sin on the one
side and obedience, on the other belonging only to voluntary
states. The division of the will between the two contradictory
moral attitudes of sin and holiness is a metaphysical impossibility." The ethical theory underlying the doctrine is here
thrown into emphasis. The man is dissolved into a series of
volitions. Each volition is isolated and looked at apart: and

---

[287] For 1842, pp. 33 ff., 41 ff. An abstract of the address and an estimate
of its teaching are given by Foster, " A Genetic History of the New England
Theology," pp. 459–463.

[288] See in general Fairchild, *The Congregational Quarterly*, April, 1876,
pp. 247 ff.

[289] We are summarizing the accounts of Fairchild and Foster, as cited.
The final words are justified by such a turn of phrase as this, from the pen
of Fairchild (p. 249): " The idea, then, of rising from a partial to a complete
obedience, from imperfect to perfect faith and love, in the sense in which
these are voluntary and responsible acts or states to be required of men, is
*incompatible with the idea of simplicity of moral action, and hence is not
admissible in the Oberlin Theology.*" The italics are ours.

[290] As cited, p. 248.

being treated as a bare volition, it is said not to be capable of a composite character. Volitions are either good or bad; and that is the end of it. But beyond the volition no man is recognized: the volition is the man, and what the volition is at any moment that the man is. As volitions are either good or bad, so then the man is. The morally grey is eliminated: only black and white are allowed to be possible. Every man is either as bad or as good as he can be in the circumstances in which he stands for the moment. There can therefore be no such thing as a partially sanctified believer; and the whole conception of progressive sanctification is excluded. "They allege," says John C. Lord, accurately,[291] "that there is no such thing as imperfect holiness, and, of course, that there is no such thing as being sanctified in part." Over against the general doctrine of the churches which denies the existence of perfect holiness, this doctrine sets the denial of the possibility of imperfect holiness. You are either perfectly holy, or you have no holiness at all. Holiness is a thing that does not admit of abscission and division. The idea is generalized into the proposition that " holiness must be supreme in degree to have the character of holiness at all " — a proposition which might appear to mean that a little sin neutralizes any amount of holiness, but no amount of holiness can affect the quality of existing sin at all, except that the very conception of progressive holiness is excluded. The Church at any given moment is therefore not made up of redeemed sinners in various stages of perfection, but of perfectly holy and perfectly wicked people standing side by side. The two classes are not stable but may be, in the individuals which compose them, continually changing places. The perfectly holy may, and do, become at any moment the perfectly wicked: the perfectly wicked may, and do, become at any moment, the perfectly holy. The average of the mass may yield a result that looks like the partly sanctified Christian as commonly conceived. But the " average Christian " has no real existence, and the average of the mass is obtained by finding the shifting center of gravity of a mass composed

[291] As cited, p. 238.

actually, in varying proportions, of perfectly holy and perfectly wicked men as units. There is no room here, therefore, for two classes of Christians, with a " second conversion " lying between them. To be a Christian at all is to be perfect: and the concern of the Christian is not to grow more perfect, but to maintain the perfection which belongs to him as a Christian and in which, not into which, he grows. What, then, he seeks after is not holiness — he has that. Nor more holiness than he has — if he has any he has all. What he seeks after is " establishment." Holiness cannot be imperfect in degree: but it can be and is imperfect in " constancy." The doctrine has been called " the pendulum theory of moral action." It supposes the man to oscillate between perfect goodness and perfect badness, and denies to him any abiding, permanent character.[292] To one observing the current of an individual life, it may bear — as the church at large does — the aspect of the manifestation of an imperfectly sanctified nature. This is illusion: it is due to the mingling in our observation of successive states of perfect goodness and perfect badness. They do not co-exist, but alternate. The one task of the Christian is to attain a state in which the fluctuation ceases and he is permanently established in holiness.[293] When that state is attained we are not merely " entirely " sanctified — that we had been, at intervals, all along — but " permanently " sanctified. That is the goal of all Christian progress — to cease from falling and remain steadily what all Christians ought to be, and indeed what all Christians are — whenever they are Christians.

The interpolation of this doctrine, as a controlling factor, into Oberlin thinking had the effect of antiquating the doctrine of perfection as previously taught at Oberlin. Cowles, it is true, simply permitted all he had written to stand as it was

[292] Cf. Foster, as cited, p. 460, and the quotation from Cochran there. Cf. also Lord, as cited, p. 239.

[293] Fairchild, as cited, p. 249: " The work required in Christian progress is . . . establishment of Christian character, and more and more complete deliverance from these interruptions of obedience, — an obedience more and more constant until it becomes permanent and suffers no interruption."

written — *litera scripta manet*. Morgan had not hitherto put his hand to the subject, and his hands were free to take up the new doctrine and work out from it as his starting point. To Mahan and Finney, who had written copiously in the earlier sense, the task was set, to adjust their even more copious later discussions to the new point of view. Mahan's method was to accept the new doctrine of course — and to pass by it with averted face on the other side of the road. The phraseology by which Fairchild describes his relation to it is carefully chosen and is the more significant because of its apparent colorlessness. " His later writings," he says,[294] " are intended to harmonize with the doctrine." They do not do so. It remains with him an unassimilated element of thought. Finney, on the contrary, to whom the doctrine was no stranger, entered upon the task of adjustment to it *con amore*. In his " Lectures on Systematic Theology " — the most extended and systematic of his writings — he has made the notion of " the simplicity of moral action " the fundamental principle of his doctrine of salvation, and as a consequence teaches, in point of fact, the perfection of all Christians from the inception of faith in them onward. This necessitates not only a readjustment of the whole trend of his " Views of Sanctification," which he largely incorporates into the new work, but a reconstruction of his entire treatment of the way of salvation, every stage in which requires radical alteration to fit it in with the new point of view. The doctrine of sanctification to which an inordinate formal place in the systematic arrangement is already given, nevertheless actually overflows even these ample bounds and swallows up the space allowed to the other saving operations. The doctrine of salvation becomes almost nothing indeed but a doctrine of sanctification. One of the results of this is that when the formal treatment of sanctification is reached, despite the copiousness with which it is dealt with, little is left to be said of it. In this exigency the term is retained and its meaning altered. " Entire sanctification " no longer stands as the end of the saving process, as the final goal towards which the Chris-

294 As cited, p. 254.

tian's heart yearns. That having become the characteristic of all believers from the moment of conversion, the term "sanctification" as the designation of one stage of salvation and that the most elaborately treated of all, has lost its content. As it must add something to what Christians already possess, and as all Christians — whenever they are Christians — possess "entire sanctification," "sanctification" comes to mean "permanent sanctification." "Sanctification," says Finney, in a vain attempt to deal with the embarrassing situation,[295] as he enters upon his discussion of "sanctification," "may be entire in two senses: (1) In the sense of present, full obedience, or entire consecration to God; and, (2) In the sense of continued, abiding consecration or obedience to God. Entire sanctification, when the terms are used in this sense, consists in being established, confirmed, preserved, continued in a state of sanctification or of entire consecration to God. In this discussion, then, I shall use the term 'entire sanctification' to designate a state of confirmed, and entire consecration of body, soul, and spirit, or of the whole being to God." As much as to say: All believers being from the very fact that they are believers entirely sanctified from the first moment of their believing, on receiving this great new gift of sanctification . . . will, now just stay sanctified. The goal that is set before Christians accordingly ceases to be to become entirely sanctified — that they already are if Christians at all — but to make their entire sanctification no longer fluctuating but permanent. Fairchild thinks [296] that Finney has not been able to maintain his new attitude on the subject in discussion, without some lapses into his earlier point of view. That would be both natural and unimportant; and the instances adduced by Fairchild appear fairly to bear out the suggestion. But it is the new attitude which dominates the entire system of doctrine — if this can be spoken of as a new attitude for Finney and not rather a reversion to an older attitude lying behind that exhibited in what we may perhaps

[295] "Lectures on Systematic Theology," 1851, p. 595. Cf. Fairchild, as cited, p. 256.

[296] As cited, pp. 256–259.

call his Mahan period.[297] And it is this new attitude which dominated the subsequent thought of Oberlin, so long as Oberlin remained perfectionist in its thought. The older point of view which it supplanted was now thought to be not quite an Oberlin point of view; and so far as it continued to exist in Oberlin — " in limited circles " we are told — was " sustained, not by the Oberlin theology or the Oberlin teaching or preaching, but by the writings and periodicals and teachings introduced from abroad, especially of the Wesleyan school." [298] To the Wesleyan period of Oberlin Perfectionism there succeeded, then, from 1841 on, a period of very distinctively Oberlin Perfectionism. And the characteristic feature of this new Oberlin Perfectionism is that it is the product of the conception known as " the simplicity of moral action."

Finney formally expounds his conception of " the simplicity of moral action " in a chapter in the " Lectures on Systematic Theology." [299] He takes his start from the contention that all moral character resides in the ultimate choice; and as this ultimate choice dominates all subordinate choices, volitions and acts, it dominates the whole life. The moral character of the ultimate choice thus gives its moral character to the entire life. As now the ultimate choice is simple and its moral character is simple, a man must be morally just what his ultimate choice is morally. That ultimate choice must be wholly moral or wholly immoral; entirely holy or entirely sinful. A man must be therefore altogether holy or altogether sinful; there are no gradations, no intermixtures, no intermediations. Every man is therefore at any given moment perfectly sinful or perfectly holy.[300] If his ultimate end is selfishness, he is perfectly

---

[297] Fairchild's opinion (p. 259) is different. He thinks Finney has not only not " adjusted his views of sanctification to his accepted doctrine as to the nature of moral action," but that " the treatise, in almost all its features, belongs to a system of theology maintaining mixed action." Finney is not an eminently consistent writer and in the matter of " the simplicity of moral action," Fairchild is very exigent.   [298] Fairchild, as cited, p. 259.

[299] Ed. 1, i. 1846, pp. 150 ff.; ed. 2, 1851, pp. 135 ff. We quote from the latter.

[300] Cf. p. 286 (also pp. 294, 296): " Moral agents are at all times either as holy or as sinful as with their knowledge, they can be."

sinful; if his ultimate end is benevolence, he is perfectly holy. There is no third condition. " Sin and holiness, then, both consist in supreme, ultimate, and opposite choices or intentions, and cannot, by any possibility, coëxist." [301] It is not intended that our holiness, or sinfulness, is as great as, in other circumstances than those in which we exist, it might be. It is only intended that it is complete and entire and as great as in our actual circumstances it can be. The holiness of God cannot be attained by a man; nor that of an angel; nor can even that of a man better placed be attained by one in lower circumstances. What holiness, or sin, is in anyone, is determined by his knowledge, by " the perceived value " of the objects of his choice. " The true spirit of the requirement of the moral law is this — that every moral being shall choose every interest according to its value as perceived by the mind." [302] " The fact is that the obligation of every moral being must be graduated by his knowledge. If, therefore, his intention be equal in its intensity to his views or knowledge of the real or relative value of different objects, it is right. It is up to the full measure of his obligation." [303] A man may thus be entirely holy extensively — that is, conformed to the law as known to him, or willing things according to their respective values as perceived by him — without being very holy intensively. He is, being such, altogether holy.

This is, obviously, only one way of lowering the demands of the law. Indeed, in one aspect, there can scarcely be said to be any such thing as the law in the case. Law is replaced by benevolence, and is fulfilled by willing the good of being as an ultimate end, chosen for its own sake. It is taught that all subordinate ends, and the executive volitions which secure them, not only ought to be, but must be and will be, determined by this ultimate end. So long as we really will the good of being as our ultimate end, we *cannot* make subordinate choices which are means to other ends. A law of mental nature gives dominion to our ultimate end. Having once adopted this ultimate end, our lives in all their details are absolutely de-

[301] P. 141.   [302] P. 140.   [303] P. 144.

termined by it. The mechanism of moral action makes that inevitable. We therefore would seem to need no law. Our ultimate choice of the good of being becomes a law which governs all our activities. It would seem to follow also that we cannot sin. Does not the mechanism of moral action determine that — working back from the ultimate choice of the good of being to the subordinate choices and executive volitions and their execution in acts? But Finney falters here.[304] We cannot sin so long as our ultimate choice of the good of being remains unchanged.[305] But we may change that, and in many cases we do change that. And then we not only can sin and do sin, but must sin and do nothing but sin. We have ceased to be perfectly holy and become perfectly sinful. So long as our ultimate end remains the good of being, our whole life in all its activities is determined by it. We are entirely holy. So soon as our ultimate end ceases to be the good of being and becomes our own selfish gratification, our whole life in all its activities is determined by it. We are entirely sinful. This is the doctrine of the simplicity of moral action as conceived by Finney.

It will be perceived at once that what we called the characterizing features of the older form of Oberlin Perfectionism in point of fact persist in this new construction. Perfection is still conceived as full obedience to the moral law. And full obe-

---

[304] See below p. 147, and note 307.

[305] In his " Lectures on Systematic Theology," 1851, p. 261 Finney says: " The carnal heart or mind cannot but sin. . . . The new or regenerate heart cannot sin." He explains the latter statement thus: " While benevolence remains, the mind's whole activity springs from it as from a fountain," — and appeals to " Make the tree good, etc." In that case we need to ask How, then, can benevolence help remaining? If while it remains all our activity springs from it as from a fountain, how can it be transmuted into its contradictory? We cannot sin so long as it remains, and it remains so long as we do not sin — for have we not sinned, and sinned the master sin of all sin, when we have ceased to make benevolence our ultimate end? We can change our master motive only by changing our ultimate end, and surely we cannot change our ultimate end under its own controlling influence which extends over all our voluntary activity. We must sin while benevolence remains in order to rid ourselves of the benevolence under the control of which we cannot sin. So far as appears, then, the regenerate can never sin again.

dience to the moral law is still measured not by the objective content of the law, but by the subjective ability of the agent. It is still taught with all emphasis that a man is perfect who does all he can do, being what he is; with the disabilities belonging, we would say, to his present moral state; they would say to his present condition of ignorance and weakness; and in the circumstances with which he is surrounded.[306] Beyond this narrow area of fundamental agreement, however, all is contradiction. This state of perfection in which the whole law of God is obeyed — so far as the agent, being what he is and as he is, can obey it — is no longer conceived as the culminating attainment of the Christian, to be reached, not by all Christians, but by some only, the *élite* of the Christian body, separated from the crowd precisely by this great attainment. It is conceived as the primary condition of all other Christian attainments, presupposed in every step of Christian living, and therefore the common possession of all Christians, without which no man is a Christian at all. We are no longer supposed to become perfect by being Christians, and pushing our Christianity to its limits; we become Christians by being perfect and it is only through the gate of perfection that we can enter Christianity at all. All Christians are then perfect: one is not more perfect than another: *ex vi verbi* an imperfect Christian is no Christian at all. There are therefore not two classes of Christians, the merely justified and the justified and sanctified also: no one is justified who is not also sanctified. Sanctifica-

---

[306] To the objection that by his doctrine the standard of holiness is lowered to the level of our own experience, Finney ("Lectures on Systematic Theology," p. 748) has the honesty to reply that it is quite true that in his opinion the standard of holiness has commonly been set too high. Much of the difficulty, he says (p. 749), "has arisen out of a comparison of the lives of saints with a standard entirely above that which the law of God does or can demand of persons in all respects in our circumstances," — " or indeed," he adds, " of any moral agent whatever." Cf. p. 516. The main difference between the Oberlin men and Christians at large turns on this contention. The Oberlin men insist that Christians may be perfect and demand that they shall be. Yet the actual holiness attained does not differ from that attained by the " common Christian." They call this attainment perfection: the others do not: their standard reaches no higher than this, that of the others stretches illimitably beyond.

tion is not a sequence of justification, but its condition; and therefore precedes it. We are not justified in order that we may be sanctified, but sanctified in order that we may be justified. There are only two classes of men, saints and sinners; and the difference between these classes is " radical, fundamental and complete." There is no room for a third class between them partaking of characteristics of both. The sinner has nothing of the saint about him; the saint nothing of the sinner. The saint is dead to sin and alive to God; and " the Bible . . . often speaks in such strong language as almost to compel us to understand it as denying that the saints sin at all; or to conclude, that sinning at all, proves that one is not a saint." [307] Is there not some faltering in that " almost "? Justification, we are told, is conditioned by sanctification, and implies complete sanctification — for God cannot accept as righteous one who is only " almost " righteous. According to the doctrine taught accordingly, all saints are entirely sanctified, are perfect, and do not sin. If they sin, that does not prove so much that they have not been saints, as that they are saints no longer. They may sin, but on sinning they cease to be saints. There are no remainders of sin in any Christian therefore to be eradicated. He is already on becoming a Christian all that he ought to be. Perfection lies behind him, not before. What lies before is only his establishment in his perfection that he may no longer fall from it; that and a growth in outlook which carries with it a

[307] " Lectures on Systematic Theology," 1851, p. 439, cf. p. 846. On pp. 470–472, Finney reverts to his definition of a saint, and having quoted I John ii. 3, 4; iii. 10; v. 1–4, remarks that " these passages understood and pressed to the letter, would not only teach, that all regenerate souls overcome and live without sin, but also that sin is impossible to them." He declines so to press them and takes as their spirit " that to overcome sin is the rule with every one who is born of God, and that sin is only the exception; that the regenerate habitually live without sin, and fall into sin only at intervals, so few and far between, that in strong language it may be said in truth they do not sin." " If at any time he is overcome, it is only to rise again." This is faltering indeed: it is flatly in the face of Finney's elaborately explained doctrine of regeneration with the underlying doctrine of " the simplicity of moral action." This requires him to say that the saintliness acquired in regeneration is incompatible with sinning and is lost by sinning.

corresponding growth in obligation and its fulfilment. Perfect
however he already is, perfect for his present outlook and according to his present obligations; and more than perfect he
cannot become.

It is obvious that one of the chief tasks which devolved on
the advocates of this new form of Oberlin Perfectionism was
the validation of the assumption that only those who are perfect can have any standing whatever in the sight of God. This
task was undertaken from the Biblical point of view by John
Morgan, who devoted to it the first of the two essays he published in *The Oberlin Quarterly Review* for 1845 — the essay
to which he gave the title of " The Holiness Acceptable to
God." This essay was so highly esteemed by Finney that he
incorporated it as a whole in his " Lectures on Systematic
Theology " [308] — thus making it a part of his own argument in
support of the contention that " sanctification is the condition
of justification." By this contention, he says, " the following
things are intended. (1) That present, full, and entire consecration of heart and life to God and his service is an unalterable condition of present pardon of past sin, and of present
acceptance with God. (2) That the penitent soul remains
justified no longer than this fullhearted consecration continues." [309] It will no doubt be observed that Finney replaces
here the term " sanctification " of the original statement, by
its synonym, " consecration." This is a frequent interchange
of terms with him and has no significance for the matter in
hand. By sanctification he means, under either designation,
just " full obedience to the known law of God." [310] Morgan

[308] Ed. 1, ii. 1847, pp. 108–155. We cite the essay from these pages. Finney
omitted it from his second edition, 1851.

[309] Ed. 1, ii. 1847, p. 107, immediately preceding the insertion of Morgan's
essay: ed. 2, 1851, p. 557.

[310] The caption of the section in which this statement occurs in ed. 1, ii.
p. 106 reads: " Sanctification is another condition of justification." This is
expanded in ed. 2, p. 555, without change of meaning, into: " Present sanctification, in the sense of present full consecration to God, is another condition,
not ground, of justification." He is only endeavoring to maintain his formal
definition of sanctification as " a state of consecration to God " (ed. 2, p. 594),
" exactly synonymous or identical with a state of obedience or conformity to

himself puts the question which he undertakes to answer thus:
"*Is any degree of holiness acceptable to God, which, for the
time being, falls short of full obedience to the divine law?*",[311]
and phrases his answer in the equally uncompromising terms:
"Nothing short of present entire conformity to the divine law
is accepted of God."[312] In employing the phrases "acceptable
to God," "accepted of God," he is not speaking abstractly of
what we might suppose to be generally pleasing to God; but
with perfect definiteness of the specific act which is commonly
called justification — of what God requires in order to that
special act of accepting man as righteous in His sight. In order
more clearly to explain his meaning, he uses accordingly such
language as "the holiness" enjoined "as a condition of justification before God";[313] "the supposition that the entire subjugation of sin is indispensable to justification."[314] The ultimate
foundation of the essay is denial of imputed righteousness, and
with it, of course, of the vicarious obedience of Christ; and the
discovery of the righteousness on the ground of which God
accepts man as righteous, in man himself. The contention
made is that God demands a perfect righteousness and man
provides it: the situation thus created being eased only by
defining benevolently what perfect righteousness requires in
each stage of human moral development. Although, however,
justification is very definitely in mind, the discussion is framed
so as to cover a wider field, and what is sought is declared to
be the determination of the degree of holiness which alone is
acceptable to God — at the moment of justification of course,
but also continuously thereafter. "We put the question into

---

the law of God" (ed. 1, ii. p. 200). "Sanctification," says he more at large
(ed. 2, p. 595), "consists in the will's devoting or consecrating itself and
the whole being, all we are and have, so far as powers, susceptibilities, possessions are under the control of the will, to the service of God, or, which
is the same thing, to the highest interests of God and of being. Sanctification, then, is nothing more nor less than entire obedience, for the time being,
to the moral law." It is sanctification, so conceived, which is affirmed to be
the condition of justification.

[311] P. 109.   [313] P. 113.

[312] P. 137.   [314] P. 129.

the most general form," we read, " intending it to apply to
both the accepted holiness of the new-born soul and the holiness of the most mature Christian." [315] We cannot be accepted
by God without this holiness; neither, having been accepted
by Him, can we remain accepted save this holiness be maintained. It is supposed that those accepted by God in justification may not remain acceptable to Him, and may therefore
fall out of that acceptance which is justification — to which
they can be restored again only by becoming again acceptable.
Only the perfect are acceptable to God; if we lose our perfection we lose our acceptance; but a recovery of perfection
recovers also acceptance. The two things, perfection and
acceptance, go together, and are inseparable.

On the basis of this exposition Morgan now asserts that
texts of Scripture which prove or appear to prove that converted persons sometimes sin, in no way embarrass his doctrine.[316] Of course, if converted persons sin, they are no longer
acceptable to God. They must cease to sin to become again
acceptable to Him. He admits that it would be fatal to His
view, " if it could be made out that the Scriptures represent
the saints as constantly sinful." He can allow for a passing
back and forward between saintliness and sinfulness; which
would be a passing in and out of acceptability, and in and out
of that actual acceptance which is justification. But he cannot
allow that one who sins can continue acceptable to God, or
accepted by Him, that is, justified. No one can be accepted by
God who has not ceased to sin; and no one can remain accepted by God except as he continues without sin. It is no
refutation of this contention, Morgan says, to show that Christians sometimes sin: it can be refuted only by showing that
they are always sinful: sinful, of course, with a voluntary sinfulness, since there is no sinfulness which is not voluntary.
" The language of the law plainly shows that it concerns itself
with nothing else than the voluntary inward state or actions
of men." " Nor is there any depravity, corruption, bias, evil
nature, or any thing else of whatever name, with which it is

[315] P. 109.   [316] P. 137.

offended or displeased, in man or devil, except the voluntary exclusion of love, or the indulgence of its opposite. Disobedience on the one hand, and obedience on the other, are the only moral entities known to the Scriptures, or of which the law of God takes the least cognizance. It demands nothing but cordial obedience — it forbids nothing but cordial disobedience." [317] This cordial obedience is perfection and less than this cannot be accepted by God. "Is it the Bible doctrine, that if a man will put away the greater part of his sin, God will, for Christ's sake, forgive him the whole?" No; the Scriptures always conjoin *repentance* with remission, and repentance is nothing but abandonment, and remission cannot be broader than abandonment. To suppose otherwise would be to make Christ "the enemy of the law and the minister of sin." [318]

This teaching, Morgan now says,[319] is not justification by works. It is "gratuitous justification by faith" — because our righteousness on the ground of which alone we are, or can be, acceptable to God — and therefore are accepted by Him — lays no ground in right for a claim upon Him for pardon of our *past* sins. Finney seeks the same result by merely drawing a distinction between condition and ground. Our righteousness is the condition, not the ground of the pardon of our past sins, and acceptance with God. The ground of our pardon is to be sought only in the pure clemency of God: but God exercises this clemency only on the condition that we shall perfectly obey His law. If we will perfectly obey His law, we become acceptable to Him, and He will graciously pardon our past sins. Not our future sins: if we commit any future sins we lose our standing in His favor and can recover it again only by again becoming perfectly obedient to His law, when these new sins, now become past sins, will also be pardoned. Our acceptance with God thus, now and always, is conditioned upon, though not grounded in, our complete obedience to the law.

Whether this distinction between ground and condition can be made to serve the purpose for which Finney invokes it, may admit of some question. Finney lays great stress upon it.

[317] Pp. 111–112.   [318] P. 152.   [319] P. 153.

There is but one "ground" or "fundamental reason," he says,[320] of our justification; and that is "the disinterested and infinite love of God." But there are many "conditions," that is to say *sine-qua-nons*, without which justification cannot take place; "men are not justified for these things, but they cannot be justified without them." This is understood by George Duffield — and Finney says with substantial accuracy — to mean that these are not things which must be performed in order to entitle us to justification, but only invariable "concomitants" of our justification.[321] In this sense Finney represents the atonement of Christ, repentance, faith in the atonement, sanctification, to be "conditions" of justification. He puts them on the same line: one of them is no more a ground, one of them is no less a condition, of justification than the others. He distinguishes, it is true, between present and future justification, but does not "conditionate" the one on repentance and faith and the other on sanctification; but the one on "present" repentance and faith and sanctification, and the other on "future" repentance and faith and sanctification. Justification and sanctification are thus no doubt made invariable concomitants. But does "concomitance" fully express their relation to one another? If it did, it would seem that sanctification would be as much "conditionated" on justification as justification on sanctification. But Finney is not only explicit but emphatic to the contrary. It is to him only an error of "some theologians" to make "justification a condition of sanctification, instead of making sanctification a condition of justification." [322] You can have sanctification without justification, but not justification without sanctification. This is a very one-sided concomitance, and means that the relation of sanctification to justification is not that of real concomitance, but of causal condition. Finney, it is true, denies with all energy that it is the proper "ground" of justification. "I think I may safely say," says he,[323] "that I never for a moment, at any period of my Christian life, held that man's

---

[320] "Lectures on Systematic Theology," 1851, p. 983.
[321] P. 983.   [322] P. 555.   [323] P. 984.

own obedience or righteousness was the ground of his justification before God. I always held and strenuously maintained the direct opposite of this." Quite so. According to his own definition of terms, there is but one " ground or fundamental reason " of justification — that is God's ineffable love. And we all proclaim, of course, with one voice, that out of the love of God alone comes that movement of His grace, the outcome of which is our justification. Only one " ground," then, in this sense. But there are " conditions," says Finney, in the absence of which God's love does not issue in justification, and which are therefore the proper grounds of His love manifesting itself in this particular mode of action. Finney says emphatically that there are four such " conditions." He clearly does not mean merely that justification is always found in company with these four things. He means that it occurs only in sequence to these four things. No atonement, no justification; but not in the same sense no justification, no atonement. No repentance and faith, no justification; but not in the same sense, no justification, no repentance and faith. No sanctification, no justification; but not in the same sense no justification, no sanctification. There is a relation here of precedence and sequence; of cause and consequence. Justification depends on these things, its occurrence is suspended on them; as they do not depend on it, their occurrence is not suspended on it. And that carries with it that justification depends on, is suspended on, " man's own obedience or righteousness."

It is instructive to observe what Finney asseverates that he " holds, and expressly teaches," that the grounds of justification are *not,* set as they are in contrast with the one thing, the love of God, which he declares that the ground of justification is. The ground of justification he asseverates [324] is not (1) the obedience of Christ for us; (2) our own obedience either to the law or to the gospel; (3) the atonement of Christ; (4) anything in the mediatorial work of Christ; (5) the work of the Holy Spirit in us. It is not anything that either Christ or

[324] P. 983.

we have done; and it is not anything that we have done or
have become under the operations of the Spirit. It is solely the
divine benevolence. The Atonement, from the point of view of
the Rectoral theory, which Finney teaches, naturally has no
adaptation to serve immediately as the ground of any act of
God. Its only immediate effect is to bring men to repentance and
faith; and thus the entire work of Christ is reduced to inducing
men to repent and believe. It is not so clear, however, that the
repentance and faith to which men are thus brought, together
with their resultant obedience, do not constitute the proper
ground of their justification in this scheme. No doubt " the
fundamental reason " of justification lies in the love of God:
nothing is required, in this scheme, to enable the benevolent
God to forgive sin — it flows spontaneously out of His benevolence alone. But the benevolent God is not free to act on
this scheme out of His benevolence alone. He has tied Himself
up with governmental obligations. The love of God cannot
fulfil itself in the actual justification of sinners, therefore, consistently with His governmental obligations, except in the case
of those who have been brought by the Atonement (serving
the purposes here of punishment) to repentance and faith,
with the consequent amendment of life which is sanctification.
This " reformation of life " is obviously in such a sense the
" condition " of justification that it may properly be called its
ground. It is not the ground of God's impulse to justify, but it
is the ground of God's actually justifying, the sinner. In it the
manifestation of His love to this or that particular sinner is
grounded. It is the ground of justification in the same sense in
which the righteousness of Christ — active and passive — is
in the Reformation doctrine of justification, namely, that in
view of which God pardons the sins of those whom He justifies
and accepts as righteous in His sight. When Finney strenuously argues that God can accept as righteous no one who is
not intrinsically righteous, it cannot be denied that he teaches
a work-salvation, and has put man's own righteousness in the
place occupied in the Reformation doctrine of justification by
the righteousness of Christ.

Finney, it must be confessed, exhibits no desire to conceal from himself the seriousness of his departure from the Reformation teaching in his doctrine of justification. One of the reasons for his constant insistence that the righteousness of man — no less than the atoning work of Christ — is only a condition, not the ground, of justification, is to escape from all implication of a forensic doctrine of justification. He fairly rages against this forensic doctrine. " Now," he exclaims of it,[325] " this is certainly another gospel from the one I am inculcating. It is not a difference merely upon some speculative or theoretic point. It is a point fundamental to the gospel and to salvation, if any one can be." It is with full consciousness, therefore, that he ranges himself over against the doctrine of the Reformation, as teaching " another gospel." And the precise point on which his opposition turns is that the Reformation doctrine, by interposing an imputation of the righteousness of Christ as the ground on which the sinner is accepted as righteous, does not require perfect intrinsic righteousness as the condition precedent of justification. This he cries out against as a doctrine of justification " in sin." " It certainly can not be true," he declares,[326] " that God accepts and justifies the sinner in his sins. I may safely challenge the world for either reason or scripture to support the doctrine of justification in sin, in any degree of present rebellion against God. The Bible every where represents justified persons as sanctified, and always expressly, or impliedly, conditionates justification upon sanctification, in the sense of present obedience to God." " Present, full, and entire consecration of heart and life to God and his service," he says again,[327] " is an unalterable condition of present pardon of past sin, and of present acceptance with God "; and " the penitent soul remains justified no longer than this full-hearted consecration continues." At an earlier point [328] he lays down the proposition that God cannot in any sense " justify one who does not yield a present and full obedience to the moral law," and, pouring scorn on any

[325] P. 558.
[326] Ed. 1, ii. p. 107; ed. 2, p. 557.
[327] Ibid.
[328] Pp. 157 ff.

" method of justification " which does not presuppose such an obedience, exclaims,[329] " What good can result to God, or the sinner, or to the universe by thus pardoning and justifying an unsanctified soul? " " If what has been said is true," he then remarks,[330] " we see that the Church has fallen into a great and ruinous mistake, in supposing that a state of present sinlessness is a very rare, if not an impossible, attainment in this life. If the doctrine of this lecture be true, it follows that the very beginning of true religion in the soul, implies the renunciation of all sin. Sin ceases where holiness begins." And he closes with an invective against those who object to such as " teach, that God justifies no one, but upon condition of present sinlessness " — than which we could have no more precise assertion that justification proceeds on the presupposition of sinlessness. The attainment of sinlessness with Finney is the first, not the last step of the religious life.

It certainly required some temerity for Finney to " challenge the world " to adduce any Scripture to support what he calls " the doctrine of justification in sin, in any degree of present rebellion against God." [331] Paul might seem to have written a great part of his epistles expressly to provide materials for meeting this challenge. One wonders how such language could have been employed by one who had in mind, say, Rom. iii. 21 ff., which is quoted in this very connection. For it is Paul's direct object in this passage to show that men, being incapable of justification from the point of view of their relation to law-works — Finney's " entire conformity to law " — are nevertheless graciously justified by God, in view of what Christ has done in their behalf — which is clearly an assertion of the substitution and imputation which Finney rejects with repugnance. Precisely what Paul says in the cardinal verses (23, 24) is that " all " — a very emphatic " all," declaring what is true of all believers without exception — that " all have sinned " — the view-point being taken from their present state as believers — " all have sinned and know themselves to be without the approbation of God " — the present

329 P. 160.   330 Pp. 164–165.   331 P. 557.

tense, middle voice, declaring a lack of which they were conscious — " and are therefore justified freely, by His grace, by means of the ransoming which is in Christ Jesus " — the ransoming wrought out in Christ Jesus being the means by which it has been brought about that God can proceed to justify sinners, conscious of their sin, gratuitously; the idea of the gratuitousness of the justification receiving the emphasis of repetition: " freely, by His grace." It is distinctly asserted here that those justified are sinners, and are conscious of standing as such under the condemnation of God at the moment when they are justified; that their justification is not in any sense in accordance with their deserving, but is very distinctly gratuitous, and proceeds from the grace of God alone; and that God can act in this gracious fashion toward them only because He has laid a foundation for it in the ransoming which He has wrought out in Christ. And the Apostle declares that this is true of all who are justified, without exception. In the most explicit language he has just declared that no flesh shall be justified by law-works — that if it is a question of presenting ourselves before God " in entire conformity to the law," every mouth is stopped and the whole world stands under the condemnation of God (iii. 19); and that the only hope of men accordingly lies in the provision by God of a righteousness which is apart from law, and is received through faith in Christ. And now he says that, having provided this righteousness in Christ, God, in view of it, justifies gratuitously those incapable of justification on their own account, that is to say, just sinners. If this is not a justification " in sin " — or as Finney expresses it somewhat more fully,[332] " while yet at least in some degree of sin " — it would be hard to say what is. Another mode of speech employed by Finney is, " while personally in the commission of sin." As with him " all sin is sinning," and there is no sin conceivable except the " personal commission of sin," all these phrases are completely synonymous with him, and what he contends for is the complete cessation of sinning on the part of the person about to be justi-

[332] P. 567.

fied. There being no such thing as " constitutional depravity,"
this leaves him perfectly holy. And it is Finney's contention
that it is only he who is in this condition, a condition of " personal, present holiness," in the sense of course of " entire conformity to the law " — for there is no constitutional holiness,
either — who can be justified. We must have ceased to sin —
and that means we must be sinless — before we can be justified. We are pronounced righteous, because we are personally
righteous. We are looked upon as in entire conformity to the
law, because we are in entire conformity to the law. This is
the precise contradiction of Paul's teaching, according to
which we have no righteousness of our own — a righteousness which is of law — but only a righteousness which is by
faith in Christ, a righteousness which comes from God on faith
(Phil. iii. 9).

It ought not to pass without explicit mention — although
it has repeatedly been incidentally adverted to already — that
Finney makes not only sanctification — entire conformity to
the moral law — but also perseverance a condition of justification. " Perseverance in faith and obedience, or in consecration
to God," he says,[333] " is also an unalterable condition of justification, or of pardon and acceptance with God." He means,
of course, that it is a condition " not of present, but of final or
ultimate acceptance and salvation." Thus instead of looking
upon perseverance as dependent on justification, he looks upon
the continuance of justification as dependent on perseverance.
In the Biblical doctrine the sinner, being justified, receives the
Spirit of holiness, through whose prevalent operations he perseveres to the end. According to Finney the justified person
remains justified so long as he perseveres in the obedience
which is the condition of his justification. In the Biblical view
it is God, in Finney's it is man, who determines the issue: the
whole standpoint assumed by Finney is that of a God responsive to human actions, rather than that of a man operated upon by divine grace. Justification is made, therefore, to
follow and depend upon " present full obedience," " entire

[333] P. 558.

sanctification," "moral perfection," and to endure only so long as they endure. We have accordingly such amazing forms of speech as these: The Christian " is justified no further than he obeys, and must be condemned when he disobeys "; " When the Christian sins, he must repent and do his first works or he will perish." On every sin the Christian is condemned and must incur the penalty of the law of God — that is to say, the Christian on every sin falls out of justification, comes back under the condemnation of the broken law, and must begin the saving process over again, *de novo*. Such passages as Rom. v. 1, 9, viii. 1, 31 ff., have had no influence on this theory whatever. The Christian, having been justified, is not at peace with God; he is not assured that, having been justified by Christ's blood, he will certainly be saved from the wrath by Him; he does not know that, since he is in Christ Jesus, there is no possible condemnation for him, and nothing can snatch him from his Saviour's hands. The point of view exploited carries with it, as George Duffield points out,[334] an odd confusion between the categories of punishment and chastisement. In the place of the dispensation of painful discipline in which the Christian, in his lapses, is represented by Scripture as living, Finney subjects him, on every lapse, to the ultimate penalties of the outraged law. He sees nothing between the perfect obedience due to God and the absolute rejection of the divine authority in high-handed disobedience; between the perfect child of God and God's declared enemy: an imperfect Christian becomes a contradiction in terms; for so soon as the Christian becomes imperfect he ceases to be a Christian — he has fallen from grace, returned to the world, and requires to do his first works over again. In attempting to reply to these strictures of Duffield's, Finney says nothing to the purpose. He only plays with the words pardon and penalty, justification and condemnation. How can Christians be pardoned once for all, and yet their emerging sins still need pardoning — or do they not need pardoning? If a Christian commits a sin — is not that sin condemnable and condemned? If a sinning Chris-

[334] Pp. 985 f.

tian suffers an infliction due to his sin, is not that a penalty? What is the use of playing with words? Use any words you choose, and it remains true — at least in the opinion of the author of the Epistle to the Hebrews (xii. 7 ff.) — that there are grievous inflictions which come from a Father's hands and prove that we are not outcasts but sons: which do not argue therefore our condemnation but our acceptance.

The closing paragraph of Finney's lecture on Justification [335] is given the form of a detached " Remark." Its purpose is to show that what he calls the " old school view of justification " is a necessary result of the " old school view " of depravity: that given the one, and the other, by necessary steps, must follow. " Constitutional depravity or sinfulness being once assumed, physical regeneration, physical sanctification, physical divine influence, imputed righteousness, and justification, while personally in the commission of sin, follow of course." This is all very true. Granted the Augustinian doctrine of sin and the Augustinian soteriology becomes a necessity, if sinners are to be saved. Our interest in it for the moment arises from the evidence it affords that Finney was perfectly well aware that his own series of opposing doctrines constituted a concatenated system, rooted in his denial of innate depravity. Out of his Pelagian doctrine of sin he had been compelled to construct a whole corresponding soteriology, and he was perfectly aware that it stood contradictorily over against the Augustinian at every point. Rejecting " constitutional depravity," that is to say, a sinfulness which goes deeper than the act and affects the " nature " itself, he has no need of any " physical " regeneration, sanctification, divine influence, and accordingly rejects them too: and as there is no reason why the sinner who is a sinner only in act and is endowed with an inalienable plenary ability to do all that he is under obligation to do, should not under the motives brought to bear on him in the gospel, cease sinning at will, and do righteousness, so there is no need of a righteousness of Christ to supply his lack; and none is provided and none imputed — the sinner's

[335] Pp. 567–568.

acceptance with God hangs solely on his own self-wrought righteousness.

There is a single sentence on another page into which Finney compresses one of the most systematic of his statements of his doctrine of justification, especially in its relation to the work of Christ. It will repay us to consider its phraseology closely. This is it: [336] " In consideration of Christ's having by his death for sinners secured the subjects of the Divine government against a misconception of his character and designs, God does, upon the further conditions of a repentance and faith, that imply a renunciation of their rebellion and a return to obedience to his laws, freely pardon past sin, and restore the penitent and believing sinner to favour, as if he had not sinned, while he remains penitent and believing, subject however to condemnation and eternal death, unless he holds the beginning of his confidence steadfast unto the end." According to this statement justification consists in pardon and acceptance, and is obtained by repentance and faith. This repentance and faith is defined as such a repentance and faith as imply the sinner's renunciation of his rebellion and return to obedience to God's laws — a manifest meiosis in which the word " imply " must be read, in accordance with the entire extended discussion, in a high sense. From all that appears this pregnantly conceived faith and repentance is the sinner's own work and is so completely in his own power that, as he has himself provided it, so he can himself withdraw it; and his continuance in the pardon and acceptance which he obtains by it depends absolutely on his maintenance of it. All that Christ has to do with the whole transaction is that by his death he secures " the subjects of the Divine government against a misconception " of God's " character and designs," and thus so far protects them against expecting relief in impossible ways. His work is given thus purely the character of revelation, and is directed to and affects of course man alone. It can affect the action of God only through the effect which it produces on men's mental attitude. It is therefore really not

[336] P. 562.

Christ's work but the attitude of men brought about by it, to which God has respect in pardoning and accepting sinners. Because Christ has secured men against a fatal misconception of God's character and designs, God can pardon and accept sinners — provided that they reform. From all that appears Christ's work has nothing more to do with bringing about their reformation than it has to do with God's pardon and acceptance of them on their reformation. Their reformation is presented only as a second condition, and we may add the only proper condition, of their pardon and acceptance. All that Christ has done is to secure them against walking in wrong paths and that only by making known to them that there are wrong paths. That they walk in the right path is their own doing. If they do, God then pardons and accepts them — for as long as they do.

The theory of the Atonement briefly indicated here is of course the common Rectoral theory, presented, not in its best form, it is true, but yet in its essentials as it is commonly presented by its advocates. How it lay in Finney's mind may be learned in its outlines from such a statement as this.[337] "The Godhead desired to save sinners, but could not safely do so without danger to the universe, unless something was done to satisfy public, not retributive justice. The atonement was resorted to as a means of reconciling forgiveness with the wholesome administration of justice." In the extended discussions, however, something is done to mitigate the arbitrariness of the transaction thus baldly outlined. An attempt is made to show that the provision of an atonement was incumbent on God as the moral governor of the world. A more sustained attempt is made to show that in view of this atonement it is incumbent on God to forgive reformed sinners and receive them into His favor. And some attempt is made to show that the atonement is the producing cause of that reformation, which is the condition of God's pardon of sinners and reception of them into His favor.

" In establishing the government of the universe," Finney

[337] P. 550.

tells us,[338] " God had given the pledge, both impliedly and expressly, that he would regard the public interests, and by a due administration of the law, secure and promote, as far as possible, public and individual happiness." This pledging of Himself to observe public justice in the administration of the universe, did not, it is true, commit Him directly to the provision of an atonement. Public justice requires directly only an even-handed administration of rewards and punishments. Yet, as " an atonement . . . would more fully meet the necessities of government, and act as a more efficient preventive of sin, and a more powerful persuasive to holiness, than the infliction of the legal penalty would do," [339] it may be fairly thought that its provision was incumbent on a God, seeking under His governmental pledge " the highest good of the public." [340] What is here called an atonement is anything which " will as fully evince the lawgiver's regard for his law, his determination to support it, his abhorrence of all violations of its precepts, and withal guard as effectually against the inference, that violators of the precept might expect to escape with impunity, as the execution of the penalty would do." [341] Whatever will do this will " as effectually secure the public interests " and therefore " as fully satisfy public justice," as the infliction of their proper penalties on offenders; and such an atonement having been offered, " public justice demands, that the execution of the penalty shall be dispensed with by extending pardon to the criminal." [342] The pardon of the offender thus becomes incumbent on God. Finney indeed inserts a condition — a very necessary condition — in his fuller statements, and thus avoids making it incumbent on God to pardon all offenders. This condition is — the repentance of the offender. " When these conditions are fulfilled, *and the sinner has returned to obedience,* public justice not only admits, but absolutely demands, that the penalty shall be set aside by extending pardon to the offender. The offender still deserves to be punished, and upon the principles of retributive justice, might be punished according to his deserts. But the public good admits and requires that upon the above conditions he should live, and hence, public justice, in compliance with the public interests and the spirit of the law of love, spares and pardons him." [343]

How the fulfilment of this condition is brought about is left somewhat at loose ends. It is usual with the advocates of the Rectoral scheme to link the work of Christ so closely with the reformation of men, as to constitute this its direct aim and effect, and indeed, to speak exactly, the atoning act itself. Finney does not appear to do this. He does, to be sure, argue that the atonement tends to produce this amendment of life — although he chooses to call it a condition only of the pardon and acceptance which results, and not their immediate ground. It presents " overpowering motives to repentance," he says,[344] and " the highest possible motives to virtue "; and it is " the great and only means of sanctifying sinners." But he does not appear to give the same systematic place to this effect of the atonement that is given to it by most advocates of the Rectoral theory. The reformation of the sinner, which with him, too, really constitutes the atoning act, seems to be thought of by him, at least relatively, independently of the work of Christ. When accomplished, the sinner, reformed though still guilty, is accepted as righteous in God's sight. This " entire consecration of the heart to God in view of all that the atonement signifies " is the same thing as what is called by Finney the sinner's regeneration, explained as consisting in a change of ultimate choice, accomplished, under the merely persuasive influence of the Spirit, by his own free will.

An impression is left in the mind of the reader by Finney's exposition of the relations of retribution and public justice that God is supposed, on assuming the duties of governor of the world, to have been compelled to subordinate — as many less absolute governors have been compelled to do — the law of absolute right to the demands of public interest; and does

[343] P. 321. The italics are ours.   [344] Pp. 326, 335, 333.

not attempt to administer the universe on any higher principle than the general " public good," meanwhile closing His
ears altogether to the absolute imperative of pure conscience.
It may be admitted that in the elaborate discrimination which
is drawn out between " retributive justice " and " public justice," it is fairly shown that what is called " public justice "
does not demand so strict a regard to abstract right and wrong
as does " retributive justice "; and therefore that God if He
were acting merely on the principle of " public justice " need
not be supposed to be meticulously careful of the absolutely
right. But that God in His moral government of the world
proceeds solely on this " public justice " and has regard only
to " public interest," it need not be said, Finney has not
shown in the least. Even though it may be said that
" public justice " demands only so and so, it by no means
follows that God who is the governor of the world will be
governed solely by that consideration. To say that " sin deserves punishment, — and must be punished — it is right, *per
se,* and therefore forgiveness is wrong, *per se,*" Finney rather
plaintively declares, would " thus set aside the plan of salvation." [345] It does set aside the " plan of salvation " as conceived by him; a plan of salvation which has no place in it for
expiation of sin, and supposes that God is looking around for
a plausible excuse for forgiving all sin, the social effect of
which can be neutralized. But it is the one basis of the plan of
salvation of the Bible, the heart of the heart of which is expiation, and which represents God as sheerly unable to forgive sin on any other ground whatever.

[345] P. 934.

IV. THE THEOLOGY OF CHARLES G. FINNEY

THE elements of Finney's conception of the Plan of Salvation are given, in a very succinct form, in a summary of what he speaks of as the " provisions of grace." [346] " God," says he, " foresaw that all mankind would fall into a state of total alienation from him and his government. He also foresaw that by the wisest arrangement, he could secure the return and salvation of a part of mankind. He resolved to do so, and ' chose them to eternal salvation, through sanctification of the Spirit and belief of the truth.' " Nothing is said of why God created a race the apostasy of which he foresaw; [347] or of what hindered His making an arrangement by which most of the apostates, or all of them, would be saved; [348] or of whether the part of mankind which He chose to salvation was a definite or indefinite part. [349] So far as this representation goes, God's entire action is determined by His creatures: He finds Himself (in His foresight) with an apostate race on His hands; an apostate race of whom He can " wisely " — a " wisely " which in Finney's scheme means ultimately " benevolently " — save only a part; and His choice of the part He will save is determined immediately by them and not Himself.

Now comes a description of God's mode of action under His decree of salvation. This action is summed up in the institution of a system of means to effect the end in view — " that is," says Finney, " with design to effect it." These means are the law, the atonement and mediatorial work of Christ, the publication of the Gospel and God's providential and moral government — and also " the gift and agency of the Holy Spirit." Of " the gift and agency of the Holy Spirit," it is said

[346] P. 693.

[347] In point of fact Finney followed New Haven here; see G. F. Wright, as cited, p. 200.

[348] It emerges in the end that Finney considers that it would have required God to change the government He had instituted as the wisest.

[349] It was in Finney's view a definite part, foreseen as those who could be saved under the wisest government.

that it is "to excite in them," that is in the part of mankind
chosen to salvation, "desire, and to work in them to will and
to do, in so far as to secure in them the fulfillment of the conditions, and to them the fulfillment of the promises." This is
followed by the assertion that grace has made sufficient provision to make the salvation of all men possible — a statement
which, as we shall see, is on this scheme somewhat barren —
and that of a portion of mankind certain: and this is followed
by the declaration that all who have the Gospel are without
excuse, if they are not saved — another barren statement on
this scheme. And now we get at the gist of the matter. "Grace,"
we read (italics ours), "has made the salvation of every
human being secure, who can be *persuaded,* by all the influences that God can *wisely* bring to bear upon him, to *accept*
the offers of salvation." The words which we have italicized
are key words in Finney's scheme of salvation. *Persuasion* —
all that God does looking to the salvation of men is confined
in its mode to persuasion. *Wisely* — the governing notion in
all God's saving activities is uniformly represented as derived
from His wisdom. *Accept* — the determining factor in man's
salvation is his own acceptance. In this whole statement the
greatest care is expended in making it clear that all that God
does toward saving men is directed to inducing the objects of
salvation to save themselves. What He does, it is affirmed, is
effective to the end in the case of those whose salvation He conceives it "wise" to "secure." [350] But so far it is left obscure

[350] We are somewhat surprised to find that Finney should have hesitated and vacillated over "Perseverance," in the face of the clearness of this
teaching, and of the corresponding representation of "permanent sanctification" as attainable, as the culminating attainment of Christian living (see,
for instance, the tract "How to Win Souls": There is nothing in the Bible
"more expressly promised in this life than *permanent sanctification*": we
may fall away from regeneration, which is entire sanctification, but not from
this permanent sanctification to which we are *sealed*: "this, remember, is a
blessing that we receive after that we believe"). He tells us, however, (p. 843)
that he did do so, although on the pressure of Scripture he finally accepts
the doctrine, and, indeed gives it an exceptionally full treatment. His rejection of a "physical" regeneration seemed to him to remove one of the
grounds for inferring it; and his rejection of what he calls a "perpetual"
justification removes another. He is thrown back thus on the Scriptural

what the principle is on which the objects of salvation, the salvation of whom He judges it wise to secure, are determined — foresight, or election.

When we turn to the lecture on election, we quickly learn that Finney's doctrine of election is just — Congruism. There are two varieties of Congruism, an Augustinian and an Anti-Augustinian. The Anti-Augustinian variety supposes that the same grace is given to all men alike, but is effective or not effective to salvation according as the hearts of men are " congruous " to it. In this variety there is no place for election, except on foresight of the salvability of men. The Augustinian variety supposes that God, respecting the free will of men, approaches them, just as in the other variety, with " suasive grace " only; but Himself adapts this grace so wisely to the hearts of those whom He has sovereignly selected to save, that they yield freely to its persuasion and are saved. In this variety election is the cause of salvation. Finney may superficially appear to be seeking some intermediate ground between these two ordinary varieties of Congruism: but in point of fact what he presents is, with some variation of form, a curiously complete reproduction of the Molinist scheme. According to him election proceeds on the foresight of salvability; but he does not suppose that the same grace is given to all men alike — although all receive " sufficient grace " — but that God employs in each case whatever grace it seems to Him wise to employ in order to accomplish His end. Those that are salvable — that is, those that are salvable under the wise government which He has established — He secures the salvation of. Those who, under this wise government, are not salvable, He leaves in their sins. Those whose salvation He undertakes to secure, because they are salvable under the wise government He has established, He brings to salvation by suasive influences of grace, adapted in each case to their special needs, and therefore certain to be effective. These are the elect. Obviously

---

declarations supported by the general doctrines of election and the initiative of grace — doctrines to which he gives a purer expression here (where he needs them) than in the residue of his system.

they are elected on the ground of their salvability — under
the wise government which God has established. There is no
sovereignty exhibited in their election itself, except in the
sense that God might have left them also in their sin; if He
were to save any, these were the only ones He could save —
under the wise government established by Him. The only
place in the whole transaction in which any real sovereignty
is shown, lies in God's having established the particular government which He has established, and which determines who
are salvable and who not. The particular government which
has been established has not been arbitrarily established. It is
determined by its wisdom. It is the wisest possible government
for God's end — which is the good of being. Seeking the good
of being, this is the government which an all-wise God must
establish. Its establishment, however, divides men into two
classes — the salvable and the unsalvable under the conditions of this wisest government. Here it is that election is determined. God elects to salvation all those who are salvable
under this wise government. Any sovereignty which may appear in this election is derived wholly from the sovereignty of
the choice of the wisest government to establish. That determined, everything else is determined with it: those that are
salvable; those that, on foresight of their salvability, are
elected to be saved; the manner of grace by which they
are brought to salvation. Proximately their election is on foresight of salvability; only ultimately can it be called sovereign
— that is through the sovereignty of the choice of the wisest
government to establish.

The determining characteristic of the elect on this view,
we presume, is that, in nature, character, situation, circumstances — in their totality, considered in all relations — the
salvation of just these and none others serves as means to
God's ultimate supreme end — the good of being. Not merely
the salvation of some rather than others, but the salvation
of just these same rather than any others, subserves this end.
" The best system of means for securing the great end of
benevolence, included the election of just those who were

elected, and no others. . . . The highest good demanded
it." [351] A slightly different turn is given to this statement, when
it is said: " The fact, that the wisest and best system of government would secure the salvation of those who are elected,
must have been a *condition* of their being elected." What is
suggested by this is, that the reason, or one of the reasons,
why just those who are elected are elected, is that they, and
not others, would be saved under the system of government
which God had in mind to establish. He was bound to elect
those and not others — or else alter the system of government
He had it in mind to establish, under which none others could
be saved: and He cannot alter this system of government because it is the wisest and best system. This brings us back
to the point of view with which we began — that the real
reason of the election of the elect is their salvability, that is,
under the system of government established by God as the
wisest. God elects those whom He *can* save, and leaves unelected those whom He *cannot* save, consistently with the
system of government which He has determined to establish
as the wisest and best. And this seems strongly to suggest that
there is an intrinsic difference between the objects of election
and others, determining their different treatment.

The dominating place which Finney gives to the idea of
wisdom in his construction will scarcely have passed unobserved. God saves all He can wisely save: the particular ones
He saves are those whom alone He can wisely save. Here is
rather a full statement: [352] " I suppose that God bestows on
men unequal measures of gracious influence, but that in this
there is nothing arbitrary; that, on the contrary, he sees the
wisest and best reasons for this; that being in justice under
obligation to *none,* he exercises his own benevolent discretion,
in bestowing on all as much gracious influence as he sees to
be upon the whole wise and good, and enough to throw the entire responsibility of their damnation upon them if they are
lost.[353] But upon some he foresaw that he could wisely bestow

[351] P. 775.   [352] P. 778.

[353] This is one of those numerous clauses which meet us in Finney's
discussions which have no meaning whatever in his scheme of thought, and

a sufficient measure of gracious influence to secure their voluntary yielding, and upon others he could not bestow enough in fact to secure this result." The upshot is that God elects all that it is wise for Him to elect; and as He elects them both to grace and glory, He saves all that it is wise for Him to save. The ground of His election of just them is that there is something in them or in their relations to His system of government of the world, which makes it wise to save them; and this is not true of the others. He does for those others too all that it is wise for Him to do, and He " has no right to do more than he does for them, all things considered." What He does for either never passes beyond mere suasion: everything depends therefore at every step on the free movement of their will. " The elect were chosen to eternal life," we read,[354] " upon condition that God foresaw that in the perfect exercise of their freedom, they could be induced to repent and embrace the gospel." If there is not asserted here election on the foresight of faith, there is asserted election on the foresight of the possibility of faith: on foreseeing that they can be induced to believe, they are elected to life, and the inducements provided. It is foreseen that the non-elect cannot be induced to believe — at least wisely — and inducements to believe are not wasted on them.

It appears that Finney wishes to make it appear that election is in some sense the cause of salvation. But he is hampered by his preconceptions. He wishes to deny that election is " arbitrary." He wishes to represent salvation as depending on the " voluntary " action of men. In order to protect this " voluntariness " of salvation, he wishes to confine all of God's saving operations within the category of persuasion. And above all and governing all he wishes to make benevolence the one spring of the divine action. The ultimate result is that, representing God as ordering the universe for

---

are thrown in therefore merely for effect. In his scheme of thought, the entire responsibility for their damnation lies upon the lost in any case — even if no gracious influences at all work on them. They have plenary ability in any case to meet all their obligations, and are fully responsible for their failure to do so.

[354] P. 780.

the one end of the production of the greatest happiness of the greatest number, he finds himself teaching that men are left to perish solely for the enhancement of the happiness of others. Reprobation is a thorny subject to handle in any case; but in Finney's handling of it its thorniness is greatly increased. He is compelled to confess of the reprobate, that " God knows that his creating them, together with his providential dispensations, will be the occasion, not the cause, of their sin and consequent destruction." Of course, God's foreknowledge of these results when He created the reprobate, necessarily involves them also in His comprehensive intention; but equally of course the sin and destruction of the reprobate were not His ultimate end in their creation. But neither are the holiness and salvation of the elect the ultimate end of God in His dealing with them. In both cases alike His supreme ultimate end lies beyond. What God has determining regard to in His dealing with both alike, says Finney, is the wise ordering of His government. He would prefer the salvation of the reprobate, if — but only if — they could be saved consistently with the wise government He has ordained. But, says Finney,[355] " He regards their destruction as a less evil to the universe, than would be such a change in the administration and arrangements of his government as would secure their salvation." They are sacrificed thus to the good of the universe, and perish not because justice demands that they perish, but because it is better for others — surely not for themselves — that they perish. This is a result of Finney's teleological ethics. And it is here that the benevolence scheme is most severely strained. It was benevolent in God, says Finney,[356] to create men who were destined to reprobation, because, " if he foresaw that, upon the whole, he could secure such an amount of virtue and happiness by means of moral government, as to more than counterbalance the sin and misery of those who would be lost, then certainly it was a dictate of benevolence to create them." We may possibly be able to bow before reasoning which is directed to show that our reproba-

[355] Pp. 786–787.   [356] P. 790.

tion is the unavoidable condition of the attainment of an end high and holy enough to justify any individual evils which are incurred in its achievement — say, the vindication of the right, the preservation of the divine integrity, the manifestation of God's righteousness, the enhancement of His glory. But it is not so easy to acquiesce when we are told that we must be miserable that others may be happy. If the happiness of being is the end to which everything is to give way, it is difficult to see why we should be excluded from our share of it. Surely at all events we must see the note of moral necessity, and not that of a mere governmental expediency, in the transaction before we can readily embrace it as just.

The ultimate reason why the entire action of God in salvation is confined by Finney to persuasion lies in his conviction that nothing more is needed — or, indeed, is possible. For the most deeply lying of all the assumptions which govern his thinking is that of the plenary ability of man. It is customary with him to assert this assumption in the form that obligation is limited by ability; that we are able to do all that we are under obligation to do; that nothing which we cannot do lies within the range of our duty.[357] He himself represents this as the fundamental principle of his teaching — "that obligation implies ability in the sense that it is possible for man to be all that he is under an obligation to be; that by willing, he can directly or indirectly do all that God requires him to do.[358] He thus relegates to a position subordinate and subsidiary to the primary fact of plenary ability even his ethi-

[357] Charles Hodge, *The Biblical Repertory and Princeton Review*, April, 1847, p. 244, says that it is "merely a dictum of philosophers, not of common people" that "I ought, therefore I can." Every unsophisticated heart and especially every heart burdened with a sense of sin says rather, "I ought to be able, but I am not." He cites Julius Müller's reply to Kant, in "Lehre von der Sünde," ii. p. 116.

[358] P. 925. Accordingly A. T. Swing, *The Bibliotheca Sacra*, July, 1900, pp. 466–467, says: "The most fundamental of President Finney's reform principles was, that human ability must be commensurate with human duty." This, he says, dominated not only his thinking but his practice: "Sinners ought to respond at once, *because they can repent if they will.*" "Historically then President Finney stands as one of the most earnest preachers of human ability " — surpassing even N. W. Taylor in this.

cal principle that moral value attaches in strictness only to the supreme ultimate intention, which gives its moral character to all else; and with it, his more fundamental ethical principle still that moral quality attaches only to deliberate acts of will. The ability which he thus ascribes to man as his inalienable possession is not merely that so-called " natural ability " which the New England divines were accustomed to accord to him, and which only recognized his possession of the natural powers by which obedience could be rendered were it not inhibited by man's moral condition. He means, on the contrary, that man has by his natural constitution as a free agent the inalienable power to obey God perfectly. " This ability," he says,[359] " is called a natural ability, because it belongs to man as a moral agent, in such a sense that without it he could not be a proper subject of command, of reward or punishment. That is, without this liberty or ability he could not be a moral agent, and a proper subject of moral government." " Moral agency," says he again,[360] " implies free agency. Free agency implies liberty of will. Liberty of will implies ability of will." And this ability of will extends " so far as the sphere of moral agency extends." The " ability to obey God " which Finney ascribes to man always and everywhere is thus, without any ifs and ands about it, just " the possession of power adequate to the performance of that which is required." [361] In possession of this inalienable ability man's salvation requires and admits of no other divine operation than persuasion.

It is a great concession from this point of view, indeed, to allow that it requires persuasion. Finney does allow this; and this is his sole concession to the supernaturalism of salvation. " From the beginning," he says,[362] men " universally and voluntarily consecrate their powers to the gratification of self," and " therefore they will not, unless they are divinely persuaded, by the gracious influence of the Holy Spirit, in any case turn and consecrate their powers to the service of God."

[359] P. 484.
[360] P. 924.
[361] P. 500.
[362] Pp. 501–502.

They will not; he will not admit that they cannot. He seems, indeed, almost inclined at times to declare that one not a Christian who supposes that " a man is unable to obey God without the Spirit's agency." The assertion of ability to obey God without the Spirit's agency is express. " The question in debate is not whether men do, in any case, use the powers of nature in the manner that God requires, without the gracious influence of the Holy Spirit, but whether they are naturally able so to use them." [363] But along with the strong assertion of their ability to do it, is an equally strong assertion of their universal unwillingness to do it, on the ground of which is erected an assertion of the necessity of the influence of the Spirit for salvation. " I admit and maintain," says Finney,[364] " that regeneration is always induced and effected by the personal agency of the Holy Spirit." " It is agreed," he says again,[365] " that all who are converted, sanctified and saved, are converted, sanctified and saved by God's own agency; that is, God saves them by securing, by his own agency, their personal and individual holiness." The mode of the divine agency in securing these efforts, however, is purely suasive. We are saved " by free grace drawing and securing the concurrence of free-will " [366] — a formula which, so far as the words go, might have a good meaning; but not in the sense which Finney puts on them, for in Finney's sense " drawing " means just teaching. Referring to John vi. 44, he says: " As the Father teaches by the Holy Spirit, Christ's plain teaching, in the passage under consideration, is that no man can come to Him, except he be specially enlightened by the Holy Spirit." Beyond the presentation of motives to action he will not permit the Spirit to go in the way of securing man's salvation. " The power which God exerts in the conversion of the soul," he says,[367] " is *moral* power." " It is that kind of power," he proceeds in explanation, " by which a statesman sways the mind of a senate; or by

[363] " Lectures on Systematic Theology," p. 501.

[364] P. 422.

[365] P. 767.

[366] P. 757.

[367] " Sermons on Important Subjects," p. 30.

which an advocate moves and bows the heart of a jury."
" All God's influence in converting men," he says again,[368] " is
moral influence. He persuades them by his word and his
Spirit." And then he adds, " If men will not yield to *persuasion,* they must be lost "; and phrases his conclusion thus:
" Sinners can go to hell in spite of God." It is certain, he declares in another place,[369] " that men are *able* to resist the utmost influence that the truth can exert upon them; and
therefore have ability to defeat the wisest, most benevolent,
and most powerful exertions which the Holy Spirit can make to
effect their sanctification." They can resist the divine influence
designed to save them because it is only of the nature of persuasion. But the same ability which is adequate to resisting
it, is adequate also to following it; and if it " secures " their
salvation, it is only by this, their free following of it. " The
fact is," says Finney,[370] " the actual turning . . . is the sinner's own act "; " the sinner that minds the flesh, can change
his mind, and mind God." In all this Finney was but repeating
the teachings of the New Divinity of which this very conception is declared by Lyman Beecher to have been the core.
" Our doctrine," says he,[371] describing the essence of the Taylorite contention, " was that GOD GOVERNS MIND BY MOTIVE AND
NOT BY FORCE." " Edwards," he adds, " did not come up to that
fair and square, Bellamy did not, and, in fact, nobody did until
Taylor and I did." Finney did also — " fair and square."

This construction of " the way of life," simple with true
Pelagian simplicity, is nevertheless complicated with some
serious difficulties. It deals throughout with a will to which
the " power to the contrary " is passionately vindicated; and
yet at two several points it asserts a certainty in the determination of the will which appears to be on this ground inex-

[368] *The New York Evangelist,* August 25, 1835, quoted in *The Literary and Theological Review,* March, 1836, p. 16.

[369] *The Oberlin Evangelist,* Lect. 21, p. 193, quoted by John C. Lord, *The Biblical Repertory and Princeton Review,* April, 1841, p. 234; cf. John Woodbridge, *The Biblical Repertory and Princeton Review,* 1842, pp. 426–472.

[370] " Sermons on Important Subjects," pp. 20, 38.

[371] " Autobiography," ii. pp. 156–157.

plicable. How shall we account for the asserted fact that the will, inalienably able to turn at its option from its sins to God, in point of fact never does and never will so turn, except under the persuasive action of the Holy Spirit? A universal will-not, like this, has a very strong appearance of a can-not. A condition in which a particular effect follows with absolute certainty, at least suggests the existence of a causal relation; and the assertion of the equal possibility of a contrary effect, unsupported by a single example, bears the appearance of lacking foundation. And when now we are told that this contrary effect, unexampled otherwise, nevertheless follows with invariable certainty, whenever the persuasive action of the Holy Spirit is exerted to that end — how can we help suspecting that the action of the Spirit in question is something more than persuasive? Let it be borne in mind that all the elect without exception are brought to God by the persuasive action of the Spirit, although many of them, it is affirmed, are much more difficult to convert than many of the non-elect would be; while on the other hand the non-elect are without exception, despite all the suasive influences which may be expended on them, left in their sins. Surely the action of the Spirit on the elect has the appearance of having a character more causal in nature than is expressed by the term persuasion. A persuasion which is invariably effective has at least as remarkable an appearance as the uncaused unanimity of action which it alone breaks, and which, it is affirmed, it alone can break. It is at least an arresting phenomenon that the human will, inalienably endowed with an equal power to either part, should exhibit in its historical manifestation two such instances of absolute certainty of action to one part — in one instance affecting the whole mass of mankind without exception, and in the other the whole body of those set upon by the Spirit with a view to their salvation. If this illustrates " the sovereign power of the agent," " the proper causality of moral agents," " the power of self-determination," [372] in the sense put on these

[372] " Lectures on Systematic Theology," pp. 493–494. On p. 490 the phrase " the will or agent " drops from Finney's pen. He identifies the will with

phrases — entirely satisfactory in themselves — by Finney
and his New Divinity colleagues, we do not see that anything
may be said to be illustrated by anything. It speaks volumes
meanwhile for the strength of Finney's conviction that man is
quite able to save himself and in point of fact actually does, in
every instance of his salvation, save himself, that he maintained it in the face of such broad facts of experience to the
contrary. How can man be affirmed to be fully able and altogether competent to an act never performed by any man whatever, except under an action of the Spirit under which he
invariably performs it?

Of course this extravagant assertion of plenary ability is
correlated with Finney's doctrine of sin. Naturally he scouts
the very idea of " original sin," whether in its broader or nar-

---

the agent, and that accounts for his misunderstanding of Edwards (p. 489)
as if Edwards argued that it is the motive and not the agent which is the
cause of voluntary action. He conceives of the motive as always " objective,"
intruding into the mind from without and determining the will, not as the
mind itself, that is the agent, in a given state of preference. " Edwards,"
says he (p. 491) " assumed that no agent whatever, not even God himself,
possesses a power of self-determination. That the will of God and of all
moral agents is determined, not by themselves, but by an objective motive."
Leave out the word " objective " and remember that the motive is just the
present self and see what becomes of that statement. Self-determination
with Finney, means arbitrary self-determination, independent of or in contradiction of the present preference, which is what other people mean by
motive. How far he was prepared to go, we may see from a remark he makes
in the course of his reply to George Duffield (p. 970). Duffield had written
as follows: " His own glorious nature, His own infinitely exalted excellence,
and not anything conceivably existing apart from, independent and irrespective of God, is that which determines His will." The actual meaning of that
sentence is that God is self-determining or a free agent. Finney, however,
comments as follows: " What does the Doctor mean? Does he mean that
God is a necessary as opposed to a free agent? That His will is necessarily
determined by His self-existent nature? If He means this, what virtue is
there in God? His nature is necessarily self-existent . . . God is not praiseworthy for having this nature, but for the voluntary use or exercise of it."
This comment invites remark at more than one point. It is enough for the
moment to say that it would be difficult more pointedly to assert that the
will is entirely independent of the nature — something which uses the nature,
by which the nature is exercised, not the instrument of the nature's self-
expression.

rower application. There is no imputation; no transmitted corruption of heart. Indeed, there is no heart to be corrupted: "heart" with Finney means just "will." [373] All sin is sinning — and sinning is a purely personal business. It would not be quite exact to say that Finney permits to Adam no influence whatever on the moral life of his descendants. He is willing to allow that they may have received a certain amount of moral injury through the physical deterioration that has come to them by evil inheritance. He even suggests that could this physical deterioration be corrected — say through a wise dietetic system — the sin into which they have fallen partly through its influence might in a generation or two disappear too.[374] Nevertheless physical deterioration and moral depravity are different things, different in kind, and must not be confused with one another. The one we may receive from our progenitors, the other can be produced only by our own moral action. It is true that in point of fact all of us suffer from moral depravity, all of us without exception. Moral depravity is with Finney as universal a fact as it is with the Augustinian doctrine. "Subsequent to the commencement of moral agency, and previous to regeneration, the moral depravity of mankind

[373] The course of reasoning by which Finney arrives at the conclusion that "the heart" in the Bible usage, "when represented as possessing moral character," means just a volition (p. 409), affords a very good example of his method. Its substance is that this must be so, since nothing but volitions possess moral character: "The very idea of moral character implies, and suggests the idea of, a free action or intention." It is plain, therefore, that in its Biblical usage, the heart "can be nothing else than the supreme ultimate intention of the soul." And it is equally plain that "regeneration" which in its Biblical usage, is a radical change of the heart, is "a radical change of the ultimate intention" — that and nothing else.

[374] It was a matter of course that S. B. Canfield, "An Exposition, etc.," 1841, pp. 23 ff., should fall foul of Finney's amazing representation that by "the flesh" the Scriptures mean bodily appetites, and that therefore the flesh may be overcome by physiological reform, under the influence of which we may look forward to a time in a few — very few — generations when "the human body" may be "nearly, if not entirely, restored to its primitive physical perfection" — and so "the flesh" will cease from troubling us. Canfield slyly remarks that the works which Paul enumerates as works of the flesh, in great part, "exist in a far greater degree in *fallen spirits* than among *men*," — and the fallen spirits have no bodies!

is universal." [375] And it is no less "total" than universal; it
manifests itself in the entirety of humanity "without any
mixture of moral goodness or virtue." [376] All men without exception are morally depraved through and through. It will
repay us to attend to Finney's account of the origin and nature of this universal total moral depravity, with which mankind is afflicted.

It will have already been observed that it is denied of the
first stages of infancy. It accordingly does not belong to mankind as such, as at present existing in the world; it is not a
racial affair. It is picked up for himself by each individual in
the process of living. An infant when he comes into the world,
is just a little animal. He has no moral nature. If he dies, he
dies as the brutes die; and his death argues no more than the
death of a brute argues.[377] " Previous to moral agency, infants
are no more subjects of moral government than brutes are ";
that is to say, apparently, they cannot be moved to action
through inducements addressed to their moral judgment.
Therefore, " their sufferings and death are to be accounted for
as are those of brutes, namely, by ascribing them to physical
interference with the laws of life and health." We suppose this
is the proximate cause of the sufferings and death of adults
also; but Finney appears to think that, in saying it of infants,
he is denying that sin has anything to do with their dying —
despite Rom. v. 12. He has as much trouble with their salvation as with their dying. He wishes to find a place for them in
the grace of Christ; [378] but it is not easy to do so, since, Paul
being witness, it was to save sinners that Christ came into
the world — and they are not sinners. And does not Finney
himself say: [379] " The fact that Christ died in the stead and
behalf of sinners, proves that God regarded them not as unfortunate, but as criminal and altogether without excuse " ?
No doubt, in saying this he had adults only in mind — but, is
it not a proposition of universal validity, and, then, how can
infants be partakers of this grace of Christ? Is it not true, as

Augustine urged to Finney's prototype, that in this view, Jesus cannot be "Jesus" to infants, because "Thou shalt call his name Jesus, for it is He that shall save His people from their sins"? Finney is reduced to arguing [380] that if Christ does not save them from "a sinful constitution," He does save them "from circumstances which would certainly result in their becoming sinners, if not snatched from them." A kindly proleptic salvation, it seems, may at least be theirs. But, very naturally, he does not seem wholly satisfied with this. He adds in a tone which may appear a little petulant: "All that can justly be said . . . is, that if infants are saved at all, which I suppose they are, they are rescued by the benevolence of God from circumstances that would result in certain and eternal death, and are by grace made heirs of eternal life. But after all, it is useless to speculate about the character and destiny of those who are confessedly not moral agents. The benevolence of God will take care of them. . . ." That sounds like very cold comfort to sorrowing parents. And in view of the fact that half of the human race die in infancy, it offers a trying puzzle to the philosophical thinker. And can we acquiesce without protest, when we are told that infants are "confessedly not moral agents"? Perhaps if we press the word "agents" — but let us substitute "beings." Are infants not moral beings? Does a man cease to be a moral being every time he goes to sleep? Are we moral beings only when we are acting, but become unmoral and only brutes whenever we are quiescent? We are told with extended explication how the infant picks up sin in the course of living: it is connected, we see, with its picking up a moral nature, too, in the course of living — though how it accomplishes this greater feat, we are not so explicitly told. At all events this is Finney's doctrine: infants are at first just little animals; after a while they pick up a moral nature; at that very moment they pick up sin also. Thus all men become depraved from the very first moment when moral agency begins with them.

Adam has nothing to do with it — despite Rom. v. 12 ff.

[380] P. 390.

No, not quite that. Adam has something to do with it, but
nothing decisive. What happens is this. These little brutes of
babies, like other brutes, of course follow their impulses. These,
being constitutional, have no moral quality. Following them,
the babies form habits of action in accordance with their impulses. This action has no moral quality. But one fair day the
babies awake to moral values, and then their whole habitual
activity at once becomes sin. Their new knowledge comes too
late to save them from this sin. Their habits of action are too
strong to be reversed by it. They are inevitably persisted in,
and thus the poor babies become totally depraved because of
habits formed before they knew any better. What Adam has
to do with it is this — because Adam sinned, and because all
after Adam have sinned — they all would inevitably have
sinned whether Adam had sinned or not — the physical nature
inherited by babies is to a certain extent disordered, and this
makes their impulse to self-gratification perhaps somewhat
more clamant than otherwise it would have been.[381] In any
case this impulse would have been strong enough to carry the
day against the new ethical knowledge which comes to them
when they become moral agents. But perhaps because of
Adam's sinning — and because of the sinning of all since Adam
— it carries the day, not with more certainty — it would certainly have carried it anyhow — but with a more energetic
effect than it otherwise would have done. Here is the way
Finney himself puts it: [382] " The sensibility acts as a powerful
impulse to the will, from the moment of birth, and secures
the consent and activity of the will to procure its gratification,
before the reason is at all developed. The will is thus committed to the gratification of feeling and appetite, when first
the idea of moral obligation is developed. This committed state

---

[381] " Lectures on Systematic Theology," p. 381: " We can also predict,
without the gift of prophecy, that with a constitution physically depraved,
and surrounded with objects to awaken appetite, and with all the circumstances in which human beings first form their moral character, they will
seek universally to gratify themselves, unless prevented by the illuminations
of the Holy Spirit."

[382] P. 397.

of the will is not moral depravity, and has no moral character, until the idea of moral obligation is developed. The moment this idea is developed, this committal of the will to self-indulgence must be abandoned, or it becomes selfishness, or moral depravity. But, as the will is already in a state of committal, and has to some extent already formed the habit of seeking to gratify feeling, and as the idea of moral obligation is at first but feebly developed, unless the Holy Spirit interferes to shed light on the soul, the will, as might be expected, retains its hold on self-gratification." And again: — " A diseased physical system renders the appetites, passions, tempers, and propensities more clamorous and despotic in their demands, and of course constantly urging to selfishness, confirms and strengthens it. It should be distinctly remembered that physical depravity has no moral character in itself. But yet it is a source of fierce temptation to selfishness. The human sensibility is, manifestly, deeply physically depraved; and as sin, or moral depravity, consists in committing the will to the gratification of the sensibility, its physical depravity will mightily strengthen moral depravity. Moral depravity is then universally owing to temptation."

We have here of course only the familiar construction of the old *Rationalismus Vulgaris;* and no more here than there is the implication of God in bringing the human race into a condition of universal depravity escaped. It was God, no doubt, who made the human race after such a fashion that its selfish impulses should get the start of its reason in the development of the child, who should therefore be hopelessly committed to sin before it knew any better. We are told of Lyman Beecher,[383] that " in commenting on the sentiment or

---

[383] " Autobiography," ii. p. 573. Nevertheless this view is taught not only by Finney but also by Beecher's friend, N. W. Taylor (*The Quarterly Christian Spectator*, June, 1829, p. 366). A child, says Taylor, enters the world with a variety of neutral appetites and desires. These are rapidly developed, and each advancing month brings them new objects of gratification. *" Self indulgence* becomes the master principle in the soul of every child, long before it can understand that this self indulgence will ever interfere with the rights, or entrench on the happiness of others. Thus by repetition is the force of

opinion which seeks to account for the fact that everyone sins,
not by alleging natural depravity, but by saying that 'the
appetites and passions are developed faster than reason; that
is, in the nature of things which *God* has constituted, the
appetites and passions *necessarily* obtain the ascendency over
reason,' Dr. Beecher said, 'It is by this theory as if God had
placed a man in a boat with a crow-bar for an oar, and then
sent a storm on him! Is the man to be blamed if in such a case
he is drowned?'" All that is accomplished by this explanation of how it comes about that man is morally depraved, is
that God and not man is made inexcusable for it. God betrays
mankind into depravity wholly arbitrarily, with no excuse, not
to say justification, for His act. All that can be said is that this
is the way God has chosen to make man. No reason is assigned,
none is assignable, for His making him in such a manner that
he must at the first dawn of moral agency become totally and
hopelessly depraved. If anyone supposes that an exoneration
for God is supplied in the circumstance that He does not
directly create depravity in the human heart, but produces it
only indirectly, through the operation of the laws of human
development which He has ordained, we are happy to say
that Finney is above such a subterfuge. He knows perfectly
well that the maxim *facit per alium facit per se* is as valid
here as elsewhere. "To represent the (human) constitution
as sinful," he argues,[384] "is to represent God, who is the
author of the constitution, as the author of sin. To say that
God is not the direct former of the constitution, but that sin
is conveyed by natural generation from Adam, who made himself sinful, is only to remove the objection one step farther back,
but not to obviate it; for God established the physical laws
that of necessity bring about this result." Well, God estab-

---

constitutional propensities accumulating a bias towards self-gratification,
which becomes incredibly strong before a knowledge of duty of a sense of
right and wrong, can possibly have entered the mind." Under the influence
of this bias, the child, when at length the commencement of moral agency
arrives, sins with a uniform certainty as great as if "the hand of Omnipotence
were laid upon the child to secure the result."   [384] P. 391.

lished the physical laws which bring it about that every child of man becomes totally depraved at the first dawn of moral agency, and, according to Finney, He did it arbitrarily, and in full knowledge of the effect and therefore with the intention that that effect should follow. On the other hand, though God is supposed in the doctrine Finney is criticizing to have attached the communication of sinfulness to Adam's posterity descended from him by ordinary generation, He is not represented as having done so arbitrarily but in a judicial sentence; so that a ground is assigned for His act and a ground in right — and Finney has not shown that this ground did not exist, or that existing, it was not a compelling ground in right. What Finney does is merely to substitute another account of universal sinfulness for this one — the Rationalistic account for the Augustinian one — and in doing so, to use a coarse expression, to jump from the frying pan into the fire. He leaves God equally responsible for human depravity, and deprives Him of all justification for attaching it to man. We do not assert that the Rationalistic account of human depravity which Finney exploits must necessarily leave God without justification for inflicting it upon man. It might conceivably be presented merely as an attempt to explain the manner in which man actually acquired a depravity to which he has been justly condemned on account of the sin of his first parents. It would still be open to fatal objections, but no longer to this one — that it represents God as arbitrarily creating the human race after a fashion which made it inevitable that every member of it should fall into hopeless moral depravity — at the first dawn of moral agency — as if the kind of humanity which He desired, intended and provided was a totally depraved humanity. But Finney does not set his theory forward as indicating the manner in which God brings a deserved punishment upon a guilty race. He energetically denies that the race on which this depravity is brought is a guilty race, or that it can be conceived as a punishment. He presents it as the account of how the human race — in all the length and breadth of it — becomes in the first instance sinful, in any sense of that word. And his object is to represent it as becoming so voluntarily — with a voluntariness, which, although embracing every individual of the race, is repeated in each individual's case in the completest isolation of distinct personal action.

A tendency is exhibited at times to neglect this more elaborate explanation of universal depravity, and to represent it as sufficiently accounted for by the formula of freedom plus temptation. All men are free agents, and all men are tempted; therefore all men sin. The formula is obviously inoperative in this crude form of its statement, unless free agency is supposed to carry with it, *per se,* helplessness in the face of temptation, and always to succumb to temptation if it is addressed to it in an enticing form. Finney is near to this crude form of statement when he writes: [385] "Sin may be the result of temptation; temptation may be universal, and of such a nature as uniformly, not necessarily, to result in sin, unless a contrary result be secured by a Divine moral suasion." He is still near it when he writes:[386] "Sin may be, and must be, an abuse of free-agency; and this may be accounted for, as we shall see, by ascribing it to the universality of temptation, and does not at all imply a sinful constitution. . . . Free, responsible will is an adequate cause in the presence of temptation, without the supposition of a sinful constitution, as has been demonstrated in the case of Adam and of angels. . . . It is said that no motive to sin could be a motive or a temptation, if there were not a sinful taste, relish, or appetite, inherent in the constitution, to which the temptation or motive is addressed. . . . To this I reply, — Suppose this objection be applied to the sin of Adam and of angels. Can we not account for Eve's eating the forbidden fruit, without supposing that she had a craving for sin?" Finney has permitted it to slip from his mind as he wrote that the problem he has in hand is to offer an account not of individuals sinning, but of the universality of sin. Free agency plus temptation may account for the possibility of sin, and may lay a basis for an account of the actual occurrence of

[385] P. 380.   [386] P. 387.

sinning in this or that case. It will not account for universal
sinning. For that, nothing less than a universal bias to sin will
supply an adequate account. That is the meaning of the statement which Finney quotes in order to repel, but so quotes as
to empty it of its meaning. Probably no one of those whom
Finney had in mind ever intended to say just that " no motive
to sin could be a motive or a temptation, if there were not a
sinful taste, relish, or appetite, inherent in the constitution, to
which the temptation or motive is addressed." What was intended to be said was, no doubt, that no motive to sin can be
a temptation with universal — that is, invariable — effect,
unless there is something in those tempted which constitutes
a bias to sin. That is true; and one of the proofs that it is true
is, that Finney, abandoning the simple formula of free-agency
plus temptation, is himself compelled in the end to assume a
bias to sin in order to account for the universality of sin. The
child, he teaches — that little brute — must be supposed to
have acquired habits of action which his moral sense, so soon
as moral agency dawns in him, pronounces to be sinful, if we
are to account for his universally succumbing to solicitations
to what he now perceives to be sin. He has acquired a bias
to what is objectively sinful, before he faces temptations to
these very things, now by his newly obtained knowledge of
right and wrong, become also subjectively sinful. That is Finney's account of universal sin. It posits a bias to sin as distinct
as that posited by the Augustinians. The difference is that the
Augustinians posit a bias brought by every man into the world
with him; Finney a bias created invariably for himself by
every man in his first essays at living.

Finney's repulsion of the Augustinian doctrine of original
sin does not turn, then, on its attributing a bias to evil, to
man, as at present constituted. He himself attributes total
depravity to man from the first moment of his becoming a free
agent, and that is the same as to say from the first moment
of his becoming man. It turns in the first instance on the
tracing by the Augustinians of the bias to evil back to Adam
— despite his own recognition of an effect of Adam's fall,

through "physical depravity," on humanity, increasing its
liability to sin. And it turns secondly on the nature of the depravity attributed by the Augustinians to man. Finney will
not hear of the predication of moral depravity to anything but
"violations of moral law" and the "free volitions by which
these violations are perpetuated." [387] " All sin," he declares,[388]
"is actual, and . . . no other than actual transgression can
justly be called sin." He knows and will know nothing therefore of a sinful " nature," or " constitution " as he likes to call
it, embodying his argument in a word. It is his psychology
which is at fault. The soul, to him, consists of its substance and
its acts; there is nothing more, and there is room for nothing
more — for such things, for example, as permanent, though
separable, dispositions. " We deny," he says,[389] " that the human constitution is morally depraved . . . because it is impossible that sin should be a quality of the substance of soul
or body. It is, and must be, a quality of choice or intention, and
not of substance." He will not allow that *tertium datur*. If sin,
he declares,[390] " be anything, it must be either substance or
action." He will allow no other than these two categories. His
psychology compels him thus to reject any and every doctrine
which appears to him to imply anything permanent in the soul,
permanently affecting its actions, except the bare soul itself.
He therefore constantly speaks as if the Augustinians thought
of the sinfulness of the soul as a modification of the soul itself
in its very substance, or else as the addition of another substance to the soul; as if, in a word, they were all Flacians. To
him on the contrary, everything which is not the substance
of the soul is one of its acts; and as he cannot attribute sinfulness to the soul itself, he therefore confines all sin to actual
sinning. The tree is not good and its fruit good: we are to be
content with the good fruits. The agent is lost in his acts, and
the practical result is pure activism. The question comes to be,
Is the man good or bad, or only his acts? Leonard Woods, in a
passage characterized by great force and simplicity of lan-

[387] P. 372.   [389] P. 391.
[388] P. 395.   [390] P. 392.

guage, at once points out and determines the exact issue. "Holiness or unholiness," says he,[391] "belongs primarily and essentially to *man himself,* as an intelligent, moral being, and to his *actions* secondarily and consequentially. . . . The connection between the character of the actions and the character of the agent is invariable. Take an unrenewed sinner. . . . It is necessary that he should be born again. *He,* the *man,* must be created anew; and if he is created anew, it will be *unto good works:* not that *good works* must be created, he himself remaining unchanged; but that *he* must be created anew, and then, as a matter of course, good works will be performed. . . . To say that regeneration *consists in* good moral exercises, that is, in loving God and obeying his commands, seems to me to be an abuse of language. It is as unphilosophical and strange, as to say, that the birth of a child consists in his breathing, or that the creation of the sun consists in his shining."

The affiliations of Finney's notion here are obviously with that Pelagianizing doctrine of concupiscence which infested the Middle Ages and was transmitted by them to the Roman Church. It differs from that doctrine at this point only in its completer Pelagianism. Like it, it conceives of man as persisting, under whatever curse it may allow the fall to have brought upon him, *in puris naturalibus;* and, in order to sustain this position, it denies moral character to all the movements of the human soul, deliberate volitions in view of moral inducements alone excepted. It was natural that the attention alike of Finney in sustaining and of his critics in assailing this contention was focused in the first instance on its bearing on those affectional movements — love, hate, malice, compassionateness — in the manifestations of which the man in the street is prone to see moral character especially exhibited. Having the courage of his convictions, Finney boldly proclaimed these affectional movements without any moral character whatever; and thus fell into a body of startling paradoxes which made him the easy mark of ridicule. John Woodbridge expounds his teaching

[391] "Works," 1851, ii. pp. 537–538.

in the following fashion: [392] " Concupiscence is reduced to the blameless, though, when they become excessive, somewhat dangerous cravings of physical appetite. Supreme self-love is declared to be an essential characteristic of intelligent moral agency, against which there is no law; which is the spring of all virtue as well as of vice; and to which no more blame can be attached than to the pulsations of the heart, or the vibrations of a pendulum. Affections, as such, have no character; they are but the innocent susceptibilities of our nature, and their most violent workings are innocent, except so far as they are produced or modified by a previous deliberate act of will. In all other cases, they are passive emotions, like the involuntary impressions made upon the brain by the bodily senses. It follows, on this principle, that love to God and hatred of him, are equally indifferent things; and that they become praiseworthy or criminal, solely in consequense of their connection with some previous purpose of the mind." What the moral man above everything has to do, is, recognizing the purely " constitutional " nature of his affectional movements, to abstract himself from them altogether, and to determine all his activities by voluntary choices made in view of the perception of the supreme intrinsic value of the good of being. To be governed in any action whatever by our constitutional affections, whatever they may be — whether what in the common estimation would be called wicked or what in that estimation would be called good, alike — is in view of the supreme obligation that rests upon us to direct our activities to the one end of the good of being, no longer merely unmoral but in the highest degree immoral. It is preferring self-gratification to that benevolence which is the sum of virtue. There is no more telling page in Charles Hodge's very telling review of the first volume of Finney's " Lectures on Systematic Theology," [393] than that in which he develops the consequences of this position. " The sin does not lie," in Finney's view, he

---

[392] " Theological Essays Reprinted from the Princeton Review," 1846, p. 436.

[393] *The Biblical Repertory and Princeton Review*, April, 1847, pp. 268 ff.

reminds us,[394] " in the nature of the feeling, but in the will's being determined by any feeling." " It matters not what kind of desire it is," Finney declares, " if it is desire that governs the will, this is selfishness," and therefore, " the choice of anything because it is desired is selfishness and sin." " Mr. Finney is beautifully consistent in all this," comments Hodge,[395] " and in the consequences, which of necessity flow from his doctrine. He admits that if a man pays his debts from a sense of justice, or feeling of conscientiousness, he is therein and therefore just as wicked as if he stole a horse. Or if a man preaches the gospel from a desire to glorify God and benefit his fellow men, he is just as wicked for so doing as a pirate. We may safely challenge Hurtado de Mendoza, Sanchez, or Molina to beat that." The illustrations which Hodge employs in this extract are not his, but Finney's own,[396] and they may help to indicate to us the thoroughness with which he cleansed our affectional movements from all moral character. Pure will plus external inducement — which may be in the way of temptation to evil, or may be in the way of incitement to good — that is all that comes into consideration in our moral judgments.

One of the gains which Finney felt himself to obtain from his denial of all " constitutional depravity," was that there was nothing left in man after his " conversion " which could act

[394] P. 271.
[395] P. 272.
[396] "Lectures on Systematic Theology," 1851, p. 266: " He may be prevented " from committing commercial injustice, " by a constitutional or phrenological conscientiousness, or sense of justice. But this is only a feeling of the sensibility, and, if restrained only by this, he is just as absolutely selfish as if he had stolen a horse in obedience to acquisitiveness." So, page 295: " If the selfish man were to preach the gospel, it would be only because, upon the whole, it was most pleasing or gratifying to himself, and not at all for the sake of the good of being, as an end. If he should become a pirate, it would be for exactly the same reason. . . . Whichever course he takes . . . with the same degree of light it must involve the same degree of guilt." By the " selfish man " in these extracts, there is not meant a man unusually selfish: " selfishness " is only the mark in Finney's nomenclature of the imperfect, as " benevolence " is of the perfect man. To act on selfish motives means with him to act on any other motives than the good of being as supreme end.

as *fomes peccati,* and sways his volitions sin-ward. He was perfectly free to admit that we must begin by denying the sinfulness of " concupiscence," if we are to end by affirming " entire
sanctification." " Those persons," he says, " who maintain the
sinfulness of the constitutional appetites, must of course deny
that man can ever be entirely sanctified in this life." From this
point of view also, he is eager to show " not only that sanctification implies merely ' present obedience,' ' right volitions
now,' and produces ' no change of our nature so that we become good in ourselves,' but that there is nothing ' in us,' antecedent to moral action, operating as the occasion of sinful
exercises, which *needs* to be eradicated or *changed* in order to
our being in a state of ' entire sanctification ' "; and " to *refute*
the doctrine, that apart from present transgressions, ' there
might be that in a person which would lay the foundation for
his sinning at a future time.' " [397] If there is nothing in us from
which we need to be saved except our " commitment to self-
gratification as the end of our being," and nothing to be in us
to which we are to be saved except a like " commitment to the
good of being as the end of our being," it is easier to believe
that the passage from the one to the other — being only
a passage from one purpose to another — may be made
absolutely at once; must be made, indeed, if made at all, absolutely at once. It is according to Finney, thus, only our purpose which " needs to be radically changed." What we call a
" wicked heart " is only a purpose; what we call a " good
heart " is only a purpose; and therefore Joseph I. Foot calls
this theology " the heartless theology " — the theology, that is,
which goes no deeper in its conception of salvation than a
simple change of purpose, which conceives that all that happens to a man when he is saved, absolutely all that happens to
him, is a change of purpose. A change of purpose is, naturally,
an act of our own, and Finney therefore not only identifies
regeneration and conversion, but polemicizes against all attempts to erect a distinction between them.[398] We regenerate

[397] The quotation is from Canfield, " An Exposition, etc.," pp. 17 ff.
[398] P. 408.

ourselves: only the man himself can " change his choice," and if he will not do it, " it is impossible that it should be changed " — " neither God, nor any other being, can regenerate him, if he will not turn." [399] It is we ourselves then who make ourselves holy, and that at a stroke. For regeneration " implies an entire present change of moral character, that is, a change from entire sinfulness to entire holiness." [400] — a " present entire obedience to God." [401] After this it is only a question of maintenance — of the maintenance of that " radical change of ultimate intention," that change from a selfish ultimate choice to benevolent ultimate choice, which we may call indifferently repentance,[402] or faith,[403] or conversion, or regeneration, or sanctification.

It is quite clear that what Finney gives us is less a theology than a system of morals. God might be eliminated from it entirely without essentially changing its character. All virtue, all holiness, is made to consist in an ethical determination of will. " What is virtue? " he asks, and answers: " It consists in consecration to the right end; to the end to which God is consecrated." [404] And " all holiness," he defines,[405] consists in " the right exercise of our own will or agency." The supreme ultimate end to which in the right exercise of our will we must direct ourselves, if we would be virtuous or holy — these things are one — is the good of being. God is of course included in this being, but only as part of the whole — Being — to which our benevolent purpose is directed. And He is just as much subject to this universal ethical law as we are. He too must make

[399] P. 413.

[400] P. 413.

[401] P. 994.

[402] P. 593: Repentance " implies a return to full obedience to the moral law "; " regeneration and repentance consist in the heart's return to full obedience, for the time being, to this law."

[403] P. 537: " Present evangelical faith implies a state of present sinlessness. . . . Its existence in the heart must be inconsistent with present sin there. Faith is an attitude of the will, and is wholly incompatible with present rebellion of the will against Christ."

[404] P. 46.

[405] P. 693.

the good of being His supreme ultimate end, on pain of becoming, as we would in like circumstances become, instead of
as holy as He can be, as wicked as He can be. We are all, He
and we, members of one ethical body, governed by one ethical
law, and pursuing a common ethical course. But since the same
law governs God and us, it is clear that we are dealing with
pure ethics, not religion. God has no religion. And since this
ethical law sets the good of being, interpreted as happiness,
as distinguished from our own happiness, described as self-
gratification, or selfishness, as the supreme ultimate end, the
choosing of which includes all virtue — God cannot be held to
be the sole or even the chief object included under the term,
"Being," the good of which is our supreme ultimate end. For
God at least to choose His own good — or happiness — solely
or chiefly as His supreme ultimate end — would not that be
that selfishness which is declared to constitute us as wicked
as we can be, instead of as holy as we can be? Finney constantly employs the double phrase, "God and the universe"
as the synonym of Being in this reference; and we may think
it possible that he wished the two elements in the composite
idea to be distributed differently in our case and in God's —
that in our case it should be God along with the universe, in
God's, the universe along of course with Himself — as even we
include ourselves in the Being whose good we seek. But can we
even imagine God taking this subordinate place in His own
eyes, attributing "greater intrinsic value" — which Finney
says is the reason why we are to seek the happiness of the
universe above our own — to the universe than to His own all
glorious Being? Must not His own glory be to Him also, as it
must be to us, His supreme ultimate end? We said that God
might be eliminated entirely from Finney's ethical theory without injury to it: are we not prepared now to say that He might
be eliminated from it with some advantage to it.[406]

[406] G. F. Wright devotes an article in *The Bibliotheca Sacra*, April, 1876,
pp. 381-392, to "Dr. Hodge's Misrepresentations of President Finney's System of Theology" — referring only to the remarks on Finney made by Hodge
in his "Systematic Theology." The first of his complaints is that Hodge in

" True religion," says Finney, in one of his numerous brief
summaries of his general views,[407] " consists in benevolence, or
in heart obedience to God." This identification of " benevolence " and " obedience " does not appear obvious to the
uninstructed mind and requires some explication. Finney discovers the intermediating idea in the following consideration.
" It," that is, religion, " consists essentially in the will's being
yielded to the will of God " — that is, no doubt, in " obedience." But he continues epexegetically: " in embracing the
same end that he embraces " — and this adoption of His end
as our end (how that sounds like Albrecht Ritschl!) may possibly be considered " benevolence." We read on: " and yielding
implicit obedience to him in all our lives, or in our efforts to
secure that end." " This," he now adds, " constitutes the essence of all true religion." In that case the essence of religion
is obedience; and it can be benevolence only as obedience may
be construed as rendered, not because it is due, but out of
good will; as if we obeyed God, not because He is God, whom
to obey is our primary obligation, but because we are good
and glad to subject ourselves to another for His pleasing.
Religion being obedience, it is distinctly a matter of will, and
also of conduct, the product of will. Voluntary subjection is
its form, although the form of this subjection is described as
the adoption of the Divine end as our own and the prosecution
of it (always under the Divine prescription) with all our
might. The adoption of the end of God as our end, and obedience to the will of God, are not quite the same conception:
they are assimilated to one another by the requirement that
we shall prosecute this end when adopted in implicit obedience to the Divine prescription. Clearly this is a religion of
law, and the heart of it is obedience: and these are ethical conceptions. Having thus made religion to consist " essentially in

---

one way or another represents Finney as " putting the universe in the place
of God." Hodge of course does not mean that Finney makes this substitution expressly, but only virtually. We think that is not an unfair statement
of the logical results of some elements of his system.

[407] P. 716.

yielding the will to God in implicit obedience " — that is, an affair of will — Finney now represents the emotional life of the religious man as, not a part, but merely a consequence of his religion. " The feelings or affections, or the involuntary emotions, are rather a consequence, than strictly a part of true religion." Faith itself can be thought of as " an essential element of true religion," only because it is " not an involuntary, but a voluntary state of mind "; that is, an act of will. Religion is thus conceived as through and through an affair of the will. " It should never be forgotten," we read,[408] " that all true religion consists in voluntary states of mind, and that the true and only way to attain to true religion, is to look at and understand the exact thing to be done, and then to put forth at once the voluntary exercise required." [409]

In the preface of his " Lectures on Systematic Theology," Finney declares [410] that the subject of the book is " Mind in its relations to Moral Law," and that what he has said on " Moral Law," and on the " Foundation of Moral Obligation " is the key to the whole. This remark seems to have a narrower reference as it appears in the first edition of the " Lectures," but clearly it refers to the whole treatise as it is repeated in the second. It may be taken as revealing Finney's own consciousness of the essentially ethical character of his treatise. It is a system of teleological ethics which he presents to us; or, to be more precise, we may perhaps say in modern phraseology, that it is a system of hedonistic as distinguished from eudaemonistic ethics, that is to say a system in which " happiness " rather than " welfare " — although of course the two ideas readily run into one another — is the ethical end, the ultimate object to be achieved by action and conduct, the standard and final criterion of what ought to be — by their tendency to achieve which therefore the ethical character of actions is to be estimated. Of course it is not " individualistic " hedonism which

[408] P. 630.

[409] Cf. Walter E. C. Wright, *The Bibliotheca Sacra,* July, 1900, p. 431: " The religion of Oberlin from the first was intensely ethical: it concerned actions far more than feelings."

[410] Ed. 1, i. 1846, pp. iv.–v.; ed. 2, 1851, pp. viii.–ix.

Finney teaches, not even merely "altruistic," to continue to use the phraseology of the modern schools, but "universalistic." The doctrine which he inculcates is that moral conduct consists in actions directed towards the happiness of all sentient being; from which it follows, to put it briefly, that happiness is the chief good and benevolence the comprehensive virtue, and actions are good or bad according as they do or do not manifest the one and promote the other.[411] If we ask what has become of the "right," in the sense of the morally excellent, conceived as good *per se,* it can only be said that it has dropped out of sight altogether. The "good" has become the "happiness" — or the "welfare" — of the whole body of sentient beings; and the "right" that which tends to this. We cannot define "happiness" — or "welfare" — so as to include the idea of the "right," except at the cost of self-contradiction. If there is any such thing as the "right" *per se,* then the right is not what tends to an end, conceived as the supreme good, but just the end itself: we cannot say that the right is what tends to the right. Thus all obligation is reduced strictly to the single obligation to choose the good of being as our supreme ultimate end. The ground of obligation is accordingly declared to be that in this ultimate end which makes it incumbent on us to choose it, namely its intrinsic value to being. "The ground of obligation," says Finney,[412] "is that reason, or consideration, intrinsic in, or belonging to, the nature of an object, which necessitates the rational affirmation, that it ought to be chosen for its own sake." There is some appearance of logomachy in this reasoning. We choose the good of being as our ultimate end: the ground of our choice of it is that it is worth choosing; that in it which makes it worth choosing is the ground of our obligation to choose it. We do not seem to be told how we know that the good of being, in the sense of its happiness, is the supremely valuable thing in the universe.

---

[411] Finney is even able to say ("Lectures on Systematic Theology," p. 951): "Were it not for the relation that virtue is seen to sustain to happiness in general, no moral agent would conceive of it as valuable."

[412] P. 42.

That is "a first truth of reason." Finney's polemic against what he calls barbarously, "rightarianism"[413] is very sharp. He takes us back to the primary sense of the word "right" and seeks to reduce even the connotation of the word itself to the "fit, suitable, agreeable to the nature and relations of moral agents." This representation, however, is only partially correct, although there is of course a sense in which right and wrong express what is straight and what is crooked. "Right" has the form of a past participle, and it is not overpressing its suggestion to say that it expresses not so much the straight as the straightened: behind it lies the idea of rule, regulation, government: it is cognate not only with regular but regal — in short it expresses "conformed to rule," with a subaudition of authority. The atmosphere out of which it comes is that of theism, not of naturalism; and the righteous man is accordingly not the man whose conduct is suitable to his nature but the man whose conduct is in accordance with law. The ethics of right is accordingly justly spoken of as "authoritative morality," the ethics which imposes itself as obligatory *per se,* and not merely on the ground of expediency calculated from its tendency to an end presumed to be a good, supposedly the supreme good. The right is not a means to something else conceived of as the supreme good, but is itself the supreme good imposed on us as our duty by an adequate authority.

This seems to Finney fundamentally wrong, and he endeavors to reduce it to absurdity. "If the rightarian be the true theory," he reasons,[414] "then disinterested benevolence is sin. According to this scheme, the right, and not the good of being is the end to, and for which, God and all moral agents ought to live. According to this theory, disinterested benevolence can never be duty, can never be right, but always and necessarily wrong. . . . If moral agents ought to will the right for the sake of the right, or will good, not for the sake of the good, but for the sake of the relation of rightness existing between the choice and the good, then to will the good for its own sake is sin. It is not willing the right end. It is willing the

413 Pp. 54 ff.   414 P. 57.

good and not the right as an ultimate end. These are opposing theories. Both cannot be true. Which is the right to will, the good for its own sake, or the right? Let universal reason answer." Undoubtedly these are opposing theories; and universal conscience might well be left to decide whether we should will the good because it is right to do so, or will the right because it tends to a good result. And in this lies the answer to the over-strained logic which Finney is plying. That we are to do the right because it is right, and not because of any tendency we perceive in it to advance the good of the universe, by no means makes the practice of " disinterested benevolence " a sin. It may be right to will the good for its own sake. But, you cry out, you cannot will the good because it is right and for its own sake at the same time. Why not, if it is right to will the good for its own sake? The universal ground of moral obligation is that we must do right. The particular ground of this special obligation lies in the value of the object chosen. The value of the object chosen — but, mind you, its *moral* value — indicates the rightness of its choice. The category of the right is not an empty category, it has content: the notion is not a purely formal one, it is concrete. One of the things which is right is benevolence. When we choose benevolence as a rule of life we do right; and it is a very twisted logic which declares that he who chooses benevolence as a rule of life must do wrong — because he ought to choose right as his rule of life. He ought. That is the very reason why he ought to choose benevolence as his rule of life. It is right.

Finney having endeavored to reduce " Rightarianism " to absurdity Charles Hodge is doubtless justified in retorting with a happier attempt on his part to reduce Finney's teleological ethics to absurdity.[415] He says it belongs to the same mintage with Jesuit " intentionalism " — " the means are justified by the end " — and recommends Pascal's " Provincial Letters " as a good book to be read at Oberlin. When stated in an abstract form the observation made by Hodge is so immediately obvious, as not to require argument for its justification. It is the

[415] *The Biblical Repertory and Princeton Review,* April, 1847, pp. 259 ff.

very essence of a system of teleological ethics that the means acquire all the moral quality which they possess from their relation as means to their end. It was the taunt that this involved, as truly as Jesuit "intentionalism," the contention that it is right to do evil that good may come, which stung Finney to his unavailing answer.[416] The point of the comparison lies in the principle common to both Jesuit "intentionalism" and Finney's teleological ethics that "whatever proceeds from right intention is right." From this the Jesuits proceeded to infer that it is therefore right to do evil that good may come. Can Finney escape the same inference? Everybody, of course, understands that a right intention is necessary to the rightness of any action. The point raised is whether that is all that is necessary. Is it true that if your intention is right, your action is right? This is the Jesuit doctrine: the rightness of the intention makes the action right. It is Finney's doctrine also. Does he not teach that all that makes any conduct right is the end to which it is directed? What Hodge wishes to carry home to the mind is that this is really a vicious principle: everywhere and in all applications vicious. While the rightness of the intention is essential to the rightness of the action, it does not of itself make the action right. The "matter" of the action, as the Schoolmen express it, must be right, too. The act must be right for "the matter" of it, as well as in the intention of it. Intrinsically good ends must be sought by intrinsically good means: neither does the good end make an evil means good, nor does a good means make the evil end good. Francis of Assisi had a good end in view when he gave alms: he wished to relieve distress. When he stole the money from his master's till to give the alms, he used bad means for his good end. The goodness of the end does not sanctify the means. The goodness of the end, in point of fact, never transmits its goodness to the means used to attain it: And this destroys at once all schemes of teleological ethics.

In reply to Hodge, Finney says a great deal which is wholly ineffective because not to the point. The one thing which he

---

[416] "Lectures on Systematic Theology," pp. 929 ff.

says to the point is that in his system the choice of the end includes in it the choice of the means. There is but one system of means which is adapted to achieve the good of being. This system of means and its appropriate end are bound together in an indissoluble unity. To choose the end is at the same time, and by the same act, to choose this system of means. We cannot do anything we will and call that a means to that end. We must do just the things which are the real means to that end, in order to secure it. The rightness of these means is given to them by their inherent relation as means to this supreme ultimate end, to which they are related as its only means. It is their inherent relation to the end with which they form one system which makes them right; and the only definition that can be given of them is that they are the fit means to the supreme ultimate end, chosen for its own sake and organically related as the supreme good to the fit means for securing it. The effect of this representation is to shift the whole matter from the subjective to the objective sphere. It amounts to saying that he acts rightly who does the things which in point of fact tend to the supreme good, not he whose actions are governed by the intention of subserving the good of God and the universe. And in thus shifting the matter from the subjective to the objective sphere, the whole character of the scheme is altered. It is no longer the supreme ultimate intention which gives its moral quality to all subordinate choices and executive volitions — which is the very essence of Finney's morals — but the intrinsically good end which cannot be secured except by the intrinsically good means in organic union with it. The good end is no longer conceived as making the means chosen to secure it good; it is conceived as related to a system of means which are themselves good and which form with the end a good system. Finney is obviously floundering here. In his system things — whether means or other things — are not good in themselves: they receive their goodness for their relation — as means or otherwise — to the supreme ultimate end, which is defined as the good of being. He cannot subintroduce here an attribution of intrinsic goodness to them:

what makes these means good is in his system solely their relation as means to the supreme ultimate end. He can, no doubt
objectify the whole system of ends and means, and bid us
conceive them — the end as the final term and all the means
leading to it — as an objective entity which as a whole is good;
a whole made up of its constituent parts all of which are good,
standing off in a sort of conceptual reality to our contemplation. And he can then say, See, there is the end; and see, here
are the means leading up to it — appropriate means, good as the
end itself is good; and see, he that chooses the end must choose
with it the whole concatenated system of means and ends;
they cannot be separated; they form one whole. But, doing so,
he is merely objectifying for the sake of visualizing it, a system which is really subjective: no such objective system exists,
in his view, in fact. He deceives himself, if he imagines that he
thus gives the means in his system any actually independent
goodness, and can properly speak of them as " good as the end
itself is good." They seem thus good only as they stand in this
objectified system, which is a purely mental construction. Out
of this objectified system they have no goodness: they acquire
goodness only by being brought into, and as they are brought
into each man's actual subjective system. It remains true that
any means, any whatever, which are brought into a system of
means looking towards the indicated end, is in Finney's view
made good by its relation as means to this end. That is intrinsic to any system of teleological ethics. And that is " intentionalism." What he teaches is, not that our good intention cannot
be secured unless we employ good means, but that our good
intention makes the means requisite for securing it good.

As the end of his long life drew near, Finney published a tract — called the " Psychology of Righteousness " —
in which he repeats in popular language the teaching of his
lifetime, thus certifying us that it remains his teaching to the
very end. Here he propounds afresh his fundamental ethical
theory and erects on its basis anew his Pelagian doctrine of
salvation. Righteousness here too is discovered only in our
ultimate choice, from which all the righteousness of subor-

dinate choices, volitions, actions derives. And our ultimate choice is righteous only when it is the choice of the good of universal being. " The moral quality, then, of unselfish benevolence is righteousness or moral rightness." "This ultimate, immanent, supreme preference is the holy heart of a moral agent. Out of it proceeds, directly or indirectly, the whole moral or spiritual life of the individual." A sinner is *ex vi verbi* a selfish moral agent: how can he attain to the righteousness which consists in his contradictory, in universal benevolence? Why, of course, by a change in his ultimate choice. " The first righteous act possible to an unregenerate sinner is to change his heart, or the supreme ultimate preference of his soul." If this is the first act, it is also the last — for it is the whole thing. The only thing that has moral character is the ultimate choice, and, the ultimate choice having become benevolence, the sinner has wholly ceased to be a sinner, and become altogether righteous. This great change is effected by the sinner " taking such a view of the character and claims of God as to induce him to renounce his self-seeking spirit and come into sympathy with God." You see, nothing but better knowledge is required; better knowledge leads to a better life. The ministrations of the Holy Ghost are, to be sure, not excluded; but the whole work of the Spirit is reduced to the mode of illumination. All that the Spirit does is to give the sinner a better view of the claims of God. " A sinner attains, then, to righteousness only through the teachings and inspirations of the Holy Spirit." " It is by the truths of the gospel that the Holy Spirit induces this change in sinful man." " This revelation of divine love, when powerfully set home by the Holy Spirit, is an effectual calling." The effect of the change thus brought about is that the sinner ceases to be a sinner, and becomes, at once on the change taking place, perfect. " A truly regenerated soul cannot live a sinful life." " The new heart does not, cannot sin. This John in his first epistle expressly affirms. A benevolent, supreme ultimate choice cannot produce selfish subordinate choices or volitions." A perfectionism is asserted here of every true Christian, from the inception of his Christianity; a perfectionism resting absolutely on the sinner's own ultimate choice.

But now we are told, to our astonishment, that this perfect Christian may *backslide*. How he manages it remains unexplained, if "the new heart does not, cannot sin," as John is said to teach — if the benevolent supreme ultimate choice which he has made cannot produce selfish subordinate choices or volitions. Finney, however, asserts it and argues it. If the change wrought in the sinner, he says, "were a physical one, or a change of the very nature of the sinner," this backsliding would indeed be impossible. But as nothing has happened to the sinner himself — as he has only been induced by better knowledge, to change his ultimate supreme purpose — there is no reason why he may not change it back again. This is of course making himself again a new heart — this time a bad one, as Adam and Eve did. Indeed, a man may "change his heart back and forth." Otherwise "a sinner could not be required to make to himself a new heart, nor could a Christian sin after regeneration." When a man has backslidden, there is nothing for him but to begin afresh and do his first work over again. In point of fact he has not "backslidden" but apostatized. And now to make the appearance of contradiction complete, we are told that "righteousness is sustained in the human soul by the indwelling of Christ through faith and in no other way"; and "purposes or resolutions" are spoken of which are not "self-originated"; but are due to the Spirit of Christ. Fortunately this antinomy, left unresolved in this brief popular tract, is abundantly resolved in Finney's earlier and more extended writings. In these writings all that is good in the whole sphere of Christian activity is ascribed without reserve both to the indwelling Christ and to the human agent; and the antinomy is resolved by the explanation that the action of the Spirit of Christ is purely suasive and the whole execution is the work of man himself in his active powers.

Take the following passages together. "It" — that is the doctrine of entire sanctification — "ascribes the whole of salvation and sanctification from first to last, not only till the soul is sanctified, but at every moment while it remains in that state, to the indwelling Spirit, and influence, and grace of Christ. A state of entire sanctification can never be attained . . . by any works of law, or works of any kind, performed in your own strength, irrespective of the grace of God. By this I do not mean, that, were you disposed to exert your natural powers aright, you could not at once obey the law in the exercise of your natural strength, and continue to do so. But I do mean, that as you are wholly indisposed to use your natural powers aright, without the grace of God, no efforts that you will actually make in your own strength, or independent of his grace, will ever result in your entire sanctification.[417] " By the assertion, that the Holy Spirit, or the Spirit of Christ, is received by faith, to reign in the heart, it is intended, that he is actually trusted in, or submitted to by faith, and his influence suffered to control us. He does not guide and control us, by irresistible power or force, but faith confides the guidance of our souls to him. Faith receives and confides in him, and consents to be governed and directed by him. As his influence is moral, and not physical, it is plain that he can influence us no farther . . . than we trust or confide in him." [418] " The Holy Spirit controls, directs, and sanctifies the soul, not by a physical influence, nor by impulses nor by impressions made on the sensibility, but by enlightening and convincing the intellect, and thus quickening the conscience." [419] Everything that the Spirit does for us is thus reduced to enlightenment; everything we receive from Him to knowledge. We are exhorted, it is true, to renounce our own strength and rely on, draw on, live by the strength of Christ. But the term "strength" here is only a figure of speech. When an attempt is made to explain what precisely is meant by such exhortations,[420] what we are told is that in the first place they are not meant " in the antinomian, do-nothing, sit-still sense " of the words. It is not to " sit down and do nothing," leaving it to Christ to do it for us. This is, so far so good. But it is not so well said when we

[417] " Lectures on Systematic Theology," p. 629. [419] P. 307.
[418] P. 306. [420] Pp. 667–668.

hear next, that what we are to do is to lean " upon Christ, as a helpless man would lean upon the arm or shoulder of a strong man, to be borne about in some benevolent enterprise." A kind of coöperation is depicted here which makes Christ merely our helper. The intention is to exploit our " natural ability," and accordingly we read soon: " This renunciation of his own strength is not a denial of his natural ability. . . . It is a complete recognition of his ability, were he disposed to do all that God requires of him." " Strength " then is distinctly the wrong word to use in this connection. We do not need Christ's strength: we have enough of our own. We need from Christ only an adequate inducement to use our own strength aright. The soul has " been too long the slave of lust ever to assert or to maintain its spiritual supremacy, as the master, instead of the slave of appetite "; and we need help in asserting ourselves. The idea of strength here intrudes again and we read that " the will or heart is so weak in the presence of temptation, that there is no hope of its maintaining its integrity, unsupported by strength from Christ," and it must therefore renounce its dependence on its own strength and cast itself on Christ. We cannot forget, however, that Christ acts on the " will or heart " only by instruction. And even here the conception continues to be only that of the use of Christ to supplement defects. The illustration employed is that of a lame man with his crutches. Christ is the believer's crutches; and we are exhorted to make these crutches, that is Christ, so much ours that we use them instinctively and can no more forget them when we essay to walk than we can forget our own feet. This is what it is to walk in Christ.

More illuminating still is a passage [421] in which Finney is attempting to discriminate his view of " the means and conditions of sanctification " from that of the " New Divinity " — from which he felt himself to have come out, or to have been thrust out. The New Divinity, he notes, like himself, rejects " the doctrine of constitutional moral depravity " — that is, of " original sin " — and consequently the doctrine of " physical

[421] Pp. 683–684.

regeneration and sanctification " — that is of "making the tree good" rather than the fruit only. But, having rejected these doctrines, its adherents, says he, have unfortunately lost sight of Christ as our sancification also. They accordingly "have fallen into a self-righteous view of sanctification, and have held that sanctification is effected by works, or by forming holy habits." Over against this very reprehensible drift of doctrine — a drift, let us say frankly, very natural in the adherents of the New Divinity — Finney wishes to reassert our dependence on Christ for sanctification. The precise thing he asserts is that sanctification is by faith as opposed to works. And then he explains: " That is, faith receives Christ in all his offices, and in all the fulness of his relations to the soul; and Christ, when received, works in the soul to will and to do of all his good pleasure, not by a physical, but by a moral or persuasive working." He cannot assert that Christ works in the soul without adding this limitation! It is in point of fact the key to his entire teaching. It too is the assertion that since Christ's only working in the soul is suasive in character, the sanctification of the soul is effected by itself. So that the only conceivable distinction between the rejected view of the New Divinity and Finney's own must be thought to lie in the answer to the question whether the works, done in both views alike by the soul itself and only by the soul itself, are done under persuasion from Christ or not. " Observe," says Finney now: " he influences the will." That is all that Christ does: He influences the will. " This," Finney continues, " must be by a moral influence, if its " — that is the will's — " actings are intelligent and free, as they must be to be holy." " That is, if he influences the will to obey God, it must be by a divine moral suasion."

Is there, really, anything, then, which distinguishes this view of the relation of sanctification in Christ from that ascribed to the New Divinity? Nothing. For the New Divinity did not at all deny that the soul was influenced in its sanctifying walk by the persuasions of the Holy Spirit. That was rather one of its contentions, the only rag of Christian doctrine it had left at this point to cover its nakedness. With all Finney's devout references to the indwelling Christ, dependence on the strength of Christ, and the like, he means nothing more. Tho only even apparent distinction between the two views lies in Finney's calling his view a sanctification " by faith," and setting it over against the other as a sanctification " by effort." And as he expounds his view, that is a distinction without a difference. He now goes on to say, however, after his chosen fashion of speech, that the soul, never in any instance obeys God " in a spiritual and true sense," " except it be thus influenced by the indwelling Spirit of Christ." And he hints that when we receive Christ in any relation, He is full and perfect in that relation — so that, we suppose, if we receive Him for sanctification, we are perfectly sanctified. This, however, is thrown in incidentally. The main thing in this exhortation is the staring Pelagianism of the whole construction. We believe in Christ for our sanctification; He then acts persuasively in our souls for sanctification; under this persuasion we act holily; that is our sanctification. It is all a sanctification of acts. We are not ourselves cleansed; but then there is no need of cleansing us, since we were never ourselves unclean. We were only a bundle of constitutional appetites, passions, and propensities, innocent in themselves, which we have been misusing through a bad will. What needs correcting is only this bad will into a good one. And the appropriate, the only, instrument for the correction of our willing is persuasion. Moved by this persuasion we " make ourselves a good heart " — we " change our mind," as the phrase goes — and that is the whole of it. It is to this that Finney reduces Christianity. And as this ready making for ourselves a new heart, makes us a perfectly holy heart, it is with this ease and despatch that according to Finney's form of perfectionism we become perfect. That is in brief the final form which Oberlin Perfectionism took.

The preaching of perfectionism with such energy and persistency by men of such intellectual force and pulpit power as Mahan and Finney and their coadjutors, of course had its effect. Oberlin naturally — college and community — became a perfectionist center. The majority of the students, perhaps also the majority of the inhabitants, were more or less deeply moved by the propaganda: many definitely adopted the new teaching and endeavored both to live it themselves and to communicate it to others. The surrounding country, especially that most closely affiliated with Oberlin in its general type of thinking — the Western Reserve of Ohio, and to the east, Western and Central New York, to the west Michigan and the North Western country — became so far infected that scattered groups of "Oberlin Perfectionists" appeared here and there through it.[422] The aggressions of the Oberlin propaganda, the threat of a wider extension of its teachings, the nature of the doctrine itself, naturally called out intense opposition. The whole region affected became the scene of violent controversy. The local periodical press of course reflected the state of feeling of the several communities. And soon the ecclesiastical courts were drawn into the debate. Presbyterian Presbyteries and Congregational Associations vied with one another in reasoned condemnations of the new doctrine. One of the remarkable circumstances connected with these official condemnations was, that as they came largely from the region of Finney's, and to a less extent of Mahan's, early ministry and revivalistic triumphs, or from regions bound closely to it by ties of common blood and feeling, they were often penned by men who had been associated with them or had at least strongly sympathized with them, in their work hitherto. They were being wounded, they complained, in the house of their friends. S. C. Aiken, who had been a pastor at Utica during Finney's great revival there and one of his chief supporters during the whole course of his revival campaigns in Central New York, was a signatory along with its actual author, S. B. Canfield, of the able refutation of Oberlin Perfectionism put out by the Presbytery of Cleveland in 1841. N. S. S. Beman, with whose collaboration Finney's remarkable revival at Troy had been

---

[422] Cf. P. H. Fowler, "Historical Sketch of Presbyterianism within the Bounds of the Synod of Central New York," 1877, p. 137: "'Oberlin Perfectionism' had considerable currency for a time, and Chenango and Cortland and other Presbyteries condemned it, and Onandaga Presbytery published an able refutation of it."

carried on, was the actual author of the uncompromising refutation put out in the same year by the Presbytery of Troy. George Duffield prepared the " Warning against Error," meaning Finney's system of teaching, which was sent forth by the Presbytery of Detroit in 1847, with the approval of the Synod of Michigan; and perhaps we may add here, although it was a private publication, that Lyman Beecher printed about 1844 a letter against perfectionism, which was thought important enough for John Morgan to answer it in *The Oberlin Quarterly Review*.[423] In the fateful year of 1841, the Presbyteries of Huron and Grand River in the Western Reserve, and of Richland near by, also passed condemnatory actions: and decided action in the same sense was taken soon afterward by the New York Presbyteries of Chenango, Cortland, Onondaga, Rochester. Further afield the Presbytery of Newark had been led to early action, and soon the Presbytery of North River; and it was not long before the Synods of New York and New Jersey [424] and of Genesee were compelled by appeals to act in the same sense. Similar action was taken by the General Association of Connecticut in 1841, by the General Association of New York in 1844, by the Genesee Association in 1844, by the Fox River Congregational Union of Illinois in 1845. The Cleveland Convention in 1844, and the Michigan City Convention of 1846 were organized on an anti-Oberlin basis; and in 1848 the American Board of Commissioners for Foreign

---

[423] A letter of Beecher's printed in his " Autobiography," ii. p. 435, bearing on perfectionism and showing no sympathy with it, may be consulted. It is interesting to observe that Beecher's son George appears to have shown, apparently in 1836, some leanings to perfectionism (" Autobiography," ii. pp. 411–415).

[424] Leonard, as cited, p. 256. Cf. Asa Mahan, " Out of Darkness into Light," p. 191, where we are told that " the Presbytery of Poughkeepsie, by a special order from the Synod of New York, deposed from the ministry two of its members, Messrs. Hill and Belden, for no other cause than the one fact that they had embraced the Oberlin error." Leonard puts the incident in 1843; Mahan dates it vaguely as somewhere about 1845: 1843 seems to be right and the Presbytery was, as Leonard gives it, North River. On the incident see further, R. Wheatley, " The Life and Letters of Mrs. Phoebe Palmer," 1876, p. 267, and for Henry Belden, see the " Princeton Theological Seminary Biographical Catalogue," 1909, p. 128. For William Hill, *ibid.*, p. 70.

Missions discharged two missionaries in Siam for holding the Oberlin doctrines. Oberlin very naturally felt itself persecuted, and its historian designates the conflict into which it was drawn as its " baptism of fire." [425]

Meanwhile, at Oberlin itself the doctrine was making a history which began with enthusiastic acceptance, and passed forward rapidly into indifference and decay. The originators of the doctrine never lost their hold upon it or their zeal for it. Finney was still teaching it up to the end of his long life (died 1875), the whole of which was spent at Oberlin. Mahan, whose connection with Oberlin was severed in 1850, after an unfortunate venture at Cleveland (1850–1854) and a more successful one at Adrian, Michigan (1855–1871), had yet fifteen years or so to spend in England in active propaganda for his favorite doctrine (died 1889). But the vogue of the doctrine at Oberlin was not very long-lived. James H. Fairchild gives us a very illuminating sketch of its fortunes there.[426] " The visible impulse of the movement," he says, " to a great extent expended itself within the first few years." Men sought and found with decreasing frequency the special experiences — " the blessing," " the second conversion " — which were connected with it as first preached. Those who went out to preach " under the influence of this fresh experience " came ultimately to permit it to drop into the background. " So far as I am informed," says Fairchild, " not one among them all continued for any length of time to be recognized as a preacher of these special views." They did not repudiate their former views; but they found that " they could preach the truth as it is in Jesus more effectively than by giving to their doctrine the odor of Christian perfection, or the higher life." Whatever their motive was, they ceased to be propagandists of perfectionism. A similar decay of interest in the doctrine was working itself out at Oberlin itself. Confidence " in the style of Christian culture, involving a special experience, which the

[425] D. L. Leonard, as cited, pp. 242 ff. The facts recited above are drawn from Leonard, pp. 256 ff.
[426] *The Congregational Quarterly*, April, 1876, pp. 244 ff.

movement introduced" grew progressively less clear and firm. This special experience — the "blessing" — was not found to be always associated with an advance in Christian attainment and character. On the contrary, it was observed that those who obtained it were apt to be among the less balanced characters of the community. Others who had not sought or found the experiences were not obviously less earnest and effective in Christian work than those who had enjoyed them. Thus the peculiar ideas and experiences connected with the "entire sanctification" movement gradually lost their appeal. Fairchild does not mention them, but there were also scandals to accentuate the decreasing sense of the value of the doctrine. The most shocking of them was probably the lamentable fall from virtue in 1842 of H. C. Taylor, "who had held prominent stations in both church and business affairs, had been a leader in 'moral reform (social purity),' and had also been numbered among the 'sanctified.'" [427]

A tendency has developed itself among recent Oberlin writers, as for example, D. L. Leonard,[428] to represent the whole history of Oberlin Perfectionism as only a temporary aberration which befell the institution in its early days. Leonard speaks of "the perfection episode," and is happy to say it is altogether a matter of the past. Oberlin has heard nothing of it for years and years — for a generation, he says, writing in 1898. He even goes so far as to suggest that perfectionism was never anything more than a "foible" at Oberlin; a "foible" like its early tendency to Grahamism, and its manual laborism and its temporary misprision of the classics. It may be condoned in those early leaders as their other foibles were condoned; it was a product of the earnestness of their purpose and of the strong determination of their high characters to holy living. Experience has shown, however, that it was a delusion. There were those who received "the blessing" and could not keep it; lapsing speedily into their old "earthy" conditions. There were those who had it, and did not seem to have profited anything by it. It was not "the best, the truest-hearted, the

[427] D. L. Leonard, as cited, pp. 261 f., cf. p. 38.   [428] As cited, pp. 236–241.

most reliable and useful disciples" who had it; they might on the contrary be " the weak-minded, the shallow, the merely sentimental." This has been the experience at Oberlin, according to Leonard. Leonard writes confessedly under the influence of Fairchild, and can scarcely be taken as bearing independent witness to anything beyond the attitude toward its early perfectionism which modern Oberlin takes. Changes have befallen Oberlin. The modern Oberlin is not the old Oberlin, and it is not merely the perfectionism of the past that has faded away.

But if, as we are told, its early perfectionism has left no trace of itself at Oberlin, that cannot be said of it elsewhere. There are great religious movements still in existence in which its influence still makes itself felt. Finney's doctrine of " the simplicity of moral action " continued to be enthusiastically taught even by his successor in the Presidency, J. H. Fairchild, although Fairchild found a way — not a very convincing way — to separate it from the " perfectionism " with which it was inseparably bound up by Finney. Mahan's lifelong propaganda of the earlier form of Oberlin Perfectionism was not barren of fruit. The " Higher Life Movement " which swept over the English-speaking world — and across the narrow seas into the Continent of Europe — in the third quarter of the nineteenth century, was not without traits which derived from Oberlin. And Mahan lived to stand by the side of Pearsall Smith at the great Oxford Convention of 1874, and to become with him a factor in the inauguration of the great " Keswick Movement," which has brought down much of the spirit and many of the forms of teaching of Oberlin Perfectionism to our own day. If Oberlin Perfectionism is dead, it has found its grave not in the abyss of non-existence, but in the Higher Life Movement, the Keswick Movement, the Victorious Life Movement, and other kindred forms of perfectionist teaching. They are its abiding monuments. Perhaps as the old Egyptian monarchs, in taking over the structures of their predecessors, endeavored to obliterate the signatures of those from whom they had inherited them, these later movements would be glad to have us forget the sources out of which they have sprung. But as the names of the earlier Egyptian kings may still be read even in their defaced cartouches, so the name of Oberlin may still be read stamped on movements which do not acknowledge its parentage, but which have not been able to escape altogether from its impress.[429]

[429] *Literature.* I. Books by Finney: — "Sermon Preached in the Presbyterian Church at Troy, March 4, 1827," 1827. "Sermons on Various Subjects," 1835 (several of these sermons were issued previously, as separate publications; and the collection was enlarged and republished in 1836 as: "Sermons on Important Subjects"). "Prevailing Prayer," 1865. "Lectures on Revivals of Religion," 1835 (many subsequent editions). "Lectures to Professing Christians" (delivered in the city of New York, 1836 and 1837), 1837 and many subsequent editions. "Skeletons of a Course of Theological Lectures," 1840. "Views of Sanctification," 1840. "Letters on Revivals," 1845. "Lectures on Systematic Theology," i. 1846; ii. 1847 (a new edition enlarged and largely rewritten was published in London, 1851; and a condensed form of the London edition was issued by James H. Fairchild in 1878). "The Reviewer Reviewed, or Finney's Theology and the Princeton Review," 1847 (incorporated in the "Lectures on Systematic Theology" of 1851). "Reply to the 'Warning Against Error,' written by the Rev. Dr. Duffield," 1848 (also incorporated in the "Lectures on Systematic Theology" of 1851). "Guide to the Savior," 1848 (other editions). "Sinners' Excuses Condemn God. A Sermon," 1849 (other editions). "Freemasonry: its Character, Claims and Practical Working," 1869. "Memoirs," 1876 (other editions). "Sermons on Gospel Themes," 1876. "Sermons on the Way of Salvation," 1891. A number of Tracts, n.d. II. Books by Mahan: — "Principles of Christian Union and Church Fellowship," 1836. "Scripture Doctrine of Christian Perfection," 1839 (ed. 2, of same year, stereotyped, from which many subsequent issues). "Abstract of a Course of Lectures on Mental and Moral Philosophy," 1840. "Doctrine of the Will," 1844. "A System of Intellectual Philosophy," 1845. "The True Believer," 1847. "Science of Moral Philosophy," 1848. "A System of Intellectual Philosophy," 1854 (revised and enlarged). "Modern Mysteries Explained and Exposed," 1855. "The Phenomena of Spiritualism Scientifically Explained and Exposed," 1855. "The Science of Logic," 1857. "Science of Natural Theology," 1867. "The Baptism of the Holy Ghost," 1870. "Theism and Anti-Theism in their Relations to Science," 1872. "Out of Darkness into Light," 1875. "Consequences of Neglect," 1876. "A Critical History of Philosophy," 1883. "Autobiography," 1882. "System of Mental Philosophy," 1882. "Introduction to the Critical History of Philosophy," 1893. "The Misunderstood Texts of Scripture Explained and Elucidated, and the Doctrine of the Higher Life thereby Verified," 1876. III. Perfectionist Publications of Other Oberlin Men. See *The Oberlin Evangelist,* 1839–1862; and *The Oberlin Quarterly Review,* 4 vols., 1845–1849. Henry Cowles, "Holiness of Christians in the Present Life," 1840. Charles Fitch, "Views of Sanctification," 1839. John Morgan, "Holiness Acceptable to God,"

1875. IV. BIOGRAPHY OF FINNEY: — G. Frederick Wright, "Charles Grandison Finney," 1891. Also — D. W. Bartlett, "Modern Agitators," 1854, pp. 151–169. Hiram Mead, "Charles Grandison Finney," in *The Congregational Quarterly*, January, 1877, pp. 1–28. H. Clay Trumbull, "My Four Religious Teachers," 1903, pp. 15–27. F. G. Beardsley, "A History of American Revivals," 1904, pp. 118–151. W. C. Wilkinson, "Modern Masters of Pulpit Discourse," 1905, pp. 283–295. V. DISCUSSIONS: A. Rand, "The New Divinity Tried, Being an examination of a sermon by the Rev. C. G. Finney, on Making a New Heart," 1832. [B. B. Wisner], "Review of 'The New Divinity Tried,'" 1832. C. Hodge, "'The New Divinity Tried,'" in *The Biblical Repertory and Theological Review*, July, 1832, pp. 278–304. A. B. Dod, "Finney's Sermons," in same, July, 1835, pp. 482–527; and "Finney's Lectures," in same, October, 1835, pp. 626–674. Anonymous Review of Finney's "Lectures on Revivals of Religion," in *The Literary and Theological Review*, 1835, pp. 667–705. Joseph I. Foot, "Influence of Pelagianism on the Theological Course of Rev. C. G. Finney, developed in his Sermons and Lectures," in same, March, 1838, pp. 38–71. Enoch Pond, "Christian Perfection," in *The American Biblical Repository*, January, 1839, pp. 44–58. N. S. Folsom, "Review of Mahan on Christian Perfection," in same, July, 1839, pp. 143–166. A. Mahan, "The Doctrine of Christian Perfection Explained," in same, October, 1840, pp. 408–428. S. B. Canfield, "An Exposition of the Peculiarities, Difficulties and Tendencies of Oberlin Perfectionism," 1841. L. Woods, "Examination of the Doctrine of Perfection, as held by Rev. Asa Mahan . . . and others," in *The American Biblical Repository*, January, 1841, pp. 166–189, and April, 1841, pp. 406–438 (also issued in book form, 1841). John C. Lord, "Finney's Sermons on Sanctification, and Mahan on Christian Perfection," in *The Biblical Repertory and Princeton Review*, April, 1841, pp. 231–250. W. D. Snodgrass, "The Scripture Doctrine of Sanctification, Stated and Defended against the error of Perfectionism," 1841. John Woodbridge, "Sanctification," in *The Biblical Repertory and Princeton Review*, 1842, pp. 426–472 (reprinted in "Theological Essays Reprinted from the Princeton Review," 1846, pp. 405–443). C. Hodge, "Finney's Lectures on Theology," in *The Biblical Repertory and Princeton Review*, 1847, pp. 237–277. G. Duffield, "A Warning Against Error," 1847. Samuel J. Baird, "A History of the New School," 1868, pp. 217–234. James H. Fairchild, "The Doctrine of Sanctification at Oberlin," in *The Congregational Quarterly*, April, 1876, pp. 237–259. G. F. Wright, "Dr. Hodge's Misrepresentations of President Finney's System of Theology," in *The Bibliotheca Sacra*, April, 1876, pp. 381–392. G. N. Boardman, "A History of New England Theology," 1899, ch. vii., pp. 275–292, "Oberlin Theology." W. E. C. Wright, "Oberlin's Contribution to Ethics," in *The Bibliotheca Sacra*, July, 1900, pp. 429–444. A. T. Swing, "President Finney and an Oberlin Theology," in same, July, 1900, pp. 465–482. Frank Hugh Foster, "A Genetic History of the New England Theology," 1907, ch. xvi., pp. 453–470, "The Oberlin Theology."

II

JOHN HUMPHREY NOYES
AND HIS " BIBLE COMMUNISTS "

JOHN HUMPHREY NOYES
AND HIS " BIBLE COMMUNISTS "[1]

I. THE ENVIRONMENT

FEW things are more noticeable, among the advocates of perfectionism from the opening of the second third of the nineteenth century, than their extreme reluctance to accept the name of " Perfectionists." Many things may no doubt have coöperated to produce this attitude. Its main occasion lay, however, in the association of the name with a particular body of perfectionists, then claiming the attention of the public, with which other perfectionists were very loath to be confused. How anxious they were not to be confused with this body may be measured by the vigor of the language in which, themselves perfectionists, they repudiate all connection with " Perfectionists." Asa Mahan, for example, writing at the beginning of this period,[2] intemperately declares that the doctrine he teaches " has absolutely nothing in common " with " Perfectionism," " but a few terms derived from the Bible." In order to distinguish his doctrine from " Perfectionism," however, he requires to describe the rejected doctrine as " Perfectionism technically so called," a mode of speech which already suggests that perfectionism, plainly understood, is —

[1] Reprinted from *Bibliotheca Sacra*, lxxviii. 1921, pp. 37–72, 172–200, 319–375.

[2] " Scripture Doctrine of Christian Perfection " (1839), ed. 7, 1844, pp. 70 ff.; cf. " Autobiography, Intellectual, Moral and Spiritual," 1882, pp. 373–374, where the antinomianism of the " Perfectionists " is exhibited. C. G. Finney, " Lectures on Systematic Theology," 1847, ii. p. 166, speaks of the " Perfectionists," as " the sect called Antinomian Perfectionists," and, " Memoirs," 1876, p. 341, describes them as a body which taught " Christian perfection, in the antinomian sense of the term "; cf. " Lectures to Professing Christians " (1837), 1880, p. 358. Henry Cowles, " Holiness of Christians in the Present Life," 1840, pp. 9 ff., separates himself decisively from " Antinomian Perfectionism."

as it really is — common ground between the two. Possibly to atone for this necessary confession of general kinship, he sweepingly declares that "Perfectionism, technically so called," is, in his judgment, "in the native and necessary tendencies of its principles, worse than the worst form of infidelity." To William E. Boardman, writing twenty years later,[3] the danger of confusion with this "Perfectionism" seems less imminent, and he is therefore able to speak of it with less passion. He is not the less determined, however, to separate himself decisively from it. This, it must be confessed, he does not accomplish, in every respect, without some apparent difficulty — describing its fundamental mystical doctrine of the indwelling Christ in terms which would not serve badly to describe the doctrine to which he himself ultimately came. It is, in point of fact, not the perfectionism of the rejected "Perfectionism" which offends him, any more than Mahan, but its antinomianism. And his real concern is to protest that not all perfectionism — not his own variety, for example — is chargeable with the antinomianism which men had been led to associate with the name through experience with the body of religionists who had arrogated to themselves, and had had accorded to them by common usage, the specific name of "Perfectionists." How firmly this special body of perfectionists had attached the general descriptive name of "Perfectionists" to themselves as their particular designation (just as other bodies of religionists have laid claim to the names of "Christians," "Disciples," and the like as their specific names), is illustrated by the survival of this special use of the term, and that in an even narrower application, alongside of its more general employment, in the definition of the word "Perfectionist" (not usually of "Perfectionism")[4] in our current English dictionaries, as well as in our Religious Encyclopædias. A very good example is supplied by John Henry Blunt's

[3] "The Higher Christian Life," 1859, pp. 64 ff. Cf. Mrs. Boardman's "Life and Labours of the Rev. W. E. Boardman," 1887, pp. 52, 58, 135, 170.

[4] The Oxford Dictionary includes this special sense also in the definition of "Perfectionism"; but not the Century, nor the Standard, nor Webster, nor Worcester.

"Dictionary of Sects, Heresies, Ecclesiastical Parties and Schools of Religious Thought" (1874). Under the head of "Perfectionists," he describes only "a licentious American sect of Antinomian Communists."[5] All other perfectionists he classes under the head of "Perfectibilists," a distinction in designation to which he did not succeed in giving currency.[6]

The particular sect to which thus the name of "Perfectionists" is reserved by Blunt is no more perfectionist than other perfectionist parties; nor did it arise under influences specifically different from those to which the perfectionist parties which have most sharply repudiated relationship with it owed their own origin, nor can it be represented as without some common interests with them. It differs from them, however, not merely in drawing off to itself and forming a separate sect instead of contenting itself with acting as leaven within existing churches; but also in the particular doctrinal system which it developed for itself, and which it utilized for the support and exposition not only of its perfectionism, but also of certain radical social theories, which, having the courage of its convictions, it presently put into practice up to a very bitter end. In this perfectionist sect, we have therefore the opportunity to observe a perfectionism working itself out in life under leadership strong enough to enable it to go its own way, along the lines of a development distinctly logical, although narrow and inconsiderate, untrammeled by considerations derived from tradition, whether religious, ethical, or social, and unaffected by the universal judgment of the community in which it lived. A great

---

[5] He adds at the end of the article that the Princeites have some affinities with this sect. For the Princeites, see the article "Agapemone" in Hastings's "Encyclopædia of Religion and Ethics," with its bibliography; W. H. Dixon, "Spiritual Wives," 1868, i. pp. 226 ff.; and a series of articles in *The British Weekly,* beginning in the number for March 22, 1889 (v. no. 125, p. 341).

[6] So also Otto Zöckler in Herzog-Hauck, "Realencyklopädie für protestantische Theologie und Kirche," ed. 3, xv. p. 130 (cf. the entry in "The New Schaff-Herzog Encyclopedia of Religious Knowledge"), and W. Köhler in Schiele und Zscharnack, "Die Religion in Geschichte und Gegenwart," iv. p. 1356.

deal of ability was expended in the elaboration of its underlying religious and social theory; an incredible audacity was shown in putting this theory into practice; and a certain amount of temporary success attended the enterprise. But the thinking embodied in it was as grotesque as it was acute; it was astuteness rather than wisdom which presided over its social organization; and the experiment had fairly reached the end of its possibilities of persistence in about a third of a century. There is much to be learned from a study of it; there is nothing about it which can fairly be represented as edifying.

The "Perfectionists" or "Bible Communists," as they otherwise called themselves, are only one of the many unwholesome products of the great religious excitement which swept over Western and Central New York in the late twenties and early thirties of the last century, finding its way in the early thirties also into New England and thence over the world. Albert Barnes defines a revival for us as "*the simultaneous conversion of many souls to Christ*"; adding, in order to give completeness to the description, "and a rapid advance in promoting the purity and zeal of christians." [7] If this were a complete description of the phenomena which may display themselves in revivals, they would always be such unmixed blessings that they could scarcely be connected with an earthly origin; and they certainly could leave behind them nothing but good effects. In point of fact, however, human elements are always mixed with them; and these human elements may on occasion be so predominant that any divine in-

---

[7] "Sermons on Revivals," 1841, p. 48. John Breckinridge, *The Biblical Repertory and Theological Review,* October, 1832, pp. 460–461, reverses the emphasis: "It is the divine influence upon *the mass* — the popular and social application of religion. It is the Spirit of God awakening, *at the same time,* to holy love, and the harmonious action, the whole body of Christians in a particular place. . . . When the real spiritual church among a people experience this deep and simultaneous renovation, it is most properly styled a REVIVAL OF RELIGION. . . . As an inseparable concomitant of a Revival of Religion among a people, is *the simultaneous conviction and conversion of many sinners.*" Charles G. Finney, "Lectures on Revivals of Religion," ed. 2, 1835, p. 437, says: "It is just as indispensable in promoting a revival, to preach to the church, and make them grow in grace, as it is to preach to sinners and make them submit to God."

gredient which may be hidden in them may be negligible. Accordingly Albert Barnes proceeds at once to speak of them, as actually experienced, as also periods of religious "excitement"; and to liken this excitement in its nature and effects to the excitement which tears men in a political campaign or sweeps them off their feet on the approach of war. Here is something quite out of the focus of his former description; for excitement, even though religious, has no necessary relation, whether as cause, accompaniment, or effect, with the converting or reviving operations of the Spirit of God. " A revival or religious excitement," Archibald Alexander tells us,[8] "may exist and be very powerful, and affect many minds, when the producing cause is not the Spirit of God; and when the truth of God is not the means of the awakening." "Religious excitements," he accordingly adds, "have been common among Pagans, Mohammedans, heretics and Papists." W. B. Sprague similarly warns us in the opening pages of his classical " Lectures on Revivals of Religion,"[9] not to "mistake a gust of animal passion for the awakening or converting operations of God's Holy Spirit." Great excitement may no doubt attend

[8] Letter of March 9, 1832, printed in W. B. Sprague, " Lectures on Revivals of Religion " (1833), ed. 2, 1850, pp. 229–235. C. G. Finney was quite aware that "excitement" had no converting effects. He chides people for supposing that when the excitement, with which revivals regularly began in his practice, subsided " the revival is on the decline " — " when, in fact," he says, " with much less excited emotion, there may be vastly more real religion in the community " (" Views of Sanctification," 1840, p. 19). He deliberately used excitement as an advertising agency (" Lectures on Revivals of Religion," 1835, Lect. xiv.; cf. the caustic criticisms of Albert B. Dod in *The Biblical Repertory and Theological Review,* October, 1835, pp. 632 ff.). " It seems sometimes to be indispensable," he remarks in the " Views of Sanctification " (p. 19), " that a high degree of excitement should prevail for a time, to arrest public and individual attention, and to draw people off from other pursuits to attend to the concerns of their souls." But so far from beneficial to the religious life is this excitement in itself, that if long continued, it would be destructive even to mental sanity: " the high degree of excitement which is sometimes witnessed in revivals of religion, must necessarily be short, or . . . the people must become deranged." The revival does not consist in this state of exalted emotion, but " in conformity of the human will to the will of God." Finney repeats all this in his " Lectures on Systematic Theology," ed. 2, 1851, p. 170.

[9] P. 11.

a true revival, but it is not part and parcel of it; and it may
be very great and yet there be no true revival at all. " It may
be an excitement produced not by the power of divine truth,
but by artificial stimulus applied to the imagination and the
passions, for the very purpose of producing commotion both
within and without." Let us remember that God declares Himself the God of order, and that disorder can therefore never be
the authentic mark of His working. If God is working where
disorder is, it is in spite of the disorder, not because of it;
the disorder is itself only the cause of evil. " A real work of
the Spirit," says Archibald Alexander,[10] " may be mingled with
much enthusiasm and disorder; but its beauty will be marred,
and its progress retarded by every such spurious mixture."
" All means and measures which produce a high degree of excitement, or a great commotion of the passions," he therefore
advises, " should be avoided; because religion does not consist
in these violent emotions, nor is it promoted by them; and
when they subside, a wretched state of deadness is sure to succeed. . . . Fanaticism, however much it may assume the garb
and language of piety, is its opposite." " The Church," he also
says, " is not always benefited by what are termed revivals;
but sometimes the effects of such commotions are followed
by a desolation which resembles the track of the tornado.
I have never seen so great insensibility in any people as in
those who had been subjects of violent religious excitement;
and I have never seen any sinners so bold and reckless in their
impiety as those who had once been loud professors, and foremost in the time of revival."

It is with these evils in mind that, in face of the possibility
that a sinner here and there may nevertheless chance to be
really converted through the action of this excitement, Joel
Hawes of Hartford declares[11] that " a sinner may be con-

---

[10] *Loc. cit.* Compare the remarkable testimony of the General Association of Congregational Churches in Connecticut in 1836 against itinerant
lecturers assuming to instruct the people over whom they had not been
called to be overseers, and itinerant evangelists rousing among them " public
excitement " (" Minutes," 1836, pp. 8, 20).

[11] Sprague, as cited, p. 282. Lyman Beecher, in his famous letter of

verted at too great an expense." No more awful arraignment of the religious excitement, which sometimes accompanies and sometimes serves as a substitute for revivals, could be phrased. In point of fact such excitement has no Christian character whatever; its affinities are, as Archibald Alexander has already reminded us, with the universal religious phenomena which Elizabeth Robins sums up under the name of mænadism,[12] a term which she defines broadly enough to make it include "all intoxicating, will-destroying excesses of religious fervor in which ' the multitude ' have taken part." When we remember the " exercises " which have often attended revivals and the moral delinquencies which have sometimes stained them, we shall be compelled with bowed heads to recognize that they too may be so perverted as to be included in her observation: — " It is a remarkable fact in the history of religion that men of widely differing creeds and countries have agreed in attaching a spiritual value to hysteria, chorea, and catalepsy on the one hand, and to a frenzy of cruelty and sensuality on the other. Diseased nerves and morals have often been ranked as the highest expression of man's faith and devotion."

The intrusion of this debasing excitement into revival movements, with the effect sometimes of destroying them altogether, sometimes of only greatly curtailing and marring their beneficent results, is ordinarily traceable to one or the other of two inciting causes. One of these is found in the character of the population among whom the revival is propagated; the other in the character of its promoters and the methods they

---

January, 1827, in " Letters of the Rev. Dr. Beecher and Rev. Mr. Nettleton, on the ' New Measures ' in conducting Revivals of Religion," 1828, p. 96, develops the idea. " The importance of the soul and of eternity is such," says he, " as that good men in a revival are apt to feel no matter what is said or done, provided sinners are awakened and saved. But it ought to be remembered, that though the immediate result of some courses of conduct may be the salvation of some souls, the general and more abiding result may be the ruin of a thousand souls, destroyed by this conduct, to one saved by it; and destroyed by it as instrumentally in the direct and proper sense of the term, as any are saved by it."

[12] *The Atlantic Monthly*, lii. October, 1883, pp. 487–497.

employ in promoting it — methods better adapted to lash the nerves into uncontrollable agitation than to bring the sinner to intelligent trust in his Saviour. Both of these causes were present and operative in the great revival movement which swept over Western and Central New York in the late twenties and early thirties of the last century.

It has been thought that the character of the population of this region, derived from that of its first settlers, laid them particularly open to fanaticism. The earliest stratum of settlers, entering the Palmyra country from Vermont in the second decade of the nineteenth century, was, we are told, of "rather unsavory fame"; and although this stratum was overlaid in the next decade by a virile, intelligent, industrious class of settlers from Eastern New York and New England, the earlier settlers remained, and by mixture with the newer comers gave a psychological character and a psychological history of its own to this region. It has been, therefore, it is said, on the one hand " a center of sane and progressive social movements," but on the other hand a veritable "hot-bed of fanaticism," and the two tendencies have entered into every possible combination with one another, some of them startling enough. It seems hardly just, however, to ascribe the whole of the evil to the earlier and the whole of the good to the later immigration. There were many men of the highest character among the earlier immigrants, and the newcomers themselves brought with them that tendency to eccentricity of opinion and extremity of temper which seems to be in the New England blood, and which has made New England, along with its intellectual and moral leadership of the nation, also unhappily the fertile seed-plot of fads and extravagances. Central and Western New York was in effect only an extended, and, because of its isolation and the hardness of its pioneer life, in these respects, an intensified New England.[13] The period, moreover,

[13] John Bach McMaster, "A History of the People of the United States," v. pp. 109, 120, points out that the Morgan excitement was limited to "the New England belt of emigration." "The whole New England belt from Boston to Buffalo fairly teemed with anti-masonic newspapers." This is a typical instance.

was one of universal excitability.[14] " The great improvement in the mechanic arts, and the wide diffusion of knowledge," says Albert B. Dod, writing in 1835, " have given a strong impulse to the popular mind; and everywhere the social mass is seen to be in such a state of agitation, that the lightest breath may make it heave and foam." Men stood in a condition of permanent astonishment. Everything seemed possible. They did not know what would come next, and thought it might be anything. They lived on perpetual tiptoe. It would have been strange if a raw population like that of Central and Western New York had retained its balance in such a time. That it did not may be observed from the long list of fanaticisms into which it fell, some of which are alluded to by the writer on whom we were drawing at the opening of this paragraph; and the waves of most of which it sent washing back into the parent New England.

" The earliest agitation which helped to reveal the unfortunate strain in the blood," he writes, " was the crusade against the Masonic Fraternity in 1826, originating in a wide-spread belief, unconfirmed by sound evidence, that one Morgan had been foully dealt with at the behest of the Order whose secrets he was accused of revealing. A single and mighty wave of indignation nearly obliterated the fraternity from that part of the United States. In the early forties the Rochester country was one of the two chief centres of the propaganda and excitement associated with the predictions of the Vermont farmer, William Miller, with respect to the approaching judgment and the destruction of the world. In western New York it became a thoroughly irrational epidemic. Men and women forsook their employments and gave themselves over to watchings and prayer. They hardly slept or ate, but in robes of white awaited the coming of the bridegroom. The result in very many cases was utter physical and mental exhaustion, ending in the horrors of insanity. . . . In the late forties the delusion of spiritualism entered upon its epidemic course with the ' Rochester rappings ' of the Fox sisters. It spread by imitation to New England, and thence to Europe, and many of the phenomena attending it, — the trance, the vision, the convulsive

[14] Frederick Morgan Davenport, "Primitive Traits in Religious Revivals," 1905, pp. 183 ff.

movement, the involuntary dancing, the many indications of mental and nervous instability — had closest affinity to the extraordinary revival effects which we have elsewhere observed. . . . I wish to remark upon one other strange and base spiritual product of this unique population. Of course it is generally known that Mormonism had its beginning in this region, but it is not so generally understood, I think, that Mormonism was literally born and bred in the unhealthy revival atmosphere which has just been described.[15] In fact the sect of so-called Latter-Day Saints might never have existed except for the extraordinary mental agitation about religious matters which pervaded Western New York in this period. Mormonism has two main roots, the one to be traced into the mental and nervous characteristics of the personality of Joseph Smith, Jr., the other into the revival environment in which he lived and moved — and neither is a sufficient explanation without the other." [16]

A population like this could be trusted to produce spontaneously all the evil fruits of spurious religious excitement. In point of fact it did so. The writer upon whom we have been drawing, speaking of the period preceding that to which we wish to direct particular attention, points out that during it " an unbridled revival activity characterized the ordinary religious life of western New York."

" Before Finney's personality issued upon the scene," he says,[17] " before any particular individual assumed the leadership, this fa-

[15] As to Mormonism, John Humphrey Noyes himself (" Dixon's Spiritual Wives," ii. p. 180), speaking of these revival excitements, says: " Mormonism, doubtless, came out of the same fertile soil. Joe Smith began his career in Central New York, among a population that was fermenting with the hope of the Millennium, and at a time when the great National Revival was going forth in its strength." Noyes was himself a product of this " great National Revival." Similarly, D. L. Leonard, writing the history of the fads and fanaticism of the time, says of Smith, that " in him were embodied the grossest type of Americanism and the most earthy and irrational impulses resulting from the intense revival fervor then prevalent " (" The Story of Oberlin," 1898, p. 118).

[16] Davenport, as cited, pp. 183–186.

[17] Evans' Mills is called by Finney himself " a burnt district." " I found that region of the country," he writes in his " Memoirs," 1876, p. 78, " what, in the western phrase, would be called, ' a burnt district.' There had been, a few years previously, a wild excitement passing through that region, which they called a revival of religion, but which turned out to be spurious. I can

natical restlessness, this tendency to spiritual commotion, was in the mind of the population, and periodically broke forth in fantastic and exciting revival. There were whole stretches of country in those parts that for generations were known as the ' burnt district,' and which Finney found so blistered and withered by constant revival flame that no sprout, no blade of spiritual life, could be caused to grow.[18] Only the apples of Sodom flourished in the form of ignorance, intolerance, a boasted sinlessness and a tendency to free-love and ' spiritual affinities.' "

But this fanaticism-loving populace was not left to the spontaneous manifestation of its tendency to religious excitement. It was sedulously incited to it by its religious leaders, and naturally its last state was no better than the first. If anyone wishes to enjoy the illusion of actually "assisting" at an average revival meeting of this period, he has only to read Mrs. Trollope's painfully realistic descriptions, alike of a town

---

give no account of it except what I heard from Christian people and others. It was reported as having been a very extravagant excitement; and resulted in a reaction so extensive and profound, as to leave the impression on many minds that religion was a mere delusion."

[18] The same figure of a "burnt district" is spontaneously used here too, to describe the effect of these later revivals. "Look at the present condition of the churches of western New York, which have become, in truth, ' a people scattered and peeled,'" writes William L. Stone, "Matthias and His Impostures," 1835, pp. 314 ff. "The time has not come to write the ecclesiastical history of the last ten years. And yet somebody should chronicle the facts now, lest in after times the truth, however correctly it may be preserved by tradition, should not be believed. . . . The writer entertains no doubt, that many true conversions have occurred under the system to which he is referring. But as with the ground over which the lightning has gone, scorching and withering every green thing, years may pass away before the arid waste of the church will be grown over by the living herbage." This sad result of their labors was not hidden from Finney himself and his coadjutors in the fomenting of these "revivals of excitement." James Boyle writes to Finney, December 25, 1834, to the following effect. "Let us look over the fields, where you and others and myself have labored as revival ministers, and what is now their moral state? What was their state within three months after we left them? I have visited and revisited many of these fields, and groaned in spirit to see the sad, frigid, carnal, contentious state into which the churches had fallen — and fallen very soon after our first departure from among them " (The Literary and Theological Review, March, 1838, p. 66). Cf. what Asa Mahan says, below, Note 29.

revival and of a camp meeting.[19] Albert Barnes warns us,[20] to be sure, against trusting the testimony of "the Trollopes, and the Fidlers, and the Martineaus" — "persons," he says, "having as few qualifications for being correct reporters of revivals of religion as could be found in the wide world." [21] It would be absurd, of course, to resort to Mrs. Trollope for the religious interpretation of revival phenomena; but the general trustworthiness of her report of revival occurrences, actually witnessed by her, is unimpeachable, when allowance is once made for the one-sidedness of her observation, due to her unsympathetic attitude. She describes only what she saw; she does not herself generalize on it. But what she describes might be seen anywhere in the western country at the time, sometimes no doubt in less, often unfortunately in much more, offensive forms.

[19] "Domestic Manners of the Americans" (1832), 1901, chapters viii. and xv.; cf. also chapter xix. The camp meeting at its best is described with great vividness by Andrew Reed in pp. 183–205 of vol. i. of his and James Matheson's "Narrative of the Visit to the American Churches, etc.," 1835. Ill and good will count for much in the two descriptions, but not for all; and Reed is not blind to the possibilities of evil intrinsic in the circumstances and methods of such assemblies. On Camp Meetings, cf. S. C. Swallow, "Camp Meetings: Their Origin, History and Utility, also their Perversion," 1878.

[20] As cited, pp. 69–70.

[21] Neither Isaac Fidler's "Observations on Professions, Literature, Manners and Emigration, in the United States and Canada, made during a Residence there in 1832," 1833 — a book which can be described only as flat, stale, and unprofitable — nor either of Harriet Martineau's two very informing books, "Society in America," 1837, and "Retrospect of Western Travel," 1838, contains any "reports of revivals of religion." Albert Barnes's coupling of them with Mrs. Trollope's volume as possible sources of misinformation as to revivals is a purely rhetorical flight. Miss Martineau does, however, tell us ("Society in America," ii. p. 344), in a few incidental words, what she thinks of "meetings for religious excitement." "The spiritual dissipations indulged in by the religious world," she pronounces more injurious to sound morals than any public amusements indulged in under modern conditions. "It is questionable," she then adds, "whether even gross licentiousness is not at least equally encouraged by the excitement of passionate religious emotions, separate from action: and it is certain that rank spiritual vices, pride, selfishness, tyranny, and superstition, spring up luxuriantly in the hotbeds of religious meetings." On the large literature of British criticism of American ways which sprang up after the War of 1812 and raged for a quarter of a century, see "The Cambridge History of American Literature," i., 1917, pp. 205 ff., with the accompanying bibliography, pp. 468 ff.

Of course we are not confined to the testimony of Mrs. Trollope and writers of her type to learn what revivals at this period were like. We have, for example, a very sympathetic summary account of them from the pen of Andrew Reed, one of two very competent observers sent in the early thirties by the Congregational Union of England and Wales, to visit the American churches.[22] Reed does not doubt that the revivals were in themselves a work of God, the results of which by and large were for His glory.[23] But neither is he able to close his eyes to the evils which accompanied them; especially the opportunity afforded by them and eagerly availed of, for vain, weak, and fanatical men to exploit for their own ends the emotional excitement which was aroused. That there were serious evils intrinsic in the very manner in which the revivals were conducted, he is compelled to recognize; but that, he says, was not after all the worst of it — " they seem to have the faculty of generating a spirit worse than themselves." " Rash measures attract rash men," he explains: [24] " and their onward and devious path is tracked by the most unsanctified violence and reckless extravagance." " They are liable to run out into wild fanaticism," he explains further.[25]

" A revival is a crisis. It implies that a great mass of human passion that was dormant, is suddenly called into action. Those who are not moved to good will be moved to the greater evil. The hay, wood, and

[22] " A Narrative of the Visit to the American Churches by the Deputation from the Congregational Union of England and Wales," by Andrew Reed, D.D., and James Matheson, D.D., 1835, ii. pp. 7–50. An admirable review of this book by Charles Hodge, from the religious and theological point of view, will be found in *The Biblical Repertory and Theological Review*, October, 1835, pp. 598 ff.; and it is well reviewed, from the general literary point of view, by W. B. O. Peabody, in *The North American Review* for October, 1835, pp. 489 ff.

[23] A more judicious or generally sympathetic account of the revivals centering in 1831 could scarcely be found than that given by Lyman H. Atwater in his article on " Revivals of the Century," *The Presbyterian Quarterly and Princeton Review*, v., 1876, pp. 703 ff. And Charles Hodge in his review of Reed and Matheson's book in *The Biblical Repertory and Theological Review*, October, 1835, pp. 598 ff., deals with the whole matter most judiciously.

[24] P. 35.

[25] Pp. 42–43.

stubble, which are always to be found, even within the pale of the church, will enkindle, and flash, and flare. It is an occasion favourable to display, and the vain and presumptuous will endeavor to seize on it, and turn it to their own account. Whether such a state of general excitement is connected with worldly or religious objects, it is too much, and would argue great ignorance of human nature, to expect, that it should not be liable to excess and disorder." [26]

These somewhat general reflections are brought nearer to the point of most interest to us by the testimony of James H. Hotchkin, the historian of Western New York, and a most cautious and sober-minded man, speaking directly out of his own experience.[27] He, too, of course, is sympathetic to the revival movement in itself. But he feels constrained to note explicitly that "circumstances have occurred in connection with these revivals, which give the most painful exhibition of the wickedness and folly of man, when, leaving the divine word, he imagines himself wiser than God." He is led by his experience to the generalization that "whenever the religious excitement has been strong, a spirit of fanaticism has been induced, and greatly hindered the good work, and marred its beauty." He has observed further that these evils have been particularly apparent, when the revival-work was carried on, not by the settled ministry, but by outsiders called in because of some fancied particular adaptation to this work. No doubt there were among these "revival men" or "revival preachers" men of true piety, whose usefulness was demonstrated by the results of their labors. Of others, however, Hotchkin declares himself "constrained to believe, that, if they were not impostors, they must have been self-deceived fanatics"; and, certainly, he declares, "their operations and influences were destructive in a high degree, and brought discredit on

[26] When Charles Hodge, as cited, pp. 608 ff., traverses some of these judgments, he does so only on the understanding that they apply to revivals as such. As to the special revival movements of Western and Central New York of this period he is of the same mind with Reed.

[27] "A History of the Purchase and Settlement of Western New York, and of the Rise, Progress, and Present State of the Presbyterian Church in that Section," 1848, pp. 159 ff.

the revival." One and another of these men are mentioned and described; and it is pointed out that while mighty men in stirring up excitement, they failed, under the test of time, in bringing men really to Christ. Thus they proved themselves to be mere religious demagogues; for does not Gustave Le Bon tell us,[28] when describing demagogues and their ways, that, "it is easy to imbue the mind of crowds with a passing opinion, but very difficult to implant therein a lasting belief"?

It is not, however, until we turn to the portion of his book in which Hotchkin records the life-histories of the individual churches that we realize the amount either of the excitement stirred up by these men or of the evil wrought by it. Yet, as he is speaking only of the Presbyterian churches, which suffered least of all the churches from this disease, we are looking through his eyes only at the outer fringes of the evil. Even in the Presbyterian churches it certainly was bad enough.[29]

[28] "The Crowd," E. T. 1896, p. 162; cf. p. 58: "The art of appealing to crowds is no doubt of an inferior order, but it demands quite special aptitudes." A correction of the over-exploitation of "crowd-psychology" (as in Davenport) may be found in Graham Wallas, "The Great Society," 1914, pp. 115–138. On the general subject of "Crowd Psychology and Revivals," see J. B. Pratt, "The Religious Consciousness," 1920, pp. 165–194.

[29] There is no more distressing description of the evil effects of these revivals on people, pastors, and evangelists, than that in Asa Mahan's "Autobiography," 1882, pp. 227 ff. The people were left like a dead coal which could not be reignited. The pastors were shorn of all spiritual power. Of the evangelists he writes as follows: — "It is with pain that I refer to the evangelists of that era. Among them all — and I was personally acquainted with nearly every one of them — I cannot recall a single man, brother Finney and father Nash excepted, who did not after a few years lose his unction, and become equally disqualified for the office of evangelist and that of pastor. The individual who, next to Mr. Finney, had the widest popularity and influence, when in the meridian of life, left the ministry, and lived and died a banker, manifesting no disposition to preach the gospel to any class of men. The individual who probably stood next to him, after a series of years of most successful labor, retired into the far Western States, and I could never learn even his whereabouts. One who was very constantly with Mr. Finney, and labored, for a time, as his successor in Chatham Street Chapel, in the City of New York, abandoned wholly the Evangelical faith. Another, a preacher of great power, first joined Noyes, the Free Lover, and then the infidel abolitionists of the Garrison school. What finally became of him I never learned. I refer to but one other case from the painful catalogue before me. This individual probably had as great power over his audiences as any that can be

One Augustus Littlejohn [30] seems to have been the evil genius

named, and multitudes were no doubt won to Christ through his influence.
. . . The last time I met that evangelist . . . he told us . . . that he had just
left a great revival and was on his way, for absolutely necessary rest, to visit
his friends in Michigan. We afterwards learned that he was going as a fugi-
tive from the legal liabilities of his vices, and he subsequently, I believe, led
a kind of vagabond life." — The first-mentioned of these evangelists we take
to be Jedediah Burchard, a most ambiguous figure. The plain facts about him
may be read in Hotchkin, as cited, p. 170, while the best that can be said of
him is said by P. H. Fowler, "Historical Sketch of Presbyterianism within
the Bounds of the Synod of Central New York," 1877, p. 236. W. F. P. Noble's
account, "A Century of Gospel Work," 1876, pp. 401 ff., is mere indiscriminate
adulation. Cf. Finney, "Memoirs," pp. 358 f. A very curious picture is given of
Burchard at work in a little book published at Burlington, Vermont, in 1836,
bearing the title: "Sermons, Addresses and Exhortations by Rev. Jedediah
Burchard: with an Appendix," by C. C. Eastman (12mo, pp. vi., 120), a very
slashing review of which by Leonard Withington will be found in *The Literary
and Theological Review* for June, 1836, pp. 228–236. The material for the book
was obtained by stenographers working not only without Burchard's permission but against his violent opposition. It seems that an earlier publication of
similar character had been made by a Mr. Streeter of Woodstock. The sermons printed in Eastman's volume, we are afraid, would no longer shock; and
we wish to record to Burchard's credit that he was no "Perfectionist." To his
young converts he says (p. 73): "You know who the perfectionists are.
Strange that there are such beings, but it is so. In the judgment of charity,
there are many who are sincere in this error. Now, my young friends, I wish
to guard you particularly against everything of this kind."

[30] A concurrence of witnesses testifies to the ineffable vulgarity, fanaticism, and unsoundness of Littlejohn's preaching, as well as to the coarseness
of his manners and the impurity of his life. Nevertheless, he retained his connection with the Presbyterian Church until, tardily, on March 18, 1841, "he
was, by the Presbytery of Angelica, deposed from the ministerial office, and
excommunicated from the church, on account of grossly immoral conduct
practised clandestinely, at various times through a long period" (Hotchkin, as
cited, pp. 171, 172). Cf. also to the same effect, P. H. Fowler, as cited, pp. 235,
note, 277; and the letter signed "Wyoming," in *The New York Evangelist*,
July 27, 1876, and reprinted thence in *The Presbyterian Quarterly and Princeton Review*, October, 1876, p. 713, note. James A. Miller, "The History of the
Presbytery of Steuben," 1897, pp. 15 f., draws on William Waith, "Recollections of an Emigrant's Family," for a description of Littlejohn. "He was a
common laborer," says Waith, "but was endowed with a natural eloquence
which gave him the complete mastery over any group that he addressed. He
would collect a gang of his fellow workmen and preach a funeral sermon over
a dead horse, or dog, that would fill the eyes of his hearers with tears. This
man professed conversion to Christianity, and began holding forth in school
houses, or in churches to which pastors would admit him, and hearts were
melted, and knees were bent in penitence, to such an extent that people

of the Presbytery of Angelica, one Luther Myrick [31] of the

thought this man 'the great power of God.' He offered himself as a candidate
for the ministry; but the older heads of the presbytery . . . were unyielding
in their opposition to his licensure. Littlejohn, however, went right on with
his fervent appeals, and converts were multiplied within the parishes of the
very pastors that opposed him. . . . The pressure upon the presbytery became
so strong that any longer to refuse licensure appeared like fighting against
God." Miller himself continues the story: " In 1830 he was licensed. In 1833
a day was set for his ordination as an evangelist. When the day came there
were charges against him of doctrinal unsoundness and imprudent conduct, and
his ordination was postponed. A month later Geneva Synod criticised the
method of his licensure and directed presbytery to re-examine him. Instead of
re-examining him for licensure presbytery ordained him. This action Genesee
Synod censured. Difficulties arose later between Littlejohn and his wife, but
presbytery exonerated him from blame and highly commended his work as
an evangelist. In 1839 there were charges against his character. Presbytery
appointed a committee to investigate, but in 1840, before that committee reported, made him moderator. About the same time presbytery refused a request of Ontario Presbytery to investigate charges against Littlejohn — not
even recording the charges on the minutes. The Synod of Genesee censured
presbytery very sharply for making him moderator while charges were pending against him, and for passing over the request of Ontario Presbytery. After
a good many other actions, in 1841 he was cited to answer definite charges of
grossly immoral conduct. There was an exhaustive trial at Almond in March,
1841. At last presbytery saw him as he was, and unanimously deposed him
from the ministry and excommunicated him from the church." This assuredly
is a case of all is *not* well that ends well.

[31] The Presbytery of Cayuga, August, 1833, warned the churches under its
care against employing Myrick because of the unsoundness of his doctrine and
the evil practical effects of his preaching. It mentions that he was at the time
under summons by his Presbytery (that of Oneida) for trial. Similar action
was taken by the Presbytery of Onondaga; and both Presbyteries entered a
complaint against him to the Presbytery of Oneida. Cf. Hotchkin, as cited,
p. 173; Fowler, as cited, pp. 137, 278; and especially, James Wood, " Facts and
Observations concerning the Organization and State of the Churches in the
Three Synods of Western New York, etc.," 1837, pp. 20–21. Myrick was a member of the Presbytery of Oneida from 1828 to 1844. The dealing of the Presbytery of Oneida with him showed the same general characteristics which
marked the dealing of the Presbytery of Angelica with Littlejohn. It must
have been quite clear from his first appearance before the Presbytery in 1825
as a candidate that he was not a suitable person to induct into the ministry.
Yet the Presbytery carried him through his trials, ordained him over a congregation with a protesting minority, and when the inevitable charges were
brought before it, dawdled with them; and finally, when at last, October 24,
1833, he was found guilty of both doctrinal errors (denying the doctrine of
Perseverance, and asserting the doctrine of Perfection) and disorderly conduct (disorganizing churches, encouraging confusion in religious meetings, de-

Presbytery of Onondaga, one James Boyle [32] of the Presbytery

faming the Presbyterian Church, slanderous and coarse language), removed the suspension imposed on him on his expressing sorrow for nothing but his "improper expressions." Next spring (February 6, 1834) he asked to be dismissed to the Black River Association; but that body would not receive him; and he thereupon simply "withdrew from the fellowship of the Presbyterian Church" (June 24, 1834), and his name was erased from the roll. He retained his residence within the bounds of the Presbytery, a Congregationalist in affiliation, and gave himself to the propagation of his perfectionist doctrine. "He is the editor of a paper," says Wood in 1837, "and by this means as well as by his preaching, is promulgating his pernicious doctrines — and I regret to add, they are embraced by a *few* in quite a number of churches, to the great grief and vexation of their brethren and pastors." "He was an enthusiast, probably sincere," Fowler sums up, "but wrought up to the point of derangement, and while gathering large assemblies and exciting them, his proper place was the asylum rather than the pulpit." It is worth noting that one of his "methods" was to report (in *The Evangelist* or *The Western Recorder*) the results of the revivals carried on by him, quite without regard to the facts.

[32] Of Boyle, Hotchkin (p. 171) says that almost every church in which he worked, though greatly enlarged in its membership by him, fell shortly into decay. He adds that he "lost his ministerial character," was "deposed from the ministry and excommunicated from the church." He "came to the Presbytery of Oneida" (as Fowler expresses it, p. 277) "with clean papers from the Methodist ministry," and on those credentials was received as a member of the Presbytery. He was a member of the Presbytery of Oneida from 1827 to 1835 — never through that period becoming a pastor of a church. In 1834 he was preaching for the Free Church of New Haven, and there imbibed perfectionist doctrines in the New Haven form. For these he was arraigned by the Presbytery in the spring of 1835 on the basis of "common fame." The charges as formulated by the Presbytery having been all admitted by him, he was suspended from the ministry April 29, 1835. The erroneous teachings thus confessed by him are these: "That under the Gospel men are wholly sinful or wholly righteous"; "that there is no security of ultimate salvation without perfect freedom from sin"; "that a pardon through Jesus Christ which covers all past sin is inseparably connected with a perfect and perpetual sanctification of the soul"; "that the licensing and ordaining of ministers by Presbyteries, Associations, and Councils is an assumption of the high prerogatives of the Church." These confessed teachings include the assertion of the notion of what is known as "the simplicity of moral action" — a man is always either as bad as he can be or as good as he can be; attach perfection immediately to justification — every saved soul is perfect; make this perfection indefectible; and assert what J. H. Noyes calls "disunionism" — the absolute independence of every minister of the word of all ecclesiastical authority. Boyle, a native of Lower Canada, was born and bred a Roman Catholic and after his career as Methodist, Presbyterian, and Perfectionist, came into connection with Gamaliel Bailey, Jr., and William Lloyd Garrison, and ran a notable course as Anti-Slavery Agitator. We find Garrison already printing in *The Liberator* of

of Geneva. These were all famous revivalists, enjoying high favor not only in Western New York, but to the East as well, and running through great careers; and only when they had wrought their ruin, did they fall at last under the ban of the church they had distracted and whose people they had harassed and misled. It is appalling to observe the number of churches of which it is recorded that they were disturbed, injured, or destroyed by the activities of these men and their coadjutors. We need not repeat these records here: let that of Manlius Center Church serve as a single example — it was, we read,[33] " torn to pieces, and became extinct, through the influence of Mr. Myrick and other errorists." We prefer to transcribe merely the long record of the experiences of the church of Conhocton,[34] as particularly instructive of the state of mind induced by the prevalent religious excitement.

" In the summer of 1832," we read, " Rev. James Boyle held with this church a protracted meeting, which was continued through a number of days. The measures which were common with him and others of that class of evangelists were employed, and a state of high excitement was produced, and many professed to be converted, and no doubt some souls really were born again. A large number were received into the church, swelling its number to one hundred and ten members. It might seem that the days of the mourning of this church were now ended, and that she must now have acquired such a measure of strength as to be able in all future time to enjoy the stated ministrations of the gospel. But such was not the case.

March 23, 1838, a letter from Boyle, which Garrison describes as " one of the most powerful epistles ever written by man," on " Clerical Appeal, Sectarianism and True Holiness," and another the next year " On Non-Resistance, — The 'Powers that Be,' Civil, Judicial and Ecclesiastical — Holiness." The former was dated from Rome, Ohio, the latter from Cincinnati, where Boyle was already working on Bailey's *Philanthropist*. In July, 1839, he became lecturing and financial agent of the Ohio Anti-Slavery Society, and we are told that Oliver Johnson said of him that " probably there was no man living whose religious views were more in harmony with Mr. Garrison's." For these facts see " William Lloyd Garrison: The Story of His Life Told by His Children," ii. 1885, pp. 286–287. It will be seen from this that what Noyes called his " disunionism " became in fact the fundamental note of his thinking.

[33] Hotchkin, as cited, p. 315.
[34] *Ibid.*, p. 470.

Very little pecuniary strength was acquired, a spirit of fanaticism was infused into the minds of many, and a state of preparation to be carried away with any delusion was induced. With respect to the converts, so called, the writer is unable to say what has become of them. He believes very few of them give satisfactory evidence of having been born again. In the winter of 1837–8, a very singular state of things existed. Mrs. —— Conn, who had been a member of the church a number of years, and highly esteemed by some, at least, as a woman of piety and activity in promoting the cause of Christ, began to take a very conspicuous part in the meetings for social and religious worship. She professed to have special communications from God, and to know the secrets of the hearts of those with whom she was conversant. She assumed an authoritative position in the church, and gave out her directions as from God himself, denouncing as hypocrites in the church all who did not submit to her mandates. She predicted the speedy death, in the most awful manner, of particular individuals who opposed her authority, and manifested a most implacable rancor against all who did not acknowledge her inspiration. In her proceedings she was assisted by a young man, who for his misconduct had been excommunicated from the church of Prattsburgh. A number of the members of the church of Conhocton were carried away with this delusion, and acknowledged Mrs. Conn as one under the inspiration of the Almighty. So completely were they infatuated, that they seemed to suppose that their eternal salvation depended on the will of Mrs. Conn. They were ready to obey all her commands, and to assert as truth anything which she should order. Some of them became permanently deranged, and one or two families were nearly broken up. Nor was this delusion confined wholly to the church of Conhocton. Mrs. Conn and her coadjutor went into the county of Wyoming, and some in that region were brought under the delusion, and received her as a messenger sent from God. Whether to view Mrs. Conn as an impostor, a wild fanatic, or a deranged person, the writer will not assume the responsibility of determining. Many circumstances would favor the idea of imposture. The writer is informed that she has become a maniac. This circumstance may favor the idea of mental aberration. But the consequences to the church were most disastrous."

One of the most distressing accompaniments of revival excitements has been a tendency which has often showed itself in connection with them to sexual irregularities. This tendency does not seem to find its account, solely at least, in the low level of culture of the populations which have furnished the materials on which these revivals chiefly worked. And it certainly is not to be confounded with the opportunity taken by evil-minded persons from the conditions created by the revivals for corrupt practices. The opportunity has been afforded and improved, the camp meetings of course supplying the most flagrant instances. R. Davidson, describing the great Kentucky revival at the opening of the century, feels bound to consecrate a section to the " too free communication of the sexes," and, although he excuses himself from giving details on account of the delicacy of the subject, he tells us plainly that dissolute characters of both sexes frequented the camps " to take advantage of the opportunities afforded by the prevailing license and disorder." [35] This, however, was only incidental to the revivals themselves. What needs to be recognized is that the nervous exaltation, which was the direct product of the revival methods too frequently employed, seems not merely to have broken down the restraints to the unchecked discharge of other than religious emotions, but to have opened the channels for their discharge, and even to have incited to it — so that, as W. Hepworth Dixon puts it in vivid phrase, " the passions seemed to be all unloosed, and to go astray without let or guide." [36] It was the participators in the revival excitement themselves who went astray. John Lyle, reviewing

[35] " History of the Presbyterian Church in the State of Kentucky, etc.," 1847, pp. 163–165. David Ramsay, " The History of South Carolina, 1670–1808," 1808, 1809, ii. p. 36, note, says temperately: — " The effects of these camp-meetings were of a mixed nature. They were doubtless attended for improper purposes by a few licentious persons, and by others with a view of obtaining a handle to ridicule all religion. . . . The free intercourse of so great a number of all ages and sexes under cover of the night and the woods was not without its temptations."

[36] " New America," ed. 4, 1867, ii. p. 146. The phrase occurs in a vivid description, which is also an arraignment, of the camp meeting, sensationally written, but not essentially untrue to fact. " In the revivalist camp," he says, " men quarrel, and fight, and make love to their neighbours' wives." " ' I like to hear of a revival,' said to me a lawyer of Indianapolis; ' it brings on a crop of cases.' "

the case of the women who had been the subjects of the " falling exercise " prior to November, 1802, found several " by the most unequivocal proofs, to have since *fallen* still more wofully; no fewer than four individuals having transgressed in the most flagrant manner." [37]

Occasion has of course been taken from such facts to confuse emotions which differ *toto cœlo.* There is actually a theory extant that the religious emotion is nothing but the sexual ecstasy misinterpreted,[38] and it is quite common to represent " the human love passion and the spiritual love passion " as lying in particularly close contiguity, if not even as " delicately interwoven." [39] There is no justification for such representations. They rest on an incredible confusion of the movements of the human soul set in the midst between two

[37] Davidson, as cited, pp. 163 f.

[38] Theodore Schroeder has made himself the persistent advocate of this notion: cf. *The American Journal of Religious Psychology and Education,* iii. 1908, pp. 16 ff.; v. 1912, pp. 394 ff.; vi. 1913, pp. 59 ff.; vii. 1914, pp. 23 ff. E. D. Starbuck says: " In a certain sense the religious life is an irradiation of the reproductive instinct " (" Psychology of Religion," 1899, p. 401). Cf. also G. Stanley Hall, " Adolescence," ii. p. 301; J. B. Pratt, as cited, pp. 108 ff.

[39] Davenport, as cited, p. 81, cf. p. 292. S. Baring Gould, " Freaks of Fanaticism," 1891, p. 268, says extremely: " The religious passion verges so closely on the sexual passion that a slight additional pressure given to it bursts the partition, and both are confused in a frenzy of religious debauch." This was already the theory of John Humphrey Noyes: " The tendency of religious unity," says he, in " Bible Communism," 1853, p. 31, " to flow into the channel of amativeness, manifests itself in revivals and in all the higher forms of spiritualism. Marriages or illegitimate amours usually follow religious excitements. Almost every spiritual sect has been troubled by amative tendencies. These facts are not to be treated as unaccountable irregularities, but as expressions of a law of human nature. Amativeness is in fact . . . the first and most natural channel of religious love." " Religious love is very near neighbor to sexual love," says he again, " and they always get mixed in the intimacies and social excitements of Revivals." " The next thing a man wants," he adds less appositely, " after he has found the salvation of his soul, is to find his Eve and his Paradise. Hence these wild experiments and terrible disasters " (W. H. Dixon, " Spiritual Wives," ed. 2, 1868, ii. p. 177). " It is a very sad fact," Dixon himself adds to this citation (p. 10), " which shows in what darkness men may grope and pine in this wicked world, that when these Perfect Saints were able to look about them in the new freedom of Gospel light, hardly one of the leading men among them could find an Eden at home, an Eve in his lawful wife."

environments, and accessible to influences alike from below and above. Not even all love of man is sex-love; no love of man is religious love; religious love is not the entirety of the religious emotion. We are in the presence here of nothing more mysterious than the obvious fact that man's emotional nature is a unit, and violent emotional discharges may readily be deflected from one to another direction. The phenomenon we are witnessing is only the familiar one of the peril of abandoning control of ourselves. When once we drop the reins and give unbridled play to our passional movements, there is no telling what the end may be. We cannot act the mænad in religion and expect our mænadism to manifest itself nowhere else. If religion becomes synonymous to us with excess, all excess is very apt to come to seem to us religious. It is in this sense only that it is true, when Baring Gould declares that " spiritual exaltation runs naturally, inevitably, into licentiousness, unless held in the iron bands of discipline to the moral law." [40] Davenport's wider generalization is truer: [41] " Wherever reason is subordinated and feeling is supreme, the influence is always in the direction of the sweeping away of inhibitive control."

It is, moreover, not merely into licentiousness that religious mænadism tends to run, but into all forms of lawless action. J. H. Noyes shows an insight unwonted to him, therefore, when he represents revivals — of course, as known to him, that is to say the revivals of " religious excitement " — as intrinsically subversive of the whole social as well as moral order. Defining them from the true mænadistic point of view, and even in language strongly reminiscent of heathen modes of speech, he declares [42] that a revival is the actual intrusion of the power of God into human affairs: that is to say, says he, it is the entrance into the complex of active causes of " the actual Deity." This entrance of " the actual Deity " into human life is conceived after the fashion of the intrusion of a universal

---

[40] As cited, p. 14.
[41] As cited, p. 28.
[42] Dixon's " Spiritual Wives," ii. pp. 176 f.

natural force, only more powerful than other natural forces.[43]
Conservatives fancy that its operations are restricted to the
conversion of souls. That, says Noyes, is absurd: you cannot
cabin and crib such a force in that way. Once set in motion,
" it goes, or tends to go, into all the affairs of life." A revolution is really inaugurated in every revival, and if it does not
overturn and reconstitute all the life of the world, that is only
because its action is prematurely checked. " Revival preachers and Revival converts are necessarily in the incipient stage
of a theocratic revolution; they have in their experience the
beginning of a life under the Higher Law; and if they stop at
internal religious changes, it is because the influence that converted them is suppressed." The term " higher law " here is
ominous: the first effect of revivals is conceived as emancipation from the laws which now govern life; and if redintegration
follows it must be under a higher law than they. They do and
always must leave social disintegration in their train.

The prominence particularly of sexual irregularities in the
train of the revivals of " religious excitement " is probably in
large part due, therefore, only to the large opportunities and
immediate temptations to irregularities of this particular order
offered by revival intimacies. The period in which the revivals
of the late twenties and early thirties took place was, moreover, one of widespread unrest with respect to the relations of
the sexes, and of relaxation of the strictness of traditional
habits; and the communistic experiments incited in the middle
years of the twenties by Robert Owen no doubt also brought

[43] This materialistic mode of conceiving God appears to have been habitual with Noyes. Commenting with much commendation on Buchanan's
experiments in Animal Magnetism — in which he sees effects not differing in
kind from Christ's miracles — he says (" The Berean," p. 77) : " Perhaps in the
progress of his investigation, Dr. Buchanan will find means to increase his
nervous powers, either by self-training, or availing himself of the power of
others. But he will never approach equality with Christ, as a practical neu-
rologist, till he establishes communication with God, the great source of vital
energy. . . . So long as mere human life is the fountain of magnetic influence,
its effects will only be proportioned to the weakness of human nature." God is
a physical force which may conceivably be tapped and drawn upon by the
practitioner of Animal Magnetism; and which, set at work in the world, will
move blindly to this or that effect.

their contribution to the result. With respect to these particular revivals, however, we must not underestimate the influence of the fantastic apocalyptical theories, by which a large part of their unhealthy excitement was produced, and which by persuading men that they no longer lived on the earthly plane or under earthly law, gave to sexual irregularities a religious sanction or even made them appear a religious duty. Being mænads, men and women committed adultery for the Kingdom of God's sake — as the victims of the atrocious Cochrane were doing in Maine and New Hampshire a short decade before,[44] and the associates of the unspeakable Matthias — himself a product of these revivals — were doing contemporaneously in New York and Sing Sing.[45] Thus arose the shocking theory of "spiritual wives" which was intimately connected with the

[44] For a brief notice of Cochrane's career, see W. L. Stone, "Matthias and His Impostures, etc.," 1835, pp. 296 ff. (repeated in part in H. Eastman, "Noyesism Unveiled," 1849, p. 400). The allusion in J. Brockway's "A Delineation of the Characteristic Features of a Revival of Religion in Troy, in 1826 and 1827," 1827, p. 59, seems to be to something in general similar: — "A sect started up, two or three years ago, in the eastern part of Vermont, putting defiance to all the laws of modesty and decency, breaking down all distinction of sex; they were too pure to be defiled by any intercourse. The civil arm was stretched out to put a stop to this outrage on humanity; and the cry was reiterated . . . 'persecution,' 'persecution.'" This was written too early to refer to Noyes and his Putney community.

[45] The story of Matthias is told at length and very temperately by W. L. Stone, "Matthias and His Impostures, etc.," 1835. See also the favorable review and abstract of Stone's book by Edward Everett, The North American Review, xli. 1835, pp. 307 ff. It is told from a different point of view by G. B. Vale, "Fanaticism, its Sources and Influence Illustrated in the Case of Matthias, etc., a Reply to W. L. Stone," 1835, and more recently by Theodore Schroeder in The American Journal of Religious Psychology and Education, 1913, pp. 59–65. Schroeder attaches a brief bibliography. There are very short notices of Matthias in Drake's "Dictionary of American Biography," and McClintock and Strong's "Cyclopædia of Biblical, Theological, and Ecclesiastical Literature," sub nom. "The imposture of Matthias, and the perfectionism of New Haven," says Albert B. Dod (The Biblical Repertory and Theological Review, October, 1835, p. 661), "are monster growths, in different directions, of the same monster trunk" — meaning the "revival of excitement," or as he, following Stone, expresses it, "the spirit of fanaticism which has transformed so many Christian communities in the northern and western parts of New York, and states contiguous, into places of moral waste and spiritual desolation."

perfectionism that constituted, after all is said, the most unwholesome product of the revival excitement. There is no reason to suppose that the "spiritual wives" at the outset were
anything other than the name, strictly taken, imports — intimate spiritual companions and fellow workers in a common
task.[46] The hot perfectionist, living in the new order, attached
to himself a like-minded female companion who shared his
labors at home and abroad; they lived together, traveled together, worked together, in a fellowship closer than and superseding that of husband and wife. It was a renewal of the
"spiritual wives" — the *agapetæ* or *virgines subintroductæ* —
of the early church; [47] but it required only a few months to run
through the development that its earlier model consumed some
centuries in traversing. What was in the first instance only an
incredible folly and dangerous fanaticism soon became an intolerable scandal and dissolute practice. "Spiritual wives" became carnal mistresses: here and there injured husbands
avenged their wrongs by physical assaults upon the clerical
offenders, and when the husband was complaisant the outraged
community was apt to treat both legal and spiritual husband
to a coat of tar and feathers and a ride on a rail.[48] Though

[46] This is the testimony of J. H. Noyes, in Dixon's "Spiritual Wives," ii.
p. 179: — "The original theory of the Saints, both at the East and the West,
was opposed to actual intercourse of the sexes as 'works of the flesh.' They
'bundled' it is true, but only to prove by trial their power against the flesh;
in other words, their triumphant Shakerism. Doctor Gridley, one of the Massachusetts leaders, boasted that 'he could carry a virgin in each hand without
the least stir of unholy passion!' At Brimfield, Mary Lincoln and Maria Brown
visited Simon Lovett in his room; but they came out of that room in the innocence of Shakerism."

[47] See especially H. Achelis, "Virgines Subintroductæ: Ein Beitrag zum vii
Kapitel Des I Korintherbriefs," 1902, or his article "Agapetæ" in Hastings's
"Encyclopædia of Religion and Ethics," i. pp. 177–180. Also Havelock Ellis,
"Studies in the Psychology of Sex," vi. 1910, pp. 151 ff. or the abstract from
him in Hastings, as cited, iii. p. 487.

[48] The classical account of the matter is of course that of W. H. Dixon,
"Spiritual Wives," ed. 2, 1868, ii. This account is written in a sensational
style, but in its substance is good contemporary history from the hands of
eyewitnesses. J. H. Noyes in his "Dixon and His Copyists" (1871), ed. 2,
1874, p. 32, tells us that, except chapters vii., viii., and xxvi.–xxxi., which
are Dixon's, the whole of the contents of the book was supplied by himself or

actually only sporadically practiced, the advocacy of this indecency was widespread in perfectionist circles. Its roots were planted in the prevalent notion that the " saints " had advanced beyond the legalities of the worldly order, and that it behooved them to be putting the freedom of the resurrection life into practice.

The perfectionism of which this deplorable practice was one of the fruits was pervasive, and everywhere it went it worked destruction. It was intensely individualistic in its temper and operated accordingly as a disintegrating force in the church organizations into which it found entrance. This effect was increased by its affiliation with a powerful unionistic movement which was vexing the churches of this region. Like other unionistic movements, this one also was much more effective for tearing down the existing organizations which stood in its way, than for realizing its own professed Utopian ends.[49] At all events ruin marked the pathway along which the combined perfectionist-unionist forces moved. Here is a typical notice: " Rev. A. Hale, from the Black River Association, distracted the church with perfectionism, and Rev. Luther Myrick with unionism. Twenty male members broke away from the church at one time as perfectionists." [50] There was an active organization, vigorously at work among the churches, calling itself " The Central Evangelical Association of New York," which consisted, as Hotchkin tells us,[51] just of " a body of Perfectionists and Unionists." The Synod of Geneva at its meeting in October, 1835, warned the ministers and churches under its charge against it, because, as it said, it " does not sustain the reputation of an orthodox body," and " the course

George Cragin, i.e. by intimate actors and witnesses in the occurrences described.

[49] Cf. P. H. Fowler, as cited, pp. 137–138: " ' Unionism ' made high pretensions to piety and charity, but was bitter towards existing denominations, and fiercely assailed them and sent forth multitudes of extemporized preachers to spit venom upon them, and to strike silently at them; and the Presbyteries stripped it of its disguise and exposed its ugliness and mischievousness."

[50] Hotchkin, as cited, p. 314.

[51] P. 313.

of proceeding adopted by most of their ministers is calculated to divide, corrupt, and distract the churches." The Synod therefore declared that it deemed it " irregular for any minister or church in our connexion, to admit the ministers of said Association to their pulpits, or in any way to recognise them, or the churches organized by them, as in regular standing." [52] Such a deliverance was necessarily a mere *brutum fulmen*. Even had it taken a more authoritative form, it was locking the door after the horse had been stolen. Nor is it easy in any event to see how the closing of Presbyterian pulpits to perfectionist agitators could have been expected to protect the people from the flames of wild religious excitement flaring up hotly in churches of other connections half a block away. The communities were small, and the people therefore in close contact and intimate intercourse with one another; the religious excitement that was raging was the property of no one denomination, but pervaded all; it was the professed object of one of the most active organizations engaged in fostering it — and the actual effect of many with no official connection with that organization — to obliterate all dividing lines and to reduce the whole Christian body to an indiscriminate mass of fanaticism.

Certainly perfectionists swarmed over the land, drawing from all churches, forming none. No doubt the ever-present fact of Wesleyan Perfectionism lay in the background and supplied everywhere a starting-point and everywhere gave a certain dignity and stability to the movement. A number of the perfectionist leaders were of Methodist origin.[53] But the

[52] Hotchkin, as cited, p. 173.

[53] Charles G. Finney, in his " Views of Sanctification," 1840, p. 136, says: " So far as I can learn, the Methodists have been in a great measure if not entirely exempt from the errors held by modern perfectionists." He is not in this, however, speaking of the sources upon which the Perfectionists drew for their membership, but of the teaching current in the Methodist Church in contrast with theirs. He does, however, add that "Perfectionists, as a body, and I believe with very few exceptions, have arisen out of those denominations that deny the doctrine of entire sanctification," — and this doubtless was true of the perfectionists he had in mind, if taken as a general fact. It was not, however, the whole truth.

most effective forces in the production of the prevalent perfectionism were derived from quite different quarters, particularly from the Pelagianizing theories of the will emanating from New Haven.[54] The perfectionism actually developed[55]

[54] This is fully argued and illustrated by Joseph I. Foot, in " An Enquiry respecting the Theological Origin of Perfectionism, and its Correlative Branches of Fanaticism," in *The Literary and Theological Review*, March, 1836, pp. 1–33. He declares that in point of fact the errors of "the New Dispensation" are practically confined to congregations in which "the New Divinity" had been taught, laying the stress especially on its assertion of human ability and its representation of regeneration, as " effected by ' divine moral suasion,' " — that is to say on its Pelagianism. " We come then to the conclusion," he sums up (p. 28), " that the system of light and motives, including its assumption respecting the human will, or heart, is the parent of perfectionism." Similarly, Ebenezer H. Snowden, writing in 1837 (*The Baltimore Literary and Religious Magazine*, iii. July, 1837, pp. 310 ff.), says of these perfectionists of Western New York that, " they are the results of the doctrine of man's ability and the new measures," and that, compared with them, " the Methodist perfectionists are very orthodox." He describes them as mystical in doctrine, antinomian in practice, and disintegrating in their relation to the churches. They hold that " do what they may, they *cannot sin;* yea, that it is as impossible for them as for God himself." They are guilty of " acts of the grossest sensuality," justifying themselves " on the principle that they can do no wrong." " They consider ministers *nuisances,* and churches *useless,* and that they ought to be torn down." Hence Samuel J. Baird, " A History of the New School," 1868, p. 224, says, speaking of Taylorism — " The system attained to its logical results in the perfectionism which sprang up, broadcast, as an after-crop, in Western New York. . . . If the divine commands are criteria of our ability, the words, ' Be ye perfect, even as your Father which is in heaven is perfect,' are an assurance that we can be perfect, as God." Cf. Lyman H. Atwater, *The Presbyterian Quarterly and Princeton Review,* July, 1877, pp. 410 ff.

[55] A good account of their origin and teaching is given by Joseph I. Foot in two publications, the one, a separate pamphlet entitled " Discourses on Modern Antinomianism, commonly called Perfectionism," and the other an article in *The Literary and Theological Review* for December, 1834, pp. 554–583, bearing the caption: " ' The New Dispensation,' or Modern Antinomianism, commonly called Perfectionism." In the latter of these he sums up their doctrine under three heads: (1) They " do not regard the moral law as obligatory on believers "; they " affirm that ' they have nothing to do and have already entered into rest.' " (2) They " profess to be personally united to Christ, or to the Holy Spirit." " They interpret the phrase, ' Christ is come in the flesh ' (in 1 Jno. iv. 2) as denoting ' his coming into their bodies, and being personally united to them.' " (3) They " declare themselves ' to be perfect, to be as holy as God.' " They expressed their views as to their relation to Christ by the terms " communication," or " commutation," by which they meant such an exchange of character with Christ that " we become as com-

ran, however, in point of fact, into mystical molds. "These Perfectionists," as a contemporary writer [56] very fairly puts it, "believe that they have the inward Christ — can do no wrong — that to the pure all things are pure — that Christ is responsible for all they do — and other such blasphemous absurdities." Their chief or, at least, their most obvious, charac-

pletely holy as He, and He as completely sinful as we." Another very prominent characteristic of their teaching was the profession to be so led by the Spirit as to supersede all dependence on the Word. " I have never known, or heard, of a disciple of the ' New Dispensation,' " says Foot (p. 565), " who did not profess either to receive immediate revelations, or to be personally united to the Deity. In the latter case, though there evidently can be no need of such revelations, they are frequently claimed. . . . They . . . regard their own sayings and epistles, as of equal authority with those of the apostles. They even declare, that the apostolic writings pertain only to their own times, and are now superseded by modern revelations." Asa Mahan, " Scripture Doctrine of Christian Perfection " (1839), ed. 7, 1844, pp. 70–73, gives rather a full account of their teachings. " (1) Perfectionism . . . in its fundamental principles, is the abrogation of all law . . . (2) In abrogating the moral law, as a rule of duty, Perfectionism abrogates all obligation of every kind. (3) Perfectionism is a ' rest ' which suspends all efforts and prayer, even, for the salvation of the world. (4) Perfectionism substitutes the direct teaching of the Spirit, falsely called, in the place of the ' word.' (5) Perfectionism surrenders up the soul to blind impulse, assuming, that every existing desire or impulse is caused by the direct agency of the Spirit, and therefore to be gratified. (6) Perfectionism abrogates the Sabbath, and all the ordinances of the Gospel, and, in its legitimate tendencies, even marriage itself." (7) Perfectionism by abrogating all law, abrogates all standards of conduct and accordingly demoralizes man. " (8) Perfectionism, in short, in its essential elements, is the perfection of licentiousness." Compare the description of the system by Henry Cowles, " Holiness of Christians in the Present Life," 1840, pp. 9 ff. The system, he says, " disclaims all obligation to obey the moral law," substituting the law of love. It " supposes the Christian to receive Christ within him, in such a way, that henceforth Christ only acts within him; and whatever himself seems to do, Christ really does. Some even suppose their own individual being to be absorbed or merged into Christ, so that themselves, as distinct persons, have ceased to exist, and all that was themselves is now Christ." It " either avowedly or virtually annihilates personal agency and responsibility." " As a consequence, mental impressions, supposed to be from the Spirit of God, are deemed perfect truth and law, paramount even to the Bible itself." " These principles lead more or less extensively, as the case may be, to the rejection of all Gospel ordinances, the disuse of prayer, and to all manner of licentiousness." Compare also the vivid description of the Antinomian Perfectionists in Charles Fitch, " Views of Sanctification," 1839, pp. 19 ff.

[56] W. L. Stone, " Matthias and His Impostures, etc.," 1835, p. 316.

teristic accordingly was less correctness in conduct than freedom in the Spirit. And this in fact constituted their main attraction to the populace. J. H. Noyes fully recognizes [57] that " some doubtless joined the standard of Perfectionism, not because they loved holiness, but because they were weary of the restraints of the duty-doing churches. Perfectionism presented them a fine opportunity of giving full swing to carnality; and at the same time, of glorying over the ' servants ' under law." Nothing was further from their intention, of course, than to submit themselves to the restraints of organization. Each wished to be a law to himself — and as far as he could compass it, a law also to everybody else. They erected what Noyes calls " disunity " [58] into a principle and denounced organization as in itself an evil — a slavery to which free men in the spirit would not submit. " To perfectionists generally," writes William A. Hinds,[59]

" the idea of discipline, organization, submission one to another, was intolerable. Were they children of the convenant, that ' gendereth to bondage '? they asked themselves, or were they called to ' stand fast in the liberty wherewith Christ had made them free '? Were they not living in the very days foretold by the prophet, when all were ' to know the Lord from the least unto the greatest,' and when no one ' should teach his neighbor or his brother, saying, Know the Lord '? ' Perfectionists,' said the eloquent James Boyle, ' stand as independent of each other as they do of any anti-Christian churches — they will not be taught of each other, as they are all taught of God, nor will they acknowledge any man as a leader or chief or any thing of the kind.' "

Such extreme individualism as is here announced cannot really maintain itself in practice. The perfectionists, too, of

[57] " The Berean," p. 460.

[58] Cf. § 68 of " The Berean," on " The Doctrine of Disunity," in which he says (in " History of American Socialisms," p. 623) he was aiming at " a theory that prevailed among Perfectionists, similar to Warren's *Individual Sovereignty*." Among the most influential of the advocates of the theory were James Boyle and Theophilus R. Gates, both of whom were closely associated with Noyes in the earlier stages of his development.

[59] " American Communities," revised edition, 1902, pp. 158–159.

course found leaders and showed sufficient coherence to hold conventions at which a common platform was proclaimed and joint undertakings inaugurated. Even centers of activity were formed from which perfectionist influences radiated after a fashion which suggested at least the beginnings of institutional organization. One of the earliest of them was established at the little cotton-mill village of Manlius, where the little Presbyterian Church (Manlius Center) was stamped out. Hiram Sheldon was recognized by the Manlius perfectionists as their leader and expositor, but there were associated with him such men as Jarvis Rider, Martin P. Sweet, and Erasmus Stone. In this coterie originated most of the extravagances which characterized the perfectionist movement. "At Manlius," says Dixon,[60] "the chosen took upon themselves the name of 'Saints.' Here they announced their separation from the world. Here they began to debate whether the old marriage vows would or would not be binding in the new heaven and the new earth." It was Albany, however, which became the real distributing center of the movement at least for the East; and the house of the Misses Annesley there became the center of the center.[61] Thence missionaries proceeded into New England and groups of perfectionists were established here and there — at Southampton, Brimfield, New Haven.[62] At

[60] "Spiritual Wives," ii. p. 9; cf. pp. 35, 48. On Hiram Sheldon and his work, compare H. Eastman, "Noyesism Unveiled," 1849, p. 31, note.

[61] Joseph I. Foot, "Discourses on Modern Antinomianism, commonly called Perfectionism," 1834, p. iv., says: "This class of religionists is found in small numbers in various places in this state. Perhaps one of the churches in Albany and those in Rochester have been more annoyed by them than any others." The occasion of his writing was the annoyance suffered from a small band of them in his own parish at Salina, Onondaga County. Cf. the general statement of C. G. Finney, "Memoirs," 1876, p. 341: "About this time, the question of Christian perfection, in the antinomian sense of the term, came to be agitated a good deal at New Haven, at Albany, and somewhat in New York city."

[62] W. H. Dixon, "Spiritual Wives," ii. p. 35. Joseph I. Foot, as cited, p. 51, note: "Females sometimes accompany these itinerant errorists, and in other cases go alone, 'to preach the Gospel,' as they call their delusions. A woman recently sowed the seeds of this heresy in Brimfield, (Mass.), where they have sprung up, as in other places, and are likely to produce bitter fruit."

Albany, of course, the same ruin was wrought as elsewhere: the churches were greatly troubled. The Fourth Presbyterian Church, E. N. Kirk's, was required to put into action extensive disciplinary proceedings; [63] and even the classroom of the little theological seminary which E. N. Kirk had established was invaded by the fanaticism.[64] We hear of its being carried from this center as far as the extreme western border of frontier Wisconsin.[63]

[63] Mrs. Boardman, "Life and Labours of the Rev. W. E. Boardman," 1887, chapter iii., tells of living at Potosi, Wisconsin, in close intimacy with an elderly woman who was one of a number of persons who had been excluded from E. N. Kirk's church in Albany on account of their perfectionism.

[64] H. Eastman, as cited, p. 31, where "a gentleman residing in Central New York" is quoted as explaining that "the lumen of Eastern New York Perfectionism is referred to John B. Foote, a theological student in Kirk's school, at Albany. Modest and timid to excess, the revival spirit soon impelled him with its deep-toned enthusiasm. Around him gathered the most devoted of the class. Mr. Kirk tried to quell the storm, but failed. The refractory students became the preachers of the new faith. To their labors most of the Perfectionism in Massachusetts and westward owes its existence." An account is given of Kirk's theological school in D. O. Mears, "Life of Edward Norris Kirk, D.D.," 1877, pp. 85 f. Against some of the names of the students in Kirk's private catalogue, we are told, is written, "Became a fanatic." John Brownson Foote, after an exemplary youth, was graduated at Williams College in 1831, and shortly afterwards, says Calvin Durfee, "Williams Biographical Annals," 1871, p. 460, was licensed to preach the gospel; but Durfee adds, apparently endeavoring to excuse the inexcusable, "Ere long he entered on an eccentric and wild career, which, in a man of his former habitual uprightness and sober good sense, could be accounted for only on the supposition that reason was dethroned." A horrible account is given by Dixon, "Spiritual Wives," ii. pp. 75 ff., — actually from the hand of Noyes — of a peculiarly obnoxious instance of the practice of "spiritual wives," in which Foote was implicated — though not as a principal. He is here represented to have become "a convert to Hiram Sheldon's doctrine of salvation from sin, and to the social theory which seems to have been connected in every man's mind with that doctrine of the final establishment of heaven on earth" — phraseology which is very distinctly that of Noyes. At a little later date (1847) we find Foote and Noyes sharing the leadership in certain Conventions of the "Western division of Perfectionists," at the head of which we are told that Foote had "for a considerable time" stood (Eastman as cited, pp. 140, 143).

II. THE BEGINNINGS

IT was into this atmosphere that John Humphrey Noyes was plunged by his conversion in August, 1831. He was an opinionated, self-assertive young man of twenty,[65] who had been graduated from Dartmouth College the year before (1830), and meantime had been studying law in his brother-in-law's office at Putney, where the family had been resident since 1823. The great revival of 1831 seems fairly to have rushed him off his feet. He took his conversion hard, yielding with difficulty; but when he yielded he yielded altogether. He himself sums up what happened in a rapid sentence, which is no more rapid, however, than the rush of the events it describes. " The great Finney revival found him," he says of himself, " at twenty years of age, a college graduate, studying law, and sent him to study divinity, first at Andover and afterward at New Haven." [66] He entered the Seminary at Andover four weeks after his conversion, and in less than three months after it he had placed himself at the disposal of the American Board of Commissioners for Foreign Missions. But nothing that organized Christianity could offer could satisfy his morbid appetite for excitement, and in a little more than two years more he had turned his back upon it all and was seeking thrills along a new path.

He has himself described for us the stages of his progress.

" After a painful process of conviction, in which the conquest of my aversion to becoming a minister was one of the critical points " — it is thus that he describes his conversion,[67] — " I submitted to

[65] He was born at West Brattleboro, Vt., September 6, 1811, the eldest son and favorite child of John and Polly (Hayes) Noyes. John Noyes was graduated from Dartmouth College in 1795, served his college as a tutor, 1797–1799 (having Daniel Webster as a pupil), began to study for the ministry, but finally entered mercantile pursuits, served in 1816 as Representative in Congress from the Southern District of Vermont. Polly Noyes (an aunt of President Rutherford B. Hayes) is described as a woman of notably strong character and deep religious spirit.

[66] " History of American Socialisms," p. 614.

[67] In his " Confessions of Religious Experience," from which the extracts

252

God, and obtained spiritual peace. With much joy and zeal I immediately devoted myself to the study of the Scriptures, and to religious
testimony in private and public. The year of 1831 was distinguished
as 'the year of revivals.' New measures, protracted meetings, and
New York evangelists had just entered New England, and the whole
spirit of the people was fermenting with religious excitement. The
millennium was supposed to be very near. I fully entered into the
enthusiasm of the time; and seeing no reason why backsliding should
be expected, or why the revival spirit might not be maintained in
its full vigor permanently, I determined with all my inward strength
to be ' a young convert ' in zeal and simplicity forever. My heart was
fixed on the millennium, and I resolved to live or die for it. Four
weeks after my conversion I went to Andover and was admitted to
the Theological Seminary."

This was a typical conversion of the "revival-of-excitement"
order, issuing not so much in sound religion as in restless activities, and filling the mind only with strong delusions — in
this case chiliastic delusions — which prepare it for everything
except sane religious development. It is interesting to observe
that, as he tells us more than once, most of those who followed
him in his further vagaries had begun with him in these.
" Most of those," he says, writing in 1847,[68] " who have become
Perfectionists " — he means the term in the narrow sense in
which it describes only his own followers — " within the last
ten years, had previously been converts and laborers in such
revivals," that is to say, had been victims, as he was, of the
" revival of excitement."

Of course no one in his inflamed state of mind could find
satisfaction at Andover. The students there were merely
Christians, and seemed to him from his exalted point of view
a good deal less than what Christians should be. In the censoriousness which naturally accompanies such exaltation of spirit
he accuses them of indifference, levity, jealousy, sensuality —

---

in the following pages, not otherwise credited, are also taken. The present one
is also to be found in the " Hand-Book of the Oneida Community," 1867,
pp. 6 f.

[68] " The Berean," p. 242. See also " History of American Socialisms," 1870,
p. 614.

of everything which as Christians they ought not to be. Only in a few who were touched with the enthusiasm of missions — Lyman, Munson, Tracy, Justin Perkins — did he find any congeniality of companionship. He was taken into a secret society which they maintained for mutual improvement, and learned from it a method of government by criticism which he afterwards employed in his communistic establishment.[69] The classroom instruction, also, was not wholly without effect upon him; in particular Moses Stuart's exegesis of the seventh chapter of Romans, and of the twenty-fourth chapter of Matthew, supplied him with points of departure from which he afterward advanced to the two hinges on which his whole system turned. He remained at Andover, however, only the single session of 1831–32. The autumn of 1832 found him at the Divinity School at New Haven. His motive for making the change, he tells us, was that at Yale, he " could devote a greater part of his time to his favorite study of the Bible "; by which he appears to mean that the classroom work at Yale was less exigent than at Andover. In any case he preferred to prosecute his study of the Bible without, rather than under, the direction of, his teacher. " I attended lectures daily," he writes, " and studied sufficiently to be prepared for examination; but my mind was chiefly directed with my heart to the simple treasures of the Bible. I went through the Epistles of Paul again and again, as I had gone through the Evangelists at Andover; and in the latter part of the time " — during which he was at Yale — " when I had begun to exercise myself in preaching, I was in the habit of preparing the matter of every sermon by reading the whole New Testament through with reference to the subject I had chosen." He also found time for many external activities. He worked among the negroes of the town and took part in the organization of one of the earliest anti-slavery societies in this country. He even became instrumental in building up a struggling church. There were about a dozen

[69] An account is given of this society and its practice of " mutual criticism " in *The Congregational Quarterly* for April, 1875, pp. 272–281; and the whole subject is dealt with at large in a pamphlet called " Mutual Criticism," published by Noyes in 1876. Cf. also *The Galaxy*, xxii. 1876, pp. 815 ff.

"revivalists" in the city, he says, and their fervor attracted him. "For," says he, "I was burning with the same zeal which I found in them (but nowhere else in the city) for the conversion of souls." As they grew in number they had organized themselves as the "Free Church," and, on Noyes's recommendation, they now invited James Boyle to preach to them. He was thus provided with church associations of the hottest revivalistic character.[70]

These new associations were not calculated to moderate Noyes's fanatical tendencies. The censoriousness which he had exhibited toward his fellow students at Andover he now turned upon Christendom at large. How many real Christians are there in Christendom? he asked himself; and he felt constrained to answer, Not many. From his higher vantage-ground he looked out upon Christianity, as exhibited in the churches, and found it fatally wanting. His missionary zeal naturally cooled: with all Christendom lying in the evil one, what were the heathen to him? He saw his task now in the Christianizing of nominal Christians; the lost condition, not of the heathen

[70] The "Free Church" was organized August 31, 1831, but was long in getting upon its feet. According to the account in the "Contributions to the Ecclesiastical History of Connecticut, etc.," 1861, p. 440, it worshiped for the first two years of its existence in the Orange Street Chapel, and then for three years in "a large hall in the Exchange building"; and "from September, 1836, in a house of worship erected for it in Church Street" (for this house of worship, see Leonard Bacon, "Thirteen Historical Discourses, etc.," 1839, p. 399). Noyes's connection with the church, falling between the autumn of 1832 and the spring of 1834, was in its days of extreme weakness, when it was worshiping first in the Orange Street Chapel and then in the Exchange building. The church remained weak until 1848, when it moved once more — from Church Street to College Street. It was not able to settle a pastor (the Rev. Mr. Ludlow) until 1837. "For the first six years of its existence," the "Contributions" above quoted record, "it had no pastor, but had the ministrations, for periods of from three to six months, of Revs. Waters Warren, Samuel Griswold, James Boyle, Dexter Clary, Austin Putnam, John Ingersoll, and the late N. W. Taylor, D.D." Here are seven men to divide six years between. Boyle's period of ministration to the church was necessarily short; and appears to have centered in the spring of 1834. He seems to have received no countenance from the Congregationalist authorities. In the "Minutes of the General Association of Congregationalist Churches in Connecticut," this church appears as vacant for 1835 and 1836; the earlier "Minutes" are not accessible to us.

but of Christians, was heavy on his heart.[71] And now his sedulous study of the Bible in careful seclusion from his natural
advisers, began to bear fruit — though he did not get so far
away from Moses Stuart as to impress us with the originality
of his thought. In the summer after his first year at Yale —
the summer of 1833 — he settled it with himself that our
Lord's second advent had already taken place; that it took
place, in fact, within a generation of His death. We say "he
settled it with himself," for his confidence in his new conclusion was characteristically perfect. "I no longer conjectured
or believed in the inferior sense of these words," he says, "but
I *knew* that the time appointed for the Second Advent was
within one generation from the time of Christ's personal ministry." Oddly enough he appears to have been led to this conclusion chiefly by John xxi. 22: "If I will that he tarry till I
come, what is that to thee?" "Here," said he, "is an intimation by Christ himself that John will live till His Second Coming; the Bible is not a book of riddles; its hidden treasures are
accessible to those who make the Spirit of Truth their guide;
and how is it possible to reconcile this intimation with the accepted theory that Christ's Second Coming is yet future?"
If we are inclined to wonder a little at the mental struggles
which Noyes seems to have undergone in reaching this conclusion, we should remind ourselves that it involved a very
considerable revolution of thought for him; and revolutions of
thought were not easy for Noyes. He had hitherto been, we
must remember, a hot chiliast, looking for the Second Coming
not only in the future, but in the immediate future; and expecting from it everything he was setting his hopes upon in his
inflamed fancy. It was a great wrench to transfer this Second
Coming back into the distant past, though, as we shall see, he
managed to soften the blow by preserving his chiliastic hopes

[71] This is the way he puts it himself: "As I lost confidence in the religion around me, and saw more and more the need there was of a re-
conversion of most of those who professed Christianity, my outward-bound
missionary zeal declined, and my heart turned toward thoughts, desires and
projects of an internal reformation of Christendom. Quality of religion, instead
of quantity, became my center of attraction."

for the impending future and carrying only the Second Coming itself back into the past.

In August of this same summer (1833) he was licensed to preach by the New Haven West Association, and spent the six weeks that intervened before the reopening of the Seminary in the autumn, preaching in a little church in North Salem, New York. He was as yet not a perfectionist; only a fanatical chiliastic revivalist — if we can use the word " only " in such a connection. But perfectionism did not lie outside the horizon of his vision. Those " New York evangelists " who broke their way into New England in 1831 — to whom he also had fallen a victim, and James Boyle among the others, who had been a Methodist and whom he had brought to New Haven, where he had formed with him a close intimacy — came from a region plowed and harrowed by perfectionism, and can scarcely have been ignorant of it; they may even have in their own persons borne more or less of its scars. He found also on his return to the Seminary some zealous young men, newly entered, who spurred him on to higher attainments in holiness. He diligently read such works as the " Memoirs " of James Brainerd Taylor [72]

[72] What is meant is the " Memoir of James Brainerd Taylor," by John Holt Rice, D.D., and Benjamin Holt Rice, D.D., which was published in 1833, and therefore was a new book, just issued from the press when Noyes came back to New Haven in the autumn of 1833. He may have been the more attracted to it from the circumstance that the book was intended especially for theological students. This " Memoir " was supplemented by " A New Tribute to the Memory of James Brainerd Taylor," 1838. Brief accounts of Taylor may be found in Appletons' " Cyclopædia of American Biography," vi. p. 45, and McClintock and Strong's " Cyclopædia of Biblical, Theological, and Ecclesiastical Literature," x. p. 231. Taylor was a young man of marked devoutness of spirit, who, having given himself to the (Congregational) ministry, was cut off before he could enter upon its work (1829). Noyes calls him " the John the Baptist of the doctrine of holiness," who came " to the very borders of the Gospel," " saw clearly the privilege and glory of salvation from sin," and " even confessed, at times, in a timid way, that he was free from sin," — but " did not know the Gospel of the primitive church, and was not born of God in the Bible sense." That is to say, he had not received " the second conversion " into " holiness " (" The Berean," § 39 pp. 271–272). Cf. Rice's judicious account of Taylor's attitude towards Christian attainments and the relation of this attitude to perfectionism in the " Memoir," pp. 84–92. There is a contemporary appreciation of the Memoir in *The Biblical Repertory and Theological Review* of 1834,

and Wesley's tract on "Christian Perfection." He naturally found himself, therefore, through the autumn and early winter months making steady and accelerating progression toward perfect holiness. No lower attainment would satisfy him, and he became ever more and more eager to reach the goal; this effort, in the end, absorbed all his energies. At last the blessing came, and he received his " second conversion."

He writes to his mother: " The burden of Christian perfection accumulated upon my soul, until I determined to give myself no rest while the possibility of the attainment of it remained doubtful. At last the Lord met me with the same promise that gave peace to my soul when first I came out of Egypt: ' if thou wilt confess with thy mouth the Lord Jesus and shalt believe in thine heart that God hath raised him from the dead, thou shalt be saved.' By faith I took the proffered boon of eternal life. God's spirit sealed the act, and the blood of Christ cleansed me from all sin." His " second conversion " consisted then in his pressing the promise of " salvation," the assurance of " cleansing from all sin," into a promise and assurance that the " salvation," the " cleansing," shall be completed as soon as begun, consuming no time and running through no process to the promised and assured end. The parallel between his first and second conversions was complete. Not only were both accomplished through the instrumentality of a single text — understood partly then, perfectly now — but in both cases alike he was driven by his temperament at once into publicity. The atmosphere of propaganda was his vital breath: he gave not a moment to meditation, testing, ripening. As, on his " first conversion," he tells us that he " immediately " devoted himself (along with the study of Scripture) " to reli-

---

written by Henry Axtell; in it the message of Taylor and of the " Memoir " alike is held to be " eminent holiness is attainable on earth." In C. G. Finney's " Lectures to Professing Christians," which were published in 1837 (ed. 1880, pp. 358–359), there is a passage curiously parallel to Noyes's account, in which, telling of his own conversion to perfectionism, Finney says he read Wesley's " Plain Account of Christian Perfection " and Taylor's " Memoir," and speaks of Taylor's biographers' concealing his tendency to perfectionism just as Noyes does.

gious testimony in private and public "; so now, on the evening
of the very day of his " second conversion," he preached at the
Free Church on the text, " He that committeth sin is of the
devil," and proclaimed the doctrine of perfect holiness — how
such a man would do it from such a text we can well imagine.
" The next morning," we are availing ourselves now of W. A.
Hinds's narrative,[73] " a theological student who heard the discourse of the previous evening came to labor with him, and
asked him directly, ' Don't you commit sin? ' The answer was
an unequivocal ' No.' The man stared as though a thunderbolt
had fallen before him, and repeated his question, and got the
same answer. Within a few hours word was passed through the
college and the city, ' Noyes says he is perfect! ' and immediately afterward it was reported that Noyes is crazy! " [74]

There is no mention made, in Noyes's account of his " second conversion," of any influences working on him in that
direction from without. We have seen that there cannot have
failed to be such. Noyes himself, however, speaks in this connection only of his study of perfectionist literature of the
Wesleyan school; to which, no doubt, we must hence give

[73] " American Communities," revised edition, 1902, p. 152. Hinds's account
of Noyes's early experiences given in this edition of his book (that in the
first edition is negligible) is derived from Noyes's " Confessions of Religious
Experience," and is the best of the accessible accounts. We have been glad
to check up our own by it and to follow its guidance with some closeness.

[74] Noyes is careful to explain that his assertion of freedom from sin
did not involve the claim that he was incapable of positive growth. " I certainly did not," he says, " at this time regard myself as perfect in any such
sense as excludes the expectation of discipline and improvement. On the
contrary, from the very beginning my heart's most earnest desire and prayer
to God was that I might be made perfect by full fellowship with the sufferings of Christ; and from that time till now, all my tribulations have been
occasions of thanksgiving, because I have regarded them as answers to that
first prayer, and as pledges of God's faithfulness in completing the work
then begun. The distinction between being free from sin on the one hand,
and being past all improvement on the other, however obscure it may be
to some, was plain to me as soon as I knew by experience what freedom
from sin really is. To those who endeavored to confound this distinction, and
to crowd me into a profession of unimprovable perfection, I said: ' I do not
pretend to perfection in externals; I only claim purity of heart and the answer
of a good conscience toward God. A book may be true and perfect in sentiment, and yet be deficient in grace of style and typographical accuracy.' "

much of the credit of the change in his views. The perfectionism which he adopted, however, when he worked himself
through, was not specifically Wesleyan in type, but was
rather of that mystical kind which was at the time prevalent
in Western and Central New York. As there was nothing in
Noyes's previous intellectual history to prepare us for this
particular mode of thinking, we naturally conjecture that he
must have derived it from the New York men, channels of
communication with whom, as we have seen, existed in abundance. A writer of the time, who shows himself in general very
familiar with what was going on, tells us explicitly that he
owed his indoctrination into perfectionism to one of the young
men who had gone astray in E. N. Kirk's school at Albany.
" Chauncey E. Dutton," we read,[75] " had breathed the afflatus.
In 1833 he left Albany and entered the theological department
at New Haven, Connecticut. Here he infused the new enthusiasm into John H. Noyes, a young man from Putney, Vermont, with whom he had become familiar. Thus began the
logos of New Haven Perfectionism." The date is right, and
the general circumstances; it was on his return to New Haven
in the autumn of 1833, Noyes himself tells us, that he found a
number of zealous young men just entering the Seminary, to
whose " constant fellowship and conversation " he attributes,
along with the Wesleyan literature which he read, his " progress towards holiness." The difficulty lies in the absence of the
name of Dutton from the general catalogue of the New Haven
Divinity School, and indeed from that of the University also.
It may be of course that a mistake has been made, only, in
connecting Dutton with the institution as a pupil. There is no
doubt that he was in New Haven not far from this time propagating his perfectionist faith. We find him there, for instance,
only a couple of years or so later on this errand, and Noyes was
in close intercourse with him a year earlier in Brimfield.[76] The
tone of Noyes's reference both to him and to his companion in

[75] Quoted in H. Eastman, " Noyesism Unveiled," 1849, p. 31, note.
[76] Noyes's own testimony to this intercourse will be found in Dixon's
" Spiritual Wives," ii. pp. 36 and 46 (cf. also pp. 25, 30, 35, 40, 48).

these ministries, Simon Lovett, however, leaves an impression that this intercourse with them belongs rather to 1835, and later, than to 1833–34. And we can scarcely avoid the feeling that he means us to gather that he was self-converted to his perfectionism.

Lyman H. Atwater, who was a fellow student of the next lower class with Noyes at Yale, seems to think of him merely as one of the Pelagianizing perfectionists who sprang up in his student days at New Haven under the teaching of Nathaniel W. Taylor. He is giving a general account of the rise of this class of perfectionists, and permits himself this bit of personal reminiscence: — [77]

" When we were students of theology, a little coterie, becoming wiser than their teachers or fellow students, strained the doctrine of ability beyond the scope contended for or admitted by its most eminent champions, to the length of maintaining, not only that all men can, but that some do, reach sinless perfection in this life, of which, so far as the students there were concerned, a trio or so were the principal confessors. The net result of the whole was that the leader, instead of going forward into the ministry, ran into various socialistic and free-love heresies, on the basis of which he founded the Putney and Oneida communities, over the latter of which he now presides. Other sporadic outbursts of the distemper appeared here and there in the Presbyterian and Congregational communions, or among separatists and come-outers from them, these often uniting with the radicals or advanced reformers of other communions."

This statement informs us that Noyes was not the only student at New Haven at the time who lapsed into perfectionism, but had a few companions, or, we may possibly suppose, converts. That his perfectionism arose simply from an overstraining of the Taylorite doctrine of ability seems, however, from his own account of it, not altogether likely; and we may perhaps not improperly suspect that Atwater has merely included him in the general movement which he was describing,

[77] *The Presbyterian Quarterly and Princeton Review,* July, 1877, pp. 410, 411.

without stopping to inquire as to any special peculiarity he may have exhibited. He himself, in giving an account of his mental and spiritual growth leading up to his conversion to perfectionism, has nothing to say of N. W. Taylor; but speaks rather of John Wesley as a guide and instructor. There was no doubt a Taylorite element in his thought,[78] which came out especially in his teaching as to the " first conversion " and as to the act of faith in general, concerning which he seems to have no other idea than that it is an act of our own in our own native powers.[79] But he certainly did not find the account of the perfection to which he supposed himself to have attained on that fateful twentieth of February, 1834, in the sheer ability of his will to do what it chose, and therefore (if it chose) to be perfect. He referred it, on the contrary, directly to the effect of communion with Christ. The affinities of his doctrine, in other words, were less Pelagian than mystical. By " the apprehension " of the facts concerning Christ and His saving work — " his victory over sin and death, the judgment of the prince of this world, and the spiritual reconciliation of God with man " — he explains,[80] believers are brought " into fellowship with Christ's death and resurrection," and made " partakers of his divine nature and his victory over the evil one." " The gospel which I had received and preached," he had written a

[78] G. W. Noyes in his tract, " The Oneida Community: its Relation to Orthodoxy " (no date; but certainly after 1912), represents Noyes and Noyes-ism as definitely Taylorite. An annotator (" F. W. F."), however, seeks to draw back a little.

[79] He does not betray any tendency, however, to minimize the divine control of the will, so only it be allowed to be merely suasive in its mode. His formula here is " if a man's own will goes with his acts, he is a free agent, however mighty may be the influences which persuade him " (" The Berean," p. 173). He illustrates thus: " God dwelt in Christ, and determined all his actions. And yet was he not free? " " There is not a professor in all the churches, whether sincere or not, who does not expect to be kept from sin in heaven by the power of God. . . . This is acknowledged to be consistent with free agency." One may ask whether something more than suasion is not suggested in this language. The doctrine, however, is the general Taylorite doctrine, and was made very familiar to the churches by its vigorous assertion by C. G. Finney.

[80] The Perfectionist, February 22, 1845: " Theses of the Second Reformation," Theses 29 and 30. Quoted by Eastman, as cited, p. 318.

few months earlier,[81] speaking directly of what had happened on February 20, 1834, "was based upon the idea that faith identifies the soul with Christ, so that by his death and resurrection the believer dies and rises again, not literally, nor yet figuratively, but *spiritually;* and thus, so far as sin is concerned, is placed beyond the grave, in 'heavenly places' with Christ." He goes on to say that three months later he felt compelled to extend this doctrine so as to make it include the redemption of the body as well as the soul — to abolish death as well as sin — by participation in Christ's resurrection so that though we will "pass through the form of dying" (sad concession to the appearance of things!) we who are believers indeed will not really die. This doctrine, not only in form but in substance, is extremely mystical.

The effect of Noyes's proclamation of his perfectionism was, naturally, the loss of the countenance of the several religious organizations with which he was connected. He was dismissed from the Divinity School and requested to withdraw altogether from the premises. The New Haven West Association, by which he had been licensed to preach the previous August, now recalled its license, " on account of his views on the subject of Christian perfection." [82] His church membership was still in the Congregational Church at Putney, and that church subsequently excluded him from fellowship " for heresy and breach of covenant " — supporting the charge apparently, however, by specifications which are drawn from his subsequent teaching.[83] His real church home was, nevertheless, the Free Church at New Haven, and a vote was passed at once by that church requesting him to discontinue all communication with its members. He represents himself as feeling very isolated. "I had now lost," he writes, "my standing in the Free Church, in the ministry, and in the college. My good name in the great world was gone. My friends were fast falling

[81] *The Perfectionist,* September 7, 1844. Quoted by Eastman, as cited, p. 343.

[82] " Contributions to the Ecclesiastical History of Connecticut; prepared under the direction of the General Association," 1861, pp. 328, 329.

[83] H. Eastman, as cited, p. 29.

away. I was beginning to be indeed an outcast. Yet I rejoiced
and leaped for joy. Sincerely I declared that ' I was glad when
I got rid of my reputation.' Some persons asked me whether I
should continue to preach, now that the clergy had taken
away my license. I replied, ' I have taken away their license
to sin, and they keep on sinning; so, though they have taken
away my license to preach, I shall keep on preaching.' " The
isolation complained of, however, had of course only relation
to, and meant no more than an enforced change in, his associates. There were plenty of perfectionists within reach, and
they of the most aggressive character. Noyes was soon, if he
were not already, in close intercourse with them. But there can
be no doubt that the effect of the announcement of his new
views was something of a surprise to him, and brought on a
crisis in his career. He tells us that in conversation with his
father one day, during the short interval between his conversion and his entering the Seminary at Andover, he had propounded an interpretation of some Scripture, concerning which
the older man uttered a warning. " Take care," said he, " that
is heresy." " Heresy or not," rejoined the son, " it is true."
" But," warned the father, " if you are to be a minister, you
must think and preach as the rest of the ministers do; if you
get out of the traces they will whip you in." " Never! " rejoined the son hotly: " never will I be whipped by ministers
or any body else into views that do not commend themselves
to my understanding as guided by the Bible and enlightened
by the Spirit." Now that the crisis had come, the " fighting
spirit " he had announced in this program did not fail him.
He had so little thought of yielding to the admonitions of his
mentors, that he rather threw himself unreservedly into the
conflict and seized the reins of leadership of the perfectionist
party. " I resolved," he says, " to labor alone if necessary, to
repair the breaches of our cause."

The immediate fruits of his propaganda at New Haven were
not altogether inconsiderable. He was able to count James
Boyle himself among his converts; and the two together carried on for a time a vigorous literary campaign, including the

publication from the summer of 1834 (the first number bears the date of August 20) of a monthly journal called *The Perfectionist*. A number of the members of the Free Church also left the church, and joined Noyes's party. Some converts were made also here and there outside of New Haven, especially in New York. Every effort was made by Noyes to compact his followers into a definite sect with its own doctrinal platform and organization. It was in this that his peculiarity consisted. We have already had occasion to point out the extreme individualism of the perfectionists of his day. Noyes was determined that he at least should not stand off by himself, but should be the head of a body which reflected his thought and obeyed his will. Everywhere he asserted his leadership; and although he was able to make it good with the completeness which he desired over only a small coterie, a certain deference appears to have been shown him in a surprisingly widely extended circle. Looking back upon these early days from a point of sight thirty years later, he tells us how they then appeared to him.

" The term Perfectionist," he tells us,[84] " was applied to two classes who came out from the Orthodox churches at about the same period. They resembled each other in many respects (both classes apprehending alike the great truth, that the new covenant means salvation from sin, the security of believers, the substitution of grace for law and ordinances, etc.), but there was yet this fundamental and important distinction: one class appropriated these doctrines in the interest of individualism, the other in the interest of unity; one class scorned the idea of subordination and discipline, the other joyfully received the idea of organization, and were willing to submit to such discipline as organic harmony should require; one class were all leaders, a regiment of officers, many of whom were for a time eloquent champions of the new truths, but the majority of them rushed into excesses which dishonored the name Perfectionist; the other class, led by J. H. Noyes, have persevered in a course of self-improvement, overcoming many obstacles, and finally have developed a system of principles and a form of practical life which at least challenge the attention of the world."

[84] " Hand-Book of the Oneida Community," 1867, p. 8.

This formal difference — organized or unorganized — was not, however, the only thing which divided Noyes's followers from outlying perfectionists. He was not only prepared to impose upon them his personal leadership, but his personal doctrinal views also. And, young man in his twenty-fourth year as he was, he had his doctrinal views even now in their formative ideas already in hand. They were evolved from the two fundamental assertions to which he had now attained — that Christ's Second Coming took place in A.D. 70, and that no one living in sin is in the proper sense a Christian. Working out the details of his system rapidly from these two underlying principles, he as rapidly developed a very acute sense of the uniqueness of his " New Haven Perfectionism." Consciousness of the points of agreement between his and other perfectionism grew faint: the settled persuasion that he, and he alone, possessed truth took possession of him. " New Haven Perfectionism," he writes in his journal,[85] " is a new religion . . . has affinity with no sect this side the primitive church. . . . As a system it is distinct from all the popular theologies." And again: [86] " New Haven Perfectionism is a doctrinal system, standing by itself, distinct from Wesleyan, New York, and Oberlin Perfectionism, as it is from non-resistance, ' come-outism,' etc." . . . " Perfectionism in other places " than in Putney, " so far as I know, (individual instances excepted,) has been mixed up with New York fanaticism, Boyleism, Gatesism, non-resistance, etc." His immediate purpose in these last words is not directly to assert doctrinal peculiarity (although that is asserted), but rather to repudiate any entanglement in the immoralities which persistent rumor was laying to the charge of perfectionists, at Southampton, Brimfield, and other places where the indecency of " spiritual wives " was in practice.

It is worth while to turn aside to point out that one of the peculiarities by which Noyes separated himself from the perfectionists of the time was that he did, in point of fact, keep

[85] *The Perfectionist,* iv. No. 4, quoted by Eastman, as cited, p. 79. We understand this to mean April, 1846.

[86] Eastman, p. 80: this apparently belongs to 1842.

himself free from complicity with this evil. He makes it quite clear that it was in his mind a characteristic of what he calls "New York Perfectionists," and he declares with the utmost emphasis that he himself never gave it the least countenance. It was brought into New England from New York, he tells us, by Simon Lovett and Chauncey E. Dutton, who circulated at Southampton, Brimfield, and afterward at New Haven itself, as a sort of missionaries; and though beginning in mere "bundling," passed on into actual licentiousness.[87] As for himself, he asseverates that he had no connection with such things — whether at Brimfield, Rondout, or New York [88] — except to reprove them.[89] It must not be imagined, however, that it was what we should call the immorality of the practice which kept Noyes thus free from this iniquity. He speaks of it as "licentiousness," it is true; but he fully shared the "antinomianism" of which it was the expression. His chief concern was that the premature practice of this antinomianism should not prejudice the spread of the doctrine. And then again, the idea of spiritual wives did not go far enough to satisfy the demands of his antinomianism. It still was held in the bonds of law. He stood for promiscuity in principle. And spiritual wives are just as incongruous to the principle of promiscuity as are "legal wives"; they are "spiritual dualism." "The only true foundation is that which Jesus Christ laid," he writes, "when he said, that in the good time coming there will be no marriage at all" — meaning not that celibacy will rule, but "promiscuity." [90]

[87] We are giving only the bare facts from the very interesting narrative printed in Dixon's "Spiritual Wives," ii. pp. 34–47.

[88] New York City seems to be meant, in contrast with Rondout; and no doubt it is the particular case of Abram C. Smith and Mary Cragin, told at great length by Mary Cragin's husband and reprinted from his narrative by Dixon, "Spiritual Wives," ii. pp. 89 ff., which is in mind in both references.

[89] "Dixon and His Copyists," p. 20.

[90] "Dixon and His Copyists," p. 31. Cf. his letter to a Mr. Hollister, of July 2, 1839 (Eastman, as cited, pp. 86–87): "About three months from the time when I received Christ as a whole Savior, my mind was led into long and deep meditation on . . . the relation of the sexes. I then came to the conclusions in which I have since *stood*. . . . So I have testified for the past five years; and every day sinks me deeper and deeper in the certainty that these are the principles of God, and his heavenly hosts."

Noyes himself tells us that he had already adopted this
theory of promiscuity in general in May, 1834,[91] that is to say,
on the very heels of his " second conversion " — or conversion
to perfectionism — and at the very beginning of his propaganda for the formation of a perfectionist sect. One gets the
impression that it held from the first in his mind the place of
an essential principle — we might even say of *the* essential
principle — of his system, while the whole doctrinal elaboration led up to it and prepared the way for it.[92] Meanwhile,
however, he kept it in the background, putting it forward only
tentatively and as men, having absorbed the doctrinal preparation, were able to bear it. As he himself expresses it: [93] " I
moulded it, protected it, and matured it from year to year;
holding it always, nevertheless, as a theory to be realized in
the *future,* and warning all men against premature action
upon it." How he was accustomed to propagate it is, no doubt,
fairly illustrated by his circumspect and veiled, and yet perfectly clear, presentation of it in a letter written in January,
1837, to his friend David Harrison of Meriden, Connecticut —
a letter which has acquired the name of " the Battle Axe
Letter " from the circumstance that Harrison, acting on a suggestion of Noyes's (who was eager to make quiet propaganda),

[91] " Spiritual Wives," ii. p. 183.

[92] Cf. what he writes in *The Spiritual Moralist* of June 13, 1842 (Eastman,
as cited, p. 89) : — " In the winter of 1834, I abandoned the popular religious
system in which I had been educated, and became a perfectionist. The change
in my views at the time, was not confined to the subject of holiness, but
extended to every department of theology and morals. . . . The subject of
sexual morality was early forced upon my attention, by its close connection
with those peculiar views of the *law,* of the *leadings* of the Spirit, and of
the *resurrection,* which are among the principal elements of my testimony
in the Perfectionist and in the Witness. Personal circumstances of an interesting character, the startling and in some instances the corrupt suggestions
of men with whom I was then connected, and a variety of scandalous reports
concerning the licentious doctrines and practices of certain Perfectionists,
conspired to urge me to a thorough examination of the matter. . . . Under
these circumstances, I meditated on the subject much of the time for two
years. My mind was particularly exercised in relation to it during several
long seasons of spiritual trial. In the winter of 1836–7 my views assumed
a definite and satisfactory form."

[93] " Spiritual Wives," ii. p. 184.

showed it to Simon Lovett (who liked it), and Lovett showed
it to Elizabeth Hawley,[94] who sent it to Theophilus R. Gates,[95]
who published the salient parts of it in his paper *The Battle
Axe* (August, 1837) — and thus forced Noyes's hand, and
drew him for the first time to make public acknowledgment
of this central element of his teaching. In this letter he
writes:—[96]

" I will write all that is in my heart on one delicate subject, and
you may judge for yourself whether it is expedient to show this
letter to others. When the will of God is done on earth as it is in
heaven, there will be no marriage. The marriage-supper of the Lamb
is a feast at which every dish is free to every guest. Exclusiveness,
jealousy, quarrelling, have no place there, for the same reason as
that which forbids the guests at a thanksgiving dinner to claim each
his separate dish, and quarrel with the rest for his rights. In a holy
community there is no more reason why sexual intercourse should
be restrained by law, than why eating and drinking should be; and
there is as little occasion for shame in the one case as in the other.
God has placed a wall of partition between the male and the female
during the apostasy for good reasons, which will be broken down
in the resurrection for equally good reasons; but woe to him who
abolishes the law of apostasy before he stands in the holiness of the
resurrection. The guests of the marriage supper may have each his
favourite dish, each a dish of his own procuring, and that without

[94] On Elizabeth Hawley, see " Spiritual Wives," ii. p. 46, as well as Eastman, as cited, p. 95.

[95] Eastman, as cited, p. 98, says of Gates that he " was not, as Noyes
asserts, a Perfectionist; but " he " certainly held doctrines in perfect keeping
with the sentiments of the Battle Axe Letter, for he approved of, and published it." Of Gates's writings we have had the opportunity of consulting only
two early books: " The Trials, Experience, Exercises of Mind, and First
Travels of Theophilus R. Gates," written by Himself, 1810; and " A Measuring
Reed to Separate Between the Precious and the Vile " (1815), ed. 2, 1819.
The former of these is a picaresque narrative of a boy's religious experiences,
as he travels on foot from New England to North Carolina and back.
The latter is made up nearly entirely of quotations from standard divines
on the works of an impenitent and the works of a penitent heart. It is not
possible to obtain from either of them Gates's matured opinions.

[96] The whole letter is printed in " Spiritual Wives," ii. pp. 52 ff.: the portion which we quote is printed also at the opening of the excellent chapter
on " The Battle Axe Letter and its History," in H. Eastman's " Noyesism
Unveiled," pp. 91 ff.

the jealousy of exclusiveness. I call a certain woman my wife; she is yours; she is Christ's; and in Him she is the bride of all saints. She is dear in the hand of a stranger, and according to my promise to her I rejoice. My claim upon her cuts directly across the marriage covenant of this world, and God knows the end."

What is proclaimed here is complete promiscuity among the perfect; those that are perfect are already living the " resurrection life." Noyes could not repudiate his letter, and, with characteristic courage, declared his purpose thenceforth to publish the doctrine taught in it from the housetop. But with his equally characteristic caution he kept it still in the background, and put in the front those doctrines which he appeared to value more and more, chiefly because they led up to this; but which meanwhile produced less scandal to talk about. A typical example of his dealing with the matter may be seen in the attempt which he makes in June, 1839,[97] to explain to a correspondent how his brand of perfectionism differed from that of the Methodists, Friends, and Asa Mahan. They all agree, he says, that " perfect holiness is attainable in this life." But the " Perfectionists " — that is, his own sect — are discriminated from the others by certain primary and also by certain secondary tenets. The primary ones he enumerates thus: " 1. Their belief that perfect holiness, when attained, is forever secure. . . . 2. Their belief that perfect holiness is not a mere privilege, but an attainment absolutely necessary to salvation. Holding this belief they of course deny the name of Christian to all other sects. . . . 3. Their belief that the second coming of Christ took place at the period of the destruction of Jerusalem." On this third point of doctrine he remarks: " Perfectionists insist upon this doctrine as the foundation of the two preceding " — that is to say it stood with them as the fundamental doctrine out of which all else is deduced. Out of it ultimately come then the " secondary consequences," adherence to which also characterized " Perfectionists." These he enumerates as " their ' Antinomianism,' their belief of a present resurrection, their peculiar views of the fashion of this

[97] Eastman, as cited, pp. 364 f.

world in respect to marriage, etc." The promiscuity for which "Perfectionists" stand is not left here, it is true, unsuggested; but it is not obtruded. It is made a mere secondary result of their most fundamental doctrines.

We perceive that Noyes, beginning in 1834 as a perfectionist among perfectionists, had rapidly drifted into an attitude of open antagonism to all perfectionists except that small number who were willing to receive from him a totally new doctrinal and ethical system, and to subject themselves to his unquestioned authority. He no longer disagrees with them only in standing for organization over against their atomizing individualism; nor indeed only in reprobating the tendency to cloak licentiousness under a show of close spiritual relationship, which was showing itself among some of them. He declares them not really Christians, and he takes infinite satisfaction in pointing out his differences from them. He exhibits, indeed, a real predilection not only for explaining the differences between the several varieties of perfectionist teaching and his own, but in general for pointing out the defects in the teaching of all whom he supposes might be imagined to have been in any way before him advocates of holiness. As to the "ordinary class of pietists in the carnal churches," no doubt, he considers it unnecessary to say anything.[98] They are "confessors and *pro*fessors of sin," and therefore certainly not Christians. He adduces David Brainerd as a "fair specimen" of the "more distinguished spiritualists of the churches," but thinks that enough has been said when it is said that "his general experience is in essence a transcript of the seventh chapter of Romans" — in which chapter is depicted, according to Noyes, a carnal not a spiritual condition. "It is evident," he says, "that he was, through life, *under conviction,* panting after freedom from sin, but never reaching it." With Brainerd, he classes Edwards, Payson, and "nearly all of those who have obtained the highest distinction for piety in the churches." James Brainerd Taylor's experience, as we have seen, he is willing to allow to have been "of a higher grade."

[98] "The Berean," Lecture 39, pp. 271 ff.

" He came apparently to the very borders of the gospel," he
says, and " *saw* clearly the privilege and glory of salvation
from sin." " He even confessed, at times, in a timid way, that
he was free from sin," and in doing so really " condemned the
routine of sinning and repenting which was the only experience
allowed or known in the churches before him." His biographers, he asserts, " suppress the clearest part of his testimony in relation to his own salvation." Nevertheless he was
only " the John the Baptist of the doctrine of holiness " and,
not knowing the gospel of the primitive church, " was not born
of God in the Bible sense." There is nothing better to say of
the Mystics — Madame Guyon, William Law. They lose themselves in a " spiritual philosophy ": Law is the best and his
" Address to the Clergy " his best book. It is he who is the real
father of the semi-perfectionism which the Methodists profess. The Methodists — like the Moravians and Shakers —
and Asa Mahan and his companions with them, fail because
they make holiness not the main point of religion but an appendix to something else, and have denied or suppressed the
most essential element of the new covenant, viz. " security."
Oberlin may stand as the illustration of a semi-perfectionism
like this: it represents the stage a man comes to when, seeking
holiness, he has a gleam of it — and stops.[99] " We," he says in
another place,[100] differentiating his " Perfectionists " from Wesleyans and Oberliners — " we believe in the ' New Covenant,'

[99] In " Dixon and His Copyists," p. 39, Noyes warns us against the account given by Dixon (" New America," ii. pp. 242 f.) of the relation between
the views of Noyes and Oberlin. It is, he says, " a ludicrous historical jumble "
in which the actual position of the two parties is reversed.

[100] " Bible Communism," 1853, p. 7. Cf. what is said in the " Hand-Book
of the Oneida Community," 1867, pp. 29–30: — " Wesley and his associates
almost succeeded in re-opening the way of holiness; but they failed. . . .
Perfect holiness was only a secondary appendage to Methodism, even in its
best days. . . . Besides, Wesley, in denying the security of the higher class,
left a dismal barrier at the upper end of the way of holiness, which broke
the communication of his church with heaven. These remarks may be applied
without much alteration to Oberlin Perfectionism, which, in respect to the
secondary place of perfect holiness, the insecurity of the higher class of
believers, and every other essential feature, is only an attempted repetition
of the system of Wesley."

which enlists soldiers *for life;* or, in other words, for *perpetual holiness."*

We must not exaggerate the success of the propaganda for his perfectionism which Noyes inaugurated at New Haven in the spring of 1834. Its success, although, as we have said, not inconsiderable, was not great; and what was gained at the outset was soon largely lost. It was not long before James Boyle cast off allegiance, and the converts from the Free Church also soon returned to it.[101] Noyes himself remained in New Haven, after his adoption of perfectionism, only a year. When he left it, in February, 1835, never to return except on occasional visits, his departure bore a somewhat dramatic appearance. Simon Lovett, he tells us,[102] had come " as a sort of missionary from the New York Perfectionists " to convert him to their ideas; but he on the contrary converted Lovett to some of his, "especially to the New Haven doctrine of the Second Coming." Lovett took him, however, to Southampton and Brimfield to make him acquainted with the groups of perfectionists which had sprung up in those places under the New York propaganda. He won his triumphs among them also, he tells us. " Their leader, Tertius Strong, succumbed to my reasonings," he says, " and soon the doctrine of the Second Coming, and what was called the ' Eternal promise,' were received on all sides with great enthusiasm." But he did not like what he saw. There was " a seducing tendency to freedom of manners between the sexes," and there was "a progressive excitement " manifesting itself. So he ran away — leaving without notice, on foot, " through snow and cold — below zero — to Putney, sixty miles distant." Thus he escaped complicity, perhaps participation, in one of the wildest follies of the perfectionist orgies; and at the same time found a new scene for his work and a revised program for his labors. He did not at once, indeed, find the new way. A period of uncertainty intervened in which he spent himself endeavoring to repair the losses that had been suffered and to build up the broken fortunes of his party. He went from place to place on this errand.

---

[101] Eastman, as cited, pp. 31, 32.   [102] "Spiritual Wives," ii. pp. 34 ff.

He was visited at Putney by old friends and fellow workers. Simon Lovett came on from Brimfield and joined him in his labors. Hard on his heels Charles H. Weld [103] came, fresh from Theophilus R. Gates (who, he said, was " pure gold "), with letters in his hands from a New York priestess, a Mrs. Carrington, full of censures of Noyes's " carnality and worldly wisdom." Noyes describes this woman as " a lady living somewhere in the State of New York, who had recently been converted to perfectionism by Weld's labors, and was soaring in the highest regions of ecstacy and boasting." He no longer had any sympathy with mere perfectionists — with Weld he finally broke, apparently violently, and certainly permanently. He was meditating other things to which perfectionism was only a stepping stone. To these other things, however, perfectionism was a stepping stone — an indispensable stepping stone — and he now gave himself, having the new vision before his eyes, with all diligence to building it up in a form suitable for what was to come.

" At this time," he says, " I commenced in earnest the enterprise of repairing the disasters of Perfectionism, and establishing it on a

[103] Charles Huntington Weld, born 1799, graduated from Yale 1822, at Andover 1824–1826, agent of the American Bible Society in Mississippi 1830, preached at Manlius, New York, for a short period, and then resided at Belleville, died Hyde Park, Mass., 1871. He appears to have been a fanatic of the purest water and so unstable nervously that he fell into convulsions on any great excitement. Noyes describes his relations to him at great length: and his description is reprinted by Allan Estlake, " The Oneida Community," 1900, pp. 22 ff. He was a licentiate of the Presbytery of Oneida from 1828 to 1836: but during the trial of James Boyle by that Presbytery in the spring of 1835 he became implicated in the same charges, and on March 10, 1836, wrote to the Presbytery returning his license as " being no longer in harmony with the doctrines of the Presbyterian Church." His younger brother, Theodore D. Weld (who married Angelica Emily Grimke), is well known as an anti-slavery agitator. He was a convert of Finney's, who gives a full account of the circumstances of his conversion in his " Memoirs," 1876, pp. 184 ff. He too was a licentiate of the Presbytery of Oneida and entered on his preparation for the ministry at Lane Seminary. But " tearing away from his moorings under the anti-slavery excitement, he returned his license to the Presbytery, abandoned the church, discarded the supreme authority of the Bible, silenced his golden-mouthed speech, folded his eagle wing and lived in the solitude and muteness of a grave " (P. H. Fowler, " Historical Sketch of Presbyterianism within the Bounds of the Synod of Central New York," 1877, p. 163).

permanent basis, not by preaching and stirring up excitement over a large field, as had been done at the beginning, nor by labouring to reorganize and discipline broken and corrupted regiments, as I had done at different places, but by devoting myself to the patient instruction of a few simple-minded, unpretending believers, chiefly belonging to my father's family. I had now come to regard the quality of the proselytes of holiness as more important than their quantity; and the quality which I preferred was not that meteoric brightness which I had so often seen miserably extinguished, but sober and even timid honesty. This I found in the little circle of believers at Putney; and the Bible School which I commenced among them in the winter of 1836–7 proved to be to me and to the cause of holiness the beginning of better days."

Although the work in which Noyes now engaged himself took the form of a " Bible School," neither his purpose nor his interest could any longer be described as theological or even as religious. That purpose and interest belonged to a transcended phase of his development. His teaching in the " Bible School," we are told, sought chiefly to confirm the pupils in "the new doctrines of Salvation from Sin and the Second Coming of Christ," and to draw corollaries from them " resulting in the discovery of many other doctrines at variance with the dogmas of the divinity doctors and commentators." [104] This is an euphemistic way of describing what was really being done. What was really being done was, by the constant inculcation, enforcement, elaboration, illustration, of Noyes's fundamental doctrines of the emancipation of believers from all restrictions of law, and their imminent entrance into the "resurrection state " in which the selfishness of " exclusive marriage " should be done away, to supply his pupils with a religious basis for the practice of sexual promiscuity and to induce them to enter upon the practice of it without shock, when the time seemed to him to have come to introduce it. Meanwhile he tells us emphatically and with some iteration that, personally he " walked in all the ordinances of the law blameless " — " till 1846 "; and that also his " face was set as a

---

[104] Hinds, as cited, ed. 2, p. 156.

flint against laxity among the Saints " — again " till 1846." [105]
His whole preoccupation was, however, all this time with sex.
" I got the germ of my present theory of Socialism," he writes
in 1867 [106] — meaning nothing other than his doctrine of
promiscuity, which he speaks of as if it carried with it his
entire socialistic theory — " very soon after I confessed Holiness, i.e. in May 1834. As that germ grew in my mind, I talked
about it. It took definite form in a private letter in 1836. It
got into print without my knowledge or consent in 1837. I
moulded it, protected it, and matured it from year to year;
holding it always, nevertheless, as a theory to be realized in
the future, and warning all men against premature action
upon it. I made ready for the realisation of it by clearing the
field in which I worked of all libertinism, and by educating our
Putney family in male continence [107] and criticism.[108] When
all was ready, in 1846, I launched the theory into practice." [109]

[105] " Spiritual Wives," ii. pp. 182–183; " Dixon and His Copyists," p. 7;
" Bible Communism," pp. 21, 23.

[106] " Spiritual Wives," ii. pp. 183, 184.

[107] By " Male Continence " is meant an obnoxious method of birth control, on the invention of which Noyes greatly prided himself, and of all
the most intimate details of which he speaks with the utmost nonchalance.
It was required to be practiced in the Association, that promiscuity might
be indulged while the burden of children — which no communism can live
under — was avoided. Noyes shows a nice choice of words when he defends
his community against the charge of " licentiousness," but never, so far as
we have observed, against that of " lasciviousness," which is perhaps in any
case the best word to use of its practices.

[108] See Note 69 above.

[109] In " Bible Communism," 1853, pp. 21–23, Noyes goes over much of
the same ground. The radical principles of his theory of the relation of the
sexes, he says here, were " early deduced from the religious system evolved
at New Haven in 1834, were avowed in print by J. H. NOYES in 1837," and
were subsequently discussed from time to time. " These principles, though
avowed . . . in 1837, were not carried into action in any way by any of the
members of the Putney Association till 1846." They have, indeed, it is added,
" never been carried into full practical embodiment, either at Putney or Oneida,
but have been held by the Association, as the principles of an *ultimate state,*
toward which society among them is advancing, slowly and carefully, with
all due deference to sentiments and relations established by the old order
of things." All that is meant by the last sentence is that the promiscuity has
been confined within the bounds of the association as yet, and has not yet
become world-wide. We read (p. 22): " The Association, in respect to prac-

Of course Noyes — for that was his custom — rationalized his preoccupation with sex. That was, he said, his necessary preoccupation after doctrine had been disposed of. " The first thing to be done," he writes more than once,[110] " in an attempt to redeem man and reorganize society is to bring about reconciliation with God; and the second thing is to bring about a true union of the sexes. In other words, religion is the first subject of interest, and sexual morality the second, in the great task of establishing the Kingdom of God on earth. Bible communists are operating in this order. Their main work from 1834 to 1846 was to develop the religion of the New Covenant and establish union with God. Their second work, in which they are now especially engaged, is the laying the foundation of a new state of society by developing the true theory of sexual morality." When this passage was written, however — say in 1848 — Noyes and his followers were not engaged in " developing the true theory of sexual morality," if by that is meant working it out theoretically. That had been the work of the preceding period. They were now putting that developed theory of sexual morality into practice — and only in this practical sense "developing " it. Nor must the general terms in which the statement is thrown be permitted to throw the reader off of the real line of thought which is being followed. It is of course perfectly true that the two great objects of human regard are religion and morality, and the two matters of first consideration in the establishment of a sound social order are our relations to God and to one another. Since man has been made male and female, it may very properly be said also that, after religion, the family is the foundation stone of society. Precisely what Noyes was engaged in doing, however, was destroying the family. The problem he had set himself

tical innovations, limits itself to its own family circle, not invading society around it, and not just or even legal complaint of such invasions can be found at Putney or Oneida."

[110] We are quoting from " Male Continence " (1872), ed. 2, 1877, p. 19, which itself quotes from "Bible Arguments," 1848, p. 27. The same position is argued more fully, but in much the same language in " Bible Communism," 1853, proposition 16, pp. 40 ff.

was nothing less than the reconstitution of human society without the family. It was precisely because of this that, in "the laying of the foundation of a new state of society," he required first of all to "develop" a new "theory of sexual morality," a theory of sexual morality, that is to say, which dispensed with the family. The theory which he developed was nothing other than that of sexual promiscuity — prudently regulated, no doubt, in its practice in the interest of the community, but not only distinctly but even dogmatically insisted upon. The development of this theory and its inculcation to his followers were actually his "main work" for ten years before 1846. Its practical application was equally actually his main work for the remainder of his active life. His mind was preoccupied thus for a whole half of a century with the details of the sexual life. The religious preoccupation was past: "The Berean," which was published in 1847, but is made up of articles reprinted from the periodicals published from 1834 on, is its monument. The economic experiment on which he ultimately embarked was dependent on the narrower matter of sex-relations in which he saw its foundation stone: for all communism is wrecked on the family, and he perceived with the utmost clearness that he must be rid of the family if he was to have communism. Accordingly he constantly speaks of his "social theory" when he means nothing more than his "sexual theory," and his book called "Bible Communism," published in 1848, was nothing more than an elaborate plea for the practice of sexual promiscuity under the name of "entire community," that is to say community not only in goods but also in women.[111]

[111] Cf. the statement in "History of American Socialisms," p. 616: "As the early experiences of the Community were of two kinds, religious and social, so each of these experiences produced a book. The religious book, called *The Berean*, was printed at Putney in 1847, and consisted mainly of articles published in the periodicals of the Putney school during the previous twelve years. The socialistic book, called *Bible Communism*, was published in 1848, a few months after the settlement of Oneida, and was the frankest possible disclosure of the theory of entire Communism, for which the Community was then under persecution."

III. THE STRUCTURE

It was in May, 1846, so Noyes tells us,[112] that "entire communism" was put into practice, and the association which had enjoyed hitherto only a progressively increasing community in goods, entered upon the enjoyment also of a community of women, and so became really "a common family." From this time every man in the association — it consisted then of from thirty to forty members, but was destined to grow to over three hundred [113] — looked on every woman in it as his wife, and every woman looked on every man as her husband. When he wished to set this arrangement over against the "legality" of the exclusive "marriage of the world," which he affirmed to be abrogated in the Kingdom of God, Noyes called it "free love." When he wished, on the other hand, to defend it against the charge of "licentiousness," he called it "pantagamy," and insisted that it was as true a marriage as the "exclusive marriage of the world" itself — only "complex marriage" instead of selfish individual marriage. The enormity of the arrangement will perhaps be best apprehended when we remind ourselves that the community was intended to include, and did, in point of fact, from the beginning include, men and women united to one another by the ties of the closest kinship. A historian of the community, having in mind apparently only the law of promiscuity which reigned in it, cries out in shocked amazement that men of apparently reputable standing could be found, as they were found, to take their wives and daughters with them into such an arrangement. We do not touch the bottom of this degradation, however, until we recall that under this engagement the father at once himself became the husband of his daughters and

[112] "Dixon and His Copyists," p. 20.

[113] The numbers given are not always exactly the same: we are following here the Hand-Book of the Oneida Community for 1875. According to that Hand-Book the members on January 1, 1849, numbered 87; February 20, 1850, 172; year later, 205; in 1875, 298. Hinds, ed. 2, p. 175, gives the numbers, January 1, 1849, 87; January 1, 1850, 174; February 20, 1851, 205; in 1875, 298; in 1878, 306.

his daughters the wives of their father. Children growing up in the community were — though they might be brother and sister — the prospective husbands and wives of one another, as well as of their own parents. Noyes himself took into the community with him from it first formation at Putney, not only his brother, who at once became therefore sharer with him in all his marital relations, but two sisters, who became at once therefore the wives of both himself and his brother.[114] We do not affirm that marital rights were ever actually exercised in such cases. Of that we know and can know nothing. Respect for humanity leads us to suppose it incredible that it could have been brought to that pass. But it is of the utmost importance that we should fully realize that this is what Noyes's pantogamy meant; that this pantogamy formed the very foundation stone of his whole system and was put fully into practice; that he was constant in proclaiming it and strict in enforcing it; and that he encouraged its free practice by teaching along with it that the sexual act was of no more significance than any other token of universal affection.

Noyes is insistent in pointing out that the freedom of intercourse inaugurated in his community was not absolutely unlimited in practice, and he appears to fancy that it may on this account escape the stigma of licentiousness and even perhaps of promiscuity. The limitations were, however, entirely of a prudential character, and had as one of their main pur-

[114] Of course his own wife and his brother's wife and his two sisters' husbands are to be added to this quartette, raising it to an octette, which constituted about a fourth (or a fifth) of the whole promiscuous community. Noyes was married on June 28, 1838, and he plumed himself vastly on having, in doing so, made it perfectly plain to his partner that the marriage was not to be interpreted as an "exclusive" union, but left room for the "complex marriage" into which he led her eight years later. We are not sure that he made it plain. The language in which he expresses himself in what is perhaps, on that hypothesis, the most remarkable proposal of marriage ever made, is studiedly ambiguous. We do not know how far the lady addressed was prepared by previous knowledge to interpret it in its extremest sense. In that sense, it is a repetition of the "Battle Axe Letter" of two years earlier. The proposal was made in a letter dated June 11, 1838, and may be read either in Eastman, as cited, pp. 133 ff., or in Dixon's "New America," ii. pp. 235 ff.

poses precisely to secure and maintain the practice of promiscuity. It is just here that the contrariety between his practice and Fourier's fancies, which he much — and rightly — urged in other relations,[115] comes most distinctly to view. Both insisted on promiscuity in the sexual relation. But with Fourier this promiscuity was a means to an end — the complete indulgence of passion; he sought, as Ralph Waldo Emerson puts it,[116] " the greatest amount of kissing that the infirmity of human constitution admitted." With Noyes, on the other hand, it was not the amount of the kissing which was the main concern, but its distribution; it was precisely promiscuity which was his end; and to secure that end everything else had to give way. For example, Fourier[117] expected the young people to pair among themselves, of course purely spontaneously — if inclination led elsewhere, inclination naturally was to have its way; and he expected these young pairs to remain faithful

[115] This contrariety is, for example, elaborately argued in " Bible Communism," 1853, p. 7, where Fourier's principle of "attraction" is rejected and the principle of "community of goods" is asserted over against it. The two systems, it is explained, begin at opposite ends. Fourier begins "with industrial organization and physical improvements, expecting that a true religion and the true relation of the sexes will be found out three or four hundred years hence." Noyes begins "with religion and reconciliation of the sexes," and expects "that industrial reform and physical improvement will follow" — and that speedily. This is said over again with even more elaboration and emphasis in "History of American Socialisms," 1870, p. 630.

[116] The Atlantic Monthly, October, 1883, p. 538. "It argued singular courage," he says, speaking of Albert Brisbane's advocacy of Fourierism — "the adoption of Fourier's system, to even a limited extent, with his books lying before the world only defended by the thin veil of the French language. The Stoic said, Forbear; Fourier said, Indulge. Fourier was of the opinion of St. Evremond; abstinence from pleasure appeared to him a great sin." "It was easy," he says again, "to foresee the fate of this fine system in any serious and comprehensive attempt to set it on foot in this country. As soon as our people got wind of the doctrine of marriage held by this master, it would fall at once into the hands of a lawless crew, who would flock in troops to so fair a game, and like the dreams of poetic people on the first outbreak of the old French Revolution, so theirs would disappear in a slime of mire and blood."

[117] Fourier's doctrine of the relation of the sexes is sufficiently explained at pp. 547 ff. of the very illuminating account of Fourier and his theories by Arthur J. Booth, printed in The Fortnightly Review, xii. 1872, pp. 530 ff. and 673 ff.

to one another at least during the ardor of their first love —
of course, again, only because natural inclination would so
determine it. Noyes apparently did not doubt that Fourier
was right in supposing that this would be the natural course
of things. But there was nothing which he more sternly repressed than any tendency among young or old to monopolize
one another, as he would say. When any such tendency manifested itself, he required each of those concerned to pair with
someone else. We learn that much suffering was caused by the
enforcement of this measure: [118] it had no other end than the
maintenance of promiscuity. It was his policy, also, to repress
all direct courtship.[119] Pairing was arranged through the intermediation of third parties, regularly the older female members of the community [120] being called upon to perform this
service. And it was a principle with Noyes to prevent ordinarily the pairing of the young with the young. Fourier suggests
that it might happen now and then that a youth would take
a fancy to, and obtain the favor of, a lady of mature age: indeed,
as A. J. Booth tells us,[121] he has recorded a thrilling incident " to illustrate how a youth, in all the ardor of virgin passion, may be irresistibly attracted by the personal charms of a
lady more than one hundred years of age." Noyes, on principle,
required the young of both sexes to pair with the old, and discouraged the pairing of the young with the young.[122] Thus, at
least on paper, the sexual relations were in Noyes's scheme
governed strictly by a principle: there was no spontaneity
about it; promiscuity in these relations was required and secured.[123] The ultimate end, of course, was the safety of the
community, which would be endangered by the formation of

[118] Cf. the statement in Charles Nordhoff, " The Communistic Societies
of the United States," 1874, pp. 276–277; also Estlake, p. 90.

[119] The general situation brought it about, however, as Estlake, p. 90,
naïvely puts it, that " life became a state of continuous courtship," both
women and men seeking always to attract one another.

[120] Cf. Nordhoff, as cited, p. 276.

[121] As cited, p. 549.

[122] Cf. Nordhoff, p. 276; Estlake, pp. 54–55.

[123] One saving clause was indeed admitted in his regulations: " persons
are not obliged, under any circumstances, to receive the attentions of those
whom they do not like " (Nordhoff, p. 276).

"monopolizing" attachments. The end of the safety of the community determined another of Noyes's regulations — the universal practice, through the community, of his method of birth control.[124] The care and expense of children would be a burden to the community, which would form a menace to its stability. Afterwards, when the community had passed through its tentative stage, the breeding of children — we use this phraseology advisedly — was undertaken on the most scientific principles. Not all the members of the community were permitted to produce children: certain ones were selected for breeding purposes, and paired with close attention to their mutual characteristics. Noyes calls this "Stirpiculture," and wrote a pamphlet [125] in the early seventies to explain its importance and the modes of its application. "Previous to about two years and a half ago," he says in this pamphlet, "we refrained from the usual rate of child-bearing, for several reasons, financial and otherwise. Since that time we have made an attempt to produce the usual number of offspring to which people in the middle classes are able to afford judicious moral and spiritual care, with the advantage of a liberal education. In this attempt twenty-four men and twenty women have been engaged, selected from among those who have most thoroughly practiced our social theory."

In one matter at least, connected with the restrictions placed on themselves by his followers in the practice of promiscuity, Noyes is far from candid. He wishes to obtain credit for them for confining their practice within the bounds of the community, and on this ground he invites us to look upon the compact which bound the community together as a true marriage — a "complex marriage," no doubt, but none the less a marriage,[126] and the community so bound together as a true

[124] Cf. "Bible Communism," chapter iv., and "History of American Socialisms," p. 632.

[125] "Essay on Scientific Propagation" (n.d.), pp. 32; Nordhoff conjectures "about 1873" for its date.

[126] An odd formal inconsistency results from Noyes's insistence, on the one hand, that *all* marriage is abolished in the Kingdom of Heaven in accordance with the Saviour's declaration that there shall be *no* marriage or giving in marriage in it (e.g. "The Berean," p. 431), and his equal insistence that

family. " Our Communities," he says,[127] " are *families,* as distinctly bounded and separated from promiscuous society as ordinary households." The bounding and separating of these communities from promiscuous society differed from the bounding and separating of families from that society, however, in being merely *de facto,* and, according to Noyes's most fervent preaching, temporary, affording only samples of what was soon to become universal and preparing the way to it. The promiscuity practiced in these communities was therefore in principle universal, and was expected soon to become in fact universal. It is therefore thoroughly disingenuous to point to its momentary confinement to the communities as if that were of its essence, and on that ground to cloak the unbridled lasciviousness of this doctrine under such names as complex marriage and complex families. In point of fact, the fundamental doctrine which Noyes taught in this relation was pure, unbounded promiscuity; and all adaptations of this doctrine to community life were afterthoughts and were conceived by him as temporary expedients. What he discovered in the spring of 1834 was that in the kingdom of heaven there is no marriage or giving in marriage whatever. What he declared in 1845 [128] was that " the abolishment of worldly restrictions on sexual intercourse, is involved in the anti-legality of the gospel," because such restrictions are " incompatible with the state of perfected freedom towards which Paul's gospel of ' grace without law ' leads." What he still teaches in 1870 [129] is that, as there is " no intrinsic difference between property in persons and property in things," the community of goods inaugurated after Pentecost carries with it community of women. " The same spirit which abolished exclusiveness in regard to money," he says, " would abolish, if circumstances allowed full scope to it, exclusiveness in regard to women and children.

---

the arrangements in his community amounted to and were in effect a binding marriage — only a " complex," not an individual marriage.

[127] " History of American Socialisms," p. 639, cf. Hinds, ed. 2, p. 183.

[128] " Bible Communism," p. 52.

[129] " History of American Socialisms," p. 625.

Paul expressly places property in women and property in goods in the same category, and speaks of them together, as ready to be abolished by the advent of the Kingdom of Heaven." The restriction of this promiscuity to the community was to Noyes an evil, an evil to be overcome, and to the over-coming of which he looked forward with fervent hope. And it was not the restriction of its practice within the communities which made these communities attractive to him, but the practice of it there. He arraigns " the law of marriage," be-cause, as he says,[130] it gives to sexual appetite only a scanty and monotonous allowance, and so produces the natural vices of poverty, contraction of taste and stinginess or jealousy." He praises [131] " a Community home in which each is married to all, and where love is honored and cultivated," precisely be-cause it " will be as much more attractive than an ordinary home, as the community out-numbers a pair " — which, put brutally, is just to say that the sexual satisfaction increases with numbers.[132] Fourier himself, to whom confessedly the free gratification of passion was everything, could not have ex-pressed his own principle with more frankness.[133]

Although this iniquity was put into practice in 1846, there seems to have been at first something tentative and veiled in the practice of it. Noyes's own expression is that it was begun " cautiously." [134] Even when done in a corner, however, such a thing is not easy to hide. And it became increasingly evident, as time went on, that the people of Putney were, in a general way, aware of what was being done and were quite disinclined to permit it to be done among them. As the antagonism rose, Noyes and his followers braced themselves to meet it. The line taken was the bold one of asserting for themselves immediate

[130] *Ibid.*, p. 628.

[131] P. 634.

[132] What is said in " Bible Communism," 1853, p. 20, taken from *The Circular,* for 1852, is scarcely consistent with what is said in " History of American Socialisms," 1870, pp. 628, 634, and is probably only an uncon-sidered apologetic assertion.

[133] In " Bible Communism," 1853, pp. 114 ff., we find a distinct minimizing of the sin of adultery.

[134] " History of American Socialisms," p. 616.

divine guidance and sanction. They apparently hoped thus to
overcome opposition by the dread authority of Deity itself: and they sank to the mountebank device of invoking
pretended miracles in support of their assertion. The crisis
drew on in the midsummer of 1847. On the evening of the
first of June, we are told by one of their number,[135] their leader
startled his assembled disciples with the question: " Is not
now the time for us to commence the testimony that the Kingdom of God has come — to proclaim boldly that God in His
character of Deliverer, Lawgiver and Judge has come to this
town and in this Association? " The significance of this question was twofold. What had been done more or less in secret
was now to be proclaimed on the housetop, and the coming
of the Kingdom of God was to be asserted because, in Noyes's
teaching, it was only in the Kingdom of God that such things
were sanctioned — " woe to him," he had cried in the Battle
Axe Letter, " who abolishes the law of apostacy before he
stands in the holiness of the resurrection." The answer returned by his followers to his question was a unanimous affirmation. " It was seen that a new and further confession of
truth was necessary; that it was the next thing before them
in the course of progress to which they had been called. *It
was unanimously adopted, therefore, as the confession and
testimony of the believers assembled, that the Kingdom of
God had come.*" This, however was mere assertion; and the
only proof of the assertion was that those who made it were
living in sexual promiscuity — which was to them an evident
concomitant of the entrance into the world of the new divine
order, but which could scarcely be counted upon to impress
the outside world in the same way. Hence the appeal to
miracles.

The star case was the healing of Harriet A. Hall, a chronic
invalid, by the combined ministrations of Noyes and Mary
Cragin on June 22. The miracles, it will be noted, did not tarry
when they were needed. The patient, says Noyes,[136] " was com-

---

[135] W. A. Hinds, ed. 2, pp. 169 ff.: we are drawing from his narrative.
[136] *The Spiritual Magazine,* October 15, 1847, cited by Eastman, pp. 185 f.

pletely bedrid, and almost blind, lying in nearly total
darkness." " From this state," he declares, " she was raised instantly, by the laying on of hands, and by the word of command, into strength which enabled her to walk, to face the
sun, to ride miles without inconvenience and with excessive
pleasure." " The cure of Mrs. Harriet A. Hall," he asserts, " is
as unimpeachable as any of the miracles of the primitive
church." On the contrary, it is as obvious a sham as any of the
thousands and thousands of sham miracles which disgrace the
annals of the church, and not of the church only but of every
popular religious movement throughout the world — differing
only from other sham miracles in bearing on its brow the brand
of fraud, as many of them do not. The part taken by Mary
Cragin [137] in this miracle — and others — is so barefacedly that

Cf. the full account of the details of the miracle by all the participants in it,
in *The Spiritual Magazine,* September 15, 1847, transcribed by Eastman, pp.
187 ff.

[137] Mary Cragin's name should not be passed by without some notice.
The accession of George Cragin and his wife (with a child) to Noyes's community was obviously felt by Noyes himself and the community at large to
be an event of great importance. Even in the brief account of the Community which he gives in his " History of American Socialisms," he notes it.
" Gradually a little school of believers gathered around him. His first permanent associates were his mother, two sisters, and a brother. Then came the
wives of himself and his brother, and the husbands of his sisters. Then came
George Cragin and his family from New York, and from time to time other
families and individuals from various places " (p. 615). The Cragins are the
only persons he mentions by name. Similarly Hinds, ed. 2, p. 157, after mentioning the accession of J. L. Skinner, who married one of Noyes's sisters,
adds: " The next important accession was that of the Cragin family, consisting of George Cragin and wife and child, in September, 1840. Mr. Cragin
had been a merchant of New York City, the General Publishing Agent of
the *Advocate of Moral Reform,* a co-laborer of John McDowall in reform
work, and a revivalist under Chas. G. Finney. His wife had been a teacher
and a Sunday-school worker in New York City and a zealous revivalist. Mr.
Noyes never had more active and willing helpers." We are not told here,
however, the whole story or that part of it which connected these people
with Noyes. This part is that, while still at work as revivalists in New York,
they became perfectionists and accepted Noyes as their leader. Then they
became inmates of the house at Rondout of Abram C. Smith, a fellow perfectionist of Methodist antecedents, who owned some such relation as their
own to Noyes. Then Smith made Mary Cragin his " Spiritual Wife," or, to
be more explicit, his mistress. Noyes, in accordance with his custom in deal-

of a play-actor, that one wonders that so shrewd a man as
Noyes permitted the details to be made public. Other miracles
followed in rapid succession; [138] and not content even with
these, others still, alleged to have been wrought previously,
were now brought forward and made public.[139] But it was all
in vain. The people were obdurate; and, having refused to
believe Noyes and his followers, would not believe though
many rose from their beds. Vigorous action was begun to rid the

---

ing with such cases, disapproved of the relation and sternly rebuked Smith.
The result was that the Cragins found their way into Noyes's community,
where Mrs. Cragin occupied the position of matron. The whole sordid story
was told at great length by Cragin himself in *The Oneida Circular* and has
been made accessible to all by being reprinted (Noyes says, " with slight
alterations ") in Dixon's " Spiritual Wives." The facts were, however, perfectly well known independently of Cragin's narrative (cf. Eastman, p. 430).
It seems probable that it is Mary Cragin whom Asa Mahan means when,
in his " Autobiography," 1851, p. 239, he tells of a " professedly Christian
woman " in New York, in, say 1835, who told him: " I attend church, not
from any good that I expect from the services, but as an example to others.
These ministers cannot teach me: I understand the whole subject already."
She had, he says, " been very active and influential in the revivals." " Years
after that," he adds, " I heard of her as a blubbering Perfectionist, practising,
it was believed, the abominations of the sect." With reference to John R.
McDowall and *The Advocate of Moral Reform,* perhaps this notice by D. L.
Leonard (" The Story of Oberlin," 1898, p. 72, cf. p. 303) will be enough:
" In 1830-4 McDowall undertook a well-meant but unwisely conducted work
in behalf of fallen women in New York, which soon ended in failure and
bitter sorrow to himself, but also out of which grew a widespread and
lasting movement for ' moral reform,' whose equivalent is found in our day
enfolded in the phrase, social purity." For a contemporary estimate of this
movement and its methods, see an article on " Moral Reform Societies " in
The Literary and Theological Review, for December, 1836, pp. 614 ff.

[138] Hinds, ed. 2, p. 170, writes thus: " Events followed this confession
in quick succession of such a character as to convince those making it that
the heavens had approved it, and welcomed them into new and more vital
relations with their spiritual superiors; and they did not hesitate to make
a present personal application of Christ's promises of miraculous power to
those who believed in him. Many of the Putney believers testified that they
had personally experienced miraculous healing, with and without the laying
on of hands." Thus, as late as 1902, it was still claimed among Noyes's followers that heaven had by visible testimonies set its seal of approval on the
promiscuity at Putney!

[139] The fullest and best account of the miracles of this date is given by
Eastman, pp. 185 ff.; cf. also Hinds, ed. 2, p. 170. Also in general Nordhoff,
p. 272.

town of the scandal. Indignation meetings were held. The
courts were set in motion; civil suits for damages were
brought; the Grand Jury found a true bill and in the indictment thus made Noyes was arraigned on specific charges of
adultery and held for trial on heavy bail. The result was, happily, the destruction of the obnoxious community at Putney.
The suspension of the publication of the community's journal
— *The Spiritual Magazine* — was compelled.[140] Immunity in
the courts was bought only at heavy cost; the civil suits were
satisfied by money payments out of court; [141] before the criminal case came on, Noyes broke bail and fled beyond the jurisdiction of the court.[142] The community itself began to scatter
and in a year or so it was gone.[143]

[140] Its publication was suspended, Nov. 23, 1847. We say suspended because it was soon resumed at Oneida Reserve. Noyes himself says in the issue
of August 5, 1848 (Eastman, p. 55) : " It is sufficient to say here, that the *immediate* cause of the suppression of our paper at Putney, was a resolution
passed at an ' indignation meeting ' of the citizens of that place, denouncing
our publication as licentious, and requiring an immediate stoppage of our
press."

[141] Eastman, p. 58.

[142] Eastman, pp. 35 ff., gives a full account of the criminal proceedings
against Noyes, and prints in full the court record.

[143] Noyes and his friends naturally retorted on the Putney people with
abuse. In the " Second Annual Report of the Oneida Association," 1850, p. 23,
it is declared that Putney does not present " an average specimen of the
civilization of the country," and " the transactions of 1847 " are characterized
as " foolish," " mean," and " brutal." It was a ground of great congratulation
to the Oneida people that they were able a few years later to find some
sort of a footing in Putney again. Hinds, ed. 2, pp. 171–172, states the facts
as follows: " In less than three years a colony of the Oneida Community
was established at Putney, which was maintained there for five years, free
from every disturbance, and many regrets were expressed when all the Community property there was sold and the final exodus of the Perfectionists
took place." An annotator of the pamphlet called " The Oneida Community;
its Relation to Orthodoxy," which appears to have been published about
1912, is not contented with so bare a statement. We read (p. 14) : — " The
inhabitants of Putney — ashamed of their bigotry and coming to appreciate
the usefulness and exalted moral goodness of the Oneida Community — soon
invited them back, and a branch of the Community thenceforth existed at
Putney (as at other places) for some years, until a policy of concentration
absorbed into the parent society at Oneida all the branches except the one
at Wallingford (Connecticut)."

It was not at all within the plans of the leaders of the Community, however, because they had been driven out of Putney, to pass out of existence. In the height of the storm at Putney, Noyes was busily preparing for the future. Not content with calling heaven to bear witness to him in manifest miracles, he was as diligently engaged during this fateful midsummer of 1847 in strengthening his interests among the children of men. He turned in his need to those " New York Perfectionists " from whom he had decisively separated himself, and whose ways he had never wearied of declaring not his ways. Nor did he turn in vain. He was treated by them with marked deference from the outset; and in the end he obtained from them the means for redintegrating his enterprise under better stars than ever. Already on July 3d we find him drawing up in an elaborate document " the testimony of the parties concerned " in his star miracle, " at the request and in presence of " the notorious John B. Foot, " for his private use " — from which it seems that Foot was at the time in Putney.[144] And in the issue of *The Spiritual Magazine* for July 15, announcement was made of the holding of two Conventions of perfectionists in Central New York, in the approaching September, " called," says Hinds,[145] for " promoting unity and co-operation between the New York and Putney believers." These Conventions were called by John B. Foot and John Corwin, and met, the earlier at Lairdsville, Oneida County, New York, on September 3, under the presidency of Jonathan Burt, and the latter at Genoa, Cayuga County, under the presidency of Foot. Noyes made them the occasion of a five weeks' tour of electioneering character through the region and, of course, was present at both Conventions as the official representative of one of the parties whose coöperation it was their avowed purpose to promote. As a result a series of resolutions, drafted by a committee of which Noyes was chairman, was passed at the later

---

[144] The document is published by Eastman, pp. 187–196.

[145] Ed. 2, p. 173. The language of the call seems to have been " for the purpose of acquaintance, acknowledgment of each other, and co-operation " (Eastman, p. 140).

Convention "without a dissenting vote." These resolutions ran: [146]

"1. Resolved, That we will devote ourselves exclusively to the establishment of the kingdom of God; and as that kingdom includes and provides for all interests, religious, political, social and physical, that we will not join or co-operate with any other association. 2. Resolved, That as the kingdom of God is to have an extensive manifestation, and as that manifestation must be in some form of Association, we will acquaint ourselves with the principles of Heavenly Association, and train ourselves to conformity to them as fast as possible. 3. Resolved, That one of the leading principles of Heavenly Association, is the renunciation of exclusive claim to private property. 4. Resolved, That it is expedient immediately to take measures for forming a Heavenly Association in Central New York. 5. Resolved, That William H. Cook be authorized, on our behalf, to visit Perfectionists throughout the state, for the purpose of stirring up their minds in relation to Association, and ascertaining the amount of men and means that are in readiness for the enterprise."

By these remarkable resolutions the perfectionists of Central New York not only committed themselves to communism in principle, but to the immediate establishment of a Communistic Association, and set measures on foot to carry out this declared purpose. We are told further that, on the passage of the resolutions, "with great fervor the strongest men of the convention came forward and pledged 'their lives, their fortunes and their sacred honor' to the enterprise proposed in the resolutions, and for the establishment of the kingdom of God in the world." [147] Noyes's appeal to men had been more successful than his appeal to God. He had secured from the New York Perfectionists action which looked to the mere transference of his establishment from Putney to New York. And that is indeed precisely what happened, but not with the smoothness and facility which appeared likely on a mere surface view of things.

[146] They are printed in full in Eastman, p. 142; and the first part of them in Hinds, ed. 2, pp. 173–174.
[147] Hinds, ed. 2, p. 174.

For there was one thing on which Noyes had not been quite candid with his New York brethren, and allusion to which is entirely absent from the set of resolutions whose passage he had secured from them. This was his doctrine of sexual promiscuity — and the relation in which it stood, in his view, to the possible formation of a Communistic Society, such as he had now committed them to. As they became aware of these things their zeal in coöperating with him in the foundation of such a society vanished. A series of resolutions, introduced by Otis Sanford of Clinton, New York, having the design of expressing sympathy and coöperation with Noyes, was passed by the earlier — the Lairdsville — Conference, with cordial unanimity. In these, entire approbation was expressed of the " general course of the press at Putney," and cordial coöperation with the Putney brethren in the circulation of their publications was promised.[148] But Noyes is compelled to add to his report of this resolution: [149] " After the close of the meetings, Otis Sanford, in consequence of discovering that I was the author of the ' Battle Axe letter ' (which he had never seen before,) retracted his assent to these resolutions." This is but a straw showing how the wind was veering around. The sentiments of the brethren, in point of fact, underwent nothing less than a revulsion, which wrecked the whole great project which had been entered upon. There were those among them who had been involved in the indecencies of " Spiritual Wifehood," but complete sexual promiscuity and that as the very foundation-stone of their society of saints, was more than, with all their antinomian tendencies, they could stomach. As an eye-witness of what was happening writes: — " As soon as they heard of cross-fellowship, and the fact that their chosen apostle was under bonds for the charge of adultery," they drew decisively back. And thus it was brought about that though by his visit to New York Noyes provided for the removal of his Community to that State, it was not with the support of the New York Perfectionists at large.

[148] Eastman, p. 141.
[149] *The Spiritual Magazine,* October 1, 1847, as quoted by Eastman, p. 141.

We must suppose that it was in very deep disappointment that Noyes returned to Putney. Certainly he returned to very great trouble. The people were inexorable: his Community was dispersed: the criminal suit against him was pending; there was no promise in the outlook. On the twenty-sixth of November he felt constrained to leave Putney forever, taking up his residence in New York City. Meanwhile, there were a few men in Central New York who, being like-minded with him, were not content to permit the resolutions passed at the September Conventions to fall wholly to the ground.[150] They could do nothing so grandiose as was contemplated in those resolutions. But they were resolved to establish a community in a small way on some such lines. These men, Jonathan Burt, Joseph C. Ackley, Daniel P. Nash, united their interests and invited Noyes to join them. This he did about the first of February, 1848, and at once took the lead in the enterprise and, indeed, as was his wont, became the dictator. The members of the old Putney Community joined him, and by the first of March the Oneida Community was fully organized. In giving an account in his " History of American Socialisms " [151] of the origins of the Community he wishes to trace them back alternately to impulses derived from the great revivals of 1831 and the experiments at Brook Farm. " Thus the Oneida Community," he says, " really issued from a conjunction between the Revivalism of Orthodoxy and the Socialism of Unitarianism." Then he descends to details: " In 1846, after the fire at Brook Farm, and when Fourierism was manifestly passing away, the little church at Putney began cautiously to experiment in Communism. In the fall of 1847, when Brook Farm was breaking up, the Putney Community was also breaking up, but in the agonies, not of death, but of birth. Putney con-

[150] " On the same day that the exodus from Putney commenced (November 26, 1847), practical movements were being made by Perfectionists of the same faith toward the formation of a Community at Oneida, Madison County, N. Y. The Putney exiles joined these brethren, and on the first day of the following March the Oneida Community was fully organized " (" Hand-Book of the Oneida Community," 1867, p. 10).

[151] Pp. 615–616.

servatism expelled it, and a Perfectionist Community just
begun at Oneida under the influence of the Putney school, received it."

After a quarter of a century of successful development, the
exodus could be described in this poetical language. It was anything but poetry at the time. Except the hospitable welcome of
Jonathan Burt [152] there was little that was inviting in the untamed woods and streams of Oneida Creek; and the first years
of the Community's residence there were comfortless and hard
enough, but also on that very account bracing and disciplining. "At first," says Hinds,[153] " the Community buildings at
Oneida consisted of two small frame dwellings, a log-hut, and
an old saw mill, once owned by the Indians. It was a dozen
years before their members got beyond the necessity of sleeping in garrets and out-houses. Though the means brought in
by the members enabled them to live tolerably well at first,
they soon learned to content themselves with the humblest
fare." The Community, however, grew rapidly in numbers and
efficiency; and ultimately, in wealth. Beginning in the spring
of 1848 with about forty members, by the first of the next
year it had eighty-seven, which it doubled in the course of the
year 1849: on February 20, 1851, there were two hundred and
five members, in 1875 two hundred and ninety-eight, and in
1878 three hundred and six.[154] Nearly a hundred and eight
thousand dollars were brought in by the incoming members
during the first nine years, of which something more than forty
thousand were sunk in living, leaving the Community on January 1, 1857, with a capital of sixty-seven thousand dollars.
Now, however, economic success began, and the industries of
the Community became profitable. These were mainly concentrated in the business of the canning of fruits and vegetables,

[152] " The gathering of the Community of Oneida was due to the hospitable invitation of Jonathan Burt, who possessed a few acres of land and a
rude saw-mill on Oneida Creek" ("Oneida Community: 1848–1901" [n.d.],
p. 6).

[153] Ed. 2, pp. 175–176.

[154] *Ibid.*, p. 175.

and the manufacture of silk and of steel traps.[155] It is not necessary to dwell on these things. Information on the industrial side of the life of the Community is easily accessible and is indeed in the possession of all. Only enough is required to be said to secure that it should be well understood on the one hand that the Oneida Community became eminently successful in the economic and industrial aspects, and on the other that the development of the Community on this side represents a new phase of Noyes's activities, peculiar to the Oneida period.

Although, of course, community of goods was a dogma with him from the beginning of his speculations, and he had put it into practice at Putney, as there was no necessity for the development of large industrial efficiency before the removal to Oneida, so there was no marked progress made toward it. There is no evidence that Noyes had specially engaged himself with the problems of economic and industrial life prior to his settlement at Oneida. At Oneida, however, he was faced with hard conditions, and, after a period of partial failure, conquered them. There is an appearance that perhaps as a result of this necessary engrossment with these problems, the center of his interests now changed, and that economic matters began to loom in his mind as intrinsically more important than the matters to which he had hitherto given himself with most predilection. Religion, sex, industry — it was along this line of advance that his mind seems to have moved; and as he appears to have come to value religion chiefly as a sanction to sexual promiscuity, so he appears to have come in the end to value sexual promiscuity mainly as a means to economic efficiency. Our meaning in saying this is not that he looked on his religious theories as the necessary foundation of his sexual theory, and on this sexual theory as the necessary foundation of any successful communism. That goes without saying. That was the very essence of his theorizing; and no doubt from the practical point of view, also, he was right — decent people

[155] Hinds, ed. 2, p. 189. Cf. further details of the work in 1868, "History of American Socialisms," pp. 642 ff.

could scarcely have been brought to follow his sexual practice save under the influence of some such religious fanaticism as he imbued them with, and very certainly no communism can stand save on the ruins of the institution of marriage. What we are saying, however, is nearly the opposite of this. It is that Noyes, as he appears at Putney to have lost interest in his religious fanaticism in his absorption in sexualism, so appears at Oneida to have to some extent lost interest in his sexualism in his absorption in his industrialism — necessary as each nevertheless was to the basis of the other. Revivalist, perfectionist, sensualist, economist — that seems to be the line of his development. Not that he ever formally abandoned either his fantastic religious theories or his gross sexual doctrine, but that, an industrial communism having been created on their foundation, and now actually existing, he seems to have come to fancy that it might continue to exist and to function without their aid.

In this he was certainly mistaken, as the event proved. It was precisely through its drawing back from these religious absurdities and sexual abominations that the community crumbled. It lasted just a generation — from 1848 to 1880: and that it was just a generation that it lasted was no accident. What it means is that it lasted so long as those were at the helm who had taken up the enterprise under the impulse of a strong fanaticism; and that it fell to pieces when the guidance came into the hands of a new generation which could not believe the things by which its fathers had lived. W. P. Garrison, writing in *The Nation* of September 4, 1879, p. 154, as the process of its dissolution was beginning, remarks with great weight:—

" That the split in regard to sexual relations has come with the second generation was only what was to be expected. Nothing but a Chinese wall and the adoption of a conventual stringency could have prevented it. . . . Nothing is surer than that the Oneida system of complex marriage was a reversion to barbarism — to ways repudiated by the race in its efforts to rise above the promiscuous intercourse of the brutes. All the attention it deserved at the hands of social philosophers was due to this fact, and to one other, that it was justified by an appeal to supernatural sanctions. . . . What is most surprising in Mr. Noyes's message to the Community is his declaration that he did not regard the hitherto existing social arrangements as ' essential parts ' of their profession as Christian Communists. He has been saying this, it appears, for a year past. But ten years ago, in his work on ' American Socialisms,' he still held to the doctrine laid down in his ' Bible Communism ' in 1848, that ' the restoration of true relations between the sexes is a matter second in importance only to the reconciliation of man to God,' and that ' the sin-system, the marriage-system, the work-system, and the death-system, are all one, and must be abolished together.' . . . Mr. Noyes has, we conceive, outlived his headship. His successor . . . is the self-appointed head of the party which has become dissatisfied with complex marriage. In other words, there is no real succession. A revolution has taken place: the Community as it was has suffered a mutilation which practically destroys its identity, and will by the coming historian be added to the list of extinct Utopias."

What was happening in the Community could not easily be better described. Noyes was growing old, and was losing his hold on the Community. Murmurings and disputings were heard on every side. The younger members had become skeptical both of Noyes's religious system and of his theory of sexual relationship,[156] and restive under control exercised over them. It was clear that a change of some sort was imperative. Noyes sought it in the first instance by retiring from the headship of the Community and putting a younger and more vigorous man in his place. The man he chose for his successor was not unnaturally his own son, Theodore R. Noyes, and he may have hoped the more from the choice because this son was a leader of the disaffected party — certainly at least with reference to the religious aspects of it.[157] The experiment was

[156] So we are explicitly told in an annotation to the extract from F.A. Bisbee's article on " Communistic Societies in the United States " in *The Political Science Quarterly* for December, 1905, printed in G. W. Noyes's " The Oneida Community: its Relation to Orthodoxy," p. 15.

[157] He himself tells us (*The Nation*, September 11, 1879, p. 173) that his father accused him of " Positivism "; and Estlake, pp. 9 ff., confirms this by

not successful, and Noyes was compelled to withdraw the appointment. The disaffection which had been smouldering was now in flames. There were some, no doubt, who were ready to acquiesce in any settlement commended to them by their "tried leader." But there were now two embittered parties shut up together within the bonds of this "family." The one "could see nothing but a skeptic in the man who had dared to develop the fruits of the spirit of Christ in any other way than through their prescribed methods of professing unqualified belief in some of the doctrines of traditional Christianity." [158] The other was made up of enthusiastic supporters of the younger Noyes, and some of these, offended by his enforced withdrawal from the leadership, themselves withdrew from the family.

At this period a new factor entered the situation — external opposition. The tardily begun and tardily culminating protest of the people of the State of New York against the toleration in their midst of such a moral offense as the Oneida Community constituted, had now at last reached the point of effective action. The soul of this protest had been for a number of years John W. Mears, then a professor in Hamilton College, and the credit of bringing it through many difficulties to a decisive issue belongs mainly to him. We may date the beginning of the end, doubtless, from the appointment by the Synod of Central New York in 1873 of a committee charged with the duty of conferring with other religious bodies and determining on what measures were feasible. And the end itself was foreshadowed when a Conference called by J. W. Mears, F. D. Huntington, E. O. Haven, A. F. Beard, and E. G. Thurber met on February 14, 1879, in the University Building at Syracuse, New York, "for the purpose," as it brusquely reported in *The Nation,* [159] " of breaking up the Oneida Community." This brusque language does not unfairly represent the temper of the

---

telling us that he had passed "beyond the pale of certain phases of Christianity."

[158] Estlake, p. 13.

[159] February 20, 1879, p. 128.

Convention. The Oneida Community was recognized as intolerable, and every sort of difficulty had been raised to dealing with it decisively. It sheltered itself under the constantly repeated assertion that no law existed under which it could be proceeded against: as the lawyers put it, you cannot prove adultery without first proving marriage, and the Oneida people were not generally married. Sentimental objections to proceeding against them were also diligently advanced. The Oneida people were good citizens, and good business men, and good neighbors, and good employers of labor; they were a model of order and sobriety and diligence: why disturb them? Their morality? Well, said *The Nation*,[160] " the Oneida theory of the relation of the sexes is odious, no doubt, but it is the product of crackbrained biblical exegesis and is sincerely held, and the sheriff can hardly kill it." All this was brushed aside by the Convention. Morality, it said, is worth as much to a community as business ability; and if no law exists by which an end can be put to such flagrant immorality as flaunts itself in the Oneida Community — why the sooner such a law is made the better. So it appointed a committee to see if new legislation was really needed to meet the case, and if so to set steps on foot to secure it. That committee met in June, enlarged its numbers and very obviously got to business. It had become clear to every eye that the Oneida Community was doomed.

This had already become so clear to Noyes himself before the Conference of February 19 met that he approached that Conference with a document, which he caused to be distributed among its members, in which he practically promised that the Community would adjust itself to any special legislation the Conference might secure. The Oneida Community should be compared with the Shakers, he pleaded, not the Mormons: its members " had always been peaceable subjects of civil authority, no seditious act ever having been charged upon them; they had never proposed to carry out their peculiar principles in defiance of the laws or of the public opinion of their neighbors; and if special legislation should be obtained

---

[160] As quoted.

unfavorable to them they would still be faithful to their record
in submission to the 'powers that be.' " [161] Possibly the Conference took heart of grace from such a promise; at any rate
its representatives proceeded on their way with increased
activity. Noyes's fear in February had increased by June —
when the Conference's Committee met — to a certain fore-
boding of evil, and that with reference to his own person as
well as with reference to the Community. He fled beyond the
jurisdiction of the New York Courts and took up his residence
in Canada, where he resided for the rest of his life.[162] From this
safe retreat he immediately (August 25, 1879) proposed to the
Community which he had left behind him a complete surrender of its obnoxious practices.

" I need hardly remind the Community," he wrote,[163] " that
we have always claimed freedom of conscience to change our
social practices, and have repeatedly offered to abandon the
offensive part of our system of communism if so required by
public opinion. We have lately pledged ourselves in our publications to loyally obey any new legislation which may be
instituted against us. Many of you will remember that I have
frequently said within the last year that I did not consider our
present social arrangements an essential part of our profession as Christian Communists, and that we shall probably
have to recede from them sooner or later. I think the time has
come for us to act on these principles of freedom, and I offer
for your consideration the following modifications of our practical platform." The modifications thus intimated, he then
propounds as follows: —

" I propose: (1) That we give up the practice of complex marriage, not as renouncing belief in the principles and prospective
finality of that institution, but in deference to the public sentiment
which is evidently rising against it. (2) That we place ourselves
not on the platform of the Shakers, on the one hand, nor of the

[161] Hinds, ed. 2, p. 197.

[162] He died, in Niagara Falls, Canada, April 13, 1886, aged 74. He was
nearly 68 when he retired to Canada.

[163] *The American Socialist*, August 28, 1879, quoted in Estlake, p. 36;
cf. Hinds, ed. 2, p. 202.

world on the other, but on Paul's platform which allows marriage but prefers celibacy. To carry out this change, it will be necessary first of all that we should go into a new and earnest study of the seventh chapter of 1 Corinthians, in which Paul fully defines his position, and also that of the Lord Jesus Christ, in regard to the sexual relations proper for the Church in the presence of worldly institutions. If you accept these modifications, the Community will consist of two distinct classes — the married and the celibate — both legitimate, but the last preferred." " What will become of communism after these modifications," he now proceeds, " may be defined thus: (1) We shall hold our property and businesses in common, as now. (2) We shall live together in a common household and eat at a common table, as now. (3) We shall have a common children's department, as now. (4) We shall have our daily evening meetings, and all of our present means of moral and spiritual improvement. Surely here is communism enough to hold us together and inspire us with heroism for a new career. With the breeze of general goodwill in our favour, which even Professor Mears has promised us on the condition of our giving up the ' immoral features ' of our system, what new wonders of success may we not hope for in the years to come? For my part, I think we have great cause to be thankful for the toleration which has so long been accorded to our audacious experiment. Especially are we indebted to the authorities and people of our immediate neighbourhood for kindness and protection. It will be a good and gracious thing for us to relieve them at last of the burden of our unpopularity, and show the world that Christian Communism has self-control and flexibility enough to live and flourish without complex marriage."

It must not be supposed from the tone of the preamble and appendix of this communication that Noyes was arguing with an unwilling Community, to secure if possible from it action to which it was indisposed. He was really yielding to what had become the general demand of the Community; but in doing so supplying them with a plausible account of their action, such as would as far as possible save their and his susceptibilities. The action of the Community on this proposal was so immediate as to appear eager. The same number of *The American Socialist* [164] which prints the proposal prints

[164] August 28, 1879.

also this action: " The above message was considered by the Oneida Community in full assembly, August 26, 1879, and its propositions accepted; and it is to be understood that from the present date the Community will consist of two classes of members, namely, celibates, or those who prefer to live a life of sexual abstinence, and the married, who practise only the sexual freedom which strict monogamy allows. The Community will now look for the sympathy and encouragement which have been so liberally promised in case this change should ever be made."

By this action, naturally, the bottom was knocked out of the agitation against the Community. That agitation was directed solely against its " immoral features," and these were now abandoned.[165] But the bottom happily was by it knocked out of the Community also.[166] It was precisely in its system of " complex marriage " that the coherence of the Community consisted; that was the cement which held it together. That gone, everything was gone. If Noyes cherished any real expectations that the Community would seek to prolong its exist-

[165] How the matter was looked at within the community may be perceived from the following passage from A. Estlake's book, pp. 42–43: " There is no law under which the Oneida Community would have been interfered with, so they were safe from any action under existing statutes; but the Presbyterian Church, led on by Professor Mears of Hamilton College, who for years had been an unswerving foe to the Community, had organised a movement, with Bishop Huntington at its head, to obtain special legislation against them at Albany. If Mears had succeeded, it is impossible to conjecture how a band of unprincipled lawyers and politicians might have robbed the members, nor to what extent ruin and hardship might have been entailed upon the aged and children of the Community. It was the leader's duty, therefore, to protect them in the best way that he could. Complications had arisen within the Community that rendered the task more difficult, but he completely disarmed the opposition from without by a graceful concession to public prejudice, and then prepared himself for consideration of the best plans that could be devised for the successful winding-up of the communistic experiment, — a winding-up which, in the very nature of things, had become inevitable."

[166] This was fully understood in the Community, and in the passage from Estlake, quoted in the immediately preceding note, is treated as intended. In winding up the Community, Noyes chose this method so as to obtain time and freedom for winding it up to the best advantage. Cf. Hinds, ed. 2, p. 205.

ence on the new " social platform " which he outlined for it, he was quickly undeceived. No celibacy for it! Before the close of the year " in addition to those cases in which there was a resumption of former marriage relations there were twenty marriages in the Community," and, the chronicler adds, " the work continued apace," and in a few years " scarcely half a dozen " remained unmarried.[167] And no more communism for it! The change here was scarcely more difficult to manage and was no less decisively carried through. By the end of the year 1880 all communistic features had been eliminated and the Community had become an ordinary joint-stock company, carrying on as such the large business enterprises which had been developed. Noyes himself, writing in 1885, enumerates for us the steps in the process by which his lifework was undone.[168] " On the 20th of August, 1879, I proposed that the practice of Complex Marriage be given up; on the 26th my proposition was adopted by the Community unanimously; on the 28th it was published to the world; and was received by the press generally with commendation. From that time the proposal of a general change from Communism to private ownership and joint-stock began to be agitated in the Oneida Community. It was discussed carefully and peaceably; and after sixteen months of study and preparation of details Communism of property was given up, as complex marriage had been before it, and on the 1st of January, 1881, the joint-stock company called the Oneida Community, Limited, took the place of the Oneida Community." There were naturally some in so large a community who regretted this final change and would fain have preserved, if not a completely communistic organization, yet as many communistic features in their organization as possible. But there seems to have been no doubt, either in the sentiment of the community at large or in the minds of their responsible leaders, that this was a case in which it is the first step that counts; and that the abandonment of " complex marriage " was in fact the abandonment of communism, and should be acted on as such.

[167] Hinds, ed. 2, p. 204.　　　　[168] *Ibid.*, p. 206.

In this they were undoubtedly right. It was in point of fact a part of their most intimate experience through a generation of communistic living that, while the obnoxious "mine" and "thine" continue valid in the most intimate relation of life, it is folly to speak of their abolition elsewhere. But though we may justly say that the experience of the Oneida Community provides an empirical demonstration of the theoretically obvious proposition that communism cannot exist apart from the aid of "complex marriage," with all its accompaniments and consequences, it by no means follows that permanency can be secured to it merely by this outrage on the deepest instincts of human nature. There are other instincts of human nature also which communism outrages, and on which all attempts to establish a communistic society must ultimately be wrecked. Property itself, for example, upon which communism makes its most immediate assault, is just as much a law of nature — or, let us say, a law of God — is just as much an ineradicable instinct of man — as marriage, with which it is indeed inextricably involved. Goldwin Smith, in an illuminating page,[169] instructs us to think of property not as an institution of human society, but as a fundamental condition of human life. "A state of things in which a man would not think that what he had made for himself was his own," he remarks, "is unknown to experience and beyond the range of our conceptions." The economical value of property may arise from the circumstance that it is "the only known motive power of production." But the right of property does not rest on this consideration of expediency, but is intrinsic in the individual's right to himself. This right he can never yield, and all attempts at communism, which are at bottom only attempts to deprive men of their ineradicable rights — to themselves and the fruits of their own activities — are bound to break to pieces in the end on these primeval instincts of the race. The persistence of the Oneida Community for a generation suggests nothing to the contrary. It was not a self-subsisting communistic state. Economically considered, it was

---

[169] "Essays on Questions of the Day," ed. 2, 1894, pp. 8 ff.

only a limited commercial association, pooling its earnings and living parasitically on the surrounding community. It not only recruited itself steadily from outside, but it depended wholly on the wider community in which it was encysted for all the necessities of living — police protection, social intercourse, trade distribution, peace, and opportunity to labor. More. It obtained the raw material for its industries from outside; it found the market for its product outside; it even came, as it grew prosperous, to draw a large part of its labor, by which its product was made, from outside. It became in fact, in principle only an employer-manufacturing concern, whose earnings were enjoyed in common by the owners, instead of divided, in this ratio or another, among them in severalty. When the time came to convert it into a joint-stock company, nothing could have been easier. Its six hundred thousand dollars of invested capital needed merely to be distributed equitably in stock among the owners, and the thing was done.

It was Noyes's contention that religion is the only foundation on which a stable communism can be reared. He does not seem to have been very exigent as to what the nature of this religion should be. The rôle which he assigned to it in his speculations [170] was to chasten and discipline the spirit for the hardships and restrictions demanded by community life. What has wrecked the communistic societies which have sprung up so luxuriantly in America has been largely, he says, the influx into them of idle, selfish, designing men. " General depravity," he says, is, according to the universal testimony of experience, " the villain of the whole story " — a truth much more profound than apparently he was intending to express. May it not be, he asks, that " the tests of earnest religion are just what are needed to keep a discrimination between the ' noble and lofty souls ' and the scamps? " The function he wished religion to serve, thus, was to act as a sieve to strain out the unfit — and a great variety of religions might serve this purpose if

[170] He has discussed the matter, e.g., in the forty-seventh chapter of his " History of American Socialisms," pp. 646–657.

only they were earnestly held. If a community could be formed
of earnestly religious men only, he thought, there might be
some hope of its members' living in harmony. He contended,
now, that these speculative views had been verified in practice.
Looking over the whole list of communistic experiments in
America he singles out those which have shown unusual
vitality. There are only eight of them; all the rest have quickly
died; these only have lived. And now, says Noyes,[171] " the one
feature which distinguishes these Communities from the transitory sort, is their religion; which in every case is of the
earnest kind which comes by recognized afflatus, and controls
all external arrangements." He wishes to draw the induction
that it is religion, and religion alone, which makes communism
possible.

Goldwin Smith, in criticism, remarks[172] that while it is true
that all the communities thus singled out by Noyes were religious, yet the list thus singled out does not include all the
communities which were religious. Others were religious too —
and died. And he might have added, had he written a little
later, that these eight have died too — for they are now all
dead, except the Shakers, who have become moribund, and
the Ephrata and Oneida communities, which survive only in
the changed form of joint-stock companies. Goldwin Smith
does add one other remark which is very much to the point.
All eight of Noyes's enduring communistic societies had one
other thing in common besides religion, though Noyes does
not note it. They all rejected marriage — " whereby," Smith
explains, " in the first place they are exempted from the dis-
uniting influence of the separate family; and in the second
place, they are enabled to accumulate wealth in a way which
would be impossible if they had children to maintain." Some
of them were strict celibates, and the others discouraged marriage; and it is much more probable that what enabled them
to endure longer than such experiments have ordinarily done
was this complete or partial elimination of the particular obstacle that stands most in the way of communistic practice,

[171] P. 655.   [172] " Essays on Questions of the Day," ed. 2, 1894, p. 372.

rather than their religion — except so far, of course, as it was from their religion that they derived the sanction for their misprision of marriage. It was this function, as we have seen, that Noyes assigned to religion in his own communistic experiment. He was insistent, no doubt, that putting first things first, religion was first with him. His communism was not mere communism standing on the "ordinary platform of communism." It was "Bible Communism," and as such very distinct from the communism, for example, of "the infidels and Owenites of twenty years ago." [173] God was a party to their communism. "Their doctrine is that of community, not merely or chiefly with each other, but with God." God as creator, is owner of all; every loyal citizen is joint-owner with God of all things.[174] But he was not content with laying such a general religious foundation as this for their structure. He shaped his religious teaching so as to provide a particular religious sanction precisely for that community in wives which he rightly saw was the prime essential to the stability of any communistic establishment.

[173] "Bible Communism," 1853, p. 83. [174] *Ibid.*, p. 11.

IV. THE DOCTRINE

It will be well for us to obtain some sort of a connected view of the religious system which Noyes taught, as a whole.[175] We have already had occasion to observe — what is obvious in itself and was very fully recognized by Noyes — that his religious system was determined by two fundamental doctrines. "The two corner-stones of doctrine, equally important, on which Communism rests," we read,[176] "are, the doctrine of Complete Regeneration, or Salvation from Sin, and the truth that the Second Coming of Christ, and the founding of his heavenly kingdom, took place 1800 years ago. The first furnishes the personal or experimental basis, the second, the historical and political." The former of these determining doctrines is unduly subordinated to the latter in the following enunciation of the "most important articles of faith" held by the Communists — no doubt because this statement is drawn up from the point of view of their social or "political" theories, and is printed in the opening pages of Noyes's formal exposition of those theories.[177] Nevertheless, the most of what was really effective in Noyes's faith appears in it, and it is worth quoting here for the pointed brevity of its enunciation of the elements of his faith with which it does deal: —

"We believe in the Bible as the text-book of the Spirit of truth; in Jesus Christ as the eternal Son of God; in the Apostles and Primitive church, as the exponents of the everlasting gospel. We believe that the Second Advent of Christ took place at the period of the destruction of Jerusalem; that at that time there was a primary resurrection and judgment in the spiritual world; that the

175 Noyes himself tells us ("History of American Socialisms," p. 616) that the "religious theory" of the Community is best read in "The Berean," 1847; and it emerges that the members of the Community looked upon "The Berean," as little less than an inspired book (see, e.g., Eastman, p. 50). There is an excellent account of Noyes's doctrinal system, derived from "The Berean," in *The New Englander*, vi. 1848, pp. 177–194, by J. P. Warren. A useful account of it will be found also in Eastman, pp. 309 ff.

176 "Hand-Book of the Oneida Community," 1867, p. 22.

177 "Bible Communism," 1853, p. 7.

final kingdom of God then began in the heavens; that the manifestation of that kingdom in the visible world is now approaching;
that its approach is ushering in the second and final resurrection
and judgment; that a Church on earth is now rising to meet the
approaching kingdom in the heavens, and to become its duplicate
and representative; that inspiration or open communication with
God and the heavens, involving perfect holiness, is the element of
connection between the church on earth and the church in the
heavens, and the power by which the kingdom of God is to be established and reign in the world."

There is no lack of comprehensive statements of Noyes's
faith. He was rather fond of framing series of articles of faith
or doctrinal theses. He prints, for example, in *The Witness* of
August 20, 1837, a full systematic statement of " What we
believe " in thirty-four articles, and again in *The Perfectionist*
of February 22, 1845, fifty " Theses of the Second Reformation." [178] Each of these fairly covers the whole ground of his
faith. We may, however, perhaps content ourselves, for such
a general glance over the entire system, with the shorter
series of articles printed in the preface to " The Berean." These
he speaks of as a " frank synopsis of the leading doctrines of
this book " — the book itself being *the* " religious book of the
Community," from which Noyes advises us " the religious
theories of the Community " may be best ascertained. A
polemic form is given these articles, and in each instance the
doctrine taught in the Community is set in its relations to the
teachings of other bodies. We omit that feature of them and
otherwise compress them; and so arrive at the following nine
heads of doctrine which may be thought fairly to comprise in
utmost brevity the system taught by Noyes. 1. God is not a
Trinity, but a Duality — Father and Son: these two are coeternal but not co-equal. This duality in the Godhead is
imaged in the twofold personality of the first man, who was
made male and female, and as Adam was to Eve, so is the

[178] These may both be read in Eastman, as cited, pp. 309 ff., 315 ff.; and the
former of them is printed in C. G. Finney, " Lectures on Systematic Theology," ii. 1847, pp. 167 ff.

Father to the Son. 2. God has foreordained all that comes to pass. Evil, however, was eternal, and hence does not fall under the divine foreordination. Its admission into God's creation, nevertheless, was foreordained; and this was done because it was necessary for the judgment and destruction of the uncreated evil. The foreordination of the reprobation of some men and the salvation of others rests on foresight of their divergent conduct. 3. In consequence of Adam's transgression all men are born under the spiritual power of Satan. But there are two essentially different classes of men. One class are of the very seed of Satan and in every sense depraved. The other class are only subjected to Satan's evil influence and therefore instinctively respond to the word of God when it comes to them. 4. The Atonement is not legal but spiritual. The death of Christ does not satisfy the demands of the law in the place of sinners. It perfects Christ in all human sympathies; destroys the spiritual power of the devil in whom all men are held captive by nature; and delivers those whom He thus wakes and releases from the condemning sin-occasioning power of the law. 5. The motives of the law and a change of purpose in the creature are necessary preparations for the second birth. But the second birth itself is a change not of purpose or acts, but of spiritual condition. It is a divorce of the human spirit from the power of Satan, and a junction of it with the Spirit of God. It is a progressive work, in the double effects of outward cleansing brought about by external moral and spiritual influences, and the inward quickening communicated by the life of Christ through faith. 6. "We agree with the most ultra class of Perfectionists, that whoever is born of God is altogether free from sin." But this complete freedom from sin is not ordinarily attained in the first stage of discipleship. Hence there is in the Church a class of persons called believers or disciples, but not "sons of God," and they are not yet free from sin. 7. Whoever is born of God will infallibly persevere in holiness unto salvation. But believers who are not yet "sons of God" may fall away. 8. Christ's Second Coming took place in connection with the destruction of Jerusa-

lem, at the end of the time of the Jews. At that time those
were judged who had been ripened for the harvest of history
by the Old Testament dispensation and the preaching of
Christ to the Gentiles. The formal judgment is yet to come,
at the end of the times of the Gentiles, bearing the same relation to the period in which we live as that former judgment
did to the precedent time. 9. Those that sow to the flesh shall
reap eternal punishment.

It is in the vague generality given to them in such brief
statements as this that Noyes's doctrines appear to their best
advantage. When taken up one by one and explicated in
their details, their combined grotesque crudity and reckless
extravagance are seen to pass all belief. He has not escaped
wholly from the hands of his teachers. Nathaniel W. Taylor
has given him the general method of his thinking; Moses
Stuart has built the piers on which he supports his dogmas;
the fanatical perfectionists of central and western New York
have supplied to him their fundamental content. But he has
rounded out the outline and filled in the chinks with material
derived from the most outlandish sources, giving to the whole
an aspect both fantastic and in the highest degree repellent.
He has been most influenced by the Shakers; or it would be
more correct to say that the whole formal nature of his system was borrowed from them. They taught, for instance, that
God is a dual person, male and female; that Adam was also
dual, having been made in God's image; that all angels and
spirits are also both male and female; and that the distinction
of sex in mankind is eternal, inhering in the soul itself. They
taught also that the Second Coming of Christ had already taken
place, that the Church has been apostate since the primitive
age and is only now, in themselves, being rebuilt; that the
Kingdom of heaven and the personal rule of God is now in
process of restoration; that the old law has been abolished;
and the direct intercourse between heaven and earth has been
renewed; that sinlessness of life is not only a possibility but an
obligation; that the use of marriage has ceased; and that
death itself has passed away and become only a change of

dress, a shedding of the visible robe of the flesh and assumption of the invisible glory of the spirit. To every one of these items of Shaker teaching Noyes presents a clear counterpart. Sometimes he simply takes the Shaker doctrine over just as he found it. More frequently he tried to fit it into his own personal lines of thinking. But even when he most alters it — as in his transformation of their celibacy into his promiscuity — the genetic connection is not wholly obscured. He has not contented himself, however, with borrowing from the Shakers. He has not disdained to pick up fragments of notions from what appears to have been his student's reading of the early history of the Church, and thus to embroider his doctrine with scraps of all sorts of outworn heresies. Thus, for example, he has thus given it especially the odd aspect of a revival of Gnostic Dualism.

The place which the dualistic principle takes in Noyes's theological constructions is nothing less than astonishing. We have seen that, following the Shakers, he conceives God as " a dual being, consisting of the Father and the Word," [179] and if he does not go on with the Shakers and proclaim Him flatly, in His duality, " male and female," he fails of this by the narrowest of margins. He speaks of the " law of duality " which is indicated in all nature and suggested by the creation of the first pair, and then of this law he declares that it " takes its rise from the constitution of God himself, who is dual — the Father and the Son — in whose image man was made, male and female, and of whose nature the whole creation is a reflection." [180] Nature being a reflection of the nature of God, we may of course learn what God's nature is from nature. " If we reason," says he,[181] " from the seen to the unseen, assuming that the essential nature of the effect is in the cause, we have proof as broad as the universe, that the Godhead is a duality; for every link of the chain of productive life, in its whole visible extent from the lowest region of the vegetable kingdom,

[179] *The Perfectionist,* February 22, 1845; Eastman, p. 315.
[180] " Bible Communism," 1853, p. 35.
[181] Eastman, pp. 324–325.

to the highest of the animal, is a duality. The distinction between male and female is as universal as vitality, and all visible evidence goes to prove that it is the indispensable condition of reproduction, i.e. of vital creation. If we find two elements in all the streams of life, why should we not infer that the same two elements are in the Fountain? " If this reasoning has any validity whatever, it proves not merely that there is a duality in the Divine Being, but that the duality takes the specific form of a differentiation into male and female. Accordingly we find Noyes saying: " We are led to the simple conclusion, that the uncreated Creator, the Head of the universe, like the head of mankind and the head of every family, though one, is yet ' twain ' (Mark x. 8); in a word, that the creation has a Father and a Mother." [182] And his formal confession of faith runs: [183] " We believe, not in the Trinity,[184] nor in the Unity, but in the *Duality* of the Godhead; and that Duality in our view, is imaged in the twofold personality of the first man, who was made ' male and female.' Gen. i. 27." He does, to be sure, add, " As Adam was to Eve, so is the Father to the Son; i.e. he is the same in nature, but greater in power and glory "; and this can hardly be understood otherwise than as confining the difference between the Father and Son substantially to one of "power and glory." And, elsewhere, he certainly argues at considerable length for this general idea.[185] Perhaps his most lucid explanation of his meaning, however, is conveyed in the following extended sentence: [186] " I do regard the Father and the Son, as two *Spirits,* who bear a similar *social* (not *physical*) relation to each other as that which exists between man and woman, one of whom is greater than the other, (as the man is greater than the woman) who love each other and have pleasure in their fellowship, (as man and woman love and have pleasure in spiritual fellowship) who

[182] *Ibid.*, p. 324.
[183] " The Berean," p. v.; Eastman, p. 325.
[184] The Holy Spirit, he says (" The Berean," p. 79), is not a " distinct person " but " an emanation " from the Father and the Son.
[185] " The Berean," p. 488; *The New Englander,* as cited, p. 180.
[186] Eastman, p. 325.

are the joint parents of all created things, (as man and woman
are the joint parents of their offspring) who are thus the prototype in whose image Adam and Eve were made." If this,
however, be all that Noyes means, there certainly is less in his
conclusion than in his premises.

If the sexual distinction in God may be understood, however, only of a differentiation in Him of those spiritual qualities
and modes of action which we associate with the two sexes
as known to us among men, the same cannot be said of any
other living beings. All other living beings besides God are
veritably male and female. This is true, for example, of the
angels. " I confess," writes Noyes,[187] " I see nothing very horrible in the idea of there being sexual distinction in the angelic
race. If the distinction of *spirits,* the twofold life, which I have
described in what I have said of God, exists in the angelic
nature, (as I believe it exists in every living thing, from God
to the lowest vegetable,) I see no very alarming reason why
that distinction should not be expressed in the bodily form
of angels as well as men." Of course this involves the assignment of a corporeal nature to angels, and this Noyes does
without hesitation, and then proceeds to interpret Gen. vi. 1,
2, Jude 6 f., of carnal sinning on their part. Not only does sex
distinction thus exist in the angels, it persists also in the disembodied souls of men. The human soul is not in Noyes's view,
however, pure spirit — which itself is thought of by him after
the analogy of what he calls " fluids," that is to say the " imponderable fluids " of the old physicists — electricity, galvan-
ism, magnetism, light, heat — and therefore at least after a
material image. It is the product of the union of this spirit, of
the increate spirit which is the breath of God, and the dust
of the ground. It is thus, he says,[188] " a *modification* of spirit,
produced by union with a material body." It takes the form
of the body and its size and parts; and receives into itself some
of the properties of matter. " As Adam's body was spiritualized
matter, so conversely Adam's soul was *materialized spirit.*"
The soul thus stands between spirit and matter. The materiali-

[187] Eastman, p. 332.   [188] " The Berean," p. 57.

zation of the spirit in the soul gives it its individuality and immortality. Had it not been thus materialized, on the release
of the spirit from the body, it would return to the abyss of
life whence it came: but it has entered in the soul into a
"materialized or partially indurated state," and so persists in
separation from the body. On the other hand, as the whole
nature of God is in " the breath of God," the spirit which enters
into the composition of the soul of man is still "in communication with God, and assimilated to him."

This dualism of sex, characterizing the mode of existence
of all animal being, is, however, far from the whole of the dualism which Noyes teaches. Beneath it he discovers an underlying ontological dualism, according to which an Eternal God
stands over against an eternal matter. And side by side with
this (not identical with it) he discovers yet another eternal
dualism, an ethical dualism dividing the realms of spirit itself
between the principle of good (which is God) and the principle of evil (which is the devil). Creation with him is not
ex nihilo, but out of preëxistent uncreated material; and if
we ask him whence this material came, he claims the right to
reply by another question — Whence did God come? [189] All
creation, however — if we can speak of creation when nothing
is really originated — is from God: it is not parcelled out between God and the devil. Not that sin or death originated "in
God, or in any of his works"; or that God has "by creation,
by decree, or by permission given birth to" evil. *" The ultimate cause of all evil is an uncreated evil being; as the
ultimate cause of all good is an uncreated good being."* [190] But
evil enters the realm of created being subsequently to its creation, God permitting it so to enter into His creation because
only in this field can He grapple with it and destroy it — an

[189] "The Berean," p. 93. It is a crotchet in his doctrine of creation that
he teaches, on the ground of Heb. xi. 3, that it was wrought by faith on God's
part. His motive for this impossible interpretation of the passage was apparently to escape having to allow that "we understand by faith." It is amazing
that Thomas C. Upham repeats this absurd exegesis of Heb. xi. 3 ("A Treatise
on Divine Union," 1857, pp. 32 ff.).

[190] "The Berean," pp. 97 ff.

authentic Manichæan trait.[191] By his fall Adam, who was a
creature of God, came under a divided dominion. " The streams
from the two eternal fountains flowed together in him. His
spiritual nature was primarily good, as proceeding from God;
but secondarily evil, as pervaded by the Devil." It seems,
however, that though propagating his offspring in his own
likeness, the two elements of " his compound character " were
distributed unevenly among them. God and the devil strove
for mastery over them, and the result was two distinct classes
of men, in one of which good, in the other evil, predominates.

" As the offspring of Adam's body was twofold, distinguished into
male and female, part following the nature of the primary, and
part the nature of the secondary parent; so the offspring of his
spiritual nature was twofold, distinguished like that nature, into
good and evil, part following the character of the primary and part
the character of the secondary spiritual element. In other words,
Adam has two sorts of spiritual children — one of them like himself, primarily of God and secondarily of the Devil, of whom Abel
was a specimen; the other, primarily of the Devil and secondarily
of God, of whom Cain was a specimen. Thus mankind are divided
spiritually into two classes of different original characters, proceeding respectively from uncreated good and evil. . . . The depravity
of mankind, then, is of two sorts. The seed of the woman are depraved, as Adam was after the fall, — not in their original individual spirits which are of God, but by their spiritual combination
with and subjection to the Devil." " On the other hand, the seed
of the serpent are depraved as Cain was, — not only by combination
with and subjection to the Devil, but by original spiritual identity
with him. They are not only possessed of the Devil, but are *radically*
DEVILS THEMSELVES." [192]

There are thus two radically different kinds of men in the world,
differing by nature, not by grace, and by their natural difference determining the difference which they manifest under

[191] In struggling with his incomplete theodicy Noyes sometimes speaks
of a necessity being laid on God " by the existence of uncreated evil " to permit evil to invade His creation. He does nothing to show in what such a
necessity is grounded, however, except by pointing to the exigencies of the
conflict between good and evil.

[192] " The Berean," pp. 104 f.

grace. To put it shortly, the one kind of man is accessible to grace, the other intrinsically inaccessible to it. " There is an *original difference* in the characters of men — a difference which is not produced by the gospel, but which exists before the gospel is heard, and is in fact the cause of the different consequences resulting from the gospel in different persons." [193] The gospel no doubt is presented to all alike, but there are some who *cannot* receive it, while others are so far " honest and good " that the Word, when it comes to them, is gladly received. They are "not *saved* by nature, but they are *adapted* by nature to be saved by grace." [194] " Human nature," says Noyes, reverting as is his wont to sexual imagery, " is a female which conceives and brings forth sin or righteousness, according as it has Satan or God for its husband " [195] — which is only a lame figure by which he means to say that those men who are in the deepest depths of their nature of God are " saved," those who are in the deepest depths of their nature of the devil are " lost." God, being a prudent person, does not attempt to save those who are by their very nature lost. The gospel, which is sent indiscriminately into the world, reaches them, of course, as well as others — though only to manifest, by its rejection, their real character. But in all the hidden operations of His Grace He confines Himself to those who are salvable, electing them to " salvation " and reprobating those whom He knows in His infinite foreknowledge to be inaccessible to His saving operations, to eternal misery.[196]

With this ontology behind him, Noyes's soteriology naturally takes the form fundamentally of the destruction of the evil principle in the world. Christ came primarily to destroy the devil, and to deliver those who have been taken captive by him from his domination — that is to say, those of them who are capable of this deliverance. He does not bear our sins; He delivers us from sin. It is Satan, not He, who bears our sins. " The penalty of all sin is actually inflicted on the devil, who is actually the author of it. Here is no evasion — no substitu-

[193] *Ibid.*, p. 112.   [195] *Ibid.*, p. 115.
[194] *Ibid.*, p. 113.   [196] *Ibid.*, pp. 106 f.

tion of an innocent person for the offender. The law has its
course. Man is saved, not because God abrogates the law or
evades it by a fiction, but because he rightfully imputes the
sins of which men are the instruments, to the devil, as their
real author." [197] If it be the devil, however, who expiates our
sins, it is Christ who delivers us from them. He does this by
entering by incarnation the very sphere in which sin reigns
and bringing there " the strength of the Godhead " " into immediate contact with the strength of the devil, in the very
field which was to be won." A twofold effect was sought and
was obtained. On the negative side men were to be freed from
the dominion of the devil; on the positive, they were to be
effectively united with God. In the place of the devil, God was
to be brought into immediate control of their lives. In order
to accomplish this double work Christ required not only to
enter this world of living men but to follow men into the world
of the dead where Satan " had his sanctuary." Here His saving
work culminated. For " the death of Christ was . . . a *spiritual* baptism into the devil, of which the corporeal crucifixion
was only an index and consummation." [198] Or more fully
stated: " Jesus Christ, by his death, entered into the vitals of
the devil, and overcame him. He thus destroyed the central
cause of sin. The effect of this act on them that believe, is to
release them from the power of sin; and on them that believe
not, to consign them with the devil to destruction." [199] Everything depends on faith; for faith is the vehicle by which Christ
— not merely the word of Christ, but Christ Himself — is received into the soul. No doubt, this reception of Christ is
mediated by the word, but the word is no mere series of sounds.
" It is a fact well known to spiritualists, that the word of every
spiritual being is an actual substance, sent forth from his inward center, carrying with it the properties of his life. It is
also a known fact that the act of believing actually receives
into the soul and spirit, the substance conveyed in the word
believed. So that communication by word from one person to
another, effects an actual junction of spirits, and conveys to

[197] " The Berean," pp. 127–128.   [198] *Ibid.*, pp. 122–123.   [199] *Ibid.*, p. 129.

the receiver a portion of the life and character of the communicator." [200] Thus by believing, we receive Christ, His
" flesh and blood " — which does not mean His material body,
but " a spiritual substance of which his material body was but
the envelope " — His " soul and spirit," belonging to " his
preëxistent state," " a spiritual body and a life within it." Receiving this, " the believer becomes a son of God and partaker
of the eternal life of the Father." Our salvation shows itself
in four great benefits which we enjoy: salvation from all sin;
security from all future sin; deliverance from external law;
independence of all human teaching. We have become one
with Christ, and thereby are freed from the evil one, and these
things are the mark of our emancipation. " We . . . say,"
says Noyes,[201] " none are, or have been, *Christians,* in the sense
in which Paul was (if his state corresponded to his preaching,)
who have not received PERFECT HOLINESS, PERFECT SECURITY,
PERFECT LIBERTY, AND PERFECT INDEPENDENCE, BY THE BLOOD
OF CHRIST."

" Holiness," says Noyes,[202] is " the principal object of the
atonement." Forgiveness is first in the order of time, but is
only a means to the end of purification. " Dividing salvation
into two great parts, viz., forgiveness of past sin, and purification from present sin, it is plainly implied in nearly all the
declarations of the Bible touching the subject, that the latter
part is the *primary,* and the former the *secondary* object of
the work of Christ." [203] There is a sense, of course, in which
such a statement might be accepted as substantially true: it is
intended here, however, in the sense in which it is the common
declaration of all perfectionists, and has as its end to convey
the idea that enjoyment of the salvation from sin wrought
out by Christ is just immediate entrance into a perfectly holy
state. Noyes does not hold, to be sure, this proposition to be
universally true. The Old Testament saints, for example, he
teaches, did not receive their salvation until the coming of
Christ; they lived not in fruition but in hope: they had not

200 *Ibid.,* p. 136.
201 *Ibid.,* p. 149.
202 *Ibid.*
203 *Ibid.,* p. 150.

yet been born of God (Christ was the first-born Son of God), but were only *heirs* of a future Sonship — only prospectively children, experimentally merely servants. When Christ came, they received their perfect holiness — both those in this and those in the spiritual world together. The disciples of Christ and apostolic believers, similarly, did not receive their salvation until the Second Coming of Christ — which took place, according to Noyes, in A.D. 70.[204] Hence the sins of Old Testament saints, disciples of Christ, apostolic believers are irrelevant as objections against the assertion that perfection is essential to the experience of salvation: we need not look for perfect men until after the Second Coming (A.D. 70).[205] Somewhat inconsistently, however, a good deal of space is given to proving that Paul was perfect.[206] Of course Noyes begins by setting aside Rom. vii. 14 ff., Phil. iii. 12 ff., I Cor. ix. 27 — this passage no doubt, rightly — II Cor. xii. 7, I Tim. i. 15, and ends with Paul's assertions of his own integrity. Ritschl could not have done it better. There are visible in the apostolic church, he says in explanation, " *two distinct classes of believers,*" immature and mature (I Cor. ii. 6), and the mature, of whom Paul was one, were " perfectly *holy.*" This class grew in number and distinctness, " till at last, when John wrote his epistles, Perfectionism was fully developed, and had become the acknowledged standard of Christian experience." Quoting the passages in I John which are ordinarily relied on in this sense, he comments: [207] " If this is not Perfectionism, we know not how, by

---

[204] " The second coming," says Noyes (" The Berean," p. 288), " was an event *in the spiritual, and not in the natural world.*" It was a spiritual manifestation " (" Paul's Prize," p. 10). It means Christ's " coming in the power of judgment, *to reckon with, reward, and punish, those to whom he delivered the gospel at his first coming* " (" The Berean," p. 276). It is the " *day of judgment for the primitive church and the Jewish nation* " — not the final judgment, for there are two judgments corresponding to the two great human families, Jews and Gentiles. " The Bible describes *two* dispensations of Christ, *two* resurrections, *two* judgments, one of which is past, the other future " (p. 333). The common view, he says, sees only the future judgment; many perfectionists see only the past.

[205] " The Berean," p. 157.

[206] *Ibid.*, pp. 162 ff.

[207] *Ibid.*, p. 159.

any human language, Perfectionism can be expressed." There is left, he admits, "one little text" (I John i. 8) — but when rightly understood this does not run athwart the others; it refers to pre-perfection sins. "We think it not uncharitable to say," he remarks, "that they who persist in construing this verse as opposed to the doctrine of salvation from sin, and in regarding it as sufficient to offset all the plain assertions, scattered through the whole epistle, that perfect holiness is the only standard of true Christianity, belong to that class of persons who 'strain at a gnat, and swallow a camel.'"

It would be hoping too much to expect that Noyes could wholly escape the universal tendency of perfectionists to explain the perfection which they assert as something less than perfect. When answering objections to his doctrine,[208] he tells us, for example, that to be perfectly holy is not necessarily to be free from infirmity. "We mean by perfect holiness," he says — adding, "using the expression in its lowest sense," — "simply that *purity of heart* which gives *a good conscience.*" This is a very ambiguous statement. Doubtless, taken strictly, the purity of heart which gives a good conscience is an absolutely pure heart — or else the conscience fails to accuse when accusation were fitting. But employing the language in its current meaning, something very far from perfect purity may be expressed by it. And that Noyes is employing the language in this lowered meaning an illustration he adduces in connection with it sufficiently proves. This is not, however, his ordinary manner of speaking of the perfection he asserts. It is rather characteristic of him to carry it to the height of its idea. In one passage,[209] for example, he expounds I John iii. 3–10 with a view to showing from the declaration, "he that committeth sin is of the devil," that the real Christian never sins at all, seeing that one sin is enough to manifest an essentially devilish character. When asked "how much men may sin and yet be Christians," he says: John answers that "men cannot sin at all and be Christians." There is no middle ground: we are "either as righteous as Christ or as wicked as the devil."

[208] *Ibid.*, pp. 170 f.   [209] *Ibid.*, pp. 182 ff.

"The children of God are perfectly holy. Sin, in every case, proves the subjects of it children of the devil." [210] John does not say, " He that committeth sin *habitually* is of the devil "; or, " He that committeth *known* sin is of the devil "; or, " He that committeth *wilful* sin is of the devil "; or, " He that committeth sin is of the devil *while committing sin.*" He says, " He that committeth sin is of the devil "; and we are to take the word of God just as it stands. " James spoke good philosophy when he said, ' He that offendeth in one point, is guilty of all.' " [211]

This insistence on the perfection of perfection is not only the usual view which Noyes expresses, but it is the natural, or rather the necessary, one for him to take, on the ground of his mystical doctrine of the procuring cause of our perfection of life which we have already seen him expounding. " Christ liveth in me " — it is all summed up in that. " The necessary consequence of that condition," he says,[212] " is perfect holiness, because Christ is perfectly holy." It belongs to the fundamental elements of his doctrine of salvation, that Christ has " destroyed the devil," and secured to God — to Himself as the saving God — the entire control of the children of the woman, hitherto living under the divided rule of God and the devil. That is what salvation consists in; and that is the reason that salvation is in the complete meaning of these words, salvation from sin. It is possible that Noyes is not quite consistent with himself, however, when he seeks to answer the question: " How is this union, by which Christ dwells in the soul, and so saves it from sin, to be effected? " At the place at the moment before us, he replies, as we have already seen him elaborately arguing elsewhere, " The witnesses of the New Testament answer with one voice — BY BELIEVING THE GOSPEL." [213] His prepossession at the moment, however, is to show that this faith is not exercised in our own strength, but is the gift of God. It is " an act of the heart of man, possible to all, and in the highest degree obligatory on all, but actually existing only where God

<hr>

210 " The Berean," p. 184.   212 *Ibid.,* p. 173.
211 *Ibid.,* p. 187.   213 *Ibid.*

in his sovereign mercy gives special grace." " He has forgiven all, and sent the Spirit of grace to all, and so has left all utterly without excuse for remaining unreconciled; but he has given *faith* only to them whom he chose in Jesus Christ before the world began." [214] It may be this teaching which he has in mind when he protests against Dixon's representation [215] of his doctrine of how we arrive at salvation from sin. Dixon says in effect that he teaches that we have only to believe, and it is done. In the passages that have been before us Noyes apparently teaches just that. But he also teaches that we do not acquire holiness directly by faith; but it as well as faith is a gift of God.

For Noyes, like other perfectionists, has a first and a second conversion. [216] Only he does not make the second a mere repetition of the first, seeking an additional blessing. It is a radically different transaction. The first is " an action or purpose of our own," " a voluntary movement." The second is an effect wrought on us. We do the one; we suffer the other. The one is " proximately our own work "; the second, " the operation of God." By the first we become disciples; by the second the children of God. It is only by the second that we receive " deliverance from all sin ": and on this teaching it is quite true that we do not merely have to believe — and it is done. Deliverance from sin is a gift of God, given to none but believers, it is true, but not acquired by faith. The inevitable question is, of course, raised whether it is imperative that these two stages in the process of salvation from sin must be traversed, or we may pass " from a state of irreligion " directly to " perfect holiness." [217] The reply is that it is at least " a *general* principle " that " men by their first conversion are introduced to sinful discipleship," and " reach perfect holiness only by a second conversion." But it is added that the facts seem to require the admission " that some have passed directly from irreligion to perfect holiness." This is translated in a new paragraph into the explanation that while in the order of nature a twofold process is necessary, the interval may be shortened so that to all in-

[214] *Ibid.*, p. 176.
[215] " New America," ii. p. 227.
[216] " The Berean," pp. 237 ff.
[217] *Ibid.*, p. 238, note.

tents and purposes no time intervenes. And it may be, it is
added, that after a while this may become the regular experience. The height of the perfection thus secured, we must remind ourselves, is manifested not only in its completeness
according to its idea, but also in its indefectibility. It is Noyes's
constant teaching — a teaching by which he differentiates his
perfectionism from that of others — that perfection once secured is secure. Thus, for example, writing of the New Covenant,[218] he tells us that, first it secures salvation from sin,
interpreting this as "perfect sanctification," and then secondly, "it secures salvation from sin forever" — adding
further that this is really to speak repetitiously, "for salvation
from sin, in the proper signification of the expression, is salvation from sin forever." It is the characteristic of the new
covenant, he says, that God secures the fulfillment of its
requirements — disposing men's hearts to fulfill them.

The second conversion is coincident — or rather is identical — with the second birth; by the one as by the other we
are said to become the children of God and free from all sin.[219]
To become sons of God by this new birth means just what
is meant by being united with Christ, as we have already seen
that idea expounded. It is, now, Christ that lives in us, and
it is no more we that live: all that we do He does through us,
and thus our total life manifestation perfectly corresponds
with His will. We are, as in this view we must be, just as perfect as Christ is. And of course we are just as spontaneous in
our holy activities as He is. As it is absurd to suppose Him
governed in His conduct by the precepts of an external law, so
it is absurd to suppose us, His children, and the organs of His
activities, to require or to be subject to an external law. The
children of Christ, just because they are perfectly holy and
perfectly secure in their holiness, are also emancipated from
the law and need not that any should teach them. Of themselves they do that which is right. Noyes naturally desires not

[218] " The Berean," pp. 142 ff.
[219] *Ibid.*, p. 226, e.g., the second birth is said to be a state of complete
salvation from sin.

to be thought of as an antinomian. It is not antinomianism
that he teaches, he says,[220] but "anti-legality." He believes
that the law — the whole law, moral as well as ceremonial —
has been abolished for the sons of God. But this does not mean
that we have escaped beyond the government of God; it
means only that the instrument through which He governs
us has been changed — from law to grace. He even says that
the "standard of holiness" which constitutes "the ultimate
object of God's government" has suffered no alteration. Only
"the measures which God chooses to employ to effect that
object" have been changed. The children of God neglect law
not because they desire to be free to sin; but precisely because
they have no desire to sin and do not require law to restrain
them from it. It is the way of holiness, not of sin, that they
pursue; and they pursue it because it has become their second
nature and they cannot do otherwise. They do not transgress
the law but have transcended it. They are not seeking "an
easy method of escaping the necessity of works," but have
found "the only and the sure foundation of such works as will
survive the fire of judgment."[221]

Now, Noyes says,[222] "regeneration or salvation from sin,"
that is perfection, "is the incipient stage of the resurrection."
We are married to Christ, he reasons,[223] and the status of the
wife, of course, follows that of the husband: since Christ has
risen from the dead, we therefore are living the resurrected
life. We have passed from the carnal into the resurrection
state; from this world into the heavenly world; our "state
and relations are as fully changed, as the idea of a translation
from earth to heaven demands." "Believers by fellowship
with Christ in his resurrection, are released from the beggarly
elements and carnal ordinances of that worldly sanctuary
which they have left." We are freed, then, from sin; and we are
freed from the law — for law "cannot carry its claims beyond

[220] *Ibid.*, p. 218.
[221] *Ibid.*, p. 178.
[222] "History of American Socialisms," p. 622, resuming "The Berean,"
p. 383.
[223] "The Berean," p. 255.

death "; and we are freed, indeed, even from death itself —
at first, from its sting, but not its form, since men were so far
within the territory of him that has the power of death that
they are slow to escape from its form; but this too is coming.
" The intent of the Gospel," we are told in another place,[224]
" was, and is, to take people out of this world into a state beyond death, in which the believer is spiritually with Christ in
the resurrection, and hence is free from sin and law, and all
the temporary relations of the mortal state." The church has
its " standing " therefore now " in a posthumous state "; a
posthumous state which may also be called " the angelic
state." In this angelic state, as is natural, different conditions
obtain from those of the carnal state in which we have hitherto
lived, and " free social relations are to be inaugurated as soon as
existing obligations can be disposed of."

When he wrote these words, Noyes was thinking of the
abolition of marriage in the " resurrection " or " angelic " state,
in accordance with Matt. xxii. 23-30, which he absurdly reads
as the proclamation of the reign of promiscuity in this state,[225]
thus throwing a lurid light on his contention that the abolishment of the law in the resurrection state is not that evil may
be done, but that good may be done spontaneously. In this
case at least the law is simply reversed and made to read, Thou
shalt have thy neighbor's wife. It is not, however, merely
a relaxation of morals which Noyes finds in the " resurrected "
state. He finds in it also, as has been already incidentally
noted, nothing less than " the abolition of death " itself —
although he recognizes that this is to come " as the last result
of Christ's victory over sin and the Devil." [226] And it is to be
noted that it is precisely through the abolition of marriage
— that is to say, the institution of promiscuity in the relations of the sexes — that the abolition of death is to come.
" Death is to be abolished, and . . . to this end, there must be
a restoration of true relations between the Sexes." [227] When

[224] " Bible Communism," 1853, pp. 75 ff.
[225] *Ibid.*, pp. 26 ff.
[226] " History of American Socialisms," p. 623.
[227] *Ibid.*, p. 629, summarizing " Bible Communism."

what he has to say on this point is weighed, the underlying
meaning appears to be that sexual promiscuity is absolutely
essential to the existence of a communistic society, and the
abolition of death is to result from the removal in a communistic society of the wearing evils which in the present mode
of social organization bring men to exhaustion and death.[228]
Remove these evils which kill man, and man will cease to die.
Communism, that is, is conceived as so great a panacea that
it not only cures all the evils of life, but brings also immortality; and there seems to be no reason for a man to die in a
communistic society. Running through the four great evils in
which he sums up the curses which afflict life in our present
social organization, Noyes says: " First we abolish sin " — that
is by entering through faith into a perfect life; " then shame "
— that is by practicing free love; " then the curse on woman of
exhausting child-bearing " — that is by using his recipe for
birth control; " then the curse on man of exhausting labor "
— that is through community labor, in the attractive association of the sexes; " and so we arrive regularly at the tree of
life." All " the antecedents of death " are removed; and so, of
course, death itself. " Reconciliation with God opens the way
for the reconciliation of the sexes. Reconciliation of the sexes
emancipates woman, and opens the way for vital society.
Vital society increases strength, diminishes work, and makes
labor attractive, thus removing the antecedents of death."
Perfectionism, free love, community in industry in happy association — take these things and you will not die. At the bottom
lies nothing other than the amazing assumption that communistic association, if you can only achieve it, will bring
immortality. All the other steps are only the means to communism.

We have permitted ourselves to be drawn aside from the
purely theological aspects of this matter by Noyes's own later
mode of speaking of it. His doctrine of the abolition of death
dates, however, from the spring of 1834, the period when he
formed his theological system; and he wrote of it frequently

---

[228] " History of American Socialisms," p. 636.

before he became engrossed in the actual experiment of communism. He gives us a full account of the origin of it in his mind in an article written in 1844.[229] On one occasion, he says, when he sat down to write, his mind wandered off to the subject of the resurrection. He explains: — " The gospel which I had received and preached was based on the idea that faith identifies the soul with Christ, so that by his death and resurrection the believer dies and rises again, not literally, nor yet figuratively, but *spiritually;* and thus, so far as sin is concerned, is placed beyond the grave, in ' heavenly places ' with Christ." This was the doctrine of the " New York Perfectionists," and, carrying it beyond its application to the cessation of sin, they derived from it their notion of " spiritual wives " as Noyes was just at this moment deducing from it his notion of sexual promiscuity. But Noyes continues: " I now began to think that I had given this idea but half its legitimate scope. I had availed myself of it for the salvation of my *soul.* Why should it not be carried out to the redemption of the *body?* . . . The question came home with imperative force — ' Why ought I not to avail myself of Christ's resurrection *fully,* and by it overcome death as well as sin? ' . . . I sought that identity with Christ by which I might realize his emancipation from death, as well for my body as for my soul; that I might with him, see death behind me — the ' debt of nature ' paid. What I sought I obtained." He plays a little with the difference between " deliverance from the spiritual power of death," and from " the act of dying." He will not affirm that he will " never die." But he asks, Why should he die? And he asserts that he is " not a debtor to the devil even in regard to the form of dying." And " this I know," he says, " that if I live till the kingdom of God comes, which I believe is near, I shall never die in fact or in form." This was written in September, 1844; and on June 1, 1847, it was solemnly declared by Noyes and his whole community, by unanimous resolution " as the confession and testimony of the believers assembled," precisely

---

[229] *The Perfectionist* of September 7, 1844, quoted by Eastman, pp. 343 ff. Eastman gives a very full account of Noyes's teaching on the subject.

" that the Kingdom of God had come." After that they were not to die.

The confidence of the possession of a deathless life, thus expressed, is grounded on a purely spiritual experience. The anticipation elaborately argued a generation later that the practice of communism would confer immortality on men, is drawn chiefly from materialistic considerations. Must we see in this difference an index of the downward growth through the years? Fantastic always, fanatic always, must we say of Noyes — he once was religious; now he is secularized? No doubt this was the direction of his growth. But there is a form of religion which is worse than any secularism: men's religions are often their worst crimes. And there are forms of secularism which approach religion in their nobility — though Noyes's secularism can hardly find a place among them. These are the salient facts to keep well in mind: All that was salacious in his secularism, Noyes found a sanction for in his religion; and all that was bad in his religion was already in it in 1834. We cannot think there ever was a time when Noyes's influence was wholesome, or when it was creditable to his associates that they had attached themselves to him or found profit or pleasure in his teachings. That he did not draw men of light and leading to him causes us no surprise. What astonishes us is that men like Charles H. Weld and James Boyle were temporarily associated with him; and that even a William Lloyd Garrison found in him something to admire and imitate. A fact so remarkable ought not to be passed by without remark.[230]

Garrison appears to have been familiar with Noyes's Perfectionist movement and an admiring reader of his journal practically from its beginning. Personal acquaintance was instituted when Noyes called on him at the anti-slavery office at Boston in March, 1837. In describing the interview, Noyes

[230] For what follows we have drawn on the detailed narrative of " William Lloyd Garrison: The Story of His Life told by his Children," ii., iii. 1885, 1889. The passages drawn upon may be easily turned up from the excellent indices. The narrative is fully documented and the references given. A brief summary account will be found in Goldwin Smith's " The Moral Crusader, William Lloyd Garrison," 1892, chapter ix.

says that he "found Garrison, Stanton, Whittier, and other leading abolitionists warmly engaged in a dispute about political matters." " I heard them quietly," he continues, " and when the meeting broke up I introduced myself to Garrison. He spoke with interest of the *Perfectionist;* said his mind was heaving on the subject of Holiness and the Kingdom of Heaven, and he would devote himself to them as soon as he could get anti-slavery off his hands. I spoke to him especially on the subject of government, and found him, as I expected, ripe for the loyalty of heaven." Noyes was not the man to fail to strike such iron when it was hot. He at once addressed Garrison a letter in which he sought to push home whatever advantage he had gained in the interview. In this letter he announced his emancipation from " all allegiance to the government of the United States," and declared war upon it — " a country which, by its boasting hypocrisy," he said, " has become the laughing-stock of the world, and by its lawlessness has fully proved the incapacity of man for self-government." " My hope of the millennium," he declared, " begins where Dr. Beecher's expires — *viz., at the overthrow of this nation.*" The times seemed to him to be ripening to the issue; which would come in a " convulsion like that of France." He calls therefore on the abolitionists to " abandon a government whose President has declared war upon them." Then turning to the special fish he wished to fry, he adds: — " Allow me to suggest that you will set Anti-slavery in the sunshine only by making it tributary to Holiness; and you will most assuredly throw it into the shade which now covers Colonization if you suffer it to occupy the ground, in your own mind or in others', which ought to be occupied by *universal emancipation from sin.* . . . I counsel you, and the people that are with you, if you love the post of honor — the forefront of the hottest battle of righteousness — to set your face toward *perfect* holiness. Your station is one that gives you power over the nations. Your city is on a high hill. If you plant the standard of perfect holiness where you stand, many will see and flow to it."

That Garrison should have been affected by this empty

rhetoric is astonishing; but he was, deeply and lastingly. Noyes's phrases and representations lingered in his memory: he quoted from them publicly, and publicly spoke of their author as " an esteemed friend," whose words had " deeply affected his mind." He even made Noyes's anti-government and perfectionist ideas his own. No wonder that the soberer friends of the anti-slavery agitation took alarm and sought to dissociate the movement from what were, and were likely to be, Garrison's personal vagaries. And little wonder that those who already were full of outrage at Garrison's " ultraisms," attributed to him this further " ultraism " — his friend and mentor's doctrine of sexual promiscuity. In doing this they were happily wrong. Garrison's infatuation for Noyes had limits, and did not carry him into this cesspool. He repudiated the imputation with passion, and was led, in the end, to explain that his perfectionism was not the perfectionism of Noyes, but that of Asa Mahan, whose book on the " Scripture Doctrine of Christian Perfection " was opportunely published in 1839. He permits to appear in *The Liberator* in December, 1839, a communication in which it is said of him: " But some say he is a Perfectionist, and believes that, let him do what he will, it is no sin. — That is false. His views on the subject of holiness are in unison with those of Mr. Mahan." That is to say, although asserting the attainability of perfection in this life, and the duty of all to attain it, he did not advance with Noyes to antinomian contentions. " If," says he, writing in self-defense in 1841, " what we have heard of the sayings and doings of the perfectionists, especially those residing in Vermont, be true, they have certainly turned the grace of God into lasciviousness, and given themselves over to a reprobate mind." But, he adds, " whatever may be the conduct of these perfectionists, the duty which they enjoin, of ceasing from all iniquity, at once and forever, is certainly what God requires, and what cannot be denied without extreme hardihood or profligacy of spirit. It is reasonable, and therefore atttainable. If men cannot help sinning, then they are not guilty in attempting to serve two masters. If they can, then it cannot be a dangerous doctrine to preach; and he is a rebel against the government of God who advocates an opposite doctrine." Thus, although Noyes contributed to that great accumulation of "ultraistic" notions which filled Garrison's mind, he could not attach him to his "sect." It is not without its interest, meanwhile, to find Garrison among the perfectionists, and indeed, to tell the whole truth, vigorously engaged in the perfectionist propaganda. It might almost be said that there was no "ultraism" current in his day which he did not in some measure embrace.[231]

[231] Noyes made the freest possible use of the press for the exposition and propagation of his theories. He maintained a periodical practically continuously from the beginning to the end of his career. This periodical bore successively the following titles: *The Perfectionist*, 1834; *The Witness*, 1836–1843; *The Perfectionist*, 1843–1846; *The Spiritual Magazine*, 1847–1850; *The Free Church Circular*, 1850–1851; *The Circular*, 1851–1871; *The Oneida Circular*, 1871–1874; *The American Socialist*, from 1875. Of separate publications emanating from the Community, the following, most of them from the pen of Noyes himself, have met our eye: — "Paul Not Carnal, or Christianity Full Redemption from Sin, exhibited in an exposition of Romans viii. 7–25," 1834; "The Way of Holiness," a Series of Papers published in *The Perfectionist*, 1838; "Salvation from Sin, the End of Christian Faith," edition seen, 1876, but often before; "The Berean: a Manual for the Help of those who Seek the Faith of the Primitive Church," 1847; "Confessions of John H. Noyes, Part First, or a Confession of Religious Experience," 1849; "First Annual Report of the Oneida Association," 1849; "Second Annual Report of the Oneida Association," 1850; "Third Annual Report of the Oneida Association," 1851; "Bible Communism; a Compilation from The Annual Reports and other Publications of the Oneida Association and its Branches; presenting, in connection with their History, a Summary View of their Religious and Social Theories," 1853 (Noyes uniformly speaks of "Bible Communism" as published in 1848: the edition of 1853 is the only one we have seen); "Hand-Book of the Oneida Community; with a Sketch of its Founder, and an Outline of its Constitution and Doctrines," 1867; "Male Continence," 1872 (we have seen only the second edition, 1877); "Essay on Scientific Propagation" (n.d.); "History of American Socialisms," 1870; "Dixon and His Copyists. A Criticism of the Accounts of the Oneida Community in 'New America,' 'Spiritual Wives' and Kindred Publications," 1871; "Home-Talks by John Humphrey Noyes," edited by Alfred Barron and George Noyes Miller; "Paul's Prize," reprint of a Home-Talk by J. H. Noyes (n.d.); "Hand-Book of the Oneida Community," 1875; "Mutual Criticism," 1876. There may be added the following: — "Faith Facts; or a Confession of the Kingdom of God and the Age of Miracles," edited by George Cragin, 1850; "Favorite Hymns for Community Singing," 1855; "The

Trapper's Guide," by S. Newhouse and other Trappers and Sportsmen, 1867; "Oneida Community Cooking, or a Dinner without Meat," by Harriet H. Skinner, 1873; "Oneida Community: 1848–1901 " (n.d); "The Oneida Community: its Relation to Orthodoxy: being an outline of the Religious and Theological Affinities of the Most Advanced Experiment in Applied Ethics ever made in any Age or Country," by G. W. N[oyes], a member of the Oneida Community from Birth (n.d. but apparently 1912). The following accounts of the Oneida Community and discussions of the principles involved, seem to be the most worthy of note: — J. P. Warren, "Putney Perfectionism," in *The New Englander*, vi. April, 1848, pp. 177–194. An excellent article. Hubbard Eastman, "Noyesism Unveiled: a History of the Sect Self-Styled Perfectionists; with a Summary View of their Leading Doctrines," 1849. A good and informing book. William Hepworth Dixon, "New America," ed. 4, 1857, ii. pp. 208–263; "Spiritual Wives," 1868, ii. Brilliant and informing, but sensational and so far inexact. Goldwin Smith, "Essays on Questions of the Day, Political and Social," ed. 2, 1894, pp. 361–384: "The Oneida Community and American Socialism," reprinted from *The Canadian Monthly* of November, 1874, and included as an appendix. Charles Nordhoff, "The Communistic Societies of the United States, etc.," 1875, pp. 257–301. Good account: a Bibliography, pp. 428–429. William Alfred Hinds, "American Communities," 1878, pp. 117–140; superseded by revised edition enlarged, 1902, pp. 144–213. Hinds was a member of the Oneida Community from an early date and writes from its standpoint. The account in the first edition is negligible; that in the second is good and informing. Allan Estlake, "The Oneida Community. A Record of an Attempt to Carry out the Principles of Christian Unselfishness and Scientific Race-Improvement," 1900. Estlake, like Hinds, was a member of the Community and writes from its standpoint; but his work is indefinitely less valuable than Hinds's. Frederick A. Bushee, "Communistic Societies in the United States," in *The Political Science Quarterly* for December, 1905. The brief biographical notices of Noyes in Appletons' "Cyclopædia of American Biography, iv. p. 543, and "The National Cyclopædia of American Biography," xi. p. 238, give an outline of his personal career: there are good brief accounts of the Community in "The New Schaff-Herzog Encyclopedia of Religious Knowledge," iii. p. 188, by W. H. Larrabee, and Hastings's, "Encyclopædia of Religion and Ethics," iii. pp. 785 f., by R. Bruce Taylor. See also Otto Zöckler, in Herzog-Hauck, "Realencyklopädie für protestantische Theologie und Kirche," xv. p. 130; and W. Köhler in Schiele und Zscharnack, "Die Religion in Geschichte und Gegenwart," iv. p. 1356.

III

THE MYSTICAL PERFECTIONISM
OF THOMAS COGSWELL UPHAM

THE MYSTICAL PERFECTIONISM
OF THOMAS COGSWELL UPHAM[1]

I. UPHAM AND HIS SECOND CONVERSION

A GREAT deal of the perfectionism which vexed the American churches through the first three-quarters of the nineteenth century was mystically colored. There is no difficulty in accounting for this. The embarrassment rather is to select out of numerous accounts which suggest themselves, the particular one which was really determining in each case. In some instances no doubt the mysticism was self-generated. A doctrine essentially mystical spontaneously presented itself to the inflamed minds of fanatics, as the basis of their pretension to peculiar holiness. The assumption of possession by the Divine Spirit is made with great ease. Even the West African savages make it. Nineteenth century Americans, however, did not live in the isolation of West African savages. They could not escape from the currents of religious sentiment which came flowing down to them through the years, even if they would. We easily underestimate the force and persistency of religious tradition, especially among what we call the submerged classes; and very especially if the tradition be in any degree fanatical and if it has been distilled into the blood through the experience of some form of persecution. The English sectaries of the seventeenth century were still living beneath the skins of many nineteenth century Americans; and there could be found inheritances even from radical mediæval sects, no doubt, if any one should dig deeply enough for them. Nevertheless, it was not to tradition that the mystical perfectionism which was continually springing up in nineteenth century Americans or-

[1] Reprinted from *The Union Seminary Review*, xxxii. 1920–1921, pp. 89–123, 196–230, 273–298, and xxxiii. 1921–1922, pp. 44–65.

dinarily owed its origin. It was to direct infection, either through personal contact or literary inculcation.

We have only, for example, to think of the Quakers. They were a compact body, universally esteemed, and exerting wide influence. Wherever this influence extended, a mystical perfectionism was commended, which the more recommended itself that it seemed to speak in much the same language that was familiar to everyone on the lips of the Methodists. There is nothing on which Quakerism has more strenuously insisted from its first origin than " a holy and sinless life," as the natural product of "that of God" which dwells within us, the " Light," the " Seed," the " Principle" of God within us, the " Christ within." When George Fox was haled before the magistrates of Derby, he was asked, he tells us, whether he "was sanctified." " I answered," he says, "'Yes; for I am in the paradise of God.' Then they asked me if I had no sin. I answered, 'Christ my Saviour has taken away my sin; and in Him there is no sin.' They asked how we knew that Christ did abide in us. I said, 'By His Spirit, that He hath given us.'"[2] The germ of the developed Quaker doctrine is already here — both in the extremity of its assertion and in its mystical basis.

The developed doctrine is set forth in barest outline by Robert Barclay, the most esteemed of the Quaker teachers, in his " Theological Theses." " This certain doctrine then being received," he writes, " (to-wit) that there is an evangelical and saving light and grace in all, . . . as many as resist not this light, but receive the same, in them is produced an holy, pure, and spiritual birth, bringing forth holiness, righteousness, purity, and all these other blessed fruits which are acceptable

[2] " George Fox: An Autobiography," edited with an Introduction and Notes by Rufus M. Jones, M.A., Litt.D., 1919, pp. 120 f. In a note on p. 85, the editor points out the persistency with which Fox asserted the fact of perfection. The basis of the assertion is made clearer by some remarks in the Introduction (p. 30): " As soon as he realized that . . . to be a man means to have a 'seed of God' within, he saw that there were no limits to the possibilities of a human life. It becomes possible to live entirely in the power of the Spirit and to have one's life made a free and victorious spiritual life."

to God; by which holy birth (to-wit, Jesus Christ formed within us, and working his works in us) as we are sanctified, so are we justified in the sight of God. . . . In whom this holy and pure birth is fully brought forth, the body of death and sin comes to be crucified and removed, and their hearts united and subjected unto the truth, so as not to obey any suggestion or temptation of the evil one, but to be free from actual sinning, and transgressing of the law of God, and in that respect perfect. Yet doth this perfection still admit of a growth; and there remaineth a possibility of sinning, where the mind doth not most diligently and watchfully attend unto the Lord." [3]

In his "Apology" Barclay expounds and argues these propositions at length.[4] The perfection asserted, he affirms, is the result of the new birth; and is, of course, "proportionable and answerable to man's measure"; but is not the less real, since "a little gold is perfect gold in its kind, as well as a great mass." It is, however, capable of growth, and also, unfortunately, liable to be lost — though he "will not affirm that a state is not attainable in this life, in which to do righteousness may be so natural to the regenerate soul, that in the stability of that condition he cannot sin." He does not profess to have himself attained that state, but he recognizes it as taught in I John iii. 9. This text, however, if it affirms anything to the purpose, affirms it not of some but

[3] The Eighth Proposition, "Concerning Perfection." We have prefixed some phrases from the two preceding Propositions in order to provide a context. We are quoting from Barclay's "An Apology for the True Christian Divinity: being an Explanation and Vindication of the Principles and Doctrines of the People called Quakers," Philadelphia, 1789, pp. 7–9. This Apology first appeared in Latin, Amsterdam, 1676, and then in English (Aberdeen?), 1678. For the doctrine, see also Barclay's "A Catechism and Confession . . . which containeth a true and faithful Account of the Principles and Doctrines, which are most surely believed by the Churches of Christ in Great Britain and Ireland, who are reproachfully called by the Name of Quakers . . ." ed. 5, London, 1716, pp. 42 ff. for the Catechism and pp. 129 f. for the Confession. The article in the Confession and the answers in the Catechism are mere centos of Scripture passages: but Barclay manages to argue the matter quite fully in the *questions* of the Catechism.

[4] "An Apology for the True Christian Divinity," as cited, pp. 241–262.

of all of those who are born of God. This inconsequence follows Barclay throughout his argument. His aim is to establish
for the children of God the possibility and frequent realization of a complete perfection in this life. His appeal is made,
however, always to considerations which altogether fail to
support the extremity of the contention. There is an underlying assumption always that a promise of perfection is void
unless fulfilled at once; or that the confession of imperfection
is an admission of lack of all grace; or that remainders of sin
in God's people argue incapacity on His part to deliver them
wholly, and derogate from the virtue of Christ's sacrifice; or
that the coëxistence of sin and holiness in an imperfectly
sanctified heart implies that there is no difference between
good and evil — which he says is the horrid blasphemy of the
Ranters; or something of the kind.

All these modes of argument reappear in our nineteenth
century perfectionists and become stereotyped in them. It is
impossible to say how far they are derived from Barclay directly or indirectly — from reading his " Apology," which
had long since become *the* Quaker " classic," and was not
suffered to mold on dusty shelves; or from contact with those
who carried forward his teaching in living tradition. Barclay
was not the first to frame them nor the only accessible source
from which they could be derived. And this may illustrate the
difficulty in determining how far Quaker influences coöperated
in producing the perfectionism of nineteenth century America.
It was there; it was a *vera causa;* but the extent of its contribution to the effect is indeterminate. Let us only remind
ourselves that Robert Pearsall Smith, and Hannah Whitall
Smith were both of Quaker birth and breeding. They received
their perfectionism directly from Methodism. But we can
hardly be wrong in assuming that they had been prepared for
receiving it by their Quaker associations. In Hannah Whitall
Smith's case this is demonstrably true. And it was she who took
the lead in their common adoption of perfectionism.[5] She re-

---

[5] *The Princeton Theological Review,* xvi. 1918, pp. 612 ff. or pp. 501 ff.
of this volume.

mained, it requires to be remarked, a Quaker all her life, and was perhaps more and more a Quaker as she grew in years.[6]

The name of William Law slips off of the pen of more than one of the perfectionist writers of nineteenth century America. Off of that of John Humphrey Noyes, for example. Noyes considers Law, whom he represents as the real father of Methodist Perfectionism, the best of the Mystical Perfectionists,[7] and his " Address to the Clergy " (1761) his best book.[8] Law is also repeatedly quoted, as he could not fail to be, by Thomas Cogswell Upham.[9] But it would be absurd to attribute to this aloof high-churchman any large influence in the production of movements to which he stood in no other connection than that of relative nearness in time. While Law gives large expression to his mysticism, moreover, he speaks only occasionally and briefly of its perfectionist corollary, and makes, there-

---

[6] *Ibid.,* xvii. 1919, pp. 61 ff. or pp. 534 ff. of this volume.

[7] William Law's " Humble, Earnest, and Affectionate Address to the Clergy " makes the pathetic appeal of not merely being his last book, but of having been completed only in the last few days before his death. In these last few pages (pp. 190 ff.), he argues the question of perfection. Christ came to save us from all sin; He saves us from all sin. Absolute freedom from sin is, therefore, not only our duty but our privilege. " He that is left under a Necessity of Sinning, as long as he lives, can no more be said to be cleansed from all Unrighteousness, than a man who must be a Cripple to his dying Day, can be said to be cured of all his lameness. What weaker Conclusion can well be made, than to infer, that because Christ was the only Man, that was born and lived free from Sin, therefore no Man on Earth can be raised to a Freedom from Sinning; no better than concluding, that because the Old Man is every one's Birth from Adam, therefore there can be no such Thing as a New Man, created unto Righteousness, through Christ Jesus, living and being all in all in him; no better Sense or Logic than to say, that because our Redeemer could not find us any Thing else but Sinners, therefore he must of all Necessity leave us to be Sinners " (pp. 197 f.). " To suppose a Man born again from above, yet under a necessity of continuing to Sin, is as absurd as to suppose, that the true Christian is only to have so much of the Nature of Christ born in him, as is consistent with as real a Power of Satan still dwelling in him " (p. 194). " That which cannot help you to *all* Goodness, cannot help you to *any* Goodness; nor can that take away *any* Sin, but that which can take away *all* sin " (p. 192).

[8] " The Berean," 1847, pp. 271 ff.

[9] For example, in his " Principles of the Interior or Hidden Life " (1843), ed. 8, 1859, p. 120. Quotations from this book are throughout from the eighth edition.

fore, only a limited appeal to those whose interests lay chiefly
in the latter region. Even Upham passes over him to find the
sources of his mystical doctrine of perfection in those Quietistic writers of the preceding century of whom Law apparently
thought as meanly as he could think of any mystic.[10] What
we find in Upham is in fact a sustained attempt to revive the
specifically Quietistic perfectionism of the seventeenth century, and to give it a new vogue in the conditions of the nineteenth century life of America. For this purpose he drew on
the whole series of Quietistic writers from Miguel de Molinos
himself to Antoinette Bourignon, and adapted them to his
purpose with the utmost freedom, not to say violence. His
attitude toward these writers was the precise opposite of Law's.
Recognizing, of course, the presence in them of the general
mystical conception in which he shared, Law, nevertheless,
repelled with the utmost disfavor the extravagances which
constituted their peculiarity and made them what we know as
Quietists. Upham, on the contrary, laid a remolding hand on
these very extravagances, and by a skillful firmness or firm
skillfulness of dealing with them, transmuted them into a
tolerable likeness to evangelical Protestantism. By this means
he built up on their basis a complete system of mystical per-

---

[10] Compare J. H. Overton, "William Law, Nonjuror and Mystic," 1881,
pp. 161–170: "Law himself . . . very rarely mentions any of this group of
mystics. There is, indeed, frequent allusion to Madame Guyon in the earlier
interviews between Law and Byrom; but the subject was obviously introduced by Byrom, who was attracted to her by her resemblance to his favourite,
Madame Bourignon. Law's remarks on both ladies are by no means complimentary. To that most lovable of men and fascinating of writers, Archbishop
Fénelon, Law hardly ever refers " (p. 161). " He expressly mentions both ' the
great Fénelon and the illuminated Guion ' as mystic writers whom he had
read, and yet we may gather, from his distinct words in one case and from his
silence in the other, that neither of them was a real favourite of his " (p. 164).
" They were, neither of them, robust enough for Law's taste " (p. 165).
" Though Fénelon was not exactly effeminate, there was a certain softness
about him . . . not at all the sort of charm to fascinate William Law "
(p. 166). " As to Madame Guyon, the very fact that she held many of Law's
sentiments would naturally make him all the more intolerant of her other
views which were likely to bring those sentiments into disrepute " (pp. 166 f.).
" As for that other mystic lady, Madame Bourignon, . . . Law constantly expressed strong antipathy to her in his conversations with Byrom " (p. 169).

fection, which stands out boldly in a certain — though not very deeply going — contrast with the other systems of perfection launched in such profusion in his day among the Protestants of New England inheritance.

Thomas Cogswell Upham came of a distinguished New Hampshire family, members of which have attained eminence in a variety of activities, through a series of generations, and not least in his own.[11] He was one of four brothers all of whom won recognition as men of conspicuous ability. He was born at Deerfield, New Hampshire, where his grandfather had served as pastor for a generation, on the 30th of January, 1799. It was in the autumn of this year (November 9) that Asa Mahan also was born. These two perfectionist leaders were, therefore, close contemporaries. The superior advantages which Upham enjoyed, however, showed themselves in his more rapid advancement. He was finishing his scholastic preparation about the time when Mahan was beginning his. He was graduated from college two years before Mahan entered; and had published his first book — an excellent translation of Johann Jahn's "Biblical Archæology" (1823) — a year before Mahan was graduated. By the time Mahan had completed his theological course (1827), Upham had already been for three years seated in the chair of Mental and Moral Philosophy at Bowdoin College — a chair which he occupied for the rest of his active life — and had published his "Elements of Intellectual Philosophy" (1827), by which his reputation as a thinker was established. On the other hand, Mahan was the first of the two to obtain the "second blessing" and to enter upon the career of a perfectionist teacher. The light that came to him in the winter of 1836–1837 did not reach Upham until 1839. Mahan wished to believe that he was the channel of its conveyance to Upham. That, however, was not the fact; and he must content himself with the honor of having in this matter of the first importance to both of them not merely overtaken Upham, but forestalled him by two or three years. He was publishing his first perfectionist book — his "Scripture

[11] See A. G. Upham, "History of the Upham Family," 1845.

Doctrine of Christian Perfection " (1839) — about the time
that Upham was just attaining perfection. Upham's first
perfectionist book — the " Principles of the Interior or Hidden
Life " (1843) — followed, however, at no more than the due
interval. It would be hard to say which one was, after this,
the more diligent in propagating their common opinions.

Dartmouth was Upham's college, and 1818 was his year
of graduation. The period of his residence there was a time of
great turmoil. During it the great Dartmouth College controversy was fought out. It was in 1815 that John Wheelock
was, after much violent debate, removed by the Trustees from
the Presidency of the College, and Francis Brown elected in
his stead. It was in 1816 that the usurping action of the Legislature, voiding all the college's vested rights, was taken. It was
on March 10, 1818, that Daniel Webster's famous argument in
the case which resulted, was made before the United States
Supreme Court, presided over by John Marshall, and through
it the sacredness of private trusts was established, as a principle of American law. The whole college, officers and students
alike, shared in the distraction of this long excitement. The
new president, Francis Brown, was broken by the strain and
died in 1820. There would seem no room in this preoccupation
for another strong emotion to enter in. Nevertheless, at the
very moment when the struggle between Trustees and President was reaching its climax,[12] in the spring of 1815, a remarkable revival of religion broke, unheralded and unexpected, upon
the college. Nathan Lord, Brown's successor in the presidency,
writing in 1832, gives an account of it.[13] " At once, and without
premonition," he says, " the Spirit of God evidently descended,
and saved the great body of the students. A general and almost
instantaneous solemnity prevailed. Almost before Christians
became aware of God's presence, and increased their suppli-
cations, the impenitent were deeply convicted of sin, and
besought instructions of their officers. The chapel, the recita-

[12] A number of the pamphlets published in this controversy are brought
together in vol. 430 of the " Sprague Collection," preserved in the Library
of Princeton Theological Seminary.

[13] W. B. Sprague, " Lectures on Revivals of Religion," ed. 2, 1833, p. 325.

tion room, every place of meeting became a scene of weeping, and presently of rejoicing; so that in a few weeks about sixty students were supposed to have become regenerate. A revival of such rapidity and power has been rarely known, and perhaps never one of such unquestionable fruits. Not one of the number of apparent converts, at that time, is known to have forfeited a Christian standing. Most of them are ministers of the gospel, a few are missionaries, and all are still using their influence for Christ."

Upham himself tells us that he " supposes " that he " experienced religion " " in connection with " this revival.[14] It is not probable that he meant by this language to throw doubt on the genuineness of the religious experience which he then enjoyed. It is not impossible, of course, that, looking back upon it from the exaltation of his " second conversion," it had lost in his mind some of its significance. It is more likely, however, that it seemed in retrospect less certain than at the moment, that what he then experienced was the inception of religious life, rather than perhaps an intensified manifestation of a life already existing. Throughout his writings he exhibits a marked distaste for religious excitement, and with it an unmistakable distrust of revivals of excitement.[15] Whether his religious life began in the revival of the spring of 1815, or not, however, it flowed on thence unbrokenly. He does not appear, it is true, to have made a formal profession of his faith, by uniting with the (Congregational) Church, until about the time of his graduation, three years later. He proceeded then, however, at once to the theological seminary at Andover, whence he was graduated in 1821. The professors under whose instruction he came at Andover were Leonard

[14] In a short account of his religious experience printed in Phoebe Palmer's " The Riches of Grace," 1854, pp. 20 ff.

[15] One of his pupils describing his personal carriage, says that " he was meek enough to inherit the whole earth ": — " A tall man of bent figure, face turned toward mother-earth, but heart lifted toward the stars, Professor Upham impressed the undergraduates of his time with the idea that the Kingdom of God is not taken by violence " (F. L. Dingley, in *The Lewiston* [*Maine*] *Journal*, February 27, 1915).

Woods, Moses Stuart, Ebenezer Porter and James Murdock; and he came in contact there (as indeed he had done at Dartmouth) [16] with many young men as fellow students who afterward achieved distinction. Among his classmates were Baxter Dickinson, afterward to be a professor in Lane and then in Auburn Seminary; Charles D. Pigeon, the capable editor of *The Literary and Theological Review;* and Alva Woods, who had a notable academic career in the South: while in the other classes in the seminary with him there were to be met such men as Orville Dewey, Jonas King, Joseph Torrey, Elias Cornelius, Francis Wayland, Rufus Anderson, Leonard Bacon. His career at Andover was a distinguished one. During the last year of his course (1820–1821) he also served as a teacher in Phillips Academy. And after his graduation he remained two years at the seminary as instructor in Sacred Literature — under Moses Stuart. The last of these years he was registered also as "resident licentiate" (1823). It was during these years that he prepared his translation of Johann Jahn's compendium on "Biblical Archæology," the first edition of which bears the date of 1823, and the fifth, stereotyped, edition came out in the fifties.[17]

Of his own interior life during this period of preparation there seems to have survived little direct record. We are not without indirect intimations, however, which warrant the pleasantest inferences. When pleading on one occasion for the union of spiritual with mental culture in the education of youth, he draws a beautiful picture of what he found in Phillips Academy, in which we can read his own heart. " In early life," he writes,[18] " I had the privilege of being associated, for

[16] George Bush, the eccentric Hebraist, William Chamberlain, subsequently Professor of the Classics at Dartmouth, Cyrus P. Grosvenor, afterwards President of New York Central College, were classmates at Dartmouth.

[17] The translation was made from the Latin one volume compend, compared with and enlarged from the German original, and furnished with additions in the form of notes. It is a very scholarly piece of work and was long in demand as a textbook in the theological seminaries.

[18] "A Treatise on Divine Union" (1851), ed. 6, pp. 342 f. The citations from this book are throughout from the sixth edition.

a short time, in an institution, where it seemed to me that
some of these views were happily illustrated. The studies
always opened in the morning and closed at night with religious services. The first half hour of every morning, in particular, was devoted to the reading of the Scriptures, the
explanatory and practical remarks of the worthy and learned
instructor, and to prayer. And it was understood by all, whatever might be the state of their own minds, that this religious
exercise was regarded by the teacher as one of preëminent
importance. When he came before his pupils on this occasion,
they did not doubt that he had first commended them to God
in private; and that of all objects which he desired and had
at heart, there was none so dear to him as their souls' salvation. Every movement was stilled; every voice hushed; every
eye fixed. And whatever might be their creed or want of creed,
their religious adhesions or aversions, such was their sympathy
with his obvious sense of responsibility and his divine sincerity, that even the hearts of the infidel and the profane
were cheerfully laid open before him; so that with their
own consent he was enabled, by means of his prayers and
warnings, to write upon them, as it were, inscriptions for
immortality. I was not a pupil in the seminary to which I
refer, but an assistant teacher; and had a good opportunity
to observe and judge. My own heart never failed to be profoundly affected; and, from what I have learned and known
of his pupils since, scattered as they have been in all parts of
the world, and engaged in various occupations, I have no
doubt that God eminently blessed the faithful labors of this
good man, and that he was permitted to realize in his instructions, to an extent not often witnessed, the beautiful union
of the culture of the heart with that of the understanding." [19]

[19] It seems probable that the teacher who is here described was John
Adams, born at Canterbury, Connecticut, September 18, 1772, graduated at
Yale in 1795, and given the degree of LL.D. by Yale in 1854; died at Jack-
sonville, Illinois, April 24, 1863. His life was passed in teaching, except that
in his later years he served as Sunday School Missionary in Illinois. He was
principal of Phillips Academy, Andover, from 1810 to 1833, including Upham's
time. There is a brief notice of him in Appletons' "Cyclopædia of American

When Upham left Andover in 1823 it was to become pastor
of the Congregational Church at Rochester, New Hampshire — his "home church" [20] — where he was ordained July
16, 1823. He remained at this post, however, only a single
year. In 1824 he received an invitation to become Professor
of Mental and Moral Philosophy and Tutor in Hebrew at
Bowdoin College, Brunswick, Maine; and accepting it, entered
upon what proved to be his life-work. He continued in the
active work of his chair from 1824 to 1867, and then, becoming
Professor Emeritus, retired to Kennebunkport, where his later
years were spent. He died in the city of New York, April 2,
1872. The literary activity which had begun at Andover was
continued with renewed vigor at Bowdoin. By the time he was
forty years old he had printed eight separate works. There
were included in these a treatise on the polity of Congregationalism (1829),[21] and a very notable plea for universal
peace, including the suggestion of a "Congress of Nations"
(1836).[22] But, as is natural, the larger place among them is

Biography." Horace E. Scudder gives an account of Phillips Academy, Andover, in *Harper's Magazine* for 1877, lv. pp. 562 ff., but the portrait is drawn
from the times of "Uncle Sam" Taylor.

[20] His father had removed from Deerfield to Rochester in his childhood (see A. S. Packard, "Address on the Life and Character of Thomas
C. Upham, D.D.," 1873, p. 6).

[21] "Ratio Disciplinae, or the Constitution of the Congregational
Churches," 1829; new ed., 1844.

[22] "The Manual of Peace, Embracing I. Evils and Remedies of War,
II. Suggestions on the Law of Nations, III. Consideration of a Congress of
Nations," 1836: the third part reprinted 1840, 1842. A. S. Packard, as cited,
pp. 10 f., gives the following, not perfectly clear, account of this work. "Having
embraced at an early period the doctrines of Peace announced and advocated with great zeal and ability by Capt. William Ladd of this vicinity,
he wrote several articles for the public press under the signature of 'Perier,'
the name of the eminent French banker and statesman. . . . These essays
were embodied in one of the four Prize Essays on a Congress of Nations,
in a volume under that title in 1840. . . . Previously, in 1836, was published
his Manual of Peace, which has been stereotyped, and both these works are
among the advertised volumes of the Peace Society." Upham characteristically
pushed his conclusions as to peace to the furthest extreme. He would not allow that war could be condoned in any case whatever. "We say, *in any case
whatever*," he writes, ("The Manual of Peace," p. 81) "because we do not

given to treatises in his own special department of instruction. These treatises, taken together, constitute a comprehensive discussion of the whole field, written with charming simplicity and directness, and manifesting a very wide acquaintance with the literature of the subject, and, with it, clear and acute thinking. The "Elements of Intellectual Philosophy" appeared already in 1827, to be followed in 1831 by "Elements of Mental Philosophy, Embracing the Two Departments of Intellect and the Sensibilities" (of which an abridged edition also was at once published),[23] in 1834 by "A Philosophical and Practical Treatise on the Will," and in 1840 by "Outlines of Imperfect and Disordered Mental Action." The inclusion of the last of these treatises in his scheme of a comprehensive discussion of mental faculty and action, may serve to suggest to us the wide range and rather popular character of Upham's method of treatment. He keeps himself always in contact with life and the common interests of life, and enlivens his pages with copious illustrations drawn from a wide acquaintance with literature. Above all the interests of religion, and very specifically of the Christian religion, are everywhere kept in view. The books have quite as much the flavor of a Christian minister instructing his people, as of a professor of philosophy, lecturing his class: they are almost as much theology as psychology.

We see at once that Upham carried his religion to Bowdoin

---

propose to make any distinction between offensive and defensive war. . . . The true doctrine is, that human life, both in its individual and corporate state, as one and as many, is *inviolable;* that it cannot be taken away for any purpose 'whatever, except by explicit divine permission; and that war, in every shape, and for every purpose, is *wrong,* absolutely *wrong,* wholly *wrong.*" Packard (p. 19) nevertheless tells us, with what exact meaning we do not know, that "he labored earnestly, as we have noticed, in the cause of peace, and yet when the cloud of civil war hung over our land, his heart was stirred within him for the salvation and integrity of his bleeding country."

[23] Cf. Packard, as cited, p. 8: "Prof. Upham at first gave lectures to his classes, and in 1827 embodied them in a work, which he called a compilation on Mental Philosophy, which in 1831 he expanded into a more original and systematic work in two volumes."

with him and did not sink it in his academic work.[24] We are
not surprised to learn, therefore, that outside the class-room
he was looked to by his pupils for guidance in their times of
religious distress.[25] We find, for instance, young Henry Boynton Smith, when, in the course of a notable revival which visited Bowdoin College in 1834, he was smitten in his conscience
and awakened to his soul's needs, turning to him especially
for counsel and direction. Smith had been bred under Unitarian influences, and his perplexities were accordingly as
much theological as practical. But it is quite clear that Upham
was no less helpful to him in his distresses than in his difficulties. " Last evening," he writes,[26] " Professor Upham came
in, and we conversed a long while. I stated to him, fully and
explicitly, my doubts, fears, hopes, and, in fine, my situation
in every respect, and he talked to me calmly and reasonably.
I am to see him again this afternoon." Then, some three weeks
later: " I talked with Professor Upham about the Trinity. Of
one thing I feel assured, that I need an infinite Saviour. Further than that, may the Lord in his mercy and wisdom guide

[24] He ceased, however, to preach. Packard, as cited, pp. 13 f., says: " Prof.
Upham came, as we have seen, from a pastorate to his professorship. But
although he had exercised the public ministry of the Word, his nervous temperament, as he alleged, did not allow frequent preaching. . . . He . . .
soon felt constrained to avoid public speaking. . . . At an early period of his
life among us his voice ceased to be heard even in the social meetings." One
of his pupils (*ibid.*, p. 17) writes of him: " His excessive nervous timidity
to my mind accounted for traits of character that awakened unfavorable
comment. He trembled at, and shrank from, public speech. He hesitated
at a bold assertion, however true. He loved the most retired, not to say
secret, ways of investigation for either practical or philosophical purposes,
more because his nerves were weak, than because his convictions were feeble
or his moral courage faint."

[25] Packard, as cited, p. 16, refers to " the unaffected, deep and earnest
interest he always manifested in the moral and religious well-being of his
fellow-men," and illustrates this remark by adding: " He was instant in season and out of season, in visiting the students at their rooms, was the first
to discern indications of awakening interest in religious concerns; was abundant in personal efforts in such seasons; was sagacious in detecting the inworking of the Divine Spirit, or the presence of the spirit of evil. . . ." He
cites instances of Upham's work of this sort.

[26] " Henry Boynton Smith. His Life and Work," edited by his wife,
1881, pp. 14, 15.

me! My prejudices were fixed in regard to this point as well
as to the innate sinfulness of men. On the latter point I am
convinced. As to the former, I know nothing but that Christ
is my Redeemer and has atoned for my sins." Young Smith
won out as we know, and was born once for all to God. What
part Upham's counsel really played in the great change we
can only conjecture. Smith's was the stronger mind of the
two, and he soon passed into the position of the teacher, not
the taught. But he retained Upham in warm friendship; and
it is clear enough that, in this episode at least, in which the
corner of the veil has been lifted that we may see him at work,
what we see in Upham is the devoted man of God.

We have thought it worth while to make this clear, because
Upham's own account of his state of mind at this time is not
altogether cheering. Of course he did not doubt his interest
in his Saviour. But he was not happy in his religious life. He
had early set a high ideal of religious attainment before himself and he was conscious of not having reached it. He advanced sometimes, he says, and then again was thrown back,
" living what may be called the common Christian life of sinning and repenting, of alternate walking with God and devotedness to the world." [27] He is looking back on himself here
from the heights of his " second conversion," and describing
his earlier experience from that more elevated point of sight:
and from the same point of sight, he suggests that the difficulty
he experienced in attaining the state he longed for was, in
part at least, due to " the discouraging influence of the prevalent doctrine that personal sanctification cannot fully take
place till death." It is plain, however, that he was not acquies-
cent in his shortcomings. Apparently, as time went on, his

[27] We are drawing, in the following account, on Upham's own narra-
tive printed in Phoebe Palmer's collection of " experiences " bearing the title:
" The Riches of Grace: or the Blessing of Perfect Love as Experienced, En-
joyed and Recorded by Sixty-Two Living Witnesses," 1854 (copyrighted
1852), pp. 20 ff. Compare her: " Pioneer Experiences; or the Gift of Power
Received by Faith. Illustrated and Confirmed by the Testimony of Eighty
Living Witnesses of Various Denominations." Introduction by Rev. Bishop
Janes, 1867.

sense of them continued ever unabated; and he seems to wish us to understand that his sense of personal danger in view of them steadily increased. This emphasis on his increasing sense of danger in view of his shortcomings makes the unpleasant impression that the righteousness of Christ was becoming to his apprehension ever less sufficient as the ground of his hope: that he was growing ever more anxious to supplement it, or supersede it, by a righteousness of his own: that he was uneasy — increasingly so — so long as he had nothing but Christ's righteousness to rest upon. It is probable, however, that he intends no more than to convey a strong impression of the distress the consciousness of his shortcomings gave him, and his consequent increasing anxiety to be completely delivered from them. He wishes us in any event to understand that anything short of complete deliverance from sin was becoming intolerable to him, and thus to prepare the way for his account of how he sought and obtained the " second blessing." If this is all that he means, however, he has expressed himself badly.

He proceeds now, in any case, to describe at considerable length, how, spurred on by his uneasiness or fear, he sought and at length found the "second blessing." "In this state of mind," he writes,[28] "I was led, early in the summer of 1839, by a series of special providences, which it is here unnecessary to detail, to examine the subject of personal holiness, *as a matter of personal realization.*" Conducting this examination, as he thought, "prayerfully, candidly and faithfully, looking at the various objections as well as the multiplied evidences," he was led to the conclusion " that God required " him " to be holy, that He had made provision for it, and that it was both " his " duty " and his " privilege to be so." " The establishment " of his " belief in this great doctrine was followed," he tells us, " by a number of pleasing and important results." One was that he " felt a great increase of *obligation to be holy.*" God required him to be holy, and God does not require impossibilities: on the contrary God's requirement of him to be holy involved " an implied promise " to give aid in the

28 " The Riches of Grace," 1854, p. 20.

accomplishment of the required result. Accordingly, " within a few days after rejecting the common doctrine, that sanctification is fully attainable only in the article of death, and receiving the doctrine of the possibility and duty of present holiness, I consecrated myself," he says, " to God, body and spirit, deliberately, voluntarily, and forever." There were no witnesses, and no formal written document; " it was a simple volition." But simple as the act was, it marked a crisis in his moral life. The date was about the middle of July, 1839, and the step taken was not in his view without a certain boldness in it: he was not perfectly instructed as yet in the way of life; he was acting " in comparative darkness," walking by faith, not by sight. It seemed, however, justified by the effects. " Two almost immediate and marked results followed this act of consecration. The one was an immediate removal of the sense of condemnation, which had followed me for many years, and had filled my mind with sorrow. The other result, which also almost immediately followed, was a greatly increased value and love of the Bible."

We have thus far been told nothing of any influence from without directing Upham to the new paths he was entering. He does speak, to be sure, of having been led by " special providences " to study the subject; and this may be taken to imply some sort of impulse received from without. The carefulness of his examination of the matter, which he emphasizes, moreover, may suggest that he sought aid where aid was to be found. There seems, however, to be a studied implication running through his whole narrative, that he went his own way and was his own guide. We reach a point now, however, where contact with those who were before him in believing his new doctrine and seeking to exemplify it in their lives, becomes decisive for his experience. He visited New York on business, he tells us, in December, 1839. That business, he says, " brought " him " into connection with certain persons who belonged to the Methodist denomination." " I was," he continues, " providentially led to form an acquaintance with other pious Methodists, and was exceedingly happy in attend-

ing a number of meetings which had exclusive reference to
the doctrine of holiness and to personal holy experience." He
made known to his new friends his own recently acquired
belief in the doctrine of holiness, and of his attitude as a
seeker of the experience: and they greatly cheered and aided
him. Precisely what they did for him, he tells us, was to remove a difficulty which stood in the way of his victorious
progress. That was his "ignorance of the important principle,
that *sanctification,* as well as justification, is by *faith.*" He had
put himself, it is true, in a favorable position to exercise this
faith, by consecrating himself to God. "But" he "had never
understood and felt the imperative necessity of this exercise,
viz., of *faith,* as a *sanctifying* instrumentality." He is explicit
that it was his "Methodist friends" who gave him his needed
instruction here. And it was because of this new point of view
solely, he intimates, that he was enabled "in some degree" —
"in a very considerable degree" — now to gain the victory.
He can date the very day when he gained it. "It was early on
Friday morning, the twenty-seventh of December." "The
evening previous had been spent in deeply interesting conversation and in prayer on the subject of holiness, and with particular reference to myself. Soon after I awoke in the morning
I found that my mind, without having experienced any very
remarkable manifestations or ecstasies, had, nevertheless,
undergone a great moral revolution. It was removed from the
condition of a *servant,* and adopted into that of a *son.* . . .
I had no ecstasy, but great and abiding peace and consolation."

Under the influence of these feelings Upham now consecrated himself anew to God; and this time he did it formally
in a written document. He still was unable to speak confidently of having actually experienced "sanctification." Consecration and sanctification are different things, although it
is possible that the latter may follow the former immediately
— God's work follows man's act. This did not occur, however,
in Upham's case. He had received great blessings — "a new
sense of forgiveness, increased love, actual evidence of adoption and sonship, clear and deeper communion with God."

But something was still lacking. He left New York about the middle of January, 1840, and at once on reaching home, " united with some Methodist brethren in establishing a meeting similar to those which had benefited " him " so much in New York, for the purpose of promoting present godliness." This meeting was open to persons of all denominations of Christians — that is, it took the form of a perfectionist propaganda. " Nevertheless," he says, that is to say, despite his earnest seeking, " I was unable for about two weeks to profess the personal experience and realization of the great blessing of holiness, as it seemed to be experienced and realized by others." Two weeks may seem to us a very short time in which to become perfectly holy. Upham felt them a long delay. The difficulty, he says, was that " while other evils were greatly or entirely removed," he was still conscious of " the remainders of selfishness." It seemed indeed as if the principle of self-love was even stimulated in him. He was no doubt not more selfish than before; but he *felt* it more. He prayed fervently for the realization in time of perfect love, though he did not fully know its nature.

On February 2, 1850 — Sabbath evening — he suffered great affliction of mind. On the next morning — Monday — he was for the first time able to say that he loved the Heavenly Father with all his soul and all his strength. This attainment once made was permanent. Ever after his heart expressed itself in this language — language, he says, " which involves, as I understand it, the true idea of Christian perfection or holiness." " There was no intellectual excitement," he tells us, " no very marked joy when I reached this great rock of practical salvation." " The soul had gathered strength from the storm it had passed through the preceding night; and, aided by a power from on high, it leaped forward, as it were, by a bound to the great and decisive mark." He was distinctly conscious of the attainment made. Those selfish exercises which had troubled him were gone; he was now sanctified. Temptations, no doubt, continued, and " it would be presumption to assert positively," he says, that there has never since been a lapse. But there certainly has been a new life, and the " wit-

ness of the Spirit," has been constant. This "witness" is not
delivered in the way of reasoning or of reflection; "it is a sort
of interior voice, which speaks silently and effectively to the
soul." There have even been times — for example, on February
14, 1840 — when "some remarkable operations on the mind"
were experienced. These are indescribable. The stress is laid,
however, on ordinary spiritual succor. His whole soul turns
from self to God, and all his longing sums itself up in the desire for union with God.

In this luminous narrative we have merely a typical
account of the attainment of the "second blessing" or the
experience of the "second conversion." It differs from other
similar accounts only in its unusually clear analysis of the
several steps or stages of the experience; perhaps these steps
or stages were more clearly marked in Upham's case than
usual. There is traced first the rise of the conviction of the
obligation to be holy; then the discovery of the way by faith
alone; and then the somewhat lagging actual attainment by
faith of the blessing. Every step was taken under Methodist
influence, or rather direction: this is explicitly noted in every
instance except the first, where we read only of the direction
of "providence." That this formed no exception to the others
— the exact nature of the providential circumstances thus
alluded to — we learn from a narrative which Mrs. Upham
gives us, in the same volume,[29] of her own experiences as she
journeyed to the same goal, some six months or so earlier.

She had been for fifteen years a professing Christian, she
says, before she found the way. " I never heard of the doctrine
of entire holiness," she explains, " *as a thing to be realized in
this life,* until February, 1839." "When I tell you," she adds
apologetically, speaking to Phoebe Palmer and her circle,
" that I do not belong to your order " — that is, to the Methodist Church — " and have never been at all associated with people of this belief, you will be able to account better for my
ignorance." We could not have a more direct assertion than
this, that the experiences she is about to relate were the only

[29] " The Riches of Grace," 1854, pp. 435 ff.

ones operative on her in her "second conversion." "In the good providence of God," she now proceeds, "I went last February"— that is, February, 1839, and we observe that she is writing within the year after the experiences narrated — "into a Methodist protracted meeting. I heard a sister there speak as I never before heard a man or woman speak. A holy composure sat on her countenance, and she seemed to me to be breathing the atmosphere of heaven. She spoke with the simplicity and love of the beloved disciple, who leaned on Jesus' bosom. I sought a private interview with her. I opened to her my heart. I told her I lived in a state of daily condemnation, and I had never indulged a hope of living above that state. Then, for the first time in my life I heard of Jesus, a present Saviour from all sin." Here we have an explicit statement that Mrs. Upham heard of the holiness doctrine for the first time from this woman. "I had only one interview with this sister," she continues, "as she left town, having been here only on a visit. Alone, unaided, except by the Spirit of God, I pursued the doctrine of heart holiness. . . . I soon became speculatively convinced, not only of the extent of God's requirements, but of the obligation and the *ability* of the Christian to fulfill these requirements in and through Jesus, who, I saw, was manifested to take away our sins." In these circumstances it was natural that she should set herself to make the attainment which she perceived to be required of her. The Bible alone was her guide. She saw and believed. Her efforts to be holy failed: but faith conquered its way. "For the last year I can say," she writes, "the life which I now live in the flesh, I live by faith in the Son of God."

Now, Mrs. Upham tells us [30] that she was led, on May 25, 1839, publicly —"at a public prayer-meeting," she says — "to declare the *greatness* of the salvation she had experienced." We will recall that Upham's examination of the matter was undertaken "early in the summer of 1839." The appearance is that Mrs. Upham's publication of her own experience constituted the "providential circumstances" which led to Up-

[30] P. 444.

ham's inquiry. Thus the only obscure point in his narrative is cleared up; and the beginning as well as the prosecution of his "second conversion" is brought under direct Methodist influence. It is quite clear that we have in the cases of Upham and his wife nothing more than instances of conversion to Wesleyan Perfectionism. All this, perfectly plain in itself, is authenticated now by an absolutely contemporary entry in Phoebe Palmer's diary of the date of January 3, 1840.[31] She tells us here that Mrs. Upham had been led by the simple testimony of a Methodist sister to seek "the blessing" and had entered into the enjoyment of it. The difficulties thrown in her way by her connection with the Congregational Church (which discountenanced the experience itself and also the speaking of women in the church) were "overcome," and Mrs. Upham bore her public testimony to her new experience. Her husband, however, held back. "For several months, he was skeptical as to his privilege in reference to this blessing," though he had come to be assured of the glory of the inheritance. He came to New York to attend to the publication of his book on "The Will," [32] and Mrs. Upham, who accompanied him, found her way to the famous Tuesday holiness-meeting for women, which for a whole generation was held in Phoebe Palmer's parlor.[33] She asked the privilege of bringing her

[31] Richard Wheatley, "The Life and Letters of Mrs. Phoebe Palmer," 1876, pp. 239 f.

[32] This seems to be not quite accurate. Upham's book on "The Will" was first published in 1834 at Portland; and although it was ultimately transferred to the Harpers, along with the rest of the series on Mental Science, it does not seem to have been issued by them as early as 1840. His work, "Outlines of Imperfect and Disordered Mental Action," designed to form the fourth part of his comprehensive treatment of mental faculty, on the other hand, was published by the Harpers in 1840; and it was doubtless in connection with this publication that he was in New York. He appears to have arranged at the same time, or not long afterward, for the taking over of the whole series by the Harpers. The Harpers, it will be remembered, were a Methodist house and fit the description which Upham gives of those he had business with.

[33] Phoebe Worrall was born in New York, December 18, 1807. She gave herself to her Saviour in childhood and adorned the doctrine she professed through a long life of abounding activity. It was on the 26th of July, 1837, that she "entered into the rest of faith, the Canaan of perfect love" (Wheat-

husband to the meeting. This was granted and some other
gentlemen were invited to be also present. Upham came and
was deeply impressed. On the following Thursday he had a
long interview with Phoebe Palmer and the next morning
entered into the rest of faith.

The close relations thus established between him and
Phoebe Palmer naturally were maintained. We find him writing to her on March 24 following, and again, in September,
in accents of deep gratitude. His experience in her parlor, he
tells her, was " in religion, the ' beginning of days ' " to him;
and Mrs. Upham declares to her (March 24), " you have
begotten him in the gospel." They are glad to inform her that
they have set up a meeting in their own house modeled after
hers, where (Mrs. Upham says, with wifely pride) Upham
spoke tenderly to the people of his great blessing.[34] There can
be no question that Phoebe Palmer looked upon Upham and
Upham looked upon himself as her pupil; and so strong was
her sense of this relation that when she found him after a
while wandering from the path in which she had placed his
feet she did not hesitate, in her capacity as instructress,
soundly to rebuke him, and to point him back to the right
way.[35]

It has seemed desirable to make the facts of Upham's " sec-

---

ley, p. 36). That day she always spoke of as " The day of days." The famous
Tuesday meetings date, however, from the combination of the ladies' prayer-
meetings of the Allen Street M. E. Church and the Mulberry Street M. E.
Church in 1835. The combined meeting was held at first in Dr. Palmer's
(Phoebe Worrall had become Mrs. Palmer) back office, but, outgrowing this
room, was taken upstairs to the parlor. It continued to be exclusively a ladies'
meeting until Upham's attendance was the occasion of its transformation
into a union meeting (Wheatley, p. 238). Phoebe Palmer, it will be seen,
had herself entered into holiness only a little over two years before she conducted Upham into it. She was for many years the editor of *The Guide to
Holiness.* She died November 2, 1874, and her life was written by Richard
Wheatley, 1876.

[34] For these items see Wheatley, as cited, p. 241. We should not forget how much it meant to Upham to speak publicly (see above, note 24).

[35] Letter to the Uphams of April 30, 1851, in Wheatley, as cited, pp.
518 f.

ond conversion " perfectly clear for several reasons. One of them
is, of course, because they are intrinsically interesting. Another is because of the importance, for the understanding of
his career, of the circumstance that his perfectionist doctrine
was fundamentally just the Wesleyan doctrine. A third is because a different and misleading representation has been made
with respect to the source from which he derived his new
knowledge. To put it brusquely, Asa Mahan has pointed to
him as a trophy of his own spear. He shows, to be sure, a
(somewhat distorted) knowledge of the circumstances; but
with that fine self-centeredness which often characterizes the
mental attitude of "selfless" saints, he reads them chiefly in
his own honor. He enjoyed Phoebe Palmer's acquaintance,[36]
and one would have wished to see him gladly leave her in
quiet possession of a feather in her cap in which she took
pride. This, however, is how he deals with the matter:[37] " The
spiritual writings of the late [38] Professor Upham, of Bowdoin
College, in the State of Maine, U. S., are 'known and read of
all men.' The manner in which he became such a fruitful
writer on such a theme was on this wise. When the peculiar
views advocated at Oberlin were spread before the public, he
took it for granted that they were wrong, and gave them no
examination. Mrs. Upham, however, was induced by a lady
friend, then residing in the family of the former, to give our
writings a careful examination — her husband, in the kindest
manner possible, often expressing his utter incredulity in
respect to the subject. Mrs. Upham at length became fully
convinced, and sought and obtained 'the sealing and earnest
of the Spirit.' The new life to which she had attained, and
that in connection with the manifest divineness of the change
wrought in her, soon arrested the attention of her husband,
and induced him also to inquire, until he was brought fully
to accept the views which the wife had embraced. It was
the example of the wife, as an epistle of Christ, that rendered

[36] Wheatley, as cited, p. 426.
[37] "Out of Darkness into Light," 1875, pp. 199 f.
[38] Upham had died shortly before — in 1872.

the husband 'the man of God' and the spiritual writer which he afterwards became."

It may be just within the bounds of possibility that the Uphams had "the Oberlin writings" in their hands during their period of stress and strain. When this period began for Mrs. Upham, in February, 1839, there were, however, no expositions of Oberlin Perfectionism generally accessible, except the two lectures on "Christian Perfection" included in Finney's "Lectures to Professing Christians" (1837) and whatever was contained in the first two or three numbers of *The Oberlin Evangelist*, which was started at the close of 1838. In these early numbers there was published, it is true, Mahan's famous address, which formed the nucleus of his little book on "Christian Perfection," which was just now on the eve of publication and which may have been in Upham's hands in the summer. It cannot be affirmed, therefore, that Mrs. Upham could not, or may not, have read these expositions, or that Upham did not read them later; and if they read them there is no reason why they should not be supposed to have received instruction from them. But in the face of their own detailed accounts of their experience, it is impossible to ascribe to these writings — even if read — any such part as Mahan assigns to them. It is perfectly clear that the Uphams were the converts, not of Oberlin, but of the Methodists.

Something more requires to be said. There is some reason to doubt whether "the Oberlin writings," had they been read, would have made an altogether favorable impression upon the Uphams. Upham himself, at any rate, was of a markedly different spirit from the Oberlin men, especially if we look upon Finney as their type; and there are numerous remarks scattered through his writings which bear the appearance at least of referring with distaste to their noisy and bustling religion. Quietness is the mark of Upham's piety.[39] " Quiet men," says he,[40] " other things being equal, are the truly strong men." He deprecates not only the religious excitement of visions and

[39] Cf. above, note 15.
[40] "The Life of Faith," 1845, p. 294.

drcams and revelations, but also the religion of nervous and
even of strong emotional manifestations. He wishes the emotions, "whenever they make their appearance," to be "so
kept under control, as never to disturb the calmness of the
perceptive and rational action of the mind." [41] It is not by way
of vagrant impulse and unregulated feeling, he says, that we
come to know God or His will. God is a God of order. It is
impossible to doubt that in some of the remarks of this kind
which he makes, the phenomena of the Finney revivals are
lying at the back of his mind. He frankly did not like them.
He would have had but little pleasure in the strong tremors
which have often moved the hearts of those who, like the
Oberlin men, saw God in the whirlwind and the storm. His
own ears listened for the still, small voice. "Fanaticism," says
he very significantly,[42] "is characterized, among other things
which help to define it, by being out of repose, by being restless, excitable, visionary, and denunciatory. . . . Granting
that he [the fanatic] has a disposition to do good, it is still
true, that he aims, although perhaps he is not distinctly conscious of it, to do God's work in man's hasty and selfish temper. . . . He is in too much of a hurry for God himself . . ."
As he wrote these words, did he not have Finney's "denunciatory revivals," as Lyman Beecher called them, in mind? "I
have sometimes thought," he says,[43] "that persons of flighty
conceptions and vigorous enthusiasm would regard the Savior,
if he were now on the earth, as too calm and gentle, as too
thoughtful and intellectual, as too free from impulsive and excited agitations, to be reckoned with those who are often considered the most advanced in religion." " It is probably through a
disregard, in part at least, of the course taken by the Savior,
. . . that we find, in all denominations of Christians, melancholy instances of persons, who are young in the Christian life,
or who are prompted by an undue confidence, exhibiting a disposition to enter prematurely, and sometimes violently, upon

[41] "The Life of Faith," 1845, p. 91.
[42] *Ibid.*, pp. 263–264.
[43] "Principles of the Interior or Hidden Life," pp. 245, 251.

measures which are at variance with the results of former experience, and with the admonitions of ancient piety."

We have not observed that Upham anywhere in his religious writings mentions the Oberlin men by name. That also may be a significant fact, for it cannot be that he remained ignorant of their writings. To other perfectionist movements preceding his own, he more distinctly alludes — sometimes very unhappily. There is an allusion, for example, to the " New Dispensation " Perfectionists,[44] with especial reference to their teaching as to the Sabbath. He rejects their teaching, but in doing so deals very gently with them themselves. " It is something worthy of notice, amongst the remarkable things of the present time," he says,[45] " that the Christian Sabbath, contrary to what would be the natural expectation in the case, is attempted to be set aside by persons who have a respect for religion, and appear to be persons of true benevolence and piety. Some of them make high claims to holiness of heart. The holiness of their hearts, as they understand it, has made all things holy. Their work is holy; their rest is holy; their recreations are holy; — everything they do, while the heart is holy, partakes of the character of the source or motive from which it proceeds. No one day, therefore, can be more holy to them than another. The Sabbath is on a footing with other days. All days are alike. This is the general train of their thought and reasoning. And it cannot be doubted, I think, that there is not only a degree of plausibility, but a portion of real truth in these views." This element of truth, he proceeds to point out, is that we must be holy on every day — the Sabbath is not different from other days in that. But it does not follow, he urges, that we are to do the very same things on every day. Each day has its appropriate activities, and our holiness consists, among other things, in doing on each day

[44] The " New Dispensation " Perfectionists swarmed, in Western and Central New York and adjacent parts of New England, in the later twenties and early thirties of the last century. For their teaching see *The Bibliotheca Sacra,* lxxviii. January, 1921, pp. 70 f., or this volume, pp. 247 f., note 55.

[45] " A Treatise on Divine Union," pp. 285 f.

what is appropriate for it. It is a holy duty to rest on the Sabbath; it is the day for public worship and social service, and it should be kept for that. No doubt the holier we are, the better we ourselves could get along without it; but also the holier we are the more we shall be impelled to preserve it, for ourselves and others. It is a good *ad hominem* argument, which he develops, but he says nothing in contravention of the fundamental antinomian assumptions of the errorists whose anti-Sabbatarianism he is repelling. They "appear to be persons of true benevolence and piety"; they are recognized as holy brethren.

It is quite possibly these same people who are in Upham's mind, when a few pages further on he astonishes us by adopting from some not clearly identified "experimental writers," and utilizes for his doctrine of the family, that notion of "correspondences" on the basis of which they had in Upham's own memory put into practice the iniquity of "Spiritual Wives." [46] "There seems," says he,[47] "to be a just and adequate foundation for the doctrine, of which we find some intimations and glimpses from time to time in experimental writers, that all holy beings have their correspondences." That is to say there is somewhere existing the completion or complement of each spiritual being, destined at the appropriate time to be revealed to it. "Then, under the attractions of mutual love, which is wiser and stronger than mere arbitrary and positive law, they unite together: — and they do it under such circumstances that it is not possible to separate them. They thus fulfill the purposes of their Maker; and realize in time a marriage, which, in spirit and essence, is eternal." "The moment that such beings are unveiled to each other as perfect correspondences, the mutual attraction, at once strengthened to its highest intensity, becomes irresistible." Perhaps, however, it is Swedenborg, rather than the "New Dispensationists," on whom Upham is drawing in proclaiming these bizarre notions, and

---

[46] *The Bibliotheca Sacra*, lxxviii. January, 1921, pp. 52 f., or this volume, pp. 244 f. The classical book on "Spiritual Wives," is W. Hepworth Dixon, "Spiritual Wives," 1868.   [47] "A Treatise on Divine Union," pp. 295, 299.

we recall that his Dartmouth classmate, George Bush, had become a vigorous Swedenborgian propagandist and may be thought of as a channel of Swedenborgian influence to Upham.[48] In any case, however, he was bound to remember the evil use to which this very notion of correspondences had been put only a few years before by men of whom he had just spoken without any manifestation of reprobation.

If it is surprising to see Upham adopt and utilize this notion of " correspondences " which had just wrought out so evil a history among the " New Dispensationites," it is more surprising still to see him adopt and utilize the general conception of the New Dispensation itself, from which these errorists derived their name. He announces his adherence to this conception, it is true, in connection with an exposition of some teaching of Madame Guyon's to the same effect,[49] but he does not so much represent himself as deriving this conception from her as according with her in it. In point of fact, the conception is very widespread among mystical perfectionists, who have been prone in every age to represent themselves as introducers of a new dispensation, the dispensation of the Holy Spirit, set over against the dispensations of the Father and the Son, conceived

[48] George Bush became a Swedenborgian in 1845, and was, at the moment (1851) when Upham was writing these words, editing the Swedenborgian journal, *The New Church Repository and Monthly Review* (1848–1855). " Memoirs and Reminiscences of George Bush," edited by W. M. Fernald, was published in 1860. There is a brief notice of him in " The New Schaff-Herzog Encyclopedia of Religious Knowledge," ii. p. 318.

[49] " Life and Religious Opinions and Experience of Madame de la Mothe Guyon," 1849, ii. pp. 52 ff. In the passage quoted from Madame Guyon, she is represented as speaking directly of martyrs for the truth. There are three different grounds of their martyrdom, she is represented as saying, corresponding to three several fundamental truths which required, one after the other, to be proclaimed and witnessed, thus constituting three successive dispensations. There was first the Old Testament dispensation, in which the existence of the one true God was proclaimed and won its martyrs. Then, in " the primitive times of the Christian Church," that Jesus Christ was crucified for sinners was proclaimed and won its martyrs. " At the present time " there are those who are " martyrs of the Holy Ghost " — who " suffer for proclaiming the great truth, that the reign of the Holy Ghost in the souls of men has come." Thus the entrance of Quietism into the world is set in the same sequence with the entrance of the old and new dispensations.

as now past. Among Upham's immediate predecessors in
America, the so-called " New York Perfectionists," as we have
already noted, derived their more descriptive name from this
doctrine; and John Humphrey Noyes himself, who no longer
held to the Millenarianism by which this conception was justified by them, yet managed to retain the conception itself. Upham's presentation of it possesses no advantages over that of
his predecessors and seems clearly to belong to the same mintage. The great doctrines of the Divine unity and of Christ crucified, he says, have been proclaimed, have had their advocates
and martyrs, and have prevailed. " But there is another great
truth, of which it may at length be said, that *its hour has come;*
— namely, that of God, in the person of the inward Teacher
and Comforter, dwelling in the hearts of his people, and changing them by his divine operation into the holy and beautiful
image of him who shed his blood for them. Christ, received by
faith, came into the world to save men from the penalty of sin;
but it has not been so fully . . . recognized that he came also
to save them from sin itself. The time in which this latter work
shall develop itself is sometimes spoken of as the period of the
reign of the Holy Ghost. It is now some time since the voice
has gone forth; an utterance from the Eternal Mind, not as
yet generally received, but which will never cease to be repeated; — Put away all sin; Be like Christ; *Be ye holy.*" And
then again: " The kingdom of the Holy Ghost has come. Its
beginnings are feeble, it is true. . . . But the signs of its full
approach are too marked, too evident, to be mistaken. . . .
Happy will it be, if its friends shall remember, that it is a
kingdom which comes without observation. . . . Behold here
the dominion of the Holy Ghost, the triumph of the true Millennium, the reign of holy love! " The reader can hardly believe his eyes when he sees Upham discovering in his perfectionist sect, which has only recently come into being (" some
time since "), — referring no doubt to the rise of Molinism
— and is now embodied in himself and his coterie, the dispensation of the Holy Ghost which has now at length, after
so long a time, dawned. We wonder whether he really imagined

that never until this sect had arisen, had the cry of, Put away all sin! been heard. And we wonder even more what judgment he intended to pass on all the perfectionist sectaries, stretching in unbroken succession from, say, Pelagius to, say, the Ranters, that they should be passed by and the dispensation of the Spirit made to begin only with his own special party. We must not leave without notice that he identifies this New Dispensation, the inauguration of which "some time since" he asserts, with the Millennium. In doing so he places himself distinctly on the plane of the Chiliastic perfectionism which had been troubling the churches for the preceding quarter of a century.

The general position taken in these amazing claims presents a curious parallel to the fundamental Montanistic assumption, and it is not strange that the opponents of Quietism were quick to take note of this fact. When A. C. McGiffert [50] writes of Montanism: "Its fundamental proposition was the continuance of divine revelation which was begun under the old Dispensation, was carried on in the time of Christ and his apostles, and reached its highest development under the dispensation of the Paraclete, which opened with the activity of Montanus," his words would require very little adjustment to adapt them to Upham's representations. Upham does not, it is true, assert that a new revelation in the strict sense has come with him and his companions. But he does assert that a new truth has come into the possession of the Church, through him and them; a new truth by means of which a new and culminating dispensation of the Kingdom of God has been introduced. Thus in a true sense he contends that in him and them the Kingdom of God has at last come. In this broad application of the parallel, Bossuet was not wrong, then, in comparing Fénelon and Madame Guyon to Montanus; [51] and the similarity cannot be evaded as Fénelon endeavored to evade it, by pleading that there were many

[50] "The Church History of Eusebius," p. 229, in "Nicene and Post-Nicene Fathers," Second Series, i. 1890.

[51] Upham, "Life of Madame Guyon," ii. p. 271.

particulars in the Montanistic teaching, and especially in the conduct of its protagonists, to which he and Madame Guyon provided no parallel. Neither Madame Guyon nor Upham were Montanists. But they shared with Montanus the fanatical assertion, that the culminating dispensation of the Kingdom of God, the dispensation of the Spirit, has been introduced only by them. It would be wrong, of course, to suppose that they derived this fanatical point of view, which they shared with the Montanists, either directly or indirectly from them. It came down to them, as we have already intimated, from quite a different source, and through a well-marked line of tradition. John the Scot, the head of the line of Western Mystics, holds it with as great clearness as Madame Guyon or Upham, although he avoids the identification of the Dispensation of the Spirit, which he conceives as still future, with himself. John continued in a very positive way — Rufus M. Jones describes his teaching thus [52] — " the idea of a progressive revelation, already taught by the Montanists. He marked out in his Commentary on the Gospel of John three stages of priesthood. The first stage — that of the priesthood of the Old Testament — was transitory, and it saw the truth only through the thick veils of mysterious types. The second priesthood, that of the New Testament, had a greater light of truth, but still obscured by symbols. The third priesthood, that which is to come, will see God face to face. To the first corresponds the laws of condemnation, to the second the law of Grace; the third will be the kingdom of God. The first assisted human nature, which was corrupted by sin; the second ennobled it by faith; the third will illumine it with direct contemplation. The Church of the present will be swallowed up by the light of the Church of the future, when souls will actually possess God by direct communion with Him by the Spirit." Joachim of Fiori repeats in effect the representations of John and still, like him, places the Dispensation of the Spirit in the future, although he looked for it in the immediate future; [53]

[52] " Studies in Mystical Religion," 1909, pp. 122 f.
[53] Jones, as cited, p. 172.

and his disciple, Gerard of San Donnino, in the famous " Eternal Gospel," fixed so firmly in the minds of "spiritual" men the idea of a coming religion of the Spirit that it never afterward died out.[54] In Amaury (Amalrich) of Bene, however, and his followers, the Dispensation of the Spirit, formerly looked forward to, has already come in himself and his coterie. " The Father, they taught, was incarnated in Abraham; the Son in the child of Mary's womb; and the Holy Spirit has become incarnated in them." And this new "reign of the Holy Spirit," now at last begun, " frees humanity from all burdens and servitude. In Him all laws and commandments are at an end." [55] It is this form of the conception, rife among the Brethren of the Free Spirit, and equally so among the Anabaptists and Ranters of seventeenth century England, which reappears in the mystical perfectionists of Western and Central New York at the end of the first quarter of the nineteenth century, and is proclaimed with the confidence of strong conviction by Upham.

Even the " New Dispensationists " do not represent, however, the extreme to which Upham was able to sink in order to find companionship in his vagaries. In a most astonishing chapter in his latest work [56] — published posthumously — he undertakes to reconstitute the Trinity into a Duality — Father and Mother instead of Father, Son, and Spirit; but a Duality which afterwards becomes a Trinity by the appearance of a Son, which is identified with — the creation, "the whole of creation from the lowest to the highest form." In order to obtain support for this precious speculation he does not scruple to appeal to the teaching of a long catalogue of heresies, ancient Gnostics, the Jewish Cabala, Mediæval Mystics, the Familists, the Philadelphians, the Shakers, and — this is the culmination of all — " the Bible Communists," that is to say, John Humphrey Noyes, the founder of the Oneida

[54] Jones, as cited, p. 175.

[55] Jones, as cited, pp. 187 f.

[56] " Absolute Religion. A View of the Absolute Religion, based on Philosophical Principles and the Doctrines of the Bible," 1873, pp. 45–67, especially pp. 64 f.

Community.[57] To this length his sense of solidarity with fellow-perfectionists had brought him in his old age. He actually sets forth the ravings of Noyes as an element in the "absolute religion," that is, in that essential, universal, and eternal religion which may harmonize with Christian teaching, but is in essence the rational faith of all men.

We should be sorry to leave the impression that these grotesque speculations are a fair sample of the substance of Upham's teaching. That is far from the fact. Upham belongs among the soberest of our perfectionist leaders. Our main purpose in the preceding paragraphs has been to suggest the extent of his knowledge of his immediate predecessors in this type of religious thinking, and the distance to which his mental sympathy with them was able to carry him — on occasions. He owed his "second conversion" wholly to Methodist influences: Phoebe Palmer, to use Mrs. Upham's figure, "begot him in the Gospel"; it was the Methodist doctrine of perfection which he desired to proclaim, and in the main did proclaim.[58] But his mind was not an empty cask into which the Methodist doctrine was poured, and that was the end of it. He was blessed, or, as he might himself say, cursed, with great intellectual curiosity; and first and last he explored many odd corners of religious thought, and usually came back with something in his hands. It is probable that he never taught the Methodist doctrine of perfection quite in its pur-

[57] "The doctrine, that the Divine Nature is dual in its personalities, and that this duality implies and includes the fact of a divine maternity, is adopted and advocated by the sect known as Bible Communists. The leading doctrines of this people are found in a work entitled 'The Berean'; a work which is characterized by acuteness of thought and reasoning, and by no small share of biblical learning" ("Absolute Religion," p. 64). Then he proceeds to quote from "The Berean" passages in support of his contention. It is not credible that Upham was unaware of the character of the sectaries to which he was appealing. Cf. *The Bibliotheca Sacra*, lxxviii. October, 1921, pp. 343–375, or this volume, pp. 308–333.

[58] A writer in *The Methodist Quarterly Review* for April, 1846, p. 260, remarks, apparently with no misgivings with respect to the non-Wesleyan element in its teaching: "There is no work in our language, not excepting our own writers, in which the doctrine of entire sanctification is more fully stated and applied than in the 'Interior Life.'"

ity — not even in those first days of his return from New York when, laying aside his dislike for public utterance, he spoke so winningly, in Mrs. Upham's opinion, in their little propagandist meetings at Brunswick. We have expressed our opinion that the writings of the Oberlin people did not furnish the subject of his study during those days of feverish examination of the nature of the Gospel requirements and provisions with reference to holiness, to which he was incited in the summer of 1839 by Mrs. Upham's adoption of the Methodist doctrine. But we have had no intention of implying that no writings on holiness were then in his hands. Upham being the man he was, that would have been inconceivable. It is very safe to say that many books on holiness were subjected to very intensive study during those difficult weeks. And it does not seem very difficult to say in general what books they in the main were. The writings of the Quietistic Mystics were certainly among them. They were not the whole of them, but they occupied the central place.

The general reason for saying this is that, when Upham comes into view after he had found his peace, he has these books in his hands. In point of fact we know no Upham after his " second conversion " but the mystical Upham. It is quite true that there was an interval of two or three years between his return from New York at the beginning of 1840 with the treasure conveyed to him by Phoebe Palmer, and the publication of his first religious book in 1843. We cannot confidently assert that there may not have been a period immediately after his finding " the blessing " in which he preached Methodist Perfectionism, unmodified by mystical infusions. But the wide acquaintance he shows with the Quietistic literature, and the abundant use he makes of it in his first book [59] — and the deep absorption in it which he manifests in its immediate succes-

[59] In the "Principles of the Interior or Hidden Life," 1843, he quotes not only from Tauler and Behmen, À Kempis and Law, but from St. Theresa, Francis de Sales, Molinos, La Combe, Madame Guyon, Fénelon, Antoinette Bourignon, and Père Lombaz. Yet this was a " popular " book, meant for the reading of " the general."

sors — suggests pushing back the beginnings of his engagement with it as far as possible.

What strikes us most strongly, however, as we glance through Upham's literary history is the greatness of the crisis which he passed through at his "second conversion." The direction of his studies and the whole character of his reading were transformed by it. We have already had occasion to point out the strength of his natural literary impulse and the abundance of his literary product. His first book came from the press contemporaneously with his own emergence from the schoolroom; and in the course of seventeen years thereafter he had published eight solid volumes on very abstruse subjects. A sudden and complete change takes place in this stream of publications on his "second conversion." The literary activity continues, but the subjects on which it expends itself are totally altered. Never again does he print a philosophical work.[60] There was a volume of poems,[61] and a volume of "Letters" from abroad.[62] But with these exceptions everything else that he printed through a long list of publications — embracing a dozen items — was not only religious in its subject, but designed specifically for "the promotion of practical holiness."[63] There are included in the list, it is true, two works which take the form of biographies — the "Life of Madame Catharine Adorna" (better known, perhaps, as St. Catharine of Genoa), 1845, and the "Life and Religious Opinions and Experience of Madame de la Mothe Guyon," 1847. But these books are biographies only in form: the didactic element dominates them, and indeed constitutes even physically the greater part of their contents. They are simply additional

[60] In 1869 he gathered the three parts of his "Mental Philosophy" into one comprehensive work in two volumes. But this resumé of old material constitutes no exception to what is said in the text.

[61] "American Cottage Life," ed. 2, 1850, ed. 3, 1852.

[62] "Letters Written from Europe, Egypt and Palestine," 1855.

[63] The language is his own in describing, in the preface to the latter (p. v.), the leading purpose of the first two of these books — "Principles of the Interior or Hidden Life" and "The Life of Faith." It may be applied to all.

commendations of Upham's perfectionist doctrine, cast in a biographical form in the hope, no doubt, of obtaining thereby a fresh appeal. All the rest of his books, published in this second period of his life, are openly pleas for "holiness," or aids to its attainment. They include the following volumes: " Principles of the Interior or Hidden Life," 1843; " The Life of Faith," 1845; " A Treatise on Divine Union," 1851; " Religious Maxims," 1854 (taken from the " Principles of the Interior or Hidden Life "); " A Method of Prayer," 1859 (an analysis of the work by Madame Guyon so entitled); " Christ in the Soul," 1872; and " Absolute Religion," 1873. It is obvious from this list of titles that Upham's real interest lay in " holiness," and his engagement with Quietistic Mysticism was secondary and ancillary to that. If he did not merely repeat the Methodist doctrine of " holiness " which he " learned more perfectly " from Phoebe Palmer, neither did he transmute it into Quietistic Mysticism. He modified his statement of it, here and there, with formulas which he borrowed from the Quietists, but for " substance of doctrine " what he taught remained steadily Wesleyan Perfectionism. So far from assimilating his Wesleyan doctrine to Quietism, he sought rather at bottom to assimilate Quietism to it. What he undertook, indeed, was nothing less in effect than the amazing task of evangelicizing Quietism. We say evangelicizing rather than Wesleyanizing, for, after all, there was a deeper lying stratum in Upham's thought than even the Wesleyan Methodism which Phoebe Palmer taught him. He was a Congregationalist before he became a Methodist Perfectionist — a Congregationalist of the " New Divinity " type, and holding the " New Divinity " firmly, though not in an extreme form. What we have to do with in him, accordingly, is a somewhat mild " New Divinity " Congregationalism, overlaid with Wesleyan Perfectionism, endeavoring to read the Quietism of Madam Guyon in harmony with itself.

II. UPHAM AND THE QUIETISTS

IT WAS a tremendous undertaking — this of evangelicizing Quietism. Fénelon had expended his genius in an attempt to Catholicize it, with a great deal less than indifferent success. Upham looks over the "Maxims of the Saints" and pronounces them in essence evangelical! The Jansenists, whom Fénelon persecuted and who had no weapon against their persecutor except their wit, wrote an epitaph for him:

"Neath two damnations, here lies Fénelon —
One for Molinos, for Molina one."

Upham seems to think that in combining Molinos-ism and Molina-ism, instead of doubling his condemnation, Fénelon escaped it altogether and became — evangelical. Something as, we suppose, the combination (in proper proportions) of oxygen and hydrogen comes out, not doubly gaseous, but a good, serviceable liquid. No doubt we must remember that Upham looked at Fénelon out of "New Divinity" eyes, and the "New Divinity" had invented for itself a doctrine of sin and grace, of dependence and freedom — indeed, of "congruism" itself — of which Molina-ism need not have been ashamed. From this point of sight, Fénelon might very well have been quoted as a brother, and Upham's fundamental mistake was in imagining the "New Divinity" to be evangelical. But it was not merely Fénelon's Molina-ism which he proclaimed evangelical, but his Molinos-ism also. And, perceiving no difference between the exquisite nicety of Fénelon's distinctions, by which he attempted to give Catholic standing to the essence of Molinos-ism, and the raw crudity of Madame Guyon's declamations, he pronounced her teaching also in substance evangelical. All Quietism was the same to him, whether read in Molinos' "Spiritual Guide," at the one end, or in Antoinette Bourignon's "Light in Darkness" at the other; and it was all in intention and effect evangelical. His method was very simple. He read all this literature with so firm a conviction that it is in intention and effect evangelical, despite the unfortunate appearance given it by its unhappy use of language, that he persistently imposed on the unwilling language his own evangelical sense so far as his own sense (the sense of the "New Divinity," with Methodist Perfectionism superposed on it) was evangelical. Thus the unevangelical language came in the end really to speak to him in evangelical accents, and he actually employs it to express his own evangelical meaning. The effect on his writings is very curious. However natural it may have become to him to express his evangelical conceptions in Quietistic language, his readers do not find it easy to read his Quietistic language in an evangelical sense. A veil of ambiguity is thrown over the page. The reader is continually disturbed by doubt as to how much or how little is intended by the mystical language which he reads; and it is much if he does not end by raising the general question whether Upham is a mystic at all, or whether he has not merely acquired a bad habit of obscurely expressing himself in mystical forms of speech.

Much of this confusion is due, however, to a more deeply lying confusion still — the confusion of inwardness in religion with evangelicalism. Evangelicalism is, of course, in its very idea, a religion of the heart. But it does not follow that all inwardness in religion is evangelicalism. That form of religion which we call mysticism is as inward as evangelicalism — in fact, more exclusively inward than it. It is in this that its appeal has always lain — and its usefulness — as a protest against the externalities of the sacerdotalism of the Romish Church. It is in it that the self-consciousness of the mystic has centered; or we might as well say plainly, his pride, a pride in which he has as heartily despised external religion as it has him. The *ethos* of the contestants in the Quietistic controversy is not badly revealed in the contemptuous name of "the new spiritualists" which the Catholics fixed on the Quietists, and in Fénelon's repudiation only of the epithet "new" — "It is not a *new* spirituality which I defend, but the *old*." It is quite in the manner of the mystics of all ages when Jacob Behmen reminds us grimly that Cain was an observer of ordinances. "Cain," he says,[64] "goes to church to offer and comes out again a murderer of his brother." The altar of God, he explains, is wherever the living knowledge of Christ is; and at that altar alone can true and acceptable offerings be made. He would not, it is true, "abolish and raze the stone churches," but he would keep us reminded of that "Temple of God which must be brought into the stone churches with us," or else the whole business of the stone church is only "a Cain's offering, both for the preacher and hearer." Nothing truer than that could well be said; and, reading it, and the like of it, after their own fashions of speech, in the Quietistic writers, we are almost ready to say with Upham, when speaking of Madame Guyon's "Method of Prayer": [65] "Its doctrines are essentially Protestant; making Faith, in distinction from the merits of works, the foundation of the religious life, and even carrying the power of faith in the renovation of our inward nature beyond what is commonly found in Protestant writers."

Such a remark rests, nevertheless, on a complete misunderstanding. Madame Guyon has nothing in common with Protestantism except the inwardness of her religion and her consequent emancipation from rites and ceremonies, on the one hand, and on the other a certain exaltation of Christ in the center of her religious life, although thinking of Him quite differently and looking to Him for quite different benefits, from Protestantism. In all that concerns the distinction between Protestantism and Romanism she is wholly Romanist. Her conception of faith is not the Protestant conception; and her notion of its function is far from the Protestant understanding of it. Nothing could be more misleading than to suggest that she opposed faith and works in the Protestant sense. What she did was to oppose faith to external works — for did she not teach an "interior religion"? But as for works in the broad sense, she taught as arrant a work religion

as other Romanists — only the works on which she depended
were not external but internal works. She suspended everything on the subjective state and looked upon personal holiness
as the condition, not the issue, of communion with God. In
describing the work of Madame Guyon among the young ladies
at Madame de Maintenon's "Female Institution" at St. Cyr,
Upham employs an expression which, if we may be permitted to press it into our service, may not only rather sharply
express to us the difference between the ordinary Romanist
teaching and that of Madame Guyon, but also suggest part of
the distinction between her teaching and that of Protestantism.
These young ladies, he says,[66] had no doubt generally been
accustomed — under the ordinary Romanist teaching — to regard "their acceptance with God as depending, in a great
degree at least, on a number of outward observances, rather
than on inward dispositions" — as Madame Guyon now
taught them to regard it. Here we have the exact fact — Madame Guyon suspended acceptance with God not on outward
observances but on inward dispositions, and it was in this sense
that she interiorized religion.

The New Testament and evangelical religion teach that
acceptance with God depends wholly on the finished work of
Christ, faith being merely the instrument by which this finished work of Christ is received and rested on. Of this fundamental principle of New Testament and evangelical religion,
as Heinrich Heppe justly points out, Madame Guyon knew
nothing. The foundation-stone, he reminds us,[67] on which the
whole evangelical consciousness is built, is the historical redemptive work of Christ. In this, faith finds, once for all, the
righteousness which avails with God. On it the believer reposes with sure confidence for his peace with God here and his
eternal felicity hereafter. It is the firm foundation on which
his whole system of faith is built. Of all this, however, Madame Guyon was altogether ignorant. The fundamental fact

[66] *Ibid.,* ii. 1849, p. 127.
[67] "Geschichte der quietistischen Mystik in der katholischen Kirche,"
1875, p. 488.

of the Gospel was not known to her as such. Everything therefore which was transacted in the person of Christ here on earth, and found its completion in Him, she transferred to the heart of the individual and had transacted over again there. It is only in this sense that she enthrones Christ in the center of her religious life. It is not the fact of the redemptive work of Christ on which she rests; and it is not the forming of Christ within, as a result of faith in this redemptive work, for which she hopes. She suspended her hope on the repetition in the soul, by its own exercises, of the experiences of Christ, until, having reproduced in itself the qualities that characterized Christ, it becomes sharer in the divine favor which rested on Him. Christ ceases in this view to be our Saviour and becomes our model. He is not Himself the Way by which we reach God, but only the Guide who shows us the way; not the blood of Christ but *imitatio Christi* has become the ground of our hope. It is not unfair to say, as Upham says,[68] that in this view religion has become "something more than [a] . . . mere ceremonial " — it has become " a life." But we must remember that "life " has two meanings — the life which is lived and the life by which it is lived; the manner in which we live and the power by which we live. And it is only in the former sense that religion is a life with Madame Guyon: after all is said and done, religion remains with her a scheme rather than a power.

It is already apparent how misleading it is to speak of Madame Guyon as recommending herself to Protestants by the honor she places on faith — "even carrying the power of faith in the renovation of our inward nature beyond what is commonly found in Protestant writers." [69] The allusion in these words is to what is represented as Madame Guyon's great discovery — a dramatic account of which is given [70] — of " sanctification by faith." This is a doctrine, we are told, which, hardly tolerable in the Protestant Church, is quite impossible

---

[68] "Life of Madame Guyon," ii. p. 128.

[69] *Ibid.*, i. p. 398.

[70] *Ibid.*, i. p. 238.

in the Romanist; but was formed in Madame Guyon's heart "by infinite wisdom," and was uttered by her "in obedience to that deep and sanctified conviction which constitutes the soul's inward voice" — uttered at the moment of its discovery and always, so that it became in a true sense her life-message. Faith, we must bear in mind, however, was in Madame Guyon's view a "work," that is to say, a virtue, a virtuous disposition, that particular virtuous disposition which above all others prepared and opened the soul for the reception of divine things. Her proclamation of sanctification by faith had a double significance, negative and positive. On the one hand, it was an assertion of emancipation from the sacerdotal means of sanctification without which in the modes of conception prevalent in the Roman Church, there could be no sanctification. It was anti-sacerdotal. On the other hand, it asserted that the condition of sanctification is an absolutely passive receptivity — and it is this state of mind which is called "faith." The soul that is empty, says Madame Guyon, is the soul that is filled, and the whole duty of man is to make and keep his soul empty. This is Quietism. In it is announced a philosophy of life under the influence of which — in the furthest extension of its application — inactivity, indifference, apathy, mental and bodily, became the idea of behavior in every department of living. Madame Guyon relates of herself with great satisfaction — Upham quoting her account with apparent approval [71] — that in a dangerous carriage-accident she sat quietly in the vehicle and made no effort to save herself. In any given instance this mode of action may or may not be in accordance with good judgment. That is not however Madame Guyon's plea. The point of her narrative is that faith in God implies and requires on all occasions complete inactivity on our part. In no circumstances of life are we called upon to act. Our duty at all times and in all spheres of activity (as we say — but how meaninglessly in this view!) is — to do nothing. "It is better to perish, trusting calmly in God's providence, than to make our escape from danger, trusting in

[71] *Ibid.*, i. pp. 140 f.

ourselves." "I would rather endure them" — any conceivable
trials — "all my life long, than put an end to them in a dependence on myself." That is to say, we must never make
any effort to save ourselves from any danger, or to relieve
ourselves from any difficulties. If the house catches on fire
we must sit quietly in it and burn up: to walk out is to distrust
God. If the boat sinks under us, we must not swim to shore,
but fold our hands and sink — "let go and let God." Here is a
fully developed philosophy of irresponsibility.

We have seen Upham felicitating the young ladies of St.
Cyr on the spiritual revival which they experienced under
the teachings of Madame Guyon. "Turned by the conversation of Madame Guyon," he says,[72] "from the outward to the
inward, led to reflect upon their own situation and wants, they
saw that there is something better than worldly vanity; and
began to seek a truer, sincerer, and higher position." There
is unfortunately some reason to fear, however, that this is
only an ideal sketch of the effect of Madame Guyon's instruction on her pupils, framed on the assumption that the
substance of what she taught them was "redemption, and permanent inward salvation by faith" — in the Protestant sense
of these words. We have a very spirited picture of what happened at St. Cyr under Madame Guyon's Quietistic teaching,
from the pen of an eye-witness — one of the inmates of the
house — a Madame du Pérou.[73] It proves to be very much
what might have been expected, as Ernest Seillière puts it,
"in a community invaded by a purely emotional morality and
Guyonese mysticism." Whatever may have been the spiritual
revolution which they experienced, the observable deport-
ment of the converts was not edifying. "These ladies," writes
Madame du Pérou, "were chilly, distant, even a little scornful,
towards those not of their party; very independent towards
their superiors and directors, very full of presumption and
pride. . . . They attended preaching as seldom as they could,

[72] "Life of Madame Guyon," ii. pp. 127 f.

[73] We are drawing from Ernest Seillière, "Madame Guyon et Fénelon,
Prècurseurs de Rousseau," 1918, pp. 143 f.

saying that it distracted them, and that they needed nothing
but God. . . . Nearly the whole house became Quietist. Nothing was talked about but pure love, abandonment, holy indifference, simplicity, in the practice of which every one
abandoned herself to her ease, and disturbed herself about
nothing, not even her own salvation. It is to this that this
alleged resignation to the will of God comes in which we can
consent as readily to our own damnation as to being saved; this
was what that famous act of abandonment that was taught consisted in. . . . These fashions of speech were so common that
even 'the Reds' (the pupils of the lowest class) employed
them; even down to the lay-sisters and the servants, nothing
was talked of but pure love. There were some who, instead of
doing their work, spent their time in reading Madame Guyon's
books, which they fancied they understood." The novices
no longer obeyed. "They fell into ecstatics. They conceived
so lively and so inconvenient an appetite for prayer that they
neglected their most necessary duties. One, instead of sweeping, stood nonchalantly propped on her broom; another, instead of attending to the instruction of the girls, lost herself in
inspiration and abandoned herself to the Spirit. The under-
mothers (of the novices) furtively assembled the illuminated
in some corner, where they fed themselves on Madame Guyon's
ideas. Under pretence of seeking perfection, they despised
the only method of attaining it. . . ." This last sentence, adds
Seillière, in comment, is the protest of Stoic-Christian ethics,
against a purely emotional ethics, founded on an irrational
feminine mysticism. In the Christian system, perfection is
conceived as absolute performance; in the Quietistic as absolute non-performance.

We are here at the heart of Quietism. But not of Quietism
alone. For Quietists are not alone among mystics in calling
upon man to " nought " himself, that he may become " nothing," and the floods of God may wash in and fill his emptiness.
This is general mystical teaching. " A man shall become as
truly poor," says Eckhart,[74] " and as free from his creature

[74] Rufus M. Jones, " Studies in Mystical Religion," 1909, p. 230.

will as he was when he was born. And I say to you, by the eternal truth, that as long as ye desire to fulfill the will of God, and have any desire after eternity and God, so long are ye not truly poor. He alone hath true spiritual poverty who wills nothing, knows nothing, desires nothing." " The soul " — Rufus M. Jones continues the quotations thus in summary — " must withdraw not only from possessions and ' works,' but it must also withdraw from all sense experience, from everything in time and space, from every image of memory, every idea of the understanding into an experience above this lower form of consciousness — an experience in which ' all things are present in one unified now and here.' " [75] The soul must become a *tabula rasa* if God is to write upon it. Similarly " ' Swester Katrei ' — Sister Katharine — called in the narrative ' Eckhart's Strasbourg Daughter,' " declares that " ' not even desire of heaven should tempt a good man toward activity.' " The story runs that " on one occasion she became cataleptic, and was being carried to burial for dead. Her confessor, just in time, discovered that it was trance instead of death, and awoke her. Katharine exclaimed: ' Now I am satisfied, for I have been dead all through.' " Jones,[76] in telling this story, speaks of it as presenting " an extreme example of morbid quietistic mysticism "; but it is difficult to perceive anything extreme about it in comparison with the ordinary Quietistic teaching; it is just the common doctrine of the Quietistic mystic uncommonly poignantly expressed. It is quite paralleled, for example, by what Jones [77] again calls " an extraordinary case " in which a " Friend of God " " got to the indifference-point to such a degree that he, ' through the power of love, became without love,' and in this state of perfect surrender, he heard a voice say to him: ' Permit Me, My beloved child, to share in thee and with thee all the riches of My divinity; all the passionate love of My humanity; all the joys

[75] " Alle miteinander in eime Blicke und in eime Punte " — " Everything merges into a single flash and into a single point."

[76] As cited, p. 222.

[77] As cited, pp. 270 f.

of the Holy Spirit,' and the 'Friend of God' replied: 'Yes, Lord, I permit Thee, on condition that Thou alone shalt enjoy it, and not I!'" Indifference must be carried to such a point as to be indifferent to the very end that is sought. There is nothing startlingly novel, therefore, in the "passivity," "indifference," "abandonment," "annihilation" which was taught by the sixteenth century Quietists and from their teaching of which they derived their name.

This teaching has its roots ultimately in the pantheistic background which underlies the whole mystical teaching. Whenever this pantheistic understratum cropped out fully upon the surface, it naturally destroyed all sense of individuality, and reduced what, to the vulgar apprehension, appeared to be separate personalities to mere momentary wavelets on the bosom of the deep of being. That, however, is pantheism, not mysticism; mysticism seeks as an attainment what pantheism posits as a fact. Mysticism, however, everywhere and always true to its pantheistic groundwork, with more or less force of assertion and clearness of expression, proclaims the necessity, for that union with the divine to which all its yearnings urge, of stripping away everything which enters into the individualization of the subject. This anti-individualistic tendency, intrinsic to mysticism, was, in the days of developed Romanism, no doubt reinforced in its effect, but also modified in its expression — often so greatly modified as to seem even superseded — by another tendency grounded in a wholly different, not to say contradictory, point of view. This is the tendency to contempt of "nature," arising out of the dualism of "nature" and "the supernatural" in the Romanist doctrine of salvation. For the ellipse of the Romanist doctrine of salvation is not thrown, as in Protestantism, around the foci of sin and grace, so much as around those of nature and the supernatural. God, it is taught, had designed man for a state higher than that of merely natural virtue and felicity and therefore had endowed him, when he left His creative hands, with a *donum superadditum* — a supplementary gift of something lying wholly outside of and beyond his nature

as man — which raised him to a plane of supernatural virtue
and supernatural felicity. It was this *donum superadditum*
which man lost in the fall; so that he fell not out of what he
ought to be by nature, but back into — mere — nature. It is it
also which is restored in salvation; so that man is brought by
salvation not into what he ought to be by nature, but into
something above all nature. Fallen man, accordingly, existing,
as it is phrased, *in puris naturalibus*, in the purity of his —
merely — natural state, just as he came from his Maker's
hands, requires no recreation that he may be able to maintain
himself in a state of natural virtue or natural felicity. Salvation
is therefore conceived in essence as delivering man not precisely from sin, but from a consequence of his sinning; not as
restoring him to the natural purity which belongs to him in the
conception of pure manhood, but as raising him above this,
to a higher purity, to which he could in any case be brought
only by the addition of something to him which does not belong to his nature as such. Human nature, as fallen, is thought
of then, not as depraved and corrupted, reduced below what
human nature as such ought to be, and needing restoration;
but as all that man as such ought to be or can be — only
functioning, as such of course, on a lower plane than by God's
supernatural gift to it, it may be elevated to. This doctrine
in intention and effect honoring human nature, as it at present
exists in the world — "fallen man," as we say — and only
holding out to its heights of attainment to which it may climb
above itself — ended, in the hands of earnest men, in dishonoring human nature as such and transferring to it the degradation which belongs to it only as fallen. Fallen human nature
having been defined as pure human nature, the characteristics
which belong only to fallen human nature — which, however
much they were denied, could not remain unfelt — were naturally transferred to pure human nature. The supernatural gifts
and felicity held out as the prize to be striven after, threw in
contrast with them the nature without them into the blackest
shadow and made it contemptible. The natural life in all its
manifestations came thus to be looked upon as not merely a

less exalted life than might be ours, but as an essentially degraded life; and a Manichaean-like misprision of the whole natural order resulted. Men longed to be delivered not from their sin but from their selves: and only in the deliverance from self could they see deliverance from sin. They became to their own apprehension all evil — in such a sense all evil, that nothing could avail for their salvation but their complete destruction. There was nothing about them or in them which could survive in the process of salvation. They forgot, in other words, that nature itself is the work of God, and that it is the restoration, not the destruction, of nature that Christ came to accomplish — that it is not the works of God but the works of the devil that He came to destroy.[78]

It is up against this double background of doctrine — Pantheizing Mysticism on the one hand, Pelagianizing Romanism on the other — that the "passivity," "indifference," "abandonment," "annihilation" of the Quietists were thrown. They meant precisely what they said; though naturally they succeeded but indifferently in attaining the states which they described. G. W. Leibnitz, writing to the Landgrave Ernest of Hesse,[79] reveals how the matter struck a competent contemporary observer. He remarks that there is very little in Molinos' "Spiritual Guide" which may not be found in other mystics — only Molinos has infused poison into their honey. He instances especially the doctrine of "annihilation." "For," says he, "the pretence of being without action, without thought, and without will — of what they call quietude, and of annihilating ourselves, so as to enter into silence and so hear God better (since He speaks within) and to receive His impressions — these things are chimeras, no rational justification of which has been given. We should have to take opium or get drunk in order to attain to such a quietude, or inactivity; which is nothing but the stupidity suitable only to brutes. The

[78] A good brief account of this Romanist doctrine (with references) may be found in H. Bavinck, "Gereformeerde Dogmatiek," ed. 2, i. pp. 369–378; see also the same author's "De Algemeene Genade," 1894, pp. 18–24.

[79] May 25, 1688, quoted by C. E. Scharling, "Michael de Molinos," German translation, 1855, pp. 115–116.

true quietude which is found in the Scriptures, in the Fathers, and in Reason, is withdrawal from the outward pleasures of sense, the better to hear the voice of God — that is to say, the inward light of eternal verities. But in order to do this we must give ourselves to meditation and devote ourselves to the learning and study of the great verities; we must consider God's perfections and direct the will to love Him — and all this is very different indeed from that irrational inactivity of the sham Quietists, whom the Jesuits are very right in combating. No matter what is said, it is not possible for a substance to cease to act. The mind is never more active than when the outer senses are silent. This is the silence and repose which the mystic sages ask for, with no notion of the mind's sinking itself into a deep lethargy. Tauler, Ruysbroek, Valentine Weigel, and other mystics, Catholics and Protestants alike, often speak of a resignation, or annihilation — of a ' collectedness.' But I suppose that they mean it in the sense I have just explained: otherwise the results would be evil, as is seen in the turn which Molinos has given to those ideas." [80] Mystics may differ from mystics in the length to which they push their fundamental contempt of nature common to them all; and this difference of degree may seem at times so great as to amount almost to a difference of kind. A man like John Tauler may stand at one extreme of the series: the Quietists stand so at the other extreme that the language which Tauler employs when expressing his reprobation of the men of the " Free Spirit," might be read almost without change as applicable to them. " They stand exempt from all subjection, without any activity upward or downward," he writes,[81] " just as a tool

[80] Leibnitz adds an anecdote which is not exactly *ad rem*, but may serve to show the way in which the matter was looked at: " I am told," says he, " that there was this kind of a Quietist in Hesse — a Reformed minister — who lewdly kissed a devout woman while she was praying: and when she resisted, blamed her for not being sufficiently abstracted and insensible to outward things." There were many stories of this kind in circulation, showing that in the general apprehension of the time, the quietude of the Quietist was complete insensibility. Compare above, the story of Swester Katrei, who was " dead all through."

[81] Rufus M. Jones, " Studies in Mystical Religion," 1909, p. 209, drawing from Preger, " Geschichte der deutschen Mystik im Mittelalter, iii. p. 133.

is passive and waits until its master wishes to use it, for it
seems to them that if they do anything then God will be hindered in His work; therefore they count themselves above all
virtues. They wish to be so free that they do not think, nor
praise God, nor have anything, nor know anything, nor love
nor ask nor desire anything; for all that they might wish to
ask they have (according to their notion). And they also think
that they are poor in spirit because they are *without any will
of their own* and have renounced all possessions. They also
wish to be free of all practice of virtue, obedient to no one,
whether pope, or bishop, or priest. They wish to be free of
everything with which the Church has to do. They say publicly that so long as a man strives after virtues, so long is
he imperfect and knows nothing of spiritual poverty, nor of
this spiritual freedom." This is the type of religion which the
Quietists commended.

It is often a great temptation, in reading the writings of
the Quietists, to think of the " nature " which they wish to
" crucify " much more in terms of what we commonly speak
of as our " sinful nature " than they themselves did; and
thus to accord to sin and deliverance from sin a far greater
prominence in their thought than it really occupies. Rufus
M. Jones offers us a very good example of the greatness of this
temptation. Fénelon, he says,[82] " is one of the noblest illustrations in the seventeenth century of the impossibility of successfully solving the problem of spiritual life on the assumption that human nature — the natural man — is absolutely
corrupt and depraved, and that God can triumph in the soul
only when the human powers have been annihilated, the assumption that God is all only when man is nothing." Fénelon,
however, made no such assumption as " that human nature
— the natural man — is absolutely corrupt and depraved."
That was Jansenist doctrine; and would have been thought of
by Fénelon, as it is by one of his biographers,[83] as misrepresenting God's world " as a sinful chaos, a shaking quagmire of
corruption, in the midst of which rises, stark and lonely, the

---

[82] *The Harvard Theological Review,* x. 1917, p. 49.
[83] Viscount St. Cyres, " Francois de Fenelon," 1901, p. 229.

storm-swept citadel of Grace." "Fénelon," himself, as this
same historian rightly tells us,[84] "was a priest who disbelieved in total depravity, and meant to make the best of human nature as it was." "Children," according to him, "are
born without any natural trend to good or evil," [85] and any sin
which they ever have is picked up by them in the course of
living: it may be much, but it may be little — it may conceivably be so little as to be none at all.[86] The niceties of the
distinctions which divide Protestant and Romanist — and
Mystic — in their several conceptions of the state of fallen
man, are apparently out of the focus of Jones's vision. When
he tells us [87] that Quietism "had its birth and its nurture in
the absolute despair of human nature which Protestant theology and the Counter-Reformation had greatly intensified ";
that "it flourished on an extreme form of the doctrine of the
ruin and fall of man — an utter miserabilism of the 'creature'"; that to it "the trail of the old Adam lies over all that
man does or thinks," and "the taint of the 'creature' spoils
all that springs from this source and fountain "; so that "nothing divine, nothing that has religious value, can originate in
man as man " — he has so confounded things that differ as
quite to reverse the real state of the case.

What is true in it all is only that Quietism is rooted in the
ordinary mystical contempt for the " creature " — we may call
this, if we will, a doctrine of the " utter miserabilism of the
creature " — and was sure that " nothing divine " — not quite

---

[84] As cited, p. 67.

[85] " Works," edition published by Leroux, 1851, 1852, v. p. 566; quoted by
Viscount St. Cyres, as cited, p. 61.

[86] Cf. H. Bavinck, " De Algemeene Genade," pp. 18-19: " In one word,
it is conceivable that a man, confined wholly within the limits of nature,
shall perfectly conform to his idea. . . . Most men, of course, are very
far from attaining a sinless, earthly, natural life; . . . But so far as the
abstract idea goes, it does not seem impossible." Again, pp. 21-22: " The
natural man of I Cor. ii. 14, is according to Rome, not the sinful man, but
the man without the *donum superadditum*. . . . This is the explanation of
the milder judgment which Rome confers on the heathen. And from it also
flows, for the Christian, the doctrine of *fides implicita,* the concessions made
in morals, the compilations of casuistry."

[87] As cited, p. 3.

" nothing that has religious value " — " can originate in man
as man." And we must here take " man as man " literally; not
man as sinner, but man as man. And it is because this is true
that it is also true, that to the Quietist the preparation for
all that is spiritual, lay in " the repose of all one's own powers,
the absence of all efforts of self-direction, of all strain and striving, the annihilation of all confidence in one's own capacities,
the complete quiet of the ' creature.' " This, however, only
because to the Quietist all that is " spiritual " is " divine,"
and cannot come, therefore, out of the " creature," but must
come out of God. We are here in the presence, in other words,
of that Romanist dualism of which we have already sought to
give an account, and which Jones himself describes very pic-
turesquely as follows: [88] " There are two levels or storeys to
the universe. One level is the realm of ' nature,' which has
passed through a moral catastrophe that broke its inherent
connection with the divine and so left it godless and ruined.
The other level is the ' supernatural ' realm where God is
throned in power and splendor as spiritual Ruler. Nothing
spiritual can originate on the level of ' nature '; it can come
only from ' yonder.' "

The Quietist's preoccupation, in other words, was not with
sin but with nature. The Protestant, whose preoccupation was
with sin, did not look for the annihilation of nature, but for
the eradication of its sin. But what the Quietist sought to be
delivered from was self. It was not a purified nature he sought
but a superior nature. To employ Madame Guyon's favorite
figure of the stream, what the Quietist wished was not that
the muddy waters which flow through it should be cleansed
but that the sea from which it came and to which it tends,
should flow up into it and replace its own waters wholly, hence
the appropriateness of Fénelon's own figure: [89] " As the sac-
ristan at the end of the service snuffs out the altar candles
one after another, so must grace put out our natural life, and
as his extinguisher, ill-applied, leaves behind it a guttering
spark that melts the wax, so will it be with us if one single

[88] As cited, p. 2.   [89] Jones, as cited, p. 49.

spark of natural life remains." Where Fénelon says "natural life" the Protestants say "sin": and the difference is polar. It would be misleading in the extreme to say that one and the other identifies sin with self, self with sin. To the Protestant when sin is gone, nature remains — the whole of nature; sin is merely an accident to nature. To the Quietist it is only when "nature" is gone that "sin" is gone; what he is thinking of chiefly when he says "sin" is that limitation of "nature" which constitutes its essential character. There is no cure for this evil but passage into the All.

In drawing up an abstract of Madame Guyon's "Spiritual Torrents," Jones points out that she takes her start from the common mystical doctrine of the "seed." "It is a primary idea of Madame Guyon," he writes,[90] "that there is a 'central depth' in the soul, which has come from God and which exhibits 'a perpetual proclivity' to return to Him, like the push of the stream back to its source in the sea." All souls are at bottom emanations from God and tend to return to their fountain. Hence, "all souls would return to their native Source, if they did not encounter the obstacle of sin, and therefore the main problem of life is the healing of the wounds of sin. There is, in her opinion, no solution short of the complete annihilation of the individual self in which sin inheres, the absolute spoiling of every particular thing to which the soul clings in its sundered selfhood. The soul must die to everything which it loves for self-sake, even to its desire for states of grace, gifts of the Spirit, supernatural communications, and salvation itself. . . . The soul must *let itself go* without thinking or willing or desiring. It must even get beyond doing virtuous actions, and reach a height where the *distinction* of actions is annulled. But the soul loses its own powers and capacities only to receive an immense capacity, like that of the river when it reaches the sea. It no longer possesses, it is possessed. It has lost 'the nothing' for 'the All.' It is perfect with the perfection of God, rich with His riches, and it loves with His love. It is one and the same thing with its Source. The divine

[90] As cited, pp. 36 ff.

life becomes entirely natural to it. It moves with the divine moving, acts as He acts through it, and its interior prayer is action." That is to say, put in simple language, the soul being by nature of the substance of God, by escaping from its individualism is reabsorbed into God. Or employing Madame Guyon's figure, the river which has flowed out from God, on flowing back to God is washed into by the tide and filled with the salt water of the Sea: the salt water has replaced the fresh and now constitutes the river, which of course now shows the qualities of sea-water.

This is the doctrine in the terms of which Upham undertook to express what, after all is said, remained in substance the Wesleyan doctrine of Christian Perfection. Naturally he did not accomplish this feat without some difficulty, in seeking to meet which he found it necessary to modify both doctrines. He did not, however, modify them equally. The modifications he introduced into the Quietistic teaching amounted to an act of violence, by which he forcibly transposed it into quite another key. The violence thus wrought on it, rendered similar violence less necessary with respect to the Wesleyan Perfectionism which he was endeavoring to express in terms of Quietistic mysticism. There were modifications made in the Wesleyan doctrine, modifications intrinsically of importance; but in the main the result was merely the expression of the Wesleyan doctrine in the language of Quietistic mysticism.

We may illustrate what is meant by this by observing at once, without delaying on minor matters, how the culminating conception of Quietism — that of union with God — was dealt with. Of course Upham took this conception over, and endeavored to make a place for it in his scheme of salvation. He attempts to do this by simply adding to the two stages of salvation provided for by the Wesleyan doctrine — those of justification and sanctification — a third, the state of "divine union." The adjustment did not turn out, however, to be so simple as, at first blush, it may have appeared; and Upham found himself not quite able to determine whether the third stage was really a third stage of the Christian's progress or only the second stage in its higher reaches. This doubt was due of course to the fact that, in taking over the conception of "divine union" from the Quietists, he had profoundly modified it, and reduced it to the level of mere sanctification. That he really so conceived it is sufficiently manifest from a sentence like this: [91] "It is taken for granted, that the subject of this higher experience has passed through the more common forms of religious experience; and has advanced from the incipient state of justification, and from the earlier gradations or steps of sanctification, to that state of *divine union*, in which he can say with a good degree of confidence, ' I and my Father are one.'" Only two stages of salvation are recognized here, "the incipient state of justification," and the completing "state of sanctification" — the latter of which, however, passes through a plurality of gradations, the culminating one of which is "divine union."

Nevertheless Upham permitted himself to use with reference to this "divine union" all the extremities of language which he found in his mystical teachers, and in doing so to give it an apparent significance far in advance of anything which sanctification can be supposed to express. On one occasion, for example,[92] he cites with approval Catharine of Genoa's repetition of the old formula, "God was made man that He might make men God," and declares that "it indicates the object at which every Christian ought to aim, and may hope to aim with success, viz. to experience inwardly and entirely the divine transformation, and to become, in the moral sense, and on the limited scale of humanity, ' God manifest in the flesh.' " This is quite shocking language, which only familiarity with it in the mystical writers enables us to tolerate. Its tendency is to obliterate the infinite distance which separates God and man, and to efface the sense of wonder and awe with which the miracle of the incarnation is contemplated. The qualification "in the moral sense, and on the limited scale of humanity," supplies no excuse for such reckless speech

[91] "A Treatise on Divine Union, ed. 6, p. 325.
[92] "Life of Madame Catharine Adorna," 1845, p. 245.

and serves only to declare its impropriety. The perversion of Scripture texts at once adduced in support, merely adds to the offense. When Paul says " I live, and yet not I, but Christ liveth in me," he means neither that "selfishness had become love," nor yet that "humanity had become divine," in him. Nor does John by declaring that we experience "an entire transformation of nature" teach "the conversion of the human and fallen into the restored and the deified," the "transformation of humanity into divinity."

A union with God so conceived cannot reasonably be explained as merely a high stage of sanctification, and Upham accordingly very categorically declares that it is not. " Divine union," he says,[93] " is to be regarded as a state of soul different from that of mere sanctification." " It is subsequent to it in time," he says; and " sustains [to it] the relation of effect." There seems to be, however, some difficulty in telling precisely what it is. It is " union," and union implies " two or more persons or beings, who are the subjects of it." We might conceive a perfectly holy soul by itself. We cannot conceive a united soul by itself. " Union, in the experimental sense of the term, is not merely holiness, but is the holiness of the creature united with the holiness of God." We seize on this language with avidity, as apparently implying that after the union as before there are two, not one; that it results in a society, not a coalescence. But we are told next that, although not sanctification, it is a necessary result of sanctification. " When the soul has reached a certain point in Christian experience, the divine union, in the moral sense of the terms " — that is the only sense, we remember, that Upham admits — " is a matter, not only of choice, but in some sense a matter of necessity." [94] That is because when we become holy God *must* love us — for He by the very necessity of His nature loves holiness, and what is more, we *must* love Him — for holiness must love holiness. This then is a necessary law of the life of pure love. " So strong is this tendency, that no obstacles can resist it. It is just as certain that they [God and holy beings] will

[93] P. 247.   [94] P. 248.

meet, and that they will become one in purpose and happiness, and one in purity and life, as that they exist." [95] Accordingly "holiness of heart implies, as a necessary consequence, union with God." [96] But have we not somehow, in the course of the discussion, lost sight of "divine union," altogether? That is, of that "divine union" which is not sanctification, but something additional to and higher than sanctification? There is nothing of which Upham is surer than that entire sanctification and "pure love" are one and the same thing: and is not the sanctified man one in purpose and one in purity with God? Is not that his very quality as entirely sanctified?

Upham, however, is not satisfied here with generalities. He who is in union with God, is through and through like God. "The soul," says he,[97] "which is fully in the experience of divine union, will harmonize perfectly with the emotions and desires of the divine mind." He apparently wishes us to take this declaration literally and even a little more than literally

[95] P. 249.

[96] P.250. A little before (p. 241) Upham had told us: " Nothing but sin can ever prevent him from entering into the most intimate union with the human mind. Let the heart be right, and he dwells there as a matter of necessity. A holy heart, whether it be in man or in angels, cannot be otherwise than a part of himself." It is Upham's consistent representation that holiness is the condition, not the effect, of union with God — its "first and indispensable prerequisite" ("Principles of the Interior or Hidden Life," ed. 8, p. 17). J. W. Yeomans (*The Biblical Repertory and Princeton Review,* xviii. 1846, pp. 285 f.), comments on this: "We are . . . instructed that this 'hidden life,' this 'greatly advanced state of religious feeling' results in a sacred and intimate union with the Infinite Mind. We are accustomed to reverse this order. . . . That successive stages of advancement in holiness should be attended with an enlivened consciousness of intimacy with God, is both conceivable and undeniable. . . . It is the conscious sympathy of like with like. It is a recognition of oneness; in which is involved the whole idea of the most intimate union conceivable between different persons. But we do not receive from the Scriptures the notion of any sacred and intimate union with the Infinite Mind which belongs rather to one true believer than to another. Every true Christian must be as intimately united to Christ as any other; and any difference among different Christians, respecting the consciousness of that union, and the manifestation of its fruits, cannot amount to a different kind of life, but only to a different degree, or conception, or manifestation of the same life."

[97] "A Treatise on Divine Union," pp. 364–366.

— for he ends by imposing on himself with his similitudes. As a movement in the ocean throbs in all the streams which are connected with it — we do not stop to inquire, Does it? — so, says he, " the desire of the Infinite mind sympathetically takes shape and develops itself in the finite mind." Wherever such union exists, " there cannot, as a general thing, be a feeling or purpose in one party, without the existence of a corresponding feeling and purpose in the other." So far does he push this declaration, that he actually draws as an inference from it the astounding representation that " when we know the thoughts of God's true people, we know God's thoughts; when we know what God's true people desire, we know what God desires; when we know what the people of God are determined to do, we know what God is determined to do." It is to advance but a step further, to declare that the movement of desire in the soul of " a child of God " is the continuation of " the distant but affiliated throbbing, of the great heart of the universe," and justifies the sure expectation of its realization. This appears to constitute the holy man a very tolerable prophet:[98] whatever he desires must come to pass. This too seems to be taken strictly: the voice of a holy man at prayer is something " not only impressive but sublime, and almost terrible " — it is " not more the voice of man than of God." Upham neglects to tell us how we are to identify the man who has become so holy as thus to be to the observer only a mirror of God's thoughts, desires, intentions; and thus leaves us unable to avail ourselves practically of his guidance and compelled to content ourselves just with the Scriptures as a guide to life. But what we need to observe is that in the midst of all this extremity of language he yet conceives of

[98] The conception of the holy man as an inspired man belongs to the common property of perfectionists. It is found also among the Quietists. Madame Guyon, Upham tells us (" Life of Madame Guyon," i. p. 377), was so near to claiming inspiration for her Commentaries that she records something like the miracle which attended the Septuagint translators as occurring in her case. Parts of her comments on Judges were mislaid and she rewrote them. When the first copy turned up again, it was found almost exactly like the second. She regarded this as evidence of divine superintendence over her writing.

the holy man only as a mirror of the divine; it is only sympathetically that the desires of the divine mind take shape in his mind. There is no union of coalescence; only a union of likeness.

Beyond a union which is sanctification, Upham never really gets. At the end of his first religious book,[99] he undertakes to explain to us what "the Unitive State" is. The "state of union," he says, is distinctly a "state of mind." Nothing like a "physical union," a "union of essence with essence physically," is expressed by the phrase, but only "a moral and religious union."[100] The fact is, he explains, that what we mean when we speak of "the Unitive State" is just a state "of close and ineffable conformity with the Divine Mind." We do not become in it one with God: we only become in it like God: and the thing we become like God in is holiness. No doubt Upham even here uses phraseology which, taken naturally, might mean more than this: he says, for example, "we unite with God." But he at once explains his meaning thus: "Holy beings recognize in each other a mutual relationship of character, and are led, by the very necessities of their nature, to seek each other in the reciprocal exercise of love." And he explains this to mean that "nothing appears to them so exceedingly good, desirable, and lovely as holiness, whenever and wherever found." Holy beings, in other words, tend to come together, and to act together, and to form with one another a union, a community, of holy beings; in other words, a social union. He speaks in precisely the same sense in the last of his books, the posthumously published "Absolute Religion."[101] "Man," he here declares flatly, "must necessarily retain his individuality." "The finite cannot be the Infinite." But he can enlarge in the sphere of his sympathies. If we say he is merged and mixed with God, has himself become "extinct," and "lost" in God — is "self-annihilated" — the "literal meaning" of these terms "must be somewhat modi-

---

[99] "Principles of the Interior or Hidden Life," ed. 8, pp. 370 ff.
[100] P. 374.
[101] 1873, pp. 263 ff.

fied." It is not meant that he is "lost," "annihilated," in his "actual self-consciousness," but only that he no longer has different "interests and hopes" from God; that he has ceased to have those "reflex acts which turn the mind too much upon our own joys and purposes." We may distinguish between the "individual," the "humanitarian," and the "holy or divine" (the double designation is significant) man. The difference between them is real, but it is a difference only in the progressive enlargement of man's benevolence and sympathies, until they embrace all Being. As to the "divine man" — " such a man, in the wide and resistless movement of the divine Spirit within him, not only transcends the restricted bounds of individualism, not only passes beyond the limits of kindred and country, but beyond those of humanity itself; and embraces not only the brotherhood of man but all existences, both those above him and those below him. Nothing but the boundlessness of existence, which is ever developing itself, nothing but the boundlessness of benevolence, which is ever pouring happiness into existences, nothing but the Infinite of creation and the Infinite of love, nothing but God himself in the widest and noblest sense of that glorious term, can meet and satisfy his measureless sympathies."

How little the conception of intimate and loving conformity with God presented here is that which Upham's Quietistic guides attached to the notion of Divine Union we may learn by simply permitting Heinrich Heppe to tell us how Madame Guyon thought of the relation of the perfected soul to God. "The state and life of the perfected soul," in her view, says he,[102] "is the most perfect simplicity of being, seeing that it is as little possible for it to distinguish itself from God as God distinguishes Himself from it. As long as the soul still possesses a perception of God, however slight, the union of the soul with God is still incomplete. When this union has reached its completeness, it ceases to be capable of perception, because then the life of God has become altogether restored to the

[102] "Geschichte der quietistischen Mystik in der katholischen Kirche," 1875, pp. 469 f.

soul, and it, having become merged in God's being, has become wholly one with God, absolutely deified. God has then become the life-atmosphere of the soul, which belongs as essentially to it as the earthly atmosphere to the body, and which the soul perceives therefore as little as the body does the atmosphere in which it lives. The perfected soul knows of God only that He exists, and that He is exclusively its life." Here are no two beings bound together only by the bonds of a mutual love, although so closely that the two hearts beat as one. The soul is not like God, but is God. God has ceased to be objective to it: it is not merely immersed in God as its atmosphere — that is an inadequate image. Madame Guyon says expressly that " the soul is not merely hidden in God, but has in God become God." [103] Why Upham thought it worth while to express his own widely divergent meaning in this language, appropriate only to another circle of thought — and indeed to insist that in doing so he was only bringing out the real meaning of the Quietistic writers — we can only conjecture, and need not be careful to inquire. The effect is to throw a veil of ambiguity over all his references to the subject.

Precisely the same method is followed by Upham with precisely the same effect in his discussion of that whole group of ideas which concern the mortification of " nature." We may find an excellent example in the chapter in " The Life of Faith " entitled " On the Relation of Faith to Inward Crucifixion." It is quite clear that it is precisely sin which Upham understands the soul to die to, in its inward crucifixion. To be inwardly crucified, says he, is " to be dead to every desire . . . which has not the divine sanction," " to every appetite and every affection, which is not in accordance with the divine law." Yet he alternatively speaks of the soul having " undergone a painful death to every worldly tie," and sets in opposition to the " new spiritual life " just " the old sensual life." And he attains his climax by means of this appeal to Tauler: " To be inwardly crucified, in the language of Tauler, ' is to cease entirely from the life of self, to abandon equally what

[103] " Lettres Spirituelles," ii. p. 187, quoted by Heppe, as cited.

we see and what we possess, our power, our knowledge, and
our affections; so that the soul in regard to any action originating in itself is without life, without action, and without
power, and receives its life, its action, and its power from
God alone.'" The governing idea of the discussion thus oscil-
lates between deliverance from sin and deliverance from self;
and after a while the two statements are brought into immediate contiguity that " holiness is something which must be
desired and sought *for itself*," and that holiness must by no
means be sought for itself but *only* for God's sake. The culmination is reached in the violent paradox that " perhaps the
most decisive mark of the truly crucified man is, that he is
crucified even to holiness itself." The explanation follows at
once: " that is to say, he desires God only, seeks God only, is
satisfied and can be satisfied with God only, in distinction from
. . . gifts or graces." [104] But why should God and His gifts be
set in opposition to one another, as if one could be taken and
the other left? Of course God is to be desired above all His
gifts; but they cannot be had, or even considered, apart. The
mystical analysis is pushed even further than this, however.
A definition of "pure divinity," as the object of the contemplation of those who are in a state of " pure love," is placed
on Madame Guyon's lips, which cuts even deeper.[105] This
" pure divinity " is God apart from His attributes. As God
is not the sum of His attributes, but the substrate of them,
it is argued that we may and should contemplate Him apart
from them all. To think of God's power is not to think of
God; to think of God's wisdom is not to think of God. And
so we may go through the whole list and arrive at last at the
" pure divinity " which lies back of all attributes. This is, of
course, mere logomachy, and is indicative only of the tendency
of this type of thought to seek after undifferentiated Being
for God — and for us. We are glad to have it noted that
Fénelon at least knew better than to reason thus. What he
says is that it is not enough to occupy ourselves *merely* with
the attributes of God, but we should think of " God considered

[104] P. 250.   [105] " Life of Madame Guyon," ii. p. 157.

as the *subject* of his attributes." " It is not infinite wisdom,
infinite power, or infinite goodness, *considered separately from
the existence of whom they can be predicated,* which it [the
soul] loves and adores; but *the God of infinite wisdom, power,
and goodness.*" [106]

The subject of " interior or spiritual solitude " is dealt with
in the same confusing way.[107] Seclusion of the body, we are
told, is not meant; nor indeed mental seclusion. What is meant
is " solitude from that in the mind, whatever it may be, which
tends to disunite and dissociate it from God." Why then, we
feel bound to ask, do we speak of " solitude," and not rather
" renunciation of sin "? The answer plainly is that it is not
renunciation of sin, after all, which is really in mind. Hence
we read at once in a fuller description that, " in the state of
interior solitude," the soul is " in a state of solitude or separation from two things in particular." And the average reader
may feel some surprise to learn that these two things are the
soul's " own desires " and the soul's " own thoughts." These
universal phrases receive, however, some limitation in the
more precise definitions: " all desire, except such as God himself animates," all thoughts " which are self-originated, and
which tend, therefore, to dissociate it [the soul] from God."
This language is of course dictated by the opposition between
" nature " and " the supernatural " which — rather than that
between sin and grace — rules the thinking of the Romanist
mystics; and on their lips is natural and even inevitable. In
Upham it is only disturbing. We should have expected from
him such phrases as, " all desire which is not conformed to the
law of holiness," " all thoughts which are not pure and ennobling." To say that we must be separated from all but God-
animated desires and God-originated thoughts is not to say
that we must be freed from sin, but that we must be deprived
of our own individuality. Accordingly, we are told that we are
not to have any thoughts that are " our own," and it is explained that " thoughts, which arise from the instigation of

[106] P. 237, quoting from the 27th of the " Maxims of the Saints."
[107] " A Treatise on Divine Union," ed. 6, pp. 238 ff.

self, and not from a divine movement, are not in harmony with
what God in his providential arrangements would desire and
choose to suggest," and are therefore " not only not from God,
but . . . constitute so many disturbing influences, which separate God from the soul." Of course the self, as it is now constituted, is corrupt; and all its thoughts and desires are corrupt.
But the remedy for this dreadful state of things which the
Scriptures offer is not the substitution of God for the self as
the source of our thoughts and desires, but the purification of
the self. The mystics, however, whom Upham is here reflecting,
did not think in terms of sin and grace but in terms of self and
God. It was not from sin but from the self itself from which
they wished to turn; not to holiness that they wished to flee
but to God. The form in which Upham presents that here is
to remind us that in its spiritual solitude " the soul is not left
alone with itself," but " with God, who is Eternal Life," a form
of statement which embodies an unusually crass paradox —
declaring that the soul enters into " solitude " by entering into
" communion." " Separation, in its spiritual application," he
therefore proceeds to tell us, is " not only seclusion, but transition " — transition to God, so as to be " not only *with* God,
but *in* him; not only in harmony of action, but in the sacred
enclosure of his being." All roads lead to Rome; and in mystical thinking all roads lead to union.

The doctrine taught in this discussion is repeated, with
perhaps some additional clearness of statement, in the chapter
in " The Life of Faith," " On the Mental State Most Suitable
to the Constant In-dwelling of the Holy Ghost." [108] Upham
says " most *suitable*," but he is soon found discussing rather
what the mental state is that is most *favorable* to the indwelling of the Holy Ghost. What he is investigating is the
mental state which we must assume, if we wish to induce the
indwelling of the Spirit. His conclusion is, " inward meekness
and quietness," and Ruysbroek and Père Lombaz are quoted to
the effect that this state of mind " gives full liberty to the Spirit
of God to act in the soul." Having thus suspended the entrance

[108] Pp. 356 ff.

of the Holy Spirit into the soul on the soul's prior action,[109]
Upham now gives himself to a description of what this " quiet
spirit " is. " The quiet mind, in this sense of the terms," says
he, " has no preference, no election, which results from the
impulse of its own tendencies. It is precisely in that situation,
being free from any desires or purposes of its own, in which
the smallest possible divine influence will give it the true direction. In other words, while it remains in this condition, it is
susceptible of being moved, only as it is moved upon by the
Spirit of God." There is no question here of sin, and the overcoming of sin by grace. We hear only of the necessity of the
mind's attaining to a state of inanition; and the doctrine
taught is that a state of complete inanition is the necessary
precondition of the impulsion of the Spirit. A soul is most
accessible to divine influence when there is no activity in it at
all. Even that is not enough; for Upham now proceeds[110] to
argue that not only is a soul so emptied prepared for the Spirit;
but the Spirit *must* enter it. If not physically, it is morally
necessary for Him to do so. He always stands at the door and
knocks; and he enters when unresisted — " whenever the
natural or selfish desire, in distinction from the sanctified desire, ceases." In these words there may lie a suggestion that
after all it is sin that is in question; but the suggestion is not
justified by the discussion in general. It is the emptiness of
the soul, not its purity, which prepares it for the Spirit. Accordingly Upham at once returns to the broad declaration;
" Our doctrine, in accordance with that of many judicious
writers on christian experience, is, that desire must cease;
otherwise the Holy Spirit cannot be *in-dwelling;* in other
words, cannot take up his abode fully and permanently in the
heart." Desire — not sin — must cease. But no: it is after all
sin that must cease. For in his quality as psychologist Upham

[109] Madame Guyon's statement, as given by Upham (" Life of Madame
Guyon," i. p. 393) is a little more arresting in form, but the same in substance. " When he finds us in this position," — the position of self-annihilation,
" nothingness " — " he finds us, not to despise and reject us, but to come into
the heart which is now made empty and clean for his reception, and to set
up his kingdom there forever."   [110] P. 361.

now goes on to explain that " there is not any such thing, and cannot be any such thing, as an absolute extinction of desire; neither in God, men, nor angels ": " desire is a necessary and unalienable attribute of every rational being." He uses the term, therefore, he says, in the sense, not that desire, but " the *natural, the unsanctified* desire has ceased." Once more then he plays fast and loose with mystical terminology, to the great discomfort of his readers and disadvantage of his meaning.

It will already have been observed that Upham has the odd faculty of suggesting the doctrine of Quietistic inaction as an undertone of his discussion, while avoiding its open assertion. We may find another instance of this mode of writing in the chapter, " On the True Idea of Spiritual Liberty," in the " Principles of the Interior or Hidden Life." [111] The text here is taken from Francis de Sales' definition of Christian Liberty — as " consisting in keeping the heart totally disengaged from every created thing, in order that it may follow the known will of God." That is true or false, according as we take it. That we may follow the known will of God, it is not necessary to keep the heart totally disengaged from every created thing. It may rather be necessary to engage it very deeply with every created thing. It is for example the known will of God that we shall love our neighbor, and we may take neighbor here universally. There is a contradiction suggested between obedience to God and natural affection which is not in the least Christian. It is easy, however, so to expound this fundamental declaration as to keep its false suggestion just under the surface, so that it is always suggesting itself, but is perhaps never openly asserted. It is easy to lay the stress on the duty of " in all cases and on all occasions doing the will of God " and of subordinating all else to it; and only subtly to suggest that we are therefore better without the love of country, or the love of parents, or of children, say, because they are apt to absorb us and so interfere with doing the will of God. Soon, however, we strike an openly false antithesis like this: " A man who is really guided by his appetites, his propensities, and even by

[111] Ed. 8, pp. 258 ff.

his affections," — those are Upham's three categories of desires — " his love of country, or any thing else other than the Spirit of God, cannot be said to be led by that divine Spirit." [112] Why not? The Spirit of God is not a fourth to this trio — appetites, propensities, affections, the Spirit of God — operating on the same plane with them, and contending with them on equal terms for the mastery of action, so that if we follow His guidance we must repel their propulsions. He works in and through them and by their propulsions accomplishes His guidance. It is by purifying them that He guides us in pure paths; by elevating them that He brings us to exalted actions. Nothing less true, accordingly, could be said than this: " In the heart of true liberty the Spirit of God rules, and rules alone; so that he who is in the possession of this liberty does nothing of his own pleasure or his own choice." On the contrary, he in whose heart the Spirit of God rules and rules alone, does all that he does of his own pleasure and of his own choice. His liberty consists precisely in its being his pleasure and his choice to do what the Spirit of God, who has made him thus free, would have him do. The law of God has been written on his heart, and he spontaneously does its commandments. The suggestions of the succeeding phraseology are accordingly quite unscriptural: " That is to say, in all cases of voluntary action, he does nothing under the impulse and guidance of natural pleasure or natural choice alone. His liberty consists in being free from self; in being liberated from the dominion of the world; in lying quietly and submissively in the hands of God; in leaving himself, like clay in the hands of the potter, to be moulded and fashioned by the divine will." The question is not whether we are in the hands of the Potter; or whether it is not our joy to be in the hands of *this* Potter; it is how this Potter proceeds in molding the clay. And we praise God that it is not by liberating us from our selves, but by liberating our selves from sin and forming them in the image of Christ, that He proceeds. What has deflected Upham's exposition from the truth is the undertone of sympathy with that false antagonism of the

[112] P. 265.

natural and the supernatural which dominates the thoughts of his Romanist teachers.

Out of the same source there rises a note of asceticism which sounds through many of Upham's discussions. We may take as an example the chapter in the "Principles of the Interior or Hidden Life" on "The Excision and Crucifixion of the Natural Life." [113] Everything here depends, of course, on what is understood by "the natural life." If a life of sin is meant, then of course it is to be excised and crucified. And Upham does, at bottom, mean just that. But he is always treading on the border line which divides this conception of the natural life from that which sees in it only a life in accordance with "pure nature." In other words, the Romanist doctrine of the natural and the supernatural constantly intrudes into his thought. It is a hard counsel when we are bidden [114] to "cut off and crucify the desire of internal consolations and comforts" — although a good meaning can be attached to it. It becomes harder when we read on: "If we would be what the Lord would have us to be, we must be willing, in the spirit of inward crucifixion, to renounce and reject all other natural desires, and all our own purposes and aims." It is some relief to learn that only "all desires and purposes which spring from *the life of nature,* and not from the Spirit of God," are meant; although the antithesis is not exact. And the relief is not lessened so far as the words go, when we read further: "In other words, it is our duty, as those who would glorify God in all things, to check every natural desire, and to delay every contemplated plan of action, until we can learn the will of God, and put ourselves under a divine guidance." But that by "natural desires" here are meant not the desires intrinsically sinful because the expressions of the "lusts of the flesh" of the "natural man," but just desires proper to us as men, is clear, since we are only to delay following them until we can ascertain whether they are in accordance with the will of God, which it is implied they may prove to be. And we now read further: "Every desire must so far lose its natural character as

---

[113] Ed. 8, pp. 213 ff.   [114] P. 221.

to become spiritually baptized and sanctified, before it can be acceptable to God." What? a desire intrinsically good, which on investigation may prove to be in accordance with God's will? Would it not be nearer the truth to say that every desire, not corrupted by sin, is already acceptable to God, in its natural character? Baptism and sanctification presuppose sin: and only sin-corrupted desires require baptism and sanctification. It is not nature but sin which needs extirpation. There floats before Upham's mind, in other words, under the ambiguity of his use of the word "nature," a condemnation of nature itself, and an aspiration not for a holy natural life, but for a purely supernatural life.

The resultant asceticism shows itself most plainly, however, when he begins to illustrate the doctrine which he has laid down. He illustrates it, for example, from the desire for knowledge.[115] The desire for knowledge is in itself innocent; but it becomes wrong when it is so "strong as to disquiet the inward nature, and thus to perplex our intercourse with God." It is to be "merged and lost, as it were, like all the other natural desires, in the supreme desire for God's glory" — "a desire which evidently is not the product of nature, but which can come from the inspiration of the Holy Ghost alone." Why the most complete possession of knowledge may not subserve God's glory, we are not told. There is no reason for setting the "natural" desire for knowledge and the "supernatural" purpose to seek God's glory in contradiction to one another, except an underlying feeling that nothing that is of "nature" is good. In point of fact the desire for knowledge and the desire for God's glory lie in consciousness side by side as alike just desires: as they emerge in consciousness we know nothing of their diverse origins and cannot discriminate between them on that ground. On an earlier page,[116] the warning against an excessive desire for knowledge is put on a different ground. We can easily know too much, it is there suggested, for our soul's good, for every enlargement of our sphere of knowledge decreases our sphere of faith. "Knowledge necessarily excludes

[115] Pp. 222 f.   [116] P. 199.

faith, in regard to the thing which is known. And we do not
hesitate to say, that ignorance with faith is, in many things, better than knowledge without it." We shall not be led astray by
the prudent adjunctive of those two last words " without it ":
they merely introduce an "undistributed middle." The doctrine announced is clearly that it is better not to know too
much, because faith is better than knowledge and we should
leave all that we can to be merely believed and not known —
and there is an unpleasant suggestion that faith flourishes better in half-light. Surely this is that voluntary humility which
did not commend itself to an apostle. As with knowledge, so
with friendship. Our friendships must be " crucified." Friends
may become idols: better shun the danger and not have too
many of them: and among friends he includes kindred —
though he does not tell us how it is best to free ourselves of
superfluous kindred. Even if our friends are "eminent Christians, so much so as to bear the very image and likeness of the
Savior himself," we must beware of loving them too much.
This is an atmosphere more Buddhist than Christian. In this
"baptism of fire," as he rightly calls it, he declares that the
natural life dies; and that thus the way is prepared for the
true resurrection and life of Christ in the soul. We are, that
is to say, not so much to cleanse the soul, as to empty it, that
Christ may enter in. "We must not think to go to heaven and
carry our natural life with us." That depends on what we mean
by our natural life. We are to continue men in heaven, we
suppose. But we are not to love the " world "? That again depends on what we mean by the " world." Certainly we are not
to delight in the world, the flesh, and the devil. But are we
not to love the world which is our "neighbor"? But we are
now told that it is " the corrupt life " of nature that we are to
renounce. And to that we agree with all our heart. The mystical ascetic strain serves only to confuse the two senses of
" nature," and so to convey to the uninstructed mind some very
dubious notions.

In some paragraphs [117] of a chapter devoted to the duty of a

[117] "Principles of the Interior or Hidden Life," ed. 8, pp. 314 ff.

primary, all-embracing, and eternal act of consecration, Upham endeavors to give currency to the mystical term and notion of "nihility," and yet keep his prescriptions in harmony with his strong New England sense of human activity. We must coöperate with God, he allows: but he adds at once that "in order to realize, personally, the conditions of divine coöperation . . . it is necessary to be, mentally, in a state of *passivity,* as it is sometimes expressed," or "more properly and truly, of *strict impartiality* before God." That is to say, we must be free and ready to go God's way, and that implies that we have none of our own: our minds are to be but mirrors reflecting His will. And we must "not only begin in our nothingness, but must be willing to remain in it." All our coöperation is really a receiving. If we work it is only God working in us. We are not inactive; but "man is justly and efficiently active" only "when he is active in communication with God, and yet remaining deeply in his own sphere of nothingness." "Man never acts to higher and nobler purpose than when, in the realization of his own comparative nihility, he places himself in the receptive position, and lets God work in him." This curious mode of expressing oneself amounts to a forced employment of mystical language, with a constantly suggested reserve. What, for example, is the function of the word "comparative" inserted before "nihility" in the sentence last quoted, except to warn against taking the language in its natural sense? We cannot quite say that all that is taught here is that we must do the will of God. It is taught also that the way to do the will of God is to inhibit our own willing and let God's willing flow into us in its stead. This is what is understood in mystical language by "the death of the will." But when Upham comes to deal with this phrase [118] he manages to reduce it, too, simply to preferring God's will to our own. Of course the will cannot cease to exist, he says — then we should cease to be men. But we must cease to will divergently from God's willing. And, it is added, so soon as we

[118] "A Treatise on Divine Union," ed. 6, p. 157.

cease to will divergently from God's willing, we shall find that we have begun to will accordingly with God's willing. When the will dies, then, it is not dead; it is not even quiescent; it is only transformed. Does it not seem a pity then to speak of this transformation and transfiguration of the will as " the death of the will "? Upham himself has the grace to say: [119] " When we use the phrase ' interior annihilation,' we of course use it in a mitigated or qualified sense " — in this sense, namely, " as meaning not an entire extinction of any principles within us, but only an extinction of certain irregularities of their action." " In other words," he adds, " it is not an absolute annihilation; but only the annihilation of any thing and every thing that is wrong; the annihilation of what the Scriptures call the ' old man,' in distinction from the ' new man, created anew in Christ Jesus.' " Of the habit of using in much the same reference the term " nothingness," he has the grace to speak [120] also with mild criticism: this terminology is " convenient," indeed, " but yet not accurate." Nevertheless, in deference to the usage of his Quietistic guides, he uses this phraseology and permits himself to speak familiarly of " the soul that has reached the centre of its Nothing " — meaning only, he explains, that it is " absolutely and forever nothing relatively to self," a statement not itself beyond serious criticism: let us at least say " relatively to sin." It is pleasing to report that before the end of the volume is reached — though only just before it is reached [121] — the true note is for once firmly struck. Upham is speaking here of the doctrine of " some advocates of Christian perfection," " especially," he says, of " some pious Catholics of former times," " that the various propensities and affections, and particularly the bodily appetites, ought to be entirely eradicated." That is the familiar " noughting of nature." No, says he, with unusual directness: No — " we are not required to eradicate our natural propensi-

[119] " Principles of the Interior or Hidden Life," ed. 8, p. 362.
[120] Pp. 365 ff.
[121] Pp. 394 f.

ties and affections, but to *purify* them. We are not required to cease to be men, but merely to become *holy* men." This is true, and it is well said. The question that forces itself constantly on the reader is, Why dally, then, with the mystical phraseology when the mystical meaning is not intended?

III. UPHAM'S DOCTRINAL TEACHING

FROM examples such as those which we have adduced, it is sufficiently evident that in taking over the language of his Quietistic teachers, Upham took over with it only in part the doctrines of which that language was the appropriate expression. His own doctrinal system was different and it becomes desirable to ascertain in outline — or at least in its salient points — what the doctrinal system is to which he elects to give expression in this extraordinary fashion.

His primary engrossment was psychological; and it is natural that the conclusions at which he arrived in that field should underlie and be constantly attended to in the development of his religious philosophy. The one of these upon which he seems most to have prided himself was the threefold distribution of mental faculty into the intellect, the sensibilities, and the will. There appears to have been a sense in which he — or certainly his friends — looked upon this distribution as a discovery of his own. Alpheus S. Packard tells an affecting story [122] of how in the early years of his work at Bowdoin, discouraged by his failure to coördinate the facts of mental action in an intelligible scheme, he was on the point of resigning his professorship and retiring beaten from his work, " when what we may term a discovery in mental science flashed upon his mind, which gave place, order and proportion to all his facts; the idea that there were in the unity of the soul three coördinate forms of activity, the intellect, the sensibilities and the will." Such a discovery at that date was, of course, only a rediscovery; and we can scarcely doubt that Upham was helped to it by at least obscure reminiscences of what he had read. He himself points out in his treatise on the Will [123] that this threefold distribution was already to be found in

[122] " Address on the Life and Character of Thomas C. Upham, D.D.," 1873, pp. 8 f.

[123] " A Philosophical and Practical Treatise on the Will," 1834, pp. 28 ff. Compare H. B. Smith, *The Literary and Theological Review*, December, 1837, p. 630.

411

Locke and Hume, in Lord Kames and Sir James Mackintosh.
It was as old in continental psychology as Tefens and Men-
delssohn, and had been given general currency there by Kant.
Sir William Hamilton is ordinarily credited with having first
clearly expounded and defined it in English, though we may
understand this as meaning only that he performed much the
same service for it among English-speaking writers as Kant
did on the continent. Among his own New England predecessors Upham might have read it very clearly set forth as early
as 1793 in Samuel West's " Essays on Liberty and Necessity ";
and he himself in 1834 [124] points to Asa Burton's " Essays on
Some of the First Principles of Metaphysicks, Ethicks, and
Theology," which was published in 1824, the very year he
went to Bowdoin — as expounding it. It was being taught,
also, contemporaneously with himself, at New Haven by N. W.
Taylor.[125] When he lays hold of it, however, he makes it very
much his own, and founds on it his whole conception of mental action. " The general division of the Mind," he says,[126]
" is into the Intellect, the Sensibilities, and the Will. The External Intellect is first brought into action; followed, in greater
or less proximity of time, by the development of the Internal.
The subsequent process of the mental action, when carried
through in the direction of the Pathematic " — that is, the
natural as distinguished from the moral — " sensibilities, is
from intellections to emotions, and from emotions to desires,
and from desires to acts of the will. When carried through in
the direction of the Moral sensibilities, it is from intellections
to emotions, (not natural but moral emotions;) and then
diverging into a different track and avoiding the appropriate
domain of the Desires, passes from emotions to feelings of
moral obligation, and from the Obligatory feelings, like the
corresponding portion of the sensibilities, to the region of the
Voluntary or Volitive nature."

[124] " A Philosophical and Practical Treatise on the Will," pp. 29 f.

[125] For West, Burton and Taylor, see F. H. Foster, " A Genetic History
of the New England Theology," 1907, pp. 232, 243, 247.

[126] " Elements of Mental Philosophy " (1831), ed. 2, 1837, ii. p. 117.
Cf. " A Philosophical and Practical Treatise on the Will," 1834, p. 24.

Thus everything culminates in willing; and Upham teaches [127] that " the will, in making up its determinations, takes immediate cognizance of only two classes of mental states, viz., Desires and Feelings of obligation." [128] What he is seeking to enunciate here is, no doubt, primarily the general manner of the will's action; but behind that there lies an intense conviction that the will is subject to law, and is no more capable of acting apart from the law to which it is subject than any other creature of God. He closes the long section of his " Treatise on the Will," [129] devoted to validating this conviction, with these eloquent words: " Let us remember, that in this simple proposition " — that the will is in its action subject to law — " we find the golden link, which binds us to the throne of God. If my will is not subject to law, then God is not my master. And what is more, he is not only not so in fact, but it is impossible that he should be so. But on the other hand, if my will is not independent, in the sense of being beyond the reach of law, then the hand of the Almighty is upon me, and I cannot escape even if I would. The searching eye of the great Author of all things ever attends my path; and whether I love or hate, obey or rebel, I can never annul his authority, or evade his jurisdiction."

There is, it is true, a certain faltering, scarcely in complete harmony with this eloquent assertion of the complete subjection of the will to law, in his enunciation of the general law of its action. He does not say that the will is determined by desires and feelings of obligation; he says that in its action it " takes cognizance " of them alone. What he means to say is that the will does not act except in the presence of or in view of motives: " the existence of motives in some form or other,"

---

[127] *Ibid.*, § 263; more at large, *ibid.*, §§ 28–30.

[128] The distinction between these two classes of mental states is stated as follows (" A Philosophical and Practical Treatise on the Will," p. 61): " Desires are founded on those emotions, which involve what is pleasurable or painful, while Obligatory feelings are exclusively based on emotions of a different kind, viz. those of approval and disapproval." These two classes, it is added, often " stand before the will in direct and fierce opposition to each other."   [129] Pp. 109–201.

he roundly asserts,[130] "is the indispensable condition of any action of the voluntary power." But he wishes to avoid asserting that the will is determined by the motive, in the presence or in view of which it acts: the motive is "nothing more than the preparatory condition, circumstance, or occasion; a sort of antecedent incident to that which takes place."[131] The will stands among the motives which have released it for action, and sovereignly chooses which of them it will follow. This free choice among the motives, Upham now declares to be necessary if we are to regard man "as a free and accountable agent." This seems to imply that if the motive really determined the volition man would not be "a free and accountable agent." And that seems to imply that the power to act — and the habit of acting — contrary to the motive is essential to free and accountable agency. If this does not separate the action of the will from the control of the desire or moral feeling (with all the machinery of intellection, emotion, and so forth, back of it) and make its action lawless, we would like to know what it does do.

Reverting to the matter at a somewhat later point,[132] Upham makes his doctrine plainer by repetition. The will never acts and cannot act in the absence of motives. "The will acts in view of motives and never acts independently of them." The motives furnish "the condition or occasion" — "the *indispensable* occasion" — on which the "ability" of the will to put forth volitions "is exerted." That is to say, the presence of the motives releases the will for action. But the motives, though they draw a circle around the will, do not determine — no one of them at least — *how* it will act. It acts "in view of motives"; yet "its acts are its own and are to be regarded and spoken of as its own." It acts "in connection with motives," and yet has "a true and substantive power in itself." "In other words," says Upham, coming at last really to the point, "although motives are placed round about it, and enclose it on every side, it," that is, the will, "has the power of choosing, (or if other expressions be preferable,) of deciding, determining, or arbitrating among them. Although it is shut up within barriers, which God himself has instituted, it has a positive liberty and ability within those barriers. Although its operations are confined within a sphere of action, which is clearly and permanently marked out by its maker [God], yet within that sphere, (the proposition of the will's subjection to law still holding good,) its acts emanate in itself." The meaning of this is apparently that not only is the will released for action only by the presence of motives soliciting its action, but the range of its action is limited by their solicitations. It cannot act in the absence of motives and it equally cannot act otherwise than as it is solicited by one or another of them. But it has the power of selecting, among the motives presented to it, that one in accordance with which it prefers to act. Its " free action " is confined within the circle of its solicitation: but within that circle it is " free." It must have a master, but it chooses its own master — from among the claimants for its service. It serves; but it gives willing service.

What now, we may ask, would happen if there were but one motive present at a given time to the will? Or what if a plurality of motives were present, but they acted in harmony with one another and drew all in the same direction? Obviously then we should have a determined will. The will released for action by the presence of motives and confined in its choice to the solicitations actually experienced, could choose only one way and would be a determined will. This is Upham's own understanding of the matter and on it he founds a prescription of the proper method to become holy in life. It is to become holy in our desires, that the desires may pull in the same direction as conscience: and that, says he, will secure the holiness of the will. " The will acts," he explains,[133] " if it acts at all, in accordance either with natural and interested motives, on the one hand, or with moral motives on the other." In a normal condition, in a man of sound mind, " the moral sense will always act right and act effectively, and will always fur-

[133] Principles of the Interior or Hidden Life," p. 211.

nish a powerful motive to the will, unless it," that is the will, " is perplexed and weakened in its action . . . by the influence of unsanctified desires." " If, therefore, the desires are sanctified, and the perplexing and disordering influence from that source is taken away, the feelings of desire and the sentiment of justice will combine their action in the same direction, and the action of the will cannot be otherwise than holy. To possess holy desires, therefore, in their various modifications, or, what is the same thing, to possess, as we sometimes express it, a holy *heart,* is necessarily to possess a holy *will.*" " *Cannot* be otherwise than holy "; " *necessarily* to possess a holy will." Whenever then, either because there is only a single motive present to the will or because the motives present and active are in harmony with one another, the will is the subject of a unitary solicitation, we have a determined will — it *cannot* do otherwise than follow the only solicitation acting upon it. The condition here described is, however, it ought now to be said, always the real state of the case. The picture of the will standing in the midst of contending motives dragging it hither and yon, is an artificial and mechanical one. The conflict of appetences is carried on, not in the will, but before the will is reached. At the moment of volition there is but one motive active — the resultant of the whole. So long as the mind is divided, the will hangs suspended: it forms no volition. Upham discusses, formally, at least twice, the old question whether the will follows the strongest motive and he parries it with the old rejoinder, that there is no criterion of what is the strongest motive except the actual action of the will. The question which is the strongest motive, it is better to understand, is one of which the will has no cognizance: it settles itself in the conflict of appetences — and only the surviving motive, or better, the resultant motive, reaches the will. What determines the will is the total subjectivity at the moment of volition. That total subjectivity is a very complex thing, but its pressure on the will is unitary.

Upham does not, however, attain a solution of his difficulties. Vacillating between the claims of "law" and those of

"freedom," he is at his wit's end. It is "freedom" that wins
the victory with him. At the bottom of his heart he knows
that man is determined in all his actions. Does he not tell us
that "if the law of universal causation in particular be not
true, there is no Deity"? [134] But on the top of his mind he is
sure that man is the master of his own action — nay, that he
controls God's action, too. His philosophical faith assures him
that God controls man; his practical belief is that God is at
man's disposal. Does he not tell us over and over again that
God can do nothing for man's moral and spiritual welfare
without man's consent? It is "undoubtedly a correct" opinion,
he declares, [135] "that it is impossible for God to operate on a
morally responsible being, for moral purposes, and with moral
virtue resulting, without a real and voluntary consent." "Man
is a moral being," he says again,[136] "endued with the power of
free choice; and . . . the divine presence cannot exist in him,
as a principle of life, except with *his own consent*." "God cannot take up his abode in the heart," he repeats with more
elaboration,[137] "he cannot become the God and ruler of the
heart, without the *consent* of the heart. This is all he wants,
and where this consent (an act which has the peculiarity of
sustaining moral responsibility without involving moral merit,)
is not given, the poor rebellious one is *left*, left to *himself*, left
of *God*." The parenthesis thrown in here is a vain attempt to
escape the imputation of teaching salvation by works. To
withhold consent brings moral ruin, expressed here in terms
of negative reprobation. Is it not wrong? And, it being wrong,
to give consent, is that not a right act? And does not a right
act "involve moral merit"? If God's entrance into the soul
depends as its condition on the soul's consent, how can it be
said that this consent — given on the soul's own motion and
in its own strength — is not a meritorious act? What is mainly
to be observed here, however, is the strength of the assertion

[134] "A Philosophical and Practical Treatise on the Will," p. 132.
[135] "Life of Madame Catharine Adorna," 1845, p. 32.
[136] "A Treatise on Divine Union," 1851, p. 355.
[137] "Life of Madame Catharine Adorna," p. 196.

418PERFECTIONISM

of the helplessness of God over against the rebellious sinner. He *cannot* save him, but must just leave him to perish.

This note is struck again in Upham's latest book.[138] There it is asserted that although God's love "is absolute and unchangeable," "freedom also, as an attribute of moral beings, is absolute and unchangeable," and cannot be violated. "God himself," we read, "who in being the absolute truth, can never fail to respect the absolute truth, and [139] will never coerce a sinner into heaven; for that would only be placing him in a deeper Hell. This would be a violation of fixed and unchangeable truths and relations. It would be an impossibility." Here is a flat assertion that it is impossible for God to determine human action without violating human freedom; and to give color to this absurd assertion, the more absurd assertion still is made that to save a sinner, without waiting for his "consent" to be saved, is coercion, and leaves him in his rebellious mind: that is to say, he is supposed to be saved without being saved.[140]

There is a chapter in the "Principles of the Interior or Hidden Life "[141] which deals in general with, if we may so express it, the locality of religious experience. In the course of it we may learn something more of Upham's view of the interrelation of the human faculties. He begins, of course, with his threefold division of Intellect, Sensibility, and Will; and with his subdivision of the Sensibilities into Emotions and Desires

---

[138] "Absolute Religion," p. 266.

[139] We suppose this "and" should be omitted, that the sentence may become correct.

[140] Enoch Pond, in a perfunctory notice of Upham's "Treatise on the Will," in *The Literary and Theological Review* for March, 1835, pp. 148–168, strangely says that the views of Upham are substantially the same as those of Edwards. The Methodists saw more truly and claimed him for their own. A writer in *The Methodist Quarterly Review* for April, 1846, p. 249 — who quotes Wilbur Fiske among others as of the same mind with him — declares that the "Treatise on the Will " "is certainly more satisfactory to the Arminian school than any of its predecessors," and adds that "it modifies quite away the Cyclopean mound of difficulty reared by Edwards." Compare in the same sense F. H. Foster, "A Genetic History of the New England Theology," p. 252.

[141] Pp. 138 ff.

— a subdivision so marked as to raise the question whether the Emotions and Desires — are not really conceived as major divisions. And he repeats here of course his view that normal mental action runs through these four states in the order in which they are enumerated. It begins with an act of intellect, which quickens emotions into activity, through which the desires are moved, and through them in turn the will. This is his constant representation. The point to be observed at present is that it is supposed that this normal course of action may interrupt itself at any point — so that the intellect may be brought into action without arousing any emotion, or emotion may be aroused without setting desire into action, or desire may burn strongly without moving the will. This notion results, of course, from a mechanical conception of mental action, the essential unity of which, as of the acting mind, is insufficiently apprehended. On the ground of this notion, however, we are told that if the intellect alone is moved by religious truth, there is no religion in that. No clearness of perception of religious realities, no amount of religious knowledge acquired and intellectually realized, is in any true sense religious — if it stops there. Even if the emotional nature responds to the new perception of religious realities, and is roused to the greatest conceivable heights of religious feeling, there is no religion, in the true sense, in that either — if it stops there. It is not until those modifications of the sensibilities which are called affections, and through them the will, are reached that anything which may properly be called religion is produced. " Any religion, or rather *pretence* of religion, which is not powerful enough to penetrate into this region of the mind, and to bring the affections and will into subjection to God, is in vain. It is an important fact, and as melancholy as it is true, that a person may be spiritually enlightened and have new views on the subject of religion, and that he may also have very raised and joyful emotions, and yet may be a slave to his natural desires." [142] Thus the mind is split into two halves — on the one side the intellect and emo-

[142] P. 141.

tions, on the other the affections and the will: and it is supposed that these two halves can stand contradictorily over
against one another — the intellect and emotions be teeming
with religious knowledge and thrilling with religious feeling,
and at the same time the desires and will be lying cold and unmoved, dead in sin. This representation is the more remarkable that what Upham is employed in depicting is not merely
the movements of the mind under nature but distinctively
under grace. What is under discussion is the saving operations
of the Holy Spirit. "We will suppose," he says,[143] "the case
of a person who is the subject of a divine operation. Under
the influence of this inward operation, he experiences, to a
considerable extent, new views of his own situation, of his need
of a Savior, and of the restoration of his soul to God in
spiritual union. The operation which has been experienced, so
far, is purely intellectual. . . . But in addition to this, we will
suppose that an effect, and perhaps a very decided effect, has
been experienced in the emotive part, which in its action is
subsequent to that of the intellect. . . . The perception of
new truth . . . gives him happiness; and the perception of its
relation to his salvation gives him still more happiness. . . .
His mouth is filled with praise. And others praise the Lord on
his account." Nevertheless, he has no religion, and is not the
subject of any "religious experience."

The faults of this representation are of two kinds — psychological and religious. The human soul is a unit and cannot
be divided thus into water-tight compartments. As the emotions cannot be aroused except through a prior movement of
the intellect, so every movement of the intellect must be felt in
the emotional nature — and through it, in those affections
which Upham calls desires and in the will. New views of truth,
if genuine, cannot fail to be felt to the extreme verge of human
action. Above all it is inconceivable that the intellect can be
illuminated by the Holy Spirit and the feelings, appropriate to
the new view of truth imparted, aroused, with no effect at all
upon "the affections and the will." The fundamental fault of

[143] P. 140.

Upham's representation lies, however, in his complete failure
to recognize any creative operation of the Holy Spirit on the
heart. He is endeavoring to account for the difference between
the growth of the seed which falls on the rocky ground and
of that which falls on the good ground — without recognizing
any difference in the soil. The reason why some who hear the
word go on to fruit-bearing, and others do not, he says, is that
the natural process of growth is arrested in midcourse in the
one case and not in the other. The reason why it does it, is —
that it does it. The truth of course is that whenever true religion starts in the intellect it does not end until it reaches
the will. We may say, if we choose, that whenever the Spirit
enlightens the intellect and arouses the emotions, He will
quicken the affections and move the will. That is true and may
be enough to say; but it is not all nor even the most fundamental thing that is true. We must add that whenever true
religion begins in the intellect it is because the Spirit of God
has moved creatively over the soul and prepared it in all its
departments of activity to respond to His Word. The account
of the difference of "temporary faith" and "saving faith" is
that in the one case there has never been any true religion at
all, and in the other there has — because in the one case the
soul has not been prepared by the Holy Spirit for the acceptance of the seed and in the other it has.

Let us observe meanwhile that the effect (it is really the
cause) of Upham's representation, is to throw all religion into
the affections and will; ultimately into what we would call the
voluntary activities of the soul. This too is a result of his
theological attitude, which in this matter has affected his
psychological construction. He is operating here with one of
the basic contentions of the "New Divinity," and what is
meant ultimately is that he thinks in terms of the will as the
sole source of all ethical and religious character. This involves,
of course, the denial of native depravity, and forms thus one
of the points of sympathy between him and his Romanist
mentors, with their doctrine of *pura naturalia*. It is upon this
element of his teaching that his pupil, young Henry Boynton

Smith, very naturally concentrates his criticism in the estimate of his psychological system which he wrote, at Upham's request, for *The Literary and Theological Review* of December, 1837.[144] Upham goes wrong, he points out, on the question of the morality of instincts, appetites, propensities, defending the view " that it is the will which gives them a moral character; that we are accountable for them only as far as they are voluntary; that in their native, instinctive action, they are innocent." In opposition Smith rightly declares that " the affections are a fount of moral character, separate altogether from deliberate volition," and appeals in support to the older New England tradition. In point of fact, so far is the will from giving character to the impulses, emotions, affections, it is they which give character to the will. An interesting inquiry might be started whether in Upham's view the deliverances of conscience in the sense of the moral sense, the organ of moral judgments, which appear in his system as motives to the action of the will, not products of it, have any moral character. The time may come in the development of the Christian life at any rate, he teaches,[145] when conscience passes into the background, because no longer needed: we are good without its aid. " The soul which is given to God without reserve," he teaches, has passed beyond the need, of course, of the reproofs of conscience. It is " clothed with innocence," and there is therefore now no condemnation for it. Madame Guyon accordingly spoke of having " lost her conscience." She had not done that: she had only transcended the need of the admonitions and reproofs of conscience, and now called out only its approving judgments. It is to be recognized, however, that it is not merely the reproofs of conscience, but its compulsory or constraining action, that holy people are said to pass beyond the need of. They do all that is right without any instigation from it, under the guidance of holy love. " It would be a work of supererogation to drive a soul which goes without driving." " Conscience itself becomes the companion and playmate of love, and hides itself in its bosom. Shielded by innocence, we

[144] Pp. 650 ff.   [145] " A Treatise on Divine Union," pp. 389 ff.

come to God without fear "— which seems to say that our
dependence is in our own, not Christ's righteousness. This appears to be as near as may be a doctrine of the abolition of
conscience in the "perfect" state: and as conscience is the
organ of our morality, the abolition of morality. We get beyond the categories of right and wrong. True, it is allowed that
conscience persists, in order to applaud. It no longer directs —
not even love: it waits on love's acts to approve them. In Upham's imaginative picture of what men are when they are
perfect, he says they are emancipated (among other things)
from conscience. Why just that? Why not say they are emancipated *to* the perfect fulfillment of all the indications of a
perfectly instructed conscience?

Love, it is clear, is the highest category of Upham's thought.
It is in his usage a synonym of God. He deals much more
sanely with the phrase, " God is love," than most teachers of
his type.[146] But he seemingly fancies that he is speaking intelligibly when he says that love is " the life of God," " that
elementary, self-moving and self-instigating principle in God
which constitutes " His life: [147] that it " makes or constitutes
God"; and is " the essential and eternal life of the divine existence, and in fact constitutes that existence." [148] In point of
fact no clear meaning can be attached to such words: these
are things which love, which is a quality of being or a mode
of action of a being, cannot be. What is true, Upham himself
tells us [149] when he defines the phrase " God is love by *essence*,"
as meaning that " love is forever and unchangeably essential
to his existence as God." God would not be what we call God
without it. It is inevitable, however, from his general point
of view that he should exalt love above all those other essential attributes, without which equally God would not be what
we call God; and should make it the sole principle of the
divine action. It was the principle, for example, of creation.

[146] *Ibid.*, pp. 99–104.
[147] *Ibid.*, p. 246.
[148] " Absolute Religion," p. 82.
[149] " A Treatise on Divine Union," p. 99.

We are told that love was the motive and the production of happiness the purpose of God in creation [150] — from which we perceive that Upham adopts that hedonistic theory of ethics prevalent in the New England of his day,[151] according to which happiness is the *summum bonum* and general benevolence, or the love of being in general, the principle of all virtue. Man is not only like other creatures the product of God's love, but, having been created in the image of God, like God a " *love* being " [152] — though this certainly cannot mean, on man's part, that love is the very substance out of which he is constituted. The image of God in man, we are told, does not consist in external form, for God has no form. Nor does it consist in intellect — " for the intellect of God embraces all things, while man can know only a part " — surely a suicidal remark, since it can scarcely be meant that man's love equals God's. Nevertheless, it is boldly said at once that God's image in man does consist " in that which constitutes, more than anything else " — this qualifying phrase seems to allow something else than love to be of the divine nature — " the element, the life, of the divine nature, namely, HOLY LOVE." As specifically a " love-being," man as he came from his Maker's hands, loved instinctively, immediately and universally. Love " flowed out " from him " in all directions, like a living stream " and suffused all his environment. It almost seems as if it were conceived as a necessary mode of action, like a natural force. " Spontaneous in its action," we are told, " acting because it had a principle of movement in itself, it did not wait for the slow deductions of reason." Did not reason, then, act spontaneously — and indeed also " instinctively, immediately and universally " — in the protoplasts as truly as love? We suppose in any case that the action of love did wait, even in the protoplasts, for the apprehension of an object,

[150] " Life of Madame Catharine Adorna," p. 112.

[151] Cf. " A Treatise on Divine Union," p. iv.: " The view which is taken of the nature of pure or holy love, namely, that in its basis it is the love of existence . . . does not essentially differ, I believe, from that which is presented by President Edwards, in his Treatise on the Nature of Virtue."

[152] *Ibid.*, pp. 109–110.

and for the perception of it as an appropriate object for this affection. We should be loath to conceive of love, even in them, as radiating from man as a center like light, say, from the sun, and playing indifferently on everything that came within its reach. Even in the protoplasts love, we presume, should be conceived as the action of an intelligent and moral being.

This exaggeration apart, however, there is a great deal that is just in Upham's description of man, on the side of his affectional nature, as he came from his Maker's hand. We agree that man came from his Maker's hand " a *love* being," spontaneously loving every sentient thing brought to his apprehension. Of course, loving God most of all — Upham says, because the amount of existence or being in God is greater than in any other being. " The law of love's movement, all other things being equal, is the amount of being, or existence in the object beloved." [153] We draw back from this quantitative mode of conceiving the matter, which is part of the mechanical representation by which love is supposed to act like a natural force — say " directly as the mass and inversely as the square of the distance." " Other things " are not equal: they never are. God is loved most of all because He is the most worthy of all beings to be loved. Directed to Him, the love of benevolence, which in Upham's scheme is the sum of all virtues, seems to pass into the love of complacency. We desire for Him nothing that He has not or is not: we would have Him be nothing but what He is: desire turned to Him becomes pure delight. And Upham describes the love of the protoplasts for the creature also much in terms of complacency, as if the creature in the world's prime scarcely stood in need of anything for the supply of which the love of benevolence could be called out. Man, he tells us,[154] " saw all things in the possession of life and beauty, and he rejoiced in all things, because all things had God in them. He loved the tree and the flower, which reflected the divine wisdom and goodness. But far more did he delight in the happiness of everything which had a sentient existence. . . . He loved them; and he gave them

[153] P. 112.   [154] P. 110.

their names. . . . His simple and pure heart flowed out" to them. It is a beautiful picture. And it is Upham's picture not only of the paradise that has been lost but of the paradise that shall be regained when once more " pure love " becomes the principle of our existence.

The sin-cursed desert lies between. As we traverse its burning sands one of our chief consolations is the providence of God. For in His providence we meet with God. " God himself," says Upham finely,[155] " is hidden in the bosom of every event." " So that we can truly say," he adds, " that no event in his providence happens, without bringing God with it, and without laying his hand upon us." It is here only — in His providences — besides the heart, that God is to be found. Neither in clouds nor in sunsets, neither in our seasons of retirement nor in our devotion, can He be found: only in these two " places " — the heart and His providence.[156] Upham is accordingly accustomed to insist on the presence of God in all happenings — except sin. He tells us, for instance,[157] that " every thing which occurs, with the exception of sin, takes place, and yet without infringing on moral liberty, in the divinely appointed order and arrangement of things; and is an expression, within its own appropriate limits, of the divine will." The conclusion he draws is that therefore " in its relations to ourselves personally and individually," whatever occurs " is precisely that condition of things which is best suited to try and to benefit our own state." Thus God is essentially present to us in every occurrence. " Faith identifies every thing with God's superintendence, and makes every thing, so far as it is capable of being so, an expression of his will, with the exception already mentioned, viz., of *sin*. And even in regard to this, faith proclaims the important doctrine that sin has, and ever shall have, its limits; and that Satan, and those who follow him, can go no further than they are permitted to go." There are curious — we had almost said amusing — reserves inserted here and there in this

[155] " The Life of Faith," 1845, p. 260; cf. p. 223.
[156] " The Life of Madame Guyon," i. p. 123.
[157] " The Life of Faith," pp. 182–184.

statement, as in others like it:[158] reserves which, if pressed, might go far toward eviscerating it. Sin is to be excepted from the control of God's providence, though limited by it: moral liberty is not to be infringed by it; there are limits to the expression of the divine will in it. Despite this display of timidity in giving expression to the whole truth, the statement shows clearly as its main matter, that Upham believed in the universal providence of God and had the courage to say so. Calvin says it better; but it is good to have it said at all, and that directly in the interests of holy living.

From this doctrine of universal providence it is very easy to draw the conclusion that submission to providence is not only a duty, but a privilege and a joy. If providence is the expressed will of God and we are His children, what other can we do than rejoice in it? All that God does is glorious: let us but observe and applaud. Upham, however, confuses the duties of submission to providence and of ordering our lives by providence, and while not neglecting to insist on the one, insists equally and very distressingly on the other. "Harmony with Providence," says he,[159] "is union with God." "The man who lives in conformity with Providence necessarily lives in conformity with God." How, we ask in perplexity, can a man do anything else than live in conformity with providence? In this particular statement Upham may be only expressing himself ill and may intend only to dissuade us from that temper which, in dissatisfaction with our lot in life, or with the events which befall us, complains of God's providential arrangements. It would be wise in that case, if, instead of saying that the natural man is out of harmony with God's providence, while to

[158] As, for example, in "The Life of Faith," pp. 440 ff. God is present in all things that occur. He is not the *originator* of them all, at least not in the absolute sense of the term. But He is "in some sense present to all things which take place"; "exercises over all events a degree of control and direction"; "every thing, which takes place, exists either by his control or by his permission"; "whatever is, has God in it; not always in the same sense; but always in *some* sense." There is some fumbling; but this general statement is aimed at the mark. And the inferences are right: all events are ordered in wisdom and goodness: God is glorified in everything that takes place.
[159] "A Treatise on Divine Union," p. 228.

the truly holy man God's providences are dear, because he
conforms to the law of providence — we should say simply
that the circumstances of life come from our Father's hands
and should be received as such. But it is not always possible to
escape from the confusing implication of Upham's prescriptions thus. " If the law of Providence were strictly fulfilled,"
he remarks in one place,[160] " it is obvious that order would at
once exist throughout the world." How can the law of providence — which is not the preceptive but the decretive will
of God — fail to be strictly fulfilled? Upham, however, proves
to have a special use of the phrase. " It should be remembered,"
he says,[161] " that Providence is one thing; the *law* of Providence is another." " Providence is God's arrangement of things
and events in the world, including his constant supervision.
The *law* of Providence, in distinction from Providence in itself
considered, is the RULE OF ACTION, which is contained in, and
which is developed from, this providential arrangement." He is
actually recommending us to derive our rule of life from an
observation of God's providential government of the world!
As if we could sweep our eye over the whole course of things
from the beginning to the end! It is the universal course of
things which constitutes the matter to be observed, and our
rule of life is to be in conformity to this universal course of
things. How this differs from the Stoic maxim of living according to nature, it is difficult to see: " some call it evolution,
others call it God." If, on the other hand, we limit the providence to which we attend to a few outstanding happenings
which appear to us divine interpositions, the law of life which
we derive from them runs great risk of betraying us into fanaticism. We may and must commit ourselves to the divine
providence: it is a joy to be in our Father's hands. We cannot
deduce from observed providences a law of life: if for no
other reason than that the observation is fatally defective.
It is the written Word and it alone — the preceptive, not the
decretive will of God — in which our divinely given rule of
life is to be found: that and that law of nature, written on the

<hr>

[160] "A Treatise on Divine Union," p. 234.   [161] P. 193.

heart, conscience. When we say, in our current speech, that we order our lives by the indications of providence, we mean something very different from that ordering them by a rule of life deduced from the observed providential order which Upham vainly commends. We mean that we adjust our lives to emerging events, and seek to do our obvious and nearest duty in every situation which successively confronts us. Stated in secular language that is to say that we order our lives in accordance with circumstances; from the religious point of view, the circumstances are recognized as ordered by God and hence we say we are led by providence. But the rule of life in these circumstances is not derived from an induction from them — and therefore not from providence — but from the law of God, written whether in His revealed Word or on the fleshly tablets of our hearts.

Great as is the perversion of the precious truth that God meets us in His providence, which is made by Upham's proposed erection of the observed order of providence into our rule of life, there is an even greater perversion which was also taught him by his Quietistic mentors. Under color of the high motive of — not submitting to providence merely — but gladly embracing it, because the hand of God is in everything and all that occurs is therefore right, Madame Guyon, and Upham following her, inculcate a very unwholesome indifference with respect to life and all that occurs in the process of living, as if it were wrong to seek to better anything. Madame Guyon, for example, boasts that her soul is entirely independent of every thing which is not God.[162] It would be content, she says, if it were alone in the world, since it does not find its happiness in any earthly attachments. Every desire has been mortified and no wishes survive. This is merely inhuman. God has made us social beings; he does not desire us to be indiffer-

---

[162] "The Life of Madame Guyon," i. p. 66. "The great principle of practical sanctification," says Madame Guyon (ii. p. 79), "is this; — *to desire nothing but what we now have, sin only excepted.* . . . When we thus have God, by accepting him in all his manifestations and doings, we necessarily have every thing." This is the very essence of Quietism.

ent to our fellows. We do not require to break all earthly attachments that we may be attached to Him. There is revealed in this attitude of indifference attachments not so much to God as to ourselves. It is the self-centered attitude by way of eminence. Of this aspect of it also a word should be spoken in this connection. Because God is in all that occurs, each thing that exists may be taken in turn as a center from which we may look out upon the all-embracing providence of God, and in relation to which we may contemplate all that occurs. It is not in itself wrong, therefore, that each individual soul should look upon all that occurs to it, and to all that circle of existence which closely surrounds it, as part of God's providential dealing with itself, and should utilize it from that point of sight. Nevertheless, some very curious — some very undesirable — results are apt to grow out of this entirely right and useful habit, when it is onesidedly indulged. It may, often does, end in erecting our individual self into something very like the focus of the universe and conceiving of everything and everybody in the circumference of the circle thrown out from ourselves, as a center, as existing for us alone. A death of someone in our circle, for example, comes to be viewed only in its relation to our own person, and is thought of as if it were brought about by the Divine Governor of the world solely for its effect upon us. We read, for instance, in Upham's " The Life of Madame Guyon," [163] of the deaths of her father and daughter, and from all that appears from the expressions of feeling quoted from Madame Guyon, or from Upham's comments, they seem to have been looked upon by her and to be recommended to our consideration by him, so prevailingly from the point of view of her own disciplining, as to suggest that they were brought about by God for no other purpose than to benefit her. " He who gives himself to God," writes Upham, " to experience under his hand the transformations of sanctifying grace, must be willing to give up all objects, however dear they may be, which he does not hold in strict subordination to the claims of divine love, and which he does not love IN

[163] i. pp. 136–137; cf. i. p. 144.

and FOR God alone. The sanctification of the heart, in the strict
and full sense of the term, is inconsistent with a divided and
wandering affection. A misplaced love, whether it be wrong
in its degree or its object, is as *really,* though apparently not
as *odiously,* sinful, as a misplaced hatred." Madame Guyon's
freedom of soul, it seems, was liable to be contracted and
shackled by domestic affections, which were but partially sanctified. So God took from her, her father and her daughter that
she might learn to love only Him and in Him. It would seem
to be quite dangerous to live within the reach of the as yet
only partially sanctified affections of a saint. In such a position we are liable to be "removed" at any time, for the benefit
of his growing holiness. Contact with him appears almost as
perilous as contact with a live wire. Madame Guyon's comments on the death of her daughter are: "What shall I say, —
she died by the hands of Him, who was pleased to strip me of
all." There is no reason for refusing to see this relation of the
child's death, or for refusing to profit by the sense that it is a
Father's hand here too that is dealing with us, fitting us for
the Sanctuary above. Only — it is distinctly unpleasant to see
the mother apparently thinking in this strain alone, or predominantly. Everything is looked at from the point of view of
its relation to a morbid preoccupation with self. And this is
the characteristic mental attitude of the mystic — a truly morbid preoccupation with his own subjective states and experiences. He looks within to find God, he says: it is with difficulty,
apparently, that he finds anything there but himself.

In the opening pages of "A Treatise on Divine Union," [164]
Upham gives a brief summary of his dogmatic system. It
proves to be, as expressed there, pure Semi-Pelagianism. Man
is "unable to help himself," but is "able nevertheless to utter
the cry of his helplessness and anguish," and thus to obtain the
help of God. Cassian could not have expressed his doctrine
better: men need grace, but not prevenient grace. They cannot
restore themselves, says Upham, repeating Cassian's doctrine,
but they can turn to God for the needed aid. It lies in our own

[164] 1851, pp. 26 ff.

choice whether we will live with God or not: though it is not in our power to live with God. We must go to God of our own free-will; and then, " God, acting upon the basis of man's free consent, becomes the life of the soul." [165] We must open " our hearts to the free and full entrance of his grace," and then, " he will become the true operator in the soul, and will give origin to all spiritual good." [166] " It is then," he says precisely to the point, " that God works in the soul." Man must " exercise voluntary acquiescence in and acceptance of the divine operation "; but it is this divine operation which works salvation. Not indeed even this apart from man's activities: man does not become quiescent after his first act of " consent ": let us call it coöperation rather: he ceases only from " independent action." Now " God becomes the *Giver*, and man the happy recipient." " We coöperate . . . with God in the work of . . . redemption," he explains more fully in another place,[167] " when we submit to this divine operation without reluctance "; or [168] man " unites with God in his own restoration, when he lets the great Master of the mind work upon him." " Lets." This of course subordinates God to man in the work of salvation; and as murder will out, so this comes out plainly in a statement like this: [169] " God acts in the holy man in connection with, and perhaps we should say, in subordination to, his own choice."

Thus Upham suspends the whole process of salvation in its inception and in all its stages alike, on our voluntary action. He is very much afraid of an " enforced " salvation, " against men's consent." " Grace, and compulsion in the administration of it," he declares,[170] " are ideas which negative each other." Grace " *implies a suitable subject for its reception*," and it is " impossible, in the nature of things, to bestow " it not only " upon a being, that has no intelligence to realize its value," but also upon one who has " no power of reception or rejection " [171] — a proposition which is not obvious, unless " grace "

[165] P. 29.   [169] P. 272.
[166] Pp. 28–29.   [170] " Life of Madame Catharine Adorna," p. 205.
[167] P. 271.   [171] P. 205.
[168] P. 270.

be arbitrarily defined as just "divine influence." In the statement we have just quoted from him, it is apparently more than
this. In others, however, he reduces it to this. In one passage,
for instance, dealing with it under this designation,[172] he very
naturally declares that neither "the application of material
force," nor of "anything . . . analogous to material force"
is implied in it. That "would obviously be inconsistent with
the nature of mind." "So far as we can perceive," he now adds
positively, "such divine influence is, and can be, only the
application of that mental force which is lodged in *motives*."
"God influences by setting motives before us." Then he quite
superfluously remarks: "God, in operating upon man by
means of motives, never violates his freedom." Upham places
himself here, we perceive, squarely on the platform of the
"New Divinity," the maxim of which (as enunciated by Lyman Beecher, for instance) was crisply expressed in the words:
"God governs men by motives, not by force." In doing so, he
brings the whole body of his mystical teachings and especially
the more Quietistic ones among them, under some obscuration.
It is more immediately important, however, here to note that
he equally embarrasses the doctrine of salvation which we
have just seen him teaching. He is no longer a Semi-Pelagian.
He has become a Pelagian. If God only persuades, something
more than "consent" on man's part seems to be requisite to
the working of effects.

Other language which he employs in the same relation incurs the same condemnation. There is the term "renunciation" for instance. Both justification and sanctification, he
tells us, involve, on our part, complete "renunciation." We
must "be willing to be saved, both from the guilt of the past
and from present sin, by God's grace" alone. Is God's grace
conceived here as merely suasive? What is being emphasized
is, it is true, that we must be willing. God respects our freedom
and unless by our own free act we put ourselves in His hands,
He will not save us. We must decide — but is it not implied
that it is He that does the work? We remember, however, the

---

[172] "Absolute Religion," 1873, p. 230.

importance which Upham attaches to our "consent" being conceived not as mere consenting, but as involving actual activities coöperative with God's saving operation. Even this, however, becomes an inadequate form of statement, when all the actual work proves to be done by us. On one occasion,[173] when defining the nature of this wonderful "consent" by which we make ourselves to differ, after telling us broadly that it is not a cessation of action, or the absence of action, but " a real or positive act on the part of the creature," he adds more specifically, that it is " an act of harmonious concurrence and coöperation with the divine act." Does it require nothing more than concurrence with an act of persuasion — or even coöperation with an act of persuasion — to recover a lost soul? Where the divine efficiency is reduced to persuasion, and the human to coöperation with this persuasion, there seems to be no power left to work salvation. We no longer have the alternatives, grace and free-will to choose between: each is in turn eliminated. We cannot trust in grace; it is mere persuasion. We cannot trust to free-will; it merely gives consent.

Of course it is the will that gets the victory. Even in his Semi-Pelagian mood, as we have just noted — where God's grace is conceived as the operating cause of salvation — the soul is represented as capable of performing and as actually performing an act of harmonious concurrence and coöperation with the divine act, even before God takes charge of the soul. What need has such a soul of salvation? If it can perform one such act, it can perform another. Or many others. Or an unbroken series of others. And are we not told that " salvation is nothing else, and can be nothing else, than harmony with God "? An unbroken series of acts of harmonious concurrence with God's acts is already salvation. What need of salvation has a soul already capable of performing and actually performing *these* acts? A soul must save itself — bring itself into harmony with God — in order that it may be saved by God, be brought into harmony with God! For, we are told, what characterizes a saved soul is the constant repetition of

[173] " The Life of Faith," pp. 73–74.

this "consentient and concurrent act," by which it freely enters into salvation.

We make ourselves a new heart immediately and at once by a volition, says Finney, and this volition is just as easy to make as any other volition — say the volition to raise our arm. No, says Upham, we make ourselves a new heart by our faith: it is faith that makes a new heart. And he seems to mean this of the direct action of faith. Of the two, Upham certainly has the advantage. "The faith of the heart, therefore," he says,[174] "is that faith, which makes a new heart; in other words, which inspires new affections; such affections, as are conformable to God's law and will." A body of new affections may, no doubt, be spoken of collectively as a new heart. And, no doubt, a strong faith (which is itself an affection) dropped into the seething caldron of this heart, may cause a new crystallization of the affections and so tend to make us a "new heart." What kind of a heart this "new heart" will be can scarcely be predicted so long as we operate with the abstract notion of "faith." In itself, without consideration of its object (no doubt such an abstraction has no existence) "faith" cannot make a "new heart." There is no faith which is not faith in something; and it is the nature of this something which gives its character to any faith which really exists; and to the "new heart" which results from its entrance into it. After all, then, it is not faith but the object on which faith rests which gives us our "new heart." Faith in God; faith in some great and good man; faith in ourselves; faith in a bad cause: the new hearts which faith can make differ among themselves *toto cælo*. Upham, of course, has, at the back of his mind, the idea of faith in God, when he says that faith gives us a new heart. Faith in what God? Faith in the tribal God of the savage? Faith in the distant God of the Deist? Or faith in the God who in Christ is reconciling the world unto Himself? The new heart that we get will depend on the God on whom our faith rests. Two things further need be said. The former is this: it is not faith only which will give us a new heart. Any alteration in

[174] "The Life of Faith," pp. 55–56.

any affection will no doubt produce a readjustment of our affections and so give us to that extent a " new heart." Faith has no monoply in this power to make a " new heart." The other is this: where shall we get this faith that is to make us a new heart? No doubt, if we will be satisfied with a very little change in our heart — and a very little change will make so far a " new heart " — we may manage to produce the requisite faith ourselves. But if we want a *really* new heart? Undoubtedly a change from unbelief to real, hearty faith in the God and Father of our Lord Jesus Christ, will profoundly transform — say, rather transfigure — the whole affectional life. But where shall we get this real and hearty faith in the God and Father of our Lord Jesus Christ? Certainly it cannot be the spontaneous product of a heart at enmity with God, filled with the mingled dread and hatred of God of the conscious criminal in the presence of his just Judge. Can such a heart trust itself, trust itself wholly and without reserve, trust itself with full confidence that we shall receive from Him nothing but good, to God? Clearly, we shall need the " new heart " before we can conceive the faith that is to make us this new heart. Faith, this faith, cannot come into existence except as the product of the new heart: the heart it enters is already the new heart. We may say that it is the first issue of the new heart and that it is through it that the reconstruction and realignment and rearrangement of the other affections are accomplished. It may be the gathering point about which they all assemble; and in this sense it may be precisely faith which makes us a new heart. But in any case, the new heart itself — faith does not make it but presupposes it.

In a remarkable chapter in his posthumous volume, " Absolute Religion," [175] Upham gives us in brief his whole philosophy of human existence, under the categories of creation and regeneration — the first and second births. God, we are told, " is the beginning or source of things," and therefore " the first or natural birth of man is and must be from the Infinite to the finite." That is man's descent into individuality; an

[175] Pp. 95 ff.

individuality in which, by necessity of nature he is "self-centered," and in which also, as we learn later, he becomes "by a moral necessity" sinful, "moral evil" being "necessarily incidental to the facts which are involved in the constitution of man's nature." [176] The second birth, now, "is a birth back from the finite to the Infinite." This is man's ascent back to his source; but, we are told, without loss of his personality. "In the first birth God may be said to make or constitute the finite, giving it the freedom and independence of a personal existence; and yet without spiritually incarnating Himself in it as an indwelling principle of that life. . . . In the second birth, the finite in the exercise of its moral freedom, which is an essential element in its personality, has accepted God in the central intimacy of its nature as its living and governing principle." Thus we learn that God brings about the first birth, man the second. The reason why it must be man who produces the second birth is "the inviolability" of man's freedom, which makes God's "spiritually incarnating Himself in it" impossible, "without a consenting action on the part of the creature." When, however, in its own freedom the creature accepts God in the central intimacy of its nature, "the human or 'earthy,' as the Scriptures call it, without ceasing to be human or earthy, but by renouncing its own centre as the source of life, and taking God as its centre, does by its own choice and in a true and high sense become divine." From the beginning God intended this issue: that was the plan. But it could not be reached otherwise than through this development — a development which began on the thrusting of man by God down into the finite — involving sin — and the rising of man up by his own free-will into the infinite, into unity "with the universal or divine personal life." Sin, which is not mentioned at all in the primary exposition of man's fundamental history, appears in this construction only as the incidental and inevitable result of man's finiteness, to be left behind, of course, when he attained the infinite, eliminated as incidentally as it arose. In essence, salvation is then our deliverance not from

[176] Pp. 105, 116.

sin, but from the finite, not the attainment of holiness, but
the achievement of the divine.

In dealing with the topic of justification and sanctification
Upham has in the first instance two objects in view. He wishes
to make it clear that sanctification is the end to which justification is the means. This is in order that he may preserve the
general contention of the perfectionists that deliverance from
the power of sin is more important than deliverance from its
guilt.[177] But he wishes equally to make it clear that sanctification is not an inevitable result of justification; as he phrases it
in one passage,[178] that " the work of sanctification " is not " absolutely and necessarily involved in that of justification." This
is in order that he may preserve the specific contention of the
perfectionists that sanctification is obtained by a separate and
independent act of faith. Justification exists only for sanctification, but it only prepares the way for it, and does not itself
involve it. It cannot be said, however, that Upham succeeds in
preserving formal consistency in his many discussions of their
relations. That these relations are not merely those of antecedence and subsequence he distinctly declares; [179] he represents sanctification as " starting on the *basis*[180] of justification "
though apparently not in the full force of this language; [181] and
he even speaks of sanctification being the *evidence* of justification.[182] There is something more than even this apparently implied in a statement like the following, which links justification
and sanctification so intimately together as hardly to escape
making them imply one another. [183] " It is important to re-

---

[177] So e.g. " The Life of Faith," pp. 164–165.

[178] " Principles of the Interior or Hidden Life," p. 173.

[179] *Ibid.*, p. 171.   [181] P. 170.

[180] The italics are ours.   [182] Pp. 171–172.

[183] " A Treatise on Divine Union," pp. 265–266. In the " Life of Madame
Guyon," ii. p. 8, Upham expounds Madame Guyon and Father La Combe as
teaching " that sanctification is the . . . true end of justification; and that the
merciful intentions of the Infinite Mind are not satisfied . . . by merely
redeeming us from hell, without making us holy." " They proclaimed," he
continues, " the doctrine of sanctification, therefore, as the true complement
and result of that of justification." This is said in a manner to involve his
agreement with the doctrine expressed.

member that there are two offers involved in that great work, which Christ came to accomplish; — the one is, forgiveness for the past, and the other is, a new life in God for the future. A new life in God, which implies entire reconciliation with God as its basis, could not be offered to man, until the penalty of the old transgression was remitted. And, on the other hand, the remission of the penalty of the past would be wholly unavailing, without the permanent restoration of a divine and living principle in man's spiritual part." We should be scarcely justified in insisting on the reiterated reference of forgiveness here to " past " sins and the valuelessness of their forgiveness apart from permanent spiritual restoration, as intended to assert that no remedy exists for sins committed after justification, or that no sins are committed after justification. One or the other of these assertions is, it is true, required to introduce perfect consistency into the statement, but all that seems to be intended is to declare that justification and sanctification are so interrelated that one implies the other. They have at any rate two things of great importance in common, which bind them together at least as the two indispensable saving operations. They are both supernatural operations: in both we ultimately receive everything from God. And in both, we receive everything through the same channel, viz. " by *faith*." [184]

We do not receive everything in both, however, " by faith " in precisely the same way, although in both instances faith may fairly be called the procuring cause. Justification is summed up in pardon or forgiveness, and from that point of view an attempt is made to show that there can be no effective pardon except by faith.[185] No doubt an offended person may pardon an offender with no reference to any state of mind the latter may be in or may enter into: pardon is free. But such an act of pardoning would have no effect upon the offender. He would not feel pardoned; and the act of pardon would not " result in mutual reconciliation, in the reciprocation of benevolent feelings, and in true happiness." The implication is

[184] " Principles of the Interior or Hidden Life," p. 169.
[185] " The Life of Faith," pp. 65 ff.

that in such circumstances pardon would do no good; it would
leave the offender just where he was before with unaltered
feelings towards the pardoner. The removal of objective penalties is left wholly out of the question: and the entire transaction is conceived as subjective. Upham now argues that on the
assumption that a pardon " which is spiritually available, one
which is desirable and valuable in the spiritual or religious
sense," " results in entire reconciliation between the parties "
— in the manner explained — therefore no pardon is conceivable among moral beings " without confidence or faith existing
on the part of such subject towards the author." Justifying
faith in this view is not faith in the atoning Saviour, but general confidence in the benevolent God; and justification takes
place *in foro conscientiæ* and not *in foro cæli*. As a *rationale*
of justification therefore this exposition wholly misses the
mark. It amounts to saying that justification is by faith because pardon can work its beneficent effects in the pardoned
one's heart only if received in confident trust, a trust which
will believe without question that the pardon is real and that
it is worth while. But justification concerns not the reception
of pardon on the part of the offender but the granting of pardon on the part of the offended. When we say we are justified
by faith, we do not mean that it is through faith that we are
enabled to enjoy the sense of pardon, though that is true also.
We mean that it is through faith that we enter the state of
pardoned ones. It is through entrusting ourselves to Christ,
that by virtue of His atoning work, we are received as pardoned sinners. However true it is, that it is only by trusting
in the pardoning God that we can enjoy the sense of pardon,
that is not the function of faith in justification; is only a
secondary effect of it. It is better to be saved than to feel
saved: and we must not confound salvation with the sense of
salvation.

The precise explanation of exactly how faith operates to
sanctify us apparently presents some difficulty to those who
are yet agreed that the doctrine of sanctification by faith is not
second either in importance or certainty to the parallel doc-

trine of justification by faith. Sometimes sanctification is spoken of as so directly by faith as to appear to imply that the state of mind which we call faith is itself sanctification, that is to say to identify faith and holiness. At other times what is meant seems to be merely that sanctification is an effect wrought by God, to whom we entrust it believingly. The latter is perhaps the prevailing manner in which Upham speaks of it; and when he does so his primary assertion is doubtless that sanctification is in some sense a supernatural effect. This, however, is not always made as clear as it might be. He can speak of the "sanctification of the heart, resting upon faith as its basis in distinction from mere works," [186] after a fashion which unhappily suggests that he is thinking of faith as a virtue and is merely giving it the precedence as an inward virtue — *the* inward virtue by way of eminence — to external acts of virtue, especially "ceremonial observances and austerities." In that case he would mean merely that this state of mind is a holy state of mind and those who possess it are holy. There is at least one passage, however,[187] in which he explains somewhat formally how faith purifies the heart of "irregular and unholy desires"; and we probably will not go wrong if we take this explanation as expressing his matured mind on the subject. Faith, he here says, purifies the heart in two ways, directly and indirectly. Directly, it lays hold of the promises of God, and so rests on God to cleanse us. Indirectly, it gives birth to love to God and this inhibits all love to the creature. Here is a comprehensive explanation, recognizing both a supernatural and a natural operation. It is not clear, however, at first sight, how these two are harmonized in the single effect. If it be "faith formed by love" — it is a Romanist conception which seems to be floating before his mind — which sanctifies us, that appears to carry with it the conception that our sanctification consists in a faith-produced love, which is only another name for holiness. In this case we do not readily see how our sanctification can be brought about by God in the fulfillment of His

---

186 "Life of Madame Guyon," ii. p. 10; cf. ii. p. 8, and i. p. 370.
187 "The Life of Faith," pp. 162 ff.

promises, except by just the fostering of faith in us by Him —
and this is done by Him in Upham's view, as we have seen, not
supernaturally, but naturally, viz. solely by presenting to us
motives to believe. There do not lack passages in which it
seems that it is precisely this which Upham means to say.
Thus, for example, he tells us,[188] that God saves us from sin by
" operating by the Holy Spirit in the production of faith in the
heart." What he means apparently is that God does not
directly eradicate sin from the heart through the creative
operation of His spirit, but attains the result by producing
faith in the heart — of course by the presentation of motives
to believe, which is the only mode of the divine operation
which Upham admits in the premises. In that case it seems
meaningless to talk of two modes of action by which faith
purifies the heart — a direct one in which it rests on the promises of God and an indirect one in which it produces the love
which is holiness. The so-called direct method is swallowed up
into the so-called indirect method: God purifies the heart only
through the faith which works by love. The rationalism of the
" New Divinity " neutralizes the mystical tendencies to supernaturalism, and we have left only that we are sanctified by
faith because faith passes into love and love is holiness. God
may graciously support and aid us in the process, but we
sanctify ourselves, and look to Him only to urge on our own
good work.

Faith, then, passes into love.[189] And love constitutes holiness. " PERFECT LOVE," says Upham,[190] " is to be regarded, on
the principles of the gospel, as essentially the same thing, or
rather as precisely the same thing, with SANCTIFICATION or
HOLINESS." To love, then, is to be holy; and perfect love is
only another name for perfect holiness. In assuming this attitude there is danger, of course, of conceiving of love as a substitute for holiness; and of supposing that if a man has love he
has all the holiness he needs. And the double peril lurks in this

[188] " The Life of Faith," p. 165.
[189] *Ibid.*, p. 53; " Principles of the Interior or Hidden Life," pp. 85 f.
[190] " Principles of the Interior or Hidden Life," p. 125.

path, of sentimentalizing the conception of the Christian life, on the one hand — fostering a tendency to conceive it in terms of emotion rather than of morality — and of directly relaxing the demands of righteousness, on the other. Upham does not wish to relax the demands of righteousness. " Immutable right," [191] says he, " has a claim and a power which entitle it to regulate every thing else. Even LOVE itself, an element so essential to all moral goodness that it gives a character and name to God himself, ceases to be love the moment it ceases to be in conformity with justice. Love that is not just is not holy; and love that is not holy is selfishness under the name of love. Every affection, therefore, however amiable and honorable it may be when it is in a right position, is wrong, and is at variance with inward holiness of life, which is not in conformity with the rule of right." Nevertheless, it can scarcely be denied that Upham in his actual treatment of the subject does not succeed in avoiding somewhat depreciating the sense of right as a principle of action in the interests of love — contrasting the religion of obligation with the religion of love, with a view to showing the superiority of the latter in the conduct of life.[192] It is a subject with respect to which some careful discrimination is necessary to its prudent treatment. The propositions which Upham defends are such as these: that in the order of nature love is the first in time — the heart naturally acts before the conscience; that it is love which determines the actions of the holy man — in fact not so much *from* as *with* conscience; that the more holy a man is the less he feels the compulsive power of conscience — and he may even feel that he has " lost his conscience." No doubt each of these propositions is true — with its proper qualification. But in their sum, they do not avail to subordinate duty to love. Love itself, indeed, is a duty; and in loving, we fulfil our obligation. When Augustine says, " Love and do what you please," it is with the maxim in his mind that love is the fulfillment of the law, in the sense that love is in order to duty, and

[191] *Ibid.,* p. 210.
[192] " A Treatise on Divine Union," pp. 130 ff.

instrument to the meeting of obligation. It is a fundamental mistake to set love and duty in opposition to one another, as if they were alternative principles of conduct. We cannot try a cause between the religion of love and the religion of duty as litigants — as if we were trying the cause between spontaneous and legalistic religion. Love should be dutiful and duty should be loving. What God has joined together, why should we seek to separate? If we could think of a love which is undutiful — that could not be thought of as an expression of religion; any more than a dutifulness without affection. What we are really doing is discussing the affectional and the ethical elements in religion and seeking to raise the question whether we prefer emotion or conscientiousness in religion. The only possible answer is — both.

Upham remarks that " the holy man does not act from mere will, against the desires of his sensitive or affectional nature, on the ground, and for the reason, that his conscience requires him to do so; but, on the contrary, acts under the impulse of holy and loving affections, affections which are the regenerated gift of God, and which sweetly carry the will with it." [193] True enough: and we remark in passing, that this is also true psychology, truer psychology than Upham always gives us. But this is only to say that in the holy man, his affections are on the side of his conscience. That is what his holiness — in part — consists in. His enlightened conscience and purified affections move together to the one holy end. But how if the affections are not purified — not so fully purified as perfectly to harmonize in their impulses with the requirements of conscience? That is the condition of all on earth: though Upham, as a perfectionist, may have reserves in allowing it. Surely then, the conscience and imperfectly purified affections will not " sweetly " move together to one end. There is a conflict — and, in the interests of holiness, which ought to govern? Surely conscience ought to govern. Upham has not shown that the affections ought to rule, against conscience, when there is a conflict; but only that it is a higher stage of holiness where

[193] Pp. 131–132.

there is no conflict, but the affections coincide with conscience. No doubt the law is then written on the heart; but it is the law that is written on the heart. And when it is the law that is written on the heart, why, then the impulses of the heart accord with the law. That is the *felix libertas boni*. As nothing but the good pleases us now, why — we can do as we please. Conscience has not been dethroned but enthroned. If we no longer feel "the compulsive power of conscience," that can only be because we so spontaneously obey conscience that we do not feel it as imperative as compulsion. The categorical imperative has not died within us: it has so prevailed as that it embodies itself in the systole and diastole of all our most intimate action. It is not merely that conscience now approves and so does not whimper against our actions. It is that it flows out "sweetly" into and through the open channels of the sanctified affections into the unreluctant will. Conscience is not superseded by love. Love has become an organ of conscience. Were it not so, it would not be holy love, and if it were not holy love neither would it be (Upham himself being witness), so far, religious love. There is no religion of love, then, which is not also, and first of all, a religion of obligation.

Having identified " sanctification, evangelical holiness, and evangelical or Christian perfection " with " perfect love," Upham undertakes to tell us what " perfect love " is.[194] It is, he says, first of all " PURE love," that is, it is free from all selfishness. It is, however, on the other hand, "relative to the capacity of the subject of it "; the perfection of a man is not that of an angel. It includes, of course, like all love, the two elements of pleasure or complacency in its object and a desire to do it good — or, since we are speaking of love to God, a desire to promote His glory, and that "in such a degree, that we are not conscious of having any desire or will at variance with the will of God." As, however, " the nature of the human mind is such, that we never can have an entire and cordial acquiescence in the will of God in all things, without an antecedent approval of and complacency in his character and administration," we

[194] " Principles of the Interior or Hidden Life," pp. 145 ff.

need only attend to the second mark of perfect love, " a will entirely accordant with and lost in the will of God." Thus Upham gets around to his definition of perfection: [195] " An entire coincidence of our own wills with the divine will; in other words, the rejection of the natural principle of life, which may be described as love terminating in self and constituting self-will; and the adoption of the heavenly principle of life, which is love terminating and fulfilled in the will of God." This view of the nature of perfect love, he says, is very important " practically, as well as theologically." There is certainly every appearance here that love is confounded with one of its effects.

In another place [196] " pure or holy love " is defined by Upham as the love which is *" precisely conformed to its object."* That is to say, it is the reaction of the subject loving to the object loved, when that reaction is precisely accordant with the loveliness of the object. " If," says he, " all objects were correctly understood by us in their character and in their claims upon us, and if our affections were *free from all selfish bias,* our love would *necessarily* be appropriate to the object, and therefore holy " — from which we learn incidentally that a necessary reaction of the affections may have moral character, a thing we would not have expected from Upham. What is directly said, however, is only that if our perceptions of the loveliness of the object are perfect, and our reaction to this perception is unaffected by any disturbing causes — we should love that object as it ought to be loved. From this point of view, it would seem, we can have a pure love of God only when our apprehension of Him, in His character and His claims on us, is perfect — when we know Him perfectly as He is in all the loveliness of His infinite loveliness — and when our souls, reacting to this perfect apprehension of Him, are perfectly free from every detracting and disturbing bias — in a word, are themselves perfect. This would appear to render what is called pure love to God impossible to creatures like us. Upham, if we understand him, seeks to meet this difficulty by affirming

[195] P. 148; cf. " Life of Madame Guyon," ii. p. 338.
[196] " Life of Madame Catharine Adorna," pp. 123 ff.

that pure love tends to purify the judgment. "The object is much more likely to present itself before the mind distinctly, and precisely as it is, in the state of pure love, than it is to present itself before the mind with entire precision, when its affections are perverted and selfish." Quite so. But this posits pure love as the condition of the apprehension which is to serve as its cause. What we get from it is then only the assertion that in order to exercise pure love, we must first be pure of heart. The question then presses very severely, How are we to become perfectly pure of heart? Upham's suggestion here [197] seems to be that we must not be too exigent in our demands on ourselves. God will have regard to our weaknesses. "All that he requires at such times is, that we should love the object just so far as it is presented to us. . . . And such love, however it may be perplexed in its operation by existing in connection with involuntary errors of judgment, he readily and fully accepts." The general conclusion then is, "that, *if we avail ourselves of all suitable aids in obtaining a knowledge of objects, and if by loving without selfishness we love them purely, we shall love them rightly or holily, and of course love them acceptably.*" This can mean nothing else than that, after all, then, pure love can exist without a perfect apprehension of its object, and without a perfect soul to react to it. Pure love need not be perfectly pure, then, to be pure love. "Perfect love," we read,[198] "as it is understood by such writers" — that is, "writers on evangelical holiness" — "to exist in truly holy persons in the present life, is a love which is free from selfishness, and which is conformed to its object, so far as a knowledge of its object is within our reach in our present fallen state." We are now flatly on the plane of the Oberlin "sliding scale," and arrive therefore in the end at nothing more than that perfection of heart — a mitigated perfection — is the condition of holy activities — a mitigated holiness. "Certain it is," he says at another place,[199] "that those who are perfected in

[197] Pp. 126–127.
[198] P. 135, he says this "perfection" is essentially the same thing as "pure love." [199] "Principles of the Interior or Hidden Life," p. 125.

love, whatever may be their infirmities and errors, and however important and proper it may be for them to make constant application to the blood of the atonement, both for the forgiveness of the infirmities of the present, and of the infirmities and transgressions of the past, are spoken of and are treated, in the New Testament, as accepted, sanctified, or holy persons." The term "transgressions" seems to be carefully avoided when the present failings of the saints are mentioned.

We are now in the midst of Upham's doctrine of perfection. We have already seen that the perfection which he teaches is a "mitigated" perfection: it may be — it is — marred by infirmities and errors; and it requires to be forgiven. And we infer from that, that it is not yet all that shall be: there is something beyond. In the second chapter of his " Principles of the Interior or Hidden Life," [200] he describes in some detail what he understands that holiness to be which constitutes its substance, and which he declares to be "the first and indispensable prerequisite " of the state of " the Interior or Hidden Life," here represented as " walking in close and uninterrupted communion with God," and elsewhere as "union with God." He begins by declaring it an obtainable state, a state actually to be enjoyed in this life. It is then defined in passing as consisting in a life free from " voluntary transgression." To this is soon added the information that it is sometimes called "evangelical or gospel holiness " in order "to distinguish it from Adamic perfection "; and a little later still, that the name of " Christian perfection " is given to it, thus identifying it with the Wesleyan doctrine of perfection. And then we are given quite an elaborate exposition of what it does *not* involve. It does not "necessarily imply a perfection of the physical system "; nor yet a "perfection of the intellect "; nor is it in every respect the same as " the holiness or sanctification of a future life " — it is subject to temptations, and it may be lost. Nor does it imply that we no longer need an atonement. We still require an atonement for " all mere physical infirmities, which originate in our fallen condition, but which necessarily

[200] Pp. 17–24.

prevent our doing for God what we should otherwise do." And also for " all unavoidable errors and imperfections of judgment, which in their ultimate causes result from sin." These things, he says, are " very different in their nature from deliberate and voluntary transgressions," which is true enough: and then he adds that nevertheless their stains can be washed away in the blood of Christ — they are sins, though only " involuntary sins." It would perhaps be more just, however, he adds, not to call them sins at all, but " imperfections or trespasses " — though they cannot be remitted without application to the blood of Christ. No doubt it is with these things in mind, he says, that some good people say that they are morally certain to sin all the time. If so, he has no quarrel with them: he means by perfection only freedom from " sins of a deliberate and voluntary nature." That is the negative side of it. Positively, " Christian perfection," or " that holiness which, as fallen and as physically and intellectually imperfect creatures, we are imperatively required and expected to exercise . . . at the present moment, and during every succeeding moment of our lives " — consists just in love.[201] He " who loves God with his whole heart, and his neighbor as himself, although his state may in some incidental respects be different from that of Adam, and especially from that of the angels in heaven, and although he may be the subject of involuntary imperfections and infirmities, which, in consequence of his relation to Adam, require confession and atonement, is nevertheless, in the gospel sense of the terms, a holy or sanctified person." [202] And this holiness is a " condition " of moral communion with God which is called the Hidden Life here and elsewhere Union with God.

Attention cannot fail to be attracted in this exposition to the stress which is put on voluntary sinning, with the involved light estimate of involuntary faults. This reflects, no doubt, the tendency of thought prevalent in the " New Divinity," but it is also the common tendency of perfectionists everywhere, who by it seek to adjust their doctrine of perfec-

[201] P. 23.   [202] P. 23.

tion to the only too manifest facts of life. It leads us only to observe therefore, that with Upham also, as with the rest, perfection is not conceived as perfection. Physical infirmities, intellectual errors, involuntary sins remain — all somehow connected with our fallen condition and therefore needing the atoning blood of Christ to wash away their stains. Perfect men are even guilty of " relatively wrong acts and feelings " [203] — whatever that may mean: can we understand it of anything but " little sins "? And they may even commit not merely sins which " result from infirmity and are involuntary," but sins " which are seen by the omniscient eye of God, but which may *not be obvious to ourselves*"; [204] " sins of ignorance," then, let us say. They need therefore " every moment " " the application of Christ's blood," and ought to confess sin, " during the whole course of the present life "; [205] and to pray in the words of the Lord's prayer, " Forgive us our trespasses." And no man " is able, either on philosophical or Scripture principles, to assert *absolutely and unconditionally,* that he has been free from sin, at least for any great length of time " [206] It is not wrong, then, to speak with some caution about our sinlessness, " merely as if " we " hoped, or had reason to hope," that we have " experienced this great blessing," and have been " kept free from voluntary and known sin." [207] If it is a question of " absolute perfection " — why, that " exists only in another world." " We are permitted to indulge the humble hope, that there may be, and that there are instances of holiness of heart on earth." But, " notwithstanding their exemption from intentional sin," " truly holy persons " do not exhibit " an obvious perfection of judgment, of expression, and of manner." [208] We gather that they may be rather trying people to live with; people whom, of course, we love, but may find it sometimes rather difficult to like.

The question of growth in holiness is often a perplexing one to perfectionists, and they solve it variously. Many are

[203] Pp. 274 ff.; cf. p. 72.
[204] P. 277.
[205] P. 275.
[206] P. 277.
[207] P. 278.
[208] " The Life of Faith," pp. 188–189.

content to say that we do not grow *into* but *in* holiness; but
that seems rather an avoidance than a solution of the question — to grow *in* holiness, surely, is to grow progressively *into*
a holiness not before this last increment of growth enjoyed.
Upham [209] calls in a distinction between *nature* and *degree*.
We already have holiness according to its *nature,* but can
grow in *degree* of holiness. The phraseology does not seem
happy; but the meaning is reasonably clear. He adduces also
the doctrine of total depravity as an illustration *e contrario:*
we are *totally* depraved, but we are not as bad as we might
be, or as we will be, if we continue in our bad course. The distinction here is that of extension and intensity. The *totus homo*
is depraved — his depravity extends to every department of his
being: there is no faculty or disposition, or appetite or propensity, or affection, into which depravity does not penetrate. But
the depravity which penetrates to every department of the
man's being is not necessarily the deepest possible depravity:
it may increase indefinitely in intensity. A drop of ink falling
into a glass of water may stain its whole volume — it is totally stained; but if you empty the whole ink well into it, it
is not more totally, but very much more deeply stained. The
difficulty is that the perfectionists, Upham included, do not
teach that we are merely extensively perfect, but insist that
we are intensively perfect also — or perfect as we can be.
Upham says here, for example,[210] that we are perfect " in our
perceptions, our feelings, and our purposes " — extensively
therefore — " to the full extent of our capability " — intensively, therefore, too. And it would seem that we must say
this, if we are to employ such a notion as " perfect." For perfect is a superlative notion and admits no growth beyond it.
There seems to be but one door of escape and Upham takes
it. To grow in perfection the perfect one must grow in capability. Our perfection depends on our knowledge, he says,
and may grow as our knowledge grows. " Evangelical holiness," he explains, is " nothing more nor less than perfect

[209] " Principles of the Interior or Hidden Life," pp. 267 ff.
[210] P. 269.

love." And "love is based in part upon knowledge, and is
necessarily based upon it." We can love no object we do not
know; and our love for a lovable object must grow with our
knowledge of it. As our knowledge grows, our capability for
loving grows and that means our capability for perfection.[211]
Of course we may raise the question whether this argument
proves that perfection expands with growing knowledge, or
that there can be no such thing as perfection until knowledge
is perfect. And beneath that lurk two further questions. Does
holiness really depend on knowledge? Do we really "know"
God? The importance of the last question lies in the circumstance that Upham does not always appear to be sure that we
can really "know" God: but sometimes speaks almost like an
earlier Mansel playing on the strings of "faith" as the organ
of the incomprehensible and of "symbolical knowledge" which
only serves the purposes of knowledge.[212]

Whatever may be the difficulties to a perfectionist of the
idea of a developing holiness, however, Upham frankly teaches
that idea, and gives it very rich expression. It is embodied, for
example, in the following eloquent description of the process
of salvation.[213] "In the day of his true restoration, therefore, God once more really dwells in man. We do not say, however, that he actually enters and takes full possession *at once.*
Just as soon as man gives his exiled Father permission to enter
as a whole God and a God forever he enters *effectually;* but
ordinarily he enters *by degrees,* and in accordance with the
usual laws and operations of the human mind. He does not
break the vessel of man's spirit, nor mar its proportions, nor
deface anything which is truly essential to it; but gradually
enters into all parts of it, readjusts it, removes the stains
which sin has made upon it, and fills it with divine light. Man's
business in this great work is a very simple one. It is to cease
all resistance, and to invite the Divine Master of the mind
to enter it in his own time and way. And even this last is

[211] Pp. 270, 273.
[212] "The Life of Faith," pp. 150–151; cf. "Absolute Religion," pp. 80–81.
[213] "A Treatise on Divine Union," pp. 266–267.

hardly necessary. God does not wait even to be invited to come, except so far as an invitation is implied in the removal of the obstacles which had previously kept him out. Man's ceasing from all resistance, and his willingness to receive God as the all in all, and for all coming time, may be regarded as essentially the completion of the work in respect to himself; but the work of God, who is continually developing from the soul new powers and new beauties, can be completed only with the completion of eternity." The most important thing to note here is that Upham casts his eye forward through all the eternities to view the ever-increasing perfection of God's servants. He is able to do this, it is true, only by the help of some adjustments. The work of perfecting them is " essentially " completed here and now. But there is something beyond. Inadequate as this provision for undying aspiration is, it is much that its existence is recognized. There is a sense in which the perfectionist doctrine is the child of aspiration. The trouble is that it permits this aspiration to be too easily satisfied and so clips its wings. Henrich Heppe points out [214] that Madame Guyon's perfectionism was in essence a revolt from that ecclesiastical perfectionism of official Roman teaching, which is embodied in the doctrine of the *consilia evangelica*. She longed for a higher perfection than that — and for a perfection not confined to an ecclesiastical order, but open to every child of God. What she was really thinking of, says Heppe, " was the perfection of the souls in heaven, who have now achieved complete union with God." Only — and this is the tragedy of it — she transferred this heavenly perfection to earth and identified it with the attainments of mere viators. Thus she abolished aspiration and corrupted the very notion of perfection in order that it might accord with the observed attainment of the saints on earth. We purchase the proud title of " perfect " here too dearly when we barter for it the hope of heaven. One of the gravest evils of the perfectionist teaching is that it tempts us to be satisfied with earthly attainments

[214] " Geschichte der quietistischen Mystik in der katholischen Kirche," p. 483.

and to forget the heavenly glory. It is an old remark that the
more saint-like a man is, the less saint-like he feels: the less
evil there is to see in him, the more evil the evil that remains
is seen to be. " The nearer we approach " to God — this is the
way R. A. Vaughan puts it [215] — " the more profoundly must
we be conscious of our distance. As, in a still water, we may
see reflected . . . the bird that soars towards the zenith —
the image deepest as the ascent is highest — so it is with our
approximation to the Infinite Holiness. . . . It appears to
us that perfection is prescribed as a goal ever to be approached,
but ever practically inaccessible. Whatever degree of sanctification any one may have attained, it must always be possible
to conceive of a state yet more advanced, — it must always
be a duty diligently to labour towards it."

It will scarcely have passed without notice that in all the
discussion of perfection and of the remnants of sinning which
continue even in the perfect to vex them, Upham says nothing of the " corruption of man's heart." He draws the distinction between " deliberate and voluntary transgressions " on
the one hand which he represents as inconsistent with perfection, and inadvertent, unintentional and other forms of
sinning, thought of as " relatively " light, on the other, which
he represents as still liable to show themselves in the perfect.
His thought of sin is all in terms of sinning; and no account at
all is taken of the underlying sinfulness of nature. This also
is no doubt due to his basal " New Divinity " consciousness,
which finds very insufficient correction in his chosen Quietistic
mentors — although they do not manifest so complete a neglect of the inner springs of evil as he does. Samuel Harris, in
a very able review of Upham's " Life of Madame Guyon," [216]
takes occasion to remark on the futility of a doctrine of perfection of mere act. Madame Guyon, he says, teaches a real
perfection, because she supposes that we may cease from sin
as well as from sinning. Here is a perfection in which we not
only do not determine to do wrong, but have no desire or

[215] " Hours with the Mystics," ii. p. 233; cf. p. 240.
[216] *The New Englander*, April, 1848, pp. 165 ff; see pp. 171–175.

tendency to do so. Nothing less than this is in any real sense perfection. A perfection of act is unimportant and without significance, if " through the remains of corrupt nature or the effects of sinful habit " — the conceptions of the old and the " New Divinity," respectively — " evil thoughts and evil desires are rushing into the soul, even though the strong hand of the will instantly seize and throttle them." That " the strong hand of the will " — itself under the control of these very propensities (the *operari* follows the *esse*) — can perform any such feat, is not shown and cannot be shown. The case is therefore worse than Harris supposes; and the real fact is that evil in the heart not only may, but must, show itself in all our acts. The conclusion he draws, however, is sound: " We are never perfect till the effects of corrupt nature and of sinful habit are eradicated, till self-denial ceases in the extinction of all tendency to selfishness and not the mere restraining of it, till we are restored to a state of spontaneous, delightful, universal coincidence with God's will. . . ." No man is perfect " till he not only refuses to gratify corrupt tendencies and desires, but till they actually cease to exist." And so he adds, the Bible teaches. The greatest error of perfectionism, he now goes on to say, is in neglecting this fact and " teaching that to be perfection which is not — it is the element of antinomianism perpetually appearing — the lowering of the standard of moral obligation, not merely to the capacity, but to the present habits and attainments of men." " We regard perfectionism as dangerous, not because it requires too much, but because it requires too little."

Upham may be supposed to escape the incidence of these remarks by the slenderness of the recognition he gives to the activity, not to say the very existence, of what Madame Guyon speaks of as " that secret power within us which continually draws us to evil." But the neglect or denial of the corruption of the heart does not abolish it; and in its presence it is futile to talk of perfection of life. In any event, however, he does not teach even a perfection of life; but endeavors to give that appearance to the life, which he presents as perfect, by minimizing the importance and evil of the transgressions of the absolute rule of life which he cannot deny that it exhibits. He then falls squarely under Harris' condemnation of "lowering the standard of moral obligation, not merely to the capacity, but to the present habits and attainments of men." Ray Palmer in a review of Upham's "Principles of the Interior or Hidden Life," published a few years earlier,[217] emphasizes the same point on which Harris principally lays his stress. There can be no perfection, he urges, which does not go through and through. "No being can be considered perfect, of whom it is true, either that his moral action is in any respect defective, or his moral nature in any respect deranged." But his own primary stress is thrown on the matter which, in Harris' discussion, holds the second place — on the confusion wrought by defining perfection as something less than perfection. When Upham complains that it is "the popular doctrine, that no man ever has been sanctified, or ever will be sanctified till the moment of death," he says, and speaks of "the common doctrine of the impossibility of present sanctification," it is not so certain that he is not paltering in a double sense. If we are to define "sanctification" as Upham defines it — as a state which admits of the continued commission "of a large class of sins" — it can hardly be doubted that all Christians devoutly believe that they not only ought to be but in many cases are sanctified now. What Upham calls "perfection" most Christians look upon as only the ordinary attainments of the Christian life — a stage in the advance towards perfection no doubt, but far short of perfection. These remarks are valid and important in their general sense, but it is not impossible to push them beyond their validity, and Palmer can hardly be exonerated from doing this. It is not quite true that the common doctrine looks upon perfection, as defined by Upham, as attainable and generally attained by sincere Christians, in this life. For although Upham admits into perfection as defined by him, "a large class of sins," yet, formally at least, he excludes from it all voluntary transgression. We may doubt whether he does this really; we may discern among the sins which he admits, some from which voluntariness is abstracted with some difficulty, not to say arbitrariness. Meanwhile all voluntary transgression is formally excluded; and so long as our hearts are corrupt we shall never escape all voluntary transgression. Not only shall we never be perfect through and through until we are perfect in heart as well as in life; but we shall never be perfect in life — not even in the highest movements of our living — until our hearts are perfect. We must not look upon sinning atomistically, as if we could sin in this act and not sin in that: sin is a quality which, entrenched in the heart, affects all of our actions without exception. It is more true, then, to say that all our voluntary, as well as instinctive acts, are sinful, than that all voluntary acts may be holy, leaving only the instinctive ones to sin. A defective psychology underlies the notion that the range of our activities may be divided between indwelling sin and intruding holiness; some of them being altogether holy and others altogether sinful. This could be true only on the false doctrine of the " will " that it does what it pleases, independently of the " nature " that lies behind it, and can therefore *vi et armis* act holily despite the constant infection of the evil of a sinful nature. Only on some such notion can we talk of the voluntary acts being holy in the presence of an unsanctified heart.

On its positive side, however, Palmer's criticisms are perfectly just. Nothing can be more important than that the conception of perfection be maintained at its height. If there is an eternal and immutable distinction between right and wrong, he argues, then " goodness must be everywhere and in all beings essentially the same. The fundamental principles of right moral action, must be the same to God and to his creatures; and there must be one rule of duty — one standard by which to test character — to angels and to men. . . . True perfection is one and the same thing in all beings." The habit of conceiving of perfection as admitting of many imperfections — *moral* imperfections, glossed as infirmities, errors and

inadvertences — not only lowers the standard of perfection
and with it the height of our aspirations, but corrupts our
hearts, dulls our discrimination of right and wrong, and betrays us into satisfaction with attainments which are very far
from satisfactory. There is no more corrupting practice than
the habit of calling right wrong and wrong right. That is the
essence of antinomianism, if we choose to speak in the language of the schools. To give it its least offensive description,
it is acquiescence in sin. And this is the real arraignment of all
perfectionist theories, Upham's among the rest. They lull men
to sleep with a sense of attainments not really made; cut the
nerve of effort in the midst of the race; and tempt men to
accept imperfection as perfection — which is no less than to
say evil is good.

The books in which Upham developed and commended
these opinions had a wide circulation, running through many
editions, through the middle half of the nineteenth century.
They were republished in England through the instrumentality of G. Pennell, Esq., a Wesleyan local preacher of large
means at Liverpool,[218] and have enjoyed there a larger popularity and exerted a more lasting influence than even in
America. They are apparently no longer, however, on the
market — except the most elaborate of them all and the one
with the most general appeal, the " Life of Madame Guyon,"
a new edition of which, with an Introduction by W. R. Inge,
was published so lately as 1905. Upham's retired life and
aversion to public speaking confined his influence to the single
channel of his published works. It can be traced in the perfectionist parties which succeeded him, but it is not dominant
in any of them; he formed no sect and built up no party of
his own. It is among the adherents of the Keswick movement
that his name remains in most honor, and that his works continue to be most sought and read. J. B. Figgis, writing the
history of that movement, represents him with Francis de
Sales, Thomas à Kempis, Molinos and Madame Guyon as

[218] Richard Wheatley, " The Life and Letters of Mrs. Phoebe Palmer,"
1876, p. 379.

one of the channels through which the " pure stream from the River of the Water of Life " has come down to us.[219] But even at Keswick it is not his which is the decisive influence. Loved by all who knew him; admired by all who came into contact with him, whether in person or in his printed works; he lived his quiet life out in a somewhat remote academic center, and has left behind him little more than the sweet savor of an honored name. Perhaps in his case we can reverse Mark Antony's maxim and say that the good he did lives after him and the evil has been largely interred with his bones.

[219] J. B. Figgis, " Keswick From Within," 1914, p. 9; cf. W. H. Griffith Thomas in C. F. Harford's " The Keswick Convention," 1907, p. 224.

IV

THE " HIGHER LIFE " MOVEMENT

THE " HIGHER LIFE " MOVEMENT [1]

THE circle of ideas summed up in the general term " Perfectionism," was first given standing in the Protestant churches through the teaching of John Wesley. The doctrine of " Christian Perfection " in which these ideas were formulated by him, very naturally therefore took from the beginning and has continued always to hold among the Wesleyans " the place of an acknowledged doctrine." Henry C. Sheldon tells us,[2] no doubt, that it has claimed " very different degrees of practical interest and advocacy from different representatives " of Wesleyanism. He even tells us that " in the present, while it is advocated by not a few after the manner of John Wesley, many in effect set it forth as rather a possible ideal to be progressively approached, than as the goal lying immediately before every well-instructed Christian, the prize of a present faith and consecration."

A somewhat earlier writer goes even further and gives us to understand that Wesleyans have never been very forward in laying claim to their " Christian Perfection " as practically exemplified in their own lives, however faithfully they may have clung to it as a distinctive and highly valued doctrine of their confession. " Hardly one in twenty of our ministers," he remarks,[3] " professes it, either publicly or privately, so far as I can learn. We preach it occasionally; but among our people its confessors are still fewer, in proportion to numbers, than in the ministry. Even among our bishops, from 1784 to the present day, confessors are as hard to find as in any other class of our people. The very princes of our Israel have been

---

[1] Reprinted from *The Princeton Theological Review*, xvi. pp. 572–622 and xvii. pp. 37–86.

[2] " History of Christian Doctrine," 1886, ii. p. 376.

[3] J. T. Crane, " Holiness the Birthright of All God's Children " (1874), ed. 2, 1875, pp. 14–15.

silent in regard to their own experience of it. The apostolic Wesley never professed it. In the sixty-fourth year of his age, and the forty-second of his ministry, he published, in one of the leading journals of London, a letter containing these words: ' I have told all the world *I am not perfect;* I have not *attained* the character I draw.' Bishop Asbury, who, if possible, exceeded Wesley in the toils and sufferings of his faithful ministry, did not profess it. The saintly Hedding, approaching the grave by lingering disease, always calm, and often joyous in view of death, was importuned to profess it, and declined. Myriads of men and women among us, whose lives were bright with holy light, saints *of whom the world was not worthy,* never professed it." However chary, nevertheless, men may have been in pointing to their own lives as illustrating the doctrine, the doctrine of " Christian Perfection " has always been the glory of Methodism; and for a hundred years or so it constituted also one of its most exclusive peculiarities.[4]

As the middle of the nineteenth century was drawing on, however, a kindred doctrine began to show itself, in a relatively independent development, among the American Congregationalists, in sequence to the increasing dissolution of the hereditary Calvinism of the American Congregational churches and the shifting of opinion here and there among them to a Pelagianizing basis.[5] Very potent influences were in operation in America during these years, moreover, tending to break down the barriers which divided the denominations from one another, and to give to doctrines hitherto distinctive

[4] J. S. Inskip, " Methodism Explained and Defended," 1851, pp. 59 ff.: " There is, however, one doctrine, in a great measure peculiar to Methodism. It is that, in which we teach the possibility of man attaining a state of grace in the present life, in which he will be made free from sin. . . . We contend this state *may be attained now* — at the present moment. . . . In this, as well as in our justification, ' we are saved by grace, through faith.' . . . Reader, thou mayest *now* believe, and *now* be saved from all thy sins." *The London Quarterly Review* for October, 1875, xlv. p. 192: " The testimony to the completeness of the Spirit's work of grace in the human soul, as an application of the atonement, has been and still is the leading peculiarity of Methodist teaching."

[5] See an illuminating page by Lyman H. Atwater in *The Presbyterian Quarterly and Princeton Review,* July, 1877, pp. 410, 411.

of one or another of them more general currency. The conditions of life, especially in the rapidly settling frontier regions of what is now called the Middle West, made it a struggle to preserve in them any form of Christianity whatever, and opened the way for the wide extension of all kinds of extravagances. In the welter of sharply contrasting notions struggling for a footing in this intellectual and social confusion, a certain advantage was enjoyed by extreme pretensions. Only those who took strong ground could hope for a hearing. And the constant interchange between the frontier and the country at large spread the contagion rapidly throughout the land. Among the other extravagances thus given great vogue was naturally a tendency to proclaim perfection a Christian duty and an attainable ideal, which none who would take the place of a Christian in this wicked world could afford to forego.

The growing influence of perfectionist ideas in the religious community at large was both marked and advanced by the publication in 1859 of W. E. Boardman's book called "The Higher Christian Life." Mr. Boardman had acquired his notions under Methodist influences in a frontier settlement,[6] and in this book he gave them wings and thus inaugurated a movement which has affected the whole Protestant world. We do not see but that Mark Guy Pearse's description of the book is perfectly just. It was, he says,[7] " perhaps the first popular treatise on this subject that won its way amongst all denominations; and its vast circulation, both in America and England, not only melted the prejudices of hosts against this subject, but made it possible for other writers to follow in the paths which he had opened, and led multitudes of timid souls out of the misty dawn into the clear shining of the sun." The movement thus begun reached its culmination in the labors of Mr. and Mrs. Pearsall Smith, out of which grew in the early years of the fourth quarter of the century the great Keswick Movement by which their formative ideas have been

[6] See the account given by Mrs. Boardman in her "Life and Labours of the Rev. W. E. Boardman" (1886), American edition, 1887, chapter iii.

[7] Mrs. Boardman, "Life and Labours of the Rev. W. E. Boardman," preface, p. vii.

spread throughout the English speaking world and continue still to be vigorously propagated. It is to W. E. Boardman and Mr. and Mrs. Smith accordingly that we must go if we wish to know what the Higher Life movement really is, and what it really means for Christian life and doctrine.

William Edwin Boardman [8] was born in Smithfield, New York, October 11, 1810, and grew up in the Susquehanna country into a rugged but very unstable manhood. After a number of business adventures he found himself in the early forties in the little mining town of Potosi in the southwestern corner of Wisconsin, seeking to mend his broken fortunes. His religious life had been of a piece with his business career. Converted in early manhood, he had passed through many violent changes before, under Methodist influences,[9] he found in the rough surroundings of Potosi "rest of heart in Jesus for sanctification," and became the head of the little " Plan of Union " church which had been gathered there largely under his influence.[10] Within two years, however, he was compelled to leave Potosi by a violent anti-slavery controversy in which he had become embroiled, and entered Lane Theological Seminary at Cincinnati in the summer of 1843 as a student of di-

[8] See " Life and Labours of the Rev. W. E. Boardman," by Mrs. Boardman, with a Preface by the Rev. Mark Guy Pearse, London, 1886; New York, 1887. There is a short appreciative sketch in Th. Jellinghaus, " Das völlige, gegenwärtige Heil durch Christum," ed. 4, 1898, pp. 718–720.

[9] This states the fundamental fact. It is not intended that influences from other quarters did not coöperate to the effect; Mrs. Boardman in the " Life and Labours of the Rev. W. E. Boardman " indicates a number of such influences — among others intimate intercourse with an elderly woman who was one of a coterie of persons who had been excluded from Dr. E. N. Kirk's church at Albany on the ground of their perfectionism. In " The Higher Christian Life," Mr. Boardman shows adequate acquaintance with all the current forms of perfectionism. Jellinghaus, p. 718, very properly says moreover: " Neither he nor his wife could understand sanctification in the Wesleyan fashion as Christian Perfection and the eradication of the old nature, and had seen people fall through misunderstanding of this doctrine into an awful fanaticism."

[10] He received his ordination at this time from the Presbytery of the United Congregational and Presbyterian Churches, meeting at a neighboring town (" Life and Labours of the Rev. W. E. Boardman." p. 65).

vinity. The three years that he passed at Lane seem to have been devoted as much to the propagation of the Higher Life teachings as to his studies. After their close he was a year at Greenfield, Indiana, and then six months at New Haven in some loose connection with the Yale Divinity School. In 1852 he went to Detroit and his name appears this year for the first time in the Minutes of the General Assembly of the (New School) Presbyterian Church, as a " stated supply." He found in Michigan what seems to have been congenial employment as a missionary of the American Sunday School Union, and was removed by that Society in 1855 to their central office in Philadelphia, to take charge of their " Students' Mission Service " — transferring at the same time his Presbyterial membership to the (Old School) Presbytery of Philadelphia. Leaving the Sunday School Union after two or three years of service, he became for a short time " stated supply " at the manufacturing town on the Jersey side of the Delaware called Gloucester City, and then, in 1859, sailed for California for his wife's health. In 1862 he returned from California and soon after entered the service of the United States Christian Commission, becoming its secretary and laboring efficiently in the organization of its work. After the Civil War he reverted for a while to business life, and then, in 1870, at last found his mission as a public agitator for the Higher Christian Life. At the same time he disappears also, in some unexplained way, from the roll of Presbyterian ministers, having held a place on that roll for nearly twenty years without ever having been settled as a pastor or continued longer than two or three years at a time in any one employment.[11]

[11] In the " Minutes of the General Assembly of the Presbyterian Church in the U. S. A.," his name appears on the roll of the (N.S.) Presbytery of Detroit of 1852, 1853, and 1854 as Agent and S.S.; of 1855 as Agent; and of 1856 as *in transitu*. It appears on the roll of the (O.S.) Presbytery of Philadelphia of 1856 as W. C.; of 1857–1858 as S.S. at Gloucester City, N. J.; and of 1859 as W. C. It appears in the Index to the " Minutes " (O.S.) of 1860, 1861, 1862, with the note " not reported," and in the " Minutes " of 1863 and 1864 as a member of the Presbytery of Stockton *in transitu*. In 1865 his name appears on the roll of the Presbytery of Philadelphia as Secretary of the

Mr. Boardman's eager and restless mind, little disciplined
and very prone to extravagances, naturally had little taste
for the humdrum work of the regular ministry, and the necessity of coöperation attending it. Having attained his three-
score years without finding comfort or stability in the ordinary
paths of ministerial labor, he appears to have thought it high
time to throw off all the shackles of the conventional paths
and to go his own untrammeled way. He stripped himself
naked for the conflict. He broke all ecclesiastical ties and stood
forth a perfectly free lance without responsibilities to anyone.
He even freed himself from worldly entanglements, and resolved, like an invading army, to "live on the country." A
born agitator, equipped both by nature and by training for
that work, we can imagine the zest with which he now cast
himself with absolute abandonment into his congenial and
wholly irresponsible task. The completeness of his separation
of himself for it and the whole-heartedness of his devotion
of himself to it are intimated to us by Mrs. Boardman in the
language of her coterie. "At this time," she writes,[12] "he felt
he had a definite call to a definite work. As in his earlier life
God had led him out into evangelistic work among the unconverted, so now He distinctly called him to evangelize among
Christians, and proclaim the Gospel of full rest in our indwelling Saviour." "It was evident now that the Lord was
drawing my husband on to a full surrender of all his time to

Christian Commission. From 1866 to 1870 he is a W. C. of the Presbytery of
Philadelphia. In 1871 he appears in the Index as residing in New York, without reference to a Presbytery. He then disappears from the "Minutes."
From Nevin's "History of the Presbytery of Philadelphia," p. 41 (of Roll)
we learn that Mr. Boardman was received by the Presbytery of Philadelphia
from the Presbytery of Detroit, April 2, 1856; dismissed to the Presbytery
of California, January 4, 1860; received from the Presbytery of Stockton
October, 1864; transferred to the Presbytery of New York, June, 1870. He does
not appear in the "Minutes" as a member of the Presbytery of New York,
but in S. D. Alexander's "History of the Presbytery of New York," p. 159,
his bare name, without data, occurs in the list of ministers belonging to the
Presbytery of New York before the Reunion. This seems to imply that he
presented the letter from Philadelphia, and was enrolled, but withdrew his
letter in less than a twelvemonth. But other conjectures are possible.

[12] "Life and Labours of the Rev. W. E. Boardman," p. 136.

this direct service among His own people; and he became so
very restful and happy in the separation from all secular work,
that whatever doubts had heretofore crossed his mind, as to
what the Lord wanted him to do, disappeared forever." [13] " It
was at this time in the same year, 1870, that the Lord called
upon us to give up all our possessions, and enter upon a life
of full trust in Him for all our temporal needs." [14] " Since that
day in which all was committed to the Lord, there has never
been an anxious thought as to how we should get on, or how
meet any debt, for the Lord has supplied us even before asking, so that we have been free as the birds, going wherever the
Father sends us, without a fear but that He would meet all
expenses in His own way." [15] " It was now necessary to work
independently of others, since it was the Lord who was to employ us. . . . No more committees or organizations, every step
must now be directed by the Lord Himself." [16]

We have overrun ourselves in the last two quotations.
They remind us that soon after Mr. Boardman had given
himself wholly to the work of public agitation in the interests
of the Higher Life, he found it desirable to make a certain
change in his methods. At first he made it his business to
organize " Conventions for Holiness," through which the
propaganda he had taken in hand might be carried forward.
An " Association for holding Union Holiness Conventions "
was formed; Mr. Boardman was made its chairman; and as
chairman it was his duty to be present at and to engineer all
the meetings. Successful conventions were held under these
auspices at Newark, Philadelphia, Washington, Wilmington
and elsewhere. But difficulties arose. The responsibilities for
and the labor of the conventions, all fell on Mr. Boardman's
shoulders: the financial returns from them were divided among
the members of the Association and yielded to no one any
large amount. Mr. Boardman thought that, the ball having
now been started rolling, it might be permitted with advantage
to roll on of itself. It might be left to others to organize con-

[13] *Ibid.*
[14] P. 142.
[15] P. 145.
[16] Pp. 145–146.

ventions of which he should be invited to take charge. As
Mrs. Boardman puts it: [17] " Organization, as has been said,
was one of my husband's greatest — ' gifts ' shall I call it?
And yet it was sometimes a hindrance, especially when the
Lord was calling to a single-handed work." The significance
of the last clause should not be missed. The event proved the
forecast just. " Many more invitations came than could be
met." [18] Conventions were held everywhere; in the East, in the
West: [19] there seemed no limit to them. " It was a blessed liberty," Mrs. Boardman exclaims,[20] " to be free from all bondage
to serve in connection with Committees or Associations "; and
how delightful thus to experience how bountifully the Father,
as their Provider, supplied every need!

There proved to be one limit, however — Mr. Boardman's
strength. He broke down from overwork in the spring of 1872.[21]
But even that brought new opportunities and new triumphs.
As one of its results Mr. Boardman found himself in the autumn of 1873 in London,[22] where Mr. R. Pearsall Smith had
been holding meetings during the spring for the propagation
of the Higher Life and was now preparing to resume them.
Mr. Boardman joined him, and during the next two years there
was written into the history of religious conventions one of its
most remarkable chapters.[23] The great evangelistic campaign
of Messrs. Moody and Sankey in England and Scotland was
now in full swing, and the Higher Life movement was, as it
were, embroidered upon it.[24] First there was that wonderful
series of " Breakfasts " in which, week after week, Mr. Smith
and Mr. Boardman met select parties of the ministers and
Christian workers of the city to talk with them about the

[17] P. 140.
[18] P. 146.
[19] Pp. 141, 146 ff.
[20] P. 150.
[21] Pp. 151 f.
[22] P. 155.
[23] An account of them written by Dr. Cullis is printed in the " Life and
Labours of the Rev. W. E. Boardman," pp. 156 ff.
[24] Messrs. Moody and Sankey landed at Liverpool June 17, 1873, and
spent two years in the campaign.

Higher Christian Life and Power for Service. These were followed by large popular meetings for the advancement of holiness, culminating in the meetings of the spring and summer of 1874, the climax of which was reached in the Conference at Broadlands in July and the great Oxford Union Meeting of the first week of September, 1874. Immense meetings of similar character were held throughout England during the next twelve months, and even the Continent was invaded by Mr. Smith with remarkable results. The climax was again reached in the great Brighton Convention of June, 1875 — after which came Mr. Smith's sad collapse. Meanwhile Mr. Boardman, after extensive tours through England and Scotland, had returned to America (early in June, 1875), but finding there no such opportunities for his propaganda as England offered him, he came back in December, 1875 to London, which he thereafter made his permanent home and the center of his activities. As late as 1880 when he had reached his three score years and ten he made an extended tour in Sweden preaching his favorite doctrine and — yes, healing the sick! For he had now taken up with this delusion, and indeed it seems to have become during the last few years of his life almost his chief concern. He apparently dates his conversion to it from a meeting with Dr. Cullis during his visit to America in the summer of 1875. It was not until the publication of his book, " The Lord that Healeth Thee," in 1881, however, that he was fairly " launched as a teacher of divine healing." The Faith-house called " Bethshan " was opened by Mrs. Baxter and Miss Murray in 1882 to accommodate the patients who resorted to him, and of it he was " both the father and the pastor." But his career as a faith healer was short: [25] he himself died February 4, 1886.

[25] Like Augustine who afterwards recognized occurrences he had witnessed at Milan as miracles — though they had not impressed themselves upon him as such at the time — Mr. Boardman now recognized as miracles occurrences in his earlier life which he had not recognized as such at the time (cf. " Life and Labours of the Rev. W. E. Boardman," pp. 63, 133). In Sweden, in 1880, he quite freely worked cures (pp. 199, 209, 213, 218, 219). He depended on the Lord entirely for his own health: " Whenever threatened with

Although he began late, Mr. Boardman became a somewhat voluminous writer.[26] It is by his first book, however, "The Higher Christian Life," published in 1859, that he is best known, and through it that he has exercised his widest influence as a leader in the Higher Life movement. It is with it primarily therefore that we are concerned.[27] It is not a good book, and the critics dealt faithfully with it.[28] They pointed out the incorrectness of its historical illustrations, the vagueness and ambiguity of its doctrinal statements, the inconsequence of its argument, the formlessness of its structure, the inelegance of its literary style. Everything they alleged against it was true. Nevertheless, the book sold, and was read, and bore fruit. Theodor Jellinghaus says that more than a hundred thousand copies of it went into circulation in America and England; that it made its author the leading teacher of the more circumspect and practical doctrine of complete sanctification; and that it was by it that access was gained for this teaching into all evangelical denominations.[29] This is a conservative statement. Mrs. Boardman describes the sale of the book as rapid beyond all precedent in books of its class — "it was impossible for many weeks to supply the demand"; and reminds us that it was reprinted in many editions in England — an edition was issued by Nisbet, another by Strachan, and

---

a bilious attack he looked directly to the Lord, and was delivered" (p. 240). A quite disagreeable story is told, pp. 227 ff., of his persuading a dwarf not to insist on the Lord giving him a normal figure, because of the advertising value of his deformity.

[26] We find the following books credited to him: "The Higher Christian Life," 1858; "He that Overcometh, or A Conquering Gospel," 1869; "Gladness in Jesus," 1870; "Faith Work; or, the Labours of Dr. Cullis in Boston," 1874; "In the Power of the Spirit, or Christian Experience in the Light of the Bible," 1875; "The Lord that Healeth Thee," 1881; "Rest for You" (a booklet). He also wrote much in periodicals.

[27] It was written when he was forty-eight years old while he was acting as "stated supply" at Gloucester City.

[28] See especially the article by Jacob J. Abbot in the *Bibliotheca Sacra and Biblical Repository* for July, 1860, pp. 508–535, and the article by John A. Todd in *The Biblical Repertory and Princeton Review* for October, 1860, pp. 608–640.

[29] "Das völlige, gegenwärtige Heil durch Christum," ed. 4, 1898, p. 719.

so forth — and that one British publisher alone sold sixty
thousand copies of it before 1874.[30] It is a mere superstition
to imagine that only good books sell well. Are Pastor Russell's
books good books? It is in literature as in music where ragtime makes a more popular appeal than Beethoven. This comparison may supply us with the proper characterization of
Mr. Boardman's book: it is a ragtime book. It is the book
of a Sunday School missionary accustomed to address himself
to the unsubtle intelligence of " the wild and woolly West."
Mrs. Boardman with pardonable wifely appreciation not
wholly without reason describes it by saying that it " sets
forth the truth in clear, simple, direct statements, illustrated
by examples." It uses a broad brush and lays on the color
thickly. Much of its appeal lies in the very coarseness of its
art. But that is not the whole truth. Its real power lies in its
fundamentally Christian tone. It exalts Christ, and it exalts
faith. And no book which exalts Christ and exalts faith will
ever fail of an immediate response from Christian hearts.

Mr. Boardman's zeal is, as he puts it, for a " *full salvation* "
through " *full trust.*" [31] What he has it in his heart to do is to
set forth Christ " as all in all for the sinner's salvation," and
to assure " the sinner who receives him as such, and abides in
him," that he has in Him " full salvation." [32] The sinner who
both " receives Him " and " abides in Him ": he who desires
a full salvation must do both these things. He must not only
enter by Christ but *walk* in Christ; Christ is not only the Door
but the Way. And we contribute as little to our walking in the
Way as we do to our entering by the Door. There are many
who expect to enter by the Door, but to walk in the Way for
themselves. They expect " to journey in the straight and narrow way by virtue of their own resolutions and watchings,
with such help from God and man as they can secure from
time to time." [33] It cannot be done. Jesus " is *The Way* and
there is no other. There is no real progress heavenward but

---

[30] " Life and Labours of the Rev. W. E. Boardman," pp. 104–105.
[31] " The Higher Christian Life," p. 45.
[32] P. 47.   [33] P. 326.

IN JESUS." Jesus is not a partial Saviour but a complete Saviour: we do not get a portion of our salvation in Him and supply the rest ourselves; In Him and in Him alone is complete salvation. " What we call experimental religion, is simply this: The sinner is first awakened to a realization of his guilt before God, and of his danger, it may be too. He really *feels*, that is, he *experiences*, his need of salvation, and becomes anxious and eager to do anything to secure it. Tries perhaps all sorts of expedients, except the one only and true, in vain. Then at last his eyes are opened to see that Jesus Christ is set forth to be his salvation, and that all he has to do is, just as he is, without one grain of purity or merit, in all his guilt and pollution, to trust in his Saviour, and now he *sees and feels*, that is, he *experiences*, that Jesus Christ is the Way, the Truth and the Life, the very Saviour he needs. In Jesus he triumphs and exults. In Jesus he revels and rejoices. Jesus is the one amongst ten thousand, the altogether lovely. The only one in heaven or on earth to be desired, filling all the orbit of his soul with faith, and hope and love. This in substance is the sum of all religious experience." [34] In Jesus Christ, our complete Saviour, there is complete salvation to be had by faith alone.

Nothing, of course, could be truer to the Gospel than this insistence on the completeness of the salvation provided in Christ and received by faith alone; and it would perhaps not be easy to say it better. It is the very essence of the Christian proclamation. The mischief is that Mr. Boardman contends that this " full salvation " received by a " full trust " in Jesus our " full Saviour," is not one indivisible salvation, but is separated into two distinct parts, received by two distinct acts of faith. This is the meaning of his dwelling so earnestly upon the necessity of not only entering by the Door but also walking in the Way. To his own consciousness, indeed, he is not dividing the two stages of salvation from one another but assimilating them to one another. He conceives it to be usual to think of them not only as separable in fact but as resting on different foundations; one on faith, the other on works. " We have one

[34] P. 50.

process for acceptance with God," he says,[35] " that is faith; and another for progress in holiness, that is works. After having found acceptance in Jesus by faith, we think to go on to perfection by strugglings and resolves, by fastings and prayers, not knowing the better way of taking Christ for our sanctification, just as we have already taken him for our justification. We see and believe in Jesus as our Atonement on earth, and our Advocate and Mediator in heaven, but we fail to see and receive him as our ever-present *Saviour from sin* now here with us in the hourly scenes of the daily journey heavenward." He is preoccupied with the vindication of faith as the sole instrument of salvation in all its stages alike. In making this vindication he is doing a good work, and for the sake of it we can bear with the play on words by which he gives a double reference to the Scriptural declaration: " The just shall *live* as well as be *made alive,* by faith," [36] and can read with patience such a passage as this: [37] " Whether the question relates to justification or sanctification the answer is the same. The way of freedom from sin is the very same, as the way of freedom from condemnation. Faith in the purifying presence of Jesus brings the witness of the Spirit with our spirits that Jesus is our sanctification, that the power and dominion of sin is broken, that we are free, just as faith in the atoning merit of the blood and obedience of Christ for us, brings the witness of the Spirit that we are now no longer under condemnation for sin, but freely and fully justified in Jesus."

Of course we have both justification and sanctification only in Jesus, and of course we have Jesus only by faith. But we cannot divide Jesus and have Him as our righteousness while not at the same time having Him as our sanctification. It is precisely this division of Jesus, however, which Mr. Boardman is insisting upon. That is his real meaning in the passage which we have just quoted. When we read it in its intended sense it is as pure a statement of the Wesleyan doctrine of the successive attainment of righteousness and holiness by separate acts of faith as Wesley himself could have penned. It is equally

[35] P. 52.   [36] P. 183.   [37] P. 94.

his real meaning in the double emphasis which he puts on the Scriptural declaration that the just shall *live* by faith. " The just shall be *made alive* first," he expounds it,[38] " and *after-wards learn to live* by faith. The just shall be *justified before God* first, and afterwards learn the way *to become just also* in heart and life, by faith " — where the " first " and " after-wards " are the really significant words. This separation of justification and sanctification as two distinct " experiences " resting on two distinct acts of faith is in point of fact Mr. Boardman's primary interest, and constitutes the foundation stone of his system. Grant him the reality of " the second conversion " by which we obtain sanctification, as distinct in principle from the first conversion by which we obtain justifi-cation, and he will not boggle over much else. Here lies the heart of his system of teaching and on the validation of this his whole effort is expended.[39]

[38] P. 191; cf. pp. 31, 183, 256.

[39] It is interesting to observe that Theodor Jellinghaus, who has a great admiration for Mr. Boardman, cannot go the whole way with him with regard to his "second conversion." " In England and America and lately also in Germany," he writes (" Das völlige, gegenwärtige Heil durch Christum," ed. 4, 1898, p. 71), " some have maintained that a converted man does not become a complete Christian, and does not become a thoroughly blessed and power-ful instrument of God's kingdom, until he receives suddenly and consciously a second baptism with the Holy Spirit. In this there is only this much truth — that a large number of men of God have experienced after their conversion, suddenly, a new deep baptism with the Holy Spirit; many of them at a time when there was suddenly brought to their remembrance and experience the cleansing power of Christ's blood and the greatness of Christ's love. But the New Testament nowhere requires for all believers a second, sudden baptism with the Holy Spirit. In most cases the deeper filling with the Holy Spirit comes gradually in sufferings, humiliations and wonderful answers to prayer, and deliverances by the deeper experience of the power of Jesus' death and resurrection. — He who teaches that every Christian must experience through a second baptism with the Holy Spirit the eradication of his sinful nature and the attainment of sinlessness, is an anti-Scriptural fanatic and errorist (*Schwärmer und Irrgeist*) . . ." In his book, " In the Power of the Spirit, or Christian Experience in the Light of the Bible," 1875, Mr. Boardman identi-fies " the Baptism of the Spirit " with " the second conversion ": " The name given it in the New Testament," he writes (p. 5), " is: ' The Baptism of the Holy Ghost.' " Compare below, note 73. The same general position is taken by Asa Mahan, " The Baptism of the Holy Ghost," 1870: see especially pp. iii–iv, 15–16. Jellinghaus, it will be noted, employs the phrase (in accordance with Matthew iii. 11) of the saving operations of the Spirit of Christ in general.

The necessity for this distinction of experiences he finds in the twofold need of the sinner and the consequent twofold provision made for his need. "And now," he writes,[40] "to account for the two distinct experiences, each so marked and important, and so alike in character, we have only to consider two facts, viz. first, that the sinner's necessities are two-fold and distinct, although both are included in the one word salvation. We express the two in the words of that favorite hymn, 'Rock of Ages,' when we sing,

> ' Be of sin the *double* cure,
> ' *Save from wrath*, and *make me pure.*' "

It will be observed that "Rock of Ages" is quoted here, not in its original form, but in that given it by T. Cotterill in 1815. Toplady himself wrote —

> " Be of sin the double cure,
> Cleanse me from its guilt and power."

We do not know the precise end sought by Cotterill in the alteration which he introduced. It may have been merely greater exactness in the rhyme. It may have been also greater exactness in doctrinal statement. Whether he meant it or not, in any event his form does make the doctrinal statement more exact. Christ's blood does something more for us than cleanse us from the guilt and power of sin: it cleanses us also from the corruption of sin. To sum up the "double cure" which it brings us as cleansing from the guilt and power of sin is therefore a fatally inadequate statement — though it is all that Mr. Boardman's successors in the advocacy of the Higher Christian Life are able to attribute to it. Whether he himself understood more to be included in the cleansing wrought by Christ's blood may require some further investigation. Suffice it to note here that he quotes the hymn in a form in which it says more; and that he speaks in this context in this more adequate language of the hymn. The " two great and equal wants of the sinner," he declares [41] to be these: " he must be *just* in the eye of the law, justified before God. And he must also be

---

[40] P. 51.   [41] P. 52.

holy in heart and life " — in heart as well as in life, observe
— " or he cannot be saved." All that it is necessary to make
ourselves sure of at the moment, however, is that Mr. Boardman explicitly represents the two things which he here describes as " being *reckoned* righteous before God, and being
made righteous in heart and life," as things which are " distinct
and different in their nature," and therefore separable in their
experience.

It is only fair to recognize at the same time that Mr. Boardman is willing to be as reasonable in the matter as it is possible
to be while yet preserving the essence of his contention. He is
willing to admit, for example, that the two " experiences " —
justification and sanctification — need not be always temporally separated. A man may be justified and sanctified at
the same time. He is even willing to admit that these two experiences need not be consciously separated — " by a gulph of
vain strugglings." [42] " Any particular kind of experience is
nowhere in the Bible made a pre-requisite of salvation. He
who really and truly believes in the Lord Jesus, will be saved
whether he has any experience at all to relate or not." [43] " Let
Jesus be received as the all in all, and that is enough! Whoever
can say, ' Jesus is mine and I am his,' that ' he is complete and
I am complete in him,' and say the truth, has the experience
whether he has an experience to relate, or not." [44] But he is
firm in asserting that we must actually have these two " experiences," both of them, if we are to be saved, and that they
are essentially distinct. Though they may possibly coalesce
in time, and though we may have nothing to relate concerning
them, yet they are distinct, necessary experiences both of
which we must have. There may therefore be — there ordinarily is — an interval between them, long or short. [45] The
second experience may be as cataclysmic as the first — it often
is even more so. In any event it must be had. " It is necessary
for all to come to the point of " distinctly " trusting in the
Lord for purity of heart to be prepared for heaven." " There

[42] P. 53.
[43] P. 205.
[44] P. 53.
[45] Pp. 199, 200.

is no other way under heaven to be purified but by faith in the
Lord. And none but the pure in heart shall see God in peace." [46]
So little is Mr. Boardman inclined to sink " the second experience" in the first, that his tendency is to exalt it above it. He
speaks of it as " the second and deeper work of grace." [47] He
declares plainly [48] that " the second is the higher stage, and
more difficult too. It is really harder to overcome sin in the
heart, than to break away from the world at first. And it is
harder to come to the point of trusting in Jesus to subdue one's
own heart entirely to himself, than to venture upon him for
the forgiveness of sin. We are slower to perceive that the work
of saving us from sin — of expelling sin from us — is Christ's,
than to see that he has already suffered the penalty of sin and
purchased our pardon."

That the second experience like the first is of faith alone
we have already seen to belong to the very essence of its conception. It is usually emphasized in antagonism to the notion,
supposed to be prevalent, that we are justified by faith but are
to be sanctified by works. No, it is asserted with emphasis, we
are sanctified also by faith. There were two classes in Peter's
audience at Pentecost, we are told in a typical passage [49] — not
only unconverted men, but men who had long enjoyed the
forgiveness of their sins. But Peter had not different messages
for them. " Peter did not say to the one, Believe in the Lord
Jesus and ye shall be converted, and to the other, Watch, pray,
struggle, read, fast, work, and you shall be sanctified. But to
one and all he said, Repent and be baptized, every one of you,

---

[46] P. 206.

[47] P. 139.

[48] P. 140. Speaking elsewhere in terms of his own experience, he writes:
" Forgiveness did not satisfy me; I wanted the dominion of sin destroyed.
Purification, not less than pardon, I saw to be required. I became thoroughly
awakened to my own wretched bondage to sin." " The wrath of God against
sin, as declared in the first of Romans, had been heavy upon me ten years
before; but now the bondage of sin, as illustrated in the seventh of Romans,
was heavier still, and I experienced the full bitterness of soul which sings out
in the cry, 'Oh wretched man that I am, who shall deliver me?' But after the
Lord led me into the rest of heart for sanctification, how sweet it was! "

[49] P. 113.

in the name of the Lord Jesus Christ, and ye shall receive the
Holy Ghost." Perhaps there is a tincture of the Quietism so
prominent in the later teaching of this trend of thought traceable here; and an illustration employed a little further on
increases the suspicion that there may be. "Suppose," we
read,[50] "when Daniel was cast into the lion's den, instead of
trusting in his God, that He would deliver him — suppose then
that in his impotence, bound hand and foot, he had made fight
with the lions, and sought deliverance by his own struggles
with those terrible beasts of prey, how long before he would
have been torn limb from limb and devoured by the hungry
monsters of the den?" The suspicion remains, however, a
mere suspicion: the obvious intent is less to discredit effort
than to exalt faith, as the alone instrument of salvation. Mr.
Boardman obviously means to conceive this faith on which
he hangs everything in its utter simplicity. It is a formula
with him, no doubt that, We must both give all and take all,
and that is obviously the "surrender" and "faith" of later
authors.[51] But Mr. Boardman perceives better than they that
these are but two aspects of one act. "True and saving faith,"
he says,[52] "is two-fold. It gives all and takes all." If both these
elements of it are not present, the act of faith is not complete,
and, in a word, no real faith has been exercised. "If it fails to
give all up to Christ, no matter how bold and clamorous it
may be in claiming the promises, it is dead and powerless. . . .
On the other hand if it fail of taking Christ for all, all its giv-
ings will be in vain and worse than in vain, ending only in
sore and terrible disappointment at last." "He who gives all
and takes all has all. He who gives but does not take, or takes
but does not give, has nothing but disappointment and
sorrow."

[50] P. 126.
[51] He uses the expression (p. 178): "They could tell him what to do —
could tell him to consecrate himself, and to believe." Again (p. 135): "Another
thing was needed as much as consecration to do the will of God, viz.: faith
in Jesus, for the power of Him who worketh in us, to work in Him both to
will and to do of his own good pleasure."
[52] Pp. 124, 125.

It results inevitably from Mr. Boardman's separation of justification and sanctification as two experiences, each the result of a special act of faith and normally occurring at different times, that he has two kinds of Christians on his hands. Naturally he is a little embarrassed when he attempts to relate these two kinds of Christians to one another and to the ultimate issues of life. One of his reviewers — Dr. John A. Todd [53] — wishing to push him to the wall, demands how true faith can be ascribed to a man, " when all the while, as our author says of Luther,[54] he ' accepts Christ as a propitiation, but rejects him as a sanctification.' " " On this principle," he cries out, " a man may be justified, and, we suppose, go to heaven — for ' whom he justified, them he also glorified ' (Rom. viii. 30) — while rejecting Christ in one of his most important offices as a Saviour. A more gross and revolting error could not well be conceived." Dr. Todd is right of course: the situation created by separating justifying and sanctifying faith and describing them as unrelated operations, is an impossible one. The Scriptures, not merely in Rom. viii. 30, but everywhere — very explicitly in Rom. vi. — join justification and sanctification indissolubly together as but two stages of the one salvation secured by the one faith in the one Christ. But Mr. Boardman has not laid himself open to the whole extremity of Dr. Todd's assault. He does teach that a man may accept Christ for justification and live through long years rejecting Him — or at least not receiving Him — for sanctification: as if a justified man, received into the divine favor and granted the Spirit of Adoption, could possibly fail to receive his Redeemer from sin for sanctification also — if that depended on a separate and special act of faith and was not rather, as it is, an inevitable result of the justification itself. But he does not teach that a man may go to heaven without having received Christ for his sanctification; that is to say, without being sanctified — for there is, as he too allows, no sanctification out of Christ. The way he attempts to meet the situation

---

[53] *The Biblical Repertory and Princeton Review,* October, 1860, xxxii. p. 625.   [54] P. 30.

is this: "How does it fare," he asks,[55] "with all those professors of religion who live on to the end of their days without
the experimental knowledge of the way of sanctification by
faith?" And the answer he gives is this: "Badly, of course, if
they are *mere* professors, and not truly converted. . . . For
they have not been justified, and therefore they cannot be either
sanctified or glorified, but will be banished from the presence
of God and the glory of his power forever. . . . But, if really
converted, then the way of sanctification by faith in Jesus will
be made plain in the evening of their earthly course." That is
to say, no man who has had only "the first conversion" can
be saved: but there is no man who has only "the first conversion." If he has "the first conversion," he certainly will
sooner or later have "the second." God the Lord will take care
of that. There are not then, after all, in Mr. Boardman's
scheme two kinds of saved men, merely justified and both
justified and sanctified men. There are only two stages in
salvation, which may come together or may be — even widely
— separated in time; but which invariably are both experienced in the saved. This is, it will be perceived, a doctrine of
"Perseverence." All those who are "really converted," says
Mr. Boardman, are ultimately saved: God will see that they
are also sanctified. But he can see no vinculum between the
two, except the bare will of God: God will not permit one who
has received Jesus Christ for justification to fail to receive
Him also for sanctification. This is undoubtedly something —
and might lead one to say, What God has joined together let
not man put asunder. But it falls gravely short of the teaching
of Scripture which connects sanctification with justification
as its necessary issue and through it the necessary issue of the
indivisible faith that lays hold on the indivisible salvation of
the indivisible Christ. From even it, however, Mr. Boardman's
successors in the teaching of the Higher Christian Life have
fallen away.

The most difficult matter in connection with Mr. Boardman's doctrine of sanctification is to make perfectly sure pre-

[55] Pp. 210, 211.

cisely what he supposes we receive in this "second conversion" which it is his main purpose to establish. He says with
great fervor that we receive in it by faith just Christ — and
Christ, says he, is enough. "Exactly what is attained in this
experience?" he asks.[56] And he answers, "Christ. Christ in all
His fulness. Christ as all in all. Christ objectively and subjectively received and trusted in. That is all. And that is
enough." But Christ, we must remember, is not received in
this experience for the first time. He had already been received
in the "first conversion," between which and this "second
conversion" the analogy is most complete.[57] When He was
received in the "first conversion" apparently that was not
enough. In the "first conversion" Christ was received only
for justification; only in the "second conversion" is He received for sanctification. Precisely what we get in Christ in
this second conversion is, then, sanctification. It is not meant
that the holiness of Christ is imputed to us in this transaction,
so that we are in Christ looked upon as holy, though we are
unholy in ourselves. Nor is it meant that the holiness of Christ
is transfused into us in it, so that we are instantaneously made
actually holy by our reception of Him for sanctification. Nor
is it merely meant, as Dr. Jacob J. Abbott, who wrestles with
the problem manfully in a review of the book in the *Bibliotheca Sacra and Biblical Repository*,[58] suggests, that we receive
in it in Christ "a proper *equivalent* for a completed sanctification." Dr. Abbott, however, in his explanation of what he
means by this comes very near to the truth — in one aspect of
it. "We have made the 'transfer' to Christ," he expounds;
"we may, therefore, in the full confidence that he will carry
on the work to its completion, dismiss trouble about our present imperfect state. We may act and feel and rejoice and triumph just as if the work was already consummated. We have
'conquered an abiding peace, and gained the full salvation.'"
Mr. Boardman certainly means to say that in receiving Christ
by faith for sanctification, we receive a power which assures
our sanctification. The actual realization in all its details of

[56] P. 58.   [57] Pp. 116 ff.   [58] July, 1860, xvii. pp. 533–534.

tho holiness thus assured us he represents as a process; and
he does not seem, at least clearly, to deny that it is realized
by us in its details by means of effort. But he asserts that it is
unfailingly realized, and he teaches that the strength by which
it is realized is not our own but Christ's. We are relieved from
all anxieties, all care, all responsibility, about our sanctification: it is in Christ's hands, and because it is in Christ's hands,
we are at peace. And being thus relieved from all anxiety
about it, we may properly be said to have it, to have it not
merely in prospect, but, in principle, in present possession —
though in a possession that progressively realizes itself in fact.

Mr. Boardman certainly means this, we say: but just as
certainly this is not all that he means. He teaches very distinctly that the sanctification which we receive in Christ does
not come all at once, but in process. Although he is concerned
to show that the analogy between the first and the second
conversions is complete, he yet is constrained to allow [59] that
there is one matter in which " the pardon of sins " which we
get in the one and " the purging of sins " which we get in the
other differ with a difference that is radical. This is that " pardon is instantaneously entire, but cleansing from sin is a process of indefinite length." It is *secured* instantaneously by the
single act of faith, just as pardon is, but the difference is that,
in the first conversion, " the work of Christ is already done the
instant the soul believes, while in the second, the work of
Christ remains yet to be done in the future after the soul believes." " In the one," he continues, " the atonement has been
made, and the moment it is accepted, the pardon is complete;
in the other, although the righteousness of Christ is perfect
in which the soul is to be clothed, yet the work of unfolding
the heart to itself in its wants, and the unfolding of Christ to
the heart from glory to glory, in his sympathizing love, and
purifying presence and power, as the soul shall be prepared to
go onward and upward from faith to faith, is a work of time
and progress." Or, as he states it in another place,[60] by the act
of faith in accepting Christ for sanctification " the soul is now

[59] P. 116.   [60] P. 59.

placed in the hands of Christ, as the clay in the hands of the potter; and by faith, Christ is received by the soul as the potter to mold it at his own sovereign will, into a vessel for the Master's own use and for the King's own table." Thus a new starting point has been gained. A new and higher level has been attained, upon which the soul hereafter moves. But — and the warning is made express and very emphatic — a *starting* point is "not the goal reached, or the mark of the prize won." There can be no doubt, then, that Mr. Boardman teaches that the sanctification which we make sure, absolutely sure, of in our "second conversion" is progressive and that we attain the goal only at the end of a long process. Nevertheless there is no reader of Mr. Boardman's book who will not feel that, when this has been said, all is not yet said. In one way or another, Mr. Boardman also certainly teaches that when we accept Christ for sanctification, we not only make our sanctification certain but obtain it at once.

The puzzle into which Mr. Boardman's readers are thrown at this point is relieved by an incidental remark which he lets drop in a letter, written in his old age to Miss Baxter, the founder of Bethshan. " I have known Him as my Saviour from my own conscious sins," he writes,[61] " as long as you have known your right hand from your left." That is to say, from the beginning of his career as a teacher of the Higher Christian Life, he has looked upon Christ as delivering His people from " all conscious sins." This is the precise key which is needed for what otherwise was in danger of appearing a sheer contradiction. What Mr. Boardman teaches, we now see clearly, is that the moment we accept Christ for sanctification we receive in Him freedom from all conscious sinning and at the same time absolute assurance in Him that He will progressively cleanse our "heart and life " in His own good time and way from all sin. There is here in other words, a double " experience," the experience of an immediate deliverance from all conscious sinning and the experience of progressive deliverance of the heart and life from all sin whatsoever. How Christ pro-

[61] " Life and Labours of the Rev. W. E. Boardman," p. 231.

ceeds in thus cleansing us gradually from all sin we have seen in descriptions already quoted: it is all summed up in the phrases [62] that He progressively unfolds "the heart to itself in its wants," and Himself "to the heart from glory to glory," leading the soul thus steadily upwards from faith to faith. That this was settled doctrine to Mr. Boardman we perceive from its reëmergence in precise form in his addresses at the great Oxford Union Meeting in 1874.[63] "In every one of us," he is there reported as saying, "there is a whole unknown world. Sin cannot be abandoned by us until it is known. The instant we know it, we lay it on Christ, and the blood cleanseth it. We learn much of it when we are wholly given over to Christ, but now we can learn only progressively. . . . Be content to accept this, that there is a world within, which unfolds as we walk in the light. We see day by day what we could not see before. But every discovered need is at once met in the Lord Jesus, our mercy-seat. Condemnation for known transgression is *not* the necessity of our existence. In Him is available victory over every temptation — not partial, but complete. If you have faith in Christ, Christ acts in you. . . ." What is declared here is not that Christ is our future Sanctifier, but our present Sanctifier, our present Sanctifier in every successive present. At every moment we are in Him free from all conscious sin; but we are led by His sanctifying grace every successive moment to be conscious of more sin that we may be in Him freed from that too — until we are at last freed from all sin. This is a very ingenious combination of a constant sense of freedom from sin in Christ with a constantly increasing deliverance from sin by Christ. It enables Mr. Boardman to declare that we have from the moment of accepting Christ for sanctification " full salvation " in Him and yet to represent the salvation we have in Him as wrought out in a process which is not complete until life itself ends.[64] Christ is at once

[62] Pp. 116 f.

[63] "Account of the Union Meeting for the Promotion of Scriptural Holiness, Held at Oxford, August 29 to September 7, 1874," pp. 120, 121.

[64] Mrs. Boardman, "Life and Labours of the Rev. W. E. Boardman," p. 174, teaches very expressly the same doctrine. "It is only as the Holy

a perfect present Saviour and a perfect prospective Saviour.
" Christ," he is able to say, therefore, with emphasis,[65] " is no
more freely offered in the faith of his atonement, than in the
assurance of his personal presence and sanctifying power!
He has not given himself to us in half of his offices freely,
then to withhold himself from us in the other half. If we are
content to take him as a half-way Saviour — a deliverer from
condemnation, merely, but refuse to look to him as a present
Saviour from sin, it is our own fault. He is a full Saviour. And
to all who trust him he gives full salvation. To all and to each."

From the point of view thus attained we are able to answer
the question also how far Mr. Boardman's teaching is " Perfectionism." He is himself anxious to dissociate it from " Perfectionism," and writes a whole chapter for that purpose.[66]
Nevertheless no other name can justly be given to it. In his

Spirit reveals self that the soul can see it. There is ever a vast territory within
to be possessed by our Lord, and He alone sees all the lurking places of this
hidden self, and He alone can show us. . . . 'If we walk in the light, as *He* is
in the light, we (Christ and we) have fellowship one with another, and the
blood of Jesus Christ His Son cleanseth us from all sin.' When we are walking, going on in the light, He reveals to us that from which we need to be
cleansed; and we learn that whatever knowledge we may have gained, and
however deep may be our communion with God to-day, it will not suffice for
to-morrow; all we have learned is only retained by the exercise of trust or
faith in the Lord moment by moment." According to this the Higher Christian
Life is a walk in Christ. We never commit known sin. But we continually
learn that what we do is sin. And learning this, we cease from it. Thus there
is a progressive cleansing from sin.

[65] P. 76.

[66] Part I, chapter v. pp. 64 ff. Mrs. Boardman, " Life and Labours of the
Rev. W. E. Boardman," pp. 52, 58, 135, 170, also vigorously repudiates " Perfectionism " from the same point of view as her husband. On p. 58 she tells
us that the experience of receiving Christ as Saviour from his sins was to
Mr. Boardman " not the end of sanctification, but the beginning of a life
of full, abiding union with Jesus." " It was a new and better starting-point
for full and real progress in all time to come, all the springs of which were
in Christ, not in himself." He was thus bound to Christ " for all future
progress " and was assured that " there would be no end of growth." On p. 170
she defends herself and her husband from the charge that they could not
use the clause in the Lord's prayer, " Forgive us our trespasses." They did
not doubt that Christians remained sinners always and always needed forgiveness. " Conscious sins " are a different matter.

view every Christian who rejoices " in full salvation through
full trust in Jesus," experiences Him as a " present Saviour "
from sin. All such (having passed out of the seventh chapter of
Romans into the eighth) " have learned that there is deliverance now here in this life through faith in Jesus. . . . They
have learned experimentally, they know, that Jesus Christ
our Lord, through faith in his name, does actually deliver the
trusting soul from the cruel bondage of its chains under sin,
now in this present time." [67] They do not look to death " as
their deliverer . . . as if death was the sanctifier or the sanctification of the children of God"; they have an adequate
sanctifier in the present Jesus. " The great difference between
the two classes " — those that have taken Jesus for sanctification, and those who have taken Him only for justification —
is that while the one has not, the other has " found Jesus, as a
present Saviour from the present power of sin," [68] and may
therefore give " thanks to God for triumphant deliverance
already wrought, through faith in our Lord Jesus Christ."
" *The very gist* of the experience " expounded, we are told
with the emphasis of italics,[69] is that those who possess it have
" an assured knowledge of the presence and power of Jesus to
deliver us from the dominion as well as the penalty of sin, and
keep us by the power of God, through faith unto salvation."
So the crowning thing which constitutes this fulness of faith
" is the apprehension, not so much of the certainty of final
salvation, as the joyful confidence of the presence of Jesus, as
a present Saviour from sin, and a present captain of salvation,
to direct us and sustain us in every conflict with Satan." Of
course it is the indwelling Christ that is here celebrated. The
source of all the Christian's confidence is that he knows " that
Jesus is with us, and that He will keep us by His own power,
and wash us in His own blood, and lead us by His own hand,
and uphold us from falling, or lift us when fallen " (pp. 279–
280). It is not in our state that we trust nor in our attainments,
but in Christ alone. " The command is not — Now you have
got into a high and holy state, so walk in *that;* But even as ye

[67] Pp. 266, 267.   [68] P. 269.   [69] P. 289.

received CHRIST JESUS, so walk in HIM." [70] But — in Christ Jesus we have attained to a state, in which, abiding in Him, we abide. And the state which we attain in Him is a state of freedom in Him from conscious sin and ever increasing freedom in Him from all sin as we are made by Him — in whose hands we are as the clay in the hands of the potter — progressively conscious of more and more of the sins of which we are ignorant, only that we may be progressively delivered from them also. If this is the state of the Christian it is a state of freedom from conscious sin and that at an ever higher and higher level of actual holiness. This is very expressly a doctrine of perfectionism. It is not taught that the Christian is absolutely perfect — but what perfectionism teaches that? It is not taught that the Christian never sins. But the Christian's sinning is made merely auxiliary and contributory to his holiness — the instrument which Christ his Sanctifier uses to elevate him continually to a higher and higher level in his perfection. In the most literal sense the Christian's sins become stepping-stones to higher things.

It ought to be added, however, that in his latest years Mr. Boardman appears to have exchanged this most ingenious form of perfectionism by which a constant, conscious perfection is maintained in the course of a steady actual growth towards real perfection, for the exaggerated mysticism which has become a characteristic doctrine of the later advocates of the Higher Christian Life. [71] We find him at least, say about 1880, writing to this effect in a letter to Miss Baxter, the founder of the Faith-Cure Home, Bethshan. "He is *the life, the All* of life," he now writes, [72] "for *body* as well as *soul, complete*. In Him *dwelleth* all fulness; we are filled full in Him. . . . Fulness, absolute fulness of life dwells in Him alone; and in us, only as He dwells in us by faith. . . . As long as we take healing *from* Him bit by bit, bits will yet be lacking. As long as we take strength from Him bit by bit, bits

[70] P. 322.

[71] See, for example, the article on "The Victorious Life" in *The Princeton Theological Review*, July, 1918, xvi. pp. 356 ff. or pp. 561 ff. of this volume.

[72] "Life and Labours of the Rev. W. E. Boardman," pp. 231–233.

of infirmities will remain. . . . He is the great Expulsor of
' the world, the flesh (self) and the Devil,' and that by His
own continual presence in us, in His own fulness, the Fulness
of God. And so He is the Expulsor of sin, sickness, weakness,
and all that can oppress, whether in spirit, soul, or body." On
this teaching, when we have Christ, Him Himself and not
merely things from Him, we have at once all: there is no more
room for growth — for Christ is past all growth and we are
" uplifted " by the Spirit into Christ and He is unfolded " in
all His fulness, the Fulness of God in us." We can no longer
be sick or weak or sinful in any, even the least degree, for
these things are incompatible with the fulness of life we receive in Christ. This extreme doctrine of the mystical indwelling may be thought to be already prepared for by a distinction
which Mr. Boardman had made a few years earlier, between
the dwelling of the Spirit *with* us and *in* us. " Our Saviour
makes this distinction," he writes (p. 90) in his book, " In the
Power of the Spirit," [73] " in connection with the promise of
the Spirit as an indwelling one, ' who *is with* you and *shall* be
in you.' The Spirit is with us to convince of sin before we are
converted and to regenerate us in the new birth; and He is
with us afterwards to work in us everything that is of God.
But this is an entirely different thing from His coming to
possess us fully for God as His temple; to purify us to God as
His peculiar possession, purchased by the blood of the Son of
God; fill us with all the fulness of God; attend us by the
might of God; and preserve us blameless unto the coming of
Christ." But it belongs distinctively to Mr. Boardman's later
years and supplants in them the clever theory by which he
reconciled, perhaps with a greater measure of success than any

[73] Published in 1875. This distinction is made in connection with an
unhappy effort to turn the phrase, the Baptism of the Holy Ghost, into a
technical term designating " the second conversion." " Conversion, therefore,"
he writes (p. 89), " and the baptism of the Spirit are separate and distinct
experiences." " There is one, only one Baptism of the Holy Ghost, though
there may be many and very great and precious renewals or refreshings by
the Spirit afterwards " (p. 32). " *The* baptism. *The* baptism, I say; not *a* baptism, but the *gift* of the Holy Ghost as an abiding, guiding, teaching, girding,
strengthening one " (p. 102). See above note 39.

THE "HIGHER LIFE" MOVEMENT 491

other theorizer of his school, the contradictory requirements
that the Christian must receive in Christ immediate sanctification, and that the Christian's sanctification must be a progressive attainment.

Of course it is easy to say that the sanctification received
at once in Christ is not a real sanctification; it is only sanctification to the consciousness of the Christian himself. This
might be expressed by saying that what the Christian receives
at once when he receives Christ for sanctification is not sanctification but peace. Here is the root of the phraseology which
speaks of this experience as obtaining "rest in Christ." But
this only uncovers to us the ingrained eudaemonism of the
whole Higher Christian Life movement. It is preoccupied with
the pursuit of happiness and tends in many ways to subordinate everything else to it. It is no accident that the title of
Hannah Whitall Smith's chief book is "The Christian's Secret
of a Happy Life." And it is no accident that Isaac M. See's
book bears the title, "The Rest of Faith." [74] Men grow weary

Isaac M. See, "The Rest of Faith," 1871. "Yes," says he in the preface, "let the book be called by that name. For that is the blessed condition
of the 'little ones' of the Lord Jesus." — The fundamental teaching of the
book runs on the familiar lines of the Higher Christian Life School. Mr. See
calls what he advocates "Scriptural holiness" (p. 62). The following brief
extracts will give the outlines of his doctrine. "*Can I be holy?* Yes, beloved,
surely you can. Otherwise the glorious God of our salvation would not have
commanded you to be holy" (p. 28, cf. p. 43). "I can be holy . . . God designed it. . . . He is able and willing" (p. 75). "It must be conceded by those
who have tried every way to become holy and have failed that the work of
our sanctification is only the Lord's. Our part in the gracious plan is — 'ONLY
BELIEVE'" (p. 43). "But observe, that though the Lord Jesus is so 'able to
save unto the uttermost,' yet He will not do our part of the work. . . . Do
your part . . . and He will do His part" (p. 48). "He, with *our full consent*
(He will not do it without), brings every power into harmony with His own
life" (p. 44). "Most positive are we, that if they will let Jesus work, they
shall know the joy of a perfect cure" (p. 51). "LET ALL GO FOR JESUS. This is
CONSECRATION — a complete, final yielding up of all we have to God, to be
succeeded by a continual remembrance that we possess nothing henceforth in
our own name" (p. 17). "He died to save us from all leaven of sin, that it
might be rooted out and cast away, and that our lives might shine with His
holiness. Any other view deprives the church of the full benefit of His death"
(pp. 32–33). "We are just as helpless to be holy as the man with the withered
arm was to stretch it out. All our works can never make us holy. . . . It is

of serving the Lord; they do not wish to fight to win the prize; they prefer to be carried to the skies on flowery beds of ease.

It will have been, no doubt, noticed that in his presentation of his notion of the Higher Christian Life Mr. Boardman has left a place for the divine initiative. The sanctification of the Christian is, in his view, in such a sense in Christ, that it is really Christ — or the Holy Spirit — who sanctifies him, according to His own plan and by means of His own working. This leaves a place for a doctrine of assurance — in which indeed, as we have seen, Mr. Boardman's doctrine of sanctification very largely consists; and for a necessarily correlated doctrine of perseverance. In these respects Mr. Boardman's mode of presenting the idea of the Higher Christian Life has an immense advantage over that which has been more common

---

done by the all-powerful Jesus, who reigns in the hearts of His people, and who delivers them from all things 'according to their faith.' . . . This simple faith is in momentary exercise. It does not believe that holiness which it receives from Christ is infallibility, for this has never been promised; but it does believe, that, as it *momentarily* looks unto Jesus, it gets the work of the Holy Spirit done within, it keeps the cleansing which it enjoyed at first, and that it is enabled to please God " (p. 85). The perfectionists' " distinguishing feature . . . is, that Jesus is so formed in them as to make it impossible for them to fall into sin. It would appear that they believe in infallibility. We have no such doctrine " (p. 54). " We confess our perfection cannot be Adamic, being conformable to our present imperfect capacities. . . . We also confess that our present graces are not angelic " (p. 55). " We are not sinners in the sense of active transgression of the law " (p. 89). " Jesus can and does keep those who intently look to Him from sinning, from breaking out into actual, known, and therefore wilful, acts of sinning " (p. 105). " I am utterly unable to see how sin can have any dominion or power, or active presence, if Jesus . . . dwell within. His presence is sin's expulsion " (p. 58). " I need not, therefore, be anxious about the amount of sin which is left, when by His reigning grace, yea, by His sure presence, I am not conscious of a single desire outside of His will, nor of a departure from Him in my ways " (pp. 58–59). " Jesus has done *two things* for us. These two things are the purchase of His precious blood; they are inseparable . . . IMPUTATION and IMPARTATION. The latter expresses His own indwelling. . . . If we try to cleanse ourselves we shall be unfit for His dwelling, but if we believe He will cleanse us, and if we give up the work to Him He will see it well done " (pp. 95–97). Here is perfectionism of conduct, confined to deliverance from conscious transgression of known law, produced by the indwelling of Christ. Its generic sameness with the perfectionism taught by the other adherents of the Higher Life school is clear and the specific difference small.

later. It seems really to suspend upon God the sanctification
of the Christian, instead of, as has been common later, suspending the sanctifying work of God on the Christian. Whether
Mr. Boardman was prepared, however, to go the whole way
here, and to recognize without reserve, with Paul, that in all
ways and in all respects it is " of God that we are in Christ
Jesus," may admit of some doubt. In his later years at least he
had fallen away from, if he had ever heartily embraced, that
pure confession. We find him at the Oxford Union Meeting in
1874,[75] saying: " ' Behold, I stand at the door and knock.'
Each one has to open. *A very little latch will keep a door fast,*
— a rusty lock will keep it very fast. You must undo the
fastenings. It is not His way to force the door." This sounds
like the familiar teaching of the Pelagianizers: Christ is dependent in His action on our pleasure, and works — can work
— only when we release Him for working. Theodore Monod on
the next page, puts the general notion at its height. " Believing, we shall have *life* through the Lord Jesus. How much life?
Precisely as much as we trust Him for. Christ is to each one
what each one expects Him to be: if nothing be expected, He
is nothing; if little, little; if much, much; if everything,
everything." If this be true, then it is not Christ who regulates
our activities, and so secures our sanctification; but we who
regulate His activities, and so secure our own sanctification.
Christ is merely the instrument at our disposal by means of
which we may sanctify ourselves — and we may use Him at
our will, little or much, inefficiently or efficiently, according
to our choice. Mr. Murray Shipley declares this in open language.[76] There is " limitless power " in Christ for us, he tells
us; and then he exhorts us: "The power *is yours* — use it! "
He even compares it to electricity and magnetism — forces
lying at our disposal, for us to use as we list. This conception
is the precise antipodes of that to which Mr. Boardman more
happily gives expression, when he tells us that the Christ
whom we receive within us by faith sanctifies us by bringing

[75] "Account of the Union Meeting for the Promotion of Scriptural
Holiness, Held at Oxford, August 29 to September 7, 1874," p. 74.   [76] P. 80

us progressively to the knowledge of the sins which we ignorantly commit and delivering us from them one after another as they emerge in our consciousness. It is a matter of
regret that it supplanted both in his own later teaching and
in the teaching of his successors that better doctrine.

His successors naturally were numerous, and varied very
much in the details of their teaching.[77] It was, however, in
Mr. and Mrs. Robert Pearsall Smith that the movement which
he had inaugurated found its most capable propagators and
it was through them that it attained its widest extension and
its most lasting influence.[78] Both Mr. and Mrs. Smith were
born and bred Quakers. They did not receive, however, their
doctrine of the Higher Christian Life from their Quaker inheritance. Mr. Smith indeed shows little or no Quaker influence in his teaching. He was through most of his active life a
member of the Presbyterian Church, though, when he appeared as the leader of the Higher Life movement in London
in 1873, he had renounced all ecclesiastical connection and
presented himself as an unattached teacher, who would fain
serve all denominations alike. Mrs. Smith, on the other hand,
remained essentially a Quaker throughout life, or, as it would

[77] Some idea of their number and character may be formed from the
volume published in 1872 with the title: "Pioneer Experiences; or the Gift
of Power Received by Faith. Illustrated and Confirmed by the Testimony of
Eighty Living Witnesses of Various Denominations." By the author of "The
Way of Holiness." Introduction by the Rev. Bishop Janes.

[78] There appear to be no objective, critical biographies of either Mr.
or Mrs. Smith accessible. There is a little sketch of Mr. Smith in German:
Möller, "R. P. Smith, ein Lebensbild"; and there is a short notice of him
in Schiele und Zscharnack, "Die Religion in Geschichte und Gegenwart,"
v. p. 727. There is also a discussion of the "Religious Experience of R. Pearsall
Smith" in The (London) Christian Observer, lxxv. 1875, pp. 830 ff., 926 ff.;
lxxvi. 1876, pp. 60 ff. See also Th. Jellinghaus, "Das völlige, gegenwärtige Heil
durch Christum" (1880), ed. 4, 1898, pp. 431, 720. Mrs. Smith gives data for
the earlier period of their religious life in "The Record of a Happy Life:
Being Memorials of Franklin Whitall Smith," 1873; and a valuable sketch
of her own development in "My Spiritual Autobiography or How I Discovered the Unselfishness of God," 1903. Her later years are depicted by her
granddaughter, Ray Strachey, in "A Quaker Grandmother," 1914.

be more accurate to say, grew steadily more and more Quaker. There is scarcely a distinctively Quaker conception which does not find expression at some time or other in her writings.[79] In her later years, even the fundamental mystical doctrine of the " divine seed " [80] is quite clearly enunciated and the characteristic Higher Life teaching developed out of it. " There is . . . in every man," she expounds,[81] " a seed of the divine life, a Christ-germ as it were. The old Quakers called it ' the witness for God in the soul,' ' that which corresponds to the divine inspeaking.' " This same seed, she explains, while in everyone, is not quickened in all. But " whenever we feel inward stirrings and longings after holiness," " the divine seed within us is being quickened." " This is the begetting of God." That is precisely Robert Barclay over again.[82] But now Mrs. Smith

[79] She herself says in her old age (" My Spiritual Autobiography," 1903, pp. 55 f.): " Nearly every view of divine things that I have since discovered, and every reform I have since advocated, had, I now realize, their germs in the views of the Society; and over and over again, when some new discovery or conviction has dawned upon me, I caught myself saying, ' Why, *that* was what the early Friends meant, although I never understood it before.' "

[80] Robert Barclay's term (cf. Charles Hodge, " Systematic Theology," i. p. 94; Hastings' " Encyclopædia of Religion and Ethics," vi. p. 143 a), as also William Law's (cf. W. R. Inge, " Christian Mysticism," 1899, p. 282). Eckhart called it " spark " (cf. Inge, p. 155; R. A. Vaughan, " Hours with the Mystics," i. p. 190). For the history of the term, see Inge, " Christian Mysticism," Index, " Synteresis."

[81] " Every-Day Religion," 1893, pp. 160 ff.

[82] Charles Hodge, as cited, thus summarizes Barclay's teaching: " This seed comes from Christ, and is communicated to every man. In some it lies as a seed upon a rock, which never shows any sign of life. But when the soul receives a visitation of the Spirit, if his influence be not resisted, that seed is vivified, and develops into holiness of heart and life; by which the soul is purified and justified. We are not justified by our works. Everything is due to Christ. He is both ' the giver and the gift.' Nevertheless our justification consists in this subjective change." To make the parallel complete, Mrs. Smith teaches the same subjective conception of justification (p. 193). Christ is our Righteousness, she says, and then she adds: " That is, the life of Christ in our souls is a righteous life." She had learned in 1858 the doctrine of Justification by Faith under Plymouth Brethren influences and held it for a time very clearly; but she came afterwards back to the Quaker doctrine (" My Spiritual Autobiography," pp. 235 ff.) and spoke of her earlier period as a past phase of belief — " in our very evangelical days " (p. 278).

goes on: "Then comes in our responsibility. We cannot create life, but we can let life live. We can 'lay hold' of it by an entire surrender to Christ, who is our life. We can accept Him as our life, and can refuse to let any other life live in us." "This, then, is how the spiritual life is to grow; that is, by surrender and faith. We must 'boycott' the old self-life, and must deal only with the spiritual life. But we must not make another mistake, and think that although we cannot beget life by our self-efforts, we are to make it grow ourselves. We are as powerless in the matter of our growth as in the matter of our begetting. Life grows of itself. It is a mighty dynamic force that only asks a chance to grow. The lily grows by the power of its inward life principle, and according to the laws of a lily's life. No amount of its own stretching or straining, nor any pulling up by others, would help its growth. It is all folly, and worse than folly, for Christians to make such mighty efforts to grow. If they would only let the Christ life within them grow, unhindered by their interference, they need have no fear of the result."

According to this, every man is born with a Christ-germ in him. It needs only quickening. There is to be no new creation, therefore, but only a rousing into activity of something already existing. The Holy Spirit quickens this Christ-germ. Then we come into play. Whether this new-born life is to live depends on us. We had no power to quicken the Christ-germ into activity. But it has no such power of life in it as to force itself on us. We have to decide whether it shall live or not. Only if we welcome it will it live. Our welcoming of it is described, however, very lamely, and is made purely negative. It consists of a duplex act, surrender and faith. That is all we have to do, but our doing it is, somehow, the essential condition of the living of the new-born life quickened in us. We must not do anything or try to do anything positive, looking to the cherishing of this new-born life. Hands off! — that is the only thing we are to do. Perceiving it to be quickened — "feeling inward strivings and longings" — we must just stand aside and let it grow. That is the condition of its growing. This purely negative act

is oddly described as "'lay[ing] hold' of it, by an entire surrender to Christ." No wonder the words "lay hold" are
put between quotation marks. "Surrendering" seems more
like letting go than taking hold. And indeed letting go is what
we are being told to do. It is miscalled "accepting" therefore.
The attitude is one of complete passivity. We have nothing to
do with the begetting of this new life and we have nothing
to do with its growth. "Life grows of itself." We feel the life
stirring in us. We know ourselves to be alive in Christ because
of it. And then, finger on lip, we softly step aside, and — let it
grow. The condition of its growth is that we should thus step
aside. That is Mrs. Smith's exposition of the Christian life.
No, it does not sound like Paul's, "Work out your own salvation." Nor like Christ's, "Strive — agonize — to enter in by
the narrow door." It is just quietistic mysticism. There is some
talk, no doubt, of our feeding our spiritual life on Christ, and
that not merely by contemplation but by following Him —
imitatio Christi. But that is a false note here, and we soon are
brought back to the declaration that our fruit-bearing is not
to be by effort, "but by spontaneous growth." We are not to
trouble ourselves about it, any more than the fig-tree troubles
itself about its fruit. Effort to bear fruit is like tying apples
on a tree: they are not the fruit of the tree unless they are
spontaneously produced.

Mrs. Smith became perfectly well aware, then, that her
teaching was in its essence genuinely Quaker teaching: and
she delighted to present it in its organic relation with Quaker
teaching. But she did not get it from the Quakers. She got
it from the Methodists. Having got it from the Methodists,
however, she recognized it as Quaker teaching also and rejoiced
in that fact.[83] "My dear father," she tells us,[84] "who was a

[83] "My Spiritual Autobiography," 1903, chapter xxix. pp. 275 ff.: "But
now at last I had got the clue, and the true inner meaning of Quakerism
dawned upon me more and more fully day by day. It was the 'way of holiness' in which they were seeking to walk. They preached a deliverance from
sin, a victory over the cares and worries of life, a peace that passes all understanding, a continual being made 'more than conquerors' through Christ.
They were in short 'Higher Life' people, and at last I understood them; and

genuine Quaker, as well as a most delightful one, owned to it.
At the earliest opportunity I told him of our new discovery,
and said, 'And now, father, is not this the secret of thy life
and the source of thy strength? Is not this the way thou hast
always lived?' I shall never forget his reply. 'Why, of course
it is, daughter,' he said, with a joyous ring of triumph in his
voice. . . .'' But "I must confess," adds Mrs. Smith,[85] "that,
although we found . . . that the Friends did actually teach
it, yet it was among the Methodists we received the clearest
light.'' Having got it from the Methodists moreover, she got it
in that distinctively Methodist form which separates justification and sanctification as two distinct experiences, and this is
the form in which she teaches it throughout the whole course
of the Higher Life Movement, though she reverted from it
later to the Quaker form. "The Methodists were very definite
about it," she writes [86] in her old age. "They taught definitely

---

now the old preaching, which once had been so confusing, became marrow
and fatness to my soul. The preaching had not changed, but I had changed.
I had discovered the missing link, and had reached that stage in my soul's
experience to which such preaching ministered" (pp. 280–281).

[84] "The Unselfishness of God," as cited by J. B. Figgis, "Keswick from
Within," 1914, p. 13. The passage occurs (with some expansion of details) on
pp. 278–279 of "My Spiritual Autobiography or How I Discovered the Unselfishness of God," 1903, which is advertised as "a new edition of 'The
Unselfishness of God.'" We infer that Mr. Figgis' quotations are taken from
the first edition of the book, or else that he has skilfully condensed the text.

[85] "My Spiritual Autobiography," p. 283.

[86] *Ibid.*, p. 283. Theodore Sippell summarizes the Quaker doctrine as
follows: "Let us open Robert Barclay's famous Apology of Quakerism. In
the eighth chapter, 'Concerning Perfection' we read: 'In whom this pure
and holy birth is fully brought forth the body of sin and death comes to
be crucified and removed, and their hearts united and subjected to the truth;
so as not to obey any suggestions or temptations of the evil one, but to be
free from actual sinning and transgressing of the law of God, and in that respect perfect: yet doth this perfection still admit of a growth; and there
remaineth always in some part a possibility of sinning, where the mind doth
not most diligently and watchfully attend unto the Lord.' This power to
live free from sin is ascribed by Barclay only to the regenerate man, in whom
Christ lives and rules, who not only reveals and punishes sin but also gives
power to cease from it. This perfection is, to be sure, no divine perfection, in
the sense that we are as pure, holy and perfect as God Himself, but only a
perfection which corresponds to the human measure. The doctrine that the

that there were two experiences in the Christian life, the first being justification, and the second sanctification, and they urged Christians not to be satisfied with justification (i.e., forgiveness) merely, but also to seek sanctification or the ' second blessing,' as they called it, as well. I should not myself express the truth in this fashion now, but at that time I must acknowledge it was most helpful." In point of fact, this distinction between justification and sanctification was the hinge on which her whole Higher Life teaching turned, as we shall have occasion to note later.

Robert Pearsall Smith was born in Philadelphia, February 1, 1827, and died in England, at the age of 72, April 17, 1899. His

---

saints can never in this life be free from sinning agrees, according to Barclay, neither with the wisdom and almightiness of God nor with His righteousness. It is in the highest degree an accusation of Christ, takes away the power of His offering and makes His coming and His service in the main matter ineffective. It is irrational and meaningless. Christ commands: ' Ye shall be holy; ' it must therefore be possible. We have the promise, ' Sin shall not rule over you.' Paul does not argue in Rom. vi. ' Ye *can* be free from sin,' but ' You *must* be free from it, because you are under grace, not under law.' This perfection or freedom from sin is obtained and made possible when the Gospel and the inner law of the Spirit are received and recognized. According to the witness of Scripture, many have received this freedom from sin — some before the law, and some under the law, and many more still under the gospel. This perfection can be lost again, through lack of watchfulness. . . . Barclay does not wish to throw into doubt that a still higher condition is attainable by man in this life, in which the right has become so a second nature to him that he in this condition cannot at all sin again. All doubt of this possibility is excluded for him by the Scriptural declaration, I John iii. 9. ' Whosoever is born of God doeth no sin, for his seed abideth in him, and he cannot sin, because he is born of God.' But Barclay modestly recognizes that he has not himself attained this degree of perfection. If now we bear in mind that regeneration, that is, the destruction of the sinful nature and the restoration of the original nature (as Adam possesed it before the fall), is accomplished according to the conception of the Quakers by a sudden instreaming of divine power and grace — then the kinship of the Quaker and the Methodist doctrines of perfection seems extraordinarily close. A difference between them must of course not be overlooked. According to the Quaker conception we receive the perfection immediately on our entrance into a state of grace; according to Wesleyans in a later stadium, namely in the ' second change.' But we should not lay too great weight on this difference in the question of their wider kinship " (*Die Christliche Welt,* xxviii. 1914, coll. 149–150).

wife, Hannah Whitall Smith, was some five years his junior
(she was born in Philadelphia in 1832) and outlived him a
dozen years, passing away in a serene old age at her English
home in her eightieth year. Both had been born into Christian
homes and had lived from their earliest years under exceptionally winning Christian influences. But it was not until the
summer of 1858 that they found their " all-sufficient Saviour,"
by a happy coincidence both on the same day.[87] The language
in which Mrs. Smith speaks of their experience of conversion
is enthusiastic. In it they came " to a knowledge of the Lord
Jesus Christ " as their " all-sufficient Saviour ": in it they " by
faith in Him were ' born again ' into the family of God." We
gather from certain " old papers " which she quotes in her
biographical sketch of her son Frank, that they entered by it
into a very happy Christian life.[88]

As the years passed, however, they became dissatisfied
with their Christian attainments. They wanted, not a future
deliverance only, but a present deliverance. For this they
strove, but with only indifferent success. Looking back on these
years Mr. Smith came to speak of them as "long and toilsome" years of "legality." Mrs. Smith fell into a most unhappy condition of questioning the justice of God, for which
she found relief only by adopting a doctrine of universal salva-

[87] This is what Mrs. Smith says explicitly in "The Record of a Happy
Life," p. 16. They "had long been seeking the truth," she says, and "were
both brought on the same day, during the summer of 1858, to a knowledge
of the Lord Jesus Christ as our all-sufficient Saviour, bearing our sins in His
own body on the tree; and by faith in Him were ' born again ' into the
family of God." In a much later book, "The Unselfishness of God," 1902
(American edition under the title of " My Spiritual Autobiography," 1903,
pp. 172 ff.), a somewhat different account is given. Mr. Smith seems to be
confusing this and his "second conversion" when in an address at the Oxford
Union Meeting in 1874 ("Account of the Union Meeting for the Promotion
of Scriptural Holiness, held at Oxford, August 29 to September 7, 1874,"
p. 168) he says: "I had been a 'religious man' for ten long and toilsome
years, when one day, in the railway carriage, I for the first time saw in the
Scripture what the blood of Christ had done for me. Reaching my journey's
end I found that my wife, in the same way from the Scripture, had, a few
hours before, also found eternal life in believing." It appears to have been
about 1867 that he found "the second blessing."

[88] See also " My Spiritual Autobiography," pp. 192 ff.

tion. " I began to feel," she says,[89] " that the salvation in which
I had been rejoicing was, after all, a very limited and very
selfish salvation, and, as such, unworthy of the Creator who
has declared so emphatically that his ' tender mercies are over
all His works,' and above all unworthy of the Lord Jesus
Christ, who came into the world for the sole and single purpose
of saving the world. I could not believe that His life and death
for us could be meant to fall so far short of remedying the evil
that He came on purpose to remedy, and I felt it must be
impossible that there could be any short-coming in the salvation He had provided." She was already arguing from the
" completeness " of Christ's salvation to effects she imagined
must therefore be included in it.

Soon she carried the argument one step farther. From her
immediately subsequent point of view, she explains: [90] " We
had . . . learned thoroughly the blessed truth of justification
by faith, and rejoiced in it with great joy. But here we had
stopped. The equally blessed twin truth of sanctification by
faith had not yet been revealed to us." This new revelation
came to them in the later sixties — we may apparently date it
in its culmination somewhere about 1867. How it came Mrs.
Smith describes in its broad outlines in " The Record of a
Happy Life," published in 1873.[91] " In the fall of the year
1866, there came as Tutor to Frank, a young Baptist theological student. He had not been long in our house, before we
discovered that he had a secret of continual victory and abiding rest of which we were ignorant. After watching him for
many months, continually impressed with the wonderful
purity and devotedness of his life, we began to ask him about
it. And he told us that his simple secret was faith. He trusted,
and Jesus delivered. He laid the care of his life, moment by
moment, on the Lord, and the Lord took it, and made his life
moment by moment what He would have it be. It was a wonderful revelation. At the same time, some of the workmen in

89 " My Spiritual Autobiography," p. 200.
90 " The Record of a Happy Life," 1873, p. 37.
91 Pp. 37 f.; cf. chapter xxvi. of " My Spiritual Autobiography."

our factory, having also come into the experience of this life
of faith, began to come to our house to talk about it; and we
all attended . . . a little evening meeting, held for the consideration and promotion of this truth." The result was at last,
that ". . . (we) were brought out into a clear knowledge of
the truth of sanctification by faith, and realized in the wondrous peace, and victory, and liberty of this new life, that we
had known before only half the gospel."

Details are added in later accounts. The Smiths were now
living at Millville, New Jersey, whither they had removed
in the autumn of 1864 to take charge of the glass-factories
there, belonging to the firm of Whitall, Tatum & Co. A little
Methodist dressmaker in the village became Mrs. Smith's
Priscilla; [92] Mr. Smith found his Aquila among the Methodist
workmen in his factory: [93] these took them unto them and
expounded unto them the way of God more carefully. The
Methodist Holiness Meetings became their resort: Inskip,
McDonald, Methodist Holiness revivalists, became to them
household names [94] — and they soon found themselves enthusiastic adherents of the Wesleyan doctrine of sanctification
by faith. There were points no doubt at which they held back.
Even in the glow of her new discovery Mrs. Smith, while crying out with fervor, " And this is the Methodist ' blessing of
holiness,' " feels bound to add,[95] " Couched by them it is true
in terms that I cannot altogether endorse, and held amid
what seems to me a mixture of error, but still really and liv-
ingly experienced and enjoyed by them." Despite these minor
reserves she was not backward in acknowledging that she
owed her new Blessing to the Methodists, and what she now
began to teach was in essence what they taught. Mr. Smith
was won to the new doctrine with more difficulty; it was Mrs.
Smith herself who put the finishing touches to his conversion.
" At first my husband felt somewhat frightened. He continually fell back on the argument that the ' old man ' must always

[92] " My Spiritual Autobiography," p. 240.
[93] " Holiness Through Faith," pp. 83 f., 64 ff.
[94] " The Record of a Happy Life," pp. 139, 141; cf. p. 186.
[95] " My Spiritual Autobiography," p. 245.

bring us into bondage. 'Impossible or not,' I said, 'it is certainly in the Bible, and I would like to know what thee thinks of Romans vi. 6. What can this mean but that the power of sin is really to be conquered, so that we no longer need to serve sin!' Startled, he exclaimed, 'There is no such passage in the Bible.' 'Oh! yes there is,' I replied, and turning to my Bible I showed it to him. With this verse, of course, he had been familiar, but it now appeared as if he had never seen it before. It brought conviction, however, and from that time he did not rest until he had discovered the truth for himself." [96] Hermann Benser is quite right therefore when he emphasizes that it was under Methodist influences that Mr. Smith attained his new point of view; [97] and Theodor Jellinghaus [98] is entirely accurate when he pronounces him a spiritual pupil of Inskip, Upham and Boardman, but equally right when he adds: "In his doctrine and mode of presenting it he agrees, however, most closely with Boardman." [99]

With his characteristic enthusiasm Mr. Smith gave himself, at once on acquiring his new views, to their zealous propagation. His chief book, "Holiness through Faith," after having appeared first in instalments in a periodical, was published in 1870. In the summer of 1871 he experienced at a Methodist Camp Meeting, in immediate response to prayer, what he understood to be "the baptism of the Holy Spirit," equipping him for fuller service. His description of that experience is

[96] "The Unselfishness of God," quoted by Figgis, "Keswick from Within," p. 12; in a more expanded form, "My Spiritual Autobiography," p. 263. Mr. Smith's own account, pp. 264 ff.

[97] Das moderne Gemeinschaftschristentum," 1910, p. 4.

[98] "Das völlige, gegenwärtige Heil durch Christum," ed. 4, 1898, p. 720.

[99] Johannes Jüngst ("Amerikanischer Methodismus in Deutschland und Robert Pearsall Smith," 1875) in his sketch of Smith's doctrine is concerned to show that the teaching of Smith and that of the Methodists are closely related. This he does very well. The fact is, however, not in dispute. The writer of the able article "The Brighton Convention and its Opponents" in *The London Quarterly Review*, xlv. October, 1875, pp. 84–128, while criticising quite freely, from the Wesleyan point of view, details in Smith's teaching, does not think of denying that the cause of the one is in essence the cause of the other: "We are . . . concerned to defend the general doctrine they teach" (p. 103).

very striking.[100] His whole being was inexpressibly filled with God, so that he was less conscious of what his senses presented to his apprehension than of what was revealed to him within and no creature was so real to his soul as the Creator Himself: losing nothing of his sense-perception, everything was yet glorified by the divine revelation. Mrs. Smith gives us a temperate account of the occurrence. " The truth came to me," she says,[101] " with intellectual conviction and delight; my husband, being more of an emotional nature, received the Blessing in true Methodist fashion, and came home full of Divine glow. He said he had retired to the woods to continue the prayer by himself. The whole world seemed transformed to him. This ecstasy lasted for weeks, and was the beginning of a wonderful career of power and blessing." It was in the power of this endowment that he appeared in London in the spring of 1873 as a world-evangelist.[102] We have already spoken of the remarkable meetings begun in London in the spring of 1873, which ran up to the great Oxford Union Meeting of August 29 to September 7, 1874. Mr. Boardman participated in them, but they were Mr. Smith's meetings; and by the time that the Broadlands Conference of July 17–23 and very especially the Oxford Union Meeting was reached, Mr. Boardman had fallen well into the background.[103] The Oxford Meeting was called by Mr. Smith, was presided over by him, was governed in all its details by him with calculated adjustment to the effect desired, and was, in a word, but an instrument of his propaganda. The effect of the meeting was nothing less than amazing; and from

[100] He tells about it in his book, "'Walk in the Light.'" Compare Mrs. Smith's "My Spiritual Autobiography," 1903, p. 288.

[101] "The Unselfishness of God," quoted by Figgis, "Keswick from Within," p. 14; in fuller form, "My Spiritual Autobiography," pp. 288 f.

[102] The phrase is Fr. Winkler's, "Robert Pearsall Smith und der Perfectionismus," second thousand, 1915, p. 17: "1873 beginnt seine Tätigkeit als Weltmissionar."

[103] Cf. Mrs. Boardman's "Life and Labours of the Rev. W. E. Boardman," 1886, p. 250, where J. E. Page, editor of The King's Highway, speaking of the Oxford Meeting, remarks of Mr. Boardman: "He was not very prominent in the meetings . . . but he did much valuable work in dealing with individuals."

it the propaganda was widened out with great energy and skill
to cover all Britain, and then carried over to the Continent.
Mr. Smith himself, on the invitation of highly-placed theologians, bore it to Berlin where, on the request of the Court-
preacher Baur, the Emperor placed the old Garrison Church
at his disposal. From Berlin he went to Basel, Stuttgart, Heidelberg, down the Rhine to Bonn, and thence to Barmen,
everywhere arousing the greatest enthusiasm and leaving
permanent results — although he could address his audiences
only through an interpreter, and could only shout to them as
his battle cry a single sentence in their own language, the
refrain of a hymn composed for the meetings by Pfarrer
Gebhardt of Zurich — *Jesus errettet mich jetzt,* " Jesus saves
me *now*." [104] Meanwhile preparations were making in England
for the holding of another great international convention
which should surpass even the Oxford Meeting. It was held at
Brighton from May 29 to June 7, 1875, when the climax was
reached. Mr. Smith again presided and again was the chief
speaker. The enthusiasm already at a high pitch was raised
still higher. Plans were laid for continuing the campaign vigorously throughout England — when suddenly it was announced that all of Mr. Smith's engagements were cancelled
and he had returned to America. That was his dramatic
definitive disappearance from public life.

What had happened to occasion this sudden withdrawal
at its very culminating point from a work enthusiastically
prosecuted was not fully made known to the public. Mr. Smith
had had a fall from his horse in 1861 which had been followed
by congestion of the brain and long-continued distressing
nervous symptoms; [105] and it was understood that it was to

[104] We are following the condensed narrative here of F. Winkler, " Robert
Pearsall Smith und der Perfectionismus," 1915, pp. 17 f.; cf. also the vivid
brief narrative of Hermann Benser, " Das moderne Gemeinschaftschristen-
tum," pp. 3 f. and especially the full contemporary account of Johannes
Jüngst, " Amerikanischer Methodismus in Deutschland, und Robert Pearsall
Smith," 1875, pp. 48 ff.

[105] "Account of the Union Meeting for the Promotion of Scriptural
Holiness, held at Oxford, August 29 to September 7, 1874," pp. 134 ff.

seek reliof from some of the *sequelæ* of this accident that he
had come to Europe in 1873.[106] It was said that a return of
this disorder now rendered a complete rest imperative. But
the public knew very well that this was not all that was to be
said. The air was full of rumors of the most disquieting kind;
Theodor Jellinghaus characterizes them as "a stream of the
most rancorous and malignant calumnies," to which no one
who has any respect for the ninth commandment should
listen.[107] The rumors were not, however, without foundation
in fact. And Mr. Smith's friends were compelled before the
end of the year to issue an explanation. This explanation was
signed by S. A. Blackwood, Evan H. Hopkins, Marcus Martin,
Donald Matheson, R. C. Morgan, Lord Radstock, J. B.
Smithers, and Henry Varley, and ran as follows: "Rumors of
an exceedingly painful character with regard to a prominent
teacher, which had for some time been in private circulation,
having now had currency given to them in your and other
papers, we consider it right, in the interests of truth, and in
justice to the person in question, to make the following statement: — Some weeks after the Brighton Convention, it came
to our knowledge that the individual referred to had, on some
occasions in personal conversation, inculcated doctrines which
were most unscriptural and dangerous. We also found there
had been conduct which, although we were convinced that it
was free from evil intention, was yet such as to render action
necessary on our part. We therefore requested him to abstain

---

[106] This is the ordinary account; but Mrs. Smith does not say this.
In her "My Spiritual Autobiography," 1903, p. 221, she writes: "In 1873 my
husband had come over to England to hold some meetings in the interests
of the Higher Life, or, what I prefer to call it, the Life of Faith. I soon followed him. . . ." This may be, however, only a comprehensive way of describing what actually took place.

[107] "Das völlige, gegenwärtige Heil durch Christum," ed. 4, p. 434. He
says he has fully discussed the matter in the first edition of his book, 1880,
and has there shown that Mr. Smith's whole fault lay in teaching privately
to some of his pupils "an extravagant esoteric doctrine of particular be-
trothal (*besonderen Verlobung*) with Jesus." We have not seen the first
edition of Jellinghaus' book, and do not know the grounds on which he
bases this opinion.

at once from all public work, and when the circumstances were represented to him in their true light, he entirely acquiesced in the propriety of this course, and recognized with deep sorrow the unscriptural and dangerous character of the teaching and conduct in question. In addition to the above, a return of the distressing attacks of the brain, from which he had previously suffered, rendered the immediate cessation from work an absolute necessity." This statement, it will be observed, makes it clear that Mr. Smith's withdrawal from the public agitation in the interests of the Higher Christian Life which was being vigorously carried on under his leadership, was not at his own instance or primarily on account of illness: his illness is brought in very pointedly as subsidiary and apparently as a subsequently arising justification of his retirement. His withdrawal was compelled by the intervention of his fellow-workers in the agitation, and that distinctly on the double ground of erroneous teaching and faulty conduct. Precisely what the nature of his " unscriptural and dangerous " teaching was, and exactly what the conduct was [108] which compelled intervention, the statement does not tell us, and a certain obscurity hangs about the matter accordingly until to-day.[109] It seems, however, to have been no secret at the time that

---

[108] We are assured by Mr. Smith's friends that this " indiscretion " in conduct " did not amount to immorality in word or act " (*The Presbyterian*, February 19, 1876, p. 9). The closing words in the following account of Mr. Smith, given by P. Kahlenbeck in Herzog-Hauck, " Realencyklopädie für protestantische Theologie und Kirche," ed. 3, v. p. 665, seem unjustifiably harsh: " About the same time with the news of the results [of Moody's preaching in Great Britain] there came another revivalist from across the ocean to Germany, Pearsall Smith, who addressed himself, however. more to those who were already believers, seeking to lead them to complete consecration to the Lord, and thus to sinlessness. He, however, after many had attached themselves to him, became in his personal life a disgrace to his doctrine."

[109] Fr. Winkler (" Robert Pearsall Smith und der Perfectionismus," ed. 2, 1915, pp. 18, 19) in closing his brief sketch of Smith's life mentions that the air was full of ugly rumors at the time when Smith broke off his work in England, but adds that the accessible sources of information do not render it possible to form a certain judgment of the truth of the matter. " Here," says he, " there is a task for investigation, and in general a satisfactory life of R. P. Smith, from the point of view of critical science, is still lacking."

Mr. Smith's dereliction was just that he had "lapsed into antinomianism,"[110] and one of the journals of the day tells us more explicitly,[111] that "the special error against which the gentlemen above named protested was the positive and unqualified assertion, that those who are 'in Christ' are no longer subject to the law of God, as the rule of their conduct; that they are lifted to a higher sphere of life, and walk in a freedom unknown to those who are strangers to the exalted experience of the new and better life."

This was the end of Mr. Smith's public career. He had yet a quarter of a century to live, a quarter of a century of suffering and seclusion after that short decade of exciting agitation and popular applause. A short, pathetic note from his wife to Mr. J. B. Figgis, one of his companions in that agitation, written in the midst of this quarter of a century (March 29, 1883) may contain the essential story of the whole of it: and it seems to us that it may bring us some aid — the aid of significant silences — to an understanding of what had happened following the Brighton Conference in 1875. "Mr. Smith's health," writes Mrs. Smith,[112] "is very poor, and he is obliged to live a very quiet and domestic life. He thinks he cannot live long, but, of course, this is something we know nothing about. Some physicians say that he has a very serious heart trouble. I believe myself that the springs of his life were sapped in 1874, and that existence can never be anything but weariness and suffering to him again in this world."

In our absorption in Mr. Smith's remarkable career we must not forget the woman by his side. We have seen her

[110] The phrase is Professor Thomas Smith's (*The British and Foreign Evangelical Review,* April, 1876, p. 251). Compare the words of Dr. Lyman H. Atwater (*The Presbyterian Quarterly and Princeton Review,* July, 1877, p. 419) who, warning his readers against the antinomian tendencies intrinsic in the Higher Life teaching, remarks: "Nor do we think it wrong or uncharitable in this connection to refer to the career of Mr. Pearsall Smith, who has been so conspicuous in Higher Life leadership."

[111] *The Presbyterian* (Philadelphia) of January 22, 1876, p. 8, where also the statement quoted above may be found. The matter is reverted to in the issue of February 19, 1876.

[112] "Keswick from Within," by the Rev. J. B. Figgis, 1914, p. 59.

finding Christ as her " all-sufficient Saviour " on the same day
with him; [113] and afterwards, when she had discovered that
she had not, after all, found Christ as her "all-sufficient
Saviour " but only as her halfway Saviour, leading him with
her into the devious pathway of "the second blessing" of
"holiness by faith." The immediately subsequent years of
eager propagation of this new-found gospel were as much hers
as his. At the great Oxford and Brighton meetings she played
almost as great a part as he did. Every day she gave a Bible
reading, ostensibly to the ladies, really to the gathering
crowds.[114] " But there were other portions of the day," writes
Mr. J. B. Figgis, of the Oxford Meeting,[115] " at which some
special speaker had the whole attention of the audience. This
was especially the case at 3 o'clock each afternoon, when Mrs.
Pearsall Smith gave a Bible Reading. Anything more impressive or delightful . . . than this series of addresses we
never remember hearing." Of the Brighton Convention he
writes: [116] " Such was the enthusiasm that each afternoon
people crowded together to listen to Bible-readings by Mrs.

[113] Here is Mrs. Smith's own account of the crisis (" My Spiritual Autobiography," pp. 179): "One day, however, a 'Plymouth Brother' friend,
hearing me tell my story, exclaimed 'Thank God, Mrs. Smith, that you have
at last become a Christian.' So little did I understand him, that I promptly
replied, 'Oh no, I am not a Christian at all. I have only found out a wonderful piece of good news that I never knew before.' 'But,' he persisted,
'that very discovery makes you a Christian, for the Bible says that whoever
believes this good news has passed from death unto life, and is born of God.
You have just said that you believe in it and rejoice in it, so of course *you*
have passed from death unto life and are born of God.' I thought for a moment, and I saw the logic of what he said. There was no escaping it. And
with a sort of gasp I said, 'Why, so I must be. Of course I believe this good
news, and therefore of course I must be born of God. Well, I *am* glad.' From
that moment the matter was settled."

[114] "Account of the Union Meeting for the Promotion of Scriptural
Holiness, held at Oxford, August 29 to September 7, 1874," p. 65: "At 4.30
Mrs. Pearsall Smith held a Bible Reading in the same room — a meeting
for ladies. Gentlemen who chose to attend were not excluded, and many
were present at this and the subsequent hours devoted to her Scripture
lessons."

[115] As cited, pp. 23–24.

[116] As cited, p. 37.

Pearsall Smith, with interest so keen that the Great Dome could not hold the numbers that came; and after the earliest days the readings had to be repeated an hour later in the Corn Exchange." She shared also, in a measure, her husband's retirement after 1875, but not with such complete, as not with such enforced, silence. Mr. Smith's literary as well as oral propaganda now came to an end.[117] Mrs. Smith, on the other hand, although from this time on she appeared only occasionally on public platforms, merely shifted her constant activity into more literary channels. Her calmness of disposition and greater facility of literary expression would have given her, in any event, a much larger hearing in this department of labor than her husband could ever have aspired to. Her book, "The Christian's Secret of a Happy Life," first published in 1875, has sold in innumerable editions, and Mr. Figgis feels able to say of it [118] that "with a wider circulation than any other book on holiness," it has had "greater effect in leading pilgrims to this River than any other writing of any other man or woman of the time, with the possible exception of some of Miss Havergal's." Of her writings in general he declares [119] that they have done "more than any publications ever written to extend the knowledge of the truth of sanctification." Through them [120] Mrs. Smith very easily becomes one

---

[117] Mr. Smith's books include "Holiness Through Faith," 1870; "'Walk in the Light,'" 1873; "Through Death to Life: the Lesson of the Sixth of Romans, with Illustrated Narratives"; "Bondage and Liberty; or, is Romans vii. to be the Continued Experience of the Christian?" and a series of booklets: "The Secret of Victory"; "Liberty in Serving Christ"; "Out of Darkness, into the Kingdom"; "A Clean Heart"; "Doers of the Word"; "Life's Great Sorrow, and its Remedy"; "Chosen to be Holy"; "'Thy Maker is Thy Husband'"; "The Way of Righteousness." He was also the editor of the periodical: *The Christian's Pathway of Power.*

[118] P. 10.

[119] P. 59.

[120] Hannah Whitall Smith's books include: "Holiness as Set forth in the Scriptures"; "The Record of a Happy Life: Memorials of Franklin Whitall Smith," 1873; "The Christian's Secret of a Happy Life," 1875; "The Veil Uplifted; or, the Bible its own Interpreter," 1886; "Every-Day Religion," 1893; "Soul Rest; or, the Joy of Obedience," 1893; "Child-Culture; or, the Science of Motherhood," 1894; "Christ Enough," 1895; "Old Testament

of the most conspicuous figures and one of the most influential factors in the Higher Life movement.

The hinge on which the whole system of Mr. and Mrs. Pearsall Smith's Higher Life teaching turns is the separation of sanctification from justification as a distinct attainment in Christ.[121] Sanctification is not thought of by them as involved in justification, and necessarily issuing from it in the unfolding of the salvation received through faith in the "all-sufficient Saviour." It is thought of, on the contrary, as a wholly new acquisition, sought and obtained by an entirely fresh act of faith. The fundamental fact of their religious experience was that they were dissatisfied with the results of their acceptance of Christ as their "all-sufficient Saviour, bearing" their "sins in His own body on the tree." [122] They felt the imperative need of a fuller salvation than that exercise of faith had as yet brought them, and they were unwilling to await God's slow methods of developing this fuller salvation through the conflicts of life. They supposed themselves to have obtained it at once by supplementing their first faith, through which they

---

Types and Teachings," 1899; "The Unselfishness of God," 1902; "Living in the Sunshine," 1906; "Difficulties of Life"; "God is Love"; "The Open Secret." There are besides a long series of booklets belonging to her earlier activity, such as: "The Way to be Holy"; "Abiding in Christ"; "The Christian's Cry"; "The Christian's Shout"; "A Word to the Wavering Ones"; "Jesus our Saviour from Sin"; "What Faith is and How to Exercise it." For a considerable period she contributed almost every month a paper to *The Christian's Pathway of Power.*

[121] Johannes Jüngst ("Amerikanischer Methodismus in Deutschland und Robert Pearsall Smith," 1875, pp. 62–66) has some admirable remarks upon this fundamental error of tearing apart two organically related things. "A justification which can endure for years without ripening true fruits of sanctification has been no justification at all in the evangelical sense. Can I talk of a fire which has been burning for years, but only to-day gives out warmth? According to both the Scriptures and the doctrine of the Church, justification and sanctification are two never to be separated twin sisters. He who is really justified and brought by Christ into the relation of a son to his God has received at the same time the impulse to sanctification, the impetus to an eternal advance. We must certainly bear in mind that the work of redemption in the Christian is a unitary whole."

[122] "The Record of a Happy Life," p. 16.

had received only justification, by an additional faith,[123] through which they received sanctification. And this they proclaimed to be really God's appointed way for the sanctification of His children. Their whole gospel consists essentially, therefore, in the proclamation of what they speak of as " sanctification by faith," by which they mean immediate sanctification by a special exercise of faith directed to that particular end. They imagine that thus they escape the necessity of awaiting the completion of salvation only in some future experience. Though it comes in two separate stages, it does not come in their view by process. Each of these stages is an immediate attainment following at once on the exercise of a faith particularly for its attainment. We are freed from the guilt of sin by one act of faith, and we are freed from the power of sin by another act of faith. It is the immediacy of the effect which is the point of chief insistence: the suspension of it on faith alone is only a means to that end. Hence the watchwords, " A present salvation " — " Jesus saves me *now!* " and " Sanctification by faith alone " — " Not by works or by effort, but by faith." [124]

This is what Mrs. Smith means when she describes the gospel which they proclaimed as " the glad tidings of a sufficiency to be found in the Lord Jesus, not only for our future salvation, but for our utmost present needs as well." [125] The present need which she has in mind is " real and present victory " over sin. And this is what Theodor Jellinghaus means when he explains [126] that the essential teaching of the Oxford Union Meeting was that " Jesus' blood, death and resurrection has delivered and delivers us not only from the guilt of sin, but also from all the power of sin, according to the Scriptures; that our sanctification comes not in parts through our efforts and self-mortifications according to the law, but through

[123] " The Record of a Happy Life," p. 37.

[124] Johannes Jüngst, as cited, p. 66, quotes a German periodical of the time, which remarks that this haste to secure " full salvation " is a sign of the times: " Get rich quick, get saved quick! "

[125] " The Record of a Happy Life," p. 37.

[126] " Das völlige, gegenwärtige Heil durch Christum," ed. 4, 1898, p. 431.

surrendering trust in Christ's redemptive power and leading."
The words are capable of a good sense, as also are the words of
his crisper statement: "Jesus is for every believing Christian
a present deliverer, who lets none sit and sigh in the bonds of
sin." But this good sense is not the sense intended. The sense
intended is that those who have been justified by faith may
attain sanctification also with equal immediacy by an equally
simple exercise of faith. This is, of course, perfectionism. The
exact variety of perfectionism that it is may be the object of
further enquiry, but it is already declared in this general statement that what is taught is some form of perfectionism. The
immediate attainment of sanctification and perfectionism are
convertible terms.

The whole whirlwind campaign conducted by Mr. Smith
from 1873 to 1875 was simply a concerted "drive" of American Perfectionism on the European stronghold.[127] It is interesting to observe the forces converging to the assault at the
Oxford Union Meeting. The presence on the platform there of
Dr. Asa Mahan, the chief figure among the Oberlin Perfectionists, by the side of Mr. Boardman and Mr. Smith, reveals
the significance of that meeting to the leaders of all types
of the perfectionist movement and their united effort to secure
through it their common ends. Whatever differences may have
existed among them in details of teaching, they were conscious
of unity among themselves and between them and their Wesleyan colleagues, in the main object in view. In point of fact,

[127] The air in London in the summer and autumn of 1875 was fairly
palpitant with the Higher Christian Life. Mrs. Julia McNair Wright "reported" the meetings for *The Presbyterian* (Philadelphia), perhaps a little
too sympathetically and yet with an eye open to excesses. Here is a vignette
or two (September 11, 1875, p. 2). She tells of "an errant American preacher"
who "preëmpted the platform," and "was long and loud" in his claims to
"complete sanctification," and "was more than righteously angry with all
who denied such a claim." She tells also of "an elderly sister" "who claimed
that even the roots of sin were dead in her heart." "We studied this sister's
case carefully," says Mrs. Wright, "and came to the conclusion that her
assertion was based, not on a fact of sanctification, but on an obtuseness of
perception. . . . She thought herself completely holy merely because her
conscience did not remonstrate where other people's consciences would have
lifted an outcry."

Dr. Mahan was in complete harmony with Mr. Smith in the essence of the matter. For him, too, sanctification — and he at least felt no hesitation in saying that he meant "perfect sanctification" — was at any moment obtainable by the Christian by a simple act of faith. For him, too, this sanctification was the work of the indwelling Christ alone. And for him, too, all effort on our part in the working of it out was excluded.[128]

Even on one point on which we might expect to find Dr. Mahan more decided than Mr. Smith there is no real difference between them, although Dr. Mahan gives to his exposition of it a somewhat greater fulness. We mean the reference to the sinner's own will of the really decisive action in every stage of his salvation, so that it may properly be said that his salvation continuously hangs purely on himself. Nothing could exceed the decisiveness of Mr. Smith's statements. The apostle Peter, referring to the case of Cornelius and his companions, speaks (Acts xv. 9) of God "purifying their hearts by faith." He is not speaking here of sanctification, it is true; but Mr. Smith takes him as if he were. The point to observe is that the passage, so understood, raises no barrier to Mr. Smith's affirming sharply, "We purify ourselves." God purifies us, says Peter; we purify ourselves, says Mr. Smith. We purify ourselves, but only by faith; and because we purify ourselves by faith, that means that we purify ourselves by using God to purify us; we by faith secure the purifying of our hearts by God. That is Mr. Smith's meaning when he says [129] — to quote the sentence fully now — "We purify ourselves, not by effort, but by faith; not by works, but by the precious blood of Christ." He does not dream of questioning that it is we that purify ourselves: it is only a question of how we do it. He goes further, and declares that even the maintenance of our purified condition depends wholly on ourselves. "This clean and humble condition, however," he continues, "is ours only

---

[128] For these elements of Dr. Mahan's teaching, see his "Scripture Doctrine of Christian Perfection," 1844, pp. 91, 92, 189, 190.

[129] "Holiness Through Faith," p. 76.

while the blood is applied by faith, for the very moment faith ceases to apply it, corruption ensues, and the same old bitter waters flow out."

It is not possible for Dr. Mahan, then, to be more decided than Mr. Smith is, in referring our sanctification wholly to ourselves as its procuring cause, at the very same moment that he is referring it to God as its effecting cause. But Dr. Mahan explains more fully how the matter is arranged.[130] The sinner, according to him, has power to "avail himself of proffered grace," to "abide in Christ." And, having this power, it is his part to exercise it; and when he exercises it he is properly said to sanctify himself — though, of course, it is the grace of which he avails himself, the Christ in whom he abides, that immediately works the sanctification. "The sinner," he says, "is able to make himself a 'new heart and a new spirit,' because he can instantly avail himself of proffered grace. He does literally 'make to himself a new heart and a new spirit,' when he yields himself up to the influence of that grace. The power to cleanse from sin lies in the blood and grace of Christ; and hence, when the sinner 'purifies himself by obeying the truth through the spirit,' the glory of his salvation belongs, not to him, but to Christ." It is our business to "yield ourselves up to the influence of grace," which is identified with abiding in Christ. "We can 'abide in Christ,' and thus bring forth the fruit required of us." But it is the grace to which we yield ourselves, the Christ in whom we abide, that is the immediate worker of the actual effect. "Herein also lies the ability of the creature to obey the commands of God, addressed to us as redeemed sinners." We cannot obey them directly by our own act, but we can obey them, indirectly, by using Christ as an instrument through which we may perform what is required of us. "'He that abideth in me, and I in him, the same bringeth forth much fruit; for without me ye can do nothing.' 'As the branch cannot bear fruit of itself, except it abide in the vine, no more can ye, except ye abide in me.' These declarations are literally and unqualifiedly true. We can 'abide in

[130] "Scripture Doctrine of Christian Perfection," pp. 92–93.

Christ,' and thus bring forth the fruit required of us. If by
unbelief we separate ourselves from Christ, we of necessity
descend, under the weight of our own guilt and depravity,
down the sides of the pit, into the eternal sepulchre." It is not
Christ in the last analysis that sanctifies us: He is merely the
instrument through which we perform this work. *Facit per
alium facit per se:* we are our own sanctifiers. Nevertheless,
Christ is the sole instrument through which we can sanctify
ourselves, and therefore faith, or " abiding in Christ," is the
sole thing we have to do in the matter. And here comes in the
Quietism of this teaching. " There is one circumstance connected with my recent experience," says Dr. Mahan,[131] " to
which I desire to turn the special attention of the reader. I
would here say, that I have forever given up all idea of resisting temptation, subduing any lust, appetite, or propensity, or
of acceptably performing any service for Christ, by the mere
force of my own resolutions. If my propensities, which lead
to sin, are crucified, I know that it must be done by an indwelling Christ. If I overcome the world, this is to be the victory, 'even our faith.' If the great enemy is to be overcome,
it is to be done ' by the blood of the Lamb.' " We sanctify ourselves; but we do it only by faith. Beyond faith there is nothing for us to do. The Christ, released for the sanctifying work
by faith, does the rest; and we must leave it to Him wholly.
In all these matters Mr. Smith's teaching simply repeats
Dr. Mahan's.

The primary zeal of these writers is naturally to establish
the completeness of the sanctification which we receive immediately on faith. This amounts in their hands, as it amounted
in the hands of the Wesleyans, to an attempt to substitute a
doctrine of Perfectionism for the doctrine of Perseverance, and
to discover the completeness of salvation in what we find in
our possession, rather than in " what we shall be," which an
apostle tells us is not yet made manifest. A very good example
of how Scripture is dealt with in this interest is supplied by
the address which Dr. Mahan delivered at the first morning

[131] Pp. 189, 190.

hour of the first full day of the Oxford Union Meeting.[132] He
seizes here upon the declaration of Heb. vii. 25, that Christ
is able to save to the uttermost them that come unto God
by Him. The idea of the "uttermost" of this passage includes
that of "glorification." As A. B. Davidson puts it ("The
Epistle to the Hebrews," p. 142): "The offering of Christ
enables men to draw near unto God; those that thus draw
near He is able to save completely, to bring them through all
hindrances to that honour and glory designed for them, which
He Himself has reached as the Captain of their salvation."
But for this Dr. Mahan has no consideration. He emphasizes
merely the strong assertion of the completeness of Christ's
salvation contained in the word, and then demands, dramatically: "Why is that power in Christ revealed, if we are not to
avail ourselves of it? Why are we told what He is able to do,
if we suppose that He is not ready to do it, or that we are
not authorized to expect it?" "Expand your hearts," he exhorts us; "expect to receive, *and receive* all that He is able
to do." "It is a great *sin*," he declares, "to 'limit the Holy
One of Israel.' *'Save to the uttermost!'* Dare to cease to
limit His power, and take Christ at His word!" The response,
of course, rises to the lips of every simple believer — that the
power of Christ to save to the uttermost is the foundation of
all our hope, and that everyone who believes in Him commits
himself to Him for this and nothing less; we do, all of us,
expect to receive and do receive it all, without limitation and
without diminution, and in this expectation, sure and steadfast, lies all our comfort and all our joy. But the revelation of
it would not need to be made to us — we would not need to
be told of it — if it were a present experience, not a matter of
hope. Nor would the revelation made in this great declaration
be true, if the measure of salvation we have already received
were all that we could look to Him for, if a complete salvation
both of soul and body were not the portion of His saints. And
certainly it would not be true if even the measure of salvation

[132] "Account of the Union Meeting for the Promotion of Scriptural
Holiness, held at Oxford, August 29 to September 7, 1874," pp. 49–52.

we have already received from Him were unstable or liable
to be lost to-morrow, its maintenance depending not on Him
but on us. The whole force of the declaration hangs precisely
upon our being as yet *viatores,* not *consummatores;* exactly
what it does is to give us assurance of the consummation. The
state of that Christian is sad indeed who must believe that
what he already is is the uttermost which Christ is able to do
for him, and that henceforth he must depend on himself.

On the afternoon of the very same day, Mr. Smith, in the
very same spirit, exhorted his hearers not to put an arbitrary
limitation on the power of God by postponing the completion
of their salvation to the end of their " pilgrimage," and so
virtually attributing to death the sanctifying work which they
ought to find rather in Christ. " Shall not Christ do more for
you than death? " he demands, and then he develops a *reductio
ad absurdum.* We expect a dying grace by which we shall be
really made perfect. How long before death is the reception of
such a grace possible? " An hour? A day? Peradventure a
week? Possibly two or three weeks, if you are very ill? One
good man granted this position until the period of six weeks
was reached, but then said that more than six weeks of such
living " — that is, of course, living in entire consecration and
full trust, with its accompanying " victory " — " was utterly
impossible! " " Are your views as to the limitations of dying
grace," he inquires, " only less absurd because less definite? "
The absurdity lies, however, only in the assumption of this
" dying grace " — Mr. Smith describes it as " a state of complete trust to be arrived at, but not until death." The Scriptures know of no such thing; they demand complete trust from
all alike, as the very first step of the conscious Christian life.
It finds its real source in the Arminian notion that our salvation depends on our momentary state of mind and will at
that particular moment. Whether we are ultimately saved or
not will depend, then, on whether death catches us in a state
of grace or fallen from grace. Our eternal future, thus, hangs
quite absolutely on the state of mind we happen (happen is
the right word here) to be in at the moment of death: nothing

behind this momentary state of mind can come into direct consideration. This absurd over-estimate of the importance of the
moment of dying is the direct consequence of the rejection of
the Bible doctrine of Perseverance and the substitution for
it of a doctrine of Perfection as the meaning of Christ being
our Saviour to the uttermost. The real meaning of this great
declaration is just that to trust in Jesus is to trust in One who
is able and willing and sure to save to the uttermost — to the
uttermost limit of the progress of salvation. Death in this conception of the saving Christ loses the factitious significance
which has been given to it. Our momentary state of mind at
the moment of death is of no more importance than our momentary state of mind at any other instant. We do not rest
on our state of mind, but on Christ, and all that is important
is that we are " in Christ Jesus." He is able to save to the
uttermost, and faithful is He that calls us, who also will do it.
He does it in His own way, of course; and that way is by
process — whom He calls He justifies, and whom He justifies
He glorifies. *He* does it; and therefore we know that our glorification is as safe in His hands as is any other step of our
salvation. To be progressively saved is, of course, to postpone
the completion of our salvation to the end of the process. Expecting the end of the process only at the time appointed for
it is no limitation upon the power of the Saviour; and looking
upon death as the close of the process is a very different thing
from looking upon death as a Saviour.

It will not require to be pointed out that the whole tendency of such arguments as we have just quoted is to establish
the immediate attainment by faith of all that can be subsumed under the term " salvation." Whatever Christ came to
give is ours to-day — not in developing, but in developed
form — for the taking. " You must agree with us," says Mr.
Smith,[133] " that whatever the Holy Spirit makes us to yearn
for, Christ came to give." Once the chief need of our soul was
pardon of our sins; we trusted Christ for it and got it. Now,
says he, substitute for pardon, " purity of heart," " holiness,"

[133] " Holiness Through Faith," p. 41.

being "filled with the Spirit," wholehearted "love to God and your neighbor," or "righteousness." Trust Christ for them and you shall have them all, in their completeness, here and now. Here is a doctrine of salvation, not by faith, but by faiths. Not content with dividing salvation into two halves, each of which is to be obtained by its own special act of faith, Mr. Smith pulverizes it into numerous distinct particles, each of which is to be sought and acquired by its own separate act of faith. The principle he lays down is that we are to trust in Christ for whatever our soul feels the need of, in each several instance, separately, and thus pile faith on faith. In this way we make our way through the Christian life by repeated acts of believing. Not only so, but it is to us in each several instance precisely according to our faith. " Full faith gives the full deliverance; partial faith the partial victory. So much faith, so much deliverance, no more, no less! "[134] It is our faith, then, which regulates our grace; and that means that it is we and not God who save. " The stream can ascend no higher than the passage that conveys its waters from the fountain. Faith is the channel. While the fountain is infinite in depth and in height, its flow is regulated by the channel opened for it." Mr. Smith himself draws the inference with reference to sanctification, and that with the emphasis of italics. " *If we would live up to the gospel standard of holiness, we must believe up to the gospel standard of faith.*"[135] This is a dismal outlook for those of " little faith," and indeed is as complete a doctrine of work-salvation as Pelagius' own. We advert to it, however, only by the way, as illustrative of Mr. Smith's general conception of " the way of life." Despite the confidence with which it is presented, it is held in subordination to the dichotomizing of salvation into justification and sanctification — each the product of its own act of faith. It may serve, however, to make clear to us that Mr. Smith supposes sanctification to be attainable in its fulness by mere faith — provided, of course, the faith is full faith. He that yearns for perfect sanctification can have it on perfect faith. " Full faith gives the full deliverance."

[134] P. 49. [135] P. 49.

Precisely how Mr. Smith conceived his full sanctification, however, it requires some further discrimination to make clear. Theodor Jellinghaus wishes us not to confound it with the "perilous" Wesleyan doctrine of a complete deliverance from sin.[136] He is right in insisting on this. Mr. Smith, like Mr. Boardman before him, teaches only that we are saved from all sinning; Wesley, that we are saved from all sin. The way Jellinghaus expresses the distinction between the two parties is this: [137] "Whereas Wesley teaches a sudden destruction (*einmaliges Ertöten*) of sin, so that every sinful motion that shows itself afterwards is a proof of the loss of this stage of Christian perfection, they" (that is, Messrs. Boardman and Smith) "teach that the Christian who hungers after deeper sanctification enters, through complete surrender and trust in the power of the blood of Christ to cleanse and preserve from all sin, into such a condition of the soul that he can continuously conquer. If he, nevertheless, stumbles again, he is to confess and repent and be cleansed again, and then enter boldly at once again into the same condition." They accordingly read I John i. 7, with an emphasis on the present tense: "If we walk in the light, the blood of Jesus Christ *cleanseth* us from all sin," and interpret it as meaning that our cleansing from sin is a continuous act. Wesley, on the contrary, read the text erroneously with a past tense: "The blood of Jesus Christ *has cleansed* us from all sin," and referred i. 8 to false teachers who denied that they were by nature sinful, needing redemption and purification by Christ. Jellinghaus goes on to say [138] that accordingly there was very little of the specifically Wesleyan doctrine heard at the Oxford Union Meeting. What was heard daily was declarations like these: "I feel my inward corruption more than ever"; "we remain in ourselves sinful and liable to sin"; "sinless perfection is pure nonsense — we do not dream of such a thing"; "no one can say I can be holy if I will"; "our strength in faith lies in the knowledge of our

[136] "Das völlige, gegenwärtige Heil durch Christum," ed. 4, 1898, p. 717.
[137] *Ibid.*, p. 721.
[138] P. 722.

own sinfulness and inability to conquer "; " you cannot be
cleansed to-day from all unconscious faults, but only from
the faults and sins which God has as yet revealed to you ";
" we are cleansed only according to our knowledge or our
light, therefore as we advance we discover sins in us hitherto
unknown, which must be destroyed "; " the sanctified Christian is not holy in his own nature, but only through a life of
faith in Christ, which makes and preserves us holy "; " it is
not sin that is dead, but we are dead to sin." All this amounts
only to saying that the precise teaching of Messrs. Boardman
and Smith is that when we receive Christ for sanctification
what we receive is a sanctifying power, able to make and keep
us holy in all our acts. In his earlier and better period Mr.
Boardman read the last clause, rather: " pledged to make and
keep us holy in all our acts." Mr. Smith reads it rather: " able
to make and keep us holy in all our acts — if we constantly
rest in perfect trust upon Him for it." Thus he throws us back
on our own activity to maintain (through Christ) our sanctification. The state itself into which we come by our trust is a
state of sanctification, of holiness, of perfection; but a state of
perfection of acts, not of heart, and so a state of perfection
which has its seat not in us but in Christ. We are perfect as
long as we abide in Christ. As Theodor Jellinghaus puts it: [139]
" It is a fundamental idea of the holiness-movement that sanctification and undisturbable peace of heart may be found and
maintained by believingly obedient rest on the sanctifying will
and gracious leading of God in Christ Jesus."

On its negative side this teaching denies that the sinful
nature is eradicated. Mr. Smith's language is not always exact
in this matter. He speaks repeatedly of " the purification of
the heart by faith " — partly, no doubt, because of his erroneous interpretation of Acts xv. 9 of sanctification. He even
sometimes speaks very confusingly of our having received " a
new nature " when we believed, though, when he does so, he is
careful to explain that the reception of this " new nature "
has not extruded the old nature. " Being born of God," he

[139] As cited, p. 435.

says,[140] "we received, in addition to the old nature (the flesh) a new nature, an actual existence begotten of God, of 'incorruptible seed.'" He even speaks in one passage, indeed,[141] most inconsistently, as if we had been changed in our very being by our union with Christ. "Shall the larger part of my being be held by Satan? Nay, henceforth it shall gravitate, not toward sin, but toward God. . . . No longer 'prone to wander,' though *liable* to it every moment, the current of our being sets toward God and not toward sin." All such language must be set down to the credit of traditional modes of expression intruding into Mr. Smith's speech. It does not express his own point of view. This he declares most explicitly. "Remember," says he,[142] "that *you* are now no better in and of yourself — only you have learned that you may dare to trust Christ for more than you ever conceived of before." He does not teach, he says,[143] "perfection in the flesh," but rather its exact antithesis. Nay, not only does there not dwell in the flesh any good thing, but "there never will be any good thing in it, or coming out of it." The Articles of the Church of England speak truly when they say, "This infection of nature doth remain, yea, in them that are regenerate." We are always to pray, "Forgive us our debts" — "for, even where we are not immediately conscious of displeasing God, there is so much in the debilitated condition of our moral nature, and in our lives, at an immense moral distance from the perfect holiness of God." The passage from which we are quoting[143] bears on its face an apologetical character. Mr. Smith is obviously defending himself from criticisms which had been made of his doctrine. His defense consists in the very emphatic denial that the "infection of nature" is eradicated or that we are ever freed wholly from sin.

He does teach, however, on the positive side, as he gives

[140] "Holiness Through Faith," p. 11.

[141] "Account of the Union Meeting for the Promotion of Scriptural Holiness, held at Oxford, August 29 to September 7, 1874," p. 186.

[142] *Ibid.,* p. 222.

[143] *Ibid.,* p. 150.

us at once to understand,[144] that we are freed from sinning.
Even here, however, a qualification is introduced. He does not
teach that we are freed from all sinning, but only from all
conscious sinning. He is willing to admit that there is a standard
of holiness above the holiness to which he contends that we may
attain. Our own perceptions of what is right and what is
wrong do not constitute a final standard: " Christ is our only
standard." " Trespass against the known will of God " is therefore only " one, but not the only, definition of sin." Under a
higher definition of sin we could not claim to be free from sin;
but under this lower definition of sin — which is one though
not the only definition of sin — we are, on believing, made
free from sin. We are not, then, " to ' continue in sin,' in the
sense of known evil." [145] " Christ came to save us from this."
This does not mean that Christ came to save us from this only.
Christ meets " in the atonement, not only all conscious guilt,
but also all unperceived evil in our moral condition or ways."
He saves us from all our guilt. But, besides saving us from our
guilt, he saves us also from all conscious sinning. " Christ came
to heal us, not to leave His Church one general hospital of
sick souls " [146] — a simile borrowed possibly from Isaac M.
See [147] and running in its implications somewhat beyond Mr.
Smith's meaning. For Mr. Smith does not deny that the Church
contains only sick souls. He only affirms that Christ, on being
appealed to for that purpose, takes away all the sickness of
which these souls are conscious. The Church may, and should,
then, contain none who are consciously sick; and the simile

[144] P. 150.

[145] P. 150.

[146] P. 151.

[147] " The Rest of Faith," 1871, pp. 14 f.: " We have heard that a certain
divine once said that the Church is an hospital where the inmates are all
sick. When they get well they are taken to heaven. The person speaking
may have believed it, but we believe the sentiment is of the devil. . . . If
so . . . then, too, the churches that are scattered here and there through
the land are only infirmaries where people come to be treated by the Great
Physician, who proceeds to cure the people by a slow process, in the meantime leaving them to the oversight of these sick ministering nurses," that is,
their pastors.

is intended to affirm strongly that this is Christ's purpose for His Church — that all its members should be free from all known sin. Christ " will give " us " not pardon only, but deliverance from the power and act of sin."

Mr. Smith thus very distinctly teaches a perfectionism. But the perfectionism which he teaches is equally distinctly a subjective, not an objective, perfectionism. It might be described as living up to the light that is in us. " It is noticeable," he says [148] " how constantly the Scripture speaks *to our consciousness,* rather than in absolute terms, carefully avoiding all metaphysical distinctions, and suiting its expressions to the realized need of the believing hearer." Accordingly we must define both sin and holiness relatively to our consciousness. Sin is " the *consciousness* of transgression of God's will "; holiness, " loving God with the whole heart, *unconscious* of any active, inward evil." What is asked of us, he explains, is not perfect faultlessness, but " a conscience void of offence "; not " absolute perfection," but living " up to the measure of to-day's consciousness." " The apostles," says he,[149] " neither claim an absolute holiness, nor open the door for a defiled conscience." He speaks on this subject from II Chron. xxix. 16, which tells us that the priests brought out of the temple all the uncleanness that *they found in it.* He emphasizes the words " all that they found." " It was ' *all that they found,*' that they carried forth," he says.[150] " We shall never know in this life the absolute purity of the Lord Jesus. We are, and ever shall be, at an immense moral distance from ' the Holy One,' but we cry to God for light to see the evil within us progressively as we are able to bear it; and we must accept strength from Him to ' carry forth ' all that in our dim vision we can see of ' filthiness out of the holy place.' " " There never was but One," he says again,[151] " who, from the cradle to the grave, was in every

---

[148] " Holiness Through Faith," p. 92: the italics are ours.

[149] " Account of the Union Meeting for the Promotion of Scriptural Holiness, held at Oxford, August 29 to September 7, 1874," p. 78.

[150] *Ibid.,* p. 60.

[151] *Ibid.,* pp. 60–62: the italics are ours.

thought, affection, and action, a complete burnt-offering. Everything in us is short of the perfect holiness of Christ. Yet we may, *up to the very furthest measure of our consciousness*, present ourselves living sacrifices, holy and acceptable to God. In each moment, as to the attitude of our souls we may, *so far as we see and know,* be wholly the Lord's, yet, with each day's increasing intelligence, being more and yet more completely the Lord's." " 'The blood cleanseth ' — is ever cleansing sin *from the conscience,* as it is progressively revealed "; which is not exactly what I John i. 7 says.

We perceive that in this conception of the nature of holiness, as living up to the light that is in us, a doctrine of progressive sanctification is developed, which is in harmony with perfectionism. The light that is in us may increase, and as it increases we rise to ever higher planes of living, but not to greater perfection. We can be perfect at each stage, while no stage is final: " there is no finality short of the Throne of God." My ignorance of God's will at each stage will permit me to act contrary to His objective will and yet maintain " the Rest of Faith," " entire consecration." " I breathe to-day," we are told,[152] " the atmosphere of the love of God, every past sin forgiven, and, through the blood of cleansing, without a present *sense* of transgression, — not a cloud to separate me from God; but I may not be able to walk to-morrow with a *clear conscience* in all the paths I tread to-day." " It follows from this," we are told again,[153] " that persons who have great light in the teaching of Scripture may be walking outwardly in advance of the sanctified but ignorant Christian, while yet the one is sinning and under a *sense* of condemnation, and the other, more ignorant but more trusting, walks with a *conscience* void of offence." A recently converted heathen, accordingly, living in a half-light, may commit many heathenish horrors and yet be none the less perfect. The standard being a subjective, not an objective one, our knowledge, not God's law, Christian perfection does not mean the fulfilling of all that

[152] " Holiness Through Faith," p. 59: the italics are ours.
[153] P. 60: the italics are ours.

God requires of a Christian, but only of all that a Christian's conscience, in its changing degrees of knowledge, requires from time to time of himself. The subjectiveness of the thought is intense, and one is tempted to apply the proverb, "Where ignorance is bliss, 'tis folly to be wise." [154]

Meanwhile Mr. Smith, on the basis of this theory of "adjusted holiness"—a phrase of W. B. Pope's—is able to declare the Christian at every stage of his development perfect; and having done that, he permits the idea of perfection to run away with him. Because the Christian is "perfect" at every stage of his development, Mr. Smith forgets that this perfection is, according to his own teaching, an imperfect perfection, perfect only to the Christian's consciousness; and that only the ultimate goal to which he is tending is objective perfection. He thinks now of an ever objectively perfect Christian advancing to a higher kind of perfection: the Christian is growing all the time, but he is growing not towards perfection —that he possesses all the time — but towards maturity. "Remember," he counsels us,[155] "that soul-health is very different from maturity. The sour apples in April are perfect. In October they are mature or 'perfected.' At the best we are but ripening, and yet I do not shrink from Scripture terms. The Bible speaks of many perfect men — 'as many as be *perfect* '—but adds, ' Not as though I were already *perfected.*' Little children are 'perfect' in all their immaturity. Do not confound an unobtainable, absolute, or divine holiness with an attainable victory over known sin. When Paul asserted, 'I know nothing against myself'—not as the ground of his justification, but of his conscience void of offence; and when John said, 'We keep His commandments and do those things that are pleasing in His sight'; they neither claimed absolute holiness nor opened a door for a defiled conscience." He is

[154] Compare the *reductio ad absurdum* of these teachings of Mr. Smith's given by Thomas Smith, *The British and Foreign Evangelical Review,* April, 1876. pp. 271–272.

[155] "Account of the Union Meeting for the Promotion of Scriptural Holiness, held at Oxford, August 29 to September 7, 1874," p. 323.

thinking here of the Christian's growth as if it were a normal growth like the ripening of an apple, at every stage perfect for that stage. It seems to have escaped his mind that a Christian's growth is a progressive cleansing from imperfections and has not "maturity" but "cleansing" as its goal. No doubt, says Johannes Jüngst,[156] properly, the growth which Mr. Smith's simile pictures to us would be the normal development of the divine life in a sinless soul; but it is not such a development that we poor sinners must pass through, and Mr. Smith also allows that we are in this world poor sinners: which is much the same thing that Lyman H. Atwater means when he declares[157] that Mr. Smith and his companions describe in such passages not such a growth as takes place on earth, but that which takes place in heaven.

But Mr. Smith has another expedient by which the perfection of the imperfect Christian can be vindicated. When expounding his doctrine of merely subjective perfection, at one point,[158] he drops this remark: "This might be termed a Christian, not a Divine, nor an angelic nor yet an Adamic 'perfection.'" That is to say, Christian perfection differs from all other kinds of perfection precisely in this, that it is not real perfection. That is a pity, if true, and provokes the jibe that one may then be a perfect Christian, it seems, without being a perfect man.[159] We are face to face here, in other words, with that Antinomian tendency which is the nemesis that follows on the heels of all forms of perfectionism. In order to vindicate the perfection of the Christian the perfection of

[156] As cited, p. 58.

[157] *The Presbyterian Quarterly and Princeton Review*, July, 1877, p. 415.

[158] "Holiness Through Faith," p. 59.

[159] Cf. Lyman H. Atwater, as cited, p. 408: "The late Bishop Janes, in his introduction to the book entitled *Pioneer Experiences*, says that, 'while entire sanctification makes us perfect Christians, it does not make us perfect men.'" The distinction between religious and moral perfection is curiously illustrated by a phrase of Mrs. Smith's ("My Spiritual Autobiography," p. 213): "I saw that God was good, not religiously good only, but really and actually good in the truest sense of that word." The notion that a being can be "religiously good" without being "really and actually good" is not a wholesome one.

his perfection is sacrificed. The cant phrase is that he is under no other law than that "of this dispensation," as if the law of holiness were a mere body of positive enactments which might vary from time to time and is not grounded in the nature of things, to say nothing now of the Nature of God Himself. Mr. Smith runs through the whole wretched story.[160] "We are not called to the standard of a different dispensation from that in which our lives are to be lived. We are not called to walk by the rule of angels, . . . nor yet even by the rule of the yet unfallen Adam. Neither is our standard that which will be ours in glorified bodies. . . . The obedience to which Christ is wooing us is not the legal obedience, a stainless perfection of knowledge and act impossible to these clouded faculties. . . . We are called to a hearty and supreme love of God, and to love our neighbour as ourselves. ' Love is the fulfilling of the law.' ' A *new commandment* I give unto you.' " " It would seem, then, that love is God's law and standard in this dispensation, and that whatever is not contrary to love does not now bring condemnation upon our conscience." "We cannot claim any perfection beyond this, that up to the furthest line of to-day's consciousness, we have the witness that we do love God and our brethren, and keep a conscience (or knowledge) void of offence." The only alleviation of this calamitous teaching is that the way is left open for growth; and it is gravely questionable whether this can consistently be done. "Each day of full obedience," we read,[161] " is a day of advancing knowledge. Yesterday's standard of walk will not answer for to-day. The past twilight did not discover some defiling bone in my tent, and it did not then bring an evil conscience; but, in the clearer light of to-day, the same contact would bring condemnation. The essential thing is not perfect light or perfect knowledge, but perfect obedience to the light and knowledge already bestowed."

In developing now this doctrine of the Christian's growth Mr. Smith sometimes speaks, as has already no doubt been

[160] " Holiness Through Faith," pp. 105 ff.
[161] P. 108.

noted, as if such a growth were not only normal for the Christian but sure to be experienced by him. The steps and stages of it seem to be represented as steps and stages through which Christ leads His children in conforming them more and more closely to His image. It nevertheless admits of some question how far Mr. Smith means to leave the impression that when once we have surrendered ourselves to Christ by faith we are in His hands and will not merely be " sanctified " by Him at once subjectively to our own consciences, but also gradually step by step " sanctified " by Him objectively, according to the standard of God's holiness. Cross-currents of doctrine affecting this matter are flowing through his mind. He wishes to throw on Christ, to whom our lives are committed in faith, the whole responsibility for their direction. He wishes to keep in the hands of the believer the whole responsibility for his experiences. The solution of the paradox which he ordinarily suggests is that we have the responsibility for being in Christ, and Christ has the responsibility for the lives of those in Him. He has difficulty, however, in working this suggestion out consistently in detail.

With respect to himself, at least, he is very emphatic that his commitment of himself to Christ was once for all. " I am of course," he says,[162] " with increasing intelligence always more completely given to God, yet as regards the deliberate, full surrender, I did it but once. Thenceforward I looked on it as a thing irrevocably done, just as we look on our marriage for life. We do not say the ' I will '; ' I give thee my troth,' of the marriage ceremony year after year, however more holy and complete may become the union of heart." The conception which informs this statement is not that of a moment by moment surrender, but of a surrender done once for all, and valid thenceforward for ever. And this conception is repeatedly thrown forward. It is very sharply asserted, with the emphasis on the divine side of the transaction — the side of " Preservation " as distinguished from " Perseverance " — in a passage

[162] " Account of the Union Meeting for the Promotion of Scriptural Holiness, held at Oxford, August 29 to September 7, 1874," p. 136.

like the following: [163] " As you definitely turned your back to
the world, and accepted pardon through Christ, so now, with
equal definiteness, give yourself to be the Lord's, wholly the
Lord's, and for ever the Lord's; to accept His will, to let Him
live your lives for you. . . . We dare to believe that He will go
on to ' perfect that which concerneth us.' We no longer faith-
lessly say, ' I shall some day fall by the hand of the enemy ';
but, rather, ' I will yet praise Him more and more.' We are
beginning to feel the power of that word, ' elect unto obedience '; and have given ourselves to a life of instantaneous,
implicit, uniform obedience to God. We do not expect to be
doing and doing this again and again, but always to recognize
that we *have done it.* Liable in each moment to fail, we expect
in the hourly miracle of grace, to be ' kept by the power of
God.' " If the sense of security expressed here seems not quite
as pure as the point of view occupied requires, and we still
hear of a constant " liability " to fail, we are glad to learn
from other passages that this liability is understood to be in
process of progressive elimination, and that it is not thought
of as " liability " to more than what is commonly called " backsliding." [164] " The old nature," we read,[165] " is liable in each
moment once more to assume its sway, and yet it may in each
moment be kept in the place of death and beneath our feet.
Faith's power over it becomes more uniform every day. There
will be conflict all along, but victory, not defeat." And
again: [166] " Should failure come, let us never delay for one
instant a full confession and restoration. Sometimes in this life
of full faith, there may come a momentary parenthesis of
failure. We must expect these, but if we stumble we will not lie
there an instant. The way back is open. ' If we confess our

[163] P. 152.

[164] Mr. Smith's assertions on this side reach their climax in the declaration he is reported to have made at the Brighton Conference: " I know no
example of a relapse from the higher life " (Herzog-Hauck, " Realencyklopädie für protestantische Theologie und Kirche," ed. 3, xxiii. p. 530, lines
29, 30).

[165] P. 321.

[166] P. 274.

sins, He is faithful and just to forgive us our sins, and to cleanse us from all unrighteousness.' He who thus claims instantaneous restoration, finds failure to fade out of the life and communion to become more and more unbroken."

Perhaps Mr. Smith's fundamental meaning here nowhere finds clearer statement than in the closing pages of " Holiness Through Faith." He is there speaking of our " abandoning " ourselves to Christ. " I like that word ' *abandon*,' " he says.[167] " It expresses the soul's attitude towards Christ. . . . It places the soul in Christ's hands, and makes Him alone responsible, if we may so speak, for all results. Our responsibility ends with the abiding: for then He Himself works in us both *to will* and to do of his good pleasure. A life of abiding is a life in which we sin not (I John iii. 6); we bear much fruit (John xv. 5); we ask what we will, and it shall be done unto us (John xv. 7); and then when He shall appear, we shall have confidence before Him at his coming." The antinomy is glaring and cannot be covered up. If, when we " abandon " ourselves to Christ, we place ourselves in His Hands, so that He becomes responsible for all results, does He not become responsible for our continued " abiding," too? But Mr. Smith intends to remove precisely that out of His responsibility and to reserve precisely that to us as the condition of Christ's keeping us. This amounts in the end, of course, to saying that He will keep us, if we will only keep ourselves: He will keep us in the way if we will only keep ourselves in the Way. Mr. Smith is, to put it in one word, teaching Quietism, not Evangelicalism. It is our will, after all, not Christ's will, that governs our lives. Christ can keep us only if we let Him keep us. We must first " abandon " ourselves to Him before He can take the responsibility for our lives. He can maintain His control of our lives only if we " abide " in Him. And at any moment we can — are " liable " to — snatch their control out of His hands.[168]

[167] Pp. 155, 156.
[168] Here is a hard saying of the Rev. D. B. Hankin's (" Account of the Union Meeting for the Promotion of Scriptural Holiness, held at Oxford, August 29 to September 7, 1874," pp. 83 f.): " I trusted the Lord as never

It is perhaps worth noting, in passing, that Mr. Smith
is not unaware that the determining place which he gives to
the will in religion requires of him a special doctrine of the
will. He even ventures upon a psychological grounding of this
doctrine. " President Edwards' teaching of the affections governing the will," he says,[169] " I believe to be untrue. The will
governs the affections. I believe in the yet older saying, that
' True religion resides in the will alone.' " His immediate purpose here is to protect his hearers from imagining that religion
consists in " frames and feelings." " Many are feeling deeply,"
he says, " but I desire to take you away from your emotions."
But in order to take them away from their emotions he propounds a purely voluntative theory of religion. This was held
to his credit when he went to Germany. Johannes Jüngst[170]
recalls that it was noted there that " he does not aim to call
out a movement of the emotions and feelings, but the will is
awakened almost in a Kantian fashion. Religion lies for him
chiefly in the will. He thanks God that it does not lie for him
in the feelings." The allusion in this closing sentence is to a
pathetic story which Mr. Smith tells at this place, of how,
when lying ill in South America, after the fall from his horse
which has already been mentioned, in the deepest nervous
depression and in the midst of powerful assaults of Satan,
he " was thankful then that religion was in " his " will." " To
all his [Satan's] attacks I said, ' I *will* believe: live or die, in
agony or in joy, I *will believe!* ' I seemed as one with his back
to a rock and beset by devils. . . . I know whereof I affirm;

before, and found Him faithful to His promises in keeping me from falling;
when I have stumbled, as I do even now sometimes, the failure is mine not
Christ's." He means that it is only when his trust fails that Christ's keeping
fails. But he also means that when his trust fails Christ's keeping fails. He
means, that is, that Christ's keeping depends on his own trusting. Christ has
promised to keep him from falling; and Christ will be faithful to that
promise — that is, will keep him from falling. Nevertheless he falls whenever he wishes to, and Christ does not keep him from doing so.
    [169] " Account of the Union Meeting for the Promotion of Scriptural
Holiness, held at Oxford, August 29 to September 7, 1874," p. 134.
    [170] As cited, p. 96.

I speak that I know, when I say God's salvation is beyond the region of our emotions." Of course there is defective analysis here and consequent self-deception. Because the "emotions" he has in mind were not the determinants of his will on this occasion, he fancies that the will is not determined by any emotions. He is not aware that in the sentence from Fénelon on which he supports himself, the term "will" includes the affections. He does not even stop to consider that when he makes religion to consist in "faith," or "trust" as he calls it here — with "no sensible religious emotion for almost months, I *did* trust God, not only for final salvation, but for a conscience void of offence" — he is placing its essence in an affection. He is only intent on suspending all religion on undetermined acts of the will. He conceives of himself as able at any time to act in either part by a sheer arbitrary choice, and, whatever Fénelon meant, Mr. Smith means to hang all religion on such arbitrary choices. He "abandons" himself to Christ, he "abides in" Christ — or he falls away from Christ by sin — all by arbitrary acts of will. It is on these arbitrary acts of will that all the divine operations in salvation depend.

For "substance of doctrine" the teaching of Mrs. Smith does not differ greatly from that of her husband. There is an occasional slight difference in modes of statement. There is also perhaps some difference in emphasis. The mystical aspects of the doctrine — especially its Quietistic elements — are more dwelt upon in Mrs. Smith's teaching. Their Quaker inheritance in general colors her presentation of their common teaching as it does not his, and this is increasingly so as the years go on. It is quite evident that Mrs. Smith found a growing pleasure in presenting her doctrine in a Quaker mold. She held also very strongly a doctrine of universal salvation, and declared that she would not be muzzled in the expression of it, although, in point of fact, it is not obtruded in her "holiness" teaching.[171] Mrs. Smith's career as a religious writer, moreover, extended over more than thirty years. It is not strange that

[171] "My Spiritual Autobiography," pp. 222 f.

she does not preserve entire consistency with herself through all these years in the details of her teaching, or perhaps the same zeal in the propagation of this or another of her peculiar conceptions. There is evidence that she not only gave up wholly in later years the separation of sanctification from justification, which was the very heart of her teaching at the height of her propaganda, but very much mitigated the assertion of perfection. Nevertheless, what she teaches on "holiness" during the Higher Life movement is what Mr. Smith teaches, and, in general, she teaches it just as he teaches it, often in precisely the same terms.

In the opening pages of her chief book, "The Christian's Secret of a Happy Life," she defines "the Higher Christian Life," to the propagation of which they had both given themselves with single-hearted devotion. "Its chief characteristics," she says,[172] "are an entire surrender to the Lord, and a perfect trust in Him, resulting in victory over sin, and inward rest of soul." The adjunction of "rest of soul" to "victory over sin" in the description of the thing sought — she says, rather, the thing obtained — is perhaps characteristic of her personal attitude. It is perhaps also characteristic of her personal attitude that the sentence is given a somewhat mechanical turn. She wishes victory over sin and inward rest of soul, and she knows how to get them. The recipe to be followed is, "entire surrender to the Lord and a perfect trust in Him." The result will follow. In a later book,[173] at least, we find her discoursing of "inevitable law" in these high spiritual matters, and announcing with reference to them the perhaps disputable proposition, that "the man who discovers the law of anything possesses a power in regard to that thing as limitless as the law itself." Mrs. Smith, now, knows the law of life: it consists in surrender and trust. We are in a position, accordingly, to control this life. These slight shades of suggestion apart, however, the sentence, in its isolation, is unexceptionable. All Christians understand that victory over sin and inward rest of soul come — and come only — by entire surrender to the

<hr />

[172] P. 37.   [173] "Every-Day Religion," 1893, p. 170.

Lord and perfect trust in Him. The sentence must be put in its setting in Mrs. Smith's system to bring out its meaning to her. That setting is supplied in part in the little autobiographical sketch which she gave the ladies in her first Bible Reading at the Oxford Union Conference.[174] "I saw," she said, "that sanctification was by faith as well as justification. That the same Saviour who delivers from the guilt of sin, delivers also from its power. And that the very righteousness which the law demanded, but failed to procure, was made possible and easy by grace. . . . It had been an unspeakable blessing to me to be delivered from the guilt of my sin, but it was infinitely more glorious to be delivered from its power. For to me the consequences of sin were not so dreadful as the fact of the sin itself." By the "fact of sin," however, she means merely the fact of sinning: it is from the power of sin, not from the corruption of sin, that she so yearns to be delivered. Accordingly she goes on to express herself thus: "The same grace that saved us must keep us. The same Saviour who bore our guilt for us must do our daily work for us also."

It is "our daily work" that she has particularly in mind. Her preoccupation is with Christianity as a This-world religion, that is to say, in contrast both with an Other-world and a Next-world religion;[175] and this preoccupation supplies the major-premise of all her argumentation. "Did He [Christ] propose to Himself," she exclaims,[176] "only this partial deliverance," which we have as yet experienced? "Was there a hidden reserve in each promise, that was meant to deprive it of its complete fulfilment?" Is a deliverance only partial, we ask, however, because it consumes time? Are promises deprived

[174] "Account of the Union Meeting for the Promotion of Scriptural Holiness, held at Oxford, August 29 to September 7, 1874," pp. 66–68.

[175] This also was no doubt a result of her Quaker training. Speaking of her girlhood, she writes ("My Spiritual Autobiography," p. 143): "The Quakers rarely touched on the future life in any way, either as regarded heaven or hell. Their one concern was as to the life of God in the soul of man now and here, and they believed that where this was realized and lived, the future could be safely left in the Divine care." Preoccupation with the present was therefore natural to her.

[176] "The Christian's Secret of a Happy Life," pp. 17 f.

of their complete fulfilment because they are not fulfilled completely before the time of their complete fulfilment arrives? Mrs. Smith is only endeavoring to excite in the minds of her readers a feeling that they must have all that is promised them at once, or else the promise has failed. She wishes to betray them into an unwillingness to await the day of redemption and meanwhile to rejoice in the earnest of the inheritance that has been given to them. She wishes them to demand, like greedy children, all the feast prepared for them in the first course; and so she exhorts them to "settle down on this one thing, that Jesus came to save you, now, in this life, from the power and dominion of sin, and to make you more than conquerors through His power." For proof, she can only say that "not a hint is given, anywhere, that this deliverance was to be only the limited and partial one with which Christians so continually try to be satisfied?" As if anybody supposes that! It is the good side of the Higher Life agitators that they manifest an active impatience with sinning. They revolt under and resent its bondage. It is a different matter to show impatience with God. And their reasoning too often runs on no other lines than these — if they are redeemed by the blood of Christ they have a right to all its fruits, and they wish them at once. They ask, "Is not Christ able to save to the uttermost?" and demand, "Why, then, does He not do it?" They are not willing to wait on God, and, unable to account for His method of saving by process, they chafe under the delay and require all their inheritance at once. This is the underlying attitude of the whole movement, and it is as manifest as anywhere else in the opening chapters of "The Christian's Secret of a Happy Life." All the Biblical assurances of the completeness of Christ's salvation are assembled, and then the demand made, Give me all of it — now. Mrs. Smith very properly explains that the whole work of our perfecting is done by God. Our part, she says, is only trusting it to Him that it may be done. Perhaps this is not precisely the same as trusting God to do it. We must not entrust it to God to be done, as we assign a job to a workman and require him to do it according to speci-

fications. We must just trust God to do it — it, as all other
things — in His own perfect way. The former attitude makes
God our instrument to do our bidding. It is the attitude of the
Higher Life movement.

There are two parts in "the work of sanctification," Mrs.
Smith teaches. There is man's part; and there is God's part.
It is man's part to place himself in God's hands for sanctification; it is God's part then to sanctify him. We say "then" to
sanctify him, for God can do nothing towards sanctifying him
until the man places himself in His hands for the purpose. "In
the divine order," says Mrs. Smith,[177] "God's working depends
upon our co-operation. Of our Lord it was declared that at a
certain place He could do there no mighty work because of
their unbelief. It was not that He would not, but He could not.
I believe we often think of God that He will not, when the real
truth is that He cannot. Just as the potter, however skilful,
cannot make a beautiful vessel out of a lump of clay that is
never put into his hands, so neither can God make out of me a
vessel unto His honor, unless I put myself into His hands. My
part is the essential correlation [she means "correlative"] of
God's part in the matter of my salvation; and as God is *sure*
to do His part all right, the vital thing for me is to find out
what my part is, and then do it." It is creditable to Mrs.
Smith's intelligence that she fully recognizes that, things being as she describes them, the vital thing in our salvation is our
part in it, not God's. The initiative — the decisive thing — lies
in our hands: if we do our part God's part follows of itself.
"When a soul is really given up to God He never fails to take
possession of it, and He then begins to work on that soul all
the good pleasure of His will" — not before. "It is like making the junction between the machinery and the steam engine," we are told.[178] "The machinery is yielded up to the
power of the engine, and the engine works it, and it goes easily
and without effort because of the mighty power that is behind

---

[177] "The Christian's Secret of a Happy Life," p. 36.
[178] "Account of the Union Meeting for the Promotion of Scriptural
Holiness, held at Oxford, August 29 to September 7, 1874," p. 291.

it." " Thus," we read, " the Christian life becomes an easy and natural life, when it is the outward development of the Divine life working within. When we give ourselves to Him He claims us, and this is where our safety lies — not in our giving, but in His taking. What we have to do is to put our will right over on His side, and then He will take possession of it, and work it for us, making us really willing to do His will." We must first, by an act of will, give Him our will, and then — but only then — He works our will for us. " And if God thus gets possession of us," we read next — " thus," that is, by an act of our will giving Him our will — " and causes us to walk in His statutes and to keep His commandments and do them, we shall find it an easy and happy thing to live in conformity with His will." " He works miracles in a man's will," we read in another place (p. 161) — " when it is put in his hands."

The primary thing to observe here is, of course, the suspension of the whole process on the human will. We say " the whole process " because it emerges that not only is God helpless to work on and in us unless and until we truly place ourselves in His hands for the purpose, but He is equally helpless to keep us in His hands when once He has undertaken the work on and in us that has been committed to Him. We must not only surrender ourselves to Him, but we must also " abide " in Him. Mrs. Smith told the ladies at the Oxford Union Meeting — using the simile of the clay and the potter again — that " the part of the clay is simply to be put into the potter's hands, *and to abide there passively*." [179] " Put yourselves then into God's hands," is the exhortation, " as clay in the hands of the potter, and trust Him. But do not take yourselves back. Having given yourselves to Him you must abide in Him — you must *stay* there. You must let Him mould and fashion you." Very strange clay this, passive in the potter's hands, to which the potter can do nothing unless it lets him! Mrs. Smith's main purpose here is to preach her gospel of passivity in the potter's hands: " The potter must do all the work." " When we have put our case in the Lord's hands our part is

[179] *Ibid.*, pp. 295–296.

simply to 'sit still,' for He will not rest until He has finished
the matter." " And we must remember this — that *if we carry
a burden ourselves the Lord does not carry it.*" [180] What we
need to note now, however, is, not the passivity itself, but the
fact that it is voluntary — not merely in the sense that we put
ourselves in the potter's hands voluntarily, but that we maintain our passive attitude in His hands voluntarily. Thus, as
we have said, everything is made to depend, not on the Potter's
will, but on our own. And it is anything but a passive will that
Mrs. Smith has in mind; she emphasizes the energy of the volition by which we place ourselves in God's hands in a very decisive fashion. Illustrating the right Christian method of
meeting the troubles and trials of life from Ps. lv. 6–8, she tells
us that we must not only *have* the wings of a dove, but must
use them if we wish to escape. " The power to surrender and
trust," she says,[181] " exists in every human soul, and only needs
to be brought into exercise." It belongs to us to bring it into
exercise. " With these two wings we *can* 'flee' to God at any
moment; but, in order really to reach Him, we must actively
use them. We must not merely want to use them, but we must
do it definitely and actively. A passive surrender or a passive
trust will not do. . . . We must do it definitely and practically, about each detail of daily life as it comes to us." Though
we are passive in God's hands and do nothing to work out our
own salvation — nothing, that is, directly — behind that passivity we are intensely active, instituting and maintaining it.
We enter into the surrendered life by an act of our own will;
it is a very definite and energetic act by which we abandon
ourselves to God. On the emergence of each trial we again act;
it is a very definite act by which we take it to God and leave
it with Him. It is not a " passive " but an " active " surrender
and trust, a very definite and decisive act. But this is all that
we do — we must not endeavor to tunnel the mountains in our
path, nor to make our way around them, we must just spread

---

[180] " Account of the Union Meeting for the Promotion of Scriptural Holiness, held at Oxford, August 29 to September 7, 1874," p. 299.
[181] " The Christian's Secret of a Happy Life," pp. 243–244.

our wings and soar over them. The wings are the symbol of
" surrender and trust "; they belong to us, and it belongs to us
to use them.

Behind this teaching lies a very definite doctrine of the will.
So important to her system does Mrs. Smith feel this doctrine
to be, that she devotes a whole chapter to it, both in " The
Christian's Secret of a Happy Life " and in " Every-Day Religion," her two most didactic volumes. In both chapters alike
her chief purpose is to separate religion from the surface play
of emotions. In order to do this, she makes religion an affair
of the will alone, and asserts that the emotions have nothing
to do with the will. You " yield " yourself to God, and that is
the end of it. " You meant it then, you mean it now, you have
really done it. Your emotions may clamor against the surrender, but your will must hold firm. It is your purpose God looks
at, not your feelings about that purpose; and your purpose, or
will, is therefore the only thing you need to attend to." [182] In
writing-in a basis for such assertions she develops a clear psychological voluntativism. The will is affirmed to be " the governing power in man's nature." " If the will is set right," we
are told,[183] " all the rest of the nature must come into harmony." And by the will is meant here simple volition. " By
the will," she explains [184] " I do not mean the wish of the man,
or even his purpose, but the deliberate choice, the deciding
power, the king, to which all that is in the man must yield
obedience." " It is," she adds, " the man, in short, the ' Ego '
that which we feel to be ourselves." And then she expounds:
" There is something within us, behind our emotions and behind our wishes, an independent self, that, after all, decides
everything and controls everything." Of course Mrs. Smith
meets difficulties here. As she works out her problem the notion
of the will she operates with vibrates between bare volition
and the total subjectivity. She is found identifying it with
what the Bible calls " the heart," " the interior self, the controlling personality of our being." [185] She is found, despite the

[182] " The Christian's Secret of a Happy Life," pp. 66 f.
[183] P. 80.　　　[184] P. 80.　　　[185] " Every-Day Religion," pp. 69, 72.

fact that the will is the king, to which all must yield obedience, speaking of a self behind the will, governing it. "I can control my will," she says; and we are exhorted "to keep the will steadily abiding in its centre, God's will." "Your part then is," she says,[186] "simply to put your will, in this matter of believing, over on God's side." What this "you" is which controls the will, which itself controls everything, and which is indeed itself the "Ego," she is helpless to explain. The will which is to control is the very will that is to be controlled. Mrs. Smith has no option here, of course; she must speak in this confusing way if she is to make — as she wishes to make — a bald volition possible to man and controlling in his destiny. I can choose to believe in that *bald* way, she affirms, when nothing seems true to me. She merely finds herself moving upward in that infinite *regressus* up which all the advocates of her notion of a determining will, itself undetermined, journey with no hope of a return. All that concerns us at the moment is to note that Mrs. Smith's whole doctrine of the Higher Christian Life is founded on this doctrine of the will. Its starting point lies in the assumption that it is always in our power just to say "I will." "The thing we are to do is to 'choose,' without any regard to the state of our emotions, what attitude our will shall take towards God." "The whole question lies in the choice of our will."[187]

The "surrender" and "trust" which "constitute our part" in "the work of sanctification," and which are the precedent conditions of God undertaking His part, are, then, always in our power. Precisely what they are is not made quite so plain. They are sometimes elaborately treated, not as two names for one thing or two aspects of a single act, but two distinct acts;[188] and we are told that we must have both "an entire surrender" and "an absolute trust." Difficulty is experienced, however, in so defining them as to establish a plain distinction. In the effort to do so "surrender" is sometimes spoken of as if

186 "The Christian's Secret of a Happy Life," p. 82.

187 "Every-Day Religion," p. 79.

188 "The Christian's Secret of a Happy Life," pp. 246 ff.

it meant merely "giving up" in the abstract — not giving up ourselves trustingly to God, but just accepting the course of life that comes to us. "Trust" then becomes the word for leaving ourselves in God's keeping. At other times the attempt to separate the two things, at least, is abandoned. In the discussion in "Every-Day Religion," [189] Mrs. Smith tells us that she prefers the term "yield" to "consecrate," to express what she means by "surrender." "Consecration" is apt, she says, to express something too active, and indeed self-glorifying; it is an Old Testament word. We may consecrate our wealth to a given object; we yield ourselves to the care of a physician. "In the one case we confer a favour; in the other we receive a favour." The idea sought to be conveyed is not that of sacrificing, but of abandoning. We yield ourselves to God as, when sick, we submit utterly to the nurse's ministrations, or, when lost, we put ourselves wholly in the hands of the guide. "To yield to God means to belong to God, and to belong to God means to have all His infinite power and infinite love engaged on our side." "Trusting," now, she very naturally adds [190] "can hardly be said to be distinct from yielding. . . . It is, in fact, the absolute correlation [she means "correlative"] to it. . . . Trusting, therefore, simply means that when we have yielded ourselves up unto the Lord, or, in other words, have made ourselves over to Him, we then have perfect confidence that He will manage us and everything concerning us exactly right, and we consequently leave the whole care and managing in His hands." So far as a distinction is here made out, it would seem to be that "surrender" is thought of as the act by which we place ourselves in God's hands, and "trust" as the succeeding state of confidence in His holy keeping of us. The point of importance, however, is not the discrimination of the words, but the establishment of the nature of the transaction which is expressed by them. This is made very clear. It is made very clear, for example, in this sort of a declaration: You have first to surrender your will into His hands — and by your will she means your liberty of choice — and He will take possession of

[189] Pp. 36 ff.   [190] P. 40.

it and work in you by His own mighty power " to will and to do of His good pleasure." [191] Having vindicated to us an ineradicable power of willing according to our own choice, Mrs. Smith now lays on us as our one duty in the use of this liberty of choice — to renounce it. The only use the religious man can put his will to is, by an energetic action of it, to work a complete exinanition of it.

Our part in sanctification — " surrender " and " trust " — having been duly done, God then does His part. His part is " to sanctify us." The effect is, of course, instantaneous. As precisely what has happened is that we have ceased to work and God has taken over the work, what results is that hereafter we do nothing and God does all. This is a doctrine of Quietistic Perfectionism. Mrs. Smith's Quietism is very explicit and very complete. No simile is too strong to express it. As we have had repeated occasion to note, a favorite illustration with her is derived from the clay and the potter. By our act of surrender we put the clay into the potter's hands. He molds it then according to His will. She expresses what happens without figure by saying as repeatedly that God takes our wills and works them for us.[192] He takes our wills, not our

[191] One of the most remarkable things in this passage (p. 72) is the use of Phil. ii. 13 in it. Henry A. Boardman, in his excellent examination of the teaching in " The ' Higher Life ' Doctrine of Sanctification," 1877, pp. 143 ff., animadverts on the violence done to this text by Mr. Smith in such passages as these: " Is not the promise worthy of confidence, that God will work in us to will and to do of His good pleasure, and if He does this, shall we not have to cease working ourselves? " — " God worketh in you to will and to do; therefore cease working." The Apostle says God worketh in you, therefore work. Mr. Smith says, God worketh in you, therefore cease working. Mrs. Smith, in some of her allusions at least, has learned to avoid this gross wresting of the text, though at the cost of a great inconsistency. " When we have surrendered the working of our wills to God," she says in " Every-Day Religion," 1893, p. 76, " and are letting Him ' work in us to will and to do of His good pleasure,' we are then called upon to ' set our faces like a flint ' to carry out His will, and must respond with an emphatic ' I will ' to every ' Thou shalt ' of His." The inconsistency of this with her Quietism is glaring. And the wresting of Paul in suspending God's working on our working instead of vice versa remains unaffected. Compare also pp. 72 and 80.

[192] For example, " The Christian's Secret of a Happy Life," p. 190: " God's way of working . . . is to get possession of the inside of a man, to take the control and management of his will, and to work it for him."

hearts or natures. The perfection that results, therefore, is a perfection of acts, not of heart or of nature. We put our wills into His hands, and He thenceforth works them for us. No, not exactly thenceforth, but as long as we leave them in His hands. It all depends on us, in the end, therefore; and that throws a fatal uncertainty over it all. At least, that is the way Mrs. Smith looks at it, from the point of view of her doctrine of arbitrary will. From our own point of view, as the heart remains unsanctified, we should have to say that it throws a fatal certainty of sinning over it all. "No safe teacher of this interior life," says she,[193] "ever says that it becomes impossible to sin; they only insist that sin ceases to be a necessity, and that a possibility of continual victory is opened before us."

The next sentence is somewhat oddly phrased. "And there are very few, if any, who do not confess that, as to their own actual experience, they have at times been overcome by at least a momentary temptation." Mrs. Smith scarcely means that it was a "momentary temptation" which overcame them: there seems no reason why a temptation which lasts but a moment should be thought to be particularly potent, and "momentary" does not appear to mean "sudden" — unexpected — and therefore unprepared for. She doubtless means that they are momentarily overcome by temptation. If so, she tells us that "few, if any," make "the possibility of continual victory" which is "opened before us" an actuality. "At times" — which must mean a plurality of times — they are at least momentarily overcome by temptation. If this be true, then their perfection is not very perfect: it is broken in upon "at times" by sin. They may be rather better in their Christian lives than the general run of Christians, but when it comes to talking of perfection they are really no more perfect than others. This is given an even stronger significance by the next sentence. "Of course," we read, "in speaking of sin here, I mean conscious, known sin." She is not speaking of "sins of ignorance," or of "what is called the inevitable sin of our nature." These things she leaves to the theologians to

---

[193] "The Christian's Secret of a Happy Life," p. 128.

discuss; she deals only in practical things — a rather cavalier way of speaking, one would think, of such tremendous realities. From this we learn, however, that the sins which she considers it possible to escape are only "conscious, known sins," and also that the sins which "few, if any," wholly escape falling into "at times" — fewer or more numerous times — are distinctively "conscious, known sins." Despite her waving aside all discussion of "sins of ignorance," she immediately enters into a discussion of them, the result of which seems to be that we can do very wrong things and not sin. Returning from this digression, she instructs us, not very consequently, that, as "the highway of holiness is not a *place* but a *way*," we may step out of the path for a moment without obliterating the path, and we may step back into the path the next moment. It is not clear to us that a "path" has any superiority over a "place" in these matters, but, as the application is obscure, that may pass. The trouble does not seem to be with the path or the place — whichever "the highway of holiness" may be compared to — but with the bad habit of stepping out of it with the assurance that we can just as easily step back again. We have certainly lost sight of perfection in the course of the discussion, except, perhaps, as a bare possibility, a possibility of which "few, if any," avail themselves. Nevertheless Mrs. Smith has no hesitation in asserting the possibility of continuous holiness, as if it were the experience of many and might easily be the experience of all. Of actually sinning she says,[194] "There is no necessity for it whatever."

Perhaps the most remarkable element in Mrs. Smith's teaching in this matter, however, comes to light when [195] she undertakes to expound the "causes of failure in this life of full salvation," that is to say, to explain why those that are perfect fall at times into sin. "The causes do not lie," she says, "in the strength of the temptation, nor in our own weakness, nor above all in any lack in the power or willingness of our Saviour to save us." They lie simply in this: that we are cherishing in our heart something which is contrary to the will of

[194] P. 142; cf. p. 242.   [195] Pp. 138 f.

God. That appears to amount, briefly, to this — that the perfect man sins because he is not perfect. She illustrates as follows: "Any conscious root of bitterness cherished toward another, any self-seeking, any harsh judgments, any slackness in obeying the voice of the Lord, any doubtful habits or surroundings, — these things or any of them, consciously indulged, will effectually cripple and paralyze our spiritual life." Which, being interpreted, declares to us that if we are living in sins — conscious sins, too, note — "any conscious root of bitterness," "consciously indulged" — why, we are liable to sin. And we are further told that we may be thus living in sin, though we seem to ourselves and to others to be triumphantly living the life of victory. What then becomes of consciousness as the norm of all?

It is not without its importance that we should note that Mrs. Smith is inclined sometimes to represent this liability to failure as an experience belonging particularly to the early stages of sanctification. She writes to her son,[196] when he had just entered upon the "higher life" of complete consecration, that it cannot be expected to be wholly unbroken. "It often happens," she says, "in the beginning of this life of faith, that there are temporary failures, and that the feet do sometimes stumble. But this need not discourage thee. Sanctification is not a thing once done, and done for ever; it is a life, a walk, and if we stumble we can get up again. It is a life of trust, moment by moment; and if for one moment we fail, that is no reason why we should not trust the next moment." It even appears that in the process of growth hinted at here the sanctification may penetrate inward from the acts to the heart. This is, no doubt, formally denied in the most vigorous words. She writes to her son in the autumn of 1871,[197] and prints it in 1873, on the very verge of the great London agitation: "But do not expect, dear boy, ever to find thy old nature any better or any nearer thy ideal; for thee never, never will. Thee thyself, that is, thy old nature, will always be utterly

---

[196] "The Record of a Happy Life," 1873, p. 88.
[197] *Ibid.*, p. 119.

vile, and ignorant, and corrupt; but Jesus is thy life now. It is with thee, ' No more I,' but Christ who liveth in thee. And is not this glorious — to lose thy own life, and find Christ's divine life put in its place? . . . Never look into thy own heart then for any sort of satisfaction or comfort. Thee will never find any goodness there, — no stocks of virtue laid up to draw upon. But thy goodness is all *in Christ*, and thee must draw it from Him moment by moment as thee needs it." The very spirit of the Higher Christian Life speaks here; and it teaches us that the sanctification received by faith does not eradicate the sinful nature: we retain the old nature of sin, apparently completely unaffected. All our sanctification is " in Christ," external to our self, and is drawn upon only for our daily need " moment by moment," that is to say, for our conduct solely, since it does not affect our nature. Despite these strong words, however, Mrs. Smith teaches [198] that the heart itself is purified by Christ's indwelling. Following a lead from her son, she represents that we may not merely be delivered when we trust, but may be kept continually trusting; and more than that — that that traitor in the camp, inbred sin, may be ousted.

" In order to know a complete and continuous victory," she says, " this inward enemy must be cast out, and the heart must be cleansed from all unrighteousness. Then, the very centre of the being having been taken possession of by Christ, and all His enemies destroyed by His presence, He reigns there supreme. And the soul finds itself ' kept by the power of God,' through an unwavering faith, which nothing jostles or dims." On this teaching a doctrine of perfection, not of act but of nature, and with it a doctrine of perseverance, might be based. Mrs. Smith justifies herself in it by adding that " this wonderful truth is taught in many ways, and under many different figures, in the New Testament. Being ' dead to sin," knowing ' the body of sin to be destroyed,' ' purifying our hearts by faith,' being ' cleansed from all unrighteousness '; all these, and many other expressions, set forth this truth, that Christ,

[198] " The Record of a Happy Life," 1873, pp. 148 f.

who was manifested to destroy the works of the devil, is able and willing to destroy his very worst work, — even that which he wrought in us when he implanted sin in our nature. And that when Christ enters there, sin must retire." Surely it is sufficiently clearly taught here that the old nature is not left untouched by the salvation of Christ. Indeed, it is even taught that Christ expels sin from our very nature, and that can mean nothing less than that we no longer have even indwelling sin, and that, in turn, can mean nothing less than the Wesleyan "entire sanctification," "Christian Perfection." "But," adds Mrs. Smith, seeking to guard herself, "but let it be understood that it is only the presence of Christ that keeps out the sin. There is no inherent purity in the heart itself. But as with light and darkness, so with Christ and sin; they cannot exist together, there is no possibility of fellowship between them. Let a room, however, presume on its light, and shut out the rays of the sun, and darkness at once fills it. So let the soul presume on its purity, and cease to let Christ abide in it, and that moment sin reigns there again supreme. The indwelling presence of Christ makes the heart pure, and keeps it pure. The indwelling presence of Christ drives out His enemies, and keeps them out. The indwelling presence of Christ destroys (or 'renders inert') the body of sin, and keeps it so; but the moment the soul lets go of Christ, or turns its eyes away from Him, that moment its old evil all returns."

It is evident that Mrs. Smith is here at her wit's end. She is trying to teach at once that our old nature is expelled by Christ and that it is not expelled; that Christ keeps us permanently, and that His keeping is only moment by moment; that our abiding in our grace rests on Christ alone, and that it depends absolutely on ourselves. It is an impossible task. She says that implanted sin is itself cast out; that Christ entering the heart expels sin from it; that there cannot be the least remnant of sin left where Christ dwells. The indwelling Christ not only makes the heart pure but keeps it pure; not only drives out His enemies but keeps them out. He destroys — but here she falters, and suggests that we may say only "renders inert"— the body of sin and keeps it destroyed. But she cannot leave it at that, although she has said it so strongly and with such variety of expression that she must leave it at that. She talks of there being no inherent purity in the heart itself — as if a heart that is pure can be pure any other way than "inherently." What she means is that it owes its purity to Christ, who dwells in it. But that makes no difference — if Christ dwells in it, and by dwelling in it "makes the heart pure and keeps it pure." Underneath all this lies the assumption that we can put Christ out of our hearts again: "The moment the soul lets go of Christ, or turns its eyes away from Him, that moment its old evil all returns." The mind reels as it tries to imagine how this can be — if, for example, Christ not only "drives out His enemies," but "keeps them out." The cart is surely put before the horse. Surely we cannot "let go of Christ," "turn our eyes away from Him," unless the old evil has already returned. A pure heart — and we are told that Christ has made the heart pure and keeps it pure — cannot do these things. And this old evil, all of which returns, where has it been all the intervening time? If it had only been "made inert," it might perhaps be revived; but that is not what the Apostle says, nor what Mrs. Smith says — both he and she say it has been "destroyed"— and she adds that Christ keeps it destroyed. Surely it cannot come back. We cannot both be kept by Christ and not kept by Him; we cannot be made pure and kept pure and not be pure. Mrs. Smith is laboring with the fundamental contradiction of her school; she wishes to teach a supernatural salvation on the basis of a fundamental naturalism. She cannot do it.

Ordinarily when Mrs. Smith speaks of progress in sanctification her preoccupation is merely to reconcile the immediate attainment of sanctification by faith and the possibility nevertheless of growth in holiness. On our part, she teaches, sanctification is secured by an act, the entrusting of ourselves to God; from the moment that we entrust ourselves to God we are holy — God sees to that. But on God's part, sanctification is produced in us by a process; God leads us up to ever higher planes in our holiness. "Sanctification," she says,[199] "is both a step of faith and a process of works. It is a step of surrender and trust on our part, and it is a process of development on God's part. By a step of faith we get into Christ; by a process we are made to 'grow up into Him in all things.' By a step of faith we put ourselves into the hands of the Divine Potter; by a gradual process He makes us into a vessel unto His own honor, meet for His use, and prepared to every good work." So far as the mere words go, the truth of the matter is stated here. But Mrs. Smith's meaning is not apprehended until we understand that she conceives man to be purely passive as the clay in the hands of the potter in the whole process, and that she conceives the growth which he experiences not to be towards perfection but in perfection. She speaks, indeed,[200] of God carrying us "through a process of transformation, longer or shorter as our peculiar case may require, making actual and experimental the results for which we have trusted." And if this were given true validity it might serve largely to correct the faults adverted to. After all is said, it certainly is God who sanctifies us: we are the clay in His hands, and He molds us as seems to Him good. And the process of transformation wrought out in our sanctification does only actualize in us what from the beginning we have trusted Christ for; it is a "working out" of our salvation. But to say this would not satisfy Mrs. Smith. She asserts that "purity of heart" is complete from the very first moment of our believing,[201] and that all our subsequent growth is in, not into, purity of heart. We are "truly pleasing to God" in every stage of our growth, though "it may require years of training and discipline to mature us into a vessel that shall be in all respects to His honor, and fitted to every good work."[202] "The lump of clay, from the moment it comes under the transforming hand of the potter, is, during each day and each hour of the process, just what the potter wants it to be at that hour or on that day, and therefore pleases him; but it is very far from being matured into the ves-

---

[199] "The Christian's Secret of a Happy Life," p. 30.
[200] P. 30.   [201] P. 34.   [202] P. 35.

sel he intends in the future to make it. The little babe may be all that a babe could be, or ought to be, and may therefore perfectly please its mother; and yet it is very far from being what that mother would wish it to be when the years of maturity shall come. The apple in June is a perfect apple for June; it is the best apple that June can produce; but it is very different from the apple in October, which is a perfected apple. God's works are perfect in every stage of their growth. Man's works are never perfect until they are in every respect complete." [203]

It could not be more strongly declared that the whole process of "sanctification," so far as it is a process, is the growth merely into greater maturity of a person already from the beginning free from sin. It is a process not towards purity, but in purity towards maturity. In point of fact, however, this process is, on one side of it, a process of progressive freeing from sin. The human "apple in June" is not merely an immature apple, it is a rotten apple. It does not merely need "to grow" in order to become the "perfected" apple of October, it has got to be remade before it becomes the perfect apple for June and is in a state to "grow" at all. Mrs. Smith cannot explain away the recreative process of sanctification by confusing the ideas of imperfection and immaturity; this "imperfection" is not a merely negative but a most positive quality. She says, very smartly,[204] that the Scriptures do not teach that we are to grow *into* grace but *in* grace. But to be "in grace" does not mean in Scripture that we are already free from sin, nor — it is time now to add — does the exhortation to "increase in grace" (II Pet. iii. 18) mean that we have no part in making the increase. It is, nevertheless, specifically to an attitude of passivity with respect to our growth that Mrs. Smith exhorts us. "Let me entreat of you, then," she says,[205] "to give up all your efforts after growing, and simply to *let* yourselves grow." That is her fundamental prescription for the Christian life, "a growth without effort." [206] The lilies, she

---

[203] P. 34.
[204] P. 173.
[205] P. 180.
[206] Pp. 183–184.

says, planted in good soil, do not strive to grow: their growing "is not a thing of effort, but is the result of an inward life-principle of growth." "All the stretching and pulling in the world could not make a dead oak grow; but a live oak grows without stretching." What we are to do, then, is merely "to get within" us "the growing life." More at large: [207] "We are to be infinitely passive, and yet infinitely active also; passive as regards self and its workings, active as regards attention and response to God." Which is explained to mean that "we must lay down all the activity of the creature, as such, and must let only the activities of God work in us, and through us, and by us." The fundamental meaning is that our only work is to get into Christ: He does the rest.

Of course Mrs. Smith finds herself in difficulties with the Scriptures here, and perhaps she could not have lighted upon a passage that would give her more difficulty in squaring her Quietism with the Scriptures than II Pet. iii. 18, with which she particularly concerns herself. Precisely what Peter does in this passage is to require Christians to engage actively in advancing in their life of faith. It is not enough for him that we plant ourselves in the garden of the Lord — and let God give the increase. Precisely what he says we are to do is "to exert ourselves" (verse 14, cf. 1–10, 15), and to exert ourselves precisely that we may be found on the great day of judgment "unsullied and faultless" in His sight. To that extent we are engaged in our own sanctification, and to that end we are (among other things) "to take care" — to take care that we are not carried away by errors, and so fall from "our own" steadfastness ("our own," notice); on the contrary, we are to "make increase" in grace, and the knowledge of our Lord and Saviour Jesus Christ, this "making increase" being put in contrast with the "taking care" not to fall, as the other half of our duty. There is no Quietism here; and Peter says he is teaching just what Paul teaches. In contrast to both Peter and Paul Mrs. Smith says we are neither to exert ourselves nor to make increase in grace. We are in grace already

[207] P. 179.

and all our growth is to be within the grace we are in, and it is to be accomplished without any effort on our part.

This, then, is the teaching of the Higher Life agitation which filled with its propaganda the third quarter of the nineteenth century. It is not a very profound teaching, and its tendency was downwards. It was more shallow in the hands of its later than in those of its earlier advocates. Perfectionism is impossible in the presence of a deep sense or a profound conception of sin. This movement proclaimed, it is true, only an attenuated perfectionism — a perfectionism merely of conduct. But this involved a correspondingly attenuated view of sin. The guilt of sin, the corruption of sin, were not denied, but attention was distracted from them and fixed on the practice of sin. This is a fatally externalizing movement of thought, and brings with it a ruinous under-estimate of the baneful power of sin. This effect was reënforced by an extreme limitation of the notion of sinning. Nothing was recognized as sinning but deliberate sinning. Ignorance or inadvertence was made the mother of holiness, and holiness was thus brought to so low a level that the meanest in Christian attainments might easily lay claim to its possession. Corresponding to this defective outlook on sin and holiness was an equally defective attitude towards God and His relation to men. None of the high attributes of God were denied, but the practical effect of the teaching was to encourage men to look upon Him as a force existing for them and wholly at their command. This degrading conception of God was not given, it is true, so crass an expression as it has received in some later developments of the same type of thought. Mrs. Smith even includes in her chief book [208] a chapter bearing the title " Is God in Everything? " in which she is fairly compelled to teach, in the mere interest of the life of faith, the fundamental fact of the universal government of God. Nevertheless, the open teaching of the whole movement is to the effect that God acts — and can act — in the matter of sanctification, as in the whole matter of

[208] " The Christian's Secret of a Happy Life," Part II, chapter xiii.

salvation, only as man, by his prior action, releases Him for action. This is not a wholesome attitude to take towards God. It tends to looking upon Him as the instrument which we use to secure our ends, and that is a magical rather than a religious attitude. In the end it inhibits religion which includes in its essence a sense of complete dependence on God.

With these defects in its outlook on God and sin, the movement naturally fostered a thin religious life. The deep things are not for it. Throes of repentance, ecstasies of aspiration, alike, are rendered unnecessary and unbecoming. Christian living is reduced to the level of common respectability. The law of God having been pushed out of sight His grace becomes obscured with it. The *summum bonum* becomes ease in Zion, and God, as He is no longer greatly feared, neither is any longer greatly loved. Nor is He trusted. Our dependence is put in our own trust, not in God, and as arrant a work-salvation results as was ever taught. The works depended upon are concentrated into the specific work of trust; but all is hung on this specific work. This is a gravely unethical proceeding. Pelagius, when he hung salvation on works, at least demanded perfect righteousness as its ground. In this teaching perfect righteousness is dispensed with, and the trust in favor of which it is dispensed with disappears with it. The type of piety engendered by the preaching of a conditional salvation is naturally in polar opposition to that engendered by the preaching of a free salvation. The correlate to a free salvation is trust; the correlate to a conditional salvation is performance. Trust and performance are contradictions. A " Do " religion and a " Trust " religion are irreconcilable. To demand trust as a condition defeats, therefore, its own object and renders the trust demanded impossible. If we are to depend on our own trust it ceases to be trust. We cannot look to ourselves for the decisive act in our salvation and at the same time be looking to God for all. Trust transformed into a work loses its quality; turned back on itself, it is obliterated.

Nevertheless, despite its leanness, the movement has persisted in its influence down to our own times. In Britain, on the

European Continent, in America, its echoes are still heard. Mrs. Smith herself, at the opening of the new century no doubt, looked back on it as in some sense a thing of the past [209]; but that was only relatively the case. We do not so quickly escape from low levels of thought and feeling. It is sadly true in spiritual as in earthly things that the poor are always with us. It is matter of congratulation that the two great movements which arose, Phoenix-like, from the ashes of the violent " Higher Life " agitation of the seventies — " The Keswick Movement " in Britain, and the " Heiligungsbewegung " in Germany — while very greatly extending the influence of its essential teaching, have, although in different degrees, mitigated some of its most objectionable features. If, however, we have a right-wing, we have also a left-wing, of Keswick teaching; and if there has been a Theodor Jellinghaus in Germany, there has also been a " Pastor " Paul. Outside the main currents of these two great movements, individual preachers of the Higher Life also are, of course, continually appearing. Among these, Albert B. Simpson attracts perhaps primary attention, not less for the extravagance of his thories than for the wideness of the influence he has exerted through his long career.[210] In the closing years of the last century the unwholesome figure of " the Tamil Evangelist," V. D. David, drew temporary notice to itself and then passed under a cloud.[211] On the other hand, James H. McConkey's little book, entitled " The Threefold Secret of the Holy Spirit " (1897), pleases by the sobriety of its spirit, although certainly, in the main,

---

[209] See J. B. Figgis, " Keswick from Within," 1914, p. vii.

[210] Among his relevant writings are: " The Christ Life "; " Walking in the Spirit "; " Life More Abundantly "; " Himself," an address delivered at Bethshan, London, 1885; " Tracts for the Times, Deeper Life Series." Compare *The Princeton Theological Review* for July, 1918, pp. 358 ff., or pp. 597 ff. of this volume, and " The New Schaff-Herzog Encyclopedia of Religious Knowledge," x. p. 430.

[211] The titles of some of his tracts are: " Scriptural Heart Cleansing "; " Practical and Scriptural Holiness "; " Have You Perfect Peace? "; " Are You a Pentecostal Christian? "; " Solution of Many Difficulties "; " How to Know the Voice of Christ "; " Is this Your Photograph? "; " Have You the Holy Ghost? " They were published by " The Church Press," Chicago.

running true to type.[212] By the side of Mr. McConkey we may perhaps be permitted to place such teachers as Matthew H. Houston, who have not escaped direct influence from Keswick.[213] From Wesley to Keswick may superficially seem a somewhat far cry. There is, no doubt, room between these

[212] James H. McConkey, "The Three-fold Secret of the Holy Spirit," ed. 2, 1897, 128 pages. Mr. McConkey writes on the general presupposition of the Arminian scheme of salvation. He looks upon Repentance and Faith, conceived as two separate acts, as the proper conditions of salvation. He even speaks of our "yielding" to the Spirit "for Regeneration," and in general as if our "yielding" were always the precedent condition of the Spirit's working. He teaches that there are two distinct and separate stages of salvation. On Repentance and Faith we enter into life, are united with Christ, and "receive the indwelling Spirit." Then on "yielding," or, more technically "surrendering," our life to God we "receive the fulness of the Spirit." Usually there is an actual interval between the two; *logically* such an interval is presupposed and the appeal of the Scriptures for the second is grounded on the asumption that the first has taken place; but *actually* the two steps *may* take place chronologically together, or with so short an interval between that it is unnoted. In the order of thought "conversion must of necessity precede consecration." But the interval should not be prolonged. "The flesh still abides in the believer," though he "*need* not walk in it." "Jesus Christ does not so much *impart* life as He *inbrings* life"; and so "the believer has no spiritual life in himself, apart from Christ Jesus." The old man is not to be amended but put off — as if the old man is not put off precisely by being amended. — Of course, the new spiritual life which is imparted is not "independent of Christ," or "apart from Christ." It will not do to represent the believer, however, as left dead: he is made alive in Christ — and it is *he* that is made alive. It is not only that he has Christ in him and Christ is living, but it is he himself that is living, for Christ has made him alive; yes, he has life in himself (John vi. 53). It is not true that "the believer is portrayed as a man in himself spiritually dead, indwelt through the Spirit by Jesus Christ, who is his spiritual life" (p. 98). He is portrayed as a man who is spiritually alive, in whom Jesus Christ the source of all his life, dwells by His Spirit. The man himself is saved, and his new holiness is *his* holiness. It is a grave error to suppose that the living Christ can dwell within us without imparting life to us. He *quickens* whom He will; and he whom He quickens, lives. — It is pleasant to observe that, in spite of his fundamental Arminianism, Mr. McConkey believes in "Perseverance."

[213] M. H. Houston, "Dr. Strickler on Perfectionism," 1904, p. 6: "I am nothing; Christ is all: his life is brought to me by the Holy Spirit, and to be filled with the Spirit is to have the fullness of Christ. The Christ life is obedience to all the commands of God, and the fullness of Christ is full, entire obedience to these commands. This is what is meant by the phrase, entire, or complete, sanctification."

limits for many distinguishable varieties of teaching. They are all bound together, however, by common fundamental conceptions of very dubious character, and it is too much to hope that we have seen the last of any one of them. Recent events only emphasize the fact that it is not merely the fittest among them which promise to survive.[214]

[214] An admirable detailed criticism of the "Higher Life" teaching will be found in Henry A. Boardman, "The 'Higher Life' Doctrine of Sanctification, Tried by the Word of God," 1877. It is also faithfully, though briefly, dealt with by John Charles Ryle, in the Introduction to his "Holiness: Its Nature, Hindrances, Difficulties, and Roots," 1877; ed. 2, 1879; often reissued. Professor Thomas Smith in an article on "Means and Measure of Holiness," in *The British and Foreign Evangelical Review* for April, 1876, pp. 251 ff., gives an excellent discussion of it; and Lyman H. Atwater, in an article on "The Higher Life and Christian Perfection," in *The Presbyterian Quarterly and Princeton Review* for July, 1877, pp. 389 ff., takes occasion from it to review the whole subject of Christian Perfection most helpfully. There is an able article in *The London Quarterly Review* for October, 1875, xlv. pp. 85 ff., on "The Brighton Convention and Its Opponents" from the Wesleyan point of view, defending the "Higher Life" teachers against their critics. From the heading of this article the titles of a number of the criticisms of the movement published in 1875 may be obtained. Valuable discussions are found also in Johannes Jüngst, "Amerikanischer Methodismus in Deutschland und Robert Pearsall Smith," 1875; Reiff-Hesse, "Die Oxforder Bewegung und ihre Bedeutung für unsere Zeit"; G. Warneck, "Briefe über die Versammlung in Brighton," 1876; Paul Fleisch, "Zur geschichte der Heiligungsbewegung," 1910; H. Benser, "Das moderne Gemeinschaftschristentum," 1910; Fr. Winkler, "Robert Pearsall Smith und der Perfectionismus," second thousand, 1915. Compare also Herman Bavinck, "Gereformeerde Dogmatiek," J. H. Kok, Kampen, 1911, iv. pp. 262 ff., and the literature there given.

V

" THE VICTORIOUS LIFE "

" THE VICTORIOUS LIFE "[1]

IT appears to have been early observed that the mills of the gods grind very slowly: and hasty spirits have been only partially reconciled to that fact by the further observation that they do their work exceedingly well. Men are unable to understand why time should be consumed in divine works. Why should the almighty Maker of the heaven and earth take millions of years to create the world? Why should He bring the human race into being by a method which leaves it ever incomplete? Above all, in His recreation of a lost race, why should He proceed by process? Men are unwilling that either the world or they themselves should be saved by God's secular methods. They demand immediate, tangible results. They ask, Where is the promise of His coming? They ask to be themselves made glorified saints in the twinkling of an eye. God's ways are not their ways, and it is a great trial to them that God will not walk in their ways. They love the storm and the earthquake and the fire. They cannot see the divine in " a sound of gentle stillness," and adjust themselves with difficulty to the lengthening perspective of God's gracious working. For the world they look every day for the cataclysm in which alone they can recognize God's salvation; and when it ever delays its coming they push it reluctantly forward but a little bit at a time. For themselves they cut the knot and boldly declare complete salvation to be within their reach at their option, or already grasped and enjoyed. It is true, observation scarcely justifies the assertion. But this difficulty is easily removed by adjusting the nature of complete salvation to fit their present attainments. These impatient souls tolerate more readily the idea of an imperfect perfection than the admission of lagging perfecting. They must at all costs have all that is coming to them at once.

[1] Reprinted from *The Princeton Theological Review*, xvi. 1918, pp. 321-373.

It was John Wesley who infected the modern Protestant world with this notion of "entire instantaneous sanctification." In saying this we are not bringing a railing accusation against him. There was no element of his teaching which afforded him himself greater satisfaction. There is no element of it which is more lauded by his followers, or upon their own possession of which they more felicitate themselves. "The current orthodoxy," they say, "limited the salvation of Christ." It had limited it "in the degree of its attainability as well as in the persons by whom it is attainable." [2] It was the achievement of Wesley to lift these limitations and to make it clear not only that the salvation of Christ is attainable by all but that it is completely attainable by all. "Knowing exactly what I say, and taking the full responsibility of it, I repeat," John McClintock solemnly asseverates,[3] in describing the result in the church which Wesley founded, "we are the only church in history, from the apostles' time until now, that has put forward as its very elemental thought . . . the holiness of the human soul, heart, mind and will." Nothing less than a new epoch in the history of the Church has thus, in the view of Wesley's followers, been introduced. "Historically," writes Olin A. Curtis,[4] "Wesley had almost the same epochal relation to the doctrinal emphasis upon holiness that Luther had to the doctrinal emphasis upon justification by faith, or that Athanasius had to the doctrinal emphasis upon the Deity of our Lord." We are merely recognizing, therefore, what is eagerly proclaimed by his followers, when we attribute to Wesley's impulse the wide prevalence in our modern Protestantism of what has come to be known as "holiness teaching." The fact is, however, in any event too plain to be overlooked. As wave after wave of the "holiness movement" has broken over us during the past century, each has brought, no doubt, some-

[2] G. G. Findlay, in Hastings' "Encyclopædia of Religion and Ethics," viii. 1916, p. 611: Article on "Methodism, Doctrine of."

[3] In an address delivered at the Methodist Centenary Celebration in New York, January 25, 1866, reported in *The Methodist* of February 3rd, 1866 and cited by O. A. Curtis, "The Christian Faith," 1905, p. 372.

[4] "The Christian Faith," 1905, p. 373.

thing distinctive of itself. But a common fundamental character has informed them all, and this common fundamental character has been communicated to them by the Wesleyan doctrine. The essential elements of that doctrine repeat themselves in all these movements, and form their characteristic features. In all of them alike justification and sanctification are divided from one another as two separate gifts of God. In all of them alike sanctification is represented as obtained, just like justification, by an act of simple faith, but not by the same act of faith by which justification is obtained, but by a new and separate act of faith, exercised for this specific purpose. In all of them alike the sanctification which comes on this act of faith, comes immediately on believing, and all at once, and in all of them alike this sanctification, thus received, is complete sanctification. In all of them alike, however, it is added, that this complete sanctification does not bring freedom from all sin; but only, say, freedom from sinning; or only freedom from conscious sinning; or from the commission of "known sins." And in all of them alike this sanctification is not a stable condition into which we enter once for all by faith, but a momentary attainment, which must be maintained moment by moment, and which may readily be lost and often is lost, but may also be repeatedly instantaneously recovered.

The latest of these waves speaks of itself by predilection as "the Victory in Christ" movement, or "the Victorious Life" [5] movement. Mr. Charles Gallaudet Trumbull, the accomplished editor of *The Sunday School Times,* has come forward as its chief promoter. We gather [6] that his conversion to the notions which he is now so eagerly propagating took place in

[5] We may conjecture — it is only conjecture — that the name is derived from I John v. 4. Mr. Trumbull, at the beginning of the tract, "Real and Counterfeit Victory," says, "Victory is a great word in the New Testament." It occurs just six times and in only four passages (Matt. xii. 20, I Cor. xv. 54, 55, 57; I John v. 4, Rev. xv. 2); and only in I John v. 4, cf. Rev. xv. 2, in this special sense. It occurs only three times in the Old Testament, all in the literal sense (II Sam. xix. 2, xxiii. 10, 12).

[6] See especially his tract, entitled, "The Life that Wins."

the summer of 1910. It was preceded by deep impressions received from certain sermons preached, unless we mistake his allusions, by President A. H. Strong and Mr. Richard Roberts.[7] The doctrine which he preaches was not derived, however, from these sermons. Its affinities, as is elsewhere correctly intimated,[8] are rather with the Keswick teaching; and behind that, of course, there lies the teaching of Mr. and Mrs. R. Pearsall Smith,[9] while back of all looms the general Wesleyan background. The chief instruments which he employs in the very active propaganda which he is prosecuting for this doctrine are his journal, *The Sunday School Times,* and the mid-summer Conferences which have been held for the past few years at Princeton. Both the one and the other have come to exist largely for its propagation. *The Sunday School Times* is now advertised as " a weekly journal of Bible Study and the Christian Life for adults, in which the truth of the Victorious Life is constantly presented and its problems are fully discussed "; as " an every week interdenominational paper for adults which seeks to share with its world-wide family of readers the riches of salvation and victory which are ours in Christ not only hereafter but here." This means no less than that the propagation of Mr. Trumbull's views on " the Victorious Life " has been deliberately made one of the definite objects of the publication of this journal. It is for this distinct purpose that " the Princeton Conference " also is carried on. This purpose is written into the articles of agreement by which that Conference is constituted, and it is constantly proclaimed with great explicitness. The aim of the Conference we are told, is " to lead men and women into a life of communion with God, vic-

---

[7] The matter is certain with reference to Mr. Richard Roberts' sermon, and the sermon — " The Life that is Christ," on Phil. i. 21 — is published by The Sunday School Times Company in tract form. That Dr. Strong was the preacher of the other sermon mentioned rests merely on a conjecture of our own.

[8] " Victory in Christ," pp, 6, 10, 239.

[9] *Ibid.,* p. 94. Hannah Whitall Smith's " The Christian's Secret of a Happy Life " is characterized as " one of the most remarkable settings forth of the victorious life you can find anywhere."

tory over sin, and fruit-bearing, through the presentation of
the Bible teaching concerning the life that is Christ." [10] Or, as it
is expressed elsewhere, "to lead Christians into a life of victory through moment by moment faith in Christ." Or, more
crisply, "Victory in Christ is what Princeton Conference
stands for." [11] Standing for that, it is to be looked on, we
are further told, as "a Rescue Mission for Christians," a
rescue mission which, it is sharply intimated, is much needed.[12]

Mr. Trumbull's teachings are most accessible in a series of
tracts, the most of which seem to have been reprinted from
the columns of *The Sunday School Times,* and may be had
from the Sunday School Times Company,[13] and in a series of
addresses, into which the substance of these tracts has been
incorporated, printed in the volume which bears the title,
"Victory in Christ: a Report of Princeton Conference 1916." [14]
"These addresses," we are told in the advertisement of the
book put out by the Sunday School Times Company, "comprise the fullest connected statement of the teachings of the
Victorious Life that Mr. Trumbull has ever given in conference work or has published." In this statement, it will be observed, Mr. Trumbull is spoken of as the recognized leader
of a movement and readers are supposed to be eager to obtain
the fullest statement of his teachings. The addresses do not,
however, supersede the tracts. Some of the tracts at least
have been revised and reissued since the publication of the
book. And not only do the tracts contain many details of

[10] "Victory in Christ," pp. 1, 5.

[11] *Ibid.,* p. 108.

[12] *Ibid.,* p. 109.

[13] These tracts include "The Life that Wins," "Is Victory Earned or a
Gift?", "What is Your Kind of Christianity?", "Real and Counterfeit Vic-
tory." We associate with them, "May Christians lose Sinful Desires?", "The
Secret of the Victorious Life," although these are not explicitly assigned to
Mr. Trumbull's own pen.

[14] Published in 1916 by "The Board of Managers of Princeton Conference," and to be had from "the Secretary of Princeton Conference, 1031
Walnut Street, Philadelphia." Mr. Trumbull's own addresses bear the titles
of "Are Ye Ignorant?", "Real and Counterfeit Victory," "What is Surrender?", "The Faith for Victory," "The Victory as a Gift," "The Victory
Tested," "Questions and Answers on Victory."

Mr. Trumbull's experience in which the movement originated
that have not been transferred to the volume; but the same
subjects are sometimes treated in the two in a somewhat
different manner and from a slightly different angle of vision —
and, in the tracts, with more freshness and vigor. It is naturally to these teachings of Mr. Trumbull's own that we go
(as we are expected to go) first, for information as to the
teachings of the Victorious Life movement. Mr. Trumbull has,
however, helpers in his task of propagating his doctrines, to
whom also we should do well to attend. Mr. Robert C. McQuilkin, who was for some years associate editor of *The Sunday
School Times,* for instance, has ably seconded his chief in the
columns of that journal. And then there are the speakers
whom Mr. Trumbull has gathered around him at the Princeton Conference, and whose addresses are included in the volume called " Victory in Christ." If these may justly be thought
of, so far as they prove to be like-minded with him, as secondary authorities for the ideas he wishes to inculcate, no doubt
the books and leaflets which he expressly recommends as
" literature on the Victorious Life " — " the best and clearest
books on the truth of the Life that is Christ, which is presented at Princeton Conference " [15] — may be appealed to in
the third rank for illustrations of his teaching. On this general
basis we purpose to found an attempt to make as clear as
possible precisely what these teachings are and what their
affinities are in the history of Christian thought. There is a
sense in which this is a work of supererogation, just as it would
be superfluous to subject each wave of the sea that washes at
our feet to a particular chemical analysis to show that it is

[15] " Victory in Christ," pp. 100, 116, and fly-leaf at the back. The books
which are thus recommended to us are: " The Christian's Secret of a Happy
Life," by Hannah Whitall Smith (which, p. 94, Mr. Trumbull describes as
" one of the most remarkable settings forth of the victorious life you can
find anywhere "); James H. McConkey's " The Threefold Secret of the
Holy Spirit "; W. H. Griffith Thomas's " Grace and Power "; A. B. Simpson's
" The Christ Life "; Frances Ridley Havergal's " Kept for the Master's Use."
The tracts recommended include those mentioned above, and certain others,
put up in a packet to be had from Mr. O. R. Heinze, Director of the Christian Life Literature Fund, 600 Perry Building, Philadelphia.

water and that the water which it is, is bitter. But on the whole it seems as if good purposes would be served by looking at Mr. Trumbull's teachings for the moment very much as if they were an isolated phenomenon and permitting them to speak for themselves.

Mr. Trumbull is accustomed to begin the expositions of his teaching by carefully explaining that justification and sanctification are two separate gifts of God, to be separately obtained, and by separate acts of faith.[16] He thus bases his entire system on Wesley's primary error, the fundamental error by which the whole of Wesley's doctrine of sanctification is vitiated. But he expresses this in any case fatally erroneous representation with a crudity, and presses it to consequences, of which Wesley was incapable. "Jesus, you know," says he,[17] "makes two offers to everyone. He offers to set us free from the *penalty* of our sin. And He offers to set us free from the *power* of our sin. Both these offers are made on exactly the same terms: we can accept them only by letting Him do it all." "Every Christian," he proceeds, "has accepted the first offer. Many Christians have not accepted the second offer." Or, as it is put in another place,[18] "Every Christian knows of and has accepted the first of these two offers," but "many a Christian does not even intelligently know of, and still more Christians have not accepted, the second of these two offers." The adverb "intelligently," somewhat oddly inserted into the last clause, is a sop to Cerberus. All Christians

[16] If sanctification, like justification, is directly "by faith," it is very odd that the Scriptures never connect it directly with faith, as Prof. Thomas Smith tellingly points out in *The British and Foreign Evangelical Review*, April, 1876, p. 253. J. V. Bartlet, Hastings' "A Dictionary of the Bible," iv. p. 394, says of sanctification, "It, too, begins and ends in faith: St. Paul might well have written ὁ ἅγιος ἐκ πίστεως ζήσεται." The fact is, however, that Paul never so wrote: nor is any equivalent found anywhere in the New Testament — not even in Acts xv. 9 or Acts xxvi. 18, which are sometimes wrongly quoted in this sense. Compare Bishop J. C. Ryle, "Holiness" (1877), ed. 5, 1900, p. xiii.

[17] In the tract, "What is Your Kind of Christianity?"

[18] Heading of the leaflet: "Scripture on the Victorious Life," expressly commended in "Victory in Christ," p. 100, note. The general statement is a staple of the literature of the movement.

of course know that our Lord delivers His people from the power as well as from the penalty of sin; they would not be Christians if they were not entrusting to Him their complete deliverance from both — and more. But few Christians find the meaning in this statement which the writer wishes to attach to it. The interjection of "intelligently" merely betrays the writer's consciousness that he is teaching a novelty, something not ordinarily believed by Christians. This novelty is, of course, the sharp separation that is made between Christ's deliverance of His people from the penalty of sin and His deliverance of them from the power of sin. These things are not merely distinguished as recognizable steps or stages in the process of the one salvation. They are definitely separated as two distinct gifts of grace, of which we may have the one and not the other, which may be — often are — perhaps generally, or almost always are — sought and obtained separately. Of this separation of them from one another, however, not only do the generality of Christians know nothing, but the Scriptures know nothing. Or rather, it is definitely and repeatedly contradicted by the Scriptures. The whole sixth chapter of Romans, for example, was written for no other purpose than to assert and demonstrate that justification and sanctification are indissolubly bound together; that we cannot have the one without having the other; that, to use its own figurative language, dying with Christ and living with Christ are integral elements in one indisintegrable salvation.[19]

[19] It only shows the desperation of the case when Mr. Trumbull seeks to break the force of the argument of Rom. vi by emphasizing the "might" in the English Version of Rom. vi. 4: "'We also must'? No, 'might.' That is where your choice comes in. You do not have to walk in newness of life. You do not have to sit in heavenly places with the Father. . . . It is only 'might.' Even to Christians, members of the body of Christ, the acceptance of this proffered privilege depends upon their free will" ("Victory in Christ," pp. 76, 77). Nothing could be worse than this. The attempted weakening of the phrase in vi. 6, "that the body of sin might *be done away*," by resurrecting the etymological sense of the Greek verb, borrowed by Mr. Trumbull from Dr. Griffith Thomas (though it may find support in Sanday-Headlam) is, however, equally bad. It has become traditional in this school: cf. Hannah Whitall Smith, "The Record of a Happy Life," 1873, p. 149; "The indwelling presence of Christ destroys (or 'renders inert') the body of sin."

To wrest these two things apart and make separable gifts of grace of them evinces a confusion in the conception of Christ's salvation which is nothing less than portentous. It forces from us the astonished cry, Is Christ divided? And it compels us to point afresh to the primary truth that we do not obtain the benefits of Christ apart from, but only in and with His Person; and that when we have Him we have all.[20]

This crass separation of sanctification from justification, as if it was merely an additional gift of grace to be sought and obtained for itself — instead of, as it is, an inseparable component part of the one salvation that belongs to all believers — lays the foundation, of course, for that circle of ideas which

---

It is needless to say that the Rev. Harrington C. Lees has led Dr. Thomas astray when ("Grace and Power," 1916, pp. 127, 128) he has induced him to substitute "handicap" for "condemnation" in Romans viii. 1. The word cannot be twisted into that meaning, and Deissmann's discussion gives no possible basis for it. We suppose that stenographers and compositors are responsible for the wonderful philology we find on p. 186 of "Victory in Christ": "That word compassion is a deep word; *paschor* means to suffer; it is something more than just sympathy; it is the Greek equivalent of that Latin word the paschal lamb, it carries the deep significance of that word." But what are we to make of this from Dr. A. B. Simpson's "Walking in the Spirit," p. 173: "The very word for love is charity, or *caritas,* and this is derived from the root *charis,* grace. So that the primary idea conveyed by the Bible term for love is, that it is a gift and not a natural quality"? The Victorious Life writers do not impress us on the philological side.

[20] This fundamental fact is admirably presented by H. Bavinck, "Gereformeerde Dogmatiek," Kok, Kampen, iv., 1911, p. 285. It could not be better stated than it is by John H. Livingston, Professor of Theology in the Seminary of the Reformed Dutch Church, in the course of two sermons on "Growth in Grace" delivered in the Collegiate Church, New York, in 1790: "We take Him for our all when first we believe; but what that fully implies, we do not, when first we believe, yet understand. To grow in grace is the unfolding of that mystery. It is experimentally to know that Christ is of God made unto us sanctification; that in the Lord we have not only righteousness, but in Him also we have strength. . . ." Cf. also the fine statement by Lyman H. Atwater, *The Presbyterian Quarterly and Princeton Review,* July, 1877, p. 393: "We receive a full salvation in Christ when we receive Him by faith; but a salvation begun here, and completed only with respect to the soul when we pass by the gate of death to the realms of glory; and with respect to the body when it shall also be raised in glory. . . ." Dr. Atwater illustrates the involution of all its stages in the one salvation — including even those which are completed beyond this life — from Rom. viii. 30.

aıe summed up in the phrase, "the Second Blessing." These are far from wholesome.[21] Among them may be mentioned, for example, the creation of two different kinds of Christians, a lower and a higher variety. With Mr. Trumbull, these two classes of Christians are "merely saved people" and "real disciples of Christ." "Thousands of saved people," he says, "are not following after Christ, are not bearing the cross, and therefore are not disciples. A Christian is one who is saved from the penalty of his sin; a disciple is one who, after being saved, becomes a learner, goes on learning more and more about Christ." [22] This does not seem to be just Christ's teaching (Matt. xvi. 24; Mark viii. 34; Luke ix. 23). And one asks in amazement, What is the penalty of sin? And what is salvation from it? Is not our sinfulness the penalty above all other penalties of sin, and is not holiness just salvation from sin? Are we not to credit Paul when he tells us that "God chose you from the beginning unto salvation in sanctification of the Spirit" (II Thess. ii. 13), and in pursuance of this His primal purpose has called us in sanctification (I Thess. iv. 7); and that therefore, saved by grace through faith, "we are His workmanship, created in Christ Jesus for good works, which God afore prepared that we should walk in them" (Eph. ii. 10)? Mr. Trumbull's distinction, however, is a necessary consequence of separating sanctification from justification, as a distinct blessing subsequently sought and obtained. As an inevitable result of it a most unpleasant note is sounded throughout the whole literature of this movement of what we cannot call anything else than spiritual pretension. These

[21] Cf. A. A. Hodge, *The Presbyterian,* April 1, 1876, p. 2: — "It is wholly a false view, never accepted by the Church, that the Christian undergoes two conversions — that he *first* accepts Christ for justification, and *afterwards,* by a separate act, accepts Him for sanctification. Justifying faith is an act of a spiritually quickened soul. It accepts Christ as a Savior from sin — not mere judicial condemnation. The removal of guilt is in order to the removal of the pollution and power of sin. The same act of faith, which accepts Christ as Priest, accepts Him as Prophet and King. He cannot be divided. No more, in any act of true faith, can forgiveness be separated from purification."

[22] "Victory in Christ," p. 87.

writers are always felicitating themselves upon not being as
other men are — " ordinary Christians," " average Christians "; and these " ordinary " or " average " Christians come
in for a good deal of little-disguised scorn. We are told by the
tract called " Subdued " that not more than one in a thousand
of converted men attain to " victory " — that is to say to the
status of " disciples." The rest are satisfied to live on a lower
plane. " When others are content with a meagre measure of
piety and power, with an ambition merely to be ' saved as by
fire,' " we read in the tract called " Victory " — " and you
claim your full inheritance in Christ — an overcomer — in
order to reign with Him — that is *victory*." It is possibly only
the language employed here that reminds us of the incident
recorded in Mat. xx. 20 ff. But it is not of humility that we
especially are made to think as we read.[23]

When Mr. Trumbull comes to tell us how Victory in Christ
is obtained, he refines on the dichotomy of Christians into the
merely saved and the victorious, and discovers yet a third
class. He speaks at times as if the Victorious life were obtained
by a perfectly simple act, just faith — as " mere salvation " is
obtained.[24] But it appears, as we read further, that the condition upon which alone it can be attained has a certain complexity. It is indeed a double condition, " surrender and faith,
' Let go, and let God.' "[25] And we learn that these two elements are not only distinguishable but separable. We may
" let go " and not yet " let God." Accordingly " the Surrendered Life is not necessarily the Victorious Life. There is no

[23] Charles Spurgeon was made to think of presumption and spoke accordingly. " It will be an ill day," he said, " when our brethren take to
bragging and boasting, and call it ' testimony to the higher life.' We trust
that holiness will be more than ever the aim of believers, but not the boastful holiness which has deluded some of the excellent of the earth into vain-
glory, and under which their firmest friends shudder for them." (Quoted in
The Presbyterian, February 19, 1876, p. 9.)

[24] Mr. Trumbull is careful to use the term obtain, not attain, in connection with the Victorious Life. "Victory," he says, " is not an *at*tainment,
it is an *ob*tainment. It is not something you get by working for, it is something that is given you, as an outright gift " (" Victory in Christ," p. 82).

[25] Tract called " What is Your Kind of Christianity? "

victory without surrender, but there may be surrender without victory." " Surrender and victory are not always the same," we read elsewhere.[26] " It is possible to be a completely surrendered Christian and a defeated Christian." There are therefore, it seems, three kinds of Christians: mere Christians — " very respectable church members "[27] — who have received nothing but freedom from the penalty of sin; "surrendered Christians " who have surrendered themselves wholly to God, but do not in some way or other " let God "; and "Victorious Christians " who have not merely given themselves " unreservedly and completely under the mastery of the Lord Jesus Christ," but know and remember that " it at once becomes His responsibility, His — I say it reverently — duty, to keep " them " from the power of sin."[28]

We confess that we find it difficult to understand how this distinction between " surrender " and " faith," between " let go " and " let God " can be given validity. We are tempted at once to pronounce it only one of the merely verbal distinctions, with no actual content, which seem to impress themselves occasionally on Mr. Trumbull's thought. Are not the merely negative and positive aspects of what is necessarily a single act erected here into two separate acts?[29] Surely " surrender," utter surrender — if it be surrender to God — is just faith. To " let go," if it be a distinctively Christian act at all, is certainly to " let God." It must be confessed, however, that the notion

[26] Tract called " Real and Counterfeit Victory," p. 9. So in " Victory in Christ " p. 100, we are told that many a " surrendered " Christian is " a defeated Christian," and that " there is no such thing as the victorious life without surrender; but there may be surrender without victory."

[27] " Victory in Christ," p. 23.

[28] Tract called " What is Your Kind of Christianity? "

[29] " Victory in Christ," p. 235: " Surrender is only half, the negative half; in order to have victory, we must add to our surrender faith." Hannah Whitall Smith, " Every-Day Religion," 1893, p. 40, remarks: " Trusting can hardly be said to be distinct from yielding," and adds: " It is, in fact, the absolutely necessary correlation [correlative?] to it. . . . Trusting, therefore, simply means that when we have yielded ourselves up unto the Lord, or, in other words, have made ourselves over to Him, we then have perfect confidence that He will manage us and everything concerning us exactly right, and we consequently leave the whole care and managing in His hands."

of " surrender," in all this school of writers, lacks somewhat in clarity. Sometimes it is so described as to reduce it in principle to merely a general attitude of renunciation, of apathetic inactivity, which has no specific reference to God and only supplies to Him an unresisting field in which He may freely work. This idea, the affinities of which are more mystical than Christian, even when it is not explicitly expressed, is felt hovering in the background in much of the exposition of " surrender " that is given us, coloring more or less deeply the conception presented. In proportion as it is present room is left, of course, for active faith following upon or in addition to it; but in that same proportion the possibility of an active faith succeeding or accompanying it is excluded. The soul cannot be in contradictory attitudes — passive and active — at one and the same time. The general drift of Mr. Trumbull's writing on the subject is to the effect that " surrender " merely opens the way for the divine action which gives " victory." This divine action which gives victory is in the most confusing way interchanged with the conception of faith, under the impression apparently that thus this faith is represented as the gift of God.[30] We even have the two simple conditions of the life of victory — " surrender and faith " — explained as meaning that " we must give Christ all there is of ourselves before He can give us all there is of Himself," [31] where Christ's giving us all there is of Himself is identified with " faith." The mediating thought seems to be that " faith " is just " letting Christ do it all," [32] — a conception which appears to differ from " surrender " itself only in having a specific reference to Christ or God.

The one thing that is clear about " surrender " is that it is something that we ourselves do: " Surrender is *our* part in Victory "; [33] and that it is the *conditio sine qua non* of the victory of God in us. No matter how the conception varies or what phraseology is chosen to express it, this one thing is presented with unfailing constancy and with the strongest

[30] " Victory in Christ," p. 235.   [32] P. 236.
[31] P. 26.   [33] " Victory in Christ," p. 100.

emphasis. Mrs. Pearsall Smith thinks that the term "abandonment" might to some minds express the idea intended better than "consecration" or "surrender"; but she insists that, under whatever designation, what is intended is an act of sheer will, by which we remove out of the way the difficulties which prevent God from blessing us, and render it possible for Him to do it.[34] One of the tracts recommended to be read by those seeking the Victorious Life — the copy at our disposal belongs to the 35th thousand — prefers the term "subdued" and develops the idea under that conception. "We must be perfectly subdued in every part of our nature to God's will and the disposition of His mind," before God can use us for good things. The synonyms employed are such as these: "this complete condition of teachable subjugation to God's Spirit"; "absolutely conquered by the Holy Ghost." It might be supposed that under a terminology of this sort, a conception would be presented which did some justice to the divine initiative. But no: it seems that even under this terminology the decisive act is still to be our own. God the Holy Spirit does not subdue us to Himself. He is dependent on us for the subduing; we must ourselves subdue, subjugate, conquer ourselves to Him, and the exhortation is actually given: "Let us get subdued in every way in everything," "so subdued that we can keep still in God and see Him work out the great bright thoughts of His eternal mind in our lives" — from which it appears that on our act of subduing ourselves to God there follows a quietism, when He takes the reins. If we will only put ourselves in connection with the electric current, then the current will flow through us and work its effects. The part of the individual is to make the connection; and that is

---

[34] "The Christian's Secret of a Happy Life," new and enlarged edition (1888), pp. 47, 48. "The power to surrender and trust," Mrs. Smith tells us, p. 243, "exists in every human soul, and only needs to be brought into exercise." "To every human being," she says in her tract on "Faith," "God has given the power to believe" — just as he has given him a hand; and "I must use, by the force of my wish, the power He has already given me." Compare the remarks on this statement by Henry A. Boardman, "The 'Higher Life' Doctrine of Sanctification," 1877, pp. 59 ff.

his indispensable part. Only after that, can God work: and after that God only works. This is the fundamental teaching of the whole school. We advert to it here, however, only incidentally: we shall return to it later.

What it is of most importance to call attention to here is the most fatal defect in Mr. Trumbull's doctrine of salvation. This is the neglect to provide any deliverance for "the corruption of man's heart." Writers of this school are never weary of representing "ordinary Christians" as ignorant of the fulness of the salvation which is in Christ. "They have learned only," says W. E. Boardman, in a typical statement,[35] "that their sins are forgiven through faith in the atonement of Jesus. They have not yet learned that Jesus through faith in His name is the deliverer from the power of sin, as well as from its penalty." Where they have met with these extraordinary "ordinary Christians" we have no power to conjecture. They are not the ordinary Christians with whom we are familiar. It certainly is not the ordinary Christian teaching that the salvation of Christ is exhausted in its objective benefits. We have already pointed out that, on the contrary, it is the ordinary Christian teaching that Christ is received at once for both justification and sanctification and cannot be received for the one without bringing with it the other. As Henry A. Boardman points out in perfectly simple terms:[36] "It is not possible that a justified sinner should be left, even for a moment, in a condition of spiritual death. . . . By one and the same act of faith, the soul takes Christ as its righteousness and its sanctification; as the ground of its hope, and the source of its new life; as the Author not only, but the Finisher, of its faith; as the spring of its vitality and growth, as really as the vine alone sustains its branches, or the head the members." Whenever one-sidedness in the conception of Christ's salvation has shown itself in the history of Christian teaching, the tendency has been apt to be to emphasize its subjective at the expense of its objective side, rather than the objective at the expense of the subjective. A few fanatical Moravians, a few

[35] "The Higher Christian Life," 1859, p. 266.   [36] As cited, p. 31.

followers of that great preacher Friedrich Kohlbrügge, stand out almost alone as inclined to sum up salvation in its objective benefits. When men have lauded justification as the *articulus stantis ecclesiae* — as " the beginning, and middle, and end of salvation," — it has not been because they denied or depreciated the other elements which go to make up a complete salvation; but because they, rightly, see them all indetachably bound up with justification and drawn inevitably in its train. It is not the " ordinary Christians " who hold to a fatally deficient conception of salvation, but the advocates of the " Victorious Life "; and strange to say, the fatal deficiency of their conception of salvation lies on the subjective side. They teach a purely external salvation. All that they provide for is deliverance from the external penalties of sin and from the necessity of actually sinning.

In Mr. Trumbull's scheme of salvation deliverance from corruption has no place.[37] The heart remains corrupt and so, no man can say, " I am without sin." [38] It is within the power of any Christian, however, if he chooses, to say " I am without sinning." Yes, " immediately and completely." Reiterated emphasis is laid on this. God offers us as " an outright gift," to be received by faith alone, " freedom immediately and completely from all the power of known sin," " immediate and complete freedom from the power of your known sins." This is " just as much a miracle," we are told, " as the miracle of regeneration," and " just as exclusively the Lord's work." This

[37] In " Victory in Christ," p. 98, Mr. Trumbull employs the phrase " this death of our sinful nature "; but he does not mean by it that our sinful nature is eradicated, but what would be more correctly expressed by " we die to our sinful nature." He is speaking with Gal. ii. 20 (see p. 86) in mind. Our sinful nature remains in us and we should always remember it lest we should become proud. " Away on toward the end of life Paul emphasized the fact that he was the chief of sinners. You must realize that in yourself you are just the same old worthless self, — as Billy Sunday has said, so black that you could make a black mark on a piece of anthracite " (pp. 121, 122). This is what we all remain at heart, though saved from " the power of sin," that is from all sinning.

[38] We are following in this exposition the tract, " What is Your Kind of Christianity? " The parallel passage to exactly the same effect in " Victory in Christ," pp. 117 f. should be compared.

remark confuses us vastly, from many points of view: for example, from this — regeneration is a change of our nature, but here is no change of nature at all. We remain corrupt sinners still: only we no longer commit sins — that is, "known sins." Not that we cannot commit sins: we can. And indeed we gather we generally do: Mr. Trumbull says he himself has committed them. Despite the miracle wrought in us, we can never say, "I can never sin again." We can always sin again if we choose. "I am not speaking," Mr. Trumbull asseverates, "of any mistaken idea of sinless perfection. It is not possible for anyone to have such a transaction with Christ as to enable him to say, either, 'I am without sin,' or 'I can never sin again.'" We are not saved from sin but from sinning, and we can be saved from sinning only moment by moment, by reëxercising moment by moment the faith by which we "let Christ" free us immediately and completely from all known sin. This freedom though immediate and complete is momentary: it lasts only for the single moment in which it is received, and its renewal for the next moment is wholly dependent on our renewal of the faith which obtains it.

At this point, however, Mr. Trumbull says the most startling thing he says throughout the whole discussion. It is his constant representation that this faith by which immediate and complete freedom from all the power of known sin (alas! that he always says "known sin") is obtained and re-obtained is our own contribution to our salvation. He can even say crisply [39] that "Christ plus my receiving" is the formula for the "hope for victory." And in his system this must needs be the case: until we exercise faith we stand outside all the saving influences of God — for are we not free agents, not to be compelled even to be saved? Here, however, he actually says in a happy lapse from his habitual and necessary teaching, though it, too, is unhappily but a momentary lapse: "But He Himself will give us that faith, and will continue that faith in us moment by moment." [40] Why, if that be true — why, most

[39] Tract on "Is Victory Earned or a Gift?"
[40] "What is Your Kind of Christianity?"

assuredly it *is* possible — nay, it is certain, and beyond all prevention — to have such a transaction with Christ that we can never sin again. For if Christ gives us the faith by which we receive immediate and complete freedom from the power — that is the commission — of all known sin; and if Christ not only gives this faith once but continues it to us moment by moment, why, this, too, is taken out of our hands, and of course we cannot sin; Christ sees to that by Himself giving us, apart from any action precedent on our part, moment by moment, the faith which secures immediate and complete freedom from all the power of known sin. If we ask in wonder how we are to account for Mr. Trumbull's lapse here from the very *cor cordis* of his doctrine — his contention in season, out of season, for the supreme autocracy of the human will — the next sentence reveals it to us: " We can and must, as Frances Ridley Havergal has so truly said, ' entrust to Him our trust.' " He has been reading Miss Havergal, and Miss Havergal is as fundamentally evangelical in the main current of her thought as Mr. Trumbull is fundamentally unevangelical in the main current of his. And he has taken over a phrase from her which is perfectly in place in the general context of her thought, but utterly out of place in the general context of his thought — which indeed throws the whole fabric of his teaching into confusion. Miss Havergal means in the excellent passage to which allusion is made,[41] to tell her readers that we are wholly in God's hands, that it is He and He alone who saves us, and that everything that enters into our salvation — our very faith by which we are united to our Saviour — is from Him and

---

[41] " Kept for the Master's Use," p. 20. " If Christ's keeping depends upon our trusting, and our continuing to trust depends upon ourselves, we are in no better or safer position than before, and shall only be landed in a fresh series of disappointments. The old story, something for the sinner to *do,* crops up again here, only with the ground shifted from ' works ' to trust. Said a friend to me, ' I see now! I did trust Jesus to do everything else for me, but I thought that this trusting was something that *I* had got to do.' . . . We can no more trust and keep on trusting than we can do anything else of ourselves." This is in direct contradiction to Mr. Trumbull's fundamental dogma — that Christ can act on us, in every instance of blessing, only on our opening the way for Him to do so, by an act of our own free determination.

Him only. Mr. Trumbull cannot mean this; his teaching is very explicit that we do our own believing in our own power, while God and Christ stand helplessly by until we choose to open the door for them to work in and on us; we cannot entrust to Him a trust which we must exercise as the condition precedent of His acting upon us at all. We merely note here that Mr. Trumbull, who manages to teach together, as we shall shortly see, autosoterism and quietism, also manages to inject an evangelical phrase into his autosoteric system — and pass on.

It is a fatally inadequate conception of salvation which so focusses attention on deliverance from the penalty of sin and from continued acts of sin, as to permit to fall out of sight deliverance from sin itself — that corruption of heart which makes us sinners. Laying onesided stress on deliverance from acts of sin — especially when these acts of sin are confined by definition to " deliberate transgressions of known law " — is too poverty-stricken a conception of salvation to satisfy any Christian heart. Christians know that their Lord has come into the world to save them from sin in all its aspects, its penalty, its corruption and its power: they trust Him for this complete salvation: and they know that they receive it from Him in its fulness. Mr. Trumbull and his associates have no doubt been betrayed into neglect or denial of our deliverance from the central thing — " the corruption of man's heart " — by a certain prudence. They are set upon the assertion of the possibility and duty for Christians of a life free from sinning. Grant them that, and they are willing to allow that their unsinning Christians remain sinners at heart. They do not appear to see that thus they yield the whole case. An astonishing misapprehension of the relation of action to motive underlies their point of view; and a still more astonishing misapprehension of the method of sanctification which is founded on this relation. To keep a sinner, remaining a sinner, free from actually sinning, would be but a poor salvation; and in point of fact that is not the way the Holy Spirit operates in saving the soul. He does not " take possession of our will and work it " — thus, despite our sinful hearts, producing a series of good acts as our life-manifestation and thereby falsifying our real nature in its manifestation. He cures our sinning precisely by curing our sinful nature; He makes the tree good that the fruit may be good. It is, in other words, precisely by eradicating our sinfulness — "the corruption of our hearts" — that He delivers us from sinning. The very element in salvation which Mr. Trumbull neglects, is therefore, in point of fact, the radical element of the saving process, and the indispensable precondition of that element in salvation which he elects to emphasize to its neglect. We cannot be saved from sinning except as we are saved from sin; and the degree in which we are saved from sinning is the index of the degree in which we have been saved from sin. Here too, as in every other sphere of activity, the *operari* follows and must follow the *esse:* a thing must be before it can act, and it can act only as it is. To imagine that we can be saved from the power of sin without the eradication of the corruption in which the power of sin has its seat, is to imagine that an evil tree can be compelled to bring forth good fruit — or that it would be worth while to compel it to do so — which is the precise thing that our Lord denies. What Mr. Trumbull in point of fact teaches is exactly what Hannah Whitall Smith ridicules in a vivid figure which she uses in a less felicitous connection: that what Christ does is just to tie good fruit to the branches of a bad tree and cry, Behold how great is my salvation! [42]

It is astonishing that nevertheless even Dr. W. H. Griffith Thomas falls in to some extent with this representation. Dr. Thomas does not forget, indeed, that we are to be delivered from the corruption of sin — ultimately. When he wishes to bring into view the whole deliverance which we have in Christ, he enumerates the elements of it thus: "Deliverance from the guilt of sin, deliverance from the penalty of sin, deliverance from the bondage of sin, and deliverance hereafter from the very presence of sin." [43] The insertion of

[42] For example, "Every-Day Religion," 1893, p. 165.
[43] "Grace and Power," 1916, p. 62.

the word "hereafter" into the last clause tells the story. We must wait for the "hereafter" to be delivered from the "presence of sin"—that is to say from the corruption of our hearts—but meanwhile we may very well live as if sin were not present: its presence in us need not in any way affect our life-manifestation. Dr. Thomas enters the formal discussion of the matter,[44] apparently, as a mediator in "the old question, 'suppression or eradication?'"[45] on this side or the other of which perfectionists have been accustomed to array themselves as they faced the problem of the sin that dwells in us. He comes forward with a new formula, by which, supposedly, he hopes that he may conciliate the parties to the dispute. "Suppression," he declares, says too little, "eradication" says too much; let us say, "counteraction," he suggests, and then we shall have the right word. Does "counteraction," however, come between "eradication" and "suppression," saying less than the one and more than the other? Does it not say less than either? Whether the "sinful principle" in us be "eradicated" or "suppressed," it is put out of action: if it be merely "counteracted," it not only remains but remains active, and enters as a co-factor into all effects. The illustration which Dr. Thomas himself uses, to make his meaning clear, is what he speaks of as the counteraction of gravitation by volition. In the same way, he says, "the lower law of sin and death can be counteracted by the presence of the Holy Ghost in our hearts." Of course volition does not directly counteract gravitation: we cannot by a mere volition rise at will upwards from the earth. What volition is able to do is to set another physical force in operation in the direction opposed to the pull or push of gravitation: and if this new physical force pulls or pushes more powerfully in a direction opposite to that in which gravitation pulls or pushes—why, the effect will be in the direction of the action of the new force, and will be determined by the amount of its superiority to the force of gravity. We throw

[44] "Grace and Power," chapter viii. pp. 131 ff.; also printed in tract form under the title of "Must Christians Sin?"
[45] The phrase is taken from O. A. Curtis, "The Christian Faith," p. 390.

a ball into the air. We have not suppressed gravity. It pulls the ball all the time. We only counteract its effect in the exact measure in which the force we apply exceeds the pull of gravity. If Dr. Thomas intends this illustration to be applied fully, it appears to imply that the "principle of sin" operates in all our acts with full power, and therefore conditions all our acts: only, the Holy Spirit dwelling in us is stronger than indwelling sin, and therefore the effect produced is determined by Him. We do not sin, not because the principle of sin in us is suppressed or eradicated, but because it is counteracted. If this be Dr. Thomas' meaning, one would think that he ought to declare not, as he does declare, that Christians need not sin, but that they cannot sin — not even to the least, tiny degree. If the Holy Spirit who is the infinite God dwells in them for the express purpose of counteracting the principle of sin in them; and if He operates invariably, in every action of the Christian; it would seem to be clearly impossible that the principle of sin should ever be traceable in the effect at all. The ball that we throw into the air will rise only a certain distance and ever more and more slowly until, its initial impulse being overcome by the deadly pull of gravity, it turns and falls back to earth. If, however, it was propelled by an infinite force, the pull of gravity, though always present, could have no determining effect on its movement. On this theory of counteraction Dr. Thomas should teach therefore not that Christians need not sin, but that they cannot sin — as indeed the passages in I John on which he immediately depends in his exposition of his view would also compel him, on his system of interpretation, to teach.

From the point of view of Scripture, however, this theory of counteraction is quite inadequate. It renders it impossible for the Christian to sin — and the Scriptures do not teach that: but it leaves the "principle of sin" in him unaltered and in full activity, and most emphatically the Scriptures do not teach that such is the condition of the Christian in this world. It surely would be better to be freed from the "principle of sin" in us than merely from its effects on our actions. And this is in fact what the Scriptures provide for. What they teach, indeed, is just "eradication." They propose to free us from sinning by freeing us from the "principle of sin." Of course, they teach that the Spirit dwells within us. But they teach that the Spirit dwells within us in order to affect us, not merely our acts; in order to eradicate our sinfulness and not merely to counteract its effects. The Scriptures' way of cleansing the stream is to cleanse the fountain; they are not content to attack the stream of our activities, they attack directly the heart out of which the issues of life flow. But they give us no promise that the fountain will be completely cleansed all at once, and therefore no promise that the stream will flow perfectly purely from the beginning. We are not denying that the Spirit leads us in all our acts, as well as purifies our hearts. But we are denying that His whole work in us, or His whole immediate work in us, or His fundamental work in us, terminates on our activities and can be summed up in the word "counteraction." Counteraction there is; and suppression there is; but most fundamentally of all there is eradication; and all these work one and the self-same Spirit. We are not forgetful that Dr. Thomas teaches an ultimate eradication; and we would not be unwilling to read his recognition of it "with a benevolent eye" and understand him as teaching, not that the eradication is not going on now, but only that the eradication which is going on now is not completed until "hereafter." That would be Scriptural. But we fear Dr. Thomas will not permit us so to read him. And, if we mistake not, this difference in point of view between him and the Scriptures is in part, the source of his misconception and misprision of the seventh chapter of Romans. That chapter depicts for us the process of the eradication of the old nature. Dr. Thomas reads it statically and sees in it merely a "deadly warfare between the two natures"; which, he affirms,[46] "does not represent the normal Christian life of sanctification." He even

---

[46] Pp. 93, 94. On the ill-treatment which the Seventh Chapter of Romans has received in general from the members of this school see some interesting remarks by H. A. Boardman as cited, chapter vii. pp. 98 ff.

permits himself to say, " There is no Divine grace in that chapter; only man's nature struggling to be good and holy by law." What is really in the chapter is Divine grace warring against, and not merely counteracting but eradicating, the natural evil of sin. To Paul the presence of the conflict there depicted is the guarantee of victory. The three things which we must insist on if we would share Paul's view are: first, that to grace always belongs the initiative — it is grace that works the change: secondly, that to grace always belongs the victory — grace is infinite power: and thirdly, that the working of grace is by process, and therefore reveals itself at any given point of observation as conflict. In so far as Dr. Thomas's representation obscures any one of these things it falls away from the teaching of the New Testament. Grace assuredly "means a new life, a Divine life, which lifts us above the natural, and is nothing else than the life of Christ Himself in His people." It is, in substance, as sanctifying grace, the occupation of our hearts by the Holy Spirit, and the undertaking by Him, not only of their renewal, but of their control. It is they alone who are " led " by the Spirit who are sons of God. But the work of the Holy Spirit in our hearts is not confined to the direction of our activities. Dr. Thomas says truly [47] that grace does not merely " educate the natural heart." But he errs when he says that " grace does not improve the old nature, it overcomes it." He errs when he teaches only that " it promises hereafter to extirpate it," but meanwhile, only " counteracts its tendencies." It is progressively extirpating it now, and that is the fundamental fact in supernatural sanctification. The sanctifying action of the Spirit terminates on us, not merely on our activities; under it not only our actions but we are made holy. Only, this takes time; and therefore at no point short of its completion are either our acts or we " perfect."

If we wish to observe to what lengths the notion may be carried, that the " old man " in us is unaffected by the intruding Spirit, we have only to turn to Mr. Robert C. McQuilkin's somewhat incoherent tract on " God's Way of Victory over

[47] P. 93.

Sin." This tract has for its professed object the inculcation of what it expresses in its subordinate title in the words: "If it isn't easy, it isn't good." That is to say, its primary purpose is to show that it is easy, not hard, to be "good," and that it is therefore wrong to say that "it's awful hard to be good." It is easy to be good because it is not we who have to be good but the Holy Spirit is ready to be good for us, and all we have to do is just to let Him. We have called the tract incoherent because, with this as its primary concern, it yet tells us, as it draws near its close, that "the Spirit-led life is not an easy life," that, on the contrary, "it is the hardest life in all this sin-cursed world." Are we not to apply to the Spirit-led life, then, the maxim, "If it isn't easy, it isn't good"? The specialty of this tract, however — and the reason we advert to it here — is the crudity with which, after a fashion more familiar to us among "the Brethren," it divides the Christian man into two ineradicably antagonistic "natures," the "fallen nature" and the "new nature." It is not only hard for a fallen man to be good, we are told, but impossible. This is not altered by his "new birth." The "new birth" does not change his "fallen nature." It only puts into him, by its side, a "new nature." Henceforth he has two natures in him, one of which can only sin, and the other of which cannot sin. The man himself — whatever the man himself, apart from his two natures, may be; he is apparently conceived as bare will — sits up between these two natures and turns over the lever as he lists, to give the one nature or the other momentary control. The two natures, we are told, have absolutely no effect on one another. "The carnal nature in the Christian is utterly evil, and is never mixed with any good." "The new nature has no effect whatever upon the carnal nature. It is utterly distinct from it and cannot mingle with it, any more than God can have sin in His nature." It does not "change the character of the evil that the carnal nature is capable of." Apparently the carnal nature of man is never in any way changed or modified; from all that appears it remains in him forever and forever just badness and unalloyed badness. At least nothing is said to

relieve that situation. Salvation does not consist in its eradication. It consists in the dominance in the life of "the new
nature" existing by its side. This "new nature" is identified,
now, with the indwelling Spirit. It is sometimes spoken of,
no doubt, as "the God-begotten nature"; but it is more frequently and properly treated as just the indwelling Spirit
Himself, and it is because it is the indwelling Spirit Himself
that it cannot sin. "It is impossible for the Spirit of God to be
anything but good and well-pleasing to God." "The sinless
and invincible Spirit of God has taken up His dwelling in us,"
we read further, "and has made it possible for us to permit
Him to win the victories over the temptations that assail."
It is disappointing to learn from this statement that when
"the invincible Spirit of God" takes up His dwelling in us, all
that He does is "to make it possible for us to permit Him"
(an odd clause that!) to win victories for us. He is not "in full
control" of us, it seems. It would indeed be truer to say, that
He is only at our disposal. Everything is after all in our own
control. "A Christian possessed of the indwelling Spirit of
God," we read with sad eyes, "may choose to walk after the
flesh." That is no doubt because he is possessed of rather than
by the Spirit of God. At any rate it belongs ineradicably to
"the Christian" to turn on the old carnal nature, or the new
Spiritual nature, as he may choose, and let it act for him. Who
this "Christian" is who possesses this power it is a little puzzling to make out. He cannot be the old carnal nature, for that
old carnal nature cannot do anything good — and presumably,
therefore, would never turn on the Spirit in control. He cannot be the new Spiritual nature, for this new Spiritual nature
cannot do anything evil — and this "Christian" "may choose
to walk after the flesh." Is he possibly some third nature? We
hope not, because two absolutely antagonistic and noncom-
municating natures seem enough to be in one man. The only
alternative seems, however, to be that he is no nature at all —
just a nonentity: and then we do not see how he can turn on
anything. Mr. McQuilkin is not wholly unaware of the difficulty to thought of the notion he is presenting. "That a Chris-

tian should possess two natures," he writes, "one wholly evil
and incapable of doing good, the other wholly good and incapable of doing evil, is a mystery, and no words of man's
wisdom can explain how these two natures exist in one personality." That surely is true.

It has already incidentally become clear how Mr. Trumbull
and his associates think of the Victorious Life. It is not lived
by the Christian, but by Christ in and through the Christian.
Immediately upon our "letting go and letting God," God in
Christ takes charge of our lives and lives them for us. The
conception is that of a true substitution of the Christ within
us for ourselves, as the agent in what are apparently our own
activities. It involves therefore a complete quietism on our
part, and nothing is more insisted upon than that we must
cease from all effort in the matter of good works. The sole
condition of Christ's thus undertaking for us is that we should
leave it absolutely to Him. A very fair compressed statement
of the whole theory is given in one or two pages in "Victory
in Christ." [48] There we are told that there are two conditions
of "the life of victory." They are declared to be "simple" and
are described as "surrender and faith." They are proper conditions; that is to say, they must precede the victorious life —
without them there can be no victorious life — but on their
occurrence the victorious life follows as a strict consequence,
immediately and in its completeness. "Surrender" is defined
as "the uttermost giving up of all that we have and all that
we are to the mastery of Jesus." It is elsewhere called accepting Christ not only as our Saviour (that has been done in justifying faith) but also as our Lord. It is putting ourselves wholly
at His disposal. It is said that Christ can do nothing for us
until this is done. His taking charge of our life can only be
by our permission. But "as soon as we have made this complete and unconditional surrender," "Christ instantly" "accepts the whole responsibility of living in us in His fulness."
This is the Christ in us, living in us, and living through us, of
other passages. What He accomplishes in us by thus living in

[48] Pp. 26, 27.

us is expressed as working " the miracle-victory over the power
of all known sin, of producing in us all the fruit of the Spirit."
This statement appears to declare a negative and a positive
effect; negatively, He frees us from all "known sin"; positively, He produces in us "all the fruit of the Spirit." Thus a
true perfection of life is produced. How we open the way for
Him to do this is more exactly explained as by telling Him
"that we *know* He *is* doing it." If this bears the appearance
of a contradiction — for how can His undertaking to do it be
conditioned on our recognition that He is already doing it?
— the difficulty is met by explaining that the basis of our
knowledge that He *is* doing it is the bare promise. It is not
introspection or experience. "We know this, not by any
changed feeling, nor by any evidence, or any proof, or any
manifestation of any sort." We must rest on the bare Word.
Christ says He *will* do it if we let Him; we, therefore know
that He is doing it when we " let go and let God "; and if we
tell Him so, "He will undertake the doing of it then and
there " — a statement in which there still seems to reside a
certain confusion between the present and future tenses.
We may let that pass, however. What is certainly taught is
that Christ wishes, of course, to take charge of our lives, but
cannot do it until we let Him. But when we absolutely trust
Him to do it — that is " the step of faith that Christ instantly
honors and blesses with His very fulness in the life." [49] We
must remember, of course, "that everything must depend
upon *Christ* and *His* work, in the matter of victory." But this,
only "after we have surrendered our lives to Him." [50] That
He does the work on which everything depends, itself depends,
that is, absolutely on us. Thus everything ultimately is in our
hands. Christ is an absolutely indispensable instrument; an
instrument without which the results could not be obtained;
we must use Him if we are to perfect our lives. But He is only
an instrument which we use. He can do nothing of Himself;
it is only as we use Him that He can work on or in us.
    The manner in which we must use Him, however, is to

[49] P. 28.   [50] P. 29.

submit ourselves entirely to Him. He can do nothing unless we call Him in to do it; but neither can He do anything when we call Him in to do it unless we put the case absolutely in His hands.[51] He will undertake nothing unless He has it all, and the "all" must be taken absolutely. The condition of the victorious life is that we must do nothing, absolutely nothing, except submit ourselves to Christ. Any attempt to do anything further not only does not help on the work of our perfecting; it absolutely hinders it. "Just remember this," says Mr. Trumbull in the tract on "Real and Counterfeit Victory": "any victory over the power of any sin whatsoever in your life that you have to get by working for it is counterfeit. Any victory that you have to get by trying for it is counterfeit. If you have to work for your victory, it is not the real thing; it is not the thing that God offers you." The notion is still further developed in the tract on "Is Victory Earned or a Gift?" What is affirmed here is that victory is "an outright gift of God," by which is meant that we can do nothing whatever to realize it. We do do something to secure it; something so necessary that unless we do it we cannot have it,[52] though Mr. Trumbull will not allow that even what we do to secure it, the "surrendering" ourselves to Christ, is an "effort"; it is just an "act of the will," he says. But certainly no "efforts" are in place in the realization of our victory over sin: we must not try not to sin.[53] "Our efforts," he explains — that is, our efforts not to commit sin — "can not only never play any part in our victory over the power of sin, but they can and

[51] Hannah Whitall Smith, "The Christian's Secret of a Happy Life," p. 48, illustrates from physicians who require patients to put themselves wholly in their care: "For, of course," said one, "I could do nothing for him unless he would put his whole case into my hands without any reserves. . . ."

[52] This, it will be observed, is the exact reversal of the Scriptural doctrine, which is to the effect that we can do nothing to secure, but much to realize the life in Christ.

[53] Paul's view was different, and therefore he continually exhorts us to efforts to realize our holiness, as for example in II Cor. vii. 1 where he urges us precisely to purify ourselves and thus to bring our holiness to its completion. W. B. Pope, "A Compendium of Christian Theology," iii. p. 39, points out that "the word indicates an end to which effort is ever converging."

do effectually prevent such victory." He is speaking, let us bear in mind, to men who have already received deliverance from the penalty of sin; they are Christian men. Now, he says, they must not try not to commit sin. All they must — all they can — do, is by an " act of the will " (which is no effort) to accept absolute freedom from the power of sin — that is, in his definition, from committing sins — as a free gift. If they try at all not to commit sins, that is the same as to attempt to coöperate with Christ in freeing them from the power of sin; it involves therefore a demand that Christ should recognize that they have had some part to play in freeing themselves from the power of sin — and Christ can never recognize that; and accordingly if we try to refrain from sinning the only result is that we prevent Christ from saving us — in that case, " Christ cannot save us from the power of sin." We are then, " to use our will to accept the gift of victory " — which we remember is no effort — but " we are not to make an effort " — any effort at all — " to win the victory." " We don't need to agonize about it; we don't need to work for it. The more we work, and the more we agonize, the more we prevent or postpone what He wants to give us now."

This is of course express quietism. Mr. Trumbull is not content to teach that we cannot cease from sinning in the power of our own will, even of our renewed will, alone; but must be dependent for our every victory over sin upon the indwelling Spirit and His gracious operations. He goes on to teach that, therefore, we must make no effort to cease from sinning, but leave it wholly to God the Spirit Himself to deliver us from sinning. He is not content to trust our conquest of sin to God in whose might alone we can conquer in this warfare. He insists that, therefore, we must refuse to fight the good fight of faith and decline to have any part in the working out of our own salvation. This, we say, is quietism; and because it is quietism, it may easily run over into antinomianism. All history teaches us how dreadfully easy it is to persuade ourselves that, if we have received as a sheer gift from Christ absolute freedom from sinning and need not concern

ourselves farther about it — then, of course, the things we do
(whatever they are) cannot be sins. Mr. Trumbull, of course,
like all of his coterie, has already taken this step [54] so far as
to deny that anything he does can have the guilt of sin, unless he knows it to be sin: only "recognized sins" are sins to
him. All experience teaches us that it is terribly easy not to
recognize sins when we see them; not to "know" sins to which
we chance to be prone, to be sins.[55] Here, too, constant vigilance is the price of safety. And therefore we find so good a
perfectionist as W. B. Pope rebuking the "too prevalent separation between the sanctification of Christian privilege as a
free gift and the ethical means appointed for its attainment," [56] and carefully explaining the two aspects in which
sanctification must be looked at,[57] and emphasizing "effort"
as entering into its very essence. "On the one hand," he says
truly, "it is a state of rest: 'filled with the Spirit,' the Christian can say, 'I can do all things through Christ which
strengtheneth me.' On the other it is a state in which the soul
is safe only in the highest exercise of the severest virtue. To its
safety its sedulity is required."

How far this Quietistic Perfectionism may be pressed, may
be observed from the tract, "May Christians Lose Sinful De-

[54] "What we maintain," writes Lyman H. Atwater, as cited, p. 403, "is,
that its advocates really take Antinomian ground; that they in one form
or another lower the standard of perfect holiness below the only perfect and
immutable standard of goodness — i.e., the divine law — to some vague and
indeterminate level, depending on and varying with the subjective states of
each person who supposes himself to be perfect."

[55] "One of Satan's devices," says Mrs. Alice E. McClure near the beginning of her tract, "An American Girl's Struggle and Surrender" (p. 4), "is
to get us to think that sin is not sin." It is a sentence well worth the consideration of those who wish to confine sins to "known sins." Mrs. McClure in
general manifests more sense of sin than most of her school (cf. pp. 12, 21, 29).
But alas! even she knows only an "if" religion. She even speaks of giving
God a "chance" and permits herself this broad generalization: "Christianity
is the only religion in which supremacy is given to the individual co-operation"
("Victory in Christ," pp. 167, 168). This is not Paul's view, "Of Him are ye
in Christ Jesus," "It is not of him that willeth." The gospel of salvation by
co-operation is not Christ's gospel.

[56] "A Compendium of Christian Theology," iii. p. 65.

[57] Pp. 59, 60.

sires?" What is contended for in this tract is not merely "instantaneous and complete deliverance from the power of sin," in the sense of from the commission of sin, but "effortless freedom from sinful impulse." We not only do not sin, and do not sin without any effort on our part not to sin, having "victory by freedom rather than victory by fight"; we do not even have any impulse to sin. We not only are not mastered by sinful passions; we do not even "feel any desire to yield to them"; "their very appeal to us can be broken and broken completely." "Effortless freedom" from all "sinful impulses" — this is the type of perfectionism that is taught; and this is a distinctly quietistic type of perfectionism. What we are to do and what we can do, is "to enter upon the very life of God: to be as He is, even in this world (I John iv. 17)": [58] not to struggle or fight against temptation but "simply let Christ dispose of it, while we stand by like onlookers." It seems that we are still to be tempted, even though we are to

[58] In "Victory in Christ," p. 110, Mr. Trumbull declares that I John iv. 17 is "perhaps the most daring word in the whole Bible" — as he might well declare it to be if it meant what he cites it in this tract as meaning. But he himself cannot so take it, and therefore at this place in "Victory in Christ" he introduces his own arbitrary limitation upon it: "That is," he says, (the italics are ours) "the same freedom for us from the power of *known sin* as God Himself has." On the next page (p. 111) he cites the passage again but takes it on this occasion (rightly) as referring to Christ, not God. The passage is a stock passage with the perfectionists in this sense, referred sometimes to God, sometimes to Christ. Thus O. A. Curtis, "The Christian Faith," 1905, p. 386: "We are prepared for the day of judgment by having this love of God made perfect in us; and this perfection of love can be achieved in this life — 'because as He is, even so are we in this world.'" So W. B. Pope, "A Compendium of Christian Theology," iii. p. 55: "The only time our love is spoken of as literally perfect, it is connected with this Supreme Pattern: 'because as He is, so are we in this world.'" The passage is in any case a very difficult one: but this perfectionist interpretation of it is certainly not the right one. The reference is to Christ, not God, and apparently to standing, not condition: what it probably teaches is that we shall stand before the judgment seat not in our own but in Christ's right. In the "Account of the Union Meeting for the Promotion of Scriptural Holiness held at Oxford, August 29 to September 7, 1874," pp. 91–92, it is cited, apparently by R. Pearsall Smith, in its right sense: — "We have learned that 'as Christ is so are we in this world,' and God sees us not as we are in ourselves, but as we stand in the Beloved." "The light which shows the evil also shows the blood."

be as God is in this world. This much is conceded to our humanity, though it is conceded arbitrarily. We are assured that we shall be tempted, and elsewhere we are told that our temptations even increase in violence. But we are to be "as God is" in having as our habitual experience His own freedom from the desire to sin under these temptations. "The simple fact is," we are told, "that whenever a life that trusts Christ as Savior is completely surrendered to Christ as Master, Christ is ready then to take complete control of that life, and at once to fill it with Himself. . . . When we surrender and trust completely we die to self and Christ can and does literally replace our self with Himself. Thus it is no longer we that live but Christ liveth in us in His Person, literally fills our whole being with Himself in actual, personal presence; and He does this not as a figure of speech, but just as literally as that we fill our clothes with ourselves." If this be the state of the case, why of course we cannot sin, or feel any impulse to sin; Christ has supplanted us as the actor in all our actions. There is indeed no "we" left; our place has been taken by Christ, and "Christ does not have to struggle against any appeal that sin makes to Him." Any temptation that may assault us is of course "defeated by Christ before it has time to draw us into a fight" — if there is any "us" left to be drawn into a fight.

What is our astonishment then to learn that it is nevertheless in our power — the power of the "us" which has been superseded by Christ as the agent in all our acts — to defeat Christ's purpose for us here. "The only thing that can prevent Him," we read — prevent Him from saving us from sinning and from doing it without our fighting against sin at all — "is either our distrust of His power, or our withdrawal of our complete surrender." When we surrender, Christ "does literally replace our self with Himself." And yet — we can still "distrust his power," "withdraw our complete surrender!" We seem forced to the conclusion that it is Christ (who is now the only agent) that distrusts His own power and withdraws our complete surrender, and we should not have thought that possiblc. But then we must remember that Mr. Trumbull has something always up his sleeve which is in his view more powerful than Christ, and which not even Christ can either suppress or supplant — something which, even though we have died to self and it is no longer we that live but Christ alone lives in us, can yet assert itself at any moment it chooses and cast Christ from the throne and assume it itself — the human will. We can only say that for ourselves we have not so learned either Christ or the human will.

There is another phrase which Mr. Trumbull uses in connection with the destruction of sinful desire in us that surprises us almost as much as this one, though from another point of view. " The victorious life," [59] he tells us, " is the life of overcoming sin by the miraculous fact that the very desire for sin is taken from you: you do not want to do anything that you know to be sin." This is indeed a miraculous fact — with the limitation that is put on it. For with this limitation it seems psychologically inexplicable. We can understand what is meant when it is said that the impulse to sinful acts is eradicated; but scarcely, when what is said is that the impulse to acts known to be sinful is eradicated. What has our knowledge of the moral character of the acts to do with a native impulse pushing towards them? Here is anger, for instance — Mr. Trumbull is rather fond of using it as an illustration. We can understand what is meant when it is said that all impulse to anger is removed. And we can understand that as soon as we come to realize how wrong anger is, we should strive against the impulse to it. But how can the discovery that anger is wrong all at once remove all native tendency to angry ebullition? This would be equivalent to saying that it is not the impulse to anger that is removed but all tendency to abstract lawlessness: and that seems something different. The appearance is created that on this teaching the whole of the moral reaction is reduced to the one category of loyalty to law; and that seems scarcely tenable. Clearly the eradication of a constitutional propension pushing towards a specific ac-

[59] " Victory in Christ," p. 84.

tion cannot be directly dependent on obtaining knowledge of
the moral character of that action. The eradication of all impulses to sinful acts is at least intelligible. The conditioning of
their eradication on our knowledge of the sinfulness of these
acts seems scarcely so. But this by the way.

The overstrained mystical doctrine of the Christ within us
on which Mr. Trumbull's quietism is founded, will not have
escaped the reader. The crassness of the language in which
he can express this doctrine may be noted perhaps as well as
elsewhere in the tract called "The Life that Wins." [60] He begins its exposition, as all his fellows begin it, by declaring
that such New Testament expressions as "Christ in you and
you in Christ, Christ our life, and abiding in Christ," "are
literal, actual, blessed fact, and not figures of speech." But
what these expressions literally say does not suffice him. He
presses on to such an unmeasured declaration as this: "At last
I realized that Jesus Christ was actually and literally within
me; and even more than that: that He had constituted Himself my very being . . . my body, mind, soul, and spirit. . . .
My body was His, my mind His, my spirit His; and not merely
His, but literally a part of Him . . . Jesus Christ had constituted Himself my life — not as a figure of speech, remember, but as a literal, actual fact, as literal as the fact that a
certain tree has been made into this desk on which my hand
rests." [61] If this amazing language is anything more than
somewhat loose rhetoric, it asserts that our individuality has
been abolished and Christ has taken its place. We are told
that He has "constituted" Himself our "very being"; and,
that he may not fail to give this assertion full validity, our
being is analyzed into its parts and we are told that Christ
has constituted Himself "our body, mind, soul, and spirit."
All these things become not only His, "but literally a part of
Him"; He has become them as literally as the tree which has
been sawn into boards of which a desk is made has been made
into that desk. Clearly "we" no longer exist; we have passed

[60] This tract has been revised as late as February, 1917.
[61] Pp. 13, 14.

away and Christ has been substituted for us: we and He are
not one and another — there is but one left and that one is
Christ. Accordingly Mr. Trumbull says: " I need never again
ask Him to help me, as though He were one and I another; but
rather simply [ask Him] to do His work, His will, in me, and
with me, and through me." The question no doubt obtrudes
itself how " we " can ask " Him " anything, when there is no
longer one and another in the case. There is in fact only one
agent left, whether to ask or to be asked, and that is Christ.
Surely He who has constituted Himself my very being, my
body, mind, soul and spirit, does not now turn around and
ask Himself to do His work, His will in me, and with me, and
through me. Nor does He need to do these things, for surely
they are things He cannot well help doing. And so the inference is sharply drawn: " When our life is not only Christ's, but
Christ, our life will be a winning life; for He cannot fail." [62]
Our only wonder is that Mr. Trumbull felt it necessary to say
this: of course, if we have passed away and Christ has taken
our place and He is the only agent in what we absurdly call our
acts, all — all, we say — that is done by " us " is really done
by Him, and must represent Him fully and not " us " at all.
That lies in the very nature of the case.

It must not be supposed that Mr. Trumbull is alone in
proclaiming this somewhat unintelligible mysticism. It is common to the whole school which he represents. When Henry A.
Boardman, a half century ago, was commenting on it, as
taught by Hannah Whitall Smith and her coterie,[63] he remarked on the onesidedness of their representation. It is purely
arbitrary, he intimates, to lay such stress on Christ becoming
to us righteousness and sanctification in such a sense as that
His righteousness and holiness are infused into us, and to say
nothing of His becoming to us wisdom, say, which is coupled
with the others in the same verse (I Cor. i. 30), in such a manner " that we become also perfectly wise with His wisdom."
" You have precisely the same authority," he says, " for claim-

[62] P. 17.
[63] " The ' Higher Life ' Doctrine of Sanctification," 1877, p. 90.

ing to be *perfect in wisdom,* on accepting Christ, that you have
for claiming to be perfect in sanctification." It will have been
seen that Mr. Trumbull does not lay himself open to this
criticism. He declares boldly that Christ has constituted Himself not only our soul and spirit, but also our mind, and even
our body; and the inevitable consequence must be drawn that
we must therefore be perfect in every one of these spheres of
life.

If Mr. Trumbull does not follow out all these inferences for
us, Dr. A. B. Simpson does; and that in writings which are
recommended by Mr. Trumbull as among " the best and clearest " " on the truth of the life that is Christ, which is presented
at Princeton Conference." [64] Take the tract, for example, called
" Himself," which is an address delivered at Bethshan, London.[65] The fundamental idea of this tract is that we may have
not only gifts from Christ, but Himself; and to have Christ
Himself is better than to have all His help, all His Blessings,
all His Gifts. When that has been said, however, the reins are
thrown on the neck of fancy and it is permitted to run away
with the idea. To have Christ is to have Him in such a sense,
we are told, that whatever Christ is becomes quite literally
ours. Not only does Christ's righteousness become our right-

[64] " Victory in Christ," pp. 100, 116, last fly leaf.

[65] The same doctrine that is taught in this tract is taught also, though
more briefly, in Dr. Simpson's " The Christ Life," which is explicitly mentioned among the best books on the subject of the Victorious Life. Bethshan
is the Faith-Cure Establishment founded in London by Mrs. Baxter and
Miss Murray in connection with W. E. Boardman, and Boardman taught the
same extravagant mysticism as Simpson: — " He is *the Life,* the *All* of life
for *body* as well as *soul, complete.* In Him *dwelleth* all fulness; we are filled
full in Him. . . . Fulness, absolute fulness of life dwells in Him alone; and in
us only as He dwells in us by faith. Fulness of life is fulness of health. Disease
is incompatible with fulness of life. His presence in us, welcomed by faith as
our fulness of life, and so of health, is really the expulsive power that rebukes
and dispels disease. The same is true of *strength.* . . . Our completeness in
Him cannot be actualized until our faith welcomes Him in whom dwells the
All-fulness, as our Fulness of life and health in the body, as well as in the
soul. . . . And the prominent work of the Spirit is just this — to uplift us
into Christ, and unfold *Him* in *all* His fulness, the Fulness of God in us."
(" Life and Labours of the Rev. W. E. Boardman," by Mrs. Boardman, 1886,
American ed. 1887, pp. 231–233).

eousness, and Christ's holiness our holiness, and Christ's wisdom our wisdom, and Christ's strength our strength, but Christ's spirit becomes our spirit, Christ's mind our mind, Christ's body our body. As Dr. Simpson was speaking on this occasion at Bethshan he very naturally laid his stress on Christ's body becoming our body — in such a sort, that, having Christ, we have bodily wholeness, not merely freedom from disease, but perfect bodily wholeness — for is not Christ's body whole? But he sweeps his hand over all the strings. He has taken Christ for his mind, for his memory, for his will also; and we learn that he therefore no longer makes mistakes, no longer forgets things, and no longer is irresolute or stubborn at the wrong places. " Christ in him " has become the real agent in all his mental and moral activities. Even his faith is not his own, but Christ's. This is especially puzzling, because he tells us elsewhere that we must " take " Christ for all these things or else we do not get them, and that this " taking " is our own act, Christ becoming our life only subsequently and consequently to it. Here he tells us, however, that not even faith must come between us and Jesus. Once he thought he should have " to work up the faith," and so he "labored to get the faith." But that did not work. " And then God seemed to speak to me so sweetly, saying, ' Never mind, my child, *you* have nothing. But *I am* perfect Power, I am perfect Love, I am Faith, I am your Life, I am the preparation for the blessing, and then I am the Blessing too. I am all within and all without, and all forever.' " And then he exclaims: " It is just having ' the Faith of God ' (Mark xi. 22, margin). ' And the life I now live in the flesh, I live ' not by faith *on* the Son of God, but ' by the faith *of the* Son of God ' (Gal. ii. 20). That is it. It is not *your* faith. You have no faith in you, any more than you have life or anything else in you. . . . You have to take His faith as well as His life and healing, and have simply to say, ' I live by the faith of the Son of God.' . . . It is simply Christ, Christ alone." [66] Christ thus does our very believing for us, and

[66] " Himself," pp. 10–12. Similarly, Hannah Whitall Smith, " Every-Day Religion," 1893, p. 153, makes Mark xi. 22 mean: " We are commanded to

we live not by faith in Him but by His faith in us. We have, indeed, "to take His faith," just as we have to take His life, and we do not quite understand what this "taking" is, if it is not already faith. As now, however, we take His faith and it becomes our faith, so we "take" His body and it becomes our body, and — as His body is now our body we are in a bodily sense, of course, whole. Dr. Simpson actually teaches this. You can "receive Christ" for your body's welfare as well as for your soul's; and when you do this, His body becomes your body. "His spirit is all that your spirit needs, and He just gives us *Himself*. His body possesses all that your body needs. He has a heart beating with the strength that your heart needs. He has organs and functions redundant with life, not for Himself but for humanity. He does not need strength for Himself. The energy which enabled Him to rise and ascend from the tomb, above all the forces of nature, was not for Himself. That marvelous body belongs to your body. You are a member of His body. Your heart has a right to draw from His heart all that it needs. Your physical life has a right to draw from His physical life its support and strength, and so it is not you, but it is just the precious life of the Son of God." "Will you take Him thus to-day?" he therefore pleads. And he promises: "And then you will not be merely healed, but you will have a new life for all you need, a flood of life that will sweep disease away, and then remain a fountain of life for all your future need." [67] Dr. Simpson knows, for he has tried it. He gives an affecting account [68] of how, learning the little secret of "Christ in you," he took Him for His bodily health too — and got not merely relief from suffering, not

---

have the same sort of faith that God has." "Romans iv. 17 describes," she says, "the sort of faith God has": He creates things by merely calling them as though they were. "How much of this creative power of faith we his children share, I am not prepared to say," she modestly adds. "But," she continues, "that we are called to share far more of it than we have ever yet laid hold of, I feel very sure." All this from a simple objective genitive! One would like to see them try their system of interpretation on Col. ii. 12.

[67] Pp. 13, 14.
[68] Pp. 16–18.

merely "simple healing," but Christ "so gave me Himself that I lost the painful consciousness of physical organs." This is what "letting go and letting Christ" means, when it is taken "literally."

There is indeed one dogma which takes precedence in Mr. Trumbull's mind to the dogma of the "Christ within us." This is the dogma of the inalienable ability of the human will to do at any time and under any circumstances precisely what in its unmotived caprice it chances to turn to. To this dogma accordingly he cheerfully sacrifices his fervently asserted dogma of the "Christ within us" while in the very act of elaborating it. With a bathos of inconsequence which would be incredible did it not stare us full in the face, he actually inserts into the assertion that Christ has "constituted Himself my very being . . . my body, mind, soul and spirit," at the place indicated by the points, this bewildering parenthesis: "(save only my power to resist Him)." How, in the name of all that is rational, can I retain a power to resist Him when I retain no body or mind or soul or spirit of my own; when I no longer exist as a distinguishable entity, but Christ has become me as literally as the tree which furnishes the wood of which a desk has been made has become that desk? Where is the seat of this power to resist Him? And how can it act — successfully act — against the only agent that acts at all? Following out his inconsequent dogma of a "power to resist Christ" remaining in the "being" which Christ has constituted Himself, however, Mr. Trumbull proceeds to beg us not to think that he is "suggesting any mistaken unbalanced theory that, when a man receives Christ as the fulness of his life, he cannot sin again." [69] How can we help thinking just that when we have been told that Christ has constituted Himself our very being, our body, mind, soul and spirit; and, seizing the reins, has become the sole agent in all our activities — He who "cannot fail"? Can Christ, who has thus become our very life, living thus in us, sin through us? And if He cannot sin through us, how can "we" sin, when it is no longer we who live, but He that lives in us?

[69] "The Life that Wins," p. 15.

To say that "the 'life that is Christ' still leaves us our free will and with that free will we can resist Christ" is to deny *simpliciter* that Christ in us has "constituted Himself my very being . . . my body, mind, soul and spirit"; that my body, mind, will — "will" is expressly mentioned — and spirit have become "not merely His but literally a part of Him." And when it is once said that "the 'life that is Christ' still leaves us our free will" and that "with that free will we can resist Christ," it is already denied *simpliciter* what is at once added — that "as I trust Christ in surrender, there need be no fighting against sin, but complete freedom from the power and even the desire of sin." How can he who is free from even the desire of sin possibly resist Christ? Is not resisting Christ sin? And if resisting Christ is sin, how can he who may at any time resist Christ be said to be free from all necessity of fighting against sin? Must he not fight against the impulse, the temptation, to resist Christ — even though in some mysterious sense, though retaining a liability to resist Christ, he has no "desire of sin"? And how can we talk of retaining the power to resist Christ if we "have learned that this freedom," from the power and even the desire of sin, "this more than conquering, is sustained in unbroken continuance as I simply recognize that Christ is my cleansing, reigning life"? [70]

Obviously, Mr. Trumbull cannot maintain both these dogmas — the dogma of the substitution of Christ for us as the agent in all our activities, and the dogma of the possession by us of an ineradicable power to resist Christ. They destroy one another, and one must give way before the other. It is not difficult to determine which is the more deeply rooted in Mr. Trumbull's thinking. It is clear that his dogma of free will is the foundation stone of all his thought, and that before it all else must give way. This is the account to give, indeed, of its emergence in this connection. He cannot refrain from throwing in a caveat in its favor, even when engaged in elaborating its contradictory — a dogma of the sole agency of Christ in all the activities of the surrendered Christian. In the

[70] P. 16.

light of Scripture, however, the one dogma, equally with the other, is wholly untenable. The Scriptures have a doctrine of free will and they have a doctrine of Christ within us. But the doctrine of Scripture on neither of these matters has anything in common with the exaggerated dogma on it which Mr. Trumbull announces. It happens that the Scriptural doctrine on both matters may be suggested by a single Scriptural phrase, which may stand for us as their symbol: make the tree good that its fruit may be good also. Christ dwells within us not for the purpose of sinking our being into His being, nor of substituting Himself for us as the agent in our activities; much less of seizing our wills and operating them for us in contradiction to our own immanent mind; but to operate directly upon us, to make us good, that our works, freely done by us, may under His continual leading, be good also. Our wills, being the expression of our hearts, continually more and more dying to sin and more and more living to holiness, under the renewing action of the Christ dwelling within us by his Spirit, can never from the beginning of His gracious renewal of them resist Christ fatally, and will progressively resist Him less and less until, our hearts having been made through and through good, our wills will do only righteousness.

Mr. Trumbull's attempt to perform the impossible feat of uniting in one system an express autosoterism and an equally express quietism naturally brings him into endless self-contradictions. He writes in *The Sunday School Times* as follows: [71] "Christ is living the victorious life to-day; and Christ is your life. Therefore stop trying. Let Him do it all. Your effort or trying had nothing to do with the salvation which you have in Christ: in exactly the same way your effort and trying can have nothing to do with the complete victory which Christ alone has achieved for you and can steadily achieve in you." That is express quietism, and we must not permit that fact to be obscured to us by our instinctive sympathy with the element of truth in quietism here thrown into observation — the purity of its supernaturalism in the mode

[71] Tract on " Is Victory Earned or a Gift? "

of salvation. Now Mr. Trumbull having proclaimed this Quietistic Gospel, he is very naturally taken to task for it from the
autosoteric point of view. How does he meet the assault? Why,
by turning right around and asserting with equal emphasis
the Autosoteric Gospel! " It is true," he writes, " that God can
save no man unless that man does his part towards salvation.
But what is man's part? It is to receive the salvation that
God offers him in Christ. . . . God forces salvation on no
one; and God has revealed to us in His Word that many reject salvation. Our wills are free to act; their action is the
accepting or the rejecting of the ' free gift of God . . . eternal
life in Christ Jesus our Lord.' " This is very bad. It is not only
that it stands in direct contradiction with what was formerly
said. It does that. There, we were to let Christ " do it all ";
here we are to do a part ourselves. The formula there was,
" Christ only "; the formula here is " Christ, plus my receiving." An unhappy attempt is, indeed, made to interpret the act
of receiving as no act: " But this act of the will, by which we
voluntarily and deliberately decide to take what God offers us,
is not what was meant, in that editorial on victory, by ' effort.' " And yet this voluntary and deliberate act of the will
is " man's part " toward salvation — and such a part that
there is no salvation except by its procurement. And surely it
cannot be pretended that a voluntary and deliberate decision,
a decision on which our salvation absolutely depends, to take
what God offers, requires no effort, and is accomplished without trying — especially by a dead man; a man into whose
heart Christ, who is our life, has not come, into whose heart,
Christ, who is our only life, cannot come unless and until the
man does this, his part, toward salvation, and does it, of course,
since Christ his only life has not and cannot come to him until
he does this his part — apart from Him and without His help.
This would be as much as to say that Christ's call to Lazarus
must needs have been ineffective until dead Lazarus, by a
voluntary and deliberate act of his will, decided to take what
God offered him in that call. What is most important to observe about Mr. Trumbull's new statement therefore is not

that it is directly contradictory to his former one — which it essays to explain — but that, very happily, it is not at all true. It is not true that " God can save no man unless that man does his part toward salvation." Man has no part to do toward salvation: and, if he had, he could not do it — his very characteristic as a sinner is that he is helpless, that he is " lost." He is very active indeed in the process of his salvation, for this activity is of the substance of his salvation: he works out his own salvation, but only as God works in him the willing and the doing according to His own good pleasure. It is not true that " God forces salvation on no man." It would be truer to say that no man is saved on whom God does not force salvation — though the language would not be exact. It is not true that the " eternal life in Christ Jesus our Lord " which is the " free gift of God " is merely put at our option and " our wills are free " to accept or reject it. Our wills are free enough, but they are hopelessly biased to its rejection and will certainly reject it so long as it is only an " offer." But it is not true that God's free gift of eternal life to His people is only an " offer ": it is a " gift " — and what God gives He does not merely place at our disposal to be accepted or rejected as we may chance to choose, but " gives," makes ours, as He gave life to Lazarus and wholeness to the man with the withered hand. It was not in the power of Lazarus to reject — it was not in his power to accept — the gift of life which Christ gave him; nor is it in the power of dead souls to reject life — or to " accept " it — when God " gives " it to them. The God in whom we trust is a God who quickens the dead and commands the things that are not as though they were.

It would be impossible that so extreme a doctrine of the autocracy of the human will as Mr. Trumbull holds, should not affect his doctrine of perfection. It does affect it, modifying and limiting it in more ways than one. It is doubtless to his doctrine of the will that it is ultimately to be traced, for example, that perfection is conceived by him as limited to deliverance from the commission of " known sins." This conception is rooted in the externalizing view of sin which finds it in the stream of acts rather than in the agent himself, and homologates the definition of sin which confines it to the deliberate violation of known law. It is a conception of perfection quite out of gear with Mr. Trumbull's mystical notion of the Christ within us and its consequent quietism. If Christ has indeed taken over our living for us and become Himself the principle of our actions, the formula that we are delivered from the commission of "known sins" loses all meaning. Known to whom? To us, who are no longer the agents in our activities? Or to Christ, who has taken all "the responsibility" for our activities? Surely there are no sins which Christ does not know to be sins. Or are we to suppose that Christ carefully adjusts Himself in the government of our lives to the measure of the knowledge of sin which we possessed — each of us — before He took us over; and will not work through us on a higher plane than that? That Mr. Trumbull, nevertheless, in expounding his doctrine of perfection, clings to this formula — "freedom from the whole power of every known sin," "freedom from all our desires for every known sin at once," [72] "it is the privilege of every Christian to live every day of his life without breaking the laws of God in known sin, either in thought, word or deed," [73] our victory "is as complete now in relation to every known sin as it ever can be; it meets all our needs and breaks the whole power of our sin" — can be accounted for only by the strength of the hold which his Pelagianizing doctrine of the will has on him. His Pelagianizing doctrine of the will is the primary element in his thought and everything else must be adjusted to it — even his doctrine of perfection.

It is no doubt from the same source also that the influences flow which prevent him from teaching a stable perfection. On his doctrine of the Christ within us he ought to teach a stable perfection. And he makes use of expressions here and there which seem to imply that the perfection which Christ's indwelling in us brings us must last. The essence of his teaching here in fact is that when we by faith entrust our lives to

[72] "Victory in Christ," p. 110.   [73] Ibid., p. 17.

Christ He undertakes for us; that after that condition is fulfilled we are to be passive — to struggle and fight no more —
to leave it to Christ, and He will do the rest. He has taught us,
indeed, that " it is *Christ's* responsibility to bring me into, and
keep me in, victory, after I have surrendered to Him absolutely." [74] But this is not the most fundamental line of his
teaching. That compels him to say, "Yet we have the responsibility, too," and that is but a weak expression of his real
meaning. Not only is our reception of the Victorious Life conditioned on an act of our own, performed in the power of our
own free will,[75] but our retention of it after it has been received is conditioned on acts of our own, ever repeated acts
of faith, performed in our own free will. Thus after all, struggle, not quiescence, becomes the mark of the Christian, though
the struggle is not to refrain from sinning, but to maintain, or
rather continually to renew, the faith on which everything
hangs. For Christ gives us but a moment by moment keeping,
conditioned on a moment by moment faith on our part. Mr.
Trumbull cannot call to his aid here — as he attempts to do —
a true saying of Dr. J. Wilbur Chapman's, which he quotes, to
the effect that "the great thing is, not how much I love
God, but how much God loves me" or the true exhortation
of Frances Ridley Havergal already mentioned, to the effect
that we are to "entrust to Him our trust." [76] These remarks
come out of a quite different fundamental attitude from his
own: a fundamental attitude which suspends our salvation
utterly on God and therefore rests wholly on His love for us
and expects faith itself only from His hands. Mr. Trumbull
on the contrary suspends our salvation on our own will —
"there is where free will comes in"; and demands action of
our own free determination as the condition precedent of all
God's benefits. "Christ never accomplishes spiritual results
in a person except through that person's will. . . . Christ does
not give a spiritual blessing to a person apart from that one's

[74] P. 237.
[75] Cf. pp. 5, 19, 26, 73, 75, 77, 115.
[76] Pp. 117, 118.

will." [77] What he actually teaches therefore is — just as John Wesley taught — an intrinsically fallible perfection, a perfection out of which it is possible for us to fall — out of which, in point of fact, we may fall any minute — if we should not even say every minute. But we can equally readily get it back at once by merely "claiming" the promise again; and then "go on in Him just as though it had never happened." "For your failure did not weaken Jesus Christ. He is just as strong after the worst failure of your life as He was before." [78] Alas! that we cannot forget that He was not strong enough before to keep us from falling — despite His own assurance that He is (Jude 24): and alas! that, having had experience of His failure, we can no more confidently entrust ourselves to Him! What Mr. Trumbull really means to say is that we should "turn always from our past, from our failure or victory, to Himself, moment by moment looking to Him." That at all events, is good advice. But Mr. Trumbull adds, strangely enough in this context, that we "will find that *He* is permanent, always able and always faithful." Is He, on Mr. Trumbull's teaching, able and faithful to keep us from falling? No: what Mr. Trumbull teaches is that we always have the power in our own free will to fall, and always have the power in the same free will to return: it all depends on our free will and *not* on His keeping. The condition of our salvation is a continually repeated, or maintained, will on our part to be saved; and the actual doctrine taught is that our life of holiness — such holiness as consists in freedom from the commission of "known sin" —

---

[77] P. 238. Mr. Trumbull goes on to say: "In sleep the will is quiescent or irresponsible. Christ forces no spiritual blessing upon a person whose will is not responding. If you go to sleep victorious you will wake up victorious; if you go to sleep defeated you will wake up defeated." To deny that God can work in us while we are asleep is the strongest possible way of saying that our wills are the decisive factors in every case. Fortunately Dr. Griffith Thomas has a better teaching (p. 162): — "God is at work when you and I are asleep; God is continually at work in us though we know it not. We must not limit his work to our consciousness of him." Here are two doctrines of God and two doctrines of man which stand as far apart as darkness and light: they are polar in their antithesis.

[78] P. 118.

depends on this continually repeated or maintained will, a moment by moment faith, exercised in our own strength. It is not of grace but of will that we are saved; it is not of God that shows mercy but of him that runs. If there is nothing else, there is free will which can always separate us from the love of God which is in Jesus Christ our Lord.

Of course Mr. Trumbull cries out in horror that it is not Christ that has failed: it is our trust in Christ that has failed: that " the only thing that can get us out of victory, when we have surrendered to Christ, is to cease to trust Him wholly." [79] But that only shows that our dependence must be in our trust, not in Christ. Christ cannot keep us in trust: but our trust can keep us in Christ. Our trust can fail — and Christ cannot or will not prevent it: our only recourse is to renew it ourselves. That fortunately we are told we can do. We can fall out of our trust apparently very easily; but happily, when that happens, we can get it back again just as easily. Life is a web, woven by the shuttle plying in and out — as it does in other webs. The under strand is sin: the upper perfection: and so we weave it day by day. " No one, of course, is having the victorious life *while* he is being defeated; but he may have had it just before, and he may have it just after, defeat. The victorious life is always a matter of the present moment. It is always and only a moment by moment victory, depending on our moment by moment faith. No one can take victory for a season." [80] We *can* have it continuously; but then — that is only *if* — if we have faith continuously. And — whether we have faith continuously — that is " up to us."

This is as express a Pelagianism as Pelagius' own. It is not the same Pelagianism as Pelagius' own. It substitutes faith for Pelagius' works and it draws on God for all saving operations. These things give it a certain specious appearance of Evangelicalism and it is doubtless in this specious appearance of Evangelicalism that the appeal of this system lies for devout men. But they do not the less make it pure Pelagianism. The antithesis to the Pelagian works is not faith, but grace;

[79] P. 238.   [80] Pp. 238, 239.

and grace is a thing that cannot be commanded by the fulfilment of conditions — *ex vi verbi* it is gratuitous. It is a poorer
Pelagianism than Pelagius' own to substitute faith for works
as a condition securing God's favor: especially if the favor
of God which is secured brings with it cessation of moral
endeavor on our part. That merely betrays the little regard
we have for righteousness and it may even be but to open
the door to antinomianism. And it is something far worse than
Pelagianism, something the affinities of which are with magic
rather than religion, which supposes that the activities of
God can be commanded by acts of men, even if these acts be
acts of faith. It is the essence of magic as distinguished from
religion that it places supernatural powers at the disposal of
men for working effects of their own choosing. It cannot be
overlooked that the whole tendency of the teaching of Mr.
Trumbull and his coterie is to place God at the disposal of
man, and to encourage man to use Him in order to obtain
results which he cannot attain for himself. This is of course
to stand things on their head, and in doing so to degrade God
into merely the instrument which man employs to secure his
objects.

The whole representation of the relations of man and God
which is given us by Mr. Trumbull and his associates is to the
effect that God is released for action at man's option. So much
stress is laid on the freedom of man that no freedom is left
for God at all. The analogy of a material force is most un-
pleasantly suggested. We happily have not met in Mr. Trumbull's expositions with such an express development of this
analogy as is given for example by Dr. A. T. Pierson who, in
his little book on "The Keswick Movement," speaks of God as
a reservoir of grace [81] on which we draw, and even permits to
himself such an objectionable phrase as "Holy Ghost power,"
— which, we are informed, is at our disposal.[82] But the fundamental conception is the same. God stands always helplessly
by until man calls Him into action by opening a channel into
which His energies may flow. It sounds dreadfully like turning

[81] "The Keswick Movement," 1903, p. 38.   [82] P. 83.

on the steam or the electricity. This representation is employed not only with reference to the great matters of salvation and sanctification in which God's operations are "secured" (or released) by our faith, but also with reference to every blessing bestowed by Him. We are not only constantly exhorted to "claim" blessings, but the enjoyment of these blessings is with wearying iteration suspended on our "claiming" them. It is expressly declared that God cannot bless us in any way until we open the way for His action by an act of our own will. Everywhere and always the initiative belongs to man; everywhere and always God's action is suspended upon man's will. We wish to make no concealment of the distress with which this mode of representation afflicts us. When Erasmus even distantly approached it and spoke of "securing" the grace of God by "some little thing" retained to human powers, Luther told him flatly that he was outpelagianizing Pelagius. Man does not "secure" the grace of God: the grace of God "secures" the activities of man — in every sphere and in every detail, of these activities. It is nothing less than degrading to God to suppose Him thus subject to the control of man and unable to move except as man permits Him to do so, or to produce any effects except as He is turned into the channels of their working at man's option. We shall not, however, dwell on this matter at length, although it is the most fundamental and most objectionable element in Mr. Trumbull's teaching.

We have now run through the constitutive elements of Mr. Trumbull's system of teaching. For, it is very distinctly a system of teaching. This system of teaching is not new in the sense that it breaks out an entirely new path. It is, as Mr. Trumbull himself very properly apprehends it, essentially a continuation of the teaching of Mr. and Mrs. Pearsall Smith, as prolonged in the Keswick movement. In this sense it is merely the latest form in which the general system of teaching represented a half-century ago by Mr. and Mrs. Smith has been presented to us. This latest form is not the best form of this system. Mr. Trumbull's mode of conceiving and presenting this general system of teaching shows a tendency not only to throw up into emphasis, but to push to extremes, the elements in it which are least tenable. We do not say that Mr. Trumbull has injected these untenable elements into this system of teaching. That would imply that they were not present in it until it came into his hands. They have on the contrary been present in it from the beginning. That, its origin in the teaching of Mr. and Mrs. Pearsall Smith secured for it. But Mr. Trumbull has "brought them out" and given them new point and new sharpness of statement, or perhaps we should better say, new baldness. Above all, he has definitely placed the system on an openly Pelagian basis. Not again, as if express Palagian conceptions have not always lain at the basis of this system. But he has given this Pelagianism complete dominance in the system, and that in a particularly objectionable form of statement. Perhaps we may sum it all up in one word by saying that in Mr. Trumbull's hands this objectionable system of teaching has run fairly to seed.

PERFECTIONISM

VOLUME I

BY

BENJAMIN BRECKINRIDGE WARFIELD

Professor of Didactic and Polemic Theology
in the Theological Seminary of Princeton
New Jersey, 1887–1921

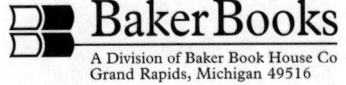

Baker Books

A Division of Baker Book House Co
Grand Rapids, Michigan 49516

PREFATORY NOTE

Rev. Benjamin Breckinridge Warfield, D.D., LL.D., Professor of Didactic and Polemic Theology in the Theological Seminary of the Presbyterian Church at Princeton, New Jersey, provided in his will for the collection and publication of the numerous articles on theological subjects which he contributed to encyclopaedias, reviews and other periodicals, and appointed a committee to edit and publish these papers. In pursuance of his instructions, this, the seventh volume, containing his articles of Perfectionism in Germany, has been prepared under the editorial direction of this committee.

The generous permission to publish articles contained in this volume is gratefully acknowledged as follows: the Pittsburgh-Xenia Theological Seminary for the article taken from *Bibliotheca Sacra,* and the Biblical Seminary in New York for the article taken from *The Biblical Review.*

The clerical preparation of this volume has been done by Messrs. Warren N. Nevius and John E. Meeter, to whom the thanks of the committee are hereby expressed.

Ethelbert D. Warfield
William Park Armstrong
Caspar Wistar Hodge
Committee.

CONTENTS

I

ALBRECHT RITSCHL AND HIS DOCTRINE OF CHRISTIAN PERFECTION

I. RITSCHL THE RATIONALIST

ALBRECHT RITSCHL AND HIS DOCTRINE OF CHRISTIAN PERFECTION

ARTICLE I

RITSCHL THE RATIONALIST [1]

THE historical source from which the main streams of Perfectionist doctrine that have invaded modern Protestantism take their origin, is the teaching of John Wesley. But John Wesley did not first introduce Perfectionism into Protestantism, nor can all the Perfectionist tendencies which have shown themselves in Protestantism since his day be traced to him. Such tendencies appear constantly along the courses of two fundamental streams of thought. Wherever Mysticism intrudes, it carries a tendency to Perfectionism with it. On Mystical ground — as, for example, among the Quakers — a Perfectionism has been developed to which that taught by Wesley shows such similarity, even in details and modes of expression, that a mistaken attempt has been made to discover an immediate genetic connection between them. Wherever again men lapse into an essentially Pelagian mode of thinking concerning the endowments of human nature and the conditions of human action, a Perfectionism similar to that taught by Pelagius himself tends to repeat itself. That is to say, history verifies the correlation of Perfectionism and Libertarianism, and wherever Libertarianism rules the thoughts of men, Perfectionism persistently makes its appearance. It is to this stream of influence that Wesleyan Perfectionism owes its own origin. Its roots are set historically in the Semi-Pelagian Perfectionism of the Dutch Remonstrants, although its rise was not unaffected by influences of a very similar character and ultimate source which came to it through the channels

[1] From *The Princeton Theological Review,* xvii. 1919, pp. 533–584.

of Anglo-Catholicism. Its particular differentiation is determined by the supernaturalization which it shares with the whole body of modifications introduced by Wesley into his fundamental Arminianism, from which Wesleyanism, in distinction from the underlying Remonstrantism, has acquired its Evangelical character.

The Perfectionist teaching of Ritschl presents a highly individual example of a Pelagianizing Perfectionism quite independent of all either Mystical or Wesleyan influences. Mysticism, with all its works, Ritschl heartily hated; Wesleyanism he, with equal cordiality, despised. But he was a Libertarian of the Kantian variety; and, going here beyond Kant — who would allow the existence of a "radical evil" in men — he would not hear of any such thing as a native bias to sin. On the contrary, every man, according to him, comes into the world with a bias to good, and with the formation of his developed moral character in his own hands. No doubt he conceived that, in the circumstances in which man lives, the moral character which every man forms for himself is inevitably an evil one. Human society therefore, in point of fact, constitutes with Ritschl too, in its phenomenal existence, a "mass of corruption"; and reacts as such on each individual as he enters it, infecting him by a sort of "social inheritance" with its evil. No actual individual thus escapes a bias to evil. But this bias to evil, as it is the product of his own free activity, is capable of being counteracted by the same power which created it. All that is needed is the formation, under a sufficiently strong inducement, of a dominating motive in the opposite direction. Acting freely under such an inducement, the individual is capable at all times (except possibly when finally hardened) of reversing his activities, revolutionizing his character, and thus, in conjunction with others similarly moved (under the influence of whom, indeed, it is that he acts) building up, in opposition to the kingdom of sin, a Kingdom of God, in which he may be "perfect."

For "substance of doctrine," this is just the ordinary Libertarian Perfectionism. But Ritschl is nothing if not original; and the peculiarities of his general system of teaching give to his Libertarian Perfectionism a specific form which presents many points of interest.

Already in his doctrine of the will Ritschl goes his own way. We have spoken of him as a Libertarian of the Kantian variety. But he does not follow Kant without dissidence. In his view of the mechanism of willing, he was as clear a determinist as Kant himself. He speaks without hesitation of "determinants" of the will and enumerates them not only as "purposes" and "intentions" but also as "dispositions," and "impulses" which he does not scruple to call "coercive" (*nöthigend*).[2] His son and biographer does not hesitate to use the strongest language in describing the quality of his determinism, outlining it in such crisp sentences as these:[3] "In the particular act of the will there is always included a necessitation (*Nöthigung*) by the motive. In case of conflict the determination follows the stronger motive. So far, every action (*Handlung*) is necessary (*nothwendig*)." Despite this clear determinism, however, Ritschl, like Kant, asserts also that the will has power to determine itself, and actually does determine itself, not only apart from but in opposition to its "determinants." It is precisely in this power that, in his view, the distinction of the human spirit consists, by which it is separated from mere nature.[4] It is the primary element therefore in that *Selbstgefühl* of which he talks so much, and by which he means not abstract self-consciousness but concrete self-esteem — our sense of our value as a self. "In this self-consciousness, and the estimate we place on self in the exalted moments of our moral willing," he tells us,[5] "we experience the might of our self-determination to the good, regardless of every obstacle whether internal or external." When this

---

[2] "The Christian Doctrine of Justification and Reconciliation," iii. E. T. 1900, pp. 251, 292. This work will be cited hereafter simply by pages. The quotations, however, it must be added, are sometimes from the German (edition 4, 1895), and hence do not follow the English Translation verbatim.

[3] "Albrecht Ritschls Leben," i. 1892, p. 350.

[4] So he frequently says; e.g. p. 513.

[5] P. 283.

almighty self-determination impinges on those coercive determinants, one would think something would be likely to happen.

Kant sought to escape the contradiction obvious here by removing this undetermined "freedom" into the "intelligible and non-empirical" region. Ritschl will have nothing to do with this evasion. He boldly declares "freedom" to be as much a matter of experience as the determination athwart of which it runs. "Freedom," he says,[6] "is not merely an idea, in accordance with which we pass judgment on our conduct, though this conduct be according to experience not free but necessitated in every act; but freedom is itself experience." Kant's doctrine, he affirms, is "theoretically unsatisfactory," because "it leaves unresolved the contradiction between the subjective claim to freedom, and the objective matter of fact of the causal nexus of action." Each action is no doubt motived, and is the necessary issue of its motive, and this naturally creates an impression that "freedom" is an illusion. "Yet in varying measures those actions are free, whose motive is a conception of a universal end, which calls a halt to the impulse which is active at the moment." It is in this formation of a universal end, acting thus as a controlling power over our impulses and inclinations, that Ritschl sees "freedom." Kant's doctrine now, he further affirms, "left no possibility open of action's directing itself according to the law produced by freedom," and thus was not only "theoretically unsatisfactory" but "practically useless." It proclaimed a universal empirical determinism. In opposition to this Ritschl asserts an experienced power of the will "to direct itself to the universal moral ultimate end."

It must be admitted that he merely asserts this power. How, under the determination of ingrained, if not innate, sinful dispositions it can possess it, is left in complete obscurity. It may be allowed that if the will, acting under the sway of sinful dispositions, is nevertheless capable of directing itself "at will" to "the all-embracing end of the King-

[6] P. 514.

dom of heaven," which includes in itself the motive of universal love, and develops out of itself the system of dispositions which involve the moral law — why, then, these dispositions thus formed might act as motives to action, just as the sinful dispositions already holding the field do, and in conflict with them might conceivably overcome them, or might blend with them, as exciting causes, of varying goodness or badness, of action. But how the sinful will can direct itself to its contrary as an end, despite the existing impulses to evil action "determining it at every step," and form these new dispositions which are to lay a restraining hand on those old dispositions, remains a mystery. It looks as if we were asked to believe that the will, which is at every step determined by dispositions, has in this instance first to create the dispositions by which it is determined, in opposition to the dispositions by which it is at every step determined. This appears to leave something to be desired as an explanation of how a possibility is "left open of action's guiding itself by the law produced by freedom." We do not wonder that Otto Pfleiderer speaks contemptuously of Ritschl's "abstract rationalistic notion of the moral will," and laughs at his representation of the human spirit "brooding as an abstract, natureless freedom over the chaos of the natural feelings and appetites — with reference to which, to be sure, it remains incomprehensible how it manages to rule over and to order them." [7]

Though all explanation of the possibility of the exercise of such an "independent power" of the will fails, however, the assertion of its reality is persistent. It is to Ritschl the condition of responsibility and the essence of the dignity of spiritual existence. Arguing against the doctrine of "original sin," [8] he declares that all ascription to ourselves of responsibility for evil — whether with respect to acts or to habits, or to propensity — depends on our recognition in our several actions of the proof-mark of "the independence of the will." This, now, he asserts, forbids looking on "the individual action as the dependent accident of a necessary power of inborn propensity."

[7] "Die Ritschl'sche Theologie," 1891, pp. 68, 79.   [8] P. 337.

The scope of this is to assert that we cannot hold ourselves responsible for an inborn disposition which is evil, or for anything that issues from it. We are responsible only for acts of "independent" willing: not then for what we are but only for what we do; or for what we are only so far as it is the result of what we do. And by these acts of "independent willing" for which and for the results of which alone we are responsible, he means very expressly empirical acts of independent willing alone. Kant, he tells us, supposed man to be afflicted with "radical evil": if we make such an assumption, we cannot ascribe responsibility to ourselves for it "except on the presupposition that it is the result of the empirical determination of the will." "For," he adds, giving the reason, "it can be derived neither from the natural origin of every man, nor from a so-called 'intelligible act of freedom'" — coupling thus Paul and Kant in a common condemnation. So far does Ritschl press this assertion of the "independence" of the will, that, applying it to God, he denies that God's will is the expression of His nature rather than, say, of His "free" purpose. To say that God wills the good because it is good — seeing that He is good in His own nature — is, he argues, to say that "God as will is subject to this righteousness as to a necessity of nature."[9] "The will," he affirms,[10] "to which its direction is given by the presupposed substantive righteousness, is not the self-determination which is becoming to God." We could scarcely have a stronger declaration that a will determined by dispositions is no will; that the only will worthy of the name determines itself. It would be unworthy of God to act otherwise than "freely" in this sense. We wonder what has become of Ritschl's psychological determinism.

We wonder also whence we are to obtain assurance of the existence of this power of "free" willing. If not from consciousness, then surely from nowhere. But Ritschl discredits the witness of consciousness in the matter. He admits that, although the particular impulses operate coercively (*nöthigend*), that does not prevent this, their coercive operation "as-

9 P. 248.   10 P. 283.

suming in the soul the form of conscious self-determination."
He is forced therefore to allow that "conscious self-determination cannot alone be the exhaustive expression of freedom." [11]
What is there to supplement it? Ritschl seems to suggest
nothing but the assumed requirement of such "freedom" of
action as he describes in order to ground responsibility, and
the dignity which it confers on spirit as distinguished from
"nature," the sphere of necessary causation. Whether on these
grounds or others, however, he asserts its existence; and that
with such vigor that, as we have seen, he pushes his psychological determinism in the mechanism of willing completely out
of sight, and stands forth as fully fledged a Libertarian as
Kant, or even as Pelagius himself.

We have already had occasion to note that Ritschl joins
in a common condemnation Paul's doctrine of original sin and
Kant's doctrine of radical evil. He will not have men come
into the world with any entail of sin from any source. But he
is not satisfied with Pelagius' idea of a will poised in indifference. "We cannot at all conceive," he says,[12] "of a will without definite direction to an end." As then he will not have
men come into the world with a bias to evil, he is compelled
to teach that they have a bias to good. This he does quite
explicitly. All attempts to educate children, he says,[13] "rest
on the presupposition that there exists in them a general,
yet still indefinite, inclination to good" — although he adds
that this inclination is without the guidance of comprehensive insight into the good and has not yet been tested in the
particular relationships of life. "This," he says, making
his meaning quite unmistakable, "is the reverse of the
inclination of the will of the child to evil and of its necessitating power, which is maintained in the doctrine of original
sin."

By this proclamation of the original goodness of children,
Ritschl escapes, however, some only, not all, of his difficulties.
Among his reasons for rejecting the doctrine of original sin is
this one — that it assumes that there is a will previous to its

[11] P. 292.   [12] P. 283.   [13] P. 337.

individual acts.[14] Is not the same assumption involved in the doctrine of original goodness? If we are to escape this assumption it would seem that we must revert to Pelagius' absurdity of an abstract will with no determination at all; and how little can be made of that we have only to watch F. A. B. Nitzsch struggling with it to learn.[15] Then, there are the facts to be faced. Do infants, in point of fact, come into the world good? " Assuredly," remarks Pfleiderer,[16] " our experience with children " gives us no justification for such an affirmation: " unless we are very blind parents indeed, we discover in them, from their tenderest years onward, that self-will which is in very fact the root and kernel of all evil." This remark, which is part of a powerful defence of the reality of original sin in the narrow sense of a native impulse to evil, has made a little amusing history, which may not be without its instructive side. Henri Schoen [17] repeats it with an added French vivacity. Ritschl, says he, has replaced the profound truth " of the innate egoism of the infant with the natural tendency to the good." "Such a theory," he adds, "does great honor to the children which Ritschl has seen grow up around him; we need to confess that those we have known do not confirm it." Constantin von Kügelgen [18] feels it necessary to go out of his way — for he himself agrees with the substance of it — to " brand Schoen's remark, which is more witty than scientific, that such a theory does great honor to Ritschl's children, as of a tone not suitable to a learned investigation." That is as it may be; but we learn meanwhile, somewhat to our surprise, that nobody seems willing to take up with Ritschl's doctrine of the goodness of infancy. Pfleiderer, Nitzsch, Schoen, von Kügelgen, Wendland,[19] men of very varied theological attitudes, all with one voice repel it. We say we learn this with some surprise, for the goodness of childhood has not only long held the place

[14] Pfleiderer, " Development of Theology," 1890, p. 187.
[15] " Lehrbuch der evangelischen Dogmatik," 1892, pp. 320, 325.
[16] " Die Ritschl'sche Theologie," 1891, pp. 66, 67.
[17] " Les origines historiques de la théologie de Ritschl," 1893, p. 151.
[18] " Grundriss der Ritschlschen Dogmatik," 1903, p. 34.
[19] J. Wendland, " Albrecht Ritschl und seine Schüler," 1899, pp. 107–108.

of a fundamental dogma among the sentimentalists, but has invaded the formal teaching of more than one type of religious thought.[20]

The greatest difficulty with which Ritschl, with his doctrine of the native goodness of man, finds himself confronted arises from the fact of man's universal sinfulness. For Ritschl fully recognizes the universality of sin and is concerned only to assert that it is the product, in every several individual, of his own voluntary action. He is constrained to admit, of course,[21] that as sin enters his life thus only by his own volition, a sinless life-development is a possibility for everyone. But this possibility is actually realized, he asserts, by no one. This is certainly a most remarkable fact for Ritschl to be compelled to recognize. We should on his ground have *a priori* expected it to be realized by most. Pfleiderer indeed declares,[22] justly enough, that "Ritschl has not . . . shown how any selfish determinations of the will at all can be explained, if there exists in the child by nature only an indefinite impulse towards good." But Ritschl asserts, as we have seen, the possession by every spiritual being of a power of quite arbitrary willing, in the teeth of any actual inclination. And there is no reason why he should not appeal to it here. Appeal to the possession of this power, however, while it may be thought to justify the assertion of the possibility, can scarcely be considered to justify the assertion of the inevitableness, of its exercise for sinning. It is not enough to account for all men without exception sinning to say that they are all able to sin. We need some account of their using their ability without exception in this particular direction. It is the duty of providing this account which is imposed on Ritschl by his

[20] Cf. a somewhat instructive column in Hastings' " Encyclopædia of Religion and Ethics," x. 513b (H. G. Wood, article on " Puritanism "), and observe the violence with which R. H. Coats (" Types of English Piety," 1912, p. 140) assaults Evangelicals because by them " blithe and happy children are scowled on in their play as being radically evil," on the ground of an innocent observation of David Brainerd's which does not go beyond Pfleiderer's.

[21] P. 378.

[22] " Development of Theology," p. 187.

teaching that all men come into the world with a bias to good and yet all men without exception sin.

The strength of Ritschl's assertion that the universality of sin is only an empirical fact, does not vacate, and is not treated by him as vacating, this duty. If he declares that " it is only by summarizing all experiences that we attain the conviction of the universal sway of sin," [23] he yet represents this universal sway of sin as something which could have been forecast not only as " possible," but even as " probable," [24] and indeed as " apparently inevitable," [25] " under the given conditions of the development of the human will." These are most astonishing representations, and seem to throw into grave doubt the primary declaration that every man comes into the world not only without impulse to evil, but with an impulse to good. The justification which is offered for them turns on further representations with regard, on the one hand, to the condition of man when he enters the world, and, on the other, to the conditions into which he enters in the world. To put it broadly, man enters the world preëminently a willing being, and, though inclined to good, too immature to be able to guide his willing wisely. And the world which he enters meets him in his immaturity with manifold temptations. The consequence is that he sins. He sins, of course, voluntarily: sin finds a necessitating (*nöthigend*) ground neither in the divine world-order, nor in man's endowment of freedom. But, so far as we can see, says Ritschl, he sins inevitably; certainly sin extends over the whole human race alike as a mode of action and a habitual propensity.[26]

The particular form which Ritschl gives this general doc-

[23] P. 378; " Unterricht in der christlichen Religion," § 28 (ed. 3, p. 26).
[24] " Unterricht," § 28.
[25] P. 380.
[26] P. 383. This teaching is fundamentally indistinguishable from that of the old Rationalism (Charles Hodge, " Systematic Theology," ii. p. 239, par. 3) and continually finds new representatives, as e.g. Miss E. M. Caillard, " Progressive Revelation," p. 77, who thinks the Fall accounted for by the fact that the self-conscious will was " newly-born and feeble," while the " animal appetites and impulses were stronger in proportion, and the will succumbed before them, becoming their slave, instead of their master."

trine calls for some remark. In the "Instruction in the Christian Religion," [27] he explains that the factors which bring the universality of sin about, are "the fact that the impulse (*Trieb*) to the unrestrained (*schrankenlos*) use of freedom, with which every man comes into the world, meets with the manifold enticements to selfishness which arise out of the sins of society." Thus it comes about, says Ritschl, that some degree of selfishness takes form in every one "even before the clearness of common self-consciousness is awakened in him." It has very naturally been pointed out [28] that the condition in which man is here represented as coming into the world is scarcely consistent with that which Ritschl ascribes to him when he represents him as endowed with an impulse (*Trieb*) to good. An impulse (*Trieb*) to good and an impulse (*Trieb*) to the unrestricted (*schrankenlos*) use of freedom are not only not the same thing; they are not even capable of conciliation. He whose action is ruled by an impulse to an unlimited use of freedom is so little the same as he whose action is ruled by an impulse to the good, that he must rather be pronounced to be without moral character altogether. Clearly, when so described, man is conceived as coming into the world merely a willing machine; will has absorbed all other faculties. And it throws a lurid light on Ritschl's real conception of the will, when we observe him, despite his expressed doctrine of psychological determinism, representing every man as beginning life as mere will, operating in a boundless manner. It sounds very well, no doubt, to hear of that high power of the spirit by which in moments of moral exaltation it can set itself to a good end, and by the sheer force of its moral energy break through the trammels of impulses and habits of evil and do the right. It has a different sound when we hear that this boasted spiritual endowment is merely our natural mode of action, without moral quality; and that all ethical development consists in curbing and shackling it in its vagrant activities. Cer-

[27] § 28; E. T. in "The Theology of Albrecht Ritschl" by Albert Temple Swing, 1901, p. 204.
[28] Nitzsch, as cited, p. 320; Wendland, as cited, pp. 107, 108.

tainly if this be the condition in which man comes into the world, he is in no sense the architect of his own fortunes. He is the helpless creature of his environment, which constitutes the mould into which, will he, nill he, he runs.

This is, in point of fact, what Ritschl's teaching comes to. According to him the universality of sin is due to the reaction of the uninformed will to the temptations of social life. In the intercourse of life man, under the temptations acting on his immaturity, becomes sinful before he knows any better. It is the temptations of human society which play here the determining rôle, and Ritschl does not scruple to say that in the environment into which man is thrust he cannot avoid sinning. Sin is "inevitable," he says, though he does not affirm this dogmatically: sin, says he,[29] is " an apparently inevitable product of the human will under the given conditions of its development." A. E. Garvie [30] seizes upon the " apparently " here with a view to breaking the force of the statement. Wrongly: it is inserted, no doubt, in order to soften the admission, but it softens it only to the ear. Dealing with the matter of original sin from the purely empirical standpoint, Ritschl declares that we observe sin to be in point of fact universal, and that this its universality, so far as he can tell, is inevitable. Its inevitableness, he further affirms, is due to the conditions under which the human will develops. These conditions he sums up in the comprehensive term " the kingdom of sin," which is his name for human society as organized in its sinful development. This kingdom of sin, he says, extends over the whole human race and binds all men together in the incalculable interplay of sinful action.[31] The conception is with him an important one, and he develops it with great fulness, and paints in very black colors the baleful influences derived from one another and from the mass, which interact on the individuals, in this evil organism. It is nevertheless just human society under the dominion of

[29] P. 380: " ein scheinbar unvermeidliches Erzeugniss des menschlichen Willens unter den gegebenen Bedingungen seiner Entwickelung."

[30] " The Ritschlian Theology," 1899, p. 300; contrast James Orr, " Ritschlianism," 1903, p. 99, note 2.

[31] P. 383.

sin that he means. Into this evil social environment every man
is thrust at birth, and by it he is, in his immaturity, moulded
to its own nature. No wonder he becomes at once, with his
impulse to unlimited use of his freedom, sinful. It is just a
matter of " social inheritance," which Ritschl substitutes for
the idea of natural inheritance. In the old antithesis of nature
and nurture, he takes the alternative of nurture; in the old
antithesis of heredity and environment, he takes the alternative of environment. His formula for universal sin is just universal freedom plus universal temptation, with the decisive
emphasis on the temptation. So decisive indeed is the emphasis
on the temptation that the suggestion is even let fall that no
resistance is made to it at all. Every man, we are told, is at
birth " put into connection with evil, against which his natural
will does not contend " at all.[32]

One of the reasons why we recoil from this explanation of
human sinfulness is that it suffers from the ugly logical disease called by the appropriately ugly name of hysteron-
proteron. This malignant " kingdom of sin," whence came it?
It is itself the creation of human sin. How can it, then, be
the creator of human sin? Unless men had sinned before there
was any kingdom of sin to infect them with its corruption,
there never would have been any kingdom of sin. The kingdom
of sin is simply the *congregatio peccatorum,* and sinners must
exist before they can congregate. They bring sin into the congregation, not take it out of it. And that means in the end that
the cause of sin must be found in something in the sinner
rather than in something in his environment. We shall have
to urge, then, still, that the formula of universal freedom plus
universal temptation is not adequate to account for universal
sin. Freedom plus temptation may be a good average receipt for
sinning: that it may be made infallible, something more is
needed. That all men are able to sin offers no sufficient account
of the use of this ability by them all without exception, under
the solicitation of temptation, for sinning. The invariability
of the result demands something else than ability to sin in

[32] " Unterricht," § 27 (ed. 3, p. 25); E. T. p. 203.

them to account for it. Ritschl, of course, could not fail to recognize so obvious a demand. He meets it by teaching that men come into the world not merely endowed with a freedom of which they have the impulse to make an unlimited use, but terribly handicapped by ignorance of the good — that good to which they have a natural inclination and to which they no doubt would therefore turn if they only knew it. " Ignorance," writes Ritschl,[33] " as experience with children teaches us, is a very important factor in the origination and development of sin. Children, when they enter into the common spirit and life, are not equipped with a knowledge of the good, or of the moral law whether as a whole or in its details. . . . Rather must they learn the value of the good only in particulars and in the special relations in which they live, since they are quite incapable of comprehending the universal good. . . . But most precisely in the case of children, the will enters into activity with the clear expectation of an unlimited effectiveness on surrounding objects and relations. In these circumstances, ignorance is the essential condition of the conflict of the will with the order of society as the rule of the good; it is also the condition of the will's setting itself in revolt against this order." . . . We perceive that from Ritschl's standpoint it is ignorance which is the true *fomes peccati*. Men do not become sinners fundamentally because they are free, though they are incredibly free; nor because they are tempted, though they are overwhelmingly tempted; but because they are ignorant.

Otto Ritschl repels the representation that all sin is to Ritschl mere ignorance.[34] Ritschl teaches, only, he says, that God regards pardonable sin as ignorance.[35] Whether there actually exists any such thing as unpardonable sin, however, Ritschl leaves an open question: he can conceive of, but will not affirm, its existence. It is not becoming in us to suppose of any of our fellow men that they have passed in their sin beyond

---

[33] Pp. 377, 378.

[34] " Leben," ii. pp. 199–200: " die Sünde sei überhaupt nur Unwissenheit."

[35] " Dass lediglich Gott die vergebbare Sünde als Unwissenheit beurtheilt."

the possibility of salvation. Some may have done so, but "whether there are such, and who they are, lies equally outside of our practical judgment and our theoretical knowledge."[36] We must therefore act on the supposition that all actual sin is in the judgment of God just ignorance.[37] Sin thus not only has its origin in ignorance, but always retains its quality as ignorance,[38] until — if it ever does so — having become invincible ignorance, it becomes also unpardonable. But though Ritschl seems thus to minimize the ethical evil of sin and the idea of its guilt evaporates in his hands, he yet deals seriously with its moral effects. He paints the moral condition of the kingdom of sin — sin in the mass, as it manifests itself in humanity at large — in sufficiently black colors. With respect to the individual, the sinful act by no means ends with itself;[39] it reacts on the will which produces it and creates a sinful propensity.[40] Thus the man who came into the world with a bias to good, acquires by his sinning a bias to evil. Ritschl explains[41] that, although sin is "no original law of the human will," it yet — "fixing itself as the resultant of particular cravings and inclinations — becomes in the individual

[36] P. 383.

[37] Pp. 379 ff.

[38] Pfleiderer, "Die Ritschl'sche Theologie," 1891, p. 68, very properly says: "It is noteworthy that Ritschl in his theory of sin, places himself wholly on the ground of the Greek intellectualism which is elsewhere so sharply condemned by him. It was Socrates, of course, who identified the evil with ignorance and therefore logically represented virtue as teachable." We shall see that to Ritschl, too, as sin is ignorance, so knowledge is the only remedy for sin.

[39] We are using here the language of Orr, "The Ritschlian Theology," 1897, p. 145. When Orr says; "Sin, in his view, not only originates in will, but consists only in acts of will," he must be interpreted in consistency with what is said in the text, and "acts of will" must include "intentions, habitual inclinations and dispositions" ("Unterricht," § 27).

[40] This is in accordance with Ritschl's general doctrine of the will — e.g. pp. 336–337: "The will, in the individual actions which are traced back to it as their ground, does not have phenomena which can exist or not exist without change in its nature; but through these actions, according to their tendency, the will acquires its kind and develops itself to a good or to a bad character."

[41] Pp. 348–349.

man the principle of the will's regulation." He therefore proceeds to speak of sin as " a personal bias (*Hang*) in the life of every individual," and is only concerned to assert that it originates as such not from our generation from a sinning ancestor, but, " so far as our observation reaches " — a rather unexpected reassertion of his empirical standpoint here — " in sinful desire and action, which, as such, finds its sufficient ground in the self-determination of the individual will."

There is such a thing then as a " law of sin " in the will, a law of sin which is nothing less than " an ungodly and selfish propensity "; and this propensity has taken possession of the " whole human race." [42] It is the result of "the necessary (*nothwendig*) reaction of every act of the will on the bent (*Richtung*) of the faculty of volition (*Willenskraft*) "; our actions being evil we could not fail through our " unrestrained repetition of selfish decisions of will " to produce " an ungodly and selfish bias." This bias may not be so strong as that which is postulated in the doctrine of " original sin "; but it is equally real, and by means of his doctrine of the kingdom of sin, with its involved interaction of sinners, consciously and unconsciously, upon one another, Ritschl labors to show that it is very strong indeed, and may conceivably become, in extreme instances, so strong that all power to the contrary is lost and man becomes in consequence incapable of salvation, since salvation in his view is the effect of free action. [43] Whether such men actually exist, as we have already noted, Ritschl declines to decide; but by declining to decide the question of fact he allows that in theory they may very well exist. And this carries with it the recognition of the possibility of sin, acting as a bias, becoming so strong as to exclude all power to the contrary. It is not altogether easy to comprehend how Ritschl, with his descriptions of the depth of the evil which pervades the kingdom of sin, preserves any individual from the full strength of this bias to evil. It must be that, after all, he thinks of sin lightly.

The same ground which we have just run over on the basis

[42] P. 383.   [43] Pp. 379-383.

of the discussion in " Justification and Reconciliation " is traversed by Ritschl again in the " Instruction in the Christian
Religion " [44] and naturally to the same effect. " Sins," we are
told here, are fundamentally " evil volitions "; but it is added,
" also the corresponding intentions, habitual inclinations and
dispositions." None of these come into the world with us;
they are all self-formed. We come into the world sinless and
pick up sin in the process of living. It is a social fact; and from
all that appears we would not become sinners, if we could be
born and reared in a sinless society. That, however, is the case
with none of us. Even he who is "born of Christian parents
into the community of Christ " is " at the same time put into
connection with evil, against which his natural will as such
does not contend." This is a statement which sets us furiously
to thinking. We wish to know why we do not contend against
the evil of the world — if we are born with a bias to good. And
we wish very much to know why, if it is our environment which
moulds us, the good environment in the "community of
Christ " does not protect us from the bad environment of the
kingdom of sin — especially if our native impulse is to good.
Ritschl, however, closes his eyes to these things, and tells us
flatly that " in every one some degree of self-seeking takes
form, even before the clearness of common self-consciousness is
awakened in him." Thus all men, without exception, become
sinners, and this means not only that they share in sinful practices, but that they are infected with a sinful bias, which conditions their whole activity. " Even the single sinful act does
not by any means come to an end with the act, but continues
to work as a disordering or perversion of moral freedom." [45]
And no one has committed only a single sinful act; and to the
multitude of his acts is added the baleful power of the community's sin. For " united sin, the opposite to the Kingdom of
God, rests upon all as a power, which at least limits the freedom
of the individual to good." From our own sinning, reinforced
by the influence of the sinful community, there thus arises a
condition of will which suggests the description of an inability

[44] §§ 27 ff.   [45] § 31.

to good. Ritschl himself phrases it thus: "This limitation of the freedom [of the individual] by his own sin and by connection with the common condition of the world is, taken strictly, a lack of freedom to good." [46] He will not allow, however, that this "lack of freedom to good" amounts to "the absolute inability to good which the Reformers" taught: though he is able to speak of sin "dominating" the individual. A. E. Garvie is therefore so far wrong when he writes [47] that Ritschl, by his denial of original sin, "does not minimise the extent or the potence of sin, but seeks to explain it by an acquired tendency instead of an inherited bias." It may seem to us that his limitation of the "potence" of sin is illogical; it does so seem to us; but he does so far limit it as to refuse to admit that it ever in fact (he allows it in theory) wholly destroys the power to will the good.

Certainly it very greatly behooved Ritschl, at the cost of whatever inconsequence, to preserve to sinful men as large an ability to good as possible. For, in his rigorous anti-supernaturalism, he has nothing to appeal to for their salvation from sin except their own wills. In the Augustinian system — which gave law to the Reformation — the depths of sin are matched by the heights of grace: by the recreation of the Holy Spirit men dead in sin are raised into newness of life. Johannes Wendland strangely fancies that he is urging a valid criticism against the Reformation doctrine of sin when he asks,[48] "Is the moral freedom of man really completely lost?" and answers, "Then there would be no possibility of deliverance; for there would be then nothing for deliverance to take hold of." The Reformation doctrine not only entails but strenuously asserts that there is nothing in sinful man on which deliverance can "take hold," and that he is therefore incapable of deliverance save by the recreation of his dead soul by the almighty power of the Holy Spirit. But Ritschl knows no soul to be recreated; and knows no Holy Spirit to recreate it; and in his anti-mystical zeal knows no immediate Divine action of any kind on the human

[46] § 30.   [48] "Albrecht Ritschl und seine Schüler," 1899, p. 104.
[47] As cited, p. 306.

will. What the human will itself in its own unaided powers cannot do for its own recovery from sin, cannot in his view be done at all.

It is Ritschl's teaching that the soul subsists only in its functions. "We know nothing," he says,[49] "of an in-itself of the soul"; and he explains his meaning by the addition of the words — "of a life of the spirit enclosed in itself, over or behind the functions in which it is active, living and present to itself as a particular entity (*Werthgrösse*)." This is not a mere *obiter dictum* but a deliberately announced doctrine, valued precisely because it excludes all talk of "mysticism" in the relations of God to man. Pfleiderer[50] charitably supposes that "when he blew this trumpet blast against all ' mysticism,' " Ritschl could scarcely have realized the radical character of the pronouncement he was making; and then draws out its consequences. It makes the unity of the soul an illusion, dissolved into the multiplicity of its functions. And it renders the hope of immortality a delusion. How can there be talk of the immortality of the soul on the basis of a doctrine which allows for the existence of no soul? What is there to hold these functions together when the body decays?[51] Garvie brings together what is the gist of these criticisms, in one comprehensive sentence. Ritschl, says he,[52] "in his denial of the metaphysical existence of the soul, and his restriction of personal life to the spiritual activities," "implicitly contradicts the unity and identity of the ' self,' the possibility of character, the certainty of immortality." In Ritschl's teaching, says Garvie again,[53] sweeping a circle with a wider radius, "God is, so to

[49] P. 21: "von einem Ansich der Seele." D. W. Simon (in his E. T. of Stählin's "Kant, Lotze, and Ritschl," p. 168, note 2) proposes to render the awkward term *Ansichsein* by the equally awkward equivalent "inseity."

[50] "Die Ritschl'sche Theologie," pp. 10 ff.

[51] We are always directed to Fr. Traub, *Zeitschrift für Theologie und Kirche*, 1894, p. 101, for a reply to Pfleiderer's strictures here. But Traub does not meet Pfleiderer's criticisms; he only asserts the right of Ritschl to his views.

[52] *Op. cit.*, contents of chap. V. sect. iii. cited by Orr, "Ritschlianism," p. 84.

[53] *Op. cit.*, p. 62.

speak, lost in His kingdom, Christ in His vocation, the soul in
its activities."

How Ritschl applies this doctrine of the non-substantiality
of the soul, may be observed as well as elsewhere, in a very
characteristic passage in which his immediate object is to defend his doctrine of the "Godhead" of Christ from the reproach that it ascribes divinity only to His will and not to His
nature.[54] Ritschl replies that there is no such distinction: the
will is the nature. When we speak of a person's character, we
mean nothing except the state of his will. A good character
is a particular state of the will — this state of the will, to wit,
the bending of the will to a good and unselfish end with sufficient decision to restrain and govern the natural impulses,
which work, presumably, for immoral or at least unmoral
ends. When the will forms and pursues a good and unselfish end
so as to subordinate and subject the natural impulses to it —
then the person is of good character. Whence, now, the will
obtains the ability thus to subordinate and subject the natural impulses to itself, or rather to a good and unselfish end
formed by itself, we are not told. That there are such impulses
requiring thus to be reduced to subjection is itself a notable
fact. Ritschl speaks of them as "the predispositions (*Anlagen*)
of the soul." He tells us that they "correspond in some way
to our bodily equipment"; and further that they are "given
to us"; and still further that they are "designated as our
nature (*Naturell*)." But now he somewhat strangely adds that
it is the allotted task of the created spirit to transform these
"predispositions of the soul" into its "obedient instruments."
We speak of this statement as strange, for surely the whole
drift of these remarks suggests that we are here contemplating
"the created spirit" as such, that is, as it comes into existence,
and not only after it has formed for itself a character, and that
an evil character. And as it comes into existence, it is in
Ritschl's teaching good, and inclines to good — to become evil
only by the action of this very will which we are here told has
as its task to obtain the mastery over these dispositions in

[54] Pp. 466 f.

order that thus a good character may be framed. Let that, however, pass. What Ritschl is teaching here primarily is that our character at any given moment is just the state of our will in that particular stage of the prosecution of this task. In proportion as we have the mastery over our predispositions and are governing them in the interests of a good end — we are good. Who or what, however, is this " we " — " the created spirit " — who thus dominates over the predispositions of the soul? Do not these " predispositions (*Anlagen*) of the soul " really constitute all the " we " that exists? Must we not have another " we," with another equipment of dispositions, before we can form a purpose antagonistic to it and dominate it in its interests? We are lost in wonder as to what it is that forms this purpose and dominates the predispositions which are " given " to us, and which are properly called our " nature." So little can Ritschl get along without a soul that he cannot conduct his discussion a single step without presupposing it.

It will have been already observed that it is not the soul of man alone which is dissolved in the acid of Ritschl's non-substantial metaphysics.[55] The being of God is dissolved in it also. As a matter of course Ritschl knows nothing of a Trinity in the Godhead. And where there is no Trinity, there can be no preëxistent Divine Christ, and no personal Holy Spirit. A. E. Garvie, who always gives Ritschl the benefit of a benevolent interpretation, whenever a benevolent interpretation can by any means be made possible, is compelled to allow that with Ritschl " the doctrine of the Trinity does not find any recognition whatever." [56] And Gustav Ecke, whose attitude toward Ritschl is as benevolent as Garvie's, is equally compelled to

[55] For an admirable summary statement of the matter see Orr, " The Ritschlian Theology," pp. 61-65.

[56] *Op. cit.*, p. 343. The defence which von Kügelgen (*op. cit.*, p. 137) offers for Ritschl is only an admission — the " Trinity " means the successive manifestations of Love in several modes of operation: " With reference to the ' denial of the dogma of the Trinity ' (so Haack) this reproach is invalidated, since the Holy Trinity, of course not simultaneously, but certainly successively, comes to manifestation in the self-revelation of God as will of love through the man Jesus, and in divine self-communication as power of God through the Holy Spirit, — wherefore naturally the immanent side of the

aver that we find as little recognition in him of a personal Holy Spirit. "According to Ritschl," he expounds,[57] "by the Holy Spirit there cannot at all be understood a kind of 'irresistible natural force' which traverses the regular course of knowledge and the normal exercise of the will. . . . When Paul makes use of the conception, he designates by it the knowledge of God as Father common to Christian believers and the knowledge of His Son as our Lord; and further the power of right conduct and self-sanctification or the formation of moral character. If the whole ethical praxis is thus deduced from the Holy Spirit, what this means is that the knowledge of God as our Father motives the disposition out of which righteousness and sanctification are produced."[58] The particular passage of Ritschl's[59] which Ecke makes use of here is a fair representative of his customary mode of speech on the subject. He is never weary of asserting that the Holy Spirit is no "stuff" and is not to be conceived in its action after the analogy of a "natural force," producing effects by its own power. And he as repeatedly explains that it is, in its real nature, just the "knowledge" which is common to the Christian community, and under the influence of which as a motive, the individual Christian sanctifies *himself* — as is particularly clearly declared in the passage expounded by Ecke. In it we are told that what Paul calls the Holy Spirit is the "power, common to Christians, of righteous conduct and of self-sanctification or moral character-formation, which finds its motive in that complete knowledge of God."[60]

Trinity gives way to the economical side on the ground of religious value-judgment."

[57] "Die theologische Schule Albrecht Ritschls," 1897, p. 293.

[58] C. von Kügelgen, as cited, pp. 114 ff., seeks to defend Ritschl against the charge — as made by Grau — that he reduces the Holy Spirit "to a function of knowledge." He is effectively answered by Leonhard Stählin in the *Neue Kirchliche Zeitschrift* for 1898 (ix. p. 506). "In spite of all his employment of the terminology which belongs to the church doctrine of the Trinity," says Stählin, "Ritschl remains a Unitarian."

[59] Pp. 533 f.

[60] P. 533.

In another typical passage [61] it is emphatically denied not only that the Holy Spirit is to be conceived as a "stuff" — which is Ritschl's way of saying a substantial entity — but equally that He is to be thought of as the "Divine means" (*göttliche Mittel*) of the regeneration of the individual. The state of regeneration or the new life may be placed in close relation to the Holy Spirit, says he; but that "is not to be understood in the sense that each individual is changed by the specific power of God after the fashion of a natural force, but that he is set in motion towards patience and humility as well as to moral activity in the service of the Kingdom of God by the trust in God as the Father of our Lord Jesus Christ which is common to all Christians." Here it is explicitly denied that it is the Holy Spirit which works that change by which we become Christians and our own trust in God is invoked in His stead. As to the Holy Spirit itself, what is meant by it is "in reference to God Himself," just "the knowledge which God has of Himself"; and with reference to the Christian community the common "knowledge of God and His counsel towards men in the world," which is the possession of the Christian community, and which, so far as it is true knowledge, of course "corresponds with God's knowledge of Himself." This last fact, namely, that the knowledge which the Christian community has of God corresponds with the knowledge that God has of Himself, is the justification of the common name given to the two knowledges — the "Holy Spirit." [62] The Holy Spirit in the meantime is defined baldly as just a "knowledge": a knowledge *of God,* no doubt, but just a *knowledge* of God. This knowledge may exist in God as subject; or in the Christian community as subject. The individual member of the community, so far as he shares in this knowledge, is affected by it in his feelings and in his acts: it becomes to him a source in him of specific emotions and activities. This is what is meant

[61] Pp. 605 f.

[62] Cf. the statement on p. 471. "The Spirit of God is the knowledge which God has of Himself, as of His self-end. The Holy Spirit denotes in the New Testament the Spirit of God so far as He is the ground of the knowledge of God and of the specific religious-moral life in the community."

by "having the Holy Spirit." The Holy Spirit is just the spirit of the community conceived as an influence, swaying the individual; that and nothing more.[63]

Commenting on the passage which has just been engaging our attention,[64] Garvie[65] seizes hold of this sentence: " As the power of the exhaustive knowledge of God common to Christian believers, the Holy Spirit is, however, at the same time the motive of the life of all Christians, which as such is necessarily directed to the common end of the Kingdom of God." On the ground of this sentence he represents Ritschl as teaching that " the Spirit is in the Christian community not only as *knowledge,* but also as the *motive* of action "; and that he explains to mean that " the *will* as well as the *mind* of God is in the community." This is quite unjustified. What Ritschl says is that " the Holy Spirit " is the motive of the life of Christians " as the power of the common exhaustive knowledge of God belonging to the believers in Christ." There is no such thing as a " Holy Spirit " conceived as will, according to Ritschl: in his view the " Holy Spirit " is only a knowledge. And it is, in any case, " knowledge " alone which can act as a " motive "; that is a thing will cannot do. Ritschl makes his meaning particularly clear in the summary paragraph in which he brings the discussion in this place to a close. Nothing objective, he says,[66] can be taught about justification and re-

---

[63] Near the close of this passage in the earlier editions (ed. 1, p. 534; ed. 2, pp. 561 f.) there were some words which have dropped out in the rewriting of the passage for the third edition, of such clearness that they naturally were much quoted by earlier writers (e.g. Hermann Weiss, *Theologische Studien und Kritiken,* 1881, p. 412; Fr. Luther, " Die Theologie Ritschl's," 1887, p. 27). It runs in ed. 2 as follows: " The Holy Spirit designates, metaphysically speaking, a *Formbestimmtheit* like justification, reconciliation and childship to God." Weiss comments: " The Holy Spirit is therefore in no way anything real or substantial, but is simply the specific form of the Christian consciousness, so far as this cherishes precisely as consciousness the specific thought of God as Father, bringing it into practice, as guiding thought, over against the conceptions and moods which arise out of the world, — as dominating motive over against the natural instincts."

[64] P. 605.

[65] *Op. cit.,* pp. 338 f.

[66] P. 607.

generation except this — " that it " (these two things are so
one with Ritschl that he uses a singular pronoun and verb)
" takes place within the community of believers in accordance
with the propagation of the Gospel and the specific onworking
of the personal peculiarity of Christ in the community." These
are its productive causes — the proclamation of the Gospel
and especially the impression made by the unique personality
of Christ. How these causes work the result Ritschl now proceeds to tell us: it takes place, he says, " seeing that there is
awakened in the individual faith in Christ, as trust in God the
Father of all, and a sense of union rooted in the Holy Spirit —
by which the entire world-view and self-judgment in the continuance of the sense of guilt for sin are dominated." That is to
say the proclamation of the gospel and the impression made
on men by the personality of Christ bring about their justification and regeneration, briefly, by awakening faith in them.[67]

Of course this is not to eliminate all " mystery " from the
process: it is only to eliminate all that is supernatural. The
words in which Ritschl says this have, it is true, been now
and then gravely misunderstood — as, for example, by Garvie.[68]
" How this state is brought about," Ritschl remarks, " eludes
all observation, like the development of the individual spiritual
life in general." He does not mean by this to suggest that there

[67] Cf. " Unterricht," § 5, note 3 (E. T. pp. 174 f.) : — " The parables
(Mark iv.), which set forth the mysteries of the kingdom in figures of the
growth of grain, etc., always signify by ' fruit ' a human product, springing
out of an individual activity called forth by the divine ' seed,' i.e., by the
impulse of the divine word of revelation." The sole divine element is the
" word of revelation." In " Justification and Reconciliation," iii. p. 175, Ritschl
seeks to defend his doctrine of justification from the charge of Pelagianism; but
his only weapon is a not altogether unjustified *tu quoque.* What interests us
here is that here again he repudiates the conception of an action on the human
spirit by the Holy Ghost as the account of the rise of faith in the soul. There
is no such thing as a " soul " in the sense of a kind of *Natur,* that is, except
as the activities of feeling, knowing, willing themselves; and grace does not
act in this fashion, on a passive recipient. When it is said that the Holy
Spirit acts upon us, what is meant, according to " Unterricht," § 46 (E. T.
p. 226) is that " the impulse to right conduct," etc., " have their criterion in the
knowledge of God as our Father which is given us in Christianity."

[68] *Op. cit.,* pp. 339, 344. Also by Gustav Ecke, " Die theologische Schule
Albrecht Ritschls," 1897, p. 63.

is, or may be, something more at work here than is merely
human — something more than knowledge acting as motive.
He means only that the manner of working by which this
knowledge produces faith, and faith justification and regeneration is, like all other operations of the human spirit, as he expressly says, something which withdraws itself from observation. Accordingly Otto Ritschl, expounding his father's doctrine
of the origin of faith, declares [69] that what he emphasizes is
that all faith, whether the one becoming a Christian is aware
of the connection or not, is called out by impulses which proceed from the Christian community as the vehicle of the
Christian proclamation. " How these influences work in individual cases " he continues, " ' eludes all observation precisely like the development of the individual spiritual life
in general ' " — quoting our present passage. Thus it
appears that this famous sentence does not, in the view of
Ritschl's son, any more than in its own apparent bearing,
refer obscurely to the possibility of some direct action of
the Holy Spirit taking place in the origin of faith; but only
to the operation of influences coming out of the community
as " bearer of the word." It is this that seems to Ritschl
mysterious.

It ought perhaps to be added that although Garvie argues
here that Ritschl means to posit an operation of God as will
on the soul in regeneration, he nevertheless proceeds at once [70]
to rebuke him precisely because he does not do this, but seeks
all the causes of the transformation wrought in what we call
regeneration in the subject of it. Garvie himself does not believe that " in the spiritual sphere " causes produce their effects
unmodified by the intrusion of free will; a mode of statement
which can mean only that he supposes that God the Holy
Spirit, operating as will, produces the effects He aims at, in the
spiritual sphere, only by the permission of the will on which
He operates. " There is a new factor," he says, " personal freedom, which either coöperates with or opposes itself to the
operative cause, and thus decisively modifies the effect " — a

[69] " Leben," ii. p. 227.   [70] Op. cit., p. 340.

remarkable assertion when we reflect that the " other factor " under consideration is Almighty God, and note that what is asserted is that the human will not only modifies but " decisively modifies " the effect which Almighty God attempts to produce. Nevertheless Garvie against Ritschl's account of the matter argues that " we are not giving a complete account of even spiritual facts, if, because of the importance of this new factor, we recognize only the effects, and refuse to inquire into the causes." " Yet this," he says, " is Ritschl's method." Surely this is to acknowledge that in his account of " regeneration " Ritschl indicates no " transcendent " cause of the effects observed; and that, in the circumstances, means that he explains the effects wholly within the sphere of human action. The phrase is now let fall [71] that in his further remarks Ritschl has no intention of " abandon[ing] this method of exclusive attention to the human activity in the spiritual life "; and the companion phrases occur,[72] that Ritschl " appear[s], at least, to deny the indwelling and inworking of the Spirit," and " in his language at least, fails to recognize the Presence and Power of God's Spirit in the individual Christian experience." Surely this is to say that so far as Ritschl has expressed himself he allows for no divine factor in the Christian life. We have nothing to go on, after all, except what he tells us. And surely he must be presumed to mean what he says.

This negative representation, however, instructive as it is in itself, yet falls unhappily short of the truth of the matter. Ritschl not only fails to mention a divine factor in regeneration; he definitely excludes it. R. A. Lipsius speaks not a bit too strongly, despite Ecke's protest,[73] when he declares [74] that " the whole course of the Christian life is explained " by Ritschl "'psychologically,' that is, empirically, without the entrance of a supernatural factor." Fr. Luther expounds the matter more fully: " There is no question in the Ritschlian theology . . . ," says he,[75] " of a new creation through the

---

[71] P. 341. [74] " Die Ritschl'sche Theologie," 1888, p. 21.
[72] P. 349. [75] Fr. Luther, " Die Theologie Ritschl's," 1887, pp. 27–28.
[73] As cited, p. 64.

Holy Spirit. The Ritschlian system has no place for a Triune personal God, and knows nothing of a salvation resting on the saving operation of this Triune God. Everything in it derives ultimately from human action. Everything is effectuated by a self-activity of a humanity associated in an ethical kingdom and abiding in the condition of nature.[76] Everything here is nature, nothing grace, everything man-work, or as the Scriptures call it, 'law-work,' nothing the work of the Holy Spirit, the Spirit of Christ, really and creatively delivering us." There is nothing on which Ritschl more insists than on what he calls the freedom of faith, by which is meant what we might rather speak of as its absolute arbitrariness. " Faith begins," says he,[77] " in harmony with the law of freedom " — and therefore its coming, he at once adds, is incapable of being predicted or foreseen. It comes, in other words, so far independently of conditions that it cannot be inferred from them. "The change of heart which is to be brought about by God's love towards sinners," he says again,[78] " must be conceived under the form of freedom of the will" — and then he immediately adds that it cannot take place therefore " when sin, regarded as enmity against God, has reached that degree of self-determination at which the will has deliberately chosen evil as its end." That is to say, man is salvable only when he is in a position to save himself. So zealous is he for this absolutely arbitrary action of the will that he even tells us [79] that " there is in no case either a mechanical or a logical necessity laid upon individuals to join themselves in faith to the existing Christian community." The language is exaggerated for effect in both members of the sentence. In excluding what he calls a " mechanical necessity " of believing, Ritschl means really to exclude the recreative operation of the Spirit, of which he always speaks in this

[76] Accordingly Fr. Luther remarks a little later (p. 29): " It is the Kingdom of God which, by the ethical communion established in it, calls out the religious-moral renewal of the heart; this is not done by the Holy Spirit."

[77] P. 577.

[78] P. 383.

[79] P. 577.

depreciatory language.[80] In excluding what he calls "a logical necessity," he may appear to be setting aside only such an inducement to believing as will leave open no rational way of escape from it; but he is actually shutting out all really determining inducements whatever. Hermann Weiss is therefore quite right when he says [81] that with Ritschl "faith is and remains so exclusively the act of freedom of the subject that the dependence of the Christian on God and Christ becomes a purely external one or an imaginary one."

We may indeed challenge the possibility — even on Ritschl's postulates — of such an arbitrary act of faith as, he asserts, takes place. For Ritschl himself, as we have seen, represents the will of sinful man as biased to evil; as so strongly biased to evil, in itself and in its conditioning in the kingdom of sin, as would lead us to suppose it incapable of the act of faith attributed to it. Ritschl himself describes the condition in which man finds himself as one of "unresolved guilt," "separation from God," "slavery to the world" — against which combination, he says,[82] we "cannot assert ourselves with our own abilities (*Mitteln*) since it is from it that we receive all the motives to our action and effort." This certainly appears to attribute to sinful man an inability to good. But we are bound to bear in mind that Ritschl constantly asserts that this inability is not absolute; and that it finally emerges that what is left to man by it is not broken fragments of ability to good but a power of willing which can be called nothing less than plenary. Freedom in this sense is the prerogative of a man as personal spirit.

Ritschl nevertheless recognizes the duty and undertakes the task of making it intelligible how sinful man performs the act which is attributed to him. Naturally a number of modes of expression are employed. What is said reduces ulti-

---

[80] Cf. e.g. p. 529: "A material, mechanical change of the sinner is altogether unthinkable," in which " the sinner is made righteous mechanically — that is, say, through the infusion of love," instancing the Roman Catholic doctrine.

[81] As cited, p. 391.

[82] P. 529.

mately, however, to an appeal to the impression made on him by the personality of Christ and the influence exerted upon him by the Christian community, "the kingdom of God"; and as the former operates only through the latter, in the last analysis his appeal is solely to the influences brought to bear on sinful man in the Kingdom of God. Here too, then, as in the matter of the origin of sin in the individual Ritschl's recourse is to "social inheritance." As there man, coming into the world with a bias to good, becomes sinful through association with those who were sinners before him; so here men living in sin and with a bias to evil become righteous through the influence of those who were righteous before them. A difficulty no doubt faces us arising from this very parallel. We have seen that, according to Ritschl, every man comes into the world inclined to good, but, even though he may be born into the Christian community, this inclination to good is invariably and "apparently inevitably" overcome by the evil influences to which he is subjected in human companionship, that is to say, in the kingdom of sin. We can scarcely avoid inferring that the influences of evil in the kingdom of sin are stronger than those to good in the Kingdom of God. And that renders it difficult to understand how men inclined to evil and long immersed in the kingdom of sin, affected deeply by its influences, and more or less hardened in sinning, can be supposed to be able to turn at once to good on entering the Kingdom of God. The solution of the difficulty lies of course in the relative unimportance in Ritschl's scheme of thought of inducements in this or the other direction, as compared with the ineradicable power of the will to turn itself in any direction whatever. No doubt thus the whole machinery which Ritschl has created — of a kingdom of sin to account for the universal sin of man, of a Kingdom of God to account for the recovery of sinful man — is made nugatory. But the robustness of his Libertarianism is thrown up into a correspondingly high light. How entirely he depends on the will to work the change by which one becomes a Christian, is luridly exhibited by the temptation to which he yields to pronounce children, and the members of backward races, incapable of making it. Christianity is only for the well-developed. Children cannot attain to it: " faith in Christ can be expected only at a riper age." [83] And Christian missions to people in a low stage of culture are at least of doubtful utility. Such peoples can be expected to embrace Christianity only when they have become more capable of entering into its ends.[84] These suggestions fall in with the great part which immaturity plays in Ritschl's idea of the origin of sin; and they are strong attestations, as they are inevitable corollaries, of the decisive part played in his doctrine by his Libertarianism.

But although the significance of " the community " is thus depressed beneath that of " the will," in Ritschl's scheme, it is not given an intrinsically unimportant rôle. It is through it that the whole " inducement to action " comes to the will. And therefore in this sense the character of the action taken can be attributed to it. Ritschl can even say [85] that the " new birth " or " new begetting by God," or " the admission into the relation of sonship to God," which " in its essence coincides with justification as well as with the bestowal of the Holy Spirit " — " all this is again the same with admission into the community." Thus he reduces the entire list of expressions apparently declaring a divine introduction of the sinner into the new life to mere figures of speech for the eminently human act of entrance into the Christian community; it is the influence of his new environment upon him which alone comes into consideration.[86] Where comprehensiveness of statement is sought, it is apt to take some such form as the following. We

---

[83] P. 599.

[84] Pp. 136 f.

[85] " Unterricht," § 47, note 1.

[86] Cf. H. Weiss, as cited, pp. 399 ff. Weiss remarks (p. 400) on Ritschl's failure to make a clear distinction between objectively belonging to the community and subjectively believing. " We have to do here," he comments (p. 403), " with an underestimate of sin, so far as it involves not merely a relation of guilt . . . but a perversion of the will and real corruption of the whole personal life in man. Therefore it is scarcely a question of a decisive conversion, and faith is conceived in the end entirely as a moral act of man's own. The religious facts present in the community, through which the individual receives his call to the Kingdom of God, suffice to call it out."

obtain "forgiveness or justification, reconciliation and adoption into Divine Sonship " — all of which are one — we read,[87]
"only as members of the religious community (*Gemeinde*) of
Christ, as the result of the incalculable and mysterious interaction between our own freedom and the determining influences
of the community (*Gemeinschaft*) — which (the community)
however, is possible, in its nature, only through Christ's unique
life-course in its well-known double aspect, and its continuous
operation through all ages." Here all that enters into the
Christian condition is represented as attained by us through
our own wills acting under influences brought to bear on us
through the Christian community. It is added no doubt that
this community itself is a creation of Christ and the influences
it exerts are transmitted from Him. But this does not introduce a new influence operative on the sinner — the influence
of Christ — distinct from that of the community. In representing the community as the vehicle of the influence of Christ it
interposes the community between Christ and the sinner, and
reduces the influence of Christ from an immediate to a mediate
one, from a possibly supernatural to a natural one. This is not
an accidental, it is the calculated, result of Ritschl's theorizing.
He has nothing more at heart than to remove man from all
direct contact with God.

It is therefore with unjustified charity in the concessive
portion of his statement, that Hermann Weiss says,[88] "It is
true, Ritschl wishes to avoid making the awaking of faith depend only on instruction or tradition — but really he is unable
to find any other way." Precisely what Ritschl wishes to do is
to separate man effectually from all direct relation to God, and
in order to do this he subordinates his relation even to Christ
to his relation to the community through which alone (never
directly and immediately) does the individual have any relation to the revelation of God in Christ and His reconciling
work. The result is naturally that throughout all Ritschl's discussions — which vainly represent themselves as seeking a
way between the Scylla of Romish and the Charybdis of Ra-

[87] P. 577. [88] As cited, p. 404, end. His vouchers are pp. 529, 567.

tionalistic conceptions — there looms (as Weiss does not fail
to point out) [89] a background of essentially deistic thinking
and the actual life of the believer is left by God wholly to himself. This is but one aspect of Ritschl's extreme anti-mystical
preconceptions, the effects of which are briefly outlined by
Henri Schoen [90] in such statements as these: " Ritschl does not
speak of a direct relation of the divine Spirit with the individual "; "The relation of man and God 'ought not to be
regarded as immediate; that would be to declare them imaginary (*eingebildet*)' "; [91] " Let it suffice us that God acts in the
bosom of His Church by the *Gospel* and by the *remembrance*
of Jesus." [92]

Jesus Christ does not live in His Church. It is only His Gospel — the memory of Him — which lives in it and works
the conversion of men. Johannes Wendland complains that
" Ritschl has never more exactly defined what the community
can give the individual, viz., only historical information." [93]
The complaint is not well-founded. Ritschl makes it superabundantly plain that it is only "knowledge" which works
through the community on the individual, though he magnifies, no doubt, the effects of this "knowledge." This is the
account to give of his reduction of the Holy Spirit just to
"knowledge"; and he looks to this "knowledge" to carry the
sinner safely out of his own sin into newness of life — to this
"knowledge" as the only thing needed to direct the will in its
"free" action to which it is at all times competent. It is curious and not a little instructive to observe how widely such a

[89] As cited, pp. 387 ff. Cf. Friedrich Nippold, " Die theologische Einzel-
schule," 1893, erste und zweite Abtheilung, p. 266, who says that Ritschl's
passionate aversion to all mysticism " brought his idea of God into undeniable
approximation to deism." This, he says, along with his Moralism, enters into
his approximation to the older Rationalism.
[90] As cited, pp. 69–70. Schoen adds (p. 70, note 2): " W. Herrmann only
draws the logical conclusion from these affirmations when he says: ' The idea
of a real relation (*Verkehr*) of the Christian with God is not Christian '
(*Verkehr des Christen mit Gott,* 1886, p. 8)."
[91] " Theologie und Metaphysik," 1881, p. 47.
[92] P. 608.
[93] " Albrecht Ritschl und seine Schüler," 1899, p. 79.

representation, fatally defective as it is, commends itself. Theodor Haering, for example,[94] accounts it a special service done by Ritschl that he gives us an answer to "the question, in what way we arrive at faith in Christ." Ritschl says — through the impression made on us by Christ of being a Revelation of God; by which there is awakened in us at the same time faith in Him and in God. Orthodoxy, says Haering, is helpless here. "To point to the mysterious working of the Holy Spirit, however justifiable this may be, is in the present connexion really an evasion of the question, not an answer." Thus he sets "the Word and Spirit," by the conjunction of which alone, "orthodoxy" teaches, is faith wrought, in antagonism to one another, as if Ritschl had the one and "orthodoxy" the other — a very significant revelation of his conception both of "orthodoxy" and of Ritschlian teaching.

Alfred E. Garvie's reasoning[95] moves on much the same lines as Haering's. Criticizing the critics of Ritschl's antagonism to all "mystical elements" in Christianity, he writes: "If there is an immediate communion with Christ, or a direct action of the Spirit, unconditioned by the historical revelation, why contend so earnestly for the defence of the New Testament, why preach the gospel in all the world, why maintain the Church and its means of grace? If Christ needs no mediation, and the Spirit uses no agency, why all this effort and testimony? The truth is, that Ritschl and his school are contending for what is recognized practically in all the Christian Churches, the dependence of Christianity on the historical revelation of God in Christ, as recorded in the New Testament." No, that is but half the truth. The whole truth is that Ritschl in contending for "the dependence of Christianity on the historical revelation of God in Christ" is not neglecting merely, but denying, the dependence of vital Christianity on the immediate operations of the Spirit of God in the heart. The appreciation of "the permanent value and universal significance of the historical revelation" which Ritschl may show

[94] "The Christian Faith," 1913, pp. 690 f.
[95] "The Ritschlian Theology," 1899, p. 149.

(so far as he shows it) must not be permitted to obscure his depreciation — his denial — of the indispensableness of the direct operations of the Spirit of God on the heart, without which even this historical revelation could have no saving effect. Garvie is pleased to play a little [96] with the expressions " direct," " immediate," as applied to the " action of the Spirit in the soul." They are not new expressions which James Orr invented: they are the vehicles through which Christians through all ages have given expression to their fundamental faith that (as a very early Christian put it) the natural man does not receive the things of the Spirit of God, and cannot know them because they are Spiritually judged. This fundamental Christian confession cannot be vacated by the remarkable suggestion that no part is left for the historical revelation to play, no place remains for the preaching of the Gospel, if there be allowed a direct action of the Spirit " unconditioned " by it. This turns things on their heads. What the New Testament teaches is rather that the saving effect of the historical revelation, of the Gospel, is conditioned by the direct action of the Spirit — a truth which, of course, Garvie has no intention of really denying.[97]

It is important that we should make clear to ourselves the completeness of Ritschl's anti-supernaturalism. It is not uncommon to make an exception to its completeness in favor of what is called the revelation of God in Christ, to which the impulse to the Christian life is traced, and the asserted supernatural character of which may therefore be supposed to give a supernatural character to the whole process of salvation. According to Hermann Weiss, for example,[98] Ritschl's system is saved from falling into " a complete Pelagianism," and the Christian faith becoming in his hands simply " a no doubt respectable but entirely insufficient trust in God in the search after virtue and consciousness of freedom," only by this cir-

---

[96] As cited, pp. 143 f.

[97] As cited, pp. 149–150. Cf. Orr's effective rejoinder to Garvie, " Ritschlianism," pp. 83, 84.

[98] *Theologische Studien und Kritiken,* 1881, pp. 414 f.

cumstance — that he " would recognize a foundation for these dispositions exclusively in a peculiar possession of the Christian community, and would refer this community as Christ's establishment to God's positive revelation or arrangement." " Herein," says Weiss, " lies the supernatural side of the system." In saying this, however, Weiss fully recognizes that the supernaturalism recognized is pushed back into the distant past, and, as God is not allowed to act directly on the individual, becomes somewhat illusive. P. Graue,[99] while occupying the same general standpoint with Weiss, is still less satisfied with the character of the supernaturalism which he recognizes in Ritschl and feels sure that it is logically insecure. Ritschl, says he, " has left standing the external revelation-fact which lies before us in the existence of Christ. That is the lure which he has thrown out to supernaturalism. From that on, the whole religious life runs on empirically-psychologically. That is his last century Rationalism. But the two do not get on together. This Rationalism swallows up that supernaturalism. How can an exception be made of Christ when in the religious life everything proceeds purely empirically? Already, now, He has for the Ritschlians (scientifically!) only the *value* of deity; already, now, it is at bottom nothing but the subjective conception of the love of God which Christ gives us; already, now, we can in this Christology speak logically neither of a deity, nor of a divinity, but only — pardon the aesthetically obnoxious term — of a God-for-us-ity of Christ. What prevents our turning away from that too? Our seeing in Christ's God-the-Father only a subjective reflection of His own loving nature, of His own moral beauty? What prevents our remaining wholly on the earth and making Him to whom the Ritschlian school still ascribes the value of deity, put up with the value of a good moral character? Our rationalizing the Son of God into the son of man? The true logic of the Ritschlian notion of revelation is a *denial* of all revelation." [100]

[99] *Jahrbücher für protestantische Theologie*, xv. 1889, pp. 338 f.

[100] Similarly Nippold, as cited, p. 265, represents Ritschl as seeking to escape from Rationalism by rejecting all natural knowledge of God and

What Graue presents here as the inevitable drift of Ritschl's teaching about Christ is really rather the gist of his teaching. Accordingly J. Wendland,[101] after surveying the grounds on which Ritschl bases his ascription of the predicate of deity to Christ, very properly declares that they do not in reality suggest that predicate. We may well understand, he says, that out of a feeling of piety for the past, unwillingness to break with the historical tradition and the custom of the Church, Ritschl should wish to retain such a title for Christ. But we can scarcely justify him in doing so, when what he means by it is nothing more than pure god-imaging (*gottebenbildlich*) humanity. "Particularly unhappy," he continues, "is Ritschl's defence of himself against his opponents who charged him with making Christ in the end nothing but a mere man. Ritschl rejoined (p. 397), 'By mere man (if I should ever use the expression) I should mean a man as a natural being (*Naturgrösse*), with the exclusion of all characteristics of spiritual and moral personality.' It follows from this that the deity of Christ is to be grounded in the characteristics of spiritual and moral personality. These, however, are not at all divine but human things." Whatever we may think of the applicability of Wendland's closing criticism, it is certainly true that Ritschl's defence of himself is in its entirety mere evasion and amounts in substance to a confession of judgment. "We, for our part," writes Leonhard Stählin justly,[102] "are unable to

---

representing the Christian community as the sole mediator of reconciliation. But, he adds, this is merely formal; in the matter of teaching "he comes near enough to the old Rationalism" to explain the polemical attitude to him of the orthodox and the only half-acceptance of the liberals. He talks of Christ no doubt as if he possessed in Him at least one supernatural datum; but from Him onward all is explained on a naturalistic, empirical-psychological basis. "All dogmatic predications dissolve in a complex of subjective-psychological notions, value-judgments and acts of will."

101 As cited, pp. 114 f.

102 "Kant, Lotze, and Ritschl," p. 221, at the close of a couple of pages of telling criticism of Ritschl's meager Christology. Similarly, J. Wendland, as cited, p. 116, points out that apart from his use of "the extravagant" expression "Godhead" of Christ and the peculiar ideal of piety which Ritschl has brought to expression in his Christology, his estimate of Jesus does not

discover anything in his Christology that raises it above the level of simple Rationalism. And the appending of the title of deity to the picture of Christ which he has drawn, is a pagan procedure for which no justification whatever is offered."

Those who insist that Ritschl teaches the proper deity of Christ [103] appear to forget that Ritschl himself declined to make any such affirmation. We do not know how "the person of Christ came into being," he says,[104] or "became what it presents itself for our ethical and religious estimation"; that "is no subject of theological investigation" — it is a problem "which transcends every kind of investigation." Only, we must not combine Him with God His Father; that explains nothing scientifically.[105] Let us content ourselves with knowing that He is that being "whose whole vocational activity forms the material of the complete revelation of God present in Him, or in whom the word of God is a human person." That is to say, what Jesus Christ is, is just the man in whom this complete revelation of God is embodied. There is no question of a preëxistence of Christ here, as indeed there could not be with Ritschl's view, whether of God or of Christ. Ritschl, it is true, employs the term "eternal" with reference to Him with great freedom.[106] He stands, we are told, in an eternal relation with God: He is the eternal object of the love of God; even the phrase "the eternal Godhead of the Son" is not shunned. But the employment of these phrases is accompanied with explanations which rob them of what might have otherwise seemed their natural meaning. Only God, he tells us, "does not become, but eternally is what He is": only He is

---

differ from that of the "Liberal Theology" — as for example that of Pfleiderer.

[103] C. von Kügelgen, as cited, pp. 64 ff. supplies a very favorable example. His contention is that with his ontology of spiritual being and his epistemological views, Ritschl could say only what he says. See also William Adams Brown, "The Essence of Christianity," 1902, pp. 260–261. Ritschl here is in effect made a mystic.

[104] P. 451.

[105] "Aber die Combination zwischen ihm und Gott seinem Vater ist eben keine Erklärung wissenschaftlicher Art."

[106] E.g. pp. 470, 471.

" of Himself." As for Christ — even theological tradition denies to Him self-existence and (in the predication of eternal generation to Him) ascribes Him to "the category of becoming in distinction from being." So far as this, says Ritschl, we may go with the traditional theology, when we speak of the deity of Christ. So far as this — that Christ is a dependent being who had His origin in time. But we can go with it no further. What Ritschl is doing is giving a new sense to the term " eternal deity," as ascribed to Christ; a new sense which would necessarily be misunderstood were it not clearly explained. It has meaning only, Ritschl says, with reference to God, not to us. " The eternal Godhead of the Son of God, in the transcription (*Umschreibung*) of it which has been given, becomes completely intelligible only as object of the divine knowledge and will, that is for God Himself." What is meant is that " Christ exists for God eternally as the same that He is manifested to us in temporal limitation." That is to say, He has always, just as He existed on earth, been the object of the divine prevision and predestination. Naturally, only of the divine. Ritschl somewhat unnecessarily adds: " But only for God; for as preëxistent Christ is for us hidden." We, not being eternal like God, can know things only under the conditions of time and space. God knows from eternity all things in one all-embracing knowledge. The mode of this knowledge is inscrutable; its objects are in a true sense real — that is to say in the eternal, timeless knowledge of God. Christ, therefore, as existing from eternity in this knowledge, has had an eternal preëxistence, in the sense of which it is more customary to speak as a merely ideal preëxistence. Of course the same could equally well be said of everything else. For anything that exists has eternally preëxisted in the divine knowledge and will. At bottom Ritschl is expounding in this passage not a doctrine of Christ's preëxistence but the doctrine of God's eternal foreknowledge and decree. This of course has not escaped notice. " Real premundane existence is thus ascribed," writes Leonhard Stählin,[107] " not to Christ, but merely to the divine will

[107] As cited, p. 207.

as directed to the establishment of the kingdom of God through Christ. As thus defined, however, the divine will is the volition of something that has yet to exist, something therefore which does not yet exist." "Ritschl," writes Henri Schoen similarly,[108] " teaches the ideal preëxistence of Christ, and Christ is for him the historical person of Jesus. But as, at bottom, a historical person preëxists really or does not preëxist at all, as there is no middle term, Jesus does not preëxist at all. What preëxists is solely the divine intention, the mercy of God. Accordingly, when Ritschl speaks to us of an ideal preëxistence of Jesus, that is only a new expression for the omniscience of God."

It is something that Ritschl thus relates Christ directly to the divine activities of foreknowledge and foreordination. It does not appear that he relates Him with similar directness to any other divine activities. How He came into being, how He came to be what He was — the bearer of the complete revelation of God, the vehicle of the complete will of God, and therefore the founder of the Kingdom of God — Ritschl warns us it is useless, even noxious, to enquire.[109] " How it was possible for such a man to come into existence," Stäh1in expounds,[110] " is a question which Ritschl declines to answer. ' So far as one desires to be a Christian, one must recognize as a fact — a given fact, a *datum* — this relation of Christ to God, declared by Himself and proved even unto death, as also by His resurrection from the dead.[111] We must refrain entirely from attempts to get behind this *datum* — to explain how it came to pass in detail, how it acquired an empirical existence. Attempts of this kind are purposeless, because they are resultless; and being resultless, it is injurious to make them.' "[112] That Ritschl was careful to leave such questions in what Orr

[108] As cited, p. 84.

[109] P. 451.

[110] As cited, pp. 214–215.

[111] On what Ritschl understood by the Resurrection of Christ see the careful statements of Orr, " The Ritschlian Theology," pp. 92, 202 f., and " Ritschlianism," pp. 96 ff.

[112] " Theologie und Metaphysik," p. 29.

calls "convenient vagueness"[113] is full of significance. The
plain fact is that his theology had no means at its disposal for
solving them.[114] With his exclusion of all direct commerce of
God with the human spirit — all "mystical fantasies" — he
has rendered all revelation in the proper sense of the word impossible, and with it all immediate divine guidance. On this
ground Christ cannot be a God-taught man; He must be explained merely as a religious genius. C. von Kügelgen, it is
true, declares[115] it is unjust to represent it as Ritschl's view,
as Lemme does, "that in Christ too the idea of the moral
world-view arose in the same way as in us all — as a consequence of a moral wish or of meditation." Did not Ritschl, he
demands, represent Jesus as "actually experiencing a religious
relation to God, theretofore non-existent, and undertaking to
introduce His disciples into the same world-view and world-
estimate?" The premise and conclusion here certainly do not
hang together. That Ritschl represents Christ as the discoverer
of a new relation to God and as able to transmit it to a following, says nothing as to his view of how Jesus acquired this new
conception of the relation of man to God. And the passage in
Ritschl to which von Kügelgen appeals[116] also says nothing
of it.

This passage says, to be sure, more to the honor of Christ
than von Kügelgen extracts from it. It says that Christ is
something more to the community which He established than
its founder and lawgiver — than "the transitory occasion of
His disciples' religion and the legislator for their conduct, who
would be a matter of indifference to them, as soon as His law
had been learned." Ritschl magnifies the abiding influence of
Jesus' person on His followers, the example which it is to them,

[113] "Ritschlianism," p. 46. "How Christ should arrive at this knowledge
of God," remarks Orr, "should possess these extraordinary endowments,
should stand in this unique relation to God and to His purpose, — in short,
should be the Person that He is, and should stand in the relation to God
and man that He does — is a mystery into which we are not permitted to
pry."

[114] Cf. Stählin, as cited, p. 314.

[115] As cited, p. 65.

[116] P. 386.

the inspiration which it brings them. " The task," he says," of the real development of the spiritual personality, cannot be conceived rightly or fully apart from the contemplation of the prototype of this human destiny. What therefore we recognize in the historically unique portraiture (*Lebensbild*) of Christ as the particular value of his existence (*Daseins*), gains through the peculiarity of this phenomenon, and through its norm-giving bearing on our religious and ethical destiny, the value of a permanent rule, since we at the same time establish that it is only through the arousing and directing power of this person that we are in a position to enter into His relation to God and to the world." [117] These remarks very greatly exalt Christ — in His functions. In this exaltation of His functions, He is separated from other men: He is the originator, they at best the imitators; He is the producer, they at best the reproducers — who apart from His inspiration can do nothing. This is not a small difference, though it be but a difference of degree: a difference of but degree all the more that it is hinted that in reproducing what He has produced we may reproduce it fully. This exaltation of Christ in His functions is even carried so far that it is connected with the predicate of Godhead — though unfortunately these high functions on which this Godhead is based are treated rather as forming its content than supplying its evidence. Nowhere do we get beyond their limit, and therefore nowhere do we get beyond a great man — say the supremely great man, who has found God and found Him completely, and by the power of His unique spiritual energy stamps His own religious image on the hearts of men.

It is necessary to revert for a moment to the hint in Ritschl's discussion to which we have just called attention in passing, that Christ's followers may become altogether like Him. Is Christianity adequately described, we may ask, as " the religion of Jesus," or is its essence to be sought rather in "faith in Christ " ? Is Jesus merely our Example, or is He also our Savior? These two antitheses are not quite identical, and we may be advanced in our understanding of Ritschl's teach-

[117] P. 387.

ing by discriminating between them. Ritschl does not wish to
teach that Jesus is only our Example. He vigorously assaults
the " advocates of the religion of Jesus," who seek to "exhaust
the significance of Jesus in the scheme of individual imitation."
They overlook, he declares, the fact that Jesus withdraws Himself from imitation "by setting Himself over against His disciples as the author of forgiveness of sins." [118] Ritschl is seeking, formally at least, to preserve to Jesus some shreds of His
function as Savior. We use this depreciatory language because
it appears that he ascribes saving functions to Jesus only so
far as there proceeds from His person an influence which
incites His followers to action and gives direction to their
action.[119] After all, therefore, he conceives of Jesus only as our
Example, except so far as he throws the emphasis on His example, less as pattern than as inspiration. Jesus affects us,
according to him, only through the impression which the contemplation of Him makes on us — the influence which He
exerts upon us; and our Christianity consists in the end, therefore, only in our repeating in our own persons what is found
first in Him — unless we prefer to split hairs with Theodor
Haering [120] and carefully explain that it is not a question of
our individual imitation of Jesus but only of experiencing in
ourselves after the fashion of a copy (*nachbildlich*) the childship to God which Jesus promises after the fashion of an
original (*urbildlich*). It remains true that the Christianity of
the Christian consists, according to Ritschl, in his presenting
in his own life-experience the "piety" which Jesus lived out
in His own person. Beyond doubt, he explains, Jesus experienced and testified to His disciples a religious relation to God
which had had no exemplification before Him, and made it
His task to lead His disciples into this same conception of the
world and judgment of self. "This religious determination of
the members of Christ's community is prefigured in the person
of the Founder and is grounded on it as the abiding power to all

[118] Pp. 2, 561 ff.
[119] P. 387.
[120] " Ueber das Bleibende im Glauben an Christus," 1880, p. 14.

imitation of Him." [121] In point of fact Ritschl therefore brings us back, for the essence of Christianity, to the repetition in His followers of just those simple elements of piety which are given originally in Jesus. His Christianity is just "the religion of Jesus." And the whole purpose of his main treatise would not be misleadingly described as an attempt to show that those conceptions pronounced by Lagarde [122] " apostolical, not evangelical " are really " evangelical " as well as " apostolical," because "rightly understood" they mean nothing more than following Jesus in thinking of God as mere love, who has no intention of punishing sin, and therefore living no longer in distrust of Him, but in trusting acceptance of His end as our end. Like Jesus, and under the impulse received from him (through the community), we are to live in faith, humility, patience, thankfulness, and the practice of love in the Kingdom of God. Doing so, we shall be divine as He, doing so, was divine. This is to Ritschl the entirety of Christianity: and this is at bottom just a doctrine of "imitation" of the "religion of Jesus."

It is mere paradox to speak of Ritschl as teaching a supernatural Christianity. " Although he lays little stress on specific miracles," writes William Adams Brown,[123] " Christianity is to Ritschl in a true sense a supernatural religion, for which no adequate preparation or explanation can be found in prechristian history." The qualification "in a true sense" really tells the story; its function in the sentence is to guard against its being understood to say that Ritschl's Christianity is a supernatural one in the ordinary sense of that term. The reason assigned for the supernaturalness of Ritschl's Christianity is, moreover, ineffective. Ritschl, to be sure, teaches that Christianity came into the world as something new; and we may for our own part believe that, properly considered, that involves its supernaturalness. But there is no reason to suppose that was Ritschl's opinion: on the contrary, he takes

[121] P. 387.
[122] " Mittheilungen," iv. 1891, p. 109.
[123] " The Essence of Christianity," 1902, p. 227.

great pains to prevent its attribution to him — and he gives
us a Christianity which, despite its sudden advent into the
world, is through and through, in its substance, modes of working, and accessories alike, purely natural. It certainly is a
meiosis to say that he "lays little stress on specific miracles."
He does not allow the occurrence of any such thing as a
" miracle." " Miracle " with him, as Orr justly tells us,[124] " is
the religious name for an event which awakens in us a powerful impression of the help of God, but is not to be held as
interfering with the scientific doctrine of the unbroken connection of nature."

Even more paradoxical than Brown's is Gustav Ecke's
representation.[125] According to him Ritschl not only has no
intention of excluding the supernatural factor from the course
of the development of the Christian life, but actually so suggests it as to compel us to perceive in it his genuine point of
view. It is allowed that he is not altogether consistent in the
matter. He only sometimes speaks as if he recognized a direct
supernatural activity underlying the Christian life, providing
indeed its producing cause; recognized it but declined to assert
it or to expound it, because, above all else that he recognized
about it, is this — that, though it is to be acknowledged, it is a
hidden mystery of which nothing whatever can be said, a kind
of *Ding an sich* behind the phenomena of the spiritual life. At
other times, it is admitted, he speaks as if there is nothing of
the sort to be recognized and the Christian life is to be explained
solely out of the natural powers of man's own spirit. Ecke now
declares that, led by considerations of a general character, he
is of the opinion that Ritschl is himself only when he speaks
in the former fashion. He apparently forgets that even to speak
in this former fashion is already to withdraw oneself wholly
from the supernaturalism of the Christian life. It is already to

[124] " The Christian View of God and the World," 1893, p. 31; see also
" The Ritschlian Theology," p. 93. Cf. Wendland, as cited, p. 61, who gives
the passages from which Ritschl's doctrine may be drawn: " Justification and
Reconcilation," E. T. iii. pp. 616–617; " Instruction," § 17, E. T. pp. 188–189;
J. d. Th., 1861, pp. 429 ff.; *Hist. Zeitschr.*, viii. 1862, pp. 97 ff.

[125] As cited, pp. 63 ff.

treat this supernaturalism, which is only conventionally allowed, as negligible; to take up an agnostic attitude over against it, which, like all agnostic attitudes, is only an indirect way of denying it. It already betrays a rationalistic conception of the processes of the Christian life as ruling the mind, and thus points to the rationalistic mode of treatment which lies by its side as representing the fundamental point of view of the author.

It is true that, after expressing, at least, a complete " agnosticism " with reference to the working of the Holy Spirit on the human spirit, and asserting the consequent necessity of confining ourselves in expounding them to a mere description of the phenomena themselves, Ritschl is able to write such a sentence as this: " In these statements the Holy Spirit is not denied, but recognized and understood." [126] And it is true that after reasserting this "agnostic" attitude in its extremest form, going so far as to declare that "nothing further can be objectively taught " about the justification and regeneration of the individual than that they follow on his acceptance of the gospel as presented to him in the Christian community, he feels justified in striking back waspishly at his critics in the assertion that he too recognizes that there are "mysteries" in the Christian life but that it is his habit when he comes across a mystery to be silent about precisely it.[127] Such declarations, however, do not point, as Ecke appears to suppose, to a fundamental supernaturalism of conception on Ritschl's part, which represents the real Ritschl; but have precisely the contrary meaning. Ritschl is able to neglect whatever supernatural elements in the Christian life he may be thought here and there to suggest that he dimly perceives, and to develop the whole story of its rise and progress without their aid. And even when his language, taken literally, may seem most clearly to carry a supernaturalistic meaning, we cannot fail to know that it is not intended to convey it. This is true for example of the instances which have just been adduced. It is certain that when Ritschl speaks of " mysteries in the religious life " he is think-

<hr>

[126] Pp. 22 f.   [127] P. 607.

ing of nothing supernatural, but only of the wonders of the natural operations of the human spirit. And it is certain that when he speaks of "recognizing and understanding" the Holy Spirit, he is not thinking of any supernatural Being — a Divine Person who acts as a Power on the persons of believers — but only of the "common spirit" of the Christian community, which in the form of a common knowledge affects the activities of the individual. Facts like these throw a lurid light on the survival in Ritschl's expositions of expressions which might otherwise be thought capable of bearing a supernaturalistic interpretation.

What these expressions indicate is not that Ritschl was of a divided mind, and spoke now in a naturalistic, now in a supernaturalistic, sense without ever being able to find a point of equilibrium. Still less do they mean that, though working out his system on naturalistic postulates, he remained at bottom a supernaturalist, and that his fundamental supernaturalism occasionally forces itself to the surface. What they mean is simply that Ritschl, though working out a purely naturalistic system, worked it out in the face of, and with a view to commending it to, a supernaturalistically minded community. He therefore clothes his naturalistic system with the terms of supernaturalism, or, to be more precise, of conservative evangelicalism. He himself thought of this procedure as a reminting of the old coin; it is not strange that the evangelical public itself looked upon it as rather counterfeiting it. In point of fact he everywhere employs the old nomenclature of a supernaturalistic theology in order to express — with whatever twisting and straining — his new naturalistic conceptions. The method cannot be said to be a happy one. Henri Schoen, who deals with it gently, points out that Ritschl borrowed, or may have borrowed, it from Hofmann, who, he thinks, in other matters also exerted a certain influence on Ritschl's development. Hofmann, says he,[128] not only compelled the Bible to teach his theology, "but inaugurated a procedure which became that of the Göttingen theologian. Persuaded that his contempo-

[128] As cited, p. 133.

raries would accept his theory more easily if it was clothed in an orthodox form, he preserved the traditional terms, redemption, expiation, satisfaction, only giving them a new sense. He did not wish, at any price, to cast off 'the uniform of his army,' that is to say, that of the orthodox party. His object, as he liked to repeat, was 'to teach old truths in a new form.' It is possible, with equal right, to reverse the formula, and say that he taught new truths, while employing old expressions. Ritschl expressed indignation at this procedure; [129] he imitated it more than once." He found, in effect,[130] " in the writings of Hofmann a valuable lesson in prudence; he could learn from them that, in order to get a truth accepted he must avoid shocking the religious feeling of his contemporaries, and that it is often useful to present new ideas under an old form, that is to say, by preserving the expressions to which pious men are accustomed. The method is dangerous; beyond question, very dangerous: we do not hesitate to repel it when the sense of truth is in danger of being blunted by it. . . ."

It cannot be denied that Ritschl deliberately adopted this method of commending his naturalistic theology to a suspicious public; or that he pressed his employment of it to an incredible extreme. It would no doubt be a mistake, however, to attribute to him a calculated intention to deceive. He obviously took pleasure in his employment of the consecrated forms of speech and no doubt persuaded himself with more or less success that he had a right to them. We have to reckon here with the peculiarities of his personality, with the special type of his piety, with the sources of his theological system.

Johannes Wendland, in an illuminating page or two, makes us aware [131] of the close connection of Ritschl's theological attitude and development with his strong and proud, angular, and self-assertive character. Hating above all things what he regarded as sentimentality and pious " gush," seeing religion

---

[129] " Justification and Reconciliation," i. p. 546.

[130] Schoen, as cited, p. 140.

[131] As cited, pp. 7 ff. Much of the contents of these closing paragraphs is drawn from this discussion.

rather in "doing" than in "feeling," and priding himself on his "practical" Christianity, he conceived it to be his mission to bring this type of Christianity to its rights as over against the tendency to emotionalism which he marked with disgust in the professionally religious. With this natural temperament, his mind turned with predilection to that ethicizing form of Christian teaching which for more than a century had been regnant in a large section of German thought, and which we know by the general name of Rationalism.[132] "In point of fact," says Leonhard Stählin justly,[133] "his system of theology is an attempt to revive in new form the antiquated principles of rationalism, and to establish them on a new basis by means of a theory of cognition suggested by Kant and Lotze, and with the help of elements drawn from Schleiermacher. . . . It is simply a reconstructed theology of the so-called faith of reason or rational faith (*Vernunftglaube*), and differs from other attempts of the same kind, not so much in substance as in form and method. . . . Matters are not altered by simply laying stress on the historical revelation through Christ, as long as Christ has no other significance than that of having first realized that which forms the content of natural religion." It is not, however, in this philosophic-theological inheritance that his theology found its starting point, although he ostentatiously presents his epistemology as its determining factor. Neither does it take its starting-point from his historical or exegetical investigations, although he ostentatiously lays extended historical and exegetical investigations at its base. His philosophical, historical, and exegetical results are all already dominated by his point of view, which has its roots in his religious peculiarity and the ideal of piety which he cherished and sought to illustrate in his person.

This type of piety he endeavored to impress on the Church as the substance of what it is to be a Christian. It was in its interest that he worked out his theology, and it was in its

---

[132] Cf. the good remarks of Julius Leopold Schultze in the *Neue kirchliche Zeitschrift,* ix. 1898, p. 214.

[133] As cited, pp. 277, 326.

interests that he turned and twisted the teaching of the Scriptures and of the great Reformers alike, in the determination to wrest from their unwilling lips support for it. Nothing could exceed the eclecticism of his procedure, except it be its violence. He takes from Scripture and Reformers alike what suits his purpose, without the least regard to its logical connection, and then fits it without mercy into his scheme. He himself naïvely betrays how he deals with the Reformers, for example, when he drops the remark: [134] " The reformatory ideas are more concealed than revealed in the theological books of Luther and Melancthon themselves." Neglecting their real teachings he gathered out from their writings such chance remarks as could be made to fit in with his own view of things, and built up from them a new Reformation doctrine which he presented as the only true one. Thus he gave the world a new Naturalism, decked out in phrases borrowed from the Scriptures and Reformers, but as like their system of thought as black is to white, and called it the true doctrine of the Bible and Reformers. This strange procedure has, under his influence, been systematized and men now tell us gravely that the essence of any movement consists of that in it which we can look upon as lasting truth — which, being interpreted, means that in it which we find conformable to our own predilections.[135] In Ritschl's own hands it was rather the result of his overbearing temper, which imposed itself upon the materials of his thought and bent them to his service. So far as this, or something like this, is the true account of the matter, it is not necessary to attribute to him any direct purpose to deceive. The result was the same.

[134] " Drei akademische Reden," 1887, p. 18.

[135] This is the procedure of W. Herrmann and A. Harnack when dealing with the doctrines of the Reformation. For the general notion see the *Harvard Theological Review,* October 1914, pp. 538 ff.

II

ALBRECHT RITSCHL AND HIS DOCTRINE OF CHRISTIAN PERFECTION

II. RITSCHL THE PERFECTIONIST

ALBRECHT RITSCHL AND HIS DOCTRINE OF CHRISTIAN PERFECTION

ARTICLE II

RITSCHL THE PERFECTIONIST[1]

IT LIES in the very nature of a naturalistic system that it should lay all its stress on the activities of the Christian life. There is nothing else on which it could lay its stress. What man himself does, the influences by which he is brought to do it, and the issue of his activities — this is the circle of topics in which what, by a strange transmutation of meaning, is still called Theology, moves. Ritschl continues to employ the terms reconciliation, justification, forgiveness, adoption, regeneration, sanctification; but they one and all denote in his hands human, not divine, acts; and his whole discussion is devoted to the elaboration of the influences under which man is brought to the performance of them, their nature, and their effects.

According to Ritschl all the influences under which man is brought to the performance of these acts are gathered up, as in their focus, in the person of Jesus Christ; or rather in the great discovery which Christ made of the real relation in which man stands to God, the effective transmission of which to His followers constituted the one object of His life.[2] This great discovery is comprehended in the one declaration that God is love and nothing but love, and therefore man has nothing to fear from Him. We do not rest under the

---

[1] From *The Princeton Theological Review*, xviii. 1920, pp. 44–102.

[2] P. 386: "Beyond doubt Jesus experienced and declared to His disciples a religious relation to God not before known, and purposed to bring His disciples into the same religious world-view and self-estimate, and under this condition into the universal task of the Kingdom of God which He knew to be set for His disciples as for Himself."

Divine condemnation; the Divine wrath does not hang over us; God intends us nothing but good; God will do us nothing but good. This is what Jesus would have us understand and act upon; and this it is by which, if we understand and act upon it, we become Christians with all that that involves. Of course what we are assured of here is that sin has no significance in the sight of God; and what we are exhorted is to treat it as without significance. Bringing us to this attitude to sin and God is the reconciling work of Jesus; our assumption of this attitude is our justification. For when we assume this attitude our distrust of God, the product of our feeling of guilt, passes away; we take our place happily by God's side; and, assured that He means us only good, we make His end our end and work with Him for its attainment.

We are obviously entangled here in a perfect network of illusions.

There is no such thing as sin. What we call sin is merely ignorance. Our feeling of guilt is therefore an illusion.[3] It is really not a sense of ill-desert for sins committed so much as a mere anticipation of the displeasure of God. We are not oppressed by the consciousness that we have done wrong; we are depressed by anxiety lest we shall receive harm. It is less regret than fear which gives it its form. This fear, however, is wholly misplaced. God feels no displeasure towards us and has no intention whatever of punishing our sin. He never has had. He experiences no movement of indignation against us; His whole emotional reaction towards us is love. Our sense of forgiveness is therefore also an illusion. There is nothing to forgive; and God has never been ill-disposed toward us. "If there is no truth in the consciousness of sin, as guilt causing alienation from God," writes Pfleiderer in an illuminating page,[4] "neither can there be any truth in the conscious-

---

[3] To be perfectly accurate we should note here that Ritschl is willing to allow that sin may become witting — in the case of the finally reprobate. As Pfleiderer ("Die Ritschl'sche Theologie," p. 69) puts it: "All sin, with the exception of the always only problematical definitive hardening, is in God's judgment only ignorance."

[4] As cited, pp. 69, 70.

ness of the annulment of guilt and alienation from God or in the forgiveness of sins. A guilt which does not exist except in man's illusory notion cannot be forgiven; a relation which has never really been interrupted cannot be restored, cannot be reconciled. The conclusion necessarily follows from the estimate of sin as an ignorance which is not deserving of wrath and does not interrupt our relation to God, that the consciousness of reconciliation or of a change from an interrupted to a peaceable relation is an illusion. There cannot occur here a change in the actual relation between man and God; the change lies only in man's conception of his relation to God so far as he is relieved from his former illusionary notion of this relation or is enlightened as to the absolute erroneousness of his sense of guilt and fear of the angry God."

In a word, Ritschl's whole doctrine of sin, guilt, forgiveness, reconciliation moves, not in the realm of realities, but in that of the subjective consciousness. Man feels himself under the Divine condemnation. He is wrong. All he needs is to be assured that he is wrong, and all is well. That is in effect Ritschl's doctrine of justification. Continuing his searching criticism Pfleiderer points out [5] that Ritschl can assign no ground for justification and that the reason is that nothing has really happened in justification. "There is no such essential difference for God between sinners and righteous that the one stands in an entirely different relation to Him from the other." "In point of fact," says he, "the key to Ritschl's doctrine of justification lies here: there is no need for a ground for the justification of the sinner simply because the sinner has never been the object of God's disfavor, but his sin has been esteemed by God only as the stage of his ignorance. Justification is therefore really nothing but the historical notification, brought about by Jesus, that God is only love and as such is not angry with sinners, and that they may therefore lay aside their fear and distrust of Him. It is no doubt assumed along with this, that those who, as members of the communion of Christ, hear this proclamation and profit by it, will be led by

[5] As cited, p. 75.

it to adopt the end of God in His Kingdom. How, however, if this assumption be too optimistic? How if it should rather be found that the proclamation of the God whose forgiveness of sins is not accorded on distinct conditions, but whom rather sin does not in the least offend, is understood and utilized by the mass of the members of the community as meaning that they need not make too much of their sin and can exercise their freedom over the world in joyous mastery of the world and enjoyment of the world, undeterred by old-fashioned scruples of conscience? Of course the Ritschlian theologians have no such meaning and purpose. But the danger of a practical consequence of this sort lies so uncommonly close in this theology that it certainly needs to be earnestly considered."

There can be no sort of question that Ritschl makes the sense which the sinner has of resting under the displeasure of God, the sense which the believer has of having been forgiven by God, illusions. "All reflections about God's wrath and pity, His long-suffering and patience, His severity and mercy," he says,[6] " are based on the religious adjustment of our individual situation with God in the form of time." A. E. Garvie[7] rightly expounds this to mean, that " subjective changes in our own spiritual state, which is conditioned by the lapse of time, are explained by us as due to objective changes in God's relation to us, although God is not Himself subject to the condition of time." But this is not all that it means. Ritschl is really employing the idea of the eternity of God to ground the denial of the presence in Him of any such emotion as wrath or any such quality as vindicatory justice, it being a maxim with him that wrath and love cannot co-exist in the same mind. However indispensable the judgments which he enumerates "may be in the context of our religious experiences," therefore, he immediately adds, " they are out of all relation to the theological determination of the whole under the viewpoint of eternity. . . . Under the theological point of view, therefore, the wrath of God and His curse on sinners yet to be reconciled, finds no validity." God's actual attitude to us is,

6 P. 322.   7 Op. cit., p. 307.

and therefore His eternal attitude has always been, just that of pure love. He feels no anger towards us, and has never felt any, and it is absurd therefore to speak of reconciling Him to us, and even more absurd to speak of reconciling His love and anger in Himself. It is true that under his own sense of guilt a sinner may imagine that God is angry with him, and, under this obsession, may even look upon the evils which befall him in the course of his life, as so many punitive inflictions. But all this is illusion. " Here," says Garvie rightly,[8] " we are concerned with a subjective representation, not an objective reality." There being no such thing as " the wrath of God revealed from heaven against every doer of iniquity," it is our sense of guilt only, not the fact of the case, which leads us to interpret the evils of life as punitive. Paul is wrong when he connects death, for example, with sin.[9] The only evil which is a real consequence of sin, is that estrangement from God which results from our sense of guilt. This experience of estrangement from God — the result of our sense of guilt — is therefore in a true sense the only "punishment" of sin.[10] " The unremoved sense of guilt is not a penal state along with others, but this is the thing itself to which all external penal evils are related only as accompanying circumstances." [11] Thus the whole of the evil of sin is swallowed up into the sense of guilt, which itself is — not the subjective reflection of an objective separation from God wrought by sin itself — but a subjective illusion as to the attitude of God towards sin, creating the feeling of a separation from God which has no existence except in our own imagination.

[8] As cited, p. 310.

[9] Pp. 358 f.

[10] Cf. Orr, " The Ritschlian Theology," p. 147: " It is this experience of separation from God which, on Ritschl's showing, is the real core or essence of the punishment of sin, so far as, *ex concessis,* the punitive idea (which rests on the rejected theory of ' rights ') is to be admitted into Christianity at all." In Ritschl's system there is no place for real punishment of sin. " If there is no wrath of God against sin," expounds Garvie (as cited, p. 310), " there can be no punishment by God of sin. This conclusion Ritschl expressly draws."

[11] P. 365.

This being true, reconciliation naturally is to Ritschl, as Friedrich Nippold phrases it,[12] "at bottom, nothing but a change of mind, though no doubt this change of mind is made possible only by the knowledge and appreciation of the divine will of love declared by Christ." And all that happens in justification — which is only a synonym of reconciliation — is, as Garvie points out,[13] "the restoration of the sinner to communion with God," or, otherwise expressed, "the removal of the separation of the sinner from God," though to be perfectly accurate we must take the nouns "restoration," "removal," not actively, but passively. The separation here spoken of is expressed, or we would better say, consists, in a "sense of guilt"; it is therefore, this "sense of guilt" which is removed. "This, however," remarks Garvie now, "would be no benefit, but an injury, unless with the sense of guilt there is also taken away the guilt, which is a real contradiction by man of God, and of his own moral destiny. As this contradiction is real, else man's sense of guilt were an illusion, so the removal is real, else man's feeling of forgiveness were a deception." This reasoning is formally sound; but as the results it ostensibly reaches are the precise contradictions of Ritschl's actual teachings, it serves only to show how completely the conceptions of sin and its removal drop out of Ritschl's teaching. Man's sense of guilt does appear in Ritschl's system as an illusion and his feeling of forgiveness does appear in it as deceptive. The guilt and forgiveness which these illusory feelings fallaciously presuppose share, of course, in their illusoriness. Ritschl knows nothing of either guilt or its removal, in the proper sense of the word guilt, in which it includes along with subjective ill-desert, also obnoxiousness to punishment.[14] The "sense of guilt" is

[12] As cited, p. 265.

[13] As cited, pp. 325 f.

[14] Orr has made the matter perfectly plain, "The Christian View of God and the World," 1893, p. 199; "The Ritschlian Theology," pp. 146 ff., 267 f.; and especially "Ritschlianism," pp. 99 ff. The strictures on Orr's representations made by A. T. Swing, "The Theology of Albrecht Ritschl," 1901, pp. 125 ff., Orr has himself dealt with adequately. Those by J. K. Mozley, "Ritschlianism," 1909, pp. 218 ff., are no more successful.

represented by Ritschl as really just distrust of God, and there is no ground for distrusting God. God does not really forgive our sins; He merely takes no account of them — His whole reaction towards us being love. He loves us continuously, with a love unconditioned by the intrusion of wrath. He experiences no change of attitude toward us, or of action toward us. We simply come to know that this is His attitude toward us; and our distrust of Him, the product of our unjustified sense of guilt, passes away. It passes away precisely because it has no ground in reality. We feel forgiven but we are not forgiven; we have merely learned that God is not " separated " from us — we have only been " separated " from Him.

What we receive through Christ according to Ritschl would be somewhat more accurately expressed therefore if we spoke of it as not forgiveness but the assurance of forgiveness.[15] Our sins are already forgiven, that is to say, overlooked: what we obtain through Christ is only knowledge of this fact.[16] We re-

---

[15] On the technical subject of " assurance " Ritschl speaks at large on p. 652. He who manifests the characteristic features of the believer — faith in God's providence, humility, patience, prayer, " combined as they are in normal fashion with the disposition to obey the moral law and with good action in one's calling " — has sufficient evidence that he is in a state of salvation. This admits of no other meaning than that our assurance of reconciliation is an inference from the observed fruits of reconciliation — including our moral state. Accordingly Ritschl tells us in the summary statement (p. 670) that " the believer experiences his personal assurance of reconciliation " in the exercise of the Christian virtues. This is a position, however, which he does not seem always to preserve.

[16] There is a certain analogy between Ritschl's representation that men are not under the wrath of God, but need only to lay aside their distrust of God and realize that they have nothing to fear from Him to be " saved," and a wide-spread type of preaching which declares all men by nature " sons of God," and " salvation " to consist in coming to understand and live according to this high character. " It is the true philosophy of history," says Phillips Brooks, " that man is the child of God, forever drawn to his Father, beaten back by base waves of passion, sure to come to Him in the end." The analogy is not completely destroyed when a universal redemption is thought of as the ground of man's favorable condition as already forgiven and requiring only subjectively to realize this forgiveness — which constitutes his salvation. It is unnecessary to point out how wide-spread this notion is: it is intrinsic in all doctrines of a " universal atonement " where the atoning fact is found in the work of Christ and not in an act of man's. A curious example

main guilty of these sins, of course, in the sense in which
Ritschl speaks of "moral guiltiness"—that is to say, we remain subjectively ill-deserving,—and we do not lose consciousness of this guilt. It would be contrary to God's truth
to pronounce us no longer guilty, and our own conscience witnesses to us that we are guilty.[17] Our sense of guilt may even
be intensified.[18] Only we are made to feel that all this makes
no difference in God's treatment of us, and so we are encouraged
no longer to hold aloof from God in distrust of His purpose towards us. What " forgiveness removes is not the sense of guilt
for past sins, but only its effect in separating from God, or the
distrust of God which attaches to it." [19] It " merely makes inoperative that effect of guilt and the consciousness of guilt,
which would appear in the abolition of the moral communion
between God and man, in their separation or mutual alienation." [20] " When God forgives or pardons sins," Ritschl now
immediately continues, " He brings His will into operation in
the direction of not permitting the contradiction — expressed
in guilt — in which sinners stand to Him, to hinder that fellowship of men with Him which He intends on higher grounds."
Forgiveness of sins thus means for Ritschl that, on God's
part, God, having ends of His own to serve, will not permit
man's sin to stand in the way of fellowship with Him; and
on man's part, man, being assured of this, lays aside his distrust of God, the natural result of his sense of guilt ("that mistrust which as an affection of the consciousness of guilt naturally separates the offender from the offended one,") and
commits himself in full trust to God's providential care. To
put the matter bluntly, God proposes on His part to take man

---

of it is mentioned by L. Ihmels, " Die tägliche Vergebung der Sünden,"
1901, pp. 39 f. in " the Bornholm movement," for which see also Herzog-
Hauck, " Realencyklopädie," *sub nom.*

[17] P. 60. " The removal of guilt and the consciousness of guilt would be
in contradiction to the validity of the law of truth for God, as also for the
conscience of the sinner."

[18] P. 544.

[19] P. 545.

[20] Pp. 63, 64.

just as He finds him; and man agrees on his part, that being done, no longer to distrust and hold aloof from God, but to trust himself to His keeping. Having no longer to look for evil from God, according to his desert, he will accept the good, which, despite his unworthiness of it, God (for ends of His own) is willing to give him. This is really Ritschl's doctrine of justification; and obviously, it is a profoundly immoral doctrine. It amounts at bottom simply to an understanding between man and God that by-gones shall be by-gones, and no questions will be asked.

Even C. von Kügelgen [21] allows that Ritschl deals too lightly with the forgiveness of sins. " That, not indeed the idea of sin, but the idea of the forgiveness of sin, is (of course unintentionally) attenuated by Ritschl on teleological grounds, seem to us easily shown. Frank says, [22] accordingly with justice, that according to Ritschl God forgives sin ' on higher grounds,' because the establishment of the Kingdom of God is His self-end, and forgiveness of sins is needed for that. Thus forgiveness of sins becomes for Ritschl at bottom a means to an end. . . ." These remarks do not, however, go to the root of the matter. What is difficult to credit is not that God has a high end in view in forgiving sins and that it is this high end which deter-

---

[21] As cited, p. 44.

[22] The reference is to Fr. H. R. Frank, " Ueber die kirchliche Bedeutung der Theologie A. Ritschl's," ed. 2, 1888, p. 14: " It corresponds with Ritschl's conception of sin, that in order to the reconciliation of man with God there is no need of an atonement by propitiation. ' When God forgives or pardons sin, He exerts His will in the direction that the contradiction, expressed in guilt, in which sinners stand to Him, shall not prevent that communion of man with Him which He purposes on higher grounds ' (p. 64). ' On higher grounds ' — because the establishment of the Kingdom of God is His self-end and forgiveness of sins is needed for it." Pursuing his theme Frank points out that in Ritschl's conception of God, no less than of sin, nothing else than this could be expected of him. " Now then," asks Frank a few pages later (p. 18), " how are we to comfort a soul that has fallen into sin and is burdened in his conscience in the presence of God? We must say to him: Dear friend, you have a wrong idea of God. God has no need of punishment and atonement. On higher grounds, namely, that He may realize the purpose of the world, which is at the same time His own purpose, He pardons sin. Be at peace, dear soul, and do not disturb yourself with such mediaeval (cf. Ritschl, *Drei akademische Reden*, p. 28) notions."

mines His action — any doctrine of forgiveness must como in the end to that; but that this forgiveness is grounded solely in this high end. Not only is God's ultimate motive in forgiving sin made to be His desire to establish a Kingdom of God; but His sole proximate justification in forgiving sins is supplied by this one motive. His forgiveness of sins is made thus a purely arbitrary act, performed for no other reason and with no other justification, than that He needs forgiven sinners for ends of His own. This, we say, is a profoundly immoral doctrine; it represents God as treating sin as no sin, which is as much as to say, failing to react to moral evil, perceived as such, as every moral being, by virtue of his very nature as a moral being, must react to it — with abhorrence and indignation. Nevertheless, as we have already seen, this representation falls in with Ritschl's actual teaching with respect to God, to whom he denies any other attribute than love and from whom he withholds specifically the attribute of vindicatory justice. It is also alone consonant with his teaching with regard to the work of Christ, to which he will not permit to be ascribed any expiatory or sin-bearing character. If he was to teach any forgiveness of sins at all, Ritschl was shut up to representing it as done by God in that purely arbitrary way in which alone, he tells us, it would be becoming for God's will to act.

An attempt is made to mitigate the immorality of the transaction, as it concerns man, by representing it as the reception by man of " eternal life " or " blessedness," and the source of great encouragement to him to undertake good works. Assured of acceptance with God, despite his sins, he, in trust in God's providence, rises, as a spiritual being, above the world, makes God's self-end his end, and, as a fellow-worker with God, labors for the building up of the Kingdom of God in the world. Having been given a new chance, he takes it. We have already seen Pfleiderer, with justified cynicism, questioning whether the proclamation of totally ungrounded forgiveness, open unconditionally to all, would naturally have this happy effect. With a similar implication Frank reminds us in this connection

of Claus Harms's comment that in the sixteenth century the
forgiveness of sins cost at least money; now, it seems, we are
to have it for nothing at all — we are just to take it for ourselves.[23] Certainly to represent forgiveness of sins as costing
absolutely nothing — either to God or to us — will scarcely
gird our loins to avoid at all costs such negligible foibles. In
any event, however, we are given here but a poor substitute for
the Holy Spirit, making His people holy by His creative action
on and in them. Yet this is what Ritschl offers us instead of
that. Readers of Ritschl are struck by nothing more strongly
than by his embarrassment in dealing with the topic of sanctification. With his passionate repulsion of all "mysticism" —
that is, of all immediate working of God upon man — he has
no instrument of sanctification but the human will, acting
"freely" under the inducement of motives.[24] Man must
sanctify himself. With his equally determined representation
of justification as purely a change of relation — it would be
better said, of attitude — to God, he repels all implication of
sanctification in justification, however that implication may
be conceived. Sanctification is an independent work of man,
taking place in a different sphere of operation. The most that
he can allow when swayed by this point of view, is that it is so
far furthered by justification that the new attitude to God
assumed in justification predisposes man to make God's self-
end his own end, and enheartens him in its prosecution. Justification may be thus, he says, the fundamental condition of the
Christian life,[25] apart from which the new life would not be
undertaken or vigorously prosecuted.[26] But it is not the direct
means of sanctification nor is sanctification its direct end.

[23] Fr. H. R. Frank, "Ueber die kirchliche Bedeutung der Theologie A.
Ritschl's," ed. 2, 1888, p. 31.
[24] Hence Fr. Luther (*Neue kirchliche Zeitschrift,* ii. 1891, p. 479) very
properly says that "according to Ritschl it is nature and not grace which
is the source of the moral activities of life."
[25] P. 535, paragraph 2.
[26] P. 546. When von Kügelgen, as cited, pp. 94 f., declares that the reproach that with Ritschl "justification has no telic relation (*Abzweck-
ung*) to the production of morally good conduct or of works" — as Lipsius
represents — is unjust, he can be justified only so far as this.

Such a representation would be to institute a "wholly apocryphal" connection between the two.[27]

The dualism between the religious and the ethical aspects of the Christian life thus brought to expression, runs through the whole of Ritschl's exposition of the Christian life and is never quite resolved. It is embodied in the famous comparison in which he pictures Christianity, not as "a circle described from a single center, but an ellipse which is determined by two *foci*"; [28] and it determines the form of his definition of Christianity, which is modified from Schleiermacher's precisely in its interests. "Christianity," says he,[29] "is the monotheistic, completely spiritual *and* ethical religion which, on the ground of the redeeming *and* Kingdom-founding life of its Originator, consists in the freedom of childship to God, includes in itself the motive to conduct out of love, aims at the moral organization of humanity, and grounds blessedness in childship to God *as well as* in the Kingdom of God." He is thinking here obviously in terms of religion and ethics set in a parallel relation to one another, with no vivid sense, at least, of their integration into a single notion. He is determined that Christianity shall not be to him "either merely a doctrine of redemption, or merely a system of morality." He insists that it is both; and in order that it may be both he continually emphasizes the two as two. He says,[30] it is true, that "dogmatics must be worked out, not purely from the idea of redemption; nor ethics purely from the idea of the Kingdom of God. . . . Each must be kept under the constitutive influence of both ideas." "Effectuation by God" supplies the form of the one; "personal self-activity" of the other. Neither can do without the other; they interact on each other. But their unity continually escapes his grasp. In the end, no doubt, the two are integrated under the scheme of means and end. Redemption is in order to the Kingdom of God; the ethical activities of the Kingdom of God manifest childship to God. But this mode of representation is reached with difficulty and is not consistently maintained.

[27] Pp. 495 ff.   [28] P. 11.   [29] P. 13.   [30] P. 14.

Means are of course always subordinate to their end. As redemption through Jesus has the Kingdom of God for its end, that means accordingly that religion is in order to morality, or, to use a parallel mode of expression employed by Ritschl, "religious dependence" is in order to "moral freedom." And that means in turn that Ritschl's system (conceiving of religion and ethics as it actually does) is at bottom less a system of theology than a system of ethics; and it is the idea of "moral freedom," which gives its form to ethics, that dominates his thought. He does indeed remind us [31] that Christianity is in the first instance a religion, and only in its specific character among religions, the ethical religion by way of eminence. Therefore, he argues, "the religious functions — trust in God, humility, patience, thanksgiving and prayer to God — in which according to Luther's teaching, the believer takes his position against the world — have precedence of the series of moral functions in which we devote ourselves directly to man." But this avails nothing; for in Ritschl's view, these "religious" functions are at most only a parallel product of man's free action, in the religious sphere, to his independent morality; and in reality only a means of his moral activity, supplying the "mood" in which alone it can be, or can be successfully, prosecuted. It is his naturalism which is determining his conceptions here. He is not talking of what God works in man in and through justification; but of how the new attitude which man assumes in what he calls justification affects him in his relations Godward and man-ward. What he presents as the religious results arising out of justification are therefore merely the motives to moral action which spring from his change of attitude. The vacillation, in which Ritschl now presents the religious aspects of the Christian life as merely the means to the moral, and now keeps the two apart as independent parallel phenomena of it,[32] may possibly be, Henri Schoen suspects,[33] if not exactly due to, yet facilitated by, a double inheritance. There is

[31] P. 527.   [33] As cited, p. 138; cf. p. 136.
[32] P. 521. "What we gain . . . is not a simple subsumption of the ethical under the religious aspect of Christianity."

Schleiermacher, after whom it was difficult to present a purely ethical theory of redemption. But there is also Kant. And if, in spite of Schleiermacher, the ethical element dominates in Ritschl's doctrine, "that is because, consciously or unconsciously, he remains more under the influence of Kant than of Schleiermacher. It is because he feared above everything to see the mystical element predominate over the will to do good, which appeared to him to be the essential factor of all religion."

We perceive that Ritschl's conception of the Christian life amounts briefly to just this: free ethical life inspired by a sense of well-pleasingness to God. Justification is viewed as the assumption of a new attitude of trust towards God and entrance, in this trust, into participation in God's aim to found an ethical Kingdom; and this Kingdom of God is viewed as the society of those animated by this motive and sharing in this endeavor. Justification thus prepares for the ethical effort; the Kingdom of God is its sphere. This free ethical life under this inspiration constitutes now Christian perfection, in Ritschl's nomenclature; that is to say, it is all that it is necessary to have in order to be a Christian — it makes us perfectly Christian though it may not make us perfect Christians.[34] Ritschl, however, is not content to leave his conception of the essence of Christianity, or Christian perfection, in this simple brevity of statement. He analyzes it, and he elaborates it. He divides, first of all, between those elements of it which

[34] William Adams Brown is quite right therefore when he tells us (" Christian Theology in Outline," 1906, p. 413) that " perfection" " as understood by Ritschl . . . is a name which describes the qualities which enter into the Christian ideal, however incomplete may be their quantitative realization in the individual." " Thus," Brown illustrates, " a man whose life is characterized by the qualities of faith, humility, patience and fidelity to his calling is perfect in Ritschl's sense of the term; since he is living in the right relation to God, however conscious he may be of occasional lapses from his own standard." And then he adds: " So defined, Christian perfection is only a name for that assurance which should characterize all true Christian living, and which is possible in every walk of life. It is the rejection of the Catholic doctrine of a double standard by which the possibility of perfection is confined to those who give themselves to the monastic life." We shall see subsequently that there is more to be said: Ritschl was not satisfied with a perfection of relation or a *perfectio partium*.

are, in his view, the direct and immediate effects of justification, and those elements of it which proceed from justification only indirectly and mediately, namely, through the mediation of the former. The former are, as we have seen, the religious, the latter the ethical elements; and we note here again that the Christian life is conceived as essentially conduct to which its religious aspect serves as means. The religious elements — Ritschl calls them religious functions — are enumerated as we have seen, as faith in the divine providence, humility, patience, prayer. They form, in their necessary unity,[35] the temper of mind or mood of the Christian, the temper of mind or mood by virtue of which he is a Christian, and because of which he becomes a worker along with God in the moralization of the world, through love.

There is nothing arbitrary in this construction. It is merely the expression in terms of the Christian life of the fundamental contents of Ritschl's doctrine of justification. He identifies justification with the forgiveness of sins, which is, positively expressed, entrance into fellowship with God. This entrance into fellowship with God involves, however, deliverance from the sense of guilt so far as the sense of guilt produces mistrust of God and separation from Him. It is necessarily accompanied therefore with peace of heart and joy. Ritschl calls this experience indifferently "blessedness" and "eternal life." And this naturally carries with it on the positive side a trust in God, which takes the place of the mistrust from which deliverance has been had. In this trust we not only accept God's providence as well for us and for the world, but are impelled to adopt God's end as our end, and to work along with Him to its accomplishment. This is all of the very essence of the experience of justification as a fact. And it is not a very complicated conception, but on the contrary, at

[35] The religious elements of Christian perfection all go together and *cannot* exist except in their combination. Ritschl says ("Die christliche Vollkommenheit," Rae's translation, pp. 148 f.) that "they are so constituted, that none of them can come up without the other; they are the various reflections shed by the religious certainty of reconciliation with God through Christ."

once very simple and quite unitary. It would not be doing serious injustice to it if we said brusquely that it is comprehended in the idea of putting ourselves by the side of God and accepting His end as our end. We put ourselves by the side of God when we not only acquiesce in the course of things which He has in His providence established for His world, but recognize it as the best course of things and best for us. This carries with it what Ritschl calls "dominion over the world," that is, superiority to its changes and chances and the subordination of it to our spiritual life. It carries with it also humility and patience and thanksgiving to God: these are the tones of mind which acquiescence in, acceptance of, and rejoicing in God's providence bring with them. Putting ourselves by the side of God in this attitude of mind, we naturally make His end our own and live for the purposes for which He has created and is now governing the world. This double attitude of believers, religious and ethical, constitutes their specific quality as believers: this is what Christianity is. In other words, this double attitude constitutes the perfection of Christians, which accordingly Ritschl defines in one of his briefer statements as consisting in "humility, faith in, and submission to God's Providence, appeal and thanksgiving to God in prayer, and fidelity in the moral vocation which is useful to the community."[36] Or again:[37] "Faith in the Fatherly providence of God, which maintains a right feeling with God through humility, and with the world through patience, and which expresses and confirms itself through prayer" — to which is to be added, on the ethical side, the faithful pursuit of our vocation.

Bearing such a relation to his doctrine of justification, Ritschl's doctrine of Christian perfection obviously embodies the essence of his religious teaching, in which his whole system culminates and into which it flows out as its issue. He himself so regarded it. He speaks of it[38] as "the practically religious

---

[36] Quoted by Garvie, as cited, p. 356.

[37] P. 652.

[38] Letter to Marcus, January 16, 1874, "Leben," ii. p. 156.

proceeds (*Ertrag*) of his theology, as also the result (*Ergebnis*) of the doctrine of reconciliation." In it is depicted what in his view Christianity actually is, the tangible, palpable, concrete Christianity of reality. Whatever else may be theory, this is the fact, the whole fact, of Christianity. He did not easily win to its full apprehension. We are given to understand that it was only at the end of his long toil in the composition of his chief treatise, that he reached perfect clearness in his understanding and statement of at least the details. In January, 1874, while the great book was in process of going through the press, he was called upon to deliver a lecture for the benefit of the Göttingen Woman's Club.[39] He chose the subject of Christian Perfection and, drawing out of the fulness of his thought what was the result of long years of labor, he found that "certain ideas which form the web of the great book, became to . . . [him] for the first time, completely clear."[40] He at once set himself to adjusting the text of his book to his new lucidity of insight, so that in it as well as in the lecture of 1874 we have his complete thought on the subject. Ritschl does not mean, of course, to say that the general conception which only thus late reached its final form was new to him. He tells us on the contrary that its fundamental elements had been for years in his mind.[41] For long, however, he had employed them only in his Theological Ethics and it was apparently not until 1873 that he discovered that they had as important a place in Dogmatics as in Ethics.[42] Perhaps it may be not without its significance that the special element of his doctrine which he himself looked upon as embodying its real significance was thus carried over from his ethical to his dogmatic system. Once carried over into the dogmatic system, it was made the most of. It is not merely the issue of the system; it pervades it. We do not have to wait to see it expounded, in its substance at least, until we read the end of the dogmatic

[39] This lecture was of course, "Die christliche Vollkommenheit: ein Vortrag," 1875.
[40] "Leben," ii. p. 156.
[41] "Leben," ii. pp. 152–155.
[42] "Leben," ii. p. 148.

volume, where the Christian life comes up for formal treatment. Its fundamental elements are already — as is natural since they are merely the effects of justification — presented in the discussion of the subjective side of justification.[43] They are even more fully presented — as again is natural — as the opposite over against which the conception of sin is adjusted.[44] They are suggested again — as again is natural, since He is the pattern of His people — when the character of Christ comes up for discussion.[45] Ritschl did not make little of his doctrine of Christian perfection, or thrust it into a corner.

Ritschl is very eager, as elsewhere, so especially here, to attach to himself the teaching of the Reformers. Nowhere else does he do so with less right. He adduces especially a passage from the Augsburg Confession, which, he intimates, can with a little interchange of what he represents as equivalent statements, be made to teach about Christian perfection precisely what he teaches.[46] The Confession is very much concerned to repel the elevation of the monastic life in contrast with that of ordinary citizens into a " state of perfection." No, it says, " the good and perfect kind of life is the kind of life which has the mandate of God," not that which has been invented by man without any commandment from God. The perfection which the Gospel teaches does not consist in a pretence of poverty and humility and celibacy, but in the fear of God and faith. It is — and this is the passage adduced by

[43] Pp. 168 ff. (177).

[44] P. 335.

[45] Pp. 389, 463, 551, 574; and see especially the letter to Diestel of May 24, 1873, printed in the " Leben " (ii. pp. 149 f.).

[46] We have only, he says, (Lecture on " Christian Perfection," E. T. *Bibliotheca Sacra,* October, 1878, p. 665) to " group these thoughts a little more systematically . . . and to combine ' reverence for God ' and ' trust in him ' into the one idea of ' humility ' "; to " substitute also ' faith in God and submission to his providence ' for ' the expectation of God's help and the contempt of death and the world ' "; and " add to these supplication and thanks to God in prayer; and lastly, faithfulness to the public demands of morality." That is to say, we have only to rewrite the statement from a fundamentally different point of view and to make it witness to a completely different conception.

Ritschl — [47] " to fear God sincerely and again to conceive great faith, and to be assured for Christ's sake that we have a placated God; to ask from God, and confidently to expect, help in all our undertakings, according to our calling; meanwhile diligently to do good works outwardly and to attend to our calling." " In these things," it is added with emphasis, " there is true perfection and the true worship of God; it is not in celibacy, or mendicancy, or dirty clothing." Here, says Ritschl,[48] there is asserted just what he teaches — "not merely . . . that faith in God's fatherly providence and prayer are the expression of our consciousness of reconciliation, but also that these functions, together with humility and the moral activity proper to one's vocation, are the expressions of *Christian perfection*." It may repay us to observe just how far this amazing assertion is justified, and precisely where the two statements part company.

This at least the Confessional statement obviously has in common with Ritschl's — it is speaking, as he ostensibly is, merely of the *perfectio partium;* of what is necessary to be a true Christian; of what enters into the idea of Christianity as essential constituent elements; of *Christianismus totus* as it itself expresses it: not of the perfect embodiment of this perfect and entire Christianity in the individual. It is in these things alone, it says, that the perfection of Christianity is to be found; we are not to seek it elsewhere. But it is not said that these things are embodied in any given life in their perfect manifestation (the *perfectio graduum*). On the contrary the Reformers very explicitly assert that they are not.[49] An-

---

[47] " Confessio Augustana," xxvii. 49, 50 (Schaff's " Creeds of Christendom," iii. 1878, p. 57).

[48] P. 647.

[49] It is a characteristic phrase of Luther's: " Christianus non est in facto sed in fieri." Similarly Calvin (on Eph. i. 16 f., 1548), " The knowledge of the faithful is never so clear that their eyes are without blearing and free from all obscurity." Our warfare, says Calvin (" Institutes," I. xiv. 13) " is terminated only by death "; then only (§ 18) is our victory perfected, " our flesh having been put off, according to which we are yet subject to infirmity." So Luther (" Lectures on Romans " of 1515) declares of the truly righteous that " they sigh, until they are completely cured of concupiscence, a release which takes place at death."

other thing in which the Confessional statement resembles Ritschl's is that in enumerating the characteristics of true Christianity it includes both religious and ethical elements and places them merely side by side. Christianity embraces, it says, both a religious attitude and ethical activities — and it adds nothing as to the relation of the two to each other. For all that is said here, that relation might be one of mere adjacency. This, Ritschl would have us believe, is the characteristic attitude of the Reformers.[50] In this, however, he is wrong and he has himself incidentally adduced some of the evidence that he is wrong.[51] The whole nature of the relation of religion to morality in the Christian system — or to speak more narrowly of the relation of justification to sanctification — may have required some time to be brought out into clear light, and may even yet in wide circles be imperfectly apprehended. But the necessary connection of the two has never been doubted in evangelical circles, and Ritschl's tendency to conceive of them in separation is only one of the results of his lapse from the evangelical position. The simple collocation of the two in the passage adduced from the Augsburg Confession means nothing more than that Melanchthon at the moment was not concerned with a closer definition of their relation. In a third matter the similarity of the passage adduced from the Augsburg Confession and Ritschl's doctrine of Christian perfection is more striking and more significant. This lies in the prominence given in the definition of Christianity on the ethical side to the great Protestant conception of vocation.[52] It is

[50] Cf. the discussion, pp. 487 ff. He discusses Luther's and Melanchthon's views in pp. 167 ff., and Calvin's, pp. 184 ff. They all, he says, were clear that both justification and sanctification follow on saving faith, but not clear as to the exact relation in which they stand to one another.

[51] Cf. p. 147 where he recognizes that both Melanchthon and Calvin teach that the believer " sees in his ability to perform good works an evidence of God's special pardon " — which certainly connects sanctification with justification.

[52] This is the way Doumergue speaks of it (" La Réformation et la Révolution," 1919, p. 35): " Then Luther, and with more logic still, Calvin, proclaimed the great idea of ' vocation ' — an idea and a word which are found in all the languages of the Protestant peoples . . . and which are lacking in

the most satisfying and the most fruitful element in Ritschl's treatment of the Christian life that he organizes its ethical side around the idea of vocation, although, of course, the conception itself cannot, in the presence of his antisupernaturalistic point of view, come fully to its rights.[53] It is a matter of course that the idea appears even in the brief allusion to the moral life of Christians in the Confession. It was a living influence in all the thought of the Reformers regarding conduct.

So soon however as we rise from the ethical to the religious aspect of the Christian life all similarity of the description of it given in the Augsburg Confession to Ritschl's conception of it completely vanishes. According to the Confession the Christian life receives its form from three fundamental reactions. These are sincere fear of God, assurance of His reconciliation through Christ, and confidence that He will answer the prayers of His people. Ritschl allows no place in the Christian life for any one of the three, and thus sets himself in diametrical opposition to the Confession's conception of the substance of Christianity. As in his system God is love and nothing but love, there is no propriety in speaking in it of a " fear," of a " serious fear," of God; phraseology which conveys, no doubt, particularly the ideas of awe, reverence, veneration, but from which the sentiment of dread — we still speak of God as a " Dread Being " — cannot be eliminated.[54] It is precisely every

---

the languages of the peoples of antiquity and in the culture of the middle ages."

[53] For example, the immediately divine appointment of each man's calling; cf. Doumergue, as cited: " Vocation is the call of God addressed to each man, whoever he may be, to charge him with a special work, no matter what. And the calls, and consequently those called, are equal among themselves. The burgomaster is God's burgomaster, the physician God's physician, the merchant God's merchant, the laborer God's laborer. Every vocation, liberal as we say, or manual, the most humble, the most lowly, or the most noble, the most glorious, according to appearances, is of divine right." Among all the wise things which Ritschl says about our vocation (cf. pp. 444, 666), he cannot quite rise to this wisest of all.

[54] Edward Young, " Centaur," p. 6 (" Works," 1757, iv. p. 108): " That dread Being we dare oppose." Cf. O. W. Holmes, " Army Hymn ": " God of all nations! Sovereign Lord! In Thy dread name we draw the sword."

idea which can be expressed by " dread " that Ritschl discards
from his conception of God. Consequently in adjusting the
Confessional statement to his own view, Ritschl passes lightly
over the phrase "serious fear of God," rendering it — not of
course in essence wrongly — "reverence (*Ehrfurcht*) for
God," and combining it — quite unwarrantably — with part of
the next clause — " trust in God " — " into," he says,[55] " humility." A "placated God" (*Deus placatus*) is of course equally
abhorrent to him as a " dread God," and for the same reason.
A God who is all love needs no placating: He has no wrath
toward sinners; and the whole of "salvation" consists in the
discovery of this fact by the sinner. Christ has not appeased
God, and the essence of His work consists, indeed, in persuading
men that God needs no appeasing. Ritschl therefore simply
sums up the entire declaration, the key declaration in the Confession, in the idea of " trust," and considers it, in combination
with the "fear of God," as we have already noted, to be
absorbed in the one notion of "humility." As little as a " placated God" does Ritschl believe in a prayer-answering God.
In his watchful zeal against all "mysticism," he will not
permit God to act directly on the human heart, and his conception of God's relation to the universe is rather deistic than
theistic. There is no way then for God to answer prayer, and
prayer is reduced accordingly to the forms of adoration and
especially thanksgiving — although, it seems, that Ritschl,
quite inconsistently, does not venture to reject petition altogether.[56] Accordingly he again divides the Confessional state-

[55] " Die christliche Vollkommenheit," 1889, p. 8 (E. T. *Bibliotheca Sacra,*
October, 1878, p. 665).
[56] Pp. 641 ff.; " Instruction ": §§ 54, 55, 78 ff. Orr (" The Ritschlian
Theology," p. 177) says: "Petitionary prayer is . . . generally excluded,
and we are taught to regard prayer as chiefly thanksgiving." That expresses
the fact. Ecke (as cited, p. 303), Haug, Lamm, omit the qualifications. Von
Kügelgen (as cited, p. 127) comes to Ritschl's defence but without effect.
From all that appears, the answer to our petitions is " limited by the reservation that the petition must accord with God's providence over us " (" Instruction," § 55); which appears to mean that we receive nothing we ask for
which we would not have received had we not asked. Even Garvie (as cited,
p. 354) allows this. He condemns Ritschl's "limitation of prayer to thanks-

ment and gravely bids us "to substitute for 'the expectation of God's help and contempt of death and the world'"—the latter phrase being derived from a passage of Luther's which he couples with the Confession—"faith in and resignation to God's providence"; to which he adds as a new item "invocation of and thanks to God in prayer." "Faith in and resignation to God's providence" are, however, not in the least the same thing as "petitioning from God and certainly expecting aid." The personal relation is gone altogether, and with it the postulation of personal action *ad rem*.[57]

The difference between the Confessional and Ritschl's conception of the Christian life, thus, is polar. In the one we have a life instinct with the sense of God in His majesty, passed in His presence as the ever present and active ruler of the universe, who is nevertheless accessible to us in our weakness, to whom therefore as to a personal supporter and helper we can go in every time of need, with full expectation of aid, because, though we are sinners, He has been reconciled to us in the blood of Jesus Christ; a life therefore suffused with the

---

giving" or the "practical exclusion of petition from it," and adds that in these circumstances that "faith in God's fatherly Providence, of which Ritschl makes so much," means "little more than acceptance of whatever God may choose to send us, without any expectation whatever that our desires will in any way be taken into account." Garvie is writing from a standpoint which would subject God to man; but he recognizes here that Ritschl's doctrine of prayer renders specific answers to petitions impossible.

[57] George Macdonald, who is not often right, is right when he says ("Robert Falconer," p. 166): "She had taught him to look up—that there was a God. He would put it to the test. Not that he doubted it yet: he only doubted whether there was a hearing God. But was not that worse? It was, I think. For it is of far more consequence what kind of a God, than whether a God or not." Of course Ritschl does not represent his far-off, silent God as a direct object of human affection. What believers love is their fellow-believers, and it is only in them that they love God, or, we may add, the exalted Christ. "For," says Otto Ritschl, describing his father's ethical teaching ("Leben," i. 1892, p. 354), "in the Johannean declarations it is 'the suppressed mediating thought that God as the unseen cannot be the immediate object of human action. Accordingly neither can Christ, as the Lord who has become unseen, be the direct object of love-expression.'" So in the "Instruction," § 6, Ritschl says: "Love to God has no sphere of activity outside of love to one's brother."

hope, the confidence, the joy which comes from the conscious-ness of pardoned sin. In the other we have a life of submission — no doubt humble, patient, even grateful, or even joyful sub-mission — to the course of things, in the belief that it is a good God that has ordained this course of things and that it must therefore be working for good. The former conception is the Christian conception. The latter — must we not call it merely pagan?

It is desirable to go somewhat more into the details of Ritschl's doctrine. Ritschl represents the sole direct effect, as it is the single proper end, of justification to be what he calls "eternal life," [58] a conception which he empties of both its eschatological [59] and its ethical content, and thinks of in terms of pure "blessedness." Its quality is given to this blessed-ness by the experience of what Ritschl calls "dominion" (*Herrschaft*) over the world, or, in other words, the sense of superiority to the changes and chances of the world which is proper to a spiritual being — or just "freedom." "The posi-tive aim of forgiveness or justification or reconciliation," says Ritschl,[60] is "that freedom of believers in communion with God which consists in dominion over the world, and is to be regarded as eternal life." And von Kügelgen expounds the meaning of his master thus: [61] "Eternal life, in the sense of Christianity, is the Christian independence . . . which in har-mony with God's providence subjects all things to itself, so that they become the means to blessedness, even though, from the external point of view, they run athwart it." This "lordship over the world," which is identical with "eternal life," and "blessedness," we see, is identical also with what Ritschl calls "faith in God's providence." We are told accord-

[58] Pp. 495 ff. Maerker subjects Ritschl's doctrine of "eternal life" to a careful examination in an article in the *Neue kirchliche Zeitschrift* for 1898 (ix. pp. 117–138), entitled "Lehrt Albrecht Ritschl ein ewiges Leben?"

[59] Von Kügelgen (as cited, p. 94) points out that Ritschl identified "eternal life" not with an extramundane consummation (*Vollendung*) but with intramundane Christian perfection (*Vollkommenheit*).

[60] P. 556. Cf. the phrases on p. 518: "reconciliation with God, or libera-tion from the world, or eternal life." These phrases are synonymous.

[61] As cited, p. 131.

ingly [62] that " the aim of reconciliation with God in the Christian sense " is " lordship over the world," and then again [63] that " in general, the form in which religious lordship over the world is exercised is faith in God's providence." The aim of reconciliation " which does not differ in substance from justification or regeneration " is then, in this intensely this-world religion, " faith in God's providence." Thus, " faith in God's providence " becomes the substance of the Christian life, the thing that makes it a really Christian life. The other elements entering into Ritschl's conception of the Christian life which are subsequently mentioned — humility, patience, thankfulness — are merely qualifications of mode, not additional constituents, of the Christian life, as thus defined. Now, we are told [64] that this " faith in Divine providence " is " normally a tone of feeling." That is to say reconciliation, justification, regeneration, have as their aim, and issue into, a purely subjective change, that and that only. We need not, because of them, find ourselves in any objectively different situation from that occupied before; we in point of fact, do not. There has come about a change only in our " tone of feeling."

Let us endeavor to make clear to ourselves precisely what this means. When it is said that Ritschl uses the phrase " eternal life " not in an eschatological sense, but of a " tone of feeling" acquired in this life, it is of course not meant merely that he teaches that the Christian does not wait until death to receive the blessings obtained through Christ, but enters into them at once on believing. What is meant is that Ritschl conceives " eternal life " after a fashion which adjusts it entirely to this life; it is in its essence in his view an attitude towards the actual course of this world. If there is anything beyond, it does not appear. " Salvation " with him, if we can speak of " salvation " with reference to his theories, is an entirely " this-world salvation." " Saving faith " is a phrase as little consonant with Ritschl's system as " salvation," and the relation of faith to justification gives him a great deal of trouble. He wishes to speak in the terms of Reformation

[62] P. 609.   [63] P. 617.   [64] P. 622.

doctrine, but he does not find it easy to determine whether faith should be represented as antecedent to justification — its condition, he would say — or as consequent on it; the best he can do is to call it its " concomitant." In point of fact, faith in his system is the substance of justification. All that justification is, is the passage from distrust to trust: this is not the way justification is obtained — this is itself justification. Justification thus is identified with faith; and the faith with which it is identified is not faith in Christ our Redeemer, nor even faith in a redeeming God, but just faith in the divine providence. The sinner having been persuaded that he can safely draw near to God despite his guilt, lays aside his distrust and draws near to God in trust. He is sure now that God, admitting him despite his guilt into fellowship with Him, will deal well with him. That is to say, he commits himself to God as Father and trusts to His fatherly love that all things will work for good to him. This is nothing more than faith in God's providence. And this faith in God's providence is declared to be itself justification, reconciliation, adoption, eternal life, all of which are synonyms.

This being so, it is astonishing to learn, as we quickly learn, that by the providence of God Ritschl has not at all in mind what that phrase would naturally suggest to the average Christian, the ever present watchful care of God; but just the established course of things, conceived of as the general ordinance of God. The world is governed by law; and God is not to be expected to interfere in any way with the working of that law, which He himself has made the governing power of the world. To trust in the providence of God, as Leonhard Stählin points out,[65] does not mean then confidence that God will " really intervene in the course of nature at individual junctures for the benefit of believers," but confidence that the actually existent order of things is not accidental, but has been ordained by God, who is our Father; and acquiescence in it as such. The established course of events is not modified by special divine action to adjust it to our needs, but we adjust

[65] As cited, pp. 228 ff.; cf. Orr, " The Ritschlian Theology," pp. 176 f.

ourselves to it, because, knowing it to be ordained of God, we know its ordering is for the best. " It is our duty . . . to see in the existing order of things the result and sway of divine providence," and to accept it in humble and patient thankfulness. There is no providence which " extends " one " whit further than the order of things as it actually exists." " Faith in the fatherly providence of God," therefore "resolves itself, on this view of the matter, into an assured confidence that reason is immanent in the actually existent order of things, and that accordingly nature is a means subordinate to spirit." No change takes place in the course of events in our behalf; the only change that takes place takes place in us. When we lay aside our distrust of God and trust in His providence, we merely assume a different attitude towards the course of events. The same things happen to us which would have happened had we not made this change of attitude towards God. But what we looked upon as against us, we now look upon as for us: what we looked upon at best as but the grinding out of blind law, at worst as the caprice of a malevolent deity, we now look upon as the expression of the will of a Father. After all is said, however, what is meant when Ritschl speaks of trusting in divine providence is nothing more than that it is the mark of the Christian that he trusts in law: he acquires a new attitude toward the actual course of things and humbly, patiently, and thankfully accepts his lot in life.

Garvie, it is true, registers a somewhat sharp dissent. " When Ritschl speaks of God's Providence," he declares,[66] " he means what he says. He does not believe in an inevitable course of nature, independent of a Personal Will, which does not do its worst with us, because we make the best we can of it. He does not give a stern fact, submission to fate, a sweet name, faith in God's Providence, by a 'poetic license,'" — and so on. This passionate language, however, is quite futile, and only betrays the confusion in its author's mind. Of course Ritschl is not supposed to be teaching a doctrine of "fate." He looks upon the course of things as having been determined

[66] As cited, pp. 350 f. Cf. the words cited in note 56.

by a Personal Will, and represents therefore this course of things as expressing a personal choice, the choice of a person whom he declares to be love and nothing but love. But he does not allow that this course of things is ever modified (no matter when the modification has been determined upon) for the individual's benefit, according to his emerging needs. It has been once for all established for the benefit of the Kingdom of God and we, for our part, are to look on it as our Father's will and understand that it is working as a whole for our good. Our trust in divine providence does not mean with Ritschl then, that we are sure that God adjusts the course of events to meet our varying individual needs. But it does mean the assurance that our loving Father has ordered the established course of things for the best, and it does mean that we, now become one with Him, have learned that that is true, and therefore accept every event as it befalls us as from His hands. This amounts to saying, when taken at its height, that we see the hand of God in all that comes to pass, the hand of our Father in everything that befalls us — whether in itself good or grievous: that in a word we look through nature in all its happenings to nature's God, even though we may see Him only far off. When taken thus at its height, faith in divine providence is no small religious achievement. It is the fundamental religious attitude towards the world: and it must enter into every worthy conception of the Christian life. It is nevertheless, as here expressed, being deistic in its tendency, a fatally inadequate conception of the nature of divine providence, and it certainly, however taken, can never be accepted as Ritschl represents it as a complete account of the essence of Christianity. "Faith in the fatherly providence of God," says Ritschl,[67] "which maintains a right feeling with God through humility, and with the world through patience, and which expresses and confirms itself through prayer, is, in general, the content of the religious

[67] P. 652. On January 1, 1874, Diestel, endeavoring to make a forecast from as yet incomplete materials of what would be the upshot of Ritschl's great work, suggests that it will be that the essence of Christianity consists in faith in God's providence. Ritschl agrees. See "Leben," ii. p. 154.

life which grows out of reconciliation with God, through Christ." That is to reduce Christianity to a merely natural religion.

From the point of view here brought to expression, Ritschl is obviously right in speaking of Christianity as consisting in a " tone of feeling." And it is natural that we should wish to ascertain somewhat closely the particular feeling which it is. We think first of all of the feeling of submission, and there does not lack phraseology in Ritschl's discussions which justifies this. But it quickly becomes evident that he does not think of the Christian's attitude towards the course of things, conceived of as the providential appointment of God, as one of bare, negative submission. It is an attitude of positive acquiescence, acceptance, adoption: the Christian makes God's appointment his own. No doubt his attitude toward the course of events conceived as God's appointment is characterized by humility with reference to God and patience with reference to the course of events itself, but it is characterized also by thankfulness. And Ritschl pours into the notion not only satisfaction, but joy. The tone of feeling which he makes Christianity consist in is distinctly an optimistic one. In the discussion which he devotes to this matter,[68] indeed, he goes far toward making it indistinguishable from the instinctive optimism of exuberant vitality, the care-free temper of the man of action prosecuting his work in the world. We are told, for example, that we have this faith in divine providence not on empirical grounds — observation does not produce it and would not confirm it[69] — but as a conviction drawn by each man from the complex of his own experiences. And yet not as a reasoned conclusion based on an analysis of our experiences; but as an instinctive conviction. It has no necessary conceptional content; it is normally a " tone of feeling " which is the expression of our " spiritual energy."[70] It may, no doubt, develop into

[68] Pp. 618 ff.

[69] P. 618: " For observation of the fortunes of others would afford just as much, or even more, ground for shaking as for supporting our own conviction."

[70] Pp. 622, 623.

clear ideas and judgments; but only if the conflicts so far inhibit action as to compel mental analysis of our struggling
spiritual energy. It is, normally, just our feeling of well-being
and of courage in the face of our circumstances. It may easily,
therefore, be confused with the mere natural courage of man
in facing the evils of life.[71] It is specifically different from this,
however, because it is not merely courage in facing the evils
of life but acceptance or rather adoption of the whole course
of things, including the evils, into our own scheme of life, because it is God's will. That is to say, it is not merely self-
assertion, but confidence in providence. And that is an attitude, says Ritschl, which is peculiarly Christian. It is an
attitude not to be found in any who have not derived it from
Christ. It was precisely this, in fact — identical as it is with
the assertion that God is love — in which Christ's discovery
consisted.[72] Thus Ritschl, having abased Christianity to a
merely natural religion, by reducing it in its essence to " trust
in the divine providence," seeks to restore it again to its uniqueness as the only " revealed " religion by declaring " trust in
the divine providence " to be solely the product of the " revelation " in Christ. This does not in any way affect the poverty
of his conception of Christianity. It merely recalls us sharply
to the realization of the extreme destitution of the religions
men have made for themselves.[73]

It is, now, this general point of view or " tone of feeling "
(*Gesinnung*) which constitutes, on the religious side, what
Ritschl calls Christian Perfection. He who is of this way of

[71] It is rather a pungent question which J. L. Schultze raises (*Neue
kirchliche Zeitschrift,* ix. 1898, pp. 238 f.) when he asks: Do all Christians
actually show the characteristics here depicted? How many possess the
energy of will here made characteristic of all? Paul himself seemed able to
live on such a plane only through Divine help. " If, however, this direct converse with God is replaced, as with Ritschl, by a mere conviction mediated
by the Christian community — if thus then the possibility of continual renewal from the source is cut off — why then, this feeling of perfection becomes nothing but an artificial fiction. Energetic characters may persuade
themselves that they possess it " — but the generality?

[72] Pp. 181, 625.

[73] Von Kügelgen, as cited, pp. 121 ff., defends Ritschl's attitude.

thinking and feeling is a Christian, and is all that he need be, from the religious point of view, in order to be all that a Christian is. But in accordance with Ritschl's dualistic conception of Christianity, there is an ethical side to Christianity also. And the ethical is so related to the religious element in Christianity that the ethical task cannot be undertaken or accomplished save under the impulse derived from the religious attitude. It constitutes, nevertheless, as the end to which the religious attitude is the means, the real substance of the Christian life, which is as much as to say the precise thing in which Christian perfection consists. How the two elements are related in the whole made up of their union, is made quite clear in an excellent summary statement of Johannes Wendland's, in the opening page of his description of Ritschl's type of piety. "With him," says he,[74] "all religion originates in man's estimate of himself as something more than a fragment of dead nature. Christianity is to him the perfected religion because man is qualified by it to become a spiritual personality, a whole in his kind. It delivers man from violent oscillations of mood between pleasure and displeasure. In the certainty that all things work for good to those who take them from the hand of God, the Christian knows how to prevail over even the evils of life in trust in God, humility, and patience. Conscientious work in his calling, whether it be a spiritual one, or one of manual labor, of low esteem among men, is for man at once the best remedy against distress, and also the way to secure that perfection which is obtainable for the Christian. Thus the personal life of the individual takes its place in the general life-purpose of the whole, which consists in erecting the Kingdom of God in the world. Man coöperates in building up God's Kingdom in every true vocational work in his appointed place. For the Kingdom of God is advanced not only by domestic and foreign missions, but marriage, family, civil society, national state are fellowships in which it is to be realized. It is through righteous conduct and neighborly love that the Kingdom of God is established." Let us see now, in more detail, how

[74] As cited, p. 8.

Ritschl presents Christianity on its ethical side and how he relates the idea of Christian perfection to it.

The ethical task of the Christian, he teaches, is determined fundamentally by his adoption of God's self-end as his own. God's self-end is the Kingdom of God.[75] This conception is not to be confounded with that of the Church. The Church is the people of God organized for the particular purpose of worship.[76] The Kingdom of God is the people of God conceived in the totality of their ethical activities, under the impulse of love.[77] The breadth of the conception enables Ritschl to subsume under it every activity of man viewed in its ethical aspect. He utilizes here, as has already been intimated, however, the Reformation conception of vocation, and thus is able to present the primary ethical task of the Christian under the rubric of faithfulness in his vocation.[78] He that is faithful in his vocation has performed his whole ethical duty in the Kingdom of God, and, being thus a whole in himself, is perfect. No doubt we may think of many other moral acts which, in the abstract, we might lay upon him as duties. But, lying outside the circle of duties belonging to him in the faithful discharge of his vocation, they do not enter into the whole which it behooves him to be in his own kind; and his failure to perform them therefore cannot be imputed to him as fault. No man

[75] See especially on Ritschl's conception of the Kingdom of God the very clear and satisfactory summary statement of Orr, " The Ritschlian Theology," pp. 119 ff.

[76] P. 284: " In order to preserve the true articulation of the Christian view of the world, it is necessary clearly to distinguish between viewing the followers of Christ, first, under the conception of the Kingdom of God, and secondly, under the conception of the *worshipping community,* or the Church. This distinction depends on the difference which exists between moral and devotional action. . . ."

[77] Pp. 610 ff. Cf. p. 285: " The same believers in Christ constitute the Kingdom of God in so far as, forgetting distinctions of sex, rank, or nationality, they act reciprocally from love, and thus call into existence that fellowship of moral disposition and moral blessings which extends, through all possible gradations, to the limits of the human race."

[78] Cf. p. 163: " . . . the Reformation principle that justification becomes matter of experience through the discharge of moral tasks, while these are to be discharged in the labors of one's vocation."

can be more than one kind of a man; or if by reason of strength he may embrace in his task more than one vocation, or if, as needs must be, a penumbra of secondary duties may gather around the governing vocation which is his special task, nevertheless the center about which the whole circle of his duties revolves remains his vocation, and it is faithfulness to this vocation and to whatever is inseparably connected with it that determines his ethical character.

We perceive that the chief concern which Ritschl shows in developing his doctrine of vocation is to utilize it so to limit the range of duty as to make it possible for the Christian man to be ethically as well as religiously perfect. The motive on which he acts here is derived from the consideration which he advances with confidence to the effect that hope of attainment supplies the only adequate spur to endeavor. " If in any activity," says he,[79] " we know ourselves beforehand unconditionally condemned to imperfection, then impulse to it is paralysed. The possibility of perfection must be held in prospect if we are to use diligence in any department of activity." On this ground, sufficiently dubious in itself — though not on this ground alone — he repels the evangelical doctrine that even in the state of grace we must always be mindful of the imperfection of our moral conduct, so that we may never be tempted to depend for our salvation on our own works, which never meet the demands of the law, but only on Christ received by faith alone. It is a contradiction, he says,[80] in any case, to tell us in one breath that we are to look away from our works to Christ because they are too imperfect to put any dependence on, and in the next that despite this their imperfection we are to depend on them as proof that we are under the action of grace. The ultimate conclusion to which he would drive us is that the Christian man's works are not subject to the judgment of the law. Before following him to this conclusion, however, we wish to point out briefly the fallacy of the reasoning from which it is drawn and the consequences of the rejection which it involves of the evangelical doctrine of the Christian's

[79] P. 662.   [80] P. 661.

unbroken sense of imperfection. The justification of this digression lies in the importance of the matter for the understanding of Ritschl's point of view. There is involved in it in one way or another, indeed, a very large part of his system; and, we may add, also the fundamental error of every form of Perfectionism.

Robert Mackintosh [81] observes that one of the leading motives of Ritschl in his dogmatic volume is his "desire to find a remedy for the Protestant perplexity regarding the assurance of salvation." And then he posits the dilemma which we have just cited from Ritschl, in somewhat different words. " Is it logical," he asks, " to bid us discover defects in all our works in order that we may rest upon God's grace, and yet to insist that we must have good works to submit lest we be moral impostors? " Why "perplexity" should be caused by such a question is inexplicable. The answer is simple. Certainly it is logical — provided salvation be a process. To find salvation in progress is as sound evidence of salvation as to find it completed — provided salvation be a supernatural work. The writers of the New Testament and the Reformers and their evangelical successors, agree in these two things — that salvation is a process and that it is a divine work. They recommend us therefore to recognize it as always here incomplete; to discover imperfection in all our works. And they recommend us equally to perceive in its discovery in us, in any stage of incompleteness whatever, the incontrovertible evidence that we are in God's hands. There can be no assurance derived from any other source than evidence that we are in God's hands; and that assurance is as firm and as vivid when the evidence is derived from the discovery that God is working, as it could be were it derived from the discovery that He had already worked, our salvation.

We are not dealing here, however, with merely an *apex logicus*. We are dealing with the very essence of Protestantism. The progressive character of salvation lies at the very heart of Protestantism's heart, because (among other things) the

[81] " Albrecht Ritschl and his School," 1915, p. 132.

Protestant doctrine of justification and its effects takes to a considerable extent its form from it. A large part of the religious value of the Protestant doctrine of justification, in its distinction from sanctification, is lost, if sanctification be not a process, the completion of which occupies the whole of life; if, that is, the injunction, "Work out your own salvation," does not apply to the whole of the Christian's walk on earth, but ought to be addressed to men only at some particular stage of their Christian experience — say, only at its beginning. For a large part of the religious value of this distinction turns on this — that the Christian's hope of salvation (his assurance) does not depend on the stage of sanctification to which he has already attained. Sanctification being a process, and a process which reaches its completion only when this life is over, the discovery of sin remaining in him at any point of his earthly life is no proof that the Christian may not nevertheless be in Christ. In proportion as it is made the Christian's duty not so much to work out his salvation continuously but to enjoy it at once in its completeness, the believer, conscious of sin, loses his confidence that he is a believer at all. If this attainment of complete salvation is made coincident with justification, all sense of continued sinfulness is a clear disproof of present salvation. The matter is only mitigated, not changed, by separating the attainment of complete sanctification in time from justification. Salvation involving taking this second step, the continued sense of sinfulness becomes evidence of failure of such portentousness as to shatter our peace and assurance. If it belongs to the Christian to be without sin, and to be without sense of sin — in this sense of the statement — then the fact of experience that we are not without sin and not without the sense of sin is pretty clear proof that we are not Christians. It is not a matter of little importance, then, that we should settle it with ourselves whether the characteristic of the Christian walk in the world is constant advance towards sinlessness, or complete present enjoyment of sinlessness. If the latter, then, gloss it as we will, no one is entitled to think of himself as a Christian, no one is justified in regarding himself as saved, unless he is in the possession of complete sinlessness. In that case the whole religious gain of the Reformation doctrine of justification in distinction from sanctification is lost, and we are thrown back again into the despairing task of determining our religious state and our future hope on the ground of our own merits.

It is no accident, therefore, that the Reformers presented the Christian life as a life of continuous dissatisfaction with self and of continuous looking afresh to Christ as the ground of all our hope. The effort of Ritschl to present the Christian life rather as a life of complete satisfaction with self tends not only altogether to undermine the entire evangelical system, but to strike a direct blow at that peace and joy of the Christian which it is his professed object to secure. For the Christian's peace and joy are not and cannot be grounded in himself, but in Christ alone. He rejoices in the sufficiency of Christ's saving work for him; his exultation is in a salvation made his despite his unworthiness of it. This joy obtains its peculiarity precisely from the coëxistence of dissatisfaction with self and satisfaction with Christ. The dissatisfaction with self does not mar it; it enhances it rather — because the more dissatisfaction we feel with ourselves the more the greatness of Christ's salvation is manifest to us, and the more our delight in it waxes. Transfer the ground of our satisfaction from Christ to ourselves, and all satisfaction becomes at once impossible — except for the shallow souls who can find satisfaction in their own hearts and in the works which proceed from them. We have returned to medieval work-salvation: the very essence of Luther's revolt turned on his inability to find satisfaction in self. We are not preaching, and Luther did not preach, a lugubrious Christianity, which is always and only preoccupied with shortcomings and failures. Of course the Christian delights in his salvation. Of course he has no impulse to depreciate what he has already received. Of course his joy is unbounded, and his peace supreme. But this only because — and only on the condition that he understands that — he has not yet "attained"; that what he has received is but the earnest of what is to come; that what he has already done or is now doing is not the ground, and what he already is is not the extent, of his hope. It belongs to the very essence of Christianity that we have not "attained"; and that is the same as saying that sanctification is in progress and there is more to come. The Christian who has stopped growing is dead; or to put it better, the Christian does not stop growing because he is not dead. Luther rightly says the Christian is not made but is in the making.

Precisely what Ritschl emphasizes, nevertheless, is that the satisfaction of the Christian has its ground in himself.[82] We gather, however, that it does not take much to satisfy a Christian: a very imperfect perfection is perfection enough to make him perfect. We have observed how Ritschl sets his main contention in direct contradiction to the evangelical doctrine of the continuous dissatisfaction of the Christian with his attainments during this life. He does not admit, however, that he is also in conflict with Scripture. In this matter at least, he contends, the Reformers were at odds with the Scriptures. The exegetical justification of this contention he seeks to supply in a passage in the closing pages of the second volume of his main work which has become famous and which has exerted a greater influence than any other portion of his discussion of the perfection of the Christian.[83] In this passage Ritschl declares that the relation in which the Reformers place the believer's supposed consciousness of continued imperfection to justification was wholly unknown to Paul. Paul, of course, knew that Christians sinned; his epistles are full of the proofs of it. But he did not at all bring these sins into relation with justification. Moreover he had a very healthful sense of his own faithfulness in his vocational activity, and asserts it against all gainsayers. Nor was his self-satisfaction official alone. We cannot do otherwise than infer, Ritschl sums

[82] Cf. p. 651: "The destination of men for perfection in Christianity may likewise be seen in the exhortation to rejoice amid all the changes of life which, in the New Testament, accompanies instruction in the Christian faith (ii. pp. 344, 350). For joy is the sense of perfection."

[83] "Rechtfertigung und Versöhnung," ed. 3, ii. 1889, § 39, pp. 365 ff.

up,[84] that " alongside of the conviction of justification through faith, a consciousness of personal moral perfection, especially of perfect faithfulness in our vocation, is possible, which is disturbed by no twinges of conscience. . . ." Paul accordingly arrogates to himself in this matter nothing which he does not accord to others. He distinctly presupposes that Christians as such possess not indeed a multiplicity of good works but a connected life-work which may properly be called good. Only John [85] among the New Testament writers strikes a different note; and the note he strikes is not fundamentally different. He teaches, it is true, that believers continue to sin and need to have continued recourse to the Forgiver of sins (I John i. 8, 9). But it does not follow that even in his teaching the self-consciousness of the Christian is to receive from this its dominant tone. Rather in this teaching also this is determined by the possibility of moral perfection. " From the pessimism with which Luther emphasized the constant imperfection and worthlessness of the moral activity of Christians, John is far removed. The sinful was to him still always only the exception in the Christian life, not the rule and an inevitable destiny." [86] As a conspectus of New Testament teaching, this representation is, of course, absurd. Nevertheless, Paul Wernle (after certain forerunners) took it up and elaborated it in his maiden book,[87] thereby opening a controversy which threshed out such questions as whether we may speak of " Paul the ' miserable sinner,' " and whether Paul knew anything of " the daily forgiveness of sins." That, however, is another story.[88]

We may suppose that Ritschl could not have been led to such a representation of New Testament teaching save as a

---

[84] *Op. cit.*, p. 370.

[85] This, of course, can be said even by Ritschl only after he has explained away such passages as Rom. vii. 14–25, Gal. v. 17, not to speak of multitudes of others which he does not notice.

[86] *Op. cit.*, p. 378.

[87] " Der Christ und die Sünde bei Paulus," 1897.

[88] Wernle, growing older and somewhat wiser, found it necessary to correct the extremities of his teaching: see the *Theologische Literaturzeitung*, xxxiv. 1909, coll. 586 ff.

result of his low view of sin as in essence just ignorance. This made it possible for him to imagine that Paul, for example, never reflected on the relation of the abounding sin which he saw in the Christian communities to the justification of these sinners, and cherished in himself a consciousness of moral perfection in conjunction with the very poignant sense of personal unworthiness to which he gives expression. Some such representation was, however, forced on him by the most fundamental elements of his system of thought, if he was to preserve for his teaching any semblance of connection with the New Testament. There is his contention, for instance, that it is impossible for God " to love " and " to hate " the same person at the same time, which lies at the very root of his whole system. He had made use of it in framing and developing his remarkable doctrine of the " wrath of God." Because God loves sinners and out of that love has chosen sinners to become sharers in His Kingdom and objects of His " redemption," it is impossible, he says,[89] to speak of the " wrath " of God with reference to sinners as such. God's wrath is turned against those sinners alone who show themselves irreconcilably enemies of His Kingdom and despisers of His love, that is to say, the finally impenitent — if there be any finally impenitent. It does not burn against sinners as such, since all are sinners, and in that case none could be the objects of His " redemptive " love; it is a purely eschatological notion. Holding firmly to this irreducible either-or — that there can be no love of God present where His wrath is in any measure active, and no wrath of God where His love is in any measure active — Ritschl could not allow that the reconciled sinner could justly suffer under a continuous sense of guilt. No clouds could be admitted to obscure the Father's countenance. The reconciled believer must not only bask in an unbroken but in an unsullied sense of the divine love. The Reformation doctrine that the Christian life is a continuous repentance, that the believer is conscious of continual shortcomings which, he knows, deserve the wrath of God, and is continually receiving unmerited forgive-

[89] Pp. 323.

ness, was not merely repugnant, but impossible to him. He
was compelled to develop a conception of the Christian life
which inferred perfection. There could be no room in it, we
do not say merely for distrust, fear, despondency, but for contrition, repentance, self-abasement. The very essence of the
Christian life is for him necessarily freedom from these things.
Precisely what "reconciliation" is to him is the discovery that
God takes no account of sin in us. Not that we are freed from
sin. But that it makes no difference whether we sin or not:
God closes His eyes to our sin. This is of course an antinomian
attitude. All perfectionist doctrines run into antinomianism.
It is intrinsic in Ritschl's low view of sin. What is at the moment important for us to note is that it enables us to understand that Ritschl is not willing to have the perfection which
he proclaims for Christians measured by the standard of the
moral law. Whatever the Christian may actually do, he is no
"sinner," and his conscience must not accuse him.

In order to sustain himself in this lamentable position
Ritschl develops an unhappy argument designed to show that
the moral law is in any event incapable of fulfilment. Not
incapable of fulfilment by sinners only, but intrinsically and
of its very nature incapable of fulfilment.[90] This because it is
in effect infinite in its demands: it claims the will simultaneously for illimitable requirements spread out through space,
and the series of claims made by each of these requirements
extends illimitably through time. The finite being is capable,
however, of only one act at a time. And since it is impossible
for him to do at once everything that falls under the category
of the good, he is under no obligation to do it. What he is required to do, in point of fact, is not to fulfil the moral law in
its abstract completeness, but to make of his life a moral

[90] P. 662: "Now the notion of good works, which find their standard
in the statutory law, is the expression of a task which not only is impracticable
on the presupposition of the continuance of sinfulness, but in and for itself
cannot be thought in connection with the characteristic of perfection."
"Therefore it is not merely sin, as evil will or as indifference, which thwarts
the quantitatively perfect fulfilment of the moral law, but this is in itself
impossible in comparison with the statutory form of the law."

whole, rounding it out in dutiful conduct in accordance with its intrinsic requirements as such a whole. It is the conception of vocation to which Ritschl appeals here to supply the limitation of duty by which it may be rendered capable of performance. "Everyone," says he,[91] "is moral in his behavior when he fulfils the universal law in his special vocation or in that combination of vocations which he is able to unite in his conduct of life." Thus, we are told, "there is excluded every moral necessity to good actions on ends which do not fit in with the individual's vocation," and the "apparent obligation is invalidated that we have to act morally at every moment of time in all possible directions."[92] The situation, however, he perceives not to be relieved in this manner. The spatial infinity is cleared away, indeed, but the temporal remains. We are moving now in one, narrow path, but there is no end to it. "Even when the fulfilment of the moral law is confined to one's own calling and what is analogous thereto, the series of good actions which are incumbent is still illimitable in time."[93] Relief can be found only in discarding all responsibility whatever to "statutory law"; that is, to externally imposed law. We "find the proximate norm which specifies for every one the morally necessary conduct in our moral vocation" itself, and thus vindicate the "autonomy of moral conduct."[94] We are under no law but such as is evolved out of our moral disposition in the course of our activities themselves: and we evolve this law, of course, only as it is needed and fulfil it as it is made. Thus, executing the particular judgments of duty as we form them, we preserve steadily, it seems, our perfection. "Under these circumstances," says Ritschl,[95] "and in this form the individual produces the moral law out of his freedom, or " — that is, in other words — "lives in the law of freedom." We are therefore under no other law but "the law of freedom," and "the universal statutory law " has no authority over us. Emancipated from all externally imposed law, we are a law to ourselves, and we recognize no other law as having dominion over us.

[91] P. 666.   [92] P. 666.   [93] P. 666.   [94] P. 666.   [95] P. 667.

It can occasion no surprise, of course, that Ritschl, with his Kantian inheritance, should proclaim this doctrine of "autonomous morality." Our interest is only in the particular form he gives it, and the use to which he puts it in expounding his views of Christian perfection. The assertion of the doctrine itself pervades the discussions of the dogmatic volume of his chief work.[96] We turn for example to its very closing sentences; [97] there all its chief elements are given crisp expression, precisely as we have drawn them out above from an earlier page. Christian perfection, he says, consists (together with the "religious functions") just in "freedom of action." In this freedom of action, the Christian, seeking the final end of the Kingdom of God, imposes on himself — "gives himself" — a "law." He gives himself this law "by the production (*Erzeugung*) of principles and judgments of duty." Thus the law which he follows, and by following which he manifests himself as what he ought to be, is his own product, developed, as means to its accomplishment, out of the aim (*Endzweck*) which he is pursuing. Not only is no "statutory law" (*statutarisches Gesetz*) imposed on him from without, but no immanent law is written on his heart by the finger of God.[98] He evolves his

[96] See especially the discussion on p. 526 where we are told that "the moral law is complete only in the reticulation of those judgments of duty which determine the necessary form of good action in each particular case," and further that "the principle of autonomy not only holds good within the circle of general moral law as such, but we act autonomously in each particular province of life. . . ." Cf. p. 650: "The saints who strive to act in the fear of God and to follow God's ways, come to know the duties incumbent on them through their disposition and not through a statutory law." We must not be misled by the superficial resemblance of language like this to the Christian doctrines of the leading of the Spirit and the writing by Him of the law of God on the heart. Ritschl knows no Holy Spirit, no immediate work of God on the heart, and indeed, no heart for God to work on. What Ritschl is doing is only adapting to his own purposes Kant's doctrine of autonomous morality, which was Kant's protest against the view of vulgar Rationalism that sin arises only from the deliberate transgression of known external law.

[97] P. 670.

[98] Ritschl strangely thinks these two things inconsistent, and blames the Second Helvetic Confession for bringing them together (p. 523). At bottom Ritschl confuses knowledge and power. He speaks as if action cannot

own rules of life — his governing principles and his determinations of duty — out of himself, solely under the guidance of the end he is seeking. In the absolute freedom of his will he chooses his own end; and that end determines his rules of living for him. These are the elements of Ritschl's ethics. God is concerned in them only so far as that He provides, through the "revelation" made by Christ, the end to which, freely adopted by them, the efforts of Christian men are freely directed — His own self-end, the "Kingdom of God." The "moral law" — we are availing ourselves here of Fr. Luther's exposition [99] — "is deduced by the men who appropriate this end out of themselves; it is a subjective product of the human moral will. It is the law which man in moral freedom gives himself so soon as he has established the advancement of the 'Kingdom of God' for himself as the self-end of his life-practice. He takes this advancement of the Kingdom of God as self-end to himself, however, so far as he has become conscious that thus his personal self-end — which he has already set before himself — is furthered. This self-end is the attainment of that moral, spiritual freedom which maintains itself triumphantly over against all hindrances from the world of nature. In 'carrying through' this 'his self-end over against the world' consists 'the blessedness of the person.' The Christian is therefore with reference to the establishment of the moral law dependent on God only in the one respect that the end of the 'Kingdom of God,' morally determining his life, is re-

---

be voluntary if directed by law — which would be as much as to say that voluntary action is necessarily lawless. That, no doubt, is much his notion of "freedom." The writing of the law on the heart does not abolish the law which is thus written on the heart. No doubt the writing of the law on the heart may be construed to mean the implantation of an independent instinct for what is contained in the law. Something like that is, apart from its "mysticism," what Ritschl supposes, not indeed to have been done to Christians, but fairly to represent what the native powers of Christians, as moral men, are capable of. The Christian will, says he (p. 526), "is guided by a free knowledge of the moral law, through which it perpetually produces that law."

[99] *Neue kirchliche Zeitschrift,* ii. 1891, p. 485; cf. also his exposition in his book, "Die Theologie Ritschl's," 1887, pp. 40 f.

vealed to him by God through Christ. Otherwise he is morally
' autonomous.' "

With this doctrine of autonomous morality Ritschl certainly seems to have found a basis on which he can pronounce
Christian men really perfect. If we create our own moral law
and create it in accordance both with our special ends in our
particular vocations, and with our particular situation at each
moment,[100] there seems no reason why, measured by that
standard, we should not be and remain "perfect." Ritschl
felicitates himself especially that with this understanding of
the matter, the moral life of the individual becomes " a whole."
If duty is limited by the demands of our vocation (together
with whatever else is associated with it), and determined by
ourselves under our conceptions of those demands, no doubt a
certain unity is acquired by our lives which gives them the
aspect of "wholes in their kinds." It is not so easy to assure
ourselves that the kinds of which they are wholes are good
kinds. Ritschl apparently would say that this is secured by
the fact that all the vocations pursued by Christian men are
pursued in subordination to the one great end of the Kingdom
of God, God's self-end communicated to us by Christ and
made ours by the new attitude which we have taken to God
in our justification. Meanwhile he exhibits a certain uneasiness here. The limitation of duty to the requirements of our
vocations no doubt reduces the multiplicity of good works in
which conduct manifests itself to an inwardly limited unity;
that is, to a " whole." " But," he adds,[101] " the whole that is so
conceived is not yet perceived to be a thing which is also externally limited," and here he reverts to a figure of speech
before employed by him: " Even if the spatial unlimitedness
of good works as measured by the universal statutory law be
set aside, yet the temporal series of actions in our moral vocation appears to be endless." Men's consciences, it seems, are
not easy in the facile solution of the question of their moral
obligation which Ritschl offers them: they are not so sure that
they have no duties which do not lie in the direct line of the

[100] P. 526.   [101] P. 667.

prosecution of their callings, and none in this line which they have not yet recognized.

There seems no particular reason why Ritschl should permit himself to be disturbed by such pricks of conscience. To conscience, which to him is only "something picked up in the course of living," [102] surely no normative authority can be ascribed. He feels bound, however, to seek to quiet its qualms. He admits that his perfect men are disturbed by a sense of shortcoming and guilt. He suggests however that this may be only the result of an undesirable "self-torturing self-scrutiny," which threatens, he complains, to "throw back the discussion on to the lines of the idea of good works from which we are trying to escape " — that is, the idea that we are really under moral obligation to do everything that is good. Conscience, the implication appears to be, ought to be kept under better control. And he has suggestions to offer in the way at least of soothing us under its assaults. We shall, no doubt, omit many actions even in the discharge of our calling which we might have performed, and we may impute their omission to ourselves as guilt and thus bring ourselves under an impression of perpetual imperfection. But consider! May we not find later that "the relaxation which we have allowed ourselves to take has served to increase our activity in our calling " ? This seems to mean that we ought to have no scruples in omitting duties if it furthers us in our calling; a sentinel, for example, we suppose, is right to sleep on his post if it refreshes him for fighting on the morrow! Moreover — can we say that all omission of useful actions that are possible is wrong? Must we not confine the condemning judgment to the omission of actions which are morally necessary? Above all, Ritschl continues in an exposition which has fallen into the commendation of a purely negative morality — must we not remember that in order to be the "whole" which constitutes Christian perfection we need not be a very big "whole" ? It is not necessary in order

[102] " Etwas im Gemeinschaftsleben Erworbenes " (" Ueber das Gewissen," 1876, p. 20). On Ritschl's doctrine of conscience see the illuminating comment of Pfleiderer, " Die Ritschl'sche Theologie," 1891, pp. 77 ff.

to be "perfect" that we shall be the biggest "whole" we can
be. We may well content ourselves with being a moderate-
sized "whole." If we are a perfect little "whole" we need not
bother over the fact that we might have been a bigger whole
had we striven harder. The point is not the quantity but the
quality. "True, a whole, too, must be a *quantum.* . . . But a
whole does not require as one of its conditions a quantitative
extension *ad infinitum.* . . . He who in the moral fulfilment
of his vocation is more indefatigable than his neighbor, merely
makes the whole possibly greater, while he also possibly imperils its existence."[103] The moral seems to be that we perhaps
would do well not to try to be too good; economy in goodness
may be a good thing; we may overreach ourselves and by
excess of goodness become bad.

We shall make no attempt to conceal our conviction that
Ritschl's effort to show that we may be "perfect," by limiting
ever more and more the sphere of our moral activities —
though it has the element of truth in it that our moral duty is
conditioned by our vocation — is not only ineffective but
immoral. At the moment, we are more concerned to point out,
however, that the attempt itself, and the manner in which it
is worked out, combine to make it superabundantly plain that
Ritschl's purpose is to represent a real moral perfection as
attainable by Christians; or in other words that Ritschl
teaches, in the proper sense of the words, a perfectionist doctrine. His method of showing that perfection is attainable is,
to be sure, to show that we can be perfect without being all
that term strictly connotes. This general method of vindicating
the attainability of perfection, however, he shares with all perfectionist teaching. His special mode of giving a color of perfection to manifest imperfection is all that is his own. He has
the courage of his convictions here too, and separates himself
from the modes adopted by others, with some decision. In particular he plumes himself greatly that he is not as other men
are in the matter of the relaxation of the law — limiting ability
by obligation and confining sin to deliberate transgression of

[103] Pp. 667, 668.

known law. Of course the typical examples of the reprobated teaching are supplied by the relaxed and relaxing teaching of the Illumination, which, says Ritschl,[104] "trifled away the Christian problem of reconciliation . . . by referring men's obligation towards God's law to the relative criterion of their internal and external situation." He adduces Töllner to whom nothing was sin but sins of "set purpose," and who taught at once that obedience to the strict law of righteousness is impossible and that in the administration of God, therefore, no absolute standard of moral perfection is applied but every man is judged according to his ability. But Ritschl does not confine his condemnation of such conceptions to them as found in the teachers of the Illumination. They are found in orthodox writers too, he says, and wherever found are offensive. They are found, too, he says,[105] in the Methodist doctrine of perfection, which also he represents as a mere evasion — "casuistry" is his word — teaching as it does that "not every transgression of the law is sin," and that "it is possible not to sin even when actually doing wrong to others." We perceive that Ritschl holds strongly that every transgression of moral law is sin and that there can be no perfection where the whole moral law is not kept. His mode of escape is to deny the validity of all "statutory law." There is no such thing as a universal moral law imposing duty in all its items on all men alike. Each man secretes for himself his own moral law, and in order to be perfect must fulfil only it in all its requirements.

We must confess that we do not see that, on the basis of this general doctrine, Ritschl can escape sharing the reproach of his fellow perfectionists — that they relax the law of God and confine sin to transgression of known law. To explain that not the entire moral law in all its range — in space and in time, he would say — applies as prescription of duty to the individual, but only those moral obligations which arise into consciousness in the process of the faithful prosecution of his vocation, is rather expressly to place himself in the same category with them. For surely this is to make "the internal and

[104] Vol. i. E. T. p. 387.   [105] P. 664.

external situation " of the individual the criterion of his duty, and to confine sin in him to the deliberate transgression of moral requirements clearly known to him. There is eliminated from his obligation the whole body of duties which the moral law, considered in its entirety, prescribes outside the special consciousness of duty developed by him in the faithful prosecution of his particular vocation. That this general moral law is a reality and constitutes the general standard of duty can hardly be denied even on the ground of a doctrine of autonomous morality. We surely are not expected to believe that each individual develops in the prosecution of his special calling not so much the section of the moral law applicable to him, but a so-called moral law, peculiarly his own, unrelated to, perhaps contradictory of, those evolved by others. These sections of the moral law, developed by individuals, must therefore in combination constitute a general moral law, the whole of which is authoritative, though it is known only in part to each individual. If this be not admitted, then there is no such thing as morality. What we call morality has become only what in each individual's case he has discovered by experience to be the most useful " trick of the trade " for him. Ritschl, then, has no advantage in the matter in question over his fellows, and his doctrine of perfection is perceived to be only another attempt to quiet the human conscience in its condemnation of the imperfections of our lives, by persuading it that its duty does not extend beyond our actual performance; and to betray it into finding satisfaction in our imperfection as if it were, in our " internal and external situation," really perfection.

It does not appear that Ritschl's doctrine of Christian perfection has reproduced itself as a whole very extensively. Its influence can be traced, however, in many quarters. We have already called attention to the controversy aroused by Paul Wernle's book on " The Christian and Sin in Paul," which took its start from Ritschl's exposition of Paul's doctrine of sin in Christians. In the wake of this controversy, it has become the fashion among a certain school of " liberal " writers to represent Paul as teaching a doctrine of perfection for

Christians. David Somerville cannot be classed with these writers; but his description of Paul's relation to sin in his "St. Paul's Conception of Christ," 1897,[106] has derived much from Ritschl's. In H. H. Wendt's "Die christliche Lehre von der menschlichen Vollkommenheit untersucht," 1882, the whole circle of Ritschl's characteristic ideas reappears, transposed into a lower key. But not only is the entire thought and expression simplified, but the asperities and exaggerations of Ritschl's doctrines are eliminated. What is left is merely the reasonable assertion that man attains in Christianity and in Christianity alone his human perfection, a perfection manifested in its completeness in Christ Himself and in His followers principally and qualitatively here, but not hereafter quantitatively. Strangely enough Paul Lobstein takes from Ritschl's treatment of Christian perfection the mould into which he pours his exposition of Calvin's doctrine of "the goal of the new life," in the last chapter of his "Die Ethik Calvins," 1877. Perhaps no more striking manifestation of a disciple's zeal could be afforded. "It is Ritschl's service," he says,[107] in explanation of his remarkable procedure, "to have investigated the idea of Christian perfection in a true Evangelical-reformed spirit, and introduced it into Christian ethics."

Ritschl's commentators naturally often express a favorable opinion of his doctrine of perfection, either as a whole or more frequently in one or another of its elements. The element in it which seems most commonly to attract favorable notice is, as it is natural it should be, the emphasis given to the notion of vocation. Garvie says shortly: [108] "This conception of Ritschl's is a very valuable one, and deserves our grateful recognition." When he comes to reproduce, however, what Ritschl's doctrine of Christian perfection is, he rather overdoes an element in it, which is already in Ritschl quite sufficiently exaggerated. "It does not mean," says Garvie, "infallibility of judgment, sinlessness of life, moral completeness; but it does mean that in his relation to God man is conscious of his own worth as a child of God, of his own claims on the grace of God, of his own independence of nature and society." The note of "humility" which is at least formally present in Ritschl's exposition is not heard here. Mozley expresses himself with even more enthusiasm of admiration than Garvie. Ritschl's handling of the subject, he says,[109] "is strikingly illuminating and of real help to piety." He particularly commends the use which Ritschl makes of the idea of vocation. This doctrine, says he, "that a man should try to be faithful to his particular vocation, and make his life a whole in its own order, and that therein lies Christian perfection, is exceedingly valuable, since it banishes the hopeless sense of imperfection, of inability even to approach the goal of effort, which must result if any one compares himself with the universal moral law, and sees perfection in conformity thereto." The lesser task is no doubt the easier: but we should be sorry to suppose that that fact abolishes the greater.

An earlier English expositor [110] — we understand it to be Archibald Duff, Jr. — throws the emphasis of his agreement upon another point. What Ritschl seeks to describe, he says, using phraseology of his own, is "what the atonement effects, what are the results of it in men," or otherwise expressed, "what a man is who has been reconciled to God through Jesus." The answer given is that such a man is "perfect." "If," he now adds, "there be men on whom God now looks with full pleasure (for what else does 'reconciled' mean?), if there be men whom God thus regards as perfect, let us know what are the characteristics of such men." Evangelical Christians, however, are not accustomed to suppose, that the fact that God looks on "reconciled" men "with full pleasure" infers their perfection. They think of Christ, and suppose that the satisfaction of God is with Him as Redeemer, rather than with them, the redeemed. They would by no means agree, therefore, that the faith of the soul "that God and it are reconciled is faith that at that moment God is satisfied with its being what it is." They suppose on the contrary, that God is so little satisfied with what the soul is that He does not

[109] As cited, p. 232.   [110] *Bibliotheca Sacra*, October, 1878, pp. 656 ff.

intend to leave it in that condition. God cannot be satisfied with any soul in which any depravity whatever remains, nor can that soul — on the hypothesis that it is a "reconciled" soul — be satisfied with itself. The truth is that this feeling of "satisfaction," the characteristic tone of mind which Ritschl demands for the believer, a demand which Duff is here echoing from him, is so far from being the mark of the Christian's life that it would be the signature of his death. Ritschl complains that unless the possibility of attaining perfection be held before Christians all impulse to effort dies in them. He forgets that dissatisfaction with their present condition supplies a much more powerful spur to effort. No doubt the Christian must be animated by hope of improvement if he is to strive with energy to advance in his course. But why this hope should take the specific form of conviction that the supreme goal of this improvement is within his easy reach at any time, if only he will take it, it is difficult to see. And should he once reach out and take it — surely that motive to exertion would at once be lost. He would then be "satisfied" and would have no motive for further effort. It is a much more powerful incitement to effort that he should know the evil of the case in which he is, the difficulty of the task which lies before him, the always increasing reward of the journey as it goes forward, and the supreme greatness of the final attainment.

We should not pass on without a further word or two suggested by the assumption which underlies Duff's remarks, that to be reconciled with God is to be perfect. There is a sense in which this is Ritschl's doctrine. But this is not the sense in which it is Duff's doctrine. And it is not the sense in which it is the doctrine of many of Ritschl's critics. We have had occasion to point out that in the interests of the "perfection" of his Christians Ritschl was ready to limit the law to which they are responsible, and in that regard cannot escape the charge of "relaxing the law." But his zeal nevertheless was precisely for morality — though a limited 'autonomous morality'"; and he never dreamed that morality could be had merely by believing, without being conquered, without effort. It is even true, as we have seen, and as Heinrich Münchmeyer, for example, is at pains clearly to point out,[111] that the Christianity of the Christian consists according to Ritschl precisely in his morality, and that whatever religion he is allowed to have is subsidiary and ancillary to his morality.

We find ourselves accordingly in substantial agreement with Münchmeyer when he writes thus: [112] " It is now clearer what the real state of the case is with Ritschl. Man is to supplement himself by God, with God's help to attain his destination by dominating as spirit the world and its influences upon him; and to labor as member of the human society at its God-appointed destiny. The first he attains through appropriation of reconciliation, the second through appropriation of the divine world-end which is directed to the Kingdom of God. It follows that for Ritschl communion with God is only a means to an end, to the end that man shall attain his destiny, which, however, does not coincide with the Kingdom of God but is only purposed, that is to say, conditioned by it. I cannot comprehend why Ritschl does not, according to his presuppositions, set forth as the destination of man, to labor, in spiritual freedom from the world, on the moral organization of humanity in the Kingdom of God — which destination he attains through the relation in which he places himself to God. In that case, the task of Christianity would of course be merely a moral one. But in any case it is not in Ritschl of a religious kind, but a rational and an ethical one, and the character of Christianity as religion is only so far preserved by him that humanity attains its rational and moral destination in dependence on God. This dependence on God would remain preserved, however, even had Ritschl more logically posited only the moral aim for Christianity. I say again, it is simply a self-deception when it is supposed that Ritschl teaches a religious and a moral destination of Christianity; in reality there is question with him only of a rational and moral destination,

---

[111] *Zeitschrift für kirchliche Wissenschaft und kirchliches Leben*, viii. 1887, pp. 95 ff.

[112] As cited, p. 109.

which however certainly cannot be set in parallelism. In reality there can be only a moral destination of Christianity according to Ritschl."

This criticism is just. Ritschl's system is a one-sided ethical system and in principle reduces Christianity to a morality. But that affords no reason why it should be met by an equally one-sided construction of Christianity as a purely religious system. This is, however, what is done by Münchmeyer in fellowship with many others, zealous for " faith " as constituting the whole substance of Christianity. Man's destination, he declares, is uniquely "communion with God," though he is forced to add that men have always felt that it was precisely sin which separated them from God, and have accordingly sought after atonement for sin. " When according to this," he asks,[113] " is man perfect? " And he answers: " When he has found his God in faith, when in faith he knows Him as his Father and himself as His child. Then his heart has peace, he desires no more. That is what the Augsburg Confession means when it places Christian perfection in 'serious fear of God and again the conceiving of great faith and confidence for Christ's sake that we have a reconciled God.' For only by the way of repentance do we come to faith in the grace of God. He who has been brought to this faith — 'I have a reconciled God' — he is perfect. And the more he grows and waxes strong in this faith, the more joyful will his heart be. Joy, however, as Ritschl says, (and in this I agree with him) is the feeling of perfection. And thus it is fully explained why Paul and the Reformers and our theologians place reconciliation so completely in the center; for by it alone is the communion with God which constitutes our perfection, made possible." Ac-

[113] As cited, p. 110. Similarly E. Cremer, " Über die christliche Vollkommenheit," 1899, pp. 21, 22: " Because the forgiveness of sins is God's whole salvation, perfect salvation — faith, which apprehends it in Christ, is perfection." " It is intelligible now why faith in Christ is perfection; it is because the forgiveness of sins is God's whole salvation, in which God's saving work reaches its goal; believers are perfect because Christ's saving work is perfect." " By designating the believer as perfect, it is emphasized that in Christ we have in the forgiveness of sins all that we need from God."

cording to this representation perfection consists entirely in
our religious relation; produced directly by reconciliation it
is just the reconciled state; and it is realized subjectively in
the soul-attitude we call faith. To be " in faith " (*im Glauben*)
is to be *ipso facto* " perfect." Good works are only the natural
activities of one in communion with God. They have no other
significance. When we sin, that is a proof that our faith has
failed; and that drives us back to faith. " So soon as the Christian has found in faith His God's heart again, he is perfect."
The perfection of the Christian, in a word, consists solely in a
relation.

In their conceptions of the nature of Christian perfection,
considered in itself, Ritschl and his followers and those of his
critics represented by Münchmeyer obviously are looking, each
at one side only of the same shield. Each holds, each denies,
half the truth. What is lacking in Münchmeyer's construction
is that he has in view only the guilt of sin. It is sin, says he,
which separates us from God: when we are relieved from sin
we are at one with God and rejoice in communion with Him.
He is thinking only of the guilt of sin: what of its pollution?
The Reformers did not make that mistake. They knew that the
blessedness of the Christian consists not only in abiding in the
presence of God but also in partaking of His holiness. They
remembered that without holiness no one shall see the Lord.
They did not oppose communion with God and holiness to
each other: they understood that these are inseparable from
each other. Ritschl is not wholly wrong in making morality the
end of Christianity: John Wesley is undeniably right when he
says that holiness is the substance of salvation. Ritschl was
right when he emphasized the moral nature of Christianity as
a religion, and saw it advancing to a Kingdom of Righteousness. He rightly wished to relate his so-called religious aspect
of Christianity to his so-called ethical aspect; and he was not
wholly wrong in looking at this relation under the rubric of
means and end. He was wrong, of course, in exalting the moral
aspect of Christianity into practically its totality; in reducing the religious aspect from the primary place it occupies in

the New Testament to almost a mere name. In his hatred of supernaturalism, he gives us no God to flee to, and no God to visit us. His total discarding of what he calls "mysticism" is really the total discarding of vital religion. His whole labor impresses the reader as a sustained effort to work out a religious system without real religion; or, with respect to our present subject, to make out an issue of justification into sanctification without any real justification to issue into sanctification and without any real sanctification for justification to issue into. The peculiarities of Ritschl's dualistic conception of Christianity and his treatment of the matters which fall under the relations of justification and sanctification arise from his determination to have only a self-moralization instead of a sanctification for believers. His antisupernaturalism rules everywhere and here, too, as in his system at large, we have only a camouflaged Rationalism. Nevertheless, it is a good witness which he bears when he testifies that there is no perfection which is not ethical. And this is the witness of the Augsburg Confession also. For Münchmeyer quotes only a part of its declaration. He omits the concern shown in it for "all our undertakings according to our vocation." And he omits the inclusion in its definition of Christian perfection itself of these words: "meanwhile diligently doing good works and serving our vocation." It is "in these things" as well as in the others "that true perfection and the true worship of God consist." There is no perfection whether *partium* or *graduum* without them in their due relations: without them no man is a Christian and no man, of course, therefore, can without them be called "perfect." [114]

[114] The sources for Ritschl's doctrine of perfection are especially his "Die christliche Lehre von der Rechtfertigung und Versöhnung," ii. ed. 3, 1889, §§ 39–40, pp. 365 ff.; iii. ed. 4, 1895, chap. ix. pp. 575 ff., and E. T. 1900, pp. 609 ff.; his lecture "Die christliche Vollkommenheit," ed. 2, 1889, and English translations in *The British and Foreign Evangelical Review,* 1875, pp. 137 ff., by John Rae, and in the *Bibliotheca Sacra,* 1878, pp. 656 ff., by E. Craigmile; and his pamphlet "Unterricht in der christlichen Religion," 1875, ed. 3, 1886, and E. T. 1901, in "The Theology of Albrecht Ritschl" by Albert T. Swing, pp. 169 ff. See also the relevant passages in O. Ritschl, "Albrecht Ritschls Leben," 1892, 1896; G. Mielke, "Das System Albrecht Ritschl's, dargestellt,

nicht kritisirt," 1894, pp. 50 ff.; J. Thikötter, " Darstellung und Beurtheilung der Theologie Albrecht Ritschl's," 1883, pp. 48 ff.; C. von Kügelgen, " Grundriss der Ritschlschen Dogmatik," ed. 2, 1903, pp. 120 ff.

The following are some of the more notable discussions of Ritschl's doctrine of perfection: — John Rae, " The Protestant Doctrine of Evangelical Perfection," in *The British and Foreign Evangelical Review*, 1876, pp. 88–107; R. Tifling, " Ueber christliche Vollkommenheit nach Ritschl," in the *Mittheilungen und Nachrichten für die evangelische Kirche in Russland*, 1878, pp. 341–362; H. Münchmeyer, " Darstellung und Beleuchtung der Lehre Ritschl's von der christlichen Vollkommenheit," in the *Zeitschrift für kirchliche Wissenschaft und kirchliches Leben*, 1887, pp. 95 ff.; Fr. Luther, " Die Theologie Ritschls," 1887, pp. 31 ff., and also " Über christliche Sittlichkeit nach lutherisch-kirchlicher Lehre und nach den Aufstellungen der neuen Schule," in the *Neue kirchliche Zeitschrift*, 1891, pp. 469 ff., 619 ff., 712 ff.; Fr. H. R. Frank, " Ueber die kirchliche Bedeutung der Theologie A. Ritschl's," ed. 2, 1888, pp. 21 ff., and also " Geschichte und Kritik der neueren Theologie," 1894, ed. 4, 1908, pp. 350 ff.; H. Weiss, " Über das Wesen des persönlischen Christenstandes " in the *Theologische Studien und Kritiken*, 1881, pp. 377 ff.; J. Köstlin, " Religion nach dem Neuen Testament," in the *Theologische Studien und Kritiken*, 1888, pp. 7 ff.; P. Graue, " Der Moralismus der Ritschl'schen Theologie," in the *Jahrbücher für protestantische Theologie*, 1889, pp. 321 ff.; M. Reischle, " Ein Wort zur Controverse über die Mystik in der Theologie," 1886; E. Vischer, " Albrecht Ritschls Anschauung von evangelischem Glauben und Leben," 1900; R. Wegener, " A. Ritschls Idee des Reiches Gottes im Licht der Geschichte kritisch untersucht," 1897, along with J. Weiss, " Die Idee des Reiches Gottes in der Theologie," 1901, chap. vi. pp. 110 ff., and J. L. Schultze, " Die Ritschlsche Theologie eine Teleologie," in the *Neue kirchliche Zeitschrift*, 1898, pp. 211 ff.; E. Cremer, " Über die christliche Vollkommenheit," 1899, pp. 7 ff.; Beyreiss, " Die christliche Vollkommenheit," in the *Neue kirchliche Zeitschrift*, 1901, pp. 526 ff.; Karl Schmidt, " Zur Lehre von der christlichen Vollkommenheit," in the *Neue kirchliche Zeitschrift*, 1905, pp. 724 ff.

III

"MISERABLE–SINNER CHRISTIANITY" IN THE HANDS OF THE RATIONALISTS

I. FROM RITSCHL TO WERNLE

" MISERABLE–SINNER CHRISTIANITY "[1] IN THE HANDS OF THE RATIONALISTS

Article I

FROM RITSCHL TO WERNLE[2]

It belongs to the very essence of the type of Christianity propagated by the Reformation that the believer should feel himself continuously unworthy of the grace by which he lives. At the center of this type of Christianity lies the contrast of sin and grace; and about this center everything else revolves. This is in large part the meaning of the emphasis put in this type of Christianity on justification by faith. It is its conviction that there is nothing in us or done by us, at any stage of our earthly development, because of which we are acceptable to God. We must always be accepted for Christ's sake, or we cannot ever be accepted at all. This is not true of us only " when we believe." It is just as true after we have believed. It will continue to be true as long as we live. Our need of Christ does not cease with our believing; nor does the nature of our relation to Him or to God through Him ever alter, no matter what our attainments in Christian graces or our achievements in Christian behavior may be. It is always on His " blood and righteousness" alone that we can rest. There is never anything that we are or have or do that can take His place, or that can take a place along with Him. We are always unworthy, and all that we have or do of good is always of pure grace. Though blessed with every spiritual blessing in the heavenlies in Christ, we are still in ourselves just " miserable sinners ": " miserable sinners " saved by grace to be sure,

---

[1] *Armesünderchristentum.* The term has become practically a technical term to express the particular attitude of the Christian towards sin in the teaching and life of the Church of the Reformation.

[2] From *The Princeton Theological Review*, xviii. 1920, pp. 269–336.

but "miserable sinners" still, deserving in ourselves nothing but everlasting wrath. That is the attitude which the Reformers took, and that is the attitude which the Protestant world has learned from the Reformers to take, toward the relation of believers to Christ.

There is emphasized in this attitude the believer's continued sinfulness in fact and in act; and his continued sense of his sinfulness. And this carries with it recognition of the necessity of unbroken penitence throughout life. The Christian is conceived fundamentally in other words as a penitent sinner.[3] But that is not all that is to be said: it is not even the main thing that must be said. It is therefore gravely inadequate to describe the spirit of "miserable-sinner Christianity" as "the spirit of continuous but not unhopeful penitence." It is not merely that this is too negative a description, and that we must at least say, "the spirit of continuous though hopeful penitence." It is a wholly uncomprehending description, and misplaces the emphasis altogether. The spirit of this Christianity is a spirit of penitent indeed, but overmastering exultation. The attitude of the "miserable sinner" is not only not one of despair; it is not even one of depression; and not even one of hesitation or doubt; hope is too weak a word to apply to it. It is an attitude of exultant joy. Only this joy has its ground not in ourselves but in our Savior. We are sinners and we know ourselves to be sinners, lost and helpless in ourselves. But we are saved sinners; and it is our salvation which gives the tone to our life, a tone of joy which swells in exact proportion to the sense we have of our ill-desert; for it is he to whom much is forgiven who loves much, and who, loving, rejoices much. Adolf Harnack declares that this mood was brought into Christianity by Augustine. Before Augustine the characteristic frame of mind of Christians was the racking unrest of alternating hopes and fears. Augustine, the first of the Evangelicals, created a new piety of assured rest in God

[3] Accordingly the first of Luther's Ninety-five Theses runs: "Our Lord and Master Jesus Christ in teaching, 'Repent,' etc., intended penitence to be the whole life of believers." Cf. *The Princeton Theological Review*, October, 1917, pp. 511 f.

our Savior, and the psychological form of this new piety was, as Harnack phrases it,[4] "solaced contrition," — affliction for sin, yes, the deepest and most poignant remorse for sin, but not unrelieved remorse, but appeased remorse. There is no other joy on earth like that of appeased remorse: it is not only in heaven but on earth also that the joy over one sinner that repents surpasses that over ninety and nine just persons who need no repentance.

The type of piety brought in by Augustine was pushed out of sight by the emphasis on human graces which marked the Middle Ages. Luther brought it back. His own experience fixed ineradicably in his heart the conviction that he was a " miserable sinner," deserving of death, and alive only through the inexplicable grace of God. What we call his conversion was his discovery of this bitter-sweet fact. He had tried to think highly of himself. He found that he could not do so. But he found also that he could not possibly think too highly of Christ. And so it became his joy to be a " miserable sinner," resting solely on the grace of Christ; and to preach the gospel of the " miserable sinner " to the world. This is the very hinge on which his Reformation turns, and of course, Luther gave expression to it endlessly in those documents in which his Reformation-work has been preserved to us.

He is never weary of setting the two aspects in which the " miserable sinner " may be viewed side by side. " These things," he says, in one place,[5] " are diametrically opposed — that the Christian is righteous and loved of God, yet is at the same time a sinner. For God cannot deny His nature, that is, cannot but hate sin and sinners, and this He does necessarily, for otherwise He would be unjust and would love sin. How then are these two contradictories both true: I am sinful and deserve the divine wrath and hatred; and the Father loves me?

[4] " Lehrbuch der Dogmengeschichte," iii. 1890, p. 59 (ed. 4, iii. p. 66; E. T. v. 1899, p. 66), " getrösteter Sündenschmerz." Cf. *The Princeton Theological Review*, January, 1905, pp. 97 ff.

[5] " Ad Gal. I 338 (1534)." The three quotations from Luther which follow are taken from J. Gottschick's article, " Propter Christum," in the *Zeitschrift für Theologie und Kirche*, vii. 1897, pp. 378–384.

Nothing at all brings it about except Christ the Mediator. The Father, He says, loves you, not because you are worthy of love, but because you have loved Me and believed that I came forth from Him. Thus the Christian remains in pure humility, deeply sensible of his sin, and acknowledging himself, on its account, to be deserving of God's wrath and judgment and eternal death. . . . He remains also at the same time in pure and holy pride, in which he turns to Christ and arouses himself through Him against this sense of wrath and the divine judgment, and believes not only that the remainders of sin are not imputed to him, but also that he is loved by the Father, not on his own account but on account of Christ the Beloved."

" A Christian," says Luther again,[6] " is at the same time a sinner and a saint; he is at once bad and good. For in our own person we are in sin, and in our own name we are sinners. But Christ brings us another name in which there is forgiveness of sin, so that for His sake our sin is forgiven and done away. Both then are true. There are sins . . . and yet there are no sins. The reason is that for Christ's sake, God will not see them. They exist for my eyes; I see them, and feel them, too. But Christ is there who bids me preach that I am to repent . . . and then believe in the forgiveness of sin in His name. . . . Where such faith is, therefore, God no longer sees sin. For thou standest there for God not in thy name but in Christ's name; thou dost adorn thyself with grace and righteousness although in thine own eyes and in thine own person, thou art a miserable sinner (*armer Sünder*). . . . Let not that, however, scare you to death. . . . Speak, rather, thus: Ah, Lord, I am a miserable sinner (*armer Sünder*), but I shall not remain such; for Thou hast commanded that forgiveness of sins be preached in Thy name. . . . Thus our Lord Jesus Christ alone is the garment of grace that is put upon us, that God our Father may not look upon us as sinners but receive us as righteous, holy, godly children, and give us eternal life."

" We, however, teach," he says again,[7] " that we are to

[6] " Werke," Erlangen ed., ii. pp. 197 f.   [7] xviii. pp. 294 ff. (1582).

learn to know and regard Him, as Him who sits there for the poor, stupid conscience, if so be that we believe on Him, not as a judge . . . but as a gracious, kind, comforting mediator between my frightened conscience and God; and says to me — You are a sinner, and are afraid that the devil will drag you by the law before the judgment seat; come then and hold fast to me, and fear no wrath. Why? Because I sit here for the very purpose that if you believe in me, I can come between you and God so that no wrath or evil can touch you. For if wrath and punishment go over you, they must first go over me, and that is not possible. . . . Therefore we are all through faith altogether blissful and safe, so that we shall abide uncondemned, not for the sake of our own purity and holiness, but for Christ's sake, because, through such faith, we hold on to Him as our Mercy-seat, assured that in and with Him no wrath can remain, but pure love, indulgence, forgiveness."

Embedded in the Protestant formularies, both doctrinal and devotional, this "miserable-sinner" conception of the Christian life has moulded the piety of all the Protestant generations. Throughout the Protestant world believers confess themselves to be, still as believers, wrath-deserving sinners; and that not merely with reference to their inborn sinful nature as yet incompletely eradicated, but with reference also to their total life-manifestation which their incompletely eradicated sinful nature flows into and vitiates. Their continued sinning, indeed, is already confessed whenever they repeat the Lord's Prayer, since, among the very few petitions included in it, is the very emphatic one: "Forgive us our trespasses." [8]

[8] Ἁμαρτίας, Luke XI. 4; ὀφειλήματα, Matt. VI. 12; "trespasses" in the Anglican "Book of Common Prayer"; "debts" in the Presbyterian "Book of Common Worship." The meaning is the same in every case, and the constant repetition of the Lord's Prayer in either form is a constant confession of continual sinning. It is admitted on all hands that Jesus did not look upon His followers as men who had ceased to sin. For recent statements from writers who would not allow as much of Paul see Weinel, "Biblische Theologie des Neuen Testaments," 1913, p. 189; and especially H. Windisch, "Taufe und Sünde," 1908, p. 534: "Miserable-sinnerism even finds support in the Bible also. Jesus, for example, by the side of the Methodist notion of conversion which He employs; by the side of the strict requirement of cleansing; recognizes the

Naturally therefore, the expositions of this prayer, designed for the instruction of the several Churches in their attitude toward God, are the special depository of pointed reminders to believers of their continual sinning. Luther, for example, incorporates a very full and searching exposition of " the Fifth Petition " into his Large Catechism, in which he affirms that "we sin daily in words and deeds, by commission and omission," and warns us that "no one is to think that so long as he lives here below he can bring it about that he does not need such forgiveness"; that, in fact, "unless God forgives without cessation, we are lost."[9] It is by his Short Catechism of 1529, however, that Luther has kept his hand most permanently on the instruction of the Churches. In it he teaches the catechumen to say that "God richly forgives me and all believers every day, all our sins," " for we sin much every day and deserve nothing but punishment."[10] In the instructions for the confessional coming from the hand of Luther which were soon incorporated into this Short Catechism, the believing penitent accordingly is told to say " I, miserable sinner (*armer Sünder*), confess myself before God guilty of all manner of sins. . . ."[11] The hold which this teaching has taken of the devotional expressions of the Lutheran Churches may be illustrated by the presence in the new Agenda of the National Prussian Church of a Confession of Sin for the whole congregation which runs thus: " We confess . . . that we were conceived and born in sin; and, full of ignorance and heedlessness of Thy divine word and will, always prone to all wicked-

---

continuance of sinning and quite like all Lutheran Christians assures His disciples of the divine clemency." So also P. Wernle, " Der Christ und die Sünde bei Paulus," 1897, p. 127, where we are told that Paul has gone far beyond Jesus, has nothing to say of no one being good, or of prayer for forgiveness, and brings the pneumatic closer to God. " It may be said that Paul thought worse of men and better of Christians than Jesus. Both the theory of original sin and the theory of the ' flesh ' are alien to Jesus, but so is the doctrine that the Christian no longer sins."

[9] See Th. Hardeland, " Der kleine Katechismus D. Martini Lutheri," 1889, p. 186; cf. H. Scholz in *Zeitschrift für Theologie und Kirche,* vi. 1896, p. 471.

[10] Hardeland, as cited, p. 137 (155 f.), and 185; P. Schaff, " The Creeds of Christendom," iii. 1878, pp. 80, 83.

[11] Schaff, as cited, p. 88.

ness and slack to all good, we transgress Thy divine commandments unceasingly in thoughts, words and deeds." [12]
Naturally it retains its place in the forms of service adopted for
"the three bodies" of American Lutherans. In the German
form [13] the Confession of Sin takes this shape: " I, poor sinful
man, confess to God, the Almighty, my Creator and Redeemer,
that I not only have sinned in thoughts, words and deeds, but
also was conceived and born in sin, and so all my nature and
being is deserving of punishment and condemnation before
His righteousness. Therefore I flee to His gratuitous mercy and
seek and beseech His grace. Lord, be merciful to me, miserable
sinner (*armen Sünder*)." The English form is to the same
effect.[14]

It is the same in the Reformed Churches as in the Lutheran:
catechisms and liturgies alike embody the confession of the
continued sinfulness of the Christian, and his continued dependence on the forgiving grace of Christ. In Calvin's Catechism the catechumen is made to declare that there is no man
living so righteous that he does not need to make request for
the forgiveness of his sins, that Christ has therefore prescribed
a prayer for forgiveness of sins for the whole Church, and that
he who would exempt himself from it " refuseth to bee of the
companie of Christes flocke: and in very deed the scriptures
doe plainlie testifie, that the most perfect man that is, if he
would alleadge one point to justifie him selfe thereby before
God, should bee found faultie in a thousand." " It is meete
therefore," it concludes, " that everie man have a recourse continually unto Gods mercie." [15] When expounding at an earlier

[12] H. Scholz, as cited, p. 472.

[13] " Kirchenbuch für Evangelisch-Lutherische Gemeinden, herausgegeben
von der Allgemeinen Versammlung der Evangelisch-Lutherischen Kirche in
Nord Amerika," 1908, p. 4.

[14] " The Common Service for the Use of Evangelical Lutheran Congregations," 1907, pp. 1–2: " Almighty God, our Maker and Redeemer, we poor sinners confess unto Thee, that we are by nature sinful and unclean, and that we
have sinned against Thee by thought, word, and deed. Wherefore we flee for
refuge to Thine infinite mercy, seeking and imploring Thy grace, for the sake
of our Lord Jesus Christ."

[15] We quote from the old English translation first printed at Geneva, 1556,
as reprinted by Horatius Bonar, " Catechisms of the Scottish Reformation,"
1866, p. 66.

point [16] the clause in the Creed, " I believe in the forgiveness of
sins," it is said that God " doeth freely forgive all the sinnes
of them which beleeve in him," the comprehensiveness of the
language is intended to include in the declaration sins committed after as well as before the inception of faith. And therefore, when good works come to be treated of,[17] it is said that
they are " not worthy of themselves to be accepted," " because
there is mixed some filth through the infirmity of the flesh,
whereby they are defiled." They are accepted by God therefore " onely because it pleaseth God of his goodnesse to love
us freely, and so to cover and forget our faultes."

The teaching of the Heidelberg Catechism is to the same
effect. We increase our guilt daily, we are told; [18] our whole
Christian life is occupied with a conflict against sin and the
devil; [19] and our best works in this life are imperfect and defiled with sin.[20] To the question whether those that have been
converted can keep God's law perfectly, it is answered explicitly, " No, but even the holiest men, while in this life,
have only a small beginning of this obedience, yet so that with
earnest purpose they begin to live, not only according to some
but according to all the commandments of God." [21] As in
Calvin's Catechism, the most comprehensive language is employed, however, in expounding the clause of the Creed on the
forgiveness of sins. " I believe, that God for the Satisfaction of
Christ," we read, "hath quite put out of his Remembrance all
my Sins, and even that Corruption also, wherewith I must
strive all my Life long." [22] And naturally the exposition of
" the Fifth Petition " of the Lord's Prayer [23] is the occasion
for repeating that we are " miserable sinners " (*arme Sünder*)
burdened not merely with the evil which always still clings to
us, but also with numerous transgressions.

Perhaps this series of truths never received crisper state-

[16] P. 26.

[17] Pp. 31 f.

[18] Q. 13.

[19] Q. 32.

[20] Q. 62.

[21] Q. 114.

[22] Q. 56. We use the old Scotch translation, Edinburgh, 1615 (Bonar, as cited, p. 132).

[23] Q. 126. (Bonar, as cited, pp. 160 f.).

ment, however, than at the hands of John Craig in his larger
Catechism (1581), on the basis whether of the article of the
Creed or of the petition of the Prayer.[24] " Why is remission of
sinnes put here? Because it is proper to the Church and members of the same. Wherefore is it proper to the Church only?
Because in the Church onely is the spirit of faith and repentance. . . . How oft are our sinnes forgiuen vs? Continually
euen unto our liues end. What need is there of this? Because
sinne is neuer thoroughlie abolished here." " What seeke we
in this fift petition? Remission of our sinnes, or spirituall
debts. . . . Should euery man pray thus continually? Yes, for
all flesh is subiect to sinne. But sometimes men doe good
thinges? Yet they sin in the best thinge they doe."

The Calvinistic liturgies naturally also reflect this universal Reformed doctrine. The Confession of Sins contained in the
liturgy which was published by Calvin in 1542 and which
passed into the use of all the French-speaking Reformed
Churches, has been universally admired. Its beauty, says
E. Lacheret, has been proclaimed with one voice; Christian
sentiment finds in it one of its purest and strongest expressions: " brief, sober, solemn, it expresses in a grave style and
penetrating tone, the grief of the penitent soul, its appeal to
the divine mercy, its desire for a new and holy life." [25] Its
opening prayer in the form in which it has been long used in
the English-speaking French Protestant Church of Charleston,
S. C., runs thus: [26] " O Lord God! Eternal and Almighty
Father! we confess before thy Divine Majesty that we
are miserable sinners,[27] born in corruption and iniquity,[28]
prone to evil, and of ourselves incapable of any good.[29]

[24] Bonar, as cited, pp. 210, 232.

[25] " La Liturgie Wallonne," 1890, p. 17.

[26] " The Liturgy, or Forms of Divine Service, of the French Protestant
Church, of Charleston, S. C." Translated from the Liturgy of the Churches of
Neufchatel and Vallangin: editions of 1737 and 1772. . . . 1853, pp. 7, 8.

[27] *Paovres pecheurs* in Calvin's form (Baum, Cunity, and Reuss, " Opera
Calvini," vi. 173): the form *misérables pécheurs* appears to have come in during the eighteenth century.

[28] " Conceived and born in iniquity and corruption " — Calvin.

[29] " Prone to evil, incapable of all good " — Calvin.

We acknowledge that we transgress in various ways [30] thy holy commandments, so that we draw down on ourselves, through thy righteous judgment, condemnation and death."

The brief Catechism of the Church of England, although very plainly presuming the continuous sinning of Christians, naturally contains nothing explicit on the subject. Whatever may be lacking in it is abundantly made up, however, in the Articles and Prayers. The Articles not only affirm that "the infection of nature" derived by every man from Adam "doth remain, yea in them that are regenerated" and has in them "the nature of sin" (ix.); but also that he can do no good works which can endure the severity of God's judgment (xii.), and very explicitly that all men, except Christ alone, "although baptized and born again in Christ, yet offend in many things; and if we say we have no sin we deceive ourselves and the truth is not in us" (xv.). They are therefore to be condemned, we are told, "which say they can no more sin as long as they live here" (xvi.). With respect to the Prayers we have only to bear in mind the Exhortation, General Confession, and Absolution with which both the Morning and Evening Services begin; or indeed only the Litany, in which specifically God's people abase themselves before Him as "miserable sinners" and beseech His forgiveness and holy keeping. The enumeration in the General Confession of the modes of sinning of which the petitioners are guilty is exceedingly comprehensive, and yet is keyed wholly to the experience of believers. In the exhortation in response to which their confession is made, they are addressed as "dearly beloved brethren," and God is designated as their "heavenly Father," from whose "infinite goodness and mercy" they are receiving and are further to look for all things requisite for the welfare of both body and soul. Yet they are represented as guilty of "manifold sins and wickedness," and are led by the minister in this Confession: "Almighty and most merciful Father: We have erred, and strayed from thy ways like lost

[30] "Without end and without cessation" — Calvin.

sheep. We have followed too much the devices and desires of our own hearts. We have offended against thy holy laws. We have left undone those things which we ought to have done; And we have done those things which we ought not to have done; And there is no health in us." Their only refuge is in the Lord; and the cry is therefore at once appended: — "But thou, O Lord, have mercy upon us, miserable offenders. Spare thou them, O God, which confess their faults. Restore thou them that are penitent; According to thy promises declared unto mankind in Christ Jesu our Lord." That is the very spirit of the "miserable sinner," as is also the closing petition of the prayer: "And grant, O most merciful Father, for His sake; That we may hereafter lead a godly, righteous, and sober life, To the glory of Thy holy Name. Amen." The note which sounds here is precisely the same as that which rings out in the Easter Litany of the Moravian Church: "We miserable sinners (*armen Sünder*) pray that Thou wouldest hear us, dear Lord and God!" [31]

It has not always been easy through the Protestant ages to maintain in its purity this high attitude of combined shame of self and confidence in the mercy of God in Christ. But even in the worst of times it has not been left without witnesses. There is Zinzendorf, for example.[32] It was in an evil day of abounding Rationalism that he rediscovered for himself and for his followers a "miserable-sinner Christianity." He gave the term as recovered by him for daily use in his brotherhood a particular coloring of his own; sentimentalized it, if we may so say; and especially made it vivid by means of a very specialized analogy. The terms "sin," "sinner," are used in German, with a less prevailing religious reference than in English, in the general sense of "offence," "culprit"; and it happens to have come about that in the popular German speech the customary designation of the condemned criminal

[31] Schaff, as cited, p. 805.

[32] Zinzendorf's doctrine of the "miserable sinner" is admirably stated by Bernhard Becker, "Zinzendorf und sein Christentum," ed. 2, 1900, pp. 296–298. See also H. Scholz, in *Zeitschrift für Theologie und Kirche*, vi. 1896, pp. 463–468.

awaiting the gallows is precisely "the miserable sinner." [33] The implication is that all the resources of such an one have been exhausted: he stands stripped, destitute, desperate before his doom. Seizing upon this accident of usage, Zinzendorf bids the Christian see in the condemned criminal the image of himself: in this thoroughly specialized sense also the Christian is a "miserable sinner." Not indeed the merely condemned criminal. He is in Christ, and for what he is in Christ is this condemned criminal snatched from the gallows by the mere clemency of one on whom he has no claim. He is therefore distinctively the pardoned criminal; and therefore his immediate preoccupation is less with the guilt from which he has escaped than with the deliverance which he has received. "The most solid distinction between an honest disciple of the no doubt still lingering old teachers who were known as Pietists, Spenerites, Halleites and a 'Brother . . .' is this: the former commonly has his misery always before his eyes and glances only for his necessary comforting to the wounds of Christ, — the latter has always before his eyes the finished reconciliation and Jesus' blood and only for his necessary humbling casts an occasional glance on his misery."

Zinzendorf pushes his simile into details and insists on the application of them all. Having J. K. Dippel's rationalizing doctrine of the Atonement in mind, he declares that the deliverance of the believer from the punishment due to his sin is accomplished in no other way than that of the thief from the gallows — not through future good behavior, but out of pure mercy. And like the thief, he owes not only his escape from the immediately impending gallows but whatever further existence is accorded to him, continuously to the mere favor of his deliverer. Thus through every moment of his life the believer is absolutely dependent on the grace of Christ, and when life is over he still has nothing to plead but Christ's blood and righteousness. Very complete expression is given to this

[33] J. and W. Grimm, "Deutsches Wörterbuch," i. 1854, p. 555: "The imprisoned and condemned criminal was called der arme Gefangne, der arme Sünder." Heath's "German and English Dictionary," 1906, p. 582: "armer Sünder, condemned criminal awaiting execution."

conception in the noble hymn, " Christ's Blood and Righteousness," some of the pungency of which is lost in John Wesley's translation of it, excellent as that translation is in transmitting the general sense. The blood of Christ, says Zinzendorf here, is his sole comfort and hope, on which alone he builds in life or in death: yea, even though by God's grace he should attain to a life of unbroken faithfulness in His service, and should keep himself clean from all sin whatever up to the grave itself — he should still, when he came to stand before the Lord, have no thought of " goodness " and " godliness," but would say only, " Here comes a sinner who depends on the great Ransom alone." The poignancy of that declaration is inadequately expressed by Wesley's

> " When from the dust of death I rise,
> To claim my mansion in the skies,
> Even then this shall be all my plea,
> Jesus hath lived and died for me."

It must not be imagined because of its hypothetical supposition in this hymn, that Zinzendorf allowed the possibility of the believer's actually living free from sin " up to the grave." Sanctification with him was most decisively held to be a process which reaches its end only when we are freed from the limitations of sense; and his rejection of all perfectionist notions is so decisive as almost to seem harsh. " Should any one say," he says, " he was in *sensu perfectissimo* done with sin, and had *hoc respectu* no longer to strive, he would be a fanatic or arrogant fool." [34] He is particularly decisive in his rejection of the Quietistic view of sanctification. That, says he, carries with it an ideal of the Christian life, with its passivity, apathy, freedom from trepidation, which can find no example in Christ. No, the believer strives against sin all his life, and is never without failings; and from his well-grounded fear of sinning arises a powerful, ever present motive to watchfulness and effort. He has nothing to depend on but Christ, and Christ is enough; but that does not relieve him from the duty

[34] Becker, as cited, p. 300, where Zinzendorf's judgment on Perfectionism is briefly but clearly stated.

of cleansing his life from sin, but rather girds his loins for the
struggle. The necessity for the continuance of the struggle
means, of course, the continuance of sin to struggle against.
As one of Zinzendorf's critics puts it: [35] " To feel himself a
' miserable sinner ' never has the meaning with him of desisting
from the moral task or of attributing less value to it than to
religious experience. On the other side it is equally excluded
that this doctrine amounts to a new form of self-torturing
after a pietistic fashion. For it is precisely against the self-
torturing of that narrow-hearted, unfruitful practice of penitence,[36] rich in illusions and disillusions, of the dominant pietism, that Zinzendorf's system is emphatically directed. It is
not his meaning that a Christian man should be of a sour
countenance, and hang his head; he hates the dejected and
grumbling piety which comes to nothing except the repetition of its dirges. He requires and exemplifies a joyous Christianity." " Miserable-sinner Christianity " is equally removed
from self-asserting and self-tormenting Christianity, which is
as much as to say from Rationalism and Pietism. It is Christ-
trusting Christianity, and casts its orbit around that center.
And when we say Christ-trusting Christianity, it must be intended not merely negatively but positively. The " miserable-
sinner Christian " not merely finds absolutely nothing but
Christ in which to repose any trust, but he actually trusts —
trusts, with all that that means — in Christ.

In those same bad days of the eighteenth century " miserable-sinner Christianity " was rediscovered also for themselves
by the English Evangelicals. We may take Thomas Adam as
an example. His like-minded biographer, James Stillingfleet,
tells us [37] how, having been awakened to the fact that he was

[35] Scholz, in *Zeitschrift für Theologie und Kirche,* vi. 1896, p. 465.

[36] *Busskampfspraxis.* What is meant is the tendency to treat the self in
accordance with the divine judgment which is recognized as impending over
it. There is a really informing article on the *Busskampf,* in C. Meusel's
" Kirchliches Handlexikon," i. 1887, pp. 618 f. See also Schiele and Zscharnack,
" Die Religion in Geschichte und Gegenwart," i. 1909, col. 1486.

[37] " Private Thoughts on Religion," by the Rev. Thomas Adam: ed.
Poughkeepsie, 1814, pp. 22 ff. There are many other editions.

preaching essentially a work-religion, he was at last led to the truth, not without some reading of Luther, it is true, but particularly by the prayerful study of the Epistle to the Romans. " He was," writes his biographer, " rejoiced exceedingly; found peace and comfort spring up in his mind; his conscience was purged from guilt through the atoning blood of Christ, and his heart set at liberty to run the way of God's commandments without fear, in a spirit of filial love and holy delight; and from that hour he began to preach salvation *through faith in Jesus Christ alone,* to man by nature and practice lost, and condemned under the law, and, as his own expression is, *Always a sinner.*" In this italicized phrase, Adam had in mind of course our sinful nature, a very profound sense of the evil of which coloured all his thought. In one of those piercing declarations which his biographers gathered out of his diaries and published under the title of " Private Thoughts on Religion," [38] Adam tells us how he thought of indwelling sin. " Sin," says he, " is still here, deep in the centre of my heart, and twisted about every fibre of it." [39] But he knew very well that sin could not be in the heart and not in the life. " When have I not sinned? " he asks,[40] and answers, " The reason is evident, I carry myself about with me." Accordingly he says: [41] " When we have done all we ever shall do, the very best state we ever shall arrive at, will be so far from meriting a reward, that it will need a pardon." Again, " If I was to live to the

---

[38] " These entries from his private diary, which were meant for no eyes but his own, bring before us a man of no common power of analytic and speculative thought. With an intrepidity and integrity of self-scrutiny perhaps unexampled, he writes down problems started, and questionings raised, and conflicts gone through; whilst his ordinarily flaccid style grows pungent and strong. Ever since their publication these ' Private Thoughts ' have exercised a strange fascination over intellects at opposite poles. Coleridge's copy of the little volume (1795) . . . remains to attest, by its abounding markings, the spell it laid upon him, while such men as Bishop Heber, Dr. Thomas Chalmers, and John Stuart Mill, and others, have paid tribute to the searching power of the ' thoughts.' " A. B. Grosart, in Leslie Stephen's " Dictionary of National Biography," i. 1885, pp. 89, 90.

[39] " Private Thoughts on Religion," as cited, p. 72.

[40] P. 74.

[41] P. 218.

world's end, and do all the good that man can do, I must still
cry 'mercy!'"[42] — which is very much what Zinzendorf said
in his hymn. So far from balking at the confession of daily
sins, he adds to that the confession of universal sinning. "I
know, with infallible certainty," he says,[43] "that I have sinned
ever since I could discern between good and evil; in thought,
word, and deed; in every period, condition, and relation of
life; every day against every commandment." "God may say
to every self-righteous man," he says again,[44] "as he did in the
cause of Sodom, 'show me ten, yea, one perfect good action,
and for the sake of it I will not destroy.'"

There is no morbidity here and no easy acquiescence in this
inevitable sinning. "Lord, forgive my sins, and suffer me to
keep them — is this the meaning of my prayers?" he asks.[45]
And his answer is: [46] "I had rather be cast into the burning
fiery furnace, or the lion's den, than suffer sin to lie quietly in
my heart." He knows that justification and sanctification belong together. "Christ never comes into the soul unattended,"
he says; [47] "he brings the Holy Spirit with him, and the
Spirit his train of gifts and graces." "Christ comes with a
blessing in each hand," he says again; [48] "forgiveness in one,
and holiness in the other, and never gives either to any who
will not take both." But he adds at once: "Christ's forgiveness
of all sins is complete at once, because less would not do us
good; his holiness is dispensed by degrees, and to none wholly
in this life, lest we should slight his forgiveness." "Whenever
I die," he says therefore,[49] "I die a sinner; but by the grace
of God, penitent, and, I trust, accepted in the beloved." "It is
the joy of my heart that I am freed from guilt," he says again,[50]

---

[42] P. 212.   [45] P. 103.   [47] P. 180.   [49] P. 209.
[43] P. 71.   [46] P. 99.   [48] P. 179.   [50] P. 216.

[44] P. 129. In the same spirit with these quotations, but with perhaps even
greater poignancy of rhetorical expression is this declaration of Alexander
Whyte's ("Bunyan Characters," iii. 1895, p. 136): "Our guilt is so great that
we dare not think of it. . . . It crushes our minds with a perfect stupor of horror, when for a moment we try to imagine a day of judgment when we shall
be judged for all the deeds that we have done in the body. Heart-beat after
heart-beat, breath after breath, hour after hour, day after day, year after year,
and all full of sin; all nothing but sin from our mother's womb to our grave."

" and the desire of my heart to be freed from sin." For both alike are from God. " Justification by sanctification," he says,[51] " is man's way to heaven, and it is odds but he will make a little serve the turn. Sanctification by justification is God's, and he fills the soul with his own fulness." " The Spirit does not only confer and increase ability, and so leave us to ourselves in the use of it," he explains,[52] " but every single act of spiritual life is the Spirit's own act in us." And again, even more plainly: [53] " Sanctification is a gift; and the business of man is to desire, receive, and use it. But he can by no act or effort of his own produce it in himself. Grace can do every thing; nature nothing." " I am resolved," he therefore declares,[54] " to receive my virtue from God as a gift, instead of presenting him with a spurious kind of my own." He accordingly is " the greatest saint upon earth who feels his poverty most in the want of perfect holiness, and longs with the greatest earnestness for the time when he shall be put in full possession of it." [55]

Thus in complete dependence on grace, and in never ceasing need of grace (take " grace " in its full sense of goodness to the undeserving) the saint goes onward in his earthly work, neither imagining that he does not need to be without sin because he has Christ nor that because he has Christ he is already without sin. The repudiation of both the perfectionist and the antinomian inference is made by Adam most pungently. The former in these crisp words: [56] " The moment we think that we have no sin, we shall desert Christ." That, because Christ came to save just sinners. The latter more at length: [57] " It would be a great abuse of the doctrine of salvation by faith, and a state of dangerous security, to say, if it pleases God to advance me to a higher or the highest degree of holiness, I should have great cause of thankfulness, and it would be the very joy of my heart; but nevertheless I can do without it, as being safe in Christ." We cannot set safety in Christ and holiness of life over against each other as contradictions, of

[51] P. 219.　　[53] P. 234.　　[55] P. 225.　　[57] Pp. 223 f.
[52] P. 242.　　[54] P. 247.　　[56] P. 231.

which the one may be taken and the other left. They go together. " Every other faith," we read,[58] " but that which apprehends Christ as a purifier, as well as our atonement and righteousness, is false and hypocritical." We are not left in our sins by Him; we are in process of being cleansed from our sins by Him; and our part is to work out with fear and trembling the salvation which He is working in us, always keeping our eyes on both our sin from which we need deliverance and the Lord who is delivering us. To keep our eyes fixed on both at once is no doubt difficult. " On earth it is the great exercise of faith," says Adam,[59] " and one of the hardest things in the world, to see sin and Christ at the same time, or to be penetrated with a lively sense of our desert, and absolute freedom from condemnation; but the more we know of both, the nearer approach we shall make to the state of heaven." Sin and Christ; ill desert and no condemnation; we are sinners and saints all at once! That is the paradox of evangelicalism. The Antinomian and the Perfectionist would abolish the paradox — the one drowning the saint in the sinner, the other concealing the sinner in the saint. We must, says Adam, out of his evangelical consciousness, ever see both members of the paradox clearly and see them whole. And — *solvitur ambulando.* " It is a great paradox, but glorious truth of Christianity," says he,[60] " that a good conscience may consist with a consciousness of evil." Though we can have no satisfaction in ourselves, we may have perfect satisfaction in Christ.

It is clear that " miserable-sinner Christianity " is a Christianity which thinks of pardon as holding the primary place in salvation. To it, sin is in the first instance offence against God, and salvation from sin is therefore in the first instance pardon, first not merely in time but in importance. In this Christianity, accordingly, the sinner turns to God first of all as the pardoning God; and that not as the God who pardons him once and then leaves him to himself, but as the God who steadily preserves the attitude toward him of a pardoning God. It is in this aspect that he thinks primarily of God and

[58] P. 220.   [59] P. 225.   [60] P. 253.

it is on the preservation on God's part of this attitude towards
him that all his hopes of salvation depend. This is because he
looks to God and to God alone for his salvation; and that in
every several step of salvation — since otherwise whatever else
it might be, it would not be salvation. It is, of course, only
from a God whose attitude to the sinner is that of a pardoning God, that saving operations can be hoped. No doubt, if
those transactions which we class together as the processes of
salvation are our own work, we may not have so extreme a
need of a constantly pardoning God. But that is not the point
of view of the "miserable-sinner Christian." He understands
that God alone can save, and he depends on God alone for
salvation; for all of salvation in every step and stage of it. He
is not merely the man then, who emphasizes justification as
the fundamental saving operation; but also the man who
emphasizes the supernaturalness of the whole saving process.
It is all of God; and it is continuously from God throughout the whole process. The "miserable-sinner Christian" insists thus that salvation is accomplished not all at once, but
in all the processes of a growth through an ever advancing
forward movement. It occupies time; it has a beginning and
middle and end. And just because it is thus progressive in its
accomplishment, it is always incomplete — until the end. As
Luther put it, Christians, here below, are not "made," but "in
the making." Things in the making are in the hands of the
Maker, are absolutely dependent on Him, and in their remanent imperfection require His continued pardon as well as
need His continued forming. We cannot outgrow dependence
on the pardoning grace of God, then, so long as the whole
process of our forming is not completed; and we cannot feel
satisfaction with ourselves of course until that process is fully
accomplished. To speak of satisfaction in an incomplete work
is a contradiction in terms. The "miserable-sinner Christian"
accordingly, just as strongly emphasizes the progressiveness of
the saving process and the consequent survival of sin and sinning throughout the whole of its as yet unfinished course, as he
does justification as its foundation stone and its true super-

naturalness throughout. These four articles go together and form the pillars on which the whole structure rests. It is a structure which is adapted to the needs of none but sinners, and which, perhaps, can have no very clear meaning to any but sinners. And this is in reality the sum of the whole matter: "miserable-sinner" Christianity is a Christianity distinctively for sinners. It is fitted to their apprehension as sinners, addressed to their acceptance as sinners, and meets their clamant needs as sinners. The very name which has been given it bears witness to it as such.

Naturally, therefore, to those who are not preoccupied with a sense of their sinfulness, "miserable-sinner Christianity" makes very little appeal. It would indeed be truer to say that it excites in them a positive distaste. It does not seem to them to have any particular fitness for their case, which they very naturally identify with the case of men in general. It appears to them to foster a morbid preoccupation with faults which are in part at least only fancied. It does scant justice, as they think, to the dignity of human nature, with its ethical endowments and capacities for self-improvement. It presents, as they view it, insufficient and ineffective motives for moral effort, and tends therefore to produce weak and dependent characters prone to acquiesce in an imperfect development, merely because they lack the vigor to go forward. Men turn away from it in proportion as they are inclined to put a high estimate on human nature as it manifests itself in the world, and especially upon its moral condition, its moral powers, its present and possible moral achievements. It is a gospel for sinners, and those who do not think of themselves as sinners find no attraction in it. It has accordingly been in every age the shining mark of attack for men of what we commonly speak of as the Rationalistic temper. It should not surprise us, therefore, that in our own age also it should have been made an object of assault by representatives of this general tendency of thought. And it is very natural that it was that arch-Rationalist, Albrecht Ritschl, who, a half century ago, drew it afresh into burning controversy.

On the basis of his Rationalistic construction of Christianity, Ritschl developed a doctrine of "Christian Perfection," in which Christians are represented as working out religious and moral perfection for themselves, by the sheer strength of their own right arm, without any help whatever from God. He developed this doctrine in express antagonism to the Reformation conception of "the miserable sinner," and he did not fail to stud his exposition of it with scornful references to that conception. It was, however, when writing-in a Biblical basis for his doctrine, in the closing pages of the exegetical volume of his great work on "Justification and Reconciliation," [61] that his polemic reached its climax. His leading purpose here is to deprive the Reformation doctrine of the support of Paul, to which it makes its chief appeal. In the teaching of the Reformers, he says, Christians are led to keep alive a sense of dissatisfaction with themselves, in order that they may the more constantly and earnestly look to Christ, and the more utterly rest on His righteousness. Paul, on the contrary, does nothing of the kind. He presents Paul's teaching both in its negative and in its positive aspect. Negatively, says he, Paul knows nothing of any provision for the forgiveness of Christians' sins; positively, he not only exhibits a very healthful satisfaction with his own moral condition, but betrays no tendency to think less well of other Christians than of himself. He did not keep his own sins constantly in mind — if he had any; and he does not teach his converts to keep their sins in mind — though his letters show us that he knew perfectly well that they had a good many. And he never connects the sins of Christians with their justification, after the manner of the Reformers; indeed, he had never reflected on the relation of the justification they had received to their subsequent sins. The justification was there; the sins were there — whenever they were there: Paul never in his thought brought the two into connection. Still less was he of a sad countenance because of these sins — whether his own or others'; on the contrary,

[61] "Die christliche Lehre von der Rechtfertigung und Versöhnung," ii. ed. 1, pp. 363 ff.; ed. 3, 1889, §§ 39 f., pp. 365 ff.

possessed of a consciousness of well-doing in his work, not unbroken sorrow for his sins — of which he betrays not a trace — but satisfaction with his condition as a Christian and with his work as an apostle, is his mood. And Ritschl does not fail to generalize from Paul's case, declaring that every man may and ought to have like Paul the consciousness of good work done — not precisely of a multiplicity of good works, but of a connected life-work that is good; and having that, he may account himself, in the Pauline sense, perfect. This work must of course be proved to be approved; but it may be proved and approved, and form a valid ground of complete satisfaction with ourselves. Satisfaction with our Christian attainments, not constant penitence for our sins — that is the Pauline conception of the Christian life.

As an account of Paul's attitude toward the sins of Christians, this leaves much to be desired. It makes the impression that he is represented as being indifferent to them, although that accords very ill with the contents of his letters. It scarcely adequately represents the preoccupation of these letters with the sins of his converts and their strenuous dealing with them, to say simply that Paul " was of course acquainted with the fact " of the imperfection of his converts.[62] He certainly does not treat the sins of his converts as negligible things. But if we ask, how it is possible that with these sins abounding about him and engaging his unceasing care, he should never have reflected on the relation of his great message of justification by faith to them, and indeed never suggests any relief for them whatever, we obtain no answer from Ritschl. There is, to be sure, a remark dropped [63] — in accordance with one of Ritschl's own doctrinal notions — to the effect that Paul kept " the two points of view, of justification by faith and the bestowment of the divine Spirit on believers, unconfused." But even if this could be pressed into a suggestion that Paul expected the sins of Christians to be eradicated by the Holy Spirit, their guilt would still be left unprovided for: and Paul would not be expected to, and does not, speak of them as if he

[62] As cited, p. 365.   [63] P. 370.

were indifferent to their guilt. Perhaps there is a veiled hint that Christians are to expiate these sins in their own persons at the judgment day. But if so it is not worked out. We are left to the unresolved contradiction that Paul, whose message revolved around the deliverance of believers from their sins, yet looked upon the sins still committed by them as negligible.

And what shall we say of Paul's alleged satisfaction with himself? Of course passages like Rom. vii. 14 ff., Gal. v. 17, in which he probes the human heart, and even uncovers his own soul for us, are set aside. Even when that is done, however, we are far from a Paul who is satisfied with his attainments and indifferent to his shortcomings; though we do have a Paul who rejoices in his salvation. It is the indifference to sin, considered as guilt, inherent in Ritschl's system of teaching, not Paul's, which is really made the basis of judgment. Ritschl wishes to make Paul say in effect that Christians may neglect their sins: it is not their sins but their salvation with which they should be concerned. But Paul will not say that. The most that Ritschl can venture to maintain, with the utmost wrenching of the text, is that Paul does not direct his converts to any remedy for their continued sinning; and that from this we may infer that he did not think it required any remedy — despite his multiplied rebukes of their sins and agonizing warnings against them! And even this he cannot assert of John. John, he allows, does provide a remedy for the sins of Christians, a remedy that directs us to the faithfulness and righteousness of God, the cleansing effect of the sacrificing Christ, the intercession of Christ.[64] John alone, therefore, says Ritschl, occupies the standpoint of the Reformers on this matter.[65] Not quite even John; for though the hard facts of experience had compelled John to modify the optimistic judgment which Paul held concerning Christians, he remained, we are told, essentially of the optimistic party, and could by no means descend to the depths of the Reformers. " John also is far removed from the pessimism with which Luther emphasized the perpetual imperfection and worthlessness (*Werthlosigkeit*) of

[64] P. 373.   [65] P. 372.

the moral activity of Christians. Sinning is for him still always the exception in the Christian life, not the rule and an inevitable fate." [66]

Ritschl's book was published in 1874. But the seed sown in it did not come to its fruitage for a quarter of a century. His representation of the attitude of the New Testament writers to the sins of Christians, did not fail of an immediate echo, of course, here and there. And it was no doubt silently moulding opinion in like-minded circles. It was not until the latter half of the last decade of the century, however, that wide interest was manifested in it. An essay or two appeared on the subject in 1896, and then, in 1897, attention was sharply attracted by an extended discussion of it in a book of unusual vigor both of thought and language written by a young man of twenty-five, just out of the University, Paul Wernle. Wernle came forward as an enthusiastic but independent pupil of Ritschl's. " So far as I see," he says,[67] " Ritschl is the sole theologian who as yet has seriously interested himself in the question of how sin in the life of Christians was thought of and dealt with by the apostles." The time had come, he thought, to go into the matter more thoroughly than Ritschl had been able to do. He devotes to it, therefore, this, his maiden book, in which he endeavors not merely to ground Ritschl's conclusions, but also to give them sharper and more complete expression. The view that he asserts (no other term will meet the case) is that with Paul — it is with Paul alone that the book concerns itself — the Christian is as such altogether done with sins, and is a sinless man, who will appear as such in the rapidly approaching judgment day; [68] and that the Reformation has so far departed

---

[66] P. 378.

[67] " Der Christ und die Sünde bei Paulus," 1897, Preface.

[68] As cited, p. 126. A certain ambiguity attaches to the word " sinless." Even Wernle does not quite venture to assert that Paul supposes himself to be free from a sinful nature; but only from sinful acts. Commenting on Gal. ii. 20, he says he does not fully understand it (p. 19), and then proceeds to say that we cannot on its ground attribute to Paul " a consciousness of sinlessness." He is speaking here of the inner nature, not of external acts, and therefore at once explains his meaning to be that " the feeling of perfection which filled Paul in so high a manner has yet its limitations in the reality of the ' flesh,'

from Pauline Christianity that it has transformed it from a religion of sinlessness into a religion of sinning.[69]

In attaching himself thus closely to Ritschl, and carrying out the suggestions made by Ritschl to their logical conclusions, Wernle perhaps somewhat neglects his chronologically closer predecessors. E. Grafe mildly rebukes him for this.[70] "The ideas brought forward here and acutely grounded," he says, " are, in great part, not altogether new, not so unheard of as the author appears to suppose. He himself recognizes with lively gratitude that A. Ritschl was the first to point energetically to the question under consideration. But other theologians also have already raised it, such as, for example, Schmiedel, Scholz, Karl, Holtzmann." Wernle was not, however, unaware of the existence of these closer predecessors. He even mentions them.[71] He writes, however, clearly, in independence of them, and those of them of any large significance in the development of the controversy antedated the publication of his book by so short an interval, that it is quite possible that it was well advanced to its completion before they became accessible to him. Two of them are of sufficient importance, nevertheless, to require that we shall give some account of them before proceeding to look into Wernle's own book. We refer to W. A. Karl and H. Scholz.

W. A. Karl[72] stands so far outside of the most direct line

---

and the delay of the ' consummation,' that is, of ' the world to come.' " Jacobi ("Neutestamentliche Ethik," 1899, p. 324) appears to have misunderstood him here to be speaking of the perfection of act — which Wernle does attribute to Paul.

[69] As cited, p. 124; cf. p. 106.

[70] *Theologische Literaturzeitung*, xxii. 1897, col. 517.

[71] Scholz, at pp. 11, 19, 53; Karl, at p. 86; Holtzmann at pp. 2, 21, 61, 87. Schmiedel's "Glaube und Dogma beim Apostel Paulus" (*Theologische Zeitschrift aus der Schweitz*, 1893, pp. 211–230), which seems likely to be the work referred to by Grafe, does not appear to be cited by Wernle; but he cites Schmiedel's Commentary on the Epistles to the Corinthians (pp. 48, 71). He cannot be reproached with lack of attention to "the most recent literature."

[72] "Beiträge zum Verständnis der soteriologischen Erfahrungen und Spekulationen des Apostels Paulus," 1896; also, "Johanneische Studien: I. Der erste Johannesbrief," 1898.

of development of the controversy that he does not derive immediately from Ritschl, and does not make it his primary object to validate Ritschl's condemnatory judgment upon the Reformation doctrine of " the miserable sinner," although he will permit as little standing-ground in the New Testament for this doctrine as Ritschl himself. Though he has thus climbed up some other way, however, he nevertheless takes his position at the head of the subsequent development, in so far as he was the first to proclaim Paul " the great idealist," who, in his incurable doctrinairism, asserted the completed sinlessness of Christians in the face of all experience.[73] His first object in his chief work — which he describes in the very military language of " obtaining the mastery of the Pauline soteriology from a new point of attack " — he tells us is to reach a unitary conception of Paul; and he seeks this, according to Wernle,[74] who does not believe that Paul can be unified, " by identifying a series of heterogeneous ideas with one another." " We can learn from this," adds Wernle, " how Paul must probably have begun had he sought after a unitary system — nothing more." This is far higher praise than we ourselves could give to Karl, who seems to us busied with imposing a system of teaching on Paul of which Paul could never have dreamed. In his work on John he proceeds to impose the system which he had already imposed on Paul, on I John also, with the object of showing that the same body of religious conceptions are present in a wider circle than that into which we enter in Paul's letters.

The chief elements of this early Christian conception-world are the idea of a real indwelling of Christ, that is, of the Pneuma (in John also of God) [75] — for the expression of which the preposition " in " forms a short formula — along with the fixed conviction that this indwelling produces in us ethical

---

[73] Cf. H. J. Holtzmann, " Lehrbuch der Neutestamentlichen Theologie," ed. 2, 1911, ii. p. 166, note 3.

[74] " Der Christ und die Sünde bei Paulus," p. 86.

[75] What is new in I John (over against Paul) is the indwelling of God as well as of Christ or the Pneuma (" Johanneische Studien," p. iv.). But this indwelling of God is not an independent indwelling but is through that of Christ (p. 99).

perfection as well as recognition of the Messiahship of Jesus
and also " parrhesistic ecstacy "; and not only guarantees but
is identical with eternal life.[76] What in this view New Testament Christianity consists in is just a mystical transformation,
referred as its cause to the indwelling of the Pneuma-Christos,
and manifesting itself in a new faith, belief in the Messiahship
of Jesus; a new conduct, ethical perfection; and ecstatic phenomena. On all three of these characteristic manifestations of
Christianity Karl lays the greatest stress. Our concernment is,
however, only with the central one. The ethical perfection
affirmed in it is asserted in its fulness. What John teaches, we
are told, is that " all Christians are entirely sinless and therefore pure and righteous as Christ Himself, that is, perfect in
love." [77] This perfection is expounded both in its relation to
forgiveness of which it proves to be the condition, and in its
relation to the indwelling of the Pneuma-Christ of which it is
represented as the immediate and necessary effect. The whole
matter is summed up in a single sentence thus: [78] " If the
Pneuma-Christ dwells in me, I am ethically renewed and thus
'righteous' in God's eyes." This " ethical renewal " which is
conceived as instantaneous and complete, is the ground of our
acceptance as righteous. "We can say briefly," says Karl,[79]
" that the word ' righteousness ' designates the ethical renewal
according to its religious value, according to the value which
it has before God." Or more crisply still,[80] " The ' righteousness
of God ' is ethical perfection."

He deals with the matter from both the objective and the
subjective point of sight. " The forgiveness of sins is accomplished," says he,[81] " with renewal of the whole man. How
would God forgive me and leave me still in my sinful misery?
How can I pardon my enemy and hold him incarcerated in his
prison? Herein I perceive forgiveness, herein it manifests
itself, completes itself, consists — that God sends me the Spirit,
renews me ethically. Our life of salvation forms a unity like all

[76] " Johanneische Studien," pp. 101, 103.   [79] *Ibid.*, p. 30.
[77] *Ibid.*, p. 103.   [80] P. 59.
[78] " Beiträge," p. 48.   [81] P. 71.

that makes claim to the word life. It consists not first in forgiveness, then in a subsequent renewal; but in the renewal I
experience also the forgiveness, and the result is full reconciliation with God." Elsewhere,[82] having declared roundly that "we
feel that our previously committed sins are forgiven only as we
are renewed," he illustrates the deliverance by urging that no
thief will believe his thefts are forgiven so long as he continues
to steal: he must stop stealing before he can have a sense of
forgiveness. No doubt men, both Protestants and Catholics,
pretend that it is otherwise, and imagine themselves to enjoy
forgiveness while they go on sinning. But this imaginary forgiveness — forgiveness to-day, to-morrow new sins — is frankly
imaginary, and we all know it. "Therefore,[83] it will not do to
say, First pardon, then ethical renewal; first the feeling of the
forgiveness of sins, then the purpose of renewal." That is not
what Paul says, and it is fundamentally wrong, as is very
easily seen. For we cannot have forgiveness without repentance; and we cannot repent without experiencing sin as sin;
and we cannot experience sin as sin without having in ourselves its contradictory with which to contrast it — the ethical
ideal. This is apparently supposed to be equivalent to saying
that we must be good before we can be forgiven. On the next
page [84] the sorites is thrown into this form: "This, then, is our
meaning: Only he can receive forgiveness of sins, who is in a
condition to be sensible of their forgiveness. Only he is sensible
of it who knows his sin. Only he knows it who is in grace.
Therefore it is not right to say, First forgiveness of sins, then
renewal; for there is no forgiveness without renewal." These
statements will not be apprehended in their full meaning unless it is understood that the "renewal" spoken of is complete renewal, "ethical perfection," and that the "forgiveness" spoken of is not supposed to accompany but to follow
on it; forgiveness is received only after we are perfect. The
process is accurately outlined as follows: [85] "Through the indwelling of Christ we are ethically renewed, and we become
an ethical new-creation. We fulfil the commandments of God.

[82] P. 51.   [83] P. 52.   [84] P. 53.   [85] P. 30.

Naturally we enter then into a new relation with Him. First, His judgment on us, then naturally His treatment of us, is changed. He esteemed and treated us before as sinners, because that is what we were; He judges and treats us now as 'righteous' because we are now become righteous before Him, that is, we are what He wants us to be."

The central Reformation doctrine is here replaced by its contradictory, and according to this teaching we should not receive forgiveness until we become glorified saints. Paul escapes this result in Karl's exposition of him by representing Christians as becoming ethically perfect immediately on their baptism, and therefore recipients of forgiveness from the inception of their Christian life. " The Apostle," says he,[86] " presupposes and does not doubt that through baptism Christ dwells in Christians. All who are baptized are ' in Christ.' *Thence* comes their sinlessness. . . . A Christian can therefore never sin again." " This indwelling of the Pneuma-Christos, however," he says again,[87] " means for us a complete ethical new-creation. ' If any one is in Christ, he is a new creature; old things have passed away, behold all has become new' (II Cor. v. 17). It cannot be otherwise than that this renewal is a complete one. For Christ, as a unitary (*geschlossene*) personality, cannot dwell in us as something only partial. A personality, a unity, suffers no division. Either we have Him wholly or not at all. If we have Him dwelling in us completely, however, there dwells in us also His moral personality. He shares with us a kind of moral infallibility. A Christian can no longer sin."

On this view all progress in Christian living is excluded; the Christian on baptism is all that he will ever be, at once. " The ethical gifts," says Karl,[88] " are not given in part, or in advancing development, but completely." Taking the matter more broadly, he undertakes to show [89] that no passages exist in Paul which suggest a development. " If Christ dwells in us at all," he says,[90] pressing his *a priori* argument, since He is an indivisible person, " He must be present in us without remainder." The charismata, being wrought by the spirits, may

[86] Pp. 96 f.   [87] P. 14.   [88] P. 24.   [89] Pp. 17 ff.   [90] P. 17.

indeed show themselves in different degrees, and if the moralization of Christians had similarly been committed to the spirits, it too might be progressive. But Paul denies the possibility of ethical development, precisely because it is the product of the indwelling Christ Himself — that it is "once for all settled by the once for all indwelling of the Pneuma-Christos — to which then the idea runs parallel that the ethical renewal, because necessary to salvation, must be always present in perfection." [91] For the Parousia hangs always trembling on the horizon, and the Christian must be always ready.

It is a sufficiently bizarre body of teaching which Karl attributes thus to Paul. And it stands in open contradiction to facts with which, as we all know, Paul was in the most observant contact. This does not deter Karl from attributing it to him. "We must of course ask," he says,[92] "whether these declarations " — the declarations concerning the sinlessness of Christians — " accord with the facts. We should think that, among the Christians of whom he could not deny that they had the Spirit, Paul would have made the experience that not all is gold that glitters, that even in Christians a notable remainder of actual sinning continued. The Corinthians, for example, might have opened his eyes in this matter. How did he adjust himself to the facts of open wickedness which he encountered? Paul never comprehended these facts. They were to him the riddle of all riddles. He stood before them with the toneless, ' Know ye not? ' . . . These are desperate passages, these numerous ' Or are ye ignorant? ' or ' Know ye not? ' sections. In them the complete perplexity of this great idealist comes to expression. . . . It is precisely when he jolts against sins, that he argues that such sins are impossible to Christians. He reasons away theoretically what stands before his eyes as facts." That is to say, that is what must be attributed to Paul on Karl's theory of his teaching. Let us hear him, however, again: [93] "We have seen that Paul's theory does not agree with the facts. It exists merely as a particular notion of the metaphysical nature and mode of existence of the Risen One,

[91] Pp. 26 f.   [92] P. 16.   [93] P. 50.

and the nature of His indwelling. This idea cannot, however,
be harmonized with the facts. That the indwelling of Christ
on the ethical side does not coincide with ecstacy, that one
can in other words be a good ecstatic and a very bad Christian
— this fact Paul did not banish out of the world by denying
it theoretically. Paul may possibly have been religiously,
ethically, psychologically and physically of such a predisposi-
tion that the glory of the Lord expanded in him all at once
like the flaring up of a great light (he himself uses this figure
in II Cor. iv. 6); it was not so with other men and it will not
be so. In his splendid enthusiasm, unselfishness and devotion
to the saving of souls, the Apostle makes on us, to be sure, the
impression that the full moral greatness of Jesus had taken up
its dwelling in him, so that Paul might have justly declared
to his opponents that he *could* no longer do an unworthy
act, because it was Christ who moved him; just as a great
musical genius may assert of himself with our approval that
it is impossible for him to write a single false harmony. But it
was a mistake in Paul to assume the same ethical completeness in every Christian ecstatic. We are not bound by the mistake, because we no longer accept his metaphysical principles.
Paul could not reason otherwise, because according to his assumption Christ dwells in us either altogether or not at all.
We think more spiritually now of the Risen One than Paul
did, and of His indwelling more as psychologically mediated.
And so it is possible for us to speak of a progress in Christ's
indwelling."

The circle of conceptions attributed by Karl to Paul stand
in no more staring contradiction with the facts of life, not
merely open to Paul's observation and thrust violently on his
attention, but copiously remarked upon in every one of his
letters, than they do with his most explicit and most elaborated
teaching. It would serve no good purpose to exhibit this in
detail. It is obvious to every reader of Paul's letters. And it is
enough here simply to point to the two formative conceptions
from which this whole system of teaching attributed to Paul
derives, and each of which stands in diametrical contradiction

to his most fundamental convictions. It is a desperate undertaking to attempt to interpret Paul as basing forgiveness on
acquired character, that is, on works. It is precisely to the destruction of that notion in all of its forms that a large part of his
life-work was devoted. It is equally unwarranted to attribute to
him the idea that renewal is instantaneously complete. That,
too, he explicitly negatives too often for citation. It is not
Paul's but Karl's reasoning, that to have Christ at all we must
have the whole Christ — which is true enough — and that
having the whole Christ is already for Him so fully to have
assimilated our nature to Himself that there remains no further
development possible — which is so far from true that it is
absurd. On these two principles hangs the entire system of
teaching ascribed to Paul. There is no need to say anything
further.

The main purpose of Hermann Scholz, in his winningly
written essay "On the Doctrine of the 'Miserable Sinner,'"[94]
is to justify Ritschl's representation of the essential difference
between the attitudes of Paul and the Reformers towards the
actual Christian life. The Reformers, says Ritschl in effect,
and Scholz after him, concentrate all their attention on the
necessary sinning of Christians, and thus give to the Christian
life the aspect of defeat and consequent endless penitence, and
to Christians themselves the character of merely perpetual
petitioners for pardon. Paul, on the other hand, say they, looks
out rather on the constant conquest of sin by Christians, and
sees the Christian life as an arena of high ethical exertions and
ever increasing ethical advance; while Christians are to him
therefore distinctively the morally strong. If the antithesis
were as here stated, *cadit quaestio:* the Reformers have no
case. But they have been deprived of their case by the removal
from the statement of their position and of that of Paul alike,
of all that each has in common with what is ascribed to the
other. Thus an artificial antagonism has been produced, and,
if you restore to each what has been omitted, the two melt
into one another. The most that can be even plausibly con-

[94] *Zeitschrift für Theologie und Kirche*, vi. 1896, pp. 463–491.

tended is that the emphasis may be thrown by each of them on different elements in the general conception of the Christian life insisted on by both: the Reformers emphasizing rather the constant penitence which belongs to Christians, Paul the constant ethical advance which is achieved by them. Scholz knows this perfectly well; and accordingly, when he comes to contrast the two, with actual appeal to the records, finds some difficulty in making out clearly the contrast between them to which he is committed.

The essay opens with an account of the doctrine of "the miserable sinner" drawn largely from Zinzendorf.[95] The definition put in the forefront [96] very fairly describes it. "The idea of 'the miserable sinner' has from of old been in ecclesiastical use in order to declare the abiding imperfection of the Christian life and the impossibility of our delivering ourselves." There is nothing apparent in that of slackness in moral effort or depression of spirits; only, what one would think a natural and necessary recognition of constant dependence on God and His grace. And Scholz is compelled to admit that in the case at least of Zinzendorf, who is used by him as its chief exemplar, the doctrine did not either inhibit ethical activity or cloud the natural joy of the Christian heart.[97] Nevertheless he deprecates the mood which it fosters. It takes all the pleasure out of our work, he says. It destroys the spur to effort. It substitutes a habit of looking for forgiveness for our actions — and expecting it as a matter of course — for the better habit of anticipating ethical results from them. Who will keep the ideal before his eyes if he knows it to be unattainable and that meanwhile it is enough that he confesses himself a "miserable sinner"? [98] Obviously Scholz has passed here beyond both his definition and his example; he is blackening the conception of "the miserable sinner" by ascribing to it traits not derivable from either.

This is even more clear, when, a little later, repudiating

<hr>

[95] Scholz had himself come out of Moravian circles and it was no doubt natural to him to turn first to Zinzendorf.

[96] P. 463.   [97] P. 465.   [98] P. 472.

the doctrine in the name of Paul, he brings against it his most summarily expressed arraignment.[99] " Accordingly the doctrine of 'the miserable-sinner' applied to the active moral life, whether as object of daily forgiveness, or as occasion for mistrust or indifference towards advance in sanctification, has no support in Paul. Of course Paul derives his Christian state exclusively from the good-pleasure of God. . . . He is never weary of emphasizing that in all the relations of our lives we are dependent on God's grace. . . . He thus represents evangelical Christianity in the whole range of its practical religious motive, as the Reformers have summed it up in the doctrine of justification; and we need not say more on that. But the special reference to daily, active sinning is lacking. In this matter he is interpreted not out of himself, but by means of alien inferences. The preponderant attention given to the doctrine of justification has dulled men's sense for the independent ethics of the Apostle; the necessary emphasizing of the natural inability of man has led to the assertion of an imperfection without measure and without end." Of course again a "miserable-sinner " doctrine such as is here described should be repelled as Scholz repels it: a doctrine which throws such stress on justification that it has lost all sense for moral action; and which has turned our continued imperfections into a " precious doctrine " to be cherished, instead of a state of sin to be striven against. We are *not* to continue in sin; moral effort is *always* demanded; and the recognition of our continued imperfection must operate as the *spur* that at every moment drives us onward. In justice to Scholz it is to be borne in mind, however, that in his own environment there are some who do appear to submerge the moral demand in continued or repeated justification, thus finding the whole meaning of Christianity, formally at least, in justification; and who fancy themselves to be maintaining the Lutheran tradition in so doing.[100] It is less in them, however, than in Scholz's transcript of Paul's teaching that the real " miserable-sinner " doctrine is to be found.

[99] P. 482.
[100] Cf. *The Princeton Theological Review,* xviii. 1920, pp. 98 ff. (i.e. pp. 102 ff. of this volume).

And when Scholz goes on to describe [101] the state of mind which ruled in Paul's day, "the miserable-sinner" finds his own very much reflected in it. " To the generation of that day, nothing was more alien than the passive knowledge of self and of sins, which makes a painful privilege or distressful business of the mournful contemplation of our perpetual imperfection, falls back therewith on the grace of God, and is just as sluggish in forming resolutions as in actual conduct. A high feeling of responsibility teaches us not to permit ourselves to be overcome by evil but to overcome evil with good (Rom. xii. 21). With this earnestness in our sense of duty, the joyful character of Christian morality thoroughly accords. Everything is thrilling with stimulation — the range of the morally attainable expands — the final success is assured." . . . That is just how the "miserable sinner" feels. Does not Scholz himself tell us so of Zinzendorf, his typical example? " That no abatement is suffered in the earnestness of sanctification and moral renewal, or in the comprehensive circle of duties included in them," he says,[102] "may be recognized all the more readily that Zinzendorf's Christocentric ethics, elsewhere made known, is characterized by richness of conception, purity of ideas, and salutary emphasis on the effort after sanctification. To feel ourselves a ' miserable sinner ' has never with him the meaning of renunciation of the ethical task, or even assignment to it of a lower value in comparison with religious experience. It is equally excluded on the other hand that this doctrine issues in a new form of self-torturing after the Pietistic fashion. It is precisely against the self-torturing of that narrow-hearted, unfruitful penitential practice of the dominant Pietism, rich in deceptions and self-deceptions, that Zinzendorf's system is directed with emphasis. He does not wish that a Christian man should be of a sad countenance, with hanging head; he hates a dejected and discontented piety, which comes to nothing but the repetition of its lamentations. He demands and exhibits a joyful Christianity."

Scholz's zeal, it cannot fail to have been perceived, is burning for the ethical character of Christianity, which he wrongly

<hr>

[101] P. 483.   [102] P. 465.

conceives to be brought into jeopardy by the point of view of
" the miserable sinner." Following Ritschl he even places justification and sanctification in contrast with each other as contradictories, of which if one be taken the other must be left.
Paul, says he,[103] never refers sinning Christians to Christ for
forgiveness, but always on the contrary to the Holy Spirit that
they may be girded for the fight. The Christian life is thus to
Scholz, in its very essence, a conflict; and as it is not a hopeless
but an auspicious conflict, it is also a constant advance towards
the good. He stands here on ground diametrically opposite to
that occupied by Karl, who, we will remember, supposes the
Christian from the very beginning perfect, just because recreated by the Holy Spirit. Scholz, on the contrary, teaches an
ethically progressive Christianity, and indeed it is precisely
for this that he is primarily solicitous, as it well became him to
be on the ground of his Ritschlian moralism. " It presupposes a high estimate of the moral powers of the gospel," says
he,[104] praising Paul, " when in general, he does not doubt a
favorable issue of the process depicted, and in particular shuns
employing the divine forgiveness as a means of soothing, to
say nothing of as a motive for correction." Paul, he says, only
incidentally and in particular instances warns against over-
confidence, but on the other hand " puts, fundamentally, in
the first rank growth, advance, progress." " Who will see in
these heroic lines," he cries,[105] " the portrait of ' the miserable
sinner ' " ? No one, of course; but only because, in painting
the figure of the strenuously advancing Christian, common to
both " the miserable-sinner Christianity " and his own fervent
moralism, he has sedulously obliterated the background upon
which it is thrown up in the one, and worked in that which is
appropriate only to the other. The divine forgiveness is not
allowed to serve either for consolation for shortcomings still
remaining or for encouragement for going onward. It is under
the incitement of the gospel proclamation alone, which can
act only " ethically," that is to say in the way of bringing inducements to bear on a free spirit, that the Christian hews his

[103] P. 476.   [104] Pp. 476 f.   [105] P. 477.

way onward in the strength of his own right arm. It is not difficult to see which of these two points of view is Paul's.

It is also easy to see that, although there is no room in Scholz's system for such a perfectionism as Karl teaches, he cherishes nevertheless a very high estimate of human prowess and human achievements, and is eager (with the help of Paul) to set it over against what he conceives to be the depreciatory view of "the miserable sinner." "Paul," says he,[106] after having drawn a picture of the shortcomings of Paul's converts, "has no scruples in designating as saints or sanctified, as the beloved of God, as the body of Christ, the temple of the Holy Ghost, the building of God, a host of men who display these obvious deficiencies in their active moral life." And then he adds: "To such an extent does reflection on God's grace, which enters into the life of believers on the one side as justifying, on the other sanctifying, and forms something new in the core of their nature, preponderate with him, that the empirical failings of moral sinfulness do not come into comparison with it." On the face of it, this statement is a recognition of the continued presence and activity of sin in Christians, and the exaltation of the power of grace — justifying, sanctifying, recreating — over it. The scope of it is merely to show by the titles which he gives them, the honor which Paul put on Christians as subjects of this grace, with a view, naturally, to withdrawing them from the depreciatory judgment supposed to be visited on them (but surely not as subjects of grace) by "miserable-sinner Christianity."

This motive is more clearly manifested, however, in the description of Paul's estimate of his own person. "It may be boldly maintained," we read,[107] "that Paul makes no express use of the predicate miserable sinner for his own person and in view of his daily life of sanctification. He would neither say with Luther, 'for we daily sin much and deserve nothing but punishment'; nor would he with Zinzendorf rest his hope before God's judgment 'on the Ransom alone.' What is to be read in II Tim. iv. 7 is spoken entirely in this sense: I have

[106] Pp. 475 f.   [107] P. 479.

fought the good fight, I have finished the course, I have kept
the faith: henceforth there is laid up for me the crown of
righteousness which the Lord, the righteous Judge will give me
at that day. His good conscience is raised above all doubt,
although with the proviso of humble deference to the final
judgment of God (I Cor. iv. 4; II Cor. i. 12; iv. 2; vi. 3 ff.); he
exhorts the brethren to walk in imitation of him (Phil. iii. 17),
and when he brings into consideration the effect of his vocational activity in his life, and the development of the inner
man, he can only triumphantly declare: We all, with unveiled
face, reflecting as in a mirror the glory of the Lord, are transformed into the same image from glory to glory, as from the
Lord of the Spirit (II Cor. iii. 18)." Shall we say that on this
showing Paul, despite his constant protest, was saved by works,
at least in part — not by " the Ransom alone " ? Shall we say
that according to it, again despite his protest, he had already
attained and was already perfect; and, different in this from
his converts whom he addresses in his letters, had already
fought his fight through to a finish and no longer was ethically
advancing? We can hardly say less than that according to it
Paul felt no lack in himself, no dissatisfaction with his attainments, and saw nothing before him but ever rising stages of
glory. And even that, although overdrawn and, as here put,
misleading, might be allowed to pass without much remark,
except for one thing — the omission of Christ.[108] If we could
look through it and see Christ behind it all; and look into

[108] It may be worth while to remind ourselves that almost as good a case
could be made for Paul's " perfection " before as after his conversion. He never
was a " sinful " man in the coarse sense. " He had been a highly moral Pharisee,
and lived the strictest of lives," as we are reminded by P. Gardner (" The Religious Experience of Saint Paul," 1911, p. 22). He tells us himself that " as
regards the righteousness which was in the law he was blameless." He does not
accuse himself of the vices which he names as having stained the lives of some
of his Gentile converts. If he seems in a passage like Tit. iii. 3 to include himself in the description, may we not say (reasons Gardner) that the " we " is
ambiguous and must we not in any case deny Titus to Paul? And is not Eph.
ii. 3 open to the same doubt? The bearing of the fundamental fact that
Paul was in any case a " good " man ought not to be neglected in interpreting
his words. The alternatives are not either " good " or " wicked," but either
" good " or " perfect."

it and see trustful dependence on Christ transfused through
it all; we might perhaps recognize Paul in it. Otherwise not:
for to him Christ was all in all and only in Christ did he have
any ground, any goal, any hope, any strength. The ground of
Paul's satisfaction was not in himself but in Christ. And that
is precisely what "miserable-sinner Christianity" means. It
does not mean that our attainments in Christian living may not
be great, or that we may not find a legitimate satisfaction in
their greatness. It means, however, that it is only as we penetrate behind these attainments, no matter how great they may
be, to their source in the Redeemer, that we find any solid
ground for satisfaction. And if our attainments meanwhile fall
in any degree short of perfection, the necessity of recourse to
their guarantor in the Redeemer becomes in that degree more
and more poignant. To Paul as to his followers there is no
satisfaction to be had in the contemplation of ourselves, since
our best attainments are imperfect, and since, because they are
experienced as imperfect, they beget in us a divine dissatisfaction which spurs us onward. Here is the paradox of "the miserable-sinner Christianity" — dissatisfaction with self conjoined
with satisfaction with Christ, in whom alone is the promise
and potency of all our possible advance.

It was immediately on the heels of Karl's and Scholz's
essays that Paul Wernle's book [109] appeared, written with such
flare and fury as to compel the attention which they had not
received. Wernle comes forward like Scholz as a follower of
Ritschl,[110] though he was too young to have been his personal
pupil; and he makes it his real task to justify by a detailed
study of Paul's Epistles, or rather of as many of them as he
will allow to Paul,[111] Ritschl's representation that the Reformation doctrine of "the miserable sinner" finds no support

[109] "Der Christ und die Sünde bei Paulus," 1897. The preface is dated
February, 1897. Scholz's essay was printed in the last *Heft* of the *Zeitschrift
für Theologie und Kirche* for 1896 and appeared probably in November. Karl's
dedication is dated January, 1896.

[110] Pp. v.; 3 f.

[111] He uses Thessalonians, Galatians, Corinthians, Romans, Philippians,
and Colossians (omitting Ephesians and the Pastorals). Karl uses only the
four great epistles and Philippians.

for itself whatever in Paul.[112] The method he pursues is that bad one very common among Teutonic investigators, of coming to the subject of study with a hypothesis already in hand, and " verifying " that hypothesis by seeing how far it can be carried through. This method leads inevitably to much twisting and turning in the effort to make the unwilling texts fit into the assumed hypothesis: and no one surely could have given us more twisting and turning than Wernle does. The Paul with which he emerges is far more Karl's Paul than Scholz's: he is indeed substantially the same Paul with Karl's. It is not easy, it is true, to obtain a perfectly unitary picture of him. He is not only presented as with the most brazen impudence asserting as fact what not only he but everybody concerned could not fail to know was not fact — as when he is said to have proclaimed all Christians, the Christians of Corinth and Galatia, for example — free from sin. He is represented also as contradicting himself flatly with the utmost ease and indifference — as when he is said to have taught that Christians are not liable to the judgment and yet to have threatened Christians sharply precisely with this judgment. He is even drawn as so developing from epistle to epistle as, in effect, to be a series of Pauls. He does not get to be really Paul in fact until the sixth chapter of Romans, and then by the third chapter of Colossians he has passed onward into still another Paul. These Pauls are all bound together, it is true, by two common traits which may be supposed to form the fundamental, as well as the abiding, elements of his character. He is always a missionary and always an enthusiast.[113]

[112] This is the way he states his problem in a general and positive form (p. 3): " The problem of the Christian life, as the Reformation raised it, and as Ritschl has posited it afresh, is this: how the Christian can be a joyful child of God, in spite of sin." The Reformation answer, By trusting our sins to Christ, he says is wrong. Paul's answer (as he reads Paul), By the immediate perfecting of the soul in baptism, is also wrong. Ritschl's answer is, By treating sinning as negligible and going on and doing your duty in your station in life. That seems in general Wernle's answer.

[113] Cf. e.g. p. 79: " For the right understanding of the Epistle to the Galatians, two factors are of decisive importance: his theory of the Christian life is the theory of a *missionary;* and its root is *enthusiasm.*"

But he only slowly becomes a moralist. Up to the sixth chapter of Romans he teaches no morality; there he teaches an immediately perfect morality; when we arrive at the third chapter of Colossians he is found teaching a progressive morality. Before the sixth chapter of Romans we have merely the missionary proclaiming justification by faith and leaving it at that; the quickly coming Parousia precludes all question of his converts' sinning — there is not time for sinning; and so they are left to the warmth of their purely religious enthusiasm in view of the rapidly approaching end. In the sixth chapter of Romans the morals of the converts have been taken up among the miraculous gifts of the Spirit; they have been recreated in their baptism into newness of life; henceforth they cannot sin; they are perfect. Yet by the third chapter of Colossians this perfection has been found sufficiently imperfect to admit of further perfecting; the converts must go on if they are to attain perfection.

It is needless to say that Wernle feels little admiration for this Paul, who seems to be ever learning and never coming to the knowledge of the truth. If the main motive of his book is to deprive the Reformers of the support of Paul, this is not because in his own view the support of Paul is of large value. The argument against the Reformers is purely *ad hominem*. If orthodox Protestantism derives comfort from the supposition that it reproduces the teaching of Paul, it must forego that comfort. For himself, however, it would be difficult to determine which Wernle thinks less well of — orthodox Protestantism or Paul. He stands apart from both, and from his superior position of critic speaks biting words of each. Nothing startled his first readers more than the contemptuous tone which he uses towards Paul. The venerable Adolf Hilgenfeld sharply rebukes his " overbearing manner " — with perhaps some increase of the sharpness because of the manifestation of this overbearing manner also toward the Tübingen school.[114] Otto

[114] *Zeitschrift für wissenschaftliche Theologie,* xli. 1898, pp. 161 ff., article "Paulus vor dem Richterstuhle eines Ritschlianers (Paul Wernle)." " The ' hard doctrinairism,' " says Hilgenfeld in closing — referring to Wernle's char-

Lorenz is full of indignation over what he calls Wernle's "swaggering attitude" toward the Apostle.[115] These are not men whom it was easy to shock with criticisms of Paul; both say things about him themselves which shock us. But they could not brook his reduction to a man of whom it could be said that he had no eye for the real, that he dealt in commonplace, high-sounding phrases of whose truth to fact he was indifferent, that when he did not wish to see a thing he did not see it, that he learned nothing from experience, did not in the least bother about the contradictions of fact, but acted steadily on the theory, " It ought to be, therefore it is."

Wernle's primary impulse was derived from what he conceived to be the unwholesome acquiescence of Protestant Christianity in sinning. What he sought in the first instance to do was to show that no warrant for this attitude was supplied by Paul from whom Protestantism felicitated itself that it derived its whole religious character. For Luther and his followers, he asserts,[116] " the riches of God's grace and of the merit of Christ are manifested precisely in the forgiveness of the ever new sins of the Christian." " It is emphasized over and over again," he says, " that the whole glory of the condition of Christians consists in this — that sin no longer condemns, that we can live in grace in spite of sin." The implication is that on the Protestant view, what we receive in Christianity is really license to sin; continuous forgiveness of sins supersedes the necessity of cessation of sinning; and the question that is raised is " whether the moral state of the Christian possesses any importance." It was not Paul who made

---

acterization of Paul's teaching — " is clearly to be recognized not in Paul of Tarsus but in Paul Wernle of Basel, who missed Ritschl's doctrine that we know nothing of sin outside the Christian community in Paul, and cannot find his way in the higher ideas of the Paul who reasons of sin and grace " (p. 171).

[115] *Protestantische Monatshefte,* i. 1897, pp. 376–378, review of Wernle's book. " Is there no other explanation of these contrasting declarations, that the Christian is free from sin and that he is not so, except the crassest self-contradiction? " " Wernle himself knows very well . . . 'that his ideas are carefully ordered and stand in a close inner connection.'" It is in truth not Paul who is self-contradictory, but Wernle himself.

[116] P. 101.

Christianity into this kind of a "sin-religion." It was Augustine who did this; he it was who first put sin and grace over against each other at the heart of Christianity, preoccupied man with the idea of sin, and presented the Christian religion as above everything else a source of consolation for men self-conscious in their sin. With Paul it was a very different story. To speak perfectly frankly Paul shows very little engagement with the subject of sin.[117] In Romans alone among his epistles does he handle the topic theoretically at all. In the other letters even the terms "sin" or "to sin" are near to lacking. In I Corinthians, for instance, the noun "sin" occurs only in three passages in the fifteenth chapter and the verb "to sin" in seven passages scattered through the letter. And yet the congregation at Corinth certainly gave sufficient occasion for speaking of sin, if Paul was specially inclined to speak of it. In Romans sin is, no doubt, made the subject of discussion in chapters i.–iii. vb. and viib. But all these discussions concern the pre-Christian situation, while in Rom. vi. sin is just dismissed altogether from the Christian life, and that in the plainest of words. When Paul thinks of sin, in other words, he is not thinking of Christians; he is thinking of something which Christians put behind them on becoming Christians. Precisely what Christians are is the men who have ceased from sinning; the relation of the condition of sin and the condition of grace is a chronologically successive one. And so, Wernle formally announces as the result of his investigations just this: [118] "That the Christian state has nothing further to do with sin; that the Christian is a sin-free man and shall appear as such before God at the rapidly approaching day of judgment."

The religion of Christians, according to Paul, says Wernle, feeds purely on God and the future. "Forgiveness of sins, comfort for sin — that belongs to the past; the Pneumatic must be done with that."[119] He has secured his forgiveness once for all in the great experience of justification, by which his life has been cut in half. We have already seen Wernle

[117] P. 124.   [118] P. 126.   [119] P. 127.

declaring that "the condition of grace follows the condition of sin in chronological succession." [120] It is precisely here, he says, that Protestantism has deserted Paul; and he expounds the matter at length. "In Protestant orthodoxy," says he,[121] "the relation of the state of grace to the state of sin is no longer conceived as one of succession. The proof of universal sinfulness has for the Lutheran dogmatician the purpose of showing the indispensableness of righteousness by faith for every moment of the life (as is very clearly set forth by Troeltsch, *Vernunft und Offenbarung bei Johann Gerhard und Melanchthon*, pp. 133 ff., 137). We should be conscious of ourselves as sinners in every moment of our Christian life, that we may ever anew feel the need of forgiveness and the imputation of Christ's righteousness. From this point of view the contrast of the 'now time' [in Rom. iii. 26] to the time of the 'sins that are past' is explained by the contrast of the Christian and pre-Christian eras, and the theme treated is why God, and how He, was gracious to the Jews already before Christ's death. For the Christian on the other hand the time of sin altogether coincides with the time of forgiveness; for Christ's death has made it possible for us to receive justification ever afresh, despite our perpetual sin." Having thus described the Protestant view, he now contrasts with it Paul's own. "It is impossible," he says,[122] "to exaggerate the divergence of this Protestant theory from Paul's meaning. Where is there in the whole body of Paul's letters a single passage in which Paul appeals to Christ's death for the continuing sins of Christians? And which letter even in the smallest degree shows the Lutheran mood as to sin and grace? In all — in absolutely all — of them the fundamental idea is this — that sins are gone, that the Christian has them no longer, since he has become a Christian. The 'now time' is precisely the Messianic age; over against it the 'sins that are past' of Rom. iii. 25 are the sins of Christians before their entrance into the community of the Kingdom of God (cf. II Pet. i. 9 and everywhere in the later literature). God has borne with them pa-

[120] P. 126.   [121] P. 94.   [122] Pp. 94 f.

tiently and passed them by up to the forgiveness through Christ's death; now, since those burdened with them have become believers in Christ, He has obliterated them. When we were still sinners, Christ died for us; now, since we have been justified by His blood, we are no longer sinners (Rom. v. [8, 9]). The 'now time' begins historically, it is true, with Christ's death and resurrection, but for every Christian it begins with his entrance into the community, with his justification. Then the sins that are past are washed away; up to then the man was a 'sinner,' now he is that no longer. Precisely from this it is clear that Paul, in Romans too, occupied the standpoint of the missionary, divided the world from the missionary's experience of conversion, and distributed sin and grace respectively to the two halves of life. He did not reflect upon how the Christian receives forgiveness in the state of grace, since he made no such supposition as that the Christian needs forgiveness in the state of grace. In Protestant orthodoxy, on the other hand, the missionary problem has fallen away, and a problem derived from the congregational life has taken its place."

It is not worth while to remark here on the violence done in this passage to Rom. iii. 25, 26. There can be no real question that Paul is distinguishing there between the two dispensations, and makes no reference whatever to the pre- and post-justification experiences of the individual Christian. It is more important at the moment to point out the emphasis with which Wernle confines the effects of justification in Paul's view to the sins committed before it has been received. If sins are committed afterwards, there is no remedy for them in justification. But he is emphatic in declaring that according to Paul, no sins are committed afterwards. The saving effect of justification continues only because Christians, having been completely saved by it once for all, need no further saving. This is how Wernle puts it: [123] " The natural man, whether Jew or Gentile, so long as he operates with works, can only bring down God's wrath on himself, and never finds of himself

[123] Pp. 95 f.

by his own activity the way to the divine salvation. In the
sight of the infallible Judge, as the Scriptures reveal Him, who
can stand before God? When it is a matter of salvation, man
can only lift his eyes and grasp the hand that is held out to
him — that is, believe. Here the missionary question has only
become the occasion for the most profound apprehension of
the religious problem. Had Paul carried this way of thinking
through, his theology would have approached that of the
Reformation, and especially Calvin's (cf. the kindred idea in
Institutes, III, 12) infinitely more closely; for how can a man
who so judges himself before God ever cease to feel himself
a sinner, who is in need of grace? But strange as it may appear
to us, Paul confined this way of thinking to the state of
the natural man, and banished it from the state of Christians. The Christian may boast (Rom. v. 2); he is the bond-
servant of God and of the righteousness (vi. 18, 22); is filled
with the fruit of righteousness (Phil. i. 11). Thus Paul has
remained to the end the missionary, who summons to the
Kingdom of God. The Christian congregations are for him
withdrawn from the world, the children of God who do righteousness. Man sins; the Christian is free from sin after his
justification."

According to this representation the entirety of salvation
not only hangs with Paul on justification, but is accomplished
in justification. But Wernle does not maintain this representation. The insistence that justification affects only the sins
" that are past " in each individual case, made even in this
very passage, renders its maintenance impossible. The life of
the Christian may be consequent on his justification, but it is
also subsequent to it; it may be lived out under the influence
of justification, it is not — and it is one of Wernle's most
peremptory assertions that with Paul it is not — lived out
under the continuous application of justification. Paul, according to him, looks upon justification as cutting the life
into two unrelated halves. What it does is to give the Christian a new start. Its only effect is wholly with the past life.
The future life — what of it? There must be something to be

said of it. We find Wernle accordingly, on an earlier page,[124] representing Protestantism as differing from Paul, precisely in its tendency to look upon justification as the entirety of salvation. Paul, it seems, had something to add to justification. "The missionary preaching of the prevenient grace of God which grants to every believer forgiveness for his previous sins, is what distinguishes Paul from the other apostles, is the peculiarly Pauline element of his theology. But this always remained with him missionary preaching; he did not revert to this side of his gospel with Christians. That great proclamation of faith and forgiveness stands with him at the beginning, and is far from being, as in Protestantism, the sum of his whole religion. Protestantism has thus — by applying this missionary preaching to the community and declaring it the whole of the gospel — passed far beyond Paul." There could not be a more distinct assertion that justification constitutes only a part, perhaps only a small part, of Paul's gospel, and concerns only the initial stage of the Christian life; it was supplemented for those who had experienced justification by an apparently copious and certainly weighty further teaching.

It is not at first apparent, however, what this further gospel for believers as distinguished from unbelievers is. It appears as if in Paul's practice, or at least in his earlier practice, it amounted to nothing more than the preaching of the duty of a moral life and exhortations to those who sinned to repent and put away sin from them. By such a representation the effect of justification is made in the sharpest way possible to be merely the giving to men of a fresh start; and Paul is made, despite the protest of his whole life, to base salvation in the most express manner on faith and works combined, or rather on works alone wrought on the basis of a clean slate attained through faith. Wernle,[125] while declaring that in point of fact Paul did proceed practically on precisely this ground — "separating justification and salvation in such a way that he bases them respectively on different conditions, the one on faith and the other on works" — yet finds himself in difficul-

[124] P. 54.   [125] P. 97.

ties in attributing this dualism to him in theory, because of his "promising salvation to every believer without any supplement or any condition." After all, then, Paul understood himself to promise a complete salvation to that faith by which justification is received; and this is sufficiently close to saying that all salvation was, in one way or another, implied in justification. His gospel was a unit, and it is to misunderstand him to divide it into unrelated or loosely related parts. "Therefore," says Wernle himself,[126] "Paul's theory of justification and salvation, what he called his gospel, is unitary and clear. It is pure proclamation of faith; faith receives salvation as well as justification. It introduces into the community of salvation and guarantees salvation to those that are in it. It needs no supplementing by works; the simple invocation of the name of Jesus at the judgment is enough." But then he adds: "But this theory, this gospel, is not the whole of what Paul taught. We meet with almost nothing of it in the letters to the Corinthians; the fear of God, sanctification, love are demanded by Paul from the believers. In I Cor. x. he directly forbids them to imagine themselves sure of salvation. That the judgment proceeds according to works is also in Rom. xiii. 14 the simple assumption. This contradiction of theory and practice is insoluble."

A consideration portion of Wernle's inability to accredit to Paul a unitary conception of salvation, is due really to his own ingrained dualism, inherited from Ritschl, with regard to justification and ethical renewal. "It is Ritschl's merit," he says,[127] "to have shown that justification has no causal relation to the moral life, that, rather, its consequences are peace with God and firm hope of acceptance at the last judgment, confidence in prayer and trust in God's providence,"[128] — in other words religious, as distinguished from ethical. "The Christian, through justification, receives a right to all the benefits of the Messianic community, without any moral trans-

---

[126] P. 99.
[127] P. 100.
[128] Ritschl, "Rechtfertigung und Versöhnung," ii. pp. 343–355.

formation being derived from it." Clearly this is a profoundly immoral doctrine to attribute to Paul, without anything so far as we have yet seen, to balance it. The Apostle, we have been told, preaches justification by faith alone, and promises to all who exercise this faith salvation in its completeness; and this is defined to include all the benefits of the Messianic community; and yet no moral transformation is included, although moral transformation is prominent among the Messianic promises. Fortunately, the Apostle is not in the least guilty of the immorality charged against him. He not only preaches morality as we have already seen with the utmost vigor, and threatens with the terrors of the judgment all doers of iniquity. He provides for the moral life of his converts as an essential part of his gospel, and that with such fulness that Wernle represents him as providing for their necessary and complete sinlessness.

It is of course the sixth chapter of Romans which comes most pointedly into consideration here; but equally of course not the sixth chapter of Romans alone, or even first. Wernle is himself compelled to admit that in Gal. v. 24 what is taught in Rom. vi. is suggested, and that in I Cor. vi. 11 it is something more than suggested. The latter passage he represents as [129] the first in which Paul gives utterance to this line of thought. " He does not yet attempt," he adds, " to make clear to himself how the sinlessness of Christians follows from the experience of baptism; he has as yet no theory of regeneration. He is merely sure that, through God's grace in baptism, past and present stand in the sharpest contrast, and sin is already broken off." " The Corinthians are to take note that the Christian life is no life at once in sin and grace, that after the once for all and unrepeatable experience of sanctification and justification, sin has simply come to an end." We are astonished, says Wernle, to read such words addressed to the sinful Corinthians. The actual situation, however, could not affect Paul's conviction " of the total separation of the Christian life and the world, and the radical significance of conversion, as he had

[129] Pp. 57 f.

experienced it in himself." " There is already exhibited here that audacious but abstract idealism, which, in the framing of theories, looks on the contradiction of experience with indifference."

As the sixth chapter of Romans itself is approached we are warned to remember the enthusiastic background and to interpret therefore from the eschatological standpoint. And then we have this remarkable passage.[130] " From the other epistles we learned that the problem of the sin of Christians had no existence for Paul whatever because of the hoped-for nearness of the Parousia. This result is not invalidated but sustained by Rom. vi. The problem does no doubt emerge, but only to be simply repelled: 'God forbid.' And the reason is the same as before; we are already living in 'the age to come,' are snatched away from the old world. We are just as certainly risen as Christ is risen; bodily death will surely pass us by. Sin is no longer anything to us, since in the next instant we receive the new sinless body. We can no longer sin, because we are men of the future." We have called this passage remarkable because it is a mass of open contradictions. The problem of sin among Christians is said to have no existence with Paul and to be raised here and argued. It is said that it is raised only to be repelled, and that it is argued to one solution out of a possible many. In point of fact, the passage is not concerned with our bodily death and resurrection and says nothing of the Parousia, whether near or distant; it is " *as if* alive from the dead " that we are to walk (verse 13). So far from sin being no concern of Christians, the passage is written because it is very much their concern. So far from its being impossible for Christians to sin because they are men of the future, the Apostle earnestly exhorts them not to sin, proves that it is grossly inconsistent in them to sin, and in the end promises them freedom from sin as an attainment of the future. From the very first verse of the sixth chapter of Romans two things subversive of Wernle's whole point of view are perfectly plain. First, that Paul is speaking to a constituency among whom sinning has not auto-

[130] P. 103.

matically ceased on their believing. "Are we to *continue* in sin?" he asks of them; and that would not have been a serious question if it had been a matter of course that they had ceased from sinning and could no longer sin. Secondly, that the grace received by them at believing did not have exclusive reference to the sins that were past. Had that been the case it would have been meaningless to ask whether they were to continue in sin that this grace *might abound*. This question involves the understanding that sins committed in the Christian life share in the same grace by which the sins of the pre-Christian life have been cancelled. Paul is contemplating a situation in which not only is it conceived that sins may occur in the life of Christians, but it is understood that, occurring in it, they receive the same treatment as the sins that are past — make drafts on the same grace, and thus "cause that grace to abound."

Wernle approaches the sixth chapter of Romans, then, with a bad case already in hand. We are afraid that we must say that he makes it worse by the way in which he deals with it. It is a typical and also a crucial instance of his mode of expounding Paul, and we shall therefore permit ourselves a considerable quotation from it.

"So far as this theory," says he,[131] speaking of the theory that the Christian on becoming a Christian becomes also automatically sinless, "is simply the expression of the personal enthusiasm of the Apostle, it still has for us something inspiring. He had experienced the radical change; for him conversion was a new creation and resurrection. And the feeling of being wholly free from the past, and of looking solely to the future — yes, even of already living in the future as a new man — was the living impetus of his great work. But the sixth chapter of Romans goes far beyond a mere confession-like expression of pure experience. It flatly asserts for every Christian what he, the Apostle, had himself experienced. After having had so many experiences of sin in the congregations, and in the midst of the very city in which the impossibil-

[131] Pp. 103 ff.

ity of a sin-free Christian life stared him daily in the face, he draws up, on the ground of a series of logical conclusions, the propositions which infer and maintain the sinlessness of Christians. After having as missionary steadily required nothing but faith, he here without more ado assumes that becoming a believer is also a break with sin, a moral renewal. What he had only suggested in Gal. v. 24 — that Christians have crucified their flesh with its passions and lusts — he expands here with manifold repetitions. He even dilates into the hyperbole, that the body of sin of baptized people is done away (vi. 6), that they are no longer in the flesh (vii. 5). No doubt he has not failed to accompany his descriptions of the Christian life always with requirements that Christians are to be what they have become. 'Reckon ye yourselves, therefore, to be dead to sin, but living for God in Christ Jesus. Let not sin therefore reign in your mortal body. Present not your members as weapons of unrighteousness in the service of sin, but present yourselves to God' (vi. 11–13, 19). What was first an experience receives the significance of an eternal obligation. It comes in the end to this — that the Christian *ought* not to give the dominion to sin, that he *ought* to refuse obedience to its lusts; but that is a subsequent supplement to the theory, which was required by observation of the congregations. The theory itself is framed like a law of nature, antecedently to all inquiry. Whether the Christian actually sins no longer — in Thessalonica, Corinth, Galatia, Rome — that gave Paul not a bit of concern. These conclusions which he draws are valid, because the presuppositions — the death of Christ, and so forth — are correct, not because experience is in their favour. As soon as this is overlooked, the whole passage loses its cogency. Paul raises the question whether the Christian still sins.[132] To say merely that it is his duty to serve God, that sin ought not to reign any longer in him, would be no answer at all. Every-

---

[132] It is doubtless unnecessary to point out that this is not the fact. The question Paul raised was not whether the Christian still sins, but whether the Christian ought still to sin. What follows in Wernle's argument is therefore from the start without force.

thing here points to the impossibility of sinning; this is declared in the propositions in the indicative. The answer that
the Christian is free from sin is *first* given. *Afterwards* his duty
is laid on him in the premises. This may no doubt seem to us
very salutary but certainly it ought not to be necessary — if
what is maintained first is true.

"In point of fact, however, the sixth chapter of Romans
yields us nothing but proof that all his experiences in his
congregations taught the Apostle nothing when he had it in
hand to repel an objection that suggested itself against his
theory. Here is pure hard doctrinairism, quite intelligible
from the Apostle's eschatological enthusiasm, but none the less
doctrinairism. Paul does not wish to see the problem of sin in
the life of Christians; therefore it has no existence. At bottom,
despite this theory, he holds the ethical and the religious together only by an assertion. For that (moral) conversion
always and everywhere coincides with becoming a believer, the
Apostle has not shown and experience had already in his time
refuted it. He could not do anything else, however, than tread
this dangerous path of postulations, because he had left the
proclamation of judgment out of his theory. If mere faith saves
and all believers are exempt from the judgment, then the
moral character of religion can be preserved only through the
postulate that justification and regeneration coincide. It remains a postulate which experience seldom verifies; but the
moral earnestness of faith is saved by it. Only by this theory
could Paul meet effectively the valid objections against his
gospel. If the believer is at the same time the regenerated,
then all reproach of moral laxity falls away. Paul is not to
blame for the difficulties and ambiguities which have thus been
imposed on Christian dogmatics. For it was his fixed belief
that the new world would come quickly and these questions
be altogether abrogated. And this would also be the sole decisive reply to the objection of vi. 1 — the destruction of the
world.

"The doctrine of the sin-free life of the Christian is the
most striking difference of the Pauline theology from that of

the Reformation. The Reformers derived from Rom. vi. the obligation to strive after sanctification, the explanation of the
perpetual *mortificatio carnis* and *resurrectio spiritus*. But the
possibility that the Christian can attain to moral perfection in
this life, they denied outright; it has since been characteristic
of sects and fanatics. There lay in this simply a historical necessity. It was out of fanaticism, that is to say, out of fixed belief
in the nearness of the Parousia, that this doctrine was generated in Paul's case too: apart from this it cannot maintain
itself. The break with this postulate of sinlessness was an act
of veracity. Since, however, the Reformers retained the Pauline
formulas, they increased the confusion and called into existence that, in spite of all idealism, false theory of regeneration
in which the question dare not be asked who is regenerate or
when and where the regeneration has taken place. And since,
following in the track of Paul, they have even more completely
set aside the proclamation of the judgment, without having,
in conversion, such a counterweight as Paul had in Rom. vi.,
they have crippled the moral power of the gospel and robbed
themselves of the simplest of the practical motives. Thus they
have at one and the same time advanced beyond Paul to the
gospel of Jesus, and yet remained behind him. It is not to the
sixth chapter of Romans alone that this applies, but it is very
clearly in evidence there."

It is after this absurd fashion that Wernle establishes his
central contention — that Paul teaches that Christians as such
are sinless, and thus stands at the opposite pole from the Reformation doctrine that Christians " sin much every day." It
is very clear from Wernle's own presentation that Paul does
not teach anything of the kind. To attribute it to him is to
bring him into open conflict, not only, as Wernle allows, with
all the facts of his observation — facts, be it noted, known to
us only from his letters — but with all the facts of his letters
as well. The Christians of Paul's letters are not sinless but
" sin much every day." The individual instances of sins
actually committed brought before us here and there in
the letters, although a significant fact, do not constitute the

main fact. The main fact is the pervasive concernment of the
letters with the moral correction and advancement of Christians. The letters are compact of imperatives. We have had
occasion to observe how Wernle attempts to meet the challenge
of these imperatives in the sixth chapter of Romans. It is
scarcely worth while, however, to endeavor to explain away
one here and there. They crowd every epistle; and this general
fact cannot be met by declaring [133] that Paul did not know
the difference between *sein* and *sollen,* so that to this man
who understood how to use the imperative better than anybody else who ever lived, " the difference between the natural
and the ethical, what we are and what we ought to be, was
hidden." After all is said, it remains true that exhortations
like these imply imperfection, effort, growth; and these things
accordingly appear as the characteristic of the Christian life as
it is brought before us in Paul's epistles. F. Winkler observes
quite to the point: [134] " We have no New Testament letter to
which there are not adjoined ethical exhortations, which set
sanctification before us in its progressive nature with the
fundamental tendency of ' Not that I have already attained or
am already made perfect, but I press on after it ' (Phil. iii.
12 ff.)." It is meaningless to attempt to explain away Phil.
iii. 12. The whole New Testament is an extended Phil. iii. 12,
and is based fundamentally on the presupposition that a holy
life is an achievement and is attained by continuous effort, the
goal of which lies ever in the future. Wernle is compelled by
his thesis to contend that nevertheless Paul does not contemplate any growth in the Christian life. The Parousia was immediately impending, says he: there was no time for growth.
The Christian must at all times be already grown, or the
Parousia would catch him unready.

The Parousia thus appears as "in the higher sense the
regulator of the Christian life." [135] " It is clear from this,"
Wernle explains, " how wholly perverse it is to talk of a *process,*

[133] Pp. 59 f.   [135] Pp. 114 f.
[134] " Robert Pearsall Smith und der Perfektionismus," 2tes Tausend,
1915, p. 12.

or a *development,* of the Christian life with Paul. He prescribes
an incessant separation from the world, and renewal of the
mind; he does not rest satisfied with conversion; nevertheless
the conception of development can only by a misunderstanding be introduced into the Pauline ethics. The nearness of the
Parousia leaves no place for it whatever; what it demands is
precisely that we be ready when the Lord comes; it makes it
difficult so much as to set before ourselves a high goal in the
distance. Therefore the ethics of Rom. xii.–xiii. passes no other
judgment on sin than the rest of the letter. Because the idea
of development is wholly absent, there is no place for it here;
there is nothing here but the either — or. He who does evil
incurs the wrath of God, and of His agent the earthly magistracy. The Christian who does evil has nothing else to expect
than the heathen; there is no forgiveness which makes his
position more endurable. The conclusion of chapter xiii. falls
in with this. He who still walks in darkness must perish when
the 'day' appears. The Christian life is a life in the clear
light of the coming day; it has nothing to hide, it needs no
twilight. It is absolutely impossible to have part in Christ and
still to do the pleasure of the flesh; that is, the Christian in
sin has secured no place whatever in the Pauline ethics. By
such a notion it would have lost its very core." No sooner,
however, has Wernle made this strong assertion that the Christian according to Paul is always "finished," always all that he
is to be, so that he may be ready for the Parousia, than he is
compelled by passages like Col. i. 5, Phil. iii. 20 f., Rom. viii.
11 ff., to allow that the Parousia does not find him finished, but
contributes something to his "glory." So long as he lives here
below he has "to contend with the remains of the old world in
his body." [136] This seems to him to be in contradiction with
Paul's general teaching, and he takes refuge as always in
the manifest inconsistency between Paul's teaching as he expounds it and the matter of fact which is always seeking
recognition at his hands: " It remains always a mere assertion
that the Christian has broken once for all with sin; experi-

[136] P. 117.

ence is always compelling corrections, exhortations and threats."

It is not, however, merely by exhortations and threats that Paul deals with the sinning Christians into contact with whom his experience brought him. He tells us of individual cases of sinning Christians with whom he dealt by discipline. They occur from the earliest epistles (II Thess. iii. 12 ff.) on, and in no case is the sin dealt with, even when of the grossest nature (I Cor. v. 5), treated, as Wernle would have us believe Paul must needs look upon it even at its lightest, as destroying the Christian character. In Gal. vi. 1 ff. this practice of discipline is generalized and made a standing Christian duty toward erring brethren, a manifest proof that it was supposed that Christian brethren might err and need to be corrected, as indeed is directly asserted. Wernle's dealing with this passage is very instructive.[137] He begins by declaring that only the lighter sins are contemplated here: an assertion borne out neither by the term employed, nor by the context: surely the nature of the faults intended is intimated in v. 19 ff. He then goes on to say that it is presupposed that at the moment of sinning, even in the case of light faults, the Christian loses the Spirit — an assertion again wholly without warrant from either the text or the context, or rather in complete disaccord with both. The term rendered " restore him " in our English version means just "correct him," " set him right." And the presupposition of the context is that, in the perpetual conflict between the flesh and the Spirit (v. 17), any Christian may, at any time, be overtaken by a fault. Wernle is merely, in the interests of his theory that a Christian cannot sin, representing every Christian that sins as no longer a Christian; and that involves, of course, a repeated passage back and forth from Christianity to the world and back again to Christianity, in the case of one who sins from time to time and is " corrected." Accordingly Wernle writes: " Thus the Christian life falls into a perpetual uncertainty, an eternal falling and rising again; it falls apart into separate pieces which are divided by periods of sin. And

[137] Pp. 75 f.

this cannot possibly be otherwise in an ethical theory based
on the Spirit. This sharp division between sinner and pneumatic draws constantly after it a pulverization of the conception of life, and leaves it dependent on each moment whether
the Christian is a sinner or a pneumatic." The bald assumption which lies at the bottom of such a deliverance — responsible for much of Wernle's false construction of Paul's teaching
— is that queer doctrine argued by Karl, merely assumed by
Wernle, that one must be all a sinner or else all a pneumatic;
that there can be no intermediation between them: in other
words that the Spirit works His effects always instantaneously
complete and never through progressive stages. There is not
only no warrant for this, but it is contradicted on every page
of Paul's letters. Then Wernle remarks that Paul speaks in
this passage no single word of "grace," or "forgiveness" —
any more than in the letters to the Corinthians: "setting
right" — that is what is suitable for the sinner. The remark
is true enough. The sinning Christian needs only to be set right
— because the forgiveness is presupposed; the Christian is
living under a dispensation of forgiveness.

That Paul teaches that Christians are living under a dispensation of forgiveness is, to be sure, precisely what Wernle
is most strenuously denying. Justification, according to his
most insistent contention, has to do in Paul only with past
sins, not future ones; there are no "future sins" — for Christians do not, cannot sin. What Paul says, however, is quite
unamenable to such an interpretation. He does not say, "There
is therefore now no sinning for those in Christ Jesus." He says,
"There is therefore no condemnation to those in Christ Jesus";
and on the face of it this means not that those in Christ Jesus
have received forgiveness for their past sins and must look out
for themselves hereafter; but that those in Christ Jesus live in
an atmosphere of perpetual forgiveness. Wernle, of course, cannot allow that. "The Reformers repeated this sentence often,"
says he; [138] "but always understood it wrongly. They interpreted it as teaching that the Christian is freed from the con-

[138] P. 109.

demnation of the law even though he should sin, because forgiveness becomes his daily portion through his faith in the
vicarious suffering of Christ: in all their sorrow for sin this
clause gave them their surest consolation. Paul, however,
grounds freedom from condemnation on this — that the Christian is freed from the law of sin and death by the law of the
Spirit of life in Christ Jesus; that therefore the demand of the
law is fulfilled in the pneumatic man. The Christian is no
longer condemned because he no longer sins up to the Parousia,
because he is a pneumatic man. Nowhere perhaps does the
difference between the two theories come so clearly to expression as in this verse. For the Reformers, everything turns on
this — that the Christian in spite of his sin, can be a joyful
child of God; for Paul, that he is delivered from his sin and
makes his entrance into his future life. It is always the intensified eschatological expectation which separates Paul from the
Reformers." It ought to be enough to point out that there is
no apparent eschatological reference in Rom. viii. 1, beyond
that which is involved in the very notion of salvation. And it
certainly ought to be enough to point out that in this passage
least of all can Paul be supposed to be teaching the perfection
of Christians. What, at bottom, Wernle makes Paul do here is
to suspend the salvation of Christians on themselves — there
is to be no condemnation only if they cease from sinning and
maintain their sinlessness up to the Parousia. And certainly
it is a desperate expedient to make Paul a patron of a work-
salvation, whether apart from or in conjunction with faith.

As the passage is treated by Wernle, however, as a kind of
crucial one, it may not be amiss to scrutinize its language a
little more closely. Paul says, " There is *therefore* now no condemnation to those in Christ Jesus," and is therefore drawing
an inference from the immediately preceding statement. That
preceding statement is, " Accordingly then the same I with
the mind serve the law of God, with the flesh, however, the
law of sin." That is to say, when Paul says, " There is therefore now no condemnation," he is inferring that there is no
condemnation from his divided mind — not from his wholly

sinless state. This clause also, however, opens with an illative particle, which carries us back to the "O wretched man that I am, who shall deliver me from the body of this death? Thanks be to God, (it is) through Jesus Christ our Lord." And that is the cry wrung from Paul by his analysis of his divided mind. Paul then certainly means to represent the "no condemnation" as his in spite of remaining sin and sinning. When now in the second verse of the eighth chapter he supports his assertion that there is no condemnation to those in Christ Jesus by declaring that "the law of the Spirit of life in Christ Jesus has freed us from the law of sin and death," he is repeating in substance what he had said in the last clause of vii. 25, with a clearer indication of the reason of the effect produced. The reason why his divided mind results in an assurance that there is no condemnation is that its division is not between equal claimants, but that one is wholly preponderant — and the preponderant one is "the Spirit of life in Christ Jesus." His mind is divided only because the Spirit of Christ Jesus has invaded it, and by invading it has freed it from the control of sin. The term employed for "freed" is not the term for "cleansed," but the term for "emancipated": it has slavery, not impurity, for its background. It is bondage to sin which is affirmed to be broken; not cleansing from sin which is affirmed to be effected. This Spirit of Christ, breaking our bondage to sin, we are told, has come to us as the result of a substitutive atonement wrought by Christ in our behalf (viii. 3); and it is explicitly declared that this atonement, condemning sin in the flesh, was "in order to the fulfilling in us of the righteousness of the law" — of "what the law has laid down as its rightful demand: the singular comprehend[ing the] . . . collective (moral) claims of right as a unity" — as H. A. W. Meyer puts it. Thus Paul teaches that our "no condemnation" in spite of our continuing sins is no ministering to evil, but has our fulfilment of the law as its necessary sequence: in other words that our justification not only covers our future as well as our past sins, but has a causal relation to our sanctification. Clearly it is the Reformers, not Wernle, who have understood Paul.

The publication of Wernle's book made something like a sensation. The subject of " the sins of Christians " was brought by it, as Hans Windisch puts it,[139] into "the foreground of theological discussion." The opinions expressed upon the subject were very varied. Many of the same general way of thinking — adherents, as Windisch would put it, of "the critical-scientific theology," or, as Fr. Winkler more distinguishingly describes them,[140] of the "history of religion wing of the modern theology " — rallied to Wernle and indeed formed a party among whom it rapidly became something like a tradition that Paul teaches in one way or another the sinlessness of Christians. Naturally, however, adverse critics were much the more numerous. Paul Feine puts it strongly when he says: [141] " This hypothesis called out almost universal contradiction, which did not remain without influence upon Wernle himself." Whether under the influence of this adverse criticism or not, Wernle did find himself ultimately unable to maintain the positions he had so violently asserted.

Already on the appearance of his " Beginnings of our Religion," [142] the old contentions by which he had startled the world had dropped out of sight. He has a chapter here on " the piety of the community and the piety of Paul himself "; and while the general portrait of Paul which he draws in it is not wholly dissimilar to his former mode of conceiving him, yet there is no repetition of the earlier book's fantastic description of him as a man sinless in his own eyes and attributing a like sinlessness to his converts — asserting it of them, rather, with the fanaticism of a doctrinaire theorist although the actual facts staring him in the face shrieked against his creed. Perhaps the nearest that he comes here to repeating those old assertions is when, in discussing the contrast between sin and grace (on which he says Paul was the first to ground piety), he declares that with Paul " sin and grace " were thought of as

[139] " Taufe und Sünde im ältesten Christentum bis auf Origines," 1908, p. 2.

[140] " Robert Pearsall Smith und der Perfektionismus," ii. 1915, p. 3.

[141] " Theologie des Neuen Testaments," 1910, p. 420, note.

[142] " Die Anfänge unserer Religion," 1901; ed. 2, 1904, pp. 250, 252 f.

successive, not contemporaneous. That is one of his old contentions and may be intended here in the old meaning; but it is
not developed here. Elsewhere he tells us in the old spirit, that,
Paul throwing the emphasis on grace and being fundamentally
a man of feeling, the danger of his point of view was ethical
sloth. This, however, says Wernle now, the Apostle struggled
against with all his might, and then instances the sixth chapter
of Romans in proof. The sixth chapter of Romans appears
here, then, as an effort on Paul's part to ethicize his congregation, and not, as in the former book, primarily as evidence
that, being in his view by necessity of their new birth holy,
they needed no ethicizing. In other words, the imperative reading of this chapter has taken the place of the indicative reading
of it insisted on in the former book.

The changes thus indicated are not small, and they were
to go further. In a few years it came about that Hans Windisch [143] did for Wernle what Wernle had done for Ritschl —
took his rapid sketch, and extended, elaborated, deepened it.
If Wernle's book is to Ritschl's paragraph or two, what, say,
our good right arm is to our little finger, Windisch's treatise is
to Wernle's book what the whole body is to the arm. Wernle
undertook to show that to Paul (the Paul of his special selection of epistles) the Christian is a sin-free man, and he paints
his Paul with a very broad brush. Windisch undertakes to
demonstrate the same proposition for the whole New Testament, and not content with the New Testament pushes his
inquiry back to Ezekiel and forward to Origen, and examines
the whole ground through a microscope. Wernle, looking apparently on Windisch's at once brilliant and labored treatise,
not as the triumphant demonstration but as the *reductio ad
absurdum* of his own thesis, out of which it grew, took occasion
from its publication to sing his *mea culpa*. Paul to him is still
fundamentally the missionary, but he is no longer supposed to
have thought Christians sinless: " Missionaries who imagine
that Christians no longer sin, are sinless men in their actual

[143] As cited.

nature," he now writes,[144] " are not known to history, have
never been known to history. Accordingly, the apparently contradictory theory must be corrected by the practice out of
which it came, and from which it is framed. A purer man of
practice than Paul, there never was; everything with him is
an 'ought' and finds its place under a life-purpose. And thus
the whole theory of sinlessness so far as it is found in him expresses nothing more than the energy of his requirements, and
the radicalness of his faith that his God will fashion something
stable out of the weak, wavering, sinking, hundred-times falling Christians. There is optimism here, of course, not only an
optimism of the backward, but of the forward view, not isolated
from experience, but deeply apprehending the sad experience
and pushing forward to the goal." He still thinks that Paul
believes it *possible* for Christians to become sinless, because
he took such expressions as " new creature," " newborn children," " second birth," seriously. Possible, but by no manner
of means necessary; all of Paul's apparent indicatives are
nothing at bottom but strengthened imperatives; when he
speaks in the sixth of Romans of an inability to sin — that is
but the strongest possible way of saying that it is very improper to sin. He still thinks Paul was no teacher of " miserable-sinner Christianity "; his object was not to comfort men
in their sins but to deliver them from them, and " he believed
in the final purification of his communities for the day of
judgment and in the salvation of all who had been called and
elected even though many would need to pass through hard
judgments." Paul's belief in election, he says, had its roots in
his radical experience of God and possession of God, which
allowed no place for a God who does His work only half way.
Lapses into sin, light or serious, are not excluded by this
mighty faith in election and grace; but grace abounds above
sin and will ultimately have its way. Those that sin Paul does
not comfort by pointing them to grace; that was forbidden
by his whole tendency as a missionary. He warns them of the

[144] *Theologische Literaturzeitung*, xxxiv. 1909, coll. 589 f.

divine judgment and calls them to repentance. They will be punished according to their sins and saved as by fire.

As we read this retractation we are almost tempted to think that Wernle has joined the company of the prophets. The ball which he had set to rolling had to roll very far, however, before it came to rest at this point.

IV

" MISERABLE–SINNER CHRISTIANITY " IN THE HANDS OF THE RATIONALISTS

II. FROM CLEMEN TO PFLEIDERER

" MISERABLE–SINNER CHRISTIANITY " IN THE HANDS OF THE RATIONALISTS

ARTICLE II

FROM CLEMEN TO PFLEIDERER [1]

TWELVE YEARS intervened between Wernle's assault on "miserable-sinner Christianity" and his retractation, and it is necessary to give some account of the course of the debate through these years. We have already intimated that one of the effects of the publication of Wernle's book was to uncover a tendency and to create a party. A tendency was uncovered among adherents of the history-of-religion school to represent Paul as claiming for himself or asserting of all Christians either express sinlessness or something very like it, and this tendency rapidly hardened into a party-contention. Men like E. Grafe, H. J. Holtzmann, Paul Schmiedel, E. Teichmann, A. Jülicher, in reviewing Wernle's book, were quick to express complete or partial agreement with its general position.[2] Carl Clemen was perhaps the first, however, to associate himself with it in an independent discussion.

Before the end of the year Clemen had published the Biblical part of his " Christian Doctrine of Sin " — the only part ever published — and he naturally included in it a section on "the dissemination of sin." [3] It had been the Biblical doctrine from the prophets down, he says, that sin is universal among men. But the possibility of overcoming it was always recognized for the future, and indeed was assumed for the past by

[1] From *The Princeton Theological Review,* xviii. 1920, pp. 399–459.

[2] H. J. Holtzmann, in the " Theologischer Jahresbericht," xvii. 1898, p. 170 and xviii. 1899, p. 187, gives references to the several reviews mentioned.

[3] " Die christliche Lehre von der Sünde: I. Die biblische Lehre," 1897, pp. 100–122.

the Priest Code and the Chronicler, and asserted for the present by Paul [4] — and he might have added also by the other writers of the New Testament since he interprets most of the post-Pauline writers in this sense (Eph. i. 4; iv. 24; v. 1; I Pet. i. 15; Jas. i. 4; I John iii. 6, 9). [5] Paul, he asserts, [6] not only sets himself up as a model and boasts of his work, but " expressly ascribes perfection to himself " — for which assertion Clemen has, however, no better proof than is afforded by the merely general, and perfectly natural, assertions of I Thess. ii. 10; I Cor. iv. 3 f.; II Cor. vi. 3 f. Paul, morever, "nowhere speaks of sins committed by him after his conversion, and nowhere refers to them the sufferings which he so often recalls, as he must have done on his . . . presuppositions, had he been conscious of any guilt whatever." [7] Apparent confessions of imperfections are only apparent — I Cor. xv. 9; II Cor. v. 2 ff.; Rom. viii. 22 f.; Gal. ii. 20.

As for Rom. vii. — of course the presents are presents; we must not make the Apostle a comedian dramatizing a distant past: but it was written in a bad hour, when the Apostle was in a gloomy mood — and therefore when he came to write the eighth chapter afterwards, he wrote in on the margin, " Thanks be to God through Jesus Christ our Lord," words which have crept since into the text. " Looked at as a whole," therefore, Rom. vii. means — what the moderns make it mean; and " in any case it has nothing to say against the freedom of Paul as a Christian in general from any consciousness of sin." [8] As to Phil. iii. 12 ff. it is not to be denied that the efforts to empty it of its confession of imperfection have been imperfectly successful, but "neither is it to be forgotten that we have to do here precisely with the last of Paul's letters to congregations, and that we find in it elsewhere also a different estimate of the Christian life from Paul's earlier one; from it therefore we can draw no conclusions for the earlier period." [9] This comment seems to convey an admission that Paul does not always teach his own sinlessness or that of his converts. In his later epistles,

[4] P. 122.   [6] P. 110.   [8] P. 112.
[5] Pp. 119 ff.   [7] P. 111.   [9] P. 113.

at any rate, he has lost the assurance which is attributed to him on the basis of his earlier ones.[10]

With reference to his converts, it is argued that in presenting himself — and indeed Christ — as their model, Paul recognizes their ability to become like him — and Christ. There are passages, also, it is asserted, in which it is " expressly declared that the Christian no longer sins." [11] Here the stress is laid on I Cor. vi. 11, Rom. v. 6, 8, and especially of course, on Rom. vi. 1 ff.; but also on Gal. iii. 27; v. 24, and finally Col. ii. 11. " In any case," the conclusion runs,[12] " the transformation which has taken place in Christians through baptism is designated here again by so strong an expression, that it appears impossible to reduce it to a reversal merely of the relative strength of good and evil, to a removal of sin from the center to the periphery, to a certain inner separation from sin — as Lütgert [13] has again of late sought to do." " I admit," Clemen adds, " that this explanation " — that is, Lütgert's — " is valid in the case of some passages . . . ; in the most of them, however, Paul speaks so clearly of the overcoming of sin through conversion, that all limitation appears to be excluded." Of course he should have added, " except the limitation of time " — but it is characteristic of this whole school of writers simply to assume that what is done in the matter of cleansing of Christians is done without any expenditure of time whatever, all at once, completely.

Clemen, then, does not press Paul's doctrine of the sinlessness of Christians quite to such extremities as Wernle, and he draws back altogether when it comes to Wernle's estimate of the Apostle himself. So far from an " abstract idealist," " doctrinaire fanatic," who flagrantly contradicts in his teaching both the facts and himself, Paul was, says Clemen, a " sober realist," who kept his eye and hand precisely on the facts.[14] There is one thing, however, he says, which Wernle has

[10] P. 119.   [14] P. 117.
[11] P. 114.
[12] Pp. 116–117.
[13] The reference is to Lütgert, " Sündlosigkeit und Vollkommenheit," 1897, pp. 38 ff.

missed in estimating Paul's dealing with sin in the churches:
when Paul charges his converts with sinning, it was only certain special sins which he ascribes to them, and otherwise he
praises them (I Thess. iv. 9 f.; I Cor. xi. 2, 17). There is no
explanation of this, says Clemen,[15] except that they had really
conquered sin in general, but had not yet learned to look upon
certain particular vices as sins. And here he draws an arrow
from Scholz's quiver. Scholz very strikingly pictures the difficulties which the newly converted heathen must have had in
comprehending the Christian standard of morality. " When we
wonder at the open transgressions of the ten commandments of
which we hear so often in the Pauline epistles," he says, " it
should not be forgotten how new and unaccustomed many of
the ethical requirements were for Christians of heathen origin;
how many hindrances to the purer moral understanding must
have arisen out of the instincts of the past. A just critic should
allow that from such a start a good advance could be recognized in spite of all wavering, falling, holding back. This is
precisely what Paul did." Certainly nothing truer could be
said. But to say this, as Clemen does through Scholz's lips, is
certainly not to say that Paul looked upon his converts as
having already attained the goal. And Clemen himself has
to admit [16] that in his later epistles at least Paul — perhaps
disheartened by the delay of the Parousia — thought of his
converts as only beginners. Their new moral life was not yet
manifest, but still " hidden " with Christ in God (Col. ii. 3);
the good work was only begun in them (Phil. i. 6); Paul himself was only beginning to know the power — it was a moral
power — of Christ's resurrection (Phil. iii. 10). The goal of
blamelessness still stood before them.

What Clemen teaches here, he repeats in the main in his
" Paul, His Life and Works," [17] though not without modifications, the most notable of which is the apparent abandonment
of the distinction between Paul's earlier and later teaching.
Justification, he teaches here, has reference, it is true, only to

---

[15] P. 118.   [17] " Paulus, sein Leben und Wirken," ii. 1904, pp. 98 ff.
[16] P. 119.

past sins, but does not on that account fail of some effect upon the future. Sins committed after we believe, we must ourselves bear the punishment of: therefore believers are sick and die — sometimes suddenly and untimely. But since they are justified, they need not commit these sins; justification brings with it the *possibility* of sanctification. Now, being justified, we can satisfy the claims of God on us, however high they may be. "We can walk in a new, holy life, because we know that our old man is crucified, therefore has paid its penalty; we can fulfill the law, after sin has been judged in the flesh." [18] The consciousness of this was very strong in Paul and he expected it to be present in others in the measure in which "he saw in the Christian in principle the new man, who actually did not sin any more at all." [19] "There was a time when we were weak and sinful, but now we are washed and sanctified, or figuratively expressed, are unleavened, so that there is no longer anything condemnable in us." This is the reason why Paul could speak of the forgiveness of sins as something past; believers have no present sins to be forgiven. Christ's intercession, however, no doubt remains, and will according to Paul's expectation be operative at the last judgment.

There is another side of the matter, however, which must not be overlooked. Although we have become new creatures in Christ, yet this life is still hidden in God. Paul considered himself not yet perfect, and did not need to be taught by experience that others were even less so. We cannot even pray as we ought and need the grace of God always. If in spite of this Paul still looked upon himself and others as without sin, the explanation is doubtless to be found in part in this — "that he did not consider every departure from the highest ideal as sin." [20] It is found further in his expectation of an early end for all things. But what chiefly comes into consideration is that "Paul and the others had with their conversion really broken with sin, so that they feel now bound to the service of

[18] P. 100.
[19] P. 101.
[20] P. 102. He supports himself in this on Gottschick, Jacoby and Titius, as cited elsewhere, and repels Max Meyer's criticism.

righteousness rather than of sin." If they were overtaken by a fault there was the hope that they would be recovered from it, and therefore could still stand unblamable at the Parousia and receive God's praise.

All this is once more said over again with the added clearness suitable to its more popular destination, in Clemen's little handbook which he calls "The Development of the Christian Religion within the New Testament," published in 1908.[21] Here too he begins by pointing out that, according to Paul, "the death of Christ blots out only our *former* sins (Rom. iii. 25) . . . and the judgment at the end of the day proceeds on the ground of *works*." No doubt even then grace will rule, but consider II Cor. v. 10. When Paul says in Rom. viii. 3 that God has judged sin in the flesh *in order that* the righteousness demanded by the law may be fulfiled in us, that proves that reconciliation so little supplants sanctification that it for the first time renders it *possible*. What is meant in Rom. vi. 7 is primarily that each one's own death has an expiatory value; as it is spoken, however, of us who have not died, it means that we are absolved from sin by the death of Jesus, and that carries with it the further idea that we are no longer to serve sin — provided that we carry with us the mediating thought, that we are brought by the forgiveness of sins into a condition in which we need not serve sin. "So long as we still had to bear our guilt, we had always to say in our battle against sin that it was of no avail how much we attained, since the old guilt always remained; now that it is done away, however, now that we have been assured of the grace and love of God, we can for the first time take up the battle against sin, and actually begin a new life." [22]

It is important to pause here to note that the only effect of forgiveness looking to sanctification which Clemen here supposes Paul to intimate, is our enheartening for the conflict with sin. There is nothing intimated as to any interior

---

[21] "Die Entwicklung der christlichen Religion innerhalb des Neuen Testaments," 1908, pp. 88 ff.

[22] P. 89.

effect of the death of Christ in the way of purifying our hearts. We are to sanctify ourselves under the inspiration of our liberation from guilt. The importance of making this clear arises from its connection with what immediately succeeds. For Clemen proceeds at once thus: " Yes, Paul assumes of his congregations that this has already happened with them, that they *have* died to sin (verse 2). Christ died for us, he says (Rom. v. 6), when we *were* still weak or sinners — now therefore we are no longer that: ye *were* slaves of sin, now however ye have become obedient from the heart to the form of teaching which ye received (vi. 17); ye have washed and sanctified yourselves (I Cor. vii. 11) or, figuratively expressed, ye are unleavened (v. 7). And now we understand why Paul, as already said, always relates reconciliation to the past sins, and speaks of forgiveness as something past (Col. iii. 13); the Christian ought actually not to sin any more at all." In this connection the deliverance from sin spoken of in this passage as already received by Christians can scarcely refer to anything more than deliverance from the guilt of sin. Their deliverance from sinning remains their own affair, wrought by their own efforts as a matter of duty under the inspiration of their forgiveness.

The sinlessness of Christians as such has become then only their duty to be sinless. And yet, just after thus explaining that all of a Christian's freedom from sin is the result of a battle against it, in obedience to the exhortations of the gospel, Clemen proceeds, just as if it was otherwise, to ask: But did not Paul have to fight against sin? Is not I Cor. ix. 27 there? And Rom. vii.? Or if Rom. vii. was written in a gloomy hour, is not Phil. iii. 12 there? And is not Paul always exhorting his readers to lay aside their sin? One thing is notable, he says: Paul has nowhere brought the death of Jesus into connection with their later sins, although he does speak once (Rom. viii. 34) of Jesus appearing before God for us. Which merely reminds us again that a Christian, having once been relieved of the burden of his guilt, is then left to take care of his own subsequent sins for himself. Then Clemen closes the dis-

cussion by telling us that we must observe three things,[23] if
we would understand Paul's position. The first of them is that
"conversion was at that time actually the beginning of a new
life; he who attached himself to the Christian community had
actually (at least in principle) broken with his past." The
second of them is that under the influence of his vivid expectation of the rapidly approaching end, "Paul could think that
the change which had taken place in these newly converted
men would protect them altogether from new sins." And the
third of them, which he says is the main one, is that Paul was
filled with "youthful faith in the divine power of the gospel
and knew nothing of the senile conception of Christianity as
'comforted sorrow for sin' (getrösteten Sündenelends)." He
hoped that his congregations would stand unblamable at the
coming of Christ. That is to say, Paul in his youthful fervor
of faith was optimistic.

It seems apparent that in the ten years of his development covered by these three books, the doctrine of the sinless
Christian lost its point in Clemen's thinking. He has abated
nothing, however, of his hatred of "miserable-sinner Christianity." "The senile conception of Christianity, as 'comforted sorrow for sin,'" is a tolerably biting characterization
to make of the type of Christianity which presumably he
identified with the doctrine of the Reformers. The excuse may
justly be offered, no doubt, that if he does identify a Christianity which could be so described with the doctrine of the
Reformers he has fallen into a mistake very prevalent in the
circles in which he moved. And it is to be remembered in his
favor that the intemperance of his language is apparently the
result of a zeal which reflects a robust sense of the duty of
moral effort. If "miserable-sinner Christianity" represents a
tendency to acquiesce in sin and to substitute constantly repeated forgiveness of sins passively accepted as inevitable, for
a manly battle against all sin and a steady advance upward
toward conquest — why, then, it fairly deserves Clemen's
characterization. Clemen has, however, tripped here over that

[23] P. 91.

facile "either — or " which catches the feet of so many of his
fellows. We do not have to choose between the alternatives of
a Christianity of mere ethical effort and a Christianity of passive submission to unopposed sinning. There is something
much better than either, between.

The defence of the Reformers against Wernle's strictures
was undertaken by a fellow Ritschlian, Johannes Gottschick,
in an effective article printed in one of the later numbers of
the *Journal for Theology and Church* for 1897.[24] The thesis of
the article is that the difference, amounting to contrariety,
which Wernle has attempted to establish between the Reformers and Paul, in their attitudes to the Christian life, is
purely imaginary; the Reformers must be recognized as the
continuators of Paulinism. The main contention of Wernle,
says Gottschick, is to the effect that " by maintaining the continuation of sinning in Christians, the Reformation has obliterated Paul's sharp separation between the state of sin and the
state of grace, and — a thing of which Paul knew nothing —
has led the Christian who has to judge himself to be a sinner
to maintain his confidence in God by means of reflection on
forgiveness in Christ; and thus justification becomes to it no
longer a single but an ever-repeated act." [25] Behind this representation, however, lie two questions of fact with reference
to Paul's teaching, simple enough to make it easy to obtain
answers to them: (1) Does the sinner remain a sinner after
justification? (2) Is the Christian's confidence in God based
on his assurance of the forgiveness of his sins in Christ?

To the first of these questions Gottschick's answer is given
in the following passage: [26] " The question is how far the
change which is given for Paul with faith and the reception
of the Spirit reaches. According to Wernle, it produces com-

[24] *Zeitschrift für Theologie und Kirche,* vii. 1897, pp. 398–460, article on
" Paulinismus und Reformation." Compare with it another article by Gottschick in the immediately preceding number of the same magazine (pp. 352–
384) entitled " Propter Christum. Ein Beitrag zum Verständnis der Versöhnungslehre Luthers."

[25] P. 403.

[26] Pp. 414 ff.

plete freedom from sin, and this is to the Apostle characteristic for the nature of the Christian; Paul, it is said, knows no
process, no development of the Christian life, but assumes that
the ideal, that which Christians ought to be, they already are,
and that the Spirit and the Christian state are lost with every
sin, even the lighter ones. The assertion that Paul takes the
ideal for the real and knows no development of the Christian
life is, however, the manifest reverse of the actual state of the
case. In all his letters the advancement, the growth, the
strengthening of the Christian life is an object of the Apostle's
exhortation and prayers." Citing then I Thess. iii. 12; iv. 10;
Phil. i. 11; I Cor. xv. 58; I Thess. iii. 13; II Thess. ii. 17; iii. 3;
I Cor. iv. 16; I Thess. i. 10; II Thess. i. 3; II Cor. x. 10; Col. i.
10, 11; I Cor. xv. 58, Gottschick adds: " These passages already
show that for Paul the Christian life is more than the actualization or even merely authentication of a condition; it is
advance and development in both the extensive and intensive
reference." Wernle, then, he continues, " has not shown that
the Christian is a *sinless* pneumatic. He admits himself that the
Apostle, in his practice, expects the recurrence of sin in the
Christian life; but he contends that in theory he ignores or
even denies it. For this he appeals to I Cor. iii. 4 and Gal. vi. 1,
passages which are to prove that to the Apostle the Christian
loses the Spirit with every sin. But I Cor. iii. 1–4 does not say
that the Corinthians . . . have *lost* what they *possessed* or
have *ceased* to be what they *were;* but that they have *not yet*
attained that stage in life in Christ, in which they should long
have stood. Although according to iii. 16 the Temple of the
Spirit, they are nevertheless not yet 'pneumatics.' To say that
Paul at iii. 16 has already 'forgotten' what he said in iii. 4
is nothing but a bad evasion. In Gal. vi. 1, too, the pneumatics
who are to restore those that stumble — who are regarded as
Christian brothers, just as the dissembling Peter and Barnabas
are in ii. 13 ff. — can be only a particular class of Christians,
and in that case were perhaps distinguished by charismata
and on that account called to such service. . . . The Christian life *cannot* be any longer a life of bold service of sin, and

need not be any longer a life of weak slavery to sin of a will wishing the good. The possibility of individual transgressions lies, nevertheless, according to Gal. vi. 1, near to everyone. What has changed is the *habitus,* the total disposition (*Gesamtcharakter*)." " And now the denial of sin in the Christian life in Rom. vi. 1 ff.! As if what is discussed there were whether in the course of the Christian life, which for Paul is self-evidently directed to a moral end, sin can *occur* — and not rather whether faith in grace and emancipation from the law are a *license* or even an *incitement* to perseverance in sin. And what Paul deduces here is not the impossibility of individual sins, but impulse and power for a life for God and righteousness in contrast with a former service of sin." On Wernle's representation that Paul's passage from the indicative to the imperative in dealing with the relations of Christians to sin — leaping, without any mediation and without noticing it, from the ethics of miracle to the ethics of will — Gottschick remarks: [27] " What appears contradictory to Wernle, is, so far as I see, only that a break with sin in principle can coexist with the necessity of admonition to contend against it, and further, that a consciousness of a nature-like propulsion can coexist with that of a spontaneous effort to obligated ends."

The question raised by Wernle, Why does not the Apostle, in dealing with the sin of Christians, comfort them with reminders of the forgiveness which lies for them in Christ as the Reformers do? would be most directly answered, no doubt, by challenging the fact which is assumed in it. It would be enough to point to a declaration like Rom. viii. 1, which, especially in its context, before and after, cannot possibly be made to refer only to the past sins of Christians, and which very eminently is of the nature of a comforting declaration. Gottschick is not prepared, however, to make just this rejoinder.[28] He prefers

[27] P. 418.
[28] P. 420: " In one matter, to be sure, Wernle is right, although his theory of the sinlessness of the Christian is not discernible in Paul: Paul did not reflect on sin as a thing which adheres to the Christian life permanently and normally and destroys its joyousness, and therefore needs a neutralizer through a continuously renewed forgiveness. And neither did he, when sin encountered

therefore to urge an argument *o concessis*, to the effect — that the forgiving grace of God is certainly everywhere presupposed in Paul.[29] Unrepentant sinners are of course dealt with by efforts to awaken their obtuse consciences and to bring them to repentance. "Even the strictest Protestant would have ventured on no other course." But, in any event, even according to Wernle himself, "faith, baptism, justification, in Paul's sense, ground a religious relation to God with the reversion of salvation." And if justification renders salvation certain, it is absurd to speak of it as absolution only from the sins that are past; it must exercise dominion over the whole life, and, if sins be committed in that life, absolve from them also. " The formula that the preaching of faith, that is, the doctrine of justification, has merely missionary significance, is conversion-theology, is therefore simply untrue, so far as it has the meaning that justification brings something only for entrance into the Christian state and the community, but not for the continuation of the Christian life in the community." [30] Wernle has himself contradicted this representation when he points out that justification guarantees salvation at the judgment-day and assures the enjoyment of future benefits, that it transfers us into the state of the "righteous" and looks therefore not merely backward to the sins that are past but forward to the heritage of the just. And Paul contradicts it no less, in passages like Rom. v. 1–11, viii. 31–39, in which he expounds the significance which being justified has for the

---

him in the community, point the sinners to the grace of God and comfort them with forgiveness. The difference between him and the Reformers appears particularly characteristically in Rom. viii. 1. There is given to him — the connection compels this view — by the experience of emancipation from the law of sin and death by the Spirit of life in Christ, the consciousness of no longer being subject to any sort of ' condemnation ' — whereas the Reformers explain the passage in such a manner that this consciousness is rather to spring from God's objective gracious judgment." Gottschick is confusing here the *proof* of " no condemnation to those in Christ Jesus," with its *ground*; or to speak broadly, assurance with salvation itself. He accordingly shows some hesitation in an attached note.

[29] Pp. 428 ff.

[30] P. 405.

believer, bringing to him triumphant confidence in God, which raises him above the trials and perils of life and assures him of salvation. According to this representation, the faith that justifies must of course remain as the motive-power of the whole life. " Faith, in Paul's sense, which supports itself on the love of God in Christ and longs for and confidently awaits life in the Kingdom of holiness and love, includes inalienably the earnest direction of the will to the moral goal." [31] Justification, however, as Paul conceives it, does not act merely as a powerful incitement to right living; it is also necessarily a constant absolvement for the sins of life. On Wernle's own representation, which allows that the faith that justifies grounds in Paul's view a religious relation with God which involves in it the reversion of salvation, it must have been included in Paul's view that the relation with God was destroyed by every sin, great or small. " Were,[32] however, that the case, all analogy suggests that simple amendment would not be thought enough, but special transactions would be required for atonement. It is only the moralism of the Enlightenment which has allayed the uneasy conscience with mere amendment. There is no trace of anything like this in Paul. Wernle himself, indeed, declares that ' Paul never, it seems, raised the question how the Christian obtains forgiveness when he sins' (p. 69). The presupposition for such an attitude can only be that he and his congregations did not feel such sins as abrogating childship to God. And that finds an excellent explanation precisely from the significance which justification (or its synonyms) has to him for the Christian life — that it does not mean only non-reckoning of past sins, but transference into the positive and perpetual condition of the children of God and heirs of His Kingdom, yes, into the already present enjoyment of its benefits. The objectivity of the electing and calling grace of God, in connection with the assurance of already enjoying a foretaste of a future benefit, accompanying to him the expression of the relatively great transformation, imparted such strength and confidence in God

[31] Pp. 413 f.   [32] P. 429.

and hope in the coming salvation, that it did not waver because of individual defeats in the struggle. And the Apostle's own judgment was not different: he only over and over again inculcated the condition which must be fulfilled, if this hope was not to deceive and this security was to be no fleshly one, — aspiration after what is above, and — the special form which this condition took over against intruding sin, — sincere and earnest repentance. Paul then does not speak of forgiveness as a continuously repeated necessary factor of the Christian life only because justification includes it once for all."

The direct contradiction in which Wernle places Paul and the Reformers in their judgments upon the Christian life — representing the one as looking upon Christians, as such, as sinless and the other as thinking of them, to put it at its height, as " all sin " — has no foundation in fact. The " optimism " ascribed to Paul by Wernle, Gottschick declares, transforms him into a " psychological monstrosity," at once " the incomparable spiritual adviser and the doctrinaire incapable of learning from experience." [33] His letters teach us that he saw things as they were and realized fully all the shortcomings of his Christians. Of course he estimated also at its true value the radical break with sin which they had made, the power they had acquired in their conversion to turn away from the old evil life and to fight their way toward the goal of Christian perfection. And this new life which had come to Christians was as little neglected by Luther as by Paul. Nothing would have shocked Luther more than any suggestion that Christians have obtained nothing by believing, except an ultimate salvation. Sinners they are, who sin daily and need daily forgiveness. But they are not as the sinners of the Gentiles; with them " sin is not as it was before, because its head has been bruised by remission of sin." [34] " They are not made but in the making," [35] but they are in the making; and that means that they are partly made. By both Paul and Luther Chris-

[33] P. 426.
[34] " Opera " (Erlangen ed.), xix. 48 [47 f.], cited by Gottschick, p. 438.
[35] xviii. 188, cited p. 440.

tians were well understood to be in the process of salvation;
but this very fact that they were and were seen to be in the
process of salvation opened the way to the possibility of a
difference in emphasis. How shall the Christian, by nature a
sinner, but now regenerated by the Spirit and justified by faith
and becoming more and more conformed to the image of God's
Son, be characterized? From the remaining sinfulness of his
nature? Or from his new creation and his now waxing holiness?
Insistence on his character as "miserable sinner," may be
exaggerated into denial or neglect of the transformation which
has taken place in him. Insistence on his character as new
creature may be exaggerated into assertion of a perfection
already attained. It would not do Wernle serious injustice to
say that in his view something like these opposite exaggerations was precisely what took place respectively in Paul and
Luther. Gottschick denies that any such exaggeration took
place in the case of either. But he is prepared to admit that a
real difference exists between Paul and Luther, arising from
their throwing their emphasis respectively in the direction of
these two opposite exaggerations.[36] He is prepared to go indeed
further than this, and to attribute to them a far-reaching difference in their definitions of sin. They both have the same
state of things before their eyes, he says,[37] a will energetically
directed to the good, which, however, is still only advancing to
perfection, and still has to contend with the temptations and
antagonisms of sin continuing to work in the periphery of the
personal life, and thus is often betrayed into manifest transgressions. "But they pass very different judgments upon it."
"This is explained," he now goes on to say, "by their applying a different standard of judgment. Paul characterized as
sin in the complex of the Christian life only notorious lapses
into sins of sensuality and selfishness; but on the other hand
he did not so regard lagging in the attainment of extensive and
intensive perfection, in trust in God, in love, in the sanctification of the whole life, which stood for him as the goal of his
Christians, nor yet the struggle with the enticements and

[36] Pp. 438, 448.   [37] Pp. 438–440.

oppositions of the flesh which made themselves felt. Luther on the other hand, with inflexible sternness pled, in opposition to the scholastic theology, for the standpoint that every falling-short precisely of this Pauline ideal of perfection — to cover which he extended the Decalogue — is condemnable sin. . . . Precisely the fact that the Christian life is a striving towards a goal is to him a proof of the continuance of sinfulness in the regenerate."

If this be true, then the Reformation has greatly refined and deepened the Pauline conception of sin. The purpose which Gottschick has in view in affirming its truth is to account for what he conceives (with Wernle) to be the greater preoccupation of the Reformation theology with sin. It has enlarged the conception of sin, he says, and, having enlarged the conception of sin, it has felt the condemnation of sin and the need of forgiveness, if not more strongly, yet more extensively than Paul. Here we have no doubt a difference with Paul, he intimates, but not a contradiction. This is the way he puts it: [38] " That Luther perpetually felt disquieted religiously by the continued conflict with the flesh and by the delay in attaining the ideal of perfection, or let us say of the Christian character, and had need of a counterpoise against this disquiet, is therefore the new thing, as compared with Paul, which remains. That, however, he found the counterpoise in justification for Christ's sake, is not an extension of the meaning given to it by Paul, beyond the beginning of the Christian life to its whole course. In Paul, too, it extends over the whole course of the Christian life; objectively as the basis of the relation of childship to God or of the right to the inheritance of eternal life; and subjectively in the humility with which the moral deliverance leads back to God and in the confidence with which protection from all inimical powers, the fatherly guidance of God, and perfecting from God are expected. It is much rather a logical application (*folgerichtige Anwendung*) of the fundamental religious conception which Paul has formulated in his doctrine of justification, to the changed judgment (required by

[38] Pp. 448 f.

the changed circumstances) on the state of things, that is to say, on the Christian life, fundamentally renewed, it is true, but still striving and growing. It is not in this as if Luther in the forgiveness of the sins of the Christian thought of a continuously repeated forgiveness of individual sins; he was just as conscious as Paul of the unity and completeness of the state of grace, given objectively with justification, or the individual promise of grace, subjectively with faith. Forgiveness, or justification, and also the absolution given in the sacrament of penance, is not with him a dispensation for a *quantum* of sins, but the reception of the *whole person* into the divine favor, the transference of it into the unitary and permanent state of grace. And it is the task of faith to raise itself, in the assurance of this, above the disquiet produced by the painful sense of continued sinfulness and by serious sins, recognized and repented of. It is on the one side included in this that it is not necessary, in the accompanying mood of humble trust in God's grace, to reflect scrupulously on daily sins; and on the other side it is not excluded that the application to particular cases of the justification which governs the whole life — since it is not a logical but an emotional one — will often enough be brought about as the restoration of a shaken or renewed consciousness of God's grace."

Among the writers on the ethics of the New Testament during this period, Hermann Jacoby [39] claims our attention at this point because of the completeness with which he associates himself with Gottschick, and that especially in the dubious views of Paul's conception of sin which we have just seen Gottschick enunciating. He was preceded by F. Mühlau,[40] whose revulsion from Wernle's whole representation was much stronger, and followed after a few years by A. Juncker,[41] writing from a modern point of view but protesting against the representation of Paul which sets his "theory" and "prac-

[39] "Neutestamentliche Ethik," 1899, pp. 320 ff., 396 ff.
[40] "Zur Paulinischen Ethik," in the "Abhandlungen Alex. von Oettingen gewidmet," 1898, pp. 220–244.
[41] "Die Ethik des Apostels Paulus," Erste Hälfte, 1904. Also "Das Gebet bei Paulus," 1905.

tice" in contradictory antagonism, and (following A. Seeberg here) maintaining on somewhat doubtful grounds the use of the Lord's Prayer by Paul and his consequent regular praying for forgiveness of sins. Jacoby, without expressly intimating any exceptions, represents himself as coinciding in Gottschick's results, and having in view for himself only to "supplement" them.[42] His presentation of their common views, however, is so clear and pointed that it will repay us to give them independent attention.

He begins his exposition of Paul's conception of the Christian's relation to sin with two affirmations.[43] The first of them is that "Paul characterizes the path of the Christian's life as a path of victory." "For a true Christian," he affirms, "there can be no such thing as a life in the service of sin; a dominion of sin, a 'reign,' 'rule' of it, is excluded (Rom. vi. 12, 13)." In Paul's view it is the other side of the Christian's "double life" that is to be emphasized; the Christian belongs to what he is to become, not to what he is leaving behind him. This is Jacoby's protest against what he conceives to be the "miserable-sinner" conception of the Christian life. It is the seamy side of the Christian life which is the subject of his own second affirmation. There is such a thing as sinful concupiscence, and it has its allurements: and we are not without a painful sense that there is something in us in sympathy with it. But, and this is the second affirmation, Paul did not range this "under the category of sin," "no consciousness of guilt grew out of the conflict for him." "He did not regard even this condition, bound up with a victorious conflict, though it contradicts the moral ideal, as sin. Falling short of the moral ideal and sinning are by no means the same thing to him. The idea of sin has for him a narrower compass." This is Jacoby's act of adherence to Gottschick's representation as to Paul's undeveloped conception of sin, and he proceeds at once to transcribe approvingly a page of Gottschick's discussion, and then to repeat and enforce its essential elements in his own language.

"No one," he says,[44] "has appreciated like Paul the conflict against the flesh in its entire greatness, in its complete difficulty. He sees the old man in his dreadful form, all the sinful lusts which move in him; he demands with uncompromising decision the putting off of this old man (Col. iii. 5–9); but the experience of these allurements is not to him sin, but suffering, an almost unendurable suffering. Out of this feeling of suffering he exclaims, O wretched man that I am, who shall deliver me out of the body of this death (Rom. vii. 24). A cry of pain out of a past continuing into the present. For though he is removed from the service of sin under the dominion of the law, the condition of suffering, which is connected with the conflict against sin, abides with him. And how far Paul knows himself to be from the goal! He has not yet reached it, he has not yet attained perfection, but with straining strength he hastens toward it. He judges the life of salvation which has been built up in the community, as only a beginning (Phil. i. 6). And it is not without anxiety that Paul looks on the path of conflict, which he must still traverse — on the temptations that he must endure (Phil. iii. 10–14). He has no doubt moreover that on this path ' transgressions ' can occur. No Christian is certain that a temptation may not overcome him; that he may not permit himself to be betrayed by the flesh into a fault (Gal. vi. 1). That declaration of the Apostle's is very important for the understanding of his view of the continuing of sin in Christians. Faults which may be thought of as sins of inadvertance can occur even in a normal Christian life, and in this sense Paul will have adopted the publican's prayer and the fifth petition of the Lord's Prayer. In this consciousness of the danger of temptation, of entanglement with lusts of the flesh, he requires from everyone who will partake of the Lord's Supper that he prove himself (I Cor. xi. 28, 31), and therefore assumes that a Christian will always find himself at his best. Paul was certainly not an enthusiast; the traits of an enthusiast are wrongly attributed to him by Wernle. But in spite of all that, it is true that Paul looked on the course of life of the Christian as a course of victory, sin as a slain foe, and the fundamental tone of his confession forms not the *Kyrie eleison* but *the Hallelujah*. Thus it ought to be in the case of every true Christian. But Paul also knows that reversions to the stage of the old man take place in the Christian life; not mere 'transgressions,' but 'sins' in the full sense of the word. To him, however, this is neither a necessary thing, nor a thing to be universally presupposed of Christians. It nevertheless does actually happen. In that case, however, the Christian state is imperiled, shaken, and must be reëstablished in the same way in which it was first begun — in the way of 'repentance,' of the 'godly sorrow' which saves (II Cor. vii. 9–11)."

According to this representation the Christian is conceived rather as capable of sinning, liable to sin, than as actually a sinner by nature and through the manifestations of that nature also an inevitable sinner in fact. Original sin is reduced to an incitement of sin, a temptation to sinning which may be successfully resisted. Even sins of inadvertence, although liable to occur in all lives, apparently need not occur in any. Sins " in the full sense of the word," we gather, are rare in truly Christian circles; and when they occur are looked upon almost as having destroyed the Christian life itself. No Christian has as yet attained his goal: he is in the making and not made. But an impression is conveyed that the goal set before Christians is in the technical sense of the words very much a " counsel of perfection." Certainly the ideal which Paul held before himself and his converts stretched far above anything he could, on Jacoby's representation, call mere cessation of sinning; and he is almost given the appearance of busying himself not with delivering himself and them from sin but with elevating himself and them into something like supermen — into a region stretching beyond what can be easily spoken of as human. The element of truth in this representation should not blind us to the serious error of it. It is the result of minimizing the amount of sinfulness still clinging to and manifesting itself in the Christian life — original sin, actual sinning — until little room seems to be left for that continued ethical development on which nevertheless Jacoby vigorously insists.

Paul, says Jacoby,[45] when expounding Paul's teaching on
the developing life of the Christian, looks on the path over
which the Christian advances from a two-fold point of view.
"It is on the one hand to him the path of effort, of personal
exertion, of his own achievement. The Apostle considers himself a combatant, who strains every nerve to win the imperishable crown, who practises self-denial to reach the goal (I Cor.
ix. 24–27). He knows that he has not yet scaled the height of
perfection (*Vollendung*), that he does not yet stand at the
goal; but he expends his whole energy upon the effort to win
it; dissatisfied (*nicht befriedigt*) with the moral stage to which
he has attained, he aspires to a higher (Phil. iii. 12–14). Thus
the moral life appears to him a perpetual struggle, which
reaches no end within the limits of earthly existence." There
was another point of view, however, from which he looked on
it. "But he looks at the same moral life," continues Jacoby,
"as a development which takes place with inner necessity, like
an organic process, which, once begun, if it is not arrested by
some accident, reaches the ends by which it is determined by
means of the action of the forces operative in it. The Christian
who sows to the Spirit, that is, lets the Holy Spirit work on him,
follows His incitement . . . reaps of the Spirit eternal life
(Gal. vi. 8)." Because he places himself in the service of God,
a moral quality "forms in him which fashions itself into
'holiness,' and has as its ultimate result eternal life, without
this quality ceasing to be a gift of God's grace; for it is the
grace of God which introduces this ethical power, carries it on,
and brings it to its conclusion (Rom. vi. 22, 23)." The main
point here is clearly and firmly stated: the Christian life is
from the ethical point of view a process, advancing continually to the as yet unattained goal; and this process has a twofold aspect, according as it is viewed from the human side, as
effort, or from the divine side, as re-creation; that is, according
as we think of the exhortation "Work out your own salvation," or of the encouragement "For it is God that worketh
in you."

[45] Pp. 396 f.

Jacoby now proceeds [46] by adducing the great passages II Cor. iii. 18, iv. 16, and warning us at the same time that, in Paul's view, "this constantly advancing procession of glory, which is grounded in childship to God, does not prevent Christians longing for a condition in which the full enjoyment of childship to God shall be possessed by them." "At present," he explains, "their childship to God is attested to them in the purely spiritual sphere, but their sensuous being is a mode of existence which in the burden of the afflictions which fall on them, in the temptations which are connected with it, contradicts the mode of existence which, according to their spiritual nature, they possess as children of God. They therefore long after the redemption of the body, after the resolution of the disharmony between the spiritual and bodily phases of their life, after the harmony in which they shall experience the complete realization of childhood to God (Rom. viii. 23, 30)." In comparison with this future condition, Paul, says Jacoby, speaks of our present blessedness as a "hidden" possession: we are pressing on towards things as yet unseen and only in the beyond shall we attain our end. "Thus the consciousness of Christians is filled with contrasting feelings and exertions. On the one side they are placed in the visible world in which they are to maintain themselves in faithfulness in their calling, in obedience to the ordinances approved by God, in sanctification of life — in a world, over against which they are nevertheless inwardly alien. On the other side they belong to a heavenly world, the powers of which are communicated only to believers, of which we can become aware, on which we lay hold, only by faith." Only when Christ appears out of that "hiddenness" in which He now works, will the inner life of Christians find an outer manifestation corresponding to Him. "To this crisis of their condition they are ripening by inner development, by constant growth, which is conditioned by the knowledge of God (Col. i. 10)."

This essentially true account of Paul's doctrine of the Christian life in the world presents the Christian life as in

[46] P. 397.

its very essence a preparation for the life to come, and as therefore in every respect now incomplete. Paul teaches not a this-world but a next-world Christianity. Everything is begun here; nothing completed. It is of the very essence of his teaching, therefore, that we are not here perfect, that, in our ethical development as well as in every other, we are only in the making. Additional point is given to this by the striking paragraph of Jacoby's discussion in which he raises our eyes from the individual to the Christian community and from the Christian community to the world — which is, after all said, God's world. The consummation of the ethical life, he tells us,[47] is not related by Paul to the individual Christian alone but to the whole Christian community. It too is in a process of God-wrought growth; it too is to be the body of Christ, the temple of the Holy Ghost. But the gaze of the Apostle is not directed to Christ's community, he now adds, as to a holy island in an unbelieving world; but to the entirety of humanity, which is to be taken up into the Kingdom of Christ. Thus, at the end of the road, every enemy shall be seen to be conquered (I Cor. xv. 26, 28), and every tongue shall confess that Jesus Christ is Lord (Phil. ii. 11).

Something like what Jacoby does for Paul is done for John by A. Titius from his more vigorously Ritschlian standpoint.[48] If, according to John, eternal life is already had here and now, it is nevertheless not here and now enjoyed in its completeness. Christianity is with John too a next-world religion: the Christian is in this life in the Way, not at the Goal (cf. the designation of Christianity as the Way in Acts xxiv. 14; xix. 9, 23). And the difference concerns every relation of life, not least the relation of Christians to sin. The world they live in is an evil world, and they are liable to temptation. "They are moreover in need of perennial (*dauernd*) cleansing (John xv. 2; I John iii. 3) and emancipation from the power of sin (John viii. 32); they must ever confess that they have sinned (I John i. 8–10) and are therefore condemned by their hearts

[47] P. 398.
[48] "Die Neutestamentliche Lehre von der Seligkeit," iii. 1900, pp. 17 ff.

(I John iii. 19, 20) and need forgiveness (I John i. 9; ii. 1, 2),"
Paul no doubt presupposes "the perpetual necessity of forgiveness of sin." But John does more than that. He emphasizes
it. "It is emphatically asserted that forgiveness of sins belongs
to the permanent life-conditions of the community, because
the notion that we do not have sin and therefore do not need
forgiveness rests in self-deception and is excluded by God's
Word (I John i. 8, 10; ii. 1b, 12). With this it accords that the
Risen One imparts to His own the right to dispose of the forgiveness of sins; this presupposes the state of forgiveness of
sins as a personal possession of the community (John xx. 23).
But also the particular conditions, under which the individual appropriation of forgiveness of sins stands, are discussed . . ."[49] Nevertheless, says Titius, with all this, there is
a difference between John — and Paul too, who, had he dealt
with these matters as fully as John does, could scarcely have
treated them differently — and Luther. It is a difference only
of degree, it is true — of the degree in which the consciousness
of sin gives its character to the Christian consciousness; but
there is none the less a difference. With John — "perpetual
incompleteness and sin are undoubtedly recognized, but it does
not make the consciousness of a relative Christian perfection
impossible; this appears rather as normal. Thus at I John ii. 1
the sin of the Christian is thought of as exceptional; and in
I John iii. 22, John xv. 7, 8, 16, the joy of prayer is conditioned by the consciousness of fulfilling God's commandment
and of doing what is pleasing to Him."[50] We do not see, however, how Luther can be interpreted as greatly differing from
this: he too supposed the Christian to be a Christian — one
who had broken with sin in principle, and though in perpetual
need of forgiveness, yet also in the perpetual joy of salvation.

In dealing with the portions of the New Testament not
connected by him with the names of Paul and John, Titius
speaks of the emergence in them of a new problem — the problem of the relation of the justification or the forgiveness of sins
obtained in baptism to the sins of Christians.[51] Paul, says he,

[49] P. 44.   [50] P. 45.   [51] Vol. iv. pp. 180 f.

had scarcely related his doctrine of justification to the continuing sin of Christians. The Apocalypse, Acts, Pastoral Epistles
— for he denies these to Paul — give no certain guidance. But,
fortunately, there is the Epistle to the Hebrews. It speaks here
plainly, and speaks strongly, "relating the forgiveness of sins
obtained by Christ to the whole life of Christians." "On the
ground of the divine will, the sanctification of Christians follows from the offering of the body of Jesus Christ once for all;
they are and remain holy (perfect tense, x. 10). By a single act
He has sanctified the people of God (xiii. 12; x. 29; cf. x. 14),
so that now all of them are holy (iii. 1; vi. 10; xiii. 24). The
application to individuals is accomplished by the sprinkling of
their hearts with the blood of Christ, and the washing of
their bodies with pure water, that is, in baptism (x. 22). The
fundamental ideas of the author place beyond doubt that he
considered, not that the forgiveness at baptism required supplementing, but that the forgiveness then once for all given
conveyed a permanent (compare the perfect, 'having been
sprinkled') relation to God not capable of destruction by sin
(within certain limits). This follows already from Christ's
offering taking the place of the entire Old Testament expiatory
system. What distinguishes the New from the Old Covenant
is that God will no longer remember sins and transgressions
(viii. 12; x. 17). From that, Hebrews draws the conclusion that
where such forgiveness is present, the sin-offering no longer is
made (x. 18). Therefore the single sin-offering of Christ expresses God's permanent readiness to forgive, not a once for
all forgiveness, but a permanent relation of forgiveness, arranged once for all in baptism . . ." "It is manifest," Titius
concludes after presenting much further evidence,[52] " that here
for the first time, the fundamental Pauline idea of justification
has received a form, in which it is capable of satisfying the
changed need, the need of assurance of permanent forgiveness
for sin." We gather that on this view the Reformation might
derive its specific quality if not from Paul, yet at least from
the author of the Epistle to the Hebrews.

[52] P. 182.

It is when treating Paul's teaching, however, that Titius formally enters into the controversy as to the sins of Christians.[53] His mode of dealing with it has close affinities with that of Jacoby. He draws back a little, indeed, from Gottschick's and Jacoby's representation that Paul's idea of sinning was a somewhat narrow one. He is willing to allow, it is true, that Paul did not think of every failure of the Christian to correspond with the highest ideal, as sin. But he is quick to warn against attributing to the Apostle the low moral standard which does not look upon the inner contradiction of the flesh as sin, and to insist upon the comprehensive breadth of his recognition of the sinful. It cannot reasonably be denied, he says,[54] that Paul considered every movement of the sensuous desire which runs athwart the divine requirements — and the divine requirements coalesce with him with the " ideal " — to be sinful. The love of our neighbor is not a mere ideal of perfection with him, but a binding requirement of the law, breach of which falls under the curse. Every action which is not accompanied with the religious assurance that it is permissible, or rather is pleasing to God, is branded by him as sin — which certainly shows an exceptional delicacy of moral judgment. Add the sharp contrasts which he draws between Spirit and flesh, light and darkness, righteousness and sin; and observe that, according to him, it is not given to men to stand neutral between these forces, but each one must take one side or the other — surely that has not the appearance of looking only on the grosser failings and faults as sin. In a word, while we need not attribute to Paul " a scrupulous and nervous anxiety of sin-consciousness," we cannot deny to him a clear and accurate and comprehensive sense of sin, as sin. We are not to suppose that he thought highly of the moral life of Christians because he thought lightly of the evil of sin. That way of answering the question raised by Wernle of whether Paul considered Christians sinners is barred.

The question no doubt would already be answered if we could follow Mühlau in considering Rom. vii. 14–25 a transcript

[53] Vol. ii. pp. 76 ff.   [54] P. 81.

of the Christian consciousness. Rejecting that interpretation of this passage does not leave us, however, in doubt as to Paul's attitude towards the Christian life. The Apostle does not look upon the salvation which has become the possession of Christians, although it is in its innermost nature really divine salvation, as, as yet the final salvation, but as incomplete, so that the position of Christians in the world is one not yet worthy of the children of God.[55] Sin and the Spirit can dwell together in the human soul — not the dominion of sin and the dominion of the Spirit, but sin and the Spirit. Neither in the seventh chapter of Romans nor anywhere else does Paul know the notion that the dominion of the Spirit is empirically compatible with the dominion of sin; nowhere does he recognize the alternation of the victorious advance of the Spirit and a retrograde moral movement, as the permanent rule of the Christian life. " But it is not less wrong, it seems to me," continues Titius,[56] " when the theory is ascribed to the Apostle — a thing which A. Ritschl did not do — that the Christian does not sin." Von Soden, Mühlau, Gottschick have brought forward much material to the contrary, but something more may be said. In saying it there is to be emphasized first of all that "not only particular observations, but precisely the whole theory of the Apostle, prove that he considered the life of Christians as sinful." That is already clear from the fact that the present state of Christians has as its characteristic the presence in them of the two opposing factors, the flesh and the Spirit. " It is, however, self-evident that the morality of conflict and strife is not the highest, but that the measure of effort required marks at the same time the measure of power which sin still possesses even in the believer. To attribute to the Apostle the notion that the Christian does not sin, means therefore, to attribute to him that he considers the inner opposition of the flesh as not sin, that is, that he operates with too low a moral standard. If, however, his norm of righteousness consists in perfect love of God and men, then every impulse repugnant to it, even though it be overcome, is sin (Rom. vii. 7); there is, however, no lack in the Christian life also of such impulses proceeding from the flesh (Gal. v. 17; Col. iii. 5); and there can be no lack of them because these lusts are the movements of our flesh (Eph. ii. 3) inseparable from our mortal body (Rom. vi. 12). If then the moral norm is not externalized after a fashion wholly incompatible with Rom. vii. 7 and with the whole inner conception of the Apostle, the fundamental fact of the existence of 'flesh' and 'Spirit' in the Christian life already brings with it the sinfulness of the life." [57] This is far from the only evidence of the fact which Titius produces, but it may serve as a sample of his reasoning. As to Paul himself, it is true that it is not easy to turn up passages in which he ascribes present sins to himself; and he speaks too of Christians, from the point of view of the Spirit which dwells in them, as sinning rather through inadvertence and through weakness than by determinate purpose. They are Christians; and sin is represented by him as an ever more and more disappearing element in the Christian life, and he presupposes a really progressive approach to the ideal of perfection (e.g. Phil. iii. 12 ff.). But sin always forms a limitation to the complete blessedness of the Christian. " And it is only in the resurrection, as the context of Phil. iii. 10–14 shows, that the goal of sinless perfection beckons." [58]

The discussion aroused by Wernle's book was thus obviously moving, from the first, even within the limits of the Ritschlian school, towards the decisive refutation of his central contention — that, according to Paul, Christians do not sin — and the consequent isolation of it as the peculiar property of those extremists who had come now to be known as the history-of-religion school. The impression is even received that, had it not been for their feeling of loyalty to their master, "the regular Ritschlians," if we may so speak of them, might have reached in the process of the discussion an unexceptionable understanding of Paul's view of the Christian life, as the as yet uncompleted product of the combined operation of the forgiving and renewing grace of God; and along with that a

[57] Pp. 81 f.   [58] P. 84.

recognition of the substantial faithfulness of the reproduction of Paul's view in the teaching of the Reformation. Their approximation to such an understanding is at times so close that their assertions of divergences from it strike the reader almost as mere eccentricities. But the main elements of what Ritschl had taught, they continue to repeat up to the end, in one form or another, although, to speak the whole truth, often with more or less complete evacuation of Ritschl's meaning, while yet always making a show of deference to his authority. We have reference here especially to the assertion that Paul does not relate justification to the sins of Christians, and indeed does not regard these sins as very serious, certainly not as serious enough to qualify their sense of their own ethical worth; and that on the other hand, the Reformers so focused attention on the perpetual sinning of Christians as to submerge all sense of or indeed effort after ethical growth in a constant search for forgiveness, so that the entirety of Christian experience was summed up for them in the sense of repeated forgiveness. The debate, of course, did not lie wholly in the hands of the Ritschlians, although they were perhaps the most active parties to it: and it must be confessed that too many of those who entered it with a view to defending the Reformation doctrine, taught, instead, a doctrine which seems to have become traditional in the Lutheran churches as the Reformation doctrine, but which, if conceived as such, would go far towards justifying the Ritschlian strictures upon the teaching of the Reformers.

An example is supplied even by the very carefully guarded discussion of Ernst Cremer.[59] It is Cremer's fundamental postulate that "forgiveness of sins" is "the whole of Christianity, full salvation."[60] And "because the forgiveness of sins is God's whole salvation, perfect salvation, the faith which apprehends it in Christ is perfection."[61] "It becomes intelligible now why faith in Christ is perfection; it is because God's for-

[59] "Über die Christliche Vollkommenheit," 1899. Compare also L. Clasen, *Zeitschrift für Theologie und Kirche*, x. 1900, pp. 439 ff., and Beyreis, *Neue Kirchliche Zeitschrift*, xii. 1901, pp. 507 ff., 621 ff.

[60] P. 40.

[61] P. 21.

giveness of sins is God's whole salvation, in which God's saving will comes to its goal; believers are perfect because Christ's
saving work is perfect." [62] " By the designation of the believer
as perfect, it is emphasized that we have in Christ in the forgiveness of sins all that we need from God." [63] The terms perfection, perfect, are, of course, used in these declarations in a
non-moral sense. We read: [64] " The idea that under Christian
perfection the final result of the so-called process of sanctification is to be understood has no point of attachment in the New
Testament." Again: " The perfection of the Christian is nowhere represented as . . . the goal that is to be attained by
him "; " it is not a particular stage of the Christian life."

If this be so, naturally the question becomes very pressing.
In what relation does the moral life stand to this experience of
forgiveness through faith? Cremer raises the question in the
first instance in this form: [65] " If the Christian has his perfection in faith in Christ, and that, just because he has in Him
forgiveness of sins — if forgiveness of sins is the whole of salvation — in what interest can then the moral requirement be
made seriously effective? " In reply he tells us that " the moral
relation cannot be so separated from the religious, from faith,
that a faith would be conceivable which does not at the same
time postulate and bring with it a moral relation ": " faith
in Christ is not possible without our attitude to the world
being decisively influenced." It is absurd to talk of going to
Christ for forgiveness of sin without a realization of the evil
that sin is, and a renunciation of it. The one is involved in
the other. That is all true enough, but it leaves us only greatly
desiring to be free from sin, without telling how our deliverance
from it may be accomplished. We are carried a step further,
however, when we are told that [66] " the salvation present in
Christ is of such a nature that it cannot be accepted in faith
except with such a transformation." But we will let Cremer
himself expound why and how this is so: " Even the minimum
of religious understanding is lacking when forgiveness of sins

[62] P. 21.   [64] P. 37.   [66] Pp. 22–23.
[63] P. 22.   [65] P. 22.

becomes suspected of being a dispensation from the moral requirement. It is a favorite notion — especially where moral perfection, or at least completeness, 'sanctification,' is demanded
with emphasis — that on deliverance from the guilt of sin,
deliverance from its power *follows* as a *second* divine gift and
human task. . . . The power of sin cannot be more strongly
experienced than when sin is experienced as guilt. Precisely
in the sense of guilt does sin exercise its enslaving dominion,
and when the sense of guilt is lacking sin is not felt as an
enslaving power and therefore the power of sin is broken when
guilt is removed. Forgiveness of sins and the gift of the Holy
Spirit are therefore one divine act; God forgives sins when
(*indem*) He gives the Spirit; the forgiveness of sins is in
itself the establishment of communion with God; a forgiveness which was not the establishment of communion with God,
gift of the Spirit, would be no forgiveness. Because, however,
forgiveness is the gift of the Spirit, essentially the entirety
of salvation is to be recognized in it. In one divine act the
power of sin is, therefore, broken along with the removal of its
guilt; in faith in the forgiveness of sins morality is inseparably
bound to religion and morality proceeds inseparably out of
religion. The establishment of the relation to God is the
removal of the relation to sin; in the instant in which the
man is bound to God, he is no longer bound to sin; the forgiveness of sins means that the one power replaces the other;
if sin has power over men, so also has God, who takes man
into fellowship with Himself; power which becomes active
in the same instant in which man yields himself to Him. In
turning to God, the relation to sin is immediately broken;
compare the exposition of Paul in Rom. vi." . . . and so
forth.

The scope of this exposition is to the effect that forgiveness of sins and the gift of the Holy Spirit as a sanctifying
power, are received by the same act of faith. And that is the
burden of Cremer's doctrine of the Christian life. "No doubt
when faith is preached," he says again,[67] "sanctification . . .

[67] P. 40.

is preached; for faith which delivers from sin is extinguished if it does not avouch its possession. . . . The preaching of forgiveness and it alone is itself the preaching of sanctification." All this is true, and is important, and as far as it goes is well put. What is lacking in it is any real explanation of how the moral life proceeds out of forgiveness, how justification necessarily carries with it sanctification. We are told that the two go together and must go together: we are told that the same faith receives both: we are told that the new relation to God involved in faith brings renewal with it, with inevitable certainty. But we are not shown how the two are immediately connected inwardly. They find their union apparently in their common relation to faith, or in their common source in a reconciled God, but not at all in an immediate relation to each other. And therefore Cremer's insistence that the "forgiveness of sins" is "the whole of Christianity, full salvation" remains unjustified, and provokes contradiction, as, despite his asseverations of the inseparable connection — involution, if you will — of moral renewal with it, leaving the ethical side of the Christian life inadequately recognized.

The tendency which seems to be guardedly suggested by Cremer comes to its full expression in an interesting article by Karl Schmidt published in the *New Church Journal* in 1905.[68] If we read him aright, sanctification with Schmidt consists really in a constantly repeated, or renewed justification; so that it might be said with the fullest meaning that in justification the entirety of sanctification is included. His apparent meaning is not merely that justifying faith brings sanctification also with it, which would be true; but that it brings complete sanctification — perfection — with it all at once. Thus every justified man is perfect; and, the extremes meeting, Schmidt and Wernle might seem to clasp hands. But Schmidt explains that he means this only "in principle" — a phrase very *caviare* to the whole Ritschlian circle. The justified man is sanctified only in beginnings, which will however certainly complete themselves in the end — provided of course that he stays justified. For he may sin; but if he sins that is because his faith has failed; and, faith failing, so does his justification. The only remedy in this condition is to refresh, renew, regain faith. Faith may, no doubt, fail not only measurably but entirely; and then we have fallen wholly out of grace. In every man without exception, however, it fails measurably over and over again. The life of the Christian is conceived thus as a continuous series of failures and renewals of faith — that is to say, of justification, and also of sanctification. This gives to it the aspect of alternations of complete sinfulness and complete sanctification; and in these alternations the Christian life is lived out. In this construction certainly the necessity of moral effort has dropped out of sight, and no place seems to be left for moral growth. Whatever morality the Christian has, comes to him without effort; and his life-history is marked, not by increasing firmness of moral purpose and strength of moral energy, to say nothing of compass of moral attainments, but only by the aimless and endless systole and diastole of his ethical vicissitudes.

If the discussions of Cremer and Schmidt take a somewhat wide range, and touch on the specific controversy about "miserable-sinner Christianity" only somewhat incidentally, the two dissertations of the Pomeranian pastor, Max Meyer, have no other reason for their existence than that controversy affords them, and make it their sole aim to test the exegetical basis and to review the conclusions of Wernle and his coadjutors. The first of these dissertations, which bears the title of "The Christian's Sin according to Paul's Letters to the Corinthians and Romans," [69] confines itself strictly to the testimony of these Epistles to Paul's attitude to the sins of Christians in general. The special question of what rôle sin plays in the life of the Apostle himself is reserved for the second dissertation, which is entitled, "The Apostle Paul as Miserable Sinner." [70] The two together thus cover the ground, and seek by

[69] "Die Sünde des Christen nach Pauli Briefen an die Korinther und Römer," 1902.

[70] "Der Apostel Paulus als armer Sünder. Ein Beitrag zur paulinischen Hamartologie," 1903.

an independent examination of the sources to reach a well-founded judgment on Paul's attitude towards sin in the life of Christians. The three things in the Christian life, as reflected to us from the pages of the Epistles to the Corinthians and Romans, on which Meyer lays stress, are its principial break with sin, its continued involvement with sin, and its progressive conquest of sin. " The Christian life," says he, therefore, is " at once both a being and a becoming, a possessing and an acquiring, an enjoying and a longing, a jubilation and a groaning." [71] The principial break with sin which has taken place is not undervalued. It is even said that " if sinning once belonged to the nature of man, it has become for the Christian henceforth unnatural." [72] But neither is it obscured that the break with sin is as yet only principial. " The new creature is nevertheless only one in principle, because one in the making." [73] " The new life is an inner, a central life, that does not yet dominate in its birth the periphery of the old life. . . . The Christian life needs therefore development in the periphery and is accordingly thought of by Paul as a process of completing and unfolding." [74] In expounding the sixth chapter of Romans, Meyer insists that it deals not with an instantaneous transaction merely but with a continuous activity. The question to which it is an answer is, Shall we continue in sin? The thing deprecated is that we may live in sin. The thing approved is that we should walk in newness of life. The passage of the discussion from the indicative to the imperative presents therefore no difficulty. " The new life is thus laid upon the baptized person as his continuous task. . . . And herein it is plainly declared that Paul looked upon the new life of the Christian as an uninterrupted process, proceeding on the ground of a single inner fact." [75]

[71] " Die Sünde des Christen," p. 77.

[72] P. 78, appealing for support to Lütgert, " Sündlosigkeit und Vollkommenheit," 1897, pp. 38 ff., and Beck, " Vorlesungen über christliche Ethik," 1892, i. pp. 244–252.

[73] P. 76.

[74] P. 77.

[75] Pp. 64 f.

The Christian life is therefore not merely a gift but also a task, not merely *Gabe,* but *Aufgabe.* "What has come into existence as a once for all determinate experience at the entrance into the Christian state, is to pervade the whole Christian life as a perpetual task." [76] The whole Christian life: there is even a hint that the Parousia itself will not find the task completed. At least, when in commenting on I Cor. i. 8 Meyer declares, "That, then, the moral development of the Christian has its crown in sinlessness at the day of the Parousia, the Apostle has not taught," [77] he does not make it clear that he has that passage only in mind. On the contrary, there is some appearance that he intends the declaration, though occasioned by the exposition of this particular passage, to have general validity. The remark is directed against Gottschick's assertion [78] that the only difference between Paul and Luther in the matter of the Christian's growth reduces to this: "that Paul hopes for the presence of perfection at the judgment day, while Luther, who understands perfection in the absolute sense, holds it to be unattainable. . . ." There underlies this assertion Gottschick's notion that Paul does not treat anything as sin among Christians except gross vices, while Luther has attained to a deeper and more refined sense of what is sinful. This notion is undoubtedly wrong. But Meyer is as certainly wrong when he seeks to remove the difference asserted to exist between Luther and Paul with reference to the state of Christians at the Parousia, by denying that Paul expected Christians to be perfect "in the day of our Lord Jesus Christ." Such an expectation, he says, "is already excluded by I Cor. vi., where Paul has recognized sin as an inevitable evil, under which the Christian community suffers." The reference here appears to be wrong, but it is the general assertion founded on it which interests us. According to it, it is Paul's doctrine that sin is an unfailing evil from which Christians suffer: it is a thing that stays by them always, from which they will never be free. If, when they stand before the Judge at the last day they are

[76] P. 77.   [78] *Zeitschrift für Theologie und Kirche,* vii. 1897, p. 446.
[77] P. 47.

" unreprovable," that is only, now Meyer continues, because they stand there in Christ Jesus and God is faithful and will fulfil the promise of their call. This remark is just, and it is no doubt a just exposition of I Cor. i. 8. But it does not follow that Paul does not teach that the conformation of Christians to their Lord, however slowly it may have proceeded, will be completed at the last day. This he teaches elsewhere with great clearness (e.g. I Thess. iii. 13; v. 23), and it is a part of his general system, the absence of which would throw it into confusion.[79]

We have laid some stress on Meyer's representation that in Paul's teaching sin is "an inevitable evil" (*unausbleibliches Übel*) in the Christian life, because he also represents that, according to Paul, sinlessness is possible to Christians. Possible, not actual; but though not actual, yet possible. Before that great experience which we call conversion, a man is under the necessity of sinning: after it, "the Christian need sin no more."[80] "The possibility of not permitting sin to occur, is, of course, present for the pneumatic."[81] Expounding Rom. vi. 12, Meyer says: "The ' obeying the lusts' need no longer occur in the Christian life. The Apostle does not mean by this, however, ' that the Christian leads a life no longer accessible to any sin' (Holtzmann). The *non posse non peccare* has no doubt ceased for the Christian, but it has not therefore already come with him to the *non posse peccare*, but at most to the *posse non peccare*."[82] We would gladly lay hold of the qualification " at most " as exhibiting at least a certain hesitation in Meyer's mind: but we fear he will not permit us to do so. He means to assert sinlessness to be possible to Christians, although illustrated by no single example. Or rather, as we shall soon find that we have to say, by only a single example. For Meyer finds

[79] Cf. the good note by T. C. Edwards on I Cor. 1. 8: " It by no means implies that a Christian can be, as Meyer says, morally defective at the day of judgment (cf. I Thess. v. 23). Rather it implies that the end of this aeon will be determined by moral reasons. The course of history is a moral development, and the cosmical development depends on that of the individual Christian."

[80] P. 78.   [81] P. 79.   [82] P. 65.

a single example in Paul himself. Were it not for this one exception we should have to say that a possibility which is never actualized is no possibility — there must be something to render it impossible if in such a multitude of instances it is never actualized. In the presence of this one exception we can only say that the possibility must be a very slight one which in so many instances has been actualized only once. Meyer's zeal in the matter is an ethical one, and is grounded in his doctrine of the will and its function in the Christian life. What has happened to the Christian at conversion is, in his view, that his will has been freed from bondage to sin, and his destiny placed in his own hands. He may sin, if he chooses; and he need not sin unless he chooses. He may sin fatally if he chooses; or he may refrain from all sinning whatever if he chooses. He stands before the two ways and can walk as he will. If he has the *posse non peccare,* he has equally the *posse peccare* — the *non posse peccare* and the *non posse non peccare* would be equally derogatory to his manhood; for has not the Spirit made him *free?* Accordingly we are told that " it is not unthinkable for Paul that even the Christians should live after the flesh," [83] and that "the eventual turning of the Christian *in malam partem* is not at all excluded." [84] Of course it is not unthinkable either that the Christian should live after the Spirit; that is his quality. And of course he may conceivably live wholly after the Spirit. But here we are called up again, for in the very act of drawing the parallel out in detail Meyer interposes: [85] " Therefore this conflict cannot possibly find its conclusion within the sphere of this life. And the Apostle has not taught that Christians stand at the end of their Christian development sinless. 'Grace' remains for them always the last word. The sinlessness of the Christian lies therefore on the other side of the earthly existence." And yet Paul was sinless! The one thing, meanwhile, of which Meyer is most sure, is that what the Spirit does is just to make us formally free; and that He is therefore not to be thought of as an " overmastering power " which acts like a " natural force of a higher order," so

[83] P. 70.   [84] P. 71.   [85] P. 80.

that "life in the Spirit is to proceed infallibly with the necessity of nature." The language here is, of course, exaggerated. It is chosen with a view to repelling the representations of Karl and Wernle. But, the exaggeration having been eliminated, there is an element of Paul's teaching of the first importance, recognized at this point by Karl and Wernle, which Meyer has not allowed for.

When Meyer comes to deal formally with the question, why Paul had nothing explicit to say to the Corinthians of the forgiveness of their sins, committed since conversion, he is more successful on the destructive than on the constructive side. He has no difficulty in showing that there is no exegetical ground for the assertion that Paul connects the forgiveness of sins so closely with baptism as to treat the merits of Christ as available only for pre-baptismal sins.[86] And he has as little difficulty in showing that the attempts to interpret Paul as reckoning as sins only the gross vices into which he could count on his Christians not falling, do not bear the test of either the exegesis of Paul's words or of the recorded facts. He is quite within the warrant of his evidence when he declares that, so far from not requiring his Christians to realize his high ideal in their lives, Paul strenuously demanded its realization by them as their obligatory task, and reckoned it sin in them when their life in the smallest respect failed to correspond with it.[87] When it comes, however, to adducing definite texts in which the forgiveness of the current sins of Christians is declared, Meyer does not appear to have made his selection with particular success. He is led therefore to suggest that Paul made only a sparing use of express references to the consolation of forgiveness, no doubt for a pedagogic reason — these raw young Christians were less in need of consolation for sins grieved over than of correction for sins indulged in. In the end he falls back, very wisely, on the general consideration that "the forgiveness of sins," that is to say that forgiveness of sins which is justification, "has with Paul the value of a permanent possession," so that the question, which it is asserted

[86] P. 33.   [87] P. 35.

Paul never raised, how the Christian when he sins receives forgiveness, obtains this as its proper answer: In the same way that he received forgiveness on becoming a Christian.[88] He has no difficulty, of course, in showing,[89] that justification in the Epistle to the Romans is treated as introducting once for all into grace, and, as H. Cremer puts it, looks both forward and backward in the great context of salvation, binding together past, present, and future into one. " God's justifying judgment" (explains Cremer more fully),[90] "is a continuous, permanent one . . . to which, therefore, even the pardoned sinner can only daily appeal afresh, for daily new and yet abiding forgiveness of his sin and guilt." It admits of no doubt that, according to Paul, justification is salvation and therefore dominates with the effects of salvation all the subsequent life of the Christian. And now, having reached this point, Meyer turns the argument around [91] and urges that this alone proves that Paul looked upon Christians as still sinning. For why should he lay such weight on the continuous importance for the Christian life of precisely justification, unless there were continuous sinning for which this justification is needed?

This argument from justification to the universal sinfulness of Christians admits of greater elaboration than is given it in this place, and receives it in the second of Meyer's dissertations. The very essence of this doctrine is that men have no righteousness of their own, but only that which is through faith in Christ, the righteousness which is of God on faith (Phil. iii. 9). That this means not only that our sole dependence is on the righteousness of God received when we believed, but also that we continue through life so far in the same condition as when we believed, that we never have any righteousness of our own on which we can depend, is clear from the eschatological reference in Phil. iii. 9–11. It was not once only that Paul and his Christians had " no confidence in the flesh "; they never had or could have confidence in the flesh, and least of all when it was a matter of entering into participation of

[88] P. 37.   [90] " Die paulinische Rechtfertigungslehre," 1899, p. 366.
[89] Pp. 54 f.   [91] P. 56.

Christ's resurrection. It has its significance that precisely in
this passage Paul proceeds to declare himself not a consummator but only a viator. He has not attained, but is pressing
on. The life that is lived here below is lived not by sight but
by faith. Accordingly he characterizes it in Gal. ii. 20 as a life
in the flesh, lived in faith, faith in his Redeemer. The question,
no doubt, arises whether the phrase " in the flesh " in this
passage implies sin. H. A. W. Meyer says it does not: "The
context does not convey any reference to the ethical character
of the ' flesh ' (as *sedes peccati*)." Max Meyer says it does;
and on the whole we think him right.[92] " Already," he writes,[93]
" that ' flesh ' and ' Spirit ' are associated " in the passage " as
two inimical powers, which stand in diametrical contradiction
with each other . . . proves that the Apostle did not consider
himself sinless. . . . The ' flesh ' with him too is still *sedes et
fomes peccati,* and is active in the ' lusts ' . . . And that Paul
has even here thought of the sin inhering in his ' flesh ' in
which he knows himself involved, in spite of his most intimate
unio mystica with Christ, we learn from this — that he, so
long as he lives ' in the flesh,' knows himself permanently united
by faith to Him who loved him and gave Himself for him. It
is Jesus' love for sinners on which he stays himself in his life
of faith. . . . According to this passage Paul not only felt the
need of comfort and new forgiveness but actually always afresh
appropriated in faith the forgiveness of sins in Christ." Meyer,
then, adduces Col. i. 14, Eph. i. 7, " we *have* forgiveness of
sins," and calling attention to the present tense, declares that
these passages show that Paul knew, for his own person also,
" a *remissio quotidiana.*" G. Hollmann [94] simply scouts this use
of these passages, and certainly it does bear some appearance
of overstraining them. But at least the passages show that the
forgiveness of sins was a blessing enjoyed, alike by Paul and
his Christians, as a continuous possession, and that this for-

[92] See also Mühlau, as cited, p. 231. On the other hand Windisch, as cited,
p. 156, holds with H. A. W. Meyer.

[93] " Der Apostel Paulus als armer Sünder," 1903, pp. 31 f.

[94] *Theologische Literaturzeitung,* xxix. 1904, col. 203.

giveness must be taken sufficiently inclusively to embrace all the sins that existed for him and them. If we cannot quite say that the passages prove that they were continuously sinning, we must at least say that they do prove that the grace of forgiveness was looked upon by them as the fundamental blessing on which they rested their whole lives long.

Meyer himself, it is to be observed, does not look upon these passages as proving that Paul and his Christians thought of themselves as continually sinning. They prove only, in his view, that Paul and his Christians thought of themselves as continually sinful. He argues strongly, as we have seen, that all others than Paul were continually sinning. But he singles Paul out as the one man who has ever lived who has realized the possibility that belongs to all Christians, of not actually sinning — a judgment which seems rather ungenerous to John and Peter and James and the rest. Paul, says he,[95] " is the greatest, next to Him who can be compared to none other." " He not only preached to his Christians, but he lived out before them, how far the Christian can advance in the battle for sanctification." If this is to be taken as meaning what it says, Paul is presented to us as illustrating the utmost moral possibility of humanity; we may just as well look upon his person as read his precepts, if we wish to learn the full duty of the Christian in the sanctification of his life. He is more completely our example than Christ Himself, because Christ went beyond — Paul only to the extreme limits of — our possibilities. There are attainments in Christ's life in which we cannot follow Him; there are no attainments possible to us whose model we do not find in Paul. It is needless to say that Paul does not present himself to us as such a universal example, when he calls on his readers to be imitators of him as he was of Christ Jesus; and it is equally needless to say that he is not brought before us in his epistles as such a universal example. Such overstraining of Paul's language is not necessary that we may do justice to his greatness, or to the really divine element in his life and in his work. Meyer is quite right when

[95] " Der Apostel Paulus als armer Sünder," p. 58.

he insists on the unity of his consciousness and refuses to separate Paul the man from Paul the apostle,[96] and to pass differing moral judgments on the two. Paul was as a man what he was as apostle: the apostleship was the sphere in which this man functioned. And after all said, Paul's apostleship was not self-sought, and was not prosecuted in his own strength. He was called by God to it, and sustained by God in it, in a definitely supernatural manner. It is not surprising that he was conscious of having done the work of the apostleship faithfully. He praises his work as well done; the praise he gives it is of course less praise of himself than of the God who strengthened him: but even so, his self-praise does not involve a claim of personal perfection even in his work. In I Cor. xv. 9 he puts himself in point of fitness for his office below all the other apostles — though he was under no illusions as to the shortcomings of some of them; and if he asserts that he has labored more abundantly than all, he ascribes that to the pure grace of God. In Eph. iii. 8 he describes himself as less than the least of all the saints, without any obvious reference to his pre-Christian life — and he knew the saints. When he calls himself in I Tim. i. 15 (if the adduction be allowed) the chief of sinners, it is not so certain that the reference is solely to his pre-Christian sins. It is not a boastful sense of his own strength, but a humble dependence on God's grace, which after all forms the basis of Paul's self-consciousness, and, as Meyer very properly remarks,[97] " if it is the triumph of the divine power in him which rules the Apostle's whole self-consciousness, then, his boasting, in which his self-consciousness finds its strongest expression, becomes intelligible; and the appearance of Paul's making himself guilty of the sin of proud exaltation, vanishes."

Meyer is no more insistent that Paul was free from actual sinning — that is his concession to his opponents in the "miserable-sinner" controversy — than he is that he remained always sinful in his "flesh," which is his concession to Paul's own teaching. He argues elaborately [98] that although Paul always felt the impulse to sin and longed to be free from it,

[96] P. 41.   [97] P. 20.   [98] Pp. 43, 44.

yet he never fell into sins of act. He bore therefore in the battle with sin the physiognomy of conquerer, and step by step drove it ever from the field. But Meyer is very strenuous in asserting the unbroken presence in Paul of this sinful "flesh." As he puts his conclusion formally: [99] "So far as the material at our disposal tells us, it must pass as an axiom that Paul in his Christian life knew sin very well, but had no acquaintance with sin in our ordinary sense. We can speak then, with reference to Paul, only of a *peccatum habituale,* not here ever of a *peccatum actuale.* Apart from the . . . possibilities of sins of inadvertence, weakness and ignorance, it was 'concupiscence' which with Paul was the constitutive characteristic of what was especially signified to him by 'sin.' On its account the Apostle has to prosecute with reference to himself continually, that 'discerning' of I Cor. xi. 31, 'cleansing' of II Cor. vii. 1. This 'concupiscence' was the constant occasion why Paul 'over and over again cried out with yearning for his deliverence from his sinful flesh.'" A position like this is scarcely more intelligible in itself than it is defensible from the records. So sharp a separation as is made between the underlying sinful nature and the body of sinful acts seems untenable. There is no sinful nature which is not active; and the activities within and the activities without are scarcely capable of such sharp division. So certainly as the *operari* follows the *esse,* so certain is it that as long as the *peccatum habituale* exists the *peccatum actuale* occurs. So far from saying that the *peccatum habituale* may lie in the background and show itself in no act, we must rather say that as long as it lies in the background it must of necessity show itself in every act. Its existence in Paul makes him in the fullest sense of the word a "miserable sinner," incapable of not sinning, because incapable of being in his acts anything but himself. Of course, if all that is meant is that Paul did not commit murder or adultery, did not steal and rob, then that is true. But we should not forget the probing touch of the Sermon on the Mount, which is Paul's touch too, as Meyer fully understands — witness his decisive repulsion of

[99] P. 51.

the attempts of Gottschick and Jacoby to attribute to Paul a coarser standard. And Meyer should not forget either, by the way, that according to him, Paul prayed, "Forgive us our trespasses." And it might even be worth while to remember the sharp saying of Samuel Rutherford about "the world's negative holiness — no adulterer, no murderer, no thief, no cozener" — which, he says, "maketh men believe they are already glorified saints." It is not necessary to do those things in order to be a "miserable sinner"; nor does the absence of such things from the life constitute us sinless.

We have just seen Meyer attributing to Paul knowledge and use of the Lord's Prayer, and we have seen formerly the same thing done by Juncker. It was inevitable that sooner or later some one would enter the controversy about the sins of Christians from this angle. This was at length done by G. Bindemann in a book entitled "The Prayer for Daily Forgiveness of Sins in Jesus' Proclamation of Salvation and in the Epistles of the Apostle Paul,"[100] published in 1902. It cannot be said that this new mode of approach brought much gain for the particular debate in progress. It was already generally allowed that Jesus did not contemplate sinless followers, so that in the first part of his discussion Bindemann can give us only a systematic arrangement of generally accepted facts. In the second part, he manages to review all the main topics which the debate had thrown into prominence, but he does this outside of his specific subject. He is compelled to allow that there is the slenderest direct ground for attributing to Paul knowledge and use of the Lord's Prayer, and indeed he bases his own conclusion that it was known to Paul ultimately on general considerations, rather than on specific references to it. He can even write:[101] "No express references to the seven petitions of the Lord's Prayer are found, and it may seem that the whole spirit of that prayer is alien to the Apostle: not petition, but thanksgiving becomes the Christian. It has even been possible

---

[100] "Das Gebet um tägliche Vergebung der Sünden in der Heilsverkündigung Jesu und in den Briefen des Apostels Paulus," 1902.

[101] P. 10.

to maintain that the Lord's directions as to prayer as they are presented in the Lord's Prayer are altogether unknown to the Apostle.[102] And in fact, for one to whom it is not from the outset on other grounds a historical impossibility that Paul should have had no knowledge of this important piece of tradition of Jesus, such knowledge is not to be indisputably proved from the epistles of Paul."

Already from this passage we perceive that the question with reference to Paul's prayers takes a wider range than merely his knowledge and use of the Lord's Prayer. In his references to prayer, we are told in this same context, the prayer of petition in general falls notably into the background in comparison with the prayer of thanksgiving, and petitions for forgiveness remain unmentioned even when the prayer of petition is spoken of. "Here Paul nowhere mentions, no matter how much occasion there was for it, the prayer for forgiveness; he neither bears witness to it for himself, nor does he recommend it to others with unmistakable clearness. This could be expected; since he is writing to congregations in which open sins, serious faults, lay publicly in sight. Even his intercessions for his congregations, the contents of which he incidentally communicates, do not enable us to determine that he prays for the forgiveness of their guilt. He prays for the growth of faith, the increase of knowledge, that they may receive in greater fulness the gifts which they already have." At a later point in the discussion this same line of remark is resumed. We read: [103] "Petition also, then, does not fail in Paul's own prayer-life. But in all the intimations concerning the content of his prayers all reference to prayers for the forgiveness of sins is lacking. We might repeatedly expect an exhortation to the congregation not to forget the prayer for forgiveness; most naturally, say, at the end of Galatians or Corinthians; but precisely here there is lacking even that general requirement of prayer, such as is found in I Thessalonians, Romans, Philippians, Ephesians,

[102] The reference is to Wernle, as cited, p. 53, to which is added Gunkel, "Wirkungen des Heiligen Geistes," [2] 1899, p. 61.
[103] P. 62.

Colossians. Other passages seem to show directly that the daily prayer for forgiveness, such as is recommended in the Lord's Prayer, does not at least take a prominent place in the Apostle's circle of ideas. In Col. iii. 13, cf. Eph. iv. 32, the readers are required to forgive one another when they have suffered injury the one from the other. But as the motive for such a willingness to forgive, there is no indication that only under this condition will their prayer for forgiveness of their own sins be heard of God — though that would be sufficiently naturally suggested by Matt. vi. 12, 14 f., Mark xi. 25, 26, Luke xi. 4. Only the fact in their own past is recalled, that their sins *have been* forgiven to his readers, the fact of washing away their sins which occurred in baptism."

Having thus sharpened the problem to the utmost Bindemann makes it his task to show in detail that despite the fact that mention of the prayer for forgiveness falls into the background in Paul's letters, Paul's whole system of teaching supposes and demands it. In that system the guilt of sin takes the most prominent place and on every page of his writings it is preëminently the guilt of sinning which is presupposed. He will not even permit it to be said that, justification being presupposed, it is, with reference to the Christian life, the power of sin which takes the place in the foreground. Having pointed out that, according to Paul, wherever the " flesh " is, there is sin, that therefore all Christians still sin, and, still sinning, are still in need of forgiveness, he continues: [104] " According to all this, it should be admitted that the prayer for the forgiveness of sins takes a place in the piety of Paul of similar importance to that which it takes in Jesus' proclamation of salvation."

Nevertheless (he proceeds to reason) precisely the significance which the contrast of "flesh " and " Spirit " with Christians possesses in the theology of Paul seems to many to lead to something different. There is an appearance as if, for the Apostle, in the estimate of sin in the Christian life, the idea of its *power* may stand in the foreground, while the idea of the

[104] P. 89.

guilt produced by it in God's sight retires into the background. Attention has accordingly been called to the fact that Paul never speaks of the importance for Christians of the forgiveness of sins obtained by Christ. Justification, forgiveness of sins, appear rather, it is said, as a possession, which believers have from the beginning on. On the other hand, it is said, the demand that Christians shall withstand the power of sin in the power of the Spirit is constantly repeated. In the description of the Christian life, interest in emancipation from the power of sin predominates with the Apostle. Here, therefore, the Apostle's teaching concerning the Spirit, which contains the really new and fruitful ideas of the Apostle, obtains the upper hand, while the juridical circle of ideas, which embraces the doctrine of justification, of faith, and so forth, seems confined wholly to the fact, lying in the past, of entrance into the Christian life. The Epistle to the Romans is, it is said, the proof of this; whereas the first five chapters are wholly dominated by the doctrine of justification, in the succeeding three which describe the life of the Christian, it is only the walk in the Spirit that is discussed. Thus the recession of prayers for forgiveness is explained, so it is said, by the concentration of the Apostle's interest on emancipation from the power of sin, whereas emancipation from its guilt, by the fundamental forgiveness of sins, which occurs once for all, is guaranteed once for all.

To this plausible representation Bindemann replies that not only does it fail to apprehend the close relations in which Paul's doctrines of justification and of the gift of the Spirit stand to one another; but it attributes to the Apostle a separation between the power and the guilt of sin, which would have been impossible to him. It would have been impossible to the Apostle to think of the power of sin, without at the same time thinking of its guilt. " It was far too serious an estimation of sin, which came to the Apostle out of his faith in God's forgiveness of sin on the ground of Christ's death, for the consciousness of guilt not necessarily to awaken with new sharpness along with the thought of Christ's act, on the occurrence of every sin that was committed in the Christian life." " Therefore," Bindemann says in conclusion,[105] "it is for Paul, too, wholly self-evident, that the Christian, considering his sin, necessarily needs the forgiveness of its guilt, and the assurance that this new sin also is forgiven and his communion with God is no longer disturbed." By such lines of thought as this, Bindemann supposes that he has shown that the preaching of Paul contains all the presuppositions which require of Christians prayer for forgiveness and manifests the sameness of the faith of Paul with that of Jesus. On this ground he thinks he may assert that Paul knew the Lord's Prayer and used it in the same sense in which Jesus gave it. "It can no longer seem strange that Paul never elsewhere " — than in the one passage in which he supposes it referred to — "mentions it, and does not oftener require it. We may hold it to be accident, if the few occasional writings which have come down to us from Paul do not give us clearer information in the matter." [106]

Ludwig Ihmels' excellent conference address on "The Daily Forgiveness of Sins"[107] occupies much the same standpoint with Bindemann's book. It itself sums up the result of its discussion in these words: [108] "We live by daily forgiveness and we praise God's mercy that we may live by it." But it adds at once: "To be sure, that we are sinners is no part of the gospel, and what we praise God's mercy for is not that we never have as yet overcome sin." That the address is preoccupied with this apologetical aspect of the question is due in part to the gibing tone of the assailants of the doctrine presented in it, and in part, no doubt, also to the circumstances that it was spoken to a company of pastors, and has as its object to advise them in their dealings with somewhat formal penitents. It is more concerned therefore to avoid appearing to give license to sinning among the indifferent, as something natural to the Christian life, which it would be useless to strive against, than it is

[105] P. 90.

[106] P. 105.

[107] "Die tägliche Vergebung der Sünden: Vortrag gehalten auf der X. Allgemeinen lutherischen Konferenz zu Lund," 1901.

[108] P. 34.

to encourage the despairing with the assurance that their sins, though many, may and will be forgiven them.

The address opens by representing opponents as saying, "Must we sin, then, in order to be orthodox?"[109] Why preach the persistence of sinning among Christians and the permanent continuance of their imperfection? The answer is, in the first instance, says Ihmels, because it is true. It is also true, of course, that it is only half the truth, and the other half must be insisted on, too. And the other half is that "wherever personal Christianity exists there necessarily is also a radical break with sin."[110] The Christian is not to be expected simply to accept his lot and adjust himself to his continued sinning as to something that has to be endured.[111] And certainly he is not to be exhorted, as some sectaries exhort him, to look on all our sinning as in such a sense already forgiven as that we need have no concern about it. That is not the attitude of the New Testament writers to the sins of Christians. Nor is it the attitude of the Reformers. The Reformation doctrine of "miserable sinners" is a doctrine of penitent sinners. It has no application to the indifferent or the secure. It offers itself only to those who, broken-hearted in repentance, look to Jesus alone as their compassionate Savior, and it tells them that for them too Jesus alone is enough. It does not tell them that they are not sinners; that would not be true, and they know it is not true; no one knows himself a sinner like a penitent sinner. It tells them that they are saved sinners — and that is the most glorious thing it could tell them.

Advising his company of pastors directly as to how the public proclamation of the perpetual forgiveness of sins is to be made, Ihmels speaks as follows:[112] "This is the gospel — that God for the sake of Jesus Christ, the Son of God, who gave Himself for our sins and rose again for our justification, will still have communion with sinners. As proclamation of

[109] P. 8. Ihmels says he takes these words from the lips of one of the leaders of the Sanctification Movement, meaning R. Pearsall Smith (" Reden," p. 99).

[110] P. 9.   [111] P. 16.   [112] P. 29.

the daily forgiveness of sins, this gospel takes the form that God will not be prevented from fostering this communion by the continuing imperfection of the Christian state. The gospel, now, belongs, however, only to the sincere. Hence it follows that consolatory preaching of the possibility and actuality of continuous forgiveness, must be accompanied — of course not in the pastoral care of the anxious, but in the general public preaching — with a plain warning against all consciously cherished sin. Consciously cherished sin makes communion with God objectively and subjectively impossible — there can be no doubt of that. Then, however, the proclamation must carefully avoid all appearance of intending to treat the Christian's continuing sin itself as a part of the gospel. It cannot, in other words, seek to quiet the Christian, lamenting over his sin, with the consolation that it cannot be otherwise, and also that it makes little difference."

It will have already been observed that the specialty of Ihmels' treatment of the general subject lies in the emphasis he throws on the duty of overcoming our sins. The forgiveness of our sins is in the interests of our overcoming them, not of our acquiescing in them. In this the whole essence of the gospel lies for him. " The whole Christian life," he says,[113] " in the sense of the Reformation is nothing but an unfolding of the communion with God and the blessedness grounded in forgiveness of sin. Therefore a forgiveness of sins, no matter how truly, as the warranty of communion with God, it may mean the whole salvation, would nevertheless be but a self-contradiction if it did not also deliver the Christian actually from sin." And what is true of the great central act of forgiveness, is true for him also of all the repeated acts of our daily forgiveness. They are in order to our constant advance in overcoming our sins. We are still imperfect; but it is perfection to which we are destined and it is through God's grace, manifested, among other things, in the forgiveness of the sins into which we fall on our way thither, that we are advanced toward it. This is the way Ihmels expresses himself on these matters: [114]

[113] Pp. 12, 13.   [114] P. 20.

"It may be said that among all assertions which are made about sanctification, there is none which is more lacking in Scriptual basis than that view according to which the divine act of justification needs to be supplemented by a later divine act of sanctification. On the other hand the Holy Scriptures certainly know of a growth in faith, which means at the same time a growth in the whole Christian life, and they know also of such Christians as they call in a special sense perfect. But let the Biblical notion of perfection be defined as exactly as it may, there are at any rate three things about which there can be no doubt. First, nothing is meant by it beyond the homely Christian state itself, accessible to all: it is rather a matter simply of perfection in this state. Secondly, the application of this conception to the individual Christian is always intended only in a relative sense. Lastly, this judgment has, moreover, nothing to do with absolute sinlessness."

Perhaps there underlies Ihmels' treatment of the Christian's advance in ethical attainment a somewhat inadequate conception of the mode of the supernatural re-creation of which it is the human manifestation. Like many of his fellows he is very much afraid of ascribing an operation to God analogous, as he would say, to the action of a natural force;[115] and is jealous above all things for "purely voluntary" action on man's part — as if the voluntariness of the human action was in any way curtailed by the underlying recreating or even "leading" action of God. When he comes to describe in detail, however, the process of the Christian's advance, the words in which he does so are at least capable of a thoroughly unexceptionable meaning. The main points in his description are that the Christian's life is a battle against remanent sin, but a battle fought under the initiation of God and with the promise of victory. "According to experience," he adds,[116] "this victory is not in this life a definitive one; the expectation of the complete overcoming of the flesh we connect with the complete deliverance from the obduracy of the world of sin and of death, and

[115] E.g. pp. 16, 36. [116] Pp. 22 f.

our immediate transference under the influence of God from face to face."

Much the same note as is struck by Ihmels is struck by Johannes Haussleiter in another conference address — on "The Christian's Consciousness of Sins"[117] — delivered in 1904. This address is indeed more intimate in tone than Ihmels', because it deals not with pastoral duty but with personal religion. Having spoken of our vivid memory of past sins, Haussleiter asks whether the change that took place in us "when we believed" has broken off all relation to the "lusts of the flesh" which formerly brought us into sin. "Were that true," he says, "the memory of the past would not be so living, so present — we might say so timeless — as it actually is. The Apostle Paul says, 'the flesh lusts against the Spirit, the Spirit, however, lusts against the flesh' (Gal. v. 17). The assertion applies to us, to Christians. We may be preserved now from many actual sins, if we let ourselves be led by the Spirit of God. But so long as we are involved in this body of death the old man does not cease to stir or to move. We have every reason to take heed to these movements and to combat them. When the Apostle gives the exhortation, 'Walk in the Spirit,' he does not add the conclusion, 'And then you will have nothing more to do with the lusts of the flesh,' but 'And then you will not *fulfil* the lusts of the flesh.' There is no longer need to fall into the gross works of the flesh and there should be no falling into them. But the impulse and the provocation to do so remain in our sinful nature, and therefore the necessity of conflict and of watchfulness abides. And therefore there abides the petition: 'Forgive us our trespasses.'"

Having next deepened our sense of the sinfulness of our misdeeds by showing how they are all specifically sins against God, Haussleiter proceeds: "There stands a declaration in the First Epistle to Timothy which has seemed to many strange. Paul writes here (I Tim. i. 15), that Christ has come into the world to save sinners, and adds: 'Among whom I *am* a chief

[117] Published in the *Allgemeine Evangelisch-Lutherische Kirchenzeitung,* xxxvii. 1904 (June 24), coll. 610 ff.

one.' Has he not miswritten? Ought he not to have written,
'Among whom I *was* a chief one?' He is certainly already
washed, sanctified, justified; he is a servant of Jesus Christ,
and His ambassador to the Gentiles. He has labored more than
the others. But that is not his merit, but the merit of grace.
Through God's grace he is what he is. But just because he
lives continuously by grace, the knowledge of his sin is ever
before him. They condition one another. Because Paul cannot
live without the Savior of sinners, he reckons himself permanently among sinners, not among sinners who wish to remain sinners and are far from God, but among those who have
experienced overpowering grace but who also know that they
need grace daily. Paul knows himself and his Savior. The Holy
Spirit has opened his eyes." "The Christian knows," we read
again, "that he is burdened with much more guilt than he
himself perceives — guilt of unrecognized results of earlier sins,
still greater guilt of sins of omission in the region of charity.
The Christian joins in the prayer of the Psalmist, 'Who can
mark how often he fails? Cleanse me from secret faults' (Ps.
xix. 13). Should he be willing consciously to increase the burden of guilt lightly? The Christian stands in daily conflict with
sins of temperament, with sins of weakness and sins of habit.
The grace of God has enough here to bear, to cleanse, to wash
away. It were a sacrilege to draw on it deliberately by conscious
transgression. God keep us, us Christians, from security! The
consciousness of sin, in the earnest sense in which we have
described it, is a means of protection."

We have moved into a totally new atmosphere when we
turn to Otto Pfleiderer. A lingering relic of the old Tübingen
school, an eager forerunner of the new history-of-religion
school, he had no more in common with the Ritschlians by
whom and with whom the controversy had in the main been
carried on, than with their "miserable-sinner" opponents.
We shall have to go back to W. A. Karl at the very beginning
of the controversy to find anything with which we can compare him, and it goes without saying that Pfleiderer owes
nothing to Karl, and that the parallel between the two has its

very narrow limits. He takes his start as is his wont from general ethnic conceptions and endeavors to interpret Paul from them, placing in this interest at the foundation of Paul's thought the universal animism of heathen mythology. The book in which Pfleiderer's views on the matter which concern us are given expression, is the second edition of his " Primitive Christianity, its Writings and Teachings." [118] The first edition of this work was published late in 1887. The second edition, " thoroughly revised and much enlarged," appeared in 1902; [119] and among the changes introduced into it were included the whole animistic background which Pfleiderer now wrote into Paul's doctrine of the Spirit, and especially the completed elaboration of that mystical conception which he had always attributed to Paul's notion of the relation of the Christian to Christ,[120] and on the basis of which he now represents Paul as inconsistent with his fundamental thought in recognizing sin as possible and actual in the Christian life.[121]

It will be observed that Pfleiderer is entirely willing to allow that Paul holds a supernaturalistic view of the Christian life. He assigns his supernaturalism, however, to an animistic inheritance. This animistic inheritance, nevertheless, has been modified by Paul in two directions. With him all the spirits had coalesced into one Spirit, the Spirit of Christ. And this Spirit operated in the Christian not occasionally only but continuously, and in particular became the productive cause of his whole ethical life. There is a recognition here of Paul's doctrine of the " leading of the Spirit," disparaged no doubt

[118] " Das Urchristenthum, seine Schriften und Lehren," (1887) 1902.

[119] An English translation was published in 1906, and the following references are to it.

[120] From the beginning of his occupation with the teaching of Paul (" Der Paulinismus," 1873, E. T. 1877) Pfleiderer had attributed to him a mystical doctrine (which he calls a Mysticism of Faith), discovering the chief of its expressions in the " in Christ " which was afterwards to be exploited by A. Deissmann (see " Der Paulinismus," pp. 197 ff.). On the early form of his doctrine of the Spirit the same reference will suffice, to which may nevertheless be added " The Influence of the Apostle Paul," 1885, pp. 69 ff. In these early expositions of the " in Christ " and the " Spirit " is to be found the germ of all that Pfleiderer teaches in 1902.

[121] Pp. 404 ff.

by its connection with animism, but nevertheless admitted in its fundamental elements. Now, Pfleiderer remarks that such a doctrine brings with it certain practical difficulties. " When the Christian life is referred back to a spiritual being of supernatural power, coming into man from without," he argues,[122] " the ethical self-determination of the human ego threatens to be suppressed, and the transformation seems to be effected in the inevitable fashion of a process of nature, in which, along with human freedom, guilt and sin would be excluded." That is to say, if we are in the hands of a supernatural power all our own activities must be supposed to be superseded and there must be attributed to the Spirit alone our entire, not merely re-creation, but life-manifestation.

Pfleiderer says that Paul, " in his ideal picture of the spiritual life under grace (Rom. vi. and viii.)," does seem to make an approach to these " inferences." " But," he adds, Paul " is practical enough to recognize fully the continuance of sin even in Christians [and] . . . attributes this to a principle of sin in the flesh which brings the ego into captivity. Over against the abstract ideal of the spiritual man who cannot sin, he sets directly the equally abstract caricature of the carnal man who can do nothing but sin (Rom. vii. 14 ff.)." Here we have, he says, " two abstractions which are doubtless meant as the opposite sides of the same condition." They are nevertheless, in Pfleiderer's opinion[123] " in fact mutually exclusive, and . . . in their opposition, split the unity of the personal life in a dualistic fashion." He thinks the " difficulty is solved," however, if, following " modern psychology," we interpret Paul in terms of " psychic conditions, motives, directions of the will, which, as they are developed out of the unity of human nature, are always held together by the unity of the personal consciousness in such a way that they form its proper content, the manifold factors of its life-activity."

As this is precisely what Paul means and says, without prejudice to his supernaturalism, we can but wonder why a self-contradiction should be thrust upon him only that it may

[122] P. 390.   [123] P. 391.

be immediately resolved. The contradiction is resolved, however, in Pfleiderer's view only for himself, not for Paul, and in his further exposition of Paul's teaching as to the Christian life it is pressed to its extremity. "A lofty idealism," we are told,[124] "appears in this description of the Christian life. The Christian is no longer in the flesh but in the Spirit; he has crucified the flesh with its lusts; the world is crucified to him and he to the world; he is risen with Christ, lives in the Spirit, possesses the Spirit of Christ. Christ himself lives in him instead of his former ego; he is a new creation; his life is hid with Christ in God; he has become a spiritual man; he is like Christ. That over such a being sin can no longer hold sway is self-evident; that is what makes it so difficult to grasp the fact that nevertheless in the actual Christian life sin is still present. The Christian, as Paul describes his character, ought properly no longer to be able to sin, since the divine Spirit is the ruling ego in him, and the sinful flesh is conquered, abolished. Yet Paul is far from drawing this obvious inference from his doctrine of the Spirit. On the contrary, all his epistles testify with what prudence and care he estimates the actual ethical condition of his churches, censures their weaknesses and sins, and exhorts them to lay aside all evil and contend unremittingly against sin. Spirit and flesh stand in constant strife with one another, and the victory of the Spirit does not come to pass by itself with the unfailing certainty of the laws of nature, but depends on whether the Christian endeavours to walk according to the standard set up by the Spirit, and mortify the deeds of the body, or allows sin again to have dominion over him."

Pfleiderer supposes here that according to Paul the flesh may defeat the Spirit — that neither justification nor the spirit of sonship secure "unconditionally" the ultimate salvation of the Christian, but that he stands or falls at the last judgment according to his works — which is certainly not Paul's teaching. But he closes the paragraph with a direct declaration that Paul did not, in any case, ignore the sins of Christians, but deals with them at large and in detail. He then

[124] Pp. 404 f.

proceeds to declare that there is a contradiction, in Paul's
presentation of the Christian life, between his doctrine of it
as Spirit-led and his doctrine of it as the scene of ethical effort.
We are accustomed, he says, to correct or to soften this contradiction by calling in the notion of development, process,
progressive advance. This is, however, declares Pfleiderer, inconsistent with the supernaturalism of the one aspect of it.
"How," he asks, "in relation to this overmastering divine
being, is there room for the free self-determination of the
human will?"[125] But the distinction which Pfleiderer draws
here — between divine control and human function — is not
Paul's. Paul's preoccupation is with "the flesh" and "the
Spirit" — the old instinct to evil, and the new power (certainly divine) to good. What Pfleiderer is asking is, how the
creature can resist the creator. His whole preoccupation is with
freedom. "Is not the new man, on this assumption," he asks,
"at bottom a will-less slave of the holy spiritual being in his
heart, as the old man was a slave of the demonic sinful being
in his flesh (Rom. vi. 16 f.)? Is he the active and responsible
subject of sanctification, or is he only the passive object for
the possession of which the two hostile powers, the holy spiritual, and the fleshy sinful, contend (Gal. v. 17)?" Why take
either horn of this dilemma, with its exclusive either — or?
Neither represents Paul, who instead of Pfleiderer's, Either
God or man, says with great clearness, Both (Phil. ii. 12, 13).

It is not without its interest to observe Pfleiderer applying
Rom. vii. 14 ff. to the Christian as a description by Paul of
one side of the Christian's condition.[126] On an earlier page,[127]
to which he here refers us, he declares of Rom. vii. 25 that it is
a "confession which is by no means to be referred to the past
of the apostle before his conversion, but pictures a present and
continuous condition." He adds, however, "but, of course, only
as regards the 'natural man,' which continues to exist even in

[125] P. 407.

[126] P. 390.

[127] Pp. 234 f. This whole passage is in the second edition added bodily to
the statement in the first edition (1887), which closes on a different note.

Christians alongside of the supernatural 'pneuma,' and is here portrayed by Paul with the same one-sided abstraction with which he elsewhere portrays the new spiritual life of Christians." "Only," says he, "from a combination of the two one-sided pictures — the dark picture in chapter vii. and the bright picture in chapter viii. — can we gather Paul's complete view of the actual concrete Christian life (cf. Gal. v. 17)." With this background of the dualism of Paul's representation behind him, Pfleiderer can now go on to declare that in Rom. viii. Paul represents believers as set free by the Spirit from all sin, meaning "not merely the removal of the guilt of sin, but also the overcoming of the power of sin." Only — it all depends on our coöperation and after all it is only an abstract picture of one side of the matter, the other side of which we have already read in chapter vii.

This is not untying the knot; it is not even cutting it; it is leaving it as tightly tied as it was before. The debate could not end in such ambiguities. We find it accordingly returning at once, for better, for worse, to the round assertions of Wernle. Only so was there hope of rescuing these assertions from their impending disintegration. Whether this rescue could in any case be accomplished we may learn by observing Windisch's valiant attempt to accomplish it.

V

" MISERABLE-SINNER CHRISTIANITY " IN
THE HANDS OF THE RATIONALISTS

III. WINDISCH AND THE END

"MISERABLE-SINNER CHRISTIANITY" IN THE HANDS OF THE RATIONALISTS

ARTICLE III

WINDISCH AND THE END[1]

THE assault on the Reformation conception of the Christian life could not end on so ambiguous a note as that struck by Pfleiderer. On the contrary, what may very properly be spoken of as the last word said in furtherance of it, was the most direct that had been said since Wernle's own, and in many respects the most forceful and telling of all. We are referring, of course, to Hans Windisch's at once brilliant and ponderous volume on "Baptism and Sin in the Oldest Christianity up to Origen,"[2] which was published in 1908. We have already pointed out the relation of the book to Wernle's published twelve years before. It came into the controversy which Wernle had provoked, very distinctly at the end, when the debate was languishing, and indeed, from the point of view of Wernle's contentions, when the battle was lost. It had much the appearance accordingly of a last vigorous attack, seeking to wring a victory out of defeat. And assuredly little was left unsaid by Windisch that could be said to rescue and save a lost cause.

What Windisch undertakes to do, to speak now of the formal contents of his volume, is to take up Wernle's proposition that to Paul Christians are in their actual nature sinless men, to justify it by a really thorough exegetical survey of the Pauline material, and then to place it in its historical connections both narrow and broad. For this purpose he traces the

[1] From *The Princeton Theological Review,* xviii. 1920, pp. 545–610.

[2] "Taufe und Sünde im ältesten Christentum bis auf Origines. Ein Beitrag zur altchristlichen Dogmengeschichte," 1908. The book, published when he was twenty-seven years old, was Windisch's first book; at least it was preceded only by his Doctor's dissertation on "The Theodicy of . . . Justin," 1906.

related conceptions with the same thoroughness through the rest of the New Testament books, and then extends the view backwards to Ezekiel and forward to Origen. He discovers preparations for the theory of the sinlessness of Christians, attributed to Paul, in the prophets' demand for repentance, in the Jewish dogma of the sinless man of the end-time, and in the sacramental rite of cleansing baptism. He follows what he thinks of as survivals of the Pauline conception through the early Patristic writings, pausing at Origen only because he discovers in him the complete dissolution of the theory of baptismal cleansing and the recognition of the natural necessity of sin, even for Christians. It is naturally, however, upon the New Testament text itself that he expends his chief effort, and he discusses this with a minuteness of detail, a fulness of exegetical comment, and a richness of illustrative remark which make the volume in effect a commentary on the entire New Testament from the point of view of its witness to the relation of the Christian life to sin. This detailed discussion of the New Testament text is of course the strength of the book; but, since its task is approached from a point of view really alien to the New Testament, it is also its weakness. Many concessions require to be made, many acts of exegetical violence are committed, much special pleading is indulged in, and it still remains necessary to declare the New Testament writers constantly inconsistent with themselves. Under whatever form it may be put forward, it is very clear that this is not really exposition. It rapidly becomes obvious to the reader that the New Testament passages which are discussed cannot be strung on the thread with which they are approached, and the most thorough of all attempts to show that to the New Testament writings the Christian is a sinless man becomes, by the very attempt to be thorough, its most thorough refutation. It becomes ever more and more plain that the text is intractable to this theory of its meaning.

We are not surprised, therefore, to observe that Wernle, reviewing the book under the spur of a wholesome sense of his own partial responsibility for its vagaries, throws into

primary emphasis the notable lack of plain, human common
sense which, despite all its diligence and acuteness, deforms
its exegesis; and the general deficiency in it of a feeling for
reality. "During the reading of great parts of the book," he
says, "we live in the labyrinth of a bewitched world, while
the simple reality of life lies without." [3] In other words,
Windisch has not shown us the plain three-dimensioned world
which the New Testament reflects; he has attempted to work
out a new two-dimensioned or four-dimensioned world, and to
impose that on the New Testament writers as their own. Naturally everything in their world, under this treatment, takes on
an artificial aspect. "What kind of a Paul is this that is
depicted," cries Wernle,[4] " a Paul for whom in the Epistles to
the Corinthians the occurrence of sin in Christianity ' obviously' and ' again ' ' makes theoretical difficulties,' who over
against the same Corinthians ' artifically creates the problem of
the sinful Christian,' who at I Cor. x. 1 ff. ' deals plainly with
the problem of sin after baptism,' who gives to his Galatians
as sinful Christians an injunction to the sinless life and sets
before them the essence of the Christian as sinlessness, whose
whole point of view is dominated by an ideal portrait of the
Christian according to which the disappearance of sin characteristically accompanies becoming a Christian? I find this Paul,
despite all the pre-Christian elucidations which Windisch adduces, a total psychological enigma; and not only he but all the
primitive Christians in the mass must have been visionaries
and dreamers if the author's closing result be right — that
Christians are in their real nature sinless men. No day perhaps
passed for them in which intelligence of faults, failings, aberrations, did not smite their eyes or ears from near and far; and
yet, for example, it was so difficult for the preacher of Second
Clement, because of his rigoristic theory of baptism, to make a
demand for repentance, that he must writhe about sadly before
he can give to Christians the exhortation to penitence demanded by the actual state of things. And why so? Because
first of all for all those Christians a theory of sinfulness was

[3] *Theologische Literaturzeitung*, xxxiv. 1909, col. 589.   [4] Coll. 587–588.

firmly established, and it was only with the presupposition of this theory that they could approach empirical reality."

In summing up at the end of his volume the results of his investigations, Windisch formulates them crisply in the words which we have just seen Wernle quoting from him. They all are comprehended, he says, in this, that he has established it as the doctrine of the primitive Church, that "Christians are in their real nature sinless men." [5] He then proceeds to develop a rationale of this doctrine, founded on the circumstance that Christianity is a historically grounded redemptive religion, in which the two matters of the first interest are the nature of the Redeemer and the nature of the redeemed. As the Redeemer is by nature without sin, so must His redeemed become sinless men. It is the burden of prophecy that all sin must be put away in order that the salvation of the Lord may come. It is the expectation which informs all apocalypses, that God will make His people sinless. Christianity comes as the fulfilment of prophecy and the realization of all the hopes founded on it, whether given expression in apocalypses or elsewhere. In it the longed for Messiah actually comes, and He brings with Him all that God's people had been taught to look for in Him; and that very especially in the special form of those expectations which sees just in sin the enemy He is to overcome. As the Messiah must be Himself without sin, so must He, in every sense of the word, save His people from their sins.

Of course all this is in substance true. But it does not follow that from this point of view Christians must be sinless; that, as Windisch expresses it, "sinless men have been on the earth ever since the sinless Messiah was sent by God" — because "the fulfilment of the hope and the realization of the requirement in the circles of the Christians have their historical starting point in the person of the Messiah Jesus." [6] The essence of the matter is contained in the simple remark that all that is here adduced leaves it still an open question how and when Christ's salvation of His people from their sins is to be supposed to reach its completion. He came into the

[5] P. 507.   [6] P. 509.

world, let us say, to save sinners; to save them from their
sins; from the guilt of their sins, from the pollution of them,
from their power, from the commission of them — from all that
they are, and from all that they bring with them in the way of
effects or consequences. But it does not follow that this whole
body of results must be supposed — or will naturally be supposed — to be brought about at once — "on faith." There is
death, for instance; it is a consequence of sin (Rom. v. 12).
There may have been some in Paul's churches who fancied
that they were to be relieved from the necessity of dying
(I Thess. iv. 13 ff.). Paul does not encourage the notion. He
points rather to the resurrection, and to the coming of Christ,
events which were to take place in the future — how far in
the future he says he does not know, but quite obviously well
in the future. It is impossible to imagine that this Paul, nevertheless, supposed that the whole process of salvation was
instantaneously completed when the act of faith was exercised.
Rather, he constantly refers its completion, and that very especially in its ethical aspects, to this same coming of the Lord
(I Thess. ii. 19; iii. 13; v. 23). It is that future event — perhaps
far future event — then, which forms the term of the salvation
of Christians; and as their salvation is precisely salvation from
sin it is only at the arrival of that event that they realize to
the full the "salvation from sin" which they receive from
Christ Jesus.

This fundamental historical fact enables us to place our
finger on Windisch's central error in his interpretation of the
New Testament writers with reference to the nature of the
Christian life. He misses the significance of the inter-adventual
period. Paul calls it "the day of salvation," which means not
merely the day in which salvation is freely offered to men, but
also, in the light of a passage like I Cor. xv. 25 f., the day during which the saving work is perfected in men and in the
world. Windisch necessarily misses this constitutive fact in
Paul's teaching because he ascribes to the New Testament
writers, Paul included, an expectation of the coming of the
Lord as immediately impending. That is not, however, their

view. Paul, for example, teaches with great fervor and con-sistency a doctrine of a prolonged period of development under the government of the exalted Jesus, through which the world advances to a glorious consummation. It is in this period of world-development that he sees his Christians living. They form its core and leaven, and he of course attributes to them individually a similar development, reaching its completion in the same great consummation. Not when He was on earth merely, but now also while He is in heaven, according to Paul's view, Jesus is actively our Savior. He is still while in heaven "saving His people from their sins"; and that not in the mass merely, but also with reference to the individual. His work of saving the individual therefore as truly as that of sav-ing the world is given the character of a process; and the end of this process for the one as for the other is to be reached only at the Parousia. That the sanctification of the Christian is a process, belongs thus to the very substance of Paul's doc-trine of salvation, and his repeated allusions to it in his writings cannot be explained away.

It is not, however, on the progressive character of the Christian's salvation from sin, itself, that this new interpreta-tion of Paul impinges with most deadly effect, but on — what is implicated in it — the continuous dependence of the progres-sively saved sinner on the living activities of the saving Christ. We are made to feel this very sharply when Windisch comes to tell us how the teaching of the Reformation differs from that of his new Paul.[7] The difference, as stated, turns, of course, on a difference in their views of the application of justification. According to Paul, we are told, we receive in justification for-giveness of our past sins only, while with Luther the forgive-ness received in it is extended to all the sins we may commit through life. This mode of statement, however, only touches the surface of the matter. Underneath it lies a conception which throws the Christian back on his own resources and withdraws from him all recourse to, as it denies of him all need of, the continued saving activities of Christ our Mediator.

[7] Pp. 524 ff.

The real dividing question comes, therefore, to be seen to be whether the Christian is always dependent on Christ and always looks to Him as His one complete Savior. According to the new intepretation of Paul, Christ earns for us only the first grace; after that we must earn eternal life for ourselves by our own work and merit. This means of course that his own works are a Christian's sole dependence. It is only, we are told, those out of Christ who have no works on which to depend, and who therefore are exhorted not to depend on their own works. Paul "in his rejection of our own works is thinking apparently only of the works of our earlier life"; while the Reformation expressly excludes present and future works also. All that we receive in Christ is thus for Paul exhausted in that "first grace"; after that we are left to our own resources. This is as much as to say that all that Christ has done for us is to start us on our way; we have to walk in the way for ourselves. We must not forget that, according to this new reading of Paul, he represents Christ as giving us a magnificent start. He not only in that "first grace" gives us forgiveness of sins but takes them away; so that all we have to do is to keep ourselves as He leaves us. It is not, to be sure, overly clear precisely what is meant by His taking away our sins; in the passage at present before us, Windisch apparently assumes that it means the cleansing of our corrupt nature — which is also what from the logical point of view it should mean. At all events it is here that the difference between this new reading of Paul and the Reformation teaching comes to its head. Windisch fixes on a phrase in the "Formula Concordiae" to give it pointed expression. We are told there that "we are and remain sinners" because of our corrupted nature, and therefore depend entirely on Christ. "This 'and remain sinners,'" says Windisch, "admirably indicates the application of the doctrine of justification which goes beyond Paul." According to Paul, we do not "remain" sinners, and accordingly do not any longer need Christ. We have got all that Christ can give us; henceforth it is our own concern. Clearly we have two different religions contrasted here. We gain by the new interpretation of Paul a more immediate perfection in our lives. We lose by it Christ out of our lives.

It would be wrong not to pause to observe that this new interpretation of Paul is really a modernization of Paul, in the theological sense of that word. One may suspect that it has its real source largely in the imputation to Paul by its authors, in more or less fulness, of their own conceptions of what the Christian life actually is. It is at all events a great step towards the modernization of Paul to relieve him of all implication in the ascription of a present saving activity to Christ. Really "modern" men do not think, of course, of allowing to even the acts of the historical Jesus any expiatory character, any "forgiveness-procuring" value. But it is a wide step toward their mode of thinking to eliminate all activities of Christ except those of the historical Jesus. When it is said that Paul knows nothing of continued saving activities by Christ after His death — that what He did while on earth serves, according to Paul, to bring about that repentance and faith which secures forgiveness and delivers from sin, and after that, it is our own concern — the exalted Christ is made as much "hidden" to Paul as He is to Ritschl, and all communion with Him is as completely eliminated from Paul's thought as it is from Herrmann's. The resultant conception of the Christian life itself, therefore, attributed to Paul is also thoroughly "modern." Man is thrown back on his own ethical activities, which are made the decisive thing in his standing or falling. All that he really obtains from Christ is a new start; the slate is washed clean for him. No doubt it is in the inspiration of this new start that he goes forward. But in the end all depends on what he has himself written on the cleansed slate. Paul is in other words thought of as teaching a "moralistic" doctrine of salvation of quite modern aspect. He is made a very respectable follower of Ritschl — or something worse.

It is this understanding of the teaching of Paul, and with him of John,[8] and indeed *mutatis mutandis,* of the whole New

___

[8] Cf. p. 508: "Paul and John are the typical and irrefutable witnesses for the dogma that the Christian is freed from sin (*entsündigt*)."

Testament, and of early Christianity in general, that Windisch sets before us at the end of his volume as the result of his investigations. It is questionable, however, whether the detailed report of these investigations, very richly set out in the volume itself, sustains this result. Windisch is himself very prompt to admit that we cannot speak with any propriety of it as the only Biblical doctrine. Indeed, from his point of view there is no such thing as " a Biblical doctrine "; many different notions concerning the Christian life may be found in the Bible. To give point to this assertion, he adds illustratively: [9] " Yes, even ' miserable-sinnerism ' is represented in the Bible. Jesus, for example, along with the Methodistic notion of repentance which He employs, along with His strict requirement of cleansing, recognises the continuance of sinning, and assures His disciples like any Lutheran Christian of the abiding favor of God." It may tend to console " miserable-sinner Christians " to know that it is admitted that Jesus is on their side. And this is not all. For Windisch is compelled to admit also that Paul himself is not able to preserve unbrokenly an attitude toward Christians which sees in them those sinless men whom he is said to proclaim them. In point of fact, it is explained,[10] the relations of Christians to sin are spoken of by Paul from three different points of view. " The *Messiah-man, cleansed by God,* is delivered from all sin and temptation. *The normal and ideal Christian* has separated himself from sin, is conscious of no new sin, and yet must, under the faithful guidance of God, be on his guard against sinful temptation. Finally the *unestablished, imperfect Christian* still occasionally commits sin, and even is still entangled in serious faults; he is still unconverted, has not yet yielded himself to the control of the Spirit, has lost the feeling of being with Christ and with His Spirit; if he is not to be destroyed he must at length repent and let the Spirit come into action, he must repent afresh and yield to Christ and to the Spirit." Needless to say the Apostle gives no hint of the existence of any such three classes of Christians. These are only three different ways in

[9] P. 534.   [10] P. 219.

which, according to Windisch, Paul is found actually dealing
from time to time with Christians. If so, we can only say that
he dealt with them very inconsistently — implying sometimes
that Christians are glorified saints, sinless and sin-proof; sometimes that they are indeed without sin but only through their
own strenuous efforts and always liable to sin; and sometimes
that they are sin-stained creatures who must bestir themselves
lest they perish. Windisch, however, very remarkably as it
seems to us, draws the conclusion from the situation thus depicted that Christians are, according to Paul, sinless beings.
" In every case," he says, " all — what has happened and what
ought to happen — tends to this: that the Christian is a sinless man." " By this ideal," he now continues, " all the Apostle's expectations are permeated. Only in two passages (I Cor.
iv. and v.) does Paul give expression to the view that God will
pardon also the Christian who has remained a sinner; these,
however, deal with disgraceful exceptions." He says two passages, apparently, only by a slip of the pen. There is nothing
in the fourth chapter of First Corinthians to satisfy the allusion, and it is clear that his mind is on merely the opening verses
of the fifth chapter. Therefore he continues: " In this single
passage Paul gives expression to a conception which presents an
individual Christian as a 'miserable sinner' who is not able to
fulfil his life-task. We may add to this, no doubt, certain oft-
recurring exhortations, which at least indirectly 'reckon with
the sin of the Christian' — exhortations to return no more evil
for evil (I Thess. v. 15; Rom. xii. 17), to forgive one another
as God has forgiven us (Col. iii. 13; Eph. iv. 32)." This is a
most inadequate adduction of the relevant material; but even
so, it is enough to show that Paul does not prevailingly deal
with Christians as if they were sinless, but assumes on the contrary that sin ever lies at their door. Windisch, however, comments as follows: " Our expositions have shown that in none
of these declarations can the proposition find support for itself
that Paul sees in sin the constant attendant of the Christian."
It is doubtless true that exhortations not to sin imply immediately only a constant liability to sin, not a constant sinning.

The distinction is, however, a rather narrow one; and one wonders whether a constant liability to sin which was never illustrated by actual sinning would naturally call out such constant exhortations against sinning.

And one wonders also whether Windisch wishes to convey the impression that in his exhortations to growth in the Christian life Paul invariably confines himself to the positive side of this growth, or the putting on of graces, and never exhorts Christians to the negative aspect of it, or the putting off of vices — always, in other words, urges the putting on of the new man, never the putting off of the old man. Obviously the implication of exhortations to put away vices may be not merely that we are liable to these vices, but that we are afflicted with them. Paul's epistles fairly swarm with such exhortations. The fact is too patent to require illustration, and it is not denied by Windisch. He founds on it indeed his representation that Paul has two inconsistent theories of cleansing from sin, the mystic and the parenetic; and in expounding this representation he actually allows that the parenetic theory implies the continuance of sinfulness in Christians.[11] "The parenesis of conversion," he says, "goes back to the phrases, 'that ye may walk in newness in life,' and 'that ye may no longer serve sin'; only, according to its intrinsic peculiarity, it presupposes subsistent sinfulness or temptability"; it is only this second theory, he says again, which "reckons with the temptability of the Christian, and in it there is even to be assumed as we have seen, an actual sin of the Christian." This admission falls short, no doubt, of allowing that Paul presupposes " continual sinning " in Christians, although that too is the real implication of Paul's continual parenesis. It must be allowed also that in dealing with the several parenetic passages Windisch does his best to transform the imperatives into indicatives. It is in its failure to enter into what may be called the prevailing parenetic tone of Paul's epistles, indeed, that Wernle finds the fundamental fault of Windisch's book. It would be truer to the real state of the case, he intimates,[12]

---

[11] Pp. 180–182. [12] *Theologische Literaturzeitung*, xxxiv. 1909, col. 588.

if instead of turning the imperatives into indicatives, the indicatives were read as nothing but strengthened imperatives. "The inability to sin in Rom. vi.," he adds illustratively, "is the strongest imperative which Paul has at his disposal, and very properly passes therefore in the end into the *impropriety* of sinning. . . . In I Cor. vi. 11, Gal. v. 24, this imperative in the form of retrospect is very evident." The idea meant to be conveyed is that Paul always writes with moral impression in view and has as his end the ethical advancement of his readers. Even his indicative statements have this as their end, and to that extent have an imperative concealed in their affirmations.

The fundamental parenesis which Windisch has to face in his endeavor to turn the exhortations rather into declarations, is of course that of the sixth chapter of Romans. He opens his exposition of this passage [13] with the remark that Paul repels the suggestion that Christians are to continue in sin — and that is the same as asserting that they are no longer to sin — and supports it by declaring that sin has become an impossibility to the pardoned man. This representation can be allowed only provided that the "impossibility" asserted be understood as a logical one. That is to say, what Paul asserts is that it is grossly inconsistent for the converted man to sin; he ought not to sin with an oughtness which should be compulsory for his whole conduct. If, however, it were a sheer impossibility in the strict sense of that word for Christians to sin Paul should have spared himself his useless argument. That he has not thus spared himself proves that sinning was not only not impossible for the converted man, but was not unexampled among converted men, or even unusual. Paul is laboring here to deter his readers from sinning: and that is the way we deal with men who still sin, not with those who have ceased sinning altogether. Windisch allows that the life, the new life, is presented in some sense as a task; but he insists with reference to the newness of life itself, that it is a sheer gift, and that the power that it brings is not an " ought " but a " can." This is of course so far true: but the point at issue is

[13] Pp. 167 f.

not the newness of life itself but the walk in this newness of life; and that is, as he is himself ready to allow, a task. He dismisses the idea, it is true, that this task includes the overcoming of hindrances; there is no conflict, no effort, no advance in the walk to which Christians are exhorted. "As little as in the case of Christ is the new walk conceived as a conflict or advance." "It is a walk on an open and level road." What is true in such statements is only that these things are not expressly notified in the words themselves, but are left to the general implication. But they are very expressly included in the general implication. The future tenses, as it is natural they should, greatly disturb Windisch. But his troubles come to their climax only when he reaches the " believe " of verse 8 and the " reckon " of verse 11. "The determination of the sense of the 'reckon,'" he says,[14] " is not easy and not certain." " I might say," he adds, " that it is the subjective conception of an objective fact, arising from the ' apprehension of Christ ' and of mystical connection with Him. To gather from it an element of pure subjectivity and of uncertainty of the objective, seems to me illegitimate. Paul would no doubt have applied ' reckon ' to the possibility of mysteriously worked circumstances." Very possibly. But he could not easily apply it to objective conditions directly known in an experience already in full enjoyment. The thing that cannot be balked is that Paul's readers had to *consider* themselves dead to sin and living to God. It was *not* to them a matter of complete present enjoyment but of faith. And then, at this point of the discussion, Windisch has to brace himself to meet as best he may the full force of the parenesis.

The memory of his struggle with the sixth chapter of Romans Windisch carries over with him to Col. iii. 5, another parenesis which gives him some trouble. Paul is dealing in the opening verses of this chapter, he tells us,[15] with the positive side of the Christians' transformation. They have been raised with Christ; and, having been raised, says Paul, their life is now hidden with Christ in God. "The glorified nature,"

[14] P. 174.   [15] P. 199.

Windisch explains, "is already present but invisible, hidden still in God's protection. It is only the revelation, not the new-creation of the 'life' that still holds back." The influence of the Jewish hopes of cleansing and glorification on Paul's thought, Windisch suggests, is visible here. "Like the apocalyptist Baruch, Paul sees cleansing and glorification together as one process." He certainly sees them together — and one result of that is that he postpones the accomplishment of the one as of the other to the manifestation of Christ our life; in the meantime it is true of both these things that they are "not yet manifest." This means naturally that as we are not free from weakness in this transition period, so we are not free from sin. Windisch, however, says: "A reference to the sinful *habitus* of the Christian is altogether lacking"; it is only asceticism that is in question, and that is spoken of with contempt. Why, however, we need to ask, does Paul throw such contempt on this asceticism? Precisely because it is useless for the purposes of moral cleansing! These practices, says he (ii. 23), "are not of any value against the indulgence of the flesh." That is the reason why he pronounces them useless to his Christians. What he conceives Christians to be in need of, therefore, is something that will aid them in their battle against "the indulgence of the flesh." Is not that to relate the matter to "the sinful *habitus*"? And is it not to say that the Christian life on earth is a process of conquering sin in its manifestations in that life — "the *indulgence* of the flesh"? Positively, no doubt, this process may find expression in seeking the things that are above, in contrast with the things of earth (iii. 1, 2). But it has a negative side too. Precisely because we have died with Christ and our life is hidden with Him in God, to be manifested in all its fulness in due season, we must bestir ourselves in the meanwhile to be prepared for its revelation. "Mortify therefore your members which are on the earth," says the Apostle (iii. 5 ff.). "Therefore!" That is a very significant "therefore," and one very unaccountable to Windisch. "The very first word 'mortify,'" he says, "shows clearly that a completely new train of thought is begun." But

Paul says " therefore." " What we have to inquire," Windisch
says, " is whether possibly there is not attempted here a connection between heterogeneous conceptions." But Paul says
" therefore "; and " therefore " does not connect " heterogeneous conceptions." Well, says Windisch,[16] it is at least not a
process of cleansing which is intimated here: look at the
aorists — " mortify," " put away," verses 5, 8. It is an abrupt
passage from sin to holiness which the Apostle has in mind.
But neither will this plea serve him. The " aorist of the strong
imperative " is too familiar a usage to be overlooked.[17] Of
course Paul wished decisive acts of moral amendment from his
Christians, and that is the reason he uses these strong aorists.
But there is no implication that the end in view could be accomplished at once. And the main point is that such an exhortation was not superfluous for Christians. Windisch seeks
to meet this, desperately we should suppose, by suggesting that
Paul was so accustomed to the use of a catechism for neophytes
that he writes down mechanically from it these exhortations,
though, of course, he had no knowledge of his readers being
guilty of any such sins. In other words, his exhortations here
are purely conventional. If so, we need to ask why it was
that he was led to transcribe just such and such sections of
the catechism for neophytes when writing to Christians. Must
we not suppose that he used the sections of the catechism which
in general were suitable to the case in hand? We do not seem
by this road to escape the implication that precisely these
exhortations were appropriate for Christians as Christians.

A similar means of escape to that which he makes use of
here Windisch essays again, when commenting on Rom. xiii. 1,
where Paul requires Christians to be good citizens and warns

---

[16] P. 200.

[17] Cf. Winer's " Grammar of New Testament Greek," Thayer's translation, 1872, p. 314. In John xiv. 15, *Keep* my commandments does not mean
keep them once for all; neither does, John xv. 4, *Abide* in me, refer to a single
act; nor, I John v. 21, *Keep* yourselves from idols, refer to a single separation of ourselves from idols; nor, Mark xvi. 15, Go and *preach,* refer to the
delivery of a single sermon. The verb in every petition of the Lord's Prayer
is an aorist, the suitable tense, as Gildersleeve says, for " instant prayer."

them that rulers are of divine appointment and that we must subject ourselves to them for conscience's sake and not merely from fear of punishment. It certainly seems to be implied here that it was conceivable that Christians, if they did not take heed to themselves, might transgress the law of the State and in doing so sin against God. This appearance Windisch does not deny. "Here," says he,[18] "the Apostle seems clearly to say that now and again sin may bring even Christians into conflict with the State." "But," he adds, "this is not so. It is not Paul the counselor of the community of believers in the Messiah who is speaking here, but the Hellenistic instructor of mankind. The Thou is man, not the Christian. The possibility that a ' Christian ' should need to be punished by the State for an offence, he did not seriously entertain; he did not intend to apply the civil law to the sin of the ' Christian.' What he wishes to make obvious to the Roman Christians is the humanitarian conception of the State, in and of itself. They are to observe in the ordinances of the State the same divine discipline to which they have subjected themselves." As Paul here forgot he was a Christian leader addressing Christians and spoke as a heathen philosopher preaching good citizenship, so, only a few verses further on he forgets himself again and speaks to his Christian readers in the forms in which he was accustomed to address his heathen audiences in his missionary preaching. The passage is Rom. xiii. 11–14, and Windisch finds it impossible to deny that Paul speaks in it to his readers as if they were still living in sin.[19] He speaks to them, he says, as if they were still unconverted people. He exhorts them in terms — "make not provision for the flesh, to fulfill the lusts thereof " — which imply that they were still capable of sinning, or, rather we should say, were still constantly sinning: "*continue not* to make provision for the flesh to fulfil the lusts thereof." The Christians are simply required to put away their vices, and the vices that are enumerated are real vices. This, precisely on the ground that they are Christians, that they had long been Christians, and that it was high time for them " to show up

[18] P. 190.   [19] Pp. 191–192.

better " as Christians. This certainly does not look as if Christians were to Paul as such sinless men. No, as Windisch complains, he treats them as if they had always up to the moment of his addressing them, lived like heathen. But Windisch grasps at the straw, that he requires of them an immediate and final break with their old sin: " Not a realizing now to be begun and gradually to be accomplished is required, but an immediate passage from sin to sinlessness." Even that straw, however, does not sustain him. He is at his wits' end. " The words," says he, " strike on us as very surprising. That a totally changed conception of the Christian State lies here, is felt by everybody. We have found the ideal carriage of the community strongly emphasized, never actual sin, but only the possibility of sin, brought into consideration, a process of renewal already brought in substantiated. Now the Christians are suddenly required to discontinue their vicious life, and yet such vices are alluded to as could confidently be supposed to have been overcome. How is this change in conception to be explained? " Windisch sees but one way. Paul was a missionary, and had acquired certain modes of speech in his missionary addresses. And here, as he was writing to the Roman Christians — " the spirit of the missionary came over him, and instead of the Christians who needed only further helpful instruction, he sees a body of lost sinners before him whom he now has to snatch with one grasp out of their sinfulness."

There is another characteristic of the passage which gives Windisch some trouble. That is the interchange of the first and second persons in it. Windisch is unwilling to allow any significance to this interchange. " Because it is the missionary that is speaking," he says,[20] " I do not think that the ' we ' is to be referred to his self-consciousness. It is a pure style-form. It gives place at once to ' you.' Since he abandons the first person precisely with ' put ye on,' it is clear that he cannot have included himself in the ' we.' " For support in this somewhat remarkable opinion he apparently appeals to A. Jülicher's comment on the passage. At least, to the sentence which ex-

[20] P. 192.

presses his opinion that the "we" is not to be referred to
Paul's self-consciousness, he appends a note which says, "compare Jülicher," with a reference to Jülicher's comment. We do
not find anything in that comment, however, which can lend
support to Windisch's representation.[21] What we find, on the
contrary, is a remark to the effect that Paul does include himself in the exhortations of verses 12b and 13, and that that fact
precludes our using verses 11, 14 to prove that there was no
trace of spiritual life in the Roman church at all. This would
be in any case an overstrained use of these verses; but the
fact that Paul includes himself in verses 12b and 13 and
does not in 11, 14, does at least show that he did not feel
it possible to associate himself with the Roman Christians
in what he has to say of them in verses 11 and 14, or at
least in verse 14 — for the "you" in verse 11 may be only
the direct address appropriate to the opening of the exhortation. The strength of the language employed is, no doubt,
throughout, as Jülicher suggests, due to a desire to move the
consciences of the Roman Christians strongly. The particular
items in the enumeration of vices in verse 13 are chosen accordingly to meet their case, actual or possible. In associating
himself with his readers in these middle clauses of the passage
the Apostle — the more forcibly that it is purely without cal-

---

[21] Jülicher's Commentary on Romans is published in J. Weiss, "Die
Schriften des Neuen Testaments." The section on Rom. xiii. 11–14 is identically the same in the first and second editions (1907, 1908). The failure of
Jülicher to support Windisch at this point is the more significant because they
occupy common ground in the contention that Paul holds that Christians are
sinless. Commenting on Rom. iv. 15, for example, Jülicher represents Paul as
meaning that "where the law is not — in the blessed present (iii. 21, 26) —
there is also no transgression and accordingly no excitation of the divine
wrath." And then he adds: "An extremely characteristic declaration of the
ideal glory in which Paul saw the condition of humanity — no more punishment because no sin." E. Kühl (*in loco*) very sharply, from his own point of
view, corrects Jülicher for this certainly very unjustified exposition and inference. It is probably enough to say that the meaning of the declaration that
"where law is not there is no transgression either" — which is no doubt a
general proposition — is *here* that the promised inheritance was in no sense
conditioned on law; it was a promise of pure grace and rested on the righteousness of faith.

culation — intimates that it is not true of bad Christians alone, but it is a universal Christian characteristic, that they must be constantly turning away from sin and reaching upwards. As Jülicher puts it: "That the awakening from sleep and the putting on of Christ must be daily repeated, with ever greater result, was to him no mystery." It is impossible therefore to escape from the implications of the passage that Christians are not sinless but sinful men, in process of making their way through the night to that day which is presented as the goal of their endeavour.

A similar instance of Paul's associating himself with his readers in an exhortation to moral improvement is found in II Cor. vii. 1b: "Let us cleanse ourselves from all defilement of flesh and spirit, perfecting holiness in the fear of God." Windisch deals with this passage very much as he deals with Rom. xiii. 11 ff. It is clearly a piece of missionary preaching which Paul more or less inadvertently delivers to his Christians. He is not thinking of any "gradual amendment," but is calling on sinful Christians to lay aside once for all, in one comprehensive act, all sin, and "to let the ideal of a truly holy walk become reality in their empirical life." [22] It is only misplaced exegetical ingenuity which would "infer from the use of the first person that the Apostle includes himself in the exhortation." "The 'we' is a friendly style form." Meanwhile, it remains inexplicable that if Christians are as such sinless men Paul could address these Christians in this fashion. The Christians whom he addresses he distinguishes at length and in the most pungent way, in the immediately preceding context, from the heathen; and exhorts them to hold themselves aloof from heathen modes of thinking and standards of conduct. He cannot possibly be reverting here to a "missionary" mode of speech more suitable to heathen than to Christians. There is no reason whatever for representing the cleansing to which Paul exhorts here as a thing which is expected to be, or that can be, accomplished suddenly, in a single stroke. The employment of "the strong aorist" — "let us cleanse ourselves" —

[22] P. 150.

only shows that the Apostle is exhorting his readers to undertake the task he is urging them to at once, vigorously and with
decisive effect; while the present participle which follows it
— "while we are bringing holiness to perfection" — shows
that the task is accomplished only through a process, — is, as
H. A. W. Meyer expresses it, "the continual moral endeavour
and work of the Christian purifying himself." And finally it is
beyond question that the Apostle includes himself in what
thus is marked out as the common task of all Christians. No
one forms an exception, at any stage of his Christian life, to the
need of purifying himself from defilement of one sort or another, affecting the flesh or the spirit, and so continuing the
perfecting of his holiness in the fear of God. And therefore,
when exhorting the Corinthians to this activity of, not keeping ourselves pure, but of making ourselves pure, the Apostle,
as Meyer puts it, with true moral feeling of the universality of
this need, places himself, the mature Christian, on an equality
with them, the immature. The Christian life is conceived here
as a continuous process of active advancement in, negatively,
purification and, positively, sanctification.

A very striking passage of the same general order meets
us in I Cor. xi. 17 ff. In the midst of Paul's rebuke of the Corinthians for irreverent conduct in connection with the Lord's
Supper, two verses (vss. 31, 32) suddenly occur in which the
second person gives way to the first: "But if we discerned
ourselves we should not be judged. But when we are judged,
we are chastened of the Lord, that we may not be condemned
with the world." The effect of this change of persons is, of
course, to give the assertion contained in these verses a greater
generality. "You," "you," "you," the Apostle had been saying, and after these verses returns to saying: here he says
"we" — not setting the two pronouns in contrast with one
another (which would require that they be expressed) but
broadening the one into the other. But why should he broaden
his statement in just these two verses? H. A. W. Meyer (and
Heinrici after him) says: "The use of the first person gives to
the sentence the gentler form of a general statement, not

referring merely to the state of things at Corinth, but of universal application." That is true of course; but it does not
fully answer the question. There is no obvious reason why just
this remark should be singled out for gentler statement. It is
not intrinsically the severest remark in the context, which
therefore called particularly for softening. The plain fact is
that, in his rebuke to the Corinthians, the Apostle introduces
this general mode of speech here because what he has to say
here no longer applies to the Corinthians only, but is true of
all Christians, himself included. Only the Corinthians had been
guilty of the specific faults mentioned in the surrounding context. But all Christians are sinners; they all require to " discern themselves "; they all fail, more or less, in that wholesome duty; thus failing, they are all chastened by the Lord,
in order that they may escape condemnation for their sins.
This is the picture which Paul draws for us here of the Christian life. A. Titius is quite right, then, when he says[23] that
Paul " in I Cor. xi. 31 f. expressly reckons himself in the number of those who are judged and disciplined by the Lord,
because they have foreborne their own proving — " although
he is at once contradicted by C. Clemen[24] and subsequently by
Windisch.[25] Windisch does not say here, however, as in former
cases which we have noted, that Paul's " we " is simply a trick
of style and means nothing. He endeavours to discover how
Paul may be supposed to associate himself with the Corinthians, without the implication that he too needed to be
brought to give proper attention to his sinning by chastening
from the Lord. The theory which he broaches is in brief this
— sufferings were sent to others to bring them to a recognition of their sins and to separation of themselves from them;
they were sent to Paul to suppress temptation to sin in him.
In associating himself with the Corinthians by his " we,"
" Paul therefore did not intend to recognize that he too was
punished by God because of his sins; he has nevertheless used

[23] " Die Neutestamentliche Lehre von der Seligkeit," ii. 1900, p. 83.
[24] " Paulus, sein Leben und Wirken," ii. 1904, p. 102.
[25] P. 139.

a 'we,' because he too in another sense reckoned himself among the 'disciplined.'"[26] This is rather a weird theory — which has no ground in the text, and indeed has nothing to recommend it except that it avoids recognizing that Paul confesses himself a sinner, who is dealt with by God as a sinner. It labors meanwhile under the disadvantage that in its effort to relieve Paul from the sins which he confesses, it involves him in a sin which he does not confess; and indeed scarcely avoids involving God Himself in sin. For is it not a sin to profess to be at one with others in a matter in which you are really radically different from them? And is it not a sin to inflict punishment where punishment is in no way deserved?

It is quite clear that Paul conceives of Christians as not yet freed from sinning. Windisch struggles hard not to admit it, although of course he struggles in vain. How hard he struggles may be revealed to us by his comment on II Cor. xii. 21. There is probably no passage in the New Testament which throws into a more lurid light the sins of which Christians may possibly be guilty. Paul, speaking to his readers with affection and addressing them as "beloved," expresses a fear lest, when he comes to them, he may find the evils which he has rebuked among them still existing, and many of the sinners whom he has reproved still unrepentant. He describes those whom he has in mind as "those who have formerly sinned," meaning those whose sinning had fallen under his rebuke on a previous occasion — as it seems without effect. Windisch [27] adopts the notion, however, that by "those who have formerly sinned" Paul means those who have sinned before their conversion (as if Paul could have imagined that there were any who had *not* sinned before their conversion), and seizes upon the words to ground a representation that Paul means to say that these sinning Christians were not Christians at all. "I may paraphrase the words," he says, "thus — they continue their heathenish sins steadily, and have not even yet repented." Paul, it seems, "looked upon such Christians as have still after baptism committed whether serious or lighter sins, as if they had

[26] P. 140.   [27] P. 151.

not yet been converted at all: sinning Christians are to him unconverted people." The fact that they sin proves that they have not yet been converted — because Christians do not sin. It is part of Windisch's theory, however, to emphasize the "not yet." They are not quite the same as heathen after all: they have been baptized, and by their baptism they have both been made capable of repentance and been obligated to repent. But they have not done so; and until they have done so, they are not Christians; and that is the reason they can still sin. That is the theory, he says, that Paul went upon. But experience compelled Paul to modify it. It was only too plain that Christians did sin. He could not think otherwise, however, than that if a real Christian sinned he would be hopelessly lost: there remained no place of repentance for him. And so Paul, out of the gentleness of his heart, represents the Christians who sin as not yet having completed the process of becoming Christians by repentance, and so as still capable of salvation. This reasoning is so incredible that we transcribe the very words in which it is presented: "The 'not yet,' however, is to be emphasized. It is precisely because of it that baptized people also are *able* to repent. When Paul describes sin as a Christian's sin, it sounds as if he were giving the sinner up for lost: the fornicator severs himself from Christ. If he intends to maintain the salvation of the sinning Christian, he changes his point of view; then the Christian has not yet entered into relation with Christ. Radically framed conceptions dominate his thought; but because within the limits of these radically framed forms a change of point of view is possible, he is able to do justice to reality. There is nothing problematical to him about the repentance of one long baptized." This certainly is beautifully simple. Paul describes Christians as sinning and repenting. Windisch says that in Paul's view Christians do not sin, or if they manage to sin, cannot repent. Hence, says he, when Paul speaks of a Christian sinning, and calls on him to repent, he really means he is no Christian. And thus, he says, Paul keeps in touch with reality. We observe meanwhile simply in passing that it is precisely the "spiritual" Christians

whom in Gal. vi. 1 Paul speaks of as liable to fall into sin; and
perhaps we may be allowed to add that in I Tim. v. 20 not
only Christians as such but even the elders among Christians
are contemplated as able to sin.

It is only Paul, not Windisch, who is deceived by this
mental legerdemain. And thus, as we have already seen, Windisch is compelled, after all is said, to pronounce Paul self-
contradictory in his modes of thinking of Christians in their
relation to sin. He does not pretend to think this contradiction a merely surface one. "Paul," he tells us,[28] "following
different influences arising from experience and observation,
brings together really incompatible things. From the mysteriously wrought cleansing, from the mystical life with Christ,
which has made men insusceptible and apathetic to the allurements of sin, there exists no passable road for logical and psychological thinking to the obligation to refuse obedience to
sinful lusts. No doubt even the theory of cleansing and renewal permits an outlook on the further life of man. But the
way in which the walk of the cleansed person is described
shows that no subsequent conversion can be added. The new
walk is not given the task to overcome old oppositions; the
new man has only to tread the road which God has opened
for him and in which God leads him. Thus Paul, in Romans,
sets the theory of baptism and the requirements of conversion
immediately together, and when he, in the later letters, unites
them, an insoluble contradiction arises, because he is trying to
think incongruities together." And yet he suggests that Paul's
entertainment of two such contradictory conceptions together
is psychologically explicable from the circumstance that in the
rite of baptism a place was found for exhortation to the neophyte to carry out in life his character as a baptized person.
"This element of human activity suggested by the theory of
baptism may offer a certain mediation between the two disparate modes of conception. It means that the instruction and
exhortation may be tendered also to the cleansed man. Presenting himself to empirical man, Paul falls involuntarily into

[28] P. 217.

the tone of the preacher of repentance." [29] Windisch does not remark on the equal inconsistency of the conjunction of the two conceptions in question in the baptismal ritual or even on the extreme inadvertence of Paul in forming his fundamental teachings.

In another passage [30] he discusses somewhat more seriously the possibility of conciliating the two theories — the mystic and the parenetic, as he calls them. The prevailing exegesis, he points out, maintains their organic unity. The God-wrought change is spoken of as a transference of the life-center, or, more frequently and more weakeningly, as a change in principle. And there is attached to it the task which is set for man. This is actually to realize in the empirical being, gradually pushing on to the outermost periphery, what God has effected in principle and in the center; or actually and really to become what we already are in principle. This conception, now, Windisch pronounces not un-Pauline if only the notion that the empirical cleansing proceeds gradually be eliminated. It becomes in this form in fact, he says, one of the theories of cleansing which he has himself brought to view as Paul's, consisting in an organic combination of the doctrine of justification and the requirement of conversion: "faith signifies an inner transformation of the spirit of man, which capacitates and impels him to put away sin by a radical break in his empirical life too." On the other hand, he continues, the mystical theory of cleansing can find no place in this mode of conceiving things. In it, deliverance from sin and the establishment of life appear as embraced in one particular definitive total process — that is to say, as effected in their completeness all at once. "The notions of dying and death are characteristic of this conception: they designate for the Christian experiences of the past and declare the impossibility of sinning in his new nature." The rejection here of the current understanding of the entire body of Paul's teaching as to the application of salvation, as forming an organic unity, declaring a salvation with the creative activity of God at its basis and human activities

---

[29] P. 218.   [30] Pp. 180–182.

working out into manifestation what God works at the center, is, it will be observed, solely in the interest of the theory that what Windisch calls the mystical conception involves the complete transformation of human nature instantaneously. That is, however, by no means the case. Paul's insistence on the radicalness of the change wrought by God's saving power in sinners, by no means carries with it the implication that the whole change is completed in the twinkling of an eye. On the contrary, the implication is always that it consumes time in its completion and engages in its processes the activities of men. It turns out that Windisch is not altogether unwilling to allow this. At the end of the paragraph he says that after all a certain conjunction between the two theories is possible, a line of connection may be laid down. And this line of connection proves to be precisely this: that " the mystical theory of cleansing too can speak of an activity of the man, of the man awakened to new life." "Only," he adds, reaching now the center of his contention, " this activity is exempted from the task of overcoming sin." Apparently then the concession amounts only to this: that in re-creating man God does not destroy him; he is still living and acting; but living and acting now as a sinless man, whereas before he lived and acted as a sinful man. He has no battle to fight, no struggle to undergo; as we are elsewhere told, the path opened up before him is a straight and smooth one.

That Paul does not so represent the Christian life, Windisch knows just as well as anybody. That is precisely the inconsistency of Paul which he is at the moment engaged in asserting. For side by side with the mystical theory of cleansing stands Paul's parenetic theory, and this presupposes " the continuous sinfulness or temptability " of Christians. " Thus there are two mutually exclusive theories which Paul opposes to the misuse of his gospel of grace; the one explains that the Christian by God's power has obtained a sinless nature — the other that through the reception of grace he is obligated and capacitated to a sinless walk. Paul sums up what he has to say as to the relations of the Christians to sin thus — they are broken off through God's power or through the energy of the man's conversion. The first mode of conception describes the Christian throughout as a man suffused with heavenly powers, detached from the natural conditions of life. Only the second theory reckons with the temptability of the Christian; in it, as we have seen, even actual sin is assumed in the Christian." [31] In this contradiction he is forced to leave Paul. He does indeed add, most unexpectedly: "Our statements would require a decisive correction, if the exposition of the seventh chapter of Romans — no longer it is true the prevailing one — which finds set forth in the conflicts portrayed in it experiences of the renewed Paul, of the renewed ego, had to be recognized as right. Then it would be convincingly proved that the Apostle ' is even inherently sinful,' yes, that he recognizes himself as a ' poor, miserable sinner.' " [32] It is not in the seventh chapter of Romans alone, however, as we have already had occasion abundantly to observe, that Paul recognizes himself as well as all other Christians as sinful. Windisch has been telling us indeed that one of the two theories of cleansing which Paul employs in his teaching on the subject implies not only the temptability but the continued sinning of Christians. If, however, the matter is to be hung on the seventh chapter of Romans we are content: it seems to us quite certain that we have in these pungent verses a revelation of the inner life of the Christian striving against sin.[33]

We certainly are conscious of no revulsion when Windisch lays stress on the greatness of the change which Paul felt himself to have experienced when he became a Christian. Neither is the language in which he describes it in itself altogether intolerable.[34] We can put a benevolent sense on such

[31] P. 181.
[32] P. 182.
[33] Windisch cites for this interpretation M. R. Engel, " Der Kampf um Römer, Kapitel 7," 1902, to which he adds F. Mühlau and L. Ihmels. This does not, however, exhaust the important names even in the " miserable-sinner " controversy. Add Max Meyer, E. Cremer, J. Haussleiter, Paul Feine, and even C. Clemen, O. Pfleiderer, A. Deissmann. Juncker leaves the matter undecided.
[34] Pp. 220 ff.

phrases as that Paul was "filled with Messianic enthusiasm,"
or even that he conceived himself "already a man of the Messianic era, transformed by the Messiah by means of a personal
revelation, a new creature, with his selfish body dead, his sinful-
lusting flesh suppressed, his sin removed." "Christ is here, the
new age has come, the man of the new age is here" — that not
unfairly expresses Paul's conviction. He did suppose that a
supernaturally wrought transformation had taken place in
him, and in all Christians. And this transformation was expressed in his life by (among other things) a sense of cleansing,
purification. He, his Christians, were no longer of the earth
earthy; their citizenship was in heaven; and they were sharers
in the heavenly character — which is without sin. We cannot
emphasize too strongly this experience. It is the strength of
Windisch's presentation that he emphasizes it — although he
emphasizes it as an "experience" rather than a fact. He tells
us what Paul thought of himself in his "enthusiasm," rather
than what Christ had done for Paul in His almighty grace.
That is the weakness of his presentation, and beyond that this
further weakness — which perhaps is, in part at least, a result
of the former — that he allows no time for the accomplishment of the great change, no process for its perfecting, no beginning and middle and end to it; but insists that because it
means a radical breach with sin, therefore from its very inception no trace of sin can be admitted to exist. As a result he is
compelled to admit that this high conception could not be sustained by Paul; that contact with life brought him disillusionment, or we must rather say, failure — for it was a matter which
concerned not abstract opinion with him but a self-judgment
which in the face of experience he could not maintain. Immediately after describing in glowing language how Paul in
his enthusiasm felt himself without sin, Windisch is forced to
add: [35] "It is true that, cast into the old course of things, he
was not able to maintain literally his enthusiastic conception.
He had to say of himself, that sin in him was not slain but put
to flight. He could represent his life to his enemies and to those

[35] P. 222.

whom he wished to win for Christ as a blameless walk according to God's working. But to his friends he revealed the secret
that the maintenance of it on its high plane cost him uninterrupted struggle." Is not this a little seventh chapter of Romans
of Windisch's own? Surely this is not the Paul who knows himself a man of the new age with his selfish body dead, his sin-
tempting flesh suppressed, his sin taken away. But Windisch
still has some fragments to save. The sin in him is not dead as
he fondly thought; he needs steadily to fight it to keep it down
— (that is the seventh chapter of Romans): but he keeps it
down. "But that he has failed, that he fails and sins, incidentally and daily, he has never conceded." He had, says Windisch, plenty of occasions to confess his sins if he had any to
confess; and other teachers — Philo, James, Clement, Clement
of Alexandria, Origen — confess that they are "miserable sinners." Why not Paul? It might be enough to answer that Paul
was not writing a confession but letters — letters dealing not
with his own conduct but with that of his readers; and that he
constantly includes himself with them when speaking of their
liability to sin. It may be better to say simply, There is the
seventh chapter of Romans — and Windisch's own little
seventh chapter of Romans which we have just had occasion to
observe. It seems to be very much a matter of standard. Probably no one thinks Paul was a "common sinner," or supposes
that he means to represent all Christians as "common sinners." But if "sin is not dead in him," then he was still a
sinner; and sin, being alive in him, affected all his activities,
none of which was what it would have been had there been
no sin in him — and so he was not only "an incidental and
daily sinner" but a perpetual sinner; and we are not surprised
to hear on his lips the "miserable sinner's" cry — O wretched
man that I am! who shall deliver me out of the body of this
death?

According to Paul, says Windisch,[36] Christianity rests on
two foundation-stones: "justified by faith, and led by the
Spirit; or without guilt because believing, and without sin be-

[36] P. 158.

cause pneumatic." His purpose is to emphasize the latter of the two, because, in his view, the Reformation has thrust it aside and elevated justification into a position of such dominance that it may be thought of as the whole of Christianity.[37] And in emphasizing the latter of the two he wishes it to be taken strictly as he has expressed it, and justice to be done to its coördination with justification. Christianity consists in these two things, not in one without the other. At an earlier point[38] he had, therefore, very properly repelled an idea advanced by Wernle and Munzinger to the effect that Paul's missionary preaching was of a purely religious character and took no account of ethics. We may learn the contrary, he says, even from his use of the single word "sanctification." For "'sanctification' is the process by which the sinful man becomes a pure personal being, perfect according to the divine model," — citing I Thess. iv. 7, II Thess. ii. 13 in illustration. Men, he continues, having received in faith the salvation to which God called them, were "by a divine act at the same time separated from the impurity which had formed their nature hitherto; there was given to them in the Holy Spirit the power to pursue a holy life removed from all immorality." "This moral transformation," he now goes on to say,[39] "is accordingly conceived as an act of God and as a task which is appointed to the believer, as the total task of his life." This statement, which is not far from Paul's actual teaching as to the Christian's sanctification, and which seems quite simple in itself, Windisch finds to contain a whole nest of antinomies. These he undertakes to "explain," not in the sense of resolving them, but of seeking an origin for each separately in Paul's inheritance — as if Paul's mind were a mere receptacle into which things were dropped to remain related to one another only by mechanical contiguity. The main matter on which we wish to lay stress now, however, is the strength of the assertion that Christianity consists no less in sanctification than in justification — a statement quite true in itself — and the use to

[37] Pp. 524, 529–531.   [38] P. 101.   [39] P. 102.

which it is put in order to discredit the Reformation doctrine
of justification.

In the section in which the teaching of Paul as a whole is
summed up, his doctrine of justification is presented in the first
instance in its relation to the sins of Christians.[40] "The doctrine of the gracious justification of the sinful man" — the
discussion begins in purely general terms, but with Paul in
view — "seems to push aside the question of the sin of the
Christian as a matter of course, as raising no problem. The
sinful man stands here on earth exposed on account of his sin
to condemnation in the rapidly approaching judgment, but
over against him stands the gracious God who does not impute
to him his enormous guilt. This judgment is assured and sealed
to him. Past and present are taken together; the view goes into
the future which will bring salvation and glory because God
forgives sin. In principle there lies at the bottom of this doctrinal conception the idea that the sin of the Christian will
be forgiven as a matter of course." Then the discussion turns
pointedly to Paul: "Paul also has so formulated it that the
sinning Christian could draw from it daily comfort and assurance; we have forgiveness in Christ and stand under grace;
Christ appears for us against every accusation." "But," it
goes on to say, adducing the contrary part — "but only once
has Paul made the general assertion that Christ's intercession
and God's justifying judgment cover every sin." We interrupt
the quotation to note in passing that it is admitted, then, that
Paul has made the assertion once. And now Windisch continues: "Never does he in an individual instance point the
sinning Christian to the forgiveness that will never be denied
him. For the most part he presents the doctrine of justification in the form in which it describes the condition of entrance
into the Christian community, in which it grounds the forgiveness of the enormous guilt that has accumulated in the past."
"Accordingly," he continues, "Paul attaches directly to it the
two other theories which have for their object the passing

[40] Pp. 213 f.

away of sin out of the empirical life of the Christian, the real
sinlessness of the normal Christian." "Paul never says, Be of
good comfort despite your sins, because they will be forgiven
you. Because they are forgiven he demands now conversion too.
And now there arises a schism of thought from the necessary
orienting of the requirement of conversion to the expectation
of judgment. Alongside the proclamation of grace, that believers will be saved from the judgment, there enters this requirement to leave off sinning because they will be judged. It
is, now, the motiving of this requirement of cleansing which
makes the sin of Christians a problem. Paul plainly declares
that sin compromises salvation — the individual sin which is
committed after conversion, after baptism." There are four
ways, Windisch now tells us, in which Paul knows how to adjust to one another the two ideas that all a Christian's sins are
forgiven and that sin is something abnormal, unsuitable in his
life, which must disappear. What he looked upon as normal
was that the Christian should commit no sins; then he would
have nothing to answer for at the judgment. If he did commit
sins he might renew his repentance and so wipe them off his
slate; or he might expiate them in suffering. In either case he
could still stand in the judgment. "Only one mode of conception reckons with the idea that a Christian remains a 'sinner,'
or that his act of repentance has failed: the condemning judgment is not spared the sinful Christian. It is grace that nevertheless saves him." [41] "Thus," Windisch now adds, "the theory
of conversion adjoined to the doctrine of grace is able to maintain the sinless character of the normal Christian, and nevertheless at the same time to reckon with the sin of the
Christian."

Surely the two propositions that Christians are as such
sinless men and that only that one of four classes of Christians which manages to maintain sinlessness may be called
normal Christians — are not identical. So soon as we allow,
as must be allowed, that the Christian proclamation includes
provision for sins committed after justification, whatever that

[41] P. 215.

provision is, we allow that the Christian man is not as such
sinless. To say that at least the " normal" Christian is sinless,
is a distinct misuse of the word "normal." Not only are Christians not presented in the Pauline epistles as, as a rule, sinless,
but they are presented as never sinless. The sinless Christian
does not meet us on Paul's pages: there, all Christians live not
by works, but by grace. What is true is that Paul presents Christians as in principle sinless: that is their fundamental character
as Christians — although it is not yet realized by them in
fact; they are all " in the making, not made." They are not
seeking to obtain salvation by being good, but striving to work
their salvation received by faith out into the goodness which
constitutes its substance. It will scarcely have escaped notice
that, after all has been said, Windisch is not able to avoid admitting that, according to Paul, justification covers the sins of
Christians also. When he attempts to set over against each
other the justifying decree on the one hand and Christians'
liability for their sins at the judgment day on the other, he is
not able to keep them from fitting into each other as parts of
one unitary conception. It is very striking to observe him, on
coming to describe his fourth class of Christians — those who
come up to the judgment day still burdened with their sins —
compelled to say that they bear their punishment, it is true,
but still are " saved by grace." When commenting on Rom.
viii. 33 — " who shall lay anything to the charge of God's
elect? " and the rest — Windisch admits that it is implied that
occasion for laying a charge against God's elect could be found,
and that in, not their pre-Christian, but their Christian life.
Their safety depends, not on the falseness of the charge supposed to be made against them, but on God's decree of justification and the saving work of Christ, which was not confined to a
single past act but embraced in it also a continued intercession.
" Here then," he says,[42] " for once the relation to the whole
life of the Christian which is intrinsic in the doctrine of justification is brought to expression." Why he should say " for
once " is not easily discerned. It is just as clearly implied in

[42] P. 188.

Rom. viii. 1. "There is therefore now no condemnation t
those in Christ Jesus," as we have had occasion to point ou
at an earlier point. It is just as clearly implied also in Rom
v. 9 ff. and Phil. iii. 9, although Windisch labors to escape the
implication in both instances. Undoubtedly in Rom. v. 9 ff
Paul grounds the future "salvation" of Christians as exclu
sively on Christ as their past justification; and argues from
the one to the other *a fortiori* — their justification carries with
it their "salvation" by necessary implication. Similarly in
Phil. iii. 9 Paul represents himself as trusting utterly at the
last day in the righteousness of God received by faith, in sharp
contrast with any righteousness of his own whatever. Passages
like these leave no room for attributing to Paul a conception
of justification which confined its effect to sins committed
before it had taken place; and as little a conception of the final
judgment which supposed it to proceed solely on the basis of
works done after justification.[43] After all said, it is the fact of
justification which according to Paul is the ruling fact in the
Christian life and the Christian destiny.

It will scarcely have escaped observation that Windisch
is apt to give expression to the difference between Paul's doctrine of justification and that of the Reformers in sharp negative propositions. In a passage which we have only recently
had before us,[44] he says for instance: "*Only once* has Paul
made the general assertion that Christ's intercession and God's
forgiving judgment cover every sin." And again: "*Never* does
he in an individual instance point the sinning Christian to the
forgiveness which will never be denied him." Similarly we read

[43] On the rather vexed question of the relation of " judgment according
to works " to " justification " see the excellent lecture by E. Kühl, " Rechtfertigung auf Grund Glaubens und Gericht nach den Werken bei Paulus,"
1904, and also the page or two (including a quotation from Chalmers) in
J. Buchanan, " The Doctrine of Justification," 1867, pp. 237 ff. Compare further
Paul Feine's discussion, " Theologie des Neuen Testaments," 1910, pp. 308 ff.,
where the literature is given, to which add James Moffat, in Hastings' " Dictionary of the Apostolic Church," ii. 1918, pp. 391 f., and G. P. Wetter, " Der
Vergeltungsgedanke bei Paulus," 1912.

[44] P. 213.

elsewhere: [45] "Paul himself *never* unambiguously *declared* that the forgiveness which the Christians experience passes over also to their new sins; he only acted on this principle." And again: [46] The attempt "to comfort the aroused *conscience* of the sinning Christians meets us *only once* in Paul." It will no doubt have been noticed that each of these statements is carefully qualified, and that nevertheless they are scarcely perfectly consistent with one another. The two pairs in which we have arranged them are so related indeed that the universal statement in each is provided with an exception in the other. The net result of the four declarations is thus that it is allowed that Paul does all the things which seem to be denied of him — even though he has done them each but once. We have here, then, not even an argument from silence, but only an argument from relative silence: which at the most might suggest that Paul and Luther threw the emphasis somewhat differently in applying their common doctrine of justification. The real import of the matter is that Windisch is aiming all the time at the one thing he most dislikes in Luther's teaching — that Christians sin daily and daily need and receive forgiveness. At this, accordingly, he directly launches his most sharply framed negative assertions. "The daily forgiving of his sins to the daily sinner," he says,[47] is "a gracious benefit which is never mentioned in Paul, and which, when it is mentioned is never related to the fundamental religious position of the Christian" — a sentence which is so prudently guarded that it seems not to wait for a companion sentence to contradict it. Again: [48] "Confessions of sins — " like Luther's when he says "we sin much every day" — "do not meet us in Paul and John (in this generality)." Should however, all that is said in these and similar assertions be granted, what do they amount to? Nothing beyond the very natural fact that in the few and brief occasional letters which have come down to us from Paul, much is left unsaid, or is only briefly and perhaps only allusively said, that nevertheless belongs to the essence of his doc-

[45] P. 518.   [46] P. 526.   [47] Pp. 525–526.   [48] P. 525.

trine, and in other circumstances and on the call of other needs
among his readers would have been said with the same fulness
and vigor that he has used in developing the aspects of his
doctrine which he was called to emphasize. Paul has given us no
systematic treatise; what he wrote he wrote in reference to the
needs of the situations he required to face. It is enough that he
has given us the doctrine of justification. We should not demand that he shall have developed systematically every element in it and given a place in his epistles to each of its possible applications in precise proportion to its systematic
importance.

The difference between Paul's position as apostle to the
Gentiles and Luther's as reformer of the Western Church, carried with it necessarily a difference in the particular application of their common doctrine on which each necessarily dwells.
In the very nature of the case it was the "former sins" of his
readers which most concerned Paul — as they most concerned
them; equally in the very nature of the case it was the present
sins of their constituents that most concerned the Reformers
— as they did their constituents. To erect this inevitable difference of interest in the varied aspects of the application of
the doctrine, into a fundamental doctrinal difference is preposterous. It is as absurd to suppose that because Paul was
absorbed in the forgiveness of past sins, he was ignorant of the
forgiveness of present sins in God's justifying grace — or even
ready to deny it — as it would be to suppose that because
Luther was eager to comfort Christians, agonizing over their
sins, by assuring them that they were forgiven them in Christ,
he was careless as to the forgiveness of sins which say, a converted Jew might have committed before conversion, or ready
even to deny that they were capable of forgiveness. It is
Wernle, however, who in a few remarkable — and very extreme
— sentences, written for another purpose, teaches us how
Luther's situation in the midst of the long established Christian community, of necessity affected the particular direction
which his interest took as he dealt with the great topics of sin
and salvation. " We have never been sinners, entering only now

by a conversion into the condition of regeneration," says he; [49] "we know absolutely nothing of sin outside the Church. The problem of the Christian life, as the Reformation framed it, and as Ritschl has stated it afresh, is this: how can the Christian be in spite of his sin, a joyful child of God?" Something like this was, we say, necessarily the form in which the problem of the Christian life presented itself more pointedly to the Reformers. As necessarily it presented itself to Paul most pointedly in the form of how the Christian could be a joyful child of God in spite of his past. In meeting the needs of their differing situations Paul and Luther inevitably dwelt most constantly on different aspects of their common doctrine. That is the whole story.

Along with Paul it is John to whom Windisch makes his principal appeal to prove that to the New Testament writers Christians are men who do not sin. "Paul and John," says he,[50] "are the typical and irrefutable witnesses for the dogma that the Christian is cleansed." And he is eager to have it understood that they are independent witnesses. That they are united in testifying "that the Christian and sin are forever separated from each other," [51] shows how firmly the idea was grounded in reality; and also, no doubt, how completely the pre-Christian conceptions on the subject were taken over into Christianity and made a part of its teaching and its life. We have seen how he has fared in his attempts to interpret Paul in this sense. His success is no greater with John, by which is meant in this connection mainly the First Epistle of John. He already finds himself in great trouble with I John i. 5 to ii. 3. Contradictory statements seem to him to be set here side by side. John represents Christians as enjoying, as such, complete actual sinlessness. And he represents them as still sinning. Windisch deals with this embarrassing situation in the following fashion. Even those declarations which assert that Christians still sin, he says,[52] "do not presuppose that we sin on and on, and consider ourselves only to be in a gradual process

---

[49] "Der Christ und die Sünde bei Paulus," 1897, p. 3.   [51] P. 277.
[50] P. 508.   [52] P. 258.

of suppression of our sinful nature (*Art*), They rather have in
view a chief act, in which we confess the sins which we *hav*
committed (perfect tense) and receive now the forgiveness o
sins and at the same time cleansing from every wickedness.
This, however, is not at all what John says. He has not a " chie
act " of confession in mind, but continuous acts of confession a
sin after sin emerges; [53] and this confession is not brought int
immediate connection with the perfect " we *have* sinned," a
Windisch's representation seems to imply, so much as with th
continuous present, " if we say we have no sin," where " sin
must mean " act of sin," standing as it does between two con
nected plurals. Nor can the perfect " we have sinned " in thi
context bear the sense which Windisch seeks to put upon it
When he continues: " ' Cleanses us from all iniquity ' must
like the preceding analogous phrase, be expounded as an *actua*
cleansing of the man, which gives his life a new character," h
is assuming the least likely sense of the word " cleansing."
Even on this view of its meaning, however, John is speakin
not of a cleansing wrought all at once, but of an energy o
cleansing resident in the blood of Christ and applied progres
sively up to the completion of the process. John in this pas
sage is assuring his readers that their sinning cannot separat
them from Christ — provided that their sinning be dealt wit
as it should be dealt with, fought against and brought t
Christ, and not covered up with lying denials. He says his whol
mind in the first verse of the second chapter: " I am writin
these things to you that ye sin not, and if any man sin " — no
" has sinned," as Windisch tendentially renders [55] — " we hav
an advocate with the Father." John obviously understood him
self therefore to be writing parenetically, and to have it as hi
end to deter his readers from sinning, and to give them com
fort when nevertheless they fell into sin. He is, in other words

[53] See Huther here: on I John i. 9, in H. A. W. Meyer's " Commentary o
the New Testament.".

[54] See R. Law, " The Tests of Life: A Study of the First Epistle of St
John," 1909, pp. 130, 165 ff.

[55] Consult Winer-Thayer, " Grammar of the . . . New Testament," 187
p. 293, and H. A. W. Meyer, " Commentary," on I Cor. vii. 11.

just a "miserable-sinner Christian." And this Windisch himself is constrained by the next clause — " for our sins, but not for ours only" — to admit. "The declaration that Christ makes propitiation for our sins," he says,[56] " generally formulated as in Col. i. 14 and Eph. i. 7, is now here for the first time expressly applied to the sins of the Christian. The general formula might include this application; that it was not unknown to Paul might be inferred from the eighth chapter of Romans. But he never spoke it out clearly and it cannot have been current with him. It is John the Pastor who first makes use of it." Having formulated this comprehensive admission, however, Windisch endeavors to save some fragments. " But even he," that is, John, he adds,[57] " does not entertain the idea of a continuous operation of the propitiatory death of Jesus, which has for its presupposition consciousness of many daily sins. He is thinking only of the occasional sinning of one and another. The fundamental characteristic of the empirical Christian life lies in the ' that ye sin not.' Sin is an exceptional occurrence in the Christian life." This is certainly to make an illegitimate use of the aorist, " that ye sin not." Of course it means that John's purpose is to deter his readers from committing acts of sin. To infer that he means at the same time that there were long intervals between these acts of sin is desperate reasoning. John says, " If we say we have no sin " — and we have seen this means acts of sin — " we deceive ourselves and the truth is not in us." Are we to suppose that he spoke these words with the reservation — " except of course during those very long intervals between sins which make our life itself a sinless one? " Or when he said, " If we say we have not sinned we make Him a liar and His word is not in us," are we to suppose that it was with the reservation — " this of course has no reference to the general tenor of our lives and refers only to the very rare slips of which we may have been guilty " ? The tone of the passage as a whole is not that Christians are sinless men who may possibly, however, be overtaken in a rare fault; but that Christians are sinful men, seeking and obtaining in

[56] Pp. 259 f.   [57] P. 260.

Christ purification from their sins and striving day by day t⟨
be more and more delivered from them. This, of course, doe⟨
not mean that sinning is according to John the characteristi⟨
mark of the Christian. Not sinning is his characteristic mark. I⟨
was as not sinning that the Christian stood out in contrast with
other men. It means only that "not sinning," when understood
in its height and depth, is a great achievement and — we shall
quote Luther's words again — "Christians are not made but i⟨
the making."

That Christians can sin and do sin, as John understood th⟨
matter, is made abundantly clear again from I John v. 16–18
where intercessory prayer in his behalf is made the duty o⟨
every Christian who "sees his brother sinning. . . ." The pas⟨
sage closes, it is true, with the declaration that "everyone wh⟨
has been begotten of God sins not," and the easiest thing to sa⟨
of the two statements is that they contradict each other. Thi⟨
is what Windisch does say. The ideal and the ideal-contradict⟨
ing reality stand here side by side. John believed Christian⟨
could not sin; John saw Christians sinning. So, at the end o⟨
his letter we find him "giving an injunction for the treatmen⟨
of sinning Christians which passes into a conspicuous confes⟨
sion of the sinlessness of the God-begotten." [58] That John i⟨
misunderstood when he is made thus flatly to contradict him⟨
self, not only within the limits of three verses, but in the gen⟨
eral drift of his whole letter, is certain. And the present tens⟨
in the declaration, "No one that is begotten of God sins,"
appears to open the way to understanding it of the general life⟨
manifestation rather than of a particular act. What John mean⟨
in that case is not that he who has been begotten of God neve⟨
commits a sin, but that not sinning is the characteristic of hi⟨
life. We may say, if we choose, that ideally, in principle, h⟨
that has been begotten of God does not sin. It is probably best⟨
to say simply that this is what it is to be one who has been be⟨
gotten of God — not to sin; and Christians who have been be⟨
gotten of God are therefore in process of becoming sinless. Tha⟨
they are not yet sinless does not prove that they have not been

[58] P. 270.

begotten of God, but that they have not yet reached their goal.

It is naturally to I John iii. 9, however, that Windisch makes his chief appeal: " No one that has been begotten of God doeth sin; because His seed abideth in him, and he cannot sin because it is of God that he has been begotten." " The most categorical assertion of the Christian conception of sinlessness in the whole New Testament," we read,[59] " is found in this passage. Like the wise man of the Stoa, like the miraculously blessed man of the Apocalypses, the Christian *cannot* sin. It is also clear that the *individual* sin is dismissed to the region of impossibility." That this is an overstatement is plain at once from the circumstances that here too as in v. 18 the verbs are in the present tense, and may not here any more than there be made to express individual acts rather than general characteristics of life. Windisch, however, appeals to the idea of "begotten of God." This must express, he rightly says, a creative act of God. "The inability to sin is therefore more than a moral, psychological, intelligible impossibility. That in the God-begotten the ethical energy could relax or occasionally intermit; that there should remain in him another nature which could come occasionally to fresh outbreak; that godly motives could mix with human-sinful impulses; that sinful acts could always be done by a Christian, without affecting the nature of his personality — all this is simply incapable of being harmonized with the conception of the begetting by God which is presented here. So also is the distinction between principial, ideal, incompatibility and empirical coexistence inadmissible. What is begotten of God is the whole man; of him it is said that he does not commit a sin, that he cannot sin. He possesses 'actual sinlessness' not alone in his 'groundwork and basis.' It is with the God-begotten which John describes here precisely as with the Messianic man of the Apocalypse of Enoch." The whole force of this very effective statement is dependent on the thoroughly unjustified assumption that it must be at once in all their fulness that all the characteristics which belong

[59] Pp. 266 f.

to a God-begotten man are manifested in one who is begotten
of God. On this mode of reasoning we should have to contend
that every man must be born an adult. The grounds on which
development is denied to the child of God and the element
of time is eliminated from his perfecting, are not stated. Once
allow, however, that he that is begotten of God requires time
for the realization of all that is included in that great designation, and that not merely in his empirical life but also in his
very being — and the overpressure of the conception of which
Windisch is guilty becomes apparent. "Of principial cleansing," he writes,[60] "of a gradual execution of the task of cleansing, there is no question with John. All the ingenious distinctions which have been made in order to apply John's words to
the present experience of the Christian, are without justification. John sums up the whole essence of the matter and all
his several declarations when he declares that he that is begotten of God does not commit sin and cannot sin." It would
seem only fair to John to remember that these phrases "does
not commit sin," "cannot sin" do not perfectly convey the
implications of his present tenses, and that he wrote I John
i. 5–ii. 2 as well as iii. 9 and v. 18.

Windisch having himself indicated Paul and John as the
two sources of his theory of the New Testament doctrine of
the Christian life, we need not follow him in his discussion of
the remaining books. We note only one or two points of special
interest in passing. The Epistle of James has a certain importance as supplying what is in his view "the first Christian
confession of sin" — meaning by that the first declaration of
the constant sinning of Christians. His reference is to James
iii. 2, "for in many things we all stumble," or "for we all
stumble much," as Windisch appears to prefer to render it.[61]
The commentators seem inclined to take the "all" comprehensively, as including all Christians. That is Windisch's view
also; and he comments on the statement thus: [62] "What is
most important is the open, comprehensive confession of sin,
in which the teacher includes himself. He had already called

<hr>

[60] P. 279.   [61] P. 292: "The Christians who all sin much."   [62] P. 288.

attention to the ease with which a man could fall into sin because of the multitude of the commandments. Now he substantiates the fact that all of us without exception are great
sinners." And not only does James thus declare all Christians
great sinners — just like the "miserable-sinner" teachers of
the Reformation — but he currently treats and addresses them
as such. "Cleanse your hearts, ye sinners" (iv. 8), is the way
he exhorts his fellow Christians. "He declares," comments
Windisch,[63] "that the Christians must cleanse themselves, because they are 'sinners.' This express designation has not been
met with by us hitherto; it appears for the first time in the
teacher who also is the first to give expression to his own consciousness of sin." There would seem to be little left in James'
"miserable-sinnerdom" to be desired, especially when we
observe that he actually did what Windisch forbade us to
conceive possible in the case of John. "Of his own will begat
He us," says James (i. 18), and Windisch comments thus:[64]
"He knows how to extol an act of God, by which the Christian has become a new perfect creature. The perception that
this begetting has not yet with those addressed penetrated into
their external life, determines him to adopt the promotion of
cleansing." It might be supposed that I Peter would be given
a place alongside of James as testifying to the universal sinfulness of Christians. It appears to assume throughout that
its readers constitute a body of "sinning saints" who require
continual spurring on to moral effort; and at iv. 8 it seems to
imply that they, one and all, commit a "multitude of sins"
which it would be well to "cover" with love. Windisch[65]
does not doubt that it is the Christian body who are expected
to "have fervent love to one another," or who are reminded, in
order to give force to this exhortation, that "love covers a
multitude of sins." But he has a way of escape here. He says
that "the multitude of sins" were all accumulated before their
conversion — which seems inadequate in the presence of the
present tenses.

The novelty which Windisch finds in the Epistle to the

[63] P. 290: cf. v. 20.   [64] P. 286.   [65] P. 240.

Hebrews (vi. 4–8 x. 26–31) and with it, in the Second Epistle of Peter (ii. 20 ff.), is the denial of the possibility of a "second repentance"; or, to express it in language of later origin, of the pardonableness of post-baptismal sins. Paul, says he,[66] never put the possibility of a new repentance in doubt; James expressly exhorts sinning Christians to come to repentance. In Hebrews on the other hand, "he who after baptism commits a serious sin or falls wholly away cannot repent afresh and receive forgiveness."[67] With II Peter, "sinning Christians are worse than never converted sinners," and "baptism is unrepeatable."[68] There are passages in both epistles which make this interpretation of their teaching difficult, or let us rather say frankly, impossible. In Hebrews there is the all-prevailing sacrifice of Christ which atones for all sins (ix. 7 ff.). In II Peter there is the express declaration that the Parousia is postponed in longsuffering specifically towards Christians, because the Lord wishes to bring all of them to repentance (iii. 9). Windisch has his way of eluding both obstacles; but we need not pause to discuss the matter here. The point of chief interest to us at the moment is that it is only in Hebrews and II Peter that he discovers such an estimate of sin in Christians that it de-Christianizes them, once and for all. In all other writers of the New Testament he himself perceives that the way is at least open for recognizing sinning Christians as still Christians. In point of fact there is no single one of them — not even the authors of Hebrews and II Peter — who does not on every page recognize sinning Christians as Christians; or rather who does not, in fact, so speak as to make it very clear that they know no other kind. That Christians have broken radically with sin; that they ought to cease from sinning absolutely; that they must give account of their sins; this they all teach. That Christians are without sin — there is none of them who teaches.

We have treated the publication of Windisch's book as bringing the "miserable-sinner Christianity" controversy to a close. But this, of course, does not mean that the general points of view urged by the protagonists of the assault on

---

[66] P. 294.   [67] P. 312.   [68] P. 254.

" miserable-sinner Christianity," and especially their reading of Paul's doctrine of the relation of the Christian to sin, ceased to be held and advocated. These things had come, however, by this time, to be recognized as merely the particular opinions of a special school of critical students and had lost their interest for the general religious public, except so far as that public was interested in the history of contemporary criticism. We need further, therefore, merely cursorily illustrate the continued expression of these opinions in the later years of the first and early years of the second decade of this century, with a view only to realizing the extent and significance of their persistence.

When Wernle in 1897 published his book on " The Christian and Sin in Paul," he expressed in its preface his indebtedness for his understanding of the Pauline theology to two of his Göttingen teachers. The terms in which he did this seem to imply that he felt no great divergence between the views he was about to publish and theirs. In point of fact, at any rate, both of the Professors in question — Johannes Weiss [69] and Wilhelm Bousset — have expressed in their own writings views very similar to his. This is particularly true of Bousset, who is found in the end chiding Wernle for playing the part of a deserter from the party.[70] " Really," he tells us in this connection,[71] " it is seriously Paul's opinion that the Christian can no longer sin. All the passages to the contrary which have been adduced have little weight " — referring especially to Rom. viii. 31 ff., Gal. ii. 20, Phil. iii. 12. Salvation is a supernatural fact to Paul: the " newness of life " in which Christians walk is nothing of their own manufacture — it is like the sunshine and the spring breezes to them; and walking in it is just basking in it. In an earlier book — " Kyrios Christos " — of which that from which we have been quoting is a defence, we are told with rather more prudence that " Paul had a sense of sin in

---

[69] " Die Christliche Freiheit nach der Verkündigung des Apostels Paulus," 1902, pp. 21 f.; also " Paul and Jesus," 1909, p. 124.

[70] " Jesus der Herr," 1916, pp. 47 ff.

[71] P. 48.

his life as an exceptional condition " — although it must be
admitted that the general description of Paul and his teaching
which is given hardly prepares us for the prudence of this statement.[72] Essentially the same representations occur also in the
article on " Paul " in Schiele and Zscharnack's encyclopædia.
" Occasionally," we there read,[73] " Paul incidentally recalls
that even in the life of the regenerated man, sin is still present;
but he looks at that, at the least, as an exception, a little
shadow in the strong light (Gal. ii. 19 f.). . . . The conception
of the Christian life as an eternal conflict in which man scarcely
advances at all, or as daily renewed conviction of the corruption of our nature and reception of the comfort of forgiveness
of sins, was alien to him. The Christianity of Paul can be understood only as the Christianity of conversion. He knows
himself to have been converted in a particular hour: his life
now, the present in its contrast with the past, appears to him
in clear, brilliant light. And he gave himself to the new life
with all the heroism of which he was capable, body and soul.
He could actually say of himself that he was conscious of no
fault (I Cor. iv. 4). It is more difficult to understand how he
could maintain this mood also with reference to his churches,
whose shadows he saw only too clearly, and strongly rebuked.
This mood with him rests, however, not only on experience,
but more on an audacious dogma — the destruction of the old
and the new birth of the new world must accompany the death
and resurrection of Christ."

Somewhat similarly to Bousset, G. P. Wetter, a Swedish
author, having the sixth chapter of Romans particularly in
mind, writes as follows: [74] " If we are delivered from the sphere
of sin, if we are dead to it — then we have nothing more to do
with it. Instead of sin, ' grace,' ' righteousness,' ' life,' are now
the life-element in which we move, whose air we breathe. The
Apostle sees everything absolutely; the one contradicts the
other. The Christian cannot sin. The fact that in the actual
life of the Christian sin obviously occurs, cannot destroy this,

---

[72] " Kyrios Christos," 1913, pp. 155 f.   [74] " Charis," 1913, p. 46.
[73] " Die Religion in Geschichte und Gegenwart," iv. 1913, coll. 1295 f.

his faith (cf. Rom. vi. 14). Paul can believe so firmly in this
new reality, because it is to him not man who produces the
new thing, but God. So often as we direct our glance to men,
nothing is as it should be. Paul, however, looks to God, and
therefore he never doubts." A. Deissmann would apparently
like to say much the same, but cannot quite do it. He too has
the sixth chapter of Romans in mind. "As a new creature,"
says he,[75] "Paul the Christian is also free from sin (Rom.
vi. 1–14). He has been loosed from sin, but is he also sinless, incapable of sinning? In theory certainly St. Paul might subscribe to the statement that the Christian does not sin (cf.
Rom. vi. 2, 6, 11). But the awful experiences of practice would
give him cause to doubt. Paul the shepherd of souls retained
a sober judgment; freedom from sin is not conceived of as
something mechanical and magical. Side by side with all his
moral exhortations to Christians to battle against sin there are
confessions of Paul the Christian himself, especially in his
letter to the Romans (particularly Rom. vii.), witnessing that
even the new-created feels at times the old deep sense of sin.
But in Christ the grace of God is daily vouchsafed to him
anew, and daily he experiences anew the renovating creative
power of that grace." It is essentially the same note that is
struck by W. Wrede. Paul, says he,[76] says we are dead, are dead
to sin, and the like, and yet every one of his exhortations implies that we are not at all dead to sin. Is there a contradiction
here? Or does Paul's language merely anticipate what is to
come? Perhaps it is best to say that what he says is true at bottom, but the external realization of this inner truth as yet lags.
This much is certainly true: " the whole Pauline conception of
salvation is characterized by suspense." This too is only a half-
truth. But there is this valuable half of the truth expressed
in it, that is much too frequently forgotten: Paul's religion
was a next-world religion, and he never dreamed that he was
experiencing here and now all that had been prepared by
Christ for him. He had the Holy Spirit already: but he him-

[75] "St. Paul," 1911, E. T. 1912, p. 156.
[76] "Paul," 1905, E. T. 1907, pp. 102 ff.

self says that what he had already in Him was only the first
fruits.

Perhaps we may look upon the statements in Weinel's
" Biblical Theology of the New Testament "[77] as representing
as fairly as possible the present state of opinion in the school
which he represents, on the attitude of the New Testament
writers to the sins of Christians. And if so, we may place by its
side two other works on the theology of the New Testament,[78]
published at about the same time and representing other
points of view. From the three together we may cherish a good
hope of deriving a well-rounded conception of the condition in
which the question at issue has been left on the dying away of
the active controversy.

It is of no significance that Weinel agrees [79] that our Lord
did not expect His disciples to be without sin but taught them
to pray, Forgive us our trespasses. That is allowed on all hands.
It is more notable that his representations of Paul's teaching [80]
also seem to yield the case, although not without reserve. "We
have seen," he says,[81] " that according to our view of Paul too,
a man's morality is the fruit of the Spirit. Nevertheless, Paul
did not hold Christians to be sinless; reality was too great a
contradiction to that. He knew of the conflict of the flesh with
the Holy Spirit even in Christians (Gal. v. 17 ff.), although
these very words of his show that he holds precisely this conflict to be surmounted: ' Ye are not under the law.' Neither did
he give repentance a place merely at the beginning of the
Christian life, but thought of it as the sole and indeed the
divinely appointed sorrow which should continue in it, II Cor.
vii. 9 f. It was, however, certainly his opinion that sin has no
rôle to play in the Christian life; and he built on that, that the
good grows in it like the fruit on the tree." This seems to be as
much as to say that Paul recognized perfectly that Christians
remained sinners, but that the Spirit was supreme in them and

[77] "Biblische Theologie des Neuen Testaments: Die Religion Jesu und
des Urchristentums," ed. 2, 1913.
[78] H. J. Holtzmann, " Lehrbuch der Neutestamentlichen Theologie," ed. 2,
1911; Paul Feine, " Theologie des Neuen Testaments," 1910.
[79] P. 189.   [80] Pp. 374 ff.   [81] P. 374.

would bring all things right in the end. For Paul was of "the fixed conviction" that no Christian can be lost. Indeed, he sometimes spoke as a universalist (Rom. xi. 32). For Christians he is, however, absolutely sure. When, at the end of the volume, Weinel comes to speak of the teaching of the latter portions of the New Testament,[82] he strikes a different note. The high attitude of Paul was no doubt long maintained — and here this is described as if it included a conviction that Christians "commit no sin, or if they commit sin, they are punished, but still are saved, though ' as by fire.' " But by and by a change came, which brought a problem with it. Apparently this was because sins increased, and that, serious sins. Peccadilloes might be passed by; they were forgiven by God and man. But what must be said of apostasy, for instance? The Epistle to the Hebrews declares that no repentance will avail. In many writings, no doubt, the problem is not raised — as in Ephesians, Colossians, I Peter. In others the strictness is relaxed somewhat — as in the Apocalypse, where one more repentance is allowed. But the problem was now raised, and passed on into the later Church to give much trouble as the problem of post-baptismal sins.

When Holtzmann published the first edition of his "Textbook of New Testament Theology" (1897) he already knew W. A. Karl's "Contributions," and cites approvingly its representation of Paul's theory of non-sinning Christians. It does not follow, of course, that he derived his idea from Karl. He appears to have been prepared to welcome it, when announced; and although he does not seem to have worked out the idea in detail prior to the publication of Karl's book, he is to be credited with independent invention of it. He speaks at any rate here in his own voice, and expounds[83] Paul as teaching "with heaven-storming idealism" that "with the passage out of the sphere of the law into the sphere of grace the dominion of sin has reached its end (Rom. vi. 14). The believer actually ceases to sin. But here too the bad reality does not correspond to the goodness of the theory. Sin works as a latent power so

[82] Pp. 628 ff.   [83] Ed. 1, ii. pp. 151 ff.

long as man lives at once in the Spirit (Rom. viii. 9) and in the
flesh (Gal. ii. 20). . . . Care is therefore always to be taken
that the flesh does not rise and make itself felt (Gal. v. 16).
Believers have, it is true, crucified the flesh once for all (Gal.
v. 24): they must, however, always slay its members afresh
(Col. iii. 5) and through the Spirit destroy the works of the
flesh (Rom. viii. 13)." The scope of this statement, it will be
seen, is that according to Paul, while Christians, being under
the control of the Spirit, are infallibly saved and from the first
are freed from sinning, yet, having still the flesh, they are continually impelled to sin and are forced to fight their way onward in ethical effort. In the second edition of his book,
published in 1911, Holtzmann has retained this passage substantially unchanged.[84] A good many alterations in its language
are made, and that for the purpose not merely of qualifying
but also of strengthening the expression; many illustrations
and supporting notes are added; but the statement remains
in its contents the same. For Holtzmann at least, therefore,
the state of the case in this controversy was not so different
after the battle had been fought from what it was before. Paul
is still thought of as defying reality — the reality about him
and the reality in his own breast — and teaching that Christians are sinless; and the evidence which Holtzmann presents
for his views does not differ in character from that which we
have already seen in other like-minded writers. His judgments
on the teaching of other New Testament writers than Paul
follow also closely those prevalent in his school. For example,
James knows nothing of Pauline sinlessness: Hebrews teaches
that only sins of weakness and ignorance are pardonable in
the baptized. It is Holtzmann's testimony, therefore, that the
contentions of his school have suffered nothing through the
controversy, but have come out of it unaffected.

Paul Feine views the matter from a very different angle,
but, although far removed in both method and judgment from
Weinel and Holtzmann, is yet in his own way not untouched
by the modern spirit. He looks upon the contentions of Wernle

[84] Ed. 2, ii. pp. 166 f.

and Windisch with their congeners as being definitely wrong.[85]
He is very emphatic that, in Paul's view, the Christian, though
a renewed man and animated by an active principle of righteousness and life, is nevertheless still a sinner. " For Paul as
for Luther," he says,[86] " this righteousness of the Christian is
neither a complete nor a meritorious one, but the effect of new
divine powers in the man. . . . So long as man is ' in the flesh,'
he is for Paul not yet freed from sin." " Even though Paul conceived the righteousness of life in the Christian, in communion
with Christ, and in the power of the Spirit, as one that is already beginning and in part also being realized," he says
again,[87] yet he is " far too sober-minded to look on Christians
to whom the ' flesh ' remains, as freed from sin. Therefore the
justified also need forgiveness of sins." There was indeed a
tendency " in the old Church " to hold that free and full forgiveness was provided by Christ for pre-Christian sins, but
not for conscious and serious sins after our reception into the
Christian community. We may possibly see a trace of this in
James (v. 20); it appears clearly in Hebrews (vi. 4 ff., x. 26 f.);
and something analogous to it in I John v. 16. There is no trace
of such a notion in Paul. He does not formally treat the question, it is true, but there is no difficulty in perceiving how he
thought. To him justification is not merely an initiatory act,
exhausting its effects on the sins that are past. He relates it
to the eternal counsel of God and the efficiency of Christ's
work of reconciliation. In it is given therefore God's definitive
judgment on man. Even sin in Christians cannot compromise
it; it remains in force despite all vacillations of the life, for
God's faithfulness does not fail and He does not repent Him
of His judgments. " Though Paul does not assert that justification includes also daily forgiveness of sins, yet at bottom
that is his meaning." [88] The passages which are adduced in
proof are the Epistle to the Galatians at large (especially iii.
and v. 4 f.), and Rom. viii. 33 f., Col. i. 14, Eph. i. 7 with an
emphasis on the present tenses. In Rom. viii. 33 f., for example,
Feine remarks that the present participles " who justifieth,"

[85] P. 420; cf. note.   [86] P. 417, note.   [87] P. 420.   [88] P. 421.

"who condemneth," as is shown also by the concluding clause "who now intercedeth for us," deal with the Christian present. "The Christian feels that he is continually subject to condemnation, that he is surrounded by inimical powers, which seek to snatch him out of the hands of God and Christ. But God's decree of justification is always valid for him and Christ equally continually appears for him when he needs help." [89] If this conception, however, is thus left only as an indispensable presupposition of Paul's it is clearly spoken out by John, who tells us plainly (I John ii. 1 f.) that when the Christian sins he has Jesus Christ the righteous as his advocate with the Father.[90] The Christian here is conceived as still sinning, and living still under the continually applied atoning power of the propitiating blood of Christ. "The walk in full Christian knowledge postulated therefore for John as truly as for Paul the confession of our sinfulness and the necessity of purification through Christ's blood." [91] Passages like iii. 6, 9, v. 18 present an ideal. "The complete ideal is shown by the Apostle — the Christian as he ought to be already here, as he will be when his abiding in God experiences no longer any intermission, and we have become God's children in the full sense. But the Christians who maintain that already here they are freed from sin, are pointed by the Apostle to still fuller moral knowledge than they possess, and to the redemption from continued sin also which is given us in this life. . . . We have no new Pentecost to expect. There is only one Pentecost. But the Holy Spirit who was then given to the Christian community as the power of Christ and the power of God, will abide forever in the community of Jesus (John xiv. 16), as earnest of the power of the heavenly life. He points us to a future perfecting even in the conditions of our moral life." [92]

The very slight effect which all this long-continued and vigorously conducted discussion of the New Testament, and especially the Pauline, conception of the relation of Christians to sin, has had on English-speaking writers is very noticeable and perhaps significant. There have been echoes of course, but

[89] P. 422.   [90] P. 684.   [91] Pp. 697 f.   [92] P. 698.

little more than echoes. Orello Cone entered the discussion at its very beginning, quite in the sense of Wernle, and with verbal allusions to Holtzmann which may indicate one of the sources of his inspiration. " For his own part," he says,[93] Paul " expresses no consciousness of sin from the time of his conversion, and no sense of the daily need of a petition for the divine forgiveness implied in the Lord's prayer. With the ' old things ' that are passed, the old sinful life, he has broken forever, and leaves them behind. . . ." What he thus held of himself, he held of others. " He regarded his fellow-believers from the point of view of his own consciousness of ' life ' in the Spirit, so far at least as his theory of their religious state was concerned. . . ." " Such expressions," Cone now goes on to comment, " lend support to the supposition that Paul's missionary preaching was religious rather than ethical, that its emphasis was placed on the mystic effects of baptism, ' on sanctification,' and on ' justification ' (I Cor. vi. 11). His expectation of the immediate coming of Christ to receive the ' justified ' believers into the kingdom may have disturbed his perspective of the course of moral struggle which actually lay before his churches. Hence the ethical-religious paradoxes." " The fact that doctrinally Paul made no provision for the sins of believers shows that he took little account of sin as a condition from which those could need to be delivered who had once been ' justified.' The atonement is not applied to them. Faith saves once only, and he who through it has become a ' new creation ' is not conceived as again needing this salvation. Paul can hardly have thought that any one of his believers would be finally rejected when Christ should come." " This ' heaven-storming idealism ' was not shaken by the apostle's experience of the moral delinquencies of his converts, which he did not fail to reprove with due energy." It is a defective apprehension of Paul's doctrine of the Spirit as the Spirit of holiness, and of the Christian's progressive sanctification by Him, which has led Cone into so bizarre a representa-

[93] " Paul: The Man, the Missionary, and the Teacher," 1898, pp. 366 f., note.

tion of Paul's conception of the relation of the Christian to sin.

Kirsopp Lake, entering the discussion, with his essay on "The Early Christian Treatment of Sin after Baptism," late enough to have Windisch behind him, takes up the most extreme ground possible as if it were a mere matter of course.[94] According to him, the whole body of the first teachers of the Church were agreed that sinning after baptism — which is the same as after believing — is unpardonable, and it was only later, when hard experience had taught them that Christians did sin after baptism, that remedies for such sins came to be suggested. The essay opens with a fundamental assertion. "The most primitive form of Christian doctrine," we read, "held that Christians, as such, were free from sin. They had been born again into a state of sinlessness, and it was their duty to see that they never relapsed again into the dangerous state which they had left; if they should fail in this duty, it was questionable whether they had any further chance of salvation." According to Hebrews, we are told, wilfully sinning Christians are hopelessly lost. We are also told that "the same point of view was that of St. Paul, but in his Epistles the question is not a matter of controversy, and it is only implied or mentioned in passing." The evidence adduced, however, concerns only the sinlessness of Christians, not the hopeless state of Christians who sin — which is the point which was raised. And the same is true of I John which is next appealed to. The latter part of the essay is concerned with the remedies proposed for sinning Christians. First rebaptism was proposed; it is polemically alluded to in Hebrews and Ephesians. Next came prayer for venial sins (I John v. 16 f.) and recourse to the advocacy of Christ (ii. 1). Then Hermas suggests penance. And possibly we may add from John xiii. 1–20, footwashing.

The most extraordinary excursion of an English-speaking

---

[94] *The Expositor*, Seventh Series, x. 1910, pp. 63–80. The essay had previously appeared in Dutch — "Zonde en Doop," in the *Theologisch Tijdschrift*, xliii. 1909, pp. 538–554. The same material is presented by H. Weinel, "Biblische Theologie des Neuen Testaments," ed. 2, 1913, pp. 628, 629.

writer into this circle of ideas, which has met our eye, however, is contained in the remarkable Kerr Lectures for 1914–1915 by W. Morgan.[95] These lectures are written distinctly from the viewpoint of the history-of-religion school, and the material which concerns us is practically a transcript of the representations of the German writers. The question of Paul's attitude towards the sins of Christians is raised in the form of, What provision does he make for post-baptismal sins? The answer is to the effect that he makes no provision for them. " The message of forgiveness in Paul's gospel stands at the beginning, and has no reference to lapses in the Christian life. For post-baptismal sins no provision is made. The believer, if he would obtain salvation, must cleanse himself from all defilement of flesh and spirit, perfecting holiness in the fear of God (II Cor. vii. 1)." [96] Paul does not shut his eyes to the fact of sin in Christians. " What we do miss, however, is a clear recognition of forgiveness as a daily need of the Christian life." [97] It is everywhere assumed " that the standing given by the justifying verdict is something permanent," but Paul " has no thought of connecting it with post-baptismal sins." Morgan finds the account of this in two circumstances — the radicalness of the change wrought by renewal, and the small place taken in Paul's consciousness by guilt. " The sense of guilt and of pardon were not the dominant notes in Paul's conversion," and " they can hardly be said to be heard at all in his life as a Christian." [98] He never confesses wrong-doing; he shows no sense of need of daily forgiveness; he never prays or teaches others to pray, Forgive us our trespasses. Precisely what Paul teaches is this: [99] " From the death and resurrection with Christ the believer comes forth a new creature. So radical is the change as described by the Apostle that one might infer that the very possibility of sin has been removed. But such an issue he certainly does not contemplate. What, however, he does teach is that the old compulsion to sin has passed and the way been

[95] " The Religion and Theology of Paul," 1917, pp. 151 ff.
[96] Pp. 152–153.
[97] P. 152.
[98] P. 154.
[99] Pp. 160–162.

opened for a sinless development. . . . His expectation is that in normal cases the Christian will advance day by day in the knowledge of Christ, practice keeping step with knowledge, until at last he apprehends that for which also he was apprehended and Christ is formed within him. That a Christian should deliberately sin appears to him not merely as an anomaly but as an enigma. . . . The contrast presented by the grey reality to this optimistic expectation cost the Apostle many a sad hour. That Christians could sin and sin badly was all too palpable a fact. The fact does not lead him to modify his view of regeneration, but it forces him to descend from the high plane of the supernatural to the humbler region of the categorical imperative. Your flesh has been crucified with Christ, he again and again insists, therefore mortify its lusts; ye have received the Spirit, walk in it. By the stress of facts he is compelled to supplement his ethic of miracle with an ethic of will. The two stand side by side unrelated." They certainly stand side by side, but why say " unrelated " ? Paul certainly relates them, as, for example, in Phil. ii. 12, 13. And why, in the interest of that spurious geneticism which is the bane of much recent criticism, represent the ethic of will as rising subsequently in time to the ethic of miracle? It is *there*, as soon as we know Paul at all (I Thess. ii. 12, iv. 1 ff., v. 14 ff.).[100]

It seems scarcely necessary to pursue this review of the ever-repeated enunciation of the same opinions farther. And if we glance over the whole course of the discussion and endeavor to estimate its results, we are surprised by their meagerness. We have already suggested that they are practically summed up in providing the most radical school of criticism with an additional tenet in their historical creed. The members of that school now characteristically affirm that, in the view of Paul, Christians are sinless men — although they one and all agree that Christians, in point of fact, are nothing of the sort. The notion was only one of Paul's fanaticisms, thoroughly intelligible in him, no doubt, his antecedents and experiences

[100] It may be reassuring to note that James Moffat in a brief review of Wernle rejects his whole point of view (Hastings' " Dictionary of the Apostolic Church," ii. 1918, p. 380b).

being considered, but nevertheless symptomatic only of his
enthusiastic temperament. On the other side no doubt the
discussion has been useful in recalling adherents of the doctrine of the Reformation as to sin in the Christian life, from
any tendency into which individuals may have fallen here and
there to lose their sense of the greatness of the deliverance
which has come to them in Christ in the profundity of their
sense of the greatness of their sinfulness. The influence of
Pietistic conceptions, emanating from more than one source,
has been very wide-spread; and wherever they have penetrated they have tended to bring with them an inclination to
give expression to the recognition of the intrinsic justice of the
divine judgment on our sinfulness, by a treatment of the self
in accordance with it. Hair shirts and flagellations are not
popular in Protestant circles; but a mood and demeanor
adapted to a deep sense of the iniquity and loathsomeness of
our sins may be thought to serve much the same purpose. The
jibe has not been wholly without justification that many have
only enough Christianity to make them miserable. There is
some evidence that the discussion of the relation of Christians
to sin which we have been viewing has operated here and there
to quicken in the minds of adherents of the Reformation doctrine the realization that Christianity makes men happy, not
unhappy, that it brings them not sin but forgiveness of sin.
In sequence to the discussion at any rate there has here and
there shown itself among adherents of the Reformation doctrine a desire to dwell rather on the blessings which Christianity brings than on the evils from which it delivers, rather
on the glories into which it ushers the believer than the burdens from which it relieves him.

We adduce only a couple of examples of quite differing
antecedents.

P. Gennrich, in the opening pages of his "Regeneration
and Sanctification with reference to the Present Currents of
Religious Life," [101] draws a very vivid picture of the sense of
new-creaturehood which filled the consciousness of the apostles

[101] "Wiedergeburt und Heiligung mit Bezug auf die gegenwärtigen
Strömungen des religiösen Lebens," 1908, pp. 5–7.

— of "the joyful avowal of the actual experience of life by everyone who had experienced, in faith in Christ, the marvellously glorious and blessed effects that proceed from life-communion with the Lord." " How movingly," he cries, " the tone of personal experience strikes upon our ear in such confessions! What the prophets of the old covenant anticipated for the people in the time of salvation, and proclaimed in God-wrought confidence in the might and mercy of their God — that God would Himself prepare for Himself a people in whom He should be well-pleased, would establish a new covenant in which sin should be forgiven and iniquity taken away, and would create in them a new spirit — that, now, might in truth and reality be experienced in themselves by all who were lifted by Christ into communion with the Father, who for Christ's sake granted them the children's right, and by Christ's Spirit created in them the sense of childship. And the experience was so transcendently great, the transformation of the whole inner and outer life-condition, which a Christian experienced who had come to faith and received baptism, was so immense, that an expression could scarcely be found which was able to compass the whole great fulness of what he had experienced and to bring himself and others quickly and impressively to the consciousness of it. This condition of new life into which the Christian knew himself to be transformed, was experienced by him as a wholly new life-state, conceivable by no human wisdom, attainable by no human art or power; as a new creative effect of the Almighty God in Christ through His Holy Spirit, who brought His almighty Becoming into the life-development of the individual even as He has brought it into the world by sending His Son; and so has worked a regeneration of humanity in Christ. In one word — it was the unanimous consciousness of the apostolic and first Christians that they were new creatures of God, born of Him to new life, *born again:* that they were now first elevated to the stage of life on which life really deserves the name of life, because it is personal life in the full sense of the word, filled with a fully satisfying content, and supported by indestructible powers, *eternal life.*" There is much in Gennrich's personal modes of thought which is not in accord with either Paul or Luther. But speaking out of his own point of view, it is very evident that he is here straining all the resources of language in the effort to give an expression, which he can hope to be something like adequate, to the greatness of the new life brought into the world by Christianity. This is the way, he says, the apostles, who did not teach the sinlessness of Christians, thought of what Christians were. This is the way Christians, taught by the apostles what their inheritance is, feel.

The second example which we shall adduce is drawn from a very different circle, and speaks to us out of a firmly grounded and historically trained Reformed consciousness. Herman Bavinck, quoting the contention of Ritschl and his successors in this discussion, to the effect that the writers of the New Testament were accustomed to speak of their salvation in accents of glorification, proceeds: [102] "There is a truth in this contention which should not be denied. The Scriptures can scarcely find words enough to describe the glory of the people of God. In the Old Testament they call Israel a priestly kingdom, elected of God, the object of His love, His portion and heritage, His son and servant perfected in beauty by the majesty of God; and in the New Testament believers are the salt of the earth, and the light of the world, born of God and His children, His elect nation and royal priesthood, partakers of His divine nature, anointed with the Holy Spirit, made by Christ kings and priests, incapable of sinning, and so forth. He who rejects the teaching of the Scriptures about sin and grace can see nothing but exaggeration in all this; such a radical change as takes place in regeneration and sanctification seems to him neither necessary nor conceivable. But the Scriptures are of a different mind; they give a high place to the Church, call it by the most beautiful names and ascribe to it a holiness and glory which make it like to God. The glorification of the Church which takes its beginning with regeneration is,

[102] "Gereformeerde Dogmatiek," ed. 2, iv. 1911, pp. 281 ff. (ed. 1, iii. 1898, pp. 559 ff.).

however, equally with justification an object of faith." It is needless to say that this recognition of the glories brought to the individual and the Church by the gospel does not in these hands in the least affect the sense of sin and ill-desert, necessary to sinners, against which as against a foil it is rather thrown up. The point which it is adduced to illustrate is merely that the fulness of this recognition of the glories of salvation — or at least the care that is taken to give it full expression — may in these instances be in part the effect of the discussion which has been in progress on the relation of Christians to sin. So far as this, advantage has been reaped from that discussion.

If now, abstracting ourselves from these individual effects of the discussion, we inquire after the real function served by this assault upon the Reformation doctrine in the great complex of the religious movements of the time, we can only say that it has operated for the support and advancement of the current perfectionist parties working in the Churches. Looked at from the point of view of the general religious movements of the time it is, indeed, in effect an attempt to supply to the contentions of these perfectionist parties a scientific exegetical basis; and it goes without saying that it is the most elaborate attempt of the kind which has ever been made. Those engaged in this attempt, of course, care nothing whatever for the current perfectionist parties in the service of which they have nevertheless expended their learning and labor. There is probably no type of current religious thought and feeling for which they have less sympathy. And they care no more for the teaching of the New Testament than they do for the perfectionist parties. Bousset, in the very act of declaring that, among modern religious tempers, that embodied in Methodistic Christianity comes nearest to the Christianity of Paul, remarks that nevertheless to modern men it is abhorrent and the Lutheran is more acceptable — whatever he may mean here by the Lutheran.[103] These scholars have performed their service for the perfectionists while pursuing a very different purpose of

[103] Schiele und Zscharnack, " Die Religion in Geschichte und Gegenwart," iv. 1913, col. 1296.

their own. But in pursuing their own purpose they have been conscious all the time of possessing in the perfectionist parties allies to whose support they could appeal. There is involved in this a judgment as to the significance of the perfectionist movement in the history of Protestant thought, a judgment which is not left to the reader to divine but is openly spoken out. The purpose with which the debate has been undertaken and carried on has been to assault the Reformation doctrine of "the miserable sinner," intensely distasteful to these men of high ethical aspirations and attainments. They saw in the perfectionist movements similar revolts against the Reformation doctrine of the Christian life and the process of salvation, and they therefore claimed in their promoters fellow workers in a common cause. They have no sense of community with them whatever in their notions of what the Christian life is, in its sources, processes, attainments, issues: but they are at one with them in their common effort to break down the Reformation doctrine and have been glad to help them in their battle, by presenting them with Paul and the rest, as their patrons — if they attached any value to that gift. And meanwhile they have derived this benefit from them in return — that they could point to them as independent witnesses to the essential correctness of their interpretation of the New Testament.

The points of connection between the two are too significant to have been neglected by either the outside observer or the inside worker. We find them therefore cursorily intimated from the very beginning of the controversy. From the one side Fr. Luther [104] already remarks of Ritschl's mode of arguing on the matter and his exegetical procedure, that they "coincide with those of Methodistic Smithism "; and later it becomes a regular custom to mark this conjunction. [105] From the other side we find the writers of the perfectionist movements quoted by the assailants of the Reformation doctrine

---

[104] " Die Theologie Ritschl's," 1887, pp. 38 f.

[105] Cf., for example, Bindemann, " Das Gebet um tägliche Vergebung der Sünden," 1902, p. 12; Ihmels, " Die tägliche Vergebung der Sünden," 1901, pp. 7-8; Feine, as cited, p. 420, note.

with a respect which is certainly notable and perhaps at times excessive. It is difficult to believe that, except as moved by a sense of party interest, Carl Clemen could have felt greatly indebted to Andrew Murray for aid in the formation of his views of Paul's attitude toward sin in his own life.[106] And it is impossible to believe that Hans Windisch felt the contributions of F. Paul to scientific religious thought very valuable.[107] The ground of the sudden interest of these ultra-"scientific" investigators in the exegetical and theological opinions of such purely "practical" writers, is that they wish to exploit the movements which these writers represent as aids in their own assault on the Reformation doctrine of sin and grace. It is for this purpose, for example, that Windisch introduces quite an elaborate account of these movements in the closing pages of his volume.[108] "There are now to be noted," says he, "some very interesting movements within the history of the Churches of the Reformation since the eighteenth century, that may perhaps be considered reactions against the Lutheran Christianity which no doubt strives against sin, but above everything consoles the pious for their sins — the person of Luther is here left out of account." These movements are named as English Methodism and above all in our day the so-called Sanctification Movement. The language in which they are introduced is very carefully guarded, but what is meant is simply that in these two movements, Methodism and what we know as the Higher Life Movement, with its continuations, we have "reactions" from the Reformation doctrine of the "miserable sinner." And accordingly we are told clearly a page or two later, where the problem of sin in the Christian life is spoken of,[109] that "Methodism and the Sanctification Movement present therefore a reaction from the solution of Christian miserable-sinnerism which is fostered in Lutheran circles." This representation is true. The perfectionist teaching of these several movements whether in its crasser or in its more guarded forms, is a revolt against the Reformation doctrine not only

---

[106] "Die christliche Lehre von der Sünde," i. 1897, p. 111.   [108] Pp. 531 ff.
[107] As cited, p. 2.				[109] P. 533.

of the continued imperfection of the Christian in this life where he enjoys only the first fruits of salvation, but of sin and grace in general, which constitutes the pivot on which the whole system of Reformation teaching turns. And we may count it among the most beneficient results of the discussion of the Biblical teaching on the sins of Christians which we have been reviewing, if we can learn from it this fact; and with it this other fact, that the appeal of these movements to the Scripture in behalf of their teaching has, in the most elaborate effort which has yet been made to validate it, completely failed. The most striking thing about the long continued attempt which has been made to prove that to Paul the Christian is a sinless man is the clearness with which it has come out that Paul knows nothing of a sinless man in this life.

VI

" DIE HEILIGUNGSBEWEGUNG "

" DIE HEILIGUNGSBEWEGUNG " [1]

A GREAT religious movement has been going on in Germany during the last half-century, to which the attention of the outside world has been far too little directed.[2] It is commonly spoken of as " The Fellowship Movement "; and the complex of phenomena which have resulted from its activities is summed up briefly as " Fellowship Christianity." [3] Paul Drews,

[1] From *Bibliotheca Sacra,* lxxvi. 1919, pp. 1–40.

[2] Paul Fleisch has gathered the material from the sources, and written the history of the movement, very sympathetically, in his " Die moderne Gemeinschaftsbewegung in Deutschland," 1st ed., 1903, pp. 159; 2d ed., 1906, pp. 304; 3d ed., 1912, pp. 605, published as " Erster Band: Die Geschichte der deutschen Gemeinschaftsbewegung bis zum Auftreten des Zungenredens (1875–1907)." The second volume appeared in 1914: " Zweiter Band: Die deutsche Gemeinschaftsbewegung seit Auftreten des Zungenredens. I. Teil: Die Zungenbewegung in Deutschland." See also his " Die gegenwärtige Krisis in der modernen Gemeinschaftsbewegung," 1905, pp. 48, and his " Die innere Entwicklung der deutsche Gemeinschaftsbewegung in der Jahren 1906, 1907," 1908. Also his " Zur Geschichte der Heiligungsbewegung: Erstes Heft: Die Heiligungsbewegung von Wesley bis Boardman," 1910, pp. 134. This last book does not seem to have been as yet completed. It is a meritorious work, but does not rest on such first-hand information as do the others. On Fleisch's standing as the fundamental historian of the movement, see Gelshorn (*Die Christliche Welt,* xix. 1905, col. 854) and Theodor Sippell (*ibid.,* xxviii. 1914, col. 235). For the understanding of the Fellowships in general and their influence on the Church life of Germany, consult the section on " Die Entfaltung der evangelischen Frömmigkeit im religiösen Gemeinschaftsleben," in G. Ecke's " Die evangelischen Landeskirchen Deutschlands im neunzehnten Jahrhundert," 1904, pp. 297–346.

[3] With some hesitation we employ the word " Fellowship " to represent the German *Gemeinschafts-* in the compounds *Gemeinschaftsbewegung, -christenthum, -kreise, -leute, -pflege,* and the like; and that carries with it the use of " Fellowship " to represent the simple noun *Gemeinschaft.* Kerr Duncan Macmillan, in his excellent brief account of the movement (" Protestantism in Germany," 1917, pp. 242 ff., 270), uses the term " Community Movement." Franklin Johnson, describing it from the report in the " Kirchliches Jahrbuch " for 1907 (" The New Evangelistic Movement in the German Church," in *The Review and Expositor,* vii. 1910, pp. 345–355), calls it the " Associations-Movement." Both of these seem awkward; and " Conventicle

in a few words of detailed description, written a decade ago
brings it rather clearly before us in its external manifestations
He says: — [4]

"The so-called 'Fellowship Movement,' which has existed now
about a generation, is a religious *lay-movement*, and that of a
power and extension such as the Evangelical Church has not seen
since the Reformation. There is no German-Evangelical National
church into which it has not penetrated. It has thrust its plow-share
even into the hard soil of the Mecklenburg Church, which is not so
easy to break up. . . . Its adherents are gathered by the Fellowship
from the circles of the so-called 'humble people': [5] artisans, craftsmen, tradesmen, railway and postal employees, waiters, servant-girls
here and there (as for example in Hesse) even peasants, and also
teachers. Added to these there are — as will not surprise those who
are acquainted with Church History — the nobility and that the
high nobility. The academically educated and the industrial workers
alone are wanting. Of course not altogether; but they form exceptions in these ranks, and do not affect the character of the whole. . .
The Fellowship is extraordinarily thoroughly and compactly organized. The particular local Fellowships are united in Provincial
associations, at the head of which stand 'Councils of Brothers'
(*Brüderräte*). Over these associations there stands the 'German
Association for Evangelical Fellowship-work and Evangelization.' [6]
There exist, however, Fellowship-circles which have not connected
themselves with this central Association. The individual associations
not seldom possess their own assembly-houses which are sometimes
so constructed that strangers attending the meetings can find lodging
or entertainment in them. The associations employ also their own

Movement," which of course inevitably suggests itself, also appears unacceptable. We need a word which, like the German *Gemeinschaft*, is "both a concrete collective and a (abstract) term of relation" (C. F. Arnold, "Gemeinschaft der Heiligen und Heiligungs-Gemeinschaften," 1909, p. 4), and which is
free from inappropriate associations in English. We are encouraged to adopt
"Fellowship" by its employment by the competent writer of the "Foreign
Outlook" in the *Methodist Review* (xciii. 1911, pp. 477–479: "The 'Fellowship
Movement' in German Protestantism").

[4] *Die Christliche Welt*, xxii. 1908, coll. 244–246.

[5] *Kleinen Leute.*

[6] *Der Deutsche Verband für evangelische Gemeinschaftspflege und
Evangelisation.*

professional-workers,[7] Bible-missionaries, colporteurs, . . . and pay
hem. . . . The professional-workers who lead the meetings have
either received no special training or have attended one of the
educational institutions which are supported by the ' Fellowship '
and in its spirit. Older instances are the Chrischona (near
Basel) and Johanneum (first at Bonn, now at Barmen) institu-
ions; latterly there have been founded the Alliance Bible-School
n Berlin (founded in 1905) and Pastor Jellinghaus' Bible-
chool Seminary at Lichtenrade, near Berlin. The Institutional
oundations are in general extraordinarily developed. The Institu-
ions serve the ends partly of foreign, partly of domestic missions.
We find hospitals, inebriate-cures, orphan-asylums, rescue-homes,
ister- (that is, deaconess-) houses and the like. They have pensions
and hotels of their own, carried on in the spirit of Fellowship Chris-
ianity, and, as it seems, with good results. Regular annual con-
erences (at Gnadau, Blankenburg in Thuringia, Frankfurt on the
Main, and elsewhere) draw thousands of visitors. There is added a
well-supported press serving, in part general, in part local needs
e.g. the *Allianzblatt, Auf der Warte, Sabbathklänge, Philadelphia,
Die Wacht, Das Reich Christi* and others). Bookstores of their own
distribute literature which is read in their circles, among which there
are many translations from the English, of course exclusively of an
edifying character. The net proceeds are devoted to ' the Kingdom
of God,' that is to say to the labors and pursuits of the Fellowship
Movement. Surveying all this — this strong organization, this reach-
ng out on all sides — we receive an impression of the power and
extension of this movement. It is of special importance that property,
and, buildings, are held. Fixed possessions always give strength,
guaranty of permanence; are the back-bone of existence. If our
National Churches should suddenly disappear from the map, the
world, to its astonishment, would become all at once aware that
behind the protecting walls and beneath the protecting roof of our
National Churches, a new lay-church of a kind of its own has grown
up which is well able to depend on its own walls and to defy the
storms of the times." [8]

[7] *Berufsarbeiter.*

[8] Cf. the vivid account of how much in evidence the Fellowship Movement is in Germany, which is given by Martin Schian in the opening pages of
his " Die moderne Gemeinschaftsbewegung," 1909. In almost every considerable town in Germany we see houses of importance bearing the inscription
" Fellowship House " or " Christian Fellowship within the National Church."

What we are looking upon in the Fellowship Movement i
the formation within the National Churches of Germany, bu
not of them, of a great German free church. We speak of it a
a church, because it is a church in everything but the name
organized under a strong and effective government, equippe(
with all the instrumentalities required for the prosecution o
the work of a church, and zealously prosecuting every variet
of Christian labor throughout the whole land. Nevertheless, i
vigorously asserts and jealously maintains its right of existenc
within the National Church, or rather within the several Na
tional Churches of the Empire. All the members of the severa
constituent Fellowships are members of the National Churche
of their several localities, fulfilling all their duties and claim
ing all their rights as such. They pay all their dues as member
of the National Churches; they are baptized, confirmed, mar
ried, buried by the pastors of the National Churches; the
are in general faithful attendants on the stated services of th
National Churches — they are careful not to hold any of thei
own special meetings during the hours of the regular Sunda
morning services — and they are ordinarily among the mos
earnest supporters of all the religious activities of the Nationa
Churches. The several Fellowships are organized as association
of members of the National Churches and hold their propert
under laws which give them this right as such. The adherent
of the Fellowship Movement, in a word, wish to be understoo(
to be just members of the National Churches who have or
ganized themselves into an Association for prosecuting, unde
the laws of their country, ends of their own — just as othe
members of the National Churches organize themselves unde
the laws of the land for prosecuting ends of their own, it ma
be a banking business or the manufacture of potash. Only, th
particular end which their Fellowship has in view is the prose-

---

Thousands of Fellowship Christians gather every summer at the Conferences
Great tents are set up in the summer on vacant lots in cities and towns, whithe
every evening through four weeks hundreds — on Sundays thousands — flock
for popular services. Every conceivable kind of subsidiary organization is employed to advance the cause. " It is no longer," he says, " a thing in a corner.'

ution of specifically religious work; and the particular reli-
ious work which they have undertaken to prosecute is just
he whole work which is proper to a church. In other words,
precisely what the Fellowship Movement has undertaken to
do is to create a new church within the old National Churches,
, veritable *ecclesia in ecclesia*, or to put it sharply from its own
point of view, a true and living Church of God within the
dead and dry shell, the necessarily dead and dry shell, of the
National Churches of the several German states.

What the Fellowship Movement is in its essence, therefore,
s a revolt from the very idea of a state church, and an attempt
o create a free church within the protecting sheath of the
National Churches of Germany. Martin Schian very properly
ums up its relation to the existing churches, accordingly, in
he formula: "External continuance in the National Church;
internal rejection of State-churchism." [9] The internal rejection
of state-churchism is complete. [10] To the adherents of this
movement it seems unendurable that the Kingdom of God,
which, its Founder declared, is not of this world, should be
under the dominion of the secular state, and should be exploited in its interests. The very constitutive principle of a
national church is abhorrent to them — that the church should
include in its ample embrace the whole body of the people as
such, that every citizen of the state by virtue of that fact
should be a member of the church, with a right to all its ordinances and participating in all its privileges. They are reproached, therefore, with having no understanding of the value
of a truly national church, of the service it can render and
must render to the community, of the blessing that is in it for
the social organism. And when they declare that the church
s an affair of religion and its organific principle must be religion and nothing but religion, they are twitted with the impossibility of running a sharp line of demarcation between the

---

[9] *Op. cit.*, p. 22; cf. also his article in *Die Christliche Welt*, xxii. 1908,
coll. 953 ff., and the remarks of Arthur Bonus, coll. 1064 ff.

[10] What is said in this paragraph is said by Paul Drews and Arthur Bonus
in the articles already cited.

religious and the irreligious. Just because religion is a matte of the inner life, the line that divides the two classes is a: invisible one, and there can be no external separation of th one from the other; nay, " the line of division between Go and the world runs through every Christian's own soul." Hov can the " real believers," " the truly converted," be distin guished that they may be united in a veritable *congregati sanctorum?* Undeterred by such criticisms the Fellowship peo ple have gone straight on organizing themselves into thei *ecclesia in ecclesia,* on the sole principle of their " decisiv Christianity," and, doing so, have become a great religiou power in the land.

They draw their justification for doing so partly from th peremptory demands of their Christian life, partly from th precepts and example of the heroes of the faith.[11] They appea to Bengel, Spener, Luther himself. In his " German Mass, Luther has laid on the consciences of his followers precisel the course which they are now pursuing. He had had his ex periences and was under no illusions as to the religious condi tion of the people at large. He would have the gospel preached to them all, of course; but he would not have " those Chris tians who are serious in their profession " content themselve with so sadly mixed a fellowship. " Let those who earnestl wish to be Christians and confess the gospel with hand and lips," he said, " enroll themselves by name and gather to gether by themselves somewhere or other in a house, to pray read, baptize, receive the Sacraments and to perform othe Christian duties." [12] Even were such sanction lacking, how ever, some such procedure were inevitable. Companionship i a human need, and birds of a feather naturally flock together Certainly men who have in common the ineffable experienc of redemption through the blood of Christ are drawn inevi tably together by the irresistible force of mutual sympath

---

[11] Cf., for this paragraph, H. Jarck, art. " Gemeinschaftsbewegung," ir Herzog-Hauck, " Realencyklopädie," xxiii. 1913, p. 529.

[12] Luther's " Werke für das Christliche Haus " (ed. by Buchwald *et al.*) vii. p. 160; cf. K. D. Macmillan, *op. cit.,* p. 50.

and love. They belong together and cannot keep apart. We may press, without any fear whatever of going beyond the mark, every possible implication of Paul's great declaration that what God "acquired with His own blood" was nothing less than a "church." There is imperious church-building power in the blood of Christ, experienced as redemption. Even the fine words of Robert Kübel[13] seem weak here — that "a converted man has an imperative need of communion with his fellows, that is with people who have passed through or are passing through a similar inner moral and religious process, a communion with brethren and sisters who sustain, cherish, protect, guard, encourage and gladden him." The converted man has not only the need of such communion; he is driven by the Spirit into seeking and finding it. We cannot think then the movement towards a Fellowship Christianity other than both natural and necessary, nor can we fail to greet it as a manifestation of life and health in the Christianity of Germany. Accustomed as we are to churches organized on the principle of personal confession of faith, it presents to our observation nothing which seems strange except its anomalous relation to the National Churches, the nearest analogy to which in our Anglo-Saxon experience is probably the position of the early Wesleyan Societies in the Church of England.[14] Theodor

---

[13] Quoted by Jarck (*loc. cit.*) from Kühn, "Das Christliche Gemeinschaftswesen," 1897, p. 15.

[14] The term *Gemeinschaft*, in its technical use to describe the local Fellowship, is defined by Paul Fleisch, the chief historian of the Movement ("Die moderne Gemeinschaftsbewegung in Deutschland," ed. 2, p. 2), as a "voluntary association of Christians in a given locality for regular meetings for the purpose of mutual edification, apart from controlling connection with the ecclesiastical authorities and government." That would do fairly well as a definition of the early Wesleyan Societies. Sippell (*loc. cit.*, col. 102) points to the practice of the Puritans of about 1600 as an earlier example. Having spoken of the Separatists, he continues: "Those Puritans who remained in the Church gave out the watchword — 'Not separation from the State Church but union of the earnest Christians and organization of them into local fellowships within the external frame of the State Church.' These were fundamentally local Fellowships independent of one another and scripturally organized, which were looked upon as the true Church of Christ. This new ideal of organization, maintaining externally connection with the State Church, was later transplanted

Jellinghaus, having in mind our British and American Churches organized on the basis of "a public confession of faith and of participation in the redemption of Christ," explains the situation very simply: "In a state church," says he,[15] "in which all through birth, baptism, and confirmation are already fully legitimated members, subject to all the dues, such a practice is of course impossible. But . . . it is possible that within the congregation circles should be formed who know that for positive (*entschiedenes*) Christianity a public confession of personal acceptance of the grace of Christ is necessary, and who seek to put this knowledge into practice." That, in one word, is the sufficient justification of Fellowship Christianity in principle.

The justification of the Fellowship Movement which is now so widely spread over Germany, with its definite historical origin and the distinctive character impressed upon it by this historical origin, is naturally not so easily managed. This movement had a very special historical origin by which a peculiar character has been given it which gravely modifies the welcome we would naturally accord it as a highly successful effort to draw together the decidedly Christian elements in the German churches, in order that, the coals being brought into contact, the fire may burn. The story is already partly told when we say simply that it is the German parallel to what we know as "the Keswick Movement" in English-speaking lands. That it may be completely told, it needs to be added that it has not been able to maintain in its development the moderation which has characterized the Keswick Movement: that it has been torn with factions, invaded by fads, and now and again shaken by outbreaks of fanatical extravagances. Like the Keswick Movement, it derives its origin from impulses received directly from Robert Pearsall Smith in "the whirl-

by Amesius to Holland and thence deeply influenced the young Pietism." On this showing, the modern German Fellowships derive straight from the English Puritans through the intermediate steps of the Reformed Churches of the Continent and the Pietists.

[15] "Das völlige, gegenwärtige Heil durch Christum," ed. 4, 1898, p. 250.

vind campaign" which he carried on in 1874–1875 in the
nterest of what we know as " the Higher Christian Life." The
Fellowship Movement has therefore from the beginning been
also a Holiness Movement, or, as they call it in Germany, a
'Sanctification Movement"; [16] and a Holiness Movement
which has run on the lines of the teaching of Pearsall Smith.
The platform on which was set up its great representative Conference — " the Gnadau Conference," founded in 1888 and
remaining until to-day the center of its public life — embraced
just these two principles: (1) " Stronger emphasis on the doctrine of Sanctification " ; (2) " Coöperation of the laity in
fellowship-work and evangelization." [17] What the Fellowship
Movement has been chiefly interested in, in other words, is
just these two things — " holiness immediately through faith,"
and lay-activity in the whole sphere of Christian work, here
distributed into its two divisions of the work of the Fellowship, which includes broadly the fostering of the Christian
life among professed Christians, and evangelization. When
C. F. Arnold wishes to sum up in a few words the sources of
its success, he naturally, therefore, phrases it thus: [18] " Much
zeal, much labor, much money have been expended on the Fellowship Movement. What makes it strong is, formally, the
voluntarist principle and the activity of the laity; materially,
the idea of sanctification by faith as a complement to justification by faith."

Naturally, Pearsall Smith did not create this movement out
of nothing. He had material to work upon. And the material
he worked upon was provided by the Pietistic Fellowships
which go back ultimately to the *ecclesiolæ in ecclesia* established by Spener in Frankfurt, with the purpose of introducing
new life into the congregations. These Fellowships, working in
more or less complete independence of their national church-

[16] *Die Heiligungsbewegung.*

[17] Hermann Benser, " Das moderne Gemeinschaftschristentum," 1910,
p. 10, and art. " Gemeinschaftschristentum," in Schiele und Zscharnack, " Die
Religion in Geschichte und Gegenwart," ii. 1910, col. 1264; also *The Methodist
Review*, xciii. 1911, p. 477.

[18] *Op. cit.*, p. 33.

organizations, had in some places, as for example in Württemberg and Minden-Ravensberg, maintained an unbroken existence from the period of Pietistic ascendency. Some of them, especially in the South and Southwest, had preserved, moreover, their peculiar Pietistic character; others were more "confessional"; while others still, especially on the lower Rhine and in the valley of the Wupper, already exhibited tendencies which we associate with the Plymouth Brethren.[19] They had experienced a revival of religious activity in the twenties and thirties, but this had now died out. Quickened into new life by the impulse received from Pearsall Smith, they supplied the mold into which the movement inaugurated by him ran. This was their contribution to the movement. They gave it its formal character, as Arnold would put it: they determined that it should be a Fellowship Movement. Its material character was impressed upon it by Pearsall Smith in the very same act by which he called it into existence. Under the impulse received from him the sense of unity of spirit among the decided Pietists was greatly strengthened, a zeal for evangelization was awakened in them, and a new doctrine of sanctification was imprinted upon them — the doctrine of immediate sanctification through faith alone.[20]

Of course it was no accident that it was precisely on the Pietistic circles that Pearsall Smith's propaganda took effect; nor did the whole effect wrought by it proceed from his own personal impulse. There was an inner affinity between the ends of the Pietistic circles and those that Pearsall Smith had in view, which laid those circles peculiarly open to his appeal. It was the cultivation of internal piety to which they addressed themselves; they had associated themselves in Fellowships for no other purpose than the quickening and deepening of the spiritual life of men already believers. It was precisely to this, their own chosen task, that Pearsall Smith summoned them,

[19] Cf. Jarck, loc. cit., pp. 528–529.

[20] Benser (op. cit., p. 5): " The movement proceeding from Smith brought three results. It straightened among the decided Pietists unity in the Spirit; it pointed to evangelization as succor for the unchurched masses; and it raised the banner of sanctification by faith alone." So also in Schiele und Zscharnack, op. cit., col. 1264.

only pointing out to them what he conceived to be a better way and promising them, walking in it, higher achievements. He did not address himself to unbelievers, seeking to bring them to Christ, but to believers, calling them to a fuller salvation than they had hitherto enjoyed, or rather, to an immediate "full salvation." The element of evangelization which entered into the movement from the first, but was, naturally in the circumstances, only gradually given full validity, was contributed to it neither by the Fellowships [21] nor by Pearsall Smith.[22] It came from without; but it came after a fashion which made it a preparation for Smith's propaganda and contributed very largely to its success. Smith's remarkable agitation in the interest of "the Higher Life" in 1874–1875 in England was embroidered on the surface, so to speak, of Moody and Sankey's great revival movement, and owed not a little of its immense effect to the waves of religious awakening set in motion by this greater and stronger movement. Those waves were already breaking on the German strand when Smith arrived there in the spring of 1875 with his message of sanctification at once by faith alone, and it was as borne upon them that his mission there was accomplished.[23] The somewhat odd result followed that he inaugurated a great evangelization movement without

[21] Jarck (*loc. cit.*, p. 529, bottom) can speak, for example, of "evangelization of the unconverted masses," "in contrast with the Fellowships which bring the converted together."

[22] Schian (*op. cit.*, p. 5) accordingly contrasts Smith with Finney and Moody by the circumstance that "his method was characterized partially by his having in view less the awakening of the unconverted than the sanctification of the already converted." Johannes Jüngst ("Amerikanischer Methodismus, in Deutschland," 1875, p. 54) tells us that he often began his addresses by explaining that he "had two messages, the one for the unconverted, the other for the children of God." "Nevertheless," he adds, "the awakening influence on the unconverted retired somewhat before a kind of inner mission for believing Christians, whom he wished to urge onward."

[23] Cf. P. Kahlenbeck, Herzog-Hauck, *op. cit.*, v. 1898, pp. 664 f.: "In the years 1873 to 1875 the American evangelist, Moody . . . and his assistant, Sankey . . . preached in Great Britain and Ireland in surprisingly successful Revival Meetings. About the same time with the news of their results there came another revivalist-preacher across the ocean to Germany, Pearsall Smith, who addressed himself, however, more to those who were already believers, seeking to lead them to complete consecration to the Lord, and thus to 'sinlessness'."

really intending to do so: he had it in mind only to bring those
already Christians to the full enjoyment of their salvation. In
another respect, also, the effect of his propaganda failed to
correspond precisely with his intention. He came proclaiming
himself even ostentatiously the member of no church, the
servant of all; and desiring to bring the blessing he felt himself charged with the duty of communicating, to Christians of
all names and connections alike.²⁴ The movement which resulted from his impulse has been rigidly confined to adherents
of the National Churches and jealously keeps itself "within

²⁴ Jüngst, in a valuable account of Smith's work in Germany, which is the
more instructive because absolutely contemporaneous, puts on Smith's lips
the following explanation of his relations to the Churches (*op. cit.*, p. 87):
"I belong to no Church at all. I wish to serve all Churches, to call in all of
them the unrepentant to conversion, the converted to sanctification, not to
loosen but to strengthen the bond between the members and the ministers in
the several Churches; I work for Christ only and His kingdom, and am far
removed from working for an individual denomination, and must wonder that
people in Germany will not at once understand my complete ecclesiastical impartiality." Remarking on an earlier page (p. 84) that "the Methodists are
obviously making Smith's affair their own," Jüngst recognizes that the answer
may be made to him: "But Smith does not make their affair his, and that
makes a great difference. Ecclesiastically, he stands in absolute objectivity.
He carries this so far in Germany that he never lodges with the members of
any particular church fellowship, but in the hotel, in order to give offence to
none, whether they belong to the Evangelical Church, to the free congregations, or to the Methodists." Jüngst adds that this behavior is well advised,
"if the movement is intended to hold open the hope of a wide extension in all
Christian circles." He permits himself to pass into conjectures as to its possible
outcome, which are very interesting in view of the actual event. Just as
Methodism ultimately crystallized into a new denomination (pp. 88 f.), "the
possibility is by no means excluded that the Oxford movement too may be
segregated and consolidated by an energetic and constructive hand into a new
ecclesiastical communion. Since, however, Smith expressly emphasizes his
unwillingness to serve any existing Church, or to form a new communion, the
more probable result will be that in addition to a revival and warming up of
the several Churches, the real fruits of the movement will be garnered by that
communion which is most closely related to the methods and the teaching of
Smith. This is, however, the Methodists, who have greeted and accompanied
his appearance with loud acclamations. Their doctrine, in essence defended by
Smith, could in Germany emerge from the small Methodistic circles and make
an impression on Evangelical congregations on a large scale, only if on the
one side it were advocated by a personality as consecrated and were presented
in a clothing, ecclesiastically speaking, as colorless, as in Smith's instance is
the case."

the Church." The Methodists, for example, who were at first inclined to claim him as their own [25] — as they had considerable color of right to do — have been effectually repelled and have learned to speak of the movement which has grown out of his propaganda with complete aloofness, and even a certain contempt.[26] If, however, in view of these circumstances, we are tempted to doubt whether Smith contributed to the movement anything more than his doctrine of immediate sanctification by faith, we should correct ourselves at once by recalling the main fact, that he contributed the movement itself. Precisely what he did was to launch in the German churches a great "Higher Life" movement. It belongs to the accidents of the situation that this Higher Life movement took form as a great Fellowship movement, only one of the features of which was its Higher Life teaching — a teaching which has, after a half-century of saddening experience, happily been permitted, it appears, to fall into the background.

There are few more dramatic pages in the history of modern Christianity than those which record the story of the prodigious agitation in the interest of " the Higher Life" conducted by Pearsall Smith in 1874–1875. The remarkable series of English meetings ran up with the most striking effect first to a preliminary and then to a final climax in the two great " international conventions," at Oxford in the first week of September, 1874, and at Brighton in the first week of June, 1875. Their permanent English monument is what we know as "the Keswick Movement." But Smith's ambition extended far beyond the conquest of England, as the " international character " which he gave to his principal meetings testifies.[27] He

[25] Jüngst (op. cit.) gives abundant proof of this.

[26] Observe the objectivity with which it is spoken of, for example, in The Methodist Review, xciii. 1911, p. 477: " If German churchmen look with some misgivings on Methodism and other ' sects ' in the Fatherland, they show a far deeper anxiety concerning the influence of the Fellowship Movement (Gemeinschaftsbewegung). For this movement aims to transform the type of doctrine and of life within the church itself. And withal it is characterized, at least in some places, by great extravagances and generally by a very narrow outlook." The statements in this extract are perfectly true.

[27] Already, at the Oxford Meeting, public intimation was given by him

mis-calculated here as little as elsewhere. The Continental
guests whom he invited to Oxford and Brighton carried the
agitation promptly over the narrow seas. There had been no
more acceptable speaker at Oxford and Brighton than Theodore Monod, whose American training and experience qualified him to address an English-speaking audience with ease
and force; and on his return to France, he diligently exercised
his office of evangelist, to which he had been lately ordained,
by holding meetings in the interest of the new doctrine of
immediate sanctification by faith at Paris, Nîmes, Montmey-
ran, Montauban, Marseilles, and elsewhere.[28] Lion Cachet[29]
became the apostle of the movement for the Low Countries,
though Holland manifested little of the desired sympathy with
it. Theodor Jellinghaus carried the good news from the Oxford
meeting back to Germany, and a year or so later Gustav
Warneck added to the favorable impression already made by
his moving letters on the Brighton Conference.[30] " The hymns
used at Oxford were translated into German and French, and
also the books on the Life of Faith. In Paris the monthly periodical, *La Liberateur*,[31] and another in Basle, *Des Christen
Glaubensweg,* were at once commenced, and devoted specially,
like the *Christian's Pathway of Power* [Smith's own journal],
to teaching the privileges of consecration and the life of
trust." [32]

In the midst of this diligently conducted general campaign,
Smith himself appeared in Germany, and that with an even

of his purpose to " carry on God's work on the Continent." (" Account of the
Union Meeting for the Promotion of Scriptural Holiness, held at Oxford,
August 29 to September 7, 1874," p. 281.)

[28] He published in 1874 his book on the new doctrine, " De Quoi il s'agit? "
[29] Cf. his book, " Tien dagen te Brighton," 1875.
[30] " Briefe über die Versammlung zu Brighton," 1876. For estimates of this
book, cf. Jellinghaus, *op. cit.,* p. 722, and Fr. Winkler, " Robert Pearsall Smith
und der Perfektionismus," 1915, p. 17. Cf. Reiff-Hesse, " Die Oxforder
Bewegung und ihre Bedeutung für unsere Zeit," 1875.
[31] Edited by Theodore Monod. It lived only from 1875 to 1879, when it
was absorbed into the *Bulletin de la mission intérieure.*
[32] " Account of the Union Meeting for the Promotion of Scriptural Holiness, held at Oxford, August 29 to September 7, 1874," p. 338.

more dramatic effect and with even more astonishing results than he had achieved in England. He was not fetched over by his followers to clinch their initial successes and advance further the cause for which they had already opened the way.[33] He was invited to Berlin by men of the highest authority, through the intervention of Court Preacher Baur,[34] and he held his meetings there so far under imperial sanction that the Emperor placed the old Garrison Church at his disposal. He was in Berlin but a few days (from March 31 to April 5, 1875), in Germany at large less than two months. He could speak no German, and addressed his audiences, therefore, only through an interpreter. And yet he roused something like enthusiasm, and left behind him a movement stamped with his spiritual physiognomy which has not yet spent its strength. Johannes Jüngst sums up the astonishing facts for us in a few straight-forward words: [35]

"His appearance filled the hall of the Clubhouse (*Vereinshaus*) as it never was filled before. Hundreds were turned away for lack of room. He spoke to the ministers; he spoke to the laity. Then he visited other cities, where his appearance was desired, and held similar meetings, especially at Basel, Stuttgart, Frankfurt and Elberfeld-Barmen. There scarcely ever streamed such masses of people to religious meetings in Germany as to his. Even the some-what disturbing circumstance that he speaks nothing but English and makes use of an interpreter seemed to act rather as an attraction than repellently."

[33] Jellinghaus, in the Preface to the first edition of his "Das völlige, gegenwärtige Heil durch Christum," 1880, says explicitly: "Against our ex-pectation and without our seeking, the dear R. P. Smith was invited to Berlin, and (although he spoke through an interpreter and is in any event a man of no special oratorical gift) made, by the power of the Holy Spirit, a deep im-pression on many hundreds of souls in many cities of Germany, such as I suppose no one ever did before in so few weeks."

[34] Schian (*op. cit.*, p. 5) puts the striking paradox of things thus: "He who would reckon himself to none of the existing Churches was invited and toasted by the strictest ecclesiastics of the German Church" — and the move-ment he founded was a strictly unecclesiastical one.

[35] *Op. cit.*, p. 52.

And Hermann Benser draws for us this vignette, that we may look intimately into Smith's mode of working in Germany: [36]

"At the hour of the evening service on the first day of April of the year 1875 a singular man stood in the pulpit of the Garrison Church in Berlin, Robert Pearsall Smith. He was preaching. — But his manner of speaking was wholly different from what men were accustomed to hear. He spoke urgently as if he wished to clutch his hearers and obtain a decision from them at once, in an instant. By his side in the pulpit there stood or sat men who interrupted the discourse with prayers and songs. Suddenly Smith cried out in the Assembly, ' Rejoice, rejoice at once! ' On Sunday, the fourth of April, he gave voice to the enthusiastic aspiration: ' My brethren, I expect this evening great things from the Lord.' He longed for the return of the Apostolic age. As the disciples of Jesus had been baptized with the Holy Spirit ten days after the Ascension, so he looked for the Baptism of the Spirit on the tenth day. In the meetings everyone who felt inwardly moved to it, led in prayer. Even women were permitted to do so, since they were all brothers and sisters with equal rights before the Lord. — Had the golden Apostolic age of spiritual power and brotherly love returned in Smith? Many entertained this hope. This makes it intelligible that a court-preacher gave Smith his welcome at the first meeting, and many pastors spoke enraptured words as if under the compulsion of a mighty Spirit. Only a few stood aloof in doubt and warned against desertion of the firm ground of Reformation doctrine."

Smith's departure did not allay the excitement which had been awakened. Jüngst describes what was going on under his eyes: [37]

" The number of Sanctification meetings in Germany increases from week to week. We cannot describe all of even the greater ones, and mention only those in Bern under Inspector Raypard of the Chrischona, in Strassburg under Pastor Haas, in Geneva, Freiburg, Basel. . . . How great the movement already is we see not only from the publication by the ecclesiastical journals of extra sheets on the phenomenon, but from the establishment by the friends of the movement of a special journal for advancing the work — *Des*

<hr />

[36] *Op. cit.*, pp. 3–4.   [37] *Op. cit.*, pp. 66, 67.

Christen Glaubensweg (Basel, Spittler) [38] — which is already at hand in the second impression."

All Germany seemed to be aroused, and Smith had done what he set out to do. He went to Germany under the determination to conquer it to the Higher Life doctrine which he had made it his life-work to propagate; and he had set forces at work which seemed to him to bear in them the promise and potency of victory. The spirit in which he went to Germany is made clear to us in an incident the memory of which Jüngst has preserved for us: [39]

" Before Smith went to Germany he was again for a while in America. There he visited the leading personalities of the Albrecht-brethren in Cleveland and described to them especially the progress of the movement in Germany (*Christl. Botschafter*, 1875, No. 7). He told them of his purpose to go to Berlin before Easter on the invitation of important ministers and laymen, and said, among other things, ' If the Lord will give the people of Berlin into my hand, as he did at Oxford ' — but corrected himself at once: ' But in the business of my God I no longer know any *if* — the Lord does it according to His word.' The *Botschafter* adds: ' He believes and doubts not. With remarkable quietness but equally decisively and confidently he speaks of the success still to be secured.' "

The state of mind in which he returned from Germany is startlingly revealed by his sudden cry one day on the platform at Brighton, " All Europe is at my feet! " The excitement which he had aroused in Germany he himself evidently shared.

Fortunately the movement inaugurated in this atmosphere of excitement fell at once into good hands. Men of combined zeal and moderation, of wide experience and trained discretion, like Theodor Christlieb, Jasper von Oertzen, Theodor Jellinghaus, took charge of it. The American Methodist evangelist Fritz von Schlümbach was employed by Christlieb in pushing the work of evangelization in northern and eastern Germany, and then by Adolf Stöcker in the slums of Berlin.

[38] Jellinghaus, writing in 1880, says its circulation was then about 8,000.
[39] *Op. cit.,* pp. 84, 85.

The organization of the movement was soon taken diligently
in hand. The "German Evangelization Association" was
formed in 1884. The Gnadau Conference was established in
1888, and out of it came in 1890 the "German Committee for
Evangelical Fellowship-work," enlarged in its scope in 1894
into "The German Committee for Evangelical Fellowship-
work and Evangelization," and transformed for legal reasons
in 1901 into "The German Philadelphia Association." Under
the leadership first of von Oertzen, then of Pückler, then of
Michielis, thirty years passed by in fruitful development.[40]
A sister alliance had in the meanwhile grown up by its side
(from 1886) — of extremer tendencies and more deeply stained
with Darbyite conceptions — holding its great conference at
Blankenburg in Thuringia.[41] Between it and Gnadau varying
relations obtained from year to year. The formation of a third
union was attempted in 1901–1902 by Dr. Lepsius, the brilliant
son of the distinguished Egyptologist, when rebuked by the
Blankenburg Alliance, of which he was a member, for some
foolish dealings with the Old Testament text; but that soon
became only an annual convention of positive theologians.
Meanwhile the Gnadau organization flourished. Very diverse

[40] C. F. Arnold's characterization, from the extremely churchly standpoint, runs as follows (op. cit., p. 32): "In the Gnadau branch the Darbyite
undercurrent was held down for a long time by the Württembergers, and up
to von Oertzen's death (1894) moderation ruled. After that, however, Graf
Pückler, supported by Graf Bernstorff and Pastor Paul, introduced a driving
propaganda. . . . Therefore the German Committee for Evangelical Fellowship-work and Evangelization was formed in 1894. In 1901 Graf Pückler sought
a greater independence for the Fellowships. . . . Since 1902 a centrifugal
movement has no doubt made itself noticeable; but an organization has been
created which stretches from East Prussia to Westphalia and from Schleswig-
Holstein to Nassau."

[41] C. F. Arnold (op. cit., p. 31) describes the characteristics of the Blankenburg branch of the Fellowship Movement. Anarchistic Darbyite tendencies
rule. The last of the nine articles of the Evangelical Alliance which declares
the preaching office, baptism, and the Lord's Supper permanent elements in
the church, is rejected. The state church is asserted to give to the Emperor
what belongs to God. Luther sowed to the flesh when he founded a state
church. All theology is worthless. The fundamental doctrine is that of the
collection of the Bride-Church, that is, extreme chiliasm. The leaders are von
Knobelsdorff, von Viebahn, Stockmayer, Kühn, Rubanowitsch.

elements were embraced in its constituency; from the soft
Pietism of the South and Southwest to the harsh fanaticism
which ruled the temper of North and East. Occasions for friction were frequent. Nevertheless, in the absorption of the Association in the pressing tasks of its extension and organization, the peace was fairly well kept until the end of the century.
With the opening of the twentieth century, however, a period
of turmoil and inward conflict set in which has shaken the
movement to its foundations and out of which it has found its
way only as through blood.

The susceptibility of the Fellowship Movement to the
worst of the evils which have torn it has been due to the circumstances of its origin and the general character then impressed upon it. It was the product of an impulse received
from without, a prolongation into Germany of a movement
originating in conditions prevalent in America after the
Civil War, and reaching Germany as the extension to the Continent of a very extravagant English upheaval. A character
both foreign — it itself would doubtless prefer that we should
say international — and enthusiastic, in the worser sense of
that term, was imprinted upon it by that circumstance from
which it has never escaped, unless indeed it has at the end
escaped from it after experiences the most humiliating. It has
always been conscious of standing in close connection with
the religious forces operating in Anglo-Saxon Christendom,
and has steadily sought to reproduce them in the conditions
of German life. Priding itself upon this connection and seeking
constantly to commend its teachings and methods on the
ground that they were teachings and methods which had already approved themselves in England and America, it has
had no just ground to complain of the reproach of " Englände-
rei " and " Methodismus " [42] which it has had to bear. Under

[42] As the term *Methodismus* has been flung at the Fellowship Christianity as a term of reproach, it has naturally been repelled, and thus a debate has
grown up as to its applicability. Jellinghaus (*op. cit.*, ed. 4, pp. 78 ff.) protests
against the use of the term and declares that there is nothing, strictly speaking,
Methodistic about the movement and the term as employed of it is only a
cloak of ignorance. In England, he says, the movement is called " the Keswick

the broad term "Methodistical" there has been included a
multitude of sins, the worst to be said of which is that the
Fellowship Movement has really been guilty of them all. For
unfortunately it has shown itself particularly sensitive to the
repeated waves of religious excitement which have swept over
Anglo-Saxon Christendom and has reproduced them with at
least equal extravagance. There is scarcely any fanatical tendency which has troubled Anglo-Saxon Christendom during
the last half-century of which the German Fellowships have
not been the prey.

Movement"; but, as that term would convey no meaning to German ears,
he proposes to call it "the Salvationist (*heilistisch*) Movement," because
what the movement proclaims is salvation — the possession of salvation, the
assurance of salvation, the present enjoyment of salvation — through joyful
acceptance of the Savior, and of free, complete, and present salvation. Jellinghaus' critics content themselves with crying out upon the linguistic enormity
of the term *heilistisch*. He, however, having the courage of his convictions,
goes on to coin a corresponding substantive and calls the movement (p. 176)
"our new Biblical Salvationism (*Heilismus*)." Friedrich Simon (*Die Christliche Welt*, xxii. 1908, col. 1144), while denying any historical ground for
calling the Fellowship Movement "Methodistic," yet wishes to take the sting
out of the term by declaring that what is called "Methodistic" in the Fellowship Movement was already recognized by Schleiermacher as natural and
right, and that whoever would deny a right in the National Church to
"'Methodistically' colored piety," in even the narrow sense, forgets the historical nexus between Luther and Spener and Zinzendorf and Wesley, and
must logically turn his back on "missions," which have their roots in Pietism
and Moravianism, and strike out of the Hymn Book and Liturgy no inconsiderable amount of their contents. — In point of fact, of course, "Methodism,"
in its narrow sense as the designation of the movement inaugurated by Wesley,
does lie in the background of the entire movement. Smith's doctrine of the
Higher Life is historically only a modification of the Wesleyan doctrine of
"Christian Perfection," and the Evangelistic methods employed by him and
conveyed by him to the Fellowship Movement were historically derived from
Methodist practice. Karl Sell (*Zeitschrift für Theologie und Kirche,* xvi. 1906,
p. 375) is not far from putting his finger on the exact point of importance when
he says that the great matter in which Methodism differs from the Pietism of
which the Fellowship Movement is a modification under the impulse of the
Evangelization Movement, lies precisely in "Methodism's ardor for saving
souls, and that quickly, in a moment." The reality and the strength of the
Methodist spirit in the Fellowship Movement is manifested in its participation
in this Methodist "suddenness" — Smith's famous *jetzt* — "Jesus saves me
now." The two most outstanding features of the movement are its twin insistence on sudden conversion and sudden sanctification. What it has stood for in

The movement from its very inception was a Higher Life movement. It was as such that Pearsall Smith launched it: and it has made its assault as such on the German Churches, seeking with constant zeal to transform their type of doctrine to this model. Fortunately the molding of the doctrinal teaching of the Fellowships fell from the first into moderate hands. Theodor Jellinghaus became their acknowledged theologian, and he gave to the Higher Life doctrine as discreet a statement as, possibly, it has ever received or is capable of receiving while remaining a Higher Life doctrine. But the seeds of a more consequent Perfectionism were always lying just under the surface ready to spring up and bear their unhappy harvest in any favorable season. Pearsall Smith had himself sown them. Did he not tell the people at Brighton that W. E. Boardman had " never broken the Sabbath of his soul " through thirty years, and did he not permit an aged minister by his side to assert roundly that he had lived for thirty-five years as purely as Jesus? [43] The seeds of a consequent Perfectionism are sown, indeed, wherever the Higher Life doctrine is preached, and must produce their harvest whenever the artificial restraints of the Higher Life discreetness are relaxed. The harvest

---

the Christian life of Germany is salvation at once on faith; complete salvation at once on faith; complete salvation at once without any delay for preparation for it and without any delay for working it out. Everybody can accept salvation at once, and at once on accepting it can possess all that is contained in it. This is really the underlying idea that gives their form to both Wesleyanism and the Fellowship Movement — although both the one and the other broke its force by separating justification and sanctification from each other. They wished to apply the epithets *instantanea, perfecta, plena, certa,* which the Old Protestantism employed of the supervention of justification on faith, to sanctification also. But they did not quite like to take the whole plunge and make every Christian absolutely perfect from the moment of believing. They both, therefore, were driven into inconsequent dealings with the relation of sanctification to justification, and with the contents of the idea of sanctification itself — designed to mitigate the extremity of the fundamental principle in its application. Meanwhile it is clear that the Fellowship Movement is not only historically, through Smith, a daughter of Methodism in the narrow sense of the word; but that it shares the most fundamental conceptions of Methodism, and from them gains its own peculiarity.

[43] So Jüngst (*op. cit.,* p. 79) tells us.

was reaped in the Fellowship Movement at the opening of the twentieth century, when " Pastor " Paul, one of the leaders of the more extravagant elements of it, came out on the platform of the Gnadau Conference itself with a full-orbed assertion of his complete holiness.[44]

The Fellowship had never constituted a homogeneous body. There had always been extravagant elements embraced in the movement. In particular the vagaries of Plymouth Brethrenism were rife in large sections of it. Not only has the great Blankenburg-Alliance Conference been from the first deeply imbued with this tendency, but also large sections of the constituency of the Gnadau Conference itself. The chiliasm which is prevalent through the whole movement takes in these circles an extreme form, and a fanatical temper is engendered by it which seems capable of everything except sobriety. Smith himself spoke of the possibility of the restoration of the spiritual gifts of the Apostolic age; even Jellinghaus was not free from this delusion; it was from the beginning an element in the movement. The Fellowships had not recovered from the turmoil roused by the outbreak of consequent Perfectionism when they received a staggering blow from the importation in the spring of 1905 of the Welsh Revival with more than the Welsh excesses. That was as nothing, however, to what befell them in the summer of 1907, when the so-called Pentecost Movement — the Los Angeles Revival [45] — shook them with

[44] " Pastor " Paul was earlier pastor at Ravenstein in Pomerania, and then, as a leader in the Gnadau Conference, organized the Fellowship Movement in Pomerania. He was very prominent in the Pentecost Movement (1907); and making Steglitz, near Berlin, his home, went out thence as an apostle of the Pentecost Movement, bearing up and down Germany in his own person the gifts of grace.

[45] This is not the place to describe this movement in detail. It is treated more or less fully, of course, in all accounts of the Fellowship Movement. See especially Paul Fleisch, " Die innere Entwicklung," usw. See also E. Edel, " Die Pfingstbewegung im Lichte der kirchliche Geschichte," Brieg, E. Captuller, 1910, pp. 122; B. Kühn, " Die Pfingstbewegung im Lichte der Heiligen Schrift und ihrer eignen Geschichte," Gotha, Ott (1913?) pp. 105. The matter is excellently treated by Paul Drews in *Die Christliche Welt*, xxii. 1908, coll. 271 ff., 290 ff., who cites the most important primary German literature; E. Buchner's article in *Die Christliche Welt* (xxv. 1911, coll. 29 ff.) gives per-

its full force. "Pastor" Paul of course was found in the thick
of it. He "spoke with tongues" more than all others; he even
sang "in tongues" — translating favorite hymns into the
supernatural speech; nay, he even subjected "the tongues"
to philological analysis and framed a sort of syllabary of
them.[46]

The humiliating performances at the "Pentecost" meetings did at least this service — they provoked a reaction. The
reaction was slow in coming: it was not until 1910 — after
three years of these disgraceful proceedings — that the Gnadau
people found strength and courage to repudiate them. There
had been polemicizing all along; but the polemics were weak
and ineffectual because conducted from a standpoint not essentially different from that of the fanatics: the whole Fellowship Movement was possessed by the convictions and hopes
of which the excesses of the Pentecost Movement were only
the legitimate expression. Time was required for the revolution
of conception which could alone bring a remedy. It was a blessing that time enough was taken for the revolution to become
radical. Hermann Benser gives us a very fair account of what
happened. With an unnecessary but not unintelligible intrusion
of German self-consciousness, confusing the just with the

---

sonal experiences with the German phenomena. F. G. Henke (*The American
Journal of Theology,* xiii. 1909, pp. 193 ff.) gives some account of the non-
German history, with references to the primary literature. See also the literature mentioned in H. Bavinck, "Gereformeerde Dogmatiek" (2d ed.), iii.
p. 568, note.

[46] Schian (*op. cit.,* p. 16) relates what "Pastor" Paul did with "the
tongues." "A special curiosity in the region of speaking with tongues is described by Pastor Paul, who has in his own little monthly magazine reported
with stenographic exactness his experiences in this field. He has not only
spoken with tongues, but also — think of it! in meaningless syllables which
he could not himself interpret! — has sung them hours at a time. Afterwards
he himself subjected his own tongues — speeches to careful investigation, and
sought to translate them, and then endeavored even to sing some well-known
religious songs 'in tongues.' 'Every song, whose melody was well enough
known to me, I could sing in tongues, and all of them every time rhymed wonderfully.' When they rhymed thus: ' ea tschu ra ta — u ra torida — tschu ri
kanka — oli tanka,' he rejoiced. 'There is more rhyme in it than in the
German words,' he said."

German and the bizarre with the English, he tells us that it had always been the desire of the men of the Gnadau Conference to keep their "Philadelphia Movement" truly German and not to permit it to become English — when he ought to have said that they wished it to remain soberly Christian and not to become (or remain) fanatically visionary. "But," he continues,[47]

" they did not immediately recognize the perils of the revivals and above all of the Pentecost Movement. For there burned in their hearts too a longing for the charismata of the Apostolic age, and the anticipation that God would perhaps grant them now to men. Only when the devastating effects of the Pentecost Movement — the extravagance of individuals and the disruption of the Fellowship circles — became palpable, did the men of Gnadau obtain clearness and power to separate themselves sharply from this kind of thing. At the Gnadau Conference at Wernigerode of this year (1910) the directory of the ' German Association for Fellowship-work and Evangelization ' unanimously repelled the Pentecost Movement. It was even declared that it was inconsistent with standing in the Association to have any fellowship in work with the Pentecost brethren. This declaration is a courageous act of great importance for the sound development of Fellowship Christianity. For it certainly has not been an easy thing for these men to renounce brethren with whom they have stood in close relations of love and esteem. But it became their conscientious duty to place walking in the fear of the Lord and building up the congregations in peace above consideration for these brethren."

By this action of the Gnadau Conference of 1910 the Pentecost Movement was not suppressed. It continued to exist; but now as a distinct movement of its own, standing apart from the general Fellowship Movement and forming a separate sect of fanatical character.[48] But the importance to the Gnadau Movement itself of its act of excision was not overestimated by Benser, writing immediately after the event. In it, it apparently meant definitively to turn its back not only on the

[47] *Op. cit.*, pp. 13, 14.
[48] Cf. *The Methodist Review*, xciii. 1911, p. 478.

Pentecost Movement and its horrible excesses, but on all in its own history which, as it now saw, led up to such things and was distinguished from them only in degree. In effect this was to cease to be distinctively a Higher Life movement and to place itself on the basis of Reformation Christianity. Its action of 1910 was followed up on January 24, 1911, by a renewed action of the directory, confirming it and even sharpening its terms: and joining with it at the same time an authoritative rejection of " Pastor " Paul's crass Perfectionism, which had already met with the disapproval of the leaders of the conference when he had aired it at the meeting of 1904. This crass Perfectionism had now become only an element in the system of fanaticism which was being exploited by the Pentecost Movement. The singling of it out for special condemnation in 1911 has signifi- cance, therefore, only for the direction in which the minds of the Gnadau brethren were moving. The two things were al- ready conjoined in some most significant remarks by Elias Schrenck on the Gnadau platform of 1910. " The children of God of today," he said, " do not have to expect a Pentecost; we *have* the Holy Spirit."

" Signs and wonders are not in and of themselves a proof of the Pentecost endowment; only such fruits of the Spirit as, according to Gal. v. 22, manifest themselves in the daily life and especially in our sufferings are evidence of the holy life of the Spirit. . . . The doctrines of the ' pure heart,' of sinlessness, have come to us from America and England, and have obscured the Biblical doctrines of sin and of justification by faith alone, in the case of many. We have need to abase ourselves deeply before the Lord because of the errors of our teaching heretofore, for which we all bear the guilt. We must cease to offer salvation to our people in three distinct stages, (1) Forgiveness of sins, (2) Sanctification, (3) the Baptism of the Spirit."

— this being the form in which the developed perfectionist doctrine of " Pastor " Paul and his coadjutors was pre- sented.[49] " This trichotomy is thoroughly un-Biblical, and,

[49] Cf. Sippell (*loc. cit.*, col. 178), who, pointing out that Methodism has always been liable to fanaticism, adds: " A sad instance of this is our present-

praise God, also thoroughly un-German." There is a healthy movement of repentance manifested here, and it did not cease until, as we have already hinted, the whole Higher Life element in the teaching of the Fellowship Movement apparently was recanted — a recantation in which Jellinghaus himself, who had devoted his life to its propagation, took part.[50] To this element in the story we must return, however, more fully later. What it is important at the moment to make plain is only that at this point in its development the Fellowship Movement has apparently made a complete *volte face*. So clear is this that Theodor Sippell, writing in 1914,[51] is inclined to look at its whole history theretofore as only its "chaotic beginnings," from which no safe conclusions can be drawn as to its future. "It cannot be denied," he says, "that a provisional stopping-point has been reached in the internal development of this movement. The new-Darbyism and fanatical currents which have exerted temporarily a prodigious influence have led in the Pentecost Movement to such deplorable aberrations, that by far the greater number of the German Fellowships have renounced them with disgust." Horrified by the realization thus forced upon them of what they have been in principle involved in, they are raising the cry with ever greater earnestness, says Sippell, that "only a return to Luther and the heritage of the Reformation can save the German Fellowship Movement from internal and external collapse."

It will no doubt be interesting to look a little more in detail at the perfectionist teaching of "Pastor" Paul, that we may observe somewhat more closely the end-point of the development of the Higher Life doctrine of the Fellowships. The discreet Perfectionism of Pearsall Smith, and of Jellinghaus, who followed even Smith at a little distance, of course

---

day Pentecost Movement, which, carrying the doctrine of Wesley further, distinguishes between the complete purification from sin and a later-occurring baptism of the Spirit, with reception of special gifts of grace — speaking with tongues, healing the sick and the like." Only, this development did not need to wait for the German Pentecost people to make it.

[50] Cf. his booklet, "Erklärungen über meine Lehrirrungen," 1912.

[51] *Loc. cit.*, col. 235.

could not achieve stability. In the nature of the case it passed
necessarily by its own intrinsic logic into consequent Perfectionism whenever it met with a temper accustomed not to
count costs but to reason straight onward without reserves.
We are not surprised to find from a hint dropped here and
there, therefore, that consequent Perfectionism was early
present in Fellowship circles. On one occasion, for example,
Jellinghaus, speaking of the fortunes, in Germany, of the
Higher Life Movement, to the propagation of which he had
given his life, feels constrained to interject a warning against
what he looks upon as a danger threatening it. " Unfortunately," he says,[52] — he is writing in 1898 —

" false anti-natural asceticism has been showing itself for a few
years back in certain very small circles, and in others an un-Biblical
exaggeration of language about sanctification, connected with a
distressing censoriousness. . . . After having for twenty-three years
taught and defended the Biblically circumspect salvationist doctrine
of sanctification, along with my beloved friend and brother Otto
Stockmayer in Switzerland, for long as its only literary advocate
in Germany, I can do no less than warn in the most earnest and
serious way against exaggerated expressions concerning the stage
of sanctification attained, which afterwards cannot be confirmed
and ratified by an actually sanctified life."

We do not know that " Pastor " Paul was in Jellinghaus' mind
when he wrote these words. But he was just the sort of man
of whom what Jellinghaus says would be true,[53] and we are

[52] *Op. cit.*, ed. 4, pp. 436–437.

[53] Benser (*op. cit.*, p. 41) assigns him his place thus: " Differences in types
of piety are produced by national character, by individual dispositions, often
not spiritually purified, or by an especially strong development of a single
trait of piety. The national character asserts itself especially in Württemberg
and in the East-German provinces. The Swabian character tends to make
Fellowship Christians who build up a sterling piety with inner sensibility and
prefer to remain in retirement rather than to appear in public. On the other
hand the East-German character, which tends in other matters also to extreme conceptions, works in the Fellowship Christianity also towards affording
glad hospitality to all sensational, out-of-the-common notions. Individual traits
of character have made Pastor Paul a fanatical Christian, with aspirations
stretching beyond all earthly limits." " Pastor " Paul belongs to the East-
German stock.

told that he had been speaking freely in this sense for some
time before he dramatically cast the matter into the arena o
public debate among the Fellowship people by his astonishing
utterances in 1904.[54]

The essential elements of the doctrine which Paul proclaimed in these utterances do not differ from those of the
ordinary Wesleyan doctrine. Like the Wesleyans, he separated
sharply between sanctification and justification, and, like them
he taught an immediate sanctification on faith, an immediate
sanctification by which our sinful nature itself is eradicated.[55]
According to his own account he ventured one day just to take

[54] *Allgemeine Evangelisch-Lutherische Kirchenzeitung*, xxxvii. 1904,
col. 606. Jellinghaus might very well, perhaps, have had Otto Stockmayer himself in view, had he attended closely to what he already had said in his address
to the Gnadau Conference of 1896 on " Die Christliche Vollkommenheit," which
Jellinghaus (p. 705, note) praises as not only admirable, but thoroughly Biblical. In that address (p. 27 of the reprint) he declares that the consciousness
that God intends to bring us into likeness to the Lamb will save us from being
satisfied with any half-way perfection: " I can be a member of the Bride only
with a holiness which can abide the eye of God, the angels and the devils,"
because what comes from God can stand in the sight of God. He afterwards
became notorious as the advocate of the possibility and duty of attaining this
perfect holiness on earth. " His favorite idea," says a writer in *Die Christliche
Welt* (xix. 1905, col. 877, note), " is the establishment of a small congregation
of the elect, in whom sanctification takes place even unto victory over death,
and makes the coming of Christ possible." Cf. Th. Hardeland, *Neue kirchliche
Zeitschrift,* ix. 1898, p. 59.

[55] Cf. Gelshorn, *Die Christliche Welt,* xix. 1905, coll. 895 f.: " On the subject of sanctification conceptions within the Fellowship Movement differ, it
must be confessed, very widely, and it is Jellinghaus who shows here to advantage — because of his moderation and prudence. While others, such as
Pückler, Brockes and Paul sharply distinguish sanctification, in point of time,
from justification, and expect it from a special baptism of the Spirit subsequently to an already accomplished justification, thinking of it therefore more
in the form of a sudden violent irruption (*Durchbruch*) while the man remains completely passive; according to Jellinghaus the beginning of sanctification comes with justification, and the filling with the Holy Ghost is a matter
inclusive of the voluntary element of faithfulness and advance in personal
surrender to Christ more and more to completion. Accordingly, also, Jellinghaus holds himself far from the folly of Perfectionism which in Paul has its
keenest advocate — Paul who in public meetings has declared that he no
more commits any sin. According to Jellinghaus the actual holiness of every
converted man consists in his holding himself free from every *conscious* or
intentional transgression of the divine law."

Jesus Christ for his sanctification, and he at once received it — in its fulness. This is the way he describes his experience in his journal — *Heiligung* — for April, 1904: [56]

"All my previous conceptions were all at once cast into ruins by it; for immediately on this faith in my new Adam, I saw and felt myself delivered from every propensity (*Hang*) to sin. Day and night passed; days and nights passed; and it was and remained in me all new. All kinds of trials constantly came upon me, but I lived in blessed newness of life. It was with me as if none of these things concerned me. What always happened to me was that I lived by the two words and the truth enclosed in them, 'Jesus only' (*Jesus wird*). The Savior became to me in a much deeper way than ever before 'actual' and 'present.' The closeness of the Father filled my horizon; and all this has remained since that time uninterruptedly my salvation. No defilement, whether through thoughts, or through ebullition of temperament, has taken place with me since then; no disturbing thing has come either by night or day between the Lord and me. I live in the blessed fact that Jesus is my new Adam from whom I expect and may expect everything. O what blessedness lies in that! I was already happy in my Jesus. Now my happiness is boundless." [57]

The theme upon which Paul addressed the Gnadau Conference at its meeting at the ensuing Whitsuntide was the

[56] We are quoting it from the *Allgemeine Evangelisch-Lutherische Kirchenzeitung*, xxxvii. 1904, col. 532.

[57] The *Allgemeine Evangelisch-Lutherische Kirchenzeitung* quotes, along with this report of "Pastor" Paul's description of his experiences, a warning comment printed by Adolf Stöcker in the pages of the journal, *Reformation:* "Of course," he says, "I do not doubt the veracity of Brother Paul in a single word. But I am full of doubt whether it is wholesome to describe in detail and justify such experiences. As personal experiences they stand far above the self-judgment of the greatest men of faith in Holy Writ. David confesses in Ps. xix. 13, 'Who can discern his errors? Cleanse Thou me from hidden faults.' And Paul denies of himself that he is already perfect. Pastor Paul, if he feels himself freed from all propensity to sin, is perfect. We have to do, therefore, in his case with a super-Biblical standpoint. Even John in the third chapter of his First Epistle does not go so far. . . . That there lies in Pastor Paul's self-declaration a great danger for himself and for the readers of his journal is certain. I recall with great sorrow Pearsall Smith, Idel, and Fries, and many others who spoke precisely like Brother Paul, and afterwards made shipwreck. God preserve Evangelical Christianity from such self-deceptions and breakdowns!"

appropriate one of " Our Task in the Kingdom of Christ is Faith." What he meant by this was to assert that faith and faith alone is our whole part in salvation: Christ does all the rest. We have only to believe; nothing else is asked of us. And we receive whatever we have faith for: according to our faith it is done unto us. Testimony to the power of faith is always grateful to Christians. The energy with which Paul testified to the power of faith met of course, as it always does, with a hearty response. But when he illustrated his meaning by declaring that from those who entrust themselves to Jesus for full redemption He takes away at once all indwelling sin, the sinful nature itself; the greater part, led by Director Dietrich, Inspector Haarbeck, and the President of the Conference, drew back. In his testimony to his personal experience he abated nothing of what he had already declared in his journal. He had taken Jesus at His word. Like other believers, he had received from Him through faith the forgiveness of sins; he had day by day been cleansed in the measure in which he had trusted; at last, because he had now trusted for this, he had been delivered from sin itself — all its allurements and impulses were gone and the promise of Rom. vi. 6 had been fulfilled to him, and from that hour, now some years back, he had seen nothing of his old Adam — to which Inspector Haarbeck somewhat dryly rejoined that it would perhaps be more to the purpose to inquire whether other people had seen nothing of him! [58] All this Paul testified had been wrought by simple faith. He had not sought to sanctify himself, but merely to let himself be sanctified. He had turned wholly from himself and only believed that the Lord had delivered him wholly and from all. At once his Ego and his old man had fallen entirely away, and sin now no longer dwells in him. [59]

It will be seen that Paul leaves nothing unsaid which would

[58] Cf. the report of the meeting of the Conference in the *Allgemeine Evangelisch-Lutherische Kirchenzeitung*, xxxvii. 1904, col. 576; also Herzog-Hauck, *loc. cit.*, p. 536; Benser, *op. cit.*, p. 36; P. Gennrich, " Wiedergeburt und Heiligung," 1908, pp. 50 ff.

[59] The language is here derived from Paul's explanation in *Heiligung*, February, 1906, pp. 12, 14, as cited by P. Gennrich, *op. cit.*, p. 50.

make the completeness of his deliverance from sin clear.[60] He argues that if God's seed is in the sanctified, if they are made by the Spirit partakers in the divine nature, then they no longer have the nature of sin, they are in this supereminent sense freed from sin. It cannot be said, indeed, he explains, that sin no longer exists for them; for, though it no longer exists in them, it exists about them. They are, then, subject to temptation; but this temptation does not arise from within them but is due solely to solicitations from without.[61] If a regenerate man had to carry his inherited evil nature about with him he would not be really free; he would be impelled to sin by his sinful nature. And if sin remains entrenched in the nature-ground of the saints up to the grave, then it is not Christ but death who is the complete deliverer; and if sin is wholly destroyed in us only at the resurrection — that is, at Christ's second coming — then, in spite of Rev. xix. 7, I Thess. v. 23, and Eph. v. 27, the soul must meet its bridegroom still in sin.[62]

Nevertheless, in defending his doctrine, Paul exhibits the usual chariness in the employment of the term "sinlessness"[63] to describe it. He wishes to distinguish between the negative idea of freedom from sin and the positive idea of incapacity to sin, and to affirm only the former. He thinks it enough to say that we do not have our freedom from indwelling sin from ourselves, but only from Christ. The regenerate man has all that he has only because he abides in Jesus and Jesus abides in him; the ground of his freedom from sin is in Jesus and not in himself — it is all of grace and not of nature or of merit.[64] We could talk of "sinlessness," he says, only if we were by virtue of our own nature free from indwelling sin — as Christ was, and as Adam was before the fall. It cannot be said that this rejection of the term "sinlessness" or the explanation by which it is justified, makes a good impression. The amount of

[60] In this discussion we are dependent on Gennrich, *op. cit.*

[61] Paul, *Reich Christi*, 1905, pp. 135 f., 144; *Heiligung*, February, 1906, p. 14.

[62] *Reich Christi*, 1905, pp. 130 f.

[63] *Sündenlosigkeit.*

[64] *Reich Christi*, 1905, pp. 140, 143.

It seems to be that Paul wishes to leave open the possibility o
his wholly sanctified Christians sinning again, and, in order to
do so, plays fast and loose with the eradication of their sinful
natures. If their sinful natures are eradicated they no longer
have them, and if they no longer have them — how do they
differ radically from Adam before the fall? It would be possible, of course, to say that the eradication of their sinful natures does not infuse into them holy natures; they have lost
the propensity to sin, but have not gained a propensity to good.
But that does not seem to be Paul's meaning: he claims for
himself apparently a holy nature: the eradication of his sinful
nature is not conceived in this sense wholly negatively — it is
equivalent to the infusion of a holy nature, even Christ Himself. Gennrich, therefore, very properly remarks,[65] that " if by
the not-sinning [the negative idea] of the regenerate man
there is meant that he has no further connection with sin, because sinning is for him something contrary to his nature
[as regenerate], and is therefore no longer conceivable in his
case — why, then, precisely what is affirmed of him is sinlessness [in the positive sense]." What Paul has really arrived at,
he goes on to say, is just the Wesleyan doctrine of Perfection,
which is repudiated by the Sanctification Movement; and,
indeed, Paul himself allows[66] that for him, as for Wesley, the
real point is, negatively, purification from all indwelling sin
and, positively, complete living to God (perfect love). Nor
does Paul escape his difficulties by transferring the ground of
our freedom from sin from ourselves to Christ. This is to confuse the cause with the effect. Our Freedom from sin, says
Paul, follows on faith and depends on abiding in Christ. Let it
be granted. What follows on faith and depends on abiding in
Christ is our own personal freedom from sin, from indwelling sin — the eradication of the sinful nature. It is easy to
understand that Paul should wish to validate even here the
familiar " moment by moment deliverance " which he had
learned from the Higher Life preachers. But Gennrich very
properly asks, Can he? If our sinful nature has been eradicated,

[65] *Op. cit.*, p. 51.   [66] *Reich Christi*, p. 130.

it is no longer there. And the reasoning becomes irresistible:
" If it belongs to the nature of the regenerate no more to sin,
because he is freed even from the last remnant of original sin
— why, then, as Heinatsch rightly remarks, there is no need for
the regenerate to have progressive purification through Christ's
blood in ever renewed surrender to Him, the 'moment by
moment deliverance.' He needs at the most a preservation in
this condition, attained once for all by complete purification,
to fall out of which would be possible only by a fall as radical
and fundamental as that of the first Adam." [67] We do not say
that the "moment by moment deliverance," dependent on a
"moment by moment surrender," is tenable even for the Perfectionism of mere conduct which alone the Higher Life people
wish to validate. For how is a lapse in faith possible to one
whose sinlessness in act is guaranteed by the Christ who has
become the source of all his life-activities? But it becomes
doubly absurd when the Perfectionism of conduct has become
a Perfectionism of nature. The plain fact is that we cannot suspend a supernatural salvation on natural activities, whether
our salvation is wrought in us all at once in its completeness or
in a long process ripening to the end — if it is wrought by
Christ, it cannot be dependent on our "moment by moment"
faith, but our "moment by moment" faith must be dependent
on it. We cannot teach both a supernatural and a natural
salvation.

As was natural, a large part of the debate called out by
"Pastor" Paul's consequent Perfectionism connects itself
with its relation to the inconsequent Perfectionism of mere
conduct, which was the official doctrine of the Fellowship
Movement. It was contended on the one side, as for example
by Heinatsch,[68] that it is an illegitimate extension of the idea
embodied in the old Sanctification Movement. On Paul's part,
on the other hand, it was vigorously asserted that it is only the
old Sanctification Movement made explicit in its necessary
contents. In this debate we must pronounce Paul right. Genn-

[67] *Op. cit.*, pp. 52–53.
[68] *Reich Christi*, 1904, p. 367, cited by Gennrich, *op. cit.*, pp. 44, 45.

rich is quite correct when he declares [69] that " in point of fac¹
the doctrines of deliverance from indwelling sin and of the
baptism of the Spirit," as taught by " Pastor " Paul, " are the
logical extension of the official doctrine of sanctification of the
Fellowship Movement — as the advocates of them rightly contended at the Gnadau Conference. . . . In them, for the firs¹
time, Jellinghaus' two requirements — deeper sanctification
greater gifts of grace — are really met for believers thirsting
after the sensible actuality of salvation." These words remind
us, however, that the debate was not left to run its course or
the simple issue of consequent or inconsequent Perfectionism
The question of the " gifts of grace " was soon complicated
with it — provided for, as we have already had occasion to note
incidentally, by a third stage in the saving process as conceived by Paul — the " baptism of the Spirit," as the culminating step following on complete justification and complete
sanctification. The Pentecost Movement broke over Germany
in 1907. " Pastor " Paul, who was already addressing the
Gnadau Conference in 1902 on Faith Healing, became at once
one of its most active promoters. The upas tree was now in
full fruit. It is not strange that men began to examine with
new anxiety into its rooting. We have already seen the issue.
At the Gnadau Conference of 1910 the Pentecost Movement
was definitely repelled and all association with it was forbidden
to the constituency of the Gnadau Conference. With it much
of the consequent Perfectionism which had been troubling the
Fellowships since 1904 was excluded. But the officials in their
formal action of January 24, 1911, went a step further, and
conjoined a definite condemnation of consequent Perfectionism with their condemnation of the Pentecost Movement —
declaring formally against " the doctrine that by faith in Christ
the abolition of the sinful nature is secured or that the believer
can attain a condition on earth in which he no longer needs
justifying grace." [70]

The end was, however, not even yet reached. Could the
fruit be discarded and the root remain in honor? It had become

_____

[69] *Op. cit.*, pp. 44, 45.   [70] Jarck, *loc. cit.*, p. 542.

:ver increasingly plain to ever increasing numbers that the
" clean heart " of the consequent Perfectionists could not be
eparated from the " clean life " of the Sanctification Movement, and the one rejected and the other kept. Among others
t had become plain to Jellinghaus himself, who had now for a
vhole generation been the trusted, almost the official, ex-
)ounder of the doctrine of the " clean life " for the Fellowship
:ircles. Perhaps we may say that this change of heart had long
)een preparing for him. He had felt himself reborn to a new
ife through the blessing which he had received at the great
)xford Meeting in 1875, and had given himself at once to the
:nthusiastic advocacy of the " Salvationist System " which
was preached by Pearsall Smith. Already in 1880 he published
iis bulky book — " The Complete, Present Salvation through
:hrist " [71] — which became at once the standard Dogmatics of
:he Fellowship Christianity. But he did not reproduce even in
t Smith's system without modification; and the modification
was in the direction of mitigation. As edition followed edition
— in 1886, 1890, 1898, 1903 — he was found moving ever,
slightly but steadily, in the direction of further mitigation.
Now, however, came the deluge. At one stroke he demolished
the work of his life and declared himself to have been running
on a wrong scent.[72] With deep pain he sees now in " the Keswick Movement," so long advocated by him, the source of all
the evils which had lately befallen Fellowship Christianity
and feels himself, because of his advocacy of " the Keswick
Movement," personally sharer in the grave responsibility for
these evils. A certain levity lies at the heart of " the Keswick
Movement "; its zeal is to assure ourselves that we are actually and fully saved, rather than to give ourselves to the repentance which is due to our sins, to the working out of salvation with fear and trembling, to heavenly mindedness, and a
life of prayer and a walk in love. It imagines that there can be

[71] " Das völlige, gegenwärtige Heil durch Christum," 1880, 1886, 1890,
1898, 1903.
[72] Cf. the accounts of Jarck, loc. cit., pp. 530–531, and Sippell, loc. cit.,
coll. 100 f.

faith without repentance and conquest of sin without moral struggle. The law, sin itself as evil desire in the regenerate, the determined fulfilment of the will of God in vital endeavor, are pushed into the background. It seeks, in a word, peace instead of righteousness, and the trail of a spiritual euthymia lies over it.[73]

But Jellinghaus did not spare himself: he even calls his book, which appeared in 1912, by the directly descriptive title of "Avowals about My Doctrinal Errors."[74] The book naturally created a sensation, but it did not at once compose the controversy. Many, of course, followed Jellinghaus' guidance here too,'as they had followed it heretofore; and the cry arose, "Back to the Reformation." Among these were the chief leaders of the Gnadau Conference. Others, however, entered the lists to defend Jellinghaus against Jellinghaus, and only sought to work out from the standpoint of the Reformation a justification for the doctrine of full present sanctification by faith alone.[75] What is most noticeable, what is most hopeful, in the

---

[73] Jellinghaus had never been blind to this aspect of the movement: only, he had treated it heretofore as an accident and not its essence. In the height of his advocacy of the movement he could write as follows (op. cit., ed. 4, pp. 434–435): "Although R. P. Smith declared often, 'I desire communion in the sufferings of Christ rather than in the joys of Christ,' yet the Biblical verities of painful co-suffering with Christ, of the sufferings of priestly-minded Christians (such as Paul describes II Cor. iii–v.; Rom. viii.; Phil. iii.; Col. i. 24) — especially of the life of persecution of the members of Christ, and of their strivings unto blood under affliction, scorn and inward mortification, retired too much into the background. Many spoke as if men were already living in the millennium, and very inadequately recognized the mighty power of anti-Christianity and therefore insufficiently also the struggle against it as a priestly task of the saints (Heb. xii. 4)." In the preceding pages (pp. 433 f.) he makes some criticisms also of Smith's methods.

[74] "Erklärungen über meine Lehrirrungen," 1912, Verlag of Prack & Co., Lichtenrode, pp. 51.

[75] Among these should be especially mentioned Ernst Heinatsch, "Die Krisis der Heiligungsbegriffes in der Gemeinschaftsbewegung der Gegenwart," 1913. While still defending Jellinghaus' former teaching, Heinatsch seeks to separate it from its inseparable Wesleyan content and from its logical issue in the Perfectionism of "Pastor" Paul. An earlier book from outside the Fellowship circles, Ernst Rietschel's "Lutherische Rechtfertigungslehre oder moderne Heiligungslehre?," 1909, should be read in this connection. Rietschel argues

lebates is that there is a return on all hands to the Reforma-
ion. As the curtain of the Great War drops on Germany and
shuts off from us further knowledge of the development of the
Fellowship Movement, we are cheered to see the promise
that, in its Gnadau branch at least, it may have definitely
urned its back on its past as a distinctively Higher Life movement and grounded its future on the Reformation doctrine of
salvation, a complete and full salvation, through faith alone.
It will be a great thing for the future of German Fellowship
Christianity if, in the welter of unwholesome tendencies, acting and reacting upon one another — the semi-rationalism of
Eisenach, the Darbyite and Chiliastic extravagance of Blankenburg, the wild fanaticism of the Pentecost people — there
shall be one center of healthy granulation at Gnadau.

that Jellinghaus has taken the wrong way to correct the later Lutheran dogmaticians: we must not borrow from the Wesleyans but return to Luther.

VII

THE GERMAN HIGHER LIFE MOVEMENT IN ITS CHIEF EXPONENT

THE GERMAN HIGHER LIFE MOVEMENT IN ITS CHIEF EXPONENT [1]

I

It was a very remarkable campaign which was conducted by Robert Pearsall Smith in Great Britain and Germany during the years 1873–1875 in the interests of what is known as "the Higher Christian Life." It has left behind it two imposing monuments. One of them, the great "Keswick Movement," is known wherever the English language is spoken. The other, a parallel movement in Germany, spoken of there as "Die Heiligungsbewegung," the "Sanctification Movement," deserves to be better known than it appears to be. It took a peculiar form, which was given it by the circumstance that it made its way primarily in, and always by means of, "the Fellowships" (*Gemeinschaften*) which had come down from the times of Pietistic ascendency, and were now given new life and set upon a career of rapid self-propagation, by the impulse received from Pearsall Smith. Thus the "Sanctification Movement" inaugurated by him became in its form a great "Fellowship Movement," which has spread throughout Germany and has extended itself everywhere in a stable organization and numerous instruments of activity. The center of its public manifestation is the great Gnadau Conference.

One of the remarkable features of this "Sanctification Movement" has been that it took its color very largely from the teachings of one man. This man was Theodor Jellinghaus, who received his Higher Life doctrine from Smith and his colleagues at the great Oxford Union Meeting for the Promoting of Scriptural Holiness, in the early days of September,

[1] From *The Biblical Review*, iv. 1919, pp. 376–406, and 561–590: published by The Biblical Seminary in New York. Copyrighted.

1874, and who returned thence to Germany having before him his life-work of propagating it. In 1880 he published the work which became very much the doctrinal text book of the movement, under the title of "The Complete, Present Salvation through Christ." [2] Through this book, in its successive editions, and the Bible school which he founded for the training of workers for the movement, Jellinghaus was able to give to the movement its doctrinal character. This doctrinal character, while following in the main, and at first very closely, the teachings of Smith, did not exactly coincide with them in all its details, and departed more and more from them as time went on, though never fundamentally. This was clearly marked in the successive editions of the book. A particular quality of its own was thus acquired by the German Sanctification Movement, which differentiated it as a distinct species of Higher Life teaching, while it retained its generic character.

Its development on these lines proceeded with great and fruitful quietness throughout the last quarter of the nineteenth century. With the twentieth century, however, a period of turmoil set in. Fanatical tendencies showed themselves, with ever increasing violence. A consequent Perfectionism endeavored to substitute itself for the moderate Perfectionism of the Higher Life teachers, and especially of Jellinghaus, the most discreet of them all. The excesses of the Welsh Revival were imported into Germany. Worst of all, the Fellowship circles were invaded by the fanaticisms of the "Pentecost Movement" — the "Los Angeles Revival," which brought ruin in their train. The ultimate result was an immense revulsion of feeling. The whole Higher Life system which had supported the doctrinal basis of the movement from its beginning was undermined and discredited. Jellinghaus himself, who had given his life to its propagation, published, in a remarkable book, his recantation of it.[3] When the Great War lowered its curtain over the land and shut off observation of the course

---

[2] " Das völlige, gegenwärtige Heil durch Christum," 1880, 1886, 1890, 1898, 1903.

[3] " Erklärungen über meine Lehrirrungen," 1912.

of religious events in it, it looked very much as if the Fellowship Movement had definitely ceased to be a Higher Life
movement and had returned with happy decisiveness to the
Reformation for its doctrinal basis.

Inclined as we thus are to look upon the Fellowship Movement as a thing of the past so far as it was distinctively a
"sanctification movement," that is to say, so far as it was a
continuation of the Higher Life Movement conveyed to Europe in 1873–1875 by Robert Pearsall Smith, it becomes desirable as a matter of history that we should make an attempt to
understand the precise character of its teaching as a "sanctification movement." It has already been pointed out that this
is practically the same thing as to undertake an exposition of
the Higher Life teaching of Theodor Jellinghaus.[4] He wrote
a number of books; [5] but it is particularly his massive volume
on "The Complete, Present Salvation through Christ" which
claims our attention here. We have already intimated that it
advances a little from edition to edition in its departure from
Pearsall Smith's teachings. It will not be necessary for us, however, to trace this advance in detail. It is not Jellinghaus'
personal growth that we are interested in; we are seeking
merely to obtain through him a clear conception of the type
of Higher Life teaching prevalent in the Fellowship Movement in Germany for the forty years from 1875 to 1914. We
shall, then, merely take the fourth edition of Jellinghaus' work,
published in 1898 — about the middle point of our period —
and observe by means of it how the matter was presented to
the Fellowships near the end of the quiet development of the

---

[4] Of course it is very possible to avoid the appearance of this, as Hermann
Benser does in his "Das moderne Gemeinschaftschristentum," 1910, pp. 24 ff.,
as also in his article on the same subject in Schiele und Zscharnack, "Die Religion in Geschichte und Gegenwart," ii. 1910, coll. 1267 f., by writing ostensibly on the Piety of Fellowship Christianity. It comes, however, to the same
thing in the end. Cf. Th. Hardeland's admirable exposition in the *Neue
kirchliche Zeitschrift*, ix. 1898, pp. 42 ff.

[5] "Das völlige gegenwärtige Heil durch Christum," (1880) 1903; "Der
Römerbrief," 1903; "Die I. Joh. Epistel," 1899; "Sieg und Leben," 1906;
"Leben aus Gott," "Erklärungen über meine Lehrirrungen," 1912. He edited
also from 1899 *Mitteilungen aus der Bibelschule*.

movement, and before the turmoil of the twentieth century set in. This is the way the adherents of the movement were being taught to think at the period of its most uninterrupted development. This is the way, in other words, in which the Fellowships connected with the Gnadau Conference have been accustomed to conceive their distinctive doctrine of full salvation through faith alone.[6]

Jellinghaus himself[7] was, in the deepest stratum of his thinking, a good Lutheran. The characteristic Lutheran doctrine of the Word, as the vehicle of the saving operations of God, remained to the end the determining element of his conception of salvation.[8] Under cover of it, he was able to teach a Pelagianizing doctrine of salvation; because, in his view, the supernatural operation conveyed in the Word brings to men only the possibility (*posse*), not also the actualization (*actio*), of that surrendering faith on which everything else is suspended. That is to say, what he teaches is that everyone who hears the Word finds himself in the exact condition in which, according to Pelagius, all are by nature; he has the *posse* for doing all that God requires of him, and the *actio* is his own responsibility.

With respect to the great doctrine of redemption his origi-

---

[6] Valuable expositions and criticisms of Jellinghaus' theology will be found in: Th. Hardeland, " Die Evangelisation mit besonderer Rücksicht auf die Heiligungsbewegung " in the *Neue kirchliche Zeitschrift,* ix. 1898, pp. 53 ff.; L. Clasen, " Heiligung im Glauben; mit Rücksicht auf die heutige Heiligungsbewegung," in the *Zeitschrift für Theologie und Kirche,* x. 1900, pp. 457 ff.; and P. Gennrich, " Wiedergeburt und Heiligung mit Bezug auf die gegenwärtigen Strömungen des religiösen Lebens," 1908. The former two use the second, the last the fifth edition of Jellinghaus' book. Cf. also Ernst Rietschel, " Lutherische Rechtfertigungslehre oder moderne Heiligungslehre? " 1909; and Paul Fleisch's series of books on the " Gemeinschaftsbewegung."

[7] Born at Schlüsselburg near Minden in Württemberg; became missionary in India in 1865; pastor at Rädnitz near Grossen on the Oder in 1873; pastor at Gütergotz, near Potsdam, in 1881; made Emeritus in 1894. He founded in 1885 the first Bible school of the Fellowship Movement and trained in it many workers; he also published, from 1899 on, *Mitteilungen aus der Bibelschule.*

[8] For example, p. 144: " The same word concerning Christ that brings Christ to our hearts, works also the power to faith in us through the Holy Spirit who dwells in it, so that everyone who *will* can believe in Christ " — that is, every hearer of the gospel who will, not everyone absolutely.

nal Lutheranism had, however, early given way under the disintegrating influences of his times. Already in his student days
at Erlangen the teaching of C. F. K. von Hofmann had taken
from him the central doctrine of the penal satisfaction of
Christ, without, however, conveying to him anything positive
in its stead. His positive doctrine of redemption, acquired
under influences emanating ultimately from J. A. W. Neander,
followed the lines of the ordinary "mystical" doctrine characteristic of the so-called "mediating theology." [9] According
to this doctrine it is not the merits of Christ which we receive
through faith, but Christ Himself; and, receiving Christ Himself, we share, in organic union with Him, all His achievements. As the last Adam, the new organic Head of the race, He
presents Himself a pure sacrifice to God,[10] dying to sin and
living to righteousness; and we who are in Him by faith die
with Him to sin and live with Him to righteousness. It is possible so to attenuate this doctrine as to reduce its contents to
nothing more than that, under the impression received from
the religious life of Christ, we too live religiously, entering
thus sympathetically into inner fellowship with Him in His
death and His resurrection. Then we have Ritschlianism; and
Gelshorn, for example, seems half inclined to claim Jellinghaus as, for substance of doctrine, of this party.[11] That, however, although not without a show of plausibility, is to do him
an injustice. It is quite clear that Jellinghaus thinks of Christ
not merely as, by the movingness of His example, inducing

[9] Those who wish to see this doctrine expressed in a form indistinguishable from Jellinghaus' may profitably read the essay on "The Work of Jesus
Christ," in F. Godet's "Studies on the New Testament," E. T. ed. 5, 1883,
pp. 148–200, to which Jellinghaus elsewhere makes admiring allusions. It was
published in 1873, nearly a year before the Oxford Meeting of 1874.

[10] Jellinghaus' doctrine of sacrifice belongs to the class of "symbolical"
theories, grounded on the hypothesis of Baer. There is no "juristically substitutive, bloody penal death"; the significance of the rite lies not in the
idea of "expiation," but in that of "drawing near." The chief matters are the
"altar" and the "blood," the symbols respectively of the presence of God
and the life of the offerer. The offerer approaches God, but being himself impure, comes into His presence through a substituted pure life. This is somehow supposed, by an organic union with the victim, to purify him.

[11] *Die Christliche Welt*, xix. 1905, coll. 890 ff.

men to imitate Him, but as releasing supernatural forces by which alone they can be assimilated to Him.

By this doctrine of redemption, it is plain, on the other hand, that a wide door was opened for the entrance of Pearsall Smith's teaching of sanctification by faith alone. It would be more exact, indeed, to say that this was already implicitly Jellinghaus' own doctrine. It only required to be explicitly stated, therefore, to command his assent. There were elements in Pearsall Smith's teaching, no doubt, which should have given him pause; and it is instructive to observe that, though these elements were received at first with the rest, it was precisely they to which he sat loosely and which he gradually eliminated from his teaching — thus no doubt loosening the hold upon him of the whole of which they were organic parts and preparing the way for his final discarding of the entire system. We may instance, as a striking example, the doctrine, fundamental to Pearsall Smith's system, as to Wesley's before him, that justification and sanctification are two separable gifts of grace to be sought and obtained separately, and standing in no other relation to one another than that the former must precede the latter. Such a conception was utterly incongruous to Jellinghaus' doctrine of redemption by organic union with Christ, instituted by a faith which receives Himself with all that that implies. It was accepted by him accordingly only to be gradually explained away, until in the end there was nothing left of it but a few encysted phrases bearing witness to a transcended phase of teaching.

From another point of view Jellinghaus was prepared to accord a welcome to the teaching of Pearsall Smith by his ten years of missionary experience in India. By it he was deeply imbued with the spirit of evangelization. The duty and profit of offering Jesus Christ to the sinner for immediate acceptance could not be doubtful to him. Nor could it be doubtful to him that this immediate acceptance of Christ brought with it enjoyment of all that is included in Christ's redemption. It is not strange that, with his doctrine of redemption, he was ready to understand this as the immediate enjoyment in its completeness of all that is included in Christ's redemption. The element of "suddenness" in Smith's doctrine was no offense to him; it rather was an attraction and fell in with his own implicit thought.

We are only surprised therefore that he tells [12] us that when "in the holiness-meetings at Oxford in September, 1874, there met him, in luminous clearness, out of the Bible, the truth that in the blood and death of Jesus not only forgiveness but also *direct and immediate* [the emphasis is his own] breaking of the power of sin, cleansing from sin, and uninterrupted victory over sin, are to be had on the surrender of faith," it was a "new truth" to him. What ought to have been new to him — and what ought not to have seemed true to him even temporarily — was the representation that these two blessings were not obtained together through "the surrender of faith," but successively by two surrenders of faith. It happens not rarely, however, that men hold to their fundamental conceptions through long periods without developing them into their implications; and, when these implications are presented to them from without, embrace them with an enthusiasm which is born not more of the convincingness of their presentation than of their reinforcement from the logical relation in which they stand to their own immanent thought. And it not rarely happens in such cases that the enthusiasm with which these conceptions are embraced, when externally presented to it, carries the mind over difficulties in the mode of their presentations, and betrays it into accepting them in forms not really in harmony with its immanent thought and incapable therefore of permanent entertainment by it.

That at any rate is what happened to Jellinghaus at Oxford. He heard asserted there in the most impressive way that we receive through faith in Jesus Christ with the same directness and immediacy as deliverance from the guilt of our sins, also deliverance from their power. He could not resist this assertion; it was a necessary implicate of his own fundamental conception of redemption. In his enthusiastic acceptance of it, he

[12] "Das völlige, gegenwärtige Heil durch Christum," 1898, p. 20.

took the assertion, naturally, as it was made to him; and it was
made to him in a form which implied not only a notion of
the relation of sanctification to justification, but a view of the
nature of justification itself which was out of harmony with
his fundamental conception of redemption and which therefore
could not be permanently held by him.

In his enthusiasm he went out and preached his new doctrine of sanctification as he had received it. That is to say, he
preached a doctrine of justification and a doctrine of the relation of sanctification to justification, which, in conjunction
with his fundamental doctrine of redemption, he could not
really believe. This could not last. The inevitable adjustments
soon began to set in. If we understand him correctly, he attributes the process of these adjustments to the period between
1883 and 1890, so that they received their record in the second
(1886) and especially in the third (1890) and subsequent
editions of his book, " Das völlige, gegenwärtige Heil durch
Christum." He conceived himself in this process to be writing
in beneath his new-found doctrine of sanctification an appropriate doctrine of redemption. He says:

" During the years 1883–1890 it became to me ever more certain
that if we have to teach according to the Scriptures that the power
of sin has been broken in the death of Christ, and life and the forces
of sanctification have been obtained for the believer in the resurrection of Christ, then we have to conceive Christ's atonement and
redemption also as a deliverance from the guilt *and* power of sin,
and as a restoration of eternal life, righteousness, sanctification and
love through His resurrection. Not the doctrine of sanctification only,
therefore, but also the doctrine of atonement and redemption through
Christ's blood and of justification and regeneration, are in need of a
Biblical purification and renovation." [13]

He misconceived, however, the direction of the process. What
he was really doing was adjusting his new-found doctrine of
sanctification to his fundamental conception of redemption. It
was the latter, not the former, which really possessed his mind
and formed the fixed point in the adjustments that were going

[13] *Op. cit.*, p. 21.

on. What he really gives us in the later editions of his book is, therefore, the Higher Life doctrine launched by W. E. Boardman and the Smiths as modified to fit the requirements of the "mediating theology" — this Higher Life doctrine in the form which it takes when preached on the basis of the "mediating theology." That is the real significance of Jellinghaus, and, under his guidance, of the German "Heiligungsbewegung" during the forty years from 1874 to 1914.

This being so, it cannot be thought in the least strange that Jellinghaus devotes a large part of his volume — at least half of it — to the vindication of the fundamental soteriological postulate of the "mediating theology," that, as we enter by faith into vital union with Christ as the last Adam, the new organic Head of humanity, we become through this faith alone sharer in all that He has wrought, in His death and resurrection, as our complete Deliverer.[14] He entitles this half of his book Justification through Christ Alone, to match the title which he gives the second half, Sanctification through Christ Alone. But this designation will be misleading to all who do not share his conception of the *ordo salutis,* based on the "mystical" idea of the nature of salvation prevalent in the "mediating theology." In this *ordo salutis* there is no place for the "justification" of the theology of the Reformation; "justification," too, becomes a purely subjective experience — the experience of forgiveness of sins as a result of vital union with the Christ who has transcended sin. It is only artificially separated, therefore, from sanctification; the two are in fact only parts of the same general experience, the experience of "participation in the Christ-life."

The two parts of Jellinghaus' book do not, therefore, in fact treat of what is commonly known as Justification and of Sanctification, or — to put it in language less open perhaps, in

---

[14] The terms *erlösen, Erlösung, Erlöser,* have, in Jellinghaus, no connotation of "redemption" in the proper sense of that term — as indeed *Lösegeld* itself has no connotation of "ransoming." They are all confined strictly by him to the general idea of "deliverance."

this atmosphere, to misapprehension — of deliverance from the guilt and deliverance from the power of sin. They treat of the experience of deliverance which the Christian has through faith in Christ, viewed, we might say, now from the point of sight of its inception, now from the point of sight of its completion, though that would be to speak far too strongly in terms of chronological sequence. Perhaps we would better say, viewed now from the point of sight of its general content, now from the point of sight of the completeness of the deliverance — in one of its aspects, singled out for special remark. What Jellinghaus actually attempts to do in the two parts of his book is to show, in the first part, that we receive by faith in Christ a complete deliverance, and, in the second part, that this complete deliverance includes in itself an immediately complete deliverance from the power of sin. The first part would have been more descriptively designated, therefore, had the title which its first chapter bears been given to it — The Complete Deliverer, or more explicitly, Complete Deliverance through Faith Alone. And the second part would have been more descriptively designated by some such title as this, Sanctification by Faith Alone an Immediately Complete Sanctification.

What Jellinghaus has undertaken in the first part of his book he has accomplished with complete success. He has triumphantly shown from the Scriptures that there is complete deliverance in Christ Jesus for all who look to Him for it in simple faith. That is the teaching of Scripture, and Jellinghaus brings it out with great fulness, energy, and convincingness. Of course, he writes from his own point of view, and adjusts the Scriptural proofs which he adduces, to meet particular ends as they emerge in the progress of his argument. It is his primary purpose, for example, to show, that in the complete deliverance which we receive by faith in Christ Jesus there is included deliverance from the power of sin as well as from its guilt. He is possessed by the odd notion that in the church doctrine of the penal satisfaction of Christ provision is made only for deliverance from guilt — justification in the Reformation sense, as he would conceive it — while the whole process of sanctification is left to be worked out by man himself under the impulse of gratitude for the forgiveness of his sins. He is zealous therefore to prove on the one hand that sanctification is a supernatural work, and on the other that it is inseparably connected with justification and is always present where justification is present. He frequently adduces the Scriptural proof of the completeness of this deliverance which we receive in Christ by faith, accordingly, with sharp application to such points as these, and always with particular emphasis on deliverance from the power of sin, and, naturally, in terms of the "mediating theology."

This in no way affects the force of that proof for the main matter. But it brings with it some very interesting results with respect to the maintenance of his own special contentions. To illustrate by a single instance, he succeeds so perfectly in proving that sanctification and justification are inseparable — that in being justified by faith we obtain also sanctification — as to leave no room for the acquisition of sanctification by a second act of faith specifically directed to that end; and thus reduces himself to the necessity of distinguishing, not between justification and sanctification as separable benefits received by separate acts of faith, but between a first sanctification coming with justification and a second and complete sanctification obtained subsequently by a detached act of faith of its own — with the further effect of making complete sanctification not an "all at once" acquisition on simple faith, but a progressive attainment received in stages. This is the more pungent that, from his point of view as a "mediating theologian," he is compelled to look upon sanctification, not as the necessary consequence of justification as in the Reformation doctrine, nor merely as the inseparable accompaniment of justification, but as identical with justification. If, when we enter into Christ by faith as the last Adam, the Head of which we are but members, we receive Him Himself, all of Him, all that He has and is, what remains to be obtained by a second act of faith as a "second blessing"?

Let us observe how Jellinghaus actually expresses himself on this fundamental matter: [15]

" The gospel becomes most simple and most intelligible when we, along with the Bible, present the whole saving-work of Christ as a deliverance, rescue, salvation for man held in sin and misery, and offer it to the simple acceptance of faith " (p. 52).

" It is a wholly one-sided quarter-gospel, when it is taught that Christ's sacrificial work accomplished no more than that He blotted out guilt and earned an imputable merit, but says nothing of this — that in Jesus' blood there are present and available for believers, hungry for righteousness and holiness, death-forces delivering from all evils, and resurrection-forces bringing all fruits of the Spirit that belong to the Kingdom of heaven " (p. 40).

" The believer seeks in Christ not only forgiveness of the guilt of sin, but also deliverance from its power and cleansing of the heart " (p. 258).

" What stands there [he is commenting on Rom. vi. 3–5] is not at all that this baptism signifies only a duty of dying daily; but what it says is that all true believers are already baptized into Jesus' death and are buried with Jesus according to the old man in this death, and therefore are free from the power of sin and uncleanliness " (p. 311).

" The Scriptures teach that forgiveness of sins, justification, the new life, cleansing and victory come of faith " (p. 259).

" Through this faith in Christ, Christ, and His righteousness, sanctification and life, which are external to us, comes into us, and becomes our possession. Yes, as soon as the man entrusts himself to Christ in faith, the Holy Spirit comes, in justification, into our heart and abides in our heart in order to testify that God, for Christ's sake, has forgiven our sins, and in order to glorify Christ in our heart, with His sanctifying death- and resurrection-power. Therefore together with justification there come also regeneration, cleansing, renovation, vivification, transference into the Kingdom of heaven, sanctification, the possession of eternal life (cf. I Cor. vi. 11, ' But ye are washed, ye are sanctified, ye are justified ') " (p. 263).

" For forgiveness of sins, justification, vivification, and sanctification fall at once together with faith " (p. 264).

[15] Unless otherwise indicated, the quotations, given with page numbers only, are from the fourth edition of " Das völlige, gegenwärtige Heil durch Christum."

" Regeneration, the new life, cleansing of heart and walk, and sanctification hang together [with justification] inwardly and inseparably (as Luther teaches clearly) " (p. 266).

" There exists therefore no justification and forgiveness of sins in Christ through faith without eternal life and regeneration in Christ; as Luther also says that where forgiveness of sins is there also is life and blessedness. He who really receives in faith forgiveness and justification in the blood, that is, in the death of the dead and risen Lord — he is also through the blood of Christ cleansed from sins and lives in Christ's life (Gal. ii. 16–21. Rom. x. 1–11, John iii. 14–16) " (p. 255).

" If we look at our deliverance thus, it becomes clear to us that John can always speak of eternal life as the immediate result of faith in Christ, and it is also manifest how, to be justified, converted, regenerated, resurrected and sanctified hang inwardly together according to the New Testament — yes, are one and the same thing " (p. 43).

It is impossible therefore that there should be faith without works: " Faith and trust are inwardly connected with faithfulness and obedience." He says expressly:

" There exists no Christian faith and trust without Christian faithfulness and obedience. So soon as I believe in Christ, I have come also to rueful apprehension of my disobedience theretofore. I trust in the Savior who was obedient up to death, that He will and can deliver me from the curse of the disobeyed commandment and from the slavery of sin, that is from disobedience. I believe, therefore, unto obedience. Everyone who believes in Christ, his Deliverer, yields himself to Christ, in order to die with Christ unto himself and his corrupt wilfulness, and to live in Jesus Christ and in obedient imitation of Him. Through the faith that is wrought by the Holy Spirit it always comes to obedience. . . . There is no faith in Christ which does not work an innermost fact and transformation, because it draws from the sanctifying life-powers of Jesus " (p. 153).

Jellinghaus undoubtedly intends that statements like these should be read as teaching that sanctification is by faith. So far are they, however, from teaching that sanctification comes from a special act of faith directed to the obtaining of it and it alone, that they rather explicitly connect sanctification with

the fundamental act of faith by which we receive the forgiveness of our sins. He cannot leave the matter at that. We find
him therefore very much preoccupied with the exact relation
of faith to sanctification. In his discussions of this subject he
sometimes speaks quite on the lines of the passages we have
already quoted, and is intent only on making the supernaturalness of salvation clear. Approaching the matter from the
standpoint of the "mediating theology" he often insists in
this interest that sanctification is something which has been
obtained for us by Christ, just like justification, objectively;
which exists therefore objectively in Christ for us, and which
is only to be taken over from Himself, as it were, as a whole.
He objects therefore to distinguishing between justification
and sanctification in such terms as "Christ for us" and
"Christ in us"; it is just as proper to speak of "Christ for
us" in connection with sanctification as in connection with
justification, and of "Christ in us" in connection with justification as in connection with sanctification. He says:

"Where the Bible speaks of sanctification through faith it means
that Christ Himself has wrought out for us our deliverance from the
power of sin, and He Himself is continuously the mighty Deliverer
and victorious Leader of believers. It is therefore a misleading representation of the doctrine of justification and sanctification when it
is said with sharp distinction that 'Christ for us' is the justification
and 'Christ in us' the sanctification of the Christian. 'Christ for
us' is the sinner's justification and forgiveness through faith; but
in the moment in which the man, in the power of the Holy Spirit,
trustingly surrenders himself to Christ as the Deliverer from sins,
Christ becomes his possession and the life of Christ comes into his
heart, so that he is not only justified but also regenerated and sanctified in Christ, so that therefore he is in Christ and Christ is in him.
. . . Precisely so is 'Christ for us,' that is, what Christ has obtained
for us by victory over the power of sin, death and the devil, or the
living, risen Jesus and His holy blood, the sole foundation and power
of our sanctification, on which we have to trust. Only because the
Christian who thirsts after sanctification has outside himself, in
Christ — the mighty Deliverer, present in the Word, who can continually wash and cleanse by His blood — a sanctifying power and

fulcrum which stands immovable, can he be confident in the midst
of his changing feelings and sure of victory. Because he thus through
the Holy Spirit surrenders himself in believing obedience to this full,
present Deliverer and all His sanctifying powers, Christ Himself
comes into his heart, and, as ' Christ in us,' becomes the heart's innermost life . . ." (pp. 540 f.).

He objects much more strenuously, however, in the same
interest of the supernaturalness of salvation, to every mode of
representation that would see in the faith which procures it
the ground or the substance of sanctification. If sanctification
is to be by works, it would be better to say so frankly, than to
say " by faith " (*im Glauben*) with the meaning that faith is
the one work which obtains it.

" Because the truth — that Christ has already wrought out and
made possible for us also our deliverance from the power of sin and
our sanctification, and offers it now *in Himself*, as the full, present
Deliverer — has been very little understood hitherto, great obscurity
and uncertainty has reigned also with respect to the doctrine of
sanctification by faith. Many teachers and textbooks, which teach
with complete decision the forgiveness of sins through naked, simple
faith alone, speak of sanctification as of a state which is gradually
brought about by the virtue of our faith and our love and gratitude.
Whereas, after the example of Luther, they repudiate with all decision, that faith as a sanctifying disposition (*Gesinnung*) justifies
and discharges from the guilt of sin or even only makes us worthy
to be received by Christ — they (as for example Thomasius) say
without hesitation that after justification faith becomes our fundamental disposition (*Grundgesinnung*) and thus sanctifies. The
Evangelical dogmatists speak with reference to sanctification not
only of a *vis receptiva* (receptive power) but also of a *vis operativa*
(self-effective power) of faith. Such a self-effective power, however,
is not possessed by faith, whether in justification or in sanctification;
all of its power comes from its object . . . , that is, from Christ "
(pp. 538 f.).[16]

In this statement justifying and sanctifying faith are, no
doubt, distinguished, but they are not separated. Jellinghaus'

[16] Cf. the parallel statement, pp. 376 f., note.

real position in this matter is made somewhat clearer by a passage which occurs on page 545. He is there speaking of the one-sidedness of the Reformation doctrine, with its stress on justification by faith alone and its neglect of the twin truth as to sanctification. He adduces in illustration a form of statement which he represents as very widespread among both Lutheran and Reformed theologians, to the effect that "justification daily repeated is sanctification." This form of statement certainly is objectionable. Justification is not, no matter how often repeated, sanctification, for the very good reason that justification directly affects only our standing while sanctification directly affects our state. In the course of the discussion, however, Jellinghaus substitutes for it the form of statement, "Justifying faith sanctifies," which he appears to treat as its equivalent, though it very certainly is not that.

The point of interest for the moment is that in criticizing this latter statement, Jellinghaus declares it to be ambiguous. It may mean, he says, this: "Justifying faith is so excellent a quality and mental attribute in a man that it sanctifies the man." He rightly says that in that sense it would be intolerable. It may also, however, happily mean this: "The same faith which lays hold of Christ for justification, lays hold of Him and experiences Him also for sanctification." In that sense, says Jellinghaus, it is "unconditionally correct"; and that he means this in the sense, not that the same kind of faith, but that the same exercise of faith, both justifies and sanctifies, he makes plain by a qualification which he at once introduces. This is to this effect: "Only, it should not be understood by it, that faith lays hold of Jesus equally along with justification in full measure for actual sanctification." Sanctification is obtained in the same act of faith by which justification is received — but not all the sanctification which is to be obtained. After this first sanctification there is a further sanctification accessible to us by a faith which is a purely sanctifying faith — a further sanctification which is in full measure.

Meanwhile the existence of any such thing as a purely sanctifying faith — and indeed the validity of the whole representation that sanctification, whether along with justification or alone, is received immediately by faith — hangs in the air. It is not until the book is three-quarters done [17] that the needed chapter on The Scriptural Proof of Sanctification by Faith is inserted. The Epistle to the Galatians is taken up first and run through. Then Jellinghaus finds himself compelled to insert a subsection with this heading: "Forgiveness of sins through faith and sanctification through faith are in the New Testament mostly taught together." That is to say, the New Testament does not ("mostly") teach justification through faith and sanctification through faith, but justification and sanctification through faith. He writes:

" When we look more closely at the Epistle to the Galatians and the whole New Testament, we find that they do not make so sharp a conceptional distinction between justification and sanctification as we are now accustomed to make, and especially, that the words ' righteous, righteousness, justify ' often include sanctification in themselves; and again in other passages the word ' sanctify ' includes forgiveness of sins and justification " (p. 567).

He illustrates the first usage by the prophetic declaration, " The just shall live by his faith," which he represents as including sanctification as well as justification, no doubt following W. E. Boardman's interpretation of it. The second he illustrates by Heb. x. 10. Then he seeks a rationale of the custom he has thus announced:

" Precisely because the apostles teach that forgiveness of sins and sanctification both take place by faith apart from works of our own, they do not need to distinguish them so anxiously. So soon, on the other hand, as a forgiveness by faith in Christ alone and a sanctification by faith and works are taught, an exaggerated distinction is necessary, such as is made by many orthodox Lutheran and Reformed Church teachers, in order that the comfort of the forgiveness of sins may be left in its abiding certainty. With the doctrine of sanctification by faith, on the other hand, the doctrine of forgiveness of sins through faith is given and established almost of itself without hair-splitting distinctions " (pp. 567 f.).

[17] Part II. chap. vii. pp. 557 ff.

He then refers us back to the first part of the volume, where, says he, " we have repeatedly shown that the apostles presented to sinners and taught a direct and immediate reconciliation with God through the surrender of faith to the justifying and purifying Deliverer. Repentant sinners are declared by them at once justified and holy, without waiting for the confirmation of their character in good works, so that forgiveness of sins rests in no way on sanctification, though it of course includes the foundation of all holiness, namely life-communion with Christ's blood." The whole drift of the chapter may be treated as summed up in the following words, which are more particularly a comment on the Epistle to the Colossians:

" As in the Epistle to the Ephesians, so also in that to the Colossians, it is taught that the believer, through the surrender of faith, has part in all that Jesus experienced, so that he has died with Christ, risen again, and has been transferred into the heavenly, the supramundane Kingdom of God. This is taught so crisply that it must be assumed that this doctrine and this conception of the Deliverer had already been proclaimed to them by Epaphras and the rest, since otherwise they would not have been able to understand it from this brief presentation. These fundamental truths were already the common property of the apostolic congregations in Asia . . ." (p. 571).

There is no evidence presented here that the New Testament represents sanctification as received immediately by faith. In point of fact there is no direct statement to that effect in the New Testament. It is to Jellinghaus' credit that he does not adduce for it either Acts xv. 9 or xxvi. 18, which are often made to do duty in this sense.[18] His strong conviction that sanctification is obtained directly and immediately by faith is a product not of his Scriptural studies, but of his " mediating theology." According to that theology, when we receive Christ by faith we receive in Him all that He is to us at once; all the benefits which we receive in Him are conceived as received immediately and directly by the faith through which

[18] He does, however, adduce Acts xv. 9 in this sense elsewhere. For Acts xxvi. 18, see p. 567.

we are united with Him and become sharers in all that He is. Justification and sanctification, for example, are thought of as parallel products of faith. This is not, however, the New Testament representation. According to its teaching, sanctification is not related to faith directly and immediately, so that in believing in Jesus we receive both justification and sanctification as parallel products of our faith; or either the one or the other, according as our faith is directed to the one or the other. Sanctification is related directly not to faith but to justification; and as faith is the instrumental cause of justification, so is justification the instrumental cause of sanctification. The *vinculum* which binds justification and sanctification together is not that they are both effects of faith — so that he who believes must have both — because faith is the *prius* of both alike. Nor is it even that both are obtained in Christ, so that he who has Christ, who is made to us both righteousness and sanctification, must have both because Christ is the common source of both. It is true that he who has faith has and must have both; and it is true that he who has Christ has and must have both. But they do not come out of faith or from Christ in the same way. Justification comes through faith; sanctification through justification, and only mediately, through justification, through faith. So that the order is invariable, faith, justification, sanctification; not arbitrarily, but in the nature of the case.

For the main matter, however, Jellinghaus' expositions of the Scriptural material are not only true, but both obvious and important. It is not exact to say that the New Testament makes no conceptional distinction between justification and sanctification. But it is true to say that it is absolutely impatient of their separation from one another, and uniformly represents them as belonging together and entering as constituent parts into the one, unitary salvation which is received by faith. The significance of Jellinghaus' exposition of the Scriptural material is that by it it is made perfectly clear that no support from the New Testament can be obtained for separating them and representing them as two distinct benefits which may be obtained apart from each other by separate acts of faith.

Jellinghaus cannot quite make up his mind, however, to renounce altogether the notion of a "second blessing." With the form in which he received this notion from his Higher Life teachers, of course, he has definitely broken. He cannot teach that we first receive justification by faith, and then afterwards receive sanctification by a different faith. He knows very well that justification and sanctification cannot, according to the New Testament, be thus separated. But from his own standpoint — of the "mediating theology" — he was prepared to look upon sanctification as obtained immediately by faith and not solely through the medium of justification; and on that ground he endeavors to save the notion, at least, of the "second blessing," by representing the distinction between the first and the second blessing as turning, not on the distinction between justification and sanctification, but on that between partial and complete sanctification. Justification and sanctification are, of course, received together, that is, some sanctification. But there is room for more sanctification. Why not say that complete sanctification remains to be obtained through a new act of faith directed to it specifically? Of course, this is just as incongruous with the fundamental postulate of the "mediating theology" as the distinction which has been discarded in its favor. According to this postulate, when we enter into "mystical union" with Christ, we receive in Him all that He is and has, all at once. He is ours and all that is in Him is ours. It may be possible to make room for a progressive realization in life of the great riches which we receive all at once in Him in principle. But for a new beginning, made by a new act of faith, scarcely. There is no room for those who are already in Christ, sharers in all that He is and has, once more, by a new act, to enter into Christ and to obtain as a second benefit from Him something entirely new.

Jellinghaus finds himself, therefore, in almost as great difficulties in validating his new doctrine of the "second blessing," according to which it is an increase in sanctification at a

definite time and in response to a definite act of faith, as he
would have been in, had he retained the old doctrine, according to which the "second blessing" of sanctification was contrasted with the "first blessing" of justification. We can
scarcely blame him in these circumstances that, in his exposition of his doctrine of the "second blessing," he moves along
a somewhat winding path. Sometimes he seems to reduce it to
merely a doctrine of progressive sanctification. Sometimes, in
order to regain its distinctiveness as a "second blessing," he
appears to be almost ready to make it merely a subjective
experience — the growing Christian's sudden realization of
what has been happening to him really in unbroken progress.
Sometimes he seems even half inclined to confine it to badly
taught Christians, in order to obtain room for a decisive change
for the better; those who begin badly naturally may have
to begin over again. But in the end he comes back to what
seems to be a decided reaffirmation of the experience, though
in a considerably attenuated form.

In one of the earlier instances of his discussion of the possibility of a sudden advance in the Christian's experience the
matter is approached through an exposition of conversion.
There is a divine side and a human side to conversion; and so
far as it is a human work, it admits of degrees, because both
the repentance and the faith which constitute this side of it
are capable of continuous deepening. From this point of view
a Christian may find himself repenting and believing over and
over again.

"Inasmuch as every increase of faith includes within itself a
deepening of repentance, the phrase 'daily repentance' may be
employed in a good sense, when what is meant by daily repentance
is not an expectation of daily repeated falls into known sins and a
weak complaining regret for them, and such a continuous condition
of spiritual weakness and lamentation is not held to be necessary.[19]

19 In contact as he was with a Pietistic community, Jellinghaus was much
exercised over the Pietistic idea of the Christian life as a "daily repentance,"
the exact antipodes of his notion that we receive by faith immediately full
sanctification — which leaves no room for daily sins to be repented of. He says

Even the child of God who is converted and is walking in sanctification should always perceive afresh and with increasing clearness how
guilty, sinful and impotent to all good he is in himself, and what grace
and power he has in Jesus. Yes, when the defects of his Christian life
are really made clear by God's Spirit to a Christian and then he finds
in faith greater unsuspected grace and gracious power in Jesus, it is
to him often as if he were newly converted. From this it may be
explained that many Christians have erroneously called by the
name of a ' second conversion ' their experience, after long stumbling,
of fuller sanctification in the power of Christ's blood through their
fuller surrender to and fuller faith in Jesus as the Deliverer
from all sins and as the compassionately leading Good Shepherd "
(pp. 287 f.).

Here an experience presenting itself to the consciousness as
revolutionary is explained as only a step in the normal advance
of the Christian in the experience of grace. Similarly, we read
at another place:

" This laying aside of sin and of the old man, as we have said,
should begin in conversion, and every converted Christian has a
right to hold himself to be dead to sin and crucified with Christ;
but nevertheless the fact is apparent that even in the Apostolic age
the majority of believers had need of an exhortation to do this.
When, however, the apostles lay such a requirement on believers,
they are not exhorting them to a half and gradual, but to an immediate and complete laying aside of sin. For what one will not
do in this matter completely and at once, that he never does rightly
and with effect. It is, however, self-evident that no matter how
thorough and decisive the renunciation is, there remains a place

---

(p. 123) that " it is utterly un-Biblical to assume that every believing Christian
falls into known sins daily and therefore must repent daily." He says it is unendurable that Christians should pray: " Forgive us the many unconscious and
conscious sins which we have done this day." " That is," he asserts, " in the
case of really converted Christians, who commit no sin with knowledge and
intention, and to whom the saying belongs, ' Rather die than to sin consciously,'
a highly unthinking mode of speech " (p. 126). He is thrown into a flutter by
every suggestion that Christians " sin daily " or that the mark of the Christian
is continuous repentance. We are to repent once for all (p. 122) and after that
— not sin. In what sense he is willing to admit the propriety of " daily repentance " the passages quoted in the text show.

for a progressive deepening: for when the degree of light on sin increases and new sins are discovered, these new sins also must be discarded and they can be laid aside only instance by instance. Where a clear knowledge of Christ's power of deliverance exists, therefore, in the beginning of conversion, and where a faithful conflict is carried on in the power of the blood of Christ — there a more spasmodic, sudden renunciation in the Christian's walk will be less in evidence. Therefore the more clearly the power of the blood of Christ to deliver is preached to souls from the beginning, and grasped by them, the more seldom will these sudden transitions, similar to ' second conversions,' occur in the life of Christians. (Just as absolutely sudden conversions are less to be expected in the case of those who grow up in good Christian nurture.) When anything like a ' second conversion ' shows itself in the life of a Christian, it is likely either that there was no accurate knowledge of the right way of salvation possessed in the beginning, or that the converted Christian had fallen into hazardous inner unfaithfulnesses and falterings. This suddenness in the renunciation of sins and deeper sanctification which is so offensive to many would occur more infrequently if the preaching of sanctification in Jesus were clearer " (pp. 499 f.).

Here certainly the " second blessing " (note the application in the last sentence) is represented not as the normal experience of the heroes of faith, but as an abnormality due either to the insufficient knowledge or to the unfaithful life of the average Christian, which may be expected to be made rarer by faithful preaching.

Of course, in these circumstances, it cannot be taught that the " second blessing " is necessary, if we are to have all that Christ has in Himself for His people. We read without surprise:

" It is quite possible, in the case of a Christian soul, that his surrender to Christ in his conversion should be so decisive and complete, and remain so true to his increasing knowledge in the course of his Christian life, and should grow so constantly, that there is no room for a temporally distinct, renewed surrender which essentially and instantaneously changes the inner condition. There is needed only a steady growth of surrender, since no partial disobedience and no partial retrogression is found here. When surrender and trust have been complete from conversion and have grown evenly side by side and soundly — then a distinct, renewed surrender, which would change the inward condition essentially and suddenly for the better, and notably advance it, would not be possible, precisely because it would be already existent " (p. 507).[20]

"We are not then to assume," we read on the next page, "that according to the Bible, a second temporally distinct event of a complete surrender must occur in the case of every believing Christian." But it is immediately added: "But according to actual experience, it is true that in the case of most believing Christians a lack of complete faith-surrender and a partial walking in self-seeking or self-sufficiency, or self-tormenting, or world-serving, shows itself in the case of most believing Christians not long after conversion and the first warmth of love." This hardly means anything else than that the need of the "second blessing" is due to the failure of the Christian to receive or use the first blessing aright: it is not an essentially different transaction communicating an essentially different blessing, but only a reparation for past failure. It therefore does not surprise us to find Jellinghaus writing as follows:

" Some have maintained in England and America, and very lately in Germany too, that a converted man does not become a complete Christian and does not become a really blessed, powerful instrument for God's Kingdom, until he has received suddenly and consciously a second baptism with the Holy Spirit. In this there is only so much true as that a great multitude of men of God have suddenly experienced, after their conversion, a new deep baptism with the Holy Spirit; many of them at a time when the cleansing power of the blood of Christ and the greatness of the love of Christ had come brightly before their eyes in knowledge and experience. But the New Testament nowhere requires a second sudden baptism with the Holy Spirit for all believers. In the case of the most, the deeper filling with the Holy Ghost comes gradually, with sufferings, humiliations and marvelous answers to prayer and deliverances, through the deeper

[20] " In the Bible," it is immediately added, not without significance, " most is said of the first surrender at conversion."

experience of the powers of Christ's death and resurrection. — He who teaches that every Christian must have the experience of the eradication of his sinful nature, and of his sinlessness, through a second baptism of the Holy Spirit, is an anti-Biblical fanatic and a victim of delusion" (p. 71).

This is in principle to discard the whole idea of the "second blessing" as taught by W. E. Boardman and the Smiths, to say nothing of John Wesley standing in the background.[21]

At the very end of his book [22] Jellinghaus devotes a page to repeating all this, led thereto by the emergence of what he himself recognizes as the most serious difficulty in the way of the contention that believers must believe again in order to become fully sanctified. This is that we read nowhere in the New Testament that believers are to receive the sanctifying power of the death and resurrection of Christ only by a second surrender. The New Testament writers always refer the duty, the right, the power, to die to sin, to the communion in the death and resurrection of Christ which has been entered into at conversion. Jellinghaus does not think of denying that this is the fact; and he feels constrained to add: " According to the Bible, there is no justification and regeneration which does not already include in itself the essential beginning of all sanctification." That is to say, in brief, the faith which justifies sanctifies — at least in the beginnings of sanctification, beginnings which include in themselves the promise and potency of all sanctification. In these circumstances he feels it necessary to add further that it cannot be denied that it is *possible* (unfortunately he underscores the " possible ") "for a Christian at once at justification and regeneration so to enter into communion in the death- and the resurrection-life of Jesus, that he has a power of victory over external and internal sins in Christ or " — he adds — " that he at least so grows gradually

---

[21] The phrase "baptism with the Holy Spirit," means with Jellinghaus just regeneration; e.g. p. 312, "the baptism with the Holy Spirit, that is, regeneration." He does not admit the propriety of its use of a new experience superinduced on regeneration and sanctification, as, for example, "Pastor" Paul used it.

[22] Pp. 691 f.

into it that there is no question of a particular second point of time for a fuller sanctification." He is compelled to go even further than this, and to say that not only is such an experience *possible* (with the underscored " possible "), but it is in certain circumstances the normal history of the soul. If the soul has been fortunate enough to enjoy from the beginning — the beginning of its life or of its Christian experience — correct instruction with respect to the way of salvation, and has given faithful and unwavering obedience throughout (perhaps we are not to read this as an impossible condition) — why, this is the normal course. He says :

" This must be set forth clearly and plainly, that we may not fall into un-Biblical artificialities and repel those who know their Bibles. *A sharp separation of two distinct sorts of sanctification, we do not find in the Bible.* It cannot be taught on Biblical grounds that we must all first be justified and regenerated, and then we must all later, at a definite time and by a sudden, definite transaction, be sanctified in complete fashion " (p. 692).

We are sorry that Jellinghaus holds back a little even in this declaration. The Bible not only does not teach that we must " all " be first justified and then by a distinct act of faith " all " be sanctified. It does not teach that any will be so dealt with. What it teaches is that justification and sanctification are but successive steps, inseparably joined together by an immanent bond, in the realization of the one salvation which is received by faith. Jellinghaus does not quite come to this point of view. He says it is *possible* for a man to be sanctified at the same time that he is justified, if — . He is thinking of sanctification not as the necessary issue of justification, included in principle in it, but as some sort of a separate entity, which the Scriptures join with it invariably, it is true, but which is not in the nature of the case its inevitable consequent. And therefore he at once qualifies even this admission — for it is after all an admission with him. " However true that is," he adds, " we may not, according to the teaching of the New Testament, and according to Christian experience, maintain that every justified man manifests and must manifest already in his life the whole sanctifying power of the death and resurrection of Christ."

That is, however, precisely what we must maintain — if we are to be true to the New Testament; that is to say, of course, if we mean it in the New Testament sense. For the words have a certain ambiguity buried in them, and Jellinghaus means them in the wrong sense, in the sense, that is, that sanctification in its completeness is received all at once at the very moment of justification. "We dare not say," he explains, "that justification and actual sanctification fall absolutely together; that he who is fully justified is sanctified in the full measure in which this is possible on earth; that he who has experienced the sanctifying power of the death and blood of Christ only in a partial way is also not yet fully justified." And then he appeals to New Testament passages in which those who are assumed to be justified are exhorted to advance in their Christian walk! Of course we dare not say anything of this sort, for sanctification is a progressive thing, as is already allowed indeed when it is pointed out that the New Testament exhorts Christians to advance in their Christian walk. Temptation to say anything of the sort can assail those only who conceive of sanctification as some kind of limited entity which can be received all at once. It is because Jellinghaus so conceives it that he is unable to accept, without qualification, what he himself recognizes as Bible teaching.

If it seems to us that the shadow of the "second blessing" to which alone Jellinghaus can cling after this is hardly worth clinging to, especially at the cost he is compelled to pay for it, that is probably because we underestimate the constraint he was under, arising from his doctrine of perfection, to preserve at least some shadow of it. His interest, it is true, does not center immediately in the "second blessing." But it does center in what he calls, in the title of his book, "full, present salvation through Christ." He wishes to teach that we may enter by faith alone into the immediate enjoyment of the whole salvation that is in Christ Jesus. Suddenness of entrance into this full salvation belongs accordingly to the essence of his doctrine. Jesus would not seem to him a complete Deliverer if we had to wait for the deliverance received in Him to be gradually accomplished in us through a long process of growth, especially if this prolonged itself throughout life. At least our experience of salvation must be at once complete on faith. That indeed is already involved in the postulate of his " mediating theology," and this is the reason of his strong insistence that sanctification too, as well as justification, must be conceived as objectively perfect and ready for us in Christ, to be taken over from Him by faith alone.

The postulates of his " mediating theology " would interpose no obstacle, it is true, to supposing that this full sanctification, objectively complete, ready for us in Christ, is taken over in the same act of faith by which we receive justification. Rather, they are really patient to no other supposition; and he finds himself in straits on this account as he seeks to save for himself even the shadow of the " second blessing " which he preserves. The Scriptures to which he appeals to justify his doctrine of the immediate reception of complete sanctification by faith, also connect this reception of complete sanctification with the same act of faith by which we receive justification. But there were powerful motives operating to prevent Jellinghaus from following in this either the postulates of his fundamental theology or the implication of his Scriptures. It is too clear to be denied, that the Scriptures are full of exhortations to men, assumed to be justified, to make advances in their holy walk, and therefore cannot mean to teach that every justified man is by the very act by which he received his justification also at once fully sanctified. It is also too clear to be denied that, in point of experience, not all who must be presumed to be justified are fully sanctified — unless we are prepared to refuse to recognize as a Christian at all any one who is not obviously perfect — a position to the intolerableness of which Jellinghaus shows himself to be keenly sensitive.

The assumption of such an attitude towards the Christian body at large would, moreover, abolish the chief religious motive which is urged in justification of the doctrine of immediate sanctification by faith — the need of encouragement for men who, having believed, yet find themselves still unde- livered from sinning, and who are ready therefore to despair of salvation itself. These men need to be assured that, despite appearances, they have not believed in vain, that their faith avails for deliverance from the guilt of sin, and the way is open still for them now to believe again for deliverance from its power. Under the stress of such considerations, that he might maintain his fundamental doctrine of immediate sanctification by faith, Jellinghaus was under necessity to preserve at least a shadow of the doctrine of the " second blessing."

II

In the former portion of this article it has been pointed out that the task which Jellinghaus set himself was, essentially, to adjust the Higher Life doctrine which he had received from Pearsall Smith to his own fundamental thinking, which ran on the lines of the so-called " mediating theology." We have seen that the primary effect was to destroy, in principle, the notion of the " second blessing," which formed the pivot of Smith's teaching; and that a semblance of this doctrine was preserved only in the interests of the idea of immediate sancti- fication by faith, which Jellinghaus found it necessary in one way or another to maintain.

It is quite true that his doctrine of the nature of the im- mediate sanctification, which we receive by faith alone, has itself also suffered somewhat from his endeavor to give it a form which may at least seem to be tolerable, in the face alike of intractable Scriptures and plain facts. He is very careful, for example, not to lift the idea of sanctification — of the " per- fection " which he supposes is received immediately by faith — too high. In endeavoring to define it moderately he some- times no doubt employs language of it, which, if taken strictly, would lead us nowhither. For instance, at one place he says:

" The Christian should and can become pure and remain pure from all sins and all impurity of a kind (welche geeignet ist) to

interrupt his inner communion with God and his peace with Jesus "
(p. 621).[23]

Of course there is no sin of conduct and no sinfulness of disposition, of whatever sort, kind, or degree, the proper effect of which is not to interrupt our communion with God and our peace with Jesus. If it does not actually interrupt our communion with God and our peace with Jesus, that can only be because our communion with God and our peace with Jesus have their ground not in our own holiness, but in Christ Himself — rest, in accordance with I John ii. on what Jesus has done for us and is doing in us, and not on any works or attainments of our own. The effect of Jellinghaus' statement is to declare that there are some sins which God will tolerate in His children and some which He will not. This seems to reintroduce the exploded distinction between mortal and venial sins, and appears to license Christians to commit a certain class of sins. In order to learn what degree of sinfulness God tolerates in His children, that is to say, what is the quality of their " perfection," however, we must go elsewhere.

We are as little advanced in our understanding of the matter when a " perfect " Christian is defined as " a Christian to whom God's Word ascribes a pure heart and holiness." [24] For, as Jellinghaus himself reminds us, God's Word ascribes a pure heart and holiness to all Christians indifferently. They are all addressed as " saints " and spoken of as " sanctified in Christ Jesus." A " saint " in Scripture is not an eminent believer — a twofold believer, a believer who has believed twice — but any believer at all. This is reinforced by the fact that the Bible seldom addresses or speaks of believers as " sinners," as we have grown accustomed to do.[25] Accordingly Jellinghaus has a certain unwillingness to use the word " perfection " only of a higher class among Christians.

[23] " Das völlige, gegenwärtige Heil durch Christum," ed. 4, p. 621. Unless otherwise indicated, all quotations with page numbers are from this work.

[24] E.g. p. 640.

[25] P. 601. The exceptions are such as in I Tim. i. 15, where Paul speaks of himself as the " chief " of sinners — referring, Jellinghaus alleges, solely to his *past;* and James iv. 8 and v. 20, which certainly refer to the present.

"All Christians from their regeneration onward can be perfect in their kind, and it therefore creates confusion when a last, highest, concluding stage of perfection is so spoken of" (p. 705).

"The word means what we now designate by the expressions 'entirely Christian,' 'rightly Christian,' 'rightly standing,' 'decisive Christian,' 'truly Christian.' As we speak without hesitation of complete, true, decisive, rightly standing Christians, we need not hesitate to say, according to the Bible, that Christians can and ought to be 'perfect'" (p. 707).

He is not denying here that there are "stages" of Christian attainment or that there is such a thing as the "second blessing." He is only arguing that "perfection" is not a word to be frightened at, and that all Christians may and ought to be "perfect." He wishes, however, to be discreet in the use of language and in the definition of conditions. And therefore he says:

"It is thoroughly Biblical to say that Christians ought and can be perfect, entire, holy, sanctified, and unblamable. But it does not at all follow that, according to the Bible, we may speak of entire sanctification, perfect holiness, complete sanctity. By uniting these words into one notion an entirely new sense arises, which does not lie in the separate words. I can call a king 'a complete king,' and 'a wise king,' and 'a righteous king' without intending to maintain that the king is 'altogether wise' and 'wholly righteous.' Similarly I can, according to the Bible, say of Christians, that they are entire, perfect, holy, pure and unblamable. But I cannot on that account appeal to the Bible when I speak of 'perfect holiness' and 'entire sanctification' and 'complete purity'" (p. 709).

Again, and more to our point:

"It is said of Christians in the Bible that they should and can be perfect, but it is not declared of the holiness or the purity of Christians that it is perfect and unsurpassable. We are not justified, then, according to the Bible in speaking of 'complete sanctification' and 'perfect holiness' with respect to Christians sanctified in the higher sense, as, after the example of Charles Wesley, many otherwise excellent theologians in England and America do. The Bible declares plainly that 'holiness' and 'perfection' belong to the complete or rightly standing Christian, this side of the grave. But that does not give us the right to speak of perfect holiness or complete holiness or even only of complete sanctification. This is to go beyond the Biblical modes of expression " (p. 709).

He is speaking here of those who have received the "second blessing." They are "perfect," but the notion of "perfection" must not be pressed too far. That is all that we learn from this discussion.

When we come to inquire what the condition thus called "perfection" precisely is, we are not left, however, without some very extended descriptions of it. It lies in the nature of the case that these should be introduced in connection with discussions of the relation of Christians to sin. There is a section, for example, on the "necessary marks of regeneration, justification, conversion, and the state of grace." [26] The chief of these marks is found not in faith but in a holy life. We read, however, in exposition of this holy life such statements as the following:

"The most important mark of regeneration for the Christian himself and also for outsiders is decisive renunciation of all and every conscious sin" (p. 327).

"Whoever of set purpose and wilfully commits sin and yet would fain be in favor with God wretchedly deceives himself in contradiction to God's clear Word" (p. 328).

All commission of wilful sin is avoidable; the power to avoid it comes with faith.

"He who is regenerated and depends on Christ in faith, has also not merely the 'good will' to desert sin, but also in Christ the power to avoid all plain, gross sin. The true Christian has the will to be obedient to Christ and also is obedient to Him; Paul therefore often designates the whole of Christianity as the obedience of faith. For there is no faith and no surrender of faith in Christ without obedience of faith. We must certainly have some doubts with respect to all those Christians who of course wish to be obedient in general but say in some particular matters, in opposition to God's will, 'I

[26] Pp. 325 ff.

cannot do that,' or 'God cannot demand that sacrifice of me'"
(p. 328).

It surely needs no argument to prove that defiant sinning is
inconsistent with a Christian profession. That there are some
sins which may be committed by a Christian, however, without forfeiture of his status as a Christian, does not seem to be
denied. It is indeed already allowed, when what is said is that
"conscious" sinning — naturally at once corrected into "pre-
meditated and wilful" sinning, which, by the way, is not at
all the same thing — cannot be thought of in a Christian's case.

A distinction is intimated here. And this distinction is
pursued. We read:

"Many now have maintained that a regenerated man must
necessarily be free also from the sins of weakness and of thoughtlessness, and from the inner stains that arise from the sinful passions of hate, jealousy, covetousness, timidity, lewdness, frivolity
and pride" (p. 329).

This is not the contention which Jellinghaus himself makes.
He says:

"Assuredly this is the aim and privilege of the regenerated
man — that he should have victory over these things too. . . .
"But [he is constrained to add] it contradicts a whole multitude
of Bible passages and also Christian experience when this is set
forth as a necessary mark of life from God and of living faith.
"The same John [he says, that is, the same John who seems to
say that a Christian does not sin at all] says in I John ii. 2, 'If any
man sin we have an advocate with the Father.' Paul says, in the
same passage in which he asserts as unconditioned fact 'that those
who do such things (that is, live in conscious open sin) shall not
inherit the kingdom of God,' of the weak condition of many Galatians (Gal. v. 15–24), 'For the flesh lusteth against the Spirit and
the Spirit against the flesh: these are contrary one to the other, that
ye do not what ye wish.'"

If there are sins, then, which a Christian cannot commit, there
are others which he may possibly commit, and we must not
deceive ourselves or judge others harshly in this matter.

" That this distinction between conscious, intentional sins which
are committed and not resisted, and unconscious sins and sins of
weakness which are hated and resisted, and by which men are overtaken, is often not kept clearly in mind is true. It is important, however, that this distinction should always be made, in order that souls
may not deceive themselves, and brethren may not be rashly and
unjustly judged " (p. 329).

But the warning is added:

" Let every Christian bear well in mind that so soon as he no
longer hates, repents, resists his sins of weakness and steadily more
and more conquers them in Christ, they become to him condemning
sins of wickedness " (p. 330).

Much the same ground is gone over again later in the volume, when the topic of " the victory over sin " is formally
taken up.[27] A beginning is made here with a survey of " the
several senses of the word ' sin.' " The word is used first, we are
told, in the sense of " conscious, intentional transgression of
God's commandment, or of conscious sins with malice." Sin
in this sense, we are told, is " wholly incompatible with Christian faith and a state of grace "; " a man who commits such a
sin either never has been a believing Christian or has fallen
out of the state of grace." [28] Such a statement is, of course,
wholly without warrant, and we are not surprised to find
Jellinghaus at once addressing himself to mitigating it. He
says, among other things, that the Bible does not permit us to
brand as " a conscious sin in the full sense, every sin with reference to which the man has some feeling that he is doing wrong "
— and instances Peter's denial as an example in point! It
emerges then, after all, that " conscious " sins are not absolutely incompatible with a state of grace, and we are glad to
read a few pages farther on a wise warning against making
too much of the element of clear consciousness in sinning:

" Accordingly it would be very dangerous to take the notion of
sin too narrowly and to make the Christian consciousness and the
conscience the sole judge of the sinfulness or rightness of conduct:

[27] Pp. 600 ff.   [28] Pp. 602 f.

it would be decisively contrary to true humility and self-knowledge
should we deny that God sees badness and evil in us and our actions
(I Cor. iv. 4, Luke xii. 47, the fifth and sixth petitions of the Lord's
prayer, Matt. vi. 12–15), which we do not see. Most 'unconscious
sins' can be traced back to our original sin, inasmuch as the human
power of discrimination with reference to God's will and between
good and evil is much weakened by it and man finds himself prone
to evil. Other unconscious sins are the result of a 'little faith' which
is displeasing to God. We must therefore humble ourselves and ask
God's forgiveness for these our hidden faults and offences also. It is
often, too, previous indifference, lukewarmness, failure in love which
is responsible for a Christian's doing something, without noting it,
that is sinful. Therefore the Roman Catholic maxim, *Invincibilis
ignorantia excusat a toto* (invincible ignorance completely excuses),
is not altogether true. It is a more important and a truer evangelical
maxim that we are to find sin not merely in individual evil deeds,
but in the evil dispositions of the heart. He who sees sin only in individual deeds, falls easily into work-righteousness and self-deception " (pp. 609 f.).

Nevertheless the distinction between "conscious" and
"unconscious" sins is so far clung to as that, whereas conscious
sinning is pronounced incompatible with Christian faith, it is
allowed that no Christian can be free from unconscious sinning
while here on earth.

" For [it is explained] so long as the Christian is not perfectly
pure and good in his own nature and is not omniscient, he will fall
into error and will, with the best intention, through error act
wrongly " (p. 610).

Nor is this all that is to be said. There is another category of
sin still to be reckoned with. We read further:

" If we should understand, however, still more broadly by sin,
'lack of conformity with the perfect holiness and purity of God,'
it is clear that the Christian can never be without sin in this world —
yes, that all that he does, even though he does it out of a pure
heart and a hearty love to God and man, would be sin or infected
with sin."

On this statement we must pause a moment, for it is a very remarkable statement — in the sense which Jellinghaus puts on it. For he is not speaking of " original sin " here, and the condition of man as fallen in Adam and a member of a sin-infected race. He is speaking of the natural constitution of man. " In this sense of holy," he says — meaning in the sense of "holy" implied in the definition of sin as " lack of conformity with the perfect holiness and purity of God " — " pure and perfect as God, Adam was not sinless even before the fall " — an assertion which he lamely supports by an appeal to I Cor. xv. 45–47, whence, he says, it follows " that Adam did not yet possess the spiritual nature and the spiritual mind of the perfected righteous man, and was therefore no doubt guiltless but still defective " — a perfect nest of confusions. " The Bible, however," he adds, " *never* uses the word ' sin ' in this sense "; and that is true if what he means is that the Bible never uses it in a sense which confuses it with the incomplete; and he adds equally truly that to give " sin " this sense would be " to erase the sharp contradiction between sin and righteousness."

It is not so clear, however, that the Bible does not use " sin " in the sense of any " want of conformity with the perfect holiness and purity of God." In point of fact, on the contrary, that is just the sense in which the Bible does statedly use the word, though it does not understand itself as thereby convicting man as man as sinner, but only as convicting man as fallen as sinner. Jellinghaus does indeed declare [29] that it is made clear that the Bible " does not use the word ' sin ' in this sense " — the sense, namely, of any " want of conformity with the perfect holiness and purity of God " — by this, " that it maintains that the Christian can walk righteously, holily, perfectly, umblamably, and not sin." But here he has overreached himself in his eagerness to make a point in favor of his Perfectionism. This representation of the condition of the Christian relative to sin is obviously just as inconsistent with a universal inherent sinfulness of mankind referred to its fall in

[29] P. 611.

Adam, as if it were referred to its nature as created by God. And Jellinghaus does not deny that man is fallen in Adam, or that, as fallen in Adam, he is inherently sinful with a sinfulness which infects him up to the grave, so that, therefore, on this account also, no man can be free from sin so long as he lives in this world.

That the fact of "original sin" could slip out of Jellinghaus' thought at this point of the discussion is no doubt evidence that it played no great part in his conception of the Christian's condition in this world. He does not think of such a thing as denying the fact of "original sin" or its infection of men throughout the whole duration of their lives on earth, even as Christians. On the contrary, he gives formal recognition to these facts.[30] He speaks freely of man's "sinful nature," calling it "the flesh," and describing it as "an evil fundamental nature (*Naturgrund*)." He declares repeatedly that this "evil fundamental nature" is not eradicated in the Christian but remains in him up to the end. He speaks of it indeed as suppressed in its activities, so that it lies as it were inert and "dead" in the background of the Christian's life. And thus he makes a place for his declaration that the Christian can be in a sense without sin, that is to say, without sinning.

"Sin in this sense ought to be crucified in the Christian and brought by Christ's blood into the condition of death, and should be held in that state, so that it cannot reign and cannot make the heart unclean, and therefore the Christian is also actually in this sense 'free from sin,' and sins not (Rom. vi.). [But he feels bound to add at once with strong emphasis:] But it *is still there* in the fundamental nature (*Naturgrund*), up to the grave, in the case of the most sanctified" (p. 607).

If it were not there, he goes on to say, those sanctified in this high degree could never fall into sin again, and their children would be born sinless.

Though crucified in Christ and slain on His cross, then, sin remains very much alive. It does not affect the Christian's

---

[30] Pp. 606 f.

activities as he walks in his holy life — and yet it lies there in the background so far affecting him that it is due to it that he can sin again, and that he does sin if he ever sins again. Our complex soul-body nature "cannot be sanctified this side of the grave in the fashion that the seed of sin in it is forever eradicated and offers no longer a handle for sin."[31] "Yes, the flesh remains in Christians unholy";[32] "the old man and the flesh are no doubt crucified by their connection by faith with the crucified one, but are not eradicated nor destroyed";[33] "the flesh with its lusts is no doubt crucified in the believer, but is still existent and in a certain sense living and always capable of being resuscitated."[34] But Christ stands between us and this, our fundamental evil nature, and makes it as if it were not our inner selves but a dead thing encysted within us.

"If the old man and the flesh are actually thus crucified and thus buried with Christ through faith in the Holy Spirit as the gospel plainly testifies (Rom. vi. 6), *then the Christian has the right to look upon the old man and the flesh as something external, from which he is actually divided and separated by the cross of Christ so long as he abides in Jesus.* He may confidently believe that Jesus' blood is nearer to him than the old man; yes, that Jesus' blood and cross stand between him and the old man as a no doubt transparent but trusty shield " (p. 625).

We perceive, then, that while a true " Perfectionism " is taught by Jellinghaus, the perfection which he teaches is, in the first place, a perfection only of acts, not of nature. In their fundamental nature (*Naturgrund*) the perfect remain sinful. In the next place this perfection of acts is not an objective perfection. The perfect man is perfect only by his own subjective standard which is always imperfect and always changing.

"He would not be unblamable and holy before God, if God would try and judge him and his works out of Christ according to the law of holiness that belongs to angels " (p. 639).[35]

[31] P. 625.

[32] Pp. 300 f.

[33] P. 627.

[34] P. 633.

[35] Cf. p. 627, where we are told that the believer " knows that the dominion of sin reaches further than his consciousness of sin." " Therefore it is," he adds,

Still further, the perfection of the perfect man is not such that even his own conscience does not accuse him. He does things which even he himself feels to be wrong, and must judge his own conduct, as he ought to judge that of others, benevolently.[36] Nor is his perfection such that he is free from sins of weakness, inadvertence, hastiness, ignorance, even if these sins are rooted in bad habits or bad judgment or bad conditions which have been created by his own former sins.

" If we must say, according to the Scriptures, that the Christian can have a clean heart and need not sin, we must nevertheless say also and emphasize in the clearest manner, that the Christian is *not* delivered by complete faith and complete surrender to Christ's sanctifying power, from all sins of ignorance, and omissions of good things which come afterwards into his consciousness; and not from errors and wrong actions which arise out of defective knowledge and insight " (p. 634).

It is even possible for the perfect man to be very imperfect in his life-manifestation in the just view of his fellow-men. There is many a man who makes a poor showing before his fellows — burdened as he is with inherited prejudices, narrowness of associations, weak memory, poor training, and handicapped by sickness or shattered nerves — who will be very differently judged in the forum of Heaven; which seems to say it is only by an exercise of mercy towards him that God can count him acceptable.

" The Christian who abides in Jesus and follows the Good Shepherd steadily, is holy, irreproachable, blameless, in the eyes

---

" also a wrong expression to speak of ' complete holiness and perfect purity, of a work free from sin and sinless, or even of the sinless perfection ' of the wholly consecrated Christian: for, according to the declarations of the apostles there is no such thing as an *objectively* ' complete holiness and purity ' of the Christian."

[36] Cf. p. 614, for example, where we are told that I John iii. 19–21 assures us of the fact that " even souls which are sanctified in a high measure, like those to whom John writes, are often entangled in things of which they are not sure whether they are brought by them into guilt and separation from God "; and then it is added: " Sanctified Christians often are burdened by a more or less clear feeling of guilt because of some particular matter, or because of their whole condition."

of his merciful Father in Christ Jesus, who requires of him, His weak child, nothing that surpasses his powers. He is, however, not irreproachable, unblamable, faultless and perfect in the eyes of his fellow-men — especially in his characteristics as pupil, maid, soldier, craftsman, artist, teacher, theologian, and the like. Men can see much that is incompetent, wrong and faulty in his works " (p. 639).

It goes without saying, of course, that moral perfection and technical perfection are different things; and we are not unwilling to allow also — as we are often exhorted to allow — up to a certain point, that moral perfection and religious perfection are not quite the same thing. But Jellinghaus is not appealing to these distinctions here; he wishes us to understand that a man may be perfect in the sight of God (who judges in full view of all the circumstances), in whom his neighbors must recognize much that is imperfect not only from the technical, but from the ethical, and not only from the ethical, but from the religious, point of view. Perfection with him is so little a matter of exact conformity to a perfect moral and religious standard that it is consistent with not only a fundamental evil nature lying in wait in the background of life, but with a multitude of actual sins, committed in ignorance, or inadvertence or haste, or out of ingrained prejudices or fixed habits of conduct, even when the commission of them is not unaccompanied with some sense of wrong-doing.[37] It must be admitted that Jellinghaus deals very tenderly with the imperfections of the perfect. And we think it must be admitted also that the model from which he has painted his portrait of the perfect man was drawn rather from the ranks of what most of us would speak of merely as sincere Christians.

Jellinghaus himself, however, insists that the portrait he has painted is that of the perfect man. We are not playing with words here. We have pointed out that Jellinghaus ex-

[37] L. Clasen, *Zeitschrift für Theologie und Kirche*, x. 1900, p. 472, very naturally remarks that there is an appearance " that Jellinghaus himself has no real confidence in his ' possibility of not sinning.' " His " no longer sinning " in point of fact means little more than the ordinary " no longer living under the dominion of sin " (p. 471).

plains that the term "perfect" is used in the Scriptures in a
sense equivalent to what we would mean if we spoke of a
"sincere" Christian. But Jellinghaus defines for himself the
sense in which he is arguing that perfection is within the reach
of Christians in this world. And the characteristic on which
he insists — despite the amount of sinning which he in the end
allows to his perfect Christian — is precisely "that they are
free from sin," that they "do not sin." We have just [38] quoted
a sentence from him in which he declares [39] that the Bible
"maintains that the Christian can walk righteously, holily,
perfectly, unblamably, and not sin." And we might quote any
number more to the same effect. Precisely what he contends
for, he tells us, is that "a continuous abiding in Christ and
continuous victory over sin" [40] — that "continuous preservation from sin in Christ" [41] — is possible for us all. And this he
must contend for if he is to save anything for his "second
blessing" at all, since he allows that it brings not a new gift,
sanctification in contrast with justification, but a new stage
of the gift of sanctification already received in the first stage
in and with justification. Naturally he makes use of the parallel
between the two transactions, after the custom of the Higher
Life writers, in order to commend and explain the second. He
begins his discussion of "sanctification and victory through
the blood of Jesus," for example, with this parallel. Jesus as a
Deliverer present in the Word "has taken away our guilt" on
simple faith.

"Similarly, or almost identically, is it with the victory over the
sins of weakness of the believer and with the attainment and preservation of a clean heart. If Christ has really broken the power of
sin in the cross and in the resurrection, and if He has become a complete, accessible Deliverer from all sins, so that sin, flesh, old man,
world, death, devil are vanquished foes *with Him,* and for everyone
who takes refuge with Him and will die to sin with Him and in His
power — then a sure victory and energetic walk in sanctification
even now is to be hoped for for believers, and looked for in faith with
assurance. If the Scriptures testify the fact that Christ is a com-

[38] Above, p. 380. [39] P. 611. [40] P. 390. [41] P. 676.

plete Deliverer from ' the power of sin and the anxieties of our own guidance,' just as plainly and clearly as the fact of deliverance from the guilt of sin, then we can be even now sure in joyful trust, and experience, that not only is the Biblical doctrine of the forgiveness of sin a good tidings of free grace for the guilt-laden, but that also the Biblical doctrine of sanctification similarly offers us as a good tidings the free grace and gift of sanctification and victory obtained for us in Christ, to be believingly accepted and possessed now, no matter how weak we are in ourselves " (pp. 438 f.).

Again:

" It is with the deliverance also from the finer power of sin precisely as it is with the deliverance from the guilt of sin. Because Christ has fully wrought out deliverance from the guilt of sin and brings it Himself in the Word, therefore the sinner who comes to himself can ' immediately ' (jetzt gleich) and ' just as he is,' receive in Christ ' through faith,' grace and forgiveness. Since now Christ has also wrought out deliverance from all the power of sin through His death and His resurrection, and is now a mighty emancipating Deliverer and Shepherd from all sins and ways of our own, the Christian who is hungering after righteousness can enter ' immediately ' according to the measure of his knowledge into this victorious power and the peace-bringing leading of Christ, and persist in this present salvation, in this continuous Now of victory and peace. For in any case it is a matter of a continuous Now and a continuing deliverance, not of a once-for-all faith and a once-for-all victory " (p. 670).

The emphasis in this statement is on the immediacy of the effect; as we received forgiveness of sins at once on our first believing, so do we receive our full deliverance from the power of sin at once on this our second believing. But, along with this, emphasis is thrown on the continuousness of both the cause and the effect. Jesus saves us now — if I believe now; and the believer is to live in a continuous believing and consequent continuous salvation. This is, of course, the well known " moment by moment " doctrine of the Higher Life teachers.[42]

The main purpose of this teaching is to prevent us from supposing that the source of our holiness is in ourselves. But

[42] A parallel passage will be found on p. 233.

it has the additional effect of denying with great emphasis that the seat of our holiness — any of it, at any time — is in ourselves. It thus makes our holiness in all its extent purely a holiness of acts, never of nature. What we obtain by faith is Christ — as a Preserver from sinful acts. By continuous faith we obtain Him continuously — as Preserver from sinful acts; and only from those particular sinful acts with which we are for the moment threatened. We do not at any time obtain Him as Savior from all possible sins, but only as Savior from the particular sinful acts for protection from which we, from time to time, need Him. Thus we are never made "holy" in any substantial sense, so that we are ourselves holy beings. And also accordingly we are never made "holy" in any conclusive sense, so that, being holy in ourselves, naturally we continue holy. This is the way Jellinghaus expresses himself:

"They [believing Christians] are not called upon to appropriate to themselves all the powers of sanctification which are present in Jesus immediately (*jetzt gleich*) and to become immediately transfigured in an especially high degree into the image of Christ; but only to trust Christ as a victorious helper and to experience His help for the needs of sanctification of which they are presently conscious, and against the foes, outer and inner, which are at the moment making themselves felt. The believing Christian should in any case never seek to have in himself a store of sanctification, but rise every morning poor, in order to depend on the present gracious powers of his rich Deliverer. The sanctified Christian remains in himself poor, absolutely poor in power and wisdom, but he has confidence that Jesus leads him in His wisdom and continually grants him the necessary powers of grace for every necessary work and struggle" (pp. 671 f.).

We are, says Jellinghaus, like a poor relation living in a rich man's house as a dependent, and receiving all he needs day by day from his benefactor, but never being made rich himself.

The purpose in view here is to emphasize our constant dependence on Christ. But this is done so unskilfully as to end in denying the possibility of our sanctification. We never are ourselves made holy; only our acts are provided for. We ask nothing and we get nothing beyond the meeting of our daily needs in sustaining our struggles on earth. As for *ourselves*, we remain unholy, apparently forever. We are told:

" Even the most sanctified Christian must confess of himself that in him, that is in his flesh, nothing good dwells " (p. 626).

That is to say that *nothing* in the way of betterment has happened to him himself. The illustration used is that a piece of iron, in itself cold and black, is in the fire hot and glowing.

" So, the Christian is in himself fleshly and can perform only works of the flesh; but in Jesus he is free from the dominion of the flesh and clean, and can also walk and behave like Jesus " (p. 626).

" Not in himself is the believer dead to sin, but in Christ; not in himself is he lively and powerful for the walk in holy love but in Christ, the saving and sanctifying head and leader " (p. 627).

But — is not hot iron hot and glowing in itself, and not merely " in the fire " by which it is made hot and glowing? There is a confusion here between the source and the seat of the heat.

" A Christian obtains [we read in a parallel passage] through regeneration or through a higher stage of sanctification not an independent holiness, not a freedom from the old man in his own strength, or such a strength of the new man that it can itself hold the flesh in death. The Christian can be pure only as a member of Christ our Head, as a branch of the vine. In himself every Christian is a branch of sinful humanity and is prone to sin. Only through implantation into Christ's death and resurrection can he be and remain holy. Separated from Christ and His purifying blood (blood signifies the life of Christ given in death and resurrection), he is sinful and has sin " (pp. 456 ff., commenting on I John i. 8).

If this be true then salvation is impossible. We are never saved. We only seem to be saved, because Christ works through us the works of a saved soul. That is not the way John conceived it, or Christ. Naturally most painful results follow from such representations. For example, our aspirations are lowered. We are never to wish or seek to be holy ourselves, but are to be content with being enabled to meet in our unholiness the temptations of the day. We lose the elevating power of a high ideal. And we are to be satisfied with never being " well-pleasing to God." Says Jellinghaus:

" When God is pleased with us, it is with what Christ works in us, not with what we in our own power and imagined goodness and wisdom do " (p. 672).

What the Scriptures teach is that we shall be more and more transformed into Christ's image until at last, when we see Him as He is, we shall be like Him, and therefore in ourselves — as He has made us — well-pleasing to God.

There is expressly included in this doctrine a provision for a progressive sanctification, along the ordinary lines of the teaching of the Higher Life Movement in this matter. We have seen Jellinghaus in passages just quoted limiting the ability of the Christian to enter " immediately " into the victorious power and peace-bringing leading of Christ, by such phrases as " according to the measure of his knowledge," [43] and " for the needs of which he is presently conscious." [44] The Christian is freed from all the sinning which at the stage of Christian knowledge to which he has attained he knows to be sinning; and as his knowledge grows so his objective sanctification increases. It is apparently also repeatedly suggested that it depends entirely on the Christian's own action whether or not he retains his hold on Christ and so continues in his sanctifying walk. Undoubtedly this is in accordance with Jellinghaus' fundamental conception of the relation of the Christian to Christ and the way of salvation. He continually suggests that our standing in Christ depends absolutely on ourselves. Those that believe in Christ, he tells us for example,[45] " have in Him forgiveness and righteousness, and also shall retain it *so long as they abide in Christ.*"

It is, he continues, like a king granting public amnesty in terms like these: He who appears within a year at a particular place, lays down his weapons, and swears fealty — to him then shall be handed an already prepared diploma of pardon,

[43] P. 670.   [44] P. 671.   [45] P. 265.

and he will remain pardoned so long as he maintains his loyalty. He tells us:

"Justification is, no doubt, a judicial sentence on God's part external to us; but it is a judicial sentence which proceeds on a relation of faith to Christ which has been entered upon, a judicial sentence, which therefore also remains valid only so long as the man remains faithful in his faith in Christ" (p. 273).

Our continued justification depends therefore absolutely on our continued faith, and the implication is that this is left wholly in our hands. Justification cannot therefore be made to cover our future sins — the sin, for example, of failing faith. The predominant mode of expression confines it to past sins — and also, almost as if it were a concession somewhat grudgingly allowed, to our present sins. We read:

"We must hold in the most definite way that to him who believes in Christ, all sins are forgiven completely and wholly through the blood of Christ. Yes, we must even understand that not only all our past sins but our present sinfulness also is forgiven us, and for Christ's sake will not be reckoned to us. . . . Luther says: 'Let everyone learn to understand and believe that Christ has given Himself not only for little and conquered, but also for great and unconquered sins'" (p. 270).

Past and present sins — one would think that they would cover all actual sinning, and that would be enough. But Jellinghaus' mind is disturbed about the sins yet future, and here he falters — justification does not cover all of them. It may perhaps be permitted to cover some of them — the less heinous of them, but not all. He writes:

"We may venture to say, then, that, when God justifies a believing soul, for Christ's sake, He forgives his past sins, his present sinfulness and the still future sins of weakness (only no sins of malice aforethought or wanton, conscious indifference and unlovingness to Jesus and the brethren)" (p. 271).

This limitation of the scope of justification as regards future sins to "sins of weakness" is of course without Biblical warrant, and equally of course without intelligible meaning. Are we to suppose that the grosser sins, though unprovided for in prospect, nevertheless when actually committed fall at once within the scope of justification (which covers present sins) and are forgiven? They are not forgiven before they are committed; but as soon as they are committed they are forgiven? Whereas the milder sins do not wait for their forgiveness until they are committed, but are already forgiven in prospect?

What Jellinghaus is really laboring for here is to make room in some way for " falling from grace." He is possessed with the fear that if he does not limit the scope of justification, at least with respect to the grosser future sins, he will give license to sin, which in the end means merely that he has more confidence in man's efforts than in God's grace. What he has succeeded in doing is only to destroy all possibility of assurance of salvation. Men are cast back on their own works, whether of faith or of conduct, for their hope of ultimate salvation. God's justification is valid only if they maintain their faith and commit no sins of malice aforethought, or of conscious indifference, or unlovingness.

There is happily, however, another current of feeling which flows through Jellinghaus' mind, disturbing the even flow of these disturbing sentiments. Christ, he tells us, has secured by His life, temptations, sufferings, death, and resurrection, this —

" that He is now, for all who give themselves to Him, a mighty, present Deliverer and Good Shepherd, who has the power not only to deliver them from the guilt and power of sin, but also to guide them surely in the way of God. This right and this might Jesus has possessed since He rose and was exalted — that He through the Holy Ghost can dwell and rule in His own " (p. 586).

In these words the negative and positive sides of Christ's sanctifying work are both emphasized; He both delivers His people from the dominion of sin and leads them in the paths of holiness. And now, we continue:

" The power of their evil self-will is broken in believers through Christ's death, so that they are ready and able to follow. And Jesus as the exalted one has also received believers as a possession given by the Father (John x. 29), so that no world-power and no nature-power can hinder Him in His leading of them: rather all things must work together for good to those that love and follow Jesus, and break out a way for them " (p. 587).

We read again:

" The apostles often bear witness to a firm conviction not only of the present state of grace of the Christians to whom they write, but also of their happy perseverance to the end " (p. 356).

And again:

" Precisely this chapter, Rom. viii., is full of the most glorious assurances not only of our present state of grace, but also of our abiding in the love of Christ up to the end " (p. 368).

Yet, he can say again in this general connection:

" Only conscious, deliberate sin and deliberate, witting desertion of the covenant of grace brings back again to the standpoint of an unconverted sinner " (p. 371).

Which affirms again the possibility of " falling from grace." Obviously Jellinghaus is in this matter of a divided mind. He himself says, as a kind of conclusion to the whole matter:

" Both are taught in the Holy Scriptures — that a branch of Christ, therefore a converted man, can be cut off again on account of unfruitfulness — and that there is a personal assurance and sealing not only of the present state of grace but also of perseverance to the end, and of faithful abiding in Jesus " (p. 378).

Jellinghaus' critics have found it difficult to make it clear to themselves precisely how he conceived sanctification to be received by faith and exactly what happens to the believer when he believes in Jesus as his complete Deliverer from the power of sin.[46] What happens to the believer is that he ceases

---

[46] What P. Gennrich (" Wiedergeburt und Heiligung," 1908, pp. 34 ff.) objects to is really the strong supernaturalism of Jellinghaus' teaching. It out-

to sin; that is to say, to commit deliberate sins; ceases to sin, that is, in the sense in which Jellinghaus understands that even the sanctified cease from sinning. No change is wrought in the believer's nature. Jellinghaus is quite vigorous in repudiating what he calls

"the unhappy error that after the reception of forgiveness of sins, we now, through an independent operation of the Holy Spirit, receive a new, independent, sanctified nature" (p. 480).

He speaks, it is true, of the cleansing of the heart, but by the heart in this connection he does not mean the nature, but only the inner springs of action; he is merely providing for the cessation of deliberate inward as well as outward sinning — our victory is over sinful desires as well as sinful transactions.[47] Now, what Jellinghaus insists upon is that this transformation of heart and life (not nature) is the direct and immediate result of faith in Christ, or rather of Christ, laid hold of by faith. He that believes receives from Christ directly and immediately — these words must be taken in their strictest meaning — freedom from sinning, inward and outward. He says:

"According to the New Testament, Christ, the crucified and risen one, is the sole ground, means and power of sanctification" (p. 535).

In further explanation, he proceeds:

"Because God is holy, He wishes to restore men to holiness. It was therefore that He sent His Son on the holy sacrificial path through death to an heavenly altar. Jesus sanctified (consecrated) Himself for the men to be delivered in His sacrificial death in order

---

rages him that Jellinghaus should say: "We are just as little to produce the Christian nature and sanctification as we produced the Adam-nature itself" ("Das völlige, gegenwärtige Heil durch Christum," ed. 5, p. 465; ed. 4, p. 468). It certainly is difficult nevertheless to understand precisely how "the blood of Christ," received by an act of faith, produces immediately a sanctification which is not of nature but of act. All that the mystical writers like Jellinghaus say in explanation is that Christ by faith in Him becomes our "organic Head," and we as His members receive all that He has and is, and therefore are in Him free from sinning. This, however, explains nothing.

47 Pp. 617, 625.

that repentant men might consecrate themselves to die and live with Christ and so be sanctified in Him in the truth. Biblical sanctification is not a self-sanctification by means of self-mortification and self-improvement, or a transformation by means of mystical operations of the Holy Spirit, but it is participation in the death and resurrection power of Jesus, or in Jesus' holiness."

So much as this his "mediating theology" compelled him to say; but he does not make it very plain how we by thus laying hold of Him by faith become "partakers of Jesus' holiness." In the passage we have been quoting he treats the subject externally under the category of "consecration." The altar sanctifies the gift, he tells; and we are thus sanctified, apparently by a kind of contact, by standing in the service of God. He only adds that in the New Testament view "this sanctification . . . must ever manifest itself as practical, or actual, cleansing and righteousness in the love of Christ"; that is, if we rightly understand it, the gift sanctified by the altar is made not merely sacred but holy — made holy because sacred, that it may be suitable for the service it renders.

This is of course to speak in figures. We seem to get somewhat closer to Jellinghaus' notion of how we actually are sanctified by the reception of Christ, our Deliverer, in faith, in those passages — they are very numerous — in which he insists that sanctification is the immediate effect of "the blood of Christ" apprehended by faith, "blood" standing as the symbol of "the death-and-resurrection-powers" of Christ.[48] By faith we participate in the dying and resurrection of our

[48] A careful statement by Martin Schian of what Jellinghaus means by "the blood of Jesus" will be found in Schiele und Zscharnack's "Die Religion in Geschichte und Gegenwart," i. 1909, col. 1701: "Through a theory of sacrifice derived from the Old Testament he opens the way to the fundamental proposition that Christ's blood means not only the death of Jesus but also the resurrected life of Jesus: in the blood of Jesus there are not merely the death-powers of Jesus, but also the eternal life-, love-, truth-, righteousness- and sanctification-giving resurrection-powers of Jesus. . . . Christ's blood is in the end nothing but a combination of the powers lying in the death and resurrection; but in other passages the blood appears apparently as something distinct by the side of the death and resurrection: it is almost a saving-power for itself."

"organic head," Christ, and therefore both die with Him to sin and rise again to holiness. In one of these passages,[49] he more elaborately explains that sanctification is the co-product of three factors — the blood of Christ, the word of Christ, and the Holy Spirit. Precisely how it is wrought by these three co-operating agents it is still not very easy to make clearly out. As the blood of Christ is communicated by the Word (the blood "im Worte" is a constant phrase) working by virtue of the Spirit inseparably connected with the Word (according to the constantly asserted Lutheran doctrine of the Word), it is na-tural to understand the idea intended to be conveyed to be that sanctification (it is, remember, a sanctification only of acts) is wrought directly by man's own volition, under the influence of the Spirit, communicated by the Word concerning the cross and resurrection. We act holily because we are incited thereto by the Holy Spirit, operating in connection with the preached gospel.

This scarcely appears, it is true, to allow full validity to the constantly repeated assertion that "the blood" of Christ immediately and directly delivers from the power of sin; [50] it appears rather to represent it as delivering from the power of sin only mediately and indirectly, namely, through the Word, the Spirit, and our own volitions acting under their influence. Nevertheless this seems to be essentially the manner in which the process of sanctification is conceived. The Word of God, or the gospel of Christ, the gospel of His blood — of His death and resurrection — testifying to the victory of Christ over sin and the devil, communicates to us, by the Spirit of God in-separably connected with it and always acting in, by and through it, the *posse* to refrain from sin and to do righteous-ness; we, in this communicated power walk now in newness of life, in Christ's life, sharers with Him in His death to sin and resurrection to life. It is not out of our own nature that we do this — our own nature is evil and evil continually; it is out of

49 Pp. 474 ff.
50 There is an amazing instance of the use of this notion in an extremely physical sense in a footnote on p. 554.

" the blood of Christ," communicated to us as a *posse* by the Spirit in the Word. The *actio* always remains, however, our own. Apparently it was thus that Jellinghaus brought together his fundamental Lutheran doctrine of the Word and the over-lying doctrine of the Mystical Union derived from the " mediating theology."

For the latter also has something of importance to communicate. What this is we may learn from the following extract. He asks:

" How now are we, then, to understand this — that the Word of God and the truth sanctifies and vivifies us and makes us free from sin? "

And he answers:

" Is this to mean merely [this emphatic ' merely ' is surely significant] that the teachings of the Bible make so deep an impression upon those who read and hear them that they are converted, and flee from sin, and love that which is heavenly? In that case [that is, if we think the effect is wrought *merely* by the natural power of the truth conveyed] the Word would give only a doctrine but not the power to regeneration and sanctification. In that case, the power to good and to victory would still come in the last analysis out of our good hearts. The Word of God and the gospel of Christ are on the contrary, such a life-giving and sanctifying power, because it is a witness of the great victory of Christ over sin and the devil, and because in the Word concerning Christ we trust in the present, mighty Deliverer. Where this Word and its declarations are now believed, there Christ is active, just because they declare true facts which authenticate themselves as true, so soon as we *believe them and act accordingly* " (p. 475).

In this passage the rationalistic doctrine, that the whole power of the preached gospel resides in the natural effect on our minds of the truths contained in it, is repudiated. But what is substituted for it seems not to be merely the Lutheran doctrine of a supernatural action of the Holy Spirit inseparably accompanying the Word — though that is reiteratedly provided for elsewhere — but the power of the great facts proclaimed in the

Word, which, when understood, believed, and acted upon, authenticate themselves as true. To believe and rest upon these facts is to believe and rest upon Christ, the Deliverer, whose work of deliverance these facts portray. And when Christ is rested upon in faith, He is active in salvation. Our sanctification thus is an immediate, supernatural work of Christ, or, as it is currently expressed with no further meaning, of "His blood." Precisely how Christ works it, however, remains in the vague mysticism of the "mediating theology."

We may be advanced a little in apprehending how these two points of view — sanctification by the Holy Spirit working in the Word, and sanctification by the "blood of Christ" operating immediately on the heart — are harmonized, if we will attend to the rather extended discussions of the manner in which what Jellinghaus calls regeneration is wrought. For regeneration with him, we will remember, is the sanctification which believers receive at their first believing, and differs from the sanctification which they receive at their second believing in nothing except in its relative incompleteness. Arguing now with reference to it that it does not come gradually, but all at once, he writes as follows:

"If regeneration were a self-improvement by faith's own power under the assistance of Christ, it would necessarily be always a very slow work. Now regeneration or the state of regeneration occurs only through Christ and in Christ and exists only in Christ, and so it can take place at once, if the sinner truly surrenders himself in trust to Christ and his sin-sick soul rests on the Crucified and Risen One. Therefore pardon, justification, sanctification and regeneration are in the Bible almost always brought into connection with the blood, that is, the death and resurrection of Jesus, for only through Christ's death and resurrection is this miracle made possible. Being regenerated means being in faith in the blood of Christ, being and becoming in the blood of Christ the Son of God justified, vivified, purified, and sanctified" (p. 303).

If in this closing definition the state of regeneration (*Wiedergeborensein*) appears to be identified with the state of faith — he who is "in faith in the blood of Christ" is in the state of regeneration, apparently with nothing further to say — that impression must be corrected by the declaration that regeneration is after all a "miracle," wrought by the death and resurrection of Jesus. It is understood, in other words, definitely as a supernatural effect. But now, we continue:

"Accordingly regeneration takes place precisely like justification, above all through Christ's cleansing and sanctifying blood, and not through the Word and the Holy Spirit alone. . . . By the Word . . . alone Jesus cannot produce regeneration; His blood (His life given in atoning death and resurrection) itself must come really into the heart, in order to vivify it and make it new. Only when the Spirit and the blood of Jesus come to actuality in the heart through faith, along with the Word, and we have died and risen with Christ, is the new birth and the new life in Christ present. If regeneration took place only through the Word and the Spirit, we could still think it an independent new life of our own in the soul, and we should be brought into the perplexity (in which so many find themselves in this question concerning regeneration) [51] of supposing ourselves bound to seek a new nature in ourselves; and, not finding it, we should fall into despair and doubt. As our regeneration and our new birth and our new life lie, however, in the blood of Jesus or in the crucified and risen Deliverer-Head, we have simply to take and hold in faith the new birth or the new life in and with Christ, our Life. We need not anxiously seek a new nature in ourselves; for since our new nature does not exist independently of our connection in faith with Christ, we shall never find in us anything that satisfies. . . . The state of regeneration is 'being in Christ' or 'being crucified and risen with Christ' or 'being in the blood of Jesus.' It can therefore also be said that Christ, the Crucified and Risen One is through our surrender in faith in the Holy Spirit, our life and our regeneration. . . . Though it is often said in the Bible that regeneration takes place through faith, that is not to be understood as if faith itself was the cause of regeneration, or even was the regeneration itself. Regeneration takes place through faith only in the sense that through faith, the Word and the Holy Spirit and Christ's death and resurrection come in us to life-giving activity and also abide in us only through faith. My faith is not my regeneration, but my faith

[51] There is an echo here of an old debate in the Fellowship circles. Cf. Gelshorn, *Die Christliche Welt*, xix. 1905, col. 855.

has laid hold of Christ, the Crucified and Risen One, the Beginning of the New Creation, the sure Guide, Shepherd and King, through the word of the Holy Ghost, as eternal life and the author of my childship to God, and holds fast to Him. The producing cause of justification, regeneration, conversion and sanctification is Christ's word, spirit, blood; faith is, on the other hand, only its receptive cause " (pp. 304–306).

It all comes back, then, to this, that regeneration — and with it sanctification — is being in Christ, the Holy One, and sharing, because we are in Him, in His holiness. Faith is the bond that unites us to Christ, and therefore it is through faith that we are in Him and have His holiness. Nothing is really explained beyond that; but the vagueness belongs not especially to Jellinghaus himself, but to the mysticism of the " mediating theology," whose conceptions he is here only repeating.

Two children clearly are striving together in the womb of Jellinghaus' mind. He is doing what he can to transmit faithfully the Higher Life doctrine he received so enthusiastically at Oxford. But his fundamental theology does not run on its lines. The result is that the Higher Life doctrine is profoundly modified. All its framework remains. We still hear of immediate deliverance from the power of sin by faith alone. We still hear of the second blessing, of cessation of sinning, of complete sanctification *now*. But the old language does not carry with it the old fulness of meaning. Everything is reduced, and the real constructive force, working under the modified explanations, proceeds not from the Higher Life conception but from the " mediating theology." Jellinghaus' " Perfectionism " thus is a more moderate " Perfectionism " than that of his Higher Life teachers. It remains, nevertheless, though a moderate " Perfectionism," yet a real " Perfectionism." It is therefore no more really acceptable than theirs. We need not, however, stay to point out in detail its inherent impossibilities. Jellinghaus has himself passed judgment on it; and, not content with passing judgment on it, he has actually executed it. Let it rest in the grave to which he has himself consigned it.

९

STUDIES IN THEOLOGY

BY

BENJAMIN BRECKINRIDGE WARFIELD

Professor of Didactic and Polemic Theology
in the Theological Seminary of Princeton
New Jersey, 1887–1921

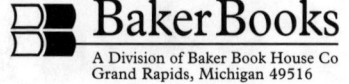

A Division of Baker Book House Co
Grand Rapids, Michigan 49516

PREFATORY NOTE

Rev. Benjamin Breckinridge Warfield, D.D., LL.D., Professor of Didactic and Polemic Theology in the Theological Seminary of the Presbyterian Church at Princeton, New Jersey, provided in his will for the collection and publication of the numerous articles on theological subjects which he contributed to encyclopaedias, reviews and other periodicals, and appointed a committee to edit and publish these papers. In pursuance of his instructions, this, the ninth volume, containing miscellaneous Studies in Theology, has been prepared under the editorial direction of this committee.

The generous permission to publish articles contained in this volume is gratefully acknowledged as follows: Funk and Wagnalls Company for the articles taken from " The New Schaff-Herzog Encyclopedia of Religious Knowledge " edited by Samuel Macauley Jackson; Charles Scribner's Sons for the article taken from the " Encyclopædia of Religion and Ethics " edited by James Hastings; The Board of Christian Education of the Presbyterian Church in the U. S. A. for the article taken from " A Dictionary of the Bible " by John D. Davis, published by The Westminster Press; The Biblical Seminary in New York for the articles taken from *The Biblical Review;* Pittsburgh-Xenia Theological Seminary for the article taken from *Bibliotheca Sacra;* and The University of Chicago Press for the article taken from *The American Journal. of Theology.*

The clerical preparation of this volume has been done by Mr. John E. Meeter, to whom the thanks of the committee are hereby expressed.

Ethelbert D. Warfield
William Park Armstrong
Caspar Wistar Hodge
Committee.

CONTENTS

v

I
APOLOGETICS

APOLOGETICS [1]

I. Significance of the Term

SINCE Planck (1794) and Schleiermacher (1811), "apologetics" has been the accepted name of one of the theological disciplines or departments of theological science. The term is derived from the Greek *apologeisthai*, which embodies as its central notion the idea of "defense." In its present application, however, it has somewhat shifted its meaning, and we speak accordingly of apologetics and apologies in contrast with each other. The relation between these two is not that of theory and practice (so e.g. Düsterdieck), nor yet that of genus and species (so e.g. Kübel). That is to say, apologetics is not a formal science in which the principles exemplified in apologies are investigated, as the principles of sermonizing are investigated in homiletics. Nor is it merely the sum of all existing or all possible apologies, or their quintessence, or their scientific exhibition, as dogmatics is the scientific statement of dogmas. Apologies are defenses of Christianity, in its entirety, in its essence, or in some one or other of its elements or presuppositions, as against either all assailants, actual or conceivable, or some particular form or instance of attack; though, of course, as good defenses they may rise above mere defenses and become vindications. Apologetics undertakes not the defense, not even the vindication, but the establishment, not, strictly speaking, of Christianity, but rather of that knowledge of God which Christianity professes to embody and seeks to make efficient in the world, and which it is the business of theology scientifically to explicate. It may, of course, enter into defense and vindication when in the prosecution of its task it

[1] Reprinted from "The New Schaff-Herzog Encyclopedia of Religious Knowledge," edited by Samuel Macauley Jackson, D.D., LL.D., i. pp. 232–238 (copyright by Funk and Wagnalls Company, New York, 1908).

meets with opposing points of view and requires to establish its own standpoint or conclusions. Apologies may, therefore, be embraced in apologetics, and form ancillary portions of its structure, as they may also do in the case of every other theological discipline. It is, moreover, inevitable that this or that element or aspect of apologetics will be more or less emphasized and cultivated, as the need of it is from time to time more or less felt. But apologetics does not derive its contents or take its form or borrow its value from the prevailing opposition; but preserves through all varying circumstances its essential character as a positive and constructive science which has to do with opposition only — like any other constructive science — as the refutation of opposing views becomes from time to time incident to construction. So little is defense or vindication of the essence of apologetics that there would be the same reason for its existence and the same necessity for its work, were there no opposition in the world to be encountered and no contradiction to be overcome. It finds its deepest ground, in other words, not in the accidents which accompany the efforts of true religion to plant, sustain, and propagate itself in this world; not even in that most pervasive and most portentous of all these accidents, the accident of sin; but in the fundamental needs of the human spirit. If it is incumbent on the believer to be able to give a reason for the faith that is in him, it is impossible for him to be a believer without a reason for the faith that is in him; and it is the task of apologetics to bring this reason clearly out in his consciousness, and make its validity plain. It is, in other words, the function of apologetics to investigate, explicate, and establish the grounds on which a theology — a science, or systematized knowledge of God — is possible; and on the basis of which every science which has God for its object must rest, if it be a true science with claims to a place within the circle of the sciences. It necessarily takes its place, therefore, at the head of the departments of theological science and finds its task in the establishment of the validity of that knowledge of God which forms the subject-matter of these departments;

that we may then proceed through the succeeding departments of exegetical, historical, systematic, and practical theology, to explicate, appreciate, systematize, and propagate it in the world.

II. Place Among the Theological Disciplines

It must be admitted that considerable confusion has reigned with respect to the conception and function of apologetics, and its place among the theological disciplines. Nearly every writer has a definition of his own, and describes the task of the discipline in a fashion more or less peculiar to himself; and there is scarcely a corner in the theological encyclopedia into which it has not been thrust. Planck gave it a place among the exegetical disciplines; others contend that its essence is historical; most wish to assign it either to systematic or practical theology. Nösselt denies it all right of existence; Palmer confesses inability to classify it; Räbiger casts it formally out of the encyclopedia, but reintroduces it under the different name of " theory of religion." Tholuck proposed that it should be apportioned through the several departments; and Cave actually distributes its material through three separate departments. Much of this confusion is due to a persistent confusion of apologetics with apologies. If apologetics is the theory of apology, and its function is to teach men how to defend Christianity, its place is, of course, alongside of homiletics, catechetics, and poimenics in practical theology. If it is simply, by way of eminence, the apology of Christianity, the systematically organized vindication of Christianity in all its elements and details, against all opposition — or in its essential core against the only destructive opposition — it of course presupposes the complete development of Christianity through the exegetical, historical, and systematic disciplines, and must take its place either as the culminating department of systematic theology, or as the intellectualistic side of practical theology, or as an independent discipline between the two. In this case it can be only artificially separated from polemic theology and other similar disciplines — if the analysis is pushed so far as to create these, as is done by F. Duilhé de Saint-Projet who distinguishes between apologetical, controversial, and polemic theology, directed respectively against unbelievers, heretics, and fellow believers, and by A. Kuyper who distinguishes between polemics, elenctics, and apologetics, opposing respectively heterodoxy, paganism, and false philosophy. It will not be strange, then, if, though separated from these kindred disciplines it, or some of it, should be again united with them, or some of them, to form a larger whole to which is given the same encyclopedic position. This is done for example by Kuyper who joins polemics, elenctics, and apologetics together to form his " antithetic dogmatological " group of disciplines; and by F. L. Patton who, after having distributed the material of apologetics into the two separate disciplines of rational or philosophical theology, to which as a thetic discipline a place is given at the outset of the system, and apologetics, joins the latter with polemics to constitute the antithetical disciplines, while systematic theology succeeds both as part of the synthetic disciplines.

III. Source of Divergent Views

Much of the diversity in question is due also, however, to varying views of the thing which apologetics undertakes to establish; whether it be, for example, the truth of the Christian religion, or the validity of that knowledge of God which theology presents in systematized form. And more of it still is due to profoundly differing conceptions of the nature and subject-matter of that " theology," a department of which apologetics is. If we think of apologetics as undertaking the defense or the vindication or even the justification of the " Christian religion," that is one thing; if we think of it as undertaking the establishment of the validity of that knowledge of God, which " theology " systematizes, that may be a very different thing. And even if agreement exists upon the latter conception, there remain the deeply cutting divergences

which beset the definition of "theology" itself. Shall it be
defined as the "science of faith"? or as the "science of religion"? or as the "science of the Christian religion"? or
as the "science of God"? In other words, shall it be regarded
as a branch of psychology, or as a branch of history, or as a
branch of science? Manifestly those who differ thus widely as
to what theology is, cannot be expected to agree as to the nature and function of any one of its disciplines. If "theology"
is the science of faith or of religion, its subject-matter is the
subjective experiences of the human heart; and the function
of apologetics is to inquire whether these subjective experiences have any objective validity. Of course, therefore, it
follows upon the systematic elucidation of these subjective experiences and constitutes the culminating discipline of "theology." Similarly, if "theology" is the science of the Christian
religion, it investigates the purely historical question of what
those who are called Christians believe; and of course the
function of apologetics is to follow this investigation with an
inquiry whether Christians are justified in believing these
things. But if theology is the science of God, it deals not with
a mass of subjective experiences, nor with a section of the
history of thought, but with a body of objective facts; and it is
absurd to say that these facts must be assumed and developed
unto their utmost implications before we stop to ask whether
they are facts. So soon as it is agreed that theology is a scientific discipline and has as its subject-matter the knowledge
of God, we must recognize that it must begin by establishing
the reality as objective facts of the data upon which it is based.
One may indeed call the department of theology to which this
task is committed by any name which appears to him appropriate: it may be called "general theology," or "fundamental
theology," or "principial theology," or "philosophical theology," or "rational theology," or "natural theology," or any
other of the innumerable names which have been used to describe it. Apologetics is the name which most naturally suggests itself, and it is the name which, with more or less accuracy of view as to the nature and compass of the discipline,

has been consecrated to this purpose by a large number of writers from Schleiermacher down (e.g. Pelt, Twesten, Baumstark, Swetz, Ottiger, Knoll, Maissoneuve). It powerfully commends itself as plainly indicating the nature of the discipline, while equally applicable to it whatever may be the scope of the theology which it undertakes to plant on a secure basis. Whether this theology recognizes no other knowledge of God than that given in the constitution and course of nature, or derives its data from the full revelation of God as documented in the Christian Scriptures, apologetics offers itself with equal readiness to designate the discipline by which the validity of the knowledge of God set forth is established. It need imply no more than natural theology requires for its basis; when the theology which it serves is, however, the complete theology of the Christian revelation, it guards its unity and protects from the fatally dualistic conception which sets natural and revealed theology over against each other as separable entities, each with its own separate presuppositions requiring establishment — by which apologetics would be split into two quite diverse disciplines, given very different places in the theological encyclopedia.

IV. The True Task of Apologetics

It will already have appeared how far apologetics may be defined, in accordance with a very prevalent custom (e.g. Sack, Lechler, Ebrard, Kübel, Lemme) as " the science which establishes the truth of Christianity as the absolute religion." Apologetics certainly does establish the truth of Christianity as the absolute religion. But the question of importance here is how it does this. It certainly is not the business of apologetics to take up each tenet of Christianity in turn and seek to establish its truth by a direct appeal to reason. Any attempt to do this, no matter on what philosophical basis the work of demonstration be begun or by what methods it be pursued, would transfer us at once into the atmosphere and betray us into the devious devices of the old vulgar rationalism, the primary fault of which was that it asked for a direct rational demonstration of the truth of each Christian teaching in turn. The business of apologetics is to establish the truth of Christianity as the absolute religion directly only as a whole, and in its details only indirectly. That is to say, we are not to begin by developing Christianity into all its details, and only after this task has been performed, tardily ask whether there is any truth in all this. We are to begin by establishing the truth of Christianity as a whole, and only then proceed to explicate it into its details, each of which, if soundly explicated, has its truth guaranteed by its place as a detail in an entity already established in its entirety. Thus we are delivered from what is perhaps the most distracting question which has vexed the whole history of the discipline. In establishing the truth of Christianity, it has been perennially asked, are we to deal with all its details (e.g. H. B. Smith), or merely with the essence of Christianity (e.g. Kübel). The true answer is, neither. Apologetics does not presuppose either the development of Christianity into its details, or the extraction from it of its essence. The details of Christianity are all contained in Christianity: the minimum of Christianity is just Christianity itself. What apologetics undertakes to establish is just this Christianity itself — including all its " details " and involving its " essence " — in its unexplicated and uncompressed entirety, as the absolute religion. It has for its object the laying of the foundations on which the temple of theology is built, and by which the whole structure of theology is determined. It is the department of theology which establishes the constitutive and regulative principles of theology as a science; and in establishing these it establishes all the details which are derived from them by the succeeding departments, in their sound explication and systematization. Thus it establishes the whole, though it establishes the whole in the mass, so to speak, and not in its details, but yet in its entirety and not in some single element deemed by us its core, its essence, or its minimum expression.

V. Division of Apologetics

The subject-matter of apologetics being determined, its distribution into its parts becomes very much a matter of course. Having defined apologetics as the proof of the truth of the Christian religion, many writers naturally confine it to what is commonly known somewhat loosely as the "evidences of Christianity." Others, defining it as "fundamental theology," equally naturally confine it to the primary principles of religion in general. Others more justly combine the two conceptions and thus obtain at least two main divisions. Thus Hermann Schultz makes it prove "the right of the religious conception of the world, as over against the tendencies to the denial of religion, and the right of Christianity as the absolutely perfect manifestation of religion, as over against the opponents of its permanent significance." He then divides it into two great sections with a third interposed between them: the first, "the apology of the religious conception of the world"; the last, "the apology of Christianity"; while between the two stands "the philosophy of religion, religion in its historical manifestation." Somewhat less satisfactorily, because with a less firm hold upon the idea of the discipline, Henry B. Smith, viewing apologetics as "historico-philosophical dogmatics," charged with the defense of "the whole contents and substance of the Christian faith," divided the material to much the same effect into what he calls fundamental, historical, and philosophical apologetics. The first of these undertakes to demonstrate the being and nature of God; the second, the divine origin and authority of Christianity; and the third, somewhat lamely as a conclusion to so high an argument, the superiority of Christianity to all other systems. Quite similarly Francis R. Beattie divided into (1) fundamental or philosophical apologetics, which deals with the problem of God and religion; (2) Christian or historical apologetics, which deals with the problem of revelation and the Scriptures; and (3) applied or practical apologetics, which deals with the practical efficiency of Christianity in the world. The funda-

mental truth of these schematizations lies in the perception
that the subject-matter of apologetics embraces the two great
facts of God and Christianity. There is some failure in unity
of conception, however, arising apparently from a deficient
grasp of the peculiarity of apologetics as a department of
theological science, and a consequent inability to permit it
as such to determine its own contents and the natural order of
its constituent parts.

VI. The Conception of Theology as a Science

If theology be a science at all, there is involved in that fact,
as in the case of all other sciences, at least these three things:
the reality of its subject-matter, the capacity of the human
mind to receive into itself and rationally to reflect this subject-
matter, the existence of media of communication between
the subject-matter and the percipient and understanding mind.
There could be no psychology were there not a mind to be investigated, a mind to investigate, and a self-consciousness by
means of which the mind as an object can be brought under
the inspection of the mind as subject. There could be no
astronomy were there no heavenly bodies to be investigated,
no mind capable of comprehending the laws of their existence
and movements, or no means of observing their structure and
motion. Similarly there can be no theology, conceived according to its very name as the science of God, unless there is a God
to form its subject-matter, a capacity in the human mind to
apprehend and so far to comprehend God, and some media by
which God is made known to man. That a theology, as the
science of God, may exist, therefore, it must begin by establishing the existence of God, the capacity of the human mind
to know Him, and the accessibility of knowledge concerning
Him. In other words, the very idea of theology as the science
of God gives these three great topics which must be dealt with
in its fundamental department, by which the foundations for
the whole structure are laid — God, religion, revelation. With
these three facts established, a theology as the science of God

becomes possible; with them, therefore, an apologetic might be complete. But that, only provided that in these three topics all the underlying presuppositions of the science of God actually built up in our theology are established; for example, provided that all the accessible sources and means of knowing God are exhausted. No science can arbitrarily limit the data lying within its sphere to which it will attend. On pain of ceasing to be the science it professes to be, it must exhaust the means of information open to it, and reduce to a unitary system the entire body of knowledge in its sphere. No science can represent itself as astronomy, for example, which arbitrarily confines itself to the information concerning the heavenly bodies obtainable by the unaided eye, or which discards, without sound ground duly adduced, the aid of, say, the spectroscope. In the presence of Christianity in the world making claim to present a revelation of God adapted to the condition and needs of sinners, and documented in Scriptures, theology cannot proceed a step until it has examined this claim; and if the claim be substantiated, this substantiation must form a part of the fundamental department of theology in which are laid the foundations for the systematization of the knowledge of God. In that case, two new topics are added to the subject-matter with which apologetics must constructively deal, Christianity — and the Bible. It thus lies in the very nature of apologetics as the fundamental department of theology, conceived as the science of God, that it should find its task in establishing the existence of a God who is capable of being known by man and who has made Himself known, not only in nature but in revelations of His grace to lost sinners, documented in the Christian Scriptures. When apologetics has placed these great facts in our hands — God, religion, revelation, Christianity, the Bible — and not till then are we prepared to go on and explicate the knowledge of God thus brought to us, trace the history of its workings in the world, systematize it, and propagate it in the world.

VII. The Five Subdivisions of Apologetics

The primary subdivisions of apologetics are therefore five, unless for convenience of treatment it is preferred to sink the third into its most closely related fellow. (1) The first, which may perhaps be called philosophical apologetics, undertakes the establishment of the being of God, as a personal spirit, the creator, preserver, and governor of all things. To it belongs the great problem of theism, with the involved discussion of the antitheistic theories. (2) The second, which may perhaps be called psychological apologetics, undertakes the establishment of the religious nature of man and the validity of his religious sense. It involves the discussion alike of the psychology, the philosophy, and the phenomenology of religion, and therefore includes what is loosely called "comparative religion" or the "history of religions." (3) To the third falls the establishment of the reality of the supernatural factor in history, with the involved determination of the actual relations in which God stands to His world, and the method of His government of His rational creatures, and especially His mode of making Himself known to them. It issues in the establishment of the fact of revelation as the condition of all knowledge of God, who as a personal Spirit can be known only so far as He expresses Himself; so that theology differs from all other sciences in that in it the object is not at the disposal of the subject, but vice versa. (4) The fourth, which may be called historical apologetics, undertakes to establish the divine origin of Christianity as the religion of revelation in the special sense of that word. It discusses all the topics which naturally fall under the popular caption of the "evidences of Christianity." (5) The fifth, which may be called bibliological apologetics, undertakes to establish the trustworthiness of the Christian Scriptures as the documentation of the revelation of God for the redemption of sinners. It is engaged especially with such topics as the divine origin of the Scriptures; the methods of the divine operation in their origination; their place in the series of redemptive acts of God, and in the process of revelation; the nature, mode, and effect of inspiration; and the like.

VIII. THE VALUE OF APOLOGETICS

The estimate which is put upon apologetics by scholars naturally varies with the conception which is entertained of its nature and function. In the wake of the subjectivism introduced by Schleiermacher, it has become very common to speak of such an apologetic as has just been outlined with no little scorn. It is an evil inheritance, we are told, from the old *supranaturalismus vulgaris,* which " took its standpoint not in the Scriptures but above the Scriptures, and imagined it could, with formal conceptions, develop a 'ground for the divine authority of Christianity' (Heubner), and therefore offered proofs for the divine origin of Christianity, the necessity of revelation, and the credibility of the Scriptures" (Lemme). To recognize that we can take our standpoint in the Scriptures only after we have Scriptures, authenticated as such, to take our standpoint in, is, it seems, an outworn prejudice. The subjective experience of faith is conceived to be the ultimate fact; and the only legitimate apologetic, just the self-justification of this faith itself. For faith, it seems, after Kant, can no longer be looked upon as a matter of reasoning and does not rest on rational grounds, but is an affair of the heart, and manifests itself most powerfully when it has no reason out of itself (Brunetière). If repetition had probative force, it would long ago have been established that faith, religion, theology, lie wholly outside of the realm of reason, proof, and demonstration.

It is, however, from the point of view of rationalism and mysticism that the value of apologetics is most decried. Wherever rationalistic preconceptions have penetrated, there, of course, the validity of the apologetic proofs has been in more or less of their extent questioned. Wherever mystical sentiment has seeped in, there the validity of apologetics has been with more or less emphasis doubted. At the present moment, the rationalistic tendency is most active, perhaps, in the form given it by Albrecht Ritschl. In this form it strikes at the very roots of apologetics, by the distinction it erects between theoretical and religious knowledge. Religious knowledge is not the knowledge of fact, but a perception of utility; and therefore positive religion, while it may be historically conditioned, has no theoretical basis, and is accordingly not the object of rational proof. In significant parallelism with this, the mystical tendency is manifesting itself at the present day most distinctly in a widespread inclination to set aside apologetics in favor of the " witness of the Spirit." The convictions of the Christian man, we are told, are not the product of reason addressed to the intellect, but the immediate creation of the Holy Spirit in the heart. Therefore, it is intimated, we may do very well without these reasons, if indeed they are not positively noxious, because tending to substitute a barren intellectualism for a vital faith. It seems to be forgotten that though faith be a moral act and the gift of God, it is yet formally conviction passing into confidence; and that all forms of convictions must rest on evidence as their ground, and it is not faith but reason which investigates the nature and validity of this ground. " He who believes," says Thomas Aquinas, in words which have become current as an axiom, " would not believe unless he saw that what he believes is worthy of belief." Though faith is the gift of God, it does not in the least follow that the faith which God gives is an irrational faith, that is, a faith without cognizable ground in right reason. We believe in Christ because it is rational to believe in Him, not even though it be irrational. Of course mere reasoning cannot make a Christian; but that is not because faith is not the result of evidence, but because a dead soul cannot respond to evidence. The action of the Holy Spirit in giving faith is not apart from evidence, but along with evidence; and in the first instance consists in preparing the soul for the reception of the evidence.

IX. Relation of Apologetics to Christian Faith

This is not to argue that it is by apologetics that men are made Christians, but that apologetics supplies to Christian men the systematically organized basis on which the faith of Christian men must rest. All that apologetics explicates in the forms of systematic proof is implicit in every act of Christian faith. Whenever a sinner accepts Jesus Christ as his Saviour, there is implicated in that act a living conviction that there is a God, knowable to man, who has made Himself known in a revelation of Himself for redemption in Jesus Christ, as is set down in the Scriptures. It is not necessary for his act of faith that all the grounds of this conviction should be drawn into full consciousness and given the explicit assent of his understanding, though it is necessary for his faith that sufficient ground for his conviction be actively present and working in his spirit. But it is necessary for the vindication of his faith to reason in the form of scientific judgment, that the grounds on which it rests be explicated and established. Theology as a science, though it includes in its culminating discipline, that of practical theology, an exposition of how that knowledge of God with which it deals objectively may best be made the subjective possession of man, is not itself the instrument of propaganda; what it undertakes to do is systematically to set forth this knowledge of God as the object of rational contemplation. And as it has to set it forth as knowledge, it must of course begin by establishing its right to rank as such. Did it not do so, the whole of its work would hang in the air, and theology would present the odd spectacle among the sciences of claiming a place among a series of systems of knowledge for an elaboration of pure assumptions.

X. The Earliest Apologetics

Seeing that it thus supplies an insistent need of the human spirit, the world has, of course, never been without its apologetics. Whenever men have thought at all they have thought about God and the supernatural order; and whenever they have thought of God and the supernatural order, there has been present to their minds a variety of more or less solid reasons for believing in their reality. The enucleation of these reasons into a systematically organized body of proofs waited of course upon advancing culture. But the advent of apologetics did not wait for the advent of Christianity; nor are traces of this department of thought discoverable only in the regions lit up by special revelation. The philosophical systems of antiquity, especially those which derive from Plato, are far from empty of apologetical elements; and when in the later stages of its development, classical philosophy became peculiarly religious, express apologetical material became almost predominant. With the coming of Christianity into the world, however, as the contents of the theology to be stated became richer, so the efforts to substantiate it became more fertile in apologetical elements. We must not confuse the apologies of the early Christian ages with formal apologetics. Like the sermons of the day, they contributed to apologetics without being it. The apologetic material developed by what one may call the more philosophical of the apologists (Aristides, Athenagoras, Tatian, Theophilus, Hermias, Tertullian) was already considerable; it was largely supplemented by the theological labors of their successors. In the first instance Christianity, plunged into a polytheistic environment and called upon to contend with systems of thought grounded in pantheistic or dualistic assumptions, required to establish its theistic standpoint; and as over against the bitterness of the Jews and the mockery of the heathen (e.g. Tacitus, Fronto, Crescens, Lucian), to evince its own divine origin as a gift of grace to sinful man. Along with Tertullian, the great Alexandrians, Clement and Origen, are the richest depositaries of the apologetic thought of the first period. The greatest apologists of the patristic age were, however, Eusebius of Cæsarea and Augustine. The former was the most learned and the latter the most profound of all the defenders of Christianity among the Fathers. And Augustine, in particular, not merely in his "City of God" but in his controversial writings, accumulated a vast mass of apologetical material which is far from having lost its significance even yet.

XI. The Later Apologetics

It was not, however, until the scholastic age that apologetics came to its rights as a constructive science. The whole theological activity of the Middle Ages was so far ancillary to apologetics, that its primary effort was the justification of faith to reason. It was not only rich in apologists (Agobard, Abelard, Raymund Martini), but every theologian was in a sense an apologist. Anselm at its beginning, Aquinas at its culmination, are types of the whole series; types in which all its excellencies are summed up. The Renaissance, with its repristination of heathenism, naturally called out a series of new apologists (Savonarola, Marsilius Ficinus, Ludovicus Vives), but the Reformation forced polemics into the foreground and drove apologetics out of sight, although, of course, the great theologians of the Reformation era brought their rich contribution to the accumulating apologetical material. When, in the exhaustion of the seventeenth century, irreligion began to spread among the people and indifferentism ripening into naturalism among the leaders of thought, the stream of apologetical thought was once more started flowing, to swell into a great flood as the prevalent unbelief intensified and spread. With a forerunner in Philippe de Mornay (1581), Hugo Grotius (1627) became the typical apologist of the earlier portion of this period, while its middle portion was illuminated by the genius of Pascal (d. 1662) and the unexampled richness of apologetical labor in its later years culminated in Butler's great "Analogy" (1736) and Paley's plain but powerful argumentation. As the assault against Christianity shifted its basis from the English deism of the early half of the eighteenth century through the German rationalism of its later half, the idealism which dominated the first half of the nineteenth century, and thence to the materialism of its later years, period after period was marked in the history of apology, and the particular elements of apologetics which were especially cultivated changed with the changing thought. But no epoch was marked in the history of apologetics itself, until under the guidance of Schleiermacher's attempt to trace the organism of the departments of theology, K. H. Sack essayed to set forth a scientifically organized " Christian Apologetics " (Hamburg, 1829; ed. 2, 1841). Since then an unbroken series of scientific systems of apologetics has flowed from the press. These differ from one another in almost every conceivable way; in their conception of the nature, task, compass, and encyclopedic place of the science; in their methods of dealing with its material; in their conception of Christianity itself; and of religion and of God and of the nature of the evidence on which belief in one or the other must rest. But they agree in the fundamental point that apologetics is conceived by all alike as a special department of theological science, capable of and demanding separate treatment. In this sense apologetics has come at last, in the last two-thirds of the nineteenth century, to its rights. The significant names in its development are such as, perhaps, among the Germans, Sack, Steudel, Delitzsch, Ebrard, Baumstark, Tölle, Kratz, Kübel, Steude, Frank, Kaftan, Vogel, Schultz, Kähler; to whom may be added such Romanists as Drey, Dieringer, Staudenmeyer, Hettinger, Schanz, and such English-speaking writers as Hetherington, H. B. Smith, Bruce, Rishell, and Beattie.

BIBLIOGRAPHY: Lists of literature will be found in F. R. Beattie's " Apologetics, or the Rational Vindication of Christianity," Richmond, 1903; in A. Cave, " Introduction to Theology," Edinburgh, ed. 2, 1896; in G. R. Crooks and J. F. Hurst, " Theological Encyclopædia and Methodology," New York, 1884, pp. 411–413; in P. Schaff, " Theological Propædeutic," 2 parts, New York, 1892–1893. Consult F. L. Patton, in *Princeton Theological Review*, ii. 1904, pp. 110 ff.; *Presbyterian and Reformed Review*, vii. 1896, pp. 243 ff. (or pp. 49 ff. of this volume). On the history of apologetics and apologetic method: H. G. Tzschirner, " Geschichte der Apologetik," Leipzig, 1805; G. H. van Senden, " Geschichte der Apologetiek,"

2 vols., Stuttgart, 1846; K. Werner, " Geschichte der apologetischen und polemischen Literatur," 5 vols., Schaffhausen, 1861–1867 (Roman Catholic); W. Haan, "Geschichte der Vertheidigung des Christenthums," Frankenberg, 1882 (popular). For early Christian apologies consult " Ante-Nicene Fathers " and " Nicene and Post-Nicene Fathers "; for discussions of these, F. Watson, " The Ante-Nicene Apologies: their Character and Value," Cambridge, 1870 (Hulsean essay); W. J. Bolton, " The Evidences of Christianity as exhibited in the . . . Apologists down to Augustine," Cambridge, 1853 (Hulsean essay); F. R. Wynne, " The Literature of the Second Century," London, 1891 (popular but scholarly); A. Seitz, " Die Apologie des Christentums bei den Griechen des IV. und V. Jahrhunderts," Würzburg, 1895. On special phases in the history of apologetics: L. Noack, " Die Freidenker in der Religion, oder die Repräsentanten der religiösen Aufklärung in England, Frankreich und Deutschland," 3 vols., Bern, 1853–1855; A. S. Farrar, " Critical History of Free Thought," New York, 1863; K. R. Hagenbach, " German Rationalism, in its Rise, Progress, and Decline," Edinburgh, 1865; A. Viguié, " Histoire de l'apologétique dans l'église réformée française," Geneva, 1858; H. B. Smith, " Apologetics," New York, 1882 (appendix contains sketches of German apologetic works); J. F. Hurst, " History of Rationalism," New York, 1902; A. H. Huizinga, " Some Recent Phases of Christian Apologetics," in *Presbyterian and Reformed Review*, vii. 1896, pp. 34 ff. Apologetical literature: F. R. Beattie, " Apologetics, or the Rational Vindication of Christianity," Richmond, 1903; W. M. Hetherington, " Apologetics of the Christian Faith," Edinburgh, 1867; J. H. A. Ebrard, " Apologetik," Gütersloh, ed. 2, 1878–1880, English translation, " Apologetics: or the Scientific Vindication of Christianity," 3 vols., Edinburgh, 1886–1887; A. Mair, " Studies in the Christian Evidences," Edinburgh, 1883; G. F. Wright, " Logic of Christian Evidences," Andover, 1880; F. H. R. Frank, " System der christlichen Gewissheit," Erlangen, 1870–1873 (ed. 2, 1884), E.T. (of ed. 2), " System of the Christian Certainty," Edinburgh, 1886; P. Schanz, " Apologie des Christentums," 3 vols., Freiburg, 1887–1888, E.T. " Christian Apology," 3 vols., New York and Cincinnati, ed. 2, 1896 (Roman Catholic); L. F. Stearns, " The Evidence of Christian Experience," New York, 1890 (the best book on the subject); A. B. Bruce, " Apologetics; or, Christianity Defensively Stated," Edinburgh, 1892; H. Wace, " Students' Manual

of the Evidences of Christianity," London, 1892; J. Kaftan, "Die Wahrheit der christlichen Religion," Basel, 1888, E.T. 2 vols., Edinburgh, 1894; C. W. Rishell, "Foundations of the Christian Faith," New York, 1899; W. Devivier, "Cours d'apologétique chrétienne," Paris, 1889, E. T. "Christian Apologetics," 2 vols., New York, 1903; A. Harnack, "What is Christianity?" London, 1901; J. T. Bergen, "Evidences of Christianity," Holland, Mich., 1902; A. M. Randolph, "Reason, Faith and Authority in Christianity," New York, 1902; the Boyle and Bampton lecture series deal exclusively with subjects in apologetics; see also under "Agnosticism"; "Antitrinitarianism"; and "Atheism."

II

CHRISTIAN SUPERNATURALISM

CHRISTIAN SUPERNATURALISM [1]

DR. JOHN BASCOM has lately told us afresh and certainly, as we shall all agree, most truly, that "the relation of the natural and supernatural" is the "question of questions which underlies our rational life." "The fact of such a relation," he justly adds, "is the most patent and omnipresent in the history of the human mind." We cannot think at all without facing the great problems which arise out of the perennial pressure of this most persistent of intellectual questions. From the first dawn of intelligence each human mind has busied itself instinctively with their adjustment. The history of human thought in every race from its earliest beginnings is chiefly concerned with the varying relations which men — in this or that stage of culture, or under the influence of this or that dominating conception — have conceived to exist between the natural world in which they lived and that supernatural world which they have ever been prone to conceive to lie above and beyond it. The most elaborate systems of philosophy differ in nothing in this respect from the tentative efforts of untutored thinking. For them, too, the problem of the supernatural is the prime theme of their investigation: and the solutions which have commended themselves to them too have been the most varied possible, running through the entire series from the one-sided assertion of the natural as absolute and complete, with the exclusion of all supernaturalism, to the equally one-sided affirmation of the reality of the supernatural alone with the entire exclusion of all that can properly be called natural. Between these two extremes of atheistic naturalism and superstitious supernaturalism nearly every

[1] Opening address delivered before the Faculty and students of Princeton Theological Seminary, September 18, 1896. Reprinted from *The Presbyterian and Reformed Review*, viii. 1897, pp. 58–74.

possible adjustment of the relation of the two factors has found some advocates. So that there is some color to Dr. Bascom's plaint that, though the proper appreciation of their relation constitutes "the summation of sound philosophy," "its final conception and statement elude us all."

Some color, but not a thorough justification. For, amid all the variety and confusion of men's ideas on this great subject, there are not lacking certain lines of direction leading to one assured goal, broadly outlined only it may be and seen only dimly through the mist of innumerable errors of detail, within which it is demonstrable that the æonian thinking of the race is always traveling: within which also it is clear that the best and most vital of that high, conscious thinking which we call philosophy finds the limits of its conceptions and the pathway of its advance. We may not fancy that every conceivable conception of the relation of the natural and supernatural has found equal favor in the unsophisticated mind of man, or has won equal support from the criticized elaborations of philosophic contemplation. No one who will permit to pass before his mental vision the long procession of world-conceptions which have dominated the human race in its several stages of development will imagine that humanity at large has ever been tempted to doubt, much less to deny, the reality or the significance to it of either the natural or the supernatural. On any adequate survey of the immanent thought of the world as expressed in its systems of popular belief, atheistic naturalism and exclusive supernaturalism exhibit themselves as alike inhuman. Atheists have existed, who knew and would know nothing beyond what their five senses immediately gave them, and naturalistic atheism has found expression in elaborate systems which have warped the conceptions of large masses of men: and in like manner a debased superstition has fallen like a pall over entire communities and for ages has darkened their minds and cursed their whole life. So there have, from time to time, appeared among men both ascetic solitaries and communistic socialists, though God has set mankind in families. The band of camp-followers on either wing of an army confuses no man's judgment as to the whereabouts of the army itself, but rather points directly to its position. Similarly a general consideration of the great philosophical systems of the world will leave us in no doubt as to the trend of deliberate pondering upon this subject. Somewhere between the two extremes of a consistent naturalism and an exclusive supernaturalism we shall assuredly find the center of gravity of the thinking of the ages — the point on which philosophy rests all the more stably that on both sides wings stretch themselves far beyond all support and hang over the abyss. Precisely where, between the two extremes, this stable center is to be found, it may be more difficult to determine — our instruments of measurement are not always " implements of precision." Assuredly, however, it will not be found where either the purely supernatural or the purely natural is excluded, and in any case it is much to know that it lies somewhere between the two extremes, and that it is as unphilosophical as it is inhuman to deny or doubt either the natural or the supernatural.

It is not to be gainsaid, of course, that from time to time, strong tendencies of thought set in to this direction or to that; and, for a while, it may seem as if the whole world were rushing to one extreme or the other. A special type of philosophizing becomes temporarily dominant and its conceptions run burning over the whole thinking world. At such times men are likely to fancy that the great problem of the ages is settled, and to felicitate themselves upon the facility with which they see through what to men of other times were clouds of great darkness. Such a period visited European thought in the last century, when English Deism set the supernatural so far off from the world that French Atheism thought it an easy thing to dispense with it altogether. " Down with the infamy! " cried Voltaire, and actually thought the world had hearkened to his commandment. The atheistic naturalism of the eighteenth century has long since taken up its abode with the owls and bats; but the world has not yet learned its lesson. An even more powerful current seems to have seized the modern world, and to be hurling it by a very different pathway to practically the same conclusion. It is to be feared that it cannot be denied that we are to-day in the midst of a very strong drift away from frank recognition of the supernatural as a factor in human life. To this also Dr. Bascom may be cited as a witness. "The task which the bolder thinking of our time has undertaken," he tells us, is "to curb the supernatural, to bring it into the full service of reason." "To curb the supernatural" — yes, that is the labor with which the thinkers of our day have burdened themselves. The tap-root of this movement is firmly set in a pantheistic philosophy, to which, of course, there is no such distinction possible as that between the natural and supernatural: to it all things are natural, the necessary product of the blind interaction of the forces inherent in what we call matter, but which the pantheist calls "God" and thinks he has thereby given not only due but even sole recognition to the supernatural. But it has reached out and embraced in its ramified network of branches the whole sphere of human thinking through the magic watchword of "evolution," by means of which it strives to break down and obliterate all the lines of demarcation which separate things that differ, and thus to reduce all that exists to but varying forms taken, through natural processes, by the one life that underlies them all. How absolutely determinant the conception of evolution has become in the thinking of our age, there can be no need to remind ourselves. It may not be amiss, however, to recall the anti-supernaturalistic root and the anti-supernaturalistic effects of the dominance of this mode of conceiving things; and thus to identify in it the cause of the persistent anti-supernaturalism which at present characterizes the world's thought. The recognition of the supernatural is too deeply intrenched in human nature ever to be extirpated; man is not a brute, and he differs from the brutes in nothing more markedly or more ineradicably than in his correlation with an unseen world. But probably there never was an era in which the thinking of the more or less educated classes was more deeply tinged with an anti-supernatural stain than at present. Even when we confess the supernatural with our lips and look for it and find it with our reasons, our instincts as modern men lead us unconsciously to neglect and in all practical ways to disallow and even to scout it.

It would be impossible that what we call specifically Christian thought should be unaffected by such a powerful trend in the thinking of the world. Christian men are men first and Christians afterwards: and therefore their Christian thinking is superinduced on a basis of world-thinking. Theology accordingly in each age is stamped with the traits of the philosophy ruling at the time. The supernatural is the very breath of Christianity's nostrils and an anti-supernaturalistic atmosphere is to it the deadliest miasma. An absolutely anti-supernaturalistic Christianity is therefore a contradiction in terms. Nevertheless, immersed in an anti-supernaturalistic world-atmosphere, Christian thinking tends to become as anti-supernaturalistic as is possible to it. And it is indisputable that this is the characteristic of the Christian thought of our day. As Dr. Bascom puts it, the task that has been set themselves by those who would fain be considered the " bolder thinkers of our time " is " to curb the supernatural, to bring it into the full service of reason." The real question with them seems to be, not what kind and measure of supernaturalism does the Christianity of Christ and His apostles recognize and require; but, how little of the supernatural may be admitted and yet men continue to call themselves Christians. The effort is not to Christianize the world-conception of the age, but specifically to desupernaturalize Christianity so as to bring it into accord with the prevailing world-view.

The effects of the adoption of this point of view are all about us. This is the account to give, for example, of that speculative theism which poses under the name of " non-miraculous Christianity " and seeks to convince the world through reasoners like Pfleiderer and to woo it through novels like " Robert Elsmere." This is also the account to give of that odd positivistic religion offered us by the followers of Albrecht Ritschl, who, under color of a phenomenalism which knows nothing of " the thing in itself," profess to hold it not to be a matter of serious importance to Christianity whether God be a person, or Christ be God, or the soul have any persistence, and to find it enough to bask in the sweet impression which is made on the heart by the personality of the man Jesus, dimly seen through the mists of critical history. This is the account again to give of the growing disbelief and denial of the virgin-birth of our Lord; of the increasingly numerous and subtle attempts to explain away His bodily resurrection; and, in far wider circles, of the ever renewed and constantly varying efforts that positively swarm about us to reduce His miracles and those of His predecessors and followers — the God-endowed prophets and apostles of the two Testaments — to natural phenomena, the product of natural forces, though these forces may be held to be as yet undiscovered or even entirely undiscoverable by men. This also is the account to give of the vogue which destructive criticism of the Biblical books has gained in our time; and it is also the reason why detailed refutations of the numerous critical theories of the origin of the Biblical writings, though so repeatedly complete and logically final, have so little effect in abolishing destructive criticism. Its roots are not set in its detailed accounts of the origin of the Biblical writings, but in its anti-supernaturalistic bias: and so long as its two fixed points remain to it — its starting point in unbelief in the supernatural and its goal in a naturalistic development of the religion of Israel and its record — it easily shifts the pathway by which it proceeds from one to the other, according to its varying needs. It is of as little moment to it how it passes from one point to the other, as it is to the electrician what course his wire shall follow after he has secured its end attachments. Therefore theory follows theory with bewildering rapidity and — shall we not say it? — with equally bewildering levity, while the conclusion remains the same. And finally this is the account to give of the endlessly varying schemes of self-salvation offered the world in our day, and of the practical neglect and not infrequent open denial of the personal work of the Holy Spirit on the heart. In every way, in a word, and in every sphere of Christian thought, the

Christian thinking of our time is curbed, limited, confined within unnatural bounds by doubt and hesitation before the supernatural. In wide circles the reality of direct supernatural activity in this world is openly rejected: in wider circles still it is doubted: almost everywhere its assertion is timid and chary. It is significant of much that one of the brightest of recent Christian apologists has found it necessary to prefix to his treatment of Christian supernaturalism a section on " the evasion of the supernatural" among Christian thinkers.

It is certainly to be allowed that it is no light task for a Christian man to hold his anchorage in the rush of such a current of anti-supernaturalistic thought. We need not wonder that so many are carried from their moorings. How shall we so firmly brace ourselves that, as the flood of the world's thought beats upon us, it may bring us cleansing and refreshment, but may not sweep us away from our grasp on Christian truth? How, but by constantly reminding ourselves of what Christianity is, and of what as Christian men we must needs believe as to the nature and measure of the supernatural in its impact on the life of the world? For this nature and measure of the supernatural we have all the evidence which gives us Christianity. And surely the mass of that evidence is far too great to be shaken by any current of the world's thought whatever. Christian truth is a rock too securely planted to go down before any storm. Let us attach ourselves to it by such strong cables, and let us know so well its promontories of vantage and secure hiding-places, that though the waters may go over us we shall not be moved. To this end it will not be useless to recall continually the frankness of Christianity's commitment to the absolute supernatural. And it may be that we shall find profit in enumerating at this time a few of the points, at least, at which, as Christian men, we must recognize, with all heartiness, the intrusion of pure supernaturalism into our conception of things.

I. The Christian man, then, must, first of all, give the heartiest and frankest recognition to *the supernatural fact.* "God," we call it. But it is not enough for us to say "God."

The pantheist, too, says "God," and means this universal frame: for him accordingly the supernatural is but the more inclusive natural. When the Christian says "God," he means, and if he is to remain Christian he must mean, a *super*natural God — a God who is not entangled in nature, is not only another name for nature in its coördinated activities, or for that mystery which lies beneath and throbs through the All; but who is above nature and beyond, who existed, the Living God, before nature was, and should nature cease to be would still exist, the Everlasting God, and so long as this universal frame endures exists above and outside of nature as its Lord, its Lawgiver, and its Almighty King.

No Christian man may allow that the universe, material and spiritual combined, call it infinite if you will, in all its operations, be they as myriad as you choose, sums up the being or the activities of God. Before this universe was, God was, the one eternal One, rich in infinite activities: and while this universe persists, outside and beyond and above it God is, the one infinite One, ineffably rich in innumerable activities inconceivable, it may be, to the whole universe of derived being. He is not imprisoned within His works: the laws which He has ordained for them express indeed His character, but do not compass the possibilities of His action. The Apostle Paul has no doubt told us that " in Him we live and move and have our being," but no accredited voice has declared that in the universe He lives and moves and has His being. No, the heaven of heavens cannot contain Him; and what He has made is to what He is only as the smallest moisture-particle of the most attenuated vapor to the mighty expanse of the immeasurable sea.

The divine immanence is a fact to the Christian man. But to the Christian man this fact of the divine immanence is not the ultimate expression of his conception of God. Its recognition does not operate for him as a limitation of God in being or activities; it does not result in enclosing Him within His works and confining the possibilities of His action to the capacities of their laws. It is rather the expression of the Christian's sense of the comparative littleness of the universe — to every part and activity of which God is present because the whole universe is to Him as the mustard seed lying in the palm of a man. An immanent God, yes: but what is His immanence in even this immense universe to a God like ours? God in nature, yes: but what is God in nature to the inconceivable vastness of the God above nature? To the Christian conception, so far is the immanent God from exhausting the idea of God, that it touches but the skirt of His garment. It is only when we rise above the divine immanence to catch some faint glimpse of the God that transcends all the works of His hands — to the truly *super*natural God — that we begin to know who and what the Christian God is. Let us say, then, with all the emphasis that we are capable of, that the Christian's God is before all else the transcendent God — a God so great that though He be truly the supporter of this whole universe as well as its maker, yet His activity as ground of existence and governor of all that moves, is as nothing to that greater activity which is His apart from and above what is to us the infinite universe but to Him an infinitesimal speck of being that cannot in any way control His life. The Christian's God is no doubt the God of nature and the God in nature: but before and above all this He is the God above nature — the Supernatural Fact. As Christian men we must see to it that we retain a worthy conception of God: and an exclusively immanent God is, after all, a very little and belittling notion to hold of Him the product of whose simple word all this universe is.

II. The Christian man, again, must needs most frankly and heartily believe in *the supernatural act*. Belief in the supernatural act is, indeed, necessarily included in belief in the supernatural fact. If immanence is an inadequate formula for the being of God, it is equally inadequate as a formula for His activities. For where God is, there He must act: and if He exists above and beyond nature He must act also above and beyond nature. The supernatural God cannot but be conceived as a supernatural actor. He who called nature into being by a word cannot possibly be subject to the creature of His will in the mode of His activities. He to whom all nature is but a speck of derived and dependent being cannot be thought of as, in the reach of His operations, bound within the limits of the laws which operate within this granule and hold it together.

Before all that we call nature came into existence God was, in infinite fullness of life and of the innumerable activities which infinite fullness of life implies: and that nature has come into existence is due to an act of His prenatural power. Nature, in other words, has not come into existence at all: it has been made. And if it was made it must have been by a *super*natural act. The Christian conception of creation involves thus the frankest recognition of the supernatural act. To the Christian man nature cannot be conceived either as self-existent or as self-made or as a necessary emanation from the basal Being which we call God, nor yet as a mere modification in form of the one eternal substance. It is a manufactured article, the product of an act of power. God spoke and it was: and the God that thus spoke nature into being, is necessarily a supernatural God, creating nature by a supernatural act. As Christian men, we must at all hazards preserve this supernaturalistic conception of creation.

There are voices strong and subtle which would woo us from it. One would have us believe that in what we call creation, God did but give form and law to a dark Somewhat, which from all eternity lay beside Him — chaining thus by His almighty power the realm of inimical matter to the divine chariot wheels of order and progress. Or, if that crass dualism seems too gross, the outlying realm of darkness is subtly spoken of as the Nothing, the power it exerts is affirmed to be simply a dull and inert resistance, while yet the character of the product of God's creative power is represented as conditioned by the " Nothing " out of which it is made. Another would have us believe that what we call nature is of the substance of God Himself, and what we call creation is but the modification of form and manifestation which takes place in the eternal systole and diastole of the divine life. Or, if this crass pantheism seems too gross, a subtle ontology is called in, matter is resolved into its atoms, the atoms are conceived as mere centers of force, and this force is asserted to be the pure will of God: so that after all no substance exists except the substance of God. As over against all such speculations, gross and subtle alike, the Christian man is bound to maintain that God created the heavens and the earth — that this great act by which He called into being all that is was in the strictest sense of the words a *creation,* and that in this act of creation He produced in the strictest sense of the words a *somewhat.* It was an act of *creation:* not a mere molding or ordering of a preëxistent substance — not a mere evolution or modification of His own substance. And in it He produced a *somewhat* — not a mere appearance or simulacrum, but being, derived and dependent being, but just as real being as His own infinite essence. In creation, therefore, the Christian man is bound to confess a frankly supernatural act — an act above nature, independent of nature, by which nature itself and all its laws were brought into existence.

Nor can he confine himself to the confession of this one supernatural act. The Christian's God not only existed before nature and is its Creator, but also exists above nature and is its Governor and Lord. It is inconceivable that He should be active only in that speck of being which He Himself has called into existence by an act of His independent power. It exists in Him, not He in it; and just because it is finite and He is infinite, the great sphere of His life and activity lies above it and beyond. It is equally inconceivable that His activities with reference to it, or even within it, should be confined to the operation of the laws which He has ordained for the regulation of *its* activities and not of *His.* What power has this little speck of derived being to exclude the operation upon it and within it of that almighty force to whose energy it owes both its existence and its persistence in being? Have its forces acquired such strength as to neutralize the power which called it into being? Or has it framed for itself a crust so hard as to isolate it from the omnipotence which plays about it and successfully to resist the power that made it, that it may not crush it or pierce it at will through and through? Certainly he who confesses the Christian's God has no ground for denying the supernatural act.

Now nothing is further from the Christian's thought than to doubt the reality and the efficiency of second causes. Just because he believes that in creation God created a *somewhat* — real substance endowed with real powers — he believes that these powers really act and really produce their effects. He thinks of nothing so little, to be sure, as to doubt the immanence of God in these second causes. It is his joy to see the hand of God in all that occurs, and to believe that it is not only by His preserving care, but in accordance with His direction, that every derived cause acts and every effect is produced. But least of all men has the Christian a desire to substitute the immediate energy of God for His mediate activity in His ordinary government of the universe which He has made. Just because he believes that the universe was well made, he believes that the forces with which it was endowed are competent for its ordinary government and he traces in their action the divine purpose unrolling its faultless scroll. The Christian man, then, is frankly ready to accredit to second causes all that second causes are capable of producing. He is free to trace them in all the products of time, and to lend his ear to the poets when they tell him that

> This solid earth whereon we tread,
> In tracts of fluent heat began,
> And grew to seeming random forms,
> The seeming prey of cyclic storms,
> Till at the last arose the man.

He only insists that in all this great process by which, he is told, the ordered world was hacked and hewn out by the great forces and convulsions of nature, we shall perceive, also with the poets, that those great artificers, " Hack and Hew, were the sons of God," and stood

> One at His right hand and one at His left,
> To obey as He taught them how.

Let us open our eyes wide to the grandeur and perfection of God's providential government; and let us not neglect to note that here too is a supernaturalism, and that in the ordered progress of the world towards that one far-off divine event we can trace the very finger of God.

But let us not fancy, on the other hand, that the providence of God any more than the immanence of God is a formula adequate to sum up all His activities. God is the God of providence: but He is much more than the God of providence. The universe is but a speck in His sight: and its providential government is scarcely an incident in the infinite fullness of His life. It is certain that He acts in infinitely varied modes, otherwise and beyond providence, and there is no reason we can give why He should not act otherwise and beyond providence even in relation to the universe which He has made. In our conception of a supernatural God, we dare not erect His providential activity into an exclusive law of action for Him, and refuse to allow of any other mode of operation. Who can say, for example, whether creation itself, in the purity and absoluteness of that conception, may not be progressive, and may not correlate itself with and follow the process of the providential development of the world, in the plan of such a God — so that the works of creation and providence may interlace through all time in the production of this completed universe? What warrant, then, can there be to assume beforehand that some way must be found for "evolution" to spring the chasms in the creative process over which even divinely led second causes appear insufficient to build a bridge? And if for any reason — certainly not unforeseen by God, or in contradiction to His ordering — there should a "rift appear in the lute," who dare assert that the supernatural God may not directly intervene for its mending, but must needs beat out His music on the broken strings or let their discord jar down the ages to all eternity? The laws of nature are not bonds by which God is tied so that He cannot move save within their limits: they are not in His sight such great and holy things that it would be sacrilege for Him not to honor them in all His activities. His real life is above and beyond them: there is no reason why He may not at will act independently of them even in dealing with nature itself: and if there be reason why He should act apart from them we may be sure that the supernatural God will so act. The frank recognition of the possibility of the supernatural act, and of its probable reality on adequate occasion, is in any event a part of the Christian man's heritage.

III. And this leads us to recognize next that the Christian man must cherish a frank and hearty faith in a *supernatural redemption.* As certainly as the recognition of the great fact of sin is an element in the Christian's world-conception, the need and therefore the actuality of the direct corrective act of God — of miracle, in a word — enters ineradicably into his belief. We cannot confess ourselves sinners — radically at breach with God and broken and deformed in our moral and spiritual being — and look to purely natural causes or to simply providential agencies, which act only through natural causes and therefore never beyond their reach, for our recovery to God and to moral and spiritual health. And in proportion as we realize what sin is — what, in the Christian conception, is the nature of that bottomless gulf which it has opened between the sinning soul and the all-holy and faultlessly just God, the single source of the soul's life, and what is the consequent mortal character of the wound which sin has inflicted on the soul — in that proportion will it become more and more plain to us that there is no ability in what we fondly call the remedial forces of nature, no capacity in growth, however skillfully led by even an all-wise providence, to heal this hurt. A seed of life may indeed be developed into abounding life: but no wise leading can direct a seed of death into the ways of life. Dead things do not climb. As well expect dead and decaying Lazarus through the action of natural forces, however wisely directed, to put on the fresh firmness of youthful flesh and stand forth a sound and living man, as a soul dead in sin to rise by natural powers into newness of life. No, the world knows that dead men do not live again: and the world's singers, on the plane of nature, rightly declare,

> One thing is certain, and the rest is lies;
> The flower that once has blown, forever dies.

If no supernatural voice had cried at the door of Lazarus' tomb, "Lazarus, come forth!" it would have been true of him, too, what the rebellious poet shouts in the ears of the rest of men,

> Once dead, you never shall return.

And if there be no voice of supernatural power to call dead souls back unto life, those who are dead in sin must needs fester in their corruption to the eternity of eternities.

One might suppose the supernaturalness of redemption to be too obviously the very heart of the whole Christian system, and to constitute too fundamentally the very essence of the Christian proclamation, for it to be possible for any one claiming the Christian name to lose sight of it for a moment. Assuredly the note of the whole history of redemption is the supernatural. To see this we do not need to focus our eyes on the supernatural man who came to redeem sinners — the "man from heaven," as Paul calls Him, who was indeed of the seed of David according to the flesh but at the same time was God over all, blessed forever, and became thus poor only that by His poverty we might be made rich — the Word who was in the beginning with God and was God, as John calls Him, who became flesh and dwelt among men, exhibiting to their astonished eyes the glory of an only-begotten of the Father — the One sent of the Father, whom to have seen was to see the Father also, as He Himself witnessed, who *is* before Abraham was, and while on earth abides still in Heaven — who came to earth by an obviously supernatural pathway, breaking His way through a virgin's womb, and lived on earth an obviously supernatural life, with the forces of nature and powers of disease and death subject to His simple word, and left the earth in an obviously supernatural ascension after having burst the bonds of the grave and led captivity captive. The whole course of preparation for His coming, extending through centuries, is just as clearly a supernatural history — sown with miracle and prophecy, and itself the greatest miracle and prophecy of them all: and the whole course of garnering the fruits of His coming in the establishment of a Church through the apostles He had chosen for the task, is supernatural to the core. Assuredly, if the redemptive process is not a supernatural operation, the entire proclamation of Christianity is a lie: as Paul declared with specific reference to one of its supernatural items, we, as Christians, " are found false-witnesses of God," " our preaching is vain," and " our faith is also vain."

Nevertheless, inconceivable as it would appear, there are many voices raised about us which would fain persuade us, in the professed interests of Christianity itself, to attenuate or evacuate the supernatural even in redemption. That supernatural history of preparation for the Redeemer, we are asked, did it indeed all happen as it is there recorded by the simple-minded writers? Are we not at liberty to read it merely as the record of what pious hearts, meditating on the great past, fancied ought to have occurred, when God was with the fathers; and to dig out from beneath the strata of its devout imaginations, as veritable history, only a sober narrative of how Israel walked in the felt presence of God and was led by His providence to ever clearer and higher conceptions of His Holy Being and of its mission as His chosen people? And that supernatural figure which the evangelists and apostles have limned for us, did it indeed ever walk this sin-stricken earth of ours? Are we not bound to see in it, we are asked, merely the projection of the hopes and fears swallowed up in hope of His devoted followers, clothing with all imaginable heavenly virtues the dead form of their Master snatched from their sight — of whom they had " hoped that it was He who should deliver Israel"? And are we not bound reverently to draw aside the veil laid by such tender hands over the dead face, that we may see beneath it the real Jesus, dead indeed, but a man of infinite sweetness of temper and depth of faith, from whose holy life we may even yet catch an inspiration and receive an impulse for good? And Peter and Paul and John and the rest of those whose hearts were set on fire by the spectacle of that great and noble life, are we really to take their enthusiasm as the rule of our thought? Are we not bound, we are asked, though honoring the purity of their fine hero-worship, to curb the extravagance of their assertions; and to follow the faith quickened in them by the Master's example while we correct the exuberance of their fancy in attributing to Him superhuman qualities and performances? In a word — for let us put it at length plainly — are we not at liberty, are we not bound, to eviscerate Christianity of all that makes it a re-demptive scheme, of all that has given it power in the earth, of all that has made it a message of hope and joy to lost men, of all that belongs to its very heart's blood and essence, as witnessed by all history and all experience alike, and yet claim still to remain Christians? No, let our answer be: as Christian men, a thousand times, no! When the anti-super-naturalistic bias of this age attacks the supernatural in the very process of redemption, and seeks to evaporate it into a set of platitudes about the guiding hand of God in history, the power of the man Jesus' pure faith over His followers' imagi-nations, and the imitation by us of the religion of Jesus — it has assaulted Christianity in the very citadel of its life. As Christian men we must assert with all vigor the purity and the absoluteness of the supernatural in redemption.

IV. And let us add at once, further, that as Christian men we must retain a frank and hearty faith in a *supernatural revelation.* For how should we be advantaged by a supernatu-ral redemption of which we knew nothing? Who is competent to uncover to us the meaning of this great series of redemptive acts but God Himself? It is easy to talk of revelation by deed. But how little is capable of being revealed by even the mighti-est deeds, unaccompanied by the explanatory word? Two thousand years ago a child was born in Bethlehem, who throve and grew up nobly, lived a life of poverty and beneficence, was

cruelly slain and rose from the dead. What is that to us? After
a little, as His followers sat waiting in Jerusalem, there was a
rush as of a mighty wind, and an appearance of tongues of
fire descending upon their heads. Strange: but what concern
have we in it all? We require the revealing word to tell us
who and what this goodly child was, why He lived and what
He wrought by His death, what it meant that He could not
be holden of the grave, and what those cloven tongues of flame
signified — before they can avail as redemptive facts to us. No
earthly person knew, or could know, their import. No earthly
insight was capable of divining it. No earthly authority could
assure the world of any presumed meaning attached to them.
None but God was in a position to know or assert their real
significance. Only, then, as God spake through His servants,
the prophets and apostles, could the mighty deeds by which
He would save the world be given a voice and a message — be
transformed into a gospel. And so the supernatural word receives its necessary position among the redemptive acts as their
interpretation and their complement.

We cannot miss the fact that from the beginning the word
of God took its honorable place among the redemptive deeds
of God. " God spake," declares the record as significantly and
as constantly as it declares that " God did." And we cannot
miss the fact that God's word, giving their meaning, their
force, and their value to His great redemptive acts, enters as
vitally into our Christian faith and hope as the acts themselves. As Christian men we cannot let slip our faith in the
one without losing also our grasp upon the other. And this is
the explanation both, on the one hand, of the constancy of the
hold which Christianity has kept upon the Word of God, and,
on the other, of the persistency of the assault which has been
made upon it in the interests of an anti-supernaturalistic
world-view. It is no idle task which has been set itself by
naturalistic criticism, when it has undertaken to explain away
the supernaturalism of this record of God's redemptive work,
which we call the Bible. This is the rock upon which all its
efforts to desupernaturalize Christianity break. It is no otiose

traditionalism which leads the Christian man to cling to this
Word of the living God which has come down to him through
the ages. It is his sole assurance that there has been a redemptive activity exercised by God in the world — the single
Ariadne's thread by which he is enabled to trace the course of
redemption through the ages. If God did not so speak of old to
the fathers by the prophets, if He has not in the end of these
days so spoken to us in His Son — He may indeed have intervened redemptively in the world, but to us it would be as if
He had not. Only as His voice has pierced to us to declare
His purpose, can we read the riddle of His operations: only as
He interprets to us their significance can we learn the wonder
of His ways. And just in proportion as our confidence in this
interpretative word shall wane, in just that proportion shall
we lose our hold upon the fact of a redemptive work of God in
the world. That we may believe in a supernatural redemption,
we must believe in a supernatural revelation, by which alone
we can be assured that this and not something else was what
occurred, and that this and not something other was what it
meant. The Christian man cannot afford to relax in the least
degree his entire confidence in a supernatural revelation.

V. And finally, we need to remind ourselves that as Christian men we must cherish a frank and hearty faith in a *supernatural salvation*. It is not enough to believe that God has
intervened in this natural world of ours and wrought a supernatural redemption: and that He has Himself made known to
men His mighty acts and unveiled to them the significance of
His working. It is upon a field of the dead that the Sun of
righteousness has risen, and the shouts that announce His
advent fall on deaf ears: yea, even though the morning stars
should again sing for joy and the air be palpitant with the
echo of the great proclamation, their voice could not penetrate
the ears of the dead. As we sweep our eyes over the world lying
in its wickedness, it is the valley of the prophet's vision which
we see before us: a valley that is filled with bones, and lo! they
are very dry. What benefit is there in proclaiming to dry bones
even the greatest of redemptions? How shall we stand and

cry, " O ye dry bones, hear ye the word of the Lord! " In vain the redemption, in vain its proclamation, unless there come a breath from heaven to breathe upon these slain that they may live. The redemption of Christ is therefore no more central to the Christian hope than the creative operations of the Holy Spirit upon the heart: and the supernatural redemption itself would remain a mere name outside of us and beyond our reach, were it not realized in the subjective life by an equally supernatural application.

Yet how easy it is, immersed in an anti-supernaturalistic world, to forget this our sound confession! Are we not men? we are asked: and is not the individuality of every human being a sacred thing? Must not each be the architect of his own fortunes, the creator of his own future — not indeed apart from the influence of the Holy Spirit, but certainly without His compulsion? Is it not mere fanaticism to dream that the very penetralium of our personality is invaded by an alien power, and the whole trend of our lives reversed in an instant of time, independently of our previous choice? Led, led certainly we may be by the Holy Spirit: but assuredly our manhood is respected and no non-ethical cataclysms are wrought in our lives by intrusive powers, not first sought and then yielded to at our own proper motion. But alas! alas! dead things are not led! Of course, the Christian is led by the Holy Spirit — and let us see to it that we heartily acknowledge it and fully recognize this directive supernaturalism throughout the Christian life. But that it may become Christian, and so come under the leading of the Spirit, the dead soul needs something more than leading. It needs reanimation, resurrection, regeneration, re-creation. So the Scriptures unwearyingly teach us. And so the Christian must, with all frankness and emphasis, constantly maintain.

The Christian man is not the product of the regenerative forces of nature under however divine a direction; he is not an " evolution " out of the natural man: he is a new creation. He has not made himself by however wary a walk, letting the ape and tiger die and cherishing his higher ideals until they become dominant in his life; he is not merely the old man improved: he is a new man, recreated in Christ Jesus by the almighty power of the Holy Spirit — by a power comparable only to that by which God raised Jesus Christ from the dead. As well might it be contended that Lazarus, not only came forth from the tomb, but rose from the dead by his own will and at his own motion, as that the Christian man not only of his own desire works out his salvation with fear and trembling, in the knowledge that it is God who is working in him both the willing and the doing according to His own good pleasure, but has even initiated that salvation in his soul by an act of his own will and accord. He lives by virtue of the life that has been given him, and prior to the inception of that life, of course, he has no power of action: and it is of the utmost importance that as Christian men we should not lower our testimony to this true supernaturalness of our salvation. We confess that it was God who made us men: let us confess with equal heartiness that it is God who makes us Christians.

Of such sort, then, is the supernaturalism which is involved in the confession of Christians. We have made it no part of our present task to enumerate all the ways in which the frank recognition of the supernatural enters into the very essence of Christianity. Much less do we essay here to discriminate between the several modes of supernatural action which Christian thought is bound to admit. We have fancied it well, however, to bring together a few of the instances in which the maintenance of the occurrence of the absolute supernatural is incumbent on every Christian man. Thus we may fortify ourselves against that unconscious yielding of the citadel of our faith to which every one is exposed who breathes the atmosphere of our unbelieving and encroaching world. The confession of a supernatural God, who may and does act in a supernatural mode, and who acting in a supernatural mode has wrought out for us a supernatural redemption, interpreted in a supernatural revelation, and applied by the supernatural operations of His Spirit — this confession constitutes the core of the Christian profession. Only he who holds this faith whole and entire has a full right to the Christian name: only he can hope to conserve the fullness of Christian truth. Let us see to it that under whatever pressure and amid whatever difficulties, we make it heartily and frankly our confession, and think and live alike in its strength and by its light. So doing, we shall find ourselves intrenched against the assaults of the world's anti-supernaturalism, and able by God's grace to witness a good confession in the midst of its most insidious attacks.

III
THE IDEA OF SYSTEMATIC THEOLOGY

THE IDEA OF SYSTEMATIC THEOLOGY [1]

The term "Systematic Theology" has long been in somewhat general use, especially in America, to designate one of the theological disciplines. And, on the whole, it appears to be a sufficiently exact designation of this discipline. It has not, of course, escaped criticism. The main faults that have been found with it are succinctly summed up by a recent writer in the following compact phrases:

The expression "systematic theology" is really an impertinent tautology. It is a tautology, in so far as a theology that is not systematic or methodical would be no theology. The idea of rational method lies in the word *logos,* which forms part of the term theology. And it is an impertinence, in so far as it suggests that there are other theological disciplinæ, or departments of theology, which are not methodical. [2]

Is not this, however, just a shade hypercritical? What is meant by calling this discipline "Systematic Theology" is not that it deals with its material in a systematic or methodical way, and the other disciplines do not; but that it presents its material in the form of a system. Other disciplines may use a chronological, a historical, or some other method: this discipline must needs employ a systematic, that is to say, a philosophical or scientific method. It might be equally well designated, therefore, "Philosophical Theology," or "Scientific Theology." But we should not by the adoption of one of these terms escape the ambiguities which are charged against the term "Systematic Theology." Other theological disciplines may also claim to be philosophical or scientific. If exegesis

[1] Reprinted from *The Presbyterian and Reformed Review,* vii. 1896, pp. 243–271.

[2] Professor D. W. Simon, D.D., "The Nature and Scope of Systematic Theology," in *Bibliotheca Sacra,* li. 1894, p. 587.

should be systematic, it should also be scientific. If history should be methodical, it should also be philosophical. An additional ambiguity would also be brought to these terms from their popular usage. There would be danger that " Philosophical Theology " should be misapprehended as theology dominated by some philosophical system. There would be a similar danger that " Scientific Theology " should be misunderstood as theology reduced to an empirical science, or dependent upon an "experimental method." Nevertheless these terms also would fairly describe what we mean by " Systematic Theology." They too would discriminate it from its sister disciplines, as the philosophical discipline which investigates from the philosophical standpoint the matter with which all the disciplines deal. And they would keep clearly before our minds the main fact in the case, namely, that Systematic Theology, as distinguished from its sister disciplines, is a science, and is to be conceived as a science and treated as a science.

The two designations, "Philosophical Theology" and "Scientific Theology," are practically synonyms. But they differ in their connotation as the terms " philosophy " and "science" differ. The distinction between these terms in a reference like the present would seem to be that between the whole and one of its parts. Philosophy is the *scientia scientiarum*. What a science does for a division of knowledge, that philosophy essays to do for the mass of knowledge. A science reduces a section of our knowledge to order and harmony: philosophy reduces the sciences to order and harmony. Accordingly there are many sciences, and but one philosophy. We, therefore, so far agree with Professor D. W. Simon (whom we have quoted above in order to disagree with him), when he says that " what a science properly understood does for a subsystem; that, philosophy aims to do for the system which the subsystems constitute." " Its function is so to grasp the whole that every part shall find its proper place therein, and the parts, that they shall form an orderly organic whole ": " so to correlate the *reals,* which with their interactivities make up the world or the universe, that the whole shall be seen in its harmony and unity; and that to every individual real shall be assigned the place in which it can be seen to be discharging its proper functions."[3] This, as will be at once perceived, is the function of each science in its own sphere. To call "Systematic Theology" "Philosophical Theology" or "Scientific Theology" would therefore be all one in essential meaning. Only, when we call it "Philosophical Theology," we should be conceiving it as a science among the sciences and should have our eye upon its place in the universal sum of knowledge: while, when we call it "Scientific Theology," our mind should be occupied with it in itself, as it were in isolation, and with the proper mode of dealing with its material. In either case we are affirming that it deals with its material as an organizable system of knowledge; that it deals with it from the philosophical point of view; that it is, in other words, in its essential nature a science.

It is possible that the implications of this determination are not always fully realized. When we have made the simple assertion of "Systematic Theology" that it is in its essential nature a science, we have already determined most of the vexing questions which arise concerning it in a formal point of view. In this single predicate is implicitly included a series of affirmations, which, when taken together, will give us a rather clear conception not only of what Systematic Theology is, but also of what it deals with, whence it obtains its material, and for what purpose it exists.

I. First of all, then, let us observe that to say that Systematic Theology is a science is to deny that it is a historical discipline, and to affirm that it seeks to discover, not what has been or is held to be true, but what is ideally true; in other words, it is to declare that it deals with absolute truth and aims at organizing into a concatenated system all the truth in its sphere. Geology is a science, and on that very account there cannot be two geologies; its matter is all the well-authenticated facts in its sphere, and its aim is to digest all these facts into one all-comprehending system. There may be rival psy-

[3] *Loc. cit.*, p. 592.

chologies, which fill the world with vain jangling; but they do not strive together in order that they may obtain the right to exist side by side in equal validity, but in strenuous effort to supplant and supersede one another: there can be but one true science of mind. In like manner, just because theology is a science there can be but one theology. This all-embracing system will brook no rival in its sphere, and there can be two theologies only at the cost of one or both of them being imperfect, incomplete, false. It is because theology, in accordance with a somewhat prevalent point of view, is often looked upon as a historical rather than a scientific discipline, that it is so frequently spoken of and defined as if it were but one of many similar schemes of thought. There is no doubt such a thing as Christian theology, as distinguished from Buddhist theology or Mohammedan theology; and men may study it as the theological implication of Christianity considered as one of the world's religions. But when studied from this point of view, it forms a section of a historical discipline and furnishes its share of facts for a history of religions; on the data supplied by which a science or philosophy of religion may in turn be based. We may also, no doubt, speak of the Pelagian and Augustinian theologies, or of the Calvinistic and Arminian theologies; but, again, we are speaking as historians and from a historical point of view. The Pelagian and Augustinian theologies are not two coördinate sciences of theology; they are rival theologies. If one is true, just so far the other is false, and there is but one theology. This we may identify, as an empirical fact, with either or neither; but it is at all events one, inclusive of all theological truth and exclusive of all else as false or not germane to the subject.

In asserting that theology is a science, then, we assert that, in its subject-matter, it includes all the facts belonging to that sphere of truth which we call theological; and we deny that it needs or will admit of limitation by a discriminating adjectival definition. We may speak of it as Christian theology just as we may speak of it as true theology, if we mean thereby only more fully to describe what, as a matter of fact, theology is found to be; but not, if we mean thereby to discriminate it from some other assumed theology thus erected to a coördinate position with it. We may describe our method of procedure in attempting to ascertain and organize the truths that come before us for building into the system, and so speak of logical or inductive, of speculative or organic theology; or we may separate the one body of theology into its members, and, just as we speak of surface and organic geology or of physiological and direct psychology, so speak of the theology of grace and of sin, or of natural and revealed theology. But all these are but designations of methods of procedure in dealing with the one whole, or of the various sections that together constitute the one whole, which in its completeness is the science of theology, and which, as a science, is inclusive of all the truth in its sphere, however ascertained, however presented, however defended.

II. There is much more than this included, however, in calling theology a science. For the very existence of any science, three things are presupposed: (1) the reality of its subject-matter; (2) the capacity of the human mind to apprehend, receive into itself, and rationalize this subject-matter; and (3) some medium of communication by which the subject-matter is brought before the mind and presented to it for apprehension. There could be no astronomy, for example, if there were no heavenly bodies. And though the heavenly bodies existed, there could still be no science of them were there no mind to apprehend them. Facts do not make a science; even facts as apprehended do not make a science; they must be not only apprehended, but also so far comprehended as to be rationalized and thus combined into a correlated system. The mind brings to every science somewhat which, though included in the facts, is not derived from the facts considered in themselves alone, as isolated data, or even as data perceived in some sort of relation to one another. Though they be thus known, science is not yet; and is not born save through the efforts of the mind in subsuming the facts under its own intuitions and forms of thought. No mind is satisfied with a bare cognition of facts: its very constitution forces it on to a restless energy until it succeeds in working these facts not only into a network of correlated relations among themselves, but also into a rational body of thought correlated to itself and its necessary modes of thinking. The condition of science, then, is that the facts which fall within its scope shall be such as stand in relation not only to our faculties, so that they may be apprehended; but also to our mental constitution so that they may be so far understood as to be rationalized and wrought into a system relative to our thinking. Thus a science of æsthetics presupposes an æsthetic faculty, and a science of morals a moral nature, as truly as a science of logic presupposes a logical apprehension, and a science of mathematics a capacity to comprehend the relations of numbers. But still again, though the facts had real existence, and the mind were furnished with a capacity for their reception and for a sympathetic estimate and embracing of them in their relations, no science could exist were there no media by which the facts should be brought before and communicated to the mind. The transmitter and intermediating wire are as essential for telegraphing as the message and the receiving instrument. Subjectively speaking, sense perception is the essential basis of all science of external things; self-consciousness, of internal things. But objective media are also necessary. For example, there could be no astronomy, were there no trembling ether through whose delicate telegraphy the facts of light and heat are transmitted to us from the suns and systems of the heavens. Subjective and objective conditions of communication must unite, before the facts that constitute the material of a science can be placed before the mind that gives it its form. The sense of sight is essential to astronomy: yet the sense of sight would be useless for forming an astronomy were there no objective ethereal messengers to bring us news from the stars. With these an astronomy becomes possible; but how meager an astronomy compared with the new possibilities which have opened out with the discovery of a new medium of communication in the telescope, followed by still newer media in the subtle instruments by which our modern investigators not only weigh the spheres in their courses, but analyze them into their chemical elements, map out the heavens in a chart, and separate the suns into their primary constituents.

Like all other sciences, therefore, theology, for its very existence as a science, presupposes the objective reality of the subject-matter with which it deals; the subjective capacity of the human mind so far to understand this subject-matter as to be able to subsume it under the forms of its thinking and to rationalize it into not only a comprehensive, but also a comprehensible whole; and the existence of trustworthy media of communication by which the subject-matter is brought to the mind and presented before it for perception and understanding. That is to say: (1) The affirmation that theology is a science presupposes the affirmation that God is, and that He has relation to His creatures. Were there no God, there could be no theology; nor could there be a theology if, though He existed, He existed out of relation with His creatures. The whole body of philosophical apologetics is, therefore, presupposed in and underlies the structure of scientific theology. (2) The affirmation that theology is a science presupposes the affirmation that man has a religious nature, that is, a nature capable of understanding not only that God is, but also, to some extent, what He is; not only that He stands in relations with His creatures, but also what those relations are. Had man no religious nature he might, indeed, apprehend certain facts concerning God, but he could not so understand Him in His relations to man as to be able to respond to those facts in a true and sympathetic embrace. The total product of the great science of religion, which investigates the nature and workings of this element in man's mental constitution, is therefore presupposed in and underlies the structure of scientific theology. (3) The affirmation that theology is a science presupposes the affirmation that there are media of communication by which God and divine things are brought before the minds of men, that they may perceive them and, in perceiving, understand them. In other words, when we affirm that theology is a science, we affirm not only the reality of God's existence and our capacity so far to understand Him, but we affirm that He has made Himself known to us — we affirm the objective reality of a revelation. Were there no revelation of God to man, our capacity to understand Him would lie dormant and unawakened; and though He really existed it would be to us as if He were not. There would be a God to be known and a mind to know Him; but theology would be as impossible as if there were neither the one nor the other. Not only, then, philosophical, but also the whole mass of historical apologetics by which the reality of revelation and its embodiment in the Scriptures are vindicated, is presupposed in and underlies the structure of scientific theology.

III. In thus developing the implications of calling theology a science, we have already gone far towards determining our exact conception of what theology is. We have in effect, for example, settled our definition of theology. A science is defined from its subject-matter; and the subject-matter of theology is God in His nature and in His relations with His creatures. Theology is therefore that science which treats of God and of the relations between God and the universe. To this definition most theologians have actually come. And those who define theology as " the science of God," mean the term God in a broad sense as inclusive also of His relations; while others exhibit their sense of the need of this inclusiveness by calling it " the science of God and of divine things "; while still others speak of it, more loosely, as " the science of the supernatural." These definitions fail rather in precision of language than in correctness of conception.

Others, however, go astray in the conception itself. Thus theologians of the school of Schleiermacher usually derive their definition from the sources rather than the subject-matter of the science — and so speak of theology as " the science of faith " or the like; a thoroughly unscientific procedure, even though our view of the sources be complete and unexceptionable, which is certainly not the case with this school. Quite as confusing is it to define theology, as is very currently done and often as an outgrowth of this same subjective tendency, as " the science of religion," or even — pressing to its greatest extreme the historical conception, which as often underlies this type of definition — as " the science of the Christian religion." Theology and religion are parallel products of the same body of facts in diverse spheres; the one in the sphere of thought and the other in the sphere of life. And the definition of theology as " the science of religion " thus confounds the product of the facts concerning God and His relations with His creatures working through the hearts and lives of men, with those facts themselves; and consequently, whenever strictly understood, bases theology not on the facts of the divine revelation, but on the facts of the religious life. This leads ultimately to a confusion of the two distinct disciplines of theology, the subject-matter of which is objective, and the science of religion, the subject-matter of which is subjective; with the effect of lowering the data of theology to the level of the aspirations and imaginings of man's own heart. Wherever this definition is found, either a subjective conception of theology, which reduces it to a branch of psychology, may be suspected; or else a historical conception of it, a conception of " Christian theology " as one of the many theologies of the world, parallel with, even if unspeakably truer than, the others with which it is classed and in conjunction with which it furnishes us with a full account of religion. When so conceived, it is natural to take a step further and permit the methodology of the science, as well as its idea, to be determined by its distinguishing element: thus theology, in contradiction to its very name, becomes Christocentric. No doubt " Christian theology," as a historical discipline, is Christocentric; it is by its doctrine of redemption that it is differentiated from all the other theologies that the world has known. But theology as a science is and must be theocentric. So soon as we firmly grasp it from the scientific point of view, we see that there can be but one science of God and of His relations to His universe, and we no longer seek a point of discrimination, but rather a center of development; and we quickly see that there can be but one center about which so comprehensive a subject-matter can be organized — the conception of God. He that hath seen Christ, has beyond doubt seen the Father; but it is one thing to make Christ the center of theology so far as He is one with God, and another thing to organize all theology around Him as the theanthropos and in His specifically theanthropic work.

IV. Not only, however, is our definition of theology thus set for us: we have also determined in advance our conception of its sources. We have already made use of the term " revelation," to designate the medium by which the facts concerning God and His relations to His creatures are brought before men's minds, and so made the subject-matter of a possible science. The word accurately describes the condition of all knowledge of God. If God be a person, it follows by stringent necessity, that He can be known only so far as He reveals or expresses Himself. And it is but the converse of this, that if there be no revelation, there can be no knowledge, and, of course, no systematized knowledge or science of God. Our reaching up to Him in thought and inference is possible only because He condescends to make Himself intelligible to us, to speak to us through work or word, to reveal Himself. We hazard nothing, therefore, in saying that, as the condition of all theology is a revealed God, so, without limitation, the sole source of theology is revelation.

In so speaking, however, we have no thought of doubting that God's revelation of Himself is " in divers manners." We have no desire to deny that He has never left man without witness of His eternal power and Godhead, or that He has multiplied the manifestations of Himself in nature and providence and grace, so that every generation has had abiding and unmistakable evidence that He is, that He is the good God, and that He is a God who marketh iniquity. Under the broad skirts of the term " revelation," every method of manifesting Himself which God uses in communicating knowledge of His being and attributes, may find shelter for itself — whether it be through those visible things of nature whereby His invisible things are clearly seen, or through the constitution of the human mind with its causal judgment indelibly stamped upon it, or through that voice of God that we call conscience, which proclaims His moral law within us, or through His providence in which He makes bare His arm for the government of the nations, or through the exercises of His grace, our experience under the tutelage of the Holy Ghost — or whether it be through the open visions of His prophets, the divinely-breathed pages of His written Word, the divine life of the Word Himself. How God reveals Himself — in what divers manners He makes Himself known to His creatures — is thus the subsequent question, by raising which we distribute the one source of theology, revelation, into the various methods of revelation, each of which brings us true knowledge of God, and all of which must be taken account of in building our knowledge into one all-comprehending system. It is the accepted method of theology to infer that the God that made the eye must Himself see; that the God who sovereignly distributes His favors in the secular world may be sovereign in grace too; that the heart that condemns itself but repeats the condemnation of the greater God; that the songs of joy in which the Christian's happy soul voices its sense of God's gratuitous mercy are valid evidence that God has really dealt graciously with it. It is with no reserve that we accept all these sources of knowledge of God — nature, providence, Christian experience — as true and valid sources, the well-authenticated data yielded by which are to be received by us as revelations of God, and as such to be placed alongside of the revelations in the written Word and wrought with them into one system. As a matter of fact, theologians have always so dealt with them; and doubtless they always will so deal with them.

But to perceive, as all must perceive, that every method by which God manifests Himself, is, so far as this manifestation can be clearly interpreted, a source of knowledge of Him, and must, therefore, be taken account of in framing all our knowledge of Him into one organic whole, is far from allowing that there are no differences among these various manifestations

— in the amount of revelation they give, the clearness of their message, the ease and certainty with which they may be in terpreted, or the importance of the special truths which they are fitted to convey. Far rather is it *a priori* likely that if there are " divers manners " in which God has revealed Himself, He has not revealed precisely the same message through each; that these " divers manners " correspond also to divers mes- sages of divers degrees of importance, delivered with divers degrees of clearness. And the mere fact that He has included in these " divers manners " a copious revelation in a written Word, delivered with an authenticating accompaniment of signs and miracles, proved by recorded prophecies with their recorded fulfillments, and pressed, with the greatest solemnity, upon the attention and consciences of men as the very Word of the Living God, who has by it made all the wisdom of men foolishness; nay, proclaimed as containing within itself the formulation of His truth, the proclamation of His law, the discovery of His plan of salvation: this mere fact, I say, would itself and prior to all comparison, raise an overwhelming pre- sumption that all the others of " the divers manners " of God's revelation were insufficient for the purposes for which revela- tion is given, whether on account of defect in the amount of their communication or insufficiency of attestation or uncer- tainty of interpretation or fatal one-sidedness in the character of the revelation they are adapted to give.

We need not be surprised, therefore, that on actual exam- ination, such imperfections are found undeniably to attach to all forms of what we may, for the sake of discrimination, speak of as mere manifestations of God; and that thus the revela- tion of God in His written Word — in which are included the only authentic records of the revelation of Him through the incarnate Word — is easily shown not only to be incomparably superior to all other manifestations of Him in the fullness, richness, and clearness of its communications, but also to contain the sole discovery of much that it is most important for the soul to know as to its state and destiny, and of much that is most precious in our whole body of theological knowledge. The superior lucidity of this revelation makes it the norm of interpretation for what is revealed so much more darkly through the other methods of manifestation. The glorious character of the discoveries made in it throws all other manifestations into comparative shadow. The amazing fullness of its disclosures renders what they can tell us of little relative value. And its absolute completeness for the needs of man, taking up and reiteratingly repeating in the clearest of language all that can be wrung from their sometimes enigmatic indications, and then adding to this a vast body of still more momentous truth undiscoverable through them, all but supersedes their necessity. With the fullest recognition of the validity of all the knowledge of God and His ways with men, which can be obtained through the manifestations of His power and divinity in nature and history and grace; and the frankest allowance that the written Word is given, not to destroy the manifestations of God, but to fulfill them; the theologian must yet refuse to give these sources of knowledge a place alongside of the written Word, in any other sense than that he gladly admits that they, alike with it, but in unspeakably lower measure, do tell us of God. And nothing can be a clearer indication of a decadent theology or of a decaying faith, than a tendency to neglect the Word in favor of some one or of all of the lesser sources of theological truth, as fountains from which to draw our knowledge of divine things. This were to prefer the flickering rays of a taper to the blazing light of the sun; to elect to draw our water from a muddy run rather than to dip it from the broad bosom of the pure fountain itself.

Nevertheless, men have often sought to still the cravings of their souls with a purely natural theology; and there are men to-day who prefer to derive their knowledge of what God is and what He will do for man from an analysis of the implications of their own religious feelings: not staying to consider that nature, "red in tooth and claw with ravin," can but direct our eyes to the God of law, whose deadly letter kills; or that our feelings must needs point us to the God of our

imperfect apprehensions or of our unsanctified desires — not
to the God that is, so much as to the God that we would fain
should be. The natural result of resting on the revelations of
nature is despair; while the inevitable end of making our
appeal to even the Christian heart is to make for ourselves
refuges of lies in which there is neither truth nor safety. We
may, indeed, admit that it is valid reasoning to infer from
the nature of the Christian life what are the modes of God's
activities towards His children: to see, for instance, in conviction of sin and the sudden peace of the new-born soul, God's
hand in slaying that He may make alive, His almighty power
in raising the spiritually dead. But how easy to overstep the
limits of valid inference; and, forgetting that it is the body of
Christian truth known and assimilated that determines the
type of Christian experience, confuse in our inferences what
is from man with what is from God, and condition and limit
our theology by the undeveloped Christian thought of the
man or his times. The interpretation of the data included in
what we have learned to call " the Christian consciousness,"
whether of the individual or of the Church at large, is a process
so delicate, so liable to error, so inevitably swayed to this side
or that by the currents that flow up and down in the soul,
that probably few satisfactory inferences could be drawn from
it, had we not the norm of Christian experience and its dogmatic implications recorded for us in the perspicuous pages of
the written Word. But even were we to suppose that the interpretation was easy and secure, and that we had before us,
in an infallible formulation, all the implications of the religious experience of all the men who have ever known Christ,
we have no reason to believe that the whole body of facts thus
obtained would suffice to give us a complete theology. After
all, we know in part and we feel in part; it is only when that
which is perfect shall appear that we shall know or experience
all that Christ has in store for us. With the fullest acceptance,
therefore, of the data of the theology of the feelings, no less
than of natural theology, when their results are validly obtained and sufficiently authenticated as trustworthy, as di-

vinely revealed facts which must be wrought into our system, it remains nevertheless true that we should be confined to a meager and doubtful theology were these data not confirmed, reinforced, and supplemented by the surer and fuller revelations of Scripture; and that the Holy Scriptures are the source of theology in not only a degree, but also a sense in which nothing else is.

There may be a theology without the Scriptures — a theology of nature, gathered by painful, and slow, and sometimes doubtful processes from what man sees around him in external nature and the course of history, and what he sees within him of nature and of grace. In like manner there may be and has been an astronomy of nature, gathered by man in his natural state without help from aught but his naked eyes, as he watched in the fields by night. But what is this astronomy of nature to the astronomy that has become possible through the wonderful appliances of our observatories? The Word of God is to theology as, but vastly more than, these instruments are to astronomy. It is the instrument which so far increases the possibilities of the science as to revolutionize it and to place it upon a height from which it can never more descend. What would be thought of the deluded man, who, discarding the new methods of research, should insist on acquiring all the astronomy which he would admit, from the unaided observation of his own myopic and astigmatic eyes? Much more deluded is he who, neglecting the instrument of God's Word written, would confine his admissions of theological truth to what he could discover from the broken lights that play upon external nature, and the faint gleams of a dying or even a slowly reviving light, which arise in his own sinful soul. Ah, no! The telescope first made a real science of astronomy possible: and the Scriptures form the only sufficing source of theology.

V. Under such a conception of its nature and sources, we are led to consider the place of Systematic Theology among the other theological disciplines as well as among the other sciences in general. Without encroaching upon the details of

Theological Encyclopedia, we may adopt here the usual four-fold distribution of the theological disciplines into the Exegetical, the Historical, the Systematic, and the Practical, with only the correction of prefixing to them a fifth department of Apologetical Theology. The place of Systematic Theology in this distribution is determined by its relation to the preceding disciplines, of which it is the crown and head. Apologetical Theology prepares the way for all theology by establishing its necessary presuppositions without which no theology is possible — the existence and essential nature of God, the religious nature of man which enables him to receive a revelation from God, the possibility of a revelation and its actual realization in the Scriptures. It thus places the Scriptures in our hands for investigation and study. Exegetical Theology receives these inspired writings from the hands of Apologetics, and investigates their meaning; presenting us with a body of detailed and substantiated results, culminating in a series of organized systems of Biblical History, Biblical Ethics, Biblical Theology, and the like, which provide material for further use in the more advanced disciplines. Historical Theology investigates the progressive realization of Christianity in the lives, hearts, worship, and thought of men, issuing not only in a full account of the history of Christianity, but also in a body of facts which come into use in the more advanced disciplines, especially in the way of the manifold experiments that have been made during the ages in Christian organization, worship, living, and creed-building, as well as of the sifted results of the reasoned thinking and deep experience of Christian truth during the whole past. Systematic Theology does not fail to strike its roots deeply into this matter furnished by Historical Theology; it knows how to profit by the experience of all past generations in their efforts to understand and define, to systematize and defend revealed truth; and it thinks of nothing so little as lightly to discard the conquests of so many hard-fought fields. It therefore gladly utilizes all the material that Historical Theology brings it, accounting it, indeed, the very precipitate of the Christian consciousness of the past; but it does not use it crudely, or at first hand for itself, but accepts it as investigated, explained, and made available by the sister discipline of Historical Theology which alone can understand it or draw from it its true lessons. It certainly does not find in it its chief or primary source, and its relation to Historical Theology is, in consequence, far less close than that in which it stands to Exegetical Theology which is its true and especial handmaid. The independence of Exegetical Theology is seen in the fact that it does its work wholly without thought or anxiety as to the use that is to be made of its results; and that it furnishes a vastly larger body of data than can be utilized by any one discipline. It provides a body of historical, ethical, liturgic, ecclesiastical facts, as well as a body of theological facts. But so far as its theological facts are concerned, it provides them chiefly that they may be used by Systematic Theology as material out of which to build its system.

This is not to forget the claims of Biblical Theology. It is rather to emphasize its value, and to afford occasion for explaining its true place in the encyclopedia, and its true relations on the one side to Exegetical Theology, and on the other to Systematics — a matter which appears to be even yet imperfectly understood in some quarters. Biblical Theology is not a section of Historical Theology, although it must be studied in a historical spirit, and has a historical face; it is rather the ripest fruit of Exegetics, and Exegetics has not performed its full task until its scattered results in the way of theological data are gathered up into a full and articulated system of Biblical Theology. It is to be hoped that the time will come when no commentary will be considered complete until the capstone is placed upon its fabric by closing chapters gathering up into systematized exhibits, the unsystematized results of the continuous exegesis of the text, in the spheres of history, ethics, theology, and the like. The task of Biblical Theology, in a word, is the task of coördinating the scattered results of continuous exegesis into a concatenated whole, whether with reference to a single book of Scripture or to a body of related books or to the whole Scriptural fabric. Its chief object is not to find differences of conception between the various writers, though some recent students of the subject seem to think this is so much their duty, that when they cannot find differences they make them. It is to reproduce the theological thought of each writer or group of writers in the form in which it lay in their own minds, so that we may be enabled to look at all their theological statements at their angle, and to understand all their deliverances as modified and conditioned by their own point of view. Its exegetical value lies just in this circumstance, that it is only when we have thus concatenated an author's theological statements into a whole, that we can be sure that we understand them as he understood them in detail. A light is inevitably thrown back from Biblical Theology upon the separate theological deliverances as they occur in the text, such as subtly colors them, and often, for the first time, gives them to us in their true setting, and thus enables us to guard against perverting them when we adapt them to our use. This is a noble function, and could students of Biblical Theology only firmly grasp it, once for all, as their task, it would prevent this important science from being brought into contempt through a tendency to exaggerate differences in form of statement into divergences of view, and so to force the deliverances of each book into a strange and unnatural combination, in the effort to vindicate a function for this discipline.

The relation of Biblical Theology to Systematic Theology is based on a true view of its function. Systematic Theology is not founded on the direct and primary results of the exegetical process; it is founded on the final and complete results of exegesis as exhibited in Biblical Theology. Not exegesis itself, then, but Biblical Theology, provides the material for Systematics. Biblical Theology is not, then, a rival of Systematics; it is not even a parallel product of the same body of facts, provided by exegesis; it is the basis and source of Systematics. Systematic Theology is not a concatenation of the scattered theological data furnished by the exegetic process; it is the combination of the already concatenated data given to it by

Biblical Theology. It uses the individual data furnished by exegesis, in a word, not crudely, not independently for itself, but only after these data have been worked up into Biblical Theology and have received from it their final coloring and subtlest shades of meaning — in other words, only in their true sense, and after Exegetics has said its last word upon them. Just as we shall attain our finest and truest conception of the person and work of Christ, not by crudely trying to combine the scattered details of His life and teaching as given in our four Gospels into one patchwork life and account of His teaching; but far more rationally and far more successfully by first catching Matthew's full conception of Jesus, and then Mark's, and then Luke's, and then John's, and combining these four conceptions into one rounded whole: so we gain our truest Systematics not by at once working together the separate dogmatic statements in the Scriptures, but by combining them in their due order and proportion as they stand in the various theologies of the Scriptures. Thus we are enabled to view the future whole not only in its parts, but in the several combinations of the parts; and, looking at it from every side, to obtain a true conception of its solidity and strength, and to avoid all exaggeration or falsification of the details in giving them place in the completed structure. And thus we do not make our theology, according to our own pattern, as a mosaic, out of the fragments of the Biblical teaching; but rather look out from ourselves upon it as a great prospect, framed out of the mountains and plains of the theologies of the Scriptures, and strive to attain a point of view from which we can bring the whole landscape into our field of sight.

From this point of view, we find no difficulty in understanding the relation in which the several disciplines stand to one another, with respect to their contents. The material that Systematics draws from other than Biblical sources may be here left momentarily out of account. The actual contents of the theological results of the exegetic process, of Biblical Theology, and of Systematics, with this limitation, may be said to be the same. The immediate work of exegesis may be compared to the work of a recruiting officer: it draws out from the mass of mankind the men who are to constitute the army. Biblical Theology organizes these men into companies and regiments and corps, arranged in marching order and accoutered for service. Systematic Theology combines these companies and regiments and corps into an army — a single and unitary whole, determined by its own all-pervasive principle. It, too, is composed of men — the same men which were recruited by Exegetics; but it is composed of these men, not as individuals merely, but in their due relations to the other men of their companies and regiments and corps. The simile is far from a perfect one; but it may illustrate the mutual relations of the disciplines, and also, perhaps, suggest the historical element that attaches to Biblical Theology, and the element of all-inclusive systematization which is inseparable from Systematic Theology. It is just this element, determining the spirit and therefore the methods of Systematic Theology, which, along with its greater inclusiveness, discriminates it from all forms of Biblical Theology, the spirit of which is purely historical.

VI. The place that theology, as the scientific presentation of all the facts that are known concerning God and His relations, claims for itself within the circle of the sciences is an equally high one with that which it claims among the theological disciplines. Whether we consider the topics which it treats, in their dignity, their excellence, their grandeur; or the certainty with which its data can be determined; or the completeness with which its principles have been ascertained and its details classified; or the usefulness and importance of its discoveries: it is as far out of all comparison above all other sciences as the eternal health and destiny of the soul are of more value than this fleeting life in this world. It is not so above them, however, as not to be also a constituent member of the closely interrelated and mutually interacting organism of the sciences. There is no one of them all which is not, in some measure, touched and affected by it, or which is not in some measure included in it. As all nature, whether mental or material, may be conceived of as only the mode in which God manifests Himself, every science which investigates nature and ascertains its laws is occupied with the discovery of the modes of the divine action, and as such might be considered a branch of theology. And, on the other hand, as all nature, whether mental or material, owes its existence to God, every science which investigates nature and ascertains its laws, depends for its foundation upon that science which would make known what God is and what the relations are in which He stands to the work of His hands and in which they stand to Him; and must borrow from it those conceptions through which alone the material with which it deals can find its explanation or receive its proper significance.

Theology, thus, enters into the structure of every other science. Its closest relations are, no doubt, with the highest of the other sciences, ethics. Any discussion of our duty to God must rest on a knowledge of our relation to Him; and much of our duty to man is undiscoverable, save through knowledge of our common relation to the one God and Father of all, and one Lord the Redeemer of all, and one Spirit the Sanctifier of all — all of which it is the function of theology to supply. This fact is, of course, not fatal to the existence of a natural ethics; but an ethics independent of theological conceptions would be a meager thing indeed, while the theology of the Scriptural revelation for the first time affords a basis for ethical investigation at once broad enough and sure enough to raise that science to its true dignity. Accordingly, a purely natural ethics has always been an incomplete ethics even relatively to the less developed forms of ethics resting on a revealed basis. A careful student has recently told us, for example, that:

Between the ethics of pagan antiquity and that of the Old Testament there is a difference of the widest and most radical kind. There is no trace of gradual transition from the one to the other. That difference is first seen in the pagan conception of God and of man's ethical relation to Him. . . . It was essentially a morality between man and man. For where man's relation to a personal God is not apprehended, anything approaching an universal ethics is impossible, and only individual virtues can be manifested. Ethics was thus deprived of its unity. . . . Morality became but a catalogue of separate virtues, and was deprived of that penetrating bond of union which it receives when the realm of human personalities is bound by innumerable links to the great central personality, God.[4]

We must not, however, on the ground of this intimacy of relation, confound the two sciences of theology and ethics. Something like it in kind and approaching it in degree exists between theology and every other science, no one of which is so independent of it as not to touch and be touched by it. Something of theology is implicated in all metaphysics and physics alike. It alone can determine the origin of either matter or mind, or of the mystic powers that have been granted to them.[5] It alone can explain the nature of second causes and set the boundaries to their efficiency. It alone is competent to declare the meaning of the ineradicable persuasion of the human mind that its reason is right reason, its processes trustworthy, its intuitions true. All science without God is mutilated science, and no account of a single branch of knowledge can ever be complete until it is pushed back to find its completion and ground in Him. In the eloquent words of Dr. Pusey:

God alone *is* in Himself, and is the Cause and Upholder of everything to which He has given being. Every faculty of the mind is some reflection of His; every truth has its being from Him; every law of nature has the impress of His hand; everything beautiful has caught its light from His eternal beauty; every principle of goodness has its foundation in His attributes. . . . Without Him, in the region of thought, everything is dead; as without Him everything which is, would at once cease to be. All things must speak of God, refer to God, or they are atheistic. History, without God, is a chaos

---

[4] W. S. Bruce, " The Ethics of the Old Testament," 1895, pp. 12–14.

[5] Cf. the ground-texts which Professor Laidlaw has placed at the head of the first division of his " The Bible Doctrine of Man," 1895: " The truth concerning the soul can only be established by the word of God." — Plato, " Timæus," 72 D. " How can the knowledge of the substance of the rational soul be sought or had from philosophy? It must surely be derived from the same divine inspiration from which the substance of the soul first emanated." — Bacon, " De Augmentis Scientiarum," lib. iv. cap. iii. § 3.

without design, or end, or aim. Political Economy, without God, would be a selfish teaching about the acquisition of wealth, making the larger portion of mankind animate machines for its production; Physics, without God, would be but a dull inquiry into certain meaningless phenomena; Ethics, without God, would be a varying rule, without principle, or substance, or centre, or regulating hand; Metaphysics, without God, would make man his own temporary god, to be resolved, after his brief hour here, into the nothingness out of which he proceeded.[6]

It is thus as true of sciences as it is of creatures, that in Him they all live and move and have their being. The science of Him and His relations is the necessary ground of all science. All speculation takes us back to Him; all inquiry presupposes Him; and every phase of science consciously or unconsciously rests at every step on the science that makes Him known. Theology, thus, as the science which treats of God, lies at the root of all sciences. It is true enough that each could exist without it, in a sense and in some degree; but through it alone can any one of them reach its true dignity. Herein we see not only the proof of its greatness, but also the assurance of its permanence. " What so permeates all sections and subjects of human thought, has a deep root in human nature and an immense hold upon it. What so possesses man's mind that he cannot think at all without thinking of it, is so bound up with the very being of intelligence that ere it can perish, intellect must cease to be." [7]

It is only in theology, therefore, that the other sciences find their completion. Theology, formally speaking, is accordingly the apex of the pyramid of the sciences by which the structure is perfected. Its relation to the other sciences is, thus, in this broader sphere quite analogous to its relation to the other branches of the theological encyclopedia in that narrower sphere. All other sciences are subsidiary to it, and

[6] E. B. Pusey, " Collegiate and Professorial Teaching and Discipline," Oxford: Parker, 1854, pp. 215, 216.

[7] A. M. Fairbairn, " Theology as an Academic Discipline," in *The Contemporary Review,* li. 1887, p. 202.

it builds its fabric out of material supplied by them. Theology is the science which deals with the facts concerning God and His relations with the universe. Such facts include all the facts of nature and history: and it is the very function of the several sciences to supply these facts in scientific, that is, thoroughly comprehended form. Scientific theology thus stands at the head of the sciences as well as at the head of the theological disciplines. The several sciences deal each with its own material in an independent spirit and supply a multitude of results not immediately useful to theology. But so far as their results stand related to questions with which theology deals, they exist only to serve her. Dr. Flint well says:

The relevant data of natural theology are all the works of God in nature and providence, all the phenomena and laws of matter, mind, and history, — and these can only be thoroughly ascertained by the special sciences. The surest and most adequate knowledge of them is knowledge in the form called scientific, and therefore in this form the theologian must seek to know them. The sciences which deal with nature, mind, and history hold the same position towards natural theology which the disciplines that treat of the composition, genuineness, authenticity, text, development, etc., of the Scriptures do towards Biblical theology. They inform us, as it were, what is the true text and literal interpretation of the book of creation. Their conclusions are the premises, or at least the data, of the scientific natural theologian. All reasonings of his which disregard these data are *ipso facto* condemned. A conflict between the results of these sciences and the findings of natural theology is inconceivable. It would be a conflict between the data and conclusions of natural theology, and so equivalent for natural theology to self-contradiction. . . . The religion of the Bible . . . is but one of a multitude of religions which have left traces of themselves in documents, monuments, rites, creeds, customs, institutions, individual lives, social changes, etc.; and there is a theological discipline — comparative theology — which undertakes to disclose the spirit, delineate the character, trace the development, and exhibit the relations of all religions with the utmost attainable exactitude. Obviously the mass of data which this science has to collect, sift, and interpret is enormous. They can only be brought to light and set in their natural relationships by the labours of hosts of specialists of all kinds. . . . Christian dogmatics has to make use of the results of natural theology, Biblical theology, and comparative theology, and to raise them to a higher stage by a comprehensive synthesis which connects them with the person and work of Christ, as of Him in whom all spiritual truth is comprehended and all spiritual wants supplied.[8]

The essence of the matter is here admirably set forth, though as connected with some points of view which may require modification. It would seem to be a mistake, for example, to conceive of scientific theology as the immediate and direct synthesis of the three sources — Natural Theology, Biblical Theology, and Comparative Theology — so that it would be considered the product in like degree or even in similar manner of the three. All three furnish data for the completed structure; but if what has been said in an earlier connection has any validity, Natural and Comparative Theology should stand in a somewhat different relation to Scientific Theology from that which Biblical Theology occupies — a relation not less organic indeed, but certainly less direct. The true representation seems to be that Scientific Theology is related to the natural and historical sciences, not immediately and independently for itself, but only indirectly, that is, through the mediation of the preliminary theological discipline of Apologetics. The work of Apologetics in its three branches of Philosophical, Psychological, and Historical, results not only in presenting the Bible to the theological student, but also in presenting to him God, Religion, and Christianity. And in so doing, it supplies him with the total material of Natural and Comparative Theology as well as with the foundation on which exegesis is to raise the structure of Biblical Theology. The materials thus provided Scientific Theology utilizes, just as it utilizes the results of exegesis through Biblical Theology, and the results of the age-long life of men under Christianity through Historical Theology. Scientific Theology rests, therefore, most directly on the results of Biblical exegesis as pro-

[8] Article "Theology," in the "Encyclopædia Britannica," ninth edition, xxiii. 1888, pp. 264 f.

vided in Biblical Theology; but avails itself likewise of all the material furnished by all the preceding disciplines, and, in the results of Apologetics as found in Natural Theology and Comparative Theology, of all the data bearing on its problems, supplied by all the sciences. But it does not make its direct appeal crudely and independently to these sciences, any more than to exegesis and Christian history, but as it receives the one set of results from the hands of Exegetics and Historics, so it receives the others from the hand of Apologetics.[9] Systematic Theology is fundamentally one of the theological disciplines, and bears immediate relation only to its sister disciplines; it is only through them that it reaches further out and sets its roots in more remote sources of information.

VII. The interpretation of a written document, intended to convey a plain message, is infinitely easier than the interpretation of the teaching embodied in facts themselves. It is therefore that systematic treatises on the several sciences are written. Theology has, therefore, an immense advantage over all other sciences, inasmuch as it is more an inductive study of facts conveyed in a written revelation, than an inductive study of facts as conveyed in life. It was, consequently, the first-born of the sciences. It was the first to reach relative completeness. And it is to-day in a state far nearer perfection than any other science. This is not, however, to deny that it is

[9] It may be useful to seek to give a rough graphic representation of the relations of Systematic Theology as thus far outlined:

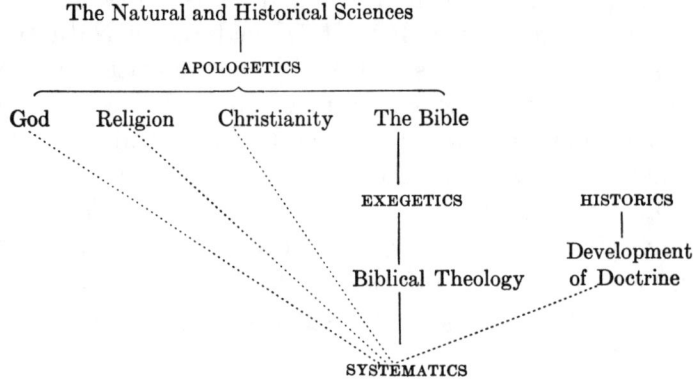

The Natural and Historical Sciences
|
APOLOGETICS

God   Religion   Christianity   The Bible
|
EXEGETICS   HISTORICS
| |
                   Development
Biblical Theology of Doctrine
|
SYSTEMATICS

a progressive science. In exactly the same sense in which any other science is progressive, this is progressive. It is not meant that new revelations are to be expected of truth which has not been before within the reach of man. There is a vast difference between the progress of a science and increase in its material. All the facts of psychology, for instance, have been in existence so long as mind itself has existed; and the progress of this science has been dependent on the progressive discovery, understanding, and systematization of these facts. All the facts of theology have, in like manner, been within the reach of man for nearly two millenniums; and the progress of theology is dependent on men's progress in gathering, defining, mentally assimilating, and organizing these facts into a correlated system. So long as revelation was not completed, the progressive character of theology was secured by the progress in revelation itself. And since the close of the canon of Scripture, the intellectual realization and definition of the doctrines revealed in it, in relation to one another, have been, as a mere matter of fact, a slow but ever advancing process.

The affirmation that theology has been a progressive science is no more, then, than to assert that it is a science that has had a history — and a history which can be and should be genetically traced and presented. First, the objective side of Christian truth was developed: pressed on the one side by the crass monotheism of the Jews and on the other by the coarse polytheism of the heathen, and urged on by its own internal need of comprehending the sources of its life, Christian theology first searched the Scriptures that it might understand the nature and modes of existence of its God and the person of its divine Redeemer. Then, more and more conscious of itself, it more and more fully wrought out from those same Scriptures a guarded expression of the subjective side of its faith; until through throes and conflicts it has built up the system which we all inherit. Thus the body of Christian truth has come down to us in the form of an organic growth; and we can conceive of the completed structure as the ripened fruit of the ages, as truly as we can think of it as the perfected result of the exegetical discipline. As it has come into our possession by this historic process, there is no reason that we can assign why it should not continue to make for itself a history. We do not expect the history of theology to close in our own day. However nearly completed our realization of the body of truth may seem to us to be; however certain it is that the great outlines are already securely laid and most of the details soundly discovered and arranged; no one will assert that every detail is as yet perfected, and we are all living in the confidence so admirably expressed by old John Robinson, "that God hath more truth yet to break forth from His holy Word." Just because God gives us the truth in single threads which we must weave into the reticulated texture, all the threads are always within our reach, but the finished texture is ever and will ever continue to be before us until we dare affirm that there is no truth in the Word which we have not perfectly apprehended, and no relation of these truths as revealed which we have not perfectly understood, and no possibility in clearness of presentation which we have not attained.

The conditions of progress in theology are clearly discernible from its nature as a science. The progressive men in any science are the men who stand firmly on the basis of the already ascertained truth. The condition of progress in building the structures of those great cathedrals whose splendid piles glorify the history of art in the Middle Ages, was that each succeeding generation should build upon the foundations laid by its predecessor. If each architect had begun by destroying what had been accomplished by his forerunners, no cathedral would ever have been raised.[10] The railroad is pushed across the continent by the simple process of laying each rail at the end of the line already laid. The prerequisite of all progress is a clear discrimination which as frankly accepts the limitations set by the truth already discovered, as it rejects

[10] "Commend me," says Coleridge, "to the Irish architect who took out the foundation stone to repair the roof" ("Anima Poetæ," 1895, p. 139). Such architects seem to be rather numerous in the sphere of theology.

the false and bad. Construction is not destruction; neither is it the outcome of destruction. There are abuses no doubt to be reformed; errors to correct; falsehoods to cut away. But the history of progress in every science and no less in theology, is a story of impulses given, corrected, and assimilated. And when they have been once corrected and assimilated, these truths are to remain accepted. It is then time for another impulse, and the condition of all further progress is to place ourselves in this well-marked line of growth. Astronomy, for example, has had such a history; and there are now some indisputable truths in astronomy, as, for instance, the rotundity of the earth and the central place of the sun in our system. I do not say that these truths are undisputed; probably nothing is any more undisputed in astronomy, or any other science, than in theology. At all events he who wishes, may read the elaborate arguments of the "Zetetic" philosophers, as they love to call themselves, who in this year of grace are striving to prove that the earth is flat and occupies the center of our system. Quite in the same spirit, there are "Zetetic" theologians who strive with similar zeal and acuteness to overturn the established basal truths of theology — which, however, can nevermore be shaken; and we should give about as much ear to them in the one science as in the other. It is utter folly to suppose that progress can be made otherwise than by placing ourselves in the line of progress; and if the temple of God's truth is ever to be completely built, we must not spend our efforts in digging at the foundations which have been securely laid in the distant past, but must rather give our best efforts to rounding the arches, carving the capitals, and fitting in the fretted roof. What if it is not ours to lay foundations? Let us rejoice that that work has been done! Happy are we if our God will permit us to bring a single capstone into place. This fabric is not a house of cards to be built and blown down again a hundred times a day, as the amusement of our idle hours: it is a miracle of art to which all ages and lands bring their varied tribute. The subtle Greek laid the foundations; the law-loving Roman raised high the walls; and all the perspicuity of France and ideality of Germany and systematization of Holland and deep sobriety of Britain have been expended in perfecting the structure; and so it grows.

We have heard much in these last days of the phrase "progressive orthodoxy," and in somewhat strange connections. Nevertheless, the phrase itself is not an inapt description of the building of this theological house. Let us assert that the history of theology has been and ever must be a progressive orthodoxy. But let us equally loudly assert that progressive orthodoxy and retrogressive heterodoxy can scarcely be convertible terms. Progressive orthodoxy implies that first of all we are orthodox, and secondly that we are progressively orthodox, that is, that we are ever growing more and more orthodox as more and more truth is being established. This has been and must be the history of the advance of every science, and not less, among them, of the science of theology. Justin Martyr, champion of the orthodoxy of his day, held a theory of the intertrinitarian relationship which became heterodoxy after the Council of Nicea; the ever struggling Christologies of the earlier ages were forever set aside by the Chalcedon Fathers; Augustine determined for all time the doctrine of grace, Anselm the doctrine of the atonement, Luther the doctrine of forensic justification. In any progressive science, the amount of departure from accepted truth which is possible to the sound thinker becomes thus ever less and less, in proportion as investigation and study result in the progressive establishment of an ever increasing number of facts. The physician who would bring back to-day the medicine of Galen would be no more mad than the theologian who would revive the theology of Clement of Alexandria. Both were men of light and leading in their time; but their time is past, and it is the privilege of the child of to-day to know a sounder physic and a sounder theology than the giants of that far past yesterday could attain. It is of the very essence of our position at the end of the ages that we are ever more and more hedged around with ascertained facts, the discovery and establishment of which constitute the very essence of progress. Progress brings increasing limitation, just because it brings increasing knowledge. And as the orthodox man is he that teaches no other doctrine than that which has been established as true, the progressively orthodox man is he who is quick to perceive, admit, and condition all his reasoning by all the truth down to the latest, which has been established as true.

VIII. When we speak of progress our eyes are set upon a goal. And in calling theology a progressive science we unavoidably raise the inquiry, what the end and purpose is towards an ever increasing fitness to secure which it is continually growing. Its own completeness and perfecting as a science — as a department of knowledge — is naturally the proximate goal towards which every science tends. And when we consider the surpassing glory of the subject-matter with which theology deals, it would appear that if ever science existed for its own sake, this might surely be true of this science. The truths concerning God and His relations are, above all comparison, in themselves the most worthy of all truths of study and examination. Yet we must vindicate a further goal for the advance of theology and thus contend for it that it is an eminently practical science. The contemplation and exhibition of Christianity as truth, is far from the end of the matter. This truth is specially communicated by God for a purpose, for which it is admirably adapted. That purpose is to save and sanctify the soul. And the discovery, study, and systematization of the truth is in order that, firmly grasping it and thoroughly comprehending it in all its reciprocal relations, we may be able to make the most efficient use of it for its holy purpose. Well worth our most laborious study, then, as it is, for its own sake as mere truth, it becomes not only absorbingly interesting, but inexpressibly precious to us when we bear in mind that the truth with which we thus deal constitutes, as a whole, the engrafted Word that is able to save our souls. The task of thoroughly exploring the pages of revelation, soundly gathering from them their treasures of theological teaching, and carefully fitting these into their due places in a system whereby they may be preserved from misunderstanding, perversion, and misuse, and given a new power to convince the understanding, move the heart, and quicken the will, becomes thus a holy duty to our own and our brothers' souls as well as an eager pleasure of our intellectual nature.

That the knowledge of the truth is an essential prerequisite to the production of those graces and the building up of those elements of a sanctified character for the production of which each truth is especially adapted, probably few will deny: but surely it is equally true that the clearer, fuller, and more discriminating this knowledge is, the more certainly and richly will it produce its appropriate effect; and in this is found a most complete vindication of the duty of systematizing the separate elements of truth into a single soundly concatenated whole, by which the essential nature of each is made as clear as it can be made to human apprehension. It is not a matter of indifference, then, how we apprehend and systematize this truth. On the contrary, if we misconceive it in its parts or in its relations, not only do our views of truth become confused and erroneous, but also our religious life becomes dwarfed or contorted. The character of our religion is, in a word, determined by the character of our theology: and thus the task of the systematic theologian is to see that the relations in which the separate truths actually stand are rightly conceived, in order that they may exert their rightful influence on the development of the religious life. As no truth is so insignificant as to have no place in the development of our religious life, so no truth is so unimportant that we dare neglect it or deal deceitfully with it in adjusting it into our system. We are smitten with a deadly fear on the one side, lest by fitting them into a system of our own devising, we cut from them just the angles by which they were intended to lay hold of the hearts of men: but on the other side, we are filled with a holy confidence that, by allowing them to frame themselves into their own system as indicated by their own natures — as the stones in Solomon's temple were cut each for its place — we shall make each available for all men, for just the place in the saving process for which it was divinely framed and divinely given.

These theoretical considerations are greatly strengthened by the historical fact, that throughout all the ages every advance in the scientific statement of theological truth has been made in response to a practical demand, and has been made in a distinctly practical interest. We wholly misconceive the facts if we imagine that the development of systematic theology has been the work of cold, scholastic recluses, intent only upon intellectual subtleties. It has been the work of the best heart of the whole Church driving on and utilizing in its practical interests, the best brain. The true state of the case could not be better expressed than it is by Professor Auguste Sabatier, when he tells us that:

The promulgation of each dogma has been imposed on the Church by some practical necessity. It has always been to bring to an end some theological controversy which was in danger of provoking a schism, to respond to attacks or accusations which it would have been dangerous to permit to acquire credit, that the Church has moved in a dogmatic way. . . . Nothing is more mistaken than to represent the Fathers of the Councils, or the members of the Synods as theoricians, or even as professional theologians, brought together in conference by speculative zeal alone, in order to resolve metaphysical enigmas. They were men of action, not of speculation; courageous priests and pastors who understood their mission, like soldiers in open battle, and whose first care was to save their Church, its life, its unity, its honor — ready to die for it as one dies for his country.[11]

In quite similar manner one of the latest critics (M. Pannier) of Calvin's doctrinal work feels moved to bear his testimony to the practical purpose which ruled over the development of his system. He says:

In the midst, as at the outset of his work, it was the practical preoccupations of living faith which guided him, and never a vain desire for pure speculation. If this practical need led [in the successive editions of the " Institutes "] to some new theories, to many fuller expositions of principles, this was not only because he now

[11] A. Sabatier, " Esquisse d'une philosophie de la religion," 1897, p. 306; cf. " The Vitality of Christian Dogmas," London, 1898, pp. 31–33.

desired his book to help students of theology to interpret Scripture better — it was because, with his systematic genius, Calvin understood all that which, from the point of view of their application, ideas gain severally in force by forming a complete whole around one master thought.[12]

Wrought out thus in response to practical needs, the ever growing body of scientific theology has worked its way among men chiefly by virtue of its ever increasing power of meeting their spiritual requirements. The story of the victory of Augustinianism in Southern Gaul, as brought out by Professor Arnold of Breslau, is only a typical instance of what each age has experienced in its own way, and with its own theological advances. He warns us that the victory of Augustinianism is not to be accounted for by the learning or dialectic gifts of Augustine, nor by the vigorous propaganda kept up in Gaul by the African refugees, nor by the influence of Cæsarius, deservedly great as that was, nor by the pressure brought to bear from Rome: but rather by the fullness of its provision for the needs of the soul.

These were better met by Christianity than by heathenism; by Catholicism than by Arianism; by the enthusiasm of asceticism than by the lukewarm worldliness of the old opponents of monachism: and they found more strength and consolation in the fundamental Augustinian conception of divine grace, than in the paltry mechanism of the synergistic moralism.[13]

Here is the philosophy, *sub specie temporis,* of the advance of doctrinal development; and it all turns on the progressively growing fitness of the system of doctrine to produce its practical fruits.[14]

[12] Jacques Pannier, "Le Témoignage du Saint-Esprit," 1893, p. 79.

[13] C. F. Arnold, "Caesarius von Arelate," 1894, p. 343.

[14] It is only another way of saying this to say with Professor W. M. Ramsay, when speaking of another of the great controversies (*The Expositor,* January, 1896 [Fifth Series, iii.], p. 52): "Difficult, however, as it is to appreciate the real character of the Arian controversy as a question of social life, on the whole we gather, I think, that the progressive tendencies were on the side of Basil, and acquiescence in the existing standard of

It may possibly be thought, however, that these lessons are ill-applied to systematic theology properly so called: that it may be allowed indeed that the separate truths of religion make themselves felt in the life of men, but scarcely that the systematic knowledge of them is of any value for the religious life. Surely, however, we may very easily fall into error here. We do not possess the separate truths of religion in the abstract: we possess them only in their relations, and we do not properly know any one of them — nor can it have its full effect on our life — except as we know it in its relations to other truths, that is, as systematized. What we do not know, in this sense, systematically, we rob of half its power on our conduct; unless, indeed, we are prepared to argue that a truth has effect on us in proportion as it is unknown, rather than in proportion as it is known. To which may be added that when we do not know a body of doctrine systematically, we are sure to misconceive the nature of more or fewer of its separate elements; and to fancy, in the words of Dr. Charles Hodge, " that that is true which a more systematic knowledge would show us to be false," so that " our religious belief and therefore our religious life would become deformed and misshapen." Let us once more, however, strengthen our theoretical opinion by testimony: and for this let us appeal to the witness of a recent French writer who supports his own judgment by that of several of the best informed students of current French Protestantism.[15] Amid much external activity of Christian work, M. Arnaud tells us, no one would dare say that the life lived with Christ in God is flourishing in equal measure: and his conclusion is that, " in order to be a strong and living Christian, it does not suffice to submit our heart and will to the gospel: we must submit also our mind and our reason." " The doctrines of Christianity," he adds:

---

morality characterized the Arian point of view. The ' Orthodox ' Church was still the champion of higher aspirations, and Basil, however harsh he was to all who differed from him, was an ennobling and upward-struggling force in the life of his time."

[15] Arnaud, " Manuel de dogmatique," 1890, p. ix.

The doctrines of Christianity have just as much right to be believed as its duties have to be practised, and it is not permissible to accept these and reject those. In neglecting to inquire with care into the Biblical verities, and to assimilate them by reflection, the Christian loses part of his virtue, the preacher part of his force; both build their house on the sand or begin at the top; they deprive themselves of the precious lights which can illuminate and strengthen their faith, and fortify them against the frivolous or learned unbelief as well as against the aberrations of false individualism, that are so diffused in our day.

In support of this judgment he quotes striking passages, among others, from Messrs. F. Bonifas and Ch. Bois. The former says: [16]

What strikes me to-day is the incomplete and fragmentary character of our faith: the lack of precision in our Christian conceptions; a certain ignorance of the wonderful things which God has done for us and which He has revealed to us for the salvation and nourishment of our souls. I discover the traces of this ignorance in our preaching as well as in our daily life. And here is one of the causes of the feebleness of spiritual life in the bosom of our flocks and among ourselves. To these fluid Christian convictions, there necessarily corresponds a lowered Christian life.

Mr. Bois similarly says: [17]

There does not at present exist among us a strongly concatenated body of doctrine, possessing the conscience and determining the will. We have convictions, no doubt, and even strong and active convictions, but they are, if I may so speak, isolated and merely juxtaposed in the mind, without any deep bond uniting them into an organism. . . . Upon several fundamental points, even among believers, there is a vagueness, an indetermination, which leave access open to every fluctuation and to the most unexpected mixtures of belief. Contradictory elements often live together and struggle with one another, even in the most positively convinced, without their suspecting the enmity of the guests they have received into their thought. It is astonishing to observe the strange amalgams which

[16] "De la valeur religieuse des doctrines chrétiennes," p. 14.
[17] *Revue théologique* de Montauban, 13e Année, p. 14.

spring up and acclimate themselves in the minds of the young theological generations, which have been long deprived of the strong
discipline of the past. This incoherence of ideas produces weakness
and danger elsewhere also, besides in the sphere of doctrine. It is
impossible but that spiritual life and practical activity should sustain also serious damage from this intellectual anarchy.

Cannot we see in the state of French Protestantism as depicted in these extracts, a warning to ourselves, among whom
we may observe the beginnings of the same doctrinal anarchy?
And shall we not, at least, learn this much: that doctrine is in
order to life, and that the study of doctrine must be prosecuted in a spirit which would see its end in the correction and
edification of life? Shall we not, as students of doctrine, listen
devoutly to the words of one of the richest writers on experimental religion of our generation,[18] when he tells us that

Living knowledge of our living Lord, and of our need of Him,
and of our relations to Him for peace, life, testimony, service, consistency, is given by the Holy Comforter alone. But it is given by
Him in the great rule of His dealings with man, only through the
channel of doctrine, of revealed, recorded, authenticated truth concerning the Lord of life.

And shall we not catch the meaning of the illustrations which
he adds:

Does the happy soul, happy because brought to the " confidence
of self-despair," and to a sight of the foundation of all peace, find
itself saying, " O Lamb of God, I come," and know that it falls,
never to be cast out, into the embraces of ever-living love? Every
element in that profound experience of restful joy has to do with
doctrine, applied by the Spirit. " O Lamb of God " would be a meaningless incantation were it not for the precious and most definite
doctrine of the sacrifice of propitiation and peace. That I *may*
" come just as I am " is a matter of pure Divine information. My
emotions, my deepest and most awful convictions, without such
information, say the opposite; my instinct is to cry, " Depart, for

[18] Principal H. C. G. Moule, in his paper entitled " On the Relations
Between Doctrine and Life," printed in " The Church and her Doctrine " (New
York: The Christian Literature Co., 1892), pp. 185–188.

I am a sinful man." The blessed doctrine, not my reveries, says, " Nay; He was wounded for thy transgressions; come unto Him." . . . And when [one] . . . draws towards the journey's end, and exchanges the trials of the pilgrimage for the last trial, " the river that hath no bridge," why does he address himself in peace to die, this man who has been taught the evil of his own heart and the holiness of the Judge of all? It is because of doctrine. He knows the covenant of peace, and the Mediator of it. He knows, and he knows it through revealed doctrine only, that to depart is to be with Christ, and is far better. He knows that the sting of death is sin, and the strength of sin is the law. But he knows, with the same certainty, that God giveth us the victory through our Lord Jesus Christ; and that His sheep shall never perish; and that He will raise up again at the last day him that has come to God through Him. All this is doctrine. It is made to live in the man by the Holy Ghost given to him. But it is in itself creed, not life. It is revealed information.

If such be the value and use of doctrine, the systematic theologian is preëminently a preacher of the gospel; and the end of his work is obviously not merely the logical arrangement of the truths which come under his hand, but the moving of men, through their power, to love God with all their hearts and their neighbors as themselves; to choose their portion with the Saviour of their souls; to find and hold Him precious; and to recognize and yield to the sweet influences of the Holy Spirit whom He has sent. With such truth as this he will not dare to deal in a cold and merely scientific spirit, but will justly and necessarily permit its preciousness and its practical destination to determine the spirit in which he handles it, and to awaken the reverential love with which alone he should investigate its reciprocal relations. For this he needs to be suffused at all times with a sense of the unspeakable worth of the revelation which lies before him as the source of his material, and with the personal bearings of its separate truths on his own heart and life; he needs to have had and to be having a full, rich, and deep religious experience of the great doctrines with which he deals; he needs to be living close to his God, to be resting always on the bosom of his Redeemer, to be filled at all times with the manifest influences of the Holy Spirit. The student of systematic theology needs a very sensitive religious nature, a most thoroughly consecrated heart, and an outpouring of the Holy Ghost upon him, such as will fill him with that spiritual discernment, without which all native intellect is in vain. He needs to be not merely a student, not merely a thinker, not merely a systematizer, not merely a teacher — he needs to be like the beloved disciple himself in the highest, truest, and holiest sense, a divine.

IV

THE TASK AND METHOD
OF SYSTEMATIC THEOLOGY

THE TASK AND METHOD
OF SYSTEMATIC THEOLOGY [1]

By "Systematic Theology" is meant that department or section of theological science which is concerned with setting forth systematically, that is to say, as a concatenated whole, what is known concerning God. Other departments or sections of theological science undertake other tasks. Whether such a being as God exists needs to be ascertained, and if such a being exists, whether He is knowable; whether such creatures as men are capable of knowing Him, and, if so, what sources of information concerning Him are accessible. This is the task of apologetical theology. These matters being determined, it is necessary to draw out from the sources of information concerning God which are accessible to us, all that can be known of God. This is the task of exegetical theology. A critical survey of previous attempts to draw from the sources of information concerning God what may be known of God, with an estimate of the results of these attempts and of their testing in life, is next incumbent on us. This is the task of historical theology. Finally we must inquire into the use of this knowledge of God and the ways in which it may be best applied to human needs. This is the task of practical theology. Among these various departments or sections of theological science there is obviously place for, or rather there is positively demanded, yet another, the task of which is to set forth in systematic formulation the results of the investigations of exegetical theology, clarified and enforced by the investigations of historical theology, which are to be applied by practical theology to the needs of man. Here the warrant of systematic theology, its task, and its encyclopedic place are at once exhibited. It is the business

[1] Reprinted from *The American Journal of Theology*, xiv. 1910, pp. 192–205.

of systematic theology to take the knowledge of God supplied
to it by apologetical, exegetical, and historical theology, scrutinize it with a view to discovering the inner relations of its several elements, and set it forth in a systematic presentation,
that is to say, as an organic whole, so that it may be grasped
and held in its entirety, in the due relation of its parts to one
another and to the whole, and with a just distribution of emphasis among the several items of knowledge which combine
to make up the totality of our knowledge of God.

It is clear at once that "systematic theology" forms the
central, or perhaps we may better say the culminating, department of theological science. It is the goal to which apologetical, exegetical, and historical theology lead up; and it provides
the matter which practical theology employs. What is most
important in the knowledge of God — which is what theology
is — is, of course, just the knowledge of God; and that is what
systematic theology sets forth. Apologetical theology puts us
in the way of obtaining knowledge of God. Exegetical theology
gives us this knowledge in its *disjecta membra*. Historical
theology makes us aware how it has been apprehended and
transmuted into life. Practical theology teaches us how to
propagate it in the world. It is systematic theology which
spreads it before us in the form most accessible to our modes
of conception, pours it, so to speak, into the molds of our
minds, and makes it our assured possession that we may thoroughly understand and utilize it. There is nothing strange,
therefore, in the common manner of speech by which systematic theology absorbs into itself all theology. In point of fact,
theology, as the science of God, comes to itself only in systematic theology; and if we set systematic theology over against
other theological disciplines as a separable department of
theological science, this is not that we divide the knowledge
of God up among these departments, retaining only some of
it — perhaps a small or a relatively unimportant portion — for
systematic theology; but only that we trace the process by
which the knowledge of God is ascertained, clarified, and ordered, up through the several stages of the dealing of the

human mind with it until at last, in systematic theology, it stands before our eyes in complete formulation.

The choice of the term " systematic theology " to designate this department of theological science has been made the occasion of some criticism, and its employment has been accompanied by some abuse. It is, no doubt, capable of being misunderstood and misused, as what term is not? It ought to be unnecessary to explain that its employment is not intended to imply that other departments of theological science are prosecuted in an unsystematic manner, that is to say, in a disorderly way and to no safe results. Nor ought it to be necessary to protest against advantage being taken of the breadth of the term " systematic," in its popular usage, to subsume under it a series of incongruous disciplines which have nothing in common except that they are all systematically pursued. What the term naturally designates is that department of theological science in which the knowledge of God is presented as a concatenated system of truth; and it is not merely the natural but the perfectly explicit and probably the best designation of this department of theological science. At all events none of its synonyms which have from time to time been in use — such as theoretical, thetical, methodical, scholastic, didactic, dogmatic theology — seems to possess any advantage over it.

The most commonly employed of these synonyms, since its introduction by Lucas Friedrich Reinhard in his " Synopsis theologicae dogmaticae," 1660, has been " dogmatic theology." This designation differs from " systematic theology " by laying stress upon the authority which attaches to the several doctrines brought together in the presentation, rather than upon the presentation of them in a system. A dogma is, briefly, an established truth, authoritative and not to be disputed. The ground of its authoritativeness is indifferent to the term itself, and will vary with the point of view of the dogmatician. The Romanist will find it in the decrees of the Church, by which the several dogmas are established. The Protestant will find it in the declarations of Scripture: " Verbum Dei," say the

Smalkald Articles, " condit articulos fidei, et praeterea nemo, ne angelus quidem." " Moderns " will attenuate it into whatever general considerations exist to commend the propositions in question to our credit, and will not pause until they have transmuted dogmas into — to put it shortly — just our " religious beliefs." " A dogma," says Dr. A. J. Headlam, " means a truth to be believed "; and it is the task of dogmatics, according to him, " to investigate, to expound, and to systematize those truths about God and human destiny, whether derived from nature or revelation, which should be believed " — a definition which, if taken literally, might seem to imply that there are some " truths " about God and human destiny — whether derived from nature or from revelation — which should not be believed. This ambiguity in the connotation of the term " dogma " is fatal to the usefulness of its derivative " dogmatic " as a designation of a department of theological science. It undertakes to tell us nothing of the department to which it is applied but the nature of the elements with which it deals; and it leaves us in uncertainty what the nature of these elements is, whether established truths or only "religious beliefs."

" Systematic theology " is attended with no such drawbacks. It properly describes the department to which it is attached, according to its own nature: it is the department in which the truths concerning God, given to us by the other departments of theological science, are systematized and presented in their proper relations to one another and to the whole of which they form parts. The authority of the truths with which it deals does not constitute its peculiarity as a department of theological science. These truths were just as authoritative as presented by exegetical theology one by one to our separate consideration, as when presented by systematic theology to our view in their concatenation with one another into a consistent whole. Their authority was not bestowed on them by their systematization; and they do not wait until presented by systematic theology to acquire authority. What constitutes the peculiarity of this department of theological science is that in it these truths are presented not one by one in isolation, but in a mutually related body — in a system. What more truly descriptive name for it could be invented than just " systematic theology "?

There are some, no doubt, to whom it may seem presumptuous to attempt to systematize our knowledge of God. If we possess any knowledge of God at all, however, the attempt to systematize it is a necessity of the human spirit. If we know so much as two facts concerning God, the human mind is incapable of holding these facts apart; it must contemplate them in relation to one another. Systematization is only a part of the irrepressible effort of the intelligence to comprehend the facts presented to it, an effort which the intelligence can escape only by ceasing to be intelligence. It may systematize well, or ill; but systematize it must whenever it holds together, in its unitary grasp, more facts than one. Wherever God is in any degree known by a being of a systematically working mind, therefore, there is a theology in the express sense of that word, that is, a " systematic theology." Only the atheist or the agnostic on the one side, the idiot or the lunatic on the other, can be without such a theology. If there is a God; if anything whatever is known of this God; if the being possessing this knowledge is capable of orderly thought — a theology in this sense is inevitable. It is but the reflection in the orderly working intelligence of God perceived as such; and it exists, therefore, wherever God is perceived and recognized. Doubt and hesitation before the task of systematizing our knowledge of God — be that knowledge great or small — is therefore not an effect of reverence, but an outgrowth of that agnostic temper which lurks behind much modern thinking.

The leaven of agnosticism underlying much of modern thought to which allusion has just been made, manifests itself more distinctly in the continuous attempt, which is more or less deliberately made, to shift the object of the knowledge which systematic theology systematizes from God to something else, deemed more capable of being really known by or more accessible to such beings as men. Theology, *ex vi verbi,* is the

systematized knowledge of God; and if God exists and any
knowledge of Him whatever is accessible to us, there must be
such a thing as a systematic knowledge of Him, and it would
seem that this would be the proper connotation of the term
"theology." Nevertheless, we are repeatedly being told that
theology is not the science of God, its object-matter being God
in His existence and activities, but the science of religion or
of faith, its object-matter being the religious phenomena
manifested by humanity at large, or observable in the souls of
believers. A whole generation of theologians, having the courage of their convictions, accordingly almost ceased to speak of
"systematic theology," preferring some such name as the
"science of faith" (*Glaubenslehre*). It was Schleiermacher, of
course, who gave this subjective twist to what he still spoke of
as "Dogmatics." Dogmas to him were no longer authoritative
propositions concerning God, but "conceptions of the states
of the Christian religious consciousness, set forth in formal
statement"; and dogmatics was to him accordingly nothing
more than the systematic presentation of the body of such
dogmas in vogue in any given church at any given time. Accordingly he classified it frankly, along with "Church Statistics," under the caption of "The Historical Knowledge of the
Present Situation of the Church." Undoubtedly it is very desirable to know what the Church at large, or any particular
branch of the Church, believes at any given stage of its development. But this helps us to a better knowledge of the Church,
not of God; and by what right the formulated results of such a
historical inquiry can be called "dogmatics" or "systematic
theology" *simpliciter* and not rather, historically, "the dogmatic system of the German Lutheran Church in the year
1821," or "the doctrinal belief of the American Baptists of
1910," it would be difficult to explain. The matter is not in
principle altered if the end set before us is to delineate, not the
doctrinal beliefs of a particular church at a particular time, but
the religious conceptions of humanity at large. We are still
moving in the region of history, and the results of our researches will be that we shall know better, not God, but man

— man in his religious nature and in the products of his religious activities. After all, the science of religion is something radically different from systematic theology. We cannot thus lightly renounce the knowledge of the most important object of knowledge in the whole compass of knowledge. Over against the world and all that is in the world, including man and all that is in man, and all that is the product of man's highest activities, intellectual and, in the noblest sense the word may bear, spiritual, there after all stands God; and He — He Himself, not our thought about Him or our beliefs concerning Him, but He Himself — is the object of our highest knowledge. And to know Him is not merely the highest exercise of the human intellect; it is the indispensable complement of the circle of human science, which, without the knowledge of God, is fatally incomplete. It was not without reason that Augustine renounced the knowledge of all else but God and the soul; and that Calvin declares the knowledge of God and ourselves the sum of all useful knowledge. Without the knowledge of God it is not too much to say we know nothing rightly, so that the renunciation of the knowledge of God carries with it renunciation of all right knowledge. It is this knowledge of God which is designated by the appropriate term " theology," and it, as the science of God, stands over against all other sciences, each having its own object, determining for each its own peculiar subject-matter.

Theology being, thus, the systematized knowledge of God, the determining question which divides theologies concerns the sources from which this knowledge of God is derived. It may be agreed, indeed, that the sole source of all possible knowledge of God is revelation. God is a person; and a person is known only as he expresses himself, which is as much as to say only as he makes himself known, reveals himself. But this agreement is only formal. So soon as it is asked how God reveals Himself, theology is set over against theology in ineradicable opposition. The hinge on which the controversy particularly turns is the question whether God has revealed Himself only in works, or also in word: ultimately whether

He has made Himself known only in the natural or also in a supernatural revelation. Answer this question as we may, we shall still have a theology, but according to our answer, so will be our theology, not merely in its contents but in its very method. By revelation may be meant nothing more than the evolution of religious ideas in the age-long thinking of the race, conceived (whether pantheistically or more or less theistically) as the expression of the divine mind in the forms of human thought. In that case, the work of systematic theology follows the lines of the psychology and phenomenology of religion; its task is to gather out and to cast into a systematic statement the metaphysical implications of the results of these departments of investigation. Or revelation may be summed up in the impression made by the phenomenon of Jesus on the minds of His believing followers. Then, what theology has to do is to unfold the ideas of God which are involved in this experience. Or, again, revelation may be thought to lie in a series of extraordinary occurrences, conceived as redemptive acts on the part of God, inserted into the course of ordinary history. In that case the task of theology is to draw out the implications of this series of extraordinary events in their sequence, and in their culmination in the apparition of Christ. Or, once more, revelation may be held to include the direct communication of truth through chosen organs of the divine Spirit. Then the fundamental task of theology becomes the ascertainment, formulation, and systematization of the truth thus communicated, and if this truth comes to it fixed in an authoritative written record, it is obvious that its task is greatly facilitated. These are not questions raised by systematic theology; nor does it belong to systematic theology to determine them. That task has already been performed for it by the precedent department of theological science which we call apologetics, which thus determines the whole structure and contents of systematic theology. The task of systematic theology is not to validate the reality, or to define the nature, or to determine the method of revelation; nor, indeed, even to ascertain the truths communicated by revelation; but to systematize these truths when placed in its hands by the precedent disciplines of apologetical, exegetical, and historical theology.

The question of the sources of our knowledge of God culminates obviously in the question of the Scriptures. Do the Scriptures contain a special revelation of God; or are they merely a record of religious aspirations and attainments of men — under whatever (more or less) divine leading? Are they themselves the documented revelation of God to man; or do they merely contain the record of the effect on men of the revelation of God made in a series of redemptive acts culminating in Christ, or possibly made in Christ alone? Are the declarations of Scripture the authoritative revelations of God to us which need only to be understood to become items in our trustworthy knowledge of God; or are they merely human statements, conveying with more or less accuracy the impressions received by men in the presence of divine manifestations of more or less purity? On the answers which our apologetics gives to such questions as these, depend the entire method and contents of our systematic theology. Many voices are raised about us, declaring " the old view of the Scriptures " no longer tenable; meaning by this the view that recognizes them as the documented revelation of God and treats their declarations as the authoritative enunciations of truth. Nevertheless men have not commonly wished to break entirely with the Scriptures. In one way or another they have usually desired to see in them a record of divine revelation; and in one sense or another they have desired to find in them, if not the source, yet the norm, of the knowledge of God which they have sought to set forth in their theologies. This apparent deference to Scripture is, however, illusory. In point of fact, on a closer scrutiny of their actual procedure, it will be discovered that " modern thinkers " in general really set aside Scripture altogether as source or even authoritative norm of our knowledge of God, and depend, according to their individual predilections, on reason, on Christian experience, corporate or personal, or on tradition, for all the truth concerning God which they will admit. The formal incorporation by them of Scripture among the sources of theology is merely a fashion of speech derived from the historical evolution of their "new" views and is indicatory only of the starting-point of their development. Their case is much the same as the Romanist's who still formally places Scripture at the base of his "rule of faith" in the complicated formula: Scripture plus tradition, as interpreted by the Church, speaking through its infallible organ, the pope — while in point of fact it is just the pope, speaking *ex cathedra,* which constitutes the actual authority to which he bows.

A striking illustration of how men cling to such old phraseology after it has become obsolete to their actual thought may be derived from a recent writer whom we have already taken occasion to quote. Dr. A. C. Headlam, whose inheritance is Anglican while his critical point of view is "modern," really recognizes no source of theological beliefs (for with him dogmatics deals with beliefs, not truths) but tradition and the living voice of the Church. Yet this is the way he describes the sources of his theology: "The continuous revelation of the Old Testament as accepted in the New, the revelation of Christ in the New Testament, the witness of Christian tradition, and the living voice of the Christian Church." The statement is so far incomplete that it omits the revelation of "nature," for Dr. Headlam allows that nature may teach us somewhat of its Maker: it includes the sources only of what Dr. Headlam would perhaps call "revealed theology." What is to be noted is that it avoids saying simply that these sources are Scripture, tradition, and the living voice of the Church, as a Romanist might have said, reserving of course the right of further explanation of how these three sources stand related to one another. Dr. Headlam has gone too far with modern Biblical criticism to accept the Scriptures as a direct source of dogma. He therefore frames wary forms of statement. He does not say "the Old Testament," or even "the continuous revelation of the Old Testament." He introduces a qualifying clause: "The continuous revelation of the Old Testament as accepted ın the New." This is not, however, to make the New Testament the authoritative norm of theological truth. Proceeding to speak of this New Testament, he does not say simply " the New Testament "; or even " the revelation embodied in the New Testament." He restricts himself to: " The revelation of Christ in the New Testament." It is not, we see, the Old and New Testaments themselves he is thinking of; he does not accord authority to either of them as is done, for example, when they are spoken of in the old phrase, " God's Word written." His appeal to them is not as the documented revelation of God, nor even, as might be perhaps supposed at first sight, as the trustworthy record of such revelations as God has given; but simply as depositories, so far, of Christian beliefs. The Scriptures, in a word, are of value to him only as witness to Christian tradition. He says explicitly: " The Scriptures are simply a part of the Christian tradition "; and he is at pains to show that Christianity, having antedated the New Testament, cannot be derived from it but must rather be just reflected in it. He does not even look upon the Scriptures as a trustworthy depository of Christian tradition. The tradition which they preserve for us is declared to be both incomplete and distorted. They cannot serve, therefore, even as a test of tradition; contrariwise, tradition is the norm of Scripture and its correction is needed to enable us safely to draw from Scripture. " It is tradition," we read, " which gives us the true proportions of apostolic teaching and practice," by which the one-sidedness of the Scriptural record is rectified. If, then, Dr. Headlam's view of the sources of dogmatics were stated with succinct clearness, undeflected by modes of speech which have become outworn to him, we should have to say that these sources are just " tradition " and " the voice of the living Church." Scripture is to him merely an untrustworthy vehicle of tradition.

Dr. Headlam is an Anglican, and when the authority of Scripture dissolves in his hands, he drops back naturally on " the Church," — its " tradition," its " living voice." Others, born under different skies, have only the authority of the

Christian's own spirit to fall back on, whether as a rationally thinking entity, or as a faith-enlightened soul. A mighty effort is, indeed, made to escape from the individualistic subjectivism of this point of view; but with indifferent success. It is not, however, to the Scriptures that appeal is made in this interest. Rather is it common with this whole school of writers that it is not the Scriptures but "the gospel" which supplies the norm by which the faith of the individual is regulated, or the source from which it derives its positive content. This "gospel" may be spoken of, indeed, as "the essential content and the inspiring soul of the Holy Scriptures." But this does not mean that whatever we may find written in the Scriptures enters into this "gospel," but rather that of all which stands written in the Scriptures only that which we esteem the "gospel" has religious significance and therefore theological value. What this "gospel" is, therefore, is not objectively but subjectively determined. Sometimes it is frankly declared to be just that element in Scripture which awakens our souls to life; sometimes more frankly still it is affirmed to be only what in Scripture approves itself to our Christian judgment. "What is a proper function of a Christian man," demands an American writer not without heat, "if not to know a Christian truth when he sees it?" — just Paul's question turned topsy-turvy, since Paul would draw the inference that whoever did not recognize his words as the commandments of God was therefore no Christian man. Sometimes, with an effort to attain a greater show of objectivity, the "gospel" is said to include all that measures up to the revelation of God in Christ. But the trouble is that the Christ which is thus made the touchstone is Himself a subjective creation. He is not the Christ of the gospel narrative, as He stands out upon the pages of the evangelists; for even in its portraiture of Jesus the Scriptures are held untrustworthy. The Jesus by which we would try Scripture is rather a reflection back upon the page of Scripture of what we conceive the revelation of God in Christ ought to be. When our very touchstone is thus a subjective creation, it is easy to estimate how much real objective authority be-

longs to the Scriptural revelation determined by it. One of
the most interesting, and certainly one of the most strenuous
attempts to preserve for Scripture a certain recognition in
theological construction from this point of view is supplied
by Julius Kaftan. Kaftan is emphatic and insistent that the
faith-knowledge which, according to him, constitutes the substance of dogmatics, takes hold upon objective realities which
are matters of revelation and that this revelation is recorded in
the Scriptures. But unfortunately he is equally emphatic and
insistent that this "revelation" witnessed by the Scriptures
is not a communication of truths, but a series of occurrences,
testified to as such, indeed, by the Scriptures (when historico-
critically dealt with), but by no means authoritatively, or even
trustworthily interpreted by the Scriptures. And therefore it is
utilizable for the purposes of dogmatics only as it is taken up
by "faith" and transmuted by faith into knowledge; which is
as much as to say that faith may, indeed, be quickened by
Scripture, but the material which is to be built into our dogmatics is not what Scripture teaches but what we believe.
"Dogmatics," we are told explicitly, "derives none of its
propositions directly from the Scriptures; . . . what mediates for Dogmatics between the Scriptures and the dogmatic
propositions, is faith." " The dogma of which Dogmatics treats
is the dogma that is recognized by the community." All of
which, it would seem, would be more clearly expressed, if it
were simply said that the source of dogmatics is not Scripture
but faith — the faith of the community.

This is not the place to vindicate the objective authority
of Scripture as the documented revelation of God. That is the
task of apologetics. What we are now seeking to make clear,
is only that, as there are apologetics and apologetics, so there
are, following them, systematic theologies and systematic theologies. Systematic theology, as the presentation of the knowledge of God in systematized form, can build only with the
materials which the precedent departments of theological science give it and only after a fashion consonant with the nature
of these materials. If our apologetics has convinced us that

we have no other knowledge of God but that given us by a rational contemplation of the world, recognized as the work of His hands; or that given us by an analysis of the convictions which form themselves in hearts fixed on Him — our procedure will take shape from the character of our sources and the modes by which knowledge of God is elicited from them. But equally if our apologetics assures us that God not only manifests Himself in His works, and moves in the hearts which turn to Him in faith, but has redemptively intervened in the historical development of the race (without this redemptive intervention lost in sin), and that not merely in acts but in words, and has fixed the record of this intervention in authoritative Scriptures, our whole procedure in systematizing the knowledge of God thus conveyed to us will be determined by the character of the sources on which we depend. Taking from the hands of apologetics the natural knowledge of God which its critical survey of the results of human science brings us, and from the hands of Biblical theology the supernaturally revealed knowledge of God which its survey of the historical process of revelation yields us, and viewing all in the light of the progressive assimilation of the body of knowledge of God by His people, through twenty centuries of thinking, and feeling, and living — systematic theology essays to cast the whole into a systematic formulation, conformed to the laws of thought and consonant with the modes of conception proper to the human intelligence.

Systematic theology is thus, in essence, an attempt to reflect in the mirror of the human consciousness the God who reveals Himself in His works and word, and as He has revealed Himself. It finds its whole substance in the revelation which we suppose God to have made of Himself; and as we differ as to the revelation which we suppose God to have made, so will our systematic theologies differ in their substance. Its form is given it by the greater or less perfection of the reflection of this revelation in our consciousness. It is not imagined, of course, that this reflection can be perfect in any individual consciousness. It is the people of God at large who are really the subject of that knowledge of God which systematic theology seeks to set forth. Nor is it imagined that even in the people of God at large, in their present imperfect condition, oppressed by the sin of the world of which they still form a part, the image of God can be reflected back to Him in its perfection. Only the pure in heart can see God; and who, even of His redeemed saints, are in this life really pure in heart? Meanwhile God is framing the knowledge of Himself in the hearts of His people; and, as each one of them seeks to give expression in the forms best adapted to human consciousness, to the knowledge of God he has received, a better and fuller reflection of the revealed God is continually growing up. Systematic theology is therefore a progressive science. It will be perfected only in the minds and hearts of the perfected saints who at the end, being at last like God, shall see Him as He is. Then, the God who has revealed Himself to His people shall be known by them in all the fullness of His revelation of Himself. Now we know in part; but when that which is perfect is come that which is in part shall be done away.

V

GOD

GOD [1]

THE English word " God " is derived from a root meaning " to call," and indicates simply the object of worship, one whom men call upon or invoke. The Greek word which it translates in the pages of the New Testament, however, describes this object of worship as Spirit; and the Old Testament Hebrew word, which this word in turn represents, conveys, as its primary meaning, the idea of power. On Christian lips, therefore, the word " God " designates fundamentally the almighty Spirit who is worshiped and whose aid is invoked by men. This primary idea of God, in which is summed up what is known as theism, is the product of that general revelation which God makes of Himself to all men, on the plane of nature. The truths involved in it are continually reiterated, enriched, and deepened in the Scriptures; but they are not so much revealed by them as presupposed at the foundation of the special revelation with which the Scriptures busy themselves — the great revelation of the grace of God to sinners. On the plane of nature men can learn only what God necessarily is, and what, by virtue of His essential attributes, He must do; a special communication from Him is requisite to assure us what, in His infinite love, He will do for the recovery of sinners from their guilt and misery to the bliss of communion with Him. And for the full revelation of this, His grace in the redemption of sinners, there was requisite an even more profound unveiling of the mode of His existence, by which He has been ultimately disclosed as including in the unity of His being a distinction of persons, by virtue of which it is the same God from whom, through whom, and by whom are all things, who is at once the Father who provides, the Son who accomplishes, and the Spirit

[1] Reprinted from " A Dictionary of the Bible," edited by John D. Davis, Ph.D., D.D., LL.D., 1898, pp. 251–253.

who applies, redemption. Only in the uncovering of this supernal mystery of the Trinity is the revelation of what God is completed. That there is no hint of the Trinity in the general revelation made on the plane of nature is due to the fact that nature has nothing to say of redemption, in the process of which alone are the depths of the divine nature made known. That it is explicitly revealed only in the New Testament is due to the fact that not until the New Testament stage of revelation was reached was the redemption, which was being prepared throughout the whole Old Testament economy, actually accomplished. That so ineffable a mystery was placed before the darkened mind of man at all is due to the necessities of the plan of redemption itself, which is rooted in the trinal distinction in the Godhead, and can be apprehended only on the basis of the Trinity in Unity.

The nature of God has been made known to men, therefore, in three stages, corresponding to the three planes of revelation, and we will naturally come to know Him, first, as the infinite Spirit or the God of nature; then, as the Redeemer of sinners, or the God of grace; and lastly as the Father, Son, and Holy Ghost, or the Triune God.

I. God, the Infinite Spirit

The conviction of the existence of God bears the marks of an intuitive truth in so far as it is the universal and unavoidable belief of men, and is given in the very same act with the idea of self, which is known at once as dependent and responsible and thus implies one on whom it depends and to whom it is responsible. This immediate perception of God is confirmed and the contents of the idea developed by a series of arguments known as the " theistic proofs." These are derived from the necessity we are under of believing in the real existence of the infinitely perfect Being, of a sufficient cause for the contingent universe, of an intelligent author of the order and of the manifold contrivances observable in nature, and of a lawgiver and judge for dependent moral beings, endowed with the sense of duty and an ineradicable feeling of responsibility, conscious of the moral contradictions of the world and craving a solution for them, and living under an intuitive perception of right which they do not see realized. The cogency of these proofs is currently recognized in the Scriptures, while they add to them the supernatural manifestations of God in a redemptive process, accompanied at every stage by miraculous attestation. From the theistic proofs, however, we learn not only that a God exists, but also necessarily, on the principle of a sufficient cause, very much of the nature of the God which they prove to exist. The idea is still further developed, on the principle of interpreting by the highest category within our reach, by our instinctive attribution to Him, in an eminent degree, of all that is the source of dignity and excellence in ourselves. Thus we come to know God as a personal Spirit, infinite, eternal, and illimitable alike in His being and in the intelligence, sensibility, and will which belong to Him as personal spirit. The attributes which are thus ascribed to Him, including self-existence, independence, unity, uniqueness, unchangeableness, omnipresence, infinite knowledge and wisdom, infinite freedom and power, infinite truth, righteousness, holiness and goodness, are not only recognized but richly illustrated in Scripture, which thus puts the seal of its special revelation upon all the details of the natural idea of God.

II. God, the Redeemer of Sinners

While reiterating the teaching of nature as to the existence and character of the personal Creator and Lord of all, the Scriptures lay their stress upon the grace or the undeserved love of God, as exhibited in His dealings with His sinful and wrath-deserving creatures. So little, however, is the consummate divine attribute of love advanced, in the Scriptural revelation, at the expense of the other moral attributes of God, that it is thrown into prominence only upon a background of the strongest assertion and fullest manifestation of its companion attributes, especially of the divine righteousness and holiness, and is exhibited as acting only along with and in entire harmony with them. God is not represented in the Scriptures as forgiving sin because He really cares very little about sin; nor yet because He is so exclusively or predominatingly the God of love, that all other attributes shrink into desuetude in the presence of His illimitable benevolence. He is rather represented as moved to deliver sinful man from his guilt and pollution because He pities the creatures of His hand, immeshed in sin, with an intensity which is born of the vehemence of His holy abhorrence of sin and His righteous determination to visit it with intolerable retribution; and by a mode which brings as complete satisfaction to His infinite justice and holiness as to His unbounded love itself. The Biblical presentation of the God of grace includes thus the richest development of all His moral attributes, and the God of the Bible is consequently set forth, in the completeness of that idea, as above everything else the ethical God. And that is as much as to say that there is ascribed to Him a moral sense so sensitive and true that it estimates with unfailing accuracy the exact moral character of every person or deed presented for its contemplation, and responds to it with the precisely appropriate degree of satisfaction or reprobation. The infinitude of His love is exhibited to us precisely in that while we were yet sinners He loved us, though with all the force of His infinite nature he reacted against our sin with illimitable abhorrence and indignation. The mystery of grace resides just in the impulse of a sin-hating God to show mercy to such guilty wretches; and the supreme revelation of God as the God of holy love is made in the disclosure of the mode of His procedure in redemption, by which alone He might remain just while justifying the ungodly. For in this procedure there was involved the mighty paradox of the infinitely just Judge Himself becoming the sinner's substitute before His own law and the infinitely blessed God receiving in His own person the penalty of sin.

III. God, the Father, Son, and Holy Ghost

The elements of the plan of salvation are rooted in the mysterious nature of the Godhead, in which there coexists a trinal distinction of persons with absolute unity of essence; and the revelation of the Trinity was accordingly incidental to the execution of this plan of salvation, in which the Father sent the Son to be the propitiation for sin, and the Son, when He returned to the glory which He had with the Father before the world was, sent the Spirit to apply His redemption to men. The disclosure of this fundamental fact of the divine nature, therefore, lagged until the time had arrived for the actual working out of the long-promised redemption; and it was accomplished first of all in fact rather than in word, by the actual appearance of God the Son on earth and the subsequent manifestations of the Spirit, who was sent forth to act as His representative in His absence. At the very beginning of Christ's ministry the three persons are dramatically exhibited to our sight in the act of His baptism. And though there is no single passage in Scripture in which all the details of this great mystery are gathered up and expounded, there do not lack passages in which the three persons are brought together in a manner which exhibits at once their unity and distinctness. The most prominent of these are perhaps the formula of baptism in the triune name, put into the mouths of His followers by the resurrected Lord (Matt. xxviii. 19), and the apostolic benediction in which a divine blessing is invoked from each person in turn (II Cor. xiii. 14). The essential elements which enter into and together make up this great revelation of the Triune God are, however, most commonly separately insisted upon. The chief of these are the three constitutive facts: (1) that there is but one God (Deut. vi. 4; Isa. xliv. 6; I Cor. viii. 4; Jas. ii. 19); (2) that the Father is God (Matt. xi. 25; John vi. 27; viii. 41; Rom. xv. 6; I Cor. viii. 6; Gal. i. 1, 3, 4; Eph. iv. 6; vi. 23; I Thess. i. 1; Jas. i. 27; iii. 9; I Pet. i. 2; Jude 1); the Son is God (John i. 1, 18; xx. 28; Acts xx. 28; Rom. ix. 5; Heb. i. 8; Col. ii. 9; Phil. ii. 6; II Pet. i. 1); and the Spirit is

God (Acts v. 3, 4; I Cor. ii. 10, 11; Eph. ii. 22); and (3) that the Father, Son, and Holy Ghost are personally distinct from one another, distinguished by personal pronouns, able to send and be sent by one another, to love and honor each the other, and the like (John xv. 26; xvi. 13, 14; xvii. 8, 18, 23; xvi. 14; xvii. 1). The doctrine of the Trinity is but the synthesis of these facts, and, adding nothing to them, simply recognizes in the unity of the Godhead such a Trinity of persons as is involved in the working out of the plan of redemption. In the prosecution of this work there is implicated a certain relative subordination in the modes of operation of the several persons, by which it is the Father that sends the Son and the Son who sends the Spirit; but the three persons are uniformly represented in Scripture as in their essential nature each alike God over all, blessed forever (Rom. ix. 5); and we are therefore to conceive the subordination as rather economical, that is, relative to the function of each in the work of redemption, than essential, that is, involving a difference in nature.

VI

PREDESTINATION
IN THE REFORMED CONFESSIONS

PREDESTINATION
IN THE REFORMED CONFESSIONS [1]

WHAT we call the Reformation was fundamentally, when looked at from a spiritual point of view, a great revival of religion; when looked at from the theological point of view, a great revival of Augustinianism. [2] It was the one just because it was the other. Revolting from the domination of ecclesiastical machinery, men found their one haven of rest in the sovereignty of God. The doctrine of Predestination was therefore the central doctrine of the Reformation. [3] In the Romish system the idea of predestination has no place, and interest in any opinions that may be held concerning it is in that communion at best but languid. Therefore Perrone, after explaining the difference between the views of the Augustinianizing Thomists and the semi-Pelagianizing Jesuits, can complacently add: " Each school has its own reasons for holding to its opinion: the Church has never wished to compose this controversy: therefore every one may, with safety to the faith, adhere to whichever opinion he is most disposed to and thinks best adapted to solve the difficulties of unbelievers and heretics." [4] The matter was very different with the Reformers. To

[1] Reprinted from *The Presbyterian and Reformed Review,* xii. 1901, pp. 49–128.

[2] Of course the term is here used of the Augustinian doctrine of grace, and not of the ecclesiastical system which finds its roots also in him.

[3] Cf. E. F. Karl Müller, " Symbolik," 1896, p. 75. What are called the formal and material principles of Protestantism belong only to developed Protestantism. The sole doctrine that from the beginning was common to all the Reformers, and that really constituted the formative principle of Protestantism, was that of predestination. It is really this that Möhler, no less than Schweizer, sees, when he seeks to trace back the contrast between Romanism and Protestantism to the emphasis on the freedom of the human will on the one side and on the sole activity of God on the other.

[4] " Tractatus de Deo uno," § 411, in his " Prælectiones theologicæ," i. 1861, p. 342. Yet, one remembers Gottschalk and Jansen.

them the doctrine of predestination was given directly in their consciousness of dependence as sinners on the free mercy of a saving God: it therefore was part of the content of their deepest religious consciousness. Calvin is historically thoroughly justified in his remark that "no one who wishes to be thought pious will dare to deny *simpliciter* the predestination by which God adopts some into the hope of life and adjudicates others to eternal death." [5] In very fact, all the Reformers were at one in this doctrine, and on it as a hinge their whole religious consciousness as well as doctrinal teaching turned. The fact is so obvious as to compel recognition even in unsympathetic circles. Thus, for instance, the late Dr. Philip Schaff, though adjusting his language with perhaps superfluous care so as to exhibit his doctrinal disharmony with the Reformers, is yet forced to give explicit recognition to the universal enthusiasm with which they advocated the strictest doctrine of predestination. " All the Reformers of the sixteenth century," he says,[6] " including even the gentle Melanchthon and the compromising Bucer, under a controlling sense of human depravity and saving grace, in extreme antagonism to Pelagianism and self-righteousness, and, as they sincerely believed, in full harmony not only with the greatest of the fathers, but also with the inspired St. Paul, came to the same doctrine of a double predestination which decides the eternal destiny of all men. Nor is it possible to evade this conclusion," he justly adds, " on the two acknowledged premises of Protestant orthodoxy — namely, the wholesale condemnation of men in Adam, and the limitation of saving grace to the present world." [7]

[5] "Institutes," III. xxi. 5.

[6] "Creeds of Christendom," i. 1877, p. 451.

[7] We should carefully note here the testimony to the necessary implication of the doctrine of "double predestination" in the evangelical system (in the doctrines of original sin and of the confinement of redemption to this life); and as well to the religious root of the doctrine — a matter of fact which Dr. Schaff repeatedly recognizes, as e.g. p. 454. It has become customary in some quarters, however, to represent it as rather a speculative than a religious doctrine. Thus Gooszen discriminates Calvinism properly so called from what he deems the milder teachings of Bullinger and the Heidelberg Catechism as the intellectualistic-speculative tendency from the soteriological-

Scarcely was the Reformation established, however, before the purity of its confession of the predestination of God began to give way. The first serious blow to it was given by the defection of Melanchthon to a synergistic conception of the saving act. As a result of the consequent controversies, the Lutheran Churches were misled into seeking to define predestination as having sole reference to salvation, denying its obverse of reprobation. "First of all," says the "Formula of Concord" (1576), "it ought to be most accurately observed that there is a distinction between the foreknowledge and the predestination or eternal election of God. . . . This foreknowledge of God extends both to good and evil men; but nevertheless is not the cause of evil, nor is it the cause of sin. . . . But the predestination or eternal election of God extends only to the good and beloved children of God, and this is the cause of their salvation." [8] The grave inconsequence of this construction, of course, speedily had its revenge; and typical Lutheranism rapidly sank to the level of Romish indifference to predestination altogether, and of the Romish explanation of it as *ex prævisa fide*.[9] Meanwhile the Reformed continued to witness a better profession; partly, no doubt, because of the greater depth of religious life induced in them by the severity of the persecutions they were called upon to undergo; and partly, no doubt, because of the greater height of religious thinking created in them by the example and impulse of their great leader — at once, as even Renan has been compelled to testify, the best Christian of his day and the greatest religious thinker of the modern world. The first really dangerous assault on what had now become distinctively the Reformed doctrine of predestination was delayed till the opening of the seventeenth century. In the meantime, though,

---

Biblical tendency: and Calvin is treated in many quarters as the reintroducer of nominalistic speculation into Protestant thought. Nothing could be more mistaken. "This," says Müller (as cited, p. 481, note 39), pointedly, "is not the language of nominalism but of faith."

[8] Article xi.

[9] This result is reached as early as Hutter (1610), in whose "Compendium" it is baldly taught that God has elected men *respectu prævisæ fidei*.

no doubt, many individual Reformed thinkers had been more or less affected by a Lutheran environment, as in the lands of German speech, or by Romish remainders, as in England, as well as no doubt by the everywhere present rationalizing spirit which ever lays its stress on man's autocracy; yet the Reformed Churches had everywhere compacted their faith in numerous creeds, in which the Reformed consciousness had expressed itself on the whole with remarkable purity. These now served as a barrier to the new attacks, and supplied strongholds in which the Reformed consciousness could intrench itself for future influence. The Arminian assault was therefore successfully met. And although, ever since, the evil seed then sown has produced a continuous harvest of doubt and dispute in the Reformed Churches; until to-day — in a new age of syncretism of perhaps unexampled extension — it threatens to eat out all that is distinctive in the Reformed Confessions: nevertheless the Reformed sense of absolute dependence on the God of grace for salvation remains till to-day the dominant element in the thought of the Reformed Churches, and its theological expression in the complete doctrine of *prædestinatio duplex* retains its place in the hearts as well as in the creeds of a multitude of Reformed Christians throughout the world.

The numerous Reformed creeds, representing the convictions of Christian men of very diverse races during a period of a century and a half (1523–1675), while on the whole falling behind the works of the great dogmaticians in the ability and fullness with which they set forth the Reformed system,[10] nevertheless form a very remarkable series of documents when looked at as the consistent embodiment of such a doctrine as the Reformed doctrine of predestination. For their own sakes, and for the sake of the great doctrine which they so persistently maintained in the face of so many disintegrating influences and

---

[10] Cf. Schweizer, "Die Glaubenslehre der evangelisch-reformirten Kirche," § 15 (i. 1844, p. 84). So of the relation of creeds and theologians in general, Dean Stanley, *Contemporary Review*, xxiv. 1874, p. 499. The Canons of Dort, the Westminster Confession, and the Formula Consensus Helvetica form exceptions in this regard.

such determined assaults, they are well worth our study. And this primary impulse to turn to them is powerfully reënforced in our own day by the circumstance that recent appeals to them seem to suggest that they have been but little investigated by the men of our generation; so that their message to us is in danger of being widely misapprehended, and sometimes, it must be confessed, even seriously misrepresented. There is a certain timeliness, therefore, as well as inherent propriety in, at this juncture, drawing out from the Reformed creeds their teaching as to predestination, and noting the essential harmony in their presentation of this great doctrine. Assuredly by such a survey the doctrine will be more deeply rooted in our thinking and love. It is possible that we may incidentally learn how to esteem the teaching on this great subject of what may well be spoken of as the consummate flower of the Reformed symbols — that Westminster Confession which it has been our happiness as Presbyterians to inherit. And along with this, we may perhaps also learn what estimate to place on the attempts which are now making more or less to eliminate from that Confession its testimony to this great central Reformed doctrine.

It will probably not be deemed impertinent if we prefix to the extracts taken from the Confessions a brief running account of the documents and their general attitude to the subject under discussion, such as may serve as a kind of introduction to reading intelligently their own words.

I

The Reformed Confessions begin, of course, with the symbolical writings of Zwingli and his Swiss coadjutors, and pass thence to those produced by Calvin and his pupils, and so on to the later documents, the work of the Reformed theologians of the latter part of the sixteenth and of the seventeenth centuries.

Zwingli himself produced four works of this character. These are the Sixty-seven Articles or Conclusions of Zurich

(1523), the Ten Bernese Theses (1528), the System of Faith ("Fidei ratio"), prepared to be presented at the Diet of Augsburg (1530), and the Exposition of the Christian Faith, addressed to Francis I, and published by Bullinger after Zwingli's death (1531). These present the Reformed faith in the first stage of its affirmation. The former two contain, indeed, only the simplest and briefest assertion of the primary elements of Protestant practice in opposition to the most prominent evils of the Romish Church: the latter two are more elaborate expositions of the Protestant belief, but are essentially of an apologetic order. No one of these documents treats professedly of predestination or election, though of course they all rest on the convictions in these matters that characterized Zwingli's thought, and in the two more elaborate documents allusions to them naturally appear. These are more direct and full in the " Fidei ratio," and occur in it in connection with the treatment of the Fall, Redemption, and especially of the Church — about which last topic the controversy with Rome of course especially raged. In the "Expositio fidei christianæ" they occur most pointedly in connection with the treatment of Good Works. In mass they are not copious, but they constitute a very clear and a tolerably full outline of the Reformed doctrine on the subject. God, we are told, has freely made appointment concerning all things, and that by a decree which is eternal and independent of all that is outside of Himself: in this decree is included the fall of man along with all else that comes to pass: and, as well, the election in Christ of some — whom He will — to eternal life; these constitute His Church, properly so called, known certainly from all eternity by Him, but becoming known to themselves as God's elect only through the witness of the Spirit in due time in their hearts, and the testimony of their good works which are the product and not the foreseen occasion of their election; and by these only are they differentiated in the external Church from the reprobates who with them may be included in its bounds.

Meanwhile the Reformation was spreading to other localities, and in proportion as the same need was felt for an

expression of the principles of the new faith which had produced the Zwinglian articles, similar articles were being elsewhere produced. The so-called Tetrapolitan Confession of 1530
owed its origin, indeed, rather to a specific demand — to the
need of a witness to the faith of the four imperial cities to be
presented, like Zwingli's " Fidei ratio," at the Diet of Augsburg; and its form and general contents were determined by
the desire of its authors (Bucer, with the aid of Capito and
Hedio) to assimilate the expression of their faith to the
Lutheran Confession presented at that Diet. It contains no
separate section on predestination, nor, indeed, does it anywhere make any clear allusion to it, though the conceptions on
this matter animating the Reformed Churches seem to underlie the sections on Justification and Good Works. Very similar
were the circumstances in which the Bohemian Confessions
(1535 and 1575) were framed: and the results are much the
same. The earliest Basle Confession, prepared by Oecolampa-
dius and Myconius (1534), on the other hand, besides asserting
the universal government of God, gives a brief paragraph in
its exposition of the doctrine of God to the subject of predestination: this affirms simply that " God before He had created
the world had elected all those to whom He would give eternal
salvation " — a sentence worthy of our note chiefly because
it is the earliest instance in the Reformed Confessions of a
separate paragraph devoted to this great subject.[11] What is
known as the Second Basle, or more properly as the First
Helvetic, Confession, prepared in 1536, under the unionistic
influences of the Strasburg Reformers (Bucer and Capito),
and in anticipation of a General Council — and therefore
under much the same conditions that gave birth to the Tetrapolitan Confession — like that document omits all direct reference to the subject of predestination. The Confessions of
Poland (1570), and Hungary, prepared under much the same
conditions, exhibit much the same sparingness of speech on

[11] A separate *paragraph,* not article: it appears as a distinct paragraph
under the general caption " Of God." The Latin translation in ordinary use
erects it into a separate " Disputation " — the Third.

the subject. Of these only the Hungarian (1557–1558) adverts to it at all, and that most explicitly only to defend God against the charge of "respect of persons." Even so, however, it tells us that all things are eternally disposed by God; and that God's election is eternal, entirely gratuitous, and therefore freely disposed according only to His own will; and that it leaves aside vessels of wrath to the endless doom justly due to their sins.

As the Reformed consciousness took firmer form in the passage of time, however, this tendency to pass lightly over the subject naturally passed more and more away. Something of the early apologetical tone in dealing with predestination doubtless still clings to the Second Helvetic Confession, which was composed by Bullinger in 1562 for his own private use, and on its publication in 1566 was rapidly very widely adopted throughout the Reformed world. Winer [12] certainly goes too far when he affirms that its presentation of predestination is so remarkable a "softening of the dogma" that "this Confession might be placed in the borderland of Predestinarianism." It is much more accurate to say with Müller that the Reformed doctrine is set forth here very clearly in its peculiarity, but with an effort to avoid giving offense: and that it is dominated not so much by doctrinal obscurity as by an ethical-practical intent.[13] The doctrine is here at length: and it is carefully and soundly stated: but there is, no doubt, apparent in its whole treatment a certain defensive attitude which seems more intent to guard it from attack than to bring out all its content with clearness and force. God is said to have determined its end to every creature and to have ordained along with the end at the same time the means by which it shall be attained. He is certainly not the author of sin, with which He is connected only as permitting it for high ends, when He could have prevented it if He had so chosen, and thus as utilizing it in the execution of His plans. His providence is

[12] "Comparative View of the Doctrines and Confessions of the Various Communities of Christendom" (E.T.), 1873, p. 168.

[13] *Op. cit.*, p. 407.

accordingly over all, though nothing finds its evil in His providence. The predestination of His saints to be saved in Christ is eternal, particular, on the ground of no foreseen merit, and assured of its end: and the election of saints to life implies the desertion of a body of reprobates. Who is elect is only *a posteriori* discoverable through men's relation to Christ; we are to judge of others in this matter with charity and are to hope well of all, numbering none rashly among the reprobates: of our own election and therefore certain salvation we may, on the other hand, be assured if we know ourselves to be in Christ and bear fruitage in a holy life. The whole substance of the doctrine clearly is here, though the stress is laid continually on its aspects as seen *sub specie temporis* rather than *æternitatis*.

The case is little different with the Heidelberg Catechism, which doubtless owes it only to its purpose as a document meant as practical milk for babes more than theological meat for mature Christians, that it has very little directly to say about so high a mystery. It is nevertheless pervaded from beginning to end with an underlying presupposition of it, and hints of the doctrine emerge oftener than is always recognized, and that both in its general and special aspects. These hints once or twice rise to explicit assertions, and when they do they leave nothing to be desired in the way of sharpness of conception. It is naturally under the doctrine of providence that general predestination is most clearly alluded to: the Eternal Father is said to uphold and govern the universe " by His eternal counsel and providence," and that effectively for His ends — " so governing all creatures that . . . all things come not by chance but by His Fatherly hand " (Ques. 26, 27). Special predestination, equally naturally, is most directly adduced in connection with the doctrine of the Church (Ques. 54): we are to believe concerning the Church " that out of the whole human race, the Son of God, by His Spirit and word, gathers into the unity of true faith, defends and preserves for Himself a communion elected to eternal life ": and further, each of us is to believe that he is " and shall ever remain a

living member of the same." Here the facts of election and
perseverance are explicitly asserted. Elsewhere we are taught
that our comfort in looking for the coming of Christ the Lord
is derived from the fact that He will " cast all His and our
enemies into eternal damnation, and will take us together with
all the elect to Himself into heavenly joy and glory " (Ques.
52); and similar comforting allusions to election are found
elsewhere (Ques. 1, 31).

Among later documents something of the circumspection
which was the natural product in the first age of unionistic
efforts on the one hand, and of desire to shield the infant
Churches from powerful enemies on the other, appears again
in a somewhat different form in what are usually called the
Brandenburg Confessions. These are the Confession of Sigismund (1614), the Leipzig Colloquy (1631), and above all the
Declaration of Thorn (1645). These are historically especially
interesting as exhibiting the general firmness with which on
the whole the Reformed held to and asserted the essentials
of their doctrine in the most untoward circumstances. The
Confession of Sigismund (1614) is a purely personal statement of the Elector's faith, published on his conversion from
the Lutheranism in which he had been bred. He explicitly confesses, under a sense of its great importance — as the basis on
which rest " not only all the other Articles, but also our salvation " itself — the eternal and gratuitous election of God — the
eternal ordination of His chosen ones, without respect to worthiness, merit or works in them, to everlasting life and all the
means thereto: as also the corresponding fact of an eternal
preterition of the rest and their preparation for the punishment which is their due. Great stress is laid on the justice
of the judgment of God in reprobation, and there is perhaps
some failure in nice discrimination between what is known
among theologians as "negative" and "positive" reprobation: the interest of Sigismund turning rather on vindicating
God from the reproach of taking pleasure in the death of sinners and claiming for Him a universal love for the world. The
statement of the Reformed doctrine at the Leipzig Colloquy

(1631) was for the avowed purpose of establishing as near an agreement with Lutheran modes of statement as could be attained without the surrender of essential truth, and the forms of statement are naturally deeply colored by this union-istic purpose. Nevertheless the entire substance of the doctrine is fairly preserved. A free, eternal election of not all but some men, particularly designed, on the ground of nothing foreseen in them, to the sole reception of the efficacious means of grace is asserted: and along with it, the corresponding eternal reproba-tion of the rest. Great care is taken to free God from construc-tive blame for the death of the wicked, and in the language in which this is done there is perhaps, as in the Confession of Sigismund, an insufficient discrimination between negative and positive reprobation.

By far the most interesting of the three Brandenburg state-ments, however, is the Declaration presented at the Colloquy of Thorn (1645). Here many of the conditions which accom-panied the statement of Protestant belief at the Diet of Augs-burg in 1530 were substantially reproduced. Reformed doc-trine was above all things to be so set forth as to attach itself to whatever latent elements of the truth might be discover-able in Romish thought. The chief points of difference from the earlier situation are due to the later date and changed times; at this period the Reformed had not only come to full consciousness of their faith, but had tasted its preciousness in times of persecution and strife. It is interesting to observe the means taken in these circumstances to commend the Re-formed doctrine to Romish sympathy. Briefly they consisted in setting it forth as simply " Augustinianism." No separate caption is devoted to predestination or to election. All that is said on these topics is subsumed quite Augustine-wise under the caption " De gratia." This caption is developed in eight calmly written paragraphs which, beginning with redemption of the helpless sinner through the sole grace of God in Christ, carries him through the stages of the *ordo salutis* — effectual calling, justification, sanctification, perseverance, final reward — all of the pure grace of God — to end in the reference of all to God's eternal purpose in election. This is followed by eighteen further paragraphs in which the whole doctrine of grace, as before positively developed, is guarded from misapprehension, and defense is offered against calumnies. Only the two last of these paragraphs concern the doctrine of election. The whole is closed with a direct appeal to Augustine and a challenge to the followers of Thomas Aquinas to recognize the Reformed doctrine as none other than that taught them by their master.

The Thoruniensian theologians thus put themselves forward distinctly as "Augustinians" and asked to be judged as such. It is nevertheless in substance a very thoroughly developed Reformed doctrine that they express under this "Augustinian" form. In their fundamental statement they refer all of God's saving activities to His eternal election as their source; deny that it itself rests on anything foreseen in its object, and derive it from mere and undeserved grace alone; and connect with it the ordination of all the means by which the predestined salvation is attained: nor do they shrink from explicitly placing over against it the preterition of the rest. In the additional paragraphs the sure issue of election in eternal life is renewedly insisted on (11), as well as the origin of the election in mere grace (17), and the fixedness of the number of the elect (17). On the other hand, some subtlety is expended in the closing paragraph on the exposition of the relation of the eternal decrees of election and reprobation to the actual character of men. It is denied that these decrees are "absolute" in the sense that they are "without any respect to faith and unbelief, to good and evil works." It is denied also, however, that faith and good works are the cause or reason of election, and doubtless by implication (though this is not said in so many words) that unbelief and sin are the cause or reason of the involved preterition. What is affirmed is that faith and good works are foreseen in the elect as "means of salvation foreordained in them by God." And that "not only original sin, but also, so far as adults are concerned, unbelief and contumacious impenitence, are not properly speaking foreordained of God, but foreseen and permitted in the reprobates themselves as the cause of desertion and damnation, and reprobated by the justest of judgments." The natural meaning of this language yields a sound Reformed sense. So far as it concerns the elect, indeed, none other is capable of being drawn from it. There is an unfortunately ambiguous use of language, however, with reference to the reprobates — as, indeed, even in the use made of the technical term "decretum absolutum" — that may easily mislead, and that the reader finds himself fearing was intentionally adopted to wrap the Reformed doctrine at this point so far in a cloud. There can be indeed no other meaning attributed to the denial that unbelief and impenitence in the reprobate are "properly foreordained"; seeing that in the Reformed conception, fully shared by these theologians, God has foreordained all that comes to pass: and while no Reformed theologian would doubt that their own unbelief and impenitence are the "meritorious cause of the desertion and damnation" of the reprobate, yet the ambiguity of the language that follows — "and are reprobated by the justest of judgments" — certainly opens the way to some misconception. The suspicion can scarcely be avoided that the Thoruniensian theologians purposely used language here capable of a double sense. While naturally suggesting an interpretation consonant with sovereign preterition (negative reprobation), it is liable to be misread as if allowing that negative reprobation itself (preterition) found a meritorious cause in men's sins, which themselves lay wholly outside the foreordination (decree) of God.

It is worthy of note that in the midst of this gingerly treatment of the matter of reprobation, these theologians yet manage to let fall a phrase in passing which betrays their Declaration into an extremity of doctrine at another point to which no other formally framed Reformed Confession commits itself.[14] The Declaration of Thorn in effect is the only

[14] The only other exception is, indeed, the "Consensus Genevensis," which is in form a polemic defense by Calvin of his doctrine of predestination against the assaults of Pighius and Georgius Siculus. In it we read (Niemeyer, "Col-

formal Reformed Confession which asserts or implies that
some of those who die in infancy are reprobated. This it does
by the insertion into the clause dealing with this topic of the
words "so far as adults are concerned." In "reprobation"
(whatever that means with them — whether both "negative"
and "positive" reprobation, or only the latter — makes no
difference in the present matter), they say, God acts on the
foresight not only of original sin, "but also, *so far as adults
are concerned,* of unbelief," etc. God then "reprobates" not
only adults on account of their sins, original and actual, but
also infants on account of original sin alone. It is exceedingly
interesting to observe a body of over-cautious men thus so intent on avoiding Scylla as to run straight into Charybdis. The
reason, however, is not far to seek. They were primarily intent
on vindicating themselves as "Augustinians" in the forum of
the Romish judgment: they wished, that is, to appeal to the
sympathies of the professed followers of Augustine in the
Roman communion: [15] while excessively careful, therefore,
with respect to the whole matter of the *prœdestinatio duplex*
they felt no reason, as professed children of the *durus pater
infantum,* to fear with respect to the fate of infants. The circumstances in which the Declaration was formed, in other
words, is responsible for its weaknesses in both directions.

---

lectio confessionum in ecclesiis reformatis publicatarum," 1840, p. 263): "If
neither original sin suffices for Pighius for the condemnation of man, nor
any place is given to the secret judgment of God, what will he do with
regard to infant children who have been taken from this life before they
could perform any such work (of charity), on account of their age? The circumstance of birth and death was certainly the same for infants who died
at Sodom and at Jerusalem, nor was there any difference in their works;
why will Christ at the last day segregate from some that stand at His right
hand, others at His left? Who does not adore here the wonderful judgment
of God, which has brought it about that some should be born at Jerusalem
whence they might soon pass to a better life, while it separated others to be
born at Sodom the gate of hell?" (Cf. p. 287.)

[15] The Augustinianism of Augustine is of course a different matter from
that of the Romish "Augustinians." The *prœdestinatio duplex* and the distinction between the two wills in God are both explicitly taught by Augustine.
If it had been to Augustine himself that the Thoruniensian divines were
appealing, their *finesse* here would have been unnecessary.

Another instance of the ambiguous use of language in the interests of their desire to come forward as simply followers of Augustine is afforded by their treatment of "perseverance" (11): in this they oddly interchange the terms "justified," "regenerate," "elect." It can scarcely be thought that they really meant to teach that the justified may "fall from grace," or that the "regenerate" are different from "the elect" — their concatenation of the "golden chain" of salvation in their fundamental statement of faith forbids that: but it is obvious that their language here is open to that misinterpretation, and we fear it must be judged that it was intended to be so in deference to current "Augustinian" modes of expression in this matter. The similar obscuration of the distinction between the *voluntas beneplaciti* and *voluntas signi* (6) has its cause in the same effort. The Declaration of Thorn, in a word, while it approves itself as a soundly Reformed document, has been drawn up with an occasional over-subtle use of language which seems intended to obscure the truth that its authors nevertheless flattered themselves was expressed: and which is therefore liable to obscure it — to other readers than those whose eyes it was first intended to blind.

The Confessions which we have thus passed in review include, it will doubtless have been observed, especially German ones. Their peculiarities, however, have no national root: they are due rather to the fact, on the one hand, that this group of Confessions embraces the earliest, tentative efforts at creed-making in the Reformed Churches, and, on the other, that the circumstances in which the German Reformed Churches were placed made them the especial prey of unionistic efforts and apologetical temptations. It is scarcely fair to expect of documents framed, as the most of the documents of this class were, expressly to commend themselves to those of other faiths, quite the same sharpness of outline that might well be looked for elsewhere. Taken as a whole and judged from the point of view of the circumstances of their origin, this is an excellent body of Reformed documents, surprisingly true to the faith of the Reformed Churches: it is, after all, rather in language than in substance that they create difficulties. Meanwhile, however, there were other Reformed Confessions being framed under other stars, and in them the Reformed conceptions came, speaking generally of them as a class, to purer because less embarrassed expression. This series begins with the Confessional writings of John Calvin. It is not to be inferred, however, either that Calvin's teaching exercised no influence on the matter or phrasing of the Confessions already adduced, or that it introduced into the Reformed Churches any new attitude toward the doctrine of predestination. On the contrary, the commanding influence of Calvin penetrated to every corner of the Reformed Churches, and is traceable in all the creedal statements framed subsequently to his appearance at Geneva. And, on the other hand, in his doctrine of predestination he proclaimed nothing not common to all the Reformed leaders. So far from advancing in it beyond the teaching of Zwingli, Zwingli's modes of expression on this high mystery seemed rather to Calvin extreme and paradoxical, if not even lacking in discretion.[16] So closely do his modes of expression regarding it resemble those of Bucer that the latest student of his doctrine of predestination [17] is inclined to believe that he derived it from Bucer. Even Bullinger, through whatever pathway of doubt and hesitation, came ultimately to full agreement with him.[18] Indeed, his doctrine of predestination was so little a peculium of Calvin's that it was originally, as we have seen, not even a specialty of the Reformed, but rather constituted the very hinge of the Reformation: and it was Luther and Melanchthon and Bucer and Peter

[16] " Zwingli's little book [" On Providence "] . . . is so full of hard paradoxes that it is as far as possible removed from that moderation which I have employed."— Calvin to Bullinger, in " Opera Calvini," ed. Baum, Cunitz, and Reuss, xiv. 1875, col. 253.

[17] Scheibe, " Calvins Prädestinationslehre," 1897.

[18] See Herzog-Hauck, " Realencyklopädie für protestantische Theologie und Kirche," ed. 3, iii. 1897, pp. 545–546, where the development, or perhaps we would better say, the librations of Bullinger's doctrine are briefly sketched. Even in the " Decades," however, Bullinger clearly defines predestination as *duplex*, or, as it is more accurately phrased, *gemina* (Parker Society edition, iv. 1851, pp. 185–186 (serm. iv.); cf. pp. 33–34 (serm. i.).

Martyr who first put it forward as the determining element in the Reformation platform. What is due to Calvin is, at most, only the final establishment of the clear, cogent, and consistent expression of it in the Reformed creeds. His systematic genius perceived from the first its central importance to the system of truth on which the Reformation was based; and he grasped it with such full and clear apprehension, that in his own writings and wherever his influence dominated it was no longer easily possible to falter either in its apprehension or its statement, and efforts to speak softly regarding it or to pare it down to fit the desires of men measurably ceased. It is on this account only that in the Confessions that derive most directly from Calvin we see the whole Reformed doctrine of predestination come most fully and consistently to its rights.

Calvin was himself the author of a considerable number of documents of symbolical character: and although the place given in them to the doctrine of predestination varies widely according to the circumstances of each case, the doctrine embodied in those which give it any full expression appears in a singularly pure form. Even the first edition of the " Institutes," published in 1536, might fairly be so far counted among the symbolical books as its publication was determined by apologetic need, and its primary purpose was to testify to the world what the faith of the French Protestants really was. In it no separate treatment was accorded to predestination and what is said on this topic emerges only incidentally, very much as in Zwingli's " System of Faith," and as in that document also most fully in connection with the doctrine of the Church. But this incidental treatment is full enough to show that there was already present to Calvin's mind all the substance of the doctrine as elsewhere developed by him. His first formal exposition of it, under its own separate caption, occurs, however, not in the " Institutes," but in the earliest of his formal symbolical writings, the " Instruction and Confession of Faith in Use in the Church of Geneva," published in April, 1537. In this document the whole of Calvin's doctrine of predestination is set forth in clear if succinct outline. The starting-point is

taken in the observed actual separation of mankind into the
two classes of the saved and lost. This distinction is carried
back at once to the secret eternal counsel of God, in which some
are predestinated to be His children and heirs of the heavenly
kingdom, while others are left to the just punishment of their
sins. The reason why God has so discriminated between men is
declared to be inscrutable by mortals, and men are dissuaded
from prying into it: it is enough for us, we are told, to know
that His action here, too, is holy and just, and therefore redounds to His praise. For the rest, it is for us to seek the
certitude of our faith in the contemplation, not of election
but of Christ, whom having we have all. On quite similar
lines runs the much more meager teaching of the " Genevan
Catechism " of 1545, in which there occur no separate questions and answers consecrated specifically to predestination,
but only incidental allusions to the subject in the answers
given under the topics of Providence and the Church. God, it
is taught, is the Lord and governor of all things, " to whose
empire all things are subject and whose nod they obey " —
even the devil and godless men, all of whom are the ministers
of His will, and are compelled even against their plans " to
execute what has seemed good to Him." The Church, it is
taught, is " the body and society of believers whom the Lord
has predestinated to eternal life," all of whom, therefore,
because elected of God, He justifies and sanctifies and will
glorify. In similar fashion even the " Consensus Tigurinus "
of 1549, which concerns itself formally with nothing but the
doctrine of the Lord's Supper, alludes, nevertheless, to election — teaching that it is only to the elect that the sacraments
actually convey grace — " for," it continues, " just as God
enlightens unto faith no others than those whom He has foreordained to life, so by the hidden power of His Spirit He brings
it about that the elect receive what is offered in the sacraments."

It is however, of course, chiefly in the " Genevan Consensus," called out in 1552 by the attacks on the doctrine of predestination made by Bolsec, that we find the fullest statement

of Calvin's doctrine of predestination which has a claim to symbolical authority. This document is not in form a Confession, but is rather a polemical treatise written in Calvin's own name and given symbolical significance only by its publication in the name of the pastors of Geneva as a fair exposition of the Genevan doctine. It is wholly devoted to the defense of Calvin's teaching on predestination, and bears the significant title: "Of the eternal predestination of God by which out of men He has elected some to salvation and left others to their destruction," — in which, as we perceive, the *prædestinatio gemina* is made the very core of the doctrine. One needs to read but a little way into the treatise to perceive how strongly and indeed even passionately Calvin insisted upon this point. The reason for this is that he looked upon election not merely as the warrant for assurance of faith, but especially as the support and stay of the alone-efficiency of God in salvation: and that he perceived, with the clearness of vision eminently characteristic of his genius, that for the protection of monergistic salvation and the exclusion of the evil leaven of synergism, the assertion of the *prædestinatio gemina* is absolutely essential. In this we see accordingly the real key to the insistence on "sovereign reprobation" in the Calvinian formularies: the conviction had become a part of the very substance of Calvin's thought that "election itself unless opposed to reprobation will not stand" — that "the discriminating grace of God" was virtually set aside as the alone cause of salvation if it were not confessed that the segregation of some to receive the just award of their sins is as truly grounded in His holy will as salvation itself in His will of grace. The extended discussion and even the polemic form of this treatise enabled Calvin powerfully to commend his doctrine to every reader, and to fortify it by full expositions of Scripture: and doubtless it is to the influence of the "Consensus of Geneva" that much of the consistency with which the *locus* on predestination was treated in subsequent Calvinistic formularies is traceable.[19] The very qualities which gave it its great influence,

[19] Cf. an interesting instance of its influence in that direction in the

however, render it difficult to extract it briefly, and we may account ourselves fortunate that we have, through a discovery by the Brunswick editors of a brief series of " articles on predestination" in Calvin's hand, a succinct statement from himself of his whole doctrine, to which, though we have no evidence that they were ever given symbolical authority, we may fairly go as to a summary of his teaching. In these he affirms that God did not create man without having previously determined upon his destiny; that therefore the fall was included in God's eternal decree; and with it, the discrimination between the elect and reprobate portions of fallen mankind; which discrimination has no other cause than God's mere will: and therefore the choice of the elect cannot rest on foreseen faith, which is rather the gift of God in the execution of His decree of salvation, granted therefore to the elect and withheld from the reprobate: as is also the gift of Christ. Rising next to the general decree, he affirms that the will of God is the first and supreme cause of all things, and yet God is not in any sense the author of sin, which is offensive to Him and will receive His punishment, though He certainly makes use of all sinners too in executing His holy purposes.

There is also a series of Confessions from Calvin's hand in which a somewhat less prominent place and thorough statement are given to predestination, though certainly there is no faltering in the conception of it which is suggested when it is alluded to. Among these would be numbered the earliest Confession of the Genevan Church (1536), if we could attribute it in whole or in part to Calvin: it is ordinarily, however, and apparently justly, assigned to Farel. In it there is no separate treatment accorded to predestination, but the keynote of Calvin's theology is firmly struck in the attribution of all good in man to the grace of God — in the acknowledgment and confession that " all our blessings are received from the mercy of God alone, without any consideration of worthiness

---

letter of Bartholomew Traheron to Bullinger, " Zurich Letters," First Series, i. p. 325, cf. 327 (cf. Schaff, " Creeds of Christendom," i. 1877, pp. 630, 631).

in us or merit of our works — for to them is due no return except eternal confusion." There is here presented in a single clause the entire premise on which rests Calvin's *prædestinatio gemina*. A Confession put by Calvin into the mouths of the students of Geneva, dating from 1559, may, however, be properly taken as a typical instance of this class. It is naturally reminiscent of the Genevan Catechism of 1545. Stress is laid in it on the divine government of the invisible spirits — whose differing fates are traced back to the divine appointment, and whose entire conduct is kept under the divine control, for the working out of His ends. In regard to special predestination emphasis is thrown on the divine origin of faith, which is confessed to be " a special gift, which is not communicated save to the elect, who have been predestinated before the creation of the world to the inheritance of salvation without any respect to their worthiness or virtue." To the same class belong also the three Confessions which Calvin prepared for the French Churches. The earliest and shortest of these is that which he seems to have drawn up in 1557 for the Church at Paris in vindication of itself against the calumnies that had been brought against it. In this there is only a brief confession that it is " of the mercy of God alone that the elect are delivered from the common perdition," and that the faith by which alone we are saved is itself a free and special gift granted by God to those to whom it seems good to Him to give it, and conveyed to them by the secret grace of the Holy Spirit. The Confession which he wrote to be presented in the name of the French Churches to Maximilian and the German Diet of 1562 is only a little more explicit. In this man's entire dependence on the undeserved mercy of God for salvation — offering no plea to God except his misery — is adverted to, and it is then affirmed that therefore the goodness of God displayed to us proceeds solely from His eternal election of us according to His sovereign good pleasure: comfort is found in this display of the divine goodness, but the fanaticism is repelled that we may rest on our election in such sort that we may neglect the means.

The third of the French Confessions drafted by Calvin after enlargement at the Synod of Paris, 1559, became the national Confession of the French Reformed Churches, and is therefore of far more significance than its predecessors. It is also somewhat fuller than they are, though following much the same line of thought. It confesses with all Calvin's clearness the universal Lordship of God and His admirable mode of serving Himself with devils and evil men, without the least participation in their evil: it draws the Christian man's comfort from the assurance of the sure protection of God over His people: it describes election as the eternal, immutable decree of God, proceeding on no foresight of works, by which He has determined to withdraw His chosen ones from the universal corruption and condemnation in which all men are plunged — "leaving," it is significantly added, "the rest in this same corruption and condemnation, to manifest in them His justice, as in the former He makes the riches of His mercy to shine forth." Of quite similar character to the Gallican Confession is the Belgic Confession (1561), the composition of the martyr hand of Guido de Brès, but in the section (16) on election somewhat revised by Francis Junius. In its statement of general predestination, indeed (13), even the language recalls that of the French Confession, whose statement it may be said only to repeat in an enriched form. The article on election, on the other hand, is somewhat less full than that in the Gallican Confession, but teaches the same type of doctrine: it is essentially an assertion of the *prædestinatio bipartita* as a manifestation at once of the divine mercy and justice.

Meanwhile across the Channel also the same influences were working. In England from 1536, when the Ten Articles — essentially Romish in contents — were published, the Reforming party were slowly working their way to a better faith, until, having at length found themselves, they published the Forty-two Edwardian Articles in 1553; of these the Elizabethan Thirty-nine Articles (1563–1571) are merely a slight revision, and in the article on Predestination a simple repetition. These "Articles of the Church of England" were prepared by a commission under the headship of Cranmer, to whom the chief share in their authorship seems to belong: but in the seventeenth Article, on Predestination, the influence of Peter Martyr seems distinctly traceable, and, whoever may have drawn it up, it may fairly be attributed in its substance ultimately to him. It confines itself to a statement of the gracious side of predestination — " predestination to life " — and it consists of two parts, in the former of which " predestination to life " is defined, and in the latter of which the use of the doctrine is expounded. The definition of " predestination to life " is made to rest on an " election " here assumed as having antecedently taken place; and to include God's eternal and " constant " (that is, unchangeable) counsel, secret to us, negatively to deliver His elect from curse and damnation, and positively to bring them by Christ to everlasting salvation. The stress is therefore laid precisely on the doctrine of " perseverance," and the surety of the whole *ordo salutis* for those so predestinated is adduced in detail in support of its general assertion. The definition is remarkable not so much for what it asserts as for what it omits, and in what it omits not so much for what it rejects as for what, though omitting, it presupposes. The exposition of the proper use of the doctrine includes a description of its effect in establishing and confirming the faith of those who use it in a godly manner, and a warning against its abuse by the carnal and merely curious; the whole closing with an exhortation quite in Calvin's manner to make the revealed rather than the secret will of God our guide to life. The whole is not only soundly Reformed but distinctly Calvinian in substance: but its peculiar method of dealing with the more fundamental aspects of the doctrine by way of allusion, as to things fully understood and presupposed, lays it especially open to misunderstandings and wrestings, and we cannot feel surprise that throughout its whole history it has been subjected to these above most other creedal statements.

In the sister Church of Scotland, in the meantime, a Confession was hastily put together by Knox and his coadjutors and adopted by Parliament in 1560, which became the legal Confession of the Reformed Church of Scotland when that Church was established in 1567. This Confession contains an Article headed "Of Election" (8), but its doctrine of predestination must be gathered not merely from the somewhat meager statements of that Article, but also from other allusions under the captions especially of Providence and the Church. It asserts the universal rule of God's providence, directing all things "to sik end, as his Eternall Wisdome, Gudnes, and Justice hes appoynted them, to the manifestatioun of his awin glorie." It traces all our salvation to "the eternall and immutable decree of God." It declares that it is of the mere grace of God that we have been elected in Christ Jesus, before the foundations of the world were laid: and that our faith in Him is wrought solely by the Holy Ghost, who works in the hearts of the elect of God, and to whom is to be attributed not only faith, but all our good works. The invisible or true Church consists, it affirms, only of God's elect, but embraces the elect of all ages: while in the visible Church "the Reprobate may be joyned in the society of the Elect, and may externally use with them the benefites of the worde and Sacraments." The whole Reformed doctrine of predestination may indeed be drawn from this Confession: but, it must be allowed, it is not set forth in all its elements in explicit statements. In this respect the earlier creed of the English Church of Geneva (1558), which is thought also to have come from the hands of Knox, is more precise: and indeed this creed differs from all other Reformed creeds in the circumstance — unimportant but interesting — that in setting forth the double predestination it speaks of the foreordination to death *first:* "God, of the lost race of Adam, hath ordained some as vessels of wrath to damnation; and hath chosen others as vessels of His mercy to be saved." By the side of the Scotch Confession it is not unfair to place also as a witness to the Confessional doctrine of Reformed Scotland so widely used a Catechism as that of John Craig, which was endorsed by the General Assembly of 1590, and for a half-century or more was the spiritual food on which the youth of Scotland was fed. In this admirable document the Calvinian doctrine of predestination is set forth with a completeness and crispness of expression that leaves nothing to be desired.

The subsequent history of the Confessional statement of predestination in England supplies a very interesting demonstration of the necessity of embodying in it, after Calvin's manner, the clear assertion of the *prædestinatio bipartita,* if the very essence of the doctrine is to be preserved. As long as a thorough Calvinism was dominant in the Church of England the inadequacy of the statement of predestination in the Thirty-nine Articles was, if not unremarked, at least the source of no danger to sound doctrine. Men in sympathy with the doctrine set forth readily read in the statement all its presuppositions and all its implications alike. Nobody of this class would question, for example, that in the mention in the last clause of " that will of God which we have expressly declared to us in the Word of God," that other will of God, hidden from us but ordering all things, was assumed — especially as, earlier in the statement, " His counsel, secret to us," is mentioned. Nobody would doubt that in " the predestination to life of those whom God hath chosen in Christ " specific individuals, the especial objects of God's electing grace, were expressly intended. Nobody would doubt that in the assertion of their choice " out of mankind," and predestination to deliverance from curse and damnation, it was peremptorily implied that there was a remainder of mankind left behind and hence predestinated unto the curse and damnation from which these were delivered. Nobody would doubt that in the assertion that these were by God's constant decree predestinated to be brought by Christ to everlasting salvation, the certitude of their actual salvation was asserted. But as soon as men in influential positions began to fall away from this Calvinistic faith, it was speedily discovered that something more than presupposition however clear, or implication however necessary, was needed in a Confessional statement which should serve as a barrier against, serious error and a safeguard to essential truth.

The evil came, in the Church of England, naturally on the heels of a renewed assertion of sacerdotalism and sacramental grace: and it entrenched itself primarily under a plea of " Augustinianism," in distinction from "Calvinism." The high doctrine of Augustine as to the grace of the sacrament of baptism was appealed to, and his distinction between the regenerate and the elect revived; the inference was drawn that participation in grace is no warrant of final salvation, and election to grace no proof of predestination to glory; and this wedge was gradually driven in until the whole Reformed system was split up. Appeal was vainly made to the declarations of the Articles — they proved too indefinite to serve the purpose. After a sharp conflict it became very evident that what was needed was a new Confessional statement in which the essential elements of the doctrine should be given explicit assertion. It was this that was attempted in what is known as "The Lambeth Articles," prepared by William Whittaker, and set forth with the approval of the archbishops and certain other ecclesiastics, in the hope of leading the thought of the Church back to better channels. It was, however, now too late. The evil leaven had eaten too deeply to be now suddenly checked. It was easy to cry out that the very attempt to frame new Articles was a demonstration that the Calvinists were introducing new doctrine. The authority of the new Articles was, moreover, not complete. They were virulently assaulted. And in the failure to establish them as a Church formulary the cause of consistent Calvinism was for the time lost in the Church of England. Meanwhile better things were to be hoped of Ireland, and when, under the leading of Usher, a series of Articles were framed for that Church the lesson taught by the course of events in the sister Church of England was taken to heart and the chapter " Of God's Eternal Decree and Predestination " was strengthened by the incorporation into it, along with the essence of the English Articles, also the new matter of the Lambeth Articles. The curb thus laid upon the inroads of error in Ireland, however, it became one of the chief objects of the English party to destroy; and this ultimately they were enabled to do and the Articles of the Church of England were quietly substituted for those of the Church of Ireland in that land also. Thus the Calvinism of the Irish Church also was fatally wounded.

The whole object and intent of the Lambeth Articles (1595) was to conserve the threatened Calvinism of the Church of England: they do not constitute a complete creed, nor even a complete statement of the doctrine of predestination and its necessary implications. They were intended merely so to supplement the statement of the Thirty-nine Articles as to guard the Reformed doctrine from undermining and destruction. They confine themselves, therefore, to asserting clearly and without unnecessary elaboration the *prædestinatio gemina,* the independence of the divine decree of election on foreseen merit in man, the definite number of the elect; the assured final condemnation of the reprobate; the perseverance of the saints; the assurance of faith; the particularity of grace; the necessity of grace to salvation; and the impotency of the natural will to salvation. Not all of these paragraphs are incorporated into that one of the Irish Articles (1615) headed " Of God's Eternal Decree and Predestination," but only such as naturally fall under that caption, while the others are utilized in other portions of the document. This particular Article is disposed in seven paragraphs. In the first a clear assertion is made of God's general decree, with a careful guarding of it against current calumnies: this is original with this document. The second paragraph sets forth in language derived from the Lambeth Articles the special decree of predestination — the *prædestinatio bipartita.* The third paragraph defines " predestination to life " in language derived from the Articles of the Church of England. The fourth explains the cause of predestination to life as, negatively, nothing in man, and, positively, the good pleasure of God alone: it is taken from the Lambeth Articles. The fifth expounds the relation of predestination to the means of grace, and is taken from the Articles of the Church of England, with the addition of a clause from the Lambeth Articles covering the fate of the reprobate. The last two paragraphs are taken with modifications from the Articles of the Church of England and set forth the use of doctrine. The whole constitutes the high-water mark of the Confessional expression of this high mystery up to this time attained in the Reformed Churches. Nothing before it had been so prudently and so thoroughly compacted. It was rightly taken by the Westminster divines as the point of departure for the formation of their own chapter on this *locus,* and to its admirable guidance is largely due the greatness of the success of the Westminster men in dealing with this mystery in such combined faithfulness and prudence.

It was not, however, only in Britain that the Reformed were called upon to defend the treasures of truth that had been committed to them, from the inroads of that perpetual foe of the grace of God which is entrenched in the self-sufficiency of the natural heart. The rise of the Arminian party in Holland was the most serious direct assault as yet suffered by the Reformed theology. It was met by the Dutch Calvinists with a successful application of the expedient, an unsuccessful attempt to apply which in somewhat similar circumstances in England gave birth to the Lambeth Articles — by the publication, to wit, of Articles supplementary to the accepted Confession of the Church, which should more specifically guard the controverted points. The product of this counter-movement in the Dutch Churches is the Canons of Dort, published authoritatively in 1619 as the finding of the National Synod with the aid of a large body of foreign assessors, representative practically of the whole Reformed world. The Canons of Dort not only, therefore, were set forth with legal authority in the Netherlands, but possessed the moral authority of the decrees of practically an Ecumenical Council throughout the whole body of Reformed Churches. Their form is largely determined by the Remonstrance to which they are formally a reply: it is therefore, for example, that they are divided into five heads; and the whole distribution of the matter, as well as the especial points on which they touch, is due to the occasion of their origin. But for the points of doctrine with which they deal they provide a singularly well-considered, prudent, and restrained Reformed formulary. The first head of doctrine deals directly with predestination, the rest with the connected points of particular redemption, inability, irresistible grace, and perseverance. The matter under each head is disposed in two parts, in the former of which the doctrine concerned is positively set forth, while in the latter the corresponding errors that had been vexing the Churches are named and refuted.

The head on Predestination contains eighteen paragraphs in its positive portion, followed by nine more in the negative part. The starting-point is taken from a broad statement of the doctrine of original sin and man's universal guilt (§ 1). Then the provisions for man's salvation are adduced — the gift of Christ, the proclamation of the gospel, the gift of faith (§§ 2–6) — and it is pointed out that the gospel has actually been sent not to all men, but only to those " whom God will and at what time He pleaseth " (§ 3), and that faith is not in the power of all, but is again the gift of God to whom He pleases. Thus the obvious distinction existing among men is traced back to the divine will, and ascribed to " that decree of election and reprobation revealed in the word of God "(§ 6). The way being thus prepared, election is next defined (§ 7) and the details of the doctrine developed (§§ 7–14); after which reprobation is defined and guarded (§§ 15–16); and the whole concludes with a section on the destiny of children dying in infancy (§ 17), and another on the proper attitude of mind in the face of these holy mysteries (§ 18). The definition of election emphasizes its eternity, immutability, and absolute freedom. Its object is said to be fallen men, and its end redemption, with all the means of grace adjoined. The unity of the decree of election and of the means of salvation is asserted (§ 8). Its relation to all good motives in the creature is carefully explained as not that of effect but of cause (§§ 9, 10). Its particularity and unchangeableness are emphasized (§ 11). Finally, the use of the doctrine, in the attain-

ment of assurance, as an incitement to good works, and for the
comforting of the people of God, is adverted to (§§ 12–14).
The decree of reprobation is then brought in as " peculiarly
tending to illustrate and recommend to us the eternal and
unmerited grace of election" and carefully defined (§ 15);
and men are warned against misusing it so as to beget within
themselves an ill-founded despair (§ 16). Little of importance
is added to this positive statement in the sections on " the
rejection of errors." These take up, one by one, the subtle
Remonstrant statements and lay them by the adduction of
appropriate Scriptures; they result only in strengthening and
sharpening the positive propositions already asserted — particularly those that concern the immutability of God's electing
counsel; its entire independence of foreseen faith or dispositions or works as causes or occasions; and its complete sovereignty in all its relations. The whole constitutes the fullest
and one of the most prudent and satisfactory expositions of
the Reformed doctrine of predestination ever given wide symbolical authority.

The Canons of Dort were adopted by the French Synods of
1620 and 1623; but soon afterward the French Churches were
disturbed by the unsettling teachings of the school of Saumur.
These teachings did not, indeed, trench upon the doctrine of
predestination in its essence. Amyraut, to whom it fell among
the innovating divines to deal with this matter, leaves nothing
to be desired in his express loyalty to the definitions that had
been the guides and guards of Reformed theology from the
beginning: he copiously defended the whole Reformed doctrine as expressed by Calvin. The following is the way his
position is set down in the " Declaration of the Faith of Moses
Amyraut with reference to the Errors of the Arminians": [20]

In the second article, what the Arminians defend is that God,
having decreed from all eternity to offer one and the same grace to
all men, that they might in the powers of free will either receive or
repudiate it; and having foreseen who would accept it and who

[20] Saumurii, 1646, pp. 6, 7.

would reject it; out of that foresight elected those whom He foresaw
would make a good use of that grace and reprobated the rest. Thus,
in their view, election is grounded in foresight of faith.

The orthodox, on the other hand, hold, that although God decreed
that all men indifferently should be invited to faith, He nevertheless
in His eternal counsel separates a given (*certum*) number of men
from the rest, to be granted a singular grace, by means of which
they may obey that invitation, and thus be led to salvation; while
all the rest, they hold, are passed by by Him in the dispensation of
that grace (*cæteros omnes ab eo in dispensatione illius gratiæ præter-
missos esse*). They add further that the reason why God has so acted
is to be traced solely to His most free good pleasure, and that there
was no reason or cause of any kind whatsoever in those whom He
elected why they should be elected; and there existed in those whom
He reprobated no cause why they should be reprobated which did
not equally exist in the others. So that election and reprobation are
equally absolute and neither rests on the prevision of anything
(*nec ulla rei cuiusquam prævisione nitatur*).

Amyraut embraces the same doctrine with the rest of the orthodox and has both explained and confirmed it with unrefuted reasons,
drawn especially from the ninth chapter of Romans, in the thirteenth
chapter of his " Defense of Calvin."

The point where the new French teachings affected the
Reformed doctrine of predestination, therefore, was not in its
substance, but in its relations — and more especially its relation in the *ordo decretorum* to the decree of the gift of
Christ. Amyraut, desiring to teach a universal atonement,
wished to place the decree of election in the order of thought
subsequent instead of prior to the decree to give Christ to
make satisfaction for sin, which satisfaction should therefore
be conditional — to wit, on the faith which is the free gift of
God to His elect. It was to meet this point of view, among
other novelties broached by the Salmurian school, that at the
beginning of the last quarter of the seventeenth century the
" Helvetic Formula of Consent " was drawn up by Heidegger
with the assistance of Turretin and Gernler (1675). Its prime
object in the " Canons " that concern predestination, therefore,
is to defend the Calvinistic order of decrees: this is set forth

there with careful precision and emphasis, and the universalism of Amyraut's construction of the gift of Christ explicitly opposed and refuted. But in stating and arguing its case, the whole doctrine of election is very carefully restated, including the details of its eternity, its absoluteness, its independence on foresight of aught in man moving thereunto, its particularity and unchangeableness, and its implication of a reprobate mass left outside the reach of saving grace by the mere fact of election. The statement may well be looked upon as a typical statement of the Calvinistic position, embodying all the points which, in the course of a century and a half of creed-making, it had been found necessary to emphasize in order to bring out the doctrine in its full outline and to protect it from insidious undermining.

It is in the midst or, more precisely, near the end of this series of creedal expressions of the Reformed doctrine of predestination that the Westminster Confession takes its place. Subsequent in date to all of them, with the single exception of the Swiss Form of Consent, it gathers up into itself the excellences of all. More particularly it is founded upon the Irish Articles of 1615, which in turn were compounded of the English Articles and the Lambeth Articles; and through them it goes back respectively to the thought especially of Peter Martyr and of John Calvin. There is nothing in it which is not to be found expressly set forth in the writings of these two great teachers: and it gives their teachings form under the guidance of the best Confessional statements precedent to its own origin. It quite deserves the high praises it has received from the hand of one of the greatest and most deservedly honored of the fathers of the modern Presbyterian Church, who speaks of it with reiterated emphasis not only as " the best and fullest expression " of the Reformed system, but as " the ablest and ripest product of that Great Reformation, which was so fruitful in symbolic literature." [21]

[21] Henry Boynton Smith, in " Faith and Philosophy," 1877, pp. 103, 147, 283. The passages in which those expressions occur are worth reading as models of the justly fervent praise which the Westminster Standards evoke from competent readers.

II

After this introductory survey of their general character, we are now prepared to set out the text of the Confessional statements of the doctrine of predestination in the Reformed Churches. We shall extract the sections specifically devoted to the subject at large, but only so much of other matter as seems needful for understanding the nature of the Confessional recognition that is really given the doctrine. The Confessions are, in general, arranged in the order in which they have been mentioned in the preceding description of them.

ZWINGLI'S FIDEI RATIO (1530) [22]

Secondly. I know that that Supreme Divinity who is my God has freely made appointment concerning all things, so that His counsel does not depend on the occasioning of any creature,[a] since it is peculiar to marred human wisdom to determine on precedent discussion or example. But God, who from eternity to eternity contemplates all that is with a single and simple regard, has no need of any ratiocination, or expectation of acts, but, equally wise, prudent, and good, freely determines and disposes concerning all things — seeing that all that is is His.[b] Hence, though He knowingly and purposely in the beginning made the man who should fall, He yet equally determined to clothe His own Son in human nature, that He might repair the fall. . . .

Thirdly. . . . The election of God, however, stands and remains firm, since those whom He elected before the constitution of the world He so elected as to choose to Himself through His Son; for He is as holy and just as He is good and merciful.[c] All His works therefore savor of mercy and justice. Election therefore properly savors of both. It is of His goodness that He has elected whom He will;[c] but it is of His justice that He has adopted His elect to Himself and joined them to Him through His Son as a victim offered to satisfy Divine justice for us. . . .

Sixthly. Of the Church, then, we think as follows: The term

[22] Translated from the text in Niemeyer, "Collectio confessionum in ecclesiis reformatis publicatarum," 1840, pp. 18 ff.

[a] West. Conf., III. i. a; ii.

[b] West. Conf., III. ii.

[c] West. Conf., III. v. a.

Church is variously used in the Scriptures. For those elect, ones whom God has destined to eternal life.[d] It is concerning this Church that Paul speaks when he says that it has no spot or wrinkle. This Church is known to God alone; for He only, according to the word of Solomon, knows the hearts of the sons of men. But, nevertheless, those who are members of this Church know themselves, since they have faith, to be elect and members of this first Church; [e] but they are ignorant with regard to other members. For it is thus written in the Acts: " And as many as were ordained to eternal life believed." Those, then, who believe are ordained to eternal life. But who truly believes no one knows but the one who believes. He then is certain that he is elected of God. For, according to the word of the Apostle, he has the Spirit as a pledge, by whom he is sponsored and sealed, and knows himself to be free and made a son of the family and not a slave. For that Spirit cannot deceive. As He declares God to be our Father, we call on Him as Father with assurance and boldness, being firmly persuaded that we shall obtain an eternal inheritance because we are sure that the Spirit of God has been poured out into our hearts. It is certain, then, that he who is thus assured and secure is elect; for those who believe are ordained to eternal life.[e] There are, however, many elect who have not faith. For the holy θεοτόκος, John, Paul — were they not elect while they were still infants or children, and even before the constitution of the world? Nevertheless, they did not know this, either from faith or from revelation. Matthew, Zacchæus, the Thief, and the Magdalene — were they not elect before the constitution of the world, though they were ignorant of the fact until they were illuminated by the Spirit and drawn to Christ by the Father? From them, then, we may learn that this first Church is known to God only, and that those only who have firm and unwavering faith know that they are members of this Church. But, once again, the term Church is used universally of all who are enrolled in the name of Christ — that is, who have given in their names to Christ, a good part of whom have openly acknowledged Christ by confession or participation in the Sacraments while still in heart they are either alienated from Him or ignorant of Him. We believe therefore that all those who have confessed the name of Christ belong to this Church. Thus Judas was of the Church of Christ, and all those that draw back from Christ. For Judas was thought by the Apostles to be not less of Christ's Church than Peter

d West. Conf., III. v. a.   e West. Conf., III. viii.

or John, since he was no less so. But Christ knew who were His and who was the devil's. There is, then, this visible Church in this world, however unfit, and all who confess Christ are in it, though many of them are reprobates.[f] For Christ depicted that charming allegory of the ten virgins, five of whom were wise and five foolish. And this Church is sometimes called elect, although it is not that first Church which is without spot; but since it is, according to man's judgment, the Church of God, on account of public confession, it is therefore called elect. For we judge those to be believers and elect who give in their names to Christ. So Peter spoke when he said, " To the elect who are scattered abroad in Pontus," etc. There by the name of elect he means all who were of the churches to which he was writing, not those only who were properly God's elect: for as they were unknown to Peter, he was not able to write to them. Finally, the word Church is used for any particular congregation of this universal and visible Church. . . .

Zwingli's Expositio Chr. Fidei (1531) [23]

[103] It is therefore by the grace and goodness of God alone, which He has abundantly poured out on us in Christ, that eternal bliss is attained. What, then, shall we say of the passage of Scripture adduced above, in which a reward is promised for a draught of cold water and the like? This to wit: That the election of God is free and gratuitous; for He elected us before the constitution of the world, before we were born. God therefore did not elect us on account of works, but He elected us before the creation of the world.[g] Our works therefore have no merit. But when He promises a reward for works it is after a human manner of speech; " for," says Augustine, " what wilt Thou, O good God, remunerate except Thine own work? For since it is Thou that workest in us both the willing and the doing, what is left for us to claim for ourselves? For . . ." etc.

The Tetrapolitan Confession (1530) [24]

III. *Of Justification and Faith.* . . . For since it is our righteousness and eternal life to know God and our Saviour, Jesus Christ; and

---

[23] Published by Bullinger, after Zwingli's death. Translated from the text in Niemeyer, p. 58.

[24] Translated from the text in Niemeyer, pp. 746 f.

[f] West. Conf., III. iii.; vii.

[g] West. Conf., III. v.

it is so impossible for this to be the work of flesh and blood that it is needful for it to be born again anew; and we cannot come to the Son except by the Father's drawing, nor know the Father except by the Son's revelation; and Paul has written so expressly that it is not of us nor of works: — it is clear enough that our works can help nothing at all toward our becoming righteous from the unrighteous ones which we were born; because that, as we are by nature children of wrath and therefore unrighteous, so we avail to do nothing righteous or acceptable to God, but the beginning of all our righteousness and salvation must needs come from the mercy of God, who out of His grace (*dignatione*) alone and the contemplation of the death of His Son offers in the first instance the doctrine of truth and His Gospel, sending those who shall proclaim it; and then, since the natural man is not at all able, as Paul says, to perceive the things of God (I Cor. ii.), makes at the same time to arise in the darkness of our hearts the ray of His light, so that we may now have faith in the proclaimed Gospel, being persuaded of its truth by the supreme Spirit, and forthwith may, enjoying the testimony of this Spirit, call upon God in filial confidence, and say, Abba, Father, obtaining thereby sure salvation according to that saying, " Whosoever shall call on the name of the Lord, shall be saved."

IV. *Of Good Works proceeding out of Faith through Love.* But we are unwilling that these things should be so understood as if we placed salvation and righteousness in the slothful thoughts of the mind, or in faith destitute of love, which is called *fides informis;* seeing that we are sure that no one can be righteous or be saved unless he loves God supremely and imitates Him zealously. For whom He foreknew, the same He also predestinated to become conformed to the image of His Son, to wit, as in the glory of a blessed life, so also in the cultivation of innocence and consummate righteousness, for we are His workmanship, created unto good works.[h] But no one is able to love God above all things, and to emulate Him with worthy zeal, except he do indeed know Him and receive the promise of all good things from Him. . . .

FIRST BOHEMIAN CONFESSION (1535) [25]

III. . . . Hence also they teach that there belong to this one God, supreme power, wisdom and goodness. There also belong to

[25] From the text in Niemeyer, pp. 789, 793 f., 796.
[h] West. Conf., III. vi.

Him alone those most excellent works, suitable to no other than Him. These are the works of creation, redemption, conservation or sanctification. They teach, moreover, that this only true God, in one essence of divinity and blessed trinity of persons, is to be ever adored, venerated and worshiped with supreme reverence, honor and praise as the supreme Lord and King of all things, regnant eternally: and from His hand alone are all things to be looked for and sought. . . .

VI. . . . They teach, moreover, that through Christ men are mercifully justified freely by faith in Christ, and obtain salvation and remission of sins, apart from all human work and merit. Likewise they teach that His death and blood alone is sufficient for abolishing and expiating all the sins of all men. . . . They likewise teach that no one can have this faith by his own power, will or choice; since it is the gift of God who, where and when it seems good to Him, works it in man through the Holy Spirit.[1] . . .

VIII. *Concerning the Holy Catholic Church,* they teach first of all that the head and foundation of the Church is Christ the Lord by His own merit, grace and truth, in whom it is built up by the Holy Spirit, the Word and Sacraments. . . .

SECOND BOHEMIAN CONFESSION (1575) [26]

III. . . . And so He is the perfect Mediator, Advocate, and Intercessor with God the Father, Reconciler, Redeemer and Saviour of our Church, which by His Holy Spirit He collects, conserves, protects, and rules until the number of God's elect shall be completed.[1] . . .

XI. . . . But such a company of good and bad men is called and is the Catholic, Christian and Holy Church, only with respect to the good fishes and wheat — that is, the elect children of God and true and faithful Christians, all of whom as a whole and without exception are holy with a holiness imputed in Christ and begun in them by the Holy Spirit; and these only God deigns to call His sheep, the community of whom is really the bride of Christ, the house of God, the pillar and ground of the truth, the mother of all the faithful and the sole ark, outside of which there is no salvation. . . .

[26] Niemeyer, pp. 828, 836.
[1] West. Conf., III. vi. b.

First Basle or Mühlhausen Confession (1534) [27]

II. *Of Creation and Providence.* We believe that God created all things by His Eternal Word, that is, by His only begotten Son; and sustains and animates all things by His Spirit, His own power: and therefore that God, as He created, so oversees and governs all things. Gen. i. 1; John i. 3; I Chron. xxix. 11, 12; Acts ii. 23.

III. *Of Predestination.* Hereupon we confess that God, before He had created the world, had elected all those to whom He would give the inheritance of eternal salvation.[j] Rom. viii. 29, 30, ix. 11–13, xi. 5, 7; Eph. i. 4–6. . . .

VI. And although man by the same fall became liable to damnation and inimical to God, God nevertheless never ceased to care for the human race. This is witnessed by the patriarchs; the promises before and after the flood; the law likewise given by God to Moses; and the holy prophets. Rom. v. 16; Gen. xii. 1, xiv. 19, 20, xv. 1; Gen. iii. 15, xxi. 12, xxvi. 3, 4, 24, xxviii. 13, 14, 15.

First Helvetic or Second Basle Confession (1536) [28]

9. *Free Will.* Thus, we attribute free will to man in such a manner that though we are conscious of both knowing and willing to do good and evil, we are able indeed of our own motion to do the evil, but are unable to embrace and pursue the good, except as illuminated by the grace of Christ and impelled by His Spirit. For God it is who works in us both the willing and the doing, according to His good pleasure.[k] And it is from God that salvation comes, from us perdition. Phil. ii.; Hos. xiii.

10. *The Eternal Counsel of God Concerning the Reparation of Man.* For this man, therefore, devoted by his fault to damnation, and incurring righteous indignation, God the Father has nevertheless never ceased to care. And this is made plain by the primal promises, and by the whole law (which arouses and does not extinguish sin) and by Christ who was ordained and set forth for this very purpose. Eph. i.; Rom. vii.

---

[27] Niemeyer, pp. 79–80; 87–89.

[j] West. Conf., III. v. a.

[28] Niemeyer, p. 117, cf. 107.

[k] West. Conf., III. vi.

The Hungarian Confession (1557–1558) [29]

Out of the Word of God we call Him Father, God and Jehovah, having life in Himself, existent from none, wanting all beginning, who from eternity without any beginning or change begot out of His own hypostasis as it were the character and splendor of His glory, the only begotten Son — through whom He from eternity foreknew and disposed all things,[1] and in the beginning created, and conserves them, and saves His elect by justifying them, but condemns the impious.[m] . . .

Thirdly, [eternity] is used of a continuous time — that is, of the period in which the world was created, of the days in which the world was made. Hence it is said: He elected us before times eternal, that is, He elected before the seven days of creation, before creation, from eternity (Eph. i. 2, 3, 5; II Tim. i. 2, 3).[n] Fourthly, it is used of the infinite salvation of the pious and the torment of the impious: and this salvation and condemnation, though they have a beginning in the elect and the vessels of wrath, nevertheless want an end. . . .

As it is impossible that things that are in direct repugnance to one another and are mutually destructive can be the efficient and formal cause of their contraries; as light is not the cause of darkness, nor heat of cold (Psalms 5, 46, 61, 66, 80, 84, 114, 135); so it is impossible for God, who is Light, Righteousness, Truth, Wisdom, Goodness, Life, to be the cause of darkness, sin and falsehood, ignorance, blindness, malice, and death; but Satan and men are the cause of all these. For God cannot *ex se* and *per se* do things that He prohibits and on account of which He condemns.[o] . . .

As He who justly renders to those who work equally an equal reward, and who gives to the undeserving, out of grace and voluntarily, what He will, is not a respecter of persons; so God had acted justly, if out of debt, according to justice and His own law, He had rendered death and condemnation as the stipend of sin to all who deserve it. And on the other hand, when for the sake of His son, out

---

[29] Niemeyer, pp. 542, 547, 549. The *title* in Niemeyer reads: " The true Confession derived from the Word of God and set forth and published with one consent, in the Synod of Czenger: I. On the one and only God . . . IX. On respect of persons in God because He saves some and hardens others."

[1] West. Conf., III. i. a.

[m] West. Conf., III. iii.

[n] West. Conf., III. v.

[o] West. Conf., III. i. b.

of the plenitude of His grace and in His freedom of will, He gives to
the undeserving righteousness and life,[p] this is not *prosopoliptis*,
that is, He is not a respecter of persons, as it is said: " Take what
is thine and what thou hast deserved and go: Is it not lawful for me
to do what I please with my own? Is it not thy eye that is evil? not
my eye, because I am good " (Matt. xx.). . . .

We confess Christ . . . as Redeemer for these reasons. . . .
Then, too, that He might make satisfaction for the life-giving mercy
of God by the omnipotence of the same Word and only begotten
Son of God, according to the eternal election made from eternity in
Christ (Eph. i.).[p]

SECOND HELVETIC CONFESSION (1562, 1566) [30]

VI. *Of the Providence of God.* By the providence of this wise,
eternal and omnipotent God, we believe that all things in heaven and
in earth and among all the creatures are conserved and governed.
. . . Meanwhile, however, we do not despise the means by which
divine providence operates, as if they were useless. . . . For God,
who has determined its own end to everything,[q] has ordained both the
principle and the means by which it shall attain its end. The Gentiles
attribute things to blind fortune or uncertain chance. . . .

VIII. *Of Man's Fall, Sin, and the Cause of Sin.* . . . We condemn, moreover, Florinus and Blastus, against whom also Irenæus
wrote, and all who make God the author of sin. . . . There is enough
vice and corruption in us for it to be by no means necessary for God
to infuse into us new and increased depravity. Accordingly when
God is said in Scripture to harden, to blind, and to give over to a
reprobate mind, it is to be understood that He does this by a
righteous judgment, as a just judge and avenger. In fine, whenever
God is said or seems to do any evil in Scripture, it is not so said
because it is not man that does the evil, but because God, who could
prevent it if He wished, in just judgment permits it to be done and
does not prevent it; or because He has made a good use of the evil
of men, as in the case of the sins of Joseph's brethren; or because
He reins in the sins, that they may not break out too widely and

---

[30] Niemeyer, pp. 474 f., 477 ff., 481 ff., 489 f.; Schaff, " Creeds of Christendom," iii. 1878, pp. 244 f., 247 ff., 252 ff., 260 ff.

[p] West. Conf., III. v.

[q] West. Conf., III. i. a.

riot.[r] St. Augustine, in his "Enchiridion," says: "In a marvelous and ineffable way, that does not take place apart from His will, which yet takes place against His will. For it would not be done, if He did not permit it to be done. Nor is it unwillingly that He permits it but willingly. Neither would the Good One permit evil to be done, were not the Omnipotent One able to bring good out of the evil."

Remaining questions — whether God willed Adam to fall, or impelled him to his fall, or why He did not prevent his fall, and the like, we account (except, perhaps, when the improbity of heretics or other importunate men compel them too to be explained out of God's Word, as has been done not seldom by pious doctors of the Church) among those curious inquiries which the Lord prohibits, lest man should eat of the forbidden fruit and his transgression be punished; but things that take place are certainly not evil with respect to the providence of God, God's will and power, but with respect to Satan and our will in opposition to God's will.[r] . . .

X. *Of the Predestination of God and the Election of the Saints.* God has from eternity freely and of His mere grace, with no respect of men, predestinated or elected the saints whom He will save in Christ,[s] according to that saying of the Apostle: "God hath chosen us in Himself before the foundations of the world were laid" (Eph. i. 4); and again: "Who saved us and called us with a holy calling, not according to our works, but according to His own purpose and grace, which was given unto us through Jesus Christ before times eternal, but is now made manifest by the appearance of our Saviour Jesus Christ" (II Tim. i. 9, 10).

Therefore, not without means,[t] though not on account of any merit of ours, but in Christ and on account of Christ, God elected us; so that those who are now ingrafted into Christ by faith the same also are elect;[u] but they are reprobates, who are without Christ, according to that saying of the Apostle: "Prove yourselves whether you are in faith. Know ye not your own selves that Jesus Christ is in you, except ye be reprobates?" (II Cor. xiii. 5).

In fine, the saints are elected by God in Christ to a sure end, which very end the Apostle sets forth when he says: [v] "He has chosen us in Him that we should be holy and without blame before Him in love; and He has predestinated us that He might adopt us

r West. Conf., III. i. b.
s West. Conf., III. v. a.
t West. Conf., III. vi. a.
u West. Conf., III. viii.
v West. Conf., III. v. a.

through Jesus Christ to Himself to the praise of the glory of His grace " (Eph. i. 4, 5, 6).

And although God knows who are His,[a] and mention is now and then made of the fewness of the elect, we must nevertheless hope well of all, and not rashly number any among the reprobates. Paul certainly says to the Philippians: " I give thanks for you all " (and he is speaking of the whole Philippian Church), " that you have come into the fellowship of the Gospel, being persuaded that He who has begun a good work in you will perfect it, as it is right for me to think this of you all " (Phil. i. 3–7).

And when the Lord was asked (Luke xiii.) whether there are few that shall be saved, the Lord does not say in reply that few or more are to be saved or lost, but rather exhorts that each should strive to enter in at the strait gate, as if He should say, It is not for you to inquire curiously about these things, but rather to endeavor to enter heaven by the straight path.[b]

Wherefore we do not approve of the wicked speeches of some who say, " Few are elected, and as it does not appear whether I am in that number of the few, I will not defraud my nature." Others say, " If I be predestinated or elected by God, nothing can hinder me from a salvation already certainly decreed, no matter what I may ever commit; but if I be in the number of the reprobate no faith or repentance either will help me, since the appointment of God cannot be changed: therefore all teachings and admonitions are useless." For to these that saying of the Apostles is opposed: " The servant of the Lord must be apt to teach, instructing them that are contrary minded, if at any time God will give them repentance unto the knowledge of the truth, that they may escape from the snare of the devil who are held captive by him to his will " (II Tim. ii. 24–26).

But Augustine also, in his work on the " Blessing of Perseverance," shows that there are to be preached both the grace of free election and predestination, and salutary admonitions and doctrines. We, therefore, condemn those who seek outside of Christ whether they are elect and what God had decreed concerning them from all eternity.[c]

For the preaching of the Gospel must be heard and faith be given it: and it is to be held indubitable that thou art elect if thou believest and art in Christ. For the Father has laid bare to us in

[a] West. Conf., III. iv.
[b] West. Conf., III. viii.
[c] West. Conf., III. viii. a.

Christ the eternal sentence of His predestination, as we have just shown from the Apostle (II Tim. i.).[d] There is to be taught, therefore, and considered before all things, how great the love of the Father toward us is that is revealed to us in Christ; and what the Lord preaches to us daily in the Gospel must be heard — how He calls and says: " Come to me, all ye that labor and are heavy laden, and I will give you rest " (Matt. xi. 28) ; " God so loved the world that He gave His only-begotten for the world, that every one who believeth in Him should not perish but have eternal life " (John iii. 16); again: " It is not the will of the Father that any one of these little ones should perish " (Matt. xviii. 14).

Let Christ then be the mirror in which we contemplate our predestination. We shall have a sufficiently clear and sure witness that we are written in the Book of Life, if we participate in Christ, and He is ours in true faith, and we His. Let it console us in the temptation of predestination, than which there is scarcely any more perilous, that the promises of God to believers are universal and that He Himself has said: " Ask and ye shall find. Every one that asketh, receiveth " (Luke xi. 9, 10) : [e] in fine, that we pray with the whole Church of God: " Our Father which art in Heaven ": and that we are ingrafted into the body of Christ by baptism, and are repeatedly fed in the Church with His body and blood to life eternal. Confirmed by these things we are commanded, according to this precept of Paul, " to work out our salvation with fear and trembling " (Phil. ii. 12).

XIII. *Of the Gospel of Jesus Christ.* . . . For God has from eternity predestinated to save the world through Christ, and has manifested this His predestination and eternal counsel to the world through the Gospel (II Tim. i. 9, 10). Whence it is clear that the evangelical religion and doctrine is the most ancient of all, among all that have ever been, are or shall be. And hence we say that they all err dreadfully and speak unworthily of the eternal counsel of God, who describe the evangelical doctrine and religion as lately arisen and a faith scarcely thirty years old.

[d] West. Conf., III. viii. a.　　　　[e] West. Conf., III. viii.

Heidelberg Catechism (1563) [31]

I, with body and soul, both in life and death, am not my own, but belong to my faithful Saviour Jesus Christ, who with His precious blood has fully satisfied for all my sins, and redeemed me from all the power of the devil; and so preserves me that without the will of my Father in heaven not a hair can fall from my head; yea, that all things must work together for my salvation. Wherefore, by His Holy Spirit, He also assures me of eternal life, and makes me heartily willing and ready henceforth to live unto Him (1).

The eternal Father of our Lord Jesus Christ, who of nothing made heaven and earth, with all that in them is, who likewise upholds and governs the same by His eternal counsel and providence, is for the sake of Christ His Son my God and my Father, in whom I so trust as to have no doubt that He will provide me with all things necessary for body and soul; and further, that whatever evil He sends upon me in this vale of tears, He will turn to my good; for He is able to do it, being Almighty God, and willing also, being a faithful Father (26).

[The providence of God is] the almighty and everywhere present power of God, whereby, as it were by His hand, He still upholds heaven and earth, with all creatures, and so governs them that herbs and grass, rain and drought, fruitful and barren years, meat and drink, health and sickness, riches and poverty, yea, all things, come not by chance, but by His fatherly hand (27).[f]

[Christ] is ordained [*verordnet*] of God the Father, and anointed with the Holy Ghost, to be our Chief Prophet and Teacher, who fully reveals to us the secret counsel and will of God concerning our redemption. . . . (31).

I look for the selfsame One . . . to come again as Judge from heaven; who shall cast all His and my enemies into everlasting condemnation, but shall take me, with all His chosen ones, to Himself, into heavenly joy and glory (52).

The Son of God from the beginning of the world to its end, by His Spirit and Word, out of the whole human race, gathers, protects

[31] Schaff, at the questions noted (iii. pp. 307 ff.). The English translation of the (German) Reformed Church of the United States is used, except in the extract from Q. 54, which is translated afresh from the German, in order to bring out the strength of the language, which is perhaps somewhat obscured in the above-mentioned translation.

[f] West. Conf., III. i.

and preserves for Himself unto eternal life, in the unity of the true faith, an elected communion; [g] and I am and ever shall remain a living member of the same (54 — Definition of the " Holy Catholic Christian Church ").

Anhalt Repetition (1581) [32]

.   .   .   .   .

Brandenburg Confessions [33]

1. *The Confession of Sigismund* (1614)

In the Article on eternal election or predestination to eternal life His Electoral Highness acknowledges and confesses that it is the most comfortable of all, on which chiefly rest not only all other Articles, but also our blessedness — that, to wit, God the Almighty, out of His pure grace and mercy, without any respect to man's worthiness, merit or works,[h] before the foundations of the world were laid, ordained and elected to eternal life all who constantly believe in Christ,[i] knows also and acknowledges them as His, and as He has loved them from eternity, so endows them also out of pure grace with justifying faith and strong endurance to the end, so that no one shall pluck them out of the hand of Christ and no one separate them from His love, and all things, good and bad alike, must work together for good to them, because they are called according to the purpose.[j] Likewise also that God has, according to His strict righteousness, eternally passed by all who do not believe in Christ, and prepared them for the everlasting fire of hell, as it stands expressly written: [k] " He who does not believe in the Son is judged already," " He who does not believe in the Son shall not see life, but the wrath of God abides (and therefore it is already) on him " — not as if God were a cause of the sinner's destruction, not as if He had pleasure in the sinner's death, not as if He were an author and inciter of sin,[l] *not as if He did not wish all to be saved,* for the contrary is to be found everywhere in the Holy Scriptures; but that the cause of sin and destruction is to be sought only in Satan and the

---

[32] Not a Reformed creed, but represents the milder " Lutheranism in opposition to the Flacian party " (Schaff). See Schaff, i. pp. 563 f.

[33] From the texts in Niemeyer: pp. 650–651, 664–666, 673–677.

[g] West. Conf., III. v.

[h] West. Conf., III. v. b.

[i] West. Conf., III. v. a.

[j] West. Conf., III. vi. a, b.

[k] West. Conf., III. vii. a, b.

[l] West. Conf., III. i. b.

godless, *who are repudiated to damnation on account of their unbelief and disobedience to God.* And moreover that *of no man's salvation is it to be doubted so long as the means of salvation are used,* because it is not known to any man at what time God will mightily call His own, or who will hereafter believe or not, since God is not limited to any time and does all things according to His pleasure. And, on the other hand, His Electoral Highness rejects all and every of such partly blasphemous and partly dangerous opinions and assertions as that we must climb up into heaven and there search out in a special register or in God's secret treasury and council chamber who are predestinated to eternal life and who not; for God has sealed the Book of Life, and no creature can pry into it (II Tim. ii. 19). Likewise [he rejects] that God has elected some, *propter fidem prævisam,* on account of foreseen faith, which is Pelagian; [m] and that *He does not desire the greater part to be saved, but condemns them absolutely, nakedly, without any cause, and therefore not on account of sin,* for certainly the righteous God has never determined on damnation except for sin,[n] and therefore the decree of reprobation to damnation is not to be regarded as an *absolutum decretum,* a free, naked decree, as the Apostle says of the rejected Jews: " Behold the branches were broken off on account of their unbelief." Again [he rejects], *that the elect may live just as they choose, and, on the other hand, nothing can help those that are not elect, no Word, no Sacrament, no piety;* for certainly from the Word of God it is clear that no good tree brings forth evil fruit, and that God has elected us that we should be holy and unblamable before Him in love (Eph. i. 4) ; and that whoever abides as a good branch in the vine of Christ brings forth much fruit; and that whosoever does not abide in Him shall be cut off as a branch and wither, and men gather them and cast them into the fire, and they must burn, as Christ the Lord Himself says (John xv. 5–6).

2. *The Leipzig Colloquy* (1631)

And although the doctrine of eternal election is not expressly treated in the Augsburg Confession, nevertheless it has seemed wise to the theologians of both sides to set forth their doctrine and meaning on this point also, concerning which there has been hitherto much strife. The Brandenburgan and Hessian theologians declare

[m] West. Conf., III. v. b.   [n] West. Conf., III. vii. b.

therefore the following to be their unanimous doctrine and belief, to wit:

That God chose from eternity in Jesus Christ out of the lost race of man, not all, but some men,[o] whose number and names are known to Him alone,[p] whom He in His own time, through the power and operation of His Word and Spirit, illuminates and renews to faith in Christ; and also enlightens in the same faith to the end and finally makes eternally blessed through faith.[q]

That He moreover found or foresaw no cause or occasion or precedent means or condition of such choice in the elect themselves — whether their good works or their faith or even the first holy inclination or emotion or consent to faith, but that all that is good in them flows originally from the pure free grace of God which is eternally ordained and given to them alone in Jesus Christ.[r]

That also God from eternity ordained and reprobated those who persevere in their sins and unbelief to eternal damnation,[s] not out of such an *absolutum decretum*, or naked will and decree, as if God either from eternity ordains or in time creates the greater part of the world or any men, without regard to their sins and unbelief, to eternal damnation, or to the cause thereof; but the reprobation as well as the damnation takes place out of His just judgment, the cause of which is in man himself, to wit, his sin, impenitence and unbelief;[t] that therefore the entire fault and cause of the reprobation and damnation of the unbelieving is in themselves; the entire cause, however, of the election and blessedness of believers is alone the pure and mere grace of God in Jesus Christ,[u] according to the word of the Lord: " O Israel! thou dost bring thyself into unhappiness: thy salvation, however, stands in me alone."

That, therefore, further, each should be assured of and should know his election and blessedness, not *a priori* from the hidden counsel of God, but only *a posteriori* from the revealed Word of God, and from his faith and the fruits of his faith in Christ;[v] and that it does not at all follow, as the wicked world mockingly misrepresents this high Article, and much less can it be taught, that " whoever is elected may persevere in his godlessness as long as he chooses, and nevertheless he must be saved," while " whoever is not

o West. Conf., III. v. a.
p West. Conf., III. iv.
q West. Conf., III. vi.
r West. Conf., III. v. b.

s West. Conf., III. vii.
t West. Conf., III. vii. b.
u West. Conf., III. v. a.
v West. Conf., III. viii.

elected, even though he should believe in Christ and live a godly life, must nevertheless be damned."

If, however, any would search and pry more deeply into this high mystery and seek for other reasons besides God's free, gracious, and righteous will why God has nevertheless actually brought to faith only some from among men who are alike by nature, and all of whom He could assuredly by His Almightiness have brought to faith and salvation, while on the other hand He has left the rest in their sins and voluntary, obstinate impenitence and unbelief: — then they [the Brandenburg and Hessian theologians] say with the Apostle: " Who art thou, O man, that would dispute with God? Has not the potter power, out of one impure mass of sin, to make one vessel to honor of pure grace, and another to dishonor of just judgment? O the depth of the riches and knowledge of God! How inconceivable are His judgments and how unsearchable His ways! Who has become His counselor? Or who has known His mind? Or who has given to Him first that it may be recompensed to him? "

[34] On the other hand the Saxon theologians declare themselves in the following fashion:

1. That God from eternity, and before the foundation of the world was laid, elected in Christ not all, but some men to eternal blessedness.

2. That the number and names of the elect are known to God alone, as the Lord says: " He knows His sheep," and, as St. Paul says: " God knows His own."

3. That God from eternity elected those of whom He saw that they in time would, through the power and operation of His Word and Spirit, believe in Christ and persevere in their faith to the end; and although the elect may for a while fall away from the grace of God, yet it is impossible that this should happen *finaliter* and persistently.

4. That God, in election, found no cause or occasion of such election in the elected themselves, not even a first holy inclination, emotion or consent to faith; but that all that is good in the elect flows originally from the pure free grace of God, which is given them in Christ from eternity.

5. That God from eternity ordained to eternal damnation and

[34] This Lutheran statement is inserted here for purposes of comparison: Niemeyer, pp. 666 f.

reprobation those only whom He knew would persevere in their sins and unbelief.

6. That this reprobation has not at all taken place out of an *absolutum decretum* or naked decree and will, as if God had condemned any one out of His sole pleasure, without regard to man's unbelief. For there was no such naked decree in God, by virtue of which He has either from eternity ordained or in time created either the greater part of mankind or even only a single man to eternal damnation or to the cause thereof.

7. That, however, although so many men are eternally lost and condemned, this happens certainly out of the just judgment of God; but the cause of this condemnation is in the men themselves, to wit, in their dominating sins, their unbelief and impenitence; that therefore the entire fault and cause of the reprobation and condemnation is in themselves, while the entire cause of the election and blessedness of believers is the pure and mere grace of God in Jesus Christ, according to the Word of the Lord: " O Israel! thou dost bring thyself into unhappiness; thy salvation, however, stands in me alone " (Hos. xiii.).

8. That each one should and may be assured of his election and blessedness, not *a priori* out of the hidden counsel of God, but only *a posteriori* out of the revealed Word of God and out of his faith in Christ; and that it does not at all follow as the wicked world mockingly misrepresents this high Article, and much less can or should it be taught that " Whoever is elected may persevere in his godlessness as long as he chooses, and nevertheless he must and will be saved," while " Whoever is not elected must therefore be damned, although he ever so surely believes in Christ or lives ever so godly a life."

9. That in this high mystery of election there are many questions mooted by men which we in this mortality cannot understand, nor answer otherwise than out of St. Paul: " Who art thou, O man, that disputest with God? " (Rom. ix.). Again: " O the depths of the riches of the wisdom and knowledge of God! How inconceivable are His judgments and how unsearchable His ways! Who has become His counselor? And who has known His mind? Or who has given to Him that it may be recompensed him? " (Rom. xi.).

10. Concerning all this the Saxon theologians have declared themselves, that they also further hold as correct and accordant with the Holy Scriptures all that is taught concerning this Article in the Book of Concord. And that God in particular chose us in

Christ, out of grace indeed, but in such a manner that He foresaw who would believe in Christ perseveringly and in verity, and whom God foresaw that they would so believe, them He also ordained and elected to make blessed and glorious.

3. *The Declaration of Thorn* (1645)

Of Grace. 1. From sin and death there is no redemption or justification through the powers of nature, or through the righteousness of the law, but only through the grace of God in Christ, who has redeemed us, when dead in sins, from wrath and the curse, by making full satisfaction by the unique sacrifice of His death and the merit of His perfect obedience for our sins, and not for ours only but for the sins of the whole world:

2. Who has efficaciously called us, when redeemed, by the Word of the gospel and the Spirit of grace, out of the kingdom of sin and death into the kingdom of grace and life; and has sealed us by the sacraments of grace:

3. Who justifies us or absolves us from sins and adopts us as sons, when we are called and are sincerely repentant, on account of the merit of Christ alone, apprehended by a living faith; and of mere grace imparted to believers, as members of Christ:

4. And likewise by the Spirit of love poured out into our hearts, daily more and more renews us to a sincere zeal for holiness and new obedience, and sanctifies us or makes us righteous and holy:

5. Who, finally, will by the same grace eternally glorify us, persevering to the end of life in faith and love, as heirs of the kingdom of heaven, not out of any merit but out of the grace promised in Christ:

6. And so also will paternally, on account of Christ, reward our good works, done by the grace of the Spirit in faith in Christ and in love, with a most abundant, nay infinite reward, beyond and above their merit:

7. Even as [w] He has from eternity elected us in Christ, not out of any foreseen faith or merit of works or disposition,[x] but out of mere and undeserved grace,[y] as well to that same grace of redemption, vocation, justification, adoption and persevering sanctification which He has given in time,[z] as to the crown of

[w] West. Conf., III. vi.
[x] West. Conf., III. v. b.
[y] West. Conf., III. v. a.
[z] West. Conf., III. vi. b.

eternal life and the glory [a] which is to be participated in by these means.[b]

8. The rest, who hold back the truth in unrighteousness and contumaciously spurn the offered grace of Christ, being rejected in righteous judgment.[c]

From this doctrine of grace, in which the whole system of our salvation is contained, thus summarily set forth:

1. We hope it is manifest that we by no means accord with Socinus, who blasphemously denies and oppugns the satisfaction and merit of Christ, and therefore the very redemption made in His blood.

2. We deny, however, that beyond the death of Christ any, even the least part, of our redemption and salvation can be attributed to sacrifices, or merits, or satisfactions, whether of saints or of ourselves.

3. We deny also that unregenerate men, by any merit of congruity, if they do what is in them to do, dispose themselves to the first grace of vocation.

4. Nor do we suspend the efficacy of the grace of vocation on the free will of man, as if it were not God by His special grace but man by his own will that makes himself to differ.

5. Yet we are falsely accused as if we denied the sufficiency for all of the death and merit of Christ, or diminished its power, when rather we teach the same that the Council of Trent set forth, Sess. 6, Cap. 3, to wit: " Although Christ died for all, all nevertheless do not receive the benefit of His death, but those only to whom the merit of His passion is communicated." The cause or fault, moreover, why it is not communicated to all we confess to be by no means in the death or merit of Christ, but in men themselves.

6. We are also falsely accused: As if we taught that not all those who are called by the Word of the gospel are called seriously and sincerely or sufficiently by God for repentance and salvation, but the most only simulatingly and hypocritically by a mere external will *signi*, with which no internal will *beneplaciti* is present, as from one who does not will the salvation of all. We most solemnly protest that we are very far removed from such an opinion, distorted against us from the ill-understood or perhaps even ill-considered words of some, and that we attribute to the Thrice-blessed God supreme

[a] West. Conf., III. v. a.　　　　　[c] West. Conf., III. vii.
[b] West. Conf., III. vi. a.

verity and sincerity in all His sayings and doings, and above all in the Word of the grace that calls to salvation, and do not imagine any contradictory wills in Him.

7. As if we denied all inherent righteousness to believers, and held that they are justified by an external imputation of the righteousness of Christ alone, which is without any internal renovation. When rather we teach that righteousness is imputed only to those that repent and believe in Christ with true faith, and at the same time by the same faith contrite hearts are vivified by the Holy Spirit, are excited to ardent love for Christ and zeal for new obedience, are cleansed from depraved passions and so the righteousness and holiness of a new life are begun and daily advanced. This only we add, that in this inherent righteousness of our own, because it is imperfect in this life, no one can stand before the just judgment of God, or trust in it, so as to be justified or absolved by it from liability to death, but through and on account of the perfect righteousness and merit of Christ alone, apprehended by a living faith.

8. As if we imagined that a man is justified by faith only, which is without works and which only believes that sins are remitted to it for Christ's sake, although it abides without any repentance for them; when rather we confess that such a faith is wholly false, and that a man is not only not justified by it, but is even more gravely condemned on account of it, as transforming the grace of God into license for sinning. What we say is that that is true justifying faith which embraces with a practical or fiducial assent the promises of the Gospel, by which remission and life in Christ are offered to the repentant, and applies it to oneself by a truly contrite heart, and which is therefore efficacious through love. We say that only it justifies; not because it is alone, but because only it apprehends the promise of the Gospel and therefore the very righteousness of Christ, through and on account of which alone we are freely, without any merit of our own, justified.

9. As if by this doctrine we took away zeal for good works, or denied their necessity; when rather it is manifest from what has already been said, that neither justifying faith nor justification itself can possibly exist in adults without sanctification and zeal in good works. And in this sense we acknowledge that they are altogether necessary for salvation, although not as meritorious causes of justification or salvation.

10. As if we held that the precepts of Christ can in no way be

kept by believers; when rather we teach that they not only can be kept, not indeed in men's own powers, but by the grace of the Holy Spirit, but also that they ought altogether to be kept by all, and that not merely by an inefficacious vow or purpose, but also by the deed itself, and that by the sincere and persevering effort of a whole life. Nevertheless, they are not and cannot be kept in this life by any one so perfectly that we can by our works satisfy the law of God and fulfill it in all respects, but have need daily to ask humbly of God, out of a sense of our imperfection and weakness, forgiveness of varied lapses and derelictions.

11. As if we held that the justified cannot even for a moment lose God's grace or the assurance of it, or the Holy Spirit Himself, though they indulge themselves in sinful pleasures; when on the contrary we teach that even the regenerate, as often as they fall into sins against their conscience, and for as long as they continue in them, do not for that time retain either living faith or the justifying grace of God, or yet the assurance of it or the Holy Spirit, but incur new liability to wrath and eternal death, and will certainly, moreover, be damned, unless they are again renewed to repentance by the operation of the special grace of God (which we do not doubt will take place in the case of the elect).[d]

12. We deny, furthermore, that faith in Christ justifies only dispositively, preparatively, initially, because, to wit, it disposes to love and other virtues, that is to say, to inherent righteousness.

13. We deny also that by that inherent righteousness of our own, we are so justified that we are absolved from liability to death by and on account of it before the judgment of God, are adopted as sons and are pronounced worthy of eternal life; in which forensic sense the word Justification is used by the Holy Ghost in this doctrine. For although there is a sound sense in which it may be said that believers are justified, that is, are made righteous and holy, by love and other infused virtues, this righteousness nevertheless is imperfect in this life and can never stand, as aforesaid, before the severe judgment of God; and this alone is what is under consideration in this doctrine.

14. Hence, also, we do not agree with those who teach that the regenerate by good works make satisfaction to the justice of God for their sins, and properly merit remission or life, and that indeed out of condignity, or out of the intrinsic worthiness of their works,

[d] West. Conf., III. vi.

or their equality with the rewards: every covenant, moreover, or promise, as some wish, being excluded.

15. Nor yet with those who teach that the regenerate can keep the law of God perfectly in this life, with a perfection not only of parts but also of degrees, so that they live without any sin, such as is in itself and its own nature mortal: and even that they can do works of supererogation transcending the perfection of the law, and by them merit not for themselves only but for others as well.

16. Nor yet with those who teach that no one without special revelation can certainly know that he has obtained the grace of God with such certitude that he cannot be mistaken; and that all ought to be always in doubt of grace. We, on the other hand, although we confess that even believers and the justified ought not rashly and securely to presume on the grace of God, and are afflicted often with various troubles and doubts, nevertheless teach out of the Scriptures that they both can and ought to strive for and by the help of the Divine grace attain in this life that certitude in which the Holy Spirit witnesses with our spirit that we are sons and heirs of God: and this testimony cannot be false, though not all who boast of the Spirit of God really have this testimony.[e]

17. Finally we teach indeed that not all men are elect, and that those who are elected are elected not out of a foreseen merit of works or a foreseen disposition to faith in them, or assent of will, but out of mere grace in Christ;[f] and that moreover the number of the elect and of the saved is certain with God.[g]

18. Meanwhile we affirm that an opinion alien to our thought is attributed to us by those who accuse us, as if we held that eternal election and reprobation is made absolutely, without any respect to faith or unbelief, or to good or evil works: whereas on the contrary we rather hold that — in election faith and obedience are foreseen in those to be elected, not indeed as cause or reason of their election, but certainly as means of salvation foreordained in them by God;[h] in reprobation on the other hand, not only original sin, but also, so far as adults are concerned, unbelief and contumacious impenitence are not, properly speaking, foreordained by God, but foreseen and permitted in the reprobates themselves as the meritorious cause of

[e] West. Conf., III. viii.
[f] West. Conf., III. v. a and b.
[g] West. Conf., III. iv.
[h] West. Conf., III. vi.

desertion and damnation, and reprobated by the justest of judgments.[1]

Accordingly on this sublime mystery of predestination, we clearly hold the same opinion which in the first instance Augustine of old asserted out of the Scriptures against Pelagius; and which the greatest doctors of the Roman Church themselves, especially the followers of Thomas Aquinas, retain to-day.

First Genevan Confession (1536) [35]

X. *All our Good by the Grace of God.* And finally that all the praise and glory may be rendered to God (as is due), and that we may be able to have true peace and quiet in our consciences, we acknowledge and confess that we receive all the blessings now recited from the mercy of God alone, without any consideration of our worthiness or the merit of our works, to which is due no return except eternal confusion; that, nevertheless, our Lord, having received us in His goodness into communion with His Son Jesus, has works which make us pleasant and acceptable with faith — not at all because they merit it, but only because, not imputing to us the imperfection that is in them, He sees in them nothing except what proceeds from His Spirit.

Genevan Confession (1537) [36]

The Apprehension of Christ by Faith. As the merciful Father offers us His Son in the Word of the gospel, so we embrace Him by faith and recognize Him as given to us. Without doubt the Word of the gospel calls all into participation of Christ, but multitudes, blinded and hardened by unbelief, reject this singular grace. Believers only, therefore, enjoy Christ, and they receive Him as sent to them, and do not reject Him as given to them: and follow Him as called by Him.

Election and Predestination. In such a difference it is necessary to consider the great secret of the counsel of God: for the seed of

[35] Probably composed by Farel, though possibly with the help of Calvin ("Opera Calvini," ed. Baum, Cunitz, and Reuss, ix. 1870, col. 696). There is no article on predestination: but all the glory of salvation is ascribed to God.

[36] From the French text ("Opera Calvini," xxii. 1880, coll. 46 f.).

[1] West. Conf., III. vii.

God's Word takes root and fructifies in those alone whom the Lord, by His eternal election, has predestined to be His children and heirs of the heavenly kingdom.[j] To all others, who are reprobated by the same counsel of God before the constitution of the world,[k] the clear and evident publication of truth can be nothing else but the savor of death unto death. Now the reason why the Lord shows mercy towards the ones and exercises the rigor of His judgment towards the others must be left to be known by Him alone; the which He has willed should be concealed from us and not without very good reason. For neither would the rudeness of our minds permit us to endure so much clarity, nor our littleness permit us to understand so much wisdom. And in fact all who seek to raise themselves to it and are unwilling to repress the temerity of their spirits, experience the truth of what Solomon says (Prov. xxv.) — that he who would search into God's majesty will be oppressed by His glory. Let us only be assured of this — that the dispensation of the Lord, although it is concealed from us, is nevertheless holy and just: for had He willed to destroy the whole human race He had the right to do it, and in those whom it withdraws from perdition, we can contemplate nothing but His sovereign goodness.[l] Therefore, let us recognize the elect to be vessels of His mercy (as they truly are), and the reprobates to be vessels of His wrath, which nevertheless is only just.[m] Let us take from the one and the other alike ground and matter for the proclamation of His glory. And on the other hand also let us not, in order to confirm the certitude of our faith, seek (as many are accustomed to do) to penetrate into the heavens and to search out what God has from eternity determined to do concerning us (which cogitation can only agitate us with miserable anxiety and perturbation): but let us be content with the testimony by which He has sufficiently and amply confirmed this certitude to us.[n] For as in Christ all those are chosen who have been foreordained to life before the foundations of the world were laid, so He is presented to us as the seal of our election if we receive and embrace Him by faith. For what is it that we seek in election except that we may participate in eternal life? And this we have in Christ: for from the beginning He has the life, and He is proposed to us for life, to the end that all who believe in Him shall have eternal life. Since then in

[j] West. Conf., III. v.
[k] West. Conf., III. iii.
[l] West. Conf., III. v.

[m] West. Conf., III. v. vi. vii.
[n] West. Conf., III. viii. a,

possessing Christ by faith we possess also life in Him we have no
need to search further into the counsel of God; for Christ is not only
a mirror in which the will of God is represented to us, but also a
pledge by which it is as it were sealed and confirmed to us.°

GENEVAN CATECHISM (1545) [37]

Q. But why do you call God [in the Apostles' Creed] *Creator*,
when to preserve and conserve the creatures in their condition is
much more grand than once to have created them?

A. It is certainly not intended by this particular that God has
so once created His works that afterwards He has laid aside care
for them. But rather it is so to be understood as that the world, as
it was once created by Him, so now is conserved by Him; and that
neither the world nor anything else stands except so far as it is sustained by His power and, as it were, His hand. Moreover, since He
thus has all things in His hands, He is constituted thereby the Supreme Governor and Lord of all. Therefore, from His being the
Creator of heaven and earth, it is proper to gather that He it is
alone who, in His wisdom, kindness, power, rules the whole course
and order of nature; who is the author at once of drought, of hail
and other storms, and as well of the calm; who in His goodness fer-
tilizes the earth and again makes it barren by withdrawing His
hand; from whom proceed both health and sickness; to whose empire, in fine, all things are subject and whose nod they obey.

Q. What are we to think, however, of the godless and of devils
— shall we say that they, too, are subject to Him?

A. Though He does not govern them by His Spirit, He nevertheless coerces them by His power as by a bit, so that they are not even
able to move, except so far as He permits to them. He makes them
also the ministers of His will, so that they are compelled, unwillingly
and against their counsel, to execute what has seemed good to Him.ᴾ

Q. What good do you derive from the knowledge of this?

A. Very much. For it would go ill with us if anything was permitted to the devils and godless men apart from the will of God;
and therefore we should never be of peaceful minds if we thought
ourselves exposed to their license. But we may rest in peace now
that we know that they are governed by the will of God and are

[37] From the text in Niemeyer: pp. 128 f., 135 f.
° West. Conf., III. viii.
ᴾ West. Conf., III. i.

held as it were in bounds, so as to be capable of nothing except by His permission: especially since God Himself undertakes to be our Tutor and the Captain of our salvation. . . .

Q. What is the *Church?*

A. The body and society of believers whom God has predestinated to eternal life.[q]

Q. Is it necessary to believe this head [of the Creed]?

A. Assuredly: unless we wish to make Christ's death otiose and to bring to naught all that has been heretofore set forth. For the one issue of it all is that there may be a Church. . . .

Q. Well, then, in what sense do you call the Church *holy?*

A. Because, to wit, whomsoever God has elected, them He justifies and builds up in holiness and innocence of life; by which His glory shines forth in them (Rom. viii. 30).[r] And it is this that Paul means when he admonishes us that Christ has sanctified the Church which He has redeemed so that it may be glorious and free from every spot (Eph. v. 25). . . .

Q. But may not this Church be otherwise known than simply believed in by faith?

A. There is certainly also a *visible* Church of God, which is marked out for us by certain notes and signs; but here we properly treat of the congregation of those whom He has adopted unto salvation by His hidden election. And that is not constantly perceptible to the eyes nor recognizable by signs.

Consensus Tigurinus (1549) [38]

XVI. [Not all who participate in a sacrament partake also in the reality.] Moreover, we sedulously teach that God does not exert His power promiscuously in all who receive the sacraments, but only in the elect. For just as He enlightens unto faith no others than those whom He has foreordained to life, so by the hidden power of His Spirit He brings it about that the elect receive what is offered in the sacraments.[r]

[Calvin's Exposition of the Heads of the Consensus]

What we say about its not being all promiscuously, but only the elect to whom has come the inner and efficacious operation of the

---

[38] From the text in Niemeyer: pp. 195, 209 f.

[q] West. Conf., III. iii. a.   [r] West. Conf., III. vi. b.

Spirit, that profit by the sacraments, is too clear to need a long discussion. For if any one wishes the effect to be common to all, apart from the passages of Scripture which refute that view, experience itself sets it aside. Therefore, as the external voice in itself by no means penetrates the heart of man, but out of many auditors only those come to Christ who are drawn inwardly by the Father: according to the saying of Isaiah, that no others believed his preaching except those to whom the grace of the Lord is revealed: so it lies in the free and gracious will of the same God to give to whom He will to profit by the use of signs. But we do not in so speaking mean that anything of the nature of the sacraments is changed, but that their integrity remains to them. For Augustine, when he restricted the effects of the Holy Supper to the body of the Church, that is, to the predestinated who are already in part justified, and now being justified and yet to be glorified, did not evacuate or diminish its power, considered in itself alone, with respect to the reprobate; but only denied that the fruit of it is equally common to all. But since there is no obstacle in the way of the reception of Christ by the reprobates except their own unbelief, the whole fault also resides in them. In fine, the representation of the sign is unavailing to no one, except him who wilfully and malignantly deprives himself. For it is very true that each receives from the signs only so much fruit as the vessel of his faith will hold. And we justly repudiate that Sorbonnic invention that the sacraments of the new law profit all who do not interpose the obstacle of a mortal sin. For it is clearly an insipid superstition to attribute to them a virtue which the merely external use of them conveys, like a canal, into the soul. And if faith must needs intervene as a means, no sane man will deny that the same God who takes away our weakness by His succor, also gives the faith which, borne up by suitable supports, mounts to Christ and becomes possessed of His favors. And beyond all controversy this certainly must needs be — that as it does not suffice for the sun to shine and to send down its rays from heaven unless first eyes are given us to enjoy its light, so the Lord will vainly shine in His eternal signs unless He makes us seeing. Yea, as the heat of the sun, which in the living and breathing body gives life, in the corpse begets a foul odor, so the sacraments, when the spirit of faith is not present, are certain to breathe a mortifying rather than a vitalizing odor. . . .

Consensus Genevensis (1552) [39]

The consent of the pastors of the Church of Geneva concerning the eternal Predestination of God, by which He has chosen from men some to salvation and has left others to their own destruction: [t] likewise concerning the Providence by which He governs human things: set forth by John Calvin [Title].

The free election of God, by which He adopts to Himself out of the lost and condemned race of men whom He will, has been taught by us here not less reverently and soberly than sincerely and without dissimulation, and has been peacefully received by the people [p. 218]. . . . And the subject is worthy of receiving the most studious attention of the children of God, that they may not be ignorant of the origin of their heavenly birth. For there are some who would foolishly blot out the election of God because the Gospel is called the power of God to every one that believes. And yet it should have come into their mind whence faith arises. The Scriptures certainly everywhere proclaim that God gives His Son those who were His own; that He calls those whom He had chosen; and that it is those whom He has adopted to Himself as sons that He regenerates by His Spirit: in fine, that those who believe are the men whom He has taught inwardly, and to whom His power has been revealed. Wherefore whoever holds that faith is the earnest and pledge of free adoption will confess that it flows from the eternal fountain of divine election. Nevertheless it is not from the secret counsel of God that the knowledge of salvation is to be sought by us. Life is set before us in Christ, who not only reveals Himself, but offers Himself to be enjoyed, in the Gospel. Upon this mirror let the gaze of faith be fixed; and let it not desire to penetrate whither access is not open [p. 219].[u] . . . As to the providence of God by which the world is ruled, this ought to be settled and confessed among all the godly — that there is no reason why men should ascribe to God a share in their sins or involve Him in any way with

---

[39] The Consensus Genevensis is written, not in compressed form, but in a diffuse and argumentative style and occupies nearly one hundred octavo pages in Niemeyer's "Collectio confessionum" (pp. 218–310). Nothing will be attempted here beyond presenting a few extracts, which it is hoped will give the substance of its teaching.

[t] West. Conf., III. iii.

[u] West. Conf., III. viii.

them in bearing the blame: [v] but whereas the Scriptures teach that the reprobate are also instruments of God's wrath, whom He partly makes teachers of patience to the faithful, and partly inflicts such punishments on as they deserve, this profane trifler contends that nothing is done righteously by God unless the reason for it lies plainly before our eyes. For taking away all discrimination between remote and proximate causes, he will not suffer the afflictions laid on holy Job to be thought the work of God, lest He should be made equally guilty with the devil and with the Chaldean and Sabæan plunderers [p. 220]. ["Dedicatory Address to the Syndics and Senate of Geneva"]

. . . Albert Pighius has endeavored . . . in the same book to establish the free will of man and to overturn the secret counsel of God by which He elects some to salvation and destines others to eternal destruction [p. 221].[w] . . . Both [Pighius and Georgius] imagine that it is placed within our freedom for each of us to introduce himself into the grace of adoption: and that it does not depend on the counsel of God who are elect or reprobate,[w] but each determines by his own will either fortune for himself: that some believe the Gospel, others remain unbelieving — that this discrimination does not arise out of the free election of God, or out of His secret counsel, but only out of the individual will of each. . . . [Pighius] further pronounces all those to think unworthily concerning God, and to attribute to Him a rigor alien to His justice and goodness, who teach that some are positively and absolutely (*præcise et absolute*) elected, others destinated to destruction [p. 222].[x] . . . It is the figment of Georgius that there has been no predestination to salvation of this or that one,[x] but God has determined a time in which He would save the whole world. . . . Thus he slips away confidently, as if it were plainly established by no Scriptural passage that some have been elected by God to salvation with the preterition of the rest [pp. 222 f.].[y] . . . What is thought by us the "Institutes" sufficiently fully testify, though I should add nothing further. At the outset I would beg my readers to bear in mind what I there suggest: That this subject is not, as it wrongly seems to some, a wordy and thorny speculation which fruitlessly wearies the mind, but a discussion solid and eminently adapted to the advancement of godliness, because it admirably builds up faith, and trains us to humility,

and rouses us to admiration of the immense goodness of God toward
us and excites us to its praise. For there is no means better adapted
to build up faith than hearing that that election which the Spirit of
God seals upon our hearts stands in the eternal and immutable good
pleasure of God, and cannot therefore be the prey of any earthly
storms, of any Satanic assaults, of any vacillation of the flesh.[z] For
our salvation is at length made sure to us when we find its cause in
the bosom of God. For thus in apprehending by faith the life manifested in Christ it is permitted to see far off, under the guidance of
the same faith, from what fountain that life proceeded. Our assurance of salvation is founded in Christ, and rests on the promises of
the Gospel. But this is no weak support, when now we hear that that
we believe in Christ is a Divine gift to us; because we were both
ordained before the beginning of the world to faith and elected to the
inheritance of eternal life. Hence that inexpugnable security —
because the Father who gave us to His Son as a peculiar possession
is stronger than all and will not suffer us to be plucked out of His
hand [p. 223]. . . . Let those clamor who will: we shall ever set
forth the praise of the doctrine we teach of the free election of God,
because except through it believers will never sufficiently understand how great the goodness of God has been towards them when
they were effectually called to salvation. . . . If we are not ashamed
of the Gospel, what is openly set forth in it we must needs confess
— that, to wit, God by His eternal good pleasure, which hangs on
no other cause, destined to salvation those whom it seemed good to
Himself, with the rejection of the rest,[a] and that those whom He
blessed with this gratuitous adoption He illuminates by His Spirit
that they may receive the life offered in Christ; while the rest are
so willingly unbelievers that they remain in darkness, destitute of
the light of faith [p. 224]. . . . But in a matter so difficult and
recondite nothing is better than to be soberly discreet. Who denies
it? But it is likewise to be looked to that it shall be the best kind of
sobriety. . . . Is this a Christian simplicity — to avoid as noxious
what God makes known? Of this, they say, we may be ignorant
without loss. As if our heavenly Teacher were not the best judge of
what and how much it were well to know [p. 226]. . . .

And that none might attribute it to faith that one is preferred
to another he [Augustine] affirms that those are not chosen who
have believed: but rather that they may believe. . . . Again, in

[z] West. Conf., III. v.   [a] West. Conf., III. iii.

another place (" Ad Bonif.," ep. 106) : " Who created the reprobate
except God? And why except because He would? Why did He will it?
Who art thou, O man, who repliest against God? " . . . But as, in
tracing the beginning of election from the free will of God, he establishes reprobation in His mere will, so he teaches that the surety of
our salvation also is founded in nothing else [p. 228].[b] . . .

The salvation of believers hangs on the eternal election of God,
of which no cause can be adduced except His gratuitous good pleasure.[b] . . . There is certainly a mutual relation between the elect
and reprobate, so that election . . . cannot stand unless we confess
that God segregated definite men, whoever it seemed good to Him,
from others. And this is expressed by the word Predestinating.[c] . . .
But to make faith the cause of election is altogether absurd.[d] . . .
" Paul asserts [says Augustine] that it is the fruit of divine election
and its effect that we begin to be holy. They then act very preposterously who subordinate election to faith." [d] . . . And Paul again
confesses that God was moved by nothing extrinsic, but Himself was
to Himself the author and cause, when He chose those as yet not created to confer on them afterward faith: " According to His purpose,"
says he, " who worketh all things according to the counsel of His
will " [p. 231].[d] . . . Now, when He pronounces that He will cast
out none from their number, but rather life is kept in security for
all, until He shall raise them up at the last day, who does not see
that final (as it is commonly called) perseverance is similarly
ascribed to the election of God? It can happen that some fall away
from faith; but those who have been given to Him by the Father,
Christ asserts to be beyond the danger of destruction. . . . Neither
should it be lightly passed by that he makes God more powerful
than all adversaries whatever, that our certainty of salvation may
not be less than our reverence for the power of God. Hence, amidst
such violent assaults, such various dangers, so many tempests and
storms, the perpetuity of our condition stands nevertheless in this —
that God will constantly preserve by the power of His arm what
He has decreed in Himself concerning our salvation [p. 235].[e] . . .

[Pighius'] last admonition is, That nothing be admitted alien to
God's infinite goodness, and by which odium rather than love would
be awakened towards Him. And so he drives with full sail against
God, if from their creation He destines any to destruction. Never-

b West. Conf., III. v.   d West. Conf., III. v.
c West. Conf., III. iv.   e West. Conf., III. vi.

theless, even if this whole doctrine should be suppressed, occasion would nevertheless never be lacking to the reprobate for either holding God in hatred or assailing Him with their sacrileges. . . . Now let those who can bear to be taught in God's school not refuse to hear with me what Paul declares plainly and with no ambiguities. He places before us the two sons of Isaac who, though both were begotten in the sacred house, almost the very temple of God, were nevertheless separated to dissimilar lots by God's oracle. The cause of this discrimination, which might otherwise have been sought in the deserts of each, he assigns to the hidden counsel of God, " That the purpose of God might stand." We hear it established by God that of the two twins He should elect one only. . . . Since Paul commends grace for this very thing, that by the rejection of the other, one was chosen, certainly what Pighius has fabricated of a universal grace falls. Paul does not simply teach that in order that election might stand Jacob was appointed heir of life, but that his brother was rejected and the right of primogeniture conferred on him.[f] It does not escape me here what some other dogs bark out, what also the ignorant mutter — that the passages cited by Paul do not treat either of eternal life or of eternal destruction. If these men, however, held the true principles of theology which ought to be trite to all Christians, they would have spoken a little more modestly. . . . The objection is that this is to be referred to the land of Canaan; and it is of this that Malachi spoke. And this would be worth listening to if God were fattening the Jews in the land of Canaan like pigs in a sty. But the meaning of the prophet is very different. For God had promised that land to Abraham as an outer symbol of a better inheritance. . . . In a word [the prophet] holds the land of Canaan as the sacred habitation of God [pp. 237 f.] . . . Add that if God foresees anything in His elect, by which He discriminates them from the reprobate,[g] Paul's argument would have been meaningless, that it was when the brothers were not yet born that it was said, of Him that calleth and not of works, The older shall serve the younger. . . . And since Paul assumes as confessed what is incredible to these good theologians, " that," namely, " all are equally unworthy, the corruption of nature is alike in all," he serenely concludes thence that it is by His own free counsel that God elects whomsoever He has elected, and not those whom He foresaw would be obedient children to Him.[g] In a word,

[f] West. Conf., III. iii. vii.   [g] West. Conf., III. v.

Paul is considering what the nature of man would be without God's election; these men are dreaming of God's foresight of what would never have been in man until He made it [p. 239]. . . . If Pighius commends the patience of God, I assert: Nevertheless in the meanwhile this remains settled — that the reprobate are separated out by the counsel of God for this end — that He may show forth His power in them.[h] And that that is not at all different from the meaning of Paul is apparent from his next illation: " Whom He will He hardens." . . . Yet the Scripture is looking especially at the beginning of the thing with which it is dealing so as to ascribe it to God only [pp. 241 f.]. . . . It is to be held, therefore, that the meaning of Paul (Rom. ix. 21) is: That God the Maker of men forms out of the same lump that is taken in hand to honor or to dishonor, according to His will; since He has elected some, not yet born, gratuitously to life, leaving others to their own destruction, seeing that all are obnoxious to it by nature.[i] For while Pighius denies any relation of the election of grace with hatred of the reprobate, I confess this really to exist, so that to the free love in which the elect are embraced, there corresponds in equal and common relation a just severity toward the reprobate (*in causa pari et communi*) [p. 245].[i]
. . . In what sense the Hebrews speak of " vessels " or " instruments," no one who is moderately instructed in the Scriptures will be ignorant. When we hear of " instruments," then God must needs go before as the head and author of the whole, then His hand is the director. But why are they called vessels of wrath, except because He exercises toward them the just severity from which He abstains with reference to others?[j] And why were they made vessels of wrath? Paul answers, In order that God might show His wrath and power in them.[j] He says, " Prepared for destruction "; whence and how, except from their first origin and by nature? — since certainly the nature of the whole human race was vitiated in the person of Adam: not that the higher counsel of God did not precede: but because from this fountain flowed the curse of God and the destruction of the human race. For it is testified that God prepared the vessels of mercy for glory. If this is special to the elect, it is certain that the rest were fitted for destruction, because to be left to their own nature was to be devoted to certain destruction. For the nonsense of some, " That they were fitted by their own proper wicked-

h West. Conf., III. vii.   j West. Conf., III. vii.
i West. Conf., III. iii. vii.

ness," is so absurd as not to deserve notice. It is certainly true that the reprobate procure to themselves the wrath of God by their depravity, and collect it on their heads with daily acceleration. But that here a discrimination which proceeds from the hidden judgment of God is dealt with by Paul is confessed. He says also, " The riches of God's grace are manifested," while on the other hand " vessels of wrath " rush to destruction. Here certainly we do not hear of what Pighius prates of — " That grace is equal to all "; but that the goodness of God is better illustrated, because He endures vessels of wrath and suffers them to come to their own end. . . . Neither otherwise can that inviolable covenant of God stand, " I am a jealous God, showing mercy to a thousand generations; a severe avenger to the third and fourth generation," than by the Lord's decreeing by His own will to whom He will grant His grace and whom He wills to remain devoted to eternal death.[k] . . . Here certainly a distinction is made among men: and it is not made on the ground of the merits of each, but on the ground of the covenant made with the fathers [p. 246]. . . . The truth of that saying of Augustine (" De prædest. sanct.," i. 2) is apparent, " Those are converted whom He Himself has wished to be converted, and these He not only from unwilling makes willing, but also from wolves sheep, from persecutors martyrs, reforming them by His mighty grace." If man's wickedness be set in opposition, it would be more mighty than the grace of God . . . if the affirmation should not be true, " He will have mercy on whom He has mercy." And Paul's interpretation leaves no doubt. For after saying (Rom. xi. 7) that the election of God was fixed, he adds, " The rest were blinded, that the prophecy might be fulfilled." I concede that the blinding was voluntary and I ascribe it gladly to their own fault (Augustine, " De bono persev.," 12). But I hear who they are that Paul excepts, — to wit, those whom it seemed good to the Lord to choose. Why, however, did He choose these rather than those? . . . He accuses them, to be sure, as they deserve. But it is wrong and foolish for any to infer from this that the origin of their hardening lies in their own wickedness, as if there were no more occult cause of this very wickedness, viz., the corruption of nature; and as if, again, they did not remain sunk in this corruption for no other reason than because in the hidden counsel of God before they were born they were not destroyed as reprobates! [pp. 247 f.] . . . This is the sum: If we

[k] West. Conf., III. iii.

admit the Spirit of God who spoke by the Apostles to be the interpreter of the Prophet, the hidden and incomprehensible judgment
of God is to be adored in its blinding the greater part of men, lest
" seeing they should see." Let there be a cessation here of all the
reasonings that can come into our minds. For if we stick fast in
man, this certainly will be first: That the Lord gives freely to those
that seek: and the rest languish in their need, the remedy for which
they do not ask. But unless what Augustine says comes to our aid
— that it is due to the Divine goodness not only that it is opened to
those that knock, but also that we knock and seek — it is not yet
sufficiently known to us what the need is under which we labor.
And if we come to the matter of help — experience evinces that that
power of the Spirit by which is brought about what needs to be
brought about is not free to all. Let no one deceive himself with
empty flatteries. Those who come to Christ were already God's sons
in His heart while they were yet in themselves enemies: and it was
because they were foreordained to life that they were given to
Christ [p. 249].[1] . . . It is not at all remarkable that Pighius should
mix up everything so indiscriminately (to use his own word) in the
judgments of God, when he does not discriminate between proximate
and remote causes. Let men look around, hither, thither, they yet
do not discover how to transfer the fault of their destruction: because its proximate cause resides in themselves. Even though they
complain that the wound is inflicted on them from without, the
interior apprehension of their mind will still hold them convinced
that the evil had its origin in the voluntary defection of the first
man. . . . If nothing then forbids either the first origin of ruin to
have begun from Adam, or each of us to discern its proximate cause
in himself, what stands in the way of the secret counsel of God, by
which the fall of man was foreordained, being afar off adored by our
faith with proper sobriety: while yet we behold as appears more
closely the whole human race bound in the person of Adam to the
guilt of eternal death and thus subjected to death? [pp. 252 f.] . . .
[Pighius] assaults that appearance of repugnancy (as it is called)
in our opinion: that inasmuch as God decreed in Himself, before
Adam's creation, what should happen to him and his posterity, the
destruction of the reprobate ought not to be imputed to sin; because
it would be absurd to make the effect prior to its own cause. But
I affirm both of those things which Pighius attacks to be true. For

[1] West. Conf., III. vi.

so far as the dissidence between these two opinions which he pretends is concerned, there certainly is none. We say that man was
created in such a state that he cannot complain of his Maker. God
foresaw Adam's fall, and assuredly it was not against His will that
He suffered him to fall. What is gained by tergiversation here? Yet
Pighius makes denial: " because the before-conceived counsel concerning the salvation of all remains stable." As if no solution was
at hand: salvation was not destined for all, otherwise than if they
should stand in their first condition. For no sane person will concede
that there was a simple and absolute decree of God that all should
attain to salvation. For it was sufficient for the just damnation of
man that, when he was placed in the way of salvation, he voluntarily
fell from it. Yet it could not be otherwise. What then? Is he thereby
freed from fault, though the seat of it all was his own will? . . .
The same also [as Augustine teaches] we too teach: that as we are
all together lost in Adam, it is by the just judgment of God that
those who perish, perish; and yet at the same time we confess that
whatever loss befell Adam was divinely ordained [pp. 253 f.]. . . .
So again the promises which incite all to salvation do not show
simply and absolutely what God has determined in His hidden
counsel, but what He is prepared to do for all who have been brought
to faith and repentance. But thus a double will is attributed to God,
who is so little variable that not even the least shadow is cast upon
Him. What would it be but to mock men, Pighius asks, if God
professes to will what He does not will? But if these two things be
read in conjunction, as they ought to be, " I desire that the sinner
should be converted and live " — that calumny is easily done away.
God demands conversion of us: and whenever He finds it, the promised reward of life is bestowed. Therefore God is said to desire life
along with repentance: and it is because He desires it that He invites
all to it by His Word. But that does not conflict with His hidden
counsel, by which He has decreed to convert only His elect. Neither
is it right to think Him variable, because He, as Legislator, publishes
to all the external doctrine of life. In this prior mode He calls all
to life: but in that other mode He leads whom He will, as a father
regenerating by His spirit, His children alone [pp. 256 f.]. . . .
Neither, assuredly, do I send men off to the hidden election of God
that they may look open-mouthed for salvation thence: but I exhort
them to flee straight to Christ in whom the salvation is set forth for
us which otherwise would have lain hidden in God. For whosoever

does not walk in the lowly path of faith — to him the election of God is nothing but a deadly labyrinth. Therefore that the remission of our sins may be assured to us, that our consciousness may rest in confidence of eternal life, that we may boldly call upon God as Father, our beginning is not at all to be made from God's determination concerning us before the creation of the world; but from the revelation of His fatherly love to us in Christ and Christ's daily preaching to us by the Gospel. There is nothing higher to be sought by us than that we should be God's children. But the mirror of free adoption, in which alone we attain so great a good — its pledge and earnest — is the Son, who came forth to us from the Father's bosom, in order that He might ingraft us into His body and so make us heirs of the heavenly kingdom [p. 261]. . . . This then is the way in which God governs His own; this the manner in which He completes the work of His grace in them. But for why He takes them by the hand, there is another higher cause: it is His eternal purpose by which He has destined them to life [p. 262].[m] . . . But as Christ will recompense to the elect the reward of righteousness, so I by no means deny that what will then be visited on the reprobate will be the penalties of their own impiety and iniquities. Neither will it be possible to elicit from our doctrine that God by His eternal counsel chose to life whom it seemed good to Him and left the others to destruction; [n] any such thing as that there are no penalties established for evil works and no reward set for good. We shall all stand before the tribunal of Christ, that each may receive according to what he has done in his body, whether good or bad. But whence comes the righteousness and holiness which shall then receive the crown, except from the regeneration unto newness of life which God works in them by His Spirit? And whence the gift of regeneration but from free adoption? . . . But the fault of our damnation resides so in ourselves that it is improper to bring alien colors to obliterate it. . . . How preposterously Pighius takes away the remote by throwing forward the proximate cause! [p. 263]. . . . The Sorbonnic Sophists prate of an ordinate will of God and another absolute one. This blasphemy, from which pious ears justly recoil, would seem plausible to Pighius and his like. But I contend on the contrary that there is so little anything inordinate in God, that there rather flows from Him whatever there is of order in the heavens and the earth. Though then we do carry forward the will of God to

[m] West. Conf., III. vi.   [n] West. Conf., III. iii.

the supremest degree, so that it is superior to all reason, far be it from us to imagine that He wills anything except with the highest reason: we believe in all simplicity that He has in His own right so much power that it behooves us to be content with His nod alone. . . . [But] did ever this monstrosity come into my mind, that God had no reason for His counsel? As I hold God to be the Ruler of the whole world, who governs and directs all things by His incomprehensible and wonderful counsel, how can any one gather from my words that He is carried hither and thither by chance, or does what He does in blind rashness? . . . The Lord has, as the reason for all His works, His own glory [pp. 264 f.] . . . There is another objection of the same nature: I deny that the elect are distinguished from the reprobate through any respect to their own deserts, since the grace of God makes, not finds, them worthy of adoption, as Augustine often says.[o] Elsewhere I deny that any injustice is done to the reprobate, since they deserve to perish. Here Pighius tumultuously vaunts himself with outspread wings: I do not, it seems, understand myself or remember what I have already said. I am so far from thinking it necessary to expend many words in my defense that it irks me to advert to it even briefly. That God prefers some to others and chooses some while passing by others — this discrimination does not hang on the worthiness or unworthiness of men.[p] Therefore it is wrong to say that those are reprobated who are worthy of eternal destruction. Although, however, in the former case there is no comparison made between the persons, and the reward of life is not afforded to worthiness, in the second case, on the contrary, the same condition is not determined for all. Add that Augustine, when he had somewhere written: "That salvation fails for no one who is worthy of it"; afterwards, in his "Retractationes," so modifies this as to exclude works and to refer acceptable worthiness to the free vocation of God. But Pighius insists "That if it be true, as I teach, that those who perish are destined to death by the eternal decree of God, the reason of which is not apparent, then they are made, are not found, worthy of destruction." I reply that there are three things here to be considered: first, that the eternal predestination of God by which, before Adam fell, He decreed what was to be, with reference to the whole human race and with reference to each and every man, was fixed and determined;[q] next, that Adam himself

[o] West. Conf., III. v.

[p] West. Conf., III. iii. v. vii.

[q] West. Conf., III. i.

was sentenced to death on account of the desert of his fall; last, that the whole of his progeny was so condemned in his fallen and lost person, that God grants the honor of adoption to those whom He freely chooses from among them. No one of these have I imagined or fabricated. Neither is it my present concern to prove any of them — this I seem to myself already to have done. I need only relieve myself of Pighius' calumny, who proudly triumphs over me as ten times over vanquished — as if these things could not be conciliated in any way whatever. Whenever predestination is discussed I have always taught and teach still to-day, that the start must be taken from this — that all the reprobate are justly left in death, since they died and were condemned in Adam;[r] that they justly perish, because they are by nature children of wrath; and therefore no one can have against God any ground of complaint of too much rigor, since they bear their guilt included in themselves. And, when we come to speak of the first man, that he, though he was created perfect, fell of his own accord; and thence it has come about that by his own fault destruction has fallen on him and his; although, of course, Adam did not fall and destroy himself and his posterity without the knowledge and thus the ordination of God, yet that in no respect operates either for alleviating his fault or for implicating God in the crime. For we must always consider that he of his own accord deprived himself of the rectitude which he had received from God, that of his own accord he gave himself into servitude to sin and Satan, that of his own accord he precipitated himself into destruction. The sole excuse alleged is that he could not escape what was decreed by God. But a voluntary transgression is enough and more than enough for guilt. And neither is the secret counsel of God, but the unobstructed will of man, the proper and genuine cause of sin. The silly complaint of Medea is justly derided in the old poet. . . . When she is conscious of her perfidy and barbarous cruelty, when the shame of her impurity smites her, she absurdly turns to occasions far remote. . . . But as to God's having knowingly and willingly suffered man to fall, the reason may be hidden, it cannot be unjust. . . . I so say that He ordained it as not to allow that He was the proper author of it [pp. 266–268].[s] . . . After Paul had taught that out of the lost mass God chose and reprobated whom it seemed good to Him, he so little set forth why and how He did it that he rather in the greatest awe broke forth into that cry:

[r] West. Conf., III. vii.   [s] West. Conf., III. i. b.

" O, the height! " (Rom. xi. 33) [t] . . . Although meanwhile I do
not in the least disapprove of what Augustine says in the twelfth
book of his " De genesi ad literam " (A, c. 4 to c. 8), when he is
adjusting all to fear and reverence toward God; yet the other part,
that God chooses whom He will out of the condemned seed of Adam,
and reprobates whom He will, as it is far better fitted to exercise
faith, so is it more likely to produce better fruit [p. 269].[u] . . .
Assuredly as the stupidity and ingratitude of men who withdraw
themselves from the help of God can never be sufficiently condemned, so is it an intolerable insult to Christ to say that the elect
are saved by Him provided that they take good care of themselves:
throwing thus an ambiguity over Christ's protection, which He
affirms is inexpugnable to the devil and all the machinations of
hell. . . . If, then, eternal life is certain to all the elect, if no one
can pluck them away, if they can be snatched away by no violence
and by no assault, if their salvation stands in the invincible might
of God, with what face does Pighius dare to break this fixed certitude? [p. 272] . . . If Pighius asks what is the source of my knowledge of my election — Christ is to me equal to a thousand witnesses;
for when we find ourselves in His body, our salvation rests in a
secure and quiet position as if it were already placed in heaven
[p. 273].

[Georgius] thinks that he argues acutely when he says (Rom.
viii. 32): " Christ is the propitiation for the sins of the whole world.
It is therefore necessary for those who would remove the reprobate
from participation in Christ to place them outside of the world."
Let us not now avail ourselves of the common solution — that
" Christ suffered sufficiently for all, efficaciously for the elect alone."
This great absurdity, by which the monk has obtained the plaudits
of his companions, has no weight at all with me. Throughout what
regions of the world soever the elect may be dispersed, John extends
to them the expiation of Christ, completed by His death. There is
nothing in this inconsistent with reprobates being mingled in the
world with the elect. There is also no place for controversy with
respect to Christ's having come to expiate the sins of the whole
world (John v. 15). But at once this solution meets us: " That
whosoever believeth in Him may not perish, but have eternal life."
For assuredly what we are now discussing is not what is the nature
of Christ's power, or what its inherent value; but to whom He offers

---

[t] West. Conf., III. vii.   [u] West. Conf., III. viii.

Himself to be enjoyed. And if possession stands in faith and faith flows from the Spirit of adoption, it follows that he only is enrolled in the number of God's children who is to be a sharer in Christ. Neither indeed does John the Evangelist set forth anything else as the office of Christ than by His death to gather together into one the children of God. Whence we conclude, that though a reconciliation is offered by Him for all, nevertheless the benefit of being gathered into the company of life belongs to the elect. But when I say that it is offered for all, I do not mean that that ambassage by which God reconciles the world to Himself (as Paul witnesses, II Cor. v. 18) extends to all: it is not even sealed, as is imagined, indifferently in the hearts of those to whom it does extend [p. 285].[v] . . .

For we do not fancy that the elect under the continuous direction of the Spirit keep a straight course: nay, we say that they often slip, wander, fall and are almost separated from the way of salvation. But because the protection of God by which they are defended is the most powerful of all things, it is impossible for them to fall into utter ruin. . . . We must confess that only those whom God illuminates by His Spirit believe; we must confess in fine that election only is the mother of faith [p. 289].

When I have said that the providence of God is to be considered together with its means, this is the sense: If any one has carried aid to those in extremity of need, this is not a human deliverance, but a divine one through the hand of man. The sun rises daily, but it is God that sends light on the world. The earth produces its fruits, but it is God that supplies the bread and into the bread instills strength for our nourishment. In a word, since the lower causes are accustomed, like a veil, to hide God from our sight, we should penetrate with the eye of faith higher, so as to discern the hand of God operating in His instruments [p. 298]. . . . In the first place, we must perceive how the will of God is the cause of all things that take place in the world, while yet God is not the author of the evil things.[w] I will not say with Augustine what I nevertheless freely allow was truly said by him, that there is in sin or in evil nothing positive. For this is a subtlety which to many is not satisfying. I assume for myself, however, another principle: That things done

by men wrongly and unrighteously are right and righteous works
of God [p. 299]. . . . That God directs by His counsel things which
seem especially fortuitous, the Scriptures plainly testify when they
say, " The lot is cast into the lap, but the determination of the
events comes from God " (Prov. xvi. 33). Similarly, if a branch
broken from a tree or an axe slipping unintentionally from the hand
of a man shall smite the head of a passer-by, Moses testifies (Deut.
xix. 5) that God has done it purposely, because He wished the man
to be killed. . . . But because the Stoic necessity appears to be
established after this fashion, the doctrine is odious to many, even
though they do not dare to condemn it as false. This was an ancient
calumny, by which Augustine complains (Lib. 2 of " Ad Bonif.,"
c. 5) that he was unjustly burdened: it ought now to be obsolete.
It is certainly highly unworthy of men of probity and ingenuousness,
who are adequately instructed. What the notion of the Stoics was is
well known. They wove their fate out of the Gordian knot of causes,
in which, since they involved God Himself, they invented " golden
chains," as the fables put it, by which they bound God and so subjected Him to the lower causes. . . . Let us leave the Stoics, then,
to their fate; for us the free will of God is the governor of all things.[x]
But to take contingency out of the world is clearly absurd. I omit
the distinctions that are employed in the schools. What I set forth
will in my judgment be simple and not at all strained, and also
suited for the usage of life. What God has determined is in such a
manner of necessity to come to pass that, nevertheless, it is not
absolutely (*præcise*) and in its own nature (*suapte natura*) a necessity. I have a familiar illustration in the bones of Christ. That
Christ assumed a body in all things like to ours the Scriptures
testify. Accordingly no sane person will hesitate to confess that His
bones were breakable. But it appears to me another and separate
question, Whether any bone of His could be broken. For that all
should remain whole and uninjured must necessarily be because it
was so determined in the fixed decree of God. I am not speaking
thus, certainly, because I object to the received forms of speech,
concerning *necessitas secundum quid* and *necessitas absoluta*, or
concerning *necessitas consequentis* and *consequentiæ;* but only that
no subtleties may stand in the way of my readers — even the least
cultivated ones — recognizing the truth of what I say. If, then, we
consider the nature of Christ's bones, they were breakable; but if,

<hr />

[x] West. Conf., III. i.

on the other hand, that decree of God which was manifested in its own time, they are no more subject to breaking than the angels are to human sorrows. Accordingly, then, as it is proper for us to consider the divinely determined order of nature, I by no means reject contingency as respects our perception.[y] And we must keep in memory what I have already laid down, that when God exercises His power through means and lower causes, it is not to be separated from them. It is a drunken notion to say that God has decreed what shall be, and therefore it is superfluous to interpose our care and effort. On the contrary, since He prescribes to us what to do and wills that we shall be the instruments of His power, let us not deem it lawful for us to separate what He has joined together.[y] . . . Therefore, so far as concerns the future, since the issues of things are as yet hidden from us, each one ought to be as intent on his duty as if nothing had been determined in any direction. Or to speak more properly, each of us ought so to hope for success in all that he undertakes at the command of God, that in the matters of which he is ignorant he conciliates contingency with the sure providence of God. . . . In a word, as the providence of God rightly understood does not tie our hands, so it not only does not impede prayer, but rather establishes it. . . . There is no exhortation more conducive to patience than our knowledge that nothing comes to pass fortuitously, but that that which has seemed good to God has taken place. Meanwhile, it does not follow that the fault of adverse things is not borne by our ignorance, or rashness, or thoughtlessness, or some other vice [pp. 299 f.]. . . . The sum, however, comes to this: Although men wanton like beasts untamed and coerced by no bonds; they are, nevertheless, governed by a secret bit, so that they cannot move even a finger except for the accomplishment rather of God's than of their own work [p. 301].[z] . . . And what Satan works is affirmed by the Scriptures to be the work of God in another aspect, inasmuch, that is, as God, by holding him bound to obedience to His providence, turns him whither He will, and thus applies his activity to His own uses [p. 302]. Considering these things honestly and soberly, there will be no doubt but that the supreme and especial cause of all things is the will of God.[z] . . . We should keep in mind indeed what I have before said: that God does nothing without the best reason: though since His will is the surest rule of righteousness, it ought to be to us, so to speak, the chief reason of all reasons. . . .

[y] West. Conf., III. i. b.   [z] West. Conf., III. i.

That Sorbonnic doctrine, accordingly, in which the Papal theologians take such pride, which attributes *potentia absoluta* to God, I detest. For it would be easier to tear away the sun's light from its heat, or its own heat from the fire, than to separate God's power from His righteousness [p. 305]. . . .

Since then it is from a righteous cause, though one unknown to us, that there proceed from the Lord the things that men perpetrate in their wickedness — although His will is the first cause of all things, I deny nevertheless that He is the author of sin.[a] Assuredly that diversity of causes which I have posited is not to be permitted to fall into forgetfulness — that there is a proximate and also a remote cause — that we may understand how great the difference is between the signal providence of God and turbulent impetuses of men. It is indeed to load us with a base and ungenerous calumny to argue that God is made the author of sin if His will is the cause of all that is done. For when a man acts unrighteously under the incitement of ambition or avarice or lust or any other depraved affection, though God works by a righteous though hidden judgment through his hand, the name of sin cannot square with Him. Sin in man is constituted by perfidy, cruelty, pride, intemperance, envy, blind self-love, or some such depraved desire. Nothing of this kind is found in God. Shimei assaults his king with monstrous petulance. The sin is clear. God uses such a minister for the just humiliation of David, and thus castigates him with such a rod. Who will accuse Him of sin? The Arabs and Sabæans make prey of the substance of others. The crime of robbery is manifest. By their violence God exercises the patience of His servant. Let there emerge from the affair the heroic confession, " Blessed be the name of the Lord," rather than profane revilings be heard. In fine, God's way of working in the sins of men is such that, when we come to Him, every spot is wiped away by His eternal purity [p. 307]. . . . There is no reason, therefore, why any one should drag God into participation in the sin, whenever any conjunction is apparent between His secret counsel and the open vice of men. Let there come to our minds continually that saying of Augustine: " Accordingly the works of God are great, exquisite in all His will, so that in a marvelous and ineffable fashion that is not done apart from His will which yet is done against His will, since it would not be done if He did not permit it: and He does not permit it unwillingly but willingly." And from this

[a] West. Conf., III. i. b.

too is refuted (" Enchir. ad Laur.," c. 100) the ignorance or else the wickedness of those who deny that the nature of God would be simple, if another will be attributed to Him besides that which is revealed by Him in the Law. Some also ask in derision, If there be any will in God which is not revealed in the Law by what name shall it be called? But those must be without understanding to whom the numerous Scriptural references which proclaim with marveling the profound abyss of God's judgments signify nothing. . . . The Scriptures are full of such examples. Shall we, therefore, impute the fault of the sins to God, or fabricate in Him a double will, so that He is at odds with Himself? But as I have already shown that He wills the same thing along with the wicked and profane but after a different manner; so we must now hold that He wills in the same manner things that are different in kind. . . . For the will by which He prescribes what shall be done and by which He avenges transgressions of His law is one and simple [pp. 308 f.].

CALVIN'S ARTICLES ON PREDESTINATION [40]

Before the first man was created God, by an eternal decree, determined what He willed should come to pass with reference to the whole human race.[b]

By this hidden decree of God it was decided that Adam should fall from the perfect state of his nature and should draw all his posterity into the guilt of eternal death.[c]

On the same decree hangs the discrimination between the elect and the reprobate: for some He has adopted to Himself to salvation; others He has destined to eternal destruction.[d]

Although the reprobate are vessels of the just vengeance of God, and again the elect are vessels of mercy, nevertheless no other cause of the discrimination is to be sought in God than His mere will, which is the supreme rule of righteousness.[e]

Although it is by faith that the elect obtain the grace of adoption, election nevertheless does not hang on faith, but is prior to it in time and in order.[f]

Inasmuch as the origination and perseverance of faith flow from

---

[40] From the text in " Opera Calvini," ed. Baum, Cunitz, and Reuss, ix. 1870, coll. 713 f. The date is not known.

[b] West. Conf., III. i. iii.

[c] West. Conf., III. i.   [e] West. Conf., III. iii. v. vii.

[d] West. Conf., III. iii.   [f] West. Conf., III. v. b.

the gratuitous election of God, so none others are truly illuminated unto faith, neither are any others endued with the Spirit of regeneration except those whom God has chosen: [g] but the reprobate must needs remain in their blindness or fall away from faith, if perchance there be any in them.[g]

Although we are chosen in Christ, nevertheless that the Lord considers us among His own is prior in order to His making us members of Christ.[h]

Although the will of God is the supreme and first cause of all things and God holds the devil and all the impious subject to His will, God nevertheless cannot be called the cause of sin, nor the author of evil, neither is He open to any blame.[i]

Although God is truly hostile to sin and condemns all iniquity in men, because it is offensive to Him, nevertheless it is not merely by His bare permission, but by His will and secret decree that all things that are done by men are governed.

Although the devil and reprobates are God's servants and instruments to carry out His secret decisions, nevertheless in an incomprehensible manner God so works in them and through them as to contract no stain from their vice, because their malice is used in a just and righteous way for a good end, although the manner of it is often hidden from us.[j]

They act ignorantly and calumniously who say that God is made the author of sin, if all things come to pass by His will and ordinance; because they make no distinction between the open depravity of men and the hidden appointments of God.[j]

GENEVAN STUDENTS' CONFESSION (1559) [41]

I confess also that God created not only the visible world, that is, the heavens and the earth and all that in them is, but also the invisible spirits, some of whom have continued in their obedience, while others by their own fault have fallen into perdition: and that the perseverance which was in the angels came from the gratuitous election of God, who continued His love and goodness to them, giving them unchangeable constancy to persist ever in good.[k] Accordingly I detest the error of the Manichees who imagined that

[41] "Opera Calvini," ix. coll. 721–726.
[g] West. Conf., III. vi. c.
[h] West. Conf., III. v. vi.
[i] West. Conf., III. i.
[j] West. Conf., III. i. b.
[k] West. Conf., III. iii.

the devil was evil by nature, and even had his origin and principle of himself.

I confess that God has so created the world as at the same time to be its perpetual Governor: so that nothing takes place or can occur except by His counsel and providence.[1] And although the devil and wicked men labor to throw everything into confusion, as do even the faithful by their sins, they cannot pervert the right order. I acknowledge that God, nevertheless, being the supreme Prince and Lord of all, turns the evil to good and disposes and directs all things, whatever they be, by a secret curb in a marvelous fashion, which it behooves us to adore in all humility, since we cannot comprehend it.[m] . . .

I confess that we are made sharers in Jesus Christ and all His benefits by faith in the Gospel, when we are assured of a right certitude of the promises which are contained in it: and as this surpasses all our powers, that we are not able to attain it except by the Spirit of God; and so, that it is a special gift, which is not communicated except to the elect, who have been predestinated before the creation of the world to the inheritance of salvation, without any regard to their worthiness or virtue.[n]

Confession for the Church at Paris (1557) [42]

We believe that it is of the mercy of God alone that the elect are delivered from the common perdition into which all men are plunged: [o] and first of all that Jesus Christ, without whom we are all lost, has been given to us as a redeemer, to bring us righteousness and salvation. . . . We believe that it is by faith only that we are made sharers in this righteousness, and also that we are illuminated unto faith by the secret grace of the Holy Spirit [seeing that we are elect in Jesus Christ],[43] so that it is a free and special gift which God grants to those whom it seems good to Him, and that not only to introduce them into the right path, but also to cause them to continue in it to the end.[p]

[42] " Opera Calvini," ix. coll. 716 f.

[43] This clause is omitted in Bonnet's text (" Lettres de Calvin," ii. 1854, p. 154).

[1] West. Conf., III. i. a.
[m] West. Conf., III. i. b.
[n] West. Conf., III. v. vi.

[o] West. Conf., III. v.
[p] West. Conf., III. vi.

CONFESSION FOR THE FRENCH CHURCHES, TO BE PRESENTED TO THE EMPEROR (1562) [44]

Thence [from original sin], we conclude that the source and origin of our salvation is the pure mercy of God: for He cannot find in us any worthiness by which He might be led to love us. We also, being evil trees, are not able to bring forth good fruit, and thus we are not able to prevent God in acquisition or to merit favor in His sight: but He looks on us in pity to show us mercy and has no other occasion to exercise His compassion on us except our miseries.[q] Accordingly we hold that this kindness which He displays toward us proceeds solely from His having chosen us before the creation of the world, and we seek no reason for His having so done outside of Himself and His good pleasure.[r] And here is our first foundation, that we are acceptable to God because it has pleased Him to adopt us as His children before we were born, and thus He has by a singular privilege withdrawn us from the common curse into which all men are plunged.[r]

But as the counsel of God is inaccessible, we confess that to obtain salvation we must needs come to the means which God has ordained: we are not of the number of those fantastics who, under the shadow of the eternal predestination of God, take no account of walking in the right path to the life that is promised us; but above all things we hold that to be the avowed children of God, and to have the right certitude, we must needs believe in Jesus Christ, because it is in Him alone that we must needs seek the whole substance of our salvation.[s]

THE FRENCH CONFESSION (1559) [45]

VIII. We believe that not only did He create all things, but that He governs and directs them, disposing and ordering, according to His will, all that which comes to pass in the world — not that He is the author of evil or that the guilt of it can be imputed to Him, seeing that His will is the sovereign and infallible rule of all right and justice;[t] but He has admirable means of so making use of devils and sinners that He knows how to turn to good the evil

[44] "Opera Calvini," ix. coll. 756 f.
[45] From the text in Niemeyer: pp. 316, 317 f.
[q] West. Conf., III. v.
[r] West. Conf., III. v. vi.
[s] West. Conf., III. viii.
[t] West. Conf., III. i. b.

that they do, and of which they bear the blame.[u] And thus, while we confess that nothing takes place without the providence of God, we humbly bow before the secrets that are hidden from us without inquiring beyond our measure; but rather applying to our benefit what is revealed to us in Holy Scripture for our peace and safety: inasmuch as God, who has all things subject to Him, watches over us with a paternal care, so that not a hair of our head shall fall without His will.[v] And yet He holds the devils and all our enemies in restraint so that they can do us no injury without His leave. . . .

XII. We believe that out of this universal corruption and condemnation wherein all men are plunged God withdraws those whom, in His eternal and immutable counsel, He has chosen, of His own goodness and mercy alone, in our Lord Jesus Christ, without respect to their works,[w] leaving the rest in this same corruption and condemnation to manifest in them His justice, as in the former He makes the riches of His mercy to shine forth.[x] For the ones are not better than the others until God distinguishes them according to His immutable counsel, which He has determined in Christ Jesus before the creation of the world;[y] neither is it possible for anyone to obtain that good for himself by his own strength, seeing that by nature we cannot have a single good motion, of either feeling or thought, until God has prevented us and disposed us to it.[z]

THE BELGIC CONFESSION (1561) [46]

Art. XIII. We believe that this good God, after He had created all things, did not abandon them to chance or fortune, but directs and governs them in such manner, according to His holy will, that nothing happens in this world without His appointment;[a] although nevertheless God is not the author of nor chargeable with the evil that occurs: for His power and goodness are so great and incomprehensible that He ordains and executes His work well and righteously[b] even when the devil and wicked men act unrighteously.[b] And as to what He does surpassing human understanding, we will

[46] From the text in Niemeyer: pp. 367 f., 370 f.
[u] West. Conf., III. i. b.
[v] West. Conf., III. viii.
[w] West. Conf., III. iii. v.
[x] West. Conf., III. iii. vii.
[y] West. Conf., III. iii.
[z] West. Conf., III. v. vi.
[a] West. Conf., III. i. a.
[b] West. Conf., III. i. b.

not curiously inquire into it farther than our capacity will admit
of, but in all humility and reverence adore the righteous judgments
of God which are hidden from us, contenting ourselves that we
are disciples of Christ, to learn only when He reveals to us by His
Word and not transgressing these limits.ᶜ This doctrine affords us
an unspeakable consolation, since we are taught by it that nothing
can befall us by chance, but by the ordinance of our good heavenly
Father, who watches in our behalf with a paternal care, holding all
His creatures subject to Him; so that not a hair of our head (for
they are all numbered) nor even a sparrow can fall to the ground
without the will of our Father. In whom we trust, knowing that
He holds the devils in restraint, and all our enemies, and that they
cannot injure us without His permission and good will.ᵈ

Art. XVI. We believe that, the whole race of Adam being thus
precipitated into perdition and ruin, by the sin of the first man,
God hath manifested Himself such an one as He is, that is to say
merciful and righteous: merciful in delivering and saving from
this perdition those whom in His eternal and immutable counsel
He has elected and chosen by His pure goodness, in Jesus Christ
our Lord, without any regard to their works; righteous in leaving
the rest in their ruin and fall wherein they have precipitated them-
selves.ᵈ [⁴⁷ Thus He declares Himself a merciful and clement God
to those whom He saves, since He owed them nothing; as likewise
He declares Himself a righteous judge by the manifestation of His
just severity towards the rest.ᵈ Nor does He do the latter any injustice. For that He saves some is not because they are better than
the rest, for all were sunk into certain ruin, and God distinguishes
and frees them according to His eternal and immutable counsel
which was established in Jesus Christ before the world was created.ᵈ
No one, then, according to this judgment, can attain to this glory
of himself, since of ourselves we are not capable of thinking any
good thing, unless God precedes us by His grace and mere goodness,
so corrupt is our nature.]

⁴⁷ The remainder (in square brackets) is not found in the French, nor in
the Latin of 1612: it is printed by Niemeyer from the Latin version of Festus
Hommius, made in 1618.

ᶜ West. Conf., III. viii.
ᵈ West. Conf., III. v. vi. vii.

Confession of the English Congregation at Geneva (1558) [48]

I believe and confesse my Lord God eternal, infinite, unmeasurable, incomprehensible and invisible . . . who by his Almightie power and wisdome hath not onlie of nothing created Heaven, Earth, and all thinges therein conteined . . . but also by his Fatherly Providence governeth, mainteineth and preserveth the same, according to the purpose of his will.[e] . . . I believe also and confesse Jesus Christ . . . who giving us that by grace which was his by nature, made us through faith the children of God . . . who . . . will come in the same visible forme in the which hee ascended, with an unspeakable Majestie, power and companie, to separate the lambes from the goates, the elect from the reprobate; so that none, whether he be alive then, or dead before, shall escape his judgement . . . yet notwithstanding it is not sufficient to believe that God is Omnipotent and mercifull, that Christ hath made satisfaction, or that the Holy Ghoste hath this power and effect, except we do apply the same benefits to our selves, who are Gods elect. I believe therefore and confesse one holy Church . . . which Church is not seene to mans eye, but only knowne to God, who of the lost sonnes of Adam hath ordeined some as vessels of wrath to damnation; and hath chosen others as vessels of his mercy to bee saved,[f] the which also in due time hee calleth to integrity of life and Godly conversation, to make them a glorious Church to himselfe [g] . . . with full assurance that although this roote of sinne lie hid in us, yet to the elect it shall not bee imputed. . . .

The Scotch Confession (1560) [49]

Art. I. We confesse and acknawledge ane onelie God, to whom onelie we must cleave, whom onelie we must serve, whom onelie we must worship, and in whom onelie we put our trust. . . . Be whom we confesse and beleve all thingis in hevin and eirth, aswel Visible as Invisible, to have been created, to be reteined in their being, and to be ruled and guyded be his inscrutable Providence,

[48] From the text in Dunlop, "A Collection of Confessions of Faith," ii. 1722, pp. 3–9.
[49] From the text in Schaff, iii. 1878, pp. 439 ff.
[e] West. Conf., III. i.
[f] West. Conf., III. iii.
[g] West. Conf., III. vi. b.

to sik end, as his Eternall Wisdome, Gudnes, and Justice hes appoynted them, to the manifestatioun of his awin glorie.[h] . . . Art. III. . . . deith everlasting hes had, and sall have power and dominioun over all that have not been, ar not, or sal not be regenerate from above: quhilk regeneratioun is wrocht be the power of the holie Gost, working in the hartes of the elect of God, ane assured faith in the promise of God, reveiled to us in his word, be quhilk faith we apprehend Christ Jesus, with the graces and benefites promised in him.[i] . . . Art. VII. We acknawledge and confesse, that this maist wonderous conjunction betwixt the God-head and the man-head in *Christ Jesus,* did proceed from the eternall and immutable decree of God, from quhilk al our salvatioun springs and depends.[j] Art. VIII. For that same eternall God and Father, who of meere grace elected us in *Christ Jesus* his Sonne, befoir the foundatioun of the warld was laide, appointed him to be our Head, our Brother, our Pastor, and great Bischop of our sauls.[k] . . . And for this cause, ar we not affrayed to cal God our Father, not sa meikle because he hes created us, quhilk we have common with the reprobate; as for that, that he hes given to us his onely Sonne, to be our brother, and given unto us grace, to acknawledge and imbrace him for our onlie Mediatour, as before is said. . . . Art. XIII. . . . the cause of gude warkis, we confesse to be not our free wil, bot the Spirit of the Lord *Jesus,* who dwelling in our hearts be trewe faith, bringis furth sik warkis, as God hes prepared for us to walke in.[l] . . . For how soone that ever the Spirit of the Lord *Jesus,* quhilk Gods elect children receive be trew faith, taks possession in the heart of ony man, so soone dois he regenerate and renew the same man.[l] . . . Art. XVI. As we beleve in ane God, Father, Sonne, and haly Ghaist; sa do we maist constantly beleeve, that from the beginning there hes bene, and now is, and to the end of the warld sall be, ane Kirk, that is to say, ane company and multitude of men chosen of God, who richtly worship and imbrace him be trew faith in *Christ Jesus,* quha is the only head of the same Kirk, quhilk alswa is the bodie and spouse of *Christ Jesus,* quhilk Kirk is catholike, that is, universal, because it conteinis the Elect of all ages, of all realmes, nations, and tongues.[l] . . . This Kirk is invisible, knawen onelie to God, quha alane knawis

[h] West. Conf., III. i. a.

[i] West. Conf., III. vi.

[j] West. Conf., III. v.

[k] West. Conf., III. vi.

[l] West. Conf., III. vi. b.

whome he hes chosen; [m] and comprehends as weill (as said is) the Elect that be departed, commonlie calld the *Kirk Triumphant*, and they that zit live and fecht against sinne and *Sathan* as sall live hereafter. Art. XVII. The Elect departed are in peace and rest fra their labours . . . they are delivered fra all feare and torment, and all temptatioun, to quhilk we and all Goddis Elect are subject in this life, and therfore do beare the name of the *Kirk Militant:* As contrariwise,[n] the reprobate and unfaithfull departed have anguish, torment, and paine, that cannot be expressed.[o] . . . Art. XXV. Albeit that the Worde of God trewly preached, and the Sacraments richtlie ministred, and Discipline executed according to the Worde of God, be the certaine and infallible Signes of the trew Kirk, we meane not that everie particular persoun joyned with sik company, be ane elect member of *Christ Jesus:* For we acknawledge and confesse, that Dornell, Cockell, and Caffe may be sawen, grow, and in great aboundance lie in the middis of the Wheit, that is, the Reprobate may be joyned in the societie of the Elect, and may externally use with them the benefites of the worde and Sacraments. . . . Bot sik as continew in weil doing to the end, bauldely professing the Lord *Jesus,* we constantly beleve, that they sall receive glorie, honor, and immortality, to reigne for ever in life everlasting with *Christ Jesus,* to whose glorified body all his Elect sall be made lyke, when he sall appeir againe in judgement.[p] . . .

CRAIG'S CATECHISM (1581) [50]

Q. What is the Church which we confess here?

A. The whole company of Gods elect called and sanctified.[p]

Q. Why is the Church onely knowne to us by Faith?

A. Because it containeth onely God's elect, which are onely knowne to himselfe.[q]

Q. When and how may we know them?

A. When we see the fruites of election and holines in them.[r] . . .

Q. Out of what fountaine doth this our stabilitie flow?

A. Out of God's eternall and constant election in Christ.[s]

[50] From Bonar's " Catechisms of the Scottish Reformation," 1866, pp. 207, 253–255.

[m] West. Conf., III. iv.

[n] West. Conf., III. vi.

[o] West. Conf., III. vii.

[p] West. Conf., III. vi.

[q] West. Conf., III. iv.

[r] West. Conf., III. viii.

[s] West. Conf., III. vi.

Q. By what way commeth this election to us?
A. By His effectuall calling in due time.[t]
Q. What worketh this effectuall calling in us?
A. The obedience of faith.[t] . . .
Q. May not this seale bee abolished through sinne?
A. No, for these giftes are without repentaunce.
Q. But many fall shamefullie from God.
A. The spirit of adoption raiseth all the chosen againe.
Q. But many are never raised againe?
A. These were never the chosen of God. . . .
Q. Where should we begin our triall?
A. At the fruites of faith and repentance. Because they are best knowne to our selves and others.
Q. What if we begin at election?
A. Then we shall wander in darkenes.[u] . . .

The English Articles (1553) [51]

XVII. *Of Predestination and Election*

Predestination to life, is the euerlasting purpose of God, whereby (before the foundacions of the worlde were laied) he hath constantlie decreed by his owne judgemente secrete to vs, to deliuer from curse, and damnation those whom he hath chosen [52] out of mankinde, and to bring them to euerlasting saluation by Christ, as vesselles made to honour: [v] whereupon,[53] soche as haue so excellent a benefite of GOD geuen unto theim [54] be called, according to Goddes purpose, by his spirite, woorking in due seasone, thei through grace obeie the calling, thei be justified frely, thei be made sonnes [55] by adoptione, thei bee made like the image of Goddes [56] oneley begotten sonne Jesu Christe, thei walke religiouslie in goode woorkes, and at length by Goddes mercie, thei atteine to euerlasting felicitie.[w]

[51] Taken from Hardwick's "History of the Articles of Religion," ed. 3, 1876, pp. 310 ff.
[52] "in Christ" subsequently added (1563, 1571).
[53] "Wherefore" later.
[54] Altered later into: "they which be indued with so excellent a benefite of God."
[55] "of God" added later.
[56] Later: "his."
[t] West. Conf., III. vi.
[v] West. Conf., III. v.
[u] West. Conf., III. viii.
[w] West. Conf., III. vi. b.

As the Godlie consideration of predestination, and our election in Christe is ful of swete, pleasaunte, and vnspeakable coumfort to godlie persones, and soche as feele in themselues the woorking of the spirite of Christe, mortifying the workes of the flesh, and their earthlie membres, and drawing vp their minde to high and heauenly thinges, aswel because it doeth greatly stablish and confirme their faith of eternal saluation to be enioied through Christe, as because it doeth feruentlie kindle their loue towardes Godde: [x] So for curious, and carnall persones lacking the Spirite of Christ, to haue continu- allie before their yies the sentence of Goddes predestination, is a moste daungerous dounefall, whereby the Deuill maie [57] thrust them either into desperation, or into a rechielesnesse of most vncleane liuing, no lesse perilous then desperation.[x]

Furthermore [although the Decrees of predestination are vn- knowne unto us, yeat] [58] we must receiue Goddes promises, in soche wise as thei bee generallie set foorth to vs in holie Scripture, and in our doinges that wille of Godde is to be folowed, whiche we haue expresselie declared vnto us in the woorde of Godde.

The Lambeth Articles (1595) [59]

1. God from eternity hath predestinated some unto life, and reprobated some unto death.[y]

2. The moving or efficient cause of predestination unto life is not the foresight of faith, or of perseverance, or of good works, or of anything that is in the persons predestinated, but the will of God's good pleasure alone.[z]

3. There is a predefined and certain number of the predestinated, which can neither be increased nor diminished.[a]

4. Those who are not predestinated to salvation shall necessarily be condemned for their sins.[b]

5. A true, lively and justifying faith, and the sanctifying Spirit of God is not extinguished, falleth not away, vanisheth not in the elect, either finally or totally.[c]

6. A man truly believing, that is endowed with justifying faith,

---

[57] Later: " doth."
[58] Subsequently omitted (1563, 1571).
[59] From the Latin text in Hardwick, p. 363.
[x] West. Conf., III. viii.   [y] West. Conf., III. iii.   [z] West. Conf., III. v. b.
[a] West. Conf., III. iv.   [b] West. Conf., III. vii.   [c] West. Conf., III. vi.

is certain with the assurance of faith, of the forgiveness of his sins and his everlasting salvation by Christ.[c]

7. Saving grace is not given, is not communicated, is not granted to all men, whereby they may be saved if they will.[c]

8. No one can come unto Christ unless it be given unto him and unless the Father draw him. And all men are not drawn by the Father that they may come unto the Son.

9. It is not placed within the will and power of every man to be saved.

THE IRISH ARTICLES (1615) [60]

Of God's Eternal Decree and Predestination

11. God from all eternity did, by his unchangeable counsel, ordain whatsoever in time should come to pass;[d] yet so, as thereby no violence is offered to the wills of the reasonable creatures, and neither the liberty nor the contingency of the second causes is taken away, but established rather.[e]

12. By the same eternal counsel God hath predestinated some unto life, and reprobated some unto death:[f] of both which there is a certain number, known only to God, which can neither be increased nor diminished.[g]

13. Predestination to life is the everlasting purpose of God whereby, before the foundations of the world were laid, he hath constantly decreed in his secret counsel to deliver from curse and damnation those whom he hath chosen in Christ out of mankind, and to bring them by Christ unto everlasting salvation, as vessels made to honor.[h]

14. The cause moving God to predestinate unto life, is not the foreseeing of faith, or perseverance, or good works, or of anything which is in the person predestinated, but only the good pleasure of God himself.[i] For all things being ordained for the manifestation of his glory, and his glory being to appear both in the works of his mercy and of his justice, it seemed good to his heavenly wisdom to choose out a certain number toward whom he would extend his undeserved mercy, leaving the rest to be spectacles of his justice.[j]

[60] Text in Schaff, Hardwick, and others.

[c] West. Conf., III. vi.
[d] West. Conf., III. i. a.
[e] West. Conf., III. i. b.
[f] West. Conf., III. iii.
[g] West. Conf., III. iv.
[h] West. Conf., III. v. a.
[i] West. Conf., III. v. b.
[j] West. Conf., III. iii. v.

15. Such as are predestinated unto life be called according unto God's purpose (his spirit working in due season), and through grace they obey the calling, they be justified freely; they be made sons of God by adoption; they be made like the image of his only begotten Son, Jesus Christ; they walk religiously in good works; and at length, by God's mercy, they attain to everlasting felicity.[k] But such as are not predestinated to salvation shall finally be condemned for their sins.[l]

16. The godlike consideration of predestination and our election in Christ is full of sweet, pleasant, and unspeakable comfort to godly persons, and such as feel in themselves the working of the spirit of Christ, mortifying the works of the flesh and their earthly members, and drawing up their minds to high and heavenly things: as well because it doth greatly confirm and establish their faith of eternal salvation, to be enjoyed through Christ, as because it doth fervently kindle their love toward God; and, on the contrary side, for curious and carnal persons lacking the spirit of Christ to have continually before their eyes the sentence of God's predestination is very dangerous.[m]

17. We must receive God's promises in such wise as they be generally set forth unto us in holy Scripture; and in our doings that will of God is to be followed which we have expressly declared unto us in the Word of God.[m]

WESTMINSTER CONFESSION (1647)

III. *Of God's Eternal Decree*

1. God from all eternity did by the most wise and holy counsel of His own will, freely and unchangeably ordain whatsoever comes to pass: yet so as thereby neither is God the author of sin, nor is violence offered to the will of the creatures, nor is the liberty or contingency of second causes taken away, but rather established.

2. Although God knows whatsoever may or can come to pass upon all supposed conditions; yet hath He not decreed anything because He foresaw it as future, or as that which would come to pass upon such conditions.

3. By the decree of God, for the manifestation of His glory, some men and angels are predestinated unto everlasting life, and others foreordained to everlasting death.

[k] West. Conf., III. vi.   [l] West Conf., III. vii.   [m] West. Conf., III. viii.

4. These angels and men, thus predestinated and foreordained, are particularly and unchangeably designed; and their number is so certain and definite that it cannot be either increased or diminished.

5. Those of mankind that are predestinated unto life, God, before the foundation of the world was laid, according to His eternal and immutable purpose, and the secret counsel and good pleasure of His will, hath chosen in Christ, unto everlasting glory, out of His mere free grace and love, without any foresight of faith or good works, or perseverance in either of them, or any other thing in the creature, as conditions, or causes moving Him thereunto; and all to the praise of His glorious grace.

6. As God hath appointed the elect unto glory, so hath He, by the eternal and most free purpose of His will, foreordained all the means thereunto. Wherefore they who are elected being fallen in Adam, are redeemed by Christ, are effectually called unto faith in Christ by His Spirit working in due season; are justified, adopted, sanctified, and kept by His power through faith unto salvation. Neither are any other redeemed by Christ, effectually called, justified, adopted, sanctified, and saved, but the elect only.

7. The rest of mankind, God was pleased, according to the unsearchable counsel of His own will, whereby He extendeth or withholdeth mercy as He pleaseth, for the glory of His sovereign power over His creatures, to pass by, and to ordain them to dishonor and wrath for their sin, to the praise of His glorious justice.

8. The doctrine of this high mystery of predestination is to be handled with special prudence and care, that men attending the will of God revealed in His Word, and yielding obedience thereunto, may, from the certainty of their effectual vocation, be assured of their eternal election. So shall this doctrine afford matter of praise, reverence, and admiration of God; and of humility, diligence, and abundant consolation, to all that sincerely obey the gospel.

WESTMINSTER LARGER CATECHISM (1647)

12. God's decrees are the wise, free, and holy acts of the counsel of His will, whereby, from all eternity, He hath, for His own glory, unchangeably foreordained whatsoever comes to pass in time, especially concerning angels and men.

13. God, by an eternal and immutable decree, out of His mere love, for the praise of His glorious grace, to be manifested in due

time, hath elected some angels to glory; and in Christ hath chosen some men to eternal life, and the means thereof: and also, according to His sovereign power, and the unsearchable counsel of His own will (whereby He extendeth or withholdeth favor as He pleaseth), hath passed by, and foreordained the rest to dishonor and wrath, to be for their sin inflicted, to the praise of the glory of His justice.

14. God executeth His decrees in the works of creation and providence; according to His infallible foreknowledge, and the free and immutable counsel of His own will.

Westminster Shorter Catechism (1648)

7. The decrees of God are His eternal purpose according to the counsel of His will, whereby, for His own glory, He hath foreordained whatsoever comes to pass.

20. God . . . out of His mere good pleasure from all eternity, elected some to everlasting life.

Canons of Dort (1618–1619) [61]

First Head of Doctrine: Of Divine Predestination

1. As all men have sinned in Adam, lie under the curse, and are obnoxious to eternal death, God would have done no injustice by leaving them all to perish, and delivering them over to condemnation on account of sin, according to the words of the Apostle (Rom. iii. 19), "that every mouth may be stopped, and all the world may become guilty before God"; (ver. 23) "for all have sinned, and come short of the glory of God"; and (vi. 23) "for the wages of sin is death."

2. But "in this the love of God was manifested, that He sent His only begotten Son into the world," "that whosoever believeth on Him should not perish, but have everlasting life" (I John iv. 9; John iii. 16).

3. And that men may be brought to believe, God mercifully sends the messengers of these most joyful tidings to whom He will, and at what time He pleaseth; by whose ministry men are called to repentance and faith in Christ crucified. "How then shall they call on Him in whom they have not believed? And how shall they believe

[61] This translation is that of the (Dutch) Reformed Church in America as given by Schaff, except in the "Rejection of Errors," which is from the Latin text given by Schaff: iii. pp. 581 ff., 556 ff., and 576.

in Him of whom they have not heard? And how shall they hear without a preacher? And how shall they preach except they be sent? " (Rom. x. 14, 15).

4. The wrath of God abideth upon those who believe not this gospel; but such as receive it, and embrace Jesus the Saviour by a true and living faith, are by Him delivered from the wrath of God and from destruction, and have the gift of eternal life conferred upon them.

5. The cause or guilt of this unbelief, as well as of all other sins, is nowise in God, but in man himself: whereas faith in Jesus Christ, and salvation through Him is the free gift of God, as it is written, "By grace ye are saved through faith, and that not of yourselves: it is the gift of God " (Eph. ii. 8) ; and, " Unto you it is given in the behalf of Christ, not only to believe on Him," etc. (Phil. i. 29).

6. That some receive the gift of faith from God, and others do not receive it, proceeds from God's eternal decree.[n] " For known unto God are all His works from the beginning of the world " (Acts xv. 18; Eph. i. 11). According to which decree He graciously softens the hearts of the elect, however obstinate, and inclines them to believe; while He leaves the non-elect in His just judgment to their own wickedness and obduracy.[o] And herein is especially displayed the profound, the merciful, and at the same time the righteous discrimination between men, equally involved in ruin; or that decree of *election* and *reprobation*, revealed in the Word of God, which, though men of perverse, impure, and unstable minds wrest it to their own destruction, yet to holy and pious souls affords unspeakable consolation.[p]

7. Election is the unchangeable purpose of God, whereby, before the foundation of the world, He hath, out of mere grace, according to the sovereign good pleasure of His own will, chosen, from the whole human race, which had fallen through their own fault, from their primitive state of rectitude, into sin and destruction, a certain number of persons to redemption in Christ, whom He from eternity appointed the Mediator and head of the elect, and the foundation of salvation.[q]

This elect number, though by nature neither better nor more deserving than others, but with them involved in one common misery, God hath decreed to give to Christ to be saved by Him, and

[n] West. Conf., III. iii.
[o] West. Conf., III. iii. v. vii.
[p] West. Conf., III. viii.
[q] West. Conf., III. v. a.

effectually to call and draw them to His communion by His Word and Spirit; to bestow upon them true faith, justification, and sanctification; and having powerfully preserved them in the fellowship of His Son, finally to glorify them for the demonstration of His mercy, and for the praise of the riches of His glorious grace: [r] as it is written, " According as He hath chosen us in Him before the foundation of the world, that we should be holy and without blame before Him in love: having predestinated us unto the adoption of children by Jesus Christ to Himself, according to the good pleasure of His will, to the praise of the glory of His grace, wherein He hath made us accepted in the Beloved " (Eph. i. 4–6). And elsewhere, " Whom He did predestinate, them He also called; and whom He called, them He also justified; and whom He justified, them He also glorified " (Rom. viii. 30).

8. There are not various decrees of election, but one and the same decree respecting all those who shall be saved both under the Old and New Testament; since the Scripture declares the good pleasure, purpose, and counsel of the divine will to be one, according to which He hath chosen us from eternity, both to grace and to glory, to salvation and the way of salvation, which He hath ordained that we should walk therein.[r]

9. This election was not founded upon foreseen faith, and the obedience of faith, holiness, or any other good quality or disposition in man, as the prerequisite, cause, or condition on which it depended; but men are chosen to faith and to the obedience of faith, holiness, etc.[s] Therefore election is the fountain of every saving good; from which proceed faith, holiness, and the other gifts of salvation, and finally eternal life itself, as its fruits and effects, according to that of the Apostle: " He hath chosen us [not because we were, but] that we should be holy and without blame before Him in love " (Eph. i. 4).[t]

10. The good pleasure of God is the sole cause of this gracious election; which doth not consist herein that God, foreseeing all possible qualities of human actions, elected certain of these as a condition of salvation, but that He was pleased out of the common mass of sinners to adopt some certain persons as a peculiar people to Himself,[u] as it is written, " For the children being not yet born, neither having done any good or evil," etc., " it was said [namely, to

---

[r] West. Conf., III. vi.
[s] West. Conf., III. v. b.
[t] West. Conf., III. vi.
[u] West. Conf., III. v. b.

Rebecca] the elder shall serve the younger; as it is written, Jacob have I loved, but Esau have I hated" (Rom. ix. 11–13); and, "As many as were ordained to eternal life believed" (Acts xiii. 48).

11. And as God Himself is most wise, unchangeable, omniscient, and omnipotent, so the election made by Him can neither be interrupted nor changed, recalled nor annulled; neither can the elect be cast away, nor their number diminished.[v]

12. The elect, in due time, though in various degrees and in different measures, attain the assurance of this their eternal and unchangeable election, not by inquisitively prying into the secret and deep things of God, but by observing in themselves, with a spiritual joy and holy pleasure, the infallible fruits of election pointed out in the Word of God; such as a true faith in Christ, filial fear, a godly sorrow for sin, a hungering and thirsting after righteousness, etc.[w]

13. The sense and certainty of this election afford to the children of God additional matter for daily humiliation before Him, for adoring the depth of His mercies, and rendering grateful returns of ardent love to Him who first manifested so great love toward them.[w] The consideration of this doctrine of election is so far from encouraging remissness in the observance of the divine commands or from sinking men into carnal security, that these, in the just judgment of God, are the usual effects of rash presumption or of idle and wanton trifling with the grace of election, in those who refuse to walk in the ways of the elect.[w]

14. As the doctrine of divine election by the most wise counsel of God was declared by the Prophets, by Christ Himself, and by the Apostles, and is clearly revealed in the Scriptures both of the Old and New Testament, so it is still to be published in due time and place in the Church of God, for which it was peculiarly designed, provided it be done with reverence, in the spirit of discretion and piety, for the glory of God's most holy name, and for enlivening and comforting His people, without vainly attempting to investigate the secret ways of the Most High.[w]

15. What peculiarly tends to illustrate and recommend to us the eternal and unmerited grace of election is the express testimony of sacred Scripture, that not all, but some only, are elected, while others are passed by in the eternal decree; whom God, out of His sovereign, most just, irreprehensible and unchangeable good pleas-

[v] West. Conf., III. iv.   [w] West. Conf., III. viii.

ure, hath decreed to leave in the common misery into which they have wilfully plunged themselves, and not to bestow upon them saving faith and the grace of conversion; but permitting them in His just judgment to follow their own way; at last, for the declaration of His justice, to condemn and punish them forever, not only on account of their unbelief, but also for all their other sins.[a] And this is the decree of reprobation which by no means makes God the author of sin (the very thought of which is blasphemy),[b] but declares Him to be an awful, irreprehensible, and righteous judge and avenger.

16. Those who do not yet experience a lively faith in Christ, an assured confidence of soul, peace of conscience, an earnest endeavor after filial obedience, and glorying in God through Christ, efficaciously wrought in them, and do nevertheless persist in the use of the means which God hath appointed for working these graces in us, ought not to be alarmed at the mention of reprobation, nor to rank themselves among the reprobate, but diligently to persevere in the use of means, and with ardent desires devoutly and humbly to wait for a season of richer grace. Much less cause have they to be terrified by the doctrine of reprobation, who, though they seriously desire to be turned to God, to please Him only, and to be delivered from the body of death, cannot yet reach that measure of holiness and faith to which they aspire; since a merciful God has promised that He will not quench the smoking flax, nor break the bruised reed. But this doctrine is justly terrible to those who, regardless of God and the Saviour Jesus Christ, have wholly given themselves up to the cares of the world and the pleasures of the flesh, so long as they are not seriously converted to God.[c]

17. Since we are to judge of the will of God from His Word, which testifies that the children of believers are holy, not by nature, but in virtue of the covenant of grace, in which they together with the parents are comprehended, godly parents have no reason to doubt of the election and salvation of their children whom it pleases God to call out of this life in their infancy.

18. To those who murmur at the free grace of election, and just severity of reprobation, we answer with the Apostle: " Nay but, O man, who art thou that repliest against God? " (Rom. ix. 20); and quote the language of our Saviour: " Is it not lawful for me to

[a] West. Conf., III. vii.　　　　　　　　[c] West. Conf., III. viii.
[b] West. Conf., III. i. b.

do what I will with mine own? " (Matt. xx. 15). And therefore with holy adoration of these mysteries, we exclaim, in the words of the Apostle: " O the depth of the riches both of the wisdom and knowledge of God! how unsearchable are His judgments, and His ways past finding out! For who hath known the mind of the Lord, or who hath been His counselor? or who hath first given to Him, and it shall be recompensed unto him again? For of Him, and through Him, and to Him are all things: to whom be glory forever. Amen." (Rom. xi. 33–36).

Rejection of the Errors

By which the Belgian Churches have for some time been troubled. Having set forth the orthodox doctrine of Election and Reprobation, the Synod rejects the errors of those —

1. Who teach, " that the will of God concerning the salvation of those who shall believe and who shall persevere in faith and the obedience of faith, is the whole and entire decree of election to salvation, and that there is nothing else revealed in the Word of God concerning this decree." For these impose on the simple-minded, and manifestly contradict the Holy Scriptures, which testify that God not only wills to save those who shall believe, but also has from eternity chosen some designated individuals to whom in distinction from the rest He will in time give faith and perseverance; as it is written, " I manifested Thy name unto the men whom Thou gavest me " (John xvii. 6); again, " And as many as were ordained to eternal life believed " (Acts xiii. 48); and, " He chose us before the foundations of the world were laid, that we should be holy," etc. (Eph. i. 4).[d]

2. Who teach, " That God's election to eternal life is various (*multiplex*); one general and indefinite, the other particular and definite; and the latter again either incomplete, revocable, nonperemptory, or conditioned, or else complete, irrevocable, peremptory, or absolute." Again, " That the one election is to faith, the other to salvation; so that the election to justifying faith can exist without a peremptory election to salvation." For this is a fancy of the human mind excogitated aside of the Scriptures, corrupting the doctrine of election and dissolving that golden chain of salvation: " Whom He did predestinate, them He also called; and whom He

[d] West. Conf., III. v.

called, them He also justified; and whom He justified, them He also glorified " (Rom. viii. 30).ᵉ

3. Who teach, " That the good pleasure and purpose of God, of which the Scriptures make mention in the doctrine of election, does not consist in this — That God has chosen certain particular individuals in distinction from others, but in this — That out of all possible conditions (among which are the works of the law), or out of the whole order of things, God has chosen the act of faith, ignoble though it be in itself, and the imperfect obedience of faith, to be the condition of salvation; and has determined graciously to take it for perfect obedience and to account it worthy of the reward of eternal life." For by this pernicious error the good pleasure of God and the merit of Christ are set aside, and men are called away from the verity of gratuitous justification and the simplicity of the Scriptures to useless questionings; and the saying of the Apostle is falsified, " God called us with a holy calling; not according to our works but according to His own purpose and grace, which was given us in Christ Jesus before times eternal " (II Tim. i. 9).ᶠ

4. Who teach, " That in the election to faith it is presupposed as a condition that a man shall rightly use the light of nature, that he shall be upright, childlike, humble, with a disposition to eternal life, seeing that election measurably depends on these things." For they savor of Pelagius and openly charge the Apostle with falsehood when he writes: " We once lived in the lusts of our flesh, doing the desires of the flesh and of the mind, and were by nature children of wrath, even as the rest: but God, being rich in mercy, for His great love wherewith He loved us, even when we were dead in trespasses, quickened us together with Christ, by whose grace ye are saved, and raised us up with Him, and made us sit with Him in the heavenly places, in Christ Jesus: that in the ages to come He might show the exceeding riches of His grace in kindness toward us in Christ Jesus: for by grace have ye been saved through faith (and that not of yourselves, it is the gift of God), not of works that no man should glory " (Eph. ii. 3–9).ᵍ

5. Who teach, " That incomplete and non-peremptory election of particular persons to salvation takes place out of foreseen faith, repentance, holiness, and piety in its beginnings and in its earlier stages; while complete and peremptory election is out of final perse-

---

ᵉ West. Conf., III. vi.   ᵍ West. Conf., III. v.

ᶠ West. Conf., III. iv. v. vi.

verance in foreseen faith, repentance, holiness, and piety: and that
this is the gracious and evangelical worthiness, on account of which
he who is elected is more worthy than he who is not elected; and
that accordingly faith, the obedience of faith, holiness, piety, and
perseverance are not the fruits or effects of an immutable election
to glory, but conditions and indispensable causes, absolutely prerequisite in those to be elected, and foreseen as if actually present."
Because this is repugnant to the whole of Scripture, which continually presses upon our ears and hearts such sayings as these: " Election is not of works, but of Him that calleth " (Rom. ix. 11) ; " As
many as were ordained to eternal life believed " (Acts xiii. 48) ;
" He chose us in Himself that we might be holy " (Eph. i. 4) ; " You
have not chosen me, but I have chosen you " (John xv. 16) ; " If of
grace, it is no longer of works " (Rom. xi. 6) ; " Herein is love, not
that we have loved God, but that He has loved us and sent His
Son " (I John iv. 10).[g]

6. Who teach, " That it is not every election to salvation that is
immutable, but, no decree of God standing in the way, some of the
elect can perish and do eternally perish." By which crass error, they
alike make God mutable and subvert the consolation of the saints
derived from the constancy of their election, and contradict the Holy
Scriptures, which say: " It is not possible for the elect to be led
astray " (Matt. xxiv. 24) ; " Christ does not lose those given Him
by the Father " (John vi. 39) ; " God also glorifies those whom He
has predestinated, called and justified " (Rom. viii. 30).[h]

7. Who teach, " That there is in this life no fruit, no sense, no
certitude of immutable election except out of a mutable and contingent condition." For besides the absurdity of speaking of an uncertain certitude, the experience of the saints stands opposed to this;
for they exult with the Apostle in the sense of their election, and
celebrate this gift of God, rejoicing with the disciples according to
Christ's admonition, that " their names are written in heaven "
(Luke x. 20): and in fine oppose their sense of election to the fiery
darts of diabolic temptations, asking, " Who shall lay anything to
the charge of God's elect? " (Rom. viii. 33).[i]

8. Who teach, " That God has not out of His mere will decreed
to leave anyone in the fall of Adam and in the common state of sin
and damnation, or to pass anyone by in the communication of the
grace necessary for faith and conversion." For this declaration

[g] West. Conf., III. v.   [h] West. Conf., III. iv.   [i] West. Conf., III. viii.

stands, " He hath mercy on whom He will; and whom He will He hardeneth " (Rom. ix. 18); and this, " To you it is given to know the mysteries of the kingdom of heaven, but to them it is not given " (Matt. xiii. 11); again, " I glorify Thee, Father, Lord of heaven and earth, because Thou hast hidden these things from the wise and understanding, and hast revealed them unto babes: yea, Father, for so it was well-pleasing in Thy sight " (Matt. xi. 25–26).[j]

9. Who teach, " That the reason why God sends the gospel to this rather than to that nation, is not the mere and sole good pleasure of God but because the one nation is better and more worthy than the other to whom the gospel is not communicated." For Moses contradicts, thus addressing the people of Israel: " Behold, unto the Lord thy God belongeth the heaven and the heaven of heavens, the earth with all that therein is; only the Lord had a delight in thy fathers to love them, and He chose their seed after them, even you, above all peoples, as at this day " (Deut. x. 14, 15); and Christ: " Woe to you Chorazin, woe to you Bethsaida, because if the mighty works had been done in Tyre and Sidon which have been done in you, they would long ago have repented in sackcloth and ashes " (Matt. xi. 21).[k]

Conclusion

And this is the perspicuous, simple, and ingenuous declaration of the orthodox doctrine . . . and the rejection of the errors, with which the Belgic Churches have for some time been troubled. This doctrine the Synod judges to be drawn from the Word of God, and to be agreeable to the confession of the Reformed Churches. Whence it clearly appears that some, whom such conduct by no means became, have violated all truth, equity, and charity, in wishing to persuade the public: " That the doctrine of the Reformed Churches concerning predestination, and the points annexed to it, by its own genius and necessary tendency, leads off the minds of men from all piety and religion;[l] that it is an opiate administered by the flesh and the devil;[l] and the stronghold of Satan where he lies in wait for all, and from which he wounds multitudes, and mortally strikes through many with the darts both of despair and security;[l] that it makes God the author of sin, unjust, tyrannical, hypocritical;[m] that it is

---

[j] West. Conf., III. iii. iv. vii.

[k] West. Conf., III. v. vi. vii.

[l] West. Conf., III. viii.

[m] West. Conf., III. i. b.

nothing more than an interpolated Stoicism, Manicheism, Libertinism, Turcism;[n] that it renders men carnally secure, since they are persuaded by it that nothing can hinder the salvation of the elect, let them live as they please;[o] and therefore that they may safely perpetrate every species of the most atrocious crimes;[o] and that, if the reprobate should even perform truly all the works of the saints, their obedience would not in the least contribute to their salvation; that the same doctrine teaches that God, by a mere arbitrary act of His will, without the least respect or view to any sin, has predestinated the greatest part of the world to eternal damnation, and has created them for this very purpose: that in the same manner in which election is the fountain and cause of faith and good works, reprobation is the cause of unbelief and impiety; that many children of the faithful are torn, guiltless, from their mothers' breasts and tyrannically plunged into hell: so that neither baptism nor the prayers of the Church at their baptism can at all profit them "; and many other things of the same kind which the Reformed Churches not only do not acknowledge, but even detest with their whole soul.

FORMULA CONSENSUS HELVETICA (1675) [62]

IV. God, before the foundations of the world were laid, formed in Christ Jesus, our Lord, πρόθεσιν αἰώνιον, an eternal purpose (Eph. iii. 11), in which, from the mere good pleasure of His will, without any foresight of the merit of works or of faith,[p] to the praise of His glorious grace He elected a certain and definite number [q] of men lying in the same mass of corruption and in common blood and therefore corrupted by sin, to be led in time to salvation by Christ, the sole Surety and Mediator, and through His merit, by the mighty power of the regenerating Holy Spirit, to be called efficaciously, regenerated, and gifted with faith and repentance.[r] And thus, determining to illustrate His glory, God decreed, first, to create man perfect, then to permit his fall, and finally to have mercy on some

[62] From the text in Niemeyer, pp. 731–734, with the aid of the English translation given by A. A. Hodge, in his " Outlines of Theology," appendix.

[n] West. Conf., III. i. b; viii.

[o] West. Conf., III. viii.

[p] West. Conf., III. v. b.

[q] West. Conf., III. iv.

[r] West. Conf., III. vi.

from the fallen, and therefore to elect these, but to leave the rest in the corrupt mass and finally to devote them to eternal destruction.[s]

V. Moreover, in that gracious decree of divine election Christ Himself also is included, not as the meritorious cause or the foundation preceding election itself, but as Himself also foreknown before the foundations of the world were laid as ἐκλεκτός, elect (I Pet. ii. 4, 6), and therefore primarily the chosen mediator for its execution and our first-born brother, whose precious merit God willed to use for conferring on us salvation with the preservation of His justice. For the Holy Scriptures not only testify that election was made according to the mere good pleasure of the divine counsel and will (Matt. xi. 26; Eph. i. 5, 9); but also derive the destination and gift of Christ, our Mediator, from the zealous love of God the Father to the world of the elect.[t]

VI. Wherefore we cannot give our suffrages to the opinion of those who teach that God, moved by φιλανθρωπία, or a sort of peculiar love for the lapsed human race, to a " previous election," intended by a certain conditioned will, velleity, or first mercy, the salvation of all and each, on a condition certainly, namely that they believe; appointed Christ as Mediator for all and each of the lapsed; and finally elected some, considered not simply as sinners in the first Adam but as redeemed in the second Adam — that is, appointed that the saving gift of faith should be bestowed upon them in time; [u] and that in this latter act alone " election properly so called " is completed. For these and all similar things are no ordinary deflections from the ὑποτυπώσει of sound words concerning divine election. The Scriptures certainly restrict the purpose of God to show mercy to men — not assuredly to all and each — but to the elect alone; [u] with the exclusion of the reprobate by name [u] — as in the case of Esau, whom God pursued with an eternal hatred (Rom. ix. 11). The same Holy Scriptures bear witness that the counsel and will of God do not change, but stand immovably, and that God in the heavens does what He wishes (Isa. xlvii. 10; Ps. cxv. 3).[v] Assuredly God is far removed from all human imperfection such as manifests itself in inefficacious affections and desires, rashness, repentance and change of counsel.[v] The appointment also of Christ as Mediator proceeds from one and the same election, equally with the salvation of those

---

[s] West. Conf., III. vi. vii.
[t] West. Conf., III. vi.
[u] West. Conf., III. vi. b.
[v] West. Conf., III. iv.

that were given to Him for a possession and an ἀναφαίρετος inheritance, and does not underlie it as its basis.

XIII. As Christ was elected from eternity as the Head, Prince and Owner of all those who are saved in time by His grace: so also was He made in time the Surety of the New Covenant for those only who were given to Him by eternal election as a people of possession, His seed and inheritance.[w] Certainly it was for the elect alone that by the determinate counsel of the Father and His own intention He encountered a dreadful death, these only that He restored to the bosom of the paternal grace, these only that He reconciled to the offended God the Father, and freed from the curse of the law.[w] For our Jesus saves His people from sins (Matt. i. 21), giving His life as the redemption price for His many sheep (Matt. xx. 24, 28; cf. John x. 15), who listen to His voice (John x. 27, 28), and for these alone also, as a divinely called priest, does He intercede, the world being set aside (John xvii. 9; Isa. lxvi. 22). Accordingly in the death of Christ the elect only, who in time are made new creatures, and for whom He was substituted in His death as a piacular victim, are regarded as having died with Him, and as justified from sin (II Cor. v. 17):[w] and the will of Christ who dies so παναρμονικῶς agrees and amicably conspires with the counsel of the Father, who gives none others but the elect to be redeemed by Him, as well as with the operation of the Holy Spirit who sanctifies and seals to a vital hope of eternal life none others but the elect, that the equal περιφορία of the Father's electing, the Son's redeeming, and the Holy Spirit's sanctifying is manifest.[w]

III

We cannot allow ourselves space to draw out in detail the harmony of the Reformed creeds in their doctrine of predestination; or even to exhibit with any fullness the combined faithfulness and discretion which characterizes them in dealing with this high mystery, which their authors felt to lie at the root of their whole system of faith, as of the whole course of the divine activities. He who will read over the series of documents, however cursorily, cannot fail to observe these

[w] West. Conf., III. vi. b.

things for himself. We permit ourselves, in concluding, only a few summary remarks.

1. We observe, then, that *the fact* of Absolute Predestination is the common presupposition of the whole body of Reformed creeds. There are a very few of them, to be sure, chiefly early brief declarations of the primary Protestant program, which lack direct allusion to it. These are such as the Sixty-seven Articles of Zurich (1523), the Ten Bernese Theses (1528), the Tetrapolitan Confession (1530), the First Helvetic (1536) and First Bohemian (1535) and the Polish or Sendomir (1570) Confessions. Even in their cases, however, the fact of predestination is often felt to lie very close in the background (as, for example, in the instances of the Sixty-seven Articles — of which the Bernese Theses are little more than an excerpt — and the Tetrapolitan Confession): and the omission of mention of it is always apparently the result of the special nature and purpose of the formulary. There are certain others of the Reformed Confessions in which predestination is adverted to, as it were, only incidentally — no separate paragraph being consecrated to its statement and formal development. This is the case with such documents as Zwingli's " Fidei ratio " (1530) and " Expositio christianæ fidei " (1531), the Genevan Catechism (1545), the Consensus Tigurinus (1549), the short creeds prepared by Calvin for the Students of Geneva (1559), the Church of Paris (1557) and the French Churches (1562), as well as the Confession of the English Exiles in Geneva (1558) and the Heidelberg Catechism (1563), to which may be added the Second Bohemian Confession (1575). The circumstance that the majority of these formularies come directly from the hand of Zwingli or Calvin himself, while the Confession of the English Exiles was written by Knox, and the Heidelberg Catechism reflects the teachings of Calvin's pupil and defender, Ursinus, already makes it clear that the lack in them of a separate treatment of predestination is due to no underestimation of the doctrine itself. This is further borne out by the circumstance that the doctrine, though adverted to only incidentally, is dealt with in these

formularies with firmness and clearness and altogether in the spirit of the most advanced Reformed teaching. It seems only an accident of their form, therefore, to be explained ordinarily [63] from the practical end held in view in their composition, leading to emphasis being laid especially on the subjective side of religious truth, that a more formal treatment of predestination was not given in these formularies also. The separation off of the topic for distinct formal assertion and treatment is found first in the First Basle or Mühlhausen Confession (1534), after which the Genevan Confession of 1537 soon follows; in the more elaborate later Confessions it is regular.

It is worth noting, however, that, in accordance with the prevailing soteriological interest in which the Confessions were composed, the treatment of General Predestination or the Decree of God is much less usual and full than that of Special Predestination or Election and Reprobation. Not rarely allusion to it fails altogether, and when it is adverted to its adduction is often purely incidental, in connection, say, with the doctrine of Providence: as a rule it is only in the more developed and extended creeds that it is set forth explicitly or with any fullness. The Westminster Shorter Catechism is perhaps unique in giving the preference to a statement of General Predestination (Q. 8) and stating Special Predestination only incidentally (Q. 20). How General Predestination is commonly dealt with may be observed by noting its treatment in Zwingli's "Fidei ratio" (1530), the Hungarian Confession (1557), the Second Helvetic Confession (1562), the Heidelberg Catechism (1563), Sigismund's Confession (1614); and among the Calvinian creeds, especially of course in the Genevan Consent, which devotes a long separate discussion to Providence (1552), but along with it also Calvin's Articles (15—), the Genevan Students' Confession (1559), the Confession of the English Exiles (1558), the Gallican Confession (1559), and the Belgic (1561) and the Scotch Confessions (1560), and especially the Irish Articles (1615),

---

[63] In the case of the Zurich Consent (1549), of course, its scope did not allow more than an incidental allusion.

from which the Westminster Confession directly derives. It
will be observed, in glancing over the treatment in these documents, that, on the one side, especial care is taken to guard
against the supposition that God, by virtue of His universal
decree, is therefore chargeable with the authorship of or moral
responsibilty for sin; and, on the other, the strongest stress is
laid upon the confidence which the child of God may cherish
in all the untoward circumstances of life that everything that
occurs is yet but the outworking of a Father's purpose and
will always conduce to good to those who are His. Even in
dealing with God's General Predestination, therefore, though
before all, of course, the motive is to do justice to the very idea
of God as the Personal Author and Governor of all, and to the
Scriptural revelation concerning the universal reach of His
purpose, yet the practical interests of the ethical construction
of sin and of the comfort of the saints largely condition and control the presentation of the doctrine. Thus it happens that the
fact of General Predestination is commonly presupposed or
incidentally alluded to rather than the doctrine fully expounded.

2. It is to be observed, next, that the whole body of these
Confessions are remarkably at one in their doctrine as to the
nature of Predestination. Little space is occupied, it is true,
with guarding the doctrine of General Predestination from the
perversion of either the coarse suspension of it on foresight or
the more subtle entanglement of it with a *scientia media* —
though Zwingli's "Fidei ratio" (1530) already strikes a
clear note here. As General Predestination is itself largely
dealt with only by presupposition and allusion, so are naturally
all questions concerning its nature. With reference to Special
or Soteriological Predestination, however, the case is different.
Its absoluteness and independence of all foreseen grounds or
conditions are copiously and emphatically asserted; the matter is treated not only positively but negatively; every conceivable ground in the creature for the decree is mentioned
in detail and expressly excluded. There is no variation in this
matter from Zwingli to the Swiss Form of Consent. To all alike

the Divine Predestination as applied to the destiny of man is
an eternal, absolute, independent, most free, immutable purpose of God, for which no cause can be assigned except His
gratuitous good pleasure; and in which no change can be
imagined, just because it is the purpose of the immutable God.
Therefore these Confessions are also at one in proclaiming the
particularity of the election of God. According to them all, it
deals, not with a variable class, but with specific individuals
which are particularly and unchangeably designed. This is the
clear assertion not only of what may be looked upon as the
stricter Calvinistic formularies, but also of those which were
laboring most heavily in the Unionistic currents. It is not
merely the Swiss Form of Consent which declares that God
" elected a certain and definite number," or the Lambeth and
Irish Articles and Canons of Dort which assert that predestination has predefined a certain number, known only to God
indeed, but capable neither of increase nor diminution: the
Second Helvetic Confession (1562) also with equal conviction
affirms that God knows who are His; the theologians at the
Leipzig Colloquy insist that both the number and names of His
elect are known to God; the authors of the Declaration of
Thorn assert that the number of the elect is certain with God.

Nor is there any difference among these Confessions in
their conception of election as in its very nature — as indeed
it is *ex vi termini* — an act specifically of *discrimination*. To
one and all alike the elect are a body of individuals, particularly and individually set upon by the inscrutable love of God,
and by this act of free and independent choice separated from
others who are thus passed by in the electing grace, and accordingly left unchosen, unelected, and therefore unblessed by the
series of acts of divine grace which follow upon election and
give it effect. In other words, for all these creeds alike *discrimination* constitutes the very essence of Soteriological Predestination. That is to say, it is a *prædestinatio gemina* that
they teach: and that again is to say that they are at one in the
conception of the necessary implication in the sovereignty
of election, of a sovereign preterition as well.

It is true enough, no doubt, that they do not all explicitly define the doctrine of sovereign preterition. We have seen that there are some of them which do not give more than a merely incidental treatment or even a mere reference to predestination at large; and others even which do not directly allude to it at all: while yet it is clear that the doctrine of predestination is a fundamental postulate of them all. Similarly, among those in which predestination is alluded to or even somewhat fully set forth, there are some which do not allude to its darker side of reprobation, or, if they allude to it, pass it by with a mere allusion. There is, for example, no explicit reference to reprobation in the following Confessions, to wit: Zwingli's Exposition of the Christian Faith (1531), the First Basle Confession (1534), the Genevan Catechism (1545), Calvin's creeds composed for the Genevan Students (1559), the Church at Paris (1557) and the French Churches (1562), the English Articles (1553), the Heidelberg Catechism (1563), and the Second Bohemian Confession (1575). It will be noted at once that some of these come from the hand of Zwingli or Calvin himself, neither of whom certainly had any desire to minimize the importance of conceiving predestination as distinctively an act of discrimination; and further, that in no one of them is election itself treated otherwise than by incidental allusion, except in the English Articles (1553) and the First Basle Confession (1534) — in the latter of which a single sentence only is given to it. Clearly the omission of allusion to reprobation is not to be interpreted in such instances as arguing any chariness as to the doctrine: it may rather be supposed to be omitted just because it is so fully presupposed. To these creeds are to be added certain others in which reprobation, though alluded to, receives no direct treatment, and is thus, while clearly presupposed, yet left without definition and guarding. These are Zwingli's " Fidei ratio " (1530), the Scotch Confession (1560), and the Second Helvetic Confession (1562). These belong, with respect to the doctrine of reprobation, in a class similar to that occupied with reference to the general doctrine of predestination by the creeds which allude to it without expounding it: and it is to be noted that the authors of these creeds — Zwingli, Knox, and Bullinger, in his later years when under the influence of Peter Martyr — cannot be suspected of any hesitation concerning the truth or importance of the *prædestinatio gemina*. Obviously the omission fully to define it is to be sought in these cases, therefore, not in doubt as to the doctrine, much less in denial of it, but, on the one hand, in such confidence in the implication of preterition in the very idea of election as seemed to render its separate statement unnecessary, and, on the other, in such engrossment with the practical aspects of the gracious side of the doctrine as led to passing lightly over all that is not immediately utilizable by the simplest Christian consciousness.

There is, therefore, a grave overstatement involved in, for example, Dr. Schaff's representation that "the Thirty-nine Articles, the Heidelberg Catechism, and other German Reformed Confessions, indorse merely the positive part of the free election of believers, and are wisely silent concerning the decree of reprobation, leaving it to theological science and private opinion": [64] and much more in the heightened form which he gives this representation later,[65] when he says that "the most authoritative" of the Reformed Creeds, "as the Helvetic Confession of Bullinger, the Heidelberg Catechism, and the Bandenburg Confessions (also the Scotch Confession of 1560) teach only the positive and comforting part of predestination, and ignore or deny a separate decree of reprobation; thus taking the ground practically that all that are saved are saved by the free grace of God, while all that are lost are lost by their own guilt." Of denial of the doctrine there can be no question here: it was certainly not denied by the authors of the documents which omit to mention it or mention it only allusively; men such as Zwingli, Calvin, Knox, Ursinus, Bullinger (at the close of his life) not only held but strenuously defended it. Of "ignoring" it, in any proper sense of that word, there can be no more question. Only in the case of the Brandenburg Confessions (which are assuredly as far as possible from

[64] "Creeds of Christendom," i. 1877, p. 454.　　　[65] P. 635.

ignoring it) can we speak even of an attempt to soften the statement of the doctrine: and the attempt in that case proceeded only by focusing attention on " positive reprobation " (concerning which some things are denied which no one of the Reformed wished to affirm of it) and withdrawing it from " negative reprobation " (of which some of the things denied of " positive reprobation " are affirmed by the Reformed system) — with the effect of betraying to the informed reader a wish to distract attention from controverted points rather than to deny any item of the Reformed faith. It is plausible only with reference to the English Articles to talk of a purposed ignoring: and even there doubtless only plausible. The broad fact is simply that the doctrine of reprobation fails to receive explicit treatment in a few of the Reformed creeds, just as predestination itself does; and that this simple omission to treat it is best explicable in the one case as in the other from the scope and special object of the creeds in question, and from the confidence of their writers in the necessary implication of the omitted doctrine in what is said. Similarly it is left unnoted in the Westminster Shorter Catechism, after the most explicit insistence on it in the Confession of Faith and the Larger Catechism — for no other reason, of course, than the different specific objects and audiences held in view in the several cases.

Certainly reprobation is treated as an essential part of the doctrine of predestination in all the Reformed creeds in which it is dealt with at all. These include not merely certain of Calvin's own compositions — the Genevan Confession (1537), the Genevan Consensus (1552), Calvin's Articles (15—), the Gallican Confession (1559); and certain others that may be thought to derive in a special way from him — the Confession of the English Exiles (1558), the Belgic Confession (1561), the Lambeth (1595) and Irish Ariticles (1615), the Canons of Dort (1618) and the Swiss Form of Consent (1675); but even such creeds as the Hungarian (1557) and the Brandenburg Confessions, Sigismund's (1614), the Leipzig Colloquy (1631) and the Declaration of Thorn (1645) which, with all their effort to soften the expression of the doctrine in its harder-looking features, do not dream of denying, ignoring, or doubting that it is, as the obverse of election, an essential element of the doctrine of predestination. In all these documents reprobation is treated as involved in the very definition of predestination as a soteriological decree, or in the doctrine of "election" itself as a selection out of a mass. It is not treated with equal detail, however, in them all. It is especially to the Genevan Confession (1537), the Genevan Consensus (1552), the Articles of Calvin (15—), the Gallican and Belgic Confessions (1559 and 1561), the Lambeth and Irish Articles (1595 and 1615), the Westminster Confession (1646), the Canons of Dort (1618), and the Swiss Form of Consent (1675) — together with the softened Brandenburg Confessions — that we must go to find its full exposition. There is, nevertheless, no reason, and indeed no room, to fancy that those documents which speak less fully of the doctrine, or do not even allude to it, occupy any other attitude towards it than the common Reformed attitude, revealed in the Confessions in which it is explicitly mentioned or fully developed. It is rather to be presumed that the common doctrine is presupposed when it does not come to explicit mention: and every indication in the creeds themselves bears this presumption out.

This constancy of the testimony of the Reformed Confessions to the *prædestinatio gemina* — that is, to the reality of a sovereign preterition by the side of and forming the foil of sovereign election — may well seem to be remarkable in the face of the universal condemnation it provoked from the controversialists of other communions. From the publication of the Form of Concord the confessional Lutheran doctrine involved the denial of a predestination to death: and Lutheran controversialists were not backward in assaulting the Reformed doctrine as in its very essence horrible. In Anglican circles, along another pathway, essentially the same result was reached: and even the best of the adherents of the new Anglicanism adopted as their own Hooker's construction of an absolute will in God for salvation but "an occasioned will" for

destruction, and made it the reproach of Calvinists that they
taught " one irrespective predestination " to death as to life.
No doubt individual theologians were more or less affected by
the very iteration and violence of these assaults; and there arose
inevitably Lutheranizers and Anglicanizers among the teachers
of the Reformed Churches. The peculiarities of the Brandenburg Confessions, for example, no doubt find their explanation in the sharpness of the conflict on German ground. But
doubtless the explanation of the constancy of the Reformed
testimony to the *prædestinatio gemina* is also in part to be
traced to the very sharpness of this conflict. The denial of
sovereign preterition was thereby clearly branded as a Lutheran error or as quasi-Augustinian Anglicanism. For the
preservation of the Reformed doctrine its affirmation was
clearly exhibited to be essential. Thus it became more and
more impossible to omit it; and after the rise of the Remonstrant controversy, quite impossible. It was therefore that
even the Brandenburg Confessions assert reprobation as an
integral part of the doctrine of predestination, and only strive
to save appearances by obscuring the distinction between
negative and positive reprobation and making denials with
reference to " reprobation " which apply only to the former.
It was therefore, also, that in the effort to save the Calvinism
of the British Churches, the *prædestinatio bipartita* was
thrown up into high relief in the Lambeth and Irish Articles
and the Westminster formularies. Hard experience had made
Calvin's judgment, that without preterition election itself
cannot stand, the deep conviction of the whole Reformed
Church: and whether at Dort or Zurich, London or Dublin, the
essence of the Calvinistic contention was found in the free
discrimination among men which was attributed to God: in
the confession that He chooses not all but some men to life
and destines the rest, therefore, to destruction. The Confession
of the English Exiles at Geneva (1558) is unique in stating
this act of discrimination so as to throw the predestination to
death in the foreground: " God of the lost sons of Adam hath
ordained some as vessels of wrath to damnation; and hath

chosen others as vessels of His mercy to be saved." But this is indicatory only of the clearness with which *discrimination* was grasped as the core of the matter. The rest follow the opposite and more natural form of statement, but are no less intent on tracing to God the actual distinction in destiny which Scripture and observation alike forced on the recognition of every thoughtful student whether of the Book or of mankind.

3. We must not fail next to observe in passing, though we shall not dwell upon it, the unanimity of these Confessions in construing the decree of God *as a unit;* that is to say, in recognizing the election to salvation as involving a predestination of all the means thereof, and correspondingly the act of preterition as involving the foreordination of all that is consequent thereto. Sometimes the unity of the decree is asserted in so many words; it is affirmed that it was in the " same decree " by which men were segregated to salvation that the means by which they should be made partakers of this salvation were ordained for them. At other times the matter is treated only by enunciating the natural sequence of things; ordination to an end implying ordination of the means to that end. But without exception the destination of men to salvation and the destination to them of the means thereto are treated as inseparably united.

4. It is, however, of more immediate interest to observe the attitude of the Reformed Confessions with respect to the *object* of Predestination. Here we are met by a greater apparent diversity than obtains in the other matters that have attracted our attention. Of the three great parties that grew up among the Reformed with reference to the object of predestination (in the sense of Soteriological Predestination) — the Supralapsarian, Infralapsarian, and Salmurian, conceiving the object of predestination respectively as unfallen, fallen, and redeemed mankind — the first and third receive no support from the Confessions. Yet all the Confessions are not Infralapsarian: nor is their attitude precisely the same towards Supralapsarianism and Salmurianism. Some of them are explicitly Infralapsarian, and none exclude, much less polemically

oppose, Infralapsarianism. None of them are explicitly Supralapsarian: many, however, leave the question between Supra- and Infralapsarianism entirely to one side, and thus open the way equally to both; and none are polemically directed against Supralapsarianism. Not only are none explicitly Salmurian, on the other hand, but those prepared after the rise of Salmurianism firmly close the door to it, while earlier ones certainly do not open it, and leave room for it, if at all, only uncertainly and by doubtful inference from chance expressions which have no direct reference to the point in controversy and are flexible to other constructions.

The explicitly Infralapsarian Confessions include the Genevan Consent (1552), the Hungarian Confession (1557), that of the English Exiles at Geneva (1558), the Gallican (1559) and Belgic (1561) Confessions, the Canons of Dort (1618) and the Swiss Form of Consent (1675), together with the Articles framed at the Leipzig Colloquy (1631). These explicitly declare that the discrimination which God made among men was made *in massa corrupta:* it is for them certain that it was out of the lost race of man that God chose some to eternal life, leaving the rest to the just recompense of their sins. By their side we may perhaps place some others, such as the Genevan Confession of 1537 and the creeds prepared by Calvin for the Genevan Students (1559), the Church at Paris (1557) and the French Churches (1562), the Confession of Sigismund (1614) and the Declaration of Thorn (1645), and perhaps also, though with less confidence, the Second Helvetic Confession (1562) and the Heidelberg Catechism (1563), as Confessions which, while not clearly implying Infralapsarianism, yet seem more or less to speak out of an underlying but not expressed Infralapsarian consciousness: this is, however, a matter of mere tone and manner, and is of course much too subtle to insist upon. In such formularies, on the other hand, as Zwingli's "Fidei ratio" (1530), the First Basle or Mühlhausen Confession (1534), the Genevan Catechism (1545), the Zurich Consent (1549), the English (1553), Lambeth (1595) and Irish (1615) Articles, and the Scotch Confession (1560), the

lines are so drawn that it is impossible to discover that there
is advantage given to either party to the debate over the other:
in the case of the Westminster Confession, which shares this
peculiarity with them, we know that this was the result of a
settled policy, and it may have been the same in some of the
others also (as in Calvin's Articles, in view of Beza's views
known to him, and in the Lambeth and Irish Articles). In
view of these facts, it is hardly possible to speak of the Reformed creeds at large as distinctly Infralapsarian, though Dr.
Schaff's language affirming that "all the Reformed Confessions . . . keep within the limits of infralapsarianism " [66] may,
so far, be adopted as well-chosen and expressive of the true
state of the case. Some Reformed Confessions explicitly define
Infralapsarianism: none assert anything which is not consonant with Infralapsarianism. On the other hand, nothing is
affirmed in the majority of the Confessions inconsistent with
Supralapsarianism either; and this majority includes several
of the most widely accepted documents. The Westminster
Confession in its careful avoidance of raising the distinction
throws itself, therefore, into a class with the majority of its
companion Confessions, inclusive of the Heidelberg Catechism
and the Second Helvetic Confession, which are certainly the
most widely accepted of Continental formularies, and of the
entire British tradition. It is a noteworthy fact that it is particularly the Genevan creeds and those formed under the
Genevan influence which are explicitly Infralapsarian; while
it is along the line of German Reformed and British influence
that the distinction is avoided, or at least not adverted to.
This is probably in part due to the prosecution of the debate
between the parties, with most vigor among the French-
speaking Calvinists and in Holland. But the effect is to throw
the Westminster Confession at this point into companionship
with the documents which have been often treated as presenting the " milder " Calvinism, but which would certainly be more
properly described as at this point setting forth rather a more

[66] As cited, p. 635: " Even," he specifies, " the Canons of Dort, the Westminster Confession, and the Helvetic Consensus Formula."

generic Calvinism. It is certainly a remarkable instance of the irresponsibility of polemics to hear, as we have recently been forced often to hear, adduced as a mark of hyper-Calvinism a feature of the Westminster method of dealing with predestination which it shares with the Second Helvetic Confession and the Heidelberg Catechism, the Confession of Sigismund and the Declaration of Thorn, the Thirty-nine Articles and the early Scotch Confession.

We restrain ourselves, however, from entering here into a comparison of the Westminster Confession with its sister documents and illustrating from them its especial type of Calvinistic teaching. It has been, to be sure, one of the chief ends we have had in view, in calling attention just at this time to the doctrine of Predestination as expressed in the Reformed creeds, to further an intelligent estimate of the teaching of the Westminster Standards on this great topic, by throwing upon it the light of its historical enunciation in the Reformed Churches. But we must rest content for the present with the general results that the whole body of Reformed creeds, including the Westminster Standards, are remarkably at one in their conceptions of this high mystery; and that the Westminster Standards in their exposition of its elements receive the support of the entire body of the Reformed creeds at every salient point. To facilitate a rough estimate of the nature and amount of the support it thus receives from them, we have marked by footnote references to the Westminster Confession the passages in them which present especially close parallels with the sections in the chapter in that formulary which deals with the decree of God. Later, we hope to return to the matter. For the present it may safely be left to the general impression which the mere reading over of the documents will inevitably make.

VII

ON THE ANTIQUITY AND THE UNITY
OF THE HUMAN RACE

ON THE ANTIQUITY AND THE UNITY
OF THE HUMAN RACE [1]

THE fundamental assertion of the Biblical doctrine of the origin of man is that he owes his being to a creative act of God. Subsidiary questions growing out of this fundamental assertion, however, have been thrown from time to time into great prominence, as the changing forms of current anthropological speculation have seemed to press on this or that element in, or corollary from, the Biblical teaching. The most important of these subsidiary questions has concerned the method of the divine procedure in creating man. Discussion of this question became acute on the publication of Charles Darwin's treatise on the " Origin of Species " in 1859, and can never sink again into rest until it is thoroughly understood in all quarters that "evolution" cannot act as a substitute for creation, but at best can supply only a theory of the method of the divine providence. Closely connected with this discussion of the mode of origination of man, has been the discussion of two further questions, both older than the Darwinian theory, to one of which it gave, however, a new impulse, while it has well-nigh destroyed all interest in the other. These are the questions of the Antiquity of Man and the Unity of the Human Race, to both of which a large historical interest attaches, though neither of them can be said to be burning questions of to-day.

The question of the antiquity of man has of itself no theological significance. It is to theology, as such, a matter of entire indifference how long man has existed on earth. It is only because of the contrast which has been drawn between the short period which seems to be allotted to human history in the Biblical narrative, and the tremendously long period which

[1] Reprinted from *The Princeton Theological Review,* ix. 1911, pp. 1–25.

certain schools of scientific speculation have assigned to the duration of human life on earth, that theology has become interested in the topic at all. There was thus created the appearance of a conflict between the Biblical statements and the findings of scientific investigators, and it became the duty of theologians to investigate the matter. The asserted conflict proves, however, to be entirely factitious. The Bible does not assign a brief span to human history: this is done only by a particular mode of interpreting the Biblical data, which is found on examination to rest on no solid basis. Science does not demand an inordinate period for the life of human beings on earth: this is done only by a particular school of speculative theorizers, the validity of whose demands on time exact investigators are more and more chary of allowing. As the real state of the case has become better understood the problem has therefore tended to disappear from theological discussion, till now it is pretty well understood that theology as such has no interest in it.

It must be confessed, indeed, that the impression is readily taken from a *prima facie* view of the Biblical record of the course of human history, that the human race is of comparatively recent origin. It has been the usual supposition of simple Bible readers, therefore, that the Biblical data allow for the duration of the life of the human race on earth only a paltry six thousand years or so: and this supposition has become fixed in formal chronological schemes which have become traditional and have even been given a place in the margins of our Bibles to supply the chronological framework of the Scriptural narrative. The most influential of these chronological schemes is that which was worked out by Archbishop Usher in his " Annales Veteri et Novi Testamenti " (1650–1654), and it is this scheme which has found a place in the margin of the Authorized English Version of the Bible since 1701. According to it the creation of the world is assigned to the year 4004 B.C. (Usher's own dating was 4138 B.C.); while according to the calculation of Petau (in his " Rationarium temporum "), the most influential rival scheme, it is assigned to the year 3983

B.C. On a more careful scrutiny of the data on which these calculations rest, however, they are found not to supply a satisfactory basis for the constitution of a definite chronological scheme. These data consist largely, and at the crucial points solely, of genealogical tables; and nothing can be clearer than that it is precarious in the highest degree to draw chronological inferences from genealogical tables.

For the period from Abraham down we have, indeed, in addition to somewhat minute genealogical records, the combined evidence of such so-called "long-dates" as those of I Kings vi. 1, Gal. iii. 17, and several precise statements concerning the duration of definite shorter periods, together with whatever aid it may be possible to derive from a certain amount of contemporary extra-Biblical data. For the length of this period there is no difficulty, therefore, in reaching an entirely satisfactory general estimate. But for the whole space of time before Abraham, we are dependent entirely on inferences drawn from the genealogies recorded in the fifth and eleventh chapters of Genesis. And if the Scriptural genealogies supply no solid basis for chronological inferences, it is clear that we are left without Scriptural data for forming an estimate of the duration of these ages. For aught we know they may have been of immense length.

The general fact that the genealogies of Scripture were not constructed for a chronological purpose and lend themselves ill to employment as a basis for chronological calculations has been repeatedly shown very fully; but perhaps by no one more thoroughly than by Dr. William Henry Green in an illuminating article published in the *Bibliotheca Sacra* for April, 1890. These genealogies must be esteemed trustworthy for the purposes for which they are recorded; but they cannot safely be pressed into use for other purposes for which they were not intended, and for which they are not adapted. In particular, it is clear that the genealogical purposes for which the genealogies were given, did not require a complete record of all the generations through which the descent of the persons to whom they are assigned runs; but only an adequate indication of the particular line through which the descent in question comes. Accordingly it is found on examination that the genealogies of Scripture are freely compressed for all sorts of purposes; and that it can seldom be confidently affirmed that they contain a complete record of the whole series of generations, while it is often obvious that a very large number are omitted. There is no reason inherent in the nature of the Scriptural genealogies why a genealogy of ten recorded links, as each of those in Genesis v. and xi. is, may not represent an actual descent of a hundred or a thousand or ten thousand links. The point established by the table is not that these are all the links which intervened between the beginning and the closing names, but that this is the line of descent through which one traces back to or down to the other.

A sufficient illustration of the freedom with which the links in the genealogies are dealt with in the Biblical usage is afforded by the two genealogies of our Lord which are given in the first chapter of the Gospel of Matthew. For it is to be noted that there are two genealogies of Jesus given in this chapter, differing greatly from one another in fullness of record, no doubt, but in no respect either in trustworthiness or in principle of record. The one is found in the first verse, and traces Jesus back to Abraham in just two steps: " Jesus Christ, the son of David, the son of Abraham." The other is found in verses 2–17, and expands this same genealogy into forty-two links, divided for purposes of symmetrical record and easy memorizing into a threefold scheme of fourteen generations each. And not even is this longer record a complete one. A comparison with the parallel records in the Old Testament will quickly reveal the fact that the three kings, Ahaziah, Joash, and Amaziah are passed over and Joram is said to have begotten Uzziah, his great-great-grandson. The other genealogies of Scripture present similar phenomena; and as they are carefully scrutinized, it becomes ever clearer that as they do not pretend to give complete lists of generations, they cannot be intended to supply a basis for chronological calculation, and it is illegitimate and misleading to attempt to use them for that purpose. The reduction for extraneous reasons of the genealogy of Christ in the first chapter of Matthew into three tables of fourteen generations each, may warn us that the reduction of the patriarchal genealogies in Genesis v. and xi. into two tables of ten generations each may equally be due to extraneous considerations; and that there may be represented by each of these ten generations — adequately for the purposes for which the genealogy is recorded — a very much longer actual series of links.

It must not be permitted to drop out of sight, to be sure, that the appearance of supplying data for a chronological calculation is in these particular genealogies not due entirely to the mere fact that these lists are genealogies. It is due to a peculiarity of these special genealogies by which they are differentiated from all other genealogies in Scripture. We refer to the regular attachment, to each name in the lists, of the age of the father at the birth of his son. The effect of this is to provide what seems to be a continuous series of precisely measured generations, the numbers having only to be added together to supply an exact measure of the time consumed in their sequence. We do not read merely that " Adam begat Seth; and Seth begat Enosh; and Enosh begat Kenan." We read rather that " Adam lived an hundred and thirty years and begat Seth; and Seth lived an hundred and five years and begat Enosh; and Enosh lived ninety years and begat Kenan." It certainly looks, at first sight, as if we needed only to add these one hundred and thirty, one hundred and five, and ninety years together in order to obtain the whole time which elapsed from the creation of Adam to the birth of Kenan; and, accordingly, as if we needed only to add together the similar numbers throughout the lists in order to obtain an accurate measure of the whole period from the Creation to the Deluge. Plausible as this procedure seems, however, it appears on a closer scrutiny unjustified; and it is the especial service which Dr. William Henry Green in the article already mentioned has rendered to the cause of truth in this matter that he has shown this clearly.

For, if we will look at these lists again, we shall find that we have not yet got them in their entirety before us. Not only is there attached to each name in them a statement of the age at which the father begot his son, but also a statement of how long the father lived after he had begotten his son, and how many years his life-span counted up altogether. If we do not read merely, " Adam begat Seth; and Seth begat Enosh; and Enosh begat Kenan "; neither do we read merely, " Adam lived one hundred and thirty years and begat Seth; and Seth lived one hundred and five years and begat Enosh; and Enosh lived ninety years and begat Kenan." What we read is: " Adam lived an hundred and thirty years, and begat a son in his own likeness, after his image; and called his name Seth: and the days of Adam after he begat Seth were eight hundred years: and he begat sons and daughters: and all the days that Adam lived were nine hundred and thirty years: and he died. And Seth lived an hundred and five years, and begat Enosh: and Seth lived after he begat Enosh eight hundred and seven years, and begat sons and daughters: and all the days of Seth were nine hundred and twelve years: and he died. And Enosh lived ninety years, and begat Kenan: and Enosh lived after he begat Kenan eight hundred and fifteen years and begat sons and daughters: and all the days of Enosh were nine hundred and five years: and he died." There is, in a word, much more information furnished with respect to each link in the chain than merely the age to which each father had attained when his son was begotten; and all this information is of the same order and obviously belongs together. It is clear that a single motive has determined the insertion of all of it; and we must seek a reason for its insertion which will account for all of it. This reason cannot have been a chronological one: for all the items of information furnished do not serve a chronological purpose. Only the first item in each case can be made to yield a chronological result; and therefore not even it was intended to yield a chronological result, since all these items of information are too closely bound together in their common character to be separated in their intention. They too readily explain themselves, moreover, as serving an obvious common end which was clearly in the mind of the writer, to justify the ascription of a different end to any one of them. When we are told of any man that he was a hundred and thirty years old when he begat his heir, and lived after that eight hundred years begetting sons and daughters, dying only at the age of nine hundred and thirty years, all these items coöperate to make a vivid impression upon us of the vigor and grandeur of humanity in those old days of the world's prime. In a sense different indeed from that which the words bear in Genesis vi., but full of meaning to us, we exclaim, " Surely there were giants in those days! " This is the impression which the items of information inevitably make on us; and it is the impression they were intended to make on us, as is proved by the simple fact that they are adapted in all their items to make this impression, while only a small portion of them can be utilized for the purpose of chronological calculation. Having thus found a reason which will account for the insertion of all the items of information which are given us, we have no right to assume another reason to account for the insertion of some of them. And that means that we must decline to look upon the first item of information given in each instance as intended to give us chronological information.

The conclusion which we thus reach is greatly strengthened when we observe another fact with regard to these items of information. This is that the appearance that we have in them of a chronological scheme does not reside in the nature of the items themselves, but purely in their sequence. If we read the items of information attached to each name, apart from their fellows attached to the succeeding names, we shall have simply a set of facts about each name, which in their combination make a strong impression of the vigor and greatness of humanity in those days, and which suggest no chronological inference. It is only when the names, with the accompanying comments, are put together, one after the other, that a chronological inference is suggested. The chronological suggestion is thus purely the effect of the arrangement of the

STUDIES IN THEOLOGY

names in immediate sequence; and is not intrinsically resident in the items of information themselves.

And now we must call attention to a characteristic of Scripture genealogies in general which seems to find a specially striking illustration in these comments. This is the habit of interposing into the structure of the genealogies, here and there, a short note, attached to this name or that, telling some important or interesting fact about the person represented by it. A simple genealogy would run thus: " Adam begat Seth; and Seth begat Enosh; and Enosh begat Kenan "; and the like, But it would be quite in the Biblical manner if there were attached to some, or even to each of these names, parenthetical remarks, calling attention to something of interest regarding the several persons. For example, it would be quite after the Biblical fashion should we have rather had this: " Adam, who was the first man, begat Seth; and Seth, he it was who was appointed as another seed in the stead of Abel whom Cain slew, begat Enosh; and Enosh, at his birth men began to call on the name of Jehovah, begat Kenan." The insertion of such items of information does not in the least change the character of the genealogy as in itself a simple genealogy, subject to all the laws which governed the formation and record of the Scriptural genealogies, including the right of free compression, with the omission of any number of links. It is strictly parenthetical in nature.

Several examples of such parenthetical insertions occur in the genealogy of Jesus recorded in the first chapter of Matthew, to which we have already referred for illustration. Thus in verse 2, the fact that Judah had " brethren " is interposed in the genealogy, a fact which is noted also with respect to two others of the names which occur in the list (verses 3 and 11): it is noted here doubtless because of the significance of the twelve sons of Jacob as tribe-fathers of Israel. Again we find in four instances a notification of the mother interposed (Tamar, verse 3; Rahab, verse 5; Ruth, verse 5; her of Uriah, verse 6). The introduction of the names of these notable women, which prepares the way for the introduction of that of Mary in verse 16, constitutes a very remarkable feature of this particular genealogy. Another feature of it is suggested by the attachment to the name of David (verse 6) the statement that he was " the King "; and to the name of Jechoniah (verse 11) the statement that his life-span fell at the time of the carrying away to Babylon: the account of these insertions being found, doubtless, in the artificial arrangement of the genealogy in three symmetrical tables. The habit of inserting parenthetical notes giving items of interest connected with the names which enter into the genealogies is doubtless sufficiently illustrated by these instances. The only point in which the genealogies of Genesis v. and xi. differ in this respect from this one in Matthew i. is that such items of information are inserted with reference to every name in those genealogies, while they are inserted only occasionally in the genealogy of our Lord. This is, however, a difference of detail, not of principle. Clearly if these notes had been constant in the genealogy in Matthew i. instead of merely occasional, its nature as a genealogy would not have been affected: it would still have remained a simple genealogy subject to all the customary laws of simple genealogies. That they are constant in the genealogies of Genesis v. and xi. does not, then, alter their character as simple genealogies. These additions are in their nature parenthetical, and are to be read in each instance strictly as such and with sole reference to the names to which they are attached, and cannot determine whether or not links have been omitted in these genealogies as they are freely omitted in other genealogies.

It is quite true that, when brought together in sequence, name after name, these notes assume the appearance of a concatenated chronological scheme. But this is pure illusion, due wholly to the nature of the parenthetical insertions which are made. When placed one after the other they seem to play into one another, whereas they are set down here for an entirely different purpose and cannot without violence be read with reference to one another. If the items of information were of a different character we should never think of reading them otherwise than each with sole reference to its own name. Thus, if they were given to show us how nobly developed primitive men were in their physical frames and read something as follows: " Adam was eight cubits in height and begat Seth; and Seth was seven cubits in height and begat Enosh; and Enosh was six cubits in height and begat Kenan "; we should have no difficulty in understanding that these remarks are purely parenthetical and in no way argue that no links have been omitted. The case is not altered by the mere fact that other items than these are chosen for notice, with the same general intent, and we actually read: " Adam lived an hundred and thirty years and begat Seth; and Seth lived an hundred and five years and begat Enosh; and Enosh lived ninety years and begat Kenan." The circumstance that the actual items chosen for parenthetical notice are such that when the names are arranged one after the other they produce the illusion of a chronological scheme is a mere accident, arising from the nature of the items chosen, and must not blind us to the fact that we have before us here nothing but ordinary genealogies, accompanied by parenthetical notes which are inserted for other than chronological purposes; and that therefore these genealogies must be treated like other genealogies, and interpreted on the same principles. But if this be so, then these genealogies too not only may be, but probably are, much compressed, and merely record the line of descent of Noah from Adam and of Abraham from Noah. Their symmetrical arrangement in groups of ten is indicative of their compression; and for aught we know instead of twenty generations and some two thousand years measuring the interval between the creation and the birth of Abraham, two hundred generations, and something like twenty thousand years, or even two thousand generations and something like two hundred thousand years may have intervened. In a word, the Scriptural data leave us wholly without guidance in estimating the time which elapsed between the creation of the world and the deluge and between the deluge and the call of Abraham. So far as the Scripture assertions are concerned, we may suppose any length of time to have intervened between these events which may otherwise appear reasonable.

The question of the antiquity of man is accordingly a purely scientific one, in which the theologian as such has no concern. As an interested spectator, however, he looks on as the various schools of scientific speculation debate the question among themselves; and he can scarcely fail to take away as the result of his observation two well-grounded convictions. The first is that science has as yet in its hands no solid data for a definite estimate of the time during which the human race has existed on earth. The second is that the tremendous drafts on time which were accustomed to be made by the geologists about the middle of the last century and which continue to be made by one school of speculative biology to-day have been definitively set aside, and it is becoming very generally understood that man cannot have existed on the earth more than some ten thousand to twenty thousand years.

It was a result of the manner of looking at things inculcated by the Huttonian geology, that speculation during the first three quarters of the nineteenth century estimated the age of the habitable globe in terms of hundreds of millions of years. It was under the influence of this teaching, for example, that Charles Darwin, in 1859, supposed that three hundred million years were an underestimate for the period which has elapsed since the latter part of the Secondary Age.[2] In reviewing Mr. Darwin's argument in his "Student's Manual of Geology," Professor Jukes remarked on the vagueness of the data on which his estimates were formed, and suggested that the sum of years asserted might with equal reasonableness be reduced or multiplied a hundredfold: he proposed therefore three million and thirty billion years as the minimum and maximum limits of the period in question. From the same fundamental standpoint, Professor Poulton in his address as President of the Zoölogical Section of the British Association for the Advancement of Science (Liverpool, September, 1896) treats as too short from his biological point of view the longest time asked by the geologists for the duration of the habitable earth — say some four hundred millions of years. Dwelling on the number of distinct types of animal existence

[2] "Origin of Species," ed. 1, p. 287.

already found in the Lower Cambrian deposits, and on the necessarily (as he thinks) slow progress of evolution, he stretches out the time required for the advance of life to its present manifestation practically illimitably. Taking up the cudgels for his biological friends, Sir Archibald Geikie [3] chivalrously offers them all the time they desire, speaking on his own behalf, however, of one hundred million years as possibly sufficient for the period of the existence of life on the globe. These general estimates imply, of course, a very generous allowance for the duration of human life on earth; but many anthropologists demand for this period even more than they allow. Thus, for example, Professor Gabriel de Mortillet [4] reiterates his conviction that the appearance of man on earth cannot be dated less than two hundred and thirty thousand years ago, and Professor A. Penck [5] would agree with this estimate, while Dr. A. R. Wallace has been accustomed to ask more than double that period. [6]

These tremendously long estimates of the duration of life on earth and particularly of the duration of human life are, however, speculative, and, indeed, largely the creation of a special type of evolutionary speculation — a type which is rapidly losing ground among recent scientific workers. This type is that which owes its origin to the brooding mind of Charles Darwin; and up to recent times it has been the regnant type of evolutionary philosophy. Its characteristic contention is that the entire development of animate forms has been the product of selection, by the pressure of the environment, of infinitesimal variations in an almost infinite series of successive generations; or to put it rather brusquely, but not unfairly, that chance plus time are the true causes which account for the whole body of differentiated forms which animate nature presents to our observation. Naturally, therefore, heavy drafts have been made on time to account for whatever

[3] Address as President of the Geological Section of the British Association, Dover meeting, September, 1899: *Science* for October 13, 1899.

[4] *Revue Mensuelle* of the Paris School of Anthropology, for January 15, 1897.   [5] Silliman Lectures at Yale, for 1908.

[6] *Nature,* October 2, 1873, pp. 462–463; cf. "Darwinism," 1889, p. 456.

it seemed hard to attribute to brute chance, as if you could admit the issuing of any effect out of any conditions, if you only conceived the process of production as slow enough. James Hutton had duly warned his followers against the temptation to appeal to time as if it were itself an efficient cause of effects. " With regard to the effect of time," he said,[7] " though the continuance of time may do much in those operations which are extremely slow, where no change, to our observation, had appeared to take place, yet, where it is not in the nature of things to produce the change in question, the unlimited course of time would be no more effectual than the moment by which we measure events in our observations." The warning was not heeded: men seemed to imagine that, if only time enough were given for it, effects, for which no adequate cause could be assigned, might be supposed to come gradually of themselves. Aimless movement was supposed, if time enough were allowed for it, to produce an ordered world. It might as well be supposed that if a box full of printers' types were stirred up long enough with a stick, they could be counted on to arrange themselves in time in the order in which they stand, say, in Kant's " Critique of Pure Reason." They will never do so, though they be stirred to eternity. Dr. J. W. Dawson [8] points out the exact difficulty, when he remarks that " the necessity for indefinitely protracted time does not arise from the facts, but from the attempt to explain the facts without any adequate cause, and to appeal to an infinite series of chance interactions apart from a designed plan, and without regard to the consideration, that we know of no way in which, with any conceivable amount of time, the first living and organized beings could be spontaneously produced from dead matter." Nothing could be more certain than that what chance cannot begin the production of in a moment, chance cannot complete the production of in an eternity. The analysis of the complete effect into an infinite series of parts, and the distribution of these parts over an infinite series of years, leaves

---

[7] "Theory of the Earth," ii. p. 205.
[8] "Relics of Primeval Life," 1897, p. 323.

the effect as unaccounted for as ever. What is needed to account for it is not time in any extension, but an adequate cause. A mass of iron is made no more self-supporting by being forged into an illimitable chain formed of innumerable infinitesimal links. We may cast our dice to all eternity with no more likelihood than at the first throw of ever turning up double-sevens.

It is not, however, the force of such reasoning but the pressure of hard facts which is revolutionizing the conceptions of biologists to-day as to the length of the period during which man has existed on earth. It is not possible to enumerate here all the facts which are coöperating to produce a revised and greatly reduced estimate of this period. First among them may doubtless be placed the calculations of the life-period of the globe itself which have been made by the physicists with ever increasing confidence. Led by such investigators as Lord Kelvin, they have become ever more and more insistent that the time demanded by the old uniformitarian and new biological speculator is not at their disposal. The publication in the seventh decade of the past century of Lord Kelvin's calculations, going to show that the sun had not been shining sixty millions of years, already gave pause to the reckless drafts which had been accustomed to be made on time; and the situation was rendered more and more acute by subsequent revisions of Lord Kelvin's work, progressively diminishing this estimate. Sir Archibald Geikie complains that " he [Lord Kelvin] has cut off slice after slice from the allowance of time which at first he was prepared to grant for the evolution of geological history," until he has reduced it from forty to twenty millions of years, " and probably much nearer twenty than forty." [9] This estimate of the period of the sun's light would allow only something like six millions of years for geological time, only some one-sixteenth of which would be available for the cænozoic period, of which only about one-eighth or forty thousand years or so could be allotted to the pleistocene age, in the course of which the remains of man first

[9] *Loc. cit.*, p. 519.

appear.[10] Even this meager allowance is cut in half by the calculation of Professor Tait;[11] while the general conclusions of these investigators have received the support of independent calculations by Dr. George H. Darwin and Professor Newcomb; and more recently still Mr. T. J. J. See of the Naval Observatory at Washington has published a very pretty speculation in which he determines the total longevity of the sun to be only thirty-six millions of years, thirty-two of which belong to its past history.[12]

It is not merely the physicists, however, with whom the biological speculators have to do: the geologists themselves have turned against them. Recent investigations may be taken as putting pre-Quaternary man out of the question (the evidence was reviewed by Sir John Evans, in his address at the Toronto meeting of the British Association, August 18, 1897). And revised estimates of the rate of denudation, erosion, deposition of alluvial matter in deltas, or of stalagmitic matter in the floors or caves have greatly reduced the exaggerated conception of its slowness, from which support was sought for the immensely long periods of time demanded. The postglacial period, which will roughly estimate the age of man, it is now pretty generally agreed, "cannot be more than ten thousand years, or probably not more than seven thousand" in length.[13] In this estimate both Professor Winchell[14] and Professor Salisbury[15] agree, and to its establishment a great

[10] Cf. the estimates of G. F. Wright, "Records of the Past," vii. 1908, p. 24. He suggests for post-Tertiary time, say 50,000 years; and adds that, even if this be doubled, there could be assigned to the post-glacial period only some 10,000 years.

[11] "Recent Advances in Physical Science," 1876, pp. 167–168.

[12] On the so-called "Planetesimal Hypothesis" of Professors Chamberlin and Moulton, which does not presuppose a molten sun and earth, these calculations which proceed on the basis of the "cooling-globe hypothesis" are of course without validity. And in recent years a somewhat despairing appeal has been made to the behavior of radium to suggest that all calculations based on rate of waste are valueless.

[13] Cf. especially articles in the *Bibliotheca Sacra* for July, 1903 (lx. pp. 572–582).   [14] *American Geologist,* September, 1902, p. 193.

[15] "The Glacial Geology of New Jersey" (Volume V of the Final Report of the State Geologist), 1902, p. 194.

body of evidence derived from a variety of calculations concur. If man is of post glacial origin, then, his advent upon earth need not be dated more than five or six thousand years ago; or if we suppose him to have appeared at some point in the later glacial period, as Professor G. F. Wright does, then certainly Professor Wright's estimate of sixteen thousand to twenty thousand years is an ample one.

The effect of these revised estimates of geological time has been greatly increased by growing uncertainty among biologists themselves, as to the soundness of the assumptions upon which was founded their demand for long periods of time. These assumptions were briefly those which underlie the doctrine of evolution in its specifically Darwinian form; in the form, that is to say, in which the evolution is supposed to be accomplished by the fixing through the pressure of the environment of minute favorable variations, arising accidentally in the midst of minute variations in every direction indifferently. But in the progress of biological research, the sufficiency of this " natural selection " to account for the development of organic forms has come first to be questioned, and then in large circles to be denied.[16] In proportion, however, as evolution is conceived as advancing in determined directions, come the determination from whatever source you choose;[17] and in proportion as it is conceived as advancing onwards by large increments instead of by insensible changes;[18] in that proportion the demand on time is lessened and even the evolutionary speculator feels that he can get along with less of it. He is no longer impelled to assume behind the high type of man whose remains in the post-glacial deposits are the first intimation

[16] Cf. V. L. Kellogg, " Darwinism To-day," 1907; R. Otto, " Naturalism and Religion," 1907; E. Wasmann, " Die moderne Biologie und die Entwicklungstheorie," ed. 3, 1906; James Orr, " God's Image in Man," 1905; E. Dennert, " Vom Sterbelager des Darwinismus," 1903.

[17] That " orthogenesis " is a fact is much more widely recognized than is the validity of Eimer's special mode of accounting for it.

[18] The recognition of the reality of these saltations — or " mutations," as De Vries inadequately terms them — is again largely independent of any particular theory with reference to them.

of the presence of man on earth, an almost illimitable series of lower and ever lower types of man through which gradually the brute struggled up to the high humanity, records of whose existence alone have been preserved to us.[19] And he no longer requires to postulate immense stretches of time for the progress of this man through paleolithic, neolithic and metal-using periods, for the differentiation of the strongly marked characteristics of the several races of man, for the slow humanizing of human nature and the slower development of those powers within it from which at length what we call civilization emerged. Once allow the principle of modification by leaps, and the question of the length of time required for a given evolution passes out of the sphere of practical interest. The height of the leaps becomes a matter of detail, and there is readily transferred to the estimation of it the importance which was formerly attached to the estimation of the time involved. Thus it has come about, that, in the progress of scientific investigation, the motive for demanding illimitable stretches of time for the duration of life, and specifically for the duration of human life on earth, has gradually been passing away, and there seems now a very general tendency among scientific investigators to acquiesce in a moderate estimate — in an estimate which demands for the life of man on earth not more than, say, ten or twenty thousand years.

If the controversy upon the antiquity of man is thus rapidly losing all but a historical interest, that which once so

[19] Cf. Hubrecht in *De Gids* for June, 1896; Otto, "Naturalism and Religion," 1907, p. 110; Orr, "God's Image in Man," 1905, p. 134. E. D. Cope, "The Primary Factors of Organic Evolution," 1896, thinks there is evidence enough to constitute two species of the genus *homo — Homo sapiens* and *Homo neanderthalensis*, to the latter of which he assigns a greater number of simian characteristics than exist in any of the known races of the *Homo sapiens*. But he requires to add (p. 170): "There is still, to use the language of Fraipont and Lohest, 'an abyss' between the man of Spy and the highest ape" — although, on his own account he adds, surely unwarrantably, "though, from a zoölogical point of view, it is not a wide one." In point of fact the earliest relics of man are relics of *men*, with all that is included in that, and there lies between them and all other known beings a hitherto unbridged "abyss."

violently raged upon the unity of the race may be said already
to have reached this stage. The question of the unity of the
human race differs from the question of its antiquity in that it
is of indubitable theological importance. It is not merely that
the Bible certainly teaches it, while, as we have sought to
show, it has no teaching upon the antiquity of the race. It is
also the postulate of the entire body of the Bible's teaching —
of its doctrine of Sin and Redemption alike: so that the whole
structure of the Bible's teaching, including all that we know
as its doctrine of salvation, rests on it and implicates it. There
have been times, nevertheless, when it has been vigorously
assailed, from various motives, from within as well as from
without the Church, and the resources of Christian reasoning
have been taxed to support it. These times have now, however, definitely passed away. The prevalence of the evolutionary hypotheses has removed all motive for denying a common
origin to the human race, and rendered it natural to look upon
the differences which exist among the various types of man as
differentiations of a common stock. The motive for denying
their conclusiveness having been thus removed, the convincing evidences of the unity of the race have had opportunity
to assert their force. The result is that the unity of the race,
in the sense of its common origin, is no longer a matter of
debate; and although actually some erratic writers may still
speak of it as open to discussion, they are not taken seriously,
and practically it is universally treated as a fixed fact that
mankind in all its varieties is one, as in fundamental characteristics, so also in origin.

In our natural satisfaction over this agreement between
Scripture and modern science with respect to the unity of
humanity, we must not permit ourselves to forget that there
has always nevertheless existed among men a strong tendency
to deny this unity in the interests of racial pride. Outside
of the influence of the Biblical revelation, indeed, the sense of
human unity has never been strong and has ordinarily been
non-existent.[20] The Stoics seem to have been the first among

[20] Cf. H. Bavinck, "The Philosophy of Revelation," 1909, pp. 137 ff.

the classical peoples to preach the unity of mankind and the duty of universal justice and philanthropy founded upon it. With the revival of classical ideas which came in with what we call the Renaissance, there came in also a tendency to revive heathen polygenism, which was characteristically reproduced in the writings of Blount and others of the Deists. A more definite co-Adamitism, that is to say the attribution of the descent of the several chief racial types to separate original ancestors, has also been taught by occasional individuals such, for example, as Paracelsus. And the still more definite pre-Adamitism, which conceives man indeed as a single species, derived from one stock, but represents Adam not as the root of this stock, but as one of its products, the ancestor of the Jews and white races alone, has always found teachers, such as, for example, Zanini. The advocacy of this pre-Adamitic theory by Isaac de la Peyrère in the middle of the seventeenth century roused a great debate which, however, soon died out, although leaving echoes behind it in Bayle, Arnold, Swedenborg. A sort of pre-Adamitism has continued to be taught by a series of philosophical speculators from Schelling down, which looks upon Adam as the first real man, rising in developed humanity above the low, beastlike condition of his ancestors. In our own day George Catlin [21] and especially Alexander Winchell [22] have revived in its essentials the teaching of de la Peyrère. " Adam," says Professor Winchell, " is descended from a black race, not the black race from Adam." The advancing knowledge of the varied races of man produced in the latter part of the eighteenth and the earlier nineteenth century a revival of co-Adamitism (Sullivan, Crueger, Ballenstedt, Cordonière, Gobineau) which was even perverted into a defense of slavery (Dobbs, Morton, Nott, and Gliddon). It was in connection with Nott and Gliddon's " Types of Mankind " that Agassiz first published his theory of the diverse origin of the several types of man, the only one of these theories of

[21] " O-kee-pa," London, 1867: he referred the North American Indians to an antediluvian species, which he called *Anthropus Americanus.*

[22] " Preadamites," Chicago, 1880.

abiding interest because the only one arising from a genuinely scientific impulse and possessing a really scientific basis. Agassiz's theory was the product of a serious study of the geographical distribution of animate life, and one of the results of Agassiz's classification of the whole of animate creation into eight well-marked types of fauna involving, so he thought, eight separate centers of origin. Pursuant to this classification he sought to distribute mankind also into eight types, to each of which he ascribed a separate origin, corresponding with the type of fauna with which each is associated. But even Agassiz could not deny that men are, despite their eightfold separate creation, all of one kind: he could not erect specific differences between the several types of man.[23] The evidence which compelled him to recognize the oneness of man in kind remains in its full validity, after advancing knowledge of the animal kingdom and its geographical distribution [24] has rendered Agassiz's assumption of eight centers of origination (not merely distribution) a violent hypothesis; and the entrance into the field of the evolutionary hypothesis has consigned all theories formed without reference to it to oblivion. Even some early evolutionists, it is true, played for a time with theories of multiplex times and places where similar lines of development culminated alike in man (Haeckel, Schaffhausen, Caspari, Vogt, Büchner), and perhaps there is now some sign of the revival of this view; but it is now agreed with practical unanimity that the unity of the human race, in the sense of its common origin, is a necessary corollary of the evolutionary hypothesis, and no voice raised in contradiction of it stands much chance to be heard.[25]

It is, however, only for its universal allowance at the hands of speculative science that the fact of the unity of the human

[23] Similarly Heinrich Schurtz, while leaving the descent of men from a single pair an open question, affirms that it is a fact that "humanity forms one great unity."

[24] It was Wallace's "Geographical Distribution of Animals" which struck the first crushing blow.

[25] Klaatsch wishes to postulate two distinct stems for man (now mingled together): see on his views, Keith in *Nature*, December 15, 1910.

race has to thank the evolutionary hypothesis. The evidence by which it is solidly established is of course independent of all such hypotheses. This evidence is drawn almost equally from every department of human manifestation, physiological, psychological, philological, and even historical. The physiological unity of the race is illustrated by the nice gradations by which the several so-called races into which it is divided pass into one another; and by their undiminished natural fertility when intercrossed; by which Professor Owen was led to remark that " man forms one species, and . . . differences are but indicative of varieties " which " merge into each other by easy gradations." [26] It is emphasized by the contrast which exists between the structural characteristics, osteological, cranial, dental, common to the entire race of human beings of every variety and those of the nearest animal types; which led Professor Huxley to assert that " every bone of a Gorilla bears marks by which it might be distinguished from the corresponding bones of a Man; and that, in the present creation, at any rate, no intermediate link bridges over the gap between *Homo* and *Troglodytes.*" [27] The psychological unity of the race is still more manifest. All men of all varieties are psychologically men and prove themselves possessors of the same mental nature and furniture. Under the same influences they function mentally and spiritually in the same fashion, and prove capable of the same mental reactions. They, they all, and they alone, in the whole realm of animal existences manifest themselves as rational and moral natures; so that Mr. Fiske was fully justified when he declared that though for zoölogical man the erection of a distinct family from the chimpanzee and orang might suffice, " on the other hand, for psychological man you must erect a distinct kingdom; nay, you must even dichotomize the universe, putting Man on one side and all things else on the other." [28] Among the manifestations of the psycho-

---

[26] E. Burgess, " What is Truth? An Enquiry concerning the Antiquity and Unity of the Human Race," Boston [1871], p. 185.

[27] " Evidence as to Man's Place in Nature," 1864, p. 104.

[28] " Through Nature to God," 1899, p. 82.

logical peculiarities of mankind, as distinguished from all other animate existences, is the great gift of speech which he shares with no other being: if all human languages cannot be reduced to a single root, they all exhibit a uniquely human faculty working under similar laws, and bear the most striking testimony to the unity of the race which alone has language at its command. The possession of common traditions by numerous widely separated peoples is only a single one of many indications of a historical intercommunion between the several peoples through which their essential unity is evinced, and by which the Biblical account of the origination of the various families of man in a single center from which they have spread out in all directions is powerfully supported.[29]

The assertion of the unity of the human race is imbedded in the very structure of the Biblical narrative. The Biblical account of the origin of man (Gen. i. 26–28) is an account of his origination in a single pair, who constituted humanity in its germ, and from whose fruitfulness and multiplication all the earth has been replenished. Therefore the first man was called Adam, Man, and the first woman, Eve, "because she was the mother of all living" (Gen. iii. 20); and all men are currently spoken of as the "sons of Adam" or "Man" (Deut. xxxii. 8; Ps. xi. 4; I Sam. xxvi. 19; I Kings viii. 39; Ps. cxlv. 12; etc.). The absolute restriction of the human race within the descendants of this single pair is emphasized by the history of the Flood in which all flesh is destroyed, and the race given a new beginning in its second father, Noah, by whose descendants again "the whole earth was overspread" (Gen. ix. 19), as is illustrated in detail by the table of nations recorded in Genesis x. A profound religious-ethical significance is given to the differentiations of the peoples, in the story of the tower of Babel in the eleventh chapter of Genesis, in which the divergences and separations which divide mankind are represented as the product of sin: what God had joined together men themselves pulled asunder. Throughout the Scrip-

---

[29] Cf. the discussion in the seventh lecture of Bavinck's "Philosophy of Revelation," 1909.

tures therefore all mankind is treated as, from the divine point
of view, a unit, and shares not only in a common nature but in
a common sinfulness, not only in a common need but in a common redemption.

Accordingly, although Israel was taught to glory in its exaltation by the choice of the Lord to be His peculiar people,
Israel was not permitted to believe there was anything in itself which differentiated it from other peoples; and by the laws
concerning aliens and slaves was required to recognize the
common humanity of all sorts and conditions of men; what
they had to distinguish them from others was not of nature
but of the free gift of God, in the mysterious working out of
His purpose of good not only to Israel but to the whole world.
This universalism in the divine purposes of mercy, already inherent in the Old Covenant and often proclaimed in it, and
made the very keynote of the New — for which the Old was
the preparation — is the most emphatic possible assertion of
the unity of the race. Accordingly, not only do we find our
Lord Himself setting His seal upon the origination of the race
in a single pair, and drawing from that fact the law of life for
men at large (Matt. xix. 4); and Paul explicitly declaring that
" God has made of one every nation of men " and having for
His own good ends appointed to each its separate habitation,
is now dealing with them all alike in offering them a common
salvation (Acts xvii. 26 ff.); but the whole New Testament is
instinct with the brotherhood of mankind as one in origin and
in nature, one in need and one in the provision of redemption.
The fact of racial sin is basal to the whole Pauline system
(Rom. v. 12 ff.; I Cor. xv. 21 f.), and beneath the fact of racial
sin lies the fact of racial unity. It is only because all men were
in Adam as their first head that all men share in Adam's sin
and with his sin in his punishment. And it is only because the
sin of man is thus one in origin and therefore of the same
nature and quality, that the redemption which is suitable and
may be made available for one is equally suitable and may be
made available for all. It is because the race is one and its
need one, Jew and Gentile are alike under sin, that there is no

difference between Jew and Gentile in the matter of salvation either, but as the same God is Lord of all, so He is rich in Christ Jesus unto all that call upon Him, and will justify the uncircumcision through faith alone, even as He justifies the circumcision only by faith (Rom. ix. 22–24, 28 ff.; x. 12). Jesus Christ therefore, as the last Adam, is the Saviour not of the Jews only but of the world (John iv. 42; I Tim. iv. 10; I John iv. 14), having been given to this His great work only by the love of the Father for the world (John iii. 16). The unity of the human race is therefore made in Scripture not merely the basis of a demand that we shall recognize the dignity of humanity in all its representatives, of however lowly estate or family, since all bear alike the image of God in which man was created and the image of God is deeper than sin and cannot be eradicated by sin (Gen. v. 3; ix. 6; I Cor. xi. 7; Heb. ii. 5 ff.); but the basis also of the entire scheme of restoration devised by the divine love for the salvation of a lost race.

So far is it from being of no concern to theology, therefore, that it would be truer to say that the whole doctrinal structure of the Bible account of redemption is founded on its assumption that the race of man is one organic whole, and may be dealt with as such. It is because all are one in Adam that in the matter of sin there is no difference, but all have fallen short of the glory of God (Rom. iii. 22 f.), and as well that in the new man there cannot be Greek and Jew, circumcision and uncircumcision, barbarian, Scythian, bondman, freeman; but Christ is all and in all (Col. iii. 11). The unity of the old man in Adam is the postulate of the unity of the new man in Christ.

VIII
ATONEMENT

ATONEMENT [1]

I. Significance and History of the Doctrine

The replacement of the term "satisfaction" (*q.v.*), to designate, according to its nature, the work of Christ in saving sinners, by "atonement," the term more usual at present, is somewhat unfortunate. "Satisfaction" is at once the more comprehensive, the more expressive, the less ambiguous, and the more exact term. The word "atonement" occurs but once in the English New Testament (Rom. v. 11, A. V., but not R. V.) and on this occasion it bears its archaic sense of "reconciliation," and as such translates the Greek term *katallagē*. In the English Old Testament, however, it is found quite often as the stated rendering of the Hebrew terms *kipper*, *kippurim*, in the sense of "propitiation," "expiation." It is in this latter sense that it has become current, and has been applied to the work of Christ, which it accordingly describes as, in its essential nature, an expiatory offering, propitiating an offended Deity and reconciling Him with man.

1. THE NEW TESTAMENT PRESENTATION

In thus characterizing the work of Christ, it does no injustice to the New Testament representation. The writers of the New Testament employ many other modes of describing the work of Christ, which, taken together, set it forth as much more than a provision, in His death, for canceling the guilt of man. To mention nothing else at the moment, they set it forth equally as a provision, in His righteousness, for fulfilling the demands of the divine law upon the conduct of men. But it

[1] Reprinted from "The New Schaff-Herzog Encyclopedia of Religious Knowledge," edited by Samuel Macauley Jackson, D.D., LL.D., i. pp. 349–356 (copyright by Funk and Wagnalls Company, New York, 1908).

is undeniable that they enshrine at the center of this work its
efficacy as a piacular sacrifice, securing the forgiveness of sins;
that is to say, relieving its beneficiaries of " the penal consequences which otherwise the curse of the broken law inevitably
entails." The Lord Himself fastens attention upon this aspect
of His work (Matt. xx. 28, xxvi. 28); and it is embedded in
every important type of New Testament teaching — as well
in the Epistle to the Hebrews (ii. 17), and the Epistles of
Peter (I. iii. 18) and John (I. ii. 2), as currently in those of
Paul (Rom. viii. 3; I Cor. v. 7; Eph. v. 2) to whom, obviously,
" the sacrifice of Christ had the significance of the death of an
innocent victim in the room of the guilty " and who therefore
" freely employs the category of substitution, involving the
conception of imputation or transference " of legal standing
(W. P. Paterson, article " Sacrifice " in Hastings, " Dictionary
of the Bible," iv. 1909, pp. 343–345). Looking out from this
point of view as from a center, the New Testament writers ascribe the saving efficacy of Christ's work specifically to His
death, or His blood, or His cross (Rom. iii. 25; v. 9; I Cor. x. 16;
Eph. i. 7; ii. 13; Col. i. 20; Heb. ix. 12, 14; I Pet. i. 2, 19;
I John i. 7; v. 6–8; Rev. i. 5), and this with such predilection
and emphasis that the place given to the death of Christ in
the several theories which have been framed of the nature of
our Lord's work, may not unfairly be taken as a test of their
Scripturalness. All else that Christ does for us in the breadth of
His redeeming work is, in their view, conditioned upon His
bearing our sins in His own body on the tree; so that " the
fundamental characteristic of the New Testament conception
of redemption is that deliverance from guilt stands first;
emancipation from the power of sin follows upon it; and removal of all the ills of life constitutes its final issue " (O. Kirn,
article " Erlösung " in Hauck-Herzog, " Realencyklopädie," v.
p. 464; see " Redemption ").

2. DEVELOPMENT OF THE DOCTRINE

The exact nature of Christ's work in redemption was not made the subject of scientific investigation in the early Church. This was due partly, no doubt, just to the clearness of the New Testament representation of it as a piacular sacrifice; but in part also to the engrossment of the minds of the first teachers of Christianity with more immediately pressing problems, such as the adjustment of the essential elements of the Christian doctrines of God and of the person of Christ, and the establishment of man's helplessness in sin and absolute dependence on the grace of God for salvation. Meanwhile Christians were content to speak of the work of Christ in simple Scriptural or in general language, or to develop, rather by way of illustration than of explanation, certain aspects of it, chiefly its efficacy as a sacrifice, but also, very prominently, its working as a ransom in delivering us from bondage to Satan. Thus it was not until the end of the eleventh century that the nature of the Atonement received at the hands of Anselm (d. 1109) its first thorough discussion. Representing it, in terms derived from the Roman law, as in its essence a " satisfaction " to the divine justice, Anselm set it once for all in its true relations to the inherent necessities of the divine nature, and to the magnitude of human guilt; and thus determined the outlines of the doctrine for all subsequent thought. Contemporaries like Bernard and Abelard, no doubt, and perhaps not unnaturally, found difficulty in assimilating at once the newly framed doctrine; the former ignored it in the interests of the old notion of a ransom offered to Satan; the latter rejected it in the interests of a theory of moral influence upon man. But it gradually made its way. The Victorines, Hugo and Richard, united with it other elements, the effect of which was to cure its one-sidedness; and the great doctors of the age of developed scholasticism manifest its victory by differing from one another chiefly in their individual ways of stating and defending it. Bonaventura develops it; Aquinas enriches it with his subtle distinctions; Thomist and Scotist alike start from it, and diverge only in the question whether the "satisfaction" offered by Christ was intrinsically equivalent to the requirements of the divine justice or availed for this purpose only through the gracious acceptance of God. It was not, however, until the Reformation doctrine of justification by faith threw its light back upon the "satisfaction" which provided its basis, that that doctrine came fully to its rights. No one before Luther had spoken with the clarity, depth, or breadth which characterize his references to Christ as our deliverer, first from the guilt of sin, and then, because from the guilt of sin, also from all that is evil, since all that is evil springs from sin (cf. T. Harnack, "Luthers Theologie," Erlangen, ii. 1886, chaps. 16–19, and Kirn, *ut sup.*, p. 467). These vital religious conceptions were reduced to scientific statement by the Protestant scholastics, by whom it was that the complete doctrine of "satisfaction" was formulated with a thoroughness and comprehensiveness of grasp which has made it the permanent possession of the Church. In this, its developed form, it represents our Lord as making satisfaction for us " by His blood and righteousness "; on the one hand, to the justice of God, outraged by human sin, in bearing the penalty due to our guilt in His own sacrificial death; and, on the other hand, to the demands of the law of God requiring perfect obedience, in fulfilling in His immaculate life on earth as the second Adam the probation which Adam failed to keep; bringing to bear on men at the same time and by means of the same double work every conceivable influence adapted to deter them from sin and to win them back to good and to God — by the highest imaginable demonstration of God's righteousness and hatred of sin and the supreme manifestation of God's love and eagerness to save; by a gracious proclamation of full forgiveness of sin in the blood of Christ; by a winning revelation of the spiritual order and the spiritual world; and by the moving example of His own perfect life in the conditions of this world; but, above all, by the purchase of the gift of the Holy Spirit for His people as a power not themselves making for righteousness dwelling within them, and supernaturally regenerating their hearts and conforming their lives to His image, and so preparing them for their permanent place in the new order of things which, flowing from this redeeming work, shall ultimately be established as the eternal form of the Kingdom of God.

3. VARIOUS THEORIES

Of course, this great comprehensive doctrine of " the satisfaction of Christ " has not been permitted to hold the field without controversy. Many " theories of the atonement " have been constructed, each throwing into emphasis a fragment of the truth, to the neglect or denial of the complementary elements, including ordinarily the central matter of the expiation of guilt itself (cf. T. J. Crawford, " The Doctrine of Holy Scripture respecting the Atonement," Edinburgh, 1888, pp. 395–401; A. B. Bruce, " The Humiliation of Christ," Edinburgh, 1881, lecture 7; A. A. Hodge, " The Atonement," Philadelphia, 1867, pp. 17 ff.). Each main form of these theories, in some method of statement or other, has at one time or another seemed on the point of becoming the common doctrine of the churches. In the patristic age men spoke with such predilection of the work of Christ as issuing in our deliverance from the power of Satan that the false impression is very readily obtained from a cursory survey of the teaching of the Fathers that they predominantly conceived it as directed to that sole end. The so-called "mystical " view, which had representatives among the Greek Fathers and has always had advocates in the Church, appeared about the middle of the last century almost ready to become dominant in at least Continental Protestantism through the immense influence of Schleiermacher. The "rectoral or governmental theory," invented by Grotius early in the seventeenth century in the effort to save something from the assault of the Socinians, has ever since provided a half-way house for those who, while touched by the chilling breath of rationalism, have yet not been ready to surrender every semblance of an " objective atonement," and has therefore come very prominently forward in every era of decaying faith. The "moral influence" theory, which in the person of perhaps the acutest of all the scholastic reasoners, Peter Abelard, confronted the doctrine of "satisfaction" at its formulation, in its vigorous promulgation by the Socinians and again by the lower class of rationalists obtained the widest currency; and again in our own day its enthusiastic advocates, by perhaps a not unnatural illusion, are tempted to claim for it the final victory (so e.g. G. B. Stevens, "The Christian Doctrine of Salvation," New York, 1905; but cf. per contra, of the same school, T. V. Tymms, "The Christian Idea of Atonement," London, 1904, p. 8). But no one of these theories, however attractively they may be presented, or however wide an acceptance each may from time to time have found in academic circles, has ever been able to supplant the doctrine of "satisfaction," either in the formal creeds of the churches, or in the hearts of simple believers. Despite the fluidity of much recent thinking on the subject, the doctrine of "satisfaction" remains to-day the established doctrine of the churches as to the nature of Christ's work of redemption, and is apparently immovably entrenched in the hearts of the Christian body (cf. J. B. Remensnyder, "The Atonement and Modern Thought," Philadelphia, 1905, p. xvi.).

II. The Five Chief Theories of the Atonement

A survey of the various theories of the Atonement which have been broached, may be made from many points of view (cf. especially the survey in T. G. Crawford, *ut sup.*, pp. 285–401; Bruce, *ut sup.*, lecture 7; and for recent German views, F. A. B. Nitzsch, "Lehrbuch der evangelischen Dogmatik," Freiburg, 1892, part 2, §§ 43–46; O. Bensow, "Die Lehre von der Versöhnung," Gütersloh, 1904, pp. 7–153; G. A. F. Ecklin, "Erlösung und Versöhnung," Basel, 1903, part 4). Perhaps as good a method as any other is to arrange them according to the conception each entertains of the person or persons on whom the work of Christ terminates. When so arranged they fall naturally into five classes which may be enumerated here in the ascending order.

1. Theories which conceive the work of Christ as *terminating upon Satan,* so affecting him as to secure the release of the souls held in bondage by him. These theories, which have been described as emphasizing the "triumphantorial" aspect of Christ's work (Ecklin, *ut sup.,* p. 113) had very considerable vogue in the patristic age (e.g. Irenæus, Hippolytus, Clement of Alexandria, Origen, Basil, the two Gregories, Cyril of Alexandria, down to and including John of Damascus and Nicholas of Methone; Hilary, Rufinus, Jerome, Augustine, Leo the Great, and even so late as Bernard). They passed out of view only gradually as the doctrine of "satisfaction" became more widely known. Not only does the thought of a Bernard still run in this channel, but even Luther utilized the conception. The idea runs through many forms — speaking in some of them of buying off, in some of overcoming, in some even of outwitting (so e.g. Origen) the devil. But it would be unfair to suppose that such theories represent in any of their forms the whole thought as to the work of Christ of those who made use of them, or were considered by them a scientific statement of the work of Christ. They rather embody only their author's profound sense of the bondage in which men are held to sin and death, and vividly set forth the rescue they conceive Christ has wrought for us in overcoming him who has the power of death.

2. Theories which conceive the work of Christ as *terminating physically on man,* so affecting him as to bring him by an interior and hidden working upon him into participation with the one life of Christ; the so-called "mystical theories." The fundamental characteristic of these theories is their discovery of the saving fact not in anything which Christ taught or did, but in what He was. It is upon the Incarnation, rather than upon Christ's teaching or His work that they throw stress, attributing the saving power of Christ not to what He does for us but to what He does in us. Tendencies to this type of theory are already traceable in the Platonizing Fathers; and

with the entrance of the more developed Neoplatonism into the stream of Christian thinking, through the writings of the Pseudo-Dionysius naturalized in the West by Johannes Scotus Erigena, a constant tradition of mystical teaching began which never died out. In the Reformation age this type of thought was represented by men like Osiander, Schwenckfeld, Franck, Weigel, Boehme. In the modern Church a new impulse was given to essentially the same mode of conception by Schleiermacher and his followers (e.g. C. I. Nitzsch, Rothe, Schöberlein, Lange, Martensen), among whom what is known as the "Mercersburg School" (see "Mercersburg Theology") will be particularly interesting to Americans (e.g. J. W. Nevin, "The Mystical Presence," Philadelphia, 1846). A very influential writer among English theologians of the same general class was F. D. Maurice (1805–1872), although he added to his fundamental mystical conception of the work of Christ the further notions that Christ fully identified Himself with us and, thus partaking of our sufferings, set us a perfect example of sacrifice of self to God (cf. especially "Theological Essays," London, 1853; "The Doctrine of Sacrifice," Cambridge, 1854; new edition, London, 1879). Here, too, must be classed the theory suggested in the writings of the late B. F. Westcott ("The Victory of the Cross," London, 1888), which was based on a hypothesis of the efficacy of Christ's blood, borrowed apparently directly from William Milligan (cf. "The Ascension and Heavenly Priesthood of our Lord," London, 1892), though it goes back ultimately to the Socinians, to the effect that Christ's offering of Himself is not to be identified with His sufferings and death, but rather with the presentation of His life (which is in His blood, set free by death for this purpose) in heaven. "Taking that Blood as efficacious by virtue of the vitality which it contains, he [Dr. Westcott] holds that it was set free from Christ's Body that it might vitalize ours, as it were by transfusion" (C. H. Waller, in the *Presbyterian and Reformed Review*, iii. 1892, p. 656). Somewhat similarly H. Clay Trumbull ("The Blood Covenant," New York, 1885) looks upon sacrifices as only a form of blood covenanting, that is, of instituting blood-brotherhood between man and God by transfusion of blood; and explains the sacrifice of Christ as representing communing in blood, that is, in the principle of life, between God and man, both of whom Christ represents. The theory which has been called "salvation by sample," or salvation "by gradually extirpated depravity," also has its affinities here. Something like it is as old as Felix of Urgel (d. 818; see "Adoptionism"), and it has been taught in its full development by Dippel (1673–1734), Swedenborg (1688–1772), Menken (1768–1831), and especially by Edward Irving (1792–1834), and, of course, by the modern followers of Swedenborg (e.g. B. F. Barrett). The essence of this theory is that what was assumed by our Lord was human nature as He found it, that is, as fallen; and that this human nature, as assumed by Him, was by the power of His divine nature (or of the Holy Spirit dwelling in Him beyond measure) not only kept from sinning, but purified from sin and presented perfect before God as the first-fruits of a saved humanity; men being saved as they become partakers (by faith) of this purified humanity, as they become leavened by this new leaven. Certain of the elements which the great German theologian J. C. K. von Hofmann built into his complicated and not altogether stable theory — a theory which was the occasion of much discussion about the middle of the nineteenth century — reproduce some of the characteristic language of the theory of "salvation by sample."

3. Theories which conceive the work of Christ as *terminating on man, in the way of bringing to bear on him inducements to action;* so affecting man as to lead him to a better knowledge of God, or to a more lively sense of his real relation to God, or to a revolutionary change of heart and life with reference to God; the so-called "moral influence theories." The essence of all these theories is that they transfer the atoning fact from the work of Christ to the response of the human soul to the influences or appeals proceeding from the work of Christ. The work of Christ takes immediate effect not on God but on man, leading him to a state of mind and heart which will be

acceptable to God, through the medium of which alone can the work of Christ be said to affect God. At its highest level, this will mean that the work of Christ is directed to leading man to repentance and faith, which repentance and faith secure God's favor, an effect which can be attributed to Christ's work only mediately, that is, through the medium of the repentance and faith it produces in man. Accordingly, it has become quite common to say, in this school, that " it is faith and repentance which change the face of God "; and advocates of this class of theories sometimes say with entire frankness, " There is no atonement other than repentance " (Auguste Sabatier, " La Doctrine de l'expiation et son évolution historique," Paris, 1901, E.T. London, 1904, p. 127).

Theories of this general type differ from one another, according as, among the instrumentalities by means of which Christ affects the minds and hearts and actions of men, the stress is laid upon His teaching, or His example, or the impression made by His life of faith, or the manifestation of the infinite love of God afforded by His total mission. The most powerful presentation of the first of these conceptions ever made was probably that of the Socinians (followed later by the rationalists, both earlier and later — Töllner, Bahrdt, Steinbart, Eberhard, Löffler, Henke, Wegscheider). They looked upon the work of Christ as summed up in the proclamation of the willingness of God to forgive sin, on the sole condition of its abandonment; and explained His sufferings and death as merely those of a martyr in the cause of righteousness or in some other non-essential way. The theories which lay the stress of Christ's work on the example He has set us of a high and faithful life, or of a life of self-sacrificing love, have found popular representatives not only in the subtle theory with which F. D. Maurice pieced out his mystical view, and in the somewhat amorphous ideas with which the great preacher F. W. Robertson clothed his conception of Christ's life as simply a long (and hopeless) battle against the evil of the world to which it at last succumbed; but more lately in writers like Auguste Sabatier, who does not stop short of

transmuting Christianity into bald altruism, and making it
into what he calls the religion of "universal redemption by
love," that is to say, anybody's love, not specifically Christ's
love — for every one who loves takes his position by Christ's
side as, if not equally, yet as truly, a saviour as He ("The
Doctrine of the Atonement in its Historical Evolution," *ut
sup.*, pp. 131–134; so also Otto Pfleiderer, "Das Christusbild
des urchristlichen Glaubens in religionsgeschichtlicher Beleuchtung," Berlin, 1903, E.T. London, 1905, pp. 164–165; cf.
Horace Bushnell, "Vicarious Sacrifice," New York, 1865, p.
107: "Vicarious sacrifice was in no way peculiar "). In this
same general category belongs also the theory which Albrecht
Ritschl has given such wide influence. According to it, the
work of Christ consists in the establishment of the Kingdom of
God in the world, that is, in the revelation of God's love to
men and His gracious purposes for men. Thus Jesus becomes
the first object of this love and as such its mediator to others;
His sufferings and death being, on the one side, a test of His
steadfastness, and, on the other, the crowning proof of His
obedience ("Rechtfertigung und Versöhnung," iii. §§ 41–61,
ed. 3, Bonn, 1888, E.T. Edinburgh, 1900). Similarly also,
though with many modifications, which are in some instances
not insignificant, such writers as W. Herrmann ("Der Verkehr
des Christen mit Gott," Stuttgart, 1886, p. 93, E.T. London,
1895), J. Kaftan ("Dogmatik," Tübingen, 1901, pp. 454 ff.),
F. A. B. Nitzsch ("Lehrbuch der evangelischen Dogmatik,"
Freiburg, 1892, pp. 504–513), T. Häring (in his "Ueber das
Bleibende im Glauben an Christus," Stuttgart, 1880, where he
sought to complete Ritschl's view by the addition of the idea
that Christ offered to God a perfect sorrow for the world's sin,
which supplements our imperfect repentance; in his later writings, "Zu Ritschl's Versöhnungslehre," Zurich, 1888, "Zur
Versöhnungslehre," Göttingen, 1893, he assimilates to the
Grotian theory), E. Kühl ("Die Heilsbedeutung des Todes
Christi," Berlin, 1890), G. A. F. Ecklin ("Der Heilswert des
Todes Jesu," Gütersloh, 1888; "Christus unser Bürge," Basel,
1901; and especially "Erlösung und Versöhnung," Basel,

1903, which is an elaborate history of the doctrine from the point of view of what Ecklin calls in antagonism to the "substitutional-expiatory" conception, the "solidaric-reparatory" conception of the Atonement — the conception, that is, that Christ comes to save men not primarily from the guilt, but from the power of sin, and that "the sole satisfaction God demands for His outraged honor is the restoration of obedience," p. 648). The most popular form of the "moral influence" theories has always been that in which the stress is laid on the manifestation made in the total mission and work of Christ of the ineffable and searching love of God for sinners, which, being perceived, breaks down our opposition to God, melts our hearts, and brings us as prodigals home to the Father's arms. It is in this form that the theory was advocated (but with the suggestion that there is another side to it), for example, by S. T. Coleridge ("Aids to Reflection"), and that it was commended to English-speaking readers of the last generation with the highest ability by John Young of Edinburgh ("The Life and Light of Men," London, 1866), and with the greatest literary attractiveness by Horace Bushnell ("Vicarious Sacrifice," New York, 1865; see below, § 7; see also article "Bushnell, Horace"); and has been more recently set forth in elaborate and vigorously polemic form by W. N. Clarke ("An Outline of Christian Theology," New York, 1898, pp. 340–368), T. Vincent Tymms ("The Christian Idea of Atonement," London, 1904), G. B. Stevens ("The Christian Doctrine of Salvation," New York, 1905), and C. M. Mead ("Irenic Theology," New York, 1905).

In a volume of essays published first in the *Andover Review* (iv. 1885, pp. 56 ff.) and afterward gathered into a volume under the title of "Progressive Orthodoxy" (Boston, 1886), the professors in Andover Seminary made an attempt (the writer here being, as was understood, George Harris) to enrich the "moral influence" theory of the Atonement after a fashion quite common in Germany (cf. e.g. Häring, *ut sup.*) with elements derived from other well-known forms of teaching. In this construction, Christ's work is made to consist pri-

marily in bringing to bear on man a revelation of God's hatred
of sin, and love for souls, by which He makes man capable of
repentance and leads him to repent revolutionarily; by this
repentance, then, together with Christ's own sympathetic expression of repentance God is rendered propitious. Here
Christ's work is supposed to have at least some (though a secondary) effect upon God; and a work of propitiation of God
by Christ may be spoken of, although it is accomplished by a
" sympathetic repentance." It has accordingly become usual
with those who have adopted this mode of representation to
say that there was in this atoning work, not indeed " a substitution of a sinless Christ for a sinful race," but a " substitution
of humanity *plus* Christ for humanity *minus* Christ." By such
curiously compacted theories the transition is made to the
next class.

4. Theories which conceive the work of Christ as *terminating on both man and God, but on man primarily and on God
only secondarily*. The outstanding instance of this class of
theories is supplied by the so-called " rectoral or governmental
theories." These suppose that the work of Christ so affects man
by the spectacle of the sufferings borne by Him as to deter men
from sin; and by thus deterring men from sin enables God to
forgive sin with safety to His moral government of the world.
In these theories the sufferings and death of Christ become,
for the first time in this conspectus of theories, of cardinal importance, constituting indeed the very essence of the work of
Christ. But the atoning fact here too, no less than in the
" moral influence " theories, is man's own reformation, though
this reformation is supposed in the rectoral view to be wrought
not primarily by breaking down man's opposition to God by a
moving manifestation of the love of God in Christ, but by inducing in man a horror of sin, through the spectacle of God's
hatred of sin afforded by the sufferings of Christ — through
which, no doubt, the contemplation of man is led on to God's
love to sinners as exhibited in His willingness to inflict all
these sufferings on His own Son, that He might be enabled,
with justice to His moral government, to forgive sins.

This theory was worked out by the great Dutch jurist
Hugo Grotius ("Defensio fidei catholicæ de satisfactiono
Christi," Leyden, 1617; modern edition, Oxford, 1856; E.T.
with notes and introduction by F. H. Foster, Andover, 1889)
as an attempt to save what was salvable of the established
doctrine of satisfaction from disintegration under the attacks
of the Socinian advocates of the "moral influence" theories
(see "Grotius, Hugo"). It was at once adopted by those
Arminians who had been most affected by the Socinian reasoning; and in the next age became the especial property of the
better class of the so-called supranaturalists (Michaelis, Storr,
Morus, Knapp, Steudel, Reinhard, Muntinghe, Vinke, Egel-
ing). It has remained on the continent of Europe to this day, the
refuge of most of those, who, influenced by the modern spirit,
yet wish to preserve some form of "objective," that is, of Godward atonement. A great variety of representations have grown
up under this influence, combining elements of the satisfaction
and rectoral views. To name but a single typical instance, the
commentator F. Godet, both in his commentaries (especially
that on Romans) and in a more recent essay (published in
"The Atonement in Modern Religious Thought," by various
writers, London, 1900, pp. 331 ff.), teaches (certainly in a very
high form) the rectoral theory distinctly (and is corrected
therefor by his colleague at Neuchâtel, Professor Gretillat,
who wishes an "ontological" rather than a merely "demonstrative" necessity for atonement to be recognized). Its history has run on similar lines in English-speaking countries.
In Great Britain and America alike it has become practically
the orthodoxy of the Independents. It has, for example, been
taught as such in the former country by Joseph Gilbert ("The
Christian Atonement," London, 1836), and in especially well-
worked-out forms by R. W. Dale ("The Atonement," London,
1876) and Alfred Cave ("The Scriptural Doctrine of Sacrifice," Edinburgh, 1877; new edition with title, "The Scriptural
Doctrine of Sacrifice and Atonement," 1890; and in "The
Atonement in Modern Religious Thought," ut sup., pp.
250 ff.). When the Calvinism of the New England Puritans

began to break down, one of the symptoms of its decay was the gradual substitution of the rectoral for the satisfaction view of the Atonement. The process may be traced in the writings of Joseph Bellamy (1719–1790), Samuel Hopkins (1721–1803), John Smalley (1734–1820), Stephen West (1735–1819), Jonathan Edwards, Jr. (1745–1801), Nathanael Emmons (1745–1840); and Edwards A. Park was able, accordingly, in the middle of the nineteenth century to set the rectoral theory forth as the " traditional orthodox doctrine " of the American Congregationalists (" The Atonement: Discourses and Treatises by Edwards, Smalley, Maxcy, Emmons, Griffin, Burge, and Weeks, with an Introductory Essay by Edwards A. Park," Boston, 1859; cf. Daniel T. Fisk, in the *Bibliotheca Sacra,* xviii. 1861, pp. 284 ff., and further N. S. S. Beman, " Four Sermons on the Doctrine of the Atonement," Troy, 1825, new edition with title " Christ, the only Sacrifice: or the Atonement in its Relations to God and Man," New York, 1844; N.W. Taylor, " Lectures on the Moral Government of God," New York, 1859; Albert Barnes, " The Atonement, in its Relations to Law and Moral Government," Philadelphia, 1859; Frank H. Foster, "Christian Life and Theology," New York, 1900; Lewis F. Stearns, " Present Day Theology," New York, 1893). The early Wesleyans also gravitated toward the rectoral theory, though not without some hesitation, a hesitation which has sustained itself among British Wesleyans until to-day (cf. e.g. W. B. Pope, " Compendium of Christian Theology," London, 1875; Marshall Randles, " Substitution: a Treatise on the Atonement," London, 1877; T. O. Summers, "Systematic Theology," 2 vols., Nashville, Tenn., 1888; J. J. Tigert, in the *Methodist Quarterly Review,* April, 1884), although many among them have taught the rectoral theory with great distinctness and decision (e.g. Joseph Agar Beet, in the *Expositor,* Fourth Series, vi. 1892, pp. 343–355; " Through Christ to God," London, 1893). On the other hand, the rectoral theory has been the regnant one among American Methodists and has received some of its best statements from their hands (cf. especially John Miley, " The Atonement in Christ," New

York, 1879; "Systematic Theology," New York, ii. 1894, pp.
65–240), although there are voices raised of late in denial of
its claim to be considered distinctively the doctrine of the
Methodist Church (J. J. Tigert, *ut sup.;* H. C. Sheldon, in
The American Journal of Theology, x. 1906, pp. 41–42).

The final form which Horace Bushnell gave his version of
the "moral influence" theory, in his "Forgiveness and Law"
(New York, 1874; made the second volume to his revised
"Vicarious Sacrifice," 1877), stands in no relation to the rectoral theories; but it requires to be mentioned here by their
side, because it supposes like them that the work of Christ has
a secondary effect on God, although its primary effect is on
man. In this presentation, Bushnell represents Christ's work
as consisting in a profound identification of Himself with man,
the effect of which is, on the one side, to manifest God's love
to man and so to conquer man to Him, and, on the other, as he
expresses it, "to make cost" on God's part for man, and so,
by breaking down God's resentment to man, to prepare God's
heart to receive man back when he comes. The underlying idea
is that whenever we do anything for those who have injured
us, and in proportion as it costs us something to do it, our
natural resentment of the injury we have suffered is undermined, and we are prepared to forgive the injury when forgiveness is sought. By this theory the transition is naturally made
to the next class.

5. Theories which conceive the work of Christ as *terminating primarily on God and secondarily on man.* The lowest form
in which this ultimate position can be said to be fairly taken,
is doubtless that set forth in his remarkably attractive way by
John McLeod Campbell ("The Nature of the Atonement and
its Relation to Remission of Sins and Eternal Life," London,
1856; ed. 4, 1873), and lately argued out afresh with even
more than Campbell's winningness and far more than his
cogency, depth, and richness, by the late R. C. Moberly
("Atonement and Personality," London, 1901). This theory
supposes that our Lord, by sympathetically entering into our
condition (an idea independently suggested by Schleiermacher,

and emphasized by many Continental thinkers, as, for example, to name only a pair with little else in common, by Gess and Häring), so keenly felt our sins as His own, that He could confess and adequately repent of them before God; and this is all the expiation justice asks. Here " sympathetic identification " replaces the conception of substitution; " sodality," of race-unity; and " repentance," of expiation. Nevertheless, the theory rises immeasurably above the mass of those already enumerated, in looking upon Christ as really a Saviour, who performs a really saving work, terminating immediately on God. Despite its insufficiencies, therefore, which have caused writers like Edwards A. Park, and A. B. Bruce (" The Humiliation of Christ," *ut sup.*, pp. 317–318) to speak of it with a tinge of contempt, it has exercised a very wide influence and elements of it are discoverable in many constructions which stand far removed from its fundamental presuppositions.

The so-called " middle theory " of the Atonement, which owes its name to its supposed intermediate position between the " moral influence " theories and the doctrine of " satisfaction," seems to have offered attractions to the latitudinarian writers of the closing eighteenth and opening nineteenth centuries. At that time it was taught in John Balguy's " Essay on Redemption " (London, 1741), Henry Taylor's " Apology of Ben Mordecai " (London, 1784), and Richard Price's " Sermons on Christian Doctrine " (London, 1787; cf. Hill's " Lectures in Divinity," ed. 1851, pp. 422 ff.). Basing on the conception of sacrifices which looks upon them as merely gifts designed to secure the good-will of the King, the advocates of this theory regard the work of Christ as consisting in the offering to God of Christ's perfect obedience even to death, and by it purchasing God's favor and the right to do as He would with those whom God gave Him as a reward. By the side of this theory may be placed the ordinary Remonstrant theory of *acceptilatio*, which, reviving this Scotist conception, is willing to allow that the work of Christ was of the nature of an expiatory sacrifice, but is unwilling to allow that His blood any more than that of " bulls and goats " had intrinsic value

equivalent to the fault for which it was graciously accepted by
God as an atonement. This theory may be found expounded,
for example, in Limborch ("Theologia Christiana," ed. 4,
Amsterdam, 1715, iii. chaps. xviii.–xxiii.). Such theories,
while preserving the sacrificial form of the Biblical doctrine,
and, with it, its inseparable implication that the work of
Christ has as its primary end to affect God and secure from
Him favorable regard for man (for it is always to God that
sacrifices are offered), yet fall so far short of the Biblical doctrine of the nature and effect of Christ's sacrifice as to seem
little less than travesties of it.

The Biblical doctrine of the sacrifice of Christ finds full
recognition in no other construction than that of the established church-doctrine of satisfaction. According to it, our
Lord's redeeming work is at its core a true and perfect sacrifice offered to God, of intrinsic value ample for the expiation
of our guilt; and at the same time is a true and perfect righteousness offered to God in fulfillment of the demands of His
law; both the one and the other being offered in behalf of His
people, and, on being accepted by God, accruing to their
benefit; so that by this satisfaction they are relieved at once
from the curse of their guilt as breakers of the law, and from
the burden of the law as a condition of life; and this by a
work of such kind and performed in such a manner, as to carry
home to the hearts of men a profound sense of the indefectible
righteousness of God and to make to them a perfect revelation
of His love; so that, by this one and indivisible work, both
God is reconciled to us, and we, under the quickening influence
of the Spirit bought for us by it, are reconciled to God, so making peace — external peace between an angry God and sinful
men, and internal peace in the response of the human conscience to the restored smile of God. This doctrine, which has
been incorporated in more or less fullness of statement in the
creedal declarations of all the great branches of the Church,
Greek, Latin, Lutheran, and Reformed, and which has been
expounded with more or less insight and power by the leading
doctors of the churches for the last eight hundred years, was

first given scientific statement by Anselm (*q.v.*) in his " Cur
Deus homo " (1098); but reached its complete development
only at the hands of the so-called Protestant Scholastics of the
seventeenth century (cf. e.g. Turretin, "The Atonement of
Christ," E.T. by J. R. Willson, New York, 1859; John Owen,
" The Death of Death in the Death of Christ " (1648), Edin-
burgh, 1845). Among the numerous modern presentations of
the doctrine the following may perhaps be most profitably
consulted. Of Continental writers: August Tholuck, " Die
Lehre von der Sünde und vom Versöhner," Hamburg, 1823;
F. A. Philippi, " Kirchliche Glaubenslehre " (Stuttgart and
Gütersloh, 1854–1882), IV. ii. 1863, pp. 24 ff.; G. Thomasius,
"Christi Person und Werk," ed. 3, Erlangen, 1886–1888, vol.
ii.; E. Böhl, " Dogmatik," Amsterdam, 1887, pp. 361 ff.; J. F.
Bula, " Die Versöhnung des Menschen mit Gott durch Christum," Basel, 1874; W. Kölling, " Die Satisfactio vicaria," 2
vols., Gütersloh, 1897–1899; Merle d'Aubigné, " L'Expiation
de la croix," Geneva, 1867; A. Gretillat, " Exposé de théologie
systématique " (Paris, 1885–1892), iv. 1890, pp. 278 ff.; A.
Kuyper, " E Voto Dordraceno," Amsterdam, i. 1892, pp. 79 ff.,
388 ff.; H. Bavinck, " Gereformeerde Dogmatiek," Kampen,
iii. 1898, pp. 302–424. Of writers in English: The appropriate
sections of the treatises on dogmatics by C. Hodge, A. H.
Strong, W. G. T. Shedd, R. L. Dabney; and the following separate treatises: W. Symington, " On the Atonement and Intercession of Jesus Christ," New York, 1853 (defective, as
excluding the "active obedience " of Christ); R. S. Candlish,
" The Atonement: its Efficacy and Extent," Edinburgh, 1867;
A. A. Hodge, " The Atonement," Philadelphia, 1867, new edition, 1877; George Smeaton, " The Doctrine of the Atonement
as Taught by Christ Himself," Edinburgh, 1868, ed. 2, 1871;
idem, "The Doctrine of the Atonement as Taught by the
Apostles," 1870; T. J. Crawford, " The Doctrine of Holy
Scripture respecting the Atonement," Edinburgh, 1871, ed. 5,
1888; Hugh Martin, " The Atonement: in its Relations to the
Covenant, the Priesthood, the Intercession of our Lord," London, 1870. See " Satisfaction."

BIBLIOGRAPHY: The more important treatises on the Atonement have been named in the body of the article. The history of the doctrine has been written with a fair degree of objectivity by Ferdinand Christian Baur, " Die christliche Lehre von der Versöhnung in ihrer geschichtlichen Entwicklung," Tübingen, 1838; and with more subjectivity by Albrecht Ritschl in the first volume of his " Die christliche Lehre von der Rechtfertigung und Versöhnung," ed. 3, Bonn, 1889, E.T. from the first edition, 1870, " A Critical History of the Christian Doctrine of Justification and Reconciliation," Edinburgh, 1872. Excellent historical sketches are given by G. Thomasius, in the second volume of his " Christi Person und Werk," pp. 113 ff., ed. 3, Erlangen, 1888, from the confessional, and by F. A. B. Nitzsch, in his " Lehrbuch der evangelischen Dogmatik," pp. 457 ff., Freiburg, 1892, from the moral influence standpoint. More recently the history has been somewhat sketchily written from the general confessional standpoint by Oscar Bensow as the first part of his " Die Lehre von der Versöhnung," Gütersloh, 1904, and with more fullness from the moral influence standpoint by G. A. F. Ecklin, in his " Erlösung und Versöhnung," Basel, 1903. Consult also E. Ménégoz, " La Mort de Jésus et le dogme de l' expiation," Paris, 1905. The English student of the history of the doctrine has at his disposal not only the sections in the general histories of doctrine (e.g. Hagenbach, Cunningham, Shedd, Harnack) and the comprehensive treatise of Ritschl mentioned above, but also interesting sketches in the appendices of G. Smeaton's " The Doctrine of the Atonement as Taught by the Apostles," Edinburgh, 1870, and J. S. Lidgett's " The Spiritual Principle of the Atonement," London, 1897, from the confessional standpoint, as well as H. N. Oxenham's " The Catholic Doctrine of the Atonement," London, 1865, ed. 3, 1881, from the Roman Catholic standpoint. Consult also: J. B. Remensnyder, " The Atonement and Modern Thought," Philadelphia, 1905; D. W. Simon, " The Redemption of Man," Edinburgh, 1889; C. A. Dinsmore, " Atonement in Literature and Life," Boston, 1906; L. Pullan, " The Atonement," London, 1906. An interesting episode is treated by Andrew Robertson, " History of the Atonement Controversy in the Secession Church," Edinburgh, 1846.

IX

MODERN THEORIES OF THE ATONEMENT

MODERN THEORIES OF THE ATONEMENT [1]

WE may as well confess at the outset that there is no such thing as a modern theory of the Atonement, in the sense in which there is a modern theory, say, of the Incarnation — the *kenosis* theory to wit, which is a brand-new conception, never dreamed of until the nineteenth century was well on its course, and likely, we may hope, to pass out of notice with that century. All the theories of the Atonement now current readily arrange themselves under the old categories, and have their prototypes running back more or less remotely into the depths of Church history.

The fact is, the views men take of the atonement are largely determined by their fundamental feelings of need — by what men most long to be saved from. And from the beginning three well-marked types of thought on this subject have been traceable, corresponding to three fundamental needs of human nature as it unfolds itself in this world of limitation. Men are oppressed by the ignorance, or by the misery, or by the sin in which they feel themselves sunk; and, looking to Christ to deliver them from the evil under which they particularly labor, they are apt to conceive His work as consisting predominantly in revelation of divine knowledge, or in the inauguration of a reign of happiness, or in deliverance from the curse of sin.

In the early Church, the intellectualistic tendency allied itself with the class of phenomena which we call Gnosticism. The longing for peace and happiness that was the natural result of the crying social evils of the time, found its most remarkable expression in what we know as Chiliasm. That no

[1] An address delivered at the " Religious Conference," held in the Theological Seminary, Princeton, on October 13, 1902. Reprinted from *The Princeton Theological Review*, i. 1903, pp. 81–92.

such party-name suggests itself to describe the manifestation given to the longing to be delivered from the curse of sin, does not mean that this longing was less prominent or less poignant: but precisely the contrary. The other views were sloughed off as heresies, and each received its appropriate designation as such: this was the fundamental point of sight of the Church itself, and as such found expression in numberless ways, some of which, no doubt, were sufficiently bizarre — as, for example, the somewhat widespread representation of the atonement as centering in the surrender of Jesus as a ransom to Satan.

Our modern Church, you will not need me to tell you, is very much like the early Church in all this. All three of these tendencies find as full representation in present-day thought as in any age of the Church's life. Perhaps at no other period was Christ so frequently or so passionately set forth as merely a social Saviour. Certainly at no other period has His work been so prevalently summed up in mere revelation. While now, as ever, the hope of Christians at large continues to be set upon Him specifically as the Redeemer from sin.

The forms in which these fundamental types of thinking are clothed in our modern days, differ, as a matter of course, greatly from those they assumed in the first age. This difference is largely the result of the history of thought through the intervening centuries. The assimilation of the doctrines of revelation by the Church was a gradual process; and it was also an orderly process — the several doctrines emerging in the Christian consciousness for formal discussion and scientific statement in a natural sequence. In this process the doctrine of the atonement did not come up for formulation until the eleventh century, when Anselm gave it its first really fruitful treatment, and laid down for all time the general lines on which the atonement must be conceived, if it is thought of as a work of deliverance from the penalty of sin. The influence of Anselm's discussion is not only traceable, but has been determining in all subsequent thought down to to-day. The doctrine of satisfaction set forth by him has not been permitted, however, to make its way unopposed. Its extreme opposite — the general conception that the atoning work of Christ finds its essence in revelation and had its prime effect, therefore, in deliverance from error — was advocated in Anselm's own day by perhaps the acutest reasoner of all the schoolmen, Peter Abelard. The intermediate view which was apparently invented five centuries later by the great Dutch jurist, Hugo Grotius, loves to think of itself as running back, in germ at least, to nearly as early a date. In the thousand years of conflict which has raged among these generic conceptions each has taken on protean shapes, and a multitude of mixed or mediating hypotheses have been constructed. But, broadly speaking, the theories that have divided the suffrages of men easily take places under one or other of these three types.

There is a fourth general conception, to be sure, which would need to be brought into view were we studying exhaustive enumeration. This is the mystical idea which looks upon the work of Christ as summed up in the incarnation; and upon the saving process as consisting in an unobserved leavening of mankind by the inworking of a vital germ then planted in the mass. But though there never was an age in which this idea failed entirely of representation, it bears a certain aristocratic character which has commended it ordinarily only to the few, however fit: and it probably never was very widely held except during the brief period when the immense genius of Schleiermacher so overshadowed the Church that it could hardly think at all save in the formulas taught by him. Broadly speaking, the field has been held practically by the three theories which are commonly designated by the names of Anselm, Grotius, and Abelard; and age has differed from age only in the changing expression given these theories and the relative dominance of one or another of them.

The Reformers, it goes without saying, were enthusiastic preachers of the Anselmic conception — of course as corrected, developed, and enriched by their own deeper thought and truer insight. Their successors adjusted, expounded, and defended its details, until it stood forth in the seventeenth century dogmatics in practical completeness. During this whole period this conception held the field; the numerous contro versies that arose about it were rather joined with the Socinian or the mystic than internal to the circle of recognized Church teachers. It was not until the rise of Rationalism that a widely spread defection became observable. Under this blight men could no longer believe in the substitutive expiation which is the heart of the Anselmic doctrine, and a blood-bought redemption went much out of fashion. The dainty Supranaturalists attained the height only of the Grotian view, and allowed only a " demonstrative " as distinguished from an " ontological " necessity for an atonement, and an " executive " as distinguished from a " judicial " effect to it. The great evangelical revivals of the eighteenth and early nineteenth centuries, however, swept away all that. It is probable that a half-century ago the doctrine of penal satisfaction had so strong a hold on the churches that not more than an academic interest attached to rival theories.

About that time a great change began to set in. I need only to mention such names as those of Horace Bushnell, McLeod Campbell, Frederick Dennison Maurice, Albrecht Ritschl, to suggest the strength of the assault that was suddenly delivered against the central ideas of an expiatory atonement. The immediate effect was to call out an equally powerful defense. Our best treatises on the atonement come from this period; and Presbyterians in particular may well be proud of the part played by them in the crisis. But this defense only stemmed the tide: it did not succeed in rolling it back. The ultimate result has been that the revolt from the conceptions of satisfaction, propitiation, expiation, sacrifice, reinforced continually by tendencies adverse to evangelical doctrine peculiar to our times, has grown steadily more and more widespread, and in some quarters more and more extreme, until it has issued in an immense confusion on this central doctrine of the gospel. Voices are raised all about us proclaiming a " theory " of the atonement impossible, while many of those that essay a " theory " seem to be feeling their tortuous way very much in the dark. That, if I mistake not, is the real state of affairs in the modern Church.

I am not meaning to imply that the doctrine of substitutive atonement — which is, after all, the very heart of the gospel — has been lost from the consciousness of the Church. It has not been lost from the hearts of the Christian community. It is in its terms that the humble Christian everywhere still expresses the grounds of his hope of salvation. It is in its terms that the earnest evangelist everywhere still presses the claims of Christ upon the awakened hearer. It has not even been lost from the forum of theological discussion. It still commands powerful advocates wherever a vital Christianity enters academical circles: and, as a rule, the more profound the thinker, the more clear is the note he strikes in its proclamation and defense. But if we were to judge only by the popular literature of the day — a procedure happily not possible — the doctrine of a substitutive atonement has retired well into the background. Probably the majority of those who hold the public ear, whether as academical or as popular religious guides, have definitely broken with it, and are commending to their audiences something other and, as they no doubt believe, something very much better. A tone of speech has even grown up regarding it which is not only scornful but positively abusive. There are no epithets too harsh to be applied to it, no invectives too intense to be poured out on it. An honored bishop of the Methodist Episcopal Church tells us that " the whole theory of substitutional punishment as a ground either of conditional or unconditional pardon is unethical, contradictory, and self-subversive." [2] He may rightly claim to be speaking in this sweeping sentence with marked discretion and unwonted charity. To do justice to the hateful theme requires, it seems, the tumid turmoil and rushing rant of Dr. Farrar's rhetoric. Surely if hard words broke bones, the doctrine of the substitutional sacrifice of the Son of God for the sin of man would long ago have been ground to powder.

[2] Bishop Foster, in his " Philosophy of Christian Experience ": 1891, p. 113.

What, then, are we offered instead of it? We have already
intimated that it is confusion which reigns here: and in any
event we cannot go into details. We may try, however, to set
down in few words the general impression that the most
recent literature of the subject makes.

To obtain a just view of the situation, I think we ought to
note, first of all, the wide prevalence among the sounder thinkers of the Grotian or Rectoral theory of the atonement — the
theory, that is, that conceives the work of Christ not as supplying the ground on which God forgives sin, but only as
supplying the ground on which He may safely forgive sins on
the sole ground of His compassion. The theory of hypothetical
universalism, according to which Christ died as the proper
substitute for all men on the condition, namely, that they
should believe — whether in its Remonstrant or in its Amyraldian form — has in the conflict of theories long since been
crushed out of existence — as, indeed, it well deserved to be.
This having been shoved out of the way, the Grotian theory
has come to be the orthodox Arminian view and is taught as
such by the leading exponents of modern Arminian thought
whether in Britain or America; and he who will read the powerful argumentation to that effect by the late Dr. John Miley,
say, for example, will be compelled to agree that it is, indeed,
the highest form of atonement-doctrine conformable to the
Arminian system. But not only is it thus practically universal
among the Wesleyan Arminians. It has become also, under
the influence of such teachers as Drs. Wardlaw and Dale and
Dr. Park, the mark also of orthodox Nonconformity in Great
Britain and of orthodox Congregationalism in America. Nor
has it failed to take a strong hold also of Scottish Presbyterianism: it is specifically advocated by such men of mark and
leading as, for example, Dr. Marcus Dods. On the Continent
of Europe it is equally widespread among the saner teachers:
one notes without surprise, for example, that it was taught
by the late Dr. Frederic Godet, though one notes with satisfaction that it was considerably modified upward by Dr. Godet,
and that his colleague, Dr. Gretillat, was careful to correct it.

In a word, wherever men have been unwilling to drop all semblance of an "objective" atonement, as the word now goes, they have taken refuge in this half-way house which Grotius has builded for them. I do not myself look upon this as a particularly healthful sign of the times. I do not myself think that, at bottom, there is in principle much to choose between the Grotian and the so-called "subjective" theories. It seems to me only an illusion to suppose that it preserves an "objective" atonement at all. But meanwhile it is adopted by many because they deem it "objective," and it so far bears witness to a remanent desire to preserve an "objective" atonement.

We are getting more closely down to the real characteristic of modern theories of the atonement when we note that there is a strong tendency observable all around us to rest the forgiveness of sins solely on repentance as its ground. In its last analysis, the Grotian theory itself reduces to this. The demonstration of God's righteousness, which is held by it to be the heart of Christ's work and particularly of His death, is supposed to have no other effect on God than to render it safe for Him to forgive sin. And this it does not as affecting Him, but as affecting men — namely, by awaking in them such a poignant sense of the evil of sin as to cause them to hate it soundly and to turn decisively away from it. This is just Repentance. We could desire no better illustration of this feature of the theory than is afforded by the statement of it by one of its most distinguished living advocates, Dr. Marcus Dods.[3] The necessity of atonement, he tells us, lies in the "need of some such demonstration of God's righteousness as will make it possible and safe for Him to forgive the unrighteous" (p. 181). Whatever begets in the sinner true penitence and impels him toward the practice of righteousness will render it safe to forgive him. Hence Dr. Dods asserts that it is inconceivable that God should not forgive the penitent sinner,

[3] In an essay in a volume called "The Atonement in Modern Religious Thought: A Theological Symposium" (London: James Clarke & Co., 1900). In this volume seventeen essays from as many writers are collected, and from it a very fair notion can be obtained of the ideas current in certain circles of our day.

and that Christ's work is summed up in such an exhibition of God's righteousness and love as produces, on its apprehension, adequate repentance. " By being the source, then, of true and fruitful penitence, the death of Christ removes the radical subjective obstacle in the way of forgiveness " (p. 184). " The death of Christ, then, has made forgiveness possible, because it enables man to repent with an adequate penitence, and because it manifests righteousness and binds men to God " (p. 187). There is no hint here that man needs anything more to enable him to repent than the presentation of motives calculated powerfully to induce him to repent. That is to say, there is no hint here of an adequate appreciation of the subjective effects of sin on the human heart, deadening it to the appeal of motives to right action however powerful, and requiring therefore an internal action of the Spirit of God upon it before it can repent: or of the purchase of such a gift of the Spirit by the sacrifice of Christ. As little is there any hint here of the existence of any sense of justice in God, forbidding Him to account the guilty righteous without satisfaction of guilt. All God requires for forgiveness is repentance: all the sinner needs for repentance is a moving inducement. It is all very simple; but we are afraid it does not go to the root of matters as presented either in Scripture or in the throes of our awakened heart.

The widespread tendency to represent repentance as the atoning fact might seem, then, to be accountable from the extensive acceptance which has been given to the Rectoral theory of the atonement. Nevertheless much of it has had a very different origin and may be traced back rather to some such teaching as that, say, of Dr. McLeod Campbell. Dr. Campbell did not himself find the atoning fact in man's own repentance, but rather in our Lord's sympathetic repentance for man. He replaced the evangelical doctrine of substitution by a theory of sympathetic identification, and the evangelical doctrine of expiatory penalty-paying by a theory of sympathetic repentance. Christ so fully enters sympathetically into our case, was his idea, that He is able to offer to God an adequate repentance for our sins, and the Father says, It is enough! Man here is still held to need a Saviour, and Christ is presented as that Saviour, and is looked upon as performing for man what man cannot do for himself. But the gravitation of this theory is distinctly downward, and it has ever tended to find its lower level. There are, therefore, numerous transition theories prevalent — some of them very complicated, some of them very subtle — which connect it by a series of insensible stages with the proclamation of human repentance as the sole atonement required. As typical of these we may take the elaborate theory (which, like man himself, may be said to be fearfully and wonderfully made) set forth by the modern Andover divines. This finds the atoning fact in a combination of Christ's sympathetic repentance for man and man's own repentance under the impression made upon him by Christ's work on his behalf — not in the one without the other, but in the two in unison. A similar combination of the revolutionary repentance of man induced by Christ and the sympathetic repentance of Christ for man meets us also in recent German theorizing, as, for example, in the teaching of Häring. It is sometimes clothed in " sacrificial " language and made to bear an appearance even of " substitution." It is just the repentance of Christ, however, which is misleadingly called His " sacrifice," and our sympathetic repentance with Him that is called our participation in His " sacrifice "; and it is carefully explained that though there was " a substitution on Calvary," it was not the substitution of a sinless Christ for a sinful race, but the substitution of humanity *plus* Christ for humanity *minus* Christ. All of which seems but a confusing way of saying that the atoning fact consists in the revolutionary repentance of man induced by the spectacle of Christ's sympathetic repentance for man.

The essential emphasis in all these transition theories falls obviously on man's own repentance rather than on Christ's. Accordingly the latter falls away easily and leaves us with human repentance only as the sole atoning fact — the entire reparation which God asks or can ask for sin. Nor do men

hesitate to-day to proclaim this openly and boldly. Scores of
voices are raised about us declaring it not only with clearness
but with passion. Even those who still feel bound to attribute
the reconciling of God somehow to the work of Christ are often
careful to explain that they mean this ultimately only, and
only because they attribute in one way or other to the work
of Christ the arousing of the repentance in man which is the
immediate ground of forgiveness. Thus Dean Fremantle tells
us that it is " repentance and faith " that " change for us the
face of God." And then he adds, doubtless as a concession to
ingrained, though outgrown, habits of thought: " If, then, the
death of Christ, viewed as the culminating point of His life
of love, is the destined means of repentance for the whole
world, we may say, also, that it is the means of securing the
mercy and favour of God, of procuring the forgiveness of
sins." [4] And Dr. (now Principal) Forsyth, whose fervid address
on the atonement at a great Congregationalist gathering a
few years ago quite took captive the hearts of the whole land,
seems really to teach little more than this. Christ sympathetically enters into our condition, he tells us, and gives expression
to an adequate sense of sin. We, perceiving the effect of this,
His entrance into our sinful atmosphere, are smitten with
horror of the judgment our sin has thus brought on Him. This
horror begets in us an adequate repentance of sin: God accepts
this repentance as enough; and forgives our sin. Thus forgiveness rests proximately only on our repentance as its ground:
but our repentance is produced only by Christ's sufferings:
and hence, Dr. Forsyth tells us, Christ's sufferings may be
called the ultimate ground of forgiveness.[5]

It is sufficiently plain that the function served by the sufferings and death of Christ in this construction is somewhat remote. Accordingly they quite readily fall away altogether. It
seems quite natural that they should do so with those whose
doctrinal inheritance comes from Horace Bushnell, say, or
from the Socinian theorizing of the school of Ritschl. We feel

[4] " The Atonement in Modern Religious Thought," as cited: pp. 168 f.
[5] Ibid., pp. 61 ff.

no surprise to learn, for example, that with Harnack the sufferings and death of Christ play no appreciable part. With
him the whole atoning act seems to consist in the removal
of a false conception of God from the minds of men. Men,
because sinners, are prone to look upon God as a wrathful
judge. He is, on the contrary, just Love. How can the sinner's
misjudgment be corrected? By the impression made upon
him by the life of Jesus, keyed to the conception of the Divine
Fatherhood. With all this we are familiar enough. But we are
hardly prepared for the extremities of language which some
permit themselves in giving expression to it. " The whole
difficulty," a recent writer of this class declares, " is not in
inducing or enabling God to pardon, but in moving men to
abhor sin and to want pardon." Even this difficulty, however,
we are assured is removable: and what is needed for its removal is only proper instruction. " Christianity," cries our
writer, " was a revelation, not a creation." Even this false
antithesis does not, however, satisfy him. He rises beyond it
to the acme of his passion. " Would there have been no Gospel," he rhetorically demands — as if none could venture to
say him nay — " would there have been no Gospel had not
Christ died? " [6] Thus " the blood of Christ " on which the
Scriptures hang the whole atoning fact is thought no longer
to be needed: the gospel of Paul, which consisted not in Christ
simpliciter but specifically in " Christ as crucified," is scouted.
We are able to get along now without these things.

To such a pass have we been brought by the prevailing
gospel of the indiscriminate love of God. For it is here that
we place our finger on the root of the whole modern assault
upon the doctrine of an expiatory atonement. In the attempt
to give effect to the conception of indiscriminate and undiscriminating love as the basal fact of religion, the entire Biblical teaching as to atonement has been ruthlessly torn up. If
God is love and nothing but love, what possible need can there
be of an atonement? Certainly such a God cannot need pro-

[6] Mr. Bernard J. Snell, in " The Atonement in Modern Religious
Thought ": pp. 265, 267.

pitiating. Is not He the All-Father? Is He not yearning for His children with an unconditioned and unconditioning eagerness which excludes all thought of "obstacles to forgiveness"? What does He want but — just His children? Our modern theorizers are never weary of ringing the changes on this single fundamental idea. God does not require to be moved to forgiveness; or to be enabled to pardon; or even to be enabled to pardon safely. He raises no question of whether He can pardon, or whether it would be safe for Him to pardon. Such is not the way of love. Love is bold enough to sweep all such chilling questions impatiently out of its path. The whole difficulty is to induce men to permit themselves to be pardoned. God is continually reaching longing arms out of heaven toward men: oh, if men would only let themselves be gathered unto the Father's eager heart! It is absurd, we are told — nay, wicked — blasphemous with awful blasphemy — to speak of propitiating such a God as this, of reconciling Him, of making satisfaction to Him. Love needs no satisfying, reconciling, propitiating; nay, will have nothing to do with such things. Of its very nature it flows out unbought, unpropitiated, instinctively and unconditionally, to its object. And God is Love!

Well, certainly, God *is* Love. And we praise Him that we have better authority for telling our souls this glorious truth than the passionate assertion of these somewhat crass theorizers. God *is* Love! But it does not in the least follow that He is nothing but love. God *is* Love: but Love is not God and the formula "Love" must therefore ever be inadequate to express God. It may well be — to us sinners, lost in our sin and misery but for it, it must be — the crowning revelation of Christianity that God is love. But it is not from the Christian revelation that we have learned to think of God as nothing but love. That God is the Father of all men in a true and important sense, we should not doubt. But this term "All-Father" — it is not from the lips of Hebrew prophet or Christian apostle that we have caught it. And the indiscriminate benevolencism which has taken captive so much of the religious thinking of our time is a conception not native to Christianity, but of distinctly heathen quality. As one reads the pages of popular religious literature, teeming as it is with ill-considered assertions of the general Fatherhood of God, he has an odd feeling of transportation back into the atmosphere of, say, the decadent heathenism of the fourth and fifth centuries, when the gods were dying, and there was left to those who would fain cling to the old ways little beyond a somewhat saddened sense of the *benignitas numinis*. The *benignitas numinis!* How studded the pages of those genial old heathen are with the expression; how suffused their repressed life is with the conviction that the kind Deity that dwells above will surely not be hard on men toiling here below! How shocked they are at the stern righteousness of the Christian's God, who loomed before their startled eyes as He looms before those of the modern poet in no other light than as " the hard God that dwelt in Jerusalem " ! Surely the Great Divinity is too broadly good to mark the peccadillos of poor puny man; surely they are the objects of His compassionate amusement rather than of His fierce reprobation. Like Omar Khayyam's pot, they were convinced, before all things, of their Maker that " He's a good fellow and 'twill all be well."

The query cannot help rising to the surface of our minds whether our modern indiscriminate benevolencism goes much deeper than this. Does all this one-sided proclamation of the universal Fatherhood of God import much more than the heathen *benignitas numinis?* When we take those blessed words, " God is Love," upon our lips, are we sure we mean to express much more than that we do not wish to believe that God will hold man to any real account for his sin? Are we, in a word, in these modern days, so much soaring upward toward a more adequate apprehension of the transcendent truth that God is love, as passionately protesting against being ourselves branded and dealt with as wrath-deserving sinners? Assuredly it is impossible to put anything like their real content into these great words, " God is Love," save as they are thrown out against the background of those other conceptions of equal loftiness, " God is Light," " God is Righteousness," " God is

Holiness," " God is a consuming fire." The love of God cannot
be apprehended in its length and breadth and height and depth
— all of which pass knowledge — save as it is apprehended
as the love of a God who turns from the sight of sin with inexpressible abhorrence, and burns against it with unquenchable
indignation. The infinitude of His love would be illustrated
not by His lavishing of His favor on sinners without requiring
an expiation of sin, but by His — through such holiness and
through such righteousness as cannot but cry out with infinite
abhorrence and indignation — still loving sinners so greatly
that He provides a satisfaction for their sin adequate to these
tremendous demands. It is the distinguishing characteristic
of Christianity, after all, not that it preaches a God of love,
but that it preaches a God of conscience.

A somewhat flippant critic, contemplating the religion of
Israel, has told us, as expressive of his admiration for what he
found there, that " an honest God is the noblest work of
man." [7] There is a profound truth lurking in the remark. Only
it appears that the work were too noble for man; and probably man has never compassed it. A benevolent God, yes: men
have framed a benevolent God for themselves. But a thoroughly honest God, perhaps never. That has been left for the
revelation of God Himself to give us. And this is the really
distinguishing characteristic of the God of revelation: He is a
thoroughly honest, a thoroughly conscientious God — a God
who deals honestly with Himself and us, who deals conscientiously with Himself and us. And a thoroughly conscientious
God, we may be sure, is not a God who can deal with sinners
as if they were not sinners. In this fact lies, perhaps, the deepest ground of the necessity of an expiatory atonement.

And it is in this fact also that there lies the deepest ground
of the increasing failure of the modern world to appreciate the
necessity of an expiatory atonement. Conscientiousness commends itself only to awakened conscience; and in much of recent theologizing conscience does not seem especially active.

---

[7] Cf. Mr. Edward Day's " The Social Life of the Hebrews," 1901, p. 207.
He is quoting apparently the late Mr. Ingersoll.

Nothing, indeed, is more startling in the structure of recent theories of atonement, than the apparently vanishing sense of sin that underlies them. Surely, it is only where the sense of guilt of sin has grown grievously faint, that men can suppose repentance to be all that is needed to purge it. Surely it is only where the sense of the power of sin has profoundly decayed, that men can fancy that they can at will cast it off from them in a " revolutionary repentance." Surely it is only where the sense of the heinousness of sin has practically passed away, that man can imagine that the holy and just God can deal with it lightly. If we have not much to be saved from, why, certainly, a very little atonement will suffice for our needs. It is, after all, only the sinner that requires a Saviour. But if we are sinners, and in proportion as we know ourselves to be sinners, and appreciate what it means to be sinners, we will cry out for that Saviour who only after He was perfected by suffering could become the Author of eternal salvation.

X

IMPUTATION

IMPUTATION [1]

I. Origin and Meaning of the Term

The theological use of the term " imputation " is probably rooted ultimately in the employment of the verb *imputo* in the Vulgate to translate the Greek verb *logizesthai* in Ps. xxxii. 2. This passage is quoted by Paul in Rom. iv. 8 and made one of the foundations of his argument that, in saving man, God sets to his credit a righteousness without works. It is only in these two passages, and in the two axiomatic statements of Rom. iv. 4 and v. 13 that the Vulgate uses *imputo* in this connection (cf., with special application, II Tim. iv. 16; Philemon 18). There are other passages, however, where it might just as well have been employed, but where we have instead *reputo,* under the influence of the mistaken rendering of the Hebrew *hashabh* in Gen. xv. 6. In these passages the Authorized English Version improves on the Latin by rendering a number of them (Rom. iv. 11, 22, 23, 24; II Cor. v. 19; James ii. 23) by " impute," and employing for the rest synonymous terms, all of which preserve the " metaphor from accounts " inherent in *logizesthai* (and *ellogein*) in this usage (cf. W. Sanday and A. C. Headlam, " Commentary on the Epistle to the Romans," iv. 3), such as " count " (Rom. iv. 3, 5), " account " (Gal. iii. 6), and " reckon " (Rom. iv. 4, 9, 10); the last of which the Revised English Version makes its uniform rendering of *logizesthai*. Even the meager employment of *imputo* in the Latin version, however, supplied occasion enough for the adoption of that word in the precise language of theology as the technical term for that which is expressed by the Greek words in their so-called " commercial " sense, or

[1] Reprinted from " The New Schaff-Herzog Encyclopedia of Religious Knowledge," edited by Samuel Macauley Jackson, D.D., LL.D., v. pp. 465–467 (copyright by Funk and Wagnalls Company, New York, 1909).

what may, more correctly, be called their forensic or " judicial "
sense, " that is, putting to one's account," or, in its twofold
reference to the credit and debit sides, " setting to one's
credit " or " laying to one's charge."

II. Three Acts of Imputation

From the time of Augustine (early fifth century), at least,
the term " imputation " is found firmly fixed in theological
terminology in this sense. But the applications and relations
of the doctrine expressed by it were thoroughly worked out
only in the discussions which accompanied and succeeded the
Reformation. In the developed theology thus brought into
the possession of the Church, three several acts of imputation
were established and expounded. These are the imputation of
Adam's sin to his posterity; the imputation of the sins of His
people to the Redeemer; the imputation of the righteousness
of Christ to His people. Though, of course, with more or less
purity of conception and precision of application, these three
great doctrines became the property of the whole Church, and
found a place in the classical theology of the Roman, Lutheran, and Reformed alike. In the proper understanding of
the conception, it is important to bear in mind that the divine
act called " imputation " is in itself precisely the same in each
of the three great transactions into which it enters as a constituent part. The grounds on which it proceeds may differ;
the things imputed may be different; and the consequent
treatment of the person or persons to which the imputation is
made may and will differ as the things imputed to them
differ. But in each and every case alike imputation itself is
simply the act of setting to one's account; and the act of
setting to one's account is in itself the same act whether the
thing set to his account stands on the credit or debit side of
the account, and whatever may be the ground in equity on
which it is set to his account. That the sin of Adam was so set
to the account of his descendants that they have actually
shared in the penalty which was threatened to it; and that the

sins of His people were so set to the account of our Lord that
He bore them in His own body on the tree, and His merits are
so set to their account that by His stripes they are healed, the
entirety of historical orthodox Christianity unites in affirming.

III. PELAGIAN OPPOSITION TO THE DOCTRINE

Opposition to these doctrines has, of course, not been lacking in the history of Christian thought. The first instance of
important contradiction of the fundamental principle involved
is presented by the Pelagian movement (see " Pelagius, Pelagian Controversies "), which arose at the beginning of the
fifth century. The Pelagians denied the equity and, therefore,
under the government of God, the possibility of the involvement of one free agent in the acts of another; they utterly
denied, therefore, that men either suffer harm from Adam's
sin or profit by Christ's merits. By their examples only, they
said, can either Adam or Christ affect us; and by free imitation
of them alone can we share in their merits or demerits. It is
not apparent why Pelagius permitted himself such extremity
of denial. What he had at heart to assert was the inamissi-
bility by the human subject of plenary ability of will to do all
righteousness. To safeguard this he had necessarily to deny all
subjective injury to men from Adam's sin (and from their own
sins too, for that matter), and the need or actuality of subjective grace for their perfecting. But there was no reason
growing out of this point of sight why he might not allow that
the guilt of Adam's sin had been imputed to his posterity, and
had supplied the ground for the infliction upon them of external penalties temporal or eternal; or that the merits of
Christ might be imputed to His people as the meritorious
ground of their relief from these penalties, as well as of the
forgiveness of their own actual sins and of their reception into
the favor of God and the heavenly blessedness. Later Pelagianizers found this out; and it became not uncommon (especially
after Duns Scotus' strong assertion of the doctrine of " immediate imputation ") for the imputation of Adam's sin to be

exploited precisely in the interest of denial or weakening of the idea of the derivation of inherent corruption from Adam. A very good example of this tendency of thought is supplied by the Roman Catholic theologian Ambrosius Catharinus, whose admirable speech to this effect at the Council of Trent is reported by Father Paul ("History of the Council of Trent," E. T. London, 1676, p. 165). Even Zwingli was not unaffected by it. He was indeed free from the Pelagianizing attenuation of the corruption of nature which is the subjective effect on his posterity of Adam's sin. With him, " original sin " was both extensively and intensively a total depravity, the fertile source of all evil action. But he looked upon it rather as a misfortune than a fault, a disease than a sin; and he hung the whole weight of our ruin on our direct participation in Adam's guilt. As a slave can beget only a slave, says he, so all the progeny of man under the curse are born under the curse.

IV. Importance of the Doctrine

In sharp contradiction to the current tendency to reduce to the vanishing-point the subjective injury wrought by Adam's sin on his posterity, the churches gave themselves to emphasizing the depth of the injury and especially its sinfulness. Even the Council of Trent acknowledged the transfusion into the entire human race of " sin, which is the death of the soul." The Protestants, who, as convinced Augustinians, were free from the Pelagianizing bias of Rome, were naturally even more strenuous in asserting the evil and guilt of native depravity. Accordingly they constantly remark that men's native guilt in the sight of God rests not merely upon the imputation to them of Adam's first sin, but also upon the corruption which they derive from him — a mode of statement which meets us, indeed, as early as Peter Lombard ("Sentences," II. xxx.) and for the same reason. The polemic turn given to these statements has been the occasion of a remarkable misapprehension, as if it were intended to subordinate the imputation of Adam's transgression to the transmission of his corrupted nature as the source of human guilt. Precisely the contrary is the fact. The imputation of Adam's transgression was not in dispute; all parties to the great debate of the age fully recognized it; and it is treated therefore as a matter of course. What was important was to make it clear that native depravity was along with it the ground of our guilt before God. Thus it was sought to hold the balance true, and to do justice to both elements in a complete doctrine of original sin. Meanwhile the recovery of the great doctrine of justification by faith threw back its light upon the doctrine of the satisfaction of Christ which had been in the possession of the Church since Anselm; and the better understanding of this doctrine, thus induced, in turn illuminated the doctrine of sin, whose correlative it is. Thus it came about that in the hands of the great Protestant leaders of the sixteenth century, and of their successors, the Protestant systematizers of the seventeenth century, the three-fold doctrine of imputation — of Adam's sin to his posterity, of the sins of His people to the Redeemer, and of the righteousness of Christ to His people — at last came to its rights as the core of the three constitutive doctrines of Christianity — the sinfulness of the human race, the satisfaction of Jesus Christ, and justification by faith. The importance of the doctrine of imputation is that it is the hinge on which these three great doctrines turn, and the guardian of their purity.

V. Socinian, Arminian, and Rationalistic Opposition

Of course the Church was not permitted to enjoy in quiet its new understanding of its treasures of doctrine. Radical opponents arose in the Reformation age itself, the most important of whom were the Socinians (see "Socinus, Faustus, Socinians"). By them it was pronounced an inanity to speak of the transference of either merit or demerit from one person to another: we can be bad with another's badness, or good with another's goodness, they said, as little as we can be white with another's whiteness. The center of the Socinian assault was upon the doctrine of the satisfaction of Christ: it is not possible, they affirmed, for one person to bear the punishment due to another. But their criticism cut equally deeply into the Protestant doctrines of original sin and justification by faith. The influence of their type of thought, very great from the first, increased as time went on and became a factor of importance both in the Arminian revolt at the beginning of the seventeenth century and in the rationalistic defection a hundred years later. Neither the Arminians (e.g. Limborch, Curcellæus) nor the Rationalists (e.g. Wegscheider) would hear of an imputation of Adam's sin, and both attacked with arguments very similar to those of the Socinians also the imputation of our sins to Christ or of His righteousness to us. Rationalism almost ate the heart out of the Lutheran Churches; and the Reformed Churches were saved from the same fate only by the prompt extrusion of the Arminian party and the strengthening of their position by conflict with it. In particular, about the middle of the seventeenth century the "covenant" or "federal" method of exhibiting the plan of the Lord's dealings with men (see "Cocceius, Johannes, and his School") began to find great acceptance among the Reformed Churches. There was nothing novel in this mode of conceiving truth. The idea was present to the minds of the Church Fathers and the Schoolmen; and it underlay Protestant thought, both Lutheran and Reformed, from the beginning, and in the latter had come to clear expression, first in Ursinus. But now it quickly became dominant as the preferable manner of conceiving the method of the divine dealing with men. The effect was to throw into the highest relief the threefold doctrine of imputation, and to make manifest as never before the dependency of the great doctrines of sin, satisfaction, and justification upon it.

VI. La Place and Later Theologians and Schools

About the same time a brilliant French professor, Josué de la Place (see "Placeus, Josua"), of the Reformed school at Saumur, reduced all that could be called the imputation of

Adam's sin to his posterity simply to this — that because of
the sin inherent in us from our origin we are deserving of being treated in the same way as if we had committed that
offense. This confinement of the effect of Adam's sin upon his
posterity to the transmission to them of a sinful disposition
— inherent sin — was certainly new in the history of Reformed
thought: Andreas Rivetus (see " Rivet, André ") had no difficulty in collecting a long line of " testimonies " from the confessions and representative theologians explicitly declaring
that men are accounted guilty in God's sight, both because of
Adam's act of transgression imputed to them and of their own
sinful disposition derived from him. The conflict of views was
no doubt rendered sharper, however, by the prevalence at the
time of the " Covenant theology " in which the immediate
imputation of Adam's transgression is particularly clearly emphasized. Thus " immediate " and " mediate " imputation
(for by the latter name La Place came subsequently to call his
view) were pitted against each other as mutually exclusive
doctrines: as if the question at issue were whether man stood
condemned in the sight of God solely on account of his " adherent " sin, or solely on account of his " inherent " sin. The
former of these doctrines had never been held in the Reformed
Churches, since Zwingli, and the latter had never been held in
them before La Place. From the first both " adherent " and
" inherent " sin had been confessed as the double ground of
human guilt; and the advocates of the " Covenant theology "
were as far as possible from denying the guilt of " inherent "
sin. La Place's innovation was as a matter of course condemned by the Reformed world, formally at the Synod of
Charenton (1644–1645) and in the Helvetic Consensus (1675)
and by argument at the hands of the leading theologians —
Rivetus, Turretin, Maresius, Driessen, Leydecker, and Marck.
But the tendencies of the time were in its favor and it made
its way. It was adopted by theologians like Wyttenbach, Ende-
mann, Stapfer, Roell, Vitringa, Venema; and after a while it
found its way through Britain to America, where it has had
an interesting history — forming one of the stages through

which the New England Theology (*q.v.*) passed on its way to its ultimate denial of the quality of sin involving guilt to anything but the voluntary acts of a free agent; and finally becoming one of the characteristic tenets of the so-called " New School Theology " of the Presbyterian Churches. Thus it has come about that there has been much debate in America upon "imputation," in the sense of the imputation of Adam's sin, and diverse types of theology have been framed, especially among the Congregationalists and Presbyterians, centering in differences of conception of this doctrine. Among the Presbyterians, for example, four such types are well marked, each of which has been taught by theologians of distinction. These are (1) the " Federalistic," characterized by its adherence to the doctrine of "immediate imputation," represented, for example, by Dr. Charles Hodge; (2) the " New School," characterized by its adherence to the doctrine of " mediate imputation," represented, for example, by Dr. Henry B. Smith; (3) the " Realistic," which teaches that all mankind were present in Adam as generic humanity, and sinned in him, and are therefore guilty of his and their common sin, represented, for example, by Dr. W. G. T. Shedd; and (4) one which may be called the " Agnostic," characterized by an attempt to accept the fact of the transmission of both guilt and depravity from Adam without framing a theory of the mode of their transmission or of their relations one to the other, represented, for example, by Dr. R. W. Landis. See " Adam "; " Atonement "; " Justification "; " Redemption "; " Satisfaction "; " Sin."

BIBLIOGRAPHY: The literature of the subject is the literature of " Sin," " Atonement," and " Justification " (*qq. v.*). Special treatment is usually given also in the systems of doctrinal theology, especially of the Calvinistic type. Consult: A. Rivetus, " Opera," Rotterdam, iii. 1660, pp. 798 ff.; R. Rüetschi, " Geschichte und Kritik der kirchlichen Lehre von . . . Sündenfall," Leiden, 1881; C. Hodge, in " Theological Essays," New York, 1846, pp. 128–217; A. Schweizer, " Die protestantischen Centraldogmen," Zürich, 1854–1856; W. Cunningham, " The Reformers and the Theology of the Reformation," Edinburgh, 1866, pp. 371 ff.; J. Buchanan, "The Doctrine of Justification," Edinburgh, 1867, pp. 279, 321–323, 334, 337; G. P. Fisher, in the *New Englander*, xxvii. 1868, pp. 468–516; J. Müller, "The Christian Doctrine of Sin," Edinburgh, ii. 1868, pp. 342 ff.; T. J. Crawford, "The Doctrine of Holy Scripture respecting the Atonement," Edinburgh, 1871, pp. 181–183, 424; R. W. Landis, "The Doctrine of Original Sin as Received and Taught by the Churches of the Reformation," Richmond, 1884; W. G. T. Shedd, "Dogmatic Theology," New York, ii. 1888, pp. 29, 42, 57–63, 192–194; H. B. Smith, "System of Christian Theology," ed. W. S. Karr, New York, 1886, pp. 283–323; R. V. Foster, "Systematic Theology," Nashville, 1898, pp. 408–413; W. A. Brown, "Christian Theology in Outline," New York, 1906, pp. 285, 290–291, 311, 362.

XI

ON FAITH IN ITS PSYCHOLOGICAL ASPECTS

ON FAITH IN ITS PSYCHOLOGICAL ASPECTS [1]

THE English word "faith" came into the language under the influence of the French, and is but a modification of the Latin "fides," which is itself cognate with the Greek πίστις. Its root-meaning seems to be that of "binding." Whatever we discover to be "binding" on us, is the object of "faith." [2] The corresponding Germanic term, represented by the English word "believe" (and the German "glauben"), goes back to a root meaning "to be agreeable" (represented by our English "lief"), and seems to present the object of belief as something which we "esteem" — which we have "estimated" or "weighed" and "approved." The notion of "constraint" is perhaps less prominent in "belief" than in "faith," its place being taken in "belief" by that of "approval." We "believe" in what we find worthy of our confidence; we "have faith" in what compels our confidence. But it would be easy to press this too far, and it is likely that the two terms "faith," "belief" really express much the same idea. [3] In the natural use of language, therefore, which is normally controlled by what we call etymology, that is, by the intrinsic connotation of the terms, when we say "faith," "belief," our minds are preoccupied with the grounds of the conviction expressed: we are speaking of a mental act or state to which we feel con-

---

[1] Reprinted from *The Princeton Theological Review,* ix. 1911, pp. 537–566.

[2] The Hebrew אמונה, האמין go back to the idea of "holding": we believe in what "holds." In both the sacred languages, therefore, the fundamental meaning of faith is "surety." Cf. Latin "credo."

[3] Cf. M. Heyne's German Dictionary, *sub voc.* "Glaube ": " *Glaube* is confiding acceptance of a truth. At the basis of the word is the root *lub,* which, with the general meaning of agreeing with and of approving, appears also in *erlauben* and *loben.*"

strained by considerations objective to ourselves, or at least to the act or state in question. The conception embodied in the terms " belief," " faith," in other words, is not that of an arbitrary act of the subject's; it is that of a mental state or act which is determined by sufficient reasons.

In their fundamental connotation, thus, these terms are very broad. There seems nothing in the terms themselves, indeed, to forbid their employment in so wide a sense as to cover the whole field of " sureness," " conviction." Whatever we accept as true or real, we may very properly be said to " believe," to " have faith in "; all that we are convinced of may be said to be matter of " belief," " faith." So the terms are, accordingly, very often employed. Thus, for example, Professor J. M. Baldwin defines " belief " simply as " mental endorsement or acceptance of something thought of, as real "; and remarks of " conviction," that it " is a loose term whose connotation, so far as exact, is near to that here given to belief." [4] He even adds — we think with less exactness — that " judgment " is merely " the logical or formal side of the same state of mind " which, on the psychological side, is called " belief." To us, " judgment " appears a broader term than " belief," expressing a mental act which underlies belief indeed, but cannot be identified with it.[5]

Meanwhile we note with satisfaction that Professor Baldwin recognizes the element of constraint (" bindingness ") in " belief," and distinguishes it clearly from acts of the will, thereby setting aside the definition of it — quite commonly given — which finds the differentia of beliefs, among convictions, in this — that they are " voluntary convictions." " There is," he says,[6] " a distinct difference in consciousness between the consent of belief and the consent of will. The consent of belief is in a measure a forced consent: it attaches

[4] Baldwin and Stout, " Dictionary of Philosophy and Psychology," i. 1901, pp. 110 and 112.

[5] Professor Baldwin does not allow any psychological distinction between " belief " and " knowledge." See *sub voc.* " Knowledge."

[6] *Ibid.*, p. 112. The passage is quoted from Baldwin, " Handbook of Psychology: Feeling and Will," 1891, p. 171.

to what is — to what stands in the order of things whether I consent or no. The consent of will is a forceful consent — a consent to what shall be through me." That is to say, with respect to belief, it is a mental recognition of what is before the mind, as objectively true and real, and therefore depends on the evidence that a thing is true and real and is determined by this evidence; it is the response of the mind to this evidence and cannot arise apart from it. It is, therefore, impossible that belief should be the product of a volition; volitions look to the future and represent our desires; beliefs look to the present and represent our findings.

Professor Baldwin does not recognize this, however, in its entirety, as is already apparent from the qualification inserted into his description of " belief." It is, says he, " *in a measure* a forced consent." He wishes, after all, to leave room for " voluntary beliefs." Accordingly, he proceeds: " In cases in which belief is brought about by desire and will, there is a subtle consciousness of inadequate evidence, until by repetition the item desired and willed no longer needs volition to give it a place in the series deemed objective: then it is for the first time belief, but then it is no longer will." " Beliefs," then, according to Professor Baldwin, although not to be confounded with acts of the will, may yet be produced by the action of the will, even while the " evidence " on which they should more properly rest, is recognized by the mind willing them to be insufficient.

We cannot help suspecting this suggestion to rest on a defective analysis of what actually goes on in the mind in the instances commented on. These appear to us to be cases in which we determine to act on suppositions recognized as lacking sufficient evidence to establish them in our minds as accordant with reality and therefore not accepted as accordant with reality, that is to say, as " beliefs." If they pass, as Dr. Baldwin suggests, gradually into " beliefs," when repeatedly so acted upon — is that not because the mind derives from such repeated action, resulting successfully, additional evidence that the suppositions in question do represent reality and may be safely acted on as such? Would not the thing acted on in such cases be more precisely stated as the belief that these suppositions may be accordant with reality, not that they are? The consciousness that the evidence is inadequate which accompanies such action (though Dr. Baldwin calls it "subtle") — is it not in fact just the witness of consciousness that it does not assert these suppositions to be accordant with reality, and does not recognize them as "beliefs," though it is willing to act on them on the hypothesis that they may prove to be accordant with reality and thus make good their aspirations to become beliefs? And can any number of repetitions (repetitions of what, by the way?) make this testimony of consciousness void? Apparently what we repeat is simply volitions founded on the possibility or probability of the suppositions in question being in accordance with reality; and it is difficult to see how the repetition of such volitions can elevate the suppositions in question into the rank of beliefs except by eliminating doubt as to their accordance with reality by creating evidence for them through their "working well." The repetition of a volition to treat a given proposition as true — especially if it is accompanied by a consciousness (however subtle) that there is no sufficient evidence that it is true — can certainly not result in making it true; and can scarcely of itself result in producing an insufficiently grounded conviction in the mind (always at least subtly conscious that it rests on insufficient evidence) that it is true, and so in giving it "a place in the series deemed objective." A habit of treating a given proposition as correspondent to reality may indeed be formed; and as this habit is formed, the accompanying consciousness that it is in point of fact grounded in insufficient evidence, may no doubt drop into the background, or even wholly out of sight; thus we may come to act — instinctively, shall we say? or inadvertently? — on the supposition of the truth of the proposition in question. But this does not seem to carry with it as inevitable implication that "beliefs" may be created by the action of the will. It may only show that more or less probable, or more or less improbable, suppositions, more or less clearly envisaged as such, may enter into the complex of conditions which influence action, and that the human mind in the processes of its ordinary activity does not always keep before it in perfect clearness the lines of demarcation which separate the two classes of its beliefs and its conjectures, but may sometimes rub off the labels which serve to mark its convictions off from its suppositions and to keep each in its proper place.

It would seem to be fairly clear that " belief " is always the product of evidence and that it cannot be created by volitions, whether singly or in any number of repetitions. The interaction of belief and volition is, questionless, most intimate and most varied, but one cannot be successfully transmuted into the other, nor one be mistaken for the other. The consent of belief is in its very nature and must always be what Dr. Baldwin calls " forced consent," that is to say, determined by evidence, not by volition; and when the consent of will is secured by a supposition, recognized by consciousness as inadequately based in evidence, this consent of will has no tendency to act as evidence and raise the supposition into a belief — its tendency is only to give to a supposition the place of a belief in the ordering of life.

We may infer from this state of the case that " preparedness to act " is scarcely a satisfactory definition of the state of mind which is properly called " faith," " belief." This was the definition suggested by Dr. Alexander Bain. " Faith," " belief " certainly expresses a state of preparedness to act; and it may be very fairly contended that " preparedness to act " supplies a very good test of the genuineness of " faith," " belief." A so-called " faith," " belief " on which we are not prepared to act is near to no real " faith," " belief " at all. What we are convinced of, we should certainly confide in; and what we are unwilling to confide in we seem not quite sure of — we do not appear thoroughly to believe, to have faith in. But though all " faith," " belief " is preparedness to act, it does not follow that all preparedness to act is " faith," " belief." We may be prepared to act, on some other ground than "faith," "belief"; on "knowledge," say — if knowledge may be distinguished from belief — or, as we have already suggested, on "supposition" — on a probability or even a possibility. To be sure, as we have already noted, the real ground of our action in such cases may be stated in terms of "faith," "belief." Our preparedness to act may be said to be our belief — our conviction — that, if the supposition in question is not yet shown to be in conformity to reality, it yet may be so. Meanwhile, it is clear that the supposition in question is not a thing believed to be in accordance with fact, and is therefore not a belief but a "supposition"; not a "conviction" but a conjecture. "Belief," "faith" is the consent of the mind to the reality of the thing in question; and when the mind withholds its consent to the reality, "belief," "faith" is not present. These terms are not properly employed except when a state of conviction is present; they designate the response of the mind to evidence in a consent to the adequacy of the evidence.

It, of course, does not follow that all our "beliefs," "faiths" correspond with reality. Our convictions are not infallible. When we say that "belief," "faith" is the product of evidence and is in that sense a compelled consent, this is not the same as saying that consent is produced only by compelling evidence, that is, evidence which is objectively adequate. Objective adequacy and subjective effect are not exactly correlated. The amount, degree, and quality of evidence which will secure consent varies from mind to mind and in the same mind from state to state. Some minds, or all minds in some states, will respond to very weak evidence with full consent; some minds or all minds in some states, will resist very strong evidence. There is no "faith," "belief" possible without evidence or what the mind takes for evidence; "faith," "belief" is a state of mind grounded in evidence and impossible without it. But the fullest "faith," "belief" may ground itself in very weak evidence — if the mind mistakes it for strong evidence. "Faith," "belief" does not follow the evidence itself, in other words, but the judgment of the intellect on the evidence.

And the judgment of the intellect naturally will vary end-lessly, as intellect differs from intellect or as the states of the same intellect differ from one another.

From this circumstance has been taken an attempt to de-fine " faith," " belief " more closely than merely mental en-dorsement of something as true — as, broadly, the synonym of " conviction " — and to distinguish it as a specific form of conviction from other forms of conviction. " Faith," " belief," it is said (e.g. by Kant), is conviction founded on evidence which is subjectively adequate. " Knowledge " is conviction founded on evidence which is objectively adequate. That " faith " and " knowledge " do differ from one another, we all doubtless feel; but it is not easy to believe that their specific difference is found in this formula. It is of course plain enough that every act of " faith," " belief " rests on evidence which is subjectively adequate. But it is far from plain that this evidence must be objectively inadequate on pain of the mental response ceasing to be " faith," " belief " and becoming " knowledge." Are all " beliefs," " faiths," spe-cifically such, in their very nature inadequately established convictions; convictions, indeed — matters of which we feel sure — but of which we feel sure on inadequate grounds — grounds either consciously recognized by us as inadequate, or, if supposed by us to be adequate, yet really inadequate?

No doubt there is a usage of the terms current — especially when they are set in contrast with one another — which does conceive them after this fashion; a legitimate enough usage, because it is founded on a real distinction in the connotation of the two terms. We do sometimes say, " I do not *know* this or that to be true, but I fully *believe* it " — meaning that though we are altogether persuaded of it we are conscious that the grounds for believing it fall short of complete objective co-erciveness. But this special usage of the terms ought not to deceive us as to their essential meaning. And it surely requires little consideration to assure us that it cannot be of the essence of " faith," " belief " that the grounds on which it rests are — consciously   or   unconsciously — objectively   inadequate.

Faith must not be distinguished from knowledge only that it may be confounded with conjecture. And how, in any case, shall the proposed criterion of faith be applied? To believe on grounds of the inadequacy of which we are conscious, is on the face of it an impossibility. The moment we perceive the objective inadequacy of the grounds on which we pronounce the reality of anything, they become subjectively inadequate also. And so long as they appear to us subjectively adequate, the resulting conviction will be indistinguishable from "knowledge." To say that "knowledge" is a justified recognition of reality and "faith," "belief" is an unjustified recognition of reality, is to erect a distinction which can have no possible psychological basis. The recognizing mind makes and can make no such distinction between the soundness and unsoundness of its own recognitions of reality. An outside observer might certainly distribute into two such categories the "convictions" of a mind brought under his contemplation; but the distribution would represent the outside observer's judgment upon the grounds of these convictions, not that of the subject himself. The moment the mind observed itself introducing such a distribution among its "convictions" it would remove the whole class of "convictions" to which it assigned an inadequate grounding out of the category of "convictions" altogether. To become conscious that some of its convictions were unjustified would be to abolish them at once as convictions, and to remove them into the category at best of conjectures, at worst of erroneous judgments. We accord with Dr. Baldwin, therefore, when he declares of this distinction that it is "not psychological." [7] The mind knows and can know nothing of objectively and subjectively adequate grounds in forming its convictions. All it is conscious of is the adequacy or inadequacy of the grounds on which its convictions are based. If they appeal to it as adequate, the mind is convinced; if they do not, it remains unconvinced. Faith, belief, is to consciousness just an act or state of conviction, of being sure; and therefore cannot be explained as something less than a con-

[7] "Dictionary of Philosophy and Psychology," i. 1901, p. 603.

viction, something less than being sure, or as a conviction indeed, but a conviction which differs from other convictions by being, if not ungrounded, yet not adequately grounded. That were all one with saying it is a conviction, no doubt, but nevertheless not quite a conviction — a manifest contradiction in terms.

The failure of this special attempt to distinguish between faith and knowledge need not argue, however, that there is no distinction between the two. Faith may not be inadequately grounded conviction any more than it is voluntary conviction — the two come to much the same thing — and yet be a specific mode of conviction over against knowledge as a distinct mode of conviction. The persistence with which it is set over against knowledge in our popular usage of the words as well as in the definitions of philosophers may be taken as an indication that there is some cognizable distinction between the two, could we but fasten upon it. And the persistence with which this distinction is sought in the nature of the grounds on which faith in distinction from knowledge rests is equally notable. Thus we find Dr. Alexander T. Ormond [8] defining " faith " as " the personal acceptance of something as true or real, but — the distinguishing mark — on grounds that, in whole or part, are different from those of theoretic certitude." Here faith is distinguished from other forms of conviction — " knowledge " being apparently in mind as the other term of the contrast. And the distinguishing mark of " faith " is found in the nature of the grounds on which it rests. The nature of these grounds, however, is expressed only negatively. We are not told what they are but only that they are (in whole or in part) different to " those of theoretic certitude." The effect of the definition as it stands is therefore only to declare that the term " faith " does not express all forms of conviction, but one form only; and that this form of conviction differs from the form which is given the name of " theoretic certitude " — that is to say, doubtless, " knowledge " — in the grounds on which it rests. But what the posi-

[8] Baldwin's " Dictionary of Philosophy and Psychology," i. 1901, p. 369.

tive distinguishing mark of the grounds on which the mode of
conviction which we call " faith " rests is, we are not told. Dr.
Ormond does, indeed, go on to say that " the moment of will
enters into the assent of faith," and that " in the form of some
subjective interest or consideration of value." From this it
might be inferred that the positive differentia of faith, unexpressed in the definition, would be that it is voluntary conviction, conviction determined not by the evidence of reality
present to our minds, but by our desire or will that it should
be true — this desire or will expressing " some subjective interest or consideration of value." [9]

Put baldly, this might be interpreted as meaning that we
" know " what is established to us as true, we " believe " what
we think we should be advantaged by if true; we " know "
what we perceive to be real, we " believe " what we should like
to be real. To put it so baldly may no doubt press Dr. Ormond's
remark beyond his intention. He recognizes that " some faith-
judgments are translatable into judgments of knowledge." But
he does not believe that all are; and he suggests that " the
final test of validity " of these latter must lie in " the sphere
of the practical rather than in that of theoretical truth." The
meaning is not throughout perfectly clear. But the upshot
seems to be that in Dr. Ormond's opinion, that class of convictions which we designate " faith " differs from that class of
convictions which we designate " knowledge " by the fact
that they rest (in whole or in part) not on " theoretical " but
on " practical " grounds — that is to say, not on evidence but
on considerations of value. And that appears ultimately to
mean that we know a thing which is proved to us to be true
or real; but we believe a thing which we would fain should
prove to be true or real. Some of the things which we thus believe may be reduced to " knowledge " because there may be

[9] In his fuller discussion in his " Foundations of Knowledge," 1900, Part
iii. chap. 1, Dr. Ormond tells us that what positively characterizes belief as
over against knowledge is, subjectively, that " the volitional motive begins to
dominate the epistemological" (p. 306), and, objectively, that the quality
of " coerciveness " (p. 307) is lacking. The two criteria come very much to the
same thing.

proofs of their reality available which were not, or not fully, present to our minds "when we believed." Others of them may be incapable of such reduction either because no such proofs of their truth or reality exist, or because those proofs are not accessible to us. But our acceptance of them all alike as true rests, not on evidence that they are true, but (in whole or in part) on " some subjective interest " or " consideration of value." Failing " knowledge " we may take these things "on faith " — because we perceive that it would be well if they were true, and we cannot believe that that at least is not true of which it is clear to us that it would be in the highest degree well if it were true.

It is not necessary to deny that many things are accepted by men as true and accordant with reality on grounds of subjective interest or considerations of value; or that men may be properly moved to the acceptance of many things as true and real by such considerations. Considerations of value may be powerful arguments — they may even constitute proofs — of truth and reality. But it appears obvious enough that all of those convictions which we know as "beliefs," "faiths " do not rest on "subjective interest or considerations of value" — either wholly or even in part. Indeed, it would be truer to say that none of them rest on subjective interests or considerations of value as such, but whenever such considerations enter into their grounds they enter in as evidences of reality or as factors of mental movement lending vividness and vitality to elements of proper evidence before the mind. Men do not mean by their "faiths," "beliefs " things they would fain were true; they mean things they are convinced are true. Their minds are not resting on considerations of value, but on what they take to be evidences of reality. The employment of these terms to designate " acceptances as true and real " on the ground of subjective interest or of considerations of value represents, therefore, no general usage but is purely an affair of the schools, or rather of a school. And it does violence not only to the general convictions of men but also to the underlying idea of the terms. No terms, in fact, lend themselves

more reluctantly to the expression of a " voluntary acceptance," in any form, than these. As we have already seen, they
carry with them the underlying idea of bindingness, worthiness of acceptance; they express, in Dr. Baldwin's phrase, a
" forced consent "; and whenever we employ them there is
present to the mind a consciousness of grounds on which they
firmly rest as expressive of reality. Whatever may be the
differentia of " belief," " faith " as a specific form of conviction, we may be sure, therefore, that desire or will cannot be
the determining element of the grounds on which this conviction rests. What we gain from Dr. Ormond's definition then is
only the assurance that by " faith " is denoted not all forms
of conviction, but a specific form — that this specific form is
differentiated from other forms by the nature of the grounds
on which the conviction called " faith " rests — and that the
grounds on which this form of conviction rests are not those
of theoretic certitude. The form of conviction which rests on
grounds adapted to give " theoretic certitude " we call " knowledge." What the special character of the grounds on which
the form of conviction we call " faith " rests remains yet to
seek.

This gain, although we may speak of it as, for the main
matter, only negative, is not therefore unimportant. To have
learned that in addition to the general usage of " faith," " belief," in which it expresses all " mental endorsement or acceptance " of anything " as real," and is equipollent with the
parallel term " conviction," there is a more confined usage
of it expressing a specific form of " conviction " in contrast
with the form of conviction called " knowledge," is itself an
important gain. And to learn further that the specific character of the form of conviction which we call " knowledge " is
that it rests on grounds which give " theoretic certitude," is
an important aid, by way of elimination, in fixing on the
specific characteristic of the form of conviction which in contrast to " knowledge " we call " faith." " Faith " we know now
is a form of conviction which arises differently to " theoretic
certitude "; and if certain bases for its affirmation of reality

which have been suggested have been excluded in the discussion — such as that it rests on a volition or a series of volitions, on considerations of value rather than of reality, on evidence only subjectively but not objectively adequate — the way seems pretty well cleared for a positive determination of precisely what it is that it does rest on. We have at least learned that while distinguishing it from "knowledge," which is conviction of the order of "theoretic certitude," we must find some basis for "faith," "belief" which will preserve its full character as "conviction" and not sublimate it into a wish or a will, a conjectural hypothesis or a mistake.

It was long ago suggested that what we call "faith," "belief," as contradistinguished from "knowledge," is conviction grounded in authority, as distinguished from conviction grounded in reason. "We *know*," says Augustine, "what rests upon *reason;* we *believe* what rests upon *authority*"; and Sir William Hamilton pronounces this "accurately" said.[10] It is not intended of course to represent "faith," "belief" as irrational, any more than it is intended to represent "knowledge" as free from all dependence on taking-on-trust. It was fully recognized by Augustine — as by Sir William Hamilton — that an activity of reason underlies all "faith," and an act of "faith" underlies all knowledge. "But reason itself," says Sir William Hamilton, expounding Augustine's dictum,[11] "must rest at last upon authority; for the original data of reason do not rest on reason, but are necessarily accepted by reason on the authority of what is beyond itself. These data are, therefore, in rigid propriety, *Beliefs* or *Trusts*. Thus it is, that in the last resort, we must, perforce, philosophically admit, that *belief* is the primary condition of reason, and not reason the ultimate ground of *belief*." With equal frankness Augustine allows that reason underlies all acts of faith. That mental act which we call "faith," he remarks, is one possible only to rational creatures, and of course we act as rational

[10] "The Works of Thomas Reid," ed. 2, 1849, p. 760 (Note A, § v.).
[11] *Loc. cit.*

beings in performing it; [12] and we never believe anything until we have found it worthy of our belief.[13] As we cannot accord faith, then, without perceiving good grounds for according it, reason as truly underlies faith as faith reason. It is with no intention, then, of denying or even obscuring this interaction of faith and knowledge — what may be justly called their interdependence — that they are distinguished from one another in their secondary applications as designating two distinguishable modes of conviction, the one resting on reason, the other on authority. What is intended is to discriminate the proximate grounds on which the mental consent designated by the one and the other rests. When the proximate ground of our conviction is reason, we call it "knowledge"; when it is authority we call it "faith," "belief." Or to put it in other but equivalent terms, we know what we are convinced of on the ground of perception: we believe what we are convinced of on the ground of testimony. "With respect to things we have seen or see," says Augustine,[14] "we are our own witnesses; but with respect to those we believe, we are moved to faith by other witnesses." We cannot believe, any more than we can know, without adequate grounds; it is not faith but "credulity" to accord credit to insufficient evidence; and an unreasonable faith is no faith at all. But we are moved to this act of conviction by the evidence of testimony, by the force of authority — rationally determined to be trustworthy — and not by the immediate perception of our own rational understandings.[15] In a word, while both knowing and believing are states of conviction, sureness — and the surety may be equally strong — they rest proximately on different grounds. Knowledge is seeing, faith is crediting.[16]

[12] Ep. 120, [i.] 3 ("Opera Omnia," Paris, ii. 1836, col. 518): "we should not be able to believe if we did not have rational minds."

[13] "De prædestinatione sanctorum," [ii.] 5 ("Opera Omnia," X. i. 1838, col. 1349).   [14] Ep. 147, [iii.] 8 ("Opera Omnia," ii. 1836, col. 709).

[15] On Augustine's doctrine of Faith and Reason see *The Princeton Theological Review*, v. 1907, pp. 389 ff. (or B. B. Warfield, "Studies in Tertullian and Augustine," 1930, pp. 170 ff.).

[16] This conception of "faith" naturally became traditional. Thus e.g. Reginald Pecock (middle of the fifteenth century) defines faith as "a knowyng

It powerfully commends this conception of the distinction between faith and knowledge, that it employs these terms to designate a distinction which is undoubtedly real. Whatever we choose to call these two classes of convictions, these two classes of convictions unquestionably exist. As Augustine puts it, " no one doubts that we are impelled to the acquisition of knowledge by a double impulse — of authority and of reason." [17] We do possess convictions which are grounded in our own rational apprehension; and we do possess convictions which are grounded in our recognition of authority. We are erecting no artificial categories, then, when we distinguish between these two classes of convictions and label them respectively " knowledges " and " beliefs," " faiths." At the worst we are only applying to real distinctions artificial labels. It may possibly be said that there is no reason in the fitness of things why we should call those convictions which are of the order of " theoretical certitude," knowledge; and those which represent the certitude born of approved testimony, faith. But it cannot be said that no two such categories exist. It is patent to all of us, that some of our convictions rest on our own

---

wherbi we assenten to eny thing as to trouth, for as mych as we have sure evydencis gretter than to the contrarie that it is toold and affermid to us to be trewe, bi him of whom we have sure evydencis, or notable likli evydencis, gretter than to the contrarie, that therinne he not lied " (" The Folewer to the Donet," f. 28, cited in J. L. Morison's " Reginald Pecock's Book of Faith," 1909, p. 85). Here we have " faith " resting on evidence; and the specific evidence on which it rests, testimony. Accordingly he defines Christian faith thus: " that feith, of which we speken now, into which we ben bounde, and which is oon of the foundementis of Cristen religioun, is thilke kinde or spice of knowyng, which a man gendrith and getith into his undirstonding, principali bi the telling or denouncing of another persoone, which may not lie, or which is God " (" The Booke of Faith," I. i. f. 9a, Morison's edition, p. 123). At the end of the discussion (f. 10a) Pecock plainly adds: " and bi this maner of his geting and gendring, feith is dyvers from other kindis and spicis of kunnyngis, which a man gendrith and getith into his undirstonding bi bisynes and labour of his natural resoun, bi biholding upon the causis or effectis or circumstancis in nature of the conclusioun or trouthe, and withoute eny attendaunce maad to eny sure teller or denouncer, that thilk conclusioun is a trouthe."

[17] " Contra academicos," iii. [xx.] 43 (" Opera Omnia," Paris, i. 1836, col. 488). Cf. " De ordine," ii. [ix.] 26 (" Opera Omnia," i. coll. 568 f.).

rational perception of reality, and that others of them rest on the authority exercised over us by tested testimony. The only question which can arise is whether "knowledge," "faith" are appropriate designations by which to call these two classes of convictions.

No one, of course, would think of denying that the two terms "knowledge," and "faith," "belief" are frequently employed as wholly equivalent — each designating simply a conviction, without respect to the nature of its grounds. Augustine already recognized this broad use of both terms to cover the whole ground of convictions.[18] But neither can it be denied that they are often brought into contrast with one another as expressive each of a particular class of convictions, distinguishable from one another. The distinction indicated, no doubt, is often a distinction not in the nature of the evidence on which the several classes of conviction rest but in — shall we say the firmness, the clearness, the force of the conviction? The difficulty of finding the exact word to employ here may perhaps be instructive. When we say, for example, " I do not *know* it — but I fully *believe* it," is it entirely clear that we are using " knowledge " merely of a higher degree of conviction than " faith " expresses? No doubt such a higher degree of conviction is intimated when, for example, to express the force of our conviction of a matter which nevertheless we are assured of only by testimony, we say emphatically, " I do not merely *believe* it; I *know* it." But may it not be that it would be more precise to say that " knowledge " even here expresses primarily rather a more direct and immediate grounding of conviction, and " faith," " belief " a more remote and mediate grounding of it — and that it is out of this primary meaning of the two terms that a secondary usage of them has arisen to express what on the surface appears as differing grades of convictions, but in the ultimate analysis is really differing relations of immediacy of the evidence on which the conviction rests? It adds not a little to the commendation of the distinction between " knowledge " and

18 " Retractationes," I. xiv. 3 (" Opera Omnia," i. coll. 52 f.).

" faith " under discussion, at all events, that it provides a starting-point on the assumption of which other current usages of the terms may find ready and significant explanations.

When we come to inquire after the special appropriateness of the employment of the terms " faith," " belief " to designate those convictions which rest on authority or testimony, in distinction from those which rest on our immediate perception (physical or mental), attention should be directed to an element in " faith," " belief " of which we have as yet spoken little but which seems always present and indeed characteristic. This is the element of trust. There is an element of trust lying at the bottom of all our convictions, even those which we designate " knowledge," because, as we say, they are of the order of " theoretic certitude," or " rational assurance." " The original data of reason," says Sir William Hamilton truly, " do not rest on reason, but are necessarily accepted by reason on the authority of what is beyond itself." " These data," he adds, " are, therefore, in rigid propriety, *Beliefs* or *Trusts*." The collocation of the terms here, " beliefs or trusts," should be observed; it betrays the propinquity of the two ideas. To say that an element of trust underlies all our knowledge is therefore equivalent to saying that our knowledge rests on belief. The conceptions of believing and trusting go, then, together; and what we have now to suggest is that it is this open implication of " trust " in the conception of " belief," " faith " which rules the usage of these terms.

There is, we have said, an element of trust in all our convictions, and therefore " faith," " belief " may be employed of them all. And when convictions are distinguished from convictions, the convictions in which the element of trust is most prominent tend to draw to themselves the designations of " faith," " belief." It is not purely arbitrary, therefore, that those convictions which rest on our rational perceptions are called " knowledge," while those which rest on " authority " or " testimony " receive the name of " belief," " faith." It is because the element of trust is, not indeed more really, but more prominently, present in the latter than in the former.

We perceive and feel the element of trust in according our mental assent to facts brought to us by the testimony of others and accepted as facts on their authority as we do not in the findings of our own rational understandings. And therefore we designate the former matters of faith, belief, and the latter matters of knowledge. Knowing, we then say, is seeing; believing is crediting. And that is only another way of saying that " knowledge " is the appropriate designation of those convictions which rest on our own mental perceptions, while " faith," " belief " is the appropriate designation of those convictions which rest on testimony or authority. While we may use either term broadly for all convictions, we naturally employ them with this discrimination when they are brought in contrast with one another.

It appears, therefore, not only that we are here in the presence of two classes of convictions — the difference between which is real — but that when these two classes are designated respectively by the terms " knowledge " and " faith," " belief " they are appropriately designated. These designations suggest the real difference which exists between the two classes of convictions. Matters of faith, matters of belief are different from matters of knowledge — not as convictions less clear, firm, or well-grounded, not as convictions resting on grounds less objectively valid, not as convictions determined rather by desire, will, than by evidence — but as convictions resting on grounds less direct and immediate to the soul, and therefore involving a more prominent element of trust, in a word, as convictions grounded in authority, testimony as distinguished from convictions grounded in rational proof. The two classes of convictions are psychologically just convictions; they are alike, in Dr. Baldwin's phrase, " forced consents "; they rest equally on evidence and are equally the product of evidence; they may be equally clear, firm, and assured; but they rest on differing kinds of evidence and differ, therefore, in accordance with this difference of kind in the evidence on which they rest. In " knowledge " as the mental response to rational considerations, the movement of the intellect is prominent to the obscuration of all else. Of course the whole man is active in " knowledge " too — for it is the man in his complex presentation who is the subject of the knowledge. But it is " reason " which is prominent in the activity which assures itself of reality on grounds of mental perception. In " faith," on the other hand, as the mental response to testimony, authority, the movement of the sensibility in the form of trust is what is thrust forward to observation. Of course, every other faculty is involved in the act of belief — and particularly the intellectual faculties to which the act of " crediting " belongs; but what attracts the attention of the subject is the prominence in this act of crediting, of the element of trust which has retired into the background in those other acts of assent which we know as " knowledge." " Faith " then emerges as the appropriate name of those acts of mental consent in which the element of trust is prominent. Knowledge is seeing; faith, belief, is trusting.

In what we call religious faith this prominent implication of trust reaches its height. Religious belief may differ from other belief only in the nature of its objects; religious beliefs are beliefs which have religious conceptions as their contents. But the complex of emotions which accompany acts of assent to propositions of religious content, and form the concrete state of mind of the believer, is of course indefinitely different from that which accompanies any other act of believing. What is prominent in this state of mind is precisely trust. Trust is the active expression of that sense of dependence in which religion largely consists, and it is its presence in these acts of faith, belief, which communicates to them their religious quality and raises them from mere beliefs of propositions, the contents of which happen to be of religious purport, to acts possessed of religious character. It is the nature of trust to seek a personal object on which to repose, and it is only natural, therefore, that what we call religious faith does not reach its height in assent to propositions of whatever religious content and however well fitted to call out religious trust, but comes to its rights only when it rests with adoring trust on a person. The extension of the terms "faith," "belief" to express an attitude of mind towards a person, does not wait, of course, on their religious application. We speak familiarly of believing in, or having faith in, persons in common life; and we perceive at once that our justification in doing so rests on the strong implication of trust resident in the terms. It has been suggested not without justice, that the terms show everywhere a tendency to gravitate towards such an application.[19] This element at all events becomes so prominent in the culminating act of religious faith when it rests on the person of God our benefactor, or of Christ our Saviour, as to absorb the prior implication of crediting almost altogether. Faith in God, and above all, faith in Jesus Christ, is just trust in Him in its purity. Thus in its higher applications the element of trust which is present in faith in all its applications, grows more and more prominent until it finishes by becoming well-nigh the entire connotation of the term; and "to believe in," "to have faith in" comes to mean simply "entrust yourself to." When "faith" can come thus to mean just "trust" we cannot wonder that it is the implication of "trust" in the term which rules its usage and determines its applications throughout the whole course of its development.

The justification of the application of the terms "believing," "faith" to these high religious acts of entrusting oneself to a person does not rest, however, entirely upon the circumstance that the element of trust which in these acts absorbs attention is present in all other acts of faith and only here comes into full prominence. It rests also on the circumstance that all the other constituent elements of acts of faith, belief, in the general connotation of these terms, are present in these acts of religious faith. The more general acts of faith, belief and

[19] "It is the nature and tendency of the word," says Bishop Moule, "to go out towards a person. . . . When we speak of having Faith we habitually direct the notion either towards a veritable person, or towards something which we personify in the mind. . . . I do not attempt to explain the fact, as fact I think it is. Perhaps we may trace in it a far-off echo of that primeval Sanskrit word whose meaning is 'to bind' . . ." ("Faith: its Nature and its Work," 1909, pp. 10–11).

the culminating acts of religious belief, faith, that is, differ from one another only in the relative prominence in each of elements common to both. For example, religious faith at its height — the act by which we turn trustingly to a Being conceived as our Righteous Governor, in whose hands is our destiny, or to a Being conceived as our Divine Saviour, through whom we may be restored from our sin, and entrust ourselves to Him — is as little a matter of " the will" and as truly a " forced " consent as is any other act called faith, belief. The engagement of the whole man in the act — involving the response of all the elements of his nature — is no doubt more observable in these highest acts of faith than in the lower, as it is altogether natural it should be from the mere fact that they are the highest exercises of faith. But the determination of the response by the appropriate evidence — its dependence on evidence as its ground — is no less stringent or plain. Whenever we obtain a clear conception of the rise in the human soul of religious faith as exercised thus at its apex as saving trust in Christ we perceive with perfect plainness that it rests on evidence as its ground.

It is not unusual for writers who wish to represent religious faith in the form of saving trust in Christ as an act of the will to present the case in the form of a strict alternative. This faith, they say, is an exercise not of the intellect but of the heart. And then they proceed to develop an argument, aiming at a *reductio ad absurdum* of the notion that saving faith can possibly be conceived as a mere assent of the intellect. A simple assent of the mind, we are told, " always depends upon the nature and amount of proof " presented, and is in a true sense " involuntary." When a proposition is presented and sufficiently supported by proof " a mind in a situation to appreciate the proof believes inevitably." " If the proposition or doctrine is not supported by proof, or if the mind is incapable, from any cause, of appreciating the proof, unbelief or doubt is equally certain." " Such a theory of faith would, therefore, suspend our belief or unbelief, and consequently our salvation or damnation, upon the manner in which truth is presented to

our minds, or our intellectual capability of its appreciation."
" To express the whole matter briefly," concludes the writer
whose argument we have been following, " it excludes the exercise of the will, and makes faith or unbelief a matter of
necessity." [20]

It is not necessary to pause to examine this argument in
detail. What it is at the moment important to point out is that
the fullest agreement that saving faith is a matter not of the
intellect but of the heart, that it is " confidence " rather than
" conviction," does not exclude the element of intelligent assent from it altogether, or escape the necessity of recognizing
that it rests upon evidence. Is the " confidence " which faith
in this its highest exercise has become, an ungrounded confidence? A blind and capricious act of the soul's due to a purely
arbitrary determination of the will? Must it not rest on a perceived — that is to say a well-grounded — trustworthiness in
the object on which it reposes? In a word, it is clear enough
that a conviction lies beneath this confidence, a conviction of
the trustworthiness of the object; and that this conviction is
produced like other convictions, just by evidence. Is it not
still true, then, that the confidence in which saving faith consists is inevitable if the proof of the trustworthiness of the object on which it reposes is sufficient — or as we truly phrase it,
" compelling " — and the mind is in a situation to appreciate
this proof; and doubt is inevitable if the proof is insufficient
or the mind is incapable from any cause of appreciating the
proof? Is not the confidence which is the faith of the heart,
therefore, in any case, as truly as the conviction which is the
faith of the intellect, suspended " upon the manner in which
truth is presented," or our " capability of its appreciation "?
In a word, is it not clear that the assent of the intelligence is
an inamissible element of faith even in its highest exercises,
and it never comes to be an arbitrary " matter of choice," in
which I may do " as I choose "? [21] For the exercise of this faith
must there not then always be present to the mind, (1) the

[20] Dr. Richard Beard, " Lectures on Theology," ii. 1871, pp. 362–363.
[21] Dr. Beard, as cited, p. 364.

object on which it is to repose in confidence; (2) adequate grounds for the exercise of this confidence in the object? And must not the mind be in a situation to appreciate these grounds? Here, too, faith is, in Dr. Baldwin's phrase, a " forced consent," and is the product of evidence.

The impulse of the writer whose views we have just been considering to make " saving faith " a so-called " act of free volition " is derived from the notion that only thus can man be responsible for his faith. It is a sufficiently odd notion, however, that if our faith be determined by reasons and these reasons are good, we are not responsible for it, because forsooth, we then " believe inevitably " and our faith is " a matter of necessity." Are we to hold that responsibility attaches to faith only when it does not rest on good reasons, or in other words is ungrounded, or insufficiently grounded, and is therefore arbitrary? In point of fact, we are responsible for our volitions only because our volitions are never arbitrary acts of a faculty within us called " will," but the determined acts of our whole selves, and therefore represent us. And we are responsible for our faith in precisely the same way because it is *our* faith, and represents us. For it is to be borne in mind that faith, though resting on evidence and thus in a true sense, as Professor Baldwin calls it, a " forced consent," is not in such a sense the result of evidence that the mind is passive in believing — that the evidence when adequate objectively is always adequate subjectively, or vice versa, quite independently of the state of the mind that believes. Faith is an act of the mind, and can come into being only by an act of the mind, expressive of its own state. There are two factors in the production of faith. On the one hand, there is the evidence on the ground of which the faith is yielded. On the other hand, there is the subjective condition by virtue of which the evidence can take effect in the appropriate act of faith. There can be no belief, faith without evidence; it is on evidence that the mental exercise which we call belief, faith rests; and this exercise or state of mind cannot exist apart from its ground in evidence. But evidence cannot produce belief, faith, except in a mind open to this evidence, and capable of receiving, weighing, and responding to it. A mathematical demonstration is demonstrative proof of the proposition demonstrated. But even such a demonstration cannot produce conviction in a mind incapable of following the demonstration. Where musical taste is lacking, no evidence which derives its force from considerations of melody can work conviction. No conviction, whether of the order of what we call knowledge or of faith, can be produced by considerations to which the mind to be convinced is inhabile.

Something more, then, is needed to produce belief, faith, besides the evidence which constitutes its ground. The evidence may be objectively sufficient, adequate, overwhelming. The subjective effect of belief, faith is not produced unless this evidence is also adapted to the mind, and to the present state of that mind, which is to be convinced. The mind, itself, therefore — and the varying states of the mind — have their parts to play in the production of belief, faith; and the effect which is so designated is not the mechanical result of the adduction of the evidence. No faith without evidence; but not, no evidence without faith. There may stand in the way of the proper and objectively inevitable effect of the evidence, the subjective nature or condition to which the evidence is addressed. This is the ground of responsibility for belief, faith; it is not merely a question of evidence but of subjectivity; and subjectivity is the other name for personality. Our action under evidence is the touchstone by which is determined what we are. If evidence which is objectively adequate is not subjectively adequate the fault is in us. If we are not accessible to musical evidence, then we are by nature unmusical, or in a present state of unmusicalness. If we are not accessible to moral evidence, then we are either unmoral, or, being moral beings, immoral. The evidence to which we are accessible is irresistible if adequate, and irresistibly produces belief, faith. And no belief, faith can arise except on the ground of evidence duly apprehended, appreciated, weighed. We may cherish opinions without evidence, or with inadequate evidence; but not possess faith any more than knowledge. All convictions of whatever order are the products of evidence in a mind accessible to the evidence appropriate to these particular convictions.

These things being so, it is easy to see that the sinful heart — which is enmity towards God — is incapable of that supreme act of trust in God — or rather of entrusting itself to God, its Saviour — which has absorbed into itself the term " faith " in its Christian connotation. And it is to avoid this conclusion that many have been tempted to make faith not a rational act of conviction passing into confidence, resting on adequate grounds in testimony, but an arbitrary act of sheer will, produced no one knows how. This is not, however, the solution of the difficulty offered by the Christian revelation. The solution it offers is frankly to allow the impossibility of " faith " to the sinful heart and to attribute it, therefore, to the gift of God. Not, of course, as if this gift were communicated to man in some mechanical manner, which would ignore or do violence to his psychological constitution or to the psychological nature of the act of faith. The mode of the divine giving of faith is represented rather as involving the creation by God the Holy Spirit of a capacity for faith under the evidence submitted. It proceeds by the divine illumination of the understanding, softening of the heart, and quickening of the will, so that the man so affected may freely and must inevitably perceive the force and yield to the compelling power of the evidence of the trustworthiness of Jesus Christ as Saviour submitted to him in the gospel. In one word the capacity for faith and the inevitable emergence in the heart of faith are attributed by the Christian revelation to that great act of God the Holy Spirit which has come in Christian theology to be called by the significant name of Regeneration. If sinful man as such is incapable of the act of faith, because he is inhabile to the evidence on which alone such an act of confident resting on God the Saviour can repose, renewed man is equally incapable of not responding to this evidence, which is objectively compelling, by an act of sincere faith. In this its highest exercise faith thus, though in a true sense the gift of God, is in an equally true sense man's own act, and bears all the character of faith as it is exercised by unrenewed man in its lower manifestations.

It may conduce to a better apprehension of the essential nature of faith and its relation to the evidence in which it is grounded, if we endeavor to form some notion of the effect of this evidence on the minds of men in the three great stages of their life on earth — as sinless in Paradise, as sinful, as regenerated by the Spirit of God into newness of life. Like every other creature, man is of course absolutely dependent on God. But unlike many other creatures, man, because in his very nature self-conscious, is conscious of his dependence on God; his relation of dependence on God is not merely a fact but a fact of his self-consciousness. This dependence is not confined to any one element of human nature but runs through the whole of man's nature; and as self-conscious being man is conscious of his absolute dependence on God, physically, psychically, morally, spiritually. It is this comprehensive consciousness of dependence on God for and in all the elements of his nature and life, which is the fundamental basis in humanity of faith, in its general religious sense. This faith is but the active aspect of the consciousness of dependence, which, therefore, is the passive aspect of faith. In this sense no man exists, or ever has existed or ever will exist, who has not " faith." But this " faith " takes very different characters in man as unfallen and as fallen and as renewed.

In unfallen man, the consciousness of dependence on God is far from a bare recognition of a fact; it has a rich emotional result in the heart. This emotional product of course includes fear, in the sense of awe and reverence. But its peculiar quality is just active and loving trust. Sinless man delights to be dependent on God and trusts Him wholly. He perceives God as his creator, upholder, governor, and bountiful benefactor, and finds his joy in living, moving, and having his being in Him. All the currents of his life turn to Him for direction and control. In this spontaneous trust of sinless man we have faith at its purest.

Now when man fell, the relation in which he stood to God was fundamentally altered. Not as if he ceased to be dependent on God, in every sphere of his being and activity. Nor even as if he ceased to be conscious of this his comprehensive dependence on God. Even as sinner man cannot but believe in God; the very devils believe and tremble. He cannot escape the knowledge that he is utterly dependent on God for all that he is and does. But his consciousness of dependence on God no longer takes the form of glad and loving trust. Precisely what sin has done to him is to render this trust impossible. Sin has destroyed the natural relation between God and His creature in which the creature trusts God, and has instituted a new relation, which conditions all his immanent as well as transient activities Godward. The sinner is at enmity with God and can look to God only for punishment. He knows himself absolutely dependent on God, but in knowing this, he knows himself absolutely in the power of his enemy. A fearful looking forward to judgment conditions all his thought of God. Faith has accordingly been transformed into unfaith; trust into distrust. He expects evil and only evil from God. Knowing himself to be dependent on God he seeks to be as independent of Him as he can. As he thinks of God, misery and fear and hatred take the place of joy and trust and love. Instinctively and by his very nature the sinner, not being able to escape from his belief in God, yet cannot possibly have faith in God, that is trust Him, entrust himself to Him.

The reëstablishment of *this* faith in the sinner must be the act not of the sinner himself but of God. This because the sinner has no power to render God gracious, which is the objective root, or to look to God for favor, which is the subjective root of faith in the fiducial sense. Before he can thus believe there must intervene the atoning work of Christ canceling the guilt by which the sinner is kept under the wrath of God, and the recreative work of the Holy Spirit by which the sinner's heart is renewed in the love of God. There is not required a creation of something entirely new, but only a restoration of an old relation and a renewal therewith of an old disposition.

Accordingly, although faith in the renewed man bears a different character from faith in unfallen man, inasmuch as it is trust in God not merely for general goodness but for the specific blessing of salvation — that is to say it is soteriological — it yet remains essentially the same thing as in unfallen man. It is in the one case as in the other just trust — that trust which belongs of nature to man as man in relation to his God. And, therefore, though in renewed man it is a gift of God's grace, it does not come to him as something alien to his nature. It is beyond the powers of his nature as sinful man; but it is something which belongs to human nature as such, which has been lost through sin and which can be restored only by the power of God. In this sense faith remains natural even in the renewed sinner, and the peculiar character which belongs to it as the act of a sinner, namely its soteriological reference, only conditions and does not essentially alter it. Because man is a sinner his faith terminates not immediately on God, but immediately on the mediator, and only through His mediation on God; and it is proximately trust in this mediator for salvation — relief from the guilt and corruption of sin — and only mediately through this relief for other goods. But it makes its way through these intermediating elements to terminate ultimately on God Himself and to rest on Him for all goods. And thus it manifests its fundamental and universal character as trust in God, recognized by the renewed sinner, as by the unfallen creature, as the inexhaustible fountain to His creatures of all blessedness, in whom to live and move and have his being is the creature's highest felicity.

In accordance with the nature of this faith the Protestant theologians have generally explained that faith includes in itself the three elements of *notitia, assensus, fiducia*. Their primary object has been, no doubt, to protest against the Romish conception which limits faith to the assent of the understanding. The stress of the Protestant definition lies therefore upon the fiducial element. This stress has not led Protestant theologians generally, however, to eliminate from the conception of faith the elements of understanding and assent. No doubt this has been done by some, and it is perhaps not rare even to-day to hear it asserted that faith is so purely trust that there is no element of assent in it at all. And no doubt theologians have differed among themselves as to whether all these elements are to be counted as included in faith, or some of them treated rather as preliminary steps to faith or effects of faith. But speaking broadly Protestant theologians have reckoned all these elements as embraced within the mental movement we call faith itself; and they have obviously been right in so doing. Indeed, we may go further and affirm that all three of these elements are always present in faith — not only in that culminating form of faith which was in the mind of the theologians in question — saving faith in Christ — but in every movement of faith whatever, from the lowest to the highest instances of its exercise. No true faith has arisen unless there has been a perception of the object to be believed or believed in, an assent to its worthiness to be believed or believed in, and a commitment of ourselves to it as true and trustworthy. We cannot be said to believe or to trust in a thing or person of which we have no knowledge; " implicit faith " in this sense is an absurdity. Of course we cannot be said to believe or to trust the thing or person to whose worthiness of our belief or trust assent has not been obtained. And equally we cannot be said to believe that which we distrust too much to commit ourselves to it. In every movement of faith, therefore, from the lowest to the highest, there is an intellectual, an emotional, and a voluntary element, though naturally these elements vary in their relative prominence in the several movements of faith. This is only as much as to say that it is the man who believes, who is the subject of faith, and the man in the entirety of his being as man. The central movement in all faith is no doubt the element of assent; it is that which constitutes the mental movement so called a movement of conviction. But the movement of assent must depend, as it always does depend, on a movement, not specifically of the will, but of the intellect; the *assensus* issues from the *notitia*. The movement of the sensibilities which we call " trust," is on the contrary the product of the assent. And it is in this movement of the sensibilities that faith fulfills itself, and it is by it that, as specifically " faith," it is " formed."

XII

THE ARCHÆOLOGY
OF THE MODE OF BAPTISM

THE ARCHÆOLOGY
OF THE MODE OF BAPTISM [1]

It is rather striking to observe the diversity which has grown up in the several branches of the Christian Church in the mode of administering the initiatory rite of Christianity. Throughout the whole West, affusion is in use. The ritual of the great Latin Church directs as follows: " Then the godfather or godmother, or both, holding the infant, the priest takes the baptismal water in a little vessel or jug, and pours the same three times upon the head of the infant in the form of the cross, and at the same time he says, uttering the words once only, distinctly and attentively: ' N, I baptize thee in the name of the Father,' — he pours first; ' and of the Son ' — he pours a second time; ' and of the Holy Ghost ' — he pours the third time." Here is a trine affusion. With the exception of the large Baptist denominations, Protestants use a single affusion. The Baptists employ a single immersion. Throughout the East a trine immersion is the rule. Although practice seems sometimes to vary whether all three immersions shall be total,[2] the Orthodox Greek Church insists somewhat strenuously upon trine immersion. The ritual in use in the Russian Church directs as follows: " And after he has anointed the whole body the Priest baptizes the candidate, held erect and looking towards the east, and says: ' The servant (handmaid) of God, N, is baptized in the Name of the Father, Amen; and of the Son, Amen; and of the Holy Ghost, Amen; now and ever, and to ages of ages, Amen.' At each invocation he immerses the candidate and raises him again." [3] Significant variations ob-

---

[1] Reprinted from *Bibliotheca Sacra*, liii. 1896, pp. 601–644.

[2] Cf. Schaff, " The Oldest Church Manual, called the Teaching of the Twelve Apostles," 1886, pp. 42–43.

[3] Bjerring, " The Offices of the Oriental Church," 1884, pp. 94 f.; cf. p. xxiv.

tain, however, among the other Oriental communions. The Nestorians, for example, cause the candidate to stand erect in water reaching to the neck, and dip the head three times.[4] The Syrians, whether Jacobite or Maronite, place the candidate upright on his feet and pour water three times over his head in the name of the Trinity.[5] The office of the Syrian Church of Jerusalem provides as follows: "The priest . . . first lets the candidate down into the baptistery. Then laying his right hand on the head of the person to be baptized, with his left hand he takes up water successively from before, behind, and from each side of the candidate, and pours it upon his head, and washes his whole body (*funditque super caput ejus, et abluit totum ipsius corpus*)." [6] In the Coptic Church the custom has become fixed for the priest to dip the body the first time up to the middle, the second time up to the neck, and the third time over the head.[7] Sometimes, however, apparently, the actual practice is that the child is dipped only up to the neck, and the immersion is completed by pouring the water over the head.[8] The Armenians duplicate the rite in a very odd way. Among them, we are told, "the priest asks the child's name, and on hearing it, lets the child down into the water, saying, '*This N, servant of God, who is come from the state of childhood* (or from the state of a Catechumen) *to Baptism, is baptized in the Name of the Father, and of the Son, and of the Holy Ghost.*' . . . While saying this the priest buries the child (or Catechumen) three times in the water, as a figure of Christ's three days' burial. Then taking the child out of the

[4] Denzinger, "Ritus Orientalium, Coptorum, Syrorum et Armenorum in administrandis sacramentis," i. 1863, p. 17; Butler, "The Ancient Coptic Churches of Egypt," ii. 1884, p. 267. Cf. the ritual in Denzinger, i. p. 381.

[5] Denzinger, *loc. cit.* Cf. Washburn, the New York *Independent*, August 7, 1884.

[6] I have quoted the words from Egbert C. Smyth (*Andover Review*, i. 1884, p. 540), who takes them from Chrystal's "History of the Modes of Christian Baptism." Cf. Denzinger, as above, p. 17, and for actual forms, pp. 277, 287, 307.

[7] Butler, "The Ancient Coptic Churches of Egypt," ii. p. 267; also Bernat, as quoted by Denzinger, *loc. cit.*

[8] Schaff, "The Oldest Church Manual," 1886, p. 43, note †.

water he thrice pours a handful of water on its head, saying, ' *As many of you as have been baptized into Christ have
put on Christ. Hallelujah! As many of you as have been
enlightened of the Father, the Holy Spirit is put into you.
Hallelujah!* ' " [9]

If we neglect for the moment the usages of minor divisions
of the Church, we may say that the practice of the Church is
divided into an Eastern and a Western mode. Broadly speaking, the East baptizes by a trine immersion; the West by
affusion. When we scrutinize the history of these differing
practices, however, we quickly learn that, with whatever unessential variations in details, the usage of the East runs back
into a high antiquity; while there are indications on the surface of the Western usage that it is comparatively recent in
origin, and survivals of an older custom persist side by side
with it. To be sure, the immersion as practised by the Protestant Baptists can scarcely be numbered among these survivals. The original Baptists apparently did not immerse; and
Dr. Dexter appears to have shown that even the first English
Baptists who seceded from the Puritan emigrants and formed
a congregation at Amsterdam, baptized by affusion.[10] It would
seem that it was by the English Baptists of the seventeenth
century that immersion was first declared to be essential to
valid baptism; and the practice of immersion by them can be
looked upon as a survival from an earlier time only in the
sense that it was a return to an earlier custom, although with
the variation of a single instead of a trine immersion. We may
more properly designate as a survival the practice of immersion which has subsisted in the great cathedral of Milan [11] —

[9] I have quoted this from Smith and Cheetham, " A Dictionary of
Christian Antiquities," i. 1875, p. 169a. But cf. Denzinger, *loc. cit.*, and for the
ritual itself, pp. 387 and 395, where, however, the order of the two halves of
the rite differs from that given above, and in both cases the actual baptism
is connected with the affusion, and the burial is separated from it.

[10] Schaff, as above, p. 53, note ‡; cf. in general Whitsitt, article " Baptists," in " Johnson's Universal Cyclopædia " (new edition, 1894).

[11] Stanley, " Lectures on the History of the Eastern Church," 1865,
p. 117; Augusti, " Handbuch der christlichen Archäologie," ii. 1836, p. 399.

a diocese in which many peculiar customs survive to remind us of its original independence of Rome. The Roman ritual itself, indeed, continues to provide for immersion as well as for affusion, the rubric reading: " If he baptizes by immersion, the priest retaining the mitre, rises and takes the infant; and being careful not to hurt it, cautiously immerses its head in the water, and baptizing with a trine immersion, says only a single time: ' *N, I baptize thee in the name of the Father, and of the Son, and of the Holy Spirit.'* " A similar survival appears in the Anglican Prayer Book,[12] the rubric in which runs as follows: " Then the priest shall take the child into his hands, and shall say to the godfathers and godmothers, ' *Name this child.*' And then, naming it after them (if they shall certify him that the child may well endure it), he shall dip it into the water discreetly and warily, saying, ' *N, I baptize thee in the name of the Father, and of the Son, and of the Holy Ghost. Amen.*' But if they shall certify that the child is weak, it shall suffice to pour water upon it, saying the foresaid words," etc. Here immersion — though a single immersion — is made the rule; and affusion appears only as an exception — although an exception which has in practice become the rule. The Prayer Book of the Protestant Episcopal Church in America accordingly parallels the two modes, the rubric reading: " And then, naming it [the child] after them, he shall dip it in water discreetly or else pour water upon it, saying," etc. A similar reminiscence of the older usage was near being perpetuated in the formularies of the British and American Presbyterian churches. John Lightfoot has preserved for us a curious account of the debate in the Westminster Assembly upon the question whether the new Directory for Worship should recognize immersion alongside of

---

[12] Cf. Augusti, as above, for somewhat similar facts as to the German churches. The first translated " Tauf-Büchlein," of 1523, and its revision of 1524, alike provided: " Da nehme er das Kind und tauche es in die Taufe "; but the Lutheran Agenda and Forms of Baptism give no precise instructions in the matter. Luther is quoted as in one passage expressing a preference for immersion (Walch, Th. x. s. 2593, cf. 2637); but the theologians (though not without exceptions) treated it as a matter of indifference (e.g. Gerhard, " Loci Theologici," t. ix. pp. 144–147).

affusion as an alternative mode of baptism, or should exclude it altogether in favor of affusion. The latter was determined upon; but Lightfoot tells us, " It was voted so indifferently, that we were glad to count names twice: for so many were unwilling to have dipping excluded, that the votes came to an equality within one; for the one side was twenty-four — the other, twenty-five." [13] The guarded clauses which finally took their places in the Westminster Directory and Confession of Faith, reflect the state of opinion in the Assembly revealed by this close vote; and, when read in its light, will not fail to operate to enshrine still a reminiscence of the earlier custom of baptism by immersion. If we will bear in mind the history of the mode of baptism in the English Church as thus exhibited in the formularies framed by her, we shall be at no loss to understand how it came about that the English Baptists desired to revive the custom of immersion, or how it happened that, in reviving it, they gave it the form of a single immersion.

Survivals such as these prepare us to learn that there was a time when immersion was as universal even in the West as in the East. In certain sections, to be sure, as in Southern Gaul and its ecclesiastical daughter, Ireland, affusion appears to have come into quite general use at a very early date. Gennadius of Marseilles (495) already speaks of the two modes of baptism as if they stood upon something like the same plane; he is comparing baptism and martyrdom, and remarks: " The one after his Confession is either wetted with the Water, or else plung'd into it: And the other is either wetted with his

[13] " The Journal of the Proceedings of the Assembly of Divines," for August 7, 1644, in Lightfoot's " Works," ed. Pitman, London, xiii. 1824, pp. 299–300. It is inexplicable how persistently the purport of this vote has been misapprehended. Even Mr. (now Professor) James Heron, in his admirable treatise, " The Church of the Sub-Apostolic Age," London, 1888, p. 140, writes: " I may remark that the vote by which the Westminster Assembly thus pronounced pouring or sprinkling legitimate was a very close one — twenty-five to twenty-four." This was not the vote by which they pronounced affusion legitimate — on that they were unanimously agreed: it was the vote by which they pronounced immersion illegitimate. Nor was the discussion upon the Confession of Faith, xxviii. 3, to which Mr. Heron refers it, but upon the Directory for Worship.

own Blood, or else is plung'd in Fire." [14] By the time of Bonaventura affusion appears to have become the common French
method; a synod at Angiers in 1175 mentions the two as on an
equal footing, while one in 1304, at Langres, mentions pouring
only. Possibly affusion first found a formal place in a baptismal
office in the case of the earliest Irish ritual, in which it is made,
as in the office of the American Protestant Episcopal Church,
alternative with immersion. [15] But it was not until the thirteenth century that it began to become the ruling mode of
baptism on the Continent, [16] and not until after the Reformation, in England. Walafrid Strabo, writing in the ninth century, speaks of it as exceptional only. Thomas Aquinas in the
thirteenth century still represents immersion as the most common and commendable way of baptizing, because of its more
vivid representation of the burial of Christ; and only recommends affusion in case the whole body cannot be wet on account of paucity of water, or some other cause — in which
case, he says, " the head in which is manifested the principle
of animal life, ought to be wet." His contemporary, Bonaventura, while mentioning that affusion was commonly used in
France, gives his own opinion as that " the way of dipping into
water is the more common and the fitter and safer." A council
at Ravenna in 1311, however, declared the two modes equally
valid; and the rubric of the baptismal service edited by Paul V
(1605–1621) treats the matter as entirely indifferent:
" Though baptism may be administered by affusion, or immersion, or aspersion, yet let the first or second mode which
are more in use, be retained, agreeably to the usage of the
churches." [17] The change was much slower in establishing itself
in England. A century before Paul V, Erasmus witnesses:

[14] " De ecclesiasticis dogmatibus," chap. lxxiv. as quoted by Wall, " History of Infant Baptism," ed. 2, 1707, ii. p. 466, whence also the following facts
are derived.

[15] Bennett, " Christian Archæology," 1890, p. 408, quoting Warren, " The
Liturgy and Ritual of the Celtic Church."

[16] Cf. Weiss in Kraus, " Real-Encyklopädie der christlichen Alterthümer,"
ii. 1886, p. 828a.

[17] Schaff, " The Oldest Church Manual," 1886, pp. 44–45.

" With us infants are poured upon; with the English, they are immersed." The first Prayer Book of Edward VI (1549) directs a trine immersion: " first, dypping the right side; secondly, the left side; the third time, dypping the face towards the fronte." Permission is first given to substitute pouring, if the sponsors certify that the child is weak, in the second Prayer Book (1552), and in the same book trine immersion is changed to single immersion. The form at present in use does not appear until the Prayer Book of Charles II (1662).[18]

There is a sense, then, in which we may say broadly that the present diversity in baptismal usage is a growth of time; and that, should we move back within the first millennium of the Church's life, we should find the whole Christian world united in the ordinary use of trine immersion. The meaning of this fact to us will be conditioned, however, by the results of two further lines of inquiry. We should inquire whether this universality of trine immersion was itself the result of ecclesiastical development, or whether it represents primitive, that is, apostolic practice. And we should inquire whether conformity to this mode of baptism was held to be essential to the validity of baptism, or only necessary to the good order of the Church.

The second of these queries is very readily answered. There never was a time when the Church insisted upon immersion as the only valid mode of baptism.[19] The very earliest extant account of baptism, that given in the " Teaching of the Twelve Apostles " (chap. vii.), which comes to us from the first half of the second century, while evidently contemplating ordinary baptism as by immersion, yet freely allows affusion in case of scarcity of water: " But if thou hast neither [living water nor standing water in sufficient quantity], pour water on the head three times, into the name of the Father and Son and Holy Spirit." " We have here," comments Harnack, " for the first time obtained evidence that even the earliest Christians had, under certain conditions, recourse to baptisms by sprinkling — a very

18 Schaff, op. cit., pp. 51–52.
19 Cf. Wall, " History of Infant Baptism," ed. 2, 1707, ii. p. 463.

important point, since it shows that the scruples about baptisms in this manner were only of late origin in the Catholic Church." [20] "You have here," comments Funk,[21] "the oldest witness for the form of affusion or aspersion in administering baptism. . . . Notice also that the author holds that form valid with certitude. . . ." From that day to this, the Church as a whole has allowed the validity of baptism by affusion, in case of necessity, whether the necessity arise from scarcity of water or from weakness of the recipient, rendering immersion a cruelty. Even the Orthodox Greek Church which, in its polemic attitude against Latin affusion, is apt to lay great stress on immersion, is yet forced to admit the validity of affusion in cases of necessity.[22] And Dr. Washburn tells us of the other Oriental churches: "While trine immersion is the general rule, none of the churches in the East insist upon this as in all cases essential. All admit that in exceptional cases other forms are valid. The Jacobites do not practice immersion at all, and the Armenians recognize the full validity of affusion or sprinkling in any case." [23]

The whole case of the validity of clinic baptism — or the baptism of the sick on their bed, ἐν τῇ κλίνῃ, whence they were called κλινικοί, clinici, and more rarely grabatarii, lectularii, or

[20] *The Contemporary Review*, 1. 1886, p. 231. Harnack's comment in his edition of the " Teaching " may be compared: " We have here the oldest evidence for the permission of baptism by aspersion; it is especially important also that the author betrays not the slightest uncertainty as to its validity. The evidences for an early occurrence of aspersion were hitherto not sufficiently certain, either in respect to their date (as the pictorial representations of aspersion; see Kraus, Roma Sotter. 2. Aufl. S. 311 f.), or in respect to their conclusiveness (Tert. de poenit. 6; de bapt. 12); doubt is now no longer possible. But scruples as to its complete validity may have been primitive in many lands; nevertheless we can appeal to Eus. Hist. eccl. vi. 46; 14, 15 for this only with reserves; while against it we may appeal to Cyprian, Ep. lxix. 12–14, and to the practice of the Orient." — " Die Lehre der Zwölf Apostel," 1884, pp. 23–24.

[21] " Doctrina duodecim apostolorum," Tübingen, 1887, p. 22 (vii. 3).

[22] Cf. Bryennios' comment on the Didache at this point; and Bapheidos as quoted by Schaff, *op. cit.*, p. 42.

[23] *The Independent*, August 7, 1884. Cf. Denzinger, *op. cit.*, pp. 17 f. Dr. Washburn had especially in mind in these words, the Greek, the Armenian, the Armeno-Catholic, and the Jacobite churches.

even *superfusi* — was canvassed by Cyprian in the third century in a manner which seems to show not only that it had been commonly practised, but also that it had not been formally challenged before.[24] He declares that clinic baptism by aspersion has all the necessary elements of baptism, so that all such baptisms are perfect, provided faith is not wanting in ministrant and recipient — the mode of the application of the water not being of essential importance. He argues that, as the contagion of sin is not washed away like the filth of the body by the water itself, there is no need of a lake for its cleansing: it is the abundance not of the water but of faith that gives efficacy to the sacrament, and God will grant His indulgence for the " abridgment "[25] of a sacrament when necessity requires it. The essential portion of Cyprian's representation runs as follows:

You have asked also, dearest son, what I thought of those who obtain God's grace in sickness and weakness, whether they are to be accounted legitimate Christians, for that they are not to be washed (*loti*), but sprinkled (*perfusi*), with the saving water. In this point, my diffidence and modesty prejudges none, so as to prevent any from feeling what he thinks right, and from doing what he feels to be right. As far as my poor understanding conceives it, I think that the divine benefits can in no respect be mutilated and weakened; nor can anything less occur in that case (*æstimamus in nullo mutilari et debilitari posse beneficia divina nec minus aliquid illic posse contingere*), where, with full and entire faith both of the giver and receiver, what is drawn from the divine gifts is accepted. For in the sacrament of salvation the contagion of sins is not in such wise washed away, as the filth of the skin and of the body is washed away in carnal and ordinary washing, as that there should be need of saltpeter and other appliances also, and a bath and a basin wherewith this vile body must be washed and purified. Otherwise is the

[24] Ep. lxix. 12–14: Hartel's edition of Cyprian's Letters, in " Corpus scriptorum ecclesiasticorum Latinorum," Vienna, III. ii. 1871, pp. 760 f. The argument is admirably abstracted by Bingham, in his " Origines ecclesiasticæ: or the Antiquities of the Christian Church," XI. xi. 5 (see the revised edition, by his great-grandson: London, iii. 1834, pp. 275 ff.).

[25] Dr. E. C. Smyth, *Andover Review*, i. 1884, p. 540, thinks this refers only to the abridgment in amount of water.

breast of the believer washed; otherwise is the mind of man purified by the merit of faith. In the sacraments of salvation, when necessity compels, and God bestows His mercy, the divine methods confer the whole benefit on believers (*in sacramentis salutaribus necessitate cogente et Deo indulgentiam suam largiente totum credentibus conferunt divina compendia*); nor ought it to trouble any one that sick people seem to be sprinkled or affused, when they obtain the Lord's grace, when Holy Scripture speaks by the mouth of the prophet Ezekiel, and says, " Then will I sprinkle clean water upon you, and ye shall be clean: . . ." [quoting further, Num. xix. 8–9, 12–13; viii. 5–7]. . . . Or have they obtained indeed the divine favor, but in a shorter and more limited measure of the divine gift and of the Holy Spirit . . . ? Nay, verily, the Holy Spirit is not given by measure, but is poured out altogether on the believer.[26]

Those who were thus baptized were often looked upon with suspicion, seeing that they were frequently such as had neglected baptism until they believed they were dying (the so-called *procrastinantes, βραδύνοντες*), and in any case had not fulfilled the full period of their catechumenate and were therefore supposed to be insufficiently instructed in Christian knowledge, and seeing that they had been brought to Christ by necessity, as it were, and not by choice and lacked the grace of confirmation and all that it was supposed to imply.[27] They were therefore denied the right to receive orders in the Church, except when a scarcity of men fitted for orders, or other necessity, forbade the strictness of this rule. This judgment concerning them is already brought to light in the letter of Cornelius on the Novatian heresy, quoted by Eusebius; [28] and the reason on which it rested is clearly expressed in the canon of the Council of Neo-Cæsarea (314; c. 12): " He that is baptized when he is sick ought not to be made a priest (for his coming to the faith is not voluntary but from necessity) unless his diligence and faith do afterwards prove commendable, or the scarcity of men fit for the office do require it." There were

---

[26] I have availed myself of the translation in " The Ante-Nicene Fathers," American edition, Buffalo, 1886, pp. 400–401.

[27] Cf. Weiss, article " Krankentaufe," in Kraus, " Real-Encyklopädie," ii. 1886, p. 223.   [28] " Hist. Ecc.," vi. 43.

reasons enough to look on those who had so received baptism with suspicion; but the validity of the baptism so conferred was not itself in doubt.[29]

As little did men doubt the propriety and validity of baptism by affusion when scarcity of water rendered immersion impossible. This is the precise case which occurs in the prescriptions of the "Teaching of the Twelve Apostles"; and that the practice of the churches continued in accordance with these prescriptions may be illustrated by a variety of references which have come down to us. For example, in the seventh century canons of James of Edessa, the priest is instructed to baptize a dying child with whatever amount of water he happens to have near him.[30]

31. *Addai.* — When an unbaptized infant is in danger of death, and its mother carries it in haste even to the field, to a priest who is at work there, where there is no stream, and no basin, and no water-vessel, if there is only water there for the priest's use, and necessity requires haste, what is proper for him to do? *Jacob.* — In necessity like this it is right for the priest, if water happens to be with him, to take the pitcher of water and pour it upon the infant's head, even though its mother is holding it in her hands, and say, " Such an one is baptized in the name of the Father and the Son and the Holy Spirit."

Indeed, so little was immersion of the essence of baptism to Syrian Christians, that we read of their mistaking for baptism in the twelfth century the blessed water of the feast of the Epiphany with which " every believer who entered the Holy Church was signed after the manner of the cross," " or sprinkled," and only thus " approached the mysteries "; so that the authorities needed to guard them from this error.[31] A body of legends from every part of the Church illustrates the same

[29] Bingham, " Antiquities of the Christian Church," XI. xi. 5; Wall, as cited, p. 43; Kraus, as cited, p. 223.

[30] See Isaac H. Hall, in *The Presbyterian Review*, ix. 1888, p. 151.

[31] It is so reported by one Mar Michael Chindisi in the introductory remarks to a twelfth century MS. of the Syriac " Hydragiologia," published by Carl von Arnhard (Munich: F. Straub). See the New York *Independent*, April 11, 1889, p. 15.

conception. There are, for example, the well-known stories of
St. Lawrence baptizing Romanus with a pitcher of water, and
of Lucillus baptizing by pouring water on the head.[32] There is
the curious story of the bishop observing the boy Athanasius
"playing at church" with his young companions and baptizing them, and the decision of the council that "as water had
been poured upon these persons" after the interrogations and
responses, the baptism was complete.[33] There is the similar
story of travelers baptizing a Jew in the desert by sprinkling
sand three times on his body, and the decision that true baptism had taken place in all but the material, with the order
that the Jew was now to be *perfusus* with it.[34] The Copts have
a story of a woman, who, in a storm at sea, drew blood from
her breast and made the sign of the cross on the foreheads of
her children with it, repeating the formula of baptism. On
arrival at Alexandria she took them to the bishop for baptism,
but the water in the font petrified to prevent the sacrilege of a
repetition of a baptism thus declared valid.[35] It is not needful
to multiply examples of such legends: they bear witness to
much popular superstition; but they bear witness along with it
to a universal allowance of the validity of baptism by affusion.

Perhaps in no way is the universality of this sentiment
more pointedly brought out, than in its easy assumption in the
discussion by the Fathers of the salvation of the apostles or of
other ancient worthies who had died unbaptized. We meet
already in Tertullian with the point of view which pervades
all the attempts to explain their salvation. "And now," he
says, "as far as I shall be able, I will reply to them who affirm
'that the apostles were unbaptized.'" He quotes some suggestions to the contrary, and continues:

Others make the suggestion, — forced enough, clearly — "that
the apostles then served the turn of baptism when, in their little

[32] Bingham, as above.

[33] Smith and Cheetham, "A Dictionary of Christian Antiquities," i.
1875, p. 167b.   [34] Smith and Cheetham, i. p. 168a.

[35] Butler, "The Ancient Coptic Churches of Egypt," ii. 1884, p. 399, cf.
p. 266.

ship, they were sprinkled and covered with the waves: that Peter himself also was immersed enough when he walked on the sea." It is, however, as I think, one thing to be sprinkled or intercepted by the violence of the sea; another thing to be baptized in obedience to the discipline of religion.[36]

He refuses, in other words, to look upon a chance wetting as baptism, but the mode in which the wetting is supposed to come raises no doubt in his mind: nor indeed is he too seriously concerned " whether they were baptized in any manner whatever, or whether they continued unbathed (*illoti*) to the end." The Syriac " Book of the Bee," on the other hand, deems it important to insist on the baptism of the apostles, and finds it in the following way:

And Mar Basilius says that on the eve of the passion, after the disciples had received the body and blood of our Lord, our Lord put water in a basin, and began to wash his disciples' feet; and this was the baptism of the Apostles. But they were not all made perfect, for they were not all pure. For Judas, the son of perdition, was not made holy; and because this basin of washing was in very truth baptism; just as our Lord said to Simon Peter, " Except I wash thee, thou hast no part with me," that is, except I baptize thee thou cannot enter the kingdom of heaven.[37]

We may take, however, Augustine's discussion of the case of the thief on the cross as our typical example of the way in which the Fathers dealt with these, to them, puzzling facts.

Accordingly, the thief, who was no follower of the Lord previous to the cross, but His confessor upon the cross, from whose case a presumption is sometimes taken, or attempted, against the sacrament of baptism, is reckoned by St. Cyprian among the martyrs who are baptized in their own blood, as happens to many unbaptized persons in times of hot persecution. For to the fact that he confessed the crucified Lord so much weight is attributed and so much availing value assigned by Him who knows how to weigh and value such

[36] " De baptismo," xii. I have availed myself of the translation in the " Ante-Nicene Christian Library," Edinburgh, i. 1869, pp. 245 f.

[37] Chap. xliii., " On the Passion of our Lord," p. 165 of the Syriac Text (as reported by Dr. Isaac H. Hall).

evidence, as if he had been crucified for the Lord. . . . There was discovered in him the full measure of a martyr, who then believed in Christ when they fell away who were destined to be martyrs. All this, indeed, was manifest to the eyes of the Lord, who at once bestowed so great felicity on one who, though not baptized, was yet washed clean in the blood, as it were, of martyrdom. . . . Besides all this, there is the circumstance, which is not incredibly reported, that the thief who then believed as he hung by the side of the crucified Lord was sprinkled, as in a most sacred baptism, with the water which issued from the wound of the Saviour's side. I say nothing of the fact that nobody can prove, since none of us knows that he had not been baptized previous to his condemnation.[38]

Such unhesitating appeals as this to " sprinkling," as confessedly true and valid baptism, if only it can be believed to have taken place, reveal to us in a most convincing way the patristic attitude towards this mode of baptism. With whatever stringency trine immersion may have been held the right and only regular mode of baptism, it is perfectly obvious that other modes were not considered invalid and no baptism. We read of those who baptized with a single immersion being condemned as acting contrary to the command of Christ,[39] or as making a new law, not only against the common practice, but also against the general rule and tradition of the Church; [40] and we find the deposition ordered of every bishop or presbyter who transgressed good order by administering baptism by a single immersion: [41] but the form or mode is ever treated as having the necessity of order and never as having the necessity of means.

Accordingly we find that the very mode of baptism against which these charges and canons were directed — that by a single immersion — was easily allowed, when sufficient occasion for its introduction arose. Trine immersion was insisted

---

[38] " On the Soul and its Origin," i. 11. I have used the translation in the " Nicene and Post-Nicene Fathers," New York, v. 1887, p. 319.

[39] Pope Pelagius in his " Ep. ad Gaudentium "; quoted by Bingham, as cited, p. 281.   [40] Sozomen and Theodoret: Bingham, *loc. cit.*

[41] " Apostolic Canons," Can. 42: Bingham, *loc. cit.*, and Kraus, *op. cit.*, p. 828.

upon on two symbolical grounds: it represented Christ's three days' burial and His resurrection on the third day; but more fundamentally it represented baptism as into faith in the three persons of the Trinity. "Rightly ye are immersed a third time," says Augustine, "ye who accept baptism in the name of the Trinity. Rightly ye are immersed the third time, ye who accept baptism in the name of Jesus Christ, who on the third day rose from the dead." The Arians in Spain, however, in the sixth century, while following the general custom of trine immersion, explained it as denoting a first, second, and third degree of divinity in the three persons named in the formula. This led some Spanish Catholics to baptize with only one immersion, in testimony to the equality of the Divine Persons in the unity of the Godhead; and when disputes arose as to this divergence from ordinary custom, Leander, Bishop of Seville, appealed for advice in his own name and in that of the other Spanish bishops to Gregory the Great. Gregory replied as follows:

Nothing truer can be said concerning the three immersions of baptism than the opinion you have yourself given, that diversity of custom does not prejudice the holy Church if the faith be one (*quod in una fide nihil afficit sanctae ecclesiae consuetudo diversa*). We use trine immersion that we may signify the mystery of the three days' burial, so that as the infant is raised three times from the water, the resurrection on the third day may be expressed. But if any one thinks this is done rather out of veneration for the Holy Trinity, neither does a single immersion in water do any prejudice to this; for, as there is one substance in three Persons, there can be nothing reprehensible in an infant's being immersed either thrice or once, — because in the three immersions the Trinity of Persons may be as well designated as in one immersion the unity of the Godhead. But seeing that now the infant is three times immersed in baptism by heretics, I think that this ought not to be done by you: lest while they multiply the immersions they divide the Godhead; and while they continue as before they glory in the victory of their custom.[42]

[42] Gregorius Magnus, "Epistolae," lib. i. ep. 41. Cf. Bingham, pp. 282 f.; Augusti, pp. 400 f.; Kraus, p. 828: *opp. cit.* I have made use of Bingham's

The application of the principle here is, of course, not to
affusion or aspersion but to single immersion; but the broad
principle that " divergent custom in unity of faith is no detri-
ment to the holy Church " is quite clearly laid down, and is
made the basis of advice which runs counter to all previous
custom. This did not mean that all canonical authority should
be broken down, or that each church should not order its affairs
by its own canons. They of Rome continued to use and to insist upon trine immersion; they of Spain, after a few years'
struggle, decreed at the Council of Toledo (633) that only a
single immersion should be used thereafter in their churches:
and though later offense was taken here and there with the
Spanish custom, yet it received the support of both German
and French synods, and the Council of Worms (868) finally
recognized both practices. But the whole incident shows perfectly clearly that a distinction requires to be drawn between
regular or canonical and valid baptism; and the passages
which have been quoted from Cyprian, Augustine, and
Gregory, when taken together, seem to show that the Church of
that age did not contemplate the possibility that difference in
mode of baptism could operate to the absolute invalidation of
the rite. We meet with no evidence from the writings of the
Fathers that baptism by affusion was held anything other than
irregular and extraordinary; but we meet with no evidence
that it was accounted void: it was even held, on the contrary,
imperative duty in case of necessity, whether on account of
paucity of water or on account of the weakness of the recipient.

---

translation. A similar instance of liberality in judgment by Gregory is the
somewhat famous case mentioned by Bede, " Historia ecclesiastica," i. 27.
When speaking of the varying Uses of the Roman and Gallican churches, he
says that " things are not to be loved for the sake of places, but places for
the sake of good things," and advises Augustine to " select " from " the
Roman, or Gallican, or any other Church," " those things that are pious,
religious, or correct; to make these up into one body, and instil them into
the minds of the English for their use." Surely this is not out of character
with Gregory's strictness of home administration, as the Abbé Duchesne
(" Origines du culte chrétien," 1889, p. 94) urges, and is closely paralleled by
the instance under discussion.

The evidence of the practice of affusion as something more than an unusual and extraordinary mode of baptism which fails us in the writings of the Fathers, seems to be provided, however, in the monumental representations of the rite. The apparent evidence of the monuments runs, indeed, oddly athwart the consentient witness of the literary remains. It may be broadly said that the Fathers, from the second century down through the patristic age, represent ordinary and regular baptism to be a rite performed on perfectly nude recipients by a form of trine immersion. In seemingly direct contradiction to this literary evidence, we read in one of the latest and most judicious handbooks of Christian archæology: " It is most noteworthy that from the second to the ninth century there is found scarcely one pictorial representation of baptism by immersion; but the suggestion is almost uniformly either of sprinkling or pouring." [43] Representations which clearly indicate immersion neither were impossible nor are altogether lacking; [44] but they bear no proportion in number to those which seem to imply the act of pouring, and when clear are usually of late date. On the other hand, representations in which affusion seems to be implied are of all ages and comparatively numerous. The fact is so obvious, indeed, that with a bald statement of it we might be tempted to conclude that the literary and monumental evidences stand in hopeless contradiction.

Any survey of the monumental evidence which would hope to be fruitful must begin with a sharp distinction between two series of representations — those which depict the historical scene of the baptism of Christ, and those which depict ordinary baptism. The treatment of neither of these subjects has

[43] Bennett, " Christian Archæology," 1890, pp. 406 f. Cf. the statement of Withrow, " The Catacombs of Rome," 1888, p. 535: " The testimony of the Catacombs respecting the mode of baptism, so far as it extends, is strongly in favour of aspersion or affusion. All their pictured representations of the rite indicate this mode, for which alone the early fonts seem adapted; nor is there any early art evidence of baptismal immersion."

[44] Cf. the example from a Pontifical of the ninth century, in Smith and Cheetham, " A Dictionary of Christian Antiquities," i. 1875, pp. 159, 171.

escaped influence from the other. Artists seeking to represent the rite of baptism have not always given a perfectly realistic rendering of the service as seen by them day after day in their own baptistery, but have allowed reminiscences of familiar representations of our Lord's baptism to affect their treatment. And on the other hand they have not been able to exclude the influence of the rite of baptism as customarily administered before their eyes, from affecting their representation of Christ's baptism. Even the most incongruous features from ordinary baptism have sometimes with great naïveté been permitted to enter into their pictured conception of Christ's baptism; thus very early our Lord is represented as of immature age, and later He is even sometimes placed in a sculptured marble font.[45] But despite the influence exerted upon one another by the two series of representations, they stand in very different relations to our present inquiry; and must be used not only separately but in different ways. Representations of the baptism of Christ have a definite historical scene to depict, and can tell us what contemporary baptism was like only accidentally and so far as the artist has forgotten himself. Representations of the rite of baptism on the other hand are available as direct witnesses of Christian usage, except in so far as they may be judged to depict what was conceived to be ideal baptism rather than what was actual at the date of their production, or to have been affected by traditional modes of representation or by influences from parallel scenes, as, for example, from the representations of the baptism of Christ. Each series may, however, have something to teach us in its own way, as to how Christians baptized in the earlier ages of the Church.

The sequence of representations of the baptism of Christ may be very conveniently examined in the plates of Dr. Josef Strzygowski's " Iconographie der Taufe Christi," to which he has prefixed a very illuminating discussion. Dr. Strzygowski cannot be acquitted, indeed, of bending his material a little

---

[45] Cf. plate viii. in Strzygowski's "Iconographie der Taufe Christi," München, 1885, and the remarks on p. 36.

here and there to fit what he is led, from the literature of that age, to expect the representation of baptism to be in each age. The purity of his induction is thus marred, and the independence of the testimony of the art-evidence to some degree affected. But he has placed in his reader's hands, both in the course of the discussion itself and in the series of representations given in his plates, ample material to guard against the slight deflection which may arise from this cause. The series of representations of the baptism of Christ begins with a fresco in the crypt of Lucina in the Roman catacombs, which seems to belong to the opening of the second century.[46] Here Christ is represented as being aided by John to step up out of the river in which He is still immersed almost up to His middle. Then, there is a somewhat enigmatical fresco in the catacomb of Praetextatus, assigned to the end of the second or beginning of the third century, which is variously interpreted as a representation of our Lord's baptism (so Garrucci and Roller) or of His crowning with thorns (so Martigny and De Rossi).[47] In this picture Christ stands, clothed, on the ground, while a second figure stretches over His head something which looks like a twig, and there is a cloud of something surrounding His head. If baptism be represented here, it is evidently conceived as a simple affusion. After the frescoes, come a series of representations on sarcophagi belonging to the early post-Constantinian age. As a type,[48] these represent Christ as a boy, naked, generally in full face, with the head turned slightly to the left towards John, and the arms hanging down. John either holds his right hand over Christ or rests it on His forehead. Jordan pours its water out of a lump of rock, hanging over Christ from behind; while a dove generally flies near the rock. Among these representations there are also some, as, for example, the sarcophagus of Junius Bassus (d. 359), in which lambs sym-

[46] Given by Strzygowski, plate i. fig. 1; De Rossi, "La Roma sotterranea cristiana," i. 1864, tav. xiv.; Roller, "Les Catacombes de Rome," i. pl. xviii. 1; Kraus, "Roma sott.," ed. 2, p. 139, fig. 18.

[47] Given by Strzygowski, plate i. fig. 4; Roller, i. pl. xviii. 2; Perret, "Les Catacombes de Rome," i. pl. lxxx.

[48] Cf. Strzygowski, as above, p. 7; for representations see plate i.

bolically take the place of persons; and either light or water or something cloc io poured from the beak of the dove on the head of the lamb which represents Christ.[49] On the cover of a fourth century sarcophagus in the Lateran,[50] John is represented as pouring water on the head of Christ from a bowl: but Strzygowski points out that this portion of the sculpture is a later restoration. The Ravenna Mosaics come next in point of time: and in the primary one of these — that in the Baptisterium Ursianum (middle of fifth century) — John is again represented as pouring water on Christ's head from a bowl; but again Strzygowski considers this feature to be due to later restoration.[51] The typical representation at this date seems to be of Christ, waist-deep in Jordan, with John's hand resting on, and the dove immediately above, His head. From the opening of the eighth century we have a new type which places a jug in the beak of the dove from which water pours upon Christ's head,[52] while from the twelfth century examples occur in which John pours water from an urn; [53] and something of this sort becomes everywhere the ruling type from the fourteenth century on.[54] As we review the whole series of representations of the baptism of Christ, we are struck with the absence from it of decisive representations of complete immersion: it may be interpreted as a series of immersions, but in any case it is strangely full of hints of incomplete immersion, which can only be accounted for by the influence of contemporary habit in baptizing upon the artist, as he attempted to depict this historical scene. It is hardly possible to understand the manner in which the artists have pictured to themselves the baptism of Christ, without postulating familiarity on their part with baptism as something else than a simple immersion.

This judgment is fully borne out by the parallel series of representation of the rite of baptism in general. This series

[49] Given in Strzygowski, i. 12.
[50] Given in Strzygowski, i. 9; Roller, ii. pl. lxvii. 3.
[51] Given in Strzygowski, i. 14.
[52] Strzygowski, viii. 1, and the discussion on pp. 35 f.
[53] Strzygowski, xiii. 9, and the discussion on p. 49, cf. note 5.
[54] Strzygowski, p. 54, and plates xv. f.

also begins in the Roman catacombs — in the so-called sacramental chapel of the catacombs of Callistus, where we have two frescoes dating from the opening of the third century.[55] In both of these the river is still presupposed — probably a trait in representing baptismal scenes borrowed from the typical instance of the baptism of Christ. Into it the neophyte has descended, but the water scarcely reaches his ankles. John stands on the adjoining ground with his right hand on the neophyte's head. In one of the pictures a cloud of water surrounds the head. In neither case is a complete immersion possible; and in one of them affusion seems to be evident. For the period after Constantine [56] we have three especially important monuments: a gravestone from Aquileia [57] on which the neophyte stands in a shallow font and water descends on him from above; a silver spoon from Aquileia [58] on which the water descends on the head of the neophyte from the beak of the dove; and a glass fragment found in the ruins of an old Roman house, representing a girl upon whom water descends from a vase, while she is surrounded with spray from it.[59] The representation of the baptism of St. Ambrose on the famous Paliotto in S. Ambrogio at Milan, comes from a later date (ca. 827). Here the recipient stands in a font up to his middle and the priest pours water on his head from a vase.[60] The later examples fall entirely in line with these earlier ones; says Kirsch: [61] " A complete immersion is not found in the West even in the first period of the middle-ages, but the form of representation which we have just noted goes over into the

[55] Strzygowski, i. 2, 3; Roller, i. pl. xxiv. 4 and 5; Garrucci, " Storia della arte cristiana," ii. 1873, tav. vii. 2.

[56] Cf. the account in Kraus, " Real-Encyklopädie," ii. pp. 837 f., from which I borrow at this point.

[57] De Rossi, " Bullettino di archeologia cristiana," 1876, tav. i. 2, and pp. 7 ff.; Garrucci, op. cit., vi. 1880, tav. 487, fig. 26.

[58] Kraus, " Real-Encyklopädie," ii. p. 342, fig. 189; Garrucci, tav. 462, fig. 8.

[59] Kraus, ii. p. 837, fig. 484; De Rossi, loc. cit., tav. i. 1; Garrucci, tav. 464, fig. 1. Cf. Strzygowski's note, p. 36 (note 2).

[60] Strzygowski, viii. 2, cf. p. 36.

[61] In Kraus, " Real-Encyklopädie," ii. p. 838.

later art with certain modifications." We need not pause to note the examples that are adduced in illustration of what seems the general course of later art-representations: our interest will naturally center in the earlier examples already cited. In them there seems to be borne an unbroken testimony to baptism by affusion.

It is, of course, impossible to believe that the literary and monumental testimony as to the mode of baptism prevalent in the patristic Church, is really as contradictory as it might at first sight seem. Reconciliation of the two lines of evidence has naturally been sought by the students of the subject; and equally naturally, in different directions. Sometimes the method adopted seems only forcibly to subject one class of evidence to the other. Dr. Withrow, for example, seems ready to neglect the literary evidence in favor of the monumental, speaking of immersion as if it were only a fourth or fifth century corruption of the earlier rite represented in the art remains, and pleading, against its primitive employment, that it is not represented in the catacombs and that the early fonts are not suitable for it — with an inclination to include among the fonts the so-called *benitièrs* or " holy-water vessels " of the catacombs.[62] On the other hand, it is not uncommon to see the monumental evidence set practically aside in favor of the literary. This is done in some degree, as we have seen, even by Strzygowski. A tendency towards it is found also even in so judicious a writer as the late Dr. Schaff,[63] who pleads that, as it is impossible to depict the whole process of baptism, we must read the monumental representations as giving only one moment in the complete trine immersion witnessed to in the contemporary literature, and not treat them as representing the whole rite — though he does not stop to tell us what part affusion plays in an ordinary immersion. The fullest and most

[62] " The Catacombs of Rome," 1888, pp. 535 ff.

[63] In the notable discussion of Baptism which he incorporated in his edition of the " Didache," as quoted above. The explanations of Garrucci, who finds in each representation a moment subsequent to the completion of baptism itself — confirmation or the like — will belong to the same class of explanations with Dr. Schaff's: and fails for like reasons.

plausible statement of this point of view is made by Victor
Schultze in his " Archäologische Studien über altchristliche
Monumente." [64] Quoting De Rossi's opinion that the baptism
of the boy depicted in the catacombs of St. Callistus with a
cloud of water about his head, is a mixed form of immersion
and affusion, he comments thus: " Such a rite, however, never
in reality existed, [65] and is seen to be an illusion from the consideration that aspersion is nothing else than a substitute for
immersion and was but gradually developed out of it. The first
traces of aspersion are found among the Gnostics, and this
circumstance, as well as the blame which Irenæus had for the
rite, are proof that the Church had not adopted aspersion in
the third century." He proceeds to remark that if the fresco is
of Tertullian's time, it must certainly represent immersion, as
that Father knows no other baptism; [66] and then explains the
scene as representing the moment when the candidate is just
rising from the water after immersion, and the water brought
up with him is streaming from his head and person; whereas,
if aspersion had been the idea of the artist, he would doubtless
have placed a vessel in the hand of the administrator, as is
done in later pictures. These very acute remarks overlook,
however, two decisive facts — the facts namely that the water
in which the youth stands is too shallow for immersion, and
that this fresco does not stand by itself but is one of a series of
representations, no one of which speaks clearly of immersion,
and many of which make aspersion perfectly clear. Such an
explanation of the one picture as Schultze offers would only
render the explanation of the series as a whole impossible. [67]

Rather than adopt either of these extreme views which
would imply the untrustworthiness of one or the other lines of
evidence, it would be easier to believe that the monumental
evidence represented the actual practice of the Church while
the literary evidence preserved the canonical form of the

[64] Wien, 1880, p. 55.

[65] Yet cf. the present-day Oriental practices as above, pp. 345 f.

[66] Yet see how broadly Tertullian deals with the matter in " De bapt.," v.

[67] Professor E. C. Smyth has criticized Schultze's theory in the *Andover
Review*, i. 1884, p. 538.

Church. It would be no unheard-of thing if the actual practice varied from the official form: indeed, we know as a matter of fact, that not only have such changes in general, but that this change in particular has usually taken effect in practice before it has been recognized in law. It was only because actual baptism had come to be by affusion that the Western Church was led in later ages to place affusion on a par in her formularies with immersion: and the same history was subsequently wrought out in the English Church. It would not be at all inconceivable, that from the beginning the actual celebration of baptism differed somewhat from the formal ritual; and this difference might well underlie the different testimony borne by the monuments as representations of what was actually done, and by the Fathers as representatives of the formal ritual. Whether and how far this hypothesis will avail or is needed for the explanation of the facts before us, may be left, however, for subsequent consideration.

We need to note, now, certain other suggestions which have been made for the harmonizing of the divergent lines of evidence, from which we shall gain more light upon the problem. Mr. Marriott,[68] for example, supposes that early baptism included both immersion and affusion, something as the modern Armenian rite does; and that the artists have chosen the moment of affusion for their representation. This acute suggestion, however, scarcely offers a complete explanation of the facts. For unless affusion was the characteristic and determining element in baptism, it will be difficult to account for the almost unvarying choice of this moment in the rite for representation. It is needful to bear in mind the unsophisticated and unconscious nature of monumental testimony; the artist, seeking to convey the idea of baptism to the observers of his picture, would choose for representation, out of mere necessity, a moment in the rite which would at once suggest " baptism " to the beholders of his work. Mr. Marriott's view does not seem, then, to remove the conflict between the literary and

[68] In Smith and Cheetham, " Dictionary of Christian Antiquities," as cited.

monumental evidence; the literary evidence represents immersion, and the monumental evidence affusion, as the characteristic feature of the rite. M. Roller has still another useful suggestion: he distinguishes localities, remarking that in the Orient and Africa, baptism may have been by " a triple immersion and a triple emersion, accompanied by a triple confession of faith in the Father, in the Son, and in the Holy Ghost," while in Rome Christians may have been for a time satisfied with " an immersion less complete." Our attention is thus at least called to the important fact that our early monumental evidence is local — confined to Rome and Roman dependencies. But again the explanation is inadequate for the whole problem: the conflict exists in Rome itself. It is not only the second and third century pictures, but also the representations from the fifth and sixth and seventh centuries and beyond, in which stress is laid on the moment of affusion. When Jerome and Leo and Pelagius and Gregory were speaking of trine immersion as of order in Rome, the artists were still laying stress on affusion.

The only theory known to us which seems to do full justice to both classes of facts — those gathered from the literature and monuments alike — is that which De Rossi has revived [69] and given the support of his great name. This supposes that normal baptism was performed in the early Church by a mode which united immersion and affusion in a single rite — not, as in the Armenian rite, making them separate parts of a repeated ritual.[70] We shall arrive, indeed, at something like this conclusion if we will proceed simply by scrutinizing the two lines of evidence somewhat sharply. We will observe, for example, that though affusion is emphasized by the monuments, it is not necessarily a simple affusion. The candidate stands in water,

[69] Kirsch, in Kraus, " Real-Encyklopädie," ii. 1886, pp. 837 f., refers us, as to the older existence of this theory, to Ciampini, " Vet. Mon.," ii. 19 ff., and remarks that it is now almost generally accepted, as e.g. by Corblet.

[70] In the *Römische Quartalschrift,* ii. 1888, pp. 106 f., De Rossi still insists that the performance of the rite by pouring was by no means exceptional in the early Church; he says that the catacombs agree with the oldest form in this matter, as given in the " Didache."

which reaches to his ankles or even to his knees in the earlier pictures, and in later ones to his waist or above. Hence Dr. Schaff says, " Pouring on the head while the candidate stands on dry ground, receives no aid from the Catacombs. . . ." [71] This is a rather extreme statement. The fresco in the catacomb of Praetextatus, if it be thought to represent baptism, would be a very early example to the contrary; [72] and symbolical representations on somewhat later monuments — as for instance that on the sarcophagus of Bassus — do not indicate water below. But if it be read only as a general remark, it is worthy of remark. The points of importance to be gleaned from the monuments are that the candidate was baptized standing, ordinarily at least standing in water, and the affusion was a supplement to the water below. And if we so read the monuments we shall find ourselves in no necessary disaccord with the literary notices. The idea in any case would be an entire bath. The candidate standing in the water, this could be accomplished either by sinking the head beneath the water or by raising the water over the head. The monuments simply bear their witness to the prevalence of the latter mode of completing the ordinance. And when we once perceive this, we perceive also that the pictured monuments do not stand alone in this testimony. The extant fonts also suggest this form of the rite. And the literary notices themselves are filled with indications that the mode of baptism thus suggested was the common mode throughout the Christian world. This is implied, indeed, in the significance attached to the baptism of the head.[73] " When we dip our heads in water as in a grave," says Chrysostom, " our old man is buried; and when we rise up again, the new man rises therewith." [74] The ritual given in the " Catechesis " of Cyril of Jerusalem (347) [75] contains the same implication; we are told that the candidates, after having con-

---

[71] "The Oldest Church Manual," as cited, p. 41, note.

[72] Cf. Roller; Garrucci; Bennett (p. 400); Smyth (p. 535, note).

[73] Cf. Schaff, "The Oldest Church Manual," pp. 33, 41.

[74] Hom. 25 on John iii. 5, as quoted by Bingham, "Antiquities of the Christian Church," XI. xi. 4 (ed. cited, iii. 1834, p. 273).

[75] Smith and Cheetham, i. p. 157.

fessed their faith, " *dipped themselves* thrice in the water, and thrice lifted themselves up from out thereof." The same may be said of the West Gothic rite for blessing the font: " God who didst sanctify the fount of Jordan for the salvation of souls, let the angel of thy blessing descend upon these waters, that thy servants being bathed *(perfusi)* therewith," [76] etc.; and in general of the occasional use of *perfusus* as a designation of the catechumen.[77] Perhaps, however, the exact nature of the literary evidence and the precision with which it falls in with this conception of the mode of ancient baptism, may be best exhibited by the adduction of a single passage, extended enough to convey the writer's point of view. We select somewhat at random the following account of baptism by Gregory of Nyssa: [78]

But the descent into the water, and the trine immersion of the person in it, involves another mystery. . . . Everything that is affected by death has its proper and natural place, and that is the earth in which it is laid and hidden. Now earth and water have much mutual affinity. . . . Seeing, then, [that] the death of the Author of our life subjected Him to burial in earth . . . the imitation which we enact of that death is expressed in the neighboring element. And as He, that Man from above, having taken deadness on Himself, after His being deposited in the earth, returned back to life the third day, so every one who is knitted to Him by virtue of His bodily form, looking forward to the same successful issue, I mean this arriving at life by having, instead of earth, *water poured on him* (ἐπιχεόμενος), and so submitting to that element, has represented for him in the three movements the three-days-delayed grace of the resurrection. . . . But since, as has been said, we only so far imitate the transcendent Power as the poverty of our nature is capable of, by having *the water thrice poured on us* (τὸ ὕδωρ τρὶς ἐπιχεάμενοι) and ascending again up from the water, we enact that saving burial and resurrection which took place on the third day, with this thought in our mind, that as we have power over the water

[76] *Ibid.*, p. 158.
[77] *Ibid.*, p. 168.
[78] " Oratio Catechetica," or, " The Great Catechism," chap. xxxv. (The " Nicene and Post-Nicene Fathers," Second Series, v. 1893, pp. 502 f.).

both to be in it and to arise out of it, so He too, Who has the universe at His sovereign disposal, immersed Himself in death, as we in the water, to return to His own blessedness.

Does it not look as if baptism was to Gregory very much what it is depicted on the monuments — an immersion completed by pouring?

We may, then, probably, assume that normal patristic baptism was by a trine immersion upon a standing catechumen, and that this immersion was completed either by lowering the candidate's head beneath the water, or (possibly more commonly) by raising the water over his head and pouring it upon it. Additional support for this assumption may be drawn from another characteristic of the patristic allusions to baptism. It is perfectly clear that baptism was looked upon by the Fathers — however much other symbolisms attached themselves to it — primarily as a bath. It is not necessary to multiply passages in support of so obvious a proposition.[79] One of the favorite designations of baptism was " the bath," and the Greeks delighted in the paronomasia which brought together the two words λουτρόν and λύτρον. It will suffice here to cite a few passages from Tertullian, merely by way of examples of what could be copiously adduced from the whole series of the Fathers: " Since we are defiled by sin," he says,[80] " as it were by dirt, we should be washed from those stains by water." " We enter then the laver *once*, — *once* our sins are washed away, because they ought never to be repeated. But the Jewish Israel bathes daily, because he is daily being defiled; and for fear that defilement should be practiced among *us* also, therefore was the definition concerning the one bathing made. Happy water, which *once* washes away; which does not mock sinners; which does not, being infected with the repetition of impurities, again defile them whom it has washed." [81] Our hands " are clean enough, which together with our whole body we once washed in Christ.

[79] Cf. Augusti, " Handbuch der christlichen Archäologie," ii. 1836, pp. 313 ff.

[80] " De bapt.," iv.　　　　　　[81] " De bapt.," xv.

Albeit Israel washed daily all his limbs over, yet he is never clean." [82] In the divers " washings " of the heathen, he tells us, they " cheat themselves with widowed waters," that is, with mere water, without the accompanying power of the Holy Ghost.[83] " Moreover," he continues, " by carrying water around and sprinkling it, they everywhere expiate country seats, houses, temples, and whole cities; at all events, at the Apollinarian and Eleusinian games they are baptized; and they presume that the effect of their doing that is their regeneration, and the remission of the penalties due to their perjuries. Among the ancients again, whoever had defiled himself with murder, was wont to go in quest of purifying waters. Therefore, if the mere nature of water, in that it is the appropriate material for washing away, leads men to flatter themselves with a belief in omens of purification, how much more truly will waters render that service, through the authority of God, by whom all their nature has been constituted! " For Tertullian, thus, the analogues of baptism were to be found in the Jewish lustrations and the heathen rites of cleansing; and so fundamental is this conception of baptism to him, that it takes precedence of every other; though these rites were performed by sprinkling they yet remain rites of the same class with baptism.

This primary conception of baptism as a cleansing bath, seems to find an odd illustration in the form of the early Christian baptisteries. When separate edifices were erected for baptism their models appear to have been drawn from the classic baths. " When the first baptisteries were built," writes Mr. G. Baldwin Brown,[84] " we have no means of knowing; but both their name and form seem borrowed from pagan sources. They remind us at once of the bathing apartments in the Thermæ, and the fact that Pliny, in speaking of the latter, twice uses the word *baptisteria,* seems to point to this derivation." If this is true, the Baptistery is emphatically the Chris-

[82] " De oratione," xiii.–xiv.
[83] " De bapt.," v.
[84] " From Schola to Cathedral," 1886, p. 146.

tian " Bath-house." Lindsay [85] adds some congruous details as
to the font itself. " The Font," he writes, " is placed in the
centre of the building, directly underneath the cupola; in the
earliest examples, as in the baptistery adjoining the Lateran, it
consists of a shallow octagonal basin, descended into by three
steps, precisely similar to the pagan bath — in later instances
it has more resemblance to an elevated reservoir.[86] The figure
of the octagon was peculiarly insisted on; even when the baptistery itself is round, the cupola is generally octagonal, and
the font almost always so. This may have been, in the first
instance, mere imitation of the pagan baths, in which the
octagon constantly occurs. . . ." Having obtained their models
of the baptistery from the surrounding heathendom, it may
possibly be that the early Christians the more readily leaned
toward completing their symbolical bath by pouring, that
that was one of the common modes of bathing among the
ancients — as appears for example in Ovid's description of
Diana's bath, " when her attendants ' urnis capacibus undam
effundunt.' " [87] But we are bound to remember in this connection that the early representations of baptism do not seem to
borrow at all from heathen representations of their purificatory
rites,[88] but exhibit, as Strzygowski points out, entire independence in treating their subject, although borrowing, of
course, the forms of the antique.

The crowning indication, however, that we have found the
true form of early Christian baptism in a rite performed on
an erect recipient, standing in water, and completed indifferently by sinking the head beneath the water or raising the

[85] "Sketches of the History of Christian Art," i. 1886, pp. 220 f. Cf.
Lundy, "Monumental Christianity," 1882, p. 385: "In these Baptismal
frescoes, the matter is obviously represented as that of a bath. . . . It was a
real washing — a thorough cleansing."

[86] The note adds that it sometimes receives the shape of a sarcophagus
in allusion to the "death unto sin" (Col. ii. 12).

[87] Marriott, in Smith and Cheetham, i. 1875, p. 168.

[88] As to these rites see Hermann, "Lehrbuch der gottesdienstlichen Alt-
ertümer der Griechen," ed. 2 (Heidelb.: 1858), p. 124, and for the few representations that have come down to us of their lustrations see "Mon. dell'
istituto," 1862, tav. lxiv. I owe these references to Strzygowski, p. 2.

water above the head, is supplied by the fact that, on assuming this as the early practice, we may naturally account for the various developments of later practice. In such a rite as this, both later immersion and affusion can find a natural starting-point; while the assumption of either a pure immersion or a pure affusion as a starting-point will render it exceedingly difficult to account for the rise and wide extension of the other mode. To point to the growing influence of the symbolism of death and resurrection with Christ attached to baptism, as making for a rite by immersion, or to the lax extension of clinic aspersion as making for a rite by affusion,[89] will no doubt help us to understand the development of either practice; but only on the assumption of a starting-point for the assumed developments such as the mode now under consideration supplies. Nor need we confine ourselves to the broad developments of the rite. The assumption of the mode suggested will account also for numerous minor elements in the later rites. It will account, for example, for the insistence still made throughout the East upon holding even the infant erect in the act of baptism. Indeed, on assuming this to have been early Christian baptism over a wide extent of territory, numerous peculiarities of Oriental services at once exhibit themselves as survivals of earlier practice. In this category belong, for instance, the Nestorian usage of thrice dipping the head of an already partially submerged candidate; the various mixtures of the two rites among the Copts and Armenians; the preservation of a partial immersion and trine affusion among the Syrians, and the like. When we add to the explanation of the apparent conflict between the early literary and monumental evidence which the assumption of this mode of baptism offers, the further explanation which it supplies of later developments in the rite, it would seem that we had discovered in it the actual form in which early Christians were accustomed to celebrate the initiatory rite of their religion.

[89] That the rise of aspersion cannot be connected with the practice of infant baptism all history shows. See this briefly indicated by Augusti, as above, p. 398.

Whether this early mode of baptism — underlying, as it would seem, all the notices and practices which have come down to us — represents truly the original mode of baptism as handed down to the Church by the apostles, requires further consideration. Our earliest literary and monumental evidence alike comes from the second century. The frescoes in the catacombs of Praetextatus and Callistus date from the end of the second century or the opening of the third — the age of Tertullian, who is probably the earliest Latin writer to whom we can appeal as a witness to the prevalent mode of baptism. In the East the evidence runs back a little further. The account of baptism given by Justin Martyr, indeed, scarcely conveys clear information as to the mode of its administration. The candidates, he tells us,[90] " are conducted to a place where there is water, and they are regenerated (ἀναγεννῶνται) after the same manner of regeneration as that in which we ourselves were regenerated. For they then make their ablution (τὸ λουτρὸν ποιοῦνται) in the water, in the name of God the Father and Lord of the universe, and of our Saviour Jesus Christ, and of the Holy Ghost." This defect is now supplied by " The Teaching of the Twelve Apostles," which, however, may in this part be little if any older than Justin. Its directions for baptism [91] run thus: " Now concerning baptism, baptize thus: Having first taught all these things, baptize ye into the name of the Father, and of the Son, and of the Holy Ghost, in living water. And if thou has not living water, baptize into other water; and if thou has not cold, then in warm. But if thou has neither, pour water thrice upon the head in the name of the Father, and of the Son, and of the Holy Ghost." It is certain, therefore, that by the middle of the second century some such mode of baptism as we have suggested — a form of immersion though not without allowance of a simple affusion in case of need — was practised in the Church. We may even be bold enough to say that at this date some such mode was probably the practice of the Church. This evidence, of course, has a retrospective value. What was the practice of the Church a decade or so

[90] " Apologia," i. c. lxi.   [91] Chap. vii.

before the middle of the second century was probably the usage also of a somewhat earlier day. But we must be chary of pursuing such a presumption too far. Christian institutions in the middle of the second century, and much more at its end, were not the unaltered institutions of the apostolic age. The bishop, for example, was already a different officer from what he was in the days when the New Testament was writing; and the Epistle of Clement of Rome witnesses to quite another church system from that which was in operation in the days of Irenæus. The " Teaching " itself, in other items of church order, brings before us a later stage of Christian life and practice than the first. The second century, in a word, marks a considerable advance on the first in the development of church usages; and it is necessary to exercise great caution in assuming what we find to be the practice of this century to be also apostolic, merely because it represents the earliest usage which we can trace.

In these circumstances we shall welcome any further line of investigation which promises to throw light on our problem, and turn therefore with some interest to inquire after the relation of Christian baptism to what is known as proselyte-baptism or the rabbinical custom of initiating proselytes into the Jewish faith by a formal and complete ablution. In this, many scholars find the original of Christian baptism, thus tracing the genealogy of the latter through the baptism of John to a well-understood and commonly practised Jewish ritual. It is argued that there is no evidence from the New Testament notices that Christ was instituting a rite that was new in the sense that its form or mode was a novelty; or that when John called on the people to come to his baptism, he needed to stop and explain to them what this " baptism " was and how they were to do it. On the contrary, it appears that Christ and John expected to be thoroughly understood from the beginning, and only implanted a new significance in an old rite, now adapted to a new use. But what could have been the older rite on which baptism was based, it is asked, except the proselyte-baptism which we find in the next age the es-

tablished practice of the Jews? If, however, Johannic and
Christian baptism were thus adopted, so far as the form of the
rite is concerned, from proselyte-baptism, a means is opened
to us for discovering how baptism was administered in the first
age of the Church which no one can venture to neglect. If we
can determine the mode of baptism in proselyte-baptism, we
raise a strong presumption that it was in this mode also that
our Lord and His apostles baptized. The path thus pointed out
is certainly sufficiently hopeful to justify our exploring it.[92]

It is scarcely possible to overstate the importance which
the rabbis attached to baptism, in the reception of proselytes.
It was held to be absolutely necessary to the making of a
proselyte; and though Rabbi Eliezer maintained that circumcision without baptism sufficed, Rabbi Joshua on the other
hand contended that baptism without circumcision was
enough, while the scribes decided that both rites were necessary. One might indeed become in some sort a proselyte without baptism; but though he were circumcised, he remained
גּוֹי until he was baptized, and children begotten in the interval
would still be מְמְזֵרִים, *spurii*. If he would become a " proselyte of
righteousness," " a child of the covenant," a " perfect Israelite,"
he must be both circumcised and baptized. The regulations
required that those purposing thus becoming Jews should first
be fully instructed in what it was to be a Jew and what the
step they were contemplating meant for them. When the time
came for their admission into the number of the covenant people, three things entered into the initiatory rite: *circumcision*,
מִילָה; *baptism*, טְבִילָה; and *sacrifice*, קָרְבָּן. Baptism was delayed

[92] Cf. an interesting discussion in Sabatier's " La Didachè," 1885, pp. 84 ff.
The direct literature on the subject is copious and easily traced. There is an
excellent guide to it, for example, in Schürer's " Jewish People in the Time
of Jesus Christ," § 31, note 302 (E.T. Div. ii. vol. ii. 1891, p. 321). Schürer
says that no one has " influenced modern opinion on the subject so much
as Schneckenburger." This may be accounted a very happy circumstance, as
Schneckenburger's book was a very solid piece of work; and we have not
been able to discover that anything has been said since which will materially modify his conclusions. His conclusions are briefly summed up in pp. 183–
186 of his book, " Ueber das Alter der jüdischen Proselyten-Taufe," Berlin,
1828.

after circumcision until the wound was healed, and meanwhile the instruction continued. When the day for it arrived, the proselyte, in the presence of the three teachers who had also witnessed his circumcision and who now served as witnesses of the baptism under the name of "fathers of the baptized," corresponding to the nature of the baptism as a "new birth," cut his hair and nails, undressed completely, and entered the water until his arms were covered. The commandments were now read to him, and, solemnly engaging to obey them, he perfected the baptism by completely immersing himself. The completeness of the immersion was of such importance that "a ring on the finger, a band confining the hair, or anything that in the least degree broke the continuity of contact with the water, was held to invalidate the act." [93] There remained now only the offering of the sacrifice, and when thus "blood was spilt" for him, the proselyte had ceased to be in any sense a heathen. In his baptism, he had been "born anew," and he came forth from the water "a new man," "a little child just born," "a child of one day." So entirely had his old self ceased, that it was held that all his old relations had passed away, the natural laws of inheritance had failed, and even those of kinship, so that it was even declared that, except for bringing proselytism into contempt among the un-understanding, a proselyte might marry without fault even his own natural mother or sister.[94]

We cannot fail to see at a glance close similarities between this rite as described in the Gemara and the rite of Christian baptism as contemporaneously administered. There is in both the instruction of the candidate both before and while in the font, the godfathers, the immersion, completed in some cases at least by self-baptism,[95] and the effect of baptism as issuing in a new creature. It is very difficult to believe that neither rite owed anything to the other. But the discovery of connection

[93] Taylor, "The Teaching of the Twelve Apostles," 1886, pp. 51, 52.

[94] Edersheim, "The Life and Times of Jesus the Messiah," ii. p. 743 (Appendix xii.).

[95] Cf. Cyril of Jerusalem, as quoted above, pp. 370 f.

between the two rites is no immediate proof that one owes
its existence to the other. It might be *a priori* possible, indeed,
that the Jewish rite was borrowed from the Christian or that
the Christian was based upon the Jewish. And we may judge
the similarity too close to admit the likelihood of their being
of wholly independent origin — despite the obviousness of a
cleansing washing as a rite of initiation and its widespread,
independent use as such among pagan religions. Yet the intermediate alternative remains that both rites may have had
their roots independently fixed in a common origin, while their
detailed similarities were the result of a gradual and only
semi-conscious assimilation taking place between similar contemporary rites through a long period, during which each
borrowed something from the other.

We will probably agree at once that it is very unlikely that
the Jews directly borrowed their proselyte-baptism from the
Christians, or even from John the Baptist, as has been maintained — the latter by Börner and others, and the former by
De Wette and others. So immediate a borrowing of so solemn
a rite is incredible, when we bear in mind the sharp antagonism which the Jews cherished towards the Christians during
this period.[96] Whether, on the other hand, the Jewish rite may
not have lain at the basis of the Christian rite requires more
consideration. Our decision in the matter will probably depend
on an answer to the stubbornly mooted question whether the
Jewish ceremony of proselyte-baptism existed when Christian
baptism was instituted. The evidence which we have drawn
upon for the description of it comes from the rabbinical literature, beginning with the Gemara. Whether this evidence, however, is valid for a period before the destruction of the Temple
admits of very serious question. Professor Schürer has recently
argued very strenuously for the existence of the Jewish rite
in the time of Christ.[97] On comparison of the actual evidence
adduced by him, however, with that dealt with, say, by Winer

---

[96] Cf. Delitzsch, in Herzog's "Real-Encyklopädie," xii. 1883, p. 299.
[97] "Geschichte des jüdischen Volkes im Zeitalter Jesu Christi," ii. 1886,
pp. 571 ff.

in his " Realwörterbuch " — where the opposite conclusion is reached — it does not appear that it has been substantially increased in the interval. The stress of Schürer's argument is laid not on these items of direct testimony — which all come to us from the second century and later — but on general considerations derived from the nature of the case. We require only a slight knowledge of Pharisaic Judaism in the time of Christ, reasons Schürer, to realize how often even a native Jew was compelled by the law to submit to ceremonial washings. Tertullian justly says, " A Jew washes daily, because he is daily defiled." A heathen was, thus, self-evidently unclean and could not possibly have been admitted into the congregation without having subjected himself to a Levitical " washing of baptism." Whatever special testimonies exist to the fact of such a requirement, they are scarcely necessary to support so conclusive a general consideration; against which, moreover, the silence of Philo and Josephus cannot avail, nor the somewhat unintelligible distinction which it is sought to erect between Levitical washings and proselyte-baptism technically so called. Winer on the other hand lays stress on the lateness of the direct testimony to the existence of proselyte-baptism and the silence of Josephus, Philo, and the oldest Targumists, while nevertheless allowing that the proselyte was, of course, compelled to submit himself to a lustration. He only denies that this lustration had already in the time of Christ become fixed, in the case of the proselyte, as no longer an ordinary lustration for the sake of ceremonial cleansing, but a special, initiatory rite, with its time, circumstances, and ritual already developed into what is subsequently known as proselyte-baptism. He thus fully answers in advance Schürer's question of wherein proselyte-baptism differs from ordinary cleansing lustration. In essence and origin, doubtless, in nothing; but very widely when considered as a ritual ceremony with its fixed laws, constituting a part, and in the minds of many the chief part, of the initiation into Judaism.

In these few words we have already hinted what seems to us the reasonable view to take of the matter. The facts seem to be that direct testimony to the existence of proselyte-baptism fails us in the midst of the second century after Christ, but that nevertheless something of the nature of a cleansing bath must be presupposed from the very beginning as a part of the reception of the proselyte. Delitzsch calls attention to a point which appears to be of importance for understanding the origin of the rite, when he adverts to the connection of this bath with the sacrifice, so that its prescription must date from a time previous to the cessation of the sacrifices. " Its origin also in itself," he remarks,[98] " presupposes the existence of the Temple, and the cleansings required by its sacrificial services, which were performed by plunge-baths; post-biblical legal language uses the word טבל (cf. II Kings v. 14, LXX ἐβαπτίσατο) for these cleansings, while the Pentateuchal Priest-code uses for them the older and vaguer term רחץ בשרו במים (e.g. Lev. xv. 5, 6, etc.). Beyond doubt cleansing by means of a plunge-bath was already from a very early time demanded of the heathen, after he had been circumcised, as a precondition of his participation in the sacrificial services. We see this from the Jerusalem Targum on Exod. xii. 44, according to which the purchased heathen slave, in order to take part in the passover, must not only be circumcised but also receive a plunge-bath. This is also presupposed in the Mishna (Pesachim viii. 8) as an existing institution, and it is only debated whether the heathen belongs to the class of the simply unclean, who through the plunge-bath became clean by the evening of the same day, or to the class of the unclean-from-a-dead-body whose uncleanness lasted seven days (cf. Lev. xv. 5, 13)." These fruitful remarks seem to us to uncover the origin of proselyte-baptism in a twofold sense. They point us back to the time when it originated; [99] but in doing so they point us also back to the thing out of which it originated. Witness to it as an important element in the rite

[98] Herzog's " Real-Encyklopädie," xii. 1883, pp. 298–299.

[99] Both Delitzsch and Plumptre (in Smith's " Dictionary of the Bible," ii. 1863, pp. 943 f.) suppose that proselyte-baptism existed in the time of Christ in a more developed form than I can admit; but they both accord, in general, with the view presented in the text.

of initiation fails, as we ascend the stream of time, in the midst of the second century: nevertheless, it presupposes the sacrifice, a preparation for which it essentially is; and therefore it must have existed in this form and meaning before the destruction of the Temple. It was on the other hand, however, only after the cessation of the sacrifices that it could become an independent element of the rite of initiation: for this, it must have first lost its reference to sacrifice and have acquired a new meaning as a symbolical "new birth." In other words, in the rite of proselyte-baptism, properly so called, we see the result of a development — a development which requires the assumption of its existence before the Temple services ceased in order that we may understand its origin, but which equally requires the assumption that the Temple services had long ceased, in order that we may understand its existing nature as witnessed to in the rabbinical writings. It could not have come into being except as the prerequisite to sacrifice; it could not have grown into its full form until its original relation to sacrifice had been partially obscured in the course of time.[100] Although we must discern its roots set in a time before the destruction of the Temple, therefore, we cannot carry the full-grown plant back into that period. It was apparently a growth of the second century after Christ; what existed in the first century, and in the time of Christ and John, was not this elaborate and independent initiatory rite, but a simple lustration not distinguishable and not distinguished from other lustrations.

If, then, we are to seek a point of departure for the rite of Christian baptism in Jewish custom, we cannot find it in the developed rite of proselyte-baptism. Proselyte-baptism and Christian baptism appear rather as parallel growths from a common root. At the base of both alike lie the cleansing lustrations of the Jewish law. It was these, knowledge of which the Baptist counted upon when he came proclaiming his "baptism." This is indeed evident, independently of what has been

---

[100] The proselytes were still required to promise to sacrifice when the Temple was restored — a survival of the third element in the rite of initiation.

urged here.[101] " The baptism of John and proselyte-baptism,"
says Delitzsch with great justice, " stand only in indirect relation to one another, in so far as one and the same idea underlies
both kinds of baptism as well as the legal lustrations in general, — the idea of the passage from a condition of moral uncleanness to a condition of purity from sin and guilt. . . .
There is no reason to assume that the baptism of John or
Christian baptism originated in proselyte-baptism, or even
that it derived only its form from it. It was, moreover, unlike the
economy of God, to build upon a Pharisaic usage and not
rather upon an ancient symbol, already sanctified by the giving of the Law on Sinai. John himself assigns the choice of
this symbolical rite to divine appointment (John i. 33). . . .
Johannic and Christian baptism have, however, in conformity
with the nature of the New Covenant as a fulfillment of the
Law and the Prophets (Matt. v. 17), over and above their
connection with the Law and the Levitical lustrations in
general as prescribed in it, also another point of connection in
prophecy, in the prediction of a future purification and sanctification through water and the Spirit (Ezek. xxxvi. 25; xxvii.
23 f.; Isa. xliv. 3; Zech. xiii. 1)." [102] This cuts to the root of the
matter. Christian baptism was not such a new thing that it
could not be understood by the disciples to whom it was committed. It had its very close connection with precedent and
well-known rites. But its connection was not specifically with
proselyte-baptism as subsequently developed into a formal rite
of initiation into Judaism; but with the cleansing lustrations
from which that in common with this sprung, and with the
prophetical predictions of Messianic cleansing.

The bearing of this conclusion upon the hope that we might
learn something of value as to the mode of primitive Christian
baptism from the mode in which proselyte-baptism was administered, is obvious. If proselyte-baptism, as known to us
with its established ritual, is of second century growth, while
the roots of Christian baptism are set, not in it, but in the
divinely prescribed lustrations and prophetic announcements

[101] Cf. e.g. Meyer and Alexander on Matt. iii. 5, 6.   [102] *Loc. cit.*

of the Old Testament, we are left without ground from this quarter for any stringent inferences as to the mode of the first administration of Christian baptism. The idea of the lustrations was bathing for the sake of cleansing; and the "many baptisms" of the Jews were performed in more modes of application of the water than one. The prophetic announcements in like manner run through all possible modes of applying the water. In any mode of application, it was complete cleansing which was symbolized. Beyond that, it would seem, we cannot proceed on this pathway.

Our archæological inquiry as to the mode of Christian baptism leaves us hanging, then, in the middle of the second century. What Christian baptism was like at that point of time we can form a tolerably clear notion of. It was a cleansing bath, usually performed by a form of trine immersion. Exceptions were freely allowed whenever dictated by scarcity of water or illness on the part of the recipient. And the usual mode of administration, certainly at Rome and probably also elsewhere, appears to have been by pouring water on the head of a candidate standing in a greater or less depth of water. A fair presumption may hold that this rite, common in the middle of the second century, represents more or less fully the primitive rite. But we dare not press this presumption very far. Take, for example, the two points of trine baptism and immersion. Are not both in the line of a natural development? Would there not be reason enough for the rise of a threefold ritual in the Christian Church in the fact that they baptized in the Triune name and that the Jews baptized by a single immersion; just as the Catholics in Spain found ground at a later period for baptizing by a single immersion in the fact that the Arians baptized by a trine immersion? Would there not be reason enough for a gradual growth of the rite to a full immersion in the fact that that form of baptism would seem more completely to symbolize total cleansing, was consonant with the conception framed of the river baptism of John, of which our Lord Himself partook, and seemed vividly to represent also that death and resurrection with Christ suggested in certain passages of the New Testament? All tho materials certainly existed for the development of such a form of baptism as meets us in the second century, from any beginning which would give the slightest starting-point for such a development. Such being the case, we appear to be forbidden to assume that second century baptism any more certainly reproduces for us primitive Christian baptism, than the second century eucharist reproduces for us the primitive Lord's Supper or the second century church organization the primitive bishop-presbyter. Where, then, it may be asked, are we to go for knowledge of really primitive baptism? If the archæology of the rite supplies ground for no very safe inference, where can we obtain satisfactory guidance? Apparently only from the New Testament itself. We are seemingly shut up to the hints and implications of the sacred pages for trustworthy information here. But the conclusion to which these hints and implications would conduct us, it is not the purpose of this article even to suggest.

XIII
THE POLEMICS OF INFANT BAPTISM

THE POLEMICS OF INFANT BAPTISM [1]

THE question of the Subjects of Baptism is one of that class of problems the solution of which hangs upon a previous question. According as is our doctrine of the Church, so will be our doctrine of the Subjects of Baptism. If we believe, with the Church of Rome, that the Church is in such a sense the institute of salvation that none are united to Christ save through the instrumentality of her ordinances, then we shall inevitably determine the proper subjects of her ordinances in one way. If, on the other hand, we believe, with the Protestant bodies, that only those already united to Christ have right within His house and to its privileges, we shall inevitably determine them in another way. All Protestants should easily agree that only Christ's children have a right to the ordinance of baptism. The cleavage in their ranks enters in only when we inquire how the external Church is to hold itself relatively to the recognition of the children of Christ. If we say that its attitude should be as exclusive as possible, and that it must receive as the children of Christ only those whom it is forced to recognize as such, then we shall inevitably narrow the circle of the subjects of baptism to the lowest limits. If, on the other hand, we say that its attitude should be as inclusive as possible, and that it should receive as the children of Christ all whom, in the judgment of charity, it may fairly recognize as such, then we shall naturally widen the circle of the subjects of baptism to far more ample limits. The former represents, broadly speaking, the Puritan idea of the Church, the latter the general Protestant doctrine. It is on the basis of the Puritan conception of the Church that the Baptists are led to exclude infants from baptism. For, if we are to demand anything like demonstrative evidence of actual participation in

[1] Reprinted from *The Presbyterian Quarterly*, xiii. 1899, pp. 313–334.

Christ before we baptize, no infant, who by reason of years is incapable of affording signs of his union with Christ, can be thought a proper subject of the rite.

The vice of this system, however, is that it attempts the impossible. No man can read the heart. As a consequence, it follows that no one, however rich his manifestation of Christian graces, is baptized on the basis of infallible knowledge of his relation to Christ. All baptism is inevitably administered on the basis not of knowledge but of presumption. And if we must baptize on presumption, the whole principle is yielded; and it would seem that we must baptize all whom we may fairly presume to be members of Christ's body. In this state of the case, it is surely impracticable to assert that there can be but one ground on which a fair presumption of inclusion in Christ's body can be erected, namely, personal profession of faith. Assuredly a human profession is no more solid basis to build upon than a divine promise. So soon, therefore, as it is fairly apprehended that we baptize on presumption and not on knowledge, it is inevitable that we shall baptize all those for whom we may, on any grounds, fairly cherish a good presumption that they belong to God's people — and this surely includes the infant children of believers, concerning the favor of God to whom there exist many precious promises on which pious parents, Baptists as fully as others, rest in devout faith.

To this solid proof of the rightful inclusion of the infant children of believers among the subjects of baptism, is added the unavoidable implication of the continuity of the Church of God, as it is taught in the Scriptures, from its beginning to its consummation; and of the undeniable inclusion within the bounds of this Church, in its pre-Christian form, as participants of its privileges, inclusive of the parallel rite of circumcision, of the infant children of the flock, with no subsequent hint of their exclusion. To this is added further the historical evidence of the prevalence in the Christian Church of the custom of baptizing the infant children of believers, from the earliest Christian ages down to to-day. The manner in which it is dealt with by Augustine and the Pelagians in their controversy, by Cyprian in his letter to Fidus, by Tertullian in his treatise on baptism, leaves no room for doubt that it was, at the time when each of these writers wrote, as universal and unquestioned a practice among Christians at large as it is to-day — while, wherever it was objected to, the objection seems to have rested on one or the other of two contrary errors, either on an overestimate of the effects of baptism or on an underestimate of the need of salvation for infants.

On such lines as these a convincing positive argument is capable of being set forth for infant baptism, to the support of which whatever obscure allusions to it may be found in the New Testament itself may then be summoned. And on these lines the argument has ordinarily been very successfully conducted, as may be seen by consulting the treatment of the subject in any of our standard works on systematic theology, as for example Dr. Charles Hodge's.[2] It has occurred to me that additional support might be brought to the conclusions thus positively attained by observing the insufficiency of the case against infant baptism as argued by the best furnished opponents of that practice. There would seem no better way to exhibit this insufficiency than to subject the presentation of the arguments against infant baptism, as set forth by some confessedly important representative of its opponents, to a running analysis. I have selected for the purpose the statement given in Dr. A. H. Strong's "Systematic Theology."[3] What that eminently well-informed and judicious writer does not urge against infant baptism may well be believed to be confessedly of small comparative weight as an argument against the doctrine and practice. So that if we do not find the arguments he urges conclusive, we may well be content with the position we already occupy.

Dr. Strong opens the topic, "The Subjects of Baptism,"[4] with the statement that "the proper subjects of baptism are those only who give credible evidence that they have been regenerated by the Holy Spirit, — or, in other words, have en-

[2] "Systematic Theology," iii. 1874, pp. 546 ff.   [4] P. 530.
[3] 1886, pp. 534 ff.

tered by faith into the communion of Christ's death and resurrection " — a statement which if, like the ordinary language of the Scriptures, it is intended to have reference only to the adults to whom it is addressed, would be sufficiently unexceptionable; but which the " only " advertises us to suspect to be more inclusive in its purpose. This statement is followed at once by the organized " proof that only persons giving evidence of being regenerated are proper subjects of baptism." This proof is derived:

(a) From the command and example of Christ and his apostles, which show: First, that those only are to be baptized who have previously been made disciples. . . . Secondly, that those only are to be baptized who have previously repented and believed. . . .

(b) From the nature of the church — as a company of regenerate persons. . . .

(c) From the symbolism of the ordinance — as declaring a previous spiritual change in him who submits to it.

Each of these items is supported by Scripture texts, though some of them are no doubt sufficiently inapposite. As, for example, when only John iii. 5 and Rom. vi. 13 — neither of which has anything to do with the visible Church — are quoted to prove that the visible Church (of which baptism is an ordinance) is " a company of regenerate persons "; or as when Matt. xxviii. 19 is quoted to prove that baptism took place after the discipling, as if the words ran μαθητεύσαντες βαπτίζετε, whereas the passage, actually standing μαθητεύσατε βαπτίζοντες, merely demands that the discipling shall be consummated in, shall be performed by means of baptism; or as when Acts x. 47, where the fact that the extraordinary power of the Holy Spirit had come upon Cornelius is pleaded as reason why baptism should not be withheld from him,[5] and

[5] This interpretation of Acts x. 47 must certaintly greatly embarrass Dr. Strong when he comes to interpret the case of the Samaritans in Acts viii. For the same falling of the Holy Ghost which was poured out on Cornelius and his friends and exhibited itself in " speaking with tongues and magnifying God " (Acts x. 46); and was made by Peter the plea why water should not be forbidden for baptizing them; not only did not precede baptism in the case of the Samaritans, but actually did not take place

Rom. vi. 2-5, which only develops the spiritual implication of baptism, are made to serve as proofs that the symbolism of the ordinance declares always and constantly a "previous" spiritual change. Apart from the Scriptural evidence actually brought forward, moreover, the propositions, in the extreme form in which they are stated, cannot be supported by Scripture. The Scriptures do not teach that the external Church is a company of regenerate persons — the parable of the tares for example declares the opposite: though they represent that Church as the company of those who are presumably regenerate. They do not declare that baptism demonstrates a "previous" change — the case of Simon Magus, Acts viii. 13, is enough to exhibit the contrary: though they represent the rite as symbolical of the inner cleansing presumed to be already present, and consequently as administered only on profession of faith.

The main difficulty with Dr. Strong's argument, however, is the illegitimate use it makes of the occasional character of the New Testament declarations. He is writing a "Systematic Theology" and is therefore striving to embrace the whole truth in his statements: he says therefore with conscious reference to infants, whose case he is soon to treat, "Those only are to be baptized who have previously repented and believed," and the like. But the passages he quotes in support of this position are not drawn from a "Systematic Theology" but from direct practical appeals to quite definite audiences, consisting only of adults; or from narratives of what took place as the result of such appeals. Because Peter told the men that stood about him at Pentecost, "Repent ye and be baptized," it does not follow that baptism might not have been adminis-

---

until a considerably later date. The Samaritans are baptized, Acts viii. 12; but the Holy Ghost had not been received by them, Acts viii. 16, and was not received until Peter and John visited them and laid their hands on them (Acts viii. 17). If the case of Cornelius proves that baptism is not administered until after the Holy Ghost is received, that of the Samaritans proves that it precedes the gift of the Holy Ghost. In truth neither passage proves the one or the other, this outpouring of the Holy Ghost referring to the *charismata*.

tered by the same Peter to the infants of those repentant sinners previous to the infants' own repentance. Because Philip baptized the converts of Samaria only after they had believed, it does not follow that he would not baptize their infants until they had grown old enough to repeat their parents' faith, that they might, like them, receive its sign.

The assertion contained in the first proof is, therefore, a *non sequitur* from the texts offered in support of it. There is a suppressed premise necessary to be supplied before the assumed conclusion follows from them, and that premise is that the visible Church consists of believers only without inclusion of their children — that Peter meant nothing on that day of Pentecost when he added to the words which Dr. Strong quotes: "Repent ye and be baptized every one of you in the name of Jesus Christ unto the remission of your sins" — those other words which Dr. Strong does not quote: "For to you is the promise and to your children" (Acts ii. 38, 39). This suppressed premise Dr. Strong adjoins in the second item of proof which he adduces; but we must observe that it is not a second item, but a necessary element in the first item which without it is invalid. In a word, when we correct the Scripture he adduces and the illegitimate use he makes of Scripture, Dr. Strong's whole argument reduces to the one item of the "nature of the Church, as a company of regenerate persons." It is only on the ground that this is the true idea of the Church that the passages quoted to prove that baptism is to be administered "only" to such as have previously repented and believed, and those quoted to prove that the symbolism of the ordinance declares a "previous" spiritual change in him who submits to it, will justify the "only" and "previous" in which lies their point. The validity of the proof he offers thus depends on the truth of the assertion that the Church consists of regenerate persons; and whether this be true or not we need not here stay to examine: certainly the texts he adduces in proof of it, as already intimated, make no approach to establishing it. We rest securely in the result that according to Dr. Strong's argument as well as our own conviction, the subjects of baptism are the members of the visible Church: and who those are, will certainly be determined by our theory of the nature of the Church.

A page or two further on [6] he takes up the question of "Infant Baptism" *ex professo*. This "we reject and reprehend," he tells us, and that for the following reasons, viz.:

(a) Infant baptism is without warrant, either express or implied, in the Scripture. . . .

(b) Infant baptism is expressly contradicted [by Scriptural teaching]. . . .

(c) The rise of infant baptism in the history of the church is due to sacramental conceptions of Christianity, so that all arguments in its favor from the writings of the first three centuries are equally arguments for baptismal regeneration. . . .

(d) The reasoning by which it is supported is unscriptural, unsound, and dangerous in its tendency. . . .

(e) The lack of agreement among pedobaptists as to the warrant for infant baptism and as to the relation of baptized infants to the church, together with the manifest decline of the practice itself, are arguments against it. . . .

(f) The evil effects of infant baptism are a strong argument against it.

Here is quite a list of arguments. We must look at the items one by one.

(a) When we ask after a direct Scriptural warrant for infant baptism, in the sense which Dr. Strong has in mind in the first of these arguments, we, of course, have the New Testament in view, seeing that it is only in the new dispensation that this rite has been ordained. In this sense of the words, we may admit his first declaration — that there is no express command that infants should be baptized; and with it also his second — that there is in Scripture no clear example of the baptism of infants, that is, if we understand by this that there is no express record, reciting in so many words, that infants were baptized. When he adds to these, however, a third contention, that "the passages held to imply infant baptism

[6] P. 534.

contain, when fairly interpreted, no reference to such a practice," we begin to recalcitrate. If it were only asserted that
these passages contain no such stringent proof that infants
were baptized as would satisfy us on the point in the absence
of other evidence, we might yield this point also. But it is too
much to ask us to believe that they contain "no reference to
the practice" if "fairly interpreted." What is a "fair" interpretation? Is it not an interpretation which takes the passages
as they stand, without desire to make undue capital of them
one way or the other? Well, a fair interpretation of these passages, in this sense, might prevent pædobaptists from claiming
them as a demonstrative proof of infant baptism, and it would
also certainly prevent anti-pædobaptists from asserting that
they have "no reference to such a practice." It should lead
both parties to agree that the passages have a possible but not
a necessary reference to infant baptism — that they are neutral
passages, in a word, which apparently imply infant baptism,
but which may be explained without involving that implication if we otherwise know that infant baptism did not exist in
that day. Fairly viewed, in other words, they are passages
which will support any other indications of infant baptism
which may be brought forward, but which will scarcely suffice
to prove it against evidence to the contrary, or to do more than
raise a presumption in its favor in the absence of other evidence for it. For what are these passages? The important ones
are Acts xvi. 15, which declares that Lydia was "baptized and
her household," and Acts xvi. 33, which declares that the
jailer was "baptized and all his," together with I Cor. i. 16,
" And I baptized also the household of Stephanas." Certainly
at first blush we would think that the repeated baptism of
households without further description, would imply the baptism of the infants connected with them. It may be a "fair"
response to this that we do not know that there were any
infants in these households — which is true enough, but not
sufficient to remove the suspicion that there may have been.
It may be a still "fairer" reply to say that whether the infants
of these families (if there were infants in them) were baptized

or not, would depend on the practice of the apostles; and whatever that practice was would be readily understood by the first readers of the Acts. But this would only amount to asking that infant baptism should not be founded solely on these passages alone; and this we have already granted.

Neither of these lines of argument is adduced by Dr. Strong. They would not justify his position — which is not that the baptism of infants cannot be proved by these passages, but much more than this — that a fair interpretation of them definitely excludes all reference to it by them. Let us see what Dr. Strong means by a " fair " interpretation. To the case of Lydia he appends " cf. 40," which tells us when Paul and Silas were loosed from prison " they entered into the house of Lydia, and when they had seen the brethren they comforted them and departed " — from which, apparently, he would have us make two inferences, (1) that these " brethren " constituted the household of Lydia that was baptized, and (2) that these " brethren " were all adults. In like manner to the case of the jailer he appends the mystic " cf. 34," which tells us that the saved jailer brought his former prisoners up into his house and set meat before them and " rejoiced greatly, having believed, with all his house, on God " — from which he would apparently have us infer that there was no member of the household, baptized by Paul, who was too young to exercise personal faith. So he says with reference to I Cor. i. 16, that " I Cor. xvi. 15 shows that the whole family of Stephanas, baptized by Paul, were adults." Nevertheless, when we look at I Cor. xvi. 15, we read merely that the house of Stephanas were the first fruits of Achaia and that they had set themselves to minister unto the saints — which leaves the question whether they are all adults or not just where it was before, that is, absolutely undetermined.

Nor is this all. To these passages Dr. Strong appends two others, one properly enough, I Cor. vii. 14, where Paul admonishes the Christian not to desert the unbelieving husband or wife, " for the unbelieving husband is sanctified in the wife, and the unbelieving wife is sanctified in the brother; else were

your children unclean; but now are they holy." This is doubtless a passage similar to the others, a passage certainly which
does not explicitly teach infant baptism, but equally certainly
which is not inconsistent with it — which would, indeed, find
a ready explanation from such a custom if such a custom existed, and therefore stands as one of the passages which raise
at least a suspicion that infant baptism underlies the form of
expression — since the holiness of the children is taken for
granted in it and the sanctification of the unbelieving partner
inferred from it — but is yet no doubt capable of an explanation on the supposition that that practice did not exist and is
therefore scarcely a sure foundation for a doctrine asserting it.
Dr. Strong is, however, not satisfied with showing that no
stringent inference can be drawn from it in favor of infant
baptism. He claims it as a " sure testimony," a " plain proof "
against infant baptism, on the grounds that the infants and
the unbelieving parent are put by it in the same category, and
(quoting Jacobi) that if children had been baptized, Paul
would certainly have referred to their baptism as a proof of
their holiness. And this in the face of the obvious fact that the
holiness of the children is assumed as beyond dispute and in
no need of proof, doubt as to which would be too horrible to
contemplate, and the sanctification of the husband or wife inferred from it. Of course, it is the sanctity or holiness of external connection and privilege that is referred to, both with
reference to the children and the parent; but that of the one
is taken for granted, that of the other is argued; hence it lies
close to infer that the one may have had churchly recognition
and the other not. Whether that was true or not, however, the
passage cannot positively decide for us; it only raises a suspicion. But this suspicion ought to be frankly recognized.

The other passage which is adjoined to these is strangely
found in their company, although it, too, is one of the " neutral
texts." It is Matt. xix. 14: " Suffer the little children and forbid
them not to come unto me; for to such belongeth the kingdom
of heaven." What has this to do with baptism? Certainly
nothing directly; only if it be held indirectly to show that in-

fants were received by Christ as members of His Kingdom on earth, that is, of His Church, can it bear on the controversy. But notice Dr. Strong's comment: " None would have ' forbidden,' if Jesus and his disciples had been in the habit of baptizing infants." Does he really think this touches the matter that is raised by this quotation? Nobody supposes that " Jesus and his disciples " were in the habit of baptizing infants; nobody supposes that at the time these words were spoken, Christian baptism had been so much as yet instituted. Dr. Strong would have to show, not that infant baptism was not practised before baptism was instituted, but that the children were not designated by Christ as members of His " Kingdom," before the presumption for infant baptism would be extruded from this text. It is his unmeasured zeal to make all texts which have been appealed to by pædobaptists — not merely fail to teach pædobaptism — but teach that children were not baptized, that has led him so far astray here.

We cannot profess to admire, then, the " fair " interpretations which Dr. Strong makes of these texts. No one starting out without a foregone conclusion could venture to say that, when "fairly interpreted," they certainly make no reference to baptism of infants. Nevertheless, I freely allow that they do not suffice, taken by themselves, to prove that infants were baptized by the apostles — they only suggest this supposition and raise a presumption for it. And, therefore, I am prepared to allow in general the validity of Dr. Strong's first argument — when thus softened to reasonable proportions. It is true that there is no express command to baptize infants in the New Testament, no express record of the baptism of infants, and no passages so stringently implying it that we must infer from them that infants were baptized. If such warrant as this were necessary to justify the usage we should have to leave it incompletely justified. But the lack of this express warrant is something far short of forbidding the rite; and if the continuity of the Church through all ages can be made good, the warrant for infant baptism is not to be sought in the New Testament but in the Old Testament, when the Church was instituted, and nothing short of an actual forbidding of it in the New Testament would warrant our omitting it now. As Lightfoot expressed it long ago, " It is not forbidden " in the New Testament to " baptize infants, — therefore, they are to be baptized." [7] Dr. Strong commits his first logical error in demanding express warrant for the continuance of a long-settled institution, instead of asking for warrant for setting it aside.

(b) If thus the first argument is irrelevant as a whole as well as not very judiciously put in its details, is not its failure well atoned for in the second one? His second argument undertakes to show that " infant baptism is expressly contradicted " by Scriptural teaching. Here, at length, we have the promise of what was needed. But if we expect stringent reason here for the alteration of the children-including covenant, we shall be sadly disappointed. Dr. Strong offers four items. First, infant baptism is contradicted " by the Scriptural prerequisites of faith and repentance, as signs of regeneration," which is valid only on the suppressed assumption that baptism is permissible only in the case of those who prove a previous regeneration — which is the very point in dispute. Secondly, " by the Scriptural symbolism of the ordinance." " As we should not bury a person before his death, so we should not symbolically bury a person by baptism until he has in spirit died to sin." Here not only that the symbolism of baptism is burial is gratuitously assumed, but also that this act, whatever be its symbolism, could be the symbol only of an already completed process in the heart of the recipient — which again is the very point in dispute. Thirdly, " by the Scriptural constitution of the church " — where again the whole validity of the argument depends on the assumption that infants are not members of the Church — the very point in dispute. These three arguments must therefore be thrown at once out of court. If the Scriptures teach that personal faith and repentance are prerequisites to baptism, if they teach that

[7] " Horæ Hebraicæ et Talmudicæ," on Matt. iii. 6 (Pitman edition of his " Works," xi. 1823, p. 58).

one must have previously died to sin before he is baptized, if they teach that the visible Church consists of regenerate adults only — why, on any of these three identical propositions, each of which implies all the others, of course infants may not be baptized — for this again is but an identical proposition with any of the three. But it is hardly sound argumentation simply to repeat the matter in dispute in other words and plead it as proof.

The fourth item is more reasonable — " By the Scriptural prerequisites for participation in the Lord's Supper. Participation in the Lord's Supper is the right only of those who can ' discern the Lord's body ' (I Cor. xi. 29). No reason can be assigned for restricting to intelligent communicants the ordinance of the Supper, which would not equally restrict to intelligent believers the ordinance of Baptism." Hence Dr. Strong thinks the Greek Church more consistent in administering the Lord's Supper to infants. It seems, however, a sufficient answer to this to point to the passage quoted: the express declaration of Scripture, that those who are admitted to the Lord's Supper — a declaration made to those who were already baptized Christians — should be restricted to those who discern the Lord's body, is a sufficient Scriptural reason for restricting participation in the Lord's Supper to intelligent communicants; while the absence of that Scripture restriction in its case is a sufficient Scriptural reason for refusing to apply it to baptism. If we must support this Scriptural reason with a purely rational one, it may be enough to add that the fact that baptism is the initiatory rite of the Church supplies us with such a reason. The ordinances of the Church belong to the members of it; but each in its own appointed time. The initiatory ordinance belongs to the members on becoming members, other ordinances become their right as the appointed seasons for enjoying them roll around. We might as well argue that a citizen of the United States has no right to the protection of the police until he can exercise the franchise. The rights all belong to him: but the exercise of each comes in its own season. It is easily seen by the help of such examples that the possession of a right to the initiatory ordinance of the Church need not carry with it the right to the immediate enjoyment of all church privileges: and thus the challenge is answered to show cause why the right to baptism does not carry with it the right to communion in the Lord's Supper.[8] With this challenge the second argument of Dr. Strong is answered, too.

(c) The third argument is really an attempt to get rid of the pressure of the historical argument for infant baptism. Is it argued that the Christian Church from the earliest traceable date baptized infants? — that this is possibly hinted in Justin Martyr, assumed apparently in Irenæus, and openly proclaimed as apostolical by Origen and Cyprian while it was vainly opposed by Tertullian? In answer it is replied that all these writers taught baptismal regeneration and that infant baptism was an invention coming in on the heels of baptismal regeneration and continued in existence by State Churches. There is much that is plausible in this contention. The early Church did come to believe that baptism was necessary to salvation; this doctrine forms a natural reason for the extension of baptism to infants, lest dying unbaptized they should fail of salvation. Nevertheless, the contention does not seem to be the true explanation of the line of development. First, it confuses a question of testimony to fact with a question of doctrine. The two — baptismal regeneration and infant baptism — do not stand or fall together, in the testimony of the Fathers. Their unconscious testimony to a current practice proves its currency in their day; but their witness to a doctrine does not prove its truth. We may or may not agree with them in their doctrine of baptismal regeneration. But we cannot doubt the truth of their testimony to the prevalence of infant baptism in their day. We admit that their day is not the apostles' day. We could well wish that we had earlier witness. We may be sure from the witness of Origen and Cyprian that they were baptized in their infancy — that is, that infant baptism was the usual practice in the age of Irenæus — a conclusion which is at once strengthened by and

[8] Cf. Cotton Mather, as quoted in Hodge, *op. cit.*, iii. 1874, p. 572.

strengthens the witness of Irenæus. But the practice of the latter half of the second century need not have been the practice of the apostles. A presumption is raised, however — even though so weak a one that it would not stand against adverse evidence. But where is the adverse evidence? Secondly, Dr. Strong's view reverses the historical testimony. As a matter of history it was not the inauguration of the practice of infant baptism which the doctrine of baptismal regeneration secured, but the endangering of it. It was because baptism washed away all sin and after that there remained no more laver for regeneration, that baptism was postponed. It is for this reason that Tertullian proposes its postponement. Lastly, though the historical evidence may not be conclusive for the apostolicity of infant baptism, it is in that direction and is all that we have. There is no evidence from primitive church history against infant baptism, except the ambiguous evidence of Tertullian; so that our choice is to follow history and baptize infants or to reconstruct by *a priori* methods a history for which we have no evidence.

(d) Dr. Strong's fourth item is intended as a refutal of the reasoning by which the advocates of pædobaptism support their contention. As such it naturally takes up the reasoning from every kind of sources and it is not strange that some of the reasoning adduced in it is as distasteful to us as it is to him. We should heartily unite with him in refusing to allow the existence of any power in the Church to modify or abrogate any command of Christ. Nor could we find any greater acceptability than he does in the notion of an " organic connection " between the parent and the child, such as he quotes Dr. Bushnell as advocating. Nevertheless we can believe in a parent acting as representative of the child of his loins, whose nurture is committed to him; and we can believe that the status of the parent determines the status of the child — in the Church of the God whose promise is " to you and your children," as well as, for example, in the State. And we can believe that the Church includes the minor children of its members for whom they must as parents act, without believing that

it is thereby made a hereditary body. I do not purpose here
to go over again the proofs, which Dr. Hodge so cogently
urges, that go to prove the continuity of the Church through
the Old and New dispensations — remaining under whatever
change of dispensation the same Church, with the same laws
of entrance and the same constituents. The antithesis which
Dr. Strong adduces — that " the Christian Church is either
a natural, *hereditary* body, or it was merely *typified* by the
Jewish people " — is a false antithesis. The Christian Church
is not a natural, hereditary body and yet it is not merely the
antitype of Israel. It is, the apostles being witnesses, the
veritable Israel itself. It carried over into itself all that was
essentially Israelitish — all that went to make up the body
of God's people. Paul's figures of the olive tree in Romans
and of the breaking down of the middle wall of partition in
Ephesians, suffice to demonstrate this; and besides these figures he repeatedly asserts it in the plainest language.

So fully did the first Christians — the apostles — realize
the continuity of the Church, that they were more inclined
to retain parts of the outward garments of the Church than to
discard too much. Hence circumcision itself was retained; and
for a considerable period all initiates into the Church were
circumcised Jews and received baptism additionally. We do
not doubt that children born into the Church during this age
were both circumcised and baptized. The change from baptism superinduced upon circumcision to baptism substituted
for circumcision was slow, and never came until it was forced
by the actual pressure of circumstances. The instrument for
making this change and so — who can doubt it? — for giving
the rite of baptism its right place as the substitute for circumcision, was the Apostle Paul. We see the change formally
constituted at the so-called Council of Jerusalem, in Acts xv.
Paul had preached the gospel to Gentiles and had received
them into the Church by baptism alone, thus recognizing it
alone as the initiatory rite, in the place of circumcision, instead
of treating as heretofore the two together as the initiatory
rites into the Christian Church. But certain teachers from

Jerusalem, coming down to Antioch, taught the brethren " except ye be circumcised after the custom of Moses ye cannot be saved." Paul took the matter before the Church of Jerusalem from which these new teachers professed to emanate; and its formal decision was that to those who believed and were baptized circumcision was not necessary.

How fully Paul believed that baptism and circumcision were but two symbols of the same change of heart, and that one was instead of the other, may be gathered from Col. ii. 11, when, speaking to a Christian audience of the Church, he declares that " in Christ ye were also circumcised " — but how? — " with a circumcision not made with hands, in putting off the body of the flesh," — that is, in the circumcision of Christ. But what was this Christ-ordained circumcision? The Apostle continues: " Having been buried with Him in baptism, wherein also ye were raised with Him through faith in the working of God, who raised Him from the dead." Hence in baptism they were buried with Christ, and this burial with Christ was the circumcision which Christ ordained, in the partaking of which they became the true circumcision. This falls little, if any, short of a direct assertion that the Christian Church is Israel, and has Israel's circumcision, though now in the form of baptism. Does the view of Paul, now, contradict the New Testament idea of the Church, or only the Baptist idea of the Church? No doubt a large number of the members of the primitive Church did insist, as Dr. Strong truly says, that those who were baptized should also be circumcised: and no doubt, this proves that in their view baptism did not take the place of circumcision. But this was an erroneous view: is represented in the New Testament as erroneous; and it is this exact view against which Paul protested to the Church of Jerusalem and which the Church of Jerusalem condemned in Acts xv. Thus the Baptist denial of the substitution of baptism for circumcision leads them into the error of this fanatical, pharisaical church-party! Let us take our places in opposition, along with Paul and all the apostles.

Whether, then, that the family is the unit of society is a

relic of barbarism or not, it is the New Testament basis of
the Church of God. God does make man the head of the
woman — does enjoin the wife to be in subjection to her husband — and does make the parents act on behalf of their
minor children. He does, indeed, require individual faith for
salvation; but He organizes His people in families first; and
then into churches, recognizing in their very warp and woof
the family constitution. His promises are all the more precious
that they are to us and our children. And though this may
not fit in with the growing individualism of the day, it is
God's ordinance.

(e) Dr. Strong's fifth argument is drawn from the divergent modes in which pædobaptists defend their position and
from the decline among them of the practice of the rite. Let
us confess that we do not all argue alike or aright. But is not
this a proof rather of the firm establishment in our hearts of
the practice? We all practise alike; and it is the propriety of
the practice, not the propriety of our defense of it, that is,
after all, at stake. But the practice is declining, it is said. Perhaps this is true. Dr. Vedder's statistics seem to show it. But
if so, does the decline show the practice to be wrong, or Christians to be unfaithful? It is among pædobaptists that the decline is taking place — those who still defend the practice.
Perhaps it is the silent influence of Baptist neighbors; perhaps it is unfaithfulness in parents; perhaps the spread of a
Quakerish sentiment of undervaluation of ordinances. Many
reasons may enter into the account of it. But how does it show
the practice to be wrong? According to the Baptist reconstruction of history, the Church began by not baptizing infants. But this primitive and godly practice declined — rapidly declined — until in the second century all infants were
baptized and Tertullian raised a solitary and ineffectual voice
crying a return to the older purity in the third. Did that decline of a prevalent usage prove it to be a wrong usage? By
what logic can the decline in the second century be made an
evidence in favor of the earlier usage, and that of the nineteenth an evidence against it?

(f) We must pass on, however, to the final string of arguments, which would fain point out the evil effects of infant baptism. First, it forestalls the act of the child and so prevents him from ever obeying Christ's command to be baptized — which is simply begging the question. We say it obeys Christ's command by giving the child early baptism and so marking him as the Lord's. Secondly, it is said to induce superstitious confidence in an outward rite, as if it possessed regenerating efficacy; and we are pointed to frantic mothers seeking baptism for their dying children. Undoubtedly the evil does occur and needs careful guarding against. But it is an evil not confined to this rite, but apt to attach itself to all rites — which need not, therefore, be all abolished. We may remark, in passing, on the unfairness of bringing together here illustrative instances from French Catholic peasants and High Church Episcopalians, as if these were of the same order with Protestants. Thirdly, it is said to tend to corrupt Christian truth as to the sufficiency of Scripture, the connection of the ordinances, and the inconsistency of an impenitent life with church membership, as if infant baptism necessarily argued sacramentarianism, or as if the churches of other Protestant bodies were as a matter of fact more full of " impenitent members " than those of the Baptists. This last remark is in place also, in reply to the fourth point made, wherein it is charged that the practice of infant baptism destroys the Church as a spiritual body by merging it in the nation and in the world. It is yet to be shown that the Baptist churches are purer than the pædobaptist. Dr. Strong seems to think that infant baptism is responsible for the Unitarian defection in New England. I am afraid the cause lay much deeper. Nor is it a valid argument against infant baptism, that the churches do not always fulfill their duty to their baptized members. This, and not the practice of infant baptism, is the fertile cause of incongruities and evils innumerable.

Lastly, it is urged that infant baptism puts " into the place of Christ's command a commandment of men, and so admit[s] . . . the essential principle of all heresy, schism, and false religion " — a good, round, railing charge to bring against one's brethren. But as an argument against infant baptism, drawn from its effects, somewhat of a *petitio principii*. If true, it is serious enough. But Dr. Strong has omitted to give the chapter and verse where Christ's command not to baptize infants is to be found. One or the other of us is wrong, no doubt; but do we not break an undoubted command of Christ when we speak thus harshly of our brethren, His children, whom we should love? Were it not better to judge, each the other mistaken, and recognize, each the other's desire to please Christ and follow His commandments? Certainly I believe that our Baptist brethren omit to fulfill an ordinance of Christ's house, sufficiently plainly revealed as His will, when they exclude the infant children of believers from baptism. But I know they do this unwittingly in ignorance; and I cannot refuse them the right hand of fellowship on that account.

But now, having run through these various arguments, to what conclusion do we come? Are they sufficient to set aside our reasoned conviction, derived from some such argument as Dr. Hodge's, that infants are to be baptized? A thousand times no. So long as it remains true that Paul represents the Church of the Living God to be one, founded on one covenant (which the law could not set aside) from Abraham to to-day, so long it remains true that the promise is to us and our children and that the members of the visible Church consist of believers and their children — all of whom have a right to all the ordinances of the visible Church, each in its appointed season. The argument in a nutshell is simply this: God established His Church in the days of Abraham and put children into it. They must remain there until He puts them out. He has nowhere put them out. They are still then members of His Church and as such entitled to its ordinances. Among these ordinances is baptism, which standing in similar place in the New Dispensation to circumcision in the Old, is like it to be given to children.

XIV

THE
DEVELOPMENT OF THE DOCTRINE
OF INFANT SALVATION

THE DEVELOPMENT OF THE DOCTRINE
OF INFANT SALVATION [1]

THE task which we set before us in this brief paper is not
to unravel the history of opinion as to the salvation of infants
dying in infancy, but the much more circumscribed one of
tracing the development of doctrine on this subject. We hope
to show that there has been a doctrine as to the salvation of
infants common to all ages of the Church; but that there has
also been in this, as in other doctrines, a progressive correction
of crudities in its conception, by which the true meaning and
relations of the common teaching have been freed from de-
forming accretions and its permanent core brought to purer
expression.

I. THE PATRISTIC DOCTRINE

It is fundamental to the very conception of Christianity
that it is a remedial scheme. Christ Jesus came to save sinners.
The first Christians had no difficulty in understanding and
confessing that Christ had come into a world lost in sin to
establish a kingdom of righteousness, citizenship in which is
the condition of salvation. That infants were admitted into
this citizenship they did not question; Irenæus, for example,
finds it appropriate that Christ was born an infant and grew
by natural stages into manhood, since " He came to save all by
Himself — all, I say, who by Him are born again unto God,
infants and children, and boys and young men, and old men,"
and accordingly passed through every age that He might sanctify all. Nor did they question that not the natural birth of the
flesh, but the new birth of the Spirit was the sole gateway for

[1] Reprinted from the pamphlet of this title published by the Christian
Literature Company of New York in 1891 (copyright now held by Charles
Scribner's Sons).

infants too, into the kingdom; communion with God was lost for all alike, and to infants too it was restored only in Christ.[2] Less pure elements, however, entered almost inevitably into their thought. The ingrained externalism of both Jewish and heathen modes of conception, when brought into the Church wrought naturally toward the identification of the kingdom of Christ with the external Church, and of regeneration with baptism. Already in Justin and Irenæus, the word " regeneration " means " baptism "; the Fathers uniformly understand John iii. 5 of baptism. The maxim of the Patristic age thus became *extra ecclesiam nulla salus;* baptism was held to be necessary to salvation with the necessity of means; and as a corollary, no unbaptized infant could be saved. How early this doctrine of the necessity of baptism became settled in the Church is difficult to trace in the paucity of very early witnesses. Tertullian already defends it from objection.[3] The reply of Cyprian and his fellow bishops to Fidus on the duty of early baptism, presupposes it.[4] After that, it was plainly the Church-doctrine; and although it was mitigated in the case of adults by the admission not only of the baptism of blood, but also that of intention,[5] the latter mitigation was not allowed in the case of infants. The whole Patristic Church agreed that, martyrs excepted, no infant dying unbaptized could enter the kingdom of heaven.

The fairest exponent of the thought of the age on this subject is Augustine, who was called upon to defend it against the Pelagian error that infants dying unbaptized, while failing of entrance into the kingdom, yet obtain eternal life. His constancy in this controversy has won for him the unenviable title of *durus infantum pater* — a designation doubly unjust, in that not only did he neither originate the obnoxious dogma nor teach it in its harshest form, but he was even preparing its destruction by the doctrines of grace, of which he was

---

[2] Irenæus, " Hær.," II. xxii. 4, and III. xviii. 7.

[3] " De bapt.," c. xii.

[4] Ep. lviii. (lxiv.).

[5] With what limitations may be conveniently read in Wall, " History of Infant Baptism," ed. 2, 1707, pp. 359 ff.

more truly the father.[6] Augustine expressed the Church-doctrine moderately, teaching, of course, that infants dying unbaptized would be found on Christ's left hand and be condemned to eternal punishment, but also not forgetting to add that their punishment would be the mildest of all, and indeed that they were to be beaten with so few stripes that he could not say it would have been better for them not to be born.[7] No doubt, others of the Fathers softened the doctrine even below this; some of the Greeks, for instance, like Gregory Nazianzen, thought that unbaptized infants are "neither glorified nor punished" — that is, of course, go into a middle state similar to that taught by Pelagius.[8] But it is not to Augustine, but to Fulgentius (d. 533),[9] or to Alcimus Avitus (d. 525),[10] or to Gregory the Great (d. 604) [11] to whom we must go for the strongest expression of the woe of unbaptized infants. Probably only such anonymous objectors as those whom Tertullian confutes,[12] or such obscure and erratic individuals as Vincentius Victor whom Augustine convicts, in the whole Patristic age, doubted that the kingdom of heaven was closed to all infants departing this life without the sacrament of baptism.

II. The Medieval Mitigation

If the general consent of a whole age as expressed by its chief writers, including the leading bishops of Rome, and by its synodical decrees, is able to determine a doctrine, certainly the Patristic Church transmitted to the Middle Ages as *de fide* that infants dying unbaptized (with the exception only of those who suffer martyrdom) are not only excluded from

[6] Cf. "The Nicene and Post-Nicene Fathers," edited by Dr. Schaff, v. 1887 ("Augustin's Anti-Pelagian Writings"), pp. lxx. f.

[7] Augustine's doctrine is most strongly expressed in "De verbis apostoli sermo xiv." (Sermo ccxciv., in "Opera," Paris, tom. v. pars ii. 1838, coll. 1738 ff.). In "De Peccat. Merit.," c. 21 (xvi.), and "Contra Julianum," v. 11, he speaks of the comparative mildness of the punishment.

[8] Cf. Wall, *op. cit.*, pp. 64 and 365.

[9] "De fide ad Petrum," c. 27.

[10] "Ad Fuscinam sororem."

[11] "Expos. in Job," i. 16.

[12] "De bapt.," c. xii.

heaven, but doomed to hell. Accordingly the medieval synods
so define; the second Council of Lyons and the Council of
Florence declare that " the souls of those who pass away in
mortal sin or in original sin alone descend immediately to hell,
to be punished, however, with unequal penalties." On the
maxim that *gradus non mutant speciem* we must adjudge
Petavius' argument [13] unanswerable, that this deliverance determines the punishment of unbaptized infants to be the same
in kind (in the same hell) with that of adults in mortal sin:
" So infants are tormented with unequal tortures of fire, but
are tormented nevertheless." Nevertheless scholastic thought
on the subject was characterized by a successful effort to mol-
lify the harshness of the Church-doctrine, under the impulse
of the prevalent semi-Pelagian conception of original sin. The
whole troupe of schoolmen unite in distinguishing between
pœna damni and *pœna sensus,* and in assigning to infants dying
unbaptized only the former — that is, the loss of heaven and
the beatific vision, and not the latter — that is, positive torment. They differ among themselves only as to whether this
pœna damni, which alone is the lot of infants, is accompanied
by a painful sense of the loss (as Lombard held), or is so negative as to involve no pain at all, either external or internal (as
Aquinas argued). So complete a victory was won by this molli-
fication that perhaps only a single theologian of eminence can
be pointed to who ventured still to teach the doctrine of
Augustine and Gregory — Gregory Ariminensis thence called
tortor infantum; and Hurter reminds us that even he did not
dare to teach it definitely, but submitted it to the judgment
of his readers.[14] Dante, whom Andrew Seth not unjustly calls
" by far the greatest disciple of Aquinas," has enshrined in
his immortal poem the leading conception of his day, when
he pictures the " young children innocent, whom Death's sharp
teeth have snatched ere yet they were freed from the sin with
which our birth is blent," as imprisoned within the brink of

[13] Petavius, " Dogmata theologica," ed. Paris, ii. 1865, pp. 59 ff.
[14] Hurter, " Theologiae dogmaticae compendium," iii. 1878, pp. 516 ff.:
tract. x. cap. iii. § 729. Wycliffe must be added.

hell, "where the first circle girds the abyss of dread," in a place where "there is no sharp agony" but "dark shadows only," and whence "no other plaint rises than that of sighs" which "from the sorrow without pain arise." [15] The novel doctrine attained papal authority by a decree of Innocent III (*ca.* 1200), who determined "the penalty of original sin to be the lack of the vision of God, but the penalty of actual sin to be the torments of eternal hell."

A more timid effort was also made in this period to modify the inherited doctrine by the application to it of a development of the baptism of intention. This tendency first appears in Hincmar of Rheims (d. 882), who, in a particularly hard case of interdict on a whole diocese, expresses the hope that "the faith and godly desire of the parents and godfathers" of the infants who had thus died unbaptized, "who in sincerity desired baptism for them but obtained it not, may profit them by the gift of Him whose spirit (which gives regeneration) breathes where it pleases." It is doubtful, however, whether he would have extended this lofty doctrine to any less stringent case.[16] Certainly no similar teaching is met with in the Church, except with reference to the peculiarly hard case of still-born infants of Christian parents. The schoolmen (e.g. Alexander Hales and Thomas Aquinas) admitted a doubt whether God may not have ways of saving such unknown to us. John Gerson, in a sermon before the Council of Constance, presses the inference more boldly.[17] God, he declared, has not so tied the mercy of His salvation to common laws and sacraments, but that without prejudice to His law He can sanctify children not yet born, by the baptism of His grace or the power of the Holy Ghost. Hence, he exhorts expectant parents to pray that if the infant is to die before attaining baptism, the Lord may sanctify it; and who knows but that the Lord may hear them? He adds, however, that he only intends to suggest that all hope

[15] "Hell," iv. 23 ff.; "Purgatory," vii. 25 ff.; "Heaven," xxxii. 76 ff. (Plumptre's translation).

[16] Cf. Wall, *op. cit.*, p. 371.

[17] "Sermo de nativitate virg. Mariae," consid. ii. ("Opera," iii. 1728, p. 1350).

is not taken away; for there is no certainty without a revelation. Gabriel Biel (d. 1495) followed in Gerson's footsteps,[18] holding it to be accordant with God's mercy to seek out some remedy for such infants. This teaching remained, however, without effect on the Church-dogma, although something similar to it was, among men who served God in the way then called heresy, foreshadowing an even better to come. John Wycliffe (d. 1384) had already with like caution expressed his unwillingness to pronounce damned such infants as were intended for baptism by their parents, if they failed to receive it in fact; though he could not, on the other hand, assert that they were saved.[19] His followers were less cautious, whether in England or Bohemia, and in this, too, approved themselves heralds of a brighter day.

III. The Teaching of the Church of Rome

In the upheaval of the sixteenth century the Church of Rome found her task in harmonizing under the influence of the scholastic teaching, the inheritance which the somewhat inconsistent past had bequeathed her. Four varieties of opinion sought a place in her teaching. At the one extreme the earlier doctrine of Augustine and Gregory, that infants dying unbaptized suffer eternally the pains of sense, found again advocates, and that especially among the greatest of her scholars, such as Noris, Petau, Driedo, Conry, Berti. At the other extreme, a Pelagianizing doctrine that excluded unbaptized infants from the kingdom of heaven and the life promised to the blessed, and yet accorded to them eternal life and natural happiness in a place between heaven and hell, was advocated by such great leaders as Ambrosius Catharinus, Albertus Pighius, Molina, Sfondrati. The mass, however, followed the schoolmen in the middle path of *pœna damni*, and, like the schoolmen, only differed as to whether the punishment of loss involved sorrow (as Bellarmine held) or was purely negative.[20] The

[18] In IV. dist. iv. q. 2: see Petavius, *op. cit.*, p. 60.
[19] Cf. Wall, p. 372.
[20] For this classification see Bellarmine, " De amissione gratiae," lib. vi.

Council of Trent (1545) anathematized those who affirm that
the " sacraments of the new law are not necessary to salvation,
and that without them or an intention of them men obtain
. . . the grace of justification "; or, again, that " baptism is
free — that is, is not necessary to salvation." This is explained
by the Tridentine Catechism to mean that " unless men be
regenerated to God through the grace of baptism, they are
born to everlasting misery and destruction, whether their
parents be believers or unbelievers "; while, on the other hand,
we are credibly informed [21] that the Council was near
anathematizing as a Lutheran heresy the proposition that the
penalty for original sin is the fire of hell. The Council of Trent
at least made renewedly *de fide* that infants dying unbaptized
incurred damnation, though it left the way open for discussion
as to the kind and amount of their punishment.[22]

The Tridentine deliverance, of course, does not exclude
the baptism of blood as a substitute for baptism of water.
Neither does it seem necessarily to exclude the application of a
theory of baptism of intention to infants. Even after it, therefore, a twofold development seems to have been possible.
The path already opened by Gerson and Biel might have been
followed out, and a baptism of intention developed for infants
as well as for adults. This might even have been pushed on
logically, so as to cover the case of all infants dying in infancy.
On the principle argued by Richard Hooker,[23] for example,
that the unavoidable failure of baptism in the case of Christian
children cannot lose them salvation, because of the presumed
desire and purpose of baptism for them in their Christian parents and in the Church of God, reasoners might have proceeded
only a single step further and have said that the desire and
purpose of Mother Church to baptize all is intention of bap-

---

c. 1 (" Opera," v. 1873, pp. 454 f.) ; and cf. Gerhard, " Loci theologici," ed.
Cotta, ix. 1769, p. 281; Chamier, " Panstratiae catholicae," iii. 1626, p. 159,
or Spanheim, " Chamierus contractus," 1643, p. 797.

[21] So Father Paul, " History of the Council of Trent," lib. ii.

[22] Perrone, " Prælectiones theologicæ . . . in compendium redactæ," i.
1861, pp. 494 ff.

[23] " Ecclesiastical Polity," V. lx. 6, in " Works," ed. Keble, i. 1844, p. 413.

tism enough for all dying in helpless infancy. Thus on Roman principles a salvation for all dying in infancy might be logically deduced, and infants, as more helpless and less guilty, be given the preference over adults. On the other hand, it might be argued that as baptism either *in re* or *in voto* must mediate salvation, and as infants by reason of their age are incapable of the intention, they cannot be saved unless they receive it in fact,[24] and thus infants be discriminated against in favor of adults. This second path is the one which has been actually followed by the theologians of the Church of Rome, with the ultimate result that not only are infants discriminated against in favor of adults, but the more recent theologians seem almost ready to discriminate against the infants of Christians as over against those of the heathen.[25]

The application of the baptism of intention to infants was not abandoned, however, without some protest from the more tender-hearted. Cardinal Cajetan defended in the Council of Trent itself Gerson's proposition that the desire of godly parents might be taken in lieu of the actual baptism of chil-

[24] Thus e.g. Dominicus de Soto expresses it ("De natura et gratia," ii. 10): "It is most firmly established in the Church that no infant apart from baptism *in re* — since he cannot have it *in voto* — enters the kingdom of heaven."

[25] This grows out of the development of the doctrines of ignorance and "invincible ignorance," the latter of which was authoritatively defined by Pope Pius IX in his Encyclical addressed to the Bishops of Italy, August 10, 1863. See an interesting statement concerning it in Newman's "A Letter to the Duke of Norfolk," on the Infallibility of the Pope. Thus while an absolute necessity for baptism *in re* is posited for the infants of even Christian parents, even though they die in the womb, on the other hand, as the law of baptism is in force only where it is known, and even an ignorance morally invincible (as among sectaries) is counted true ignorance, not even an intention of baptism is demanded of the heathen or of certain sectaries. Gousset, "Théologie Dogmatique," ed. 10, Paris, 1866, i. pp. 548, 549, 551, ii. pp. 382 f., may be profitably consulted in this connection. Among the heathen thus the old remedies for sin are still probably valid; St. Bernard says (quoted approvingly by Gousset), "Among the Gentiles as many as are found faithful, we believe that the adults are expiated by faith and the sacrifices; but the faith of the parents profits the children, nay, even suffices for them." If the fathers are saved, why not the children? Might not a Christian's infant dying in the womb be said to be "invincibly ignorant"? Why need the "law of baptism" be so inflexibly extended to *it?*

dren dying in the womb.[26] Cassander (1570) encouraged parents to hope and pray for children so dying.[27] Bianchi (1768) holds that such children may be saved *per oblationem pueri quam Deo mater extrinsecus faciat.*[28] Eusebius Amort (1758) teaches that God may be moved by prayer to grant justification to such extra-sacramentally.[29] Even somewhat bizarre efforts have been made to escape the sad conclusion proclaimed by the Church. Thus Klee holds that a lucid interval is accorded to infants in the article of death, so that they may conceive the wish for baptism.[30] An obscure French writer supposes that they may, " shut up in their mother's womb, know God, love Him, and have the baptism of desire." [31] A more obscure German conceives that infants remain eternally in the same state of rational development in which they die, and hence enjoy all they are capable of; if they die in the womb they either fall back into the original force from which they were produced, or enjoy a happiness no greater than that of trees.[32] These protests of the heart have awakened, however, no response in the Church,[33] which has preferred to hold fast to the dogma that the failure of baptism in infants, dying such, excludes *ipso facto* from heaven, and to seek its comfort in mitigating still further than the scholastics themselves the nature of that *pœna damni* which alone it allows as punishment of original sin.

And if we may assume that such writers as Perrone, Hurter, Gousset, and Kendrick are typical of modern Roman theology throughout the world, certainly that theology may be said to have come, in this pathway of mitigation, as near to posit-

---

[26] In 3 part. Thomae, q. 68, art. 2 et 11.

[27] " De baptismo infantium."

[28] " De remedio . . . pro parvulis . . . sine baptismo morientibus."

[29] " Theolog. moralis," II. xi. 3.

[30] " Katholische Dogmatik," iii. 1845, pp. 151 f. (cap. ii. zweiter Abschnitt, § 1).

[31] De la Marne, " Traité métaphysique des dogmes de la Trinité," Paris, 1826.

[32] Hermesius, *Zeitschrift für Phil. und kath. Theologie*, Bonn, 1832.

[33] Cf. Vasquez, in 3 P. s. Th. disp. cli. cap. 1; Hurter, *op. cit.*, iii. 1878, pp. 516 ff.; Perrone, " Prælectiones theologicæ," vi. 1839, p. 55.

ing salvation for all infants dying unbaptized as the rather intractable deliverances of early popes and later councils permit to them. They all teach, of course (as the definitions of Florence and Trent require of them) — in the words of Perrone[34] — "that children of this kind descend into hell, or incur damnation"; but (as Hurter says[35]), "although all Catholics agree that infants dying without baptism are excluded from the beatific vision and so suffer *loss*, are *lost* (*pati damnum, damnari*); they yet differ among themselves in their determination of the nature and condition of the state into which such infants pass." As the idea of "damnation" may thus be softened to a mere *failure to attain,* so the idea of "hell" may be elevated to that of a natural *paradise*. Hurter himself is inclined to a somewhat severer doctrine; but Perrone (supported by such great lights as Balmes, Berlage, Oswald, Lessius, and followed not afar off by Gousset and Kendrick) reverts to the Pelagianizing view of Catharinus and Molina and Sfondrati — which Petau called a "fabrication" championed indeed by Catharinus but originated "by Pelagius the heretic," and which Bellarmine contended was *contra fidem* — and teaches that unbaptized infants enter into a state deprived of all supernatural benefits, indeed, but endowed with all the happiness of which pure nature is capable. Their state is described as having the nature of penalty and of damnation when conceived of relatively to the supernatural happiness from which they are excluded by original sin; but when conceived of in itself and absolutely, it is a state of pure nature, and accordingly the words of Thomas Aquinas are applied to it: "They are joined to God by participation in natural goods, and so also can rejoice in natural knowledge and love."[36] Thus, after so many ages, the Pelagian conception of the middle state for infants has obtained its revenge on the condemnation of the Church. No doubt it is not admitted that this is a return to Pelagianism; Perrone, for example, argues that

[34] "Prælectiones theologicæ . . . in compendium redactæ," i. 1861, p. 494, No. 585.

[35] *Op. cit.,* p. 517, No. 729.

[36] Perrone, i. p. 495; cf. ii. 1861, p. 252.

Pelagius held the doctrine of a natural beatitude for infants as one unrelated to sin, while " Catholic theologians hold it with the death of sin; so that the exclusion from the beatific vision has the nature of penalty and of damnation proceeding from sin." [37] Is there more than a verbal difference here? At all events, whatever difference exists is a difference not in the doctrine of the state of unbaptized infants after death, but in the doctrine of the fall. In deference to the language of fathers and councils and popes, this natural paradise is formally assigned to that portion of the other world designated " hell," but in its own nature it is precisely the Pelagian doctrine of the state of unbaptized infants after death. By what expedient such teaching is to be reconciled with the other doctrines of the Church of Rome, or with its former teaching on this same subject, or with its boast of *semper eadem,* is more interesting to its advocates within that communion than to us.[38] Our interest as historians of opinion is exhausted in simply noting the fact that the Pelagianizing process, begun in the Middle Ages by assigning to infants guilty only of original sin liability to *pœna damni* alone, culminates in our day in their assignment by the most representative theologians of modern Rome to a natural paradise.

IV. The Lutheran Doctrine

It is, no doubt, as a protest against the harshness of the Romanist syllogism, " No man can attain salvation who is not a member of Christ; but no one becomes a member of Christ except by baptism, received either *in re* or *in voto,*" [39] that this Pelagianizing drift is to be regarded. Its fault is that it impinges by way of mitigation and modification on the *major* premise, which, however, is the fundamental proposition of Christianity. Its roots are planted, in the last analysis, in a conception of men, not as fallen creatures, children of wrath,

[37] *Op. cit.,* i. p. 495, No. 590.

[38] See some of the difficulties very mildly stated in Hurter, *loc. cit.*

[39] The words are Aquinas' (p. 3, q. 68, art. 1); see them quoted and applied by Perrone, *op. cit.,* ii. p. 253, No. 99.

and deserving of a doom which can only be escaped by becoming members of Christ, but as creatures of God with claims on Him for natural happiness, but, of course, with no claims on Him for such additional supernatural benefits as He may yet lovingly confer on His creatures in Christ. On the other hand, that great religious movement which we call the Reformation, the constitutive principle of which was its revised doctrine of the Church, ranged itself properly against the fallacious *minor* premise, and easily broke its bonds with the sword of the word. Men are not constituted members of Christ through the Church, but members of the Church through Christ; they are not made the members of Christ by baptism which the Church gives, but by faith, the gift of God; and baptism is the Church's recognition of this inner fact. The full benefit of this better apprehension of the nature of that Church of God membership in which is the condition of salvation, was not reaped, however, by all Protestants in equal measure. It was the strength of the Lutheran movement that it worked out its positions not theoretically or all at once, but step by step, as it was forced on by the logic of events and experience. But it was an incidental evil that, being compelled to express its faith early, its first confession was framed before the full development of Protestant thought, and subsequently contracted the faith of Lutheranism into too narrow channels. The Augsburg Confession contains the true doctrine of the Church as the *congregatio sanctorum;* but it committed Lutheranism to the doctrine that baptism is necessary to salvation (art. ix.) in such a sense that children are not saved without baptism (art. ix.),[40] inasmuch as the condemnation and eternal death brought by original sin upon all are not removed except from those who are born again by baptism and the Holy Ghost (art. ii.) — that is, to the doctrine that the necessity of baptism is the necessity of means. In the direction of mollifying interpretation of this deliverance, the theologians urge: 1. That the necessity affirmed is not absolute but ordinary, and binds man and not God. 2. That as the assertion

[40] " Or outside the Church of Christ," as is added in ed. 1540.

is directed against the Anabaptists, it is not the privation, but the contempt of baptism that is affirmed to be damning. 3. That the necessity of baptism is not intended to be equalized with that of the Holy Ghost. 4. That the affirmation is not that for original sin alone anyone is actually damned, but only that all are therefor damnable. There is force in these considerations. But they do not avail wholly to relieve the Augsburg Confession of limiting salvation to those who enjoy the means of grace, and as concerns infants, to those who receive the sacrament of baptism.

It is not to be held, of course, that it asserts such an absolute necessity of baptism for infants dying such, as admits no exceptions. From Luther and Melanchthon down, Lutheran theologians have always taught what Hunnius expressed in the Saxon Visitation Articles: " Unless a person be born again of water and the Spirit, he cannot enter into the kingdom of heaven. *Cases of necessity are not intended, however, by this.*" Lutheran theology, in other words, takes its stand positively on the ground of baptism of intention as applied to infants, as over against its denial by the Church of Rome. " Luther," says Dorner,[41] " holds fast, in general, to the necessity of baptism in order to salvation, but in reference to the children of Christians who have died unbaptized, he says: ' The holy and merciful God will think kindly upon them. What He will do with them, He has revealed to no one, that baptism may not be despised, but has reserved to His own mercy; God does wrong to no man.' "[42] From the fact that Jewish children dying before circumcision were not lost, Luther argues that neither are Christian children dying before baptism;[43] and he comforts Christian mothers of still-born babes by declaring that they should understand that such infants are saved.[44] So Bugenhagen, under Luther's direction, teaches that Christians' children intended for baptism are not left to the hidden

[41] " History of Protestant Theology " (E.T.), i. 1871, pp. 171 f.

[42] " Werke," xxii. 872 (Dorner's quotation).

[43] " Com. in Gen.," c. 17: " Exegetica opera latina," Erlangen, iv. 1829, p. 78.

[44] " Christliches Bedenken."

judgment of God if they fail of baptism, but have the promise of being received by Christ into His kingdom.[45] It is not necessary to quote later authors on a point on which all are unanimous; let it suffice to add only the clear statement of the developed Lutheranism of John Gerhard (1610–1622): [46] "We walk in the middle way, teaching that baptism is, indeed, the ordinary sacrament of initiation and means of regeneration necessary to all, even to the children of believers, for regeneration and salvation; but yet that in the event of privation or impossibility the children of Christians are saved by an extraordinary and peculiar divine dispensation. For the necessity of baptism is not absolute, but ordinary; we on our part are obliged to the necessity of baptism, but there must be no denial of the extraordinary action of God in infants offered to Christ by pious parents and the Church in prayers, and dying before the opportunity of baptism can be given them, since God does not so bind His grace and saving efficacy to baptism as that, in the event of privation, He may not both wish and be able to act extraordinarily. We distinguish, then, between necessity on *God's* part and on *our* part; between the case of *privation* and the *ordinary* way; and also between infants born *in* the Church and *out* of the Church. Concerning infants born out of the Church, we say with the apostle (I Cor. v. 12, 13), 'For what have I to do with judging them that are without? Do not you judge them that are within? For them that are without God judgeth.' Wherefore, since there is no promise concerning them, we commit them to God's judgment; and yet we hold to no place intermediate between heaven and hell, concerning which there is utter silence in Scripture. But concerning infants born in the Church we have better hope. Pious parents properly bring their children as soon as possible to baptism as the ordinary means of regeneration, and offer them in baptism to Christ; and those who are negligent in this, so as through lack of care or wicked contempt for the sacrament

[45] See for several such quotations brought together, Laurence, "Eight Sermons Preached before the University of Oxford," Bampton Lectures, 1804, ed. 1820, pp. 271 f. Also Gerhard as in next note.

[46] Ed. Cotta, ix. 1769, pp. 282 ff.

to deprive their children of baptism, shall hereafter render a very heavy account to God, since they have 'despised the counsel of God' (Luke vii. 30). Yet neither can nor ought we rashly to condemn those infants which die in their mothers' wombs or by some sudden accident before they receive baptism, but may rather hold that the prayers of pious parents, or, if the parents are negligent of this, the prayers of the Church, poured out for these infants, are clemently heard and they are received by God into grace and life."

From this passage, too, we may learn the historical attitude of Lutheranism toward the entirely different question of the fate of infants dying outside the pale of the Church and the reach of its ordinances, a multitude so vast that it is wholly unreasonable to suppose them simply (like Christians' children deprived of baptism) exceptions to the rule laid down in the Augsburg Confession. It is perfectly clear that the Lutheran Confessions extend no hope for them. It is doubtful whether it can even be said that they leave room for hope for them. Melanchthon in the "Apology" is no doubt arguing against the Anabaptists, and intends to prove only that children should be baptized; but his words in explanation of art. ix. deserve consideration in this connection also — where he argues that "the promise of salvation" "does not pertain to those who are without the Church of Christ, where there is neither the Word nor the Sacraments, because the kingdom of Christ exists only with the Word and the Sacraments." [47] Luther's personal opinion as to the fate of heathen children dying in infancy is in doubt; now he expresses the hope that the good and gracious God may have something good in view for them; [48] and again, though leaving it to the future to decide, he only expects something milder for them than for the adults outside the Church; [49] and Bugenhagen, under his eye, contrasts the children of Turks and Jews with those of Christians, as not sharers in salvation because not in Christ.[50]

[47] "Opera," in "Corpus reformatorum," xxvii. 1859, p. 533.
[48] Cf. Dorner, *op. cit.*, i. p. 172.
[49] Cf. Laurence, *op. cit.*, pp. 272 f.
[50] *Ibid.*, p. 272.

From the very first the opinion of the theologians was divided on the subject. 1. Some held that all infants except those baptized in fact or intention are lost, and ascribed to them, of course — for this was the Protestant view of the desert of original sin — both privative and positive punishment. This party included such theologians as Quistorpius, Calovius, Fechtius, Zeibichius, Buddeus. 2. Others judged that we may cherish the best of hope for their salvation. Here belong Dannhauer, Hulsemann, Scherzer, J. A. Osiander, Wagner, Musæus, Cotta, and Spener. But the great body of Lutherans, including such names as Gerhard, Calixtus, Meisner, Baldwin, Bechmann, Hoffmann, Hunnius, held that nothing is clearly revealed as to the fate of such infants, and they must be left to the judgment of God. 3. Some of these, like Hunnius, were inclined to believe that they will be saved. 4. Others, with more (like Hoffmann) or less (like Gerhard) clearness, were rather inclined to believe they will be lost; but all alike held that the means for a certain decision are not in our hands.[51] Thus Hunnius says: [52] " That the infants of Gentiles, outside the Church, are saved, we cannot pronounce as certain, since there exists nothing definite in the Scriptures concerning the matter; so neither do I dare simply to assert that these children are indiscriminately damned. . . . Let us commit them, therefore, to the judgment of God." And Hoffmann says: [53] " On the question whether the infants of the heathen nations are lost, most of our theologians prefer to suspend their judgment. To affirm as a certain thing that they are lost, could not be done without rashness."

This cautious agnostic attitude has the best right to be called the historical Lutheran attitude. It is even the highest position thoroughly consistent with the genius of the Lutheran system and the stress which it lays on the means of grace. The drift in more modern times has, however, been decidedly in the direction of affirming the salvation of all that die in infancy,

[51] This classification is taken from Cotta (Gerhard's "Loci," ix. p. 282).

[52] " Quæst. in cap. vii. Gen."

[53] See Krauth, " The Conservative Reformation and its Theology," 1872, p. 433.

on grounds identical with those pleaded by this party from the beginning — the infinite mercy of God, the universality of the atonement, the inability of infants to resist grace, their guiltlessness of despising the ordinance, and the like.[54] Even so, however, careful modern Lutherans moderate their assertions. They affirm that " it is not the doctrine of our Confession that any human creature has ever been, or ever will be, lost purely on account of original sin";[55] but they speak of the matter as a " dark " or a " difficult question,"[56] and suspend the salvation of such infants on an "extraordinary" and "uncovenanted" exercise of God's mercy.[57] We cannot rise to a conviction or a "faith" in the matter, but may attain to a "well-grounded hope," based on our apprehension of God's all-embracing mercy.[58] In short, the Lutheran doctrine seems to lay no firm foundation for a conviction of the salvation of all infants dying in infancy; at the best it is held to leave open an uncontradicted hope. We are afraid we must say more; it seems to contradict this hope. For should this hope prove true, it would no longer be true that "baptism is necessary to salvation," even *ordinarily;* the exception would be the rule. Nor would the fundamental conception of the Lutheran theory of salvation — that grace is in the means of grace — be longer tenable. The logic of the Lutheran system leaves little room for the salvation of all infants dying in infancy, and if their salvation should prove to be a fact, the integrity of the system is endangered.

V. ANGLICAN VIEWS

A similar difficulty is experienced by all types of Protestant thought in which the older idea of the Church, as primarily an external body, has been incompletely reformed. This may be

[54] Cf. the statements in Cotta, *loc. cit.,* and Krauth, *loc. cit.*

[55] Krauth, *op. cit.,* p. 429.

[56] *Ibid.,* pp. 561–563.

[57] *Ibid.,* pp. 430, 438.

[58] Krauth, " Infant Baptism and Infant Salvation in the Calvinistic System," 1874, p. 22.

illustrated, for example, from the history of thought in the
Church of England. The Thirty-nine Articles, in their final
form, are thoroughly Protestant and Reformed. And many of
the greatest English theologians, even among those not most
closely affiliated with Geneva, from the very earliest days of
the Reformation, have repudiated the " cruel judgment " of
the Church of Rome as to the fate of infants dying unbaptized.
But this repudiation was neither immediate, nor has it ever
been universal. The second of the Ten Articles of Henry VIII
(1536) not only declares that the promise of grace and eternal
life is adjoined to baptism, but adds that infants " by the sacrament of baptism do also obtain remission of their sins, the
grace and favor of God, and be made thereby the very sons and
children of God; insomuch as infants and children dying in
their infancy shall undoubtedly be saved thereby, and else
not." The first liturgy embodied the same implication. The
growing Protestant sentiment soon revised it out of these
standards.[59] But there have never lacked those in the Church
of England who still taught the necessity of baptism to salvation. If it can boast of a John Hooper, who speaks of the " ungodly opinion, that attributeth the salvation of men unto the
receiving of an external sacrament," " as though the holy
Spirit could not be carried by faith into the penitent and sorrowful conscience, except it rid always in a chariot and external
sacrament," and who (probably first after Zwingli) taught that
all infants dying in infancy, whether children of Christians or
infidels, are saved; [60] it also has counted among its teachers
many who held with Matthew Scrivener that Christ's " death
and passion are not communicated unto any but by outward
signs and sacraments," so that " either all children must be
damned, dying unbaptized, or they must have baptism." [61]
The general position of the Church up to his day is thus con-

[59] For an outline of the history see Schaff, " Creeds of Christendom," i.
1877, p. 642; cf. Laurence, *op. cit.*, pp. 176 f.
[60] " Answer to the Bishop of Winchester's Book," 1547, in the Parker Society's " Early Writings of Bishop Hooper," 1843, pp. 129, 131.
[61] " Course of Divinity," London, 1674, p. 196.

ceived by Wall: [62] " The Church of England have declared their Sense of the [that is, baptism's] Necessity, by reciting that Saying of our Saviour, John iii. 5, both in the Office of Baptism of Infants, and also in that for those of riper Years. . . . Concerning the everlasting State of an Infant that by Misfortune dies unbaptized, the Church of England has determined nothing, (it were fit that all Churches would leave such Things to God) save that they forbid the ordinary *Office for Burial* to be used for such an one: for that were to determin the Point, and acknowledge him for a Christian Brother. And tho' the most noted Men in the said Church from Time to Time since the Reformation of it to this Time, have expressed their Hopes that God will accept the Purpose of the Parent for the Deed; yet they have done it modestly, and much as Wickliff did, rather not determining the Negative, than absolutely determining the Positive, that such a Child shall enter into the Kingdom of Heaven." If this is all that can be said of the children of the faithful, lacking baptism, where will those of the infidel appear? Many other opinions — more Protestant or more Pelagian — have, of course, found a home for themselves in the bosom of this most inclusive communion, but they are no more characteristic of its teaching than that of Wall. It is only needful to remember that there are still many among the clergy of the Church of England who, retaining the old, unreformed view of the Church, still believe " that the relationship of sonship to God is imparted through baptism and is not imparted without it "; [63] though, of course, many others, and we hope still a large majority, would repudiate this position as incredible.

VI. THE REFORMED DOCTRINE

It was among the Reformed alone that the newly recovered Scriptural apprehension of the Church to which the promises were given, as essentially not an externally organized body but

[62] " History of Infant Baptism," ed. 2, 1707, p. 377.
[63] " Tracts for the Times," by members of the University of Oxford, ii. 1839, No. 67.

the people of God, membership in which is mediated not by the external act of baptism but by the internal regeneration of the Holy Spirit, bore its full fruit in rectifying the doctrine of the application of redemption. This great truth was taught alike by both branches of Protestantism, but it was limited in its application in the one line of teaching by a very high doctrine of the means of grace, while in the other it became itself constitutive of the doctrine of the means of grace. Not a few Reformed theologians, even outside the Church of England, no doubt also held a high doctrine of the means; of whom Peter Jurieu may be taken as a type.[64] But this was not characteristic of the Reformed churches, the distinguishing doctrine of which rather by suspending salvation on membership in the invisible instead of in the visible Church, transformed baptism from a necessity into a duty, and left men dependent for salvation on nothing but the infinite love and free grace of God. In this view the absolutely free and loving election of God alone is determinative of the saved; so that how many and who they are is known absolutely to God alone, and to us only so far forth as it may be inferred from the marks and signs of election revealed to us in the Word. Faith and its fruits are the chief signs in the case of adults, and he that believes may know that he is of the elect. In the case of infants dying in infancy, birth within the bounds of the covenant is a sure sign, since the promise is " unto us and our children." But present unbelief is not a sure sign of reprobation in the case of adults, for who knows but that unbelief may yet give place to faith? Nor in the case of infants, dying such, is birth outside the covenant a trustworthy sign of reprobation, for the election of God is free. Accordingly there are many — adults and infants — of whose salvation we may be sure, but of reprobation we cannot be sure; such a judgment is necessarily unsafe even as to adults apparently living in sin, while as to infants who " die and give no sign," it is presumptuous and rash in the extreme.

The above is practically an outline of the teaching of

[64] See his views quoted and discussed by Witsius, " De efficacia et utilitate baptismi," in " Miscellanea sacra," ii. 1736, pp. 513 ff.

Zwingli. He himself worked it out in its logical completeness, and taught: 1. That all believers are elect and hence are saved, though we cannot know infallibly who are true believers except in our own case. 2. All children of believers dying in infancy are elect and hence are saved, for this rests on God's immutable promise. 3. It is probable, from the superabundance of the gift of grace over the offense, that all infants dying such are elect and saved; so that death in infancy is a sign of election; and although this must be left with God, it is certainly rash and even impious to affirm their damnation. 4. All who are saved, whether adult or infant, are saved only by the free grace of God's election and through the redemption of Christ.[65]

The central principle of Zwingli's teaching is not only the common possession of all Calvinists, but the essential postulate of their system. They can differ among themselves only in their determination of what the signs of election and reprobation are, and in their interpretation of these signs. On these grounds Calvinists early divided into five classes: 1. From the beginning a few held with Zwingli that death in infancy is a sign of election, and hence that all who die in infancy are the children of God and enter at once into glory. After Zwingli, Bishop Hooper was probably the first [66] to embrace this view.[67] It has more lately become the ruling view, and we may select

[65] Zwingli's teaching may be conveniently worked out by the aid of August Baur's valuable "Zwinglis Theologie," especially vol. ii. (Halle, 1889). Zwingli's doctrine of original sin had practically no influence on this question.

[66] The adverb is used advisedly. Calvin is often held to have believed that all infants dying such are saved. For a careful statement of this opinion see especially the full and learned paper of Dr. Charles W. Shields, in The Presbyterian and Reformed Review for October, 1890 (i. pp. 634–651). To us, however, Calvin seems, while speaking with admirable caution, to imply that he believed some infants dying such to be lost. See e.g. his comment on Rom. v. 17, and his treatises against Pighius, Servetus, and Castellio. Dr. Schaff repeatedly speaks of Bullinger as agreeing in this point with Zwingli — on what grounds we know not unless the note in "Creeds of Christendom," i. 1877, p. 642, note 3, is intended to direct us to the passages quoted by Laurence as such. But these passages do not seem to support that opinion; and in a diligent search in Bullinger's works we find nothing to favor it and much to negative it.

[67] See reference ante, p. 129.

Augustus Toplady [68] and Robert S. Candlish as its types. The latter, for example, writes: [69] " In many ways, I apprehend, it may be inferred from Scripture that all dying in infancy are elect, and are therefore saved. . . . The whole analogy of the plan of saving mercy seems to favour the same view. And now it may be seen, if I am not greatly mistaken, to be put beyond question by the bare fact that little children die. . . . The death of little children must be held to be one of the fruits of redemption. . . ." 2. At the opposite extreme a very few held that the only sure sign of election is faith with its fruits, and, therefore, we can have no real ground of knowledge concerning the fate of any infant; as, however, God certainly has His elect among them too, each man can cherish the hope that his children are of the elect. Peter Martyr approaches this sadly agnostic position (which was afterward condemned by the Synod of Dort), writing: " Neither am I to be thought to promise salvation to all the children of the faithful which depart without the sacrament, for if I should do so I might be counted rash; I leave them to be judged by the mercy of God, seeing I have no certainty concerning the secret election and predestination; but I only assert that those are truly saved to whom the divine election extends, although baptism does not intervene. . . . Just so, I hope well concerning infants of this kind, because I see them born from faithful parents; and this thing has promises that are uncommon; and although they may not be general, *quoad omnes*, . . . yet when I see nothing to the contrary it is right to hope well concerning the salvation of such infants." [70] The great body of Calvinists, however, previous to the present century, took their position between these extremes. 3. Many held that faith and the promise are sure signs of election, and accordingly all believers and their children are certainly saved; but that the lack of faith and the promise is an equally sure sign of reprobation, so that all the children of unbelievers, dying such, are equally certainly

---

[68] " Complete Works," new edition, 1857, pp. 645 f.
[69] " The Atonement: its Efficacy and Extent," 1867, pp. 183, 184.
[70] " Loci communes," i. 1580, p. 439a (classis IV. loc. viii. § 16).

lost. The younger Spanheim, for example, writes: " Confessedly, therefore, original sin is a most just cause of positive reprobation. Hence no one fails to see what we should think concerning the children of pagans dying in their childhood; for unless we acknowledge salvation outside of God's covenant and Church (like the Pelagians of old, and with them Tertullian, Epiphanius, Clement of Alexandria, of the ancients, and of the moderns, Andradius, Ludovicus Vives, Erasmus, and not a few others, against the whole Bible), and suppose that all the children of the heathen, dying in infancy, are saved, and that it would be a great blessing to them if they should be smothered by the midwives or strangled in the cradle, we should humbly believe that they are justly reprobated by God on account of the corruption (*labes*) and guilt (*reatus*) derived to them by natural propagation. Hence, too, Paul testifies (Rom. v. 14) that death has passed upon them which have not sinned after the similitude of Adam's transgression, and distinguishes and separates (I Cor. vii. 14) the children of the covenanted as holy from the impure children of unbelievers." [71]

4. More held that faith and the promise are certain signs of election, so that the salvation of believers" children is certain, while the lack of the promise only leaves us in ignorance of God's purpose; nevertheless that there is good ground for asserting that both election and reprobation have place in this unknown sphere. Accordingly they held that all the infants of believers, dying such, are saved, but that some of the infants of unbelievers, dying such, are lost. Probably no higher expression of this general view can be found than John Owen's. He argues that there are two ways in which God saves infants: " (1) by interesting them in the covenant, if their immediate or remote parents have been believers. He is a God of them and of their seed, extending his mercy unto a thousand generations of them that fear him; [72] (2) by his grace of election, which is most free, and not tied to any conditions; by which I

---

[71] " Opera," iii. 1703, coll. 1173 f., § 22.

[72] It is, perhaps, worth noting that this is the general Calvinistic view of what " children of believers " means. Cf. Calvin, " Tracts," iii. 1851, p. 351.

STUDIES IN THEOLOGY

make no doubt but God taketh many unto him in Christ whose parents never knew, or had been despisers of, the gospel." [73]

5. Most Calvinists of the past, however, have simply held that faith and the promise are marks by which we may know assuredly that all those who believe and their children, dying such, are elect and saved, while the absence of sure marks of either election or reprobation in infants, dying such outside the covenant, leaves us without ground for inference concerning them, and they must be left to the judgment of God, which, however hidden from us, is assuredly just and holy and good. This agnostic view of the fate of uncovenanted infants has been held, of course, in conjunction with every degree of hope or the lack of hope concerning them, and thus in the hands of the several theologians it approaches each of the other views, except, of course, the second, which separates itself from the general Calvinistic attitude by allowing a place for reprobation even among believers' infants, dying such. Petrus de Witte may stand for one example. He says: " We must adore God's judgments and not curiously inquire into them. Of the children of believers it is not to be doubted but that they shall be saved, inasmuch as they belong unto the covenant. But because we have no promise of the children of unbelievers we leave them to the judgment of God." [74] Matthew Henry [75] and our own Jonathan Dickinson [76] may also stand as types. It is this cautious, agnostic view which has the best historical right to be called the general Calvinistic one. Van Mastricht correctly says that while the Reformed hold that infants are liable to reprobation, yet " concerning *believers'* infants . . . they judge better things. But *unbelievers'* infants, because the Scriptures determine nothing *clearly* on the subject, they judge should be left to the divine discretion." [77]

The Reformed Confessions with characteristic caution re-

[73] " Works," ed. Goold, x. 1852, p. 81 (ed. Russell, v. 1826, p. 137).
[74] " Catechism," q. 37.
[75] " Miscellaneous Works," 1830, p. 940.
[76] " Sermons and Tracts," 1793, p. 205.
[77] " Theoretico-practica theologia," 1724, p. 308.

frain from all definition of the negative side of the salvation
of infants, dying such, and thus confine themselves to emphasizing the gracious doctrine common to the whole body of Reformed thought. The fundamental Reformed doctrine of the
Church is nowhere more beautifully stated than in the sixteenth
article of the Old Scotch Confession, while the polemical
appendix of 1580, in its protest against the errors of "antichrist," specifically mentions "his cruell judgement againis infants departing without the sacrament: his absolute necessitie
of baptisme." No synod probably ever met which labored under
greater temptation to declare that some infants, dying in infancy, are reprobate, than the Synod of Dort. Possibly nearly
every member of it held as his private opinion that there are
such infants; and the certainly very shrewd but scarcely sincere methods of the Remonstrants in shifting the form in which
this question came before the synod were very irritating. But
the fathers of Dort, with truly Reformed loyalty to the positive declarations of Scripture, confined themselves to a clear
testimony to the positive doctrine of infant salvation and a
repudiation of the calumnies of the Remonstrants, without a
word of negative inference. "Since we are to judge of the will
of God from His Word," they say, "which testifies that the
children of believers are holy, not by nature, but in virtue of
the covenant of grace in which they together with their parents
are comprehended, godly parents have no reason to doubt of
the election and salvation of their children whom it pleaseth
God to call out of this life in their infancy" (art. xvii.).
Accordingly they repel in the Conclusion the calumny that the
Reformed teach "that many children of the faithful are torn
guiltless from their mothers' breasts and tyrannically plunged
into hell." [78] It is easy to say that nothing is here said of

[78] The language here used has a not uninteresting history. It is Calvin's
challenge to Castellio: "Put forth now thy virulence against God, who hurls
innocent babes torn from their mothers' breasts into eternal death" ("De
occulta Dei providentia," in "Opera," ed. Amsterdam, viii. pp. 644-645).
The underlying conception that God condemns infants to eternal death seems
to be Calvin's; but the mode of expression is Calvin's *reductio ad absurdum*
(or rather *ad blasphemiam*) of Castellio's opinions. Nevertheless the

the children of any but the "godly" and of the "faithful";
this is true; and therefore it is *not* implied (as is so often
thoughtlessly asserted) that the contrary of what is here
asserted is true of the children of the ungodly; but nothing is taught of them at all. It is more to the purpose to observe
that it *is* asserted that the children of believers, dying such, are
saved; and that this assertion is an inestimable advance on
that of the Council of Trent and that of the Augsburg Confession that baptism is necessary to salvation. It is the confessional doctrine of the Reformed churches and of the Reformed
churches alone, that all believers' infants, dying in infancy,
are saved.

What has been said of the Synod of Dort may be repeated
of the Westminster Assembly. The Westminster divines were
generally at one in the matter of infant salvation with the
doctors of Dort, but, like them, they refrained from any deliverance as to its negative side. That death in infancy does
not prejudice the salvation of God's elect they asserted in the
chapter of their Confession which treats of the application of
Christ's redemption to His people: "All those whom God hath
predestined unto life, and those only, he is pleased, in his appointed and accepted time, effectually to call, by his Word and
Spirit, . . . so as they come most freely, being made willing
by his grace. . . . Elect infants dying in infancy are regenerated and saved by Christ, through the Spirit who worketh
when, and where, and how he pleaseth." [79] With this declaration

---

Remonstrants allowed themselves in their polemic zeal to apply the whole
sentiment to the orthodox, and that, even in a still more sharpened form —
viz., with reference to *believers'* children. This very gross calumny the Synod
repels. Its deliverance is subjected to a very sharp and not very candid
criticism by Episcopius ("Opera," I. i. p. 176, and specially II. p. 28).

[79] Westminster Confession of Faith, X. i. and iii. The opinion that a
body of non-elect infants dying in infancy and not saved is implied in this passage, although often controversially asserted, is not only a wholly unreasonable opinion exegetically, but is absolutely negatived by the history of the
formation of this clause in the Assembly as recorded in the "Minutes," and
has never found favor among the expositors of the Confession. David Dickson's (1684) treatment of the section shows that he understands it to be directed against the Anabaptists; and all careful students of the Confession

of their faith that such of God's elect as die in infancy are saved by His own mysterious working in their hearts, although incapable of the response of faith, they were content. Whether these elect comprehend all infants, dying such, or some only — whether there is such a class as non-elect infants, dying in infancy, their words neither say nor suggest. No Reformed confession enters into this question; no word is said by any one of them which either asserts or implies either that some infants are reprobated or that all are saved. What has been held in common by the whole body of Reformed theologians on this subject is asserted in these confessions; of what has been disputed among them the confessions are silent. And silence is as favorable to one type as to another.

Although the cautious agnostic position as to the fate of uncovenanted infants dying in infancy may fairly claim to be the historical Calvinistic view, it is perfectly obvious that it is not *per se* any more Calvinistic than any of the others. The adherents of all types enumerated above are clearly within the limits of the system, and hold with the same firmness to the fundamental position that salvation is suspended on no earthly cause, but ultimately rests on God's electing grace alone, while our knowledge of who are saved depends on our view of what are the signs of election and of the clearness with which they may be interpreted. As these several types differ only in the replies they offer to the subordinate question, there is no " revolution " involved in passing from one to the other; and as in the lapse of time the balance between them swings this way or that, it can only be truly said that there is advance or retrogression, not in fundamental conception, but in the clearness with which details are read and with which the outline of the doctrine is filled up. In the course of time the agnostic view of the fate of uncovenanted infants, dying such, has given place to an ever growing universality of conviction that these

understand it as above, including Shaw, Hodge, Macpherson, and Mitchell. The same is true of all schools of adherents to the Confession. See e.g. Lyman Beecher, in the *Spirit of the Pilgrims,* i. 1828, pp. 49, 81; cf. also Philip Schaff, " Creeds of Christendom," i. 1877, p. 795.

infants too are included in the election of grace; so that to-day few Calvinists can be found who do not hold with Toplady, and Doddridge, and Thomas Scott, and John Newton, and James P. Wilson, and Nathan L. Rice, and Robert J. Breckinridge, and Robert S. Candlish, and Charles Hodge, and the whole body of those of recent years whom the Calvinistic churches delight to honor, that all who die in infancy are the children of God and enter at once into His glory — not because original sin alone is not deserving of eternal punishment (for all are born children of wrath), nor because they are less guilty than others (for relative innocence would merit only relatively light punishment, not freedom from all punishment), nor because they die in infancy (for that they die in infancy is not the cause but the effect of God's mercy toward them), but simply because God in His infinite love has chosen them in Christ, before the foundation of the world, by a loving foreordination of them unto adoption as sons in Jesus Christ. Thus, as they hold, the Reformed theology has followed the light of the Word until its brightness has illuminated all its corners, and the darkness has fled away.

VII. "Ethical" Tendencies

The most serious peril which the orderly development of the Christian doctrine of the salvation of infants has had to encounter, as men strove, age after age, more purely and thoroughly to apprehend it, has arisen from the intrusion into Christian thought of what we may, without lack of charity, call the unchristian conception of man's natural innocence. For the task which was set to Christian thinking was to obtain a clear understanding of God's revealed purpose of mercy to the infants of a guilty and wrath-deserving race. And the Pelagianizing conception of the innocence of human infancy, in however subtle a form presented, put the solution of the problem in jeopardy by suggesting that it needed no solution. We have seen how some Greek Fathers cut the knot with the facile formula that infantile innocence, while not deserving of supernatural reward, was yet in no danger of being adjudged to punishment. We have seen how in the more active hands of Pelagius and his companions, as part of a great unchristian scheme, it menaced Christianity itself, and was repelled only by the vigor and greatness of an Augustine. We have seen how the same conception, creeping gradually into the Latin Church in the milder form of semi-Pelagianism, lulled her heart to sleep with suggestions of less and less ill-desert for original sin, until she neglected the problem of infant salvation altogether and comforted herself with a constantly attenuating doctrine of infant punishment. If infants are so well off without Christ, there is little impulse to consider whether they may not be in Christ.

The Reformed churches could not hope to work out the problem free from menace from the perennial enemy. The crisis came in the form of the Remonstrant controversy. The anthropology of the Remonstrants was distinctly semi-Pelagian, and on that basis no solid advance was possible. Nor was the matter helped by their postulation of a universal atonement which lost in intention as much as it gained in extension. Infants may have very little to be saved from, but their salvation from even it cannot be wrought by an atonement which only purchases for them the opportunity for salvation — an opportunity of which they cannot avail themselves, however much the natural power of free choice is uninjured by the fall, for the simple reason that they die infants; while God cannot be held to make them, without their free choice, partakers of this atonement without an admission of that sovereign discrimination among men which it was the very object of the whole Remonstrant theory to exclude. It is not strange that the Remonstrants looked with some favor on the Romish theory of *pœna damni*. Though the doctrine of the salvation of all infants dying in infancy became one of their characteristic tenets, it had no logical basis in their scheme of faith, and their proclamation of it could have no direct effect in working out the problem. Indirectly it had a twofold effect. On the one hand, it retarded the true course of the development of doctrine, by leading those who held fast to Biblical teaching on original sin and particular election, to oppose the doctrine of the salvation of all dying in infancy, as if it were necessarily inconsistent with these teachings. Probably Calvinists were never so united in affirming that some infants, dying such, are reprobated, as in the height of the Remonstrant controversy. On the other hand, so far as the doctrine of the salvation of all infants, dying such, was accepted by the anti-Remonstrants, it tended to bring in with it, in more or less measure, the other tenets with which it was associated in their teaching, and thus to lead men away from the direct path along which alone the solution was to be found. Wesleyan Arminianism brought only an amelioration, not a thoroughgoing correction of the faults of Remonstrantism. The theoretical postulation of original sin and natural inability, corrected by the gift to all men of a gracious ability on the basis of universal atonement in Christ, was a great advance. But it left the salvation of infants dying in infancy logically as unaccounted for as original Remonstrantism. *Ex hypothesi,* the universal atonement could bring to these infants only what it brought to all others, and this was something short of salvation — viz., an ability to improve the grace given alike to all. But infants, dying such, cannot improve grace; and therefore, it would seem, cannot be saved, unless we suppose a special gift to them over and above what is given to other men — a supposition subversive at once of the whole Arminian contention. The assertion of the salvation of all infants dying in infancy, although a specially dear tenet of Wesleyan Arminianism, remains therefore, as with the earlier Remonstrants, unconformable to the system. The Arminian difficulty, indeed, lies one step further back; it does not make clear how *any* infant dying in infancy is to be saved.[80]

[80] The prevailing view in the Methodist Episcopal Church is probably that infants are all born justified. The difficulties of this view are hinted by a not unfriendly hand in the *Cumberland Presbyterian Review* for January, 1890, p. 113. The best that can be said toward placing the dying infant " in the same essential condition as that into which the justified and regenerate adult is brought by voluntary faith," may be read from Dr. D. D. Whedon's pen in the *Methodist Quarterly Review* for 1883, p. 757. It is inconsequent; and its consequences are portentous to Arminianism — or shall we say that God does not determine who are to die in infancy?

The truth seems to be that there is but one logical outlet
for any system of doctrine which suspends the determination of
who are to be saved upon any action of man's own will, whether
in the use of gracious or natural ability (that is, of course, if
it is unwilling to declare infants, dying such, incapable of salvation); and that lies in the extension of "the day of grace"
for such into the other world. Otherwise, there will inevitably
be brought in covertly, in the salvation of infants, that very
sovereignty of God, "irresistible" grace and passive receptivity, to deny which is the whole *raison d'être* of these schemes.
There are indications that this is being increasingly felt among
those who are most concerned; we have noted it most recently
among the Cumberland Presbyterians,[81] who, perhaps alone of
Christian denominations, have embodied in their confession
their conviction that all infants, dying such, are saved. The
theory of a probation in the other world for such as have had
in this no such probation as to secure from them a decisive
choice has come to us from Germany, and bears accordingly a
later Lutheran coloring. Its roots are, however, planted in the
earliest Lutheran thinking,[82] and are equally visible in the
writings of the early Remonstrants; its seeds are present, in
fact, wherever man's salvation is causally suspended on any
act of his own. But the outcome offered by it certainly affords
no good reason for affirming that all infants, dying such, are
saved. It is not uncommon, indeed, for the advocates of this
theory to suppose the present life to be a more favorable opportunity for moral renewal in Christ than the next.[83] Some,
no doubt, think otherwise. But in either event what can assure
us that *all* will be so renewed? We are ready to accept the
subtle argument in Dr. Kedney's valuable work, "Christian
Doctrine Harmonized,"[84] as the best that can be said on the
premises; for although Dr. Kedney denies the theory of "future
probation" in general, he shares the general "ethical" view

[81] *Cumberland Presbyterian Review*, ii. 1890, p. 369; cf. p. 113.
[82] Cf. e.g. Andreæ, "Actis Colloq. Montisbelligart," pp. 447, 448; and
note Beza's crushing reply.
[83] Cf. "Progressive Orthodoxy," 1886, p. 76.
[84] Vol. ii. 1889, pp. 90 ff.

on which it is founded, and projects the salvation of infants dying in infancy into the next world on the express ground that they are incapable of choice here. He assures us that they will surely welcome the knowledge of God's love in Christ there. But we miss the grounds of assurance, on the fundamental postulates of the scheme. If the choice of these infants, while it remains free, can be made thus certain *there*, why not the same for all men *here?* And if their choice is thus made certain, is their destiny *determined* by their choice, or by God who makes that choice certain? Assuredly no thoroughfare is open along this path for a consistent doctrine of the salvation of all those that die in infancy. But this seems the only pathway that is consistently open to those, of whatever name, who make man's own undetermined act the determining factor in his salvation.[85]

VIII. THE DOCTRINAL DEVELOPMENT

The drifts of doctrine which have come before us in this rapid sketch may be reduced to three generic views. 1. There is what may be called the *ecclesiastical doctrine,* according to which the Church, in the sense of an outwardly organized body, is set as the sole fountain of salvation in the midst of a lost world; the Spirit of God and eternal life are its peculiar endowments, of which none can partake save through communion with it. Accordingly, to all those departing this life in infancy, baptism, the gateway to the Church, is the condition of salvation. 2. There is what may be called the *gracious doctrine,* according to which the visible Church is not set in the world to determine by the gift of its ordinances who are to be saved, but as the harbor of refuge for the saints, to gather into its bosom those whom God Himself in His infinite love has selected in Christ Jesus before the foundation of the world in whom

[85] The Rev. D. Fisk Harris, himself a Congregational minister (" Calvinism Contrary to God's Word and Man's Moral Nature," 1890, p. 107), tells us that a view not essentially differing from Dr. Kedney's " seems to be the prevailing view of Congregationalists." This he states thus: " All dying infants become moral agents after death. Exercising a holy choice they ' are saved on the ground of the atonement and by regeneration.' "

to show the wonders of His grace. Men accordingly are not saved because they are baptized, but they are baptized because they are saved, and the failure of the ordinance does not argue the failure of the grace. Accordingly, to all those departing this life in infancy, inclusion in God's saving purpose alone is the condition of salvation; we may be able to infer this purpose from manifest signs, or we may not be able to infer it, but in any case it cannot fail. 3. There is what may be called the *humanitarian doctrine*, according to which the determining cause of man's salvation is his own free choice, under whatever variety of theories as to the source of his power to exercise this choice, or the manner in which it is exercised. Accordingly, whether one is saved or not is dependent not on baptism or on inclusion in God's hidden purpose, but on the decisive activity of the soul itself.

The first of these doctrines is characteristic of the early, the medieval, and the Roman churches, not without echoes in those sections of Protestantism which love to think of themselves as " more historical " or less radically reformed than the rest. The second is the doctrine of the Reformed churches. These two are not opposed to one another in their most fundamental conception, but are related rather as an earlier misapprehension and a later correction of the same basal doctrine. The phrase *extra ecclesiam nulla salus* is the common property of both; they differ only in their understanding of the " ecclesia," whether of the visible or invisible Church. The third doctrine, on the other hand, has cropped out ever and again in every age of the Church, has dominated whole sections of it and whole ages, but has never, in its purity, found expression in any great historic confession or exclusively characterized any age. It is, in fact, not a section of Church doctrine at all, but an intrusion into Christian thought from without. In its purity it has always and in all communions been accounted heresy; and only as it has been more or less modified and concealed among distinctively Christian adjuncts has it ever made a position for itself in the Church. Its fundamental conception is the antipodes of that of the other doctrines.

The first step in the development of the doctrine of infant salvation was taken when the Church laid the foundation which from the beginning has stood firm, *Infants too are lost members of a lost race, and only those savingly united to Christ are saved.* In its definition of what infants are thus savingly united to Christ the early Church missed the path. All that are brought to Him in baptism, was its answer. Long ages passed before the second step was taken in the correct definition. The way was prepared, indeed, by Augustine's doctrine of grace, by which salvation was made dependent on the dealings of God with the individual heart. But his eyes were holden that he should not see it. It was reserved to Zwingli to proclaim it clearly, *All the elect children of God, who are regenerated by the Spirit who worketh when, and where, and how He pleaseth.* The sole question that remains is, Who of those that die in infancy are the elect children of God? Tentative answers were given. The children of God's people, said some. The children of God's people, with such others as His love has set upon to call, said others. *All those that die in infancy,* said others still; and to this reply Reformed thinking and not Reformed thinking only, but in one way or another, logically or illogically, the thinking of the Christian world has been converging. Is it the Scriptural answer? It is as legitimate and as logical an answer as any, on Reformed postulates. It is legitimate on no other postulates. If it be really conformable to the Word of God it will stand; and the third step in the development of the doctrine of infant salvation is already taken. But if it stand, it can stand on no other theological basis than the Reformed. If all infants dying in infancy are saved, it is certain that they are not saved by or through the ordinances of the visible Church (for they have not received them), nor through their own improvement of a grace common to all men (for they are incapable of activity); it can only be through the almighty operation of the Holy Spirit who worketh when and where and how He pleaseth, through whose ineffable grace the Father gathers these little ones to the home He has prepared for them.

XV

ANNIHILATIONISM

ANNIHILATIONISM [1]

I. Definition and Classification of Theories

A TERM designating broadly a large body of theories which unite in contending that human beings pass, or are put, out of existence altogether. These theories fall logically into three classes, according as they hold that all souls, being mortal, actually cease to exist at death; or that, souls being naturally mortal, only those persist in life to which immortality is given by God; or that, though souls are naturally immortal and persist in existence unless destroyed by a force working upon them from without, wicked souls are actually thus destroyed. These three classes of theories may be conveniently called respectively, (1) pure mortalism, (2) conditional immortality, and (3) annihilationism proper.

II. Pure Mortalism

The common contention of the theories which form the first of these classes is that human life is bound up with the organism, and that therefore the entire man passes out of being with the dissolution of the organism. The usual basis of this contention is either materialistic or pantheistic or at least pantheizing (e.g. realistic); the soul being conceived in the former case as but a function of organized matter and necessarily ceasing to exist with the dissolution of the organism, in the latter case as but the individualized manifestation of a much more extensive entity, back into which it sinks with the dissolution of the organism in connection with which the individualization takes place. Rarely, however, the contention

[1] Reprinted from "The New Schaff-Herzog Encyclopedia of Religious Knowledge," edited by Samuel Macauley Jackson, D.D., LL.D., i. pp. 183–186 (copyright by Funk and Wagnalls Company, New York, 1908).

in question is based on the notion that the soul, although a spiritual entity distinct from the material body, is incapable of maintaining its existence separate from the body. The promise of eternal life is too essential an element of Christianity for theories like these to thrive in a Christian atmosphere. It is even admitted now by Stade, Oort, Schwally, and others that the Old Testament, even in its oldest strata, presupposes the persistence of life after death — which used to be very commonly denied. Nevertheless, the materialists (e.g. Feuerbach, Vogt, Moleschott, Büchner, Häckel) and pantheists (Spinoza, Fichte, Schelling, Hegel, Strauss; cf. S. Davidson, " The Doctrine of Last Things," London, 1882, pp. 132–133) still deny the possibility of immortality; and in exceedingly wide circles, even among those who would not wholly break with Christianity, men permit themselves to cherish nothing more than a " hope " of it (S. Hoekstra, " De Hoop der Onsterfelijkheid," Amsterdam, 1867; L. W. E. Rauwenhoff, " Wijsbegeerte van den Godsdienst," Leiden, 1887, p. 811; cf. the " Ingersoll Lectures ").

III. Conditional Immortality

The class of theories to which the designation of " conditional immortality " is most properly applicable, agree with the theories of pure mortalism in teaching the natural mortality of man in his entirety, but separate from them in maintaining that this mortal may, and in many cases does, put on immortality. Immortality in their view is a gift of God, conferred on those who have entered into living communion with Him. Many theorists of this class adopt frankly the materialistic doctrine of the soul, and deny that it is a distinct entity; they therefore teach that the soul necessarily dies with the body, and identify life beyond death with the resurrection, conceived as essentially a recreation of the entire man. Whether all men are subjects of this recreative resurrection is a mooted question among themselves. Some deny it, and affirm therefore that the wicked perish finally at death, the children of God alone attaining to resurrection. The greater part, however, teach a resurrection for all, and a "second death," which is annihilation, for the wicked (e.g. Jacob Blain, "Death not Life," Buffalo, 1857, pp. 39–42; Aaron Ellis and Thomas Read, "Bible versus Tradition," New York, 1853, pp. 13–121; George Storrs, "Six Sermons," New York, 1856, pp. 29 ff.; Zenas Campbell, "The Age of Gospel Light," Hartford, 1854). There are many, on the other hand, who recognize that the soul is a spiritual entity, disparate to, though conjoined in personal union with, the body. In their view, however, ordinarily at least, the soul requires the body either for its existence, or certainly for its activity. C. F. Hudson, for example ("Debt and Grace," New York, 1861, pp. 263–264), teaches that the soul lies unconscious, or at least inactive, from death to the resurrection; then the just rise to an ecstasy of bliss; the unjust, however, start up at the voice of God to become extinct in the very act. Most, perhaps, prolong the second life of the wicked for the purpose of the infliction of their merited punishment; and some make their extinction a protracted process (e.g. H. L. Hastings, "Retribution or the Doom of the Ungodly," Providence, 1861, pp. 77, 153; cf. Horace Bushnell, "Forgiveness and Law," New York, 1874, p. 147, notes 5 and 6; James Martineau, "A Study of Religion," Oxford, ii. 1888, p. 114). For further discussion of the theory of conditional immortality, see "Immortality."

IV. Annihilationism Proper

Already, however, in speaking of extinction we are passing beyond the limits of "conditionalism" pure and simple and entering the region of annihilationism proper. Whether we think of this extinction as the result of the punishment or as the gradual dying out of the personality under the enfeebling effects of sin, we are no longer looking at the soul as naturally mortal and requiring a new gift of grace to keep it in existence, but as naturally immortal and suffering destruction at the hands of an inimical power. And this becomes even more apparent when the assumed mortalism of the soul is grounded not in its nature but in its sinfulness; so that the theory deals not with souls as such, but with sinful souls, and it is a question of salvation by a gift of grace to everlasting life or of being left to the disintegrating effects of sin. The point of distinction between theories of this class and " conditionalism " is that these theories with more or less consistency or heartiness recognize what is called the " natural immortality of the soul," and are not tempted therefore to think of the soul as by nature passing out of being at death (or at any time), and yet teach that the actual punishment inflicted upon or suffered by the wicked results in extinction of being. They may differ among themselves, as to the time when this extinction takes place — whether at death, or at the general judgment — or as to the more or less extended or intense punishment accorded to the varying guilt of each soul. They may differ also as to the means by which the annihilation of the wicked soul is accomplished — whether by a mere act of divine power, cutting off the sinful life, or by the destructive fury of the punishment inflicted, or by the gradual enervating and sapping working of sin itself on the personality. They retain their common character as theories of annihilation proper so long as they conceive the extinction of the soul as an effect wrought on it to which it succumbs, rather than as the natural exit of the soul from a life which could be continued to it only by some operation upon it raising it to a higher than its natural potency.

V. Mingling of Theories

It must be borne in mind that the adherents of these two classes of theories are not very careful to keep strictly within the logical limits of one of the classes. Convenient as it is to approach their study with a definite schematization in hand, it is not always easy to assign individual writers with definiteness to one or the other of them. It has become usual, therefore, to speak of them all as annihilationists or of them all as conditionalists; annihilationists because they all agree that the souls of the wicked cease to exist; conditionalists because they all agree that therefore persistence in life is conditioned on a right relation to God. Perhaps the majority of those who call themselves conditionalists allow that the mortality of the soul, which is the prime postulate of the conditionalist theory, is in one way or another connected with sin; that the souls of the wicked persist in existence after death and even after the judgment, in order to receive the punishment due their sin; and that this punishment, whether it be conceived as infliction from without or as the simple consequence of sin, has much to do with their extinction. When so held, conditionalism certainly falls little short of annihilationism proper.

VI. EARLY HISTORY OF ANNIHILATIONISTIC THEORIES

Some confusion has arisen, in tracing the history of the annihilationist theories, from confounding with them enunciations by the earlier Church Fathers of the essential Christian doctrine that the soul is not self-existent, but owes, as its existence, so its continuance in being, to the will of God. The earliest appearance of a genuinely annihilationist theory in extant Christian literature is to be found apparently in the African apologist Arnobius, at the opening of the fourth century (cf. Salmond, " The Christian Doctrine of Immortality," Edinburgh, 1901, pp. 473–474; Falke, " Die Lehre von der ewigen Verdammnis," Eisenach, 1892, pp. 27–28). It seemed to him impossible that beings such as men could either owe their being directly to God or persist in being without a special gift of God; the unrighteous must therefore be gradually consumed in the fires of Gehenna. A somewhat similar idea was announced by the Socinians in the sixteenth century (O. Fock, " Der Socinianismus," Kiel, 1847, pp. 714 ff.). On the positive side, Faustus Socinus himself thought that man is mortal by nature and attains immortality only by grace. On the negative side, his followers (Crell, Schwaltz, and especially Ernst Sohner) taught explicitly that the second death consists in annihilation, which takes place, however, only after the general resurrection, at the final judgment. From the Socinians this general view passed over to England where it was adopted, not merely, as might have been anticipated, by men like Locke ("Reasonableness of Christianity," § 1), Hobbes ("Leviathan"), and Whiston, but also by Churchmen like Hammond and Warburton, and was at least played with by non-conformist leaders like Isaac Watts. The most remarkable example of its utilization in this age, however, is supplied by the non-juror Henry Dodwell (1706). Insisting that the "soul is a principle naturally mortal," Dodwell refused to allow the benefit of this mortality to any but those who lived and died without the limits of the proclamation of the gospel; no "adult person whatever," he insisted, "living where Christianity is professed, and the motives of its credibility are sufficiently proposed, can hope for the benefit of actual mortality." Those living in Christian lands are therefore all immortalized, but in two classes: some "by the pleasure of God to punishment," some "to reward by their union with the divine baptismal Spirit." It was part of his contention that "none have the power of giving this divine immortalizing Spirit since the apostles but the bishops only," so that his book was rather a blast against the antiprelatists than a plea for annihilationism; and it was replied to as such by Samuel Clarke (1706), Richard Baxter (1707), and Daniel Whitby (1707). During the eighteenth century the theory was advocated also on the continent of Europe (e.g. E. J. K. Walter, "Prüfung wichtiger Lehren theologischen und philosophischen Inhalts," Berlin, 1782), and almost found a martyr in the Neuchâtel pastor, Ferdinand Olivier Petitpierre, commonly spoken of by the nickname of "No Eternity" (cf. C. Berthoud, "Les quatre Petitpierres," Neuchatel, 1875). In the first half of the nineteenth century also it found sporadic adherents, as e.g. C. H. Weisse in Germany (*Theologische Studien und Kritiken,* ix. 1836, pp. 271–340) and H. H. Dobney in England ("Notes of Lectures on Future Punishment," London, 1844; new edition, "On the Scripture Doctrine of Future Punishment," 1846).

VII. Nineteenth Century Theories

The real extension of the theory belongs, however, only to
the second half of the nineteenth century. During this period
it attained, chiefly through the able advocacy of it by C. F.
Hudson and E. White, something like a popular vogue in
English-speaking lands. In French-speaking countries, while
never becoming really popular, it has commanded the attention of an influential circle of theologians and philosophers (as
J. Rognon, " L'Immortalité native et l'enseignement biblique,"
Montauban, 1894, p. 7; but cf. A. Gretillat, " Exposé de théologie systématique," Paris, iv. 1890, p. 602). In Germany, on the
other hand, it has met with less acceptance, although it is
precisely there that it has been most scientifically developed,
and has received the adherence of the most outstanding names.
Before the opening of this half century, in fact, it had gained
the great support of Richard Rothe's advocacy (" Theologische
Ethik," 3 vols., Wittenberg, 1845–1848; ed. 2, 5 vols., 1867–
1871, §§ 470–472; " Dogmatik," Heidelberg, II. ii. 1870, §§ 47–
48, especially p. 158), and never since has it ceased to find
adherents of mark, who base their acceptance of it sometimes on
general grounds, but increasingly on the view that the Scriptures teach, not a doctrine of the immortality of the soul, but
a reanimation by resurrection of God's people. The chief names
in this series are C. H. Weisse (" Philosophische Dogmatik,"
Leipzig, 1855–1862, § 970); Hermann Schultz (" Voraussetz-
ungen der christlichen Lehre von der Unsterblichkeit,"
Göttingen, 1861, p. 155; cf. " Grundriss der evangelischen
Dogmatik," 1892, p. 154: " This condemnation of the second
death may in itself, according to the Bible, be thought of as
existence in torment, or as painful cessation of existence. Dogmatics without venturing to decide, will find the second conception the more probable, biblically and dogmatically ");
H. Plitt (" Evangelische Glaubenslehre," Gotha, 1863); F.
Brandes (*Theologische Studien und Kritiken*, 1872, pp. 545,
550); A. Schäffer (" Auf der Neige des Lebens," Gotha, 1884;
" Was ist Glück? " 1891, pp. 290–294); G. Runze (" Unster-

blichkeit und Auferstehung," Berlin, i. 1894, pp. 167, 204:
" Christian Eschatology teaches not a natural immortality for
the soul, but a reanimation by God's almighty power. . . .
The Christian hope of reanimation makes the actualization of
a future blessed existence depend entirely on faith in God ");
L. Lemme ("Endlosigkeit der Verdammnis," Berlin, 1899, pp.
31–32, 60–61); cf. R. Kabisch (" Die Eschatologie des Paulus,"
Göttingen, 1893).

The same general standpoint has been occupied in Holland, for example, by Jonker (*Theologische Studiën*, i.). The
first advocate of conditionalism in French was the Swiss pastor, E. Pétavel-Olliff, whose first book, " La Fin du mal," appeared in 1872 (Paris), followed by many articles in the
French theological journals and by " Le Problème de l'immortalité " (1891; E. T. London, 1892), and " The Extinction
of Evil " (E. T. 1889). In 1880 C. Byse issued a translation of
E. White's chief book. The theory not only had already been
presented by A. Bost ("Le Sort des méchants," 1861), but
had been taken up by philosophers of such standing as C.
Lambert (" Le Système du monde moral," 1862), P. Janet
(*Revue des deux mondes*, 1863), and C. Renouvier ("La
Critique philosophique," 1878); and soon afterward Charles
Sécretan and C. Ribot (*Revue théologique*, 1885, No. 1)
expressed their general adherence to it. Perhaps the more distinguished advocacy of it on French ground has come, however, from the two professors Sabatier, Auguste and Armand,
the one from the point of view of exegetical, the other from
that of natural science. Says the one ("L'Origine du péché
dans le système théologique de Paul," Paris, 1887, p. 38):
" The impenitent sinner never emerges from the fleshly state,
and consequently remains subject to the law of corruption and
destruction, which rules fleshly beings; they perish and are
as if they had never been." Says the other (" Essai sur l'immortalité au point de vue du naturalisme évolutioniste," ed. 2,
Paris, 1895, pp. 198, 229): " The immortality of man is not
universal and necessary; it is subject to certain conditions, it
is conditional, to use an established expression." " Ultrater-

restrial immortality will be the exclusive lot of souls which have arrived at a sufficient degree of integrity and cohesion to escape absorption or disintegration."

VIII. ENGLISH ADVOCATES

The chief English advocate of conditional immortality has undoubtedly been Edward White whose " Life in Christ " was published first in 1846 (London), rewritten in 1875 (ed. 3, 1878). His labors were seconded, however, not only by older works of similar tendency such as George Storrs's " Are the Wicked Immortal? " (ed. 21, New York, 1852), but by later teaching from men of the standing of Archbishop Whately ("Scripture Revelations concerning a Future State," ed. 8, London, 1859), Bishop Hampden, J. B. Heard ("The Tripartite Nature of Man," ed. 4, Edinburgh, 1875), Prebendary Constable ("The Duration and Nature of Future Punishment," London, 1868), Prebendary Row ("Future Retribution," London, 1887), J. M. Denniston ("The Perishing Soul," ed. 2, London, 1874), S. Minton ("The Glory of Christ," London, 1868), J. W. Barlow ("Eternal Punishment," Cambridge, 1865), and T. Davis ("Endless Suffering not the Doctrine of Scripture," London, 1866). Less decisive but not less influential advocacy has been given to the theory also by men like Joseph Parker, R. W. Dale, and J. A. Beet ("The Last Things," London, 1897). Mr. Beet (who quotes Clemance, " Future Punishment," London, 1880, as much of his way of thinking) occupies essentially the position of Schultz. "The sacred writers," he says, "while apparently inclining sometimes to one and sometimes to the other, do not pronounce decisive judgment" between eternal punishment and annihilation (p. 216), while annihilation is free from speculative objections. In America C. F. Hudson's initial efforts ("Debt and Grace," Boston, 1857, ed. 5, 1859; "Christ Our Life," 1860) were ably seconded by W. R. Huntington ("Conditional Immortality," New York, 1878) and J. H. Pettingell ("The Life Everlasting," Philadelphia, 1882, combining two previously

published tractates; " The Unspeakable Gift," Yarmouth, Me.,
1884). Views of much the same character have been expressed
also by Horace Bushnell, L. W. Bacon, L. C. Baker, Lyman
Abbott, and without much insistence on them by Henry C.
Sheldon ("System of Christian Doctrine," Cincinnati, 1903,
pp. 573 ff.).

IX. Modifications of the Theory

There is a particular form of conditionalism requiring
special mention which seeks to avoid the difficulties of annihilationism, by teaching, not the total extinction of the souls
of the wicked, but rather, as it is commonly phrased, their
" transformation " into impersonal beings incapable of moral
action, or indeed of any feeling. This is the form of conditionalism which is suggested by James Martineau ("A Study of
Religion," Oxford, ii. 1888, p. 114) and by Horace Bushnell
("Forgiveness and Law," New York, 1874, p. 147, notes 5
and 6). It is also hinted by Henry Drummond ("Natural Law
in the Spiritual World," London, 1884), when he supposes
the lost soul to lose not salvation merely but the capacity for
it and for God; so that what is left is no longer fit to be
called a soul, but is a shrunken, useless organ ready to fall away
like a rotten twig. The Alsatian theologian A. Schäffer ("Was
ist Glück?" Gotha, 1891, pp. 290–294) similarly speaks of the
wicked soul losing the light from heaven, the divine spark
which gave it its value, and the human personality thereby
becoming obliterated. " The forces out of which it arises break
up and become at last again impersonal. They do not pass
away, but they are transformed." One sees the conception here
put forward at its highest level in such a view as that presented by Professor O. A. Curtis ("The Christian Faith," New
York, 1905, p. 467), which thinks of the lost not, to be sure,
as " crushed into mere thinghood " but as sunk into a condition " below the possibility of any moral action, or moral concern . . . like persons in this life when personality is entirely
overwhelmed by the base sense of what we call physical fear."

There is no annihilation in Professor Curtis' view; not even relief for the lost from suffering; but it may perhaps be looked at as marking the point where the theories of annihilationism reach up to and melt at last into the doctrine of eternal punishment.

BIBLIOGRAPHY: An exhaustive bibliography of the subject up to 1862 is given in Ezra Abbot's Appendix to W. R. Alger's " Critical History of the Doctrine of a Future Life," also published separately, New York, 1871; consult also W. Reid, " Everlasting Punishment and Modern Speculation," Edinburgh, 1874, pp. 311–313. Special works on annihilationism are J. C. Killam, " Annihilationism Examined," Syracuse, 1859; I. P. Warren, " The Wicked not Annihilated," New York, 1867; N. D. George, " Annihilationism not of the Bible," Boston, 1870; J. B. Brown, " The Doctrine of Annihilation in the Light of the Gospel of Love," London, 1875; S. C. Bartlett, " Life and Death Eternal: A Refutation of the Theory of Annihilation," Boston, 1878. The subject is treated in S. D. F. Salmond, " The Christian Doctrine of Immortality," Edinburgh, 1901, pp. 473–499; R. W. Landis, " The Immortality of the Soul," New York, 1868, pp. 422 ff.; A. Hovey, " The State of the Impenitent Dead," Boston, 1859, pp. 93 ff.; C. M. Mead, " The Soul Here and Hereafter," Boston, 1879; G. Godet, in *Chrétien évangélique*, 1881–1882; F. Godet, in *Revue théologique*, 1886; J. Fyfe, " The Hereafter," Edinburgh, 1890; R. Falke, " Die Lehre von der ewigen Verdammnis," Eisenach, 1892, pp. 25–38. On conditional immortality, consult W. R. Huntington, " Conditional Immortality," New York, 1878; J. H. Pettingell, " The Theological Tri-lemma," New York, 1878; *idem*, " The Life Everlasting: What is it? Whence is it? Whose is it? A Symposium," Philadelphia, 1882; E. White, " Life and Death: A Reply to J. B. Brown's Lectures on Conditional Immortality," London, 1877; *idem*, " Life in Christ: A Study of the Scripture Doctrine on . . . the Conditions of Human Immortality," London, 1878. Further discussions may be found in the appropriate sections of most works on systematic theology and also in works on eschatology and future punishment. See, besides the works mentioned in the text, the literature under " Immortality."

XVI

THE THEOLOGY OF THE REFORMATION

THE THEOLOGY OF THE REFORMATION [1]

CHARLES BEARD begins his Hibbert Lectures on The Reformation with these words: " To look upon the Reformation of the sixteenth century as only the substitution of one set of theological doctrines for another, or the cleansing of the Church from notorious abuses and corruptions, or even a return of Christianity to something like primitive purity and simplicity — is to take an inadequate view of its nature and importance." He wishes us to make note of the far-reaching changes in human life which have been wrought by what we call the Reformation, to observe the numerous departments of activity which have been at least affected by it, and then to seek its cause in something as wide in its extension as its effects. He himself discovers this cause in the " general awakening of the human intellect," which had begun in the fourteenth century and was being " urged on with accelerating rapidity in the fifteenth." In his view the Reformation was merely the religious side of what we speak of as the Renaissance. " It was the life of the Renaissance," he affirms, " infused into religion under the influence of men of the grave and earnest Teutonic race." He even feels justified in saying that, in the view he takes of it, the Reformation " was not, primarily, a theological, a religious, an ecclesiastical movement at all."

That there is some exaggeration in this representation is obvious. That this exaggeration is due to defective analysis is as clear. And the suspicion lies very near that the defect in analysis has its root in an imperfect sense of values. To point us to the general awakening of the human intellect which was in progress in the fifteenth century is not to uncover a cause; it is only to describe a condition. To remind us that, as a result

[1] Reprinted from *The Biblical Review,* ii. 1917, pp. 490–512 (published by The Biblical Seminary in New York; copyrighted).

of this awakening of the human intellect, a lively sense had
long existed of the need of a reformation, and repeated attempts had been vainly made to effect it, that men everywhere
were fully alive to the corruption of manners and morals in
which the world was groveling, and were equally helpless to
correct it, is not to encourage us to find the cause of the Reformation in a general situation out of which no reformation had
through all these years come. The question which presses is:
Whence came the power which achieved the effect — an effect
apparently far beyond the power of the forces working on the
surface of things to achieve?

There is no use in seeking to cover up the facts under
depreciatory forms of statement. It is easy to talk contemptuously of the "substitution of one set of theological doctrines
for another," as it would be easy to talk contemptuously of the
substitution of one set of political or of sanitary doctrines for
another. The force of the perverse suggestion lies in keeping
the matter in the abstract. The proof of the pudding in such
things lies in the eating. No doubt it is possible to talk indifferently of merely working the permutations of a dial-lock,
regardless of the not unimportant circumstance that one of
these permutations differs from the rest in this — that it
shoots the bolts. The substitution of one set of theological
doctrines for another which took place at the Reformation was
the substitution of a set of doctrines which had the promise
and potency of life in them for a set of doctrines the issue of
which had been death. What happened at the Reformation, by
means of which the forces of life were set at work through the
seething, struggling mass, was the revival of vital Christianity; and this is the *vera causa* of all that has come out of that
great revolution, in all departments of life. Men, no doubt,
had long been longing and seeking after "a return of Christianity to something like primitive purity and simplicity."
This was the way that an Erasmus, for example, pictured to
himself the needs of his time. The difficulty was that, rather
repelled by the Christianity they knew than attracted by
Christianity in its primitive purity — of the true nature of

which they really had no idea — they were simply feeling out
in the dark. What Luther did was to rediscover vital Christianity and to give it afresh to the world. To do this was to
put the spark to the train. We are feeling the explosion yet.

The Reformation was then — we insist upon it — precisely
the substitution of one set of theological doctrines for another.
That is what it was to Luther; and that is what, through
Luther, it has been to the Christian world. Exactly what
Luther did was for himself — for the quieting of his aroused
conscience and the healing of his deepened sense of sin — to
rediscover the great fact, the greatest of all the great facts of
which sinful man can ever become aware, that salvation is by
the pure grace of God alone. O, but, you will say, that resulted
from Luther's religious experience. No, we answer, it was primarily a doctrinal discovery of Luther's — the discovery of a
doctrine apart from which, and prior to the discovery of which,
Luther did not have and could never have had his religious
experience. He had been taught another doctrine, a doctrine
which had been embodied in a popular maxim, current in his
day: Do the best you can, and God will see you through. He
had tried to live that doctrine, and could not do it; he could
not believe it. He has told us of his despair. He has told us how
this despair grew deeper and deeper, until he was raised out of
it precisely by his discovery of his new doctrine — that it is
God and God alone who in His infinite grace saves us, that He
does it all, and that we supply nothing but the sinners to be
saved and the subsequent praises which our grateful hearts
lift to Him, our sole and only Saviour. This is a radically different doctrine from that; and it produced radically different
effects on Luther; Luther the monk and Luther the Reformer
are two different men. And it has produced radically different
effects in the world; the medieval world and the modern world
are two different worlds. The thing that divides them is the
new doctrine that Luther found in the monastery at Wittenberg — or was it already at Erfurt? — poring over the great
declaration in the first chapter of the Epistle to the Romans:
" The righteous shall live by faith." Émile Doumergue puts the

whole story into a sentence: " Two radically different religions give birth to two radically different civilizations."

Luther himself knew perfectly well that what he had done for himself, and what he would fain do for the world, was just to substitute a new doctrine for that old one in which neither he nor the world could find life. So he came forward as a teacher, as a dogmatic teacher, as a dogmatic teacher who gloried in his dogmatism. He was not merely seeking for truth; he had the truth. He did not make tentative suggestions to the world for its consideration; what he dealt in was — so he liked to call them — " assertions." This was naturally a mode of procedure very offensive to a man of polite letters, like Erasmus, say, who knew of nothing that men of culture could not sit around a well-furnished table and discuss together pleasurably with open minds. " I have so little stomach for ' assertions,' " he says, striking directly at Luther, " that I could easily go over to the opinion of the sceptics — wherever," he smugly adds, " it were allowed me by the inviolable authority of the Sacred Scriptures and the decrees of the Church, to which I everywhere submit, whether I follow what is presented or not." For this his Oliver he certainly got more than a Roland from Luther. For Luther takes occasion from this remark to read Erasmus a much-needed lecture on the place of dogma in Christianity. To say you have no pleasure in " assertions," he says, is all one with saying you are not a Christian. Take away " assertions," and you take away Christianity. No Christian could endure to have " assertions " despised, since that would be nothing else than to deny at once all religion and piety, or to declare that religion and piety and every dogma are nothing. Christian doctrines are not to be put on a level with human opinions. They are divinely given to us in Holy Scripture to form the molds in which Christian lives are to run.

We are in the presence here of what is known as the formal principle of the Reformation. The fundamental meaning of it is that the Reformation was primarily, like all great revolutions, a revolution in the realm of ideas. Was it not a wise man who urged us long ago to give especial diligence to keeping our hearts (the heart is the cognitive faculty in Scripture), on the express ground that out of them are the issues of life? The battle of the Reformation was fought out under a banner on which the sole authority of Scripture was inscribed. But the principle of the sole authority of Scripture was not to the Reformation an abstract principle. What it was interested in was what is taught in Scripture; and the sole authority of Scripture meant to it the sole authority of what is taught in Scripture. This of course is dogma; and the dogma which the men of the Reformation found taught in Scripture above every other dogma, so much above every other dogma that in it is summed up all the teaching of Scripture, is the sole efficiency of God in salvation. This is what we call the material principle of the Reformation. It was not at first known by the name of justification by faith alone, but it was from the first passionately embraced as renunciation of all human works and dependence on the grace of God alone for salvation. In it the Reformation lived and moved and had its being; in a high sense of the words, it is the Reformation.

The confusion would be ludicrous, if it were not rather pathetic, by which the correction of abuses in the life whether of the Church or of society at large, is confounded with the Reformation. Luther knew perfectly well from the beginning where the center of his Reformation lay, and did not for a moment confound its peripheral effects with it. Here, indeed, lay the precise difference between him and the other reformers of the time — those other reformers who could not reform. Erasmus, for example, was as clear of eye as Luther to see, and as outspoken as Luther to condemn, the crying abuses of the day. But he conceived the task of reform as a purely negative one. The note of his reform was simplicity; he wished to return to the " simplicity of the Christian life," and, as a means to that, to the " simplicity of doctrine." He was content with a process of stripping off, and he expected to reach the kernel of true Christianity merely by thoroughly removing the husk which at the moment covered and concealed it. The assumption being that true Christianity lay behind and beneath the corruptions of the day, no restoration was needed, only un-covering. When he came to do the stripping, it is true, Erasmus found no stopping-place; he stripped not only to the bone but through the bone, and nothing was left in his hand but a "philosophy of Christ," which was a mere moralism. Peter Canisius, looking at it formally, calls it not inaptly, "the theology of Pyrrhus." Luther, judging it from the material standpoint, says Erasmus has made "a gospel of Pelagius." Thus at all events Erasmus at once demonstrated that beneath the immense fabric of medieval Christianity there lay as its sustaining core nothing but a bald moralism; and by dragging this moralism out and labeling it "simple Christianity," has made himself the father of that great multitude in our day who, crying: Back to Christ! have reduced Christianity to the simple precept: Be good and it will be well with you.

In sharp contrast with these negative reformers Luther came forward with a positive gospel in his hands; "a new religion" his adversaries called it then, as their descendants call it now, and they call it so truly. He was not particularly interested in the correction of abuses, though he hewed at them manfully when they stood in his way. To speak the whole truth, this necessary work bored him a little. He saw no pure gospel beneath them which their removal would un-cover and release. He knew that his new gospel, once launched, had power of itself to abolish them. What his heart was aflame with was the desire to launch this new gospel; to substitute it, the gospel of grace, for the gospel of works, on which alone men were being fed. In that substitution consisted his whole Reformation.

In his detailed answer to the Bull of Excommunication, published against him in 1520, in which forty-one propositions from his writings were condemned, Luther shows plainly enough where the center of controversy lay for him. It was in the article in which he asserts the sole efficiency of grace in salvation. He makes his real appeal to Scripture, of course, but he does not neglect to point out also that he has Augustine with him and also experience. He scoffs at his opponents' pretensions to separate themselves from the Pelagians by wire-drawn distinctions between works of congruity and works of condignity. If we may secure grace by works, he says, it means nothing that we carefully name these works works of congruity and refrain from calling them works of condignity. " For what is the difference," he cries, " if you deny that grace is from our works and yet teach that it is through our works? The impious sense remains that grace is held to be given not gratis but on account of our works. For the Pelagians did not teach and do any other works on account of which they expected grace to be given than you teach and do. They are the works of the same free will and the same members, although you and they give them different names. They are the same fasting and prayers and almsgiving — but you call them works congruous to grace, they works condign to grace. The same Pelagians remain victors in both cases."

What Luther is zealous for, it will be seen, is the absolute exclusion of works from salvation, and the casting of the soul wholly upon the grace of God. He rises to full eloquence as he approaches the end of his argument, pushing his adversaries fairly to the ropes. " For when they could not deny that we must be saved by the grace of God," he exclaims, " and could not elude this truth, then impiety sought out another way of escape — pretending that, although we cannot save ourselves, we can nevertheless prepare for being saved by God's grace. What glory remains to God, I ask, if we are able to procure that we shall be saved by His grace? Does this seem a small ability — that he who has no grace shall nevertheless have power enough to obtain grace when he wishes? What is the difference between that, and saying with the Pelagians that we are saved without grace — since you place the grace of God within the power of man's will? You seem to me to be worse than Pelagius, since you put in the power of man the necessary grace of God, the necessity of which he simply denied. I say, it seems less impious wholly to deny grace than to represent it as secured by our zeal and effort, and to put it thus in our power."

This tremendous onslaught prepares the way for a notable

declaration in which Luther makes perfectly clear how he thought of his work as a reformer and the relative importance which he attached to the several matters in controversy. Rome taught, with whatever finessing, salvation by works; he knew and would know nothing but salvation by grace, or, as he phrases it here, nothing but Christ and Him crucified. It was the cross that Rome condemned in him; for it was the cross and it alone in which he put his trust. " In all the other articles," he says — that is to say, all the others of the forty-one propositions which had been condemned in the Bull — " those concerning the Papacy, Councils, Indulgences, and other non-necessary trifles (*nugae!*)" — this is the way in which he enumerates them — " the levity and folly of the Pope and his followers may be endured. But in this article," — that is, the one on free will and grace — " which is the best of all and the sum of our matter, we must grieve and weep over the insanity of these miserable men." It is on this article, then, that for him the whole conflict turns as on its hinge. He wishes he could write more largely upon it. For more than three hundred years none, or next to none, have written in favor of grace; and there is no subject which is in so great need of treatment as this. " And I have often wished," he adds, " passing by these frivolous Papist trifles and brawls (*nugis et negotiis*), which have nothing to do with the Church but to destroy it — to deal with this."

His opportunity to do so came when, four years afterward (1524), Erasmus, egged on by his patrons and friends, and taking his start from this very discussion, published his charmingly written book, " On Free Will." It is the great humanist's greatest book, elegant in style, suave in tone, delicate in suggestion, winning in its appeal; and it presents with consummate skill the case for the Romish teaching against which Luther had thrown himself. Separating himself as decisively if not as fundamentally on the one side from Pelagius and Scotus — in another place he speaks with distaste of " Scotus his bristling and prickly soul " — as on the other from the reformers — he has Carlstadt and Luther especially in mind

— Erasmus attaches himself to what he calls, in accordance with the point of view of his time, the Augustinian doctrine; that is to say, to the synergism of the scholastics, perhaps most nearly in the form in which it had been taught by Alexander of Hales, and at all events practically as it was soon to be authoritatively defined as the doctrine of the Church by the Council of Trent. To this subtle doctrine he gives its most attractive statement and weaves around it the charm of his literary grace. Luther was not insensible to the beauty of the book. He says the voice of Erasmus in it sounded to him like the song of a nightingale. But he was in search of substance, not form, and he felt bound to confess that his experience in reading the book was much that of the wolf in the fable, who, ravished by the song of a nightingale, could not rest till he had caught and greedily devoured it — only to remark disgustedly afterward: " Vox, et praeterea nihil."

The refinements of Erasmus' statements were lost on Luther. What he wished — and nothing else would content him — was a clear and definite acknowledgment that the work of salvation is of the grace of God alone, and man contributes nothing whatever to it. This acknowledgment Erasmus could not make. The very purpose for which he was writing was to vindicate for man a part, and that the decisive part, in his own salvation. He might magnify the grace of God in the highest terms. He might protest that he too held that without the grace of God no good thing could be done by man, so that grace is the beginning and the middle and the end of salvation. But when pressed to the wall he was forced to allow that, somewhere in " the middle," an action of man came in, and that this action of man was the decisive thing that determined his salvation. He might minimize this action of man to the utmost. He might point out that it was a very, very little thing which he retained to human powers — only, as one might say, that man must push the button and grace had to do the rest. This did not satisfy Luther. Nothing would satisfy him but that all of salvation — every bit of it — should be attributed to the grace of God alone.

Luther even made Erasmus' efforts to reduce man's part in salvation to as little as possible, while yet retaining it at the decisive point, the occasion of scoffing. Instead of escaping Pelagianism by such expedients, he says, Erasmus and his fellow sophists cast themselves more deeply into the vat and come out double-dyed Pelagians. The Pelagians are at least honest with themselves and us. They do not palter, in a double sense, with empty distinctions between works of condignity and works of congruity. They call a spade a spade and say candidly that merit is merit. And they do not belittle our salvation by belittling the works by which we merit it. We do not hear from them that we merit saving grace by something " very little, almost nothing." They hold salvation precious; and warn us that if we are to gain it, it can be at the cost only of great effort — " tota, plena, perfecta, magna et multa studia et opera." If we *will* fall into error in such a matter, says Luther, at least let us not cheapen the grace of God, and treat it as something vile and contemptible. What he means is that the attempted compromise, while remaining Pelagian in principle, yet loses the high ethical position of Pelagianism. Seeking some middle-place between grace and works, and fondly congratulating itself that it retains both, it merely falls between the stools and retains neither. It depends as truly as Pelagianism on works, but reduces these works on which it nevertheless depends to a vanishing-point. In thus suspending salvation on " some little thing, almost nothing," says Luther, it " denies the Lord Christ who has bought us, more than the Pelagians ever denied Him, or any heretics."

To the book in which Luther replied to Erasmus' " On Free Will," matching Erasmus' title, he gives the name of " On the Enslaved Will." Naturally, the flowing purity of the great humanist's Latinity and the flexible grace of his style are not to be found here. But the book is written in sufficiently good Latin — plain and strong and straightforward. Luther evidently took unusual pains with it, and it more than makes up for any lack of literary charm it may show by the fertility of its thought and the amazing vigor of its language. A. Freitag, its latest editor, characterizes it briefly, in one great word, as an "exploit" (*Grosstat*), and Sodeur does not scruple to describe it roundly as "a dialectic and polemic masterpiece"; its words have hands and feet. Its real distinction, however, is to be sought in a higher region than these things. It is the embodiment of Luther's reformation conceptions, the nearest to a systematic statement of them he ever made. It is the first exposition of the fundamental ideas of the Reformation in comprehensive presentation, and it is therefore in a true sense the manifesto of the Reformation. It was so that Luther himself looked upon it. It was not because he admired it as a piece of "mere literature" that he always thought of it as an achievement. It was because it contained the *doctrinae evangelicae caput* — the very head and principle of the evangelical teaching. He could well spare all that he had ever written, he wrote to Capito in 1537, let them all go, except the "On the Enslaved Will" and the "Catechism"; they only are right (*justum*). He is reported in the "Table Talk" (Lauterbach-Aurifaber) to have referred once to Erasmus' rejoinder to the book. He did not admit that Erasmus had confuted it; he did not admit that Erasmus ever could confute it, no, not to all eternity. "That I know full well," he said, "and I defy the devil and all his wiles to confute it. For I am certain that it is the unchangeable truth of God." He who touches this doctrine, he says again, touches the apple of his eye.

We may be sure that Luther wrote this book *con amore*. It was not easy for him to write it when he wrote it. That was the year (1525) of the Peasants' Revolt; and what that was in the way of distraction and care, anguish of mind and soul, all know. It was also the year of his marriage, and has he not told us with his engaging frankness that, during the first year of his married life, Katie always sat by him as he worked, trying to think up questions to ask him? But what he was writing down in this book he was not thinking out as he wrote. He was pouring out upon the page the heart of the heart of his gospel, and he was doing it in the exulting confidence that it was not his gospel merely but the gospel of God. He thanks Erasmus for giving him, by selecting this theme to attack him upon, a respite from the wearing, petty strifes that were being thrust continually upon him, and thus enabling him to speak for once directly to the point. "I exceedingly praise and laud this in you," he writes at the end of his book, "that you alone, in contrast with all others, have attacked the thing itself, that is, the top of the question (*summam caussae*), and have not fatigued me with those irrelevant questions about the papacy, purgatory, indulgences and such like trumperies (*nugae*) rather than questions — in which hitherto all have vainly sought to pursue me. You and you alone have seen the hinge of things and have aimed at the throat; and for this I thank you heartily."

It was in no light, however buoyant, spirit, however, that Luther entered upon the discussion. In a very moving context he writes: "I tell you and I beg you to let it sink into the depths of your mind — I am seeking in this matter something that is solemn, and necessary, and eternal to me, of such sort and so great that it must be asserted and defended at the cost of death itself — yea, if the whole world should not only be cast into strife and tumult, but even should be reduced to chaos and dissolved into nothingness. For by God's grace I am not so foolish and mad that I could be willing for the sake of money (which I neither have nor wish), or of glory (a thing I could not obtain if I wished it, in a world so incensed against me), or of the life of the body (of which I cannot be sure for a moment), to carry on and sustain this matter so long, with so much fortitude and so much constancy (you call it obstinacy), through so many perils to my life, through so much hatred, through so many snares — in short through the fury of men and devils. Do you think that you alone have a heart disturbed by these tumults? I am not made of stone either, nor was I either born of the Marpesian rocks. But since it cannot be done otherwise, I prefer to be battered in this tumult, joyful in the grace of God, for the sake of the word of God which must be asserted with invincible and incorruptible courage, rather than in eternal tumult to be ground to powder in intolerable torment under the wrath of God." This was the spirit in which Luther sustained his thesis of " the enslaved will." It is the spirit of " Woe is unto me if I preach not the gospel." It is the gospel which he has in his hands, the gospel for the world's salvation, and necessity is laid upon him to preach it.

The gospel which Luther had it thus in his heart to preach was, to put it shortly, the gospel of salvation through the grace of God alone. There are two foci around which this gospel revolves: the absolute helplessness of man in his sin; the sole efficiency of grace in salvation. These complementary propositions are given expression theologically in the doctrines of the inability of sinful man to good, and of the creative operation of saving grace. It is the inability of sinful man to good that Luther means by his phrase " the enslaved will." Neither he nor Erasmus was particularly interested in the psychology of the will. We may learn incidentally that he held to the view which has come to be called philosophical determinism, or moral necessity. But we learn that only incidentally. Neither he nor Erasmus was concerned with the mechanism of the will's activity, if we may be allowed this mode of speech. They were absorbed in the great problem of the power of sinful man to good. Erasmus had it in mind to show that sinful man has the power to do good things, things so good that they have merit in the sight of God, and that man's salvation depends on his doing them. Luther had it in his heart to show that sinful man, just because he is sinful and sin is no light evil but destroys all goodness, has no power to do anything that is good in God's sight, and therefore is dependent utterly on God's grace alone for salvation. This is to say, Luther was determined to deal seriously with sin, with original sin, with the fall, with the deep corruption of heart which comes from the fall, with the inability to good which is the result of this corruption of heart. He branded the teaching that man can save himself, or do anything looking to his own salvation, as a hideous lie, and "he launched point-blank his dart at the head of this lie — taught original sin, the corruption of man's heart."

Erasmus, of course, does not fail to put his finger on the precise point of Luther's contention. He complains of the new teachers that they "immensely exaggerate original sin, representing even the noblest powers of human nature as so corrupt that of itself it can do nothing but ignore and hate God, and not even one who has been justified by the grace of faith can effect any work which is not sin; they make that tendency to sin in us, which has been transmitted to us from our first parents to be itself sin, and that so invincibly sin that there is no commandment of God which even a man who has been justified by faith can keep, but all the commandments of God serve no other end than to enhance the grace of God, which bestows salvation without regard to merits." It outraged him, as it has outraged all who feel with him up to to-day — as, for example, Hartmann Grisar — that Luther so grossly overdraws the evil of "concupiscence," and thus does despite to that human nature which God created in His own image. Luther was compelled to point out over and over again that he was not talking about human nature and its powers, but about sin and grace. We have not had to wait for Erasmus to tell us, he says, "that a man has eyes and nose, and ears, and bones, and hands — and a mind and a will and a reason," and that it is because he has these things that he is a man; he would not be a man without them. We could not talk of sin with reference to him, had he not these things; nor of grace either — for does not even the proverb say: "God did not make heaven for geese"? Let us leave human nature and its powers to one side then; they are all presupposed. The point of importance is that man is now a sinner. And the point in dispute is whether sinful man can be, at will, not sinful; whether he can do by nature what it requires grace to do. Luther does not depreciate human nature; his opponents depreciate the baleful power of sin, the necessity for a creative operation of grace; and because they depreciate both sin and

grace they expect man in his own powers to do what God alone,
the Almighty Worker, can do.

He draws out his doctrine here in a long parallel. " As a
man, before he is created, to be a man, does nothing and makes
no effort to be a creature; and then, after he has been made and
created, does nothing and makes no effort to continue a
creature; but both these things alike are done solely by the will
of the omnipotent power and goodness of God who without
our aid creates and preserves us — but He does not operate
in us without our coöperation, seeing that He created and preserved us for this very purpose, that He might operate in us
and we coöperate with Him, whether this is done outside His
kingdom by general omnipotence, or within His kingdom by
the singular power of His Spirit: So then we say that a man
before he is renovated into a new creature of the kingdom of
the Spirit, does nothing and makes no effort to prepare himself for that renovation and kingdom; and then, after he has
been renovated, does nothing, makes no effort to continue in
that kingdom; but the Spirit alone does both alike in us, recreating us without our aid, and preserving us when recreated,
as also James says, ' Of His own will begat He us by the word
of His power, that we should be the beginning of His creation '
(he is speaking of the renewed creature), but He does not
operate apart from us, seeing that He has recreated and preserved us for this very purpose that He might operate in us and
we coöperate with Him. Thus through us He preaches, has
pity on the poor, consoles the afflicted. But what, then, is
attributed to free will? Or rather what is left to it except
nothing? Assuredly just nothing." What this parallel teaches is
that the whole saving work is from God, in the beginning and
middle and end; it is a supernatural work throughout. But
we are saved that we may live in God; and, in the powers of
our new life, do His will in the world. It is the Pauline, Not
out of works, but unto good works, which God has afore prepared that we should live in them.

It is obvious that the whole substance of Luther's fundamental theology was summed up in the antithesis of sin and

grace: sin conceived as absolutely disabling to good; grace as absolutely recreative in effect. Of course he taught also all that is necessarily bound up in one bundle of thought with this great doctrine of sin and grace. He taught, for instance, as a matter of course, the doctrine of " irresistible grace," and also with great purity and decision the doctrine of predestination — for how can salvation be of pure grace alone apart from all merit, save by the sovereign and effective gift of God? A great part of " The Enslaved Will " is given to insistence upon and elucidation of this doctrine of absolute predestination, and Luther did not shrink from raising it into the cosmical region or from elaborating it in its every detail. What it is important for us at the moment to insist upon, however, is that what we have said of Luther we might just as well, *mutatis mutandis*, have said of every other of the great Reformers. Luther's doctrine of sin and grace was not peculiar to him. It was the common property of the whole body of the Reformers. It was taught with equal clarity and force by Zwingli as by Luther, and by Martin Bucer and by John Calvin. It was taught even, in his earlier and happier period, by that " Protestant Erasmus," the weak and unreliable Melanchthon, who was saved from betraying the whole Protestant cause at Augsburg by no staunchness in himself, but only by the fatuity of the Catholics, and who later did betray it in its heart of hearts by going over to that very synergism which Luther declared to be the very marrow of the Pope's teaching. In one word, this doctrine was Protestantism itself. All else that Protestantism stood for, in comparison with this, must be relegated to the second rank.

There are some interesting paragraphs in the earlier pages of Alexander Schweizer's " Central Doctrines of Protestantism," in which he speaks of the watchwords of Protestantism, and points out the distinction between them and the so-called formal and material principles of Protestantism, which are, in point of fact, their more considered elaboration. Every reformatory movement in history, he says, has its watchwords, which serve as the symbol by which its adherents encourage

one another, and as the banner about which they gather. They
penetrate to the very essence of the matter, and give, if popular, yet compressed and vivid, expression to the precise pivot
on which the movement turns. In the case of the Protestant
revolution the antithesis, Not tradition but Scripture, emerged
as one of these watchwords, but not as the ultimate one, but
only as subordinate to another in which was expressed the contrast between the parties at strife with respect to the chief
matter, how shall sinful man be saved? This ultimate watchword, says Schweizer, ran somewhat like this: Not works, but
faith; not our merit, but God's grace in Christ; not our own
penances and satisfactions, but the merit of Christ only. When
we hear these cries we are hearing the very pulse-beats of the
Reformation as a force among men. In their presence we are
in the presence of the Reformation in its purity.

It scarcely requires explicit mention that what we are, then,
face to face with in the Reformation is simply a revival of
Augustinianism. The fundamental Augustinian antithesis of
sin and grace is the soul of the whole Reformation movement.
If we wish to characterize the movement on its theological
side in one word, therefore, it is adequately done by declaring
it a great revival of Augustinianism. Of course, if we study
exactness of statement, there are qualifications to be made.
But these qualifications serve not to modify the characterization but only to bring it to its utmost precision. We are bidden
to remember that the Reformation was not the only movement
back toward Augustinianism of the later Middle Ages or of its
own day. The times were marked by a deep dissatisfaction
with current modes of treating and speaking of divine things;
and a movement away from the dominant nominalism, so far
back toward Augustinianism as at least to Thomism, was
widespread and powerful. And we are bidden to remember that
Augustinianism is too broad a term to apply undefined to the
doctrinal basis of the Reformation. In its complete connotation it included not only tendencies but elements of explicit
teaching which were abhorrent to the Reformers, and by virtue
of which the Romanists have an equal right with the Prot-

estants to be called the true children of Augustine. It is suggested therefore that all that can properly be said is that the Reformation, conceived as a movement of its time, represented that part of the general revulsion from the corruptions of the day — the whole of which looked back toward Augustine for guidance and strength — which, because it was distinctively religious in its motives and aspirations, laid hold purely of the Augustinian doctrines of sin and grace, and built exclusively on them in its readjustments to life.

We may content ourselves with such a statement. It is quite true that the Reformation, when looked at purely in itself, presents itself to our view as, in the words of Fr. Loofs, " the rediscovery of Christianity as religion." And it is quite true that purely Augustinian as the Reformation is in its conception of religion, it is not the whole of Augustine that it takes over but only " the Augustine of sin and grace," so that when we speak of it as a revival of Augustinianism we must have in mind only the Augustinianism of grace. But the Augustinianism of grace in the truest sense represents " the real Augustine "; no injustice is done to historical verity in the essence of the matter when we speak of him as " a post-Pauline Paul and a pre-Lutheran Luther." We have only in such a phrase uncovered the true succession. Paul, Augustine, Luther; for substance of doctrine these three are one, and the Reformation is perceived to be, on its doctrinal side, mere Paulinism given back to the world.

To realize how completely this is true we have only to look into the pages of those lecture notes on Romans which Luther wrote down in 1515–1516, and the manuscript of which was still lying in 1903 unregarded in a showcase of the Berlin Library. Luther himself, of course, fully understood it all. He is reported to have said in his table talk in 1538 (Lauterbach): " There was a certain cardinal in the beginning of the Gospel plotting many things against me in Rome. A court fool, looking on, is said to have remarked: ' My Lord, take my advice and first depose Paul from the company of the Apostles; it is he who is giving us all this trouble.' " It was Paul whom Luther was consciously resurrecting, Paul with the constant cry on his lips — so Luther puts it — of "Grace! Grace! Grace!" Luther characteristically adds: "In spite of the devil" — "grace, in spite of the devil"; and perhaps it will not be without its value for us to observe that Luther did his whole work of reëstablishing the doctrine of salvation by pure grace in the world, in the clear conviction that he was doing it in the teeth of the devil. It was against principalities and powers and spiritual wickednesses in high places that he felt himself to be fighting; and he depended for victory on no human arm. Has he not expressed it all in his great hymn — the Reformation hymn by way of eminence? —

> A trusty stronghold is our God . . .
> Yea, were the world with devils filled.

XVII

THE NINETY-FIVE THESES IN THEIR THEOLOGICAL SIGNIFICANCE

THE NINETY-FIVE THESES IN THEIR
THEOLOGICAL SIGNIFICANCE [1]

" A POOR peasant's son, then a diligent student, a humble
monk, and, finally, a modest, industrious scholar, Martin
Luther had already exceeded the half of the life-time allotted
to him, when — certainly with the decision characteristic of
him, but with all the reserve imposed by his position in life and
the immediate purpose of his action — he determined to subject the religious conceptions which lay at the basis of the
indulgence-usages of the time to an examination in academic
debate." [2] This singularly comprehensive and equally singularly accurate statement of Paul Kalkoff's is worth quoting because it places us at once at the right point of view for forming
an estimate of the Ninety-five Theses which Luther, in prosecution of the purpose thus intimated, posted on the door of
the Castle-Church at Wittenberg on the fateful October 31,
1517. It sets clearly before us the Luther who posted the
Theses. It was — as he describes himself, indeed, in their
heading [3] — Martin Luther, Master of Arts and of Theology,
Ordinary Professor of Theology in the University of Wittenberg. And it indicates to us with equal clearness the nature of
the document which he posted. It consists of heads for a discussion designed to elucidate the truth with respect to the
subject with which it deals — as again Luther himself tells us
in its heading. We have to do here in a word with an academic

[1] Reprinted from *The Princeton Theological Review*, xv. 1917, pp. 501–
529.

[2] P. Kalkoff, " Luther und die Entscheidungsjahre der Reformation," 1917,
p. 9.

[3] For the Theses see any standard edition of Luther's " Works ": e.g. " D.
Martin Luthers Werke," Weimar edition, i. 1883, pp. 233–238. Cf. " Works of
Martin Luther," Philadelphia, i. 1915, pp. 29–38; and Philip Schaff, " History
of the Christian Church," vi. 1888, pp. 160–166.

document, prepared by an academic teacher, primarily for an academic purpose. All that the Theses were to become grows out of this fundamental fact. We have to reckon, of course, with the manner of man this Professor of Theology was; with the conception he held of the function of the University in the social organism; with the zeal for the truth which consumed him. But in doing so we must not permit to fall out of sight that it is with a hard-working Professor of Theology, in the prosecution of his proper academical work, that we have to do in these Theses. And above everything we must not forget the precise matter which the Theses bring into discussion; this was, as Kalkoff accurately describes it, the religious conceptions which lay at the basis of the indulgence traffic.

Failure to bear these things fully in mind has resulted in much confusion. It is probably responsible for the absurd statement of A. Plummer to the effect that " Luther began with a mere protest against the sale of indulgences by disreputable persons." [4] One would have thought a mere glance at the document would have rendered such an assertion impossible; although it is scarcely more absurd than Philip Schaff's remark that the Theses do not protest " against indulgences, but only against their abuse " [5] — which Plummer elaborates into: " Luther did not denounce the whole system of indulgences. He never disputed that the Church has power to remit the penalties which it has imposed in the form of penances to be performed in this world." [6] To treat the whole system of indulgences, as proclaimed at the time, as an abuse of the ancient custom of relaxing, on due cause, imposed penances, is to attack the whole system with a vengeance.

The general lack of discernment with which the Theses have been read is nothing less than astonishing. It is not easy to understand, for instance, how T. M. Lindsay [7] could have been led to say that they are " singularly unlike what might

[4] A. Plummer, " The Continental Reformation," 1912, p. 98.

[5] " History of the Christian Church," vi. 1888, p. 157.

[6] *Op. cit.*, p. 98.

[7] " A History of the Reformation," ed. 2, i. 1912, p. 228.

have been expected from a Professor of Theology." " They lack," he tells us, " theological definition, and contain many repetitions which might have been easily avoided." He speaks of them as simply unordered sledge-hammer blows directed against an ecclesiastical abuse: as such utterances as were natural to a man in close touch with the people, who, shocked at the reports of what the pardon-sellers had said, wished to contradict some of the statements which had been made in their defense. One does not know how Lindsay would expect a professional theologian to write. But certainly these Theses lack neither in profundity of theological insight nor in the strictest logical development of their theme. They constitute, in point of fact, a theological document of the first importance, working out a complete and closely knit argument against, not the abuses of the indulgence traffic, and not even the theory of indulgences, merely, but the whole sacerdotal conception of the saving process — an outgrowth and embodiment of which indulgences were. The popular aspects of the matter are reserved to the end of the document, and are presented there, not for their own sake, but as ancillary arguments for the theological conclusion aimed at. E. Bratke is right in insisting on the distinctively theological character of the Theses: they were, he says truly, " a scientific attempt at a theological examination "; and Luther's object in publishing them was a clearly positive one. " Not abuses," says Bratke rightly, " nor the doctrine of penance, but the doctrine of the acquisition of salvation, it was, for which Luther seized his weapons in his own interests and in the interests of Christianity." [8]

Bernhard Bess [9] may supply us, however, with our typical example of how the Theses should not be dealt with. He wishes to vindicate a Reformatory importance for them; but he has difficulty in discovering it. They do not look very important at first sight, he says. Everybody who reads them for the first time has a feeling of disappointment with them. Even

[8] E. Bratke, " Luther's 95 Thesen," 1884, pp. 275 and 279; cf. p. 273.
[9] " Die 95 Thesen Luther's und der Anfang der Reformation," in *Protestantische Monatshefte*, v. 1901, pp. 434 ff.

theologians well acquainted with the theological language of the times have trouble in forming a clear notion of what they are about — what they deny, what they affirm. The few plain and distinct propositions as to the true penitence of a Christian and the forgiveness of sins, are buried beneath a mass of timid inquiries, of assertions scarcely made before they are half-recalled, of sentences which sound more like *bon mots* than the well-weighed words of an academical teacher, of citations which only too clearly betray themselves as mere padding. Everything is found here except the clear, thoroughly pondered, and firmly grounded declarations of a man who knows what he is at. Naturally, in these circumstances, it has proved difficult for others to discover what Luther had it in mind here to say. A layman, on first reading these propositions, will understand little more than that the abuses with which the preaching of indulgences was accompanied, are here condemned. There have been learned theologians who have seen so little in them, that they have felt compelled to seek the motive for their publication outside of them. Catholics have found it in the jealousy of the Augustinian monk of the Dominican Tetzel; or in the fear that the indulgences offered by Tetzel should put out of countenance those connected with the Castle-Church at Wittenberg and its host of relics. Protestants have been driven back upon the notion that Luther is assaulting only the gross abuses of Tetzel's preaching — abuses which, however, better knowledge shows did not exist: Tetzel did not exceed his commission. Compelled to go behind Tetzel, A. W. Dieckhoff finds the ground of Luther's assault on indulgences in the rise of the doctrine of attrition by which all earnestness in repentance was destroyed and sin and salvation had come to be looked upon so lightly that moral seriousness was in danger of perishing out of the earth. Others, of whom Bess himself is one, call attention rather to the difference between indulgences in general and the Jubilee indulgences: the Jubilee indulgences alone are attacked by Luther — the Jubilee indulgences which had become a new sacrament, as John of Paltz declares, and a new sacrament of such power as to threaten to absorb into itself the whole saving function of the Church, and to substitute itself for the gospel, for the cross.

We are moving here, no doubt, on the right track, but we are moving on too narrow-gauged a road, and we are not moving far enough. We must distinguish between the immediate occasion of Luther's protest and its real motive and purport. The immediate occasion was, no doubt, Tetzel's preaching of the Jubilee indulgences in his neighborhood. But what Luther was led to do was to call in question, not merely the abuses which accompanied this particular instance of the proclamation of the Jubilee indulgences, or which were accustomed to accompany their proclamation; and not merely the peculiarities of the Jubilee indulgences among indulgences; and not even merely the whole theory of indulgences; but the entire prevalent theory of the relation of the Church as the institute of salvation to the salvation of souls. Thus the Theses become not merely an anti-indulgence proclamation but an anti-sacerdotal proclamation. And therein consists their importance as a Reformation act. Luther might have repelled all the abuses which had grown up about the preaching of indulgences and have remained a good Papalist. He might have rejected the Jubilee indulgences, *in toto*, and indeed the whole theory of indulgences as it had developed itself in the Church since the thirteenth century, and remained a good Catholic. But he hewed more closely to the line than that. He called in question the entire basis of the Catholic system and came forward in opposition to it, as an Evangelical.

That this could be the result of a series of Theses called out in opposition to the preaching of Jubilee indulgences is in part due to the very peculiarity of these indulgences. They included in themselves the sacrament of penance; and their rejection, not in circumstantials only but in principle, included in itself the repudiation of the conception of salvation of which the sacrament of penance was the crown. When Luther affirmed, in Theses 36 and 37, the culminating Theses of the whole series: "Every truly contrite Christian has plenary remission from punishment and guilt due to him, even without letters of pardon. Every true Christian, whether living or dead, has a share given to him by God in all the benefits of Christ and the Church, even without letters of pardon " — there is included in these " letters of pardon," expressly declared unnecessary, the whole sacerdotal machinery of salvation; and Luther is asserting salvation apart from this machinery as normal salvation. Reducing the ecclesiastical part in salvation to a purely ministerial and declaratory one, he sets the sinful soul nakedly face to face with its God and throws it back immediately on His free mercy for its salvation.

The significance of the Theses as a Reformation act emerges thus in this: that they are a bold, an astonishingly bold, and a powerful, an astonishingly powerful, assertion of the evangelical doctrine of salvation, embodied in a searching, well-compacted, and thoroughly wrought-out refutation of the sacerdotal conception, as the underlying foundation on which the edifice of the indulgence traffic was raised. This is what Walther Köhler means when he declares that we must recognize this as the fundamental idea of Luther's Theses: " the emancipation of the believer from the tutelage of the ecclesiastical institute "; and adds, " Thus God advances for him into the foreground; He alone is Lord of death and life; and to the Church falls the modest rôle of agent of God on earth — only there and nowhere else." " The most far-reaching consequences flowed from this," he continues; " Luther smote the Pope on his crown and simply obliterated his high pretensions with reference to the salvation of souls in this world and the next, and in their place set God and the soul in a personal communion which in its whole intercourse bears the stamp of interiorness and spirituality." Julius Köstlin puts the whole matter with his accustomed clearness and balance — though with a little wider reference than the Theses themselves — when he describes the advance in Luther's testimony marked by the indulgence controversy thus: " As he had up to this time proclaimed salvation in Christ through faith, in opposition to all human merit, so he now proclaims it also in opposition to an external human ecclesiasticism and priesthood, whose acts are represented as conditioning the imparting of salvation itself, and as in and of themselves, even without faith, effecting salvation for those in whose interests they are performed." [10]

How, in these circumstances, Philip Schaff can say of the Theses, " they were more Catholic than Protestant," [11] passes comprehension. He does, no doubt, add on the next page, " The form only is Romish, the spirit and aim are Protestant "; but that is an inadequate correction. They are nothing less than, to speak negatively, an anti-sacerdotal, to speak positively, an evangelical manifesto. There are " remainders of Romanism " in them, to be sure, for Luther had not worked his way yet to the periphery of his system of thought. These " remainders of Romanism " led him in after years to speak of himself as at this time still involved in the great superstition of the Roman tyranny (1520), and even as a mad papist, so sunk in the Pope's dogmas that he was ready to murder anyone who refused obedience to the Pope (1545). But these strong expressions witness rather to the horror with which he had come to look upon everything that was papist than do justice to the stage of his developing Protestantism which he had reached in 1517. The remainders of Romanism imbedded in the Theses are, after all, very few and very slight. Luther was not yet ready to reject indulgences in every sense. He still believed in a purgatory. He still had a great reverence for the organized Church; put a high value on the priestly function; and honored the Pope as the head of the ecclesiastical order. It is even possible to draw out from the Theses, indeed, some sentences which, in isolation, may appear startlingly Romish. We have in mind here such, for example, as the sixty-ninth, seventy-first, and seventy-third. It is to be observed that these are consecutive odd numbers. That is because they are mere protases, preparing the way, each for a ringing apodosis in which the gravamen of the assertion lies.

[10] " The Theology of Luther," i. 1897, p. 218 (Hay's translation, from the second German edition).
[11] *Op. cit.,* p. 157.

Luther has reached the stage in his argument here where he has the crying abuses connected with the preaching of indulgences in view. He declares, to be sure, " It is incumbent on bishops and curates to receive the commissaries of the apostolical pardons with all reverence." But that is only that he may add with the more force: " But much more is it incumbent on them to see to it with all their eyes and to take heed to it with all their ears that these men do not preach their own dreams instead of the commission of the Pope." He proclaims, it is true, " He who speaks against the truth of apostolic pardons, let him be anathema and accursed." But that is only to give zest to the contrast: " But he who exerts himself against the wantonness and license of speech of the preacher of pardons, let him be blessed." If he allows that " the Pope justly fulminates against those who use any kind of machinations to the injury of the traffic in pardons," that is only that he may add: " Much more does he intend to fulminate against those who under pretext of pardons use machinations to the injury of holy charity and truth." If Luther seems in these statements to allow the validity of indulgences, that must be set down to the fault of his antithetical rhetoric rather than of his doctrine. These protases are really of the nature of rhetorical concessions, and are meant to serve only as hammers to drive home the contrary assertions of his apodoses. Luther has already reduced valid indulgences to the relaxation of ecclesiastical penances, and curbed the Pope's power with reference to the remission of sin to a purely declaratory function. " The Pope has neither the will nor the power to remit any penalties, except those which he has imposed by his own authority or by that of the Canons. The Pope has no power to remit any guilt except by declaring and approbating it to have been remitted by God." These two Theses (5 and 6) cut up sacerdotalism by the roots.

We must be wary, too, lest we be misled by Luther's somewhat artificial use of his terms. He persistently means by " indulgences," " pardons," not the indulgences which actually existed in the world in which he lived — which he held to be

gross corruptions of the only real indulgences — but such indulgences as he was willing to admit to be valid, that is to say,
relaxations of ecclesiastically imposed penances; and he repeatedly speaks so as to imply that it is these which the Pope
really intends — or at least in the judgment of charity ought
to be assumed really to intend — by all the indulgences which
he commissions. Even more persistently he means by "the
Pope," not the Pope as he actually was, but the Pope as he
should be; that is to say, a " public person " representing and
practically identical with the ecclesiastical Canons. Thus,
when he declares in the forty-second Thesis that " it is not
the mind of the Pope that the buying of pardons is comparable
to works of mercy," he explains in his " Resolutions " (1518)
that what he really means is that the Canons do not put the
two on a par. " I understand the Pope," he says,[12] " as a public
person, that is, as he speaks through the Canons: there are
no Canons which declare that the value of indulgences is comparable to that of works of mercy." At an earlier point he had
said with great distinctness (on Thesis 26), " I am not in the
least moved by what is pleasing or displeasing to the supreme
Pontiff. He is a man like other men; there have been many
supreme Pontiffs who were pleased not only with errors and
vices but even with the most monstrous things. I hearken to the
Pope as pope; that is when he speaks in the Canons and speaks
according to the Canons, or when he determines with a Council: but not when he speaks according to his own head — for
I do not wish to be compelled to say, with some whose knowledge of Christ is defective, that the horrible deeds of blood
committed by Julius II against the Christian people were the
good deeds of a pious pastor done to Christ's sheep." [13] The
Pope to Luther was thus an administrative officer: not precisely what we should call a responsible ruler, but rather
what we should speak of as a limited executive. The
distinction he draws is not between the Pope speaking *ex
cathedra* and in his own private capacity; it is rather between
the Pope speaking of himself and according to his mandate.

[12] " Luthers Werke," Weimar edition, i. 1883, p. 599.   [13] P. 582.

Only when the Pope spoke according to his mandate was he the Pope, and Luther repeatedly in the Theses ascribes to the " Pope " what he found in the Canons, and denies to the " Pope " what the actual Pope was saying and doing, because it was not in the Canons. To him the Pope was not so much authoritative as what was authoritative was " the Pope."

What Luther found it hardest to separate himself from in the Catholic system, was the authoritative ministration of the priest, God's representative, to weak and trembling souls. The strength and purity of the evangelicalism of the Theses is manifested in nothing more decisively than in their clear proclamation of the dependence of the soul for salvation on the mere grace of God alone. But Luther could not escape from the feeling that, in some way, the priest had an intermediating part to play in the application of this salvation. This feeling finds its expression particularly in Thesis 7: " God never remits guilt to anyone at all, except at the same time He subjects him, humbled in all things, to the priest, His vicar." In the exposition of this Thesis in the " Resolutions " he has much ado to discover an essential part in salvation for the priest to play. When the dust clears away, what he has to say is seen to reduce to this: " The remission of God, therefore, works grace, but the remission of the priest, peace." [14] We may be saved without the priest, but we need his ministration to know that we are saved. The awakened sinner, by virtue of the very fact that he is awakened, cannot believe that he — even he — is forgiven, and needs the intermediation of God's representative, the priest, to assure him of it. The mischief is that Luther is inclined, if not to confuse, yet to join together these two things, and to treat salvation itself as therefore not quite accomplished until it is wrought *in foro conscientiae* as well as *in foro coeli.* " The remission of sin and the donation of grace is not enough," he says,[15] " but there is necessary also the belief that it is remitted." It makes no difference to him, he says, whether you say that the priest is the *sine qua non* or any other kind of cause of the remission of sin: all that he is exigent for

[14] P. 542. [15] P. 543.

is that it be allowed that in some way or other the priestly absolution is concerned in the remission of sin and guilt.

He will have, however, no *opus operatum;* and despite this magnifying of the part of absolution in salvation, he puts the priest firmly in his place, as a mere minister. It is after all not the priest, by virtue of any powers he may possess, but the man's own faith which in his absolution brings him remission. " For you will have only so much peace," he declares,[16] " as you have faith in the words of Him who promised, ' whatsoever you loose, etc.' For our peace is Christ, but in faith. If anyone does not believe this word, he may be absolved a million times by the Pope himself, and confess to the whole world, and he will never come to rest." " Forgiveness depends not on the priest but on the word of Christ; the priest may be acting for the sake of gain or of honor — do you but seek without hypocrisy for forgiveness and believe Christ who has given you His promise, and even though it be of mere frivolity that he absolves you, you nevertheless will receive forgiveness from your faith . . . your faith receives it wholly. So great a thing is the word of Christ, and faith in it." [17] " Accordingly it is through faith that we are justified, through faith also that we are brought to peace — not through works, penances, or confession." [18] There is no lack even here, therefore, of the note of salvation by pure grace through faith alone. There is only an effort to place the actual experience of salvation in some real connection with the ministrations of the Church. And underlying this there is a tendency to confuse salvation itself with the assurance of it. Both these points of view lived on in the Lutheran churches.

The part played, in the line of thought just reviewed, by Luther's conception of evangelical repentance ought not to be passed over without notice. This conception is in a sense the ruling conception of the Theses. The Christian, according to Luther, is a repentant sinner, and by his very nature as a repentant sinner must suffer continuously the pangs of repentance. By these pangs he is driven to mortifications of the

[16] P. 541.   [17] Pp. 543 f.   [18] P. 544.

flesh and becomes even greedy of suffering, which he recognizes as his appropriate life-element. So strong an emphasis does Luther place on suffering as a mark of the Christian life, indeed, that he has been sometimes represented as thinking of it as a good in itself, after the fashion of the mystics. Walther Köhler, for example, cries out, " The whole life a penance! Not only as often as the Church requires it in the confessional, no, the Christian's whole life is to be a great process of dying, ' mortification of the flesh ' — up to the soul's leaving in death its bodily house. . . . The mystical warp is visible in this through and through personal religion." [19] This, however, is a misconception. Luther is not dealing with men as men and with essential goods; he is speaking of sinners awakened to a knowledge of their sin, and of their necessary experience under the burden of their consciousness of guilt and pollution. He is giving us not his philosophy of life in the abstract, but his conception specifically of the Christian life. This, he says, is necessarily a life of penitent pain. In the fundamental opening Theses, he already points out that suffering, the suffering of rueful penitence, necessarily belongs to every sinner, so long as he remains a sinner — provided that he remains a repentant sinner. Without this compunction there is no remission of sin (36); with it there is no cessation in this life of suffering. The very process of salvation brings pain: no man, entering into life, can expect anything else for the outer man but " the cross, death, and hell " (58); nor does he seek to escape them, but he welcomes them rather as making for his peace (40, 29). And so, preaching " the piety of the cross " (68), Luther arrives at length at those amazing closing Theses in which, invoking a curse on those who cry, " Peace, peace! " when there is no peace, and pronouncing a blessing on those who call out, " The cross, the cross! " — though it is no real cross to the children of God — he declares that Christians must strive to follow Christ, their Head, through pains, deaths, and hells, and only thus to enter heaven through many tribulations — rather than, he adds, striking at the indulgence

[19] See " Martin Luther und die deutsche Reformation," ed. 2, 1917, p. 35.

usages, "through the security of peace." There is a note of *imitatio Christi* here, of course; but not in the mystical sense. Rather there speaks here a deep conviction that the Christian life is a battle, a struggle, a strenuous work; and a great cry of outrage at the whole tendency of the indulgence system to ungird the loins, and call men off from the conflict, lulling their consciences into a fatal sleep. Luther is not dreaming here of the purchase of heaven by human suffering or works. He has a Christian man in mind. He is speaking of the path over which one treads, who, in his new life, is journeying to his final bliss. Clearly he does not expect to "lie down" on the grace that saves him. He looks at the Christian life as a life of strenuous moral effort. His brand of "passive" salvation is all activity.

Its lack of moral earnestness was to earnest minds the crowning offense of the system of indulgences. In the midst of a system of work-salvation it had grown up as an expedient by means of which the work might be escaped and the salvation nevertheless secured. The "works" could not, to be sure, be altogether escaped: there must be something to take their place and represent them. That much the underlying idea of work-salvation demanded. That something was money. The experience of young Friedrich Mecum (we know him as Myconius) may instruct us here. As a youth of eighteen he heard Tetzel preach the indulgences in 1510 at Annaberg. He was deeply moved with desire to save his soul. He had no money, but had he not read, posted on the church door, that it was the wish of the holy Father that from now on the indulgences should be sold for a low price and even indeed given gratis to those unable to purchase them? He presented himself at Tetzel's dwelling to make his plea. The high commissary himself he could not see; but the priests and confessors in the antechamber pointed out to him that indulgences could not be given, and if given would be worthless. They would benefit only those who stretched out a helping hand. Let him go out and beg from some pious person only so much as a groschen, or six pfennigs — and he could purchase one for that. This was

not mere heartlessness. It was intrinsic to the system. An indulgence was a relaxation of penance, and penance was payment: provision might be made for less payment but not for
no payment at all. At the bottom of all lies the fundamental
notion that salvation must be paid for: it is only a question of
the price. Indulgences thus emerge to sight as a scheme to
evade one's spiritual and moral debts and to secure eternal
felicity at the least possible cost.

We need not insist here on the peculiarities of the Jubilee
indulgences with which Luther was most immediately concerned, and the characteristic feature of which was that it
included the sacrament of penance within itself. All indulgences in their developed form made a part of the sacerdotal
system and worked in with the sacrament of penance: they
were not offered to the heathen but to Christians, to men,
that is, who had been baptized and had access to the ordinary
ghostly ministrations. The fundamental idea embedded in
them — of which they are, indeed, the culminating illustration
— is that the offices of the Church may be called in not merely
to supplement but to take the place of the duties of personal
religion and common morality: they thus put the capstone on
sacerdotal religiosity. It may be a coarse way of putting it, to
say that in this system a man might buy his way into heaven;
that he might purchase immunity for sin; that he might even
barter for license to sin. But with whatever finessing the direct
statement may be avoided, both in theory and practice it
amounts to that. Baptism, penance, indulgence — these three
provisions taken together provide a method by which a man,
through the offices of the Church, might escape every evil
consequence of his sin, inborn and self-committed; and by
the expenditure of only a little ceremonial care and a little
money, assure himself of unmerited salvation. He who is baptized is brought into a state of grace and through penance may
maintain himself in grace — and, in the interests at once of
the comfort of weak souls and of the power of the Church,
the efficacy of penance is exalted, despite the defects of contrition and the substitution for it of mere attrition. Relieved

by these offices of the eternal penalities of their sin, indulgences now come in to relieve men of their temporal penalties.
Both the eternal and the temporal penalties being gone, guilt
need not be bothered with: hell and purgatory having both
been abolished, guilt will take care of itself. Thus a baptized
man — and all within the pale of the Church are baptized
— by shriving himself, say, every Easter and buying an indulgence or two, makes himself safe. The Church takes care
of him throughout, and it costs him nothing but an annual confession and the few coins that rattle in the collection box.
Adolf Harnack sums up the matter thus: " Every man who surrenders himself to the Catholic Church . . . can secure salvation from all eternal and temporal penalties — if he act with
shrewdness and find a skilful priest."

It was one of the attractions of the indulgences which
Tetzel hawked about that they gave the purchaser the right
to choose a confessor for himself and required this confessor
to absolve him. They thus made his immunity from all punishment sure. Marvelous to say, the vendors of indulgences were
not satisfied with thus selling the justice of heaven; they
wished to sell the justice of earth, too. Luther, it is true, in a passage in his " Resolutions " [20] denies that " the Pope " " remits
civil or rather criminal penalties, inflicted by the civil law," but
he adds that " the legates do do this in some places when they
are personally present "; and in another place he betrays why
he wishes to shield " the Pope " from the onus of this iniquity,
saying that " the Pope " cannot be supposed to have the power
to remit civil penalties, because in that case " the letters of indulgence will abolish all gibbets and racks throughout the
world " — that is to say, would do away altogether with the
punishment of crime. In point of fact the actual as distinguished from Luther's ideal Pope did issue indulgences embodying this precise provision, and those sold by Tetzel were
among them. Henry Charles Lea remarks upon them thus:
The power to protect from all secular courts " was delegated
to the peripatetic vendors of indulgences, who thus carried

[20] " Luthers Werke," Weimar edition, i. 1883, p. 536.

impunity for crime to every man's door. The St. Peter's indulgences, sold by Tetzel and his colleagues, were of this character, and not only released the purchasers from all spiritual penalties but forbade all secular or criminal prosecution. . . . It was fortunate that the Reformation came to prevent the Holy See from rendering all justice, human and divine, a commodity to be sold in open market." [21]

It is very instructive to observe the superficial resemblance between the language in which the indulgences were commended and that of the evangelical proclamation. Both offered a salvation that the recipient had not earned by his works, but was to receive from the immense mercy of God. " We have been conceived . . . in sin " — Tetzel's preaching is thus summarized by Julius Köstlin — " and are wrapped in bands of sin. It is hard — yea, impossible — to attain salvation without divine help. Not by works of righteousness which we have done, but of His mercy, has God saved us. Therefore . . . put on the armor of God." [22] The attractiveness of indulgences arose from this very thing — that they offered to men relief from the dread of anticipated punishment and reception into bliss, on grounds less onerous than the " works of righteousness " or " merit-making " involved in the ordinary church system. To the superficial view this could be given very much the appearance of Luther's doctrine of justification by faith. In both the pure mercy of God to lost and helpless sinners could be pointed to as the source of the salvation offered. In both the merits of Christ could be pointed to as the ground of the acceptance of the sinner. The Romanists included in their " Treasure " also, it is true, the merits of the saints, and Luther therefore couples the two in Thesis 58, although telling us in his " Resolutions " that the saints have no merits to offer, and if they had they would do us no good. It does not go deeply enough to say that the difference between the

[21] " The Cambridge Modern History," i. 1902, p. 662.

[22] " The Theology of Luther," i. 1897, p. 223 (Hay's translation, from the second German edition).

two proclamations lies in this — that Luther demands for this free salvation faith alone, while Tetzel proposes to hand it over for money down — in accordance with the quip attributed to Cardinal Borgia, that God desires not the death of sinners, but that they shall pay and live. The fundamental difference between the two doctrines is the fundamental difference between evangelicalism and sacerdotalism. Evangelicalism casts man back on God and God only; the faith that it asks of him is faith in God's saving grace in Christ alone. Sacerdotalism throws him into the hands of the Church and asks him to put his confidence in it — or, in the indulgences, very specifically in the Pope. He is to suspend his salvation on what the Pope can do — whether directly by his own power or in the way of suffrage — transferring to his credit the merits of Christ and His saints. This difference is correlated with this further one, that the release offered in the indulgences was from penalty, that sought in evangelicalism very distinctly from guilt. Transposed into positive language, that means that in the one case desire for comfort and happiness holds the mind, in the other a yearning for holiness. The one is non-ethical and must needs bear its fruits as such. The other tingles with ethicism to the finger tips. The mind, freed by its high enthusiasm from debilitating fear of suffering, is fired to unceasing endeavor by a great ambition to be well-pleasing to God. The gulf which separated Luther and the proclamation of indulgences and compelled him to appear in opposition to it was therefore radical and goes down to the roots of the contradictory systems of doctrine. It was not the abuses which accompanied this proclamation which moved him, though they shocked him profoundly. It was indeed not the indulgences themselves, but what lay behind and beneath the indulgences. J. Janssen is perfectly right, then, when speaking of the abuses of the traffic, he writes: " It was not, however, especially these abuses which occasioned Luther to his procedure against indulgences, but the doctrine of indulgences itself, particularly the church doctrine of good works which was con-

trary to his conceptions about justification and the bondage
of the human will." [23]

The Roman Curia had no difficulty in perceiving precisely
where Luther's blow fell. The lighter forces rushed, of course,
to the defense of the peripheral things: the papal authority,
the legitimacy of indulgences. The result was that, as Luther
says in the opening words of " The Babylonish Captivity,"
they served as teachers for him and opened his eyes to matters
on which he had not perfectly informed himself before. He
had preserved reverence for the Pope as head of the Church.
They taught him to look upon him as Antichrist. He had not
wished totally to reject indulgences. " By the kind aid of
Sylvester and the Friars," he now learned that they could
properly be described only as " the mere impostures of Roman
flatterers, by which they took away both faith in God and
men's money." [24] In his " Assertio " of the Articles condemned
by Leo's Bull, written in the same year (1520), he, with mock
humility, retracts his statement, objected to, to the effect that
indulgences were pious frauds of believers — a statement apparently borrowed from Albert of Mainz who calls them pious
frauds by which the Church allured believers to pious works
— and now asserts that they are just impious frauds and impostures of wicked popes. [25] But the Curia in its immediate
action went deeper than these things. When Luther appeared
before Cardinal Cajetan in October, 1518, the representative
of the Pope laid his finger on just two propositions which he
required him absolutely to recant. These were the assertion in
the fifty-eighth Thesis that the merits of Christ work effectually without the intervention of the Pope and therefore
cannot be the " Treasure " drawn upon by the indulgences;
and an assertion in the " Resolutions " on the seventh Thesis
to the effect that the sacraments do not work effectively unless
received by faith. Obviously in these two propositions is em-

[23] J. Janssen, " Geschichte des deutschen Volkes," ii. 1886, p. 75.
[24] " Luthers Werke," ed. Weimar, vi. 1888, p. 497. Cf. " Works," Philadelphia, ii. 1916, p. 170.
[25] " Werke," vii. 1897, p. 125.

bodied the essence of evangelicalism: salvation the immediate gift of Christ; faith and faith alone the real instrument of reception of grace.

Cajetan's entire dealing with Luther consisted in insistence on his recanting just these two assertions. Luther gives a very amusing account of an undignified scene in which Cajetan pressed him to recant the fifty-eighth Thesis, on the basis of an Extravagant of Clement VI's. He would listen to no explanations, but simply demanded continuously, pointing at the Extravagant, "Do you believe that or do you not?" At last, says Luther, the Legate tried to beat him down with an interminable speech drawn from "the fables" of St. Thomas, into which Luther a half score of times attempted in vain to break. "Finally," he proceeds in his description, "I too began to shriek, and said, 'If it can be shown that that Extravagant teaches that the merits of Christ are the treasure of indulgences, I will recant, according to your wish.' Great God, into what triumphant gestures and scornful laughter he now broke out! He seized the book suddenly and read furiously and snarlingly until he came to the place where it says that Christ purchased a treasure by His suffering, etc. Here I said, 'Listen, reverend Father, note well the words — "He purchased." If Christ purchased the treasure by His merits, it follows that the treasure is not the merits, but that which the merits have purchased — that is the keys of the Church. Therefore my thesis is true.' Here he became suddenly confused; and since he did not wish to appear confused he jumped violently to other subjects and sought to have this forgotten. But I was (not very respectfully, I confess) incensed, and broke out thus: 'Reverend Father, you must not think that Germans are ignorant of grammar also; "to be a treasure" and "to purchase" are different things.'" [26]

We must confess that Luther escaped by the skin of his teeth that time. Fortunately he had better reasons for contending that the Scriptures do not teach the doctrine in ques-

[26] From his letter to George Spalatin, written at Augsburg, October 14, 1518: E. L. Enders, "M. Luther's Briefwechsel," i. 1884, pp. 246–247.

tion than that Clement and Sixtus do not. In his written
answer to Cajetan he deals with the matter more seriously.
He argues the question even there, however, with the understanding that his business is to show that his Thesis is not in
disharmony with the papal teaching; and he not very safely
promises to adopt as his own whatever the Pope may declare
to be true, a promise which two years afterwards he could not
have repeated. On the real evangelical core of the Thesis,
however — that the merits of Christ work grace independently
of the Pope — and on the second proposition which he was
required to recant — that the sacraments are without effect
in the absence of faith — he was absolutely unbending. He
throws his assertion concerning faith, moreover, into such a
form as to make it include assurance — a matter of some
interest in view of the presence of a phrase or two in the Theses
and in the letter to Albert of Mainz enclosing a copy of them to
him, which might be incautiously read as denying the possibility of assurance, but which really mean only to deny that
assurance can be derived from anything whatever except
Christ alone. What he declares to Cajetan to be " absolutely
true," is " that no man can be just before God except alone
through faith "; and therefore, he adds, " it is necessary that
a man certainly believe that he is just and not doubt that he
receives grace. For if he doubt it, and is uncertain of it," he
argues, " then he is not just but opposes grace and casts it
away from him." [27]

What Luther is eager to do is, not to leave men in uncertainty as to their salvation, but to protect them from placing
their trust in anything but Christ — certainly not in letters of
pardon (Thesis 32: " Those who believe that through letters
of pardon they are made sure of their own salvation, will be
eternally damned along with their teachers "), or in the assurances of any man whatever, no matter what his assumed
spiritual authority may be (Thesis 52: " Vain is the hope of salvation through letters of pardon, even if a commissary — nay,

[27] " Luthers sämmtliche Schriften," Walch edition, xv. 1899, col. 578;
cf. " Werke," Weimar edition, ii. 1884, p. 13.

the Pope himself — were to pledge his soul for them "): but just as certainly not in their own contrition (Thesis 30: " No man is sure of the reality of his own contrition, much less of the attainment of plenary remission " — a thesis which Luther declares in the " Resolutions " not to be true in his sense but only in that of his opponents). " May all such teaching as would persuade to security and confidence (*securitatem et fiduciam*) in or through anything whatever except the mercy of God, which is Christ, be accursed," he cries out in the " Resolutions " when speaking of Thesis 52.[28] " Beware of confiding in thy contrition," he says when commenting on Thesis 36 — and the comment is needed, lest the unwary reader might suppose that Thesis to counsel this very thing — " or of attributing the remission of sins to thy sorrow. God does not look with favor on thee because of these things, but because of thy faith with which thou hast believed His threatenings and promises and which has wrought such sorrow." " Guard thyself, then," he says again (on Thesis 38), " against ever in any wise trusting in thy contrition, but only in the mere word of thy best and most faithful Saviour, Jesus Christ: thy heart can deceive thee, He cannot deceive thee — whether thou dost possess Him or dost desire Him." [29]

How pure the evangelicalism here expressed is may be perceived by reading only a few lines of the positive comment on the great central Theses 36, 37. " It is impossible that one should be a Christian without Christ; but if anyone has Christ, he has with Him all that is Christ's. For the holy Apostle speaks thus — . . . Rom. viii. 32: ' How shall He not with Him also give us all things? ' " " For this is the confidence of Christians, and the joy of our consciences, that by faith our sins become not ours but Christ's, on whom God has put our sins and He has borne our sins — He who is the Lamb of God that taketh away the sin of the world. And again all Christ's righteousness is ours. For He lays His hands upon us and it is well with us; and He spreads His robe over us and covers us — the blessed Saviour forever, Amen! " " But since this sweet-

[28] " Werke," ed. Weimar, i. 1883, p. 604.   [29] P. 596.

est participation and joyful interchange does not take place except by faith — and man cannot give and cannot take away this faith — I think it sufficiently clear that this participation is not given by the power of the keys, or by the benefit of letters of indulgence, but rather is given before and apart from them by God alone; as remission before remission, and absolution before absolution, so participation before participation. What participation then does the Pope give in his participation? I answer: They ought to say as was said above of remission in Thesis 6, that he gives participation declaratively. For how they can say anything else I confess I do not understand." [30] " Why then do they magnify the Pontiff because of the keys and think of him as a terrible being? The keys are not his, but rather mine, given to me for my salvation, for my consolation, granted for my peace and quiet. In the keys the Pontiff is my servant and minister; he has no need of them as a Pontiff, but I." [31] Through all it is faith that is celebrated. " You have as much as you believe." [32] The sacraments are efficacious not because they are enacted, but because they are believed. Absolution is effective not because it is given, but because it is believed. Only — the penitent believer needs the authoritative priestly word that he may believe that he — even he — can really be sharer in these great things. " Therefore it is neither the sacrament, nor the priest, but faith in the word of Christ, through the priest and his office, that justifies thee. What difference does it make to thee if the Lord speak through an ass or a jenny, if only thou dost hear His word, on which thou dost stay thy hope and rest thy faith? " [33]

It is not, however, only in a sentence here and there that the evangelical note is sounded in the Theses. What requires to be insisted upon is that they constitute in their entirety a compact and well-ordered presentation of the evangelical position in opposition to sacerdotalism. This presentation was called out by the preaching of indulgences and takes its form from its primary reference to them. But what it strikes particularly at is the sacerdotal roots of indulgences, and what it

[30] P. 593.   [31] P. 596.   [32] P. 595.   [33] P. 595.

sets in opposition to them is the pure evangelical principle. It must not be imagined that these Theses were hastily prepared merely to meet a sudden emergency created by Tetzel's preaching at Jüterbog. Luther had preached on indulgences on the same day, October 31, of the preceding year, and in the midsummer (July 27) before that. And — this is the point to take especial note of — the Theses repeat the thought and much of the language of these sermons. They are therefore the deliberate expression of long-meditated and thoroughly matured thought; in substance and language alike they had been fully in mind for a year and more. The " Resolutions," published the next year — and manifesting next to no advance in opinion on the Theses which they expound — show that Luther was thoroughly informed on the whole subject and had its entire literature at easy command. His choice of October 31, the eve of All Saints' Day, for posting the Theses, has also its very distinct significance. This choice was determined by something more than a desire to gain for them the publicity which that day provided. All Saints' Day was not merely the anniversary of the consecration of the church, elaborate services on which were attended by thousands. It was also the day on which the great collection of relics accumulated by the Elector was exhibited; and to the veneration of them and attendance on the day's services special indulgences were attached. It was, in a word, Indulgence Day at Wittenberg; and that was the attraction which brought the crowds thither on it. Luther, we have just pointed out, had preached a sermon against indulgences on the preceding October 31. On this October 31 he posts his Theses. The coincidence is not accidental. The Theses came not at the beginning but in the middle of his attack on indulgences, and have in view, not Tetzel and his Jubilee indulgences alone, but the whole indulgence system. That the preaching in Germany of the Jubilee indulgences was the occasion of Luther's coming forward in this attack on indulgences, he tells us himself. He explains somewhat objectively how he was drawn into it, when writing to his ecclesiastical superior: " I was asked by many strangers as well as friends, both by letter and by word of mouth, for my opinion of these new not to say licentious teachings; for a while I held out — but in the end their complaints became so bitter as to endanger reverence for the Pope." [34] Similarly he declares in the " Resolutions ": " I have been compelled to lay down all these positions because I saw that some were infected with false opinions, and others were laughing in the taverns and holding up the holy priesthood to open ridicule, because of the great license with which the indulgences are preached." This is not to say, however, that in meeting this call upon him, Luther was not moved by a deeper-lying motive and did not wish to go to the bottom of the matter. When writing privately to his friends he did not hesitate to say as early as the middle of February, 1518, that " indulgences now seem to me to be nothing but a snare for souls and worth absolutely nothing except to those who slumber and idle in the way of Christ," and to explain his coming forward against them thus: " For the sake of opposing this fraud, for the love of truth, I entered this dangerous labyrinth of disputation." [35]

The document itself however is the best witness to the care given to its preparation and to the depth of its purpose as an anti-sacerdotal manifesto. There are no signs of haste about it, and, in point of fact, the question is argued in it from the point of sight of fundamental principles. In its opening propositions, Luther begins by laying down in firm lines the Christian doctrine of penitence. It is, he says, of course the very mark of the penitent sinner that he is penitent; and of course he can never cease to be penitent so long as he is, what as a Christian he must be — a penitent sinner. His penitence is not only fundamentally an interior fact: but if it is real, it manifests itself in outward mortifications. This being what a Christian man essentially is, what now has the Pope to do with the penalties which he suffers — which constitute the very substance and manifestation of the penitence by virtue

[34] To Jerome Scultetus, Bishop of Brandenburg: Enders, " Briefwechsel," i. 1884, p. 148.

[35] To Spalatin, February 15, 1518: Enders, " Briefwechsel," i. 1884, p. 155.

of which he is a penitent as distinguished from an impenitent
sinner? Luther's answer is, Nothing whatever. With reference
to the living he declares that the Pope can relieve a man only
of penalties of his own imposing; with respect to penalties of
God's imposing he has only a declarative function. With reference to the dying, why, by the very act of dying they escape
out of the Pope's hands. There is, of course, purgatory. But
purgatory is not a place where old scores are paid off; but a
place where imperfect souls are perfected in holiness; and
surely the Pope neither can nor would wish to intermit their
perfecting. Clearly, then, it is futile to trust in indulgences.
There is nothing for them to do. They cannot release us from
the necessity of being Christians; and if we are Christians, we
can have no manner of need of them. In asserting this, Luther
closes this first and principal part of the document — constituting one third of the whole — with the great evangelical
declarations: " Every truly contrite Christian has of right
plenary remission of penalty and guilt — even without letters
of pardon. Every true Christian, whether living or dead, has
given to him by God, a share in all the benefits of Christ and
the Church — even without letters of pardon " (Theses
36, 37).

Having thus laid down the general principles, Luther now
takes a new start and points out some of the dangers which
accompany the preaching of indulgences. There is the danger
that the purchase of indulgences should be made to appear
more important than the exercise of charity, or even than the
maintenance of our dependents. There is the danger that the
head of the Church may be made to appear more desirous of
the people's money than of their prayers. There is the danger
that the preaching of indulgences may encroach upon or even
supersede the preaching of the gospel in the churches. After
all, the preaching of the gospel is the main thing. It is the true
treasure of the Church: indeed, it is the only treasure on which
the Church can draw. The section closes with some pointed
antitheses, contrasting the indulgences and the gospel: the indulgences which make the last to be first and seek after men's

riches, and the gospel which makes the first to be last and
books after those men who are rich indeed: indulgences are
gainful things no doubt, but grace and the piety of the cross
— they belong to the gospel.

A third start is now taken, and Luther sharply arraigns the
actual misdeeds of the preachers of pardons and their unmeasured assertions (*licentiosa praedicatio*). Of course the commissaries of the apostolical pardons are not to be excluded
from dioceses and parishes: they come with the Pope's commission and the Pope is the head of the Church. But bishops
and curates are bound to see to it that the unbridled license of
their preaching is curbed within the just limits of their commission. As it is, they have filled the world with murmurings
and it is not easy to defend the Pope against the sharp questions which the people are asking. Luther adduces eight of
these questions as specimens: they constitute a tremendous
indictment against the whole indulgence traffic from the point
of view of practical common sense, and are all the more effective because repeated out of the mouth of the people. They
are such as these: If the Pope has the power to release souls
from purgatory, why does he not, out of his mere charity, release the whole lot of them, and not dole their release out one
by one for money? If souls are released from purgatory by
indulgences, why does the Pope keep the endowments for
masses for these same souls, after they have been released?
Why should the money of a wicked man move the Pope to
release a soul from purgatory more than that soul's own deep
need? Why does the Pope treat dead Canons as still alive and
take money for relaxing them? Why does the rich Pope not
build St. Peter's out of his own superfluity and not tax the
poor for it? What is it, after all, that the Pope remits to those
whose perfect contrition has already gained their remission?
What is the effect of accumulating indulgences? If it is the
salvation of souls and not money that the Pope is after, why
does he suspend old letters of pardon and put new ones on
sale? Such searching arguments as these, Luther justly says,
cannot be met by a display of force: they must be answered.

Then he brings the whole document to a close with some fervent words renouncing a gospel of ease, crying Peace, peace! such as the indulgences offer: and proclaiming the strenuous gospel of the cross: "Christians should be exhorted to strive to follow their Head, Christ, through pains and deaths and hells, and thus to trust to enter heaven rather through many tribulations than through the security of peace."

It belongs to the general structure of the document — advancing as it does from the principles which underlie the indulgence traffic, through the dangers which accompany it, to its actual abuses — that its tone should grow sharper and its attack more direct with its progress. Luther's argumentative purpose and his rhetorical instinct have no doubt co-operated to produce this result. It suited the end he had in view to present the indulgences as a species under a broader genus. But also it pleased his rhetorical sense so to manage his material as to have it grow in force and directness of assertion steadily to the end, and to close in what deserves the name of a fervent peroration. The calm, detached propositions of the first section pass in the second into a series of rhetorical repetitions, and these give way as the third section is approached to stinging antitheses. Nevertheless the real weight of the document lies in its first section, and it is by virtue of the propositions laid down there that it is worthy of its place as the first great Reformation act, and the day of its posting is justly looked upon as the birthday of the Reformation.

The posting of these Theses does not mark the acquisition by Luther of his evangelical convictions. These had long been his — how long we hardly know but must content ourselves with saying, with Walther Köhler, that they were apparently acquired somewhere between 1509 and 1515. Neither does their posting mark the beginning of the evangelical proclamation. From at least 1515 Luther had been diligently propagating his evangelicalism in pulpit and chair, and had already fairly converted his immediate community to it. He could already boast of the victory of "our theology" in the university, and the town was in his hands. What is marked by the posting of these Theses is the issuing of the Reformation out of the narrow confines of the university circles of Wittenberg and its start on its career as a world-movement. Their posting gave wings to the Reformation. And it gave it wings primarily by rallying to its aid the smoldering sense of outrage which had long been gathering against a gross ecclesiastical abuse. This would not have carried it far, however, had not the document in which it was thus sent abroad had in it the potency of the new life.

"What is epoch-making in the Theses," writes E. Bratke,[36] " is that they are the first public proclamation in which Luther in full consciousness made the truth of justifying faith as the sole principle of the communication of salvation, the theme of a theological controversy, and thus laid before the Church a problem for further research, which afterwards became the motive and principle of a new development of the Christian Church, yes, of civilization in general." What Bratke is trying to say here is true; and, being true, is vastly important. But he does not say it well. Luther had often before proclaimed the principle of justifying faith in full enthusiasm, to as wide a public as his voice could reach. It happens that neither faith nor justification is once mentioned in the Theses. It is in the Lectures on Romans of 1515–1516 that the epoch-making exposition of justification by faith was made, not in the Theses. Nevertheless, it is true that the Theses are the express outcome of Luther's new "life principle," and have as their fundamental purpose to set it in opposition to "human ecclesiasticism and sacerdotalism." And it is true that the idea of justification by faith underlies them throughout and only does not come to explicit expression in them because the occasion does not call for that: Luther cannot expound them (as in the "Resolutions") without dwelling largely on it. The matter would be better expressed, however, by saying that Luther here sets the evangelical principle flatly in opposition to the sacerdotal. What he here attacks is just the sacerdotal principle in one of its most portentous embodiments — the teaching that

[36] *Op. cit.,* p. 315.

men are to look to the Church as the institute of salvation for all their souls' welfare, and to derive from the Church all their confidence in life and in death. What he sets over against this sacerdotalism is the evangelical principle that man is dependent for his salvation on God and on God alone — on God directly, apart from all human intermediation — and is to look to God for and to derive from God immediately all that makes for his soul's welfare. In these Theses Luther brought out of the academic circle in which he had hitherto moved, and cast into the arena of the wide world's conflicts, under circumstances which attracted and held the attention of men, his newly found evangelical principle, thrown out into sharp contrast with the established sacerdotalism. It is this that made the posting of these Theses the first act of the Reformation, and has rightly made October Thirty-first the birthday of the Reformation.

XVIII

EDWARDS AND THE
NEW ENGLAND THEOLOGY

EDWARDS AND THE
NEW ENGLAND THEOLOGY [1]

JONATHAN EDWARDS, saint and metaphysician, revivalist
and theologian, stands out as the one figure of real greatness
in the intellectual life of colonial America. Born, bred, passing
his whole life on the verge of civilization, he has made his
voice heard wherever men have busied themselves with those
two greatest topics which can engage human thought — God
and the soul. A French philosopher of scant sympathy with
Edwards' chief concernment writes: [2]

There are few names of the eighteenth century which have obtained such celebrity as that of Jonathan Edwards. Critics and historians down to our own day have praised in dithyrambic terms the
logical vigor and the constructive powers of a writer whom they
hold (as is done by Mackintosh, Dugald Stewart, Robert Hall, even
Fichte) to be the greatest metaphysician America has yet produced.
Who knows, they have asked themselves, to what heights this
original genius might have risen, if, instead of being born in a half-
savage country, far from the traditions of philosophy and science,
he had appeared rather in our old world, and there received the
direct impulse of the modern mind. Perhaps he would have taken a
place between Leibniz and Kant among the founders of immortal
systems, instead of the work he has left reducing itself to a sublime
and barbarous theology, which astonishes our reason and outrages
our heart, the object of at once our horror and admiration.

Edwards' greatness is not, however, thus merely conjectural. He was no " mute, inglorious Milton," but the most
articulate of men. Nor is it as a metaphysician that he makes

[1] Reprinted from the " Encyclopædia of Religion and Ethics," edited by
James Hastings, M.A., D.D., v. 1912, pp. 221–227. Used by permission of the
publishers, Charles Scribner's Sons.

[2] Georges Lyon, " L'Idéalisme en Angleterre au XVIIIᵉ siècle," Paris,
1888, pp. 406 f.

his largest claim upon our admiration, subtle metaphysician as he showed himself to be. His ontological speculations, on which his title to recognition as a metaphysician mainly rests, belong to his extreme youth, and had been definitely put behind him at an age when most men first begin to probe such problems. It was, as Lyon indeed suggests, to theology that he gave his mature years and his most prolonged and searching thought, especially to the problems of sin and salvation. And these problems were approached by him not as purely theoretical, but as intensely practical ones. Therefore he was a man of action as truly as a man of thought, and powerfully wrought on his age, setting at work energies which have not yet spent their force. He is much more accurately characterized, therefore, by a philosopher of our own, who is as little in sympathy, however, with his main interests as Lyon himself. F. J. E. Woodbridge says:[3]

> He was distinctly a great man. He did not merely express the thought of his time, or meet it simply in the spirit of his traditions. He stemmed it and moulded it. New England thought was already making toward that colorless theology which marked it later. That he checked. It was decidedly Arminian. He made it Calvinistic. . . . His time does not explain him.

Edwards had a remarkable philosophical bent; but he had an even more remarkable sense and taste for divine things; and, therefore (so Woodbridge concludes, with at least relative justice), "we remember him, not as the greatest of American philosophers, but as the greatest of American Calvinists."

I. THE PERIOD OF EDWARDS' PREPARATION

It was a very decadent New England into which Edwards was born, on 5th October 1703. The religious fervor which the Puritan immigrants had brought with them into the New World had not been able to propagate itself unimpaired to the third and fourth generation. Already in 1678, Increase Mather

---

[3] *The Philosophical Review,* xiii. 1904, p. 405.

had bewailed that " the body of the rising generation is a poor, perishing, unconverted, and (except the Lord pour down His Spirit) an undone generation." [4] There were general influences operative throughout Christendom at this epoch, depressing to the life of the spirit, which were not unfelt in New England; and these were reinforced there by the hardness of the conditions of existence in a raw land. Everywhere thinking and living alike were moving on a lowered plane; not merely spirituality but plain morality was suffering some eclipse. The churches felt compelled to recede from the high ideals which had been their heritage, and were introducing into their membership and admitting to their mysteries men who, though decent in life, made no profession of a change of heart. If only they had been themselves baptized, they were encouraged to offer their children for baptism (under the so-called " Half-Way Covenant "), and to come themselves to the Table of the Lord (conceived as a " converting ordinance "). The household into which Edwards was born, however, not only protected him from much of the evil which was pervading the community, but powerfully stimulated his spiritual and intellectual life. He began the study of Latin at the age of six, and by thirteen had acquired a respectable knowledge of " the three learned languages " which at the time formed part of the curricula of the colleges — Latin, Greek, and Hebrew. Before he had completed his thirteenth year (September 1716), he entered the " Collegiate School of Connecticut " (afterwards Yale College). During his second year at college he fell in with Locke's "Essay concerning Human Understanding," and had more satisfaction and pleasure in studying it, he tells us himself,[5] " than the most greedy miser finds, when gathering up handfuls of silver and gold, from some newly discovered treasure." He graduated at the head of his class in 1720, when he was just short of seventeen years of age, but remained at

---

[4] H. M. Dexter, " Congregationalism . . . in its Literature," New York, 1880, p. 476, note 36.

[5] Dwight's " Memoir," prefixed to his edition of Edwards' " Works," i. 1829, p. 30.

college (as the custom of the time was) two years longer (to
the summer of 1722) for the study of Divinity. In the summer
of 1722 he was "approbated" to preach, and from August
1722 until April 1723 he supplied the pulpit of a little knot of
Presbyterians in New York City.[6] Returning home, he was
appointed tutor at Yale in June 1724, and filled this post with
distinguished ability, during a most trying period in the life
of the college, for the next two years (until September 1726).
His resignation of his tutorship was occasioned by an invitation to become the colleague and successor of his grandfather,
Solomon Stoddard, in the pastorate of the church at Northampton, Mass., where, accordingly, he was ordained and installed on 15th February 1727.

By his installation at Northampton, Edwards' period of
preparation was brought to a close. His preparation had been
remarkable, both intensively and extensively. Born with a
drop of ink in his veins, Edwards had almost from infancy
held a pen in his hand. From his earliest youth he had been
accustomed to trace out on paper to its last consequence every
fertile thought which came to him. A number of the early
products of his observation and reflection have been preserved,
revealing a precocity which is almost beyond belief.[7]

----

[6] See E. H. Gillett, "History of the Presbyterian Church," revised edition, Philadelphia, pp. 38 f.

[7] On this ground, indeed, Lyon, for example, refuses to believe in their
genuineness. It is futile to adduce the parallel of a Pascal, he declares; such
a comparison is much too modest; the young Edwards united in himself
many Pascals, and, by a double miracle, combined with them gifts by virtue
of which he far surpassed a Galileo and a Newton; what we are asked to believe is not merely that as a boy in his teens he worked out independently a
system of metaphysics closely similar to that of Berkeley, but that he anticipated most of the scientific discoveries which constitute the glory of the
succeeding century.

It is well to recognize that Lyon has permitted himself some slight exaggeration in stating his case, for the renewed examination of the MSS. which
he, and, following him, A. V. G. Allen asked for, has fully vindicated the
youthful origin of these discussions. (See especially Egbert C. Smyth, "Some
Early Writings of Jonathan Edwards, 1714–1726," in "Proceedings of the
American Antiquarian Society," New Series, x. 1896, pp. 212 ff.: 23d October,
1895; also The American Journal of Theology, i. 1897, p. 951; cf. H. N. Gardiner, "Jonathan Edwards: a Retrospect," 1901.) There is, for instance, a ban-

It is in these youthful writings that Edwards propounds his spiritualistic metaphysics, and it is chiefly on the strength of them that he holds a place in our histories of philosophy. His whole system is already present in substance in the essay " Of Being," which was written before he was sixteen years of age. And, though there is no reason to believe that he ever renounced the opinions set forth in these youthful discussions — there are, on the contrary, occasional suggestions, even in his latest writings, that they still lurked at the back of his brain — he never formally reverts to them subsequently to his Yale period (up to 1727).[8] His engagement with such topics belongs, therefore, distinctively to his formative period, before he became engrossed with the duties of the active ministry and the lines of thought more immediately called into exercise by them. In these early years, certainly independently of Berkeley,[9] and apparently with no suggestion from outside beyond what might be derived from Newton's explanations of light and color, and Locke's treatment of sensation as the source of ideas, he worked out for himself a complete system of Idealism, which trembled indeed on the brink of mere phe-

---

tering letter on the immateriality of the soul, full of marks of immaturity, no doubt, but equally full of the signs of promise, which was written in 1714–1715, when Edwards was ten years old. There are some very acute observations on the behavior of spiders in spinning their webs which anticipate the results of modern investigation (on these observations, see Egbert C. Smyth, *The Andover Review,* xiii. 1890, pp. 1–19; and Henry C. McCook, *The Presbyterian and Reformed Review,* i. 1890, pp. 393–402), and which cannot have been written later than his thirteenth year. There are, above all, metaphysical discussions of " Being," " Atoms," and " Prejudices of Imagination," written at least as early as his junior year at college, that is to say, his sixteenth year, in which the fundamental principles of his Idealistic philosophy are fully set out. And, besides numerous other discussions following out these views, there is a long series of notes on natural science, filled with acute suggestions, which must belong to his Yale period. It is all, no doubt, very remarkable. But this only shows that Edwards was a very remarkable youth.

[8] Cf. President T. D. Woolsey, " Edwards Memorial," Boston, 1870, pp. 32–33; and E. C. Smyth, " Proceedings of the American Antiquarian Society," as cited, p. 232; H. N. Gardiner, p. 117.

[9] So E. C. Smyth and H. N. Gardiner, *locc. cit.;* it is now known that he had not read Berkeley before 1730 (F. B. Dexter, " The Manuscripts of Jonathan Edwards," Cambridge, 1901, p. 16).

nomenalism, and might have betrayed him into Pantheism
save for the intensity of his perception of the living God.
"Speaking most strictly," he declares, "there is no proper
substance but God Himself." The universe exists "nowhere
but in the Divine mind." Whether this is true "with respect
to bodies only," or of finite spirits as well, he seems at first to
have wavered; ultimately he came to the more inclusive
opinion.[10]

Edwards was not so absorbed in such speculations as to
neglect the needs of his spirit. Throughout all these formative
years he remained first of all a man of religion. He had been
the subject of deep religious impressions from his earliest boyhood, and he gave himself, during this period of preparation,
to the most assiduous and intense cultivation of his religious
nature. "I made seeking my salvation," he himself tells us,

---

[10] He could write of the rise of a new thought: "If we mean that there
is some substance besides that thought, that brings that thought forth; if it
be God, I acknowledge it; but if there be meant something else that has no
properties, it seems to me absurd" (*American Journal of Theology*, i. 1897,
p. 957). Of "all dependent existence whatsoever" he comes at last to affirm
that it is "in a constant flux," "renewed every moment, as the colors of
bodies are every moment renewed by the light that shines upon them; and
all is constantly proceeding from God, as light from the sun" ("Original
Sin": "Works," 4 vol. edition, New York, ii. 1856, p. 490). He did not mean
by this, however, to sublimate the universe into "shadows." He was only
attempting to declare that it has no other substrate but God: that its reality
and persistence are grounded, not in some mysterious created "substance"
underlying the properties, but in the "infinitely exact and precise Divine
Idea, together with an answerable, perfectly exact, precise and stable Will,
with respect to correspondent communications to Created Minds, and effects
on their minds" (Dwight, i. p. 674). He is engaged, in other words, in a
purely ontological investigation, and his contention is merely that God is
the *continuum* of all finite existence. He is as far as possible from denying the
reality or persistence of these finite existences; they are to him real "creations," because they represent a fixed purpose and an established constitution
of God. (On Edwards' early Idealism, see especially Egbert C. Smyth, *American Journal of Theology*, i. 1897, pp. 959 f.; G. P. Fisher, "Discussions in History and Theology," New York, 1880, pp. 229 f.; H. N. Gardiner, *op. cit.*,
pp. 115–160; J. H. MacCracken, "The Sources of Jonathan Edwards's Idealism," in the *Philosophical Review*, xi. 1902, pp. 26 ff.; also G. Lyon, *loc. cit.*;
and I. W. Riley, "American Philosophy: the Early Schools," New York,
1907.)

" the main business of my life." [11] But about the time of his graduation (1720) a change came over him, which relieved the strain of his inward distress. From his childhood, his mind had revolted against the sovereignty of God: " it used to appear like a horrible doctrine to me." Now all this passed unobservedly away; and gradually, by a process he could not trace, this very doctrine came to be not merely a matter of course to him but a matter of rejoicing: " The doctrine has very often appeared exceedingly pleasant, bright, and sweet; absolute sovereignty is what I love to ascribe to God." One day he was reading I Tim. i. 17, " Now unto the King, eternal, immortal, invisible, the only wise God, be honor and glory, for ever and ever, Amen," and, as he read, " a sense of the glory of the Divine Being " took possession of him, " a new sense, quite different from anything " he " ever experienced before." He longed to be " rapt up to Him in heaven, and be as it were swallowed up in Him for ever." [12] From that moment his understanding of divine things increased, and his enjoyment of God grew. There were, no doubt, intervals of depression. But, on the whole, his progress was steadily upwards and his consecration more and more complete. It was this devout young man, with the joy of the Lord in his heart, who turned his back in the early months of 1727 on his brilliant academic life and laid aside forever his philosophical speculations, to take up the work of a pastor at Northampton.

II. Edwards the Pastor

Edwards was ordained co-pastor with his grandfather on 15th February 1727, and on the latter's death, two years later, succeeded to the sole charge of the parish. Northampton was relatively a very important place. It was the county town, and nearly half of the area of the province lay within the county. It was, therefore, a sort of little local capital, and its people prided themselves on their culture, energy, and independence

---

[11] Dwight, i. p. 59.   [12] *Ibid.*, p. 60.

of mind. There was but the one church in the town, and it was probably the largest and most influential in the province, outside of Boston. It was not united in sentiment, being often torn with factional disputes. But, under the strong preaching of Solomon Stoddard, it had been repeatedly visited with revivals. These periods of awakening continued at intervals during Edwards' pastorate; the church became famous for them, and its membership was filled up by them. At one time the membership numbered six hundred and twenty, and included nearly the entire adult population of the town. Stoddard had been the protagonist for the laxer views of admission to Church-ordinances, and early in the century had introduced into the Northampton church the practice of opening the Lord's Supper to those who made no profession of conversion. In this practice Edwards at first acquiesced; but, becoming convinced that it was wrong, sought after a while to correct it, with disastrous consequences to himself. Meanwhile it had given to the membership of the church something of the character of a mixed multitude, which the circumstance that large numbers of them had been introduced in the religious excitement of revivals had tended to increase.

To the pastoral care of this important congregation, Edwards gave himself with single-hearted devotion. Assiduous house-to-house visitation did not, it is true, form part of his plan of work; but this did not argue carelessness or neglect; it was in accordance with his deliberate judgment of his special gifts and fitnesses. And, if he did not go to his people in their homes, save at the call of illness or special need, he encouraged them to come freely to him, and grudged neither time nor labor in meeting their individual requirements. He remained, of course, also a student, spending ordinarily from thirteen to fourteen hours daily in his study. This work did not separate itself from, but was kept strictly subsidiary to, his pastoral service. Not only had he turned his back definitely on the purely academic speculations which had engaged him so deeply at Yale, but he produced no purely theological works during the whole of his twenty-three years' pastorate at Northampton. His publications during this period, besides sermons, consisted only of treatises in practical Divinity. They deal principally with problems raised by the great religious awakenings in which his preaching was fruitful.[13]

It was in his sermons that Edwards' studies bore their richest fruit. He did not spare himself in his public instruction. He not only faithfully filled the regular appointments of the church, but freely undertook special discourses and lectures, and during times of " attention to religion " went frequently to the aid of the neighboring churches. From the first he was recognized as a remarkable preacher, as arresting and awakening as he was instructive. Filled himself with the profoundest sense of the heinousness of sin, as an offense against the majesty of God and an outrage of His love, he set himself to arouse his hearers to some realization of the horror of their condition as objects of the divine displeasure, and of the incredible goodness of God in intervening for their salvation. Side by side with the most moving portrayal of God's love in Christ, and of the blessedness of communion with Him, he therefore set, with the most startling effect, equally vivid pictures of the dangers of unforgiven sin and the terrors of the lost estate. The effect of such preaching, delivered with the

---

[13] Such, for instance, are the " Narrative of Surprising Conversions," published in 1736, the " Thoughts on the Revival of Religion in New England in 1740," published in 1742, and that very searching study of the movements of the human soul under the excitement of religious motives called " A Treatise concerning Religious Affections," published in 1746. Then there is the " Humble Attempt to Promote Explicit Agreement and Visible Union of God's People in Extraordinary Prayer for the Revival of Religion," published in 1749, which belongs to the same class, and the brief " Account of the Life of the Rev. David Brainerd," published in the same year. There remains only the " Humble Inquiry into the Rules of the Word of God, concerning the Qualifications requisite to a Complete Standing in Full Communion in the Visible Church of God," published in 1749, along with which should be mentioned the defense of its positions against Solomon Williams, entitled " Misrepresentations Corrected and Truth Vindicated," although this was not published until somewhat later (1752). No doubt there was much more than this written during these score or more of years, for Edwards was continually adding to the mass of his manuscript treasures; and some of these voluminous " observations " have since been put into print, although the greater part of them remain yet in the notebooks where he wrote them.

force of the sincerest conviction, was overwhelming. A great awakening began in the church at the end of 1735, in which more than three hundred converts were gathered in,[14] and which extended throughout the churches of the Connecticut valley. In connection with a visit from Whitefield in 1740 another wave of religious fervor was started, which did not spend its force until it covered the whole land. No one could recognize more fully than Edwards the evil that mixes with the good in such seasons of religious excitement. He diligently sought to curb excesses, and earnestly endeavored to separate the chaff from the wheat. But no one could protest more strongly against casting out the wheat with the chaff. He subjected all the phenomena of the revivals in which he participated to the most searching analytical study; and, while sadly acknowledging that much self-deception was possible, and that the rein could only too readily be given to false " enthusiasm," he earnestly contended that a genuine work of grace might find expression in mental and even physical excitement. It was one of the incidental fruits of these revivals that, as we have seen, he gave to the world in a series of studies perhaps the most thorough examination of the phenomena of religious excitement it has yet received, and certainly, in his great treatise on the " Religious Affections," one of the most complete systems of what has been strikingly called " spiritual diagnostics " it possesses.

For twenty-three years Edwards pursued his fruitful ministry at Northampton; under his guidance the church became a city set on a hill to which all eyes were turned. But in the reaction from the revival of 1740–1742 conditions arose which caused him great searchings of heart, and led ultimately to his separation from his congregation. In this revival, practically the whole adult population of the town was brought into the church; they were admitted under the excitement of the time and under a ruling introduced as long before as 1704 by Stoddard, which looked upon all the ordinances of the church, in-

[14] More than five hundred fifty members were added to the church at Northampton during Edwards' pastorate (see Solomon Clark, " Historical Catalogue of the Northampton First Church," 1891, pp. 40–67).

cluding the Lord's Supper, as "converting ordinances," not presupposing, but adapted to bring about, a change of heart. As time passed, it became evident enough that a considerable body of the existing membership of the church had not experienced that change of heart by which alone they could be constituted Christians, and indeed they made no claim to have done so. On giving serious study to the question for himself, Edwards became convinced that participation in the Lord's Supper could properly be allowed only to those professing real "conversion." It was his duty as pastor and guide of his people to guard the Lord's Table from profanation, and he was not a man to leave unperformed a duty clearly perceived. Two obvious measures presented themselves to him — unworthy members of the church must be exscinded by discipline, and greater care must be exercised in receiving new applicants for membership. No doubt discipline was among the functions which the Church claimed to exercise; but the practice of it had fallen much into decay as a sequence to the lowered conception which had come to be entertained of the requirements for church membership. The door of admission to the Lord's Supper, on the other hand, had been formally set wide open; and this loose policy had been persisted in for half a century, and had become traditional. What Edwards felt himself compelled to undertake, it will be seen, was a return in theory and practice to the original platform of the Congregational churches, which conceived the Church to be, in the strictest sense of the words, " a company of saints by calling," among whom there should be permitted to enter nothing that was not clean.[15] This, which should have been his strength, and which ultimately gave the victory to the movement which he inaugurated throughout the churches of New England,[16] was in his own personal case his weakness. It gave a radical ap-

[15] According to the organic law of the Congregational churches (the Cambridge Platform), "saints by calling " are "such as have not only attained the knowledge of the principles of religion, and are free from gross and open scandals, but also do, together with the profession of their faith and repentance, walk in blameless obedience to the word."

[16] Cf. H. N. Gardiner, " Selected Sermons of Jonathan Edwards," New York, 1904, p. xii.

pearance to the reforms which he advocated, which he himself was far from giving to them. It is not necessary to go into the details of the controversy regarding a case of discipline, which emerged in 1744, or the subsequent difficulties (1748–1749) regarding the conditions of admission to the Lord's Supper. The result was that, after a sharp contest running through two years, Edwards was dismissed from his pastorate on 22d June 1750.

III. Edwards the Theologian

By his dismissal from his church at Northampton, in his forty-seventh year, the second period of Edwards' life — the period of strenuous pastoral labor — was brought to an abrupt close. After a few months he removed to the little frontier hamlet (there were only twelve white families resident there) of Stockbridge, as missionary of the " Society in London for Propagating the Gospel in New England and the Parts Adjacent " to the Housatonic Indians gathered there, and as pastor of the little church of white settlers. In this exile he hoped to find leisure to write, in defense of the Calvinistic system against the rampant " Arminianism " of the day, the works which he had long had in contemplation, and for which he had made large preparation. Peace and quiet he did not find; he was embroiled from the first in a trying struggle against the greed and corruption of the administrators of the funds designed for the benefit of the Indians. But he made, if he could not find, the requisite leisure. It was at Stockbridge that he wrote the treatises on which his fame as a theologian chiefly rests: the great works on the Will (written in 1753, published in 1754), and Original Sin (in the press when he died, 1758), the striking essays on " The End for which God created the World," and the " Nature of True Virtue " (published 1765, after his death), and the unfinished " History of Redemption " (published 1772). No doubt he utilized for these works material previously collected. He lived practically with his pen in his hand, and accumulated an immense amount of written matter — his " best thoughts," as it has been felicitously called. The work on the Will, indeed, had itself been long on the stocks. We find him making diligent studies for it already at the opening of 1747; [17] and, though his work on it was repeatedly interrupted for long intervals,[18] he tells us that before he left Northampton he "had made considerable preparation, and was deeply engaged in the prosecution of this design." [19] The rapid completion of the book in the course of a few months in 1753 was not, therefore, so wonderful a feat as it might otherwise appear. Nevertheless, it is the seven years at Stockbridge which deserve to be called the fruitful years of Edwards' theological work. They were interrupted in the autumn of 1757 by an invitation to him to become the President of the College of New Jersey, at Princeton, in succession to his son-in-law, Aaron Burr. It was with great reluctance that he accepted this call; it seemed to him to threaten the prevention of what he had thought to make his life-work — the preparation, to wit, of a series of volumes on all the several parts of the Arminian controversy.[20] But the college at Princeton, which had been founded and thus far carried on by men whose sympathies were with the warm-hearted, revivalistic piety to which his own life had been dedicated, had claims upon him which he could not disown. On the advice of a council of his friends,[21] therefore, he accepted the call and removed to Princeton to take up his new duties, in January 1758. There he was inoculated for smallpox on 13th February, and died of this disease on 22d March in the fifty-fifth year of his age.

The peculiarity of Edwards' theological work is due to the

[17] Letter to Joseph Bellamy, 15th January 1747, printed by F. B. Dexter, "The Manuscripts of Jonathan Edwards" (reprinted from the "Proceedings of the Massachusetts Historical Society," March 1901), p. 13; letter to John Erskine, 22d January 1747, reconstructed by Dwight, i. pp. 249–250, but since come to light ("Exercises Commemorating the Two-Hundredth Anniversary of the Birth of Jonathan Edwards, held at Andover Theological Seminary, October 4 and 5, 1903," Andover, 1904, p. 63 of the Appendices).

[18] Dwight, i. pp. 251, 270, 411.

[19] Ibid., pp. 411, 507, 532, 537.

[20] Ibid., p. 569.

[21] Dwight (i. p. 576) was not able to ascertain all the facts concerning this council; Ezra Stiles, "Literary Diary," New York, iii. 1901, p. 4, supplies interesting details.

union in it of the richest religious sentiment with the highest intellectual powers. He was first of all a man of faith, and it is this that gives its character to his whole life and all its products; but his strong religious feeling had at its disposal a mental force and logical acuteness of the first order; he was at once deeply emotional, and, as Ezra Stiles called him, a " strong reasoner." His analytical subtlety has probably never been surpassed; but with it was combined a broad grasp of religious truth which enabled him to see it as a whole, and to deal with its several parts without exaggeration and with a sense of their relations in the system. The system to which he gave his sincere adhesion, and to the defense of which, against the tendencies which were in his day threatening to undermine it, he consecrated all his powers, was simply Calvinism. From this system as it had been expounded by its chief representatives he did not consciously depart in any of its constitutive elements. The breadth and particularity of his acquaintance with it in its classical expounders, and the completeness of his adoption of it in his own thought, are frequently underestimated. There is a true sense in which he was a man of thought rather than of learning. There were no great libraries accessible in Western Massachusetts in the middle of the eighteenth century. His native disposition to reason out for himself the subjects which were presented to his thought was reinforced by his habits of study; it was his custom to develop on paper, to its furthest logical consequences, every topic of importance to which his attention was directed. He lived in the " age of reason," and was in this respect a true child of his time.[22] In the task which he undertook, furthermore, an appeal to authority would have been useless; it was uniquely to the court of reason that he could hale the adversaries of the Calvinistic system. Accordingly it is only in his more didactic — as distinguished from controversial — treatise on " Religious Affections," that Edwards cites with any frequency earlier writers in support of his positions. The reader must guard himself,

[22] Cf. the discussion of Edwards' "rationalism," by Jan Ridderbos, " De Theologie van Jonathan Edwards," 1907, pp. 310–313.

however, from the illusion that Edwards was not himself conscious of the support of earlier writers beneath him.[23] His acquaintance with the masters of the system of thought he was
defending, for example, was wide and minute. Amesius and
Wollebius had been his textbooks àt college. The well-selected
library at Yale, we may be sure, had been thoroughly explored
by him; at the close of his divinity studies, he speaks of the
reading of " doctrinal books or books of controversy " as if it
were part of his daily business.[24] As would have been expected,
he fed himself on the great Puritan divines, and formed not
merely his thought but his life upon them. We find him in his
youth, for instance, diligently using Manton's " Sermons on
the 119th Psalm " as a spiritual guide; and in his rare allusions
to authorities in his works, he betrays familiarity with such
writers as William Perkins, John Preston, Thomas Blake, Anthony Burgess, Stephen Charnock, John Flavel, Theophilus
Gale, Thomas Goodwin, John Owen, Samuel Rutherford,
Thomas Shephard, Richard Sibbes, John Smith the Platonist,
and Samuel Clark the Arian. Even his contemporaries he knew
and estimated at their true values: Isaac Watts and Philip
Doddridge as a matter of course; and also Thomas Boston, the
scheme of thought of whose " View of the Covenant of Grace "
he confessed he did not understand, but whose " Fourfold
State of Man " he " liked exceedingly well." [25] His Calvin he
certainly knew thoroughly, though he would not swear in his
words; [26] and also his Turretin, whom he speaks of as " the
great Turretine "; [27] while van Mastricht he declares " much

---

[23] Hopkins tells us that " he had an enormous thirst for knowledge, in
the pursuit of which he spared no cost or pains. He read all the books, especially books treating of theology, that he could procure, from which he could
hope to derive any assistance in the discovery of truth." From his youth up,
however, he disliked a display of learning. In his earliest maxims, by the
side of " Let much modesty be seen in the style," he sets this other: " Let it
not look as if I was much read, or was conversant with books, or with the
learned world " (Dwight, i. pp. 41 f.).

[24] Dwight, i. p. 93.

[25] *Ibid.*, p. 242.

[26] Preface to the treatise on the Will, Dwight, ii. 1829, p. 13.

[27] " Works," 4 vol. edition, iii. 1856, p. 123, note.

better " than even Turretin, " or," he adds with some fervor,
" than any other book in the world, excepting the Bible, in my
opinion." [28] The close agreement of his teaching with that of
the best esteemed Calvinistic divines is, therefore, both conscious and deliberate; his omission to appeal to them does not
argue either ignorance or contempt; it is incident to his habitual manner and to the special task he was prosecuting. In
point of fact, what he teaches is just the " standard " Calvinism
in its completeness.

As an independent thinker, he is, of course, not without
his individualisms, and that in conception no less than in expression. His explanation of the identity of the human race
with its Head, founded as it is on a doctrine of personal identity which reduces it to an " arbitrary constitution " of God,
binding its successive moments together, is peculiar to himself.[29] In answering objections to the doctrine of Original Sin,
he appeals at one point to Stapfer, and speaks, after him, in
the language of that form of doctrine known as " mediate
imputation." [30] But this is only in order to illustrate his own
view that all mankind are one as truly as and by the same
kind of divine constitution that an individual life is one in its
consecutive moments. Even in this immediate context he
does not teach the doctrine of " mediate imputation," insisting rather that, Adam and his posterity being in the strictest
sense one, in them no less than in him " the guilt arising
from the first existing of a depraved disposition " cannot at
all be distinguished from " the guilt of Adam's first sin ";
and elsewhere throughout the treatise he speaks in the terms of
the common Calvinistic doctrine. His most marked individualism, however, lay in the region of philosophy rather than of
theology. In an essay on " The Nature of True Virtue," he
develops, in opposition to the view that all virtue may be
reduced ultimately to self-love, an eccentric theory of virtue

[28] Letter to Joseph Bellamy, 15th January 1747, printed by F. B. Dexter,
op. cit., p. 13.
[29] " Works," 4 vol. edition, ii. 1856, pp. 489 ff.; Dwight, ii. pp. 555 f.
[30] " Works," 4 vol. edition, ii. pp. 483 f.; Dwight, ii. pp. 544 f.

as consisting in love to being in general. But of this again we hear nothing elsewhere in his works, though it became germinal for the New England theology of the next age. Such individualisms in any case are in no way characteristic of his teaching. He strove after no show of originality. An independent thinker he certainly claimed to be, and "utterly disclaimed a dependence," say, "on Calvin," in the sense of "believing the doctrines he held because Calvin believed and taught them."[31] This very disclaimer is, however, a proclamation of agreement with Calvin, though not as if he "believed everything just as Calvin taught"; he is only solicitous that he should be understood to be not a blind follower of Calvin, but a convinced defender of Calvinism. His one concern was, accordingly, not to improve on the Calvinism of the great expounders of the system, but to place the main elements of the Calvinistic system, as commonly understood, beyond cavil. His marvelous invention was employed, therefore, only in the discovery and development of the fullest and most convincing possible array of arguments in their favor. This is true even of his great treatise on the Will. This is, in the common judgment, the greatest of all his treatises, and the common judgment here is right.[32] But the doctrine of this treatise is precisely the doctrine of the Calvinistic schoolmen. "The novelty of the treatise," we have been well told long ago,[33] "lies not in the position it takes and defends, but in the multitude of proofs, the fecundity and urgency of the arguments by which he maintains it." Edwards' originality thus consists less in the content of his thought than in his manner of thinking. He enters into the great tradition which had come down to him, and "infuses it with his personality and makes it live," and "the vitality of his thought gives to its product the value of a unique creation."[34] The effect of Edwards' labors was

[31] Dwight, ii. p. 13.

[32] Cf. F. J. E. Woodbridge, in *The Philosophical Review,* xiii. 1904, p. 396; and G. Lyon, *op. cit.,* p. 412.

[33] Lyman H. Atwater, *The Biblical Repertory and Princeton Review,* xxx. 1858, p. 597.

[34] H. N. Gardiner, "Selected Sermons," 1904, p. xviii.

quite in the line of his purpose, and not disproportionate to
his greatness. The movement against Calvinism which was
overspreading the land was in a great measure checked, and
the elimination of Calvinism as a determining factor in the
thought of New England, which seemed to be imminent as he
wrote, was postponed for more than a hundred years.[35]

IV. The New England Theology

It was Edwards' misfortune that he gave his name to a
party; and to a party which, never in perfect agreement with
him in its doctrinal ideas, finished by becoming the earnest
advocate of (as it has been sharply expressed[36]) " a set of
opinions which he gained his chief celebrity in demolishing."
The affiliation of this party with Edwards was very direct.
" Bellamy . . . and Hopkins," says G. P. Fisher,[37] tracing the
descent, " were pupils of Edwards; from Hopkins, West derived his theology; Smalley studied with Bellamy, and Emmons with Smalley." But the inheritance of the party from
Edwards showed itself much more strongly on the practical
than on the doctrinal side. Its members were the heirs of his
revivalist zeal and of his awakening preaching; they also
imitated his attempt to purify the Church by discipline and
strict guarding of the Lord's Table — in a word, to restore the
Church to its Puritan ideal of a congregation of saints.[38]
Pressing to extremes in both matters, as followers will, the
" Edwardeans " or " New Divinity " men became a ferment
in the churches of New England, and, creating discussion and
disturbances everywhere, gradually won their way to dominance. Meanwhile their doctrinal teaching was continually
suffering change. As Fisher (p. 7) puts it, " in the process of

[35] Cf. Williston Walker, " Ten New England Leaders," 1901, p. 232.

[36] Lyman H. Atwater, p. 589; cf. J. Ridderbos, pp. 320 f.

[37] " A Discourse Commemorative of the History of the Church of Christ
in Yale College during the First Century of its Existence," New Haven, 1858,
p. 36.

[38] On the " rigidity " of the New Divinity men in " Church administration " and " discipline," see the interesting details in Ezra Stiles's " Diary,"
iii. 1901, pp. 273 f., 343 f., 358 f.

defending the established faith, they were led to recast it in new forms and to change its aspect." Only, it was not merely the form and aspect of their inherited faith, but its substance, that they were steadily transforming. Accordingly, Fisher proceeds to explain that what on this side constituted their common character was not so much a common doctrine as a common method: " the fact that their views were the result of independent reflection and were maintained on philosophical grounds." Here, too, they were followers of Edwards; but in their exaggeration of his rational method, without his solid grounding in the history of thought, they lost continuity with the past and became the creators of a " New England theology " which it is only right frankly to describe as provincial.[39]

It is a far cry from Jonathan Edwards the Calvinist, defending with all the force of his unsurpassed reasoning powers the doctrine of a determined will, and commending a theory of virtue which identified it with general benevolence, to Nathaniel W. Taylor the Pelagianizer, building his system upon the doctrine of the power to the contrary as its foundation stone, and reducing all virtue ultimately to self-love. Taylor's teaching, in point of fact, was in many respects the exact antipodes of Edwards', and very fairly reproduced the congeries of tendencies which the latter considered it his life-work to withstand. Yet Taylor looked upon himself as an " Edwardean," though in him the outcome of the long develop-

[39] Cf. Woodbridge, in *The Philosophical Review,* xiii. 1904, pp. 394 f. The men who worked out this theological transmutation were men of high character, great intellectual gifts, immense energy of thought, and what may almost be called fatal logical facility. Any people might be proud to have produced in the course of a century such a series of " strong reasoners " on religious themes as Joseph Bellamy (1719–1790), Samuel Hopkins (1721–1803), Stephen West (1735–1819), John Smalley (1734–1820), Jonathan Edwards, Jr. (1745–1801), Nathaniel Emmons (1745–1840), Timothy Dwight (1752–1817), Eleazar T. Fitch (1791–1871), and Nathaniel W. Taylor (1786–1858) — all, with the single exception of the younger Edwards, graduates of Yale College; not to speak of yet others of equal powers, lying more off the line of direct development, like Leonard Woods (1774–1854), Bennet Tyler (1783–1858), Edward D. Griffin (1770–1837), Moses Stuart (1780–1852), Lyman Beecher (1775–1863), Charles G. Finney (1792–1875), Leonard Bacon (1802–1881), Horace Bushnell (1802–1876), and Edwards A. Park (1808–1900).

ment received its first appropriate designation — the " New Haven Divinity" Its several successive phases were bound together by the no doubt external circumstance that they were taught in general by men who had received their training at New Haven.

The growth of the New Divinity to that dominance in the theological thought of New England from which it derives its claim to be called " the New England Theology " was gradual, though somewhat rapid. Samuel Hopkins tells us that at the beginning — in 1756 — there were not more than four or five " who espoused the sentiments which since have been called ' Edwardean,' and ' New Divinity'; and since, after some improvement was made upon them, ' Hopkintonian,' or ' Hopkinsian ' sentiments." [40] The younger Edwards still spoke of them in 1777 as a small party.[41] In 1787, Ezra Stiles, chafing under their growing influence and marking the increasing divergence of views among themselves, fancied he saw their end approaching.[42] In this he was mistaken: the New Divinity, in the person of Timothy Dwight, succeeded him as President of Yale College, and through a long series of years was infused into generation after generation of students.[43] The " confusions " Stiles observed were, however, real; or, rather, the progressive giving way of the so-called Edwardeans to those

[40] E. A. Park, " Memoir of the Life and Character of Samuel Hopkins, D.D.," Boston, 1854, p. 237; Fisher, " A Discourse," as cited, p. 80.

[41] Ezra Stiles, ii. 1901, p. 227; Fisher, *loc. cit.*

[42] " It has been the Ton," he writes (Ezra Stiles, iii. pp. 273–275), " to direct Students in divinity these thirty years past or a generation to read the Bible, President Edwards', Dr. Bellamy's, and Mr. Hopkins' Writings — and this was a pretty good Sufficiency of Reading." But now, " the New Divinity Gentlemen are getting into Confusion and running into different sentiments." " The younger Class, but yet in full vigor, suppose they see further than these Oracles, and are disposed to become Oracles themselves and wish to write Theology and have their own Books come into Vogue." He thought these " confusions " the beginning of the end.

[43] Young Theodore D. Woolsey in 1822 can speak of " Hopkinsianism " as " a sort of net which catches all but the Presbyterian eels who slip through." It had become, he says, " a general term which comprehends all who are not Arminians and disagree with Turretin on the atonement " (*Yale Review,* i. 1912 [January], p. 246).

tendencies of thought to which they were originally set in opposition.[44] The younger Edwards drew up a careful account of what he deemed the (ten) "Improvements in Theology made by President Edwards and those who have followed his course of thought."[45] Three of the most cardinal of these he does not pretend were introduced by Edwards, attributing them simply to those whom he calls Edwards' "followers." These are the substitution of the Governmental (Grotian) for the Satisfaction doctrine of the Atonement, in the accomplishment of which he himself, with partial forerunners in Bellamy and West, was the chief agent; the discarding of the doctrine of the imputation of sin in favor of the view that men are condemned for their own personal sin only — a contention which was made in an extreme form by Nathaniel Emmons, who confined all moral quality to acts of volition, and afterwards became a leading element in Nathaniel W. Taylor's system; and the perversion of Edwards' distinction between "natural" and "moral" inability so as to ground on the "natural" ability of the unregenerate, after the fashion introduced by Samuel Hopkins [46] — a theory of the capacities and duties of men without the Spirit, which afterwards, in the hands of Nathaniel W. Taylor, became the core of a new Pelagianizing system.

The external victory of the New Divinity in New England was marked doubtless by the election of Timothy Dwight to the Presidency of Yale College (1795); and certainly it could have found no one better fitted to commend it to moderate men; probably no written system of theology has ever enjoyed

[44] We note Hopkins already conscious of divergence from Edwards' teaching — a divergence which he calls an "improvement." Ezra Stiles tells us (iii. pp. 273 f.) that in 1787 the New Divinity men were beginning to "deny a real vicarious Suffering in Christ's Atonement," and were "generally giving up the Doctrine of *Imputation* both in *Original Sin* and in *Justification*"; and some of them, "receding from disinterested Benevolence, are going into the Idea that all holy Motive operates as terminating in personal Happiness," — a very fair statement of the actual drift.

[45] Published in Dwight, i. pp. 613 ff.

[46] Cf. G. N. Boardman, "A History of New England Theology," New York, 1899, p. 50.

wider acceptance than Dwight's "Sermons."[47] But after Dwight came Taylor, and in the teaching of the latter the downward movement of the New Divinity ran out into a system which turned, as on its hinge, upon the Pelagianizing doctrines of the native sinlessness of the race, the plenary ability of the sinner to renovate his own soul, and self-love or the desire for happiness as the spring of all voluntary action. From this extreme some reaction was inevitable, and the history of the so-called "New England Theology" closes with the moderate reaction of the teaching of Edwards A. Park. Park was of that line of theological descent which came through Hopkins, Emmons, and Woods; but he sought to incorporate into his system all that seemed to him to be the results of New England thinking for the century which preceded him, not excepting the extreme positions of Taylor himself. Reverting so far from Taylor as to return to perhaps a somewhat more deterministic doctrine of the will, he was able to rise above Taylor in his doctrines of election and regeneration, and to give to the general type of thought which he represented a lease of life for another generation. But, with the death of Park in 1900, the history of "New England Theology" seems to come to an end.[48]

LITERATURE: A. A list of Edwards' works is given by Dwight, i. pp. 765 f.; S. Miller, 254 ff.; and Ridderbos, 327 ff. (opp. cit. infra). A brief bibliography will be found in Allen, op. cit. infra, pp. 391 ff. The first edition of Edwards' Works was in 8 vols., ed. S. Austin, Worcester, Mass., 1808–1809. This edition has been frequently reproduced in 4 vols.: New York, 1844, 1852, 1856, 1863, 1881. A new and enlarged edition in 10 vols., ed. S. E. Dwight, vol. i. being a Memoir, appeared at New York, 1829. An edition was published at London in 8 vols., 1837, to which 2 supplementary vols.

---

[47] Cf. G. P. Fisher, "A Discourse," as cited, p. 37: "No work on systematic divinity has had such currency and authority in Great Britain, at least outside the established Church of England, as the Sermons of Dr. Dwight. In that country they have passed through not less than forty editions."

[48] Cf. F. H. Foster, "A Genetic History of the New England Theology," Chicago, 1907, pp. 543–553 ("Conclusion"), where the fact is fully recognized, though the reasons assigned for it are questionable.

were added, Edinburgh, 1847. Later British editions are: London, 1840, with Dwight's Memoir and an Essay by H. Rogers; London, 1865 (Bohn), in 2 vols. Additional writings of Edwards have been published: " Charity and its Fruits," ed. Tryon Edwards, London, 1852 (subsequently reissued under the title " Christian Love, as Manifested in the Heart and Life," ed. 6, Philadelphia, 1874); " Selections from the Unpublished Writings of Jonathan Edwards," edited with an introduction by A. B. Grosart, Edinburgh, 1865; " Observations concerning the Scripture Economy of the Trinity," edited with an introduction by Egbert C. Smyth, New York, 1880; " An Unpublished Essay of Edwards on the Trinity," edited with an introduction by George P. Fisher, New York, 1903; " Selected Sermons of Jonathan Edwards," edited with an introduction and notes by H. N. Gardiner, New York and London, 1904 (contains one new sermon).

B. For life, etc., see S. Hopkins, " The Life and Character of the late Reverend . . . Mr. Jonathan Edwards," Boston, 1765, Northampton, 1804; S. E. Dwight, " Memoir," being vol. i. of his edition of the " Works " (see above), New York, 1829; S. Miller, " Life of Jonathan Edwards," Boston, 1837 and 1848 (vol. viii. of first series of Jared Sparks's " The Library of American Biography "); A. V. G. Allen, " Jonathan Edwards," Boston and New York, 1889; Williston Walker, " Ten New England Leaders," Boston and New York, 1901, pp. 215–263; idem, " A History of the Congregational Churches in the United States," New York, 1894, chaps. vii. viii. ix.; Joseph Tracy, " The Great Awakening," Boston, 1842.

C. The most comprehensive survey of Edwards' theological teaching is given by Jan Ridderbos, " De Theologie van Jonathan Edwards," The Hague, 1907; see also G. P. Fisher, " Discussions in History and Theology," New York, 1880, pp. 227–252; Noah Porter, " The Princeton Review . . . and the Edwardean Theology," in The New Englander, xviii. 1860, pp. 737 ff.; H. N. Gardiner, " Jonathan Edwards: a Retrospect," Boston and New York, 1901; " Exercises Commemorating the Two-Hundredth Anniversary of the Birth of Jonathan Edwards, held at Andover Theological Seminary," Andover, 1904.

D. The New England Theology should be studied in the works of its chief exponents. Lives of many of them are also accessible. See also F. H. Foster, " A Genetic History of the New England Theology," Chicago, 1907; G. N. Boardman, " A History of New

England Theology," New York, 1899; C. Hodge, " Princeton Essays,"
first series, 1846, pp. 285–307, second series, 1847, pp. 206 235,
" Essays and Reviews," 1856, pp. 539–633; Lyman H. Atwater, *The
Biblical Repertory and Princeton Review*, xxvi. 1854, pp. 217–246,
xxx. 1858, pp. 585–620, xxxi. 1859, pp. 489–538, xl. 1868, pp. 368–
398; Edwards A. Park, " The Atonement," Boston, 1859; G. P.
Fisher, " Discussions in History and Theology," pp. 285–354; H. B.
Smith, " Faith and Philosophy," New York, 1877, pp. 215–264.

XIX

CHARLES DARWIN'S RELIGIOUS LIFE: A SKETCH IN SPIRITUAL BIOGRAPHY

CHARLES DARWIN'S RELIGIOUS LIFE: A SKETCH IN SPIRITUAL BIOGRAPHY [1]

THERE was a great deal of discussion in the newspapers, about the time of Mr. Darwin's death, concerning his religious opinions, provoked, in part, by the publication of a letter written by him in 1879 to a Jena student, in reply to inquiries as to his views with reference to a revelation and a future life; [2] in part by a report published by Drs. Aveling and Büchner of an interview which they had had with him during the last year of his life. [3] Of course the appearance of the elaborate " Life and Letters " by his son [4] has now put an end to all possible doubt as to so simple a matter. Mr. Darwin describes himself as living generally, and more and more as he grew older, in a state of mind which, with much fluctuation of judgment from a cold theism down the scale, never reaching, however, a dogmatic atheism, would be best described as agnosticism. [5] But the " Life and Letters " does far more for us than merely determine this fact. " In the three huge volumes which are put forth to embalm the philosopher's name," as *Blackwood* somewhat flippantly expresses it, " he is observed like one of his own specimens under the microscope, and every peculiarity recorded, for all the world as if a philosopher were as important as a mollusc, though we can scarcely hope that a son of Dar-

[1] Reprinted from *The Presbyterian Review*, ix. 1888, pp. 569–601.

[2] First published in the *Deutsche Rundschau*, then in the Separat-Ausgabe of Professor Haeckel's paper: " Die Naturanschauung von Darwin, Goethe und Lamarck," p. 60, note 17. Afterward also in English journals: see *The Academy*, Nos. 545, 546, 547, 548 (xxii. 1882).

[3] *The National Reformer* for October 29th, 1882.

[4] " The Life and Letters of Charles Darwin, including an autobiographical chapter." Edited by his son, Francis Darwin. In three volumes. London: John Murray, 1888. Seventh thousand, revised. All references in the present paper are to this edition.

[5] " Life and Letters," i. p. 304: written in 1879.

win's would commit himself to such a revolutionary view." [6]
The result of this excessively minute description, and all the
more because it is so lacking in proportion and perspective, is
that we are put in possession of abundant material for tracing
the evolution of his life and opinions with an accuracy and
fullness of detail seldom equaled in the literature of biography. For example, although the book was not written in
order to depict Mr. Darwin's " inward life," it is quite possible
to arrange out of the facts it gives a fairly complete history
of his spiritual changes. And this proves unexpectedly interesting. Such men as Bunyan and Augustine and St. Paul himself have opened to us their spiritual growth from darkness
into light, and made us familiar with every phase of the struggle by which a spirit moves upward to the hope of glory. Such
a writer as Rousseau lifts for us a corner of the veil that hides
from view the depths of an essentially evil nature. But we
have lacked any complete record of the experiences of an essentially noble soul about which the shades of doubt are slowly
gathering. This it is that Mr. Darwin's " Life " gives us.

No one who reads the " Life and Letters " will think of
doubting the unusual sweetness of Mr. Darwin's character. In
his school-days he is painted by his fellow students as " cheer-
ful, good-tempered, and communicative." [7] At college, we see
him, through his companions' eyes, as " the most genial, warm-
hearted, generous, and affectionate of friends," with sympathies alive for " all that was good and true," and " a cordial
hatred for everything false, or vile, or cruel, or mean, or dishonorable " — in a word, as one " pre-eminently good, and
just, and lovable." [8] A co-laborer with him in the high studies
of his mature life sums up his impressions of his whole character in equally striking words: " Those who knew Charles
Darwin," he says, " most intimately are unanimous in their
appreciation of the unsurpassed nobility and beauty of his
whole character. In him there was no ' other side.' Not only

---

[6] *Blackwood's Edinburgh Magazine,* cxliii. 1888, p. 105.

[7] Rev. John Yardley, in the *Modern Review,* July, 1882, p. 504.

[8] " Life and Letters," i. p. 166.

was he the Philosopher who has wrought a greater revolution in human thought within a quarter of a century than any man of our time — or perhaps of *any* time — . . . but as a Man he exemplified in his own life that true *religion*, which is deeper, wider, and loftier than any Theology. For this not only inspired him with the devotion to Truth which was the master-passion of his great nature; but made him the most admirable husband, brother, and father; the kindest friend, neighbour, and master; the genuine lover, not only of his fellow-man, but of every creature." [9] Mr. Darwin himself doubted whether the religious sentiment was ever strongly developed in him,[10] but this opinion was written in his later years, and the context shows that there is an emphasis upon the word " sentiment." There was, on the other hand, a truly religious coloring thrown over all his earlier years, and the fruits of religion never left his life. But, nevertheless, there gradually faded out from his thought all purely religious concepts, and there gradually died out of his heart all the higher religious sentiments, together with all the accompanying consolations, hopes, and aspirations. On the quiet stage of this amiable life there is played out before our eyes the tragedy of the death of religion out of a human soul. The spectacle is none the less instructive that it is offered in the case of one before whom we gladly doff our hats in true and admiring reverence.

The first clear glimpse which we get of the future philosopher, as a child, is a very attractive one. He seems to have been sweet-tempered, simple-hearted, conscientious, not without his childish faults, but with a full supply of childish virtues. Here is a pretty picture. Being sent, at about the age of nine years, to Mr. Butler's school, situated about a mile from his home, he often ran home " in the longer intervals between the callings over and before locking up at night. . . . I remember in the early part of my school life," he writes, " that I often had to run very quickly to be in time, and from being a fleet runner was generally successful; but when in doubt I prayed

[9] Dr. W. B. Carpenter, in the *Modern Review*, July, 1882, pp. 523, 524.
[10] " Life and Letters," i. p. 311 (1876).

earnestly to God to help me, and I well remember that I attributed my success to the prayers and not to my quick running, and marvelled how generally I was aided." [11] Thus, heaven lay about him in his infancy. But he does not seem to have been a diligent student, and his school-life was not altogether profitable; his subsequent stay at Edinburgh was no more so; and before he reached the age of twenty it seemed clear that his heart was not in the profession of medicine to which he had been destined. In these circumstances, his father, who was a nominal member of the Church of England, took a step which seemed from his point of view, no doubt, quite natural; and proposed that his son should become a clergyman.[12] "He was very properly vehement," the son writes, " against my turning into an idle sporting man " — as if this was a sufficient reason for the contemplated step. The son himself was, however, more conscientious. " I asked for some time to consider," he writes, " as from what little I had heard or thought on the subject I had scruples about declaring my belief in all the dogmas of the Church of England; though otherwise I liked the thought of being a country clergyman. Accordingly I read with care ' Pearson on the Creed,' and a few other books on divinity; and as I did not then in the least doubt the strict and literal truth of every word in the Bible,[13] I soon persuaded myself that our Creed must be fully accepted." [14]

This step led to residence at Cambridge, where, however, again the time was mostly wasted. The influences under which he there fell, moreover, were not altogether calculated to quicken his reverence for the high calling to which he had devoted himself. " The way in which the service was conducted in chapel shows that the dean, at least, was not over zealous. I have heard my father tell [it is Mr. Francis Darwin who is writing] how at evening chapel the Dean used to read alternate

[11] " Life and Letters," i. p. 31.

[12] *Ibid.,* i. p. 45.

[13] An interesting indication that in Mr. Darwin's mature judgment the Bible does teach the doctrines of the Creed.

[14] " Life and Letters," i. p. 45.

verses of the Psalms, without making even a pretence of waiting for the congregation to take their share. And when the
Lesson was a lengthy one, he would rise and go on with the
Canticles after the scholar had read fifteen or twenty verses." [15]
Nor were his associates at Cambridge always all that could
be desired: from his passion for sport he " got into a sporting
set, including some dissipated low-minded young men," with
whom he spent days and evenings of which (he says) he should
have felt ashamed.[16] Fortunately, he had other companions
also, of a higher stamp,[17] and among them preëminently Professor Henslow, who united in his own person the widest
scientific learning and the deepest piety, and with whom he
happily became quite intimate, gaining from him, as he says,
" more than I can express." [18] Best of all, Henslow was accustomed to let his light shine, and talked freely " on all subjects,
including his deep sense of religion." [19] Accordingly, as we are
not surprised to learn, it was with him that Mr. Darwin wished
to read divinity.[20] Not that he was even now ready to enter
with spirit upon his preparation for his future work. A touching letter to his friend Fox, written in 1829, on the occasion
of the death of the latter's sister, shows that his heart at this
time knew somewhat of the consolations of Christianity. " I
feel most sincerely and deeply for you," he writes, " and all
your family; but at the same time, as far as any one can, by
his own good principles and religion, be supported under such
a misfortune, you, I am assured, will know where to look for
such support. And after so pure and holy a comfort as the Bible
affords, I am equally assured how useless the sympathy of all
friends must appear, although it be as heartfelt and sincere,
as I hope you believe me capable of feeling." [21] But he still had
conscientious scruples about taking Orders. A fellow student
writes (1829): " We had an earnest conversation about going
into Holy Orders; and I remember his asking me, with refer-

[15] *Ibid.*, i. p. 165.
[16] *Ibid.*, i. p. 48.
[17] *Ibid.*, i. p. 49.
[18] *Ibid.*, i. p. 188.

[19] *Ibid.*, i. p. 188.
[20] *Ibid.*, i. p. 171.
[21] *Ibid.*, i. pp. 177 f.

ence to the question put by the Bishop in the ordination service, 'Do you trust that you are inwardly moved by the Holy Spirit, etc.,' whether I could answer in the affirmative, and on my saying I could not, he said, 'Neither can I, and therefore I cannot take Orders.'"[22] And certainly the lines of his intellectual interest were cast elsewhere. Only under the pressure of his approaching examinations was he led to anything like professional study. On such occasions, however, he showed that his mind was open to impression. "In order to pass the B.A. examination," he writes, "it was also necessary to get up Paley's 'Evidences of Christianity,' and his 'Moral Philosophy.' This was done in a thorough manner, and I am convinced that I could have written out the whole of the 'Evidences' with perfect correctness, but not of course in the clear language of Paley. The logic of this book and, as I may add, of his 'Natural Theology,' gave me as much delight as did Euclid. The careful study of these works, without attempting to learn any part by rote, was the only part of the academical course which, as I then felt and as I still believe, was of the least use to me in the education of my mind. I did not at that time trouble myself about Paley's premises; and taking these on trust, I was charmed and convinced by the long line of argumentation."[23] Despite such occasional pleasure in his work, when, on leaving Cambridge, the offer of a place in the Beagle expedition came, and his father objected to his taking it that his proper clerical studies would be interrupted, Josiah Wedgwood was able to argue: "If I saw Charles now absorbed in professional studies, I should probably think it would not be advisable to interrupt them; but this is not, and, I think, will not be the case with him. His present pursuit of knowledge is in the same track as he would have to follow in the expedition."[24] By this representation, his father's consent was obtained, although, with that long-sighted wisdom which his son always regarded as his distinguishing characteristic, he "considered it as again changing his profession."[25] And so,

[22] "Life and Letters," i. p. 171.
[23] Ibid., i. p. 47.
[24] Ibid., i. p. 199.
[25] Ibid., i. p. 197.

indeed, it proved. Mr. Darwin's estimate of the sacredness of a clergyman's office improved somewhat above what it was when he was ready to undertake it, if he could sign the Creed, because the life of a country clergyman offered advantages in a sporting way.[26] He writes in 1835 to his friend Fox, almost sadly: " I dare hardly look forward to the future, for I do not know what will become of me. Your situation is above envy: I do not venture even to frame such happy visions. To a person fit to take the office, the life of a clergyman is a type of all that is respectable and happy." [27] But though, perhaps because, his feeling toward the clerical office had grown to be so high, he no longer thought of entering it. He writes in his Autobiography that this intention was never " formally given up, but died a natural death when, on leaving Cambridge, I joined the Beagle as naturalist." [28]

The letter to Fox which has just been quoted is a sufficient indication that it was not his Christian faith, but only his intention of taking Orders that was dying out during the course of his five years' cruise. Other like indications are not lacking.[29] We are, therefore, not surprised to read: " Whilst on board the Beagle I was quite orthodox, and I remember being heartily laughed at by some of the officers (though themselves orthodox) for quoting the Bible as an unanswerable authority on some point of morality." [30] Nevertheless, his defection from Christianity was during these years silently and, as it were, negatively preparing in the ever increasing completeness of his absorption in scientific pursuits, by which he was left little time for or interest in other things. And on his return to England, the working up of the immense mass of material which he had collected during his voyage claimed his attention even more exclusively than its collection had done. Thus he was given occasion to occupy himself so wholly with science that

[26] *Ibid.*, i. p. 45.
[27] *Ibid.*, i. p. 262.
[28] *Ibid.*, i. p. 45.
[29] Cf. his words of appreciation of missionary work, *ibid.*, i. p. 264. See also i. p. 246.
[30] " Life and Letters," i. pp. 307 f.

there was not only no time left to think of his former intention of entering the ministry — there was little time left to remember that there was a soul within him or a future life beyond the grave. Readers of the sad account which Mr. Darwin appended at the very end of his life [31] (1881) to his autobiographical notes, of how at about the age of thirty or thereabouts his higher æsthetic tastes began to show atrophy, so that he lost his love for poetry, art, music, and his mind more and more began to take upon it the character of a kind of machine for grinding general laws out of large collections of facts, will not be able to resist the suspicion that this exclusive direction to one type of thinking was really, as he himself believed, injurious to his intellect as well as enfeebling to his emotional nature, and lay at the root of his subsequent drift away from religion.

It was an ominous conjunction, that simultaneously with the early progress of this "curious and lamentable loss of the higher æsthetic tastes," a more positive influence was entering his mind which was destined most seriously to modify his thought on divine things. "In July [1837]," he tells us, "I opened my first note-book for facts in relation to the Origin of Species, about which I had long reflected." [32] The change that was passing over his views as to the manner in which species originate is illustrated by his biographer by the quotation of a passage from his manuscript "Journal," written in 1834, in which he freely speaks of "creation," which was omitted from the printed "Journal," the proofs of which were completed in 1837 — a fact which "harmonizes with the change we know to have been proceeding in his views." [33] We raise no question as to the compatibility of the Darwinian form of the hypothesis of evolution with Christianity; Mr. Darwin himself says that "science" (and in speaking of "science" he has "evolution" in mind) "has nothing to do with Christ, except in so far as the habit of scientific research makes a man cautious in admitting evidence." [34] But if we

---

[31] "Life and Letters," i. pp. 100 ff.   [33] Ibid., ii. p. 1.
[32] Ibid., i. p. 68.   [34] Ibid., i. p. 307.

confine ourselves to Mr. Darwin's own personal religious history, it is very clear that, whether on account of a peculiarity of constitution or by an illogical train of reasoning or otherwise, as he wrought out his theory of evolution, he gave up his Christian faith — nay, that his doctrine of evolution directly expelled his Christian belief. How it operated in so doing it is not difficult dimly to trace. He was thoroughly persuaded (like Mr. Huxley [35]) that, in its plain meaning, Genesis teaches creation by immediate, separate, and sudden fiats of God for each several species. And as he more and more convinced himself that species, on the contrary, originated according to natural law, and through a long course of gradual modification, he felt ever more and more that Genesis "must go." But Genesis is an integral part of the Old Testament, and with the truth and authority of the Old Testament the truth and authority of Christianity itself is inseparably bound up. Thus, the doctrine of evolution once heartily adopted by him gradually undermined his faith, until he cast off the whole of Christianity as an unproved delusion. The process was neither rapid nor unopposed. He speaks of his unwillingness to give up his belief and of the slow rate at which unbelief crept over him, although it became at last complete.[36] Drs. Büchner and Aveling report him as assigning the age of forty years (1849) as the date of the completion of the process.[37] Of course, other arguments came gradually to the support of the original disturbing cause, to strengthen him in his new position, until his former acceptance of Christianity became almost incredible to him. A deeply interesting account is given of the whole process in the Autobiography.[38] "During these two years," he says — meaning the years when his theory of evolution was taking shape in his mind — "I was led to think much about religion. . . . I had gradually come by this time, i.e. 1836 to 1839, to see that the Old Testament was no more to be trusted than the sacred books of the Hindoos. The question then continually rose before my mind and would not be banished, — is it

[35] *Ibid.*, ii. p. 181.

[36] *Ibid.*, i. pp. 308 f.

[37] *National Reformer*, xl. 1882, p. 292.

[38] "Life and Letters," i. pp. 307–309.

credible that if God were now to make a revelation to the
Hindoos, he would permit it to be connected with the belief
in Vishnu, Siva, etc., as Christianity is connected with the Old
Testament? This appeared to me to be utterly incredible."
Here is the root of the whole matter. His doctrine of evolution
had antiquated for him the Old Testament record; but Christianity is too intimately connected with the Old Testament to
stand as divine if the Old Testament be fabulous. Certainly,
if the premises are sound, the conclusion is inevitable. Only
both conclusion and premises must shatter themselves against
the fact of the supernatural origin of Christianity. Once the
conclusion was reached, however, bolstering arguments, pressing directly against Christianity, did not fail to make their
appearance: the difficulty of proving miracles, their antecedent incredibility, the credulity of the age in which they profess to have been wrought, the unhistorical character of the
Gospels, their discrepancies, man's proneness to religious enthusiasm [39] — arguments, all of them, drawn from a sphere in
which Mr. Darwin was not a master, and all of them, in
reality, afterthoughts called in to support the doubts which
were already dominating him. How impervious to evidence he
at last became is naively illustrated by the words with which
he closes his account of how he lost his faith. He says he feels
sure that he gave up his belief unwillingly: "For I can well
remember often and often inventing day-dreams of old letters
between distinguished Romans, and manuscripts being discovered at Pompeii or elsewhere, which confirmed in the most
striking manner all that was written in the Gospels. But I
found it more and more difficult, with free scope given to my
imagination, to invent evidence which would suffice to convince me." [40] When a man has reached a stage in which no
conceivable historical evidence could convince him of the
actual occurrence of a historical fact, we may cease to wonder

[39] See them in full, "Life and Letters," i. p. 308. It is interesting to observe that they all circle around miracles, evincing that Mr. Darwin found
difficulty in persuading himself that these miracles did not take place.

[40] "Life and Letters," i. pp. 308, 309.

that the almost inconceivable richness of the actual historical evidence of Christianity was insufficient to retain his conviction. He ceases to be a judge of the value of evidence; and that he has resisted it is no proof that it is resistible; it is only an evidence of such induration of believing tissue on his part that it is no longer capable of responding to the strongest reagents.

Here, then, approximately at the age of forty, we have reached the end of one great stage of Mr. Darwin's spiritual development. He was no longer a Christian; he no longer believed in a revelation. We see the effect in the changed tone of his speech. Mr. J. Brodie Innis reports him as saying that he did not attack Moses, and that he could not remember that he had ever published a word directly [41] against religion or the clergy.[42] But in his private letters of this later period he certainly speaks with scant respect of Genesis [43] and the clergy,[44] if not also of religion,[45] and he even gradually grew somewhat irreverent in his use of the name of God. We see the effect still more sadly in his loss of the consolations of religion. It is painful to compare his touching, if somewhat formal and shallow, letter of condolence to his friend Fox, written in 1829, which we have already quoted, with the hopeless grief of later letters of similar origin. He lost a daughter whom he tenderly loved in 1851, and his " only consolation " was " that she passed a short, though joyous life." [46] When Fox lost a child in 1853, his only appeal is to the softening influence of the passage of time. " As you must know," he writes him, " from your own most painful experience, time softens and deadens, in a manner truly wonderful, one's feelings and regrets. At first it is indeed bitter. I can only hope that your health and that of poor Mrs. Fox may be preserved, and that time may do its work softly, and bring you all together, once again, as the happy family, which, as I can well believe, you so lately formed." [47] What a contrast with " the pure and holy comfort

[41] Note the word "directly."

[42] "Life and Letters," ii. pp. 288 f.

[43] Ibid., ii. p. 152.

[44] Ibid., i. p. 340.

[45] Ibid., ii. p. 143.

[46] Ibid., i. p. 380.

[47] Ibid., i. p. 388; cf. iii. p. 39, note ‡, written in 1863.

afforded by the Bible "! Already he was learning the grief of those who " sorrow as the rest who have no hope." Whether his habitual neglect of the Sunday rest and of the ordinances of religion was another effect of the same change it is impossible to say, in our ignorance of his habits previous to the loss of his Christian faith. But throughout the whole period of his life at Down, we are told, " week-days and Sundays passed by alike, each with their stated intervals of work and rest," while his visits to the church were confined to a few rare occasions of weddings and funerals.[48]

But the loss of Christianity did not necessarily mean the loss of religion, and, as a matter of fact, in yielding up revealed, Mr. Darwin retained a strong hold upon natural religion. There were yet God, the soul, the future life. The theory which he had elaborated as a sufficient account of the differences that exist between the several kinds of organic beings, including man, was, however, destined to work havoc in his mind with even the simplest tenets of natural religion. Again we raise no question as to whether this drift was inevitable; it is enough for our present purpose that in Mr. Darwin's case it was actual.[49] To understand how this was so, it is only necessary for us to remember that he had laid hold upon " natural selec-

[48] " Life and Letters," i. pp. 127, 128.

[49] In the case of many others it has not proved inevitable, as e.g. in the case of Dr. W. B. Carpenter, whose opinion is worth quoting here, because his general conception of the relation of God to the universe seems to be very similar to what Mr. Darwin's originally was. " To myself," he writes, in an interesting paper on " The Doctrine of Evolution in its Relations to Theism " (*Modern Review,* October, 1882, p. 685), " the conception of a continuity of action which required no departure to meet special contingencies, because the plan was all-perfect in the beginning, is a far higher and nobler one than that of a succession of interruptions. . . . And in describing the process of evolution in the ordinary language of Science, as due to ' secondary causes,' we no more dispense with a First Cause, than we do when we speak of those Physical Forces, which, from the Theistic point of view, are so many diverse modes of manifestation of one and the same Power. Nor do we in the least set aside the idea of an original Design, when we regard these adaptations which are commonly attributed to special exertions of contriving power and wisdom, as the outcome of an all-comprehensive Intelligence which foresaw that the product would be ' good,' before calling into existence the germ from which it would be evolved."

tion " as the *vera causa* and sufficient account of all organic forms. His conception was that every form may vary indefinitely in all directions, and that every variation which is a gain to it in adaptation to its surroundings is necessarily preserved by that very fact through the simple reaction of the surroundings upon the struggle for existence. Any divine guidance of the direction of the variation seemed to him as much opposed to the one premise of the theory as any divine interference with the working of natural selection seemed to be opposed to the other; and he included all organic phenomena, as well mental and moral as physical, in the scope of this natural process. Thus to him God became an increasingly unnecessary and therefore an increasingly incredible hypothecation.

The seriousness of this drift of thought makes it worth while to illustrate it somewhat in detail. During the whole time occupied in collecting material for and in writing the " Origin of Species " Mr. Darwin was a theist,[50] or, as he expressed it on one occasion: " Many years ago, when I was collecting facts for the ' Origin,' my belief in what is called a personal God was as firm as that of Dr. Pusey himself." [51] The rate at which this firm belief passed away was slow enough for the process to occupy several years. He tells us that his thought on such subjects was never profound or long-continued.[52] This was certainly not the fault, however, of his friends, for from the first publication of his development hypothesis they plied him with problems that forced him to face the great questions of the relation of his views to belief in God and His modes of activity. We get the first glimpse of this in his correspondence with Sir Charles Lyell. That great geologist had suggested that we must " assume a primeval creative power " acting throughout the whole course of development, though not uniformly, in order to account for the supervening, say, of man at the end of the series. To this Mr. Darwin replies with a decided negative. " We must, under present knowledge," he

[50] " Life and Letters," i. p. 313.
[51] *Ibid.*, iii. p. 236 (1878).
[52] See e.g. i. pp. 305, 306 (1871).

wrote, " assume the creation of one or of a few forms in the same manner as philosophers assume the existence of a power of attraction without any explanation. But I entirely reject, as in my judgment quite unnecessary, any subsequent addition ' of new powers and attributes and forces,' or of any ' principle of improvement,' except in so far as every character which is naturally selected or preserved is in some way an advantage or improvement; otherwise it would not have been selected. If I were convinced that I required such additions to the theory of natural selection, I would reject it as rubbish. . . . If I understand you, the turning-point in our difference must be, that you think it impossible that the intellectual powers of a species should be much improved by the continued natural selection of the most intellectual individuals. To show how minds graduate, just reflect how impossible every one has yet found it, to define the difference in mind of man and the lower animals; the latter seem to have the very same attributes in a much lower stage of perfection than the lowest savage. I would give absolutely nothing for the theory of Natural Selection, if it requires miraculous additions at any one stage of descent. I think Embryology, Homology, Classification, etc., show us that all vertebrata have descended from one parent; how that parent appeared we know not. If you admit in ever so little a degree, the explanation which I have given of Embryology, Homology and Classification, you will find it difficult to say: thus far the explanation holds good, but no further; here we must call in ' the addition of new creative forces.' " [53] A few days later he wrote again: " I have reflected a good deal on what you say on the necessity of continued intervention of creative power. I cannot see this necessity; and its admission, I think, would make the theory of Natural Selection valueless. Grant a simple Archetypal creature, like the Mudfish or Lepidosiren, with the five senses and some vestige of mind, and I believe natural selection will account for the production of every vertebrate animal." [54]

Let us weigh well the meaning to Mr. Darwin's own

[53] *Ibid.,* ii. pp. 210 f., written October 11th, 1859.   [54] *Ibid.,* ii. p. 174.

thought of these strong assertions of the competency of natural selection to " account " for every distinguishing characteristic of living forms. It meant to him, first, the assimilation of the human mind, in its essence, with the intelligence of the brutes; and this meant the elimination of what we ordinarily mean by " the soul." He only needed to have given " the five senses and some vestige of mind," such as exists, for instance, in the mud-fish, to enable him by natural selection alone, with the exclusion of all " new powers and attributes and forces," to account for the mental power of Newton, the high imaginings of Milton, the devout aspirations of a Bernard. How early he consciously formulated the extreme form of this conclusion it is difficult to say; but we find him in 1871 thanking Mr. Tylor for giving him new standing ground for it: " It is wonderful how you trace animism from the lower races up to the religious belief of the highest races. It will make me for the future look at religion — a belief in the soul, etc. — from a new point of view." [55] Accordingly, the new view was incorporated in the " Descent of Man," published that same year.[56] And Dr. Robert Lewins seems quite accurately to sum up the ultimate opinion which he attained on this subject in the following words:

Before concluding I may, without violation of any confidence, mention that, both *viva voce* and in writing, Mr. Darwin was much less reticent to myself than in this letter to Jena. For, in an answer to the direct question I felt myself justified, some years since, in addressing to that immortal expert in Biology, as to the bearing of his researches on the existence of an " *Anima*," or " Soul " in Man, he distinctly stated that, in his opinion, a vital or " spiritual " principle, apart from inherent somatic energy, had no more *locus standi* in the human than in the other races of the Animal Kingdom — a conclusion that seems a mere corollary of, or indeed a position tantamount with, his essential doctrine of human and bestial identity of Nature and genesis.[57]

[55] *Ibid.*, iii. p. 151.
[56] " The Descent of Man," i. pp. 62 ff.
[57] *Journal of Science*, xix. 1882, pp. 751 f.

It was but a corollary to loss of belief in a soul, secondly, to lose belief also in immortality. If we are one with the brutes in origin, why not also in destiny? Mr. Darwin thought it "base" in his opponents to "drag in immortality," in objection to his theories; [58] but in his own mind he was allowing his theories to push immortality out. His final position as to the future of man he gives in an interesting passage in the autobiographical notes, written in 1876. He speaks there of immortality as a "strong and almost instinctive belief," but also of the "intolerableness" of the thought that the more perfect race of the future years shall be annihilated by the gradual cooling of the sun, pathetically adding: "To those who fully admit the immortality of the human soul, the destruction of our world will not appear so dreadful." [59] Accordingly, when writing to the Jena student in 1879, after saying that he did not believe that "there ever had been any revelation," he adds: "As for a future life, every man must judge for himself between conflicting vague probabilities." [60] Thirdly, his settled conviction of the sufficiency of natural selection to account for all differentiations in organic forms deeply affected Mr. Darwin's idea of God and of His relation to the world. His notion at this time (1859), while theistic, appears to have been somewhat crassly deistic. He seems never to have been able fully to grasp the conception of divine immanence; but from the opening of his first notebook on Species [61] to the end of his days he gives ever repeated reason to the reader to fear that the sole conceptions of God in His relation to the universe which were possible to him were either that God should do all things without second causes, or, having ordained second causes, should sit outside and beyond them and leave them to do all things without Him. Beginning with this deistic conception, which pushed God out of His works, it is perhaps not strange that he could never be sure that he saw Him in His works; and when he could trace effects to a "natural cause" or group a body of phenomena under a

[58] "Life and Letters," ii. p. 228. [60] *Ibid.*, i. p. 307.

[59] *Ibid.*, i. p. 312. [61] *Ibid.*, ii. p. 9 (1837).

"natural law," this seemed to him equivalent to disproving the connection of God with them.[62] The result was that the theistic proofs gradually grew more and more meaningless to him, until, at last, no one of them carried conviction to his mind.

Sir Charles Lyell was not left alone in his efforts to clarify Mr. Darwin's thinking on such subjects; soon Dr. Asa Gray took his place by his side and became at once the chief force in the endeavor. Nevertheless, Mr. Darwin outlines already in a letter to Lyell in 1860 [63] the arguments by which he stood unto the end. " I must say one more word," he writes, " about our quasi-theological controversy about natural selection. . . . Do you consider that the successive variations in the size of the crop of the Pouter Pigeon, which man has accumulated to please his caprice, have been due to ' the creative and sustaining powers of Brahma? ' In the sense that an omnipotent and omniscient Deity must order and know everything, this must be admitted; yet, in honest truth, I can hardly

[62] We have seen that Dr. W. B. Carpenter refuses to be held in Mr. Darwin's logic, although with him holding to a somewhat deistic conception of the divine relation to the process of development. " Attach what weight we may to the *physical* causes which have brought about this Evolution," he insists, " I cannot see how it is possible to conceive of any but a Moral Cause for the endowments that made the primordial germ susceptible of their action " (*loc. cit.*, p. 680). " And in the so-called *laws* of Organic Evolution, I see nothing but the orderly and continuous working-out of the original Intelligent Design " (p. 681). Dr. W. H. Dallinger also begins with a similar conception (comparing God's relation to the universe to the relation to his work of a machinist who constructs a calculating machine to throw numbers of one order for a given time and then introduce suddenly a new series, " by prevised and preordained arrangement "), and yet refuses the conclusion. " Evolution," he argues, " like gravitation, is only a method; and the self-adjustments demonstrated in the ' origin of species ' only make it, to reason, the clearer, that variation and survival is a method that took its origin in mind. It is true that the egg of a moth, and the eye of a dog-fish, and the forearm of a tiger *must* be what they are to accomplish the end of their being. But that only shows, as we shade our mental eyes, and gaze back to the beginning, the magnificence of the design that was *in*volved in nature's beginning, so as to be *e*volved, by the designed rhythm of nature's methods." See the whole passage in his eloquent Fernley lecture for 1887, on " The Creator, and what we may Know of the Method of Creation " (London: T. Woolmer, 1887), pp. 61 f.

[63] " Life and Letters," ii. pp. 303, 304.

admit it. It seems preposterous that a maker of a universe should care about the crop of a pigeon solely [64] to please man's silly fancies. But if you agree with me in thinking such an interposition of the Deity uncalled for, I can see no reason whatever for believing in such interpositions in the case of natural beings, in which strange and admirable peculiarities have been naturally selected for the creature's own benefit. Imagine a Pouter in a state of nature wading into the water, and then, being buoyed up by its inflated crop, sailing about in search of food. What admiration this would have excited — adaptation to the laws of hydrostatic pressure, etc. For the life of me I cannot see any difficulty in natural selection producing the most exquisite structure, *if such structure can be arrived at by gradation,* and I know from experience how hard it is to name any structure towards which at least some gradations are not known. . . . P. S. — The conclusion at which I have come, as I have told Asa Gray, is that such a question, as is touched on in this note, is beyond the human intellect, like 'predestination and free will,' or the 'origin of evil.'" There is much confused thought in this letter; but it concerns us now only to note that Mr. Darwin's difficulty arises on the one side from his inability to conceive of God as immanent in the universe and his consequent total misapprehension of the nature of divine providence, and on the other from a very crude notion of final cause which posits a single extrinsic end as the sole purpose of the Creator. No one would hold to a doctrine of divine " interpositions " such as appears to him here as the only alternative to divine absence. And no one would hold to a teleology of the raw sort which he here has in mind — a teleology which finds the end for which a thing exists in the misuse or abuse of it by an outside selecting agent. Mr. Darwin himself felt a natural mental inability for dealing with such themes, and accordingly wavered long as to the attitude he ought to assume toward the evidences of God's hand in nature. Thus he wrote in May, 1860, to Dr. Gray: " With respect to the theological view of the question. This is

[64] How much of the argument depends on this word!

always painful to me. I am bewildered. I had no intention to write atheistically. But I own that I cannot see as plainly as others do, and as I should wish to do, evidence of design and beneficence on all sides of us. There seems to me too much misery in the world. I cannot persuade myself that a beneficent and omnipotent God would have designedly created the Ichneumonidæ with the express intention of their feeding within the living bodies of Caterpillars, or that a cat should play with mice. Not believing this, I see no necessity in the belief that the eye was expressly designed. On the other hand, I cannot anyhow be contented to view this wonderful universe, and especially the nature of man, and to conclude that everything is the result of brute force. I am inclined to look at everything as resulting from designed laws, with the details, whether good or bad, left to the working out of what we may call chance. Not that this notion *at all* satisfies me. I feel most deeply that the whole subject is too profound for the human intellect. A dog might as well speculate on the mind of Newton. Let each man hope and believe what he can. Certainly I agree with you that my views are not at all necessarily atheistical. The lightning kills a man, whether a good one or bad one, owing to the excessively complex action of natural laws. A child (who may turn out an idiot) is born by the action of even more complex laws, and I can see no reason why a man, or other animal, may not have been aboriginally produced by other laws, and that all these laws may have been expressly designed by an omniscient Creator, who foresaw every future event and consequence. But the more I think the more bewildered I become; as indeed I have probably shown by this letter." [65] The reasoning of this extract, which supposes that the fact that a result is secured by appropriate conditions furnishes ground for regarding it as undesigned, is less suitable to a grave thinker than to a redoubtable champion like Mr. Allan Quartermain, who actually makes use of it. "At last he was dragged forth uninjured, though in a very pious and prayerful frame of mind," he is made to say of a negro whom he had

[65] "Life and Letters," ii. pp. 311, 312.

saved by killing an attacking buffalo; "his 'spirit had certainly looked that way,' he said, or he would now have been dead. As I never like to interfere with true piety, I did not venture to suggest that his spirit had deigned to make use of my eight-bore in his interest." [66] Dr. Gray appears to have rallied his correspondent in his reply, on his notion of an omniscient and omnipotent Creator, foreseeing all future events and consequences, and yet not responsible for the results of the laws which He ordains. At all events, Mr. Darwin writes him again in July of the same year: "One word more on 'designed laws' and 'undesigned results.' I see a bird which I want for food, take my gun and kill it — I do this *designedly*. An innocent and good man stands under a tree and is killed by a flash of lightning. Do you believe (and I really should like to hear) that God *designedly* killed this man? Many or most people do believe this; I can't and don't. If you believe so, do you believe that when a swallow snaps up a gnat that God designed that that particular swallow should snap up that particular gnat at that particular instant? I believe that the man and the gnat are in the same predicament. If the death of neither man nor gnat are designed, I see no good reason to believe that their *first* birth or production should be necessarily designed." [67] We read such words with almost as much bewilderment as Mr. Darwin says he wrote them with. It is almost incredible that he should have so inextricably confused the two senses of the word "design" — so as to confound the question of intentional action with that of the evidences of contrivance, the question of the existence of a general plan in God's mind, in accordance with which all things come to pass, with that of the existence of marks of His hand in creation arising from intelligent adaptation of means to ends. It is equally incredible that he should present the case of a particular swallow snapping up a particular gnat at a particular

---

[66] Dr. Flint seriously refutes this strange reasoning, which he justly speaks of as "irrational," and only explicable in "sane minds" from the exigencies of foregone conclusions, in his "Theism," lecture vi. (ed. 3, pp. 189 f.).

[67] "Life and Letters," i. pp. 314, 315.

time as (to use his own words) "a poser," when he could scarcely have already forgotten that all Christians, at least, have long since learned to understand that the care of God extends as easily to the infinitely little as to the infinitely great; that the very hairs of our head are numbered, and not one sparrow falls to the ground unnoted by our Heavenly Father. Yet this seems to him so self-evidently unbelievable, that he rests his case against God's direction of the line of development — for this is really what he is arguing against here — on its obvious incredibility.

And he found it impossible to shake himself free from his confusion. In November of the same year he wrote again to Dr. Gray: "I grieve to say that I cannot honestly go as far as you do about Design. I am conscious that I am in an utterly hopeless muddle. I cannot think that the world, as we see it, is the result of chance; and yet I cannot look at each separate thing as the result of Design. To take a crucial example, you lead me to infer . . . that you believe 'that variation has been led along certain beneficent lines.' I cannot believe this; and I think you would have to believe, that the tail of the Fantail was led to vary in the number and direction of its feathers in order to gratify the caprice of a few men. Yet if the Fantail had been a wild bird, and had used its abnormal tail for some special end, as to sail before the wind, unlike other birds, every one would have said, 'What a beautiful and designed adaptation.' Again, I say I am, and shall ever remain, in a hopeless muddle." [68] The reader is apt to ask in wonder if we would not be right in thinking the fantail's tail a "beautiful and designed adaptation," under the circumstances supposed. Mr. Darwin actually falls here into the incredible confusion of adducing a perversion by man of the laws of nature, by which an animal is unfitted for its environment, as an argument against the designed usefulness of these laws in fitting animals to their environment. We might as well argue that Jael's nail was not designedly made because it was capable of being adapted to so fearful a use; that the styles of Cæsar's

[68] *Ibid.*, ii. pp. 353, 354.

assassins could not have been manufactured with a useful intention. Nevertheless, in June, 1861, Mr. Darwin writes again to Dr. Gray: "I have been led to think more on this subject of late, and grieve to say that I come to differ more from you. It is not that designed variation makes, as it seems to me, my deity of 'Natural Selection' superfluous, but rather from studying, lately, domestic variation, and seeing what an enormous field of undesigned variability there is ready for natural selection to appropriate for any purpose useful to each creature." [69] And a month later he writes to Miss Julia Wedgwood: "Owing to several correspondents I have been led lately to think, or rather to try to think over some of the chief points discussed by you. But the result has been with me a maze — something like thinking on the origin of evil, to which you allude. The mind refuses to look at this universe, being what it is, without having been designed; yet, where one would most expect design, viz. in the structure of a sentient being, the more I think on the subject, the less I can see proof of design. Asa Gray and some others look at each variation, or at least at each beneficial variation (which A. Gray would compare with the rain-drops [70] which do not fall on the sea, but on to the land to fertilize it) as having been providentially designed. Yet when I ask him whether he looks at each variation of the rock-pigeon, by which man has made by accumulation a pouter or fantail pigeon, as providentially designed for man's amusement, he does not know what to answer; and if he, or anyone, admits [that] these variations are accidental, as far as purpose is concerned (of course not accidental as to their cause or

[69] "Life and Letters," ii. p. 373.

[70] Mr. Francis Darwin indicates in a note that Dr. Gray's metaphor occurs in the essay "Darwin and his Reviewers" ("Darwiniana," p. 157): "The whole animate life of a country depends absolutely upon the vegetation, the vegetation upon the rain. The moisture is furnished by the ocean, is raised by the sun's heat from the ocean's surface, and is wafted inland by the winds. But what multitudes of rain-drops fall back into the ocean — are as much without a final cause as the incipient varieties which come to nothing! Does it therefore follow that the rains which are bestowed upon the soil with such rule and average regularity were not designed to support vegetable and animal life?"

origin), then I can see no reason why he should rank the accumulated variations by which the beautifully adapted woodpecker has been formed, as providentially designed. For it would be easy to imagine the large crop of the pouter, or tail of the fantail, as of some use to birds, in a state of nature, having peculiar habits of life. These are the considerations which perplex me about design; but whether you will care to hear them, I know not." [71] The most careless reader of this letter cannot fail renewedly to feel that while what was on trial before Mr. Darwin's thought was not the argument " from design " so much as general providence, yet he falls here again into the confusion of confining his view of God's possible purpose in directing any course of events to the most proximate result, as if it were the indications of design in a given organism which he was investigating. If, however, it is the existence of a general and all-comprehending plan in God's mind, for the working out of which He directs and governs all things, that we are inquiring into, the ever recurring argument from the pouter and fantail pigeons is irrelevant, proceeding as it does on the unexpressed premise that God's direction of their variations can be vindicated only if these variations can be shown to be beneficial to the pigeons themselves and that in a state of nature. It is apparently an unthought thought with Mr. Darwin that the abundance of variations capable of misdirection on man's part for his pleasure or profit, while of absolutely no use to the bird in a state of nature, and liable to abuse for the bird and for man in the artificial state of domestication, may yet be a link in a great chain which in all its links is preordained for good ends — whether morally, mentally, or even physically, whether in this world or in the next. This narrowness of view, which confined his outlook to the immediate proximate result, played so into the hands of his confusion of thought about the word " design " as from the outset fatally to handicap his progress to a reasoned conclusion.

The history of his yielding up Christianity, because, as he

[71] " Life and Letters," i. pp. 313, 314.

said, "it is not supported by evidence " [72] — that is, because its appropriate evidence, being historical, is of a kind which lay outside of his knowledge or powers of estimation — was therefore paralleled by his gradual yielding up of his reasoned belief in God, because all the evidences of His activities are not capable of being looked at in the process of a dissection under the simple microscope. We have seen him at last reaching a position in which no evidence which he could even imagine would suffice to prove the historical truth of Christianity to him. He was fast drifting into a similar position about design. He writes to Dr. Gray, apparently in September, 1861: "Your question what would convince me of Design is a poser. If I saw an angel come down to teach us good, and I was convinced from others seeing him that I was not mad, I should believe in design. If I could be convinced thoroughly that life and mind was in an unknown way a function of other imponderable force, I should be convinced. If man was made of brass or iron and no way connected with any other organism which had ever lived, I should perhaps be convinced. But this is childish writing." [73] And so indeed it is, and in a sense in which Mr. Darwin scarcely intended. But such words teach us very clearly where the real difficulty lay in his own mind. Life and mind with him were functions of matter; and he could not see that any other concause in bringing new births into the world, could be witnessed to by the nature of the results, than the natural forces employed in the natural process of reproduction. He believed firmly that indiscriminate variation, reacted upon through natural laws by the struggle for existence, was the sufficient account of every discrimination in organic nature — was the *vera causa* of all forms which life took; and believing this, he could see no need of God's additional activity to produce the very same effects, and could allow no evidence of its working. "I have lately," he continues in the letter to Dr. Gray just quoted, " been corresponding with Lyell, who, I think, adopts your idea of the stream of variation having

[72] *National Reformer,* October 29th, 1882.
[73] " Life and Letters," ii. p. 377.

been led or designed. I have asked him (and he says he will hereafter reflect and answer me) whether he believes that the shape of my nose was designed. If he does I have nothing more to say. If not, seeing what Fanciers have done by selecting individual differences in the nasal bones of pigeons, I must think that it is illogical to suppose that the variations, which natural selection preserves for the good of any being, have been designed. But I know that I am in the same sort of muddle (as I have said before) as all the world seems to be in with respect to free will, yet with everything supposed to have been foreseen or pre-ordained." [74] And again, a few months later, still laboring under the same confusion, he writes to the same correspondent: " If anything is designed, certainly man must be: one's 'inner consciousness' (though a false guide) tells one so; yet I cannot admit that men's rudimentary mammæ . . . were designed. If I was to say I believed this, I should believe it in the same incredible manner as the ortho-dox believe the Trinity in Unity. You say that you are in a haze; I am in thick mud; . . . yet I cannot keep out of the question." [75] One wonders whether Mr. Darwin, in examining a door-knocker carved in the shape of a face, would say that he believed the handle was " designed," but could not admit that the carved face was " designed." Nevertheless, an incised outline on a bit of old bone, though without obvious use, or a careless chip on the edge of a flint, though without possible use, would at once be judged by him to be " designed " — that is, to be evidence, if not of obvious contrivance, yet cer-tainly of intentional activity. Why he could not make a similar distinction in natural products remains a standing matter of surprise.

The years ran on, however, and his eyes were still holden; he never advanced beyond even the illustrations he had grasped at from the first to support his position. In 1867 his " Variation of Animals and Plants under Domestication " appeared, and on February 8th of that year he wrote to Sir Joseph Hooker: " I finish my book . . . by a single para-

[74] *Ibid.*, ii. p. 378.   [75] *Ibid.*, ii. p. 382.

graph, answering, or rather throwing doubt, in so far as so little space permits, on Asa Gray's doctrine that each variation has been specially ordered or led along a beneficial line. It is foolish to touch such subjects, but there have been so many allusions to what I think about the part which God has played in the formation of organic beings, that I thought it shabby to evade the question." [76] In writing his Autobiography in 1876, he looks back upon this "argument" with pride, as one which " has never, as far as I can see, been answered." [77] It has a claim, therefore, to be considered something like a classic in the present discussion, and although it does not advance one step either in force or form beyond the earlier letters to Dr. Gray and Sir Lyell, we feel constrained to transcribe it here in full: " An Omniscient Creator," it runs, " must have foreseen every consequence which results from the laws imposed by Him. But can it be reasonably maintained that the Creator intentionally ordered, if we use the words in the ordinary sense, that certain fragments of rock should assume certain shapes so that the builder might erect his edifice? If the various laws which have determined the shape of each fragment were not predetermined for the builder's sake, can it with any greater probability be maintained that He specially ordained for the sake of the breeder each of the innumerable variations in our domestic animals and plants; — many of these variations being of no service to man, and not beneficial, far more often injurious, to the creatures themselves? Did He ordain that the crop and tail-feathers of the pigeon should vary in order that the fancier might make his grotesque pouter and fantail breeds? Did He cause the frame and mental qualities of the dog to vary in order that a breed might be formed of indomitable ferocity, with jaws fitted to pin down the bull for man's brutal sport? But if we give up the principle in one case — if we do not admit that the variations of the primeval dog were intentionally guided in order that the greyhound, for instance, that perfect image of symmetry and vigor, might be formed — no shadow of reason can be assigned for the

[76] " Life and Letters," iii. p. 62.   [77] Ibid., i. p. 309.

belief that variations, alike in nature and the result of the same general laws, which have been the groundwork through natural selection of the formation of the most perfectly adapted animals in the world, man included, were intentionally and specially guided. However much we may wish it, we can hardly follow Professor Asa Gray in his belief ' that variation has been led along certain beneficial lines,' like a stream ' along definite and useful lines of irrigation.' If we assume that each particular variation was from the beginning of all time pre-ordained, the plasticity of organization, which leads to many injurious deviations of structure, as well as that redundant power of reproduction which inevitably leads to a struggle for existence, and, as a consequence, to the natural selection or survival of the fittest, must appear to us superfluous laws of nature. On the other hand, an omnipotent and omniscient Creator ordains everything and foresees everything. Thus we are brought face to face with a difficulty as insoluble as is that of free will and predestination." [78] We read with an amazement which is akin to amusement the string of queries with which Mr. Darwin here plies his readers, as if no answer were possible to conception but the one which would drive " the omnipotent and omniscient Creator " into impotency and ignorance, if not into non-existence. An argument which has never been answered! Why should it be answered? Is it not competent to any man to string like questions together *ad infinitum* with an air of victory? " Did the omnipotent and omniscient Creator intentionally order that beetles should vary to so extreme an extent in form and coloration solely in order that Mr. Darwin might in his enthusiastic youth arrange them artistically in his cabinet? Did he cause the blackthorn to grow of such strong and close fiber in order that Pat might cut his shillalah from it and break his neighbor's head? Did Mr. Darwin himself write and print these words in order that his fellows might wonder why and how he was in such a muddle? " But there is really no end to it, unless we are ready to confess that an ob-

---

[78] "Variation of Animals and Plants under Domestication," authorized edition, ii. 1868, pp. 515 f.

ject may be put to a use which was not " the end of its being ";
that there may be intentions possible beyond the obvious
proximate one; and that there is a distinction between an
intentional action and a contrivance. The fallacy of Mr. Darwin's reasoning here ought not to have been hidden from him,
as he tells us repeatedly that he early learned the danger of
reasoning by exclusion; and yet that is exactly the process
employed here.

Dr. Gray did not delay long to point out some of the confusion under which his friend was laboring.[79] And Mr. Wallace
shortly afterward showed that there was no more difficulty in
tracing the divine hand in natural production, through the
agency of natural selection, than there is in tracing the hand
of man in the formation of the races of domesticated animals,
through artificial selection. In neither case does there confront
the outward eye other than a series of forms produced by
natural law; and in the one case as little as the other is the
selecting concause of the outside agent excluded by the unbroken traceableness of the process of descent.[80] But Mr. Darwin was immovable. One of the odd circumstances of the case
was that he still felt able to express pleasure in being spoken
of as one whose great service to natural science lay " in bringing back to it Teleology." [81] Yet this did not mean that he
himself believed in teleology; and in his Autobiography written in 1876 he sets aside the whole teleological argument as
invalid.[82]

[79] With reference to the first simile of the extract Dr. Gray pointedly
urged: " But in Mr. Darwin's parallel, to meet the case of nature according
to his own view of it, not only the fragments of rock (answering to variation)
should fall, but the edifice (answering to natural selection) should rise,
irrespective of will or choice! " Mr. Darwin (" Life and Letters," iii. p. 84)
calls this " a good slap," but thinks it does not essentially meet the point.
Mr. F. Darwin (*loc. cit.*) answers it lamely by observing that according to
his father's parallel natural selection should be the *architect,* not the *edifice.*
Do architects get along without " will or choice "?

[80] " Life and Letters," iii. p. 116.

[81] *Ibid.,* iii. p. 189: " What you say about Teleology pleases me especially,
and I do not think that any one else has ever noticed the part." This was
written June 5th, 1874. See iii. p. 255, and ii. p. 201.

[82] *Ibid.,* i. pp. 309, 310.

Nor was the setting aside of teleology merely the discrediting of one theistic proof in order to clear the way for others. The strong acid of Mr. Darwin's theory of the origin of man ate into the very heart of the other proofs as surely, though not by the same channel, as it had eaten into the fabric of the argument from design. We have already seen him speaking of the demand of the mind for a sufficient cause for the universe and its contents as possessing great weight with him; and he realized the argumentative value of the human conviction, arising from the feelings of dependence and responsibility, that there is One above us on whom we depend and to whom we are responsible. But both these arguments were, in his judgment, directly affected by his view of the origin of man's mental and moral nature, as a development, by means of the interworking of natural laws alone, from the germ of intelligence found in brutes. We have seen how uncompromisingly he denied to Lyell the need or propriety of postulating any additional powers or any directing energy for the production of man's mental and moral nature. In the same spirit he writes complainingly to Mr. Wallace in 1869: " I can see no necessity for calling in an additional and proximate cause in regard to man." [83] This being so, he felt that he could scarcely trust man's intuitions or convictions. And thus he was able at the end of his life (1881) to acknowledge his " inward conviction . . . that the Universe is not the result of chance," and at once to add: " But then with me the horrid doubt always arises whether the convictions of man's mind, which has been developed from the mind of the lower animals, are of any value or at all trustworthy. Would anyone trust in the convictions of a monkey's mind, if there are any convictions in such a mind? " [84] It is illustrative of Mr. Darwin's strange confusion of thought on metaphysical subjects that he does not appear to perceive that this doubt, if valid at all, ought to affect not only the religious convictions of men, but all their convictions; and that it, therefore, undermines the very theory of man's origin, because of which it arises within him. There is

[83] *Ibid.*, iii. p. 116.   [84] *Ibid.*, i. p. **316.**

not a whit more reason to believe that the processes of physical research and the logical laws by means of which inferences are drawn and inductions attained are trustworthy, than that these higher convictions, based on the same mental laws, are trustworthy; and the origin of man's mind from a brutish source, if fatal to trust in one mental process, is fatal to trust in all the others, throwing us, as the result of such a plea, into sheer intellectual suicide.

In discussing these human convictions Mr. Darwin draws a sharp distinction between those which appeared to him to rest on feeling and that which springs from the instinctive causal judgment and demands a sufficient cause for the universe, and which, as he judged it to be " connected with reason and not with the feelings," " impressed him as having much more weight." To the argument from our Godward emotions he allows but little value, although he looks back with regret upon the time when the grandeur of a Brazilian forest stirred his heart with feelings not only of wonder and admiration but also of devotion, and filled and elevated his mind.[85] He sadly confesses that the grandest scenes would no longer awaken such convictions and feelings within him, and acknowledges that he is become like a man who is color-blind and whose failure to see is of no value as evidence against the universal belief of men. But he makes this remark only immediately to endeavor to rob it of its force. He urges that all men of all races do not have this inward conviction " of the existence of one God ";[86] and then attempts to confound the conviction which accompanies the emotions which he has described, or more properly which quickens them, and to the reality and abidingness of which they are undying witnesses, with the

[85] This paragraph is a report of what Mr. Darwin says, writing in his Autobiography in 1876: see "Life and Letters," i. pp. 311, 312.

[86] Mr. Darwin writes more guardedly here than in his "Descent of Man," i. 1871, p. 63, where he declares, chiefly on Sir John Lubbock's authority, that there are " numerous races " who have no idea of " one or more gods, and who have no words in their languages to express such an idea." Professor Flint, in his "Antitheistic Theories," lecture vii., with its appropriate appendixes, has sifted this question of fact, with the result of showing the virtual universality of religion.

emotions themselves, as if all "the moving experiences of the soul in the presence of the sublimer aspects of nature" were resolvable "into moods of feelings." [87] He does more; he attempts to resolve all such moods of feeling essentially into the one "sense of sublimity"; and then assumes that this sense must be itself resolvable into still simpler constituents, by which it may be proved to be a composite of bestial elements, and to witness to nothing beyond our brutish origin. [88] "The state of mind," he writes, "which grand scenes formerly excited in me, and which was intimately connected with a belief in God, did not essentially differ from that which is often called the sense of sublimity; and however difficult it may be to explain the genesis of this sense, it can hardly be advanced as an argument for the existence of God, any more than the powerful though vague and similar feelings excited by music." [89] Here is reasoning! Is it then a fair conclusion that because the "sense of sublimity" no more than other similar feelings is itself a proof of divine existence, therefore the firm conviction of the existence of God, which is "intimately connected with" a feeling similar to sublimity, is also without evidential value? It is as if one should reason that because the sense of resentment which is intimately connected with the slap that I feel tingling upon my cheek does not essentially

[87] See this criticism properly pressed by Dr. Noah Porter, in *New Englander and Yale Review,* for March, 1888, p. 207.

[88] The elements which in his view unite to form a religious emotion are enumerated for us in the "Descent of Man," i. p. 65: "The feeling of religious devotion is a highly complex one, consisting of love, complete submission to an exalted and mysterious superior, a strong sense of dependence, fear, reverence, gratitude, hope for the future, and perhaps other elements." How, in these circumstances, he can speak of his state of mind, involving "feelings of wonder, admiration, and devotion" ("Life and Letters," i. p. 311), as one which "did not essentially differ from that which is often called the sense of sublimity," is somewhat mysterious. But we must remember that even this complex of emotions was, in Mr. Darwin's view, distantly approached by certain mental states of dogs and monkeys. Nevertheless, the whole drift of the passage in the "Descent of Man" is to credit the results of man's reasoning faculties as he progressed more and more in the power to use them; while the drift of the present passage is to discredit them.

[89] "Life and Letters," i. p. 312.

differ from that which is often called the sense of indignation, which does not any more than other like feelings always imply the existence of human objects, therefore the tingling slap is no evidence that a man to give it really exists! How strong a hold this odd illusion of reasoning had upon Mr. Darwin's mind is illustrated by an almost contemporary letter to Mr. E. Gurney, discussing the origin of capacity for enjoyment of music, which he closes with the following words: "Your simile of architecture seems to me particularly good; for in this case the appreciation almost must be individual, though possibly the sense of sublimity excited by a grand cathedral may have some connection with the vague feelings of terror and superstition in our savage ancestors, when they entered a great cavern or gloomy forest. I wish," he adds, semi-pathetically, "some one could analyse the feeling of sublimity." [90] He seems to think that to analyze this feeling would be tantamount to letting our conviction of God's existence escape in a vapor.

He ascribed much more weight to the conviction of the existence of God, which arises from our causal judgment, and it was chiefly under pressure of this instinct of the human mind, by which we are forced to assign a competent cause for all becoming, that he was continually being compelled "to look to a First Cause having an intelligent mind in some degree analogous to that of man," and so "to deserve to be called a Theist." But as often "the horrid doubt . . . arises whether the convictions of man's mind," any more than those of a monkey's mind from something similar to which it has been developed, "are of any value or at all trustworthy." [91] The growth of such doubts in his mind is not traceable in full detail; but some record of it is left in the letters that have been preserved for us. For example, in 1860 he wrote to Dr. Gray: "I cannot anyhow be contented to view this wonderful universe, and especially the nature of man, and to conclude that everything is the result of brute force." [92] Again, "I

---

[90] "Life and Letters," iii. p. 186, written July 8th, 1876.
[91] *Ibid.*, i. p. 316: written in 1881.   [92] *Ibid.*, ii. p. 312.

cannot think that the world, as we see it, is the result of chance." [93] Again, in 1861, he writes to Miss Wedgwood: "The mind refuses to look at this universe, being what it is, without having been designed." [94] At this time he deserved to be called a theist. In 1873 he writes, in reply to a query by a Dutch student: " I may say that the impossibility of conceiving that this grand and wondrous universe, with our conscious selves, arose through chance, seems to me the chief argument for the existence of a God "; but immediately adds: " But whether this is an argument of real value, I have never been able to decide." [95] And in 1876, after speaking of " the extreme difficulty or rather impossibility of conceiving this immense and wonderful universe, including man with his capacity of looking far backwards and far into futurity, as the result of blind chance or necessity," he immediately adds: " But then arises the doubt, can the mind of man, which has, as I fully believe, been developed from a mind as low as that possessed by the lowest animals, be trusted when it draws such grand conclusions? " [96] Nearly the same words, as we have seen, were repeated in 1881.[97] And he appears to have had this branch of the subject in his mind rather than teleology, when, in 1882, he shook his head vaguely when the Duke of Argyll urged that it was impossible to look upon the contrivances of nature without seeing that they were the effect and expression of mind; and looking hard at him, said: " Well, that often comes over me with overwhelming force; but at other times it seems to go away." [98]

What, then, became of his instinctive causal judgment amid these crowding doubts? It was scarcely eradicated. He could write to Mr. Graham as late as 1881: " You have expressed my inward conviction . . . that the Universe is not the result of chance." [99] But " inward conviction " with Mr. Darwin did not mean " reasoned opinion " which is to be held and de-

[93] *Ibid.,* ii. p. 353.
[94] *Ibid.,* i. pp. 313 f.
[95] *Ibid.,* i. p. 306.
[96] *Ibid.,* i. pp. 312 f.

[97] *Ibid.,* i. p. 316.
[98] *Ibid.,* i. p. 316.
[99] *Ibid.,* i. p. 316.

fended, but "natural and instinctive feeling" which is to be corrected. And he certainly allowed his causal judgment gradu ally to fall more and more into abeyance. In his letter to the Dutch student, in 1873, he knew how to add to his avowal that he felt the impossibility of conceiving of this grand universe as causeless, the further avowal, "I am aware that if we admit a first cause, the mind still craves to know whence it came, and how it arose," [100] and thus to do what he could to throw doubt on the theistic inference. And he also knew how to speak as if the agnostic inference were reasonable and philosophical, everywhere maintaining his right to assume living forms to begin with, as a philosopher assumes gravitation,[101] by which, as he is careful to explain, he does not mean that these forms (or this form) have been "created" in the usual sense of that word, but "only that we know nothing as yet [of] how life originates"; [102] and writing as late as 1878: " As to the eternity of matter, I have never troubled myself about such insoluble questions." [103] Nevertheless, it is perfectly certain that neither Mr. Darwin nor anyone else can reject both creation and non-creation, both a first cause and the eternity of matter. As Professor Flint truly points out, "we may believe either in a self-existent God or in a self-existent world, and must believe in one or the other; we cannot believe in an infinite regress of causes." [104] When Mr. Darwin threw doubt on the philosophical consistency of the assumption of a first cause, he was bound to investigate the hypothesis of the eternity of matter; and until this latter task was completed he was bound to keep silence on a subject on which he had so little

[100] "Life and Letters," i. pp. 306, 307.

[101] E.g. ii. p. 210.

[102] *Ibid.*, ii. p. 251.

[103] *Ibid.*, iii. p. 236.

[104] "Theism," ed. 3, p. 120. See also note xxii. p. 390: "Creation is the *only* theory of the *origin* of the universe. Evolution assumes either the creation or the self-existence of the universe. The evolutionist must choose between creation and non-creation. They are opposites. There is no intermediate term. The attempt to introduce one — the Unknowable — can lead to no result; for unless the Unknowable is capable of creating, it can account for the origin of nothing." The whole note should be read.

right to speak. Where his predilection would carry him is
plain from the pleasure with which he read of Dr. Bastian's
Archebiosis in 1872, wishing that he could "live to see" it
"proved true." [105] We are regretfully forced to recognize in
his whole course of argument a desire to eliminate the proofs
of God's activity in the world; "he did not like to retain God
in his knowledge."

Further evidence of this trend may be observed in the tone
of the addition to the autobiographical notes which he made,
with especial reference to his religious beliefs, in 1876, and in
which he, somewhat strangely, included a full antitheistic
argument, developed in so orderly a manner that it may stand
for us as a complete exhibit of his attitude toward the problem of divine existence. In this remarkable document [106] he
first discusses the argument from design, concluding that the
"old argument from design in Nature, as given by Paley,
which formerly seemed to me so conclusive," fails "now that
the law of natural selection has been discovered." He adds
that "there seems to be no more design in the variability of
organic beings, and in the action of natural selection, than in
the course which the wind blows," and refers the reader to the
"argument" given at the end of "Variation of Animals and
Plants under Domestication," as one which has never been
answered. Having set this more detailed teleology aside, he
next examines the broader form of the argument from design,
which rests on the general beneficent arrangement of the world,
and concludes that the great fact of suffering is opposed to the
theistic inference, while the prevailing happiness, in conjunction with "the presence of much suffering, agrees well with
the view that all organic beings have been developed through
variation and natural selection." Next he discusses the "most
usual argument" of the present day "for the existence of an
intelligent God," that "drawn from the deep inward conviction and feelings which are experienced by most persons." He
speaks sadly of his own former firm conviction of the existence
of God, and describes how feelings of devotion welled up

[105] "Life and Letters," iii. p. 169. [106] *Ibid.*, i. pp. 307–313.

within him in the presence of grand scenery; but he sets the
argument summarily aside as invalid. Finally, he adduces the
demands of the causal judgment, in a passage which has already been quoted, but discards it, too, with an expression of
doubt as to the trustworthiness of such grand conclusions when
drawn by a brute-bred mind like man's. His conclusion is formulated helplessness: "The mystery of the beginning of all
things is insoluble by us; and I for one must be content to remain an Agnostic." It was out of such a reasoned position that
he wrote in 1879: "In my most extreme fluctuations I have
never been an Atheist in the sense of denying the existence of
God. I think that generally (and more and more as I grow
older), but not always, that an Agnostic would be the more
correct description of my state of mind." [107] Nor can we help
carrying over the light thus gained to aid us in explaining the
words written to Jena the same year: Mr. Darwin "considers
that the theory of Evolution is quite compatible with the belief
in a God; but that you must remember that different persons
have different definitions of what they mean by God." [108] It
would be an interesting question what conception Mr. Darwin,
who began with a deistic conception, had come to when he
reached the agnostic stage and spoke familiarly of "what is
called a personal God." [109]

By such stages as these did this great man drift from his
early trust into an inextinguishable doubt whether such a
mind as man's can be trusted in its grand conclusions; and by
such reasoning as this did he support his suicidal results. No
more painful spectacle can be found in all biographical literature; no more startling discovery of the process by which
even great and good men can come gradually to a state of
mind in which, despite their more noble instincts, they can but

> Judge all nature from her feet of clay,
> Without the will to lift their eyes to see
> Her Godlike head, crowned with spiritual fire,
> And touching other worlds.

[107] "Life and Letters," i. p. 304. [109] *Ibid.*, iii. p. 236 (1878).
[108] *Ibid.*, i. p. 307.

The process that we have been observing, as has [110] been truly said, is not that of an *ejectment* of reverence and faith from the system (as, say, in the case of Mr. Froude), or of an *encysting* of them (as, say, with Mr. J. S. Mill), but simply of an *atrophy* of them, as they dissolve painlessly away. In Mr. Darwin's case this atrophy was accompanied by a similar deadening of his higher emotional nature, by which he lost his power of enjoying poetry, music, and to a large extent scenery, and stood like some great tree of the forest with broadreaching boughs, beneath which men may rest and refresh themselves, but with decay already marking it as its own, as evidenced by the deadness of its upper branches. He was a man dead at the top.

It is more difficult to trace the course of his personal religious life during this long-continued atrophying of his religious conceptions. He was not permitted to enter upon this development without a word of faithful admonition. When the " Origin of Species " was published in 1859, his old friend and preceptor, Professor A. Sedgwick, appears to have foreseen the possible driftage of his thought, and wrote him the following touching words: " I have been lecturing three days a week (formerly I gave six a week) without much fatigue, but I find by the loss of activity and memory, and of all productive powers, that my bodily frame is sinking slowly towards the earth. But I have visions of the future. They are as much a part of myself as my stomach and my heart, and these visions are to have their antitype in solid fruition of what is best and greatest. But on one condition only — that I humbly accept God's revelation of Himself both in His works and in His word, and do my best to act in conformity with that knowledge which He only can give me, and He only can sustain me in doing. If you and I do all this, we shall meet in heaven." [111] The appeal had come too late to aid his old pupil to conserve his Christian faith; it was already long since he had believed that God had ever spoken in word and he was

---

[110] F. W. H. Myers, in the *Fortnightly Review,* January, 1888, p. 103.
[111] " Life and Letters," ii. p. 250.

fast drifting to a position from which he could with difficulty believe that He had spoken in His works. It is not a pleasant letter that he wrote to Mrs. Boole in 1866, in reply to some very respectfully framed inquiries as to the relation of his theory to the possibility of belief in inspiration and a personal and good God who exercises moral influence on man, to which he is free to yield. The way in which he avoids replying to these questions almost seems to be irritable,[112] and is possibly an index to his feelings toward the matters involved. Nevertheless, his sympathy with suffering and his willingness to lend his help toward the elevation of his fellow men remained; he even aided the work of Christian missions by contributions in money,[113] although he no longer shared the hopes by which those were nerved who carried the civilizing message to their degraded fellow beings. Why, indeed, he should have trusted the noble impulses of his conscience, and been willing to act upon them, when he judged that the brutish origin of man's whole mental nature vitiated all its grand conclusions, it might puzzle a better metaphysician than he laid claim to be satisfactorily to explain; but his higher life seems to have taken this direction, and it is characteristic of him to close the letter to the Dutch student, written in 1873, with such words as these: " The safest conclusion seems to be that the whole subject is beyond the scope of man's intellect; but man can do his duty." [114] But when there is no one to show us any truth, who is there to show us duty? If our conscience is but the chance growth of the brute mind, hemmed in by its environment and squeezed into a new form by the pressure of a fierce and unmoral struggle for existence, what moral imperative has it such as deserves the high name of " duty "? [115] Certainly

---

[112] " Life and Letters," iii. pp. 63, 64.

[113] *Ibid.*, iii. pp. 127, 128.

[114] *Ibid.*, i. p. 307.

[115] What Mr. Darwin actually taught as to the moral sense may be conveniently read in the third chapter of the " Descent of Man." " This sense," he says, " as Mackintosh remarks, ' has a rightful supremacy over every other principle of human action; ' it is summed up in that short but imperious word *ought,* so full of high significance " (i. 1871, p. 67). But what gives this " im-

the argument is as valid here as there. But by the power of so divine an inconsistency, Mr. Darwin was enabled as citizen, friend, husband, and father to do his duty. He had no sharp sense of sin; [116] but so far as duty lay before him he retained a tender conscience. And thus, as he approached the end of his long and laborious life, he felt able to say: " I feel no remorse from having committed any great sin, but have often and often regretted that I have not done more direct good to my fellow creatures "; [117] and again, as the end came on, we learn that " he seemed to recognize the approach of death, and said, ' I am not the least afraid to die.' " [118] And thus he went out into the dark without God in all his thoughts; with no hope for immortality; and with no keenness of regret for all the high and noble aspirations and all the elevating imaginings which he had lost out of life.

---

perious word *ought*" so rightful a supremacy? Mr. Darwin teaches that "the moral sense is fundamentally identical with the social instincts" (pp. 93 f.), and that "the imperious word *ought* seems merely to employ the consciousness of the existence of a persistent instinct, either innate or partly acquired," so that "we hardly use the word *ought* in a metaphorical sense when we say hounds ought to hunt, pointers to point, and retrievers to retrieve their game" (p. 88). He has, indeed, "endeavored to show that the social instincts — the prime principle of man's moral constitution — with the aid of active intellectual powers and the effects of habit, naturally lead to the golden rule, ' As ye would that men should do to you, do ye to them likewise; ' and this lies at the foundation of morality" (pp. 101, 102). But this is not because the golden rule is any more truly "moral" than any other rule. "Any animal whatever, endowed with well-marked social instincts, would inevitably acquire a moral sense or conscience, as soon as its intellectual powers had become as well developed, or nearly as well developed, as in man" (pp. 68, 69); but not necessarily "exactly the same moral sense as ours" (p. 70). For instance, bees so developing a moral sense would develop one which required it as a duty to murder their brothers and fertile daughters. Thus the moral law has no more sanction than arises from its being the best mode of conserving the common good, as it is known in present conditions; and its very opposite might be as moral and as imperious under changed conditions. Mr. Darwin's own tender conscience was thus, in his own eyes, nothing more than the dissatisfaction that arose from an unsatisfied inherited instinct (p. 69)!

[116] How inevitable this was may be seen from the temperate discussion of the relation of naturalistic evolution to the sense of sin, in John Tulloch's " The Christian Doctrine of Sin," lecture i.

[117] "Life and Letters," iii. p. 359 (1879).

[118] *Ibid.*, iii. p. 358.

That we may appreciate how sad a sight we have before us, let us look back from the end to the beginning. We stand at the deathbed of a man whom, in common with all the world, we most deeply honor. He has made himself a name which will live through many generations; and withal has made himself beloved by all who came into close contact with him. True, tender-hearted, and sympathetic, he has in the retirement of invalidism lived a life which has moved the world. But is his death just the death we should expect from one who had once given himself to be an ambassador of the Lord? When we turn from what he has done to what he has become, can we say that, in the very quintessence of living, he has fulfilled the promise of that long-ago ingenuous youth who suffered some- thing like remorse when he beat a puppy, and as he ran to school "prayed earnestly to God to help him"? Let us look upon him in the light of a contrast. There was another Charles, living in the world with him, but a few years his senior, whose childhood, too, was blessed with a vivid sense of the nearness of heaven. He, too, has left us some equally simple-hearted and touching autobiographical notes; and from them we learn that his, too, was a praying childhood. "As far back as I can remember," he writes, " I had the habit of thanking God for everything I received, and asking Him for everything I wanted. If I lost a book, or any of my playthings, I prayed that I might find it. I prayed walking along the streets, in school and out of school, whether playing or studying. I did not do this in obedience to any prescribed rule. It seemed natural. I thought of God as an everywhere-present Being, full of kindness and love, who would not be offended if children talked to Him. I knew He cared for sparrows." [119] Thus Charles Hodge and Charles Darwin began their lives on a somewhat similar plane. And both write in their old age of their child- hood's prayers with something like a smile. But how different the quality of these smiles! Charles Darwin's smile is almost a sneer: " When in doubt," he writes, " I prayed earnestly to God to help me, and I well remember that I attributed my

[119] "The Life of Charles Hodge," by his son, A. A. Hodge, 1880, p. 13.

success to the prayers and not to my quick running, and marvelled how generally I was aided." [120] Charles Hodge's smile is the pleasant smile of one who looks back on small beginnings from a well-won height. "There was little more in my prayers and praises," he writes, "than in the worship rendered by the fowls of the air. This mild form of natural religion did not amount to much." [121] His praying childhood was Charles Darwin's highest religious attainment; his praying childhood was to Charles Hodge but the inconsiderable seed out of which were marvelously to unfold all the graces of a truly devout life. Starting from a common center, these two great men, with much of natural endowment in common, trod opposite paths; and when the shades of death gathered around them, one could but face the depths of darkness in his greatness of soul without fear, and yield like a man to the inevitable lot of all; the other, bathed in a light not of the earth, rose in spirit upon his dead self to higher things, repeating to his loved ones about him the comforting words of a sublime hope: "Why should you grieve? To be absent from the body is to be with the Lord, to be with the Lord is to see the Lord, to see the Lord is to be like Him." [122] The one conceived that he had reached the end of life, and looked back upon the little space that had been allotted to him without remorse, indeed, but not without a sense of its incompleteness; the other contemplated all that he had been enabled to do through the many years of rich fruitage which had fallen to him, as but childhood's preparation for the true life which in death was but dawning upon him.[123]

[120] "Life and Letters," i. p. 31.

[121] "Life," p. 13.

[122] "Life," p. 582.

[123] Since this paper was put into type a new letter of Mr. Darwin's on his religious views has come to light, which adds, indeed, nothing to what we already knew, but which is so characteristic as to deserve insertion here. It is dated March 11th, 1878, and runs as follows: "Dear Sir: I should have been very glad to have aided you in any degree if it had been in my power. But to answer your question would require an essay, and for this I have not strength, being much out of health. Nor, indeed, could I have answered it distinctly and satisfactorily with any amount of strength. The strongest argu-

ment for the existence of God, as it seems to me, is the instinct or intuition which we all (as I suppose) feel that there must have been an intelligent beginner of the Universe; but then comes the doubt and difficulty whether such intuitions are trustworthy. I have touched on one point of difficulty in the two last pages of my 'Variation of Animals and Plants under Domestication,' but I am forced to leave the problem insoluble. No man who does his duty has anything to fear, and may hope for whatever he earnestly desires. — Dear Sir, yours faithfully, Ch. Darwin." (See *The British Weekly* for August 3d, 1888.)

XX

THE LATEST PHASE OF
HISTORICAL RATIONALISM

THE LATEST PHASE OF HISTORICAL RATIONALISM [1]

FIRST ARTICLE

I. "DOGMA," AND "EXTERNAL AUTHORITY"

MR. G. A. SIMCOX, reviewing Dr. Liddon's recently published "Life of Pusey," tells us that Dr. Pusey "developed into a great tactician, who kept an academical majority together in face of all manner of discouragement from outside." [2] Nothing is more remarkable, indeed, than the prosperity of Dr. Pusey's leadership, and the success with which he impressed his peculiar modes of thinking upon a whole church. The secret of it is not to be found, however, in any "tact" which he may be supposed to have exercised — as we might be led to suspect by the mere sound of the word "tactician." Dr. Pusey had as great a capacity for blundering as any man who ever lived; and one wonders how his cause could survive his repeated and gross errors of judgment. "What strikes us rather," says Mr. Simcox truly, "is how many false moves he made, and how little harm they did him." The secret of it is found in his intensity, steadfastness, and single-hearted devotion to what he believed to be divine truth. The mere "tactician" has always ultimately failed, since the world began. The blunderer who lays himself a willing sacrifice upon the altar of what he believes to be the truth of God has never wholly failed. This is true even when truth has been misconceived. The power of truth is the greatest power on earth. Next to it, however, is the power of sincere, earnest, and steadfast conviction.

[1] Reprinted from *The Presbyterian Quarterly,* ix. 1895, pp. 36–67 and 185–210. The sections marked I., III., IV., V., VI., appeared earlier in *The Presbyterian Journal,* of Philadelphia; the section marked II., in *The Presbyterian Messenger,* of Pittsburgh; and the section marked VII., in *The Sunday-School World,* of Philadelphia. The section marked VII. has been copyrighted by the American Sunday-School Union, and can be had at their house at 1122 Chestnut street, Philadelphia, in tract form.

[2] *The Academy* for October 28, 1893 (xliv. p. 368).

Dr. Pusey himself lays open to us the secret of his power, in a letter written to Dr. Hook in the period of the deepest depression of the fortunes of " the party." " I am quite sure," he says, " that nothing can resist infidelity except the most entire system of faith; one said mournfully, ' I could have had *faith;* I cannot have *opinions.*' One must have a strong, positive, objective system which people are to believe, because it is true, on authority out of themselves. Be that authority what it may, the Scriptures through the individual teaching of the Spirit, the Primitive Church, the Church when it was visibly one, the present Church, it must be a strong authority out of one's self." [3] Here is the most successful leader of modern times telling us the principles that gave force to his leadership. What do they prove to be? Two: the steadfast, consistent proclamation of an " entire system of faith," strong, positive, objective, which people are required to believe on the simple ground that it is true; and the foundation of this system upon an external authority, an " authority out of one's self." All experience bears Dr. Pusey out. The only propagandism that has ever won a lasting hold upon men has been the bold proclamation of positive, dogmatic truth, based on external, divine authority; and the only power that can resist the infidelity of our day is the power of consistently concatenated dogmatic truth, proclaimed on the authority of a fully trusted, " Thus saith the Lord."

The value of positive truth proclaimed on the basis of divine authority, is not to be measured, of course, simply by its usefulness in propagating Christianity. It has an individual importance which is far greater. Without it Christianity would not be able to acquire or maintain empire over the soul. Adolphe Monod points out, for example, how dependent we are for all adequate conceptions of sin upon the dogmatic teachings of " external authority." " Our own personal meditations," he tells us,[4] " will never reveal to us what sin is; and here I particularly feel the necessity and the reality of the

---

[3] H. P. Liddon, " Life of Edward Bouverie Pusey," ii. 1893, p. 489.
[4] " Farewell to his Friends and to the Church," 1858, p. 56.

inspiration and Divine authority of the Scriptures, because we should never have learned to know what sin is, unless we learned it from obedience to an outward authority superior to us, independent of our secret feelings, upon which we ought certainly to meditate with study and fervent prayers. But enlightened truth comes from above, is given by the Spirit of God, speaking with the authority of God himself; for we must begin by believing the horror that sin ought to inspire, before we are capable of feeling it." And he points out equally how dependent we are for a proper basis for faith on the same " external authority." " The more I study the Scriptures," he says,[5] " the example of Jesus Christ, and of the Apostles, and the history of my own heart, the more I am convinced that a testimony of God, placed without us and above us, exempt from all intermixture of the sin and error which belong to a fallen race, and received with submission on the sole authority of God, is the true basis of faith." " If faith," he says,[6] " has not for its basis a testimony of God to which we must submit, as to an authority exterior to our own personal judgment, superior to it, and independent of it, then faith is no faith." That this witness is true, the heart of every Christian may be trusted to bear witness. But for the moment we may fix our attention on the more external fact already adverted to, that the only basis of an appeal to men which can at all hope to be prevalent is positive truth commended on the credit of " external authority."

What is ominous in the present-day drift of religious thought is the sustained effort that is being made to break down just these two principles: the principle of a systematized body of doctrines as the matter to be believed, and the principle of an external authority as the basis of belief. What arrogates to itself the title of " the newer religious thinking " sets itself, before everything else, in violent opposition to what it calls " dogma " and " external authority." The end may be

[5] " Life and Letters of Adolphe Monod," by one of his daughters, E.T. London, 1885, pp. 357–358.

[6] *Ibid.*, p. 224.

very readily foreseen. Indefinite subjectivism or subjective indifferentism has no future. It is not only in its very nature a disintegrating, but also a destructive, force. It can throw up no barrier against unbelief. Its very business is to break down barriers. And when that work is accomplished the floods come in.

The assault on positive doctrinal teaching is presented to-day chiefly under the flag of " comprehension." Men bewail the divisions of the Church of Christ, and propose that we shall stop thinking, so that we may no longer think differently. This is the true account to give of many of the phases of the modern movement for "church union." Men are tired of thinking. They are tired of defending the truth. Let us all stop thinking, stop believing, they cry, and what a happy family we shall be! Look into Mr. David Nelson Beach's recent book (1893), which he calls " The Newer Religious Think-ing," but which seems to us to be rather a plea for unthinking irreligion, and see how clearly this is its dominant note. He tells us that God is no more a respecter of religions than of persons; that the doctrine of the Trinity is a mere philosophy and ought no longer to stand between brethren; that access to God is no longer to be represented as exclusively " as a matter of terms," through Christ. In a word, the lines that separate evangelical from " liberal " Christianity, and those that sepa-rate distinctive Christianity from the higher heathenism, are to be obliterated. We are no longer to defend anything that any religious soul doubts. We are to recognize every honest worshiper as a child of God, though the God he worships may be but another name for force or for the world.

We find the seeds of this movement towards " comprehen-sion " in the most unlikely places. Even Dr. Schaff, in his latest book, represents himself as occupying a position in which not only Arminianism, Lutheranism, and Calvinism, but also Ra-tionalism and Supranaturalism, are reconciled. It is essentially present wherever the concessive habit of dealing with truth has taken root. For what is the " concessive " method of con-troversy but a neat device by which one may appear to con-

quer while really yielding the citadel? It is as if the governor
of a castle should surrender it to the foe if only the foe will
permit him to take possession of it along with them. On this
pathway there is no goal except the ultimate naturalization of
Christianity, and that means the perishing of distinctive
Christianity out of the earth. Dr. Pusey calls attention to the
fact that the Rationalists of Germany were the descendants
not of the unbelievers of former controversies, but of the " defenders " of Christianity. The method of concession was tried,
and that was the result. The so-called " defenders " were found
in the camp of the enemy.

Along with this attack on distinctive truth goes necessarily
an accompanying attack on " external authority in religion."
For if there be an " external authority," that which it teaches
is true for all. This canker, too, has therefore necessarily entered our churches. It exists in various stages of development.
It begins by rejecting the authority of the Bible for minor
matters only — in the " *minima*," in " circumstantials " and
" by-passages " and " incidental remarks," and the like. The
next step is to reject its authority for everything except " matters of faith and practice." Then comes unwillingness to bow
to all its doctrinal deliverances and ethical precepts; and we
find men like Dr. DeWitt, of New Brunswick, and Mr. Horton,
of London, subjecting the religious and ethical contents of the
Bible to the judgment of their " spiritual instinct." Then the
circle is completed by setting aside the whole Bible as *authority;* perchance with the remark, so far as the New Testament is concerned, that in the apostolic age men depended
each on the spirit in his own heart, and no one dreamed of
making the New Testament the authoritative word of God,
while it was only in the later second century that the canon
was formed, and " external authority " took the place of " internal authority." This point of view comes to its rights only
when every shred of " external authority " in religion is discarded, and appeal is made to what is frankly recognized as
purely human reason: we call it then Rationalism. It is only
another form of this Rationalism, however, when it would

fain believe that what it appeals to within the human breast is not the unaided spirit of man, but the Holy Ghost in the heart, the Logos, the strong voice of God. In this form it asks, " Were the Quakers right? " and differs from technical Rationalism only in a matter of temperature, the feelings and not the cold reason alone being involved: we call it then Mysticism.

Of course men cannot thus reject the Bible, to which Christ appealed as authoritative, without rejecting also the authority of Christ, which is thus committed to the Bible's authority. Accordingly, we already find not only a widespread tendency to neglect the authority of Christ on many points, but also a formal rejection of that authority by respectable teachers in the churches. We are told that authority is limited by knowledge, and that Christ's knowledge was limited to pure religion. We are told that even in matters of religion He accommodated Himself, in the form at least of His teachings, to the times in which He lived. Thus all " external authority " is gradually evaporated, and men are left to the sole authority each of his own spirit, whether under the name of reason or under the name of the Holy Spirit in the heart. As each man's spirit has, of course, its separate rights, all basis for objective doctrine thus departs from the earth.

The attitude of mind which is thus outlined constitutes the most dangerous, because the most fundamental, of heresies. Distinctive Christianity, supernatural religion, cannot persist where this blight is operative. It behooves the Church, if it would consult its peace or even preserve its very life, to open its eyes to the working of the evil leaven. Nor will it do to imagine that we shall have to face in it only a sporadic or temporary tendency of thought. It is for this tendency of thought that the powerful movement known in Germany as Ritschlism practically stands. And it has already acquired in America the proportions of an organized propaganda, with its literary organ, its summer schools, its apostles and its prophets. It is something like this Ritschlite Rationalism that Professor George D. Herron teaches in his numerous works, as the coming form of Christianity. It is something like it that Mr. B. Fay Mills is propagating in his evangelistic tours. It is something like it that *The Kingdom* is offering to the churches; and that those whom that newspaper has gathered to its support are banded to make a force in the land. Surely there is clamant need to inform ourselves of its meaning and its purposes.

II. RITSCHLITE RATIONALISM

" Rationalism " never is the direct product of unbelief. It is the indirect product of unbelief, among men who would fain hold their Christian profession in the face of an onset of unbelief, which they feel too weak to withstand. Rationalism is, therefore, always a movement within the Christian Church; and its adherents are characterized by an attempt to save what they hold to be the essence of Christianity, by clearing it from what they deem to be accretions, or by surrendering what they feel to be no longer defensible features of its current representations. The name historically represents specifically that form of Christian thought which, under the pressure of eighteenth century deism, felt no longer able to maintain a Christianity that needed to appeal to other evidences of its truth than the human reason; and which, therefore, yielded to the enemy every element of Christian teaching which could not validate itself to the logical understanding on axiomatic grounds. The effect was to reduce Christianity to a " natural religion."

The most recent form of Rationalism, the Ritschlite, partakes, of course, of the general Rationalistic features. In its purely theological aspect, its most prominent characteristic is an attempt to clear theology of all " metaphysical " elements. Otherwise expressed, this means that nothing will be admitted to belong to Christianity except facts of experience; the elaboration of these facts into " dogmas " contains " metaphysical " elements. For example, the Ritschlite defines God as love. He means by this that the Christian experiences God as love, and this much he therefore knows. Beyond that, he cannot define

God; since all question of what God is in Himself, as distinguished from what God is to us, belongs to the sphere of "metaphysics," and is, therefore, out of the realm of religion. Similarly, the Ritschlite defines Christ as Lord, and declares that the saying of Luther, *Er ist mein Herr,* includes all that we need to believe concerning Christ. He means by this that the Christian experiences Christ as his master, bows before His life and teaching, and therefore knows Him as Lord. But beyond what he can verify in such experiences, he knows nothing of Him. For example, he can know, in such experience, nothing of Christ's preëxistence, and cannot control anything told us about it by any available tests; he can know nothing of Christ's present activities by such experience; but he can know something of the power and worth of His historical apparition, in such experience. All that is outside the reach of such verification belongs to the sphere of "metaphysics," and is, therefore, out of the realm of religion. The effort is to save the essence of Christianity from all possible danger from the speculative side. The means taken to effect this is to yield the whole sphere of "metaphysical" thought to the enemy. The result is the destruction of the whole system of Christian doctrine. Doctrine cannot be stated without what the Ritschlite calls "metaphysical elements"; a theory of knowledge underlies, indeed, the Ritschlite construction of "Christianity without metaphysics itself." But, however inconsistently, the Ritschlite contention ultimates in an "undogmatic Christianity." Theology, we are told, is killing religion.

But Christianity as it has come down to us is very far from being an undogmatic Christianity. The history of Christianity is the history of doctrine. Ritschlite Rationalism must, therefore, deal with a historical problem, as well as with a speculative and a practical one. What is it to do with a historical Christianity which is a decidedly doctrinal Christianity? Its task is obviously to explain the origin and development of doctrinal Christianity in such a manner as to evince essential Christianity to be undogmatic. Its task, in a word, is historically to explain doctrinal Christianity as corrupted Christianity; or, in other words, to explain the rise and development of doctrine as a series of accretions from without, overlying and concealing Christianity. Ritschlism, in the very nature of the case, definitely breaks with the whole tradition of Christian doctrine, from Justin Martyr down. Adolf Harnack, one of the most learned of modern church historians, has consecrated his great stores of knowledge and his great powers to the performance of the task thus laid upon his school of thought.

The characteristic feature of Harnack's reconstruction of the history of Christian dogma, in the interests of Ritschlite Rationalism, is to represent all Christian doctrine as the product of Greek thought on Christian ground. The simple gospel of Christ was the gospel of love. On the basis of this gospel the ancient world built up the Catholic Church, but in doing so it built itself bankrupt. That is, the ancient world transferred itself to the Church; and in what we call church theology we are looking only at the product of heathen thinking on the basis of the gospel. To make our way back to original Christianity, we must shovel off this whole superincumbent mass until we arrive at the pure kernel of the gospel itself, hidden beneath. That kernel is simple subjective faith in God as Father, revealed to us as such by Jesus Christ.

These new teachings have been variously put within the reach of the American churches. Professor Mitchell, of Hartford Seminary, has given us a translation of Harnack's "Outlines of the History of Dogma." Mr. Rutherfurd has published a translation of Moeller's "History of the Christian Church," in which Harnack's views are adopted and ably reproduced. Williams and Norgate, the great "liberal" publishing-house of London, are issuing a translation of Harnack's great "History of Dogma." The writings of Edwin Hatch, the Oxford representative of Ritschlism, have had a wide circulation on this side of the sea. But of late years something more has come to be reckoned with within the American churches than such literary importations. Young American students, visiting German universities, have returned home enthusiastic devotees of the "new views." They have been commended to them by

the immense learning of Harnack; by his attractive personality
and his clear and winning methods of presenting his views; by
the great vogue which they have won in Germany; and possibly by a feeling on their own part that they offer a mode of
dealing with the subject which will lessen the difficulty of the
Christian apologist in defending the faith. The less faith you
have to defend the easier it is apt to seem to defend it. At all
events, it is a fact that the historical Rationalism of the
Ritschlite is now also an American movement and needs to be
reckoned with as such. There are in particular three recent
American publications in which the influence of Harnack's
rationalizing reconstruction of Christian history is dominating,
to which attention ought to be called in this connection: The
first of these is a very readable "Sketch of the History of the
Apostolic Church," by Professor Oliver J. Thatcher, formerly
of the United Presbyterian Seminary at Allegheny, but now of
the University of Chicago. Another is the very able Inaugural
Address, delivered by Professor Arthur C. McGiffert at his
induction into the chair of Church History at Union Theological Seminary, New York, which deals with the subject of
"Primitive and Catholic Christianity." The third is a lecture
by the Rev. Dr. Thomas C. Hall, of Chicago, pronounced before the students of Queens University, Kingston, Canada, and
bearing the title of "Faith and Reason in Religion." Anyone
who will take the trouble to look into these publications will
soon become convinced of the importance of observing what
the American churches are now being taught by the pupils of
Harnack as to the origin of Christianity.

It will then, doubtless, repay us to look for a moment into
this matter. The best way to do so is doubtless to analyze
briefly one of these three publications. We select for the purpose Dr. McGiffert's brief and admirably clear paper. And in
the following pages we shall attempt to give as clear an account
of its contents as the necessity for succinctness will allow.

Dr. McGiffert begins with a few remarks on the function of
church history and the duty of the historian of the Church.
The object of the whole of church history is, he tells us, to

enable us to understand Christianity better, and to fit us " to
distinguish between its essential and non-essential elements." [7]
And the special task of the historian is to " discover by a careful study of Christianity at successive stages of its career
whether it has undergone any transformations and, if so, what
those transformations are " (p. 17). It is not the duty of the
historian to pass judgment on the value of any assimilations
or accretions which Christianity may be found to have made.
That is the theologian's work. The historian's is only to make
clear what belonged to the original form of Christianity and
what has been acquired by it, in its process of growth, in its
environment of the world. Dr. McGiffert gives us to understand, however, that, in his opinion, the value of an element of
our system is not to be determined merely by its origin:
whether it belonged to original Christianity or has been acquired by it from the world. Its right to a place in the Christian
system is to be determined solely by what we deem its vital
relation to, or at least its harmony with, Christianity itself.

He chooses as his subject, the portrayal of " the most vital
and far-reaching transformation that Christianity has ever
undergone — a transformation, the effects of which the entire
Christian Church still feels, and which has in my opinion done
more than anything else to conceal Christianity's original form
and to obscure its true character " (p. 18). This is the transformation of the primitive into the Catholic Church; and it
was " practically complete before the end of the second century of the Church's life." He points out that it would be too
much to attempt to explain such a momentous transformation
in all its features in the limits of a single discourse. He confines
himself, therefore, to indicating and explaining as fully as the
time at his disposal permitted, the *change of spirit* which constitutes the essence of the transformation.

He begins with a picture of the primitive, that is, of the
apostolic Church. Its spirit was " the spirit of religious individualism, based upon the felt presence of the Holy Ghost "
(p. 19). That is to say, it was the universal conviction of the

[7] " Primitive and Catholic Christianity," 1893, p. 16.

primitive Church that every Christian had, in the indwelling of the Holy Spirit in him, a personal source of inspiration at his disposal, to which he could turn in every time of need. There was, therefore, no occasion for an authority for Christian teaching, external to the individual's own spirit; and there had arisen no conception, accordingly, as yet, of a " rule of faith," or of a " New Testament Canon." The only authority that was recognized was the Holy Spirit; and He was supposed to speak to every believer as truly as He spoke to an apostle. There was no instituted Church, and no external bond of Christian unity. There were some common forms of worship, and Christians met together for mutual edification; but their only bond of union was their common possession of the Spirit of God and their common ideal and hope. There was no intervening class of clerics, standing between the Christian and the source of grace; but every Christian enjoyed immediate contact with God through the Spirit. Such was the spirit of the primitive Church — of the Church of the apostles and of the Church of the post-apostolic age, for there was no change of spirit on the death of the apostles. The Church of the second half of the second century believed itself as truly and exclusively under the authority of the indwelling Spirit as the apostolic Church and as the apostles themselves. On historic grounds, we can draw no distinction between the apostolic and post-apostolic ages on the ground of supernatural endowment.

The change of spirit which marks the rise of the Catholic Church took place, then, in the second century. In general terms, it was the result of the secularization of the Church and of the effort of the Church to avoid such secularization. Among the heathen brought into the Church in the second century, gradually more and more men of education were included. Among these were some philosophical spirits of a Platonizing tendency, who brought into the Church with them a habit of speculation. Their speculative theories they represented as Christianity, and they appealed to the authority of the apostles in their favor. Thus arose the first theologizing in the Christian Church; the Gnostics were the first creed-builders within the limits of the Church and the first inventors of the idea of apostolic authority, and of the consequent conception of an apostolic Christian canon. And it was in conflict with them that the Church, for her part, first reached the conception of apostolic authority and of an apostolic canon, and gradually developed the full conception of authority which gave us finally the full-fledged Catholic Church.

The steps by which this transformation was made were three: " First, the recognition of the teaching of the Apostles as the exclusive standard and norm of Christian truth; second, the confinement to a specific office (viz., the Catholic office of bishop) of the power to determine what is the teaching of the Apostles; and third, the designation of a specific institution (viz., the Catholic Church) as the sole channel of divine grace " (p. 29). The transformation was, it will be seen, complete. The spirit of free individualism under the sole guidance of the indwelling Spirit, which characterized the primitive Church, passed permanently away. The spirit of submission to " external authority " took permanently its place. The transformation to Catholicism means simply, then, that the Church had emptied itself of its spiritual heritage, that it had denuded itself of its spiritual power, and that it had invented for itself, and subjected itself to, a complete system of " external authority." The first step was to recognize the exclusive authority of apostolic teaching. Thus Christians laid aside their privilege of being the constant organs of the inspiration of the Holy Ghost, and framed for themselves a " rule of faith " (Creed) and a New Testament Scripture (Canon). The next step was to confine to a particular office the power to transmit and interpret that teaching. The believer was thus permanently denied not only the privilege of receiving divine revelations, but also the right to interpret for himself the revelations received and transmitted by the apostles. The last step was to confine the transmission of grace itself to the organized Church, so that out of it there could be no salvation. Thus the believer's last privilege was taken from him; he could no longer possess anything save as through the Church. When this last step was completed, the Catholic Church was complete.

No " transformations " of the Church have taken place since this great transformation. Changes have occurred, and changes which may seem to the casual observer of more importance. But, in fact, the Church is still living in the epoch of the Catholic Church. The Reformation was, indeed, an attempt at a real " transformation," and it has wrought a real " transformation " upon as much of the Church as has accepted it. It was a revival of the primitive spirit of individualism, and a rejection of " external authority." But the Reformation has affected only a small portion of the Church; and it was, even for the Protestant Churches, only a partial revival of the primitive spirit. It " did not repudiate, it retained the Catholic conception of an apostolic Scripture canon — a conception which the primitive Church had entirely lacked " (p. 42). Thus it has retained the essential Catholic idea of an " external authority." But the Reformers sought to bring this idea into harmony with the primitive conception of the continued action of the Holy Spirit in the hearts of true believers; and it is by this fact alone that Protestants can be justified in retaining the Scriptures as a rule of faith and practice. The true statement of the Protestant position, therefore, is not, That the word of God contained in the Scriptures of the Old and New Testaments is the sole and ultimate standard of Christian truth. It is, " That the Spirit of God is the sole and ultimate standard for Christian truth — the Spirit of God who spoke through the Apostles and who still speaks to his people " (p. 43); it is, That " the Holy Spirit, which voices itself both in the teaching of the Apostles and in the enlightened Christian consciousness of true believers," is " the only source and standard of spiritual truth " (p. 42).

This is, as briefly as possible, the gist of Dr. McGiffert's Address. Two things are to be especially noted in it: First, the whole development of a Christian " authority " — the rise alike of the very conception of authority as attributed to the apostles, and of the conception of a New Testament canon —

is assigned to post-apostolic times. The Church of the apostles, and the apostles themselves, knew nothing of an authoritative Christian teaching. Thus all Christian doctrine is a human product, and of no real authority in the Church. And, secondly, the Christian Scriptures are in no sense the authoritative rule of faith and practice which we have been taught to believe that they are. The apostles who wrote them did not intend them as such. The Church which received them did not receive them as such. The Protestant Churches can be justified in declaring them such, only provided they do not mean to erect them over the Christian spirit — " the Christian consciousness of true believers " — but mean only to place them side by side with it as co-source of the knowledge of Christian truth. This is, of course, to deny " authority " to the New Testament *in toto*. If we are to follow Dr. McGiffert, therefore, we are to renounce all doctrinal Christianity at a stroke, and to reject all " authority " in the New Testament, on pain of being un-primitive and unapostolic. These things are, according to his conception, parts of the accretion that has gathered itself to Christianity in its passage through the ages.

This, then, is the question which the introduction of the Ritschlite historical Rationalism has brought to the American churches. Are we prepared to surrender the whole body of Christian doctrine as being no part of essential Christianity, but the undivine growth of ages of human development, the product of the " transformations " of Christianity, or, as Dr. T. C. Hall phrases it with admirable plainness of speech, the product of the " degradations " of Christianity? Are we pre-pared to surrender the New Testament canon, as the invention of the second century Church to serve its temporary needs in conflict with heresy? Once more, Dr. Hall gives us an ad-mirably plain-spoken account of what, on this view, was ac-tually done when the canon was made: " The need of an infallible authority to interpret a code gave rise to the fiction of apostolic authority, at first confined to written and spoken messages, and later imbedded in an organization, and inherited by its office-holders." Are we prepared to represent the authority of the apostles, as imbedded in their written words and preserved in our New Testament, as a "fiction"? This is the teaching of the new historical Rationalism; and it is with this teaching that the Church has now to reckon.

Let us now enter a little more into detail as to the meaning of this new teaching; and in order to do this, let us examine more fully one or two of the fundamental positions of Dr. McGiffert's Address. And first of all let us look a moment at

III. Dr. McGiffert's Theory of Development

The learning, the ability, and the skill in the presentation of its material, which characterize Dr. McGiffert's Inaugural Address, will occasion surprise to no one. These things have been confidently expected of the accomplished annotator of Eusebius. There will be many, doubtless, however, who will be surprised to find the fundamental thought of so learned an address, delivered by a Presbyterian professor, to be the presentation of Christianity under the form of a development, of a sort not merely outside the ordinary lines of Protestant thinking, but apparently inconsistent with the most fundamental of Protestant postulates.

When the body of revealed truth was committed into the hands of men, it of course became subject to adulteration with the notions of men. As it was handed down from age to age, it inevitably gathered around it a mass of human accretions, as a snowball grows big as it rolls down a long slope. The importance of that committal of the divine revelation to writing, by which the inspired Scriptures were constituted, becomes thus specially apparent. The "word of God written" stands through all ages as a changeless witness against human additions to, and corruptions of, God's truth. The chief task of historical criticism, in its study of Christianity, becomes also thus very apparent. Dr. James M. Ludlow, who delivered the charge to the new professor, and whose charge is printed along with the Address, does not fail to point this out. Because "what the truth receives in the way of admixture from the passing

ages it is apt to retain," therefore he charges the new professor
to remember that " the most pressing demand upon historical
criticism " is " to separate from essential Christianity what the
ages have contributed " (p. 8).

The Reformation was, in this sense, a critical movement.
The weapon it used in its conflict with the pretensions of Rome
was historical criticism. The task it undertook was to tear off
the medieval and patristic swathings in which Christianity
had become wrapped in the course of the careless ages, and to
stand her once more before men in her naked truth, as she had
been presented to the world by Christ and His apostles. " The
fittest and most suggestive criticism we can to-day pass on
Catholicism," says Adolf Harnack justly, " is to conceive it as
Christianity in the garb of the ancient world with a medieval
overcoat. . . . What is the Reformation but the word of God
which was to set the Church free again? All may be expressed
in the single formula, the *Reformation is the return to the
pure gospel;* only what is sacred shall be held sacred; the
traditions of men, though they be most fair and most worthy,
must be taken for what they are — viz., the ordinances of
man."

The principle on which Protestantism proceeded in this
great and salutary task had two sides, a negative and a positive
one. On the negative side, it took the form that every element
of current ecclesiastical teaching or of popular belief, which,
on being traced back in history, ran out before Christ's authoritative apostles were reached, was to be accounted a spurious accretion to Christianity and no part of Christianity itself.
On the positive side, and this is the so-called " formal principle
of Protestantism," it took the form that everything enters as
an element into the Christian system that is taught in the
Holy Scriptures, which were imposed on the Church as its
authoritative rule of faith and practice by the apostles, who
were themselves appointed by the Lord as His authoritative
agents in establishing the Church, and were endowed with all
needed graces and accompanied by all needed assistance from
the Holy Spirit for the accomplishing of their task. This is

what is meant by that declaration of Chillingworth which has passed into a Protestant proverb: " That the Bible, and the Bible only, is the religion of Protestants." And this is what is meant by the Westminster Confession when it asserts that " the whole counsel of God, concerning all things necessary for His own glory, man's salvation, faith, and life, is either expressly set down in Scripture, or by good and necessary consequence may be deduced from Scripture: unto which nothing at any time is to be added, whether by new revelations of the Spirit or traditions of men " (i. 6). This is the corner-stone of universal Protestantism; and on it Protestantism stands, or else it falls.

This " formal principle " of Protestantism, of course, does not deny that there has been such a thing as a " development of doctrine." It does not make its appeal to the early Church as the norm of Christian truth; and it does not imagine that the first generation of Christians had already sounded all the depths of revelation. It makes its appeal to the Scriptures of God, which embody in written form the teaching of Christ through His apostles upon which the earliest as well as the latest Church was builded. Protestantism expects to find, and does find, a progressive understanding and realization of this teaching of Christ in the Church. The Reformers knew, as well as the end of the nineteenth century knows, that there is a sense in which the Nicene Christology, the Augustinian Anthropology, the Anselmic Soteriology, their own doctrine of Justification by Faith alone, were new in the Church. They thought of nothing so little as discarding these doctrines because they were " new," in the only sense in which they were new. They rather held them to constitute the very essence of Christian truth. They believed in " the development of true Christian doctrine," and looked upon themselves as raised up by God to be the instruments of a new step in this development. Following the Reformers, Protestants universally believe in " the development of true Christian doctrine "; but, as Dr. Ludlow pointedly and truly adds, " not the growth of its revelation, for that we believe was made complete in the

New Testament, but its development in the conception of men " (p. 5).

This " development in the conception of men " Protestants are very far from supposing ever to take place, in ever so small a one of its stages, without the illuminating agency of the Holy Spirit. They affirm the activity of the Spirit of revelation in the Church of God continuously through all the ages. And they attribute to His brooding over the confused chaos of human thinking every step that is taken towards a truer or a fuller apprehension of God's saving truth. But they know how to distinguish between " the inward illumination of the Spirit of God," by virtue of which Christian men enter progressively into fuller possession of the truth which was once for all delivered unto the saints, and " new revelations of the Spirit," by virtue of which men may suppose that additions are made to the substance of this truth.

Despite Dr. Ludlow's faithful warnings in the charge which he laid upon him, Dr. McGiffert appears to have failed to make this distinction. In opposition to the fundamental Protestant principle, he teaches that the true system of Christianity has gradually come into existence during the last two millenniums through a process of development. He conceives of " Christianity " (the word has somewhat of the character of an " undistributed middle " in his use of it) as having been planted in " the days of Christ " only in germinal form. From this original germ it has grown through the ages, not merely by unfolding explicitly what was implicitly contained in it, but also by assimilating and making its own elements from without, elements even of late and foreign origin. " The fact that any element of our system is of later growth than Christianity itself does not necessarily condemn it, nor even the fact that it is of foreign growth " (p. 18). For " guarantee of truth " is not given by " general prevalence " or by " age " (as if the question of its tracing to the apostles were a question of mere age!) ; but the " right [of any element] to a place within the Christian system " is vindicated " only by showing its vital relation to, or at least its harmony with, Christianity itself " (p. 18). Though present-day Christianity contains elements " of late and foreign origin," elements which materially modify the forms of expressing the spirit of primitive Christianity, conceptions even which the primitive Church (i.e. the Church of the apostles) " certainly lacked," it may not be the less pure Christianity on that account. It may even be the more pure Christianity on this very account: it may " mark a real advance " on primitive Christianity.

For we must bear constantly in mind that the right of any elements " to a place within the Christian system " is vindicated solely by their power to express the Christian spirit. This is the true test alike of elements of late and foreign origin and of the elements which entered into primitive Christianity itself. When speaking of the former, Dr. McGiffert makes a significant addition to his sentence so as emphatically to include the latter also. " By the degree to which they give expression to that spirit " (i.e. " the Christian spirit "), he says, " is the value of such elements, *and of all elements,* to be measured." " If they contribute to its clear, and just, and full expression," he adds, " they vindicate their right to a place within the Christian system; if they hinder that spirit's action, they must be condemned " (p. 42). Thus we learn that there were in primitive Christianity itself — the Christianity of " the days of Christ " and of His apostles — both essential and nonessential elements; elements of permanent and universal worth, and others of only temporary and local significance; and the criterion for distinguishing between them is our own subjective judgment of their fitness to express " the Christian spirit " — of course, according to our own conception of that spirit.

Thus Professor McGiffert takes emphatic issue with both sides of the fundamental Protestant principle. As over against its assertion that the whole counsel of God is set down in Scripture, " unto which nothing at any time is to be added," he declares that it is a " pernicious notion that apostolic authority is necessary for every element of the Christian system " (p. 33); and that elements of even late and foreign origin can

" vindicate their right to a place within the Christian system "
" by showing their vital relation to, or at least their harmony
with, Christianity itself " (p. 18). That is to say, the test of a
distinctively Christian truth is not that it is part of that body
of truth which was once for all delivered to the saints, as all
Protestantism, with one voice, affirms; but whether it seems
to us to harmonize with what we consider that Christianity is
or ought to be. A subjective criterion thus takes the place of
the objective criterion of the written word of God.

Accordingly, as over against the fundamental Protestant
principle that " the Holy Scriptures of the Old and the New
Testaments are the word of God, the only rule of faith and
obedience " (Larger Catechism, Q. 3), Professor McGiffert
declares that the teaching of the apostles is not " the sole
standard of truth " (p. 33). He is willing to allow, indeed, that
the teaching of the apostles was regarded by the primitive
Church, and may be rightly regarded by the modern Church,
as " a *source* from which [may] . . . be gained a knowledge
of divine truth " (p. 32). But that it is " the only rule," or
" *standard,*" he will not admit; or even that it is more than *a*
" source " along with others. For he tells us that Protestants
can be justified " in retaining the Scriptures as a rule of faith
and practice " (p. 43) only on the condition that they join
with the Scriptures for this function " the enlightened Christian consciousness of true believers," affirming the two to be
alike the organs of the Holy Ghost, " the only source and
standard of spiritual truth " (p. 42). " The true statement of
the Protestant position," he adds, " is not that the Word of
God, contained in the Scriptures of the Old and New Testaments, but that the Spirit of God is the sole and ultimate
authority for Christian truth — the Spirit of God who spoke
through the Apostles *and who still speaks to his people*"
(p. 43). If this be so, the Reformers, the first Protestant divines, and the Reformed Confessions, including our own Standards, were not only ignorant of the " true statement of the
Protestant position," but in ineradicable opposition to it.
When the Shorter Catechism (Q. 2) asserts that " the word of

God which is contained in the Scriptures of the Old and New Testaments is the only rule " it speaks with the intention and effect of confining the " word of God," which it declares to be " the only rule," to the Scriptures, and of thereby excluding not only the " word of God " which the Romanist affirms to be presented in objective tradition, but also the " word of God " which the mystic affirms that he enjoys through subjective illumination. And, therefore, the Confession of Faith explicitly explains its assertion that " nothing at any time is to be added " to the " whole counsel of God " " set down in Scripture," by adding: " whether by new revelations of the Spirit or traditions of men " (i. 6). A theory of development on a mystical basis is no less in open contradiction to the " formal principle of Protestantism " than one on a Romish basis.

We have spoken only of Dr. McGiffert's formal theory of development, and have pointed out its inconsistency with the " formal principle " of Protestantism. The material development which, under this formal theory, he would ascribe to Christianity, he does not draw out in the present Address. The Address is consecrated, no doubt, to the depicting of one of the greatest changes which Christianity has undergone; but this change is not one which appears to Dr. McGiffert to commend itself, according to the tests he lays down, as a proper development of Christianity. The material changes in Christianity which are brought to our attention by the Address, therefore, are not illustrations of his theory of development, but are instances of the progressive deterioration of Christianity in its environment of the world. Let us, however, attend for a moment to them.

IV. DR. McGIFFERT'S THEORY OF THE TRANSFORMATIONS OF
CHRISTIANITY

" The subject of study in Church History, as in all the theological sciences," Professor McGiffert tells us in the opening of his Inaugural Address, " is Christianity itself." The church historian's aim is, therefore, " to contribute to a clearer and fuller understanding of Christianity." In the prosecution of this aim he must learn to distinguish between the " essential and non-essential elements " of Christianity, " between that in it which is of permanent and universal worth, and that which is of only temporary and local significance " (p. 16). He must, further, make it his special task " to discover by a careful study of Christianity at successive stages of its career whether it has undergone any transformations, and, if so, what those transformations are " (p. 17). One would think, as we have already pointed out, that the purpose of this discovery would be to obtain knowledge of what belongs really to Christianity, so that the accretions which have gathered to it from without may be rejected, and the original form of that deposit of faith once for all delivered to the saints may be recovered. But Professor McGiffert excludes all passing of judgment on results from the sphere of the historian as such. The historian's business is merely to present a complete picture of the transformations that Christianity has undergone. The theologian comes after him, and estimates the value and meaning of the assimilations and accretions which the historian's labor has brought to light. But Dr. McGiffert, as we have seen, cannot resist the temptation so far to desert this rôle of pure historian as to tell us on what such an estimation must turn. It must not turn, he tells us, on the question of the originality of this element or that in the Christian system, but solely on its ideal harmony with the Christian spirit. Doubtless, the " theologian " who comes after him, however, along with the whole body of Christian people, may be trusted to disagree with him in this pronouncement. It is the Christianity of Christ and His apostles alone that they will care to profess; and they will thank the historian for tracing out the transformations of Christianity, chiefly because his work will enable them to recover for their souls the Christianity which Christ and His apostles taught.

Dr. McGiffert devotes his Inaugural Address to the discussion of a single one of these " transformations " of Christianity, the one which he believes to be the "most vital and far-reaching transformation that Christianity has ever undergone," the "transformation of the primitive into the Catholic Church" (p. 18). This transformation, which was "practically complete before the end of the second century of the Church's life," was so radical that it has "done more than anything else to conceal Christianity's original form and to obscure its true character"; and it has been so powerful and far-reaching in its influence that "the entire Christian Church still feels" the effects of it. In fact, in Dr. McGiffert's view, it gave to the greater portion of the Church what has proved to be its permanent form. In it the spirit of primitive Christianity permanently disappeared (p. 28), and the spirit which still rules the Catholic Church permanently entered. The Catholic Church is still living in the period inaugurated then (p. 40), the Greek and Roman Churches being but localizations of the one Church which had existed in undivided form for some centuries before their separation.

Since this great "transformation" of the primitive into the Catholic Church, therefore, there have been no "transformations" of Christianity. There have been changes. And these later changes have often been such as to "impress the casual observer more forcibly, and seem to him more worthy of notice," than this great fundamental transformation itself. He will think of "the cessation of persecution with the accession of Constantine, and the subsequent union of Church and State; the preaching of Christianity to the barbarians of western and northern Europe; the development of the Greek patriarchate and of the Roman papacy; the formation of the elaborate liturgies of the eastern and western Churches; the rise of saint and image worship, of the confessional and of the mass; the growth of monasticism, which began with renouncing the world and ended with subjugating it; the development of Nicene trinitarianism, of the Chalcedonian Christology, of the Augustinian anthropology and of the Anselmic theory of the atonement" (pp. 18–19). And as he thinks of these, he may think them "of greater historical significance than any changes which took place during the first two centuries." But he will be mistaken. The transformation of the primitive into the Catholic Church, which took place in the course of the second century, was a far more fundamental change than any of these subsequent changes, or than them all taken together.

Before this great transformation, it was the free spirit of primitive Christianity that reigned; after it, the Church was a completely secularized institution. For the secularization of the Church " was not due, as has been so widely thought, to the favors shown the Church by the Emperor Constantine, or to the ultimate union of Church and State. The Church was in principle secularized as completely as it ever was long before the birth of Constantine. The union of Church and State was but a ratification of a process already complete, and is itself of minor significance " (p. 38). Of all subsequent movements only that one which we know as the Reformation was sufficiently radical to promise a new " transformation." This movement was in essence a revival of the spirit of primitive Christianity, and it did open a new epoch in the Church, so far as it produced its effects. But unfortunately Protestantism has affected only a part, and that the smaller part, of the Church. The Church at large is still living in the epoch which was inaugurated by the great " transformation " which took place in the second century.

If, then, we speak of the " transformations " of Christianity we must have our eye fixed upon changes which took place before the great transformation that gave birth to the Catholic Church — changes greater and more radical than any that have occurred subsequent to that event. In the days of the Church's strenuous youth, it rapidly passed through a series of " transformations " of fundamental importance, much, we suppose, as the stages of babyhood, childhood, boyhood, youth, and manhood are all run through in some twenty restless years, to be followed by an extended period of unchanged manhood for the better part of a century. If we understand Dr. McGiffert, he would count, including the Reformation, some four such transformations in all, three of which were suffered by

Christianity during the first two centuries of its existence. In other words, by the time that two hundred years had rolled over it the introduction of alien ideas had three times fundamentally transformed the gospel of Christ. In quick succession there were presented to the world each largely effacing its predecessor, first the Gospel of Love, which Christ preached; then the Gospel of Holiness, which ruled in the primitive Church; then the Gospel of Knowledge, announced by the Greek spirit, not so much converted by, as converting, the Church; and finally, the Gospel of Authority, the proud self-assertion of the Catholic Church. Last of all, after ages of submission, the primitive spirit once more rises in what we call Protestantism, and revolting against authority proclaims anew the Gospel of Individualistic Freedom.

Let us look a little more closely at Dr. McGiffert's conceptions of these several " transformations."

1. Christ's Christianity " was, above all, ethical; the Sermon on the Mount strikes its key-note." According to Christ, " the active principle of love for God and man . . . constituted the sum of all religion " (p. 24). Christ came, in other words, not teaching a dogma, but setting an example of a life of perfect love; proclaiming the Kingdom of God, founded on the fundamental principle of love for God and man; and announcing the law of the Kingdom in such language as that preserved for us in the Sermon on the Mount. It was His example of holy love which reveals God to the world as Father; and all the emphasis of His teaching was laid on the principle of love.

2. But Christianity extended; and, as it grew, it changed its environment from the Jewish to the Gentile world. This change induced in it " certain modifications, which were of permanent significance " (p. 21). These modifications centered in a change of emphasis of fundamental importance, by which, " in consequence of the conception of the immediate and constant presence of the Holy Spirit, and in opposition to the moral corruptness of the age, the element of personal holiness or purity naturally came more and more to the front, and in-

creasingly obscured the fundamental principle of Christ "
(p. 24). This is the Christianity of the primitive Church, or
the Church of the apostles, though the latter name is the less
descriptive one, inasmuch as the death of the apostles and the
close of the apostolic age introduced no change of spirit, but
the Church of the first half of the second century remained in
principle the same Church as that of the last half of the first
century.

When Dr. McGiffert speaks of the consequent obscuration
of " the fundamental principle of Christ " as " increasing," he
seems to refer to the effect of the introduction into the Church,
early in the second century, of the educated classes of society.
Wherever the influence of Stoicism predominated among these,
they readily assimilated with the spirit which already characterized the primitive Church. For with the Stoics " the ethical
element came to the front, and religion lost its independent
significance, having no other value than to promote virtue by
supplying it with a divine basis and sanction." This tendency,
we are told, " was in entire harmony with that of the Hebrew
mind and of early Christianity in general " (p. 25). Primitive
Christianity, therefore, was simply an ethical system with a
changed ethical ideal from that of Christ — laying the emphasis on holiness rather than on love. It was, in a word, a " Society for Ethical Culture," with a background of monotheism,
and looking to Jesus as its founder and example. " It is true
that, from the beginning, belief in one God and in Jesus Christ
was demanded of all converts, but such belief was commonly
taken for granted — the formula of baptism itself implied it
— and all the emphasis was laid upon the ethical element "
(p. 31).

3. With the introduction of the educated classes into the
Church, however, another class of philosophers came in besides
the Stoics — a class which brought in a speculative tendency
grounded in Platonism, and which began to lay stress on *knowledge*. Christianity seemed to these thinkers only a *revelation;*
and accordingly they busied themselves at once with its rational investigation and elucidation. Here appeared the first

Christian theologians, and they gave the Church, for the first time, a " theology." In their hands arose the first Christian creeds; through their work Christianity became for the first time a system of belief. The transformation of Christianity which they wrought did not come without throes and conflicts. Nevertheless, so far as this it did come; and its coming is marked later on by the approval and adoption by the Church of " the speculative theology of the great fathers and doctors." In this sense " the spirit of Gnosticism . . . lived on and finally won a permanent place within the Church " (pp. 27, 28). Here is a transformation as great as it is possible to conceive: the " Society for Ethical Culture " becomes an institution for the propagation of a body of truth.

4. But the temporary dualistic form in which the speculative spirit first entered the Church could not, and did not, find acceptance. And " it was in the effort to repudiate it that steps were taken which resulted " in that momentous transformation, to the description of which Dr. McGiffert gives his Address — the transformation into the Catholic Church. These efforts to repudiate Gnosticism involved an appeal to authority, and the essence of this great transformation consists, therefore, in the substitution of the idea of external authority for the individualistic spirit of earlier Christianity. " The spirit of Catholicism . . . means submission to an external authority in matters both of faith and of practice, and dependence upon an external source for all needed spiritual supplies " (p. 21).

Three steps are counted in this transformation: " First, the recognition of the teaching of the Apostles as the exclusive standard and norm of Christian truth; second, the confinement to a specific office (viz., the Catholic office of bishop) of the power to determine what is the teaching of the Apostles; and third, the designation of a specific institution (viz., the Catholic Church) as the sole channel of divine grace " (p. 29). When the transformation was complete, therefore, the whole Catholic machinery of " external authority " had been invented, and the last vestige of spiritual freedom had been crushed out.

But its earlier stages included the invention of the very first
and simplest forms of " external authority " to which Christians bowed, the first recognition of the authority of the apostles as teachers, and the rise of the very conception of an
apostolical Scripture canon. The greatness of the transformation that is asserted can be properly estimated only by remembering that it thus includes, not only the completion of
the full Catholic system, but, at the other extreme, the very
earliest conception of a Christian " external authority " at all.
Before this change, Christians had no external law; by virtue
of the Holy Spirit dwelling in them, each was a law unto himself. The change consisted in the finding of an external Christian authority. This was found first in the teaching of the
apostles, either as written in their extant books (and hence
arose the idea of a New Testament), or as formulated in clear,
succinct statements (and hence arose the idea of a rule of faith,
and of creeds). That it was found afterwards in the bishop,
considered as the living representative of the apostles, and
still later in the organized Church as the institute of salvation, constitutes only a minor matter. The finding of an " external authority " at all was the main thing, and constituted
a tremendous transformation in the spirit and the nature of
Christianity. This great transformation took place in the course
of the second century. Before that there was no external Christian authority at all.

5. It was only after ages of submission to external authority that a partial revival of the individualistic spirit of primitive Christianity arose in the Protestant Reformation. By the
Protestants " the Catholic principle was definitely rejected "
(p. 40); " but elements of Catholicism were retained which
materially modified the forms of that spirit's [the revived
spirit of primitive Christianity] expression, and which have
served to make the Protestant a different thing from the
primitive Church " (p. 42). In so far as Protestantism restored
to the individual his spiritual rights, and " made the Holy
Spirit, which voices itself both in the teaching of the Apostles
and in the enlightened Christian consciousness of true be-

lievers, the only source and standard of spiritual truth," it is a revival of the spirit of primitive Christianity. But in so far as it did not repudiate but "retained the Catholic conception of an apostolic Scripture canon — a conception which the primitive Church had entirely lacked," it remains in bondage to the Catholic conception of "external authority." The true statement of the Protestant position is not, then, "That the word of God, contained in the Scriptures of the Old and New Testaments . . . is the sole and ultimate authority for Christian truth." That is Catholic. But it is, "That the Spirit of God is the sole and ultimate authority for Christian truth — the Spirit of God who spoke through the Apostles and who still speaks to his people" (p. 43). No doubt the voice of the Spirit must always accord with itself, and we may, therefore, allow that the genuine teaching of the apostles is also true; for they, too, had the Spirit. But the true Protestant spirit finds "authority" in the Holy Ghost alone; and He speaks in the hearts of Christians to-day as truly as He ever did to the apostles. It cannot, then, come under bondage to the "external authority" of the apostolic teaching. In a word, the specific Quaker position is the only true Protestant one.

Now there is much that occurs to us to say of this scheme of the "transformations" of Christianity which Dr. McGiffert presents. That in the course of the ages Christianity did undergo very real "transformations" there is, of course, no reason to deny. And no Protestant will doubt that, of these, the most complete and the most destructive to the conceptions of primitive Christianity was that great transformation which gave the world the Catholic Church, with its claim to all the authority of heaven for the execution of its will. But it is another question whether Dr. McGiffert's characterization of the several "transformations" which he thinks Christianity has undergone — or even his characterization of that great "transformation" alone which produced the Catholic Church — is just and accordant with the facts. Had we space at our disposal we think we could show that it is not, in a single instance. It can be shown that Jesus did much more than introduce into the world a new ethical ideal, founded on the active principle of love. A whole dogmatic system underlies and is presupposed in even the " Sermon on the Mount "; and Jesus represented Himself continuously as the bearer of a revelation of truth. It can be shown that the primitive Church — the Church of the apostles — was something far other and more than a " Society for Ethical Culture." A complete system of doctrinal truth was authoritatively taught it by the apostles, as the basis of all ethical endeavor. It can be shown that " the Catholic Church " was not the inventor of " external author- ity," the first stage in the development of the Church to assign " authority " to the teaching of the apostles, and the first to frame the conception of an apostolic Scripture canon. The authority of the apostolic teaching and of the apostolic canon was fully recognized from the beginning, and constituted, in- deed, the very corner-stone of the fabric of the Church. It can be shown, finally, that Protestantism is not Quakerism; and that the Protestant principle does not coördinate " the teach- ing of the Apostles " and " the enlightened Christian conscious- ness of true believers," as co-sources of equal rank of the knowledge of God's truth and will; but appeals to the Holy Spirit speaking in the Scriptures as the Supreme Judge in all matters of religious truth. But these are obvious matters, and may be safely left without formal proof.

It will be more instructive to permit our attention to rest for a moment on some of the effects of Dr. McGiffert's teach- ings. Its effect upon our estimate of and interest in the apostolic writings and teachings — our " New Testament Scrip- tures " in a word — is illustrated in an enlightening manner by a remark of Dr. McGiffert's own. He is pointing out the " stu- pendous significance " of the invention, by the second century Church, of the conception of an apostolic Scripture canon. He remarks upon what he judges " pernicious " in its results; mainly this, that men are led to think that they must have apostolic authority for every element of the Christian system. This he offsets by pointing out an advantage we have received from the change of attitude towards the apostles. " To it is

largely due, on the other hand," he says, " much of the knowledge of the apostolic age which we possess, for had the original
conception of continuing divine revelations been retained,
there would have seemed little reason for preserving apostolic
writings and traditions " (p. 33). Just so. And if this conception, which Dr. McGiffert thinks the original one, should be
now "revived," will there not seem now as little reason to preserve and study the apostolic writings? On Dr. McGiffert's
notion of a continuous, direct access of every believer to the
revealing Spirit for all needed truth, of a growing revelation
which has left the Biblical revelation in the rear, so that it is
a " pernicious notion " that we must have its authority for all
the elements of our Christian system, why should we bother
ourselves with those old and outworn writings of the apostles?
They are useless in the presence of the Spirit in our hearts;
nay, they may (possibly have) become even *Nehushtan*
(II Kings xviii. 4). So opposite are his principles to the true
Protestant principle, that the most precious possession of
Protestantism, the Bible, could not be deemed other than a
clog upon the free operation of the Spirit of God, were his
views to prevail.

It is interesting to ask, further, why Dr. McGiffert makes
so much of "primitive" and "original" Christianity. All the
early "transformations" of original Christianity are represented by him as evils, and Protestantism is a good only
because it partly restores, and only so far as it restores, "primitive Christianity." But, on his principles, what is " primitive
Christianity " to us? Have we not the Spirit as truly as those
old believers, including the apostles? And are not the revelations of the Spirit to the Church *progressive,* " as truth may be
needed," so that it " is a pernicious notion that apostolic authority is necessary for every element of the Christian system "? When we turn our eyes back longingly to the primitive
Church, are we not deserting the principle of spiritual independence, and betraying a craving for apostolic authority lingering in our breast? Ought we not to go to the Spirit in our
hearts instead of to the " primitive Church," or to the apostles,

or to Christ Himself, for our knowledge of the truth, as well as for our encouragement in embracing it, and for our support and stay in proclaiming and defending it? To look back, thus, to the past, is it not to hanker after the leeks and onions of Egypt?

We are told that the whole conception of authority in religion is unprimitive and the invention of the second century, in the effort of the Church to conquer its temporary heresies. If we wish to be "primitive," if we desire to be followers of the apostles, we must cast off all "external authority," and especially must we cast off the fancy that the teaching of the apostles is authority. But why should we wish to be "primitive," or desire to be followers of the apostles? It can only be because, in feeling after the authority we have lost, we instinctively look to them as authoritative teachers whom we can trust. We cannot question the truth of their teaching (p. 29). But in matters of truth, authority consists precisely in the possession of unquestionable truth. How can we fail, then, to recognize and appeal to the authority of this unquestionable truth taught by the apostles, as the standard to which all so-called teachings of the Spirit in the heart shall be conformed? According to Professor McGiffert, however, such an appeal to the authority of the apostles is itself unapostolic. To go back to the apostles is to renounce the authority of the apostles; it is to renounce every "external authority," for they knew nothing of an "external authority," and to submit everything to the internal authority of the Holy Spirit, who speaks in every Christian's heart. This is what the apostles teach us. Is not this to cut the limb off on which he is sitting? He appeals to the authority of the apostles in order to destroy the authority of the apostles. This seems to us a most illogical proceeding. It appears to us that we ought either to renounce all appeal to authority, and cast ourselves wholly on the Holy Spirit in the heart as the sole revealer of truth, or else, making our appeal to the authority of the apostles, roundly to accept their authority as supreme.

To this, indeed, it must come. We cannot have two supreme

standards. Either the Holy Spirit in the heart is the norm of truth and the deliverances of the apostles must be subjected to what we consider His deliverances (and then we have Mysticism cooling down into Rationalism), or else the apostolic revelation is the norm of truth, and the fancied deliverances of the Spirit in our heart must be subjected to the apostolic declarations (and then we have Protestantism). There can be no doubt which view is Confessional. The Westminster Confession (i. 10), for example, tells us distinctly that the Supreme Judge is the Holy Spirit speaking in Scripture and that all private judgments are to be subject to it. There can be as little doubt which is apostolic. The Apostle Paul, for example, demands that the reality of all claims to be led by the Spirit shall be tested by their recognition of his claim to speak authoritatively the word of God (I Cor. xiv. 37). Nor can there be much doubt which is rational. Is it still asked: What difference does it make what the Apostle Paul says, if we have the revealing Spirit as truly as he had it? This much, at any rate, we must reply: If his words were really not authoritative they were not even true, for he asserts them to be authoritative. And if the words of Paul and his fellow apostles were not true, we do not even know whether there be a Holy Spirit. It is on the authority of the New Testament alone that we know of the existence of a Holy Spirit, or of His indwelling in the hearts of Christians; that we are justified in interpreting inward aspiration as His leading. If their authority cannot be trusted we have no Holy Spirit. After all, we must build on the foundation of the apostles and prophets, Christ Jesus Himself being our chief corner-stone, or we build on the sand.

Second Article

In the first part of this paper we undertook to give some general account of the new historical rationalism which is being now introduced to the American churches by certain enthusiastic pupils of Adolph Harnack; and then, for its better elucidation, began a somewhat fuller exposition of one or two of the more fundamental positions assumed by Dr. A. C. McGiffert in his Inaugural Address, in his advocacy of it. We pointed out in that section of our paper Dr. McGiffert's conception of Christianity as a development, and gave some account of the " transformations " which he conceives Christianity to have undergone since its origination by Christ. The most important of these " transformations " he represents, certainly with the best of right from his point of view, to be that from the primitive to the Catholic Church, to the better understanding of which his Address is devoted. For our better estimation of the significance of his teaching here, we should next consider more closely:

V. Dr. McGiffert's Theory of the Primitive Church

One of the most striking passages in Dr. McGiffert's Inaugural Address is that in which he draws a picture of " primitive Christianity " as it is conceived by him, preliminary to expounding what he calls the momentous " transformation of the primitive into the Catholic Church, of the Church of the Apostles into that of the old Catholic fathers " (p. 19). That important changes did take place in the spirit, teaching, and organization of the Church during the first two centuries of its life is, as we have said, of course, undoubted. Whether these changes were, however, of the nature which Dr. McGiffert represents them to have been is a different matter, and depends

619

very largely upon the truth of his picture of " primitive Christianity." We desire now to look for a moment at this picture.

He sums up his conception of " primitive Christianity " in the brief formula: " The spirit of primitive Christianity is the spirit of religious individualism, based upon the felt presence of the Holy Ghost " (p. 19). There are combined in this statement the recognition of a fundamental truth of the first importance and the assertion of a fundamental error of the utmost seriousness. The truth is, that all vital Christianity was conceived by the apostles and their first converts as the product of the Holy Spirit working upon the hearts of men. The error is, that the result of this conception was " religious individualism " in Dr. McGiffert's sense, that is, in the sense that each individual Christian felt and asserted himself to be, by virtue of his possession of the Spirit, a law unto himself, independent of the objective revelation of God's will through the apostles, of the objective means of grace provided in the ordinances of the Church, and of the objective discipline exercised by the organized Christian societies; which three things Dr. McGiffert brings together under the somewhat contemptuous designation of " external authority." The diligent reader of those documents of " primitive Christianity," which we call the New Testament, will scarcely need to be told that the effect of the work of the Holy Spirit upon the hearts of Christians is represented in them to be to draw and to bind Christians to these " external authorities," not to array them against them.

It is impossible to exaggerate the emphasis which is placed, in these primitive documents, upon the presence of the Holy Spirit in the hearts of believers as the indispensable condition of their becoming or remaining Christians. They were Christians by virtue of their new relation to Christ. Christ was preached to them, and that as crucified; the truth concerning Him was made known to them, and accepted by them. They were Christians because they accepted Him as their Prophet, Priest, and King. But no man could say Jesus is Lord but in the Holy Spirit. It was only by the work of the Holy Spirit, therefore, that Christians were made Christians, and He remained the immanent source of all spiritual life. It was this feature of the new covenant which had engrossed the attention of Joel when he foresaw the glories that should come. It was this great promise that the dying Master had presented as the comfort of His people. It was by the visible and audible descent of the Spirit that the Church was constituted on that first great Pentecost. It was by receiving the Spirit that men became Christians, in the Spirit that they were baptized into one body, by His presence within them that they were made the sons of God, and by His leading that they were enabled to cherish the filial spirit. Christians were taught to look to the Spirit as the source of every impulse to good and of every power to good. In Him alone was the inspiration, the strength, the sphere of the Christian's whole life.

The presence of the Spirit of God in the apostolic Church was, moreover, manifested not merely by the spiritual graces of Christians, of every one of which He was the sole author, but also in a great variety of miraculous gifts. It is no exaggeration to say that the apostolic Church was a miraculous Church. It is not easy to overestimate the supernatural character of either our Lord's ministry or the apostolic Church. When the Son of God came to earth, He drew heaven with Him. The signs which accompanied His ministry were but the trailing cloud of glory which He brought from heaven, which is His home. His own divine power, by which He began to found His Church, He continued in the apostles whom He had chosen to complete this great work; although their use of it, as was fitting, appears to have been more sporadic than His own. And they transmitted it, as a part of their own miracle-working and the crowning sign of their divine commission, to others, in the form of what the New Testament calls " spiritual gifts," that is, extraordinary capacities produced in the primitive communions by direct gift of the Holy Ghost. The number, variety, and diffusion of these " spiritual gifts " are, perhaps, quite commonly underestimated. The classical passage concerning them (I Cor. xii.-xiv.) only brings before us a chance picture of divine worship in an apostolical church; it is the ordinary church service of the time, and we have no reason to suppose that essentially the same scenes would not be witnessed in any one of the many congregations planted by the apostles in the length and breadth of the world. The exception would be a church without, not a church with, miraculous gifts. Everywhere the apostolic Church was marked out among men as itself a gift from God, by manifesting its possession of the Spirit through appropriate works of the Spirit: miracles of healings and power, miracles of knowledge and speech. The apostolic Church was characteristically a miraculous Church.

In such circumstances, it would seem very difficult to exaggerate the supernatural claims of the " primitive Church." But Dr. McGiffert has managed to do so. How he has managed to do so, and with what serious consequences to the fundamental bases of our religion, it will now be our duty to point out.

1. He exaggerates the supernatural character of the apostolic Church, in the first place, by representing the enjoyment of the " spiritual gifts " in it as absolutely universal. This is the constant assumption of the Address, and is expressed in such statements as this: " It was the universal conviction of the primitive Church that every Christian believer enjoys the immediate presence of the Holy Spirit. . . . The presence of the Spirit . . . meant the power to work miracles, to speak with tongues, to utter prophecies " (p. 19). " The consciousness of the possession of supernatural gifts " is made, accordingly, the characteristic of the primitive Christian.

But, widespread as the supernatural gifts were in the apostolical Church, they were not universal. They were the characteristic of the apostolical Church, not of the primitive Christian. The circumstances attending the conversion of the Samaritans are recorded for us, in the eighth chapter of Acts, apparently for the very purpose of teaching us this. The first converts were all brought into the Church by the apostles, and the primitive Christians themselves were, it appears, in danger of supposing that the possession of miraculous gifts was the mark of a Christian. Therefore, it was ordered that the conversion of the Samaritans should take place through non-apostolic preaching, that all men might learn (and Simon among them) that " it was through the laying on of the hands of the Apostles that the Spirit was given." In a word, the miraculous gifts are, in the New Testament, made one of the " signs of an Apostle." Where he conveyed them they existed; where he did not convey them they did not exist. In every case where there is record of them they are connected with apostles; usually they are conferred by the actual laying on of the apostles' hands. In no recorded instance are they conferred by the laying on of the hands of one not an apostle. In fine, the supernatural gifts of the apostolic Church are attestations of the apostles' commission and authority. By detaching them from the apostles, and representing them as the possession of the primitive Christian as such, Dr. McGiffert depreciates the apostles relatively to other Christians, and assimilates Christians as such to the apostles. He can gain no authority for this from the New Testament record.

2. The seriousness of this error is exhibited so soon as we note the stress which Dr. McGiffert lays, among the supernatural gifts, on the special gift of revelation as the universal possession of primitive Christians. This, again, is the constant assumption of the Address, and comes to expression in such statements as this: " Christian believers had . . . from the beginning . . . believed themselves in immediate contact with the Holy Spirit and had looked chiefly and directly to him for revelations of truth, as such truth might be needed " (p. 33). Accordingly, we are told that the original conception was that of continuing divine revelations; and the "communion with God through the Holy Ghost," enjoyed by the primitive Christians, is spoken of as involving the reception of "revelations immediately from him " (p. 21); and this is sharply emphasized by contrasting it with " the submission to an external authority in matters both of faith and of practice," which characterized later times. In a word, Dr. McGiffert teaches that the primitive Christian as such, by virtue of his

communion with God through the immediate presence of the Holy Spirit within him, needed no source of knowledge of God's truth and will external to himself: "The Holy Spirit was in the Church, imparting all needed truth and light" (p. 29), and spoke as truly to the other Christians as to the apostles themselves.

Certainly, however, this is not the state of affairs reflected in those documents of the primitive Church gathered into our New Testament. In them the gifts of prophecy, interpretation, revelation, do not appear as the universal possession of Christians as such. They are expressly confined to some, to whom the Spirit has imparted them as He distributes His gifts severally to whom He will. In them, the authority over all Christians of the apostolic declarations of truth and duty is expressly and reiteratingly affirmed, and is based upon the possession of the Spirit by the apostles in a sense in which He was not common to all believers. In them, so far from the apostolic word being subjected to the test of the Spirit in the hearts of all Christians, it is made the test of their possession of the Spirit. In a word, in them the " external authority " of the revelation of truth and duty through the apostles is made supreme; and the recognition of it as supreme is made the test of the presence of the Spirit in the heart of others (I Cor. xiv. 37). Neglecting the whole body of apostolic assertion of authority, and the proof of the acceptance of that authority by the whole body of Christians which pervades the New Testament, Dr. McGiffert represents the common gift of the Holy Spirit to Christians as constituting every Christian a law to himself, and so depreciates the apostles and the apostolic word relatively to other Christians, and assimilates Christians as such to the apostles. He can obtain no warrant for this from the New Testament.

3. The seriousness of this error is still further increased by the circumstance that Dr. McGiffert extends what we may call the supernatural age of Christianity, or what a writer of the same school of thought with himself calls " the Spirit-permeated community," far beyond the limits of the apostolic

period. He expressly tells us that no change of spirit took place synchronously "with the passage of Christianity from the Jewish to the Gentile world," nor yet synchronously "with the death of the Apostles and the close of the apostolic age " (pp. 21, 22). " The Church of the first half of the second century," he tells us, "believed itself to be just as truly under the immediate control of the Spirit as the apostolic Church. There was the same consciousness of the possession of supernatural gifts, especially of the gift of prophecy. . . . No line, in fact, was drawn between their own age and that of the Apostles by the Christians of the early second century. They were conscious of no loss, either of light or of power " (p. 22). " The only authority which was recognized," we are told again, " was the Holy Spirit, and he was supposed to speak to Christians of the second century as truly as he had ever spoken through the Apostles " (p. 33). Accordingly, we are told that it is only on *a priori* or dogmatic grounds, not on historical ones that a line can be drawn between the apostolic and postapostolic ages, so as to " emphasize the supernatural character of the former as distinguished from the latter " (p. 22).

This is again, however, certainly not the impression which the contemporary records make on the reader. Those records do draw the line very sharply between the apostles and any leaders, however great, of the second century Church. To the apostles alone, the Christians of this age conceived, did Jesus give "authority over the gospel," as Barnabas phrases it.[8] They alone were conceived of as in such a sense the mouthpieces of Christ that Ignatius, for example, could say that " the Lord did nothing without the Father, either by Himself or by the apostles." [9] It does not mark the personal humility of the men, but the recognized proprieties of the case, when Polycarp, for instance, wrote to the Philippians: " These things, brethren, write I unto you . . . because you invited me; for neither am I, nor is anyone like unto me, able to follow the wisdom of the blessed and glorious Paul "; [10] or

[8] Ep. 8.

[9] " Epistola ad Magnesios," 7.

[10] " Ad Philippenses," 3.

when Ignatius wrote to the Romans: " I do not enjoin you as Peter and Paul did; they were apostles, I am a convict." [11] From the beginning, therefore, the writings of the apostles are appealed to by name, quoted as " Scripture " along with, and with equal respect with, the Old Testament, and bowed to with reverence and submission. No one apparently dreamed of claiming that equality with the apostles which Dr. McGiffert ascribes to every Christian, as a channel of knowledge concerning divine things; everybody submitted to the " external authority " of their writings.

Nor do these records permit us to believe that the supernatural gifts extended into the second century in an unbroken stream. Who can fail to feel the gulf that yawns between the clear, detailed, and precise allusions to these gifts that meet us in the New Testament, and the vague and general allusions to them which alone are found in the authentic literature of the second century? As was long ago pointed out triumphantly by Conyers Middleton, the early second century is almost bare of allusions to contemporary supernatural gifts. The apostolical Fathers contain no clear and certain allusions to them. And so characteristic of the age is this sobriety of claim, that the apparently miraculous occurrences recorded as attending the martyrdom of Polycarp, in the letter of the church of Smyrna, are an acknowledged bar to the admission of the genuineness of the document; and it is only on purifying the record of them, some as interpolations, some as misinterpretations, that Dr. Lightfoot, for example, thought himself warranted in assigning to it as early a date as A. D. 155. When references to supernatural gifts occur, as in Justin and Irenæus, they are couched in general terms, and suggest rather a general knowledge that such gifts had been common in the Church than specific acquaintance with them as ordinary occurrences of the time. The whole evidence in the matter, in a word, is just what we should expect if these gifts were conferred by the apostles, and gradually died out with the generation which had been brought to Christ by their preaching. The copious stories

[11] " Ad Romanos," 4.

of supernatural occurrences in writings of the third and later centuries have their roots, not in the authentic literature of the second century, but in the apocryphal Gospels and Acts. Dr. McGiffert can obtain no warrant from the contemporary records for his assimilation of the Christians of the early second century to the apostles, and his consequent depreciation of the apostles, both in their personal authority and in the authority of their written word, relatively to the Spirit-led Christian, as such.

4. The whole effect, and, we ought, perhaps, also to say the whole purpose, of the speculatively reconstructed picture of "primitive Christianity" which Dr. McGiffert gives us, is to destroy the supreme authority of the New Testament in the Church as the source and norm of truth and duty, and to reduce Christianity to a form of mystical subjectivism.

Dr. McGiffert admits, indeed, inconsistently with his fundamental conception but consistently with historical fact, that "from the very beginning, the Jewish Scriptures, to which Christ and his Apostles had so frequently appealed, had been appropriated by the Christian Church" (p. 28), although not, possibly, in their native sense. He admits, also, that the truth of apostolic teaching was unquestioned, and that "the Apostles were universally recognized as the divinely commissioned and inspired founders of the Church" (p. 29); and because they were thus looked upon, "their teaching was . . . everywhere regarded as a *source* from which might be gained a knowledge of divine truth" (p. 32).

But he very justly points out that thus to look upon the teaching of the apostles as one of the sources from which a knowledge of truth may be obtained is a "very different thing from making the teaching of the Apostles the sole *standard* of truth," and "ascribing to their teaching exclusive normative authority" (pp. 32–33). Accordingly, he is able to tell us that "the primitive Church had entirely lacked" "the Catholic conception of an apostolic Scripture canon" (p. 42); that the Church attained the conception of an authoritative "apostolic Scripture canon" only deep in the second century and as a piece of borrowed goods from Gnostic heresy; that the early Church needed no New Testament, "especially since the Holy Spirit was in the Church imparting all needed truth and light" (p. 29); and accordingly that "the only authority which was recognized was the Holy Spirit, and he was supposed to speak to Christians of the second century as truly as he had ever spoken through the Apostles" (p. 33).

The ideas thus attributed to the "primitive Church" are the ideas of Dr. McGiffert; and therefore he tells us that the Protestant churches do not speak the truth when they make "the word of God, contained in the Scriptures of the Old and New Testaments," "the sole and ultimate authority for Christian truth" (p. 43), since the Spirit of God is this sole and ultimate authority — as He speaks still to His people as well as formerly through His apostles (p. 43). He tells us, therefore, plainly, that the Holy Spirit still reveals Himself to the members of the several churches "if they keep themselves in touch with him, as truly as to members of the primitive Church" (p. 39), and that is, as we have seen, "as truly as he had ever spoken through the Apostles" (p. 33).

Thus the upshot of Dr. McGiffert's speculative reconstruction of the primitive Church is to set aside the authority of the New Testament altogether, and to enthrone in its place the supreme authority of an "inner light." This is most excellent Quaker teaching, but it is a direct onslaught upon the very basis of Reformed, and, indeed, of the whole Protestant, theology. It seems to be incumbent upon us, therefore, to scrutinize with some care, before we bring these observations on Dr. McGiffert's teaching to a close, what he has to say regarding the origin of the New Testament.

VI. Dr. McGiffert's Theory of the Origin of the New Testament Canon

The task of Dr. McGiffert's Inaugural Address, as we have seen, is to trace the steps in what he thinks "the most vital and far-reaching transformation that Christianity has ever undergone" — "the transformation of the primitive into the

Catholic Church, of the Church of the Apostles into that of
the old Catholic fathers " (pp. 18, 19). One of the steps in this
" momentous transformation " — a step which is justly spoken
of as " of stupendous significance," if it can be made good that
it constituted a part of a transformation which took place in
the Church of the second century — is represented to be no
less a one than this: " the recognition of the teaching of the
Apostles as the exclusive standard and norm of Christian
truth " (p. 29). In this was included, as one of its chief elements, what may be called, without exaggerating Dr. McGiffert's conception, the invention by the second century Church
of the New Testament canon. We must now give some consideration to this astonishing representation.

According to Dr. McGiffert, the primitive Church " entirely lacked " the " conception of an apostolic Scripture
canon " (p. 42). Its spirit was in fact wholly alien to such a
conception. Its spirit was " a spirit of religious individualism,
based upon the felt presence of the Holy Ghost " (p. 19). As
all Christians possessed the Spirit, He was " the only authority
which was recognized "; and He was supposed to speak to all
Christians "as truly as he had ever spoken through the
Apostles " (p. 33). The apostles were no doubt " reverenced "
as " divinely guided and inspired " (p. 32); they "were universally recognized as the divinely commissioned and inspired
founders of the Church " (p. 29); and " their teaching was
consequently everywhere regarded as a *source* from which
might be gained a knowledge of divine truth " (p. 32). But we
will remember that we are very justly told that " that is a very
different thing from making the teaching of the Apostles the
sole *standard* of truth, a very different thing from ascribing to
their teaching exclusive normative authority " (pp. 32–33).
All Christians were as truly " in immediate contact with the
Holy Spirit " as the apostles; to Him directly and not to the
apostles they looked " for revelations of truth, as such truth
might be needed " (p. 33); and having Him always with them,
and having, moreover, along with Him, the Old Testament,
they " needed no New Testament " (p. 29).

But Gnosticism arose, and the Church joined in combat

with it. In the effort to repudiate the spirit of Gnosticism it
was that steps were taken which resulted in the disappearance
of that spirit of individualism which was the spirit of the
" Church of the Apostles," and the introduction of " the spirit
of Catholicism," " which means submission to an external
authority in matters both of faith and of practice " (p. 21).
Three steps were taken towards this consummation. The first
of these was " the recognition of the teaching of the Apostles
as the exclusive standard and norm of Christian truth "
(p. 29). And in this step were included the formation of a New
Testament canon, and the formation of an apostolic rule of
faith.

" The Gnostics were the first Christians to have a New
Testament." In seeking to commend their bizarre doctrines,
they were led to appeal to the authority of the apostles transmitted orally or in writing. " Hence they felt themselves impelled at an early date to form a canon of their own, which
should contain the teachings of Christ through his Apostles,
which should, in other words, be apostolic " (pp. 29–30). This
was a new thing in Christendom. But no one could deny that
what the apostles taught was true; the apostles, as well as
other Christians, had the Spirit. The Gnostics' appeal to
apostolic authority could be met, therefore, only by determining what was truly apostolic. Thus " the Church reached the
conception of an authoritative apostolic Scripture canon and
of an authoritative apostolic rule of faith " (p. 29). " Thus it
was led to gather into one whole all those writings which were
commonly regarded as of apostolic origin; in other words, to
form an authoritative and exclusive apostolic Scripture canon,
which all who wished to be regarded as Christian disciples
must acknowledge, and whose teachings they must accept."
" The conception of an apostolic Scripture canon had arisen,
and the appeal to that canon had been widely made before the
close of the second century " (p. 30).

This is the account which Dr. McGiffert gives of the creation of the New Testament canon. It will be seen that it is very
comprehensive. It includes an account of the origin of the

ascription of "authority" to the apostolic teaching; an account of the rise of the very conception of an apostolic canon of Scripture; an account of the collection into such a canon of the writings " commonly regarded as of apostolic origin "; and an account of the imposition of this body of collected writings upon the Church as its law of faith and conduct. It includes an account, in a word, of the whole " stupendous transformation," from a state of affairs in which every Christian man, by virtue of the Holy Spirit dwelling in him, was a law to himself, and knew no external apostolic authority at all; to a state of affairs when, " under the stress of conflict, they resigned their lofty privileges and made the Apostles the sole recipients (under the new dispensation) of divine communications, and thus their teaching the only source (the Old Testament, of course, excepted) for a knowledge of Christian truth, and the sole standard and norm of such truth " (p. 33). This whole stupendous transformation from beginning to end is included in the course of the second century, that is, belongs to distinctly post-apostolic times. And it was due to the pressure of the Gnostic controversy, and, indeed, was a following by the Church of Gnostic example. In a word, the ascription of any " authority " as teachers to the apostles at all, and the very conception and existence of a New Testament canon, and much more the erection of such a canon as, along with the Old Testament, the exclusive standard of faith and practice, were no part of primitive or apostolical Christianity at all. They were inventions of the second century Church, as expedients the better to meet its difficulties in controversy.

What is to be said of this theory of the formation of the New Testament canon?

1. This is to be said, in the first place: That the cause which is assigned for this stupendous transformation is utterly inadequate to bear its weight.

We are asked to believe that a Church which had hitherto known nothing of apostolic authority, and much less of a canon of authoritative apostolic writings, but had depended wholly upon the living voice of the ever present Holy Spirit speaking to Christians as such, suddenly invented this whole machinery of external authority, solely in order to meet the appeal of the Gnostics to such an external authority. That is to say, in conflict with the Gnostic position, the Church deserted its own entrenched position and went over to the Gnostic position, horse, foot, and dragoons. The Church, we are told, made its sole appeal to the internal authority of the Holy Spirit, speaking in the hearts of living Christians. The Gnostics appealed to the external authority of the apostles, and were the first to do so. If the situation was in any measure like this, the Church was assuredly entitled to meet, and most certainly would have met, this heretical appeal to external authority with the declaration that the Holy Spirit of God which it had was greater than the apostles which the Gnostics claimed to have; and that the living and incorruptible voice of that Spirit in the hearts of Christians was more sure than the dead, corruptible word of the apostles. Yet instead of doing this we are told that the Church weakly submitted to the Gnostic imposition of an external authority upon it, and made its sole appeal to it. This construction is an impossible one. The facts that the Gnostics appealed to apostolic authority, and especially to a body of authoritative apostolic writings as against the Church, and that the Church appealed to apostolic authority and to an apostolic canon as against the Gnostics, do not suggest that the Gnostics were the first to appeal to apostolic teaching and to make a New Testament; but rather prove that the authority of apostolic teaching and of the apostolic writings was already the settled common ground on which all Christians of all names stood.

This is not to be met by saying that just what we have supposed the Church would do in the circumstances assumed was done — by the Montanists. The Montanists were not the Church; but from their first origin were in violent conflict with the Church. Nor did the Montanists represent a revival of the primitive spirit. The main reason for fancying so arises from the exigencies of the theory at present under discussion; and they were certainly not recognized as doing so by the men of their time best qualified to judge of their affiliations. They are uniformly represented as smacking more of Phrygia than of Palestine, more of Cybele than of Christ. Nor yet did they essay to do what in these circumstances we should have expected the Church to do; but something very different indeed. They, too, accepted the external authority of apostles and canon. They themselves rested in this external authority, and did not seek to add to the deposit of truth handed down by it. They claimed only to " develop " the " practical " side of Christianity; and that not by means of a universal teaching of the Spirit, but by means of the sporadic continuance of the specific prophetic office, and by a series of requirements laid by this external authority upon the consciences of men.

Nor is the case met by the remark that the surrender of the Church to the point of view of the Gnostics in this matter of external authority no doubt does presuppose " a partial loss of the original consciousness of the immediate presence of the Holy Spirit " (p. 37). Of course it does; if such an original consciousness ever existed in the sense intended. The point at issue is whether any such " original consciousness," in the sense intended, ever existed. The point urged is that if this consciousness existed it could not but have shown itself in the conflict against Gnosticism. The point yielded is that it must indeed have already been " partially lost." The point claimed is that there is no proof, then, that it ever existed, but every proof that the Gnostics and the Church stood on common ground in their common appeal to " external authority."

2. It is to be said, secondly, that the origin of this stupendous transformation is assigned by this theory to a most unlikely source.

The Gnostics were not just the people whom we can naturally suspect of the invention of the idea of an external apostolic authority. They are known in history as men of speculative intellect, pride of knowledge, rationalistic methods. They are known in history as rejecters of external authorities, not as the creators of them. It is allowed that the Old Testament had from the beginning been accepted by the Church as the authoritative voice of God. The Gnostics repudiated the Jewish Scriptures. Marcion is represented to us, by every contemporary witness, as a man who discarded part of the New Testament canon which had come to his hand; and he certainly mutilated and curtailed the books of his " Apostolicum." To such men as these we can scarcely ascribe the invention of the fiction of an apostolic canon. That they held and appealed to such an " external authority " can be accounted for only on the supposition that this was already the settled position of the Church, which they sought to rationalize and so to reform.

3. It is to be said, thirdly, that to assign the origin of the New Testament canon to the Gnostics is to contradict the whole body of historical testimony which has come down to us as to the relation of the Gnostics to the New Testament canon.

The Fathers, to whose refutation of them we are indebted for well-nigh our whole knowledge of the Gnostics, are unanimous in representing them as proceeding with the church canon as their point of departure, not as first suggesting to the Church the conception of a canon. They differed among themselves, we are told, in their mode of dealing with the Church's canon. Some, like Marcion, used the shears, and boldly cut off from it all that did not suit their purposes; others, like Valentinus, depended on artificial exegesis to conform the teaching of the apostles to their own views. For all alike, however, an authoritative apostolic canon is presupposed, and to all alike this presupposed authoritative apostolic canon constituted an obstacle to their heretical teachings, and accordingly would not have been presupposed by them could it have been avoided.

4. And this leads to saying, fourthly, that this whole theory of the formation of the New Testament canon involves a serious arraignment of the trustworthiness, or, as we should rather say plainly, the truthfulness, of the whole body of the great Church Fathers who ornament the closing years of the second century.

Take such a man, for instance, as Irenæus. It is positively impossible to believe that anything like the origination of, or any essential change in, the New Testament canon occurred in his lifetime without charging him with conscious falsehood in his witness concerning it. For Irenæus not only testifies to the existence and estimate as divinely authoritative of the New Testament at the close of his life, but repeatedly asserts that this same New Testament had enjoyed this same authority from the apostles' day. Now, Irenæus was already a young man when Marcion provided his followers with his mutilated New Testament. He had himself sat as a pupil at the feet of John's pupil, Polycarp, in Asia Minor. He had served the church of Lyons as presbyter and bishop. He had kept in full communication with the churches both of Ephesus and of Rome. And he tells us that so strict had been the Church's watchfulness over its New Testament that not even a single text of it had been corrupted. It avails nothing to say that, nevertheless, many texts had been corrupted. Irenæus could be mistaken in some things; but in some things he could not be mistaken. If such a thing as the New Testament had been invented in his own day he could not have been ignorant of it. Here the dilemma is stringent: either Irenæus has borne consciously false witness, or else the Church in Ephesus, in Rome, and in Gaul, already had in the days of Marcion the same New Testament which it is confessed that it had at the close of the century. And practically the same argument might be formed on the testimony of Clement of Alexandria, Tertullian, Theophilus of Antioch, or, indeed, the whole body of the church writers of the close of the second century.

5. It is to be said, still further, that the whole theory of the origin of the New Testament canon in post-apostolic circles is inconsistent with the acknowledged position of the Church during this period.

It is acknowledged that from the beginning the Church received the Old Testament at the apostles' hands as the word of God (p. 28). From the beginning, therefore, the Church had an "external authority," and possessed already the idea of a "canon." How could it help adding to this authoritative teaching the writings of the apostles, whom, as is admitted, it "recognized as the divinely commissioned and inspired founders of the Church " (p. 29), and whom it reverenced " as divinely guided and inspired" (p. 32)? The whole dealing of the Church with the heresies of the day betrays the fact that apostolicity and authority were to it synonymous terms. Every step which Dr. McGiffert traces in the opposition to these heresies is an outgrowth of this conception, and is recognized by Dr. McGiffert as an expression of this conception. Apostolicity was indeed the war-cry in all the Church's battles; and yet we are asked to suppose that this was a *borrowed* war-cry — borrowed from its enemies!

6. Finally, it is to be said that there is quite as much evidence from this whole period of the Church's possession and high estimate of the New Testament, as the nature of the literary remains from the time would warrant us in expecting.

It is nothing to the point to say that we cannot, with full historical right, speak of a New Testament "canon" until deep in the fourth century, since this word was not applied to the New Testament in this sense until then; or that we cannot, with full historical right, speak of a " New Testament " until late in the second century, for not until then was this name applied to it. We are not investigating the history of names, but of things. The term "instrument" which Tertullian applies to the New Testament is just as good a designation of the thing as the term " canon " that Jerome uses. And there was an earlier name for what we call the " New Testament " than that now hoary and sacred title. Over against " The Law and the Prophets," which was the name then given the Old Testament, men had a " Gospel and Apostles," which was the name they gave the New Testament. And as they commonly called the one half of the canon briefly " The Law," so they called the other half for similar reasons " The Gospel." The name still remains in Augustine; it is the common name for the New Testament in the second century. It was clearly already in use in the days of Ignatius, and of the authors of the so-called second epistle of Clement and the epistle to Diognetus. New Testament books are among the

" Oracles " in the days of Papias and of the author of II
Clement. To Polycarp, Ephesians was already along with
Psalms in " the sacred letters." To Barnabas, Matthew was
" Scripture "; and indeed, already to I Timothy Luke was as
much " Scripture " as Deuteronomy (I Tim. v. 18), and to
II Peter Paul's letters as much Scripture as " the other Scriptures " of the Old Testament. Dr. McGiffert gives some hint
(p. 27), indeed, that he may deny that I Timothy was a letter
of Paul's, or even a product of the first Christian century.
Whether he would make II Peter also of post-Gnostic origin,
he does not tell us. But too many adjustments of this kind will
need to be made to render it " historical " to deny that the
Church had an authoritative New Testament from the beginning of its life.

What color of historical ground remains, then, for the
asserted " stupendous transformation " in the Church during
the second century, by which it acquired not only the actual
possession but the very conception of an apostolic Scripture
canon?

There is, first of all, this fact: that in the latter part of
the second century the evidence that the Church possessed a
New Testament canon first becomes copious. But this is not
because the Church then first acquired a canon; the evidence
is retrospective in its character and force. It is simply because
Christian literature of a sort which could bear natural testimony to the fact first then becomes abundant. It is a great
historical blunder to confound such an emergence of copious
testimony with the historical emergence of the thing testified to.

Then, secondly, there is doubtless this fact: that in its
controversies with the Gnostic sects the Church was thrown
back upon its New Testament and its authority as before it
had never had occasion to be. When the gospel was preached
to Jews and Gentiles the simple story was told; and there was
no occasion to appeal to books, save in the former case to the
prophecies of the Old Testament. When Christianity was de-

fended before Jews or before Gentiles, the common ground of appeal was necessarily restricted to the Old Testament and to reason; and any allusion to Christian books was necessarily only by the way and purely incidental. But when new gospels were preached, then the appeal was necessarily to the authority of the authoritative teachers of the true gospel. There is a sense, then, in which it may be said that, in these controversies, the Church "discovered" its New Testament. It learned its value; it investigated its contents with new zeal and new insight; in the process it strengthened its sense of its preciousness and authority.

Harnack in one place uses phraseology in describing what took place with the New Testament in the second century, which, if we could only be allowed to take it in its strict verbal meaning, would express the exact truth. The transformation, he tells us, must be looked upon as " a change in interest in the Holy Scriptures brought about by the Gnostic and Montanistic conflict." This is just what happened. But this is not what Harnack and his followers demand of us to believe to have happened. They demand that we shall believe that in these controversies the Church created these " Holy Scriptures " of the New Testament. They do so without historical warrant, and in doing so they destroy the New Testament as " Holy Scriptures "; that is, they reduce its authority as " Holy Scriptures " to the authority of the second century Church, which they would have us believe created it " Holy Scripture " in its controversies, and which, indeed, as they would teach us, even created some of the books themselves (e.g. I Timothy) out of which this " Holy Scripture " was constituted.

How, then, are we to conceive the formation of the New Testament canon? After so much said as to how we are not to conceive it, it is but right that before we bring this paper to a close we should try to place clearly before us the actual process of its formation. Let us now essay to do this in the simplest and most primary way.

VII. The Formation of the Canon of the New Testament

In order to obtain a correct understanding of what is called the formation of the canon of the New Testament, it is necessary to begin by fixing very firmly in our minds one fact, which is obvious enough, and to which attention has been already called, but the importance of which in this connection cannot be overemphasized. That is, that the Christian Church did not require to form for itself the idea of a " canon," or, as we should more commonly call it to-day, of a " Bible " — that is, of a collection of books given of God to be the authoritative rule of faith and practice. It inherited this idea from the Jewish Church, along with the thing itself, the Jewish Scriptures, or the " Canon of the Old Testament." The Church did not grow up by natural law; it was founded. And the authoritative teachers sent forth by Christ to found His Church carried with them as their most precious possession a body of divine Scriptures, which they imposed on the Church that they founded as its code of law. No reader of the New Testament can need proof of this; on every page of that book is spread the evidence that from the very beginning the Old Testament was as cordially recognized as law by the Christian as by the Jew. The Christian Church thus was never without a " Bible " or a " canon."

But the Old Testament books were not the only ones which the apostles (by Christ's own appointment the authoritative founders of the Church) imposed upon the infant churches as their authoritative rule of faith and practice. No more authority dwelt in the prophets of the old covenant than in themselves, the apostles, who had been " made sufficient as ministers of a new covenant "; for (as one of themselves argued) " if that which passeth away was with glory, much more that which remaineth is in glory." Accordingly, not only was the gospel they delivered, in their own estimation, itself a divine revelation, but it was also preached " in the Holy Ghost " (I Pet. i. 12); not merely the matter of it but the very words in which it was clothed were " of the Holy Spirit "

(I Cor. ii. 13). Their own commands were, therefore, of divine authority (I Thess. iv. 2), and their writings were the depository of these commands (II Thess. ii. 15). " If any man obeyeth not our word by this epistle," says Paul to one church (II Thess. iii. 14), " note that man, that ye have no company with him." To another he makes it the test of a Spirit-led man to recognize that what he was writing to them was " the commandments of the Lord " (I Cor. xiv. 37). Inevitably, such writings, making so awful a claim on their acceptance, were received by the infant churches as of a quality equal to that of the old " Bible," placed alongside of its older books as an additional part of the one law of God, and read as such in their meetings for worship — a practice which, moreover, was required by the apostles (I Thess. v. 27; Col. iv. 16; Rev. i. 3). In the apprehension, therefore, of the earliest churches, the " Scriptures " were not a *closed* but an *increasing* " canon." Such they had been from the beginning, as they gradually grew in number from Moses to Malachi; and such they were to continue as long as there should remain among the churches " men of God who spake as they were moved by the Holy Ghost."

We say that this immediate placing of the new books, given the Church under the seal of apostolic authority, among the Scriptures already established as such was inevitable. It is also historically evinced from the very beginning. Thus, the Apostle Peter, writing in A.D. 68, speaks of Paul's numerous letters, not in contrast with the Scriptures, but as among the Scriptures, and in contrast with " the *other* Scriptures " (II Pet. iii. 16), that is, of course, those of the Old Testament. In like manner, the Apostle Paul combines, as if it were the most natural thing in the world, the Book of Deuteronomy and the Gospel of Luke under the common head of " Scripture " (I Tim. v. 18): " For the Scripture saith, ' Thou shalt not muzzle the ox when he treadeth out the corn ' [Deut. xxv. 4]; and, ' The laborer is worthy of his hire ' [Luke x. 7]." The line of such quotations is never broken in Christian literature. Polycarp [12] in A.D. 115 unites the Psalms and Ephe-

[12] " Epistola ad Philippenses," 12.

sians in exactly similar manner: "In the sacred books, . . . as it is said in these Scriptures, ' Be ye angry and sin not,' and ' Let not the sun go down upon your wrath.' " So, a few years later, the so-called second letter of Clement, after quoting Isaiah, adds (chap. 2): " And another Scripture, however, says, ' I came not to call the righteous, but sinners,' " quoting from Matthew, a book which Barnabas (*circa* 97–106 A.D.) had already adduced as Scripture. After this such quotations are common.

What needs emphasis at present about these facts is that they obviously are not evidences of a gradually heightening estimate of the New Testament books, originally received on a lower level, and just beginning to be tentatively accounted Scripture. They are conclusive evidences, rather, of the estimation of the New Testament books from the very beginning as Scripture, and of their attachment as Scripture to the other Scriptures already in hand. The early Christians did not, then, first form a rival " canon " of " new books " which came only gradually to be accounted as of equal divinity and authority with the " old books "; they received new book after new book from the apostolical circle, as equally " Scripture " with the old books, and added them one by one to the collection of old books as additional Scriptures, until at length the new books thus added were numerous enough to be looked upon as another *section* of " the Scriptures."

The earliest name given to this new section of Scripture was framed on the model of the name by which what we know as the Old Testament was then known. Just as it was called " The Law and the Prophets and the Psalms " (or " The Hagiographa "), or, more briefly, " The Law and the Prophets," or, even more briefly still, " The Law," so the enlarged Bible was called " The Law and the Prophets, with the Gospels and the Apostles," [13] or, more briefly, " The Law and the Gospel " (so Claudius Apollinaris, Irenæus); while the new books separately were called " The Gospel and the Apostles," or, most briefly of all, " The Gospel." This earliest name for the new

[13] So Clement of Alexandria, " Stromata," vi. 11: 88; Tertullian, " De præscriptione hæreticorum," 36.

Bible, with all that it involves as to its relation to the old and briefor Bible, is traceable as far back as Ignatius (A.D. 115), who makes use of it repeatedly.[14] In one passage he gives us a hint of the controversies which the enlarged Bible of the Christians aroused among the Judaizers: "When I heard some saying," he writes,[15] "'Unless I find it in the *Old* [*Books*] I will not believe the *Gospel*,' on my saying, 'It is written,' they answered, 'That is the question.' To me, however, Jesus Christ *is* the Old [Books]; His cross and death and resurrection, and the faith which is by Him, the undefiled Old [Books], by which I wish, by your prayers, to be justified. The priests, indeed, are good, but the High Priest better," etc. Here Ignatius appeals to the "Gospel" as Scripture, and the Judaizers object, receiving from him the answer, in effect, which Augustine afterwards formulated in the well-known saying that the New Testament lies hidden in the Old, and the Old Testament is first made clear in the New. What we need now to observe, however, is that to Ignatius the New Testament was not a different book from the Old Testament, but part of the one body of Scripture with it; an *accretion,* so to speak, which had grown upon it.

This is the testimony of all the early witnesses, even of those which speak for the distinctively Jewish-Christian churches. For example, that curious Jewish-Christian writing, "The Testaments of the Twelve Patriarchs" ("Benjamin," 11), tells us, under the cover of an *ex post facto* prophecy, that "the work and word" of Paul, that is, confessedly, the Book of Acts and Paul's epistles, "shall be written in the Holy Books," that is, as is understood by all, made a part of the existent Bible. So, even in the Talmud, in a scene intended to ridicule a "bishop" of the first century, he is represented as finding Galatians by "sinking himself deeper" into the same "book" which contained the Law of Moses ("Babl. Shabbath," 116 a and b). The details cannot be entered into here. Let it suffice to say that, from the evidence of the frag-

14 E.g. "Ad Philad.," 5; "Ad Smyrnæos," 7.
15 "Ad Philadelphenses," 8.

ments which alone have been preserved to us of the Christian writings of that very early time, it appears that from the beginning of the second century (and that is from the end of the apostolic age) a collection (Ignatius, II Clement) of " New Books " (Ignatius), called the " Gospel and Apostles " (Ignatius, Marcion), was already a part of the " oracles " of God (Polycarp, Papias, II Clement), or " Scriptures " (I Timothy, II Peter, Barnabas, Polycarp, II Clement), or the " Holy Books," or " Bible " (" The Testaments of the Twelve Patriarchs ").

The number of books included in this added body of New Books, at the opening of the second century, cannot, of course, be satisfactorily determined by the evidence of these fragments alone. From them we may learn, however, that the section of it called the " Gospel " included Gospels written by " the apostles and their companions " (Justin), which there is no reason to doubt were our four Gospels now received. The section called " The Apostles " contained the Book of Acts (" The Testaments of the Twelve Patriarchs ") and epistles of Paul, John, Peter, and James. The evidence from various quarters is, indeed, enough to show that the collection in general use contained all the books which we at present receive, with the possible exceptions of Jude, II and III John, and Philemon; and it is more natural to suppose that failure of very early evidence for these brief booklets is due to their insignificant size rather than to their non-acceptance.

It is to be borne in mind, however, that the extent of the collection may have — and, indeed, is historically shown actually to have — varied in different localities. The Bible was circulated only in hand-copies, slowly and painfully made; and an incomplete copy, obtained, say, at Ephesus in A.D. 68, would be likely to remain for many years the Bible of the church to which it was conveyed, and might, indeed, become the parent of other copies, incomplete like itself, and thus the means of providing a whole district with incomplete Bibles. Thus, when we inquire after the history of the New Testament canon, we need to distinguish such questions as these: (1)

When was the New Testament canon completed? (2) When did any one church acquire a completed canon? (3) When did the completed canon, the complete Bible, obtain universal circulation and acceptance? (4) On what ground and evidence did the churches with incomplete Bibles accept the remaining books when they were made known to them?

The canon of the New Testament was completed when the last authoritative book was given to any church by the apostles, and that was when John wrote the Apocalypse, about A.D. 98. Whether the church of Ephesus had a completed canon when it received the Apocalypse, or not, would depend on whether there was any epistle, say that of Jude, which had not yet reached it, with authenticating proof of its apostolicity. There is room for historical investigation here. Certainly the whole canon was not universally received by the churches till somewhat later. The Latin Church of the second and third centuries did not quite know what to do with the Epistle to the Hebrews. The Syrian churches for some centuries may have lacked the lesser of the Catholic Epistles and Revelation. But from the time of Irenæus down, the Church at large had the whole canon as we now possess it. And though a section of the Church may not yet have been satisfied of the apostolicity of a certain book, or of certain books, and though afterwards doubts may have arisen in sections of the Church as to the apostolicity of certain books (e.g. of Revelation), yet in no case was it more than a respectable minority of the Church which was slow in receiving, or which came afterwards to doubt, the credentials of any of the books that then, as now, constituted the canon of the New Testament accepted by the Church at large. And in every case the principle on which a book was accepted, or doubts against it laid aside, was the historical tradition of apostolicity.

Let it, however, be clearly understood that it was not exactly apostolic *authorship* which constituted a book a portion of the " canon." Apostolic authorship was, indeed, early confounded with canonicity. It was doubt as to the apostolic authorship of Hebrews, in the west, and of James and Jude, which seems to underlie the slowness of the inclusion of these books in the "canon" of certain churches. But from the beginning it was not so. The principle of canonicity was not apostolic authorship, but *imposition by the apostles as "law."* Hence Tertullian's name for the "canon" is "*instrumentum*," and he speaks of the Old and New *Instrument* as we would of the Old and New Testament. That the apostles so imposed the Old Testament on the churches which they founded as their "instrument," or "law," or "canon," can be denied by none. And in imposing new books on the same churches, by the same apostolical authority, they did not confine themselves to books of their own composition. It is the Gospel according to Luke, a man who was not an apostle, which Paul parallels in I Tim. v. 18, with Deuteronomy, as equally "Scripture" with it, in the first extant quotation of a New Testament book as Scripture. The Gospels which constituted the first division of the New Books — of "The Gospel and the Apostles" — Justin tells us, were "written by the apostles and their companions." The authority of the apostles, as founders of the Church by divine appointment, was embodied in whatever books they imposed on the Church as law, not merely in those which they themselves had written.

The early churches received, as we receive, into their New Testament all the books historically evinced to them as given by the apostles to the churches as their code of law; and we must not mistake the historical evidences of the slow circulation and authentication of these books over the widely extended Church for evidence of slowness of "canonization" of books by the authority or the taste of the Church itself.

XXI

MYSTICISM AND CHRISTIANITY

MYSTICISM AND CHRISTIANITY [1]

RELIGION is, shortly, the reaction of the human soul in the presence of God. As God is as much a part of the environment of man as the earth on which he stands, no man can escape from religion any more than he can escape from gravitation. But though every man necessarily reacts to God, men react of course diversely, each according to his nature, or perhaps we would better say, each according to his temperament. Thus, broadly speaking, three main types of religion arise, corresponding to the three main varieties of the activity of the human spirit, intellectual, emotional, and voluntary. According as the intellect, sensibility, or will is dominant in him, each man produces for himself a religion prevailingly of the intellect, sensibility, or active will; and all the religions which men have made for themselves find places somewhere among these three types, as they produce themselves more or less purely, or variously intermingle with one another.

We say advisedly, all the religions which men have made for themselves. For there is an even more fundamental division among religions than that which is supplied by these varieties. This is the division between man-made and God-made religions. Besides the religions which man has made for himself, God has made a religion for man. We call this revealed religion; and the most fundamental division which separates between religions is that which divides revealed religion from unrevealed religions. Of course, we do not mean to deny that there is an element of revelation in all religions. God is a person, and persons are known only as they make themselves known — reveal themselves. The term revelation is used in this distinction, therefore, in a pregnant sense. In the un-

[1] Reprinted from *The Biblical Review*, ii. 1917, pp. 169–191 (published by The Biblical Seminary in New York; copyrighted).

revealed religions God is known only as He has revealed Himself in His acts of the creation and government of the world, as every person must reveal himself in his acts if he acts at all. In the one revealed religion God has revealed Himself also in acts of special grace, among which is included the open Word.

There is an element in revealed religion, therefore, which is not found in any unrevealed religion. This is the element of authority. Revealed religion comes to man from without; it is imposed upon him from a source superior to his own spirit. The unrevealed religions, on the other hand, flow from no higher source than the human spirit itself. However much they may differ among themselves in the relative prominence given in each to the functioning of the intellect, sensibility, or will, they have this fundamental thing in common. They are all, in other words, natural religions in contradistinction to the one supernatural religion which God has made.

There is a true sense, then, in which it may be said that the unrevealed religions are "religions of the spirit" and revealed religion is the "religion of authority." Authority is the correlate of revelation, and wherever revelation is — and only where revelation is — is there authority. Just because we do not see in revelation man reaching up lame hands toward God and feeling fumblingly after Him if haply he may find Him, but God graciously reaching strong hands down to man, bringing him help in his need, we see in it a gift from God, not a creation of man's. On the other hand, the characteristic of all unrevealed religions is that they are distinctly man-made. They have no authority to appeal to, they rest solely on the deliverances of the human spirit. As Rudyard Kipling shrewdly makes his "Tommy" declare:

The 'eathen in 'is blindness bows down to wood and stone,
'E don't obey no orders unless they is 'is own.

Naturally it makes no difference in this respect whether it is the rational, emotional, or volitional element in the activities of the human spirit to which appeal is chiefly made. In no case are the foundations sunk deeper than the human spirit itself, and nothing appears in the structure that is raised which the human spirit does not supply. The preponderance of one or another of these activities in the structure does, however, make an immense difference in the aspect of that structure. Mysticism is the name which is given to the particular one of these structures, the predominant place in which is taken by the sensibility. It is characteristic of mysticism that it makes its appeal to the feelings as the sole, or at least as the normative, source of knowledge of divine things. That is to say, it is the religious sentiment which constitutes for it the source of religious knowledge. Of course mystics differ with one another in the consistency with which they apply their principle. And of course they differ with one another in the account they give of this religious sentiment to which they make their appeal. There are, therefore, many varieties of mystics, pure and impure, consistent and inconsistent, naturalistic and supernaturalistic, pantheistic and theistic — even Christian. What is common to them all, and what makes them all mystics, is that they all rest on the religious sentiment as the source of knowledge of divine things.

The great variety of the accounts which mystics give of the feeling to which they make their appeal arises from the very nature of the case. There is a deeper reason for a mystic being "mute" — that is what the name imports — than that he wishes to make a mystery of his discoveries. He is "mute" because, as a mystic, he has nothing to say. When he sinks within himself he finds feelings, not conceptions; his is an emotional, not a conceptional, religion; and feelings, emotions, though not inaudible, are not articulate. As a mystic, he has no conceptional language in which to express what he feels. If he attempts to describe it he must make use of terms derived from the religious or philosophical thought in vogue about him, that is to say, of non-mystical language. His hands may be the hands of Esau, but his voice is the voice of Jacob. The language in which he describes the reality which he finds within him does not in the least indicate, then, what it is; it is merely a concession to the necessity of communicating with the external world or with his own more external self. What he finds within him is just to his apprehension an "unutterable abyss." And Synesius does himself and his fellow mystics no injustice when he declares that "the mystic mind says this and that, gyrating around the unutterable abyss."

On the brink of this abyss the mystic may stand in awe, and, standing in awe upon its brink, he may deify it. Then he calls it indifferently Brahm or Zeus, Allah or the Holy Spirit, according as men about him speak of God. He explains its meaning, in other words, in terms of the conception of the universe which he has brought with him, or, as it is more fashionable now to phrase it, each in accordance with his own world-view. Those who are held in the grasp of a naturalistic conception of the world will naturally speak of the religious feeling of which they have become acutely conscious as only one of the multitudinous natural movements of the human soul, and will seek merely, by a logical analysis of its presuppositions and implications, to draw out its full meaning. Those who are sunk in a pantheistic world-view will speak of its movements as motions of the subliminal consciousness, and will interpret them as the surgings within us of the divine ground of all things, in listening to which they conceive themselves to be sinking beneath the waves that fret the surface of the ocean of being and penetrating to its profounder depths. If, on the other hand, the mystic chances to be a theist, he may look upon the movements of his religious feelings as effects in his soul wrought by the voluntary actions of the God whom he acknowledges; and if he should happen to be a Christian, he may interpret these movements, in accordance with the teachings of the Scriptures, as the leadings of the Holy Spirit or as the manifestations within him of the Christ within us the hope of glory.

This Christian mysticism, now, obviously differs in no essential respect from the parallel phenomena which are observable in other religions. It is only general mysticism manifesting itself on Christian ground and interpreting itself accordingly in the forms of Christian thought. It is mysticism which has learned to speak in Christian language. The phenomena themselves are universal. There has never been an age of the world, or a form of religion, in which they have not been in evidence. There are always everywhere some men who stand out among their fellows as listeners to the inner voice, and who, refusing the warning which Thoas gives to Iphigenia in Goethe's play, " There speaks no God: thy heart alone 'tis speaks," respond like Iphigenia with passionate conviction, " 'Tis only through our hearts the gods e'er speak." But these common phenomena are, naturally, interpreted in each instance, according to the general presuppositions of each several subject or observer of them. Thus, for example, they are treated as the intrusion of God into the soul (Ribet), or as the involuntary intrusion of the unconscious into consciousness (Hartmann), or as the intrusion of the subconscious into the consciousness (Du Prel), or as the intrusion of feeling, strong and overmastering, into the operations of the intellect (Goethe).

According to these varying interpretations we get different types of mysticism, differing from one another not in intrinsic character so much as in the explanations given of the common phenomena. Many attempts have been made to arrange these types in logical schemes which shall embrace all varieties and present them in an intelligible order. Thus, for example, from the point of view of the ends sought, R. A. Vaughan distinguishes between theopathic, theosophic, and theurgic mysticism, the first of which is content with feeling, while the second aspires to knowledge, and the third seeks power. The same classes may perhaps be called more simply emotional, intellectual, and thelematic mysticism. From the point of view of the inquiry into the sources of religious knowledge four well-marked varieties present themselves, which have been given the names of naturalistic, supernaturalistic, theosophical, and pantheistic mysticism.

The common element in all these varieties of mysticism is that they all seek all, or most, or the normative or at least a substantial part, of the knowledge of God in human feelings, which they look upon as the sole or at least the most trustworthy or the most direct source of the knowledge of God. The differences between them turn on the diverging conceptions which they entertain of the origin of the religious feelings thus appealed to. Naturalistic mysticism conceives them as merely " the natural religious consciousness of men, as excited and influenced by the circumstances of the individual." Supernaturalistic, as the effects of operations of the divine Spirit in the heart, the human spirit moving only as it is moved·upon by the divine. Theosophical mysticism goes a step further and regards the religious feelings as the footprints of Deity moving in the soul, and as, therefore, immediate sources of knowledge of God, which is to be obtained by simple quiescence and rapt contemplation of these His movements. Pantheistic mysticism advances to the complete identification of the soul with God, who is therefore to be known by applying oneself to the simple axiom: " Know thyself."

Clearly it is the type which has been called supernaturalistic that has the closest affinity with Christianity. Christian mysticism accordingly, at its best, takes this form and passes insensibly from it into evangelical Christianity, to which the indwelling of the Holy Ghost — the Christ within — is fundamental, and which rejoices in such spiritual experiences as are summed up in the old categories of regeneration and sanctification — the rebegetting of the soul into newness of life and the leading of the new-created soul along the pathway of holy living. From these experiences, of course, much may be inferred not only of the modes of God's working in the salvation of men but also of the nature and character of God the worker.

The distinction between mysticism of this type and evangelical Christianity, from the point of view which is now occupying our attention, is nevertheless clear. Evangelical Christianity interprets all religious experience by the normative revelation of God recorded for us in the Holy Scriptures, and guides, directs, and corrects it from these Scriptures, and thus molds it into harmony with what God in His revealed Word lays down as the normal Christian life. The mystic, on the other hand, tends to substitute his religious experience for the objective revelation of God recorded in the written Word, as the source from which he derives his knowledge of God, or at least to subordinate the expressly revealed Word as the less direct and convincing source of knowledge of God to his own religious experience. The result is that the external revelation is relatively depressed in value, if not totally set aside.

In the history of Christian thought mysticism appears accordingly as that tendency among professing Christians which looks within, that is, to the religious feelings, in its search for God. It supposes itself to contemplate within the soul the movements of the divine Spirit, and finds in them either the sole sources of trustworthy knowledge of God, or the most immediate and convincing sources of that knowledge, or, at least, a coördinate source of it alongside of the written Word. The characteristic of Christian mysticism, from the point of view of religious knowledge, is therefore its appeal to the " inner light," or " the internal word," either to the exclusion of the external or written Word, or as superior to it and normative for its interpretation, or at least as coördinate authority with it, this "inner light" or "internal word" being conceived not as the rational understanding but as the immediate deliverance of the religious sentiment. As a mere matter of fact, now, we lack all criteria, apart from the written Word, to distinguish between those motions of the heart which are created within us by the Spirit of God and those which arise out of the natural functioning of the religious consciousness. This substitution of our religious experience — or " Christian consciousness," as it is sometimes called — for the objective Word as the proper source of our religious knowledge ends therefore either in betraying us into purely rationalistic mysticism, or is rescued from that by the postulation of a relation of the soul to God which strongly tends toward pantheizing mysticism.

In point of fact, mysticism in the Church is found to gravitate, with pretty general regularity, either toward rationalism or toward pantheism. In effect, indeed, it appears to differ from rationalism chiefly in temperament, if we may not even say in temperature. The two have it in common that they appeal for knowledge of God only to what is internal to man; and to what, internal to man, men make their actual appeal, seems to be determined very much by their temperaments, or, as has been said, by their temperatures. The human soul is a small thing at best; it is not divided into water-tight compartments; the streams of feeling which are flowing up and down in it and the judgments of the understanding which are incessantly being framed in it are constantly acting and reacting on one another. It is not always easy for it to be perfectly clear, as it turns within itself and gazes upon its complex movements, of the real source, rational or emotional, of the impressions which it observes to be crystallizing within it into convictions. It has often been observed in the progress of history, accordingly, that men who have deserted the guidance of external revelation have become mystics or rationalists largely according as their religious life was warm or cold. In periods of religious fervor or in periods of fervid religious reactions they are mystics; in periods of religious decline they are rationalists. The same person, indeed, sometimes vibrates between the two points of view with the utmost facility.

It is, however, with pantheism that mysticism stands in the closest association. It would not be untrue, in fact, to say that as a historical phenomenon mysticism is just pantheism reduced to a religion, that is to say, with its postulates transformed into ends. Defenses of mysticism against the inevitable (and true) charge of pantheizing usually, indeed, stop with the announcement of this damaging fact. "Lasson," remarks Dean Inge as if that were the conclusion of the matter instead of, as it is, the confession of judgment, "says well, in his book on Meister Eckhart, 'Mysticism views everything from the standpoint of teleology, while pantheism generally stops at causality.'" What it is of importance to observe is that it is precisely what pantheism, being a philosophy, postulates as conditions of being that mysticism, being a religion, proposes as objects of attainment. Mysticism is simply, therefore, pantheism expressed in the terms of religious aspiration.

This is as true within the Christian Church as without it. All forms of mysticism have no doubt from time to time found a place for themselves within the Church. Or perhaps we should rather say that they have always existed in it, and have from time to time manifested their presence there. This must be said even of naturalistic mysticism. There are those who call themselves Christians who yet conceive of Christianity as merely the natural religious sentiment excited into action by contact with the religious impulse set in motion by Jesus Christ and transmitted down the ages by the natural laws of motion, as motion is transmitted, say, through a row of billiard balls in contact with one another. Yet it would only be true to say that mysticism as a phenomenon in the history of the Church has commonly arisen in the wake of the dominating influence in the contemporary world of a pantheizing philosophy. It is the product of a pantheizing manner of thinking impinging on the religious nature, or, if we prefer to phrase it from the opposite point of view, of religious thought seeking to assimilate and to express itself in terms of a pantheizing philosophy.

The fullest stream of mystical thought which has entered the Church finds its origin in the Neoplatonic philosophy. It is to the writings of the Pseudo-Dionysius that its naturalization in the Eastern Church is usually broadly ascribed. The sluice-gates of the Western Church were opened for it, in the same broad sense, by John Scotus Erigena. It has flowed strongly down through all the subsequent centuries, widening here and there into lakelets. The form of mysticism which is most widely disturbing the modern Protestant churches comes, however, from a different source. It takes its origin from the movement inaugurated in the first third of the nineteenth century by Friedrich Schleiermacher, with the ostensible purpose of rescuing Christianity from the assaults of rationalism by vindicating for religion its own independent right of existence, in a region " beyond reason." The result of this attempt to separate religion from reason has been, of course, merely to render religion unreasonable; even Plotinus warned us long ago that " he who would rise above reason falls outside of it."

But what we are immediately concerned to observe is the very widespread rejection of all "external authority," which has been one of the results of this movement, and the consequent casting of men back upon their "religious experience," corporate or individual, as their sole trustworthy ground of religious convictions. This is, of course, only "the inner light" of an earlier form of mysticism under a new and (so it has been hoped) more inoffensive name; and it is naturally, therefore, burdened with all the evils which inhere in the mystical attitude. These evils do not affect extreme forms of mysticism only; they are intrinsic in the two common principles which give to all its forms their fundamental character — the misprision of "external authority," and the attempt to discover in the movements of the sensibilities the ground or norm of all the religious truth which will be acknowledged.

"Mystics," says George Tyrrell, "think they touch the divine when they have only blurred the human form with a cloud of words." The astonishing thing about this judgment is not the judgment itself but the source from which it comes. For Tyrrell himself as a "Modernist" held with our "experientialists," and when he cast his eye into the future could see nothing but mysticism as the last refuge for religion. "Houtin and Loisy are right," he writes; "the Christianity of the future will consist of mysticism and charity, and possibly the eucharist in its primitive form as the outward bond. I desire no more." The plain fact is that this "religious experience," to which we are referred for our religious knowledge, can speak to us only in the language of religious thought; and where there is no religious thought to give it a tongue it is dumb. And above all, it must be punctually noted, it cannot speak to us in a Christian tongue unless that Christian tongue is lent it by the Christian revelation. The rejection of "external authority" and our relegation to "religious experience" for our religious knowledge is nothing more nor less, then, than the definitive abolition of Christianity and the substitution for it of natural religion. Tyrrell perfectly understood this, and that is what he means when he speaks of the Christianity of the future as reduced to "mysticism and charity." All the puzzling facts of Christianity (this is his view) — the incarnation and resurrection of the Son of God and all the puzzling doctrines of Christianity — the atonement in Christ's blood, the renewal through the Spirit, the resurrection of the body — all, all will be gone. For all this rests on "external authority." And men will content themselves, will be compelled to content themselves, with the motions of their own religious sensibilities — and (let us hope) with charity.

There is nothing more important in the age in which we live than to bear constantly in mind that all the Christianity of Christianity rests precisely on "external authority." Religion, of course, we can have without "external authority," for man is a religious animal and will function religiously always and everywhere. But Christianity, no. Christianity rests on "external authority," and that for the very good reason that it is not the product of man's religious sentiment but is a gift from God. To ask us to set aside "external authority" and throw ourselves back on what we can find within us alone — call it by whatever name you choose, "religious experience," "the Christian consciousness," "the inner light," "the immanent Divine" — is to ask us to discard Christianity and revert to natural religion. Natural religion is of course good — in its own proper place and for its own proper purposes. Nobody doubts — or nobody ought to doubt — that men are by nature religious and will have a religion in any event. The *sensus divinitatis* implanted in us — to employ Calvin's phrases — functions inevitably as a *semen religionis*.

Of course Christianity does not abolish or supersede this natural religion; it vitalizes it, and confirms it, and fills it with richer content. But it does so much more than this that, great as this is, it is pardonable that it should now and then be overlooked. It supplements it, and, in supplementing it, it transforms it, and makes it, with its supplements, a religion fitted for and adequate to the needs of sinful man. There is nothing "soteriological" in natural religion. It grows out of the recognized relations of creature and Maker; it is the creature's response to the perception of its Lord, in feelings of dependence and responsibility. It knows nothing of salvation. When the creature has become a sinner, and the relations proper to it as creature to its Lord have been superseded by relations proper to the criminal to its judge, natural religion is dumb. It fails just because it is natural religion and is unequal to unnatural conditions. Of course we do not say that it is suspended; we say only that it has become inadequate. It requires to be supplemented by elements which are proper to the relation of the offending creature to the offended Lord. This is what Christianity brings, and it is because this is what Christianity brings that it so supplements and transforms natural religion as to make it a religion for sinners. It does not supersede natural religion; it takes it up in its entirety unto itself, expanding it and developing it on new sides to meet new needs and supplementing it where it is insufficient for these new needs.

We have touched here the elements of truth in George Tyrrell's contention, otherwise bizarre enough, that Christianity builds not on Judaism but on paganism. The antithesis is unfortunate. Although in very different senses, Christianity builds both on Judaism and on paganism; it is the completion of the supernatural religion begun in Judaism, and it is the supernatural supplement to the natural religion which lies beneath all the horrible perversions of paganism. Tyrrell, viewing everything from the point of view of his Catholicism and dealing in historical as much as in theological judgments, puts his contention in this form: " That Catholicism is Christianized paganism or world-religion and not the Christianized Judaism of the New Testament." The idea he wishes to express is that Catholicism is the only tenable form of Christianity because it alone is founded, not on Judaism, but on " world-religion." What is worthy of our notice is that he says " world-religion," not " world-religions." He is thinking not of the infinite variety of pagan religions — many of them gross enough, none of them worthy of humanity ("man's worst crimes are his religions," says Dr. Faunce somewhere, most strikingly) — but of the underlying religion which sustains and gives whatever value they possess to them all.

Now mysticism is just this world-religion; that is to say, it is the expression of the ineradicable religiosity of the human race. So far as it is this, and nothing but this, it is valid religion, and eternal religion. No man can do without it, not even the Christian man. But it is not adequate religion for sinners. And when it pushes itself forward as an adequate religion for sinners it presses beyond its mark and becomes, in the poet's phrase, "procuress to the lords of hell." As vitalized and informed, supplemented and transformed by Christianity, as supplying to Christianity the natural foundation for its supernatural structure, it is valid religion. As a substitute for Christianity it is not merely a return to the beggarly elements of the world, but inevitably rots down to something far worse. Confining himself to what he can find in himself, man naturally cannot rise above himself, and unfortunately the self above which he cannot rise is a sinful self.

The pride which is inherent in the self-poised, self-contained attitude which will acknowledge no truth that is not found within oneself is already an unlovely trait, and a dangerous one as well, since pride is unhappily a thing which grows by what it feeds on. The history of mysticism only too clearly shows that he who begins by seeking God within himself may end by confusing himself with God. We may conceivably think that Mr. G. K. Chesterton might have chosen his language with a little more delicacy of feeling, but what he says in the following telling way much needs to be said in this generation in words which will command a hearing. He had seen some such observation as that which we have quoted from Tyrrell, to the effect that the Christianity of the future is to be a mere mysticism. This is the way he deals with it:

Only the other day I saw in an excellent weekly paper of Puritan tone this remark, that Christianity when stripped of its armor of dogma (as who should speak of a man stripped of his armor of bones) turned out to be nothing but the Quaker doctrine of the Inner Light. Now, if I were to say that Christianity came into the world

specially to destroy the doctrine of the Inner Light, that would be
an exaggeration. But it would be very much nearer the truth. . . .
Of all the conceivable forms of enlightenment, the worst is what
these people call the Inner Light. Of all horrible religions the most
horrible is the worship of the God within. Anyone who knows anybody knows how it would work; anyone who knows anyone from the
Higher Thought Center knows how it does work. That Jones should
worship the God within him turns out ultimately to mean that Jones
shall worship Jones. Let Jones worship the sun or moon, anything
rather than the Inner Light; let Jones worship cats or crocodiles, if
he can find any in his street, but not the God within. Christianity
came into the world firstly in order to assert with violence that a
man had not only to look inward, but to look outward, to behold
with astonishment and enthusiasm a divine company and a divine
captain. The only fun of being a Christian was that a man was not
left alone with the Inner Light, but definitely recognized an outer
light, fair as the sun, clear as the moon, terrible as an army with
banners.

Certainly, valuable as the inner light is — adequate as it
might be for men who were not sinners — there is no fate
which could be more terrible for a sinner than to be left alone
with it. And we must not blink the fact that it is just that, in
the full terribleness of its meaning, which mysticism means.
Above all other elements of Christianity, Christ and what
Christ stands for, with the cross at the center, come to us
solely by " external authority." No " external authority," no
Christ, and no cross of Christ. For Christ is history, and
Christ's cross is history, and mysticism which lives solely on
what is within can have nothing to do with history; mysticism
which seeks solely eternal verities can have nothing to do with
time and that which has occurred in time. Accordingly a whole
series of recent mystical devotional writers sublimate the
entire body of those historical facts, which we do not say
merely lie at the basis of Christianity — we say rather, which
constitute the very substance of Christianity — into a mere set
of symbols, a dramatization of psychological experiences succeeding one another in the soul. Christ Himself becomes but

an external sign of an inward grace. Read but the writings of John Cordelier. Not even the most reluctant mystic, however, can altogether escape some such process of elimination of the external Christ; by virtue of the very fact that he will not have anything in his religion which he does not find within himself he must sooner or later " pass beyond Christ."

We do not like Wilhelm Herrmann's rationalism any better than we like mysticism, and we would as soon have no Christ at all as the Christ Herrmann gives us. But Herrmann tells the exact truth when he explains in well-chosen words that " the piety of the mystic is such that at the highest point to which it leads Christ must vanish from the soul along with all else that is external." " When he has found God," he explains again, " the mystic has left Christ behind." At the best, Christ can be to the mystic but the model mystic, not Himself the Way as He declared of Himself, but only a traveler along with us upon the common way. So Miss Underhill elaborately depicts Him, but not she alone. Söderblom says of von Hügel that Jesus is to him "merely a high point in the religious development to which man must aspire." " He has no eye," he adds, " for the unique personal power which His figure exercises on man." This applies to the whole class. But much more than this needs to be said. Christ may be the mystic's brother. He may possibly even be his exemplar and leader, although He is not always recognized as such. What He cannot by any possibility be is his Saviour. Is not God within him? And has he not merely to sink within himself to sink himself into God? He has no need of " salvation " and allows no place for it.

We hear much of the revolt of mysticism against the forensic theory of the atonement and imputed righteousness. This is a mere euphemism for its revolt against all " atonement " and all " justification." The whole external side of the Christian salvation simply falls away. In the same euphemistic language Miss Underhill declares that " nothing done for us, or exhibited to us, can have the significance of that which is done *in* us." She means that it has no significance for us at all. Even a William Law can say: " Christ given *for* us is neither more nor less than Christ given *into* us. He is in no other sense our full, perfect, and sufficient Atonement, than as His nature and spirit are born and formed in us." The cross and all that the cross stands for are abolished; it becomes at best but a symbol of a general law — *per aspera ad astra.* " There is but one salvation for all mankind," says Law, " and the way to it is one; and that is the desire of the soul turned to God. This desire brings the soul to God and God into the soul: it unites with God, it coöperates with God, and is one life with God." If Christ is still spoken of, and His death and resurrection and ascension, and all the currents of religious feeling still turn to Him, that is because Christians must so speak and feel. The same experiences may be had under other skies and will under them express themselves in other terms appropriate to the traditions of those other times and places. That Christian mysticism is Christ mysticism, seeking and finding Christ within and referring all its ecstasies to Him, is thus only an accident. And even the functions of this Christ within us, which alone it knows, are degraded far below those of the Christ within us of the Christian revelation.

The great thing about the indwelling Christ of the Christian revelation is that He comes to us in His Spirit with creative power. *Veni, creator Spiritus,* we sing, and we look to be new creatures, created in Christ Jesus into newness of life. The mystic will allow, not a resurrection from the dead, but only an awakening from sleep. Christ enters the heart not to produce something new but to arouse what was dormant, what has belonged to man as man from the beginning and only needs to be set to work. " If Christ was to raise a new life like His own in every man," writes Law, " then every man must have had originally in the inmost spirit of his life a seed of Christ, or Christ as a seed of heaven, lying there in a state of insensibility, out of which it could not arise but by the mediatorial power of Christ." He cannot conceive of Christ bringing anything new; what Christ seems to bring he really finds already there. " The Word of God," he says, " is the hidden treasure of every human soul, immured under flesh and blood, till as a

day-star it arises in our hearts and changes the son of an
earthly Adam into a son of God." Nothing is brought to us;
what is already in us is only "brought out," and what is
already in us — in every man — is "the Word of God."
This is Christ mysticism; that is to say, it is the mysticism in
which the divinity which is in every man by nature is called
Christ — rather than, say, Brahm or Allah, or what not.

Even in such a movement as that represented by Bishop
Chandler's Cult of the Passing Moment, the disintegrating
operation of mysticism on historical Christianity — which is
all the Christianity there is — is seen at work. Bishop Chandler himself, we are thankful to say, exalts the cross and thinks
of it as a creative influence in the lives of men. But this only
exemplifies the want of logical consistency, which indeed is
the boast of the school which he represents. If our one rule
of life is to be the spiritual improvement of the impressions
of the moment, and we are to follow these blindly whithersso-
ever they lead with no steadying, not to say guidance, derived
from the great Revelation of the past, there can be but one
issue. We are simply substituting our own passing impulses,
interpreted as inspirations, for the one final revelation of God
as the guide of life; that God has spoken once for all for the
guidance of His people is forgotten; His great corporate provision for His people is cast aside; and we are adrift upon the
billows of merely subjective feeling.

We see that it is not merely Christ and His cross, then,
which may be neglected, as external things belonging to time
and space. God Himself, speaking in His Word, may be forgotten — in "the cult of the passing moment." We are reminded that there have been mystics who have not scrupled
openly to contrast even the God without them with the God
within, and to speak in such fashion as to be understood (or
misunderstood) as counseling divesting ourselves of God Himself and turning only to the inwardly shining light. No doubt
they did not mean all that their words may be pressed into
seeming to say. Nevertheless, their words may stand for us
as a kind of symbol of the whole mystical conception, with the

exaggerated value which it sets upon the personal feelings and its contempt for all that is external to the individual's spirit, even though it must be allowed that this excludes all that makes Christianity the religion of salvation for a lost world — the cross, Christ Himself, and the God and Father of our Lord and Saviour Jesus Christ who in His love gave His Son to die for sinners.

The issue which mysticism creates is thus just the issue of Christianity. The question which it raises is, whether we need, whether we have, a provision in the blood of Christ for our sins; or whether we, each of us, possess within ourselves all that can be required for time and for eternity. Both of these things cannot be true, and obviously *tertium non datur*. We may be mystics, or we may be Christians. We cannot be both. And the pretension of being both usually merely veils defection from Christianity. Mysticism baptized with the name of Christianity is not thereby made Christianity. A rose by any other name will smell as sweet. But it does not follow that whatever we choose to call a rose will possess the rose's fragrance.

LIST OF OTHER STUDIES IN THEOLOGY

I. APOLOGETICS

AGNOSTICISM. (Article in " The New Schaff-Herzog Encyclopedia of Religious Knowledge," i. pp. 87–88. Funk and Wagnalls Company, New York, 1911.)

ATHEISM. (Article in " The New Schaff-Herzog Encyclopedia of Religious Knowledge," i. pp. 346–347. Funk and Wagnalls Company, New York, 1911.)

CHRISTIAN EVIDENCES: HOW AFFECTED BY RECENT CRITICISMS. (*The Homiletic Review*, xvi. August, 1888, pp. 107–112.)

II. EXEGETICAL THEOLOGY

THE GREEK TESTAMENT OF WESTCOTT AND HORT. (*The Presbyterian Review*, iii. April, 1882, pp. 325–356.)

THE PROLEGOMENA TO TISCHENDORF'S NEW TESTAMENT: A REVIEW. (*The Expositor*, 3d series, i. 1885, pp. 142–150.)

INTRODUCTION TO ACTS AND THE PASTORAL EPISTLES. (" The Temple Bible." J. B. Lippincott Company, Philadelphia, 1902.)

SOME CHARACTERISTICS OF THE BOOK OF ACTS. (*The Bible Student*, v. January, February, March, 1902, pp. 13–21, 72–80, 130–136.)

SYLLABUS ON THE SPECIAL INTRODUCTION TO THE CATHOLIC EPISTLES. (W. W. Waters, Publisher, Pittsburgh, 1883.)

SYNOPSIS OF ST. PAUL'S EPISTLE TO THE ROMANS. (Appendix to " Syllabus on the Special Introduction to the Catholic Epistles," pp. 197–211.)

ON THE POST-EXILIAN PORTION OF OUR LORD'S GENEALOGY. (*The Presbyterian Review*, ii. April, 1881, pp. 388–397.)

MESSIANIC PSALMS OF THE NEW TESTAMENT. (*The Expositor*, 3d series, ii. 1885, pp. 301–309.)

THE SCENES OF THE BAPTIST'S WORK. (*The Expositor*, 3d series, i. 1885, pp. 267–282.)

THE READINGS Ἕλληνας AND Ἑλληνιστάς, ACTS XI. 20. (*Journal of the Society of Biblical Literature and Exegesis*, 1883, pp. 113–127.)

SOME DIFFICULT PASSAGES IN THE FIRST CHAPTER OF II CORINTHIANS. (*Journal of the Society of Biblical Literature and Exegesis*, December, 1886, pp. 27–39.)

THE DATE OF THE EPISTLE TO THE GALATIANS. (*Journal of the Society of Biblical Literature and Exegesis*, 1884, pp. 50–64.)

SOME EXEGETICAL NOTES ON I TIMOTHY. (*The Presbyterian Review*, viii. July, October, 1887, pp. 500–508, 702–710.)

JAMES. (Article in "A Dictionary of the Bible," by John D. Davis, 2d ed., pp. 337–338. The Westminster Press, Philadelphia, 1903.)

JUDE. (Article in "A Dictionary of the Bible," by John D. Davis, 2d ed., pp. 406–407. The Westminster Press, Philadelphia, 1903.)

PETER. (Article in "A Dictionary of the Bible," by John D. Davis, 2d ed., pp. 569–571. The Westminster Press, Philadelphia, 1903.)

AMAZEMENT. (Article in "A Dictionary of Christ and the Gospels," edited by James Hastings, i. pp. 47–48. Charles Scribner's Sons, New York, 1908.)

ASTONISHMENT. (Article in "A Dictionary of Christ and the Gospels," edited by James Hastings, i. p. 131. Charles Scribner's Sons, New York, 1908.)

CHILDREN. (Article in "A Dictionary of Christ and the Gospels," edited by James Hastings, i. pp. 301–305. Charles Scribner's Sons, New York, 1908.)

RENEWAL. (Article in "The New Schaff-Herzog Encyclopedia of Religious Knowledge," ix. pp. 487–488. Funk and Wagnalls Company, New York, 1911.)

CHRIST'S "LITTLE ONES." (*The Bible Student and Teacher*, i. September, 1904, pp. 515–525.)

ST. PAUL'S USE OF THE ARGUMENT FROM EXPERIENCE. (*The Expositor*, 5th series, i. 1895, pp. 226–236.)

THE CENTURY'S PROGRESS IN BIBLICAL KNOWLEDGE. (*The Homiletic Review*, xxxix. March, 1900, pp. 195–202.)

REVIEW OF FIVE EDITIONS OF THE DIDACHE. (*The Andover Review*, iv. December, 1885, pp. 593–599.)

TEXT, SOURCES, AND CONTENTS OF "THE TWO WAYS" OR FIRST

SECTION OF THE DIDACHE. (*The Bibliotheca Sacra*, xliii. January, 1886, pp. 100–161.)

TEXTUAL CRITICISM OF "THE TWO WAYS." (*The Expositor*, 3d series, iii. February, 1886, pp. 156–159.)

NOTES ON THE DIDACHE. (*Journal of the Society of Biblical Literature and Exegesis*, June, 1886, pp. 86–98.)

THE DIDACHE AND ITS KINDRED FORMS, WITH ESPECIAL REFERENCE TO THE PAPER OF DR. MCGIFFERT. (*The Andover Review*, vi. July, 1886, pp. 81–97.)

SOME RECENT APOCRYPHAL GOSPELS. (*The Southern Presbyterian Review*, xxxv. October, 1884, pp. 711–759.)

III. SYSTEMATIC THEOLOGY

THE RIGHT OF SYSTEMATIC THEOLOGY. (*The Presbyterian and Reformed Review*, vii. July, 1896, pp. 412–458. Also published in book form by T. & T. Clark, Edinburgh, 1897.)

THE INDISPENSABLENESS OF SYSTEMATIC THEOLOGY TO THE PREACHER. (*The Homiletic Review*, xxxiii. February, 1897, pp. 99–105.)

RECENT RECONSTRUCTIONS OF THEOLOGY, FROM THE POINT OF VIEW OF SYSTEMATIC THEOLOGY. (*The Homiletic Review*, xxxv. March, 1898, pp. 201–208.)

ANTITRINITARIANISM. (Article in "The New Schaff-Herzog Encyclopedia of Religious Knowledge," i. pp. 203–205. Funk and Wagnalls Company, New York, 1911.)

PROFESSOR HENRY PRESERVED SMITH ON INSPIRATION. (*The Presbyterian and Reformed Review*, v. October, 1894, pp. 600–653.)

GOD'S PROVIDENCE OVER ALL. (*The King's Own*, vi. July, 1895, pp. 671–675.)

THE PRESENT DAY CONCEPT OF EVOLUTION. (Published by the College Printing Office, Emporia, Kansas, n. d.)

REPENTANCE AND ORIGINAL SIN. (*The Union Seminary Magazine*, x. February, 1899, pp. 169–174.)

THE FOUNDATIONS OF THE SABBATH IN THE WORD OF GOD. (An address delivered at the Fourteenth International Lord's Day Congress held in Oakland, California, July 27–August 1, 1915, published in "Sunday the World's Rest Day," pp. 63–81. Doubleday, Page & Company, New York, 1916. Also pub-

lished in *The Free Presbyterian Magazine*, Glasgow, January, February, March, 1918, pp. 316–319, 350–354, 378–383.)
BAPTISM. (Article in " The New Schaff-Herzog Encyclopedia of Religious Knowledge," i. pp. 446–450. Funk and Wagnalls Company, New York, 1911.)
How SHALL WE BAPTIZE? (*The Methodist Quarterly Review*, lx. October, 1911, pp. 641–660.)
CHRISTIAN BAPTISM. (Pamphlet published by the Presbyterian Board of Publication and Sabbath School Work, Philadelphia, 1920.)

IV. HISTORICAL THEOLOGY

THE BIBLE THE BOOK OF MANKIND. (A paper read at the World's Bible Conference, held at the Panama-Pacific Exposition, San Francisco, California, August 1–4, 1915. Published as " Centennial Pamphlet No. 1," by the American Bible Society, New York, 1915.)
DARWIN'S ARGUMENTS AGAINST CHRISTIANITY AND AGAINST RELIGION. (*The Homiletic Review*, xvii. January, 1889, pp. 9–16.)
AFRICA AND THE BEGINNINGS OF CHRISTIAN LATIN LITERATURE. (*The American Journal of Theology*, January, 1907, pp. 95–110.)
THE POSTURE OF THE RECIPIENTS AT THE LORD'S SUPPER: A FOOTNOTE TO THE HISTORY OF REFORMED USAGES. (*Journal of the Presbyterian Historical Society*, xi. June, 1922, pp. 217–234.)
THE RELATION OF THE PRESBYTERIAN PRINCIPLE TO THE HISTORIC EPISCOPATE. (*Methodist Review*, lxxi. November, 1889, pp. 845–850.)
How PRINCETON SEMINARY GOT TO WORK. (*Journal of the Presbyterian Historical Society*, ix. June, 1918, pp. 256–266.)
THE EXPANSION OF THE SEMINARY, A HISTORICAL SKETCH. (Pamphlet published at Princeton, 1914.)

V. MISCELLANEA

SPIRITUAL CULTURE IN THE THEOLOGICAL SEMINARY. (*The Princeton Theological Review*, ii. January, 1904, pp. 65–87.)
THE RELIGIOUS LIFE OF THEOLOGICAL STUDENTS. (An address

SECTION OF THE DIDACHE. (*The Bibliotheca Sacra,* xliii. January, 1886, pp. 100–161.)

TEXTUAL CRITICISM OF " THE TWO WAYS." (*The Expositor,* 3d series, iii. February, 1886, pp. 156–159.)

NOTES ON THE DIDACHE. (*Journal of the Society of Biblical Literature and Exegesis,* June, 1886, pp. 86–98.)

THE DIDACHE AND ITS KINDRED FORMS, WITH ESPECIAL REFERENCE TO THE PAPER OF DR. MCGIFFERT. (*The Andover Review,* vi. July, 1886, pp. 81–97.)

SOME RECENT APOCRYPHAL GOSPELS. (*The Southern Presbyterian Review,* xxxv. October, 1884, pp. 711–759.)

III. SYSTEMATIC THEOLOGY

THE RIGHT OF SYSTEMATIC THEOLOGY. (*The Presbyterian and Reformed Review,* vii. July, 1896, pp. 412–458. Also published in book form by T. & T. Clark, Edinburgh, 1897.)

THE INDISPENSABLENESS OF SYSTEMATIC THEOLOGY TO THE PREACHER. (*The Homiletic Review,* xxxiii. February, 1897, pp. 99–105.)

RECENT RECONSTRUCTIONS OF THEOLOGY, FROM THE POINT OF VIEW OF SYSTEMATIC THEOLOGY. (*The Homiletic Review,* xxxv. March, 1898, pp. 201–208.)

ANTITRINITARIANISM. (Article in " The New Schaff-Herzog Encyclopedia of Religious Knowledge," i. pp. 203–205. Funk and Wagnalls Company, New York, 1911.)

PROFESSOR HENRY PRESERVED SMITH ON INSPIRATION. (*The Presbyterian and Reformed Review,* v. October, 1894, pp. 600–653.)

GOD'S PROVIDENCE OVER ALL. (*The King's Own,* vi. July, 1895, pp. 671–675.)

THE PRESENT DAY CONCEPT OF EVOLUTION. (Published by the College Printing Office, Emporia, Kansas, n. d.)

REPENTANCE AND ORIGINAL SIN. (*The Union Seminary Magazine,* x. February, 1899, pp. 169–174.)

THE FOUNDATIONS OF THE SABBATH IN THE WORD OF GOD. (An address delivered at the Fourteenth International Lord's Day Congress held in Oakland, California, July 27–August 1, 1915, published in " Sunday the World's Rest Day," pp. 63–81. Doubleday, Page & Company, New York, 1916. Also published in *The Free Presbyterian Magazine*, Glasgow, January, February, March, 1918, pp. 316–319, 350–354, 378–383.)

BAPTISM. (Article in " The New Schaff-Herzog Encyclopedia of Religious Knowledge," i. pp. 446–450. Funk and Wagnalls Company, New York, 1911.)

HOW SHALL WE BAPTIZE? (*The Methodist Quarterly Review*, lx. October, 1911, pp. 641–660.)

CHRISTIAN BAPTISM. (Pamphlet published by the Presbyterian Board of Publication and Sabbath School Work, Philadelphia, 1920.)

IV. HISTORICAL THEOLOGY

THE BIBLE THE BOOK OF MANKIND. (A paper read at the World's Bible Conference, held at the Panama-Pacific Exposition, San Francisco, California, August 1–4, 1915. Published as " Centennial Pamphlet No. 1," by the American Bible Society, New York, 1915.)

DARWIN'S ARGUMENTS AGAINST CHRISTIANITY AND AGAINST RELIGION. (*The Homiletic Review*, xvii. January, 1889, pp. 9–16.)

AFRICA AND THE BEGINNINGS OF CHRISTIAN LATIN LITERATURE. (*The American Journal of Theology*, January, 1907, pp. 95–110.)

THE POSTURE OF THE RECIPIENTS AT THE LORD'S SUPPER: A FOOTNOTE TO THE HISTORY OF REFORMED USAGES. (*Journal of the Presbyterian Historical Society*, xi. June, 1922, pp. 217–234.)

THE RELATION OF THE PRESBYTERIAN PRINCIPLE TO THE HISTORIC EPISCOPATE. (*Methodist Review*, lxxi. November, 1889, pp. 845–850.)

HOW PRINCETON SEMINARY GOT TO WORK. (*Journal of the Presbyterian Historical Society*, ix. June, 1918, pp. 256–266.)

THE EXPANSION OF THE SEMINARY, A HISTORICAL SKETCH. (Pamphlet published at Princeton, 1914.)

V. MISCELLANEA

SPIRITUAL CULTURE IN THE THEOLOGICAL SEMINARY. (*The Princeton Theological Review*, ii. January, 1904, pp. 65–87.)

THE RELIGIOUS LIFE OF THEOLOGICAL STUDENTS. (An address

delivered at the Autumn Conference at Princeton Theological Seminary, October 4, 1911. Published as a pamphlet at Princeton, 1911.)

TRUE CHURCH UNITY: WHAT IT IS. (*The Homiletic Review,* xx. December, 1890, pp. 483–489.)

THE PROPOSED UNION WITH THE CUMBERLAND PRESBYTERIANS. (*The Princeton Theological Review,* ii. April, 1904, pp. 295–316.)

PRESBYTERIAN DEACONESSES. (*The Presbyterian Review,* x. April, 1889, pp. 283–293.)

SOME PERILS OF MISSIONARY LIFE. (*The Presbyterian Quarterly,* xiii. July, 1899, pp. 385–404.)

KIKUYU, CLERICAL VERACITY AND MIRACLES. (*The Princeton Theological Review,* xii. October, 1914, pp. 529–585.)

SANCTIFYING THE PELAGIANS. (*The Princeton Theological Review,* i. July, 1903, pp. 457–462.)

DREAM. (Article in " A Dictionary of Christ and the Gospels," edited by James Hastings, i. pp. 494–498. Charles Scribner's Sons, New York, 1908.)

" EDITORIAL NOTES " and reviews of current theological literature under the heading, " CURRENT BIBLICAL THOUGHT," in *The Bible Student,* i.–viii. 1900–1903.

CRITICAL REVIEWS

BY

BENJAMIN BRECKINRIDGE WARFIELD

*Professor of Didactic and Polemic Theology
in the Theological Seminary of Princeton
New Jersey, 1887–1921*

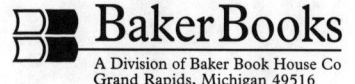 Baker Books

A Division of Baker Book House Co
Grand Rapids, Michigan 49516

PREFATORY NOTE

Rev. Benjamin Breckinridge Warfield, D.D., LL.D., Professor of Didactic and Polemic Theology in the Theological Seminary of the Presbyterian Church at Princeton, New Jersey, provided in his will for the collection and publication of the numerous articles on theological subjects which he contributed to encyclopaedias, reviews and other periodicals, and appointed a committee to edit and publish these papers. In pursuance of his instructions, this, the tenth (and last) volume, containing a selection from those of his Critical Reviews which appeared in *The Presbyterian and Reformed Review* and *The Princeton Theological Review*, has been prepared under the editorial direction of this committee.

The clerical preparation of this volume has been done by Mr. John E. Meeter, to whom the thanks of the committee are hereby expressed.

Ethelbert D. Warfield
William Park Armstrong
Caspar Wistar Hodge
Committee.

CONTENTS

vi CONTENTS

CONTENTS

The Natural History of the Christian Religion. By William Mackintosh, M.A., D.D. Glasgow: James Maclehose & Sons; New York: Macmillan & Co. 1894.[1]

Some fifteen years ago, the religious world was startled by the appearance of a volume bearing the simple title of " Scotch Sermons, 1880." It was a collection of twenty-three sermons by thirteen " clergymen of the Church of Scotland," and was designed to acquaint the public with " a style of teaching " which the editor thought was " increasingly prevalent amongst the clergy of the Scottish Church," and which made it its object so to present " the essential ideas of Christianity " as to show that they are " in harmony with the results of critical and scientific research." A good object, surely. The trouble with these sermons, however, was that they did not seek to consider the results of recent " critical and scientific research " in the light of the revealed truth of God, and to exhibit the harmony of all truth, whether derived from revelation or from nature; but, taking their point of view from current theorizing, pared down " the essential ideas of Christianity " to fit the assumed " results of the most recent critical and scientific research." The volume was appropriately estimated by Dr. A. A. Hodge in the issue of *The Presbyterian Review* for January, 1881 (ii. pp. 212-214). " The collection, as a whole," he said, " is utterly valueless, except as ' specimens of a style of teaching ' which is said to ' increasingly prevail amongst the clergy of the Scottish Church.' Neither the learning nor the logic of these sermons avails to throw light upon any other subject of human interest under the sun. And neither the hearing nor the reading of such discourses could ever avail to promote any other valuable practical quality than that of patience. Some of these sermons do not contain any statements absolutely opposed to the essential truths of Christianity, but not one sets forth any doctrine or duty which can be in any special sense classed as Christian."

One of the writers represented in the volume was the Rev. William Mackintosh, D.D., of Buchanan, who contributed two sermons

[1] *The Presbyterian and Reformed Review*, vi. 1895, pp. 507-522.

on the text, " Whatsoever a man soweth, that shall he also reap "
(Gal. vi. 7). With reference to these sermons, but more especially
the latter of them, Dr. Hodge remarks: " Rev. William Mackintosh,
D.D., Buchanan, discourses concerning the ' renovating power of
Christianity.' He asks: ' What is the Gospel good for? What title has
it to that designation? What service does it render? ' (p. 162). This
he answers thus: ' The problem of human life — the task appointed
to us — is our deliverance from the sway of our lower nature, our
surrender to the control of our higher nature. The powers by which
we are enabled to accomplish this task are three. *First*. Our own
higher nature itself. *Secondly*. The beneficent constitution of things
in general, their tendency in favor of what is good. *Thirdly*. These
two factors are brought into full operation by the revelation to our
consciousness, of that which was implicitly contained in them of the
Divine good-will, or paternal relation towards us, given us by
Christ ' (pp. 171–173). That is, all that Christ does for us is to
assure us of God's good-will. With this encouragement we save ourselves, by the use of natural powers acting under natural conditions."
Dr. Mackintosh's sermons, in a word, fairly illustrated the hint of
the editor of the volume, that the sermons included in it belong to a
class which are seeking to bring " the essential ideas of Christianity "
into " harmony with the results of critical and scientific research."
He himself describes his aim in them in such words as these: " Our
endeavour has been to show what modifications of the popular construction of Christianity are needed to bring it into harmony with
the laws of mental physiology " (p. 172). " The light which science
sheds upon human destiny " is the light in which he would walk. And
" science " with him is above all the investigation of physical nature: it is from this sphere that he would borrow his governing idea.
" In these later times," he tells us with extreme naïveté, " science,
in its researches into the material world, has lighted everywhere upon
the traces of an all-pervading continuity " (p. 145) ; and this being
true, we may now " confidently postulate " " the existence in the
moral and spiritual worlds of an analogous principle." Wherefore,
that a step may be taken towards the reconciliation of faith and
science he devotes these sermons to showing that " the principle of
continuity obtains in the moral sphere no less than in the material,
and rules the succession of religious as of other phenomena " (p. 145;
cf. p. 134).

The former of the two sermons is occupied with an attempt to demonstrate this "law of moral continuity." "The law of the spiritual harvest," we are told, "is that evil is the natural," nay, the inevitable, "product of evil; that nothing either good or evil ever perishes of itself, but must, in some way, influence, or enter as an element into, the future" (p. 146). This is an article of natural religion, and "underlies Christianity as much as does the existence and unity of God, or any other article of natural religion" (p. 134). It cannot be " shaken or removed by any subsequent revelation " ; it is rather one of the tests of the truth of systems (p. 134). If we speak of God's judgment on sin, we must still think merely of this direct and infallible action of moral continuity, "without the intervention of any supplementary or epicyclical contrivance" (p. 139) : for " the judgment of God is only another name for the natural and inevitable consequence of our lives " (p. 143). Divine judgment is therefore continuous and progressive, and all supernatural action is out of place in it: no divine fiat can interfere with moral development here or hereafter. "Such interference on the day of judgment is as inadmissible, because as inconsistent with human liberty, and with an inviolable order, as at any other crisis in the history of man " (p. 140). No, it is impossible to remove sin by a sovereign or forensic fiat: " the chain of moral sequence . . . is carried on in unbroken continuity" (p. 144) — we are under the operation of a universal law which acts, like all law, uniformly.

Under such circumstances we may well ask, What service, then, can the gospel render? The second sermon essays to offer a reply. "The gospel," we are told, "does not profess to exempt us from the law of . . . moral continuity " (p. 146), although it does show us the way from evil to good (p. 147). Certainly it does not offer us a supernatural change. But even physiology knows something of reversal of process; and there is a latent spiritual force within us to which the gospel may appeal. The dominance of sin indeed never becomes absolute and undisputed; so that the better principle has within itself the potency of a reactive force. Doubtless after evil habit has become confirmed, the better principle may seldom or never be led so to act by the mere sense of duty or moral obligation: it needs some new hope or new affection to arouse it. But under the stimulus of " the revelation to our mind of the paternal character of God, and of the gracious relation in which He stands to us," it is capable of very energetic reaction (pp. 153, 163, 165, 168). Thus a complete revolution is produced in our feelings and relations towards Him, and our religious life is elevated to a higher level (p. 153). " The problem of human life " then, " — the task appointed to us — is our deliverance from the sway of our lower nature, our surrender to the control of our higher nature. The powers by which we are enabled to accomplish this task are three: *First.* Our own higher nature itself, which is never wholly effaced, and which reacts against the evil, and makes us receptive of all the higher influences that may be brought to bear upon us from without. *Secondly.* The complex of all those higher influences — the beneficent constitution of things in general, their tendency in favor of what is good, which operates upon us more or less, even when we are unconscious of it. . . . *Thirdly.* These two factors for the accomplishment of the Divine purpose are consummated, or brought into full operation, by the revelation to our consciousness of that which was implicitly contained in them, but of which we had otherwise remained unconscious; by that revelation, we mean, of the Divine good-will, or paternal relation towards us, by which Christ has reënforced our better nature, enabling us to be intelligent fellow-workers with God in our conflict with evil, and giving a higher aim to our life. . . . It is . . . through our reason, through our conviction that God wills the triumph of our better nature, that we are animated to a triumphant forth-putting of its latent energies " (pp. 153–156).

So viewed, it is apparent that " the gospel can only be regarded as a revelation or discovery to man of a method of salvation which had always been possible in the nature of things " (p. 157); and doubtless many have used it apart from what we call the gospel (pp. 156, 157, 159). The gospel is not some new power which comes to our salvation; it is only an instrumentality to stir us up to save ourselves: " it will be distinctly apparent that the gospel can be a means of supplanting evil by good, only by discovering and evoking powers which had always existed. . . . The gospel deserves its name simply because it teaches and persuades us to cease from evil and to do well; to change the seed which we sow, and thus to obtain a better harvest " (p. 158). We call ourselves Christians, not because we fancy Christ has saved us by some sort of " expiation," but simply because we have obtained our knowledge of God as Father, which calls out our latent reaction against sin, " in some historical connection with the impulse given by Christianity " (p. 156). All that Christ did for us, " in the strict and literal sense, was to reveal to us the infinite placability of the Divine nature "

(p. 158; cf. pp. 161, 162–163, 170). His teaching amounts to no more than " that nothing stands in the way of those who desire to break off their sins by righteousness, except the outward and inward opposition, which has been arrayed by the law of recompense against their better endeavours " (p. 167) ; and His work amounts only to this teaching. We may reverence His memory " as Mediator between God and man "; but only in the sense that " He it was who, from the depths of His own experience, imparted to men the knowledge of God as our Father in heaven; whose property it is to forgive the trespasses of His children, and to incline their feet into the path of righteousness " (p. 170). How " humanity rose at length in Christ to the thought of God's absolute goodness " would be inexplicable to us, were it not that we have reason to believe that God has impressed on creation itself evidences of " His design to secure the triumph of what is good, and to deliver us from evil " (p. 155). But humanity in Christ having obtained this knowledge of the divine paternity, it is able in its power to react against sin and sow its seed unto righteousness. And so the very law of moral continuity will operate to bring it to moral perfection.

It is evident that Dr. A. A. Hodge was thoroughly justified in finding nothing either novel or distinctively Christian in this teaching. It is just the purest form of Socinian thought. The Unitarian layman, Mr. George William Curtis, gives perfectly clear expression to the same conceptions in that confession of his faith which leads his biographer to say that to him " conscience " (not Christ) was " the divinely appointed saviour of the world " : " I believe in God, who is love; that all men are brothers; and that the only essential duty of every man is to be *honest,* by which I understand his absolute following of the conscience when duly enlightened " (" George William Curtis," by Edward Cary, 1894, pp. 7, 334, 339). Dr. Mackintosh could not express his own doctrine better: even down to the emphasis on honesty, it is quite the same. " Only he who feels that a necessity is laid upon him of bearing his own burden, and helping others to bear theirs," says Dr. Mackintosh, " may hope to grow into that noblest work of God, the simply honest man, the genuine disciple of Christ " (p. 172). To be simply honest is to be Christ's genuine disciple: not to depend on Him for " escaping responsibility for our vices." In this case, of course, any pagan may be a " genuine disciple of Christ." How entirely apart from all that is distinctively Christian Dr. Mackintosh's whole scheme of doctrine is, indeed, may be illustrated for us by a remark of Mr. Edmund Gosse, in his interesting " portrait " of Walter Pater. " When I had known him first," he says, " he was a pagan, without any guide but that of the personal conscience; years brought gradually with them a greater and greater longing for the supporting solace of a creed " (*The Contemporary Review*, lxvi. 1894, p. 805). Dr. Mackintosh is dominated on the contrary by a desire " to reduce the dimensions of dogma," to strip off everything from his creed but the one article of " moral continuity " (p. 170). Walter Pater, in other words, was moving upwards from his paganism to Christianity: Dr. Mackintosh had moved down from the heights of Christian truth to a merely pagan position. This is fairly illustrated again by an incident recorded by Dr. Denney, in his recent " Studies in Theology " (New York, 1895, p. 130). He tells us of a Hindu society, which was formed for much the same object which Dr. Mackintosh doubtless thinks he has secured in his sermons — " to appropriate all that is good in Christianity without burdening itself with the rest." " Among other things which it appropriated, with the omission of only two words, was the answer given in the Westminster Shorter Catechism to the question, What is repentance unto life? Here is the answer. ' Repentance unto life is a saving grace, whereby a sinner, out of a true sense of his sin, and apprehension of the mercy of God in Christ, doth with grief and hatred of his sin turn from it unto God, with full purpose of, and endeavour after, new obedience.' The words the Hindus left out were *in Christ;* instead of ' apprehension of the mercy of God in Christ,' they read simply, ' apprehension of the mercy of God.' . . . . They were acute enough to see [continues Dr. Denney] that in the words they left out the whole *Christianity* of the definition lay. . . . I entirely agree with their insight. If the mercy of God is separable from Christ, independent of Christ, accessible apart from Christ, ... there is no need and no possibility of a Christian religion at all." In a word, salvation by repentance and amendment is not Christianity — just because Christianity is specifically salvation by Christ. The essence as well as the glory of Christianity is that it provides for sinful man *a Saviour.*

We have dwelt thus fully on Dr. Mackintosh's contributions to the volume of " Scotch Sermons " because the treatise at present before us stands in such express relation to the earlier sermons that a

clear apprehension of their teaching will greatly conduce to an understanding of this treatise. It is not merely that the present work
occupies the same standpoint with the sermons and proclaims the
same meager teaching, although now as "the religion of Jesus"
rather than as the doctrine of Paul. It is that it is in effect a serious
attempt to supply a rational basis for the teaching of the sermons.
The sermons taught that the essence of Christianity is, Every man
his own saviour. But they left the truth of this teaching dependent
on Dr. Mackintosh's assertion. He said, This is Christianity; this
is God's method of dealing with the soul; this is what Paul and Jesus
teach us. But it was obviously not what Christians believed to be
Christianity; what the creeds of the Churches set forth as God's
method of dealing with the soul; what the founders of Christianity
proclaimed as its substance; what the records of the New Testament
represent as the teaching of either Paul or Jesus. In what alembic
and by the aid of what reagents Dr. Mackintosh had been able to
reduce Christianity to this "essence" remained hidden from his
readers. On further reflection, he himself preceived that he had
run beyond his warrant (p. 149): Paul, at least, taught a "heterosoteric" doctrine — to use E. von Hartmann's term. Otherwise,
however, his original conception remained unchanged; and remained
hanging in the air. After fourteen years, he gives the world at
last an attempt to supply a foundation for his teaching. This is the
real function of the present volume. It sets forth the conception of the
origin and development of Christianity, which alone will harmonize with his teaching as to the nature of Christianity. He had taught
that Christianity provided only for a natural salvation. Conformably to this he now argues that it is merely a natural religion, and,
being a natural religion, can have had no other than a natural origin.
The task which the author has set before himself in this volume is,
thus, none other than to account for the rise of Christianity as a
purely natural religion. There is no lack of frankness or of
thoroughness in the manner in which this task is approached and
prosecuted. "The attempt made in this volume," he says, is "to
trace the origin of Christianity to the common religious instinct,
working under the influence of natural forces and amid historical
conditions" (p. v.). More specifically it attempts "to show that
Christianity took its rise in a great spiritual and religious movement
among the Jewish people, or in a great transformation of Jewish
ideas effected by Jesus, and spreading from him to his disciples; and

to find in that movement and in certain favouring circumstances and historical conditions, without looking beyond to any supernatural or transcendental causes, an explanation of the whole relative phenomena " (p. 4). Dr. Mackintosh means by the phrase, " the whole relative phenomena," all that it is capable of expressing. At no point and through no channel does he allow that anything above nature has entered into the formation of Christianity. Not in the person of Jesus Himself, and not in aught that preceded or followed Him. Jesus was no doubt the founder of Christianity; but His rising to whatever height of thought He attained, is entirely explicable from " the reaction of his mind upon the inherited and environing conditions, social and spiritual, present in Judea in his day " (p. vii.). All that had gone before was merely a natural spiritual and religious development, providing these inherited and environing conditions. All that came after was merely the progressive mythical and dogmatic corruption of the teaching of Jesus, through the working upon it of the imaginative and ratiocinative faculties of His followers.

Now of course Dr. Mackintosh does not suppose that the records of Christianity represent it as the merely natural religion which he conceives it to be. He freely admits that the account of the origin and nature of Christianity given in these records, if treated as trustworthy, would entirely justify the common conception of Christianity as supernatural both in origin and method. He even declares that if Christianity be the merely natural religion which he supposes, its genesis " must have differed widely, nay, enormously, from that which can possibly be gathered from a literal or textual exegesis, and an unsceptical study of the New Testament " (p. 586). He declares it therefore to be evident that " something more than a sound exegesis and hermeneutic will be needed to extract from " " the primitive records," " the proximate facts regarding the origin and development of the Christian system," if that origin and development are to be conceived as purely natural. " We have only to make the attempt," he adds, " to find that we cannot effect the removal of the supernatural element, as if it were a mere appendage or external fixture, so as to leave the residuum standing as it was. That element is, so to speak, chemically combined with the history, and can be discharged only by a process which involves a change or dissolution of the entire fabric, or, if this be thought to be an exaggerated representation, let us say rather that it is an element woven like a strand into the texture of the history, so as to be removable only by a general disturbance and dislocation of the evangelical narrative " (p. 45).

But if the case be such, surely it is incumbent on us to inquire, on the one hand, whence arises the justification for the attempt to remove so pervading and determining an element out of the primitive records, and, on the other, after the fabric has been dissolved, whence can be derived the clue for the recombination of the elements, into a new and now purely natural history of the origin and development of Christianity. Our author seeks his justification in the postulate of the impossibility of the supernatural. On the assumption of the impossibility of the supernatural, the supernaturalistic account of the origin of Christianity given in its primitive records cannot be true, and necessity is laid upon us to attempt to conceive its origin as a natural development. The clue for the reconstruction of the history, on the other hand, is sought at the hands of modern criticism : " the history, be it observed, being such as is arrived at by submitting the canonical records to the ordeal and sifting of modern criticism " (p. vi.). By the aid of these two assumptions — the assumption of the impossibility of the supernatural and the assumption of the validity of all the conclusions of the extremest type of modern criticism — Dr. Mackintosh supposes that he can reconstruct the history of the origin of Christianity so as to exhibit it as a purely natural religion. It would be too gross a circle to suppose that thus Christianity is directly proved to be a natural religion. What is apparently in Dr. Mackintosh's mind is that the success of his reconstruction of the origin and development of Christianity under these assumptions will react to give him increased confidence in the assumptions themselves. He seems to point to the consistency, the naturalness, the likelihood of his construction of the history as an evidence of its truth, and thus as an evidence that Christianity is not a supernatural religion. Why this should need evidencing if the supernatural is really impossible, is not, however, easy to see.

It must be admitted, to be sure, that Dr. Mackintosh does not make clear to us why we must assume the supernatural to be impossible. We are told that " the critical necessity of getting rid of the supernatural element " is so " imperative," that it justifies any conjectural reconstruction of the history which accomplishes it (p. 262). But when we inquire what this imperative necessity rests upon we never get much beyond the simple dictum that it is "in accordance with the demands of modern science." In the brief passage which is given to the formal treatment of the subject, this declaration is somewhat expanded (pp. 19 ff.). We are told that "science has brought into view certain considerations which strongly imply the impossibility of any infraction of the immanent laws of existence"; that it has found in every department of existence which it has investigated, "that all occurrences, phenomena, and sequences bear invariable witness to the control of law and to the sway of order — that what is called divine action never operates irrespective of such order, or otherwise than naturally — i.e., through, or in accordance with such order": and that therefore, "modern thought holds, in the form of a scientific conviction, what was matter of surmise or divination to a few of the leading minds in ages long past, viz., that the universe is governed by immutable laws inherent in the very nature and constitution of things — by laws which are 'never reversed, never suspended, and never supplemented in the interest of any special object whatever'" (pp. 23, 24). The stringency of the steps in this reasoning does not lie, however, on the surface. How we can infer from any study of the ordinary course of things, however protracted, prolonged, or complete, that an extraordinary event never occurs, and much more that it can never occur, it is not easy to see. An extraordinary event is by definition outside the ordinary course: and whether it occurs or not is not a matter of inference from the ordinary course, however completely investigated and understood, but a matter of observation; while whether it can occur or not is certainly not a matter of inference from its observed non-occurrence, but must rest on some principle deeper than experience can supply. The fact is that the impossibility of the supernatural can be affirmed only on a priori grounds, and no theist is entitled to affirm it. We may hold it to be improbable to the verge of the unprovable, but its possibility is inherent in the very conception of God as the personal author and governor of the universal frame. And if it is possible, then its actual occurrence is simply a question of experience and a proper subject for testimony. So soon, however, as it is once admitted that the actual occurrence of the supernatural is a proper subject for testimony it will be hard to contend that such wealth and variety of testimony as is available for the occurrence of supernatural events in the origin of Christianity can be mistaken. This, Dr. Mackintosh himself understands.

" When a critic like Küenen," he remarks, " professes to believe, or not to dispute, the possibility of miracle in the abstract, and to be willing to leave that as an open and unsettled question, but at the same time shows himself very exacting as to the evidence for the miraculous element in Christianity as a whole, or for the miraculous works recorded of Jesus in particular, and declares that the evidence for these does not satisfy his canons of credibility, the likelihood is that, unconsciously to himself, there is an *arrière pensée* in his mind equivalent to the denial of the possibility of miracles; at least, that is the impression which the rigour of his criticism will make on the minds of others " (p. 23). An instinct for safety, therefore, leads him to deny the possibility of miracles. " Indeed," he exclaims, " it is easy to see that to grant the possibility of miracle in the abstract, is to surrender the whole position to the orthodox theologian. To say the very least, it is to place the supernatural character of Christianity among the things which cannot be disproved " (p. 22). But however inconvenient this fact may be for those who are determined to deny the reality of the supernatural in Christianity, it hardly supplies a philosophical basis for asserting the impossibility of miracles. Miracles remain a matter of observation and testimony. And if anything can be proved by testimony, the supernatural origin and nature of Christianity must be held to be proved.

It is possible, of course, to demur that this testimony evaporates in the caldron of modern criticism: and we must remember that our author, along with the impossibility of miracles, assumes the truth of the conclusions announced by this criticism. To him the Biblical accounts are not history but philosophy — the crude philosophy of men who could not but share in the errors and superstitions of their age. The true course of the history can be obtained only by seeking the kernel of fact concealed within this philosophizing envelope. " The religious movement as it went on from age to age created for itself a miraculous history, just because it knew not how otherwise to place itself on record." But " underlying the miraculous records of the Old and New Testaments there is the secret history of that great, non-miraculous religious movement which was of secular duration and ran through many stadia." " The historical records do not so much show the phases of the religious evolution as rather the religious standing of the writers who compiled them as a vehicle for the utterance and propagation of their own religious ideas." It is the task of " what is called the ' higher criticism,' " to eliminate these crude conceptions of the Biblical writers, and " trace and follow out the course of the underlying history " (p. 6), the result being, of course, the substitution of a non-miraculous for a miraculous account of the origin of Christianity. That Dr. Mackintosh's anti-supernaturalism cannot get along without this critical reconstruction of the Biblical histories, is obvious enough, and is clearly recognized by himself: " The volume which is here placed before the public could not possibly have been written until the new criticism had so far done its work, and may be regarded as an outcome of that great movement " (p. v.). It is only on the assumption of the full conclusions of the extremest form of this criticism that his work can claim consideration at all. To plead this critical reconstruction, however, as a support to his anti-supernaturalism, would involve a peculiarly gross form of the *argumentum in circulo*. The very principle of this criticism in the form in which alone its results would be available for such a purpose, is the denial of the supernatural; and results which depend on the rejection of the supernatural can scarcely be made a support for its rejection. Nor is an appeal to these critical results calculated to add strength to his case. They are themselves matters of pure assumption. Dr. Mackintosh simply adopts them and nowhere seriously attempts to justify them. No one else has succeeded in justifying them. Not only are they wholly without historical evidence; they possess no historical probability, they supply no natural historical sequence, and they cannot be made to coalesce with known historical facts or to fit into the known historical framework. A scheme which requires the assumption of their truth, stands condemned as impossible by its association with a congeries of such impossibilities. It is perhaps worth while to observe further, that even if these critical conclusions were admitted in their full extent as assumed, they would still fail to rid Dr. Mackintosh of the most stringent testimony to the supernatural. This is true even of that form of the supernatural which consists in miraculous occurrences in the origin of Christianity. The confessedly genuine epistles of Paul, by themselves, bear a testimony which cannot be gainsaid to the occurrence of supernatural events at the foundations of Christianity, culminating in that greatest of all supernatural events, the resurrection of Jesus. It is true equally of that form of the supernatural which consists in the manifested glory of the divine founder of Christianity. No critical reconstruction of

Christian literature has yet availed — none which does not destroy not merely its texture but the very threads of which it is woven can avail — to eliminate from it its ineradicable testimony to the supernatural impression of that unique figure, or to the supernatural impulse that streams from it. It is the testimony not merely of one of His disciples, but of every line of Christian record and of every event of Christian history: " We beheld His glory, a glory as of an only begotten of the Father, full of grace and truth." Still less will the whole body of assumed critical results avail to rid Dr. Mackintosh of that form of the supernatural which is equally an offense to him — a supernatural salvation, wrought out by Jesus and offered by Him through His followers to the world. When the most violent forms of critical reconstruction have done their worst, the results still embalm for us a Jesus who is and who claims to be a Redeemer and a Saviour, who does not proclaim an " autosoteric " but a " heterosoteric " salvation. Dr. Mackintosh, indeed, is constrained to admit as much. The critical residuum brought to his hands requires still further criticism that he may obtain from it an unmiraculous Jesus who requires men to save themselves and does not undertake to save them. The Jesus and the Christianity which Dr. Mackintosh offers us, therefore, is not the product of even the most radical criticism, but simply the creation of his own mind. What he believes to be sober, Jesus may be allowed to teach: but beyond the line of his own judgment as to sobriety of doctrine, no record can convince him that Jesus taught. " So long as we credit Jesus with sobriety of judgment, our guiding principle of criticism, viz., the rejection of the supernatural element, forbids us to regard these sayings as genuinely his " (p. 64). Here is Dr. Mackintosh's principle of criticism. It may not seem unlikely that if we are to make our Jesus on the pattern of our own souls, we may have to content ourselves with an unmiraculous Jesus. But if we are to have the Jesus of historical testimony, in any degree, we cannot escape acknowledging a supernatural Jesus — who Himself came from heaven and brings a message from heaven of redemption in His blood.

May not, then, the results of Dr. Mackintosh's reconstruction of the origin and development of Christianity serve as their own sufficient testimony? It is on this possibility that Dr. Mackintosh apparently places his dependence. He seems to say, Look at this picture of how Christianity was prepared for, how it was originated, how it was developed, how it was corrupted; and see if its naturalness, coherency, consistency do not justify the presuppositions on which the picture is founded. The plausibility of the suggestion arises from the happy use which is made of hypothesis in all forms of scientific investigation: the positing of a supposition, the deducing of the results which would follow on the assumption of its truth, the comparison of these results with observed fact, the establishment of the truth of the original supposition by the conformity of the results with known fact and the discovery through their suggestion of further facts not hitherto observed. The fallaciousness of such an appeal to this method as is at present proposed, however, is too glaring to require to be shown. Here the proposed assumptions are not suggested by the observed phenomena, but are dragged in from without and lack all inherent probability; the results they yield by deduction confessedly differ enormously from the facts as witnessed by testimony; their assumption does not put us in the road to the discovery of independent evidence of their truth, but sets us in opposition to the whole body of evidence. The sole appeal is made to the inner consistency of the results; and this obviously, so far as it exists, is an artificial product and the inevitable effect of the process by which they are obtained. Such an appeal, indeed, involves the grossest confusion between the verisimilitude of fiction and the verity of fact. If valid in a case like the present, it would be valid to demonstrate the objective reality of the whole *mise en scène* and action of every successful fiction: the " wizard of the north " would become a " creator " in the strictest sense, and his product would no longer be romances but actualities; and the objective reality of the world of *Flat-Land* would require to be affirmed. Self-consistency and " naturalness " may be carried to the point of that " inevitableness " which is the mark of the action of the best fiction, and they argue only the genius of the author: actuality is not reached on this road. After all, history is not an *a priori* but an *a posteriori* science, and the test of reality in its sphere is nothing else than conformity to fact as experienced and witnessed. Even then, did Dr. Mackintosh's reconstruction of the history of the origin and development of Christianity possess the qualities of self-consistency, naturalness, " inevitableness " to the highest conceivable degree, it would remain a mere idle sketch of what might have been on certain contingencies; it might fairly be contemplated by him with sadness as what he could well wish might have occurred — the poet tells us that " the saddest words of tongue or pen " are these, " It might have been "; but it could gain thence no claim whatever to be considered as what was.

What, then, are we to say of the claims of his reconstruction to be the actual history of the rise and development of Christianity, when we are obliged to deny to it, as we are, even this inner consistency and naturalness? It is only when stated generally and in the vague that it has the least verisimilitude. It sounds quite attractive to speak of Christianity as taking its rise " in a great spiritual and religious movement among the Jewish people," so that " Judaism and Christianity denote the successive stages of one long evolution of religious thought and sentiment ": to represent the phase of this development which is specifically called Christianity, to have " been founded, proximately, in the great religious experience which befell Jesus in its purest form " and to have been " reflected in his life and teaching "; and to explain " that that experience was transmitted and propagated to the minds of his disciples, not, however, in its pure and original form, but through the medium of the impression made by the personality of Jesus on their emotional nature; and that that impression, acting on their imaginative and ratiocinative faculties, was what gave to Christianity the mythical and dogmatic construction which is presented to us in the New Testament and in the creeds of the Churches " (p. 4). But so soon as an attempt is made to fill in these vague outlines with a detailed history of the progress of this great religious movement — as it passed from heathenism into Judaism; through the various stages of the religion of Israel into Christianity; from the religion of Jesus to the doctrine of Paul and the mythology of John: all appearance of verisimilitude passes away and we are asked to leap all sorts of historical chasms and to assume repeatedly the most impossible sequences, in order that not a natural but a contra-natural evolution may be substituted for a supernatural history. The author enters, of course, into the labors of his predecessors and founds his attempted reconstruction of the history of this secular development on the assumed results of the critical schools of Wellhausen and Reuss, of Weizsäcker and Pfleiderer. All the historical impossibilities for which these schools are responsible in their efforts to eliminate the supernatural from the history of the Christian religion lie then, from the beginning, at his door. But these are not enough. From their results he merely takes his starting-point, and proceeds to cleanse the history of the last remnants of the evil leaven of supernaturalism and with it of the last traces of verisimilitude. Everything now hangs in the air: the most stupendous events, turning the whole course of the world's history, spring causelessly into existence; historical Christianity itself becomes a mighty beneficent force released out of a fermentation of delusion, error, and fraud.

We are dealing here with a mass of details which it is impossible to transfer to our pages in justification of our remarks, much more to examine with any fullness. We are reduced to the adduction of an illustration or two. Consider, for example, then, the lame and impotent explanation which is offered of the undeniable identity of the Christ of prophecy with the Christ of history. " In this fulfilment . . . we do not see the evidence of a prophetic fore-knowledge of events which took place five or six hundred years after the prophets lived; for that would manifestly be a supernatural prevision. But yet, the correspondence between the prophetic embodiment of the ideal, and the general features of the life of Jesus as reported by the synoptists, is so close, that no sane person can regard it as purely accidental. We therefore explain the fulfilment to ourselves as due fundamentally to the evolution of that religious idea of which Israel and the early Church were the organs " (p. 329). In other words, the correspondence between the prophets and synoptists is due to the simple fact that they shared the same ideal, and therefore expressed their ideal alike: the actual Jesus had nothing to do with either picture. " ' The prophets impersonated their ideal, while the Church idealized the person,' thus between them completing the circle of thought " (p. 330). That we may escape the admission of the supernatural here, therefore, we are asked to conceive the whole fundamental portrait of Jesus, even as given by the synoptists, as myth.

Consider again the explanation that is offered of the conversion of Paul. " Our explanation, then, of the Apostle's conversion is that it was occasioned by the moral and spiritual ideas introduced into his mind by contact and intercourse, though of a hostile kind, with the little band of men whom he persecuted. . . . When speaking of the doctrine of Jesus, we pointed out that it was his discovery of the evangelic view of the religious relation which satisfied him, that he himself, as the discoverer of that relation, was the promised Messiah. And our position now is that St. Paul, conscious of having derived this view, however mediately and indirectly, from Jesus, was satisfied that his claim to be the Messiah was well founded. The moment of Paul's conversion was just the moment at which, after much inward debate and misgiving, the evangelic view as taught by Jesus took absolute possession of his mind. As by a flash of inward light, he recognized the immense import of that new relation which formed the core of that teaching. The doctrine was so novel, so revolutionary in the religious sphere, of such startling range and gravity, and of such beneficent consequence to himself, that he readily believed all that the disciples alleged of the resurrection of him who had revealed it. . . . In the moment of crisis, when the new ideas gained the upper hand, it would appear to him as if Jesus had wrestled and prevailed, and cast him to the ground. The light, the fall, and the voice were but the form into which his sense of mental illumination and of subjugation by one who was stronger than he had thrown itself. And when he afterwards reflected on that wonderful experience, it would seem to him as if the struggle which had gone on within him had been brought to an issue by an act of self-manifestation on the part of Jesus, by an act of condescension to him personally, if not on his account, yet to him as a chosen instrument to transmit ' the benefit' to others " (pp. 370–372). In this subjective experience of Paul's, Dr. Mackintosh bids us find the sole " sight " of the " risen Jesus " on which the deathless conviction of His resurrection which animated the primitive disciples could be founded.

We say the " sole ' sight' of the ' risen Jesus,' " although we read in this paragraph itself of Paul's accepting the doctrine of the resurrection at the hands of those who were disciples before him. For, when we turn to the earlier passage where the origin of the belief in the resurrection on the part of the earlier disciples is treated, we learn that their language as to a " resurrection " is represented as purely figurative, and that they are supposed to have made no pretension of having seen even an apparition; but that now Paul is thought to have erroneously imputed his own experience to them. In such a passage as I Cor. xv. 1 ff., then, the Apostle simply misrepresents the matter when he attributes " Christophanies " essentially like his own to others. The query, of course, inevitably arises, How, granting that Paul may have so misconceived the facts at first, is it conceivable that he should not soon have been set right? Dr. Mackintosh thinks it enough to reply that it is not at all likely that Paul and Peter ever found out their difference. " It is by no means likely that the conference of the two men would turn upon the nature of their experiences. St. Paul's mind would be prepossessed with the idea that the experience of Peter and his companions had been the same with his own, and he would feel no curiosity upon the subject, nor think of scrutinizing the details. On the other hand, Peter had by this time, we presume, accepted the sensuous representation of that experience in place of the real explanation; or, for the sake of convenience, he had adopted the figurative mode of describing it, and would naturally suppose that St. Paul in any allusion which he might make to a vision, might only be referring to a similar experience and employing that figurative style of expression which seemed to come naturally to all who spoke of that crisis of the spiritual life " (pp. 364 f.). The desperation of this hypothesis of mutual misunderstanding and of no intercourse between Paul and his fellow disciples on the foundations of his faith — especially in face of the explicit historical statements of his epistles — is evident on its face, and is illustrated by the looseness of its hold on Dr. Mackintosh's own mind. Shortly afterwards it suits his purpose, in a new turn of the argument, to assume the exact contrary: and the existence of this previous passage, or its essential place in the central argument of the book, does not prevent him from writing: " But as, by the time that the Apostle wrote his great Epistles, he had conversed with the earlier apostles, and no doubt with many of the first disciples, there is, to say the least, a huge unlikelihood that he could have remained ignorant of the leading events of the life of Jesus. It is hardly conceivable that he should not have taken care to inform himself as to the earthly life and teaching of one whom he adored as the Lord from heaven. His omission to do so would argue a state of mind so incurious and indifferent as to be unnatural and incomprehensible " (p. 377). And yet, though he professes to be informed as to Christ's resurrection appearances, we are to believe that he was not so informed, and never felt the need of becoming so!

We are at the center of Dr. Mackintosh's argument, we say, when we envisage his account of the rise of the belief in the resurrection of Jesus, and it may repay us to consider what he expects us to believe with reference to it. That no such resurrection ever took place is of course given at once, in his fundamental postulate of the impossibility of the supernatural. That not even a subjective vision occurred in the case of any but Paul, we have already incidentally seen to be his contention. How then does he account for the rise of that belief in the resurrection of the Master which was the dominat-

ing force in Christianity from the very beginning? The answer is
to be found in observing that he subtly transmutes the problem into
the essentially different one of how the disciples regained their belief
in Jesus' Messiahship after the deadly blow inflicted by His death.
Then he operates with platitudes like these: " the human mind is
endowed with marvelous elasticity " and " does not willingly surrender itself to despair," so that a reaction is sure to supervene
shortly after any deep depression. This inherent tendency of the
mind was reinforced by the impression made on His disciples by
Jesus, " which was too deep to be effaced by a single blow." And
this was further reinforced by the great impression made by the
nobility of His death, so that it is truer to say that the cross glorified
Christ than that He glorified the cross. " The spiritual sense of the
disciples had been so far trained and educated by their intercourse
and association with Jesus as to discern the hidden ' glory ' of the
cross — i.e., of the death of Jesus upon it. No act of his life ' became
him ' or exalted him so much in their eyes, or so revealed his true
greatness, as his death. It was not the Christ who, in the first instance, transfigured the cross, but the cross which transfigured the
Christ. . . . The mode and spirit in which Jesus laid down his life
was what above all else transfigured him in the eyes of his disciples
and confirmed his claim to be the Messiah or the Christ " (p. 278).
The reaction from their sensuous hopes which was consequent on
Christ's death clarified their vision, and led them on to look for a
spiritual kingdom, in which Jesus, though dead, might still reign:
" When Jesus died, it was to the disciples inconceivable that a life of
such divine beauty should have lapsed. . . . All that had been
visible of him, all that was mortal of him, had been consigned to the
tomb; but this undeniable fact could not prevent the rising conviction that the spirit within him had escaped, and soared into a new
life in a higher and happier sphere. *The sudden birth of this conviction in the minds of the disciples we hold to have been the true.
Christophany, the apotheosis of Jesus* " (pp. 285 f.). The disciples,
then, did not suppose that Jesus had in any physical sense "risen
again "; this was but a figurative mode of expressing their own
resurrection to new hope: " What then actually took place on a day
or days immediately subsequent to the crucifixion was, not that
Jesus rose again from the dead, but that the disciples, commencing
with Peter, emerged suddenly, as in a moment, from the more than
sepulchral gloom, into which they had been plunged by the death of

Jesus, and in which it seemed as if the light of faith had been forever extinguished " (p. 287). Thus the resurrection of Jesus is transmuted into simply the rise of a new hope in the minds of the disciples, unattended by any event in any way extraordinary. The subsequent discussion is occupied with an attempt to show how this hope propagated itself, and how it was, through a figurative use of language, altered into a belief in a physical resurrection.

It must not be overlooked what an important part the nobility of Christ's death on the cross plays in this construction. It was the cross that transfigured Christ to His first disciples. It was the cross that glorified Him to them. It was by the mode and spirit in which He laid down His life that His claim to be the Messiah was confirmed to them (p. 278). It is probably a vice inseparable from the mode of argumentation adopted in this volume that elsewhere, when the needs of the argument require it, precisely the contrary is asserted with reference to the effect of Christ's crucifixion upon His followers. " The crucifixion," we read (p. 374), " was in fact a sort of puzzle to the disciples, which, however, did not shake their faith in him as the Messiah, and in the truth of his doctrine and the reality of his resurrection." It was " an offense " which they could only hope would be removed by a glorious second coming. It is difficult to see how the cross could have been both one of the chief causes of the continued faith of Christ's first followers in His Messiahship and a difficulty to their faith in Him as the Messiah; both an offense and Christ's chief glory. But it is not very difficult to see how it happens that it is alternately represented as each in turn by our author. By the one representation he seeks to help himself over the difficulty of explaining, as a mere subjective fact, the rise of belief in Christ's resurrection in the hearts of His dejected followers, left forlorn by their Master's death. By the other representation, he seeks to help himself over the difficulty of explaining, as a Pauline invention, the rise of faith in Christ as a Redeemer, who died that we might live. For the former purpose he enlarges on the grandeur of Christ's death on the cross and its potent effect in enheartening His followers. For the latter purpose he enlarges on the offense of the cross to the first disciples, that the emphasis placed on it in Paul's theology may be made to appear singular. In spite, then, of the declaration on the one page that it was the cross which "above all else " " confirmed Jesus' claim to be the Messiah " to His first followers, he does not hesitate to say on another that they " maintained their faith in the Messiahship of Jesus, *in spite* of his ignominious death," while " he became the Messiah for Paul *in consequence* of it " (pp. 450 f.). So slight a hold on reality has Dr. Mackintosh's whole construction.

Could anything indeed possibly be more " unreal " than this whole explanation of the rise of faith in Christ's resurrection? The chasm that yawns between despair and enthusiasm is to be bridged over. Our author proposes to bridge it by postulating — nothing. Nothing occurred, he says: the disciples simply recovered their tone. They preached the resurrection: their followers believed in it. They themselves did not: they were merely using figurative language. By this figurative language they meant to express only their own recovery of hope. If we ask what occurred to mediate their recovery of hope and to lead them so to express it, he replies simply, nothing occurred. Nothing occurred! Nothing occurred at the root of the greatest revolution in the human heart and in the history of mankind the world has ever seen. No sun arose between that black Friday and that glorious Sunday to account for the new splendor which illuminated the world. Nothing occurred to create the Christian Easter and the Christian Sabbath. Nothing occurred to deflect the whole course of human life, to ring out the old and ring in the new, to implant in man new hopes, new ideals, new life. There is nothing in " Alice in Wonderland," half so incredible, half so contrary to the " order of nature." As certain as it is that new life and hope came to the disciples' hearts on that Sunday morning, as certain as it is that through this new life and hope Christianity sprang into existence, as certain as it is that Christianity still persists in the world, so certain is it that *something occurred* in Jerusalem on that Sunday morning, of so stupendous a nature as to bear in its bosom the promise and potency of all these stupendous results.

Not only, however, is Dr. Mackintosh's construction thus incapable of being carried through on any simple and consistent view of the history; it is incapable of being carried through without the imputation of dishonest intention and deed to the chief actors in the development of the Christian religion. This imputation is again already involved, of course, in Dr. Mackintosh's adoption of the conclusions of the most radical forms of modern criticism as the foundation of his structure: for those conclusions include no little imputation of fraud to the writers of the Biblical books. But Dr. Mackintosh is compelled to go yet farther in the same pathway.

Not only is it found by him impossible to exonerate the procedure of the fourth evangelist in the forum of the modern conscience (pp. 532, 543), but Jesus Himself must stand convicted in the same court, guilty of one of the worst faults of religious innovators — the employment of familiar language to hide the novelty of a new proclamation (p. 140). The accusation is softened as far as possible: such conduct is represented as perhaps a virtue — certainly as but " the following of an instinct common to all religious reformers." But it remains an accusation of the use of a deception from which the truly honest man will shrink. A naturalistic origin for Christianity, it seems, cannot be obtained, save at the cost of something more important than even historical verity: it involves also the ruin of the moral character of its founders and builders. This surely cannot be held to be a recommendation of the construction, derived from the character of the results obtained by it.

But if Dr. Mackintosh's assumptions have nothing in themselves to recommend them, and are not confirmed by the results obtained on the supposition of their truth, where shall we go to find support for his construction of Christian history? He himself points out that his attempt to provide Christianity with a naturalistic account of its origin may have an alternative issue. " Either it may discredit the supernaturalistic theory of Christianity; or it may go far, in the way of a *reductio ad absurdum*, to demonstrate the untenableness of the anti-supernatural theory." The marked ability and unwonted thoroughness with which he has prosecuted his task — shrinking from no extremity of conclusion legitimately involved in his premises — offer certainly an unusual opportunity for a fair comparison between the two theories. No one possessed of any historical insight ought to hesitate an instant in deciding between them. The naturalistic construction is renewedly exhibited here as historically incredible: things do not happen so, cannot happen so in a world where the law of adequate causes rules. The intrusion of supernatural causes into the affairs of men may be difficult to believe: the multiplication of contra-natural effects in a chain of ever increasing complexity is impossible to believe. Dr. Mackintosh's volume thus acts, " in the way of a *reductio ad absurdum*, to demonstrate the untenableness of the anti-supernatural theory." The reader must conclude that Christianity cannot be explained as a natural religion: the " common religious instinct, working under the influence of natural forces," is inadequate to its production. But Dr. Mackintosh not only assumes, as we have seen, but solidly argues, that the supernatural origin and the supernatural nature of Christianity stand or fall together. The anti-supernaturalistic assumption must operate all through or nowhere. If it is admitted in the matter of the origin of Christianity, it must involve, as is shown in a very lucid Appendix, an anti-supernaturalistic construction also of the person of Jesus, of the nature of His work, and of the method of salvation. The converse is, of course, equally true. It would be difficult to refute the representation which Dr. Mackintosh makes of the implication of the Divinity of Christ in the conception of His work as expiatory (pp. 415, 416). His real starting-point, for this volume, it will be remembered, did not lie in a conviction of the naturalistic origin of Christianity, but in a conviction of the naturalistic character of the saving process (pp. 212, 149, note). The real object of the book is to support this conviction. That he may believe that " salvation " under Christianity is " autosoteric," he seeks to show that Christianity is itself a human product. The failure to show the latter will necessarily react on the possibility of believing the former. A supernatural Christianity is as unconformable with an " autosoteric " salvation, as a natural Christianity is with a " heterosoteric " salvation. The attempts to seek a middle ground, Dr. Mackintosh's trenchant logic grinds to powder: and here is likely to be found the chief service that his book will render. He who ponders the argument as he has wrought it out with such boldness and care, is likely to rise from its perusal with the conviction that the whole leaven of Socinian thought on the mode of salvation has gone to its judgment with Dr. Mackintosh's attempt to construct an anti-supernaturalistic Christianity. If we begin, for example, with the soteriological conceptions of McLeod Campbell, or let us rather say specifically of Dr. John Young — for it is from something like these, it would seem, that Dr. Mackintosh took his starting-point — we must logically proceed to something like Dr. Mackintosh's conceptions of the origin and history of Christianity. Conversely, if the most elaborate attempts to conceive Christianity as in origin a purely natural religion go up in smoke, the fires which consume them must inevitably eat their way back to the correlated conceptions of the method of salvation.

The failure of Dr. Mackintosh's effort to construe Christianity as a natural religion, however, will react on his attempt to explain

Christian salvation as " autosoteric " in other and more direct ways also, as well as by this logical correlation. For it must be evident that the failure of the attempt to explain away the supernatural in the origin of Christianity, will discredit beforehand the use of the same methods which are relied on for that result, to explain away the expiatory nature of Christ's saving work. The contrast which Dr. Mackintosh seeks to erect, in dealing with this matter, between " the religion of Jesus " and " the doctrine of Paul," is a purely artificial one, with no ground in fact. All of Christ's followers understood Him to teach that He came into the world to save the world by the outpouring of His blood: all the records of His teaching represent Him as offering Himself as a ransom for sin: the sacramental ordinances which He instituted for His Church embody the sacrificial and cleansing nature of His work in vivid object lessons. This witness cannot be eliminated. If we are to credit any historical testimony, it is quite certain that Jesus represented Himself as rendering the Father placable to sinful man by His own expiatory work, and not as merely discovering the Father's inherent " infinite placability." And if we are to credit Jesus in this, Dr. Mackintosh himself being judge, He must needs be more than man, and Christianity, as instituted by Him, is a supernatural religion, not merely as originating in supernatural acts, but also as supported by supernatural sanctions, and as operating in supernatural modes and with supernatural powers. The failure to explain away the supernatural in the origin of Christianity not only, however, discredits the process of explaining away this testimony, it also removes the motive to refuse credit to the testimony of Jesus to His redemptive work in what Dr. Mackintosh calls " the dogmatic or supernatural sense." It does indeed even more, as we have seen: it leaves this as the only conception of the nature of His work which will harmonize with the origin of Christianity, now shown to be supernatural, and therefore predisposes us to credit it. Supernatural pomp and display accompanying the advent of Jesus might have been unnecessary, unsuitable, incredible, if all that He came to do was to teach anew what men by feeling after had often before discovered without His teaching, and would often again discover without His teaching. But if He came truly as a redeemer of a lost race, to reverse the course of history and restore to men the favor of God, then it was fitting that He should bring heaven to earth with Him. So Dr. Mackintosh perceives; and we do not see that the argument can be resisted by

which he exhibits it. He rightly therefore acts on the assumption
that if salvation is " autosoteric," Christianity must be a natural
religion, and must have its origin like other natural religions only
in the religious instincts of men. And if we act rightly it must be
on the parallel assumption that since Christianity, as is renewedly
exhibited in this volume, cannot be construed as a merely natural
religion in origin, neither can the salvation it offers men be construed
as " autosoteric." Dr. Mackintosh has bravely thought himself
through and correlated the parts of his system: the result is that in
the collapse of a part the whole system is involved.

THE TRADITIONAL TEXT OF THE HOLY GOSPELS VINDICATED AND
    ESTABLISHED. By the late JOHN WILLIAM BURGON, B.D. Edited
    by Edward Miller, M.A. London: George Bell & Sons; New York:
    Macmillan & Co. 1896.
THE CAUSES OF THE CORRUPTION OF THE TRADITIONAL TEXT OF THE
    HOLY GOSPELS. By the late JOHN WILLIAM BURGON, B.D. Edited
    by Edward Miller, M.A. London: George Bell & Sons; New York:
    Macmillan & Co. 1896.
SOME THOUGHTS ON THE TEXTUAL CRITICISM OF THE NEW TESTA-
    MENT. By GEORGE SALMON, D.D. London: John Murray. 1897.
ADVERSARIA CRITICA SACRA. By FREDERICK H. A. SCRIVENER, M. A.,
    D.C.L., LL.D. Cambridge: University Press; New York: Mac-
    millan & Co. 1893.
THE OLD SYRIAC ELEMENT IN THE TEXT OF CODEX BEZAE. By
    FREDERIC HENRY CHASE, B.D. London and New York: Macmil-
    lan & Co. 1893.
THE SYRO-LATIN TEXT OF THE GOSPELS. By FREDERIC HENRY CHASE,
    B.D., D.D. London and New York: Macmillan & Co. 1895.
FOUR LECTURES ON THE WESTERN TEXT OF THE NEW TESTAMENT.
    By J. RENDEL HARRIS, M.A., D.Litt. (Dubl.). London: C. J.
    Clay & Sons; New York: Macmillan & Co. 1894.[1]

THE most solid and immediately effective work done of late years
on the text of the New Testament is doubtless that which the veteran
New Testament scholar, Dr. B. Weiss, has lavished upon the deter-

[1] *The Presbyterian and Reformed Review*, viii. 1897, pp. 779–790.

mination of the actual text, the first fruits of which he gave us in
his study of the text of the Apocalypse published in 1891 (see this
Review, iii. 1892, p. 543), followed by similar studies of the text of
the Catholic Epistles (1892), Acts (1893), and Paul (1896). The
thoroughness of these studies is what would be expected from their
distinguished author; and it is satisfactory to observe that, though
he proceeds by a method of his own and exhibits a rare independence
in both processes and conclusions, the results at which he arrives
are in general confirmatory of those reached by the great editors of
the text who have immediately preceded him (cf. Dr. C. R. Gregory's
extended paper on Weiss's labors, published in the initial number of
The American Journal of Theology, i. 1897, pp. 16 ff.). But though
to this extent it must needs be said that the center of gravity of
textual study of the New Testament has once more " left the shores
of England," this is in no other sense true. The impulse given by
the epoch-making publication of Dr. Hort's " Introduction," so far
from having expended itself, may be said to be only now issuing in
its natural results: and the list of titles given above bears witness to
the facts not only that textual problems still engage the attention of
British scholars, but also that recent English work on textual criticism is largely devoted to questions which have been raised by Dr.
Hort's theories.

Dr. Scrivener's final volume is the only one of the list the whole
contents of which are not in this sense the outgrowth of Dr. Hort's
work. Its object is rather to preserve, for the benefit of the public,
the critical collections of one of the most painstaking and deservedly
honored of the scholars of our generation, accumulated, as he pathetically tells us, " during the broken and scanty leisure of forty
years," and, at length, in weak health and dimness of sight, passed
" laboriously through the press." The very title which he gives them
modestly labels them as but the contents of a critic's " wastebook."
As everybody acquainted with Dr. Scrivener's work will understand,
this modest description in no wise implies that the work he offers to
the public is not supremely well done of its kind. The volume is
made up of a collation of Evan. 556, by which its affinities with 13,
69, 124, 346 are exhibited; a collation of a number of cursive copies
of the Gospels, and of a number of the early printed editions; a collation of some MSS. of the Apocalypse; and the full text of a few
fragments of Old and New Testament texts. In all, some sixty-three
documents are here reported on; and though the value of the whole

may not be very great, it is a welcome addition to our detailed knowledge of the documents.

The two volumes published by Mr. Miller from Dean Burgon's remains remove us at once from the calm atmosphere of the cloister into the arena where contending theories strive for the mastery. " It seemed like waking up after fifteen years' sleep," remarks Dr. Salmon, " to find, on looking at the new theological publications, that the controversy, Burgon versus Westcott and Hort, was still raging " (p. 1). It is inevitable, however, that the controversy should continue to " rage " until it is fought to a finish. The question at issue between the parties to it is the fundamental question of the textual criticism of the New Testament; and it is well that it should not be allowed to pass out of public sight so long as there is a single thing which is even plausible remaining to be said upon either side. Certainly the purity of Dean Burgon's motives, the enthusiasm of his research, the breadth and accuracy of his scholarship, and the vigor of the style in which he was accustomed to present his views, would make us loath to miss anything he might have had it in mind to say on so fundamental a problem. And it is certainly not those alone who hold with him in this controversy that are the losers by the incompleteness of the great project on which he was employed when death cut him off and added " another name to the . . . melancholy list of unfinished work." " He had been engaged," says Dr. Scrivener (p. vi.), " day and night for years, in making a complete index or view of the manuscripts used by the Nicene (and ante-Nicene) Fathers, by way of showing that they were not identical with those copied in Codd. ℵ and B, and, inasmuch as they were older, they must needs be purer and more authentic than these overvalued uncials." The accomplished fragment of this uncompleted enterprise, filling sixteen thick volumes, is now in the British Museum, to make us grieve that the mind that directed the work was not spared to see it finished and to estimate its teaching. No doubt, disappointment was in store for him. The problem of the use of such *collectanea* is something other than Mr. Miller at least conceives it, and would involve work and reach results essentially different from what we have outlined for us in the hopelessly slight chapters in which he attacks the problem of " The Antiquity of the Traditional Text " (I. chaps. v. vi. vii. viii.). Dr. Scrivener appears to have foreseen the difficulty. For though he tells us (p.vi.) that the effect of even this fragmentary collection " on the stability of the opposite system is direct and cannot be shaken," he adds in a postscript (following p. ci.) the salutary warning: "The Dean's capital argument arising from the fact that the text used by Patristic writers is often purer than primary manuscripts written one or two centuries younger than they . . . needs, of course, much care in its application, and can only be insisted on when the context renders it quite clear what the reading before the elder writer actually was."

Besides this vast collection of Indexes to the Fathers, a large body of fragmentary papers were placed in Mr. Miller's care, together with the text of a recension of the Gospels. Mr. Miller has piously undertaken to raise out of these materials a monument to his friend's memory, and hopes ultimately to give us: (1) the text of Dean Burgon's recension of the Gospels, concerning which he informs us that it departs from the Received text in the Gospel of Matthew in about a hundred and fifty cases (I. p. 5); (2) the portion of the Indexes to the Fathers which relates to the Gospels, as some indication of the extent of " his *apparatus criticus* in that province of Textual Criticism, in which he has shown himself so *facile princeps*, that no one in England, or Germany, or elsewhere, has been as yet able to come near him " (I. p. viii.) — Mr. Miller meaning, in the copious adduction of patristic quotations as witnesses to the text; and (3) a treatise in two volumes in which an explanation is made of Dean Burgon's system, and his general case against the recent editors and in favor of the " Traditional Text " is presented. He has begun with this last-named item and the two handsome volumes now before us are the result. Unfortunately, the material left for them was in a very fragmentary state, and Mr. Miller has been obliged to supplement it continually. He has succeeded, however, in forming out of it a tolerably complete presentation of Dean Burgon's position, with a good body of that illustrative material in the way of the discussion of special readings which no one ever knew how to make more effective.

Dean Burgon was incapable of writing a dull page, and there is much that is valuable as well as interesting in these two volumes. Especially would we not willingly miss the charming discussions of individual readings at length, such as those of the " honeycomb " of Luke xxiv. 42, the " vinegar " of Matt. xxvii. 34, the " rich young man," and " the Son of God " of Mark i. 1, which are gathered into an Appendix to Vol. I, and the numerous briefer discussions scattered through Vol. II. culminating in the long Appendix on the pericope concerning the adulteress. It is not merely that these discussions give us a completer and more sifted view of the witnesses for the readings discussed, and bring together a mass of interesting information as to the use and understanding of these texts in the early Church; nor is it merely that they reopen the question as to the right reading in a number of very important passages of Scripture, and sometimes present considerations which cast doubt upon or reverse previous decisions — as we think is the case in a number of instances, as for example in Acts xx. 24; Mark vi. 22; Matt. xxvii. 17; Titus ii. 5 (see Vol. II. pp. 28, 32, 54, 65). Such detailed discussions as these perform the far more salutary office of keeping us aware that every reading in the New Testament requires to be discussed separately and to be determined on the merits of its own evidence. It may be true that, as Dr. Salmon complains (p. 33), a certain " servility " has been exhibited in the acceptance of Dr. Hort's results, and it may well be that his theory as to the history of the text and of the consequent general value of the several MSS. and other witnesses has not only been embraced sometimes with " servility," but applied often with a dull mechanicalness which is wholly alien to its very nature. But nothing can be more certain than that Dr. Hort's determinations of the relative value of witnesses are determinations of average values only, and that nothing could more sadly confound the whole system of criticism which he has given the world than to treat them as absolute and invariable. It may possibly be true that he himself used his materials a little too mechanically in the actual framing of his text, and that there may be some color to the reproach that he looked upon B as an infallible voice proceeding from the Vatican and upon the combination B‭ℵ as a manifest deliverance from heaven itself: it may possibly be true, also, that others, following him, have dismissed with too cavalier a contempt all the readings of the mass of the MSS. and have shown a disposition to prefer nonsense to sense when it was BℵACD which babbled it. But such extremes of treatment of the authorities are not only not inherent in Dr. Hort's system, but are distinctly contradictory to his system. Neither on genealogical considerations, nor on considerations derived from the verdict of internal evidence of groups, can we suppose that everything in B or Bℵ, or in the " Neutral " or the " Neutral + Western " *stirps* is genuine, and everything in the later uncials and cursives or in the earlier Fathers is corrupt. This whole method of criticism is founded rather on averages and probabilities. The combination Bℵ, on genealogical principles, carries us back to an exceptionally good MS., but not to a perfect one: a perfect MS. never existed, and even a very bad one may sometimes correct the best. The group of MSS. classed as " Neutral," by the test of internal evidence of groups, evinces itself as exceptionally good; and that classed as " Western " exhibits itself as exceptionally bad. But the one group remains human — and *humanum est errare;* and the other group remains a group of witnesses to the New Testament text, and is not transformed into a body of MSS. of another work — and it therefore may sometimes give good witness. In a word, there is not only left place here for exceptions, but exceptions are to be expected. Discussions of individual passages like those which Principal Brown and Dean Burgon gave us, therefore, must be expected to bear good fruit and to aid substantially in the better settlement of the text. The discovery of the exceptions to the validity of the general rules for applying the testimony may, indeed, be even said to be now the chief task of the actual work of the textual criticism of the New Testament. It is with no reserves, therefore, that we can welcome the rich discussions of separate readings such as Dean Burgon's writings bring us.

Nor do we need to make reserves in welcoming the discussion which he gives us of the main grounds of difference in critical principles between himself and Dr. Hort. We do not, it is true, expect to see made good the principles advocated by Dean Burgon and Mr. Miller (with whom Dr. Scrivener only partially agreed, cf. I. p. 35). There is, of course, much that they contend for with which we are in hearty accord. That, for example, all witnesses to the text are to be taken into consideration and the restored text built upon the broad basis of the whole testimony, who will doubt? But who can doubt, either, that in taking all witnesses to the text into consideration, each is to receive a valuation proportionate to its relative importance and weight? And here we touch upon the real difference between the two schools. It is found in the relative value and weight which they severally ascribe to the two great groups of MSS. — represented roughly the one by the oldest uncials, BℵACD, and the other by the great mass of codices. Accordingly the controversy is often said to be between the older few and the later many, as if the one party were determined in their preference chiefly by a predilection for antiquity, and the other by a predilection for numbers. Were this the case it would surely be an interminable controversy — for *de gustibus non disputandum*. But, of course, each offers a more rational basis for his procedure. Dr. Hort follows the old uncials not merely because they are the oldest MSS. which have come down to us, but because he thinks the text which they present is the most trustworthy and the best text, exhibited as such under the tests of genealogical evidence and the internal evidence of groups. Dean Burgon follows the mass of copies, not merely because of their overwhelming numbers, but because he thinks the text they present the most trustworthy transmission, evinced as such by the richness and fullness and variety of its attestation — coming from all ages, all parts of the Church, all classes of witnesses — and by the fact that, in the conflict of texts in the Church, it was this text which drove all competitors from the field and established itself as the single text recognized by the Church and (what appears to him an unavoidable corollary from this fact) by the Church's God, who surely may be supposed to have busied Himself in His providence with preserving to His Church in its purity the Word He had bestowed upon it by His inspiration. The grounds of Dr. Hort's preference, if with great succinctness and somewhat abstractly, yet clearly and unmistakably, were set forth in his "Introduction." We have lacked hitherto anything like an adequate presentation of the grounds of the preference of the school represented by Dean Burgon. It is to be regretted that the hand that planned this presentation was not permitted to complete it: even after the pious care expended by Mr. Miller upon the fragments left in his hands, the arguments retain an incompleteness unavoidable in the circumstances. But they enable us to see clearly the basis of the contention of the school they represent, and thus draw the issue between the two schools more exactly than ever before. In doing this, they distinctly advance the controversy towards its conclusion.

It may be suspected that Dean Burgon was nerved for the gigantic task of indexing the Fathers, partly, by the mistaken notion that the preference for the primary MSS. of the school he was opposing turned chiefly on their superior antiquity: he wished to turn its flank by showing that the Fathers who wrote at a date earlier than that of the origin of these MSS. familiarly used a different text. So far, we may say with Dr. Salmon, that "he might have spared himself much of this trouble if he had known how freely the facts which he brings forward were acknowledged by WH ": he has engaged so far in " contradicting what had not been asserted, and laboriously proving what had not been denied " (p. 16). But in another aspect this investigation of the antiquity of the " Traditional Text " is an essential element in Dean Burgon's case. For the head and front of Dr. Hort's offending relatively to the " Traditional Text " is that he denies to it the rights of an original witness altogether, and explains it as a text which has not simply " grown," but has been " made " — assigning to its manufacture a somewhat definite date. If it can be shown to have been in existence and in common use prior to the date thus assigned for its origin, this contention, at least, of Dr. Hort's falls to the ground. It would not follow, indeed, that the " Traditional Text " is a preferable text to that transmitted by the primary uncials; but it could no longer be put summarily out of court as no simple witness to the contents of the autographs, but a critically constructed text of the third or fourth century. Our authors have therefore laid out their strength on what they call " the Pre-manuscriptural Period, — hitherto the dark age of Sacred Textualism," and they fancy that they have " abundantly established the antiquity of the Traditional Text, by proving the superior acceptance of it during the period at stake to that of any other " (I. pp. ix. and x.). Their argument, however, is vitiated by a series of fatal misapprehensions. Dr. Hort does not doubt that the " Traditional Text " was already predominant in Chrysostom's day, or that it was in existence probably a century earlier. Nor does he doubt that the elements out of which it was composed existed before its formation; he does not think of it as a pure invention of its originators — a kind of New Testament freely composed out of the whole cloth by the Antiochian critics. Nor does he consider that the text which he derives from the primary uncials (if one wishes so to describe it) was the text in predominant use up to the date which he assigns for the origin of the " Traditional Text." It does not avail to set aside his conclusions relative to the " Syrian Text," therefore, to show that certain elements of it were in currency long before the date which he assigns for its origination, or were in far more predominant use than the corresponding elements which enter into his own text. What we need, and what we do not in the least get, is some evidence that that composite entity which he calls the " Syrian Text " antedates the date he assigns for its origination, or (in order to satisfy the contention of our authors) antedates the origination of the text presented in the primary uncials.

For our authors are not content with an assault on Dr. Hort's construction of the history of the transmission of the text: they set over against it an antagonistic construction of their own. And it is just in this that the value of their contribution to the settlement of the controversy lies, since thus the precise alternative is laid clearly before us. The really telling objection to Dr. Hort's construction, heretofore, has been, that his whole theory stands or falls with a piece of wholly speculative history. It assumes a formal revision of the text of the New Testament, carried through with skill and completeness, by which its whole complexion was changed, and yet for which there is not a scintilla of historical evidence. This, it has been plausibly said, is incredible, and can be admitted on no other than purely inferential grounds. This form of attack on Dr. Hort's construction is abandoned by our authors. That the New Testament text passed through some such history as is outlined by him they explicitly allow. Mr. Miller, for instance, tells us (I. p. 197) that:

" The Tradition of the Church does not take shape after the model of a stream or streams rolling in mechanical movement and unvaried flow from the fountain down the valley and over the plain. Like most mundane things, it has a career. It has passed through a stage when one manuscript was copied as if mechanically from another that happened to be at hand. Thus accuracy except under human infirmity produced accuracy; and error was surely pro-creative of error. Afterwards came a period when both bad and good exemplars offered themselves in rivalry, and the power of refusing the evil and choosing the good was in exercise, often with much want of success. As soon as this stage was accomplished, which may be said roughly to have reached from Origen till the middle of the fourth century, another period commenced, when a definite course was adopted, which was followed with increasing advantage till the whole career was fixed irrevocably in the right direction. The period of the two Gregories, Basil, Chrysostom, and others, was the time when the Catholic Church took stock of truth and corruption, and had in hand the duty of thoroughly casting out error and cleansing her faith."

Is there not here allowed, in full conformity with Dr. Hort's construction of the history, (1) a period of naive copying, with growing corruption; (2) a period of critical discrimination, " from Origen to the middle of the fourth century "; and (3) a period of the dominance of the critically chosen text? And is it not the problem of criticism, in such circumstances, to get behind this critically chosen to the naively transmitted text — that is, of course, to get to the text which underlies the total transmission?

Not, however, to press the implications of chance passages like this, in which, after all, more may be conceded than the writer would like to be held to, the mode in which our authors draw the lines of the debate implies the admission of some such history as that which Dr. Hort has suggested. For the very center of their contention rests on the supposition that there was a quasi-ecclesiastical critical revision of the New Testament text consummated in the period between Origen and Eusebius. Only, they represent the primary uncials and not the " Traditional Text " as the product of this revision: and it is therefore that they would discard the testimony of these primary uncials, which present, as they say, a " fabricated text," not a text which has grown up naturally in the ordinary course of copying, but a text which has been deliberately framed, and that not merely with critical but with sinister intent and effect. " Inadvertency," we are told, " may be made to bear the blame of some omissions: it cannot bear the blame of shrewd and significant omissions of clauses, which invariably leave the sense complete. A systematic and perpetual mutilation of the inspired Text must needs be the result of design, not of accident " (II. p. 23). Accordingly it is deemed to be in no other way than by the assumption of deliberate heretical depravation, possible " to account for such systematic mutilations as are found in Cod. B, such monstrous additions as are found in Cod. D, such gross perturbations as are continually met with in one or more, but never in all, of the earliest Codices extant, as well as in the oldest Versions and Fathers " (II. p. 201). Therefore they recognize in B and א " the characteristic features of a lost family of (once well known) second or third-century documents, which owed their existence to the misguided zeal of some well-intentioned but utterly incompetent persons who devoted themselves to the task of correcting the Text of Scripture, but were entirely unfit for the undertaking " (I. p. 234). " The fact is," we are told, " that B and א were the products of the school of philosophy and teaching which found its vent in semi-Arian or Homoean opinions " (I. p. 160). They are therefore among " the most corrupt copies in existence " (I. p. 25) ; " a reading vouched for by only B א C is safe to be a fabrication " (II. pp. 30 f.) ; and the proper mental attitude towards B is one of " habitual distrust "

(II. p. 27). Now the result of this theory of the origination of the text presented by the primary uncials in a formal revision by which a " corrected text " characterized by abridgment was given the world by " some person or persons of great influence and authority," " in the age immediately succeeding that of the Apostles " (II. p. 22, note), is to draw the issue between Dr. Hort and Dean Burgon with unwonted sharpness. It is by it admitted that the differences between the " Traditional Text " and that of the primary uncials are not fully accounted for by the simple unwary corruption of copying: a formal revision has taken place. The issue is, Which text — that of the uncials or that of tradition — is the " corrected text," and which is the simply transmitted text? When the issue is drawn thus exactly, its decision cannot lie far off.

We know the grounds on which Dr. Hort relies for the decision of this question. He attempts to show by a critical examination of the " Syrian Text " that it presents the features of a composite text and that it presupposes the text of the primary uncials: that this latter text is one of the constituent elements out of which it was made. He attempts to show historically that the " Syrian Text," in its characteristic features, runs out, as we ascend the stream of time, in the early fourth or third century. He attempts to show by internal evidence of groups that the " Syrian Text " is inferior to that of the primary uncials. The grounds on which our present authors rely for their decision of the question are given in these volumes. They seek to rebut some of Dr. Hort's arguments: by an attempt to meet his critical argument from the phenomena of " conflation " as exhibited in the " Syrian Text "; by an effort to show out of the earlier Fathers the early prevalence of elements which enter into the " Syrian Text "; and by an exhibition of the subtle beauty of a number of " Syrian " readings. As positive grounds for their preference they appeal on the one hand to the curtailed and " clipped " character of the text presented by the great uncials, which they endeavor to show to be both deliberate and heretical in purpose and thus to discredit their witness; and on the other hand to the widespread and varied testimony to the " Traditional Text," and above all to the fact that it is the " Traditional Text " and thus must be considered, rationally, to have the presumption in its favor and, religiously, to represent the providentially preserved Word of God.

We would not willingly underestimate any item of the case for the " Traditional Text " thus presented. But we are bound to bear witness that after an honest attempt to weigh it impartially, in its entirety and in its several parts, it seems to us to halt fatally. We cannot indeed fail to be impressed when we read such a statement as this: " The advocates of the Traditional Text urge that the Consent without Concert of so many hundreds of copies, executed by different persons, at diverse times, in widely sundered regions of the Church, is a presumptive proof of their trustworthiness, which nothing can invalidate but some sort of demonstration that they are untrustworthy guides after all " (I. p. 17; cf. p. 33). But we observe that its whole force turns on the phrase " Consent without Concert," which is the very point in dispute. Dr. Hort seems to have shown that the consent is due just to concert, and his exhibition of that fact, as yet unrebutted, transfers the presumption at once to the older though fewer witnesses, which, on the test of internal evidence of groups, evince themselves also as the better. So, again, we are far from accounting the appeal to Providence either illegitimate or without force. We do believe that God has in His Providence been active in preserving His inspired Word to His Church. We do not believe that, after giving the Scriptures of Truth to mankind, He " straightway abdicated His office; took no further care of His work; abandoned those precious writings to their fate " (I. p. 11). But just because we believe in God's *continuous* care over the purity of His Word, we are able to look upon the labors of the great critics of the nineteenth century — a Tregelles, a Tischendorf, a Westcott, a Hort — as well as those of a Gregory and a Basil and a Chrysostom, as instruments of Providence in preserving the Scriptures pure for the use of God's people. Dean Burgon and Mr. Miller are able to reconcile with their appeal to Providence the early prevalence of a corrupt text which needed purifying in the fourth century: why cannot they reconcile with it also a further purification of this same text in the nineteenth century? The fact is, their point of view is determined not so much by a religious as by an ecclesiastical presumption. And when we probe their fundamental principle to the bottom, it is found to rest really on a high doctrine of the Church. Their prime consideration is, in a word, that " a certain exhibition of the Sacred Text — that exhibition of it with which we are all most familiar — rests on ecclesiastical authority " (p. 13). Their confidence in the " Traditional Text " is due to their view that that text " rests on the authority of the Church Catholic "; and they are

strenuous in its defense because they cannot believe that the " probat
of the Orthodox . . . Christian bishops " through so many years
can be mistaken (p. 14) : and therefore they fully recognize that the
force of their appeal can be felt in its fullness only by " Churchmen."
" How Churchmen of eminence and ability, who in other respects
hold the truths involved in Churchmanship," they exclaim (p. 59),
" are able to maintain and propagate such opinions " as those advocated by Dr. Hort, " without surrendering their Churchmanship, we
are unable to explain." In a word, the root of the opinions here set
forth as to the purity of the " Traditional Text " of the New Testament is to be found, not in considerations drawn from the history of
the transmission of that text or from a critical estimate of the relative value of its actual witnesses, but in considerations which lie
outside of the text itself and its own history in a general doctrine of
the *continuous* authority of the Church, which itself rests on a special
theory of the Church peculiar to certain sections of the Christian
body. There is truth therefore in the judgment sometimes expressed
that the two schools of criticism may be not inaptly discriminated
as the Catholic and Protestant schools, a truth that lies deeper than
what was in the mind of Dr. Salmon when he speaks of Dr. Hort's
text as " a thoroughly Protestant New Testament " (p. 86). It may
be doubted, at least, whether a thoroughgoing Protestant could find
sufficient grounds for adopting Dean Burgon's conclusions; in any
event the reasons which are only secondary with Dean Burgon and
Mr. Miller must needs in his case be palmary, while what is determining in their case is out of court with him.

To decline the leadership of Dean Burgon and Mr. Miller is not
quite the same, however, with throwing oneself unreservedly into
the arms of Dr. Hort, as Dr. Salmon's little book shows us. His
remarks were occasioned, in a sense, by the publication of Mr.
Miller's earlier volume; and they take up its note in so far as they
are mainly critical of Dr. Hort. But they in no wise echo its contentions. Dr. Salmon has no expectation of ever seeing Burgon " set on
his legs again " (p. 33) ; he is " unable to accept his principles " and
feels no confidence in his mode of conducting an investigation (p. 5).
But he thinks that " in Dr. Hort's work will be found some rash decisions which calmer followers will regard as at least doubtful "
(p. 33). His tone and manner of setting forth his own doubts as to
certain of Dr. Hort's positions are so unobtrusive and modest and
withal so winsome, that we are led to ask ourselves whether, as Dr.

Salmon sometimes seems to think that clever advocacy supplies a ground for doubting the validity of the conclusions commended by it, we would not do well to stop our ears at once to his siren voice. With some of his criticisms on Dr. Hort's methods we find ourselves at all events at once in substantial agreement. With the strictures which he makes, for example, upon Dr. Hort's " question-begging nomenclature " (p. 43), we cannot help sympathizing; the " Old Syrian " version would have been just as " old " under a less controversy-inviting name; the " neutral " text just as " neutral " under a more " neutral " title. We are also in sympathy with Dr. Salmon's animadversions on Dr. Hort's overfreedom in conjectural emendation (p. 81); and, with more reserve, with his condemnation of his overstrained critical tendency to omissions in framing his text. The criticisms on Dr. Hort's account of the origin of the " Syrian Text " (pp. 73 f.), by which his theory is not rejected but simplified, we have also read with much general agreement.

With reference to the more important strictures which Dr. Salmon brings against Dr. Hort's procedure, we must express, however, more hesitation. The one of these concerns the end which Dr. Hort set before himself, viz., to get back to the autographic text. This Dr. Salmon considers far too ambitious a project (p. 40). The other, which is closely related to this, concerns the neglect of the Synoptic problem on Dr. Hort's part. Dr. Salmon thinks that Dr. Hort ought not to speak of " the individual words of the individual author " with reference to compositions like the Synoptic Gospels (p. 104); and criticizes Dr. Hort's words elsewhere where he speaks of " the genuine text of the extant form of St. Matthew," as if the two forms of expression involved an inconsistency. The confusion seems to us, however, to be Dr. Salmon's own. Surely, no matter how the Synoptics came into being, each of them, as a completed work, bearing traces of individuality in the object, methods, and modes of speech of its author (or " compiler," if you will), had an " autograph "; and it is to the recovery of this that textual criticism looks as its goal. To be sure, if we hold that our present Gospels were not " made " in any sense, but " grew," — are but the products of gradual accretion, silently and undirectedly made — in that case it would be a misnomer to speak of their having had " an autograph." But though Dr. Salmon speaks (p. 148) as if something in a minor way like this may have happened with reference to them, he surely would not push such a hypothesis so far as to confound the oral and written stages of Gospel composition. The expression of the judgment, moreover, that Westcott and Hort have actually not attained the autographic text, but have given us only the text of an early Alexandrian MS. of probably the early third century (p. 52, cf. p. 155), and that their method could lead them to nothing else, ought not to carry with it the *dictum* that the autographic text is unattainable and that it is too ambitious to seek it. In any event, we find ourselves out of harmony with Dr. Salmon in both of these main contentions. Nor can we go with him in his partial accord with Blass's theory of a twofold recension of Luke — Gospel and Acts — as the explanation, so far, of the origin of the " Western Text."

But on approaching the problem of the origin of the " Western Text," it behooves us to take account of the remaining titles set at the head of this review. If the problem as to the origin and value of the " Syrian Text " may rightly be said to be the fundamental problem of the textual criticism of the New Testament, the problem of the origin and value of the " Western Text " may equally rightly be said to be its cardinal problem. To the investigation of this problem, therefore, much of the most acute and painstaking work of scholars has of late been given; and the books by Dr. Chase and Dr. Harris named above are among the most recent fruitage of these labors. Four chief theories as to the origin of the " Western Text," as Dr. Harris tells us (p. vii.), are now in the field. There is Resch's theory, " that the bifurcation in the primitive text of the New Testament is due to independent translations from a Semitic document (probably Hebrew)." There is Blass's theory that, in the Lucan writings at least, " they are due to the issue of two separate drafts from the hand of the original writer." These two theories have in common that they look upon the " Western Text " as having similar if not equal claims to originality with the rival transmission, and in sharing this common conception they share inevitable failure. For if there is anything certain in the textual criticism of the New Testament, it is that the " Western Text " is a corrupted text. A Semitic influence may well be traced at the root of the whole New Testament transmission: the men who wrote the New Testament were Jews; it may very well be that the men who first copied its books were Jews, or, when Gentiles, Semites of the first center of Gentile Christianity, Antioch: who shall say what depth of Semitic stain the various lines of transmission may not have received before they got well out of Semitic hands and from under Semitic influences

— influences which were not localized, but were, if not dominant, yet certainly present in the first age in every Christian church in the world? Knowledge of additional incidents, and of additional details of the recorded incidents, in the life and work of our Lord and His apostles, may very well have been current in more centers of Christian teaching than one; and may very well have found their way into the text of Gospels and Acts, giving a color of authenticity to many a gloss. But any careful examination of the peculiarities of the " Western Text " will show again, as it has often shown heretofore, that they have distinctly the character of corruptions and not of original inheritances. " We thus arrive at the conclusion," Dr. Harris says in the last of his " Four Lectures " (which is devoted to this subject), " that ' the glosses in the Codex Bezae show signs of having been inserted from the margin ' . . . and further ' the displacement which is observable in certain of the glosses, is a strong though not a conclusive argument, against the theory that those glosses formed a part of a primitive redaction of the text ' " (p. 81). If we may thus summarily set these two first theories aside and assume that the " Western Text " is a corrupt text, and that the only problem regarding it is to account for and trace the origin of this corruption, we have in the books of Dr. Chase and Dr. Harris exceptionally happy advocacy of the two most likely hypotheses, viz., that this corruption is derived from Syriac and that it is derived from Latin influences, entering into and corrupting the original text.

Dr. Harris was first in this very inviting field of investigation. In his brochure on " The Diatessaron of Tatian," published as long ago as 1890, he was evidently testing the hypothesis that in the Diatessaron we might discover a source of the " Western " corruption. Failing to obtain standing ground for such a hypothesis, he turned to the opposite quarter and in his " A Study of Codex Bezae," published the next year, sought to explain the " Western Text " as due to corruption derived from the influence of a Latin version upon its parallel Greek text. In the enthusiasm of discovery he naturally at first pushed this theory to extremes, as he now candidly allows (p. viii.). But he still contends that much is explained by " reaction on the Greek text from the primitive Latin translations," adding " as well as, occasionally, from the Syriac Version " (p. viii.). The general theory of the origination of the " Western Text " substantially through Syriac corruption, which Dr. Harris had thus early discarded, has been enthusiastically taken up by Dr. Chase, and is advocated in detail in the two volumes named above. Dr. Harris' " Lectures," with which our list of titles closes, contains a series of sprightly criticisms on the more recent deliverances upon the subject, with a view to defending himself from criticisms made, orienting himself relatively to the work done, and in general advancing the subject. The first lecture explains why he cannot take Resch's advice and go back to Credner's crudities; the second criticizes Dr. Chase's book on the Acts; the third treats of Corssen and Blass on the " Western Text " of Acts; and the last investigates the character of the glosses in the " Western Text " of Acts.

We shall not enter here into any detailed account of the investigations and conclusions of either Dr. Harris or Dr. Chase. They are both engaged in pioneer work, and, as the one has found, so the other will find, need to abate the extremity of his claims. For, in his enthusiasm, Dr. Chase, too, announced in his former volume that he had discovered " the true solution of the problem of the Western Text " — or of the " Syro-Latin " text as he now wishes it called. That Syriasms are found in the " Western Text " we believe has been shown, as that Latinisms are found in it has also been shown; but the problem of the " Western Text " is a great problem and, as befits a great problem, its solution lags. That hopeful advances towards its solution are being made, and that valuable contributions towards its solution are offered both by Dr. Chase and Dr. Harris, is thankfully to be recognized; that it never was so near to its solution as now seems likely enough. But when it is solved, it will surely be found that so complex a problem has not an absolutely simple solution, but that a variety of factors have entered into its making and must be unraveled for its explanation. Some of these days, however, Dr. Harris will no doubt surprise us again, and this time, doubtless, with its real solution. Meanwhile there is no place to which one can go for more stimulating notes on the problem than to his brilliant brochures upon it (cf. this *Review*, ii. 1891, p. 688; iii. 1892, p. 543; and *The Critical Review*, ii. 1892, p. 130).

A DICTIONARY OF THE BIBLE: dealing with its Language, Literature
and Contents, including the Biblical Theology. Edited by JAMES
HASTINGS, M.A., D.D. Vol. I: A — Feasts. New York: Charles
Scribner's Sons; Edinburgh: T. & T. Clark. 1898.[1]

THE first volume of Dr. William Smith's "Dictionary of the
Bible" was published at the end of 1863, and was reissued in
America four years later in a thoroughly revised form, under the
editorial care of Dr. H. B. Hackett and Mr. Ezra Abbot. Before the
close of the year 1870, the four volumes of the American edition
were in the hands of the public. Of course there were other works of
the kind in the field, the most valuable of which were probably Dr.
Patrick Fairbairn's "The Imperial Bible-Dictionary" (2 vols.,
London, 1866) and Dr. W. Lindsay Alexander's edition of Kitto's
"Cyclopædia of Biblical Literature" (3 vols., Philadelphia, 1866).
McClintock and Strong's "Cyclopædia of Biblical, Theological, and
Ecclesiastical Literature," the publication of which was begun in
1867, sought to occupy so much wider a field that it hardly came
into direct competition with the specific "Bible Dictionaries." It is
true to say, at all events, that the "American Smith" immediately
took its place on the tables of scholarly American ministers and
students of the Word as the standard work of the kind. That place
it has worthily and almost undisputedly held ever since. Meanwhile
a generation of years has passed, and in these days of restless research a generation is a very long time, in which many changes of
opinion must needs occur, and some not inconsiderable advance in
knowledge may haply be made. It is easy, to be sure, to overestimate
the "increase of knowledge" that has come with "the process of the
years." Augustine points out that all the knowledge best worth
having is acquired by the human animal in its infancy: it is the
puling metaphysician who accomplishes the task set us by the oracle
and learns to know himself, and, wiser than he may afterward become, separates off from himself the external world, and discovers
about him other spirits like himself: it is in our earliest youth that
we learn to think and speak and read: and what are all other acquisitions but relatively unimportant growths of these fruitful roots?

---

[1] *The Presbyterian. and Reformed Review,* ix. 1898, pp. 515–520. For review of vol. ii. cf. *ibid.,* xi. 1900, pp. 174 ff.; vol. iii., *ibid.,* xii. 1901, pp. 151 ff.;
vol. iv., *ibid.,* xiii. 1902, pp. 641 ff.; extra vol., *The Princeton Theological
Review,* iii. 1905, pp. 136 ff.

Similarly what is best worth knowing about the Bible has not been reserved for the aging Church of the last third of the nineteenth century to discover. It is all duly set down in our Smith and Kitto and Fairbairn, and in our Calmet, too, and in whatever before that served to inform men what the Bible is, what it contains, and what one must know in order to understand and appreciate its message. Whatever else the last thirty years have discovered, they have not discovered the Bible, nor anything about the Bible of the first importance. Nevertheless the diligent labors of Bible students during this period have not been in vain: a considerable body of fresh information has been accumulated, sometimes of a corrective, sometimes of a supplementary character. The time has fully come to garner this new material and put it within the reach of all.

The most natural way of doing this was to build on the old foundations, and we were accordingly promised a revised edition of Smith. After the publication of its first installment, however, that project seems to have fallen through. In its stead, we have been bidden to look for two completely new Bible Dictionaries. The one of these, projected first by Prof. W. Robertson Smith, is being completed under the editorship of Prof. T. K. Cheyne, with the assistance of Dr. J. Sutherland Black; and its first part is announced to appear in the approaching October. It is expected to occupy what is known as a very " advanced " standpoint; to scorn " average opinion " and start out from " the latest that has been written " on each subject; and to apply the " most exact scientific methods " and thoroughgoing critical solvents to all that is Biblical. The other of our two promised Dictionaries, undertaken by the great firm of Messrs. T. & T. Clark, of Edinburgh, was understood to be laid out on less extreme lines and to aim at presenting rather what is known about the Bible than the latest conjectures concerning it by the least sober of scholars. It has outstripped its rival in speed of preparation, and its first volume now lies before us. Those who had looked forward to it, however, as throughout a reliable guide to what is really known of Biblical matters will be in some measure disappointed. The editor speaks of the care that has been exercised to exclude " unaccepted idiosyncrasies " from its pages. The success of the effort has been only partial. The trouble has been in the standard assumed. " Unaccepted " is a good word, but its value can be estimated only when we ask further, By whom? " Unaccepted " by a narrow circle of critical scholars which has acquired temporary vogue among us, has been the practical answer. And the consequences are that the sober reader finds the book characterized by the abundance of idiosyncrasies which crowd its pages and is offended by its apparent lack of coherence as a whole; and that the distinction between the two new Bible Dictionaries sinks at last very much into a question of details. The interval that separates the two is indeed just the interval that divides from one another the two Oxford colleagues, Drs. Cheyne and Driver. There is no need to minimize this interval; it is perceptible: but there is no difference in principle between the two; it is only a matter of a little more or a little less. The Edinburgh Dictionary both profits and loses by the difference. It loses by it in internal consistency and unity and in stability and hold upon the future — for, after all, the "moderate criticism" which it has elected to represent wavers between two opinions and must advance in one direction or the other through rapid changes; while for an extremer scepticism there is always a constituency — few perhaps but fit — it being true in this sphere too that the "poor we have always with us." It profits by it, in so much as the frying pan, after all said, *is* a better place than the fire; and in so much as the essentially mediating and inconsistent character of the standpoint of "moderate criticism" which it assumes has naturally justified the insertion of many articles of a more conservative tendency (although these are mostly on the "safe" topics, that is, on such subjects as impinge only indirectly on matters of "criticism") and especially has demanded a tolerably conservative attitude in matters connected with the New Testament. Despite its unsatisfactory critical point of view, accordingly, this new Dictionary is not only a rich record of, but also an important contribution to our present knowledge of the Bible: it has been edited with the highest skill and gathers in the most scholarly manner the results of modern research into Biblical matters: it is full, thorough, learned, and bids fair to be the student's *vade mecum* for the next few years.

From the book-maker's point of view, the new Dictionary has been modeled on "Chambers's Encyclopædia," and its page is a very close reproduction of that of that work. Perhaps the impression of the type is a little less clear, and certainly it falls short of "Chambers" in the matter of illustrations. Here indeed is the weakest point of the new Dictionary from a formal point of view. The illustrations are very few (only some forty-four separate figures occur in this whole volume, and only two articles — "Agriculture" and

" Dress " — can be called " illustrated " at all), and also (we fear
we must add) very poor. The Preface tells us that " the illustrations
. . . are confined to subjects which cannot be easily understood
without their aid." We should never have discovered for ourselves
that this was the principle that governed their occurrence. Could we
not, then, have been spared the odd inksplotch which is labeled
" A ' Lodge in a Garden of Cucumbers ' " (p. 532) ? We could not, on
the same ground perhaps, ask to be relieved from the " Cedar from
the Besherri Grove " (p. 364), but we have our doubts whether it
illustrates anything. This Cedar of Lebanon and the Porcupine
(p. 304) are the only natural history subjects that are figured. In
our judgment every animal and plant mentioned in the Bible should
have been presented to the eye. In the matter of illustrations the new
Dictionary falls lamentably not only behind what was to be expected
of it, but also behind its predecessors.[2]

The strength of the volume lies in what we may speak of as the
scholarly character of its contents. Here we are specially struck with
the admirable quality of the numerous short articles, particularly
those on the obsolete and obsolescent words of the English Versions,
which are mostly written by the editor and leave nothing to be
desired. The proper names of the Bible are very thoroughly worked
out, and a special word of commendation is due to the geographical
terms. The same is to be said of the ethnological, geological, and
natural history articles, the last of which, forming a very notable
series of some sixty articles, we are proud to say are from the pen
of an American scholar, Dr. George E. Post, professor in the American College at Beyrout. Along with Dr. Post some thirteen other
American writers appear in this volume. Of these Dr. Willis J.
Beecher has contributed the largest number of articles, which seems
to be partly due to his having undertaken the article " Giant " (to

---

[2] The following are the only illustrations in the volume: Articles " Agriculture," seven figures (pp. 49–51) ; " Amulets," eight figures (p. 89) ; " Anklets "
(p. 99) ; " Art," two figures (p. 158) ; " Axe," two figures (p. 206) ; " Bag," two
figures (p. 232) ; " Balance " (p. 234) ; " Battering-Ram " (p. 258) ; " Bell "
(p. 269) ; " Bit " (p. 303) ; " Bittern " (p. 304) ; " Bonnet " (p. 310) ; " Brick "
(p. 326) ; " Cedar " (p. 364) ; " City " (p. 446) ; " Cosmogony " (p. 503) ;
" Cucumber " (p. 532) ; " Dead Sea " (p. 575) ; " Drawer of Water " (p. 621) ;
" Dress," thirteen figures (pp. 624–628) ; " Ear-rings " (p. 633) ; " Engraving "
(p. 704) ; " Eye " (p. 814). Under the letter A alone, Smith has some sixty-two
illustrations, and they are both far better selected and far better executed
than those that meet us here.

appear in the next volume) with all subsidiary titles; we have from him at any rate the following twelve articles: " Anak," " Arba," " Avva," " Beth-Dagon," " Dagon," " Delilah," " Drunkenness," " Dwarf," " Ekron," " Emerods," " Emim," " Ephes-Dammim." Needless to say these are thoroughly satisfactory, the most extended one — that on " Drunkenness " — being a useful historical study of a rather neglected subject. Dr. Ira M. Price contributes seven articles: " Abrech," " Accad," " Assurbanipal," " Bayith," " Belshaz- zar," " Chaldæa," " Evil Merodach " — chiefly, as will be seen, on subjects connected with Assyriological learning. Four articles come from the hand of Prof. J. H. Thayer: " Abba," " Bar," " Eli, Eli, Lama Sabachthani," and " Ephphatha," all of which concern the Aramaic element in the New Testament. Three each are contributed by Profs. F. C. Porter, E. L. Curtis, G. T. Purves, and H. Porter. Prof. Frank C. Porter's contribution consists of the extended and valuable article " Apocrypha," along with short accompanying notes on Achior and Chelod: Prof. Curtis' of the important articles on the Chronology of the Old Testament and Daniel, man and book; all written from the standpoint of the presently fashionable sceptical criticism, the historical character of the book of Daniel being denied and indeed even the historical existence of a " Daniel " left in doubt. Prof. H. Porter writes about " Cupbearer," " Distaff," and " Dye- ing "; and Prof. Purves most satisfactorily on " Crown," " Diadem," and " Darkness." Two articles each are contributed by Profs. W. A. Brown (" Cross," " Excommunication "), B. B. Warfield (" Doubt," " Faith "), and Lewis W. Batten (" Ezra," and " Ezra-Nehemiah " — from the standpoint of the sceptical criticism). Dr. Selah Merrill contributes a short note on Chorazin; Prof. J. Poucher a long ac- count of Crimes and Punishments; and Prof. Francis Brown a long article on Chronicles, in which with great minuteness he gathers together all that can tend to break down confidence in the historical trustworthiness of the books — his general conclusion being that " it is plain that the character of the Chronicler's testimony, when we can control it by parallel accounts, is not such as to give us reason to depend on it with security when it stands alone." In all, the American contribution to the Dictionary consists of some one hun- dred and four articles. It is not such as to render the book an " inter- national " book; but in point of scholarship it is a creditable aid to a British enterprise; and to it is due some of the longest and most important articles in the volume — such as those on " Apocrypha " (thirteen pages), "Chronology of Old Testament" (six pages), "Chronicles" (eight pages), "Crimes and Punishments" (seven pages), "The Book of Daniel" (six pages), "Faith" (twelve pages). Perhaps we can scarcely speak of it as fairly representative of American scholarship: American Old Testament scholarship, for example, is not only prevailingly but overwhelmingly "conservative," or, as it would be better called, historical, while the adherents of the school of sceptical criticism are here thrown prominently forward. Nevertheless, from the standpoint of the Dictionary, it cannot be said that American aid has been despised, and certainly the American contribution does not in quality fall below the general standard of the work.

Fullness and thoroughness being among the objects which the editor has set before himself, quite a number of the articles have been allowed to "extend to considerable length." We have counted some seventy-five which extend to a length exceeding two pages, that is to say about three thousand words, each. One article — Mr. C. H. Turner's comprehensive paper on the Chronology of the New Testament — attains the dimensions of a treatise, filling twenty-two of these large pages. Two others exceed fifteen pages each, viz., Prof. Hommel's notable paper on Babylonia, and Mr. Crum's perhaps equally notable paper on Egypt. Prof. Hommel's paper on Assyria almost equals in length and quite equals in value the paper on Babylonia. Other papers exceeding ten pages are Mr. Headlam's careful study of the book of Acts (ten pages), Prof. Porter's article on the "Apocrypha" (thirteen pages), Prof. Stewart's article on "Bible" (thirteen pages), Mr. Gayford's article on "Church" (fifteen pages), Mr. White's article on "David" (thirteen pages), Mr. Strong's admirable paper on "Ethics" (twelve pages), and Prof. Warfield's paper on "Faith" (twelve pages). Some twelve more papers exceed seven pages: Dr. Plummer's "Baptism," Prof. Francis Brown's "Chronicles," Mr. Kilpatrick's "Conscience," Principal Robertson's "I Corinthians," Prof. Poucher's "Crimes and Punishments," Prof. Ryle's "Deuteronomy," Prof. Lock's "Ephesians," Prof. Davidson's "Eschatology of the Old Testament," Mr. Charles's "Eschatology of the Apocryphal and Apocalyptic Literature," Prof. Salmond's "Eschatology of the New Testament," Mr. Thackeray's "Books of Esdras," and Prof. Bernard's "Fall." Fifteen others exceed five pages, viz., Prof. Mayor's "Brethren of the Lord," Prof. Curtis' "Chronology of the Old

Testament," Principal Robertson's " II Corinthians," Principal
Whitehouse's " Cosmogony," Prof. Davidson's " Covenant," Prof.
Curtis' " Book of Daniel," Mr. Mackie's " Dress," Prof. Peake's
" Ecclesiastes," Prof. Kennedy's " Education," Mr. Forbes Robin-
son's " Egyptian Versions," Mr. Strachan's " Elijah," Mr. Harford-
Battersby's " Book of Exodus," Prof. Skinner's " Ezekiel," and
Principal Harding's " Feasts and Fasts."

It will not fail to be observed how many of the titles thus
incidentally mentioned concern matters of Biblical Theology. The
effort to give proper treatment to these subjects forms one of the
special features of this Dictionary. We have noted in the volume
such articles as the following which fall under this head: " Adoption " (J. S. Candlish, one and one-half pages); " Angel " (A. B.
Davidson, four pages); " Anger (Wrath) of God " (J. Orr, one
page); " Ascension " (J. Denney, one and one-half pages); " Assurance " (A. Stewart, one-quarter page); " Atonement " (J. O. F.
Murray, one and one-half pages); " Baptism " (A. Plummer, seven
pages); " Blessedness " (W. F. Adeney, one-half page); " Brotherly
Love " (J. Denney, one-half page); " Calling " (J. Macpherson,
one-fifth page); " Chastening " (J. Denney, three-quarters page);
" Christology " (J. Agar Beet, three pages); " Church " (S. C.
Gayford, fifteen pages); " Communion " (J. A. Robinson, two
pages); " Conscience " (T. B. Kilpatrick, seven and one-half pages);
" Conversion " (J. S. Banks, one-half page); " Corruption " (J.
Massie, one-third page); " Cosmogony " (Owen C. Whitehouse, six
pages); " Covenant " (A. B. Davidson, six pages); " Creed "
(J. Denney, one page); " Curse" (J. Denney, one and one-half
pages); " Demon, Devil " (Owen C. Whitehouse, four and one-half
pages); " Election " (J. O. F. Murray, four pages); " Eschatology
— Old Testament " (A. B. Davidson, six pages); " — Apocrypha "
(R. H. Charles, eight pages); " — New Testament " (S. D. F.
Salmond, seven and one-half pages); " Ethics " (T. B. Strong, twelve
pages); " Faith " (B. B. Warfield, twelve pages); " Fall " (J. H.
Bernard, seven pages); " Fasting " (V. H. Stanton, one and two-
thirds pages); " Fear " (W. O. Burrows, one-half page). Many of
these articles are admirable; all of them are carefully written;
some of them are adequate. But they certainly are not consentient;
and our pity follows the man who seeks to learn what the teaching
of the Bible is by reading consecutively these topics in the Dictionary. The individualistic and idiosyncratic character of the

volume comes out here no more strongly than elsewhere; but it is disturbingly present here as elsewhere; and it makes the reader wonder what the editor can mean by speaking of the book as a whole as " reliable and authoritative." If Dr. Orr is " reliable and authoritative " on the " Wrath of God," for example (as he certainly is), then Dr. Murray cannot possibly be " reliable and authoritative " on the " Atonement " — for he leaves no place for wrath in God. And if we rise beyond the question of mere harmony among the several writers, and ask after some general standard of doctrinal truth which has governed the admission of views, we shall ask in vain. All sorts of theological conceptions here struggle together and label themselves alike " Biblical." We can only say that as in criticism the standard of the book is mainly what can only be described as " sceptical," in theology it is mainly " Socinianizing " — though both terms must be taken here, of course, not in their precise, but in their broader connotations. It cannot be said, either, that the space allowed for the treatment of the topics under the rubrics of Biblical Theology is at all nicely proportioned to their relative importance. Surely, in any case, for example, the space allotted to the topics of Atonement and Baptism is not adjusted to the relative importance of the subjects. Nor indeed is the list of topics treated as complete as it might well be. We miss for instance any proper discussion of such topics as Creation and Fatherhood — the cross-references given in neither case fill the need. And we miss altogether such entries as Absolution, Age (the present and to come), Apocatastasis, Apostasy, Asceticism, Bearing Sin, Benediction, Beelzebub, Birth (new), Blood of Christ, Ceremonial, Communion, Conception (miraculous), Consummation, Descent to Hell, End (other than the mere term), Eternity, Exaltation, Example. In the interests of fullness and accessibility such topics should not be passed over.

We have set down frankly the impression the new Bible Dictionary has made on us at first sight. Space would fail us to undertake detailed criticism of the separate articles. Its characteristic mark seems to be accuracy, and it is obviously a book which has information to give with a lavish hand. The student will seldom consult it in vain: though he may sometimes refuse its leading, he will be always stimulated and instructed by its presentation. It is a book, moreover, which will beyond doubt improve with acquaintance. We congratulate the editors and publishers alike on the successful launching of so great an enterprise.

THE MAKING OF RELIGION. By ANDREW LANG, M.A., LL.D. London, New York and Bombay: Longmans, Greene & Co. 1898.[1]

IN HIS dedicatory letter to Principal Donaldson, Mr. Lang intimates that these chapters on the early history of religion " may be taken as representing the Gifford Lectures " delivered by him; " though in fact," he adds, " they contain very little that was spoken from Lord Gifford's chair." Unsystematic, diffuse, repetitious, desultory, " jotty," the whole discussion, nevertheless, not only is clothed with that piquant literary quality which Mr. Lang gives his writings, but is also of undeniable scientific importance.

The object of the book is to discuss afresh the origin of the two fundamental beliefs which lie at the base of what we call " Religion " — the belief in God and the belief in the immortality of the soul. If these beliefs arose, comments Mr. Lang, " in actual communion with Deity (as the first at least did, in the theory of the Hebrew Scriptures), or if they could be proved to arise in an unanalysable *sensus numinis*, or even in ' a perception of the Infinite ' (Max Müller), religion would have a divine, or at least a necessary source. To the Theist, what is inevitable cannot but be divinely ordained; therefore religion is divinely preordained; therefore, in essentials, though not in accidental details, religion is true. . . . But if religion, as now understood among men, be the latest evolutionary form of a series of mistakes, fallacies, and illusions, if its germ be a blunder, and its present form only the result of progressive but unessential refinements on that blunder, the inference that religion is untrue — that nothing actual corresponds to its hypothesis — is very easily drawn " (p. 51). The latter view has attained among anthropologists almost the position of a fixed truth. The current teaching is briefly that man first derived the conception of " spirit " from the phenomena of sleep, dreams, shadow, trance, and hallucination; that his first worship was directed to the souls of his dead kindred and to spiritual existences fashioned on the same lines; and that, as the result of a variety of processes, these " spirits " prospered until they became gods, and at last one of them became supreme: thus " the ideas of God and of the soul are the result of early fallacious reasonings about misunderstood experiences " (p. 1). Even so, Mr. Lang is not prepared to acknowledge that " religion " may be lightly set aside as only

[1] *The Presbyterian and Reformed Review*, ix. 1898, pp. 744–749.

a huge blunder. " All our science itself is the result of progressive refinements upon hypotheses originally erroneous, fashioned to explain facts misconceived." Why may not our religion likewise, " even granting that it arose out of primitive fallacies and false hypotheses," have yet " been refined, as science has been, through a multitude of causes, into an approximate truth " (p. 51)? But it seems more directly to the point to ask whether the current teaching is accordant with the facts. Mr. Lang thinks that it is not. And it is the object of this book to show that in two crucial points it is not; or, as he more coyly expresses it, that " there are two points of view from which the evidence as to religion in its early stages has not been steadily contemplated " (p. 2). He proposes to reopen the matter at these two points and to raise anew the two questions: Whether man arrived at belief in the existence of a " soul " solely through a misinterpretation of such simple phenomena as those of sleep and dreams; and whether man attained the conception of God through an evolution from the idea of " spirit." To both questions he returns a negative reply. And it is the purpose of his book to validate these two negative replies.

Mr. Lang justly points out that the two positions thus taken up by him are independent of each other. The establishment of them both would be, of course, the ruin of the presently dominant theory of the origin of religion. But the establishment of both is not essential for that result. It might well be that man arrived at the notion of " spirit " through a misinterpretation of the phenomena of dreams and the like, and yet, if his idea of God is not a development of his doctrine of " spirit," this fact would have no bearing on the validity of his doctrine of God. Mr. Lang unites the discussion of the two questions in this volume thus, not because they are essential to one another, but because he conceives that the developed idea of religion, as prevalent among the higher races at present, is a complex of the two ideas of the immortality of the soul and of the existence of an infinite moral Ruler and Judge. He is, therefore, at pains to investigate the origins of both ideas. His book thus falls into two very different portions. In the first he seeks to bring forward indications that " the savage theory of the soul may be based, at least in part, on experiences which cannot . . . be made to fit into any purely materialistic system of the universe " (p. 2). In the second he presents evidence which shows that the idea of God was not dependent on or derived from the idea of

" spirit," but was of wholly independent origin, and was capable of a very high development apart from the aid of the idea of " spirit " — though, of course, this idea supplied a formula by which the Mighty Being already envisaged could be more adequately conceived, as well as an elevating conception of man's own nature. The importance of thus separating the idea of God from that of " spirit " is obvious. But we do not see why the idea of immortality also may not equally validly and with equal advantage be separated from that of " spirit." Men believed in God, as Mr. Lang shows, without the aid of any metaphysical conception of " spirit." Why might they not equally readily have believed in their own future existence apart from a conscious elaboration of a doctrine of " spirit " ? It is also a question worth asking at this point, What does Mr. Lang mean by " spirit " ? In this query we may indeed place our finger on a weak point in the book. Mr. Lang does not seem to keep clearly before him any consistent definition of this term, fundamental though it is to his whole argument. He seems to use it prevailingly as equivalent to " ghost," and to conceive it merely negatively as over against solid matter. Indeed, as we read his pages we are reminded of the old scholastic pleasantry which replied to the query, " What is matter? " " Never mind " ; and to the query, " What is mind? " " No matter." But what " spirit " *is* as distinguished from what it is *not*, Mr. Lang does not seem to stop to consider. If, however, " spirit " means, positively, nothing but thinking, feeling, willing being — that is, if it is practically a synonym for " person " — then, of course, every person has the idea of " spirit " (undeveloped of course) given in the most immediate and intimate action of his self-consciousness: and the idea of a personal Ruler is already the idea of a spiritual God and, as well, the idea of the continued life of a person is already the idea of spiritual immortality. The metaphysical development of this conception is, to be sure, a different matter. We are, meanwhile, confused, and we think Mr. Lang confuses himself, by his undefined usage of the term. We think, had he clearly discriminated the differing connotations of the word, he would have argued that the idea of " spirit " (=ghost) was no more necessary to the belief in immortality than it is to the belief in God: and would have sought (and found) evidence of early belief in continued life and in future rewards and punishments either before or certainly apart from the emergence in thought of any developed metaphysics of

" spirit." Certainly, at all events, such a state of mind is not uncommon to-day. The whole first section of Mr. Lang's book, thus, appears to us unnecessary to his avowed purpose. It is not required to show that men arrived at the conception of " spirit " by a valid pathway in order to obtain a valid starting-point for belief in immortality. In the order of developing thought, the idea of immortality would rather precede that of " spirit " in this sense: men would naturally believe in their own future existence before they fully wrought out a theory of the mode of that existence. Nevertheless we are grateful for the chapters which investigate the possible and the actual grounds on which savage men may have come to the conviction of the existence of a something in man different from his bodily organism which they could speak of as " that in men which makes them live," and which they pictured as subject of experiences beyond the confines of the merely bodily life.

The professed purpose of these chapters is to offer evidence that the inference drawn by primitive man that he possessed a " soul " did not necessarily rest on phenomena which readily admit of a materialistic explanation. Mr. Lang marshals an array of supernormal experiences asserted to occur among savage races, on the basis of which such an inference would not seem so absurd as it is commonly represented. He then parallels these asserted supernormal experiences with similar ones, occurring not among savages, but among the cultured races of the modern world, and subject to the investigation of trained scientific intellects, with the effect of raising the question whether they are to rank merely among asserted experiences, or must not rather be believed to have actually occurred. " If so," he observes, " the savage philosophy and its supposed survivals in belief will appear in a new light," and it may at least be wise " to suspend our judgment, not only as to the origins of the savage theory of spirits, but as to the materialistic hypothesis of the absence of a psychical element in man " (p. 71). The discussion of these points leads Mr. Lang into a very obscure region — into the region of hypnotism, clairvoyance, crystal-gazing, hallucinations, prophetic dreams, and the like. It is too much of a jungle for unwonted feet to tread. But we think he fairly makes out his point that there *are* supernormal experiences in this obscure region which are as yet insoluble on the ordinary assumptions of materialism. The evidence will, of course, appeal to different minds with different degrees of force — and indeed to the same mind at different times very differently. Personal experience of or first-hand acquaintance with similar phenomena will count for much in the estimate put upon the narrative of such experiences in the case of others. But for ourselves we do not see how it can be successfully denied that such supernormal events as Mr. Lang relates occur. What interpretation is to be put on them is a different story. The savage man has been prone to explain supernormal knowledge of the remote, for example, by the assumption of the wandering of the separable soul temporarily from the body. Mr. Lang seems now and again to suggest that it may be explained as a telepathic communication from one mind to another. Others fall back on the assumption of common participation in the universal *fühlende Seele,* or on common contact with the Absolute. The savage man's theory does not seem the worst of these guesses — rather than accept any of which we prefer to remain (like Mr. Lang) without a theory, meanwhile abiding content with the conviction that there are experiences that come to the human animal which shake the foundations of the materialistic hypothesis. " No more than any other theory, nay, less than some other theories, can it account for the psychical facts which, at the lowest, we may not honestly leave out of the reckoning " (p. 172).

The great success of the volume is attained, however, in the discussion of the second of the questions to which it is devoted. Here, by an array not of strange experiences drawn from a dubious borderland, but of plain and open facts, Mr. Lang demonstrates that so far from belief in a moral Supreme Being being the last result of a slow evolution, due to the action of advancing thought upon the original conception of ghosts, it occurs (often apart from the conception of ghosts) in the lowest known grades of savagery in a strikingly pure and complete form, and is so widely spread as to suggest its aboriginal universality. The novelty of this exhibition is perhaps not so great as Mr. Lang thinks, though it is doubtless very novel, indeed, in the scientific circles for which he specially writes; but the importance of his solid contribution to the establishment of the fact cannot easily be overestimated. After his marshaling of illustrative cases drawn from every part of the world and his luminous discussion of the relations of their theism to the other beliefs of savages, it would seem that the crudities of the Animistic theory of the origin of the idea of God are forever antiquated. " The savage Supreme Being," says Mr. Lang, " with added power, omniscience, and morality, is the idealisation of the savage, as conceived of by himself, *minus* fleshly body (as a rule), and *minus* Death. He is not necessarily a ' spirit,' though that term may now be applied to him. He was not originally differentiated as ' spirit ' or ' not spirit.' He is a Being, conceived of without the question of ' spirit ' or ' no spirit ' being raised; perhaps he was originally conceived of before that question could be raised by men. . . . In the original conception he is a powerful intelligence who was from the first: who was already active long before, by a breach of his laws, an error in the delivery of a message, a breach of ritual, or what not, death entered the world. He was not affected by the entry of death, he still exists " (pp. 203 f.). In a word, the Supreme God of the lowest races, who stands behind and above their Animism and Fetishism and even his own mythology (p. 198), has not been conceived metaphysically but religiously: he was not primarily a " spirit " — he was and remains the Eternal, Omniscient, Ethical Creator, Ruler and Judge of all things. No wonder that Mr. Lang is impelled to exclaim: " These high gods of low savages preserve from dimmest ages of the meanest culture the sketch of a God which our highest religious thought can but fill up to its ideal " (p. 208). To the origin of this conception he devotes little discussion, contenting himself with hints that he would reject the assignment of it to a special primeval revelation and would look with favor on the supposition that it represents an instinctive operation of the causal judgment seeking an adequate cause for the universe — to which he doubtless would not object to adding the action of that sense of dependence and responsibility which seems native to man as man. Its history he is inclined to trace in a progressive degeneration incident to the very advance of culture, the *vera causa* of which he discovers in the " attractions which animism, when once developed, possessed for the naughty natural man " (p. 281). He tentatively suggests that four stages in this history may be traced, represented by (1) the Australian unpropitiated Moral Being; (2) the African neglected Being, still somewhat moral; (3) the relatively Supreme Being involved in human sacrifice, as in Polynesia; and (4) the Moral Being reinstated philosophically, or as in Israel (p. 329). Whether, however, these stages can be made out or not, the mass of evidence offered for the main proposition is overwhelming; and we think Mr. Lang has shown with a clearness and force which should convince the most recalcitrant that the conception of a Supreme Being, the cause of all existences and the moral ruler of the world, is native to the human race, is possessed by even its lowest representatives, and can only with difficulty be eradicated or even obscured.

It is natural, of course, that Mr. Lang should wish to see how far his conclusions "can be made to illustrate the faith of Israel." His closing chapter is given to this subject. Perhaps it is not the most satisfactory portion of his book. Mr. Lang is as chary of the directly supernatural as most men of science of the day. But, apart from this, his remarks on the Israelitish religion and its course are most suggestive. He naturally looks upon the belief in Jehovah as "a shape of the widely diffused conception of a Moral Supreme Being, at first (or, at least, when our information begins) envisaged in anthropomorphic form, but gradually purged of all local traits by the unexampled and unique inspiration of the great Prophets" (p. 294). "Had it not been for the Prophets," he remarks, "Israel, by the time that Greece and Rome knew Israel, would have been worshipping a horde of little gods, and even beasts and ghosts, while the Eternal would have become a mere name — perhaps, like Ndengei and Atahocan and Unkulunkulu, a jest. The Old Testament is the story of the prolonged effort to keep Jehovah in His supreme place. To make and to succeed in this effort was the *differentia* of Israel. Other peoples, even the lowest, had, as we prove, the germinal conception of a God. . . . ' But their foolish heart was darkened ' " (p. 220). Upon the current "critical" theories of the origin of Jehovah-worship, Mr. Lang accordingly pours a well-deserved scorn. "Have critics and manual-makers," he exclaims, "no knowledge of the science of comparative religion? Are they unaware that peoples infinitely more backward than Israel was at the date supposed have already moral Supreme Beings acknowledged over vast tracts of territory? Have they a tittle of positive evidence that early Israel was benighted beyond the darkness of Bushmen, Andamanese, Pawnees, Blackfeet, Hurons, Indians of British Guiana, Dinkas, Negroes, and so forth? Unless Israel had this rare ill-luck (which Israel denies) of course Israel must have had a secular tradition, however dim, of a Supreme Being " (p. 312). The uniqueness of the religious history of Israel does not then consist in the mere fact of its Theism, but in the preservation and on the whole steady elevation — not, of course, without periods of decline and degeneration (which Mr. Lang paints far too black, p. 283) — of this universal high Theism. In the account to be given of " the historically unique genius of the Prophets " by whose instrumentality Israelitish Theism was thus preserved and developed, Mr. Lang certainly falters: the divine purpose was exhibited in it, he is driven to admit; but beyond that single admission he will not go. But of the fact he is clear: here is a unique experience among the races of men — the progressive broadening and deepening of primitive Theism in one race, under the influence of a series of unparalleled religious teachers until a greater than all the prophets came to birth. And the uniqueness of the experience of Israel is all the more marked because of the relative indifference of Israel to the second stream of influence which, in Mr. Lang's theory, enters into the formation of religion in our modern conception of that term. " The great Prophets of Israel, and Israel generally, were strangely indifferent to that priceless aspect of Animism, the care for future happiness, as conditioned by the conduct of the individual soul " (p. 329). " They carried Theism to its austere extreme — ' though He slay me, yet will I trust in Him ' — while unconcerned about the rewards of Animism " (p. 295). And so it seems that " early Israel having, as far as we know, a singular lack of interest in the future of the soul, was born to give himself up to the developing, undisturbed, the theistic conception, the belief in a righteous Eternal " (pp. 332 f.).

We may not find here quite all that we could wish: but surely we find what is fundamental in the Christian conception of the history and mission of the religion of Israel, and the germ of much else. One feels that Mr. Lang needs only to give a somewhat more detailed study to the development of that religion, to be forced to posit something more than what we may speak of as natural inspiration in the Prophets, for example, in order to account for their unique work. And one is strengthened in such a feeling by reading such a treatise, for instance, as Giesebrecht's " Die Berufsbegabung der alttestamentlichen Propheten." Giesebrecht is quite as keen as Mr. Lang can be, to account as far as possible for the prophetic teaching on natural grounds, that is, without the assumption of direct supernatural revelation; and his postulation of a natural *Ahnungsvermögen* as the basis of the Prophetic phenomena would, one would think, be attractive to Mr. Lang. But a reader of Mr. Lang's acuteness would soon discover that even Giesebrecht does not succeed in accounting for the Prophetic phenomena by eliminating all direct supernatural communication from them; and we fancy his candor would gradually lead him to the conviction that there is a deep discrimination between religions that he has not yet clearly made, which nevertheless the facts require — a discrimination by which, over against those religions which are the product of men's reaching up after God if haply they may grasp Him, is set the religion which is the product of God's reaching down to men if haply He may restore them to communion with Himself.

ENCYCLOPÆDIA BIBLICA. A Critical Dictionary of the Literary, Political and Religious History, the Archæology, Geography, and Natural History of the Bible. Edited by the Rev. T. K. CHEYNE, M.A., D.D., and J. SUTHERLAND BLACK, M.A., LL.D. Vol. I: A to D. New York: the Macmillan Company; London: Adam & Charles Black. 1899.[1]

THE scholarly world has for some years been aware that there was in preparation a new Bible dictionary, originally projected by the late W. Robertson Smith, and after his death taken in charge by Prof. T. K. Cheyne and Dr. J. Sutherland Black, destined to be the mouthpiece of the newer criticism in its most radical form. The appearance of the first volume has disappointed none of the expectations which had been formed concerning it. The vigorous scholarship and indefatigable industry of Dr. Cheyne and the skill and experience of Dr. Black as an editor of encyclopædias justly led the public to look for a notable work at their hands. It is a notable work that lies before us. Every page is instinct with living learning, poured out without stint on every subject which naturally comes into view in a dictionary of the Bible. And it is safe to say that on no encyclopædia ever published has there been expended such a wealth of expedients to make it the handy, useful book of reference which it is the very mission of an encyclopædia to be. It is possible even that in both matters the thing is overdone. It requires a number of pages to put the reader in possession of the abbreviations, symbols, typographical devices, systems of cross-

---

[1] *The Presbyterian and Reformed Review,* xi. 1900, pp. 516–522. For review of vol. ii. cf. *ibid.,* xii. 1901, pp. 459 ff.; vol. iii., *ibid.,* xiii. 1902, pp. 460 ff.; vol. iv., *The Princeton Theological Review,* i. 1903, pp. 645 ff.

reference by the employment of which the book has been reduced
in size and increased in handiness; and the average reader may be
somewhat appalled as he contemplates the necessity of mastering
this new language before he advances to the work itself. And he
certainly will not read far into the latter before he will recall the
familiar distinction between knowledge and wisdom and will begin
to desiderate less of mere learning and more of good judgment in
the matter laid before him: after all, he who consults a Bible dictionary is commonly more in search of safe guidance to the knowledge of the truth than desirous of spending his time in learning some
new thing. When once he is adjusted, however, to these two conditions, he will no longer be disappointed in the book. He will
certainly find the type too small (though it is remarkably clear),
and he will often find the articles too compressed: both of these
faults he will recognize, however, to be in the right direction. He
will assuredly not find the book characterized by sobriety and restraint in criticism or by trustworthiness or reverence in its dealing with the Biblical material: he was not entitled to expect this
in a work the very keynote of which has ever been announced as
" advanced criticism," and that as interpreted by Dr. Cheyne.
But he will discover himself in possession in this book of a mass of
information as to all archæological, geographical, and physical matters connected with the Bible which it would be difficult to surpass
elsewhere; and with a complete conspectus of the most recent conjectures as to its literary, political, and religious history, which will
interest him extremely, and doubtless prove not less instructive than
interesting. He justly expected all this in Dr. Cheyne's dictionary:
he receives it in Dr. Cheyne's dictionary.

For this is distinctly, and in a sense in which the other large
dictionaries of the Bible are not, the dictionary of one man, and
that one man Dr. Cheyne. It is somewhat important to note this
fact clearly. For in the pious regard which the editors pay to the
memory of the late Prof. W. Robertson Smith and the anxiety they
exhibit to give due credit to his initiative — to which the " Encyclopædia " owes its origin — the impression is apt to be obtained that
it is in some true sense Dr. W. Robertson Smith's dictionary of the
Bible. Except, however, that it is in a fashion the carrying out of a
project contemplated by him and by men whom he trusted and to
whose hands he committed the task, it is in no sense Dr. W. Robertson Smith's dictionary. Confessedly the positions taken up in the

dictionary are not those which Prof. Smith taught during his lifetime. Dr. Cheyne only contends that they are such as Prof. Smith —
who was always in the van of critical opinion — would have taught
had his life been prolonged to the close of the century. It is an
opinion which Dr. Cheyne is quite entitled to hold. Certainly
Prof. Smith occupied a position which in principle leaves nothing to
choose between it and Dr. Cheyne's own: and if with prolonged
life he had not " advanced " step by step with Dr. Cheyne in the
application of their common principles this would have been due
not to less radicalism of fundamental postulates on his part, but
only to differences between the two in habits of mind, spirit, and
mode of applying common presuppositions. We do not ourselves
think that Prof. Smith could have failed to " advance " steadily
toward the goal toward which Dr. Cheyne's own face is turned.
Whether he would have embraced the same body of opinions which
Dr. Cheyne publishes in this dictionary — which is proclaimed
with some flourish to be Prof. Smith's own — may on the other hand
be very seriously doubted. Prof. Smith's criticism was in principle
all that Dr. Cheyne could desire: but he was a very serious-minded
man, and liked to have some show of sober reason for his opinions.
That these reasons were sound, that the apparently wide inductions
on which he established his opinions were trustworthy, we are the
last to believe. That Dr. Cheyne's patronizing air to his " more
moderate colleagues," as only radical critics in the making, has a
certain justification we do not question. But meanwhile it is true
that Dr. Cheyne's critical methods have none of the apparent caution which characterized Prof. Smith's procedure, and that his
critical opinions have none of the air of grounded judgments which
Prof. Smith knew how to throw around his.

Nor can it even be said that what Prof. Smith intended or what
Prof. Smith did has fared very well at the hands of the editors of the
actual dictionary. This is certainly not precisely the dictionary
Prof. Smith projected, if we are to believe the account of his purposes which Dr. Cheyne gives us in his Preface. And certainly the
material which Prof. Smith left behind him has been treated in the
most cavalier fashion. It appears to have been Prof. Smith's purpose to republish, in a revised and completed form, his own contributions to Biblical learning printed in the " Encyclopædia
Britannica," and to supplement these with such articles as were
necessary to complete the scheme of an " Encyclopædia Biblica ":

and much work seems to have been done in the preparation of the briefer articles for this purpose. Almost none of this work has been given a place in the dictionary as published. The articles contributed to the " Encyclopædia Britannica " have not been revised and republished. Only in the single instance of " Chronicles," cared for by the comparatively sober hand of Dr. Driver, has this been done. The famous article " Bible " (spoken of in the Preface somewhat shortly as " inevitably provisional ") has simply been passed by. New articles on " Canticles " and " David " by Dr. Cheyne, written from wholly different standpoints, have been substituted for those by Prof. Smith bearing these titles. While the minor articles " Angel," " Ark," " Baal," " Decalogue " have taken practically no account of what Prof. Smith had said on these themes in the " Britannica." The article " Baal " is signed indeed " W. R. S. — G. F. M.," but stands in no internal relation whatever to the " Britannica " article; while the only connection which the new article " Ark " has with Prof. Smith arises from the incorporation into it of a short extract from his " Bennett Lectures." Besides occurring along with Dr. Driver's initials at the end of the article " Chronicles," and along with those of Dr. Moore at the end of that on " Baal " (in this latter case one scarcely sees why), the initials " W. R. S." appear very infrequently in the pages of the volume — only, so far as we have noted in a somewhat hasty glance through its pages, at the end of the short and unimportant articles, " Abez "; " Adoni-Zedek "; " Adversary "; " Baalis "; " Barkos "; " Beth-Marcaboth "; " Bidkar." In a word, the only places where Prof. W. Robertson Smith is honored in this volume are the Dedication and Preface: in the body of the work he has practically no place and receives very scanty respect.

The book is distinctly therefore, we say, not Prof. Smith's, but Dr. Cheyne's. A very large part of it is written by Dr. Cheyne's own hand. It is, indeed, a marvel of industry and scholarship that one man could have written so much, so much to the point, and so much so learnedly and acutely as Dr. Cheyne has written for this volume. It deserves to be accounted one of the wonders of the literary activity that marks the close of the nineteenth century. And even what has not been actually penned by Dr. Cheyne bears for the most part the impress of his peculiar genius and reflects his modes of thought and feeling. He has had, of course, the choice of his collaborators in his own hands, and these have naturally been

selected from the men most nearly akin to himself; and a large part
of the work has been done by younger men, trained by himself, and
working in the spirit with which he has indoctrinated them. The
result is that we not only have " advanced criticism " in this new
" Encyclopædia," but distinctively what we may perhaps be permitted to call without offense " Cheyneyesque " advanced criticism;
and this is a variety which is certainly not marked by sobriety of
judgment, but will strike most men — though they be " advanced
critics " themselves — as sometimes erratic and often ungrounded.
Thus even Dr. C. N. Toy — who of course welcomes the book as
in the main learned and conscientious — feels impelled to enter a
caveat against its overfree resort to conjecture and the overboldness
of its use of emendation of the texts with which it deals (*The
American Historical Review*, v. 1900, p. 545). And Julius Wellhausen,
in his biting way, does not hesitate to rebuke it for addiction to the
employment of most doubtful data as if they were of historical value
(*Deutsche Literaturzeitung*, xxi. 1900, coll. 9–12). Perhaps a transcript of a short section of Wellhausen's notice will exhibit, better
than anything that we could ourselves say, this characteristic of
the work. He remarks:

" The Dictionary projected by W. Robertson Smith was to be
' no mere collection of useful miscellanea,' but ' a survey of the contents of the Bible as illuminated by criticism.' To this his successors
and especially the Chief Editor, Cheyne, have addressed themselves.
The distinguishing characteristic of the work, at least so far as the
Old Testament articles are concerned, is ' advanced criticism.' To
the substantial indications of this belong: (1) the bold emendation
and dissection of the Old Testament transmission, combined when
necessary with subjective divination; (2) that conception of the
general history of religion, of English origin, which was applied to
Semitic antiquity by W. Robertson Smith, and has been lately applied to classical antiquity also by E. Rohde; (3) the effort to cast
light on the Old Testament from Egypt and especially from Assyria
and Babylonia. In the article on ' Bela,' written by Cheyne, we
meet with the following with regard to the list of Edomitish kings
in Genesis xxxvi. In *v.* 32 we must read probably ' Bela b. Achbor '
instead of ' Bela b. Beor,' and certainly ' his city was Rehoboth,'
instead of ' his city was Dinhabab.' The city of Rehoboth lay in
the North Arabian land of Musri. Thence came Bela and Saul, and
also Mehetabel, the daughter of Matred, the daughter of Mezahab
(*v.* 39). For ' Matred ' is a corruption of ' Misran,' ' Mezahab ' of
' Misrim,' and ' Misrim ' is merely a variant of ' Misran '; both
represent the land of Musri. What unexpected gains for the under-

standing and correcting of the oldest Hebrew tradition spring thus from the discovery of this land in the cuneiform inscriptions! Not less fresh and important light as to the Ark is derived from the article ' Ark of the Covenant,' also written by Cheyne. It had never left, we learn, the land of the Philistines, up to David's day, but had only been transferred from a temple to a private house — and that, indeed, the house of Obed-edom in Gath; thence, however, David brought it up after a victory which he won over the Philistines. For it is certainly too incredible that David should have intrusted it in Jerusalem to the guardianship of a Philistine resident there. This is a convincing consideration, as Kosters also saw — with whom Cheyne agrees. Although I feel myself now, I confess, too old to follow such a lofty flight, it is nevertheless very pleasing to me to find here so full and faithful a portrayal of that latest phase of ' advanced criticism ' which has hitherto been in some respects wholly unknown to me."

What strikes Profs. Toy and Wellhausen as bizarre and unbalanced may surely be looked upon without offense by others as registering something other than the ascertained and securely established facts of modern Biblical learning.

Of course the book, despite the dominance of Dr. Cheyne's hand, is not all of a piece. His touch is visible constantly; but all his helpers are naturally not of precisely one mind. In particular he complains in the Preface that " the literary and historical criticism of the New Testament is by no means as far advanced as that of the Old Testament " — which may be well taken as an expression of regret that he was not able to obtain New Testament scholars who were willing to treat their text with the license with which he himself and his pupils dealt with that of the Old Testament. In some instances at least, however, his complaint is only partially justified by the event. The most copious writer on New Testament subjects in this volume is Prof. Paul W. Schmiedel, of Zürich, whose contributions — " Acts of the Apostles "; " Alphæus "; " Apollos "; " Barjesus "; " Barnabas "; " Christian " (name of); " Clopas "; " Community of Goods "; " Cornelius "; " Council of Jerusalem " — would make a small volume; and assuredly they are sufficiently arbitrary and ungrounded, one would think, to please the most exacting of " advanced critics." But within the limits of " advanced criticism " there are of course the necessary grades of opinions to be recognized which always accompany the work of a variety of writers. Only in such rare cases as the article on the Epistles to the Corinthians by Dr. William Sanday and the ecclesiastical articles by Dr. J. Armitage Robinson is anything like a cautious voice raised. The body of helpers Dr. Cheyne has gathered around him, though selected very broadly from a geographical point of view (the work plumes itself on its "international" character), in a word, form a rather narrow coterie of like-minded scholars.

Some fifty-three writers are represented in the volume before us. Of these some thirty-two are British, fifteen Continental, and six American. Prof. Lucien Gautier, of Lausanne, writes an excellent article on the "Dead Sea"; and we confess that his name seems as out of place among its companions as do those of Profs. Sanday and Robinson. Prof. Tiele, of Leiden, and the late Prof. Kosters, also of Leiden, have been called on to write on their specialties. But the foreign contingent is mostly German: Benzinger ("Atonement" [Day of], "Circumcision," "Golden Calf," etc.); Bousset ("Antichrist," "Apocalypse"); Budde ("Canon of Old Testament"); Guthe ("Dispersion"); Jülicher ("Colossians and Ephesians"); Kamphausen ("Book of Daniel"); Marti ("Chronology of the Old Testament," "Day," etc.); Eduard Meyer ("Adonis," etc.); Nöldeke ("Amalek," "Arabia," "Aram," "Aramaic," etc.); Schmiedel (as above); von Soden ("Aretas," "Chronology of the New Testament," etc.); Zimmern ("Creation," "Deluge"). The six American writers have not been called upon for much very important work. The most copiously represented is Prof. George F. Moore, of Andover, whose articles, besides the extended paper on "Deuteronomy," chiefly concern matters of the neighboring idolatry ("Abimelech"; "Adoni-Bezek"; "Adoni-Zedek"; "Asherah"; "Ashtoreth"; "Asylum"; "Baal"; "Bezek"; "Chemosh"; "Cherethites"; "Dagon"; "Deuteronomy"). Prof. Morris Jastrow, Jr., of the University of Pennsylvania, writes the important article "Canaan"; Prof. Nathanael Schmidt, of Cornell University, that on "Covenant"; Prof. Francis Brown, of Union Theological Seminary, New York, contributes two short notes, on "Carites" and "Dedan"; Prof. Robert W. Rogers, of Drew Theological Seminary, one on "Chiun and Siccuth"; and Prof. W. Max Müller, of the Reformed Episcopal Seminary, Philadelphia, four articles connected with his Egyptological studies — "Baal-zephon" (§ 2), "Brick," "Camel" (§ 3), and "Candace." The mass of this American material is not very considerable, but its quality is equal to that derived from any other quarter.

Of two classes of articles a special word may perhaps be fitly said. The first of these includes those in the domain of New Testament Geography. These, as a body, appear distinctly inferior to the corresponding articles in Old Testament Geography. This is not because they are not full of learning; they are packed with information, often of a sort difficult easily to lay hands upon elsewhere. But it is because they are badly adjusted to their purpose. The majority of them are from the pens of Prof. George Adam Smith, of Glasgow, whose interests lie in Old Testament study, and of Mr. W. J. Woodhouse, Lecturer in Classical Philology at Bangor, whose interests lie rather in the classical than the Biblical region. The result is as might have been anticipated: they tell us much, but not as the New Testament student would fain have it told him, and often not what the New Testament student most needs to know. The other class of articles we wish to speak particularly of includes those of Dr. J. Armitage Robinson on prevailingly ecclesiastical subjects — " Apostle "; " Baptism "; " Bishop "; " Canon "; " Church "; " Deacon." These have been very much spoken against in some quarters as deeply dyed in Anglicanism and producing the strange anomaly of the conjunction in one " Encyclopædia " of the utmost radicalness of criticism with ecclesiastical teaching which cannot stand the test of the slightest critical examination. This conjunction would not, indeed, be unwonted; from Richard Simon's day it has ever been normal in certain quarters — and, indeed, when men feel the authority of the Scriptures breaking to pieces beneath their feet under the action of their critical postulates, it is not strange that they should temporarily grasp at the straw of " the Church." But in the present instance the criticism is so exaggerated as to appear to us thoroughly unjustified. Dr. J. Armitage Robinson does not write entirely without bias — perhaps nobody does; and his bias is an Anglican one. But he writes not only with adequate scholarship, but with so balanced a judgment and such transparent candor, that his papers stand out in this " Encyclopædia " as a shining light in the midst of a dark place.

His article on " Canon," indeed, we consider thoroughly bad: it begins with an *a priori* construction of the origin and early history of the New Testament Canon which is at war with all the facts and has not even *a priori* probability to recommend it: and this, of course, the careful collation of certain of the historical facts that follow does little to redeem. Those on " Church " and " Baptism " would rouse little remark, one way or another: the stress in the former is laid upon the point of the unity of the Church, and little reference is made to the deeper conception which has gained for itself the name of the "invisible Church"; while in the latter the discussion of the formulas of baptism is hardly satisfactory, but the general drift of the article is sober and balanced. In the article "Apostle" there is apparent a lack of grasp upon the more fundamental question of the apostolic authority. But the two articles on the most controverted topics — "Bishop" and "Deacon" — are really very good indeed, excellent instances of well-wrought-out statements of the essential facts, not written throughout without some bias, to be sure, but with careful guarding against the influences of personal traditions, and on the whole marking a successful effort to attain and state the truth without fear or favor. On all the main matters involved these two articles are distinctly on the right side. It would indeed be difficult to find anywhere a more accurate statement of the New Testament evidence than that given in the "General Conclusions" of the former article (§ 7, col. 580); and on the chief points — that the bishop is a development from the presbyterate by differentiation of function and not from the apostolate by localization of service, that the government of the local Church was in the hands of a plurality of presbyters with the bishops at their head, and that the diaconate was not a ministry of the word but a local ministry of subordinate, chiefly eleemosynary service — these articles are thoroughly sound and thoroughly non-Anglican. Indeed, were we to search the "Enclyclopædia" through for examples of pure and unbiased scholarship, intent only on discovering and setting forth the facts, we are not sure that we should find anything with a better claim upon our recognition than these carefully studied articles.

It is not possible to go into further details in reviewing a book of this kind. Perhaps enough has been said to suggest its general character. In comparison with the new "Dictionary of the Bible," publishing simultaneously under the editorship of Dr. James Hastings, it is more compressed, and more radically destructive in its criticism. It omits, moreover, not only all that large mass of explanations of the language of the Authorized Version which is so striking a feature in Dr. Hastings' work, but also all the professed treatment of topics of Biblical Theology which is almost the most characteristic feature of Dr. Hastings' work. To us, we do not hesitate to say it, Dr. Hastings' work is far the more trustworthy and the more really scientific and the more valuable book. And we say this with our eyes fully open both to the immensity of learning packed away in the " Encyclopædia Biblica," which makes it an indispensable guide to those who wish to know the latest facts discovered in Biblical archæology and as well the latest guesses hazarded in the way of the reconstruction of the Biblical history; and also to the sad fact that Dr. Hastings' work is itself filled with the " results " of a Biblical criticism which differs from that which vitiates the whole substance of Dr. Cheyne's less in principle than in stage of development. It remains true, however, that Dr. Hastings' work is by far the more sober and by far the more trustworthy, as well as the more comprehensive of the two. But the two, remarkable products of our day of minute learning as they are, leave the way still open for a really satisfactory " Dictionary of the Bible " — a " Dictionary of the Bible " written from the standpoint of established faith in the trustworthiness of the Bible — its trustworthiness in its account of itself, in its account of the origin, nature, and development of the religion whose history it records, and in its account of the facts, doctrinal, ethical, and historical alike, which it recounts. Dr. Cheyne declares not without some superciliousness that his book is based on a criticism that " identifies the cause of religion with that of historical truth." Of course. So is everybody's. The point of difference turns on what we deem " historical truth ": and that is largely determined by the processes by which we suppose it can be attained. What we need is a " Dictionary of the Bible " which is sound in its views of historical truth and which does not wreck the cause of religion by insisting on adjusting it to a history which is at bottom, as Wellhausen puts it, " Weissagung aus den Eingeweiden." Who will give us, now, a " Dictionary of the Bible " which renounces speculation and sets out the *facts?*

JEAN CALVIN. Les hommes et les choses de son temps. Par E. DOU-
MERGUE. Tome Premier: La Jeunesse de Calvin. Lausanne:
Georges Bridel et Cie, Éditeurs. 1899.[1]

CALVIN has had to wait long for an adequate biography. But this
first volume of the work projected by M. Emile Doumergue, of
Montauban, gives us hope that he will have it ere the fourth century
since his birth runs wholly out.

We are not forgetful or unappreciative of those who have already
labored in this field. How many they are any good bibliography will
exhibit — say, for example, the select list given by Dr. Schaff at the
head of his treatment of " The Reformation in French Switzerland "
in the seventh volume of his " History of the Christian Church."
How good they are everyone who has sought to know this greatest
man — nay, as Renan was compelled to recognize, this greatest
Christian — God has given the modern Church, has had ample
opportunity to appreciate. There has been left us little excuse for
not knowing John Calvin. The description of the wealth of our
means of information with which M. Ant. J. Baumgartner opens
his admirable lectures on " Calvin Hébraïsant et Interprète de
l'Ancien Testament " is no more than just. A considerable number
of really good biographies of Calvin already exist — biographies
which seem to leave almost nothing to be desired — Henry's (1835–
1844), Bungener's (1862), E. Stähelin's (1863), Kampschulte's
(1869–1899), Lefranc's (1888). These have been supplemented by
the publication of his correspondence by Jules Bonnet (1854),
Herminjard, and the Strasburg Editors; by the great Strasburg
edition of his works with its illuminating prefaces; and by an incredible number of special essays and articles. " Thanks to his
biographies," remarks M. Baumgartner, " we have seen cleared
up many an obscure point, many a detail of his life as youth,
student, mature man; thanks to his commentaries we are better
prepared than ever to appreciate the astonishing, multifarious, almost superhuman activity of this supernaturally courageous man,
this *vere theologus,* this incomparable theologian, as Melancthon
fitly called him. . . . His latest biographies enable us to penetrate
deeply into his inner life; and make it possible for us to witness his

---

[1] *The Presbyterian and Reformed Review,* xi. 1900, pp. 713–718. For review
of vol. ii. cf. *The Princeton Theological Review,* ii. 1904, pp. 344 ff.; vol. iii.,
ibid., v. 1907, pp. 333 ff.; vol. iv., *ibid.,* x. 1912, pp. 501 ff.

early studies, to see in action the factors which produced his first works, and the unrolling of the diverse phases through which his spiritual or intellectual development passed." He concludes: " We should not be wrong, therefore, to be satisfied with what we know." Yet he at once adds a " nevertheless." And we must echo this " nevertheless."

It is possible, to be sure, to exaggerate this " nevertheless." Dr. A. Pierson certainly exaggerates it when, in the Preface to the first part of his " Studien over Johannes Kalvijn," he represents mere " studies " about him and not a complete biography of him as alone possible as yet; and speaks of the present duty of the historian as the renunciation of the legends set forth by Henry, Merle d'Aubigné, Stähelin, and not wholly eliminated from even the, in many ways, admirable work of Kampschulte; and the careful and patient eduction of the truth from the authentic records — or at least the demonstration that the riddles of this life are incapable of resolution. As if no one had trodden this hard pathway of detailed investigation before himself; and as if such painstaking investigation could result only in revolutionary conceptions of the course of this life! Before Pierson and after Pierson such studies have been vigorously prosecuted, and our knowledge of Calvin's life has been correspondingly enriched. The older biographies had already made use of the results of many of them. Much has, how-ever, been acquired since, and thus an adequate biography has re-mained a desideratum up to to-day and grown daily ever more a desideratum.

It is one of the reasons we have for hoping that M. Doumergue is about to give us this adequate biography that he has neglected none of the " studies over John Calvin " that have hitherto been made. Everything seems to be in his control. And controlling all that has been hitherto brought to light he has added investigations of his own: and better than that, he has brought to his task a clear intelligence and a trained literary habit; a detailed knowledge not only of the whole compass of the literature concerning Calvin — earlier and later — but of the times in which he lived and the currents of thought in which he was formed and amidst which he labored; and as well an acute as well as calm faculty of judgment. Above all he has brought apparently a keen and instinctive sym-pathy with the personality he is depicting. We do not know how fully this sympathy extends to the doctrinal and ethical teachings of Calvin — subsequent volumes of the work will determine this; but this first volume enables us to say that if M. Doumergue is able to write as sympathetic an account of Calvin's labors in Geneva and of his theological teaching as he has written of his youthful development and his preparation for his work, he will give us at length an adequate biography of Calvin. There will no doubt remain details which will require further investigation: there will no doubt be expressed historical judgments which will need correcting: the really definitive treatise on no subject will ever be written. But if the promise of this first volume is fulfilled in the remaining four we shall have a portrait of the greatest of the Reformers which will adequately present his grand figure before the eyes of every sympathetic reader.

It will doubtless have been already noted that the book has been planned on a scale which, so far as bulk in concerned, ought to be adequate. Here are nearly six hundred and fifty quarto pages devoted to " the youth of Calvin." For the depicting of his entire life five such great volumes are to be subsidized. It is a veritable monument which M. Doumergue is raising to the memory of the greatest of theologians. And everything has been done to make this monument, even in its externalities, worthy of the memory it is to enshrine. The publishers have spared no expense and no pains to turn out a perfect piece of work — the best of paper, the best of type, the best of presswork vie here with the best of editing to produce a volume that it is a pleasure to the eye to look upon and to the hand to handle. Archæological knowledge and artistic skill have combined to illustrate it richly and illuminatingly. The illustrations alone almost suffice to carry us back into the sixteenth century and to place us among the scenes, in the midst of the companions, in the presence of the literary products, in contact with which Calvin's youth was passed. Already in this we see revealed one side of M. Doumergue's furnishing for the task he has undertaken. M. Doumergue is evidently an enthusiastic archæologist. No archæological detail escapes his keen sight or fails to set him throbbing with enthusiasm. Perhaps his antiquarian zeal is even a little excessive. Perhaps when he reaches, for example, his chapter on " Protestant Paris in the Sixteenth Century," his ardor runs a little away with him and he almost forgets his Calvin for a season in his engrossment with the old streets and old houses and their multifarious associations. All this, to be sure, is in accordance with his theory of how a biography should be written: he would fain present to us not a dead abstraction called " Calvin " but a concrete living man in the midst of the rich life in which he was immersed. And certainly his archæological enthusiasm has borne good fruit in adorning the volume and throwing a local atmosphere around the portrait that is painted. The life of the sixteenth century stares us in the face here on every page, and even he who runs cannot fail to read it off from the beautiful cuts which are lavished everywhere. And let no one imagine that because M. Doumergue is an archæologist he is therefore dull. He appears incapable of writing a tiresome line, whatever may be his subject. Indeed, if the book errs in the matter of its style, it errs in precisely the opposite direction. It is the temperament of the dramatist, of the orator, of the journalist, rather than that of the antiquary which is revealed to us in these sparkling, lively, ever moving pages, full of literary art and Gallic vivacity. The touch is light with French gayety, the disposition of the material lucid with French clarity, the story is told with the verve and liveliness of which only a French pen is capable. There is not a dull line from the beginning of the volume to the end of it, and he is a poor reader who, having begun it, will not be content to stay until he reads through to the last page.

This volume treats, as we have said, of the youth of John Calvin; and it treats of it in the full light of all that has been brought to knowledge upon this obscurest period of his life. Of course the investigations of Lefranc and the studies of Lecoultre and of Herminjard are largely used: but the whole mass of recent discussion also has been thoroughly winnowed and a keen intelligence is brought to bear upon its criticism and utilization. The period covered by the volume extends from the birth of the Reformer in 1509 to the publication of the first edition of the " Institutes " in 1536. Along with his personal development, of which we get a picture even more vivid and even more winning than that offered by Lefranc himself, we have all the currents of thought of his time and all the influences that played upon him — Humanism, Faber Stapulensis and the religious movement of which his teaching was the source, and all the reformatory impulses that were aroused in the France of the day — fully depicted for us. We are shown the Noyon of his boyhood, the Paris of his youth, the Orleans and Bourges of his opening manhood, the France of his years of persecution, the Bâle of his refuge, and all the streams of intellectual and religious life that

were flowing through them: and then we are shown the young
Calvin moving through them all and thrown out into relief against
them all, until we almost feel as if we had lived his life with him
and might well claim him as our boyhood's friend.

And let us note the phrase which we have thus unpremedi-
tatedly used to describe the impression the picture of the youthful
Calvin, as limned by M. Doumergue, makes on us. We feel as we
read this flowing but precise narrative which so vividly brings his
figure before us, we say, as if we might well claim him as our own
boyhood's *friend*. For it is distinctly a friendly, attractive, lovable
youth who is here presented to us, one whom we look upon distinctively as a friend — whom to look upon is to love. We have been
taught to think of another kind of Calvin — even in his youth:
somber, sour, forbidding, inaccessible, almost a hater of the human
race (as other Christians before him have been slanderously designated). We have been told that the iteration and severity of the
denunciation he visited upon his young companions earned everywhere their disgust, and won for him at their hands the unenviable
nickname of " The accusative case." It is only a part of the Romish
legend — fully exploded by Lefranc and now again by Doumergue.
A serious-minded youth he was, of course, and one filled with a
gracious piety and schooled in a strict morality: he was certainly
no Rabelais rioting among his companions — but as certainly he
was neither an anchorite nor an accuser of his associates. Born to
a competency, reared in the company of the great and the cultured, living on terms of frank and free intercourse with the
choicest spirits of his time, the young Calvin reveals himself to
us as an open-minded, affectionate young man of irreproachable
morals, decent habits, and frank manners — somewhat sensitive
perhaps but easy to be entreated, and attracting not merely the
admiration but also the lasting affection of all into contact with
whom he came. He finds his Biblical prototype not in Elijah or in
John the Baptist but distinctly in that other John who was at
once a " son of thunder " and the " apostle of love." This is how
M. Doumergue sums up the chief results attained by his minute
study of Calvin's life among his fellows during these years of
preparation:

" Thus he journeys from place to place, from north to south and
from south to north, through France and through the churches, seeing, hearing, observing, noting, enriching his heart and his conscience

not less than his understanding with all that he encounters among men as well as in libraries; a prodigy of work, of rigorous self-denial (*ascétisme*), and yet full of youthfulness, highly esteemed, always welcomed. All circles dispute for him, and on all he exercises that mysterious influence, that irresistible power of seduction and attraction which is one of the most characteristic signs of the sovereignty of genius. All who know him love him; and those who love him cannot resist the wish, or let us say the necessity, of seeing him again. They leave, one after another — Noyon: his brother, his sister, his successor in the chaplaincy of the *Gésine*, his successor in the curacy of Pont l'Evêque, and the King's lieutenant, Laurent of Normandy; — Paris: his master Mathurin Cordier, his fellow pupils of the house of Montmor, his friends the Cops, his friends the Budés; — Orleans: the sons of his friend Daniël; — Bourges: the Colladons; — Angoulême: his host himself who cannot be separated from him; — Poitiers: Véron, the *procureur* Babinot, the lecturer in the Institute, Saint-Vertumien: a strange enough procession, but one which attests the fascination exercised upon hearts by one whom men have dared to reproach with not being able to feel or inspire affection " (p. 515)!

In a word the legend of Calvin's hard and unlovable disposition, on any real acquaintance with his life, goes up in the same smoke with those other legends — the product with it of the malignant imagination of hate — which have pictured him as of low extraction and of criminal habits — branded for nameless vice at Noyon, convicted of theft at Orleans, and a victim of all sorts of evil passions.

One of the chief preoccupations of M. Doumergue in studying the early years of Calvin is naturally the preparation it formed for his subsequent labors. The hand of Providence is indeed so clearly revealed in the training of the future Reformer that it has ever been the subject of admiring remark: Dr. M'Crie, for example, has written a very striking page or two on it in his posthumous work on the " Early Years of John Calvin " (pp. 2, 22, 77, 78). The more careful study of his early years only increases the impression of the singular preparation which they formed for his subsequent career: and M. Doumergue does not permit this side of his task to escape him. The words we have just quoted from him, indeed, are a portion of an eloquent passage in which he sums up the elements of this preparation. It was certainly long, he remarks, but assuredly also most marvelous.

" Driven from Noyon by the plague while still little more than a child, he falls in with the best teacher of Latin of the age, Mathurin

Cordier, who waits before leaving Paris to teach him. Then at Orleans he falls in with the best master of Greek of the age, Melchior Wolmar, who seems to have come from Germany, whither he is about to return, in order to inculcate his method upon him: two incomparable masters who prove incomparable instructors. Not content with teaching him the languages they speak to him also of the Gospel of Christ.

" It was for him, it seems, that the Middle Ages had preserved its somber college of Montaigu, so that before it disappeared it might initiate him into all the secrets of an irresistible dialectic. For him too it was that modern times had hastened to establish the College of France, that he might attend its first lectures and later rank among the masters of Humanism.

" And on the benches of these schools, while his cousin, Robert Olivétan, is pressing him to read the Bible, he almost had opportunity to elbow Loyola, who pronounced the vow of Montmartre, and Rabelais, who wrote *Gargantua:* the Jesuitical spirit and the Gallic spirit, the two inspirations of the anti-Calvinistic opposition.

" And even this is not enough: here is our young man encountering the most illustrious professors of law, — l'Estoile, who is still at Orleans, and Alciat, who is just arrived at Bourges. They mold his mind to that kind of precise, exact, realistic thinking which permits him to be not merely the theologian but the legislator of the Reformation.

" Nevertheless Providence had not yet accomplished more than half its task. What is intellect without life? And these wonderful years of study are at the same time wonderful years of experience. The Church takes care to reveal to him all its failings, all its most secret vices. It gives him personal experience of its weaknesses and its hardnesses. It endows him abusively with its benefices; it casts him unjustly into prison; it obliges him to rescue the dead body of his father from its anathemas. While yet a babe he commences to visit the bizarre relics of Ourscamp; later he looks upon the episcopal disorders at Angoulême; he listens to the legends of Poitiers; and just as he is leaving France, the Franciscans are still playing before his eyes the farce of Orleans, that he may sound the lowest depths of a superstition which ends in vulgar trickery.

" But by the side of the shadow destined to repel him shines the light destined to attract him. If Calvin was the pupil of Béda, chief of the Sorbonnic band, he is also the *protégé* of the friends of Le Fèvre d'Etaple, the Cops and the Budés, and he passes through all the stages of the Fabrician movement. He allies himself intimately with Gérard Roussel, and the venerable Le Fèvre prolongs his life to more than a century that he may be able to give him his blessing at Nérac. Similarly before enduring his martyrdom, Estienne de la Forge receives him into his house and permits him to learn the piety and heroism of the nascent Church, while Quintin, chief of Libertines, and Servetus, chief of Antitrinitarians, present themselves in Paris to horrify the young doctor with their dangerous heresies."

Then follows the description of the enchanting personality which the young man bore through all these experiences, which we have already quoted. This was the youthful David — intellectually and morally fair of eyes and goodly to look upon — whom God had chosen to overthrow those new Goliaths, the King, the Pope, the Emperor, and to conduct Protestant Christianity to its destined victory: and this was the way God chose to prepare him for his great work.

We have quoted M. Doumergue as saying that the young Calvin "passed through all the phases of the Fabrician movement," and the remark bids us pause to call brief attention to the most interesting controverted question which is treated in the whole volume. This concerns of course the conversion of Calvin. It has become customary to date the conversion of Calvin in 1532 or later. M. Doumergue enters the lists with great spirit for an earlier date, and would carry it back, say, to 1528. We cannot go here into the reasons pro and con. It may well be that too much stress is laid by M. Doumergue on the necessity of a development of Calvin's religious life through stages, if not slow, at least not unprepared: Calvin himself speaks of his conversion as "sudden." It may well be that a little of that Gallic spirit which is such an ornament to Frenchmen attaches itself to his argumentation and that he is a shade overzealous for the purely French origination of French Protestantism. But certainly he marshals the facts and inferences with amazing skill, and the result of his construction is to leave an impression on the mind of the reader which is very strong that Calvin was no stranger to the new doctrines through his years of study at Orleans and Bourges, and that if we are still to speak of a "conversion" as late as 1532 it must be in the purely spiritual sense. Long before this he assuredly had known and yielded intellectual assent to the central elements of the new teaching.

We know it is a very inadequate introduction to our readers that we are giving M. Doumergue's notable book. Our consolation is that we shall have subsequent occasion, on the appearance of the remaining volumes, to call attention to it anew. The first volume exhibits it as a piece of solid historical work, fortified by ample citations of the sources, and presented in a charmingly direct and readable narrative style. No one can pretend hereafter to know John Calvin who does not take account of M. Doumergue's full, rich, and thoughtful study of his life and work. We look forward with the greatest eagerness to the appearance of the subsequent volumes, and we can wish nothing better for them than that they may prove as thorough and illuminating for their own periods as this first one is for the years of Calvin's youth.

OUR BIBLE AND THE ANCIENT MANUSCRIPTS. By FREDERIC G. KEN- YON, M.A., D.Litt., Hon. Ph.D. With Twenty-six Facsimiles. Second Edition. Eyre and Spottiswoode, etc. 1896. Third Edition, revised and enlarged, with Twenty-nine Facsimiles and an Ap- pendix on Recent Biblical Discoveries. 1898.

THE PALAEOGRAPHY OF GREEK PAPYRI. By FREDERIC G. KENYON, M.A., Hon. Ph.D. (Halle), Hon. D. Litt. (Durham). With Twenty Facsimiles and a Table of Alphabets. Oxford: At the Clarendon Press. 1899.

HANDBOOK TO THE TEXTUAL CRITICISM OF THE NEW TESTAMENT. By FREDERIC G. KENYON, Assistant Keeper of Manuscripts, British Museum. With Sixteen Facsimiles. London: Macmillan and Co., Limited; New York: The Macmillan Company. 1901.[1]

THE publication of Dr. Kenyon's " Handbook to the Textual Criticism of the New Testament " furnishes a fit occasion for bringing together for cursory remark the chief contributions he has hitherto made to the better or wider understanding of the history and state of the text of the New Testament. We have accordingly associated with this latest of his works on the subject two earlier publications, one more popular, one more scientific in its scope, to both of which the present volume bears a somewhat close relation. We have observed the attribution to him of yet another volume which would naturally fall into the same series — a collection of " Facsimiles of Biblical Manuscripts in the British Museum " (1900): but this happens not to have fallen in our way. There is also, of course, the somewhat long list of his editions of Greek texts from the British Museum papyri, which more remotely bear upon his work on the problems of the New Testament text. These began, it will be remembered, with almost the unexpectedness of an ex- plosion, in the simultaneous publication in 1891 of the text and translation of Aristotle's " Constitution of the Athenians " and

[1] The Presbyterian and Reformed Review, xiii. 1902, pp. 463–473.

the volume of " Classical Texts from Papyri in the British Museum," containing fragments of Demosthenes, Herodas, Homer, Hyperides, Isocates, etc. Certainly here was an achievement for a young man under thirty, whose scientific expression hitherto had been practically confined to the preparation of the earlier parts of the " Catalogue of Additions to the Department of Manuscripts in the British Museum " (1888–1893). A separate facsimile edition of Herodas and an edition of the " Orations of Hyperides against Athenogenes and Philippides " (1892) quickly followed. Later there was added an edition of the Odes of Bacchylides (1897), while other papyri fragments have been from time to time given to the world through the periodical press (*Class. Rev.*, vi. 436; *Rev. de Phil.*, xvi. 181, xxi. 1; *Journal of Philology*, xxi. 296; *Mélanges Weil*, 1898, p. 243), and still others in those beautiful volumes, " Greek Papyri in the British Museum, Catalogue with Texts " — the first of which with one hundred fifty plates appeared in 1893, and the second with one hundred twenty-three plates in 1898. In the comprehensive Introduction to this last-named work, we find much which has been drawn upon — with appropriate amplifications and modifications, of course — in the books which we have placed at the head of this article, and to this extent this " Catalogue " might readily be looked upon as part of Dr. Kenyon's direct preparation for writing his latest book, with which we are now more immediately concerned. But it is not unfair to treat the whole series as bearing witness rather to Dr. Kenyon's general palæographical learning, and thus as only indirectly facilitating the preparation of his treatise on New Testament Textual Criticism. With the two earlier books, which we have placed at the head of this article, the case is different: in different ways and degrees, it is true, but equally really, both stand immediately at the root of the " Textual Criticism " and contribute directly to its pages. It might almost be said, in fact, that this treatise is but an amplified, enriched, and scientifically heightened recension of the portion of " Our Bible and the Ancient Manuscripts " dealing with the New Testament text, which, among other additions, has incorporated also the cream of " The Palaeography of Greek Papyri," so far as it is applicable to the New Testament.

It is not our purpose, however, to revert to these volumes more than is necessary to call attention to them and place them in their right relation to the volume more particularly in hand. The earlier of them is a remarkably successful attempt to put into the hands of educated Bible readers a readable and accurate account of how the Bible has come down to us. It opens with three general chapters on Variations in the Bible Text, The Authorities for the Bible Text, and The Original Manuscripts of the Bible. The Hebrew Text and the Versions of the Old Testament are then treated in two chapters; and these are succeeded by three in which the Text, Manuscripts, and Versions of the New Testament are dealt with. A single chapter is given to the Vulgate in the Middle Ages: and then the book closes with two chapters tracing the fortunes of the English Bible, in its Manuscript and Printed Forms. No pretension is made to originality: the book is frankly based on the work of others, which it only proposes to popularize. It's note is sobriety and judiciousness. Only in a single matter has it gone astray by accepting bad guidance. This is a very serious matter in itself, though here of less importance because forming no essential part of the book: it concerns the account given of the origin and history of the Canon, both Old Testament and New (cf. pp. 27, 95). One wonders, again, that Dr. Kenyon, of all men, with his first-hand knowledge of papyrus documents, should not have known in 1898 how the papyrus-paper was manufactured (p. 19: the matter is set right in the later books — " Papyri," p. 15; " Handbook," p. 19). But (with the exception of the matter of the Canon) they are only minute flaws that can be picked in this good book. It easily takes rank with the best popular expositions we have.

The treatise on " The Palaeography of Greek Papyri " stands at the opposite pole from " Our Bible and the Ancient Manuscripts " in point of originality. This is original or nothing: it pretends to be only an essay, but it undertakes to break entirely new ground. Though strictly scientific in contents, it is so clearly written and marshals its material with such skill that its interest is by no means dependent solely on its novelty. The brief opening chapter, entitled " The Range of the Subject," contains a welcome *précis* of the history of the recovery of papyrus documents, chiefly from the sands of Egypt. The second chapter summarizes what is known of papyrus as a writing material, and provides what we may call the archæology of the subject. The palæography of the non-literary papyri is briefly surveyed in the third chapter; this branch of the general subject being passed over succinctly because it is not new. The proper subject of the book is reached in the fourth and fifth chapters, in which the palæography of the literary papyri is for the first time worked out systematically. Finally the transition to vellum is described in a sixth chapter, and some useful tables and lists are added in an Appendix. The quality of sobriety and judiciousness which characterized the more popular volume are equally in evidence in this, and gives an air of fine restraint to the whole which vastly adds to the comfortable confidence of the reader: he is easily persuaded that he is in the hands of a competent and safe guide and passes on from page to page in a docile spirit. For a book breaking new ground this is a noticeably modest and eminently satisfying one.

On turning to the " Handbook to the Textual Criticism of the New Testament," one notes at once the same qualities of style, tone, manner which characterized its predecessors. It is an eminently well-written book: it is a markedly calm and sober book: it is a thoroughly well-informed book. The same tone of moderation and good judgment which met the reader in the former volumes delights him here also. It is a positive pleasure to read these quiet, judicious pages, so free from all special pleading, and so aloof from all whimsical extravagances. One feels assured from the outset that he is getting a fair summary of the present attainment of the art in which he is being instructed. Perhaps he will miss a little the individual note; will feel the lack of the stimulus that attends enthusiastic advocacy; and will scarcely avoid receiving an impression that he is getting an essentially outside view of the subject — something like the summing up of a judge in a case in which he has had no personal part to play. His consolation will be that he feels himself in the hands of a fair-minded and well-informed judge whose guidance he can trust.

The eminent sobriety of the book is at once brought to the attention of the reader in the opening chapter, where the function of criticism is expounded. He will note for example with satisfaction the circumspect position taken up with reference to the practice of conjectural emendation (pp. 2, 6, 14–15). It is " a process precarious in the extreme, and seldom allowing any one but the guesser to feel confident in the truth of its results." " Where documentary evidence is plentiful, conjecture will be scarce; but where the former is wanting, the latter will have to try to take its place to the best of its ability. In the case of the New Testament the documentary evidence is so full that conjecture is almost excluded."

" Where the evidence is so plentiful and varied as it is for the New Testament, the chances that the true reading should have been lost by all are plainly very much smaller. . . . It is universally agreed . . . that the sphere of conjecture in the case of the New Testament is infinitesimal; and it may further be added that for practical purposes it may be treated as non-existent. No authority could be attached to words which rested only upon conjecture." This is eminently prudent. But the reader may be pardoned for wondering whether it goes to the bottom of the matter. He will certainly desiderate some account of the nature of the conjectural process and the natural limitations of its use. This he does not get.

For it will not suffice him to be told that exceptionally plentiful or early attestation will exclude it. If he is a receiver of letters, he knows from his own experience that autographs themselves constantly contain errors which conjecture both can and must remove. If he is a reader of popular literature, he knows from repeated observation that such errors may persist through a million copies issued in scores of editions. He has himself corrected hundreds of them. He opens, we will say, the fifth volume of the English Translation of Harnack's " History of Dogma," at chapter vi. (p. 274), and he reads in the title of the chapter of " The Cralovingian Renaissance." Will he hesitate to correct this at once to " Carlovingian "? A few lines lower down he reads of " the Neoplatonic type of thouoht ": and with as little hesitation corrects the errant second " o " into a " g." He turns the page and on p. 277 the word " activitv " meets his eye and is at once made " activity ": and when a little lower down he reads " the king-emperor of the Franks and Romans was the successor of Augustine and Constantine," he as promptly corrects the " Augustine " into " Augustus." Nor does he hesitate on p. 285 when he reads that " Christ was as man sacrificed for sakes " to insert " men's " before " sakes," nor a little lower down to change the order of the words " the then Incarnation " to " then the Incarnation." Neither does he do all this with fear and trembling, but with confidence and assurance.

Nor will he be satisfied by being told that the sacred text is too holy to be thus corrected by conjecture. If it is obviously wrong he will be apt to think it too holy not to be corrected, whether by conjecture or what not, so only it be corrected. He takes up, for example, the Brevier 16mo edition of the Revised New Testament, issued at the Cambridge University Press in 1881, and at I Cor. iii. 5, he reads:

" What then is Apollos? and what is Paul? Ministers through whom ye Lord believed; and each as the gave to him." Because this is a sacred text, will he decline to transfer the word " Lord " to its proper place before the word " gave "? Or he takes up the " Editio critica minor ex viii. maiore desumpta " of Tischendorf, published in 1877, and on p. 945 he runs into mere nonsense, due to the misplacement of a whole line from the first to the seventh place on the page. Sacred as the text is, he is not likely to wait to consult the MSS. before he readjusts the lines and goes on his way in entire confidence both in his readjustment and in the authority of the text as readjusted. Or if he takes up the Barker and Bill Bible of 1631 and reads at Exod. xx. 14, " Thou shalt commit adultery," will he decline to insert at once the " not " so obviously required, or to act on the thus amended text, because forsooth " no authority can be attached to words which rest only upon conjecture "? Would he have to wait until he consulted other copies (which are happily extant and accessible in these cases) before he gave full confidence to such conjectures and assigned full authority to them? We must not confuse the authority due to the Biblical text with the method of procedure by which the Biblical text is ascertained. When once ascertained, it has the authority that belongs to it as the Biblical text: and the only valid question is, Whether it is really ascertained. This question clearly has nothing to do with the nature of the text ascertained, but purely with the nature of the processes by which it is ascertained. Processes that are valid for the ascertainment of a secular are equally valid for the ascertainment of a sacred text, and it has no bearing on their validity that the texts when thus validly ascertained have the imperative of law in them, or the authority of God's holy word.

Enough has doubtless been said, however, to make it manifest that appeals to the sacredness of the New Testament text, to the multitude of its depositories, to the antiquity of its attestation, do not really touch the question of the applicability of conjectural criticism to it. There are limits to the successful use of conjectural emendation: but Dr. Kenyon's comfortable remarks do not even hint to us what they are or where they are to be found. Roughly speaking, they may be suggested by the broad remark that a bad text may be successfully emended by conjecture; a good text, not. That is to say, in proportion as a text is really bad — in proportion as gross errors are sown thickly through it — in that proportion does conjectural emendation find its opportunity; just as anyone, looking over a "dirty proof-sheet," will find numerous opportunities to correct it without consulting the " copy " — errors of spelling, errors of grammar, errors of transposition, omission, insertion, and the like. On the other hand, in proportion as a text is good, in that proportion does the sphere of the safe application of conjectural emendation shrink. This is because in a good text all the grosser errors have been eliminated, and such errors as remain belong to a different order: it is no longer a question of mere blunders of careless reproduction but a subtle question of style or meaning — and here tastes differ and the fear lies near at hand that we are not correcting the scribe but the author himself, and hence not restoring but corrupting his text. The reason why the New Testament text is inaccessible to conjectural emendation is then, not because we have so many witnesses to it, nor because we have such early witness to it, nor yet because it is so sacred — though each of these facts doubtless enters, in its own way, into the production of the correctness which has secured the result — but shortly because it has been so excellently transmitted to us. The New Testament text, as it comes into our hands, is so good a text that there has been eliminated from it the *fomes conjecturæ*.

Even here, however, we need to make distinctions. The New Testament text as it lies in any given single manuscript is certainly not removed from correction by conjecture; it rather gives occasion for even the easiest and most obvious conjectures. No manuscript in existence is free from a set of *incuria* which any and every reader of it will correct as he reads — just as he will correct the *incuria* of any printed book, as we illustrated above from a few pages of Harnack's " History of Dogma." If we needed to print the New Testament from a single codex — as many of the classical authors have been from time to time printed — we should need cursorily to correct it, as we cursorily correct them, by conjecture pure and simple, without raising any question about the propriety of the process. When we speak of the inapplicability or the practical inapplicability of conjectural emendation to the New Testament text, we are having in mind not that text as it lies actually in this or that single document, but an already emended text derived from a comparison of witnesses and already editorially revised. And the reason why this already castigated text is inaccessible to conjectural emendation is simply because it is so good a text that the opportunity for conjectural emendation has been removed. Still another distinction, however, must be made at this point. If the New Testament text is removed by its excellence from the chance of emendation by conjecture, it is still not removed from the application of conjectural criticism. No text can be too good to be criticized: the only proof we can have of its excellence is through criticism. The autograph itself, if we had it, and whatever approach to the autographic text we may have attained by our most careful and wise use of the documentary evidence, must be subject to the further critical scrutiny of our best powers to betray its shortcomings or certify its correctness. The last resort in any process of criticism, bestowed on any text whatever, is just conjectural criticism. That is to say, the final step in settling any text is the careful scrutiny of the text as provisionally determined, with a view to learning whether it commends itself to the critical judgment as the very text of its author. This is essentially the application of the conjectural process to the entire text: and it is just as essentially this if no errors are detected by the process or no remedies for detected errors suggested, as it would be if it were found still full of difficulties and impossibilities, cures for which we proceed to suggest. So far is it then from true to say that conjectural criticism has no place in the text of the New Testament, and that we must have some surer foundation for the authoritative Word of Life than conjecture can supply, that it would be truer to say that the final establishment of every word of the New Testament is due to the application of this mode of criticism, and that it is on its authority that our ultimate confidence is built that what we have in our hands is the veritable Word of Life that God has given us through His servants the apostles. It may sound paradoxical: it is in truth a paradox of just the same order as the fundamental philosophical truth that all knowledge is built on faith: and it is just as true as that undeniable proposition. No more can the documentary critic boast himself as over against the " conjectural critic," than can the sensationalist boast himself over the " believer."

We have permitted ourselves to run beyond all reason in these remarks on conjectural criticism because we have fancied they might so illustrate the matter as to permit us to say more intelligibly what we wish to say in the way of criticism of Dr. Kenyon's book. We have already remarked that he seems to approach the subject of the textual criticism of the New Testament a little too much from the outside — as if he had not after all entered sympathetically into its processes. We wish to add that accordingly far too preponderant a place is in this volume given to the *externalia* of the art with which it deals. Dr. Kenyon tells us all about the Manuscripts, and the Versions, and the Patristic quotations; he tells us all about the history of the art in the past; he outlines the present state of the textual problem as it is discussed in the schools: and all with admirable skill. Nobody could do it better. But as to the art of textual criticism itself — the reader will rise from the book but little wiser than he opened it. He has not read a page without pleasure; he has not read a page without profit; he has not read a page without admiration. For all that Dr. Kenyon has set out to tell us, we could not have had a better guide. But Dr. Kenyon has not elected to tell us how we must proceed in undertaking the great and, to each of us, indeed necessary task of actually criticizing the text of the New Testament. He informs us (pp. 15, 16) that " the function of the textual critic is, first, to collect documentary evidence, and, secondly, to examine it and estimate its value." There is not a word about applying it to the actual formation of the text! Accordingly, he goes on to say: " The object of the present volume is to show what has been done in both these directions." It is no part of its object, then, to teach us how to exercise the art of textual criticism. Its point of view is purely historical and at most it provides us with an estimate of a condition attained. " In chapters ii.–vi.," he proceeds, " an account will be given of the available textual material — the copies of the New Testament in the original Greek, the ancient translations of it into other languages, and the quotations from it which are found in the early writers of the Christian Church. The materials having been thus passed in review, an attempt will be made in chapters vii. and viii. to summarise what has hitherto been done in the way of using these materials, to discuss the principal theories now current with regard to the early history of the New Testament text, and to estimate the general position of the textual problem at the present day." This is an exact record of the contents of the volume. All this is done and done admirably. But when all this is done there yet remains the whole subject of the textual criticism of the New Testament. In a word, Dr. Kenyon's volume is devoted to the *externalia* of the subject and treats these *externalia* exceedingly well. He does not profess to do more. He does not do more.

It will be observed that our criticism of the volume turns rather on what it does not contain than on what it does contain. The volume is indeed somewhat remarkable for its omissions. There are minor surprises in this regard as well as the great surprise we have tried to suggest. We read over the Table of Contents: I. The Function of Textual Criticism; II. The Autographs of the New Testament; III. The Uncial Manuscripts; IV. The Minuscule Manuscripts; V. The Ancient Versions; VI. Patristic Quotations; VII. Textual Criticism in the Past; VIII. The Textual Problem. Where shall we find what we may call the archæology of the subject discussed? Where shall we look for some sufficing account of various readings, their ordinary character, their several modes of origination? Where shall we discover the proper modes of dealing with these variations outlined: the different kinds of evidence, internal, whether intrinsic or transcriptional, and external, in its various modes of application? What has become of the Lectionaries? But we pause in the long list of inevitable questions. Compare the Table of Contents of a contemporaneously appearing primer on " The Text of the New Testament " — almost in its contents as defective as this — we mean the Rev. K. Lake's contribution to the " Oxford Church Text Books " (London, 1901) — and we shall see at least how odd it is that some of these topics are not formally recognized as substantial constituents of a " Handbook to the Textual Criticism of the New Testament." Mr. Lake's table runs: The Object and Method of Textual Criticism; The Apparatus Criticus of the New Testament — the Greek MSS., the Versions, Patristic Quotations, Liturgical Evidence; Chapter Divisions and Stichometry; History of Modern Criticism; The Western Text.

No doubt some of the topics left unrecognized in Dr. Kenyon's Table of Contents are nevertheless to be found tucked away in some corner or other of the book. The Index helps us to discover an incidental mention of the Lectionaries among the pages devoted to the Minuscule MSS. (pp. 109, 122). Some classes of variations and some canons of criticism are cursorily mentioned and even criticized in the opening chapter on " The Function of Textual Criticism." Some archæological and palæographical details are given in connection with the descriptions of the MSS. And perhaps some suggestions as to the method of procedure in criticism may be picked up in the course of the historical remarks that occupy the concluding chapters. But this only advises us that there is not only an insufficiency in the treatment of these things, but also a confusion of formal arrangement of the material. This formal confusion emerges even in the captions of the chapters. What are we to make of the caption of the second chapter, for instance: " The Autographs of the New Testament "? Of course this chapter does not treat of " the autographs of the New Testament." It is, on the contrary, a very illuminating description of the first period of " The Manuscript History of the New Testament " — the period during which it was propagated on papyrus, a period of which Dr. Kenyon has a special right to speak with authority and on which he writes most interestingly and instructively. It is with something like irritation that we see hidden under such a misleading title this admirable chapter, in some respects the most welcome in the volume, outlining as it does the history of the New Testament for nearly four centuries and adding a new chapter to that history from first-hand knowledge.

Next after this chapter on the Papyrus period, the two closing chapters of the book are likely to commend themselves to the reader. The intermediate chapters leave little to be desired in the presentation of their own subjects: but they are necessarily more of the nature of compilations and have less of the attraction of novelty. The penultimate chapter surveys the history of textual criticism in the past; the last one, under the title of " The Textual Problem," really summarizes recent discussion regarding the families of text precised by Dr. Hort. Both turn as on a pivot upon Dr. Hort's textual theory, and provide a most useful account of the debates that have raged of late around it, — especially with reference to the origin and value of the so-called " Western " text — giving a singularly judicial summing up of the results so far. Dr. Kenyon finds Dr. Hort's working out of the history of the text essentially unaffected by more recent investigation. His own view he represents as " substantially the same as that of Hort, though with some modifications." He outlines it as follows: " The early history of the New Testament text presents itself to us as an irregular diffusion of the various books among the individuals and communities which embraced Christianity, with few safeguards against alteration, whether deliberate or unintentional. To that stage, which follows very soon on the production of the original autographs, belong the various readings, early in their attestation yet comparatively rarely convincing in themselves, which we call the δ-text, and which Hort terms ' Western,' and Blass (in the case of the two books of St. Luke) ' Roman.' In Egypt alone (or principally) a higher standard of textual fidelity prevailed, and in the literary atmosphere of Alexandria and the other great towns a comparatively pure text was preserved. This has come down to us (possibly by way of Origen and his pupils) in the Codex Vaticanus and its allies, and is what we have called the β-text, and what Hort calls ' Neutral.' Another text, also found in Egyptian authorities, and differing from the last only in minor details, is that which we call the γ-text, and Hort ' Alexandrian.' Finally there is the text which, originating in the neighbourhood of Antioch about the end of the third century, drew together many of the various readings then in existence, and with many minor editorial modifications developed into a form which was generally adopted as satisfactory throughout the Eastern Church. This is the a-text of our nomenclature, Hort's ' Syrian '; the text which monopolised our printed editions until the nineteenth century, but which is now abandoned by all but a few scholars " (pp. 309–310). Dr. Kenyon rightly represents this as substantially Dr. Hort's construction of the history.

The modification of Dr. Hort's position which he thinks recent research points to consists in a slight abatement of the hegemony which Dr. Hort ascribed to the " Neutral " text, and a consequent admission of the probability that " among much that is supposititious there is also something that is original " preserved in the " Western " text. Put in this general way there is nothing in this proposition which Dr. Hort could ever have thought of denying: as Dr. Kenyon at once points out, instancing the case of the readings which Dr. Hort awkwardly called " Western non-interpolations." Apparently what Dr. Kenyon means to suggest is simply that more " Western " readings may ultimately have to be accepted as over against " Neutral " readings than Dr. Hort supposed. Certainly this may well be true; it may easily be true under Dr. Hort's reading of the history of the text. But it is worth while to keep in mind that it was not alone on " genealogical " principles that Dr. Hort's preference for the " Neutral " text was based. It was equally on the verdict of " internal evidence of classes " and " internal evidence of groups." And here we must call attention to the neglect of these powerful instruments of criticism of which both Dr. Kenyon and Mr. Lake are guilty in their exposition of Dr. Hort's theory of criticism. They seem to have focused their attention so exclusively on Dr. Hort's genealogical distribution of the texts that they have permitted to slip out of view his exposition of the critical processes which he calls by these names. No doubt there are faint echoes of them left even in

Dr. Kenyon's exposition: but they are so faint that they give no
proper account of themselves and pass practically off the stage
altogether. The consequence is that Dr. Hort's theory appears as
practically only a theory of the history of the text, and even his
genealogical method falls back into practically little more as an engine of criticism than Dr. Tregelles' " comparative criticism." It is
much more than this; and supplies, by its attention to the force of
attestation consisting of cross-witnesses, an organon of a value not
known before his day. When further reinforced by the results of his
" internal evidence of groups " and " internal evidence of classes "
it has a value and decisiveness which no reader of Dr. Kenyon's account of it would be likely to perceive. The essence of the matter
may be summed up in a word by saying that Dr. Hort trusts his
" Neutral " text so fully not merely because he adjudges it the
earliest and most carefully transmitted text, but because he has
thoroughly tested it and finds it in any case supereminently the best
text. The " Western " text is treated as a corrupt text, not in forgetfulness of its early and wide distribution, but because on testing it
betrays itself, whatever its origin, intrinsically a depraved text. Dr.
Hort has solid reasons to give for this judgment: it is a pity to
permit these reasons to fall out of notice and to treat the question
as if it were chiefly one of age and distribution and external attestation.

  This neglect of the elaborate processes of " internal evidence of
groups " and " internal evidence of classes " in the exposition and
estimate of Dr. Hort's theory is symptomatic of the age as well as
peculiarly characteristic of the external tone of Dr. Kenyon's book.
Dr. Kenyon almost seems to fancy that we can get along in reconstructing the text of the New Testament very much with the external
evidence alone. Nothing could be more mistaken. The use of internal
evidence, recognized or unrecognized — both intrinsic and transcriptional — accompanies every step of the process, and it is not the
least of the merits of Dr. Hort's method that this constant dependence of critical procedure on internal evidence is drawn out from
obscurity and made explicit. Had Dr. Kenyon given us such a chapter as no one could have written better and as ought to have been
included in his excellent treatise, on the methods and processes, the
philosophy and the practice of criticism, he would have been forced
to acknowledge and expound the place of internal evidence in every
step of the work; and he could never have left his readers in igno-

rance of the large part it plays in Dr. Hort's methods and the unavoidably constant use made of it by every critic who actually forms a text. Neither could he have left his readers supposing that the ultimate question of the " Western " text is the question of its origin rather than the question of its value. We do not know when, where, or how it came into being; but there is an organon of criticism in our hands by which, pending the settlement of these questions, we can already assure ourselves that it is not the original text of the New Testament, just because it can be shown to be a corrupt text — the most corrupt text, in fact, that has ever had a large circulation in the Church.

It does not follow, naturally, that the question of the origin of the " Western " text is of little interest or of little importance. It has rightly become the leading question of post-Hortian investigation. But the very character of the text itself excludes, from the beginning, all hypotheses concerning its origin which would make it out to be the original text of the New Testament. We do not ourselves see why the most likely hypothesis of its origin may not be found in a modifi- cation of Prof. Ramsay's theory of its origination in a revision by an Asiatic scribe, or, to speak more exactly, in a multiplication and dis- tribution of his *glossator*. In his admirable chapter on the Papyrus period of the New Testament transmission, Dr. Kenyon draws a vivid picture of how we must suppose that the New Testament cir- culated in this period. He has, wholly unnecessarily, introduced into this account some highly unsupported and insupportable views as to the origin and history of the New Testament canon (pp. 23, 39–40, 270). There never was a time when the New Testament books were " regarded as ordinary books and not as sacred " — at least if we are to let history decide the question for us. There never was a time when the text, because so looked upon, was treated with a certain contempt by those who yet valued it sufficiently to copy it. The character of the monuments of the text is enough to assure us of that — choose we even designedly the worst text extant as a witness. But there was a time when the multiplication of the New Testament manuscripts was in the hands not of professional " publishers," but of private zeal: when it was circulated from hand to hand and, as it were, subterraneously, as believer after believer sought and obtained this or that fragment of it for his own use — a single book or, at most, group of books — possibly laboriously copied by himself from a companion's cherished exemplar, almost certainly secured painfully at the hand of some amateur copyist. This mode of propagating itself belonged to that " servant form " which the New Testament shares with Christianity itself and Christianity's Founder; it must needs so make its way among the humble of the earth, whose names are written in heaven.

Consider how the Book of Acts, for instance, thus passed from hand to hand — laboriously, unskillfully, but most lovingly copied out by unwonted fingers on the cheapest of material, from the cherished manuscript of some humble Christian " evangelist " or " prophet " perchance — long carried in his bosom, often thumbed with clumsy, work-worn fingers, rubbed, frayed, annotated with loving care to mark its sense and preserve items of information picked up here and there and thought fitted to illuminate the narrative, perhaps even to enrich it. How could such a text as the " Western " fail to grow up in such circumstances? In a region like the Mediterranean littoral from Cæsarea to Rome, full of humble Christians of whom some had known Paul (many, those who had known Paul) and all knew something of an intimate character of this or that locality or of the origin and history of this or that church touched on in the narrative — can it surprise us that the text so framing itself should be filled with bits of authentic information possessing every mark of original and first-hand knowledge? Consider how notes first put into the margin by a Mnason or a Tychicus, or some one who had known such " ancient believers," would be cherished by the humble copyist who was " privileged " to transcribe them. And consider at the same time how less " authentic " annotations would inevitably become confused in the course of time with these. For ourselves we do not see how a text like the " Western " text of Acts could fail to grow up in the conditions in which this book was certainly circulated through the first four hundred years. And the character of the " Western " text of Acts is in our judgment the standing and shining testimony, not to the license with which the text of the book was treated, but to the amazing care with which it was dealt with, the real reverence with which it must have been handled. It is, after all is said, a great wonder that the text did not come out of these four centuries of private multiplication mangled and mauled beyond recognition. Nothing could have preserved it so pure except such a reverential handling as comported with its sacred character.

In a word the glossator who made the " Western " text — which is not a uniform text in all documents representing it, it must be remembered, but has its local and temporal variations — may well have been the Christian community itself from Jerusalem to Rome, working with " local knowledge " at its disposal as well as with loving zeal. The " Western " text in this view would be just the " popular " text of the first four centuries. Alongside of it would coexist, of course, what we may venture, for the sake of a distinction, to call the " ecclesiastical " or the " official " text, provided we do not read into these terms later connotations: we mean a text propagated for the use of churches rather than of individuals, and therefore much more carefully, or perhaps we should rather say effectually, guarded, copied doubtless by professional hands, taken from old and well-preserved copies in use in mother-churches and the like. This transmission would continue a line of descent for the text of a more " aristocratic " and of a more trustworthy kind, and would naturally provide a text to which other texts in circulation would stand related as either corrupt popular parallels or artificial scholastic revisions. If we do not mistake we have in this general scheme the real nature of the " Neutral," " Western," and " Alexandrian " texts suggested. And looking at the whole problem from some such point of view, no discovery of the antiquity of the " Western " text, its wide extension, the exactness and air of original information of many of its distinctive readings, and the like, can disturb us: it is all just what we should expect and we are thoroughly prepared for it. It is all full of interest to us: all full of instruction: historically we expect to profit much from it: but we shall be slow in preferring the " popular " text to the " official " text.

Meanwhile, let us repeat that even with the " Western " text in view, we can scarcely emphasize too strongly the excellence of the transmitted text of the New Testament. Dr. Kenyon has some admirable remarks in his opening chapter on the superiority of the New Testament transmission to that of classical authors, in point both of number of witnesses and relative closeness of testimony. Its superiority in exactness of textual transmission is even more marked. Dr. Hort's estimate is that in seven-eighths of the New Testament we have the actual autographic text in hand, and in nine hundred and ninety-nine thousandths of it practically so. This is no exaggeration. We may read nine hundred and ninety-nine words consecutively with the comfortable feeling that we are reading the author's own words: and then we may put our finger on the thousandth word and estimate precisely the amount of doubt that attaches to it and the amount of difference in sense that would result in the settlement of the doubt in any possible way. This is of the providence of God, and ought to be recognized as such. What actually printed text is nearest to the autographic text, it may meanwhile be somewhat difficult to decide. We certainly should not with Dr. Kenyon recommend the text that underlies the Revision of the English Bible made in 1881, as a standard text for common use. This text does not even pretend to provide a standard text: but is essentially a compromise text altered from the Receptus only where compulsion was laid on the Revisers. Mr. Weymouth's or Dr. Nestle's " resultant " text would be better: Westcott and Hort or Weiss better still. What the practical worker really needs is a good text, say Westcott and Hort's; a good digest of readings, either full or such as is given in Dr. Hort's " Introduction " or Dr. Sanday's " Appendix "; and a brief practical outline of how to use the evidence, such as is given, for example, at the end of Dr. Hort's first volume. So equipped even the beginner may hopefully enter into the work of scrutinizing the text of the New Testament. If now he wishes to know all the important things about the *externalia* of the art of textual criticism as applied to the New Testament, what can he do better than add this admirable volume of Dr. Kenyon's? Only he must not expect to get out of it anything very helpful outside the limits of the *externalia*. For Dr. Kenyon has not designed to put, and has not put, anything beyond the *externalia* into it.

St. Augustine and His Age. By Joseph McCabe. New York and London: G. P. Putnam's Sons. 1903 (published December, 1902). [*Also:* London: Duckworth & Co. 1902.] [1]

Mr. McCabe was formerly known as the Very Reverend Father Anthony of the Order of Saint Francis. He came, however, happily to see the error of his monastic ways, and very properly gave them up. Discharging thus his duty to himself, he has further discharged it to humanity by revealing some of the abuses of the monastic system in two somewhat pungent and very profitable volumes pub-

[1] *The Princeton Theological Review,* i. 1903, pp. 305–312.

lished during the closing years of the last century — " Twelve Years in a Monastery," and " Life in a Modern Monastery." With the opening of a new century he has turned to new themes, and we are already his debtors for two interesting essays in Christian biography — one dealing with " Peter Abelard," published in the midsummer of 1901, and the other, this " St. Augustine," published but little more than a year afterwards. We would gladly forget his past distresses and rejoice only in his present gifts. But Mr. McCabe will not permit this. He drags his past on with him and persists in writing his biographical studies from the point of view of what he himself calls the " escaped monk." In the study of Abelard, this was of little importance: Mr. McCabe's monastic experiences perhaps even prepared him the better to understand Abelard and his times. In this study of Augustine, it has brought something very like ruin.

Our complaint is not merely that Mr. McCabe occasionally obtrudes reminiscences of his own experiences into his biographical sketches. This is a fault of taste. After all, we go to a life of Augustine to learn about Augustine and not about the author; and it is for the moment a matter of indifference to the reader that the author has, say, been injuriously spoken of (as e.g. p. 201) for having followed his bent and exposed the abuses of a mode of life he once shared. But there is not very much of this in the book and it could not in any event seriously injure its value.

Our complaint is not even merely that Mr. McCabe has brought with him into the broader life he now enjoys a cynical temper and a carping spirit which warp his judgment and deform his pages. Surely the bitterness he is constantly exhibiting against " ecclesiastics " and " hagiographers " is somewhat superfluous. And it is not rendered more engaging by the circumstance that he includes under these complimentary designations well-nigh the whole body of his predecessors in the study of his subject — so that there runs through his book a vein of scorn of previous biographers of Augustine. " Mr. Marcus Dods," for example, is an " ecclesiastic " and hence represents the facts of Augustine's life " in safe terms " (p. 38). The picture that " most of his ecclesiastical biographers " draw of Augustine's unregenerate days — though transcribed from Augustine's own account — is mere " pretense " (p. 54). When the biographers follow Ambrose's version of a matter they are " trustful hagiographers " (p. 113). Certain articles in Smith and Wace's " Dictionary of Christian Biography " are recommended as " choice specimens of the literary art of tempering justice with mercy, which is so admirably cultivated by the ecclesiastical writer" (p. 312). Drs. Milman and Smith are satirically characterized as "safe commentators"; and it is added: "If we *must* have our Gibbon served up with an abundance of ecclesiastical sauce, it is at least time there was an improvement in its quality" (p. 111). This kind of thing is really very bad, and it is unfortunately pervasive (cf. e.g. pp. 58, 146, 206, 222, 281, 355, 397, 413). And the unhappy facility of innuendo thus exhibited is permitted to cut much deeper than merely into the credit of previous students of the subject. "It is probable," Mr. McCabe tells us, "that Manicheism did no more than Christianity towards the purification of the Empire" (p. 64). "It is impossible," he says with a truly monkish skill of suggestion, "to discuss here what probability there was of Mithraism absorbing Christianity instead of Christianity absorbing Mithraism" (pp. 105 f.). Similarly, "whether it be that 'Plato wrote a human preface to the Gospels,' as De Maistre said, or that the evangelists wrote a human appendix to Plato, as others think, it is hardly our duty to inquire here" (pp. 158 f.). Speaking of Augustine's commentaries on Genesis, he drops the incidental remark: "One reads them with a feeling of pity now that Mr. Sayce and other reputable scholars have told us whence these stories were copied" (p. 217, cf. pp. 362, 379). Possibly some piquancy may be added to the page by this mode of writing. It will scarcely add to the confidence with which the reader will commit himself to the guidance of the author. But even such faults may possibly belong to the form rather than to the substance of a book.

Our real complaint begins when we note that Mr. McCabe's whole presentation of Augustine's life and character is affected by his point of view, and that not merely in tone and proportion but also in its very substance. He has given us a very different Augustine from the Augustine of what we may call, to please Mr. McCabe, "the hagiographic tradition" — that is to say, of history, as that history is set down in contemporary accounts (including Augustine's own narrative in his "Confessions") and embodied in contemporary records. He looks at Augustine through spectacles which have distorted his figure out of all proportion — throwing up into great prominence subordinate elements in his character and unimportant aspects of his life, and obscuring the really significant features. Augustine was above all else and before all else the "reformer of

Christian piety," as even Harnack puts it — " even Harnack," for as Prof. West truly points out (*Presbyterian and Reformed Review,* xii. 1901, p. 183), Harnack does not himself do justice in his thought of Augustine to his " personal religion." He revolutionized the whole conception of the truly " Christian life " and introduced into Christendom a completely new ideal of Christian feeling and aspiration. Of all this Mr. McCabe has not a word to say. Of the real significance of Augustine's doctrine of Grace for his own inner life and for the history of thought, he betrays no conception. Here is Hamlet with Hamlet left out with a vengeance. On the other hand the wholly insignificant matter of Augustine's attitude towards marriage and his deflected opinions about the sexual passion are thrown out into a prominence beyond all reason. It might be unjust to say that every nasty story and every morbid expression is sought out and exploited to Augustine's discredit. But a very undue emphasis is certainly thrown on this aspect of Augustine's life and teaching.

Even such distortions of the figure he is drawing do not constitute, however, Mr. McCabe's worst fault as a biographer of Augustine. The fact seems to be that the whole portrait that is presented is dominated by the conception that its tendency was distinctly downward, and that, taken in its entirety, it was fraught with evil rather than good for the Church and the world. To secure this effect Mr. McCabe is at considerable pains first to discredit Augustine's own account of the evil of his early life and then systematically to depreciate the attainments of his later life. His was, it seems, a bright and essentially good boyhood and his young manhood blossomed out into a high-minded devotion to " reason." But then, alas, he fell under the domination of " authority." Reason gradually ceased to be his " darling " (p. 207, cf. pp. 233, 479). He steadily became more and more a dupe to silly miraculous stories (p. 466), a contemner of all that is valuable in life (p. 213), a slave to the ecclesiastical machine, an intolerant controversialist who stopped at no means to secure the defeat of his opponents (pp. 214, 232) — if not a blasphemer, yet certainly a persecutor and injurious. " The bloody pages of mediæval history rise before us as we dwell on his later ideas " (p. 398). Thus Augustine's progress according to Mr. McCabe was the opposite of Paul's: his development, like that of the Church itself, according to Harnack, was a " pathological " process. It is quite likely that (like Harnack, in the parallel case) Mr. McCabe might deny this and declare that " on the whole " there was, in his view, an " advance." We should be forced to reply (as in the case of Harnack) that he has not so depicted it. The reader takes away from his book the distinct impression that Augustine grew steadily a worse man and a more evil influence as he grew older.

If we ask after the account we are to give of this low view of Augustine's character and work, we must probably make a distinction. Ultimately, it seems to us, it must be traced to Mr. McCabe's point of view as an " escaped monk." He has approached the study of Augustine with a poignant hatred of the monachism of which Augustine was one of the founders in the West — with all that monachism implies of depreciation of the earthly life and its delights and duties alike: and with an equal hatred of the great ecclesiastical system of which monachism has ever been a part and a stay and of which Augustine's teaching, on one of its sides, has supplied a chief theoretical support. This side of Augustine's character and teaching has loomed so big before him as to obscure all else. Augustine the monk, Augustine the ecclesiastic: this is the Augustine he has known and this is the Augustine he has painted. This Augustine he has sought to portray with truth and justice: but he could not think Augustine the monk and ecclesiastic an admirable figure. Above all, he was consumed with zeal to set forth the monk and ecclesiastic as essentially unlovely and essentially injurious to all the higher ideals of living. Accordingly he has given us an Augustine who gradually grows hard and evil before our eyes under the influences of those erroneous — those destructive — views of life and religion, under the influence of which the Christian world has ever since grown harder and harder and more and more corrupt. This is as much as to say, of course, that Mr. McCabe's sketch of Augustine's life is not an essay in pure biography, but is essentially a polemic treatise. It is another assault of the " escaped monk " upon the system from which he has, doubtless through throes and suffering, separated himself. In his first books he gave us a picture of the working of monasticism in modern life: in his " Peter Abelard " he gave us a picture of monastic life in its mediæval conception: in his " St. Augustine " he gives us a picture of the working of the monastic idea in its inception. If he had only put his book forward as a study of such evil tendencies as entered into Augustine's life it would not be so bad. There were these evil tendencies in Augustine's life, and they ought not to be minimized or neglected. Cromwell was right in demanding that the artist should paint truly the wart on his nose. But it would hardly do to look at the wart through a microscope and paint it and it alone in this exaggerated light in all its hideous rugosities, and label it " Cromwell." It is something like this that Mr. McCabe has done to Augustine.

The process by which Mr. McCabe has been able to persuade himself that he was drawing a true portrait of Augustine supplies us with a not inapt illustration of " higher-critical " methods. He tells us in the Preface that his attempt is " to interpret by the light of psychology rather than by that of theology," or, as he otherwise expresses it, that he has " brought to the story a saving tincture of Pelagianism ": that he has " tried to exhibit the development of Augustine as an orderly mental and moral growth." This, of course, involves the elimination of all " supernaturalism " — say, in this instance, obvious divine leading and cataclysmic conversion. The account given of his spiritual development by Augustine himself in what Mr. McCabe calls " his seductive *Confessions* " is therefore set aside at once as " perverse." A very harsh judgment is passed, in fact, on the " Confessions." They " may be fine literature, but they contain an utterly false psychology and ethics " (p. 24). In them, Augustine is " sternly bent on magnifying his misdeeds " (p. 39). Something like this is said by others also, as, for example, by Harnack and Boissier and with the same general intent. But they speak far less extremely than Mr. McCabe and never dream of carrying " reconstruction " practically so far. The only documentary evidence being thus discredited, the way is open to give to Augustine an " orderly mental and moral growth " — that is, of course, to attribute to him such a development as on the whole seems to the special biographer natural in the circumstances. There is assigned to him, therefore, a noble heathen youth, breaking down into a sort of weariness toward early middle life, under the stress of which he flees to " authority " for refuge, and then progressively deteriorates to the end.

It is rather odd to observe how different the constructions of this " orderly " life are in different hands under this method. To make the life " orderly," that is, to give it the appearance of a continuous development in one natural line, Boissier and Harnack represent Augustine as having been essentially a Christian from his infancy. There is no " Prodigal son " here, says Harnack. " Rather do the *Confessions* portray a man brought up from youth by a faithful mother in the Christian, that is, in the Catholic faith." Boissier takes his start from that wonderful conversation which the converted Augustine held with his dying mother at Ostia, when he seemed borne by the mystic breath of her devotion up to heaven itself. " I picture to myself," he says, " experiences on his part of something of the same sort in his infancy, while his mother talked to him of Christ, as she tried to make a perfect Christian of him and spoke to him words he could never forget." Seeking precisely the same end, Mr. McCabe pursues a precisely opposite course. Monnica, he tells us, showed no particular zeal in imbuing the early years of her son with Christian principles, and her later devotion can be supposed to have had only some indirect influence on the course of his development. He grew up frankly heathen: and betrays in the " Confessions " some embarrassment with respect to her early neglect (p. 10). It was not until he was about twenty that his mother " entered upon the long and passionate devotion to her son's conversion which has earned for the simple, ignorant woman an immortal place amongst the mothers of men " (pp. 66–67). Even then, the low-born (p. 194), ignorant, but earnest woman had her limitations as a religious guide. She did not object very much to Augustine cherishing a concubine, but she objected very much indeed to his cherishing a heresy (p. 66). From all which it appears that the picture drawn of Monnica is as much " lowered " in tone as that drawn of Augustine himself.

The mention we have just made of Augustine's concubine leads to raising the question whether the treatment Mr. McCabe gives this certainly sufficiently disgraceful episode in Augustine's life is thoroughly judicious. His attaching himself to a single mistress and living in faithfulness to her for fourteen years is rightly pointed to as implying " (for those days) a rare moderation of character " (p. 40). To say this is, however, probably inadequate. The truth seems to be fairly expressed in the words of Dr. Marcus Dods that are scoffed at on an earlier page (p. 38), viz.: that in this union Augustine formed " a connection which was not matrimonial in the strict sense." That is to say, it *was* matrimonial in a secondary sense, fully recognized as legitimate by the Lex Julia and Papia Poppæa, and entailing no moral dereliction, though of course not ranking in social standing with " connections that are matrimonial in the strict sense " (cf. Plumptre, in Smith and Cheetham's " Dictionary of Christian Antiquities," i. 1875, p. 422; Moyle, in Smith's " Dictionary of Greek and Roman Antiquities," i. 1890, p. 526; Leonhard,

in Pauly-Wissowa, " Real-Encyclopädie der classischen Altertums-
wissenschaft," iv. 1 [siebenter Halbband], 1900, coll. 835 ff.). It
was, in a word, a form of marriage, adapted to the case of women
of the lower classes, who could not legally become wives of citizens
of Rome. So fully was it recognized as a legitimate relationship that
there was a strong tendency to give it ecclesiastical sanction. A
Synod at Toledo, A.D. 400, for example, decreed: " If anyone who
has a believing wife has [also] a concubine, let him not communicate. But let not him who has no wife, but instead of a wife has a
concubine, be repelled from communion; only let him be content
with union with one woman, whether wife or concubine, according
to his pleasure: but let him that lives with others be rejected, until
he desists and is restored through penitence " (Mansi, " Sacrorum
conciliorum nova et amplissima collectio," iii. 1901, col. 1001; cf.
Loofs, in Herzog, " Realencyklopädie für protestantische Theologie
und Kirche," ed. 3, ii. 1897, p. 261). Here we have simply a repetition
in an ecclesiastical ordinance of the existing civil law and the general
judgment of society. It doubtless represents the usage in Africa in
the fourth century, and indeed is thought by many to represent the
usage of the whole Church up at least to the fifth century (cf. Herzog, as cited, x. 1901, p. 746). Perhaps a due recognition of this fact
will account for any winking at the relation which Monnica may be
supposed to have exhibited — although the remark of Mr. McCabe
(p. 66) that " she seems to have accepted his companion without a
murmur " appears to be only an inference from the silence of the
" Confessions."

Such unions, however, though irreproachable under the law of
the Empire and involving no moral degradation in the estimation of
the highest heathen circles — in which, accordingly, there was more
or less tendency among the Christians themselves to acquiesce —
nevertheless were discouraged in the Church. When Augustine came
to prepare for baptism it appears to have been treated accordingly
as a *conditio sine qua non* that this connection should be brought to a
close. It seems to be thoroughly out of place, therefore, to animadvert
on Augustine's coldness and insensibility towards the companion of
all these years, when he prepared to put her from him and to take a
wife as a preliminary to baptism (p. 143). In the first place he was
not insensible: he tells us that there was left on her departure " a raw
and bloody wound in his heart where she had lain." In the next
place, he seems to have had no choice. In accepting Christianity he

accepted its code of moral law: and he did not accept Christianity
in a cold and calculating spirit but under the stress of a great religious and moral upheaval. That he did not solve the problem by
marrying his concubine, as Mr. McCabe suggests might have been
the proper course, probably in no way argues that he had " no sense
whatever of obligation to the woman who had shared his life for
fourteen years " (p. 143). It is explained by Mr. McCabe's own
remark immediately following: " Evidently, she belonged to a much
lower condition of life than his own." " Let a concubine," says the
" Apostolical Constitutions " (viii. 32), " who is a slave of an unbeliever, and confines herself to her master alone, be received [to
baptism]; but if she be incontinent with others, let her be rejected.
A believer who has a concubine, — if she be a slave, let him cease
[from her] and take a wife legitimately: if she be free, let him take
her as his legitimate wife; and if he does not, let him be rejected."
If we may suppose these regulations fairly to represent the usage at
Milan at the end of the fourth century — no very violent supposition — they explain Augustine's case as neatly as the recently
recovered Laws of Hammurabi fit into all the plications of the episode of Hagar. We need only presume that Augustine's concubine
was of servile or equivalent condition to bring his action into exact
harmony with the regulations.

Mr. McCabe has indeed said (p. 42): " It does not seem likely
that Augustine's mistress was a slave "; though he needs to add that
nothing whatever is told us about her social position and, as we have
seen, he allows at a later point, that she was " evidently " of a much
lower condition of life than Augustine. That Augustine treated her
as a slave is evidence enough, in such circumstances, to justify the
supposition that she was a slave. Certainly the parting was not unattended with the deepest emotion on both sides. Augustine tells us
that she went away " vowing to God " to keep herself free from
future connections. This is surely a fine and pathetic touch. Mr.
McCabe treats it with incredible coarseness. Because the " hagiographer " — including in this case M. Boissier! — generally considers
that the meaning is that she entered a nunnery, Mr. McCabe, with
his customary " anti-hagiographic " fury, actually contends that it
probably means that she went away cursing and swearing! " *Vovens
tibi*," he says, " may very well mean that ' she vowed and swore
[every African, including Augustine, swore habitually] she would
have nothing more to do with men '; either in anger or in her great

love for Augustine" (p. 147, note). Surely every simple-hearted reader — we use the epithet inviting Mr. McCabe's scorn — will perceive that a serious vow to God alone can be meant. With such an instance as this before us of the lengths Mr. McCabe can go in his " anti-hagiographic " rage, it is hardly necessary to seek further illustrations of the lowering effect it has had on the picture he is painting of Augustine under its influence.

The book is very free from minor slips in statements of fact. There is a perfectly blind note on p. 449 on the relations of Augustinian and Calvinistic doctrine. There occurs a note on p. 499 in which a curious slip which Dr. Hodgkin made in the first edition of his " Italy and her Invaders," relative to the opponent with whom Augustine deals in the " Opus imperfectum " is mentioned: in his second edition Dr. Hodgkin corrected it duly, as also other slips of the same kind that deformed the first issue. On p. 292 we meet the odd phrase " Christian Presbyterians " — as designating a body including M. de Pressensé " and others ": we have not fathomed the designed implication. On p. 41 Paulinus of Pella is quite decisively represented as the grandson of Ausonius: the point is still, perhaps, disputable. On p. 380 it is doubtless the insufficiently overseen printer who has foiled the author's evil counsel by giving us בְּקֵבָה for נְקֵבָה. But a truce to such things. We shall mention only one more for the sake of the curious interest that attaches to it. On p. 416 Mr. McCabe speaks of the attribution of Pelagius' Commentary on Paul's Epistles to Gelasius and " then . . . to Jerome himself, the most bitter opponent and critic of its real author," as " a unique and precious fact in the history of heresy." Did Mr. McCabe bear in mind that the " Confession of Faith " presented by Pelagius to Innocent was actually admitted into the " Libri Carolini " at the close of the eighth century as Augustine's; and indeed was produced as Augustine's in 1521 A.D. by the Sorbonne against Luther? There is really no limit to which ignorance cannot go in the confusion of doctrines — as the Presbyterian Church has lately had much occasion to observe!

Let us not close without a word of appreciation of what is praiseworthy in the book. If the portrait which it gives us of Augustine is distorted, it is yet sharply drawn and brings to notice real traits of his character which may now and again be obscured by the " hagiographer." The book may very profitably be read, therefore, along with the " hagiographers " and may supply a useful supplement to

them: though assuredly some of the " hagiographers " — say, Tille-
mont, Bindermann, Böhringer, or Rauscher — must needs be read
along with it as a corrective, if we are not to be altogether misled in
our estimate of Augustine. It certainly is a very easy book to read:
the style is pleasantly flowing and though deformed by cynical turns,
yet attractive and picturesque. There does not seem to lie behind its
narrative as careful study of the sources as lay behind the narrative
of the " Peter Abelard," but Mr. McCabe, as we have said, makes
few slips in matters of fact and writes out of a considerable acquaintance with the ecclesiastical life of the fourth and fifth centuries. A high degree of literary skill is exhibited and much historical
feeling. If Mr. McCabe can only bring himself to write in a purely
historical spirit, we feel sure he has a great service to render to the
Churches.

THE ATONEMENT AND THE MODERN MIND. By JAMES DENNEY, D.D.
New York: A. C. Armstrong & Son. 1903.[1]

AFTER Dr. Denney's valuable study of " The Death of Christ "
in the New Testament (reviewed in this *Review,* i. 1903, pp. 492 ff.)
this interesting little volume is most welcome. It performs an important service in vindicating the essence of the Atonement of Christ,
culminating in His death, as a substitutionary offering to God. Its
sturdy defense of the objective work of Christ and its significance
for human salvation commends it powerfully to the reader whose
heart is set on the Christ of the New Testament. Nothing could sum
up better the great reality than the penultimate sentence: " It is the
goal of our life to be found in Him; but I cannot understand the man
who thinks it more profound to identify himself with Christ and
share in the work of redeeming the world, than to abandon himself
to Christ and share in the world's experience of being redeemed."
The true note of Bible religion rings in that: this is, after all, not
fundamentally a religion of imitation but of trust. And what could
be better than the retort made to those who are accustomed to insist
that there is no Atonement in the parable of the prodigal son, that
there is no Christ in that parable either? So that, if we are to take

that parable as the quintessence of the gospel, it will be a gospel without Christ as well as without expiation.

That this high note dominates the volume we rejoice to recognize: that it is not sustained without faltering throughout the volume, we suppose is due as much as to any other one circumstance to the point of view from which it is written. " The Atonement and the Modern Mind " is the title given to the volume. What is " the modern mind "? Perhaps we ought not to ask that question after listening to Dr. Denney describe in such detail and with such brilliancy of touch precisely what it is, or rather precisely what he takes it to be. We rise from this discussion, however, with the conviction that Dr. Denney has not escaped the common tendency to project one's own mind, or to spread out one's own associates, into " the general," and to mistake this for " the modern mind." Important a factor in life as Glasgow has become, however, it is not the world: neither is semi-sceptical Britain the world: nor yet even civilized Europe. There is after all but one " mind " to be considered, and this is the human mind; and the human mind is fundamentally much the same in modern times as it has always been, and is accessible to much the same rational and emotional appeal. The fact of the matter is that Dr. Denney writes here — as elsewhere — under the narrowing and clogging influences of the " Apologetical School," which Dr. Bruce unfortunately founded in Glasgow. If he could only shake himself free from these deadening traditions, cease to fancy that he must adapt the gospel to this or that temporary and local manifestation (or degree) of unbelief, refrain from mixing a constant apologetical leaven with the Bread of Life, whether as expounded exegetically from the page of Scripture or enforced didactically in constructive exposition, and give us the pure, positive truth as it lies in Scripture and is assimilated from it by his own strong and devout mind and heart — then we should get something worth while from Dr. Denney!

It is to be hoped that it is due merely to the faltering way in which, from his apologetical standpoint, Dr. Denney sets forth his doctrine of the Atonement in order to adjust it to " the modern mind," that we cannot quite make out whether his theory of the Atonement rises essentially above what is known in history as the Grotian or Rectoral theory. Perhaps as concise a statement of the chief elements of his theory as anywhere in the volume is given on pp. 112–113. " The New Testament," we read there, " teaches that forgiveness is mediated to sinners through Christ, and specifically through His death: in other words, that it is possible for God to forgive, but possible for God only through a supreme revelation of His love, made at infinite cost, and doing justice to the uttermost to those inviolable relations in which alone, as I have already said, man can participate in eternal life, the life of God Himself — doing justice to them as relations in which there is an inexorable divine reaction against sin, finally expressing itself in death." When the terms in this passage are explained in accordance with their use elsewhere in the volume it seems to be fairly the Rectoral theory of the Atonement that is in mind. Accordingly, it is taught at once that the Atonement of itself only renders the forgiveness of sins possible: what renders it actual in the case of any sinner is an act on his own part. " It is possible on these terms, and it becomes actual as sinful men open their hearts in penitence and faith to this marvellous revelation, and abandon their lives unreservedly to the love of God in Christ who died for them " (p. 113). " Substitution " is taken in this theory thus in a notably lowered sense. As our substitute, Christ merely " stands in the midst of us, the pledge of God's love " — " a divine challenge to men which is designed to win our heart." It is only " when men are won — when that which Christ in His love has done for them comes home to their souls — when they are constrained by His infinite grace to the self-surrender of faith " — that we can say He is become our " representative." God may make Him our Substitute: only we ourselves can make Him our Representative. From which it would appear that, at the decisive point, we are our own saviours. This may be very gratifying to the " modern mind ": it is intolerable to the Christian heart.

The greatest flaw in Dr. Denney's teaching, however, is that it proceeds upon an essentially " rationalistic " basis — we use the word in the historical and not in the vulgar opprobrious sense of it. He does indeed tell us that " the Christian religion is a historical religion, and whatever we say about it must rest upon historical grounds "; and that we owe what we know of the Atonement to the testimony of Christ which is " in the last resort the testimony of Scripture." But he goes at once forward to add that we do not receive the things thus historically mediated to us and testified to us by Scripture on the authority of Scripture. There can be, it seems, no such thing for the mind as " blank authority." " It cannot believe things — the things by which it has to live — simply on the word of Paul or John," nay, " it can just as little believe them simply on the word of Jesus." " Truth is the only thing that has authority for the mind, and the only way in which truth finally evinces its authority is by taking possession of the mind for itself." The Atonement is to be accepted, therefore, " not on the authority of any person or persons whatever, but on the authority of the truth in it, by which it has won its place in our minds and hearts." We prize the Scriptures because of this truth we find in them, not the truth because we find it in Scripture. Certainly Christian Wolff would have welcomed such teaching, despite the different metaphysics underlying it, as indistinguishable from his own. When we read it, we wonder only that Dr. Denney has been able to set forth so high a theory of the Atonement: and we wonder greatly how he expects to convince any man that the theory he sets forth is true. He does not know that there was a teacher sent from God named Jesus except on testimony that to us in the last resort is the bare testimony of Scripture: he does not know that this man died for our sins except simply on the word of this Jesus: he does not know that this death was acceptable to God and atones for sin, or how it atones for sin, or how it is made available for us — or anything that enters into the essence of the transaction — except on the bare authority of Scripture. He does not know one-tenth part of what he has told us about the Atonement, and what he insists upon as constituting its very heart, except on the faith of these very Scriptures to which he will accord no real authority. When at the close of the book he tells us, to clinch the matter, " And I am very sure that in the New Testament " the exercise of trust in Christ " is first and fundamental," it appeals to *us;* but we resent it a little from *him. He* has given himself no right to urge that argument. We are deeply thankful that Dr. Denney expounds the Atonement to us so richly and so truly. But we look at his foundations and can see no reason why he should be so sure he is right; and we see no reason why to-morrow he may not expound to us something else — which may happen then " to find him " — with equal confidence and equal inconsequence. We are as sure as he can be that we cannot get along without heart experience and that certitude which can come from nothing but the witness of the Holy Spirit in the heart. We wish he saw as clearly as we do that neither can we get along without the " external authority " — *authority*, we say — of revelation, embodied in the Holy Scriptures. That is, if we are to be and to abide Christian men, in all the meaning of that term.

THE DOCTRINE OF THE ATONEMENT, AND ITS HISTORICAL EVOLUTION. And RELIGION AND MODERN CULTURE. By the late AUGUSTE SABATIER. Translated from the French by Victor Leuliette, B.-ès-L. (Paris), A.K.C. London: Williams & Norgate; New York: G. P. Putnam's Sons. 1904.[1]

No ONE who has ever read ten lines of the writings of the late Prof. Auguste Sabatier but will have been impressed with the grace of his style and the truly Gallic attractiveness of his method of opening and presenting a subject. His learning seemed only to adorn, his polemic zeal only to add zest to, what seemed always primarily a piece of literature. Whatever else he was he was always eminently readable. The two essays which combine to make up the little volume at present before us are like the rest of his writings in these things. They are like the rest of his writings also in the poverty-stricken thinness of the religious conceptions which they present to us as the only form in which Christianity can hope to live — or rather must expect to die — in the conditions presented by modern culture.

The second of these essays is really an address which was delivered at the Religious Science Congress at Stockholm, September 2, 1897. It undertakes to elucidate precisely the problem of the relations of religion and modern culture. These relations, we are told, are summed up in the one word " conflict." The principle of modern culture is expressed in the single term " autonomy " — that is to say, " the unconquerable assurance of the human mind, in its present advanced state of development, that it possesses within itself the norm of its life and of its thought " (p. 169). It, of course, scouts the " heteronomy " in which traditional religion entrenches itself. Traditional religion, on the other hand, too timid to trust the human soul to its inherent religious instinct, and clinging in one way or another to " external authority," profoundly distrusts the efforts of the human spirit, characterizing every department of modern culture, to realize its independence. What is to be done and what is the outlook for the future? Prof. Sabatier counsels cessation of the external conflict, and points with hope to the mutual interpenetration of religion and culture.

At this point, we delight to say, we are heartily at one with Prof. Sabatier; and the section of the address in which he pictures the coming reconciliation through mutual internal influence, is a beauti-

[1] The Princeton Theological Review, iii. 1905, pp. 506–509.

ful expression of a noble conception, and as well, as we shall be happy to believe, a true forecast of the ultimate issue. " To the violent and sterile conflict which we have just described there succeeds the closest and most active solidarity " (p. 212). Scientific men having become religious, the science they produce will exhibit the traits of their religion. Religious men having become scientific, the religion they serve will take on the forms of rational and intellectually defensible expression. " Being an inner inspiration, a deepseated life, kindled within the soul itself by the spirit of God, piety will not act from without upon science in order to curb it beneath a strange law; it will not impose its methods or assign its limits to science, still less will it dictate its conclusions. But it will call forth and maintain, within the heart of the scientist, the sacred flame of the religious, that is to say, absolute love of truth " (p. 212). Similarly religion will manifest itself as " in communication and close touch with human culture " (p. 218). It is the vision of the lion and lamb lying down together: and, we praise God for it, it is a vision that is to be realized.

It is all the more regrettable that, when we look closely at Prof. Sabatier's personal expectation — perhaps we would better say, individual prophecy — of the precise manner in which this great end shall be attained, we discover that the side of the lion where he looks (and hopes) to see the lamb lie down is the inside. He tells us, indeed, that religion is to borrow nothing from culture, but to go its own way to its own perfect development. But he conceives that religion in its perfect development will possess nothing that culture can take the least interest in. The process by which religion is to make itself " agreeable to the general culture of modern times " is a process of " freeing itself from worn out forms and old ideas." And to Prof. Sabatier every form and idea is old and worn out except the pure products of the religious sentiment itself. The Socinian criticism, the Rationalistic assault, the demands of Modern Culture, these, in Prof. Sabatier's apprehension, are the successive instruments by means of which religion has been progressively purified; and the pure religion he commends to us as the religion of the future is accordingly just a highly sentimentalized natural religion. He expresses this dreary conclusion in terms so gracious and so suggestive that we scarcely realize that it is merely bald natural religion that is commended to us. We read almost without shock of the doctrines of the Trinity, of the Person of Christ, of the Sacrificial Atonement as so much " Christian mythology " which has " broken down beneath the blows of the rationalism of the eighteenth century " (pp. 221 f.). Under the sense of the beauty of the conception of piety which describes it as " the sensitiveness of the heart for God," we almost fail to catch what is meant when we are told that " the permanent Christian consciousness will be the religious consciousness of man, induced by the experience of filial piety wrought in the soul of Christ " (p. 204). It is with all the more shock that we realize in the end that when Prof. Sabatier commends to us the religion of Jesus, he means rather the religion which Jesus had than the religion that has Jesus.

The earlier of the two essays affords an illustration of how fully Prof. Sabatier in the religion he commends to modern men was prepared to do without Jesus and all that Jesus has stood for in the religion He founded. Its subject is the doctrine of the Atonement, and its method is what Prof. Sabatier calls " the historical method." That is to say, it is dominated by the assumption that when you have worked out the historical development of a doctrine you have " explained " that doctrine — which in the view of writers of this class is the same as to say you have explained it away. The object of this essay is to trace " the historical evolution of the doctrine of the Atonement," with a view to rendering any doctrine of Atonement incredible. The first half of it is occupied with the Biblical conceptions of Atonement; the last half with the ideas that have been entertained by the teachers of the Church. The one class of conceptions is treated as of as little authority as the other: and it is not unassuring to those of us who believe in a doctrine of Atonement on the authority of Scripture, to observe from such an exposition as is here given us that it can be got rid of only along with the authority of Scripture. When we are told that the sacrifices of the Old Testament are of merely human origin and significance, for example, it comforts us somewhat to learn that it has to be allowed that the author of the Epistle to the Hebrews (a treatise we admire even more than we do Prof. Sabatier's) thought very differently. And when we are told that the idea of substitution is crude and impossible, it brings us some consolation to learn that confessedly it is positively contained in the teaching of Paul, a writer in whose view we cannot help placing some confidence with respect to such a matter.

The essay is professedly a historical one. Perhaps it is not wrong in us to take interest in it, therefore, chiefly from the historical point of view. Its main interest to us at all events arises not from any help it brings us for understanding the Atonement, but from the information it gives us of what Prof. Sabatier was accustomed to teach concerning the Atonement. For it cannot be without very great significance to those living in this modern age to have so authoritative an exposition of what it is that is commended to us by the leaders of the new thought as to the essence of Christianity. Let us say at once, however, that we find nothing particularly new in Prof. Sabatier's doctrine of the Atonement. He himself is conscious that it is the outcome of the Socinian and Rationalistic criticism, and in point of fact it merely reproduces the characteristic view of these schools of destructive criticism, driven to the last extremity.

According to Prof. Sabatier the gospel is summed up in the parables of the prodigal son and of the publican (p. 123), and he makes it the reproach of the orthodox that they find only a part of the gospel in these parables and seek a supplement for them in other passages of Scripture. Accordingly " God needs neither mediation nor satisfaction " (p. 120). " The Father is satisfied if the prodigal son, confessing his sins and condemning his errors, earnestly repents and returns to his Father's house " (p. 120). " In order to accomplish the work of the salvation of sinners, Jesus then had no need to influence God, whose love has taken and forever retains the initiative of forgiveness. God has no need to be brought back to man and reconciled with him " (p. 125). Christ's entire work consists, therefore, in reconciling man to God, " in bringing about in the individual and in humanity the state of repentance in which alone the forgiveness of the Father can become effective " (p. 126). For the only thing God asks and can ask as the ground of forgiveness of the sinner is simply repentance on the sinner's part. " Forgiveness for the sinner who repents from the bottom of his heart: such is the message of the Gospel. What constitutes the superiority of the Christian conception of the Father is precisely that it rises above the feeling of retaliation and vengeance, and that it wills not the death of the sinner, but his conversion and life. What *satisfaction* does the Father in the parable require in order to forgive his repentant son who returns to him? " (p. 112). " From one end of the Gospel to the other, forgiveness of sins is promised simply to repentance and faith, because, in the inner life of the soul, repentance and faith are in reality the beginning of the defeat and destruction of sin " (p. 120). It is not taught indeed that " repentance is the cause of the forgiveness of sins ": " this cause," it is remarked, " is none other than the love of the Father for His children." " But repentance is the necessary and sufficient condition "; and " it is impossible to conceive God the Father rejecting one of His children who returns to Him, condemning himself, deploring his sins, and craving forgiveness " (p. 124). Repentance, in one word, " is salvation itself " (p. 127). " There is no atonement other than repentance " (p. 127). From which it would seem to follow that the atoning act is the act of man, not of Christ, and that Christ's whole work consists in bringing man to perform this atoning act of repentance.

How Christ accomplishes this, is that He so touches our hearts as to make us grieve over our evil entreatment of our loving Father. In this work of touching our hearts, no doubt, His passion and death have their high part to play. But we must not fancy that they in any way affect God and stand in any sense in His sight as a reason or ground of His acceptance of our persons. " The death of Christ is an essentially moral act, the significance and value of which proceed solely from the spiritual life and the feeling of love which it reveals " (p. 110). " The cross is the expiation for sins only because it is the cause of repentance to which remission is promised " (p. 127) ; and there is no other atonement than this repentance (p. 127). Jesus is, then, only in a modified sense our Saviour. Indeed, though He has done what He did supremely, what He did has no uniqueness about it — it is in kind no other than what many others than Himself have done and are still doing. " The work of Christ ceases, then, to be isolated and incomprehensible " (p. 131) ; " the sufferings and death of the righteous and of the good operate in the same way as the passion of Christ upon the conscience of the wicked ; . . . which signifies that they help to produce that state of repentance in which the forgiveness of sins and the work of salvation devised by the divine mercy may be realized " (p. 133). Not merely Paul then, who claims (Col. i. 24) a part in this work, " to the scandal of all future orthodoxies " (p. 133), but " all God's servants " have stood by the side of Jesus, as along with Him and in the same sense (though not in the same degree) in which He is, our saviours. Christianity thus emerges before us " as the religion of universal redemption by love " (p. 134).

The point that ultimately focuses our attention as we read Prof. Sabatier's exposition emerges in this last declaration. Christianity, we are told, is the religion " of universal redemption by love." *Whose* love? Even the old Socinianism would reply, as a matter of course,

God's love. Not so Prof. Sabatier. With him, it is everybody's love. He has, in a word, transmuted Christianity into bald Altruism; in his soteriological theory he has substituted the universe of sentient creatures for God and His Christ. Such, he tells us, " are the authentic data of the Christian consciousness ": and with this he would stop. The deeper basis he declines to probe. " But if the philosophic mind would go further and ask whence proceeds this supreme law of the moral world which has made self-denial, disinterested self-sacrifice, and brotherly love the ransom of sin and the means of its progressive destruction, we may well be led to confess our inability to answer " (p. 135). Perhaps, then, the reader may be excused if he takes leave to doubt whether there is any justification in reason or Scripture for representing " brotherly love " as " the ransom of sin " — especially if his own Christian consciousness (taught, no doubt, by the Scriptural declarations) declines to add its seal to it. If we are to rest on an *ipse dixit* we may without offense, perhaps, prefer the *ipse dixit* of our Lord Himself (Matt. xx. 28) and of the Apostle Paul (I Tim. ii. 6, Titus ii. 14) that our Lord is Himself our Ransom, because He has given His life for us.

Prof. Sabatier's new Christianity has too much the appearance of old infidelity to attract us. And when he tells us that it is only in some such form as this that Christianity can hope to persist in the conditions of modern culture — the watchword of which is " autonomy " — we should be dull indeed if we did not apprehend that the meaning of this, translated into terms of more brutal frankness, is simply that there is no place for Christianity in the modern world. " Altruism " — yes, we may wonderingly admit that altruism works and on a basis of pragmatism may find a place for itself, though we are at a loss for an ultimate justification of it to " reason." But " Christianity " — well, certainly as Christianity has been heretofore understood (except by the Socinians and Rationalists), there can be no place for it. Do not the eighteen centuries of this " heteronomic " Christianity which have been lived out in the world, then, give an indication that it too " works "? And are we so sure that it will not find a justification for itself in " reason " — provided that " reason " has not been hopelessly warped by too great hospitality to the assaults of Socinian and Rationalistic criticism? The fact is that the *ipse dixit* of Prof. Sabatier weighs no more than that of Faustus Socinus or of Julius Wegscheider, and we see no reason for listening in him to what we should pay no attention to in them.

Bible Problems and the New Material for their Solution.
By T. K. Cheyne, D. Litt., D.D. London: Williams & Norgate;
New York: G. P. Putnam's Sons. 1904.[1]

The "Crown Theological Library," of which this volume forms
the eighth number, is a new propaganda of what in our modern
nomenclature is miscalled "liberal" Christianity. The most of the
essays hitherto published in it are translations from the German
and French of characteristic papers by such men as Friedrich
Delitzsch, Harnack, Herrmann, Pfleiderer, Lobstein, Réville,
Sabatier. They give the series the appearance of an attempt to
naturalize in lands of English speech the variety of "liberal"
Christianity now so flourishing on the continent of Europe. An occasional paper of English authorship has, however, been included.
Among these certainly none can put in a better claim to either repre-
sentativeness or readableness than this sprightly essay by Dr.
Cheyne. Were it only on the score of literary delight no one ought
to miss anything which Dr. Cheyne writes. The fine patience with
which he bears with the intellectual backwardness of the uninstructed multitude whom he considers it his duty to correct; the
tender solicitude with which he chides his fellow laborers in the
field of Biblical criticism for their slowness of heart to believe all
that this prophet has spoken; the depth of the interest which he
exhibits in the religion which he makes it his business sedulously
to undermine; the carefully chosen phraseology with which he gloves
the hand with which he crushes; the childlike frankness with which
he confesses his own great attainments and achievements, and congratulates the Christian world on its possession in these confused
days of a guide to truth who unites within himself such clearness of
sight, loftiness of aim, courage and tenderness — is it not all most
engaging? When we add to these fascinations of manner the rich
residuum of facts which the prudent reader may always strain out
from Dr. Cheyne's imaginative constructions, and the stimulus
which he is sure to receive from contact with so widely-read a
scholar, it will be readily understood with what pleasure each succeeding publication of Dr. Cheyne's is received by a very broad
public.

The present essay is an expansion of a lecture delivered before
a society called "The Churchmen's Union," and is couched through-

[1] *The Princeton Theological Review*, iii. 1905, pp. 674–678.

out in the tone of a heart-to-heart talk from a churchman to his fellow churchmen, with whom he feels heartily at one in all that is of the deepest concern, though not perhaps insensible that it has fallen to him to become the leader of his brethren to a better outlook than may possibly at present obtain among them. He describes the task which he undertakes as " partly an exposition of new facts, partly a plea for a bolder style of Biblical criticism, justified and invited by those facts " (p. 5). This bolder Biblical criticism which he wishes to commend has its application not merely to the Old Testament, but also, and chiefly in this lecture, to the New. The new facts to which he appeals are the facts unearthed by recent Oriental archæology. In effect the lecture is a plea for the employment of the results of recent research in the field of Oriental archæology not merely to the elucidation but the reconstruction of the Biblical records — in both Testaments. Their bearing on the understanding of the Old Testament has been more fully recognized and therefore is here less fully entered upon: their bearing on the understanding of the New Testament it is therefore made the business of the greater part of the lecture to insist upon. " In short " — the lecturer himself thus sums up this part of his contention — " there are parts of the New Testament — in the Gospels, in the Epistles, and in the Apocalypse — which can only be accounted for by the newly-discovered fact of an Oriental syncretism, which began early and continued late. And the leading factor in this is Babylonian " (p. 19). The purpose of the lecture may be, therefore, not unfairly described as an attempt to popularize the application of Pan-Babylonism for " accounting for " the New Testament as well as for the Old — although, of course, " Pan-Babylonism " must be understood here in no narrow sense, but rather, in accordance with Dr. Cheyne's effort to do justice to the entire range of recent Oriental investigation, broadly enough to include the entirety of ancient Shemitic culture.

The contention of the lecture with respect to the Old Testament is, in brief, that " it is a fact, which cannot be argued out of existence, that we have recently acquired two new keys to the Old Testament, by which great problems are being brought nearer to a solution." One of these, he continues, " is furnished by a critical Assyriology, soon, we may hope, to be reinforced from South Arabia; the other, by a more methodical textual criticism " (p. 185). Why anyone should attempt " to argue out of existence " such a fact as is here asserted, we cannot ourselves imagine. No one doubts the value of " a critical Assyriology " to Old Testament interpretation; and certainly one of the chief desiderata of Old Testament criticism is " a more methodical textual criticism " — for nothing has brought greater or more deserved reproach upon the reigning school of Old Testament textual criticism than its subjective arbitrariness. Dr. Cheyne is simply confusing in his thought the recognition accorded to " the two keys to the Old Testament " he instances, and the reception given to the use which he himself has made of these keys. The heartiest recognition of the value of " a critical Assyriology " " reinforced from South Arabia " is entirely consistent with a most decisive rejection, for both method and result, of Dr. Cheyne's attempt to apply what he deems the results already attained by these branches of investigation to the problem of the interpretation of the Old Testament. And the most convinced conviction of the clamant need of a " more methodical textual criticism " of the Old Testament, happily, need not commit us to the acceptance of Dr. Cheyne's textual criticism of the Old Testament: it may, on the contrary, be the very reason why we cannot accept Dr. Cheyne's textual criticism, either in methods or in results. There is much that Dr. Cheyne says about the textual criticism of the Old Testament with which we find ourselves in full agreement. We agree, for example, that the ascertainment of the traditional text or texts and the ascertainment of the true text are two different problems, and ought to be kept separate. We agree, moreover, that the ascertaining of the texts that underlie the Massoretic and the Septuagint transmissions is the prior duty, to which succeeds the further duty of " approximating as closely as possible to the true text " that lies underneath both transmissions. We agree, moreover, that much of the current criticism of the text is arbitrary and subjective and can lead us nowhither. We feel no impulse to demur to the declaration that further criticism of the text must take " account of Winckler's discovery of Musri and Kûs in the inscriptions." But we should be sorry to think that this agreement in obvious principles would commit us to the acceptance of the new Bible which Dr. Cheyne has written on the basis of his Jerahmeel theory, or even of the new Psalms which he has produced by the help of a criticism which seems to us in its subjectivity and arbitrariness to surpass all that has gone before it — though that, of course, is saying a good deal.

The real purpose of the volume is to carry into the New Testament — somewhat *vi et armis*, it must be confessed — the " Pan-

Babylonism " which has already become an old story in Old Testament criticism. Its fundamental thesis is that " facts of Oriental archæology (including mythology) may hopefully be brought into connection with the New Testament " (p. 61) ; or, to be more specific, that " the form of the most peculiar and difficult New Testament statements can only be accounted for by the newly-discovered fact of the all-pervading influence of Oriental and more particularly Babylonian and Persian systems of belief " (p. 62). When stated in this broad manner there is nothing, of course, in principle to be objected to this thesis. The New Testament writers were men of their time, and wrote, of course, in language and modes of statement formed under the influence of the ideas of their time. It would be strange if there were discoverable in their thought and speech no traces of systems of belief which could with any show of right be called " all-pervading." The mischief lies in Dr. Cheyne's definition of what he calls " peculiar and difficult New Testament statements," and his determination of the line which divides the " form " of these statements from their " essence." The particular " peculiar and difficult statements " which he adduces as illustrations of his thesis are the New Testament accounts of " the Virgin-birth of Jesus Christ, His Descent into the nether world, His Resurrection, and His Ascension." As the result of his discussion he suggests that " on the ground of facts supplied by archæology, it is plausible to hold that all these " " four forms of Christian belief " " arose out of a pre-Christian sketch of the life, death, and exaltation of the expected Messiah, itself ultimately derived from a widely current mythic tradition respecting a solar deity " (p. 128).

We must observe the slight difference in language between this last-cited proposition and the one formerly cited. There Dr. Cheyne spoke of the possibility of accounting for the " form " of certain " New Testament *statements* " from the influence of certain Oriental beliefs: now he speaks of these Oriental myths supplying an account of the " form " of certain " Christian *beliefs*." It is, in fact, the latter and far more serious proposition which his arguments are directed to justify. His contention is not that the New Testament writers tended to express the facts of the virgin-birth, the descent into hell, the resurrection, and the ascension of our Lord in language which had been formerly employed to express certain Oriental myths, and which therefore preserved a certain coloring derived from them. It is rather that Christians had already, when the New Testament was written, come through the influence of these myths to express their fundamental ideas in terms of a virgin-birth, descent into hell, resurrection, and ascension. The fundamental ideas so expressed, therefore, have in themselves no implication of a virgin-birth, descent into hell, resurrection, ascension as actually occurring: these things all belong to the mythical form and are to be accounted for, not as things that really happened and are therefore recounted in the narrative, but as modes of conception inherited from immemorial mythological stories, running back, for the most part, to Babylon for their original forms. What the real nature is of " the essential Christian truths " which are enshrined in these mythical forms as in their " suitable caskets," and to which the faith " of the Christian is pledged," Dr. Cheyne indicates to us only with brevity — his main object in this lecture being to show whence the forms were derived, not what the substance is. In his most succinct statement he tells us that " the chief of them are, — the uniqueness of the personality of the Lord Jesus, and the immense worth of His act of absolute self-sacrifice; then, by inference, the indestructibleness of His personality, its perpetual redemptive capacity, and its identity with that manward aspect of the Divine Nature, so full of mingled grandeur and compassion, which, by early efforts of theological thought, acquired the names of the Messiah, the Son of God, the Word of God " (p. 129). It is only (or at least chiefly) these few starved and hunger-bitten dogmas that he recognizes as the substance of those " forms " of Christian belief.

Dr. Cheyne, of course, tells us that there is nothing disparaging to the Christian beliefs in his theory. He means, of course, the Christian beliefs he has just enumerated as " the essential Christian truths " enshrined in these mythological caskets. He would scarcely say that there is nothing in his theory disparaging to the Christian's beliefs of a virgin-birth, descent into hell, resurrection, and ascension for Christ. At least those who will read, even with the best will, his equation of the Messiah and Michael and Marduk, and of the virgin-mother with the mother who was virgin only in the sense that she was not a wife, will scarcely credit that Dr. Cheyne supposes that there is nothing in his theory disparaging to the Christian belief in the virgin-birth of our Lord and Saviour. But these beliefs are in his theory not Christian beliefs, but only the forms in which the real Christian beliefs have become enshrined as men have sought to give them expression, limited as they were by the modes of expression accessible or familiar to them. If any chance still to look upon such beliefs as themselves " Christian beliefs," " essential Christian truths," which enter into the very fabric of Christianity (as all of the Lord's apostles did, and the Lord Himself as reported by them), why then, of course, he must recognize that the Christianity of which they are essential parts is shattered by Dr. Cheyne's theory. The most interesting part of Dr. Cheyne's theory thus comes to be the conception of the essential truths of Christianity — of the nature, that is, of the Christian religion — which it embodies and, if it should prove to be sound, necessitates. These essential truths — we have already enumerated them — constitute in effect Dr. Cheyne's Confession of Faith. Do they constitute also Christianity? Certainly not — as Christianity has been hitherto understood, whether by its founders, or its propagators, or its adherents. The upshot of Dr. Cheyne's theory, then, is that it offers us a new Christianity — a Christianity independent of such old forms of belief as the virgin-birth, the descent into hell, the resurrection, the ascension.

Is this new Christianity an improvement on the old Christianity? That is the great question. That is to say, for Dr. Cheyne. It is not an important question for the rest of us. For judging by the evidence that is here presented for it, it is not apt to become the Christianity of very many others, at least of those who are used to give a reason for the faith that is in them. But Dr. Cheyne's main interest, one would think, since this has become his Christianity, would naturally center in the query whether this is an adequate Christianity. And one would think that, trained as he has been as a " Churchman," Dr. Cheyne might well cherish serious doubt on that point. The new Christianity he offers us is certainly not the Christianity one would expect from a good Churchman — whose professed creed is the Thirty-nine Articles, incorporating as they do " the Three Creeds "; and whose ordinary vehicle of public worship is the Book of Common Prayer. Of course, the modes of expression — and even the conceptions expressed — found in these documents may also be represented as mere " forms," quite as well as the modes of expression — and conceptions expressed — found in the Scriptures. But two questions will arise here — one for us, and one for Dr. Cheyne. We should ask where this interpretation of modes of expression and conceptions expressed as mere " forms " — husks concealing a kernel — is to end? Whether it may not be ultimately applied even to the essential truths of Christianity which Dr. Cheyne himself still enumerates as such? Dr. Cheyne should ask, and one would think should ask seriously, whether, if his representation be true, Socinianism has not at length won its tardy victory? For after all Dr. Cheyne's new Christianity is just old Socinianism.

THE BIBLE, ITS ORIGIN AND NATURE. The Bross Lectures, 1904. By the Reverend MARCUS DODS, D.D. New York: Charles Scribner's Sons. 1905.[1]

BY THE munificence of the late William Bross, a considerable sum of money has been placed in the hands of the " Trustees of Lake Forest University," the proceeds of which they are charged to use to create a literature of exposition and defense of the Christian religion. It is specified, among other particular objects that should be sought under this general commission, that an effort is to be made " to demonstrate the divine origin and authority of the Christian Scriptures." It was quite natural, therefore, that among the earlier works called out under the stimulation of this bequest, there should be one on the origin and nature of the Bible. It may be doubted, however, whether Dr. Dods's lectures are calculated to meet perfectly the expectation aroused by language which speaks of a demonstration of the divine origin and authority of the Christian Scriptures. Dr. Dods, of course, believes that the Scriptures are a product of a movement of life and thought which originated in a divine impulse, and that there is much that is divine, and therefore authoritative, in them — that their main burden and central message, in fact, is divine. But around this central core, he believes that much that is human in origin and far from authoritative in effect has been woven like a widely extended web, or shall we say like the coma of a comet that surrounds, partly transmitting, partly obscuring, the light of the nucleus.

In this Dr. Dods is but a respresentative of a general tendency which is at the moment very active in Christendom. Men everywhere, deeply affected by the assault which has been made in our

[1] *The Princeton Thelogical Review,* iv. 1906, pp. 109–115.

day, perhaps with unexampled vigor and subtlety, upon the Christian system as a divine revelation, and especially upon the Christian Scriptures as the vehicle of that revelation, have sought to ease the situation by casting away what they have deemed the husk in the hope of saving what appeared to them the kernel. They have commended to us, therefore, a new and reduced Christianity, documented in a new and reduced body of Scriptures. Dr. Dods is by no means an extreme representative of this tendency. But *gradus non mutant speciem*. In this book also he appears before us as the " concessive " apologist, the " mediating " theologian, and begs to put in our hands a Bible, which, in his view, is much more rationally conceived in its origin and nature than the old Bible was, and therefore, in his opinion, may be much more successfully defended. We certainly shall not deny that a certain measure of ease may be purchased for the defender by simply declining to defend; although it is not always certain that, so long as what we consider the citadel is to be defended, its defense is made really easier by the surrender of what we may deem outposts but which may prove to be approaches. We gladly recognize that Dr. Dods would fain defend what both he and we look upon as the citadel. But we find it impossible to admit that what he would yield as indefensible outposts are either indefensible or can be yielded safely or loyally. We rejoice that we have a fuller and richer Christianity than Dr. Dods feels bound to proclaim, and Scriptures far more divine in their origin and nature than he is inclined to admit. We believe that the defense of this richer Christianity and these more completely divine Scriptures is not only possible but imperative, if we would preserve Christianity in the world. And we believe their defense to be logically easier than that of the lowered views which Dr. Dods would commend to us. We do not believe that half-truths are more easily defended than whole ones; and we look upon the " concessive apologetics " which Dr. Dods represents as inimical to Christianity, and all the more to be firmly resisted because its assault is more insidious and therefore more dangerous than open attack.

Ask Dr. Dods what the Scriptures are and he will tell you, A body of books which we set apart from all others and assign a place of supremacy because they " are all in direct connection with God's historical revelation which culminated in Christ " (p. 23). Like all Dr. Dods's definitions (it is inherent in the position he occupies) this is — inadequate. If we should say the Bible is the documentation of God's self-revelation for the purpose of human salvation, that would be a more adequate description of the internal characteristic of the Scriptures — expressing, indeed, their unifying principle. But the plain fact is, to put it in briefest terms, that the Scriptures are the *corpus juris* of Christians imposed on them as such by competent authority. This competent authority is proximately the apostles, acting as Christ's authoritative agents in founding His Church. Thus apostolicity (in the sense of apostolic imposition, not authorship) is and always has been the principle of canonicity. There is no gain in blinking this plain fact, and seeking to transmute it into some more immanent principle. The Christian Church is a manufactured article; it was founded; and its character was impressed on it and its law imposed on it by its founders. Of course we may ask why the apostles imposed just this particular body of books on the churches which they established as Christ's authorized agents in founding His Church. And doubtless, in pursuing this inquiry, we shall ultimately reach the principle that these books stand together as constituting the " canon " which the apostles gave the Church, because they constitute as a whole the documentation of God's revelation of Himself for salvation. But nothing could be more confusing than to confound this internal principle of unity with the external principle of canonicity, though good men, as, for example, Luther, have in every age been guilty of the confusion — with the most unfortunate results. Throughout its whole history authentication as God's law for His Church has been the proximate ground of the reception of the canon, although, of course, throughout the whole history of its formation organic participation in the revelatory process has been the principle of the constitution of the canon. And it is on the same ground that the canon must continue to be received if received at all. It is a grave error to represent this rational procedure as a desertion of the principle which governed the fathers of the Reformed Churches. They, as little as we, sought to determine the " canon " — which is a matter of history — on the basis of the *testimonium Spiritus Sancti* — which is a matter of experience: on that basis is determined not the " canon " but " the Word of God." From his standpoint Dr. Dods very naturally finds the method of the Reformed doctors a little confusing: but the confusion is his, not theirs. They treated the Scriptures as a unit because the Scriptures are a unitary apostolic

book; and they then asked if this book " found them." Discovering
that it did, they recognized it as " the Word of God." Of course, Dr.
Dods may say that apostolicity cannot justly be claimed for all
these books. That is a matter of opinion, concerning which we
differ with him and concerning which the fathers of the Reformed
Churches differed with him. That the body of the apostles imposed
a Bible on the Church is not disputable; that this Bible contained
all the books, and no others, which our present Bible contains we
consider historically substantiated: that this collection as a whole
is " the Word of God " is experimentally verifiable. This strikes
us as a much more reasonable method of dealing with the matter
than Dr. Dods's fluctuating way, which involves a confusion between the historical question of what constitutes the canon and the
vital one of what is the Word of God to me — analogous to the
common confusion of the Scriptures as the *principium cognoscendi*
and the Scriptures as the means of grace.

Let us, however, revert to the primary definition which Dr. Dods
gives of the Bible as constituted of books which we set apart from
all others and give a place of supremacy because they " are all in
direct connection with God's historical revelation which culminated
in Christ." What is to be observed here is that all that Dr. Dods
can say of Scripture is that it is " in direct connection with " revelation: and that the adjective " historical " which he attached to
" revelation " is not to be read as distinctive, but as descriptive.
That is to say, Dr. Dods believes in no other than a " historical "
revelation; what he teaches is that God reveals Himself only in the
sequence of historical events, while Scripture is only one product
of this revelation, working through human minds. The theory, as
will at once be perceived, is that which was given great vogue in the
middle of the past century by the attractive presentation of it by
Richard Rothe, and which has been more recently commended, with
some caution but much earnestness, to English readers by the late
Prof. A. B. Bruce. As commonly presented, its essence is that it
confines revelation to the series of divine acts in history, while it
treats inspiration as the correlate of revelation, or, as Dr. Dods
prefers to phrase it, its " complement " (p. 97) — the action of the
Divine Spirit on the human spirit by virtue of which the latter
" perceives, appreciates, accepts, and in certain cases records the
revelation of God." In this view the Bible is no part of the revelation (though why the production of the Scriptures may not be con-

ceived as an element in the series of the redemptive acts of God
it is hard to perceive), but is simply its record; and its record,
so far as appears, in purely human strength — apart, that is, from
the effects of that so-called inspiration by which in Dr. Dods's
view men are enabled sympathetically to receive and possibly to
record revelation. " The essential elements in revelation," explains
Dr. Dods, " have been understood and interpreted by men." " In the
Bible we have that selected revelation which inspired men have accepted and seen fit to record." " God has revealed Himself, and the
leading facts of this revelation are recorded for us in the Bible, and
from these facts we can gather what God wishes us to know about
Him and how He wishes us to think of Him " (pp. 96, 97). In other
words, all that we commonly know as " direct revelation " is denied
or retired to the background: revelation is made to consist in an immanent action of God through man by virtue of which a series of
events are produced which are then perceived and interpreted by
human spirits prepared for their task by a corresponding action of
God upon them enabling them to see and appreciate these events
aright. The latter divine activity is then called inspiration. Inspiration has, therefore, no direct concern with the record; it is
distinctly not graphical but personal.

We shall not pause to point out how little support this construction has in the letter of Scripture itself. Scripture represents revelation, normative revelation, as through the medium of speech, or at
least in a mode best represented by speech. " Thus saith the Lord "
is its typical expression. And Scripture assigns inspiration not to
the person but to the written product: to it, it is " every Scripture "
— or, as it is probable we should translate it, " the entire Scripture " — that is given by inspiration of God. Let us pause only
to call attention to the lowered supernaturalism of the theory; and
also to the inconsequence of the reasoning by which it is supported.
" What has been the method of revelation? " asks Dr. Dods. " Our
answer to this question," he replies, " depends upon our idea of
God. If we believe in God as immanent in the world and man, then
we shall necessarily believe that God reveals Himself through
human sensitiveness to the Spiritual and inquiry after Him. If we
believe in God as merely transcendent, we shall think of Him as
moving man from without " (pp. 78–79). Now, why has Dr. Dods —
shall we say subintroduced? — the little word " merely " into the
last clause, by the introduction of which the exact parallelism of this

clause with the preceding one is broken? In point of fact, " merely " must stand in both clauses if they are to be taken, as they are treated here, as true disjunctives. And, in point of fact, Dr. Dods actually reasons throughout the volume on a presupposition which tends to treat God as " merely " immanent and as operating in the world solely " through human sensitiveness to the Spiritual " — though we thankfully recognize that in dealing with the miraculous element in the Gospels a higher note is struck. Indeed, he at once goes on to say in our present passage: " In the one case revelation will be internal and natural; in the other it will be external and super-natural," — and proceeds to point out that " belief in the immanence of God tends to abolish the distinction between the natural and the supernatural." It is this tendency, showing itself everywhere, which leads Dr. Dods to pare down the supernatural character of the Bible; it is it which lies at the root of his denial of the infallibility of the Bible — or of its " literal infallibility " as he elects to call it, in the effort to save for the Bible, even on his theory of its origin and nature, a sort of infallibility in a single sphere.

How inadequately Dr. Dods thinks of the supernatural element in the Bible may be observed as well as elsewhere at the point where, in an attempt to break the force of the Bible doctrine of inspiration, he cries out with emphasis (in opposition to the direct testimony of Scripture) that it is not the book but " the *man* who is inspired " (p. 117). But where does Dr. Dods suppose that this man that is inspired came from? He apparently imagines that he is given by the world — or by himself — and that God comes to him, finds him as he is, and does the best He can with so poor and inadequate an instrument. It is " with all his natural powers and idiosyncrasies " that " he becomes the organ of the Spirit " — as if, *therefore*, the product would necessarily be different from what the Spirit might have made it if only He had had a better instrument! " Inspiration does not lift the inspired person out of all his limitations, but uses him as he is, and all his faculties as they are," he asserts, with no pause to consider, that all these natural powers and idiosyncrasies, all these faculties and capacities, that make the man, are them-selves, down to the last one of them, of God; that the man himself is what God made him and what God made him precisely for this end, that through him He might give this precise word to men; that God the almighty ruler of the world does not have to put up with the best man He can find and agree to abide the result, but first forms the man to suit His purpose, and then uses him to accomplish His purpose, and so produces through him precisely what He wills. It is, ultimately, this defective sense of the divine, even in its immanent working, which lies at the root of our modern tendency to depress the supernatural; and the evidences of it face us everywhere. Thus, for example, we find Dr. Dods using such language as this: " God was compelled " (p. 85), " It was useless for Christ to die until . . ." (p. 86), — as if God were under the domination of men and needed to wait on man and walk warily lest He should get beyond His tether. It is amazing that any thinking man could imagine that by such shallow expedients as this language embodies, the great problem may be solved of why God Almighty operates in this world by process. The current employment of such language is the saddest indication of how far the men of our day have lost the vision of God, and of how prone they are to operate in their thinking with the will of man as really the prime factor of importance in the world's history. It surely is no wonder, therefore, that, even though but a little under the influence of this modern blight, Dr. Dods should show himself throughout these lectures working under the fatal confusion of man's thought of God with God's revelation of Himself, and that he should accordingly be continually treating the record as the record of how man (under whatever divine impulses) had come to conceive of God rather than of how God from time to time revealed Himself to man.

We have written somewhat desultorily, but we hope we have made it clear that the fountain of Dr. Dods's inadequate conception of Scripture as the documentation of God's revelation of Himself for salvation, lies in his inadequate conception of the modes of the divine operation in the world — in a word, in his chariness with regard to the supernatural. He wishes apparently as little supernatural a book as he can, as a Christian man, manage to get along with. The writers of Scripture, it is undeniable, held the diametrically opposite view. There was no antecedent opposition to the supernatural in their minds. They lived in a supernaturalistic atmosphere. They saw God in everything and above and over everything. And they give us a frankly supernatural book. Dr. Dods says that it is not the book but the man that is inspired: Paul says that every, or all, Scripture is God-breathed. Dr. Dods says that much of Scripture is of little or no spiritual value; Paul says it all is profitable to make the man of God perfect. Dr. Dods says that whole stretches of it are untrustworthy for historical or other not directly spiritual purposes, and no part of it is untouched by human fallibility; the writers of the New Testament say as the end of all strife, " It is written! " and Jesus Himself says that when we adduce Scripture we adduce what cannot " be broken." It is possible that in a matter of fact like the infallibility of Scripture, however, Scripture will not, on Dr. Dods's view, be implicitly trusted. We must at least ask, however, how he will practically get along with his fallible Scriptures. He gives his strength to proving that, fallible as they are, they yet preserve a true picture of Christ, and that Christ, once given us, becomes the criterion of Scripture. Now, of course, this is the main thing. The Scriptures exist to give us Christ; and when they have brought us to Christ they have performed their fundamental function. No human being who knows the Scriptures and has by them come to Christ will deny that. But what Christ is this that we shall get from our fallible Scriptures? We know the Christ which the infallible Scriptures give us: and every lineament of that divine-human form is precious to us. Shall we be able to retain this form in all its lineaments on the basis of a fallible Scripture? How much of it goes, with the infallibility of Scripture? Nothing essential, says Dr. Dods: and we might conceivably be willing to content ourselves with the Christ he preserves for us. But what about the Christ that Wernle gives us? or Wrede? or Oscar Holtzmann? or Auguste Sabatier? or Réville? or Brandt? or Harnack? Which Christ of the fallible Scriptures shall we be ultimately forced to put up with? Will He become to us at length only a vague figure who lived in Galilee nineteen centuries ago and made a religious impression on His followers of such depth that it has propagated itself down to our day? And when we have got our Christ from Scripture, what Scripture will that Christ in turn give us? The Christ the Scriptures as they stand give us, is the Christ that said of Scripture, " It cannot be broken." Everywhere throughout the whole extent of the Scriptural representation, it is this attitude that He holds to Scripture. It seems quite clear that this is not the Christ that Dr. Dods would have us receive from Scripture; or at least, if we receive Him, it is clear that he would not have us accept His Scriptures at His estimate. It appears that we are to estimate Scripture not by His teaching, then, but by His " standard." That He was conscious of no incongruity of Scripture with His standard — even that is not to weigh decisively with us.

We are to do our own judging: we are easily to reject all that does not approve itself to our estimate as measuring up to Him. It may seem to some of us, indeed, that we thus come into grave danger of discrediting the very Christ we have received. But as we have received Him only from a fallible Scripture, perhaps we may be justified in adjusting Him when received to our own ideals. Many pursue this method. But in that case what warrant, other than our own subjective conception, have we for the Christ we finally adopt and make the criterion of Scripture? And if we are to make the Scriptures that give us the Christ and then make the Christ which gives us back the Scriptures — it will be hard if we do not ultimately find ourselves arrived at the goal for which we set out.

Subjectivism is, in truth, the gulf into which all our modern theorizers inevitably fall. Dr. Dods no more escapes it than the others. What he really gives us is therefore an ideal sketch — a " program," is it not, that they call it? — of what he would like to be the principle of the canon, the nature of revelation, the function of inspiration, the extent of infallibility, and the like; of what he would find it commodious, in accordance with his preconceived opinions as to God and the world, to hold and teach and defend on these matters. For what is really the principle of the canon, the nature and method of revelation, the effect of inspiration, the infallibilty of Scripture, — for the facts, hard or comforting as we may esteem them — we must go elsewhere. That what Dr. Dods could wish were the facts approaches much nearer to what they are than what they are represented as being by many others, sharers with him in the modern prepossessions against the supernatural — though adopting them more exclusively or developing them more consequently than he — we very gladly recognize. Dr. Dods still believes in the general historical trustworthiness of the Gospels; and, although unwarrantably assailing their trustworthiness in many details (on, let us say it frankly, very frivolous grounds), yet sturdily and successfully defends the essential historical soundness of their narrative, and especially the trustworthiness of the portraiture of our Lord which they present. Dr. Dods even believes in and defends the reality of the miraculous element in the life of Christ as it is depicted by the evangelists. These are great things to say of one who is so much affected by the modern spirit which, as he himself tells us, is swayed by nothing more profoundly than " the presupposition of the incredibility of miracles " (p. 134), and to which the presence of a supernatural element in a narrative is enough to condemn it at once as unhistorical. We rejoice that Dr. Dods would preserve to us at least a supernatural Redeemer, even if he draws back before too supernatural a Bible. We could wish, of course, that he had gone on and done as much justice to the supernaturalism of revelation and inspiration and the resultant Scriptures as he has to the supernaturalism of the person and work of our Lord. As it is, he inevitably seems to us to have handled these matters far too lightly and to have presented only, as he himself remarks of Prof. Huxley in a similar case, " another demonstration that the ablest man may sometimes be satisfied with touching but the surface of a subject."

THE CHRISTIAN DOCTRINE OF SALVATION. By GEORGE BARKER STEVENS, Ph.D., D.D., LL.D. New York: Charles Scribner's Sons. 1905.[1]

DR. STEVENS, although since 1895 Professor of Systematic Theology in Yale Divinity School, has hitherto been known to the wider public chiefly as a writer upon themes of Biblical Theology, the fruit, doubtless, of his studies while he was Professor of New Testament Criticism and Interpretation in the same University (" The Pauline Theology," 1892; " The Johannine Theology," 1894; " The Theology of the New Testament," 1899; " The Teaching of Jesus," 1901). There was no doubt a little volume of not very great significance called " Doctrine and Life " published in 1895. And more to the point, there was always a strong dogmatic tone in the professed Biblical studies, and there were always intruded into them not merely a dogmatic method, but large elements of purely dogmatic discussion. And as Dr. Stevens has been very much of a dogmatist from the beginning, so he has from the beginning been very much the dogmatist he exhibits himself in the present volume. From his earliest publication the same tendencies of thought which meet us here in their full flower were already present. Already in the volume on " The Pauline Theology " (1892), for example, the divine righteousness is resolved into the divine love, and the doc-

trines of " original sin " and " satisfaction " are rejected. Even the
same methods of argumentation and the same insufficiency in the
statement of opposing views which characterize the present volume
are already noticeable in that. We must confess to some surprise,
therefore, at the chorus of astonishment which has greeted the appearance of this volume. Doubtless, Dr. Stevens' theological conceptions have somewhat ripened during the interval which separates
it from its predecessors, and in the process of his special studies
for it, but this is very much the kind of book on " the Atonement "
which any reader of his former works should have expected to
receive from Dr. Stevens.

We shall not profess to have found the volume pleasant reading.
The polemic tone in which it is cast from beginning to end, strident
from the commencement, finishes by becoming rasping. It is not
obvious that the opinions thus endlessly controverted have been
sympathetically appreciated. It is not even obvious that the trouble
has been taken thoroughly to understand them. Certainly they are
not always stated in their completeness; and they are not seldom
refuted in mere caricature. The reader acquires an unpleasant feeling as he proceeds in the volume that the language of scorn, rising
even to vituperation, is now and again depended upon to do the
work of argument. Dr. Stevens does not like the doctrine of " penal
satisfaction." Not liking it, he is entitled to argue against it, and
(if he can) to refute it. It may be questioned, however, whether its
refutation is advanced by declaring that it makes God a Shylock
(p. 410) whose most distinguishing characteristic is " his appetite
for revenge " (p. 331 *et seq.*). And it seems more than questionable
whether this procedure is justified by the open declaration that the
advocates of such a doctrine are past arguing with. Take, for example, this sentence: " It seems to me that one who can adopt the principle which underlies the penal theory of our Lord's sufferings —
that God is so just that He cannot forgive the guilty until He has
first punished the innocent — thereby renders himself inaccessible
to all considerations of equity and morality " (p. 383). In Dr.
Stevens' view sin itself, in its most complete development, does not
reduce man to so hopeless a condition (p. 316): he remains always
accessible to appeal and open to conviction. It is inconceivable that
he really considers his Christian opponents in worse case than the
worst of sinners. His language is the language of simple vituperation.

The book is laid out, on lines usual in such treatises, in three parts. These parts would commonly be described as occupied successively with laying the Biblical foundation, tracing the historical development, erecting the dogmatic construction. These descriptions appear, however, to apply to Dr. Stevens' three parts only in a somewhat modified sense.

The discussion of the First Part (pp. 1–135), for example, seems devoted less to laying firmly a Biblical basis for a doctrine of Atonement than to removing all Biblical basis for such a doctrine. In Dr. Stevens' view there are almost as many Biblical doctrines of Atonement as there are Biblical writers: which is as much as to say that there is no Biblical doctrine at all. He does not deny that the " theory of penal satisfaction " is taught in the Bible. He intimates rather that it is taught by Paul; although when he expounds Paul's teaching for us, it takes in his hands much more of the appearance of the governmental theory (p. 60). He seems not very averse to allowing even that it may be implied in certain sayings attributed to our Lord in even the Synoptic narrative. But on that very account he doubts the authenticity of these sayings. And he does not feel bound to believe all that Paul taught. He is a modern man, and can no more " think in terms of late Jewish theology " (as Paul did) than he " can think in terms of pre-Socratic philosophy " (p. 74). He claims the right, then, to distinguish " between the specifically Christian and the characteristically Jewish or rabbinic in Paul " (p. 75). Making this distinction, he ascribes Paul's doctrine of a substitutive atonement, of a " propitiation of God " (p. 61, note), to his Jewish inheritance; and rejects it from the possibilities of thought. " The men of to-day can no more appropriate the outward forms of Paul's Jewish thought respecting expiation than they can adopt the cosmology or demonology which he derived from the same source " (p. 74). " What is Pauline? What is Scriptural? Is every conception of which Paul made use a necessary part of his religion, and of ours, — physical death due to sin, our sin due to Adam's, Christ's speedy, visible return to earth? As I have frequently intimated, it seems to me that no fruitful investigation of the beginnings of Christian theology can be made without recognizing the distinction between the contingent thought-forms of the first Christian thinkers and the essential religious life and fundamental Christian certainties concerning God and the experience of salvation which they were seeking to expound and to philosophize " (p. 131). The upshot of his discussion

of " the Biblical basis of the doctrine," therefore, is to free himself
from the trammels of much of the Biblical teaching. Only the teaching of Jesus, it seems, is to be implicitly trusted: and that, not the
entire teaching attributed to Jesus, but only the Synoptic tradition
of His teaching: and not even that in its completeness, but only
so much of it as Dr. Stevens' criticism spares.

In the historical section of his treatise (pp. 136–261) Dr. Stevens
does not attempt " to write the history of the doctrine of salvation
in the Church "; but quite properly confines himself to outlining
" the principal types of theory which have obtained in Christian
thought regarding the specific problem of atonement." These types
of theory he conceives to be fundamentally three, which may be
roughly designated by the names of the doctrine of " Satisfaction "
and the " Governmental " and " Moral Influence " theories. The
first two of these he discusses in their founders, Anselm and Grotius,
and in their modern representatives of various kinds, under the
names of " modern penal satisfaction theories " and " modern ethical
satisfaction theories." He devotes no separate chapter to the
founders or early representatives of the Moral Influence theory,
but, adverting to Abelard and the Socinians only incidentally in
the chapters devoted respectively to Anselm and Grotius, reserves
what he has to say of this third type of theory to a final chapter
on " modern ' subjective ' theories." It cannot be said that the
several theories which come up for discussion in this series are dealt
with dispassionately. The tone is severely critical throughout; and
the object seems to be not so much to estimate the elements of truth
discoverable in each as to clear the way for a passionate advocacy
of the Moral Influence theory. The instability of the compromising
Grotian theories is recognized (see especially p. 531), and the real
opponent of the " ' subjective ' theories " is perceived to be the doctrine of Satisfaction. To discredit this doctrine becomes, thus, the
chief purpose of these chapters. So engrossed is Dr. Stevens with
this task that he does not stop to state the doctrine in its completeness before he refutes it; and thus falls into a carping habit which
expends its criticisms upon isolated and, we must add, often misconceived elements of the doctrine. He is aware that although
Anselm struck out the fundamental statement of the doctrine, it did
not come to its rights until it received restatement at the hands of
the post-Reformation divines. This has not led him, however, to any
careful exposition of the doctrine as taught by the post-Reformation

divines. He prefers to close the matter with a scornful allusion to " that period of Protestant scholasticism and hyperorthodoxy," and its " provincial extravagances," which " have no right to the name of orthodoxy in the comprehensive use of that term " (p. 252). The result is that his polemic is vitiated by its lack of comprehension. The most astonishing oversights are committed; the doctrine attacked is scored for lacking elements which really lie at its very core; and the whole polemic misses its mark and degenerates into an amusing, perhaps, but certainly most ineffectual criticism of detached modes of expression. Though the doctrine of Satisfaction is rooted in the infinite love of God, Dr. Stevens, in criticism of it, elaborately argues out in opposition to it the necessary origin of the saving work of God in His love (p. 246), and ostentatiously compliments an advocate of it here and there as " damagingly admitting " this common proclamation of the whole body of its adherents. Though Christ's " active obedience " enters as an essential element into the doctrine — as even F. A. B. Nitzsch (" Lehrbuch der evangelischen Dogmatik," 1892, pp. 468, 484), to whom he defers much, would have told him — he blames the doctrine for a total neglect of the whole side of Christ's work which consists in His sinless and holy life in the world. Though it is of the very essence of the doctrine that Christ purchased by His Satisfaction both release from the dominion of sin and a title to holiness, together with the only prevalent instrument of sanctification, the Holy Spirit, he reproaches it with not correlating justification and sanctification in a vital and adequate way. Though the peculiarity of the doctrine of Satisfaction among attempts to explain the nature of the work of Christ lies in its conception of the reconciliation wrought by Him as mutual, he assaults it as making nothing of the attractive power of the manifestation of the love of God in Christ, the force of the demonstration of God's righteousness made on the cross, the moving influence of the perfect example of our Lord's holy life. In a word, Dr. Stevens is in such haste to thrust the doctrine of the Satisfaction of Christ out of the way, that he does not stay to grasp the doctrine itself, but is ever hastily thrusting aside something else which his hands have seized. The consequence is that naturally he is never satisfied that he has thrust it aside. He tells us over and over again that it is all over with the doctrine of Satisfaction; and yet he is ever returning to slay afresh the slain. He cannot get done with it. And finally he seeks his comfort in the assertion that it never needed any slaying anyhow: it long since died of itself. " It has been, at no period, entirely unchallenged; it has had its rivals and its critics, until now, at last, there is scarcely a reputable theologian anywhere who ventures to come forward in its defense " (p. 251). He calls F. A. B. Nitzsch and private letters from Kaftan and Ménégoz to witness that it has disappeared from the European Continent, and adds his own assurance that it has equally disappeared from Britain and America — at least in " noteworthy " publications (p. 187). He declares that, " for better or for worse, this theory is moribund " (p. 187), is " obsolescent " (p. 260), and finds practically no place " in the literature of investigation, in the theological monographs and doctrinal systems which are attracting attention and exercising widespread influence to-day " (p. 261). In short, he is continually assuring his readers that the doctrine of Satisfaction is already out of the way, and yet he is perpetually returning to the charge and elaborately refuting it. Is it not unseemly thus to hack a corpse? And is it not strange that as the book comes to its close (p. 531) this poor dead theory — and by this time, one would think, not merely safely dead but sufficiently mangled — is still set forth as living, between which and the Moral Influence theory alone " lies the choice " (" forever irreconcilable theories "); and the reader is recommended — if he is not convinced by this volume that the Moral Influence theory is the truest and most satisfactory — to go on and read Dr. W. N. Clarke's " Outline of Christian Theology " and Dr. T. V. Tymms's " The Christian Idea of Atonement " ? It sounds very much as if the weary combatant would say, " I have done my best to kill this thing; but it won't stay killed: now I lay down my sword " (shall we say " my hacked sword " ?) " and leave the task to my fellow combatants: perhaps they may succeed where I have failed."

Throughout the whole Third Part of the volume (pp. 262–536) — which is entitled " Constructive Development of the Doctrine " — the polemic element continues to occupy a large space. But in the fourteen chapters which constitute this part an attempt is made to elaborate and commend the special form of the Moral Influence theory to which the work is consecrated. This task involves a survey of a great number of the topics of theology; and they are expounded — if we may be permitted to use a general term in a general sense — in what must be spoken of generally as the Socinian sense. The doctrines of historical Christianity are, in other words, reduced, here, at least " to their lowest terms." We thankfully recognize that there are many expressions scattered through the discussion which show that this is not Dr. Stevens' inheritance, and that he has not adjusted himself perfectly to the lowered views of the doctrines which he is, nevertheless, in the main, commending. He can even criticize a treatise on the Atonement on the ground of its want of " scripturalness " (p. 243). If he objects to Anselm's phrase which ascribes to God " outraged dignity," he can himself speak of His " affronted love " (p. 275). If he scouts the analysis which distinguishes between justification and sanctification, he yet claims its benefit in distinguishing between the forgiveness of sin and the removal of its moral consequences (pp. 355–356): " Forgiveness is but one factor in salvation "; " the pardon of sin is never conceived in Scripture in separation from the cleansing, life-bestowing action of the divine Spirit "; " forgiveness is a name for the beginning or restoration of right personal relations," etc. If the conception of guilt is minimized almost to the vanishing-point, it yet is explicitly retained (pp. 319, 337, 355) — although race-guilt is denied and no guilt is allowed to stand in the way of acceptance with God. Nevertheless it must be regretfully allowed that Dr. Stevens ' theology is of a piece — as indeed all theologies must be, since, as Dr. Orr has tellingly pointed out afresh (" God's Image in Man," 1905, pp. 7, 8, 12, 13, 23), it is impossible to hold the Socinian doctrine of Atonement and not hold along with it a Socinianizing doctrine of everything else — of God, of sin, of the person of Christ, of the application of salvation.

We are not asserting that Dr. Stevens " does not believe in the deity of Christ." But we are constrained to admit that no reader of the chapter in this volume on " The Personality of the Saviour " could venture to affirm that it is taught in it. There seems to us in this chapter (we trust we are mistaken) a notable falling off from the position (already somewhat unsatisfactory) in his " Theology of the New Testament." There, Dr. Stevens represented " the metaphysical Sonship," the " ontological deity " of Jesus, rather as an inference we draw from the ethical facts or the data of our Lord's manifestation than as an element of His own consciousness: but he at least expressed his own earnest conviction of its reality. Here, although we are told that " the divinity of Christ is presupposed in the Christian view of His Saviourhood " (p. 298), we are also bidden to magnify " the moral and religious significance of His person " and be careless what " its metaphysical background " may be. Men may have " tried to exalt Him by ascribing to Him all manner of metaphysical characteristics and powers," but what " the Gospels place in the forefront of their portraiture is just His moral completeness, His perfectly filial consciousness, His stainless, untainted holiness " (p. 290). Just how much or just how little this may mean the reader may be puzzled to determine. Nor will he feel sure that things can stand at this point. For he can scarcely fail to note with blanching countenance the attenuated grounds on which alone Dr. Stevens can rest an assertion of moral completeness, perfect filial consciousness, untainted holiness for Jesus. With the feeble hold he has on the trustworthiness of the Scripture records, as he partly perceives himself, there is no sufficient reason to be derived from them for so great a conclusion: and to say that " the divinity of Christ " — does that mean His " metaphysical deity "? — " is presupposed in the Christian view of His Saviourhood " may not suffice one who does not hold to " the Christian " but to " the Socinian " " view of His Saviourhood." This " view of His Saviourhood " has not been historically correlated with a clear and firm faith in the " metaphysical deity " of Jesus.

On another matter we feel less hesitancy in speaking decisively. Dr. Stevens exhibits a remarkable sensitivity to the " charge " that the Moral Influence theory of the Atonement implies a lowered view of sin (pp. 267–268, 390, 392, etc.). One does not wish to be offensive: but is not the truth of the " charge " not only inherent in the case, but also plain matter of fact and universally recognized? Is Dr. Orr bringing a railing accusation against his brethren when he says (" God's Image in Man," p. 11): " It is a truism that, with defective and inadequate views of sin, there can never be an adequate doctrine of redemption: it is, in fact, precisely because so many superficial views of sin are abroad, that there is at the present time so general a recoil from the Biblical declarations on the need and reality of atonement." Certainly if we needed an *a posteriori* proof of the truth of this dictum, we should not need in order to supply it to go farther than Dr. Stevens' own chapter on " The Sin from which Christ Saves " in this volume. Of course, no one supposes that either Dr. Stevens or any other advocate of these lower views of " the Atonement " does not think sin a bad thing, a very bad thing: or that they cannot discourse eloquently about its badness.

But no one who reads this chapter can doubt that Dr. Stevens does not think sin so bad a thing as it has been thought by the advocates of those " provincial extravagances " of the " era of Protestant polemic scholasticism," which included among them the doctrines of original guilt, total depravity, and inability. It is, in fact, part of the very purpose of this chapter to discard these " extravagances," " exaggerations ": and in calling them " extravagances," " exaggerations," Dr. Stevens advertises his own view as, relatively to them, a " lowered " view. It surely cannot be offensive, then, to say that it is only because this " lowered " view of sin and its effects on man is Dr. Stevens' view, that his view of the Atonement seems to him adequate. If he held the " exaggerated " view " taught, for example, by Augustine and Edwards, and embodied in the Westminster Confession," he would not be able to content himself with his view of the Atonement.

It can scarcely be necessary to prolong this notice in order to explain in detail what Dr. Stevens' view of the Atonement is. He did not leave it to this point in his treatise first to avow it: and we have not been able to follow his treatise thus far without repeatedly suggesting it. Let it suffice to say it is simply a form of the very prevalent Moral Influence theory, and like all forms of this theory finds the atoning fact, the actual thing which brings man into right relations to God, not in Christ or in anything which Christ was or taught or did, but in man's own act of repentance and return to God — Christ's whole function consisting in inducing man to repent and return to God. It is only by a figure of speech therefore that it can be said that " Christ gives us repentance and so remission " (p. 354). For how does He " give " it? Only by " making us to feel and know our sin, and showing us the sure way to escape from it." There is nothing upon which Dr. Stevens waxes more passionate than upon man's inalienable power to repent, " to heed and respond to the gospel invitation " (p. 316). On this view one may well ask, What then becomes of those who lived and died before Christ came? Only two views are possible. Either they are hopelessly lost, or else Christ's work is not necessary to salvation. The former alternative Dr. Stevens, of course, does not take; he even (absurdly enough) tries to fix it on the " Satisfaction theory " (p. 379). The latter is, then, inevitable to him: and he boldly embraces it in a theory of what he calls " Eternal Atonement " (chap. x. pp. 433 ff.), in which he teaches that " the word ' atonement ' represents a process and not a merely single event — that it designates the operation in history of certain laws or forces of the divine life which are perpetually operative, an action of God in relation to sin and salvation which has been continuous throughout human history " (p. 433). Thus our Lord's " saving mission is a transactional expression of eternal atonement " (p. 440) : " the earthly life and suffering of Christ are the historic form of an eternal reality, a perpetual process " (p. 442). All of which, being interpreted, means that it is not what Christ did on earth which grounds salvation, but " the dateless passion of God on account of sin "; and that " God is, by His very nature, a sin-bearer." Why, then, the mission of Christ? Why His sufferings and death? There is a chapter (chap. viii.) on this too. It's axiom is that " Christ came to realize in the world the ends of God's holy love " (p. 401). " Christ did not come to procure, but to proclaim and bestow forgiveness " (p. 386). In any event that He did not come earlier leaves it certain that what He did in the world was not necessary for the salvation of man — that nothing He did in the world was essential to salvation. If the world did not need His work for so many ages, it can have stood in no need of it at all. Search and look: it is inherent in the very nature of the Moral Influence theory to depreciate the importance of the mission of Christ. He becomes only one Saviour among many (Bushnell, Sabatier). His work is really unessential to salvation. Undeniably this is not the Biblical view. Undeniably it is not the view of the Christian centuries. Is it a view tolerable to the Christian heart? The plain fact is that the lowered views of the Atonement now becoming so prevalent are unconformable to all the presuppositions of the Christian faith, and involve a reconstruction which will ultimately transform it into a merely natural religion.

GOD'S IMAGE IN MAN, AND ITS DEFACEMENT, IN THE LIGHT OF MODERN DENIALS. By JAMES ORR, D.D. London: Hodder & Stoughton. 1905.[1]

DR. ORR'S " Stone Lectures " were listened to in Princeton with great pleasure. Their publication in this handsome volume will

[1] The Princeton Theological Review, iv. 1906, pp. 555–558.

carry to a wider audience their fine exposition of the fundamentals of Christian anthropology and their vigorous protest against a tendency, apparently growing among us, " to wholesale surrender of vital aspects of Christian doctrine at the shrine of what is regarded as ' the modern view of the world ' " (p. vi.). What renders this protest most valuable is that it is particularly directed against weak evasions of the issue raised by the conflict between the Christian view of the world and that " congeries of conflicting and often mutually irreconcilable views " which is commonly spoken of as the " modern view." Dr. Orr has the courage to recognize and assert the irreconcilableness of the two views and the impossibility of a compromise between them; and to undertake the task of showing that the Christian view in the forum of science itself is the only tenable one. This task he accomplishes with distinguished success: and this is the significance of the volume.

The material is divided into six lectures. In the first of these the issue is stated, and the actual irreconcilability of the two views demonstrated. The Biblical doctrine of God, man, and sin is set sharply over against the " evolutionary " view of them, the exaggerations sometimes found on both sides are cleared away, and the residuary conflict made plain. The second lecture, proceeding to details, sets the Bible and the new views of the nature of man over against one another, and shows that no scientific facts really endanger the Bible doctrine that man differs in kind and not merely in degree from the lower creatures. In the third lecture it is shown that the extreme evolutionary theories have broken down before the advance of knowledge, and that, on the data of science itself, man stands forth as the product not of nature but of a Higher Cause intruded into nature. The fourth lecture extends this argument with especial reference to the mental nature of man. In the fifth lecture the great question of sin is grappled with, and the Biblical view of sin as a racial fact rooted in voluntary action on the part of the creature is powerfully commended. Finally, in the sixth lecture, the Biblical account of death as non-natural to man and the result of sin is defended: and the bearing of the whole discussion on the entirety of the Christian system explained. At the end a body of valuable material is collected in a series of Appendixes which support, and in some instances advance, the positions taken in the text of the lectures.

What impresses the reader of these admirable lectures most is their fine balance. In the statement neither of the Biblical doctrine nor of the "modern view," nor in their comparison, is there any exaggeration. The two are just calmly set over against one another and investigated in their bases and relations. Perhaps the most striking feature of the exposition of the Biblical doctrine is the just insistence upon the unity of man as "a being composed of body and soul in a unity not intended to be dissolved." A firm grasp upon this element of the Biblical doctrine notably clears the air. It not only puts in their right aspects death and the resurrection — the former as the product of sin and the latter as the necessary fruit of redemption from sin: but it throws the whole question of the origin of man into a new light. It perhaps may not be too much to say that the hinge of the Biblical anthropology lies here: and that the argument of Dr. Orr turns upon his clear appreciation of it. Next to this, we are struck perhaps by the searching analysis and account of sin given in the fifth lecture. The question arises, as we read, why sin cannot be characterized, in contradistinction to that "love" in which the fulfillment of the law consists, as just "lovelessness" or, in its positive manifestation, "hate." This would be only another way — whether a better way or not may be open to question — of reducing sin to the principle of selfishness.

Some striking minor points in Dr. Orr's arguments should also be mentioned. Among these is his suggestion (p. 152) of the impossibility of disparate development of mind and body, with the inference he draws from it that, therefore, it can scarcely be credited that the body of man was formed by the accumulation of insensible variations from a brutish original, and the soul made all at once by a divine fiat for the completed man. Body and mind must go together: and a great brain with a little mind is just as unthinkable as a little brain with a great mind. The argument does not seem to be available, however, as against a theory of evolution *per saltum*. If under the directing hand of God a human body is formed at a leap by propagation from brutish parents, it would be quite consonant with the fitness of things that it should be provided by His creative energy with a truly human soul. And this leads us to say that the precise point in the question of evolution is, after all, not whether the new forms proceed from older ones, whether by or without the directing hand of God; but whether the forces concerned in the production of the new forms are all intrinsic in the evolving stuff. Man may "breed" many varieties of pigeons, fowls, sheep;

and the varieties he " breeds " may often come *per saltum*. But they all find their account in the forces operating in the materials dealt with: his directing hand cannot be traced in the chain of efficient causes, all of which are discoverable in the evolving stuff. Accordingly, under man's hand we can have nothing but an " evolution," an unrolling — a drawing out into new forms of what was potentially present in the evolving material from the beginning. If this were all that God does, there would be no " creation " in the case whatever. We do not quite understand, therefore, Dr. Orr's remark on p. 87, to the effect that " evolution " and " special creation " are not mutually exclusive, whether as terms or as things. Surely " evolution " means just " modification"; and " creation " just " origination ": and surely " modification " and " origination " are ultimate conceptions and mutually exclude one the other. You cannot " originate " by " modifying "; you cannot " modify " by " originating." Whatever comes by " evolution " that certainly cannot arise by " creation "; and whatever is " created " certainly is not " evolved." The old definition of " creation " as the making of something *partim ex nihilo, partim ex materia naturaliter inhabili — ex materia inhabili supra maturæ vires aliquid producere,* — is certainly the sound one. Unless the thing produced is above what the powers intrinsic in the evolving stuff are capable of producing (under whatever divine guidance), the product is not a product of " creation " but of " providence." And " providence " can never do the work of " creation." Dr. Orr fully understands this and argues therefore that the apparition of man implies the intrusion of a new cause, that it is a creation, strictly so called: and this is what makes the remark on p. 87 inexplicable. Let man have arisen through the divine guidance of the evolutionary process, there is no creative act of God, but only a providential activity of God, concerned in his production, unless there has been intruded into the process the action of a cause not intrinsic in the evolving stuff, causing the complex product to be something more than can find its account in the intrinsic forces, however divinely manipulated. Evolution can never, under any circumstances, issue in a product which is specifically new: " modification " is the utmost that it can achieve — " origination " is beyond its tether.

One of the most pregnant passages in the volume is that (p.188) in which it is briefly demonstrated that for a moral being to exist in a non-moral condition is really for it to exist in an immoral condition. We may in the abstract distinguish actions into those that are right, wrong, and indifferent. But there are no indifferent acts: in the concrete all acts are good or bad. So we may in the abstract speak of conditions which are moral, non-moral, and immoral. But for a moral being, a state of non-morality is a state of immorality. Such a being is either good or bad; never neither good nor bad. This simple demonstration cuts up by the roots the whole Pelagian standpoint.

As we have already pointed out, Dr. Orr's whole treatment of sin is very sane and satisfactory. Only, we demur to what seems to us the overemphasis of the fact of " heredity," taken in the strict sense, in this connection. We hear indeed of " the representative principle " (p. 277), and the " inheritance " of death is apparently hung upon it. But the transmission of sin appears to be hung at least mainly upon the principle of " heredity " (e.g. pp. 235, 242). This seems to us a mistake, and to involve us in many unnecessary difficulties, as, for example, the difficulty of accounting for our " inheritance " of specifically Adam's first sin (why not Eve's? and why not the sins of all our ancestors?) and the difficulty of accounting for our Lord's failure to " inherit " sin. We are burdened with the guilt of Adam's first sin and have received its penalty. Surely that is enough. We do not need to defend the theory of the " inheritance " of acquired qualities in order to account for it; the principle of representation is enough. And we do not need to insist that a son tends to inherit the moral character of his parents, which (on the broad question) certainly is not borne out by common experience: the children of the pious are not uniformly pious nor are those of the vicious uniformly vicious, and assuredly few would contend that the specific forms in which piety and vice are manifested are on the average transmitted. It seems much better, then, to follow what appears to us the simple Scriptural representation, and to say that we partake in Adam's sin because he was our representative, and that he was constituted our representative because he was our father and was naturally indicated as such for that office.

We have in these remarks, we think, noted everything with respect to which we should feel disposed to question even Dr. Orr's modes of developing his subject. Perhaps a query may be placed also against his remarks (pp. 153–154) on the difficulty created for a purely evolutionary theory by the necessity of the production of not a single instance, but of a pair of human beings. We do not feel this difficulty as strongly as Dr. Orr appears to feel it. Why should there be a pair? Nothing is more common in the experience of breeders than the origination of a new type through an individual sport. And what is the difficulty of obtaining a pair or more of the same fundamental type? *Ex hypothesi* the new variation is slight; and that implies the coexistence of many individuals of almost equal advantages. And nothing is commoner in the experience of breeding than the production from the same parentage of a succession of individuals of the same or nearly the same " sporting " characters. Perhaps also a query may be placed over against the strong statement (p. 257) to the effect that " there is not a word in Scripture to suggest that animals . . . came under the law of death for man's sin." The problem of the reign of death in that " creation " which was cursed for man's sake and which is to be with man delivered from the bondage of corruption, presses on some with a somewhat greater weight than seems here to be recognized. But these are matters of no importance to the march of the general argument of the book. The book is a distinct contribution to the settlement of the questions with which it deals, and to their settlement in a sane and stable manner. It will come as a boon to many who are oppressed by the persistent pressure upon them of the modern point of view. It cannot help producing in the mind of its readers a notable clearing of the air.

CHRISTIAN LIFE IN THE PRIMITIVE CHURCH. By ERNST VON DOB-SCHÜTZ, D.D. Translated by the Rev. George Bremner, B.D., and Edited by the Rev. W. D. Morrison, LL.D. London: Williams & Norgate; New York: G. P. Putnam's Sons. 1904.[1]

THE task which Prof. von Dobschütz has set himself in this attractive volume is to present an exact and detailed picture of the moral condition of Christians during the first century of the Church's existence (A.D. 30–A.D. 130). Perhaps the title under which the book is published is a little too broad. There are two sides to what we commonly know as " Christian life " — a Godward and a manward side, or perhaps we may better say a religious and a moral side. It is the latter of these to which Prof. von Dobschütz confines his survey. The mystical side of the Christian life he puts out of sight. What he undertakes to investigate is its ethical manifestation. He is not attempting, however, a history of Christian Ethics in the first age: he has nothing to do here with the teaching of the apostles and their successors. What he is essaying is to determine the actual practice of Christians during the first century of their existence in the world. The question he raises is, What kind of people were these early Christians? He wishes to determine by an exact and detailed study whether the Christians did or did not introduce into the world actual moral health: whether they were, or were not, " good men."

The answer Prof. von Dobschütz returns to his question is an affirmative one. The early Christians were good people. As over against the background of heathen immorality — even of Jewish formalism — they stand forth as lights in the world. They not only taught a high and searching morality: they lived it. He thinks it worth while to emphasize this answer and to substantiate it by an exhibition of the evidence for it drawn out with convincing detail. For it is not the answer which has of late been universally given. At an earlier period, indeed, it was customary to idealize the first Christian communities. Of late, however, too black a picture has often been painted. Hausrath, for example, " from all sorts of statements gleaned in the darkest corners and dipped in the deepest hues " has drawn " a picture so gloomy that one is compelled to wonder where Christianity ever found the power to conquer the ancient world " (p. vii.). In his view the worst of Christian Churches of to-day " approaches the ideal of the Sermon on the Mount more closely " (p. 363) than the best of the second century. If we understand Prof. von Dobschütz, he believes Hausrath has exaggerated both the end-terms of the development. He agrees perfectly with Hausrath that Christianity has developed from the beginning until now — if not steadily yet substantially — in moral fiber and moral manifestation. Only he believes it started at a higher level and (probably) has reached at the present a lower level than Hausrath maintained. The difference between the earliest Christianity and the latest in point of moral attainment is less in his view than in Hausrath's. It is the purpose of this volume to show that it started at a higher level and to establish the height of this level.

In Prof. von Dobschütz's view — a view which in our judgment he substantiates — the level from which it started was very high. " It is astonishing," he remarks at the end of his survey of the condition of the Pauline Churches as reflected in Paul's letters — " it is astonishing what Christianity in a relatively short time made out of these motley and confused heathen groups; earnest men working out their salvation with fear and trembling, saints fully aware of the moral tasks of their consecration. If their judgment was often immature, their goodwill and vigour were great " (p. 137). Of course the ideal was not realized, least of all by every Christian. " But," Prof. von Dobschütz remarks as he closes his survey of the whole century, " offences against it were exceptions, and have less significance, as they awoke at once the moral consciousness of the spiritual leaders and of the congregations. If even one half of the Christians lived as we have described, something great was already achieved. Certainly more of them did. The discipline exerted by this majority was, apart from other considerations, an invaluable moral achievement " (p. 371). The actual morality of the Christians constituted and constitutes to Prof. von Dobschütz's mind, indeed, its best apologetic. " It is the most effective proof of the truth of Christianity " (p. xiii.). It was so in those early ages themselves: the Apologists appeal, as they were thoroughly entitled to appeal, to what Christians were as a proof of their divine calling. The heathen — Pliny, Lucian, Celsus — were compelled even, against their will, to witness to the correctness of the picture the Apologists drew. As a fact, it was not the superiority of Christianity's dogmatic system, nor even of its ethical teaching which constituted its power. It was (and it is) the superiority of its life. " Stoicism and Neoplatonism after all produced moral thoughts of great beauty and purity, thoughts which are more imposing to superficial contemplation than the simple commandments of Christianity. Yet neither of them could enable artisans and old women to lead a truly philosophical life. Christianity could and did; the apologists point triumphantly to the realisation of the moral ideal among Christians of every standing. That was due to the power which issued from Jesus Christ and actually transformed men " (p. 379). It was in this sign that Christianity conquered, and in it that it must ever conquer, when conquer it will and does.

Prof. von Dobschütz's method is to pass the literary remains of the period from A.D. 30 to A.D. 130 in review, reproducing the moral condition of the Churches as reflected in them, in the form of a

running comment. This method has some obvious advantages. Not
least among them is to be accounted the vividness and life it enables Prof. von Dobschütz to impart to his pages. The result is that
he has given us a most engaging book, and the attention of the reader
is held unflaggingly to the end. We have been especially attracted
by the portrayal of the situation underlying the Shepherd of Hermas
in the final chapter. But this method is attended also with some disadvantages. Among these is that it tempts the writer to overload
his pages with material not germane or only remotely germane
to his subject. Prof. von Dobschütz has not escaped this danger, and
his successive chapters read often more like studies in the general
situation of the Churches addressed in the several epistles or presupposed in the documents he analyzes, than like specific investigations into the moral condition of the primitive Churches; in a word,
like sections in Biblical or Patristic Introduction. The reader finds
it almost as much of a task to gather from his flowing and interesting pages a clearly-cut and sufficing account of the morals of the
early Christians as it would be to derive this from the original
documents themselves. It is a graver matter that it throws into
exaggerated prominence an inconvenience which would, no doubt,
attend any mode of studying such a subject — we mean the influence on the result of the author's individual opinions as to
problems of literary history. The consecution of the New Testament books, for example, and the authenticity, authorship, and
provenience of them — in this mode of presenting the material —
become very important matters indeed, and dominate not only the
structure of the volume but the outline of the picture presented in
it of early Christian morals.

This is a specially important matter to us, since we do not at
all share Prof. von Dobschütz's opinions as to the problems of New
Testament Introduction. There is nothing in them, to be sure,
peculiar to Prof. von Dobschütz; his views are just the views prevailing in the extremer wing of modern critical reconstruction of the
literary history of the New Testament. And no one could expect
him (as he himself suggests in the Preface) to include a justification
of his views on literary history in this volume. But the value of the
volume to all who do not share these views is seriously impaired
by the unnecessary prominence given them in its structure; and this
the more since Prof. von Dobschütz strives to present his material
not statically but dynamically — that is to say, in perspective, with

an indication of what he deems the development of Christian morals through the century of which he treats. Obviously divergent views of the consecution of the witnessing documents will work havoc here. If Colossians is to be treated as Paul's; and Ephesians as an imitation of it from the hands of the next generation; and the Pastorals as ecclesiastical documents of a generation later — why, clearly the picture of " the development of morals " (if any such development can be traced) will be different from that derived from these documents conceived as the product of a single pen and of a period covering only five or six years. From the latter point of view the confident tracing of a development as witnessed by these documents must seem to rest on an illusion supported by overstrained niceties of interpretation. And in any case Prof. von Dobschütz cannot be acquitted of this fault. When no marked distinction is discovered in the moral condition of Christians as pictured in Philippians, and that pictured in the two Epistles to the Thessalonians; and yet a significant development is traced between the moral assumptions underlying Colossians and Ephesians, it seems obvious that the scales employed do not give equal weights.

We rise from the perusal of Prof. von Dobschütz's book, accordingly, with a great sense of indebtedness to the author and with much spoil in our hands: but we rise from it also with a conviction that there are some things in it which are not derived from the sources. We feel confident that if Prof. von Dobschütz had begun simply by investigating the moral condition of the Churches underlying each document in turn, and then had compared these results and combined them in a single account, he would have spoken less of a regular development through the century; and certainly he would have put the documents into classes differing somewhat from the arrangement he has given them, in what seems to us, so far as the New Testament documents are concerned, not only an unhistorical but also an unnatural order. And, then, had he presented the material thus gained under rubrics derived from the moral categories, instead of in the quasi-chronological order he has preferred, derived from his personal opinions as to the consecution of the documents, his readers would have gained from him not only a truer but a much clearer and more convincing conception of the state of Christian morals during the first Christian century. In a word, in our judgment, Prof. von Dobschütz's study of the morals of the early Church suffers from his wrong views of the composition of the documents with which he deals; and suffers from this unduly on account of the method of presentation which he has adopted.

At the close of the volume, a series of " Notes " (six in all) are printed, in which some interesting ancillary questions are discussed in a more scholastic way than was consonant with the more popular style of the body of the work. One of these is devoted partly to a justification of the author's view of Paul's curse upon the incestuous man at Corinth; this view we do not find it possible to share. The most important of them is an attempt — the author emphasizes that it is only an " attempt " — to survey the terms employed in early Christian literature to express moral ideas. This is a valuable contribution to a department of study hitherto much neglected: and it may be commended to students as a beginning of importance in a new line of research. The book is fairly well translated, and reads in general smoothly and clearly. The proof-reading is not immaculate. There is even an appearance (perhaps it is only appearance) of assigning a new work to Ignatius with the title of " Heresy " (p. 246), even a treatise to our Lord bearing the designation of " Life of Poverty " (p. 265; what is really meant appears — though even then somewhat awkwardly — upon p. 376).

SOME DOGMAS OF RELIGION. By JOHN McTAGGART ELLIS McTAG-GART. London: Edward Arnold. 1906.[1]

DR. McTAGGART presents us in this volume with a reasoned plea for atheism. His atheism is based neither upon materialism nor upon a complete scepticism, but upon an idealistic metaphysic. The particular form of idealism to which he holds is that which (as he supposes) underlay the systems of Fichte, Hegel, and Lotze; and which conceives reality as ultimately consisting of a harmonious system of self-existent selves: it may perhaps be designated idealistic pluralism. He does not in this volume set forth the grounds on which he holds to this metaphysic. It is not its purpose to establish his metaphysical basis. It is its purpose to examine the evidence for the great trilogy of natural religion — God, Freedom, Immortality — with a view to determining whether this evidence is ade-

[1] The Princeton Thelogical Review, v. 1907, pp. 288–294.

quate. The method of the reasoning is, therefore, critical, and its trend is negative. Dr. McTaggart holds, indeed, that there exist arguments of sufficient strength to justify a belief in human immortality. But these are not the arguments which are commonly relied upon, but reduce to those which establish the idealistic theory of the fundamental nature of reality. And as it is not the purpose of this volume to determine the fundamental characteristics of reality these arguments are not adduced. All that is done is, by a critical examination of the arguments ordinarily relied upon in disproof of immortality, to remove objections out of the way, and then to suggest that, as the really telling arguments for immortality are metaphysical rather than moral, they tend to commend to us a doctrine of eternity rather than of immortality — a doctrine of preëxistence as truly as of postexistence, for human beings — Dr. McTaggart himself being inclined to construe this eternity of existence in terms of transmigration. With his fundamental conception of reality as a system of selves, freedom presents no necessary inconsistency, provided this freedom be not construed out of relation to the law of causality. Accordingly, if we understand him aright, Dr. McTaggart argues for the doctrine of human freedom ordinarily called the freedom of self-determination, but called by him, in accordance with a distribution of theories of his own, the freedom of self-direction; although it is possible that he may push his determinism to a mechanical extreme. This chapter is chiefly notable for its clear and convincing refutation of the theory of indeterminism. It is in its examination of Theism, however, that the interest of the volume culminates. There is no suggestion of a God inherent in Dr. McTaggart's fundamental metaphysic: and he finds no reason to believe in a God in the lines of argument usually relied on to prove His existence. He feels quite certain that there is no such God as the higher Theism demands — an omnipotent Creator and Director of all. To him all existent reality is eternal and ultimate (p. 234) — and there is therefore no place for a Creator, and the Divine Being, if such exists, is limited by the coexistence of the rest of existing reality. He might find a place for a non-omnipotent, non-creative God — if there was only valid evidence of His existence. But he discovers none. "There seems to me," he says, "only one reason why we should not believe in his existence — namely, that there is no reason why we should believe in it" (p. 260). The issue of the whole discussion is therefore that the slate is clean: we have no guidance on these great subjects of God, Freedom, Immortality except the implications of our metaphysical theory. And as in Dr. McTaggart's view a true metaphysic conceives reality as an eternal self-existent system of selves, a true religion, founded on this metaphysic, will do without a God, but will allow a self-determined freedom and an immortality construed as eternity *a parte ante* as well as *a parte post*. Meanwhile all non-metaphysicians are warned off the religious terrain. No man is justified in holding opinions on these great subjects save as the result of metaphysical study. Religion is therefore for the metaphysician alone. " And thus we are driven to the conclusion that, whether any religion is true or not, most people have no right to accept any religion as true " (p. 293). We may regret this, but we may in part console ourselves with the reflection (among others) " that the man who has no religion cannot have a bad one " (p. 294).

As Dr. McTaggart's purpose in this volume is not to establish conclusions but to clear away conclusions illegitimately established, we should perhaps attend more to his critical method than to what we may incidentally learn of his positive opinions. The progress of his discussion is as follows. He first undertakes to demonstrate the importance of dogma, or rather its indispensableness to religion. Next he endeavors to show that the customary arguments relied on for the establishment of religious dogma are illegitimate. Taking up then the three great dogmas, he examines in turn the ordinary basis for belief in Immortality, Freedom, and God, and finds it in all cases inadequate; indicating, however, as he goes on, that there exists nevertheless good reason in his metaphysical assumption for belief in immortality and freedom, defined in accordance with its requirements, but not for belief in God. Summing up, finally, he contends that there remains nothing but our metaphysical determinations to rely upon for the establishment of dogma. The dialectic employed by Dr. McTaggart in his destructive reasoning is very sharp and clear-cut, but not seldom also very formal, descending at times into purely verbal reasoning and even to something not far removed from what has been not very euphoniously called " choplogic." Great reliance is placed upon definition and the verbal analysis of definition; and it would go hard with any logician if he could not put into his definition precisely what he purposed subsequently to bring out of it by analysis. Dr. McTaggart's logical sense is very acute, and with much of his reasoning the reader will be carried convincingly along: but it not seldom fails to convince because it fails in content. We cannot take space here to illustrate either its excellences or its defects. These may, however, be sufficiently suggested by some desultory remarks on one or two points of primary importance to Dr. McTaggart's argument.

Dr. McTaggart considers " that no man is justified in a religious attitude except as a result of metaphysical study " (p. 292). This judgment rests, however, ultimately on Dr. McTaggart's definition of religion. If religion be so defined as to make it rest on metaphysical conclusions, it should require less than an octavo volume to determine it to be unjustifiable in one who has made no metaphysical study. According to Dr. McTaggart, religion is that " state of mind " which " may best be described as an emotion resting on a conviction of a harmony between ourselves and the universe at large " (p. 3). If this be true, it is clear that no one is entitled to possess a religion until he has contemplated " the universe at large," and has attained a conviction that he himself is in " harmony " with it. Yet it is notorious (and Dr. McTaggart is at once compelled to admit it) that men are religious who have no conception whatever of a " universe at large "; and that others are religious whose most fundamental conviction is that they are out of harmony with the universe as they conceive it. Why make so long and devious a circuit to get at a fundamental trait of human nature? Why not recognize at once that religion is simply the reaction of the human spirit in the presence of (add the qualification " real or imagined " if you will) higher powers, perceived as such? Here is a perfectly simple definition which covers all the instances. It may indeed be argued — and successfully argued — that these " higher powers " must be personal since nothing less than personal can be higher than persons; and indeed that they must be one, since the involved attributes are singular; in a word that religion can come to its rights only in Theism, which is in and of its very nature Monotheism. But religion may exist without coming fully to its rights: else it could not exist at all as a " state of mind " of creatures like us. And we need only to recognize that systems like Buddhism which are formally atheistic, and thinkers like Spinoza and Hegel, who think of the higher power in relation to which they perceive themselves as standing, as impersonal, conceive this higher power imperfectly and are absorbed in the contemplation of this or that aspect of it, as, for example, its immensity, its all-inclusiveness, its universal operation, — to understand that their response to its perception may be essentially religious. Religions thus differ from religions as the conceptions entertained by their subjects of the nature of the higher powers which are their objects differ, and as the conceptions entertained by their subjects of their own relations to these higher powers differ. When these higher powers are conceived as persons, as they are explicitly almost invariably and, one may say, implicitly always (and that seems the significance of Mr. Dickinson's remark quoted on p. 10 that religious emotion is dependent on the universe being " greatly and imaginatively conceived "), then the sense of dependence which lies at the root of all religion (because it grows out of the perception of powers as " higher ") is completed by a sense of responsibility (because these powers are perceived as " personal," that is, as moral agents) ; and the response of human nature will take form from the moral judgment which the subjects of religion pass upon themselves. Religions become thus fundamentally religions of fear or religions of hope; and the conceptions, emotions, and usages developed by them take form as one or the other of these emotions preponderates in them. Religion is not, therefore, so much " that particular happiness which comes from the belief that we are in harmony with the universe " (p. 9), as rather that particular state of mind which grows out of the conviction that there are higher powers upon our relations with whom our happiness depends. Happiness does not lie, therefore, at the root of religion, as is contended by both Dr. McTaggart and Mr. Dickinson, to whom no attitude towards the " universe " is religious unless it brings with it " rest and peace and happiness "; but is rather the end sought in religion — by various means according to the place of each religion in the scale of religions. Religion therefore is not based on a precedent conviction of a harmony already existing, but rests on a desire for harmony earnestly sought after. And above all, it is not based on a conviction of harmony existent between us " and the universe at large," but on a desire to secure harmony between us and " the higher powers," however conceived. The attempt to substitute the " universe " for " God " in the conception of religion, which characterizes both Dr. Mc-Taggart's and Mr. Dickinson's definitions, is simply an outgrowth of their own philosophy and contradicts the entire phenomenology of religion. It is not " the universe " perceived as over against himself which is the source of man's religious ideas, emotions, actions. It

is distinctly "the higher power," contemplated ordinarily distinctly as personal, and one may believe always obscurely so conceived or else the religious reaction does not follow. This broad fact of human religion becomes thus itself a witness to God. Resting on no metaphysical reasoning it presupposes no "metaphysical study." It is the immediate reaction of the human spirit to a part of its environment, and it becomes thus a guide to metaphysical reasoning rather than waits upon its results. It is only if we shut our eyes to what is and embody in our definitions our metaphysical theories that we can draw out of those definitions conclusions inconsistent with a valid religious experience and a sound religious conviction quite independent of metaphysical study.

It is perhaps especially in his argument against the validity of Theism that Dr. McTaggart's vice of purely verbal argumentation becomes most glaring. The hinge of his argument here, it is not too much to say, is his doctrine of omnipotence. Omnipotence, he would have us understand, means a power to which, and to the exercise of which, no limitation of any sort whatever can be conceived. "An omnipotent person," he says, "is one who can do anything" (p. 202): "there is nothing that an omnipotent being cannot do" (p. 166). It is scarcely credible, but Dr. McTaggart does wish us to believe that this implies that an omnipotent being must be conceived as able to make the sum of two and two five or a thing to be and not be at the same time! And on the basis of this absurdity he gravely reasons that an omnipotent being could not be a person and could not have the benefit of the ordinary theodicy in view of the evil in the world — or indeed, even of the teleological argument for His existence, because forsooth the employment of means is in and of itself inconsistent with omnipotence! "There is nothing," says he, "that an omnipotent being cannot do. . . . A really omnipotent being cannot be bound by the law of Contradiction. If it seems to us absurd to suggest that the law of Contradiction is dependent on the will of any person, we must be prepared to say that no person is really omnipotent" (p. 166). "If he is bound by" the law of Identity, or "by the law of Contradiction and the law of Excluded Middle," "he is not omnipotent" (p. 203). Of such a God it may not be supposed that He has permitted sin to exist, in order that a greater good may be attained; for "any good result which might follow from the sin and the punishment could be obtained by such a God, in virtue of his omnipotence, without the sin or the punishment " (p. 165). Nay, such a God cannot be supposed to use means at all, for, *ex hypothesi*, means have no worth in themselves, but owe their entire value to their supposed necessity in attaining a valuable end. But an omnipotent God cannot require means to attain any end: " and therefore it would be inconsistent with his wisdom to use them, since they are of no value except to get an end which he could get as well without them " (p. 201). Not only then can He have the benefit of no theodicy which turns on a doctrine of means: but the teleological argument if valid in the discovery of means is His refutation — if means have been used, it is no omnipotent God who has used them. Now, all this, we say, is quite astonishing. When we affirm omnipotence we affirm unlimited power, it is true, but we affirm only unlimited power. The omnipotent person is a person whose power has no limits. He can do all that He wills. But certainly this unlimited power imposes no limits upon His other attributes — His wisdom, say, or His goodness. It is not necessary in order to be omnipotent to be an idiot or a devil. By virtue of His omnipotence such a being can accomplish all He will: all that is the object of power is in His power. But it does not follow that He may therefore will the foolish or the wicked: foolishness and wickedness raise no question of power but of wisdom and of goodness. The law of Contradiction, for instance, does not belong within the sphere of power: its place is in the sphere of wisdom; and it is no limitation of the omnipotent God's power to say that He is incapable of folly. It is not a limitation of His power which renders it impossible for Him to make the sum of two and two five: it is the perfection of His reason. One might as well talk of a steam engine being made strong enough to draw an inference, as of omnipotence possessing such might as to transcend the law of Excluded Middle. These things are things which are unrelated to power: and concerning which power has no function. And the same is true of the employment of means in order to secure ends. There is here no question of power but of wisdom. If the ends are more wisely secured by means than by power, then it is the part of wise omnipotence so to secure them. If the ends are outside the ends of power, then no omnipotence can make the first step towards securing them. The plausibility of Dr. McTaggart's argument here seems to depend entirely on its generality and abstractness. Some ends are objects of power, and it may seem strange that an omnipotent being should reach them by means rather than by immediate act. There may be reasons why He should: but these reasons lie outside the ends themselves. Other ends, however, are obviously unattainable by power, because they are not objects of power. And it happens that the specific ends sought in the creation of the universe and in its government are not only supposed by the framers of theodicies, but also are in themselves intrinsically of this last sort. It is not within the power of omnipotence, for example, to secure a manifestation of the divine justice and grace without objects of such kind that upon them justice and grace may be secured. These things do not belong in the sphere of " power." The reason why God is supposed not to attain that better thing which is attained by the presence of sin in the universe, without sin, is not, then, because He is supposed to lack in power, but because the attainment of this end in itself requires sin as its condition. We may accord with Dr. McTaggart in his criticism of special theories which have been advanced. We agree with him that the attempt to make the presence of sin the inevitable result of the creation of free agents or the inevitable result of government by general laws, and so justifiable in God's universe, is a failure. But it does not follow that the very idea of a theodicy derived from the use of sin as a means to a glorious end otherwise unobtainable is inconsistent with the conception of an omnipotent God, because forsooth omnipotence can have no need of means. Omnipotence has the same need of means for the attainment of ends not themselves the direct product of force as impotence itself has: and omnipotence abnegates none of its prerogatives when it subjects itself to the government of wisdom, goodness, and truth. To affirm that God is omnipotent is not to assimilate Him to the hurricane or the volcano which blindly acts in all its power on all occasions; but to affirm that infinite righteousness, holiness, goodness, and love is served by equally infinite power — that whatever God wills, He can execute, and that therefore the infinite holy, righteous, and good Will will work its ends, and that in its own time and way, according to what is the absolute Best.

From these specimens the quality of Dr. McTaggart's reasoning may be not unfairly judged. Let it suffice to say further merely that the charm of his style carries the reader over many a doubtful argument. With his criticism upon the current reasoning by which Immortality is established or supposed to be established, we find ourselves very much in sympathy. Only, as our metaphysical presuppositions differ fundamentally from his, we differ substantially with him in the relative estimate we put upon the several varieties of reasoning which are employed. To the metaphysical reasoning we attach little value: to the moral, more: but we should not be greatly disturbed were all of it pronounced inconclusive. " We have a more sure word of prophecy "; and it is Jesus Christ who has " brought life and immortality to light." No doubt it may seem below the dignity of metaphysics to consider facts of experience in determining a question like this. But plain men often find the empirical establishment of facts very great aids to belief. Thinking as we do of souls as manufactured articles, and of the ultimate nature of reality as something very different from a " joint stock company," we have no tendency to construe immortality in terms of eternity *a parte ante* as well as *a parte post* — the less so, that it is precisely upon the metaphysical arguments for immortality that we lay the least stress. With respect to Freedom, we go very fully with Dr. McTaggart, if we correctly understand him, although there are some of his arguments which do not appeal to us, and we consider him more successful in refuting indeterminism than in meeting the objections to determinism — because, chiefly, of the intrusion of his peculiar metaphysical views into this portion of the discussion. So soon as he enters formally upon the discussion of Theism, we part company with him *in toto*. Here everything seems to us unreal and deformed by verbal subtleties; and the conclusion arrived at impresses us as already given in the metaphysical presupposition rather than as derived from the critical process. The discussion may be recommended to students, however, as a good whetstone for their wits.

THE AUTHORITY OF CHRIST. By DAVID W. FORREST, D.D. Edinburgh: T. & T. Clark. 1906. New York: Imported by Charles Scribner's Sons.[1]

THERE is a story told of an impetuous and somewhat headstrong cavalry leader in our great Civil War which is brought back to our memory by Dr. Forrest's book. He had just ordered a daring charge, when he was interrupted by an aide-de-camp, riding furiously and

bringing imperative orders from the general in command, to draw
back. " Of course I obey my superior officer," he said, with no attempt to conceal his chagrin. " But," he at once added, his face
clearing up, " Mr. Aide-de-camp, this is a very remarkable order,
which I find it difficult to understand. And how do I know it has
not suffered some ' sea-change ' in its transmission through you?
And, indeed, how do I know ' the old man ' is quite himself this
morning? " " Men," he said, turning to his forces, "charge! " The
authority of Christ, says Dr. Forrest, is of course final. It has in
all ages been acknowledged by the Christian Church to be final
(p. 1, cf. pp. 101, 392). But it certainly is not always easy to ascertain precisely the bearing of either His commands or His example
(pp. 160, 393) ; and in point of fact men have repeatedly and in great
masses and through long periods gone astray in their appeal to His
authority. Nor is it easy to be sure that some of the phrases transmitted to us " have not come to us coloured by later reflection "
(p. 399): His disciples certainly misunderstood Him in some of
His utterances and modified them to suit their own convictions
(pp. 312, 317, 319), and though " the question of subsequent modification or interpretation touches " different parts of His teaching
with more or less force, it is legitimate on all occasions to raise it
(p. 292). And in any event Jesus' own outlook was bounded by the
horizon of a man of His own time, race, and social and intellectual
opportunities. The mysteries that press on us pressed similarly on
Him. The mystery of suffering, for example — " we have no reason
to suppose " that the data required for its solution " lay within
Christ's purview more than within ours " (p. 141). " The *detailed*
course of the kingdom in the world " was " inscrutable " to Him as
to us; because " the influences that determined it were infinitely
complex," and above all the factor of the free human will comes
in to modify all forecasts (p. 300, cf. p. 312). It is not difficult for us
to convict Him even of positive errors. No doubt He shared the
current opinion which attributed the 110th Psalm to David, and
the later chapters of Isaiah to Isaiah (p. 69). Nor did He err only
in matters of Biblical criticism. " His teaching in many of its parts
is coloured by temporary Jewish influences " (p. 96): even the
Parables, at least those " that portray the final judgment," are
affected by " suggestions from Jewish traditional belief " (p. 292).
Thus we are carried through the whole sorites and — despite the
occasional accidental dropping of such a phrase as " Christ teaches

with authority " (p. 331) — the only conclusion that can be reached is that no such " authority " can justly be assigned to the teaching of Christ as has " in all ages been acknowledged by the Christian Church " (p. 1). As we read we are inevitably reminded of Nelson at St. Vincent, vociferously protesting his subjection to his admiral's authority, but taking great care to clap his glass to his blind eye, and, crying out " I see no signal," to go his own way.

And here we must emphasize the phrase " his own way." For we must not suppose that Dr. Forrest puts aside the authority of Jesus in favor of that of the Scriptures. As he says himself, generalizing on an individual instance: " He who believes that Christ's thought had its limitations will not think that Peter's knowledge in such a matter was infallible " (p. 330, cf. p. 413). " Is it at all likely," he demands, " that the Apostle was commissioned to reveal an eschatological truth which was concealed from the Lord Himself, or which He deliberately refrained from proclaiming? " We do not pause here to point out that according to John's representation (John xvi. 12-13) precisely this might seem very likely; or to point out that according to Dr. Forrest's own principles there seems no good reason why the later writer, after mature reflection and the teaching of experience, might not have known better than Jesus. What we are concerned to point out here is that so far from falling back from Christ's authority upon that of the Holy Ghost speaking through the apostles, it is one of Dr. Forrest's aims in setting aside the authority of Christ to escape also from the authority of Scripture. It is, in fact, just because Christ's authority authenticates the Scripture that Christ's authority is onerous to him. He sweeps the field clean and leaves himself logically without any " external authority " at all. And he succeeds very fairly in living practically up to this logical result (pp. 372, 382, 421, cf. pp. 2, 64, 68). There is, of course, an appeal here and there to Scriptural teaching as if there were some good reason why we should not outrun the " scriptural warrant " for this or that (p. 50). But this occasional slip is explicable usually from the influence of long habit and from a sense of the force of the appeal upon those addressed. There is exhibited no great tendency to defer to the detailed teaching of John or Paul or Peter: but rather a suggestion here and there of an underlying hesitancy in appealing to it. At one point, no doubt (p. 330), there seems to be a hint let fall that we may appeal from any one apostle to " the common primitive faith " as a better basis of confidence. What is not shared by all or a plurality of the apostles, we are told, "according to every sound canon of biblical criticism," "can only rank as a theologoumenon" of the individual; and as not "forming part of the common primitive faith" fails, by implication, of normative authority (p. 330). The New Testament, however, is treated on the whole as but a product of the Church (p. 383) which can possess no higher authority than belongs to the Church — even though it comes from "the creative period of the Christian faith" (p. 421). We say truly, then, that Dr. Forrest strips himself of all "external authority," and stands forth as, in some sense, autonomous. Has he not the Spirit as truly as any of the apostles? And does not the promise of guidance into all the truth belong to him as really as to them? And does there not lie behind him a much longer and a much wider experience than lay behind them — through which the Church has learned many things?

We have thought it best to begin thus by stating briefly the central and determining line of thought of Dr. Forrest's volume, that we may have before us at once the principles which have controlled his thought, and the issue to which he would conduct us. We may properly revert now, however, to the manner in which these principles and conclusions find utterance. Dr. Forrest takes for his subject "The Authority of Christ": and his end is to determine the sphere in which that authority — shall we say is available or shall we say is extant? — and its "character" — or shall we say its mode of operation? — within that sphere. In one word, Dr. Forrest's purpose is to investigate the limits of Christ's authority both extensively and intensively. In what sphere is He authoritative? he asks; and then, How authoritative is He in that sphere? He cannot be said to proceed in his discussion in a right line: nor does the book give the impression of a unity. One gets the suggestion as he reads that it may have been composed piecemeal, at perhaps disconnected periods, and not in all its parts with the same precise end prominently in view and with the same definitions and presuppositions vividly in mind. Nevertheless the whole is bound together in some sort of unity by the fact that the whole treats in one way or another of the authority of Christ: and if at one time there seems an implicit recognition underlying the discussion of the plenary authority of our Lord's declarations and only a zeal to provide against their misapplication, while at another there seems a tendency to deny at least absolute authority to His declarations themselves, the reader still is able, with a little care, to find his way amid the resulting ambiguities. If we may be allowed a conjecture as to the composition of the book, we may perhaps suppose that it originated in a strong feeling on Dr. Forrest's part that "the authority of Christ" has been and is frequently much too lightly asserted; and has accordingly been invoked for a multitude of points of view and conceptions, usages, and practices for which no colorable warrant can be found in the recorded teaching and example of Jesus. Here is, for example, a portentous sacerdotal system like that of the Church of Rome. Or here is an impracticable scheme of conduct like that propounded by Tolstoy. Or here is a thoroughly indefensible withdrawal from public life and avoidance of the common duties in which our complicated modern social organization enmeshes us. Or here is an innumerable body of particular crochets more or less offensive to sane thought. And for all of them alike "the authority of Christ" is confidently appealed to. The case obviously calls for a serious examination of the basis on which "the authority of Christ" is claimed for these things, and Dr. Forrest has felt this obligation and has given us a series of excellent chapters in which the interpretation of Christ's precepts and the general bearing of His teaching is searchingly examined and illustrated. It is a dreary mass of crass and often evident misinterpretations and misapplications of Christ's words which he has to expose.

If Dr. Forrest had stopped at this point, although there would certainly remain points of detail which would invite criticism, he would have made us all his debtors. But unfortunately there are a number of instances in which the authority of Christ is invoked for matters not to Dr. Forrest's mind, with regard to which it cannot be denied that the recorded words or example of Jesus warrant the appeal. And Dr. Forrest has unhappily permitted himself to be misled on their account into an attempt to discredit the authority of Christ. He pleads that we must not raise the dilemma in men's minds " as to whether the acceptance of His authority is compatible with loyalty to truth " in any region of their investigation (p. 2): and he does not seem to perceive, or at least does not stay at this point sufficiently to consider, that if this principle is given universal validity it amounts to saving Christ's authority in name while discarding it in fact throughout the whole range of knowledge. Under its pressure, he seeks to escape the dilemma, first, by throwing doubt upon the exact transmission of our Lord's words and example; and next by invoking a theory of the incarnation by which the authority of His teaching and example, even when fully before us, is reduced to the vanishing-point. The book thus becomes a sustained attempt to throw off the authority of Christ altogether; and by this driftage of the argument its own unity is, as we have said, seriously marred. For what is the use of arguing at great length that the teaching and example of Christ have been misapplied by this or that class of reasoners or body of Christians, if we are not quite certain what the teaching and example of Christ are, and they have no authority at any rate? The assertion in the opening chapters of the book of a theory of the incarnation which robs the teaching and example of Christ of all authority, antiquates beforehand the argument of the later chapters that the teaching and example of Christ have often been grossly misinterpreted by those who have appealed to them. The argument of these later chapters proceeds on a major premise which has already been discredited, and can command our attention only if the assertion of the former chapters is rejected by us. The gravamen of the case the book seeks to make out certainly lies therefore in its opening chapters, in which Dr. Forrest attempts to expound the incarnation as in its very nature voiding the authority of Christ; and that attempt must therefore claim our previous attention. We think this unfortunate, for the excellence of the volume lies in its later chapters, in which the proper use of Christ's authority is studied. But we have no choice. Both the logic of the case and Dr. Forrest's own arrangement of his matter demand of us to seek the crux of the volume in its opening chapters and its theory of the incarnation.

This theory of the incarnation is nothing other than that kenotic theory which, after enjoying a remarkable vogue in the middle of the last century, has in more recent years fallen very much out of credit, as continued discussion has thrown more and more into light its inherent weaknesses, or rather impossibilities — metaphysical, exegetical, theological, and religious. Respectable in the hands of its first propounders as an attempt to do justice to Christological data neglected by the Lutheran construction in which they had been bred, it has lost the respect of men when it has become only a fig-leaf to hide the nakedness of those who, fallen from their first estate of trust in the God-man, yet shrink from standing forth in a bare naturalistic conception of the person of Jesus. It is thus, unfortunately, that it appears in Dr. Forrest's pages, as in those of most of its remaining advocates. Dr. Forrest declines to enter into the deep questions which such a theory necessarily brings with it. "It is quite futile," he says, "to seek to disparage the idea of the Son's self-limitation by asking what became of His cosmical function during the incarnate period" (p. 95). And then he enumerates a number of the suggestions which have been made to meet this and similar difficulties raised by the kenotic assumption, with the general implication that any of them will do well enough — although no one of them has yet been invented which does not fatally infringe upon either the Christian doctrine of the Trinity or our fundamental conception of God. With these things, however, Dr. Forrest does not concern himself. His concern is rather with the right of men to hold to be false, what the Son of Man recognized as true. Says he: "The frank recognition that such was the character of the Son's incarnate state is a prime necessity for Christian faith at the present time. For this age is pre-eminently one of historical research, bent on discovering as far as possible the actual facts of the past. Now it has been demonstrated beyond dispute that there are sayings of our Lord which, taken literally, seem to conflict with established results of biblical investigation, and that His teaching in many of its parts is coloured by temporary Jewish influences. When Professor Pfleiderer, on grounds such as these, ridicules the notion that Christ is a 'final definitive authority,' the only right reply is: We do not claim that Christ's word is final in all spheres. . . . We can only gain for Christ His true place and essential significance by plainly recognizing, not only that the limitations are there, but that they are the inseparable accompaniments of a historical Incarnation" (pp. 96–97). Which, being interpreted in the brutal language of the streets, means just that we cannot in the face of modern research sustain the claim of Christ to "authority." Dr. Forrest would, in- deed, distinguish and say, except in the "sphere of faith and con- duct" (p. 3) — or, as he puts it here: "We do claim that He has embodied in His person and in the principles He has expounded the final revelation of religious truth and practice, of 'what man is to believe concerning God, and what duties God requires of man'" (p. 97). The care with which this language is chosen should not, however, pass unobserved. Even in "the sphere of faith and con- duct" Dr. Forrest is not prepared to claim absolute and indefectible authority for every utterance of Jesus. "His teaching in many of its parts is coloured by temporary Jewish influences," and we shall need to take these into account in applying it to our own times: and this " revelation " of religious truth and practice does not find its embodiment so much in spoken words enunciating final doctrine and promulgating final precepts, as in lives quickened by the Spirit He has sent and efflorescing under His influence into true thinking and high acting. There is, thus, at least a tendency in Dr. Forrest's discussion to reduce the authority of Christ to His immanent action on the conscience of the race, or of His Church. " That He constantly confronts us with an obligation which presses down upon us from the Unseen " constitutes " what we call the authority of Christ " (p. 7). This seems to mean that Christ is the incarnate conscience of the race; and His authority consists in the coincidence of His demands on us with the demands of our religious and moral nature. " He quickens the impulses and resolves " of our moral and religious nature, and we respond to it in a higher outlook and upward aspiration —

> " Then a sense of law and beauty,
>   A face turned from the clod —
> Some call it Evolution
>   And others call it God."

Dr. Forrest calls it Christ: and sees here Christ's authority manifested. It is thus that Dr. Forrest adjusts his profound reverence for Jesus as the " final authority " of Christians and his inability to find in His recorded teaching a final authority for his thinking and acting. It is always painful to disturb such adjustments: and the more painful as it becomes evident that the adjustment is in the individual an expedient to retain as much as is possible to him of the higher truth. But what choice have we? In this sphere too the maxim will be found to have in all its absoluteness its inevitable application: " Ye cannot serve two masters."

Dr. Forrest's impulse to the adoption of the kenotic theory of the incarnation seems then to be rooted in mental perplexity in view of the conflict between some of Jesus' utterances or points of view and some suggestions of recent research. This perplexity is voiced in such phrases as this: " If Christ is declared by us to guarantee the accuracy of what is scientifically disproved, or at least improbable in the last degree, we are much more likely to imperil His claim than to establish the disputed point " (p. 69). And certainly we may be permitted to suspect that the dogmatism with which the elements of the kenotic theory are asserted and the fundamental postulates of the Chalcedonian Christology are discarded, is a reflection of the terrror with which the dilemma Dr. Forrest finds himself in inspires him — the terror lest all trust in Christ be destroyed in wide circles by the conflict between His utterances and recent theory. But Dr. Forrest seeks support for his theory from Scripture. Why he should be exigent in this matter is not very apparent, in view of the weak hold which the authority of Scripture has upon him, particularly in its historical element, the only element on which he can depend for the dramatization of our Lord's life on earth, from which he derives his chief support in advocating the kenotic theory of His incarnation. But, permitting that to pass, Dr. Forrest has persuaded himself that the Scriptures give us, both in their didactic teaching and in the portrait they draw of Jesus in the Gospels, a kenotized Christ; and he supports himself on this their supposed testimony. We cannot say, however, we have found anything very new or particularly strong in the exegetical argument with which he has favored us.

To the great passage, Phil. ii. 6 ff., he consecrates two long passages (pp. 98 ff. and 338 ff.) — one of them a formal discussion in the kenotic interests: and, of course, he says many things in both of them which command our attention and exhibit his own careful study of the passage. But in neither discussion can he be said to have advanced the matter in hand. The more formal discussion (pp. 98 ff.) even acquires a somewhat unpleasant flavor from the sustained effort made in it to rid it of its two most obvious theological implications — that of the unbroken persistence of the Son of God " in the form of God " after His incarnation, and that of the consequent coexistence in the incarnate Son of " two natures." It is quite certain that in the phrase ἐν μορφῇ θεοῦ ὑπάρχων, the participle embodies the conception of continuance and, therefore, declares not merely that Jesus was before His incarnation " in the form of God " but also that He retained that " form of God " after His incarnation. The sixth verse indeed, as its tense-forms unmistakably indicate, lays the basis in one broad negative statement for the entire positive statement given in verse seven, and there analyzed into two parts — not less, then, for the " He humbled Himself " than for the " He emptied Himself." The unbroken continuance of our Lord " in the form of God " is therefore of the very essence of the assertion; and it is it which governs the choice of the language throughout the entire passage. It is this that accounts not only for the λαβών and the γενόμενος (in both instances), but also for the ἐν ὁμοιώματι and the σχήματι, which have seemed to many "to point to an apparent rather than to a real Incarnation" only because the ruling idea of the passage, that Christ Jesus always continued to be — because He was by nature and could not but be — "in the form of God," has been lost sight of. It was because He continued in His incarnation to be "in the form of God," that He is said, not to have come to be in "the form of a servant," but to have *taken* "the form of a servant": there was here no exchange of one "form" for another, but an addition of one "form" to another; as the ecclesiastical language has accurately phrased it, there was an "assumption." Accordingly He is said, not to have "become man," but to have "become in the likeness of men." The docetic inference had been excluded by the "He *took* the *form* of a servant"; there is no illusion here, but a real assumption of the "form," that is, of the characterizing quality, of all that belongs to, the servant's nature. The transmutation notion is now excluded by the assertion that He did not, in assuming humanity, "become man" exactly, but only "became in the likeness of men": He remained much more than He seemed; though His humanity was a real humanity, really "assumed," and He lived in the sight of man within the limits of this humanity so as to appear only man, this was not all — He remained "in the form of God" all the time as well, and therefore was only "in the likeness of men."

Whatever He did therefore as man — within the limits of the humanity He had assumed — He did voluntarily, by an ever fresh act of voluntary self-abnegation. His dying, for instance — that was not an inevitable sequence of His incarnation, but an additional act of voluntary self-devotion. He who is and remains "in the form of God" may properly at any and all times claim and exercise His right of "being on an equality with God" the deathless one, and not die: and this possibility and right is wholly unaffected by the fact that He has assumed into union with Himself "the form of a servant," and thus has made it possible for Him to act here too "in the likeness of men." Accordingly we are told, in order that the example of our Lord in His self-abnegation may be exhibited in its full extent, that "being found in fashion as a man," "He humbled Himself" — it is a voluntary act of His own, not an inevitable consequence of His changed nature, no longer in His power to do or to prevent; and that He did this "by becoming" — it is a change to the unnecessary, not a submission to the inevitable, that is signalized by the term "by becoming subject even unto death." Death, then at least — and all that led up to and accompanied and issued from death in His subjection to human conditions — was not the unavoidable and irresistible consequence of His incarnation, coming of itself as the necessary lot of the nature He had, not assumed, but become; but an additional act of humiliation voluntarily entered into in the prosecution of His mission by Him who, just because He remained "in the form of God," had no necessary part in death, but might well have held to His inherent right to be in this matter also, on "an equality with God." Not only is at least this much so imbedded in the passage that it cannot by any artifice of exegesis be driven out of it, but it constitutes the main and emphasized teaching of the passage, on which hangs its whole value to Paul in his exhortation to his readers to look not to their own things but each also to the things of others, and thus to have the mind in them which was in Christ Jesus.

The meaning of the passage to us, then, is precisely that, according to Paul, the Son of God did not lay aside His divine "existence form" in "becoming man," but, retaining in full possession all that characterizes God as God and makes Him that specific Being we call God (for that is the significance of "being in the form of God"), took to Himself also all that characterizes a servant as a servant and makes Him that specific being we call a servant; and having so done, willed to live out a servant's life in the world, subjecting Himself from moment to moment, by uncompelled and free acts of His unweakened will, to the conditions of the life which, for His own high ends, He willed to live, and manifesting Himself thus to man as "in the likeness of men," "in fashion as a man," though He was all the time Lord of all. This is, of course, the precise antipodes, the express and detailed contradiction, of the entire kenotic construction. It is the assertion of the dual nature of our Lord: for according to it the humanity of our Lord was something added to (λαβών) His divine nature, not something into which His divine nature was transmuted. And this includes of course the assertion that within the person of Christ there are two "minds"; though both matters are denied by Dr. Forrest with intense dogmatism. "No matter how real may be the affinity of divine and human nature, these two diverse methods or forms of operation can by no possibility coexist within the same conscious personality" (p. 89, cf. pp. 51, 91) ; " there was but one mind, that of the Word made flesh " (p. 58, cf. pp. 53, 90). It is also the assertion of the retention, in the incarnate state, in possession and use, of the whole body of divine attributes, which in their sum make up " the form of God "; although this too is not only denied but scoffed at by Dr. Forrest. He complains of those who occupy the same position here with Paul, that they " calmly transfer " " what is true of the Son in His timeless existence " " to Him in the period of His humiliation, as if the continuity of His absolute attributes were self-evident " (p. 65, cf. pp. 51, 53, 59). It is further the assertion that the controlling factor in our Lord's whole earthly manifestation, as well as in His entire life-history, is His divine nature, since it was He who was in the form of God who not only " emptied Himself " by taking the form of a servant, thus becoming in the likeness of men; but also, being found in fashion like a man, humbled Himself by becoming subject even unto death and that the death of the cross; although this too Dr. Forrest sharply denies (pp. 91–92).

But above all for our present purpose — for this is the hinge on which the whole kenotic controversy turns — it is the assertion that our Lord's life of humiliation on earth was a continuous act of voluntary self-abnegation, in which He by the strong control of His absolute will to live within the bounds of a human life, moment by moment denied Himself the exercise of His divine attributes and prerogatives in all that concerned His mission, because He had come to do a work and for the doing of it it behooved Him thus to do; and not the unavoidable natural development of a purely human life incapable as such of escaping the changes and chances which are necessarily incident to humanity. By this assertion Paul sets aside at one stroke the whole kenotic contention, to which it is essential to hold that in our Lord's life of humiliation " there was not merely " (as Bishop O'Brien puts it in words adopted and utilized by Dr. Forrest, p. 93) " a voluntary suspension of the exercise " " of all His infinite attributes and powers," " but a voluntary *renunciation of the capacity of exercising them,* for the time." And not only Paul, we may add, but the whole Gospel narrative as well, to which Dr. Forrest would make his appeal, as if it dramatized Christ's life on earth as not only a purely human one but a helplessly human one. A very simple test will exhibit this. Let any simple reader of the Gospels be asked whether their narrative leaves upon his mind the impression that Jesus' life and acts were determined for Him by the necessary limits of a well-meaning but weak humanity; or were not rather the voluntarily chosen course of a life directed to an end for the securing of which He daily denied Himself the exercise of powers beyond human forces. No simple reader of the Gospels will be easily persuaded that Jesus' life was what it was because He had for the time lost the capacity to act in superhuman powers: that it was, for example, lack of power rather than lack of will which withheld Jesus either from making the stones bread at the demand of the tempter (else where was the temptation?), or from coming down from the cross when challenged thereto by the scoffing multitude. But when we have assured ourselves that the limitations within which Jesus' life were cast were voluntary from day to day and act to act — and not the necessary sequence of a change which had once for all befallen Him at His incarnation — we have cut up the kenotic theory by the roots.

The advocate of the kenotic theory who, under the condemnation of the Epistles, seeks comfort from the Gospels, certainly has a claim upon our pity. No one of the evangelists, assuredly, shares his conception. To one and all alike Jesus is God manifest in the flesh, and to each and all alike a divine manifestation is both a *manifestation* and a manifestation of *what is divine.* " Even the oldest Gospel," says that Bousset whom Dr. Forrest repeatedly quotes as if he were an " authority " in such matters, — on this occasion indeed speaking truly — " even the oldest Gospel is written from the standpoint of faith; already for Mark Jesus is not only the Messiah of the Jewish people, but the miraculous eternal Son of God whose glory shone in the world. And it has been rightly emphasized that in this regard our three first Gospels are distinguished only in degree from the fourth." And again: " In the faith of the community, which is shared already by the oldest evangelist, Jesus is the miraculous Son of God in whom men believe, whom men set wholly by the side of God " (" Was wissen wir von Jesus," 1904, pp. 54, 57). It would be hard if writers, writing for the express purpose of depicting a divine Being manifesting His deity in His daily course, should have so missed their mark as to have presented us rather with a portrait in which only a human life is manifested. That they have not done so is obvious to every reader of their Gospels. And when Dr. Forrest attempts to make it appear that they have done so, he not only wilfully shuts his eyes to one whole half of their representation, but sets himself in direct contradiction to their whole portraiture of

Jesus. It is he, not they, who tells us that Jesus had a " bounded outlook," was " subject to all the influences of His immediate surroundings," and even in His " perfection " was not " absolute " but " conditioned " (pp. 11, 12). In their view Jesus' outlook had no limits, He was master of all circumstances, and His perfection was just the perfection of God. So far from Jesus' " perfection " being to them " conditioned, not absolute," " derived, not creative," negative, not positive (" His sinlessness means that He did not at any point of His progressive experience deflect from the specific ideal of service set before Him by God," p. 12), it was just the realization in a human life of the perfection which constitutes the ethical content of the idea of God (Matt. v. 48), asserted by Jesus as His own possession as the Son of God (cf. Volkmar Fritzsche, " Das Berufsbewusstsein Jesu," 1905, pp. 31–32). According to the evangelists thus Jesus' perfection is the manifestation of the τελείωσις of God in flesh: a manifestation made under the conditions of human growth, it is true, but a *manifestation,* and a manifestation precisely of the τελείωσις of the absolute God. Others needed daily to seek from God forgiveness of their unceasing sins: He, needing no forgiveness, is the dispenser of forgiveness to others, and even commits to others the right to remit sins. As self-evident as is the evil of all others (Matt. vii. 11), so self-evident is it that " doing the work of the Father " brings them into unison with Him (Matt. xii. 50): since whatever the Father has, in that does He share (Matt. xi. 27).

It surely is hopeless to appeal to evangelists seeking to present this conception of Jesus, in order to validate a theory that in the days of the flesh He was phenomenally mere man with no capacity left Him for divine activities. Of course they represent Him as growing in wisdom, and as therefore at every stage of His growth lacking in complete knowledge and perfected wisdom: as subject to changing emotions — and there might have been included, only there does not chance to be included, in this, the experience of the emotion of surprise; as making inquiries and learning by experience. All this belongs to another side of His complex personality — the human side, which the evangelists, though they do not dwell upon it so fully or make its validation so much the end of their writing, yet are as far from obscuring as His divine dignity and powers. If we begin with the dogmatic announcement, " There was but one mind in Christ," naturally — *cadit quaestio.* If there was but one mind in Christ, then certainly He could not have been at one and the same time the subject of knowledge and ignorance, He could not have been at once God and man. But then, the whole Gospel narrative becomes at once a mass of contradictions: contradictions which cannot be voided by resolutely shutting our eyes to one and that the main line of representation and focusing attention on the lower and less emphasized series. Thus we are brought, to say nothing more, into flagrant contradiction with the main purpose and general trend of the evangelical narrative. It is designed to set forth Jesus to us in His divine majesty: to it He is the manifestation of God in the flesh. To Dr. Forrest, He reveals nothing but human limitations in His life. " Confessedly, what we desire to discover is the revelation which God has been pleased to give us in Jesus Christ. We see that in certain instances Christ is represented as characterised by limitations. Of what value is it to say that, while these existed for Him in one sense, they did not exist in another? The sphere in which they did *not* exist is, *ex hypothesi,* outside the range of the revelation " (pp. 55 ff., cf. p. 79). It is worth while to insist on this and similar passages. For they are not chance utterances but belong to the essence of the situation. What we have to interpret is a double series of parallel facts. The means of interpretation adopted is neglect of one whole series and exclusive validation of the other. The result is that all that is left to be said of Jesus in the days of His flesh is that He was subject to human limitations.

Let us not blink this shocking result. All that Christ was, in the days of His flesh, was, according to this conception, that limited nature whose outlook was bounded, which was accessible to temptation and was the subject of moral growth (p. 79). This was absolutely all there was to Him. Behind this there were no depths in that personality. The Scriptures tell us that God's outlook is boundless, that He is essentially perfect, that He is not tempted of evil. In what sense was this Jesus, then, who was nothing beyond and above the nature whose outlook was bounded, which suffered temptation and was the subject of moral growth — and who therefore was not in any recesses of His being perfect as God is perfect — in what sense was this Being God? Dr. Forrest wishes to recognize Him as God. In order to recognize this Being as God, however, he must redefine Deity and in redefining it he must define it away. The ultimate difficulty of all theories of the class that he is defending is thus brought before us. Having set their hearts on a merely human Christ, and yet feeling unwilling to yield up frankly the divine Christ of the Gospel revelation, they end by debasing the idea of God to the human level; so that in the end we lose not only our divine Christ but God Himself. That simply is not God which is imperfect, and in process of perfecting by means of temptation. If this is all that Christ is, then Christ is not God; and Dr. Forrest continues to call Him such only by stress of old habit and by a willing delusion. Dr. Forrest seeks to make capital (pp. 94, 95) out of the consent of the humanitarian theorizers with the orthodox in their perception of the absurdity of the kenotic hypothesis. If it is any comfort to him to cry out against the upper and nether mill-stones grinding together, he ought not to be denied that small comfort. It ought, however, not to seem unnatural that every consistent thinker — whether his consistency is of belief or of unbelief — should think ill of a theory which inconsistently wishes to be both at once.

We cannot illustrate here in detail the straits into which Dr. Forrest is brought by his attempt to interpret the Christ of the Gospels as a mere limited human being in His phenomenal manifestation. It admits of no doubt, for instance, that the evangelists represent Him as sharer in the whole extent of the divine knowledge, differentiated from the prophets (with whom Dr. Forrest confuses Him, p. 7, though He never calls Himself a mere prophet) just in this — that to the prophets God reveals some items of knowledge, while His Son shares in all He knows (Matt. xi. 27). We have lately had occasion to point this out, however (see Hastings' " Dictionary of Christ and the Gospels," article " Foresight "), and will not here go over the ground again. Let us take the sole example we can allow ourselves, then, from another sphere — that of the divine power which the evangelists ascribe to Christ; but which Dr. Forrest in the interests of his theory denies to Him, insisting that He wrought His mighty works, like other instruments of God's will, only by means of the power of God graciously exerted, now and again, in His behalf. In the course of his argument he necessarily, however, comes across this phenomenon of the Scriptural representation: that Jesus in working a miracle says, " I will: be thou clean "; " I say unto thee, arise "; while His disciples say, " In the name of Jesus of Nazareth "; " Jesus Christ maketh thee whole." In face of this contrast Dr. Forrest knows nothing better to urge than this paradox: that " the emphasis which He puts on His own personality is an assertion, not of His independence of the Father, but of the entireness of His dependence upon Him "! By this he apparently

hopes he will persuade us that the distinction here drawn only means
that Christ was more dependent — more perfectly dependent, he
would say — on an exterior power for the working of His miracles
than His apostles even!

Surely no one will contend that the Son is " independent " of the
Father; much less that the Mediator of the Covenant, in His covenanted work, acts " independently " of the Father. Here is only one
of those " undistributed middles " which are as characteristic of
Dr. Forrest's reasoning as the misplaced " only " is characteristic
of his style: for the whole plausibility of his paradox here depends
on the ambiguity of the use of the words " dependent " and " independent." The plain man will be slow to believe, however, that the
contrast between the " I will " of Jesus and the " Jesus Christ
maketh thee " of His disciples, is not a contrast between the relatively independent action of the Lord and the relatively dependent
or instrumental action of the apostles, in the matter of working
miracles. It is nothing less than obvious, indeed, that the difference in
the modes of statement means that the power by which the miracles
of Jesus were wrought was in some high and true sense His own
power, while that by which those of the apostles were wrought
was not in this high and true sense their own power. So far from
it being possible to say that Jesus " was not the worker of His own
miracles," we must go on to say that, according to this representation, He was the worker not only of His own but also of those of
His disciples as well. The whole series — His and theirs alike —
was His work. Is this a false testimony of the authors of the
historical books of the New Testament? Jesus Christ on earth or in
heaven — but whether on earth or in heaven, the same Jesus Christ
incarnate — is the real source of the power by which the miracles,
whether of His own or of His disciples' working, were wrought: and
what is really significant of the record is that it takes pains by its
" I will " and " Jesus Christ maketh thee whole," to say this of
all alike. There is no such distinction then in the minds of these
writers as that which Dr. Forrest draws between the earthly and
the exalted Christ, in respect to this question. Of course this is not
to say that God the Father was not concerned in the working of
these miracles, and that they were wrought " independently " of
Him: that the Man Jesus was not conscious of resting on the
Father's power, or of doing merely the Father's will: that in all
His mediatorial work He did not act as the " Sent of the Father " —

as His " delegate," if you will. These are deeper questions than can be touched upon in this notice: but it is surely already super-abundantly evident that they are not to be lightly set aside, as if there were no profound problems here of the interrelations of the Persons of the Godhead — by the shallow expedients at the disposal of a kenotic theory. Enough that here too, as at every other point, the kenotic theory runs precisely athwart the most emphatic deliverances of the Gospel narratives.

In the failure of the kenotic theory on which he bases his whole argument, the entire structure of Dr. Forrest's attempt to reduce the authority of our Lord in sphere and character alike, of course falls to the ground. It will scarcely do to say that God is authoritative only in the spheres of faith and conduct. It is, of course, open to Dr. Forrest to follow his Bousset and his companions, and assail the trustworthiness of the Gospel report of Christ's teaching and life. We have already seen that he exhibits a tendency here and there to find in the evangelic report the intrusion of the later reflection of the community. We cannot believe, however, that he is prepared to carry this to such lengths as, like Bousset, to disengage from the Christ of faith as presented in the evangelists a Christ of fact who was merely man, and perhaps something less than an average man; much less to such lengths, as, with Pfleiderer, to lose the real Christ altogether behind the veil of the Christ of faith. The retention of the Christ of the evangelists in any recognizable form, however, entails the retention of the Christ of authority — authority in His declarations as well as in the religious impression He made, and in His declarations in all spheres as well as in those of faith and conduct. Of this Christ, it is illegitimate to speak, as Dr. Forrest speaks of his kenotic Christ, as if He were liable to repeat in His teaching Jewish errors (p. 69), and not quite able to forecast the future in which His authority might be wrongly applied. There remains to us, of course, the whole duty of carefully weighing His words and example and of seeking to apply them only according to His will. Whatever value Dr. Forrest's book possesses to us will be found to lie in its earnest attempt to perform this work in several departments of thought and action. He has, of course, not been able in even this serious and careful discussion to place himself on a plane which is above criticism: but he has led us through a study of the relation of Christ's teaching to individual and corporate duty which is cast in a high note and cannot fail to interest every reader.

We must not neglect to say frankly before closing, nevertheless, that in tho course of his discussion Dr. Forrest occasionally hints at theological positions which we cannot share and which on another occasion we should like to traverse — such as, for example, his very defective doctrine of providence in connection with an exaggerated doctrine of freedom (pp. 139, 140, 142, 143, 146), or his conception of the gift of the Spirit without distinction of His miraculous endowment of the apostles and His indwelling in the people of God, or, indeed, his fundamental conception of Christianity as summed up in "the filial spirit" (pp. 153, 202). Nor would we neglect to say equally frankly that we deprecate the apparently confused way in which certain findings of modern criticism are here and there utilized, as if they stood apart item from item and did not form a part of a closed system of anti-supernaturalistic interpretation. But on none of these things can we dwell now. We shall only stay to say in a word that Dr. Forrest's second work does not seem to us to fulfill the promise of his first one: but exhibits him as embarking upon a line of thought from advancing in which his well-wishers will heartily pray he may be saved.

WHAT IS RELIGION? By WILHELM BOUSSET. Translated by F. B. Low. New York and London: G. P. Putnam's Sons. 1907. (London: Williams & Norgate.)[1]

PROF. BOUSSET tells us that "the object of this little book is" to help us "to understand the meaning of the phenomenon which we call religion" (p. 6). It is the phenomenon which he undertakes to expound; that is to say, he deals directly with the phenomenology rather than with the philosophy or the psychology of religion. In other words, his method is historical. He traces what he conceives to be the history of the development of religions from their beginning in the first vague manifestations of the religious aspirations of man to their culmination, we do not say in Christianity, but in the liberal Christianity of the twentieth century; and through this medium of history he seeks to convey to the reader a conception of what religion is.

[1] The Princeton Theological Review, vi. 1908, pp. 479–484.

Prof. Bousset's book is, therefore, historical in form. But it is not primarily historical in purpose. As there are some novels which are written " for the novel's sake," and some which are written " for a purpose "; so there are some histories which are written for the history's sake and some histories which are written " for a purpose." And Prof. Bousset's history of religions is of the latter class. He does not trace the varied forms of religion which have been prevalent among men merely that he may make these forms known to us; nor even that through them and their sequence he may make the development of religion known to us; nor even that through this development he may make what religion as religion is known to us. His real purpose, dominating his whole undertaking, is that he may make Christianity — naturally, as he conceives Christianity — known to us. The book, therefore, very properly culminates in two long chapters on the Nature and the Future of Christianity, for which in point of fact the whole of the preceding chapters have been written and to which they lead up. In a word, Prof. Bousset's little book is a study of the nature and prospects of Christianity from the point of view not so much of " comparative religion " or of the " history of the religions," as of the so-called " comparative-religion " or " history-of-religion " (*religionsgeschichtliche*) school. It is in other words an attempt to explain Christianity, in its entirety, as a religion among religions, the product like other religions of the religious nature of man.

Prof. Bousset is quite frank and quite emphatic in the expression of his point of view upon the main matter at issue — whether, to wit, Christianity is just a religion among religions, the product, like all other religions, of the religious nature of man. Nor does he wait for his exposition of the course of religious development to suggest this, or to establish it. He announces it already in his Introduction, practically as a postulate; and sets out on his exposition of the course of religious development, therefore, with his goal well in view. The distinction so often drawn between " revealed and natural religion " — as if, forsooth, " the religion of the Old and New Testaments is revealed religion," and " all others are natural religions, the product of man's thought or imagination " — is in his opinion thoroughly untenable — " impossible " is his word (p. 8) — and, indeed, " irreligious and Godless " (p. 7). For not only is it not accordant with the principle of historical evolution, but it implies a " narrow-minded and melancholy view of the history of humanity."

This mode of speech is determined by the shock which it gives Prof. Bousset that anyone should suppose God to have allowed " the nations " " to go their own way " without guidance from Him, the implication being that all religion is the product in a sense of " revelation." Elsewhere his thought swings around the opposite focus of the ellipse. The thinking of men imbued with modern culture, he tells us, " rests upon the determination to try to explain everything that takes place in the world by natural causes; or — to express it in another form — it rests upon the determined assertion of universal laws to which all phenomena, natural and spiritual, are subject " (p. 283). " Historical science," accordingly, " puts before itself the object of explaining all intellectual events by reference to a universal law " (p. 288). There is, no doubt, always " the riddle of personality and individuality " which enters everywhere into the fabric of history; but this is not the same thing as — or in any way analogous to — the intrusion of a supernatural factor. The " halo of the supernatural " which has in the past " clung around ' sacred history ' " has been disrupted. We can now believe only in an evolution of religion shaping itself in accordance with " the universal evolution of civilization," and it is in consequence no longer possible to " believe in a Divine revelation, in the old acceptance of the term, which restricted revelation to one special province " (p. 289). Thus we see the curve of the ellipse turn back on itself. When we speak of " the natural course of events " and of " the direction of Divine revelation," we are speaking of one and the same thing, and the upshot of it is that Christianity is no more " revealed " than any other religion and is just as much a product of human thought and imagination as any other religion. It takes its place among other religions as just one of them — the purest form, the highest and most perfect, religion has yet reached: but certainly not the only true religion, " but simply the most complete species of the genus " (p. 9).

It is to exhibit this of Christianity that Prof. Bousset has written his book. As was natural, he takes his start from the beginning. Religion being natural to man, there never was a time when men did not have religion; or if we, from the evolutionary standpoint, must say that " there must be some point of time when religion had its beginning," that point of time must be placed so early that " wherever human life advanced a stage religion was evolved " (p. 2). Its first beginnings were no doubt of a low character — corresponding to the low intellectual and social development of its creators. Prof. Bousset puts " animism " at the basis of all religious development; and then traces the gradual evolution of religious conceptions and practices from it, in stages running *pari passu* with the development of social organization, up through tribal and natural to universal religions. Prof. Bousset is a scholar of wide reading and an expositor of decided gifts; and much that he tells us of these several phases of religious construction is well conceived and well told. But by means of it all he is working his way steadily onward to an explanation of the religion of the Bible — or, from his point of view, we should say, of the religions of the Old and New Testament writings in their several stages — as of purely natural origin. He is careful, therefore, to insert accounts of the successive stages of religion which he thinks he finds set forth progressively in the several strata of the Biblical books in their proper places in the advancing evolution. And so he comes at last to the origin of Christianity.

Christianity, like certain other high religions of " reform " character in this, owes its origin, of course, to the impulse received from a great personality, the greatest religious personality the world has (as yet) seen. An element of inexplicability is thus introduced into it; for who can read the riddle of powerful personalities? But this does not prevent our perceiving that it grew naturally out of the soil of its own time. What Jesus did may indeed be summed up almost entirely in one word: He simplified the developed Judaism of His day. The Jewish Rabbis are quite right in saying that everything that Jesus taught may be found taught beforehand in Judaism. The proper retort is to acknowledge that the Rabbis had said all that Jesus said — and to add that " unfortunately they said so much else besides " (p. 217)! What Jesus did was not to add to their teaching but to subtract from it. The note of His teaching was simplification. He freed religion from rationalism, ceremonialism, legalism, and scribism. And doing so, He gave us Christianity. For the Christianity of Jesus is just the Judaism of His day freed from these elements and thus reduced to the simple doctrine of God as Father, who forgives the sins of men, because He is good.

The Christianity of Jesus, we say: but not the Christianity we know, or indeed the Christianity a modern man can accept. For the development of religion did not stop with Jesus. After Jesus came, for example, Paul. And Paul's Christianity is not the Christianity of Jesus. For one thing, the Christianity of Paul worships Jesus, and

Jesus worships God alone. For another thing, the Christianity of Paul talks of an atoning sacrifice, of which Jesus knew nothing. For yet another thing, the Christianity of Paul has incorporated into it sacramental acts, to all which that of Jesus is a stranger. Nor did the development stop with Paul. After Paul came Old Catholicism; and after Old Catholicism, Mediævalism; and after Mediævalism the Reformation; and after the Reformation has come — or at least is coming — Modernism. And it is not the Christianity of Jesus or the Christianity of Paul — or even the Christianity of the Reformation, great as is the advance of the Christianity of the Reformation on all preceding Christianities — which can lay claim to being the highest of religions, but the Christianity of Modernism now at last assuming firm outlines and a stable form. The old order has changed and given place to a new: " since the Reformation the whole structure of human life has entirely altered, and history and experience teach us that when this happens religion assumes other forms " (p. 271). A new Christianity conformable to the data supplied by modern culture is, therefore, now called for.

" The narrow Pauline idea of redemption, which was developed by St. Augustine and strengthened anew by Luther " (p. 275), must go. We must " no longer speak of the ' divinity ' of Christ " (p. 279). And with the " divinity " of Christ must go all its corollaries — primarily the self-contradictory doctrine of the Trinity. The idea of an atonement and of a vicarious sacrifice, of course, goes too (p. 282). And indeed the whole conception of the supernatural which has hitherto ruled — which contradicts not only " our whole mode of thought " but also " our changed belief in God " (p. 285): and with this idea of supernaturalism must go also not only the whole notion of an inspired book, but also of a special revelation (p. 289). This is not to return to the Christianity of Jesus. The Christianity of Jesus lies at the root of Christianity; it does not appear at its apex. Jesus believed in the supernatural: we cannot (p. 286). We cannot accept His demonology or His eschatology (p. 292). Even much of Jesus' moral teaching is too one-sided or ascetic to be possible to a modern man (p. 295). It is ours not slavishly to copy but to grow. " We take our stand by Jesus " only in the Parable of the Lost Son and " on the ground of the absolutely simple conviction that God is to be found in the good, and that faith in the Heavenly Father includes moral deeds and moral work in the human community." Here is the creed of the Christianity into which all the

religious development of all the ages meets and coalesces: " God
the Father; life in accordance with His will, spent in joyful work
for the service of the world; forgiveness of sins and eternal hope "
(p. 298).

We must bear in mind that it is this Christianity which Prof.
Bousset has in view when he tells us that Christianity is the last
and best of religions and that the future of religion is bound up in it.
What place does Christ take in this Christianity? None whatever.
He is merely the impressive religious personality back to whose
impulse is traced the development which has issued, after two thousand years, in it. If we can say of the Jewish Rabbis that they taught
all that Christ taught, but the mischief of it is that they taught
so very much more: so we must say of Christ that if He taught all
of this " abiding " Christianity, the mischief again is that He taught
so very much more. Why call this new Christianity by His name
any more than call this Christianity Judaism? He did not more
" simplify " Judaism than our moderns are " simplifying " Christianity. And let us particularly note what this new " simplification "
reduces us to. It is just God, morality, immortality. " God the
Father "; " life in accordance with His will, spent in joyful work
for the service of the world "; " forgiveness of sins and eternal
hope." Is there any religion which does not embrace these three
elements of " natural religion "? No doubt the conception of God, the
conception of morality, the conception of immortality which are
commended to us bear the traces of Christian teaching. It is God
" the Father." It is life " in the service of the world." It is " forgiveness of sins." We are thankful that it is proposed to retain this much
of the contribution of Jesus and of His accredited apostles to the
religion of the world. But it is worth while to observe that when
Christianity is reduced to a " natural religion " in its origin, it is
reduced also to a " natural religion " in its contents: it shrinks at
once to the meager contents of the familiar trilogy, of God, morality, and immortality.

The main question of course recurs, Has Prof. Bousset succeeded
in reducing Christianity to a " natural religion " in its origin? He
has certainly put together an account of the origin and development
of religion, into which he has interspersed an account of the origin
and development of the religions of the Scriptural narrative, including Christianity, in all its developments, on the assumption that
it is equally with all the rest a " natural religion." But this is

merely Prof. Bousset's historical argument for the naturalistic origin
of Christianity. He says, in effect, " See, if this be conceived to be
the way religion has come into existence and developed itself in the
course of the ages, then Christianity may be conceived to be a
growth of nature." The " if " here is, however, a mighty one and
covers an immense assumption, or rather a whole series of immense
assumptions. Behind it lies the assumption of the validity of all the
results of the Graf-Wellhausen critical reconstruction of the history
of the development of the Old Testament religion; and of all the
results of " the history-of-religion " critical reconstruction of the
history of the New Testament development. Behind it lies the assumption of the invalidity of all the evidence of the divine origin
of the religion of the Bible, of the divine mission of Christ, of the
revelation of truth through His Spirit to the apostles: in a word,
of the whole body of the claims of the founders of Christianity, substantiated as those claims are by a mass of the most varied evidence.
In one word, behind it lies the simple assumption of the naturalistic
origin of Christianity. Prof. Bousset's essay amounts, therefore,
merely to this declaration: " See, if Christianity is merely a natural
religion, this is the way it must be conceived to have come into
existence." The argumentative value of his presentation will reduce,
therefore, simply to this: that a self-consistent scheme of the origin
of Christianity as a natural religion can be constructed. For the
testing of the value of this presentation as an argument, we should
have, therefore, to examine into the self-consistency of the presentation primarily; then into the legitimacy of the combinations that
are made, the exactness of the facts which are marshaled, and the inclusiveness of the explanations which are offered.

This is not the place to enter into such a detailed examination.
But it is not out of place to remark simply that in none of these items
is Prof. Bousset's presentation in our opinion impeccable. In addition to the primal assumption to which we have adverted, his presentation is burdened with a mass of minor assumptions. The facts
are adjusted to fit the thesis, instead of the thesis inferred from the
facts. And the whole presentation takes, therefore, merely the form
of a plausible effort to justify a foregone conclusion. If this is in its
details at least the course of the development of religion we must
assume in case Christianity be deemed a natural religion, we can
only say that Christianity cannot be deemed a natural religion.
It does not naturally emerge out of its environment as here presented.

DARWINISM TO-DAY. By VERNON L. KELLOGG. New York: Henry
Holt & Co. 1907. With good analytical Table of Contents and
an (insufficient) Index.[1]

A BOOK like this has long been greatly needed: and this ever
increasing need is admirably met by this volume. Of course, Prof.
Kellogg writes from his own point of view, and he would not be
human if he did not leave some things to be desired. Readers of his
book should supplement it by reading also some such book as
Rudolph Otto's "Naturalism and Religion"; as readers of Otto's
book should certainly supplement it by reading Prof. Kellogg's.
If what Otto has to say, for example, upon teleology, and the relation
of teleology to mechanical explanations of phenomena, will help
the reader to correct Prof. Kellogg's unreasonable objection to all
that he calls "mystical" in our world-view, Prof. Kellogg will
on the other hand give him a far richer knowledge of, if not a
deeper insight into, the great debate which has been going on of
late upon the factors and processes of the development of organized forms. No one can have been unaware of this debate or of
the gradual modifications it has been working in the attitude of the
scientific world to the traditional Darwinian conceptions. But the
general reader has lacked adequate guidance to an exact estimate of
the drift of the discussion, and has been liable to be left in a state
of mental confusion or to be unduly swayed by the latest advocate
of a special line of theory he may have chanced to read. A comprehensive survey of the whole field of the debate from the hand of a
competent guide is what he has needed. And this is what Prof. Kellogg has given us in this volume.

Prof. Kellogg wisely begins at the beginning — with a lucid
account of what Evolution means, in general, and what that particular theory of Evolution known as Darwinism really is. And he
rightly finds the differentiation of Darwinism, specifically so called,
in the Selection Theories — or, let us say, that we may keep our
eyes fixed on the real pivot of it all, in the theory of Natural Selection. Keeping this central point well in sight, he next gives his readers
a careful and clear account, in no way glozing its extent or its seriousness, of the widespread revolt of biological investigators during
the last few decades against the principle of Natural Selection —
against ascribing to it the whole work of species-forming, and even

[1] *The Princeton Theological Review*, vi. 1908, pp. 640–650.

at times against ascribing to it any effectiveness or capacity for species-forming. Having thus exhibited the attack on Darwinism in its full reach and force, he next, with equal care and fullness, recounts the defense which has been made of it — a defense sometimes very strong, but always involving certain concessions which go to modify or even to transform the rôle which is ascribed to Natural Selection in the molding of forms. This leads naturally to a survey of the new theories of species-forming which have been suggested, whether as auxiliary to the theory of Natural Selection, designed to supply its deficiencies, or as alternative to it, designed to supplant it. This survey has not been carried through without betraying Prof. Kellogg's own predilections; the volume naturally closes, therefore, with a chapter on Darwinism's Present Standing, in which the results of the debate are summed up and Prof. Kellogg's own conclusions outlined. These conclusions may be briefly stated in these two sentences (p. 374): " Darwinism, as the all-sufficient or even most important causo-mechanical factor in species-forming and hence as the sufficient explanation of descent, is discredited and cast down." " Darwinism, as the natural selection of the fit, the final arbiter in descent control, stands unscathed, clear and high above the obscuring cloud of battle." That is to say, Prof. Kellogg recognizes in Natural Selection a true cause, actually working in nature, to the control of which the stream of descent is subjected, so that when we look at the whole course of development, we see it moving on under its guidance. But he recognizes also that Natural Selection rather works on the stream of descent than produces it, and accounts rather for the general channel in which it flows, than for itself, whether in its main character or many of its minor characteristics. He evidently conceives himself as standing midway between the contending extremes, allowing to Natural Selection a most important function in species-forming, but denying to it the omnipotence which the Neo-Darwinians are prone to ascribe to it.

The place of Darwin in the history of the evolutionary theories is determined by the fact that he first pointed to a *vera causa*, actually working in the world, to which could be plausibly ascribed the production of the various forms which occur in the animated universe. The essence of his suggestion consisted in the very simple proposition that if multitudes more beings are born into the world than can possibly live in it, it will be inevitable that those which are least fitted to live in it will be crowded out, which will result naturally in the survival of the fittest in each generation. Thus there will come about the gradual molding of organized beings to fit their environment. The strength of the theory lies in its simplicity, and its apparent appeal to nothing but recognized facts. We all know that overproduction is the law of life. We all know that no two individuals are precisely alike. We are all prepared to allow that in the struggle for existence which seems inevitable in these circumstances it will be the fittest among these unlike individuals which survive. We are equally prepared to admit that, as " like begets like," the fittest will reproduce in their offspring their fitnesses. Who, then, can deny that in the course of innumerable generations going on thus, very considerable modifications from the original stock might be produced? Is there not given here, then, an adequate account of the whole course of development of animate forms?

Certainly the theory looks very simple and convincing. But so soon as we transfer it from the region of imaginary construction to that of fact, difficulties arise. Many of the objections which have been urged against it seem to us, to be sure, to be little justified. These are largely directed against its consistency or completeness as a logical construction. From this point of view, however, as it seems to us, the theory is unassailable. When, for example, it is objected — as it has been persistently objected — that it provides only for the survival of the fittest, not for the production of the fittest; that it leaves unexplained the whole matter of the cause of variation and particularly of the causes of the actual variations which occur; that it has no account to give of the opportune appearance of the variations needed, or of the repeated consecution of variations in the same direction in the line of actual descent — and the like: the mark seems to us to be completely missed. The Darwinian theory does not need to concern itself with the origin of the fittest, the cause of variation, the causes of the specific variations which occur, or their opportuneness or consecution. It is logically complete in the simple postulates of variation, struggle for existence, the survival of the fittest. If we admit, as all must admit, that no two individuals are ever exactly alike, then we must admit that some of these individuals are more fit to exist than others; that is given in the very fact of difference. We need not concern ourselves with how the " fitness " arises; relative fitness is inherent in the mere fact of difference. Neither need we concern ourselves with the objection that relative fitness in some particulars in a given individual may be offset by relative unfitness in other particulars. To estimate in these circumstances which organism is on the whole most fit to survive might puzzle us: it cannot puzzle Nature, which acts simply along the line of the resultant. Wherever two individuals exist it is inevitable that one will be " fitter " than the other: wherever thousands or millions of individuals, generically alike, come into being, there necessarily exist among them some, few or many, who will be " fitter " than the rest. And if these thousands or millions of individuals come into being in such circumstances that the great majority of them must needs be crowded out, the survival of the " fittest " seems certain; and as this process goes on through generation after generation, the line of descent must follow the line of relative fitness.

Logically unassailable as the theory is, however, so soon as we presume that this process has actually gone on, we find ourselves faced with many difficulties. The difficulties are important — or let us frankly say, as it seems to us, are destructive of the theory. But they do not lie against the logical completeness (and therefore the plausibility) of the theory, but rather against its actual working power. It may be suspected that it is often an underlying sense of these factual difficulties, subtly modifying the objector's point of view as to the conditions of the problem to be solved, which accounts for the pressing of the (really ineffective) logical difficulties. These real difficulties raise such questions as these: What reason is there to believe that the struggle for existence in animate nature is severe enough rigorously to eliminate in each generation all but the fittest to survive? What reason is there to suppose that the differences by which (as we all must agree) individuals are discriminated from one another, are great enough to form telling factors in the struggle for existence, even supposing it to exist in the rigor which the theory postulates? What reason is there to suppose, even if the variations are great enough to furnish a handle for selection and the struggle for existence is severe enough to weed out all but the fittest in each generation, that this process, continued from generation to generation, will result in any great modification of type, and the successive generations will not rather fluctuate around a center, as variation itself fluctuates around this center, and thus on the whole the type remain stationary? Or if there is marked on the whole an increasing divergence from the original type as the line of descent advances through the fittest of each generation — a general divergence on the whole amid much fluctuation (which seems the most that, on the theory, can be possibly postulated) — what reason is there to suppose that this divergence could advance very far in the time at disposal? And above all, what reason is there to suppose that this slowly increasing divergence produced by the survival in each generation of only the " fittest " — through the many fluctuations to this side and that which, on the hypothesis, must occur — could in the time at disposal produce the infinite variety of animate forms which has actually come into being? Or, to put the question in its sharpest form, could not only bridge the gulf which separates the amœba from man, but bridge it by a steady upward advance — upward, that is, not merely in the sense of ever more and more perfect adjustment to the environment, nor even in the sense of progress " from homogeneity to heterogeneity," to ever greater complexity of structure, but measured by an absolute standard of value? For this is what has really happened, if the palæontological record has anything at all to tell us; and it has happened, if any trust at all can be placed in the calculations of the physicists, with a rapidity which confounds thought. The formal completeness of the logical theory of Darwinism is fairly matched, therefore, by its almost ludicrous actual incompetence for the work asked of it.

Of course, this has become ever more and more apparent as time has passed, and workers in the relevant fields of research have escaped somewhat from the obsession of the specious plausibility of the Selection Theory and looked more squarely in the face of the problems to be solved. Here and there, no doubt, as was inevitable, there has been a disposition exhibited to gloze its inefficiency, and to " cure " its defects by ineffective remedies. A recent instance of this is noted by Prof. Kellogg, when he records (p. 55) Prof. Ray Lankester's appeal to the properties of radium as offsetting the physicists' calculations as to the time available for the possible existence of life on the earth. If, Prof. Lankester argues, the sun contained a fraction of one per cent of radium, that would offset its estimated loss of heat and, " upsetting all the calculations of the physicists," give us the thousands of millions of years which are needed (on the Darwinian hypothesis) " to allow time for the evolution of living things." When men catch at straws like this to

buttress their theories with, it becomes clear what a strawy foundation they are building on. Nor would the concession of the thousands
of millions of years needed (but not obtained) relieve the difficulties
of the case, which have led biologist after biologist to suggest supplementary theories designed to meet the failure of the main
theory in this or that aspect of it, or, in ever increasing numbers
as time has gone on, to propose alternative theories, and in extreme
instances to assume an attitude of opposition to the doctrine of
descent altogether. Thus De Vries's theory of " mutations " may be
supposed to be ultimately due to the feeling that " natural selection "
must have marked variations to work on; Eimer's theory of " orthogenesis " to the feeling that some account must be given of the
advance of development along a straight line; Nägeli's theory of
a " principle of perfection " in organisms to the recognition of the
steady advance of the line of evolution towards something that looks
very much like a goal.

The result of it all is that Darwinism, specifically so called —
that is, as a particular theory accounting for the differentiation of
organic forms — stands to-day not merely as Prof. Kellogg somewhat too gently puts it (p. 5), " seriously discredited in the biological world," but practically out of the running. Even the most
extreme Neo-Darwinians (like Weismann) have been compelled to
supplement it by auxiliary theories which altogether change its
complexion. It is quite true also, on the other hand, however, that
nothing has come to take its place; as Prof. Kellogg truly puts it
(p. 375): " these bitter antagonists of selection are especially unconvincing when they come to offer a replacing theory, an alternative explanation of transformation and descent." The real state of
the case seems to be that the deficiencies of the Darwinian hypothesis
have come to be widely recognized and numerous suggestions have
been made, which severally provide for, or seek to provide for, this
or the other of these deficiencies. But no one of these will serve
any better than Darwinism itself serves — possibly not even so well
as Darwinism serves — as a complete " causo-mechanical " explanation of the differentiation of organic forms. Each severally —
all in combination (so far as they can be combined) — still leave
something, and something essential, to be desired. The problem still
presses on us; a great variety of suggestions are being made to
solve it; it remains as yet unsolved.

What most impresses the layman as he surveys the whole body of

these evolutionary theories in the mass, is their highly speculative
character. If what is called "science" means careful observation
and collection of facts and strict induction from them of the principles governing them, none of these theories have much obvious
claim to be "scientific." They are speculative hypotheses set forth
as possible or conceivable explanations of the facts. This is fully
recognized by Prof. Kellogg. "What may for the moment detain
us, however," he says (pp. 18 f., cf. p. 382), "is a reference to the
curiously nearly completely subjective character of the evidence
for both the theory of descent and natural selection. . . . Speaking
by and large we only tell the general truth when we declare that
no indubitable cases of species-forming or transforming, that is,
of descent, have been observed; and that no recognized case of natural selection really selecting has been observed. . . . The evidence
for descent is of satisfying but purely logical character; the descent
hypothesis explains completely all the phenomena of homology,
of palæontological succession, of ontogeny, and of geographical
distribution; that is, it explains all the observed facts touching
the appearance in time and place on this earth of organisms and the
facts of their likenesses and unlikenesses to each other. . . . The
evidence for the selection theory . . . also chiefly rests on the logical
conclusion that under the observed fact of over-production, struggle
is bound to occur; that under the observed fact of miscellaneous
variation, those individuals most fortunate in their variations will
win in the struggle; and, finally, that under the observed fact of
heredity, the winners will transmit to their posterity their advantageous variations, all of which inter-acting facts and logically derived processes will be repeated over and over again, with the result
of slow but constant modification of types, that is, formation of new
species " (cf. pp. 92, 394). What is thus true of the theory of descent
in general and the specific theory of selection put forward to account
for this descent, is equally — often far more — true of the auxiliary and substitutionary theories which have been suggested to fill
out the deficiencies of the latter or to supplant it (cf. pp. 382, 391).
These are often hyper-speculative theories, which have only this
to recommend them to our consideration — that *if* they be conceived
to represent fact they may supply an explanation of the facts of
observation. Thus far, there is no other reason than this for supposing them to represent fact. And it is obvious that a vivid imagination may supply many competing theories of this hypothetical

sort and all of them prove subsequently to have no basis whatever in reality. The lay reader may be excused if, reading over the outlines of these several theories, he is oppressed with a sense of their speculative character; in a word, of their unreality. For ourselves we confess frankly that the whole body of evolutionary constructions prevalent to-day impresses us simply as a vast mass of speculation, which may or may not prove to have a kernel of truth in it. All that seems to us to be able to lay claim to be assured knowledge in the whole mass is that the facts of homology and of the palæontological record suggest that the relation of animate forms to one another may be a genetic one. So soon as we come to attempt to work out for ourselves a theory of the factors and process of the differentiation of these forms, we are in the region of pure speculation and can claim for our constructions nothing more than that the facts leave them tenable. Whether they ought to be held as well as are capable of being held, we seem to lack all direct evidence.

The next thing that most strongly impresses the lay reader is the amazing zeal which is exhibited by our biological workers for these speculative theories. It is not merely that every man has his theory and sets great store by it, however speculative it may be. It almost seems at times that facts cannot be accepted unless a " causo-mechanical " theory be ready to account for them: which looks amazingly like basing facts on theory rather than theory on facts. Prof. Kellogg himself is no stranger to this state of mind. He is at least repeatedly telling us of this or the other contention that it is unacceptable because no " causo-mechanical " theory explaining its operation is forthcoming. It almost seems at times as if it were " causo-mechanical " theories rather than facts that our biological investigators are on the lookout for. And let us note well, that it is a " causo-mechanical " theory alone that satisfies them. There must be no " mysticism " involved; we had almost said no " mysteries." They seem to say to us that nature is as plain as a book and has no secrets which are intrinsically secrets, but only secrets in the sense that they are not yet found out. But above all, they not only seem to say — but, if we are to take Prof. Kellogg for an example, do say — that there must be no loophole left in our explanations for the intrusion of even directive forces from without. It is enough for Prof. Kellogg to condemn a theory out of hand, if it involves the recognition — or the suspicion — of the working in animate nature of forces deeper — or higher — than physico-chemical ones. Accordingly the Neo-Vitalism which is playing its part in the biological circles of Germany is set aside with a bare word. " Bütschli has well pointed out," we read, " that Neo-Vitalism is really only a return to the old ' vital principle ' belief, and that we are now, and have been ever since our practical giving up of the vital principle notion, making steady progress in the explanation of life-forms and life-functions on strictly mechanical and physico-chemical grounds " (pp. 226–227). Even when it is introduced " under a pseudo-scientific guise," therefore — as, no doubt, for instance by Driesch, who in positing " an extra-physico-chemical factor " (which he calls " psychoid "), yet is careful to represent it as " an attribute of, or essential kind of potentiality pertaining to, organized living substance " — the assumption of the interworking into the phenomena of organic life of anything above " physico-chemical " forces is treated as out of the question. The whole animate universe is to be explained on the basis of these forces alone, and no theory of it is even to be taken into serious consideration which is not ready with a " causo-mechanical " explanation on these grounds. Here is a chance sentence, for example, which seems to indicate in a word the settled point of view of Prof. Kellogg himself certainly and apparently of those whom he naturally represents: " Nägeli's automatic perfecting principle is an impossibility to the thorough-going evolutionist seeking for a causo-mechanical explanation of change " (p. 387).

This amounts, it will be seen, to a definitely polemic attitude — of a rather extreme kind — towards teleology. It is true that teleological language is sometimes employed. In the immediate context of the sentence just quoted, Prof. Kellogg speaks of the occurrence of " determinate or purposive change." But this is only an instance of that " personifying language " which is the bane of naturalistic writers. What he means is that " the simple physical or mechanical impossibility of perfect identity between process and environment in the case of one individual and process and environment in the case of any other " will automatically produce such a variety in individuals as will result in " the change needed as the indispensable basis for the upbuilding of the great fabric of species diversity and descent." That is to say, he is here only saying that the simple fact of unlikeness between individuals — so that no two individuals are precisely alike — provides materials for selection to work on and precludes the necessity — on Darwinian ground — of inquiring into the causes of variation or seeking out a principle of orthogenesis. There will always be " a fittest " at hand. We have already pointed out the sense and limits in which this contention is valid. What is here interesting us is that this is all that Prof. Kellogg means by " determinate or purposive change." His polemic attitude towards all real teleology in the evolutionary process — to the intrusion into it of the guidance of purpose, properly and not abusively so called — we will not say is betrayed, it is expressed, over and over again in this volume. In criticizing the type of theory represented by Nägeli and Korschinsky which assumes " a special tendency towards progress " in the organism — " an inner directive force," an " inner law of development " — for instance, Prof. Kellogg writes (p. 278) : " It is needless to say that but few biologists confess to such a belief. However much in the dark we may be regarding the whole great secret of bionomics, however partial and fragmentary our knowledge of the processes and mechanism of evolution, such an assumption of a mystic, essentially teleologic force wholly independent of and dominating all the physico-chemical forces and influences that we do know and the reactions and behaviour of living matter to these influences which we are beginning to recognize and understand with some clearness and fulness — such a surrender of all our hardly won actual scientific knowledge in favour of an unknown, unproved, mystic vital force we are not prepared to make. As Plate well says, such a theory of orthogenesis is opposed, in sharpest contrast, to the very spirit of science." Again (p. 376) : " Modification and development may have been proved to occur along determinate lines without the aid of natural selection. I believe they have. But such development cannot have an aim; it cannot be assumed to be directed toward advance; there is no independent progress upward, i. e., toward higher specialisation. At least, there is no scientific proof of any such capacity in organisms. Natural selection remains the one causo-mechanical explanation of the large and general progress toward fitness; the movement toward specialisation; that is, descent as we know it." Still again, criticizing von Kölliker (p. 330) : " He included in his general theory of heterogenesis a basic plan of progressive evolution. Such a conception has in it too much ontogenic orthogenesis; it is too redolent of teleology for present-day biology." Teleology itself is seen then to be the *bête noire* of biology as represented by Prof. Kellogg. " Certainly," we are told (p. 375), " no present-day biologist is ready to fall back

on the long deserted standpoint of teleology and ascribe to heterogenesis or orthogenesis an auto-determination toward adaptiveness
and fitness." " Definitely directed variation " he may with Weismann allow to exist (p. 199) ; " but not predestined variation running
on independently of the life conditions of the organism as Nägeli
. . . has assumed " (cf. p. 381). As he expresses it with the polemic
edge well turned out, in another place (p. 377): " Nor can any
Nägelian automatic perfecting principle hold our suffrage for a
moment unless we stand with theologists on the insecure basis of
teleology." That is to say, the ultimate objection to Nägeli's " principle of perfection " is — just that it is too much like teleology — the
" teleology of the theologists." In other words, the scandalon is precisely teleology, in any form.

Now all this is very depressing. The anti-teleological zeal of Mr.
Darwin is well known: the vigor with which — as, for instance, in
his correspondence with Asa Gray — he repelled the intrusion of
teleology into his system betrays his fundamental thought. The
anti-teleological implication of Darwinism, taken in its strictness —
when it becomes a system of pure accidentalism — is obvious. But
it could have been hoped that we had got by now well beyond all
that. Some lack of general philosophical acumen must be suspected
when it is not fully understood that teleology is in no way inconsistent with — is rather necessarily involved in — a complete system
of natural causation. Every teleological system implies a complete
" causo-mechanical " explanation as its instrument. Why, then,
should the investigators of the " causo-mechanical " explanation
array themselves in polemic opposition to the very conception of
governing purpose? Above all, why should they make the test of the
acceptability of theories, the recognition or non-recognition by them
of teleological factors? This gives the disagreeable appearance to
the trend of biological speculation — we do not say of biological
investigation — that it is less interested in science for science's sake,
that is, in the increase of knowledge, than it is in the validation of
a naturalistic world-view: that it is dominated, in a word, by
philosophical conceptions, not derived from science but imposed
on science from without. Of course, there are many workers in the
biological, as in other scientific fields, to which this will not apply.
And it may well be contended that the drift of thought among
investigators in these fields is precisely towards the recognition
of the mystery of life and life-processes, of their inexplicability on

purely physico-chemical grounds, of the necessity of the assumption
of the working of some higher directive force in the advance of
organic development — in a word, towards just that vitalism and
teleology which Prof. Kellogg scouts, not as excluded by observed
fact or by proved theory, but as inconsistent with " the scientific
spirit " — which seems as much as to say with an *a priori* philosophical attitude. In the meanwhile, however, it seems clear that
much of our scientific thought is still under the control of a very
definite anti-teleological (which is as much as to say an a-theistic,
for teleology and theism are equipollent terms) prejudice.

We should be sorry to close even so desultory a notice of a
book so competent and so informing on a note of blame. After all,
the book is not an anti-teleological treatise; and though its allusions
to the hypothesis of teleology in organic nature are disturbing, they
are only allusions. What the book undertakes to do is to " present
simply and concisely . . . the present-day standing of Darwinism
in biological science," and to outline " the various auxiliary and
alternative theories of species-forming which have been proposed
to aid or to replace the selection theories " (p. iii.). And this it does
well, with thorough knowledge, with sufficient fullness, and with
adequate exactness. Prof. Kellogg exhibits here great skill in expounding and much penetration in criticizing the several views
which have been advanced, and commends his own views to us by
their moderation and balance. He impresses us as a safe guide to the
history both of evolutionary speculation and of biological research.
Readers desiring to know the present state, whether of knowledge or
of opinion, in this sphere of research, cannot do better than to resort
to his comprehensive and readable volume.

NATURALISM AND RELIGION. By Dr. RUDOLF OTTO. Translated by
    J. Arthur Thomson and Margaret R. Thomson. Edited with an
    Introduction by Rev. W. D. Morrison, LL.D. New York: G. P.
    Putnam's Sons; London: Williams & Norgate. 1907.[1]

DR. OTTO is introduced by his English editor to his new audience
as " a thinker who possesses the rare merit of combining a high

[1] *The Princeton Theological Review*, vii. 1909, pp. 106–112.

philosophic discipline with an accurate and comprehensive knowledge of the science of organic nature." The appearance of the name of Prof. Thomson on the title-page of the book as translator, may be taken as an additional guarantee of the scientific competency of the author. The book itself fully meets the expectations so aroused. We do not, indeed, share the author's philosophical standpoint; and still less can we homologate the theological conceptions which may occasionally be read between the lines. But there can be no question that the book is ably thought and attractively written; or that its author is exceptionally well informed in the current scientific discussion of Germany, and is exceptionally well equipped to expound it alike in its details and in its general drift. As a result we have in the book an admirable survey of recent German speculation on the origin and nature of the world and man, and a strong and convincing defense of the right of religion in the face of modern thought.

Dr. Otto calls his book " Naturalism and Religion," and explains its purpose as " in the first place, to define the relation, or rather the antithesis, between the two; and, secondly, to endeavour to reconcile the contradictions, and to vindicate against the counter-claims of naturalism, the validity and freedom of the religious outlook " (p. 1). Or, as he somewhat more crisply expresses it at a later point, " to define our attitude to naturalism, and to maintain in the teeth of naturalism the validity and freedom of the religious conception of the world " (p. 278). The real subject of the book is, therefore, Naturalism; and its real purpose is to assert over against Naturalism the right of religion. Its primary purpose, in other words, is polemic rather than constructive. It is less concerned with the positive exposition and development of the religious conception of the world than with the vindication of the right of a religious conception of the world. Of course Dr. Otto has not written so much without suggesting what, in his view, the religious conception of the world includes. He has even formally outlined and briefly expounded and even argued its elements. But neither the strength nor the mass of the book is given to it, but is expended rather on a careful critical survey of current forms of Naturalism, with a view to exhibiting its essential failure. From our point of view the value of the book is immensely increased by this circumstance. For Dr. Otto's philosophical and even theological conceptions would necessarily dominate his positive construction of the world-view to which he would give the name of religious. And, as we have already explained, we do not particularly care for Dr. Otto's philosophical or theological views. But in his exposition and criticism of Naturalistic theories he is moving on ground common to all who would cherish a religious world-view of any sort. And here we can follow his lucid expositions and his trenchant criticisms with unalloyed satisfaction.

Dr. Otto's philosophical standpoint is that of a convinced Kantian idealism, or perhaps we ought rather to say he is a disciple of that mixed product of Kant and Jacobi, Jacob Friedrich Fries, who has lately been disinterred in Germany and given at least some semblance of renewed vitality. Although he doubtless transcends Fries's anti-teleological view of nature, some slight echo of it may perhaps be detected in his willingness to admit that a direct study of nature will not yield a teleological view of it. The Friesian leaven is more in evidence, however, in his view of religion as rooted primarily in a sense of mystery, upon which he then engrafts, to be sure, the sense of dependence in which religion centers, and the conception of teleology in which, we may say, it culminates. The peculiar extension he gives to the implications of the feeling of dependence, by which he derives from it the assurance not only that man, the subject of this ineradicable and surely not misleading feeling, is a contingent being, but that so is the whole world itself, has, perhaps, its roots in the same idealism. The external world which is our creation, can scarcely be less dependent than the beings whose creation it is. One gets the impression that Dr. Otto's objection to Naturalism turns less on the obliteration by Naturalism of the distinction between matter and mind, than on Naturalism's attempt to work this obliteration the wrong way about. The external world from which Naturalism would explain mind, he would rather explain from mind. And so it comes about that as the argument runs on it seems almost to become rather a plea for spiritualism than for what we commonly speak of as a religious interpretation of the world. Its thesis almost appears to be summed up in the striking and strikingly true remark (p. 283) that " mental science, from logic and epistemology up to and including the moral and æsthetic sciences, proves by its very existence, and by the fact that it can not be reduced to terms of natural science, that spirit can neither be derived from nor analysed into anything else." At this point, however, we are a little puzzled by the rushing in of another current of Dr. Otto's thought, which almost sweeps away this spirit, the substantial existence of which he seems to have so firmly established.

We must not talk, it seems, of its "substantial nature" (p. 330) —
that is "a matter of entire indifference" (p. 331); what concerns
us is only its "incomparable value" (p. 331). "What lives in us . . .
is not a finished and spiritual being . . . but something that only
develops and becomes actual very gradually" (p. 298). Whence it
comes . . . who can tell? Or whither it goes? All we know of it is,
lo! it is here. And, that it is the manifestation of something that is.
"There is no practical meaning in discussing its 'origin' or its
'passing away,' as we do with regard to the corporeal. Under certain
corporeal conditions it is there, it simply appears. But it does not
arise out of them. And as it is not nothing, but an actual and effectual
reality, it can neither have come out of nothing nor disappear into
nothing again. It appears out of the absolutely transcendental, associates itself with corporeal processes, determines these and is
determined by them, and in its own time passes back from this world
of appearance to the transcendental again" (p. 358). Is this only
another way of saying that "the soul that rises with us, our life's
star, hath had elsewhere its setting, and cometh from afar"? Or
does it, as we much doubt, mean much more than this? Decidedly
Dr. Otto's philosophy needs watching. And we may be glad it does
not form the staple of his book but only lies in its background.

What forms the staple of his book is the exposition and criticism
of Naturalism. Naturalism, he tells us, exists in two forms, naive
and speculative. And speculative Naturalism entrenches itself in
two great contentions, the one embodied in the Darwinian doctrine
of evolution, the other in the mechanical theory of life. To the exposition and criticism of these two great contentions of Naturalism
Dr. Otto accordingly devotes himself. To the Darwinian theory
chapters 4 to 7 (pp. 85–186) are given; to the mechanical theory of
life, chapters 8 to 11 (pp. 187–359). The discussion in both cases is
full, the exposition clear, the criticism telling.

In dealing with the Darwinian theory, Dr. Otto very properly
distinguishes between the theory of descent in general and the
specific form given this theory by Darwin's hypothesis of the indefiniteness of variations and the survival of the fittest in the
struggle for existence. The former, he points out, has maintained its
ground, or perhaps we may even say has strengthened its stakes.
Dr. Otto intimates, almost as a matter of course, his own adhesion
to it. The latter, on the contrary, has become in the estimate of wide
circles, not merely suspect, but even disproved. Dr. Otto intimates

that he himself will have none of it. But it is precisely in this peculiarly Darwinian theory of "natural selection" that the virus of
Naturalism in current evolutionary speculation is prominent. The
theory of descent is in no sense specifically Darwinian: it is far
older than Darwin and remains the conviction of multitudes who
are definitely anti-Darwinian. What is specifically Darwinian is
the appeal to the factors of overproduction, indefinite variation,
struggle for existence and consequent elimination of the unfit and
the survival of the fittest as containing in themselves the true account of the modifications which have produced the multitudinous
forms of life. Thus teleology was reduced to an illusion and suitability substituted in its place: utility became the one sufficient
creator of all that is living. The widespread dissatisfaction with,
and even rejection of, this account of organic development which
marks the present state of discusion may be taken as at the same
time, therefore, a refutation of the Naturalism which underlies
it, because it is an exhibition of the inadequacy of mere utility to
account for all things. As investigation has gone on it has become
clearer and clearer to numerous students of the subject that variations do not occur indifferently in every direction, but turn up
opportunely. As Du Bois-Reymond expressed it in his vivid way,
Nature's dice are loaded; not accidentalism but purpose rules her
acts. The greater organism of the animate world grows apparently
like the lesser organism of the individual being along fixed lines by
definite steps to determined ends. "Natural selection" may have a
part to play in the process: but it is in wider and wider circles
coming to be believed that it is a very subordinate part. It can work
on only what is given it; and it does not seem to have indefinite
variations in every direction to work on, but, rather, very definite
variations in one direction. The goal attained is, therefore, not determined by it, but by the inherent tendency of the developing organism. So, at least, an increasing number of students of nature
are coming to think.

Dr. Otto's method is marked by a very large infusion of the concessive spirit. He betrays no tendency to drive antitheses into
contradictions; and he does not permit the cause of teleology in
nature to be identified with the extremest anti-Darwinian opinions.
On the contrary, he is quick to point out that purpose has no quarrel
with means; and can live, therefore, under the strictest reign of law.
It is not law which is fatal to purpose, but chance. Nay, says he,

" absolute obedience to law, and the inexorableness of chains of sequence are, instead of being fatal to ' teleology,' indispensable to it." " When thére is a purpose in view," he argues, " it is only where the system of means is perfect, unbroken, and absolute, that the purpose can be realised, and therefore that intention can be inferred " (p. 83). Accordingly, therefore, he considers it possible to embrace in a teleological interpretation " the whole system of causes and effects, which, according to the Darwin-Weismann doctrine, have gradually brought forth the whole diversity of the world of life, with man at its head " (p. 150). For why may not this be looked upon " as an immense system of means," intricate no doubt, but working to its end with inevitable necessity — which may therefore be the manifestation of intention (p. 151)? At a later point, when dealing with the mechanical theory of life, he reverts to the same line of remark to show that mechanism has in it nothing inconsistent with purpose (pp. 222–223). Mechanism may be only the way in which purpose realizes itself. Of course, the danger here is that we may fall thus into a deistic conception of the method of what we theologically call " Providence." But this does not seem necessary, even when the whole of what we call nature is conceived as " a machine." Though the guiding hand of purpose be conceived as everywhere and at all times immediately operative, nevertheless the whole account of the several phenomena would be found in the efficient, not in the final causes. In no case are the final causes to be conceived as additional efficient causes producing with them a resultant effect. They are and remain only final causes and operate only through and by means of the efficient causes. Each phenomenon finds its whole account when severally considered, accordingly, in its efficient causes. It is therefore indifferent to purpose whether the events which occur under its government occur as products of mechanical or free causes. " Providence," then, which is but another way of saying " purpose," is as consistent with a mechanical theory as with any other theory of life: because " purpose " is not discerned in the separate phenomena but in their combination. Romanes was quite right, therefore, when he regretfully said of his earlier mistake in ruling purpose out of the universe: " I had forgotten to take in the whole scope of things, the marvelous harmony of the all." Dr. Otto is anxious that his readers shall not make the analogous mistake of supposing that because a thing is " caused " it is therefore not " intended." He does not imagine, of course, that in this vindication of teleology in relation to mechanism, he has done all that is necessary to validate the religious view of the world. He rightly supposes, however, that he has by it done something to remove some current objections to the religious view of the world; for there are still some who imagine that when they say mechanism they deny purpose. How far the alleged mechanism rules is another question.

The most striking feature of Dr. Otto's method is, however, his employment of exposition as argument. His book thus becomes a mirror of current thought on the subjects with which he is dealing. The inherent weakness of the Darwinian construction of the factors of evolution, for example, he exhibits less by direct argument of his own against it than by a running exposition of the course of evolutionary thought in latter-day Germany. The first impression the reader gets from this survey is of the uncertainty of the conclusions which are from time to time announced. He soon perceives, however, that amid the apparent confusion there is a gradual and steady driftage in one direction, and that that direction is away from Darwin's conceptions. Whatever in the end he may come to think of Darwin's theory in its application to nature, he receives a strong impression that it is fairly illustrated in this section of human research and thought. Here is certainly exhibited indefinite variation in all directions, struggle for existence, and — let us hope — the survival of the fittest. It may become us to bear in mind, to be sure, that the survival of the fittest is not quite the same as the survival of the true. It may be only the survival of the theory that fits in best with the presuppositions and prejudices of the times. Nevertheless truth is strong; and we can scarcely doubt it will (finally) prevail. And one gets the impression that, in this case, what seems likely to prevail in the meantime is the truth, and that this truth is hostile to the anti-teleological schematization of Darwin; and, indeed, to his whole construction of the main factors of evolution. Indeed, it seems at times as if the new investigators were inclined to react from " natural selection " a shade too violently, and not content with assigning *Darwinismus* to the *Sterbebett* were determined to deny to " natural selection " not only any real effectiveness or capacity for species-forming, but even reality itself. Dr. Otto avoids this extreme. He not only recognizes its operation in nature as a *vera causa* but points out that its obvious reality and actual working is the main cause of the attractiveness of the theory which found in it the one great agency in species-forming (pp. 156–157). Nevertheless, he holds firmly with the more recent thought, which discovers for it only a very subordinate rôle to play in nature; and he points out with great clearness that its dethronement and the substitution for it of theories of evolution dominated by the recognition of inherent tendencies in the organism and progression along right lines, is the definite relegation of Naturalism too to the *Sterbelager*, so far as it had entrenched itself in the doctrine of evolution.

In dealing with the mechanical theory of life, Dr. Otto employs much the same method which he uses in dealing with the doctrine of evolution. Here, too, he avoids dogmatism and relies largely on the effect a mere tracing of the history of research is fitted to produce. For the progress of investigation has been away from the mechanical view of life. We have lived to see the dawn of a new age of " vitalism "; and even where the name is scouted and the thing deprecated, the edges of the old mechanical theory have become very frayed. On the basis of present-day thought, Dr. Otto is justified in emphasizing the mystery of life and in pointing decisively to the supremeness of mind, so making way for the religious view of the world from this point of sight also.

Enough has doubtless been said to manifest the high value we place on Dr. Otto's discussion. It would be difficult to find elsewhere in such brief compass so full and lucid a survey of the recent German literature on evolution and the nature of life. And it would be, we are persuaded, impossible to find another work of such compressed form in which the failure of Naturalism as a theory of the world is more tellingly argued.

THE CHRIST OF THE CROSS: or the Death of Jesus Christ in its relation to Forgiveness and Judgment. By Rev. J. GIBSON SMITH. Wellington, N. Z.: Gordon & Gotch (London: Gordon & Gotch). 1908.[1]

MR. SMITH's object in this strongly and even fervently written volume is to propose what he takes to be a new theory of the Atone-

[1] *The Princeton Theological Review*, vii. 1909, pp. 141–152.

ment. It is not, however, as new as he takes it to be. It is in point of fact one of tho most prevalent theories of the Atonement in this age of lowered conceptions of the guilt of sin, and heightened conceptions of man's own part in the saving process. Stated in its barest outline, it is the theory that the ground on which God receives sinful man back into His favor is just man's own repentance and faith, while the part of Christ is simply to induce acceptable repentance and faith in man. This is, of course, only a form — one of the highest forms, certainly — of the so-called " Moral Influence " theory (see " The New Schaff-Herzog Encyclopedia," i. 1908, p. 352b).

Mr. Smith, to be sure, formally repudiates the " Moral Influence " theory — as he states it, that is; and that means, in one of its special forms (p. 57: " as thus stated "). But his own theory is only another mode of stating essentially the same view. He thinks he draws away from the " Moral Influence " theory (of course, in the unacceptable form of it which he outlines) in two particulars — inasmuch as he gives an essential place in his theory to the death of Christ, and makes this death " answer to some demand in the nature of God, as well as to some need in man " (p. 57). The wariness of this language should not pass, however, without observation. If an essential place is given to the death of Christ, it is not that the salvation of the sinner is grounded in the death of Christ; it is grounded in the sinner's own repentance and faith and nothing more. The necessity which is vindicated for the death of Christ arises merely out of the sinner's need of influences issuing from the death of Christ to produce in him such repentance and faith as will be acceptable to God. And if the death of Christ may be said in this indirect way to " answer to some demand in the nature of God," it directly meets no demand of the nature of God at all. It operates only to secure from man the repentance and faith which meet the demand of God's " holy mercy." The death of Christ thus terminates solely on man, affecting him; and not at all on God, affecting Him —save through the effect it works in man, by inducing in man acceptable repentance and faith.

Mr. Smith does occasionally, to be sure, incidentally use language which may seem to imply or assert that the death of Christ has an effect on God. Thus, we read (p. 54) of a " remission of sins on the ground of the death of Christ," and again (p. 36), of " obstacles to man's forgiveness in God " which Christ has come and removed. But these perhaps not unnatural reversions to the common language of Christianity must naturally be interpreted according to the terms of his own theory. And according to the terms of his theory Christ's work does not terminate on God supplying the ground on which He forgives sins, and does not remove any obstacles on God's part to the forgiveness of sin. In his view there is on God's part no obstacle to man's forgiveness, and God requires no death of Christ, or anything else of the kind, to enable Him to remit sin. All that is required to enable God's free mercy to flow forth to sinful man, is that the conditions of forgiveness necessarily imposed by a holy God on sinners should be fulfilled (pp. 106 f.). And Christ's work does not fulfill these conditions. It terminates wholly on man, enabling him to comply with the necessary conditions of acceptance with God and so be saved. " Therefore," we read (p. 106), " even though there is mercy eternally in God, and even though God requires no satisfaction to His retributive justice before He can show mercy, yet the mercy of God must remain eternally unavailable for sinful man unless, through the mediatorship of a Saviour from sin, he is enabled to comply with the conditions which God's holiness must always impose upon God's mercy." Man, in other words, is his own saviour, though, of course, only as empowered thereto by Christ. God accepts man only on the fulfillment by himself of conditions of salvation, not on the fulfillment of any conditions by Christ. Christ's whole work is to enable man to save himself: and only as man, thus enabled, saves himself can he be saved. The function which Christ performs in the saving process is not, then, that He does anything for man, but that He enables man to do all that it is necessary to do for himself.

This line of thought is very familiar. It is, moreover, the natural line of thought for one who occupies the general theological standpoint of Mr. Smith. Mr. Smith has turned his back upon the governing conceptions of his Reformed forefathers, and adopted instead the point of sight of their Arminianizing opponents. He considers himself in doing so only to be rising out of the " earth-born mist " of " fatalism," and to be according to men only " the full possession of their moral freedom " (p. 97). That is to say, in plain English, Mr. Smith takes his starting-point in a Pelagianizing anthropology; his position relatively to the condition of the human race being as nearly as possible that of historical Semi-Pelagianism (pp. 125–127). Man being thus conceived to need only incitement to enable him to do all that God requires of him, God is, on the other hand, conceived as requiring no satisfaction for guilt, but freely extending mercy to all who return to Him in acceptable repentance and faith. The resultant soteriological scheme travels thus in an ellipse around the two foci of the divine offer of mercy up to the uttermost (p. 215), and the free dealing accorded to this offer by man. Man may accept this offer; and the power to accept it is native to him; he needs divine aid only to work fully out to their complete issues the results of his acceptance of it. Or man may reject this offer, and may not in any mechanical or miraculous fashion be deprived of his power to reject it, even up to " the point of the Breaking-Strain of the Soul " — beyond which he can but reject it, and before which, of course, he may equally readily accept or reject it. His destiny being thus determined by his own choice, he who accepts God's proposals of mercy will on this acceptance, being united by faith with Christ, be, through spiritual discipline received from Christ, more and more enabled to repent and believe, and on this beginning be accepted by God on the guarantee of Christ that this imperfect repentance and faith will ultimately ripen into perfect. There would seem to be implied here a doctrine of " Perseverance," and, though this is nowhere explicitly asserted, it is everywhere implied and frequently stated in less theological language. Otherwise the scheme is the familiar Arminian one and has nothing to distinguish it from what we hear on every side of us, every day. And Mr. Smith's acumen is to be commended for perceiving that in this scheme there is no place for a doctrine of expiatory atonement; and for seeking another doctrine more conformable to his general theological point of view. If God's mercy is " free " and man's will is " free " in the senses of " freedom " ascribed to them respectively by this type of thought, a doctrine of expiatory atonement is an impertinence. And this is one of the most telling evidences of the falsity of the system. For the doctrine of an expiatory atonement is undoubtedly taught in the Scriptures, and no scheme of salvation can be the true one which, we will not say can find no place for it, but does not make it central.

Mr. Smith, of course, would deny that a doctrine of expiatory atonement is taught in the Scriptures. And it is in his effort to support this denial, if anywhere, that original material is presented by his book. He finds five " large tracts of Scripture which at least seem to be opposed to the theory " of " satisfaction to justice " in the blood of Christ (pp. 23 ff.). Three of these he subsequently, however (very justly), abandons — apparently as raising only *prima facie* objections to the expiatory doctrine of the Cross — and hangs his case on the other two (pp. 66 ff.). These, which he speaks of as " two great, important, perfectly plain, and intelligible truths " of Scripture, hitherto neglected, he calls " the Truth of the Crime of the Crucifixion " and " the Truth of the Coming Judgment " (pp. 66–67). These two plain facts of Scripture, that the Crucifixion of the Lord of Glory was a terrible, " a unique and transcendent " crime, and that there looms before men a yet future judgment in which God's righteousness will be manifested in retributive justice — he represents as utterly inconsistent with the expiatory theory of the Cross. " The former truth," he declares (p. 81), " leads us to reject that theory because it is *impossible* — for how can God's most holy justice be satisfied through the commission of a crime on the person of His Son, or through the Son's submitting to have a crime committed upon His person? The latter truth calls upon us to reject the expiatory theory, because it is *unnecessary*, for how can it have been necessary that God's retributive justice, which is, in the future, to be satisfied to the full in the final Judgment, should already have been satisfied to the full upon the Cross? " A great portion of his volume is occupied with the elaboration and enforcement of these contentions, and he quite properly places one of them, in a quotation from Mr. W. L. Walker's " The Spirit and the Incarnation," in its forefront as the motto of the whole. The entire argument, indeed, turns on them as on its hinge and stands or falls with them. And yet — can it be necessary to point out the confusions on which both of them rest?

When Mr. Smith declares, " It is simply inconceivable that the crucifixion of Christ can be, at one and the same moment, a terrible crime which God is bound to regard as a crime, and also a means of satisfying God's retributive justice " (p. 73) — what can the astonished reader do but pause in wonder and ask, Why? Why does not the philosophy of Gen. 1. 20 — " And as for you, ye meant evil against me; but God meant it for good, to bring to pass, as it is this day, to save much people alive " — apply here as it applies throughout God's dealings with men? Of course, Mr. Smith cannot sustain his own contention. He finds himself compelled to admit that the Scriptures declare that " the death of Christ was divinely appointed, and foretold, that Jesus endured it of His own free will, and that it was a death for sin, by which the salvation of believing sinners was secured " (p. 73); that in that death " the purposes of God were carried out " (p. 76), and the like. From which it emerges that the difference between him and those whom he opposes here does not concern the question whether the same transaction may be on man's part a crime deserving punishment and on God's part a vehicle of blessing for the race, but solely the question of what particular purpose of God is accomplished by this particular crime of the Cross. The tentative attempt to distinguish between *indirect* and *direct* utilization of man's crimes by God for the attainment of His ends (p. 92) may be neglected here as not directly applied by Mr. Smith to this question, and, indeed, as obviously not applicable to it. The plain fact is that Mr. Smith's whole contention at this point is but an attempt to confuse the reader's judgment by directing and holding his attention to the moral quality of the human acts involved in the crucifixion of Christ, to the exclusion of contemplation of the tremendous purpose of God in that great transaction. To say (p. 78) that it is " the supposition of the expiatory theory " " that there was practically no crime in the Cross at all, and that God's justice was satisfied thereby " is to set in collocation things which stand out of all relation to one another. Rather, on the supposition of the expiatory theory there was an immense crime committed in the crucifying of Christ, and God's justice was satisfied thereby.

When we say, however, that God's justice was satisfied thereby we are hard on the heels of Mr. Smith's second " great tract of Scriptural truth " which he represents as inconsistent with the doctrine of satisfaction in the blood of Christ — the Truth, as he calls it, of the Coming Judgment. By this he means simply that if Jesus satisfied the divine justice on the Cross, then there can remain no more remembrance of sin, and accordingly there can be left no place for a Coming Judgment. Did we not have it here repeatedly flaunted in our face, it would be incredible that anyone could fail to distinguish between the satisfaction rendered on the Cross for Christ's people and the judgment which still hangs over those who are " without." It is quite true that those who are in Christ Jesus do not come into judgment; but how that abolishes the judgment impending over those who are not in Christ, it is, we do not say difficult, but impossible, to see. What has blinded the eyes of Mr. Smith here is no doubt the strength of his revulsion from the Reformed doctrine of a " definite atonement," and his consequent zeal for a so-called " universal atonement." He is quite right in insisting that a universal satisfaction for sin on the Cross would have abolished all impending judgment. There is a certain validity, therefore, in his reiterated assertion that if, " according to the expiatory theory, God's retributive justice " (*simpliciter*) " was satisfied on the Cross," if there was made on it " a complete satisfaction of retributive justice," so that " God's retributive justice has *already* been satisfied to the full upon the Cross " (p. 74), there cannot remain any real judgment for the future. But it is safe to say no one but convinced Universalists — who do abolish all future judgment and usher all into eternal life — has ever taught such a universal atonement as this. The most convinced advocates of the so-called " universal " satisfaction for sin, Arminian as well as Calvinist, have made it hypothetical, conditioned in its efficacy on faith, so that its expiatory value inured only to believers, and a place of judgment remained for all unbelievers. We do not say that this hypothetical scheme will work: we do not think it will, and we commend recent Arminian thinkers for seeing that it will not work and discarding it. What we do not commend in them is that in discarding it they discard the expiatory doctrine and set themselves to invent lowered views of the atonement more conformable to Arminian principles. The unconformableness — which we believe to be real — of Arminian principles with the Biblical doctrine of the substitutive satisfaction of Christ, is the condemnation, not of that doctrine, but of the Arminian principles which cannot be united with it in a consistent system of truth. But all this aside, what Mr. Smith has set up in his universal expiatory atonement which satisfies the divine retributive justice *simpliciter*, leaving no retribution for the future, is a man of straw. Nobody holds to such a doctrine. Nobody holds that Christ has rendered satisfaction for the sins of any but " believers," whether these believers be conceived as the elect of God, who believe because God has bought them by the precious blood of His Son, or whether they be conceived as sinners who, by believing, have made themselves the beneficiaries of the atoning sacrifice of the Son of God. A satisfaction, however, for the sins of believers, cannot be said in any way to affect the necessity or the ethical value of the proclamation of a coming judgment for those who do not believe. Surely, if it is only by such confusions as these that the expiatory doctrine of the Cross can be attacked, it lies safely entrenched behind the mass of direct Scriptural evidence by which it is established.

The positive side of Mr. Smith's argument for his theory of the Atonement is no more solid than its negative side. What he has undertaken to commend to us in the stead of the expiatory doctrine of the Church is a theory of salvation on the ground of our own repentance and faith, induced in us by a work of Christ undertaken and accomplished for this end — that He might lead us perfectly to repent of our sins and believe in God our Saviour. For the validation of such a theory it would be necessary to show, (1) that repentance and faith can avail to ground acceptance of sinners by God; (2) that a repentance and faith such as can avail with God can be exercised by sinful men; and (3) that the work of Christ was directed towards and was adapted to and was efficient for the production in sinful men of a repentance and faith such as may avail with God. It cannot be said, however, that Mr. Smith has shown any of these things.

The first of them he does not even attempt to show. He simply assumes it, remarking lightly (pp. 107 ff.) that as a self-respecting man will certainly require repentance and faith as conditions precedent to his own bestowals of forgiveness on any brother man who has sinned against him, so God will demand the same conditions " with this infinite difference, that God must demand, not a relatively true repentance and a relatively genuine faith, but a *perfect repentance* and a *perfect faith* " (p. 109). Much effort is expended to show that this at least must be demanded by God — that nothing but a perfect repentance and a perfect faith will suffice; but no effort is made to show that this will suffice with God. That is just assumed. After the late Prof. Moberly's acute and sustained argument of this point — even which we can but judge ineffective — one would have anticipated that no subsequent writer would be able to pass it over. But cardinal point as it is to the whole theory, Mr. Smith leaves it a mere assumption that repentance and faith can avail to commend a sinner to God; and an assumption, let us add, which is at variance at once with all Scripture, all experience, and all the dictates of natural justice. In point of fact, for example, no man ever does, and no man ever contends that we ought to, " forgive," that is, absolve from punishment, criminals, say, on mere repentance: else no murderer who seriously repents of his crime would be hanged. The speciousness of his argument here depends on treating sin for the nonce merely as something personally offensive to God, rather than as something morally wrong.

This initial difficulty, or rather impossibility, having been, we will not say transcended, but put out of sight, Mr. Smith's theory is im-

mediately face to face with another equally intractable. How can
sinful man render to God the repentance and faith which a holy God
must require before extending mercy? We have seen that Mr. Smith
is insistent in asserting — properly enough — that this repentance
and faith must be perfect. Dr. McLeod Campbell cut the knot by
affirming that Christ Himself, sympathetically identifying Himself
with sinful man, offered up to God in his stead a perfect repentance.
Mr. Smith, however, — very properly again — rejects this expedient
as inoperative (pp. 61, 120). Where, then, is sinful man to get this
perfect repentance and faith, accept anything less than which God
cannot " without denying Himself " (p. 109)? Mr. Smith is no
Pelagian and cannot say that it is the ineradicable privilege of every
man to be perfect whenever he chooses. He is rather at pains to show
that " natural men," though capable of repenting and believing (for
Mr. Smith is a Semi-Pelagian), are not capable of such repentance
and faith as God — the All-holy One — is able to accept as enough
(p. 110). Here, clearly, we are at an *impasse*.

Mr. Smith gets over this *impasse* by teaching that God accepts
the promise for the performance. After all, then, God does accept our
imperfect repentance and faith (though He cannot do so " without
denying Himself "), because He foresees that this imperfect repentance and faith is after a while to become perfect. " The Scripture doctrine deals with possibilities that will by and by become actualities,
and which, in the sight of Him who is the Alpha and the Omega, are
as good as actualities already " (p. 44). " It is because God, who sees
the end of all things in their beginnings, sees that great day as though
it were present now, that He is able, in entire consistency with His
holiness, to grant forgiveness of sins to the sinful man who is united
by faith to the Christ of the Cross " (p. 180). " It is because God
finds in the faith of the Christian believer this certainty of becoming,
in the end, perfect, assured knowledge that sin is worthy of death,
that He is able, in entire consistency with His holiness, to bestow a
full and free forgiveness on the sinner whose faith unites him to the
Christ of the Cross " (pp. 194 f.). There is, of course, here confusion
worse confounded. The question raised is, On what ground can God
accept sinful man into His favor? The answer returned is that there
can be no other ground than a perfect repentance and faith. It is
admitted, however, that no man can render this perfect repentance
and faith until after he has been received into the divine favor and
as a result of that favor. It is the product in him of the Holy Spirit

received in Christ, and, if we do not misunderstand the author, is never realized in this life (e.g. p. 284). It is actually taught, however, that God receives man into His favor on the ground of this perfect repentance and faith foreseen as certainly to be realized by him who is in Christ (e.g. p. 267). That is to say, man is received into the divine favor on the ground of the foreseen product of that favor! Of course, this is only a roundabout way of saying that sinful man is accepted by God on the ground of his weak and imperfect faith and repentance by which he becomes united with Christ, through whom he is enabled gradually to perfect his repentance and faith. Stripped of its labored verbiage, in other words, Mr. Smith's elaborate theory reduces simply to the common Arminian doctrine. Man's imperfect faith and repentance is the proper ground of his acceptance with God, who graciously accepts it as perfect and undertakes to make it perfect through spiritual influences brought to bear on man in Christ.

Thus we are brought to the part which Christ, according to Mr. Smith's theory, plays in the salvation of sinful man. Put briefly, this is the part of producer and guarantor of the perfect repentance and faith in man, on the ground of which alone a holy God can receive sinful man into His favor. The whole of Christ's work is, according to Mr. Smith, devoted to this end — that He may qualify Himself to impart and then may actually impart to sinners the perfect repentance and faith on the ground of which alone a holy God can accept them as His children; while meanwhile he guarantees to the holy God this perfect repentance and faith on the part of those who believe in Him. " The holy God is able to accept " the sinner " as one of His own children, because he is united by faith to a Saviour, who is now able, because He has acquired through His experience on earth a perfect human hatred of sin, and a perfect human love of righteousness, and a perfect human knowledge of God, to communicate these eternal possessions of His to all human beings who believe in Him, and thus to enable them in the end to comply to the uttermost with the conditions of divine mercy. God therefore knows that the Saviour is an all-sufficient surety for the ultimate perfection of all who trust in Him. . . . And therefore God, who sees the end of all things in their beginnings, is able even here and now to reckon as righteous every true believer in Jesus Christ " (p. 267).

In such passages as this — which are rather frequent — there are brought together in commodious succinctness all the essential elements of the theory. These concern (1) the qualification of Christ

to communicate a perfect repentance and faith to those who believe
in Him; (2) the method of communication by which the perfect
repentance and faith are imparted by Christ to those who believe
in Him; (3) the capacity of Christ in the meanwhile to act as
guarantor of this perfect repentance and faith in His people.

It is to the first of these elements of his theory that the author
addresses himself with most fullness, and we may say predilection.
The whole volume may be said without unfairness, indeed, to be a
sustained attempt to show that Christ " has through His death on
the Cross become eternally qualified to impart through the Holy
Spirit to all who believe in Him a perfect human hatred of sin, a
perfect human love of righteousness, and a perfect human knowledge
of God " (p. 267). The presupposition is that a divine, or an angelic,
hatred of sin, love of God, knowledge of God is incommunicable to
man (p. 149). If these things were to be communicated to man,
therefore, it behooved the Son of God to become man, that in the
way of a true and pure human experience He might acquire a hatred
of sin, and a love of righteousness, and a knowledge of God, which,
while perfect, should be truly human, and thus capable of being
communicated to man. This is the account, according to Mr. Smith,
of the incarnation and the sufferings of the Son of God — and
what He did and all that He endured were necessary to the acquisition by Him in human experience of these great possessions (e.g. p.
164). What the essential difference is between a perfect hatred of sin,
love of righteousness, and knowledge of God in the divine heart —
or in an angel's heart — and in a man's heart, which renders the
former incommunicable to those who are expected to be perfect even
as their Father in Heaven is perfect, to be imitators of God, sharers
in the divine nature, and partakers of His holiness, and to have the
same mind in them that was in Christ Jesus when He was in the
form of God and might well have clung to His equality with God —
while the latter is communicable to them — the author does not
stay to tell us.

Nor, indeed, does he make it very clear how this humanly acquired hatred of sin, love of righteousness, and knowledge of God
which he declares to be alone communicable, is actually communicated to those who believe in Christ. He tells us, certainly, broadly,
that it is " imparted through the Holy Spirit " (pp. 221, 267, 283–
284), and by a " process of spiritual discipline " (pp. 194, 207), but
he does not go into details here. He does, indeed, make it plain that in

his view there is no " irresistible " activity of the Spirit contemplated. The Holy Spirit, it seems, in taking the things of Christ and showing them to man does not operate " by way of force or of overwhelming demonstration to the senses," nor " in such a way that men could not, if they chose, quench the Spirit; but by reasonable and spiritual persuasion, so that those who did not accept the salvation offered in Christ might do so of their own free and deliberate choice " (p. 283). " God Himself," therefore, " cannot render it certain that every man shall accept His offered mercy " (p. 213). Man's " moral freedom " must be preserved at all hazards! Thus the impartation by Christ to men of perfect repentance and faith cannot be a prevalent impartation. It is of the nature of a tender rather than of a true communication. We are told, therefore, that it is effected through, first, a revelation of the Truth, and next an impartation — doubtless through suasion only — of a spiritual power (p. 259). We read accordingly (p. 124): " He is able to declare the truth with certainty, authority, and assurance, and so [italics ours] produce in sinful man that all-essential, God-acceptable faith which, when it attains its culmination, ceases to be any longer merely faith, but is transmuted into certain and assured spiritual knowledge." This truth is " sympathetically communicated and willingly received " (p. 229), and it is only " by accepting the crucified Christ as their Saviour " that men " are enabled to become partakers of that perfect human hatred of sin and that perfect human love of righteousness which Christ through the Cross has acquired," and that God may possess for them " a guarantee that in the end they shall be freed from all complicity with sin, and made worthy to enter fully into His holy kingdom " (p. 203).

Only, we miss the ground of this guarantee. If the Spirit's work is only suasive, and no recreating power is exerted, how are men who, by reason of sin, *cannot* repent and believe perfectly, to be made able to do so? Can suasion overcome an *inability?* And how can we call an act of mere suasion a true " communication "; or in such circumstances declare that the Saviour, who is able no doubt to supply " all the spiritual gifts " necessary to sinful man's perfection, in the way of proffer, is able also to guarantee the acceptance and improvement of these gifts by sinful man? Do we not find ourselves in the unfortunate position of being compelled to say, not merely that " God Himself cannot render it certain that every man shall accept His offered mercy " (p. 213), but that God Himself cannot render it certain that any man shall accept it? And by parity of reasoning, so far from God knowing " that there is not one of the Saviour's flock that will not in the end be presented before Him wholly spotless and clean " (p. 267), are we not compelled to say that He cannot know that any one will be so presented before Him? If the Saviour of the world is to be limited in His saving work to what is euphemistically described as doing " the best possible for man, by saving him while still respecting his freedom of will " (p. 155), it is absurd to speak of Him as able to " guarantee to the God of all holiness that the man who was truly His should at once, in some degree, and at last perfectly, become partaker of that perfect, holy, human hatred of sin and that perfect, holy, human love of right-eousness which He, as the Sinless Man, by suffering sin to do its utmost worst upon Him, and thereby fulfilling to the uttermost the will of the Father, had made His own forever " (pp. 165 f.). If the very principle of our construction is to preserve to men as moral agents a moral freedom which in its very definition is made to in-volve uncertainty, we can obtain no certainty by assuming the play upon these men of any merely moral inducements.

We perceive, then, that Mr. Smith's theory of the Atonement fails at every salient point. Proclaiming salvation solely on the ground of perfect repentance and faith, it fails to show that perfect re-pentance and faith will avail with God, or can be supplied by man, or can be communicated to man by Christ. It stands indeed more com-pletely bare before its task than is usual with theories of its class. Dr. Moberly had something at least specious to say of the atoning power of repentance and faith. Dr. McLeod Campbell had a perfect repentance to offer in the sympathetic expression of repentance by Christ. The Germans, with their inheritance from the Lutheran doc-trine of the " Means of Grace," have something plausible to urge of the revolutionary effect of the Cross when brought home in its true meaning to the hearts of men — which the Andover divines were not slow to avail themselves of. Of none of these expedients to give a superficial appearance of completeness to his theory does Mr. Smith, however, avail himself. His theory is certainly not really weakened by this refusal to invoke the aid of unavailing expedients. But it stands out more barely in its essential inefficiency through their absence; and its ineffectiveness is perceived with more startling distinctness. Its main difficulty is, however, no other than that on which all other autosoteric theories are wrecked — and that is just

its autosoteric character. If man can save himself or must save himself, he does not need a Saviour. And if nevertheless it is urged that
he does need the work of Christ to induce him or to enable him to
save himself, new difficulties at once emerge.

For example, what are we to say of those who lived before
Christ, on whom, therefore, no influences from the Cross could play?
Mr. Smith declares boldly that Christ " came that He might become
eternally qualified to be the Saviour not of Jews only, but of the
whole world — of all generations of men, past, present, and to
come " (p. 173). But we can only reply, Such an effect, on his theory,
were impossible. Does he not in the very assertion declare that
Christ came in order to *qualify* Himself to become a Saviour — and
that His saving power *arises* from effects " produced in His own
being and character *by His experiences in the midst of sinful men* " ?
And does he not over and over again tell us that the saving effects
of Christ's work depend on influences which were incapable of working except after the saving work was accomplished (cf. p. 267: " is
now able "), and which play not on God but on men? Now, if
Christ came as the God-provided substitute for sinners and expiated
the guilt of our sins on the tree, why, of course, God could act upon
this great satisfaction in prospect as well as in retrospect: for God's
promissory note is as good as the money down. But if He came to
qualify Himself to communicate to men a spiritual power attained
by Himself only in the course of His earthly work — why, of
course, this communication cannot be made until He is qualified to
make it and it can be made only to those who are exposed to those
influences which spring from it. The universal loss of the entire
human race before Christ is the inevitable result of finding the saving fact in an action of man's own will under influences streaming
from the Cross.

We do not put this consideration forward, of course, as the
matter of main importance: but only as an incidental result which
may bid us pause and think. The matter of main importance is,
naturally, that no man at all can ever be saved by such an Atonement — because man is *ex hypothesi* incapable in his sin-bred
inability of responding, in a saving act of faith and repentance, to
any inducements brought to bear on him from the Cross. He needs
not merely inducements to action but recreating grace, and an
Atonement which purchases for him the recreating Spirit as well as
the proffer of mercy. It is here that the true opposition between the

two views lies. It is the old opposition between " grace " and " free will." " I am at present reading our Erasmus," wrote Luther six months before he inaugurated the Reformation movement by nailing his theses on the door of the Schloss-Kirche at Wittenberg: " I am at present reading our Erasmus, but my heart recoils more and more from him. . . . The human is to him of more importance than the divine. . . . Those who ascribe something to man's freedom of will regard these things differently from those who know only God's free grace." Here we have the real hinge of the Reformation announced to us; and the core of the gospel. There is an impassable gulf fixed between those who hang the efficacy of Christ's work upon the " free " action of man's will, and those who ascribe all to God's free grace. They are of different religions.

We have noted an occasional misprint in Mr. Smith's volume — for example, p. 173, line 4, " alienable " for " inalienable." We may be permitted to suppose, therefore, that the *monstra* " true and proper incarnate man," " sinless incarnate humanity," " Sinless Incarnate Man," " sinless incarnate humanity," occurring on pp. 151–152, are to be attributed to the printer.

ENCYCLOPÆDIA OF RELIGION AND ETHICS. Edited by JAMES HAST-INGS, M.A., D.D., with the Assistance of JOHN A. SELBIE, M.A., and other scholars. Vol. I: A–Art. New York: Charles Scribner's Sons; Edinburgh: T. & T. Clark. 1908.[1]

THE first volume of Dr. Hastings' new " Encyclopædia " makes a very handsome appearance. The type and the column are apparently the same as in the " Dictionary of the Bible " and the " Dictionary of Christ and the Gospels "; and we are sorry to say we cannot commend this type, which seems to make a singularly severe demand upon the eyes. But by the omission of the ruling around the page and an increase in the width of the margin, and above all by a change in the paper, a much clearer and more at-

[1] *The Princeton Theological Review,* vii. 1909, pp. 326–332. For review of vol. ii. cf. *ibid.,* viii. 1910, pp. 271 ff.; vol. iii., *ibid.,* ix. 1911, pp. 640 ff.; vol. iv., *ibid.,* x. 1912, pp. 467 ff.; vol. v., *ibid.,* xi. 1913, pp. 494 ff.; vol. vi., *ibid.,* xii. 1914, pp. 502 ff.; vol. vii., *ibid.,* xiii. 1915, pp. 275 ff.; vol. viii., *ibid.,* xiv. 1916, pp. 649 ff.; vol. ix., *ibid.,* xvi. 1918, pp. 110 ff.; vol. x., *ibid.,* xvii. 1919, pp. 312 ff.

tractive page is secured than in the earlier " Dictionaries " Moro is done also to render the use of the " Encyclopædia " convenient. The list of authors who have contributed to the volume contains an intimation of the articles written by each. This is an excellent innovation. A still more excellent innovation is the printing of a page (p. xv.) of topic-headings, which do not occur in the " Encyclopædia," but the topics represented by which are treated under other heads. This will enable the reader to find " Aben Ezra," for example (under " Ibn Ezra "), or " Adventism " (under " Chiliasm "), or " Affinity " (under " Blood Relationship "), and not hastily conclude that the " Encyclopædia " has overlooked such topics. The articles are ordinarily, moreover, divided into numbered sections, with headings in black type; and sometimes a summary of their contents is given at the outset in a sort of " table of contents." These expedients place the substance of the articles more readily at the command of the reader.

The cosmopolitanism of scholarship is illustrated anew by the list of writers whom Dr. Hastings has called to his aid in the preparation of the matter of the volume. Nearly two hundred have been engaged on the work. About a sixth of these are Americans (some thirty-three); about a tenth Germans (some twenty); something over a twelfth Frenchmen (some fourteen); while a few more are derived from still other foreign sources — two or three each are Dutchmen, Belgians, Finns, Scandinavians, Hindoos; and there are also Armenians, Japs, and even an Apache Indian. It belongs also to the emancipation of scholarship from conventional bonds that we meet in this list of presumable authorities on questions of religious and moral erudition such names as Mrs. Rhys Davids, Catherine Julia Gaskell, Mary Alicia Owen, Mary Mills Patrick, Bertha Maud Horack Shambaugh, Florence Melian Stawell. *Place aux dames!* It is a principle Dr. Hastings seems to have acted on when he gave Miss Shambaugh twenty-one columns in which to tell about the " Amana Society " — a type of religious thought the influence of which is apparently confined within the narrow limits of eighteen hundred souls. Dr. Hastings in his Preface offers no doubt an explanation of this generous allotment of space to an insignificant movement; but it is questionable if the explanation will not read to most of us more as an apology than as a justification.

The question of the proportionate distribution of space in a book like this is to be sure one of the most difficult which confronts an editor. It certainly is not a simple question. There are many other things which have to be considered besides the relative importance of the topics; and all judgments of the relative importance of the topics are not likely to agree. For the critic to object to the editor's assignment of space commonly means little more, therefore, than that he and the editor think differently in the matter. Even so, however, it is not unfair to say that Dr. Hastings' assignments of space seem sometimes bewildering. There are few greater topics than Art, and there is a great deal that is very important said in the two great articles " Architecture," " Art," in this volume. But the volume, which covers nearly the whole of the letter A, has only nine hundred pages in it; and nearly one hundred ninety of these — about one-fifth of the whole — are given to these two topics " Architecture " and " Art." In an " Encyclopædia " specifically of religion and ethics, that strikes us as excessive. This is not the only instance in which the special character of the " Encyclopædia " seems to be lost sight of. Here is an article — a most excellent article — for example, on " A Priori," extending to sixteen columns, much of it cast into fine type. There are applications of the *a priori*, no doubt, both to ethics and religion: but does the article itself, or the topic itself, fall naturally into either category? And here is an admirable article on " Aristotle, Aristotelianism," one of the shorter articles — shorter, though one of them is on " Arianism " and another on " Arminianism," both of which, if they do not deserve well of religion, yet loom large in the history of that religion which we call Christianity — which seem to keep " Architecture " and " Art " from running into each other and absorbing the volume. Aristotelianism also has certainly played a great part in the history of that same religion: but we hear nothing of that here, though, to be sure, we are bidden to look for " Scholasticism," where no doubt the story will be told. Aristotle, too, had an ethical system, which is very appropriately (and finely) outlined here, but not as if it were the main matter of concernment. In short, the article is just what an article on " Aristotle, Aristotelianism " ought to be — in a general encyclopædia, or an encyclopædia of philosophy or of classical biography. It has no particular adjustment to this special " Encyclopædia." And here is a good short article on " Anæsthesia "; we have profited from reading it — but we have looked in vain in it for any allusion to or connection with ethics or religion. The editor, it will be seen, has interpreted the scope of the " Encyclopædia " broadly. This has its advantages — and its disadvantages. We get much more in the book than the title gives us right to expect — much of which, perhaps, as it was not to be looked for in this " Encyclopædia," will possibly not be looked for in it. But, as a consequence, we get perhaps less than the title might lead us to expect — the articles more properly falling in its special field being unduly compressed to make room for those which possibly might just as well be reserved for another place.

Among the topics which seem out of place in this " Encyclopædia " are those on the technical terms of evolutionary speculation — unless, indeed, we are to conceive " Evolution " a religion. Such articles are those on " Accommodation," " Adaptation " — even " Abiogenesis " (to which are given *two* articles of the same general import, with an additional cross-reference to yet a third, " Biogenesis," which must cover again much the same ground). Both authors who write on " Abiogenesis " would apparently commend it to us as the formula for the origin of life, Prof. J. A. Thompson with caution and scientific hesitancy, Mr. Edward Clodd with bold assertiveness. Mr. Clodd does not indeed tell us, as another recent writer does, with unconscious repetition of the Greek myth, that the atmosphere quickened the sea and begot life — and prove it, as the author in question does, by a chemical analysis of the alleged parents. " The elements contained in sea-water," we read in this remarkable statement, " are sodium, calcium, magnesium, potassium, chlorine, sulphur, carbon, hydrogen, oxygen, and iron. The composition of the air is nitrogen, oxygen, and carbon. *The elements contained in living matter are these identical things.* In the heavy carbonated air above, and in the solvent water on the land beneath, there lay in mobile contiguity the essential elements of living matter." " We see, then, for there is no other way out of it, that not only did the air and water at the beginning of things contain in contiguity the elements of living matter, but that these elements did naturally unite to form this living matter." Mr. Edward Clodd, on the contrary, contents himself with the broad declaration, as one " generally accepted by biologists," that " in its passage from the nebulous to the more or less solid state, our globe reached a temperature and general conditions which made possible the evolution of the organic from the inorganic." It would be interesting to know what this temperature was, and what were these " general conditions." But though " the inter-relation between living and lifeless matter is a fundamental canon of the theory of Evolution, which recognizes no break in continuity," it has apparently no evidence for it as yet available, except the theory of evolution itself. This freedom of speculative construction is not confined, however, to evolutionary biology. It has invaded history and archæology as well. How little the declarations of the Scriptures can stand against it may be observed from such articles as those on " Adam," " Antediluvians," " Ark." Prof. Kennett, who writes the last of these, thinks he knows what was in the Ark much better than so late a writer as the Deuteronomist. It was the brazen-serpent! The Ark was originally the box in which a snake was kept, which the Israelites worshiped, and there was subsequently substituted for it " the bronze seraph, or, to call it by the name by which it is generally known, the brazen serpent." It was, in a word, the shrine of the serpent — the god of fertility. These be thy gods, O Israel! Fortunately, Prof. Kennett's pseudo-scientific speculations are no more authoritative than Mr. Clodd's: there is no more reason for believing that the Ark was the shrine of the serpent than that life is the product of " a certain temperature " and " certain general conditions."

It gives the reader an odd impression, we may remark in passing, to turn over a few pages and read the article " Adaptation " in close conjunction with these on " Abiogenesis." Evolution, we learn, is simply a process of " Adaptation." The fittest in every generation survives; that is to say, there is a constant progress towards more perfect adaptation. Why, then, one may well ask, has there not been a tolerable adaptation attained long ago? Or, remembering " Abiogenesis," we may rather ask, Why was there not a perfect adaptation from the beginning? If the living organism is in the first instance the spontaneous production of the " environment " it is inconceivable that it should not begin by being in perfect adaptation to it. How could the environment produce an organism out of adaptation to itself? And starting thus in perfect adaptation to its environment, how could the living organism ever get out of this adaptation to the environment of which it is not only at the start but throughout merely the expression? From start to finish the " environment " is but the mold in which the organism is cast, and the cast surely must repeat the features of the mold. If the mold changes the cast changes with it, that is all: and it is not so much a question of " adaptation " which implies a certain independence of mold and cast, as of simple reproduction. The evolutionary idea here resembles very closely what we read of Alice in the Looking Glass, who, we remember, had to run with all her might just to keep standing still. And here another difficulty faces us. This living organism which is in the first instance the spontaneous product of its environment and must therefore begin in perfect adaptation to its environment — of which it is indeed but the expression; and which continues ever but the product of its environment and should therefore steadily express its environment and change only as it changes that it may abide in complete adaptation to it — does nothing of the sort. On the contrary, it from the beginning spurns the slime (of which it is just the expression) and soars upwards and advances steadily to higher and higher things! That is what has happened. The law of development of organic forms has not been to ever closer and closer adaptation to the environment. They began ("abiogenesis" being postulated) in perfect adaptation to the environment. The law of their development has been to ever fuller, richer, more elevated manifestations of what looks very much like a new thing with forces all its own, which struggles with its environment and conquers it; which ends, indeed, by adapting its environment to itself. This is not the behavior of crystals, say, which form themselves in pools of evaporating sea-water; and dissolve again and reform afresh as the water is alternately diluted by the rain or wasted by the sun — but never stand over against the mother-water and insist on going their own way. It is all very puzzling — on the postulates of the thoroughgoing evolutionism of Mr. Clodd, which Mr. Clodd tells us is the doctrine (unuttered or expressed, we may suppose) of all biologists.

Let us return, however, to our "Encyclopædia," which goes out of its way to teach these puzzling things. The mass of the articles, of course, are those which one would naturally look for in an "Encyclopædia of Religion and Ethics," and so far as can be judged the vocabulary is very full. Nearly every name of importance in the history of religion and ethics will be found here, either the subject of a separate article or referred to in more general discussions: and if an index of names is supplied the "Encyclopædia" will be a very full guide to the leaders of religious and ethical thought. The major topics of religious and ethical import are all treated: and, what is more noticeable, a place has been found for a wealth of minor topics — down even to such as "Accidie" and "Action Sermon." There are some unexpected omissions, however, among these minor topics:

for example, our eye catches the heading " Accommodation," and in an " Encyclopædia of Religion and Ethics " we naturally expect to find it a discussion of the ethics of so-called " accommodation " in teaching. It proves to treat, however, only of evolutionary and psychological " accommodation." We wonder whether, when " Economy " comes to be dealt with, it will be only a " political " (or perhaps " household ") economy, to the exclusion of ethical, that will be touched on?

We have been ourselves, naturally, interested particularly in the articles which deal with topics belonging to the history of the Christian religion, and especially to the history of Christian thought. There are many of these, some comprehensive and some more particular, and in the main they are sufficiently careful and full, although as a class they do not show a very firm grasp of either the substance or the development of doctrine. Two of them we have already mentioned, as among the shorter articles somewhat in danger of being crushed out of sight between the great articles, " Architecture," " Art " — those on " Arianism " and " Arminianism." These are very fair samples of all of their class. " Arianism " is dealt with quite externally, in the main correctly enough, but without insight. No one could derive from the article any real comprehension of the place of Arianism in the history of Christian thought, or of the internal development of the doctrine. Arminianism, on the other hand, is, from the point of view of a convinced Arminian, very fairly presented. The article is rambling, not to say repetitious, and not very exact in its statements, but, on the whole, leaves on the mind a generally clear view of the nature of Arminianism. It opens, to be sure, with an amazing account of the Calvinistic doctrine of the decree. Dr. Lindsay, in the article on " Amyraldism," had already spoken of this, if not wisely yet not altogether without prudence. But here we hear of the " decree of salvation " being " antecedent to the Fall " (not to the decree of the Fall) ; and of this being a party position, that is, Supralapsarian; while the characteristic of Infralapsarianism is the " connecting the Fall with the permission of God, instead of with His foreordination." Confusion could not easily be more confounded. Of course, no Calvinist imagines that a decree of God was made subsequent to any event in time; and all Calvinists hold that the Fall was permitted, and that it was also foreordained. The difference between Supralapsarianism and Infralapsarianism was (and is) merely whether in the order

of thought the foreordination of the Fall (which both teach) as a
thing permitted to occur (which both teach) precedes or follows the
foreordination of some men to life and some men to death (which
both teach). Why will men persist in writing on such themes so
mechanically that they do not even consider the meaning of the
terms they employ? The language elsewhere in the article and that
even in matters of the first significance is often very misleading.
Thus, for example, we read: " The Remonstrance is first negative,
stating the five Calvinistic articles in order to reject them." " *The*
five Calvinistic articles " — by no means. What was stated was five
articles selected by the Remonstrants from the Calvinistic doctrinal
sum, to be attacked by them. Proceeding, we read that the Synod
of Dort " promulgated five heads of doctrines of its own." What
was done by the Synod was to set forth clearly its own doctrine with
respect to the five points of Calvinistic teaching brought into dispute
by the Remonstrants. Not only are the Thirty-nine Articles of the
Church of England claimed as almost Arminian, but it looks as if
even the Lambeth Articles were represented as substantially Arminian: at least the sentence referring to them (p. 811a, at bottom)
is ambiguous. It is allowed that Arminianism has no definite theological distinctness, and yet Arminius is ranged by the side of
Athanasius and Augustine as one of the three greatest leaders in
theological definition (p. 809a, top). Athanasius, it seems, has determined the doctrine of God; Augustine, the doctrine of man;
Arminius, the essential relations between God and man!

The article on " Abelard " is informing and appreciative — too
appreciative. That on " Anselm " (by the same writer) is brief and
sketchy, and in its remarks on the " Cur Deus Homo " is dominated
by prejudice. No adequate understanding of the doctrine of Satisfaction is shown; though it is rightly denied that it owes its form
to the influence of Teutonic law. The Atonement seems to have
proved a thorny subject to the contributors to this " Encyclopædia."
For example, the otherwise very excellent brief article on " Acceptilation " sharply criticizes Turretine for the phrase: " We
admit no Socinian acceptilation." Turretine is, however, quite
within his rights in this phrase: the Socinian doctrine of the Atonement, which holds that God forgives sinners their debt without any
payment at all, being precisely described by the term " acceptilatio."
It may be another matter whether Socinus himself employs the
term " acceptilatio " to describe his doctrine. Grotius says he does

(but not in chap. iii. of his " Defensio," as is here stated, but in chap. vi.), and the author of the article, following Crell, says he does not. We have not looked the matter up. But in any event Grotius does not misrepresent Socinus' meaning, but quite accurately defines the meaning of " acceptilatio " (Amsterdam edition of 1679, p. 320a) — telling us that " acceptilatio " is used even where no payment precedes, is opposed to some payment, and is figuratively defined as an imaginary payment. It would be difficult to catch Grotius napping in the matter of significance of law-terms, whatever we may think of his own doctrine of the Atonement. It is not the Socinian but the Scotist doctrine of the Atonement which is abusively described by the term " acceptilatio," as our author tells us, and ought thereby have been saved from his mistaken criticism of Grotius and Turretine.

Among the best of the articles of the class we are speaking of is that on Thomas Aquinas, although its encomium is somewhat excessive. The same must be said of the estimate of Origen in the excellent comprehensive article on " Alexandrian Theology," by the side of which the equally excellent one on " Antiochene " must be placed. The article on the " Albigenses " is thoroughly good, and that on the " Anabaptists " is also very satisfactory. There are very few articles in this volume on specifically doctrinal points. Among them those on the " Anger " or " Wrath " of God and on " Annihilation " are perhaps the most outstanding. The former is, however, a carefully rather than profoundly thought article, though it has much in it that is suggestive. Among articles of another class, we have not been attracted to that on " Agnosticism "; and still less to that on " Absolute," which seems to us a little pretentious. The article on " Apologetics " does not appear to us to be quite adapted to its place in the " Encyclopædia." Most readers would expect to find in it an account of " Apologetics," its idea and place in the theological encyclopædia, method, history. Instead it is an attempt to outline a system of apologetics — an attempt sure to prove unsatisfactory, if for no other reason than the limitations of space.

A notice of a work of this kind as it passes from article to article may easily run to an inordinate length. We have probably said enough to suggest the general features of the volume before us. It is comprehensive, learned and, so far as we have been able to test it, interestingly written. It is to be followed by nine or eleven more,

220 CRITICAL REVIEWS

and it is already evident that the completed work will be a welcome
and valuable addition to our encyclopædic literature.

GESCHICHTE DER AUTOBIOGRAPHIE. Von GEORG MISCH. Erster
Band: Das Altertum. Leipzig und Berlin: B. G. Teubner. 1907.[1]

THIS considerable volume is only one of three which shall contain a comprehensive history of autobiography. The work was undertaken in response to an offer of a prize for such a history, made
through the Prussian Academy of the Sciences in 1900 (" Sitzungsberichte der Königlich Preussischen Akademie der Wissenschaften,"
1900, p. 55). Two manuscripts were presented — the one written
more from the point of view of purely literary history (a history,
therefore, of autobiographies), the other from a more philosophico-
social standpoint (a history, therefore, more of autobiography).
The prize fell to the latter (" Sitzungsberichte," etc., 1905, p. 686) ;
and it is this treatise, the first part of which now lies before us.
Although only a fragment of the whole work, this first part has
nevertheless a completeness of its own. It gives us the entire history
of autobiography in the old world. It has indeed a higher claim to
unity than this merely external fact may suggest. For the history of
autobiography in the old world is not merely the history of the
inception and development of autobiographical writing through a
definitely marked literary period. It is the history of the growth of
this literary form from its first tentative beginnings to its culmination; for this literary form reached its culmination as the old world
was passing away. We can say even more than that. Both as a
purely literary mode and as the expression of individuality autobiography attained its climax in a single work, which came into
existence just as the old world was dying. The history of autobiography in antiquity may almost be read, therefore, as the history
of the production of a single great work — the long preparation for
it, ending in the finished product. And this is really the ground of
our deepest interest in this history. For this one great work into
which all these lines of preparation, so carefully traced by Dr. Misch,
issue, is Augustine's " Confessions." The history of autobiography

[1] *The Princeton Theological Review,* vii. 1909, pp. 500–510.

in antiquity may be looked at, then, as at bottom only an orderly study, in a genetic way, of Augustine's " Confessions." All that goes before them but leads slowly up the long slope to these heights. All that comes after rests in their shadow.

No one who reads Dr. Misch's detailed study of the origin and development not merely of autobiographical forms, but of autobiographical life-expression, will fail to feel this. Dr. Misch feels it himself, and from the beginning of his work keeps his readers' eyes set on the " Confessions " as the goal to which all tends. He is eager that it shall not be inferred from the circumstance that complete autobiographies in the strict sense scarcely attract attention in the Græco-Roman literature until the time of Augustine, that they were a new invention of that age. In point of fact, he insists, the bases for all the autobiographical developments of this age were laid in antiquity, " and Augustine's work is not a beginning but a completion " (p. 9). It is a part — a very large part — of his task to trace out the lines of development through which autobiography thus slowly came to its rights. He begins at the beginning, by pointing out the autobiographical form which is taken in the Assyrio-Babylonian and Egyptian inscriptions. He fully recognizes, however, that the creation of true autobiography depends on the development of personality and the individualistic habit of looking at things. This he finds to have arisen first on Greek soil and to have received its first impulse from the introspection fostered by the Socratic self-consciousness, reinforcing our natural need of self-expression and desire to be understood — not to say to be admired. Nevertheless autobiographical writing was slow in working out its inevitable destiny. Throughout the whole period of Greek culture up to the birth of Christ, it held only a very secondary place in literature. Only in the one species of political autobiography have we anything like a complete series of works of this order either preserved or witnessed to us. Beyond this, the cultivation of this literary form was in the hands of the rhetoricians, and it was from this subordinate region of life that the first Greek autobiography worthy of its name — the so-called " Antidosis " of Isocrates — has come down to us (B.C. 353). In this artificial defense of himself against an imaginary opponent, the rhetorician, in full consciousness of the novelty of his task, undertook, for the benefit of the ill-informed and of future generations, to depict his own character, his course of life, and his training: to make known the truth concerning himself, and

to set out " an image of his mind and of his whole life "; fondly
hoping thus " to leave behind him a monument to himself more lasting than statues of brass." The example thus set by Isocrates was
not, however, at once widely followed. At least there have come down
to us, for the space of some three hundred years, outside of the
steady succession of political autobiographies from Alexander down,
little or no traces of autobiographical writing. After the time of
Cicero, however, the stream began to flow with gradually increasing
fullness, and by the second century after Christ we find ourselves in
the presence of an astonishing variety of autobiographical forms.
Here side by side appear Hadrian's " Vita," Galen's treatises on his
own books, Marcus Aurelius' " Meditationes," the romance of
Apuleius with its autobiographical conclusion, the " sacred orations "
of Ælius Aristides, the subject of which is his daily communion in
his sickness with the deity, the visions of the martyr Perpetua and
numerous Hellenizing histories of conversion like those of Justin
and Cyprian.

One of Socrates' immediate pupils, Antisthenes, on being asked
what he had gained from philosophy, replied, " the power to hold
converse with my soul." Yet throughout all the centuries alike of
Hellenic and Hellenistic culture few attempts seem to have been
made to create a literary form of self-inspection. The history of his
development which Cicero gives in his " Brutus " is perhaps the
completest attempt at self-analysis which was made before Augustine
(p. 196). From Cicero the line of the evolution of the literary expression of self-consciousness ran through Marcus Aurelius' " Meditationes," to culminate in connection with Hellenistic Mysticism, in
the lyrics of Gregory of Nazianzum and the soul-history of Augustine
(p. 48). From the second Christian century on, there appears in particular a whole series of what we may call " conversion-histories."
These move at first in the purely intellectualistic region, but more
and more lay stress not merely on the result but the process. Rhetoricians, moral philosophers, Christian Apologists all supply examples. It became the fashion for a would-be teacher, as a device
of argumentation, to tell of his own conversion to the philosophical
standpoint which he would fain commend. Perhaps the most striking
illustration of this fashion is supplied by Dio Chrysostom, the best
of the cynico-stoic traveling preachers of the first century. He had
had an uncommonly deep experience of transition, itself not uncommon at the time, from mere rhetoricism to practical philosophy;

and on the basis of his varied experiences as a cynic apostle, he delivered in Athens on his return from exile his great oration περὶ φυγῆς, in which he commends his experiences as a guide to life (p. 293). The narration of his conversion given by Justin Martyr at the opening of his " Dialogue with Trypho " is of essentially the same type: it is intended as an illustration of the insufficiency of heathen philosophy drawn from his own experience. And the matter is not essentially altered when, in the next century, the climax is no longer a merely intellectual surrender to a new teaching, but is traced to the divine grace and attributed to the effect of baptism — as in Cyprian's letter to Donatus. Here too belongs the autobiographical sketch which Hilary prefixed to his " De Trinitate," as a description of how he came to be a believer in the true God, whom he commends to his readers. Aristides of Smyrna claims to have invented, in his ἱεροὶ λόγοι (A.D. 170–179), a new form of those religious orations which it was customary to deliver at religious feasts, in honor of the divinity which was being celebrated. The novelty of his performance consists, however, only in transferring the real motive of the discourse from the glorification of the deity — the materials for which might be gathered from other spheres than his own experiences — to the most intimate portrayal of the orator's own personality. Sick in body and soul, he had cast himself on the mercy of Asclepios, and now wishes to tell all the healing operations of the god of which he had been made the recipient. Thus throughout the whole Hellenistic and Hellenistic-Roman period — say from 250 B.C. to 250 A.D. — the stock of autobiography (growing out of roots set in the Attic period) was flourishing and throwing out abundant branches to this side and that. Its flowering-time was, however, not yet.

That came only in the changed conditions of the fourth century after Christ, as the old world was passing away and men, in the dissolution of the social fabric which had seemed so stable, were driven back upon themselves. Seven hundred years after Isocrates had first invented autobiography as a rhetorical form, the last of the great heathen rhetors, Libanius, opens the series of great autobiographies of the flowering-time of this species of literature (p. 357). From the century and a half beginning with, say, 360 A.D., more non-political autobiographies are known to us than from all the preceding years put together. And in what variety do they come! And how wide a sphere of interest do they sweep! " Now we could fancy we were holding converse with a monk or a feudal lord of the Middle Ages, now we see before us a later humanist, now we hear the tone of romantic lyricism, and Augustine's work in its tendency to the philosophical grounding of the life-whole recalls the type of the newer autobiography since Rousseau " (p. 357).

" In the seventh decade of the fourth century there falls the notable autobiography (now lost) written in the mixed style of the moral romance, by the converted Spaniard Acilius Severus, the title of which, ' Peira or Catastrophe,' has been preserved for us by Jerome. The leader of the Syrian Church, Ephrem († 373), wrote at about the same time autobiographical ' Confessions.' From the last famous representative of pure Rhetordom, the ' heathen ' Libanius, to whom one of the greatest Christian preachers in the Greek tongue, John Chrysostom, went to school, we have a long autobiography, ' Bios or of my own Tyche '; nor is it without religious significance. His friend and admirer, the Emperor Julian, . . . was certainly prevented only by his early death from putting together his life in an independent representation. Then the new epoch in autobiography vigorously announced itself in Gregory of Nazianzum, the poet among the Church Fathers: his great autobiographical poems from the eighth and ninth decades of the century, the product of ecclesiastical controversy and solitary contemplation, have internal form and beauty; and his subjective religious lyric, nourished on metaphysical speculation, stands over against the historical portion of Augustine's ' Confessions ' as another typical form of the expression of personal religion. About A.D. 400 Augustine's book appeared. It made an epoch only in the West, since it was the Western culture alone which was able to bear Augustine's spirit and to enrich itself from him. In the East, the development proceeds in the autobiographical species, too, along the antique way, and precisely because the working of genius is here not in question, the further constructions from this time, which nevertheless have their place in the general evolution, illustrate the necessity in the course of things. Along with Gregory, there appears in the Greek Church the Neoplatonic-Christian bishop Synesius of Cyrene; he too built out of his metaphysics a personal religious poem and in a special work, ' Dio or of my own Life,' he delineated his conduct of his life (about 406). And that it was not in Gregory alone that the mighty conflicts of the Church awoke a sympathetic subjective echo, we are advertised by the title ' Tragoedia,' by which was designated the autobiographical work of a heresy-hating Bishop of Constantinople who was cast out as a heresiarch, Nestorius — a work (about 432) of which we can now ascertain only that there was room in it for the justification of his own teaching, and for the communication of records after the fashion of the church history writing of the day. But even in Latin Christendom, Augustine's ' Confessions ' were not

the end of the antique development; side by side with direct imitations of this work there were still composed in Southern Gaul and
Ireland autobiographies of quite individual types. And while the
Hellenistic traditions were still making themselves independently
felt, — in autobiographical opening poems and in the end even in a
great antique phenomenon, in Boëthius' ' Consolation of Philosophy '
(524) — Augustine himself in the evening of his life produced still
something new in this department, in his ' Retractations ' (427) "
(pp. 347–348).

We have transcribed this rather long passage because it sets
Augustine's " Confessions " for us in the midst of its congeners and
helps us to realize how much, in the matter of form at least, it belongs to its time. There was no lack of analyses of the human soul
in that period: it was rather the epoch of searching studies of men
— in history, biography, and romance. " The age in which Augustine's ' Confessions ' came into being must be thought of as flooded
with such soul-portraitures " (p. 110). Nor was it an age in which
men were backward in speaking frankly of themselves. Witness, for
example, the autobiographical opening verses not only of an Ausonius, but of a hymn-writer like Prudentius; and the autobiographical *prolaliae* of a Hilary. Or witness rather the smug satisfaction
with which Jerome closes his work on " The Illustrious Men "
with an account of himself. It is not because Augustine's " Confessions " do these things that they are so remarkable and great: it is
because they do these things so remarkably and greatly. Needless
to say that Dr. Misch fully appreciates the unique greatness of
the " Confessions " among other books of their order which have
come down to us from antiquity — or perhaps we should rather say
among other books of what Dr. Misch looks upon as of their order.
For we cannot for ourselves admit that the " Confessions " are
exactly described when they are called an autobiography or a self-
portraiture, or an analysis of the writer's soul, or even a history
of his conversion. The " Confessions " contain these things rather
than are them. It is often a nice question, no doubt, whether a book
of autobiographical contents shall be classed as strictly an autobiography or not. But the question does not seem to be so very
nice a one, when the book to be classified is only in part of autobiographical contents, and even in its autobiographical contents
does not seem to be governed by a strictly autobiographical motive.
Only nine or ten of the thirteen books of the " Confessions " contain
any autobiographical material at all, and as Dr. Misch duly points

out (p. 424), a " full half of the autobiographical part of the work deals with one period of only four years — the time in which Augustine's conversion fell; the entire period of youth up to Augustine's twenty-eighth year being compressed into a first briefer part." It would appear more appropriate, therefore, to speak of the book as a " conversion-narrative " than as an autobiography, and to find its forerunner as such in Dio Chrysostum's περὶ φυγῆs and its analogies in the *prolaliae* of Justin and Tatian and Hilary and Augustine himself in his earliest and most Hellenistic writings, composed at Cassiciacum. Dr. Misch seems occasionally almost on the point of so classifying it, inadequate as such a characterization of the book obviously would be. And he frankly allows not only that Augustine's fundamental purpose lies outside the autobiographical narrative, which is really only ancillary to it, but that a very large portion of the contents of the book are out of place in an autobiography and mar the unity of the work considered as such. " The essential and conscious purpose of Augustine," he writes (p. 414), " does not lie in the narration of his individual experiences, but in the arousing of religious affections and ideas." Again (p. 415): " He not only interposes in the life-history philosophical speculations, the unfathomable problems of which are resolved into questions addressed to God, but he adjoins to it as its last part — filling more than a quarter of the whole — purely didactic discussions, which, strung on the thread of the first chapter of Genesis, enlarge in turn on God, the Trinity, the creation of the world." Such topics, Dr. Misch very properly remarks, one would expect to find discussed in a dogmatic rather than in an autobiographical treatise, and in their treatment he thinks the form of " confession " can be only artificially kept up. Dr. Misch has, of course, his own way, if not of justifying, at least of accounting for and so far of condoning the inclusion of this incongruous matter in an autobiography. Augustine passes at the eleventh book, it seems, for example, into a " confession of his knowledge and ignorance " — surely a topic sufficiently autobiographical. This appears much the same as to say with Dr. Gibb and Mr. Montgomery in their recent edition of the " Confessions " (p. 332) that what Augustine does here is to pass from the description of his religious and moral condition to outlining " what might be called, in modern phraseology, his ' theological position.' " Would it not be better frankly to allow that neither these closing books — constituting " more than a quarter of the whole " work — nor much else in the " Confessions " can be brought without forcing into the legitimate scope of an autobiography or yet of a " conversion-history " ? And that, therefore, the " Confessions," despite the wealth of autobiographical material which they contain, and despite the central place taken in them by Augustine, are not strictly speaking either an autobiography or a " conversion-history "?

In point of fact, the subject of the " Confessions " is not Augustine's self, nor were they written to make himself known; though they were so written as to make him known and to enable him to say that the first ten books are about himself. This Dr. Misch partly perceives, not merely in recognizing that in the autobiographical details which Augustine incorporates into the " Confessions " he has a purpose beyond " the narration of his individual experiences," and in describing that purpose as " the awaking of religious affections and ideas," but also in discovering at the bottom of the " Confessions " the underlying purpose (securing their unity) not to make known the soul alone, but the soul and God. This Dr. Misch interprets as Neoplatonic mysticism. He wishes us to find " the fundamental religious sentiment of the ' Confessions ' " in " the yearning of the mystic for cessation, rest, eternity " (p. 416), and its great end, in the depicting of the hidden working of God in all that is, and the rising of the soul towards and its losing itself in God. " For this," says he (pp. 417–418):

" For this is the kernel of the inner form: the several component parts are not brought together according to the rhetorical rule of pleasing variety, but the nature of the connection is the result of a firm structure, and this fundamental form itself is not simple, but issues from the higher unity which comprehends in itself the contradictions which are resolved in it. God and man draw apart from one another in the phenomena of life and in the description of these phenomena, and yet remain always bound together; in the hymns of longing and love their perfect unity sounds forth. The form does not wish to follow the historically given psychological reality of the individual existence, but will make perceptible that which is in truth going on in the objective reality: this reality lies in a metaphysical Beyond, out of which the narrated history, like a variegatedly agitated color-play, proceeds without separating itself from it — and the Beyond itself lies not in a transcendental distance, but in the continual presence of God's person, who embraces even erring souls with His love and is to be found by their will. Thus the history of the soul which the first ten books of the ' Confessions ' depict and explain, receives its unitary structure through a Neoplatonic-Christian monotheistic mysticism, which conceives the relation of God with the soul at once as uniform presence and as historical process. The inner form is two-voiced, comparable to the relation of two lines, one of which, symbolizing the Being of God, goes smoothly and quietly on from eternity to eternity, while the other, in broken, ultimately ascending course, pictures the struggle and striving of the soul towards its divine source and end; the two, however near they may approach each other, can never in any natural way come together, until the unfathomable experience of unity with God brings the resolution of all contradictions."

We certainly do not agree with Dr. Misch in this neoplatonization of the " Confessions " — as we do not agree with him in his too generous estimate of the amount of Neoplatonism Augustine carried over into Christianity with him and the consequent relation of his first Christian writings to his later ones. But there is involved in Dr. Misch's construction, however obscurely, recognition of the fact that Augustine is not primarily writing of himself in the " Confessions," but at least of the relation of God to his soul, or let us say, better, of the dealings of God with his soul. The true subject of Augustine's " Confessions " is not himself but God, and his real object in writing them was not that men might know him in all the depths of his being — though he does reveal himself in them in all the depths of his being: but that men might know God and learn from His dealings with Augustine the wonders of His Grace. Its fundamental note is therefore not even that great declaration, " Our hearts are restless till they find their rest in Thee," fundamental as this note is to the whole fabric of the " Confessions "; but may be summed up, in Augustine's own language, in the two words *Ab Eo,* " From Him! " And therefore Dr. Misch is perfectly right when he writes (p. 424): " All gifts of nature, even his mother herself and the nourishing of his infancy, are derived from the superabundance of Grace. It belongs to the nature of a pragmatic biography to carry the life-history as far back as possible, to the very generation itself: but in this case the exposition proceeds not from the natural derivation but from the metaphysical obscurity which surrounds the origin of the soul: and thus the narrator can advance regularly without a break from the introductory prayer." And therefore it was also that the " Confessions " from the first wrought so powerfully in the world as a religious force — even on Augustine himself, both when writing them and whenever he reread them (p. 414). They focused men's eyes on God, the God of Grace, and worked in them that frame of mind which lies at the root of all true religion — utter dependence on God.

We have permitted our attention to drift somewhat away from Dr. Misch's book to Augustine's. Our excuse is that it is Dr. Misch's aim to direct our attention to Augustine's book. We must return, however, for a moment, before closing, to Dr. Misch's volume. His analysis of Augustine's " Confessions " as the culminating autobiography of the old world, filling some forty pages, is very able and suggestive. We have already indicated that there are some things in his view of the " Confessions " with which we cannot agree. There are many more to which our assent is very hearty; and the discussion as a whole is very informing. It is immediately preceded by chapters on the general tendencies of autobiography in this age of declining antiquity, and especially on the lyrics of Gregory of Nazianzum. In these chapters we are made acquainted with all the similar works which immediately preceded Augustine's — including his own " Soliloquies." In a closing chapter the final shoots of the tree of antique autobiography are described to us — particularly the " Eucharisticos Deo " of Paulinus of Pella, the " Confession " of St. Patrick, Augustine's own " Retractations," and last of all Boëthius' " Consolation of Philosophy." One or two quotations may perhaps help us to catch the note in which Dr. Misch brings his survey of autobiography in antiquity to a close:

" Thus Augustine's ' Confessions ' have entered as an active force into Time. They are one of the few books which in all periods in which spiritual life has existed in the West have been much read; the verbal expression of inward conditions has been influenced by Augustine up to our own day. He himself at the end of his life bore witness to the effect of his autobiography upon his contemporaries, and subordinated to it in point of effectiveness all his other writings, which were nevertheless of extraordinary influence. ' No one of my works has found a wider circulation, or more eager reading, than the books of my Confessions.' And already in the succeeding decade there appeared literary imitations of it: they continued among the newer peoples, ending by passing outside the religious sphere to coöperate in the development of spiritual history in the world's literature. The continuity of autobiography in the West rests in large part on the effect of this one work " (pp. 440–441).

" No fewer than four autobiographical works with the title ' Confessio ' or ' Thanksgiving,' ' Eucharisticos,' are known to us from the century following the ' Confessions ' (about 400). Three of their authors come from Southern Gaul; there had long existed there a lively literary impulse and rhetorical training held its place, unaffected by Christianity, into the time of the Ostrogoths, so that this province of the disintegrating western empire attained at last the leadership in the decadent literature " (pp. 442–443).

" This was the first wave of Confessions, which swept over the West and laid hold even of an unlettered man in the far North. He who gave rise to it was a great writer without a fellow in the Latin tongue since Cicero and Tacitus. Summoning all his art, Augustine related to the human race the history of the spirit; the spiritual development reached its goal with his conversion and the self-biography ended with the question, What am I now? — the answer to which gave a poetic delineation of the inner form of the religious life, which had hitherto been a closed book. To narrate his further life-history, his administration as bishop and his ecclesiastico-political acts, which would seem to be the natural ending of his autobiography, time — so the ' Confessions ' explain — was too precious. What was left was his writings: in them he conceived was gathered up his work which belongs to God and the world. They gave him occasion for a special biographical work [the " Retractations "], which coming from another attitude towards life, exhibits the self-delineation of later antiquity from a new side " (p. 455).

" What an immense undertaking it is, however, for a leading mind to take its own product again as material for treatment and to compact it into an ultimate whole! We think of Goethe, whom the idea of a history of his works, taken up as a consequence of a collected edition, drove onwards to the great product of an evolutionary-historical biography in ' Dichtung und Wahrheit.' Or of Vico's ' Vita,' which, remaining in the narrower limits of the exposition of his life-work, made for the first time in this type of authors the notion of a natural development fruitful for biography " (p. 456).

" Here again, as in the ' Confessions,' Augustine could borrow the outward form from literature. Independent treatises on their own books are encountered by us among the Hellenistic autobiographies, and it is no doubt simply an accident of transmission that this species is met with only in isolation, in the cases of Galen and Cicero. Hellenistic traditions were still operative in the epoch of Augustine; this is evident precisely for the lesser sorts of author-autobiography. The autobiographical opening poem appears not only in an Ausonius, but even in the hymn-poet Prudentius, who expected a future reward for his pious verses and accordingly transmuted the enconiums with which these autobiographies customarily ended into hopes for heaven; the biographical *prolaliae* in didactic writings served in Hilary and the young Augustine to display the spiritual development of the author, and Saint Jerome did not deny himself in his book on ' The Illustrious Men,' the addition at the end of his own self, with name, origin and catalogue of writings " (p. 459).

" Philosophy in person appeared to Boëthius. She bears the appearance of antiquity: her self-woven garment is faded, soiled and torn, but an inexhaustible youth and radiant eyes shine from her awe-inspiring countenance. She had once in her freedom pointed out to the Greeks the way to make men known in their personality; while still a maiden she was able to give to the best a consciousness of themselves. Autobiography was as deeply indebted to her as to religion which found the divine kernel in men as ' life.' And the ' Consolatio philosophiae ' along with Augustine's ' Confessions ' stands, with Dante, under the foundations of the ' Vita nuova ' " (pp. 465 f.).

It is with such words that Dr. Misch ends the first volume of his survey of the history of autobiography.

REVELATION AND INSPIRATION. By DR. REINHOLD SEEBERG. London and New York: Harper and Brothers. 1909.[1]

PROF. REINHOLD SEEBERG is one of the leaders of that school of recent German thought the object of whose research is a " Modern Positive Theology," or, as Prof. Grützmacher, another of its leaders, prefers to phrase it, a " Modern-positive Theology." We are happily relieved from all necessity of explaining to the readers of this *Review* the nature of this " Modern Positive Theology," by the admirable exposition of it which was given by Dr. C. W. Hodge in the April number. It will suffice now to remind ourselves that, as its very name advises us, it attempts to be at once " modern " and " positive." It wishes first of all to be " modern "; but in being " modern " it does not wish to break utterly with the historical faith of the Church — it wishes so far to remain " positive." In one word, its purpose is — as Prof. Grützmacher's mode of phrasing its chosen self-designation perhaps most clearly suggests — to " modernize " the historical faith of the Church. The particular elements of that faith which Prof. Seeberg undertakes to " modernize " in the booklet now before us, are the doctrines of Revelation and Inspiration. In its German form this booklet constitutes the seventh and eighth " Hefte " of the fourth series of the well-known " Biblische Zeit-

[1] *The Princeton Theological Review*, viii. 1910, pp. 679–688.

und Streitfragen " which have been publishing for the last five or six yoars " zur Aufklärung der Gcbildctcn." Bclonging to thc fourth year of this publication, this booklet appeared in 1908, and is now (1909) offered afresh for the enlightenment of the English educated public. It would fain show them that " the opinion that the Bible is a religious book is compatible with strict historical criticism of its contents "; that it is possible " to avoid the errors of the old doctrine " of Revelation and Inspiration " while not surrendering any of its material value." From the language of this statement it is already apparent that Prof. Seeberg is concerned to preserve the religious value of the Bible; but it is also apparent that he supposes that its " religious " can somewhat sharply be distinguished from its " historic " contents, and the one be taken and the other left.

The task which Prof. Seeberg has set before himself is not a new one. It is rather the task which everyone who has not liked " the old doctrine " of Revelation and Inspiration has set before himself for the last hundred years; " the kernel and the husk " has been the watchword of a century's criticism and reconstruction of Christian doctrine. Anything new Prof. Seeberg has to offer must be sought, therefore, in the particular manner in which he attempts to separate the kernel from the husk, and in the particular elements in " the old doctrine " which he accounts respectively kernel and husk. Even here, however, diligent search will be needed for the detection of anything specifically new. He tells us certainly that he has " attempted to outline the main features of a new theory of Inspiration "; and there are, no doubt, new elements discoverable in the details of his treatment of the subject. But in essence this " new theory " proves to be just the old theory which Richard Rothe set forth so winningly in his " Zur Dogmatik " a half century ago (1869) that it has infected the great body of subsequent thinking. The earnestness with which Prof. Seeberg works out his theory, however; the evident seriousness of his purpose to secure to Christianity a really revelatory character; and the modifications he has introduced into Rothe's theory for the furtherance of this end; will justify dropping out of sight for the moment the affiliation of his theory with Rothe's and seeking to learn from his own development of it how " the Modern Positive Theology " would have us think of the Bible, and what it would have us understand by the two great terms, " Revelation " and " Inspiration."

Prof. Seeberg's purpose requires of him two tasks, a negative and a positive one. He must clear the ground by showing that " the old theory of inspiration " must be " definitely abandoned," " in all its forms and details." And, then, on this cleared ground he must build up the structure of his " new theory of inspiration," " avoiding the errors of the old doctrine " but retaining all in it " of material value." In prosecuting the former of these two tasks he follows the ordinary lines of the destructive criticism with which we have long been only too familiar, and repeats all its most glaring faults. The notions which have become traditional in so-called " critical circles " as to the formation of the Biblical Canon, the ground of the authority of the Bible, the trustworthiness of the Biblical record, are assumed, and " the old theory " condemned for its lack of accord with them. There is no need to dwell on this destructive side of the argument. There is nothing distinctive in it; it is conventional in the extreme. We pause only to advert briefly to a few isolated points.

The whole elaborate " critical " theory of the slow establishment of the New Testament books into a position of authority — the formation of a New Testament Canon — is here renewedly exploited, although it is already refuted by the innocent admission that these New Testament writings were given to the Church by their authors as authoritative documents: " As the authors of the Epistles were apostles, or at least men gifted with the Spirit, these letters were *also* [the reference is to " the so-called Synoptic Gospels "] regarded as authoritative documents, *as indeed they were intended to be* (e.g. I Cor. vii. 40) " (p. 11; italics ours). The authoritative New Testament was imposed on the Church by its founders, not evolved by the Church in the course of its controversies; and the same is true *mutatis mutandis* of the Old Testament. The entire labored theory of the development of the Canon, of Old and New Testament alike, which has been worked out by the " critical " school is an invention which flies flat in the face of all the facts.

The old Protestant doctrine of the *testimonium Spiritus Sancti* to the authority of the Scriptures is, as is usual among the "critical " writers, misconceived in the interests of a merely subjective grounding of the authority of the Scriptures: " Calvin gave them Luther's subjective foundation " (p. 24). To students of Calvin it is needless to say he did nothing of the kind. What Prof. Seeberg, in common with the entire " critical " school, has done is to confuse the *testimonium Spiritus Sancti* to the contents of Scripture with the

testimonium Spiritus Sancti to the divine origin and authority of
Scripture. Dropping out the latter altogether, he endeavors to represent Calvin and the Reformers in general as basing their absolute
assurance of the divine origin and authority of Scripture on the
former. That, closely related as these two testimonies of the Spirit
are, Calvin did not confuse them, the readers of this *Review* do
not need to have pointed out to them afresh (see number for April,
1909, pp. 262 ff.). Suffice it to say that Calvin would have agreed
with Prof. Seeberg's declaration that " it is sheer nonsense to
say that the accuracy of a genealogical table, for instance, or of
the number of years of a king's reign, or of a miraculous story, or of
the date of the composition of a book is [immediately at least]
guaranteed by that living witness of the Holy Spirit " in us which
gives us " inward assurance of the grace of God, of the Divine
presence of Christ, of sin and forgiveness of sins, of virtuous impulses, in short, of the religious and moral truths of Scripture "
(pp. 25–26). But Calvin also taught, what Prof. Seeberg has not
yet learned, that the Spirit witnesses also to the divine origin and
authority of Scripture in all its extent, through the nöetic effects of
His regenerating grace, by which the renewed spirit is enabled and
led to perceive and estimate in their full validity the *indicia* of
divinity in the Scriptures, and so to recognize the hand of God in
the book of God. The odd thing is that the view which Prof. Seeberg
wrongly attributes to Calvin and scores as absurd as Calvin's, proves
to be very much his own view. In polemic against Calvin (wrongly
interpreted) he declares (p. 26) that the " course of religious experience can never lead us to any certain conclusions with reference
to the several historical facts related by Scripture." Unless we have
greatly mistaken his meaning, however, it is precisely on the basis
of the course of religious experience and on nothing else, that he
himself rests our certainty with reference to the great facts of
revelation (pp. 111–114). His argument for their reality runs indeed
expressly thus: we have a certain religious experience; this religious
experience is the product of the teaching of Scripture; this teaching implies the reality of certain facts; " the reality of these facts
and words is thereby guaranteed " (p. 112) — that is to say, they
are guaranteed ultimately by our own religious experience, and
everything is thus made to hang on an " analysis of the nature of
religious experience " (p. vii.). Of this, however, more later.

Prof. Seeberg eases his task of refuting " the old theory of inspiration " by always speaking of this " theory " (it is the " theory " of Christ and of His apostles) in its least acceptable and, we may add, least accepted form. To him it is always the theory of " dictation," taking " dictation " in its most literal sense, in which revelation and inspiration are identified, and men are supposed to be employed by God as mere implements which contribute absolutely nothing to the product, not even as much as a flute contributes to the tone of the music played on it. Accordingly he is able, appealing to I Cor. i. 16, to cry out: " No one would regard such a confession of ignorance as inspired by the Holy Spirit " (p. 27). Certainly no one could suppose ignorance to be the *result* of inspiration. But why should not confession of an ignorance which is real be made under the inspiration of the Holy Spirit? Is He not the Spirit of Truth? " To what purpose," he demands again, " should God inspire ideas which men already possessed " (p. 27). But why speak of " inspiring " ideas at all? Ideas are not " inspired " but " revealed," to employ Prof. Seeberg's distinction. Certainly ideas which are wrong could not be incorporated into an inspired body of teaching; but it is not so evident that only ideas which are directly revealed could be incorporated into such a body of teaching. Accordingly, it is only against the extremest theory of mechanical dictation that it is valid to argue that the use of sources by the inspired writers is fatal to inspiration (p. 31). The " hand of the writer may be held by the Holy Spirit " so that he writes only what the Spirit wills, and yet he proceed in his work precisely as an uninspired writer would, seeking the same ends. We have no intention, however, of following Prof. Seeberg into the details of his argument. We merely point out the serious fault in it that it is so framed as to give the impression that " the old theory of inspiration," with which the detailed credit of the Bible is bound up, is the theory of verbal dictation, rejecting which we are free to adopt some such theory as Prof. Seeberg's own. This is not the state of the case. Few have ever taught the theory of verbal dictation, though no doubt a Quenstedt, for example, did; it is certainly by no means characteristically the " old theory of inspiration "; and between it and such a theory as Prof. Seeberg proposes there stretches a great gulf, in our passage through which we shall encounter many other theories, which would need to be examined and set aside before such a one as his could come into serious consideration. Prof. Seeberg eases his task unduly when he presents the theory of dictation (which practically nobody holds) and his own theory (which nobody ought to hold) as the alternatives between which his readers must choose.

It is time we turned, however, to Prof. Seeberg's positive construction.

This runs, as we have already had occasion to note, on fundamentally the same lines as Rothe's. According to Rothe God "manifests" Himself in a series of marvelous historical acts and dispositions; for the understanding of which He "inspires" chosen men by an internal action of His Holy Spirit on their heart and mind. Similarly, according to Prof. Seeberg, revelation consists in the series of the divine acts by which God redeems the world; in a word, in the "history of salvation (*Heilsgeschichte*)"; while inspiration consists in the operation of the Spirit of God on the hearts and minds of particular men, by means of which they are enabled to understand these divine acts and so to make them operative in the minds of men. "Revelation," says he with concise directness, "is not the imparting of certain abstract ideas to the human race; revelation is history" (p. 39): and revelation being thus just history, the way "God reveals Himself to the human spirit" is "through His guidance of the course of historical evolution" (p. 41). Two things need, however, to be borne in mind here that we may not do injustice to the theory. It is not "the entire stream of historical development" which we have in mind when we speak of revelation, but the "small section of history which we call the history of salvation (*Heilsgeschichte*)" (p. 116). And words too may be deeds: "the thoughts and words evoked by God in the actors who are part of this history" are themselves elements in this history (p. 41), so that "utterances directly caused by God" may be counted in among "the historical facts caused by God" (p. 59) and prophecy becomes "itself direct revelation," introducing as it does, "new words of God into history" (p. 77). Revelation remains thus, however, speaking generally, just the historical development of redemption; facts, not words. But facts must be understood and put into words to become operative. And this is the function of inspiration, which is "simply the influence of the Spirit directed to produce the understanding of the given facts of revelation" (p. 59). "Revelation," we read, "itself consists of historical facts caused by God" (p. 59); "Inspiration consists in the fact that the Spirit of revelation creates in His first witnesses the right, sufficient and efficacious understanding of revelation" (p. 57). Again: "We understand, therefore, by inspiration . . . certain effects worked by the Spirit of God in the souls of the prophets and the first witnesses of Christ through which they were enabled to understand revelation — its facts and its words — and make it intelligible " (p. 69). Revelation, therefore, strictly taken as such (for the exact meaning of the term is not constant in Prof. Seeberg's discussion), would remain inoperative if it were not supplemented by inspiration (p. 52). " The Spirit of God," we read (p. 57), " produces, in the first place, the revelation or the facts of salvation (*Heilstatsachen*) in word and deed. Now this revelation is to become historically operative in humanity. For this purpose it is necessary that witnesses to it should arise who recognize and can express its nature in a way that will make it operative. It is the Spirit that works in revelation who, by special stimulus (*Wirkung*), brings forth in the first witnesses this understanding whereby revelation can be made historically operative. And it is the production of this understanding which we characterise as *inspiration*."

The chief thing we observe in this construction is that it provides only for the acquisition of divine truth, not at all for its communication. " Revelation " and " Inspiration " are both absorbed in the attainment of truth by its chosen witnesses; nothing is left to safeguard its transmission to others. We have reached the prophet by their means; we have not reached the Scriptures. For us, however, the prophet exists only in the Scriptures: the Scriptures lie between us and the prophets. What does it advantage us if God has revealed Himself in a series of redemptive acts and His Spirit has enabled chosen witnesses to understand and interpret these acts, unless these inspired interpretations and these revealing acts are trustworthily communicated to us? It may soothe us to be told that the Scriptures are " the literary monument which tells us " of the divine " deeds which have led men to salvation " and of the divine " knowledge of salvation " to which certain men of old have attained; that they are " a special effect of revelation," " a literature precipitated, so to speak, by the process of revelation through history " and " thus indirectly themselves also revelation " (p. 45). But will all this satisfy us? What we wish to know is whether these Scriptures are a *trustworthy* record of these revelations. And this question presses upon us with greater persistency since Prof. Seeberg, in clearing the ground of " the old theory of inspiration," has assured us and endeavored to prove to us, that the Scriptures are not

always trustworthy either in their record of facts or in their inculcation of principles — that, for example, they contain statements
which are " notoriously false," presuppose antiquated cosmologies,
perpetuate popular errors (like the belief in demoniacal possession),
set forth outgrown world-views and even present absurd interpretations of facts and prophecies (pp. 26–29). It is in his endeavor to
meet this question that Prof. Seeberg is perhaps most individual.

He assures us that despite their many faults as a general historical record — let " criticism " do its worst as to that — the Scriptures can be fully trusted precisely as a record of revelation; so
fully trusted that, possessing as we do no other understanding of
the revelation-history and its thoughts than that deposited in the
Scriptures, we may safely take the contents of the Scriptures as the
expression of the divine revelation for us (p. 45). The ground on
which this assurance is based has a sufficiently Pragmatistic appearance. It is in brief that Scripture serves all the purposes of
revelation to us and therefore is revelation. The complex of ideas
presented to us by the Scriptures works in us a remarkable inward
experience, in which we find ourselves in the living presence of
God. And " since we experience in the thoughts of Scripture a Divine
effect, we characterise it on the ground of experienced faith as Divine
revelation " (p. 48). It is " a judgment of our faith " to which we
thus give expression; and this judgment carries us very far. It not
only assures us that the Bible is a revelation, but it guarantees to
us the historical character of the facts of which this revelation is
an interpretation. When we experience the ideas based on these facts
as true, this assuredly should carry with it the reality of the facts
on which these ideas are based (p. 49). To the elucidation of this
point a whole section is given (pp. 111–114). " Inspiration," we are
told (p. 112), " was an effect of the operation of the Spirit of God,
through which a man learned to understand the nature of the facts
given him. From this it follows, however, that so far as inspired
knowledge can be gained from a fact or a word, this fact and this
word are guaranteed as actual. If God produces knowledge by means
of certain particular facts, these facts must needs also be produced
by God. The more paradoxical and miraculous these facts are the
more certain is this conclusion. If then the apostles through God's
Spirit gained inspired knowledge from the resurrection of Christ,
the actuality of the resurrection is thereby established for everyone
who feels the witness of the Spirit in the Bible. If the words of Jesus

and the oracles spoken through the prophets have become the object of inspired understanding, then for the religious view their reality is proved thereby." We need only bear in mind that this guarantee does not extend to the minute details of historical occurrence, or to the verbal accuracy of texts, but is available only for the establishment of the reality of the great facts of salvation (*Heilstatsachen*) and ideas of revelation (*Offenbarungsgedanken*) to feel assured that we have in it a thoroughly satisfactory criterion of reality.

It can scarcely escape us that precisely what we have here is an attempt to discover a basis for confidence in the great facts recorded in the Bible and the great ideas set forth in it without implication of the historical trustworthiness or of the authority of the Bible itself. The basis of confidence is shifted from the Bible to Christian experience, or what we used to call " the Christian Consciousness," and the Bible is made to play the rôle only of vehicle of transmission. The whole conception of an authoritative book is set aside and we are to accept in the Bible only what Christian experience validates. It is asserted on the other hand, however, that Christian experience validates all the great " salvation facts " and " revelation ideas " brought to us by the Bible. There is of course nothing new in this general position; but it is well worth carefully noting as indicatory of the place in the history of thought of the Modern-positive Theology. By it the Modern-positive Theology takes its place as only a part of that general tendency which has been long operative in the German churches, to substitute, as the seat of authority for the Christian man, his own inner experience for the infallible book which the Reformers substituted for the infallible Church: in other words it is only the latest outcome of that great subjectivistic movement of thought inaugurated by Schleiermacher.

Nothing could be further from our wish, of course, than to deny or doubt the validity of " the argument from experience," which at its height is only another name for the *testimonium Spiritus Sancti* to the contents of revelation. There is such a thing as the " assurance of salvation "; and this assurance of salvation does validate the great " salvation facts " and " revelation ideas " brought to us by the Bible, and is not dependent on a precedent confidence in the trustworthiness of the Bible: to the Spirit-prepared heart these great facts and ideas are their own credentials. But this is not to say we can get along very well, then, without a Bible. After all it

was from the Bible that we got these great facts and ideas to which
our " Christian experience " sets its seal that they are real and
true; and the authoritative Bible, if it is not the *prius* of this " Christian experience," may well prove to be its *posterius*. In point of
fact, no one doubts that the doctrine of the detailed authority of
the Scriptures — their " inspiration " in the old sense — belongs to
the " high doctrines " of Christianity, and does not underlie our
first confidence in its fundamental facts, which rests rather on the
general historical trustworthiness of the Biblical record. But it is
another question whether Christianity, as a system of truth, can
dispense with this " high doctrine," and can even get along without
the general historical trustworthiness of the Bible record, abandoning it to a naturalistic " historical criticism " and contenting itself
meanwhile with an appeal to " Christian experience." For one thing,
this were to shift the Christianity which we are to teach from an
objective to a subjective foundation, and to limit its content to the
few " vital " truths which " find " us, with the ultimate elimination
of all objective basis for these " vital " truths themselves and the
relegation of them for their content as well as for their validation to
the subjective experience itself. For we must not conceal from ourselves, for another thing, that a procedure such as is proposed will
necessarily introduce a schism into our mental life which cannot be
permanent and which can have but one issue. What is the use of our
telling ourselves that our experience of religious effects arising from
the ideas gained by the apostles in fellowship with the risen Christ,
guarantees for us the fact of His resurrection " for the religious
point of view " (p. 112, cf. p. 49), if our critical examination of the
historical record convinces us that in point of fact Christ did not rise
from the dead, for the scientific point of view? We cannot continue
to believe on the warrant of our religious experience what we know
to be contrary to fact on the verdict of our scientific investigation.
Unless we are prepared to accept the validation of the facts and
ideas brought to us by the Bible on the faith of " religious experience " as the validation of the trustworthiness of the Bible as a
record of facts and ideas, we shall be driven for our entire Christianity into the most unreal subjectivism. But so soon as we adopt
the former attitude, our " religious experience " becomes a testimony not only to the facts and ideas which " find " us but to the
trustworthiness of the Biblical record which brings us these facts
and ideas, and the first step is taken in the validation of an authoritative Bible. This first step taken, others will necessarily follow, and

we shall soon find ourselves in the possession of an objectively and not merely subjectively established Christianity. And we shall find ourselves in possession of this objectively established Christianity ultimately precisely because we shall find in our hands an authoritative Bible, and for no other reason whatever. What the ground of the Bible's authority is, what is the nature of the divine operations by which it is communicated to the Bible, what is its extent, and what is its degree — such questions as these may still remain open to investigation. But the Bible's authority having been once established we may be disposed and indeed required to listen to its own testimony on these subsequent matters; and if its own testimony is followed we shall have as a result nothing other than the " old Protestant theory " of inspiration. It really admits of no question that the Bible conceives itself the product of the Divine Spirit in such a sense that it is the pure expression of His mind and will. And nothing is more certain than that the Bible stands forth in the world at once as a great spiritual fact, and an interpretation of this fact; that this is a fact which " finds " us and produces in our hearts spiritual effects. Does not the maxim hold here too that unique spiritual effects infer unique spiritual causes? And if our religious experience quickened by the Scriptures and their message fails to validate the great fact of the Bible, how can we plead it as the validation of other facts implicated in it?

What Prof. Seeberg has sought to do, it will be observed, is to supply a reasoned basis for the common notion that the Scriptures are authoritative only in spiritual matters — " for faith and practice " as the phrase goes — and for all else may be freely delivered over to the hand of the destroyer. Our confidence in what the Scriptures transmit to us, he says, is grounded in our religious experience; and therefore, he seems to say, we have ground for confidence only in that element of Scripture which religious experience directly validates. There are therefore two sides to Prof. Seeberg's argument, a positive and a negative side, and the trouble is that the negative side fits ill in with the positive side. Conceived as an attempt to show that in Christian experience we have a basis for confidence in the great Christian facts and ideas which underlie and give form to that experience, we may find help and comfort in it. Conceived as an attempt to show that, having in Christian experience this basis for confidence in the great Christian facts and ideas, we may dispense with an authoritative Bible, we can look upon it only as an assault upon the foundations of the Christian faith. The former

element is the " Positive," the latter the " Modern " element in the
" Modern Positive Theology "; and they do not agree together.
The one is fundamentally Supernaturalistic and the other fundamentally Naturalistic; and a Supernaturalistic Naturalism or Naturalistic Supernaturalism is a contradiction no less in fact than in
terms. If in a supernaturalistically created Christian experience we
have a guarantee of the truth of the great revelation-ideas brought
to us by the Bible and constituting its substance, and of the reality as
well of the great salvation-facts with which these ideas are connected in the Bible as their interpretation, then we have in this
Christian experience a guarantee of the trustworthiness and authority of the Bible which records these facts and develops their
meaning. And if we will not admit the validity of this guarantee
in the one case, we cannot put confidence in it in the other: the
" scientific " considerations which lead us to reject it in the one
may compel our rejection of it in the other also. The question which
really faces us in both cases alike is, What is the real state of the
evidence? Not abstractly, Is the positive evidence of religious experience or the negative evidence of " scientific " investigation most
conclusive? But concretely, Is the positive evidence of religious experience or the negative evidence of " scientific " investigation most
conclusive in this case? We cannot set each off by itself and follow
both, each with one-half of the soul. Nor can we decline the task
of estimating the weight of the evidence as a whole, by shutting our
eyes to one or the other variety of the evidence, or attending to them
only alternately. Christianity is neither a mere philosophy nor an
empty illusion: it is objectively real and subjectively operative, and
finds its rooting both in its inspired record and in its spiritual efficacy.

LE PROBLÈME DE DIEU ET LA THÉOLOGIE CHRÉTIENNE DEPUIS LA
RÉFORME. Par VICTOR MONOD. I. Étude historique. Foyer Soli-
dariste: Saint-Blaise, près Neuchâtel (Suisse); Roubaix, 123,
Boulevard de Belfort. 1910.[1]

M. VICTOR MONOD is profoundly disturbed by the condition of
current opinion upon the nature and activities of God. The idea of

[1] *The Princeton Theological Review*, ix. 1911, pp. 149–156.

God he thinks has perhaps never before been made the object of more intense and widespread study. But the issue of the prolonged debates of recent centuries has been little more than an immense confusion. Nearly every thinking man has formed a different conception of the Divine Being for himself. " In the teaching of the Churches heterogeneous philosophies and contradictory religious aspirations are juxtaposed or superficially amalgamated " (p. 3). The question is raised whether " the Christian doctrine of God is essentially amorphous and irrational or is only compromised to-day by lack of critical spirit and of historical knowledge in some of its adherents " (p. 4). M. Monod's convictions lie in the line of the latter alternative, and he naturally wishes to do his part to clarify the atmosphere. The task he has undertaken is essentially a dogmatic one. But it has its natural if not necessary historical approach. " To draw out in order," he explains, " the solutions of the problem of God which have been proposed by the great theologians, to set them in the historical framework which explains them, to indicate how they have been engendered by successive corrections or reactions, to discriminate, in a word, the vital necessity to which the succession of divers theological systems has responded; these have appeared to me the indispensable preliminaries of a methodical study of the question " (p. 4). Accordingly he gives us now this " historical study," while the dogmatic construction to which it is to lead us up waits a more convenient season. He does not feel bound, however, to pass in review in this " historical study " the whole history of the idea of God, in detailed exposition. He is not writing a history of the idea of God but a historical introduction to his own forthcoming attempt to put together a competent exposition of the idea of God. He therefore confines his survey to the historical antecedents of his own construction.

In point of fact, M. Monod confines his survey of the history of the idea of God to two epochs, the sixteenth and the nineteenth centuries; and in these two epochs to two great outstanding movements of thought, the Reformation, or better, the Reformed theology, and the Kantian criticism. The conceptions of God characteristic of these two great movements of thought he sets over against one another in sharp antithesis, discriminating them under the contrasting designations of " God as sovereign " and " God as a moral person." The antithesis obviously is a false one; the two designations are not mutually exclusive. It is also historically unjust: the Reformed theology throws an emphasis upon the moral personality of God which cannot be exceeded, and the moral personality of God is not the most outstanding feature of the conception of God developed by the Kantian movement. M. Monod himself cites Calvin as declaring that God is good by a necessity as stringent as that by which He is God, and that it would be easier to sever the light of the sun from its heat than to separate God's power from His righteousness; while the very stress which the Reformed theology places on the will of God is a stress on His personality, since he who says will says person. And M. Monod himself points out how the moral character of God evaporates in, for example, the thought of M. Ch. Secrétan in the face of the demand of " absolute freedom " for Him. The real distinction between the Reformed and the Kantian movements in their relation to the idea of God lies quite apart from the question of His moral personality, although, of course, it concerns very distinctly the question of His sovereignty. The difficulty with Kantian speculation has been indeed to find any place for God at all in its scheme of things. Beginning with calling in God only as a postulate of the moral imperative, it ends by limiting His action in the interest of human freedom. The whole tendency of the Kantian thought is spoken out when M. Secrétan remarks: " There seems no place in the world for both man and God " (p. 146); and M. Monod's dilemma is from the Kantian standpoint a very real one: Render with Calvin all glory to God and man is reduced to nonentity; vindicate with Kant all man's liberty and all man's dignity and you have (with Schleiermacher) no use for God save, perhaps, for the Judgment Day. The issue that is drawn between the Reformed thought of the sixteenth and the Kantian thought of the nineteenth century is not between a sovereign and an ethical God; it is between God and man. And the movement from the one to the other is a veritable revolution by which God is dethroned and man elevated to His place as the center of the universe. M. Monod puts it not unjustly in a passage which we gladly quote entire (p. 108): " Just as for Copernicus the earth so far from being a pivot about which the stars revolve, describes an ellipse around a fixed sun, so for Kant the objects which constitute the external world so far from determining knowledge are subject to laws impressed by the mind. This figure can be adapted to indicate the way in which the Kantian theology sets itself in opposition to the theology of the sixteenth century. God is no longer the central star of the religious domain; He is only a satellite, a postulate of the mind. The point of departure is the thinking sub-ject, his rights and his needs; the nature and the attributes of God can be determined only as functions of the exigencies of the human being. And the whole effort of Kant bears on a point which theolo-gians of the sixteenth century had not thought to investigate: In what is God necessary to man? Is the existence of God legitimated by the needs of reason? " In a word the sixteenth century conceived man as the creation of God, existing for God and serving His ends; men now are prone to think of God as, if not exactly the creation of man, yet as existing for man and serving man's ends. The center of the universe has shifted; and God has become as has been, per-haps wittily, perhaps bitterly, said, very much a domestic animal which man keeps, as he does his horse or his cow, to meet certain specific needs of his being.

About half of M. Monod's volume is given to an exposition of each of these two types of thought concerning God. The latter half, dealing broadly speaking with the Kantian notions, under the rubric of " God as a moral person," appears to us the more penetrating and satisfactory piece of exposition, chiefly because it seems to us the more sympathetically worked out. The master-thought of this move-ment is shown to be the conception of the greatness of man: " the idea that man so far as he is man and because he is man has right to the free efflorescence of his personality and can recognize as legitimate no authority which is not judicially constituted " (p. 102). This master-thought is traced in its enunciation to Kant, to whom God exists only as a moral postulate and only so far as His existence may be made consistent with what Kant deemed the necessities of the moral responsibility of man. So determining has the conception of " freedom " thus conceived become in modern thought that M. Monod incidentally drops the remark, as if it were a matter of course, that since Kant " liberty and morality have become so in-dissolubly bound together that Luther's and Calvin's doctrine of the subject-will has become merely an incomprehensible curiosity to the contemporary consciousness " (p. 121). After Kant, no doubt, there comes Schleiermacher, in whose system there is no place for any other liberty than " that of Spinozistic spontaneity, autonomous vitality," the capacity of " reaction upon finite beings which exert a certain determination on man, and of determining them in turn " (p. 133) ; and who led in the interest of the religious feeling a reac-tion towards a kind of spurious Calvinism which would preserve a divine sovereignty without emphasis upon the divine personality. "God, for Schleiermacher," we read (pp. 130 f.), "is therefore a mysterious master of whom we know only one thing, — that He commands and that we ought to obey. He is an active Being and not a dead Law, but He is not less an abstract Being, with no name and no countenance, known only by the hand which He presses against us. The Sovereign God of Calvin, the Monarch of good-pleasure and individual feeling is gone; but on the celestial throne there still remains in austere idealization the Scepter, the Baton of command." But Schleiermacher does not mark the end of the series. After Schleiermacher comes Secrétan — Secrétan to whom " freedom " is at once the first and the last word of philosophy, a " freedom " for man which admits of no limitations and a corresponding " freedom " for God which enables Him to keep out of the way of this " free " man — by virtue of which He is infinite only if He wishes it, and can be finite as well if He wishes it, knows what He wishes to know and is ignorant of what He wishes to be ignorant of. " If God is God," says Secrétan, " it is only because He wills it " (p. 148). Thus Secrétan finds his way out of the great difficulty of his school of thought by pressing to its extreme its primal postulate. It has been common to say that if " freedom " be defined as this school defines freedom, then we have to choose between a " free " humanity and a " free " Deity; both cannot be " free " in this sense, which knows no difference between freedom and ability. Secrétan replies that the difficulty disappears if only you make God free enough, if only you ascribe to Him " absolute liberty," a liberty which is capable of everything; for, then, He would be free not to be God, or even to abnegate His freedom itself. " Secrétan, we see," remarks M. Monod (pp. 148 f.), " commences by attributing to the absolute Being a fathomless freedom and sovereignty, but he adds that the day on which pure freedom resolves itself into an act, the day on which creation takes place, the reign of Law, of Relation, of Determinism commences." For M. Monod's present purpose, Secrétan has spoken the last word which has yet been spoken in the way of solving " the problem of God " — that is to say, in the effort so to conceive God that man may be left " free," in the exaggerated sense of freedom assumed by this school. But this last word has not, he thinks, solved the problem; and the way is open for another attempt to reach a true conception of God — a conception which shall do better justice to both sides of the problem, the side rooted in man's sense of dependence as well as that rooted in his sense of freedom. For the terms in which this solution may be worked out, however, we shall have to wait for the dogmatic discussion which, M. Monod promises us, shall follow this historical sketch. We may, indeed, already perceive that what M. Monod proposes to do is to set over against " God as sovereign " and " God as moral person " alike the conception of " God as Father." This is, of course, to introduce another false antithesis, and to substitute tropical for scientific treatment. But despite these drawbacks with respect to method it is quite possible that M. Monod may give us in his dogmatic treatment a very happy solution of the problem of the conception of God. We are content to wait to see.

Meanwhile we note that M. Monod already recognizes that there is another side to the problem besides that of human " freedom " and " responsibility " so insisted on by the Kantian thinkers. This other side of the problem is that which forms the burden of the Reformed theology; and M. Monod has begun his book with a survey of it as given expression in that theology. We have already intimated, however, that we do not think this survey as illuminating, because not as sympathetic, as that given of the Kantian theories. It would seem that with all his desire to do justice to that sense of dependence on God which is the psychological reflection of the Divine Sovereignty, M. Monod is to some extent preoccupied with the current over-estimate of man in his present condition in the world, which has its ultimate roots in a defective sense of sin. He himself very fairly describes this current point of view when, speaking of the surprise with which the modern man hears Calvin describe the doctrine of predestination as " sweet and savory," he offers this account of it: " The reason is that the condition of man does not appear to us as tragically horrible as it does to the Calvinists; we are surprised at the rejection of the lost, the Reformed of the sixteenth century were astonished rather at the salvation of the elect " (pp. 57 f.). This is but to say that a Pelagianizing estimate of man in his powers, achievements, and present condition cannot accord with an Augustinian soteriology; the current estimate of man is distinctly Pelagianizing and therein lies the whole account of its ineradicable opposition to the Reformed theology. Borne along to some extent, doubtless, by this current of modern thought, M. Monod finds himself out of tune with the Reformed soteriology, and most of all with its emphasis on predestination; and finding himself out of tune with it, he is not quite able to comprehend it, much less to do full justice to it.

He recognizes, indeed, the religious value and the practical motive of the Calvinistic doctrine of the divine sovereignty; he even exaggerates this aspect of it, by representing it as a product of religious experience in such a sense as to give it only a subjective grounding, in this connection misconceiving the doctrine of the *testimonium Spiritus Sancti*. " We see," he remarks (p. 15), " that while scholasticism limited its art of persuasion to two processes, reasoning and the citation of an inspired text, the Reformation made appeal to a third authority, . . . the inward witness of the Holy Spirit." The " witness of the Holy Spirit " was not to the Reformers, however, in any sense a " third authority " operating apart from (perhaps in opposition to) reason and the Scriptures — as anyone may satisfy himself by merely reading the anti-Anabaptist chapters in Calvin's exposition of it at the opening of the " Institutes "; but a power of God clarifying reason in its use of the Scriptures and acting only confluently with them. M. Monod's partial sympathy with the Reformed doctrine as an expression of religious experience is therefore itself a symptom of his real lack of complete sympathy with it; and when he goes into its particulars his lack of complete sympathy is manifested in not infrequent failures to enter fully into its spirit which betray him into certain errors of judgment regarding it. There occur even occasional lapses in apprehension of declarations of the advocates of the view he is controverting, which lead him into no doubt unconscious but nevertheless regrettable misrepresentations of their contentions. Thus for example the " De dono perseverantiae," xx. is cited (p. 59) as an avowal on the part of Augustine that " it was the Pelagian controversies which caused him to defend the doctrine of election in its integrity." What Augustine really says is precisely the contrary, namely, that before the controversy broke out he had taught the whole doctrine of election with clearness and emphasis, and had been compelled by the controversy only to do more laboriously and abundantly what he was doing in any event. Immediately after quoting Zanchi's clear statement of his *ordo decretorum* (which is, on this occasion at least, expressly Infralapsarian: " creation, fall, election, redemption "), and while in act of inveighing against Zanchi's scholasticism, M. Monod shows so little care for the niceties of the subject as to attribute to Zanchi Amyraut's *ordo decretorum*. " Once, once only," he cries, " God has thought of man and assigned him his destiny. Thenceforward everything is evolved with the rigor of a mathematical theorem: creation, fall, redemption, election, reprobation, crimes and virtues, prayers and blasphemy, all has been willed, foreseen, foreordained by God " (p. 81). Are then the differences which separate Supralapsarian, Infralapsarian, and Postredemptionist too small to hold a place in the mind of one who consigns them all alike to the oblivion of an incomprehensible past?

It is naturally, however, when M. Monod undertakes professedly to report the objections to predestination that his failure of sympathy with the doctrine works most havoc in his reasoning. Here we have arrayed all the old uncomprehending arguments: predestination deprives the work of Christ of all significance, it menaces the authority of the moral law, it dissipates the guilt of man, and the like. What underlies everything, however, is failure to realize that predestination is never supposed to determine ends apart from means. It would for example be as intelligible to argue that when a king has determined to take a city he may at once intermit all concern about armies and engines of war — the determination will take the city; or that when a physician has determined to cure a patient, he may safely neglect to administer the remedies — the determination will cure the patient; as that when God has determined to save His people, all significance in the work of Christ, the only means by which the determined salvation is to be accomplished, is taken away. How reasoners like M. Monod are pursued by this incomprehensible uncomprehendingness is oddly illustrated in a footnote in which he wishes to ascribe to Luther himself, that sound and fervent predestinarian because sound and fervent believer in God and His grace, the objection to predestination that " it renders singularly vain and futile the work of Jesus Christ." We quote this footnote (pp. 66 f.) in full: " This was the objection of Luther. Towards 1542 he wrote: ' I hear that the nobles and great people emit such criminal talk about predestination as to say, If I am predestinated I shall be saved whether I do well or ill, and if I am not I shall be damned. I shall gladly combat this impious language if my uncertain health will permit me. If this talk were sound, the incarnation of the Son of God, His passion, His resurrection and all that He has done for the salvation of the world would be abolished. What end would be served by the prophets and all the Holy Scriptures? What by the Sacraments? Let us cast off and trample under foot this talk ' — *Commentary on Gen. xxvi. Opera*, Witebergae. 1580. Vol. vi. 353. — How far we are here from the affirmations of the

De Servo Arbitrio! " Needless to say, the words quoted from Luther have no such implication as M. Monod puts on them. In them Luther promises that if only the infirmities of his health permit, he will confute those who abuse the doctrine of predestination, saying, " If I am predestined, I shall be saved no matter whether I do well or ill; if I am not I shall be damned." To give a brief hint of the line his confutation will take, Luther adds that if such talk were sound " the incarnation of the Son of God, His passion, His resurrection and all that He has done for the salvation of the world would be abolished " — the prophets and the whole of the Sacred Scriptures, the sacraments would be useless; wherefore, says he, we should reject and trample under foot such prating. What Luther says in this none too vigorous language is, as we all at once perceive, simply that if predestination is perverted into a predestination of ends apart from all means — so that those predestinated to life will live no matter what they do — then the significance of all means is taken away and this is tantamount to abolishing Christ and all His work, the Scriptures and all the Means of Grace, since these are the means by which the predestined end is attained. But he says this only in objection to a manifest perversion of the doctrine of predestination, and in vigorous defense of the doctrine of predestination. And when M. Monod cries out upon it, " How far we are here from the affirmations of the *De Servo Arbitrio*," he merely betrays how far he himself is from understanding not Luther merely whom he quotes (perhaps at second-hand; possibly through the deflecting medium of Luthardt) and the " De Servo Arbitrio " which he refers to, but the whole Reformed doctrine of predestination which he is in act of expounding and criticizing. Luther speaks here in complete and even enthusiastic accord with the affirmations of the " De Servo Arbitrio," and can be misunderstood only by writers who, not being in agreement with Luther, are determined to make Luther be in agreement with them.

We have no intention, however, of indulging in a series of petty criticisms of the details of M. Monod's exposition of the Reformed doctrine. We have merely wished to illustrate by a few instances taken at random from his pages a vein of failure in comprehension which runs through them and vitiates their conclusions. There is much in his exposition and criticism meanwhile that is worthy of remark — particularly, if we may specify, his connection of the political and religious thinking of the times. We can only express the conviction that if M. Monod had approached the study of the Reformed theology with the sympathy with which he has approached the study of the post-Kantian movement, he would have found an acceptable doctrine of God less a problem to his thought, because he would have found it already worked out for him in that great body of Augustinian thinking which has been the possession of the world for nearly a millennium and a half. The *scandalon* of this body of thinking has ever been, and is, that it thinks of God as God, and will not have His glory diminished by the exaltation of man. M. Monod himself says (p. 84): " The error of Calvinism was, above all, that it did not recognize the specific character and unique value of the human person." The charge is quite untrue. Calvinism fully recognizes the high value of human personality. But Calvinism certainly does not allow that the human person has power to set itself by the side of the Divine. And the retort is just that the error of anti-Calvinism has always been, and continues to be, that it does not recognize the specific character and unique value of the Divine person. M. Monod sometimes speaks as if he would charge Calvinism with wiping out the gulf which separates man from the beasts that perish. It does not do that. Calvin teaches rather that man is raised infinitely above the brutes by that *sensus deitatis* which is ineradicably imprinted on his nature, and by reason of which he aspires to immortality (e. g. " Institutes," I. iii. 1, 3; v. 4). But Calvinism resists and will continue to resist every effort to wipe out the greater gulf which separates the creature from his Creator. We have said advertently " greater gulf." For we stand with Calvin, or rather with Augustine, — for Calvin is quoting Augustine here (" Opera Calvini," ed. Baum, Cunitz, and Reuss, viii. col. 286) — when he declares that " he is assuredly mad who does not ascribe to God a far greater preëminence above himself than he allows to the human race above the beasts." And we stand with Calvin when (still after Augustine) he adds that what is most becoming in the sheep of God's flock is quiet submission to His will; and when he adjoins, now on his own behalf, that this would assuredly be more fitting than, after the example of Pighius, to substitute man for God and demand that each man should earn his own destiny on the ground of his own virtues. The " problem of God " is to be solved for the twentieth century as for all that have preceded it, not by deifying man and abasing God in his presence, but by recognizing God to be indeed God and man to be the creation of His hands,

whose chief end it is to glorify God and to enjoy Him forever. And
this is as M. Monod truly perceives, just Calvinism.

CHRISTOLOGIES ANCIENT AND MODERN. By WILLIAM SANDAY, D.D.,
LL.D., Litt.D. Oxford University Press, American Branch. 1910.[1]

PUBLICITY is one of the striking characteristics of our times.
Our Village Improvement Societies, demanding the removal of all
fences, are but a symbol of a universal temper. Perhaps Dr. Sanday
is the first scholar, however, who has deliberately elected to do his
studying in the public view. He has, as it were, knocked down the
walls of his study, and, taking his seat in the open, invited all that
pass by to observe him writing his great book on the Life of Christ.
It is pleasant to be taken thus into a great scholar's confidence; and
we have all profited by the series of charmingly written volumes
in which Dr. Sanday has laid before us the processes of his preliminary studies for his great task. The volume now before us, he
tells us, is probably the last of these, and it does not yield in interest
to either of its predecessors. We confess, however, to a certain decrease in the interest with which we look forward to the work to
which they lead up, as we have read one after the other of these
preliminary studies. They pass in review a great mass of modern
research, and whatever they touch upon they illuminate. It would
be difficult to find a more sympathetic survey of the recent literature
of Gospel criticism or a more useful guide to the intricacies of modern constructions of the person of Christ. But it is possible for width
of sympathy itself to become a snare; there are other qualities than
breadth of importance to a teacher of fundamental religious truth;
and it is not strange that the term " latitudinarianism " has even
acquired an evil connotation. As we have reread, one after the other,
Dr. Sanday's preliminary studies, while our admiration of the extent of his learning and the clearness of his comprehension of the
currents of recent thought has steadily grown, misgivings have
grown with it of the firmness of his grasp on the fundamental problems which must underlie and give its body to a Life of Christ which
would do justice to the deposit of faith. It was distinctly not reas-

[1] *The Princeton Theological Review,* ix. 1911, pp. 166–174.

suring to observe the nature of the hospitality which he accorded in the earliest of these volumes to certain very wiredrawn hypotheses as to the personality of the author of the Fourth Gospel. It was not more reassuring to observe the nature of the commendation which he gave in the second of them to Albert Schweitzer's brilliant, in some respects surely epoch-making, but sadly negative history of what Schweitzer's translators call, not unfairly from their point of view, " the quest of the historical Jesus." Nor does reassurance come with the present volume, with the feebleness of its hold upon the Biblical and Historical Christologies, its readiness to fly for refuge to doubtful modern speculations as supplying the key to the mystery of our Lord's person, its determination to have a Jesus who in all His earthly manifestations was, phenomenally, " strictly human." If the outline given on pp. 179 ff. of what Dr. Sanday calls " the working of our Lord's consciousness," in which is briefly traced His career from the cradle to the grave, is to furnish, as seems likely, the schematization of the coming Life of Christ, the mold which is to determine the lines of its structure, then, we may as well say frankly at once, we shall have no interest in the new Life of Christ whatever. For then it will be nothing but one more of those " reduced " Lives of Christ, of which the world has already too many, the writers of which, deserting the testimony of the sources, have as Renan puts it " imputed themselves to their victim," and, creating a Jesus after their own image, permitted Him to function only within the limits of their own consciousness. It will be a matter of sincere regret if, after the warnings of even a Wrede and a Schweitzer, Dr. Sanday should only again " psychologize " the Life of Christ.

The title of the present volume — " Christologies Ancient and Modern " — might lead one to expect to find it a historical sketch of Christological thought in the Church, or perhaps a critical discussion of the chief Christological theories which have been current in the Church. It is not quite either of these. Its leading motive is rather the suggestion of a new Christological theory, the Christological theory which is to underlie the forthcoming Life of Christ. Even so, however, the general drift of ancient Christological thought up to Chalcedon, and the chief forms of German Christological construction of the last century are lightly sketched, to form a background against which the new suggestion may be thrown out. These sketches are drawn, of course, by the hand of a master, although only leading principles are brought out, with no attempt to enter into details. In these circumstances probably we ought not to scrutinize with too much care the occasional details which are rapidly alluded to. Otherwise we might question the description of Tertullian's Trinity, without qualification, as " what is called an ' economic Trinity ' " (p. 26), and we should certainly demur to the rendering of his οἰκονομίας sacramentum by " the mystery of the divine appointment " (p. 25). Dr. Sanday himself at a later point uses the term " economy " in Tertullian's sense, when (p. 45) he speaks of projecting " our ideas of Personality into the internal economy of the Godhead " — which, by the way, is precisely what Tertullian was in the act of doing, when he wrote the passage which Dr. Sanday quotes. The language which is used in speaking of the Chalcedonian formula (pp. 52–55) again does not seem to us to retain perfect exactness. The Chalcedonian fathers would seem to have done all they could to save themselves from the charge of conceiving the Two Natures as " separable and separate," when they solemnly declared that they were united ἀδιαιρέτως, Leo's " agit utraque natura quod proprium est *cum alterius communicatione* " would seem to preclude the supposition that these two natures were conceived as " operating distinctly "; and the emphatic " without confusion, without conversion " of the decree, would certainly appear to render it impossible to describe it as allowing " by a system of mutual give-and-take " " for the transference of the attributes from one nature to the other " — which is a characteristic feature not of the Chalcedonian but of the Old-Lutheran Christology. Nor do we think it happy (p. 104) to take over Paul's words in II Cor. v. 19 in the form, " God was in Christ, reconciling the world to Himself," without remark, as a fair expression of the Ritschlian view of Christ's person. We suppose it to be unquestionable that these words, as they stand in Paul's epistle, have a Soteriological rather than Christological content, and should be read, " God was, in Christ, reconciling the world with Himself," or to put its full point upon it, " It was God who was reconciling the world with Himself in Christ "; and it is hardly desirable to perpetuate a perversion of an apostolical phrase by making it in its perverted use the vehicle of a special Christological hypothesis. Small incidental matters of this kind, however, are scarcely more worth adverting to than the incapacity the American publishers show (pp. 27, 40, 51, 121) to print a Greek phrase correctly, a matter which must be especially mortifying to Dr.

Sanday and his British publishers alike, to whom such things are unwonted.

The center of interest in the volume lies not in its historical but in its constructive aspect, in " the tentative modern Christology " which it outlines. This is dominated by a gently expressed but perfectly firm refusal of the doctrine of the Two Natures on the one side, and a fixed determination, on the other, to have a Jesus who, phenomenally at least, shall be " strictly human." It will go without saying, of course, that if there be not Two Natures in the person of Christ, then there can be but one; and He must be conceived, therefore, either as a purely divine Nature as Person, or as a purely human Nature as Person. In the former case we shall be landed inevitably, of course, in some form of Docetism; in the latter as inevitably in some form of Humanitarianism. Dr. Sanday, as is his gracious wont, speaks kindly of the Docetists, and seeks and finds the element of truth which they saw and endeavored to conserve. But he does not cast in his lot with them. Neither (very properly) will he consort with the Kenotists who think to have in a one-natured Jesus both God and man, on the theory that a shriveled God is a man, and that Jesus, who was nothing but a man, may be thought to have been God before He shrunk into human limits — thus losing really both Natures in the attempt to make one two. There is nothing left for Dr. Sanday, therefore, but a pure Humanitarianism. His historical sense, however, and his Christian heart will not permit him to think of Christ " merely as man." He feels compelled to recognize deity in Him as well as humanity. But not deity alongside of the humanity. Why not, rather, he suggests, deity underlying and sustaining the humanity — as deity underlies and sustains all humanity? Then we may think of Christ as " strictly human "; but, as man differs from man in the richness and fullness with which the divine that underlies his being surges up in him and enters into his consciousness, and Jesus stands in this incomparably above all other men, we may think of Him as incomparably the divine man. Thus Dr. Sanday would cut the knot of the Christological problem. Obviously, what he gives us is at best only a new Nestorianism, a Nestorianism stated in terms of modern speculation; Jesus Christ is a man in whom God dwells in a fullness in which He does not dwell in other men. At worst, what he gives us is a devout Humanitarianism, a Humanitarianism stated in terms of mystical contemplation: the doctrine of the Incarnation gives place to a theory of Divine Immanence, and Jesus Christ is just the God-filled man.

The basis of Dr. Sanday's suggested Christology, we perceive, is a mystical doctrine of human nature. Support for this mystical doctrine of human nature he seeks, we must now note, in recent speculations as to the subliminal self. Nobody doubts, or has ever doubted, that mental processes take place below the threshold of consciousness. And nobody doubts that God operates on the human soul, as we say, " beneath consciousness." The peculiarity of Mr. Myers' doctrine of the " subliminal consciousness " — as it is mis-leadingly called, for how can we speak of unconscious consciousness? — to which Dr. Sanday attaches himself, is that this " subliminal consciousness " is supposed to be not merely the larger but the nobler part of the self. " The wonderful thing is," writes Dr. Sanday (p. 145), " that while the unconscious and subconscious processes are (generally speaking) similar in kind to the conscious, they sur-pass them in degree. They are subtler, intenser, further-reaching, more penetrating. It is something more than a metaphor when we describe the sub- and unconscious states as more ' profound.' It is in these states, or through them, that miracles are wrought . . ." Our subconscious states and operations are not subnormal, or even normal, but supernormal. Nay, they are even divine; for beneath our subliminal selves lies the ocean of the Infinite, and, as we are open at the bottom, the tides of the Infinite wash in. If we pass down deep enough into our subliminal being, then, we shall find God; or, if the tides of the Infinite wash in high enough, they will emerge in our consciousness. Dr. Sanday pictures our human con-sciousness " as a kind of ' narrow neck ' through which everything which comes up from the deeps of human nature has to pass " (p. 176). This " narrow-necked vessel," he tells us, has an opening at the bottom. " Through it there are incomings and outgoings, which stretch away into infinity and in fact proceed from, *and are,* God Himself " (p. 178, italics ours). " That," he adds most naturally, " is the ultimate and most important point . . . Whatever there may be of divine in man, it is in these deep dim regions that it has its abiding-place and home." Accordingly he refuses to follow Sir Oliver Lodge when that scholar speaks of this " larger and dominant entity " and greater self which is " still behind the veil," as " not anything divine but greater than humanity." " I should not like to put upon it this limitation," says Dr. Sanday (p. 193). Dr. Sanday apparently supposes that the conception of human nature thus enunciated will homologate with the Biblical doctrines of divine influence, of the indwelling Spirit, of the framing of Christ in us. It will not. Its affiliations are rather with pantheizing Mysticism, if we ought not to say outright, with Pantheism — that is if, as we suppose, the distinction of Pantheism from Mysticism lies in its postulating as an ontological fact what Mysticism proposes as an attainment of effort.

On the basis of this mystical view of humanity, Dr. Sanday suggests that we may frame our conception of the Person of Christ. With Him, too, as with us, whatever there is of divine must be looked for in the subliminal regions. As " the proper seat or *locus* of all divine indwelling, or divine action upon the human soul, is the subliminal consciousness," so " the same, or the corresponding, subliminal consciousness is the proper seat or *locus* of the Deity of the Incarnate Christ " (p. 159). It is safe to transfer the analogy of our human selves to Him so far at least as to understand that whatever there was of divine in Him it was in " these deep dim regions " that it had " its abiding-place and home " (p. 178) and in coming up into consciousness " must needs pass through a strictly human medium " (p. 165). " We have seen," writes Dr. Sanday (pp. 165 f.), " what difficulties are involved in the attempt to draw as it were a vertical line between the human nature and the divine nature of Christ, and to say that certain actions of His fall on one side of this line and certain other actions on the other. But these difficulties disappear if, instead of drawing a vertical line, we draw rather a horizontal line between the upper human medium, which is the proper and natural field of all active expression, and those lower deeps which are no less the proper and natural home of whatever is divine. This line is inevitably drawn in the region of the subconscious. That which was divine in Christ was not nakedly exposed to the public gaze; neither was it so entirely withdrawn from outward view as to be wholly sunk and submerged in the darkness of the unconscious; but there was a sort of Jacob's ladder by which the divine sources stored up below found an outlet, as it were, to the upper air and the common theatre in which the life of mankind is enacted." The precise meaning of this is perhaps not altogether clear. What it seems to say is that the difference between our Lord and us lies fundamentally here — that the Infinite washes into His subliminal self more constantly and more freely than into ours; and so, though His life, " so far as it was visible, was a strictly human life," yet " this human life was, in its deepest roots, directly continuous with the life of God Himself " (pp. 167 f.). " If St. Paul could quote and endorse the words of a pagan poet claiming for the children of men that they are also God's offspring," Dr. Sanday goes on to expound; " and if they are this notwithstanding that they are confined in the body as creatures of perishable clay; if in spite of these limitations it may still be said of them that in God they ' live and move and have their being,' might not the same be said in a yet more searching and essential sense of Him who was Son in a more transcendent and ineffable mode of being than they? " Dr. Sanday assures us that there is ample room left here for the Homoousion, " whatever the Homoousion means." We suppose he means that we may understand, if we will, that the whole of that " self-determination of the Godhead " which we call " the Son " may have invaded the subliminal recesses of the being of Jesus, as the Infinite washes in varying measures into all of us. But even so, does the man Christ Jesus differ from us, into the subliminal being of all of whom the Infinite washes in varying measures, otherwise than in degree? And how does this conception of Jesus separate itself essentially from that, say, of Ernest Renan who writes as follows (" Vie de Jésus," ed. 3, 1863, p. 75)? " The men who have most highly understood God . . . have felt the divine in themselves. In the first rank of this great family of true sons of God, Jesus must be placed. Jesus had no visions; God does not speak to Him from without; God is in Him; He feels Himself with God, and He draws out of His own heart what He says of His Father. He lives in the bosom of God and enjoys constant intercourse with Him; He does not see Him but He hears Him . . . He believes Himself in immediate relation with God, He believes Himself God's Son. The highest consciousness of God which has ever existed among men, was that of Jesus." Surely this is as eloquently said as that: does it not also present as lofty a conception of Jesus' relation to the Divine Being?

We are not endeavoring to convey the impression that Dr. Sanday's attitude towards our Lord's Person is the same as Renan's. He tells us expressly that it is not. It would be monstrous to doubt Dr. Sanday's complete loyalty of heart to the true deity of Christ, which he constantly asserts in the face of all gainsayers. But it is quite another question whether the mode of conceiving the Person of our Lord which he tentatively puts forward for our consideration conserves the true deity of Christ. We cannot think it does. Dr. Sanday very properly discriminates contemporary Christian thought into two main types which he calls " full Christianity " and " reduced Christianity," each of which has a Christology of its own. The Christology which he has worked out here in outline only, distinctly belongs to the type which he calls " reduced Christianity." How could it help doing so when it is insisted that the humanity of our Lord must be taken in such real earnest that His life " so far as it was visible " must be conceived as " a strictly human life " and His consciousness (Dr. Sanday says His " human consciousness " but in the circumstances the adjective seems decidedly otiose) as " entirely human," and yet the application to Him of the Chalcedonian conception of the Two Natures is firmly declined? No adherent of the doctrine of the Two Natures will fall a whit behind Dr. Sanday in the seriousness with which he takes the humanity of our Lord: the true and perfect humanity of the Lord is as real and as precious a part of the doctrine of the Two Natures as is His true and perfect deity. To the adherent of the doctrine of Two Natures as truly as to Dr. Sanday " the human consciousness of the Lord " is " entirely human." But to him " the human consciousness of the Lord " is not the entirety of His consciousness, and he will not say that " whatever there was of divine in Him, on its way to outward expression whether in speech or act " (why not say " in thought " too?) " passed through, and could not but pass through, the restricting and restraining medium of human consciousness " (p. 167). For the adherent of the doctrine of the Two Natures is determined to take the deity of the Lord in real earnest also; and this is not taking the deity of the Lord in real earnest but is subjecting it to the yoke of the humanity. When Dr. Sanday says, therefore, " If whatever we have of divine must needs pass through a strictly human medium, the same law would hold good even for Him " (p. 165), the adherent of the doctrine of the Two Natures draws back. This could be only if our Lord were not only human as we are, but divine also only as we are. We may indeed say this of His human nature, in which the Spirit dwells as He dwells in us, only without measure while He dwells in each of us according to his measure. But we must not leave Christ's divine nature (which we have not) wholly out of account! He is not merely the most perfectly God-indwelt man who ever was — though He is that.

He is God as well. And He is God first and man only second Why should He who is God and the Living God, infinitely full of the incomparable activities which we call divine, on assuming a human nature into personal union with Himself forthwith become incapable of life-expression save through " the restricting and restraining medium of human consciousness "? If we begin with the categories of purely human activities and proceed by confining the activities of our Lord to these, whatever else we include or exclude in our conception of Christ, we exclude the idea of God *manifest* in the flesh. The adherent of the Two Natures has this advantage over all such constructions of the Person of Christ as this which Dr. Sanday proposes — that in doing justice to the humanity of Christ (and none can surpass him in the earnestness with which he takes the humanity of Christ), he does justice also to His deity.

The doctrine of the Two Natures, it must be confessed, is not very much in favor in the circles of modern scientific theology. Dr. Sanday, though himself turning away from it, finds himself impelled by his mere sense of justice to say a good word for it as not, after all, so black as it is painted. There are many causes which concur to produce this widespread indifference or rejection of it. Among them there should not be permitted to fall out of sight this very potent one — the change in men's attitude to the Bible. For the doctrine of the Two Natures is a synthesis of the entire body of Biblical data on the Person of Christ, and a synthesis which has been worked out in the crucible of life, not in that of mere intellectual inquiry. Work so done is done for all time. The principle of the Chalcedonian formulation does full justice to the entire body of the Biblical data: but men are no longer seeking to do full justice to the entire body of the Biblical data. The Bible has fallen to pieces in their hands, and they are impatient of an effort to synthetize all its points of view, as an artificial attempt to induce a fictitious unity in a variegated array of unrelated notions. What each successive investigator is endeavoring to accomplish is to penetrate behind the superincumbent mass of Biblical ideas to discover, if he may, not the common truth which binds them all together and finds trustworthy if partial expression in each, but the lost truth which has been covered up and hidden under them all and can be recovered only by tearing them away and laying bare the forgotten reality beneath. The Bible having been lost, the Christ of the Bible has naturally been lost also; and each thinker is left very much to his own imagination to picture how it were fitting that God should become man. Meanwhile it is certain that we know absolutely nothing of the facts of Christ's life or its manifestations except what the New Testament writers tell us, and on many grounds their account of it and of its *rationale* is far more apt to be true to the reality than any we can invent for ourselves to-day. If we are searching for the real Jesus we shall find Him nowhere else than in the New Testament writings, and we can have few better proofs that we have found Him than is furnished by this fact — that all the representations of the New Testament writings are capable of so simple and so complete a synthesis as is provided in the doctrine of the Two Natures. In it all the Biblical data are brought together in a harmonious unity in which each finds recognition and from which each receives its complete exposition. The key which unlocks so complicated a lock can scarcely fail to be the true key: and when the key is once in our hands we may turn the argument around and from the details of the key authenticate the wards of the lock into which it fits. That all the data of the New Testament synthetize in the doctrine of the Two Natures authenticates these data as component elements of the Great Reality, because it were inconceivable that so large a body of varying and sometimes apparently opposite data could synthetize in so simple a unifying conception were they not each a fragment of a real whole.

PERSONALITY IN CHRIST AND IN OURSELVES. By WILLIAM SANDAY, D.D., LL.D., Litt.D. New York: Oxford University Press, American Branch. 1911.[1]

DR. SANDAY's "Christologies Ancient and Modern," published last year, was reviewed in this journal for January, 1911, pp. 166–174. His purpose in that book was, he tells us, to suggest a " tentative modern Christology." The " modernness " of the Christology he suggested consists in two things. First, it deserts the historical Christology of the Two Natures and proposes to us a Christ who is, phenomenally at least, of only a single nature, and that nature purely human. Secondly, it seeks to explain what is divine in Christ

[1] *The Princeton Theological Review*, ix. 1911, pp. 686–689.

by pointing to the " subliminal self " which underlies the conscious self of every man, and explaining that even in common men this " subliminal self " is invaded by divine influences — or rather washed into by the divine — and may well be supposed in Christ's case to have been so invaded in a unique measure. Thus, as was pointed out in our review of the book, the divine-human Christ of the New Testament, and of historical Christianity deriving from the New Testament, was reduced to a purely human Christ, in whom God dwelt, though in a fuller measure, just as He dwells in all men.

In the pamphlet now before us, Dr. Sanday gives us a supplement, or perhaps we may rather say a complement, to the " Christologies Ancient and Modern." As the title of the pamphlet advises us, its interest lies in the philosophical basis which that volume proposed to us rather than in the Christological structure erected on it. The pamphlet consists of two lectures delivered in November, 1910, in which an effort is made to ascertain precisely what personality is in man, with a view to preparing the way for Dr. Sanday's doctrine of the subliminal self as the *locus* of divine influences; and a " retrospect " in which he passes in review such of the criticisms of the " Christologies Ancient and Modern " as he considers especially worthy of remark, chiefly or wholly, again, with reference to the philosophical side of that work. As will be seen, the Christology suggested in that work passes largely out of sight in this supplementary material. This we think a pity. Partly because we do not find Dr. Sanday's further remarks on the philosophical basis of his new Christology very helpful; and partly because the purpose of the book was, after all, to suggest a new Christology, and the Christology suggested ought to hold, and in our own case, we frankly admit, does hold the place of chief interest.

It must be confessed that the few allusions to Christology which are found in the pamphlet are distinctly discouraging. In reading the book, one could not help hoping that, in the enthusiasm of propounding a new theory of the Person of Christ, Dr. Sanday might have failed to observe all its implications, and especially its reduction of Christ to merely a divinely endowed man. But our startled eyes can scarcely miss taking up from the pamphlet phrases and even paragraphs which, though few, seem only too clearly to intimate that Dr. Sanday's conception of the Incarnation is fatally inadequate, that the Incarnation is reduced in his thought of it to mere inhabitation, and that, indeed, to all appearance it is confused with the indwelling of the Holy Spirit.

Already at the opening of the first lecture we hear the Incarnation spoken of as " the meeting of Human and Divine " (p. 4), in a context which suggests that its specific character is not fully allowed for. But it is towards the end of the second lecture that the most disturbing phraseology occurs. It is not merely that inexact language is employed. Such a phrase as " His incarnate nature " (p. 47), for example, as Dr. Sanday uses it, is distinctly untheological. In strict speech it can mean nothing but our Lord's Divine Nature: which is the one Nature in His Person of which incarnation can be affirmed. But Dr. Sanday does not mean by it His Divine Nature, in distinction from His Human Nature; but apparently uses the phrase to speak of our Lord's total Being as some sort of composite. What clear sense can be attached to the term " incarnate " in the phrase does not appear. If our Lord has but a single nature and that nature is human, to qualify this nature by the epithet " incarnate " seems merely a very loose and misleading way of saying that Christ's human nature is in some way more divine than that of other men. " Incarnate " has sunk to be little more than an honorific epithet, notifying us that in Christ we are dealing with a particularly divinitized man.

A couple of pages further on Dr. Sanday cites Paul's great words: " Nevertheless I live, yet not I; but Christ liveth in me "; and pronounces them the enunciation of an ideal which " never has been, and never will be, completely realized." Paul, however, is not here proclaiming an ideal but describing an experience; and an experience cannot but be realized. Not only Paul, but every Christian, in point of fact, realizes this experience; and no one is a Christian at all of whom it cannot be affirmed, each no doubt in his own measure; for it is only another way of saying that the Spirit of Christ dwells in us and takes the guidance of our lives, and " if any man have not the Spirit of Christ, he is none of His." But Dr. Sanday comments on it as follows: " If we could conceive of it as realized we should say, not that there were two Gods, but that there were two Incarnations " (p. 49). This comment is not perfectly clear to us; we do not understand what the import of the negative clause is. But it seems certainly to imply this much: that in Dr. Sanday's mind a perfect indwelling would be an incarnation — the ideal of Paul carried to its complete realization is what Dr. Sanday understands by Incarnation. "Incarnation" is, therefore, in its mode an indwelling.

On the immediately preceding page (p. 48) he tells us this explicitly. There is only one God, he tells us, and only one Divine; and the Holy Spirit who dwells in us is the same Holy Spirit who dwelt in Christ. What is the difference, then, between Christ and us? "The difference," he tells us, "was not in the essence, nor yet in the mode or sphere, of the indwelling, but *in the relation of the indwelling to the Person*" (italics his). The "Divine influences" working alike in Him and in us "do not *hold and possess*" our person, "as the Deity within Him *held and possessed* the Person of the incarnate Christ" (italics again his). Then, does the fact that the Holy Spirit (Dr. Sanday explicitly mentions the Holy Spirit as the indwelling agent), dwelling alike in us and in Him, "held and possessed" His Person — "meaning the whole Person — each several organ and faculty — but especially the central core of Personality, the inner, controlling, and commanding Person " — as He does not "hold and possess" ours, constitute our Lord "the incarnate Christ "? "Incarnation," we perceive, is reduced explicitly to the indwelling of the Holy Spirit: Christ is just the man in whom the Holy Spirit dwells without measure. Needless to say, here is a complete evacuation of the meaning of the term "incarnate "; and equally needless to say, here is a complete evacuation of the conception of incarnation. Christ is merely a man in whom the Holy Spirit dwells in greater measure than He dwells in other men. He is not God and man; He is not even God in man; He is man with God dwelling in Him — as, but more completely, God dwells in all men.

Now, of course, the Scriptures teach that the Holy Spirit does dwell in Jesus Christ, and they teach that the Holy Spirit that dwells in Him is the same Holy Spirit that dwells in us, and that He dwells in Him after the same fashion in which He dwells in us, only beyond measure in Him, while He dwells in us each according to his measure. But the Scriptures do not confound this indwelling of the Holy Spirit in the human nature of Christ with the Incarnation. This indwelling is, according to the Scriptures, additional to the Incarnation, and fits the human nature which is assumed into personal union with the divine in the Incarnation for its great companionship. The substitution of this indwelling of the Spirit in Jesus Christ for the Incarnation is just the elimination of the In-

carnation altogether: Christ's Divine Nature is cut away from Him
and His Spirit-indwelt Human Nature is presented to us as the
whole Christ. How this differs in essence from Socinianism and
Ebionism, it would certainly be interesting to learn.

If we may be permitted conjecturally to penetrate behind what
lies on the face of Dr. Sanday's pages and attempt to discover the
origin of the error which has led to these conclusions, we should be
inclined to find it in a conception of the incarnating act as the entrance of God into a man, or a human nature, so that God, so to
speak, clothed Himself in human nature. Such is not the conception
of Scripture. According to Scripture God the Son did not at the
incarnation enter into a man, but took a human nature up into
personal union with Himself. Accordingly " assumption " is the
theological term to describe the act; and it would be truer to speak
of the human nature of Christ as existing in God than of God as
existing in it. Jesus Christ is primarily not a man in whom God
dwells, but God who has assumed into personal union with Himself
a human nature as an organ through which He acts. Even historically, the term Incarnation does not mean the insertion of
Deity into flesh, or humanity. *Incarnari, incarnatus, incarnation*
are just the Latin equivalents of σαρκόομαι, σαρκωθείς, σάρκωσις (cf.
Irenæus, " Adv. Haer.," I. x. 1, III. xix. 1) and mean just " to be
made flesh," " made flesh," " making flesh." The impression which
has grown up among us that reads the sense of the insertion
into flesh into them, is just a " disease of language," and is perhaps responsible for more bad thinking on the Incarnation than we
realize.

This pamphlet has been incorporated into a new edition of the
" Christologies Ancient and Modern " (1911).

CHRISTUS. Die Anfänge des Dogmas. Von Professor D. JOHANNES
WEISS, Heidelberg. Religionsgeschichtliche Volksbücher für die
deutsche christliche Gegenwart. Tübingen. 1909. Verlag von
J. C. B. Mohr (Paul Siebeck).
CHRISTOLOGIE DES URCHRISTENTUMS. Von JOHANNES WEISS (in
Schiele's " Die Religion in Geschichte und Gegenwart," i. 1909,
coll. 1711 ff.).

266 CRITICAL REVIEWS

PAULUS UND JESUS. Von JOHANNES WEISS. Berlin: Verlag von
Reuther und Reichard. 1909.
JESUS IM GLAUBEN DES URCHRISTENTUMS. Von JOHANNES WEISS.
Tübingen: Verlag von J. C. B. Mohr (Paul Siebeck). 1910.
JESUS VON NAZARETH. Mythus oder Geschichte? Eine Auseinander-
setzung mit Kalthoff, Drews, Jensen. Von JOHANNES WEISS.
Tübingen: Verlag von J. C. B. Mohr (Paul Siebeck). 1910.
DIE GESCHICHTLICHKEIT JESU. Von Professor JOHANNES WEISS
und Professor GEORG GRÜTZMACHER. Tübingen: Verlag von J. C.
B. Mohr (Paul Siebeck). 1910.[1]

THERE is no representative of contemporary German thought
with respect to the criticism of the Gospel history and the origins
of Christianity who is better worth listening to than Johannes Weiss.
Of a temper but little less radical than William Wrede himself, he
approaches Wrede also in sharpness of vision, independence of spirit,
and bluntness of speech. He may perhaps even not unfairly be
looked upon as Wrede's successor as the *enfant terrible* of the
" liberal " school. The very thoroughgoingness of his naturalism
makes him bold; he abandons without fear entrenchments which
have become habitual to " liberal " thought, and frankly declares
untenable contentions which " liberals " have been accustomed to
treat as key-positions; he is so secure in his naturalism, it seems,
as scarcely to feel the need of any protection for it whatever. As
we read his treatises we are sensible of coming into contact with a
vigorous mind, stored with learning, bent on understanding the origin
of Christianity and its record — understanding them, of course, as
a naturalistic mind understands " understanding," which means just
the discovery of the complex of causes and conditions out of which
they naturally proceeded and the processes by which they naturally
came into being; but nevertheless understanding them — in which
is involved also the exact ascertainment of the precise things which
are to be naturalistically accounted for. In both stages of this proceeding he is very instructive to us. In his attempts to determine
the exact things which are to be explained from natural causation,
he displays a very unusual clearness and acuteness of perception
and becomes a not unwelcome guide to many points of difficult
exegesis and historical construction. In his attempts to naturalize
the things thus determined, he makes unwontedly plain to us the

---

[1] *The Princeton Theological Review*, ix. 1911, pp. 332–342.

violence of the assumptions on which alone the naturalization of the origins of the Christian religion can be accomplished.

By some chance it was bought about that Johannes Weiss gave repeated expression to his views on the great subject of the Christology of the New Testament during the early months of 1909. Then came the publication of Arthur Drews's " Die Christusmythe," and in the early months of 1910 the sudden bursting into flame of the fire that it had kindled and that had been smoldering for the preceding year. Of course Johannes Weiss, in company with his fellow " liberals," was drawn into this controversy, by which the entire structure of the " liberal " Christology was thrown violently on the defensive; and in his effort to treat a sensational subject unsensationally he was led to give another expression to his Christological conceptions. Thus, we have from him a series of little volumes put forth within the limits of a twelvemonth, in which his ideas concerning Jesus and the development during the New Testament period of the thought of His followers concerning Him, are stated over and over again with different audiences in view and with different and even opposite antagonists in mind. We cannot complain that we are left in any doubt as to how he himself thinks of Jesus or as to how he thinks Jesus' first followers thought of Him.

The first book upon our list, entitled " Christ: the Beginnings of the Dogma," appears in the well-known series of " liberal " handbooks publishing under the general title of " History-of-Religion Peoples' Books for the Present-Day Christianity of Germany," and is accordingly of a semi-popular character. It undertakes to describe the development of the doctrine of the Person of Christ through the New Testament period under the successive rubrics of " the Belief of the Primitive Community," " Paul," and " the Christology after Paul "; and in doing this, it seeks to preserve a strictly historical point of view. It opens with these words: " ' What think ye of Christ? Whose Son is He? ' — so still runs to-day the burning question by which our church is split up, many earnest Christians disquieted, and not a few conscientious men hindered from entering into a close relation to the Person of Jesus and His religion. No attempt will be made in the following pages to give a definitive reply to this question: the author feels no call whatever to obtrude his convictions in this matter on others. He certainly thinks it would be desirable, however, that even those who are not theologians, so far as they are earnest inquirers and not afraid of a little labor, should come to clearness as to what the earliest witnesses to our religion really *teach* with respect to the Person of Christ, what the old difficult and obscure terms ' Son of God ' and ' Son of Man,' ' Lord ' and ' Messiah ' really meant at first, and what convictions of belief the oldest confessors intended to express by them." Of course the historical objectivity announced in this declaration is not preserved in the discussion itself (or, for that matter, throughout this declaration itself), as indeed it could not be. The author is soon found reading his own faith back into the primitive Christian community and, indeed, making his booklet a historical argument for his own point of view. In another one of the little volumes, indeed, — that entitled " Paul and Jesus " (pp. 4–5) — he drops the mask entirely and openly pleads the cause of his personal Socinianism against that Christianity which he confesses to be, and to have been since the beginning, dominant. " Primitive Christianity," he says there, " is — at least in one part of it — Christ-religion, that is, there stands at its center an inner relation of faith to the exalted Christ. This form of religion has throughout the millenniums passed as the real Christianity, and there are still to-day innumerable Christians who know and wish no other form of faith. They live in the most intimate communion of soul with the ' Lord,' pray to Him and long to see Him face to face. Alongside of this there flows another religious stream which is no longer able to find a religious relation to the exalted Christ and has its full satisfaction in permitting itself to be led to the Father by Jesus of Nazareth. Both forms of religious life stand in our church side by side; it were to be wished that they would tolerate one another and that the preaching of the Gospel should not suffer violence from either of them. I make no concealment of my profession, along with the majority of recent theologians, of the second of these views, and my hope that this view will gradually become dominant in our church. But as a historian I must say that it is widely different from the ruling view of primitive Christianity, from the Pauline view. On the other hand, however, I must decidedly maintain that the historical Jesus, as far as we can perceive Him, saw His task in drawing His followers into the direct experience of sonship with God, without demanding any place for Himself in their piety."

The second publication on our list is the article on " The Christology of Primitive Christianity " in Schiele's new religious Cyclopædia. It follows the same lines as the first — of which it is in point of fact only a somewhat condensed repetition, coinciding with it often in its very language.

From these two the fourth — " Jesus in the Faith of Primitive Christianity " — differs only in that it professes to give account of the varieties not of doctrinal but of religious attitude towards Jesus which follow one another in the New Testament development. We read in its introductory words: " The task which my theme sets me, is not to describe the origin of the *doctrine* of Christ in primitive Christianity: it is not the oldest forms of confession and systems of belief which are the subject of this recital. I wish to try to show what place Jesus occupied in the *religion* of the earliest Christians, how their religious life stood related to Him, and what they got from their faith in Him for their practical life-task." The schematization of this new theme, however, turns on the same pivot as before — " the weighty religious personality of Paul "; and the chief forms of the religious relation to Jesus are held to be determined by the circumstance whether they are or are not affected by the influence of Paul's modes of feeling and expression. There are treated in turn, therefore, " belief in Jesus before Paul, Paul himself, and the post-Pauline piety, especially that of John." It has been found impossible, moreover, of course, to describe religious attitudes save in terms of religious conceptions; so that what we get is, after all, another account of the varieties of doctrinal attitude towards Jesus, reflected in the pages of the New Testament, differing from its companions only in its greater warmth of tone and the greater generality of its treatment. And even these differences are due doubtless as much to the original end for which this brochure was prepared, as to its particular subject. It was delivered as an address to the Thirteenth Conference of Christian Students held at Aarau in March, 1909, and was published first in the Proceedings of that Conference, whence it has been reprinted in this pamphlet.

The pamphlet on " Paul and Jesus " is also a reprint, in this case in enlarged form, from an article which appeared in the *Monatschrift für Pastoraltheologie*. It does not, however, like the " Jesus in the Faith of Primitive Christianity," bear its original practical purpose stamped upon its face. In form it is a purely critical inquiry in which Weiss orients himself on the question of Paul's relation to Jesus, particularly with reference on the one side to Wrede's radicalism — by which Paul was made the real founder of what we know as Christianity, a wholly new phenomenon, far more unlike Jesus

than Jesus was unlike the higher forms of Jewish piety — and on
the other, to the replics to Wrede of men like Kölbing, Kaftan, and
Jülicher. Needless to say that Weiss's attitude is far nearer to
Wrede's than to that of Wrede's critics. Although he recognizes
a much closer relation of Paul to Jesus, and a much more profound
influence upon Paul by Jesus — insisting even (for purposes of his
own, especially in order to render the naturalization of the appearance of Jesus on the road to Damascus easier) on a personal acquaintance of Paul with Jesus — he is yet as emphatic as Wrede himself
in conceiving Paul's Christianity as essentially a different religion
from that of Jesus, as at bottom not a development but a transformation of it: " I therefore cannot agree that Paul's Christology and
doctrine of Atonement was fundamentally only a further spinning
out of a thread already begun by Jesus; and from the point of view
of the historian, I hold the sharp exaggerations of Wrede more right
than the softenings of his opponents " (p. 8). In making this position
good he necessarily requires to review the development of Christological doctrine in the early Christian community, so that there is
much material in this pamphlet too which runs parallel to the discussion in its companions and Weiss is quite right in speaking of the
series as, conceived from an internal point of view, a single work,
whose several sections mutually illuminate one another.

   The last two documents in our list — entitled respectively, " Jesus
of Nazareth: Myth or History? " and " The Historicity of Jesus "
— are separated from their fellows by the circumstance that their
face is turned in an opposite direction and they make it their task
to vindicate the views common to the whole series against a sudden
attack from the rear. The little pamphlet on " The Historicity of
Jesus " is of weighty enough contents to claim our especial attention
did it stand alone. But the contribution to it of Johannes Weiss is
little more than a succinct and gracefully worded repetition of the
main conclusions to which he gives more extended expression in the
larger document which lies before us under the name of " Jesus of
Nazareth," and with this larger treatise in our hands we may neglect the smaller. As our present concern is with Weiss's views, we
may also pass over with only a word Georg Grützmacher's lecture
combined with his in the smaller publication. It is an interesting
discussion from the point of view of the historian, of Drews's new
religion, and a very strong reassertion as over against Drews's (and
also, of course, the Social-Democratic) view of the origins of Chris-

tianity, of the principle that great religious movements are always rooted in great religious personalities, and every great religion has and must have a personal founder. With so much hint of the contents of the smaller pamphlet we may be permitted to turn from it to the larger. This gives us the manuscript basis of two lectures delivered in Berlin in the height of the excitement aroused by the exploitation of the assault upon the historicity of the man Jesus, of which Arthur Drews had become the popular exponent. But it attempts very much more than the mere refutation of this assault, as indeed it needed to do, if it was to have any substance. For the assault itself, it must be acknowledged, is in itself pitiably weak, and required rather to be exposed than answered. Its exposure is certainly admirably managed by Johannes Weiss, though it is, no doubt, drawn out to an inordinate length — for which he duly apologizes in his Preface. When he had pointed out that the fundamental trouble with Jensen is that he cannot read, expressed his sincere sympathy with Drews for his severe attack of " mythologitis, complicated with that infantile ailment etymologitis," and courteously given utterance to the hope that W. B. Smith's mathematics may be better than his theology, — he had perhaps said all that needed to be said in their direct refutation. The contention of these writers that Jesus never existed cannot by any possibility be true, and the grounds they urge in its defense are a mere mass of crudities. The " positive " theologians of Germany have therefore very properly simply passed them by unnoticed. The " liberal " theologians are not, however, in a position to do this. For, however absurd the central contention of the new school is, and however weakly it is supported, it yet lies on the face of things that the method employed by the new school in defense of it is just the method of the " liberal " theologians themselves — their method " reduced to absurdity " no doubt, but nevertheless in all essentials the same method. It has lain in the necessity of the case, therefore, that the " liberal " theologians should orient themselves carefully with reference to the new views; and this is what Weiss undertakes in this book.

In one of his footnotes (p. 16) Weiss somewhat tartly remarks, that despite his respect for Schmiedel, he must say he might have been in better business than in giving W. B. Smith's book on " The Pre-Christian Jesus," a send-off by providing it with a preface. But Schmiedel did much more than give Smith's book a " send-off " by providing it with a preface. He very distinctly suggested in that preface that Smith's method is the "scientific" method, and his results therefore worthy of respectful consideration. Weiss himself does not find himself in a position to object in principle to the method (p. 14), or indeed to reject in the mass the results, of this new radicalism. He esteems Kalthoff's method, indeed, above that of Drews or Jensen; but this seems mainly due to Kalthoff's restriction of himself largely to generalities without proceeding to those details in the handling of which the absurdities of Drews and Jensen are most amusingly manifested. And he may distinguish between their results as more or less acceptable; but in the fundamental contentions of the new speculators he more or less fully shares. They cannot assert with more energy than he does, for example, that the whole Christ-theology of the Church is mythical. He is not even in a position to offer effective opposition when they declare that this mythical Christ-theology is the aboriginal Christian theology, behind which there is — nothing. He does indeed for himself declare that there is behind it a more primitive Christianity, a Christianity to which Jesus is just a man who has been exalted after His death to world-dominion — an "adoptionist Christology," as it is the fashion to call it. But he discovers this more primitive view by very unconvincing methods of dealing with the records, all of which, he is compelled to admit, already present the higher Christology. As the result of Weiss's own criticism of the documents it is plain enough that the adherents of Jesus from the beginning held Him to be just God manifest in the flesh; and Weiss himself has been led by this fact to seek and find a pre-Christian basis for their high Christology. He still supposes, indeed, that this was first brought into Christain circles by Paul; but there seems no reason why, if it were in the air, others than Paul might not have been affected by it, even indeed Jesus Himself, who, Weiss does not doubt, believed in His own Messiahship and might very well have believed therefore even on naturalistic grounds in His "transcendental" Messiahship. In any event, the plain truth is that when Drews asserts roundly that "the Jesus of the oldest Christian communities is not, as is commonly thought," — that is, in "liberal" circles — "a deified man, but a humanized God" ("Die Christusmythe," 1910, p. 211), he announces a fact which cannot be successfully denied, and it is the announcement of this indefeasible fact which gives all its force to the movement which he represents. One would think that, already trembling on the verge of the recognition of this

fact on his own account, Weiss would in the face of its new assertion, now from the radically naturalistic and no longer " positive "
side, simply admit it and adjust his theories to it.

But the establishment of this fact, we must observe, is nothing
less than the death-blow of the old " liberalism." The fundamental
contention of the old " liberalism " is not merely that Jesus was a
mere man, but that He was only gradually deified in the thought
of His followers. The "liberal " theologians may conceal for a time
the seriousness of the blow they have received by crying out loudly
upon the fantastic element of the new speculation — its attempt to
eliminate the figure of Jesus altogether and to hang the whole account of the origin of Christianity on a myth. Any number of pamphlets, however, on " the burning question," " Did Jesus ever live? "
will not extricate them from their difficulties. It has been driven
home to men's consciousness afresh that Christianity is rooted not
in the deification of a man but in the incarnation of a God, and whatever else may come out of the controversy it will no longer be
possible for the bald Socinianism which has dominated German
theological thought for a generation or two to rule the minds of men.
Negative theology must find a better way of accounting for the
origin of Christianity than by the religious impression made on
men's hearts by the happy, holy life of the man Jesus who trusted
Himself wholly to the love of His Father. The transition, as we have
said, ought not to be difficult for men like Johannes Weiss who
already stands so near to the new platform that a very short step
indeed would place him fairly on it. He already believes that "there
was already existing among Jews and heathen alike *before* the
appearance of Jesus a Christology, that is a doctrine of the Messiah,
or at least the materials for a Christology, and at the moment when
the Messiah was found in the person of Jesus, the scattered elements,
which lacked only a combining middle-point, gathered together like
a crystal about its core " (" Christus," pp. 4–5; Schiele's " Die Religion," col. 1713). He already believes that this fact accounts for
the rapidity of the development of a high Christology among the
followers of Jesus. And he already thus reduces the rôle of Jesus
in the production of this high Christology to that of a mere occasion
for the crystallization of elements already in solution in contemporary thought. A very little earlier dating of the process would
enable him to free himself from his unjustified assumption of a
precedent " adoptionist " Christology; and it should not require a

very much further attentuation of the rôle of Jesus in it to dispense with His " impression " altogether. And then, what would he have more than Kalthoff or Drews or Jensen — except a little sounder scholarship and a little more reasonable mode of picturing the origin and growth of the " Christ-myth "?

Meanwhile, however, Weiss throws himself along with his fellow " liberals " valiantly into the not difficult task of defending " the historical Jesus " from the assaults of Kalthoff and Drews and Jensen. And incidentally, while doing so, he makes clearer his own views as to the origins of Christianity and its records. It is exceedingly pleasant to see him in the unwonted rôle of an apologist; and it must be confessed that he plays the part very well. They tell us that it came to such a pass in ancient Rome that two augurs could not meet one another without smiling. But Weiss can develop quite a sound method of criticism in the face of Jensen and Kalthoff and Drews with no apparent shamefacedness. We read for instance (pp. 83–84) this: " In theological investigation there are especially in dominant operation two manias. First, there is the tendency, before the understanding of a narrative in itself has been acquired, to go off in search of what lies behind it — for the mythological, astral, or even political antecedents. . . . I do not at all deny the value of such a world-embracing history of ideas, but it is hard to carry it out in a really scientific manner, and it is of doubtful value to trace back to primitive forms of thought complicated, refined, and individual phenomena. . . . Secondly, there all too often intrudes between the source and the reader a really morbid scepticism. . . . If it is unscientific to give credence to a writer on his mere word, it is just as unscientific to refuse credence to a source where what it relates is wholly unexceptionable merely because it could no doubt possibly be fabulous. . . . Over against our evangelical tradition, not merely the miraculous stories, there is arrayed to-day a mood of what I can call nothing else but distrust, which in no way arises from the matter itself, but from an excess of critical feeling, which goes often enough hand in hand with a touching lack of critical sense. . . ." If only Weiss would follow his own prescription! For this is the same Weiss who, having framed for himself a pretty scheme of the development of the Christological thought of the Church — a scheme which supposes Jesus to have made no claims to a divine dignity for Himself, but His followers first to have exalted Him, after His death, to the side of God as world-ruler, then, under the influence of Stoic ideas to have made Him a kind of secondary God (Paul), and finally to have put Him quite on a level with God (John) — on finding that the entire body of New Testament writers present a Jesus who was divine and claimed to be divine, seeks to wrest from them unwilling testimony to an "earlier" view of which they themselves know nothing and vigorously contradict; on finding no "direct evidence" of an "adoptionist Christology" among Christ's earliest disciples endeavors to make indirect evidence of its early prevalence out of records which certainly did not bear this meaning to those who have transmitted them to us; on finding Paul openly declaring Christ to be nothing less than God over all, just, without a scintilla of objective ground for doing so, throws out the text in which Paul makes this declaration as "inconceivable" in Paul's mouth — that is, discordant with Weiss's theory of what Paul ought to have said ("Christus," p. 29)! In other words, he sustains his radical position only by neglecting his own prescribed methods of sound critical procedure. Thus he seems to hang between two destinies. Either he must continue to use the methods common to him and his more radical opponents, and then he can scarcely escape their extremities of negation. Or else he must follow the sounder methods he tells them they ought to follow, and then he can surely not fail ultimately to reach "conservative" conclusions. It appears to be only a new instance of the old difficulty: "I see the good; the evil I pursue."

In would be interesting to call attention to the numerous matters of importance to the understanding of early Christian Christology on which Weiss speaks in these treatises with his usual point and force. This notice is, however, already long; and perhaps it will suffice, after what has been already said, simply to transcribe, in concluding, the opening and closing words of the two formal presentations of his views upon the early development of Christological thought. In these passages, he himself sums up the substance of his findings.

The opening words we take in the form in which they occur in the article in Schiele's Cyclopædia (coll. 1712 f.):

"It is a burning question for science as well as for the Church: On what does the belief of Christianity in the Son of God, in His deity, in His names 'Lord' and 'Son of Man' rest? How did this belief come into being? The older theology did not see any problem in this question; for it was self-evident to it, that the belief of the early Christians merely gave clear expression to what Jesus Himself had witnessed of Himself. The primitive Christian Christology was, therefore, only the fit description of what was actually given in the Person of the Lord. The newer theology, since it strives to conceive the historical personality of Jesus ever more clearly as purely human, feels a problem here. How was it possible that the early Christians should so unhesitatingly and with such assurance transfer a fullness of divine predicates to a personality the human traits of which are still recognizable by us? And — to sharpen the problem — how can it be explained, that so lofty and developed a doctrine did not work itself out in a long development, but lies before us essentially complete already in the oldest literary witnesses, the epistles of Paul? The newer theology answers: this rapid development of Christology to its highest and farthest-reaching expression has its ground in this — that, already before the appearance of Jesus a Christology existed among Jews and Hellenists alike, that is to say, a doctrine of the Messiah, or at least the materials for a Christology; and at the moment when the Messiah was discovered in the Person of Jesus, the scattered elements, which had lacked only a combining center, gathered together like crystals around their core. There was hardly needed any particular reflection; the same expressions which had been in use previously of the future Messiah, were applied at once to the present Messiah — of course with the adjustments which were required by what was peculiar to Jesus, especially by His death on the cross; and the Christology was in substance complete. But there never was a Jewish doctrine of the Messiah, however completely worked out, which had power to transmute the longings for a better future into the joyful assurance that the fulfillment of the hope had come. And all Hellenistic speculation about the highest middle-being between God and man could never awaken the clear and inspiring conviction that the divine Logos was present in a particular, well-known, heart-winning personality. This transformation of speculation into religious intuition, of a Messiah-idea into a Jesus-figure — this combination of hitherto disconnected elements of conception into a fixed middle-point — presupposes a power of attraction of which we cannot form a strong enough notion. What a powerful indirect or direct influence must Jesus' personality have exerted upon the souls of His adherents, that they should have believed such things about Him and have been ready to die for this belief! Thus there lies at the basis of the doctrine of Christ, at every stage of its development, a belief in Jesus which we must sympathetically feel, even though often enough it seems choked by speculation."

The closing words we take in the form in which they occur in the tractate, " Christus " (pp. 87–88):

" We have traveled over a long road: from the Jewish-Christian idea of a political Messiah to the doctrine of the heavenly Messiah

and Son of God; from the adoptionistic exaltation-Christology to the
doctrine of the preëxistent 'Man' and 'Son of God,' and to the
Logos-Pneuma-Christ; through the difficult questions of the incarnation to the conception and presentation of the Gospels. The total
impression has been that primitive Christianity made use of already
existing forms and ideas, in which to bring to expression, in a
manner capable of being understood by all, and yet at the same time
absolute and determinative, the overwhelming impression made by
the Person of Jesus. Predicates were sought out which declared
that there were contained in Him the ideal, and the highest religious
goods. To the men of old time the predicate of deity offered itself
continually for this purpose. In varied forms this was applied to
Jesus. Thus, however, the problem was raised that nevertheless the
true humanity which was perfectly clearly preserved in memory and
tradition, should not be lost. The efforts to find a solution, which
were made, are altogether incomplete and only create new questions.
A chain of inexpressibly complicated and in the highest degree unhappy controversies attached itself to this, until the famous
compromise-formula of 'one Person in two Natures' was invented,
which can never give satisfaction, no matter how acutely it may be
thought out. For the question must be continually raised afresh
how it can be imagined that Godhood and manhood can be united
in a single earthly person. For the modern man striving earnestly
and longingly after clearness and certainty all these Christological
formulas have already about them something strange and foreign,
because they are products of the utterly different soil of ancient
thought. What was altogether easy for an ancient man to conceive,
that a man should be in reality an incarnate God — as, for example,
the Roman emperor or Antiochus Epiphanes — or that a Plato
might be the Son of a God, cannot make entrance into our minds,
because we feel much too sharply the unpassable boundary line that
divides the divine and the human. From all the stammering attempts
to express the nature of Christ in formulas, we can learn only how
mighty the personality must have been which has inspired men to
such a faith, stirred their phantasy after such a fashion, and occupied
their thought through thousands of years. The less we are able to
understand and adopt the Christology the more strongly are we
thrown back upon the Person of Jesus. To understand Him, to receive our impression from Him, to let ourselves be drawn by Him
into His life with the Father — this is more important than to find
a formula of confession, in which we may be at once dogmatically
correct and historically true."

These words are surely very pathetic. For what is their burden
but just this: we are modern men, and as modern men simply cannot believe in a divine Christ; but we cannot do without Jesus and
will therefore think of Him as greatly as we can — as a truly heroic

man. Meanwhile what is most strongly borne in on us as we read is that Weiss does not find his merely human Jesus in the records but imposes him on the records. The whole effort of the newer theology, he says, is " to conceive the historical personality of Jesus ever more clearly as purely human." The test of all conceptions of Christ is, Do they offer us a merely human Christ? The one thing that cannot be allowed is that that Man who walked the earth and has created the new world, was in any respect more than man. At all hazards we must not allow that God has entered in this Man into the sphere of human life. The rock of offense is the Incarnation: and anything is more credible than that. When we make our Socinianism the major premise of all our reasoning, is it strange that what we take out of our premises as our conclusion is just Socinianism?

THE CHRIST OF THE GOSPELS. 41st Fernley Lecture. By the Rev. W. W. HOLDSWORTH, M.A. London: Charles H. Kelly. 1911.[1]

MR. HOLDSWORTH's Fernley Lecture makes a book of excellent quality. If we cannot quite say that it brings a contribution to our knowledge of the great subject with which it deals, we must at least find it a thoughtful and readable discussion of this great subject in the light, and to some extent under the dominance, of modern views. Its subject is " The Christ of the Gospels." But this subject is construed somewhat broadly. Mr. Holdsworth himself outlines the task he undertakes as follows (p. 18): " We are not concerned here with the efforts of the Church, nor with the degree of success it attained. Our investigation is with the Records upon which the Church has been built up. What is the doctrine of the Person of our Lord which is given to us in the New Testament? How did it come to find a place in those writings? The double question calls for at least an outline statement from the writings as a whole, and then for some measure of historical criticism of the Four Gospels. When we have thus considered the Records, it may be possible to build up from the writings such a statement of our Lord's Person as will present Him once again to His Church as the one true object of

[1] *The Princeton Theological Review,* x. 1912, pp. 481–488.

her adoration; the God-Man, in fellowship with whom a man may find the very fullness of his life."

We perceive that Mr. Holdsworth has a constructive purpose in view; his object is to reach a new statement of the doctrine of the Person of Christ which will " once again " present Him acceptably to the Church's adoration. The phraseology suggests that he feels dissatisfied with the statements of this doctrine with which the Church has hitherto been compelled to content itself, as well as that he recognizes that in discarding them the Church has fallen away also from its proper attitude to its divine Lord; he hopes by a restatement to help the Church to recover its lost ground. The method by which he hopes to attain this object is a critical re-examination of the Evangelical records; thus he expects to obtain a basis for interpretation which will yield a truer view of the Person of the Lord than either the new or old views which have hitherto been prevalent. He quite properly, however, supposes that this new interpretation can be most hopefully made in the light of a general view of the teaching as to our Lord's Person of the New Testament as a whole. Accordingly, after a short Introduction, he begins with a rapid survey of " The Christology of the New Testament," which is very well done indeed, and shows a true historical sense, a clear expository talent, and a thoughtful mind. From this he passes to a somewhat lengthy discussion of what he calls " The Gospel Record," that is, to a critical investigation of the origin and historical character of our Gospels. Here he does not appear to us to move with such sure step, and seems to speak more as a reporter of the views of others adopted by himself with scarcely sufficient basis of individual consideration. Finally, in four chapters entitled respectively " The Synoptic Jesus," " The Johannine Christ," " The Higher Synthesis — Jesus Christ," and " The Gospel Message " he presents his constructive view of the Christ of the Gospels, and offers it as the solution of the difficulties created by modern conditions and as a new point of crystallization for the Church's adoration of its Lord. Along with much that is strikingly said and winningly argued here, we cannot help thinking that Mr. Holdsworth is least successful in this part of his task. The conception he offers us of " the God-Man " is vague, and in danger of running off into a subjectivity which affords little support to faith.

Precisely what the view of Christ's Person which Mr. Holdsworth would commend to us is, remains a little difficult to determine. He is constant in his affirmation of the true deity of Christ. And he does not always shun the language of the Chalcedonian Christology. He can speak of " incarnation " (p. 222) as if he were using the term in its historical sense; and indeed of the " incarnation "meaning " the union of two natures, human and divine " (p. 41). He can even employ the precise Chalcedonian affirmation and declare that it is the teaching of the Gospels and the sole firm foundation for faith. " If our faith is to have a sufficient objective we want exactly what is offered us in the Gospels — a true humanity and a complete divinity united in one Person " (p. 237). Yet he can speak of this same doctrine as creating " a fatal dualism " in our Lord's Person (p. 211), and as " representing our Lord as governed by two distinct personalities which, if they do not conflict, at any rate alternate " (p. 138). He declares that " no explanation yet offered as to how perfect God and perfect man could attain to a unity of consciousness in one Person can be considered sufficient " (p. 210). Nothing but a " complete fusion " of the two natures would satisfy him: " It is possible that the Christian Church will never be able to frame a definition that will perfectly express the complete fusion of two natures, one human and one divine " (p. 194). Accordingly he can write such a passage as the following (p. 132): " We may even accept without fear of loss or compromise in that which has interpreted us to ourselves, and filled us with living hope, that to our Lord Himself the consciousness of a true humanity, simple and undivided, preceded the recognition within Himself of Deity. Nothing but confusion and vagueness of thought awaits us if we allow ourselves to think that the God He was came before His consciousness from the earliest days. The puerilities of the Apocryphal Gospels are a sufficient warning to us of the penalties which the Church will pay if any attempt be made to confuse or divide the complete Personality of our Lord by positing in Him a clear sense of inherent Deity from the first. We do not gain, but lose, when we thus divide the Person of Jesus." This is surely a remarkable passage from any point of view: among the others, however, not least from a logical point of view. The assertion is distinct that our Lord was both God and man: the implication is express that in later life He was fully conscious of being both God and man: we are warned, nevertheless, not to suppose that he could have possessed this consciousness of being both man and God in early life: the reason assigned is that this would be to " divide the Person of Jesus." Why, meanwhile, it

should " confuse or divide the complete Personality of our Lord "
to " posit in Him a clear sense of inherent Deity " " at the first,"
any more than at the last, remains dark. Light begins to dawn only
when we begin to suspect that Mr. Holdsworth does not intend his
Chalcedonian language in a Chalcedonian sense. When he speaks
of " the union of two natures, human and divine " in Christ, he
does not seem to mean that these two natures are two distinct
natures; he seems to mean that they are just one nature, which is
both human and divine. He does not seem to mean that Christ has
a human nature and a divine nature; he seems to mean that Christ
has a nature which is both human and divine. And what he seems
to mean in the passage before us is that this single nature, in reality
as divine as it was human, — or divine because it was human — as
it could not be perceived by others, so could not perceive itself, to
be divine until it had reached its perfection of development. Perhaps
it is even implied that it is not divine except in its perfect development. It is our Lord's perfect humanity that is His deity.

Let us hope we are misreading Mr. Holdsworth's meaning. There
are passages which would lend some color to such a hope. He speaks,
as we have seen, of " two natures " in Christ, and of their " union "
to form " one Personality." We read (p. 41) : " It is evident from
such passages as we have been considering that to St. Paul the
Incarnation meant the union of two natures, human and divine "
(cf. p. 29). We read again (p. 47) : " No candid critic of such writings can deny that the faith of the first disciples gathers around
one who was to them both perfectly human and perfectly divine."
And yet again (p. 48) : " For them the human and the divine had
made one Personality, unique and consummate." There are other
passages which might easily fall in with these, as when we read
that (italics his) " it was *through His humanity* that His first
disciples learned to discover in Him a divinity before which they
bowed in worship " (p. 131), that " the Synoptic writers, in de-
lineating the humanity of our Lord, lead up to His divinity "
(p. 164), and even that " the humanity they had depicted made an
interpretation in terms of divinity inevitable " (p. 165) — though
we begin to wonder why any *humanity* can demand interpretation
in " terms of divinity," and this wonder is increased when we read
in similar language that " when we find in Him a perfect humanity
we are close upon the Deity which transfigures, indeed, but never
destroys it " (p. 133), which appears to imply that a perfect hu-

manity approaches divinity. And our hope is quite dashed when we read plainly that "perfect manhood" "stamps Him as divine" (p. 141), and that "a manhood so complete" as His can be "accounted for only in terms of Deity" (p. 157). In such expressions the separating lines that divide humanity and deity seem quite washed out and the underlying conception seems to be that to be complete and perfect man is to be God. And therefore it is, doubtless, that instead of speaking of our Lord's divine-human Person Mr. Holdsworth prefers to reverse the terms and to speak of His "human-divine Person" (p. 215). We regretfully conclude therefore that there is floating before his mind a conception which enables him to speak of our Lord as divine as well as human, because He is perfectly and completely human. We gladly confess, however, that this conception seems to remain somewhat vague to him and that his recognition of the true deity of our Lord is far more significant of his attitude to Him than the explanation which he seems to suggest of how it is that He can be God as well as man. It is not reassuring, nevertheless, to see him appeal in the end with sympathy to the modes of representation of Wilhelm Herrmann and Albrecht Ritschl.

The lack of clearness in the presentation of his conception of the Person of Christ attends also occasionally Mr. Holdsworth's less important statements. On pp. 30–31, for instance, he cites Rom. ix. 5 in this somewhat odd and misleading paraphrase: "As concerning the flesh He is of the patriarchs, but in Himself He is God blessed for ever" — precisely what he means to convey by which it somewhat puzzles us to determine. He adds immediately: "There is good reason for believing that in one passage (Col. ii. 3) the true reading directly gives to Christ the name ' God,' but even if we do not press the reading of the Vatican MS. in this passage," etc. From the context, we suppose that Rom. ix. 5 is cited as "directly giving to Christ the name God" — as it well might be. The succeeding words therefore are very confusing to the reader, and not less so that it does not appear that the name "God" is directly given to Christ in Col. ii. 2, and especially not in the reading of B, where χριστοῦ seems to stand in apposition to τοῦ μυστηρίου τοῦ θεοῦ and not to τοῦ θεοῦ alone. Again, after reading on p. 154 that "the language used" in Matt. xi. 25–30 "indicates the preëxistence of the Messiah" (why, by the way, "the Messiah" here?), with a supporting footnote from Dr. W. C. Allen's "Commentary on

St. Matthew," it is rather confusing to read on p. 164 that the Synoptics know nothing of the preëxistence of Christ, and this is introduced only by John in his account of Christ's self-testimony. Of course every time the Synoptics represent Christ as calling Himself " the Son of Man " they record an implication of a claim to preëxistence, and the implication of preëxistence is not easily excluded from His recorded representations of His earthly life as a mission to which He has come forth (Mark i. 38) or upon which He has been sent (Luke iv. 43). We cannot think, either, that the suggestion that there was no recognition of our Lord's divinity among the disciples until after His resurrection (p. 49; we are stating the point more strongly than Mr. Holdsworth does) is quite consistent with the general representation in the volume with regard to our Lord's claims and His disciples' apprehension of them. It was not merely " in the light of Easter Day and of Pentecost " that His followers " knew that ' this Jesus ' was ' the very God ' " (p. 48). What could His disciples have understood Him to mean by the great declaration of Matt. xi. 25–30, which Mr. Holdsworth understands to involve a distinctly divine claim, and also asserts not to stand as a " rock in the sky " in the Synoptic Gospels (pp. 152 f.)? What meaning could they attach to such a declaration as that of Mark. xiii. 32? What was floating before Peter's mind when he made his " great confession " (Matt. xvi. 16) with its double designation of his Master as not only " the Christ," but " the Son of the living God " — even though we may agree that in its full reach it " was scarcely understood even by the man who made it " (p. 132)? What meaning did His followers attach to His response to the solemn adjuration of the High Priest (Matt. xxvi. 63–64)? We do not ask here what meaning they could attach to the culminating enunciation of essential deity by our Lord recorded in Matt. xxviii. 19, because that was spoken after His resurrection and may take its place therefore side by side with Thomas' high ascriptions in John xx. 28 — and for another reason also, to which we shall immediately advert.

This is the unhappy readiness which Mr. Holdsworth occasionally exhibits to throw doubt on the trustworthiness of the records in their reports of our Lord's sayings. This is of course incidental to his critical position over against the Evangelical documents, which, as we have already hinted, seems to us artificial and secondary. He does not hesitate to argue for the relative priority of one account

as over against another on grounds which posit the modification of
the language attributed to Jesus in accordance with the changing
beliefs of His reporters (p. 61). The small place which such argumentation takes in his pages in comparison with what we have grown
accustomed to in writers of less conservative instincts, does not
affect the principle on which alone it can rest. Thus he is not at
all averse to supposing that there is " a considerable element of
subjectivity " to be found in our Lord's discourses as reported by
John, which, though given " in the vivid form of direct speech,"
yet present us the Master's teaching only as " enlarged and interpreted by the recording apostle " (p. 121). This same " subjectivity " he carries also into the Synoptic reports. Thus, in
particular (p. 122): " It has often been pointed out that the words
of the great commission (Matt. xxviii. 19) do not read like that
which we have been accustomed to find given as sayings of Jesus in
the earlier Gospels. The baptismal formula is more like an expansion made when baptism was more of a sacrament than it was
in the days of Jesus, and when the Doctrine of the Trinity was seen
to be an inevitable deduction from our Lord's teaching of His own
relation to the Father. That there was an underlying ' saying ' of
Jesus thus amplified few will wish to deny, and as the words
appear in the earliest MSS. and versions without any suggestion of
hesitation, they cannot be considered an interpolation from later
times. It appears, however, in the form of a divinely directed expansion of some simpler phrase. The gift of the Spirit at Pentecost
had thrown a flood of light upon the Person of our Lord and upon
His relation to the Father, and in that light the injunction of our
Lord was interpreted. The great commission is not less authoritative
because it contains an interpretation of a command which was
probably simpler in expression though equally profound in meaning." Such criticism is essentially frivolous. Jesus could not have
said what is here put into His mouth; for what is here put into His
mouth belongs to the ecclesiastical usages and the doctrinal
formulation of a later time. But He doubtless said something of
importance (if only we had it!) ; and we may accept even the injunctions of a later time as " authoritative." Meanwhile there is no
reason in the world for transferring what Matthew ascribes to Jesus
to the later community, except unwillingness on the part of the
critic to believe that Jesus could have established " the sacrament
of baptism " and could have announced that doctrine of the Trinity

which all men afterwards (but not Jesus) could see "to be an inevitable deduction from our Lord's teaching of His own relation
to the Father." In a word, the critic's ungrounded theory of the
development of doctrine in the first years of Christianity — a theory
which denies to our Lord the capacity to draw "inevitable deductions " from His own claims — becomes a Procrustean bed on which
he measures the trustworthiness of all documentary evidence; and
that is as much as to say that he imposes his hypothetical construction on the records instead of drawing his constructions from the
records. From which we may perceive that whatever we may say of
the subjectivity of Matthew's account of our Lord's saying, we cannot deny the intense subjectivity of Mr. Holdsworth's interpretation of Matthew's account.

Mr. Holdsworth's general critical attitude is that of the present
dominant school of Gospel-criticism, set forth, however, in as genial
and reverent a tone as it admits of. We suppose very few will go
with him in the hearty acceptance he accords to Dr. Arthur Wright's
highly artificial hypothesis of successive editions of Mark as the
true account of the phenomena of the Synoptic tradition. There are
also, of course, other individualisms in his treatment of the critical
problem. But these are unimportant. What he gives is in general
merely a very clear exposition of current views, supported after the
usual fashion. Though he knows and praises Dr. Lightfoot's " admirable discussion of the word *logia*," he can still tell us that when
Papias says that " Matthew composed his logia in the Hebrew
tongue, and each man interpreted these as he was able," he " evidently means that St. Matthew collected and arranged a considerable
number of the sayings of Christ which were floating about the
Christian Church " (p. 75). He can still tell us also " that there
can be no doubt that the earlier use of the word [ιολόγν] was in the
sense of what we know as an ' oracle,' that is, a short condensed
utterance " (p. 77). Is a " short condensed utterance " what we
know as an " oracle "? Or is an " oracle," with us, not rather, a
sacred, an authoritative utterance? In any event the latter is what
λόγιον was to the Greeks. The word is not (in usage at least) a
diminutive, and it has no implication of brevity. Its implication is
that of divinity. And Papias' statement does not represent Matthew
as " collecting sayings of Christ " but as " composing his Scriptures." Mr. Holdsworth, even in the company of the great host of
New Testament scholars who do the same, should not confound

λόγια with λόγοι. The simplicity with which he does so may be perceived by comparing the footnote on p. 74 with the text. In passing
we may call attention to what seems to us a remarkable sentence
on p. 58: " But the appearance of logia preserved upon pieces of
papyrus shows that there were documents at a very much earlier
stage of Church history than is indicated by the more ordered collections which we have in the first Gospel." We pass the employment
of the term " logia " to denote the " sayings " of Christ found on
certain fragments of papyrus: it was the term adopted by Messrs.
Grenfell and Hunt and though unfortunately adopted and misleading in its use, yet finds some justification in the authoritative manner in which these " sayings " are put forward. But do any of these
scraps of papyrus antedate (" very much earlier ") A.D. 70, before
which Matthew was written, or that earlier date at which the " Discourses " used by Matthew were put together? Is there any reason
to imagine that the collection of " sayings " which they draw upon,
antedates the " Discourse-source " which Matthew draws upon and
which must have been put together within the first decade or so after
the Crucifixion?

We must not give the impression that Mr. Holdsworth's book is
compact of errors. On the contrary it is a very unusually good book
of its kind; so good — so reverent and so generally " positive " in
its point of view — that it is worth while pointing out in what respect it fails to sustain its high level. It will be read with pleasure
by everyone who will enjoy a generally sound and telling presentation of the evidence of the deity of our Lord, derived from the
records. And there are scattered through it remarks of unwonted
insight and helpfulness. We esteem one of these the suggestion
(p. 42) of the source from which Luke may have obtained the
speeches of Peter which he incorporates in the early chapters of
Acts. Why not from Mark? Mark was a companion of Peter's, and
also of Paul's, where Luke must have come into contact with him.
And those who think that Mark's Gospel underlies Luke's (we are
not of that number) can scarcely refuse to allow that Mark's reports
may also underlie what Luke gives us of Peter's speeches. The
whole treatment of the Christology of Peter's speeches (pp. 42 ff.) is
suggestive. We shall give ourselves the pleasure, however, of referring to only a couple of passages which show the delicacy and
precision with which Mr. Holdsworth is able to deal with burning
questions in modern church life. There is, for instance, the question

of " social betterment." Could anything more neatly hit off the truth than this? " The reproach has been flung at the Church that sometimes ' the modern priest is more concerned for the unemployed than for the unrepentant.' That the gospel of Jesus Christ contains a definite social reference and prospect few will wish to deny. In accepting and using the language of Jewish eschatology our Lord shows that He, too, has a social and political promise for the world. *But the material good is always a secondary product of the kingdom* " (p. 245, italics ours). The world is to be bettered through its conversion — otherwise not: the preaching of the gospel is therefore the prime instrument of social betterment. Then there is the question of " church union." " We are justified, then, in seeking the unity which all desire, not along the lines of organic unity, nor in any system of Church orders, however revered they may have become, and however charged they may be with historic association, but wherever the presence of its one Lord is realized. Where two or three are gathered together in His name, there He is in the midst; and it is impossible for any one, unless blinded with prejudice, to deny that it is the presence of the Christ that makes the Church " (p. 249). These, too, are golden words, and a golden day will dawn for the churches when their leaders cease to seek unity in anything else than " in Christ." There are few names in which more crimes against the Church of Christ have been committed, and are being still committed in our day — not least on mission ground — than the name of " unity." A show of organized strength in the face of the world is everywhere being made to take the place of the only real strength, which comes out of loyalty to Christ and His Word. Everywhere men are busy building a big house over a divided family and reck nothing of that divided heart which can prosper in nothing.

DIE BEDEUTUNG DER GESCHICHTLICHKEIT JESU FÜR DEN GLAUBEN. Von ERNST TROELTSCH, Dr. phil. et theol. Tübingen: Verlag von J. C. B. Mohr (Paul Siebeck). 1911.[1]

TROELTSCH's chief merit as a writer on theological themes lies in his straightforward downrightness. Among the sentimentally in-

---

[1] *The Princeton Theological Review*, x. 1912, pp. 647–654.

consistent naturalists which crowd the ranks of "modern" theologians, he shines forth as the consistent naturalist, who will have nothing to do with half-measures. In the Lecture which at present lies before us there is, however, a greater appearance of "halfness" than is customary with him. He is clear that religion is a natural phenomenon; and that Christianity as truly as any other religion is a natural phenomenon. He sees no reason why in the natural development of human life and culture Christianity may not be transcended, and a different religion take its place. He, therefore, will not affirm the "eternity" of Christianity. But he sees no immediate prospect of the replacement of Christianity by a new religion. He is sure that Christianity is so related to the culture of the Mediterranean basin that so long as that culture endures, so long will Christianity endure. And he writes to show that the historicity of Jesus is essential to Christianity. Thus the thesis of his Lecture is the indispensableness of the historicity of Jesus for faith. And yet, he will not admit that this indispensableness is absolute. What is indispensable for faith now may cease to be indispensable hereafter. Who knows whether the culture of the Mediterranean basin is the ultimate culture? Who, then, can know whether the religion which is bound up with the culture of the Mediterranean basin is the ultimate religion? Meanwhile we know that for the culture of the Mediterranean basin Christianity is the only possible religion; and that for Christianity the historicity of Jesus is indispensable. This is the ground on which Troeltsch stands.

The Christianity which, in Troeltsch's view, is the only possible religious expression of the culture which has been developed in the Mediterranean basin, and to which he wishes to show that the historicity of Jesus is indispensable is, of course, not historical, or, as it is more willingly called in some quarters, "traditional" Christianity. For any Christianity the object of whose faith is a divine Christ, and the center of whose gospel is the saving work of this divine Christ "propitiating God and thus freeing men from the consequences of their infection by original sin," to raise question of the historicity of Jesus by whom this redemption has been wrought, were nonsense. "From this standpoint the raising of this question would be nothing else than to display the death-certificate of the whole of Christianity" (p. 5). The same is true of those "mixed forms" which "share the fundamental change which the Christianity of the modern world has suffered, — the transmutation of the real miracle of redemption wrought out in a historical act, into an ever new redemption through the knowledge of God " — but who " connect this redeeming faith-knowledge with the knowledge and recollection of the historical personality of Jesus, which here comes into consideration, however, with respect to neither its miracles, nor its separate declarations, but the total effect of the religious personality " (p. 11). "This," continues Troeltsch, "is the view, founded by the later, ecclesiastical Schleiermacher, which has been presented with most emphasis by Ritschl and Herrmann. For Schleiermacher it is the suggestive power of the personality, which, working on through the mediation of His community, and conspicuous in the portrait of the Gospels, conquers the religious inefficacy, unconquerable everywhere outside the sphere of Jesus' influence, and creates the might, certitude, joy and permanence of the knowledge of God. What apart from the faith-creating influence of Christ remains mere idea and presentiment, becomes by means of this personal influence continued in the community victorious and effective force. With Ritschl the same idea is referred less to the suggestive power of the personality than to the authority of Jesus, producing assurance of the forgiveness of sins. Christ by this authority makes Himself Lord and King of the Kingdom of God, or of the Kingdom of God-trusting capacity of life, and it is by the knowledge of Him mediated by the community that there comes the assurance without which sinful man dared not, and may not dare, to believe in God's sin-pardoning grace. With Herrmann the humiliating and exalting fact of the personality of Christ is a historical reality which only the evil and impenitent will can deny, just as it is only the believing will, yearning after God and convicted of its sin, that sees it. It is this fact alone that gives the courage to believe in God as sin-pardoning grace, and with it, the bright delight in and power to all the goods conformable to conscience, while he who cannot become sure of this fact of God falls into doubt, or soothes himself in scepticism and loses the habit of religious needs. It is clear that in all these cases, Christianity is a thought of God, an idea, a faith-knowledge of the true nature of things. All notion of a historical redemptive miracle happening once, and of the foundation of an institute of grace carrying it on, is lacking. But the idea is still, in its efficiency, bound to the historical personality of Christ, by which alone power or certitude is lent it, and the idea so strengthened made the property of a community united in the recollection of Christ. The presupposition for such a mode of thought, besides the silent assumption of the knowableness of the religious personality of Jesus and its effectiveness by means of the mediation of the tradition and the abiding community, is the essential incapacity of men who do not know Christ for hearty faith in God. ' Without Christ I should be an atheist ' — that is the express or silent necessity which is here assumed for men who do not know Christ. The consequence corresponds to the presupposition which places Christianity in sharp contrast with extra-Christian humanity. The Kingdom of God, or the Christian community, or the Church as the object of faith, or the redemption-connection proceeding from Christ — that is the sole region of redemption, and the necessary, eternally abiding collection of the redeemed in the Kingdom of Christ. It will last till the end of humanity, and will extend unto eternity as the collection of humanity in the religious communion of absolute salvation and of absolute truth made possible by Christ " (pp. 11–13). Evidently those who think thus cannot raise a question of the historicity of this Christ without self-stultification.

There can be no question, then, of the historicity of Jesus except among truly modern thinkers who know, like David Friedrich Strauss (in his Christian period), how to distinguish between the principle of Christianity and the Person of Christ (p. 10) ; and who have learned that " in the first instance Christianity is a living faith in God, new at every moment, and that redemption is an ever new work of God in the soul through the operation of faith in God: or, otherwise expressed, that Christianity is a particular faith in God, a peculiar knowledge of God with its corresponding mode of life, or, as it is called, a religious idea or a religious principle " (pp. 5–6) — not, however, necessarily intellectually or philosophically conceived. On this ground there is no historical work of salvation postulated in the background, and there is no inner necessity for the assumption of a historical Jesus. And it is not strange that men standing on this ground should be moved by the increasingly radical conclusions of the historical criticism of the Gospel narratives to raise the question whether it is any longer necessary — or possible — to give significance to Jesus for faith. In ever wider circles there is a feeling growing up that the riddle of the Gospels is incapable of solution, and that the figure of Jesus is fading from sight. And even though it be recognized that the more radical conclusions that are sometimes drawn are unjustified, can faith in God be really inseparably connected with a historical object subject to such critical doubt? " Must it not rather be made inwardly independent of all essential relation to historical elements which in any case are subject to science and which, under scientific examination, show a form so far removed from the religious life of to-day " (pp. 4–5)? " Thus there is to remain, then, nothing but a purely historical-factual and a pedagogical-symbolical significance of the Person of Jesus for the Christian idea! We are to come back to Lessing's declaration of the third Gospel, or to Ibsen's representation of the third kingdom, where religious faith maintains and propagates itself without historical supports, purely by its own purifying and redeeming force, and is to develop itself in connection with the totality of life, freely, out of its own inner depths! " (p. 23). " That in very fact," remarks Troeltsch, " seems to be the outcome of it all " — and then he adds a " But . . ."

But — this is never the way religion exists or propagates itself in the world. There is no clearer result of the history of religions and religious psychology than that what is essential in religion is not dogma or idea, but cultus and communion. " The third kingdom where in religion each stands off to himself and the spirit develops itself in perfect freedom and isolation in the individual, will probably never come, any more than the state and society which rest simply on the natural coalescence of individual interests or reasons " (pp. 28–29). There will never be a really active Christianity apart from communion and cultus; and " as we need cultus and communion so also we need Christ as the head and point of union of the community. For the Christian knowledge of God has absolutely no other means of producing union and making itself visible, and lectures on the philosophy of religion will never create and never propogate a real religion " (p. 31). " So long as there exists a Christianity in any sense whatever, it will be bound up with the central place of Christ in worship " (p. 29). It is idle, therefore, Troeltsch declares, to talk of a Christianity without Christ, and if criticism ever really disproves the historicity of Jesus or even abolishes all real knowledge of Him — that is the end of Christianity. On religio-historical grounds a Christless Christianity is an impossibility: " Christianity, in the central position of the personality of Jesus, does not have a distinguishing peculiarity which separates it from all other religions and renders redemption possible to it alone, but only fulfills in this a general law of the life of the human spirit, though after a fashion peculiar to itself " (p. 42).

To those who suppose that the historicity of Jesus may go and His personality be retained as " a symbol," which will serve the same purpose as a rallying-point as His reality, Troeltsch has this to say: " But the state of the case being such, certainly a real and principial indifference regarding the historico-critical questions is impossible. No doubt Jesus is in this sense the symbol of Christian faith in general. But those who imagine that for such a symbol a rooting in historical fact is a matter of indifference, and that the great work of the history of religions is precisely the mythical embodiment of ideas, are for their own person far removed from entering into and giving themselves inwardly with enthusiasm or practical labor to a faith-circle, the idea of which is embodied by this mythical symbol. They merely impute to believers, that they, in their humbler limitation, may be altogether content with a mythical symbol. Such imputations, as those for example made by Samuel Lublinski, are nothing more than examples of those æstheticizing toyings with reality which are so common nowadays, where the æsthete purposes to the believer that he shall satisfy his life-hunger on a mystical symbol, because he himself considers that what has to be quieted in the case is not at all a real hunger for conviction and certainty, but only a playful demand of the fantasy. For one who really belongs inwardly to the Christian life-world, it is impossible to hold that the center and head of the community, the point of reference of all worship and of all apprehension of God, is simply a myth, no matter how beautiful it may be. As God is to him not notion and possibility but holy reality, so will he stand with this, his symbol of God, also on the firm ground of real life. It is for him of true importance that an actual man lived, strove, believed and conquered thus, and that from this actual life there has flowed a stream of power and certainty down to him. The symbol is to him a real symbol only because behind it there stands the figure of a preëminent actual religious prophet, by means of whom he not only comes to the knowledge of God, but on whom he stays and strengthens himself in his own uncertainty, as he requires now and again support in a superior personal-religious authority, and reiteratedly experiences it in life. This is what is legitimate in Herrmann's talk of the ' fact of Christ.' What is under consideration, however, is not that the assurance of salvation of the individual can be won only by becoming assured of Jesus, but that there can be no productive and strengthening life-coherence of the Christian spirit without gathering about Jesus, and a gathering about Jesus must also go back to a real living life if it is to have real power and veracity " (pp. 31–33).

The point of Troeltsch's contention thus is that religion is after all a social affair and consists at bottom in associated worship, and this associated worship requires for its persistence a rallying-point which must be envisaged as real. So soon as the reality of this rallying-point is doubted, the whole religious life centering in it crumbles. Christianity can persist, therefore, only as the historicity of Jesus, its rallying-point, remains beyond question in Christian circles. The historicity of Jesus is not given in the persistence of Christianity; it is rather its presupposition and depends, like all other questions of historicity, on the results of historical research. But whenever — if ever — the results of historical research prove unfavorable to it, then the death-knell of Christianity is sounded. It is precisely here that Troeltsch separates himself with most decisiveness from what he calls that mediating type of thought represented by Schleiermacher, Ritschl, Herrmann, and their followers; and in separating himself from them refuses to find in Christianity the ultimate religion and therefore to claim for Jesus the place of eternal redeemer of men. " If the central position of Jesus," he reasons, " is established by means of the miracle of a power and assurance which overcomes all weakness and incapacity to faith born of original sin, then the religion of humanity must always remain Christianity, and all religious communion in all eternity must turn about the center of the person of Christ. Then, with Schleiermacher, Christ will be designated the second Adam, or with Ritschl, He and His community will be represented as the essential-purpose of God, identical with the world-purpose, and from the one as from the other a bridge can be thrown over to the old Christology of Nicæa and Chalcedon. But if it is to be established upon universal social-psychological necessities, then there can be inferred from it only, that so long as the special Christian prophetic piety persists — bearing in itself the Stoa and Platonism and so much more besides — all possibility of a community and a cultus, and with them all real power and propagation of belief, is bound to the central position of Christ in faith " (pp. 47–48). How long this specific Christian piety will persist is, no doubt, another question; and it is a question a prudent man will not be quick to give a response to. Enough for us that it is bound up with the culture of the Mediterranean basin, and for us who are the products and the vehicles of that culture another form of religion is meanwhile impossible. Christianity will abide as long as the culture of which we are the exponents abides; and so long as Christianity abides, Christ must hold the central place in faith, and that as a really existent and historical person. This is the last word of social-psychological research.

We shall not enter into any extended criticism of Troeltsch's position. The problem which he raises is a purely academic one. It amounts in effect to asking how small a place can be assigned to Christ in our religious life and His historicity yet remain indispensable. Troeltsch's contention is that though His rôle be reduced to that of a mere symbol, a symbol of the peculiar faith in and knowledge of God which constitutes our religion, for the fulfillment of even this attenuated rôle He yet requires to have really existed. This may be true; if true, it may be interesting; but it is altogether without practical importance. For Troeltsch does not pretend that the Christianity — if it can justly be called Christianity — which looks upon Jesus as a mere symbol is playing any large part in the religious life of the world. He does indeed tell us that " die Gegenwart " is turning with avidity to this reduced Christianity: that there are not a few to whom Jesus has become only " the historical starting-point of the Christian life-world, and His portrait only of pedagogical importance or a symbol of Christianity "; and that, if everything does not deceive us, such a point of view is destined to become very much more widespread in the circles of German culture than it now is (p. 17). But he also tells us that it is not manifesting any great productive power, and gives little promise of a great future; " that in fact almost all the religiousness of to-day draws its life from modifications of the strong religious treasures propagated in the churches and in them alone " (p. 23). So long as all the vital and productive religion in the world is manifested in connection with the historical (or, if you will, " traditional ") forms of Christianity, we need not concern ourselves greatly with the question whether the historicity of Jesus is indispensable also for the more advanced (or debased) forms of " Christianity " (if the word be allowed) which are without vitality or probable future. We only note, with whatever satisfaction the facts are fitted to give us, that in Troeltsch's opinion religion cannot flourish or propagate

itself, in the conditions of our Mediterranean culture at least, apart
from the recognition of the historicity of Jesus, and that the historicity of Jesus is in any event an assured fact, and indeed that
the fundamental character of His teaching is beyond question
(pp. 4, 38). We have our own opinion here, which goes much further
than Troeltsch would allow, and we believe our opinion is firmly
grounded; but we are not without interest when we learn that even
to an extremist like Troeltsch " the decisive importance of the personality of Jesus for the origin and formation of Christianity," and
" the religious-ethical ground character of the preaching of Jesus "
are " established with certainty " (p. 38). We are pleased to hear
such an extremist declare that the " allegation of the non-existence
of Jesus is without doubt a monstrous thing, and also the allegation
of the impossibility of knowing the fundamental traits of His preaching is a great exaggeration " (p. 4). We wish we could hear him
go on and declare that doubt of the true deity of Jesus is also a
monstrous thing, and denial of His great atoning act a gross absurdity. Were his opinions determined by purely historical considerations, he could so declare; and so declaring, would understand how
nonsensical the raising of the question whether the historicity of
Christ is indispensable to Christianity is; for he would understand
that a Christianity which knows nothing of a Divine Christ or of
an Atoning Death of Christ is just not Christianity at all. The
question of the indispensableness of Christ to Christianity is in a word
just the question of the nature, or, as it is now fashionable to phrase
it, of " the essence," of Christianity. A Christless Christianity is no
more a contradiction in words than a non-atoning Christ is a contradiction in fact; Christianity involves the acknowledgment not
of Christ *simpliciter* but, as Paul insists, specifically of " Christ
as crucified."

JESUS CHRISTUS IN DER GESCHICHTE. Von D. EBERHARD VISCHER.
Tübingen: Verlag von J. C. B. Mohr (Paul Siebeck). 1912.[1]

EBERHARD VISCHER always writes interestingly, and this Address — for it is an Address, delivered at a Conference of Christian

students — is no exception to the rule. In substance it is a popular presentation of the argument developed at length and with more scientific stringency in his well-known article on " Historical Certainty and Faith in Jesus Christ," published in the *Zeitschrift für Theologie und Kirche* for 1898 (viii. pp. 195–260). Although, therefore, it declares on its title-page that it is a " Contribution to the Drews- and Jatho-Debates," it has only the slightest connection with these debates. They are mentioned only that the reader may be counseled to let them alone and go behind them. No doubt Drews and Jatho may be answered point by point. But what then? The real question still remains untouched. For it is Vischer's " conviction, that by this labor, necessary and meritorious as it is, the difficult questions raised by Drews and his predecessors are by no means answered; that, on the contrary, precisely by this defense the real problem which is in debate, is made a burning one — the question, to wit, of how a historical personality, which, because it belongs to history, shares also the lot of all that is historical and passes more and more into the past — of how such a personality can possess at the same time abiding significance, can be for humanity the guide, who guides them, despite all the changes of times and relations, most surely and most directly to the eternal Ground of all Being and Becoming. It is precisely by a defense which follows the doubts of the historicity of Jesus step by step, which takes up every consideration urged against the sources which come into account and tries its weight, that it first becomes thoroughly clear what it means that Jesus Christ too is a historical object " (pp. 6–7). What is historical belongs to time, nay, rather to a time; and as times succeed times, it fades more and more into the past, to which, indeed, it inherently belongs, bearing its character and meeting perhaps it needs, but certainly not ours upon whom a new heaven and a new earth have dawned. Jesus Christ as a historical object cannot escape this twofold result of His very historicity. He becomes only a shadowy figure in the fading past; and what may be discerned of Him through the mists of time belongs distinctly to the past, separated from our modern world by a deep chasm. " What has this historical Jesus, this figure of a Jewish Rabbi in His indefiniteness and in the limitations of His times, in common with what Christianity has believed and confessed itself to possess in Christ? How can the significance which a great part of mankind has ascribed, and continues to ascribe, to Jesus for its relation to God, be combined with the knowledge that Jesus is a historical object, and all that is historical is transitory? This is the real religious problem which comes into discussion in this controversy over the historical Jesus " (pp. 8–9).

Having thus posited the problem, Vischer addresses himself to solving it. At the outset, he is concerned that we shall adopt the right method. It is usual to begin with an investigation of the oldest tradition concerning Jesus, first of all of the conception of Christ of the earliest Christian community, and to ask, first, how far this is credible, and then how far we can recognize to-day a guide in this Jesus shown to be historical. This, Vischer considers a bad way: we shall scarcely go through with it without subjecting the results of our researches to a certain amount of manipulation to make them fit our needs. He recommends to us, therefore, an opposite way. Let us begin, he says, with the other end — with what Jesus Christ has been and is to men, and proceed backwards from that to what He was as a historical figure. " Let us turn from the investigators who dispute over the trustworthiness of the oldest tradition, to the company of those who from the times of the first disciples until to-day have gathered about Jesus Christ as their Lord. What have they always believed that they found in and through Christ? And whence have they drawn this assurance, confident in which many have gone to their death? " (p. 10). The argument which he proposes, it will be seen, is that from effects to their cause; and the principle on which he proceeds — a principle fully developed, and defended at length, in the earlier article to which we have already adverted (*Zeitschrift für Theologie und Kirche*, 1898) — is that not only a sound, but the only sound, method of reaching absolute certainty as to past things is through observation of their present effects. Of past personalities and events necessarily implied in present conditions we may have true certainty; of all other past things only a greater or less degree of probability may be attained.

Proceeding on this principle Vischer passes in rapid review what we may call the sequences of Jesus in history and emerges at length in the following conclusion. " If now, after this journey through history, after this survey of what the Christian community, yes, humanity in general, have received from Jesus, and ever anew receive from Him, we turn back to the problem from which we started out, we have now found the right standpoint for replying to the questions contained in it. Now, at length we are in a position to give

a clear and distinct answer to the question as to the historicity of
Jesus. And it is certainly not too much to say that the arguments
brought against it appear to us now simply ridiculous. Not because
we now — as no doubt we are accustomed to hear — occupying the
standpoint of faith, have no need to give heed to the objections of
historical science, but because we have struck out the method by
which alone we can attain to a real, complete knowledge of historical objects, the method, to wit, of inference from the collective,
still tangible, effects to their causes. Undoubtedly it is altogether
right when, in order to obtain an assured judgment as to Jesus, all
the testimonies to Him that lie before us, in and out of the Bible,
are examined in the most exact manner, according to the methods
which the historian applies in all his investigations; the Gospels,
before all, as well as the Epistles of Paul, and the well-known passages in Tacitus, Pliny and Suetonius. Only so will we guard
ourselves from substituting, on the ground of actual and alleged religious experiences, phantasies for the historical actuality . . . We
would not, then, by an appeal to the Christ of faith juggle with the
Christ of history. But neither would we neglect when dealing with
Jesus what seems to us a matter of course in the case of every other
great man. To the still existing vestiges from which we can and must
infer the greatness or nature of a historical phenomenon, there belong, not merely the oldest written testimonies which give an account
of it, but, much more, its work and the effects which proceed from
it. It would be a remarkable historian who should carefully collect
all the notices about Dante, and search the whole history of his times
for traces of his existence, and not put himself under the influence
of the ' Divina commedia,' but leave it to one side unheeded . . . Of
course, the greater a personality is, the more important he is for the
history of mankind, so much the more impossible is it for any rightly
to comprehend his actuality and personality except those who stand
under his influence, and possess the organs to feel the imperishable
power of his work. That is true again of a Dante and a Goethe, of
a Giotto and a Bach, of a Francis of Assisi and a Luther as well
as of a Jesus. And we are asking no exceptional treatment for Him,
when we reply to those who combat His historicity: Only when we
attend to Jesus' effects in history and experience them in ourselves
are we in position to decide this question. It is therefore quite intelligible when to the plain Christian who lives in the gospel, the
conflict over the historicity of Jesus seems absurd. Only after we

have traced the effects of Jesus through history and taken account of what the Christian community believes it possesses in Christ, and why it believes it possesses it, do we understand also how far Jesus Christ, in spite of being a historical man, affected in many respects by the limitations of His time, of His people, and of His locality, yet can possess abiding religious significance " (pp. 34–38).

What it is important to observe here is that Vischer is not arguing that the Christ of faith may be indifferent to historical assault. He is seeking the certitude of history, not of faith. And he is arguing that history gives us a Jesus whose existence is not merely probable, in however high a degree, but absolutely certain; certain with the certainty of the axiom that every effect must have a cause. His method is to point out that historical certainty does not wait upon the criticism of the witnessing documents, but may be grounded in quite other considerations; nay, wherever it exists, indeed, must always rest on other considerations — on the observation, in a word, of historical effects. Had history preserved for us no single intimation of the existence of Dante, the existence of the " Divina commedia " would compel — not suggest — his postulation. And had historical records preserved for us no single intimation of the existence of Jesus Christ — or, what comes to the same thing, should historical criticism obliterate every existing intimation of His existence — there exist in the world effects, quite as palpable as the " Divina commedia," which compel — not suggest — His postulation. What the consideration of these effects gives us is not probability, however high, but certainty. Of course the estimation of the effects and the discovery of the nature of their cause implies a certain capacity of appreciation. To infer a Raphael from the Sistine Madonna, a Beethoven from his Sonatas, a Dante from the " Divina commedia," implies specific endowments in the observer; likewise to infer from the effects which He has wrought in the world a Jesus Christ, has its implication also of endowments in the observer. This circumstance, however, no more in the one case than in the other, destroys the validity of the inference. It only directs us to its proper organs. Nor does Vischer desire by this appeal to the witness of the effects to set aside the appeal to the critically examined sources. So far as, under criticism, they yield a positive result, they supply, according to him, the details as to the personality inferred from His effects in the world. There could have been no " Divina commedia " had there been no Dante; but it is from the historical notices of Dante that we draw our portrait of Dante. Our certainty that there was a Jesus is drawn from the effects He has wrought in the world; what manner of Jesus He was, we are to go to the criticized testimonies which have come down to us to tell us. To put it coarsely, our certainty of the existence of Jesus is given us in the effects He has wrought in the world; our conception of what this Jesus thus certified to us was is given us in the critically reconstructed records.

To put it thus coarsely does injustice to Vischer's position. It does not seem to do as much injustice to it, however, as it ought to. It can scarcely be contended that the inference from effects is only to the existence of a cause, without involving anything as to the nature of that cause; the qualitative is as stringent as the merely quantitative inference. It is not the existence of merely a man, but of a genius, and of a genius of quite specific gifts, that we infer from the " Divina commedia," the Sistine Madonna, the Sonatas of Beethoven. What from the effects Christ has wrought in the world? Vischer himself tells us (p. 11) that, in whatever various ways men may have expressed it, the one thing which Jesus Christ has meant to all the world, in all ages, may be summed up in the one word, God. What, then, if the criticism of the sources gives us, as the Jesus that really lived, not God but man? In his eagerness not to juggle away " the historical Jesus " in the interests of the Christ of faith, and in his fear that men shall set their phantasies in the place of the historical actuality in their thought of Jesus, Vischer does not here do justice to his own principle of interpretation. When we survey the effects of Jesus in the world we are compelled to infer as cause, not some Jesus merely, but a Jesus of a very particular quality, of a quality which alone could be the cause of these effects. And that Jesus is not the Jesus which Vischer would commend to our acceptance on the basis of the criticism of the sources. How, after his survey of these effects, he can still recommend us to see in Jesus merely a man is a standing wonder. No matter what Jesus criticism extracts from the sources, the Jesus which actually was is the Jesus which is required to account for His effects in the world. Or rather, no criticism of the sources can be sound which eliminates from them the Jesus which corresponds to the effects which He has wrought in the world; for it is undeniable, that the Jesus which lies on the face of the sources is the very Jesus who appears in these effects. It will not do to attempt to account for the presence of the Divine Jesus in the historical records on the ground that it is a natural creation of those who have felt the effects of Jesus, and to substitute for Him another Jesus who stands in no recognizable relation to these effects. What needs to be accounted for is not the rise of the Divine Jesus in the consciousness of His first followers, but the fading of the Divine Jesus out of the consciousness of so many of His later followers. It is this last estimate of Him which stands in contradiction with the observed effects He has left in the world.

We wonder, in this connection, what Vischer can mean by words like these (p. 25): "Yea, even the death on the cross, this frightful enigma (*furchtbare Rätsel*), for the solving of which the deepest thinkers have ever afresh labored . . ." To Vischer Jesus Christ, though bringing to the world a revelation of God which has revolutionized the world, was after all only a Rabbi of Nazareth, who cannot Himself, but only God who has revealed Himself in Him, be our comfort and support in life and in death (p. 39). Why should the death of such a one, even on the cross, be a frightful enigma, to which profound thinkers devote continual labor in the hope of reaching a solution of it? Is there any enigma in a good man who throws himself athwart the religious prejudices of a fanatical people, falling a victim to their hate? What is there in Jesus' death more than in that of Socrates, which will justify us in speaking of it as a "frightful enigma," which ever presents itself to the investigation of profound thinkers, in the hope that, mayhap, they may fathom its mysteries? On Vischer's view of who and what Jesus was there is no mystery here whatever; no enigma to solve. What should a Galilean Rabbi do, but, after awhile, die? And what could a good man do other than die a martyr to his cause? And what could be more natural than that the zealots for the law should slay Him who made Himself greater than Moses and the Prophets and clothed Himself (with whatever meaning) with those prerogatives of God, the forgiveness of sins on earth, the judgment of the world? (On the inevitableness of Jesus' death on Vischer's presuppositions, see the instructive exposition of Julius Kaftan, "Dogmatik," ed. 4, pp. 570–572.) And as for the cross, how else could He have managed to die by judicial sentence, just then and there? If there be an enigma here to study, a mystery worthy of the thought of men of thought, it is because there is something more in Jesus than a Rabbi of Nazareth, and something more in His death than the natural end which a Rabbi of Nazareth who called down on Himself the wrath of His fanatical compatriots would make. That there was something more both in Him and in His death is certain, with that historical certainty which, Vischer insists, resides in the necessary implication of an adequate cause in observed effects. We wish he himself had followed his argument until he had uncovered precisely what this something more is.

THE DOCTRINE OF THE PERSON OF JESUS CHRIST. International Theological Library. By H. R. MACKINTOSH, D.Phil., D.D. Edinburgh: T. & T. Clark; New York: Charles Scribner's Sons. 1912.[1]

PROF. MACKINTOSH tells us in his Preface that he has designed his book " chiefly as a student's manual," and (that it may serve that end) that he has wished to make it " cover with a fair measure of completeness, the whole field of Christology." This seems to promise us a plain, objective, comprehensive treatise. But we are afraid these qualities are scarcely those which most strikingly characterize it. The language in which it is written is overloaded, burdened with superfluous qualificatives, and, though often brilliant, often also not very exact. The presentation is individualistic to its finger-tips. And comprehensiveness of treatment is sought chiefly by prefixing to the constructive discussion — the author calls it, significantly, " the reconstructive statement " — an equally long survey of the " history of Christological doctrine." Under this heading we class together the first two Books, which are entitled respectively " Christology in the New Testament " and " History of Christological Doctrine," because, though formally distinguished, their subject-matters are dealt with much after the same fashion. They together occupy two hundred and eighty-four pages, leaving for the " reconstructive statement " the remaining two hundred and fifty pages.

Perhaps we ought to give some illustration of the looseness of the language of which we have complained. We begin with the simplest forms. On p. 43 our attention is directed to the " sugges-

[1] The Princeton Theological Review, xi. 1913, pp. 141–156.

tion that in the earliest faith two forms of faith in Christ went side by side, in peaceful rivalry: that to which He was but a prophet and forerunner, and that to which He already appeared as authentically Divine in majesty and redeeming power." It is then very correctly remarked that no such division of opinion is traceable in the New Testament, but it is surprisingly added (italics his) : " Both estimates were held by *all* Christians." What is intended is clear enough and very true: but what is actually said is, strictly taken, nonsense — for no one could possibly have combined the beliefs that Jesus was both " *but* a prophet " and that He was God. The fatally pleonastic " but " wrecks the precision of the statement. Similarly we read on p. 108 of " St. John's usage of the title ' Son of Man,' " whereas the fact of course is that John never uses that title, but only quotes Christ as using it; on p. 118, in an exposition of the Prologue to John, that it declares of the Logos that " He was from the beginning," when what it really declares of course is that *in* the beginning He already was, which is something very different; on p. 125, that the apostolic habit of praying to Christ may be regarded " as the practical ' deifying ' of Jesus," whereas the truth is that Jesus was not held to be God because He was prayed to but was prayed to because He was held to be God; on p. 129, that it was possible for the first Christians " to accentuate either Christ's Divine unity with, or His personal distinction from, the Father," where the adjective " Divine " is quite without meaning; on p. 228, that according to Thomas Aquinas the two natures of our Lord " are not so much united, as brought into a common relation to the Logos," which after some reflection may no doubt be made to yield its meaning, but is a very awkward way of expressing it; on p. 266, that according to Thomasius the Logos by His exinanition " became capable of forming the centre of a single personal Life," as if He had not formed the center of a single personal life from all eternity; on p. 318, that the " influence " of Jesus has in every age " continued to reconcile men with God," an expression which we would be loath to believe fairly embodied Prof. Mackintosh's conception of the work of Christ; on p. 323, that the Greek idea of salvation naturally led to defining our Lord's Person " in terms of substance, not spirit," an instance of an inveterate habit of false antithesis; on p. 386, with respect to the attribution of " an impersonal humanity " to our Lord, that " we are rightly told that the truth against which the phrase is designed to safeguard is this, that the humanity of our Lord had no *independent personality*," where, however, the disturbing "against" is probably a printer's error [2]; on p. 397, with reference to Mark xiii. 32, that if Jesus "could thus be ignorant of a detail connected in some measure with His redemptive work, the conclusion is unavoidable that in secular affairs His knowledge was but the knowledge of His time" — certainly as fine a specimen of *non sequitur* as could easily be turned up anywhere. We have purposely chosen these instances from statements of no great intrinsic importance: they illustrate better on that account a fault of style.

But the fault illustrated invades the most important statements also, in which overstatement, incomplete antithesis, disturbing adverbial and adjectival qualificatives abound. Take such a sentence as this, for example: "God and man are one, but the unity results not from the formal juxtaposition of abstract natures, but from spiritually costly experiences of reciprocal possession and coalescence" (p. 371). What is a "*formal* juxtaposition of *abstract* natures"? Had Prof. Mackintosh said simply "juxtaposition of natures," his meaning would have been clear, though question might still be raised of the justice of the use of this expression to describe the orthodox doctrine of the Person of Christ. But what a "formal" juxtaposition of natures is, and how "abstract" natures can be juxtaposed, whether formally or any other way, we must profess our inability to imagine. We are equally puzzled to divine what it means to say that the unity of God and man in the Person of the exalted Jesus "results from experiences of reciprocal possession and coalescence." Where "reciprocal possession and coalescence" are experienced, one would think unity already given — not requiring yet to be constituted. And when we remember that in Prof. Mackintosh's view, as we shall see, there never existed in Jesus Christ — certainly not prior to His exaltation — any two factors (God and man) to experience "reciprocal possession and coalescence," we shall begin to realize how loose and unmeaning the expression is. Take another example. We read (p. 270): "If we hold with conviction that Jesus is one in whom God Himself enters humanity" (this is itself a fatally ambiguous expression) "then He does so either with all His attributes unmodified, or in such wise as to manifest only those qualities which are compatible with a real human life." The false disjunction is flagrant. God may enter the human race by assuming into per-

---

[2] We have not observed many printer's errors: p. 150, line 2, "second" for "third"; p. 216, "Julius of Halicarnassus" for "Julian."

sonal union with Himself a human nature without any modification taking place in any of His divine attributes (this in point of fact is precisely what did take place) ; and yet manifest ordinarily, in His life " in the flesh " only those of His divine qualities which are compatible with the real human life which by virtue of His assumed human nature He willed to live.

Perhaps, however, a longer passage will give us a better insight into Prof. Mackintosh's methods of sentence building. We will take one from pp. 455–456. " It is, of course, true," we read, " that Christ, both in His own mind and in that of the apostles, stands in positive relations to the Divine fore-knowledge. But we do not exhaust the special connection of Christ with God by relating Him merely to the Divine *thought*. So far He is on the same plane as the creatures." Here there is a quite clear declaration that Christ in common with the creatures was the object of the divine foreknowledge (and therefore has not existed eternally), and with it an intimation that He differs from the creatures in being something more than the object of the divine foreknowledge. The statement, therefore, at once follows that this something more is that He — and by immediate inference, not they — is the object also of the divine *will*. But in accordance with Prof. Mackintosh's usual manner, he cannot make this statement simply. Qualifying clauses are introduced, and qualifying clauses of such a character as confuse the antithesis and indeed go far towards abolishing it. What we actually read is: " The filial connection is so close that we must also think Christ as eternally related, and related as an eternal fact, to the *will* of God — as the timeless object of His producing and sustaining love." What the disturbing intercalated phrase " and related as an eternal fact " means and what its function in the antithesis is, are not immediately clear. Any fact, eternally contemplated as such in the thought of God and eternally decreed as such in the will of God, might be appropriately designated, perhaps, on that account " an eternal fact," that is, a fact which has from all eternity been certain to occur. But this does not seem to exhaust the meaning of the phrase as here used. It seems to be intended to designate Christ, as distinguished from the creatures, a fact which has existed eternally not merely in the thought of God, nor merely in the will of God, but also in actuality. But thus the antithesis is confused. The main declaration of the sentence is that Christ differs from the creatures in being the object not merely of the eternal divine thought but also of the eternal divine *will*. The assertion that He differs from them further in, unlike them, existing eternally in actuality is inserted in the midst of this declaration without preparation for it and in such a manner as to confuse the consecution of thought. Things are not bettered by the addition of the explanatory clause — " as the timeless objects of His producing and sustaining love " — although the qualification " timeless " here attached to " object " confirms the explanation of the phrase " an eternal fact " as a declaration of the eternal actual existence of Christ. For the eternal Christ which was formerly said to be the eternal object of the divine thought, and has just been said to be the eternal object also of the divine will, and that so as to exist coeternally with this will, is now said, not merely to be also the " timeless object " of the divine love, but also to owe His existence and His persistence in being alike to that love. What would appear to be meant is that the love of God eternally produces and sustains in being as its timeless object Him whom we know as Christ in accordance with the eternal will and, behind that, the eternal thought of God. So far have we traveled from the simple antithesis which differentiates the temporal Christ from the creature as the object not merely of the thought but also of the will of God; and we begin to suspect that that fundamental antithesis was never intended to be drawn at all, and that Prof. Mackintosh did not have it in his mind to deny that creatures are eternally the object of the divine will as well as of the divine thought (which nevertheless his words do emphatically deny), but only wished to deny to them the eternal actual existence which he affirms for Christ. Be that as it may, having now ascribed Christ to the love of God as His producing and sustaining cause, Prof. Mackintosh passes at once away from this idea again and reverts to the mere " thought and will of God." He proceeds: " The thought and will of God cannot be conceived save as imparting reality to Christ." This can scarcely mean that God cannot be conceived as a thinking and willing being save as bringing into being the man Christ, as a phenomenon in time and space. It appears to be Prof. Mackintosh's mode of stating the old argument that a duality in the Godhead is given in the very idea of a self-conscious and loving God, an argument to which, we may remark in passing, he does not seem elsewhere to accord quite conclusive force. If so, we perceive how completely he has passed in the course of a few sentences from the phenomenal Christ with which the paragraph began to the noumenal Christ. The concluding sentence carries on this new line of thought. " Or, to put it otherwise," we read, " the Father revealed in the Son cannot be thought as fully real in abstraction from the Son in whom alone we apprehend Him." The change of terms here from " Christ " to " Son " is no doubt the sign that now the phenomenal Christ has been definitely left in the background, although to Prof. Mackintosh, " Son " is not always elsewhere — at least primarily — the designation of the preincarnate person. We appear to have arrived nevertheless at the thesis that God, if He is to " be thought as fully real," must be thought of as dual — Father and Son. We apprehend Him only in the Son in whom He is revealed; and in abstraction from the Son we cannot think of Him as real. Even here, however, we are haunted with a doubt whether a new idea is not intended to be subtly suggested — the Ritschlian principle that we know God only through Christ. On the whole, nevertheless, we seem by searching to have found out the author's thought. But we have had to search for it.

The intelligent reading of a book written after this fashion is not an easy task. We are not always sure it is a rewarding one. Logical consecution not having always presided over its composition, it does not easily yield its meaning to logical analysis. We are tempted again and again to take it " in the vague " and to depend for the ascertainment of its meaning on the general impression it leaves on the mind — much, for example, as we take the illusive writings of, say, Maeterlinck. The thought seems to be so congested in Prof. Mackintosh's pregnant sentences that it refuses to flow out liquidly to the reader.

And even when we reach the thought our difficulties are not all over. Prof. Mackintosh says many good things well and strongly. We have noted numerous passages where truths of importance, often truths disputed in circles with which Prof. Mackintosh manifests a certain sympathy, are stated with clearness and force. And the drift of the whole discussion is on the side of the angels. But the points of view from which Prof. Mackintosh approaches his task and the presuppositions with which he endeavors to accomplish it, gravely compromise his results, or rather, if we are to speak quite frankly, render it from the first impossible that he should succeed in reaching a satisfying solution of the problems which it offers. Even when he is endeavoring to state facts which are generally allowed, it is impossible for him, with his presuppositions, to state them so as to be generally acceptable. This is perhaps sufficiently illustrated by the very first affirmation he makes. The authors of the New Testament, he tells us (p. 2), " are eventually " (not a very well chosen adverb here, one would think) " one in their view of Christ." " Two certainties are shared in common by all New Testament writers: First, that the life and consciousness of Jesus was in form completely human; second, that this historic life, apprehended as instinct with the powers of redemption, is one with the life of God Himself. In Christ they find God personally present for our salvation from sin and death." This is Prof. Mackintosh's substitute for saying that throughout the New Testament our Lord is looked upon and presented as both God and man. It is a very poor substitute: it fails indeed to make it clear that the New Testament recognizes Him as either God or man, and in its positive statements it stands in no relation whatever to New Testament teaching. Nothing could be more untrue than to say that " the life and consciousness of Jesus " are represented in the New Testament as " in form completely human." It would be nearer the truth to say that the whole New Testament is written to show that neither the life nor the consciousness of Jesus was even in form completely human. John expressly tells us this of himself: and, as Prof. Mackintosh recognizes (p. 5, note), even Mark draws Jesus " as He appeared to contemporaries, *living out the truth of Divine Sonship*" (italics ours). Not forgetting, Prof. Mackintosh adds, it is true, " the human limitations of this Divine personality," but as he supports this only by a passage (vi. 5) which, as he subsequently himself explains (p. 14), does not in the least support it, we may be justified in leaving the qualification out of account. How can it be said of one who is reported as declaring, " Verily, verily, I say unto you, Before Abraham was I am " (John viii. 58), that His consciousness is represented as " completely human "? Nay, how can Prof. Mackintosh tell us in one breath that the consciousness of Jesus is represented throughout the whole New Testament as " in form completely human," and almost in the next breath (p. 29) remark on " the unconditioned character of His self-consciousness " as depicted even in the Synoptic Gospels as a rock on which low views of His Person even in the days of His flesh inevitably make shipwreck? Is an " unconditioned self-consciousness " "in form completely human "? We cannot withhold the expression of our sympathy for Prof. Mackintosh in the difficulties he experiences in attempting to impose his *a priori* schematization of the Person of our Lord on a New Testament text obviously so impatient of it. Neither is it the New Testament view that the " historic life " of Jesus Christ, that is to say, we suppose, the life He lived in what the Epistle to the Hebrews calls the days of His flesh, " is one with the life of God Himself." They represent it rather as a life in a true sense alien to the life of God, a life altogether unnatural to Christ as God, a life of humiliation, characterized by obedience, whereas it belongs to God to reign (Phil. ii. 7 f.). Nor is the matter helped by the insertion *more suo* of the qualifying clause, " apprehended as instinct with the powers of redemption." This is not a New Testament phrase and it represents a point of view which is not a New Testament point of view. Jesus Christ according to His own testimony came into the world on a ministry of mercy and redeems men by giving His life as a ransom for their sins. It is redolent of a totally different conception to say that His life on earth " was instinct with the powers of redemption "; and if His life on earth were apprehended as thus " instinct with the powers of redemption," this would not justify us in pronouncing it on that account " one with the life of God," and in point of fact the majority of those who so apprehend it do not therefore consider it " one with the life of God." To find " God personally present for our salvation from sin and death " in Christ is not to find Christ God, and those who have made this and like phrases their shibboleths do not in point of fact find Christ God. If this were all that could be said for the New Testament conception of Jesus on His divine side, then nothing is said which might not be said of any good man in and through whom God works for the salvation of sinful men. That it is not all that must be said Prof. Mackintosh knows very well, and tells us in detail in his subsequent treatment of the conception of Christ presented in the several portions of the New Testament. It is all the more to be regretted that he permits his *a priori* schematization of the Person of the Lord to confine his statement here of the common New Testament doctrine to such a doubtful minification. Obviously we shall not find our way a step in Prof. Mackintosh's book unless we keep clearly in mind the presuppositions of his speculative doctrine of the Person of Christ. Those presuppositions color all his thought and all his expressions, and make the book merely a historico-speculative presentation and defense of his particular " reconstruction."

We shall confine ourselves in what follows to some remarks on three of the fundamental presuppositions which Prof. Mackintosh brings with him to his attempt to expound the doctrine of the Person of Christ, and which condition or rather determine his entire conception of that doctrine. These concern his ontology of spiritual being — if " ontology " is the right word to use in connection with his conception of the nature of spirit; his point of view with reference to the Christian doctrine of the Two Natures of our Lord; and his opinions with reference to Kenosis.

Prof. Mackintosh gives his adherence to a very explicit, and we may add somewhat extreme, voluntarism in his conception of the nature of spirit (cf. pp. 113–114, 166, 188, 221, 304, 334, 416, 421, 422, 424, 500). " There is in the universe," he declares (p. 114), " nothing more real than will, the living energy of spirit; nothing more concrete and actual, whether it be in God or man." Again, " To the modern mind will is the very core and essence of personality " (p. 188). And more explicitly still, " The ultimate and central reality of things is Will " (p. 417). Prof. Mackintosh does not mean by these declarations merely to assert the primacy of the will among the constitutive attributes of personality. He means to replace the conception of " substance " by the conception of " will " in representing to himself the being of spirit. When he comes to form a conception of the Person of Christ, therefore, he has no divine " nature " and no human (spiritual) " nature " by the union of which in one person he can think of it as constituted. He has nothing on which to fix his thought but the Divine Will and a human will. He has no other formula for a divine-human Christ, then, except the affirmation of the identity of Christ in will with God. " What the believer wishes to assert is not that Christ is manifestly superhuman and so far partially Divine, but that His will, the personal energy which moved in Him, is identically the will of God " (p. 422). " Let men perceive that in Christ there stands before them One who in spiritual being — that is, in will and character — is *identical* " (italics his) " with God Himself, that in Him we have to do with nothing less than the Eternal, and at once it becomes plain that revelation can go no further " (p. 424). Does the deity of Christ consist then merely in the identity of His will with God's? Prof. Mackintosh would deprecate the qualification " merely ": identity of will with God is identity with God, for God is just Will. " If behind all will and thought there exists in God a mysterious incognizable substance, not to be described in terms familiar to human experience, but representing the point through which the thread of cosmic relations passes and constituting the inmost essence of the Divine life, then indeed the oneness of Christ with God " — on the hypothesis that it is a oneness of will — " is after all only relative " (pp. 113 f.). But if will is not " something less and lower than ultimate reality " (p. 113) — then, " if we are inspired by Christian faith to affirm that Jesus Christ is identical with God in will — a Will manifested in His achievement — we have reached a point beyond which no advance is possible; for in ethical terms, the highest terms available, we have affirmed His ontological unity with God in a sense generically different from that which is predicable of man as man " (p. 304). We may " speak," indeed, " loosely of making *our* wills one with God's " (p. 417), and we certainly do not mean that thereby we become really one with God. But this is not all we mean when we speak of Christ's will being one with God's: we do not mean *this* " partially, or intermittently, or by way of metaphor; it is one identically " (p. 417) ; we mean that " the self-conscious active principle of the Son's life " (we interrupt the quotation to ask if this change in terminology is not significant) " subsisted in perfect and identical union with the Father " (p. 417). There can be no doubt, then, that Prof. Mackintosh wishes, under his new point of view, to teach the real deity of Christ, as identity in Will with God. " In every conceivable sense in which this is a *true* estimate of His Person, it also is a metaphysical estimate," he remarks (p. 304), in defense of himself against the reproach that he is teaching a merely (he would object again to the term " merely ") ethical view of Christ's deity. It is another question, however, whether the constructon he offers us really gives us a divine Christ. He himself is constrained to add, immediately after the last quotation we have made from p. 417: " This of course does not carry us once more beyond the moral relations of love and trust; that were to de-ethicise Sonship all over again. What is meant is that these relations must be interpreted at their full value — as significant of truth proper, not mere metaphors — and when we take them so, it appears that essentially (which means not in virtue of some ineffable substance, but in that central Will by which personality is constituted) Christ is one with God." This is a blind saying. If we do not get beyond the moral relations of love and trust in asserting Christ to be one with God, it seems an abuse of language to speak of this union as " essential." And in any case to speak of Christ's

unity with God as a unity not in " substance " (we pass the gratuitous characterisation of this " substance " as " some ineffable substance " as only another instance of Prof. Mackintosh's mannerism)
but only in " Will," has its dangers. We do not affirm that a doctrine
of real incarnation is impossible if spiritual being be defined as just
will; but undoubtedly this ontology presents grave difficulties to
thought in construing the idea of incarnation, and Prof. Mackintosh
does not appear to us to have overcome these difficulties. With all
his manifestly good intentions he may prove to have given us a
Christ who is rather ethically like God than a Christ who is God.

That Prof. Mackintosh has not succeeded in speaking always
in the terms of his ontology is not surprising. To conceive will without a subject of which it is the will is not easy: to speak of it otherwise than as someone's will is impossible. This difficulty is not to
be covered up by contrasting the rival ontologies as " metaphysical " and " ethical " or even as " quantitative " and " qualitative "
conceptions of God. When we are asked to think of God rather as
" Purpose " than as " Infinite Thing or Quantity " (p. 500), or " to
put aside the category ' substance ' and construe the facts freshly
in terms of personality " (p. 334), or to " place the reality of God "
rather in His " will and character " than in an " inscrutable and
unethical substance " (p. 421), or not to assume " that substance
as a category is higher and more adequate than Subject " (p. 416),
it is a poor reader who does not fully understand that there is only
an attempt being made to " rush " his judgment by calling names.
The question is not whether God is to be conceived as a Thing or a
Person, Substance or Subject, but whether He is to be conceived as
Person or mere Attribute, as Subject or mere Activity. When Prof.
Mackintosh equates " Subject " with " intelligent conscious Will,"
and this in turn with " personality, or self-consciousness," he is
only hastily gathering fig-leaves to conceal the nakedness of the
idea of bare Will, which he affirms that God is. How can there be
Will save as the will of some Subject, self-consciousness without a
self to be conscious of itself; and what is an " intelligent conscious
Will " except a short way of saying an intelligent, conscious, voluntary Agent? No doubt Person is the highest of all categories, and
Purpose is the constitutive quality of Person; but we confound
all thought if we wish to make this Purpose the Person rather than
the Person's. To evaporate God into His activities or functions is
simply to abolish God and can end in nothing but Ritschlian phe-

nomenalism. Some of Prof. Mackintosh's historical judgments may illustrate further the difficulties into which his voluntarist ontology may bring him. Expounding Origen's Christology he mentions that father's ascription to the Son of *homoousia* with the Father and then adds (p. 166): " It is quite in harmony with this homoousia that Origen should elsewhere describe the Son as ' begotten of the Father's will,' for in the spiritual realm no contrast exists between will and substance." [3] Again, speaking of Athanasius (p. 188), he remarks: " We should put differently his point that God is Father ' by nature, and not of will,' for to the modern mind will is the very core and essence of personality." A point of view which obliterates the distinction between Arian and Athanasian is certainly a powerful solvent. It is perilous to attempt to construct the doctrine of the Trinity held by any thinker from fragmentary remarks. But it is difficult to understand what sort of a doctrine of the Trinity can be built up on Prof. Mackintosh's postulates, and we have read his final chapter, which is entitled " Christ and the Divine Triunity," without receiving full enlightenment. The one thing he seems to be sure of (cf. also pp. 452–454) is that the eternal distinctions in the Godhead are not, in any very intelligible sense at least, distinct persons.

If the distinct Persons of the doctrine of the Trinity present a difficulty to Prof. Mackintosh's thought which he seems scarcely to know what to do with, the Two Natures of the doctrine of the Person of Christ present to it an impossibility which he knows very well what to do with, and against which he therefore turns his direct polemic (cf. pp. 14, 29, 46, 73, 85, 127, 155–157, 164, 214, 228, 236–237, 293–299, 371). To one who, as Prof. Mackintosh does, acknowledges Christ to be truly God, there would seem no escape from recognizing two natures in the constitution of His person — that is, of course, unless the extremest docetism is embraced and His bodily nature is treated as an illusion. Prof. Mackintosh enunciates, it is true, with apparent approval the proposition, " All that is Divine in Christ is human, and all that is human, Divine " (p. 214); but he will scarcely extend this to our Lord's body. We must suppose his vigorous denial of two natures to Christ to refer

---

[3] The remark is borrowed from Loofs, as a footnote advises us. Loofs (" Leitfaden zum Studium der Dogmengeschichte," ed. 3, 1893, p. 124) writes: " This is not contradicted by the description of the Logos as υἱὸς ἐκ τοῦ θελήματος τοῦ πατρὸς γεννηθείς (citat Justinianus L. XXI, p. 482, note 3), for in the purely spiritual realm ἐκ τοῦ θελήματος and ἐκ τῆς οὐσίας are no contrasts."

therefore only to the spiritual side of His person. Even here, no doubt, he admits that at least an appearance of duality has always been recognized and must be recognized. " He was always viewed as both things — heavenly Divine Spirit, and true man who had suffered and died," he tells us (p. 127). He even writes (p. 85): " As a matter of fact, the duality is simply indissociable from the Christian view of Jesus. Faith is conscious of the personal presence of God in Him; it is therefore inevitable that He should be regarded alike in a Divine or eternal aspect — implying somehow a real pre-existence — and in an aspect for which He fulfils His mission under the conditions of time." But he insists that this duality concerns merely " two *aspects* " (italics his) " of a single concrete life " (p. 295) ; and he fulminates loudly against and cheerfully caricatures what he calls the false " hypostatisation " (it is not precisely the term we should have expected) of these aspects into " distinctly function-ing substantialities which may be logically estimated or adjusted to each other, or combined in unspiritual modes " (p. 295). Thus, he insists, " an incredible dualism " is introduced into our concep-tion of the Person of Christ, which substitutes for " that perfect unity which is felt in every impression of Him " (p. 294) a " formal juxtaposition of abstract natures " (p. 371) that " leaves a pro-foundly disappointing impression of unethical mystery and even, in a sense, duplicity " (p. 294): " no longer one," our Lord is thus " divided against Himself." Moreover, he insists, an impossible impersonal " human nature " is thus assumed to lie back of the personality " enjoying some kind of real being apart from the unify-ing or focal Ego " (p. 295). This is of course mere caricature. The doctrine of the Two Natures does not suppose that there ever existed or ever could exist an impersonal human nature, and never dreamed of attributing any kind of reality to any human nature apart from " the unifying Ego." To say that the denial that the human nature assumed into personal union with Himself by the Logos possessed an *independent* personality, reduces it " in itself " " to unconscious and impersonal elements " (p. 207, cf. pp. 386–387) is only to play with words. No one ever imagined a " human nature " which was or could be " unconscious and impersonal." The con-junction of a human nature with a divine nature in one conscious and personal subject no doubt presents an insoluble problem to thought. But this is just the mystery of incarnation, without which there is no incarnation; for when we say incarnation we say Two

Natures — or can there really be an incarnation without a somewhat which becomes incarnate and a somewhat in which it becomes incarnate? And it is really indisputable (despite Prof. Mackintosh's caveats) that the Two Natures are everywhere presupposed in the New Testament, which simply cannot be interpreted in its allusions to our Lord without their aid, and in which there are passages like Phil. ii. 6, where they are frankly mentioned. The successful explanation of how Christ could be both " of the Israelites as concerning the flesh," and " God over all " (Rom. ix. 5), and yet not of two natures, is a task we do not envy any man who undertakes it. It does not help to this explanation, of course, to declare Christ's humanity only modified deity — the preëxistent Son of God transformed into a man — so that the " Two Natures " are after all but one nature, for that finds the source of His humanity in the bosom of God, whereas Paul finds it in the Israelitish race, or more specifically in the seed of David (Rom. i. 3). We might no doubt take a roundabout way and explain that the Son of God became incarnate only through the mediation of the whole line of our Lord's Israelitish ancestors. It would be hard in that case to be sure to vindicate for Jesus Christ a more express deity than belonged in common with Him to each of the long line through which Luke, let us say, traces Him back to end at last in the words, " which was the Son of God." But if that difficulty were only got over we might explain the rest by serving ourselves with a rather odd formula of which Prof. Mackintosh seems fond (e.g. p. 365, cf. p. 469) and say that thus the incarnation was with Him " immediate, though by no means unmediated." On the whole, however, we think it easier, and in every way more satisfactory, just to follow the New Testament teaching and accept the doctrine of the Two Natures.

Prof. Mackintosh prefers, however, to explain our Lord's humanity as modified deity, and thus comes forward as a belated champion of the Kenotic theories (for references, see Index, *sub voc.* " Kenosis "). He finds what he calls " the profoundest motive operating in the Kenotic theories " — it certainly is the nerve of their appeal to the devout mind — in what he speaks of as " the wondrous nature and subduing magnitude of the Divine sacrifice " (p. 265): " they wished to throw into strong relief the exceeding greatness of the step downwards taken by the Son of God when for our sakes, though rich, He became poor." In this, however, they possess no advantage over the common doctrine. And in the very act of emphasizing this motive Prof. Mackintosh himself seems to allow that the fundamental motive of the Kenotic theories was rather " to signalise the reality and integrity of our Lord's manhood," and elsewhere he more justly explains that " it was precisely the wish to read the divinity of Christ through His true humanity which inspired the Kenotic theories of His person " (p. 421). In point of fact the Kenotic theories owe their origin to a determination to see in Jesus Christ " in the days of His flesh," phenomenally at least, nothing more than a human being; and it is therefore that Albrecht Ritschl described them as merely *verschämter Socinianismus*. It is from this point of view that Prof. Mackintosh takes his start, insisting that Jesus was not merely purely man but a man of His time whose life on earth (we emphasize the telling words) was " a distinctively human phenomenon, moving *always* within the lines of an authentically human mind and will " (p. 400) and indeed, as Dr. Sanday expresses it, " presenting *all* the outward appearance of the life of any other contemporary Galilean " (p. 398). So obvious does Prof. Mackintosh consider this that he even affirms that " were it conceivable that we were forced to choose . . . between the conviction that Jesus preserved true manhood in all its parts, and the assurance that He was the Son of God come in flesh for our salvation, our plain duty would be to affirm His humanity and renounce His deity " (p. 395). Certainly on this ground the Kenotic argument is conclusive, if Jesus is nevertheless held to be God and the doctrine of the Two Natures is discarded. If Jesus is God and nothing but God, and yet on earth was man and nothing but man, why then, of course, it must be that God has been metamorphosed into man; it is a truism that " no human life of God is possible without a prior self-adjustment of deity " (p. 470). This is the whole of the argument which is presented with much elaboration (cf. especially pp. 469–470). The difficulties with it are naturally, that Jesus is not represented in the New Testament — the sole source of our knowledge of His person — as in His essential being God and nothing but God; nor is His life on earth there presented as, in Prof. Mackintosh's sense, " unequivocally human " (p. 469); and the conception of a metamorphosis of God into a man which is assumed is as Albrecht Ritschl declared it to be (" Justification and Reconciliation," E. T. 1900, pp. 409–411) " pure mythology." The particular manner in which this metamorphosis was accomplished in Prof. Mackintosh's opinion was not as supposed by Thomasius,

by the abandonment by the Son of some of His attributes, explained
for the purpose to be merely " relative " (such as His omnipotence,
His omniscience, His omnipresence), while others, designated " immanent " or " essential " (such as His holiness and His love) were
retained; but by the "transposition" or "modification" (both
terms are used) of *all* His attributes (p. 477). The Son, it is explained, continues, as incarnate, to possess " *all* the qualities of
Godhead " (the italics are Prof. Mackintosh's), only now " in the
form of concentrated potency rather than of full actuality, δυνάμει
rather than ἐνεργείᾳ." No explanation is suggested of how, when
God thus ceases to be God, He yet remains God — for does not the
very idea of God involve not only the conception of immutability,
against the emphasis of which Prof. Mackintosh vainly inveighs
as if it were rather immobility, but also the conception embodied
in the Scholastic phrase of " actus purus "? One who is only potentially God is certainly not acually God, as indeed Prof. Mackintosh
naively confesses when he writes the sentence, " What Christ is by
potency, with a potentiality based on His personal uniqueness, God
is actually for ever " (p. 479). God to be God must be all He can be
actually, and He must be all this " actually for ever." When He
ceases to be actually what God is, He ceases of course to be God.
How far Prof. Mackintosh is prepared to press his idea of the reduction of God in Christ is revealed to us startlingly by a phrase let
fall on p. 470: " We are faced by a Divine self-reduction which
entailed obedience, temptation, and death "; and that this is not a
chance inadvertence we may learn from its virtual repetition ten
pages later: " Prayer and death are the seals of His oneness with
us " (p. 480). It must be carefully observed that what is said here
is not that the Divine Subject, by assuming into personal union
with Himself a human nature, became a sharer in the obedience,
temptation, and death, which belong to humanity; but that God
Himself, not by a " fictitious " *communicatio idiomatum* but in His
own Being, obeyed, was tempted, died. God Himself not merely
acquired knowledge slowly and by effort, felt temptation and learned
obedience by that which He suffered, but endured the last indignity
of death! One would question whether Prof. Mackintosh really means
what he says, did he not with such persistence insist that the Infinite
became just finite in Christ, or as he himself expresses it, " descended
into the sphere of finitude " (p. 481). " Only one limit to God's
presence in Him remained," he tells us (pp. 414 f.) — " the limit

of finitude "; so clear is he that Jesus Christ is just a finite being. And yet He is just God! We must confess that Prof. Mackintosh permits to himself language in all such matters which dazes us. He tells us that " it belongs to deity, not indeed to be immutable, but to be eternal " (p. 423), and we mark the statement as giving us at least one stable feature of deity by which we can recognize it when we see it. But we soon read of the " Eternal passing into time," and thereby losing knowledge in the eternal form and requiring to retain it, if He retains it at all, as " discursive and progressive " (p. 477, cf. p. 470) ; and soon afterwards we meet with the declaration that time and eternity are not essentially disparate. If " God and man are not definable as opposites " so also " time is susceptible of eternity " (p. 503) — a declaration the meaning of which we confess is dark to us.

The oddest thing about Prof. Mackintosh's Kenoticism, however, is that he seems to think he has a Biblical basis for it. He does not depend, indeed, " on two or three isolated passages in St. Paul " (p. 469), and it is well he does not, as not even two or three passages suggesting or even allowing it can be discovered. He seems to think that Jesus is dramatized in the Gospel narratives as living an exclusively human life, " moving always " (note the " always " again) " within the lines of an experience humanly normal in constitution, even if abnormal in its sinless quality " (pp. 469 f.). Were this so, it would be very remarkable; for certainly the evangelists did not intend so to depict Him. John assuredly not; and just as assuredly not the Synoptists, as Prof. Mackintosh indeed appears to recognize (p. 5, note 1). And surely it were remarkable that that long line of acute and diligent scholars who for a century and more have been engaged in " the quest of the historical Jesus " have not up to to-day found it out. Then were their long quest over. What a poor showing Prof. Schmiedel, for example, makes, with his meager list of nine " pillar-passages," presenting, as he tells us, an unmistakably human Jesus, and presenting this human Jesus, as he tells us again, in definite *contradiction* to the whole drift of the narrative — if the whole narrative really presents us with nothing but a normally human Jesus! Will Prof. Mackintosh, by a stroke, stultify the whole long, laborious struggle of the Liberal critics — " from Reimarus to Wrede " — to discover a merely human Jesus beneath the narrative of the Gospels? If there is one thing that is certain, it is that the Gospels know nothing, in any of their parts, of a normally human Jesus: their whole effort is to place before us in vivid dramatization a distinctively superhuman Jesus.

We are neither insensible nor unappreciative of the elements of value in Prof. Mackintosh's work. We heartily recognize that its fundamental note is adoration of the divine Saviour. But it must be frankly recognized that its theoretical construction of the doctrine of the Person of Christ is quite impossible. It ought by now to be clearly understood that no resting place can be found in a half-way house between Socinianism and orthodoxy. We cannot have a Christ purely divine in essence and purely human in manifestation. And what on this ground can be made of the exalted Christ? Does He remain after His ascension to heaven the purely human being He was on earth? Or does He, on ascending where He was before, recover the pure deity from which He was reduced that He might enter humanity? In the one case we have no divine Christ, in the other no human Jesus, to-day: and the Christian heart can consent to give up neither. Prof. Mackintosh takes the latter of the alternatives, and greatly magnifies the place of the Resurrection " as a ' crisis ' in the constitution of Christ's person " (pp. 370–371). The exalted Lord in heaven has become as our Saviour indistinguishable from the Father. Is He still man? Prof. Mackintosh wishes us to believe that He is — how, since His humanity belonged to, nay *was,* His humiliation, he does not, he cannot explain. " There is now," he says, " a Person in whom the focus of a human life is become indissolubly one with the last reality of being, so that the heart of man and the heart of God beat in the risen Lord with one pulsing movement, one indistinguishable passion to save and bless " (p. 371). This is rhetoric. In cold fact, the exalted Lord, having laid aside the modifications of deity by virtue of which He entered into the sphere of finite life, has necessarily laid aside His humanity (which was only this modified deity), and that He was once man can be to Him only a memory. Ritschl pointed out that on the Kenotic postulates " Christ, at least in His earthly existence, has no Godhead at all." It requires to be pointed out now that in the form which Prof. Mackintosh gives these postulates, He has in His exalted state no manhood at all — except always His body! Of course Prof. Mackintosh does not wish this result. He strives manfully to escape or at least to gloss it. It is unavoidable. And it is because such results as these are unavoidable on his postulates that we think that these postulates are as unacceptable to truly Christian feeling as they are repugnant to right reason and in contradiction to the whole drift of revelation.

FOUNDATIONS. A Statement of Christian Belief in Terms of Modern Thought. By Seven Oxford Men — B. H. STREETER, R. BROOK, W. H. MOBERLY, R. G. PARSONS, A. E. J. RAWLINSON, H. S. TALBOT, W. TEMPLE. London: Macmillan and Co., Limited. 1913.[1]

THE character of this book is fairly intimated by its title. The "Seven Oxford Men" who have written it describe themselves as young men; and, as young men, they conceive their place to be in the advance-line of progress. They feel their responsibility to the church to which they belong; they are loyal in heart to that church; but they consider that the nature of their responsibility is of a different kind from that of older men. It may be the part of older men to conserve what has been attained; to the younger men belongs the task of leading on to what is yet to be acquired; their responsibility is "the responsibility of making experiments." And the times in which we find ourselves living call loudly for experiments. They are times of transition. The Victorian age is gone; and the assumptions on which Victorian religion was built up have been dissipated. What was thought to be the bed-rock has become shifting sand. A new world has come into being, a new world which is asking questions. The repetition of old answers can serve no purpose. New answers must be framed, and these answers must be couched in the "terms of modern thought." Young men, children of the new age, cannot breathe "the atmosphere of pre-'critical' and pre-Darwinian religion." They think in other terms; they must at least attempt to express what they think in the terms of the thought-world in which they live. And, indeed, to be perfectly frank, if Christianity cannot be expressed in terms of this new thought-world, Christianity is doomed. Men of the time are under the stress of a great obligation, therefore, at least to attempt to pour the old wine of Christianity into the new bottles of modern thought.

Adventuring upon this necessary task of transfusion, our "Seven

[1] *The Princeton Theological Review*, xi. 1913, pp. 526–538.

Oxford Men " present us with nine trial essays. They " do not profess to have covered the whole field." They have confined themselves to the problems which seemed to them the most fundamental, or on which they felt they had something to offer. And they speak modestly of what they offer: it is not put forward as the solution, but only as a contribution towards the solution of the problems they have approached. The nine essays which are given, after a general exposition of the modern situation calling for restatement of fundamental principles, treat in turn of " the Bible," " the Historic Christ," " the Interpretation of the Christ in the New Testament," " the Divinity of Christ," " the Atonement," " the Church," " the Principle of Authority," " God and the Absolute." Probably only a coterie of Anglican writers — among Protestants at least — would have hit upon just this series of topics, when dealing with Christian fundamentals; could have chosen to write of the Church, for example, instead of the Holy Spirit, or could have separated " the Principle of Authority " so far from " the Bible " and attached it so closely to " the Church." Certainly the " Critical " preoccupation is very prominent. And one will naturally wonder how, in this age of Psychological investigation, even so short a series of fundamental problems could be outlined without including a single topic belonging to the subjective life — not Sin, for example, or any of the great stages or steps of the recovery of the soul from sin to holiness. The disclaimer of all pretension to have covered the whole field must no doubt be borne in mind here; as must also the fact that the book is not altogether silent on these great subjects. If they are not made the subjects of separate essays, they come up for discussion incidentally, sometimes for rather full discussion. Sin for instance is discussed as fully as its own proper subject in the essay on " the Atonement," and the essay entitled " the Interpretation of the Christ in the New Testament " is almost a brief sketch of New Testament Theology. Meanwhile the precise series of topics selected for professed discussion is worthy of remark, as is also the order in which they are discussed. Some explanation is given in the brief Introduction of the rather odd postponement of the discussion of the existence of God to the end. This amounts to saying that it was thought best to examine in the light of modern knowledge the actual sources from which Christians have derived their conception of God before the validity of the belief in God itself was brought to the question. This would seem a natural ordering of the material if a negative conclusion all along the line were aimed at; it seems to us an unnatural order since it is a positive conclusion that is aimed at.

No one will doubt that Christians of to-day must state their Christian belief in terms of modern thought. Every age has a language of its own and can speak no other. Mischief comes only when, instead of stating Christian belief in terms of modern thought, an effort is made, rather, to state modern thought in terms of Christian belief. The writers of this volume seem not to have escaped this danger. They are preoccupied with modern thought and appear to suppose that Christianity must be assimilated to it. They open their Introduction by telling us that " Christianity " as well as " its traditional theology " originated in a past of outworn conditions; and they apparently intimate as the condition of the survival of " Christianity " that " its theology " shall not be " out of harmony with science, philosophy, and scholarship." This is, of course, to lay down an impossible condition, if " Christianity " is to be supposed to have any determinate content. For " science, philosophy, and scholarship " are not stable but varying entities, and nothing but a most habile chameleon could manage to keep in harmony with them from age to age. Of course what is meant is our own " science, philosophy, and scholarship " — which seems to be only a naive way of transferring the claim of infallibility from " Christianity " and " its theology " to ourselves. Nothing is more certain, however, than that a " Christianity " and a " theology " which are closely in harmony with the " science, philosophy, and scholarship " of to-day will be out of harmony with the " science, philosophy, and scholarship " of to-morrow. After all, is it not enough to ask that " Christianity " and " its theology " shall be in harmony with truth? And if it is to be in harmony with truth, must it not be out of harmony with all the half-truths, and quarter-truths, and no-truths, which pass from time to time for truth, while truth is only in the making? A " Christianity " which is to be kept in harmony with a growing " science, philosophy, and scholarship," beating their way onward by a process of trial and correction, must be a veritable nose of wax, which may be twisted in every direction as it may serve our purpose.

The question is of course a question of standard. Is our standard Christianity? Or is our standard our own " science, philosophy, and scholarship," that is to say, the congeries of notions which we have taken up as the outcome of the impact upon us of the results of modern investigation, deeply or shallowly, widely or narrowly, understandingly or misunderstandingly assimilated? If we hold Christianity to be true, we shall naturally sit loosely to the " science, philosophy, and scholarship " of any passing moment, so far as it seems to traverse the truth of Christianity, and look forward to the better day when trial and correction shall be over and the unity of truth shall be vindicated by its manifested harmony. If we do not hold Christianity to be true, we shall naturally substitute for it the findings of the momentarily accepted " science, philosophy, and scholarship " as at least provisionally the most likely hypothesis. What is a standing puzzle is why we should wish to call by the name of " Christianity " these provisional findings of our " science, philosophy, and scholarship " substituted for it. If " Christianity " has no stable meaning, the name has no content: it is in the strictest sense of the word an empty name. It is a purely formal designation for whatever may chance in any age or in any company to be the sum of the conclusions presumed for the moment to be commended by " science, philosophy, and scholarship." Coteries at one in nothing save in the lack of the thing, may be at each other's throats in strife over the monopoly of the name. Would it not be better to allow that " Christianity " is a historical entity and has a definite content? And then, when we have drifted away from this historical entity with its definite content, just frankly to acknowledge that we are to that extent no longer " Christians "? That was, for example, what Strauss did. But that is not now the fashion. Men nowadays cheerfully give up the substance, but never the name of Christianity. Rudolf Eucken asks, " Can we still be Christians? " and answers with emphasis, Of course! but the " Christianity " we embrace must be a very different Christianity from that which has hitherto borne the name. So also Ernst Troeltsch declares himself still a " Christian " (a " free Christian "), though his " Christianity " has been so " refashioned " that it has become nothing more than an " immanent theism," the quintessential extract of the religious development of mankind, which still clings to the name of Jesus only because it needs a rallying-point and a name to conjure with. We are not suggesting that the writers of our present volume have drifted away from Christianity as have Rudolf Eucken and Ernst Troeltsch. But we are suggesting that they have in common with such writers the tendency to employ the term " Christianity " to express not a historical entity of fixed content, but just what they may themselves

happen to believe. They have lost to this extent an objective standard of what Christianity is.

How completely they have lost an objective standard of what
Christianity is appears at once from the first essay proper in the
book — that on "the Bible." It is written by Mr. Richard Brook.
Its central contention is that the Bible has no "authority." It is
simply the record of the religious experience of its writers. These
writers were no doubt religious geniuses, and their religious experience is therefore in a sense normative. "We go to the Bible in
order to deepen and correct our religious lives by the aid of the
Biblical writers" (p. 66). "And so I go to the Bible, as others have
gone before me, to learn from those who have heard God speak,
seeking by their help to see the vision they saw, and finding in their
words inspiration and power" (p. 71). In this sense we may still
speak of the "authority" of the Bible. "Yet it still remains true
that the ultimate appeal for each is to his own experience" (p. 59).
The Bible may inspire, it cannot directly instruct: we go to it
specifically for religion, not for, say, theology (p. 68). The theology
of the Bible is necessarily very inadequate: our own may be — one
would think, must be — better: "in some ways our theology may
be more adequate than that of St. Paul" (p. 68). But not our religion. We may, nay must, kindle our flame from Paul's, but we can
interpret the implications of the fire once enkindled in our hearts
better than he could. "We can learn more religion from the humblest
saint," we are told, "than from the greatest theologian" (p. 68), but
this is only half of what is meant to be conveyed to us: the point
is the entire separation of saintliness from theology, and the other
half of the lesson we are expected to draw from the illustration is
that we cannot learn theology even from the greatest saint. For
religion "we may, or rather we must go to St. Paul," for example,
but we may safely neglect his theology. Theology is "the intellectual
interpretation" of religion, and we must needs do our own interpreting, and we feel ourselves better equipped for the task than
Paul was.

Clearly all this rests on a fatally false conception of the relation
of religion and theology. "Theology," we are told crisply, "is the
science of religion" (p. 38). This, however, it of course just is not.
Ex vi verbi it is the science of God. It most decidedly is not "the
reflexion upon religious experience, the attempt to interpret, to
understand and to systematise it." That is what "the science of

religion " is — quite a different thing from " theology." What theology is, is reflection on God and on all that we know concerning God. It is not then the product of religion any more than — or indeed as much as — religion is the product of it. What it precisely is, is the product in the intellect of the same body of facts of which religion is the product in the life: religion and theology are parallel and interactive products of the same body of facts and are too intimately related to be separated (cf. p. 379). One would like to see religion defined without involving theology. Is not religion the reaction of the human spirit in the presence of God? And how is the human spirit to be in the presence of God except by intellectual apprehension? By as much as man is an intelligent being, by that much he cannot react to objects unperceived. Perception, ripening into conception, underlies all religious reaction; and as is the perception ripening into conception, so is the religion. Otherwise we should be committed to the proposition that fetishism is as good a religion as Christianity. For precisely that in which fetishism differs from Christianity is its theology: take away the differences in the conception of deity and you take away the differences in the religious functioning. Mr. Brook is not so far from adopting this view as could be wished. " The same religious experience will be differently interpreted, not only at different times," he reasons in his endeavor to lay a basis for refusal to be governed by the " theology " of the Biblical " writers " (p. 38), " but even by different individuals at the same time. The Professor and the Blacksmith, in so far as they are religious, may have the same religious experience, but their 'theological' views, their 'thoughts' about God, are and must be widely different." Why not, instead of the Professor and the Blacksmith, say the Christian and the Fetishworshiper: *gradus non mutant speciem?* Is it not because the Professor and the Blacksmith are surreptitiously supposed both to be Christians, that is, to have the same " theology " underlying and giving form to their religious experience? In point of fact the Professor and the Blacksmith, though both have religion, will not and cannot have the same religious experience save as they have the same theological conceptions. If one conceives of God as a stock or a stone and the other as an infinite moral person, their religious reaction and the whole complex of their religious experience will be utterly different. Religion, in all its manifestations, waits, like all other human functioning, on the operation of ideas: here too the line of action is from perception, through emotion, to volition. And nothing can be more certain than that if the theology of the Bible is discarded, the religion of the Bible is discarded with it. We shall certainly have religion: we cannot avoid that: man is a religious animal. But our religion will not be the religion of the Bible unless — among other elements of it — our religious conceptions, that is, our theology, be the religious conceptions, that is to say, the theology, of the Bible. It is the gravest kind of self-deception to imagine — to bring the matter to its sharpest point — that we can discard the religious conceptions of Paul, or of Jesus, and remain of the same religion as Paul or Jesus, because forsooth we feel that we too, like them, are religious beings and function religiously. Christianity is not a distinctive interpretation of a religious experience common to all men, much less is it an indeterminate and constantly changing interpretation of a religious experience common to men; it is a distinctive religious experience begotten in men by a distinctive body of facts known only to or rightly apprehended only by Christians.

As this rejection of all external authority in religious conceptions is principial, it should extend to the authority of Christ also. There are indications that it does so. Jesus is declared to have been not only " not formally impeccable " (though " actually sinless ") but also " in nowise exempted from such intellectual limitations, or even (within the spheres of science and history) from such erroneous conceptions of fact, as were inseparable from the use of the mental categories of the age and generation among whom He came " (p. 368). It is even allowed, though guardedly, that His ethical teaching was conditioned by the shortness of His view: " Doubtless had the Master explicitly contemplated the centuries of slow development still awaiting humanity, the actual form and phrasing of many a precept would have been different. Doubtless, too, He would have let fall a word or two on the creative moral value of institutions like the Family and the State " (p. 109). There is even a shocking paragraph in which Jesus' whole view of His work is represented as a " venture of faith," as if it were a speculative invention of His mind to explain " the facts of the world," that is to say, the experiences to which He was subjected: " Because He believes in the goodness of God, Jesus Christ is sure that His death cannot mean either the end of His life or the ruin of His work. His faith leads Him to see in the apparent failure of His ministry the vindication of the teaching of Deutero-Isaiah as to the redemptive value of suffering, and therefore He sees in the Cross the salvation of mankind, and beyond the Cross the triumph of His risen life " (p. 51). " Doubtless," it is added, " this was a venture of faith, but essentially it was a venture which faith was bound to make." No compelling reasons are given why we should feel bound to make the venture with Him; why the theological interpretation of the facts of His life made after this fashion by a man of His " intellectual limitations " should be authoritative to us.

The essay on " the Divinity of Christ " (which is by Mr. William Temple) opens with a couple of sentences which, taken in themselves, announce an important truth, that, duly considered, might correct the tendencies of thought to which we have adverted — though Mr. Temple employs them for quite a contrary purpose. They are: " The central doctrine of Christianity has been made unduly difficult by the way in which believers inevitably tend to state it. It is really a doctrine about God; but it is made to appear as if it were primarily a doctrine about a historic Person, who lived at the beginning of our era." In themselves these words might be taken to mean that in thinking of Christ we should always take our start from His Divine Nature and work out from that as our — as it was His — starting-point: though Mr. Temple himself takes the opposite course. In his attempt to construct a doctrine of the Person of Christ it is from the voluntarist standpoint that Mr. Temple works; and he fails precisely as voluntarists are accustomed to fail, by giving us a Christ who seems to be divine only as one can be said to be divine who is one in purpose with God. It is already ominous that he is constrained to tell us that Paul of Samosata was the first to attempt a construction on this presupposition (p. 226). He hopes to escape the ruin wrought by Paul by refusing to distinguish between Will and Substance (p. 247): to the voluntarist " Will is the only Substance there is in a man; it is not a part of him, it is just himself as a moral (or indeed ' active ') being." It may be doubted, however, whether he really escapes. It does not make Christ God to say that, while His " Will, as a subjective function, is of course not the Father's Will," yet " the content of the Wills — the Purpose — is the same " (p. 248); that " what we see Christ doing and desiring, that we thereby know the Father does and desires." This only makes Christ (so far) like God. And what shall we do with a passage like this (pp. 248 f.): " He is the Man whose will is united with God's. He is thus

the first-fruits of the Creation — the first response from the
Creation to the love of the Creator. But because He is this, He
is the perfect expression of the Divine in terms of human life.
There are not two Gods, but in Christ we see God. Christ is identically God; the whole content of His being — His thought, feeling,
and purpose — is also that of God. This is the only ' substance ' of
a spiritual being, for it is all there is of him at all. Thus, in the
language of logicians, formally (as pure subjects) God and Christ
are distinct; materially (that is in the content of the two conscious-
nesses) God and Christ are One and the Same. The human Affections
of Christ are God's Affections; His Suffering is God's; His Love is
God's; His Glory is God's." This is undoubtedly to exalt Christ:
does it exalt Him as more than the greatest of the sons of men?
Is it not an illusion to suppose that thus the true deity of Christ
is vindicated? Let us assume whatever ontology of spiritual being
we choose: let us declare that Will is the essence of spirit — if that
is not a contradiction in terms. But let us not suppose that thus we
abolish the distinction between distinct Subjects. That the contents
of Christ's will is the " same " as the contents of God's will, His
purpose the " same " as God's purpose, does not identify Him with
God. If it did, then, when two men " have the same thought or the
same purpose " they would be " merged into one another "; and it
is not enough to say, in order to escape this, that the identity in
their case " extends to a very small part of the content of consciousness, while in the case " of Christ and God, " it extends to the whole "
(p. 250). We are in danger here of juggling with the ambiguities of
" identical," whether as *homoousios* or *homoiousios*. To justify the
position taken it would seem that one must accept the postulate that
all spirit is one, and individualization is the result only of differences
in the " content " of that will which constitutes its being. When the
" content " — the " purpose " — becomes one, the artificial (and
temporary) barriers are broken down and spirit becomes confluent.
Unless this pantheism is permitted to lie unacknowledged behind our
thought, to speak of Christ as identical with God in content of will —
in purpose — does not seem to be to speak of Him as divine.

It is part of the " modernness " of these essays that they are very
chary in acknowledging the occurrence in our Lord's life — or in the
origins of Christianity in general — of what we have been accustomed to call miracles. More than one of the writers carefully define
miracles away. " The best definition of a miracle," we read (p. 167,

cf. p. 138) " is that it is something which when we are confronted
by it compels us to say, ' This is the Lord's doing, and it is marvellous in our eyes ': it is no less marvellous if after our first sense
of wonder has calmed down we are enabled to see a little further
into the divinely-ordered process by which the event was brought
about." The Virgin-birth is not discussed (cf. p. 81). The Resurrection is elaborately explained away by Mr. B. H. Streeter (pp.
127–141) in the interests of the " objective vision hypothesis," and
while it is obvious that some of his colleagues agree with him, we
are glad to learn (p. 135) that not all of them do. Mr. Streeter can
even say (p. 132) : " I know of no living theologian who would maintain a physical *Ascension* in this crude form, yet so long as emphasis
is laid on the physical character of the *Resurrection* it is not obvious
how any refinement of the conception of ' physical ' really removes
the difficulty." He is certainly right in thus bringing together the
Ascension and Resurrection — both are physical or neither is: and
we think him right in declaring that if they are in any sense physical
no refinement of the conception of " physical " will help. In the
meanwhile it must be borne in mind that the totality of the testimony is to a physical resurrection. There is not only the empty
tomb, which Mr. Streeter but lamely accounts for; but the whole
account of the resurrection appearances, culminating in the explicit
declaration of our Lord recorded in Luke xxiv. 39 (of which Mr.
Streeter makes no use), is to be reckoned with — as well as Paul's
clear exposition that our resurrection-bodies which are to be like
Christ's are veritable " bodies " and are composed of " flesh "
(I Cor. xv. 39, 40).

Where the conception of the Person of Christ is so inadequate
the conception of His Work is not likely to be less so. We are not
surprised to find accordingly that only a " subjective " Atonement is
admitted by some of the writers. This seems to be the position of
Mr. Temple. In the essay on " the Atonement," which is by Mr.
W. H. Moberly, however, a somewhat higher doctrine is taught —
the doctrine developed by Dr. R. C. Moberly in his well-known
and powerfully reasoned " Atonement and Personality," in which
penitence is made to do the work of expiation and Christ's work is
summed up in vicarious penitence, whatever that can be. Mr.
Moberly accordingly speaks of " moral transformation " as if it
could " constitute an atonement for sins," that is, as if, " in removing
the cause of estrangement " it removed, " as it were automatically,

the estrangement between God and man " (p. 293). He recognizes indeed that man's own penitence would be inadequate; not, he adds, " because it is *merely* penitence (*i.e. only* a change of character), but because it is *incomplete* penitence (*i.e.* only a *partial*, and therefore very probably a transitory, change of character) " (p. 295). Thus we escape out of a purely " subjective " atonement — which is a blessing. But all that is offered objectively is a vicarious penitence of Christ, which is perfect and complete — not indeed in itself but in and with its effect in inducing penitence in us: " vicarious penitence is only redemptive when it succeeds in becoming more than vicarious " (p. 310). So firmly grounded is Mr. Moberly in his theory that he even permits himself to write: " if vicarious penitence is unmeaning and impossible, the problem of atonement is insoluble; for penitence that is not vicarious, the unsupported penitence of the sinner himself, is never complete or whole-hearted " (p. 308) — from which we learn that not only in his view *can* penitence atone, but *only* penitence can atone! Having referred the atoning efficacy in Christ's work thus to His " vicarious penitence," Mr. Moberly is naturally greatly embarrassed in having Christ's death on his hands, to which, rather, the New Testament writers — and indeed Christ Himself — as well as the historical Church refer it. After some pages of discussion he arrives at the point where, as he says, " we can dimly see how the fact of sin and the requirements of holiness made it necessary that Jesus should die " (p. 313)! The method of Mr. Moberly's essay (a method we do not like) is to set over against each other the " liberal " and the " conservative " views and to seek an " inclusive " view as presumably better than either. It is noticeable that in stating the " conservative " view there is repeated intrusion of elements drawn not from the doctrine of Satisfaction as expounded by the great teachers of the Church, but from the Grotian or Governmental Theory (pp. 288, 302, 305). The " conservative " view thus does not get a fair hearing, and is made the object of criticisms which do not touch it. As the essay draws to its close Mr. Moberly addresses himself to answering some objections which seem to lie against the whole idea involved in the Christian doctrine of the Atonement. Among them he raises this one — that provision is made by it for only a fraction of the human race (p. 331). " How can we possibly believe in a divine scheme of salvation for the human race which ' leaves whole continents out of its ken ' ? " In other words, if Christ is the Saviour of the world, must He not save the world? Mr. Moberly acknowledges that he has "no complete answer" to this objection, but he thinks he can "see the direction in which an answer is to be sought." This answer is, in brief, that we do not need to know Christ to be Christ's, supplemented by the suggestion that Christ can do His saving of the world in the next world (p. 332)! The Scriptures, it is needless to say, have a very different answer. We infer that Mr. Temple agrees in principle with his colleague here, from the circumstance that we find him endeavoring from a wrong point of view to grasp the idea of the "invisible Church," putting into it the heathen sages also, "each in his degree" — whatever that may mean (p. 341).

It is in dithyrambic strains that Mr. Temple speaks of the Church, making use at times of forms of speech to which it is difficult to attach an exact meaning. Some particularly remarkable results are attained by his endeavor to give to language struck out originally from a view of the Eucharist which he does not share, validity from his new point of view as to the "sacrifice of Christ." Jesus is veritably in the Eucharist as beauty is in a great picture, though it is not every eye which can see Him there. "His sacrifice is perpetual": once only in the history of men has its whole nature been set forth, "but the sacrifice itself, which is His obedience and the submission of His will, is eternal" (p. 344). There is a devotion and a mystical ecstacy which is altogether admirable throbbing through his words, but the fire which glows in them has not been kindled at Calvary. Noble words are spoken about the communion of the saints into which we enter at the Eucharist (pp. 343 f.): our hearts are quickened by the vision which is summoned up of the saints of all ages gathered with us around the table of the Lord, participants with us in the body that was broken and the blood that was shed for us. But the underlying thought is not that of the altar. There seems to be something bizarre in suggesting that the phrase which calls the Church "the Body of Christ" is "probably taken from the Eucharist" (p. 340, cf. p. 185). Surely "This is my body" refers to Christ's literal, not figurative body — to Christ, that is, not to His disciples. They did not eat themselves in symbol! The latter part of the essay on the Church is filled with shrewd good sense, and exhibits a clear perception of the nature and value of Church unity.

In Mr. Rawlinson's essay on "the principle of Authority" a careful comparison is made between various views. It is a pity that

Congregationalism is taken as the proper representative of Protestantism in the matter of Church organization and authority. It is as insular as Anglicanism itself: and has no existence outside of lands of English speech. A world-wide polity like Presbyterianism would have afforded a much truer representative type. Take for example the idea of " the invisible Church." If the twenty-fifth chapter of the Westminster Confession — or its parallel in any of the representative Reformed confessions — had been in Mr. Rawlinson's mind he could scarcely have written as he has written on pp. 394–395, 404. In the very interesting discussion of the origin of the Christian ministry which is attached to this essay the ordinary confusions into which Anglican writers of liberal tendencies fall are not escaped. When Mr. Rawlinson says that the " ministry appears to have very early assumed the form of a bishop, presbyters, and deacons to each eucharistic assembly," he seems unaware that, though he defines the individual church in different terms from those that would be natural to a Presbyterian, he has described precisely the Presbyterian polity. When he goes on to say that " the modern diocese is virtually an expansion of the primitive congregation by means of the delegation to presbyters of functions originally episcopal " (p. 422), he is very lightly springing wide chasms. The bishop, the presbyter, the deacon — and the officering of the local church — have each and every one of them suffered a sea-change which has transmuted them into something different from what they are, say, in the Pastoral Epistles — which Mr. Rawlinson, by the way, treats with strange neglect. From a " pastor " of a congregation, the Bishop has become the ruler over many congregations. The Presbyter has ceased to be a co-ruler with the Bishop; and shrinking from a plurality in each congregation to a singularity, has become a pastor. The Deacon from " a server of tables " has lost all connection with the local church and become an inchoate Presbyter. The local church instead of possessing a Bishop, a college of Presbyters, and a college of Deacons, has left to it only a single Presbyter. In other words from Presbyterian the church has become Episcopal — and that is a total transformation.

The final essay, — on " God and the Absolute " — by Mr. W. H. Moberly, is the longest in the volume, and while very able is also very unsatisfying. It is in effect an attempt to interpret the doctrine of God in terms of the absolutist philosophy. It with difficulty escapes sheer pantheism, if indeed it does escape it. It is a hard saying

to be told that " God Himself must be religious " (p. 512), even
though this is transmuted into the declaration that, being a Trinity,
He " can know God." It is a harder one to be told that " the union
of God and man is necessary to the full reality of either " (cf.
p. 520), or that God could not still remain God without creation,
incarnation, and atonement (p. 511). It is perhaps even a still harder
one to be told that " the world and its history is essential to the very
Life and Being of God " (cf. p. 341).

Throughout the whole volume there is apparent a spirit of
readiness to weigh and appreciate points of view other than that
which may be thought hereditary with its authors. What is more
remarkable, this open-mindedness is manifested not merely towards
what is commonly known as " liberalism " but also towards what
is known in average Anglican circles as " sectarianism." For party-
spirit apparently dies more hardly than Christian principle. We have
known men who were cheerfully willing to give up the deity of
Christ but not baptism by immersion alone; and latitudinarian Anglicanism has perhaps been more common than a truly tolerant one:
even our modern " Evangelicals " are solicitous to be understood to
be " good churchmen." No one would mistake the writers of this
volume for anything but Anglicans. There are indications that they
might even be classed as " High Anglicans ": Mr. Temple for example pleads for prayers for the dead and the invocation of saints
(p. 346) ; and remnants show themselves here and there of that smug
self-felicitation on the position of Anglicanism midway between
Romanism and Protestantism, which betrays so many Anglicans into
the notion that the coming unity of Christendom must crystallize as
Anglican. But few books have emanated of late from Anglican
circles in which is manifested a greater readiness to consider the
positions of writers of other communions of Christian men, or to
weigh afresh the distinctive contentions of traditional Anglicanism.
We take it that a remark like the following is typical of the general
mental attitude of the volume. " In its strictest and most traditional
form the theory of an original Apostolic succession has perhaps
broken down; but the liberalized restatement of it, which is to be
found in the writings of Duchesne and Batiffol abroad and the
present Bishop of Oxford at home, is at least a tenable interpretation
of the evidence as viewed in the light of certain antecedent presuppositions " (p. 383). We may think it still too much to say even
so much as this, and question whether the view still clung to is com-

patible with the facts. But we recognize the openness of mind which is manifested in the position assumed. And this, we take it, is the most encouraging feature of the volume.

We have dealt with the volume not as a collection of separate essays but as a single whole, because we are asked to do so (p. viii.). There is a good Index.

MYSTICISM. A Study in the Nature and Development of Man's Spiritual Consciousness. By EVELYN UNDERHILL. London: Methuen and Co., Ltd. [1911.]

THE MYSTIC WAY. A Psychological Study in Christian Origins. By EVELYN UNDERHILL. London and Toronto: J. M. Dent & Sons, Ltd. 1913. New York: E. P. Dutton & Co.

IMMANENCE. A Book of Verses. By EVELYN UNDERHILL. London: J. M. Dent & Sons, Ltd. New York: E. P. Dutton & Co. [1912.]

THE MIRACLES OF OUR LADY SAINT MARY: brought out of divers tongues and newly set forth in English. By EVELYN UNDERHILL. New York: E. P. Dutton & Co. 1906.[1]

THE primary object of this notice is to give some account of Miss Underhill's " The Mystic Way," in which she formally presents her views of the origin and nature of Christianity. We have associated with this book in the heading, however, the titles of such others of Miss Underhill's publications that have come into our hands as are serious in form, in order that " The Mystic Way " may be seen in its setting. We should not like to suggest that Miss Underhill's novels by which she has been previously known — " The Grey World," 1904, " The Lost Word," 1907, " The Column of Dust," 1909 — were written without serious purpose or are without significance as disclosures of her mind and of the direction of her studies. On the contrary they already reveal to us the intensity of her engagement with what is loosely called the mystical aspects of life, and no doubt embody, in an imaginative form, much of what she would consider symbolically at least wholesome instruction for our sense-preoccupied world. In " The Grey World " we are told how the neurotic son of a London tailor, dying in a hospital, catches

a glimpse, as he passes through it to his next incarnation, of that
" grey world " which lies behind this, and lived in consequence
throughout his next earthly life with the curtain which hides that
world from our view worn rather thin. It is a Dean's son, who is
the hero of " The Lost Word "; and we are shown in it how, brought
into intimate contact from his earliest years with the symbolism
and mysterious romance of a great cathedral, he found his way,
despite the insistent pull of earthly passion, into dimly apprehended
relations with an unseen permanent existence where he held communion with the great artistic spirits of the past. In " The Column
of Dust " we learn how a bookseller's clerk in London summons a
spirit, who, however, refusing to be used by her, uses her rather,
and how out of it all sacrificial love comes to its rights. In all
three alike Miss Underhill seeks her inspiration in præternatural
themes, and manifests a profound preoccupation with the supernatural, not to say the morbid, phases of life. From these novels
alone we might assure ourselves that here is a writer who is ready to
insist seriously that there are more things, not in heaven merely but
here on earth, than are dreamed of in our starveling five-senses
philosophy: and indeed that the most real things which surround
us are not those which we touch with our clumsy fingers and gaze
at with our dull eyes and taste with our gross tongues. It is not a
matter of surprise that such a writer should come forward at length
as a serious eulogist of Mysticism.

Among Miss Underhill's serious writings we need not delay long
over her little volume of verses. In the greater number of the pieces
included in it an attempt is made to give expression to mystical
moods. These do not seem to us the most successful. Strange to say
Miss Underhill's muse does not appear to move easily in such moods.
We quickly gain the impression also that verse is not her most happy
medium of expression. There are some lofty conceptions; there is
much fine language; here and there a well-turned phrase meets us;
we can smile at a conceit like that embodied in " The Idol "; we can
respond to the stirring counsel of " Memento, Homo "; we can thrill
with the grim lesson of " The Backward Glance." But the volume
leaves us cold — and uninstructed. Little more need be said of the
collection of " The Miracles of Our Lady Saint Mary." For all that
appears on the surface, a purely literary motive might have presided over its production. Here is a byway of mediæval literature
but little trodden by recent feet. Not merely students but amateurs

" of mediæval manners and Christian mythology " may find interest in exploring it. Certainly Miss Underhill has done her work well and made this sufficiently dreary series of folk-stories and hagiographs as attractive as possible. There is a sentence near the close of the brief but competent Introduction, however, which may suggest that she may have had a deeper than a merely literary purpose in seeking to give new life to the Mary-legends. Speaking of the mediæval attitude towards the Virgin she remarks upon the " simple and familiar friendship, mystical adoration, and unfailing trust " which were given to " Goddes Moder and oures " by those who, as she phrases it, " were in every sense her children." And then she adds that it is " the aim of this book " " to drag back," not only the " literary expression " of this sentiment " from the shadow-land to which it has retreated," but the " sentiment " itself. May we infer that Miss Underhill has had, then, a directly religious motive in seeking to revive the knowledge of the Mary-legends?

It is not altogether easy to make quite sure of Miss Underhill's precise religious standpoint. On the basis of her two solid works on Mysticism alone — which embrace her professed contribution to religious discussion — we might readily think of her as a Modernist Romanist. We do not suppose we do her injustice at any rate in imagining her in congenial society when in the company of, say, Friedrich von Hügel or George Tyrrell. Many of their points of view she certainly holds in common with them; some of their suggestions she works out in detail; and, if we mistake not, the ultimate issue of her religious thought is very much theirs — perhaps, we may add, in somewhat extreme expression. The whole argument of the work which is more especially in our mind as we write — " The Mystic Way " — might be represented as the detailed explication of a tendency apparent in von Hügel (it is no doubt present in more or less strength in all Mystical writers), to which Söderblom calls sharp attention — the tendency, we mean, to think of Jesus as only a high-point in the religious development of humanity, which attracts the eye of men and to which we must also aspire, while there is withheld from Him all truly creative effects on the religious life of the world. Perhaps it is not right to hold George Tyrrell too closely to everything he wrote in even the last years of his singularly ununified career. But he seems to have meant it seriously when in the early days of the last year of his life he declared: " Houtin and Loisy are right, the Christianity of the future will consist of mysticism and charity, and possibly the Eucharist in its primitive form as the outward bond: I desire no better." Perhaps even Mysticism no doubt seemed to him something less than solid ground: " Mystics think they touch the divine," he explains in one of his moods of scepticism, " when they have only blurred the human form with a cloud of words." The precise effect of Miss Underhill's discussion of " The Mystic Way," in any event, is to place her in the same category with Houtin and Loisy and Tyrrell as here expounded. She reduces Christianity to simple Mysticism.

The background of the volume called " The Mystic Way " is provided by Miss Underhill's *magnum opus,* the elaborate volume on " Mysticism." This volume is brilliantly written. All the resources of a trained literary art are expended upon it, and its pages are not only illuminated with numerous well-chosen extracts from the Mystical writers who are thus permitted to tell in their own quaint and often singularly impressive language exactly what they are, but are also gemmed with vivid phrases caught from the Mystics and used by Miss Underhill in her own composition with exquisite skill. Above all it is written with a verve and enthusiasm which impart to it an *élan* (as Miss Underhill would call it, in deference to Bergson) that sweeps the reader well-nigh off his feet. It is divided into two parts, called respectively " The Mystic Fact " and " The Mystic Way," in the former of which an attempt is made to tell what Mysticism is in contrast with other tendencies, while in the latter the several steps and stages of the Mystical process are described in detail. The effect is that we have what Mysticism is elaborately explained to us twice over, and one would think it must be the reader's own fault if he rises from the book without a clear conception of exactly what it is that Miss Underhill at least would have him think Mysticism to be. It is an indication of the fluidity of the notion — perhaps also of the almost incurable ambiguities of the current usages of the term — that one requires, even so, to pause and consider before he is quite sure of the precise limits of the sense in which Miss Underhill employs it.

Formal definition of the term begins for us already in the Preface. " Broadly speaking," we read there (p. x.), " I understand it to be the expression of the innate tendency of the human spirit towards complete harmony with the transcendental order; whatever be the theological formula under which that order is understood." This is " broadly speaking " indeed. By the final clause, Mysticism is at once separated from all " positive religions " whatever; and (as we are immediately told) it is made matter of indifference to the experience of " mystic union " in which it " attains its end," whether that union is conceived to be with " the God of Christianity, the World-Soul of Pantheism, the Absolute of Philosophy " (p. x.). " Attempts to limit mystical truth — the direct apprehension of the Divine Substance — to the formulae of any one religion," we are accordingly told later (p. 115), " are as futile as the attempt to identify a precious metal with the die which converts it into current coin." It is upon the little word " innate," however, that the hinge of the definition turns. Mysticism is " the expression of the *innate* tendency of the human spirit towards complete harmony with the transcendental order." In other words it is " natural " religion; and it is therefore that it is quite independent of all possible conceptions of that " only Reality," which is here called " the transcendental order." Let philosophers call it " the Absolute "; let theologians call it " God "; think of it as Personal Spirit, think of it as the impersonal ground of Being, think of it how you choose: the human spirit moves by its own intrinsic gravitation towards it, and this gravitation towards it is Mysticism. Obviously " Mysticism " is used here as but a name for the inherent native religiosity of the human spirit.

Subsequent formal definitions advance us but little beyond this. Thus, for example, when at a later point Miss Underhill is again (as in the Preface) animadverting upon the loosenesses of the current usages of the term, she emerges with this crisp assertion (p. 86): " Mysticism, in its pure form, is the science of ultimates, the science of union with the Absolute, and nothing else." She does indeed go on to declare that " the mystic is the person who attains to that union, not the person who talks about it "; that it is not a matter of " knowing about " but " Being " (she spells it with a big B); but she seems already to have closed that question by defining it as " science " — for " science " is " knowing about " *ex vi verbi*. When, among sciences, she declares Mysticism to be this particular science, namely, " the science of ultimates," she seems to identify it with what we are accustomed to call Metaphysics; but that she can scarcely mean this is manifest from the parallel phrase which she immediately adjoins: " the science of union with the Absolute " — for certainly Metaphysics is not that. What is apparently meant to be asserted is that Mysticism is the systematized knowledge of "union with the Absolute"; or, since the emphasis is thrown on the practical side, perhaps we may say (as we speak of "pugilistic science") that Mysticism is expertness, acquired skill in attaining "union with the Absolute."

Accordingly as this discussion approaches its end Miss Underhill reformulates her definitions thus (p. 97): "Mysticism, then, is not an opinion: it is not a philosophy. It has nothing in common with the pursuit of occult knowledge. It is not merely the power of contemplating Eternity. It is the name of that organic process which involves the perfect consummation of the Love of God: the achievement here and now of the immortal heritage of man. Or, if you like it better — for this means exactly the same thing — it is the art of establishing his conscious relation with the Absolute." What was formerly declared to be a "science" has now become explicitly an "art": but in varying the term we do not escape from the thing — behind the "art" the "science" necessarily lies. Miss Underhill says the Mystic is the man who has attained to union with the Absolute. Let us be more modest and say that the Mystic is the man who professes, or supposes himself, to have attained to union with the Absolute. Then Mysticism surely may be fairly described as that congeries of notions which are presupposed or implicated in this profession; or, if we choose, in the practice of the art by which this end is supposed to be attained. It would seem, therefore, that it must inevitably embrace a doctrine of the Absolute; a doctrine of the relation of the human spirit to this Absolute; a doctrine of the possibility of the human spirit attaining "union with the Absolute"; a doctrine of the nature of this "union with the Absolute" which the human spirit may attain. Here certainly there is "an opinion," or rather a body of opinions; and certainly there is here "a philosophy," and, we are afraid we shall have to add, what, despite the vagueness which may be allowed to cling to the several notions involved, looks very much like that specific philosophy which we know as Pantheism. It is notorious that in the history of religious thought the types which it has been commonly agreed to speak of as Mystical have ordinarily been associated with Pantheistic or at least Pantheizing conceptions: the very language of Mysticism has been dictated to it by Pantheism, and it is therefore in any event difficult for the Mystic to express himself without at least seeming to declare himself a Pantheist. Miss Underhill has reduced this Pantheizing implication to a minimum in her formal

definitions. Therefore in the one now before us she avoids even
declaring that Mysticism is the "science of union with the Absolute." Instead, she says that it is the process by which man enters
into the conscious enjoyment of the love of God — by which, she
truly says, he " achieves " " his immortal heritage ": and in the
alternative clause she explains that what Mysticism seeks is
the establishment of " conscious relation with the Absolute." Obviously these are carefully chosen phrases. If we were to abide by the
breadth of their suggestion Mysticism would be what indeed Miss
Underhill calls it (p. x.), just " the science or art of the Spiritual
life." Every " other-worldly-minded " man would be a Mystic.

Clearly Mysticism, however, is not defined by merely declaring
that it is the " art of establishing conscious relation with the Absolute." Its peculiarity resides rather in the nature of the process by
which it seeks this end and the nature of the condition in which,
when it is achieved, it finds this end accomplished. There are other
views proposed to us of what " the immortal heritage of man "
consists in, and of how it may be achieved. There is, to go no further,
Christianity, which thinks that it can point the way to the enjoyment of " the perfect consummation of the Love of God," and finds
the Way in Christ. Mysticism is not sufficiently defined by simply
declaring that it differs from all these by — " doing the trick."
Many have essayed to penetrate to " the Reality behind the veil,"
says Miss Underhill (p. 4) : " but if we may trust the reports of the
mystics — and their reports are given with a strange accent of certainty and good faith — they have succeeded where all these others
have failed, in establishing immediate communication between the
spirit of man, entangled as they declare amongst material things,
and that ' only Reality,' that immaterial and final Being, which some
philosophers call the Absolute, and most theologians call God."
It is a great claim — if only it can be substantiated. Its substantiation is, however, the last thing the Mystic seems to think of. " We
have seen," writes Wilhelm Fresenius (" Mystik und geschichtliche
Religion," 1912, p. 82), " how the Mystic has never posited the
question of the substantiation of religion, has never made inquiry
into its moral right, into its truth, but his soul has been filled with
the search after the experience of the Eternal. And when he has
found this Eternal, when he has felt this Imperishable, then he is
content, the fact of this feeling establishes for him its right. Why
does the question not now spring forth of the ' How ' of this feeling,

the investigation into whether this feeling may not rest on illusion —
that is, in the forum of the moral judgment? " So soon, however, as
the substantiation of its great claims is seriously attempted Mysticism, it is evident, must emerge from vague phrases and define
itself sharply in its method and aim. It is unfortunate, then, that in
her definitions Miss Underhill falls into the very common habit
of using to describe it terms so wide that they provide no differentiation at all. How persistently this bad method is followed by writers
on the subject may be illustrated by the definition given by O. C.
Quick in two recent articles in the *Journal of Theological Studies.*
" Mysticism," he says, " is the claim made by the soul to the apprehension of a wider reality in no sense mediated by the data of
sense-perception " (xiv. 1913, p. 2; cf. xiii. 1912, p. 164). If that
were an adequate definition, Mysticism would be merely spiritual
apprehension: and all who believe in the accessibility of spirit to
spirit would be Mystics. Even William James's well-known definition (" The Varieties of Religious Experience," 1902, p. 508) is
better — for at least it is discriminating. He finds the " nucleus of
agreement " among all Mystics in the feeling of the subject that
his higher self is " conterminous and continuous with a More of the
same quality, which is operative in the universe outside of him,
and which he can keep in working touch with, and in a fashion get
on board of and save himself when all his lower being has gone to
pieces in the wreck." Clearly on this conception Mysticism is
fundamentally Pantheistic, and therefore Quick criticizes it. It is
not inclusive, he says, of Christian Mysticism through which there
runs a profound feeling of " infinite otherness " from God; and he
goes on to insist that Mysticism embraces every and " any direct
consciousness of God's presence and nature " (*Journal of Theological
Studies,* xiii. 1912, p. 172). By thus broadening the skirts of Mysticism to enclose all " sense " of God, we may of course rid it of
its Pantheistic stamp; but the question is whether we are not merely
merging it thus into a wider category. What it concerns us to take
note of here, however, is merely that this is Miss Underhill's method.
To her the typical form of Mysticism is Christian Mysticism, as
manifested especially in the great Mediæval Saints. She is therefore
careful to define it so as to make it include them; and she then
proceeds to expound it from them as its purest examples.[2] This

---

[2] Perhaps G. Siedel, " Die Mystik Taulers nebst einer Erörtering über der
Begriff der Mystik," 1911, has fallen into the same trap. " Tauler's Mysticism,"

seems to stand the whole matter upon its head. It is not in virtue
of their Christianity that the Christian Mystics are Mystics: Miss
Underhill, as we have seen, herself allows that their Mysticism is
quite independent of their Christianity. We might better say that
it is in despite of their Christianity; and that therefore Mysticism in them is modified by their Christianity just so far as their
thought and practice is determined by their Christianity. They are
Mystics not by virtue of what they have in common with other
Christians, but by virtue of what they have in common with other
Mystics — with Al Ghazzali, say, for instance, or with 'Attar and
Sadi and Jalálu'd Din, or to sum it all up in one word, say, with
Plotinus. And what they have in common with these other Mystics
is precisely Pantheizing tendencies of thought. Miss Underhill would
have us believe that Mysticism appears always in the train of great
periods of abounding culture; it is the consummate flower of human
culture (p. 541). We think it truer to say that it appears always in
the train of periods of the dominance of a Pantheizing philosophy:
it is the effect in the religious mind of prevalent Pantheizing thought.

Miss Underhill allows (though this is far from all that she
allows) that the Mystics at least speak the language of Plotinus
(p. 544). So true is this, that even she, though set upon cleansing
the idea of Mysticism from the smudge of Pantheism (e.g. pp. 38,
119), yet herself speaks the language of Plotinus, if indeed she stops
with that. Though she may on occasion therefore insist that in his
achieved " union with the Absolute," the Mystic does not lose his
identity in God, but " in the Mystic this union is conscious, personal
thought "; and even indeed that what the Mystic " calls ' Union with
God ' is only his utter identification with the interests of the spiritual life " — she naturally cannot maintain this point of view, and
everywhere lapses into language with quite other implications. For,
as Fresenius (*op. cit.*, pp. 50–51) reminds us, it is of the very essence
of Mysticism to maintain the immediate presence of the divine in

---

he tells us (p. 130), " is the assurance, obtained through a particular discipline,
that the Divine Subject has entered into the human subject, expressed philosophically by means of the Thomist-scholastic doctrine of the vision of the
essence of God, experienced in a Christian way as the assumption of man into
the intertrinitarian life of God." Assuming Tauler to be the purest example
of a Mystic he asserts that the universal " formula of the only right and
possible idea of Mysticism " is " the revival (*Aufleben*) of another subject in
man " (p. 129).

man, needing only to be recognized and felt; and it is therefore that it is by the way of " contemplation " that the Mystic bids us seek and find God. Miss Underhill herself tells us that " the whole claim of the Mystics ultimately depends on man's possession of pure being in ' the spark of the soul ' " (p. 119, note 4) — " pure being " being but a synonym for the Absolute. Accordingly she tells us that there is a point " where Subject and Object, desirous and desired, are *one* " (p. 86). Or more elaborately: " That there is an extreme point at which man's nature touches the Absolute: that his ground, or substance, his true being, is conterminous with the Divine Life which constitutes the underlying reality of things; this is the basis on which the whole Mystic claim of possible union with God must rest " (pp. 65–66). And again: " The Mystics find the basis of their method not in logic but in life: in the existence of a discoverable ' real,' a spark of true being, within the seeking subject which can, in that ineffable experience which they call the ' act of union,' fuse itself with and thus apprehend the reality of the sought Object. In theological language, their theory of knowledge is that the spirit of man, itself essentially divine, is capable of immediate communion with God, the One Reality " (p. 28).

That in this " ineffable experience " called " the act of union," something more is achieved than merely the identification of our- selves " with the interests of the spiritual life " — something very much like the identification of ourselves with God — emerges from such statements as the following: " All pleasurable and exalted states of Mystic consciousness in which the sense of I-hood persists, in which there is a loving and joyous relation between the Absolute as object and the self as subject, fall under the head of Illumination " (p. 282). " The real distinction between the Illuminative and the Unitive life is that in Illumination the individuality of the subject — however profound his spiritual consciousness, however close his com- munion with the Infinite — remains separate and intact " (p. 295). " No doubt there were hours in which St. Catherine's experience, as it were, ran ahead; and she felt herself not merely lit up by the Indwelling Light, but temporally [temporarily?] merged in it. . . . Her normal condition of consciousness, however, was clearly not yet that which Julian of Norwich calls being ' oned with bliss '; but rather an intense and continuous communion with an objective Reality which she still felt to be distinct from herself. . . . Cath- erine, then, is still a spectator of the Absolute, does not feel herself to be *one* with it " (p. 297). Clearly, then, when the " Unitive Life " itself is attained it is no longer a mere " communion " with the Absolute, but in some more intimate sense a " union " with it, by virtue of which the " oneness " of the two is experienced as a fact.

That the achievement of this union with the Absolute should be represented by some Mystics at least (p. 496) as "deification " can occasion no surprise. These Mystics certainly do not bate their breath when they speak of it: Miss Underhill herself calls their language with respect to it " blunt and positive " (p. 501). " If we are to allow," she writes, however, " that the Mystics have ever attained the object of their quest, I think we must also allow that such attainment involves the transmutation of the self to that state which they call, for want of exact language, ' deified.' The necessity of such transmutation is an implicit of their first position: the law that ' we behold that which we are, and are that which we behold.' Eckhart, in whom the language of deification assumes its most extreme form, justifies it upon this necessity. ' If,' he says, ' I am to know God directly, I must become completely He and He I: so that this He and this I become and are one I ' " (p. 502). It is easy to point out that these same Mystics nevertheless protest that by this transmutation the creature does not really become God; and that others prefer the figure of marriage with God to that of deification to express the " mystic union " which they seek in common. But this is only to say that they are Christians as well as Mystics, and that their Christianity modifies their Mysticism: it does not throw doubt upon but rather establishes the fact that the truly — unmodified — Mystical doctrine involves the identification of the creature with the deity. And that for a much deeper reason than the merely epistemological one pointed out by Miss Underhill in the passage just quoted from her (p. 502), or even than that general one adduced by E. Lehmann in the following instructive passage (" Mystik im Heidentum und Christentum," in " Aus Natur und Geisteswelt," No. 217, p. 4; E.T. p. 7): " What constitutes the main distinction between mysticism and other piety is that the ordinary pious man has above everything an eye for that which *distinguishes* him from God: for his insignificance in contrast with God's greatness, for his finiteness in contrast with God's infinity and eternity, for his sinfulness in contrast with God's holiness. In their feeling of this distinction men remain clearly conscious of their humanity and look upon their God as something peculiar, different from themselves. Of this distinguishableness of God, however, the Mystic will know nothing. God is to him indistinguishable as He is incomprehensible, invisible and infinite and therefore all-embracing. No one is in a position to draw a sharp line between humanity and deity; and therefore this line is capable of being crossed and man accordingly can attain this union." Behind this somewhat negative attitude there lies the positive conviction of the Mystic that there exists in himself a native spark of " pure Being " which is in and of itself divine, and that it is his part to blow this spark into a flame that he may become truly himself in the consciousness that he is really God. " The achievement of reality, and deification," says Miss Underhill (p. 503), " are then one and the same thing: necessarily so, since we know that only the divine is the real." Accordingly " the Mystic Way " begins " by the awakening within the self of a new and embryonic consciousness; a consciousness of divine reality, as opposed to the illusory sense-world in which she was immersed " (p. 536). There is nothing more fundamental to the whole Mystical consciousness than the conviction that what we shall see when we retreat into the " cell of self-knowledge " is just that Reality which stands to it for God.

One of the natural results of thus conceiving oneself is inevitably a certain intellectual and spiritual pride. The Mystic has a hearty contempt for his fellow men, who are still shut in by " the hard crust of surface-consciousness," and who know only " the machine-made universe presented by the cinematograph of sense," from which he has escaped (pp. 536–537). For himself — he has been made aware of Reality and has come from out of the cave of illusion, to live hereafter on the supersensual plane (p. 147). According to Miss Underhill the whole external world in which we live is not only of our own creation but is miscreated by us — being but the product of our deceiving senses: nay, each man creates an exclusive world for himself, since the senses of no two men act precisely alike; or rather, each man creates successively a series of exclusive worlds of his own, since his senses never function twice precisely alike; and we have only to imagine what would happen if our senses were " arranged upon a different plan " (p. 7) — if for example, as William James suggests, we heard colors and saw sounds — or if " human consciousness changed or transcended its rhythm " (p. 37), to understand in how illusory a world it is that the ordinary man lives. Quite so: if our senses were radically different and " the rhythm of our human consciousness " were radically changed, we should undoubtedly be in a different world — for our senses could not be different nor could the " rhythm of our consciousness " be changed unless we were in a different world. We may find it a pleasant exercise to speculate on what kind of a world would be involved if we had radically different senses or the world-movement proceeded in a radically different rhythm: as we may work out, for example, the nature of a world in which two and two would make five and in which space would have only two or as many as four dimensions. So, holding a key in our hands, we may find a diversion in mentally picturing the changes that would be involved in the wards of the lock by radical differences in the notches on the bit of the key. Meanwhile our senses, the stream of our consciousness, are thus and not otherwise; and that means that the world of which we are a part, and correlated to which we are by means of our senses, and of the movement of which we are aware in the " rhythm of our consciousness," is thus and not otherwise. We may as well " accept the universe ": for it is this universe that is; and to be out of harmony with it is only to be intellectually, morally, and spiritually mad. It is the condemnation of Mysticism that it must begin by declaring that the world of appearance is illusion and that the rhythm of normal consciousness is a mere jangling, out of tune with reality.

But the Mystic has no more contempt for the man in the street who persists in accepting the world for what he knows it to be, than for what he calls " popular Christianity," as a religion fit only for the man who " lives in the world of sense." For himself he lays claim to a higher plane of religious functioning. " Thus," we read, " in spite of persistent efforts to the contrary, there will always be an inner and an outer Church: the inner Church of the Mystics who *know*, the outer Church which, operating beneficently it is true, but — roughly speaking — upon the magical plane, only *knows about* " (p. 199). The Mystic has got beyond " prayer," for instance, " as understood by the multitude, with all its implications of conventional piety, formality, detailed petition — a definite something asked for, and a definite duty done, by means of extempory or traditional allocutions addressed to the anthropomorphic Deity of popular religion " (p. 366). He has also got beyond the great redemptive acts of God by which God has intervened in the world to lay an objective basis for the salvation of sinners: each and every one of these — the Incarnation, the Atonement, and the rest — is seen by him to be a symbol of a subjective experience which takes place in his own soul. " The one secret, the greatest of all," Coventry Patmore is quoted as saying (p. 141), "is the doctrine of the Incarnation, regarded not as an historical event which occurred two thousand years ago, but as an event which is renewed in the body of every one who is in the way to the fulfilment of his original destiny." The Mystic, Miss Underhill explains, does not so much deny that the Incarnation is a historical event, as merely look by preference upon it as a symbol of inward experience. And " thus," she adds (p. 142), " the Catholic priest in the Christmas Mass gives thanks, not for the setting in hand of any commercial process of redemption, but for a revelation of reality " — citing in support a passage from the Roman Missal which certainly only in isolation can be pressed into her meaning. Similarly, we read in a little Mystical manual which has come into our hands written quite in Miss Underhill's spirit (" The Path of the Eternal Wisdom: A Mystical Commentary on the Way of the Cross," by John Cordelier [manifestly a pseudonym], London, John M. Watkins, 1911) : " The Cross-bearer of the Universe as He passes in our midst does not act *for* us but *in* us: by an enhancement of our energies, a call to us to use our vitality in greater or less self-regarding efforts " (p. 63).

There is probably nothing in the treatment of Christianity by the Mystical writers which is more offensive than this sublimation of the great constitutive facts — in which the very heart of Christianity is to be found — into symbols of subjective transactions. An unusually inoffensive statement of what is attempted is given in the following explanation by a recent writer (H. Erskine Hill, *The Expositor*, August, 1913, p. 192) : " To most men the transitory is the real world, and hence its events and facts assume an absurdly exaggerated importance. To the mystic, on the other hand, the real world is the spiritual, and nothing that happens under conditions of time and space can be anything but reflections. For example, he would not say that the salvation of the world depended on what happened on Calvary, but that what happened on Calvary made manifest once for all the eternal Sacrifice on which the salvation of the world depends. He does not think of the Virgin Birth at Bethlehem as the coming of the eternal Christ into the world, but as the manifestation to the world that He is there all the time." It may be, as we are told, that this is "the lifting up of the Son of Man 'out of the earth' which will draw all men unto Him." It is abolishing the scandal of the Cross and removing the offense of the Incarnation by the simple expedient of pushing them both out of sight. He who thinks that the importance of the Incarnation and the Atoning Sacrifice as transactions in time and space is capable of "absurd exaggeration," or doubts that the Eternal Christ came into the world through the Virgin's womb, thus assuming flesh for our redemption, or that the salvation of the world depends absolutely on what happened at Calvary, has assuredly lost all sense of Christian values. He may remain a Mystic, but he has ceased to be in any intelligible sense a Christian.

We have no intention of following Miss Underhill further into the intricacies of her rich and closely packed discussion. We have thought it worth while, at the cost of whatever space it might require, to attempt to get a somewhat clear conception of precisely what she represents Mysticism to be, because thus the significance of her volume entitled "The Mystic Way," with which we are now more immediately concerned, may be most easily and clearly displayed. For, having thus expounded Mysticism in its nature in the one book she simply turns in the other and says, It is just this Mysticism which what we know as Christianity really is. "The Mystic Way" is, in other words, nothing but an elaborate attempt to explain Christianity as natural religion; and as that particular variety of natural religion which is known as Mysticism, the nature of which Miss Underhill has even more elaborately expounded in her work called "Mysticism." "The Mystic Way" is indefinitely the thinner work of the two. It gives no such impression as "Mysticism" does of being the fruit of long and loving absorption in its subject. It seems rather to be the product of an impulse; to have been somewhat hastily composed; and to resemble a lawyer's brief got up for an occasion and betraying no very large-minded survey or deep consideration of its subject. There is a certain extremity in its contentions, a certain pressure put on the facts which are adduced, a certain overanxiety to make out a case, a certain — to speak frankly — appearance of special pleading combined with insufficient familiarity with the subject-matter, which are at least not so apparent in the other volume. We cannot quite say the volume reads like an afterthought, for all that is said here lies implicitly in the earlier volume and there are not lacking hints in it

of what was to come; but the explication of the implications as to
Christianity of the earlier volume in the later one has proved a
task for which Miss Underhill was not quite prepared and indeed
has brought her sharply up against a barrier which is to be removed
only by an act of supreme violence. To this extent the second volume, while intended as a corollary to the first, is in actual fact a
refutation of it.

The thesis sustained in " The Mystic Way " is, as we have just
said, that what we know as Christianity is simply a great irruption
of Mysticism. What it sets out to prove is accordingly that Jesus
was only a Mystic of exceptional purity and energy; that Paul,
John, all the great leaders of early Christianity were just so many
outstanding Mystics; and that all the phenomena which accompanied the origin of Christianity and have been thought to be
supernatural in character, are just Mystical phenomena, and may
be paralleled in the experiences of other Mystics and thus shown
to be natural — natural, that is, to Mystics. In the elaboration of
this proof the Synoptical record of the life and teaching of Jesus
is subjected to a detailed examination with a view to the explanation of all the phenomena as Mystical; and then the teaching of
Paul and of " the Fourth Evangelist " is poured into the same
molds. This is followed by some account of " three of the special
forms taken by the Mystical impulse in the early Church," with an
Appendix on " St. Macarius the Great of Egypt." And finally, an
attempt is made to show that the whole underlying spirit of the
liturgy of the Mass is Mysticism. The point of view and method
of the discussion are given expression in the Preface in the following words: " The examination of Christian origins from the psychological point of view suggests that Christianity began as a Mystical
movement of the purest kind; that its Founder and those who succeeded Him possessed the characteristically Mystical consciousness,
and passed through the normal stages of Mystical growth. Hence
its nature is best understood by comparison with those lesser Mystical movements in which life has again and again asserted her
unconquerable instinct for transcendence; and the heroic personalities through whom the Christian vision of reality was first
expressed, are most likely to yield up the secret of their ' more
abundant life ' when studied by the help of those psychological
principles which have been deduced from the general investigation
of the Mystical type " (p. viii.). It is important to observe that

what is proposed here is an essay in comparative religion; that Christianity is defined as just a Mystical movement; and that it is placed in its proper position among Mystical movements as only one of the class, so that its explanation may properly be sought from the general characteristics of its class.

We say it is important to observe this. For there is an odd suggestion made here and there, that Christian Mysticism may be set off in a class by itself, and separated by a great gulf from other Mysticism — a gulf so wide that one might think that there could be no bridge of inferences cast over it from one to the other. " We are still too often told," we read on the page immediately preceding that from which we have just quoted, " that Christian Mysticism is no integral part of Christianity; sometimes, even, that it represents an opposition to the primitive Christian ideal. Sometimes we are asked to believe that it originated from Neoplatonic influence; that Pagan blood runs in its veins, and that its genealogy goes back to Plotinus. Far from this being the case, all the doctrines and all the experiences characteristic of genuine Christian Mysticism can be found in the New Testament; and I believe that its emergence as a definite type of spiritual life coincides with the emergence of Christianity itself, in the person of its Founder " (p. vii.). Accordingly, exaggerating beyond all recognition the very natural differentiation of Christian Mysticism from other types of Mysticism made by James Leuba and Henri Delacroix, as they confine their study for the moment to this particular class of Mystics, Miss Underhill is ready to proclaim that " the Christian Mystic " " represents, so far as the psychical nature of man is concerned, a genuine species apart " (p. vii.), " constitutes a true variation of the human species " (p. 41). This is not figurative language. Miss Underhill really wishes us to greet in the Christian Mystic the actual superman. As in the age-long process of evolution the emergence of intelligence introduced a new kind of being and set the factors of evolution on a new plane, she explains, so the emergence of the Christian Mystic has again introduced in evolving humanity a new kind of being and raised humanity to yet a new plane. Miss Underhill is never tired of telling us therefore that the Christian Mystic is not merely morally or religiously different from other men, but is in the strictest sense a new " biological species." " Here we see, in fact," she asserts (p. 11), " creative evolution at work; engaged in the production of species as sharply marked off from

normal humanity as 'normal' humanity supposes itself to be
marked off from the higher apes. The *élan vital* here takes a new
direction, producing profound modifications which, though they
are for the most part psychical rather than physical, yet also entail
a turning of the physical machinery of thought and perception to
fresh uses — a cutting of fresh paths of discharge, a modification
of the normal human balance of intuition and intelligence." "If
this be so," she remarks again (p. 6), "the spiritual evolution of
humanity, the unfolding of its tendency towards the Transcendental
Order, becomes as much a part of biology as the evolution of its
stomach or its sense."

This "fortunate variation" which has befallen humanity as the
ultimate (so far) outcome of a process which has been "continuous
from the first travail of creation even until now," it must be carefully observed, has come to it only at the advent of Jesus Christ.
"And I believe," we read, "that its emergence as a definite type
of spiritual life coincides with the emergence of Christianity itself,
in the person of its Founder" (p. vii.). Again: "The first full and
perfect manifestation of *this* life, this peculiar psychological growth,
in which human personality in its wholeness moves to new levels
and lives at a tension hitherto unknown — establishes itself in the
independent spiritual sphere — seems to coincide with the historical
beginnings of Christianity. In Jesus of Nazareth it found its perfect
thoroughfare, rose at once to its classic expression; and the movement which He initiated, the rare human type which He created,
is in essence a genuinely biological rather than merely credal or
intellectual development of the race. In it, we see life exercising her
sovereign power of spontaneous creation: breaking out on new
paths" (p. 35). And still again: "More and more as we proceed
the peculiar originality of the true Christian Mystic becomes clear
to us. We are led towards the conclusion — a conclusion which rests
on historical rather than religious grounds — that the first person
to exhibit in their wholeness the spiritual possibilities of man was
the historic Christ; and to the corollary, that the great family of
the Christian Mystics — that is to say, all those individuals in
whom an equivalent life-process is set going and an equivalent
growth takes place — represents to us the substance of things
hoped for, the evidence of things not seen, in respect of the upward
movement of the racial consciousness. This family constitutes a
true variation of the human species . . ." (p. 41). If these and such

deliverances mean anything, they mean that with Jesus Christ something new came into the world, something so new that all that had been in the world before it is inadequate to its explanation. And yet Miss Underhill proposes to treat it as only an instance of " the Mystical type," and on the ground that it manifests " the characteristically Mystical consciousness " to explain it from general Mysticism of which it is obviously only a specific manifestation!

The expedient by which Miss Underhill escapes from the *impasse* into which she has brought herself by her isolation of Christian Mysticism as a new creation in the world, is as remarkable as the exaggerations by which she has brought herself into it. Having separated Christian Mysticism off from all other so-called Mysticisms as something (in the " biological " sense) specifically different, she cheerfully proceeds at once to mix it up again with them all. Here is the passage in which she does it (p. 42) : " This new form of life, as it is lived by the members of this species, the peculiar psychic changes to which they must all submit, whatsoever the historic religion to which they belong, may reasonably be called Christian; since its classic expression is seen only in the Founder of Christianity. But this is not to limit it to those who have accepted the theological system called by His name. ' There is,' says Law, ' but one salvation for all mankind, and that is the Life of God in the soul. God has but one design or intent towards all Mankind, and that is to introduce or generate His own Life, Light, and Spirit in them. . . . There is but one possible way for Man to attain this salvation, or Life of God in the soul. There is not one for the Jew, another for a Christian, and a third for the Heathen. No; God is one, human nature is one, salvation is one, and the way to it is one.' We may, then, define the Christian life and the Christian growth as a movement towards the attainment of this Life of Reality; this spiritual consciousness. It is a phase of the cosmic struggle of spirit with recalcitrant matter, of mind with the conditions that hem it in. More abundant life, said the great Mystic of the Fourth Gospel, is its goal; and it sums up and makes effective all the isolated struggles toward such life and such liberty which earlier ages had produced." If we understand this paragraph (in which Christ ceases to be the first to become only the classic expression of Christian Mysticism) it amounts to saying that we may fairly call by the name of Christian Mysticism, any spiritual movement in which we may discover those characteristics which we have discovered in the movement which we have designated by that name. And this would seem to amount to nothing less than saying that the element common to all Mystical movements is not their Mysticism but their Christianity! It is a complete *bouleversement* of values. Something was originated by Christ. We will say it was Mysticism. But Mysticism obviously was not originated by Christ; it exists apart from Him, it existed before Him. But that can be remedied by recognizing all Mysticism by virtue of our agreement that Mysticism was originated by Christ, as Christian! If Christianity is just Mysticism, why of course Mysticism is Christianity, and Christianity, since Mysticism has nothing to do with Him, has nothing to do with Christ.

We do not intend to enter into the details of Miss Underhill's elaborate explaining away of the whole supernatural element of Christianity in her effort to transmute it into just Mysticism, to her reduction of the prophet to " a spiritual genius," of Paul's mighty works to " a growth of automatic powers," of the Son of Man to " the forward-marching spirit of humanity." There is nothing distinctive about the processes she employs or the conclusions she reaches. We may briefly allude only to her dealing with what she calls " the confused poem of the resurrection " as an instance in point. The only fact that emerges clear from it, she tells us, is that " a personal and continuous *life* was veritably recognized and experienced: recognized as belonging to Jesus, though raised to ' another beauty, power, glory,' experienced as a vivifying force of enormous potency which played upon those ' still in the flesh ' " (p. 149). This cannot be accounted for, she thinks, on purely subjective lines. The thing seized upon was " the indestructibility and completeness of the new, transfigured humanity; the finished citizen of the Kingdom of God " (p. 150). The vision then was " of a *whole man;* body, soul and spirit transmuted and glorified — a veritable ' New Adam ' who came from heaven " (p. 151). And it was of course by the intuition, not the senses, that he was " seen " (p. 152). Certainly, no such " whole man " existed as the Jesus that was seen. As the Ascended Christ (p. 233), so naturally the Resurrected Christ was " discarnate." All this, of course, we have heard before: Miss Underhill's rationalism is certainly of the commonest garden variety. Take this amazing specimen (p. 219, note 2), relatively to the employment of " John " to designate the author

of the Fourth Gospel: "I retain for convenience' sake this traditional name, which may well be that of the actual author: 'John'
was a common name in Christian circles." Surely enough there are
five hundred and ninety-five "Johns" listed in Smith and Wace.
But what made "John" so favorite a name "in Christian circles"?
And how does Miss Underhill know that "John" was a common
name in Christian circles at about the time the Fourth Gospel was
written, say at the turning-point of the first and second centuries?
None of Smith and Wace's five hundred and ninety-five "Johns"
belong to that period except one ("The Presbyter John") — and
he was not invented until later. The irruption of "Johns" in Christian circles means an earlier date by a generation for the Gospel of
John; for it is not allusions to John in other books but the writings
attributed to him which have made the name of John precious to
Christians.

That there are elements — fortunately extensive, even dominating elements — in that historical phenomenon which we know as
"Christian Mysticism" that derive from Christ and what He
brought into the world, of course no one will deny. It is these elements which constitute this Mysticism that particular variety of
Mysticism which we call Christian Mysticism, and which justify,
or rather require, that it should be studied apart, as Henri Delacroix
has done in his excellent volume on "Les grands mystiques Chré-
tiens" (1908), which Miss Underhill misquotes in her efforts to
make Christian Mysticism out to be a wholly new creation in the
world. We shall all approve of Delacroix's going to the great Christian Mystics by preference to learn what Christian Mysticism is, lest,
as he says, he should see only the lower characteristics of it and so
miss the greatness of these great men. And we shall all approve also
of his going rather to those of them who have lived and practised
Mysticism than to those who have merely written about it. But we
shall not doubt any more than he doubts that a doctrine underlies the
practice of even these practical Mystics, or that this doctrine by
virtue of which they are Mystics derives not from Christ but from
Plotinus. "No doubt," he writes, "— and we shall show it in this
book — doctrine intervenes in experience, and there is, to speak it
out, no great Mystic who has not grounded his experience in a doctrine and who has not up to a certain point made doctrinal preoccupations intervene in the constitution of his experience. . . . We have
shown that throughout the whole course of Christianity there has

been an almost continuous Mystical doctrine deriving from Neo-platonism. . . . We shall find it again as a substructure and an implicit theory in the Mysticism of experience " (p. iv.). In a sense the source of all of Miss Underhill's woes is her determination that Christian Mysticism, as it is Mysticism, shall find its starting-point in Christ and not in Plotinus. " Above all," she writes, " we shall be in conflict with those who . . . consider the Mystical ele-ment in Christianity to be fundamentally unchristian and ulti-mately descended from the Neoplatonists " (p. 58). Nevertheless it was she herself who, when not so deeply intoxicated with this theory, told us that " Christian philosophy, especially that Neo-platonic theology which, taking up and harmonizing all that was best in the spiritual intuitions of Greece, India and Egypt, was developed by the great doctors of the early and mediæval Church, supports and elucidates the revelations of the individual Mystic as no other system of thought has been able to do" (" Mysticism," p. 125); that " we owe . . . above all to Dionysius the Areopagite, the great Christian contemporary of Proclus, the preservation of that mighty system of scaffolding which enabled the Catholic Mys-tics to build up the towers and bulwarks of the City of God " (p. 125).

Least of all can any one deny that there is a sense, a wide sense, a sense too wide for the historical meaning of the term Mysticism, in which Christianity is mysticism. It is of the very essence of Christianity that God has immediate access to the human soul and that the Christian enjoys direct communion with God: it is of the very essence of Christianity that it is in Christ that every Christian lives and that it is Christ who lives in every Christian. If there is nothing that shocks the Christian more in Mysticism than its tend-ency to seek God apart from Christ — as W. Herrmann says, " to leave Christ behind " (" Communion of the Christian with God," E.T. 1913, p. 30), he is equally shocked when Herrmann on his own part declares: " We cannot speak of a communion with the exalted Christ " (p. 291). We shall not turn our backs on Mysticism there-fore to throw ourselves into the arms of that Ritschlianism in which Miss Underhill, perhaps rightly, sees the most determined modern enemy of all mysticism. But neither need we in revolt from Ritsch-lianism cast ourselves into the arms of that Mystical individu-alism which would throw man back on what we have seen Miss Underhill speaking of as the " revelations of the individual " (" Mysticism," p. 125). There are some words of Herrmann's which, deeply vitiated though they are by his inadequate view of the person and work of our Lord, and of the relation of the Christian to Him, may yet bring us a needed warning here. " The Christian," says he (p. 193), " can never even wish that God should specially appear to him or speak down to him from heaven. He receives the revelation of God in the living relationships of Christian brotherhood, and its essential contents are that personal life of Jesus which is visible in the Gospel, and which is expounded by the lives of the redeemed." It certainly is not merely in the communion of saints that we have communion with God; it is not only in and through the community of Christian men that we receive the impression of the living Christ; " the personal life of Christ," that is, the aroma of His holy personality lingering behind Him in the world, does not constitute the essential contents of the revelation of God; the whole conception of the work of Christ and of the substance of the gospel here outlined is in direct contradiction with what the gospel itself proclaims. But it is true that the Christian ought to be, and will be, satisfied with the revelation of God in Christ, and cannot crave special and particular revelations, each one for himself. The one revelation of His grace which God has given to His people in His Son is enough for the needs of all and floods the souls of all with a sense of its completeness and its all-sufficiency. As Dr. A. Kuyper beautifully expresses it, God the Lord does not feed His people each by himself but spreads a common table of the abundant supply of which He invites His whole family to partake. But just because the common supply is enough for all, He gives in it personal communion with Him, the Master of the feast, to each and all; and in that communion abundance of life. " Humanity," says A. H. Strong ("Philosophy and Religion," 1888, p. 225) finally " is a dead and shattered vine, plucked up from its roots in God, and fit only for the fires. But in Christ, God has planted a new vine, a vine full of His own divine life, a vine into which it is His purpose one by one to graft these dead and withered branches, so that they may once more have the life of God flowing through them and may bear the fruits of heaven." " It is a supernatural, not a natural, process," he adds. And it is only " in Christ," we may add with the utmost emphasis.

MYSTIK UND GESCHICHTLICHE RELIGION. Von WILHELM FRESENIUS,
Lic. theol. Göttingen: Vandenhoeck und Ruprecht. 1912.[1]

LICENTIATE FRESENIUS is an admiring pupil of W. Herrmann, and
has written this little book apparently for the purpose of defending
the so-called " historical " conception of religion, held by Herrmann
in common with his fellow Ritschlians, against the " mystical "
conception of religion which is now again becoming very widespread.
According to the so-called " historical " conception of it, religion is
not a native possession of the human soul; it is something which
meets man in the course of the process of living. It is an experience
— an *Erlebnis*, something that occurs to him — which some day
befalls him — *begegnet*, encounters him — when he finds himself
face to face with goodness manifested in a personal life with such
power that he cannot choose but utterly surrender himself to it.
Religion is thus a fact which occurs in a human life, a transaction,
a transaction of the man's own; yet it is rather produced in him
than by him — through the might of the goodness revealed to his
observation. " A man cannot make religion for himself; nor can he
acquire it by labors or performances of any kind whatsoever — he
can neither earn it by works nor excogitate it by brooding. It has
always itself laid claim to be a gift of God to man. Therefore, the
only path to religion lies in observing and marking the experiences
of our own life, if perchance there may speak to us in them a power of
love and goodness which we cannot withstand. Experiences arise
in our own life, however, only in our commerce with other men,
with personalities in whom we are able to put trust, that is, from
whom we receive the impression that they have risen above purely
instinctive life to personal being. By their means we are turned to
that which raised them out of their nothingness. We Christians
accordingly speak of the Christian community as that with the
existence, vitality and historical power of which the possibility of
religious life is for us indissolubly bound up. And it is therefore
that we designate religion, because it is attached to human intercourse and its historical, personal root, as historical religion "
(p. 64). Religion, in this view, therefore arises in the soul of man
in particular conditions of time and space, under influences brought
to bear upon him from without — under the influences, to be more
specific, of other personalities which impress him as good. In the

[1] *The Princeton Theological Review*, xii. 1914, pp. 332–340.

formal definitions which Fresenius frames (p. 63), "religion is the experience which the morally thinking man makes, when the power of the good so encounters him that he must surrender himself to it utterly"; and (p. 65) "the Christian religion is the experience which the morally thinking man makes of the Person of Jesus, when the power of the good so encounters him in it, that he must surrender himself to it utterly."

With this conception of religion as evoked in man by a quite specific experience, which comes to him from without, the Mystical contention that we must look within ourselves to find God stands obviously in direct contradiction. "It is the characteristic of all Mysticism," Fresenius remarks in bringing this contradiction to view, "that it maintains the immediate presence of divine life in man, which needs only to be recognized and felt, — and it is therefore that in all mysticism it is contemplation which self-evidently forms the best way to God — while historical religion has always presented itself as the *new* life, which comes into being by the action of person on person and is not already (even though hiddenly) present in man" (pp. 50–51). It is not strange therefore that Fresenius looks with alarm upon the irruption of Mystical ideas which seems at present in progress and posits the problem which is raised by this irruption in such phrases as these — " whether we are to be saved from the religious exigencies of our day by giving our attention to historical religion, to the gospel of Jesus as the Reformers understood it, or by sinking ourselves into the feeling of infinity and by speculatively contemplating that which lives in our souls by nature " (pp. 54–55). For Fresenius emphasizes that what the Mystic finds in the soul is merely its natural endowment. " We have heard religion — or rather its Mystical form —," he says, " compared with the contemplation of nature and art; what we experience and feel in the enjoyment of nature, in gazing on a beautiful painting, in listening to a symphony by a master, that — so we have been told — is essentially related to religion, or rather is religion's self, because it is the apprehension and feeling of the eternal and imperishable. But just as surely as the enjoyment of nature and art can evoke mysticism, just so surely is the infinite which is felt in it not the God of religion. For Christian piety at least, God is not the Eternal, Imperishable which we feel, but the Power for Good which comes into contact with us, above time and eternity, in the personalities who evoke confidence (*Zutrauen*) in us, — which

Power is not maintained by us to be God, but manifests itself to us as God. Where, however, God is sought and found in indefinite feelings, in experiences of the infinite, there He is nothing but a name for the unknown and incomprehensible which arouses that feeling. Man then humbles himself before a power which he does not know, but which, if he will not give himself the lie, he postulates, and from which he then, since he cannot get along without them, arbitrarily forms conceptions — which perhaps, however, are actually derived from historical religion " (p. 82).

Obviously the debate between the Ritschlian, as represented by Fresenius, and the Mystic turns primarily upon the question of what, when the Mystic sinks himself into himself, he finds there. The Mystic says he finds God. The Ritschlian says he finds nothing but an indefinite and indefinable feeling of the infinite which he arbitrarily dubs God. This question at once, however, passes into another: the question of the conception of God. To the Mystic, Fresenius intimates, God is simply Immensity; to the Ritschlian He is the Good: to the former therefore He is a mere thing, to the latter He is a Person — for when we say " good " we say Person. As over against all Mystical phantasies, therefore, the Ritschlian stands for " the personal God, who drawing near to us in religious experience, calls us to ethical, personal life " (p. 88). This great transaction takes place, of course, at a given point of time and thus the Ritschlian stands for what he calls " historical religion." " Thus over against *historical* religion which springs out of personal life-experiences in the social organism there stands history-less Mysticism which forgets the social organism in arbitrarily produced feelings and phantasies " (p. 89). That the contradiction of these conceptions may be felt in its full force, however, the phenomenalism which rules the Ritschlian conception must be borne in mind. To this phenomenalism Fresenius manages to advert even in this brochure (p. 73), speaking with some contempt of the old Lutheran dogmaticians who still believe in a substantial soul (it is " the thing in itself," he remarks in parenthesis) and, over against this human soul, in a substantial God. As they did not find the real nature of man in his activities, he complains, so they did not find God " in particular activities, in historical acts and personal operations " but postulated a somewhat behind these activities of which they endeavored to frame some conception and which they sought afterwards to bring somehow into connection with historical facts.

For the " soul " of man he would substitute a series of activities
under the conception of " Life " (*Leben*), and correspondingly for
the substantial God he would substitute a series of activities also
known as " Life " (*Leben*). And as God consists only in His activities, of course He can be known only in His activities, and it is idle
to seek Him as lying inert in the human heart.

It certainly were hard choosing between two such one-sided conceptions of God — a God who is bare Immensity (or " Reality," as
it is the irritating habit of the Mystics to call Him), or a God who is
bare Activity. Fortunately we are shut up to no such option. Nor
can the question of what may be found in the human soul be thought
to be closed by the unfortunate fact that many of those who have
turned their contemplation in upon it have found there apparently
nothing but a vague sense of immensity. There are mystics and
mystics. Indeed Fresenius, as he addresses himself to the study of
mysticism and the possibility of there being a mystical element in
religion, is oppressed no more by the multitude of the mystics who
require to be taken account of than by the immense variety of definitions of mysticism which claim attention. *Quot homines, tot sententiae.* To ease his task Fresenius selects three recent writers of
importance, whom he considers fair representatives of divergent
types of Mystical thought and endeavors to derive from a study of
them a working notion of what Mysticism stands for at the moment
at least. These are Friedrich von Hügel, Nathan Söderblom, and
Georg Klepl. To the first of these thinkers " Mysticism is the specifically Catholic ideal of piety " (p. 10) ; to the second it is " the
essential content of Christianity, and that precisely of Protestant
Christianity " (p. 28) ; to the third (he does not employ the term) it
is the abiding basis of all possible religion in these sophisticated
times. As the result of his induction Fresenius strangely arrives at
the conclusion that, as a phenomenon in the Christian Church at
least, Mysticism is distinctively Catholic or at least Catholicizing.
He had no doubt thrown Söderblom out of consideration, somewhat
arbitrarily one would think, because of his identification of mysticism with the general supernatural element in Christianity. But one
would suppose that Klepl — who does not, however, consider himself a Mystic — was as far as possible from a Catholicizing conception of religion.

The truth seems to be that Fresenius has not in the end been
able to emancipate himself from his traditional Ritschlian concep-

tion here. Ritschl, Harnack, Herrmann are cited in support of his finding (p. 85) and the volume closes with a quotation from the well-known pages of Harnack's " History of Dogma " (E.T. vi. 1899, pp. 99 f.) in which he warns evangelical Christians off from too complete a sympathy with Mysticism — merely because of their delight in the warm spiritual life which it exhibits — on the ground that it is essentially Catholic and cannot be Protestantized. Despite so great an array of authority we cannot help thinking this finding a mistake. The evangelical Christian may be well put on his guard against Mysticism — to which he cannot unreservedly give himself, as Harnack truly observes, " if he has made clear to himself what evangelical faith is "; and no doubt the legalism and formalism of the Romish teaching have ever been powerful contributory causes to the production of Mysticism in the Catholic Church. But it finds its impelling cause clearly elsewhere and therefore it is not even exclusively an intra-Christian phenomenon. We can scarcely deny the name of Mystic to Plotinus or Jalálu 'd Din, to Greek or Persian, Muslim or Hindu saint. In the actual definition of Mysticism to which Fresenius comes, if it be considered merely as a definition of Mysticism within the limits of the Catholic Church, we may nevertheless find our way. " Mysticism," says he, " is the ideal of piety which is necessarily formed on the basis of a legalistic, Catholic or Catholicizing conception of religion, by men, weary of the burden of ecclesiastical tradition and cold formalism, who seek after a personal experience and assurance of faith, and, utilizing religious tradition and customs as means to their end, find the goal of their search in an indefinite and indefinable feeling of the eternal which is arbitrarily maintained to be God " (pp. 83–84). *Mutatis mutandis* the same might be said for Mysticism in the Protestant Churches, or for Mysticism among the Mohammedans or the Hindus. Everywhere Mysticism avails itself of the forms of religion and the theological formulas under which it grows up as means: everywhere it lays hold of the sense of the immense and the eternal which it finds in the soul. It remains still a question, however, whether its discovery of God through this feeling of the immense and the eternal is altogether arbitrary.

To go at once to the root of the matter, what Mysticism really is, is, at bottom, just natural religion. That its form has been given it so prevailingly — perhaps we ought to say, constantly — by the influence of Pantheizing thought may be treated here as acci-

dental; though it must be confessed that it has much the look, historically, of an essential characteristic, in which case we should
have to define Mysticism as Pantheizing natural religion. Meanwhile we are not to be driven or tempted from the position that
men are by nature religious and will in any event have a religion;
that there has been ineradicably implanted in them a *sensus deitatis*
(as Calvin has taught us to call it) which inevitably becomes a
semen religionis. Fresenius himself is compelled to allow the presence in man of " a religious disposition, or an inborn religious
capacity " which provides the psychological possibility of religion
(p. 60); and he freely admits that this " capacity for religion " has
enabled multitudes to become actually religious under influences
wholly unknown to us (p. 16). His contention only is that it must
be called into action by influences coming from without and of a
personal-ethical kind: it never, according to him, functions independently so as to produce religion. The Mystic, on the contrary,
insists that it normally effloresces into actual religion whenever opportunity is given it to function. The difference here is fundamental
and rests on divergent ontologies. If it be reduced to the single
question of whether God approaches man only from without,
through the medium of other personalities acting upon him by the
way of a so-called " ethical " appeal; or rather Himself forms a
part of man's spiritual environment in contact with whom man exists
and of whom he has immediate experience, we must pronounce the
Mystic certainly in the right. And this we may surely do without
prejudice to complete rejection of the entire Pantheizing coloring
of the common (or shall we say constant?) Mystical presentation.
The mischief of Mysticism lies not in its claim to find God through
the ineradicable natural instincts of the soul but in its persistent
effort, being natural religion, to substitute itself for supernatural religion, that is to say, for Christianity. The relation of
Christianity to natural religion seems to be very frequently, we
might even say commonly, misconceived. They are not two religions,
lying side by side of one another, of which one must be taken and
the other left: whether with the Ritschlian we take Christianity
(or rather, what they mistake for Christianity) and leave natural
religion, or with the Mystics we take natural religion and leave
Christianity. As what is called special revelation is superinduced
upon and presupposes what is called general revelation, and these
two form one whole, so Christianity is superinduced upon and pre-

supposes natural religion and forms with it the one whole which is the only sufficing religion for sinful man. Although Mysticism is not Christianity, therefore, Christianity is mysticism. There are multitudes of Mystics who are not Christians, but there is no Christian who is not a mystic — who does not hold communion with God in his soul, and that not merely as the God of grace by virtue of whose recreative operations he is a Christian, but as the God of nature by virtue of whose creative, upholding, and governing operations he is a creature. We may or may not be able to make out a historical claim to the name of Mysticism to express this Christian mysticism; the name may be preëmpted by something essentially different and any attempt to rescue it to this nobler usage may be productive only of confusion. We may think it futile to distinguish, as has often been attempted (von Hügel quotes the distinction from Rauwenhoff, as Charles Hodge quoted it from Nitzsch), between *Mystik* and *Mysticismus*, as designations respectively of the "white" and the "black" Mysticism. But the name apart, the thing lies at the very foundation of the Christian religion: there is no Christian religion where there is no inward communion with God.

As Christianity is mysticism without being Mysticism, so also is it a historical religion without being "Historical Religion" in the sense of Fresenius and his school. In calling religion "historical" Fresenius and his school mean nothing more than that its origin in every individual case is to be sought and found not in some innate disposition of the man but "in his own history," that is, as he explains (p. 21), "in the experiences of his life, in the effects of living personalities, in occurrences which can maintain their right before his clear ethical judgment." Their minds are not at all on the great historical occurrences by which the God of Grace has intervened in the sinful development of the race by redemptive acts — the incarnation, the atonement, the outpouring of the Holy Ghost — but merely on the life-experience of the individual man, in the course of which, they affirm, religion is brought to him as one item in the temporal series of his experiences. Of the great redemptive acts of God by which Christianity is constituted and by virtue of which, lying at its heart, it is a "historical religion" they will know as little as the Mystic himself. To them, too, all religion, inclusive of Christianity, as a, or the, religion, is independent of all occurrences of the past and is purely a present experience of man. They differ with the Mystic here only in making it an experience, not of man's native life of feeling, but of his presently acting ethical will.

When remarking on this matter Fresenius carefully explains that "the deepest difference " between von Hügel the Mystic and Herrmann, the advocate of "historical religion," "lies here in this: that Hügel seeks to assign its place in the soul-life of man to religion as a given entity (psychological method), while Herrmann exhibits its origin in the spiritual-ethical life of man and establishes it as a power which works from person to person and is therefore historical (historical, systematic method) " (p. 21). So eager is he not to be misunderstood, by the use of the term "historical " here to imply some recognition of the historical elements of Christianity as that term is ordinarily understood, that he attaches a note to the word to explain that he, like Wobbermin (*Zeitschrift für Theologie und Kirche*, xxi. 1911), distinguishes between the two German terms *geschichtlich* and *historisch* and applies only the former, but never the latter, to his Christianity. To him Christianity has ceased to be a "historical" (*historische*) religion and the "faith" which he calls by that name is absolutely independent of all "historical" (*historische*) facts. This includes even the fact of Jesus. We must not be misled here by the place which "the Person of Jesus " holds in the "Christianity" of Herrmann and of course also in that of his pupil Fresenius. Fresenius has been at pains to explain to us that it is the *geschichtliche* Jesus, not the *historische* Jesus, that is here in question. It is a matter of indifference to him and all those of his way of thinking whether there ever existed any *historische* Jesus: all that is important is that we shall have a genuine "experience " of Jesus, that He should come to us *geschichtlich*, that is, in a real encounter with our soul. This constitutes Him to us the point of inspiration needed to awaken us to religious life and it is indifferent to us whether He really ever lived on earth (*Zeitschrift für Theologie und Kirche*, xxii. 1912, pp. 244–268). Not merely have the incarnation, the atonement, the outpouring of the Spirit — all the redemptive acts of God — gone; the "historical Jesus " may go too. On no fact of the past whatever can Christianity rest: it is purely for each man an experience of his own.

Certainly no Mystic could cut himself more completely loose from the historical elements of Christianity than is done here. And, by virtue of the fact that all that makes Christianity that specific religion which we call Christianity lies precisely in these historical elements, the neglect or rejection of them is the rejection of Christianity. The whole life-work of Herrmann may have been to show how a man of our day may still be a Christian; but unfortunately he has done this by adapting what he calls Christianity to the point of view of the "man of our day," and the outcome is that he solves the problem by dissolving Christianity. The " historical religion " which Fresenius offers us is therefore no more Christianity than the Mysticism of the most extreme of the Mystics, and brings us not a single step closer than it to a real Christianity. Of course if the whole difference between Mysticism and " historical religion " were reduced to the single question of whether Christianity is the product of the native religious sentiment or comes to man from without and is embraced by an act of his own ethical will, we should have unhesitatingly to give the right to " historical religion." We have not had to wait for the Ritschlian school to learn that faith comes by hearing; or that as believing implies hearing so hearing implies a preacher. By virtue of the very circumstance that Christianity is a historical religion and is rooted in facts which have occurred in the world and through which the redemption which has come into the world has been wrought out, it must be communicated. And nothing is more sure than that there can be no Christianity apart from the working upon the heart of these historical facts as proclaimed, appreciated, and embraced in confident faith. The action of the ethical will in laying hold upon the Saving Christ is of the essence of Christianity and there is no Christianity without it.

What Fresenius brings into contrast in his discussion is, then, merely two extremely one-sided conceptions of religion: the religion of the mere feelings and the religion of the bare ethical will. Neither has any claim to the name of Christianity. For Christianity is a historical religion and neither of these conceptions of religion has any essential connection with history. The religion of the mere ethical will is just as purely a merely natural religion as is the religion of the mere feelings. The Christian may therefore stand by and watch the conflict of these standpoints with interest indeed but without concern. Each tendency — " Mysticism," " Historical Religion " — is engaged in validating elements of the religious life, which enter into and find their due place in Christianity. But not only is each fatally one-sided in its exclusive insistence upon its own element of religious experience, but both in combination fall far short of even a complete account of natural religion; and neither has any place whatever in its system of thought for that supernatural religion which alone can avail for the needs of sinful men. The problem which presses on us is not whether, in the religious conflicts of our time, we should turn for rest and peace to " Mysticism " or to " Historical Religion " — to the religion of the feelings or to the religion of the ethical will: but whether there is not some more comprehensive religion which will take up into itself and engage the whole man, intellect, sensibility, and will alike, and meeting him in his actual condition of weakness and corruption and guilt, rescue him from his lost state and renew him in all the elements of his being, to present him to God a new man. After all said Christianity remains the only religion which meets the case.

MYSTICISM IN CHRISTIANITY. By the Rev. W. K. FLEMING, M.A., B.D. London: Robert Scott; New York and Chicago: Fleming H. Revell Company. 1913.

MYSTICISM AND MODERN LIFE. By JOHN WRIGHT BUCKHAM. New York and Cincinnati: The Abingdon Press. [1915.] [1]

THESE two books illustrate a movement of recent thought which both of them are eager that we should recognize as in progress. This is a movement towards a reawakened interest in Mysticism, and even toward a reversion to it as a satisfying religious point of view. Such a movement was for religious men inevitable in the prevalent decay of confidence in the Christian revelation. For Mysticism is religion, and supplies a refuge for men of religious mind who find it no longer possible for them to rest on " external authority " — as George Tyrrell both expounded and illustrated for us. Once turn away from revelation and little choice remains to you but the choice between Mysticism and Rationalism. There is not so much choice between these things, it is true, as enthusiasts on either side are apt to imagine. The difference between them is very much a matter of temperament, or perhaps we may even say of temperature. The Mystic blows hot, the Rationalist cold. Warm up a Rationalist and you inevitably get a Mystic; chill down a Mystic and you find yourself with a Rationalist on your hands. The history

---

[1] *The Princeton Theological Review,* xiv. 1916, pp. 343–348.

of thought illustrates repeatedly the easy passage from one to the other. Each centers himself in himself, and the human self is not so big that it makes any large difference where within yourself you take your center. Nevertheless just because Mysticism blows hot, its " eccentricity " is the more attractive to men of lively religious feeling. But it is just as scornful as Rationalism of the supernatural, of " external revelation," of historical foundations for religion. Face to face with the supernatural revelations recorded in the Christian Scriptures, it reduces them to " mystical phenomena," and assimilates them to the experiences of a Plotinus, or of a Sadi. Face to face with the historical foundations of Christianity, it treats them as symbols of transactions which take place within the souls of men. It is of the very essence of Mysticism to find God within the circle of the individual's experience. So soon as any other " way " of coming into " contact " with God is proposed than by sinking into ourselves, Mysticism is radically deserted. And because not the perception of God but God Himself is found in the human soul, and by implication in every human soul, God is ultimately confounded with the human soul: at his deepest depths man is God. No doubt, being a religion and not merely a philosophy, " unification " is presented by Mysticism as an achievement rather than as a postulate. And no doubt we may learnedly distinguish between Pantheism and Panentheism, between Pantheism and Negativism. All such efforts to escape from the coils of the serpent, however, are futile. Mysticism, in its fundamental basis of underlying conception, is just Pantheizing Anti-supernaturalism. And such it has shown itself — in greater or less purity of manifestation — in its entire historical development.

This is what Mysticism, with a capital M, is. Spell it with a lower-case m, and we may possibly broaden it out into only another name for natural religion. As it is religion, it is of course when so understood admirable. As it remains natural religion, it is equally of course, for fallen men, inadequate. Its relation to Christianity is that of natural religion to the religion of revelation. It goes without saying that it finds " for itself in Christianity a field of the richest and most fruitful soil." This is saying too little. We must say that only in Christianity can it attain its true development and complement. For Christianity is not an unnatural religion disputing the field of religion with natural religion. It is natural religion reinforced by supernatural republication and sanctions, and completed by the addition of what is needed for a religion for men in the un-natural condition induced by sin. It takes up natural religion into itself and gives it the power to come to its rights while it enlarges it by adding to it the supernatural religion needed for sinful man. But it goes equally without saying that mysticism, understood as natural religion, is not, in some of its less complete developments, confined to the soil of Christianity. Just because it is natural re-ligion it is present wherever human nature is present and functions religiously; and we do not need Schleiermacher to teach us that there is no human self-consciousness which is destitute of the God-consciousness. Of course, then, " it has been at the root of any and every religion worthy of the name, in its original and indefectible ' feeling after God, if haply it may find Him.' " Wherever man exists he is " in contact " with God: and wherever men are " in con-tact " with God they may " know " Him if only they will attend to Him " in contact " with whom they are. We may even use the word " know " in its full sense. We see no reason to dispute Plotinus' dictum that God to be known must be " seen " or " felt." If God be a mere hypothesis, however fully that hypothesis is verified, He can scarcely be said to be " known." That He is we may be sure; but to know that God is, is not yet to " know " God. We may acquire after a while good reason to believe that Mars, say, is inhabited: that would not warrant us in saying that we " know " the beings whose bare existence we have found reason to believe in. God is known only by those who being " in contact " with Him have looked upon Him with that eye of the soul to which He is visible. If this be mysticism, we are all mystics: not merely Augustine with his doctrine of the intelligible world and the *sensus internus* by which it is perceived, but Calvin also with his doctrine of the *sensus deitatis* which is the *semen religionis*. But it certainly is not Mys-ticism in any historical sense of that term.

The fault of books like those now before us is that they confound Mysticism (which is Pantheizing Anti-supernaturalism) with mys-ticism (conceived as conscious living, moving, and having our being in God) and then interpret Christianity in terms of the re-sultant confused idea. The effect is to desupernaturalize and de-historicalize Christianity, and to reduce it to a merely natural religion, or rather to substitute merely natural religion for it. Christ is ranged with other masters; and the Christianity which He died to give to the world is explained as already in the possession of men before and quite apart from Him; as lying always, in fact, at the disposal of men in the depths of every man's own heart. This is the fundamental point of view which lies beneath and gives their ground-color to both of the books now before us, though it manifests itself in the discussions of each, of course, in a degree and manner of its own. Mr. Fleming's book is historical in form. Its task is to present a succinct account of the manifestations of Mystical thought and of the Mystical attitude in the historical development of Christianity. His mind is on Mysticism with a capital M, and he represents its presence in the Christian life and thinking of the ages as the saving salt by virtue of which Christianity has been made, and maintained, as a religion. Mr. Buckham's book has more the form of a discussion of principles. Some of the chapters which constitute it were written originally for separate publication and the unity of the volume suffers somewhat from this fact. But a sufficient internal unity is given to the whole by the common purpose, pervading all parts alike, to assimilate Mysticism and Christianity to one another. This assimilation is effected by first interpreting Mysticism in terms of Christianity — the stages of " the Mystic Way," for example, are expounded in a fashion which may enable the Christian to " receive it " but scarcely the Mystic to recognize it as his own — and then interpreting Christianity in terms of Mysticism. What comes out as a result is something which is neither Mysticism nor Christianity, but a good deal more the former than the latter. Anti-doctrinal zeal is a fundamental trait of both books; their misprision of evangelical teaching and practice is marked; their hatred of Calvinism and all its works intense, though not very intelligible, or indeed even intelligent. Observe this list of names brought together by Mr. Buckham as not very commendable for the theology they represent: " Arius, Pelagius, Abelard, Dominic, Socinus, Calvin, the Westminster Divines, Priestley "!

It is interesting to observe what Mr. Buckham makes of Christianity in his determination to give it a common denominator with Mysticism. In one passage, he formally expounds " the essence of Christianity." We do not quarrel with him that, in his anti-dogmatic zeal, he seeks primarily the essence of Christianity as spiritual experience. What we quarrel with him for is the particular spiritual experience which he segregates as constituting the specific essence of Christianity. This he phrases as " a filial communion and coöperation with God, so deep and real as to transform life." Obviously, there is nothing specifically Christian in this. "This spirit came through Jesus," he says. But then he adds immediately: "Not that it is absolutely new with Jesus." He adds again, indeed: "But it was so intense and fructifying as to exercise an almost " — this " almost " is intensely revealing — " creative influence upon those who came to share it with and through Him." But this does not remove the fatal fact that nothing exclusively Christian is discovered in " the essence of Christianity." Christianity may bring what it brings with a special poignancy of appeal; but it is a matter of degree not of kind after all. So Pelagius said that men could be saved apart from Christianity as truly as by Christianity, only they could be saved more easily under Christianity: just as a boat would convey you from Carthage to Italy by sail more easily to yourself than if you had to row it across — but you could row it across all right if you had to. Christianity is a good religion; no doubt the best religion; but you can do very well without it.

But, now, how did Mr. Buckham arrive at this remarkable " essence " for Christianity? By historical induction, it seems. " It is only as we grasp that which is common in Christian experience, in the first century and in our own, and in all that intervene, that we understand the essence of Christianity," he tells us. And then he tells us, that proceeding after this fashion he finds the essence of Christianity what we have seen. Did anybody ever reason with more delightful circularity? We presume that the spiritual experience of those alone who possess the essence of Christianity is truly Christian experience; and we presume equally that the essence of Christianity is the spiritual experience of those only who are truly Christians. We may know who are truly Christians by observing who have truly Christian experience; and we may know what truly Christian experience is by observing what is the experience of those who are truly Christians. Or, shall we say rather that the spiritual experience common to all who *call* themselves Christians is " the essence of Christianity "? If only a single man from the time of Christ until to-day who has called himself a Christian and has not been truly a Christian be included in this induction, the conclusion is vitiated. We should get not what is common to all Christians, but what is common to Christians and non-Christians. This is what has happened to Mr. Buckham. He gives us not the essence of Christianity, which is a specific religion, but the essence (from his point of sight) of religion. And that is the reason why after saying that this "filial communion and coöperation with God," to be Christian, must be "so deep and real as to transform life," he immediately, bethinking himself of the other religions with which Christianity is confounded in his thought, qualifies this and says of it that it is only "an *almost* creative influence."

We have noted that Rationalism does not lie any too far away from Mysticism. Mystics sometimes betray a tendency to Rationalistic turns of thought. Mr. Buckham does not altogether escape. Does God send trouble? is a question which seems quite to bowl over his attempt to interpret the universe in terms of God. In reporting the attitude of the Mystic towards "the disasters and ills" of life he interjects a remark on his own account to the effect that these disasters and ills of life "are acts of nature rather than of God, or His only as belonging to a world that is His." What wretched dualism have we here? Mr. Buckham seeks to salve his defection by intimating that Mysticism at least does not go so far astray here as Evangelicalism — that *bête noire* both of himself and Mr. Fleming. "Evangelicalism," he tells us, "went too far" in the direction of attributing the dark and the storm to the sending of God and interpreting "the lightning javelins of fate" as "hurled by His hand." The Mystic has not urged, he affirms, that disasters are direct acts of God, and especially not that they have been sent with punitive intent: he has only endeavored to utilize trouble when it comes for his own purification and perfection. All this is obviously not only unevangelical, but irreligious, if we can make a distinction here. He who does not see the hand of God in all that befalls him is a Rationalist more extreme than even such an extreme Rationalist as Wilhelm Herrmann. He has not only torn God out of his heart (where the Mystic finds Him), but even out of the universe (where the mere Theist must see Him).

"The experience of the mystics as a whole," writes Mr. Buckham, "offers a striking exemplification of the saying of Christ as to the life of the Kingdom consisting in a *renewed childhood.*" What saying of Christ is this? Mr. Buckham seems conscious that there is something wrong here; for he immediately adds, "Not that such a life has the weaknesses and limitations of childhood, but, rather, its vision, its faith, its confiding communion." Has childhood — infancy would be the truer term — "vision, and faith, and confiding communion"? The mistake here is not to be condoned merely because it has become so common. The kingdom of heaven is not an infantile estate in which the immature alone may be at home; nor is it a children's paradise. Men are not to renew their childhood in it, but to put away childish things. We rise not sink into manhood, and the kingdom of heaven consists not in reduced men but in enlarged men — built up into the fullness of the stature of manhood in Christ. What our Lord said was not that life in the kingdom consists in a renewed childhood, but that no man can enter the kingdom save as an infant enters the world, naked and bare of all claim on his own behalf, utterly dependent on God for all and receiving all from His mere grace. It is to that state that we are to turn, humbling ourselves, if we are to enter the kingdom. To receive the kingdom as a gratuity from God is a very different thing, however, from using it as a *crèche*.

We may of course speak of a " mystical aspect of Christianity," and we may even speak of " the doctrine or rather the experience of the Holy Ghost," as " the real truth of mysticism." The term " Christ-mysticism " may have a good meaning. But in the ambiguity of the word " mysticism " all such modes of speech may also be gravely misleading. If it be true as R. C. Moberly said it was true, that " had only all Christians understood, and lived up to their belief " in the Holy Ghost, " they would all have been mystics," it is certainly not true, what he immediately adds, " or, in other words, there would have been no ' mysticism.' " All Christians not only might have been, or may be, but actually are " mystics " in the sense of the former clause: communion with God is of the very essence of Christianity: Paul tells us in so many words, that " if any man hath not the Spirit of Christ he is none of His." No man is a Christian who has not the experience of the indwelling Christ. But " Mysticism " is still with us and is another matter. This is a Pantheizing anti-supernaturalistic religiousness which must not be permitted to come to us in the sheep's-clothing of " essential Christianity " on the ground that it is only another name for " spiritual inwardness." It is most decidedly something very different from that.

THE CHRISTIAN DOCTRINE OF MAN. By H. WHEELER ROBINSON,
M.A. Edinburgh: T. & T. Clark. 1911.[1]

THE task which Mr. Robinson has set before himself, put briefly,
is the restatement in modern terms of the essential features of
Christian anthropology. He occupies, however, the very modern
standpoint which conceives everything as in a flux. What the Christian doctrine of man is, is therefore not a fixed thing but an ever
changing — perhaps Mr. Robinson would prefer to say, an ever
developing — quantity. It must be conceived as process, and
studied as history. Even " its statement in terms of to-day can
be no more than a cross-section of this continuous development "
(p. 2). There is no way of stopping the flow and obtaining once for
all a precipitate. We can tell what Christian men used to think
about man — what the writers of the New Testament thought, and
how, standing on the shoulders of the writers of the Old Testament,
they came to think it; what the Christian men of any subsequent
age thought and how, standing on the shoulders of the preceding
ages, they came to think it. We can tell what the Christian men
of to-day think, and how, in the midst of the influences which play
upon them they have come to think it. But who can tell what the
Christian man of to-morrow will think? And above all who can
isolate from the steadily flowing stream, we will not merely say
the constant elements, the elements which, up to to-day, have
remained characteristic of Christian thought, but the permanent
elements, the elements which will always remain characteristic of
Christian thought? The weakness of the genetic method to which
Mr. Robinson commits himself is revealed in such questions. We
may speak of the Christian doctrine of man " beginning historically
with the life and teaching of Jesus Christ "; we may represent the
whole subsequent historical development as but " the record of the
germination and growth of the seed sown by Jesus Christ "; we
may declare that it has never " lost its vital continuity with Him
who is its source "; we may praise it for its power to slough off
what is outworn and to assimilate new elements which in the enlarging knowledge of the increasing years present themselves to it.
But what we cannot gloze is that we have on this ground lost all
right to speak of any such thing as the Christian doctrine of man.
There have already been many doctrines of man held temporarily

[1] The Princeton Theological Review, xii. 1914, pp. 151–161.

by Christians, and for aught we know there will be many more. Unless we can lay our hands upon a continuous teaching character-istic of all who are Christians, bearing the mark not only of constancy so far, but of permanency forever, it is idle to talk about " the Christian doctrine of man." There is no such thing.

What is needed to give us a really Christian doctrine of man is obviously an authoritative standard of Christian doctrine. And Mr. Robinson has no such authoritative standard of Christian doctrine. The only authority which he ultimately recognizes is just his own personal decisions as to what were right and fitting (pp. 273–274). If we say, with our fathers, that the Scriptures are authoritative, clearly their authority rests on the inspiration of their writers, and the inspiration of their writers is reducible to " the Christian experience created in them by the Spirit of God." But we have Christian experience as well as they and from the same source. " The potential authority of the Scriptures becomes actual over us only through the continuity of this experience within us, as mediated by the historic society." That is to say, we company with Christians; by our association with them a Christian ex-perience is begotten in us which we refer to the Spirit of God; we see this same Christian experience reflected in the Scriptures; and so far, but only so far, we recognize them as authoritative. This, Mr. Robinson speaks of as a " unity of the historical and individual consciousness " which " goes back," he declares, " at last to the Spirit of God, on whom both depend." Thus he transmutes the " Schriftprinzip " of the fathers into a " Geistprinzip," but a " Geistprinzip " which reduces at last to a mere " Selbstprinzip." For he proceeds: " This is the religious expression of what is more than a pragmatic appeal to consciousness; we may put it philo-sophically by saying that the only rational appeal to authority is ultimately an appeal to intrinsic truth." Whatever manifests itself to us as intrinsically true we accept as true. It is its self-evidencing quality which authenticates it to us. This is the language of Lessing and the old Rationalism. Only, by it, they reduced what could be accepted as true to rational axioms. Mr. Robinson does not wish to do that. " We appeal," he says, " to the intrinsic truth, the self-evidencing credibility of the experience which runs through Bible, and Church, and the life of the Christian man to-day." There is something else, in his view, in man, the source of sound convictions of truth, besides the bare rational faculty: but there is no other source of sound convictions of truth than what is in man. We accept as true only what evinces itself to us, being what we are, as true on intrinsic grounds: only what is self-evident to us. The Scriptures have no authority to us; their contents are accepted by us only so far as they accredit themselves to us on intrinsic grounds. Even the testimony of Jesus is without authority to us. This does not mean that we have no reverence for Jesus or fail to recognize His uniqueness among men. " We may emphasize as we may, and ought, the closeness of His relation to the ideals of Israel, the intimate interweaving of His thought as well as His life with all the tendencies of His time; we may recognize the limitations to His power in the defeat of His hopes for Israel, and the limitations to His knowledge, as in the eschatological outlook of some at least of the discourses ascribed to Him in the Synoptic Gospels; the fact remains that there is a uniqueness in His own consciousness of Himself, in the historic presentation of His personality in the New Testament, and in His influence on the subsequent centuries of human life, that forbids us to regard Him as simply one of ourselves " (p. 279). It only means that whatever we think of Him, we cannot always think well of what He teaches us, and therefore cannot accept His deliverances as authoritative enunciations of truth. " Not only did the Light of the World shine first on Semitic faces, and flash its glory to us from the jewels of Oriental parable and paradox, but, in the humility of the Incarnation, the divine Thought was moulded to the pattern of Jewish conceptions. In particular, the eschatology of the Gospels is distinctively Jewish, and its influence on Christian thought has been out of all proportion to the worth of its forms. Scientific conceptions of the world and of the limits of its material destiny have replaced the panorama of Jewish apocalypse in the modern man's imaginative forecasts; the ultimate questions lie beyond both modern and ancient forms " (pp. 80–81). We may manage perhaps to believe in Jesus; we cannot always believe Him. We have no authoritative guide to truth except our own personal judgment, depending, as Mr. Robinson would add, on the Spirit of God.

When Mr. Robinson begins his book on " The Christian Doctrine of Man " with two chapters on "The Old Testament Doctrine of Man " and " The New Testament Doctrine of Man " respectively, we must understand, therefore, that he is not seeking and finding in the Old and New Testaments a doctrine of man which

shall be normative for Christian thought, but only writing the first
two chapters of the history of Christian thought concerning man —
tracing its roots in Hebrew soil, observing its first blades as they
shoot up from that soil in the teaching of Jesus and His first
disciples. He is even at pains to warn us in the opening words of
the former of these chapters not to fancy we can get authoritative
guidance for our thinking from the data with which it deals. "The
object of this chapter," he says (p. 4), "is to collect and interpret
the evidence afforded by the Old Testament as to the ideas of
human personality current amongst the Hebrew (or Jewish) people.
It is customary to refer to the result as 'The Old Testament Doctrine of Man,' and the custom is here retained for the sake of convenience; but it must not be supposed that any formal statement
of belief on these matters is contained in the literature itself, much
less that the title is intended to suggest that the results of our inquiry
are necessarily binding for Christian faith." A much greater wrong
is done to the Old Testament, however, by this method of approaching it than merely voiding it of its authority. It does not profess
to be a record of the ideas current among the Hebrew (or Jewish)
people. It professes to contain a revelation from God to the Hebrew
(or Jewish) people. And though of course much can be learned from
it of the ideas current among the Hebrew (or Jewish) people, this is
from its own point of view merely incidental, while its main communications are from quite another source. To lump both elements of
its contents together as ideas current among the Hebrew (or Jewish)
people is already to discredit the Old Testament in its most fundamental assertions. Mr. Robinson does it, however, an even greater
wrong than this. He insists, not only on interpreting it " on the plane
of 'natural' development," but actually on assimilating its teaching (against its own loudest protest, since Israel proclaims itself a
unique nation in contrast with heathen nations) to that of ethnic
thought. The euphemistic way in which he expresses this fell purpose to stifle all that is unique in the Old Testament is this: "The
Bible is here studied simply as ancient literature, and simply in the
light of ancient thought." The meaning of this is that the start is
taken from "primitive thought" as that thought is ascertained by
the anthropologists in their study of so-called "primitive peoples,"
and the Old Testament is forced into its grooves. Thus, if the Old
Testament tells us that God, having formed man of the dust of the
ground, " breathed into his nostrils the breath of life and man be-

came a living soul," we are at once told that we have here "the common idea of the breath-soul, which is so frequent in animistic thought, and indeed provides a name for animism (Latin, *anima*) " (p. 15). If the solidarity of the human race is assumed in the Old Testament, we are told that we meet here only that idea of " corporate personality " which is so widespread an item of " primitive psychology " (pp. 8, 27, etc.). If the Old Testament proclaims the great fact that the Spirit of God acts immediately upon the spirit of man, we are reminded of " the ancient conception of the accessibility of personality to all manner of external influences, not exercised through the natural sense-organs," and are asked to think of " telepathic powers " ascribed to all, of " the phenomena of fetishism and totemism, demonology and witchcraft, of a vast world of possible outside influences extending (for the Hebrew) right up to the Spirit of God " (p. 7; cf. p. 10). The interpretation of the Old Testament, in this sense, " simply in the light of ancient thought," means nothing less than the degradation of the Old Testament; and we cannot wonder that when after such evisceration of its teaching the contributions of the Old Testament to dogmatic thought come to be summed up (pp. 55–60) little is left but to deny that it supplies any basis for the doctrines of the universality of sin, inborn sinfulness, or a racial fall.

The New Testament is as little authoritative for Mr. Robinson as the Old Testament. But he shows himself, nevertheless, deeply interested in its correct exegesis, and expounds its teaching under the three rubrics of the Synoptic Gospels, the Pauline Epistles, and the Johannean writings, far beyond the direct needs of his special topic. With many of his exegetical findings we find ourselves in full accord: many of them seem to us, on the other hand, perverse and the outgrowth of zeal, say, to be rid of such doctrines as those of the fall of the race in Adam, original sin, and what Mr. Robinson calls " total depravity," under the impression apparently that by that term man is declared to be as bad as he can be. " Jesus," he tells us, " has no concern in tracing sin back beyond the will of the individual, but short of this He will in no case stop " (p. 94). He does not mean that Jesus finds sin only in the actual volition, as distinguished from the disposition of the heart: he recognizes that Jesus always carries sin " back past the external act to the inward disposition." He only means that Jesus says nothing of a fall in Adam. He does not even admit that Paul does. Speaking of

Rom. v. 12–21, he remarks: "The present passage certainly supplies no clear proof that he did, or exegetes would not be so divided as they are on this crucial point of exegesis" (p. 119). Paul, he strongly contends, teaches in Rom. vii. 7–25 the "doctrine of the fall of each man through the weakness of his physical nature," and takes "no account of the pseudo-historic Adam other than is implied in the fact that he was the first to fall in this way" (p. 118). Making thus every man the Adam of his own soul, we can hardly suppose him to ascribe in Rom. v. 12–21 any further direct influence of "Adam's act upon racial sin than belongs externally to the example and unique place in history of that act" (p. 120). The exegesis of this latter passage is very sinuous; and as a result Paul is made out a pure Pelagian. At least, however, he is allowed to teach the universality of sin as did Jesus before him; and that should have protected Mr. Robinson from certain remarks on Luke xiii. 1–5: "Jesus expressly refuses to allow any inference to be drawn from a calamity to the guilt of the sufferer" (p. 95, note); and John ix. 2–3: "It should be noted that Christ explicitly rejects the view that present suffering is necessarily the punishment of sin" (p. 139, note 3); generalized on another and equally mistaken basis: "Suffering, as the Book of Job has taught us, does not necessarily imply sin; but sin must necessarily imply suffering" (p. 310). The truth is that what we are taught by these passages is only that it is not possible for us to point out the particular ground of any particular instance of suffering: that sin does not underlie all suffering they do not in the least suggest. Side by side with his difficulties with "total depravity" (some very remarkable remarks upon Jesus' teaching with regard to it are to be found on p. 93), Mr. Robinson's difficulties with the Biblical doctrine of predestination should be mentioned — seeing that these difficulties appear also to root in his extreme zeal for human "freedom." It should not fail to be observed that he is already compelled to recognize the complete sovereignty of God as the Old Testament view (p. 63) — a recognition not really broken by the attempt to set up "two conditioning facts," in the goodness of God and the freedom of man (p. 64). When he reaches Paul he is still harping on the "double truth" of the grace of God and the freedom of man, with a view to leaving an impression that though Paul never even saw that they needed reconciling, and much less suggests any reconciliation of them, they are yet wholly irreconcilable. In Mr.

Robinson's own mind (surely not in Paul's) there is nothing for it but that the divine factor should give way to the human. The history of the Christian doctrine of man subsequently to the New Testament is traced in the chapters bearing respectively the titles of "Dogmatic Anthropology" and "The Contributions of Post-Reformation Science and Thought." The former of these traces the history through the Reformation period, the latter thence to our own day. The discussions of the former period are presented as dominated by the contrast between grace and free will; those of the latter by the problem of personality. Both chapters are ably written and are full of interesting detail. The discussion of the Augustinian-Pelagian debate is particularly well done; and the exposition of the revived Augustinianism of the Reformers is clear and decisive. It is wrong, however, to say that the doctrine of "immediate imputation" comes into Protestant theology late. It is Zwingli's doctrine, the formal characterization of which (p. 223) is misleading: it is only the guilt of "inherited" corruption, not "the guilt of Adam's first sin" which Zwingli doubts. It is wrong again to speak of Calvin's doctrine of predestination as "supra-lapsarian" (p. 225); Calvin was explicitly infralapsarian. But the trouble here lies doubtless in the widespread misapprehension of the meaning of these terms. It is absurd, of course, to repeat from Fairbairn that "Calvin was as pure, though not as conscious and consistent, a Pantheist as Spinoza": Calvin's theism was exceptionally pure and conscious. And it is equally absurd to repeat the inconsiderate charge against Calvin of Scotist elements of thought; Calvin stood, in his thought of God, at the opposite extremity from Scotism. We do not know what to make of a clause like this: "Pre-scientific supernaturalism, so far as it subordinated the events of Nature to the control of God, glorified divine wilfulness and human self-importance" (p. 238). Surely no one will deny that "the events of Nature" "are subordinated to the control of God": and surely that God controls "the events of Nature" does not carry with it the necessity of "wilfulness" on His part. If what is meant is merely that before the age of "the reign of law" men ventured to believe that God would intervene in the affairs of the world for the benefit of His people, why, it is to be said, that there is every warrant in Scripture and Reason — and surely in "Christian Experience" — for believing that yet, and that in any event the denial of it is expressed in unnecessarily violent terms. We have gained

immensely, of course, from the growth of scientific knowledge and
in nothing more than in the deeper conception of the orderliness of
the world which it has brought us: but this gain would be dearly
bought if it separated us further from God, and left us in the hands
rather of a machine. To be sure that all the events of Nature, and
of History as well, are under the direct control of God cannot give
us a "piecemeal" and "erratic" world. Law and God are not
contradictories and if they were, it were better to choose God than
Law for our portion. The chief interest in this chapter culminates,
however, in the discussion of "evolution," which enters in during
this period as a factor of importance in man's thought of man. The
current ineptitudes in dealing with this subject reappear here. We
cannot speak of evolution as relating "simply to the method of
man's creation" (p. 242): evolution cannot *create* — it presents a
substitute for creation, and undertakes to show us how man may
come into being without being created, by just, as Topsy says,
"growing." Nor can we follow when we are bidden to look forward
to further evolution with hope for ourselves, especially when this
is connected with some thought of personal immortality (pp. 243–
244). The doctrine of evolution has no hopeful message for us concerning our individual future; it teaches us to look not beyond
death but beyond ourselves for what is more nearly to approach
the longed-for goal. But of this we shall have something to say later.

The volume not only closes but culminates in its last chapter, for
which we may believe the whole was written. It is entitled, " The
Christian Doctrine of Man in Relation to Current Thought "; but
what it is is the systematic statement " in modern terms " of what
the writer believes to be " the essential features of Christian anthropology " (p. 344). In the light of the whole history outlined in
the preceding pages, he now essays to gather up what a Christian
man finds himself permitted by modern thought to think of man.
He sums it all up in five propositions: man has worth to God as
spiritual personality; he is an individual self, possessing moral
freedom and responsibility; sin is that which ought not to be; man
is dependent on divine aid for the realization of spiritual possibilities; personal development must be defined in terms of social relationship. Personality, Freedom, Sin, Society — these are the topics
which engage attention; and the interacting factors which determine conclusions are fundamentally the doctrines of evolution on
the one hand, and of human autonomy on the other. Mr. Robinson's

acceptance of the doctrine of evolution is quite decided and goes the whole way; but it can scarcely be said to be without misgivings. He apparently rejoices to be able to say that " modern views of the Bible and of the origin of the race remove Adam's transgression from the data of the problem," say, of the universality of sin (p. 269), but he is still compelled to add that evolution " still leaves us with an unsolved mystery of iniquity," which, he holds, " throws us back on personal freedom " (p. 302). He will not admit indeed that any other explanation of the universal sinfulness which our observation informs us of is tolerable than just that of personal freedom. " The search for explanation, other than freedom, springs from an inadequate view of personality " (p. 304). But Mr. Robinson knows as well as we do that freedom will not account for universality of action: he finds his exit from the difficulty as others do — by denying sin to be sin and affirming that only that is sin which is " freely " done by man. " The general conclusion is that whilst we may speak of the whole mass of evil tendencies in the race, transmitted from one generation to another by heredity, organic and social, as alien to the divine purpose for man, we must not call it sin in the full sense, since, apart from personal freedom appropriating it, it lacks the essential element of guilt. . . . Admittedly, this view of the facts leaves unexplained the universality of sin; yet if there be such a thing as real personal freedom, how can we ever go behind it, without denying its reality? " (pp. 306–307).

This is not all, however, which Mr. Robinson is willing to sacrifice to his unreasonable theory of freedom. To make room for it he is ready to curtail the omnipotence of God and His universal providence. God must have " limited Himself " when He created " finite personality, possessing moral freedom " (pp. 334 ff.) ; and the divine providence, while no doubt its " general purpose " shall be realized, must " leave room for the contingency which is a mark of human action " (p. 336). The predestination which lies behind particular providence is of course also denied, but strangely enough a particular foreknowledge is still allowed to God, on the remarkable ground that what God foreknows is unknown to us and thus cannot fetter our choice. " Thus there is full scope for human contingency; for divine foreknowledge does not enter as an operative force into our volitional activity " (p. 337). How foreknowledge differs in this from foreordination is not explained to us. What God has foreordained is certainly as hidden from us as what He foreknows: and His foreordinations therefore enter as little as His foreknowledge as operative factors into our volitional activity. Of course we shall infallibly choose what God has foreordained that we shall choose. But no less shall we infallibly choose what He has foreknown that we shall choose: otherwise it could not be *foreknown*. The choice is as certain in the one case as the other; and the choice is as free in the one case as the other. Of course Mr. Robinson is not to be expected to be affected by such considerations. He is not even affected by the fully recognized fact that the quality of freedom which he demands for moral responsibility cannot be justified on psychological analysis (p. 292), — so that he is compelled to say, " On the level of psychological analysis, freedom " — that is such a " freedom " as he demands — " seems impossible ": though he adds, " On the level of moral personality, freedom " — that is this kind of " freedom " which he has in mind — " is essential." We have no reason to believe this last assertion, however, except on the authority of its assertion. The plain fact is that it demands a kind of freedom for the grounding of moral responsibility which not only does not exist, but is not moral at all. God surely is a moral personality and immensely responsible; but He certainly does not possess a kind of " freedom " by virtue of which He may choose independently of the " set " of His nature. It is absurd to say we have no moral responsibility, unless we have equal power to choose as we choose and to choose as we do not choose.

The difficulties of the evolutionary scheme, taken as a complete account of the universe, seem to culminate in such facts as these: the presence among existences of living beings, among living beings of persons, among persons of the divine-man, Jesus Christ. If evolution itself is called on to give an account of these things, we must posit life as latent in the non-living, personality as latent in the impersonal, deity as latent in the undivine. The alternative is to suppose that life, personality, the divine are introduced from without — and that is to break away from the evolutionary principle as the sole organon of explanation. We are not quite sure that Mr. Robinson preserves throughout his discussions complete consistency in this matter. But ordinarily at least he takes his courage in his hands and goes the whole way with the evolutionary demands. We may feel considerable satisfaction as we begin to read this sentence (p. 278) : " Whilst all personality is dependent on evolution for the clay of its physical manifestation, all personality must transcend the course of such physical evolution by the inbreathed breath of spiritual life." So far, it looks as if Mr. Robinson intended to allow for an intrusion from without at the point of the production of personality. But our satisfaction is at once dashed by the addition of this closing clause: " though that breath of God go back to the very beginnings of life." The " breath of God " producing spiritual life was then, according to him, already present, though no doubt only latently present, through the whole series of nonpersonal living-beings. And there is no reason for stopping at the beginnings of life: it must have been equally present, though only latently present, also in the non-living existences that lie behind life. Similarly, with reference to Jesus Christ, we read (pp. 279–280): " From such conceptions it is not far to the recognition of all human personality as the partial manifestation of the pre-existent Son of God; *i.e.* the supra-naturalistic element we have recognized in all personality is spiritually akin to its one transcendent manifestation in Jesus Christ." And again (p. 280): " If it be asked how such an Incarnation be conceivable in connection with the acceptance of evolution, the answer is not an appeal to supernatural birth (*necessary* to Augustinianism only), but to the presence of personality in and amid the working of natural law in the case of every man." The Incarnation is, then, not a new beginning except in the sense that every new species is a new beginning; it is a new form taken on by what is old — actually present in the evolving stuff beforehand. Accordingly Mr. Robinson quotes here with evident emphasis on the comparison made, Illingworth's words (" Lux Mundi," ed. 1904, p. 152), to the effect that the coming of Christ " introduced a new species into the world — a Divine man transcending past humanity, as humanity transcended the rest of the animal creation, and communicating His vital energy by a spiritual process to subsequent generations of men." If we read Mr. Robinson aright here, then, he would posit the divinity which was " brought out " in Jesus as already latent in all personality, in all living beings, in the non-living existences which lie back of all. Jesus Christ is not an intrusion of the Divine into the human race; he is merely a modified man, as man is a modified beast, and a beast is a modified thing. All that is patent in Him was latent beforehand not only in us, but in the amœba and in the sea-water. Such a theory has express affinities with Manichæanism and Gnosticism, with their extraction of the spiritual and the divine from entanglement with matter; it brings into clear view the Pantheistic background of the evolutionary philosophy (as lucidly expressed by, say, Le Conte); but it is not recognizable as Christian.

Another difficulty which is thrust upon Mr. Robinson by his evolutionism — we have already adverted to it briefly — concerns the outlook for the future. Mr. Robinson strenuously argues for personal immortality — that is for the immortality of the soul, for, being rather of Plato than of Paul, he has doubts of resurrection; is not "death the natural fate of the bodily organism"? He cannot be content "with an ultimate philosophy which does not carry up all these values and personality itself into God as their home and source and hope" (pp. 287–288). But on evolutionary ground, is this reasonable? Is it even to be desired? From the evolutionary point of view Christ is a new species, as different from present humanity as humanity is different from the beast. From Him as starting-point a new kind may come into being, a new kind which after a while (it did not happen so with Christ) may win to itself deathlessness. But what of those who lived before this new species had its birth? What of those who have lived since it made its appearance in the world, but have manifestly fallen behind it in the qualities of the new life? What of all mankind up to to-day, no one individual of whom has been quite a Christ? We might as well confess it frankly — evolution has no hope to hold out for personal immortality. It bids us look forward to an ever bettering race, not to an ever bettering individual. It tells us to see in the individual a stepping stone to a higher individual to come, built up upon its ruins in the survival of the fittest. How can it promise eternal survival to the unfit? And to what of the unfit will it promise it? If we are to project into eternity the unripe to abide forever, instead of seeing an ever increasing succession of the riper and yet riper — how far down the scale of unripeness does immortality extend? If the merely personal — not yet the divine — has in it the power of an endless life, why not also the merely living — not yet personal? Is not the logic of the matter shut up to this alternative: since from the bottom up all that is to come is latent in the evolving stuff, and hidden in the amœba itself (or the clod, for the matter of that) there already exists, although not yet manifested, all the divinity that is in the Christ — all is immortal and "the spirit" that is in every form that ever existed shall live on forever; or else the immortality which crowns all is not attained until the end of the process is reached — which is not yet. We must not permit the fundamental fact of the evolutionary principle to pass out of sight, that the goal to which all tends is not to be found in the future of the individual, but in the successors of the individual. On an evolutionary basis, immortality must mean the persistence of the evolving stuff in every higher manifestation, and cannot mean the persistence of the unripe individual itself. When Mr. Robinson proclaims then the immortality of the soul, and of all souls, and indeed the ultimate perfection of every soul — for Mr. Robinson would fain " trust the larger hope " and believe in the ultimate blessedness of all (p. 338) — he is drawing his faith and his high hopes from some other than an evolutionary fountain. And to be perfectly frank we do not see that Mr. Robinson has left himself any fountain from which he can draw them. Evolution, plus the autonomy of man, with some sense of wrong-doing and ill-desert and a more or less vague feeling of the goodness of God, constitute but a poor basis for any eschatology. In point of fact we cannot form any sure expectation of what is in store for us, unless God has told us of it. Where no authoritative revelation of God is allowed, no express eschatology is attainable.

THE CHRISTIAN TRADITION AND ITS VERIFICATION. By. T. R. GLOVER. New York: The Macmillan Company. 1913. (Being the Eighth Course of the Angus Lectures, 1912.)

THE NATURE AND PURPOSE OF A CHRISTIAN SOCIETY. By T. R. GLOVER. Third Edition. London: Headley Brothers. 1912. (Being the Fifth of the Swarthmore Lectures, 1912.) [1]

UNDER the title of " Life and Letters in the Fourth Century," Mr. Glover published some dozen or more years ago (1901) fifteen studies of typical figures and movements in the literature of that century in which heathenism was dying and the Church was advancing to take its place as the governing force of the Roman world. It is a delightful volume full of insight and marked by great delicacy of touch and it gave us great pleasure to say as much, in re-

---

[1] *The Princeton Theological Review*, xii. 1914, pp. 277–283.

viewing the book in *The Presbyterian and Reformed Review* (xiii. 1902, pp. 664–666). When, a few years later (1907), he was called upon to deliver the Dale Lectures in Mansfield College, Oxford, Mr. Glover was well advised to adopt for them the same method of treatment which he had so successfully used in his earlier volume. The subject he chose was " The Conflict of Religions in the Early Roman Empire," and the resulting volume (1909) contains ten graphic studies of the various forms of religion which jostled each other in the opening centuries of the Christian era, presented, as he says, " not in the abstract, but as they show themselves in character and personality." This too is a delightful volume, vivid and illuminating. There are essays on the Roman Religion, the Stoics, and Plutarch; on Celsus and Clement of Alexandria and Tertullian; on the Conflict of Christian and Jew and the struggle between " Gods and Atoms." In the midst of them there stand essays also on " Jesus of Nazareth " and " The Followers of Jesus." These are not the best essays in the book. Mr. Glover is essentially a humanist; his interest lies in literature and the expression of personality in literature; his charm consists in his lightness of touch, the daintiness of his handling of his material, a certain fastidious humor which is poured over all. These are not the qualities which fit one best to deal with Jesus of Nazareth or those first missionaries of the cross who, " in deaths oft," broke a way through the ingrained prejudices of the old world's life and thought for the entrance of Christianity. Nor are Harnack and von Dobschütz and Weinel, Wernle and Pfleiderer, Wellhausen and Bousset, nor even Prof. Burkitt, and certainly not Mr. Conybeare, the best guides to the understanding of the beginnings of Christianity or the person of its founder.

Not that Mr. Glover fails in appreciation of the human personality of Jesus, or of the new spirit which animated His followers. He only fails to appreciate that there was anything more than a human personality in Jesus or that His followers were animated by any other spirit than may be summed up in the immense impression made upon them by Jesus' human personality. In his attempt to portray this human personality he says many fine and beautiful things about Jesus; many of the traits which really characterized Him he catches and knows how to throw vividly forward. He understands His uniqueness and the uniqueness of the religion He founded, and has such things as this to say about it: " As its opponents were quick to point out, — and they still find a curious pleasure in rediscovering it — there was little new in Christian teaching. Men had been monotheists before, they had worshipped, they had loved their neighbors, they had displayed the virtues of Christians — what was there peculiar in Christianity? Plato, says Celsus, had taught long ago everything of the least value in the Christian scheme of things. The Talmud, according to the modern Jew, contains a parallel to everything that Jesus said — (' and how much else! ' adds Wellhausen). What was new in the new religion, in this ' third race ' of men? The Christians had their answer ready. In clear speech, and in aphasia, they indicated their founder. He was new " (p. 116). But of the real uniqueness of Jesus Christ and of the religion which He founded — of the redemption of the world in His blood (" the blood of God," Paul calls it), of the regeneration of the world by His Spirit (" the Spirit of Jesus " is, with Mr. Glover, but His influence, His character " repeating itself in the lives of men and women ": pp. 139–140), Mr. Glover has no sense. And therefore his chapters on " Jesus of Nazareth " and " the Followers of Jesus " flat dreadfully among the more sympathetic studies which otherwise fill the volume. Jesus Christ is too high for him: he cannot attain to Him. Accordingly there creeps over one as he reads these chapters something of the feeling of unreality and insufficiency, though happily in indefinably less degree, that assaults the soul as we read the pages of, say, Renan. As an expounder of the color and movement of life in the ages of transition from heathenism to Christianity, Mr. Glover moves with firm step and shows unending skill: when he passes to expound Jesus Christ and His gospel he has got beyond his *métier*.

It seemed to be needful to say some such things as these about a volume which we are not now reviewing, because we may thus be enabled to make clear, in the fewest possible words, the exact nature and character of the volumes which we are reviewing. In them Mr. Glover turns aside from the portrayal of the ideas and personalities of the later classical period to undertake the exposition and defense of fundamental Christianity and of its function in the world. It will scarcely be necessary for us to say that these volumes are therefore of indefinitely less value than the former ones. Of course, in these too Mr. Glover writes interestingly: probably he could not write uninterestingly if he tried. He writes here, it is true, with what seems almost exaggerated simplicity of diction. It would appear that he is determined to be thoroughly understood by " the general." But all the old brightness is here. Indeed, many of the old bright sayings are here, for Mr. Glover has permitted himself in perhaps an unusual measure to treat his former (Dale) Lectures as a mine from which to derive gems for the ornamentation of the plainer pages of his later (Angus and Swarthmore) Lectures. The reader of the former volume, at all events, continually meets in the pages of the later ones fine turns of speech which are already familiar to him; mingled, no doubt, with others which are here new, derived from other fields of learned and loving research. Here, too, Mr. Glover, as is natural, writes largely *en historien*. This is his point of view. He has swept the wide horizon with widely opened eye and stands forward to tell his less fortunate brethren, as simply as may be, how Christianity appears to him and what seems to him to be its function in the world. We are bound to say also that the " reduced " view of the Person of Christ and of the essence of His work as an atoning sacrifice, which was thrown clearly, if even then prudently, up to observation in the more scientific Dale Lectures, retires into the background in the more popular Angus and Swarthmore Lectures; or perhaps we may even say recedes out of sight. It is doubtful if the cursory reader of these Lectures, while he might feel that not always all was said that might well be said, would detect any tendency to transpose the great music of Christ and His gospel into a lower key. The whole treatment is instinct with reverence for Christ, and that not merely as the historical source of the whole movement which we call Christianity but as its moving factor still; everywhere there is evident the most complete dependence on the Holy Spirit; and the fervor of Christian love glows on every page.

Behind the deep devotion to the person of Jesus which is everywhere manifest, we do not easily see that, after all, this Jesus is to Mr. Glover no more than a good man, who was not a " mediator between God and man, making atonement " in His blood (" Conflict," p. 156) ; whose death on the cross was only " a pledge of His truth," " making possible our reconciliation with God " (p. 139); and whose entire function it has been to reveal to us with new poignancy the great fact that God is our Father (p. 142). Who could imagine that beneath the constant references to the Holy Spirit as the power of a new life in Christians, there lies nothing but a reference to the " influence of Jesus " " repeating itself in the lives of men and women " (p. 140), which though Paul may call it " the

holy spirit " (note the lower-case initials) we may speak of perhaps as " the Christian instinct " (p. 150)? And certainly when we
read the appeals to the Great Commission we are hardly prepared
to understand that it is extremely doubtful (" Conflict," p.
114) whether this Commission is allowed by Mr. Glover, we will not say
merely to be an utterance of our Lord's, but even to be a genuine
portion of Matthew's Gospel. We read at the end of his Swarthmore
Lecture these moving words: " We have found the nature and purpose of a Christian Society, and we can sum it up in familiar words:
' Go ye into all the world, and preach the gospel to every creature ';
and, if we obey, we in our turn shall be able to speak of ' the Lord
working with us, and confirming the word with the signs following ' " (p. 85). It is not likely that Mr. Glover attaches any
authority to either text which he here cites: it is not likely that
he believes either to be a genuine part of the Gospel in which it is
now found. His bringing them together in this solemn passage may
help us to form an estimate of how much significance we may attach to his citation of the Great Commission as if it were of importance to Christians; and also of his method of dealing with his
audiences. Clearly in these Lectures Mr. Glover has not wished to
wound the sensibilities of his hearers by any suggestion of critical
hesitations, or of doctrinal doubts. He has wished to speak to them
on the basis of whatever of Christian belief — and more, of whatever of Christian sentiment — remained common to him and them.
No doubt his justification of this course would be that Christianity
after all is a life, not a dogma: and no doubt this justification is
valid — to a certain extent. Thus, at all events, the Lectures gain
immensely in usefulness as addressed to Christian audiences: they
may be read with profit by all. But they lose equally in significance
— unless we are to read them as signs of the decay of Christianity
as a doctrine and of its persistence merely as a traditional sentiment, seeking still to justify itself as such by its fruits. We wonder
if Mr. Glover does not feel as he delivers such Lectures much as
he portrays Plutarch as feeling as he argued for the old religion
which he looked out upon with saddened eyes in its decay — that
" delightful man of letters," as Mr. Glover describes him, " so full of
charm, so warm with the love of all that is beautiful, so closely knit
to the tender emotions of ancestral piety — and," Mr. Glover adds,
comparing him with Seneca, " so unspeakably inferior in essential
truthfulness " (" Conflict," p. 111).

It was highly appropriate that the distinguished son of Dr. Richard Glover should be called upon to deliver a course of the Angus Lectures; and the general tone of the Lectures which he has delivered on that Baptist foundation is a testimony to the Christian training which he received in the Baptist manse at Bristol in which he was bred. The subject chosen — " The Christian Tradition and its Verification " — gives large opportunity for the manifestation of a Christian heart, and the opportunity is taken. The verification of the Christian tradition is sought in experience; and the effort of the lecturer is to give to his hearers some sense of the immense mass of experience the Church of Jesus Christ has accumulated of Him; with the hope that by its contemplation they will be led on to experiment and by experiment to the discovery of " what life in Truth is." The Lectures are six in number and are entitled in their order: The Challenge to Verification, the Use of Tradition, the Significance of the Christian Church, the Experience of the Early Church, Jesus in the Christian Centuries, and the Criticism of Jesus Christ. The practical note is everywhere dominant, but it is no unintellectual Christianity that Mr. Glover recommends. As he elsewhere expresses it (" Conflict," p. 125): " It is only the sentimentalism of the Church that supposes the flabby-minded to be at home in the Kingdom of God: Jesus did not." What Mr. Glover aims at is the consecration of all human powers to the service of Christ: " action," he says, " is impossible without some working theory, and this very fact drives earnest men into speculation " (p. 37). He suggests, indeed, in a somewhat Sphinx-like saying, that " Jesus Christ is not a teacher to be quoted " (p. 31); but what he seems to mean is that His words are not to be repeated merely but lived. If he gives too secondary a place in the Christian life to the life of the mind (which is emphasized in the declaration that we must love the Lord our God, as with our whole " heart " and " soul," so also therefore of course with our whole " mind " — " the whole *understanding*, all the powers of thought and will," as Meyer explains it), he yet insists on the life of the mind. And he places Christ at the center. " The plain fact is that, in the long run, despair is at the heart of every religion without Christ; and if man or woman is to get through the world at all, it must be by the hardening or deadening of the more sensitive parts of human nature. Marcus Aurelius' *Diary* is a sort of breviary of despair " (p. 63). " One thing has always stood out clearly sooner or later. Whenever the

Church at large, or any church in particular, has committed itself to any scheme of thought that has lessened the significance of Jesus Christ, it has declined. Error always tells; and the error of over-estimating Jesus Christ ought to have told by now, but the experience of the Church so far suggests that it has no real reason to dread any danger from over-estimating Him, but rather that the danger has always come from obscuring or abating His significance. It is, I think, worth while to reflect upon what this involves. The faith has been tested in every compromise that Christians have attempted, and if it is still held, it is with some warrant " (pp. 86–87). Good apologetics, that! Can we have read Mr. Glover wrong, when we have read him as " obscuring and abating the significance of Christ," both in His Person and in His work? We could wish he had known " Jesus Christ and Him as crucified " better, and Wilhelm Herrmann less well!

The Swarthmore Lecture runs somewhat on the lines of the third of the Angus series. Its leading topic is the significance of the Christian Church, and its keynote is perhaps struck in some such words as these: " We do not enough value the fact that the story of the Christian religion is the story of personality influenced by personality — re-birth constantly the product of the influence of the re-born " (p. 27). There may be an echo of Wilhelm Herrmann in this and we are glad therefore to read on the next page: " The blessing comes from a higher source, but the broken bread is given by human hands " — followed by some illuminating remarks. We do not wonder that surprise has been felt that this particular topic was chosen for a lecture addressed to Friends. Mr. Glover defends his choice of topic in an interesting Preface, the upshot of it being (if we understand him) that Friends especially need instruction on the Church. This is probably true; at all events it is instruction on the Church that Mr. Glover gives them — and he does it very well. Beginning with the inheritance we have in the Christian Church, he ends with the duty of the Church to the world, while between the two he expounds the relation of the individual to the Church. In the center of all, here too he sets Jesus Christ. " From the very beginning and ever onwards right in the centre of all their thoughts, the Christian communities have had Jesus Christ, the Son of God, in whom God was, reconciling the world unto Himself. He has been the leaven within the Church, disruptive, propulsive, recreating and stirring, the permanent life, the guaran-

tee and promise of a future that shall progressively transcend the
past

> No dead fact stranded on the shore
> Of the oblivious years,

but the living Christ, always recognized, and owned and loved by
the Church. The great function of the Church has been to witness to
Him, and to bring the world face to face with Him " (pp. 42–43).
We ask again, Can we have misread Mr. Glover when we read him
as holding to a " reduced " Christ? For the rest, we call attention to
two small points. One is the comma, in the first sentence we have
quoted, after the phrase " in whom God was." This gives a particular interpretation to II Cor. v. 19 — an interpretation which, indeed,
is wrong, but which seems notable on Mr. Glover's lips. The other
concerns the allusion to the Parable of the Leaven, in which an interpretation of that Parable which Mr. Glover repeats in more than
one of his series of Lectures, is adverted to. This interpretation conceives that Parable as teaching not so much, as it has been customary to expound it, the hidden, pervasive growth of the Kingdom
in the world, as the seething fermentation of life which takes place
in the Church of Christ — in the individual man and in the community. The leaven, says Mr. Glover, *works;* and in its working
bubble after bubble *breaks;* the breaking of the bubbles is not an
indication that the end has come, but that there is *life* at work
behind them. The interpretation again is wrong; but again it is not
without its significance on Mr. Glover's lips.

We must not close without pointing to a passage in each of the
Lecture-courses which has pleased us vastly. In the Swarthmore
Lecture we point to the section on " Grace " (pp. 33–37) — " ' the
greatest of all the Catholic doctrines,' Renan said " (p. 33). In
the Angus Lectures we point to the passage on the phrase " From the
foundation of the World " (pp. 135–140), — in which is enshrined
" the great fact of God's love as antecedent to all things — of
Christ as the embodiment of purposeful love — of the universe itself
in all its range as a Cosmos indeed, inspired and achieved by love,
and subservient in its last detail to love " (p. 139).

JESUS. Von W. HEITMÜLLER, D. u. Professor der Theologie in Marburg. Tübingen: J. C. B. Mohr. 1913.[1]

THIS volume contains a reprint of the Article " Jesus Christ " in the third volume (1912) of the encyclopædia published under the name of "Die Religion in Geschichte und Gegenwart"; together with an Address on "Jesus of Nazareth and the Way to God" delivered on March 11, 1913, at the seventeenth meeting (at Aarau) of the Conference of Swiss Christian Students.

The occasion of the publication of the volume is not without its interest. The Theological Faculty of the University of Marburg has for some time been in controversy with the Prussian *Kultusministerium* over the appointments made from time to time to its professorships. One fruit of this controversy was a pamphlet — his opponents call it a *Brandschrift* — by Jülicher bearing the title of "Die Entmündigung einer preussischen theologischen Fakultät." Notice was taken of this pamphlet in the Prussian Chamber of Deputies, and in the course of some remarks upon it the Freiherr von Schenk of Schweinsberg, who happened to be not only a deputy of the Chamber but also President of the *Konsistorialbezirk Kassel,* within the bounds of which the University of Marburg is situated, took occasion to comment also, with some sharpness, on Heitmüller's Article "Jesus Christ" (April 5, 1913). This is what he said:

" I am constrained to show you by means of a scientific work to what such a critical tendency can lead. I will be quite brief and, with the permission of the President, will read from the scientific work, ' Die Religion in Geschichte und Gegenwart,' only the following sentences from the Article Jesus Christ, II, Particular Questions in the Life of Jesus. ' For the Jewish conception there lies immediately comprehensible in the idea of "the Son," that God stands to Jesus in a special relation of trust and love; as "the Son" Jesus knows Himself as before all other men the object of the special love of God. As we must understand from the context, He knows Himself as the Son precisely because He knows God in a unique fashion and God has made Him the vehicle of Revelation. Vehicle of a unique revelation, the Son absolutely — we are almost appalled (*erschrecken*) by the loftiness of this consciousness. It is certainly in no way a divine consciousness, but yet a vocational consciousness which almost oversteps the bounds of humanity and evacuates all the human experience which is otherwise manifested — with ref-

[1] *The Princeton Theological Review,* xii. 1914, pp. 315–324.

erence to which we might ask indeed whether it can be made consistent with soundness and clarity of mind.' (Hear, hear! and for
shame! from the Right.) ' Here is the point at which the figure of
Jesus becomes mysterious, almost unearthly to us. But ' . . .
Now comes the But, for were the author to stop at this point and
not proceed to this But, I am convinced that he, like any professor
who propounds such teaching, must be liable to have a process
entered against him for blasphemy (deputy Heckenroth, very true!)
or at least for overstepping his professorial privileges. The text
being read proceeds: ' But we have scarcely the right to distrust
the essential contents of our passage, Matt. xi. 25 to 27, and that
the less that the whole manner of conceiving the significance of
Jesus (Revealer) which meets us here corresponds very little with
the modes of thought of the primitive community.' Gentlemen,
I am constrained to place my finger upon this point, because I say
to myself, Here is an absolutely essential point, which must receive
attention, for here there comes to an end what is otherwise spoken
of as a theological tendency; here there meets us a point of view
which is absolutely different from what we otherwise speak of as
the Christian point of view (very true! from the Right). We are
not dealing here with two tendencies, but with two world-views
(very true! from the Right), with two completely diverse religions.
They cannot be forced under the shibboleths of ' positive ' and
' liberal ' or dealt with from the standpoint of party politics. . . .
Gentlemen, no indulgence can be shown to such things — even under
the mantle of freedom of teaching (*Lehrfreiheit*). I am convinced,
if we enter upon such a pathway, that we must ultimately reach
the point where it must be said, What is here offered to the people
has nothing in common with Christianity except the name, but
intrinsically nothing more. The monistic conception of life is making way among ever wider circles of our people, not merely among
the professors at the universities, among the educated and learned —
no, it is already penetrating into very wide circles of all ranks, and
the more deeply our population descends on the downward sloping
road of the monistic conception of life, the more firmly and steadily
must the *Kultusminister,* as the first counselor of the throne, take
his stand upon the high Christian world-view, and give expression
to this his point of view in his decrees and acts. . . .''

To the man in the street these must seem very sensible and
straightforward remarks. But they naturally gave great offense at
Marburg. The venerable Herrmann at once protested against them
in behalf of his colleagues, in an open letter addressed to von Schenk
and published in *Die Christliche Welt* for May 1, 1913 (No. 18),
and Heitmüller has felt compelled by them to lay the Article attacked
before the wider audience before which he was incriminated, as his
sufficient defense. In republishing thus this Article Heitmüller adds

to it the Swiss Address as offering " a practical-religious supplement " to it. The Article is a scientific statement of what we historically know of Jesus. The Address deals with " the complex of the much discussed questions which concern the significance of the historical Jesus for faith." The two together may supply us, their author thinks, with some suggestion at least of his whole attitude, scientific and religious, towards Jesus.

The line which Heitmüller takes in reply to von Schenk is apparently a simple denial that he can justly be charged with ascribing to Jesus an unsound mind. He therefore contents himself at this point with a simple reference to a passage in his Article in which he expressly declares that the attempt to represent Jesus as of unsound mind has not succeeded. This passage (p. 89) runs as follows: " As assured data of the tradition, we have the vocational consciousness transcending the limits of the prophetic and the fact that Jesus laid claim to the Messianic dignity in some sense or other. That these two facts raise difficult psychological questions, scarcely needs to be emphasized. And when of late the mental soundness of Jesus has been questioned, and He has been presented as a pathological subject, this attempt has at least a possible point of attachment here. It has not succeeded and it can never succeed. The poet of the parables, the framer of the proverbs, was as sound as ever man was. And in this sound consciousness we find that content! Much can be brought forward to mitigate the puzzle; we are in no position to solve it." It is right to recall, however, that von Schenk does not represent Heitmüller as declaring Jesus to have been of unsound mind. He represents him as saving himself from that by a " But." The gist of his representation appears to be that Heitmüller deals frivolously with the charge that Jesus was of unsound mind and seems indeed to treat it as a preferable hypothesis to the ascription of a divine self-consciousness to Him: that he even appears to suggest that had Jesus' mysterious self-consciousness been but a little more exalted than he allows it to have been, we should have had to admit that He was of unsound mind. And this representation we can scarcely deny to be fairly justified.

The self-consciousness of Jesus is manifestly the crux of Heitmüller's presentation of Him. He declares it roundly to be merely human. " That the self-consciousness of Jesus," he says (p. 68), " was through and through a human one, will be regarded as self-evident by every one who without hindrance from ecclesiastical dogma, makes use of the sources and of the historical criticism which is indispensable with reference to them." But in the palmary passage, which von Schenk cites (p. 71), it is only by dealing most drastically with Matt. xi. 27 (which is there under discussion) and violently reconstructing its text after the unfortunate example of Harnack, that he can reduce the lofty self-consciousness there ascribed to Jesus to something which he can pronounce human; and he seems indeed only barely able to pronounce even what he makes it soundly human. A little later he speaks of " this self-consciousness which far transcends all human experience and seems to lift its subject out of the series of men " (p. 118); and again at the end of the Article (p. 148) of " that extraordinary vocational consciousness transcending all human analogies, which, if we regard it as sound, can be represented only as an intimation that in this man in peculiar measure a creative, or as the pious man puts it, a divine life has entered into history." The constant recurrence of the suggestion that this self-consciousness may be thought to be unsound — or is thought by some to be unsound — may serve the purpose of conveying to the reader a keen sense of its exaltation. It also, however, leaves the impression on the reader's mind that in Heitmüller's view Jesus' self-consciousness just falls short of being unsound; and that, even after he has reduced it far below its actual representation in such an unassailable passage as Matt. xi. 27. The conviction unavoidably forms itself, accordingly, that Heitmüller, after all said, finds himself with a Jesus on his hands whose self-consciousness is so little " through and through human " that he does not quite know what to do with it, and is compelled to allow that those who pronounce it a deranged self-consciousness have some show of justification, even after he has reduced it from the actual representation of it in, say, Matt. xi. 27. And, if this reduction be not allowed — as it cannot be allowed — what then? We cannot see that Heitmüller safely escapes from the antithesis, *aut Deus aut non sanus;* and since he will not have the *Deus* at any cost, that he has any just ground of complaint against von Schenk's charges. He does seem upon the verge of assigning to Jesus a diseased self-consciousness (and that is all that von Schenk charges) and he appears to save himself from this result only by dealing with extreme violence with his texts.

The vigor of Heitmüller's Socinianism in his conception of Jesus' person has already become evident. He will not hear of Jesus being anything else than a man and a man of His times. How he obtains this purely human Jesus from records which present a very different Jesus lies in that mystery of " Liberal criticism " with which we are so familiar nowadays: Heitmüller's critical methods differ in nothing from those current in the " Liberal " circles of which he is an ornament, and require the less to be adverted to here in detail that we have recently had occasion to explain them pretty fully in this *Review* (xi. 1913, pp. 218 ff.). By means of this " criticism " very drastically applied, he manages to extract from records which present to us a divine Jesus, a purely human figure; from records which present to us a supernatural Son of God surrounded by an aureole of miracle, a simply natural man who wrought no miracle. Not at Nazareth only, but throughout His career, He could do no mighty work, though He laid His hand on a few sick folk and healed them. Jesus had an impressive personality and may be credited with " faith-cures " (p. 67) ; it was from this beginning that tradition, certainly very rapidly, transmuted Him into " the Aesculapius of His people " (p. 60). But the historian can allow to Him no real " miracle " (p. 61). When " the historian " is done with the records, indeed, we find ourselves with very much less real knowledge of Jesus in our hands than we could wish. Heitmüller desires to separate himself, it is true, from that overstrained scepticism with reference to the knowledge of Jesus which he recognizes has been of late far too common even among theologians (p. 153). But he recoils from the other extreme also, which would have it that we know Jesus " as if He were one of our contemporaries " (p. 154). The way in which he would express himself is this (p. 41) : " What we can attain by this procedure is certainly far less than we could wish. It of course does not suffice for writing a Life of Jesus; but neither is it enough even to sketch a portrait of His character or of His activity. There are individual traits of the portrait of Jesus which we distinguish, some of them clearly, some of them only in obscure outlines; there is often lacking the unifying bond and if we are prudent and desire to proceed with surety we will do well to make very little use of complementary and psychologizing inferences. On the other hand what we can grasp historically is not little and it includes what is most important. Whether the Christian can found his faith on it is a question which it is not the historian's business to answer and the Christian should not raise it."

It must be admitted that Heitmüller is not very exigent with reference to the historical foundations of a Christian's faith. That is a matter which is more fully discussed in the Lecture at Aarau; but there are some odd hints regarding it even in the encyclopædia Article which it may repay us to take note of in passing. When discussing the story of the Virgin-birth, he determines it to be an invention of Gentile Christians on the model of the heathen myths of divinely-begotten men, possibly in misapprehension of the proclamation of Jesus as the " Son of God " (pp. 45–46). Yet he can tell us (p. 43) that " the question as to the right of the faith which comes to expression in it, is not strictly speaking at all subject to the judgment of the historian." The historian, it seems, can only " determine whether this faith showed itself early or late, and in whom it is found in the primitive Christian community." The plain man is apt to think that when it has been shown by the historian that the belief that Jesus was born of a virgin stands on a par with the similar belief as to Plato, it is already determined that it has no right to exist. At an earlier point the distinction here suggested is drawn broadly out (pp. 12–13). " The pious man, even the simplest and most unlearned, on sinking himself believingly in these faith-laden accounts, finds the Jesus who kindles faith and whom faith needs. But the historian who does not ask what Jesus means for faith, but would fain ascertain and present what can be known of Jesus' life, acts, and nature by means of the generally recognized instruments and methods of scientific research, is able only through infinitely toilsome and complicated investigation to establish the treasure which is hidden in these writings on really sure reports. The chief question for him, before he uses them, is that which concerns the historical value of these sources." Is not this " the chief question " for the man who seeks spiritual life in them too? We observe that even Heitmüller says that the pious man finds what he seeks in the Gospels only when he sinks himself in them *believingly* (*bei glaübiger Versenkung*). Can he ponder *believingly* upon accounts whose historical truth he suspects or denies? To recommend the pious man to kindle his faith by narratives which he knows or suspects to be fables is a frivolity which must avenge itself in the degradation of faith into empty sentimentality.

The state of the case is not really altered by Heitmüller's view that though the Evangelical narratives are not historically trust-worthy we come into contact in them with Jesus' "creative per-sonality." How can we come into contact with Jesus' "creative personality" in accounts of words which He did not speak and deeds which He did not do? Meanwhile, we are led by this remark to observe Heitmüller's point of sight. According to him, though we obtain from the Evangelical narratives very little knowledge about Jesus, we do obtain from them a very vital knowledge of Jesus. Not that they enable us to form a clear conception of His whole personality. We may regret this; but we may congratulate ourselves that what is most important lies within our reach — a sufficient insight into His religious character, at least in its funda-mental traits. "No doubt insight into its development is here too almost wholly denied to us, and thus we lack an important key to its full understanding. But we discover nevertheless its outlines and the chief elements of it" (p. 107). There are (apart from Jesus' acts) two sources for our knowledge of it: His words, and the re-ligious life of the primitive Christian community, quickened by Him, from which we can argue back to the personality which in-spired it (p. 108). Through these means we come into touch with the really creative thing in Jesus, which was just Himself. "The secret of His efficacy from His death on rests in His personality, which received its peculiar stamp from that extraordinary vocational con-sciousness, leaving all human analogies behind, which, if we regard it as sound, can be taken only as an indication that in this man a life, in peculiar measure creative — the pious man says, divine — has entered into history. Filled with life in and with God, sustained by this enigmatical consciousness, Jesus' personality has become — that is its significance — a 'power of God' from which ever new streams and surges of religious power have proceeded and proceed, the inexhaustible source of religious life, out of which Christianity still to-day draws" (p. 148).

In these few words there is compressed a brief exposition of Heitmüller's whole conception of the function of Jesus, of Heit-müller's entire "Christianity." Elsewhere he merely expands it, as, for example, thus (pp. 105–106):

"The pious zeal of the dominant ecclesiastical party and the pru-dent calculation of the magistracy had won in the unequal conflict with the bold Galilean prophet. In the gibbet at Golgotha they had prepared an abrupt ending of the history of the Messiah Jesus.

Yet at and with Golgotha this history really began: the history of
Jesus in His community, which has not reached its end even to day.
And this history leaves no doubt of the answer which is to be given
to the historian's question, Where the original and creative element,
the effective force of the manifestation of Jesus is to be sought, in
what its world-historical significance is grounded. Not in His
sacrificial death on the cross, as dogma has determined. Nor yet,
as modern opinion wishes, in His teaching or preaching, which is
called by predilection, ' the gospel.' It needs only a glance into the
beginnings of the Christian community to perceive the truth. The
disciples had in their enthusiasm hoped that Jesus should redeem
the people Israel. Their hope was shattered by Golgotha. Like
sheep who have lost their shepherd they were scattered, without
guides, without hope. But in a little while we find them again in
Jerusalem, at first behind closed doors, then, however, in the streets.
At first they whispered it in the ear — then, however, they proclaimed it from the housetops: that Jesus is nevertheless the
Messiah. Rapidly the little band of simple Galilean men and
women became a company which was feared and persecuted and yet
thus only increased. What turned these fishermen and peasants into
missionaries, these fainthearted and stupidly fleeing disciples into
heroes, the little community into the mustard-seed whose branches
should soon shade the whole earth? What was the mark of this
community? The knowledge of the preaching of Jesus? The no-
doubt valuable new information on religion and ethics which it
contains? Certainly not. But *the personality of Jesus.* To Him
the hopes and the thought of this band attached themselves, from
Him it looked for everything in life and death; that He would come
was its hope, its prayer that He would come soon. Jesus, *He Himself,* was the power which wrought here, not some kind of knowledge
or other, which He had discovered and proclaimed; not some kind
of transaction or other which He had wrought. Jesus Himself is the
' gospel.' His personality was what was new and creative, that entered into history, animated the community, and has worked itself
out in humanity."

This is eloquently said, but certainly not truly. On the face of
it, it was the resurrection of Jesus from the dead, not His " personality," which reanimated His overwhelmed followers. Heitmüller, by the way, has strangely little to say of Jesus' resurrection:
apparently he does not consider it even worth refuting, as he refutes,
say, the Virgin-birth. But he had nevertheless, immediately before
the passage which has been quoted, said this: " After a short time,
we see His Galilean adherents back in Jerusalem; they proclaimed
that Jesus was nevertheless the Messiah, that He was risen from
the dead. This, however, belongs no longer to the history of the

'historical Jesus,' but to that of the primitive Christian community " (p. 104). On the face of it it was not " the personality " of Jesus that conquered the world, but the glad-tidings that God was reconciling the world with Himself in Christ — a text which Heitmüller misquotes (p. 169). Paul, for example, preached not Christ *simpliciter* but Christ " as crucified." Nor was Paul the first to preach this. There is no " double gospel " in the records of the New Testament; and it was Jesus Himself who declared that He had come to give His life a ransom for many — a text which Heitmüller vainly strives to rob of its true content and bearing (p. 117). It is not by the influence of His " creative personality " but by His blood of the covenant which is shed for many that Jesus has redeemed the world.

These ideas of course recur in the Aarau Address, the precise purpose of which is to show that — and how — Jesus may still be the — or a — way to God. This Address begins, like a sermon, with a text; and this text is taken from the words of Philip, " Lord, show us the Father, and it sufficeth us." In Heitmüller's view (for he makes as strangely little of Sin here as of the Resurrection in the encyclopædia Article) the one thing needful is that we should " see the Father," that is, in his sense, realize God as Father. What Jesus does is merely " to show us the Father," that is, by the impression made on us by His religious personality lead us to be, like Him, religious-minded. He is not the only one who can show us the Father: there are other ways of finding God and many there be who go to Him by them. We should not lose our faith, then, even were He to vanish out of history: should He prove a mere myth, we could still find our way to the Father. But Jesus is a Way to God; and we, in our surroundings, can not only best find our way to God by Him but the loss of Him as the inspirer of our faith would be a great loss indeed.

In developing these ideas Heitmüller begins by pointing out that the starting-point in all seeking after God must be found in our hearts. But only the starting-point. We cannot attain complete, victorious certitude of God, clearness as to that which He means for us, in isolation. " Generality, paleness, indeterminativeness, characterize the religious experiences which we make in ourselves, in independence. They are without blood and sap, without triumphant, compelling power, without concrete content. Content and convincing, emancipating power are received by them, they become revelation of

God, *only* and *first* when they fall in with a powerful experience of
God outside of us, only by contact with the stream of religious life
which surrounds and flows about us " (p. 158). Now, the religious life
which thus surrounds *us* is in its peculiar form Christian — goes
back to Christ as its source. " Not in all cases — that we wish to
recognize — but certainly for the most part, when men meet us
with living faith in God, we hear that they owe to Jesus ultimately
the best that is in them " (p. 161). Thus Jesus meets us in the way
and serves as the rallying-point for the religious-minded. " His
figure is the symbol and vehicle of all religious goods and knowledge " (p. 162). And as time has gone on the richness of this symbolism has become ever greater. Into it has been interwoven all
that the later generations of the Christian community have experienced, and thus " the traits of His figure have been deepened, the
outlines of its form here and there have been altered " — there have
been contributions made to it by a Paul or a Luther or a Schleiermacher — and " thus Jesus, or what men have taken and still take
for Him, the source and symbol and type of the Christian community's experience of God, as a whole," becomes indirectly and
mediately, through His community, the way to God for us (p. 162).
This, however, is not all: throughout Christian history, Christian
faith has been powerful, rich, and clear in proportion as Jesus has
been clearly laid hold of, and thus He has been also directly and
immediately the way to God for many (p. 163). " This is certain —
we wish to say it once more: that it is in any case not necessary
that for men of the present day Jesus should be directly the guide
to God, that the religious life of the individual should relate itself
immediately and constantly to Jesus, be determined by Him, correct itself with reference to Him. There are other media of revelation, other ways to God. God lets Himself be found, experience of
God can grow and gain power, through the community — and indeed also through the religious life outside the community " (p. 163).
But all through the Christian ages, nevertheless, " Jesus, the historical form of Jesus of Nazareth, has been the immediate way to
God *for many*," and He can still be such for us. It is a mistake to
think of Jesus as wholly a figure of the past. " Jesus belongs in any
event also to the *present* — in His effects. In manifold reflections and
radiations He reaches in His effects up to our day. And we have to
deal with *that* Jesus, who in His effects can be a *part of our reality*,
not with the various fragments and externalities which are no doubt

important for the historian, and belong to His person, not with His several conceptions and ideas, with His view of the world and of nature and the like, but with His entirety, His personality, His essence, with that which has worked and works " (pp. 164–165). If we ask where we are to find this really historical Jesus, " not the symbol and vehicle of the Christian religion, but the historical form of Jesus, of course that which is operative in history " — we must certainly say, not in the presentation of exact research. " The historian who works with the instruments and methods of exact research, and for good or evil must confine himself to them, can certainly even with the richest sources, grasp and set forth only details, particular traits, of a historical figure, not its personality. Here, however, we can have to do only with the indefinable, mysterious somewhat which we call personality — *it* is the source of the effects which proceed from a man. The personality is not, however, grasped by the instruments of exact history alone " (we beg the reader not to omit to mark this " alone "); " it is true even of the men with whom we live that we recognize and grasp their personality, their real nature, not through exact observation of details; they can be perceived only by the inner eye, intuitively understood — *experienced* " (pp. 165–166). There is perpetrated in this representation a complete reversal of the facts of life: if anything in life is certain, it is certain that it is precisely by the intense observation of details, often no doubt done unconsciously, and by their vital synthesis that we arrive at that vivid sense of personality which moves us in others. But working on this false analogy Heitmüller proceeds. Thus also we grasp the personality of Jesus by coming into contact with Him as He has lived in history; best of all in the narratives of Scripture (though Scripture, we have been told, does not depict Him as He really was!), when read — almost a lost art nowadays — simply and at large. Thus we meet with a character to which religion is first and God is all. Gazing upon this personality, we do not acquire indeed a faith *in* the history of Jesus, but we acquire faith by *means* of the history of Jesus (p. 175). No doubt, we do not see Jesus as He was, but only as He has been interpreted to us — by a Luther, by a Schleiermacher. " But what Paul, Augustine, Francis of Assisi, Luther, and Schleiermacher experienced by means of Jesus, and on which we also nourish ourselves, was nevertheless also an effect of the historical Jesus." " And what if now," Heitmüller proceeds to ask, " it were proven that Jesus was only the reflection and the cult-figure of a community? It has not been proven — but even if proven, then, what comes to the individual from the history of Jesus in the Gospels — which in that case would be a history of the oldest Christian community — by means of reception of it and living into it, bears in itself its own inner necessity and truth. No doubt, among other things we must in that case refrain from relating ourselves to Jesus and by this we would lose much. Above all for the times of inward uncertainty and weakness in our life with God, we should not be able to find support in this — that this manner of experiencing God has been actually a reality in its purity and compelling power in a man. It would be a great loss, but certainly not destructive of faith itself" (p. 176). After this clear declaration that Jesus may indeed be useful but cannot be necessary to faith ("Christian faith," mind you!) Heitmüller has little more to add except this positive declaration with which his Lecture closes: "Jesus' significance is a purely one-sided and limited one, and on that very account a very great and abiding one: it rests on the absolute forcibleness of His consciousness of God, which precisely for this reason makes Him the revelation of God for others, and in the apprehension of God as holiness and love. Thus He is a source of power; from which there ever proceed new waves and surges of that faith in God, the exposition and further development of which remains the task left to the exigencies and gifts of the different generations — to the Spirit who takes of the things of Jesus (John xvi. 12 ff.). Our generation too has had its particular task. But we too, like all generations, may with Philip turn to Jesus with the confident request: 'Lord, show us the Father, and it sufficeth us'" (pp. 177–178).

We have transcribed the argument of this Lecture with perhaps unnecessary fullness, because it seems to be put forward by Heitmüller as his defense against the charge that what he teaches is "Christianity" only in name, and has nothing but the name in common with anything that has hitherto been known by that name. Clearly it offers no sufficing defense against that charge. Under the name of "Christianity," indeed, it is clear that Heitmüller teaches a religion which stands in so external a relation to Christ, that it can get along very well without Him, and appeals to Him only to enable it to do a little more easily perhaps, perhaps a little more thoroughly, what it would be quite able to do even though He never existed. Jesus is an encouragement, an incitement, an in-

spiration to religious endeavor: nothing more. Obviously this has
nothing but the name in common with the Christianity which sees
in Jesus Christ not merely a revelation of God as Father, but the
reconciliation of God to sinful man. Here, as von Schenk truly
says, are not two varieties of "Christianity," but two different
religions, and the only question is, which of these two religions is
Christianity. We know which is the Christianity of Jesus, of Paul,
of all the New Testament writers, who all alike present Christ as
offering in His blood a ransom for the sins of the world. This is
not the "Christianity" of Heitmüller. We cannot profess to be
of both parties here. They stand in crass contrariety to one another
and we must choose between them; and choosing between them,
we must frankly declare of which of these two religions we are.

THE CHRISTIAN FAITH: A SYSTEM OF DOGMATICS. By THEODORE
HAERING, D.D. Translated from the second revised and en-
larged German edition, 1912, by John Dickie, M.A., and George
Ferries, D.D. Two volumes. London and New York: Hodder and
Stoughton. 1913.[1]

HAERING'S "Der christliche Glaube" was published in the
autumn of 1906, and was briefly but sufficiently noticed in this
Review for January, 1908 (pp. 166–167), by Dr. C. W. Hodge.
The appearance of an English translation of its second edition —
which was published in 1912 — would in itself call for nothing more
than an intimation of that fact, with some remarks, perhaps, upon
the nature and extent of the changes introduced into the second
edition, and the quality of the English rendering. On the former
matter there is no need to enter into detail: the changes made are
rather of the nature of expansions than of alterations. Of the latter
matter we cannot speak with entire satisfaction. The sense of the
original is doubtless conveyed in the translation. But the clearness
with which the original was credited by its German readers ("marvelously perspicuous" is Titius' characterization of it) is certainly
conspicuously absent from the translation; and all the charm which
they also attribute to the book as a popular religious discussion is

[1] *The Princeton Theological Review*, xii. 1914, pp. 667–685.

dissipated. We have found the reading of the English version somewhat heavy going.

An adventitious importance has been given to the English translation, however, by the unmeasured (and let us say at once, gravely misleading) praise which has, on the occasion of its appearance, been lavished on the treatise. An influential journal, widely circulated in both hemispheres, for example, announces it as " theology at its best." Had the proper qualification been inserted, and the book announced merely as Ritschlian theology at its best, little exception would need to be taken to the characterization. Haering's theology is exceptionally good Ritschlian theology. But no Ritschlian theology can be really good theology. Ritschlianism would not be unfairly described as the form taken in the later years of the nineteenth century by Socinianism, squeezed into the molds of Neo-Kantian philosophizing. And in the nature of the case, Socinian theology is bad theology, no matter in what philosophical garb — and, we may add, no matter with what religious fervor — it may be set forth. Haering brought to the exposition of Ritschlianism a warm religious nature, deeply steeped in Swabian Pietism, and, from the publication of his maiden-book (" Ueber das Bleibende im Glauben an Christus," 1880) in the first days of " the movement " (the first literary symptom of the existence of " the school " was the publication in 1876 of Herrmann's " Die Metaphysik in der Theologie "), he has been diligently engaged in pouring the new wine into these old bottles. The wine has in the process no doubt taken on some of the flavor of the bottles, but the bottles have certainly burst. Despite the many modifications it has received at his hands — all of them, happily, in the direction of a fuller recognition of essential Christian truth — and despite the profoundly religious tone which he has cast over the whole exposition, what Haering gives us remains just Ritschlianism, and that is to say just Socinianism — Ritschlianism, Socinianism in the richest religious expression possible to them, perhaps, but Ritschlianism, Socinianism still.

When we say Ritschlianism, however, we say not only Socinianism but Socinianism in a decadent form. A quarter of a century has elapsed since Albrecht Ritschl died (1889), and the stir which his theological teaching began to make during the last decade of his life has already quieted down, and the movement which he inaugurated has largely merged in the general course of unevangelical thought. Perhaps it would be too much to say that his system has been already " relegated to the ineffectual past," for there still remain with us men of mark — among whom Haering holds a conspicuous place — who have drawn a great part of their inspiration from it. But these are mostly men somewhat advanced in life; and it is not without its pathetic side to witness the publication by them, in their declining years, of system after system of a dogmatics, which, to put it brusquely, has had its day. There may not be wanting, indeed, some indications that the true state of the case is not altogether concealed from themselves, and that, in presenting their several transcripts of the Ritschlian system, they write consciously as much as historians of thought as they do as religious teachers. Haering, for example, not only makes no pretense of writing " definitive dogmatics," but even asserts roundly that there cannot be any such thing: " the dogmatics of any one generation," he repeatedly declares, " comes in the next to belong only to the history of dogma " (e.g. p. 21). He has even erected what he calls " the mutability of dogmatics " itself into a dogma, and finds for it crisp gnomic expression. " Theologies," he remarks (*Zeitschrift für Theologie und Kirche*, xx. 1910, p. 166), " change as doth a garment, and only the gospel abides."

In utterances like this there is obviously betrayed, however, much more than mere distrust of the permanence of one's own system in act of being expounded. What is uncovered is a veritable despair of dogmatics as such; or, to put it in its true light, a profound disbelief in the real — or " universal," as it is fashionable to phrase it — validity of what is yet somewhat oddly called religious knowledge. It is the same point of view which finds expression in the rampant individualism of Haeberlin's declaration that the results of dogmatics " can never be the same for all theologians, just because and so long as the forms of piety which are described are not the same " (*Schweizerische theologische Zeitschrift*, xxiii. 1906, pp. 17 f.); or in Herrmann's even more disintegrating representation, which not only gives to each man his own necessarily peculiar dogmatics but will not permit any man to have a self-consistent dogmatics even for himself, since each several one of his " ideas (*Gedanken*) of faith " will necessarily bear traces of the peculiar occasion out of which it individually arose (" Die Kultur der Gegenwart," I. iv. 1906, pp. 616 ff.). The root of these disturbing deliverances is pointed out by Herrmann himself when he warns his brother Ritschlians off from the notion that a universally valid expression of faith is possible, on the ground of the inseparable correlation of that assumption with that conception of revelation which sees in it a supernatural communication of truth (*Zeitschrift für Theologie und Kirche*, xvii. 1907, p. 29). Only an objective revelation of truth can supply a basis for an objectively valid dogmatics. And as the Ritschlians will not have an objective revelation of truth, they are in no position to give us anything better than individualistic, which is to say, subjective dogmatics.

Haering, of course, as a good Ritschlian points to revelation as the source of all religious knowledge. But to Haering, of course, as to his fellow Ritschlians, revelation is not " propositional " but purely " personal." To Christians at least (p. 144), it is summed up in the " personal life " of Christ (p. 293). Nothing can exceed the emphasis with which Haering insists upon this. " The revelation of God in Christ," he tells us (p. 262), " is the source, norm and basis of all Christian religious knowledge." Again (p. 317): " The revelation of God in Christ is the ground and norm of all religious knowledge." Further (p. 317): " As revelation is the ground, so is it the norm, of Christian knowledge of God, as regards its content and compass, as well as its nature." As regards its content, God is what He reveals Himself to faith in Christ as being. As regards its compass, God is nothing except what He is according to His revelation of Himself in Christ. The Christian *Glaubenserkenntnis* is, in a word, as is repeatedly asserted, *ganz und gar* the knowledge of the revelation of God in the " personal life " of Christ. No mode of statement is omitted which could emphasize the exclusiveness of the personal revelation in Christ as the source of Christian religious knowledge. But as this revelation is " personal " and not " propositional " it requires to be interpreted. The instrument by which the personal revelation of God in Christ is received and translated into religious knowledge is described as " faith." Sometimes, indeed, Haering speaks of the revelation in Christ as if it directly produced " faith ": " the revelation of God in our religion," he says (p. 201), " is a revelation which produces faith, i.e. trust." But this is at once varied to the somewhat different form of statement, that God's " revelation consists in a self-attestation capable of producing personal trust." What is meant is apparently that God's manifestation of Himself in Christ is of such a sort that faith may find a basis for the knowledge of God in it — if it will. For Haering is very

jealous of what he looks upon as the " freedom " of faith, and will
not have the knowledge of God thrust upon any man by sheer
revelation. In his view there are therefore two factors which must
coöperate in the production of religious knowledge — Revelation
and Faith: and only in their conjunction can religious knowledge
arise. " It is a revelation which faith has to interpret, and it is faith
which has to interpret the revelation " (p. 421). Revelation alone
cannot give religious knowledge; and, though neither can faith alone
give it, yet it is faith which works up into knowledge what in revelation is only the raw material for it. If without revelation there is
no object of knowledge, without faith there is not only no subject
able to assimilate this knowledge, but no " knowledge " as yet to
be assimilated. Religious " knowledge " is the product of a voluntary " faith " working upon a " revelation " which at the most is a
mere " manifestation." On the face of it, here is a purely subjective
theory of religious knowledge.

Haering, it is true, makes some effort to escape from this subjectivity; to avoid making faith, in effect, the creator of its own
object. We find him, for example, vigorously asserting that " judgments of value," in the sense in which that concept is employed by
him and his fellows, include in themselves " judgments of being."
He strongly protests, indeed, against the representation that a
value-judgment leaves the reality of the object of it undetermined
(pp. 65 ff.). He protests further against the representation that the
reality of its object is affirmed only on the ground of its value; that
it is, in other words, an assumption or postulate resting on subjective experience. This appears to mean that a judgment of value
presupposes the recognition of the reality of the object whose value
is affirmed, and the recognition of it on some other ground than its
value. Nevertheless, when an instance in point comes under discussion, and we are told dutifully (p. 67) that " the validity of judgments of faith " — here the judgment of value concerning God —
" depends on the living conviction that the supreme reality in
question " — that is, God — " manifests itself," it is at once added,
" but only to one who consents to recognize its reality as of value
for him personally, not in the irresistible way in which the laws
of logic demand recognition." The fat is obviously again in the
fire. The will is brought in as the decisive factor in conviction: such
a conviction is distinctively a voluntary conviction, and in this
differs from the conviction wrought by logical reasoning, which, in

contrast with it, is a compulsory conviction. This surely implies that the conviction in question is purely personal — that is to say " subjective " — and cannot impose itself on another — that is to say is not of universal validity. On what grounds could we impose on others convictions which even with ourselves we recognize as not imposed but as voluntary? Another, obviously, shares such convictions, if he shares them at all, also only voluntarily; that is by a purely personal, subjective act. The process by which the individual obtains a religious conviction, then, it would seem, is that by a voluntary act he recognizes value for himself in the object before his mind; and when it thus, by this voluntary act on his part, acquires value to him, it becomes " real " to him in a " living conviction." On the face of it, this is an extraordinary thing for it to do. But in any case, have we not here a purely subjective process? The ground adduced for the alleged reality of the object certainly appears to be its recognized value to the subject. And that value surely to all appearance is attributed to the object, not because of any compulsion of recognized fact, but by a voluntary act of the subject's own. That a " living conviction " of " reality " can arise in this fashion is sheerly incredible. All convictions, of whatever kind, are the product of course of evidence, and are not producible at will; and each conviction naturally rests on evidence fitted to produce that particular conviction. Judgments of being must rest, therefore, on evidence of reality, not on " recognition of value "; as indeed we have seen Haering himself compelled to allow — in words.

These remarks have brought us to the center of Haering's doctrine of Faith. It is not easy, to be sure, to determine precisely what he means by faith, despite the fundamental place held by this conception in his system. One reads the inordinately long Apologetical Introduction to his treatise with suspended mind, looking, and ever looking in vain, for some clear definition of the exact sense in which the ever recurring " faith " is employed: and the want is not supplied even in the section of the Dogmatic part of the volume which expressly treats of Faith. It emerges, however, with sufficient clearness that faith is with Haering distinctively " voluntary conviction." It is without significance for our present point that he sometimes broadens his definition so as to include feeling as well as volition in the source of faith; as in the (for the elucidation of Haering's view) pregnant sentence: " Faith, on the ground of determinations (*Entscheidungen*) of the volitional and emotional spirit, in coöperation with the historical self-revelation of God, is sure of a reality which is inaccessible to theoretic understanding (*Erkennen*), compulsory knowledge (*zwingendes Wissen*) " (p. 257). As " voluntary conviction," he is never weary (as in the sentence just quoted) of setting " faith " over against " compulsory knowledge," a thoroughly misleading opposition (cf. the, no doubt insufficient, strictures of Titius, *Theologische Rundschau*, x. 1907, p. 378), which nevertheless forms the hinge of his whole treatment. According to this distinction, convictions which we cannot choose but have are knowledge; convictions which we have or not as we choose are faith. He even occasionally falls into the unhappy habit of setting " knowledge " and " faith " unqualifiedly in contradiction to one another, as if either we could believe what we know to be false, or that need not be true which we know. Thus in speaking of reservation in prayer with respect to earthly things, he remarks (p. 536), " It does not spring from faith, but from fear of the power of knowledge "; and again he tells us (p. 540) that certain reservations in defining miracles result from a feeling that " a decision on the point has already been pronounced in another quarter, from the side of knowledge." In such contrasts " faith " is in danger of appearing purely arbitrary. In any event Haering makes its complete voluntariness so of its essence that he exhibits an almost morbid fear lest its " freedom " should be curtailed. " Compulsion," he declares (p. 209), is " the greatest enemy of all faith." God can propound faith to us, but He cannot produce it in us: He can only ask " whether we bestow our trust on Him in Jesus," " whether we are willing to let ourselves be laid hold of by His love revealed in Jesus." So alien is compulsion to faith, indeed, that it is laid down as axiomatic, that " in the interest of faith " there cannot be any revelation which " compels assent on grounds of logical necessity "; and even that " there cannot be any testimony to " a revelation, " so homogeneous in itself and so uniformly authoritative, that it is not left to the believing community to fix the grade of authority which shall belong to each part of the record." The very nature of the divine revelation with which faith deals is thus accommodated to the nature of faith as necessarily voluntary: God Himself cannot " rush " the jealously guarded defenses of its voluntariness. In the sphere of knowledge, in a word, compulsion may rule — we must accept what presents itself to us as true: throughout the whole realm of faith, freedom reigns — what we accept here we accept at our own option. Faith thus comes forward in Haering's system as a contribution which we ourselves bring to the production of religious knowledge. There can be no religious knowledge without faith, and faith lies in our own power. Whatever religious knowledge we have we work up at our own option out of non-compulsory materials. The function of faith in the production of religious knowledge is, indeed, so magnified that it almost seems at times as if it were supposed to bring something to its objects which lends them a reality not possessed by them in themselves.

This is not to be obscured by representing what is meant as merely that it is only to religious susceptibility that religious data appeal. It has become quite common nowadays to say that the whole object of Ritschl and his followers in their doctrine of " value-judgments " and " faith " is to maintain that only one with religious susceptibility is competent to form a judgment in religious matters. If this were the case, certainly no writers could write more misleadingly or indeed more trivially. No one has ever doubted that only a religious being can apprehend religious truth, as no one has ever doubted that only a moral being can apprehend moral truth; or — to push the matter to its conclusion — that only a rational being can apprehend truth at all. It requires as special an endowment to know that two and two make four as it does to apprehend the excellence of virtue or to perceive the beauty of holiness. But that it is not this truism which Ritschl and his followers wish to express by their doctrines of " value-judgments " and " faith " is plain from the circumstance that it does not cover the ground claimed by their contentions. We do not need to go further here than to ask: what becomes then of this immense emphasis on the voluntariness of faith? Our religious susceptibility is not subject to the control of will. Does the susceptibility which responds to the moral quality of a virtuous act, or which, say, is sensitive to the music of a sonata of Beethoven, either exist or not, only at our option? By virtue of the presence of the susceptibility in the subject the object is apprehended more adequately than otherwise it would be — that is all. Nothing is apprehended which is not " there " independently of its apprehension, and no increase of reality is brought to the object by its more complete apprehension. Value-judgments, judgments of appreciation, in other words, are not substitutes for judgments of being but supplements to them:

they are superinduced on them and make only for more adequate knowledge of what is already less adequately known on other grounds. The blight of Haering's conception of faith as an essentially voluntary act affects his whole system, and vitiates even his most promising concessions to an objectively valid Christianity. The function he assigns to revelation, for example, as a factor in the production of religious knowledge carries with it necessarily a strong assertion of the actual historical existence of Jesus Christ, the personal revelation of God; and an equally strong assertion of the historical trustworthiness of our records of Him. Haering therefore explicitly recognizes that, since Jesus Christ is the source and basis of Christian faith, " for all others than those contemporary with that historical revelation which produces faith, there must be historical primary sources of information (*geschichtliche Urkunden,* ' historical records ') regarding it " (p. 279). Though he does not go the length of Kähler's " whole Biblical Christ," in positing the object of faith, he cannot satisfy himself with Herrmann's meager and vague " inner life of Jesus." He argues that we must be historically assured of much about Jesus before He can serve as a revelation of God to us. To Kähler's astonishing declaration that there is not a single fact concerning the historical Jesus of which we can be historically sure, he opposes the recognition that " a certain measure of historical credibility (*Glaubwürdigkeit*) is indispensable, and its place can be taken by no amount (*Gewalt*) of religious value " (p. 281). That Jesus may work upon us as a revelation of the love of God we must know Him; and to know Him — seeing that He is a historical figure — we must have trustworthy historical accounts of Him. Haering even goes so far as to include in the trustworthy historical knowledge that we must have of Him, the knowledge of Him as the conqueror of death. He therefore makes the trustworthiness of the accounts of the " resurrection " of Jesus — as to the " fact " of it only, however, not as to its " mode," as he too explains in the customary effort to deny the resurrection while seeming to allow it — neccessary to the creation of Christian trust in the complete sense. Indeed, he seems almost inclined to throw his circle out more widely still, and to bring (contrary to his fundamental principle) the preparatory " revelation " of the Old Testament itself into the compass of the grounds of faith, and even the march of God's providence in the world, and nature itself — when viewed from "the storm-free center of the revelation of Jesus." But no sooner do we begin to congratulate ourselves on such apparently notable concessions than we are rudely called back to the qualifications which eviscerate them all.

If Haering is willing to say flatly that "it is all over with faith" if it can be shown that "Jesus is only a creation of faith" (p. 217), he will not say that faith cannot exist unless it can be shown that Jesus is not a creation of faith: he will allow that "knowledge" can destroy "faith," he will not allow that "faith" needs the aid of "knowledge," or indeed can profit by "knowledge." No sooner does he declare, then, that faith requires the historicity of Jesus for its validity than he begins to qualify. We must ask after the message of historical trustworthiness which history can supply, and which faith may demand. And Haering's contention is that history can neither supply nor faith ask certainty — but only probability. No doubt, he sometimes speaks as if he were only denying that history can supply or faith demand precise "demonstration," in the strict sense of that word as the designation of a mode (not degree) of proof. But his real meaning goes further than that. "If the tradition concerning Jesus possessed compelling credibility (*zwingende Glaubwürdigkeit*)," he argues (p. 217), "we should have what we have elsewhere had to renounce in the name of faith, on account of faith's very nature — that intelligent men would be compelled to believe, or rather, not to believe, but to recognize as indisputable fact. On the contrary, there is no such compulsion in the sphere of history, so soon as we pass beyond the establishment of external facts and simple connections." The statement is, perhaps, not perfectly clear in all its suggestions; but this much seems plain — history does not yield facts which intelligent persons, conversant with the historical evidence, are compelled to accept as facts — beyond at least certain external facts in their external connection. History presents to us (beyond this) only data which we may (however intelligent and however well-informed historically) accept or reject with good conscience — at our option.

History does not make, for example, the reality of Jesus Christ — such a Jesus Christ as may be recognized as a revelation of the love of God — so certain that every intelligent man, conversant with the historical evidence, must assent to it as indisputable. All that history can bring us, as Haering goes on to explain (p. 218), is a sufficiently high probability (*Wahrscheinlichkeit*) to enable the

" religiously susceptible " " to surrender themselves to the impression of this person " " with a good conscience." If the religiously susceptible man makes this venture of faith, he may indeed attain through this to a certainty of the existence of this Jesus. But assuredly, then, the certainty he thus attains is the product of his faith, not of the historical evidence — since, says Haering, this certainty " but for that surrender would be unattainable " (p. 218). We seem here perilously near to making Jesus — the Jesus in whom we find the revelation of the love of God — " only the creation of faith ": and, in that case, Haering himself being witness, " it is all over with faith." Haering does, indeed, go on to say that the purely historical evidence of the existence of this Jesus must be sufficient to compel the man who will not accept it " to admit, in order to maintain a good scientific conscience, that he is kept from giving his assent, not by compelling grounds of a historical character, but by a theory of the universe opposed to the Christian " (p. 218). Apparently this means that though there cannot be compelling grounds in history for affirming that Jesus existed — the Jesus in which faith sees the revelation of the love of God — neither must there be compelling grounds discoverable in history for affirming that He did not exist. History is not to say the decisive word as to the fact, one way or the other. All that can be asked of history — all that history can give — is room for believing in Jesus, on other grounds — grounds apparently of " religious susceptibility." Historical evidence cannot establish it; but historical evidence must not exclude it. It may be proper to ask here how the history which cannot give compelling evidence of the existence of such a Jesus, can be supposed to be possibly able to give compelling evidence that He did not exist. Are not these equally historical facts? If we deny that history is capable of making the existence of such a character certain, do we not in that very act deny that it is capable of making His non-existence certain? And is not the upshot simply then, that history cannot give any certainty in such a matter at all; and our actual conviction with respect to it, whether positive or negative — must rest upon and be the product of our own subjectivity? In a word, does not Haering appear here in a purely anti-historical rôle? What, then, becomes of his theory of religious knowledge, which requires for its production the two factors of " revelation " and " faith "? If the " revelation " itself depends for its reality on the " faith "; and without " faith " can be looked upon only as a possibility not absolutely refuted by objective historical evidence — are we not on the plane of a pure subjectivity? Is not, in any express sense, the Jesus in which " faith " finds the revelation of the love of God, in that case, the creation of " faith " itself?

We have other misgivings also about the revelation of God in Jesus Christ, upon which Haering hangs the entirety of the Christian's religious knowledge. We can for our own part cheerfully allow that the revealing Christ is more convincingly accessible to us in the historical records than Haering will admit. We could grant him what he cannot accept from us, then — a thoroughly trustworthy access to Christ. But how can we be assured that the holy love of God is revealed to us in this Christ's " personal life "? Haering scouts all external evidence, such as that of miracles and the like, and presents instead this: " the drawing near on God's part in a historical personality must prove itself real, through God's inmost being revealing itself in His whole life and work " (p. 205). We are to know that this life and work is a revelation of God (otherwise unknown) not because it is convincingly attested as such, but just because " God's inmost being reveals itself in the whole life and work." Circular reasoning could scarcely be more bold. How can we know that God's inmost being is revealed in this person's whole life and work, unless we already know God and know what His inmost being is? And what in that case becomes of our complete dependence on the revelation in Christ for our knowledge of the God of holy love? Haering continues: " God's will of love towards sinners must confront us in the work of this personality, in a manner so effectual, that His work can be experienced as the work of God, and consequently excite in us trust in the love of God." But how can we recognize God's will of love for sinners in the work of this personality unless we previously know of God's will of love for sinners? The question becomes indeed a very pressing one, on Haering's ground, What reason have we for believing that God is love? — though he gives us to understand that the entirety of his theology is summed up in that proposition. According to Haering we can know nothing of God except by revelation, and this revelation is for Christians (for non-Christians there are hints that a substitute may be found) wholly included in the personal life of Christ. Not in what Christ teaches, nor in the details of what He did; but in the general drift of His life as historically transmitted to us (in a probable record) and received in a religiously susceptible soul. But how can this general drift of Jesus' life, even though transmitted to us with entire trustworthiness in history, reveal even to the religiously susceptible that God is love? On Evangelical ground the revelation of the love of God in Christ is clear enough; for herein is love, not that we loved God, but that He loved us and sent His Son to be the propitiation for our sins; for God commendeth His own love towards us, in that, while we were yet sinners, Christ died for us. But on Haering's ground? On Haering's ground we have no other reason for believing that God is love, except that Jesus Christ lived and wrought in that firm belief — if indeed we can assure ourselves, amid the uncertainties of historical testimony, that He did so live and work. It is as subject of faith — Himself exercising perfect trust in God — that He becomes the producer of faith in us. We believe that God is love for no other reason than that Jesus believed that God is love. Is it more than a case of spiritual contagion? And is such spiritual contagion enough to base our whole hope in life and death upon? Haering is perfectly right when he declares that we can postulate " pardoning love " to the Righteous God as a fact, only on the basis of an actual revelation. But he will admit no revelation in word. Where, on his ground — without any Divine Son of God and without any Atonement wrought in His blood — do we get any actual revelation in fact of the pardoning love of God? In his view Jesus was sinless: how, in His " personal life " — not in His teaching — does He manifest to us specifically " the pardoning love " of God?

Obviously we are at the center of Haering's Christology when we raise such questions. Like all good Ritschlians it is the work of Christ which chiefly interests Haering and he accordingly (like all the rest) begins with it, and only infers from what he supposes Christ to do, what he is willing to allow that Christ is. The work of Christ is all included for him in this — that He reveals God to us as holy love, though, as we have seen, it puts him on his mettle to make out that He does this. Of course, everybody knows that from the beginning Haering has stood out among the Ritchlians as the one among them all who was striving to formulate the most adequate doctrine of Atonement. Gustav Ecke, pointing out the shortcomings of the teaching of Ritschl and Gottschick (the most completely Ritschlian of the Ritschlians), feels able to speak of " the surmounting of these shortcomings by Haering." And indeed Haering must be given the credit of having made effort after effort to find some

" objective aspect " for Christ's work on Ritschlian assumptions
(" Ueber das Bleibende im Glauben," 1880; " Zu Ritschls Versöhnungslehre," 1888; " Zur Versöhnungslehre," 1893). What he has
put forward with this end in view, however, he has had steadily to
retract (a fair brief account of the course of his thought here may be
read in Bensow, " Die Lehre von der Versöhnung," 1904, pp. 106 ff.),
until in the present volumes not a vestige — or perhaps we may say
literally just a vestige — of it remains. He still divides the work
of Christ, viewed as regards its content, into His prophetic and His
priestly work; and describes the former as wrought by Christ " as
God's personal Revelation of Himself for us," and the latter as
wrought by Him as " our Representative before God." He thus
appears as still fain to discover some Godward side to Christ's work.
But he discovers none. The best he can do is to represent that God is
pleased with the perfection of Christ's revelation of His holy love
to men. How this redounds to our credit remains meanwhile, as
Wendt points out (*Theologische Literaturzeitung*, xxxii. 1907, coll.
646-647), unexplained; and we may add inexplicable.

As Haering still speaks thus of a " priestly " work of Christ, in
which He " represents " us before God, so, continuing his careful use
of old categories which have lost all their content to him (he actually
orders his treatise on the Trinitarian categories of " Faith in God
the Father," " Faith in Jesus Christ, the Son of God," " Faith in
the Holy Spirit of God and Christ," though he does not in the least
believe in the Trinity), he still speaks also of a " kingly " work of
Christ. His exposition of the work of Christ is thus cast in the
familiar molds of His office-work as Prophet, Priest, and King, while
yet there is assigned to Him none other than His " prophetic " work.
The kingly work of Christ is the work of the exalted Christ, and
that Haering throws stress on this work of the exalted Christ stamps
him at once as belonging to the Ritschlian " Right." Though he thus
asserts his belief in a continued saving work for the exalted Christ,
however, Haering is careful not to let it be supposed that he considers such a belief an essential element of the Christian religion:
he thus preserves a place among good Christians for his fellow
Ritschlians of the " Left," who will not hear of any saving work
for the " hidden " exalted Christ (p. 660). And in his own Ritschlian
fear of mysticism (no " Christ Mysticism " for him) he is careful to
confine this work of the exalted Christ within very narrow limits
and not to permit it to add anything of importance to His work on

earth — not advancing here in substance of teaching beyond what he had already taught in his earliest work (1880). When he describes "the work of the exalted Lord" as consisting solely "in the fact that He makes His historical work on earth operative" (it is meanwhile not made clear *how* He does this), he is only remaining true to the necessary implications of Christ's saving work as he conceives it, which he makes to consist wholly in the revelation of the love of God to us through His trustful life in complete recognition of that love.

When we think of the exalted Christ we naturally think of that Resurrection by which, according to the Scriptures, He entered upon His glory. Haering's dealing with the Resurrection is very characteristic. He adverts to it twice (pp. 211 ff., 627 ff.), and then leaves us not quite certain what he believes with respect to it. He allows that it is essential to complete Christian faith to hold that, when the disciples "saw the Lord, they were not self-deceived, that He actually showed Himself to them as the Living One" (p. 211). All theories of merely "subjective vision" must then be rejected (p. 629). Beyond this, however, he will not go. He too wishes to draw a distinction between "the fact" and "the mode" of the resurrection; and thus to cover up the actual denial of all "resurrection" by those who talk of an "objective vision" — or, as Haering prefers to phrase it, "a vision which has an objective basis." His chief concern is that all should agree that it is unimportant what we think became of the dead body, so only we understand that the person Jesus did not at death pass wholly out of existence — as if we could talk of a "resurrection" of what never died, or as if Jesus' disciples required assurance that He, like other men, still lived after that experience which we call death. We may infer that Haering attaches great importance to this attitude towards the question of our Lord's resurrection from the circumstance that he repeats it in his booklet, called "Persönlich-Praktisches aus der christlichen Glaubenslehre" (1911), and there expresses his thanks to his theological friend Max Reischle for "well-considered and pious words" on "the mode and manner" of the resurrection of Christ, to which "nothing essentially new has been added since" (p. 108). What Reischle has to say on the matter, however, whether in his articles in the seventh and eighth volumes of the *Zeitschrift für Theologie und Kirche* or in his later "Christliche Glaubenslehre in Leitsätzen" (ed. 2, 1902), is merely that while the resurrection experiences of the disciples cannot be scientifically proved not to have been a delusion, yet they are assured facts of faith, though even to faith " the question as to the *how* " of them remains unanswerable. That is to say, we can be sure only " *that* the crucified One really lives as the Lord of His kingdom and revealed Himself to His disciples as the Living One." What Haering thinks so fine in Reischle, therefore, is only his teaching that we cannot be sure that Christ ever rose from the dead, but we need not concern ourselves about that — all that is important is that His spirit did not die with the body and that He has entered into His glory.

With the idea of the exalted Christ there is associated the thought of prayer to Him, and Haering is accordingly led at this point to face this question (p. 665). He treats it with the chary caution with which he deals with all such matters. He permits us to pray to Christ; but he adds: " All invocation of Jesus is . . . adoration of God who is revealed to us in Him." That is to say, we do not invoke Jesus as He is Himself God, but only as an intermediary through whom God reaches us and we Him. The notion has its affinities with Karl Thieme's insistence that Christ deserves our adoration because of His " representative unity " with God.

With this introduction Haering proceeds formally to discuss the " Divinity of Christ " (pp. 667 ff.). He is willing for himself to employ the term, " Divinity " of Christ — but only as an indication that " saving faith " embraces God and Jesus in one act of confidence; and so, " in the view of saving faith " Jesus " belongs on the side of God." But, we may add, no more truly than " as He who reveals God, He belongs really to us " (p. 669). Just because He is the revelation of God, we are told, He " is not God; otherwise He would not be a revelation of God " (p. 670). Accordingly, throughout the whole treatise, Jesus is treated frankly as a human being, in his nature not different from us, His brethren.

It would naturally be supposed that with this view of Jesus' nature, Haering would make as short work of the notion of the pre-existence of Christ as, say, his fellow Ritschlian, H. H. Wendt, in his contemporaneously published " System der christlichen Lehre," whose " Dynamistic Monarchianism " differs from Haering's only in its greater frankness of expression. Strange to say, however, Haering appears to feel compelled to attribute some sort of preëxistence to Jesus. We say he appears to do so; for despite the somewhat lengthy discussion given to the matter, it is not made perfectly clear. He

speaks of the preëxistence of Christ as one of the *Grenzgedanken
unsrer Glaubenserkenntnis*, " limitative-notions of our faith-
knowledge " — a truly Germanic phrase which our translators render, not with complete lucidity, " conceptions that mark the limit of
the knowledge which we have of faith " (p. 695). Precisely what
Haering means by a " limitative-notion " is not, however, obvious,
and little light is thrown upon it by his explanations (pp. 704 ff.).
These close with these words: " The *logical right* of the notion may
be maintained by its friends in the measure in which they take it
seriously that it is really a limitative-notion, one which surpasses the
power of our knowledge — this being understood in the sense of the
theory of knowledge of the Critical Philosophy, which does not maintain limits of knowledge arbitrarily but recognizes those that really
lie therein " (pp. 705–706). We are apparently referred here to Kant,
who employs the term — or rather its cognate, *Grenzbegriff* — on a
single occasion, of " the inconceivable something behind the phenomenon." " Finally, however, the possibility of such *noumena* is
wholly incomprehensible, and what lies outside the sphere of phenomena is (for us) empty, that is, we have an understanding which
extends itself *problematically* further than that, but no intuition
(*Anschauung*) — and not even a conception of a possible intuition,
by means of which objects outside the field of sensibility are given
to us and the understanding can extend beyond this in an *assertory*
way. The concept (*Begriff*) of a noumenon is therefore only a
limitative-concept (*Grenzbegriff*), intended to confine the claims
of sensibility within proper bounds, and therefore only of negative
use. It is nevertheless not arbitrarily invented, but hangs together
with the limitations of the sensibility — without being able to posit
anything positive beyond the limits of the sensibility " (" Kritik der
reinen Vernunft," ed. 1, p. 235). Accordingly, Rudolf Eisler (" Wörterbuch der philosophischen Begriffe," i. 1910, p. 462) tells us that
" Kant understands by a limitative-conception (*Grenzbegriff*) a
conception which sets limits to, circumscribes, the claims of sensibility, and which at the same time leads to the limits of our knowledge, inasmuch as it posits something to thought without being able
to define it qualitatively, positively." For himself, Eisler broadly
defines limitative-conceptions (*Grenzbegriffe*) as " conceptions
which contain as content the existence of a transcendent object,
without embracing (adequately) along with that its qualities; or
conceptions which lead to the confines of the knowledge whose con-

tents are valid at once for the subjective and for the objective
reality." If we are to be governed by these definitions, it would seem
that we must understand Haering, in representing the preëxistence
of Christ as a limitative-notion, to be declaring it something which
we must declare to be real, while yet we renounce all claim to comprehend what it is.

But if we will turn to the discussion of the same matter by Otto
Kirn (" Grundriss der evangelischen Dogmatik," ed. 1, 1905, p. 92;
ed. 2, 1907, p. 99; ed. 3, 1910, p. 107) — with whom in general Haering shows strong affinities — we will discover that the representation
of the preëxistence of Christ as a limitative-conception (*Grenzbegriff*) is consistent, among Ritschlian theologians, with denial of,
not its comprehensibility merely, but its reality as well. The passage is instructive enough to justify giving it in its entirety. " The
Logos idea," says Kirn, " contains thus the ultimate explanation of
the historical manifestation of Christ; but it gives us no knowledge
of *His prehistoric being*. Logos means revelation, and the revelation
of God to us belongs to history. The attempt to speculate upon the
hypostatic distinction of the Logos from the Father, leads inevitably
to subordinationistic ideas which do not do justice to the Christian
faith. For only communion through Jesus Christ with God — in the
most unlimited sense of the word — preserves to the Christian
revelation its absoluteness and to the Christian salvation its certainty. The *Sonship of Christ* to God also enables us to illuminate
the life-connection of the historical Jesus with God, but not the eternal, intradivine life-process which forms the basis of the historical redemptive revelation. The attempt to pass beyond these limits, such as
is made by means of the notion of the eternal generation of the Son,
yields nothing further, but only reduplicates the faith-knowledge
oriented to history. The idea of *preëxistence* forms therefore a
limitative-conception (*Grenzbegriff*) of our theological thought. It
declares that the historical Christ has eternally His central and universal place in God's will of salvation, and that the content of His
life, His redemptive holy love, comes from God and is an eternal
content of the supernatural life of God. We would, therefore, more
correctly speak of the *super-historical* character of the revelation of
God in Christ than of the *pre*-historical existence of Christ with the
Father." Here the preëxistence of Christ is represented as a " limitative-conception " and yet explained as only " ideal," as the phrase
goes. An elaborate argument is devoted to showing precisely that

Christ did not exist "really" before His earthly career began. It does not follow, therefore, that Haering intends to represent the preexistence as real, from the mere fact that he calls it a "limitative-notion."

Nor are all our hesitancies at once dissipated by the circumstance that Haering explicitly speaks of it as "real." The Ritschlians (perhaps Haering conspicuously among them) are so accustomed to employ phraseology consecrated by long usage in novel senses or in new applications, that it behooves us to scrutinize their language closely before accepting it in what may seem to us its obvious meaning. Not to go beyond this very matter of the preëxistence of Christ, H. H. Wendt, on the low ground of his frankly acknowledged Dynamistic Monarchianism, can still find an element of truth in the doctrine of the preëxistence of Christ, and can still speak of this preëxistence as "real," not "ideal." "We have," he remarks, "merely not to refer the idea of real, eternal preëxistence to the historical man Jesus Christ as a whole, but to that which was divine in Him, to the Holy Spirit which He bore in Himself. And this eternal preëxistence of the Holy Spirt is not a *personal* preëxistence, like that of the Logos in the Athanasian conception. *Real* preëxistence was not possessed by the ' Son.' For ' Son ' of God is not the Holy Spirit but the personal man Jesus in which the Holy Spirit showed Himself operative. Of this man we can only affirm *ideal* preëxistence; that He as mediator of the redemptive revelation, which was to lead to the establishment of the Kingdom of God, belonged to the eternal redemptive plan of God and was the object of God's loving prevision and provision " ("System der christlichen Lehre," ii. 1907, p. 379). It is no doubt sufficiently bizarre to speak of the eternity of the God who employed the man Jesus as His organ as, in any sense, a "real preëxistence" of Jesus Himself. But this is the way the Ritschlians employ language.

Coming nearer home to Haering, we may profitably observe how the question of our Lord's preëxistence is dealt with by his life-long theological friend, his fellow Swabian, Max Reischle. Reischle feels able to speak of " an eternal Being of Jesus Christ " after a fashion wholly incomprehensible to us, and is able to connect this with the idea of the Logos, thought of, however, not as a distinct hypostasis in the Godhead but only as " an aspect, tendency, mode of operation of the Divine Being Itself." " If, however, we raise the question," he proceeds, " whether we are to carry into the eternal Being of the θεὸς λόγος, also the personal life of the historical and exalted Christ, distinct from that of the Father " (for it is only to the historical and exalted Christ that a distinct hypostasis is allowed, p. 62), " only so much as this can be said: Since the action of the Logos is intelligible to us only with respect to and in the person of Jesus Christ, we can never in our faith think away this personality from the conception of the Logos; but we must always think, as of the eternal God as Father of Jesus Christ, so also of the eternal Logos or of that eternal self-determination in God, as related to Jesus Christ. But what the nature of this relation is, we are, as finite beings, incapable of penetrating, and still more of making it the starting-point in an explanation of the incarnation of Jesus." " Thus," he adds, " we are in the question of the eternal origin of Jesus Christ, ever again brought back to this — the believing recognition, not only *back of*, but *in* His earthly personal life, and in the activities of the exalted one, of the eternal Divine Being determining the time-course " (" Christliche Glaubenslehre in Leitsätzen," ed. 2, 1902, pp. 119–120). There is a distinct refusal here to allow to Christ any personal preëxistence, and the reduction of His preëxistence to that of the impersonal Logos inseparably connected with Him in our thought, while the meagerness of this result is partially covered up by a suggestion that we are, as finite creatures, incapable of understanding such relationships, and a reference to the manifest presence of the eternal God with Jesus Christ. If our necessary thinking of God as Father of Jesus Christ, he intimates, does not carry with it the consequence that God was always the Father of Jesus Christ, neither does our necessary thinking of the Logos in connection with the person, Jesus, carry with it the consequence that the Logos was always connected with that person.

The impulse to suspect that Haering's doctrine of the preexistence of Jesus may also evaporate under our gaze into some such mist as this, arises not only generally from its astonishing incongruity with the scheme of his teaching as a whole, but more particularly from the immense difficulty of taking it literally in the face of his decisive rejection of the doctrines of the Trinity on the one hand and of the Two Natures of our Lord on the other. With him God is a monadic divine person and Jesus is a monadic human person, and on those postulates it seems impossible to construe to thought a real personally preëxistent Christ. He cannot be thought of as a personal distinction in the Godhead; for there are no personal distinctions in the Godhead. He equally cannot be thought of as some sort of a "middle-being": whatever else Jesus is to Haering, He is a genuine man, a human being with all the qualities of humanity. Will he then project Him back into eternity as some kind of a "heavenly man," despite his strong asseveration that He "belongs to us"? The monstrosity of these notions in the general context of Haering's thought bids us pause before we take his words at their face value. Is it not more probable that like his fellow Ritschlians here he has some subtle meaning in mind, which does not appear on the surface of his words, especially since he tells us that his advocacy of the preëxistence of Christ will commend itself in proportion as we accept the notion strictly as a "limitative-notion," that is to say, as something quite incomprehensible to us? Meanwhile, it must be admitted that he seems to ascribe to Christ as a fact, whatever we are to say of the mode, a real personal pre-existence. " This *limitative-notion,*" he says, " may be formulated " ("by those who accept it" seems to be added in the later text) " as follows: the love of God, effective to us in Christ as the Son, is so truly love of God, effective self-revelation of His nature, that it is eternally directed to Him, the vehicle of this eternal love, not only in the sense of ideal preëxistence — to Him as the temporal-historical correlate of the eternal love of God — but also apart from His earthly existence, as love of the Father for the Son, in the mystery of the eternal life of God, or then, accordingly, because no other word stands at our disposal, in real preëxistence; and — this the other side of the same notion — this Son, eternally loved by God, is, as sent by the Father into the world, so come into the world by an act of love of His own " (p. 704). It certainly seems to be said here not only that God's love for the Son is eternal, but that the Son whom God loves is eternal; not only that the Son was sent into the world by God, but that He came into the world by an act of His own. All things considered it does not appear strange that Haering's confidence in such a "limitative-notion" should not seem quite complete. He speaks of its "advocates," to be sure, as "convinced." But he agrees that they must not "make assent to it an essential element of saving faith itself " — that is to say, of the necessary content of the Christian religion — "but," he adds in the later revision of his text, " shall rather leave open the possibility that, in the progress of knowledge with regard to the Christian salvation, it may be superseded " (p. 707).

We have been interested to observe how Haering's critics, sharing his general Ritschlian point of view, understand him on this matter. A. Titius (*Theologische Rundschau*, x. 1907, p. 460) seems merely to record the fact that Haering holds such an opinion. "The doctrine of Christ's real preëxistence," he writes, "is accepted" by Haering, "with respect to its kernel indeed as a 'providentially supplied limitative-notion'" (p. 449), but along with that also not as an 'essential element of saving faith itself' (p. 451)." H. H. Wendt (*Theologische Literaturzeitung*, xxxii. 1907, col. 647) seems to drop a sly suggestion that Haering's recognition of a real preëxistence for Christ may possibly be classed in Haering's view along with that knowledge which passes away. "With circumspect reserve," he writes, "Haering permits the New Testament ideas of the real preëxistence of Christ to pass as limitative-notions, which the Christian community may retain, 'so as to lose nothing of the mystery of God's revelation of love in Christ, until in other conditions of existence a more perfect knowledge of it discloses itself' (p. 449)." E. Günther ("Die Entwicklung der Lehre von der Person Christi im XIX Jahrhundert," 1911, pp. 330–331) deals with the matter at more length, but also, it seems, with a slight undertone of sarcasm. "Perhaps the most difficult point in Haering's Christology," he says, "is his doctrine of *preëxistence* as a '*limitative-notion.*' If he advances beyond the so-called ideal preëxistence this is wholly from motives derived from religion and the New Testament. The ideas of the love of the Father who gives the Son and of the humble self-surrender of the Son who came into the world by an act of love of His own, are to him too valuable to be relinquished (p. 449). The origin of the Pauline and Johannine Christology is also a problem for Haering, which, however, is not capable of being solved — or perhaps is already solved — from analogies and connections derived from Comparative Religion (pp. 443–448). But he who will not abandon the notion of the real preëxistence should give it expression on the one side only as the ultimate culmination of the immediate conceptions of faith, and on the other with the conscious reservation that there can exist for us in this region no knowledge (p. 450). We may conjecture that in this reference many will rather be disposed to speak of the limits of thought than of 'limitative-thoughts' (*die Gedankengrenze als Grenzgedanken*). They will, however, be gladly ready with Haering 'without curtailment of their particular gift, encouraged rather by a noble rivalry, weary of mere negations, to unite in a real affirmation ' (p. 452)." Whatever they may think of the procedure, neither Titius, Wendt, nor Günther appears to doubt that Haering intends to teach a real personal preëxistence for Christ.

We shall not follow the details of Haering's system further. With his reduction of the person of Christ to the dimensions of a mere man (despite that " rock in the sky " of a problematical incomprehensible preëxistence), and of the work of Christ to merely impressing men with the conviction that God is " holy love " (despite the ineffective efforts to discover in this some value to God) ; with his reduction of God Himself to mere Love — whatever that may mean — (despite the incongruous insistence against his master, Ritschl, that " righteousness " and " wrath" have a place in the Divine nature) : it is easy to understand what a " reduced Christianity " he sets forth. The fundamental difficulty lies of course in the lack of " external authority." It is not to be wondered at that one who, having discarded the authority of the revelation of God embodied in the Scriptures, finds his task as a theologian only in " giving expression to the religious interpretation of the gospel which is attainable at the period " at which he writes, — that is, who seeks his guidance not in a sure word of God but in shifting public opinion — should be able to set forth only a meager and lowpitched-system of doctrine. Or that he should sit rather loosely to what he does give us. Certainly there is observable in the teachings of such writers, and not least in Haering, a certain " elasticity," as it has been euphemistically phrased. He has his own faith-judgments; but so also have others: why should he demand exclusive recognition for his own? So, to take examples only from matters which have come before us, Haering will not " dogmatize " on the " mode " of the resurrection of Jesus; on the saving activity of the exalted Christ; on the employment of the term " divinity " with reference to Christ; on even his poverty-stricken notion of some sort of preëxistence for Christ. In his hands Christianity takes on the appearance of a highly elastic cord in rapid vibration; there may be a solid cord somewhere, but all that appears to sight is a vague and tenuous lozenge of unstable and unsubstantial material. Despite the parade of apologetical substructure a sense of unreality gradually grows upon the reader as he proceeds through the volumes, and he closes them with the feeling that he has not been given a solid system of Christian doctrine; not even a " gospel " — a body of glad-tidings — which Haering would no doubt prefer that it should be; but only a collection of the more or less plausible religious opinions of a good man conscious of lacking any firm ground for his feet.

SOME LOOSE STONES. Being a Consideration of Certain Tendencies in Modern Theology Illustrated by Reference to the Book called "Foundations." By R. A. KNOX. Second Impression. London and New York: Longmans, Green, and Co. 1913.[1]

MR. KNOX is a member of that coterie of young Oxford Fellows out of which come the " Seven Oxford Men " who wrote the Liberal Manifesto called " Foundations " (see the notice of it in this *Review*, xi. 1913, pp. 526–538 [or pp. 320–334 of this volume]). Not being of their way of thinking and, naturally, being aware of the approaching publication of the book, he greeted its birth with a brilliant satire, parodying Dryden's " Absalom and Achitophel," under the somewhat lurid title of " Absolute and Abitofhell." There were those who thought that if the book was to be attacked at all, it would better be seriously attacked; a proposition the universal validity of which would not have been allowed, to be sure, by John Calvin, say, or Pierre Viret — though we are not sure that Mr. Knox would care to support himself on the judgments of precisely these great men. At any rate, having enjoyed his burst of laughter, Mr. Knox has turned to earnest remonstrance and has written this volume of criticism in which he traverses the main positions taken up by the authors of " Foundations." He still, however, conceives himself to be engaged rather with the writers of " Foundations " than with their doctrines; or rather, perhaps we should say, he conceives himself to be engaged with their doctrines primarily not on their own account but as expressions of the personalities of their propounders. He insists that he is not writing a theological book: he is rather occupied, he suggests, in " a study in psychology " (p. vii.). What interests him particularly is the psychology — the " far more intricate psychology," he says, than that of " the Prophets, or of the Apostles, or of the Fathers, or of the Schoolmen " — of " the modern theologian." The most wonderful thing about our wonderful " modern theology " to Mr. Knox is, apparently, that there are people who can think that way.

Even the attitude of the Modern Theologian to his task seems to Mr. Knox an odd one. The Modern Theologian is apparently less concerned in the discovery of precisely what is true about Christianity, than in the ascertainment of how much can be made easily to pass as true among " modern men." He seems oppressed by the mass of scientific opinion around him; but what daunts him is not so much the effect of this scientific opinion on his own faith, as " its effect on the faith of other people." Therefore, there enters into all his work an apologetic tone which produces even " at times a cynical indifference to abstract truth." " For we are not concerned, now, to find how we can represent truth most adequately, but how we can represent it most palatably. We ask of a doctrine, not, ' Is it sound?,' but, ' Couldn't we possibly manage to do without it? '; not, ' Is it true?,' but, ' Can I induce Jones to see it in that light? ' " (p. 9). Jones has been to College and has heard of Hegel. He is a good man: " *anima naturaliter Christiana,* and all that." But when it comes to Christian doctrine, Jones has difficulties. Concessions are in order: it will not do to estrange Jones's " modern mind "! Mr. Knox is outraged by such an attitude. " The great argument used now against any theological proposition," he breaks out (pp. vii. f.), " is not, that it is untrue, or unthinkable, or unedifying, or unscriptural, or unorthodox, but simply, that the modern mind cannot accept it. It is the modern mind that accepts this, and rejects that, that expresses itself in terms of A rather than in terms of B, that thinks along these lines rather than along those, that shrinks, or ratifies, or demands. And after reading a few paragraphs of such ostensibly psychological discussion, I find myself sorely tempted to exclaim, in an equally psychological spirit: ' If the modern mind has really got all these peculiar kinks about it, then, in Heaven's name, let us trepan it.' "

Even this, however, is, according to Mr. Knox, not the worst of the matter in the case of the authors of " Foundations." The Jones to whom they are so assiduous in adjusting their teaching is a " back number." " In a word, our objection is, not that Jones is unreal, or unimportant, or unrepresentative, but that he is sixty " (p. 11). It was forty years ago that Jones went to College: and the strenuous efforts which the authors of " Foundations " are making " to convert our great-uncles " must strike the really " modern mind " as a

CRITICAL REVIEWS

sad anachronism. The world has moved in this generation: *tempora mutantur, nos et mutamur in illis.* This " modern mind " to fit it into the queer corners of which the authors of " Foundations " are so busy whittling down Christianity, always an impertinence, has become fairly non-existent. Jones has receded into the background; and his grandchildren are of a very different temper. They wish no " accommodations " of doctrine made for them. " I have never met (outside of Senior Common Rooms) any demand from questioners for restatement or accommodation of my beliefs to theirs: they want rather to know what the Church does say, in order to see whether they can accommodate their beliefs to mine " (p. 13). " Against all this complicated process I am convinced that the cry of the average man is, ' Tell me what you do believe and always have believed . . . and then I will see about it ' " (pp. 15–16). " The modern mind does not want pulp. It wants something that it can close its teeth on " (p. 18). " More dogma is wanted, pulpitfuls of it." The actual mind of the day demands not quieting compromises but clearly-cut differentiations and consequent consistency of convictions.

The fundamental difficulty of the Modern Theologian leading him to sit loosely to Christian truths lies, Mr. Knox thinks, in his method of approach to them. He approaches them by way of hypothesis instead of by way of presupposition, or *a posteriori* rather than *a priori.* Looking at them only as so many propositions proposed for consideration, and approaching them (professedly) wholly without prepossessions, he sets to work framing hypotheses, on the ground of which they may be accounted for. Obviously any number of conflicting hypotheses may be framed: there are few bodies of alleged facts which may not find some kind of explanation on any one of a score or of a hundred hypotheses. And at the last resort, there always remains the simple explanation of the amazing report brought by the child: " the little boy lied " (more or less). There is no limit to the number of hypotheses which may be suggested to account for any body of alleged facts, except the limits of the fertility of the imagination. And there are no final grounds of discrimination between the several hypotheses proposed. More than one will account for the facts on the assumption that it is true. And each man becomes enamored of his own hypothesis and twists the facts to make them accord with it. We soon find ourselves in the midst not merely of a confused mass of hypotheses but also of a confused mass of doubted facts; and we seek in vain for a firm footing. Everything, however, is different if we approach a body of truths presented for our acceptance with presuppositions rather than hypotheses in our hands. Presuppositions are solid things, on which we can take our stand. We already believe, say, in God, and in a personal God who acts purposively; and in a God of love who intervenes in a sinful and miserable world for its salvation. We bring these things with us as facts of which we are assured, not as hypotheses which we are testing; and what a different aspect is taken on by the body of Christian doctrine! Now everything is clear, and solid and sure. And the difference hangs, says Mr. Knox in effect, wholly on the difference in standpoint.

Mr. Knox, it will be seen, is an " authoritarian." And that is well. We cannot get along in this world of fact without authority. Without authority we may assure ourselves, it may be, of what must be; we cannot be assured of a single thing that merely is. And Christianity, as a historical religion, is a religion of facts and is therefore built up, in all that makes it that specific religion which we call Christianity, on authority. We may be theists without authority but not Christians. The blows which Mr. Knox strikes in the name of authority are without doubt fatal and he does especially good service when he exposes the inconsequence of the attempt to substitute religious experience for authority as the foundation of conviction. " As a matter of modernist psychology," he writes, " this appeal to experience is very interesting. The modernist will not allow himself to be regarded as in any way prejudiced in favour of one particular theological system. He therefore collects together the testimony of innumerable other people, primitive Bishops, mediæval nuns, and contemporary charcoal-burners, who were and are, beyond any shadow of dispute, prejudiced theologians — prejudiced by what they believed upon a basis of purely traditional authority. And the result of this appeal is served up as if it were the most modern of all critical investigations, an essay in psychology. But if a priori assumptions are to play no part in modern theology, spiritual experience must play no part in modern theology, for spiritual experience is based on a priori assumptions " (pp. 193–194). " The whole argument from experience," he comments, " seems to rest on the assumption that you can first make people believe, on the strength of Bible documents or inherited tradition, certain clearly defined dogmas; and then, when they have got accustomed to this way of thinking, you can come and knock away the supports

CRITICAL REVIEWS

on which the belief rests, Biblical or traditional, and say, ' We have now proved the truth of these doctrines, because we have reared on them so splendid an edifice of faith ' " (p. 190).

Valid, however, as is Mr. Knox's appeal to authority; and sound as is his contention that authority lies at the basis of all Christian faith; it must be confessed that he gives no adequate account either of the ground or the nature of the authority to which he makes appeal. His argument thus hangs in the air, and the impression is created that the authority on which Christianity rests is accepted by its votaries by a purely arbitrary act of will. This is indeed, to all appearance, true in Mr. Knox's own case; otherwise, we surely would catch in his numerous allusions to it some hint of a rational basis of his acceptance of authority. He is, it would seem, just a " traditional " Christian and is inclined to give validity to the traditional Christianity which he accepts, chiefly one would imagine, despite his solid refutation of that ground of faith, because of the beneficent results of his acceptance of it. He would scarcely expect us to take literally " the crude metaphor " by which he attempts to illustrate his attitude to Scripture and Tradition (pp. 33–34): " You have a motor-car with two headlights, each throwing out its rays obliquely in either direction. The hedge on each side is illuminated by one lamp only, but in the centre of the road the two lights converge, and mark out a triangular area of brilliant clearness. The two lights of Scripture and Tradition (if we may pursue this crude metaphor) may be said in the same way to provide sufficient guidance for our course only where they overlap. Beyond this area, speculation is at liberty to botanize in the hedgerows." If we were really to " pursue this crude metaphor " Mr. Knox would have left himself no authority at all. If neither Scripture nor Tradition has any authority by itself — and he apparently deprives each severally of authority — they cannot have any authority when combined — on the principle at least in which Mr. Knox tells us he was brought up (p. 190), viz. that 0 + 0 yields still 0. Authority is not a thing of degrees: it is either absolute or non-existent. He must therefore look upon either Scripture or Tradition as by itself authoritative if their combination is to be authoritative. And it is quite clear that it is to Tradition, not to Scripture, that Mr. Knox really accords authority. When he says therefore, " It is only at the points where Scripture and ecclesiastical tradition combine to form a defined doctrine, that he " — he who thinks with Mr. Knox — " pretends to stand on sure ground, in virtue of a presupposition " (p. 33), we can but understand him to mean that his faith rests not on Scripture *simpliciter*, but on Scripture, as interpreted by Tradition — that is to say, that he finds his authority not in Scripture at all but in Tradition; in other words, that he is a traditionalist in the sense of the Church of Rome. Authority to him thus spells Tradition, and Tradition spells " Church," and " Church " spells practically Rome. Mr. Knox in a word is a High Anglican, indistinguishable in his theory of authority from the general doctrine on this subject of the Roman Church, except, perhaps, for a little drawing back when the place of the Pope in the definition of dogma comes into consideration (cf. p. 193). His pleading for a commanding place for authority in religion is largely vitiated, therefore, by the circumstance that his own view of the nature, seat, and ground of authority in religion is baseless and untenable.

This fundamental inconsequence in his own point of view does not prevent Mr. Knox, however, from exposing the inconsequences of the " Modernist " point of view, as illustrated in the authors of " Foundations," in a very trenchant manner. In successive chapters he traverses the greater number of the essays in " Foundations " and points out in them tendencies of method and treatment which annul their conclusions. He speaks himself of having dealt only very cursorily with Mr. Moberly's essay on the Atonement. But we are not sure that the strictures on this essay do not constitute the best piece of criticism in the volume. The notion that our Lord offered for us a " vicarious penitence " is very properly scored. Can there be such a thing as " vicarious penitence "? If there can be, can it take away sin? And if it can take away sin, must it not be because it, as suffering, is " *actually allowed to count* in the eye of divine justice as satisfaction for sins which we have committed "; and if this is so, how does it avoid the criticism that " it is immoral that the sufferings of one man should be accepted as satisfaction for the sins of another " (pp. 162–163)? The essence of the matter is touched in a passage like the following: " But this surely is clear, that if we are to hold the full traditional view of the Atonement, we must suppose that the brand left by our sins is not twofold, but threefold. They leave a mark on our own souls — true. They leave a mark on the lives of men around us — true. But over and above all this, they leave a mark in the book of life, a black mark on our records, which no human penitence can efface. There is an objective disturbance in

the moral order which our sins have created, and only one thing
could right it, the Sacrifice of Christ, to which we have contributed
not a jot or a tittle on our own part. And there can be neither
Catholicism nor Evangelicalism where the fact is not realized"
(pp. 170–171). Some of the remarks on the deity of our Lord and
the Incarnation are equally pungent, and that whether the attempt
to substitute the category of will for that of substance in construing
the one doctrine or the notion of kenosis in construing the other,
is under discussion. To be " of the same mind " with one another
is not to have numerically only one " mind " among us; and when
two beings will the same thing it is not clear that they are therefore
but one. And if anything such as the Kenotists assert happened at
the Incarnation we certainly cannot say that Jesus was God, but
only that He was a man who once had been God. The Virgin-birth
and the Empty Tomb (though Mr. Knox stumbles sadly with
reference to our Lord's resurrection-body) and the Ascension are all
dealt with in adequate fashion. Mr. Knox is willing even to become
aggressive here. " Mr. Streeter says he knows of no living theologian
who would maintain a physical Ascension in this crude form. I have
no claim to be a theologian. I can only say that as a person of ordinary education I believe, as I hope for salvation, in this literal
doctrine; I believe, that whatever change may have glorified the
Risen Body when it passed beyond the cloud into a new mode or
sphere of existence, the earth has ever since the Ascension been the
lighter by so many pounds' weight, and the sum of matter in the
world the less by so many cubic inches of volume " (p. 85). Such
" materialism " may shock some ears: but the issue ultimately
comes to just that.

There are, of course, other passages with which we feel less satisfaction. We do not quite go with Mr. Knox in his dealing with
miracles; especially in his inability to separate between Biblical
and Ecclesiastical Miracles. We certainly do not go with him in
his treatment of Scripture: especially in his discussion of the
eschatological utterances of our Lord. His Romeward tendencies
— which are numerous and decisive — are an offense to us. His
obsession of " freedom " is equally regrettable. Even here, however, he shows his characteristic courage and in the interests
of " free-will " cheerfully denies that we have any solid ground
for anticipating the conversion of the world. Enough: there is
much in Mr. Knox's book which is crude and unconsidered. But

this cannot destroy its general value as an exposure of the weaknesses of " modernism "; and it is in this that its significance lies. It is an earnest and successful plea to reasonable men to draw back from these shifting shoals where " we have to be reassured by a yearly statement from Dr. Sanday, comparable to the weather report, as to ' what we may still believe ' " (p. 35), and to plant our feet firmly on the rock. The fine air of conviction which suffuses it, and the brightness of the style, should give the book a wide circulation and, we trust, will give it, in its main message, large acceptance.

DIE BEICHT IM ZUSAMMENHANGE MIT DER SAKRALEN RECHTSPFLEGE IN DER ANTIKE. Von FRANZ STEINLEITNER, Dr. phil. Leipzig: Kommissionsverlag der Dieterich'schen Verlagsbuchhandlung, Theodor Weicher. 1913.[1]

" THE following essay," says the author, " moves in the frontier region between philosophy and theology, in the field of the history of religion."

Hermann Usener and his school have led the way to the study of the problems in the history of religion presented by that period " when young Christianity entered upon its victorious course in the slippery field of the religious syncretism and theocracy of vanishing antiquity, and introduced into the history of mankind a completely new epoch of its spiritual life " (p. 5). Franz Cumont in his great Mithras-works and, after him, Hugo Hepding in his studies on the Attis-worship, have shown us how to illuminate dark subjects by collecting the scattered material from every quarter and subjecting it as a whole to intelligent scrutiny. The road having been opened by such competent hands, it has been diligently walked in; investigation into " the chaos of ideas and religious usages of that period of strong religious agitation " has been pushed steadily on. We need recall but such leading names as A. Dieterich, Anrich, Reitzenstein, Wendland, and the essays published in the " Archiv für Religionswissenschaft," in the " Religionsgeschichtlichen Versuche und Vorarbeiten," and, in part, in the Zeitschrift für die neutestamentliche Wissenschaft und die Kunde des Urchristentums. As a result

we understand as never before the vital contact in which the world
of antiquity, which was passing away, and the rising world of Christianity stood with one another; how " the two worlds, however
inimicably they envisaged one another and bitterly struggled with
one another, were nevertheless inseparably bound together "; how
" the Christian spirit, liberated from Judaism, formed a new body
for itself out of the members of dying antiquity, and thus the spirit
of Greece and the religiousness of the Orient, stamping themselves
on Christian ideas and usages, won new life for themselves and lived
in Christian clothing " (p. 5).

When we remember, however, that the earliest Christianity
gained its adherents largely from the lower classes, and afterwards
established itself preëminently in the region in which the old popular
religions most flourished, it will be perceived that in the investigation of the process of the Hellenization of Christianity, the study of
the popular religions can least of all be neglected. " Along with the
popular religion of Greece, whose usages were concentrated in the
Mysteries, the Oriental religions come into consideration, and not
least among them the Phrygian worship, which was spread throughout the whole of Asia Minor, and whose inscribed and sculptured
monuments are found scattered over the whole of the Roman Empire " (p. 6). In these circumstances it has seemed to the author
eminently worth while to attempt to gain a better knowledge of the
popular religious ideas and usages of the Phrygian and Lydian cults.
As a contribution to that end, he has selected a particular element
in their religious usages for investigation, the institution of Confession. " Whether and how far this sacrament of the Church is to be
considered an inheritance from old Oriental piety and beliefs may
be left meanwhile out of consideration. The fact is that this cult-
institution existed in the Oriental religions which strove with Christianity for the dominion of the world, and everywhere in the Roman
Empire set themselves in the longest and most lasting opposition
to its victory " (p. 6).

The material for his investigation Dr. Steinleitner finds in a considerable body of Lydian and Phrygian inscriptions of the class
commonly called Votive or Expiatory Inscriptions, coming from the
second and third Christian centuries, supplemented by some inscriptions from Knidos of the first or second century before Christ, and
a few literary notices. This material he gathers together from all
sources, reprints, and reëdits with an adequate commentary. This

constitutes the first part of his work (pp. 7–74). The second part
(pp. 75–123) is an essay, founded on this collected material, on
" Confession in Antiquity." This essay really constitutes a very
interesting exposition of the theology of the inscriptions and gives
us a valuable insight into the religious ideas which ruled the minds
of the people of Asia Minor near the opening of the Christian era.
The first chapter treats of " the relation of man to deity in the
Lydian-Phrygian religion "; the second of " sin and punishment
according to the Lydian and Phrygian Expiatory-Inscriptions ";
the third of " religious administration of justice in Lydia and
Karia "; the fourth of " Confession in the cults of Asia Minor ";
while the fifth adds a section on " a confession in the mysteries of
Samothrace and the Isis-worship."

When Dr. Steinleitner comes to sum up at the end (pp. 121 ff.)
the results of his discussion, he naturally lays his stress on the chief
object which he had in view, namely, the establishment of the existence of a regular institution of Confession in the primitive religion of Lydia and Phrygia, " in which the sinner confessed his sin
before the priest as the representative of the deity in order to propitiate the deity and thus to become free from sickness and want,
the consequences of the sin." Other elements of the old religion,
however, interest us more: most of all its conception of deity as both
all-powerful and as intimately concerned with human life in all its
manifestations. " If we sum up briefly what has been said," remarks Dr. Steinleitner at the end of the discussion of this matter,
" the religion and life of the Lydian and Phrygian people in its
lower strata appears as dominated by the belief that the deity is
the absolute lord and owner of his worshiper, but no ruthless tyrant,
like, say Baal in the Syrophoenician religion, but certainly the
τύραννος or κύριος and yet also the greatest benefactor and the
righteous judge, from whose hand the believer receives blessing
and calamity as a child receives its mother's caresses and its father's
chastisements " (pp. 81–82). Dr. Steinleitner seems to consider this
conception of deity one-sided in its emphasis on the power and all-
pervading activity of God. It seems to us a conception which does
great credit to its sharers.

One of the results of it was to develop a series of epithets for
the deity which expressed its power and rulership, and among these
epithets κύριος was prominent. " The title κύριος, which meets us
in this inscription," says Dr. Steinleitner on one occasion (p. 60),

438   CRITICAL REVIEWS

" is a divine predicate, conceived in a genuinely Oriental fashion
and thoroughly intelligible in the Eastern world, that occurs in
Thrace, Asia Minor, Syria and Egypt, and that found also its way
into the religious language of Christianity." Christianity did not
derive its employment of κύριος as an epithet of God — or as a
standing designation of Christ — from the folk-religions of the
Orient: it is well to know, however, that the heathen converts to
Christianity could find no difficulty in catching the high implications
of the term as used by Christians.

Another result of this conception of God was the highly supernaturalistic coloring given by it to the whole view of life. " A further
characteristic of the Lydian-Phrygian religiousness and of its view of
the relation between God and man," writes Dr. Steinleitner (pp. 80–
81), " is the belief in epiphanies of the deity in which the deity reveals
its might suddenly and unexpectedly to believers, a belief shared, no
doubt, with the Lydians and Phrygians by other stocks of Asia
Minor. The notion of the epiphany of a god or demonic being is
primitive Greek, and was possessed also by other peoples. But between the idea and significance of the ἐπιφάνεια of the deity or of
a demon in the popular belief of the Greeks and divine appearances
in the belief and conception of the peoples of Asia Minor and the
Orient, this difference exists — that the appearance of the deity for
the pious Oriental on the ground of his belief in an absolute dependence on the deity, extending to all situations in life, and of its
constant care for the health of his soul, which shows itself in atonements, expiations and all kinds of asceticism, means not only a
beneficent intrusion into the life of the individual or the establishment of a community, but also an *experience of religion,* in the
mystical sense, in which he lives and moves." Dr. Steinleitner
wishes, it is true, very illegitimately to apply this point of view at
once to the conversion of Paul in a naturalistic psychological explanation of the supernatural features of the narrative. Paul was
anything but a cold casuist, like his Pharasaic companions; his religiously readily excitable character, his inward faith, his vital
mysticism can at bottom find its roots only in the Anatolian inheritance of the former tent-weaver of Tarsus. We must consider
also the whole mystical nature of the Apostle: he experienced other
ecstatic conditions and could relate " visions and revelations of the
Lord." " Out of these psychological and religious foundations, which
Paul had brought with him from his Anatolian home with its old

traditions of visible epiphanies of the deity, and its ever new experience of the δυνάμεις of gods and demons in ecstasies and visions,
we may perhaps explain his experience of Christ before Damascus
as an ecstatic, visionary occurrence " (p. 81, note 2). But even such
a bizarre use of it as this does not destroy the value to the student
of the New Testament of the fact here made evident that " ἐπιφάνεια
is in this religious language the *terminus technicus* for a sudden and
unexpected appearance of the deity, in order to help its worshipers
in time of need and misfortune " (p. 19). When Paul speaks of the
glorious epiphany of our great God and Saviour, Jesus Christ, he
was using language which had a perfectly determinate meaning for
his readers.

It is perhaps natural that in inscriptions of this kind the only
sins which are mentioned are breaches of the rules of the cult, by
which breaches the deity is supposed to be offended, and it may not
be quite justified to infer from this fact that the Lydian-Phrygians
had no consciousness of distinctly ethical faults as sin. There is a
tendency apparent to extend the responsibility for acts of sin beyond the individual who actually commits them to his group; and
there is an instance of vicarious satisfaction for a fault — a brother
undertaking the task for a sister. There is even an instance in which
the sin appears to be carried back of the sinful act to the sinful wish.
On the whole, however, we get little help to the understanding of
New Testament language from this section. We note only that the
word for sinning is ἁμαρτάνω (ἁμαρτία occurs, but not frequently).
We lay no stress on the mention of an " unpardonable sin." And we
do not find ourselves particularly interested in the treatment of
sickness (ἀσθένεια) as the punishment of sin, or of the use of
κολάζειν and κόλασις with apparent preference for the notion of punishment.

The most valuable contribution which these inscriptions make to
the interpretation of the New Testament is due to the appearance
in one of them — perhaps in two others — of the term λύτρον, to
express the means by which immunity from the consequences of a
fault was secured from the deity. For naturally the confession of the
fault to the priest did not complete the making of satisfaction for
it. The climax and completion of the expiatory process was formed
rather by the erection of a tablet on which the sin and its punishments with the name of the sinner were notified, and that by requirement of the god. The ordinary expression for this command to

make expiation in the Lydian inscriptions is ἐπιζητεῖν, although sometimes ἀπαιτεῖν also occurs. In the case of the particular inscription which we have mentioned, however, we read λύτρον κατ' ἐπιταγὴν Μηνὶ Τυράννῳ καὶ Διὶ 'Ογμηνῷ καὶ τοῖς σὺν αὐτῷ θεοῖς. The interpreters have puzzled themselves over this λύτρον. Sir William Ramsay and Perdrizet take it in the sense of εὐχή ; Buresch leaves to it its sense of "ransom" but scarcely knows what then to do with the inscription. Steinleitner with too great deference to A. Deissmann, as we think, starts with the idea of the price of emancipation for a slave, and thinks that we must assume that a man was supposed to come into bondage to the deity by sin and required to be ransomed out by this expiatory offering. We see no reason why we should travel so roundabout a pathway to so simple a conclusion. The λύτρον simply indicates the expiatory tablet as the price paid to the god for immunity for the fault committed. And thus we have before us a special use of λύτρον, parallel to the special use of it which Deissmann has so fully illustrated as the emancipation-price of slaves, in which it is used as the immunity-price of faults in the service of deity. The point of interest is that we have here a usage of λύτρον very closely akin to the sense in which it and its derivatives are employed in the New Testament — in our Lord's great saying in Mark x. 45, Matt. xx. 28, for example, and in the apostolic doctrine of "Redemption." When we read for example in Heb. ix. 15 of a "ransoming of trangressions" we are moving in the same circle of ideas as when we read in this inscription: "Artemidorus the son of Diodotus and Amia, together with his six kinsmen, knowing and unknowing, a ransom according to command, to Mēn Tyrannus and Zeus Ogmenus and the gods with him" (p. 36). This is "a ransom of sin": it is a price paid (though not of silver or gold) by means of which is obtained "the remission of sin" (Eph. i. 7, Col. i. 14).

DICTIONARY OF THE APOSTOLIC CHURCH. Edited by JAMES HASTINGS, D.D. Vol. I: Aaron — Lystra. New York: Charles Scribner's Sons; Edinburgh: T. & T. Clark. 1916.[1]

WITH this "Dictionary of the Apostolic Church" presumably the series of Biblical Encyclopædias which was begun by Dr. Hast-

ings' " Dictionary of the Bible " will be brought to completion. The
first volume of the " Dictionary of the Bible " was issued in 1898;
the last volume of this " Dictionary of the Apostolic Church," the
first of which is now before us, will scarcely be issued much before
the middle of 1917. Twenty years, or thereabouts, will have been
consumed, therefore, in the preparation and publication of the series. The intermediately published " Dictionary of Christ and the
Gospels " was supposed to have been keyed to a little more popular
note than the general " Dictionary of the Bible." It apparently was
therefore found by a larger public of more practical value; and a
call was made for another work which should do for the rest of the
New Testament what that Dictionary had done for the Gospels.
The present work is the answer to this call. It should be noted, however, that it is not precisely a Dictionary of the rest of the New
Testament. There are circles in which the New Testament is losing its uniqueness, and the editors of this Dictionary live within
those circles. They think in terms not of the delivery of the
revelation of God, and its assimilation, but of periods of the developing Church. They present us with a Dictionary, therefore, not
of the *Apostolicum,* as the ancients would have called it, dividing
the New Testament into " the Gospels and the Apostles," but of
"the history of the Church as far as the end of the first century."
Here the Epistles of Clement of Rome, Barnabas, Ignatius, the
Shepherd of Hermas, the Didache — although it is not pretended
that all of these fall within the first century — are set ostentatiously
by the side of the Epistles of Paul, the Acts of the Apostles, and the
Apocalypse of John; the Apocryphal Gospels and Acts and Apocalypses are added; and we are invited to contemplate the first
Christian century in the total mass of the literature to which it
gave birth. This has hardly been done in the practical interests of
ministers of the Word, requiring help in preparation for their
ministrations in the sanctuary.

As is his wont, Dr. Hastings has gathered to his aid in the
preparation of this Dictionary a large company of competent scholars. About a hundred writers take part in it. Among them there are
seven Continental scholars (P. Batiffol, E. von Dobschütz, H. Jordan, O. E. Moe, A. von Schlatter, A. Thumb, J. de Zwaan) — four
of whom, it will be observed, are Germans: these contribute in all
thirteen articles, none of which, however, except Schlatter's stimulating article on the Holy Spirit, lies at the center of things. Besides
five scholars who reside in Canada, eight of the writers are Amer-

icans. These are C. A. Beckwith, S. J. Case, J. A. Faulkner, S. Mathews, A. T. Robertson, G. L. Robinson, A. C. Zenos — and our own Dr. Vos, who contributes the articles on Brotherly Love, Goodness, Joy, Kindness, Longsuffering, Love. The American writers contribute some twenty-six articles in all, but again none of these lies at the center of things. Dr. A. T. Robertson might have made his articles on such topics as Bond, Debt, Deliverer, Destruction important, but he has chosen rather to work formally and briefly.

There are naturally included in the scope of this Dictionary general articles on the several books of the New Testament, from Acts to Revelation. A general article on " Gospels " has been added, supplemented by isagogical material in the article on Luke (the person). These, along with such ancillary material as that supplied by such articles as those on Epistle, Letter, Dates, provide a tolerably complete Introduction to the New Testament Books. The general tone of this Introduction is sufficiently " Liberal," although many " Conservative " opinons are mixed in. Take the question of the dates of the Synoptic Gospels, for instance. W. C. Allen, who writes the article " Gospels," is inclined to very early dates — Mark in the neighborhood of 45, Matthew about 50, and Luke between 47 and 60. Similarly A. C. Zenos seems not disinclined to assign Mark to about 60, Luke to about 61, and Matthew to about 68. Even Kirsopp Lake (p. 20) does not seem quite sure that Luke was written later than 70, and this would carry with it an earlier date for at least Mark. The Book of Acts, Lake would still date in the decennium 90–100; he speaks of Harnack's argument for its early date as onesided and expects a reaction from it; and he is still inclined to represent Acts as dependent on Josephus (pp. 20, 721). With respect to this last point it is a satisfaction to be able to point to the excellent article on Josephus, by E. von Dobschütz, whose solid refutation of the dependence in question reads almost as if it had been written with direct reference to Lake's argument for its likelihood. We note in passing that von Dobschütz opposes the recent tendency to pronounce the famous passages in Josephus which mention Christ to be genuine.

When we turn to the theological side of the Dictionary our attention is naturally attracted first to the great articles on God, Christ, and the Holy Spirit. The article on God is written by Dr. A. J. Maclean, a Bishop of the Scottish Episcopal Church, to whom we owe quite a number of other theological articles. It is conceived in excellent spirit and is written with clearness and force. It is valuable in this Dictionary, among other things, for its correction of many details in the article on " Christ, Christology," where that article shows overdeference to modern " critical opinions." For, as is natural, its strength is given to the doctrine of the Trinity and that involves discussion of, say, the deity of Christ and the passages in which it is expressed. Perhaps we should say that there is a slight uncertainty of touch exhibited here and there, as, for example, with reference to the idea of " Subordination," which is too easily accepted from the language of the traditional formularies and not independently grappled with. It is odd that the appended " Literature " does not mention a single work on the specific subject of the article, that is, the apostolic doctrine of God. We could wish that the purely empirical fact that the term " God " appears in the pages of some of the Epistles of the New Testament as the personal name of the Father, in contrast to " Lord " and " Spirit " as the personal names of the other persons of the Trinity, had been expressed in some other way than in the sentence: " It must be borne in mind that, when the name ' God ' is used *absolutely,* without pronoun or epithet, it is never, with one possible exception, applied explicitly to the Son as such or to the Spirit as such " (p. 460). A careless reader may easily take out of this sentence more than the facts stated in it warrant.

The article on the Holy Spirit is written by Prof. A. Schlatter, who employs in it a reconstructive method of expounding the apostle's doctrine. This inevitably introduces a speculative element into the exposition, which makes it very stimulating but does not always command assent. The presuppositions of Schlatter intrude and it becomes the task of the reader to untangle the two threads of the Biblical teaching and the theologian's own thought. As is Schlatter's habit, he says many very searching things in the progress of his exposition, and numerous detached passages may be cited from the article in which important truths are given exceptionally exact and pungent statement. The paragraph on the effect of the operation of the Spirit on the body (p. 576) is an instance in point — but it is too long to quote here. Take instead this brief statement of the Spirit's action in saving men — which constitutes an excellent description of what the old theologians call " Effectual Calling ": " The Spirit gives man the power of choice, makes his volition effective, and induces him to bring his will into subjection to the

Divine Law " (p. 575). Or take this pregnant criticism on Perfectionism: " As the perfectionist finds complete satisfaction in the communion with God bestowed upon him by the Spirit, his hope for the future dies away (I Cor. xv. 12, II Tim. ii. 18); for naturally such a religious attitude could have no final ideal standing supreme above present attainment. It thus tended to arrest that forward process into which Saint Paul had brought his churches (Phil. iii.) " (p. 581).

We regret that we cannot speak with satisfaction of Prof. C. Anderson Scott's article on " Christ, Christology " (twenty-two pages) — which should be the central article of the volume. Dr. Scott's critical harness clanks about him dreadfully as he moves, and he does grave injustice to the writers he is expounding by what seems to be sheer inability to enter sympathetically into their thought. The result is that he forces them not only into inconsistency with one another but also into inconsistency with themselves; and, having wrought his will upon it, holds their thought up before us in shreds. Paul, according to him (p. 195), " held with equal conviction and emphasis two propositions which seem contradictory: ' There is one God and Father of all, who is above all and through all, and in you all '; and ' Christ is God for me.' " He adds: " perhaps they find their synthesis in that saying which is at once the simplest and profoundest account of the whole matter: ' God was in Christ reconciling the world unto Himself ' (II Cor. v. 19) " — which involves, of course, a wrong understanding of II Cor. v. 19, as of much else besides. And this is what he says of John: " It is in this document where the human nature of the Son and His dependence on the Father are asserted with the strongest emphasis that His Divinity is for the first time expressly acknowledged (i. 1; xx. 28). If John thus leaves an unsolved problem for posterity to attack it is better to recognize that it is so " (p. 199). But, that Johannes Weiss says so, is really no good reason for asserting that John left an unsolved problem for posterity to attack. Why should we deny to the apostolic writers the synthesis which is essential to give the harmony to their thought in which it evidently serenely moved, merely because our own halting minds, poisoned with carping criticisms, the very reason of existence for which is to break in upon their serene harmony, fail to see it with their clarity of vision?

Dr. Scott tells us, it is true, that " St. Paul had no doctrine of the Trinity." But he tells us this only because he is endeavoring at the moment to show that Paul had no doctrine of a hypostatically distinct Spirit. Paul, according to him, identified Christ and the Spirit, and " the Spirit of God, or Holy Spirit, was for him (apart from the identification with the Risen Christ) the energy of the Divine nature " (p. 189). We congratulate the readers of this Dictionary that they only have to turn over to Schlatter's article on the Holy Spirit to learn better (p. 574b: " 3. The Spirit sent by Christ "), and have only to turn to Allen's remarks on the Trinitarian formula in Matt. xxviii. 19 (p. 475a) to be set right on the main matter. We revert for a moment, however, to the citations we have just made from Dr. Scott. He declares that " the divinity of Christ is for the first time expressly acknowledged " by John, and yet he declares that Paul held with complete conviction and asserted with emphasis, " Christ is God for me." The saving clause to enable Dr. Scott to make a synthesis of his own words lies of course in the words " for me." Paul was convinced, it seems, that Christ was God " for him," but not that He was God for other people. This subjectivizing of Paul's assertions about Christ is thoroughly unjustifiable. Paul does not tell us what Christ was " for him "; he tells us what in his view Christ was. Dr. Scott tells us, it is true, with the emphasis of formal announcement: " St. Paul never gives to Christ the name or description of ' God ' " (p. 194). But he tells us this again only because he cannot see that such a statement could be made consistent with Paul's monotheism, although at the end, we have seen, he has to admit that Paul did hold in conjunction his monotheism and the conviction that Christ was God — " for him." In point of fact, however, Paul does give to Christ both the name and the description of God. He gives Him the name of God for example in Rom. ix. 5, and not the bare name of " God " merely, but the description of " God over all "; he gives Him the name of God in Titus ii. 13, and again not merely the name of " God " but the description of " our great God and Saviour." He describes Him as God in Acts xx. 28, in Phil. ii. 8 ff., and in Col. ii. 13 ff., and in numerous places besides. No doubt Dr. Scott has his own way of explaining away all such descriptions. But this is to be set to the charge of his exegesis: they cannot be explained away. If we are to be permitted to put an artificial meaning on every statement which is inconsistent with a generalization which we wish to foist upon an author, no author's meaning is safe and it becomes a folly to write.

The quality of Dr. Scott's exegesis may be gauged by observing the curious interpretation which he gives of Rom. i. 4. He represents Paul as teaching here that as born of the seed of David Jesus had been "Χριστὸς κατὰ σάρκα and υἱὸς θεοῦ in the Messianic sense "; " but after and in consequence of the Resurrection, He has entered upon the status of Son of God in an exalted form, set free from ' the likeness of (weak and) sinful flesh ' " (p. 189). This should mean, ex vi verborum, that to Paul Christ while on earth was but " the fleshly Christ " and only became the spiritual Son of God after and in consequence of the Resurrection. The passage certainly does not mean this; and no doubt this is something more than Dr. Scott would have it mean. Where, however, does Paul speak of Jesus being or being conceived as Χριστὸς κατὰ σάρκα? Not at Rom. ix. 5 or II Cor. v. 16 where alone the terms are brought together. It is safe to say that it would have been simply impossible for Paul to speak of Jesus as Χριστὸς κατὰσ άρκα. And where does Paul suggest that Christ in His exaltation has been set free from " the likeness of sinful flesh "? That would be to teach that Christ was incarnate only upon earth and ceased to be incarnate in His exaltation. When he comes formally to expound Rom. viii. 3, Dr. Scott discards the translation " sinful flesh " in favor of " sin's flesh "; that is, if we understand him, he wishes to take the genitive as genitive of possession rather than of characterizing quality. He explains that this " flesh " is not conceived by Paul as originally or inherently sinful — as Jülicher, for example, will have it, saying " there never was any other kind " — but has become so " historically and experimentally " (p. 192). This is well, so far as it goes: but the point is that " flesh " has thus, according to Dr. Scott, become " an appanage of sin " in all its manifestations. Now Christ took this flesh, flesh as the possession of sin. " The σάρξ which He assumed was truly human flesh; it was, for such it had come to be historically, ' sin's flesh ' — flesh that was in the grasp of sin " (p. 193). In being made in the likeness of sin's flesh, therefore, Christ took flesh that was in the grasp of sin, flesh " as it was conditioned by sin, tyrannized and enslaved by it." This would seem to be inconsistent with the term " likeness " here, and flat in the face of such a phrase as meets us, say, in II Cor. v. 21. But Dr. Scott does not mean to say that Paul teaches that the flesh which Christ took was actually sinful. He supposes that he meets the difficulty by saying: " He ' knew no sin ' (II Cor. v. 21), and yet in His case the σάρξ was the medium of

sin's assault upon Him." Obviously the conclusion does not match the premises. And what is the use of erecting a problem to be solved in this way?

The difficulty of stating statistical facts with exactness and without misleading implications is proverbial. Dr. Scott does not escape scatheless. He makes these statements with respect to what he, not altogether exactly, speaks of as Luke's use of Χριστός in the early chapters of Acts, with a view to illustrating the writer's constant consciousness of its official sense. " He never employs it," he says, " as a proper name. His name for our Saviour is either ' Jesus' or ' the Lord'; and Χριστός when it stands alone always means ' Messiah.' This is specially significant in passages where ' Christ' and ' Jesus' occur together, in apposition; e.g. iii. 20, ' that He may send the Messiah who has been before appointed — Jesus '; v. 42, xvii. 3, xviii. 5, xviii. 28, ' showing by the Scriptures that Jesus was the Messiah ' " (p. 178). He speaks of these three facts as " completely attesting " the primary fact asserted, namely, that Luke always uses Χριστός with its official sense in mind. But we observe at once that the first of the three statements is inexact. To make it exact, the qualifying clause employed in later statements must be inserted. It is true only that Χριστός " when it stands alone " does not occur as a proper name. It does occur as a proper name in conjunction with other designations: " Jesus Christ " (viii. 12, ix. 34, x. 36, 48), " Jesus Christ, the Nazarene (iii. 6, iv. 10), " the Lord Jesus Christ " (xi. 17), " our Lord Jesus Christ " (xv. 26). And its occurrence as a proper name in these compounds renders the inexact statement misleading. They show that " Christ " has so fully taken the place of a proper name in the consciousness of the community that even such compounds could be formed. Dr. Scott's second statement thus becomes also inexact and misleading. It is true that " Lord " is the ruling designation of Jesus in Acts; " Jesus " on the other hand is comparatively sparingly employed, and only in particular circumstances which rendered it peculiarly natural to employ it: it occurs sometimes in conjunction with not only " Lord " (" the Lord Jesus ") but " Christ " itself (" Jesus Christ ") or both (" the Lord Jesus Christ "). It is no doubt a tardy remembrance of the use of " Jesus " along with " Christ " which compels the qualified form of the assertion in the second half of this second statement: " and Χριστός *when it stands alone always means Messiah.*" It only rarely, however, stands alone; and when it does so, it is chiefly in such statements as " showing by the Scriptures that Jesus was the Christ " — which are scarcely *ad rem*. Even the last of the three statements thus becomes misleading. Some of the passages cited in it are not from the first part of Acts. Only those passages are adduced in which the order is " Christ Jesus " (xvii. 3 certainly belongs in any event to a different category), not those in which the order is " Jesus Christ." And the possibility that " Christ Jesus " in iii. 20 and v. 42 as well as in xxiv. 24 (the omission of which from Dr. Scott's list seems to show that he does not consider it to the point) may be a proper name, as it frequently is in the Epistles, is not allowed for. The statistics of the occurrence of Κύριος in I and II Thessalonians, p. 187b, are marred by the same kind of inexactness of statement. Decidedly, the reader would do well to scrutinize these statistical statements before drawing inferences from them in support of propositions.

If we do not like Dr. Scott's article on " Christ, Christology," we like Dr. A. S. Martin's articles on " Grace " and " Justification " even less. It would probably have been impossible to discover a person more unfitted to deal with these subjects sympathetically. The treatment of Grace is vitiated from the beginning by the determination of the writer to set man over against God as His fellow, not to say — as a personal spirit like Him — His equal. Coöperation becomes thus the formula for the relation of the two, and a coöperation which ever tends to a certain equalization. Grace is not merely given; it is taken. God and man work together to all effects, God's willingness to help being matched by man's willingness to be helped. It is a case of mutual love, the love of God to man meeting the love of man to God, and the conjunction of the two issuing in a common effect. Accordingly there is nothing " infallible " or " irresistible " in grace: it is merely God's side of a mutual activity — which is barren, and to say the truth, not even instituted, until and unless man's side is in evidence also. All this is, of course, quite un-Biblical. When Paul declares, for example, on the one side, that man is carnal, sold under sin, and on the other, that sin shall not rule over those who are not under law but under grace, he certainly allows for the voluntary activities of men, but as certainly he presents the grace that comes to them gratuitously as both " infallible" and " irresistible." " Sin *shall not* rule over you "; it is a definite promise of what shall be. " *For* ye are under grace ": the reason is defined; grace is a power which irresistibly brings the result. What Martin has done is to transform the almighty power of God which creatively works its effect into a mere influx of immanently acting influence, which in concourse with the human soul, as a second cause, makes towards an end. The article " Grace," in these circumstances, becomes not one on Grace itself, that is, the divine activities in saving the soul, but on " the grace-filled life," that is, the growth of the human soul under the divine influences. Everything is subjectivized — translated into terms of human action. This is sometimes nothing less than absurd. Take this definition of Election: " Election expresses the soul's experience and certainty of saving grace " (p. 510). Or this definition of Grace itself: " Grace is a sense of God's favor."

We are not sure that it is possible — we are sure that it is very difficult — to obtain from Martin's discussion of Justification any clear conception of how he really thinks it is accomplished. Take the section, for example, in which he sums up what he conceives to be meant by " the new righteousness " in Paul's teaching — that is to say, in his own. We are told (p. 671) that we cannot " stand before God's righteousness " on the basis of a self-righteousness which is the righteousness of the Law. Then we are told that " there is another righteousness, never lost sight of under the old Law, which has now appeared in Jesus Christ " and is " by Him made ours." But we seek in vain to learn what this " other righteousness " is, or how it is made ours by Christ. We are told that it is " presented in Christ "; that " it awakes in the sinner penitence and faith — a love of Christ's holiness, a hatred of his own sinfulness "; and that it does this " by God's grace." We are told that the very thing provided in it is a provision " to bridge the chasm between God and sin." But we are not told what it is. And when an effort is made to point out how it " bridges the chasm between God and sin " it is in this, if not confused, certainly confusing sentence: " In Christ God gives His own righteousness, which is the end and meaning of all faith." What is " the end and meaning of all faith "? God's own righteousness? Or the gift of God's own righteousness in Christ? And what is this righteousness of God's own, which He gives in Christ, and which, or the gift of which, is the end and meaning of all faith? Until we know that we are told nothing and we are not in the least told that. We are only told that " he who receives it " — whatever this mysterious " it " is — " *in initio* receives it virtually *in extenso;* such is the mode of God's gift of it."

This sounds so good that we are the more anxious to know what " it " is. And fortunately we strike now a stream of lucid writing, which, however, does not obviously relate itself to what has been said before. " The condition of possible or future righteousness," we read, " is the right attitude or intention of mind towards the actual present righteousness. It is possible to justify or accept as right only that attitude which at the time is the nearest right possible for the person. In the initial moment of contrition, the only possible and right posture of the sinner is that consciousness of himself which could not be the beginning of his hatred of sin if it were not to the same extent the beginning of a love of holiness. Where this exists in love and sincerity, even though it be but the beginning of an infinite process, it is possible and right to accept and treat as right that which as yet is only a first turning to and direction towards right (cf. I John i. 8–10)." This is an admirably clear statement of the doctrine, not indeed of Paul, but of current modern Pelagianism, which bases God's acceptance of the sinner on the sinner's own righteous conduct, but (here is where it differs from fifth century Pelagianism), in concession to the imperfection of the sinner's righteousness, supposes that God accepts the will for the deed, takes the beginnings in anticipation of the completion, is willing, in other words, to accept the sinner's note of hand in lieu of the cash down, as the purchase price of His favor. But that " other righteousness " presented in Christ, described as " God's own righteousness given in Christ," " which is the end and meaning of all faith " — what has it to do with this Pelagian scheme? God demands from man a righteousness of his own, and graciously accepts its first motions as if the completion were already present — that is all we have here.

Martin does make some effort to institute a connection between our righteousness and Christ. But it seems lame and ineffective. He proceeds (p. 671): " Thus the righteousness of faith " — we have not heard before of any " righteousness of faith " but our righteousness is suddenly called by this name — " thus the righteousness of faith begins with our sense of sin and experience of impotence, and God's loving acceptance of this repentance in us is the condition, starting-point, and earnest of a righteousness in us which is maintained and increased through Christ's," — it is the possessive case and hence means " Christ's righteousness " — " in whom we see revealed all the presence and power of God in us, and in consequence all the power in ourselves necessary to its actual attainment and possession." We can attach no other meaning to this sentence except this: that we begin our own righteousness with a sense of sin and experience of impotence; that God lovingly accepts this repentance as the condition, starting-point, and earnest of a righteousness of our own (" in us ") ; that we then see all the presence and power of God " in us " — that " in us " is very disturbing! — revealed in Christ, which apparently means that we see already manifested in Christ all that we hope to be, that complete righteousness of which we as yet have only the beginnings; that this is equivalent in some way unexplained (" consequently ") to seeing in Him " all the power in ourselves necessary to its actual possession " — " its " being apparently the complete righteousness already manifested in Christ and begun in us; and finally, that this sight of these revelations in Him " maintains and increases our faith." This seems to mean nothing more than that the righteousness which we begin in ourselves and which is accepted by God as the promise and potency of a completed righteousness yet to come, is maintained and increased by the inspiration of Christ's example: we see in Him what we fain would be, and that inspires us to become it. Accordingly Martin continues: " Faith in Christ as our righteousness can justify us because it is based on the one condition in ourselves of becoming righteous — a loyal disposition — and the one power without ourselves to make us righteous — the righteousness of God." We do not profess to understand that sentence; but it seems to be explicated by the next one which runs: " The grace of God in Christ makes the sinner righteous, by enabling him to make himself righteous. It starts the process by regarding and treating as righteous the penitent believer." Thus, out of all the confusion, we get — mere Pelagianism. And this is represented as the doctrine of Paul!

No doubt Martin would not confess himself a Pelagian. And it is very true that he frequently makes use of expressions which are inconsistent with the complete Pelagianism of this reasoned statement of doctrine. The main point to insist on, therefore, is his lack of clarity. And perhaps it is well to note that he is not very exact in his history of doctrine. At one point in the article on Grace (p. 512), he undertakes to discriminate Pelagianism, Augustinianism, and Semi-Pelagianism. He does it thus: " In the Pelagian view, grace precedes and assists the *natural* (unregenerate) will; in the

Augustinian, grace prepares and assists the *regenerate* will; in the Semi-Pelagian, grace is not operative at all till man's will (*indifferent*) brings it into play." Did anyone ever hear such confusion? We are tempted to conjecture that the terms Pelagian and Semi-Pelagian have accidently got interchanged. But that correction will not cure all the faults of the statement. It is hopelessly incompetent.

That we should meet with this bald Pelagianism here should not in the least surprise us. Pelagianism is the anthropological aspect of that "reduced Christianity" which calls itself "modern Liberalism." It is, therefore, very much in evidence in this Dictionary which is tinctured everywhere with this "Liberalism." We open it, for example, at the article "Hardening." This is written by Prof. James Strahan. We find him struggling unsuccessfully with the ascription of "hardening" to God. The reason is simply that he does not believe in a "Fall." He does not recognize that man stands before God as a guilty creature, who already deserves all the punishment which may befall him. He quotes Hermann Schultz as saying, "Nor does any one doubt that it is an effect intended by God, when, at a certain stage in sin, His revelation makes the heart harder" (p. 522) — and in quoting this saying approvingly he undermines his whole labored argument (and Schultz's as well) — if indeed man be a sinner. Every man is always, the Scriptures being witness, at that stage of sin that any manifestation of God makes his heart harder; and it requires a creative operation by the Spirit of God to beget in him a new life. Dr. Strahan is a professor in the M'Crea-Magee Presbyterian College, Londonderry, Ireland; and Dr. Martin is a minister of the Church of Scotland and was formerly an examiner in Divinity in Edinburgh University. We have sometimes fancied that it is the men of these better traditions who have fallen most hopelessly under the newer "reduced" influences. We were glad, accordingly, to see that the article on the Freedom of the Will has been committed to a good Wesleyan, Prof. W. F. Lofthouse. When we read it, we were gladder still. We may not agree with everything Prof. Lofthouse says: but there is nothing shallow here. The article is written not only with solid learning but with true insight, and at least touches the full truth. Prof. Lofthouse knows not only his own philosophy but his Paul. His article is like an oasis in a dry land.

DICTIONARY OF THE APOSTOLIC CHURCH. Edited by JAMES HAST-
INGS, D.D. Vol. II: Macedonia — Zion, with Indexes. New
York: Charles Scribner's Sons; Edinburgh: T. & T. Clark.
1918.[1]

THIS concluding volume of Dr. Hastings' "Dictionary of the
Apostolic Church" is the product of the labors of about a hundred
scholars. Five of these are from the Continent, and a dozen are
Americans. The material contributed by the Continental scholars
is not large in amount nor of the first importance. P. Batiffol writes
on Polycarp; E. von Dobschütz on Philo; H. Jordan on Writing;
O. E. Moe on Moses; A. von Schlatter on Paraclete. The American
writers are C. A. Beckwith, S. J. Case, J. A. Faulkner, W. M. Groton,
K. Kohler (who, although a Jew, has been intrusted, among others,
with so intimately Christian a subject as "Shepherd"), A. T.
Robertson, G. L. Robinson, T. G. Soares, G. Vos, B. B. Warfield,
and A. C. Zenos. Of these the largest contributions have been made
by the late Prof. Groton of the Episcopal Divinity School, Philadelphia, and Prof. Case of the University of Chicago. Prof. Groton
writes the long (thirteen pages) and valuable article on "Mystery,
Mysteries," which will serve admirably as a succinct introduction
to the study of this obscure subject. Besides some shorter articles
("Seed," "Theudas," "Tribute") Prof. Case writes the long
articles (nineteen pages in combination) on "Peter" and the
"Epistles of Peter." The even longer article on "Paul" (twenty-one
pages) is written by Prof. James Stalker, an old hand at the subject. Articles on such topics legitimately occupy large space in a
Dictionary of the Apostolic Church. When we say Peter and Paul
we almost say Apostolic Church — as the narrative of the Book
of Acts may suggest to us. There are other long articles in the volume, however, the scope of which passes so far beyond the Apostolic
Church as to set the reader to wondering as to the principle on which
they have been admitted. There is, for example, Prof. James Moffatt's article on "War." It is an altogether admirable treatise on
the attitude of the early Church to war. It quickly, however, gets
beyond anything that can be called the Apostolic Church and does
not stop till it reaches Augustine. And there is Principal Thomas
Lewis' excellent article on "Persecution." It finds no stopping-
place short of the Reformation.

[1] The Princeton Theological Review, xvii. 1919, pp. 500–512.

It is the policy of this Dictionary to interpret the phrase "Apostolic Church" purely temporally. It means to it merely the Church of the first century. It is an incidental good result of this bad point of view that besides articles on the New Testament books we get admirable articles on what we may perhaps still speak of as subapostolic writings, and indeed on Jewish writings dating from a time somewhere about the Apostolic Age. We have not only articles on Polycarp (P. Batiffol) — poor Papias is left out — and the Odes of Solomon (A Mingana), but also articles on Philo (E. von Dobschütz), Sirach and Wisdom (D. S. Margoliouth), the Psalms of Solomon (G. B. Gray), the Testaments of the Twelve Patriarchs (A. L. Davies), and Sibylline Oracles (James Moffatt). It may no doubt be said that a knowledge of these writings is important, both as regards their language and their thought, for a complete understanding of the Apostolic Age. Such a plea would be much more valid for the Jewish writings antedating the apostolic times than for the subapostolic writings. There is really no good reason for including subapostolic writings in a Dictionary of the Apostolic Church. The gulf between the two groups of writings is as wide as that which divides any two groups of writings, contiguous in time, known to history. If we needed any proof of that, it would be supported by the result of attempting to smelt the two groups together in this Dictionary. For, if the excellence of the articles on the several subapostolic books tends to lead us to condone their intrusion into the Dictionary, the case is far different with the habit of tacking on to article after article on apostolic teaching on this or that subject, a paragraph on the teaching of the subapostolic writers on it also. If this begins by being amusing, it ends by becoming wearisome. There is no section of the history of doctrine less exhilarating than that which deals with the subapostolic Fathers. It was a true saying of a great man long ago that they would be better named supapostolic babies. No matter how close they stand to one another in time, the apostolic and the subapostolic writers cannot be compressed into the same category. The attempt to do so is a blunder.

Underlying the attempt to wash out the boundary line which separates between the apostolic and subapostolic writings, and the consequent habit of speaking of the latter as "first century writers outside the New Testament," a low view of the inspiration and authority of the New Testament writings is usually discoverable, and in general a chariness with respect to the immediately supernatural in the origins of Christianity. Of course one would not require to look long before he found something of this sort among the hundred or so writers who have coöperated in the preparation of this volume. On the whole, however, even those whose personal views leave little place for an authoritative Scripture or for direct supernaturalism appear to have sought to write objectively. Prof. A. R. Gordon, of M'Gill University, who writes the good article on "Scripture," seems to doubt whether the Christian can take the Old Testament, in its own sense, as authoritative to him, but he nevertheless tells us frankly that "the high Jewish theory of the inspiration of Scripture is fully accepted in the New Testament," where the words of Moses, David, Isaiah and the other prophets are "attributed directly to God" and are looked upon as the final norm alike of faith and of conduct. In the article "Miracles" by Bishop Maclean, we meet on the other hand with an attempt to explain miracles away, which was rather unexpected in this quarter. Many of the "miracles" recorded in the New Testament, we are told, are clearly not miracles in the strict sense; many which seemed miracles to those who witnessed them we can now see were not really miracles; many more, the natural mode of working which, that even we may not yet see, no doubt those who come after us will see. Perhaps "the theory of 'relative miracles' propounded by Schleiermacher" may commend itself to us. "This theory substitutes for a contravention of nature a miraculous knowledge. Certain persons had a greater hold upon the secrets of nature than their contemporaries." "But," it is added, "this was by a divine interposition"; and is not the essential thing, as Dr. Sanday says, "the divine act"? What is troubling Bishop Maclean is the conception of nature as an absolutely closed system, in which everything that occurs must be the product of its own intrinsic forces operating normally; no intrusion from without is possible, or, at least, can be admitted to have ever occurred. Doubtless God made it; but having made it, He never afterwards has interfered with its mechanical working, for any purpose whatever. Whatever occurs is "natural." Of course Bishop Maclean seizes hold of that remark of Augustine's — which has frequently before been as gravely misused as he misuses it — that a "portent" happens not against nature but against "known nature." On the repeated occasions when he made this remark Augustine was not reducing our conception of miracles to merely " natural " events but elevating and enlarging our conception of " nature." There is a " nature," he says, above the nature spread out for our observation, the " nature," to wit, of the Divine Decree: for everything that God wills becomes by that act a natural thing to occur although it does not occur by means of the " natural " forces: it cannot be said to be " unnatural " though it be " supernatural," for the constitutive fact of all nature is the will of God. It is enough to dispose of Bishop Maclean's theory of " relative miracles " to ask what is the difference, on its basis, between a miracle and a trick, between the miracles of Moses before Pharaoh, say, and those of the Egyptian magicians? Despite his reduction of miracles to tricks, we observe, Bishop Maclean is concerned to show that the Apostolic Age was marked by abounding miracles, while the Post-Apostolic Age lacked them.

Perhaps the best way to obtain a fair conception of the quality of a book like this is to take some one general subject and observe how it is treated in its several parts by the various writers to which they have been committed. We choose the broad subject of Salvation for this purpose. There is a general article on " Salvation, Save, Saviour," by Principal Darwell Stone, of Pusey House, Oxford. It seems to be a fair example of what such an article should not be. It consists in the main of statistics of no great significance, and an analysis of Dr. Stone's own doctrine of salvation supported item by item by proof-texts bent to its service. It is certainly only a crochet which denies that " save " in James v. 15 refers to bodily healing. On the other hand Prof. A. T. Robertson of the Louisville Baptist Seminary gives us in the article " Mediation, Mediator " a refreshingly clear, straightforward, and instructive account of the apostolic teaching on the saving work of Christ. The skillful grammarian is always in evidence and the exact meaning of the sacred writings is sought and brought out with very telling effect.

A group of articles bearing on the expiatory work of Christ — " Ransom," " Sacrifice," " Propitiation," " Reconciliation " — has been committed to Prof. Frederic Platt of the Wesleyan College at Birmingham. The short article on " Ransom " covers the ground fairly well, and reaches the eminently just conclusion expressed at the end, that by the employment of this term it is implied that " life in the higher sense " has been lost by man, and he " has no means of buying it back "; but " Christ has laid down His life as a price or means of redemption by which the forfeited possession was

restored " (p. 298). The article on " Sacrifice " is much longer and
more thorough, but is marred by its presupposition of the modern
critical view of the composition of the Old Testament and the development of Old Testament religion, and by its estimating the
whole Biblical material from this point of sight. A certain continuity
in the development of the notion of sacrifice from the most primitive
conceptions to that of developed Christianity is assumed. It is even
supposed (p. 431) that traces of all the main theories of primitive
sacrifice which have been broached by speculators may be discovered in the New Testament; and the necessity of choosing between them in our search for the original significance of sacrifice is
avoided by the suggestion that all of them may have been held in
those primitive ages the influence of which was still felt by the
men of the New Testament. It is more reasonably declared, however (p. 431), that " the one constant element in primitive sacrifice
persisting to apostolic times that modern research, both anthropological and psychological, seems to warrant is that sacrifice appears
to have pleased the object of worship and secured the favor of
deity — i.e. it was ' propitiatory ' in the broadest sense." It is
recognized that, at the time the Levitical system was formed, the
" piacular or expiatory sacrifice " had become prominent. " It was
the expiatory type that constituted the daily sacrifices — the continual burnt-offering — up to apostolic times; it was regarded as
most perfectly embodying, through its vicarious character, the
sacrificial idea " (p. 432). That having been said, there seems no
reason for the hesitation regarding the conception attributed to
sacrifices in later Judaism, at least so far as the Judaism contemporary with the apostles is concerned. It is allowed that Christ
referred to His death as sacrificial; that " at a very early period,"
that is, in the Apostolic Age, the death of Christ was regarded as
expiatory; and that " this sacrificial interpretation of His death is
imbedded in subsequent types of apostolic teaching " (p. 434) —
that Peter sharply asserts the vicarious nature of the sufferings of
Christ, Paul " clearly regards the death of Christ as substitutionary," and the Epistle to the Hebrews and the Epistles of John
make use of the same conception. Nevertheless there is some hag-
gling over the question whether the Apostolic Church is to be said
to have regarded Jesus' death as sacrificial or only to have employed sacrificial language illustratively of His death. We gain an
impression that if the Scriptures were more definitely authoritative

to Prof. Platt his conclusions would possess a more decided character. The just decisiveness with which A. B. Bruce's suggestion is
repelled (p. 434b), that Paul's ideas of Christ's sacrifice were colored
more by the analogy of Greek and Roman human sacrifices than
by that of the Levitical system, is the more welcome that more
hospitality seems to be shown to this suggestion in the article on
" Propitiation " (p. 283a). That article suffers from diffuseness and
from an attempt to draw nice distinctions of somewhat doubtful
validity. It insists, for example, that the classical and pagan use
of the Greek " term must not be carried over into the New Testament," with a vigor which can scarcely fail to seem excessive, when
it emerges that " although such phrases as ' propitiating God ' or
God ' being propitiated ' are foreign to apostolic teaching, the
Pauline view relates the propitiation to God as recipient " (p. 282a).
To give any plausibility to the distinction, such exaggerated language requires to be used as this: " The idea of directly appeasing
one who is angry with a personal resentment against the offender
. . . is foreign to biblical usage " (p. 281) — which is of course
true, but concerns less the usage of the word than the conception
of the deity. The attempt to distinguish between the usages of
Paul, " the Johannine writer," and the author of Hebrews is equally
futile. The fact is that the usage of words of this stem in the New
Testament is too meager to supply a basis for such speculations. It
does not make a pleasant impression when, after we have been told
that the verb " propitiate " is construed in classical Greek regularly
with the accusative of the person propitiated, it is added, " this
construction is never used by apostolic writers." This can hardly
be a significant fact when the verb occurs only twice in the New
Testament. In the Septuagint it occurs in the banned construction
and that with God as its object (Zech. vii. 2). Certainly the God of
Christians is a different kind of person from the gods of the heathen,
but we can never so " ethicize " the conception of propitiation as to
rid it of the implication that it removes obstacles in Him (and not
merely in us) to His favorable regard of us. That Prof. Platt does
not himself think that we can, we learn with more distinctness from
the article on " Reconciliation." In it (p. 301b), he even uses such
language as this: " God's anger is real; it is not simply official as
the hostility of a law-giver in the presence of a law-breaker; it is
personal, but not a fitful personal resentment. . . ." He goes on to
tell us, it is true, in quite modern fashion, that it is but the seamy

side of love — " love's crowning sign, not its contradiction " — but this appears to be merely the repetition of a conventional mode of speaking and scarcely represents any very clear thought. We are glad to say that Prof. Platt very decidedly represents the fundamental reconciliation wrought by the blood of Christ to have been the reconciliation of God. He feels bound to insist, however, strenuously and at length, that the transaction is mutual. This is not so plain as far as the direct Scriptural representations as to our Lord's " reconciling work " are concerned. If any are inclined to adduce the passive imperative of II Cor. v. 20 in this connection, they may profitably consult the passive imperative of Eph. v. 18. Prof. Platt misconstrues the " in Christ " of II Cor. v. 19 after the fashion now so common, and founds some pretty theologizing on his misconstruction.

A large number of the elements that enter into the conception of Salvation come in for discussion in Prof. James Moffatt's long and brilliant article on " Righteousness," chiefly of course from the point of view of Paul's teaching. Prof. Moffatt touches nothing which he does not illuminate, and everyone will be his debtor for this searching and stimulating discussion. There are naturally some things he says, with which we should be compelled to take issue. We are thankful to be able to say, however, that with the larger part of the discussion we are heartily in agreement, and that we find many important truths enunciated in it in unwontedly sharp and telling language. This is the way in which at the opening of the section on the " technical Pauline use of the term ' God's righteousness ' " (p. 376) he sums up the content of the several passages which deal with that notion: " What is common to all is the presupposition that this righteousness, this state of acceptance with God, this right relationship between the righteous God and sinful man, is brought about by God. It is not the goal of a laborious quest of man for God. The initiative is with Him. That is what the genitive signifies." We will not deny ourselves the pleasure of quoting further one or two crisply phrased truths. " Because the Christian is sure of final acquittal, he is to live up to it. Or, to put it in an antithesis: he is not to be saved because he is good, he is to be good because he is justified " (p. 380b). " To be justified by faith was God's gift. But it was more than a gift; it was a vocation, a career — Aufgabe as well as Gabe " (p. 392a). Every reader of this article will find himself instructed.

We have already with Prof. Moffatt's article passed over from articles dealing with the procuring of salvation to those in which its application is expounded. At the head of these stands the late Prof. T. Nicol's (of Aberdeen) excellent article on " Predestination." He is perhaps unduly exercised over the antinomy between predestination and free will, and repeats the banal comment, now widely current, on the change in voice in Rom. ix. 22, and in his short article on " Reprobate " he unhappily even enlarges on this matter. This comment only illustrates the straits in which those find themselves who would fain discover some hint in Scripture of a fundamental distinction in the nature of the Divine decree as it concerns the several classes of men. The article as a whole, however, is both well conceived and well worked out, and even with respect to the antinomy mentioned the right note is struck. " Whilst St. Paul . . . affirms the doctrine of absolute predestination to life, he asserts no less clearly the truth of human responsibility " (p. 263). That is the truth, accurately expressed. Prof. W. F. Lofthouse, of the Wesleyan College, Birmingham, the author of the good article on the Freedom of the Will in the first volume of this Dictionary, writes here an article on the " Will " in the apostolical writings which we find interesting rather than satisfactory. We shall not be easily persuaded to look on faith as " unswerving attention " (whatever may be the psychological effects which may be shown to result from sustained attention) rather than confident entrusting of ourselves to Christ. " If the attention is concentrated " on Jesus conceived as the Son of God, says Prof. Lofthouse, expounding the notion of faith in I John, " the universe of evil around him is powerless to harm the Christian " (p. 680). We demur to this representation of the nature and working of faith even with reference to the teaching of I John, and much more with reference to its presentation in the New Testament at large. Prof. Lofthouse is much occupied with the relation of God's will to man's in the processes of salvation. He sums up the matter very fairly. Man's will, he says, " acts properly only when it is roused and directed by Divine grace. The necessity for its exercise will never be superseded; but the more it is exercised under Divine control, the more it becomes God's will in man, and the more it becomes man's own will, acting at last in complete freedom " (p. 680b). But he is disturbed about the initial act of salvation. " Man's will appears to be clearly called for," he says, " by such passages as II Cor. v. 20, ' Be ye reconciled to God,' but against them Rom. ix. 18 may be quoted . . ." (p. 679). If we are to be saved by grace, he argues, we are also to be saved through faith; and if the one might lead us to suppose we are to be merely passive in salvation, the latter " shows that this is very far from being the case." We must mind, however, our prepositions — " by " and " through " convey the notification of different and not inconsistent relations; and with respect to passivity and activity, we must distinguish times — a famous old formula speaks accurately, regarding the initiation of salvation, of man being " altogether passive therein until — ." We have already pointed out how easily the passive imperative in II Cor. v. 20 is misunderstood. We are not exhorted there to lay aside our enmity to God, and even less to secure from God the laying aside of His enmity to us. The means by which God is reconciled to men is not their faith but the blood of Christ. We need not wonder that we find it difficult to express the passive imperative with accurate simplicty in translation. A phrase like this (Eph. v. 18), " Be ye filled in the Spirit," requires paraphrasing. Prof. Lofthouse writes also the article on " Repentance." It is a distinctly disappointing article. It is written under the influence of preconceptions which the Biblical statements, conceived as they are only as references to the subject by early preachers, have no power to dispel. The rich literature on the subject is almost entirely passed by in the appended Literature.

According to Prof. D. S. Adam of Melbourne, who writes on " Union with God," salvation consists essentially in the complete expression of the Divine Logos in man, who, as made in the image of God, furnishes " a form of being capable of expressing the Divine Logos in fullness of measure," and by his sin only conditioning the nature " of the task which the perfect Son of man and Son of God, when He appeared on earth, had to undertake " (p. 631). He is very careful not to commit the apostolic writers to the doctrine of the Trinity, and is equally careful to commit them to such doctrines as the institution of " a certain metaphysical union between man and God, in virtue of creation "; the necessity of the incarnation independently of sin; and the redemption of man through the union of the Logos with him in the incarnation. We are in a different atmosphere in Prof. T. G. Soares' (of Chicago University) article on " Regeneration." He seeks to throw the New Testament doctrine up against a background supplied by Jewish Apocalypticism and the heathen mystery religions. But he is very much afraid of sacramentalistic and magical conceptions slipping in; and labors so hard to " ethicize " the notion as to go far towards desupernaturalizing it. He gets the cart before the horse in his interpretation of such passages as I John v. 1, iv. 7, ii. 29, in which, in John's meaning, the begetting from God is not the effect but the cause of faith, love, righteousness. The reader is confused by a repeated odd use of the word " status " as if it expressed nature rather than relation. An appearance is created as if Prof. Soares' conception of regeneration vibrated between that of justification and that more commonly connected with the term regeneration, and as if he may perhaps wish to wipe out this distinction. The article on " Sanctification " (as also that on " Saints ") is written by Mr. Robert H. Strachan, Minister of the Presbyterian Church at Cambridge. " Sanctify, sanctification " are to him terms of relation, not of condition, much less of process. " Holy " really means sacred, and " to sanctify " means to make sacred, and " sanctification " the state of having been made sacred. As this is a thing God does, it is done absolutely and all at once. " Our moral progress is not a growth into holiness out of a state of comparative unholiness. That would be to negative the Christian gospel. Rather it is a growth *in* holiness. The act that makes us holy is done once and for all " (p. 452). In itself, therefore, sanctification has nothing to do with ethical conduct. It means merely that we belong to God. But as the God we belong to is an ethical Being, belonging to Him involves ethical conduct on our part. Sanctification thus necessitates ethical conduct and this conduct may be progressively ethical. The standard of this ethical conduct is not, however, " statutory " law, but the Christ within us. The ethics of the saints is autonomous; precisely what they are as saints is freemen in Christ Jesus. " All legal statutes are out of place in the Christian life." Even the teaching and example of Christ are subject to our critical scrutiny. " This is dangerous doctrine," says Mr. Strachan himself. But he comforts himself by adding: " All great doctrines are dangerous." At another point he quotes Paul's declaration that the law is good and holy and righteous. This, he says, however, illustrates only one side of Paul's teaching; it has reference only to those whose walk as saints has only begun — to babes in Christ. " Obedience to law is good for those to whom God says only ' Thou shalt ' or ' Thou shalt not ' . . . For the Christian, for ' those that are sanctified,' the ' law ' of sin and death is done away altogether, and obedience to the law of God is merged in a higher and nobler

loyalty to the God and Father of Jesus Christ, and above all in' a
sense of supreme indebtedness" (p. 452). It is true, of course, that
the Christian has a more constraining motive to " conformity with
God " than even the commands of God's holy law; and it is
true also, of course, that the recreating Spirit is by His recreation
of him writing the law of God on his heart, so that he becomes
more and more a law to himself: but the law of God must remain ever his standard, and the words of Christ must be always
valid, that not one jot or one tittle of it shall pass away until
all of them are accomplished. It would be harsh to speak of Mr.
Strachan's teaching as antinomian — but that way antinomianism
lies.

The article " Perfect, Perfection " by Principal J. G. Tasker of
the Wesleyan College, Birmingham, confines itself to tracing the
usage of the words in the New Testament. This it does very interestingly. The article on " Perseverance " by Mr. A. S. Martin
of Aberdeen on the other hand enters fully into the subject and
gives it a treatment which is excellent in conception and eloquent
in presentation. The paragraph near the beginning on the antinomy
of preservation and perseverance — or, as Mr. Martin phrases it,
of the religious and the moral aspects of the matter — is especially
finely worked out. " The more dependent the spiritual sense," he
says (p. 186), " the more intense the moral independence." It is a
good saying when we are told later that to the religious man " any
attempt to claim for man ability or sufficiency " " must appear as
nothing less than religious illiteracy " (p. 188). And it is an equally
good saying when we are told that the Christian *agonistes* is " slack
in no element of its manifold nature " (p. 190) but throws all that
he has and is into the good fight. There is a little wavering at the
end as to the relation of God and man in the work. God has the
initiative in salvation. But " He waits on the start of our effort."
This, it appears, is because " our effort is the beginning of His gift,
the first stirring of ' the grace that is in us ' from Him, and which
can be ours in no other way." " And so," it is added, " after the
start, throughout the whole of our moral growth, every new stirring
in us is of our effort *and* of His gift and increase (Phil. ii. 12). We
are never from first to last simply quietistic receivers of something
infused." The statement is not free from ambiguity and does not
carry its broad meaning with certainty. But it awakens a fear that
its spiritual affiliation may be with Erasmus, rather than with

Luther — and Paul. Every saving work of God actifies the soul, but no saving work of God waits on the soul's activities.

We shall not follow the treatment of the elements of salvation into the eschatological field. There are important articles on topics which fall in this region, which invite remark — articles for example on " Resurrection," " Parousia," " Paradise," " New Jerusalem." We have already occupied, however, as much space as is at our disposal. And perhaps enough has already been said to convey a fair conception of the character of the discussions which fill the volume.

THE DOCTRINE OF THE ATONEMENT. By J. K. MOZLEY, M.A. New York: Charles Scribner's Sons. 1916.[1]

MR. MOZLEY has packed an immense amount of detail into these two hundred and odd small pages, and has done so without in the least overweighting them. The book is written in a charming style, clear and pointed; and so far as its two main sections are concerned — those on the Biblical material and on the history of the doctrine — it is not only informing but illuminating. We do not think Mr. Mozley has done justice to himself in the third — the constructive — section. He devotes only twenty of his two hundred and twenty pages to it, and although he enhearteningly tells us that we cannot live without a doctrine of the Atonement, he ventures only to give us, not a doctrine, but merely suggestions " towards a doctrine." The worst of it is that the reader is apt to think in the end that this is just as well. The doctrine to which the lines of suggestion laid down appear to point, seems to be of a surprisingly low order — for Mr. Mozley: lower than the doctrine which he himself finds suggested by Paul, or by our Lord Himself, or by the fifty-third chapter of Isaiah. A book on the Atonement, which, after two thousand years of Christian living and thinking and teaching, manages to come to a close without telling us just what the Atonement is, can scarcely be thought other than a portent: but it is better so than that such a book should seek dogmatically to impose upon its readers, as the issue of all these years, a wholly inadequate doctrine of the Atonement.

[1] *The Princeton Theological Review,* xv. 1917, pp. 467–476.

The notion of Atonement which Mr. Mozley suggests may possibly lie at the end of our search after a doctrine, could we penetrate far enough, may perhaps be shadowed out in the following two sentences. Christ's death has a relation to sins not His own, which implies an intervention that amounts to a mediation between God and man. As the result of this mediation, the situation as between God and man changes. In expounding the notion thus vaguely expressed, Mr. Mozley lays stress primarily on sin's desert of punishment, a punishment which is at bottom retributive; and on the penitent soul's recognition of the justice of its punishment and yearning after the removal of that estrangement from God which is the primary effect of sin. The divine response to this penitence, he tells us, is forgiveness; and if we cannot quite equate forgiveness with the cancellation of punishment, we can say that it cancels a situation, that it changes punishment from retributive to restorative. Suffering, we are now told, always implies sin. The sufferings of Christ, therefore, who, we must bear well in mind was not Himself a sinner, but the Son of God, must therefore stand in relation to sin and could not leave things as they were. They altered the nature of the reference of suffering and death to sin; they so transformed death to us, indeed, that it loses its character as judgment: " the element of judgment, universal in death, spends itself in the Cross " (p. 216).

This may be expressed, says Mr. Mozley, " by saying that Christ bore penal sufferings for us and in our stead." We do not discover in his further exposition, however, any adequate justification of this excellent mode of expression. What we get instead is an explanation of how Christ is related to the race, by virtue of which His acts stand in a quite unique relation to the action of the race. Mr. Mozley does not think of Christ's humanity as " inclusive " or " generic." His mind rests rather, in accordance with modern feelings of solidarity, on the " almost limitless reaction of individuals and their acts upon other personalities " (p. 217). Apparently this carries us no further than the notion that Christ's saving work is accomplished by His so affecting men as to lead them " to identify themselves by way of aspiration with the work of Christ." This enables Mr. Mozley to say of this " work of Christ," that it is not the work of man but Christ's own work; though he adds as if that were the significant point, " it is also not the work of a divine non-human redeemer, but of Christ as Man fulfilling human obligations " (p. 218). The upshot, then, seems to be no more than that Christ, entering the human race and sharing with it the sufferings and death which had come to it as the punishment of sin, transmutes suffering and death for this race from retributive to restorative, and in the reactions of personality on personalities quickens men to identify themselves with " His work " — which seems scarcely to mean more than to imitate His lofty attitude towards life and its evils.

If we have not misunderstood Mr. Mozley's exposition of it, we can hardly look upon the theory of Atonement which he thus tentatively suggests as more than an elevated form of what is known as " the moral influence theory," the nerve of which is the reaction of Christ's personality on the lives of His fellow men. The actual atoning fact appears to be discovered not in what Christ does, nor even in what He is — but in what men do under the inspiration of His life among them. And therefore the discussion is brought to a close with such questions as these (p. 218) : " Is there anything immoral if God looks at men's inchoate moral achievements and forgives their moral shortcomings, that is, their sins, in the light of the moral completeness of Christ's life? If He reckons faith as righteousness, when in the act of faith man recognizes the moral obligations that press upon him for fulfilment, confesses his own failures, admits the justice of punishment as that which he has deserved, and at the same time points to the complete fulfilment of the law, the complete confession of God's holiness, and the voluntary endurance of penal suffering and death by Christ from within humanity? " Translating these questions into affirmations, there is suggested here that God, looking at men's inchoate moral achievements, forgives their moral shortcomings, that is, their sins, — for so sin is inadequately defined — and that He does this " in the light of " — whatever that may mean, but scarcely " on the ground of " — " the moral completeness of Christ's life." It is suggested again that God reckons faith as righteousness in certain circumstances, namely, when in the act of faith man recognizes the moral obligations that press upon him for fulfillment, confesses his own failures, admits the justice of punishment as that which he has deserved, and at the same time points to Christ's complete fulfillment of the law, complete confession of God's holiness, and voluntary endurance of penal suffering and death from within humanity.

Why men should thus point to Christ's holy life and to His death, as if God's action with respect to men could or should be affected by them, remains unexplained. Why the fact that Christ's sufferings and death come from " within humanity," should be adduced when only the modern notion of solidarity is in question, as a ground for God's dealing with humanity otherwise than according to its strict deserts, remains unexplained. How Christ's suffering and death can be spoken of as penal, is only lamely explained. We cannot wonder then that Mr. Mozley can only add by way of conclusion: " We go beyond what we have a right to assert if we say with Anselm that God was bound by the satisfaction which Christ provided and the merit which He won to treat man after a particular manner; but we have a right to say that it is neither unreasonable nor immoral that He should do so." Is not this a confession that no basis has been laid for firm confidence in salvation " for Christ's sake "? And is not even the negative conclusion presented too bold? Would it after all be reasonable — would it be moral — for God to accept men as righteous in His sight on the grounds here stated? The questions which have vexed all the ages start into sight: Is repentance an adequate ground for the forgiveness of sin? Is man able in his own strength to repent adequately of his sin? We would fain read Mr. Mozley's phrases: " in the light of the moral completeness of Christ's life," pointing " to the complete fulfilment of the law, the complete confession of God's holiness, and the voluntary endurance of penal suffering and death by Christ from within humanity," — as indicative of the attribution to Christ of some real law-keeping and penalty-paying on behalf of man. But, with the best will in the world, we have been unable to find in his expositions just warrant for doing so. We are ever driven regretfully back upon the recurring fear that Mr. Mozley's suggestions for a possible doctrine of the Atonement reduce in the last analysis to the presentation of man's own repentance plus an unjustified appeal to Christ's life and death (unjustifiedly spoken of as " penal "), as having taken place " within humanity," as the ground of forgiveness. The fundamental idea seems to be that repentance secures forgiveness; and the fundamental effect of Christ's life and death seems to be conceived as awakening men to repentance. So far as appears, the interposition of Christ — His mediating intervention — has this for its sole effect: and the attempt to suggest for it a Godward operation also seems to have failed. This, as we have already mentioned, is, according to Mr. Mozley's own expositions, below what the Scriptures teach in all their parts: and we believe it to be below also what Mr. Mozley himself wishes to teach. It seems to us perfectly clear that he must allow to our Lord's life and death a much more distinct substitutive character and a much more distinct propitiatory effect upon God if he would raise the theory to which his suggestions point above the rank of a purely subjective one.

It is with great pleasure that we turn back from Mr. Mozley's unfortunate constructive chapter to the brilliant chapters in which he expounds the Biblical teaching with respect to atonement. There are three of these: one on the Old Testament; one on the testimony of the Synoptic Gospels; and one on the New Testament interpretation, dealing with the rest of the New Testament. They are all marked by an adequate command of the literature of the subject, a clear, critical, and independent judgment and luminous exposition. The tendency of them all is to vindicate for the Biblical writers a consistent testimony to the need and provision in Christ of an objective atonement. The chapter on the "testimony of the Synoptic Gospels" is an especially admirable piece of writing, well-informed, sympathetic, penetrating. The account given in it of the consistently eschatological school of Gospel criticism, the discussion of the "ransom" passage, and, perhaps in a somewhat less eminent degree, that of our Lord's words at the last supper, are particularly instructive and leave us with an impression which cannot easily be dissipated that Jesus did represent His death as having the effect of an expiation of sin.

Even in these admirable chapters, however, we meet with some odd uses of language, which are forerunners perhaps of the failure in constructing a doctrine of Atonement in the end. Thus in discussing the Old Testament foundation Mr. Mozley distinguishes very sharply not only between "substitution and vicarious punishment" on the one hand and atonement on the other, but between propitiation and expiation. He is willing to admit that the Old Testament sacrifices were expiatory, but not propitiatory, much less vicarious or substitutionary. This is a series certainly of very delicate distinctions, and the distinctions are as unusual as they are delicate. We have been accustomed to hear of a propitiation without expiation, but scarcely of an expiation without propitiation: and it is difficult to comprehend how expiation of sin can be made through the medium of another's death, and substitution and vicarious punishment be avoided. It is already evident that Mr. Mozley uses current terms in not quite their current meanings — and that is at least confusing. His notion appears to grow out of the idea that sacrifices are essentially gifts — gifts intended, not to appease, but to make amends: gifts, that is to say, speaking in the language of the older theories of sacrifice, not of the order of bribes but of the order of fines. He quotes Piepenbring approvingly (p. 22) to the effect that " expiatory sacrifice " is " like every other sacrifice, a corban, a gift ": " a guilty person " offers it to God " to make amends." In his own language, he explains that " the sacrificial system assumes that sin makes a barrier between man and God; and that before the covenant relationship with Jahveh, which the individual normally enjoys as a member of the covenant people, can be restored, the sin must be covered or wiped out. For that Jahveh Himself has made provision, and the final act of reparation is the presentation and sprinkling of the blood, the most sacred of all earthly things, as the equivalent of life " (pp. 22–23). The most notable thing about this definition is what we may call its prudence. Precisely what sacrifice is, it is difficult to learn from it: or what really removes the barrier which sin has erected between men and God. We are told that, for its removal, " sin must be covered or wiped out," — the two meanings assigned to *kipper* by differing schools of philologists being both prudently allowed for. We are told that God has made provision for this, but are not told what the precise nature of this provision is: we are only told what the final (may we take this as equivalent to essential?) act of " reparation " is. Are we to take " reparation " here as descriptive of what is accomplished by the " covering " or " wiping out " of the sin of the earlier clause, or as what is accomplished by the presentation and sprinkling of the blood? And how is " reparation " wrought in either case? The definition is vague at the crucial point, and covers under generalities questions which must be faced and settled if the sacrificial system of Israel is to be understood. The reader is just about to conclude that nothing is discovered in Old Testament sacrifices except " making amends," and that this is paralleled by the prophetic demand of nothing but repentance, when he is happily pulled up by a ringing denial that repentance and amendment sum up prophetic religion and finds himself reading with delight a good exposition of the fifty-third chapter of Isaiah which brings clearly out the conception of vicarious punishment embedded in that passage.

Somewhat similarly in the chapter on " the New Testament interpretation " we find Mr. Mozley boggling at the word " punishment " as a description of Paul's view of the sufferings of Christ. He is willing to allow that Paul holds these sufferings to be " penal." " For St. Paul," he says, " there is a penal element in the Cross " (p. 72). " Christ on the Cross," he (with agreement) quotes Feine as saying, " has endured what mankind had to expect." But he will not allow the word " punishment " in this connection. This seems rather wiredrawn. What is the difference in the fundamental connotation of punishment and penalty? Apparently two difficulties lie in Mr. Mozley's mind. He does not wish to say that Christ suffered precisely what we should have suffered had we borne the penalty of our own sins. And he does not wish to make Christ's sufferings punishment to Him. He has no question that Christ's sufferings were vicarious; and he has no difficulty with the idea of substitution. But he balks at saying that Christ " was vicariously punished." He agrees (with Herrmann) that " St. Paul thinks of Christ as suffering what we should have suffered." But he adds at once that His sufferings " had not the same quality or character as ours would have had," and commends Bey- schlag for declaring that " Jesus does not die the eternal death which we as sinners have deserved " (p. 73). He agrees (with Jülicher) that according to Paul " God reckons Christ's sufferings to mankind as punishment endured by it." But he adds at once, " That is not to equate suffering and punishment." " St. Paul's doctrine is not one of atonement and expiation through punishment, but rather of ex- piation instead of punishment, in which respect he anticipates Anselm." We may speak, he says through the medium of a quotation from Pfleiderer, of Paul teaching, not that Christ suffered " vicarious punishment," but certainly that He suffered death vicariously; not that He suffered this as a punishment, but that He endured it as a penalty. If the thought arises unbidden in our minds that we are very close to logomachy here, we correct it at once by perceiving happily that Mr. Mozley is only, very properly although not very clearly, attributing to Paul the doctrine of " satisfaction." The doctrine of " satisfaction " denies that Christ's sufferings had " the same quality or character as ours." What it affirms is that they had the same value. It denies that He died the eternal death that we sinners deserved. What it affirms is that His sufferings and death had the same value in the sight of God that our eternal death would have had. According to it, in this sense Christ did not bear our punish- ment, but something which took the place of our punishment. There was " a vicarious quittance of the penalty "; but this was wrought by paying it. Similarly with all his denials Mr. Mozley allows that according to Paul what was done by Christ was penal and what He endured was penalty. It must be confessed, however, that only a few pages after thus expounding Paul as teaching the doctrine of " satisfaction," Mr. Mozley, by an odd inconsequence, lapses for a moment in seeking to reproduce Paul's thought (p. 79) into phrases made familiar to us by the Rectoral theory.

Mr. Mozley is not the first writer on the history of the doctrine of the Atonement who has found pitfalls dug for him by the differing conceptions of the Atonement indicated by the Scholastic terms — ultimately derived from the Roman law — solution, satisfaction, acceptilation, acceptation. He is probably not primarily responsible for the confusion of the last two in the Index, in which there is but one entry " acceptatio," the references under which refer indifferently to *acceptatio* and *acceptilatio* in the text. But this confusion in the Index only follows the confusion in the text. Mr. Mozley blames Grotius for accusing Socinus " of applying the word *acceptilatio* to the remission of sins," and adds, " whereas his own theory has no coherence at all apart from the Scotist idea, to which the term acceptilation is technically applied, that God can fix a value as He will " (p. 155). And he speaks of Dr. Dale's well-known treatise as containing much which recalls Grotius " and the theory of *acceptilatio*, that Christ's sufferings were not the actual penalties of sin, but were accepted by God in place of, or as of equal value with, those penalties " (p. 179). Grotius may be wrong in saying that Socinus himself calls his theory by the name of *acceptilatio*, but he does Socinus no injustice in describing it as a theory of *acceptilatio;* and though we ourselves might agree that Grotius' own theory is little better than Socinus' in this respect, Grotius would have repudiated this imputation with vigor, and (being learned in the law) would have opened his eyes with wide surprise to hear acceptilation identified with " the Scotist idea that God can fix a value as He will." Has he not himself carefully explained to us that acceptilation is applied in law to discharges which are made without any payment at all, and has he not sharply separated his own theory from complicity with such notions, because, as he says, it provides for " some payment "? Scotus, of course, does not use the term *acceptilatio* of his theory, though he freely employs *acceptatio*, a term in such general use, to be sure, that it can scarcely be called a technical law-term: and Grotius would have so little denied that he himself taught an *acceptatio*, that he proclaims that fact with full voice when he gives the name of *satisfactio* to his theory. It is one of the things which Mr. Mozley does not seem quite to apprehend that when we say satisfaction we have already said acceptation; that acceptation is of the very essence of satisfaction; and that the difference between the Church doctrine of the "satisfaction" of Christ and the Scotist theory of " acceptation," as it has become the habit to speak of it, does not turn on the presence or absence of " acceptation " in the transaction — " acceptation " occurs in both views — but on the part assigned to this " acceptation " in the two views severally. The constitutive fact of the doctrine of " satisfaction " is that the reparation " accepted " by God is held to be *per se* equivalent to the obligation resting on the sinner. The characteristic feature of Scotist theory, on the other hand, is that the reparation provided is declared to possess no intrinsic equivalence to the obligation, but to be " accepted " by God in its place by an act of gracious will. The whole zeal of the satisfactionists is expended throughout all the centuries of debate in this matter on insistence upon this difference: and " equivalence " becomes thus their most insistent watchword. A " satisfaction," *ex vi verbi*, is the rendering of an equivalent; not the very thing in obligation (that would be *solutio* in the strict sense) nor something merely " accepted " in lieu of the obligation (that would be *acceptatio* in the Scotist sense) but, in distinction from both, a real *equivalent*.

Through failure to hold in mind these distinctions Mr. Mozley sometimes goes astray in his criticism of theories and writers. For example, it is questionable whether a remark like the following does not miss the mark: " Thomas, apparently, does not keep to the Anselmic distinction *aut satisfactio aut poena*. Rather does he think of ' satisfaction by the legal penalty merited and duly borne,' and so of penal expiation " (p. 138). Every satisfaction is an alternative to penalty: the infliction of the precise penalty would be *solutio* (in the strict sense), not *satisfactio*. Anselm's *aut* . . . *aut* brings this out, that lying in the line of his argument. When on the other hand the interest shifts and the purpose is to bring out that what was offered was a real satisfaction (and not something arbitrarily accepted in lieu of a real satisfaction), the insistence is transferred to the complete equivalence of what Christ bore to the penalty incurred. Accordingly what Aquinas is insistent for is that " he properly satisfies for our offense, who exhibits to the offended one what he loves equally or more than he hates the offense." " The passion of Christ," he says accordingly, " was not only a sufficient but a superabundant satisfaction for the sins of the human race " (p. 136). To insist thus that what Christ bore in His satisfaction was in no respect less than the *poena* incurred by sinners is in no way inconsistent with saying that what He offered to God was a *satisfactio*, not the *poena* itself. It is only a slightly different mode of employing terms. Anselm also is at pains to show that the *satisfactio* offered by Christ was fully equivalent in value to the *poena* the place of which it took. Aquinas is as clear as Anselm that the *satisfactio* offered by Christ was not the *poena* itself but took the place of the *poena* to which we were bound by our sin.

The matter may perhaps be better illustrated by Mr. Mozley's remarks on John Owen and Richard Baxter, to neither of whom is he able quite to do justice, precisely because his apprehension of the implications of " satisfaction " is not altogether perfect. It is true that the personal attitude of the two men towards Grotius is different; but it is unfair to represent Baxter on that account as holding the Grotian rather than the strictly penal view of the atonement. When Baxter " denies that Christ paid the same penalty as was due from men, and contends that the idea of satisfaction can be preserved only if Christ paid an equivalent, but not the same, penalty, with avowed approval of the Grotian *satisfactio non est solutio eiusdem* " (p. 157), he is standing squarely on the ground of " satisfaction " — and the assertion that " satisfaction is not the payment of the very thing," is " Grotian " in no other sense than that Grotius, as a jurist, of course knew the legal commonplaces and repeats them on occasion. It is on the selfsame ground of " satisfaction " that Owen equally squarely stands. The difference between the two amounts only to this: that Baxter's zeal is to show that Christ's work, being a *satisfactio*, is not a *solutio* in the strict sense; while Owen's zeal is to show that Christ's work, being a *satisfactio*, is not an *acceptatio* in the Scotist sense. In his righteous zeal — it is a very righteous zeal — Owen does modify the language ordinarily employed by satisfactionists, and insists that Christ made payment *eiusdem* and not merely *tantidem*, although, as he of course adds, not *per eundem;* and even asserts that His satisfaction discharges *ipso facto*. He explains, however, that by his *idem* he means merely full equivalence — " there is a sameness in Christ's sufferings with that in the obligation in respect to essence, and equivalency in respect of attendancies," — and that by *ipso facto* he means, not " apart from God's acceptance," but " without any further conditions " — intending to exclude Grotius' insertion of a condition, not absolutely procured by Christ, on the performance of which alone by the sinner would Christ's satisfaction take effect on him. Owen departs from the doctrine of satisfaction by his strong insistence on one side of its contention as little as Baxter does by his equally strong insistence on its other side. They both stand firmly on the fundamental Christian doctrine of " the satisfaction of Christ," a doctrine which magnifies at once the infinite grace of God in the forgiveness of sins for Christ's sake (which is what Baxter had in mind to assert) and the perfection of the satisfaction for our sins wrought by Christ (which is what Owen had in mind to assert).

Mr. Mozley writes with an obvious desire to be not only fair but sympathetic and generous in his presentation of and judgments on the opinions he reviews. Of course he speaks from his own stand-point, and that means that he must distribute his commendations and condemnations from the point of view of his particular notion of the nature of our Lord's atoning work. We do not know that satis-factionists have much ground for discontent with the judgment he passes on their position — or at least on their position as reproduced by what he calls " the rigid American school of half a century ago." He names here Charles Hodge, A. A. Hodge, W. G. T. Shedd, and A. H. Strong in his earlier, and in our judgment better, teaching. And this is what he says of them: " Given their premises as to the inspiration of Scripture, and the validity of a perfectly precise method of deduction with the use of hard and fast ideas, and their conclusions afford little scope for logical disintegration " (p. 177). We surely ought to be satisfied to have it recognized that this doc-trine which we teach as Scriptural is Scriptural — provided Scripture be trusted wholly in what it says and its teachings be drawn from it by a perfectly precise method. When Mr. Mozley adds that never-theless the conclusions thus arrived at are morally disquieting, that seems to us, in the circumstances, an arraignment of the moral char-acter of the Scriptures from which they are derived by precise de-duction: and we console ourselves by recalling that when Paul taught these same conclusions (we shall remember that Mr. Mozley at one point interprets Paul as we have seen in terms of the doctrine of " satisfaction "), the Pharisees and the Libertines united in de-claring them immoral. Paul himself did not seem to think so.

No small part of the value of Mr. Mosley's volume is given it by the wideness of his survey of the history of the doctrine. He has not permitted his view to be narrowed to any coterie or to any single class of writers. Not only writers of every age and land, but, what is more unusual, writers of every ecclesiastical connection and type of thought, are given equal attention, and are treated with like care and interest. Mr. Mozley does not conceal his predilections; but his sympathies are wide, and, we rejoice to say, are most warm for the more deeply Christian types of thought. The book thus acquires a distinctly conservative tone and despite what seems to be the deficiencies of the constructive doctrine of Atonement outlined in it, will make for sane and sound views.

VAN DEN EEUWIGEN VREDE TUSSCHEN WETENSCHAP EN RELIGIE. Rede uitgesproken op den 26en Maart 1920 ter herdenking van den 284en geboortedag der Utrechtsche Universiteit. Door den Rector Magnificus Dr. H. VISSCHER. Utrecht: Drukkerij Universitas. 1920.

PROFESSOR VISSCHER'S RECTORALE REDE. Door Dr. H. W. VAN DER VAART SMIT. Overdruk van het *Gereformeerd Theologisch Tijdschrift*, 1920. Baarn: Drukkerij Oranje Nassau, R. K. v. d. Berg. 1920.[1]

IT IS a somewhat exigent position in which a theologian finds himself, when, as Rector Magnificus of a great University, he faces "the four faculties" for the purpose of delivering to them his Rectoral Address. There are many points of view represented among his hearers; and some of them are quite intolerant of anything which he, as a theologian, may have to bring before them. In his Rectoral Address Prof. Visscher has chosen the rôle of peace-maker. Looking out upon a hard-bestead world, he bespeaks the coöperation of all in the pressing task of saving Western civilization from the dissolution with which he appears to think it threatened.

Prof. Visscher seems fairly to groan within himself as he surveys the social unrest of the day. The times are out of joint. The whole world is suffering from a one-sidedness of development which has destroyed the spiritual equilibrium — and is not harmonious growth the condition of social health? True, progress has hitherto been made, not on a straight line of advance, but as a ship tacks back and forth in its course. But the leg of *Diesseitigkeit* on which the social ship in our Western world is now sailing seems to Prof. Visscher an inordinately long one; and he trembles lest it should prove that the ship has lost its bearings and may never get back on the balancing tack of *Jenseitigkeit*. Indeed, he does not wish it to do just this. The leg of *Jenseitigkeit* is itself only a tack. He wishes the ship to cease all tacking and sail straight onward, in the teeth of whatever wind, directly to its goal.

Why should not science and religion, for example, live in harmony, each contributing its part to the spiritual health of mankind? Each has its own sphere, and each has only to keep its own place and the harmony is complete. And surely their harmonious coworking is a clamant duty of the times. " For the salvation of Western humanity there rests on science and religion the most pressing call to work in harmony for the regeneration of civilization. Science has the task of subjecting nature to the scepter of reason, in order thus to make it ancillary to the full development of human life. But because of its very nature, it is unable of itself to bring about this ripe result. The happiness of the peoples is not the product of it alone. Quite the contrary. It is social health alone that secures the happiness of the people. And it is religion, which sheds the light of eternity on human life, that is the wellspring of moral strength. Science and religion are the two spiritual powers which in harmonious coöperation can save the peoples of civilization. Or is it possible to save them? If the social movement continues to refuse to take the factor of religion up into itself, the destruction of our civilization is certain, and science, too, will go down in the common ruin."

It is under the impression of so great a need, and with so high a purpose in view, that Prof. Visscher undertakes the discussion of the relations of science and religion. He is at bottom pleading for the right of religion to a part in the social development of the day. This plea, however, takes the form of an attempt to show that science, properly conceived and properly presented, cannot possibly invade the field of religion, nor religion the field of science. Thus the discussion becomes formally a discussion of the relations of science and religion; and much is very richly and much is very wisely said of the relations of these two spiritual forces to one another as they have actually wrought in the life of mankind. The discussion suffers somewhat, however, from a vacillation in the use of the terms, which no doubt it would be difficult to avoid in any case with terms so loose and general — too loose and general to lend themselves to exact discriminations. It is so managed, moreover, that it seems at times on the point of becoming a discussion of the relations between knowledge and faith, if not between intellect and feeling. It is too obvious to require argument, however, that we cannot out of hand identify, on the one hand, intellect, knowledge and science, and, on the other, emotion, faith and religion. Both science and religion are products of the human spirit and the human spirit does not function thus in sections. It is, however, the attempt to bring into comparison precisely these two things, " science and religion," that works the most mischief. We might bring, say, research and religion into relation, or " science " in some narrowed sense, and theology; but " science " in the narrowed sense in which Prof. Visscher understands that term and " religion" in the purely subjective sense which Prof. Visscher strangely puts upon " religion," move in such different spheres that they are unrelatable — there is no *tertium comparationis* between things so disparate. You might as well talk of instituting relations between the planet Neptune and the League of Nations.

We have noted that Prof. Visscher narrows the conception of " science " for the purpose of his discussion. By it he means merely physical science. But physical science is far from being all the science there is. There is, for example, as we have suggested, theology. Theology is as truly a science as physical science; it is as truly a product of the intellect; it deals as truly with facts; it is as truly a knowledge. It is theology, the science, not religion, the life, which should be set in comparison with physical science. The thrusting of " religion," so understood, into its place has the effect of depriving it of — or at least of obscuring — its fact-content. Of " religion " it may be possible to say — what could not be said of theology — that it is only a manner — perhaps only an emotional manner — of looking at facts with which as facts " science " alone has to do, so that " science " and " religion " cannot possibly come into conflict. It is " science " alone which determines facts while it is the sole function of " religion " to suffuse these facts, given to it by " science," with a glow of transcendental emotion. It is a melancholy page which Prof. Visscher writes under the influence of this point of view, when he attempts to illustrate it by examples. Had he drawn his examples from natural religion his mistake might have been less glaring. But he draws his examples from revealed religion. The effect is that he seems to require Christianity to surrender to natural science — for it is of " natural science " alone that he speaks — all question of facts, while it confines itself to a " valuation of them in relation with God." This appears to abolish all supernaturalism from the fact-basis and fact-content of Christianity. For the " science " to which is assigned the determination of the facts which will be allowed actually to have occurred, is defined not only as a science which cannot know anything of God — for whom it has no organ — but a science which can take cognizance of nothing which does not proceed mechanically.

The actual examples considered are drawn from the creation of the world, miracles, answers to prayer, the resurrection of Christ. Of the creation of the world we are simply told that science which knows nothing of origins and confines itself to the phenomena lying before it, has nothing to do with it. We gather, however, that neither has Revelation. It is a mistake to read the creation narrative as a statement of fact; it merely gives expression to the purely religious valuation (*waardeering*) of the cosmos. For the rest, we prefer to transcribe Prof. Visscher's own words. " Lessing," he says, " declared that ' miracle is faith's most darling child.' And are not science and miracle in conflict? In point of fact science recognizes no miracle. But that does not yet bring it into conflict with religion. Because the chemist subjects bread to exact analysis — does that prevent the pious man from receiving his food from God's hand? Necessity teaches man to pray and to the petitioner the deliverance comes as an answer to his prayer. Does this forbid a scientific explanation of the occurrence? But let us come to the most critical matter of all. The Crucified One is proclaimed as risen from the grave. Is there any place for resurrection in exact science? Whenever it shall be brought before it as a phenomenon. Not before. And then it will have to investigate it as a physiological problem. But it is precisely here that the difference comes clearly to view. In the world-order of religion, life and death are not conceived as physiological processes, but are religious-ethical values (*waarden*). The resurrection is for religion an element in the great regenerative process which, by God's creative act, is producing out of this world-order a new heaven and a new earth."

Despite the reassuring tone of its closing words, the reader may be pardoned if he receives from this paragraph a very unpleasant impression. There is an appearance at least that the actual occurrence of strictly miraculous events in the foundation of Christianity is denied. Miracles and providential answers to prayer seem to be brought into the same category. The one, as the other, appears to be conceived at best as the product of the concursive action of God; at worst, as only a subjective way of looking at facts wholly " natural " alike in their nature and in the mode of their production. And what shall we say of the manner in which the resurrection of Christ is dealt with? " Science," we are told, can have nothing to do with it until it is presented to it as a " phenomenon." Is it not precisely as a phenomenon that it lies in the sight of all men — an occurrence in space and time verified by the senses? And has not even the " physiological problem " been adequately determined? Has it not been established on unexceptionable observation that the resurrection-body, like that which was laid in the grave, was a body of flesh and bones? When now it is immediately added that life and death are not conceived in the religious world-order as physiological processes, but as religious-ethical values, can we escape a distressed feeling that religion — precisely the Christian religion — is in danger of being politely bowed out of the world of fact? Precisely what characterizes Christianity, however, among the religions, is that it is a " historical religion," that is, a religion whose facts are its doctrines; which does not consist in a " tone of feeling," a way of looking at things — as for example the perception of a Father's hand in all the chances and changes of life — but has to tell of a series of great redemptive acts in which God the Lord has actually intervened in the complex of nature and the stream of history in a definitely supernatural manner. If these facts are denied as actual occurrences in time and space, Christianity is denied; if they are neglected, Christianity is neglected. Christianity is dismissed from the world of reality, and evaporated into a sentiment — " an iridescent dream."

We have no wish to be read as asserting that Prof. Visscher intends to deny, or is ready to neglect, the series of great redemptive acts of definitely supernatural character, which are constitutive of Christianity. We are only pointing out that an impression to that effect is inevitably created by the sharp contrast in which he places science as the only organ of objective reality and religion as moving in a purely subjective sphere. Whatever may be said of religion as a general world-phenomenon, native to the spirit of man, that religion which is Christianity is inseparably bound up with its " facts," and stands or falls with their objective reality. Any science which leaves no place for these facts, as such, is not neutral but antagonistic to Christianity; and between that science and this religion there must be not eternal peace but eternal war. Prof. Visscher apparently supposes that he escapes this result by so defining science as to exclude facts of supernatural origin from its ken. Facts of supernatural origin, however, are not different in nature from other facts. There is no reason to suppose that the chemical composition of the wine made at Cana or the physical properties of the loaves and fishes with which our Lord fed the multitudes — or of His resurrection-body, for that matter — differed from those of " natural " wine and bread and bodies. If facts like these have actually occurred in time and space, they necessarily come under the scrutiny of that science whose function is to give an account of phenomena. Prof. Visscher seems, however, to have made a mode of escape for himself — by confining the function of science to pure description. He tells us, it is true, that the knowledge for which this science seeks is a knowledge of relations, and he even declares with some formality that " its object can be nothing else than the world, as it presents itself as a system of relations to the knowing subject." When we say relations, however, we have already said metaphysics; and if among the relations determined there is included not merely that of antecedence and consequence, but of cause, we are already embarked on an inquiry which cannot stop short of origins. Prof. Visscher tells us, however, not only that everything which exists behind phenomena lies beyond the sphere of his science, but that this science must repel the conception of a supernatural, mystical, non-mechanical factor and confine itself to the world in which " everything proceeds mechanically." If he really means us to understand the science with which he deals after this fashion — as strictly limited to the world of mechanical causation, of which it undertakes nothing more than a descriptive account — it may not be impossible to contend that its failure to take cognizance of the supernatural facts constitutive of Christianity in no way dismisses them from objective reality. It may be the result merely of the limitations of a purely descriptive science which does not take cognizance, even descriptively, of the whole field of objective reality, but only of that portion of this field which is governed by mechanical necessity. In this case it might be true enough that " all the results of this exact science are consistent with religion," because the world of religion " is a different and a wider world than the system of relations which exact science," so conceived, " builds up with immense labor." An eternal peace may well be declared between the two, bought not at the cost of religion — the fact-content of Christianity — but at the cost of science.

Whether this limited conception of science, as seeking only a descriptive account of mechanical reality, can be maintained is another question. Certainly, in any case, the science with which Prof. Visscher proclaims religion to be eternally at peace, has never, whether in the limitations which he puts upon it, or in the perfection which he ascribes to its deliverances, existed on sea or land. He is not unaware of course of the subjective side of science; but he appears to neglect it in the prosecution of his discussion, and to identify the science of which he speaks with the objective system of realities itself, which he apparently imagines to be perfectly reflected in the human intellect. Thus he seems to think of science as the pure product of the pure intellect of a pure humanity working purely. We shall get no such science as that until the world of reality is reflected in the consciousness of the perfected humanity of the completed palingenesis. The science and religion of perfected humanity will of course be in harmony. What we have in the meantime, however, is only the distorted reflection of reality in warped intellects, dimmed by imperfections and clouded by prepossessions. Could we listen directly to the teaching of that " beautiful Maiden bearing the torch of enlightenment," to whom Prof. Visscher introduces us, we should of course yield to it instant and complete obedience. But this " calm-eyed Science " is not to be encountered in the Market-place, and is not to be met with in the Rialto. She speaks to us only in the voices of her servants, and each of them has his own — well, say personal equation. After all is said, the voices of the scientists are not the voice of Science. And no inability which religion — the Christian religion — may show to live in peace with the one can argue disharmony with the other. No more here than elsewhere can millennial conditions be anticipated. There is no conflict between science and religion: they are not only, as Prof. Visscher declares, two expressions of our spiritual life, but two revelations of God. But conflict between science and religion will continue so long as we toil and moil in the present distress; they are only expressions of our spiritual life, and in these days of our tribulation our spiritual life is faulty in all its expressions. It is only when that which is perfect is come, that here too imperfection shall put on perfection.

There is no help for it, then; science and religion must just strive together until both the one and the other lie perfect in the minds of the perfected. Principially, there is no conflict between them: actually, the conflict is without cessation. There is no menace in this struggle. What would be ominous would be if the struggle should cease, especially if it should cease through either one or the other losing heart or selling its soul for a patched-up peace. We take it that the gist of Prof. Visscher's Address is to call on religion to recognize science's right to exist, to call on science to recognize religion's right to exist. If we may so read it, we shall all heartily echo the call. Of course neither will wait for the permission of the other to exist. Whether we accord them permission or not, both exist side by side, not only in the social organism, but in every man's own soul. The problem is their adjustment to one another. In the soul of the individual and in the community of mankind alike, the adjustment can be attained only through conflict. As they wrestle together each is more and more purified and perfected; each grows ever stronger. Now the one may seem to get the advantage; now the other. But through the struggle both push steadily onward. The advance is a zig-zag progress, but it is ever advance. At the end lies the goal; the goal, not of one but of both; then the struggle ceases because both emerge from it perfect. Science too is a builder in the Kingdom of God, and along with religion advances its coming. No less truly than religion itself, it is a son of God, and works as He has taught it how.

It is not surprising that the ambiguities of Prof. Visscher's treatment of his theme have caused distress to those who have been accustomed to look to him for guidance and support. Acute expression is given to this distress in the remarks on the Address by Dr. van der Vaart Smit. As he reads it, it dismisses from Christianity the whole element of direct supernaturalism. We cannot deny that there is far too much color of justification for such an interpretation of it. It is true, moreover, that Prof. Visscher seems to impose on himself with the phrase " exact science," that he conceives too narrowly of science as purely " materialistic-mechanistic," that he has forgotten

theology in his absorption with " religion." Still we hope that the intended meaning of the Address is not that which Dr. Smit finds in it. Prof. Karl Heim contributed to the " Studies on Systematic Theology " presented a year or two ago to Theodor von Haering, on his seventieth birthday, a very interesting sketch of the history of the doctrine of " The Double Truth." In it he tells the story of a young instructor in the University of Paris, in 1247, John Brescain by name, who, holding a professorship alike in the Faculty of Arts and the Faculty of Theology, thought it right to teach Averroism in the one, with its denial of individual immortality and the resurrection, and Christianity in the other, with its affirmation of both. His case proved not to be singular: a whole party developed itself at the University of Paris, which declared that such things were true *secundum fidem catholicam* but not *secundum philosophiam* — as if, says the Episcopal Rescript, *sunt duae contrariae veritates.* We are not insinuating that Prof. Visscher holds to the doctrine of " the double truth," or lives under its shadow; but we think that the state of mind in the University of Paris in the thirteenth century may afford us a not unsuggestive parallel to such a complete disassociation of science and religion as Prof. Visscher seems to wish to carry through.

INDEX OF AUTHORS